HEBREW-ENGLISH EDITION OF THE BABYLONIAN TALMUD

SEDER MO'ED

SHABBATH

תלמוד בבלי

מסכת
שבת

עם פירוש רש״י ותוספות
ובצירוף תרגום ופירוש והערות באנגלית

על ידי
אהרן מרדכי פרידמאן

בעריכת
יחזקאל (איזידור) אפשטיין ז״ל

דפוס שונצין
שנת להחזיר העטרה ליושנה לפ״ק
לונדון

HEBREW-ENGLISH EDITION OF THE BABYLONIAN TALMUD

SHABBATH

TRANSLATED INTO ENGLISH WITH NOTES AND GLOSSARY BY

RABBI DR H. FREEDMAN, B.A., PH.D.

UNDER THE EDITORSHIP OF

RABBI DR I. EPSTEIN, B.A., PH.D., D.LIT.

FOREWORD BY

DR J. H. HERTZ

LATE CHIEF RABBI OF THE BRITISH EMPIRE

INTRODUCTION BY

THE EDITOR

THE SONCINO PRESS

LONDON · JERUSALEM · NEW YORK

ISBN 0-900689-90-0

PUBLISHERS' NOTE

This HEBREW-ENGLISH EDITION of THE SONCINO TALMUD is being published to facilitate the easier reference to the original text by scholars and students.

The Soncino Press is privileged to be able to include the Novellae of Rabbi Moshe Feinstein o.b.m., on Tractate Shabbath (© Copyright 1973 Judaica Press Ltd), and we wish to thank Judaica Press Ltd. for permission to include this original material.

The Publishers wish to express their sincere thanks to Rabbi Dr. M. Ginsberg, M.A. for his painstaking care in examining the entire text and making the necessary corrections for the preparation of the Tractates in this series.

It has been necessary to duplicate some of the original Hebrew-Aramaic pages in this Tractate where the text has been of such length as to require more than one page of English translation.

MANUFACTURED IN THE UNITED STATES OF AMERICA

FOREWORD

BY

THE VERY REV. THE CHIEF RABBI

Dr J. H. HERTZ

SABBATH, FESTIVAL AND FAST IN JUDAISM

Sabbath and holyday, festival and fast—round these is spun the web of ordinances constituting the Order Mo'ed. What significance did the Rabbis give them for the spiritual life of the Jewish people?

THE SABBATH

The Rabbis made the Sabbath the very centre of the Jewish religion, a perennial fountain of idealism and regeneration in Israel. They instituted the *Kiddush* prayer, praising God for the gift of the Sabbath, to celebrate its coming in; and the *Habdalah* blessing, praising God for the distinction between the Sabbath and the six weekdays, to mark its going out. In addition to being a day of rest, the Sabbath was to be 'a holy day, set apart for the building up of the spiritual element in man' (Philo). Religious worship and religious instruction—the renewal of man's spiritual life in God—form, according to them; an essential part of Sabbath observance. We, therefore, sanctify the Sabbath by a special Sabbath liturgy, by statutory Lessons from the Torah and the Prophets, and by attending to discourse and instruction given by religious teachers. The Sabbath has thus proved the great educator of Israel in the highest subject of all, namely, the laws governing human conduct. The effect of these Sabbath prayers and Synagogue homilies upon the Jewish people has been incalculable. Leopold Zunz, the founder of the New Jewish Learning, has shown that almost the whole of Israel's inner history since the close of the Bible times can be traced in the development of these Sabbath discourses on the Torah. Sabbath worship is still the chief bond which unites Jews into a religious Brotherhood. Neglect of such worship injures the spiritual life of both the individual and the community.

By keeping the Sabbath, the Rabbis tell us, we testify to our belief in God as the Creator of the Universe; in a God who is not identical with Nature, but is a *free Personality*, the Creator and Ruler of Nature. The Talmudic mystics tell that when the heavens and earth were being called into existence, matter was getting out of hand, and the Divine Voice had to resound, 'Enough! So far and no further!' Man, made in the image of God, has been endowed by Him with the power of creating. But in his little universe, too, matter is constantly getting out of hand, threatening to overwhelm and crush out soul. By means of the Sabbath, called זכרון למעשה בראשית, 'a memorial of Creation', we are endowed with the Divine power of saying 'Enough!' to all rebellious claims of our environment, and are reminded of our potential victory over all material forces that would drag us down.

The Sabbath, as conceived by the Rabbis, is the supreme example of the hallowing of life under the sanctifying influence of the Law. That sacred day more than any other institution, has moulded Jewish family life with its virtues of chastity, charity, love, peace; virtues nowhere surpassed, rarely equalled. Amid all the misery and slavery that for so many centuries were the lot of Israel, once a week the home of the humblest Jew was flooded with light. The Sabbath banished care and toil, grief and sorrow. On that day, the despised and rejected of men was emancipated from the oppression and tribulation and degradation of this world; he felt himself a prince, a member of a great, eternal, holy people.

The Rabbis attached to the Sabbath a number of minute regulations which make its complete observance a matter of no small difficulty. In all ages—from early Christian times to the present day—ignorant and unsympathetic critics have stigmatized these minutiae as an intolerable burden and asserted that they make the Sabbath not a day of rest but one of sorrow and anxiety. Such a view shows a complete misunderstanding of the spirit in which the Rabbis approached their task. It was their love for the Sabbath which led them to exert all their ingenuity in discovering ways of differentiating it from other days and making it more thoroughly a day of rest, a day in which man enjoys some foretaste of the pure bliss and happiness which are stored up for the righteous in the world to come. And the Jewish people received it from them in the same spirit. Let a hostile witness—a German Protestant theologian of anti-Semitic tendencies—testify what the Rabbinic Sabbath is to the loyal Jew.

> 'Anyone who has had the opportunity of knowing in our own day the inner life of Jewish families that observe the Law of the fathers with sincere piety and in all strictness, will have been astonished at the wealth of joyfulness, gratitude and sunshine, undreamt of by the outsider, with which the Law animates the Jewish home. The whole household rejoices on the Sabbath, which they celebrate with rare satisfaction not only as the day of rest, but rather as the day of rejoicing. Jewish prayers term the Sabbath a "joy of the soul" to him who hallows it: *he* "enjoys the abundance of Thy goodness". Such expressions are not mere words; they are the outcome of pure and genuine happiness and enthusiasm' (R. Kittel).

By means of the Rabbinic expansion of the kinds of forbidden work on the Sacred Day, and as the outcome of the gigantic intellectual labour on the part of generations, nay centuries, of Sopherim, Tannaim, and Amoraim in the elucidation of these laws, there arose the choicest spiritual edifice in the realm of Judaism—the Sabbath Day of Jewish history. Without the observance of the Sabbath, of the olden Sabbath, of the Sabbath as perfected by the Rabbis, the whole of Jewish life would disappear. And only if the olden Sabbath is maintained by those who have lost or abandoned it, is the permanence of Israel assured.

PASSOVER

What epoch-making significance the Rabbis ascribed to the Exodus is clearly shown by the constant recurrence in the prayers of the expression, 'in memory of the going forth from Egypt'. 'The Exodus from Egypt is not only one of the greatest events and epochs in the history of the Jews, but one of the greatest events and epochs in the history of the world. To that successful escape, Europe, America and Australia are as much indebted as the Jews themselves. And the men of Europe, the men of America, and the men of Australia might join with us Jews in celebrating that feast of the Passover'. (C. G. Montefiore). The Rabbis deemed it a sacred task to keep alive the memory of that event, and the full understanding of its significance, in the mind of the Jewish people. And in the performance of this task, with sound psychological insight they began with the mind of the young. Out of a mere hint in the Biblical text, they evolved the wonderful Seder service, with its irresistible appeal to the interest and curiosity of the intelligent child. Of all the ceremonies of the Jewish religion, there is perhaps none so well calculated as the Seder to awaken the Jewish consciousness in the child, at the same time that it brings home to the adult with unique force the unbroken continuity of Jewish history.

One phrase in connection with Passover was the subject of heated controversy in early Rabbinic times between the Pharisees and Sadducees. The latter took the word '*sabbath*' (Lev. XXIII, 15)[1] in its usual sense, and maintained that the '*Omer* was to be brought on the morrow of the first Saturday in Passover. The Pharisees argued that '*sabbath*' here means, 'the day of cessation from work'; and the context shows that the Feast of Unleavened Bread is intended; therefore, the '*Omer* was to be brought on the sixteenth of Nisan. This is supported by the Septuagint which renders 'on the morrow of the first day', and by Josephus. The offerings of the sheaf took place on the sixteenth, the first busy work-day of the harvest, in relation to which the preceding day might well be called a *Sabbath* or rest-day, though not all labour was prohibited. This is alone compatible with the context, and is free from the objections to which all the other opinions are open (Kalisch).

FEAST OF WEEKS—SHABU'OTH

One of the three agricultural festivals is the feast of the first harvest חג הקציר. Jewish tradition, however, connects it with the Covenant on Mount Sinai, and speaks of the festival as זמן מתן תורתנו 'the Season of Giving of our Torah', the date of which is not expressly mentioned in the Torah but is calculated by the Rabbis from statements in the text to have been on the sixth day of the third month. Hence its association with the Feast of Weeks, which became the Festival of Revelation.

Its name in Talmudic literature is not Shabu'oth, but almost invariably '*Aẓereth* 'the concluding festival' to Passover. 'We count the days that pass since the preceding Festival, just as one, who expects his most intimate friend on a certain day, counts the days and even the hours. This is the reason why we count the days that pass since the departure from Egypt and the anniversary of the Lawgiving. The latter was the aim and object of the exodus from Egypt' (Maimonides). In other words, the Deliverance from bondage was not an end in itself; it was the prelude to Sinai (Ex. III, 12). Liberty without law is a doubtful boon, whether to men or nations.

FEAST OF TABERNACLES

In Rabbinic literature, it is known as '*the* Feast', because, as the time of the harvest, it would naturally be a period of rejoicing and holiday-making. It really consists of two groups; the first seven days, Tabernacles proper; and the eighth day, '*Aẓereth*. The seventh day of Tabernacles became in later times an echo of the Day of Atonement and was known as Hoshanah Rabbah; and the 'second day' of '*Aẓereth* assumed the nature of a separate Festival under the name of Simḥath Torah, Rejoicing of the Law, the day on which the annual reading of the Torah was completed and restarted.

ROSH HASHANAH

As the seventh day in the week was a holy day, so the seventh month was the holy month in the year. It is, therefore, not surprising that the New Moon of the seventh month should be a Festival of special solemnity. In later times, it was known as Rosh Hashanah, New Year's Day. But unlike the New Year celebrations of many ancient and modern nations, the Jewish New Year is not a time of revelry, but an occasion of the deepest religious import.

'A day of blowing the horn', i.e., *Shofar*, the ram's horn. The sound of *Shofar* consisting, as handed down by Tradition, of three distinctive *Shofar*-notes—*teḳi'ah*, *shebarim*, *teru'ah*—has been looked upon from times immemorial as a call to contrition and penitence, as a reminder of the *Shofar*-sound of Sinai; and the Day of Memorial, the beginning of the Ten Days of Repentance עשרת ימי תשובה which culminate in the Day of Atonement, as a time of self-examination and humble petition of forgiveness. 'The Scriptural injunction of the *Shofar* for the New Year's Day has a profound meaning. It says: Awake, ye sleepers, and ponder over your deeds; remember your Creator and go back to Him in penitence. Be not of those who miss realities in their pursuit of shadows and waste their years in seeking after vain things which cannot profit or deliver. Look well to your souls and consider your acts; forsake each of you his evil ways and thoughts, and return to God so that He may have mercy upon you' (Maimonides).

YOM KIPPUR

This Day, set aside for penitence, and moral regeneration, is the only one for which the Torah prescribes fasting—which is the intensest form of devotion and contrition. The Fast is to demonstrate to the sinner that man can conquer all physical cravings, that the spirit can always master the body. The abstention from all food and from gratification of other bodily desires, however, must be accompanied by deep remorse at having fallen short of what it was in our power to be and to do as members of the House of Israel. Without such contrite confession accompanied by the solemn resolve to abandon the way of evil, fasting in itself is not the fulfilment of the Divine command and purpose of the Day of Atonement.

Repentance, Prayer and Beneficence—these can change the whole current of a man's life and destiny, and lead to perfect atonement.

'Happy Israel', Rabbi Akiba exclaimed—'before Whom do ye purify yourselves, and Who is it that purifieth you? Your Father Who is in Heaven'. Note that the initiative in atonement is with the sinner. He cleanses himself on the Day of Atonement by fearless self-examination, open confession and resolve not to repeat the transgressions of the past year. When our Heavenly Father sees the abasement of the penitent sinner, He—and not the High Priest or any other Mediator—sprinkles, as it were, the clean waters of pardon and forgiveness upon him. 'The whole philosophy of monotheism is contained in this rallying-cry of Rabbi Akiba' (Hermann Cohen).

Confession of sin is the most essential and characteristic element in the services of the Day of Atonement; 'every one entreating pardon for his sins and hoping for God's mercy, not because of his own merits but through the compassionate nature of that Being Who will have forgiveness rather than punishment' (Philo). The Confession is made by the whole Community collectively;

(1) E.V. '*day of rest*'.

and those who have not themselves committed the sins mentioned in the Confession regret that they were unable to prevent them from being committed by others (Friedländer).

'From all your sins before the Lord shall ye be clean'. Thereon Rabbi Eleazar ben Azaryah founded the sublime teaching: 'For transgressions of man against God, the Day of Atonement atones (given repentance on the part of the sinner); but for transgressions against a fellowman the Day of Atonement does not atone, unless and until he has conciliated his fellowman and redressed the wrong he has done him'. The Confession deals almost exclusively with moral trespasses against our fellowmen. Especially numerous are the terms denoting sins committed with the tongue—falsehood, slander, frivolous and unclean speech. The Rabbis, who certainly did not underrate ritual offences, deemed moral shortcomings to be infinitely graver, and hence confined the Confession to them. Repentance can give rebellious sins the character of errors; i.e., by his penitence the sinner shows that his wilful sins were largely due to ignorance, and hence are treated by God as if they were 'errors'.

The Day of Atonement survived the High Priesthood; nay, it gained in inwardness and spiritual power with the passing of the sacrificial system. 'The fasting and humiliation before God, the confession of sins and contrition for them, and fervent prayer for forgiveness, were even before the destruction of the Temple the reality in regard to the Day of Atonement, of which the rites in the Temple were but a dramatic symbol' (Moore). The Rabbis had stressed the Prophetic teaching that without repentance no sacrificial rites were of any avail. With the cessation of sacrifices, therefore, repentance was left as the sole condition of the remission of sins. 'In our time when there is no Temple and no Altar for atonement, there is repentance. Repentance atones for all iniquities' (Maimonides). The Day of Atonement, the Rabbis further declare, will never pass away, even if all other Festivals should pass away. And indeed as long as Israel does not lose its soul, so long shall the Day of Atonement remain.

* * *

The volumes of Seder Mo'ed have again been planned on the same lines as those of the previous Orders in regard to Text, rendering and cultural Notes. The Editor and his collaborators have again performed with consummate skill a task of stupendous difficulty, and the standard of scholarship and accuracy set in the previous volumes has been fully maintained. The Publishers also have left nothing undone to render the Soncino Seder Mo'ed in every way a worthy continuation of their Seder Neziḳin and Seder Nashim.

J. H. HERTZ

London, 16 Sivan 5698
15 June 1938

INTRODUCTION TO *SEDER MO'ED*

BY

THE EDITOR

GENERAL CHARACTER AND CONTENTS

Mo'ed, which is the name given to the second 'Order' of the Babylonian Talmud, deals with the 'appointed seasons', the feasts and fasts and holy days of the calendar, which have always constituted a highly distinctive feature of Jewish life. The Pentateuch enumerates six such seasons—the Sabbath, the three pilgrimage Festivals, and the Days of 'blowing of the trumpet' and atonement. To these were added subsequently, by the religious authorities of the people, certain holidays and fast days of lesser sanctity, instituted to commemorate outstanding occasions of joy or sorrow in later Jewish history. Each of these had its own distinguishing mark or ceremony, the rules and regulations for which are exhaustively discussed in the appropriate tractates of Seder Mo'ed.

The term 'Mo'ed' ('appointed season') by which this Order has always been known is probably derived from Lev. XXIII, 2 where it is used in introducing the laws of the Festivals including the Sabbath. It might be observed that the designation 'Mo'ed' is in the singular, as distinct from the plural forms used to designate the other Orders, e.g., Nashim, Neziḳin, etc. It has been suggested that the singular is here specially used to avoid the confusion that might arise through the employment of the plural Seder Mo'adim (or Mo'adoth) denoting as it does in Rabbinic literature the Order of the Calendar.[1] The opinion may, however, be hazarded that it is because the Sabbath and the Festivals constitute one complete cycle of Jewish observance that preference has been given to the singular form.

The 'Order' is divided into twelve tractates arranged according to the separate editions of the Mishnah in the following sequence:[1]

SHABBATH (Sabbath) 24 Chapters. Rules and regulations for observing the Sabbath rest. Includes also the laws of Ḥanukkah.

'ERUBIN (Blendings) 10 Chapters. Regulations enabling freedom of movement beyond certain prescribed limits on Sabbaths and Festivals.

PESAḤIM (Paschal Lambs) 10 Chapters. Laws of destroying leaven on Passover, of bringing the Paschal lamb and of the *Seder* service.

SHEḲALIM (Shekels) 8 Chapters. On the contributions for the upkeep of the Temple and the regular sacrifices.

YOMA (The Day) 8 Chapters. Regulations for the Day of Atonement, with an historic description of the ceremonies carried out by the High Priest on that day.

SUKKAH (Booth) 5 Chapters. Regulations of the 'booth' on the Feast of Tabernacles and the taking of the four plants.

BEẒAH (Egg) 5 Chapters. Lays down the limitations within which food may be prepared on Festivals.

ROSH HASHANAH (New Year) 4 Chapters. Rules for proclaiming New Moon, for the New Year liturgy and the blowing of the *shofar* (trumpet).

TA'ANITH (Fast) 4 Chapters. Rules for the fast days, whether fixed or occasional, whether private or communal.

MEGILLAH (The Scroll) 4 Chapters. Rules for reading the Book of Esther on Purim; also the regulations for the reading of the Torah in public worship.

MO'ED ḲAṬAN (Minor Feast) 3 Chapters. Regulations governing work on the intermediate days of Passover and Tabernacles; also contains the laws of mourning.

ḤAGIGAH (Festival-Offering) 3 Chapters. Regulations regarding voluntary offerings on Festivals. Contains the famous digression on the esoteric teaching of the Torah.

In the printed editions of the Babylonian and Jerusalem Talmud there are deviations from this order of succession.[1] In view of these divergencies it is idle to search for any logical sequence in the arrangement of the several tractates within the 'Order'. Significant in this connection is the fact that already in the days of Sherira Gaon there was no uniformity in this respect in the Academies; and the Gaon, in his famous *Epistle*, written in 987 C.E., is at pains to explain why a particular sequence was followed in his Academy.[2] Generally speaking the tractates are arranged in accordance with the respective number of chapters in each, the largest taking precedence; and such variations as do occur are in most cases where the number of the chapters in the tractates is equal.

RELIGIOUS AND MORAL SIGNIFICANCE OF THE 'APPOINTED SEASONS'

The Sabbath, declare the Talmudic Sages, is equal in importance to all the precepts in the Torah.[1] An evaluation of the Sabbath will accordingly involve as preliminary some explanation of the significance of the Torah. Briefly stated, the foremost meaning of the word Torah is teaching. The primary purpose of the Torah which God gave to Israel is educative. Its aim is the idealization of all earthly action and the bringing of all detail of life into touch with the divine.

The laws of the Torah are divided into two classes—socio-moral and religious. They consist in other words of precepts concerning the relations between man and God and precepts governing the relations between man and man. Precepts that affect directly our fellowman are regarded as socio-moral. Those regulating the cult and ritual are religious. These differences in the laws, however, involve no contradiction in the unity of the Torah. For what is not moral law, is law helping thereto, or means of educating thereto, although the connection may not be evident in all cases.

SABBATH

The Sabbath stands at the boundary between the moral and the religious signification of the Torah. In the law of the Sabbath is thus to be found the quintessence of Judaism. It is both 'a memorial of the work of the beginning', and 'of the going out of Egypt'. Its socio-ethical character is well illustrated in Deuteronomy (V, 12-15): *Observe the Sabbath day, to keep it holy as the Lord thy God commanded thee. Six days shalt thou labour, and do all thy work; but the seventh day is a Sabbath unto the Lord thy God, in it*

a (1) V. Baneth, E., *Die sechs Ordnungen der Mischna, Seder Mo'ed*, p. 168.

b (1) This arrangement rests on the order given by Maimonides in his introduction to his commentary on Zera'im.

c (1) In the current editions of the Babylonian Talmud the tractates appear in the following order: Shab., 'Er., Pes., Beẓ., M.Ḳ., Ḥag., R.H., Yoma, Suk., Ta'an., Sheḳ., Meg. In J.T., Yoma precedes Sheḳ.; and Ḥag., M.Ḳ. For other variations v. Strack H., *Introduction to the Talmud and Midrash* (Philadelphia 1931) p. 365. (2) The sequence given by him follows that of Maimonides. Though, strange to say, neither in the Spanish nor French Recension of the *Epistle* is there any reference to Megillah, Mo'ed Ḳaṭan and Ḥagigah. V. Ed. Lewin, M.B. p. 33.

d (1) V. Ḥul. 5*a*; J. Ber. I, 5; J. Ned. III, 14; Ex. Rab. XXV, 12.

thou shalt not do any manner of work, thou, nor thy son, nor thy daughter, nor thy man-servant, nor thy maid-servant, nor thine ox, nor thine ass, nor any of thy cattle, nor thy stranger that is within thy gates; that thy man-servant and thy maid-servant may rest as well as thou. And thou shalt remember that thou wast a servant in the land of Egypt, and the Lord thy God brought thee out thence by a mighty hand and by an outstretched arm; therefore the Lord thy God commanded thee to keep the Sabbath day. Here we have the emphasis on the social significance of the Sabbath as the symbol of the emancipation of the slave who must rest on the day when the Israelites rest. It is further worthy of note that the Hebrew word *'as well as thou'* כמוך is the same as that used in
a the injunction to love thy neighbour as thyself[1] (Lev. XIX, 18). The wording of the Sabbath law in Deuteronomy clearly shows that the Sabbath is designed to make secure the equality of all men in spite of the differences in their social position. This is indeed a clear testimony to the fundamental connection of Sabbath with morality.

The religious significance of the Sabbath is emphasized in Exodus (XX, 8-11) where it is presented as the symbol of the creation as well as the end of creation. This aspect of the Sabbath makes it not merely a day of rest, of cessation of labour, but a Holy Day. *'Therefore the Lord blessed the day of Sabbath and sanctified it'*, a phrase which is conspicuously absent from the Deuteronomic version.

The proper observance of the Sabbath in testimony to the Creator and His creation demands the sanctification of objects as well as of life.[2] This does not imply a flight from the holy pleasures of life: *Thou shalt call the Sabbath a delight, the holy of the Lord, honourable* (Isa. LVIII, 13). But it does mean a surrender to the Creator of all such activities as shut in man's outlook during the working days of the week and blind him in consequence to his actual relations to God and to his fellowman.[3] Hence the many restrictions of the Sabbath day regarding the handling of objects (*Mukẓeh*, v. Glos.) as well as action and movement, which form the major part of the laws discussed in this 'Order'. By such a surrender to God man testifies that the world and all that is therein is God's. 'He who observes Sabbath testifies to Him at Whose word the world came into existence'.[4] The sanctification of the Day of Rest makes the Sabbath into a day in which man is free to attend to the claims of his relations to God and to his fellowman. *Blessed be the man that keepeth the Sabbath from profaning it and keepeth his hand from doing evil* (Isa. LVI, 2). The Sabbath thus becomes a day of religious inwardness and moral regeneration.

FESTIVALS

The same twofold significance is found in the Festivals. The three pilgrimage Festivals, Passover, Tabernacles and Pentecost, commemorating the mighty acts at the Exodus that culminated in the Revelation at Sinai and the national experiences of Israel during their wandering in the desert, combine the religious and the social aspects of the Torah. The former finds expression in the special ceremonies and rites attached to each of the Festivals, proclaiming the sovereignty and overruling providence of God, and the latter in the Festival rejoicings in which the stranger, the
b orphan and the widow were to be invited to participate.[1]

DAY OF ATONEMENT AND NEW YEAR

But the most striking expression of the close connection between the religious and social aspects of the Law is found in the Day of Atonement. The Day of Atonement is the chief of all Festivals not excepting the Passover Festival. The Bible describes the day as one given up to fasting and solemn sacrifice. The high priest atoned for himself, then for the priests, lastly for all Israel. Yet an old Mishnah[2] tells us that the Atonement-day was at the same time a day of national rejoicing. Young men and young women held bride-shows. The richer young women had to dress in plain white linen in order not to outshine the poorer—a piece of consideration, which is as yet conspicuously absent from the polished societies of modern times. In the evening all went to the house of the high priest who made a feast for all his friends. The culminating act was the sending of the scapegoat into the wilderness and the pronouncement of the pardon of the people. In later days when the sacrificial system ceased, the Day of Atonement still retained its twofold significance. While the fasting and abstention from other bodily requirements spelled contrition, confession and repentance for all trespasses both ritual and moral, the liturgy of the day, significantly enough, practically excluded from the confession ritual trespasses. Moreover, the reconciliation of man with God was made dependent on the reconciliation of man with man. Closely linked with the Atonement-day is the New Year day, both being periods of Divine Judgment and days of self-scrutiny and
c moral regeneration,[1] in which too the socio-moral and religious aspects of the Torah are merged into one.

MINOR FEASTS AND FASTS

And not only the appointed seasons prescribed by the Torah possess this twofold signification of Jewish feast and fast; it is found equally in all the holidays and fasts of lesser sanctity instituted by the religious leaders of later generations: Purim with the Megillah reading and the distribution of 'gifts to the poor'[2] as special features of the feast; and the four minor fasts with their insistent message of the love of 'truth and peace',[3] alike show the inseparableness in the Jewish conception of morals and religion. And similarly the rain-fasts were like the minor fasts on which they were patterned. The various regulations of the rain-fasts described in Ta'anith were primarily designed to rouse the people to contrition and to make amends for any social wrongs of which they might have been guilty.[4] The only feast in which the blending of the moral and religious is absent is Ḥanukkah (the Feast of Dedication). But Ḥanukkah is strictly speaking not a Feast. The eight days of Ḥanukkah, except for the kindling of lights and the recital of *Hallel* and other liturgical additions, are but ordinary working days and do not bear the stamp of *Yom Tob*.[5] Nevertheless, later Jewish piety introduced the moral note characteristic of

a (1) V. Cohen H., *Religion der Vernunft aus d. Quellen d. Judentums* (1929) p. 182. (2) V. Bialik, *Sefer ha-Shabbath*, p. 518. (3) Cf. Huxley, A., *Ends and Means*, p. 298: 'We fail to attend to our true relations with ultimate reality and, through ultimate reality, with our fellow beings, because we prefer to attend to our animal nature and to the business of getting on in the world'. (4) Mekilta, *Yithro*, 8.
b (1) V. Deut. XVI, 11 and 14. Cf. Maimonides, *Guide for the Perplexed*, III, 53: 'They (the festivals) promote the good feelings that men should have to each other in their social and political relations'. (2) V. Ta'an. 26*b*.
c (1) Cf. Sherira Gaon, *Epistle*, loc. cit. (French Recension): 'New Year is like the harbinger (כמעביר קול) of the Day of Atonement'. (2) V. Esth. IX, 22. (3) Zech. VIII, 19. (4) V. Ta'an. 16*a* and Büchler, A. *Maimonides VIII Centenary Memorial Volume* (Soncino Press) p. 13ff. (5) The technical term by which a Jewish festival is designated. This term occurs in connection with Purim (Esth. IX, 22) and on this basis Purim was to be treated according to an old Baraitha as a day on which all work was prohibited (v. Meg. 5*b*). Although this restriction was not made absolute, the established custom to the present day is to abstain from non-urgent manual labour on Purim (v. *Shulḥan Aruk* O.Ḥ. 696, 1). True it is that this term occurs also in connection with Ḥanukkah, v. Shab. 22*b*, but the phrasing there makes it quite clear that it is designated as *Yom Tob* only in respect of *Hallel* recital and thanksgiving ימים טובים בהלל והוראה Cf. with this the phrase ימי יום טוב in Esth. loc. cit. It is a noteworthy fact that but for a bare reference to the Ḥanukkah light, the Ḥanukkah feast is ignored by the Mishnah; for the reason v. Naḥmanides on Gen. XLIX, 10.

Jewish festivals in the celebration, and made the distribution of charity a feature also of this festival.[1]

METHOD AND SCOPE

Text. The Text used for this edition is in the main that of the Wilna Romm Edition. Note has, however, been taken of the most important variants of manuscript and printed editions some of which have been adopted in the main body of the translation, the reason for such preference being generally explained or indicated in the Notes. All the censored passages appear either in the text or in the Notes.

Translation. The translation aims at reproducing in clear and lucid English the central meaning of the original text. It is true some translators will be found to have been less literal than others, but in checking and controlling *every line* of the work, the Editor has endeavoured not to lose sight of the main aim of the translation. Words and passages not occurring in the original are placed in square brackets.

Notes. The main purpose of these is to elucidate the translation by making clear the course of the arguments, explaining allusions and technical expressions, thus providing a running commentary on the text. With this in view resort has been made to the standard Hebrew commentators, Rashi, the Tosafists, Asheri, Alfasi, Maimonides, Maharsha, the glosses of BaḤ, Rashal, Strashun, the Wilna Gaon, etc.[2] Advantage has also been taken of the results of modern scholarship, such as represented by the names of Graetz, Bacher, Weiss, Halevy, Levy, Kohut, Jastrow, Obermeyer, and—happily still with us—Krauss, Büchler, Ginzberg, Klein and Herford among others, in dealing with matters of general cultural interest with which the Talmud teems—historical, geographical, archaeological, philological and social.

Glossary and Indices. Each Tractate is equipped with a Glossary wherein recurring technical terms are fully explained, thus obviating the necessity of explaining them afresh each time they appear in the text. To this have been added a Scriptural Index and a General Index of contents.

In the presentation of the tractates the following principles have also been adopted:

(i) The Mishnah and the words of the Mishnah recurring and commented upon in the Gemara are printed in capitals.

(ii) תנן introducing a Mishnah cited in the Gemara, is rendered 'we have learnt'.

(iii) תניא introducing a Baraitha, is rendered 'it has been (or was) taught'.

(iv) תנו רבנן introducing a Tannaitic teaching, is rendered 'Our Rabbis taught'.

(v) Where an Amora cites a Tannaitic teaching the word 'learnt' is used, e.g., תני רב יוסף, 'R. Joseph learnt'.

(vi) The word tanna designating a teacher of the Amoraic period (v. Glos.) is written with a small 't'.

(vii) A distinction is made between הלכה כ... referring to a Tannaitic ruling and הלכתא כ... which refers to the ruling of an Amora, the former being rendered 'the *halachah* is ...' and the latter, 'the law is ...'

(viii) R. stands either for Rabbi designating a Palestinian teacher or Rab designating a Babylonian teacher, except in the case of the frequently recurring Rab Judah where the title 'Rab' has been written in full to distinguish him from the Tanna of the same name.

(ix) רחמנא, lit., 'The Merciful One', has been rendered 'the Divine Law' in cases where the literal rendering may appear somewhat incongruous to the English ear.

(x) Biblical verses appear in italics except for the emphasized word or words in the quotation which appear in Roman characters.

(xi) No particular English version of the Bible is followed, as the Talmud has its own method of exegesis and its own way of understanding Biblical verses which it cites. Where, however, there is a radical departure from the English versions, the rendering of a recognized English version is indicated in the Notes. References to chapter and verse are those of the Massoretic Hebrew text.

(xii) Any answer to a question is preceded by a dash (—), except where the question and the answer form part of one and the same argument.

(xiii) Inverted commas are used sparingly, that is, where they are deemed essential or in dialogues.

(xiv) The archaic second person 'thou', 'thee' etc. is employed only in *Aggadic* passages or where it is necessary to distinguish it from the plural 'you', 'yours', etc.

(xv) The usual English spelling is retained in proper names in vogue like Simeon, Isaac, Akiba, as well as in words like *halachah Shechinah, shechitah*, etc. which have almost passed into the English language. The transliteration employed for other Hebrew words is given at the end of each tractate.

(xvi) It might also be pointed out for the benefit of the student that the recurring phrases 'Come and hear:' and 'An objection was raised:' or 'He objected:' introduce Tannaitic teachings, the two latter in contradiction, the former either in support or contradiction of a particular view expressed by an Amora.

ACKNOWLEDGMENTS

Once again I have the pleasure of expressing my warmest appreciation of the industry and scholarship which the several collaborators have brought to bear upon their work.

To Mr. Maurice Simon, M.A., who has assisted in many directions, and to my dear wife for her invaluable help in many ways, I would express my especial thanks.

I should also like to pay personal tribute to Mr. J. Davidson, the Governing Director of the Soncino Press, for the care and self-sacrificing devotion with which he has seen Seder Mo'ed through the press.

* * *

With the publication of this 'Order' we are approaching the completion of the Soncino Edition of the first complete and unabridged English translation of the Babylonian Talmud. Only those who have been closely connected with it can appreciate the exacting and strenuous nature of the task. I tender my humble thanks to the Almighty God for having given me strength to carry through, amidst other labours, my heavy share of the work, and on behalf of all those who have been concerned with this publication I offer the traditional prayer: יהי רצון מלפניך ד׳ אלהינו כשם שעזרתנו לסיים סדר מועד כן תעזרנו להתחיל סדרים אחרים ולסיימם. May it be Thy will, O Lord our God, even as Thou hast helped us to complete the Seder Mo'ed so to help us to begin the other Sedarim, 'Orders', and complete them.

I. EPSTEIN

Jews' College, London.
Sivan 24, 5698
23 June, 1938

(1) V. אורה היים, מגן אברהם, 670. (2) These names are referred to more fully in the list of Abbreviations at the end of each Tractate.

INTRODUCTION

TO

TRACTATE SHABBATH

Shabbath is the first treatise of Mo'ed, the second Order of the Talmud. It contains 157 folios divided into 24 chapters, and is the second longest Tractate of the Talmud, being exceeded only by Baba Bathra, which runs to 176 folios.

As its name implies, the Tractate deals with the laws and regulations of the Sabbath. It is obvious that an institution of such far-reaching importance, which is indeed one of the foundations of Judaism and for the violation of which Scripture prescribes the supreme penalty,[1] had to be carefully defined, and its observance precisely determined. To this task the Rabbis devoted themselves in the present treatise.[2]

The Biblical data are furnished by the following passages: Gen. II, 2-3; Ex. XVI, 22 *seq.*; XX, 8-11 (the Fourth Commandment); XXIII, 12; XXXIV, 21; XXXV, 2-3; Num. XV, 32 *seq.*; Deut. V, 12-15 (the Fourth Commandment in the Deuteronomic revision); Jer. XVII, 21 *seq.*; Amos VIII, 5; Neh. X, 32 and XIII, 15 *seq.* From an analysis and examination of these we learn that the following labours are forbidden: baking and seething; gathering manna and bringing it in; harvesting and ploughing (and perhaps the labours associated with these); kindling; bearing burdens and carrying into a town (Jerusalem) or out from a private house; buying and selling; treading winepresses, and lading asses.[3] But of course, mere chance references, as many of these are, could not be regarded as exhausting the labours forbidden on the Sabbath, and a scientific investigation was necessary for the full understanding of its observance.

It will help to an understanding of the Tractate to know the principles upon which the Rabbis based their definition of labour, and the various categories of forbidden work which they distinguished. The *locus classicus* for determining the meaning of 'work' was found by them in Ex. XXXV. There the instructions to build the Tabernacle are preceded by a short passage dealing with the prohibition of labour on the Sabbath which is apparently superfluous. The Rabbis accordingly interpreted it as intimating that whatever work was required in the building of the Tabernacle constituted 'work' which is forbidden on the Sabbath. Acting on this principle they drew up a list of thirty-nine 'principal' labours, which they extended by adding 'derivatives', i.e., such as partook of the nature of the 'principal' labours.

In addition to the foregoing they forbade other actions (*shebuth*) on the Sabbath which while not falling into the categories of either 'principal' labours or 'derivatives' were nevertheless felt not to harmonize with the sacred and restful nature of the Sabbath. And finally, they prohibited the handling of certain articles under the term '*mukẓeh*' (lit., 'set apart').

It would be too wearisome to give a detailed summary of each of the twenty-four chapters. Suffice it to say that with the exception of the first Mishnah a definite order of sequence may be discerned. Thus the Tractate commences with the things which may not be done on Friday, goes on to discuss the oils and wicks which may be used in kindling the Sabbath lights; the things in which food may be stored for the Sabbath; the ornaments which may be worn, and then the enumeration of the thirty nine 'principal' labours, in the seventh chapter. The following nine chapters consist of definitions of these labours, while from Chapter XVII until the end a number of miscellaneous subjects are dealt with, including those things which are forbidden as a '*shebuth*' or under the heading of '*mukẓeh*'. A special chapter (XIX) is devoted to circumcision on the Sabbath.

A considerable portion of the Tractate consists of *Aggadah*. It is difficult to make a selection from the rich store of Rabbinic legend, sentence, apologue and aphorism in which the Tractate abounds, but perhaps special attention might be drawn to the following: Prayer must be preceded by preparation; the judge who judges truthfully becomes a partner with God in the Creation; the Sabbath is God's gift to Israel; the story of Ḥanukkah (the Feast of Lights); the attempt to exclude Ecclesiastes and Ezekiel from the Canon; the heathens who wished to embrace Judaism on certain conditions and Hillel's famous epitome of Judaism—'What is hateful to thee do not do to thy neighbour'; R. Simeon b. Yoḥai's criticism of the Roman Government and his flight; 'truth' is God's seal; Rome was founded when Solomon married Pharaoh's daughter; God's stipulation that the world was to return to chaos unless Israel accepted the Torah; Israel's joy in accepting it and Moses' fight to obtain it—an appreciation of the fact that God's kingdom on earth can be established only after struggle; the Torah is the cause of the nations' hatred of Israel; why Jerusalem was destroyed; schoolchildren are God's anointed; and finally, 'Repent one day before thy death' and the necessity to be ready at all times to appear before God illustrated by the parable of the wise and the foolish men invited to the king's feast. In that desire to be at harmony with God, which is the core and essence of Judaism, the Rabbis found the spiritual significance of the sacredness of the Sabbath.

H. FREEDMAN

(1) In actual practice this was hedged about with so many restrictions as to make its application virtually impossible. (2) On the relationship between 'Shabbath' and 'Beẓah' (or Yom Tob) v. Halevi, *Doroth Harishonim*, I, 3, p. 253. (3) In these texts too the sanctity of the Sabbath is stressed, the persons who benefit by this day of rest, and the reasons for same. In connection with the last it may be mentioned that while Gen. II, 2-3 and Ex. XX, 8-11 state God's resting after the Creation as the reason, in Deut. V, 12-15 the Sabbath is based on Israel's bondage in Egypt and their eventual liberation. Thus the Sabbath emphasizes God's Creation of the world on the one hand, and freedom as an essential right of man on the other.

PREFATORY NOTE BY THE EDITOR

The Editor desires to state that the translation of the several Tractates, and the notes thereon, are the work of the individual contributors and that he has not attempted to secure general uniformity in style or mode of rendering. He has, nevertheless, revised and supplemented, at his own discretion, their interpretation and elucidation of the original text, and has himself added the footnotes in square brackets containing alternative explanations and matter of historical and geographical interest.

ISIDORE EPSTEIN

מסכת
שבת

SHABBATH

CHAPTER I

a *MISHNAH*. [2a] THE CARRYINGS OUT[1] OF THE SABBATH[2] ARE TWO WHICH ARE FOUR WITHIN, AND TWO WHICH ARE FOUR WITHOUT.[3] HOW SO? THE POOR MAN STANDS WITHOUT AND THE MASTER OF THE HOUSE WITHIN: [i] IF THE POOR MAN STRETCHES HIS HAND WITHIN AND PLACES [AN ARTICLE] INTO THE HAND OF THE MASTER OF THE HOUSE, OR [ii] IF HE TAKES [AN ARTICLE] FROM IT AND CARRIES IT OUT, THE POOR MAN IS LIABLE,[4] AND THE MASTER OF THE HOUSE IS EXEMPT.[5] [AGAIN,] [i] IF THE MASTER OF THE HOUSE STRETCHES HIS HAND WITHOUT AND PLACES [AN OBJECT] IN THE POOR MAN'S HAND, OR [ii] TAKES [AN OBJECT] THEREFROM AND CARRIES IT IN, THE MASTER IS LIABLE, WHILE THE
b POOR MAN IS EXEMPT.[1] [iii] IF THE POOR MAN STRETCHES HIS HAND WITHIN AND THE MASTER TAKES [AN OBJECT] FROM IT, OR PLACES [AN OBJECT] THEREIN AND HE CARRIES IT OUT, BOTH ARE EXEMPT; [iv] IF THE MASTER STRETCHES HIS HAND WITHOUT AND THE POOR MAN TAKES [AN OBJECT] FROM IT, OR PLACES [AN ARTICLE] THEREIN AND HE CARRIES IT INSIDE, BOTH ARE EXEMPT.[2]

GEMARA. We learnt elsewhere:[3] [False] oaths are two which

a (1) Lit., 'outgoings'. (2) I.e., the acts of transporting objects from private to public ground or *vice versa*, which are forbidden on the Sabbath. Tosaf. observes that the phraseology, 'outgoings,' (יציאות) instead of the more usual 'carryings out' (הוצאות) is based on Ex. XVI, 29: *let no man go out of his place on the seventh day*. L. Blau in *MGWJ*., 1934 (*Festschrift*) p. 122, n. 2 is inclined to reject this, and conjectures that 'outgoings' (יציאות) is the original Hebrew for 'carrying out,' and its present use indicates the extreme antiquity of this Mishnah. (3) I.e., by Biblical law two acts of carrying out are interdicted to the person standing in a private domain ('within') and two to the person standing in public ground ('without'); to each two the Rabbis added another two, thus making 'TWO WHICH ARE FOUR.' Tosaf. is much exercised with the question why this is taught at the beginning of the Tractate, instead of in the seventh chapter, where all the principal forbidden acts of the Sabbath, including this, are enumerated, and offers various answers. L. Blau, op. cit., p. 124f maintains that this was originally part of the Mishnah of Shebu. I, 1, which is quoted at the beginning of the Gemara (*infra*), where a number of subjects, having no inner connection, are grouped together by the catchphrase 'two which are four.' As an aid to the memory each subject was then put at the head of the Tractate to which it refers. (4) For desecrating the Sabbath. (5) Because the poor man performs the two acts which *together* constitute 'carrying out' in the Biblical sense, viz., he removes an object from one domain and replaces it in another. (When he withdraws the object into the street, holding it in his hand, he is regarded as having deposited it in the street.) The master, on the other hand, is quite passive, performing no action at all.

b (1) In both cases here the master performs the two acts, the poor man being passive. Thus there are two Biblically forbidden acts for each.—'Liable' means to a sin-offering, if the acts are committed unwittingly, or to death (in theory, hardly in practice) if committed knowingly, and can apply here only to a Biblical interdict. (2) In iii and iv each performs one act only, *either* removing from one domain *or* depositing in another. This is Rabbinically forbidden, and involves no liability. (When the master places an object into the poor man's outstretched hand, which is already in the house, he, and not the poor man, is regarded as having removed it from the private domain.) (3) Shebu. I, 1.

יציאות

*השבת שתים שהן ארבע בפנים ושתים שהן ארבע בחוץ כיצד העני עומד בחוץ ובעל הבית בפנים אפשט העני את ידו לפנים ונתן לתוך ידו של בעל הבית או שנטל מתוכה והוציא העני חייב ובעל הבית פטור: פשט בעל הבית את ידו לחוץ ונתן לתוך ידו של עני או שנטל מתוכה והכניס בעל הבית חייב והעני פטור: פשט העני את ידו לפנים ונטל בעל הבית מתוכה או שנתן לתוכה והוציא שניהם פטורין ב*פשט בעל הבית את ידו לחוץ ונטל העני מתוכה או שנתן לתוכה והכניס שניהם פטורין:
גמ' *תנן התם שבועות שתים שהן ארבע
ידיעות

יציאות השבת. הוצאות שמרשות לרשות האמורות לשבת ובגמ' מפרש דהכנסות נמי קא קרי יציאות הואיל ומוציא מרשות לרשות: שתים שהן ארבע בפנים. לאותן העומדים בפנים שתים מן התורה הוצאה והכנסה דבע"ה ובפ' הזורק (לקמן צו:) ברישיה נפקא לן מויצו משה ויעבירו קול במחנה וגו' לא תפיקו מרה"י לר"ה להביא נדבה למחנה לויה ויום השבת היה כדיליף התם ועל שתים אלו חייב חטאת על שגגתו ועל זדונו כרת ועל התראתו סקילה וכן בכל מלאכת שבת: שהן ארבע. מדבריהם הוסיפו שתים לאסור לכתחלה ואם עשה פטור ולקמן מפרש להו ואזיל: ושתים שהן ד' בחוץ. שתים מן התורה הוצאה והכנסה דעני העומד בחוץ ושתים מדבריהם כשהמלאכה נעשית על ידי שנים זה עוקר וזה מניח לכתחלה אסור ואם עשה פטור כדיליף בגמרא (דף ג.) שנים שעשאוה פטורים: פשט העני את ידו. וחפץ בתוכה: ונתן לתוך ידו דבעה"ב. דעביד ליה עקירה ברה"ר והנחה ברה"י: או שנטל מתוכה והוציא. החפץ והניח בר"ה דעביד ליה עקירה [ברה"י] והנחה [ברה"ר]: העני חייב. שעשה מלאכה שלמה והרי שתים מן התורה לעומד בחוץ: ובעל הבית פטור. פטור לגמרי ואפי' לכתחלה מותר דהא לאו מידי עבד והכי מפרש בגמ' (דף ג.): פשט בעה"ב כו' בעה"ב חייב. והרי שתים מן התורה לעומד בפנים: פשט העני את כו'. דעביד ליה עקירה ונטל בעה"ב מתוכה והניח בפנים ועביד ליה בעל הבית הנחה: או שנתן לתוכה. דעביד ליה בעל הבית עקירה והוציא העני והניח: שניהם פטורין. שלא עשה האחד מלאכה שלימה אבל אסורין לעשות כן לכתחלה שמא יבואו כל אחד ואחד לעשות מלאכה שלימה בשבת הרי שתים מדבריהם אחת לעני בחוץ ואחת לבע"ה בפנים וא"ת שנים הן לכל אחד ואחד עקירה לעני ועקירה לבע"ה הנחה לעני והנחה לבע"ה לקמן פריך לה ומשני דלא חשיב אלא עקירות שהן תחלת המלאכה ואיכא למימר שמא יגמרנה:
גמ' תנן התם. במסכת שבועות: שבועות שתים. שבועות של ביטוי להרע או להיטיב שתים הן להתחייב עליהן קרבן עולה ויורד האמור בפרשה (ויקרא ה) דנפקי מלהרע או להטיב דמשמע להבא אוכל ולא אוכל: שהן ארבע. יש לך לרבות עוד שתים מריבוי הכתוב לכל אשר יבטא האדם לרבות לשעבר אכלתי ולא אכל לא אכלתי ואכל:
ידיעות

יציאות השבת שתים שהן ארבע. הקשה ריב"א דדיני הוצאות שבת היה לו לשנות גבי אבות מלאכות אחר פרק כלל גדול לקמן (דף עג.) דהתם קתני אבות מלאכות מ' חסר אחת וקתני הוצאה לבסוף והוה ליה להתחיל כסדר בדברים דמיירי בע"ש מבעוד יום כגון לא יצא החייט במחטו סמוך לחשיכה אין שורין דיו וסממנין ואין צולין בשר ואח"כ במה מדליקין וכירה ובמה טומנין שהם דברים הנוהגים עם חשיכה ואח"כ במה בהמה ובמה אשה יוצאה דברים הנוהגים בשבת עצמו ושוב אבות מלאכות של שבת ודרך התנא לשנות כסדר זה כמו שמצינו בפסחים דמתחיל בליל י"ד ושוב בי"ד ושוב בשחיטת פסחים שהוא בין הערבים ואחר כך שונה מאכילת פסחים שהוא בלילה וכן ביומא מתחיל בז' ימי קוד' יה"כ ואח"כ בעיה"כ ואח"כ ליל יה"כ ותירץ דהוצאה חביבא ליה לאקדומי משום דממשנה זו שמעינן כמה דברים הוצאה והכנסה דעני ועשיר ודבעי' עקירה והנחה ושנים שעשאוה פטורין וידו של אדם חשובה לו כד' על ד' וידו של אדם אינה לא כרה"י ולא כרה"ר ור"ת מפרש דדבר ההוה רגיל הש"ס לשנות תחילה וכן במס' ב"ק (דף ב.) השור והבור המבעה וההבער ולא *נקט כסדר הפרשה וכן מפרש רב האי גבי ד' צריכין להודות בפרק הרואה (ברכות דף נד:) דלא נקט הש"ס כסדר הפסוק ועוד מפרש ר"ת דפתח ביציאות משום דבעי למימר לא יצא החייט במחטו אע"ג דלא שנה המלבן משום אין נותנין כלים לכובס ולא המעביר משום במה טומנין הוצאה הוצרך לשנות טפי משום דמלאכה גרועה היא כמו שאפרש: **יציאות**. הוצאות הוה ליה למתני' אלא נקט יציאות לישנא דקרא אל יצא איש ממקומו (שמות טז) ודרשינן מינה (עירובין דף יז:) הוצאה אל יצא עם הכלי ללקט המן: **שתים** שהן ארבע בפנים. כן נראה כמו שמפרש רש"י כאן דמבפנים היינו לבעה"ב העומד בפנים ובחוץ היינו לעני העומד בחוץ שתים הוצאות והכנסות דחיוב שהן ד' הוצאות והכנסות דפטור ובשבועות* פרש"י בפנים היינו הכנסות פנים שנים דחיוב דעני ודעשיר ושנים דפטור ובחוץ היינו הוצאות חוץ* ואין נראה מדפירש מילי דעני לחוד ומילי דעשיר לחוד משמע כפי שפירש כאן ולפי' דהתם לא היה לו לערב הוצאות והכנסות יחד ומיהו שמא לפי שהיה צריך להאריך אם היה בא לפרש הוצאות לבד [והכנסו' לבד] מ"מ אין נראה לרביט אלחנן מדקאמר בגמרא דיקא נמי דקתני יציאות וקמפרש הכנסות לאלתר ולא דייק מדקתני בפנים: **פשט** בעה"ב את ידו כו'. תימה לר"י אמאי צריך למתני תרתי דעני ודבעה"ב וכן ברישא שבועות דמפרש בגמרא (דף ג. ושם) שתים דעני ודבעל הבית מה שייך לקרותו שתים מה לי עני מה לי עשיר ונראה לר"י דאיצטריך לאשמעי' משום דהוצאה מלאכה גרועה היא דמה לי מוציא מרה"י לרה"ר מה לי מוציא מרה"ר לרה"י ולא הוה גמרינן הוצאה דעני מבעה"ב ולא בעה"ב מעני ותדע מדאיצטריך תרי קראי בהוצאה כדנפקא לן ברישא הזורק (לקמן דף צו: ושם) מויכלא העם מהביא ובספ"ק דעירובין (דף יז:) נפקא לן מקרא אחרינא דדרשינן אל יצא איש ממקומו אל יוציא *והתם פירשתי והיינו משום דמלאכה גרועה היא איצטריך תרוייהו חד לעני וחד לעשיר *וכן בכל תולדות דאבות מלאכות לא חיישינן שיהא במשכן אלא אבות בלבד ובתולדות דהוצאה בעי' שיהא במשכן דתנן בהזורק (דף צו.) שתי גזוזטראות זו כנגד זו המושיט והזורק מזו לזו פטור היו שתיהן בדיוטא אחת הזורק פטור והמושיט חייב שכך היתה עבודת לוים וברישא הזורק (ג"ז שם:) נמי בעי הזורק ד' אמות ברה"ר מנלן ודחיק לאשכוחינהו במשכן עד דמסיק כל ד"א ברה"ר הלכתא גמירי לה וכל אלו תולדה דהוצאה נינהו ולא אבות שאין אבות אלא מ' חסר אחת וגבי הכנסה נמי אמרינן בפ' במה טומנין (לקמן מט:) הם העלו קרשים מקרקע לעגלה אף אתם אל תכניסו מרה"ר לרה"י* וא"ת כיון דהכנסה היתה במשכן מה צריך תו לקמן בהזורק (דף צו:) לפרושי דסברא הוא מה לי אפוקי מה לי עיולי דהזורק ד' אמות ברה"ר משמע דלאי הוה משכחת לה במשכן הוה ניחא ליה אע"ג דהתם ליכא סברא וי"ל דאיצטריך סברא להכנסה דבעה"ב דלא הוה במשכן דהם העלו קרשים כו' היינו הכנסה דעני דמהמחא בקרקע היו עומדים שהוא רה"ר ואם תאמר כיון דאיכא סברא אמאי איצטריך בבמה טומנין למימר דהכנסה היתה במשכן וי"ל דתנא ליה איידי דבעי למיתני הם הורידו קרשים מעגלה ואתם אל תוציאו כו' אע"ג דהוצאה נפקא לן מקרא איצטריך למיתני שהיתה במשכן משום דקתני ברישא בברייתא אין חייבין אלא על מלאכה שכיוצא בה היתה במשכן ואם לא היה מוצא הוצאה במשכן הייתי מחייב בכל מלאכות הדומות למלאכה גמורה אע"פ שלא היה במשכן כמו בהוצאה והא דאסמוך קרא דשבת למלאכת המשכן הוה דרשינן למילתא אחריתי: **שבועות** שתים שהן ארבע. ברישא שבועות (דף ג.) מפרש שתים אוכל ולא אוכל דכתיב בהדיא להרע או להיטיב דהיינו להבא שהן ד' אכלתי ולא אכלתי דאתי מדרשא והא דלא מפר' שהן ד' אזרוק ולא אזרוק והוה אתיא כולה כר' ישמעאל ולא הוה צריך לאוקומי בתרי תנאי משום דמתני' בפ"ג (דף יט:) תנן בהדיא שהן ד' אכלתי ולא אכלתי וא"ת אמאי לא קתני שתים שהן שמונה [אוכל ולא אוכל] אכלתי ולא אכלתי אזרוק ולא אזרוק זרקתי ולא זרקתי ונראה דלכך פירש רש"י ברישא שבועות דאינו שונה אלא דבר וחילופו ור' יצחק תירץ דלא נקט אלא אכלתי ולא אכלתי משום דפליג ר' ישמעאל והוי רבותא טפי אבל אזרוק ולא אזרוק דמודה ר"י לא חש למיתני וא"ת וגבי שבת אמאי קתני שתים שהן ד' ותו לא ליתני נמי מושיט ומעביר מרשות היחיד לרשות היחיד דרך רה"ר דחייב כדאמר לקמן (דף צו:) וזורק מרשות היחיד לרשות הרבים ומרה"ר לרה"י וי"ל דלא קתני אלא הכנסה *דדמיא להוצאה שהוא מרה"י לרה"ר לאפוקי מושיט ומעביר שהוא מרה"י לרה"י וזריקה נמי לא דמיא להוצאה שזה בהולכה ביד וזה בזריקה:
ידיעות

שבועות ה.
לקמן צג.
שבועות ב.
[ועי' תוספות פסחים סה: ד"ה הוצאה]

עין משפט נר מצוה

אזהרה בכלל דיני שבת כתב סמיי' פ"א מהל' שבת הלכה ג וז"ל כל מקום שנאמר שהעושה דבר זה פטור הרי זה פטור מן הכרת ומן הסקילה ומן הקרבן אבל אסור לעשות אותו דבר בשבת ואיסורו מד"ס

א א מיי' פי"ב מהלכות שבת הלכה ט ופי"ג שם הלכה ב סמג לאוין סה טוש"ע א"ח סי' שמז:

ב ב מיי' שם הל' ו:

רבינו חננאל

יציאות השבת שתים שהן ארבע בפנים כו'. גמ' תנן התם בתחלת שבועות. שבועות שתים שהן ארבע. ידיעות הטומאה שתים שהן ארבע. יציאות השבת שתים שהן ארבע. מראות נגעים שתים שהן ארבע. ואקשי' אמאי התם במסכת שבועות לא קתני בענין שבת שתים

[עי' מהר"ם]

[דף ב. ודף ה. ושם ד"ה שתים]

[ת"י]

והתם פריך מי כתיב אל יוציא והיינו משום כצ"ל רש"ל

מצאתי כתוב בגליון ת"י וז"ל ופי"ל שתים שתי הוצאות דחיוב ופטור שהן ארבע הכנסות דחיוב ופטור עכ"ל ואין נראה דבירושלמי בעי מה שנים כו' ומסיק ב' לחיוב וב' לפטור ע"ש. [דבור זה שייך לתוס' לעיל ד"ה שתים שהן ארבע אחר פירש"י לפני ואין נראה ט']

דדמיא לגמרי להוצאה כצ"ל

ידיעות הטומאה שתים שהן ארבע (א) *מראות נגעים שנים שהן ד' יציאות השבת שתים שהן ארבע *מאי שנא הכא דתני ב' שהן ד' בפנים וב' שהן ארבע בחוץ ומאי שנא התם דתני שתים שהן ארבע ותו לא הכא דעיקר שבת הוא תני אבות ותני תולדות התם דלאו עיקר שבת הוא אבות תני תולדות לא תני אבות מאי נינהו יציאות ויציאות תרי הויין וכי תימא מהן לחיוב ומהן לפטור והא דומיא דמראות נגעים קתני מה התם כולהו לחיובא אף הכא נמי כולהו לחיובא אלא אמר רב פפא הכא דעיקר שבת הוא תני חיובי ופטורי התם דלאו עיקר שבת הוא חיובי תני ופטורי לא תני חיובי מאי נינהו יציאות יציאות תרתי הויין שתים דהוצאה ושתים דהכנסה והא יציאות קתני אמר רב אשי תנא הכנסה נמי הוצאה קרי לה ממאי מדתנן *המוציא מרשות לרשות חייב מי לא עסקינן דקא מעייל מרה"ר לרה"י וקא קרי לה הוצאה וטעמא מאי כל עקירת חפץ ממקומו תנא הוצאה קרי לה אמר רבינא מתניתין נמי דיקא דקתני יציאות וקא מפרש הכנסה לאלתר ש"מ רבא אמר רשויו' קתני רשויו' שבת שתים: א"ל רב מתנה לאביי הא תמני הויין תרתי סרי הויין וליטעמיך שיתסרי הויין א"ל הא לא קשיא בשלמא בבא

ידיעות הטומאה. האמורות בקרבן עולה ויורד (ויקרא ה) או נפש כי תגע וגו' ואמרינן במס' שבועות (פ"א דף ז ע"ב) שאין הכתוב מדבר אלא בטומאת מקדש וקדשיו שלאחר שנטמא אכל קודש או נכנס למקדש וילפינן התם (דף ד') שאינו מתחייב אלא בידיעה תחלה וידיעה בסוף והעלם בינתיים כגון שידע שנטמא ונעלם ממנו טומאה ואכל קדש ומשאכל ידע שאכלו בטומאה שתים הן ממשמעות הכתוב (שם) ונעלם ממנו והוא טמא משמע שנעלם ממנו טומאה אבל זכור הוא שאכל קדש ושזה מקדש הרי שתים העלם טומאה לגבי קדש והעלם טומאה לגבי מקדש: שהן ארבע. יש לך לרבות עוד שתים מריבוי ונעלם ונעלם ב' פעמים לרבות את הזכור לטומאה אבל נעלם ממנו קדש כסבור שחולין הן או נעלם ממנו מקדש: מראות נגעים. ליטמא בהן שנים הן שאת ובהרת: שהן ארבע. מריבוי ספחת שהוא משמע טפילה כמו ספחני נא אל אחת וגו' (שמואל א ב) מרבה טפילה לזו ולזו תולדה לשאת ותולדה לבהרת ושנו חכמים בהרת עזה כשלג שניה לה כסיד ההיכל שאת כלמר לבן שניה לה כקרום בילה מראה לשון זכר הוא משום הכי תני שנים שהן ד': תני אבות ותולדות. יציאות והכנסות שהיציאות אבות הן דמויעבירו קול במחנה (שמות לו) לא משמע אלא הוצאות אלא מסברא אמרינן (בריש הזורק דף צו:) מכדי מרשות לרשות קפיד קרא מה לי אפוקי מה לי עיולי: תרתי הויין. דעני ודבעל הבית ומאי שהן ארבע דקתני התם: מהן לחיוב ומהן לפטור. יציאות דעני ודבעל הבית לחיוב ויציאות שתים של פטור שתי עקירות של הוצאה כגון פשט בעל הבית ידו מלאה לחוץ ונטל עני מתוכה הרי פטור של בעל הבית דקחשיב ליה תנא דמתני' וכגון פשט העני ידו ריקנית לפנים ונתן בעל הבית לתוכה הרי פטור שני של הוצאה (ס"א של עני) שהוא אסור לכתחלה דגזרינן שמא יעשה הנחה על עקירתו והיינו שהן ד' דקתני התם: הא דומיא דמראות נגעים קתני לה מה התם כולהו לחיובא. שבאיזו מהן שנטמא בה ונכנס למקדש חייב ולהכי פריך ממראות נגעים דאילו שבועות וידיעות פלוגתא היא דאיכא מ"ד בשבועות (דף כה') אינו חייב אלא על העתיד לבא ובידיעות נמי איכא למ"ד (שם דף יד:) אינו חייב אלא על העלם טומאה: חיובי תני. כדמפרש לקמיה ב' הוצאות וב' הכנסות וכולן לחיוב ביחיד שעשאם עני לבדו או בע"ה לבדו: חיובי מאי נינהו יציאות. כלומר יציאות קתני דמשמע הוצאה לכך מתמה הי מחיובי קתני ע"כ יציאות לחודייהו ותרתי הוא דהויין ומשני הכנסות נמי קתני בהדייהו: מדתנן המוציא מרשות לרשות. קחשיב מנין אבות מלאכות בפרק כלל גדול: מי לא עסקינן כו'. דהא ע"כ אהכנסה נמי חייב כדקתני מתני' העני חייב וקתני המוציא: מתניתין. דהכא נמי דיקא דהכנסה נמי קרי הוצאה: דקתני יציאות. ועל כרחך לא מצית מפרש לה דיציאות לחודייהו קאמר ומאי שהן ארבע חיובי ופטורי דהא מפרש הכנסה ברישא דקתני כילד פשט העני את ידו לפנים דהיינו הכנסה וקתני לה בפירושא דיציאות אלמא הכנסה נמי קרי לה הוצאה: רבא אמר. דקשיא לך לישנא דיציאה בין הכא בין התם רשויות קתני רשויות שתים רשות היחיד ורשות הרבים שהן ארבע בפנים כו' כלומר ועל ידיהן יש לך ארבע איסורין בפנים וכנגדן בחוץ ומהן לחיוב ומהן לפטור והאיך דשבועות כולהו לחיובא כדאוקימנא: תרתי סרי הויין. ארבעה חיובי ותמניא פטורי שתי עקירות לעני בלא הנחה ושתי הנחות בלא עקירה וכן לבעל הבית כגון פשט העני את ידו מליאה לפנים ונטל בעל הבית מתוכה הרי עקירה לעני והנחה לבעל הבית או שנתן לתוכה והוציא הרי עקירה לבעל הבית והנחה לעני וכן פשט בעל הבית כו' כדקתני לה: שיתסרי הויין. דאיכא למיחשב נמי הנך פטורי דמיתנו גבי חיובי העני חייב ובעל הבית פטור וכן בעל הבית חייב והעני פטור:
בבא

ידיעות הטומאה כו'. וא"ת ואמאי לא קתני העלמות שתים שהן ד' העלם טומאה ואכל קדש או נכנס למקדש שהן ד' העלם קדש והעלם מקדש והוה אתי שפיר דלא מצי למיפרך הני תמני הויין כדפריך אידיעות וי"ל דנקט ידיעות כדמפרש התם (פ"ב ד' יד:) ידיעות קמייתא דליתנהו בכל התורה כולה קחשיב בתרייתא דאיתנהו בכל התורה לא קחשיב א"נ ידיעות בתרייתא דמייתי לידי קרבן קחשיב ולההיא לישנא דידיעות קמייתא קחשיב לא שייך למיתני גבי שבועות ושבת ידיעות שבועות וידיעות שבת ולאידך לישנא נמי דקאמר ידיעות בתרייתא דמייתי לידי קרבן קחשיב לא תנא בהו ידיעות כיון דחילוק שתים שהן ארבע משכחת באיסורא גופיה אבל גבי טומאה החילוק דשתים שהן ארבע איט בא אלא מחמת הידיעה: מראות נגעים וכו'. ברוב ספרים גרס שנים שהן ד' וכן בשילהי המזבח מקדש (זבחים פח:) ברוב ספרים גרס מראות נגעים ר' דוסא אומר שלשים וששה עקביא בן מהללאל אומר שבעים ושנים דממראה יאמר מראות כמו ממחנה מחנות וכי היכי דכתיב ועתה הייתי לשני מחנות (בראשית לב) ה"נ קתני שפיר מראות שנים ואע"ג דהתם חשיב כולי האי והכא לא חשיב אלא ב' שהן ד' התם חשיב פתיכין ונגעי אדם וראש וזקן ונגעי בתים והכא לא חשיב אלא לבנות כדתנן במס' נגעים (פ"א מ"א) ומייתי לה בפ"ק דשבועות (דף ה') בהרת עזה כשלג שניה לה כסיד ההיכל כו'*: התם דלאו עיקר שבת אבות תני ותולדות לא תני. וא"ת והא במראות נגעים תני אבות ותולדות כדמפרש בשבועות שהן ארבע שאת ותולדתו בהרת ותולדתו אף על גב דהתם לאו עיקר נגעים הוא וי"ל דלא דמי דתולדות דנגעים כתיבי ותולדות דשבת לא כתיבי: והא דומיא דמראות נגעים קתני. הא דנקט מראות נגעים טפי משבועות וידיעות משום דאינהו גופייהו לא ידעינן דהוו להו כולהו לחיובא אלא משום דדומיא דמראות נגעים קתני דבכולהו איכא פלוגתא בר ממראות נגעים: התם דלאו עיקר שבת הוא חיובי תני פטורי לא תני. לא הוה צריך לומר משום דלאו עיקר שבת הוא אלא משום דדומיא דמראות נגעים קתני דהוו כולהו לחיובא אלא משום דצריך לשניי הכא דעיקר שבת תני חיובי ופטורי קמסיים נמי התם דלאו עיקר שבת הוא וגם המקשה לא הקשה דליתני התם כי הכא כיון דידע דדומיא דמראות נגעים קתני אלא פריך דליתני הכא שתים שהן ד' ותו לא: *וכי תימא מהן לחיוב ומהן לפטור. רש"י לא פי' כאן לפי שיטתו שבסמוך דעקירות קחשיב ולפי שיטתו היה לו לפרש שתים לפטור בעקירות דבעה"ב: והא יציאות קתני. לא פריך אלא אמתני' דשבועות דהוה כולהו לחיובא ולא משכחת אלא שתים אבל במתני' דהכא משכחת לה כולהו ביציאות כגון שלא יהיו כולם לחיובא שתים דהוצאה שיש בה חיוב חטאת ופטור אבל אסור דאתי לידי חיוב חטאת שהן ד' פטור אבל אסור דלא אתי לידי חיוב חטאת ופטור ומותר בעני וכן בעשיר לפירוש ריב"א בסמוך ולהכי לעיל כי משני הכא דעיקר שבת הוא תני אבות ותולדות לא הוה מצי למיפרך והא יציאות קתני: מי לא עסקינן דקא מעייל מרה"ר לרה"י. ובפ"ק דשבועות (דף ה:) פריך ואימא דקא מפיק מרה"י לרה"ר ומשני א"כ ליתני המוציא לרה"ר מאי מרשות לרשות אפילו מרה"ר לרה"י וא"ת ומ"ש דתני תולדה דהוצאה ולא תני שום תולדה דכל שאר אבות ותירץ ריב"א דבכל שאר תולדות אם היה רוצה לשנותם היה צריך להאריך בלשונו אבל הכנסה דקרויה הוצאה כוללה עמו בקוצר: וקמפרש הכנסה לאלתר. וא"ת ואמאי לא דייק מכח דלא משכחת ארבע בפנים וד' בחוץ בלא הכנסות וי"ל דמשכחת להו כדפירשתי לעיל א"כ דמהא לא הוה שייך למימר מתני' נמי דיקא דמאי אולמא מההיא דשבועות דקיימא עלה דהתם נמי לא משכחת כולהו לחיובא אא"כ תחשוב הכנסות בכלל: רשויות קתני. רשויות שתים שהן ארבע פירוש דשתים קאי ארשויות רשות הרבים ורשות היחיד וקשה לריב"א דאם כן לא הוה ליה למיתני ושתים שהן ארבע בחוץ אלא שתים שהן ארבע בפנים וארבע בחוץ שתים למה לי ופירש ריב"א רשויות שבת יש בהן שני חיובים שהן ד' בפנים וב' חיובים שהן ד' בחוץ ויציאות נראה לריב"א דהוי כמו תוצאות דאשכחן רשויות דאקרי הוצאות דכתיב (במדבר לד) והיו תוצאותיו הימה ומתרגמינן רשוותיה:
בבא

רבינו חננאל

שהן ארבע בפנים ושתים שהן ארבע בחוץ. והכא קתני שתים שהן ארבע בפנים ושתים שהן ד' בחוץ. ושנ[ינן] הכא דעיקר שבת [תני] אבות ותולדות כו' [וגר]חת. ושני רב פפא הכא דעיקר שבת תני חיובי ופטורי. התם חיובי תני דומיא דשבועות. וידיעות הטומאה ומראות נגעים משום הכי פטורי לא תני התם. ואקשי' תוב והא תרתי אינון הוצאה דעני והוצאה דבעל הבית. ושני שתים דהוצאה כדאמרן. ושתים נמי דהכנסה אחת דעני ואחת דבעה"ב הוצאה קרי לה. ופירשה רב אשי לטעמא ואמר האי תנא כל עקירת חפץ ממקומו כיון שמוציאו ממקום למקום אפילו הכנסה קרי לה הוצאה. וסייעיה רבינא ואמר דייקא דמתניתין הכי דקתני יציאות השבת וקא מפרש בתחלתדבריו פשט העני את ידו לפנים שהיא הכנסה ש"מ ההכנסה הוצאה קרי לה. רבא אמר שרשויות שבת שתים קתני. הוצאה והכנסה דעני. הוצאה והכנסה דבעה"ב. אקשי' תוב ד' בפנים וד' בחוץ הא תמניא ואנן תנינן י"ב. וכי תימא לטעמיך י"ו הויין

[ועי' תוס' שבועות ג. ד"ה מראות]

הגהות הב"ח

(א) גמ' ידיעות הטומאה שתים שהן ארבע יציאות השבת שתים שהן ארבע מראות נגעים שנים שהן ארבעה מאי שנא הכא:

רש"ל מוחק כל דיבור זה

מסורת הש"ס

נגעים פ"א מ"א

שבועות ה.

לקמן צו.

are four:[4] [2b] the forms of consciousness of uncleanness are two which are four;[5] the appearances of leprosy are two, which are four;[6] a the carryings out of the Sabbath are two which are four.[1] Now, why is it taught here, TWO WHICH ARE FOUR WITHIN, AND TWO WHICH ARE FOUR WITHOUT; whereas there it is [simply] stated, 'two which are four,' and nothing else?—Here, since the Sabbath is the main theme, [both] principal [forms of labour] and derivatives are taught;[2] but there, since the main theme is not the Sabbath, principal labours only are taught, but not derivatives. What are the principal labours?—carryings out! But the carryings out are only two?[3] And should you answer, some of these involve liability, and some do not involve liability[4]—surely it is taught on a par with the appearances of leprosy: just as there all involve liability,[5] so here too all involve liability?—Rather said R. Papa: here that the Sabbath is the main theme, acts of liability and non-liability are taught;[6] there, since the Sabbath is not the main theme, only acts of liability are taught, but not of exemptions.[7] Now, what are the cases of liability—carryings out? But the carryings out are [only] two?[8]—There are two forms of carrying out and two of carrying in. But 'carryings out' are taught?—Said R. Ashi: The Tanna designates b 'carrying in' too as 'carrying out.'[1] How do you know it?—Because we learnt: If one carries out [an object] from one domain to another, he is liable. Does this not mean even if he carries [it] in from the public to a private domain, and yet it is called 'carrying out.' And what is the reason?—Every removal of an article from its place the Tanna designates 'carrying out.' Rabina said: Our Mishnah too proves it, because CARRYINGS OUT are taught, yet straightway a definition of carrying in is given; this proves it. Raba said: He [the Tanna] teaches [the number of] domains; the domains of the Sabbath are two.[2]

R. Mattenah objected to Abaye: Are there eight?[3] but there are twelve![4]—But according to your reasoning, there are sixteen![5] Said he to him, That is no difficulty: as for the first clause, it is

(4) In Lev. V, 4-7 (q.v.) a variable sacrifice (vv. 6-7) is imposed for taking a false oath (v. 4 is so explained). '*To do evil, or to do good*,' is interpreted as meaning that one swears, 'I will eat,' or 'I will not eat,' which are the two referred to, viz., a positive or a negative oath relating to the future. These are further increased to four by including similar oaths relating to the past: 'I ate', or 'I did not eat.' (5) In Lev. V, 2f, 5-7 a variable sacrifice is also decreed for transgressing through uncleanness. According to the Talmud (Shebu. *7b*) this refers to the eating of holy food, e.g., the flesh of sacrifices, and entering the Temple while unclean. Further, liability is contracted only if one was originally aware of his uncleanness, forgot it, and ate sacred food or entered the Temple, and then became conscious of it again. Thus there are two, viz., forgetfulness of uncleanness when eating sacred food, and same when entering the Temple. To these another two are added: forgetfulness of the sacred nature of the food and forgetfulness of the sanctity of the Temple while being aware of one's uncleanness. (6) The two are '*a rising*' and '*a bright spot*' (Lev. XIII, 2), which, in order to be unclean, must be snowy white and white as wool respectively. To these the Rabbis added, by exegesis, the whiteness of the plaster of the Temple and the whiteness of the white of an egg respectively—in each case a darker shade.

a (1) BaH, on the basis of the text in Shebu. I, 1, reverses the order of the last two. (2) Labours forbidden on the Sabbath are of two classes: (i) principal labours (*aboth*, lit., 'fathers') and (ii) derivatives (*toledoth*, lit., 'offsprings'), which are prohibited as partaking of the nature of the principal labours. Both are regarded as Biblical. Carrying out from private into public ground is a principal labour, while the reverse is a derivative thereof (*infra 96b*). (3) Viz., that of the poor man who takes an article from the houseowner's hand, and that of the master of the house who puts an article into the poor man's hand. Where then are the 'two which are four?' (4) I.e., two carryings out impose liability, as in preceding note, and another two are forbidden yet do not involve liability. Viz., if the poor man stretches his hand within, receives an article, and withdraws it; likewise, if the master of the house puts forth his hand with an object which the other takes, as explained on *supra 2a*, n. a5 on the Mishnah.—Thus there are 'two which are four,' all referring to carrying out. (5) To the purificatory sacrifices of a leper (Lev. XIV). (6) V. notes on Mishnah. (7) Two instances of carrying out, and two of carrying in, as explained in the Mishnah. (8) Though there is liability for carrying in, the Mishnah in Shebu. speaks only of 'carryings out.'

b (1) Employing 'carrying out' in the wider sense of transporting between private and public ground. (2) I.e., in respect of the Sabbath we recognize two domains, public and private, carrying between which is prohibited. On account of these two four acts are forbidden to a person standing within and four to a person standing without, and that is the meaning of 'TWO WHICH ARE FOUR,' both here and in Shebu. (Rashi). Riba explains it differently.—Actually four domains are distinguished (*infra 6a*), but these are the principal two. (3) 'TWO WHICH ARE FOUR WITHIN, AND TWO WHICH ARE FOUR WITHOUT.' (4) In addition to the four acts which involve liability, there are eight which do not. Viz., two acts of removal by the poor man without depositing, i.e., if he stretches his hand into the house and the master takes an object from him, or the master puts his hand without and the poor man places an object in it. Reversing these, we have two acts of depositing by the poor man without removal. These four, again, are also to be viewed from the standpoint of the master of the house, which gives eight in all. (5) For the two actions which involve liability for the poor man are likewise to be regarded from the standpoint of the master of the house, and *vice versa*, which yield another four.

well: [3a] he does not teach what involves no liability and is [also] permitted.[6] But the last clause, where no liability is involved, yet it is forbidden, is indeed difficult.[7] (But is there in the whole [of the laws relating to] Sabbath [an action described as involving] no liability [yet] permitted: did not Samuel say: Everything [taught as] involving no liability on the Sabbath, involves [indeed] no liability, yet it is forbidden, save these three, which involve no liability and are [also] permitted: [viz.,] the capture of a a deer,[1] the capture of a snake, and the manipulation of an abscess?[2]—Samuel desires to say this only of exemptions where an act is performed; but as for exemptions where no act [at all] is done, [of such] there are many?)

Yet still there are twelve?—Non-liable acts whereby one can come to the liability of a sin-offering are counted; those whereby one cannot come to the liability of a sin-offering are not counted.[3] 'BOTH ARE EXEMPT?' But between them a [complete] action is performed!—It was taught: [*And if anyone*] *of the common people sin unwittingly, in doing* [*any of the things etc.*]:[4] only he who performs the whole of it [a forbidden action], but not he who performs a portion thereof. [Hence] if a single person performs it, he is liable; if two perform it, they are exempt. It was stated likewise: R. Ḥiyya b. Gamada said: It emanated[5] from the mouth of the company[6] and they said: '*In doing*': if a single person performs it, he is liable: if two perform it, they are exempt.

Rab asked Rabbi: If one's neighbour loads him with food and drink, and he carries them without, what is the law? Is the removing[7] of one's body like the removing of an article from its place, and so he is liable; or perhaps it is not so? He replied: He is liable, and it is not like his hand.[8] What is the reason?—His

(6) E.g., if the man without extends his hand and places an article into the hand of the man within, the latter commits no action at all, being passive throughout, and, as far as the Sabbath is concerned, he does nothing forbidden. (7) Why these are not counted as separate actions, as explained in n. 4.

a (1) V. *infra* 106b end and 107a. (2) V. *infra* 107a. (3) Stretching out one's hand with an article from a private to a public domain or *vice versa* may involve a sin-offering, viz., by depositing the said article in the new domain. But acceptance can never lead to this (Riba). (4) Lev. IV, 27. (5) Lit., 'it was cast forth'. (6) Of scholars—i.e., it was generally ruled. (7) Lit., 'uprooting'. (8) For, as stated in the Mishnah, if an article is placed in one's hand and he withdraws it, he is exempt.

בבא דרישא *פטור ומותר לא קתני אלא בבא דסיפא דפטור אבל אסור קשיא מי איכ' בכולי שבת פטור ומותר והאמר שמואל *כל פטורי דשבת פטור אבל אסור בר מהני תלת דפטור ומותר צידת צבי °וצידת נחש ומפיס מורסא כי איצטריך ליה לשמואל פטורי דקא עביד מעשה פטורי דלא קא עביד מעשה איכא טובא מ"מ תרתי סרי הויין פטורי דאתי בהו לידי חיוב חטאת קא חשיב דלא אתי בהו לידי חיוב חטאת לא קא חשיב שניהן פטורין והא אתעבידא מלאכה מבינייהו *תניא ר' ויקרא ד אומר °מעם הארץ בעשותה העושה את כולה ולא העושה את מקצתה יחיד ועשה אותה חייב שנים ועשו אותה פטורין איתמר נמי א"ר חייא בר גמדא נזרקה מפי חבורה ואמרו בעשותה יחיד שעשאה חייב שנים שעשאוה פטורין: בעי מיניה רב מרבי הטעינו חבירו אוכלין ומשקין והוציאן לחוץ מהו עקירת גופו כעקירת חפץ ממקומו דמי ומיחייב או דילמא לא א"ל ג'חייב ואינו דומה לידו (א) מאי טעמא גופו נייח ידו לא נייח א"ל

רש"י

בבא דרישא. העני חייב ובעל הבית פטור ובעל הבית חייב והעני פטור דפטור מחטאת ומותר לכתחלה דהא לאו עקירה עבד ולא הנחה עבד [שהאחר] הניחה בידו: פטור אבל אסור. פטור מחטאת אבל אסור מדבריהם לכתחלה: צידת צבי וצידת נחש ומפיס מורסא. כולהו בפ' ר"א אומר האורג בסיפיה והתם מפרש טעמייהו מנא ליה בהו דפטור ומותר: מורסא. קויסטור"א: מפיס. עולר שתפתח ותצא הליחה: כי איצטריכא ליה. לאשמעינן דפטור ומותר בהנך דלית בהו מעשה כגון הני תלת ותו ליכא: איכא טובא. כגון הנך דבבא דרישא: פטורי דאתי בהו לידי חיוב חטאת. °כגון עקירות שהן תחלת המלאכה דאיכא למגזר דילמא גמר לה אבל הנחות לא מצי למיתי לידי חיוב חטאת דהא ליכא עקירה גבי האי וארבע דקתני בכל חד תרתי דחיובא ועקירה דפטורא דתרתי נינהו פשט העני ידו מלאה לפנים הא חדא או שנתן לתוכה בע"ה וידו של עני היתה ריקנית הא תרתי וכן באידך ורבותי' אומרים פשיטות יד לפנים [לגבי שניהם] בין מלאה בין ריקנית היא תחלת המעשה וההוא הוא דקחשיב דהוו להו תרתי בעני ותרתי בבע"ה: כל חיוב ופטור במסכת שבת בחטאת קאי ובשוגג: מעם הארץ בעשותה. גבי חטאת כתיב: הטעינו חבירו. שהיה גופו ברה"י והטעינו חבירו דאיהו גופיה לא עקר מידי: אוכלין ומשקין. אורחא דמילתא נקט דבר הצריך לשבת ודרך בני אדם להתעסק בהן בשבת: עקירת גופו. שעקר את רגליו מן הבית לאחר שטענו: ואינו דומה לידו. הפשוטה לפנים וגופו לחוץ ונתן בע"ה לתוכה דפטר ביה תנא דמתני' אף לעני שהוציאה. ידו לא נייח. הלכך כי הוציאה לא עקר מידי ואין דרך הוצאה בלא עקירה והנחה: גופו נייח. ע"ג קרקע והוית עקירה. ל"א ידו בתר גופו גרירא ל"ג דיתירא היא:

בר

תוספות

בבא דרישא פטור ומותר. וא"ת והא קא עבר אלפני עור לא תתן מכשול ואפילו מיירי שהיה יכול ליטלו אפילו לא היה בידו דלא עבר משום לפני עור דמושיט כוס יין לנזיר מוקי לה בפ"ק דמס' עבודת כוכבים (דף ו:) דקאי בתרי עברי דנהרא °מ"מ איסור דרבנן מיהא איכא שחייב להפרישו מאיסור ואפילו אי מיירי בנכרי דלא שייך לפני עור מיהו איסור דרבנן מיהא איכא כדתניא בשילהי פירקין (דף יט.) נותנין מזונות לנכרי בחצר כלבו ויצא אין נזקקין לו משמע דווקא כשהנכרי בחצר אבל אם עומד בחוץ ופושט ידו לפנים משמע דאסור ליתן להדיא ע"מ להוציא ויש לומר דמיירי בנכרי והחפץ של נכרי דאפילו מכניס ומוציא כל היום אין כאן איסור כלל כיון שאין החפץ של בעל הבית*: בר מהני תלת. הקשה ר"ת הא איכא הא דתנן בפרק במה מדליקין (לקמן כט:) המכבה את הנר מפני שהוא מתירא כו' ואם בשביל החולה שיישן פטור ומוקי לה בחולה שיש בו סכנה וא"כ הוא פטור ומותר דאין לך דבר שעומד בפני פקוח נפש ותירץ דהא מלתא דפשיטא היא ולא איצטריך ליה לשמואל לאשמעי' כדמשני בסמוך דלא איצטריך ליה לאשמעי' פטורי דלא קעביד מעשה וצד נחש מיירי בדליכא סכנה שיוכל להנצל בענין אחר אלא משום צערא שרו ליה רבנן כמו במפיס מורסא וכן מוכח בריש פרק שמונה שרצים (שם קז:) דצד נחש לאו משום סכנה פטור דהא מוקי לה כר"ש דאמר מלאכה שא"צ לגופה פטור עליה וע"ק לר"י והא איכא הא דתני' בפ' במה אשה (שם סב:) ר"א פוטר בכובלת ובצלוחית של פלייטון והוא פטור ומותר דהא בברייתא אחרת קתני התם ר"א יוצאה אשה בכובלת לכתחלה ותירץ ר"י בשם ר' אברהם דלא חשיב שמואל אלא פטורים השנויין במשנה דצד צבי משנה היא בהאורג (שם ד' קז:) הצד נחש ומפיס מורסא משנה היא בעדיות (פ"ב מ"ה) ולספרים דגרסי בפ' במה אשה (שם ד' סב.) איידי דאמר ר"מ חייב חטאת א"ל איהו פטור אבל אסור פי' דר"א קאמר לר"מ לדבריך נמי לכל היותר לא יהא אלא פטור אבל אסור לפי גרסא זו אתי שפיר: הצד נחש. הקשה בה"ג דשמואל אדשמואל דהכא סבר שמואל מלאכה שאינה צריכה לגופה פטור כר"ש ומשום צערא דגופא שרי ובפ' כירה (לקמן מב.) אמרינן בדבר שאין מתכוין סבר לה כר"ש במלאכה שאינה צריכה לגופה סבר לה כר"י ותירץ ר"ת דשמואל קאמר דלר"ש דאמר מלאכה שאינה צריכה לגופה פטור בהני תלת פטור ומותר כמו שמוכיח שמואל בסוף האורג (שם קז.) דודאי פטור ומותר קאמר °וליה לא ס"ל כר"ש ומיהו לדידן קי"ל כר"ש דרבא דהוי בתרא סבר כותיה בריש נוטל (שם קמא:) (*): ומפיס מורסא. בעדיות (פ"ב שם) תנן אם לעשות לה פה חייב ואם להוציא ממנה ליחה פטור וא"ת היכי מתחייב הפתיחת פה דמורסא הא אמרינן לקמן בפ' חבית (ד' קמו.) כל פתח שאינו עשוי להכניס ולהוציא אינו פתח ותירץ ר"ת דהאי נמי עשוי להכניס אויר ולהוציא ליחה: פטורי דאתי לידי חיוב חטאת. מה שפירש"י דעקירות קחשיב אינו נראה לר"י חדא דעקירה בלא הוצאה אינה אלא טלטול בעלמא ואין בה דררא דחיוב חטאת כלל ועוד דלפי' הקונט' קחשיב לבע"ה ג' יציאות והכנסה אחת ולעני ג' הכנסות והוצאה אחת ועוד דלא חשיב תרתי לפטור דעני באחת ודעשיר באחת כדחשיב חיובא ברישא ומפרש ריב"א דאתי לידי חיוב חטאת היינו אותו שפושט את ידו ומכניסה או מוציאה דכוותה בבא דרישא חייב חטאת והכא פטור לפי שלא עשה כל המלאכה שחיסר ממנה מעט או עקירה או הנחה והביא ראיה מירושלמי דקאמר לא אתיא מתני' אלא פטור שכנגד החיוב ומשום הכי לא חשיב אלא פטור של אותו שכנגדו חייב למעלה בבבא דרישא כגון פשט העני את ידו לפנים כו' וקתני העני חייב פטורה דידיה חשיב בבבא דסיפא בפשט העני את ידו לפנים וכו' וכן לבע"ה: שניהם פטורין והא איתעבידא מלאכה מבינייהו. אינו קאי אמתני' שהרי רישא דשניהם פטורין דהיינו פשט העני את ידו לפנים קבעי לקמן (ד' ד.) אלא קאי אמאי דקאמר פטורי דאתי בהו לידי חיוב חטאת קחשיב אבל חטאת לית בהו אלא שניהן פטורין כדקתני מתני' ואמאי והא איתעבידא מלאכה מבינייהו ולא פריך שיתחייב הראשון דאין סברא דע"י השני שעשה הנחה וגמר המלאכה יתחייב הראשון אלא אשני קא פריך שיתחייב לפי שעל ידו נגמרה המלאכה: בעשותה. בכל הספרים גר' העושה את כולה ולא העושה מקצתה יחיד שעשאה חייב שנים שעשאוה פטורין פשטיה דקרא נראה דבעשותה קאי אנפש אבל הש"ס דריש ליה אמלאכה כלומר בעשות אותה וכולה מיירי בזה עוקר וזה מניח ואינו אלא כפל מלה וליכא למימר דב' איירי בב' שעשאוה בבת אחת דבפרק המצניע (לקמן צג. ושם) משמע דצריכי תרי קראי לזה עוקר וזה מניח ולב' שעשו מלאכה בבת אחת ועוד דבאיתמר נמי דקאי אמתניתין נמי קאמר האי לישנא יחיד ועשה אותה וכו' אך קשה דבפרק המצניע (שם) משמע דזה עוקר וזה מניח נפקא מנפש או מאחת והכא נפקא לה מבעשותה קשה לר"י מדמצרכינן קרא לפטור משמע דזה עוקר וזה מניח היה במשכן ובפרק המצניע (צג. שם) נמי פוטר ר"ש זה אינו יכול וזה אינו יכול אע"פ שהיה במשכן כגון ב' שנושאין את הארון ובירושלמי פרק הזורק אהא דתנן שתי גזוזטראות ברשות הרבים כו' היו שתיהן בדיוטא אחת המושיט חייב אמר רב חמא בשם ר' מיישא ובלבד על ידי ב' ופריך בכל אתר אמרת ב' שעשאוה פטורין וכאן אמרת חייבין ומשני שכך היתה עבודת הלוים והשתא מה בכך שהיתה במשכן מ"מ הוי ליה לפטור מושיט כיון דשניהם עושין אותה ונראה לר"י דבמושיט אין זה עוקר וזה מניח אלא המושיט עשה עקירה והנחה ולא קשיא ליה בירושלמי אלא אמה שאינו מחייב מושיט אלא כשחבירו מקבל מידו אבל אם המושיט מניחו על רשות היחיד [אחר] פטור ובכל מקום על ידי חבירו פטור [טפי] כגון ב' שעשאוה וכאן אינו מתחייב אלא על ידי חבירו: איתמר נמי כו'. תימה דמייתי סייעתא משמעתא לברייתא ובפרק קמא דקדושין (ד' ו:) פריך יהודה ועוד לקרא וי"ל דנזרקה מפי חבורה דקאמר היינו חבורה של תנאים ור"י תירץ משום דברייתא דלעיל לא מתניא בי ר' חייא ור' אושעיא(א): עקירת גופו כעקירת חפץ דמי או לא. נראה לר"י דהכי נמי מצי למיבעי לענין (ב) הנחה כגון שהוציא חפץ לר"ה ועמד שם לפוש ולא הניחו ע"ג קרקע אם הנחת גופו הוה כהנחת חפץ או לא וממתני' דקתני או שנטל מתוכה והוציא העני חייב ליכא למיפשט דאיכא לאוקמא שהניחו ע"ג קרקע וא"ת (ג) ואמאי לא פשיט ממתניתין (ד' יא:) דקתני לא יצא החייט במחטו סמוך לחשכה שמא ישכח ויצא ואי עקירת גופו לאו כעקירת חפץ דמי אמאי לא יצא בה הא לא מצי למיתי לידי איסור דאורייתא וי"ל דאפ"ה אסרו רבנן: מאי טעמא ידו לא נייח. נראה לר"י כלשון אחר דגרס ידו דבתר גופו גרירא ולמאי דגרס נמי ידו לא נייח מפרש ר"י דהיינו משום דבתר גופו גריר ורש"י פי' ידו לא נייח ע"ג קרקע משמע אפי' הוא וידו במקום אחד ונתן לו חבירו לתוך ידו והוציא פטור ואין נראה דבכל ענין שהטעינו חבירו בין על כתפו בין על ידו והוציא חייב דהא קתני או שנטל מתוכה והוציא חייב אלמא הנחת חפץ ביד בע"ה שהוא וידו ברשות אחת הויא הנחה מדחייב העני שעקר מיד בע"ה וכיון דהויא הנחה כשעוקר גופו עם זה שבידו הרי עוקרו ממקום הנחה:

(*) [וע"ע תוס' זבחים לג. ד"ה במלאכה:]

היה

עין משפט נר מצוה

ג א מיי' פי"ג מהל' שבת הלכה ז טור שו"ע א"ח סי' שמו:

ד ב מיי' שם הל' ט:

א"נ י"ל דמ"מ לאיסור שבת פטור ומותר [ת"י]

רבינו חננאל

ד' פטורי דרישא דלית בהן מעשה כלל דפטור ומותר נינהו לא חשיב להן. לפיכך לא קשיא לי. ושמואל נמי דאמר כל פטורי דשבת פטור אבל אסור לבר מהני תלתי צידת צבי יצידת נחש ומפיס מורסא. דפטור ומותר לא אמר אלא במידי דאית בהו מעשה וליתא מלאכה גמורה. אבל כי הני לית בהו [מעשה] כלל לא אמר מכל מקום י"ב הוין. פי' בבא (ודישא) [דרישא] קתני פשט העני את ידו לפנים ונתן לתוך ידו של בעל הבית העני חייב בעה"ב פטור. כי נמצא שעקר מרשות הרבים והכנים והניח ברה"י לפיכך חייב חטאת. אבל בעה"ב שלא עקר כלל וגם לא הניח אלא העני הוא בא והניח לתוך ידו של בעה"ב פטור ומותר דהא בעה"ב לא עשה מעשה כלל. הנה שתים אחת לחיוב ואחת לפטור. או שנטל העני מתוך ידו של בעה"ב והוציא עני חייב שנמצא כי עקר מרה"י והניח לרה"ר אבל בעה"ב שלא עקר ולא הניח פטור ומותר. הנה העני עוד חייב ובעה"ב פטור. נמצאו שתים אחרות וכן כיוצא בבא שניה בעה"ב חייב שתים והעני פטור בשתיהן נמצא בהני תרתי בבי ח'. ד' מנהון חיובי חטאת. וד' מנהון פטורין (ותרין) [ומותרין] לגמרי דהא לית בהו מעשה כלל וכיון דלית בהו מעשה כלל (וכיון דלית בהו מעשה) בהני ד' לפיכך לא חשיב להו האי תנא ובבא תליתאה פשט העני את ידו לפנים ונטל בעה"ב מתוכה. נמצא העני עקר ובעה"ב הניח שניהם עשו מעשה מיהו ולא אחד מהן עשה מעשה כולו אלא מקצתו וקיימא לן שנים שעשו מלאכה פטורין לפיכך שניהם פטורין. הנה שתים לפטור אחד העני ואחד בעה"ב. ועוד קתני סיפא או שנתן בעה"ב חפץ לתוך ידו של עני והוציאו העני שניהם פטורין. נמצאו בעה"ב עקר בפנים והעני הניח מבחוץ לפיכך שניהם פטורין. הנה שתים אחרות. וכן נמצא בה בבבא ד' פטורי כיוצא באלו נמצאו שיתסרי בד' בבי. הסר מהם ד' ראשונים דפטור ומותר דלית בהן [מעשה] דלא חשיב להו נשתיירו י"ב. והיאך שנינו ד' בפנים וד' בחוץ שהן ח' בלבד. ושנינו פטורי כיוצא דאתי בהן לידי חיוב חטאת הוא חשיב התנא. אבל פטורי דלא אתי בהן לידי חיוב חטאת לא קתני וזה פירושו פשט העני את ידו לפנים שיש בה חפץ שעקרו מרה"ר והכניסו לרה"י ולא הניחו וכיון שלא הניחו אין לו [אלא] אסור ואילו הניחו היה חייב פטור אבל אסור דאתי לידי חיוב חטאת אבל בעה"ב שנטל חפץ מידו של עני אע"פ שעשה מעשה ואסור מידו לא אתי לידי חיוב חטאת לעולם. שאין*) בו דרך כדי שעקר. כבר עקרו העני ולא נשאר לו מה לעשות

*) אולי צ"ל שאין כאן דרך כדי לעקור שכבר עקרו העני וכו'

מסורת הש"ס

רש"ע

לקמן דף קז.

לקמן דף נג:

ס"א רש"ע

הגהות הב"ח

(א) גמ' מ"ט ידו לא נייח גופו נייח א"ל ר' חייא:

גליון הש"ס

גמ' ולא העושה. עיין סנהדרין דף סב ע"א ברש"י ד"ה ולחכן ובכאר בבא שם: רש"י ד"ה פטורי דאתי וכו' כגון עקירות. עיין שבועות דף יד ע"ב תוס' ד"ה ארבע שהן: תוס' ד"ה בבא דרישא וכו'. מ"מ איסור דרבנן מיהא איכא. עי' טורי אבן בחגיגה דף יג ע"א בד"ה אין מוסרין: תוס' ד"ה הצד נחש וכו' וליה לא ס"ל כר"ש. עיין סנהדרין דף פד ע"ב תוס' ד"ה מאן שמעת ליה:

(א) ועי' תוס' ב"ב סא. ד"ה ואיבעית וכו' ולומר ר"י דהתם לא קפיד אלא אלשון ועוד וכו' וקצ"ע

(ב) ורשב"א פי' דהנחה פשיטא ליה ואם ה"ב בעי על עקירה כדפריך לקמן דלמא הנחה לא בעי אבל עקיר' כפי ת"י:

(ג) ורשב"א ממחלק בין עקירה להנחה (ת"י) ק"מ כתב במ"ס אך מ"מ קשה לי לפ"ה כיון דהוי הנחה אע"ג דלא נייח על גבי קרקע אפי' הוציא ידו מליאה לחוץ או לפנים יתחייב אלא ודאי משום כשידו דוקא ברשות אחרת לא הוי הנחה כדפרש"י משו' דבתר גופו גרירא ולר"י דלא מחלק בין עקירה להנחה קשה לי אמאי לא פשיט ממתניתין דעקירת גופו כעקירת חפץ כי היכי דהנחת חפץ ביד בעה"ב שהוא וידו ברשות א' הוי הנחה וי"ל דגבי הנחה מודה הקונטרס שיש חילוק אבל בעקירות דחשיבי טפי אפי' הוי ידו ברשות שהוא שם לא הוי עקירה כיון דלא נח ע"ג קרקע [תוס' ישנים]:

עין משפט
נר מצוה

ה א מיי' פ"ד מהל' פ"ח הלכה ו :

ו ב ג מיי' פי"ג מהל' שבת הל' כ סמ"ג לאוין סה טוש"ע א"ח סי' שמח וש"ע :

א"ל ר' חייא לרב *°בר פחתי לא אמינא לך *כי קאי רבי בהא מסכתא לא תשייליה במסכתא אחריתי דילמא לאו אדעתיה דאי לאו דרבי גברא רבה הוא כספתיה דמשני לך שינויא דלאו שינויא הוא השתא מיהת שפיר משני לך דתניא היה טוען אוכלין ומשקין מבעוד יום והוציאן לחוץ משחשיכה חייב לפי שאינו דומה לידו: אמר אביי פשיטא לי ידו של אדם אינה לא כר"ה ולא כרה"י כר"ה לא דמיא מידו דעני כרה"י לא דמיא מידו דבע"ה בעי אביי ידו של אדם מהו שתעשה ככרמלי' מי קנסוה רבנן לאהדורי לגביה או לא ת"ש היתה ידו מלאה פירות והוציאה לחוץ תני חדא אסור להחזירה ותני אידך מותר להחזירה מאי לאו בהא קמיפלגי דמר סבר ככרמלי' דמיא ומ"ס לאו ככרמלית דמיא לא דכ"ע ככרמלית דמיא ולא קשיא כאן למטה מעשרה כאן למעלה מעשרה ואיבעית אימא אידי ואידי למטה מעשרה ולאו ככרמלית דמיא ולא קשיא כאן מבעוד יום כאן משחשיכה מבעוד יום לא קנסוה רבנן משחשיכה קנסוה רבנן אדרבה איפכא מסתברא ב מבעוד יום דאי שדי ליה לא אתי לידי חיוב חטאת ליקנסו' רבנן °משחשיכ' דאי שדי ליה אתי בהו לידי חיוב חטאת לא ליקנסו' רבנן ומדלא קא משנינן הכי *°תפשוט דרב ביבי בר אביי דבעי רב ביבי בר אביי הדביק פת בתנור התירו לו לרדותה קודם שיבא לידי חיוב חטאת או לא התירו תפשוט דלא התירו °הא לא קשיא ותפשוט ואיבעית אימא לעולם לא תפשוט ולא קשיא כאן בשוגג כאן במזיד בשוגג לא קנסוה רבנן במזיד קנסוה רבנן ואיבעית אימא אידי ואידי בשוגג °והכא *בקנסו שוגג אטו מזיד קמיפלגי מר סבר קנסו שוגג אטו מזיד ומר סבר לא קנסו שוגג אטו מזיד ואיבעית אימא לעולם לא קנסו ולא קשיא ג כאן לאותה חצר
כאן

היה טוען אוכלין ומשקין מבעוד יום כו'. כשעמד לפוש משחשכה איירי דבלא עמד לא מיחייב אע"ג דעקירת גופו כעקירת חפץ דמי לא בטלה עקירה ראשונה כדאמר לקמן (ד' ה:) המפנה חפציו מזוית לזוית ונמלך עליהן להוציאן פטור שלא היתה עקירה משעה ראשונה לכך נקט מבעוד יום לאשמעינן דעקירת גופו כעקירת חפץ דמי דאי הוה נקט טוען עצמו משחשכה ועמד לפוש לא היה משמע מידי דאפילו אי עקירה והנחת גופו לא הויא עקירה והנחה חייב משום עקירה ראשונה: מהו שתעשה ככרמלית. כגון שהוציא ידו מלאה לחוץ ולאהדורה אבל בע"א לא דהא תנן בפרק בתרא דעירובין (ד' צח:) עומד אדם ברה"י ומטלטל ברה"ר ולא הויא כרמלית אלא לענין רשות שהגוף שם שדומה יותר לשתי רשויות: מי קנסוה רבנן לאהדורה. נראה לר"י דגרס מי אסרוה ולא גרס מי קנסוה דלקמן בסמוך כי מוקמא דלאו ככרמלית דמיא אמרינן דאסור להחזירה משום קנס ושמא הא דעבדוה ככרמלית נמי הוי קנסא וכ"מ דאסור בשוגג *מבעוד יום: כאן למעלה מי'. וא"ת למעלה מי' לכתחלה נמי מותר להוציאה דהוי מקום פטור וי"ל דקמ"ל דאפילו הוציאה מתחלה דרך מטה מי' מותר להחזירה למעלה מי' ולא קנסינן ליה: התירו לו לרדותה. ואע"ג דאמרינן בר"ה בפרק י"ט (ד' כט: ושם) כל מלאכת עבודה לא תעשו וגו' יצאו תקיעת שופר ורדיית הפת שחכמה היא ואינה מלאכה מ"מ מדרבנן אסורה כדאמר בכל כתבי הקדש (לקמן קיז: ושם) ולא ירדה במרדה אלא בסכין וכן תקיעת שופר אסור מדרבנן דתנן בפ"ב דר"ה (ד' לג.) אין מעכבין התינוקות מלתקוע משום חינוך הא נשים מעכבין*: ואיבעית אימא לעולם לא תפשוט. נראה לר"י דל"ג לעולם לא תפשוט דאע"ג דאיכא שינויא אחרינא דלא תיקשי שני ברייתות אהדדי עדיין איכא למיפשט דרב ביבי מבני בית המדרש מדלא משני איפכא מכלל דלא התירו ולרשב"א נראה דשפיר גריס ליה דממאי דלא משני איפכא ליכא למיפשט דסברי בני בית המדרש דלא התירו דהא דלא משני איפכא לפי שאין נראה סברא לעולם לומר משחשיכה לא קנסוה מבעוד יום קנסוה דאי משחשיכה לא קנסוה שוב אין לומר מבעוד יום קנסוה דהוי כחוכא ואטלולא ואע"פ שאין שייך טעם משחשיכה לומר כמבעוד יום ולעיל ה"פ מדלא משנינן הכי לפי שאין נראה להם סברא לומר כן והוצרכו לומר משחשיכה קנסו מבעוד יום לא קנסו כדי לדחות שלא לפשוט בעיא דאביי א"כ תפשוט בעיא דרב ביבי אע"ג דאיכא למידחי בשינויא קמא ואי בעית למפשט דאביי נאמר כשינויא בתרא וזיל הכא קמדחי ליה כו' מ"מ חדא מינייהו מיפשטה ממה נפשך והשתא א"ש דקאמר ואב"א לעולם לא תפשוט לא דאביי ולא דרב ביבי: *בשוגג לא קנסוה. ומיירי מבעוד יום דהשתא ליכא למפשט דרב ביבי וא"ת מבעיא קמא נמי נפשוט בעיא דרב ביבי דלא התירו דלמטה מי' אסור להחזירה ואפילו מוקמי' מבעוד יום הא פירשתי דאי מבעו"י לא התירו כ"ש משחשיכה וי"ל דאין לפשוט דהתם מה שלא התירו משחשיכה אע"ג דאתי לידי חיוב חטאת היינו משום מבעו"י דלא שייך טעם זה אבל גבי רדיית הפת לעולם אימא דהתירו:
כאן

בר פחתי. *בן גדולים: לא תשייליה. כלומר שאין לבו למס' זו שמא יתביישו: מבעוד יום. דהיינו דומיא דהטעינו חבירו בשבת דהכא והכא ליכא עקירה דאיסור גביה: שאינו דומה לידו. הפשוטה לפנים וגופו לחוץ ונתן חברו לתוכה: אמר אביי פשיטא לי. ממתניתין דידו של אדם הפשוטה לרשות אחרת אינה נגררת אחר גופו לגמרי להיות כרשות שהוא עומד בה בין שהוא רשות היחיד בין שהוא רשות הרבים: כרה"ר לא דמיא מידו דעני. דקתני מתני' דכי נטל בע"ה מתוכה פטור: וכרה"י לא דמיא. אם פשוטה לרשות הרבים: מידו דבע"ה. דקתני נטל עני מתוכה פטור: בעי אביי. השתא דחזינן דלאו בתר גופו שדינן לה לענין איחיובי מדאורייתא אלמא איפלוג רשותא מי אחמור עלה רבנן למיהוי כרמלית דהיכא דהושיט ידו מלאה לרשות אחרת לא יחזירנה אצלו ותהא כך פשוטה עד שתחשך דכיון דלאו בתר גופו גרירא נעשית לה רשות אחרת מדרבנן דגזור רשות מדבריהם לשבת שאסור להכניס ולהוציא ממנו לרה"י ולרה"ר ושמו כרמלית כדתניא בפרקין (דף ו.) ד' רשויות לשבת כרמלית *לשון יערו וכרמלו שאינו לא הילוך תמיד לרבים ולא תשמיש רה"י: מי קנסוה. הואיל והתחיל בה באיסור: למטה מי'. רה"ר הוא קנסוה רבנן ושויוה כרמלית דלא ליהדרה: למעלה מי'. דאויר מקום פטור הוא כדתנן בהזורק (לקמן ק.) הזורק ד"א בכותל למעלה מי' טפחים כזורק באויר ופטור דלא הוי רה"ר למעלה מי' הלכך לא קנסוה דלאו איסורא עביד: ואיבעית אימא אידי ואידי למטה מי' טפחים ולאו ככרמלית דמיא. למהוי רשות לעצמה: כאן מבע"י. הושיטה מבע"י מחזירה משתחשך דלאו רשות לעצמה היא אלא בתר גופו גרירא: כאן משתחשך. הושיטה משחשיכה קנסוה ולא שתהא רשות לעצמה דא"כ אף מבעוד יום מיתסרא אלא קנסא בעלמא: מבע"י דאי שדי ליה. כלומר היכא דהושיטה מבעוד יום שאם תאסרנה להחזירה וישליך מידו החפץ כדי להקל טרחו לא אתי לידי חיוב חטאת דלא הוי עקירה בשבת אלא הנחה לחודיה ואיסורא דרבנן הוא דהיכא דעשה מקצתה וכדתנן שניהן פטורין אבל אסורין קנסוה רבנן שלא יחזירנה אבל היכא דהושיטה משחשכה דאי שדי ליה מידו על ידי קנס שתאסרנו להחזירה נמצא מתחייב חטאת אם שוגג הוא דעביד ליה עקירה והנחה לא קנסוה רבנן דמוטב שלא נקנסנו משנגרום לבא לידי חילול שבת דאורייתא ומדלא חיישת להכי תפשוט בעיא דרב ביבי דלא נמנעו חכמים מלהעמיד דבריהם מפני חשש שמא לא יעמוד האדם בהם ויעשה איסור חמור: הדביק פת בתנור. בשבת בשוגג ונזכר שהוא שבת קודם שתאפה וקיימא לן (לקמן דף קיז:) דרדיית הפת שבות היא שהיא חכמה ואינה מלאכה: התירו לו. את האיסור מדבריהם וירדנה קודם שתאפה ויתחייב משום אופה שהוא אב מלאכה או לא התירו לרדותה ולהוציאה מן התנור: בשוגג לא קנסוה רבנן כו'. ודרב ביבי לא תפשוט מהכא לא לאיסור ולא להיתר דהאי דלא קנסוה בשוגג לאו משום חששא דדילמא שדי להו מידיה הוא אלא משום דלא עבד איסורא במזיד וחזרת ידו אינה אפילו שבות אי לא משום קנסא והכא לא קנים אבל רדיית הפת שבות הוא וגזרה במכין ומשום קודם שיבא לידי חיוב חטאת לא בטלו גזירתם ולאיסור נמי לא תפשוט מדקנסו במזיד דהתם ליכא למיחש דילמא לישדינהו שיתחייב מיתת בית דין אבל הכא אי קנסינן ליה מלרדות על כרחיך יתחייב מיתת בית דין:
לאותה

מסורת הש"ס

[ברכות יג: וש"נ]

[ישעיה י]

גליון הש"ס

גמ' בר פחתי עיין לקמן דף כט ע"א: שם משחשיכה דאי שדי לי' וכו'. עיין עירובין ד"כ ע"א תוס' ד"ה לא יעמוד: שם תפשוט דרב ביבי וכו'. עי' ב"ק דכ"ג ע"א תוס' ד"ה תפשוט: שם הא לא קשיא וכו'. זבחים דף פז ע"ב: שם והכא בקנסו שוגג וכו'. עירובין דס"ח ע"ב וד"ק ע"א וגיטין דף נ"ג ע"א: רש"י ד"ה בר פחתי בן גדולים. מלשון הכתוב זרובבל פחת יהודה (חגי א) ומלשון המשנה הפחו' והסגני' (בכורים פ"ג מ"ג):

וא"ת היכי תפשוט הא דרב ביבי וודאי אתי לידי חיוב חטאת וי"ל דהכא נמי וודאי דא"א לו נתפוס שם ידו כל היום א"נ כ"ל להשוות דרב ביבי אף על גב דאתי וודאי לידי חיוב חטאת מ"מ איכא חדא עיטותא דהיכא איסור ברדיה והכא נמי אע"ג דלא אתי וודאי לידי חיוב חטאת ליכא איסור בחזרה [ת"י]:

נ"ל או מבעוד יום רש"ל וכ"מ גורס ומבע"י

*) [ועי' תוס' ר"ה כ"ט: ד"ה לרדיית הפת ועי' ערוך ערך רדה]

[עירובין סה: גיטין עג:]

בה"ג כתוב שדיבור זה עם דלעיל הוא דיבור אחד

רבינו חננאל

לעשות יותר ממה שעשה. והמעשה שעשה הנחה איכא עקירה ליכא הלכך הוא פטור אבל אסור. כיוצא בה בעה"ב שעקר חפץ מרה"י ונתנו לתוך ידו של עני והוציאו העני והניחו ברה"ר בעה"ב שעקר מרה"י ואילו הוציאו והניחו ברה"ר היה חייב חטאת חשיב ליה. אבל העני שהניח דלא אפשר ליה לאיתחובי כי האי גונא חטאת לא קתני ליה. כללו של דבר העוקר אתי לידי חיוב חטאת אילו הניח שהנחה אחר עקירה היא. אבל המניח לא אתי לידי חיוב חטאת לעולם שכבר נעקר מקודם. ולא נשאר למניח מה לעשות. נמצאו בבבא ד' פטורי ב' מהן יתכן שיבוא לידי חיוב חטאת. וב' מהן לא. וכן בבבא דסיפא ד' כיוצא בהן. נמצאו בהני ד' בבי י"ו. ד' מנהון חייב חטאת. וד' מנהון פטור ומותר. וד' מנהון פטור ולא אתי בהו לידי חיוב חטאת. וד' מנהון אתי בהו לידי חיוב חטאת. והאי תנא ד' דאית בהן חיוב חטאת. וד' פטורי דאתי בהן לידי חיוב חטאת קתני הני אחריני דפטור ומותר ופטורי דלא אתי בהו לידי חיוב חטאת לא קתני ועלתה השמועה יחיד שעשה חייב. שנים שעשו פטורין: ירושלמי מנין שההוצאה נקראת מלאכה שנאמר ויצו משה ויעבירו קול במחנה לאמר וגו'. בעא מיניה רב מר' הטעינו חבירו אוכלין ומשקין ברה"י והוציאו לחוץ מהו עקירת גופו כעקירת חפץ ממקומו דמי וחייב או לא. א"ל חייב ואינן דומה לידו דמתניתין שהנותן לתוכה, מוציא שניהם פטורים. מ"ט ידו לא ניהא בתר גופיה גרירה. ומקום שגופו עומד שם ידו חשיבה. כי אם יעתק הגוף ידו נמשכת עמו. וכיון שהגוף בחוץ כמו כן היד בחוץ חשיבה והנה לא עקר מרה"י אבל בעת שהגוף בפנים גופו נייח ובעי עקירה. ואם נתנדנד כאילו עקר והוציא חייב שנמצא כל מעשה בידו הוא עקר מבפנים והוא הוציא והניח וכ"ש אם הוא משא כבד. אמר אביי ידו של אדם אינה חשובה כרה"י מידו דעני הנתונה בחוץ*). שאילו היתה כרשות היחיד לא היה בעה"ב הנוטלו מתוכה חייב. ועוד אילו היתה כרה"ר לא נתחייב העני הנוטלו מתוכה והוא בבית חייב וכיון ד אמר אביי ידו של אדם אינה לא כרה"ר ולא כרה"י הוצרך לשאול מהו שתיחשב ידו ככרמלית ואם הוציאה בשבת בחפץ מותר לו להחזירה. כיון
שלא

*) בש"ס הגי' להיפך כרה"י לא דמיא מידו דבעה"ב וגי' רבינו המוה ואולי ט"ס נפל בדבריו וכ"צ

body is at rest[9] whereas his hand is not at rest.[10] [3b] Said R. Ḥiyya to Rab: Son of illustrious ancestors! Have I not told you that when Rabbi is engaged on one Tractate you must not question him about another, lest he be not conversant with it. For if Rabbi were not a great man, you would have put a him to shame, for he might have answered you incorrectly.[1] Still, he has now answered you correctly, for it was taught: If one was laden with food and drink while it was yet day,[2] and he carries them out after dark, he is culpable, because it is not like his hand.[3]

Abaye said: I am certain that a man's hand is neither like a public nor like a private domain:[4] it is not like a public domain—[this follows] from the poor man's hand;[5] it is not like a private domain—[this follows] from the hand of the master of the house.[6] Abaye propounded: Can a man's hand become as a *karmelith*:[7] did the Rabbis penalize him not to draw it back to himself, or not?—Come and hear: If one's hand is filled with fruit and he stretches it without—one [Baraitha] taught: He may not draw it back; another taught: He may draw it back. Surely they differ in this: one Master holds that it [the hand] is like a *karmelith*, and the other holds that it is not? No. All agree that it is like a *karmelith*, yet there is no difficulty: the one [refers to a case where it is] below ten [handbreadths], and the other [where it is] above ten [handbreadths].[8] Alternatively, both [Baraithas refer] to [a hand] below ten, and [hold that] it is not like a *karmelith*, yet there is no difficulty: one [speaks of a case] while it is yet day; the other, when it is already dark [the Sabbath has commenced]. [If he stretches out his hand] while it is yet day, the Rabbis did b not punish him;[1] if after sunset, the Rabbis punished it. On the contrary, the logic is the reverse: [if he stretches out his hand] by day, so that if he throws it [the article] away he does not come to the liability of a sin-offering,[2] let the Rabbis penalize him; but if [he does it] after nightfall, so that if he throws it away he incurs the liability of a sin-offering, the Rabbis should not punish him. Now, since we do not answer thus,[3] you may solve R. Bibi b. Abaye's [problem]. For R. Bibi b. Abaye asked: If a person places a loaf in an oven,[4] do the Rabbis permit him to remove it before he incurs the liability of a sin-offering, or not?[5] Now you may deduce that they do not permit it![6] That is no difficulty, and indeed solves it! Alternatively, you cannot solve it, after all: [and reply thus],[7] The one Baraitha refers to an unwitting, the other to a deliberate act. Where it is unwitting, the Rabbis did not punish him[8] for it; where it is deliberate, they punished.[9] Another alternative: both [Baraithas] refer to an unwitting act, but here they differ as to whether they [the Rabbis] punished an unwitting [offender] on account of a deliberate one: one Master holds that they did punish an unwitting [offender] on account of a deliberate one; the other, that they did not punish an unwitting [offender] on account of a deliberate one. Another alternative: after all, they did not punish [the one on account of the other], yet there is no difficulty. The one [Baraitha] means into the same courtyard;

(9) Hence the article upon his body is likewise at rest, and he effects its removal. (10) On the ground: hence he does not actually remove the article from its place.

a (1) Lit., 'he would have given you an answer which is not an answer.' (2) I.e., before sunset on Friday. (3) As explained above. (4) If a man stands in one and stretches out his hand into the other, the hand is not accounted the same as his body, to have the legal status of the domain in which the body is. (5) For the Mishnah states that if the Master takes an article from the poor man's hand stretched within he is exempt. (6) If the poor man takes an object from it, he is not liable. (7) V. *infra* 6a. A *karmelith* is part of a public domain which is but little frequented, therefore regarded as neither public nor private ground; by Rabbinical law one may not carry from a *karmelith* to a public or a private domain, or *vice versa*. Now, as we have seen, when one stretches out his hand into another domain, it does not enjoy the body's status. Yet does it occupy the intermediate status of a *karmelith*, and since it holds an object, its owner shall be forbidden to withdraw it until the termination of the Sabbath? (8) V. *infra* 100a. If the hand is within ten handbreadths from the ground it is in a public domain, and therefore the Rabbis ordered that he must not withdraw it. But if it is above, it is in a place of non-liability; hence he is not penalized.

b (1) Lit. 'it' sc. his hand. They did not compel him to keep his hand stretched out till the termination of the Sabbath. (2) Since he does not perform a complete forbidden act on the Sabbath. (3) This reversed answer. (4) Lit., 'sticks a loaf to (the wall of) an oven.' (5) If it remains in the oven until baked he incurs a sin-offering for baking on the Sabbath. On the other hand, it is Rabbinically forbidden to remove bread from the oven on the Sabbath. How is it here? (6) Since the reverse answer is not given, we see that the Rabbis do not abrogate their interdict even when it leads to a liability to a sin-offering. (7) To reconcile the two Baraithas. (8) V. n. b1. (9) Thus this has no bearing on R. Bibi b. Abaye's problem.

a [4a] the other, into a different courtyard.[1] Even as Raba asked R. Naḥman: If a person holds a handful of produce in his hand and he extends it without,[2] may he withdraw it into the same courtyard? He replied, It is permitted. And what about another courtyard? Said he to him, It is forbidden. And what is the difference?—When you measure out a measure of salt for it![3] There his intention is not carried out; here his intention is carried out.[4]

[To revert to] the main text: 'R. Bibi b. Abaye propounded: If one places a loaf of bread in an oven, do they permit him to remove it before he incurs the liability of a sin-offering or not?' R. Aḥa b. Abaye said to Rabina: What are the circumstances? Shall we say [that he did it] unwittingly and he did not remind himself;[5] then whom are they to permit?[6] Hence it must surely mean that he did afterwards become aware thereof;[7] but then would he be liable? Surely we learnt: All who are liable to sin-offerings are liable only if the beginning and end [of the forbidden action] are unwitting. On the other hand, if his problem refers to a deliberate action, he should have asked [whether he may remove it] before he comes to an interdict involving stoning![8]—R. Shila said: After all, it means unwittingly; and [as to the question] 'whom are they to permit?', [the reply is], Others. R. Shesheth demurred: Is then a person told, 'Sin, in order that your neighbour may gain thereby?'[9] Rather, said R. Ashi, after all it refers to a deliberate act; but say [in the b problem], before he comes to an interdict involving stoning.[1] R. Aḥa son of Raba recited it explicitly: R. Bibi b. Abaye said: If one places a loaf in an oven, he is permitted to remove it before he comes to an interdict involving stoning.

IF THE POOR MAN STRETCHES HIS HAND WITHIN. Why is he liable? Surely removal and depositing must be from [and into] a place four [handbreadths] square,[2] which is absent here?[3]—Said Rabbah: The author of this [Mishnah] is R. Akiba, who maintains: We do not require a place four by four. For we learnt: If one throws [an article] from one private domain to another and public ground lies between: R. Akiba holds him liable; but the Sages hold him not liable. R. Akiba holds: We say, An object intercepted by [air] is as though it rested there;[4] while the Rabbis maintain: We do not say, An object intercepted by [air] is as though it rested there. Shall we say that Rabbah is certain that

a (1) When one stands in a courtyard, which is private ground, and stretches his laden hand into the street, he may withdraw it into the same courtyard, but not into an adjoining one and drop the article there. (2) I.e., into the street. (3) A jesting remark: then I will tell you the difference. (4) If he stretches out his hand into the street he wants to remove the produce from that courtyard. Hence he may draw it back into the same, when his intention remains unfulfilled, but not into an adjoining courtyard, whereby his intention would be carried out. (5) Before it was completely baked, that it was the Sabbath, or that baking on the Sabbath is forbidden. (6) Being unaware of anything wrong, he does not come to ask. (7) Before it was baked. (8) Which is the penalty for the deliberate desecration of the Sabbath, and not 'before he incurs the liability of a sin-offering'? (9) Can one be told to infringe the minor injunction of removing bread from an oven in order to save his neighbour from the greater transgression of baking on the Sabbath?

b (1) From this it is obvious that R. Bibi's original question was merely whether he is permitted to remove it or not. 'Before he incurs etc.,' was a later addition, which R. Ashi emends. The same assumption must be made in similar cases. V. Kaplan, *Redaction of the Talmud*, Ch. XIII. (2) Removal from one domain and depositing in the other necessitates in each case that the object shall rest upon a place four handbreadths square. (3) A person's hand does not fulfil this condition. (4) Hence when it crosses public ground it is as though it rested there, and so liability is incurred.

כאן לחצר אחרת כדבעא מיניה רבא מר"נ היתה ידו מלאה פירות והוציאה לחוץ מהו להחזירה לאותה חצר א"ל מותר לחצר אחרת מהו א"ל אסור ומאי שנא לכי *תיכול עלה כורא דמילחא התם לא איתעבידא מחשבתו הכא איתעבידא מחשבתו: גופא בעי רב ביבי בר אביי הדביק פת בתנור התירו לו לרדותה קודם שיבוא לידי חיוב חטאת או לא התירו א"ל רב אחא בר אביי לרבינא היכי דמי אילימא בשוגג ולא אידכר ליה למאן התירו °ואלא לאו דאיהדר ואדכר *מי מחייב והתנן *כל חייבי חטאות אינן חייבין עד שתהא תחלתן שגגה וסופן שגגה אלא במזיד קודם שיבא לידי איסור סקילה מיבעי ליה אמר רב שילא לעולם בשוגג ולמאן התירו לאחרים מתקיף לה רב ששת *וכי אומרים לו לאדם חטא כדי שיזכה חבירך אלא אמר רב אשי לעולם במזיד ואימא קודם שיבא לידי איסור סקילה רב אחא בריה דרבא מתני לה בהדיא אמר רב ביבי בר אביי °הדביק פת בתנור התירו לו לרדותה קודם שיבא לידי איסור סקילה: פשט העני את ידו: אמאי חייב *והא בעינן עקירה והנחה מעל גבי מקום ד' על ד' וליכא אמר רבה הא מני ר"ע דאמר לא בעינן מקום ארבעה על ארבעה *דתנן הזורק מרשות היחיד לרשות הרבים ורשות הרבים באמצע רבי עקיבא מחייב וחכמים פוטרים ר"ע סבר אמרינן *קלוטה כמי שהונחה דמיא ורבנן סברי לא אמרינן קלוטה כמי שהונחה דמיא למימרא דפשיטא ליה לרבה דבקלוטה כמי שהונחה דמיא

ובתוך

רש"י

לאותה חצר. שהוא עומד בתוכה מותר להחזירה אבל לחצר אחרת הסמוכה לה אסור לזורקה: לכי תיכול עלה כורא דמילחא. בבדיחותא אהדר ליה כשתמדוד לי כור של מלח אומר לך טעמו של דבר לישנא אחרינא לכשתאכל עליה כור של מלח לא תוכל להשוותם זו לזו: מחשבתו. שנתכוון לפנותה מחצר זה לא נתקיימה הלכך לא גזרו אבל לחצר אחרת נתקיימה מחשבתו וגזור דילמא זימנא אחריתי שדי להו לרה"ר: ולא אידכר. קודם אפייה על שגגתו שהיא שבת או שמלאכה זו אסורה: למאן התירו. הא לא מסיק אדעתיה לבא לישאל על כך: ואלא דאיהדר ואידכר. קודם אפייה: מי מחייב. חטאת באפייתו: תחלתה וסופה. תחלת המלאכה וסופה לא נודעה לו שגגתו עד שנגמרה עבירה: לאחרים. אחר שראה ובא לפניו לישאל לרדותה קודם שיבא חבירו לידי חיוב חטאת: וכי אומרים לו לאדם. לא וחטא איסור קל כדי שלא יתחייב חבירך עונש חמור: בהדיא. סקילה ובלשון פשיטותא ולא בלשון בעיא מתני רב אחא בריה דרבא מילתא דרב ביבי: מעל גבי מקום ד'. דהוי חשוב למיהוי הנחתו הנחה ועקירתו עקירה וידו לאו מקום ד' הוא וקתני לה מתני' בין לעקירה בין להנחה דקתני ונתן לתוך ידו של בעל הבית הרי הנחה או שנטל מתוכה הרי עקירה: קלוטה. החפץ הואיל ונקלט באוירה של רשות הרבים כמי שהונחה בתוכו הוא ואע"ג דלא נח:

תוספות

כאן לחצר אחרת. ואסור להחזירה דקתני לא להחזירה אלא קאמר אלא להחזירה לחצר אחרת: ומאי שנא. בזו כנגד זו איירי דבדיוטא אחת שנא ושנא דאיכא איסור חיוב חטאת דמושיט מרה"י לרה"י דרך רה"ר א"נ בדיוטא אחת וכגון שאין מפסיק שם רה"ר:

ואלא דאהדר ואידכר מי מחייב. תימה דלישני אימא לידי (חיוב) איסור חטאת כדקאמר בסמוך קודם שיבא לידי איסור סקילה:

וכי אומרים לו לאדם חטא בשביל שיזכה חבירך. והא דאמר בכל מערבין (עירובין לב: ושם) רבי סבר ניחא ליה לחבר דליעבד איסורא קלילא ולא ליעבד עם הארץ איסורא רבה התם כדי שלא יאכל ע"ה טבל על ידו דאמר לי' מלא לך כלכלה של תאנים מתאנתי אבל הכא שלא נעשה האיסור על ידו אין אומרים לו חטא אפי' איסור קל שלא יבא חבירו לידי איסור חמור ואומר ריב"א דאפי' למדביק עצמו אין לפשוט מכאן להתיר דהתם עדיין לא נעשה האיסור ומוטב שיעשה איסור קל ולא יעשה איסור חמור על ידו אבל הכא המעשה של איסור כבר נעשה וממילא יגמור לא יעשה אפי' איסור קל בידים והא דתנן בהשולח (גיטין דף מא: ושם) מי שחציו עבד וחציו בן חורין כופין את רבו ועושה אותו בן חורין ואע"ג דבהאי פירקא (דף לח:) א"ר יהודה כל המשחרר עבדו עובר בעשה דלעולם בהם תעבודו שאני פריה ורביה דמצוה רבה היא כדמשני התם בר"א שנכנס לבה"מ ולא מצא שם י' ושחרר את עבדו להשלימו לי' מצוה דרבים שאני ועוד י"ל דדוקא היכא דפשע קאמר וכי אומרים לו לאדם חטא כדי כו' ואתי שפיר הא דאמרי' בריש תמיד נשחט (פסחים דף נט. ושם) דאתי עשה דפסח שיש בו כרת ודחי עשה דהשלמה וקא עברי כהנים בעשה דהשלמה ומקריבין למחוסר כפורים כפרתו כדי שיביא פסחו וכן בפרק בתרא דעירובין (דף קג: ושם) כהן שנמצא בו יבלת חבירו חותכה לו בשיניו אע"ג דהוי שבות וגבי חציה שפחה וחציה בת חורין שנהגו בה מנהג הפקר וכפו את רבה בהשולח (גיטין דף לח:) משום שהיתה מחזרת וממציאה עצמה לזנות ודומי' לאנוסין *והוי נמי כמצוה דרבים:

קודם שיבא לידי איסור סקילה. וא"ת מאי בעיא היא זו אם התירו לרדותה פשיטא שלא ישמע לנו אם נאסור לו ותי' ריב"א *דאם לא התירו לא מיחייב סקילה כיון שמניח מלרדות ע"י מה שאנו אוסרין לו וכן בפסחים בס"פ האשה (דף צב. ושם) ערל הזאה ואיזמל העמידו דבריהם במקום כרת אלמא לא מיחייב כרת הואיל ורבנן הוא דאסרי ליה למיעבד פסח וא"ת והיכי אתי לידי חיוב סקילה והא התראת ספק הוא דבשעה שהדביק פת בתנור שמא היה בדעתו לרדותה קודם שיבא לידי איסור סקילה ומה שלא רדה שמא שכח ההתראה ותי' ריב"א דכיון שהדביק תוך כדי דבור של התראה °ובודאי תאפה אם לא ירדנה לאו התראת ספק הוא °דודאי לא היה בדעתו לרדות קודם אפייה ולא הוי התראת ספק אלא בלוקח אם על הבנים למ"ד בפ' ואלו הן הלוקין (מכות דף טו.) בטלו ולא בטלו דשמא לא ישבור כנפיה או לא ישחטנה ועכשיו שמשבר כנפיה אין יכולין להתרותו דלא הויא התראה אלא על הלאו והלאו כבר עבר וכן בשבועה שלא אוכל ככר זו אם אוכל זו ואכליה לאיסוריה והדר אכליה לתנאיה דכשמתרין בו בשעת אכילת איסור עדיין מחוסר מעשה אכילה של תנאי קודם שיתחייב מלקות אבל הכא כשמדביק פת בתנור אין האפייה מחוסרת מעשה:

מתני' לה בהדיא. אית ספרים דגרסי בעי רב ביבי ומתני בהדיא בבעיא דרב ביבי איסור סקילה:

והא בעינן עקירה והנחה מעל מקום ד'. אומר ר"ת דאין רגילות להניח החפץ בפחות מד' וכן היה מסתמא במשכן ועוד אומר ר"י דאל יצא איש ממקומו משמע דקאי נמי אחפץ כלומר ממקומו של חפץ דרשינן בעירובין (פ"ה ד' יז:) דאל יצא אל יוציא אע"ג דפשטיה דקרא קאי אמקומו של אדם דהיינו ד' אמות מ"מ משמע נמי מקום החפץ ואין מקום חשוב בפחות מד':

*אבל למעלה מי' ד"ה פטור. יש להוכיח קצת מכאן דמושיט חייב נמי למטה מי' דאם תמצא לומר פטור לפי שלא מצינו במשכן מושיט למטה מי' שהעגלות היו גבוהים י' א"כ לימא הכא אבל למעלה מי' ד"ה חייב דילפינן זורק ממושיט אבל עתה דמושיט חייב למטה מי' אז לא מצי למימר למעלה מי' ד"ה חייב דא"כ למטה מי' מ"ט פטור זורק ומיהו אינו הוכחה דלא מצי למימר דלכ"ע ילפינן זורק ממושיט דא"כ הא דתנן לקמן בהזורק (דף צו.) היו שתיהן בדיוטא אחת הזורק פטור והמושיט חייב אלמא לא ילפי' זורק ממושיט אמאן תרמייה ותדע דהא כי נמי נימא דמושיט חייב למטה מי' הוי מצי למימר דלכ"ע ילפי' זורק ממושיט ובדיוטא אחת בין למטה מי' בין למעלה מי' ד"ה חייב ופליגי למטה מי' בזו כנגד זו דמר סבר אמרינן קלוטה כמי שהונחה דמיא ומר סבר לא אמרינן אלא דלא מצי למימר דלכ"ע ילפינן זורק ממושיט משום מתני' דהזורק ולמאי שנפרש בסמוך אתי נמי שפיר דלא נקט הכי:

דרבי עקיבא סבר ילפי' זורק ממושיט. וא"ת והא ע"כ זורק מרשות היחיד לרה"י דרך רשות הרבים לא היה במשכן דאם היה במשכן מה צריך למילף ממושיט ומ"ט נמי דרבנן דפטרי וכיון דלא היה במשכן אמאי מחייב ר"ע דבתולדה דהוצאה שהיא מלאכה גרועה אין לנו לחייב אלא דוקא אותן שהיו במשכן כדפרישית לעיל (ד' ב:) וי"ל דר"ע סבר דזורק דמי טפי למושיט ממאי דדמו שאר תולדות להוצאה:

אבל למטה מי' ד"ה חייב דאמר קלוטה כמי שהונחה. °כשהחפץ בידו של עני או של בעה"ב לא שייך קלוטה דהא כשנותן בעה"ב לתוך ידו והוציא לא מחייב תימה לר"י אם ברייתא היא בשום מקום דבעינן הנחה על גבי מקום ד' וכדמשמע קצת בסמוך דא"ר זירא הא מני אחרים היא משמע דפליגי רבנן עליה אם כן היכי קאמר הכא ד"ה חייב אם כן ההיא ברייתא מני ונראה דלא קשה מידי שיעמיד ר"ע ורבנן כמתניתין ולא כההיא ברייתא דניחא ליה להעמיד מתני' ככ"ע:

דאמרינן קלוטה כמי שהונחה דמיא. וקשה לר"י דמאי פריך למימרא דפשיטא ליה לרבה מנא ליה דפשיטא ליה לרבה אי משום דקאמר הא מני ר"ע היא היינו משום דלר"ע אית ליה ממה נפשך קלוטה כמי שהונחה דמיא אבל אליבא דרבנן מספקא ליה ולהכי לא הוה מצי למימר הא מני רבנן היא ואם היינו אומרים הא דקאמר לעיל רבי עקיבא סבר קלוטה כמי שהונחה דמיא ורבנן כו' הכל מדברי רבה היא הוה אתי שפיר אך אין נראה שיהא מדברי רבה ואומר ר"י דהכי פירושו והא מיבעיא בעי לרבה וכיון דאיכא לספוקי בפלוגתייהו איכא נמי לספוקי דילמא לכולי עלמא לא אמרינן קלוטה כמי שהונחה ובזו כנגד זו לכ"ע פטור כי פליגי

בדיוטא

עין משפט נר מצוה

ז א מיי' פי"א מהל' שבת הלכה יט ופ"ב מהל' שגגות הלכה א סמג עשין ריג:

ח ב מיי' פ"ג שם הל' י"ח ופ"ט הל' ה' ופ' כ"ב מהלכות שבת הלכה א סמג לאוין סה טוש"ע א"ח סי' רנד סעיף ו:

ט ג מיי' פי"ג מהל' שבת הלכה א ופי"ד הלכה יד סמג שם טוש"ע א"ח סי' שמה סעיף יט יעוין סי' שמח:

קשה לרשב"א דכי אידכר נמי יכול לבוא לידי חטאת אם שכח לנסוף קודם שנאפה הפת כדמוכח ס"פ הזורק ואומר מהר"ת דהא לא שכיח שיחזור וישכח [תוס' ישנים]

רבינו חננאל

שלא הניח החפץ אי לא. תני חדא מותר להחזירה ותניא אידך אסור. ושקלינן וטרינן ואסקינן הא דתני מותר להחזירה באותה חצר ופירשה רב נחמן באותה חצר שהוציאה ממנה שהרי לא עשה כלום כי לא נעשית מחשבתו. שרצה להשליכן לחצר אחרת ולא עלתה לו מחשבתו. והא דתני אסור להחזירה בחצר אחרת שהרי אם יחזירנה לחצר אחרת הרי נעשית מחשבתו ולפיכך אסור. בעיא דרב ביבי בר אביי תירצה רב אשי הכי הדביק פת בתנור בשבת במזיד התירו לו לרדותה קודם שתיאפה שלא יבא

תימה למהר"ר שמואל ממירבורא א"כ מאי קא מיבעיא כיון דבין התירו בין לא התירו לא מחייב פשיטא דלא יתירו וי"ל דנ"מ אם התירו דמחייב אם לא ירדה א"כ כיא גופא קא מיבעי' ליה התירו דאם לא יתירו מחייב ול"ד להניא דפסחים כיון דפשע או לא התירו דלא מחייב אע"ג דפשע מתחלה בשאה מיהא אינו מניח מלרדות אלא ע"י שאסרו לו חכמים [תוס' ישנים] [שייך לע"ב]

רב נסים גאון

פרק א אבל למעלה מעשרה דברי הכל פטור ולא ילפי' זורק ממושיט. עיקרו במשנה בפרק הזורק (דף צו) היו שתיהן בדיוטי אחת הזורק פטור והמושיט חייב שכך היתה עבודת הלוים ב' עגלות זו אחר זו ברה"ר משיטין את הקרשים מזו לזו אבל לא זורקין ולפום דהויין

מסורת הש"ס

[עירובין לו. חולין יב. קיב.]

לקמן קב.

מנחות מח. [קידושין נה:] ועי' בעירובין לג:

[עי' תוס' לקמן ז. ד"ה וטח]

לקמן צו

[שם ז. גיטין עט. ב"ק ע:]

[תוס' גיטין מח: סוף ד"ה כופין כתבו ועוד מצוה דרבים שאני ג"ש ועי' תוס' פסחים פח: ד"ה כופין]

גליון הש"ס

גמ' ואלא לאו דאהדר ואידכר מי מחייב. עיין שו"ת תולדות אדם המיוחסו' לרמב"ן סי' ר"ה: תוס' ד"ה קוד' שיבא וכו' ובודאי תאפה אם לא ירדנה. עיין גיטין דף לג ע"א תוס' ד"ה ואפקעינהו בא"ד דודאי לא היה בדעתו לרדות מל' זה משמע דמש"ה לא הוי התראת ס'. והלא ממש"כ אח"כ וכן בשבועה לא אוכל זה אם אוכל זה. משמע דשלא אוכל זו אם לא אוכל זו לא הוי התראת ס' כיון דמחוסר מעשה אף דלא שייך לומר דהיה בדעתו שלא לאכלו דהא אפילו בהיפוך מראה דעתו לאכלו: תוס' ד"ה אבל למטה וכו' כשהחפץ בידו. ע"ל לב ע"

ובתוך עשרה פליגי והא מיבעיא בעי לה רבה דבעי רבה *למטה מי' פליגי ובהא פליגי דר"ע סבר *קלוטה כמי שהונחה דמיא ורבנן סברי לא אמרינן קלוטה במי שהונחה דמיא אבל למעלה מי' דברי הכל פטור ודכ"ע לא ילפינן זורק ממושיט או דילמא למעלה מי' פליגי ובהא פליגי דר"ע סבר ילפינן זורק ממושיט ורבנן סברי לא ילפינן זורק ממושיט אבל למטה מי' דברי הכל חייב מאי טעמא אמרינן קלוטה כמי שהונחה דמיא הא לא קשיא בתר דאיבעי הדר איפשיטא ליה *דסבר ר"ע קלוטה כמי שהונחה דמיא ודילמא הנחה הוא דלא בעיא הא עקירה בעיא אלא אמר רב יוסף הא מני רבי היא הי רבי אילימא הא ר' דתניא *זרק ונח ע"ג זיז כל שהוא רבי מחייב וחכמים פוטרין התם כדבעי' למימר לקמן כדאביי *דאמר אביי הכא באילן העומד ברה"י ונופו נוטה לר"ה וזרק ונח אנופו דר' סבר אמרי' *שדי נופו בתר עיקרו ורבנן סברי לא אמרי' שדי נופו בתר עיקרו אלא הא ר' *דתניא זרק מרה"ר לרה"ר ורה"י באמצע *ר' מחייב וחכמים פוטרין ואמר רב יהודה אמר שמואל מחייב היה ר' שתים אחת משום הוצאה ואחת משו' הכנסה אלמא לא בעי עקירה ולא הנחה ע"ג מקום ד' על ד' הא איתמר עלה רב ושמואל דאמרי תרווייהו

לא

ובתוך י'· דאילו למעלה מי' לאו אויר ר"ה הוא אלא אויר מקום פטור הוא ואפי' קלוטה ליכא: זורק ממושיט· דאילו במושיט מרה"י לרה"י דרך ר"ה אפי' למעלה מי' קיימא לן בפ' הזורק דחייב דיליף מעגלות של מדבר שמושיטין את הקרשים מזו לזו והן רה"י וביניהם ר"ה ולא היו זורקים אותן שלא יתקלקלו: ודילמא הנחה הוא דלא בעיא· מדקתני ר"ע מחייב אבל עקירה בעי מעל גבי מקום ד' מדלא קתני ר"ע מחייב שתים אחת משום הוצאה ואחת משום הכנסה: זרק· מר"ה מתחלת ד' לסוף ד' ונח' ע"ג זיז מכל שהיוצא מן הכותל קרי זיז: רבי מחייב· אלמא דלא בעי הנחה על מקום ד': שדי נופו בתר עיקרו· והוי כמונח בר"ה על מקום ד' דעיקר מחשב ליה לנוף: מחייב היה ר' שתים· דהוי כאלו נח ברה"י וחזר ונעקר משם והכניס לר"ה אלמא לא עקירה בעי ולא הנחה בעי ע"ג מקו' ד':

מקורה

בדיומא אחת דר"ע סבר ילפי' זורק ממושיט ורבנן סברי לא ילפינן אלא דרבה לא חש לפרש כל הבעיות ועוד אומר ר"י דהא דקאמר הש"ס אבל למטה מעשרה ד"ה חייב דאמרינן קלוטה כמי שהונחה הייט לרבנן אבל לר"ע קלוטה לאו כמי שהונחה דמיא ומחייב משום דילפינן זורק ממושיט דאי סבר כמי שהונחה דמיא *לא הוה מצי למילף זורק ממושיט דהא לא דמיא כלל דכיון דכמי שהונחה דמיא הוי [זורק למעלה מעשר'] כזורק מרה"י למקום פטור וממקום פטור לרה"י ולא דמי כלל למושיט שהוא מרה"י לרה"י ורה"ר באמצע אלמא ע"כ כיון דסבר ילפינן זורק ממושיט סבר קלוטה לאו כמי שהונחה דמיא והשתא אתי שפיר דפריך למימרא דפשיטא ליה כו' ואתי נמי שפיר דלא מצי למימר לעיל אבל למעלה מי' ד"ה חייב דילפינן זורק ממושיט דלר"ע לא מצי למילף כיון דסבר כמי שהונחה דמיא וכן משמע קצת דהא רב חסדא בעי נמי בהזורק (לקמן דף צז·) כמו רבה דהכא ואי הא דקא מסיים קלוטה כמי שהונחה דמיא קאי נמי אדר"ע היכי מצי למימר לרב חסדא דלכ"ע כמי שהונחה דמיא ולקמן בפירקין (דף ח·) משמע דדוקא ברה"י לא בעי רב חסדא הנחה ע"ג מקום ארבעה ומיהו רשב"א פירש בסמוך אף ברה"ר לא בעי רב חסדא מקום ד': **ודילמא** הנחה הוא דלא בעיא הא עקירה בעיא· פירש"י דדייק מדלא מחייב ב' אחת משום הוצאה ואחת משום הכנסה וקשה *דילמא הא דלא מחייב ב' משום דלא מחייב אתולדה במקום אב ועוד דבסמוך קאמר רב יהודה מחייב היה רבי ב' אע"ג דקתני סתם רבי מחייב ה"נ לר"ע מנ"ל דלא מחייב שתים ונראה לפרש דפריך הא עקירה בעיא דילפינן ממשכן מתיבתן שהיו נוטלין בהן ארבע על ארבע ונותנין ליד עושי המלאכה ולפי מה שפירשתי לעיל דדרשינן מאל יצא איש ממקומו אתי נמי שפיר דבעקירה מיירי: **אלא** א"ר יוסף כו'· קשה לרשב"א מה צריכין רבה ורב יוסף להעמיד המשנה כתנאים והא סבירא להו בפ"ב דעירובין (ד' צט· ושם) דמחשבתו משויא ליה מקום דקאמר התם רב יוסף השתין ורק חייב חטאת ופריך והא בעינן מקום ד' וליכא ומשני מחשבתו משויא ליה מקום דאי לא תימא הכי הא דאמר רבה זרק בפי כלב או בפי כבשן חייב וכו' ותי' ר"ת דהא דאמר מחשבתו משויא ליה מקום היינו היכא דלא ניחא לי' בענין אחר אלא בענין זה כמו משתין ורק שאינו יכול להשתין או לרוק בענין אחר וכן זרק בפי כלב שרצונו שיאכלנו הכלב או שישרוף העץ בכבשן ול"ג התם ונח בפי כלב דנח משמע דאין כוונתו לכך אבל הכא אינו חושש אם מקבל בידו או בכלי אחר והא דאמר לקמן (ד' ה.) ה"א ה"מ היכא דאחשבה לידו אע"ג דניחא ליה שיקבלנו בע"א כמו בידו הייט משום דקאמר דידו של אדם חשובה לו כד' על ד' אבל בשאר דברים לא משוי ליה מחשבתו אלא היכא דלא ניחא ליה בע"א: **זרק** ונח ע"ג זיז כל שהוא ר' מחייב· וא"ת אכתי תקשה לך דילמא הנחה הוא דלא בעיא הא עקירה בעיא וי"ל דבלאו הכי פריך שפיר אבל קשה לספרים דגרסי לקמן בהזורק (ד' צז·) על מילתא דרב יהודה דאמר בסמוך מחייב היה רבי שתים ויתיב רב חסדא וקא קשיא ליה למימרא דמחייב רבי אתולדה במקום אב וכו' א"ל רב יוסף מר אדר' מתני לה וקשיא ליה אנן אדר' יהודה מתניגן לה לדברי ר"י דאמר חייב ב' אבל לר' לא מחייב ב' דלא מחייב ר' אתולדה במקום אב אם כן מה תירץ רב יוסף הא מני ר' היא אכתי תקשה דילמא הנחה הוא דלא בעי הא עקירה בעי וי"ל דסבר רב יוסף דדוקא אקלוטה דר"ע דליכא הנחה כלל איכא למיפרך הא עקירה בעי אבל אר' דבעי הנחה ע"ג זיז כל שהוא ה"ה דלעקירה סגיא בכל שהוא ומיהו להש"ס בסמוך לית ליה סברא דרב יוסף דפריך אדרבי זירא דילמא אחרים בעו עקירת מקום ד' ולא סגיא בכל שהוא כמו בהנחה ולר"ת נראה דגרסינן בהזורק יתיב רב יוסף וקא קשיא ליה א"ל רב חסדא וכו' ואתי שפיר דרב יוסף הוה מתני דברי רב יהודה אדר' ובסמוך דפריך והא איתמר כו' הוה מצי למיפרך הא דקשיא ליה לרב יוסף בהזורק (שם:) דרבי לא מחייב אתולדה במקום אב דתניא ר' אומר דברים הדברים אלה הדברים וכגירסת ר"ת נראה דלהוות גירסא דמתני רב יוסף מילתא דרב יהודה דמחייב ב' ארבי יהודה קשה דרב יוסף אדרב יוסף דהתם אומר בהדיא רבה ורב יוסף דאמרי תרווייהו לא מחייב ר"י אלא אחת ויש לדחות דרב יוסף משמי' דרב יהודה קאמר (*) ורב יהודה מחייב שתים וליה לא סבירא ליה: **באילן** העומד ברה"י ונופו נוטה לרשות הרבים· הכא בשמעתין הוה מצי לאוקמי באילן שעיקרו ונופו כולו קאי ברה"י ויש בעיקרו ד' דרבי סבר שדי נופו בתר עיקרו וחשיבא מקום ד' ורבנן סברי לא אמרינן שדי נופו בתר עיקרו ולא הוי מקום ד' דברה"י נמי סברא שמעתין דבעינן מקום ד' על ד' מדאמר בסמוך תני טרסקל שבידו הא תינח ברה"י משמע דברה"י נמי מהדרינן לאשכוחי מקום ארבע אלא נקט בכה"ג משום דמילתא דאביי איתמר בפרקין אמילתא דרב חסדא דאמר נעץ קנה ברה"י וזרק ונח על גביו אפילו גבוה מאה אמה חייב ופריך לימא דרב חסדא דאמר כרבי ומשני דברה"י כ"ע לא פליגי כדרב חסדא והכא באילן העומד ברה"י ונופו נוטה לרה"ר ומיירי אפילו אין בעיקרו ד' דרבי סבר שדי נופו בתר עיקרו דהויא כרה"י וחייב אע"ג דלא הוי מקום ד' כדרב חסדא ורבנן סברי לא אמרינן שדי נופו בתר עיקרו אבל קשה אמאי לא משני אביי לקמן באילן העומד כולו ברה"ר ויש בעיקרו ד' דרבי סבר שדי נופו כו' וחשיב מקום ד' ולרבנן לא הוי מקום ד' דברה"ר מודה רב חסדא דבעינן מקום ד' דברה"י דווקא קאמר רב חסדא כדמשמע לקמן דקאמר ברשות היחיד כולי עלמא לא פליגי כדרב חסדא ויש לומר דברה"ר לא מצי לאוקמי דאי הנוף למטה מג' לא הוו פטרי רבנן אע"ג דליכא ד' דכארעא סמיכתא היא ואי למעלה מג' לא הוה מחייב ר' דכרמלית היא אם רחב ארבע או מקום פטור אם אינו רחב ד' ולרשב"א נראה דברשות הרבים נמי משכחת לה למימר שדי נופו בתר עיקרו כגון שעיקרו פחות משלשה או גבוה ט' ורבים מכתפים עליו דהוו רה"ר ונופו עולה למעלה מג' דלרבי הוי נוף רשות הרבים דשדינן ליה בתר עיקרו לשויא רה"י ולרבנן לא הוי כרה"ר והא דלא מוקי ליה אביי הכי *משום דרב חסדא לא בעי מקום ד' גם ברשות הרבים דמ"מ ורב חסדא נקט רשות היחיד משום דבעי לאשמעינן אפילו גבוה מאה אמות משום דרה"י עולה עד לרקיע ואיידי דנקט איהו רשות היחיד נקט נמי בתר הכי ברה"י כ"ע לא פליגי כו' ולמאי דמוקי לה אביי לקמן אליבא דרב חסדא הא דנקט זיז כל שהוא דהא אפי' ברוחב ד' נמי פליגי אומר רשב"א דנקט כל שהוא לאשמעינן משום למעלה מי' דאי הוי רחב ד' הוי רה"י ולא הוו פטרי רבנן*)(אי אין) גדיים בוקעין תחתיו אי סברי כר' יוסי בר' יהודה בהזורק (לקמן ד' קא·) ואין נראה לר"י דמשמע דמשום רבותא דר' נקט לה ואומר ר"י דאי הוה נקיט זיז סתמא הוה סלקא דעתך דמיירי ברחב ארבע וטעמא דר' לאו משום שדי נופו בתר עיקרו אלא ה"א דסבר כרבי יוסי בר"י דנעץ קנה ברה"ר ובראשו טרסקל להכי נקט כל שהוא לאשמעינן דטעמא דרבי משום שדי נופו כו' ורש"י שפירש כאן משום שדי נופו בתר עיקרו והוי כמונח ברשות הרבים ע"ג מקום ד' אי אפשר להעמידה דאי למטה מג' לא בעי רחב ד' לכ"ע ולמעלה מג' לא הוי רה"ר אם לא נעמיד בדבילה שמנה וטח בצד הנוף:

לא

ז"ל אפילו

זאינה כוכחה דלא אמר קלוט' כמי שהונחה דמיא אלא להחמיר דאי להקל נמי אמרו א"כ זורק ד"א ברה"ר היכי משכחת לה [תוס' ישנים]

רבינו חננאל

לידי איסור סקילה או לא שהאופה מאבות מלאכות היא*) ולא אפשיטא. וקשי' לן מכדי רדיית הפת חכמה ואינה מלאכה. דגרסי' בפ' כל כתבי הקדש תנא דבי שמואל כל מלאכת עבודה לא תעשו. יצא תקיעת שופר ורדיית הפת שהיא חכמה ואינה מלאכה. וכיון שאינה מלאכה אמאי לא פשטי בה להיתרא. וקבלנו מרבותינו כי בעיא זו להתיר לו בפטור ומותר היא לפיכך לא איפשיטא וי"א כי רדיית הפת האפויה היא חכמה ואינה מלאכה. אבל דרדייתה בעודה עיסה קודם שיקרמו פניה מלאכה היא. הלא תראה הפת האפויה אפשר לרדותה בסכין וכיוצא בה. אבל העיסה אי אפשר לרדותה אלא בידים שנמצא כמו לש ועורך. ומתקן הוא ואינו מקלקל. ולפיכך לא הזכירו במקום הזה. הא דתנא דבי שמואל כלל ללמד כי אינו דומה זה לזה כלל:

פיסקא פשט העני את ידו לפנים אקשי' והא בעינן עקירה והנחה מעל גבי מקום ארבעה וליכא דהא כל חיובי שבת לא מחייבי עד שיעקור ממקום ד' ויניח במקום ד' ואוקמה רבה לר' עקיבא דסבר קלוטה באויר כמי שהונחה בקרקע דמיא. דתנן מרה"י לרה"י ורה"ר באמצע ר' עקיבא מחייב וחכמים פוטרין. ודחינן ודילמא הנחה ע"ג מקום ד' לא בעי אבל עקירה מע"ג מקום ד' בעי דהא לא שמעי' ליה לר' עקיבא מהא מתניתין אלא בהנחה בלבד. אלא אמר רב יוסף ר' היא כו'· ונדחת

*) מדברי רבינו וי"ל אלו נראה קצת דמפרש דגם רב אחא בריה דרבא מחני להא דרב ביבי בלשון בעיא ודלא כפרש"י רק דמתני בהדי בעי רב ביבי דמיירי במזיד ודו"ק:

רב נסים גאון

אבות המלאכות ילפי מםלאכות המשכן כמו שאמרו בפרק במה טומנין (דף מט) אין חייבין אלא על מלאכה שביוצא בה היתה במשכן וכו' והיתה עבודת הלוים בעגלות שמושיטין את הקרשים ולא זורקין גם כן המושיט בשבת מגוזטרא לגוזטרא שהן בדיוטא אחת חייב והזורק פטור ועל העיקר הזה אמרו לא ילפינן זורק ממושיט:

מסורת הש"ס

[לקמן לז.]

[ב"ק ע: לעיל ע"א וש"נ]

כ"ל נהי דסבר

[לקמן ז:]

שם דף ח.

[שם ב"מ קיח:]

לקמן לז.

[גיטין עט.]

אין זה קושיא כ"כ דהא לא קאמר דלא עקירה ודאי בעי אלא דילמא קאמר [תוס' ישנים]

דרבי יהודה כצ"ל

לא נתיישב לי דה"מ למימר דפליגי דלא הוי נופו ברה"ר ולרבנן מקום פטור או כרמלי' הוא ועוד דה"מ אביי למימר איפכא באילן העומד ברה"ר ונופו נוטה לרה"י אלא

תדא מיניהו נקט דברשות אחד לא מצי לאוקמי דלרבנן הוי עיקרו רה"י ונופו כרמלית או מקום פטור ולר' הוי רבותא טפי דאפי' נופו לגמרי ברשות אחר שדי נופו בתר עיקרו [תוס' ישנים]

they differ as to whether an object intercepted is considered at rest, [4b] and when it [crosses the public domain] within ten handbreadths [of the ground]?[5] But surely Rabbah asked a question thereon. For Rabbah propounded: Do they disagree when it is below ten, and they differ in this: R. Akiba holds, An object intercepted is as through it rested, while the Rabbis hold that it is not as though it rested; but above ten all agree that he is not liable, all holding that we do not derive throwing from reaching across?[6] Or perhaps they disagree when it is above ten, and they differ in this: R. Akiba holds, We derive throwing from reaching across, while the Rabbis hold, We do not learn throwing from reaching across; but below ten all agree that he is liable. What is the reason? We say that an object intercepted is as though it rested?—That is no difficulty: after propounding, he solved it that R. Akiba holds that an object intercepted is
a as though it rested.[1]

But perhaps he [R. Akiba] does not require depositing [on a place four handbreadths square], yet he may require removal [from such a place]?[2] Rather, said R. Joseph, the author of this [Mishnah] is Rabbi. Which [ruling of] Rabbi [intimates this]? Shall we say, This [ruling of] Rabbi: If one throws [an object][3] and it comes to rest upon a projection,[4] of a small size,[5] Rabbi holds him liable; the Sages exempt him? [But] surely there, as we will state below, it is in accordance with Abaye. For Abaye said: The reference here is to a tree standing in private ground while its branch inclines to the street, and one throws [an article] and it comes to rest upon the branch,[6] Rabbi holding, We say, cast the branch after its trunk;[7] but the Rabbis maintain: We do not rule, Cast the branch after its stock?—Rather it is this [ruling of] Rabbi. For it was taught: If one throws [an article] from public to public ground, and private ground lies between: Rabbi holds him liable; but the Sages exempt him. Now, Rab Judah said in Samuel's name: Rabbi imposed a twofold liability, one on account of carrying out and one on account of carrying in:[8] this proves that neither removal nor depositing requires a place four by four. But surely it was stated thereon, Rab

(5) For the space above ten does not rank as public ground. (6) If one reaches over an object from private to private ground across public ground, even if it is above ten handbreadths, he is liable.

a (1) Var. lec.: . . . he solved it. Granted that R. Akiba holds, An object intercepted is as at rest, yet perhaps (etc., continuing text as in next paragraph). (2) This objection reverts to Rabbah's answer that our Mishnah agrees with R. Akiba. (3) In the street. (4) A bracket moulding, or anything which projects from the wall of a house; both the house and the projection are private ground. (5) Lit., 'whatever (size) it is'. I.e., very small, less than four square. (6) Which is a projection of the tree. (7) Hence it is private ground, and therefore liability is incurred.—The tree as a whole is regarded, and so we have 'a place four by four.' (8) When the object enters the air space in a private domain, there is 'carrying in' from public to private ground; when it leaves it and re-enters the public domain, there is 'carrying out' from private to public ground. Since the man's act has caused both, he is liable twice over.

and Samuel both assert, [5a] Rabbi imposed liability only in the case of a covered-in private domain, for we say that a house is as
a though it were full,[1] but not in one which is uncovered. And should you answer, Here too [in our Mishnah it speaks of] it as covered, [I might retort] that is well of a covered private ground, but is one liable for a covered public ground? Did not R. Samuel b. Judah say in the name of R. Abba in the name of R. Huna in Rab's name: If one carries an article four cubits in covered public ground, he is not liable, because it is not like the banners of the wilderness?[2]—Rather, said R. Abba, the authority of this is the 'others.'[3] For it was taught: Others say: If he stands still in his place and catches it, he [the thrower] is liable; if he moves from his place and catches it, he [the thrower] is exempt.[4] [Now it states], 'If he stands in his place and catches it, he [the thrower] is liable',—but surely there must be depositing on an area four [handbreadths square], which is absent! Hence this proves that we [i.e., 'others'] do not require a place four by four. Yet perhaps only depositing [on such an area] is not required, but removal [from such] may be necessary? And even in respect to depositing too: perhaps it means that he spread out his garment and caught it, so that there is also depositing [on such an area]?—Said R. Zera: Our Mishnah also means that he removes it [the article] from a basket and places it in a basket, so that there is depositing too [in a place four square]. But HIS HAND is stated?—Learn: a basket in HIS HAND. Now, that is well of a basket in a private
b domain; but a basket in public ground ranks as a private domain?[1] Must we then say that it does not agree with R. Jose son of R. Judah? For it was taught: R. Jose son of R. Judah said: If one fixes a rod in the street, at the top of which is a basket, [and] throws [an article] and it comes to rest upon it, he is liable.[2] For if it agrees with R. Jose son of R. Judah, WHERE THE MASTER OF THE HOUSE STRETCHES HIS HAND WITHOUT AND PLACES [AN OBJECT] IN THE POOR MAN'S HAND, why is he LIABLE? Surely he [merely] carries it from private ground to private ground!—You may even say [that it agrees with] R. Jose son of R. Judah: There it is above ten [handbreadths];[3] here it is below ten.[4] This[5] presented a difficulty to R. Abbahu: Is then 'a basket in his hand' taught: surely HIS HAND [alone] is stated! Rather, said R. Abbahu, it means that he lowered his hand to within three handbreadths [of the ground] and accepted it.[6] But HE STANDS is taught![7]—It refers to one who bends down. Alternatively, [he is standing] in a pit; another alternative: this refers to a dwarf. Raba demurred: Does the Tanna trouble to inform us of all these![8] Rather, said Raba, A man's hand is accounted to him as [an area] four by four. And thus too, when Rabin came,[9] he said in R. Johanan's name: A man's hand is accounted to him as [an area] four by four.

R. Abin said in the name of R. Elai in R. Johanan's name: If one throws an article and it alights on his neighbour's hand, he is liable. What does he inform us? [that] a man's hand is accounted to him as [an area] four by four! But surely R. Johanan already stated it once?—You might argue: That is only when he himself
c accounts his hand as such,[1] but where he does not account his hand as such,[2] I might say [that it is] not [so]. Therefore we are informed [otherwise].

R. Abin said in R. Elai's name in the name of R. Johanan: If he [the recipient] stands still in his place and catches it, [the thrower] is liable; if he moves from his place and catches it, he [the thrower] is exempt. It was taught likewise: Others say: If he stands still in his place and catches it, he [the thrower] is liable; if he moves from his place and catches it, he [the thrower] is exempt.[3] R. Johanan propounded: What if he throws an article and himself moves from his place, and catches it? What is his problem?[4]—Said R. Ada b. Ahaba: His problem concerns two forces in the same man: are two forces in the same man accounted as the action of one man, hence he is liable, or perhaps they count as the action of two men?[5] The question stands over.

R. Abin said in R. Johanan's name: If he puts his hand into his neighbour's courtyard and receives [some] rain, and then withdraws it, he is liable. R. Zera demurred: What does it matter whether his neighbour loads him[6] or Heaven loads him; he himself did not effect removal?—Do not say, he [passively] receives rain, but, he catches it up.[7] But removal must be from a place four [square], which is absent?—Said R. Hiyya son of R. Huna: E.g., he catches it up [as it rebounds] from the wall. But
d even on the wall, it does not rest there?[1]—It is as Raba[2] said [elsewhere], It refers to a sloping wall; so here too it refers to a sloping wall. Now, where was Raba's [dictum] said?—In con-

a (1) Of articles—i.e., it is accounted as though lacking air space entirely, and immediately an object enters therein, we regard it as lying on the ground. (2) It is stated *infra* 49b and 96b that the definition of what constitutes forbidden work on the Sabbath is dependent on the work that was done in connection with the Tabernacle in the wilderness. Carrying was necessary, and so carrying an article four cubits is work. But there it was done under the open sky; hence Rab's dictum, and the same applies here. By 'banners of the wilderness' is meant the whole disposition and encampment of the Israelites, and they did not have any covered-in public ground. (3) In Hor. 13b 'others' is identified with R. Meir. (4) If A throws an article in the street to B, and B catches it while standing in his place, A is liable, because he is regarded as having both removed and deposited it. But if B moves away and catches it, A did not effect its deposit, since it does not lie where it would have done on account of his throw.

b (1) Why then should he be liable in respect of carrying out? (2) For it ranks as private ground, v. *infra* 101a. (3) Then it ranks as private ground. (4) Then it is public ground. (5) Explanation of R. Abba. (6) Everything within three handbreadths is regarded as the ground itself on the principle of *labud* (v. Glos), and thus the hand becomes a place four square. (7) And he would have to be sitting for his hand to be so low. (8) Surely he does not state a law which requires all these conditions. He should rather have taught: If the poor man spreads out his garment, etc. (9) From Palestine to Babylon. Rabin and R. Dimi were two Palestinian Amoraim who travelled between the Palestinian and the Babylonian academies to transmit the teachings of one to the other.

c (1) If one intentionally deposits an article in his neighbour's hand, or takes an article into his own, in each case he accounts the hand as a resting place, i.e., an area four square. (2) I.e., when it merely chances to alight on a man's hand. (3) V. notes *supra*. (4) On what grounds should he be exempted: did he not remove it from one place and deposit it in another? (5) The throw is one manifestation of his force: the catch arrests that force and is in the nature of a counter act; hence they may be regarded as performed by two people, which involves no liability. (6) In which case the Mishnah declares him exempt. (7) Actively. This is assumed to mean that he intercepts the flow of rain, beating it with one hand into the other.

d (1) The side of a wall—it being assumed that an ordinary vertical one is meant—affords no resting place for the rain, whereas removal must be from a place where it can stay. (2) Rashal reads: Rabbah.

לא מחייב רבי אלא ברשות היחיד מקורה דאמרינן °ביתא כמאן דמליא דמיא אבל שאינו מקורה לא וכ"ת הכא נמי במקורה התינח ברשות היחיד מקורה בר"ה מקורה מי חייב *והאמר רב שמואל בר יהודה אמר רבי אבא א"ר הונא אמר רב המעביר חפץ ד' אמות בר"ה מקורה פטור לפי שאינו דומה לדגלי מדבר אלא א"ר זירא הא מני אחרים היא דתניא אחרים אומרים עמד במקומו וקבל חייב עקר ממקומו וקבל פטור עמד במקומו וקבל חייב הא בעינן הנחה על גבי מקום ד' וליכא אלא שמע מינה לא בעינן מקום ארבעה ודילמא הנחה הוא דלא בעינן הא עקירה בעינן והנחה נמי דילמא דפשיט כנפיה וקיבלה דאיכא נמי הנחה אמר רבי אבא מתניתין (א) כגון (שקבל בטרסקל) והניח ע"ג טרסקל דאיכא נמי הנחה והא ידו קתני תני טרסקל שבידו התינח טרסקל ברשות היחיד אלא טרסקל שבר"ה רה"י הוא לימא דלא כרבי יוסי בר' יהודה דתניא *רבי יוסי בר' יהודה אומר נעץ קנה בר"ה ובראשו טרסקל זרק ונח על גביו חייב דאי כר' יוסי בר' יהודה פשט בעל הבית את ידו לחוץ ונתן לתוך ידו של עני אמאי חייב מרה"י לרה"י קא מפיק אפילו תימא רבי יוסי בר' יהודה התם למעלה מי' הכא למטה מי' קשיא ליה לר' אבהו מי קתני טרסקל שבידו והא ידו קתני אלא א"ר אבהו כגון ששלשל ידו למטה מג' וקבלה והא עומד קתני בשוחה ואיבעית אימא בגומא ואב"א בננס °אמר רבא איכפל תנא לאשמעינן כל הני אלא אמר רבא **ידו של אדם חשובה לו כד' על ד' וכן כי אתא רבין א"ר יוחנן ידו של אדם חשובה לו כד' על ד' א"ר אבין א"ר אילעאי א"ר יוחנן ג'זרק חפץ ונח בתוך ידו של חבירו חייב מאי קמ"ל ידו של אדם חשובה לו כד' על ד' והא אמרה ר' יוחנן חדא זימנא מהו דתימא ה"מ היכא דאחשבה הוא לידיה אבל היכא דלא אחשבה הוא לידיה אימא לא קא משמע לן א"ר אבין א"ר אילעאי א"ר יוחנן ד'עמד במקומו וקיבל חייב עקר ממקומו וקיבל פטור תניא נמי הכי אחרים אומרים עמד במקומו וקיבל חייב עקר ממקומו וקיבל פטור בעי ר' יוחנן זרק חפץ ונעקר הוא ממקומו וחזר וקיבלו מהו מאי קמבעיא ליה אמר רב אדא בר אהבה שני כחות באדם אחד קא מבעיא ליה שני כחות באדם אחד כאדם אחד דמי וחייב או דילמא כשני בני אדם דמי ה'ופטור תיקו א"ר אבין א"ר יוחנן הכנים ידו לתוך חצר חבירו וקיבל מי גשמים והוציא חייב מתקיף לה ר' זירא מה לי הטעינו חבירו מה לי הטעינו שמים איהו לא עביד עקירה לא תימא קיבל אלא קלט והא בעינן עקירה מעל גבי מקום ד' וליכא אמר רבי חייא ברי' דרב הונא כגון שקלט מעל גבי הכותל על גבי כותל נמי והא לא נח כדאמר *רבא בכותל משופע הכא נמי בכותל משופע והיכא איתמר דרבא אהא דתנן

היה

רש"י

מקורה. שיש לה גג: כמאן (ב) דמלי. דבר שתוס מכל לד הוי כמלא חפלים עד גגו דאין אוירו חשיב אויר הלכך כל הנזרק לתוכו הוי כמונח: התינח רה"י. דבע"ה אלא רשות הרבים דעני מי מוקמת ליה במקורה: לדגלי מדבר. וכל מלאכות דשבת ממשכן גמרי לקמן מדנסמכה פרשת שבת לפרשת משכן בויקהל: הא מני. דלא בעי מקום ד' אחרים היא: עמד במקומו. זרק חפץ וקבלו אחר עמד המקבל במקומו וקבל: חייב. הזורק דאיהו עבד עקירה והנחה: עקר. המקבל ממקומו ורץ לקראת החפץ וקבלו: פטור. הזורק דלא איתעביד הנחה מכחו: דפשיט כנפיה. *פרס בגדו דהוי ד': טרסקל. כל: רשות היחיד הוא. ואמאי מחייב משום הולאה: לימא. מתניתין דלא חשיב ליה רה"י דלא כרבי יוסי ברבי יהודה: וזרק. מרשות הרבים: ונח על גביו חייב. דאע"ג דלמטה לא הוי קנה רחב ד' הואיל ובראשו ארבע אמרינן גוד אחית מחילה והוי רה"י גמור: למעלה מי'. הוי רה"י הואיל ורחב ד': שלשל. השפיל כמו *היה משלשל בחבל: למטה מג'. דהויא כקרקע: והא עומד קתני. העני עומד בחוץ והא יושב הוא: בשוחה. כופף עלמו: ואיבעית אימא. בעומד בגומא וידו סמוכה לשפתה: איכפל תנא כו'. טרח התנא בכל זאת ולא היה לו להודיעם דמוליא מרשות לרשות חייב אלא על ידי דברים הללו שאין דרכן בכך לתני פשט כנף בגדו לפנים דהוי ד': היכא דאחשבה. זה העושה מלאכה נתכוון לתתה ליד חבירו כי מתניתין: אבל היכא דלא אחשבה. שהלכה ונחה מעלמו ביד חבירו דהאי דזריק לא אחשבה ליד חבירו לאנוחה בגווה דלא נתכוון לכך: עמד. המקבל במקומו וקבל: חייב. הזורק: פטור. הזורק דלא עביד הנחה: מאי קמיבעיא ליה. מאי ספיקא איכא מאיזה טעמא יפטור הא עבד עקירה והנחה: כשני בני אדם דמיא ופטור. דהוו להו שנים שעשאוה דכיון שלא הניח החפץ לילך עד מקום הילוכו ולנוח אלא רץ אחריו ועכבו הויא ליה עקירה קמייתא בלא הנחה: מה לי הטעינו חבירו. דפטר ליה תנא דמתניתין דקתני או שנתן לתוכה והוליא שניהן פטורין: לא תימא קיבל. פשט ידו וירדו לתוכה דלא עבד מעשה: אלא אימא קלט. השתא סלקא דעתך כשהיה הקילוח יורד הכה בידו אחת וקבלו בחברתה דעבד ליה עקירה:

קורא

תוספות

לא מחייב ר' אלא ברשות היחיד מקורה. נראה לרשב"א דמשמע ליה מדלא נקט מרשות היחיד לרה"י ורשות הרבים באמצע כמו בפלוגתא דר"ע ורבנן והיא דגיטין פ' הזורק (ד' עט: ושם) גבי היתה עומדת על ראש הגג וזרקו לה כו' וקאמר כמאן כרבי דאמר קלוטה כמי שהונחה דמיא לא סברי דרב ושמואל דהכא דאמרי דלא חייב ר' אלא ברשות היחיד מקורה ולדידהו צריך לשנויי דהתם משום איגטורי כדמשני התם אליבא דרבנן אפילו תימא רבנן כי פליגי רבנן לענין שבת אבל הכא משום איגטורי כו':

אמאי חייב מרה"י לרה"י קא מפיק. ואפילו משום מושיט ובדיוטא אחת לא מחייב °לפי הירושלמי דמצריך שיקבלנו שני מידו:

כאן למטה מי'. וא"ת נהי דרשות היחיד לא הוי ר"ה נמי לא הוי אלא ככרמלית כמו עמוד גבוה שלשה ורחב ד' ואמאי חייב ויש לומר דאין כרמלית בכלים כמו שפירש רש"י לקמן גבי היתה קופתו מונחת כו' קשה לר"י מה עלה על דעתו של המקשן דע"כ ידע דמתניתין מיירי למטה מי' בלא פירכא דר' יוסי בר' יהודה *דכל למעלה מי' הוי מקום פטור ולא מחייב לכ"ע וא"כ מאי פריך מרבי יוסי ברבי יהודה הא מילתא דפשיטא היא דלמטה מי' לא הוה רה"י דהא תנן לקמן בהזורק (לקמן ד' צט.) חולית הבור והסלע שהם גבוהים י' ורחבים ד' הנוטל מהן והנותן על גבן חייב פחות מכן פטור ופשיטא דרבי יוסי ברבי יהודה לא איירי אלא למעלה מי':

כגון ששלשל ידו למטה מג' וקבלה. וקסבר רבי אבהו דאגד יד שמיה אגד דאי לא הוי שמיה אגד מאי איריא דנטל עני מתופה אפילו נתן בעה"ב לתוכה יהא חייב העני כשהוליא כיון דיד העני מיירי נמי דהוה למטה מג' דמסתמא יד בעה"ב ויד עני איירי בענין אחד דהא כי נטל מתוך ידו של בעה"ב דהוי למטה מג' הויא יד עני נמי למטה מג' ובכהאי גוונא אפילו נותן בעה"ב לתוך יד העני יהא חייב: בגומא. צריך לפרש בגומא שהיא רשות הרבים כגון שרבים משתמשים בה למ"ד תשמיש על ידי הדחק שמיה תשמיש (לקמן ד' ח:) או בענין שמהלכים שם רבים אבל גומא שהיתה כרמלית או מקום פטור כיון שגופו שם ידו שהיא פשוטה לרשות הרבים לא הויא כרה"ר דבתר גופו גריר אע"פ שהיא למטה מג' כיון דסבר אגד יד שמיה אגד כדפי':

ה"מ היכא דאחשבה לידיה. וא"ת ולימא הך ולא ההיא דלעיל וי"ל דה"א דוקא לענין הנחה חשובה כד' על ד' אבל לגבי עקירה לא:

כשני בני אדם דמי ופטור. פי' כי היכי דבשני בני אדם פטור הראשון משום דלא עבד כלל הנחה ה"נ כיון שחטפו מהילוכו ולא הניח החפץ ללכת עד מקום הילוכו לא הויא הנחה דלא נח מכח הזורק או דילמא כאדם אחד דמי וכיון דעביד עקירה והנחה חייב ולא דמי לשנים שעשאוה ור"ח גריס איפכא כשני בני אדם דמי וחייב דאמר לעיל עמד במקומו וקבל חייב וה"נ כי קבלה הוא עצמו ולא חטפה מהילוכו ליחייב דהא איתעביד מחשבתו או דילמא כאדם אחד דמי ופטור דהוי כמו שטתן מימינו לשמאלו דאע"פ שהעבירה ד' אמות פטור:

היה

עין משפט נר מצוה

י א מיי' פי"ג מהל' שבת הלכה ג:

יא ב ג ד מיי' שם הלכה טו:

אמר מהר"ש דמפיקרא ס"ד דמתני' איירי למעל' מי' ושולי הכלכלי' למטה מי' ול"ל גוד אחית והוי שולי הכלכלה רשות הרבים [תוס' ישנים]

רבינו חננאל

ואוקמה ר' זירא כאחרים. דתניא אחרים אומרים עמד במקומו וקיבל אפי' בידו חייב. ש"מ לא בעי מקום ד'. ודחינן כגון שפשט כנפיה וקיבלה דאית בכנפיה מקום ד'. ואמרי' מתני' נמי כגון שקיבלה בטרסקל שבידו שיש בו ד'. פי' טרסקל טאבק. איני והא קיי"ל דטרסקל ברשות הרבים רה"י היא. נימא דלא כר' יוסי ב"ר יהודה. אפי' תימא ר' יוסי ב"ר יהודה היא מתני' והתם דתני נעץ קנה ברה"ר והניח בראשו טרסקל [וזרק] מרה"ר ונח על גביו חייב כשהיה טרסקל זה נתון למעלה מי' שאין רה"ר למעלה מי'. מתני' בטרסקל שבידו למטה מי' ודחי' לה ר' אבהו להא ואוקמה הוא כגון ששלשל ידו למטה מג' וקיבלה. דכל פחות מג' כלבוד דמי. וכאלו בקרקע הניח והאי העני עומד בשוחה כדכתיב (ישעיה ס) והלכו אליך שחוח. והוא פי' כפוף כדכתיב (שם נח) הלכוף כאגמון ראשו. פי' בגומא בור כדכתיב דופר גומץ. גומץ וגומא הכל אחד הוא. ננס קצור בקומתו. ותדוש אלו כולם. ואוקמא רבא הכי. ואמר האי סבר ידו של אדם חשובה לו כד' על ד'. וכן א"ר יוחנן

רב נסים גאון

אמר ר' אבהו כגון ששלשל בידו למטה מג' וקיבלה ועיקר דבריהן במשנה אבל בתוספתא במס' כלאים ועירובין וסוכה אמרו כל פחות מג' כלבוד דמי ואם היתה ידו של עני סמוכה לארץ בפחות מג' לדברי ר' אבהו והניח בעל הבית בתוכה הרי אלו כאילו הניח בארץ ובמקום שיש בו ד' חייב וכבר אמרנו בברכות בפרק ג' (דף כה) כל פחות מג' כלבוד דמי והלכתא גמירי לה כמו שאמרו בפרק הזורק (דף צז) ואמרו עוד בעירובין ובסוכה לגוד וללבוד ולדופן עקומה:

מתקיף

מסורת הש"ס

לקמן צח.

ד"ה כנף

[מכות ז.]

לקמן קא. עירובין לג:

כתובות לא:

גיטין רבה

הגהות הב"ח

(א) גמ' אמר ר' אבא מהני' נמי כגון (שקבלה בטרסקל) תא"מ ונ"ב ס"א שעקר' מטרסקל: (ב) רש"י ד"ה כמאן דמלי דמי דבר:

גליון הש"ס

גמ' ביתא כמאן דמליא כו'. עירובין ד' עו ע"ב: שם אמר רבא איכפל הנא לאשמעינן וכו'. זבחים עו ע"א. וק"ל דדילמא מש"ה נקט ידו דאיירי ע"כ בלמטה ומוכח מזה דאגד יד שמיה אגד: תוס' ד"ה אמאי חייב וכו' לפי הירושלמי וכו' הובא לעיל ג ע"א תוס' ד"ה בעשותה:

עין משפט
נר מצוה

יב א מיי' פי"ג מהל' שבת הלכה כא סמג לאוין סה טוש"ע א"ח סי' שנג סעיף א:
יג ב מיי' שם טוש"ע שם סעיף ב:
יד ג ד ה ו מיי' פי"ג מהל' שבת הלכה ד ופ"ח מהלכות טומאת אוכלין הלכה ג:
טו ז ח מיי' פי"ג מהל' שבת הלכה ח:
טז ט שם הלכה י:
יז י שם הלכה יב:

נראה דאם מהלך כעומד דמי וכלי בידו וכא א' ושם בכלי דדמי למניח אגוז בכלי וכלי צף ע"ג המים אבל רוכב או מניח ע"ג אדם דמי לאגוז ע"ג מים [ת"י]

[ועיין תוס' מעילה יג. סד"ה בשלמא]

*היה "קורא בספר· על האיסקופה ונתגלגל הספר מידו גוללו אצלו "היה קורא בראש הגג ונתגלגל הספר מידו עד שלא הגיע לי' טפחים גוללו אצלו משהגיע לי' טפחים הופכו על הכתב והוינן בה אמאי הופכו על הכתב *הא לא נח ואמר רבא בכותל משופע אימור דאמר רבא בספר דעביד דנייח מים מי עבידי דנייחי אלא אמר רבא "כגון שקלט מע"ג גומא גומא פשיטא מהו דתימא מים ע"ג מים לאו הנחה הוא קמ"ל ואזדא רבא לטעמיה דאמר רבא מים ע"ג מים היינו הנחתן אגוז ע"ג מים לאו היינו הנחתו בעי רבא *אגוז בכלי וכלי צף ע"ג מים בתר אגוז אזלינן והא נייח או דילמא "בתר כלי אזלינן והא לא נייח דנייד תיקו "שמן שצף ע"ג יין מחלוקת ר' יוחנן בן נורי ורבנן *דתנן "שמן שצף ע"ג יין ונגע טבול יום בשמן לא פסל אלא שמן בלבד ר' יוחנן בן נורי אומר שניהם מחוברים זה לזה א"ר אבין א"ר אילעאי א"ר יוחנן "היה טעון אוכלים ומשקין ונכנס ויוצא כל היום כולו אינו חייב עד שיעמוד אמר אביי "והוא שעמד לפוש *ממאי מדאמר מר "תוך ד' אמות עמד לפוש פטור לכתף חייב חוץ לד' אמות עמד לפוש חייב לכתף פטור מאי קמ"ל שלא היתה עקירה משעה ראשונה לכך הא אמרה רבי יוחנן חדא זימנא *דאמר רב ספרא א"ר אמי א"ר יוחנן (א) "המעביר חפצים מזוית לזוית ונמלך עליהן והוציאן פטור שלא היתה עקירה משעה ראשונה לכך אמוראי נינהו מר אמר לה בהאי לישנא ומר אמר לה בהאי לישנא: ת"ר *המוציא מחנות לפלטיא דרך סטיו חייב ובן עזאי פוטר בשלמא *בן עזאי קסבר מהלך כעומד דמי אלא רבנן נהי נמי דקסברי מהלך לאו כעומד דמי היכא אשכחנא כה"ג דחייב א"ר ספרא א"ר אמי א"ר יוחנן מידי

רש"י

קורא בספר. כל ספרים שלהם עשוים כמגילה: ונתגלגל הספר מידו. וראשו אחד בידו: גוללו אצלו. ובפרק בתרא דעירובין מוקים לה באיסקופת כרמלית כגון גבוה ג' ורחבו ד' ורשות הרבים עוברת לפניו דאי נפל כוליה מידיה ומהדרי ליה מרה"ר לאיסקופה לאו חיוב חטאת איכא הלכך השתא דראשו אחד בידו ואין כאן עקירה אפילו משום שבות נמי לא גזור: היה קורא בראש הגג. שהוא רה"י: ונתגלגל הספר מידו. וראשו אחד בידו: עד שלא הגיע. ראש התחתון: לי'. התחתונים שהוא אויר ר"ה גוללו אצלו: הגיע לי'. אסור לגוללו דגזור רבנן משום שבות היכא דאוגדו בידו אטו היכא דנפק מידיה כוליה דלא לייתיה דאיכא חיובא דאורייתא: הופכו על הכתב. כתבו לצד הכותל והחלק כלפי ר"ה שלא יהא מוטל כל כך בבזיון: והא לא נח. ואמאי אסור לגוללו אצלו: משופע. בולט מלמטה ומצר מלמעלה דנח ליה על אותו שיפוע: מי עבידי דנייחי. אלא בדבר שיש לו תוך: מהו דתימא. לאו היינו הנחתן דתהוי עקירתו עקירה דהא ניידי ואזלו: קמ"ל. דהיינו הנחתן ועקירתן עקירה: שמן שצף ע"ג יין. ועקר השמן והוליאו לר"ה וה"ה ע"ג מים לענין שבת אבל לענין תרומה לא סגי דלא נקט יין: מחלוקת רבי יוחנן ורבנן דתנן שמן. של תרומה שצף ע"ג יין. של תרומה: טבול יום. פוסל את התרומה מן התורה ביבמות בפ' הערל (דף עה·): לא פסל אלא שמן בלבד. לפי שאינו חבור זה לזה ושמן פסול הוא ולא טמא הילכך לא פסיל ליה ליין ולענין שבת נמי הוי כדבר אחר הצף על המים דלאו היינו הנחתו: היה טעון אוכלין ומשקין. משמע שלא טענו לכך אלא היה טעון ברה"י כדי להוליכו מזוית לזוית (ב) (או מבעוד יום) ומשעקר רגליו נמלך ויצא ונכנס כל היום כולו: אינו חייב עד שיעמוד. ואח"כ יעקור עלמו ללאת דעמידת גופו ודאי (ג) כעמידת חפץ דמי הלכך כי עמד ועקר ע"מ ללאת מיחייב אבל בלא עמידה ליכא עקירה אלא עקירה ראשונה והיא לא היתה ע"מ ללאת והתורה לא חייבה אלא מלאכת מחשבת וגמרינן ממשכן שיתכוין לעשות המלאכה אבל לא יודע שהוא שבת או כסבור שמלאכה זו מותרת: והוא שעומד לפוש. לנוח ההיא הויא עמידה ועקירה דבתרה הוי עקירה אבל עומד לכתף לתקן משאו על כתיפו לאו עמידה היא: מדאמר מר. רבה דהוא רביה דאביי: תוך ד' אמות. המעביר ד' אמות ברה"ר ועמד תוך ד' אמות לפוש וחזר והשלים והניח או עמד שם: פטור. שלא העביר ד' אמות בעקירה אחת ואם לכתף עמד בתוך הד' אמות וכשהשלים ד' אמות הניח או עמד שם לפוש חייב (ד) ועמידה דתוך ד' לאו עמידה היא שהיתה לכתף: חוץ לד' אמות. המעביר ד' אמות שלימות ועמד חוץ לד' אמות אם לפוש עמד הוי הנחת גופו כהנחת חפץ ואם לכתף עמד אין זו עמידה ואם נטלה אחר מידו אחרי כן שניהם פטורין: אמוראי נינהו. ר' אלעאי ור' אמי: מר אמר לה בהאי לישנא ומר אמר לה בהאי לישנא. ומיהו ר' יוחנן חדא זימנא אמרה: חנות. רה"י: פלטיא. רחבה והוא רה"ר: דרך סטיו. מקום איצטבאות שיושבים סוחרים ושם כרמלית עליה דלאו להילוכה הוא כרה"ר: חייב. הואיל ולא עמד בסטיו לפוש אין כאן הנחה אלא בפלטיא: ובן עזאי פוטר. כדמפ' קסבר מהלך כעומד דמי ונמלא נעקר מרה"י ומונח בסטיו ועוקר (ה) מסטיו ומניח ברה"ר: היכא אשכחן כה"ג. דמפסקא רשותא אחריתי מיחייב דילמא לא חייב' רחמנא אלא במוליא מרה"י לר"ה בהדיא:

תוספות

היה קורא בספר על האסקופה. ואם תאמר ולרבא בפרקין דלא גזר בכרמלית גזירה לגזירה גבי לא ילא החייט במחטו (לקמן ד' יא:) מאי איריא ספר אפילו כל מילי נמי שרי באגדו בידו כיון דאפילו באין אגדו בידו לא אסור אלא מדרבנן ואי אפשר לאוקמה אלא באסקופת כרמלית כדמסיק אביי בפרק בתרא דעירובין (דף צח· ושם) וי"ל דנקט ספר לאשמעינן אפילו ספר אם אין אגודו בידו אסור לאפוקי רבי שמעון דאמר התם כל דבר שהוא משום שבות אינו עומד בפני כתבי הקודש: בכותל משופע. אור"י דאיירי כגון שרבים מכתפים עליו דהוי רה"ר: אגוז ע"ג מים לאו היינו הנחתו. ואע"ג דאמרינן בפ"ק דב"מ (דף ט: ושם) ספינה מינח נייחא ומיא הוא דקא ממטי לה לגבי קנין שאני דלא אקרי חצר מהלכת דחצר ילפינן מיד *ויד נמי איהו דקא מסגי תותא וקא ממטי לה אבל הכא ממשכן ילפינן ושם לא היה מכתמא אלא כדרך שמניחים חפצים בני אדם ובעי אגוז בכלי וכלי צף ע"ג מים אם הוא דרך כך להניח חפצים או לא אע"ג דודאי לאו כמונח דמי דקי"ל רכוב כמהלך דמי ובריש פרק בתרא (דף קנג·) משמע נמי דאם נותן על אדם כשהוא מהלך דלא חשיב הנחה *דקאמר מניחו עליה כשהיא מהלכת ונוטל ממנה כשהיא עומדת ואמרינן נמי בהמוליא (לקמן דף פ.) הוליא דיו כשיעור שתי אותיות וכתבן כשהוא מהלך חייב כתיבתם זו היא הנחתם משמע דוקא כתבן שהניחן במקום שישארו שם לעולם אבל אם שפך לכלי אחר לא חשיב הנחה כיון שהוא מהלך: רבי יוחנן בן נורי אמר שניהם כו'. מדנקט טבול יום ולא נקט שני משמע דשמן חשיב משקה דשני אחר מטמא משקין להיות תחלה וכן משמע בפ"ק דפסחים (דף יד: ושם) ומה שקשה ממנחות פירשתי שם בפסחים: בשלמא לבן עזאי מהלך כעומד דמי. קשה לר"י מה לריך להאי טעמא לימא בשלמא לבן עזאי לא אשכחנכה"ג דמיחייב כדפריך מהא טעמא לרבנן דאי משום דמודה בזורק קאמר האי טעמא הא אכתי לא ידע דמודה בזורק דאי ידע לפרוך נמי לבן עזאי אזורק ומושיט היכא אשכחן כו' ותירץ ר"י דה"ק בשלמא לב"ע אפילו משכחת כה"ג במשכן פטור דמהלך כעומד דמי אלא לרבנן תקשה היכא אשכחן כו' *ובירושלמי פריך על דעתיה דבן עזאי אין אדם מתחייב על ד' אמות ברה"ר לעולם דיעשה כמי שהונחה על כל אמה ואמה ויפטר ומשני משכחת לה בקופץ והש"ס דידן לא חשיב לה פירכא כדאמר בהזורק (לקמן דף נו:) דד' אמות ברה"ר הלכתא גמירי לה ולהכי לא מקשה עלה וכן קלוטה לר"ע אע"ג דכמי שהונחה דמיא בזורק ד' אמות ברשות הרבים חייב ולא אמרינן כמי שהונחה תוך ד' אמות ברשות הרבים וריב"א מספקא ליה כיון דבד' אמות ברשות הרבים *)לא אמר מהלך כעומד דמי אף על גב דבעלמא כעומד דמי לבן עזאי אם חייב לבן עזאי אפילו עמד לפוש תוך ד' אמות אם לאו וכן אם לא עמד חוץ לארבע אמות כגון שנטלה אחר מידו אם אמרינן מהלך כעומד דמי חוץ לד' אמות אם לאו וכן קלוטה לרבי עקיבא אם אמר כמי שהונחה דמיא חוץ לארבע אמות אפילו קלטה אחר או כלב או שנשרפה כיון דתוך ארבע אמות לא אמרינן נראה לרשב"א לרבי יוחנן דאמר לעיל המפנה חפציו מזוית לזוית ונמלך עליהם והוליאן פטור לית ליה דבן עזאי דלבן עזאי דאמר מהלך כעומד דמי הוה חייב וכן מוכח בהדיא בריש אלו נערות (כתובות דף לא. ושם): מידי

*) הא ליכא למימר דלית ליה מהלך כעומד דמי בשום מקום כי הכא ד:פסק סטיו חשיב כמונח דאי טעמא משום הפסק כרמלית א"כ זורק ומושיט נמי ליפטר אלא ודאי גם לרס"י או איפכא נמי אית ליה מהלך כעומד דמי לבד מד"א בר"ה הלכתא גמירי לה אבל מודה בזורק ומושיט רק במהלך פליג ש"מ טעמא לא משום הפסק כרמלית אלא משום דמהלך כעומד דמי בכל מקום והמוליא מרה"י לרה"ר כיון דנכנס לרה"ר חייב אבל עומד ברה"י ומושיט או זורק אינו חייב עד שתנוח לבן עזאי [תוס' ישנים]

מסורת הש"ס

עירובין צח: [קג.]
[עירובין צח.]
לקמן פ.
ג"ז שם עירובין צח: טבול יום פ"ב מ"ה
[רש"ל אבל עומד לכתף פטור]
כתובות לא. ע"ש עירובין כג:
לקמן לא:
[כתובות לא: עירובין לח.]

הגהות הב"ח

(א) גמ' אמר ר' יוחנן המפנה חפציו מזוית לזוית ונמלך: (ב) רש"י ד"ה היה טעון וכו' מזוית לזוית ומשעקר רגליו כצ"ל ותיבת או מבעוד יום נמחק: (ג) ד"ה אינו חייב וכו' גופו ודאי כהנחת חפץ דמי וכו' מחשבת דגמרי' ממשכן (ד) ד"ה פטור וכו' לפוש חייב דעמידה דתוך ד' וכו' היא כיון שהיתה לכתף: (ה) ד"ה ובן עזאי וכו' בסטיו ונעקר מסטיו ומונח:

רבינו חננאל

זרק והלכה ונחה בתוך ידו של חבירו חייב. וא"ר יוחנן עמד במקומו וקיבל. כגון שזרק לחבירו (כבו מה) חייב בזה שנעשית מחשבתו. נעקר ממקומו אחרי שזרק שקיבלה פטור הזורק שהרי לא נצטרכה כוונתו לקבל באותו מקום שמילא באה לידו. בעי ר' יוחנן זרק ונעקר הוא ממקומו וקיבל מהו שנמצא הוא שזרק הוא עצמו שקיבל. שני טחותיו הללו שזרק ושנעקר וקיבל כשני בני אדם דמו וחייב. או דילמא אפי' הכי אדם אחד הוא לא נעקר ממקום[זה]ו הונח במקום אחר אלא מקום העקירה הוא מקום הנחה. כי שניהם כאדם אחד הן. ועלתה בתיקו. הא דא' משום ר' יוחנן הכניס ידו לחצר חבירו וקיבל מי גשמים והוציאן חייב אתינן לאוקמה כגון שקלט מי גשמים הללו ולא כשהן יורדין אלא מעל גבי הכותל משופע דנחו ע"ג הכותל כגון הא דא' בסוף עירובין בהא דתנן היה קורא בראש הגג ונתגלגל הספר מידו כו' כד נח זה הספר ע"ג כותל משופע ודחינן אימור דא' רבה בספר דעביד דניח. מיא מי עבידי דניחי. ואוקמא רבא כגון שקלט מע"ג הגומא ונמצא המוציאו לרה"ר שקלט ממקום ד' רבא לטעמיה דאמר רבא מים ע"ג מים היינו הנחתן אגוז ע"ג מים לאו היינו הנחתו. כגון שעקר והוציא אגוזים מרה"י ונתנם ע"ג מים ברה"ר עקירה איכא הנחה ליכא. בעי רבא הוציא ונתן אגוז בכלי והכלי נתון במים מהו. בתר אגוז אזלינן והא נח חייב. או דילמא בתר כלי אזלינן והא לא נח ועלתה בתיקו. הוציא שמן ונתנן ע"ג [יין] מחלוקת ר' יוחנן בן נורי ורבנן דתנן בפרק (כ' דטב"י) שמן שצף ע"ג יין ונגע טבול יום בשמן לא פסל אלא שמן בלבד. ור' יוחנן בן נורי אמר שניהם חיבור לתנא קמא לא נח. לר' יוחנן בן נורי נח כמו המים שאמרנו מים ע"ג מים היינו הנחתו פי' לפרש. כגון שיגע במשוי שעליו ומתכוין לעמוד להתרוח ולנוח כדי שיסור יגיעו זה חשוב כאילו יניח המשא שעליו. וכל כי האי גונא הוי הנחה. אבל לכתף שכוונתו לתקן המשאו שעל כתיפו פטור דכמהלך דמי ולא עקר ולא הניח. הא דא"ר יוחנן המתכוון לפנות חפצים מזוית לזוית ונמלך עליהן והוציאן פטור. שלא היתה עקירה בכוונה להוציאן לחוץ במקום חיוב אלא לזוית שאין שם חיוב ועיקרו באלו נערות וכבר פירשנוהו שם. פי' סטיו אצטבא. והוא איקרביסא ועשין כי האי גוונא בפני החנויות ועל זה שנינו בחיצונה המוציא מחנות לפלטיא דרך סטיו חייב ובן עזאי פוטר. ספק זהו

גליון הש"ס תוס' ד"ה אגוז. ויד נמי איהו דמסגי תותא. תמוה לי הא כנוהן גט ביד עבדו אמרינן דהוי חצר מהלכת והא הוי דומיא דידו. אע"כ דאמרינן דומיא דידו דא"א להלוך ממנו דסקונה ותמיד ידו אצלו כך בעי' חצר שאינה מהלכת ממנו דסקונה ולע"ג:

nection with the following. For we learnt: [5b] If he is reading a scroll on a threshold, and it rolls out of his hand,[3] he may rewind it to himself.[4] If one is reading on the top of a roof,[5] and the scroll rolls out of his hand,—before it comes within ten handbreadths [of the ground] he may wind it back himself;[6] if it comes within ten handbreadths, he must turn the written side inwards.[7] Now, we pondered thereon: why must he turn the written side inwards, surely it did not come to rest?[8] and Raba answered: This refers to a sloping wall.[9] Yet may it not be argued that Raba said this [only] of a scroll, whose nature it is to rest [where it falls]; but is it the nature of water to rest?[10] Rather, said Raba, [R. Joḥanan spoke of a case] where he collected [the rain] from the top of a [water] hole. 'A hole'! But then it is obvious?—You might argue, Water upon water is not at rest;[11] [therefore] he [R. Joḥanan] informs us [that it is].

Now Raba follows his opinion. For Raba said: Water [lying] upon water, that is its [natural] rest; a nut upon water, that is not its [natural] rest.[12] Raba propounded: If a nut [lies] in a vessel,
a and the vessel floats on water,[1] do we regard the nut, which is at rest,[2] or the vessel, which is not at rest, since it is unstable? The question stands over.

In respect to oil floating upon wine R. Joḥanan b. Nuri and the Rabbis differ. For we learnt: If oil is floating upon wine[3] and a *ṭebul yom*[4] touches the oil, he disqualifies the oil only. R. Joḥanan b. Nuri said: Both are attached to each other.[5]

R. Abin said in R. Elai's name in the name of R. Joḥanan: If one is laden with food and drink and goes in and out all day,[6] he is liable only when he stands still.[7] Said Abaye: Providing that he stands still to rest.[8] How do you know it?—Because a Master said: Within four cubits, if he stops to rest, he is exempt; to shoulder his burden, he is liable?[9] Beyond four cubits, if he stops to rest, he is liable;[10] to rearrange his burden, he is exempt. What does he [R. Joḥanan] inform us—that the original removal was not for this purpose?[11] But R. Joḥanan stated it once. For R. Safra said in R. Ammi's name in R. Joḥanan's name: If one is carrying articles from corner to corner [in private ground] and then changes his mind and carries them out, he is exempt, because his original removal was not for this purpose?—It is dependent on Amoraim: one stated it in the former version; the other stated it in the latter
b version.[1]

Our Rabbis taught: If one carries [an article] from a shop to an open space via a colonnade,[2] he is liable; but Ben 'Azzai holds him not liable. As for Ben 'Azzai, it is well: he holds that walking is like standing.[3] But according to the Rabbis, granted that they hold that walking is not like standing, yet where do we find liability for such a case?[4]—Said R. Safra in the name of R.

(3) Into a public domain skirting it. (4) This refers, e.g., to a threshold three handbreadths above the ground and four handbreadths square. This constitutes a *karmelith* (v. *supra* 3b, n. a7), and even if it entirely falls out of his hand it is only Rabbinically prohibited to carry it back; hence here that he retains one end there is not even that. (5) Which is a private domain. In the East all roofs were flat and put to use; *T.A.* I, p. 33. (6) Because only the first ten handbreadths above the street surface count as public ground. (7) He must not draw it back, since it has entered public ground, so he reverses it, because it is degrading for a scroll to lie open with its writing upward. (8) Hence he should be permitted to roll it back. (9) V. 'Er., 100 *b* and notes. (10) It does not stay even on a sloping wall. (11) The article must be removed from a place where it may be regarded as naturally at rest, e.g., a stone lying on the ground. (12) And if one picks it up and carries it without, he is not liable.

a (1) And he lifts up both and carries them out. (2) In the vessel. (3) Both of *terumah*. (4) V. Glos. He renders *terumah* (q.v. Glos.) unfit for food. (5) And both become unfit. Thus in respect to the Sabbath too: the Rabbis hold that the oil is not at rest upon the wine, whereas R. Joḥanan b. Nuri holds that the oil is at rest upon the wine. The same applies to oil floating upon water: wine is mentioned on account of the quotation, as there is no *terumah* of water. (6) From private to public ground. (7) And then goes in or out; this alone constitutes removal. He was laden in the first place to carry the stuff from one part of a private domain to another, and if he goes out instead it is not removal, since when the food was moved at first there was no intention of carrying from a private to a public domain; v. *supra* 3a. (8) But if he stops merely to rearrange the burden, it is all part of his walking. (9) One is liable for carrying an article four cubits over public ground, providing that he himself removes it from the first spot and deposits it on the other in one intentional single act. Now stopping to rest constitutes depositing, and when he restarts there is a new removal; consequently if he stops to rest within four cubits he is not liable, since he does not carry it four cubits. But stopping to rearrange the burden does not constitute depositing; hence, when he does eventually stop after four cubits, he has effected removal and depositing in one single act and therefore he is liable. Similarly, in R. Abin's case, he would not be liable when stopping to rest the first time, for the food he carried in and out was not carried in a single act of removal and deposit (v. n7); but he would be liable if he went in and out after his rest. (10) On the same grounds as before, but since the stop is after four cubits, its results are the reverse. Hence, if he stops to rearrange his burden, he is still engaged in walking, and should another relieve him of it before he stops to rest, both are exempt. (11) Viz., to carry it without, and so he is not liable.

b (1) R. Joḥanan did not teach both, but amoraim reporting his words gave different versions of what he did state. (2) The shop is private ground, the open space is public ground, and the colonnade ranks as a *karmelith*, being occupied by stall holders and not frequented as a public thoroughfare. (3) When he walks through the colonnade it is as though he stood there. Hence he performs two separate actions: (i) carrying an object from private ground to a *karmelith*; (ii) carrying an object from a *karmelith* to public ground. Neither of these imposes liability. (4) In Scripture, by analogy with the Tabernacle (v. *supra* 5a, n. a2) we find liability only for direct transference from private to public ground.

Ammi in R. Joḥanan's name: [6a] Compare it to one who carries an article in the street: there, surely, though he is not liable as long as he holds it and proceeds, yet when he lays it down he is liable; so here too, it is not different. How compare! There, wherever he puts it down it is a place of liability; but here, if he deposits it in the colonnade, it is a place of non-liability? Rather compare it to one who carries an article [in the street] exactly four [cubits].[5] There, surely, though he is exempt if he deposits it within the four cubits, yet when he deposits it at the end of the four cubits he is liable; so here too, it is not different. How compare? There it is a place of exemption [only] as far as this man is concerned, but to all others[6] it is a place of liability; but here it is a place of exemption for all? Rather compare it to one who carries [an object] from private to public ground through the sides of the
a street:[1] there, surely, though he is exempt if he lays it down in the sides of the street, yet when he lays it down in the street [itself] he is liable; so here too it is not different.

R. Papa demurred thereto: That is well according to the Rabbis, who maintain that the sides of the street are not regarded as the street; but according to R. Eliezer [b. Jacob][2] who rules that the sides of the street are regarded as the street, what can be said?—Said R. Aḥa son of R. Iḳa to him: Granted that you know R. Eliezer [b. Jacob] to rule that the sides of the street are regarded as the street where there is no fencing;[3] but do you know him [to rule thus] where there is fencing?[4] Hence it[5] is analogous to this.

R. Joḥanan said: Yet Ben 'Azzai agrees in the case of one who throws.[6] It was taught likewise: If one carries [an object] from a shop to an open place through a colonnade, he is liable, whether he carries [it] out or carries [it] in; or whether he reaches it across or throws it. Ben 'Azzai said: If he carries it out or in, he is exempt; if he reaches it across or throws it, he is liable.

Our Rabbis taught: There are four domains in respect to the Sabbath; private ground, public ground, *karmelith*, and a place of non-liability. And what is private ground? A trench ten [handbreadths] deep and four wide, and likewise a wall ten [handbreadths] high and four broad,—that is absolute private ground.[7] And what is public ground? A highroad,[8] a great public square,[9] and open alleys,[10]—that is absolute public ground. One may not carry out from this private to this public ground, nor carry in from this public to this private ground; and if one does carry out or in, unwittingly, he is liable to a sin-offering; if deliberately,
b he is punished by *kareth*[1] or stoned.[2] But the sea, a plain, a colonnade, or a *karmelith*, ranks neither as public nor as private ground:[3] one must not carry [objects] about[4] within it and if he does, he is not liable; and one must not carry out [an object] thence into public ground or from the public ground into it, nor carry [an object] from it into private ground or from the private ground into it; yet if he does carry out or in, he is not liable. As to courtyards with many owners[5] and blind alleys,[6] if an *'erub* is made, they are permitted; if an *'erub* is not made, they are forbidden.[7] A man standing on a threshold[8] may take [an object] from the master of the house, or give [it] to him, and may take [an object] from the poor man or give [it] to him; providing however that he does not take from the master of the house and give to the poor man or from the poor man and give it to the master of the house;[9] and if he does take and give, the three are exempt. Others state, A threshold serves as two domains: if the door is open, it is as within; if shut, it is as without. But if the threshold is ten [handbreadths] high and four broad, it is a separate domain.[10]

The Master said: 'That is [absolute] private ground.' What
c does this exclude?[1]—It excludes the following [view] of R. Judah. For it was taught: Even more than this did R. Judah say: If one owns two houses on the opposite sides of the street,[2] he

(5) Lit., 'from the beginning of four to the end of four'. (6) To whom the limit of four cubits terminates at this particular spot.

a (1) E.g., if the wall of a private courtyard fronting on the street is broken through, the place of the wall is called the sides of the street. In 'Er. 94b (quoted below) it is disputed whether this is private or public ground; yet when one carries an object into the street through the breach he is certainly liable. (2) b. Jacob is omitted in 'Er. 94b and Keth. 31a. (3) Rashi: stakes against which vehicles rub to protect the wall. (4) And yet if one carries through the breach into the street he is liable. (5) The case of the colonnade. (6) From a shop to an open place through a colonnade: he is then liable. (7) Even if they are in a public thoroughfare. A house, of course, is also private ground. (8) Jast.: a camp. (9) Or, an open place. (10) I.e., open at both ends into streets.

b (1) If he was not formally warned. (2) If formally warned. (3) The former, because they are not for the general passage of the multitude; the latter, because they are not enclosed. It should be observed that 'public ground' does not mean any ground that is open to the public, but that which is actually frequented by the masses. (4) Lit., 'carry and give,' across a distance of four or more cubits. (5) I.e., a courtyard into which many houses open and which itself abuts on the street. The inhabitants of these houses own the courtyard in common and must pass through it into the street. (6) These too are provided with courtyards through which the inhabitants pass into the streets. (7) For *'erub* v. Glos. If the separate householders make an *'erub*, e.g., each contributing a little flour for baking a large loaf, all the houses and the courtyard into which they open are counted as one domain, and carrying between them is permitted. Again, if all the courtyards are thus joined by an *'erub*, carrying is permitted between the courtyards themselves and between them and the blind alley on which they abut. (8) This is less than four handbreadths square, and is a place of non-liability, i.e., not a separate domain at all, but counted with public or private ground indifferently. (9) This is a Rabbinical measure, lest one treat the Sabbath lightly and carry direct between public and private ground. (10) Like the trench or wall mentioned above. It is private ground, yet not part of the house, and carrying between the two is prohibited.

c (1) The emphasis suggests that only that is private ground. (2) Facing each other.

מסורת הש"ס

עין משפט נר מצוה

מידי דהוה אמעביר חפץ ברה"ר התם לאו אע"ג דכמה דנקיט ליה ואזיל פטור כי מנח לי' חייב ה"נ ל"ש מידמי התם כל היכא דמנח ליה מקום חיוב הוא הכא אי מנח ליה בסטיו מקום פטור הוא אלא מידי דהוה אמעביר חפץ מתחלת ד' לסוף ד' התם לאו אע"ג דאי מנח ליה בתוך ד' אמות פטור כי מנח ליה בסוף ד' אמות חייב ה"נ ל"ש מי דמי התם לגבי דהאי גברא מקום פטור הוא לכ"ע מקום חיוב הוא הכא לכ"ע מקום פטור הוא אלא מידי דהוה אמוציא מרה"י לרה"ר דרך צדי רה"ר התם לאו אע"ג דאי מנח ליה אצדי רה"ר פטור וכי מנח ליה ברה"ר חייב ה"נ ל"ש מתקיף לה רב פפא הניחא לרבנן *דאמרי צדי רה"ר לאו כרה"ר דמי אלא לר' אליעזר *(בן יעקב) דאמר צדי רה"ר כרה"ר דמי מאי איכא למימר א"ל רב אחא בריה דרב איקא אימור דשמעת לר"א *(בן יעקב) דאמר צדי רה"ר כרה"ר דמי היכא דליכא חיפופי אבל היכא דאיכא חיפופי מי שמעת ליה הלכך להא דמיא *א"ר יוחנן ומודה בן עזאי בזורק תניא נמי הכי *המוציא מחנות לפלטיא דרך סטיו חייב אחד המוציא ואחד המכנים (א) ואחד הזורק ואחד המושיט בן עזאי אומר המוציא והמכנים פטור המושיט והזורק חייב: *ת"ר ד' רשויות לשבת רה"י ורה"ר וכרמלית ומקום פטור ואיזו היא רה"י חריץ שהוא עמוק י' ורחב ד' וכן גדר שהוא גבוה י' ורחב ד' זו היא רה"י גמורה ואיזו היא רה"ר סרטיא ופלטיא גדולה ומבואות המפולשין זו היא רה"ר גמורה אין מוציאין מרה"י זו לרה"ר זו ואין מכניסין מרה"ר זו לרה"י זו ואם הוציא והכנים בשוגג חייב חטאת במזיד ענוש כרת ונסקל אבל ים ובקעה ואיסטווניות והכרמלית אינה לא כרה"ר ולא כרה"י ואין נושאין ונותנין בתוכה ואם נשא ונתן בתוכה פטור ואין מוציאין מתוכה לרה"ר ולא מרה"ר לתוכה ואין מכניסין מרה"י לתוכה ולא מתוכה לרה"י ואם הוציא והכנים פטור חצרות של רבים ומבואות שאינן מפולשין עירבו מותרין לא עירבו אסורים אדם עומד על האיסקופה נוטל מבעה"ב ונותן לו נוטל מעני ונותן לו ובלבד שלא יטול מבעה"ב ונותן לעני מעני ונותן לבעה"ב ואם נטל ונתן שלשתן פטורים אחרים אומרים איסקופה משמשת ב' רשויות בזמן שהפתח פתוח כלפנים פתח נעול כלחוץ ואם היתה איסקופה גבוהה י' ורחבה ד' ה"ז רשות לעצמה: אמר מר זו היא רה"י למעוטי מאי למעוטי הא דר' יהודה *דתני' יתר על כן א"ר יהודה מי שיש לו ב' בתי' בשני צדי רה"ר עושה לחי

רש"י

מידי דהוה אמעביר חפץ ברה"ר · יותר מד' אמות וכל כמה דלא מנח ליה פטור וכי הניחו חייב ואע"ג דאיפסיק הילוכא ביני וביני: מתחלת ד' לסוף ד' · אמות מלומלמות: לכולי עלמא מקום חיוב · אם יטלהו חוץ לד' ויניחהו כאן שהרי העבירו ד' שלימות: אצדי ר"ה. מרה"י לר"ה (ג) כגון חצר שנפרץ לר"ה דהוי מקום המחילה לצדי ר"ה ופליגי בה ר' אליעזר ורבנן בעירובין בפ' כל גגות ואמרי רבנן דלאו כר"ה דמו ואפ"ה כי אפיק מרה"י לר"ה דרך שם חייב: היכא דליכא חיפופי. כגון ההיא דעירובין: היכא דאיכא חיפופי. גיצלים יתדות קטנות לפני הכותל שיתיפו שם עגלות וקרונות ולא יחופו בכותל ויפילוהו: מי שמע' ליה · דהוי ר"ה ואפילו הכי כי מפיק לר"ה דרך שם חייב: בזורק · מחנות לפלטיא דרך סטיו דחייב דהא לא נח בכרמלית מידי: המכנים והמוציא פטור · דמהלך כעומד והא נח גופו בכרמלית: ד' רשויות · כולהו מפרש ליה: גדר · כותל שהוא גבוה י' ורחב ד' הוי רה"י: סרטיא · מסילה שהולכין בה מעיר לעיר: פלטיא: רחבה של עיר ששם מתקבלין לסחורה: ומבואו' · של עיר רחבים י"ו אמה: המפולשין · משני ראשיהן *לפלטיא: ענוש כרת · בלא התראה: ונסקל · בהתראה: בקעה · שדות הרבה קנפי"א בלע"ז: איסטוונית · שלפני החנויות שיושבים שם סוחרים: והכרמלית · לקמיה פריך אטו כל הני ים ובקעה לאו הייני כרמלית דקתני הנא לעיל: אינן לא כרשות היחיד · משום דדמיא לרה"ר דאין להם מחיצות: ולא כרה"ר · דאינן דומין לדגלי מדבר דלאו להילוכא דרבים עבידי: אין נושאין ונותנין בתוכן · כלומר אין מטלטלין בהן אלא בתוך ד' משום דדומין לר"ה וגזרו בהן רבנן אטו ר"ה: ואם הוציא והכניס פטור · וזו היא כרמלית האמורה למעלה: חצר של רבים · שפתוחין לחצר בתים רבים והחצר פתוחה לרה"ר ובני הבתים יוצאים דרך החצר לרה"ר: ומבואות שאינן מפולשין · שראשו אחד סתום וחצרות פתוחין לו ובני החצרות יוצאין דרך מבוי לרה"ר: עירבו. כל הבתים של חצר יחד בפת וכן לענין המבוי אם עירבו החצרות הפתוחות לו ביחד: מותרים · להכניס ולהוציא מן הבתים לחצר וכן מן החצרות למבוי: לא עירבו אסורין · מפני שהבית מיוחדת לבעליה והחצר רשות לכולן ונמצא מוציא מרשות לרשות אע"פ שבתיקן רה"י לעשות סייג לתורה להרחיק (ג) שלא יוציא מרה"י לרה"ר והך מילתא לאו מחילוק ד' רשויות היא דבין עירבו בין לא עירבו רה"י היא והמוציא מתוכו לרה"ר חייב: אדם עומד על האסקופה נוטל מעני העומד בחוץ ונותן לו כו' · וזה מקום פטור שהוזכר למעלה שאינו חשוב רשות לעצמו לפי שאינו רחב ד' כדמפר' לקמן ובטל אגל רה"י ואגל רשות הרבים: ובלבד שלא יטול כו' · דמזלזל באיסורי שבת לכתחלה לגרום הוצאה מרה"י לרה"ר וגזירה דילמא אתי לאקולי ולאפוקי להדיא מרה"י לרה"ר: משמשת שתי רשויות · פעמים שהיא משמשת בתורת רה"י ופעמים כרה"ר ולקמיה מפרש לה בשילהי כולהי שמעתא: הרי זו רשות לעצמה · אע"פ שהיא מרה"י כדאמרינן לעיל בגדר גבוה י' ורחב ד' הויא רשות בפני עצמה ואין מוציאין מן הבית לתוכה ולקמן מפרש טעמא: בשני צדי רה"ר · זו כנגד זו: לחי

תוספות

מידי דהוה אמעביר חפץ בר"ה · ה"ל למנקט המוציא דאיירי ביה לעיל דכל כמה דלא מנח ליה מיפטר אלא משום דבתר הכי נקט מעביר נקט ליה נמי השתא ובכל עניני העברה בר"ה קאמר:

התם כל היכא דמנח ליה מקום חיוב הוא · ומוציא ומושיט ומעביר ד"א בר"ה דרך למעלה מי' דחייב אע"ג דאי הוה מנח ליה *למעלה מי' פטור מ"מ תחתיו במקום שמהלך מקום חיוב הוא אבל סטיו הקרקע נמי מקום פטור הוא:

מידי דהוה אצדי ר"ה · וא"ת מה פשוט לן יותר דרך צדי ר"ה מדרך סטיו וי"ל דדרך בית שיש לפניו לדין וכן היה מסתמא במשכן:

היכא דאיכא חיפופי כו' · ותימה בפ' כל גגות (עירובין צד: וסם) פריך ולפלוג בצדי ר"ה דעלמא פירוש ואמאי פליגי בחצר שנפרצה ומשני אי הוי פליגי בעלמא ה"א כי פליגי רבנן עליה ה"מ היכא דאיכא חיפופי אבל היכא דליכא חיפופי מודו קמ"ל משמע דר"א נמי פליג בדאיכא חיפופי וי"ל דה"ק קמ"ל דהיכא דליכא חיפופי דוקא פליגי אבל היכא דאיכא חיפופי מודה רבי אליעזר אי נמי ההיא סוגיא כרב פפא דהכא דלא מחלק:

המושיט והזורק חייב · וא"ת אמאי מודה במושיט וזורק כיון דלא יליף דרך סטיו מדרך צדי לענין (ד) מעביר ה"נ לא נילף בזורק ומושיט וי"ל דלבן עזאי מעביר דרך צדי נמי פטור אע"ג דהיה במשכן משום דמהלך כעומד דמי אבל זורק ומושיט דרך סטיו יליף מזורק ומושיט דרך צדי:

ארבע רשויות לשבת. ק' לרשב"א ליתני ה' רשויות דהא קרפף יותר מבית סאתים שלא הוקף לדירה הזורק מר"ה לתוכו או איפכא חייב ואין מטלטלין בו אלא בד"א וי"ל דההיא רה"י גמור אלא לענין דאין מטלטלין בו אלא בד"א עשאוה ככרמלית והרי כבר שנה רה"י וכרמלית ולהכי נמי לא תני חצר שלא עירבו*:

כרמלית · בירושלמי בריש שבת תני ר' חייא כרמל רך (*ומלה) לא לח ולא יבש אלא בינוני ה"נ כרמלית אינו לא כרה"י ולא כר"ה:

יתר על כן א"ר יהודה · הכי מיתני' בתוספתא פרק ז' דעירובין אחד חלון שבין ב' חצרות ואחד חלון שבין שני בתים כו' וגשרים ונפשות ור"ה מקורה מטלטלין תחתיו בשבת דברי ר' יהודה יתר על כן א"ר יהודה כו פירוש יתר ע"כ בשני בתים משני צדי ר"ה דאף על גב דליכא למימר פי תקרה יורד וסותם כ.זו בגשרים ונפשות ור"ה מקורה דישא אפ"ה עושה ונותן באמצע דקסבר ר"י ב' מחילות דאורייתא כדאמרן בפ' כל גגות (עירובין צה.) וא"ת אמאי לא מייתי הכא מתני' דכל

ע"ש; מסורת הש"ס; הגהות הב"ח; גליון הש"ס:

יח א מיי' פי"ד מהל' שבת הלכה טו סמג לאוין סה טוש"ע א"ח סי' שמו סעיף א:

יט ב מיי' שם הלכה ומוש"ע א"ח שם:

כ ג מיי' שם טוש"ע שם סעיף ב:

כא ד מיי' שם טוש"ע שם סעיף ז:

כב ה מיי' פ"א מהל' שבת הלכה ב:

כג ו מיי' פי"ד שם הל' ו סמג שם טוש"ע א"ח סי' שמה סעיף יד:

כד ז מיי' שם הל' יא וסמג שם טוש"ע א"ח סי' שמו סעיף ב:

כה ח מיי' שם הלכה יג טוש"ע שם ס"א:

כו ט מיי' פ"א מהלכות עירובין הל' ה סמג עשין דרבנן א טוש"ע א"ח סי' שמו וסי' שסו סעיף א:

בעירובין ובכתובות לא נזכר בן יעקב]

כז י מיי' פי"ז מהל' שבת הלכה א סמג שם טוש"ע א"ח סי' שסג סעיף ב:

תוספתא שבת פרק א

[ועי' תוס' עירובין ד"ה ומאי]

[נ"ל ומלא וכן הערוך ועי' תוס' מנחות סו:]

עירובין לד: כתובות לא.

[ליתא] ס"א לאטרי

עירובין לח.

הגהות הב"ח

(א) גמ' ואחד המכנים ואחד המושיט ואחד הזורק בן עזאי: (ב) רש"י ד"ה אצדי רה"ר מרה"י לרה"ר כגון: (ג) ד"ה לא עירבו וכו' לתורה להרחיק הלכם מן העבירה שלא יוציא: (ד) תוס' ד"ה המושיט וכו' מדרך צדי לענין מעביר ה"נ לא נילף וכו' וי"ל דלבן עזאי מעביר דרך צדי:

גליון הש"ס

תוס' ד"ה התם וכו' למעלה מי' פטור. עיין לקמן קב ע"א תד"ה והילכך:

לקמן קיז. עירובין ו. [יב: כב. כה.]

רבינו חננאל

זהו כרמלית. לבן עזאי כאילו עומד בסטיו. שנמצא מוציא מכרמלית לרה"ר ואף על פי אחר ולא מהר חייב ואמרי מידי דהוה אמוציא דרך צדי רשות הרבים התם לאו אע"ג דאי מנח ליה בצדי רה"ר פטור. כי ספיק לה לרה"ר חייב הכא נמי כך הוא דאית להתרא בותל שהוא צדי רה"ר. חיפופי. פי' אבנים. יוצאות מן הקיר כדיים כדי שלא יחופו והחכבו הבהמות ובני אדם העוברים בו ויהרסוהו. דאמי' לר' אליעזר דאמר צדי רה"ר כרה"ר הן היכא דאיכא חיפופי דברי הכל לאו כרה"ר נינהו. א"ר יוחנן מודה בן עזאי שהזורק מחנות לפלטיא דרך סטיו חייב. תניא נמי חכי אחד הזורק ואחד המושיט ואחד המוציא ואחד המכנים מחנות לפלטיא דרך סטיו חייב. בן עזאי אומר המוציא והמכנים פטור המושיט והזורק חייב. מ"מ לא אמרי' קלוטה כמו שהונחה: ת"ר ד' רשויות לשבת. רה"י

רב נסים גאון

מתקיף לה רב פפא הנידא לרבנן דאמרי צידי רשות הרבים לאו כרשות הרבים דאמו אלא לר' אליעזר דאמר כרשות הרבים דאמו מאי איכא למימר ופליגא דר' אליעזר ורבנן במס' עירובין בפרק כל גגות העיר (דף צד) דתנן חצר שנפרצה לרה"ר המכניס מתוכה לרה"י או מרה"י לתוכה חייב דברי ר' אליעזר וחכמים אומרים מתוכה לרה"ר ומרה"ר לתוכה פטור ואמרי' בגמ' ואיבעי תימה בצידי רה"ר קמיפלגי דר' אליעזר סבר צידי רה"ר כרה"ר דאמו ורבנן סברי צידי רשות הרבים לאו כרה"ר דאמו: הבקעה בימות החמה רשות היחיד לשבת ורשות הרבים לטומאה בימות הגשמים רשות היחיד לכאן ולכאן פירשו בתוספתא במסכת טהרות בפרק המסוכן [פ"ז] אלו הן ימות החמה משתעקר תבואה מתוכה ואלו הן ימות הגשמים משתרד רביעה שנייה ומפורש הרביעה במסכת תענית (דף ו) בפ' א':

עין משפט
נר מצוה

כח א מיי' פי"ז מהל' שבת הלכה לג:

כט ב מיי' פי"ד מהל' שבת הלכה א:

ל ג ד מיי' פ"כ מהל' אבות הטומאות הל' ו:

לחי מכאן ולחי מכאן או קורה מכאן וקורה מכאן ונושא ונותן באמצע אמרו לו אין מערבין רשות הרבים בכך ואמאי קרו ליה גמורה מהו דתימא כי פליגי רבנן עליה דרבי יהודה דלא הוי רה"י ה"מ לטלטל אבל לזרוק מודו ליה קמ"ל: אמר מר זו היא רה"ר למעוטי מאי למעוטי אידך דרבי יהודה *דתנן רבי יהודה אומר אם היתה דרך רה"ר מפסקתן יסלקנה לצדדין [א]וחכמים אומרים אינו צריך ואמאי קרו ליה גמורה אידי דתנא רישא גמורה תנא נמי סיפא גמורה ולחשוב נמי מדבר דהא תניא איזו היא ר"ה סרטיא ופלטיא גדולה ומבואות המפולשין [ב]והמדבר אמר אביי לא קשיא כאן בזמן שישראל שרויין במדבר כאן בזמן הזה: אמר מר אם הוציא והכניס בשוגג חייב חטאת במזיד ענוש כרת ונסקל בשוגג חייב חטאת פשיטא במזיד ענוש כרת ונסקל אצטריכא ליה הא נמי פשיטא הא קמ"ל כדרב דא"ר *מצאתי° מגלת סתרים בי רבי חייא וכתוב בה איסי בן יהודה אומר אבות מלאכות מ' חסר אחת ואינו חייב אלא אחת איני *והתנן אבות מלאכות מ' חסר אחת והוינן בה מנינא למה לי ואמר רבי יוחנן *שאם עשאן כולן בהעלם אחת חייב על כל אחת ואחת אלא אימא אינו חייב על אחת מהן והא קמ"ל האמהנך דלא מספקן: אמר מר אבל ים ובקעה והאיסטוונית והכרמלית אינן לא כרה"י ולא כרה"ר ובקעה אינו לא כרה"י ולא כרשות הרבים והא *תנן [ג]הבקעה בימות החמה רה"י לשבת ורה"ר לטומאה בימות הגשמים רה"י *(לכאן ולכאן) אמר עולא לעולם כרמלית הויא ואמאי קרי לה רה"י לפי שאינה רה"ר [ד]רב אשי אמר כגון

לחי מכאן ולחי מכאן· בשתי פאות של אחד מן הבתים להיכר בעלמא דקסבר רבי יהודה ב' מחיצות הוו רה"י מדאורייתא והא איכא שתי מחיצות מעלייתא מחיצות של ב' בתים: מהו דתימא כי פליגי רבנן עליה דר' יהודה· בברייתא ואמרי אין מערבין רה"ר בכך למהוי רה"י ה"מ לטלטל שיהא מותר לטלטל בתוכה כדקתני אין מערבין רה"ר בכך דגזור בה משום דדמי לרה"ר: אבל לזרוק· שהזורק מרה"ר לתוכה מודו ליה דחייב דשתי מחיצות דאוריי' ושם רה"י עליה: קמ"ל גמורה. כלומר זו היא שנגמרו מניין מחיצות שלה שיש לה מחיצות מכל צד כגון חריץ וכן גדר דאמרינן מד' לדדין גוד אסיק פני המחיצה על ראשו ונמלא ראשו מוקף מד' לדדין וחללו ד' אבל דרבי יהודה לא נגמרו מחיצות שלה למניינן ולאו רה"י היא כלל: מפסקתן· לפסי בירָאות בפרק ב' דעירובין דהקילו חכמים משום עולי רגלים בבור בר"ה והבור עלמה רה"י שהיא עמוקה י' ורחבה ד' והממלא מתוכה ומניח על שפתה חייב והקילו חכמים לעשות ד' פסין וביניהן י' אמות דהוי חללו רה"י למלאות מן הבור וקאמר ר' יהודה אם היתה דרך רה"ר מפסקתן יסלקנה מביניהן דאתו רבים ומבטלי מחילתה והתם רמינן דרבי יהודה אדרבי יהודה דלעיל דאמר נושא ונותן באמצע דלא אתו רבים ומבטלין מחילות ורבנן אדרבנן ומשנינן לה: אינו צריך· והיינו דקתני זו היא רה"ר אבל הילוך דרבים לבין הפסים לא הוי רה"ר הואיל ואיכא שם ד' מחילות: ומאי גמורה· הכא ליכא למימר מהו דתימא כדלעיל דעיקר עשייתן משום לטלטל בתוכו וקאמרי רבנן אינו צריך דרשות היחיד היא אפילו לטלטל וכ"ש דהזורק לתוכה מרה"ר חייב: בזמן שהיו ישראל במדבר· חשיבא רה"ר: בזמן הזה· אינו מקום הילוך לרבים דהולכי מדברות לא שכיחי: חייב חטאת פשיטא· כיון דתנא חדא רה"י וחדא רה"ר ניתני סתמא ואם הוציא והכניס חייב ואנא ידענא דשגגתו חטאת דהא שבת זדונו כרת הוא: הא נמי פשיטא· דבהתראה סקילה ממקושש: מגילת סתרים· שהסתירוה. מפני שלא ניתנה ליכתוב וכששומעין דברי יחיד חדשים שאינן שנוין בב"ה וכותבין אותן שלא ישתכחו מסתירין את המגילה: אינו חייב אלא אחת· השתא משמע אם עשאן בהעלם אחד שלא נודע לו בין כל אחת ואחת שחטא אינו חייב אלא אחת דכל חילול דשבת גוף אחד של עבירה הוא: מנינא למה לי· ליתני אבות מלאכות הזורע והחורש כו' למה לי לאשמעי' מניינא הא מני להו ואזיל: חייב על כל אחת ואחת· ובא להודיענו סכום החטאות שאדם חייב באיסורי שבת בהעלם אחד ואשמעינן מ' חסר אחת הן ותו לא שאפי' עשה תולדותיהן עמהן אינו מביא על התולדה היכא לעשאה עם אביה דה"ל כעושה וחוזר ועושה דכול' חדא עבירה היא: אינו חייב על אחת מהן· אחת יש בהן שאינו חייב עליה מיתה ולא פי' (רבי) איזו היא ואשמעי' תנא דמתני' דקתני נסקל דהא הולאה והכנסה מהנך דלא מספקן היא דעל זו לא אמר איסי בן יהודה: בימות החמה· שאין בה זרעים: רה"י לשבת· דהא לאו הילוך לרבים הוא שאין רבים מסתלקין מן המסילה לילך בשדה: רה"ר לטומאה· וספקו טהור דהא לאו מקום סתירה הוא שיש בני אדם נכנסים לה דספק טומאה לטמא מסוטה גמרינן לה והתם סתירה כתיב ונסתרה והיא נטמאה דבמקום סתירה טמאה היא לבעלה מספק ומכאן אתה דן לשרץ: בימות הגשמים· שהיא זרועה אין אדם נכנס לה: לעולם כרמלית הויא· והזורק מרה"ר לתוכה אינו חייב:

כגון

דכל גגות (עירובין צב.) דקתני התם ועוד אמר רבי יהודה מערבין למבוי המפולש וי"ל דמתני' איכא לפרושי דמערבין בצורת הפתח וקסבר ג' מחילות דאורייתא א"כ ה"א דמתני' איירי במבוי המפולש לרה"ר אבל אין ר"ה עוברת לתוכה להכי מייתי הברייתא דיתר על כן דאפי' רה"ר (גמורה) עוברת בה מטלטלין ע"י לחי או קורה משום דשתי מחילות דאורייתא ואע"ג דבפ"ק דעירובין (דף י.) אמתני' דהרחב מי' אמות ימעט משמע דלכל היותר לא התיר רבי יהודה אלא עד י"ג אמה ושליש °היינו מדרבנן אבל מדאורייתא אפי' ברוחב י"ו אמות מטלטלין דאית ליה ב' מחילות דאורייתא דע"כ צ"ל דרבי יהודה איירי ברה"ר גמורה שבוקעין שם רבים כדמוכח בפ"ק דעירובין דף ו: ושם) גבי כילד מערבין רה"ר ושם פירשתי* וא"ת והא מדקתני סיפא דמבואות המפולשין הוו רה"ר שמעי' שפיר לאפוקי מדר' יהודה דאית ליה ב' מחילות דאורייתא דלדידיה מבואו' המפולשות לא הוו רה"ר כיון דאיכא שתי מחילות וי"ל דמסיפא לא הוה שמעינן לאפוקי מדר' יהודה דה"א טעמא דרבי יהודה משום· דקסבר לחי וקורה משום מחילה דאיכא מאן דסבר הכי בפ"ק דעירובין (דף טו:) להכי אצטריך למתני' זו היא רה"י גמורה *למעוטי דר' יהודה דלא הוי רה"י דלחי וקורה לא חשיב מחילה:

ואמאי קרי ליה גמורה כו' מהו דתימא· אומר ר"י דלשון גמורה אדרבה איפכא מסתברא זו היא רה"י גמורה אבל זו אינה רה"י גמורה אבל היא רה"י קצת ורש"י ישבה בדוחק (א) לפי הגמרא:

כאן בזמן שישראל שרויין במדבר· משמע קצת דאינה ר"ה אלא א"כ מצויין שם °ששים רבוא כמו במדבר:

בשוגג חייב חטאת פשיטא· כיון דאשמעינן דהאי הוי רה"י והאי הוי ר"ה פשיטא דהמוליא מזה לזה בשוגג חייב חטאת:

הא קמ"ל כרב כו'· מכאן מדקדק ר"י דלא קתני איסי אינו חייב על אחת מהן אלא אסקילה אבל חטאת חייב על כולם דאי קאי אחטאת א"כ כי פריך בשוגג חייב חטאת פשיטא הו"ל לשנויי הא קמ"ל כרב דהא דמשני במזיד ענוש כרת ונסקל אילטריכא ליה לא משני מידי ומעיקרא ודאי לא היה ידע דמיירי בסקילה מדפריך מדר' יוחנן דמיירי בחטאת והיינו משום דאינו חייב אלא אחת לא מצי לאוקמי בסקילה דאטו בתרי קטלי קטלינן ליה אבל כי קמפרש דאינו חייב על אחת מהן קאמר איסי אז ידע שפיר דלא איירי איסי אלא בסקילה דלא פליג אמתני' דכלל גדול (לקמן עג:) דקתני מנייא למימר דחייב על כל אחת ואחת ואתי שפיר הא דבריש פרק כלל גדול (שם סט·) קאמר ארבי יוחנן דאמר שאם עשאן כולם בהעלם אחת חייב כו' דידע לה לשבת במאי ומפרש דידע לה לתחומים ואליבא דר"ע ולא מצי למימר דידע לה בדאיסי דהא אכולהו חייב חטאת וכן פירש בקונטרס ולקמן בריש הארק (דף צו:) מייתי לדאיסי לענין סקילה ולא מישתמיט בשום מקום לאתויי לענין חטאת והא דאמרינן לקמן בריש פרק בתרא (דף קנד.) לרמי בר חמא דילמא הכי קאמר כל שחייבין על שגגתו חטאת חייבים על זדונו סקילה אומר ריב"א דאליבא דרמי בר חמא אתיא ההיא ברייתא דלא כאיסי דלאיסי איכא דוכתא דחייב חטאת ולא סקילה:

ואמר רבי יוחנן שאם עשאן כולם בהעלם אחת כו'· אין לריך לפרש דפריך דמסתמא לא פליג איסי עלה אלא מדברי איסי נמי יש לדקדק כן מדקתני מניינא כדדייק לקמן בכלל גדול (דף עג:):

לא

רבינו חננאל

ורה"ר כרמלית ומקום פטור. פשיטא היא זו הברייתא וגם פירשוה הראשונים ממני. איזו היא רה"י חריץ עמוק י' טפחים ורחב ד'. וכן גדר גבוה י' ורחב ד' זו היא רה"י גמורה (הבז) זו היא למעוטי הא דתני ר' יהודה מי שיש לו ב' בתים בשני צדי רה"ר עושה לחי מכאן וכי זה אינו רה"י לא לזרוק וכ"ש לטלטל. סרטיא ופלטיא ומבואות המפולשות זו היא רה"ר גמורה למעוטי הא דר' יהודה. דתנן בעירובין בפסי ביראות. ר' יהודה אומר אם היתה דרך הרבים מפסקתה יסלקנה לצדדין קמ"ל דאע"ג דלא סילקה אינה כרה"ר: אמר מר והוציא מרה"י זה לרה"ר זה בשוגג חייב חטאת במזיד בלא התראה ענוש כרת בהתראה נסקל פשיטא לא נצרכה אלא להא דאמר רב מצאתי במגילה סתרים בי ר' חייא וכתיב בה איסי בן יהודה אומר אבות מלאכות ארבעים חסר אחת אינו חייב על אחת מהן נכנא חייב על אחת בפני עצמה בספק זולתי המוציא מרשות לרשות דלא מספקא חיוב. דתני בהדיא בשוגג חייב חטאת במזיד חייב כרת ונסקל הא דתנן בטהרות פ"ו הבקעה בימות החמה רה"י לשבת ומטלטלין בה רה"ר לטומאה וק"ל ספק טומאה ברה"ר טהור בימות הגשמים שמלאה מים ואין אדם נכנס לתוכה רה"י לזה ולזה. משני עולא לעולם הבקעה כרמלית היא.

יראה

נד"ס וכי תימא

ולא בעי למימר דזו היא רה"י גמורה למעוטי דרבנן דאם היה רה"ר מפסקתן זו היא רה"ר למעוטי אידך דרבנן דמי שיש לו שני בתים דלא הוי רה"ר דלחי וקורה משום מחילה דזהו לא מיסתבר יעוד ליתא ליה עפי לאוקמי כרבנן [ת"י]

ב"ב קנג: טהרות פ"ו מ"ו

[בטהרות אי' לכך ולכך]

מסורת הש"ס

עירובין [כ.] כב.

לקמן צו:

לקמן סט. ע: עג: [צו:]

הגהות הב"ח

(א) תוס' ד"ה ואמאי וכו' ורש"י ישבה בדוחק (לפי הגמרא) תא"מ וכ"ב ס"א לפירוש גמורה:

*בקשה ריב"א ומאי קמ"ל ר"י מתני' היא לקמן סז: ומי דקמ"ל בהעלם זה וזה בידו לאי בשבת בכרכת והזיד בלאו כדלקמן דף ע: א"כ קמ"ל דלא כאיסי דאף בדאיסי חייב חטאת [ת"י]

גליון הש"ס

גמ' דאמר רב מצאתי מגלת סתרי בי ר"ח. ב"מ צב ע"א: תוס' ד"ה יותר היינו מדרבנן. ולא זכיתי להבין הא מה דקתני ומקן לחי כו' ונושא ונותן באמצע היינו נמי מדרבנן דמדאורייתא ל"צ דהא סבר ב' מחיצות דאורייתא: תוס' ד"ה כאן כו' ששים רבוא כו' עי' עירובין ע"ח תוד"ה כיצד:

can place [6b] a board or a beam at each side[3] and carry between them.[4] Said they to him: A street cannot be made fit [for carrying] by an *'erub* in this way.[5] And why is it called 'absolute' [private ground]?—You might argue, The Rabbis differ from R. Judah, [maintaining] that it is not private ground only in respect of carrying [therein]:[6] but in respect of throwing[7] they agree with R. Judah:[8] hence we are informed [otherwise].

The Master said: 'That is [absolute] public ground.' What does this exclude?—It excludes R. Judah's other [ruling]. For we learnt: R. Judah said: If the public thoroughfare interposes between them, it must be removed to the side; but the Sages maintain: It is unnecessary.[9] And why is it called 'absolute?'—Because the first clause states 'absolute', the second does likewise. Now, let the desert too be enumerated, for it was taught: What is public ground? A high-road, a great open space, open alleys and the desert?—Said Abaye, There is no difficulty: The latter means when the Israelites dwelt in the desert; the former refers to our
a own days.[1]

The Master said: 'If one carries out or in, unwittingly, he is liable to a sin-offering; if deliberately, he is punished by *kareth* or stoned.' 'Unwittingly, he is liable to a sin-offering': but it is obvious?—It is necessary [to state] 'If deliberately, he is punished by *kareth* or stoned.' But that too is obvious?—We are informed the following, in agreement with Rab. For Rab said, I found a secret scroll[2] of the school of R. Ḥiyya wherein it is written, Issi b. Judah said: There are thirty-nine principal labours, but one is liable only [for] one. Yet that is not so? for we learnt: The principal labours are forty less one: and we pondered thereon, Why state the number?[3] And R. Joḥanan answered: [To teach] that if one performs all of them in one state of unawareness,[4] he is liable for each separately! Rather, say thus: for one of these he is not liable; and so we are informed here that this one [*sc.* carrying] is of those about which there is no doubt.

The Master said: 'But the sea, a plain, a colonnade, and a *karmelith* rank neither as public nor as private ground.' But is a plain neither private nor public ground? Surely we learnt: A plain: in summer it is private ground in respect to the Sabbath and public ground in respect to uncleanness;[5] in winter it is private ground in both
b respects![1]—Said 'Ulla: After all it is a *karmelith;* yet why is it called private ground? Because it is not public ground.[2] R. Ashi

(3) Of one of the houses. (4) R. Judah holds that two partitions facing each other render the space between private ground by Biblical law. The outside walls of the houses are two such partitions, while the two are added to mark out this particular space and distinguish it from the rest of the street. (5) V. 'Er., *6b* and notes. (6) Forbidding it as a precautionary measure, lest one carry in public ground too. (7) An object from other private ground into this. (8) That liability is incurred, because by Biblical law two partitions constitute private ground. (9) A well ten handbreadths deep and four broad in a public highway is private ground, as stated above; consequently, if one draws water and places it at the side, he desecrates the Sabbath. Therefore the Rabbis enacted that it should be surrounded by boards, even at some distance, and placed at intervals, providing that there is not a gap of more than ten cubits between any two; this renders the whole private ground, as though it were entirely enclosed. But R. Judah maintains that if the actual road taken by travellers lies between these boards, it destroys its character as private ground and makes it public ground in spite of the boards, and therefore it must be diverted. The emphasis in our Baraitha—*that* is public ground—is to reject this view of R. Judah.

a (1) When it is not frequented. (2) מגלת סתרים. Rashi: When a scholar heard a new law which had no authoritative tradition behind it and was thus rejected by the schools, he committed it to writing for fear that he might forget it, and kept it secret. Weiss, *Dor,* II, 189 thinks that the scroll contained views which R. Judah ha-Nasi had desired to exclude from his authoritative compilation, and therefore it was kept concealed.—On these lines a very considerable portion of the Baraitha would have had to be kept secret! Kaplan, *Redaction of the Talmud,* p. 277 suggests that the concealed scroll contained laws which were unsuited for unrestricted publicity. He also suggests that the phrase may not mean 'concealed' but written in a 'concealed', i.e. esoteric style. But there is nothing particularly esoteric about the style of the law quoted here. V. also Levi, *Wörterbuch* s.v. (3) Since they are all stated separately. (4) I.e., he is unaware throughout that these are forbidden on the Sabbath. (5) In summer it is not sown, hence a few may pass through it, yet not many will trouble to leave the highway. Hence carrying therein is permitted. With respect to uncleanness, it is a general principle that if a doubt arises in a *strictly* private place, a stringent ruling is given, and the article or person concerned is unclean; if it arises in a public i.e., not a strictly private place, we are lenient. Hence, since the plain is not strictly private, it ranks as public ground.

b (1) Since it is sown, no stranger enters therein. (2) And as the main purpose of that Mishnah is to draw a distinction between the Sabbath and uncleanness, that is sufficient, without pointing out that it is a *karmelith.*

said: [7a] E.g., when it has barriers,[3] and [this is] in accordance with the following dictum of 'Ulla in R. Johanan's name: An enclosure more than two *se'ahs* [in area][4] which is not enclosed in attachment to a dwelling place,[5] even if it is a *kor* or two *kor* [in area],[6] if one throws [an article] therein [from public ground] he is liable. What is the reason? It is a partitioned area, but it lacks inhabitants.[7] Now, as for R. Ashi, it is well that he does not explain it as 'Ulla;[8] but why does 'Ulla not explain it in accordance with his own dictum?—He answers you: if it has barriers, is it called a plain: [surely] it is an enclosure! And R. Ashi?[9]—'Private ground' is taught.[10]

'And a *karmelith*.' Are then all these [sea, plain and colonnade] too not *karmelith?*—When R. Dimi came,[1] he said in the name of R. Johanan: This is necessary only in respect of a corner near a street[2]: though the masses sometimes press and overflow therein,[3] yet since it is inconvenient for [general] use, it ranks as a *karmelith*.

When R. Dimi came, he said in R. Johanan's name: [The place] between the pillars[4] is treated as a *karmelith*. What is the reason? Though the general public walk through there, since they cannot proceed with ease,[5] it is as a *karmelith*. R. Zera said in Rab Judah's name: The balcony in front of the pillars is treated as a *karmelith*. Now, he who stated thus of [the ground] between the pillars,—how much more so the balcony![6] But he who mentions the balcony—only the balcony [ranks as a *karmelith*], because it is inconvenient for [general] use, but not [the ground] between the pillars, which is convenient for [general] use.[7] Another version: but [the place] between the pillars, through which the public occasionally walk, is as public ground.

Rabbah b. Shila said in R. Hisda's name: If a brick is standing upright in the street, and one throws [an article][8] and it adheres to its side, he is liable; on top, he is not liable.[9] Abaye and Raba both state: Providing that it is three handbreadths high, so that the public do not step on it;[10] but thorns and shrubs, even if not
b three [handbreadths] high.[1] Hiyya b. Rab maintained: Even thorns and shrubs, but not dung.[2] R. Ashi ruled: Even dung.

Rabbah, of the school of R. Shila, said: When R. Dimi came,[3] he said in the name of R. Johanan: No *karmelith* can be less than four [handbreadths square].[4] And R. Shesheth said: And it extends[5] up to ten. What is meant by, 'and it extends up to ten?' Shall we say that only if there is a partition ten [handbreadths high] is it a *karmelith*, not otherwise;[6] but is it not? Surely R. Gidal said in the name of R. Hiyya b. Joseph in Rab's name: In the case of a house, the inside of which is not ten [handbreadths in height] but its covering makes it up to ten, it is permitted to carry on the roof over the whole [area];[7] but within, one may carry only four cubits![8] But what is meant by 'and it extends up to ten?' That only up to ten is it a *karmelith*, but not higher.[9] And even as Samuel said to Rab Judah, Keen scholar![10] In matters concerning the Sabbath do not consider[11] aught above ten. In what respect? Shall we say that there is no private ground above ten? Surely R. Hisda said: If one fixes a rod in private ground[12] and throws [an article from the street] and it alights on the top, even if it is a hundred cubits high, he is liable, because private ground extends up to heaven! [7b] But [if it means]

(3) I.e., it is enclosed by a fence, wall, etc. Though the Rabbis treat it as a *karmelith* in so far that carrying therein is forbidden, it is nevertheless private ground by Biblical law, and carrying between it and public ground involves liability. It is in that sense that the Mishnah designates it a private domain. (4) *Se'ah* is primarily a measure of capacity; by transference it is used as a surface measure on the basis that two *se'ahs'* seed require an area of five thousand square cubits. (5) V. Rashi: *Aliter:* which is not enclosed for living purposes. (6) 1 *kor* = 6 *se'ahs*. (7) An enclosed place is private ground by Biblical law, whatever its size. Now, if it is attached to a dwelling (or enclosed for living purposes), e.g., a house stood in a field and then the field, upon which one of the doors of the house opens, was enclosed, it remains private ground by Rabbinical law too. But if it is not connected with a house, it is private ground only up to the area of two *se'ahs;* beyond that one may not carry therein by Rabbinical law. Since, however, it is private ground by Biblical law, if one throws an article into it from public ground he is liable, and to this the Mishnah quoted refers when it states that a plain is private ground. (8) Viz., that the Mishnah means that it is a *karmelith*, because he prefers to explain it in accordance with 'Ulla's other dictum. (9) That being so, why does he not accept 'Ulla's explanation? (10) Which is definitely not a *karmelith*.

(1) V. *supra* 5a, n. b9. (2) At which stood a house the front of which the owner had thrown open to the public. (3) When the street is very crowded. (4) Pillars were erected in public squares or markets, upon which traders hung their wares. (5) Lit., 'directly'. On account of the numerous pillars, which were not always in a straight line. (6) Which is even less convenient.—The balcony was used as a stand for traders' stalls. (7) In his opinion. (8) Across a distance of at least four cubits. (9) When an article lies in the street and is less than ten handbreadths high and four square it is a place of non-liability; but that is only in respect of what can be put to a well-defined, natural use; e.g., the top of a low wall or of a brick, upon which articles may be placed. But the side of a wall or a brick can only give accidental service, as in the example, and in that case everything less than *ten* handbreadths high is as the street itself, and so when one throws an article and after traversing four cubits it cleaves to the side of the brick, it is as though it fell in the street, and he is liable. But the top, which, as explained by Abaye and Raba, is three handbreadths high, constitutes a separate domain—a place of non-liability. (10) Then it is not part of the street; v. preceding note. [Whether the surface area of the brick has to be four square handbreadths v. Tosaf. a.l.].

b (1) Rank as a separate domain, because people avoid stepping on them. (2) People wearing thick shoes may step upon the former; but dung is avoided. (3) V. *supra* 5a, n. b9. (4) If it is, it is not a *karmelith* but a place of non-liability. (5) Lit., 'takes hold'. (6) I.e., an enclosed space less than two *se'ahs* in area and not attached to a house (v. *supra* n. b7) is a *karmelith* only if its fencing is ten handbreadths high. (7) The roof is ten high, and therefore private ground. (8) Since it is unfit for a dwelling, its walls are disregarded and it ranks not as a private domain but as a *karmelith* (R. Han.). This is the reverse of our hypothesis. (9) If its top is more than ten handbreadths above ground level it is not a *karmelith*. (10) Or, man of long teeth. (11) Lit., 'be'. (12) A rod is generally less than four handbreadths square.

כגון דאית לה מחיצות וכי הא דאמר עולא א"ר יוחנן *קרפף יותר מבית סאתים שלא הוקף לדירה ואפילו כור ואפילו כוריים הזורק לתוכו חייב מ"ט מחיצה היא אלא שמחוסרת דיורין בשלמא רב אשי לא אמר (א) כדעולא אלא עולא מ"ט לא אמר כשמעתיה אמר לך אי דאית לה מחיצות בקעה קרי לה קרפף היא ורב אשי °רה"י קתני: והכרמלית אטו כולהו נמי לאו כרמלית נינהו כי אתא רב דימי א"ר יוחנן לא נצרכה אלא לקרן זוית הסמוכה לרה"ר דאע"ג דזימנין דדחקי ביה רבים ועיילי לגוה כיון דלא ניחא תשמישתיה כי כרמלית דמי כי אתא רב דימי א"ר יוחנן בין העמודין נידון ככרמלית מ"ט אף על גב דדרסי בה רבים כיון דלא מסתגי להו בהדיא ככרמלית דמיא אמר ר' זירא אמר רב יהודה איצטבא שלפני העמודים נידון ככרמלית למ"ד בין העמודים כ"ש איצטבא למ"ד איצטבא איצטבא הוא דלא ניחא תשמישתיה אבל בין העמודים דניחא תשמישתיה לא לישנא אחרינא אבל בין העמודין דזימנין דדרסי ליה רבים כרה"ר דמיא אמר רבה בר שילא אמר רב חסדא לבינה זקופה ברה"ר וזורק וטח בפניה חייב על גבה פטור אביי ורבא דאמרי תרוייהו והוא שגבוה שלשה דלא דרסי לה רבים אבל *היזמי *והיגי אע"ג דלא גבידי שלשה וחייא בר רב אמר אפילו היזמי והיגי אבל צואה לא ורב אשי אמר אפילו צואה אמר רבה דבי רב שילא כי אתא רב דימי אמר רבי יוחנן *אין כרמלית פחותה מארבעה ואמר רב ששת ותופסת עד עשרה מאי ותופסת עד עשרה אילימא דאי איכא מחיצה עשרה הוא דהוי כרמלית ואי לא לא הוי כרמלית ולא והאמר רב גידל אמר רב חייא בר יוסף אמר רב בית שאין בתוכו עשרה וקרויו משלימו לעשרה על גגו מותר לטלטל בכולו °בתוכו אין מטלטלין בו אלא ד' אמות אלא מאי ותופסת עד י' דעד י' הוא דהויא כרמלית למעלה מי' טפחים לא הוי כרמלית וכי הא דא"ל שמואל לרב יהודה שיננא לא תיהוי במילי דשבתא למעלה מי' למאי הלכתא אילימא דאין רשות היחיד למעלה מי' והאמר רב חסדא *נעץ קנה ברשות היחיד וזרק ונח על גביו אפילו גבוה מאה אמה חייב מפני *שרה"י עולה עד לרקיע

אלא

כגון דאית לה מחיצות. ואשמעינן דאע"ג דהיקפה יותר מבית סאתים ולא הוקף לדירה שאין ביתו סמוך לה קודם היקף ולענין לטלטל לתוכה הויא ככרמלית כדאמרינן בעירובין שאין מטלטלין בו אלא בד' אפ"ה דאורייתא רה"י היא והזורק מרה"ר לתוכה חייב: כדעולא. דאמר מחיצה היא לקרות רה"י אלא שמחוסרת דירה לכך אסורה לטלטל מדרבנן והא דקתני רה"ר לטומאה כגון שיש פתחים במחיצותיה ונכנסין בה *ויוצאין בה: עולא. דאמר אמאי קרי לה רה"י כו' מ"ט לא אמר כגון דאית לה מחיצות ורה"י גמורה קאמר וניזיל בתר שמעתיה דאמר הזורק לתוכו חייב: ורב אשי. אמר לך רה"י קתני וכרמלית לא קרי לה תנא רה"י: אטו כולהו. הנך ים ובקעה ואיסטווניות לאו זו היא כרמלית דהוזכר במנין רשויות הא קתני איטו לא כרה"י ולא כרה"ר ואין מוליכין כו' ש"מ זו היא רשות שלישי: לא נצרכה. כרמלית דקתני אלא לאוסופי כרמלית אחריתי כגון קרן זוית שנכנס בו בית לתוכו והניח מקרקעו לרה"ר: לא ניחא תשמישתיה. שאין יכולין להכנס לה להדיא דרך הילוכו אי נמי בית שפניו עומד באלכסון שזויתו אחת סמוכה לרה"ר והשניה משוכה מרה"ר ולפנים זוית הבולטת מעכבת את הרבים מליכנס בהדי' בתוך כניסה של זוית האחרת: בין העמודים. שהיו עמודים ברחבה ותולין בהם התגרים פרגמטיא וגם איצטבאות היו לפניהם לישב שם התגרים: לא מסתגי להו להדיא. שהיו עמודים הרבה באורך ורוחב וזה שלא כנגד זה: לבינה. סתם לבינה ארכה ורחבה ג' ואין לעביה שיעור יש מהן עבות ויש מהן דקות: וטח על פניה. כגון דבילה שמינה או טיט: חייב. אם זרק ד"א דהוי כמונח ברה"ר דכל למטה מי' רה"ר הוא ובלבד שינוח (או) למטה מג' דהוי כקרקע או באויר כי האי דנדבקה בכותל וכדאמרינן במתני' לקמן הזורק ד' אמות בכותל למטה מי' טפחים כזורק בארץ וחייב וכי אמר למטה מי' ברוחב ד' כרמלית וכשאין רחב ד' מקום פטור היינו בתשמיש המסוים כגון גב לבינה וראש כותל או עמוד דהני מסתיים תשמישתייהו אבל אויר כגון פני הכותל דבר הנדבק בו לא הוי רשותא לנפשיה אלא אי למטה מי' הוא הוי רה"ר גמור ואי למעלה מי' הוא דלא שלטי ביה רבים הוי אוירא בעלמא מקום פטור כדתנן למעלה מי' טפחים כזורק באויר ופטור: על גבה פטור. כדמוקי לה אביי ורבא בגבוהה ג' דלא דרסי בה רבים דהוי מקום לעצמה: היזמי. דורנא"י: היגי. אינגלטי"ר: אע"ג דלא גבוה ג'. הוי מקום פטור לעצמו דלא דרסי בה רבים עליה שלא יזוקו: אפילו היזמי והיגי. דדרסי עליה בסנדליהון אבל צואה אע"ג דלא גבוה לא דרסי עלה ורב אשי אמר אפילו צואה: ה"ג אין כרמלית פחותה מד'. רוחב ואי לא מקום פטור הוא ומותר לכתחלה להוציא משם לרשות הרבים ולרה"י: ותופסת. בגובה עד י' ולקמיה מפרש לה: אילימא דאי איכא מחיצה י' כו'. כגון בקעה המוקפת גדר והיא יתירה על בית סאתים ולא הוקפה לדירה: וקירויו משלימו. עובי קירויו: על גגו. דגבוה י' הוי רה"י ומותר לטלטל בכולו: אלא בד'. דכיון דלא גבוה המחיצה י' הוי כרמלית אלמא איפכא שמעינן לה: דעד י' הוי כרמלית. אויר של בקעה או של ים או של קרפף יתר על בית סאתים תופס את שמו עד י' אבל למעלה מי' אין שם כרמלית על אוירו בדבר שאינו מסויים כגון פני לבינה או פני כותל או קלט מן האויר למעלה מי' מותר להוציא לכתחלה משם לרה"י ולרה"ר דאין שם כרמלית עליו כי היכי דאויר למעלה מי' ברה"ר לאו רה"ר הוא כדתנן לקמן למעלה מי' כזורק באויר גבי כרמלית נמי לאו כרמלית הוא ובדבר מסויים כגון ראש עמוד וגב לבינה ליכא לאוקמיה דאי אית ביה ארבע פשיטא דלמעלה מעשרה לא הוי כרמלית דהא אפילו עמוד ברשות הרבים רשות היחיד הוא ואי דלית ביה ארבע ולמטה מעשרה מי הוי כרמלית הא קאמר אין כרמלית פחותה מארבע ואי בדקאי בכרמלית וכיון דלית ביה ד' הוי *שם הכרמלית עליו אם כן מצינו חומר בכרמלית מרשות הרבים דאילו ברשות הרבים כי האי גוונא מקום פטור הוא ובטל ומותר לרשות הרבים ולרשות היחיד ואנן אמרינן בשמעתין דהאי תופסת עד י' מקולי רשות הרבים הוא הלכך לא מיתוקמא אלא באוירא: אילימא. דאין רה"י שולטת בחלל באויר למעלה מי' אלא מקום פטור הוא ובטל אף לגבי רה"ר: נעץ קנה. סתמיה אין רחב ד': וזרק. מר"ה ונח על גביו: חייב. כמונח ע"ג קרקע דלא בעי הנחה על גבי מקום ד' ברה"י כדמפרש לקמיה בשמעתין: עד לרקיע. כל אויר שכנגד רה"י בין אויר חלל בין אויר עמוד בר"ה גבוה י' ורחב ד' כנגדו עד לרקיע שם רה"י עליו:

אלא

לא נצרכה אלא לקרן זוית. לא בעי למימר דאיצטריך לגלויי דרה"ר משום דלר"א כרה"ר דמי ואפילו אית בהו חיפופי או שמא מספקא ליה אי מודה להו רבי אליעזר אם לאו: אבל בין העמודים. כרה"ר דמי אע"פ שאין בין עמוד לעמוד ט"ז אמות הוי רה"ר כיון שבני רה"ר בוקעין בה וחוץ לבין עמודים °רחב שש עשר אמה: וטח בפניה חייב. אומר ר"ת דאם נח למעלה משלשה צריך שיהא בפניה ארבעה על ארבעה ומה שמודבק בפני הלבינה חשוב כמונח עליה אע"פ שאינו אלא באויר וכן הא דתנן למטה מי' כזורק בארץ ומוקי לה רבי יוחנן בדבילה שמינה היינו טעמא נמי דכיון שנדבק בפני הכותל שהוא רוחב ד' על ד' חשוב כמונח עליו וריב"א פי' דאף למעלה מג' לא בעי שיהא בפני הלבינה וכותל ד' על ד' דכיון שרואה את הקרקע חשיב כמונח ע"ג קרקע וקשה לר"י דלעיל (דף ד.) כי פריך אמתניתין דפשט ידו והא בעיא עקירה והנחה מע"ג מקום ארבע לוקי מתניתין במחזיק החפץ בענין זה שרואה את פני הקרקע: אילימא דעד עשרה הוא דהוי כרמלית ואי לא לא הוי כרמלית. פרש"י כגון בקעה המוקפת גדר והיא יתירה על בית סאתים ולא הוקף לדירה וקשה לר"י דהא רשות היחיד היא בין לעולא בין לרב אשי ולא הוי צריך לאתויי מרב גידל ועוד דהיכי קאמר ואי לא לא הויא כרמלית והרי ים ובקעה אין להן מחיצות ונראה לר"י דהכי פירושו אילימא עד דאיכא מחיצות י' היינו אויר הראוי למחיצות עשרה לאפוקי בקעה מסוככת בפחות מי' על גבי קונדסין דלא הוי כרמלית כיון דאין גבוהה י' והוי מקום פטור ומותר לטלטל בכולו והאמר רב גידל כו':

ואם

עין משפט נר מצוה

לא א מיי' פט"ו מהל' שבת הלכה א סמג לאוין סה טור שו"ע א"ח סי' שמו וסי' שנח:

לב ב ג מיי' פי"ד מהל' שבת הלכה ד טוש"ע א"ח סי' שמה סעיף יד:

לג ד מיי' שם הל' ו:

לד ה ו מיי' שם הלכה ז טוש"ע א"ח סי' שמה סעיף י:

לה ז ח מיי' שם הל' ד טוש"ע שם סעיף יא:

רבינו חננאל

והא דתנן רה"י כלומר אינה רה"ר. רב אשי אמר (וקאמר) בבקעה דאית לה מחיצות מדקתני רשות היחיד: קרן זוית הסמוכה לרה"ר ואיצטבא שלפני העמודים ככרמלית נידונין. כל שאין גבוה מן הקרקע ג' טפחים כגון ליבני וכיוצא בה כרה"ר דמי. וכל הגבוה ג' טפחים ואין בו רחב ארבעה וזרק ונח על גביו פטור חוץ מן הזורק ונח על פי הכלב או בפי הכבשן או בידו של אדם וכיוצא בהן המפורשות בהמוצא תפלין משום דמחשבתו משויא להו מקום ומפורש בהמוצא. תפלין כי האי גונא דכל פחות מג' בארץ כארץ חשיב. וא"ר יוחנן אין כרמלית פחותה מד' ותופסת עד י' טפחים אבל למעלה מי' מקום פטור הוא והכי פירושא בפ' הזורק כי הא דאמר שמואל לרב יהודה שיננא לא תיהוי במילי דשבתא למעלה מעשרה ואוקימנא בכרמלית ואקילו בה רבנן מקולי רה"י דאי איכא מקום ד' על ד' הוא דהויא כרמלית ואי לא מקום פטור הוא מקולי רה"ר נמי דעד י' הויא כרמלי' למעלה מי' לא הויא כרמלית אלא מקום פטור. הא דרב גידל דאמר בית שאין בתוכו עשרה טפחים וקירויו

גליון הש"ס

גמ' קרפף יותר מבית סאתים כו' הזורק לתוכו חייב. עי' לקמן פ ע"א ברש"י ד"ה והוא שיש חיוב כו' וד' לט ע"ב ברש"י ד"ה מוקף לכרמלי' וצע"ג: שם רה"י קתני. וע"ש בטהרות פ"ו מ"ז שבילי בית הגלגל רה"י לשבת ושם מ"י איסטוונית רה"י לשבת וצ"ע: שם בתוכו אין מטלטלין וכו'. עי' עירובין פט ע"א תוס' ד"ה במחיצות: תוס' ד"ה אבל בין העמודים כו' רחב ט"ז אמה. עי' עירובין ו ע"ב תוס' ד"ה וכי תימא:

מסורת הש"ס

עירובין סז:

ס"א ותניא פ"ק דעירובין חצר שהרבים נכנסין בו ויוצאין בו

הגהות הב"ח

(א) גמ' רב אשי לא אמר כעולא אלא עולא מ"ט:

פי' סנה והוא אילן סרק

[עירובין סז.]

פי' קוליס

גיטין עט. ע"ש [עירובין לג: לד:]

שם אויר כרמלית עליו כצ"ל רש"א

[גמרא]

אלא דאין רה"ר למעלה מי' מתני' היא *דתנן הזורק ד' אמות בכותל למעלה מי' טפחים כזורק באויר למטה מי' טפחים כזורק בארץ אלא אכרמלית דאין כרמלית למעלה מי' ואקילו בה רבנן מקולי רה"י ומקולי רה"ר מקולי רה"י דאי איכא מקום ארבעה הוא דהויא כרמלית ואי לא מקום פטור בעלמא הוא מקולי רה"ר דעד י' טפחים הוא דהויא כרמלי' למעלה מי' טפחים לא הויא כרמלי': גופא אמר רב גידל אמר רב חייא בר יוסף אמר רב *בית שאין תוכו י' וקרויו משלימו לי' על גגו מותר לטלטל בכולו בתוכו אין מטלטלין בו אלא בד' אמות אמר אביי ואם חקק בו ד' על ד' והשלימו לי' מותר לטלטל בכולו מאי טעמא הוי חורי רה"י וחורי רה"י כרה"י דמו דאיתמר חורי רה"י כרה"י דמו חורי רה"ר אביי אומר כרה"ר דמו °רבא אומר לאו כרה"ר דמו א"ל רבא לאביי לדידך דאמרת חורי רה"ר כרה"ר דמו מ"ש מהא דכי אתא רב דימי א"ר יוחנן לא נצרכה אלא לקרן זוית הסמוכה לרה"ר ותיהוי כחורי רה"ר התם לא ניחא תשמישתיה הכא ניחא תשמישתיה תנן *הזורק ד' אמות בכותל למעל' מי' (א) כזורק באויר למטה מי' טפחים כזורק בארץ והוינן בה מאי כזורק בארץ והא לא נח וא"ר יוחנן בדבילה שמינה שנו ואי ס"ד חורי רה"ר כרה"ר דמו למה לי לאוקמה בדביל' שמינה לוקמה בצרור וחפץ ודנח בחור °זימנין משני לה שאני צרור וחפץ דמיהדר ואתי זימנין משני לה בכותל דלית ביה חור ממאי מדקתני רישא זרק למעלה מי' טפחים כזורק באויר ואי ס"ד בכותל דאית ביה חור אמאי כזורק באויר הא נח בחור וכי תימא מתני' דלית בהו ד' על ד' והאמר רב יהודה א"ר חייא *זרק למעלה מי' טפחים והלכה ונחה בחור כל שהוא באנו למחלוקת ר"מ ורבנן דר"מ סבר *חוקקין להשלים ורבנן סברי אין חוקקין להשלים אלא לאו ש"מ בכותל דלית ביה חור שמע מינה: גופא אמר רב חסדא נעץ קנה ברשות היחיד וזרק ונח על גביו אפי' גבוה מאה אמה חייב מפני שרה"י עולה עד לרקיע לימא רב חסדא דאמר כרבי דתניא *זרק ונח ע"ג זיז כ"ש ר' מחייב וחכמים פוטרים (אלמא לא בעינן מקום ד' על ד')

אמר

[רש"י]

אלא . דאין אויר רה"ר למעלה מי' והוי אוירא מקום פטור : מתני' היא . ולמה ליה לשמואל לאשמעינן : הזורק ד' אמות . ברה"ר ונדבק בכותל כגון דבילה שמינה כדמוקי לה לקמן : כזורק באויר . ופטור דלאו ברה"ר נח והה"י נמי לא הוי אלא דבר המסויים ורחב ארבע : כזורק בארץ . וחייב דאויר רה"ר משנח משהו הוי הנחה ולא דמי לנח על דבר המסויים למטה מי' דההוא חשיב למיהוי רשות חשוב לעצמו או כרמלית או מקום פטור ולא הויא הנחה ברה"ר: אכרמלית. כדפרישית: ואקילו בה רבנן . לעיל קאי אדרב דימי ורב ששת דאקילו בה רבנן בכרמלית הואיל ואיסורה מדבריהם אקילו בה : מקולי רה"י ורה"ר · רב דימי אשמעינן מקולי רה"י כי היכי דרשות היחיד ליתיה פחות מרחב ד' והמכניס מרה"ר עליו פטור כרמלית נמי לא הוי ומותר לכתחלה להכניס מרשות הרבים ומרה"י עליו ורב ששת אשמעינן למקולי רה"ר נמי אקילו עלה דאינה תופסת באויר למעלה מי' כרה"י אלא למטה מי' כתורת רה"ר : חקק בו . בקרקע הבית באמצעיתו ארבעה באורך ורוחב : והשלימו . במקום חקק לחלל י' גבוה עד הקירוי נעשה כל הבית כולו חורי רה"י כמו כותלי רה"י והם חורים כלפי רה"י שהם כרה"י והכי נמי כיון דנגד החקק רה"י גמור אינך הוי פיאות של תשמישי רה"י: חורי רה"ר. חורים שהכותלים כלפי רה"ר : לאו כרשות הרבים דמו .· אלא רשות לעצמן הן ואם רחבים ד' הוי כרמלית ואי לא הוי מקום פטור : לא נצרכה . והכרמלית דתני בברייתא אוקמוה רב דימי בקרן זוית כו' : תיהוי כחורי רשות הרבים . ואמאי הויא כרמלית : והא לא נח . וכי חזרה נפלה לתוך ד' אמות דעל כרחך כשמכה בכותל קופלת. לאחוריה : ושאני צרור וחפץ גרסינן . כלומר בכותל דאית ביה חור ואפילו הכי לא אוקמיה ר' יוחנן בדנח בחור משום דלאו אורחייהו דצרור וחפץ לנוח ע"י זריקה במקום שנופלין שם : אמאי כזורק באויר הא ה"ל מרה"ר לרה"י דהוה ליה גבוה י' ורשות לעצמו : רבי מאיר ורבנן . במסכת יומא גבי מזוזה : רבי מאיר סבר . דבר שאין בו שיעור ויש שם עובי ורחב לחקוק ולהשלים לכשיעור אמרינן כמאן דחקוק דמי והכא נמי לרבי מאיר חוקקין להשלים וחייב וסתם משנה ר' מאיר : דאמר כרבי . דלא בעי הנחה על גבי מקום ד': זרק ונח כו' . קס"ד מרה"ר לרה"י :

וטפו

[תוספות]

ואם חקק בו ד' על ד' . וקשה לריב"א מ"ש מסוכה דאינה גבוהה י' דאמר בפ"ק דסוכה (דף ד·) חקק בה להשלימה לי' אם יש משפת חקק ולכותל ג' טפחים פסולה פחות מג' כשרה והכא מהני חקיקה אפילו מופלגת מן הכותל הרבה *ותירץ דשאני התם גבי סוכה דבעינן שיהיו מחיצות סמוכות לסכך דילפינן התם (דף ו:) מחיצות מבסכת בסכת בסכות כדאמרי' התם *הרחיק הסיכוך מן הדפנות פסולה ולהכי בעינן שיהא פחות מג' דצריך לצרף הגידוד של חקק למחיצות כדי שיהיו סמוכות לסכך שכנגד הנקב ואע"ג דדופן עקומה מכשרת עד ד' אמות מתרץ לה הש"ס *ה"מ היכא דאיכא מחיצות מעלייתא אבל הכא דלשויה מחילה בפחות מג' מצטרף הגידוד עם המחיצות דהויא סמוך לסכך טפי לא מצטרף*: **התם** לא ניחא תשמישתיה . ולדי רה"ר לרבנן לאו כרה"ר דמי אע"ג דניחא תשמישתיה טפי מקרן זוית דהא אפילו ר"א דפליג בלדי רה"ר מודה בקרן זוית כדפריש' לעיל אפ"ה . לא הוי כחורי רה"ר דחורי רה"ר ניחא תשמישתיה טפי : **והלכה** ונחה בחור כל שהוא באנו למחלוקת רבי מאיר ורבנן . תימה לר"י דבפרק קמא דעירובין (דף יא: ושם) בכיפה דפליגי בה ר"מ ורבנן אמרינן התם דלא אמרינן חוקקין להשלים לר"מ אלא בים ברגליה ג' וגובהה י' פי' גבוה ג' טפחים שיש בהן רחב ד' אבל אין ברגליה ג' או שאינה גבוה מי' לא אמרינן °וא"כ היכי אמרינן הכא חוקקים להשלים לר"מ בחור כל שהוא ואומר ר"י דאיירי בחורין שדרכן לעשות בשעת הבנין שמפולשין לרה"ר ובנד רה"י הם רחבים ד' אבל לא מלד רה"ר ולכ"ע הוי חור רה"י דהא חורי רה"י כרה"י דמי ולא פליגי אלא לשויה מקום ד' על ד' דלרבי מאיר חוקקין להשלים והוי כד' על ד' אבל ממש בחור כל שהוא אפילו ר"מ מודה דלא אמרינן חוקקין להשלים וכן משמע בירושלמי דגרסינן התם על דעתיה דר"מ בין שיש שם ד' בין שאין שם ד' רואין את הכותל כגמום ודוקא אותם שלמעלה מי' חשיבי חורי רה"י אבל שלמטה מעשרה אין בני רה"י משתמשין שם מפני בני רשות הרבים שמשתמשין בהן וה"פ וכ"ת דלית ביה ד' ואע"ג שהם חורי רה"י הוי כזורק באויר לפי שלא נח על מקום ד' והאמר רב יהודה כו' והא דלא מוקמינן מתני' בחור כל שהו ממש דלא אמרי' חוקקין לכ"ע הייט משום דסתם חורים כך הם ועוד דע"כ הוצרך לאוקמי בדביל' שמינ' דבחור כל שהוא ממש דלא אמר ביה חוקקין להשלים ליכא לאוקמי' דא"כ למטה מי' אמאי כזורק בארץ והא לא נח ע"ג מקום ד' ואל"ל כפרש"י דפריך מכח דסתם מתני' ר"מ היא אלא ע"כ אי מיירי בחור כל שהוא שאינו רחב ד' צריך לאוקמה כר"מ דאמר חוקקין להשלים דלרבנן אמאי למטה מי' כזורק בארץ ויש ליישב פירש"י דהוצרך לפ' משום דסתם מתני' ר"מ קפריך דאי לאו הכי הוה ליה למפרך בהדיא וכ"ת דלית ביה ד' למטה מי' אמאי כזורק בארץ :

אמר

עין משפט נר מצוה

לו א ב טוש"ע א"ח סי' שמה סעיף טו :

[ועי' תוס' סוכה ד: סד"ה פחות מבלבה]

[דף יז.]

לז ג מיי' פי"ד מהלכות שבת הלכה י סמג לאוין סה טוש"ע שם סעיף ד :

לח ד מיי' שם הלכה י טוש"ע שם סעיף יג:

[שם ד.]

לט ה מיי' שם הל' יח טוש"ע שם סעיף י :

מ ו מיי' שם הלכה יז טוש"ע שם סעיף ה :

ונ"ל דהכא יש מחיצות גבוהות מבחוץ וא"צ לצרף הגידוד אלא דאין אויר י' וכשמקק דאיכא אויר י' במקום אחד הוי רה"י אבל בסוכה צריך לצרף הגידוד וביותר מג' לא מצטרף [תוס' ישנים]

רבינו חננאל

משלימו לעשרה על גגו מותר לטלטל בכלו כי כרה"י הוא חשוב . דאמרי' בכי האי גונא גוד אסיק מחיצתא . בתוכו אין מטלטלין בו אלא בד' אמות . מ"מ כיון דלא חזי לדירה אין המחיצות מועילות. אלא כמו שאין שם מחיצות דמו : **אמר** אביי אם חקק בו ד' על ד' מותר לטלטל בכל הבית . מ"מ אלו הארבעה שיש בגובהן עשר הן הבית והשאר חשובין כחורין . וקי"ל חורי רה"י כרה"י דמו . חורי רה"ר אביי אמר כרשות הרבים דמו ורבא אמר לאו כרשות הרבים דמו . והלכתא כרבא. הא דא' רב חסדא נעץ קנה ברה"י אפי' מאה אמה וזרק מרה"ר ונח על גביו חייב. נימא כר' אמרה דתניא זרק ונח ע"ג זיז כל שהוא ר' מחייב וחכמים פוטרין

רב נסים גאון

הא דאמר רב יהודה אמר רב אמר ר' חייא זרק למעלה מעשרה והלכה ונחה בחור כל שהוא באנו למחלוקת ר' מאיר ורבנן ושמועה זו בפרק הזורק (דף ק) ותניא נמי הכי זרק למעלה מי' והלכה ונחה בחור כל שהוא ר' מאיר מחייב וחכמים פוטרים ותמצא בירור השמועה במס' עירובין בפרק א' (דף יא) אשכחית רב ששת לרבה בר שמואל אמר ליה תאני מר סידי בצורת פתח אמר ליה תנינא כיפה רבי מאיר מחייב במזוזה וחכמים פוטרין דר' מאיר סבר חוקקין להשלים ולדבריו אם נחה בחור כל שהוא חייב ורבנן סברי אין חוקקין להשלים ואם נחה בחור כל שהוא פטור עד שתנוח בחור שיש בו ד' ועוד תמצא בפרק א' מן מסכת יומא (דף יא) (ובמסכת שבת בפרק המוצא תפילין) [עירובין דף קא] תנו רבנן פתחי גינה בזמן שיש להן בית שער מבפנים כו' ואמרו אמר אביי לעולם דלית ביה ד' ויש בו להוק להשלימו לד' ובהא פליגי דר' מאיר סבר חוקקין להשלים ורבנן סברי אין חוקקין להשלים :

מסורת הש"ס

לקמן צו: ק.

[לק.: לט: ק.]

[ג"ז שם.ע"ש]

[לקמן ק.] יומא יא: [עירובין יא: לג: קא:]

[לעיל ד:]

רש"ל מ"ז

הגהות הב"ח

(א) גמ' למעלה מעשרה טפחים כזורק באויר והוינן בה אמאי כזורק :

גליון הש"ס

גמ' רבא אומר לאו כרה"ר דמו . עיין עירובין פז ע"ב וברש"י שם ברה"ר והוי: שם זימנין משני לה. כעין זה נדרים מח: תוס' ד"ה והלכה ונחה כו' וא"כ היכי אמרינן הכא חוקקים כו' . עי' חולין קטו ע"א תוד"ה אגן:

ומנין

that there is no public ground above ten,[13] it is our Mishnah! For we learnt: If one throws [an article] four cubits on to a wall above ten handbreadths, it is as though he throws it into the
a air;[1] if below ten, it is as though he throws it on to the ground.[2] Hence he must refer to a ***karmelith***, [teaching] that there is no ***karmelith*** above ten. And [R. Dimi and R. Shesheth inform us that] the Rabbis treated it with the leniencies of both private and public ground. 'With the leniencies of private ground': that only if [it measures] four [handbreadths square] is it a ***karmelith***, but if not it is simply a place of non-liability. 'With the leniencies of public ground': only up to ten is it a ***karmelith***, but above ten it is not a ***karmelith***.

[To revert to] the main text: 'R. Gidal said in the name of R. Ḥiyya b. Joseph in Rab's name: In the case of a house, the inside of which is not ten [handbreadths in height] but its covering makes it up to ten, it is permitted to carry on the roof thereof over the whole [area]; but within, one may carry only four cubits.' Said Abaye: But if one digs out four square [handbreadths][3] and makes it up to ten, carrying over the whole is permitted. What is the reason? [The rest] is [as] cavities of a private domain, and such are [themselves] a private domain.[4] For it was stated: The cavities of a private domain constitute private ground. As to the cavities of a public domain,[5]—Abaye said: They are as public ground; Raba said: They are not as public ground.[6] Said Raba to Abaye: According to you who maintains that the cavities of public ground are as public ground, wherein does it differ from what R. Dimi, when he came, said in the name of R. Joḥanan: 'This is necessary only in respect of a corner near to the street',[7]—yet let it be as cavities of a public domain?—There the use thereof is inconvenient; here the use thereof is convenient.

We learnt: If one throws an article four cubits on to a wall, above ten handbreadths, it is as though he throws it into the
b air; if below ten, it is as though he throws it on to the ground.[1] Now we discussed this: why 'as though he throws it on the ground'; surely it does not rest [there]?[2] And R. Joḥanan answered: This refers to a juicy cake of figs.[3] But if you maintain that the cavities of public ground are as public ground, why relate it to a juicy cake of figs; relate it to a splinter or any article and it is a case where it alighted in a cavity?—Sometimes he answered him, A splinter or any other article are different, because they fall back;[4] sometimes he answered him: The reference must be to a wall not possessing a cavity.—How do you know it?—Because the first clause states: If one throws above ten handbreadths, it is as though he throws it into the air. Now if you imagine that this refers to a wall with a cavity, why is it as though he throws it into the air; surely it came to rest in the cavity?[5] And should you answer, Our Mishnah [refers to a cavity] that is not four square,—surely did not Rab Judah say in R. Ḥiyya's name: If one throws [an article] above ten handbreadths and it goes and alights in a cavity of any size,[6] we come to a controversy of R. Meir and the Rabbis, R. Meir holding, We [imaginarily] hollow it out to complete it,[7] while the Rabbis maintain, We do not hollow it out to complete it.[8] Hence it surely follows that the reference is to a wall without a cavity. This proves it.

[To revert to] the main text: 'R. Ḥisda said: If one fixes a rod in private ground and throws [an article from the street] and it alights on the top, even if it is a hundred cubits high, he is liable, because private ground extends up to heaven'. Shall we say that R. Ḥisda holds with Rabbi?[9] For it was taught: If one throws [an object] and it alights upon a projection of whatever size; Rabbi holds

(13) I.e., anything above ten handbreadths from ground level is not treated as public ground.

a (1) He is not liable. (2) And since it traverses four cubits, he is liable.—Why then need Samuel state it? (3) I.e., he lowers the level of four square handbreadths of the ground. (4) Cavities in a wall bounding private ground rank as private ground. Here, the lowered portion is true private ground, and the rest is regarded as cavities in an imaginary wall surrounding it. (5) I.e., in a wall fronting a street. (6) But constitute a separate domain. If four handbreadths square, they are a ***karmelith***; if less, a place of non-liability. (7) V. *supra* 7*a*, notes; it is there accounted as a ***karmelith***.

b (1) Mishnah, *infra* 100*a*. (2) Since it must rebound at least slightly, the final distance is less than the four cubits that is the least for which a penalty is incurred. (3) Which sticks. (4) Lit., 'come again'. Even if they do not rebound. (5) Which, if four handbreadths square, is private ground. (6) I.e., less than four square. (7) Where the wall is thick enough, we regard the small cavity as enlarged to four square, and liability is incurred. (8) And since the Mishnah under discussion is anonymous, it reflects R. Meir's view; v. Sanh. 86*a*. (9) That depositing upon a place four handbreadths square is not required.

him liable; the Sages exempt him! [8a]—Said Abaye: In the case of private ground none differ, agreeing with R. Ḥisda. But here the reference is to a tree standing in private ground, while a branch inclines to the street, and one throws [an article] and it alights on the branch: Rabbi holds, We say, Cast the branch after its trunk; but the Rabbis maintain, We do not say, Cast the branch
a after its trunk.[1]

Abaye said: If one throws a bin[2] into the street, [even] if it is ten [handbreadths] high but not six broad, he is liable; if six broad, he is exempt.[3] Raba said: Even if it is not six broad, he is [still] exempt. What is the reason? It is impossible for a piece of cane not to project above ten.[4] If he overturns it,[5] mouth downwards, [and throws it], then if it is a shade more than seven [in height] he is liable; if seven and a half, he is exempt.[6] R. Ashi said: Even if it is seven and a half, he is liable. What is the reason? The walls are made for their contents.[7]

'Ulla said: If there is a column nine [handbreadths high] in the street, and the public rest and rearrange their burdens thereon,[8] and one throws [an object] and it alights upon it, he is liable. What is the reason? It if is less than three, the multitude step
b upon it;[1] from three to nine, they neither walk upon it nor arrange their burdens upon it;[2] nine, they certainly re-arrange their burdens upon it.[3] Abaye asked R. Joseph: What of a pit?[4]—He replied: The same holds good of a pit. Raba said: It does not hold good of a pit. What is the reason? Service through difficulty is not designated service.[5]

R. Adda b. Mattenah raised an objection before Raba: If one's basket is lying in the street, ten [handbreadths] high and four broad,[6] one may not move [an object] from it into the street or from the street into it; but if less, one may carry; and the same applies to a pit. Surely that refers to the second clause?[7] —No: to the first clause.

a (1) V. *supra 4b* for notes. (2) Jast.: a large *round* vessel, receptacle of grain, water, etc. (3) A circle with a diameter of six is the least (roughly) in which a square of four can be inscribed. Now, as stated above (6a), an object four square is a separate domain itself, and no liability is incurred for throwing one domain into another. (4) Since it is ten handbreadths high, it is impossible that the top and bottom canes of the circumference shall be absolutely even and straight, and so something must project above ten from ground level, which is a place of non-liability, not public ground. But in order to incur liability the *whole* of the article thrown must rest in public ground. (5) Where it was less than six handbreadths broad (Rashi). (6) It is a principle that the walls of an object are regarded as extending beyond its opening down to the ground itself as soon as that opening comes within a shade less than three handbreadths from the ground. V. Glos. s.v. *labud*. Hence, when this overturned bin, which is a shade more than seven in height (and certainly if less), enters within just under three handbreadths from the ground and is regarded as already resting on the ground, the whole is within ten from the ground, and therefore he is liable. But if it is slightly taller than this it is partly above ten; hence there is no liability. (7) I.e., to enable it to be used as a receptacle, and not to create an imaginary extension downwards. (8) It being of the exact height to facilitate this.

b (1) And it is therefore part of the street. (2) It is too low for the latter purpose. (3) And since it is thus put to public use, it is part of the thoroughfare. (4) Nine deep. (5) It can only be used with difficulty; therefore it is not part of the street. (6) As such it is private ground; v. *supra 6a*. (7) *Sc.* on nine handbreadths.

*אמר אביי ברה"י דכ"ע לא פליגי כדרב חסדא אלא הכא באילן העומד ברה"י ונופו נוטה לרה"ר וזרק ונח אנופו דרבי סבר אמרי' *שדי נופו בתר עיקרו ורבנן סברי *לא אמרי' שדי נופו בתר עיקרו: אמר אביי ג זרק כוורת לרה"ר גבוהה י' ואינה רחבה ו' חייב רחבה ו' פטור רבא אמר ג אפי' אינה רחבה ו' פטור מ"ט אי אפשר לקרומיות של קנה שלא יעלו למעלה מעשרה כפאה על פיה שבעה ומשהו חייב שבעה ומחצה פטור רב אשי אמר אפי' שבעה ומחצה חייב מ"ט מחיצות לתוכן עשויות: *אמר עולא ד עמוד תשעה ברה"ר ורבים מכתפין עליו וזרק ונח על גביו חייב מ"ט פחות משלשה מדרס דרסי ליה רבים משלשה ועד תשעה לא מדרס דרסי ליה ולא כתופי מכתפי תשעה ודאי מכתפין עילויה א"ל אביי לרב יוסף גומא מאי אמר ליה וכן בגומא רבא אמר ה בגומא לא מ"ט תשמיש על ידי הדחק לא שמיה תשמיש איתיביה רב אדא בר מתנא לרבא היתה קופתו מונחת ברה"ר גבוהה עשרה ורחבה ד' אין מטלטלין לא מתוכה לרה"ר ולא מרשות הרבים לתוכה פחות מכן מטלטלין וכן בגומא מאי לאו אסיפא לא ארישא איתיביה נתכוון

רש"י

ונופו נוטה לרה"ר וזרק· מתחילת ד' לסוף ד' ונח אנופו: שדי נופו כו'· דחשיב אגב עיקרו דאית ביה ד' ודרב חסדא דלא כרבי ודלא כרבנן לישנא אחרינא אמר אביי בדרב חסדא דהוי ברה"י אפי' רבנן מודו וכי פליגי רבנן בשדי נופו בתר עיקרו הוא דפליגי: כוורת· עגולה היא: גבוהה י'· כלומר אפי' גבוהה י' אם אינה רחבה ו' באמצעיתה חייב דאכתי חפץ בעלמא הוא ואינה רשות לעצמה דלא הוי רשות דאורי' אלא גבוהה י' ורחבה ד' על ד' כדאמרי' בעירובין (דף נא·) דכל שיעורין דשבת צריך הן ואלכסונן ודבר עגול כי מרבעת לה מתוכו ומפקע עיגול שסביב הריבוע לא משכחת ביה ד' מרובעים אי לא הוי עיגולו קרוב לששה כדאמרינן גבי סוכה העשויה ככבשן (סוכה פ"א דף ז:) דעל כרחיך צריך שתמלא בתוכו אלכסון של ד' על ד' וכל טפח בריבועו טפח ותרי חומשי באלכסונו הרי ה' טפחים וג' חומשין ואביי לא דק ולחומרא הוא דלא דק והפרישו מאיסור שבת אף ע"ג דיש כאן אלכסון באינה רחבה ששה מחייב ליה מדרבנן עד דאיכא ששה אבל ודאי לענין קרבן לא מייתי אי הויא ה' טפחים וג' חומשין דהוי כזורק רשות: רחבה ו' פטור· דהוי רשות לעצמה ואנן ממשכן גמרינן שהיו זורקין מחטיקן במלאכתן זה לזה *ולא היו זורקין רשויות וא"ת כדלא גבוהה עשרה נמי רשות לעצמה היא דהא שמה כרמלית ההיא לאו מדאורייתא הוה רשות אלא מדרבנן ולא להקל על דברי תורה בא כגון זו שיפטר מחטאת: אי אפשר· הואיל וגבוהה י' שלא יהא בה קרומיות מן הקנים שגבוהים מחבריהם של ערב· ועולין למעלה מי' שהוא אויר מקום פטור וכיון דלא ניחא כולה ברה"ר לא הויא הנחה לאיחיובי: כפאה על פיה· וזרקה אאינה רחבה ו' קאי: ז' ומשהו חייב· אם גבוהה ז' ומשהו עדיין חייב וכ"ש פחותה מכן אלא אפילו גבוהה ז' ומשהו דאיכא למימר הואיל ומחיצותיה למטה וקיי"ל הלכה למשה מסיני דאמרינן לבוד (א) אכתי כולה ניחא ברה"ר דכי מטיא פחות מג' סמוך לקרקע ואמר בהן לבוד והויא הנחה אכתי כולה באויר רה"ר היא וחייב: אבל גבוה ז' ומחצה· וה"ה לשני משהויין פטור דמכי מטא לפחות מג' סמוך לקרקע אמרינן לבוד במחיצותיה והרי היא כמונחת כמאן שוליה למעלה מעשרה ואינה נוחה כולה ברה"ר ובשלא כפאה ליכא למימר לבוד דלא אמרינן לבוד אלא במחיצות והא מילתא בין לאביי בין לרבא דאביי נמי מודה דבעינן הנחה כולה ברשות הרבים אלא דאביי לא חשיב קרומיות אבל בהא מודה דבלא קרומיות איתא למעלה מי': לתוכן עשויות· להניח בהן דבש ולא לכופן כלפי מטה הלכך אין כאן תורת לבוד: תשעה· דוקא נקט דחזי לכתופי דאיתו לא גבוה ולא נמוך: וזרק· מתחלת ד' לסוף ד': מכתפי עילויה· וכיון דצריך לרבים רה"ר הוא *בין רחב בין קצר: גומא· עמוקה ט': מאי· גבי רה"י דעשרה תניא לעיל (דף ו·) עומקה כגובהה דקתני חריץ עמוק י' ורחב ד' רשות היחיד הכא מאי אי אמרי' מנחי ביה בני רה"ר חפצים שבידם עד דהדרי ואתו דרך שם ושקלי ליה וכמאן שצריכים לו רבים הלכך רשות הרבים הוא: ה"ג רבא אמר גומא לא מ"ט תשמיש ע"י הדחק לא שמיה תשמיש הלכך לאו צורך רבים הוא אלא כרמלית הוא: אין מטלטלין. דהוי רה"י לעצמה: פחות מכן· או בגובה או ברוחב מטלטלין וא"ת פחות מי' ורחבה ד' כרמלית היא לא גזור רבנן לבטולי מתורת כלים הואיל וכלי הוא: מאי לאו· האי וכן אסיפא נמי קאי דפחות מכן מטלטל לכתחלה אלמא רה"ר חשיב ליה ואוקמא בעמוק ט' דמשתמשין בו קצת: לא ארישא· אגבוהה י' ורחבה ד' דהוי רה"י קתני וכן בגומא:

תוספות

אמר אביי הכא באילן העומד כו'· תימה לר"י דטפי ניחא ליה למימר דפליגי בדרב חסדא ורב חסדא כרבי דלשנויה דאביי דלא שייכא פלוגתייהו בדרב חסדא כ"ש דקשה לרב חסדא דהא איכא ברייתא לקמן בהזורק (דף ק· ושם) דלא כרב חסדא דפליגי רבנן ורבי אליר בזורק למעלה מעשרה ונח בחור כל שהוא דר"מ מחייב משום דאמרי' חוקקין להשלים והוי כמונח ע"ג מקום ד' וחכמים פוטרין אלמא כולהו מודו דבעינן מקום ד' ברה"י ושמא י"ל דטעמא דרב חסדא דלא בעי' מקום ד' ברה"י משום דאמרי' ביתא כמליא דמי וחשיב כמונח על גבי מקום ארבעה אבל בכותל בעינן שיהא בחור ד' על ד':

רחבה ששה פטור· פר"ח דדוקא נקט ששה דדופני הכוורת יש בהן שני חומשין וצריך שיהא אויר ד' בתוך הכוורת וגבוה י' אף ע"ג דאין אויר גבוה י' אלא עם השולים מצטרפין עם האויר לענין גובה דהלכתא גידוד ה' ומחילה ה' מצטרפין (עירובין דף נג· ושם) אף על גב דרש"י פי' דגידוד ה' ומחילה ה' הייט שעשה מחילה ה' על בור עמוק ה' אין פירושו נראה דהא תנן (שם פ"י דף נט: ולקמן דף נט.) בור וחוליתו מצטרפין ואם כן היכי פליג רב חסדא לומר אין מצטרפין כיון דמתניתין היא ובכל גגות (עירובין נג:) אמרינן בהדיא דמודה רב חסדא בתחתונה הואיל ורואה פני י' אלא צריך לפרש דגידוד ה' ומחילה ה' הייט שעשה מחילה ה' על תל גבוה ה' ואין נראה פירוש ר"ח דהא עובי חוליות הבור מצטרף נמי לחלל הבור לארבעה משום דחזי למינח עליה מידי ולהשתמש כדאמר בפ' חלון (עירובין דף עח.) גבי מלאו כולו ביתדות אלא נ"ל הא דנקט הכא ששה לא דק כדפירש"י: **רחבה** ששה פטור. שהכוורת עצמה נעשית רה"י כשתנוח והוי כזורק מרשות היחיד לרה"י דרך רה"ר דפטור כדאמר לעיל (דף ד·) דלא יליף זורק ממושיט ואפילו לר' עקיבא דאמר קלוטה כמי שהונחה דמיא הכא פטור דכל מקום שהיא מונחת חשיב רה"י* השתא משמע דפשיטא ליה לאביי דחשיבא כאילו נחה אחר שנעשה רה"י ובפ' הזורק (לקמן צט:) בעי ר' יוחנן בור ט' ועקר ממנו חוליא והשלימו לי' והניחו ברה"ר עקירת חפץ ועשיית מחילה בהדי הדדי קאתו ומיחייב או לא ואת"ל כיון דלא הויא מחילה י' מעיקרא לא מיחייב בור י' ונתן לתוכו חוליא ומעטו מהו הנחת חפץ וסילוק מחילה כו' וא"כ אביי דפשיטא ליה במחללת דמבטל מחילתה דקאמר התם בור ברה"ר עמוק י' ורוחב ח' וזרק לתוכו מחללת וחלקו פטור משום דהשתא לא הויא רוחב ד' וכ"ש דפטור בעשיית מחילה משום דכיון דלא הויא מחילה עשרה מעיקרא לא מיחייב וא"כ הכא הוי ליה לחיובי מהאי טעמא כיון דלא הויא מחילה מעיקרא הרי נח ברשות הרבים וחייב וי"ל דטעמא דאביי משום דלא חשיב לא עקירה ולא הנחה כי אתי בהדי הדדי והכא נמי לא חשיבה הנחה כיון דהנחה ועשיית מחילה בהדי הדדי קאתו והא דפשיטא ליה לרבי יוחנן טפי בעשיית מחילה מבסילוק מחילה הייט משום דדילמא עקירה בעינן שתהא חשובה אבל בהנחה לא: **כפאה** על פיה· נראה לריב"א דארחב ששה קאי וכי איכא שבעה ומשהו חייב דכשמגיעות המחילות תוך שלש אין המחילות גבוהות י' ועובי השולים אין מצטרפין דבעינן מחילה הרואה את אויר הכלי שיהא גבוה י' ואע"ג דהיכא דכוורת גבוה י' מצטרפין השולים להיות על גבו רה"י כדאמר לעיל גבי בית שאין תוכו י' כו' וכיון דעל גבו רה"י פטור הזורק מ"מ כיון דאין גבוה י' אלא מחמת לבוד אין אויר פחות מג' מצטרף אלא א"כ יהיו המחילות גבוהות י' לבד השולים דלא אמרינן לבוד אלא במחיצות כדפירש בקונטרס תדע דבשולים למטה לא אמרי' לבוד: **שבעה** ומחלה פטור· דכשמגיעות המחילות תוך ג' יש שם מחילות עשרה לבד השולים והרי הוא רשות היחיד וחשיב כנח בתוכה שעה ושוב אינו מתחייב אע"ג דלאחר מכן טפל לארץ ובטל ממנה רה"י ונעשה כמונח ברה"ר אבל אינו רחב ו' אפי' ז' ומחלה חייב דלא אמרי' לבוד אלא במחילות ומחילות לא חשיבי אלא כשיש שם רחב ד' אבל כשאינו רחב ד' הרי הוא כשאר חפצים דעלמא ולא אמרינן לבוד: **אי** אפשר לקרומיות של קנה שלא יעלו למעלה מי'. ולאביי לא חשיב קרומית ליחשב אגודו במקום פטור: **אמר** ליה וכן בגומא· נוכל

ועוד דכל למעלה פטר ר"ע [תוס' ישני]

ולא נהירא דאשכחן מיהא שהיו מוליאין רשויות כגון ארון ומזבחות [תוס' ישנים]

[לעיל ד:] | [שם וש"נ] | [עירובין נג.]

עין משפט נר מצוה

מא א מיי' פי"ד מהל' שבת הלכה יז:
מב ב מיי' שם הל' טוש"ע א"ח שנה סעיף ו:
מג ג מיי' שם הלכה סמג לאוין סה:
מד ד מיי' שם הלכה סמג שם טוש"ע סעיף יוד:
מה ה שם סעיף יא:

הגהות הב"ח

(א) רש"י ד"ה ז' ומשהו וכו' הלכה למשה מסיני דאמרי' לבוד אפי' הכי חייב דכי מטיא כצ"ל ותיבת אכתי כולה ניחא ברה"ר ימחק:

גליון הש"ס

רש"י ד"ה רחבה שהיו זורקין מחטיהן· עי' לקמן צו ע"ב דלמסקנא אמרינן דלא מצינו שהיו זורקין מחטין ושם ד"ה מכתפין עליה בין רחב בין קצר. עי' לקמן נא ע"ב תד"ה אי וכ"ש:

רבינו חננאל

אמר אביי ברה"י כ"ע לא פליגי דרה"י עולה עד לרקיע. והכא באילן העומד ברה"י ונופו נוטה לרה"ר וזרק מרה"ר ונח ע"ג נופו ר' סבר אמרינן שדי נופו בתר עיקרו ומרה"ר לרה"י זרק דהא יש בעיקר האילן ד' ורבנן סברי כיון דנופו ברה"ר נוטה מרה"ר לרה"ר זרק ולא אמרינן שדי נופו בתר עיקרו וקי"ל כחכמים: **אמר** אביי זרק כוורת לרה"ר גבוה עשרה ורחבה ששה פטור כו' חזינן לרבותא מגאונים. פי' שמועה זו. וכן אמרו כוורת זו עשויה מחוצלת של קנים והיא עגולה והיא צריכה ששה מפני שתחתיה לא יעשה משווה מרובע אלא מגלגל. ובהיות בין זוית לזוית ד' טפחים והוא משופע ועולה ימצא יתרונו ב"ט. ואילו היתה מרובעת משווה לא הצריכה אלא רוחב ד"ט. ולא הצריכה ו"ט אלא במשופע כדי שימצא בה ד' משוון: ואנן קיבלנו מרבנן זכר אדונינו לברכה כי כוורת זו היא עגולה וצריך להיות חללה *)ו' טפחים על ו' טפחים מרובעות כדי להיחשב מקום רשות בפני עצמה. ואילו לא היה לה חלל **)ד' על ד' דיי לה מיהו כיון שיש בה חלל אינה חשובה רשות בפני עצמה עד שיהו בחללה ד' על ד' טפחים מרובעות וכוורת זו עם כתליה יש בה ו' טפחים על ו' טפחים מה' אצבעות בטפח נמצאו בה ו' אצבעות חסר אצבע עובי כותלה סביבותיה כשתסיר ממנה בעובי הכל אצבע לכל רוח נמצא חללה כ"ח אצבע על כ"ח אצבע וכל אצבע היא חומש טפח שכן יסדנו החשבון חמש אצבעות בטפח וקיימא לן בהדיא בחשבון מדוקדק כל אמתא ברבועא אמתא ותרי חומשי באלכסונא כשתחלק אלו כ"ח אצבעות לד' טפחים לכל טפח ה' אצבעות וב' אצבעות יתרון האלכסון על המרובע יבא ז' אצבעות לכל טפח נמצאו כ"ח אצבעות ד' טפחים על ד' טפחים חללה של כוורת בלא תוספת ובלא גירעון ולא אמרנו ה' אצבעות בטפח ממש אלא לפי שנוח למתלמד לבא החשבון הזה בלבו. אבל אם תעשהו ו' טפחים לפי חשבון תוציא עובי הכתלים אלו דברי אביי ורבא אמר אפילו אין רחבה ו' פטור אי אפשר לקרומיות של קנים שלא [יעלו] למעלה מי' וקי"ל דלמעלה מי' אין צריך ד' על ד' אלא אפי' קנה עולה למעלה מי' טפחים וזרק ונח על גביו פטור· כפאה על פיה וזרק אם גבוהה ז' ומשהו חייב כי ז' ומשהו וג' חסר משהו הרי עשרה ובעת תשלום למחיצות עשרה נחה על הקרקע לפיכך חייב. אבל אם הוא שבעה וחצי ושלשה פחות משהו הנה עשרה ועוד נמצאת בעת שנוחה בארץ גבוהה מי' טפחים ואין רה"ר למעלה מי' ונמצא כמוציא מרה"ר לרה"י. רב אשי אמר אפי' ז' ומחצה חייב שהמחיצות לתוכה הן עשויות ומבפנים אתה צריך ו' טפחים בזמן שנחה קרקעיתה בארץ והמחיצות עולות בי' טפחים אבל מהופכת נמצאת שנחה ע"ג קרקעיתה בהגעת קרומיות של קנים בארץ בפחות מעשרה טפחים וחייב: **אמר** עולא עמוד תשעה ברשות הרבים ורבים מכתפין עליו וזרק ונח על גביו חייב מ"ט דכל פחות מג' רבים דורסין אותו וכארץ חשוב לפיכך הזורק ונח על גביו חייב מג' ולמעלה אינו נדרס שיותר הוא מכדי הרחק (ידו) [רגליו] של אדם בפסיעות וגם אין מכתפין בו שאין גבוה עד הכתף לפיכך אינו תשמיש הרבים כלל ואינו כרשות הרבים אלא הוא ככרמלית השוב לפיכך פטור. אבל אם זה העמוד גבהו תשעה טפחים וודאי רבים מכתפין עליו וכרשות הרבים הוא. והזורק מרשות הרבים ונח על גביו פטור. והזורק מרשות היחיד ונח על גביו חייב. גומא פחות מעשרה מאי. רב יוסף אמר דין הגומא כדין העמוד גומא ט' טפחים ברה"ר היא כמו העמוד. רבא אמר גומא לא מ"ט הילוך ע"י הדחק שמיה הילוך. אבל תשמיש ע"י הדחק לאו שמיה תשמיש. לפיכך אינה כרה"ר. ומותבינן עליה דרבא מהא היתה קופתו מונחת ברה"ר גבוהה י' ורחבה ד' אין מטלטלין מתוכה לרה"ר ולא מרה"ר לתוכה. כלומר כרה"י היא. פחות מכאן מטלטלין וכן בגומא מאי לאו אפחות מיכן קתני וכן בגומא כלומר מטלטלין מתוכה לרה"ר כי כרה"ר היא כמו עמוד ט' טפחים. ומשני לא כי קתני וכן בגומא אגבוה י' ורחבה ארבע קתני ואסיקנא

*) נראה פשוט דצ"ל וצ"ל חללה ד' טפחים על ד' טפחים וכן מסיק אח"כ בסמוך וכ"ה בתוס' כמו. **) נראה דצ"ל ואילו לא היה לה חלל כלל דיי לה.

עין משפט
נר מצוה

מו א מיי' פ"ו מהלכות עירובין הל' ט סמג עשין דרבנן א טוש"ע א"ח סי' תט סעיף ב:

כמו בקופה מיהו האי וכן דקיימים ביה לפ"ז לאו דוקא כצ"ל רש"ל

מז ב מיי' פכ"ד מהל' שבת הלכה י טוש"ע א"ח סי' שז סעיף כב וסי' שמג:

[וע"ע תוס' חולין לו: ד"ה ואי אשמעינן ותוס' סנהדרין סג: ד"ה וטבול יום ותוס' זבחים יז. ד"ה סג"ה וכו' וקצ"ע בתוס' יבמות כג. ד"ה ואי אשמועינן]

מח ג מיי' פי"ד מהל' שבת הלכה כד:

מט ד מיי' פי"ג מהל' שבת הלכה יא:

נ ה מיי' פי"ד מהלכות שבת הלכה יז סמג לאוין סה טוש"ע א"ח סי' שמו סעיף א:

נא ו מיי' שם הל' טו:

נב ז מיי' פי"ב מהל' שבת הלכה יד:

מסורת הש"ס

נתכוון לשבות ברה"ר והניח עירובו בבור למעלה מי' טפחים עירובו עירוב למטה מי' טפחים אין עירובו עירוב היכי דמי אילימא בבור דאית ביה עשרה ולמעלה דדלאי ואותביה ולמטה דתתאי ואותביה מה לי למעלה ומה לי למטה הוא במקום אחד ועירובו במקום אחר הוא אלא לאו בבור דלית ביה עשרה וקתני עירובו עירוב אלמא תשמיש על ידי הדחק שמיה תשמיש זמנין משני ליה הוא ועירובו בכרמלית ואמאי קרי לה רה"ר לפי שאינה רשות היחיד וזמנין משני ליה [א]הוא ברה"ר ועירובו בכרמלית ורבי היא *דאמר [ב]כל דבר שהוא משום שבות לא גזרו עליו בין השמשות ולא תימא דחויי קא מדחינא לך אלא דוקא קאמינא לך *דתנן [ג]אם היה רקק מים ורשות הרבים מהלכת בו הזורק לתוכה ד' אמות חייב וכמה הוא רקק מים פחות מי' טפחים ורקק מים שרה"ר מהלכת בו הזורק לתוכו ד' אמות חייב בשלמא רקק רקק תרי זימני חד בימות החמה וחד בימות הגשמים וצריכא דאי אשמעינן בימות החמה דעבידי אינשי לקרורי נפשיהו אבל בימות הגשמים אימא לא ואי אשמעינן בימות הגשמים אגב דמטניף מקרי ונחית אבל בימות החמה לא צריכא אלא הילוך תרי זימני למה לי אלא לאו ש"מ הילוך על ידי הדחק שמיה הילוך תשמיש על ידי הדחק לא שמיה תשמיש ש"מ אמר רב יהודה [ד]האי זירזא דקני רמא וזקפיה רמא וזקפיה לא מיחייב עד דעקר ליה אמר מר *אדם עומד על האסקופה נוטל מבעה"ב ונותן לו נוטל מעני ונותן לו האי אסקופה מאי אילימא *אסקופת רה"ר נוטל מבעל הבית הא מפיק מרה"י לרה"ר ואלא אסקופת רה"י נוטל מן העני הא קא מעייל מרה"ר לרה"י אלא אסקופת כרמלית נוטל ונותן לכתחלה סוף סוף איסורא מיהא איתא [ה]אלא אסקופה מקום פטור בעלמא הוא כגון דלית ביה ד' על ד' וכי הא *דכי אתא רב דימי אמר רבי יוחנן מקום שאין בו ד' על ד' טפחים מותר לבני רשות היחיד ולבני רשות הרבים לכתף עליו ובלבד שלא יחליפו אמר מר ובלבד שלא יטול מבעל הבית ונותן לעני מעני ונותן לבעל הבית [ו]ואם נטל ונתן שלשתן פטורין לימא תיהוי תיובתא דרבא *דאמר רבא [ז]המעביר חפץ מתחילת ד' לסוף ד' ברשות הרבים אע"פ שהעבירו
דרך

נתכוון לשבות ברה"ר · המערב עירובי תחומין עירובו קונה לו שביתתו שם שיוכל לילך משם לכל רוח אלפים כאילו שבת שם וצריך שיתכוון לקנות שביתתו במקום שיוכל לאכול שם עירובו אם היה רוצה לאוכלו שמתוך כן מועיל לו עירובו לקנות שביתה דמקום פיתא גורם דהתם שייך איניש ואע"פ שהוא בתוך העיר כשקדש היום: למעלה מי' טפחים עירובו עירוב · קס"ד דיכול ליטלו בשבת: אי נימא בבור דאית ביה י' · עמוק: ומאי למעלה דדלאי ואותביה · שהגביהו והניחו למעלה מי' מקרקעיתו של בור: ומאי למטה דתתאי ואותביה · שהשפילו והניחו למטה מי' התחתונים אמאי עירובו עירוב הרי הבור רה"י הוא משפת אוגנו ולמטה וכל שמונח בו ברה"י הוא מונח וכיון דנתכוון שתהא שביתתו ברה"ר ולא הניח עירובו על שפת הבור נמצא הוא במקום אחד ועירובו במקום אחר ואינו יכול להוציאו מרה"י לרה"ר לאוכלו: אלא לאו · האי למעלה מי' דקתני בבור דלית ביה י' וה"ק אם קרקעיתו של בור למטה מי' דהוי הבור חללו י' והוי רה"י אין עירובו עירוב כל מקום שהונח שם ואם קרקעיתו של בור למעלה מי' דה"ל חללו פחות מעשרה עירובו עירוב ולא חשיב ליה כמונח בכרמלית אלמא תשמיש לרבים חשיב ליה: הוא ועירובו בכרמלית · כגון שהיה בור זה בבקעה ונתכוון לשבות על שפתו ובור נמי כיון דלא עמוק י' כרמלית הוא: ואמאי קרי ליה · נתכוון לשבות ברה"ר: לפי שאינה רה"י · דאילו הואי האי בור בחצר אפילו עמוק י' עירובו עירוב: וזמנין משני ליה · רה"ר דוקא קתני ובור שהוא פחות מי' כרמלית הואי כדאמרינן דלא שמיה תשמיש ודקשיא לך היכי מצי מפיק ליה על כרחיך קניית עירוב בין השמשות איתא כשקדש היום והוא ספק יום ספק לילה: ור' היא דאמר · בעירובין (דף לד:) דשבות שגזרו חכמים באיסורי שבת לא גזרו עליה אלא בשבת ודאי ולא בין השמשות הלכך מכרמלית לרשות הרבים שבות בעלמא הוא ובין השמשות ראוי ליטלו משם ולאוכלו לפיכך קנה עירוב: ולא דחויי קא מדחינא לך אלא דוקא קאמינא לך · דלא שמיה תשמיש לרבים: רקק · גרוויל"א ומים צפין עליו: ורשות הרבים מהלכת בו · שעוברין בתוכו רקק ברגליהם: פחות מי' · שאין המים עמוקים י': חייב · שהוא כרשות הרבים גמורה: אלא הילוך תרי זימני למה לי · ליתני בסיפא ורקק מים שברה"ר הזורק לתוכו חייב רה"ר מהלכת בו לאשמועינן דבעינן שיהא צורך לרבים למה לי הא מרישא שמעינן ליה אלא להכי הדר תנייה דוקא שיהא הילוך לרבים דאף על גב דע"י הדחק הוא שמיה הילוך אבל אם היה צורך רבים לתשמיש לא חשיב רשות לרבים: זירזא דקני · חבילה של קנים ארוכים: רמא וזקפיה רמא וזקפיה · הוליכו אמות הרבה ברשות הרבים כענין הזה שלא נטלו כולו מן הקרקע אלא זקפו והשליכו וחזר וזקפו והשליכו אין זו עקירה: אסקופת רשות הרבים · כגון אסקופת מבוי שאין עליה תקרה ואין גבוה ג' מן הקרקע ולחי של מבוי לפנים הימנה: רשות היחיד · כגון עומדת תחת התקרה או לפנים מן הלחי או גבוהה י' ורחבה ד': אסקופת כרמלית אינה גבוהה י' אלא רחבה ד' היכי קתני נוטל לכתחילה סוף סוף איסור דרבנן איכא: ומקום פטור · מקום שאין בו ארבע על ארבע הוא מקום מסויים שיש לו ראש רחב קצת וגבוה ג' ועומד סמוך לרשות היחיד ולרה"ר והכי מוקים לה בעירובין בגבוה ג': ובלבד שלא יחליפו · והכי נמי קתני לעיל ובלבד שלא יטול מן העני ויתן לבעל הבית:
דרך

יכול לומר דוקא בגומא היינו כלומר אפי' (א) גבוה ט' הוי רה"ר דמכתפין בה ע"י הדחק וכ"ש פחות מתשעה דיותר נוח להשתמש בה וכן משמע בסמוך דקאמר אברייתא דמייתי מאי לאו וכן בגומא אסיפא משמע דכל פחות מי' מטלטלין *כמו בקופה: ואי אשמועינן בימות הגשמים כו' · בבריתא חדא סגיא דאי תנא חדא זימנא רקק הוה מוקמינא ליה בדדמי ליה להכי תנא תרי זימני רקק אלא כיון דמשכחת בריתא עביד כאילו תנא בברייתא בהדיא רקק בימות החמה ורקק בימות הגשמים*:

לא מיחייב עד דעקר לי' ממקומו · תימה מאי קמ"ל פשיטא דלא מיחייב כיון דלא עקר ועוד מה שייך הכא הך מילתא וי"ל דקמ"ל דאע"ג דדרך להוליכם בענין זה שאינן קלין לנושאן והוי כמו עומד לכתף (ב) דאמרי' לעיל (דף ה:) דחייב אפ"ה פטור ומשום דלעיל איירי בכיתוף עמוד ט' ברה"ר ורבים מכתפים עליו נקט ליה הכא ודוקא רמא וזקפיה דכשהניח ראשו האחד חוץ לד' אמות עדיין ראשו השני מונח בתוך ד' וכשחזר ומשליך ראשו [הב'] חוץ לד' אמות עדיין אינו מתחייב דהוי כמגרר החפץ עד שהוציא ראש החפץ חוץ לד' אמות והניחו דאע"פ שחוזר ומושכו לחוץ פטור שלא נעשית המלאכה בבת אחת אבל אם מגרר זירזא דקני בבת אחת עד חוץ לד' אמות או מרה"י לרה"ר חייב כדאמרינן (לקמן המצניע דף צה:) בגונב כיס בשבת היה מגרר ויוצא פטור משום דאיסור שבת ואיסור גניבה באין כאחד ואומר ר"י דאם מגלגל חבית ד' אמות ברה"ר או מרה"י לרה"ר חייב דהוי כמו מגרר דאינו נח כלל אבל מגלגל תיבה שהיא מרובעת פטור דהוי כמו רמא וזקפיה דא"א שלא תהא נחה קצת:

לימא תהוי תיובתא דרבא כו' · פרש"י (ג) אע"פ שהעבירו למעלה מי' דהוי מקום פטור ולא נהירא דא"כ ה"ל למיפרך מרבנן דאמרי (לעיל דף ה:) המוציא מחנות לפלטיא דרך סטיו חייב ומאי פריך נמי לימא תהוי תיובתא דרבא לימא הא רבנן קיימי כוותיה ועוד דבהמוצא תפילין (עירובין דף צח:) תנן עומד אדם ברה"י ומטלטל ברה"ר ובלבד שלא יוציא חוץ לד' אמות ודייק בגמרא הא הוציא חייב חטאת לימא מסייע ליה לרבא דאמר רבא המעביר כו' ולפי' הקו' מה ענין זה לזה לכך נראה כפי' ר"ח דמפ' שהעבירו דרך עליו שהעבירו *לפניו נגד גופו דה"א כיון שהגיע כנגדו הוי כמונח ונמצא שלא העביר ד' אמות יחד ומשני התם לא נח דאין זה הנחה *[דרך עצמו]:
אף

[לעיל ו.]

סוס מאי למימר דע"כ אסקופה מקום פטור הוא דהא לאכתי לא תני מקום פטור ומיהו בהא נמי לא פי' דגבוה ג' ואינו רחב ד' דא"כ לא בא לפרש איזהו מקום פטור ושמא מרישא שמעינן ליה עמוד גבוה י' ורחב ד' דהוי רה"י אבל אין רחב ד' הוי מקום פטור [ת"י]

לפניו מימינו לשמאלו נגד גופו כצ"ל רש"ל

גי' רש"ל

עירובין לג: לד: לה. [עח.]

לקמן ק:

עירובין ס. פח. פה: קא:

עירובין צח: ע"ש צט. ע"ש

הגהות הב"ח
(א) תוס' ד"ה אמר ליה וכו' כלומר אפי' נמוך ט' הוי רה"ר דמשתמשים בה על ידי הדחק: (ב) ד"ה לא וכו' כמו עומד לכתף תוך ד' אמות דאמרי' לעיל: (ג) ד"ה לימא וכו' פירש"י. נ"ב עי' פרק המוצא תפילין דף צח תוס' ד"ה וסאמר:

רבינו חננאל

ואסיקנא הילוך ע"י הדחק שמיה הילוך. תשמיש ע"י הדחק לאו שמיה תשמיש כרבא והא דאמר רב יהודה זירזא דקני פי' חבילת קנים רמא וזקפה כגון שהיתה מוטלת [ע"ג הקרקע] והגביה הקצה האחת והאחרת מונחת ע"ג קרקע. והעמידה והשליכה אפי' כל היום לא נתחייב שהרי לא הגביהה כלל ואינו חייב עד דעקר ומנח הנחה היא: הא דא"ר יוחנן מקום שאין בו ד' על ד' טפחים מותר לבני רה"ר ולבני רה"י לכתף עליו ובלבד שלא יחליפו מרשות זה לזה ועל זה הדרך העמדנו זו הברייתא דתניא אדם עומד על האסקופה נוטל מבעל הבית ונותן לו נוטל מן העני ונותן לו ובלבד שלא יטול מבעל הבית ויתן לעני ולא מן העני ויתן לבעל הבית כגון זה הוא שא"ר יוחנן שלא יחליפו. ולא יטול מבעל הבית ויתן לעני כו' ואם נטל מבעה"ב ונתן לעני או מן העני ונתן לבעה"ב פטור. ואמרי' נימא תהוי תיובתא דרבא

רב נסים גאון

וזמנין משני ליה [הוא] ברה"ר ועירובו בכרמלית ור' היא דאמר כל דבר שהוא משום שבות לא גזרו עליו בין השמשות ועיקר דבריו של ר' בברייתא במס' עירובין בפרק בכל מערבין (דף לג) דתניא נתנו באילן למעלה

He raised an objection: [8b] If one intends to take up his Sabbath abode in a public ground, and places his *'erub*[8] in a pit above ten handbreadths, it is a valid *'erub*;[9] if below ten handbreadths, it is not a valid *'erub*. How is this meant? Shall we say, [he placed it] in a pit ten [handbreadths] in depth, and 'above' means that he raised [the bottom] and set it [the *'erub*] there;[10] and 'below' means that he lowered it[11] and set it there: what is the difference between above and below? He is in one place and his *'erub*
a in another![12] Hence it must surely refer to a pit not ten deep,[1] and it is taught, it is a valid *'erub*, which proves that use with difficulty is regarded as use?[2] Sometimes he answered him: Both he and his *'erub* were in a *karmelith*,[3] and why is it called public ground? Because it is not private ground.[4] And sometimes he answered him: He was on public ground while his *'erub* was in a *karmelith*, this agreeing with Rabbi, who maintained: Whatever is [interdicted] as a *shebuth*[5] was not forbidden at twilight.[6] And do not think that I am merely putting you off, but I say it to you with exactitude.[7] For we learnt: If there is a water pool and a public road traverses it, if one throws [an object] four cubits therein, he is liable. And what depth constitutes a pool? Less than ten handbreadths. And if there is a pool of water traversed by a public road, and one throws [an object] four cubits therein,[8] he is liable. Now, as for mentioning this pool twice, it is well; one refers to summer and the other to winter, and both are necessary. For if we were informed [this about] summer, [it might be said the reason] is because it is the practice of people to cool themselves;[9] but in winter I would say [that it is] not [so]. And if we were informed this of winter, [it might be said the reason] is because becoming mud-stained[10] it may happen that he goes down [into the water]; but in summer [I would say that it is] not [so]; thus both are necessary. But why mention 'traversing' twice? Hence it must surely follow that a passage under difficulties[11] is regarded as a [public] passage, whereas use
b under difficulties is not regarded as [public] use.[1] This proves it.

Rab Judah said: In the case of a bundle of canes: if one repeatedly throws it down and raises it,[2] he is not liable unless he lifts it up.[3]

The Master said: 'A man standing on a threshold may take [an object] from or give [it] to the master of the house, and may take [an object] from or give [it] to the poor man.' What is this threshold? Shall we say, a threshold of a public road?[4] [How state that] he 'may take [an object] from the master of the house'? Surely he [thereby] carries [it] from private to public ground! Again, if it is a threshold of a private domain—[how state that] 'he may take [an object] from the poor man'? Surely he [thereby] carries [it] from public to private ground? Or again if it is a threshold of a *karmelith*,[5]—[how state that] 'he may take or give' [implying] even at the very outset? But after all, the prohibition does exist.[6] Rather it must mean a threshold which is merely a place of non-liability, e.g., if it is not four [handbreadths] square. And [it is] even as what R. Dimi, when he came,[7] said in the name of R. Johanan: A place which is less than four square, the denizens both of public and private ground may rearrange their burdens upon it, provided that they do not exchange.[8]

The Master said: 'Providing that he does not take from the master of the house and give to the poor man or the reverse, and if he does take and give [from one to the other], the three are exempt.' Shall we say that this refutes Raba? For Raba said: If one carries an object full four cubits[9] in the street, even if he

(8) V. Glos. (9) Lit., 'his *'erub* is an *'erub* . . . his *'erub* is not an *'erub*.' On the Sabbath one may not go more than two thousand cubits out of the town. This, however, may be extended by placing some food (called an *'erub*) at any spot within the two thousand cubits on Friday; by a legal fiction that spot becomes the Sabbath abode, since he can now eat his meal there, and from there he is permitted to walk a further two thousand cubits in any direction. This food must so be placed that it is permissible to take it on the Sabbath. (10) E.g., he placed a small board on the bottom and the food upon it. (11) E.g., by removing some of the earth at the bottom. (12) The whole of that pit being ten deep, it is private ground (*supra 6a*), and no object in it, even if raised to the very edge, may be taken out into the thoroughfare. Hence the *'erub* is inaccessible, and therefore invalid.—'He is in one place'—*sc.* in public ground, 'and his *'erub* in another,'—in private ground.

a (1) 'Above' and 'below' referring to the bottom of the pit. (2) For otherwise it would not be regarded as public ground. (3) E.g., the pit was in a plain; *supra 6a*. (4) Cf. *supra 6b*. (5) V. Glos. This includes carrying between public ground and a *karmelith*. (6) On Friday, because it is doubtful whether twilight belongs to the day (Friday) or night (the Sabbath), while a *shebuth* itself is not a stringent prohibition. Hence he could have taken out his food at twilight, which is just the time when the *'erub* acquires that spot for him as his resting place for the Sabbath. (7) Viz., that service with difficulty is not regarded as public use. (8) I.e., it travels four cubits before it alights. (9) Hence it is open for public use. (10) Through travelling. (11) As when the public road traverses a pool.

b (1) This is deduced from the emphasis on 'traversing'. (2) Thus moving it: yet he does not actually lift it entirely from the ground at any moment. (3) Lit., 'removes it' completely from the ground. (4) Rashi: e.g., one leading to an alley. (5) Being four handbreadths square but less than ten high, so that it does not rank as private ground. (6) Of carrying between a *karmelith* and public or private ground, though its infringement is not punishable. (7) V. *supra 5a*, n.b9. (8) Using it as a means of transport between public and private ground. (9) Lit., 'from the beginning of four to the end of four.'

carries it [9a] across [or, over] himself,[10] he is liable.[11]—There it does not come to rest [in the place of non-liability], whereas here
a it does.[1]

'Others state, A threshold serves as two domains: if the door is open, it is as within; if the door is shut, it is as without.'[2] Even if it has no stake?[3] But R. Ḥama b. Goria said in Rab's name: That which lies within the opening requires another stake to permit it.[4] And should you answer that [the reference is to a threshold which] is not four square: surely R. Ḥama b. Goria said in Rab's name: That which lies within the opening, even if less than four square, requires another stake to permit it!—Said Rab Judah in Rab's name: The reference here is to the threshold of an alley, half of which [threshold] is covered and half uncovered, the covering being toward the inner side: [hence] if the door is open, it is as within; if the door is shut, it is as without.[5] R. Ashi said: After all, it refers to the threshold of a house, and e.g., where it is covered over with two beams, neither being four [handbreadths wide], and there are less than three [handbreadths] between them, while the door is in the middle: if the entrance
b is open, it is as within, if shut, it is as without.[1]

'But if the threshold is ten [handbreadths] high and four broad, it is a separate domain.' This supports R. Isaac b. Abdimi. For R. Isaac b. Abdimi said, R. Meir[2] used to teach: Wherever you find two domains which are really one, e.g., a pillar in private ground ten high and four broad, one may not re-arrange a burden thereon, for fear of a mound in a public domain.[3]

(10) Rashi: above his hand; i.e., through space more than ten handbreadths from the ground, which is a place of non-liability. R. Ḥan. and Tosaf.: from the right to the left hand, i.e., across his body. (11) On Rashi's interpretation the difficulty is obvious: carrying an object via a place of non-liability is the same as transferring it from public to private ground by way of a threshold, which is a similar place, yet Raba rules that the former imposes liability, whereas the Baraitha states that the three are exempt. According to R. Han. and Tosaf. the difficulty appears to be this: when a person passes an object from one hand to another, his own body not moving, he is in a similar position to this man who stands on the threshold and takes the one and gives to the other, himself not moving, and its passing his stationary body in the former case is the same as when in the latter case it is laid down on the threshold; so, at least, one might argue. (Tosaf. a.l. s.v. ליטא and in 'Er. 98a s.v. והאמר).

a (1) Hence in the case posited by Raba we disregard the method of its passage and condemn him for carrying an object four cubits in the street. (2) Rashi: this is now assumed to refer to a threshold lying at the opening of a blind alley between it and the public road. An alley was made fit for carrying by planting a stake at the side of the opening, which by a legal fiction was regarded as a complete partition stretching right across, and it is understood that this threshold is excluded from the partitioning influence of a stake, which was fixed at the inner side of the threshold. Tosaf. explains it somewhat differently. (3) On the outer side; v. preceding note. (4) 'That which . . . opening' is understood to mean the threshold, it being assumed that the stake is fixed on its inner side, so that the threshold does not come within its influence and therefore it must be enclosed, as it were, and converted into private ground before carrying therein is permitted. This contradicts the Baraitha. (5) This alley was rendered fit for carrying not by a stake but by a beam across its front (v. 'Er. 11b); and it was also furnished with a door or gate at its opening. Now, the threshold referred to here lies in front of the door, while the beam overhead covers the inner half of the threshold. If the door is open (it opened inwards) the whole threshold is counted as part of the alley, and so it is permitted; if it is closed, the threshold is shut out, and even the portion under the beam is forbidden.

b (1) The entrance was covered over from above; if the cover was a single beam four handbreadths wide, everything beneath it, including the threshold, is permitted, as imaginary partitions are assumed to descend from the sides of the beam parallel to the house and enclose the entrance. But this assumption is not made when the beam is less than four in width. Again, when two beams are less than three handbreadths apart, the whole, including the space, is regarded as one, on the principle of *labud*, providing that there is nothing between them to break their imaginary unity. Now, the reference here is to a threshold in the middle of which the door is set. If this entrance is open, nothing breaks the unity above, and since the width of the two beams plus the space between is four cubits, the threshold is permitted. But if it is shut, the door coming between the two beams above forbids the assumption that they are united, and by corollary, the imaginary existence of partitions; hence the threshold remains forbidden. (2) Who is the 'others' mentioned as authors of this teaching, v. *supra* 5a, n. a3. (3) Of the same size; since such constitutes private ground, one may not move an article from it into the street, and so even when situated in private ground it is also forbidden, lest one lead to the other.

דרך עליו חייב התם לא נח הכא נח: *אחרים אומרים *אסקופה משמשת שתי רשויות בזמן שהפתח פתוח כלפנים פתח נעול כלחוץ ואף על גב דלית ליה לחי *והאמר רב חמא בר גוריא אמר רב תוך הפתח צריך לחי אחר להתירו וכי תימא דלית ביה ד' על ד' והאמר רב *חמא *בר גוריא אמר רב תוך הפתח אע"פ שאין בו ד' על ד' צריך לחי אחר להתירו אמר רב יהודה אמר רב הכא באיסקופת מבוי עסקינן חציו מקורה וחציו שאינו מקורה וקירויו כלפי פנים פתח פתוח כלפנים פתח נעול כלחוץ רב אשי אמר לעולם באיסקופת בית עסקינן וכגון שקירה בשתי קורות שאין בזו ארבעה ואין בזו ארבעה ואין בין זו לזו שלשה ודלת באמצע פתח פתוח כלפנים פתח נעול כלחוץ: *ואם היתה איסקופה גבוהה י' ורחבה ד' הרי זו רשות לעצמה מסייע ליה לרב יצחק בר אבדימי דאמר רב יצחק בר אבדימי אומר היה רבי מאיר *כל מקום שאתה מוצא ב' רשויות והן רשות אחת כגון עמוד ברה"י גבוה י' ורחב ד' אסור לכתף עליו גזירה משום תל ברה"ר:

מתני'

רש"י

דרך עליו. שהגביהו למעלה מי' דלא שליט ביה אויר רה"ר והוי מקום פטור: חייב. כי הדר אנחיה ואע"ג דדרך מקום פטור אזל: לא נח. במקום פטור והויא ליה עקירה מרה"ר והנחה ברה"ר: הכא נח. במקום פטור ביד העומד על האסקופה: פתח פתוח כו'. קס"ד במבוי שהכשירו בלחי ולחיו לפנים מן האסקופה והיינו דקא מתמה ואע"ג דלית ליה לחי מבחוץ והא אמר רב חמא כו': תוך הפתח. של מבוי דהיינו רחב האסקופה: צריך לחי אחר להתירו. שהלחי המתיר את המבוי סתמיה נגד האסקופה וזקוף עליה וקסבר אסור להשתמש נגד הלחי אלא מחודו הפנימי ולפנים הוי היכר המחיצה: וכ"ת דלית ביה רחב ד'. במשך עובי החומה לפיכך אינה רשות לעצמה ומותר להשתמש כנגד הלחי מחודו החיצון שהוא שוה לאסקופה אצל רה"ר ואין לך לחי גדול מעובי החומה שמכאן ומכאן שבהם המבוי ניתר: הכא באסקופת מבוי עסקינן. כדקאמרת אבל לא במבוי שהכשרו בלחי אלא במבוי שהכשרו בקורה וקורת המבוי שיעור רחבה טפח בפ"ק דעירובין (דף יג:) והאסקופה ועובי הפתח מסתמא רחבים הם נמצא חציו של עובי הפתח מקורה וחציו אינו מקורה וכגון שהניח הקורה כלפי פנים לצד המבוי הלכך פתח פתוח כלפנים מחוד החיצון של קורה ולפנים וסבר לה כמ"ד מותר להשתמש תחת הקורה או משום טעם ההיכרא מלבר כדמפרש פלוגתייהו בעירובין (דף ה:) אי משום דקורה משום מחיצה דאמרינן חודה החיצון יורד וסותם: פתח נעול. והדלת שוקף בפני האסקופה הפנימית וכל האסקופה חוץ לדלת כלחוץ ואפילו תחת הקורה דכיון דנסתם המבוי בטלה לה קורה וליכא למימר יורד וסותם דכל מחיצה שאין בין חלל המחיצות ד' אינן מחיצות ולא שייכא בהו תורת גוד אחית ולהכי לא אוקמא באסקופת בית דסתם בית פתח שלו יש לו משקוף מלמעלה ונמצא עובי הפתח כולו מקורה ואפילו פתח נעול אמרינן יורד וסותם שהרי יש בחלל עביו ד' מן הדלת לסתימת פי התקרה וה"ה דמצי לאוקמא כולו מקורה אלא שאין ברחב עביו ד' אלא משום דסתם עובי החומה אינו פחות מד': באסקופת בית. שכולו פתח מקורה והיינו טעמא דפתח נעול כלחוץ כגון שקירה עובי הפתח בשתי קורות דאילו תקרה שיש בה ד' אמרינן בה יורד וסותם ותו לא אתי נעילת דלת ומבטל למחיצה ואפילו הוא שוקף באמצעיתו דלא דמי למבוי דקירת מבוי קצרה היא ולא הוכשרה אלא למבוי הלכך פתח נעול בטלה מתורת קורה דהא אזל ליה מבוי אבל תקרת ד' לא בטלה ירידת סתימתה בנעילת דלת דהלמ"מ הוא גוד ולבוד ודופן עקומה במקום ד' והכא טעמא משום דשתי קורות הא שאין בזו ארבע ולא בזו ארבע ולא ביניהן ג' והדלת מתוקן להיות נעל באמצע הלכך פתח פתוח כלפנים דכיון דאין ביניהם ג' אמרינן לבוד והוי כחדא ופיה החיצון יורד וסותם דהא השתא אית בה ד': פתח נעול כלחוץ. כיון דבאמצע הוא נמצא הוא מפסיק ביניהן ומחלקן זו מזו שאינן נראות יחד לומר בהן לבוד וליכא למימר בחיצונה פיה יורד וסותם דהא לית בה ד': ואם היתה אסקופה גבוהה י' כו'. סיפא דמילתא דאחרים דברייתא דלעיל והדר נקיט לה לפרושה כמו אמר מר: רשות לעצמה. ואין מטלטלין בה אפילו מן הבית ואף על גב דשניהם רה"י: אומר היה ר"מ. דהוא אחרים כדאמרינן בהוריות*: והן רשות אחת. דשניהן רה"י אלא שזה נמוך וזה גבוה: כגון עמוד ברה"י כו'. אסור לכתף עליו מן החצר: משום תל ברה"ר. גבוה י' ורחב ד' דהוי רשות היחיד דאיכא חיובא דאורייתא מרשות הרבים לכתף עליו:

מתני'

תוספות

אע"ג דלית ליה לחי כו'. פרש"י דס"ד דמיירי באסקופת מבוי שהכשירו בלחי ולא נהירא מדקאמר בסמוך לעולם באסקופת בית אלא נראה דמיירי בכל אסקופה בין דמבוי בין דבית בין דחצר ונקט אע"ג דלית ליה לחי משום מבוי דבית וחצר אינו ניתר בלחי וקורה אלא בפסים א"נ נקט לחי משום דבית וחצר נמי ניתרין בלחי מכאן ולחי מכאן ומיירי דקיימא אסקופה כנגד עובי החומה דהיינו בין לחיים שהוא תוך הפתח והדלת עומדת אצל עובי החומה של צד פנים ולהכי פתח פתוח כלפנים שאותו עובי רה"י גמורה היא שיש לה ג' מחיצות ב' מחיצות מעובי החומה ושלישית לצד פנים אע"פ שמצד רביעית היא פרוץ במלואו אפ"ה כיון שהפתח פתוח בטל אותו עובי למה שבפנים שיש לו ד' מחיצות פתח נעול כלחוץ דכיון שהוא נעול אינו בטל למה שבפנים והוי כנפרץ במלואו למקום האסור ולאו דוקא כלחוץ דהא רה"י גמורה היא מדאורייתא כיון שיש לה ג' מחיצות ואסור לטלטל משם ולחוץ אלא קרי כלחוץ לפי שאינה כלפנים ואסור לטלטל מבפנים לעובי הפתח דרך נקב אם יש בדלת א"נ יש לייתב כלחוץ כגון שפתוח לכרמלית אבל באסקופה כולה ברה"ר חוץ לעובי החומה ליכא לאוקמא דאי לאו גבוה ג' אפילו פתח פתוח הויא כלחוץ דהוי רה"ר ואי גבוה ג' ורחבה ד' כרמלית היא ולא הויא לא כלחוץ ולא כלפנים ואם אינה רחבה ד' מקום פטור הוא ולעולם הוא כלפנים וכלחוץ ואי קיימא כולה לפנים א"כ לעולם הוא כלפנים וא"ת כיון דמיירי באסקופת בית א"כ מאי פריך אע"ג דלית ליה לחי והא אסקופת בית מסתמא מקורה הוא ואית לן למימר פי תקרה יורד וסותם ואור"י דע"כ באינו מקורה איירי דבמקורה אפילו פתח נעול נמי כלפנים: תוך הפתח אע"פ שאין בו ד' צריך לחי אחר להתירו. וא"ת לרבא דמוקי לה בפ' קמא דעירובין (דף ט. ושם) דהיינו דוקא בפתוח לכרמלית משום דמצא מין את מינו ונעור לוקי הכא בפתוח לרה"ר ולאביי נמי דלא מפליג התם בין פתוח לכרמלית בין פתוח לרה"ר נוקי באסקופה גבוה ג' דבפ"ק דעירובין (ג"ז שם) מוקי אביי הא דצריך לחי אחר להתירו בדליכא אסקופה ג' או בדליכא אסקופה כלל ואמאי דחיק רב לשנויי בע"א וי"ל דלא מצי לאוקמי הכי דא"כ אפילו נעול נמי כלפנים וכי קאמר וכי תימא דלית ביה ד' הוה מצי למיפרך א"ה אפילו נעול נמי: אמר רב יהודה אמר רב הכא באסקופת מבוי עסקינן. דוקא באסקופת מבוי פתח פתוח כלפנים כיון שהקורה ראויה להתיר את המבוי אע"פ שמבוי זה א"צ לקורה שהרי יש לו ד' מחיצות שהפתח והדלת ברביעית מ"מ כיון שראויה להתיר את המבוי מצטרף יחד והוי כאילו מקורה ד' טפחים אבל באסקופת חצר ובית כיון שהקורה אינה ראויה להתיר שם אפילו פתח פתוח הוי כלחוץ הואיל ואינו מקורה אלא חציה ודוקא נקט הכא חציו מקורה דבכולה מקורה אפילו נעול כלפנים דסתם אסקופה שהיא תוך הפתח רחבה ד' אף על גב דאוקי אסקופה דאיירי בה ת"ק באינה רחבה ד' התם מיירי בעומדת חוץ לעובי הפתח ודוקא קירויו כלפי פנים אבל כלפי חוץ אפילו נעול הוי כלפנים דקסבר רב חודו החיצון יורד וסותם כדמסיק בפ"ק דעירובין (דף ה:) וה"ה דהוי מצי למנקט טפח א' מקורה וקירויו באמצעו בלבד שיהא פחות מארבע מחודו החיצון של אותו טפח עד הדלת*: גזירה משום תל ברה"ר. אומר ר"י דמבית לעלייה לא אסר ר"מ לטלטל דלא יבא לטלטל בכך מרה"ר לעלייה דמינכר מחיצתא ולא טעו אינשי בהכי אלא דוקא תל ברה"י גזר אטו תל ברה"ר דליכא מחיצות ובריש כל גגות (עירובין דף פט: ושם) מפרש דלא אמר ר"מ אלא כגון עמוד ואמת הריחים דקביעי אבל לא מכתשת ודברים המטלטלים ואומר ר"י דאע"ג דקי"ל כר"מ בגזירותיו אפילו לגבי רבים כדמוכח בריש אע"פ (כתובות ד' נז.) גבי הא דאמר ר"מ אסור להשהות אשתו אפי' שעה אחת בלא כתובה הכא אין הלכה כר"מ דבפ' כל גגות (עירובין ד' פט. ושם) פסקינן בהדיא הלכה כר"ש דפליג עליה וקאמר א' גגות וא' חצרות וא' קרפיפות רשות אחת הן לכלים ששבתו בתוכן ושרי לטלטל מגג לחצר:

לא

אמר מהר"ם ה"מ לאוקמא וקירויו כלפי חוץ וכגון שהדלת עומדת באמצע עובי הפתח אבל הקירוי אלא דרך הדלת לעמוד כולה בפנים והא דלא אוקימנא בלחי כדס"ד וכגון שהלחי באמצע האסקופה ואין משם עד הדלת ד' שמא לפי שאין דרך להעמיד לחי באמצע האסקופה אלא או בפנים או בחוץ או כמו שתירץ מהר"ם דלחי הוי משום מחיצה ואפילו נעול הוי כלפנים ואע"ג דליכא ד' כמו תקרת ד' דאפילו נעול יורד וסותם [תוס' ישנים]

עין משפט נר מצוה

נב א ש"ע א"ח סי' שמו סעיף ג בהג"ה:

רבינו חננאל

ושנינן הא דרבא (בדנח) [בדלא נח] לפיכך חייב והא (בדלא נח)[בדנח]. פי' דרך עליו שהעבירו על עצמו מימינו ומשמאלו. הא דאחרים דאמרי אסקופת משמשת ב' רשויות פשוטה היא:

ס"א תנן בר רבא

מסורת הש"ס

[לעיל ו.]

עירובין ט.

[שם]

[לעיל ו.]

[עירובין שם:]

[הוריות יג:]

נג א מיי' פ"ו מהל' תפלה הלכה ה סמג עשין יט טוש"ע א"ח סי' רלב סעיף ב וטוש"ע ח"מ סי' ה סעיף ד:
נד ב ש"ע א"ח סי' רלה סעיף ב:
נה ג ד מיי' שם והל' ו סמג שם טוש"ע א"ח סי' רלב סעיף ב:

מתני' *לא ישב אדם לפני הספר סמוך למנחה עד שיתפלל לא יכנס אדם למרחץ ולא לבורסקי ולא לאכול ולא לדין *ואם התחילו אין מפסיקין [ג]מפסיקין (*לקרות ק"ש) ואין מפסיקין לתפלה: **גמ'** הי סמוך למנחה אילימא למנחה גדולה אמאי לא האיכא שהות ביום טובא אלא סמוך למנחה קטנה אם התחילו אין מפסיקין נימא תיהוי תיובתא דר' יהושע בן לוי דאמר ר' יהושע בן לוי *כיון שהגיע זמן תפלת המנחה אסור לאדם שיטעום כלום קודם שיתפלל תפלת המנחה לא לעולם סמוך למנחה גדולה ובתספורת בן אלעשה ולא למרחץ לכולא מילתא דמרחץ ולא לבורסקי לבורסקי גדולה ולא לאכול בסעודה גדולה ולא לדין בתחלת דין רב אחא בר יעקב אמר [ד]לעולם בתספורת דידן לכתחלה אמאי לא ישב גזירה שמא ישבר הזוג ולא למרחץ להזיע בעלמא לכתחלה אמאי לא גזירה שמא *יתעלפה ולא לבורסקי לעיוני בעלמא לכתחלה אמאי לא דילמא חזי פסידא בזביניה ומטריד ולא לאכול בסעודה קטנה לכתחלה אמאי לא דילמא אתי לאמשוכי ולא לדין בגמר הדין לכתחלה אמאי לא דילמא חזי טעמא וסתר דינא [ה]מאימתי התחלת תספורת אמר רב אבין משיניח מעפורת של ספרין על ברכיו ומאימתי התחלת מרחץ אמר רב אבין משיערה מעפרתו הימנו ומאימתי התחלת בורסקי משיקשור בין כתיפיו ומאימתי התחלת אכילה רב אמר משיטול ידיו ור' חנינא אמר משיתיר חגורה ולא פליגי *הא לן והא להו אמר אביי הני חברין בבלאי למאן דאמר *תפלת ערבית רשות כיון דשרא ליה המייניה לא מטרחינן ליה ולמ"ד חובה מטרחינן ליה והא תפלת מנחה דלכולי עלמא חובה היא ותנן אם התחילו אין מפסיקין ואמר רבי חנינא משיתיר חגורו

התם

רש"י

מתני' לא ישב אדם לפני הספר. להסתפר: סמוך למנחה. קודם למנחה: עד שיתפלל. שמא ישכח ולא יתפלל והא אפילו בחול נמי והא דתני הכא משום דדמי להא דתני גבה לא יצא החייט במחטו ע"ש עם חשכה שמא ישכח ויצא משתחשך: ולא יכנס. סמוך למנחה: לא למרחץ כו'. וטעמא דכולהו משום שמא ימשך עד שיעבור זמן תפלה: ואם התחילו. אחת מכל אלו: אין מפסיקין. אלא יגמור ואח"כ מתפלל ובגמרא (דף י.) מפרש בדאיכא שהות לגמור קודם שיעבור הזמן: מפסיקין לק"ש. דאיתא מדאורייתא: ואין מפסיקין לתפלה. ובגמרא (דף יא.) פריך הא תנא ליה רישא: **גמ'** מנחה גדולה. התחלת זמן תמיד של בין הערבים מכי מתחיל להעריב דהיינו מחצי שבע ולמעלה דהא חצי שש וחצי שבע חמה עומדת בראש כל אדם וקודרת כנגדה למטה ואינה נוטה לשום צד ומחצי ז' ולמעלה נוטה ברקיע למערב סמוך למנחה מהתחלת שבע: מנחה קטנה. בט' ומחצה שהיו רגילין שלא לאחרו יותר מכן כדאמרי' בתמיד נשחט סמוך לה מתחילת י': אם התחילו אין מפסיקין. בתמיה ויעבור הזמן לימא תהוי תיובתא כו' דקתני הכא יגמרו סעודתם: בן אלעשה. חתנו של רבי היה ופזר מעות ללמוד תספורת של כ"ג [נדרי' נא.] שהיה מספר כל ראשו ולא לגמרי אלא מניח כל השערות קצת כדי שיהא ראשו של זה בצד עיקרו של זה והייט כמוס יכסמו [את ראשיהם] (יחזקאל מד) ומימשיך טובא: בורסקי גדולה. עורות הרבה ובתחלת תקונן: לכולא מילתא דמרחץ. לחוף ראשו ולהשתטף בחמין ובצונן ולהזיע: שמא ישבר הזוג. של מספרים ויהא צריך לחזור אחר זוג אחר: למרחץ. נמי לא תימא לכולא מילתא דמרחץ אלא להזיע בעלמא: יתעלפה. פשמי"ר בלע"ז: לעיוני בעלמא. שאין זה תחלת עשייתה ואפ"ה לכתחלה לא יכנס לה סמוך למנחה גדולה: דילמא חזי פסידא בזביניה. שמא נתקלקלו בתוכה העורות: ומטריד. ילטער ויהא טרוד בלערו ולא יתפלל: וסתרו דינא. יסתרו מה שפסקו ויחזרו בהן וחוזר להיות תחלת הדין: מאימתי התחלת תספורת. דנימא שוב אין מפסיק כדתנן אם התחילו כו': מעפורת. סודר ונותנו על ברכיו שלא יפול השער על בגדיו: משיערה מעפרתו הימנו. סודרו הוא ראבון להפשטת בגדיו: משיקשור בין כתפיו. את בתי זרועותיו שקורין ברלייר"א: הא לן והא להו. *בני בבל היו חוגרין את עצמן בחוזק וכשאוכלין צריכין להתירם ובני ארץ ישראל לא היו נוהגין כן בהתרת חגורה קודם נטילת ידים: למאן דאמר *תפלת ערבית רשות. במסכת ברכות (דף כז:) מפני שהיא כנגד הקטר חלבים ואימורים שאין מעכבין כפרתן: לא מטרחינן ליה. להפסיק אלא יגמור ואחר כך יתפלל: ולמאן דאמר חובה כו'. בתמיה:

לא

תוספות

לא ישב אדם לפני הספר סמוך למנחה עד שיתפלל. והא דאמר בערבי פסחים (דף צט: ושם) ערבי שבתות וערבי ימים טובים לא יאכל עד שתחשך היינו אפילו התפלל לא יאכל כדמפרש התם כדי שיכנס לשבת כשהוא בתאוה אבל לא התפלל אפילו בשאר ימים נמי אסור כדאמר הכא: **ואם** התחילו אין מפסיקין. אפילו התחילו באיסור כדמוכח בסוכה (דף לח.) גבי מי שבא בדרך ואין בידו לולב נוטלו על שולחנו ופריך למימרא דמפסיקין והא תנן אם התחילו אין מפסיקין ולא משני דהכא בהתחילו בהיתר וגבי לולב התחילו באיסור דמלפרא זמניה הוא וה"נ משמע בגמ' דקאמר כיון דשרי המייניה לא מטרחינן ליה ויתיישב נמי הא דקשה בגמרא גבי לימא תהוי תיובתא דריב"ל: **אין** מפסיקין. ודוקא בדאיכא שהות [ז]ביום להתפלל כדמשמע בגמרא דקאמר במנחה לא שכיח שכרות משמע דאין לו להפסיד תפלת מנחה ובסוכה (ג"ז שם) בהדיא מוקי מתני' בדאיכא שהות דמשני אמה שהבאתי לעיל הא דאיכא שהות והא דליכא שהות:

לימא תהוי תיובתא דר' יהושע בן לוי. משמע ליה דאפילו התחיל מפסיק מדאמר אסור לטעום (א) וא"ת לוקי מתניתין בהתחיל בהיתר דאשכחן גבי הבדלה (ע"פ דף קז.) דקאמר כמי כי האי לישנא אסור לאדם *לטעום כלום קודם שיבדיל ואפ"ה משמע אם התחילו בהיתר אין מפסיקין דקאמר התם *הכי אמר רב הבדלה אינה קובעת וה"מ דקבעי ואכלי אבל אתחולי מעיקרא לא מתחלינן ויש לומר דאם התחילו אין מפסיקין משמע ליה אפילו התחילו באיסור כדפירש במתני':

בתספורת של בן אלעשה כו'. נראה דהכי הלכתא ושרי סעודה קטנה במנחה גדולה עד זמן תפלה ודוקא סעודה גדולה כגון סעודת אירוסין ונשואין וסעודת מילה אסור ודלא כרב אחא בר יעקב דאסר אפילו סעודה קטנה סמוך למנחה גדולה דהלכה כלישנא קמא דהתם לן הש"ס ורב אשי שהוא בתרא סידר את הש"ס והלכתא כותיה לגבי רב אחא בר יעקב ואמאי דאמר לקמן מאימתי התחלת דין אין להוכיח דמתניתין איירי בתחלת הדין דלא כרב אחא דאיכא למימר דקאי אאם התחילו אין מפסיקין ומיהו סמוך למנחה קטנה אסור אפילו סעודה קטנה ואם התחילו מפסיקין ואע"ג דהש"כ אי לאו דר' יהושע בן לוי הוה מוקי לה בסעודה קטנה וסמוך למנחה קטנה ואם התחילו אין מפסיקין ולא קי"ל כר' יהושע בן לוי כדאמר בפרק תפלת השחר (ברכות כח:) מ"מ כיון דמסיק סתם הש"ס הכי משמע דבהא דאם התחילו מפסיקין קיימא לן כוותיה. ודוקא בהא דאמר דאסור לטעום אפילו פירות לא קיימא לן כוותיה: **הא** לן והא להו. פי' בקונטרס בני בבל היו חוגרים עצמם בחוזק וכ"מ בסמוך מדקאמר הני חברין בבלאי למ"ד תפלת ערבית רשות מכי שרא המייניה לא מטרחינן ליה ורבי חנינא שהיה בא"י היה אומר לתלמידיו שהיו מבבל ורב שהיה מבבל אומר לתלמידיו שהיו מא"י לפי שדרכן היה להתרחק שלא היו יכולין לעסוק כל כך בביתם וקשה דבפרק כיצד מברכין (שם דף מד.) בסופו קאמר רב חסדא אמר על הארץ ועל פירותיה ור' יוחנן אמר על הארץ ועל הפירות ואמר התם לא פליגי הא לן והא להו מתקיף לה רב נחמן ארב חסדא איכנו אכלי ואנן מברכינן ומאי פריך [ו]לימא רב חסדא אומר לתלמידיו שהיו מארץ ישראל ווי"ל דקים ליה שבאותה שעה לא היו לפניו תלמידים מארץ ישראל*:

למ"ד תפלת ערבית רשות לא מטרחינן ליה. וא"ת תיפוק ליה משום ק"ש וי"ל כגון שקרא ק"ש ונראה לר"י אפילו למאן דאמר תפלת ערבית רשות אין לבטלה בחנם אלא בשביל שום צורך כמו בשרא המייניה דהכא או אם יש שום מצוה שאינה עוברת יעשה המצוה ולא יתפלל אע"פ שהמצוה אינה עוברת אבל בחנם אין לבטלה תדע שהרי יעקב תקנה ולמה יש לבטלה בחנם ועוד דאמרינן בפרק תפלת השחר (שם כו: ושם) שהיא כנגד הקטרת אברים שהיא כל הלילה דלא מעכבי כפרה אלא מצוה ה"נ תפלת ערבית מצוה ואין להאריך:

התם

רבינו חננאל

מתני' לא ישב אדם לפני הספר סמוך למנחה עד שיתפלל. אתינן לאוקמה סמוך למנחה גדולה שהוא ט' שעות ומחצה ולמעלה. ובתספורת בן אלעשה שצריך שהות הרבה: כדגרסי' בסנהדרין ס"פ כהן גדול כסום יכסמו את ראשיהם תנא כמין תספורת *לוליאנית תספורת יחידתא היא כלומר שתהיה הראש מכוסה בשיער כזר ראש זה השיער נוגע בעיקר השיער שלמעלה הימנו תניא א"ר לא לחנם פיזר בן אלעשה את מעותיו אלא כדי להראות את התספורת כהן גדול. ובא רב אחא בן יעקב ודחאה ואוקמה למתני' בתספורת דידן וגזירה שמא ישבר הזוג שצריך לתקנו. מאימתי התחלתה משיניח מעפורת של ספרין על ברכיו: **ולא** יכנס למרחץ להזיע בעלמא. ולכתחילה אמאי לא גזירה שמא יתעלפה. ומאימתי התחלתו משיערה מפרתו. ולא לבורסקי. לעיוני בעלמא. ולכתחלה אמאי לא דילמא חזי בהן פסידא וצריך לתקנתינהו ומאימתי התחלתו משיקשור בין כתיפיו. ולא לאכול בסעודה קטנה. ולכתחלה אמאי לא דילמא אתי לאמשוכי. מאימתי התחלת סעודה רב אמר משיטול ידיו ר' חנינא אמר משיתיר הגורו ולא פליגי בני א"י שמהלכין אזורי חלצים עד שיתירו הגורתם. ובני בבל משיטול ידיו. וי"א בני בבל מהלכין אזורי חלצים ועלייהו אמרו משיתיר הגורו ובני א"י נטילת ידים: **ולא** לדין בגמר דין ולכתחלה אמאי לא דילמא מוספי טענתא וסתרי לדין

*) עי' ערוך ערך לולייני'

רב נסים גאון

למעלה מי' טפחים אין עירובו עירוב: **מנחה** גדולה מו' שעות ומחצה ולמעלה ומנחה קטנה מט' שעות ומחצה ולמעלה ופירושם במסכת ברכות בפרק תפלת השחר (דף כו): **תספורת** בן אלעשה מפורשת בפ' סנהדרין בפרק כהן גדול (דף כב) מאי כסום יכסמו את ראשיהם תניא כמין תספורת לוליאנית מאי תספורת לוליאנית אמר רב יהודה אמר שמואל תספורתא יחידאה היכי דמי אמר רבה ראשו של זה בצד עיקרו של זה שאלו את רבי איזהו תספורת של כהן גדול אמר להן צאו וראו תספורת של בן אלעשה תנא ר' אומר לא לחנם פיזר בן אלעשה את מעותיו אלא כדי להראות תספורת של כהן גדול: **אמר** ועירי הבריין בבלאי למאן דאמר תפלת ערבית רשות רבי יהושע הוא דסבר כי תפלת ערבית רשות כמו שאמרו בברכות בפרק תפלת השחר (דף כז) תפלת ערבית רבן גמליאל אומר חובה ר' יהושע אומר רשות:

רב

מסורת הש"ס

סוכה לח.
[נ"ל לק"ש כ"א במשנה שבהרי"ף ורא"ש וכן כפרש"י דהכא וכפיסקא דלקמן יא.]
ברכות כח:
[ברכות ה: מד. יומא כח: סוכה נו. מח. בילה ס. יד: תענית ד: קדושין כט: ב"מ קז. ב"ב קמז.]
[ועי' תוספות ברכות מד. ד"ה איכנו ותוס' קידושין כט: סד"ה פא]

הגהות הב"ח

(א) תוס' ד"ה לימא וכו' אסור לטעום כלום וא"ת:

פי' יתלוש [ובערוך ערך עלף גרס יתעלף פי' לשון עייפות כמו על ראש יונה ויתעלף ועי' רש"י חולין ג: ד"ה נתעלף]:

לפניש שם הגי' שיאכל
[דף קה.]
ברכות ד: ס:

גליון הש"ס רש"י ד"ה הא לן וכו' בני בבל היו חוגרין וכו'. מליט כן ביחזקאל כג טו שאמר על בבל חגורי אזור במתניהם: תוס' ד"ה הא לן וכו' וי"ל דקים ליה וכו'. וכעין זה לקמן לב ע"א תד"ה ורמי דאביי וכו' ולקמן קט ע"ב תד"ה הכנמא זעירי. ובעירובין כט ע"א תד"ה מאי אולמא ובפסחים קא ע"ב ברשב"ם ד"ה לקבעו. ובחולין נד ע"א תד"ה וחזיא לדר"מ ובשבועות מז ע"א תד"ה הלכתא מאי ובמנחות ע"א תד"ה מ"מ דר"י. ובנדה מד ע"ב תד"ה שלשים יום וביבמות פ' ע"ב תד"ה כיון. ובב"ק כט ע"ב תד"ה כי פליגי. ובב"ב קח ע"א תד"ה הלב. ובנדרים כב ע"ב בר"ן ד"ה מ"ש. ושם כו ע"א בר"ן ד"ה ולר"ס. ובמרדכי פרק בתרא דיבמות במתני' דאין מעידין אלא עד ג' ימים:

MISHNAH. [9b] ONE MUST NOT SIT DOWN BEFORE A BARBER NEAR MINḤAH[4] UNTIL HE HAS PRAYED: NOR MAY HE ENTER THE BATHS OR A TANNERY, NOR TO EAT NOR TO
a A LAWSUIT;[1] YET IF THEY BEGAN, THEY NEED NOT BREAK OFF.[2] ONE MUST BREAK OFF FOR THE READING OF THE SHEMA', BUT NOT FOR PRAYER.[3]

GEMARA. Near what *minḥah?*[4] Shall we say, near the major *minḥah?* But why not, seeing that there is yet plenty of time in the day? But if near the minor *minḥah:* YET IF THEY BEGAN, THEY NEED NOT BREAK OFF? Shall we say that this is a refutation of R. Joshua b. Levi? For R. Joshua b. Levi said: As soon as it is time for the *minḥah* service one may not eat[5] anything before he has recited the *minḥah* service.—No. After all [it means] near the major *minḥah,* but the reference is to a hair-cut in the fashion of Ben Elasah.[6] [Similarly.] NOR [MAY HE ENTER] THE BATHS [means] for the complete process of the baths; NOR A TANNERY, for tanning on a large scale; NOR EAT, at a long meal [of many courses]:[7] NOR FOR A LAWSUIT, at the beginning of the trial.

R. Aḥa b. Jacob said: After all, it refers to our mode of hair-cutting: and why must he not sit down [for it] at the very outset?
b For fear lest the scissors be broken.[1] [Similarly] NOR TO THE BATHS [means] merely for sweating; [and] why not [do this] in the first place? For fear lest he faint [there].[2] NOR A TANNERY, merely to inspect it:[3] [and] why not at the very outset? Lest he see his wares being spoilt, which will trouble him.[4] NOR TO EAT [means even] a small meal: [and] why not at the very outset? Lest he come to prolong it. NOR TO A LAWSUIT, for the end of the trial; [and] why not [enter] at the very outset? Lest he see an argument to overthrow the verdict.[5]

What is the beginning of a hair-cut?[6]—Said R. Abin: When the barber's sheet is placed on one's knees. And when is the beginning of a bath? Said R. Abin: When one removes his cloak.[7] And when is the beginning of tanning? When he ties [an apron] round his shoulders. And when is the beginning of eating?—Rab said: When one washes his hands; R. Ḥanina said: When he loosens his girdle. But they do not differ: the one refers to ourselves [Babylonians]; the other to them [Palestinians].[8] Abaye said: These Babylonian scholars, on the view that the evening service is voluntary,[9] once they have undone their girdle [to eat], we do not trouble them;[10] but on the view that it is obligatory, do we trouble them? But what of the *minḥah* service, which all agree is obligatory, and still we learnt, YET IF THEY BEGAN, THEY NEED NOT BREAK OFF; whereon R. Ḥanina said, [That means]

(4) The afternoon service.

a (1) Lest he forget about the service. This refers to weekdays, and is taught here because of its similarity to the next Mishnah on 11a. (2) For the service—providing that there will still be time when they finish. (3) The *Shema'* ('hear') is the name of the Biblical passages Deut. VI, 4-9; XI, 13-21; Num. XV, 37-41 the first of which commences with that word *shema'* (*Hear O Israel, the Lord our God the Lord is One*). The 'prayer' *par excellence* is the 'Eighteen Benedictions.' Both the *shema'* and the service must be recited daily, but the former is regarded as a Biblical obligation whereas the latter is a Rabbinical institution (v. Elbogen, *Jüdische Gottesdienst,* 27ff; *J.E.* art. Shemoneh Esreh); hence the activities mentioned in the Mishnah must be interrupted as soon as it is time to recite the *shema'*, even though it can be recited later, but not for the 'service.' (4) The Talmud distinguished two times for *minḥah:* the major, i.e., first *minḥah,* at 12·30 p.m. and the minor, i.e., the late *minḥah,* from 3·30 to sunset, which was calculated as at 6 p.m. but the service was not generally delayed after the minor *minḥah,* i.e., after 3·30. V. Elbogen, op. cit. pp. 98ff; *J.E.* XVIII, 59*b*. (5) Lit., 'taste'. (6) The son-in-law of R. Judah ha-Nasi; he cropped his hair closely in the manner of the High Priest, v. Sanh. 22*b*. This was a long process and if one commenced it even before the major *minḥah* he might be too late for the service. (7) For descriptions of long meals and short meals v. *T.A.* III, pp. 28f.

b (1) And by the time another pair is procured it may be too late for the service. (2) Or, be overcome by weakness. (3) Even not to superintend the whole process. (4) And make him forget about the service. (5) Which will necessitate starting afresh. (6) So that it shall be unnecessary to break it off for the service. (7) I.e., when he starts undressing. (8) Rashi: the Babylonians were tightly belted, so they loosened the girdle before eating; but for the Palestinians this was unnecessary. R. Ḥan. reverses it. (9) It is disputed in Ber. 27*b* whether the evening service is compulsory or voluntary. (10) To refrain from their meal until they have prayed.

when he loosens his girdle? [10a]—There,[11] drinking is rare; here it is usual.[12] Alternatively, as for *minhah*, since it has a fixed time,
a one is afraid[1] and will not come to transgress; but as for the evening service, since there is time for it all night, he is not afraid, and may come to transgress.

R. Shesheth demurred: Is it any trouble to remove the girdle![2] moreover, let him stand thus [ungirdled] and pray?—Because it is said, *prepare to meet thy God, O Israel.*[3] Raba son of R. Huna put on stockings and prayed, quoting, '*prepare to meet* etc.' Raba removed his cloak,[4] clasped his hands and prayed, saying, '[I pray] like a slave before his master.' R. Ashi said: I saw R. Kahana, when there was trouble in the world, removing his cloak, clasp his hands, and pray, saying, '[I pray] like a slave before his master.' When there was peace, he would put it on, cover and enfold himself and pray, quoting, '*Prepare to meet thy God, O Israel.*'[5]

Raba saw R. Hamnuna prolonging his prayers.[6] Said he, They forsake eternal life and occupy themselves with temporal life.[7] But he [R. Hamnuna] held, The times for prayer and [study of the] Torah are distinct from each other. R. Jeremiah was sitting before R. Zera engaged in study; as it was growing late for the service, R. Jeremiah was making haste [to adjourn]. Thereupon R. Zera applied to him [the verse], *He that turneth away from hearing the law, even his prayer is an abomination.*[8]

When is the beginning of a lawsuit? R. Jeremiah and R. Jonah—
b one maintains: When the judges wrap themselves round;[1] and the other says: When the litigants commence [their pleas]. And they do not differ: the latter means when they are already engaged in judging;[2] the former, when they are not already engaged in judging.

R. Ammi and R. Assi were sitting and studying between the pillars;[3] every now and then they knocked at the side of the door and announced: If anyone has a lawsuit, let him enter and come. R. Ḥisda and Rabbah son of R. Huna were sitting all day [engaged] in judgments, and their hearts grew faint,[4] [whereat] R. Ḥiyya b. Rab of Difti[5] recited to them, *and the people stood about Moses from the morning unto the evening;*[6] now, can you really think that Moses sat and judged all day? when was his learning done? But it is to teach you, Every judge who judges with complete fairness[7] even for a single hour, the Writ gives him credit as though he had become a partner to the Holy One, blessed be He, in the creation.[8] [For] here it is written, '*and the people stood about Moses from the morning unto the evening*'; whilst elsewhere it is written, *and there was morning, and there was evening, one day.*[9]

Until when must they [the judges] sit at judgment?—R. Shesheth said: Until the time of the [main] meal [of the day]. R. Ḥama observed, What verse [teaches this]? For it is written, *Woe to thee, O land, when thy king is a child, and thy princes eat in the morning! Happy art thou, O land, when thy king is the son of nobles, and thy princes eat in due season, for strength, and not for drunkenness!*[10] [i.e.,]
c in the strength of the Torah and not in the drunkenness of wine.[1]

Our Rabbis taught: The first hour [of the day][2] is the mealtime for gladiators;[3] the second, for robbers;[4] the third, for heirs;[5] the fourth, for labourers;[6] the fifth, for all [other] people. But that is not so, for R. Papa said: The fourth [hour] is the mealtime for all people?—Rather the fourth hour is the mealtime for all [other] people, the fifth for [agricultural] labourers, and the sixth for scholars. After that it is like throwing a stone into a barrel.[7] Abaye said: That was said only if nothing at all is eaten in the morning; but if something is eaten in the morning, there is no objection.[8]

R. Adda b. Ahabah said: One may recite his prayers [the Eighteen Benedictions] at the baths. An objection is raised: If one enters the baths in the place where people stand dressed,[9] both reading [the *shema'*] and prayer [the Eighteen Benedictions] are permissible, and a greeting of 'Peace'[10] goes without saying; and one may don the phylacteries there,[11] and it goes without saying that he need not remove them [if already wearing them]; Where people stand both dressed and undressed, a greeting of 'Peace' is permissible, but reading and praying are not; it is not necessary to remove the phylacteries [which one is already wearing], but one may not don them at the outset; In the place where people stand undressed,[12] a greeting of 'Peace' is not permissible there[13] and reading and praying goes without saying; the phylacteries must be removed, and it goes without saying that they must not be donned!—When R. Adda b. Ahabah made his statement it referred to baths in which no one is present. But did not R. Jose b. Ḥanina say: The baths of which they [the Rabbis] spoke are even those in which none are present; the privy closet of which they spoke[14] means even such as contains no excrement?—Rather, when R. Adda
d stated [his ruling] it was in reference to new [baths].[1] But surely [this is just what] Rabina propounded: What if a place is designated for a privy closet; is designation recognized or not?[2] and it was not solved. Now did not the same [query of his] apply to baths?[3]—

(11) At *minḥah* time. (12) It was not customary to drink much by day; but the evening meal was often prolonged through drinking; therefore, on the view that the evening service is obligatory, one must refrain from his meal even if he has removed his girdle.

a (1) Careful not to overstep it. (2) Surely you cannot maintain that by that slight act he has commenced his meal. (3) Amos IV, 12. When it is customary to wear a girdle, it is not fitting to pray without one. (4) Rashi: divested himself of his costly upper cloak as a mark of humility. (5) On these preparations for prayer cf. *MGWJ*. 1935 Vol. 4, pp. 330f. (6) Though the general order and contents of the service, e.g., the Eighteen Benedictions (v. Elbogen, op. cit. pp. 5, 27: צלי and צלותא refer to these) was settled, the actual text was left to each individual (ibid. pp. 41 *seqq.*), and R. Hamnuna may have thus prayed at great length; or perhaps this length was due to devotional intensity. (7) They spend time in prayer which might be more usefully employed in study: the former, which is a petition for health, sustenance, etc., he called temporal life—not with great exactitude, as it also contains prayers for knowledge, repentance, and forgiveness. This is interesting as shewing the high place occupied by study as a religious observance in itself. (8) Prov. XXVIII, 9.

b (1) In their praying shawls (*tallith*), that they might be duly impressed with the solemnity of dispensing justice. (2) Having started earlier with a different suit. (3) Of the Beth Hamidrash. (4) Rashi: they grieved at not being able to study. Or literally, because they had not eaten all day. (5) A town probably to be indentified with Dibtha, in the vicinity of Wasit on the Tigris; Obermeyer, p. 197. (6) Ex. XVIII, 13. (7) Lit., 'who judges a true judgment according to its truth'. V. Sanh., *7a*, n. c8. (8) Lit., 'work of the Beginning'. (9) Gen. I, 5. The deduction is based on the similarity of the phrases used in both cases. — Thus, according to Rashi's first reason for their faintness (v. n. 4) he comforted them with the assurance of great reward. According to the second, he told them that they were not bound to sit and judge all day. (10) Eccl. X, 16f.

c (1) Translating: thy princes, viz., judges, do not eat the first thing in the morning, but sit and judge until the proper time for eating. (2) Which was reckoned from six a.m. to six p.m. (3) Whose diet required special attention (Jast.); or perhaps, circus attendants. (4) Rashi in Pes. 12*b*: both are rapacious, hence they eat so early; but robbers, being awake all night, sleep during the first hour of the day. (5) Not having to earn a living, they can eat earlier than others. (6) In the field. (7) Rashi: no benefit is derived. (8) To postponing the main meal. (9) In the outer chamber. (10) Lit., 'enquiring after one's Peace.' (11) In Talmudic times these were worn all day, not only at the morning service as nowadays. (12) In the inner chamber. (13) V. *infra*. (14) In the same connection.

d (1) I.e., which had never been used, but merely designated for baths. (2) Does designation subject the place to the laws appertaining to a privy? (3) But surely he could have solved it on the latest interpretation from R. Adda's ruling.

התם לא שכיחא שכרות הכא שכיחא שכרות א"נ במנחה כיון דקביעא לה זימנא מירתת ולא אתי למפשע ערבית כיון דכולא ליליא זמן ערבית לא מירתת ואתי למפשע מתקיף לה רב ששת טריחותא למיסר המייניה ועוד ליקו הבי וליצלי "משום שנא' °הכון לקראת אלהיך ישראל *רבא בר רב הונא "רמי פוזמקי ומצלי אמר הכון לקראת וגו' רבא "שדי גלימיה "ופכר ידיה ומצלי אמר כעבדא קמיה מריה אמר רב אשי חזינא ליה לרב כהנא כי איכא צערא בעלמא שדי גלימיה ופכר ידיה ומצלי אמר כעבדא קמי מריה כי איכא שלמא °לביש ומתכסי "ומתעטף ומצלי אמר הכון לקראת אלהיך ישראל רבא חזייה לרב המנונא דקא מאריך בצלותיה אמר *מניחין חיי עולם ועוסקים בחיי שעה והוא סבר זמן תפלה לחוד וזמן תורה לחוד ר' ירמיה הוה יתיב קמיה דר' זירא והוו עסקי בשמעתא נגה לצלויי והוה קא מסרהב ר' ירמיה קרי עליה ר' זירא °מסיר אזנו משמוע תורה גם תפלתו תועבה מאימתי התחלת דין רב ירמיה ורבי יונה חד אמר משיתעטפו הדיינין וחד אמר משיפתחו בעלי דינים "ולא פליגי הא דעסקי ואתו בדינא הא דלא עסקי ואתו בדינא רב אמי ורב אסי הוו יתבי וגרסי ביני עמודי וכל שעתא ושעתא הוו טפחי אעיברא דדשא ואמרי אי איכא דאית ליה דינא ליעול וליתי רב חסדא ורבה בר רב הונא הוו יתבי בדינא כולי יומא הוה קא חליש לבייהו תנא להו רב חייא בר רב מדפתי °ויעמד העם על משה מן הבקר עד הערב וכי תעלה על דעתך שמשה יושב ודן כל היום כולו תורתו מתי נעשית אלא לומר לך *כל דיין שדן דין אמת לאמיתו אפילו שעה אחת מעלה עליו הכתוב כאילו נעשה שותף להקדוש ברוך הוא במעשה בראשית כתיב הכא ויעמד העם על משה מן הבקר עד הערב וכתיב התם °ויהי ערב ויהי בקר יום אחד "עד מתי יושבין בדין אמר רב ששת עד זמן סעודה אמר רב חמא מאי קרא דכתיב °אי לך ארץ שמלכך נער ושריך בבקר יאכלו אשריך ארץ שמלכך בן חורים ושריך בעת יאכלו בגבורה ולא בשתי בגבורה של תורה ולא בשתייה של יין *תנו רבנן שעה ראשונה מאכל לודים שניה מאכל לסטים שלישית מאכל יורשין רביעית מאכל פועלים חמישית מאכל כל אדם איני והאמר רב פפא רביעית זמן סעודה לכל אדם אלא "רביעית מאכל כל אדם חמישית מאכל פועלים ששית מאכל ת"ח מכאן ואילך כזורק *אבן לחמת אמר אביי °לא אמרן אלא דלא טעים מידי בצפרא אבל טעים מידי בצפרא לית לן בה אמר רב אדא בר אהבה מתפלל אדם תפלתו בבית המרחץ מיתיבי *הנכנס לבית המרחץ "מקום שב"א עומדין לבושין יש שם מקרא ותפלה ואין צריך לומר שאילת שלום ומניח תפילין ואין צריך לומר שאינו חולץ מקום שבני אדם עומדים *ערומים ולבושין יש שם שאילת שלום ואין שם מקרא ותפלה ואינו חולץ תפילין ואינו מניח לכתחלה מקום שבני אדם עומדין ערומים אין שם שאילת שלום ואין צריך לומר מקרא ותפלה והולץ תפילין ואין צריך לומר שאינו מניחן כי קאמר רב אדא בר אהבה במרחץ שאין בו אדם *והא אמר רבי יוסי בר חנינא [י] מרחץ שאמרו אע"פ שאין בו אדם בית הכסא שאמרו אע"פ שאין בו צואה אלא כי קאמר רב אדא "בחדתי והא מבעיא בעא ליה רבינא *הזמינו לבית הכסא מהו יש זימון או אין זימון ולא איפשיטא ליה לאו הוא הדין למרחץ לא דילמא שאני

לא שכיחא שכרות. אין דרך להשתכר מבע"י לפיכך גומר ויתפלל אבל בלילה עשוי להשתכר בסעודתן: הכון לקראת אלהיך · התנאה לפניו: רמי פוזמקי · טוען אנפילאות חשובים ברגליו ובלע"ז קאלצו"ס: שדי גלימא · משליך אדרתו מעליו שלא יראה כחשוב: ופכר ידיה · חובק ידיו באצבעותיו כאדם המצטער מאימת רבו: חיי עולם · תורה · תפלה צורך חיי שעה היא לרפואה לשלום ולמזונות: נגה · איחר: מסרהב · ממהר לעמוד: דיינין מתעטפין בטליתן · כשפותחין בדין מאימת שכינה ושלא יפנו ראשן לכאן ולכאן ותהא דעתן מיושבת עליהם: עסיקי ואתו · בדין אחר וכבר מעוטפים הן וכשנגמר אותו דין בא לפניהם דין אחר סמוך למנחה הויא התחלתן משיפתחו בעלי הדין בטענות דהכא ליכא למימר משיתעטפו: עמודי · שעליית בית המדרש נשען עליהם: חליש לבייהו · מצטערין שלא עסקו אותו היום בתורה: תנא להו חייא בר רב · שגדול שכר הדיינים ולא יצטערו ול"נ דאין זה [משמעות] לשון לבייהו אלא לשון חלש דעתייהו ולשון חלש לבייהו לשון תענית הוא שלא סעדו כל היום תנא להו חייא בר רב שאין צריכין לישב ולידון כל היום אלא מקצת היום ומה שאמר מן הבקר עד הערב מדרש הוא שחשוב הדבר כמעשה בראשית שנאמר בו ערב ובוקר: שמלכך · דייק שהדיין קרוי מלך שנאמר מלך במשפט יעמיד ארץ (משלי כט): לודים · אומה שקורין קליגם ואוכלי אדם הן והם רעבתנין: מאכל יורשים · יורשי און רב שלא טרחו בו ואין עסוקים ודואגין לשוט אחרי מזונות ולעסוק במלאכה: כזורק אבן לחמת · קשה לגוף ולי נראה לא קשה ולא יפה: מרהגאות שלהן ג' חדרים היו לו פנימי לאמצעי ולהסתפף אמצעי שיורד לתוכו מן המרחץ ולובש חלוקו ויוצא לחיצון וגומר לבישתו וכא שם שעה מגיעת המרחץ: עומדים ערומים · פנימי: מקרא · ק"ש: ערומים ולבושים · אמצעי שיוצא בו ערום וממהר לכסות את עצמו ויוצא לחיצון: וחולץ תפילין · מראשו ואין צ"ל שאם אוחזן בידו בתיק שלהן שאינו מניח והא דתני ואין צ"ל כו' איידי דבעי למיתני מציעתא ואינו מניח ואינו חולץ שאמצעי לא כמרחץ גמור הוא ומקצת תורת מרחץ עליו הלכך היו בראשו אין צריך לחלוץ היה אוחזן אסור להניחן שם בראשו אלא יוצא לחיצון ומניחן: אף על פי שאין בו צואה · ספיעה משם: בחדתי · שלא רחץ בו אדם מעולם אלא בהזמינו לכך: בהני

התם לא שכיחא שכרות · וא"ת דבריש פ' בתרא דתענית (דף כו: וכם) אמרינן שחרית ומוסף דכל יומא לא שכיח שכרות לא גזרינן מנחה ונעילה דשכיח שכרות חיישינן אלמא גם במנחה שכיח שכרות וי"ל דהתם לענין נשיאת כפים שאני דאפילו לא שתה אלא רביעית אסור לישא את כפיו:

טריחותא למיסר המייניה ועוד ליקו הכי ולילי ומשני משום שנאמר הכון לקראת אלהיך ישראל. °ולא חייש לשנויי קושיא קמייתא מכאן שצריך לאזור חלציו כשמתפלל ובמחזור ויטרי מפרש דטעם דבעינן אזור שלא יהא לבו רואה את הערוה ודוקא להן שלא היה להם מכנסים לכך היו צריכים לאזור בשעת תפלה אבל לדידן שיש לנו אבנט של מכנסים אין אנו צריכין לאזור: רמי פוזמקי · מכאן יש להוכיח שאין להתפלל יחף אלא בט' באב ויו"כ: אי איכא דאית ליה דינא ליעול · משמע דעדיף דין מתלמוד תורה והא דאמרי' בפ' בתרא דמ"ק (דף יז:) גבי ההוא דטרקיה זיבורא ושכיב עיילוהו למערתא דחסידי ולא קבלוהו למערתא דדייני וקבלוהו התם בדיינין שאינן מומחין שפעמים נוטין אחר השוחד: דין אמת לאמיתו · לאפוקי °*דין "מרומה: שאני

[עי' ב"ב דף ח ע"ב]

נז א טוש"ע א"ח סי' לח סעיף ב:
נח ב מיי' פ"ה מהל' תפלה הלכה ה סמג עשין יט טוש"ע שם סעיף ה:
נט ג מיי' שם טוש"ע שם סעיף י:
ס ד מיי' שם הלכה ד סמג שם טוש"ע א"ח סי' לה סעיף ג·
סא ה מיי' שם ופ"ג מהל' ציצית הלכה יא טוש"ע א"ח סי' לא סעיף ו ובהג"ה וסי' כד סעיף א:
סב ו מיי' פ"ג מהלכות סנהדרין הלכה ז ופ"ו מהלכות תפלה הל' ו סמג עשין לז טוש"ע א"ח סי' רלב סעי' ב וטוש"ע ח"מ סי' ה סעי' ה:
סג ז מיי' פ"ג מהל' סנהדרין הל' א סמג עשין לז טוש"ע ח"מ סי' ה סעיף ג:
סד ח ט מיי' פ"ג מהל' ק"ש הלכה ג טוש"ע א"ח סי' קנז [וסי' פד]:
סד [י] [מיי' שם הל' ב טוש"ע א"ח סימן פג סעיף א]
סה כ מיי' פ"ג מהל' ק"ש הלכה ג טוש"ע א"ח סי' פד וסי' מה סעי' ב [ברי"ף כאן וכפ"ג דברכות ד' כ. וכן ברא"ש כאן ושם סי' נז]

[כגון חמת יין שהוא חסר וזורק לתוכו אבן שיתמלא וזה לא מעלה ולא מוריד וטוב היה שימלאהו יין של"ס והביאו המג"א סי' קנז סק"ג]

מס' ד"א פ"י ע"ש ול"ע

רבינו חננאל

ומאימתי התחלת דין. אי הוו עסקי בדינא אחרינא משיפתחו בעלי הדין טענותיהן ואי לא משיתעטפו הדיינין: עד מתי יושבין בדין עד זמן סעודה. ואסיקנא ארבע זמן סעודה לכל היא: כל דיין שדן דין אמת לאמתו אפי' שעה אחת מעלה עליו הכתוב כאילו סייע במעשה בראשית מ"ט במעשה בראשית כתיב ויהי ערב ויהי בוקר והכא כתיב ויעמוד העם על משה מן הבוקר עד הערב: פיסקא עד שיתפלל. אריב"ל כיון שהגיע זמן תפלת המנחה אסור לאדם שיטעום קודם שיתפלל תפלת המנחה אין הלכה כי הא דריב"ל וכבר פירשנוה בברכות בפ' תפלת השחר: אמר רב אשי חזינא ליה לרב כהנא דכי איכא צערא [בעלמא] שדי גלימיה וכסי ידיה ומינח כרעיה כעבדא לקמיה מריה ומצלי. וכד איכא שלמא לביש ומכסי ומעטף ומצלי אמר הכן לקראת אלהיך ישראל. וכן ראוי לעשות: אמר רב אדא בר אהבה מתפלל אדם במרחץ. ואותיבנא עליה מהא הנכנס למרחץ. מקום שבני אדם עומדים לבושים יש שם מקרא קריית שמע ותפלה ואין צריך לומר שאילת שלום ומניח שם תפלין ואין צ"ל שאינו חולץ. מקום שבני אדם עומדים ערומים ולבושים יש שם שאילת שלום ואין שם קרית שמע ולא תפלה ולא תפלין ואם היה לביש אותם *)חולצן מקום שב"א כולן עהומין אין שם שאילת שלום ואין צ"ל ק"ש ותפלה וחולץ תפלין אחד מרחץ ואחד ביהכ"ס. ושנינן כי קאמר רב אדא במרחץ חדש ואשמעי' דהזמנה במרחץ לאו מילתא היא אבל הזמנה בביהכ"ס לא איפשיטא ונקטינן לה לאיסורא:
*) לפנינו בגמרא הגי' אינו חולץ תפילין ונראה דט"ס נפל בדברי רבינו וצ"ל כאמת אין חולצין.

אמר

ע"ז רבה
[לקמן נג. ביצה טו: תענית כח.]
סנהדרין ז. מגילה טו:
פסחים יב: ע"ש
תוספתא ברכות פ"ב (לקמן קנ: ע"ז מד: זבחים קב: קידושין לג:)
ברכות כו: ע"ש
שם נדרים ז.

גליון הש"ס גמ' לביש ומתכסי. עי' ברכות ל ע"ב: תום' ד"ה טריחותא וכו' ול"ה לשנויי קושיא קמייתא וכו'. וכעין זה פסחים עח ע"א וכמו שכתב המהרש"א שם ובכתובות לה ע"א תד"ה התם איתו דאפסיד ובזבחים ע"א תד"ה דלמא. וברמב"ן פ"ב דב"ב במלחמות ד"ה ועוד כו' אלא אמר רבינא: ד"ה דין אמת וכו' לאפוקי דין מרומה. עי' מגילה ע"ו ע"ב תוד"ה הדן וב"ב ח' ע"ב:

עין משפט
נר מצוה

סו א מיי' פ"ז מהל' ק"ש הל' ה טוש"ע א"ח סי' פה סעיף ב :

סז ב מיי' פ"ו מהל' נחלות הלכה יג סמג עשין לו טור ח"מ סי' רפב:

שאני בית הכסא דמאים: אין שם שאילת שלום מסייע ליה לרב המנונא משמיה דעולא דאמר אסור לאדם שיתן שלום לחבירו בבית המרחץ משום שנאמר °ויקרא לו ה' שלום אלא מעתה הימנותא נמי אסור למימר בבית הכסא דכתי' °האל הנאמן וכ"ת ה"נ והאמר רבא בר מחסיא אמר רב חמא בר גוריא אמר רב *שרי למימר הימנותא בבית הכסא התם שם גופיה לא איקרי הכי דמתרגמינן אלהא מהימנא הכא שם גופיה איקרי שלום דכתיב ויקרא לו ה' שלום: ואמר רבא בר מחסיא אמר רב חמא בר גוריא אמר רב הנותן מתנה לחבירו צריך להודיעו שנאמר °לדעת כי אני ה' מקדשכם *תניא נמי הכי לדעת כי אני ה' מקדשכם א"ל הקב"ה למשה מתנה טובה יש לי בבית גנזי ושבת שמה ואני מבקש ליתנה לישראל לך והודיעם מכאן ארשב"ג הנותן פת לתינוק צריך להודיע לאמו מאי עביד ליה אמר אביי *שאיף ליה משחא ומלי ליה כוחלא והאידנא דחיישי' לכשפים מאי אמר רב פפא שאיף לי' מאותו המין איני *והאמר רב חמא *(בר) חנינא הנותן מתנה לחבירו א"צ להודיעו שנאמר °ומשה לא ידע כי קרן עור פניו בדברו אתו לא קשיא הא במילתא דעבידא לאגלויי הא במילתא דלא עבידא לאגלויי והא שבת דעבידא לגלויי מתן שכרה לא עביד לגלויי רב חסדא הוה נקיט בידיה תרתי מתנתא דתורא אמר כל מאן דאתי ואמר לי שמעתתא חדתא משמיה דרב יהיבנא ליה ניהליה א"ל רבא בר מחסיא הכי אמר רב הנותן מתנה לחבירו צריך להודיעו שנאמר לדעת כי אני ה' מקדשכם יהבה ניהליה אמר חביבין עלך שמעתתא דרב כולי האי א"ל אין א"ל היינו דאמר רב מילתא אלבישיהו יקירא א"ל אמר רב הכי בתרייתא עדיפא לי מקמייתא ואי הוה נקיטנא אחריתי יהיבנא לך: *ואמר רבא בר מחסיא אמר רב חמא בר גוריא אמר רב °לעולם אל ישנה אדם בנו בין הבנים שבשביל משקל שני סלעים מילת שנתן יעקב ליוסף יותר משאר בניו נתקנאו בו אחיו ונתגלגל הדבר וירדו אבותינו למצרים: ואמר רבא בר מחסיא אמר רב חמא בר גוריא אמר רב לעולם יחזור אדם וישב בעיר שישיבתה קרובה שמתוך שישיבתה קרובה עונותיה מועטין שנאמר °הנה נא העיר הזאת קרובה לנוס שמה והיא מצער מאי קרובה אילימא קרובה דמקרבא וזוטא והא קא חזו לה אלא מתוך שישיבתה קרובה עונותיה מוצערין א"ר *אבין מאי קרא דכתיב °אמלטה נא שמה נ"א בגימטריא נ' וחד הוי ושל סדום נ' וב' ושלותה כ"ו

ויקרא — שופטים ו
דברים ז
שמות לא
שם לד
בראשית יט
שם

רש"י

שאני בית הכסא דמאים · ושם מגונה עליו מש"ה מספקא לן בהזמנתו : ויקרא לו · גדעון להקב"ה ה' שלום : הימנותא . להזכיר אמונה בבית הכסא : צריך להודיעו · מתן פלוני אתן לך וזהו דרך כבוד דשמא יתבייש לקבלה ומתוך כך מתרצין בדברים ואינו בוש תורה אור בדבר וכן אם נתנה בביתו שלא מידיעתו צריך להודיעו שמידו באה לו שמתוך כך יהא אוהבו : לדעת כי אני ה' וגו' · להודיעם אני בא שאני רוצה לקדשם : שייף ליה משחא · ישפשפנו בשמן בין עיניו דבר הנראה שתשאלנו אמו מי עשה כן ויאמר לה התינוק פלוני עשה וגם פת נתן לי : ומלי ליה כוחלא · נותן כחול סביב עינו וכן לשונו בתלמוד : לכשפים · שתחשדנו שכשפו : לאגלויי · מי נתנו לו : מתן שכרה כו' · והוא הודיעם [ע"י משה] בעל פה מה שכרה : רב חסדא · כהן הוה *כדאמרינן (ברכות פ"ו דף מד.) גבי עיר אחת היתה בא"י ובה שמונים זוגות אחים כהנים הנשואים שמונים זוגות אחיות כהנות ובדקו מסורא עד נהרדעא ולא אשכחו אלא תרתי בנתיה דרב חסדא דהוו נסיבי לרמי בר חמא ולמר עוקבא בר חמא : הוה נקיט תרתי מתנתא דתורא · זוג של זרוע לחיים וקיבה שנתנה לו ורשאי להאכילן לישראל ואע"ג דרב חסדא בח"ל הוה לא ילפינן מהכא דמתנות נוהגות בזמן הזה דהאידנא נהוג עלמא כתלתא כסבי (ברכות דף כב·) כרבי יאשיה בכלאים וכרבי יהודה בטבילת בעלי קריין לת"ת וכרבי אלעאי בראשית הגז שהיה אומר אינו נוהג אלא בארץ וכן מתנות בימי רב חסדא אכתי לא נהוג כר' אלעאי ובימי ר"נ בר יצחק נהוג כוותיה בראשית הגז לא במתנות והשתא קא חזינא דנהוג אף במתנות וכי היכי (א) דלאחזו במנהג בראשית הגז בימי ר"נ ולא מחינא בהו ונהגנא כולא כוותיה השתא דנהוג אף במתנות לא משנינן מנהגא : חדתא · חדשה שלא שמעתיה: מילתא אלבישי' יקירא · מעיל דמיו יקרים למי שרגיל ללובשו כלומר לפי שאתה תלמידו של רב ורגיל בשמועותיו אתה מחזר אחריהם : משקל ב' סלעים · לאו דוקא נקט בתלמידי רבינו יצחק הלוי מצאתי כתונת פסים סביב פס ידו נתן מילת ולא כל הכתונת : שישיבתה קרובה · שנתיישבו בה מקרוב כלומר עיר חדשה: דמקרבא · לנוס שם : וזוטא · ולא צריכין אתם להקפיד על קיומה : הא קא חזו לה · למה ליה למימר להו : שישיבתה קרובה · שנה אחת קדמה לה סדום כדמפרש של סדום חמשים ושתים דע"כ בוני מגדל בארץ שנער היו ולא היה ישוב בעולם אלא באותה בקעה כדכתיב (בראשית יא) ויהי כל הארץ שפה אחת וגו' ויהי בנסעם מקדם ומשם נפוצו למקומות אחרים כשנתפלגו ובנו להם עיירות ומשנתפלגו עד שחרבה סדום אינו אלא חמשים ושתים שנה שהרי בסוף ימי פלג נתפלגו הארצות כדתניא בסדר עולם אמר רבי יוסי נביא גדול היה עבר שקרא בנו פלג כי בימיו נפלגה הארץ ואם תאמר בתחלת ימיו והלא יקטן אחיו קטן ממנו והוליד משפחות ונתפלגו ואם תאמר באמצע ימיו לא בא הכתוב לסתום אלא לפרש כתן לך סימן ולא תדע באיזו משנותיו אלא בסוף ימיו לא ותשוב שנותיו של פלג ונמצא שנה שמת בה היא שנת מ"ח לאברהם וכשחרב סדום שנת צ"ט לאברהם שהרי בו ביום נתבשרה שרה ולשנה אחרת ילדה ואברהם בן מאת שנה וגו' (שם כא) : ושלותה . האמורה בה גאון שבעת לחם ושלות השקט היה לה וגו' (יחזקאל טז) וכתיב נתיב לא ידעו עיט לא הדריכוהו וגו' (איוב כח) : עשרים

תוספות

שאני בית הכסא דנפיש זוהמא · תימה בסוף פ"ק דנדרים (דף יז·) גרס בעי רבינא הזמינו לבית הכסא והזמינו לבית המרחץ מהו אלמא במרחץ נמי מיבעי ליה ויש שמוחקין אותו שם מן הספרים משום הך דהכא ומיהו יש לקיים שם הגיר' והכא ה"פ מאי לאו כי היכי דלא איפשיטא ליה מבית הכסא ה"נ לא איפשיטא ליה מבית המרחץ ומשני שאני בית הכסא דנפיש זוהמיה להכי לא איפשיטא ליה אבל מרחץ בתר דבעיא הדר פשטא א"נ הזמינו לבית המרחץ אינו מדברי רבינא אלא הש"ס הוא דמסיק שאינו רוצה לחלק וכן יש בכמה מקומות : דמתרגמינן אלהא מהימנא · תימה דשלום נמי מתרגמינן דעבד ליה שלום וי"ל דהתם קראו שלום על שם שהוא עושה שלום דאי לא קראו שלום אלא בעי למימר ה' שלום ה' העושה לו שלום א"כ ה"ל למימר ה' שלומו : הנותן מתנה לחברו צריך להודיעו · ודוקא במתנה שנותן לו ע"י אהבה שאין המקבל מתבייש אבל הנותן לדקה שהמקבל מתבייש מתן בסתר יכפה אף (משלי כא) : יהבה ניהליה · דמותרת לזרים כפירוש הקונטרס והכי מוכח בפרק הזרוע (חולין קלב·) והא דאמר בפ"ב דכתובות (דף כה·) חזקה לכהונה חילוק מתנות כגון שמעיד לו דבתורת כהונה יהבה ניהליה : ה"ג נתגלגל הדבר וירדו אבותינו למצרים · ואע"ג דבלאו הכי נגזר דכתיב (בראשית טו) ועבדום וענו אותם שמא לא היה נגזר עליהם עינוי כ"כ אלא ע"י זה שהרי ארבע מאות שנה התחילו *קודם שנולד יצחק ל' שנים : וישל סדום כ"ב שנה·כמו שמוכיח בקונ' שהיה אברהם בן מ"ח שנה כשנבנית סדום ושלותה כ"ו שנים משמע שהיה אברהם בן ע"ג כשהרג את המלכים ובסדר עולם משמע שהיה בן ע"ה שנה כשהכה את המלכים דקאמר התם אברהם אבינו כשנדבר עמו בין הבתרים בן ע' שנה היה שנאמר ויהי מקץ שלשים שנה וגו' וחזר לחרן ושהה שם ה' שנים שנאמר ואברם בן חמש שנים ושבעים שנה בצאתו מחרן וגו' ואותה שנה שיצא מחרן שנת רעב היתה ירד למצרים ושהה שם ג' חדשים בא וישב לו באלוני ממרא היא שנה שכבש את המלכים ולפ"ז לא היתה שלותה אלא כ"ד וצריך לומר שהיתה בשלוה ב' שנים בתחלה: ולא

ביצה טז.

ג"ז שם

גירסת רש"ל משנולד יצחק והשאר נמחק [ועי' בשל"ה דף קסא. כמלה שמורה ד"ס ברוך שמר וכו' ביאור יפה בדברי תוס' כללו] ועי' מהרש"א

מסורת הש"ס

עי' רש"י חולין מד: ד"ה רב חסדא ומה שרמזתי שם

[ביצה טז. ע"ש]

[נ"ל ברבי]

מגילה טז:

כ"ה א"ר יצחק ישיבתה של צוער נ"א שנה

הגהות הב"ח

(א) רש"י ד"ה הוה נקט וכו' וכי היכי דלאחזוק במנהג בראשית הגז :

רבינו חננאל

אמר רב המנונא אסור ליתן שלום לחבירו בביהכ"ס שהשם גופיה איקרי שלום שנאמר ויקרא לו ה' שלום אבל לומר נאמן בבית הכסא מותר שאינו שם שנא' האל הנאמן ומתרגמי' אלהא מהימנא : אמר רב הנותן מתנה לחבירו צריך להודיעו שנאמר לדעת כי אני ה' מקדשכם . והני מילי במילתא דלא עבידא לאיתגלויי. אבל במילתא דעבידא לאיתגלויי לא . שנאמר ומשה לא ידע כי קרן עור פניו : אמר רב לעולם אל ישנה אדם בנו אחד משאר בניו . שהרי בשביל ב' סלעים מילת שהוסיף יעקב אבינו ליוסף נתקנאו בו אחיו ונתגלגל הדבר וירדו אבותינו למצרים : אמר רב לעולם יחזור אדם וישב בעיר שישיבתה קרובה [שמתוך שישיבתה קרובה] עונותיה מועטין א"ר חנן מאי קרא שנאמר הלא מצער היא ותחי נפשי כלומר מצער עתה בקרוב נתיישבה . א"ר יצחק ישיבת צוער נ"א שנה היתה שנאמר אמלטה נא שמה נא בגימטריא הכי הוו . ישיבתה של סדום נ"ב שנה הוה שהיתה מוקדמת לצוער שנה ושלותה כ"ו דכתיב שתים עשרה שנה עבדו את כדרלעומר ושלש עשרה שנה מרדו הרי כ"ה שנה ובארבע עשרה למרידה בא כדרלעומר והחריבה נמצאת שלותה כ"ו שנים ותשלום נ"ב לישיבתה :

רב נסים גאון

רב חסדא הוה נקט מתנתא דתורא בידיה. רב חסדא כהן הוה ותמצא במסכת ברכות בפרק כיצד מברכין (דף מד) אמר ר' יצחק עיר אחת היתה בארץ ישראל וגופנא שמה והיו בה שמונים זוגים אחים כהנים לשמנים זוגות אחיות כהנות ובדקו רבנן מסורא ועד נהרדעא ולא אשכחו אלא תרתי בנתיה דרב חסדא כו' ואע"ג דאינהי כהנתא אינהו לא כהני :

רבא

No. Perhaps [10b] a privy is different, because it is offensive.[4]

'A greeting of 'Peace' is not permissible there'. This supports the following dictum of R. Hamnuna on 'Ulla's authority: A man may not extend a greeting of 'Peace' to his neighbour in the baths, because it is said, *And he called it, The Lord is peace.*[5] If so, let it also be forbidden to mention, By faith![6] in a privy, for it is written, *the faithful God?*[7] And should you answer, that indeed is so: but Raba b. Meḥasia said in the name of R. Ḥama b. Goria in Rab's name, By faith! may be mentioned in a privy?—There the Name itself is not so designated, as we translate it, God is faithful; but here the Name itself is designated 'Peace', as it is written, *and he called it, The Lord is Peace.*[8]

Raba b. Meḥasia also said in the name of R. Ḥama b. Goria in Rab's name: If one makes a gift to his neighbour, he must inform him [beforehand], as it is written, *that ye may know that I the Lord sanctify you:*[9] It was taught likewise: *That ye may know that I the Lord sanctify you:* The Holy One, blessed be He, said to Moses, I have a precious gift in My treasure house, called the Sabbath, and desire to give it to Israel; go and inform them. Hence R. Simeon b. Gamaliel said: If one gives a loaf to a child, he must inform his mother. What shall he do to him?[10]—Said Abaye, He must rub him with oil and paint[11] him with kohl.[12] But nowadays that we
a fear witchcraft what [shall be done]?[1]—Said R. Papa: He must rub him with the self-same kind.[2] But that is not so, for R. Ḥama son of R. Ḥanina said: If one makes a gift to his neighbour, he need not inform him, as it is said, *and Moses did not know that the skin if his face shone by reason of His speaking with him?*[3]—There is no difficulty: the one refers to a matter which is likely to be revealed; the other, to one which is not likely to be revealed. But the Sabbath is a matter which stood to be revealed!—Its reward did not stand to be revealed.[4]

R. Ḥisda was holding two [priestly] gifts of oxen in his hand.[5] Said he, 'Whoever will come and tell me a new dictum in Rab's name, I will give them to him.' Said Raba b. Meḥasia to him, Thus did Rab say: If one makes a gift to his neighbour he must inform him, as it is said, *'that ye may know that I the Lord sanctify you'*. Thereupon he gave them to him. Are Rab's dicta so dear to you? asked he. Yes, he replied. That illustrates what Rab said, he rejoined, A garment is precious to its wearer.[6] Did Rab indeed say thus! he exclaimed; I rate the second higher than the first, and if I had another [priestly gift] I would give it to you.

Raba b. Meḥasia also said in the name of R. Ḥama b. Goria in Rab's name: A man should never single out[7] one son among his other sons, for on account of the two *sela's* weight of silk, which Jacob gave Joseph in excess of his other sons, his brothers became jealous of him and the matter resulted in our forefathers' descent into Egypt.[8]

Raba b. Meḥasia also said in the name of R. Ḥama b. Goria in Rab's name: A man should always seek to dwell in a city but recently populated, for since it is but recently populated its sins are few, as it is said, *behold now, this city is near* [kerobah] *to flee to, and it is a little one.*[9] What is meant by '*kerobah*'? Shall we say that it is near and small? But surely they could see that for themselves!
b Rather [he meant,] because it has been recently populated[1] its sins are few. R. Abin said: What verse [supports this]? *Oh, let me* [na] *escape thither:*[2] the numerical value of *na* is fifty-one;[3] but Sodom [had been in existence] fifty-two [years],[4] whilst its

(4) Hence mere designation may suffice there, yet be ineffective in respect to baths. (5) Judg. VI, 24. The form of the greeting was 'Peace unto thee,' 'What is thy peace?' (6) By my word! A term of asseveration. (7) Deut. VII, 9. (8) 'Faithful' is an adjective; 'peace' is a predicative substantive referring to God. (9) Ex. XXXI, 13. (10) To the child, that his mother may know. (11) Lit., 'fill'. (12) A powder used for painting the eyelids.—His mother, seeing this, will enquire who did it, and so the child will tell her about the loaf too.

a (1) The mother may think that the child was put under a spell. (2) Of whatever he gives him. (3) Ex. XXXIV, 29. (4) And this Moses was bidden to do. (5) He was a priest, v. Ber. 44a. The 'gifts' are the priestly dues, viz., the shoulder, jaws and the maw. (6) And you, being Rab's disciple, cherish his sayings. (7) Lit., 'distinguish'. (8) Lit., 'and the matter was rolled on and our forefathers descended' etc. (9) Gen. XIX, 20.

b (1) Likewise expressed by *kerobah*. (2) Gen. XIX, 20. (3) Heb. נא; every letter in Hebrew is also a number. (4) According to a calculation in *Seder Olam*, an ancient chronological work.

peace [11a] [lasted] twenty-six [years], as it is written, *Twelve years they served Chedorlaomer, and thirteen years they rebelled. And in the fourteenth year*, etc.[5]

Raba b. Meḥasia also said in the name of R. Ḥama b. Goria in Rab's name: Every city whose roofs are higher than the synagogue will ultimately be destroyed, as it is said, *to exalt the house of our God, and to repair the ruins thereof*.[6] Yet that refers only to houses; but as for towers and turrets, we have no objection. R. Ashi said: I achieved for the town of Meḥasia[7] that it was not destroyed.[8] But it was destroyed![9]—It was not destroyed as a result of that sin.

Raba b. Meḥasia also said in the name of R. Ḥama b. Goria in Rab's name: [Let one be] under an Ishmaelite but not under a 'stranger';[10] under a stranger but not under a *Gueber*;[11] under a Parsee but not under a scholar; under a scholar but not under an orphan or a widow.[12]

Raba b. Meḥasia also said in the name of R. Ḥama b. Goria in Rab's name: Rather any complaint, but not a complaint of the bowels; any pain, but not heart pain; any ache, but not head ache; any evil, but not an evil wife!

Raba b. Meḥasia also said in the name of R. Ḥama b. Goria in Rab's name: If all seas were ink, reeds pens, the heavens parchment, and all men writers, they would not suffice to write down the intricacies of government. Said R. Mesharshia, What verse [teaches this]? *The heaven for height, and the earth for depth, and*
a *the heart of kings is unsearchable.*[1]

Raba b. Meḥasia also said in the name of R. Ḥama b. Goria in Rab's name: Fasting is as potent against a dream as fire against tow.[2] Said R. Ḥisda: Providing it is on that very day. R. Joseph added: And even on the Sabbath.[3]

R. Joshua son of R. Idi chanced on the home of R. Ashi. A third grown calf[4] was prepared for him and he was invited, 'Master, partake somewhat.' 'I am engaged in a fast,' he replied. 'And do you not accept the ruling of Rab Judah who said: One may borrow his fast and repay it?'[5] 'It is a fast on account of a dream,' he answered, 'and Raba b. Meḥasia said in the name of R. Ḥama b. Goria in Rab's name: Fasting is as potent against a dream as fire against tow; and R. Ḥisda said, Providing it is on that very day; and R. Joseph added: And even on the Sabbath.'

YET IF THEY BEGAN, THEY NEED NOT BREAK OFF. ONE MUST BREAK OFF FOR THE READING OF THE SHEMA', [BUT NOT FOR PRAYER]. But the first clause teaches, THEY NEED NOT BREAK OFF?—The second clause refers to study.[6] For it was taught: If companions [scholars] are engaged in studying, they must break off for the reading of the *shema'*, but not for prayer. R. Joḥanan said: This was taught only of such as R. Simeon b. Yoḥai and his companions, whose study was their profession; but we[7] must break off both for the reading of the *shema'* and for prayer. But it was taught: Just as they do not break off for the service, so do they not break off for the reading of the *shema'*?—That was taught in reference to the intercalation of the
b year.[1] For R. Adda b. Ahabah said, and the Elders of Hagrunia[2] recited likewise: R. Eleazar b. Zadok said: When we were engaged in intercalating the year at Yabneh,[3] we made no break for the reading of the *shema'* or prayer.

MISHNAH. A TAILOR MUST NOT GO OUT WITH HIS NEEDLE NEAR NIGHTFALL,[4] LEST HE FORGET AND GO OUT,[5] NOR A SCRIBE WITH HIS QUILL; AND ONE MAY NOT SEARCH HIS GARMENTS [FOR VERMIN], NOR READ BY THE LIGHT OF A LAMP.[6] IN TRUTH IT WAS SAID, THE ḤAZZAN[7] MAY SEE WHERE THE CHILDREN READ,[8] BUT HE HIMSELF MUST NOT READ. SIMILARLY IT WAS SAID, A ZAB MUST NOT DINE TOGETHER WITH A ZABAH,[9] AS IT MAY LEAD TO SIN.[10]

GEMARA. We learnt elsewhere: One must not stand in private ground and drink in public ground, or on public ground and
c drink in private ground;[1] but if he inserts his head and the greater part [of his body] into the place where he drinks, it is permitted;

(5) Ibid. XIV, 4f. During the twelve years of servitude, the thirteen of rebellion, and the fourteenth of war, they were not at peace; this leaves 26 years of peace before its destruction. (6) Ezra IX, 9. Thus, when '*the house of our God*' is exalted, the ruins are repaired; the present saying is its converse. (7) A famous town near Sura on the Euphrates (Obermeyer, p. 188) which possessed an academy of which R. Ashi was the principal. (8) By not permitting houses to be built higher than the Synagogue. (9) There is evidence that Meḥasia was still standing in the second half of the seventh century; consequently the destruction mentioned here must have been a partial one; ibid. p. 290. (10) Var. lec.: Edomite. Jast.: rather under Arabic dominion than under Byzantium. (11) Parsee, v. Git., 17a, n. a2. (12) A scholar is quick to punish; and God himself punishes an affront to an orphan or widow.

a (1) Prov. XXV, 3. (2) Dreams were believed portents foreshadowing the future, though, as seen here, the evil they foretold might be averted. Cf. Ber. 55-58. B.B. 10a; Yoma 87b *et passim*. Though R. Meir said, 'Dreams neither help nor harm,' (Hor. 13b) we find that he was warned against a certain innkeeper in a dream (Yoma 38b). (3) Though otherwise fasting is forbidden on the Sabbath, a dream-fast is permitted. (4) So Rashi in 'Er. 63a. (5) If one vows to fast, he may 'borrow,' i.e., postpone it and subsequently 'repay,' i.e., keep it later. (6) Lit., 'words of Torah.' (7) Who interrupt our studies for business.

b (1) The Jewish year consists of twelve lunar months. As this is about eleven days shorter than the solar year, an additional month was periodically intercalated, and when the Intercalatory Board deliberated the question of prolonging the year, they did not interrupt themselves for the *shema'* or the service. (2) A town in immediate proximity to Nehardea on the Euphrates. By the middle of the fourth century Nehardea was already on the decline and many scholars preferred to live in Hagrunia, as shown by the phrase, the Elders (i.e., the leading scholars) of Hagrunia. Obermeyer, pp. 265-267. (3) The famous town N.W. of Jerusalem which R. Joḥanan b. Zakkai made the chief academical centre and the seat of the Sanhedrin after the fall of the Jewish state in 70 C.E. (4) Of the Sabbath. (5) In the evening. (6) Lest the light flickers and he tilts the lamp that the oil should flow more freely, which is forbidden on the Sabbath. (7) Lit., 'supervisor.' In the Talmudic period the word did not denote synagogue reader, as in modern times, but was applied to various functionaries, e.g., the person who supervised children's studies in the synagogue, the beadle, the court crier, and the janitor at academical debates. Possibly the same man combined a number of these functions. V. Soṭ., 41a, n.c4. (8) V. Gemara. (9) On *zab* and *zabah* v. Glos. (10) Viz., intimacy, which is forbidden.

c (1) On the Sabbath. He must not put his head into the other domain, lest he draw the drinking cup to himself, thus transferring an object from one domain to another.

עשרים ושש דכתיב שתים עשרה שנה עבדו את כדרלעומר . אין זו שלוה וי"ג מרדו אין זו שלום שהיו בהן מלחמות הרי כ"ה שנים ושנת כ"ו נהרג כדרלעומר והיתה בשלוה כ"ו הנותרים מכ"ב : לרומם בית אלהינו · ועל ידי כן זכינו לתת לנו גדר ביהודה : קשקושי ואברורי . *בירניות ומגדלים:

ולא תחת חבר · פירש בקונטרס חבר פרסיים ול"נ דפרסיים היו בבבל מימות כורש כדפירש"י בפ"ב דגיטין (דף יז·) וחברים בימי רבי יוחנן אתו לבבל כדאמר בהבא על יבמתו (יבמות סג:) ועוד דאמרינן בקדושין (עב·) הראני פרסיים דומין לחיילות בית דוד הראני חברין דומין למלאכי חבלה משמע דחברי אומה אחרת היא והא דאמר בפרק ב' דגיטין (דף יז·) אתא חברא שקל שרגא מקמייהו אמר רחמנא או בטולך או בטולא דבר עשו למימרא דבני אדומים מעלי מפרסיים והתניא אלהים הבין דרכה וגו' ידע הקב"ה שאין ישראל יכולים לקבל רוב גזרותיו של עשו הרשע עמד והגל' אותם לבבל לאו משום דחברים היו פרסאי אלא עיקר היו הפרסיים והחברים שביניהם היו כפופין להן ומשני הא מקמי דאתו חברי לבבל היו פרסאי מעלו מרומאי והא דקאמר או בטולך או בטולא דבר עשו בתר דאתו חברי לבבל בימי ר' יוחנן כדמוכח בהבא על יבמתו (יבמות סג:) והרשיעו את הפרסיים דרומיים מעלי מפרסאי ורש"י פירש שם דאתו חברי לבבל פרסיים בימי כורש ול"נ כדפרישי' דהא בימי רבי יוחנן אתו חברי ופרסיים בימי כורש ודמוכח בקדושין (דף עב·) דלאו אומה אחת הן והר"ר יעקב מקורביל (ג) *מפרש דחברים היו משרתים מפרסיים דומים למלאכי חבלה לפי שלובשים בגדים שחורים ורחבים והיינו דשקל הכומר שרגא להביא לע"ז שלהן :

כגון אנו מפסיקין בין לקריאת שמע בין לתפלה · והא דאמר ליה רבי זירא לרבי ירמיה *מסיר אזנו משמוע תורה וגו' וי"ל תורתו היתה אומנתו או עדיין לא היתה שעה עוברת :

כגון רבי שמעון בן יוחי וחבריו · והא דאמר לקמן (דף לג:) כי הוה מטי *(זמן תפלה) לביש ומכסי ומצלי ההוא מצלי היינו ק"ש :

בעיבור שנה · שלא יתקלקלו המועדות :

שמא ישכח ויצא · אליבא דרבא דאמר לא גזרי גזירה לגזירה אין לפרש שמא ישכח המחט דאפילו יצא ליכא איסור דאורייתא כדאיתא בפ"ב דב"ק (דף כו:) הכיר בה ושכחה לענין שבת פטור מלאכת מחשבת אסרה תורה אלא שמא ישכח את המחט להצניעו עד שיהיה שבת ולבסוף כשיזכור את המחט ישכח שהוא שבת ויצא :

לא יעמוד אדם ברה"ר וישתה ברה"י · בהמוצא תפילין (עירובין דף צט·) מוקי לה בחפצים הצריכים לו ודברי הכל פי' אפי' רבנן דאמרי עומד אדם בר"ה ומטלטל ברה"י הכא מודו דכיון דצריך לשתות איכא למיחש שמא יביאם אצלו וא"ת השתא נמי כי יכניס ראשו ורובו אמאי שרי הא מפיק מרה"י לרה"ר שלוקח ברה"י ונחית בבטנו ברה"ר דהכי אמר התם השתין מים ורק חייב חטאת ויש לומר דבליעתו היינו הנחתו ואין לחוש במה ששב ונכנסים לתוך מעיו כדאמר (לקמן דף פ·) הוציא דיו לכתוב ב' אותיות וכתבן כשהוא מהלך חייב דכתיבתן זו היא הנחתן ואתי שפיר הא דפרק אמרו לו (כריתות דף יג:) יש אוכל אכילה אחת וחייב עליה ד' חטאות ואשם אחד רבי מאיר אומר אף אם היתה שבת והוציאו בפיו חייב והשתא היכי תני ר"מ הוצאה דלא מחייב עלה עד שתנוח במעיו בהדי הנהו דמחייב

רב אשי ראש ישיבה היה במתא מחסיא ומנעם מלהגביה בתיהם יותר מבהכ"נ: תחת ישמעאל· לשמשו: ולא תחת נכרי. אדומים שהיו רשעי' יותר: חבר· (א) אומה מבני פרסיים: תלמיד חכם · אם יקניטו יעניטו וכן יתום ואלמנה מפני שדמעתן מצויה : חולי . הוא חולי ארוך המטונה והולך ומתיש כח כגון אשתא וחולי הראש : כאב · הוא ההולך ובא כגון כאב שן כאב מכה : מיחוש · חששא בעלמא לפי שעה וקל : חללה של רשות · עומק לבם שהוא צריך להיות לו לב לכמה מדינות למס הקצוב ולכמה מלחמות ולכמה משפטים והכל ביום אחד : עיגלא תילתא · (ג) שלישי לבטן שהוא משובח מפני שהבהמה בקטנותה אינה עדיין בכחה והולד ראשון ושני אינו בריא : והא תנא ליה רישא אם התחילו אין מפסיקין · וגבי תפלה קיימינן ולמה ליה למיהדר למיתני ואין מפסיקין לתפלה : אתאן לדברי תורה · ומילתא אחריתי נקט: חברים העוסקין בתורה מפסיקין · תורתן לקריאת שמע דזמנה דאוריי' ובשכבך ובקומך ואין מפסיקין לתפלה : אבל אנו הואיל ומפסיקין תורתנו לאומנתנו כ"ש שנפסיק לתפלה : עיבור שנה · שהיו עולים שבעה לעלייה ונושאין ונותנין אם השנה ראויה וצריכה להתעבר כדאמר בסנהדרין (יא:) על האביב ועל פירות האילן ועל התקופה:

מתני' שמא ישכח ויצא· משתחך: ולא יפלה את כליו · מבער כנים מבגדיו דמתרגמינן בערתי פליתי (דברים כו) ולקמן (יב.) מפרש טעמא: ולא יקרא לאור הנר · בספר שמא יטה הנר להביא השמן לפי הפתילה שידלק יפה ונמצא מבעיר בשבת : החזן · חזן הכנסת המקרא שבעה הקוראים בתורה ופעמים שאינו יודע היכן צריכין לקרות למחר ורואה היכן קורין תינוקות של בית רבן בשבת זו והן קורין בסדר לאור הנר בבית הכנסת ויודע שהיא פרשה של שבת זו ל"א חזן מלמד תינוקות ורואה היכן יתחילו למחר והיכא יסיימו פרשיותיהן : כיוצא בו · לעשות הרחקה לעבירה אמרו : לא יאכל הזב עם הזבה · וכ"ש טהור עם הזבה : מפני הרגל עבירה · מפני שמתוך שמתיחדין יבא לבעול זבה שהיא בכרת : גמ' לא יעמוד אדם . *)ברה"י ויושיט פיו וראשו לרה"ר לאחוז כלי ולשתות גזרה שמא יוציא הכלי אליו ונמצא מתחייב חטאת :

*) בדפ"א הגי' ברה"ר וכו' לרה"י

תורה אור

כ"ו דכתיב °שתים עשרה שנה עבדו את כדרלעומר ושלש עשרה שנה מרדו ובארבע עשרה שנה וגו' : ואמר רבא בר מחסיא אמר רב חמא בר גוריא אמר רב *כל עיר שגגותיה גבוהין מבית הכנסת לסוף חרבה שנאמר °לרומם את בית אלהינו ולהעמיד את חרבותיו וה"מ בבתים אבל *בקשקושי *ואברורי לית לן בה אמר רב אשי אנא עבדי למתא מחסיא דלא חרבה והא חרבה מאותו עון לא חרבה : ואמר רבא בר מחסיא אמר רב חמא בר גוריא אמר רב תחת ישמעאל ולא תחת נכרי תחת נכרי ולא תחת חבר תחת חבר ולא תחת תלמיד חכם תחת ת"ח ולא תחת יתום ואלמנה : ואמר רבא בר מחסיא אמר רב חמא בר גוריא אמר רב כל חולי ולא חולי מעים כל כאב ולא כאב לב כל מיחוש ולא מיחוש ראש כל רעה ולא אשה רעה : ואמר רבא בר מחסיא אמר רב חמא בר גוריא אמר רב אם יהיו כל הימים דיו ואגמים קולמוסים ושמים יריעות וכל בני אדם לבלרין אין מספיקים לכתוב חללה של רשות מאי קראה אמר רב משרשיא °שמים לרום וארץ לעומק ולב מלכים אין חקר : *ואמר רבא בר מחסיא אמר רב חמא בר גוריא אמר רב יפה תענית לחלום כאש לנעורת אמר רב חסדא ובו ביום ואמר רב יוסף אפי' בשבת רבי יהושע בריה דרב אידי איקלע לבי רב אשי עבדי ליה עיגלא תילתא אמרו ליה לטעום מר מידי אמר להו בתענית יתיבנא אמרו ליה ולא סבר ליה מר להא דרב יהודה דאמר *רב יהודה לוה אדם תעניתו ופורע א"ל תענית חלום הוא ואמר רבא בר מחסיא אמר רב חמא בר גוריא אמר רב יפה תענית לחלום כאש לנעורת ואמר רב חסדא ובו ביום ואמר רב יוסף אפי' בשבת : ואם התחילו אין מפסיקין מפסיקין לק"ש : הא תנא ליה רישא אין מפסיקין סיפא אתאן לדברי תורה דתניא °חברים שהיו עוסקין בתורה מפסיקין לק"ש ואין מפסיקין לתפלה א"ר יוחנן לא שנו אלא כגון ר"ש בן יוחי וחביריו שתורתן אומנותן אבל כגון אנו מפסיקין לק"ש ולתפלה והתניא כשם שאין מפסיקין לתפלה כך אין מפסיקין לק"ש כי תני ההיא בעיבור שנה דאמר רב אדא בר אהבה וכן תנו סבי דהגרוניא אמר רבי אלעזר בר צדוק כשהיינו עוסקין בעיבור השנה ביבנה לא היינו מפסיקין לא לקריאת שמע ולא לתפלה : **מתני'** לא יצא החייט במחטו סמוך לחשכה °שמא ישכח ויצא ולא הלבלר בקולמוסו ולא יפלה את כליו *ולא יקרא לאור הנר באמת אמרו החזן רואה היכן תינוקות קוראין אבל הוא לא יקרא כיוצא בו לא יאכל הזב עם הזבה מפני הרגל עבירה : **גמ'** תנן התם לא *יעמוד אדם ברה"י וישתה ברה"ר בר"ה וישתה ברה"י אבל אם הכניס ראשו ורובו למקום שהוא שותה מותר וכן

ברכות יד. | עזרא ט | משלי כה | תענית יב: | לקמן קמט. | עירובין כ. ע"ש לט. ע"ש

עין משפט נר מצוה

סח א מיי' פי"א מהל' תפלה הל' ג טוש"ע א"ח סי' קג סעיף ג :
סט ב טוש"ע שם :
ע ג מיי' פי"א מהלכות תענית הלכה יב סמג עשין דרבנן ג טוש"ע א"ח סי' רכ סעיף ב [וברי"ף כאן ובפ"ק דתענית ד' קע"ב. וברא"ש כאן ובפ"ט דברכות סי' ה' ובפ"ק דתעני' סי' טז]:
עא ד מיי' שם טוש"ע או"ח סי' תקסח סעיף ב:
עב ה מיי' וסמג שם טוש"ע א"ח סי' רפח סעיף ד :

[בלשון ישמעאל מגדל] ואמר רבינו יעקב דהני גגין דידן כקשקושי דמיין לפי שאין משתמשין עליהן כמו שהיו רגילין להשתמש על גגותיהן בימי חכמים ולפ"ז א"צ להגביה בהכ"נ יותר משאר גגין [תו"י]

עג ו מיי' פ"ד מהלכות נדרים הלכה טז סמג לאוין רמב טוש"ע א"ח סי' תקסח סעיף ב :
עד ז ח מיי' פ"ב מהל' ק"ש הלכה ה ופ"ו מהל' תפלה הל' ח סמג עשין יט טוש"ע א"ח סי' קו סעי' ג :
עה ט מיי' פ"ב מהל' ק"ש הלכה ה :

[וכן מפרש הערוך בערך חבר]

עו י מיי' פי"ט מהל' שבת הלכה כו סמג לאוין סה טוש"ע א"ח סי' רנב סעיף ו :
עז כ מיי' פט"ו מהל' שבת הלכה ב סמג שם טוש"ע א"ח סי' שנ סעיף א :

[לעיל י:ד.]

[פ"ל עידן צלויי]

רבינו חננאל

וכל עיר שגגותיה גבוהות מבהכ"נ סופה ליחרב שנאמר לרומם בית אלהינו ולהעמיד את חרבותיו . אמר רב אשי [אנא] עבדי למתא מחסיא שהגבהתי [את בית] הכנסת למעלה מכל גג דלא ליחרב מהאי עון *)לעולם: אמר רב תחת נכרי ולא תחת ישמעאל. תחת ישמעאל ולא תחת חבר שהן רעים כדגרסי' ביבמות (סג:) תחת חבר ולא תחת ת"ח . כלומר אין בו כח להציל מיד הרשעים בזרוע רמה . וכ"ש יתום ואלמנה : אמר רב כל חולי ולא חולי מעיים . כל כאב ולא כאב לב . כל מחוש ולא מחוש ראש : אמר רב יפה תענית לחלום כאש בנעורת . אמר רב חסדא ובו ביום אמר רב יוסף ואפי' בשבת . ואינו תענית חלום . זה שאמר רב לוה אדם תעניתו ופורע אלא שקבל עליו מעצמו להתענות בו. ואפי' אם אירע בו אונס לוה ופורע . ודייקינן מהא דגרסי' בתעניות צערא קביל עליה כי הא שמעי' היכא דאירע בו [אונס]. אמר רב לוה אדם תעניתו ופורע ותענית חלום בין כך ובין כך לא: אם התחילו אין מפסיקין (בו) [כו']. ואוקימנא סיפא איצטריך לדברי תורה. דתניא חברים שהיו עסוקין בתורה מפסיקין לק"ש ואין מפסיקין לתפלה. א"ר יוחנן לא שנו אלא כגון רשב"י וחביריו שתורתן אומנותן אבל כגון אנו מפסיקין אפי' לתפלה והא דתניא כשם שאין מפסיקין לתפלה כך אין מפסיקין לק"ש ההיא בעיבור שנה תניא דא"ר אלעזר ב"ר צדוק כשהיינו עסוקים בעיבור שנה ביבנה לא היינו מפסיקין לא לק"ש ולא לתפלה : מתני' לא יצא החייט במחטו סמוך לחשכה כו' . ירושל' [לעיל בהלכה ב'] ממה דתנינן מנחה ותני לה ר' חייא חשיכה . הדא אמר אפילו חשיכה דתנינן בתרה מנחה היא : תנן התם בסוף עירובין לא יעמוד אדם ברה"י וישתה ברה"ר ולא ברה"ר וישתה ברשות היחיד אא"כ הכניס ראשו ורובו למקום ששותה
*) אולי כיון רבינו בתיבת לעולם לגז"כ התוס' בחידושיו לשבת בתוספתא שעשה רב אשי שלא תחרב היינו שלא תהא נשארת בחורבנה לעולם כשעתיד הקב"ה לחזור בתי צדיקים לישובן וכדאיתא בברכות ל"ח ב' תחזור גם היא לישובה . והיינו דכתיב ולהעמיד את חרבותיו ע"ש ודו"ק :

הגהות הב"ח

(א) רש"י ד"ה חבר אומה. נ"ב ורש"י בפ' כיצד דף מה ע"א חברי פי' אומה שהיתה עם פרסים : (ב) ד"ה עגלא תלתא שלישי. נ"ב ובעירובין דף סג. דחה רש"י פי' זה בעצמו : (ג) תוס' ד"ה ולא תחת וכו' והר"ר יעקב מפרש דחברים כומרים מפרסיים דומי' למלאכי חבלה:

גליון הש"ס גמ' חברים שהיו עוסקין בתורה מפסיקין לק"ש. עי' מ"ק ט ע"ב תוס' ד"ה כאן במצוה וכו' ול"ע ועמד בזה הרלנ"ח בתשובותיו : מתני' שמא ישכח ויצא. עיין לעיל ג ע"א תוס' ד"ה עקירת גופו : תוס' ד"ה כגון ר"ש וחבריו. מצלי היינו קריאת שמע. עיין ברכות טו ע"א תוס' ד"ה אמאן :

עין משפט נר מצוה

עח א מיי' פי"ב מהל' שבת הלכה ב סמג לאוין סה טוש"ע א"ח סי' שנ סעיף א:

עט ב מיי' פי"ה מהל' מעשר הלכה טו:

פ ג מיי' פי"ט מהל' שבת הלכה כו סמג לאוין סה טוש"ע א"ח סי' רנב סעיף ז:

פא ד ה מיי' שם הלכה כא סמג שם טוש"ע א"ח סי' שא סעיף יג:

פב ו מיי' שם הל' כב טוש"ע שם סעיף יב:

פג ז מיי' פי"ג מהל' טומאת אוכלין הל' ג:

[גמרא]

וכן בגת *איבעיא להו כרמלית מאי אמר אביי היא היא רבא אמר **היא גופה גזירה ואנן ניקום ונגזור גזירה לגזירה אמר אביי מנא אמינא לה דקתני וכן בגת מאי גת אי רשות היחיד תנינא אי רשות הרבים תנינא אלא לאו כרמלית רבא אמר וכן בגת לענין מעשר וכן אמר רב ששת וכן בגת לענין מעשר *דתנן שותין על הגת בין על החמין בין על הצונן ופטור דברי ר' מאיר ר' אלעזר בר' צדוק מחייב וחכ"א על החמין חייב על הצונן פטור *מפני שהוא מחזיר את המותר תנן לא יצא החייט במחטו סמוך לחשיכה שמא ישכח ויצא מאי לאו דתחובה לו בבגדו לא דנקיט ליה בידיה ת"ש לא יצא החייט במחטו התחובה לו בבגדו מאי לאו בערב שבת לא כי תניא ההיא בשבת והתניא לא יצא החייט במחטו התחובה בבגדו בע"ש עם חשיכה הא מני רבי יהודה היא דאמר אומן דרך אומנתו חייב *דתניא לא יצא החייט במחטו התחובה לו בבגדו ולא נגר בקיסם שבאזנו ולא סורק במשיחה שבאזנו ולא גרדי באידא שבאזנו ולא צבע בדוגמא שבצוארו ולא שולחני בדינר שבאזנו ואם יצא פטור אבל אסור דברי ר"מ ר' יהודה אומר אומן דרך אומנתו חייב ושאר כל אדם פטור תני חדא לא יצא הזב בכיסו ואם יצא פטור אבל אסור ותניא אידך לא יצא ואם יצא חייב חטאת אמר רב יוסף לא קשיא הא ר"מ הא ר' יהודה א"ל אביי אימור דשמעת ליה לרבי מאיר במידי דלאו היינו אורחיה במידי דהיינו אורחיה מי שמעת ליה דאי לא תימא הכי אלא *מעתה הדיוט שחקק קב בבקעת בשבת לר"מ הכי נמי דלא מחייב אלא אמר רב המנונא לא קשיא כאן בזב בעל שתי ראיות כאן בזב בעל ג' ראיות מ"ש זב בעל שתי ראיות דחייב דמיבעי ליה לבדיקה זב בעל ג' נמי מיבעי ליה לספירה לא נצרכא אלא לבו ביום והא מיבעי ליה כדי שלא יטנפו כליו א"ר זירא האי תנא הוא דאמר °כל אצולי טינוף לא קא חשיב דתנן *הכופה קערה על הכותל אם בשביל שתודח הקער' הרי זה בכי יותן אם בשביל

שלא

רש"י

וכן בגת · לקמיה מפרש לה: כרמלית · כגון בקעה דמדרבנן הוא דאסור להכניס ולהוציא: מהו · לעמוד ברה"י או ברה"ר ויושיט ראשו לכתחלה לתוכו וישתה: היא היא · כשם שאסרנו זו במשנתנו כך זו אסורה: היא גופה · אפי' יוציא הכלי מתוכה לרשות היחיד או מתוכה לרה"ר מדרבנן בעלמא הוא: ואנן ניקום ונגזור · הושטת ראשו אטו הוצאת כלי: אי נימא רה"י · כגון גבוה י' וקאמר דלא יעמוד ברה"ר וישתה לתוכה תנינא: ואי רה"ר · כגון אינה גבוה ג': לענין מעשר · דשתיה על הגת ממש שלא עקרו משם להוציאו חוצה הויא שתיית עראי ופטור ממעשר כל זמן שלא ירד לבור שהוא גמר מלאכתו למעשר אבל להוציאו משם הוי קבע שאין בדעתו להחזיר המותר ואע"ג דלא נגמר מלאכתו למעשר אסור: בחמין · שמזגו בחמין שוב אינו ראוי להחזיר המותר שלא יחמיץ את היין מחמת החמין: מאי לאו דתחובה בבגדו · שאין דרך הוצאה בכך ואפי' הוציאה לרשות הרבים משחשכה שבות בעלמא הוא וקא גזור סמוך לחשכה אטו חשכה אלמא גזרינן לאיסור שבת גזירה לגזירה: כי תניא ההיא · בשבת עצמה דחדא גזירה היכא גזירה תחובה בבגדו אטו היכא דמפיק בידים: אומן · המוציא דרך אומנתו שהוא רגיל לצאת לפרקים כן בחול חייב דהשתא לדידיה ליכא אלא חדא גזירה דגזרינן סמוך לחשכה אטו חשכה: בקיסם שבאזנו · קיסם ארוך ושוה כעין סרגלא שמשרטטין בה ספרים שקורין ויר"א בלע"ז ובו משוין את הנסרים כדרך נגרים שלנו משוים בנטיית קו ולי נראה שכל השנויין כאן אינו אלא שנותנין אותו בני האומנות עליהן בצאתם לשוק כדי שיכירו מאיזו אומנות הוא וישכרוהו למלאכה: סורק · בגדים שקורין פילי"ש: במשיחה · הוא קושר הקוצים שקורין קרדונ"ש וגם את הבגד תופר ומחבר בו ב' ראשין כשמותחו על יתדות האומנות לחובטו במקלות לזקוף את שערו: אירא · הוא נמר או נמר גפן שסותם בו פי הקנה לאחר שהניח בתוכו פקעויות הערב ומשייר בנקב מלא חוט לאריג וזורקו לקנה והפקיע מתגלגל לתוכו ולצאת אינה יכולה שנסתם הנקב: דוגמא · מעט צמר צבוע אדום ומעט צבוע שחור וכן בכל מיני צבע שמראה בהם דוגמא לאחר כזה תרצו או כזה תרצו: כיס · שעושין לזב וקושרו לפי האמה לקבל בו את הזוב: הא רבי יהודה · דזו דרך הוצאתו בחול: במידי דלאו היינו אורחיה · כגון כל אלו השנוין למעלה אין דרך הוצאתו אלא ביד אפילו לאומן אלא בשעה שהוא רוצה להכריז לעצמו שהוא אומן אבל כיס לזב אין דרך הוצאתו אלא בכך מי שמעת ליה דפטור: דאי לא תימא הכי · דמודה ר"מ במי שכל דרכו בכך: הדיוט שחקק קב בבקעת · הואיל ואינו אומן ואין דרך חקיקה בכך הכי נמי דפטור לרבי מאיר א"כ לא מחייב ר' מאיר בשבת אלא אומנין אלא על כרחיך הואיל וכל דרך חקיקתו של זה בכך מיחייב והכא נמי הואיל וכל דרך הוצאה זו לזה בכך חייב: זב בעל שתי ראיות · חייב לפי שהכיס צריך לו לבדוק עצמו אם יראה עוד שלישית ויהיה זב גמור לקרבן וכיון דצריכה לו הויא ליה לדידיה דרך הוצאתו בכך: מיבעי ליה לספירה · דכתיב (ויקרא טו) וכי יטהר הזב וספר לו שבעת ימים ז' נקיים וצריך הוא לכיס לברר לו היום בנקיות שאילו יראה באחד מהן יסתור את הכל דבעינן רצופין דכתיב לטהרתו טהרה אחת לכולן שלא תהא טומאה מפסקת ביניהן: לבו ביום · באותו יום שבת ראה הראיה שלישית דשוב אינו צריך לכיס כל אותו היום שאין אותו יום ממנין הנקיים: לא חשיב · הלכך לאו דרך הוצאה היא לו: כפה קערה על הכותל · שיורדין גשמים עליו: הרי הוא בכי יותן · דאחשבינהו להנך משקין הראה בדעתו שצריך להן ואע"ג דלא ניחא ליה נפילה שנפלו על הפירות לאחר זמן הוי מוכשרין דתנן (מכשירין פ"א) כל משקה שתחלתו לרצון אע"פ שאין סופו לרצון מכשיר:

שלא

תוספות

דמחייב בשעת בליעה אלא אהוצאה מחייב נמי בשעת בליעה כדפרישית ורש"י תירץ בענין אחר בהמוצא תפילין (עירובין דף צט:) ובפ"ב דעירובין (דף כ: ושם) פירשתי ונראה דאע"ג *דהלכה כר"מ בגזרותיו בהא דאמר לא יעמוד ברה"ר ומטלטל ברה"י או איפכא לית הלכתא כוותיה אלא כרבנן דשרו כדמוכח בהמוצא תפילין (שם דף צח:) דאמר מתני ליה רבי חנינא בר שלמיא לחייא בר רב קמיה דרב לא יעמוד כו' א"ל שבקת רבנן ועבדת כר"מ:

אמר אביי מנא אמינא לה דגזרינן גזירה לגזירה °דוקא בהוצאה גזר אביי וכל הנהו דמייתי ראייה איירי בהוצאה אבל בעלמא לא גזר דהא בריש ביצה (דף ג.) פריך אביי למאן דגזר ביצה שנולדה בי"ט אטו פירות הנושרים היא גופה גזירה ואנן ניקום ט':

אלא לאו כרמלית · ואע"ג °דאין כרמלית בכלים האי גת כיון דמחובר לקרקע לא שמיה כלי:

ואם יצא פטור אבל אסור דברי ר"מ · והא דתנן בפרק במה אשה (לקמן דף סב·) ואם יצאה אשה במחט הנקובה חייבת חטאת התם לגמרי דרך הוצאה בכך וכן גבי הא דאמר ר"מ אם (א) שכח והוציאה בפיו חייב התם נמי דרך להוציא המאכל בפה:

כל אצולי טינוף לא קא חשיב · אע"ג דהוי אורחי' בכך כיון דלא הוי אורחיה אלא משום אצולי טינוף לא חשבינן הוצאה כי אורחיה תדע דהא הכופה קערה בשביל שלא ילקה הכותל אינו בכי יותן אע"ג דניחא ליה שנופלים המים ברחוק מן הכותל ע"י הקערה כיון דלא ניחא ליה אלא משום אצולי טינוף לא חשבינן ניחותא לגבי הכשר ה"נ לא חשיב הוצאה כי אורחיה ופריך התם לא ניחא ליה בהני משקין כלל הכא ניחא ליה בהאי כיס לקבולי בי' זיבה ובכה"ג שמקבל מים לאצולי טינוף חשוב משקה לרצון כדמוכח מסיפא וכי היכי דחשיב משקין המתקבלין אע"ג דלאצולי מטינוף (ב) משום דאחשבינהו קבלתן ה"נ חשיב כיס המקבל זיבה לאצולי מטינוף הוצאה כי אורחיה:

ושבתוכה

רבינו חננאל

וכן בגת: איבעיא להו מהו לעמוד בכרמלית וישתה ברה"י או ברה"ר אע"פ שאינו מכנים ראשו ורובו למקום שהוא שותה. אמר אביי היא היא כלומר אסור. רבא אמר היא גופה גזירה להכניס ראשו ורובו למקום ששותה משום חששא שמא יוציא מרשות לרשות ליקום וניגזור בכרמלית לחיבולהכנים ראשו ורובו העומד (ברה"י) [בכרמלית] ושותה (בכרמלית) [ברה"י] למקום ששותה אמו עומד ברשות [הרבים] ושותה ברה"י שהוא עצמו גזירה גזרינן עליה שמא יוציא מרשות לרשות אלא מותר בכרמלית ובקש להביא ראיה לדבריו מסיפא דקתני וכן בגת. כלומר הגת ככרמלית הוא ואסור. ודחה רבא ואמר האי דקתני וכן בגת לענין מעשר. והכי קאמר כשם שהעומד ברה"ר ושותה ברה"י אינו מותר לו לשתות אא"כ יכנים ראשו ורובו למקום שהוא שותה. שאם ישאר לו מים מותר להחזירן למקומן כן בגת לענין מעשר אינו מותר לו לשתות מן היין שבגת קודם שיעשר אלא אם הן צונן שיתכן לו להחזיר המותר. אבל בחמין שמפסידין היין ואי אפשר לו להחזיר המותר אסור לו לשתות שכיון שמזגו בחמין נקבע למעשר ואסור ואקשי' עליה דרבא מהא דתנן לא יצא החייט במחטו שהוא גזירה לגזירה כי זו המחט היא תחובה לו בבגדו וגזרי' עליה שלא יצא בה בבין השמשות שמא יצא בה במחט התחובה בבגדו בשבת. וגזרינן בה בשבת שמא יצא במחטו בידו. ושני רבא הכי הא דתנן לא יצא החייט במחטו כשאוחז המחט בידו. וגזרינן עליה בין השמשות שמא יוציאה בשבת דחדא גזירה היא והא דתניא בהדיא במחט התחובה לו (והברייתא דתניא במחט התחובה לו) בבגדו העמידה בשבת עצמה וגזירה שמא יוציאנה בידו דחדא גזירה היא והא דתניא בהדיא במחט התחובה לו בבגדו ע"ש עם חשיכה אוקמא כר' יהודה דאמר אומן דרך אומנתו חייב כלומר החייט במחט התחובה לו בבגדו כאחד המוציאה בידו דלאו גזירה לגזירה היא: תני חדא לא יצא הזב בכיס שלו ואם יצא פטור אבל אסור ותניא אידך לא יצא ואם יצא חייב חטאת קשיין אהדדי ופריק רב יוסף לא קשיא הא ר' מאיר הא ר' יהודה ונדחת זו גם פירק רב המנונא דהא דקתני פטור בזב בעל שלש ראיות והא דקתני חייב חטאת בזב בעל ב' ראיות ליה כיס שאם יראה אחרת חייב קרבן דחינן דגם בבעל ג' ראיות בעי כיס שאם יספור ימים טהורים וראה אח"כ סותר כל הימים הטהורים וחוזר לחשוב מאותו היום ולהבא ז' ימים טהורים ואח"כ יטהר. כגון שראה זוב בו ביום בשבת ולא ספר ימים טהורים עדיין ואין צריך כיס לסתירה. ודחינן אם אין שם צורך הכיס לסתירה צריך לו כדי שלא יטנפו כליו. ודחה רב זירא ואמר האי תנא אצולי מטינוף לא חשיב ליה מלאכת מחשבת וכי האי תנא דהכופה קערה על פי הכותל:

רב נסים גאון

רבא אמר גזירה היא ותיקו לגזור גזירה לגזירה היא וגזירה הזכורה בפרק עושין פסין (עירובין כ) גזירה דילמא חזי ליה לאיבוס דמיקלקל ושקיל ליה לדוולא ומפיק ליה וחזאי ליה לאידך גיסא נמי דמיקלקל ומנח ליה ומפיק ליה מרה"י לרה"ר. ואיתא במס' יום טוב בפ' המביא כדי יין (דף לה) אמרו כל דבר שמותרו חוזר לא קבע וכן השותה על הצונן פטור מן המעשר מפני שמחזיר את המותר. אלא אמר רב המנונא לא קשיא כאן בזב בעל ב' ראיות וכאן בזב בעל ג' ראיות ומה הפרש בין זב הרואה ב' ראיות ובין זב הרואה ג' ראיות זכור במשנה בפ' מגילה נקראת (דף ח) אין בין זב הרואה שתי ראיות לרואה ג' אלא קרבן ובתלמוד ברור הדבר ופירש מן הכתוב מנה הכתוב שתים וקרא טמא דכתיב (ויקרא טו) איש איש כי יהיה זב מבשרו זובו טמא הוא הזכיר הזיבה ב' פעמים וכן אמר טמא ודן עליו ליטמא בב' ראיות וחזר ואמר (שם) וזאת תהיה טומאתו בזובו רר בשרו את זובו או החתים בשרו מזובו טומאתו היא מנה הכתוב ג' וקרא טמא הזכיר הזיבה ג' פעמים וכן אמר טמא ואם בב' ראיות דן עליו ליטמא ובג' ראיו' אינו דין שיהא טמא שעד שלא ראה ג' ראה ב' ומאי (כו) אהני לן האי קרא אחרינא וגמרי' מרבנן פירושא דיליה ב' ראיות לטומאה וג' לקרבן ובמשנת זבין בפ' ב' ראה ראייה ראשונה בודקין אותו וכו' ר' אליעזר אומר אף בשלישית בודקין אותו מפני הקרבן. וכן עוד לדבריהן זב בעל שלש ראיות נמי מיבעי ליה לסתירה *) עיקר דיליה בקרא לפום מאי דגמרינן בפירושיה והוא שאמר הכתוב (ויקרא טו) וכי יטהר הזב מזובו וספר לו שבעת ימים ואמרו בתורת כהנים שבעת ימים יכול בין סמוכין בין מפוזרין ת"ל לטהרתו שתהא טהרתו אחת כלומר צריך שיהיו ימי הטהרה רצופין כדי שלא תפסיק טומאה ואם יראה במקצתן זיבות הרי סתר כל מה שעברו עליו מימי הספירה וחייב לספור אחר שיטהר מטומאה ז' ימי טהרה מתחלה עד שימלאו לו כולם בטהרה והוא טהור ובמשנת זבין בפרק א' אמרו אבל אם ראה אפי' יום ז' סתר שלפניו ובמסכת נדה בפרק המפלת (דף כב) אמר ליה גזירת הכתוב היא זיבה נמי סותרת כל ז' צהצוחי זיבה לא סתרה כל ז' ובפ' בנות הכותים (נדה דף לג) בעי רמי בר חמא פולטת שכבת זרע שתסתור בזיבה רואה היא וכו' וליטעמיך זב גופיה היכי סתר אחרי טהרתו אמר רחמנא שלא תהא טומאה מפסקת ביניהן אלא מאי אית לך למימר שלא תהא טומאה זיבה מפסקת ביניהן ובפ' כל הזבחי' (ד' כט) אמרו אמר לו ר' עקיבא מצינו בזב וזבה ושומרת יום כנגד יום שהן בחזקת טהרה וכיון שראו ובסוף הפרק הא' מן כריתות (דף ח) אמרו הא קמ"ל דווקא דראה בלילי ח' אבל ביממא דז' לא דקתני ראייה שהיא סותרת אין מביאה לידי קרבן ובפסחים בפ' כיצד צולין את הפסח (ד' פא) ובנזירות בסוף פ' נזיר (ד' עו) אמרו תאני ר' אושעיא אבל הרואה זב בשביעי סותר שלפניו ורבינסכמו אלה ובנזיר אמרו עוד הראשונים יפלו מי שיש לו אחרונים סותר כו' כי טמא נזרו הטומאה סותרת הכל ואין התגלחת סותרת

לא

*) [לפנינו בגמ' איתא לספירה]

מסורת הש"ס

עירובין לט: [ביצה ג. וש"נ]

עירובין שם מעשרות פ"ד מ"ד

[הך טעמא מפני שהוא מחזיר כו' ליתא במשנה דמעשרות רק בעירובין]

תוספתא פ"א

[עי' מה שפירש בערוך ערך קב]

חולין קז. מכשירין פ"ד מ"ג

הגהות הב"ח

(א) תוס' ד"ה ואם יצא וכו' ר' מאיר אם היתה שבת והוציאה בפיו: (ב) ד"ה כל וכו' אע"ג דלאצולי מטינוף הן משום:

גליון הש"ס

גמ' כל אצולי טינוף וכו'. עי' לקמן דף ע"ב וכו'. תוס' ד"ה אמר אביי וכו' דוקא בהוצאה וכו'. עי' עירובין ע"ב ע"א ד"ה אלא

[11*b*] and the same applies to a wine vat.[2] The scholars propounded: What of a *karmelith?*[3]—Abaye said: It is precisely the same. Raba said: That itself[4] is only a preventive measure:[5] are we to arise and enact a preventive measure[6] to safeguard[7] another preventive measure![8]

Abaye said, Whence do I say it? Because it is taught, and the same applies to a wine vat. Now what is this wine vat? If private ground, it has [already] been taught: if public ground, it has [also] been taught. Hence it must surely refer to a *karmelith*. Raba said: 'And the same applies to a wine vat' is [stated] in reference to tithes; and R. Shesheth said likewise, 'And the same applies to a wine vat' refers to tithes. For we learnt: One may drink [wine] over the vat in [a dilution of] both hot or cold [water], and is exempt [from tithing]: this is R. Meir's view. R. Eleazar son of R. Zadok holds him liable. But the Sages maintain: For a hot [dilution] he is liable; for a cold one he is exempt, because the rest is returned.[9]

We learnt: A TAILOR MUST NOT GO OUT WITH HIS NEEDLE NEAR NIGHTFALL, LEST HE FORGET HIMSELF AND GO OUT.
a Surely that means that it is stuck in his garment?[1]—No: it means that he holds it in his hand.[2] Come and hear: A tailor must not go out with a needle sticking in his garment. Surely that refers to the eve of Sabbath?—No; that was taught with reference to the Sabbath. But it was taught, A tailor must not go out with a needle sticking in his garment on the eve of the Sabbath just before sunset?—The author of that is R. Judah, who maintained, An artisan is liable [for carrying out an object] in the manner of his trade.[3] For it was taught: A tailor must not go out with a needle stuck in his garment, nor a carpenter with a chip behind his ear,[4] nor a [wool] corder with the cord in his ear, nor a weaver with the cotton[5] in his ear, nor a dyer with a [colour] sample round his neck, nor a money-changer with a *denar*[6] in his ear; and if he does go forth, he is not liable, though it is forbidden: this is R. Meir's view.[7] R. Judah said: An artisan is liable [for carrying out an object] in the manner of his trade, but all other people are exempt.

One [Baraitha] taught: A *zab* must not go out with his
b pouch;[1] yet if he goes out he is not liable, though it is forbidden. And another taught: A *zab* must not go out with his pouch, and if he goes out he is liable to a sin-offering!—Said R. Joseph, There is no difficulty: the former is R. Meir; the latter R. Judah. Abaye said to him. When have you heard R. Meir [to give this ruling], in respect to something which it is not natural [to carry thus]; but have you heard him in respect to something which demands that mode [of carrying]? For should you not say so, then if an unskilled worker hollows out a measure from a log on the Sabbath, would he indeed be exempt on R. Meir's view?[2] Rather, said R. Hamnuna, there is no difficulty; the one refers to a *zab* who has had two attacks,[3] the other to a *zab* who has had three attacks.[4] Now, why does a *zab* of two attacks differ in that he is liable? [Presumably] because he requires it for examination![5] But then a *zab* of three attacks also requires it for counting?[6] It holds good only for that very day.[7] Yet still he needs it to prevent the soiling of his garments?—Said R. Zera, This agrees with the following Tanna, who maintains, The prevention of soiling has no [positive] importance.[8] For we learnt: If one overturns a basin on a wall, in order that the basin be washed [by the rain], it falls within [the terms of], '*and if it* [water] *be put* [etc.]';

(2) This is now assumed to mean that one must not stand in either a public or private ground, as the case may be, and drink from the vat. (3) May one stand in public or private ground and drink in a *karmelith*, or *vice versa?* (4) The prohibition of actually transporting an object between a *karmelith* and public or private ground. (5) V. *supra 6a* on *karmelith*. (6) *Sc.* the prohibition of standing in one domain and drinking in another. (7) Lit., 'for'. (8) Surely not. (9) The vat is the utensil into which the expressed juice of the grapes runs, whence it descends into the pit beneath. Once it is in the pit its manufacture as wine is complete, and it is liable to tithes, before the rendering of which nothing at all may be drunk. But while it is yet in the vat its manufacture is not complete, and so a little wine may be drunk even before the rendering of the tithes. That, however, is only if it is drunk directly over the vat; if it is taken out, that action itself confers upon it the status of finished wine, and the tithes, etc., must first be given. Thus, when it is taught, 'and the same applies to a wine vat', it means that if one drinks wine from the vat, he is regarded as taking it away, unless he has his head and greater part of his body in the vat, and must render the tithes before he drinks.—Wine was not drunk neat, but diluted with water; if it is diluted with cold water, the rest can be poured back into the vat; if with hot water, it cannot, the hot mixture injuring the rest. R. Meir holds that in both cases, since he does not take it away from the vat, he can drink a little without tithing; R. Eleazar b. R. Zadok rejects this view. The Sages agree with R. Meir if it is diluted with cold water; if it is diluted with hot, since the rest cannot be returned into the vat, it is as though it were carried away, and therefore may not be drunk.

a (1) Then even carrying it out on the Sabbath is only Rabbinically forbidden as a preventive measure, lest one carry in general, and yet he must also not go out before the Sabbath as a preventive measure lest he go on the Sabbath itself. Thus we have one preventive measure to safeguard another in respect to the Sabbath. (2) This is Biblically forbidden on the Sabbath. (3) And this is such; thus he regards it as Biblically forbidden. (4) Rashi: this was the sign of his trade, and he wore it that he might be recognized and offered employment. (5) Krauss in *T.A.* I, p. 249 and p. 281 a.l. translates: a small distaff, carried behind the ear as an indication of a man's trade. (6) A coin. (7) He regards these as unnatural ways of carrying, whereas Scripture prohibits only the natural mode of any particular form of labour.

b (1) To receive his discharge. (2) Because he did not do it in a professional manner? Surely not, for if so only a skilled worker will be liable for doing something of his own trade. Hence it must be that a person is liable for doing any labour in the manner natural *to himself*, and the same applies to a *zab* and his pouch. (3) Lit., 'sights'—of discharge. (4) When a *zab* has had three attacks he must bring a sacrifice (Lev. XV, 13-15). Consequently, after two attacks he needs this pouch to see whether he has a third (which otherwise may pass unknown to him), and since he needs it that is the natural way for him to carry it, and therefore he is liable. (5) As in last note. (6) After he ceases to discharge he must count seven consecutive days of cleanness, i.e., in which there is no discharge (ibid.): a single attack during this period necessitates counting afresh from the following day. Hence he too needs this pouch for that period. (7) I.e., he is not liable only if he had the third attack on that Sabbath itself; he does not need the pouch then, as in any case he commences counting only on the next day. (8) I.e., when a thing is done not for its own sake but to prevent something from being soiled, it is not regarded as a positive act and involves no liability.

if in order [12*a*] that the wall be not damaged [by the rain], it
a does not fall within [the terms of] '*and if it be put* [etc.]'[1] But how compare! There he does not want that fluid at all, whereas here he needs this pouch to receive the discharge.[2] This can only be compared to the second clause: If a tub[3] is placed so that the dripping [of water] should fall therein, the water which rebounds or overflows is not within [the meaning of] '*and if* [*water*] *be put*'; but the water inside it is within [the meaning of] *and if* [*water*] *be put!*[4]—Rather, said both Abaye and Raba, There is no difficulty: the one is according to R. Judah; the other agrees with R. Simeon.[5]

The School of R. Ishmael taught: A man may go out with his *tefillin*[6] on the eve of Sabbath near nightfall.[7] What is the reason? Because Rabbah son of R. Huna said: One must feel his *tefillin* every now and then, [inferring] *a minori* from [the High Priest's] headplate. If in the case of the headplate, which contained the Divine Name[8] only once, yet the Torah said, *and it shall always be on his forehead*,[9] [i.e.,] his mind must not be diverted from it; then with the *tefillin*, which contain the Divine Name many times,
b how much more so! therefore he is fully cognizant thereof.[1]

It was taught: Ḥanania said: One must examine[2] his garments on Sabbath eve before nightfall. R. Joseph observed: That is a vital[3] law for the Sabbath.[4]

ONE MAY NOT SEARCH HIS GARMENTS [FOR VERMIN] etc. The scholars propounded: [Does this mean], ONE MAY NOT SEARCH HIS GARMENTS by day, lest he kill [the vermin], and would this agree with R. Eliezer, (for it was taught, R. Eliezer said: If one kills vermin on the Sabbath, it is as though he killed a camel);[5] while ONE MAY NOT READ BY THE LIGHT OF A LAMP, lest he tilt it? Or perhaps, both are [forbidden] lest he tilt [the lamp]?[6]—Come and hear: One may not search [his garments] nor read by the light of a lamp. But is it stronger than our Mishnah?[7] Come and hear: One may not search his garments by the light of a lamp, nor read by the light of a lamp, and these are of the *halachoth* stated in the upper chamber of Ḥananiah b. Hezekiah b. Garon.[8] This proves that both are on account lest he tilt [the lamp]; this proves it.

Rab Judah said in Samuel's name: [It is forbidden] even to distinguish between one's own garments and his wife's [by lamp light]. Said Raba: That was stated only of townspeople;[9] but those of country folk[10] are easily distinguished. And [even] in the case of townspeople this was stated only of old women;[11] but those of young women are readily distinguishable.

Our Rabbis taught: One must not search [his garments] in the street out of decency. In like way R. Judah—others state, R. Nehemiah—said: One must not cause himself to vomit in the street, out of decency.

Our Rabbis taught: If one searches his garments [on the Sabbath] he may press [the vermin] and throw it away, providing that he does not kill it. Abba Saul said: He must take and throw it away, providing that he does not press it. R. Huna said, The *halachah* is, he may press and throw it away, and that is seemly, even on
c weekdays. Rabbah killed them, and R. Shesheth killed them.[1] Raba threw them into a basin of water. R. Naḥman said to his daughters, 'Kill them and let me hear the sound of the hated ones.'[2]

It was taught, R. Simeon b. Eleazar said: Vermin must not be killed on the Sabbath: this is the view of Beth Shammai; while Beth Hillel permit it. And R. Simeon b. Eleazar said likewise on the authority of R. Simeon b. Gamaliel: One must not negotiate for the betrothal of children [girls],[3] nor for a boy, to teach him the book[4] and to teach him a trade,[5] nor may mourners be comforted, nor may the sick be visited on the Sabbath:[6] that is the ruling of Beth Shammai; but Beth Hillel permit it.

Our Rabbis taught: If one enters [a house] to visit a sick person [on the Sabbath], he should say, 'It is the Sabbath, when one must not cry out, and recovery will soon come.' R. Meir said, [One

a (1) V. Lev. XI, 38. Foodstuffs, e.g., grain, fruit, etc., cannot become unclean unless moisture has fallen upon them after being harvested; also, this moisture must be such as the owner of the foodstuffs desires. Now, in the first instance the rain was desired; hence, even if it rebounds from the basin on to the fruit, it is regarded as desired moisture, though it was not wanted for the latter, and the fruit is henceforth liable to uncleanness. But in the second it was not wanted at all, and therefore does not render the fruit liable. This proves that an action to prevent another thing from being soiled (here, to save the wall from damage) has no positive value. (2) And precisely because he needs the pouch he should be liable. (3) Or kneading trough. (4) The latter is desired, and therefore if it comes into contact with fruit the fruit is liable to uncleanness, but the water that squirts or overflows is not desired. This shows that when a man's intentions are fulfilled, the action is of positive value; so here too, he carries the pouch with a definite intention, which is fulfilled. Hence he should be liable! (5) R. Judah maintains that one is culpable for an act even if that which necessitates it is undesired; while R. Simeon holds that there is no liability for such. Thus, here the carrying of the pouch is necessitated by the discharge, but the discharge itself is certainly unwanted. (6) V. Glos. phylacteries. (7) In Talmudic times the phylacteries were worn all day and in the street, but not on the Sabbath. (8) Lit., 'mention'. (9) Ex. XXVIII, 38.

b (1) And need not fear that he will go out with them after nightfall. (2) Lit., 'feel'; to see whether there is anything attached to them or in them. (3) Lit., 'great'. (4) In general, steps must be taken before the Sabbath to avoid the desecration of the Sabbath. (5) I.e., it is a complete labour, and forbidden. (6) In which case HE MAY NOT SEARCH HIS GARMENTS at night only. (7) The same question of interpretation arises here. (8) V. Mishnah *infra* 13*b*. (9) Rashi: being idle, the men wear wide garments like women's. (10) Land workers. (11) Whose garments were more alike those of men.

c (1) Even on the Sabbath (Rashi). (2) Of their death? (3) On marrying young v. *T.A.* II, pp. 28f. (4) I.e., for his elementary education. The obligation of a child's education lies primarily upon his father (Ḳid. 30*a*), and was left to him originally, public instruction being given to adults only. By the reforms of R. Simeon b. Sheṭaḥ and Joshua b. Gamala elementary schools were set up for children from the age of six or seven and upwards (J. Keth VIII, *ad fin.*). From this passage we may conclude that the system of engaging private teachers was also in vogue in the education of girls, v. Kid., 29*b*, n. b1 and Ned., 35*b*, n.a2. It may be observed that only boys are referred to here. (5) This was definitely obligatory upon the father; Kid. 29*a*. (6) Both are too sad for the Sabbath.

שלא ילקה הכותל אינו בכי יותן מי דמי התם לא קא בעי להו להני משקין כלל הכא קא בעי להו להאי כים לקבולי ביה זיבה הא לא דמיא אלא לסיפא *עריבה (א) שירד דלף לתוכה מים הניתזין והנצפין אינן בכי יותן ושבתוכה הרי זה בכי יותן אלא אביי ורבא דאמרי תרוייהו ל"ק הא *ר' יהודה והא ר' שמעון תני דבי רבי ישמעאל [ב]יוצא אדם בתפילין בע"ש עם השיכה מאי טעמא כיון *דאמר רבה בר רב הונא [ג]חייב אדם למשמש בתפילין כל שעה ושעה ק"ו מציץ מה ציץ שאין בו אלא אזכרה אחת אמרה תורה °והיה על מצחו תמיד (שמות כח) שלא יסיח דעתו ממנו תפילין שיש בהן אזכרות הרבה על אחת כמה וכמה הלכך מידכר דכיר להו תניא חנניא אומר [ד]חייב אדם למשמש בבגדו ע"ש *עם חשכה אמר רב יוסף הלכתא רבתי לשבת: לא יפלה את כליו כו': איבעיא להו לא יפלה את כליו ביום שמא יהרוג ורבי אליעזר היא דתניא אמר רבי אליעזר *ההורג כינה בשבת כאילו הורג גמל ולא יקרא לאור הנר שמא יטה או דילמא תרוייהו שמא יטה ת"ש אין פולין ואין קורין לאור הנר °מי אלימא ממתניתין ת"ש *אין פולין לאור הנר ואין קורין לאור הנר *אלו מן ההלכות שאמרו בעליית חנניה בן חזקיה בן גרון [ה]ש"מ דתרווייהו שמא יטה ש"מ אמר רב יהודה אמר שמואל [ו]אפילו להבחין בין בגדו לבגדי אשתו אמר רבא לא אמרן אלא דבני מחוזא אבל דבני חקליתא מידע ידעי ודבני מחוזא נמי לא אמרן אלא דזקנות אבל דילדות מידע ידיעי ת"ר אין פולין ברה"ר מפני הכבוד כיוצא בו אמר *(רב) [נ"א רבי] יהודה ואמרי לה רבי נחמיה אין עושין אפיקטויזין ברה"ר מפני הכבוד ת"ר *המפלה את כליו מולל וזורק ובלבד שלא יהרוג אבא שאול אומר נוטל וזורק ובלבד שלא ימלול אמר רב הונא [ז]הלכה מולל וזורק וזהו כבודו ואפי' בחול רבה מקטע להו ורב ששת מקטע להו רבא שדי להו לקנא דמיא אמר להו רב נחמן לבנתיה קטולין ואשמעינן לי קלא דסנוותי תניא *רשב"א אומר אין הורגין את המאכולת בשבת דברי ב"ש [ח]וב"ה מתירין וכן היה רשב"א אומר משום רשב"ג אין משדכין את התינוקות לארס ולא את התינוק ללמדו ספר וללמדו אומנות ואין מנחמין אבלים° ואין מבקרין חולין בשבת דברי בית שמאי [ט]וב"ה מתירין: ת"ר הנכנס לבקר את החולה *) אומר שבת היא מלזעוק ורפואה קרובה לבא ור"מ אומר יכולה היא שתרחם

*) [נ"ל בשבת אומר וכו']

רבי

רש"י

שלא ילקה כו' · דהיינו אלולי טינוף לא חשיב ליה הך כפיי': מי דמי · (ב)הא לא ניחא ליה בהנך משקין כלל וברצונו לא ירדו והאי נמי דכפיית קערה חשיבא ליה אבן חשיבותא דמשקין בעינן וכפייה זו אינה אלא לגלות עליהן שאינו חפץ בהן אבל הכא לענין שבת אחשיבותא דהוצאה קפדינן והך הוצאה דכים חשיבא דקא מיבעי ליה להציל על בגדיו: הא לא דמיא · ע"כ אם להכשר זרעים באת לדמויה לא תדמיה אלא להך: שירד דלף לתוכה כו' · משנה היא במסכת מכשירין (פ"ד משנה ה) השנויה אחר הסיפא דהכופה את הקערה והכי תנן עריבה שירד הדלף לתוכה כו' הניחה שירד הדלף לתוכה מים הניתזין והנצפין ב"ש אומרים בכי יותן וב"ה אומרים אינם בכי יותן נטלה לשופכה אלו ואלו מודים שהן בכי יותן ומ"מ יש לשמוע מהך סיפא כדגרסינן בספרים (וכב"ה) נתנה לעריבה זו שירד הדלף לתוכה אע"ג דאלולי טינוף הוא אפילו הכי מדלא כפאה גלי דעתי' דאחשבינהו לקבלן והוו חשובים אותן שבתוכה והך הוצאה נמי אחשבה לקבולי בהאי כים האי זיבה אע"ג דזיבה לא ניחא ליה אבן לחיובי אהוצאת זיבה לא מהדרינן אלא אהוצאת כים: הניתזין · למרחוק: והנצפין · מלמעלה כשהיא מלאה: אינן בכי יותן · דלא ניחא ליה בהו: הא רבי יהודה · דאמר מלאכה שאינה צריכה לגופה שברצונו לא תעשה ואינו צריך לעיקר (תחלתה)[תכליתה] כי הכא שאינו צריך לזיבה זו שעל ידה בא הכים הזה ואעפ"כ חייב עליה ופלוגתייהו בהמצניע (לקמן דף צג:) גבי מוציא המת במטה חייב ואע"ג דהוצאת המת לא ניחא ליה ביה ור"ש פוטר: עם חשיכה · ולא חיישינן דילמא נפיק בהו משתחשך: והיה על מצחו תמיד · קרא יתירא הוא להך דרשה דהא כבר קבע ליה מקום והיה על מצח אהרן: למשמש בבגדו · שלא יהא כרוך בשום דבר פן יוליאנו: הלכתא רבתי · דבר גדול יש כאן להפרישו מאיסור שבת: שמא יהרוג · וביום נמי עסקינן ולאור הנר דמתני' אלא יקרא קאי: כהורג גמל · כלומר דגדול מאד: או דילמא · לאור הנר דקתני אתרוייהו קאי ותרוייהו שמא יטה אבל ביום שפיר דמי: מי אלימא ממתניתין · דקתני לאור הנר בסוף ואפ"ה מספקא לן דאיכא לפלוגי בהו ולמימר דלאור הנר אלא יקרא קאי הכא נמי איכא למימר דאין פולין אפילו ביום ולאור הנר אאין קורין קאי: ת"ש · דקתני לאור הנר בתרווייהו: בני מחוזא · מפנקי ולא עבדי מלאכה ובגדיהם רחבים כשל אשה וצריכים עיון: מידע ידעי · שבגדי האנשים קצרין שעוסקין בשדות במלאכה ושל נשים רחבים בתי יד שלהן: דזקנות · קצרים במקלות ושל אנשים מטוגנין רחבים ודומין זה לזה וגזרינן שמא יטה: אבל דילדות · רחבים הרבה ואין של אנשים דומין להם: ברה"ר · בחול: מפני הכבוד · של עוברין שלא ימאסו: אפיקטויזין · הקאה גומיטא בלע"ז כך מצאתי: מולל וזורק · בשבת מולל להתיש כחן שלא יחזרו אליו ובלבד שלא ימלול בדוחק ויהרוג דסבירא ליה הריגת כינה שבות ואבא שאול כר"א ומחייב חטאת הלכך גזרינן מלילה שלא יהרוג: מקטע להו · הורגן ובשבת: לקנא · ספל: מאכולת · כינה: מתירין · כדמפרש טעמא בפרק שמונה שרצים (לקמן דף קז:) מאילים מאדמים דמשכן מה אילים פרים ורבים אף כל שפרה ורבה וכינה אינה פרה ורבה אלא מבשר אדם היא שורצת: וכן היה רבי שמעון בן אלעזר אומר · דבהני נמי פליגי ב"ש וב"ה: אין משדכין · בשבת משום ממצוא חפצך: וב"ה מתירין · °דקא סברי חפצך ולא חפצי שמים: ואין מנחמין · משום דמצטער עם המצטערין: שבת היא מלזעוק · צריך (ג) להרחיב דעתם בתנחומים שלא יצטערו: יכולה היא שתרחם · אם תכבדוה מלהצטער בה:

בתוך

תוספות

ושבתוכה הרי זה בכי יותן · אין זה במשנה אלא שהש"ס מדקדק מדנקט הניתזין והנצפין אינן בכי יותן משמע הא שבתוכה הרי הן בכי יותן: **שמא** יהרוג · פירש הרב יוסף מאורליינ"ש דכינה היינו שחורה הקופצת דכתיב ויך את עפר הארץ והיה לכנים (שמות ח) ודרך שחורה הקופצת לצאת מן הארץ ובזאת נחלקו עליו רבנן אבל פרעוש היא הכינה הרוחשת וחייב עליה אפילו לרבנן כדאמרי' בפ' שמונה שרצים (לקמן דף קז: ושם) ואין נראה לר"ת דאמרינן במדרש *אף כי אנוש רמה אלו כנים שבראש (ד) ובנדה פ"ב (דף כ:) שלח לה מסריקותא מקטל קלמי ופי' בקונטרס מסרק להרוג כנים ואין דרך שחורה הקופצת להיות בראש ועוד בברכות (פ"ז דף נה:) אמרינן ממהדורי מילי ומסמרטוטי קלמי ודרך כנים לבנות הרוחשות להיות בסמרטוטי מבגדים ישנים ועוד דפרעוש אמר לקמן בפרק שמונה שרצים (דף קז:) שהוא פרה ורבה וכינה הרוחשת אינה פרה ורבה אלא באה מזיעת אדם לכך נראה לר"ת דשחורה הקופצת היא פרעוש וחייב עליה לכ"ע וכינה הרוחשת שרי להרוג כב"ה המתירין ובקונטרס נמי פירש בסמוך דרבה מקטע להו בשבת: **מי** אלימא ממתניתין · והפושט ס"ד דברייתא דרכה לפרש טפי ממתניתין ועוד דבברייתא קתני אין פולין ואין קורין משמע טפי דקאי לאור הנר אתרוייהו מבמתני' דקתני ולא יפלה את כליו: **אפילו** להבחין בין בגדו לבגדי אשתו · דרכן היו להיות שוין מכאן נראה לאסור להבחין בין בגדו לבגדי חברו לאור הנר: **נוטל** וזורק ובלבד שלא ימלול · נראה לפרש דאבא שאול כרבנן וגזר מלילה דכינה אטו מלילה דפרעוש ומלילה דפרעוש שמא יהרוג וכולה חדא גזירה היא ורש"י פי' דכר' אליעזר סבירא ליה וקשה דמשמע דרבי אליעזר סבירא ליה דלפלות נמי אסור דקאמר לעיל לא יפלה שמא יהרוג ור' אליעזר היא ומיהו י"ל דלעיל לא קאי הכי: **רבה** מקטע להו · מפרש ריב"א בחול וקאי אדרב הונא דקאמר זהו כבודו אפילו בחול ואנן סמכינן אפרש"י דפי' בשבת וקיימא כבית הלל דשרו בסמוך:

רבי

מסורת הש"ס

[לקמן עג: וש"נ]

יומא ז: מנחות לו:

[עי' תוס' מנחות לו: ד"ה אי קסבר]

לקמן קז:

[לקמן יג:]

[שם אי' ואלו]

[נ"א רבי]

הגהות הב"ח

(א) גמ' אלא לסיפא עריבה שנתנה שירד דלף: (ב) רש"י ד"ה מי דמי בתם לא ניחא: (ג) ד"ה שבת היא מלזעוק צריך (להרחיב) הז"מו"כ ס"א להכריע: (ד) תוס' ד"ה שמא וכו' רימה אלו כני' שבראש ואין דרך שחורה הקופצת להיות בראש ובנדה פ"ב וכו' להרוג כנים ועוד בברכות כצ"ל:

גליון הש"ס

גמ' מי אלימא ממתניתין וכו'. לקמן דף פג ע"א עירובין דף פט ע"ב: שם ואין מבקרין חולין וב"ה מתירין. עי' לקמן קנ ע"א תוס' ד"ה ואמר ר"א: רש"י ד"ה וב"ה מתירין דקסברי חפציך וכו'. לקמן דף קנ ע"א:

עין משפט נר מצוה

פב א מיי' פי"ב מהל' טומאת אוכלין הלכה ח:

פג ב מיי' פי"ט מהל' שבת הלכה כו סמג לאוין סה טוש"ע או"ח סימן רנב סעיף ו:

פד ג מיי' שם ופ"ד מהלכות תפילין הל' יד סמג עשין כב טור שו"ע או"ח סימן כח סעיף א:

[קהלת פסוק ברכות הטובה]

פה ד מיי' פי"ט מהל' שבת הלכה כו סמג לאוין סה טוש"ע או"ח סימן רנב סעיף ז:

פו ה מיי' פ"ה מהל' שבת הלכה יד סמג שם טוש"ע או"ח סימן ערה סעיף א:

פז ו מיי' שם הלכה טו טור שו"ע שם סעיף יא:

פח ז ח מיי' פי"א מהל' שבת הל' ג סמג שם טוש"ע או"ח סימן שטז סעיף ט:

פט ט מיי' פכ"ד מהל' שבת הלכה ה סמג שם טוש"ע או"ח סי' שו סעיף ו וסימן רפז:

רבינו חננאל

ואיפרכא הא דרבי זירא ואמרינן מי דמי הכים דזב לקערה בכותל כו' ואוקמינה אביי ורבא הא דקתני חייב ר' יהודה דסבר מלאכה שאינה צריכה לגופה חייב עליה והא דקתני פטור לר' שמעון דאמר מלאכה שאינה צריכה לגופה פטור עליה וקיי"ל כר' שמעון: תני דבי שמואל יוצא אדם בתפלין ע"ש עם חשיכה. מ"ט כיון דאמור רבנן חייב אדם למשמש בתפלין בכל שעה ק"ו מציץ ומה ציץ שאין בו אלא אזכרה אחת אמרה תורה תמיד תפלין שיש בהן אזכרות הרבה עאכו"כ הלכך מדכר דכיר להו. תניא חנניא [אומר] חייב אדם למשמש בבגדו ערב שבת עם חשיכה אמר רב יוסף הלכתא רבתי לשבת וכן הלכה: **לא** יפלה את כליו איבעיא להו שמא יטה או שמא יהרוג כנים ומתניתין רבי אליעזר היא דקתני ההורג כינה בשבת והוא הפרעוש כהורג גמל בשבת ופשטנא לא יפלה שמא יטה את הנר. אמר רב יהודה אמר שמואל אפילו להבחין בין בגדו לבגדה והני מילי בבני מחוזה ובזקנות אבל בילדות בגדיהן מידע ידיען שהרחבות ודבבני חקליאתא נמי מידע ידיען: **תנו** רבנן אין פולין ברשות הרבים ואין עושין אפיקטויזין ברה"ר

רב נסים גאון

לא קשיא הא ר' יהודה דאמר מלאכה שאינה צריכה לגופה חייב עליה והא ר' שמעון דאמר מלאכה שאינה צריכה לגופה פטור עליה אבל עיקר דבריו של ר' שמעון במשנה בפרק המצניע (דף צג) דתנן וכן כזית מן המת וכזית מן הנבילה וכעדשה מן השרץ חייבין ור"ש פוטר ובגמ' אמרי פוטר היה ר"ש אף במוציא את המת לקוברו וזאת ההוצאה מלאכה שאינה צריכה לגופה היא לפי שזה שהוציא כלים מרשות לרשות לא לצורך נפשו הוציא לא לאכלו ולא ליהנות ממנו ולזאת נקראת מלאכה שאינה צריכה לגופה שאם חס ושלום יהיה זה המת סרוח או זאת הנבילה סרוחה ואין יכול לעמוד עמה מפני הריח הרע אז ר' שמעון מודה שאם הוציאה חייב חטאת מפני שהיא באותה שעה נעשית מלאכה שצריכה לגופה ופרק אמר ר' עקיבא (דף ל) תנו רבנן המוציא ריח רע כל שהוא ובגמ' דבני מערבא אמרי את המת במטה חייב דברי הכל ולא כן תאני אף ריח רע כל שהוא ואמר ר' לא ור' שמעון מודה ליה אבל דברי ר' יהודה כבר אמר בעל ההלכות גדולות בהלכות שבת כופין את הקערה על הנר בשביל שלא יאחוז בקורה ועל צואה של קטן ועל עקרב שלא תישך אמר ר' יהודה מעשה בא לפני רבן יוחנן בן זכאי ואמר חושש אני לו מחטאת הא דאמרי' בכל דוכתא ר' יהודה דאמר מלאכה שאינה צריכה לגופה חייב עליה לא אשכחנן לה (עיקבא) [עיקרא] אלא מן האי ומאי דכי פליגי תנא קמא ור' יהודה בהא מתניתא במלאכה שאינה צריכה פליגי דקא אמרינן איכא דמתני לה אהא הצד נחש בשבת ומתעסק שלא ישכנו פטור ואם לרפואה חייב מאן תנא אמר ר' יהודה ר' שמעון היא דאמר מלאכה שאינה צריכה לגופה פטור עליה וקא פשטינן ליה להוא דפטור ומותר מהא ועל עקרב שלא תישך אלמא כי פליגי במתני' במלאכה שאינה צריכה לגופה תנא קמא דאמר כופין קסבר מלאכה שאינה צריכה לגופה פטור עליה ור' יהודה קאמר חייב עליה ומעשה נמי אתא לקמיה רבן יוחנן בן זכאי ואסר וכתב אדוננו האי ז"ל דהני מילי דכתיבן בהלכות רביאתא דבתר רבנן סבוראי פרישו להו ותמצא במסכת כריתות בפרק ספק אכל חלב בסופו (דף כ) תנו רבנן החותה גחלים בשבת להתחמם בהם והבעירו מאיליהן תני חדא חייב ותניא אחריתי פטור הא דתניא פטור קסבר מלאכה שאינה צריכה לגופה פטור עליה והא דתניא חייב קסבר מלאכה שאינה צריכה לגופה חייב עליה והתנאי שהזכרתי על דברי ר' שמעון שאם יהיה ריח רע והוציאו חייב דאת כך מצאתי בפי' אדוננו האי ואלו דבריו ומדקדקי רבנן בהאי דקא מיפטר המוציא את המת הני מילי דלית ליה ריחא דאי אית ליה ריחא נמצאת הוצאתו מלאכה שצריכה לגופה ותניא בפרק אמר ר' עקיבא בסופיה המוציא ריח רע כל שהוא ואית לה להא מילתא סייעתא בתלמוד ארץ ישראל ומילתא מוכחא היא עד הנה דברי גאון נ"ע ואני עיינתי בתלמוד ארץ ישראל וכתבתי ממנו ההלכה שהוקדם זכרה וכפשטן של דברים יראה סיוע גדול לאותו הפרש שפרשתי אבל כשתעיין בסוף הדברים שנאמרו לשם מודה ר' שמעון כו' לא הויא סייעתא אבל סמכתי על דברי אותם הגאונים ז"ל:

רבי יהודה אומר המקום ירחם עליך ועל חולי ישראל רבי יוסי אומר המקום ירחם עליך בתוך חולי ישראל שבנא איש ירושלים בכניסתו אומר שלום °וביציאתו אומר *שבת היא מלזעוק ורפואה קרובה לבא ורחמיו מרובין ושבתו בשלום כמאן אזלא הא דאמר רבי חנינא °מי שיש לו חולה בתוך ביתו צריך שיערבנו בתוך חולי ישראל כמאן כר' יוסי ואמר רבי חנינא בקושי התירו לנחם אבלים ולבקר חולים בשבת אמר רבה בר בר חנה כי הוה אזלינן בתריה דרבי אלעזר לשיולי בתפיחה זימנין אמר המקום יפקדך לשלום וזימנין אמר (ליה) רחמנא ידכרינך לשלם היכי עביד הכי *והאמר רב יהודה °לעולם אל ישאל אדם צרכיו בלשון ארמי *ואמר רבי יוחנן כל השואל צרכיו בלשון ארמי אין מלאכי השרת נזקקין לו °שאין מלאכי השרת מכירין בלשון ארמי °שאני חולה דשכינה עמו *דאמר רב ענן אמר רב מנין ששכינה *סועד את החולה שנאמר °ה' יסעדנו על ערש דוי תניא נמי הכי °הנכנס לבקר את החולה לא ישב לא על גבי מטה °ולא על גבי כסא אלא מתעטף ויושב לפניו מפני ששכינה למעלה °מראשותיו של חולה שנאמר ה' יסעדנו על ערש דוי *ואמר רבא אמר רבין מנין שהקב"ה זן את החולה שנאמר ה' יסעדנו על ערש דוי: ולא יקרא לאור הנר: *אמר רבה °אפילו גבוה °שתי קומות ואפי' שתי מרדעות ואפילו עשרה בתים זו על גב זו חד הוא דלא ליקרי הא תרי שפיר דמי והתניא לא אחד ולא שנים אמר ר' אלעזר לא קשיא °כאן בענין אחד כאן בשני ענינים אמר רב הונא °ובמדורה אפי' עשרה בני אדם אסור אמר רבא °אם אדם חשוב הוא מותר מיתיבי *לא יקרא לאור הנר שמא יטה אמר ר' ישמעאל בן אלישע אני אקרא ולא אטה פעם א' קרא ובקש להטות אמר כמה גדולים דברי חכמים שהיו אומרים לא יקרא לאור הנר ר' נתן אומר קרא והטה וכתב על פנקסו אני ישמעאל בן אלישע קריתי והטיתי נר בשבת לכשיבנה בהמ"ק °אביא חטאת שמנה א"ר אבא שאני ר' ישמעאל בן אלישע הואיל ומשים עצמו על דברי תורה כהדיוט תני חדא שמש בודק כוסות וקערות לאור הנר ותניא אידך לא יבדוק לא קשיא °כאן בשמש קבוע כאן בשמש שאינו קבוע ואי בעית אימא הא והא בשמש קבוע ולא קשיא הא בדמשחא והא בדנפטא איבעיא להו שמש שאינו קבוע בדמשחא מהו אמר רב הלכה °ואין מורין כן ור' ירמיה בר אבא אמר הלכה ומורין כן ר' ירמיה בר אבא איקלע לבי רב אסי קם שמעיה קא בדיק לנהורא דשרגא אמרה ליה דביתהו ומר לא עביד הכי אמר לה שבקיה כרביה ס"ל: באמת אמרו החזן כו': והאמרת רישא רואה מאי לאו לקרות לא °לסדר ראשי פרשיותיו וכן אמר רבה בר שמואל אבל מסדר הוא ראשי פרשיותיו וכולה פרשה לא

מיתיבי

בתוך חולי ישראל. שמתוך שכוללן עם האחרים תפלתו נשמעת בזכותן של רבים: שבנא איש ירושלים. אדם גדול היה בירושלים ושמו שבנא: רחמיו. של הקב"ה מרובים: שבתו בשלום. נוחו בשבתכם לשלום: בקושי התירו. מפני שמצטער: בתפיחה. בחולה: זימנין אמר לה. בלשון קדש וזימנין אמר לה בלשון ארמי והא לאו לענין שבת נקט: דשכינה עמו. ואין המתפלל צריך שיזדקקו לו מלאכי השרת להכניס תפלתו לפנים מן הפרגוד: סועד. סומך בתשות כחו ומשום רבינו יעקב סוער תרגומו של פוקד כלומר מבקר כמו ואת אחיך תפקוד לשלום (שמואל א יז) ומתרגמי' ואת אחיך תסער לשלם ולהך לישנא גרסינן אל תקרי יסעדנו אלא יסערנו: מתעטף. מאימת שכינה כאדם היושב באימה ואין פונה לצדדין: ואפי' גבוה. דליכא למיחש להטייה דכיון דגזור לא פלוג למילתייהו: הא תרי שפיר דמי. שאם יבא להטות יזכירנו חברו: בשני ענינים. בשתי פרשיות הואיל וכל אחד מעיין לעצמו אין מכיר במעשה חבירו: במדורה. מדורת אש גדולה אסור דהואיל ויושבין רחוק זה מזה ועוד שזגבות האודים סמוכים להם אין זה מכיר בבא חבירו להבעיר ולחתות: מותר. לקרות לאור הנר שאינו רגיל להטות נר בחול מפני חשיבותו: שמש קבוע. לא יבדוק מפני שאימת רבו עליו אם ימצא בהן דבר מגונה ובודקן יפה וחיישינן להטייה: שאינו קבוע. לא רמיא עליה כולי האי: הא והא בשמש קבוע גרסי': בדנפטא. שהוא מסריח מותר לבדוק לאורו דלא אתי להטות: שמש שאינו קבוע בדמשחא מאי. כיון שאינו קבוע אינו מטה אפילו בחול והלכך בשבת מותר או דילמא בדמשחא הואיל ולא מאים דרכו להטות בחול הוא: הלכה. דמותר: ואין מורין כן. שלא יזלזלו: קם שמעי'. דר' ירמיה דהוא שמש שאינו קבוע בבית רב אסי: אמרה ליה דביתהו. דרב אסי לרב אסי מר לא עביד הכי: כרביה. ר' ירמיה דאמר הלכה ומורין כן: ראשי פרשיות. ומרילן בפיו שמתוך שראש הפרשה שגורה בפיו הוא נזכר בכולה למחר ומסייע את שבעה הקורין בנקודה וטעמיה בלחש:

ואימת

רבי יהודה אומר המקום ירחם עליך כו'. ק' לר"ת מה מועלת תפלה לר' מאיר ור' יהודה דקאמר בפ"ק דר"ה (ד' טז· ושם) הכל נידונים בר"ה וגזר דין שלהם נחתם ביוה"כ דברי ר"מ ר' יהודה אומר הכל נידונין בר"ה וגזר דין של כל אחד ואחד נחתם בזמנו בפסח על התבואה ואדם ביום הכפורים ר' יוסי אומר אדם נידון בכל יום ואמר התם אמר רב יוסף כמאן מצלינן האידנא אקצירי ואמריעי כר' יוסי משמע דלר"מ ולר' יהודה לא מהניא צלותא וי"ל דהכא בשבת שבין ר"ה ובין יוה"כ איירי ולפי מאי דמשני התם איבעית אימא כדר' יצחק דאמר ר' יצחק יפה צעקה לאדם בין קודם גז"ד כו' אתי הכא שפיר: שבנא איש ירושלים°. ר"ת לא גרים שבנא דשבנא רשע הוה ולא מסקינן בשמיה דשם רשעים ירקב כדאמר בפרק אמר להם הממונה (יומא דף לח:) אלא גרס שכנא דהוי נמי שם אדם כדאמר בסוטה (דף כא·) אלא כשכנא (א) אחי הלל ונראה לר"י דשפיר גרס שבנא דאטו אם אחד רשע ושמו אברהם לא נקרא בשם זה אחר ואשכחן דתרי שבנא הוו כמו שמוכיח בישעיה (כב) דכתיב שבנא אשר על הבית וכתיב וקראתי לעבדי לאליקים וגו' וממשלתך אתן בידו וכתיב בתר הכי (שם לו) ויבא אליו אליקים אשר על הבית ושבנא הסופר משמע דשבנא אשר על הבית כבר מת והיה אליקים במקומו ושבנא הסופר היה אחר*: שאין מלאכי השרת מכירין בלשון ארמי · לבד מגבריאל כדאמר בסוטה בריש אלו נאמרין (דף לג·) דאמר מר בא גבריאל ולמדו שבעים לשונות ליוסף ותימה °דאפי' מחשבה שבלב כל אדם יודעים ולשון ארמי אין יודעים: לא ישב על גבי מטה ולא על ספסל. נראה דדוקא כשחולה שוכב בנמוך שלא ישב גבוה ממראשותיו של חולה: רבי נתן אומר קרא והטה. הכא ובמכות (דף ה:) גבי יהודה בן טבאי שהרג עד זומם ובהאשה רבה (יבמות דף נו:) גבי הא שנקרעה ס"ת בחמתן לא פריך ומה בהמתן של צדיקים אין הקב"ה מביא תקלה כו' אומר ר"ת דלא פריך בשום מקום אלא גבי אכילת איסור שגנאי הוא לצדיק ביותר וההוא דערבי פסחים (פסחים דף קג: ושם) דר' ירמיה אישתלי וטעים קודם הבדלה והנהו דמס' ר"ה (דף כא·) דקאמר בסים תבשילא דבבלאי בצומא רבה דמערבא התם לא הוה מאכל איסור אלא השעה אסורה ובבראשית רבה *אמרינן ר' ירמיה שלח לר' זירא חד טרסקל דתאנים ומסיק בין דין לדין מתאכל תאנתא בטבלא הא קאמר עלה ר' אבא בר זימנא בשם ר' אליעזר זעירא אם הראשונים מלאכים אנו בני אינש ואם הם בני אינש אנו כחמורים ולא כחמורו של ר' פנחס בן יאיר*: שמש שאינו קבוע בדמשחא מאי. ללישנא בתרא מבעי ליה ור"ת גרים הא והא בשמש שאינו קבוע איבעיא להו שמש קבוע בדמשחא מאי דשמש שאינו קבוע בודק יפה שלא יעבירוהו אבל קבוע לא מרתת שיעבירוהו בשביל כך כיון שהוקבע כבר:

מיתיבי

רבינו חננאל

מפני הכבוד · אמר רב הונא הלכך מולל וזורק חוץ כבודו ואפי' בחולי · תניא ר' שמעון בן אלעזר אמר משום ר' שמעון בן גמליאל אין הורגין את המאכולת בשבת ואין משדכין על התינוקת לארסה ועל התינוק ללמדו ספר ואומנות ואין מנחמין אבלים ואין מבקרין את החולה דברי ב"ש וב"ה מתירין בכולן · ת"ר המבקר חולה בשבת אומר שבת היא מלצעוק ורפואה קרובה לבוא: רבי יהודה אומר יכולה היא שתרחם עליו ועל כל חולי ישראל. רבי יוסי אומר המקום ירחם עליך בתוך חולי ישראל: כמאן אמר רבי חנינא מי שיש לו חולה בתוך ביתו יערבנו בתוך חולי ישראל כר' יוסי וכמאן (אמרי')[מצלי']האידנא אקצירי ומריעי כר' יוסי דאמר אדם נידון בכל יום ומפורש בר"ה פ"א. שבנא איש ירושל' בכניסתו אומר שלום ביציאתו היה אומר שבת היא מלצעוק ורפואה קרובה לבוא ורחמיו מרובין אחינו שבתו לשלום א"ר חנינא בקושי התירו לנחם אבלים ולבקר חולים בשבת משום דחיישינן שמא יבקש עליו רחמים בצרה ובצעקה · רבי אלעזר כד הוה שאיל בתפיחה אמר ליה המקום יפקידך לשלום וזמנין אמר ליה רחמנא ידכרך לשלם · ואפילו בלשון ארמי שפיר דמי דשכינה עמו · דתניא הנכנס לבקר חולה לא ישב ע"ג מטה ולא (בכפא) [בכסא] ולא בספסל אלא מתעטף ויושב לפניו מפני שהשכינה עליו שנאמר ה' יסעדנו על ערש דוי ואמר (רבי) [רבין] אמר רב מנין שהקב"ה זן את החולה שנא' ה' יסעדנו על ערש דוי: ולא יקרא לאור הנר אמר (רבא) [רבה] ואפי' גבוה ב' קומות או ב' (מרועות) [מרדעות] או אפילו כמה בתים זה על גבי זה אסור וקיי"ל (כרבא) [כרבה] דאע"ג דבפרקין שואל אדם מחבירו אוקימנא להא דרבה כתנאי כיון דסתם לן תנא כוותיה דתנן מונה אדם את אורחיו ואת פרפריותיו מפיו אבל לא מן הכתב לא חיישינן להא מחלוקת דברייתא וכבר פירשנוה שם דהלכתא כרבה: לא יקרא דייקינן ממתניתין דוקא חד אבל תרי שרי והני מילי בענין אחד אבל בתרי עניני אסור דחיישינן שמא יטה ואפילו אדם חשוב ממעשה דר' ישמעאל*: ירושלמי תני רבי חייא אבל מסתכל מה שבכוס ומה שבקערה ואינו חושש · לא יקרא אמר שמואל לא שנו אלא אחד אבל שנים מאחר שיכולין למחות זע"ז מותר: תני חדא השמש בודק הקערות וכוסות לאור הנר ותניא אידך לא יבדוק וסניין דשמעתא בין שמש קבוע בין שמש שאינו קבוע בודק כוסות וקערות לאור הנר. ודחקא בנפטא דמאים ונפיש נהוריה ולא אתי לאצלויי ביה אבל בדמשחא שמש שאינו קבוע ודאי אסור שמש קבוע פלוגתא והלכתא בודק ואין מורין כן: פיס' באמת [אמרו] החזן רואה וכו' · ואסיק' אבל מסדר הוא לתינוקות ראשי פרשיות:

*) לפנינו בגמ' אדרבה מסיק דאדם חשוב מותר ומר' ישמעאל אין ראיה ואולי דרבינו היה לו גי' אחרת בסוגיא וצ"ע.

עין משפט נר מצוה

צא א ב מיי' פכ"ד מהל' שבת הלכה ה סמג לאוין סה טוש"ע או"ח סימן רפז וטוש"ע יו"ד סימן שלה סעיף ו:

צא ג טוש"ע או"ח סימן קא סעיף ד:

צב ד טוש"ע יו"ד סי' שלה סעיף ה:

צג ה מיי' פי"ד מהל' אבל הלכה ו סמג עשין ב טור שו"ע שם סעיף ג:

צד ו מיי' פ"ה מהלכות שבת הלכה יד סמג לאוין סה טוש"ע או"ח סי' ערה סעיף א:

צה ז מיי' שם טור שו"ע שם סעיף ב ג:

צו ח שם סעיף ה:

צז ט שם סעיף ד:

צח י כ מיי' שם הלכה טז טור ש"ע שם סעיף יב:

צט ל מיי' שם הלכה טו טור שו"ע שם סעיף ט י:

ועי' תוס' יומא לח: ותוספות כתובות קד: ד"ה שני]

מסורת הש"ס

ס"א שלום

סוטה לג.

[כסוטה אי' דאמר]

נדרים מ. ע"ש

[נ"ל סר את החולה שנאמר ה' יסעדנו קרי בי' יסערנו פי' סר סער]

[שם ע"ש]

לקמן קמט. [תוספת' פ"א]

תוספתא פ"א

וכ"ה לקמן קיב:

הגהות הב"ח

(א) תוס' ד"ה שבנא וכו' אלא כשכנא והלל כצ"ל ותיבת אחי נמחק:

גליון הש"ס גמ' שאין מלאכי השרת כו'. עי' בתמים דעים להראב"ד סימן קפ"ד: שם ולא ע"ג כסא. גירסת הרי"ף והרא"ש ולא ע"ג שרפרף ולא ע"ג מקום גבוה: שם מראשותיו של חולה שנאמר וכו'. עיין ברש"י בחומש פרשה ויחי בפסוק וישתחו ישראל על ראש המטה: שם אפילו גבוה ב' קומות. עי' ברא"ש פ"ב דעירובין סימן ג': שם אביא חטאת שמנה וכו' עי' יבמות דף ו ע"ב תוס' ד"ה לא אינו:

תוס' ד"ה שבנא וכו'. ר"ת ל"ג כו' עי' כתובות דף קיד ע"ב תוסד"ה ב' דייני וכו' ומגילה דף י ע"ב תוס' ד"ה רבה בר עופרן: שם ד"ה שאין אפילו מחשבה. ועי' בס' משכיל לדוד להרב מהר"ם פאדווה על פירש"י בתורה פ' ויגש ד"ה ויבא בשם משנת חכמים למהר"ם חאגיז ז"ל:

should say,] 'It [the Sabbath] may have compassion.'[7] [12b] R. Judah said, 'May the Omnipresent have compassion upon you and upon the sick of Israel.' R. Jose said, 'May the Omnipresent have compassion upon you in the midst of the sick of Israel.' Shebna, a citizen of Jerusalem, on entering would say 'Peace'; and on leaving, 'It is the Sabbath, when one must not cry out and healing will soon come, His compassion is abundant and enjoy the Sabbath rest in peace.' With whom does this dictum of R. Ḥanina agree: One who has an invalid in his house should combine
a him with other Jewish sick?[1] With whom? — With R. Jose.

R. Ḥanina also said: It was [only] with difficulty that comforting mourners and visiting the sick was permitted on the Sabbath.[2]

Rabbah b. Bar Ḥanah said: When we followed R. Eleazar to inquire after a sick person, sometimes he would say to him, [in Hebrew], 'The Omnipresent visit thee in peace'; at others, he said, [in Aramaic], 'The Omnipresent remember thee in peace'. But how might he do thus: did not Rab Judah say, One should never petition for his needs in Aramaic; and R. Joḥanan said: When one petitions for his needs in Aramaic, the Ministering Angels do not heed him, for they do not understand Aramaic?[3] —An invalid is different, because the Divine Presence is with him. For R. 'Anan said in Rab's name, How do you know that the Divine Presence supports an invalid? Because it is written, *The Lord supports him upon the couch of languishing*.[4] It was taught likewise: One who enters [a house] to visit the sick may sit neither upon the bed nor on a seat, but must wrap himself about[5] and sit in front of him,[6] for the Divine Presence is above an invalid's pillow, as it is said, *The Lord supports him upon the couch of languishing*. And Raba said in Rabin's name: How do we know that the Holy One, blessed be He, sustains the sick? Because it is said, *The Lord supports him on the couch of languishing*.

NOR MUST HE READ BY THE LIGHT OF A LAMP. Rabbah said: Even if it is as high as twice a man's stature, or as two ox-goads
b [height],[1] or even as ten houses on top of each other.[2]

One alone may not read, but for two [together] it is well?[3] But it was taught: Neither one nor two!—Said R. Eleazar, There is no difficulty: the former refers to one subject; the latter to two.[4] R. Huna said: But by [the light] of an open fire even ten people are forbidden.[5] Said Raba: If he is an important man,[6] it is permitted.

An objection is raised: One must not read by the light of a lamp, lest he tilt [it]. Said R. Ishmael b. Elisha, 'I will read and will not tilt.' Yet once he read and wished to tilt. 'How great are the words of the Sages!' he exclaimed, 'who said, One must not read by the light of a lamp.' R. Nathan said, He read and did tilt [it], and wrote in his note book, 'I, Ishmael b. Elisha, did read and tilt the lamp on the Sabbath. When the Temple is rebuilt I will bring a fat sin-offering.'[7]—Said R. Abba: R. Ishmael b. Elisha was different, since he treated himself as an ordinary person in respect to religious matters.

One [Baraitha] taught: An attendant may examine glasses and plates by the light of a lamp; and another taught: He must not examine [them]! There is no difficulty: one refers to a permanent attendant, the other to a temporary one.[8] Alternatively, both refer to a permanent attendant yet there is no difficulty: one
c refers to [a lamp fed with] oil, the other to naphtha.[1]

The scholars propounded: What of a temporary attendant and a [lamp fed with] oil?—Rab said: There is the *halachah*, but we do not teach thus.[2] R. Jeremiah b. Abba said: There is the *halachah* and we teach it so. R. Jeremiah b. Abba chanced to visit R. Assi. Now, his[3] attendant arose and examined [the glasses] by candlelight.[4] Thereupon his [R. Assi's] wife said to him [R. Assi], 'But you do not act thus!' 'Let him be,' he answered her, 'he holds with his master.'[5]

IN TRUTH IT WAS SAID, THE ḤAZZAN etc., But you say in the first clause, [HE] MAY SEE; surely that means to read?[6]—No: to arrange the beginnings of the sections.[7] And Rabbah b. Samuel said likewise: But he may arrange the beginnings of the sections.

(7) The due observance of the Sabbath will bring recovery in its wake.
a (1) I.e., pray for him as one of many. (2) Because both induce grief, which is contrary to the spirit of the Sabbath, which is 'a day of delight.' (3) Angels were held to mediate between God and man, carrying the prayers of the latter to the Former (Tobit XII, 12, 15). This is not to be compared with prayer to or worshipping angels, from which Judaism is free. 'Not as one who would first send his servant to a friend to ask for aid in his hour of need should man apply to Michael, or Gabriel, to intercede for him; but he should turn immediately to God Himself, *for 'whosoever shall call on the name of the Lord shall be delivered'*. (Joel III, 5; Yer. Ber. IX, 13a. Many Rabbinical authorities disapprove even of invoking angels as mediators, as shown by the passage quoted; v. Zunz, *S P*. p. 148.) (4) Ps. XLI, 4.—Hence he does not need the angel's intercession. (5) In a spirit of reverence. (6) In Ned. 40a the reading is, 'upon the ground.'
b (1) Probably twice the height of an ass and its saddle. (2) Though the lamp is inaccessible and cannot be tilted, the Rabbis enacted a general measure without distinctions. (3) This follows from the use of the singular in the Mishnah. But when two read, each may remind the other should he wish to tilt the lamp. (4) When both are reading the same subject in the scroll, each can remind the other. But if they are occupied with different subjects, neither thinks of his companion. (5) Each sits at a distance from the other, and any one may forget himself and stir up the fire. (6) Who is not accustomed even on weekdays to trim the lamp. (7) This shows that the prohibition applies even to a great man like R. Ishmael b. Elisha. (8) The former is more careful, and may tilt the lamp to see whether there is the least grease on the crockery; hence he must not examine them by a lamp.
c (1) The latter emits an unpleasant odour, and so one naturally refrains from tilting. (2) It is permitted, but this must not be publicly diffused. (3) R. Jeremiah's. (4) In R. Assi's house; he was not of course a permanent attendant. (5) The light of naphtha (or of a candle) is the same as the light of an oil-fed lamp. (6) How then explain BUT HE HIMSELF MAY NOT READ? (7) In ancient times the Pentateuch portion which was part of the Sabbath service was read by a number of worshippers (on Sabbaths, seven), whilst the *ḥazzan* prompted them.

But not the whole section? [13*a*] An objection is raised: R. Simeon b. Gamaliel said: School children used to prepare their [Biblical] portions and read by lamplight?—[There is no difficulty]: I can answer either [that it means] the beginnings of the sections; or that children are different: since they are in awe of their teacher, they will not come to tilt it.

SIMILARLY . . . A ZAB MUST NOT DINE, [etc.]. It was taught, R. Simeon b. Eleazar said: Come and see how far purity has spread in Israel! For we did not learn, A clean man must not eat with an unclean woman, but A ZAB MUST NOT DINE TOGETHER WITH A ZABAH, AS IT MAY LEAD TO SIN.[9] Similarly, a *zab*, a *parush*[10]
a may not dine with a *zab*, who is an *'am ha-areẓ*,[1] lest he cause him to associate with him. But what does it matter if he does cause him to associate with him? Rather say [thus]: lest he offer him unclean food to eat. Does then a *zab* who is a *parush* not eat unclean food?[2]—Said Abaye: For fear lest he provide him with unfit food.[3] Raba said: The majority of the *'amme ha-areẓ* do render tithes, but [we fear] lest he associate with him and he provide him with unclean food in the days of his purity.[4]

The scholars propounded: May a *niddah*[5] sleep together with her husband, she in her garment and he in his?[6]—Said R. Joseph, Come and hear: A fowl may be served together with cheese at the [same] table, but not eaten [with it]: this is Beth Shammai's view. Beth Hillel rule: It may neither be served nor eaten [together]![7]—There it is different, because there are no [separate] minds.[8] It is reasonable too that where there are [separate] minds it is different, because the second clause teaches, R. Simeon b. Gamaliel said: Two boarders[9] eating at the same table, one may eat meat and the other cheese, and we have no fear.[10] But was it not stated thereon, R. Ḥanin b. Ammi said in in Samuel's name: This was taught only when they do not know each other;[11] but if they do, they are forbidden? And here too they know each other!—How compare! There we have [separate] minds but no
b unusual feature;[1] but here there are [separate] minds and an unusual feature.[2]

Others state, Come and hear: R. Simeon b. Gamaliel said: Two boarders may eat at the same table, one meat and the other cheese. And it was stated thereon, R. Ḥanin b. Ammi said in Samuel's name: This was taught only if they do not know each other, but if they do, it is forbidden; and these two know each other!—[No.] There we have [separate] minds but nothing unusual, whereas here there are [separate] minds and an unusual feature.

Come and hear: A ZAB MUST NOT DINE TOGETHER WITH A ZABAH, LEST IT LEAD TO SIN![3]—Here too there are [separate] minds but nothing unusual.

Come and hear: *And hath not eaten upon the mountains, neither hath lifted up his eyes to the idols of the house of Israel, neither hath defiled his neighbour's wife, neither hath come near to a woman who is a* niddah:[4] thus a woman who is a *niddah* is assimilated to his neighbour's wife: just as his neighbour's wife, he in his garment and she in hers is forbidden, so if his wife is a *niddah*, he in his garment and she in hers is forbidden. This proves it. Now, this disagrees with R. Pedath. For R. Pedath said: The Torah interdicted only intimacy of incestuous coition, as it is said, *None of you shall approach to any that is near of kin to him, to uncover their nakedness.*[5]

'Ulla, on his return from the college,[6] used to kiss his sisters on their bosoms; others say, on their hands. But he is self-contradictory, for 'Ulla said, Even any form of intimacy is forbidden,[7] because we say, 'Take a circuitous route, O nazirite, but do not approach the vineyard.'[8]

c [It is taught in the] Tanna debe Eliyahu:[1] It once happened that a certain scholar who had studied much Bible and Mishnah[2] and had served scholars much,[3] yet died in middle age. His wife took his *tefillin* and carried them about in synagogues and schoolhouses and complained to them, It is written in the Torah, *for that is thy life, and the length of thy days:*[4] my husband, who

(8) [This proves that children may read on Friday night by lamplight? Our Mishnah affords no such proof as it could refer to children who read in disregard of the prohibition, v. Tosaf. a.l.]. (9) But there was no need to interdict the first, because even Israelites ate their food only when it was ritually clean (though under no obligation) and would not dine together with an unclean woman, *sc.* a *niddah* (v. Glos.) in any case. (10) Lit., 'separated,' v. next note.

a (1) Lit., 'people of the earth', 'the rural population'; the term is synonymous with ignoramus and law breaker, for living on the land they were only partially accessible to the teachings of the Rabbis, and in particular were negligent of ritual purity and the separation of tithes. Those who held aloof from them (separatists) were known as *perushim* (sing. *parush*), who were very particular in matters of purity and tithes; v. also Glos. s.v. *ḥaber*. (2) Whatever he eats is unclean, since his contact defiles food. (3) I.e., food from which the priestly and Levitical dues were not rendered. (4) If he is a visitor, he will continue even when he becomes clean. (5) V. Glos. (6) Taking precaution to avoid all bodily contact. Intimacy, of course, is forbidden: do we fear that this may lead to it? (7) And the *halachah* is always as Beth Hillel. They may not be served lest they be eaten together, and by analogy the answer to our problem is in the negative. (8) There is no one to restrain the diner from eating the fowl and the cheese together. But here each may restrain the other.

(9) Or travellers lodging at an inn. (10) The assumed reason is that each restrains the other. (11) Then one does not take from the other.

b (1) Lit., 'change'. There is nothing on the table to remind one diner that he must not eat of his neighbour's. (2) Viz., that they take care to avoid all bodily contact. (3) And the same applies here. (4) Ezek. XVIII, 6. (5) Lev. XVIII, 6. 'Incest' in the Talmud includes adultery.—The same applies to a *niddah*. (6) The term *Be Rab* denotes either the great Academy founded by Rab or college in general. (7) With consanguineous relations, such as a sister. (8) A nazirite must not eat grapes or drink wine (v. Num. VI, 1-3); as a precaution he is forbidden even to approach a vineyard. The same reasoning holds good here.

c (1) This is the Midrash consisting of two parts, 'Seder Eliyahu Rabbah' and 'Seder Eliyahu Zuṭa'. According to the Talmud Keth. 106*a* the Prophet Elijah taught this Midrash, the Seder Eliyahu, to R. 'Anan, a Babylonian Amora of the third century. Scholars are agreed that the work in its present form received its final redaction in the tenth century C.E., though they are not agreed as to where it was written. V. Bacher, *Monatsschrift*, XXIII, 267 *et seqq.*; in *R.E.J.* XX, 144-146; Friedmann, *Introduction to his edition of Seder Eliyahu.* (2) *Ḳara* refers to the study of the Bible; *shanah* to the study of the Mishnah. (3) 'Serving scholars', i.e., being in personal attendance on scholars, was one of the requisites of an academical course. (4) Deut. XXX, 20.

תורה אור

מיתיבי *רשב"ג אומר התינוקות של בית רבן היו מסדרין פרשיו' וקורין לאור הנר אי בעית אימא ראשי פרשיותיו ואי בעית אימא אשאני תינוקות הואיל בואימת רבן עליהן לא אתי לאצלויי: גכיוצא בו לא יאכל הזב: *תניא ר"ש בן אלעזר אומר בוא וראה עד היכן פרצה טהרה בישראל שלא שנינו לא יאכל הטהור עם הטמאה אלא לא יאכל הזב עם הזבה מפני הרגל עבירה כיוצא בו לא יאכל זב פרוש עם זב עם הארץ שמא ירגילנו אצלו וכי מרגילו אצלו מאי הוי אלא אימא שמא יאכילנו דברים טמאין אטו זב פרוש לאו דברים טמאין אכיל אמר אביי גזירה שמא יאכילנו דברים שאינן מתוקנין ורבא אמר *רוב עמי הארץ מעשרין הן אלא שמא יהא רגיל אצלו ויאכילנו דברים טמאין בימי טהרתו איבעיא להו נדה מהו שתישן עם בעלה היא בבגדה והוא בבגדו אמר רב יוסף ת"ש *העוף עולה עם הגבינה על השלחן ואינו נאכל דברי ב"ש ב"ה אומר לא עולה ולא נאכל שאני התם דליכא דיעות ה"נ מסתברא דהיכא דאיכא דיעות שאני דקתני סיפא *רשב"ג אומר שני אכסניים אוכלין על שלחן אחד זה אוכל בשר וזה אוכל גבינה ואין חוששין ולאו אתמר עלה *אמר רב חנין בר אמי אמר שמואל לא שנו אלא שאין מכירין זה את זה אבל מכירין זה את זה אסורים וה"נ מכירין זה את זה נינהו הכי השתא התם דיעות איכא שינוי ליכא הכא איכא דיעות ואיכא שינוי איכא דאמרי ת"ש רשב"ג אומר שני אכסניים אוכלין על שלחן אחד זה בשר וזה גבינה ואתמר עלה אמר רב חנין בר אמי אמר שמואל לא שנו אלא שאין מכירין זה את זה אבל מכירין זה את זה אסור והני נמי מכירין זה את זה נינהו התם דיעות איכא שינוי ליכא הכא איכא דיעות ואיכא שינוי ת"ש לא יאכל הזב עם הזבה משום הרגל עבירה ה"נ דיעות איכא שינוי ליכא ת"ש °אל ההרים לא אכל ועיניו לא נשא אל גלולי בית ישראל ואת אשת רעהו לא טמא ואל אשה נדה לא יקרב מקיש אשה נדה לאשת רעהו מה אשת רעהו הוא בבגדו והיא בבגדה אסור דאף אשתו נדה הוא בבגדו והיא בבגדה אסור ש"מ *ופליגא דר' פדת דאמר ר' פדת לא אסרה תורה אלא קורבה של גילוי עריות בלבד שנאמר °איש איש אל כל שאר בשרו לא תקרבו לגלות ערוה *עולא כי הוי אתי מבי רב הוה מנשק להו לאחוותיה אבי חדייהו ואמרי לה אבי ידייהו ופליגא דידיה אדידיה דאמר עולא האפי' שום קורבה אסור *משום לך לך אמרי נזירא סחור סחור לכרמא לא תקרב: תני דבי אליהו *מעשה בתלמיד א' *ששנה הרבה וקרא הרבה ושימש תלמידי חכמים הרבה ומת בחצי ימיו והיתה אשתו נוטלת תפיליו ומחזרתם בבתי כנסיות ובבתי מדרשות ואמרה להם כתיב בתורה °כי הוא חייך ואורך ימיך בעלי ששנה הרבה וקרא הרבה

רש"י

ואימת רבן עליהן. אין פושטין יד לשום דבר ואפי' בחול אלא על פי רבן: פרצה. גברה כמו ופרצת ימה וקדמה (בראשית כח): שלא שנינו לא יאכל טהור עם הטמאה. מפני הערוה לפי שלא הוצרכו לכך שכולן אוכלין חוליהן בטהרה היו ולא היו אוכלין עם נשותיהן טמאות: אטו זב פרוש לאו דברים טמאין קאכיל. והלא כל מגעו טמא: מעשרין הן. ולא גזרי' גזירה לגזירה: שתישן עם בעלה. במטה כגון שהוא טמא דליכא למיחש משום טהרה או בזמן הזה שאין בו טהרה מי חיישי' להרגל עבירה או דילמא כיון דאיכא היכרא מדכר דכירי: על השולחן. שאוכל עליו מותר להניח בשר העוף אצל הגבינה דקסברי בית שמאי בשר עוף בחלב לאו דאורייתא ולא גזרי' העלאה אטו אכילה: ואינו נאכל. עמו: וב"ה אומרים כו'. ש"מ דאסור: דליכא דיעות. שני בני אדם שיזכירו זה לזה וה"ה נמי דמצי לשנויי דליכא שינוי להיכרא ומיהו דעדיפא נקט דאפי' דיעות ליכא: שאין מכירין. דלא אתי חד למשקל מדחבריה ומיכל: אבל מכירין. אסור ואשה ובעלה [נמי] מכירין זה את זה וש"מ דאסור: שינוי ליכא. שאוכלין בדרך אכילה: איכא שינוי. שאין דרך לישן אלא בקירוב בשר כדכתיב שארה כסותה ועונתה ואמר מר שאר זה קירוב בשר שאם אמר אי אפשי אלא היא בבגדה והוא בבגדו יוציא ויתן כתובה במס' כתובות (פ"ד דף מח.): אל ההרים לא אכל. בפרק אלו הן הנשרפין בסנהדרין (דף פא.) מפרש ליה שלא נתפרנס בזכות אבות שלא הוצרך לכך לפי שהוא צדיק: מה אשת רעהו כו'. דאסור לן יחוד מן התורה בקדושין (פ"ד דף פ.) מאחיך בן אמך: ופליגא. דרב יוסף דפשט מדרשה דהאי קרא לאיסור אדרבי פדת: גילוי עריות. תשמיש ממש ושאר קורבה ואפי' קירוב בשר מדרבנן והיא בבגדה אפי' מדרבנן ליכא למגזר:

ושימש

תוספות

מיתיבי התינוקות של בית רבן מסדרין פרשיותיהן כו'. אומר הר"ס לפי' הקונטרס שפי' במתני' החזן רואה היכן התינוקות קורין לאור הנר הא דלא פריך ליה ממתני' משום דאיכא למימר דקורין באיסור ואין מוחין בידם אבל הכא דקתני מסדרין משמע שמותרין לעשות כן: רבא אמר רוב עם הארץ מעשרין הן. וא"ת האמרי' בפרק בתרא דסוטה (דף מח.) שיוחנן כהן גדול גזר על הדמאי לפי ששלח בכל גבול ישראל וראה שלא היו מפרישין אלא תרומה גדולה בלבד וי"ל דה"ק שלא היו מפרישין כולם אלא תרומה גדולה אבל רובן היו מעשרים והא דחשו הכא טפי למיעוט מבמקום אחר משום דהויא מיעוט דשכיח טובא והיו הרבה נכשלים ומה שקשה דאביי אדאביי ודרבא אדרבא מפורש בפ"ב דכתובות (דף כד. ושם) גבי חיישינן לגומלים: מה אשת רעהו הוא בבגדו והיא בבגדה אסור. והתם סברא הוא לאסור לפי שיצרו תוקפו ומתגבר עליו ביותר ורש"י פי' אפי' ביחוד נמי אסור מדאורייתא ואין נראה דמשמע דרוצה לאסור יחוד בנדה תימה דיחוד דאסור מן התורה לא ילפי' מאשת איש ושרי בנדה כדכתיב סוגה בשושנים (סנהד' פ"ד לז.) והוא בבגדו והיא בבגדה דלא הוי אפי' באשת איש אלא מדרבנן אסור בנדה מהיקשא טפי הוה לן למיסר יחוד מהיקשא ולמישרי הוא בבגדו והיא בבגדה בלא יחוד כגון שפתח פתוח. לר"ר מסוגה בשושנים*: ופליגא דר' פדת דא"ר פדת לא אסרה תורה אלא כו'. תימה מנא ליה דפליגי דילמא מדרבנן אסור אפי' הוא בבגדו ורש"י דפירש כאן כיון דמדאורייתא לא אסור אלא תשמיש ממש מדרבנן לא אסור אלא קירוב בשר לא נהירא דמסתמא לא פליגי אמתני' דלא יאכל הזב עם הזבה ועוד וכי לית ליה דאשת רעהו הוא בבגדו והיא בבגדה אסור ומפרש ר"ת דפליגא דר' פדת דכיון דלא אסרה תורה אלא קריבה של גילוי עריות בלבד א"כ אין לנו לאסור ולגזור אלא כעין שאסר הכתוב דהיינו דיעות בלא שינוי כגון לא יאכל הזב עם הזבה אבל הוא בבגדו והיא בבגדה דאיכא דיעות ושינוי לא יסבור ר' פדת דאפי' באשת איש הוא בבגדו והיא בבגדה שרי ור"י פי' ופליגא דר' פדת כיון דאית ליה דלא שייך לשון קריבה אלא בגילוי עריות ממש וא"כ ואל אשה נדה לא יקרב היינו תשמיש ממש שוב אין ללמוד בהיקש מאשת איש לאסור הוא בבגדו כו' לאפוקי לשון קריבה ממשמעותו ודוחק הוא דהא אשת רעהו לא טמא משמע תשמיש ממש ואפילו הכי אסרי' הוא בבגדו והיא בבגדה: ופליגא דידיה אדידיה. והוא היה יודע בעצמו שלא יבא לידי הרהור שצדיק גמור היה כדאמרינן בפרק ב' דכתובות (דף יז) *דרב אחא בר אהבה מרכיב לה אכתפיה ומרקד א"ל רבנן אנן מהו למעבד הכי א"ל אי דמיא לכון כי כשורא לחיי ואי לא לא והספר לא חש לפרש ולהאריך כאן למה היה עושה:

בימי

עין משפט נר מצוה

ק א ב מיי' שם הלכה טו טור שו"ע שם סעיף ז:

קא ג מיי' פי"א מהלכות איסורי ביאה הלכה יח ופי"ו מהלכות טומאת אוכלין הלכה יא סמג לאוין קיא טוש"ע יו"ד סימן קצה סעיף ג:

קב ד מיי' פי"א מהלכות א"ב שם טוש"ע שם סעיף ו:

קג ה מיי' פכ"א מהל' איסורי ביאה הלכה ו סמג לאוין קכו טוש"ע אה"ע סימן כא סעיף ז:

רבינו חננאל

כיוצא בו לא יאכל הזב עם הזבה. בוא וראה עד היכן פרצה [טהרה] בישראל*) כיוצא בו לא יאכל זב פרוש עם זב עם הארץ שמא יהי רגיל אצלו ויאכילנו בימי טהרתו דברים טמאים אבל לדברים שאינם מתוקנים לא חיישינן דאמר רבא רוב עמי הארץ מעשרין הן. איבעיא להו נדה מהו שתישן עם בעלה היא בבגדה והוא בבגדו ובעי רב יוסף למפשטא מהא דתנן בשחיטת חולין פרק כל הבשר העוף עולה עם הגבינה על השולחן ואינו נאכל כו' ונדחה זו ופשטנ' מהא דכתב ואת אשת רעהו לא טמא ואל אשה נדה לא יקרב. מקיש אשתו נדה לאשת רעהו מה אשת רעהו הוא בבגדו והיא בבגדה אסור אף אשתו נדה כיוצא בהן. ואף על גב דפליגא דר' פדת ומהא עובדא נמי דההוא דקרא ושנה

*) נראה דחסר כאן וצ"ל שלא שנינו לא יאכל טהור עם הטמאה אלא לא יאכל הזב עם הזבה.

[פסחים מ: ב"מ נב. ע"ז יז. נח: נט. יבמות מו.]

רב נסים גאון

מיתיבי רבן שמעון בן גמליאל אומר תינוקות מסדירין פרשיותיהן לאור הנר זאת התיובתא פירקו עליה ב' פירוקין בתלמודנו ובתלמוד ארץ ישראל פירקו פירוק אחר חביב רציתי לכתבו בכאן וכך אמרו אילין בעו דיספי בוצינא ואילין לא בעי דיספי בוצינא ופי' דבריהם כי התינוקות יתרחקו מן הקריאה ויאהבו שיכבה הנר ואנו בטוחים בהן כי הם לא יטו את הנר ולפיכך הותר להם לקרות לאור הנר דליכא למיחש שמא יטו אבל החזן לא יקרא דחיישינן שמא יטה לפי שלא ירצה שיכבה הנר לפיכך מבטלין התינוקות מן הקריאה: בוא וראה עד היכן פרצה טהרה בישראל פירשו בגמ' דבני מערבא כי זו הטלה למדנוה ממה שאמר הכתוב (בראשית ל) כי מעט אשר היה לך לפני ויפרץ לרוב כלומר מרוב שמשמרין ישראל הטהרות ורוב שמזדהרין מליגע ומליקרב לדבר שגורם לטומאה:

סלא

מסורת הש"ס

תוספתא פ"א

שם

לקמן כג. כתובות כד. גיטין סא: [חולין לה: מנחות לא.]

חולין קד: עדיו' פ"ה מ"ב

[חולין קז:]

[שם]

יחזקאל יח

ע"ז יז.

ויקרא יח

ע"ז שם

[אדר"נ פ"ב]

[באדר"נ פ"ב אי' שקרא הרבה ושנה הרבה וכו' וכ"א בכרי"ף והרא"ש]

דברים ל

[כתובות שם אי' רב אחא]

קד א מיי' פי"א מהלכו' א"ב הלכה יח סמג לאוין קיא טוש"ע יו"ד סימן קצה סעיף ג:

קה ב מיי' שם טור שו"ע שם סעיף יד:

תורה אור

ושימש תלמידי חכמים הרבה מפני מה מת בחצי ימיו ולא היה אדם מחזירה דבר פעם אחת נתארחתי אצלה והיתה מסיחה כל אותו מאורע ואמרתי לה בתי בימי נדותך מה הוא אצלך אמרה לי חס ושלום °אפי' באצבע קטנה לא נגע [בי] בימי לבוניך מהו אצלך אכל עמי ושתה עמי וישן עמי בקירוב בשר ולא עלתה דעתו על דבר אחר ואמרתי לה ברוך המקום שהרגו °שלא נשא פנים לתורה שהרי אמרה תורה °ואל אשה בנדת טומאתה לא תקרב (ויקרא יח) כי אתא רב דימי אמר מטה חדא הואי במערבא אמרי אמר רב יצחק בר יוסף סינר מפסיק בינו לבינה:

מתני' ואלו מן ההלכות שאמרו בעליית חנניה בן חזקיה בן גרון שעלו לבקרו נמנו ורבו ב"ש על ב"ה וי"ח דברים גזרו בו ביום:

גמ' א"ל אביי לרב יוסף אלו תנן או ואלו תנן ואלו תנן הני דאמרן או אלו תנן דבעינן למימר קמן תא שמע *אין פולין לאור הנר ואין קורין לאור הנר ואלו מן ההלכות שאמרו בעליית חנניה בן חזקיה בן גרון ש"מ ואלו תנן ש"מ: ת"ר מי כתב מגילת תענית אמרו חנניה בן חזקיה וסיעתו שהיו מחבבין את הצרות אמר רשב"ג אף אנו מחבבין את הצרות אבל מה נעשה שאם באנו לכתוב אין אנו מספיקין ד"א אין שוטה נפגע ד"א אין בשר המת מרגיש באיזמל איני *והאמר רב יצחק קשה רימה למת כמחט בבשר החי שנא' °אך בשרו עליו יכאב ונפשו עליו תאבל (איוב יד) אימא אין בשר המת שבחי מרגיש באיזמל אמר רב יהודה אמר רב *ברם זכור אותו האיש לטוב וחנניה בן חזקיה שמו שאלמלא הוא נגנז ספר יחזקאל שהיו דבריו סותרין דברי תורה מה עשה העלו לו ג' מאות גרבי שמן וישב בעלייה ודרשן: ושמנה עשר דבר גזרו: מאי נינהו שמנה עשר דבר *דתנן אלו פוסלין את התרומה האוכל *אוכל ראשון והאוכל אוכל שני והשותה משקין טמאין *והבא ראשו ורובו במים שאובין וטהור שנפלו על ראשו ורובו שלשה לוגין מים שאובין *והספר והידים והטבול יום והאוכלים והכלים שנטמאו במשקין (פסחים יט:) מאן תנא האוכל אוכל ראשון והאוכל אוכל שני מפסל פסלי טמויי

לא

רש"י

ושימש תלמידי חכמים · להסבירו סתומות המשנה וטעמיה והוא הנקרא תלמוד : נדותיך · כל שבעה של ראייה ראשונה : ליבוניך · כגון זבה שסופרת שבעה נקיים משפסקה וצריכה להיות לובשת לבנים לבדיקה שמא תראה ותסתור ספירתה : בנדת טומאתה · ועד שתבא במים לטבילה היא בנדתה דמרבינן מתהיה בנדתה בהוייתה תהא עד שתבא במים בתורת כהנים*: מטה חדא הואי · רחבה ולא קירוב בשר הואי וסבר דשרי בהכי: סינר · פורצינ"ט שהיא חוגרת בו ומגיע ממתנים ולמטה :

מתני' ונמנו ורבו · באו למנין ונמצאו של ב"ש מרובין : גמ' ה"ג ואלו תנן הני דאמרן או דלמא אלו תנן הני דבעינן למימר קמן · ואלו קאי אדלעיל לא יפלה את כליו ולא יקרא לאור הנר ואלו מן ההלכות כו' או דילמא אלו תנן וקאי לקמן ואין שורין דיו: ת"ש · דאתרתי קמייתי קאי אבל אינך לאו משמונה עשר דבר נינהו ולקמן בגמרא מפרש להו : מגילת תענית · לפי שאר כל משנה וברייתא לא היו כותבין דאסור לכתבם וזו נכתבה לזכרון לדעת ימים האסורין בתענית לכך נקרא מגלה שכתוב במגלת ספר : מחבבין את הצרות · שנגאלין מהן והנס חביב עליהן להזכירו לשבחו של הקב"ה וכותבין ימי הנס לעשותן יום טוב כגון אלין יומין דלא להתענאה בהון כו': אין אנו מספיקין · לפי שהן תדירות · *ל"א אין אנו מספיקין מלעשות י"ט בכל יום : אין שוטה נפגע · אין פגע רע בא עליו כלומר אינו מכיר בפגעיו כך כמה נסים באים לנו ואין אנו מכירין בהן: בשר מת שבחי · הגדל באדם החי מחמת מכה או מחמת כויה אינו מרגיש באיזמל כשחותכין אותו : דברי תורה · כגון נבילה וטרפה וגו' לא יאכלו הכהנים הא ישראל אוכלים וכגון וכן תעשה בשבעה בחודש היכן נרמז קרבן זה בתורה : גרבי · למאור ולמזונות : דרשן · כדדרשינן להני קראי במנחות (דף מה·) דמשום דאשתרי מליקה בחטאת העוף גבייהו הוצרך להזהירם על מליקת חולין שהיא נבילה: האוכל אוכל ראשון · מן התורה אין אוכל מטמא אדם האוכלו חוץ מנבלת עוף טהור אבל נבלת בהמה לא כדאמר במסכת נדה (פ"ה דמ"ב:) מי שאין לו טומאה אלא באכילתה יצאתה זו שיש לה טומאה קודם שיאכלנה וכ"ש אוכל ראשון שאינו אב הטומאה אבל הן גזרו באותו היום כדמפרש טעמא לקמן בכולהו ושיעורן לפסול את הגויה בחצי פרס בפרק יום הכפורים (יומא ד' פ:) והתם נמי לא אמר הנא לטומאת גויה דלאו דאורייתא ומצאתי בספר ערוך* משונה טומאה זו מטומאה דאורייתא דסגי לה בטבילה לתרומה דלא בעיא הערב שמש דתניא בספרי אין האוכל אוכלים טמאין ולא השותה משקין טמאין טמא טומאת ערב : והבא . לאחר שטבל מטומאתו במים שאובין בו ביום : וטהור . גמור שנפלו על ראשו כו' : והספר . כל כתבי הקודש תורה נביאים וכתובים פוסלין תרומה במגען : והידים . סתמן קודם נטילתן : וטבול יום . ולקמן פריך טבול יום מדאורייתא הוא : והאוכלין והכלים שנטמאו במשקין . לקמן בעי לה : מאן תנא . מי הוא האומר כן : פסלי · את התרומה ואותה תרומה לא תפסול אחרת שוב במגעה :

לא

תוספות

בימי ליבוניך מהו אצלך · לא משום שיש לחלק בין נדות לליבון דהא אמר ר"ע בפרק במה אשה יוצאה (לקמן דף סד:) הרי היא בנדתה עד שתבא במים אלא לפי שידע אליהו בכך היה המעשה ור"ח ורש"י פירשו בפרק אע"פ (כתובות דף סא· ושם) גבי שמואל מחלפא ליה דביתהו בידא דשמאלא היינו בימי ליבונה אין נראה כדפירשתי ור"ת פירש שהיו רגילים לטבול שתי טבילות אחת לסוף שבעה לראייתה שהיא טהורה מדאורייתא בהך טבילה ואחת לסוף ימי ליבון לכך היה מיקל אותו האיש ורש"י היה נוהג איסור להושיט מפתח מידו לידה בימי נדותה ונראה לר"י שיש סמך מסדר אליהו דקתני אמר לה שמא הבאת לו את השמן שמא הבאת לו את הפך ומיהו התם מסיים ונגע ביך באצבע הקטנה ומפרק אע"פ (שם) דאמר אביי מנח' ליה אפומיה דכובא ורבא מנח' ליה אבי סדיא אין ראיה כי שמא דוקא במזיגת הכוס שיש חיבה יותר כדאמר התם אבל שאר דברים לא ומהכא דקאמר אכל עמי ושתה עמי יכול להיות שלא הקפיד אלא על השכיבה : מטה חדא הואי · ופלטי בן ליש שנעץ חרב בינו לבינה (סנהדרין פ"ב דף יט:) איכא למימר שרחוק ממנה היה ביותר והיה פתוח לרה"ר שלא היה משום יחוד או שמא סבר כשאול שלא היתה מקודשת לדוד ומחמיר על עצמו היה מלבא עליה : רש"י גרים [וכן ר"ת] ואלו תנן הני דאמרן ומביא ראיה דאומר במדרש (פ' משפטים) כל מקום שנאמר ואלה מוסיף על הראשונים אלה פסל את הראשונים ועל המדרש קשה לר"י דאלה דברי הברית (דברים כח) קאי אמה שכתוב למעלה : ש"מ ואלו תנן · דלא קתני בתר הכי כדקתני במתניתין : אוכל ראשון ואוכל שני · אי תנן אוכל ראשון לחוד לא הוה ידעינן מיניה אוכל שני ואי תנא אוכל שני הוה אמינא דאוכל ראשון נמי טמויי מטמא* : והשותה משקין טמאים · לא שייך בהו ראשון ושני דלעולם משקין תחלה הוו אע"ג דאכתי לא נגזר כמו שאפרש בסמוך מ"מ היה בדעתם לגזור מיד וצריכא לאשמעינן משקין ואוכלין כדאמר בסמוך דהך דמשקין לא שכיח ואי תנא משקין ה"א דוקא משקין דחמירי אבל אוכל לא פסיל כלל : והבא ראשו ורובו במים שאובין · וא"ת תיפוק ליה שהוא טבול יום וי"ל דנפקא מינה דאפילו העריב שמשו פוסל עד שיחזור ויטבול : וטהור שנפלו על ראשו כו' . וא"ת מ"ש דבטהור לא גזרו כ"א בנפל ולא גזרו נמי בביאה כמו בטבול יום ונראה לר"י דבטהור לא רצו לגזור יותר אלא דוקא בנפילה כמו שרגילים להפיל עליהם מים שאובים אחר שטבלו במים סרוחים כדאמר בסמוך והיו נותנים עליהם ג' לוגים מים שאובים [וע"ע תוס' גיטין טז: ד"ה הבא]:

רבי

*ואי תני משקי' ואוכל שני ה"א דמיירי במשקי' שני' אבל אוכל ראשון ה"א דמטמא ואע"ג דהמשקין לעולם תחלה הוי אכתי לא נגזר ועי"ד אוכל ראשון דהוי ראשון דאוריי' ה"א דחמור ממשקין שהם תחלה רק מדרבנן [תוס' ישנים]

רבינו חננאל

ושמש ת"ח הרבה ומת בחצי ימיו ושאל אליהו את אשתו בימי (נדותיך) [לבתיך] מהו אצלך. פירוש בז' ימי נקיים[והיא](ואף)אמרה לו אכל עמי ושתה עמי וישן עמי בקירוב בשר ולא עלה על דעתו דבר אחר אמר לה ברוך המקום שהרגו שלא נשא פנים לתורה שנא' ואל אשה כנדת טומאתה לא תקרב.במערבא אמרי כך אמרה לו מטה חדא הוה וסינר מפסיק ביניהם : פשטנא ממתניתין דתני אין פולין לאור הנר ואין קורין לאור הנר אלו מן ההלכות שאמרו בעליית חנניא בן חזקיה בן גרון ש"מ אלו תנן שכבר הזכרנום ולא מה דבעו למימר לקמן:ת"ר מי כתב מגילת תענית אמרו חנניה בן חזקיה בן גרון וסייעתו שהיו מחבבין להזכיר ימי צרות בשמחה . ארשב"ג אף אנו כו' שאלמלא הוא נגנז ספר יחזקאל שדבריו סותרין דברי תורה פירוש יש בספר יחזקאל דברים שנראין כאילו סותרי ד"ת כגן קרבנות המועדים והנוכות וכיוצא בהן . ובא חנניא בן חזקיה ודרשן כגון (הכתוב כת"י*) ונתברר שספר יחזקאל והתורה שוין : פיס' שמונה עשר דברים גזרו בו ביום ואלו הן דתנן פוסלין את התרומה האוכל אוכל ראשון והאוכל אוכל שני כו' פי' אוכל ראשון הוא שנגע בו השרץ ואוכל שני הנוגע במשקין במה שנגע בו השרץ אבל אוכל לא שאין אוכל מטמא אוכל ושניהם אליבא דר' יהושע האוכל אותם שני הוא ופוסל את התרומה דתנן בטהרות פרק ב' ר' יהושע אומר האוכל אוכל ראשון ואוכל שני שני והשותה משקין טמאים שאלו כולן פוסלין גופו של אדם כדתנן במעילה פרק ד' כל האוכלין מצטרפין לפסול את הגויה כבחצי פרס פירוש אוכלין טמאים . וכל המשקים פירוש הטמאין מצטרפין לפסול את הגויה ברביעית' [והבא ראשו ורובו במים שאובין] וטהור שנפלו על ראשו ועל רובו ג' לוגין מים שאובין פוסלו בתרומה פי' לולי שאמר כי בטהור טומאתו לא עמדה בטמא שלא טיהרוהו . גזרו על הספר מפני שהיו מצניעין אוכלין של תרומה גבי הספרים והיו העכברים באין על האוכלין ומפסידין הספרים . ידים מפני שהן עסקניות חיישינן דילמא נגעו בטומאת הלכך גזרו בהו טומאה ומתחלה גזרו על הידים הנוגעות בספר להיות פוסלין התרומה כדי שלא יהו מצוין ליגע ס"ת אלא במפה וגזרו נמי על האוכלין שנטמאו מן המשקין שנטמאו מחמת ידים שיפסלו התרומה גזירת משום משקין שנטמאו מחמת שרץ . ועל הכלים שנטמאו במשקין הבאים מחמת שרץ גזירה משום זב . טבול יום אסיק' טמי מכאן טבול יום ואסיק' שלמה תיקן טומאה לידים לקדשים והלל ושמאי גזרו לתרומה נמי ולא קבילו מינייהו אתו תלמידיהן גזרו וקבילו מנהון אמר רב יהודה בי"ח דבר נחלקו ובי"ח גזרו ואסיק' בי"ח שנחלקו בו ביום לטהר תרשו :

*) אולי צ"ל הכתוב ביחזקאל מ"ד.

[וכ"א לקמן סד:]

[לעיל יב.]

ס"א אינו וככל פירוש אחד

לקמן קנג. ברכות יח:

חגיגה יג: מנחות מה.

זבין פ"ה מי"ב

[פי' מאכל כמו ויהן אוכל בעריס בפרשת מקץ ועי' תוס' פרק ב' דסוכה כ"ח:]

[ערך גוף]

read [Bible], learned [Mishnah], [13b] and served scholars much, why did he die in middle age? and no man could answer her. On one occasion I[5] was a guest at her house,[6] and she related the whole story to me. Said I to her, 'My daughter! how was he to thee in thy days of menstruation?' 'God forbid!' she rejoined; 'he did not touch me even with his little finger.' 'And how was he to thee in thy days of white [garments]?'[7] 'He ate with me, drank with me and slept with me in bodily contact, and it did not occur to him to do other.' Said I to her, 'Blessed be the Omnipresent for slaying him, that He did not condone on account of the Torah![8] For lo! the Torah hath said, *And thou shalt not approach unto a woman as long as she is impure by her uncleanness*.'[9] When R. Dimi came,[10] he said, It was a broad bed. In the West [Palestine] they said, R. Isaac b. Joseph said: An apron interposed between them.[11]

MISHNAH. AND THESE ARE OF THE HALACHOTH WHICH THEY STATED IN THE UPPER CHAMBER OF ḤANANIAH B. HEZEKIAH B. GARON, WHEN THEY WENT UP TO VISIT HIM. THEY TOOK A COUNT, AND BETH SHAMMAI OUTNUMBERED BETH HILLEL; AND ON THAT DAY THEY ENACTED EIGHTEEN
a MEASURES.[1]

GEMARA. Abaye said to R. Joseph: Did we learn, THESE ARE or AND THESE ARE? Did we learn AND THESE ARE [viz.,] those that we have stated [in the former Mishnah]; or did we learn THESE ARE [viz.,] those that are to be stated soon?[2]—Come and hear: One may not search his garments by the light of a lamp, nor read by the light of a lamp; and these are of the *halachoth* stated in the upper chamber of Ḥananiah b. Hezekiah b. Garon. This proves that we learnt, AND THESE ARE;[3] this proves it.

Our Rabbis taught: Who wrote *Megillath Ta'anith*?[4] Said they, Ḥananiah b. Hezekiah and his companions, who cherished their troubles.[5] R. Simeon b. Gamaliel observed: We too cherish our troubles, but what can we do? For if we come to write [them down], we are inadequate.[6] Another reason is: a fool is not assailed.[7] Another reason: the flesh of the dead does not feel the scalpel. But that is not so, for did not R. Isaac say, Worms are as painful to the dead as a needle in the flesh of the living, for it is said, *But his flesh upon him hath pain, And his soul within him mourneth*?[8]—Say: The dead flesh in a living person does not feel the scalpel.

Rab Judah said in Rab's name: In truth, that man, Ḥananiah
b son of Hezekiah by name, is to be remembered for blessing:[1] but for him, the Book of Ezekiel would have been hidden,[2] for its words contradicted the Torah.[3] What did he do? Three hundred barrels of oil were taken up to him and he sat in an upper chamber and reconciled[4] them.

AND ON THAT DAY THEY ENACTED EIGHTEEN MEASURES. What are the eighteen measures?—For we learnt: The following render *terumah* unfit:[5] one who eats food of the first degree or the second degree, or who drinks unclean liquid;[6] one who enters with head and the greater part of his body into drawn water;[7] a clean person upon whose head and the greater part of his body there fell three *logs*[8] of drawn water; a Book;[9] one's hands;[10] a *ṭebul yom*;[11] and food or utensils which were defiled by a liquid.[12]

Which Tanna [holds that] one who eats food of the first or

(5) Elijah, the supposed author of the Tanna debe Eliyahu; v. n. 1. (6) Elijah was believed to visit the earth and speak to people. (7) When a *niddah's* discharge ceased, she donned white garments and examined herself for seven consecutive days, which had to pass without any further discharge of blood before she became clean. During this time she was forbidden to her husband. (8) He showed no unfair favouritism because of the man's learning. (9) Lev. XVIII, 19. (10) V. *supra* 5a, n. b9. (11) But they were not actually in bodily contact.

a (1) Scholars are divided as to when this took place. Z. Frankel, *Darke ha-Mishnah* assigns it to the beginning of the division of the two schools. Graetz maintains that it took place about four years before the destruction of the Temple; Weiss favours the last generation before the destruction, not long after the death of Agrippa I. V. also Halevi, *Doroth*, I, 3, 580 *seq*. (2) Lit., 'before us'. The actual eighteen were forgotten in course of time—hence Abaye's question. (3) Since the *halachoth* quoted are given in the previous Mishnah. (4) 'The scroll of fasting', containing a list of the days on which fasting is forbidden. Thirty-five days are listed; on fourteen public mourning was forbidden, whilst fasting was prohibited on all. V. *J.E.* VIII, 427. (5) I.e., the days of victorious release from their troubles, and declared them minor festivals. (6) Every day marks the release from some trouble. (7) I.e., he does not perceive the troubles which surround him. So we too do not perceive our miraculous escapes. (8) Job XIV, 22.

b (1) Lit., 'for good'. (2) The technical term for exclusion from the Canon. (3) E.g. Ezek. XLIV, 31; XLV, 20, q.v. (4) Lit., 'expounded them'. (5) For *terumah* v. Glos. 'Unfit' denotes that it may not be eaten on account of defilement, but does not defile any other *terumah* by its contact; 'unclean' denotes that it defiles other food too by its touch. (6) Various degrees of uncleanness are distinguished. The greatest of all is that of a human corpse, called the prime origin (lit., 'father of fathers') of uncleanness; this is followed in successively decreasing stages by 'origin' (lit., 'father') of uncleanness, first, second, third and fourth degrees of uncleanness. When an object becomes unclean through contact with another, its degree of defilement is one stage below that which defiles it. By Biblical law unclean food or drink does not defile the person who eats it; but the Rabbis enacted that it does, and so he in turn renders *terumah* unfit by contact.—Ordinary unsanctified food (*ḥullin*) does not proceed beyond the second degree; i.e., if second degree *ḥullin* touches other *ḥullin* the latter remains clean; but if it touches *terumah*, it becomes a third degree. Again, *terumah* does not go beyond the third degree (hence it is then designated 'unfit', not 'unclean' in respect of other *terumah*); but if it touches flesh of sacrifices (*heḳdesh*) it renders this unfit, and it is called 'fourth degree'. (7) Water which had passed through a vessel, as opposed to 'living water', i.e., well water, river water, or rain water collected in a pit. (8) 1 *log* = 549,4 cu.centimetres; v. *J.E.* Weights and Measures. (9) Any of the Books of the Bible. (10) Before washing. (11) V. Glos. (12) All these render *terumah* unfit—they are all discussed in the Gemara.

of the second degree [merely] renders unfit [14a] but does not a defile?[1]—Said Rabbah b. Bar Ḥanah, It is R. Joshua. For we learnt: R. Eliezer said: One who eats food of the first degree is [himself defiled in] the first degree; of the second degree, is [defiled in] the second degree; of the third degree, is [defiled in] the third degree.[2] R. Joshua said: One who eats food of the first or of the second degree is [defiled in] the second degree;[3] of the third degree, [he enters] the second degree in respect of *hekdesh*,[4] but not in respect of *terumah*,[5] this referring to *ḥullin* subjected to the purity of *terumah*.[6]

When one eats food of the first or of the second degree, why did the Rabbis decree uncleanness in his case?—Because one may sometimes eat unclean food [*ḥullin*] and take a liquid of *terumah* and put it in his mouth and thus render it unfit.[7] When one drinks unclean liquid, why did the Rabbis decree uncleanness in his case?—Because he may sometimes drink unclean liquid and take food of *terumah* and put it in his mouth, and thus render it unfit. But it is the same thing![8]—You might argue, The first is usual but not the second:[9] therefore he informs us [that it is not so].

And one who comes with his head and the greater part of his body] into drawn water, why did the Rabbis decree uncleanness in his case?—Said R. Bibi in R. Assi's name: Because originally people performed *ṭebillah*[10] in collected pit water, which was stagnant [noisome], and so they poured drawn water upon them-b selves.[1] [But when] they began to make this a fixed [law], the Rabbis imposed uncleanness thereon. What is meant by 'a fixed [law]?'—Abaye said: They maintained, Not this [pit water] purifies, but both together purify. Said Raba to him, Then what did it matter, seeing that they did perform *ṭebillah* in this [the pit water]? But, said Raba, they maintained, Not this [the pit water] purifies but that [the drawn water].[2]

And a clean person upon whose head and the greater part of his body there fell three *logs* of drawn water, why did the Rabbis decree uncleanness in his case? For if not this, the other would not stand.[3]

And why did the Rabbis impose uncleanness upon a Book?—Said R. Mesharsheya: Because originally food of *terumah* was stored near the Scroll of the Law, with the argument, This is holy and that is holy.[4] But when it was seen that they [the Sacred Books] came to harm,[5] the Rabbis imposed uncleanness upon them.[6]

'And the hands'?—Because hands are fidgety.[7] It was taught: Also hands which came into contact with a Book[8] disqualify *terumah*, on account of R. Parnok['s dictum]. For R. Parnok said in R. Joḥanan's name: One who holds a Scroll of the Law naked[9] will be buried naked. 'Naked!' can you really think so? Rather said R. Zera, [it means] naked without good deeds.[10] 'Without good deeds!' can you really think so?[11] Rather say, naked, without that good deed [to his credit].[12]

Which was first enacted? Shall we say that the former was

a (1) V. *supra* 13b, n. b5. (2) Hence, when he eats defiled food in the first degree, he *defiles terumah*, not merely renders it unfit (v. *supra* 13b, nn. b5 and b6). (3) Hence in both cases he merely renders *terumah* unfit. (4) Flesh of sacrifices. (5) If he touches *hekdesh* he defiles it in the third degree, being regarded himself as second degree in respect thereto; but he does not affect *terumah* at all. (6) People (particularly *perushim*, v. *supra* 13a, n. a1) voluntarily treated *ḥullin* as *terumah*; then it could become unfit in the third degree, but not otherwise (v. *supra* 13b, n. b6), and this is the only way in which it is possible for a person to eat *ḥullin* of the third degree, v. Ḥul. 33b. (7) For it may touch the food still in his mouth. Unfit *terumah* may not be eaten. (8) Both being based on the same reason, the second is a corollary of the first and need not be stated. (9) So that a Rabbinical measure is not required in the second case. (10) I.e., took a ritual bath to be purified of defilement.

b (1) The correct reading appears to be: three *logs* of drawn water; v. Marginal Gloss to cur. edd. (2) This would lead to the neglect of proper *ṭebillah*. (3) A general measure had to be enacted that three *logs* of drawn water defiled a person, whether it came upon him by his intention or accidentally. Had the Rabbis drawn a distinction, the former too would have remained unobserved. (4) Hence it is fitting that they be placed together. (5) The food attracted mice, which naturally injured the Books too. (6) To put an end to the practice. (7) They are active and apt to touch things. Hence unless their owner has taken care that they should not touch a ritually unclean object after he washed them, they are treated as unclean. (8) Lit., 'which come on account of a Book.' (9) Without its wrapping. (10) As though he had never performed a good deed or fulfilled a precept. (11) Surely that act does not nullify all his meritorious deeds! (12) If he took it for study or to wrap it up after the public reading—likewise a 'good deed'—it is not accounted to him (Tosaf.). Tosaf. also observes that presumably this applies to any of the Books of the Bible.—The reference is to the actual parchment; but there is no objection to the modern practice of elevating the uncovered Scroll whilst holding it by the rollers on which it is wound. The Sephardi Jews, i.e., the descendants of the Spanish Jews, have the entire parchment of the Scroll from end to end shielded with silk or cloth.

לא מטמו אמר רבה בר בר חנה ר' יהושע היא דתנן *ר' אליעזר אומר האוכל אוכל ראשון ראשון ואוכל אוכל שני שני אוכל שלישי שלישי ר' יהושע אומר [א]האוכל אוכל ראשון ואוכל שני שני שלישי שני לקודש ואין שני לתרומה בחולין שנעשו על טהרת תרומה [ב]אוכל אוכל ראשון ואוכל אוכל שני מ"ט גזרו ביה רבנן טומאה *דזימנין דאביל אוכלין טמאין ושקיל משקין דתרומה ושדי לפומיה ופסיל להו שותה משקין טמאין מ"ט גזרו ביה רבנן טומאה דזימנין דשתה משקין טמאין ושקיל אוכלין דתרומה ושדי לפומיה ופסיל להו היינו הך מהו דתימא *הא שכיחי והא לא שכיחי קמ"ל [ג]והבא ראשו ורובו במים שאובין מ"ט גזרו ביה רבנן טומאה א"ר ביבי אמר רב אסי שבתחלה היו טובלין במי מערות מכונסין וסרוחין והיו נותנין עליהן *מים שאובין התחילו ועשאום קבע גזרו עליהם טומאה מאי קבע אמר אביי שהיו אומרים לא אלו מטהרין אלא אלו ואלו מטהרין אמר ליה רבא מאי נפקא מינה הא קא טבלי בהנך אלא אמר רבא שהיו אומרים לא אלו מטהרין אלא אלו מטהרין *וטהור שנפלו על ראשו ורובו שלשה לוגין מים שאובין מ"ט גזרו ביה רבנן טומאה דאי לא הא לא קיימא הא [ד]וספר מ"ט גזרו ביה רבנן טומאה אמר רב משרשיא שבתחלה היו מצניעין את אוכלין דתרומה אצל ס"ת ואמרו האי קדש והאי קדש כיון דקחזו דקאתו לידי פסידא גזרו ביה רבנן טומאה [ה]והידים מפני שהידים עסקניות הן תנא [ו]אף ידים הבאות מחמת ספר פוסלות את התרומה משום דר' פרנך *דא"ר פרנך א"ר יוחנן [ז]האוחז ס"ת ערום נקבר ערום ערום ס"ד אלא א"ר זירא ערום בלא מצות בלא מצות ס"ד אלא אימא ערום בלא אותה מצוה הי גזור ברישא אילימא הא גזור ברישא כיון

[מקוואות פ"ג מ"ד] [גיטין ס.]

רש"י

לא מטמו · את התרומה להיות שניה והיא תחזור ותפסול אחרים: האוכל אוכל ראשון. נעשה גופו ראשון ומטמא את התרומה להיות שנייה והיא תחזור ותפסול שלישי: שני. פוסל ואינו מטמא: שלישי. אינו פוסל תרומה במגעו אבל הקדשים פוסל ובפ"ב דשחיטת חולין מפרש טעמא דתרוייהו: ר' יהושע אומר האוכל אוכל ראשון הוי שני וכן האוכל אוכל שני הוי שני. והתם מפרש טעמא מאי שהשני עושה שני ע"י משקין דמשקין אפי' הן שניים נעשין תחלה ועושין מגען שני ואף כאן החמירו בשני לעשות האוכלו כיוצא בו: שלישי שני לקדש. האוכל אוכל שלישי עושה גופו שני לקדש והתם מפרש טעמא דהאי אוכל שלישי חולין שנעשו על טהרת תרומה הוא וטהרתן טומאה היא אצל הקדש הלכך שמירה דידה לאו שמירה היא לענין קודש וחיישינן באוכל שלישי דידיה דילמא ראשון הוא והאוכלו שני: בחולין שנעשו על טהרת תרומה. כלומר באיזו חולין אתה מוצא אוכל שלישי בחולין שנעשו על טהרת תרומה דאילו חולין גרידא לא משכחת בהו שלישי: מאי טעמא גזור. באדם האוכל שיהא טמא: ופסיל להו. והתורה הזהירה על התרומה לשמרה בטהרה דכתיב (במדבר יח) את משמרת תרומתי לפיכך גזרו באוכל אוכלין טמאין שלא יהא רגיל אצל תרומה: הא' שכיחא. שאדם שותה עם אכילתו: והא לא שכיחא. שיהא אוכל עם שתייתו: ה"ג היו טובלין במי מערה סרוחים מכונסין. שיש בה מ' סאה מי גשמים שהם כשרים לכל טמא חוץ מזב לבדו דכתיב ביה מים חיים: והיו נותנין עליהן. על גופן מים שאובין להעביר סרחון המקוה: התחילו. הטובלין ועשו השאובין קבע לפיכך גזרו על השאובין טומאה לטמא אדם אחר טבילתו אבל אין מטמא שום אוכל ומשקה אלא אם כן נטמאו בשרץ: לא אלו. דמקוה לבדה מטהרין אלא אלו ואלו מטהרין דמתוך שהורגלו הכל בכך לא היו יודעין שלהעביר הזוהמא היו השאובין באין אלא לטהר: מאי נפקא לן מינה. כיון שכולן טובלין תחלה במקוה מאי איכפת לרבנן אם עשאוה הטובלין קבע אחר טבילה: אלא אלו מטהרין. וחיישינן דילמא אתי לבטולי תורת מקוה וטובלין בשאובין והתורה אמרה אך מעין ובור מקוה מים וגו' (ויקרא יא): מ"ט. הא לאו לאחר טבילה הוה: אי לאו· דגזור אף על הטהור לא קיימא גזירה הבא אחר טבילה דאמרי מ"ש האי מהאי: לידי פסידא· עכברים מצויין אצל אוכלין ומפסידים את הספר אבל בחולין לא הוצרכו לגזור דבלאו הכי נמי לא היו נותנין חול אצל קדש: עסקניות הן. ונוגעין בבשרו ובמקום טנופת וגנאי לתרומה בכך ונמאס לאוכלין כשנוגע בה בידים מסואבות ורבותינו מפרשים חיישינן שמא נגעו [ידיו] בטומאה [ונטמא] וקשיא לי אם כן ניחוש שמא נגע באב הטומאה ונמצא ראשון ויטמאנה ועוד מאי שנא ידים לחודייהו בכל גופו נגזור לפסול תרומה שמא נגעו ידיו בטומאה ונטמא כל גופו ועוד לא תסגי להו בנטילה אלא בטבילה: ספר תורה ערום. אלא על ידי מטפחת: אילימא הא. דסתם ידים גזור ברישא: *הא תו למה לי. הך מי נפקא מכלל סתם ידים: *) אלא הא גזור ברישא. דסתם ידים·לא גזרו (סמוך) לנטילתן מגע לתרומה:

*) ס"א הא גזרו סמוך לנטילתה מגע התרומה רש"ל.

תנא

אף הידים הבאות מחמת ספר. מדקתני אף משמע דעל הספר גזרו תחלה ואח"כ על הידים הבאות מחמת ספר וכיון דסתם ידים לבסוף גזרו כדאמר לקמן א"כ ידים הבאות מחמת ספר בו ביום גזרו דהא בין גזירה דספר לגזירה דסתם ידים גזרו עליהם וא"כ הוה טפי מי"ח דבר ואם נאמר דעל הידים הבאות מחמת ספר לא באותו פרק גזרו אלא מקודם לכן הוה אתי שפיר אך לשון אף לא משמע כן ועוד לא יתכן שגזרו על הידים ועדיין ספר עצמו לא היה פוסל את התרומה:

האוחז ספר תורה ערום· קלת משמע דלאו דווקא ספר תורה דהא כל כתבי הקדש תנן במסכת ידים* °שמטמאין את הידים:

בלא אותה מצוה. אם אוחזו ללמוד בו אין לו שכר של אותו לימוד ואם בשביל לגוללו אינו מקבל שכר על הגלילה:

כיון

תוספות

רבי יהושע אומר האוכל אוכל ראשון ושני שני. בפ"ב דחולין (דף לד· ושם) מפרש טעמא משום דמלינו שני עושה שני על ידי משקין וא"ת מאי צריך התם להאי טעמא נימא דלהכי שני עושה שני כדמפרש בסמוך בגמרא משום דזימנין דאכיל אוכלין טמאין ושדי משקין דתרומה כו' וי"ל משום גזירה דתרומה אין לנו לעשות אוכל שני שני אם לא שמלינו כזה משום דדמי לחוכא ואיטלולא: **זמנין** דאכיל אוכלין טמאין כו'. אומר ר"ת דפסול גוייה הנזכרת בכל מקום דאמרי' (בעירובין פ"ח דף פב: ושם) וחצי חציה לפסול את הגויה דהיינו שיעור שני בילים ולמ"ד בילה ומחצה לאו היינו גזירה דהכא דמהך טעמא דהכא אפילו כבילה פסול אלא פסול גויה גזירה קדמוניות היתה וגזרו שלא יהיו באים לטעות ולומר כמו שמותר לאכול תרומה אחר אוכלים טמאין אע"פ שנוגע התרומה באוכלין טמאין שבמעיו כך מותר להגיע תרומה לאוכלין טמאין מבחוץ ולכך גזרו דהאוכל אוכלין טמאים כחצי פרס שיהא גופו נפסל מלאכול בתרומה אבל *ע"י מגע לא גזרו ודוקא כחצי פרס אבל כבילה ליכא למטעי שנשאר בין השינים ונחסר קודם שיגיע למעיו וכיון דאפקי מכבילה אוקמי אחצי פרס אבל גזירה דהכא גזרו שיפסול אף למגע ואף בכבילה משום טעמא דמפרש *תדע דגזירה קדמוניות היתה דביומא בפ' בתרא (דף פ: ושם) ס"ד למימר דפסול גויה דאורייתא וכי"ח דבר היו כולם בקיאים ואיך .היו טועים לומר דהיא דאורייתא דא"כ חסר להו: **ושקיל** משקין דתרומה ושדי לפומיה ופסיל להו· ואע"ג דמשקים תחלה הוו כדאמר (פרה פ"ח משנה ז) כל הפוסל את התרומה מטמא משקין להיות תחלה הכא דקאמר ופסיל להו משום דלאכי קודם י"ח דבר לא גזרו להיות משקין תחלה כמו שאפרש: **תנא** אף הידים הבאות מחמת ספר. והא דלא מייתי מתני' דמסכת ידים (פ"ג מ"ה) כל כתבי הקדש מטמאין את הידים משום דמלינו למימר דה"מ לקדש להכי מייתי בהייתא דקתני בהדיא תרומה וא"ת ומאי אריא ידים הבאות מחמת ספר משום דר' פרנך אפילו מחמת כל פסולי תרומה נמי כדתנן במסכת ידים (פ"ג משנה ב) כל הפוסל את התרומה מטמא את הידים להיות שניות °וי"ל דהיינו דווקא לקדש· דומיא דיד דמטמא את חברתה שאינו אלא לקדש כדמוכח בחגיגה (דף כד:) ופ"ב דחולין (דף לד:ושם) דקאמר מלינו שני עושה שני על ידי משקין הוי מלי נמי למימר דמלינו דע"י ספר שני עושה שני ושמא כשראה שלא קבל רבי אליעזר תשובתו במשקין חזר והשיב לו מכתבי הקדש*:

תנא אף הידים כו'· וא"ת הא דתנן (ידים פ"ג מ"ב) היד מטמא חבירתה ד"ר יהושע אמרו לו כו' א"ל מצינו כתבי קודש כו' א"ל אין דנין דברי סופרים מד"ת ולא מד"ס ע"ש והשתא היכי מייתי ראיה מכתבי קודש שהן שני ומטמאות ידים אף לתרומה ליד דלא מטמא חבירתה רק לקידש וי"ל דאינו חושש רק להשיב על סברתם שאמרו דאין שני עושה שני ועוד נראה לפרש דהסיפא דכתבי קודש היינו דוקא לקודש ולאו היינו גזירה דהכא דידים הבאות מחמת ספר דר' פרנך ומה שמקשה וכי לית להו לרבנן האוכל אוכל שני כיון דאין דנין דברי סופרים מד"ת ולא מד"ס נראה היכא דאיכא טעמא אית להו לרבנן שני עושה שני *כגזירה הבאות מחמת ספר משום דר' פרנך והאוכל אוכל שני כדמפרש כאן זימנין דאכיל אוכלין טמאים ושדי משקין דתרומה לפומיה (ת"י):

עין משפט נר מצוה

קה א ב מיי' פ"ח מהל' שאר אבות הטומאות הלכה י:

קו ג מיי' שם פ"ט הלכה א:

קז ד שם הלכה ה:

קח ה ו מיי' שם ופ"ח הלכה ח:

קט ז מיי' פי' מהלכ' ס"ת הלכה ו טור ושו"ע או"ח סימן קמז סעיף א וטור שו"ע יו"ד סימן רפב סעיף ד

אבל למגע כו'

וריב"א מפרש דפסול גויה היינו גזירה דהכא ולא גזרו אכבילה לפי שאין אדם נמנע לשתות עד שיאכל חצי פרס ומשקין טמאים שצריך רביעית משום דמדאוריי' לא מטמו אחרים אלא ברביעית. כפירים [ס"י]

גליון הש"ס

תוס' ד"ה תנא אף הידים וכו' וי"ל היינו דוקא לקדש וכו'· עי' פסחים יט ע"א תוס' ד"ה שאין טומאת ידים: תוס' ד"ה כאותו ס"ת וכו' שמטמאין את הידים. עי' מגילה ז ע"א ברש"י ד"ה אינה מטמאה. ועי' תוס' סוטה יז ע"א ד"ה לא על טלות כסוכ"ד:

מסורת הש"ס

סוטה ל. חולין לג: טהרות פ"ב מ"ב

[עי' תוס' חולין לג: ד"ה האוכל]

ס"א למימר ה"א משקין דתמירי מטמו [תוס' ישנים]

[ע"ל ג' לוגין מים וכו' כן גי' הרא"ש בסוף מס' זבין ועי' תוי"ט שם ובן היא גירס' תוס' בגיטין טו. ד"ה והבא וכו' ע"ש וכן מ"מ גירסת תוס' לעיל יג: ד"ה וטהור וכ"ג תוס' כ"ב סו: ד"ה מכלל]

מגילה לב. ע"ש מסכת סופרים פ"ג [הלכה טו]

[ועי' תוס' חגיגה כה: ד"ה דתנן וכו']

רש"ג

[ידים פ"ג]

עייד לג"ב

ידים פ"ג

רים מ"ז

עין משפט
נר מצוה

קי א מיי' פ"י מהלכות אבות הטומאות הלכה א:

קיא ב מיי' פ"ח שם הלכה י:

קיב ג מיי' פ"ז שם הלכה ב:

קיג ד מיי' פ"ח שם הלכה ח:

וה"ה דה"מ למיפרך א"כ טמויי נמי ליטמו לר"ע דאית ליה שני עושה שלישי בחולין [ת"י]

ס"מ לשמיי דקודם גזרו אתלויה אע"פ שאין אנו יודעין מתי דהא על ו' ספיקות שורפין תרומה ע"כ קודם לכן גזרו אתלויה אע"פ שלא מצינו אלא דעדיפא מיניה פריך [תוספות ישנים]

גליון הש"ס

גמ' דאמר רב הונא בג' מקומות נחלקו וכו' עיין חגיגה דף טז ע"א תוס' ד"ה יוסי בן יועזר: שם ונטילת ידים וכו' רש"א מוחק ונטילת: תוס' ד"ה ואילו וכו' ובשאר י"ח דברים נחלקו ולמחר הושוו וכו' וכדאיתא כה"ג חולין דכ"ה ע"ב לא נחלקו לא עמד ר"מ במחלוקת:

כיון דהך גזור ברישא הא תו למה לי אלא הך גזור ברישא והדר גזור בכולהו ידים וטבול יום *טבול יום דאורייתא הוא דכתיב °ובא השמש וטהר (ויקרא כב) סמי מכאן טבול יום והאוכלין שנטמאו במשקין במשקין דמאי אילימא במשקין הבאין מחמת שרץ דאוריי' נינהו דכתיב °וכל משקה אשר ישתה (שם יא) אלא ב במשקין הבאין מחמת ידים וגזירה משום משקין הבאין מחמת שרץ והכלים שנטמאו' במשקין כלים דאיטמאו במשקין דמאי אילימא במשקין דזב דאוריי' נינהו דכתיב °וכי ירוק הזב בטהור (שם טו) *מה שביד טהור טמאתי לך אלא ג במשקין הבאין מחמת שרץ וגזירה משום משקין דזב וידים תלמידי שמאי והלל גזור שמאי והלל גזור דתניא יוסי בן יועזר איש צרידה ויוסי בן יוחנן איש ירושלים גזרו טומאה על ארץ העמים ועל כלי זכוכית *שמעון בן שטח תיקן כתובה לאשה וגזר טומאה על כלי מתכות שמאי והלל גזרו טומאה על הידים וכ"ת שמאי וסיעתו והלל וסיעתו והאמר רב יהודה אמר שמואל י"ח דבר גזרו ובי"ח נחלקו ואילו הלל ושמאי לא נחלקו אלא בג' מקומות °דא"ר הונא *בג' מקומות נחלקו ותו לא וכ"ת אתו אינהו גזור לתלות ואתו תלמידייהו וגזרו לשרוף *והאמר אילפא *ד ידים תחלת גזירתן לשריפה אלא אתו אינהו גזור ולא קבלו מינייהו ואתו תלמידייהו גזרו וקבלו מינייהו ואכתי שלמה גזר *דא"ר יהודה אמר שמואל בשעה שתיקן שלמה עירובין °ונטילת ידים יצתה בת קול ואמרה °בני אם חכם לבך ישמח לבי גם אני (משלי כג) °חכם בני ושמח לבי ואשיבה חורפי דבר (שם כז) אתא שלמה

תוספות

כיון דהך גזור ברישא הא תו למה לי · ואם תאמר והא נפקא מינה לנוגע בספר מיד אחר נטילה ולא הסיח דעתו ואפילו הכי ידיו טמאות משום דרבי פרנך ויש לומר דמשום הא לא היו גוזרין המילתא דלא שכיחא היא שיגע בספר מיד אחר נטילה ומיהו השתא דגזור ידים מחמת ספר ברישא אפילו נוגע סמוך לנטילה גזרו עליה שלא חלקו:

סמי מכאן טבול יום · לא מן המשנה אלא דלא הוי ממנין י"ח דבר:

משקין הבאים מחמת שרץ · דאורייתא נינהו *לרבי עקיבא פריך דאית ליה בפרק קמא דפסחים (ד' יד:) משקין לטמא אחרים דאורייתא: **דכתיב** וכל משקה אשר ישתה · האי קרא במשקין הבאין מחמת כלי איירי ומשקין הבאין מחמת שרץ אתיא בק"ו מינה ואם תאמר ומאי פריך דאורייתא נינהו נימא דיו לבא מן הדין להיות כנדון ולא ליהוי אלא שני כמשקין הבאין מחמת כלי והאוכלין הנוגעין בהן לא פסלי תרומה וי"ל דאין דבר הנוגע בשרץ שלא יהא ראשון ובפ"ק דפסחים (ג"ז שם) הארכתי יותר:

אלא במשקין הבאין מחמת ידים · וא"ת ומה הוצרכו לגזירה זו דכיון דגזרו דידים פוסלות את התרומה א"כ משקין שנגעו בהן הוי תחלה דכל הפוסל את התרומה מטמא משקין להיות תחלה וי"ל דהאוכלים שנטמאו במשקין היינו · גזירה דכל הפוסל את התרומה ועד השתא לא נגזרה והא דקאמר במשקין הבאים מחמת ידים ה"ה מחמת כל פוסלי תרומה והא דקמהדר ר' יהושע לרבי אליעזר (חולין פ"ב דף לד·) מצינו שהשני עושה שני ע"י משקין ואע"ג דהשתא לא נגזרה מ"מ היה דעתן לגזור מיד:

אלא במשקין הבאים מחמת שרץ · אומר ר"י דה"ה דהוה מצי למנקט משקין הבאים מחמת ידים שגם הם מטמאים כלי לפסול תרומה כדאמר בברכות בפרק אלו דברים (דף נב·) ב"ש אומרים נוטלים לידים ואחר כך מוזגים את הכוס שאם מוזגים תחלה יטמאו משקין שאחורי הכוס מחמת ידים ויחזרו ויטמאו את הכוס אלא נקט משקים הבאים מחמת שרץ לאשמעינן דאפילו הנך לא הוי אלא מדרבנן:

שמאי והלל גזור · לא בעי לשנויי דשמאי והלל גזור בידים הבאות מחמת ספר ולא בסתם ידים דגזרו טומאה על הידים סתמא קתני דמשמע כל סתם ידים: **ואילו** שמאי והלל לא נחלקו אלא בג' דברים בלבד · ואם תאמר לימא דבג' דברים נחלקו ועמדו במחלוקתם ובשאר י"ח דברים נחלקו °ולמחר הושוו כדמשני לקמן כי פריך והא איכא בוצר לגת כו' הא שתיק ליה הלל לשמאי להכי לא מני לה בהדי ג' דברים וי"ל דלא דמי להתם דהבוצר לגת שתיק ליה הלל לשמאי והודה לו מיד באותו מעמד להכי לא חשיב אבל הכא דכל היום נחלקו ולא הושוו עד למחר לא הוה ליה למימר לא נחלקו ואע"ג דקצת משמע שהיו שמאי והלל עצמן ביום שגזרו י"ח דבר (דהא) כי היכי דקתני (דף יז·) גבי בוצר לגת אותו היום היה הלל כפוף ויושב לפני שמאי כו' וה"נ קתני בתוספתא דשבת גבי י"ח דברים מ"מ צריך לומר דשני מעשים הוו:
אלא

רש"י

ובא השמש וטהר · ומקמי הכא לא ואוקמינן להאי קרא בתרומה ביבמות בפ' הערל (ד' עד:) ואפי' לנגיעה אשכחן קרא התם *כל כלי אשר יעשה מלאכה בהם במים (א) וגו' והאי נגיעה היא ובעינן הערב שמש אלמא פסיל בנגיעה דאי לא פסיל למאי קרי ליה וטהר השתא מכלל דמעיקרא לא הוי טהור גמור והאי כלי לאו בר אכילה הוא ומיהו טמויי לא מטמינן דהא לאו טמא איקרי: סמי מכאן · הסר מכאן: מחמת שרץ · שנטמאו בשרץ: דאורייתא היא · שהמשקין ראשון והאוכל שני ופוסל תרומה להיות שלישי: דכתיב וכל משקה וגו' · ואע"ג דהאי במשקין הבאין מחמת אויר כלי חרס כתיב דהא כתיב לעיל מיניה כל אשר בתוכו יטמא מכל האוכל כלומר אם יש בתוכו אוכלין או משקין והני שניים נינהו שהכלי היה ראשון והם שניים והאוכל הנוגע בהן אינו פוסל את התרומה (א"ה) הא גמרינן משקין הבאין מחמת שרץ מינייהו בק"ו ובפ"ק דפסחים (דף יח:) וכיון דמקבלי טומאה מדאורייתא ממילא עבדי לאוכל שני דהכי גמרינן סדר טומאה התם דמשקה מטמא אוכל ואוכל משקה דלא משכחת רביעי בקדש אלא בהכי דהא אין טומאה עושה כיוצא בה לא להיות אוכל מטמא אוכל ולא משקה מטמא משקה ולא אוכל ומשקה מטמאין כלים דאין כלי מיטמא אלא באב הטומאה: מחמת ידים · לפני נטילה דגזרו רבנן בידים וכן בשאר כל פוסלי תרומה השויין לטמא משקין. להיות תחלה: גזירה משום משקין הבאים מחמת שרץ · דאשכחן בהן שהן ראשונים דאורייתא והא דגזור בכל טומאת משקין להיות תחלה ולא גזור נמי באוכלין גזירה משום אוכל הבא מחמת שרץ היינו טעמא דאחמיר רבנן במשקין משום דעלולין לקבל טומאה שאינן צריכין תיקון הכשר להביאן לידי טומאה אבל אוכלין צריכין תיקון נתינת מים להכשירן לקבלת טומאה כל הכשר שבש"ס לשון תיקון: משקה הזב · היוצא ממנו רוקו וזובו ומימי רגליו: וכי ירוק הזב וגו' · וכבס בגדיו אלמא אב הטומאה הוא לטמא אדם ובגדים דהיינו כלים ושאר משקין היוצאין ממנו גמרינן מרוק מה רוק מתאסף תחלה ואח"כ יוצא אף כל מתעגל ויוצא כגון מימי רגליו: מה שביד טהור טמאתי לך · אינו צריך כאן דטומאת משא ילפינן מיניה לרוק במסכת נדה (פ"ז דף נה:): אלא בבאין מחמת שרץ. דלאו אב הטומאה הן והכלי אינו מקבל טומאה אלא מאב הטומאה כדתניא בפסחים (דף כ·) יכול יהו כל הכלים מיטמאים מאויר כלי חרס ת"ל מכל האוכל וגו' אוכל ומשקה מיטמא מאויר כלי חרס כו' אלמא לא אתי כלי טמא ומטמא ליה וכ"ש אוכל ומשקה וגזור רבנן דליטמא לענין תרומה משום משקה זב וזבה שהן אב הטומאה: על ארץ העמים · ומשום ספק קברות שלהן דנכרי מטמא במגע ובמשא ואהל לרבנן *ולרבי שמעון נמי דאמר אין מטמאין באהל מטמאין הן במגע ובמשא ורקב: ועל כלי זכוכית · דלא כתיב באורייתא טומאה: תיקן כתובה · שיהא כותב לה כל נכסי אחראין לכתובה לפי שהיה מייחד לה כתובתה וכשהיה כועס עליה אומר לה טלי כתובתיך וצאי בכתובות בסוף האשה שנפלו (דף פב:): וגזרו טומאה על כלי מתכות · לקמן מפרש: שמאי וסיעתו כו' · והם עצמן היו עם תלמידיהם במחלוקת של י"ח דבר: ובי"ח דבר נחלקו · כלומר אותם י"ח שגזרו במחלוקת היו אלא שנמנו ונמצאו ב"ש רבים: שלשה מקומות · לקמן מפרש: לתלות · תרומה על מגען לא אוכלין ולא שורפין: לשריפה · שיהו שורפין תרומה עליהן: שלמה גזר · דכתיב (קהלת יב) ואזן וחקר שעשה אזנים לתורה כלומר סייג והרחקה ככפיפה זו שנוטלין אותה באזנים ואין נוגעין בה: עירובין · אזנים להוצאת שבת שאסור להוציא מרשותו לרשות חבירו ואע"פ ששניהם רה"י:
ולמחר

מסורת הש"ס
[שם עה.] [נדה נה:] [לקמן טז: ועי' כתובות פב:] [לקמן טז.] [שם:] עירובין כא: ע"ש [יבמות סא.]

הגהות הב"ח
(א) רש"י ד"ה ובא השמש וכו' אשר יעשה מלאכה בהם במים יובא וטמא עד הערב וטהר וגו' והאי נגיעה:

a first enacted?[1] [14b] But since this was first enacted, why was the other too needed?—Rather the latter was first decreed, and then it was enacted in respect of all hands.

'And a *ṭebul yom*.' But the law of *ṭebul yom* is Biblical, for it is written, *and when the sun is down, he shall be clean;* [*and afterwards he shall eat of the holy things*,[2] i.e., *terumah*]?—Delete *ṭebul yom* from here.

'And food which was defiled through liquid'. Through liquid of which [uncleanness]?[3] Shall we say, through liquid which was defiled by a [dead] reptile:[4] then its law is Biblical,[5] for it is written, *and all drink that may be drunk* [*in every such vessel shall be unclean*]?[6]—Rather it means through liquid defiled by the hands, and it is a preventive measure on account of liquid defiled by a reptile.[7]

'And vessels which were defiled by liquid'. Vessels which were defiled by liquid of which [uncleanness]?[8] Shall we say, by the liquid of a *zab*? But that is Biblical, for it is written, *and if the zab spit upon him that is clean;* [*then he shall wash his clothes, and bathe himself in water*],[9] [meaning] what is in the clean man's hand have I declared unclean unto thee![10] Rather it refers to liquid defiled by a reptile, and it is a preventive measure on account of the
b fluid of a *zab*.[1]

'And the hands'. Did then the disciples of Shammai and Hillel[2] decree this: [Surely] Shammai and Hillel [themselves] decreed it! For it was taught, Jose b. Jo'ezer of Ẓeredah[3] and Jose b. Joḥanan of Jerusalem[4] decreed uncleanness in respect of the country of the heathens and glassware.[5] Simeon b. Sheṭaḥ instituted the woman's marriage settlement[6] and imposed uncleanness upon metal utensils.[7] Shammai and Hillel decreed uncleanness for the hands. And should you answer, [It means] Shammai and his band and Hillel and his band [of scholars];[8] surely Rab Judah said in Samuel's name: They enacted eighteen measures, and they differed on
c eighteen measures,[1] whereas Hillel and Shammai differed only in three places; for R. Huna said, In three places they differed, and no more! And should you answer, They [Hillel and Shammai] came and decreed that it be suspended,[2] while their disciples came and decreed that it be burnt:[3] surely Ilfa said: The original decree concerning hands was for burning?—Rather, they [Hillel and Shammai] came and decreed it, yet it was not accepted from them; then their disciples came and decreed, and it was accepted from them.[4]

But still, Solomon decreed it! For Rab Judah said in Samuel's name, When Solomon instituted *'erubin*[5] and the washing of the hands, a Heavenly Echo came forth and declared, '*My son, if thine heart be wise; My heart shall be glad, even Mine*';[6] and '*My son, be wise, and make My heart glad, That I may answer him that reproacheth*

a (1) Viz., that hands in general are unclean. (2) Lev. XXII, 7. (3) I.e., how did this liquid itself become unclean? (4) Lit., 'which come on account of a reptile'. (5) *Sc.* that this food disqualifies *terumah*. (6) Ibid. XI, 34. Though that refers to a liquid defiled through an earthenware vessel, the Talmud deduces in Pes. 18*b* that the same holds good if it is defiled by a reptile. Now, the latter is original ('father of') uncleanness; the fluid is first degree, and the food is second degree, and therefore it renders *terumah* the third degree, i.e., unfit (v. *supra* 13*b*, n. b6), and all this is *Bibilical* law, not a Rabbinical enactment. (7) The latter is Biblical; but if the former were not declared unclean, it would be thought that the latter is not unclean either. (8) How did the liquid itself become unclean? (9) Ibid. XV, 8. (10) This interpretation is not really germane to the difficulty which arises directly from the verse; v. Rashi. Since the clothes are to be washed etc., the saliva must rank as original ('father of') uncleanness, for only such defiles garments and man. The vessels therefore defiled by the saliva (or any fluid emanating from a *zab*) are unclean in the first degree, and defile *terumah* by Biblical law.

b (1) The former is unclean in the first degree, and by Biblical law does not defile vessels (v. previous note); nevertheless the Rabbis enacted that it shall defile vessels, which in turn render *terumah* unfit, lest it might be confused with the fluid of a *zab*, which will also be held incapable of defiling vessels. (2) As is implied by the terms Beth Shammai, Beth Hillel. (3) A town in Persia; Neub. *Géogr.* p. 275. (4) Two Rabbis of the early Maccabean period (second century B.C.E.); together they formed the beginning of the *Zugoth* (duumvirate) which governed Jewish religious life until Hillel and Shammai. It may be observed that the title 'Rabbi' is not prefixed to their names: the famous letter of Sherira Gaon to Jacob b. Nissim, quoted by Nathan b. Jeḥiel in the *'Aruk* (s.v. אביי) declares that this title dates from the time of R. Joḥanan b. Zakkai only. (5) The former, to stem the emigration of Jews from Palestine consequent upon the troublous times of the Maccabees; and the latter probably because glassware was manufactured in those countries, or because they learnt at that time that its manufacture was similar to that of earthenware; Weiss, *Dor.* I, 105. (6) When a woman married, she brought a dowry to her husband, which was returnable if he divorced her. Originally the security for the return of the dowry was deposited with her father. This went through a number of changes until Simeon b. Sheṭaḥ enacted that the husband should trade with the dowry and mortgage all his effects for its repayment, the purpose being to make divorce more difficult. This is the meaning of the present passage, not that he actually instituted the marriage settlement itself; J. Keth. end of chapter VIII, and Weiss, *Dor.* I, 144 and note a.l. (7) This is discussed below. (8) I.e., enacted the eighteen measures.

c (1) I.e., these eighteen measures which they enacted jointly were originally subjects of controversy between them (Rashi). (2) I.e., that the hands are only suspected of uncleanness, and if they touch *terumah* it is 'suspended', and may neither be eaten, as clean, nor burnt as unclean. (3) Ruling that the hands are definitely unclean, not merely suspected. (4) The need for renewing some of the early Rabbinical enactments, to which reference is made in the present discussion, arose through the interdict which the Sadducees laid upon their observance; Weiss, *Dor*, 1, 143*f*; cf. Halevi, *Doroth*, I, 3, pp. 584 *seq*. (5) V. Glos. and *supra* 6*a*, n. b7. (6) Prov. XXIII, 15.

me'?[7] [15a]—Solomon came and decreed in respect of holy things,[8] while they came and instituted [it] in respect of *terumah*.

[To revert to] the main text: 'Rab Judah said in Samuel's name: They enacted eighteen measures, and differed in eighteen measures.' But it was taught: They were in agreement?—On that day they differed and [only] on the morrow were they in agreement.[9]

[To revert to] the main text: R. Huna said: In three places Shammai and Hillel differed: Shammai said: *Ḥallah*[10] is due from a *ḳab* [of flour]; Hillel said: From two *ḳabs*: but the Sages ruled neither as the one nor as the other, but a *ḳab* and a half is liable to *ḥallah*. When the measures were enlarged, they said, Five quarters of flour are liable to *ḥallah*. R. Jose said: [Exactly] five are exempt; just over five are liable.[1]

And the second?—Hillel said: A *hin* full of drawn water renders a *miḳweh* unfit. (For one must state [a dictum] in his teacher's phraseology). Shammai maintained: nine *ḳabs*. But the Sages ruled neither as one nor as the other, until two weavers[2] came from the dung gate of Jerusalem and testified on the authority of Shemaiah and Abṭalion that three *logs* of drawn water render a *miḳweh* unfit, and the Sages ratified their words.[3]

And the third?—Shammai said: All women, their time suffices them; Hillel maintained: From examination to examination; even if this covers many days; but the Sages ruled neither as the one nor as the other, but a full day[4] reduces [the time] between examination and examination, and [the time] between examination and examination reduces a full day.[5]

And are there no more? But there is [this]: Hillel said: One shall
b lay [hands]; while Shammai ruled that one must not lay [hands]?[1]—R. Huna spoke only of those concerning which there is no dispute of their teachers in addition.[2] But there is also [this:] When one vintages [grapes] for the vat [i.e., to manufacture wine], Shammai maintains: It is made fit [to become unclean]; while Hillel ruled: It is not made fit.[3]—That is excepted, for there Hillel was silenced by Shammai.[4]

'Jose b. Jo'ezer of Ẓeredah and Jose b. Joḥanan of Jerusalem decreed uncleanness in respect of the country of the heathens and glassware.' But the Rabbis of the 'eighty years' decreed this? For R. Kahana said, When R. Ishmael son of R. Jose fell sick, they [the Rabbis] sent [word] to him, 'Rabbi, tell us the two or three things which you stated [formerly] on your father's authority.' He sent back, 'Thus did my father say: One hundred and eighty years before the destruction of the Temple the wicked State [*sc.* Rome] spread over Israel.[5] Eighty years before the destruction of the Temple uncleanness was imposed in respect of the country of the heathens and glassware. Forty years before the destruction
c of the Temple the Sanhedrin went into exile[1] and took its seat in the Trade Halls.[2] (In respect to what law [is this stated]?—Said R. Isaac b. Abdimi, To teach that they did not adjudicate in laws of fines.[3] 'The laws of fines' can you think so![4] But say: They did not adjudicate in capital cases.)[5] And should you answer, They [Jose b. Jo'ezer and Jose b. Joḥanan] flourished during these eighty years too: surely it was taught: Hillel and Simeon [his son], Gamaliel and Simeon wielded their Patriarchate during one hundred years of the Temple's existence;[6] whereas Jose b. Jo'ezer

(7) Ibid. XXVII, 11. (8) That the hands must be washed before eating e.g., flesh of sacrifices. (9) V. Halevi, *Doroth*, I, p. 600 for a discussion of a variant which he considers correct. (10) V. Glos.

(1) 1 *ḳab* = four *logs* = 2197,4 cu.cm. The controversy centres on the interpretation of *'your dough'* in Num. XV, 20. The Talmud does not state when the measures were enlarged, but the enlargement was by one fifth, i.e., one 'Sepphoric' *log* (which was the name of the new measure) = one and one fifth Jerusalem *log*, as the old one was called; v. 'Ed., Ch. I, Mish. 2, n. 3. (2) V. Halevi, op. cit., p. 122, n. 59. (3) A *miḳweh* (v. Glos.) must be filled with 'living' water, as opposed to 'drawn' water, i.e., water drawn in vessels, and it must contain not less then forty *se'ahs*. The controversy refers to the quantity of drawn water which, if poured into the *miḳweh* before it contains forty *se'ahs* of 'living' water, renders it unfit. The *hin* is a Biblical measure, equal to twelve *logs*. The passage 'for one must state (a dictum) in his teacher's phraseology' is difficult, and various interpretations have been advanced. They are discussed by Halevi in *Doroth*, I, 3, 95-7, who explains it thus: The teachers referred to are not Shemaiah and Abṭalion, Hillel's masters in Palestine, but his Babylonian teachers (unnamed). Now *hin* is not the usual Mishnaic term but Biblical. This, however, was sometimes preferred to Babylonian because it was constant, whereas the Babylonian measure varied in different places (cf. *J.E.* XII, 488 s.v. Cab.). Thus Hillel said a *hin* full instead of twelve *logs*, in order to be faithful to his teacher's phraseology. V. 'Ed., Ch. I, Mish. 2 and notes. (4) Lit., 'from time to time', the technical phrase for a twenty-four hour day. (5) A menstruous woman defiles whatever food she touches. Shammai maintains that this is only from when she discovers her discharge, but not retrospectively. Hillel holds that since her discharge may have been earlier, though she has only now observed it, her uncleanness is retrospective to when she last examined and found herself clean. Thus Shammai said, Their time, *sc.* when they actually find that they are unclean, suffices them and it has no retrospective effects; whilst Hillel rules, They are retrospectively unclean from the present examination to the last. The Sages make a compromise: she is retrospectively unclean for twenty-four hours or from the last examination, whichever is less. V. 'Ed., IV, 1 and notes.

b (1) When a man brings a freewill-offering, part of the ritual consists in his laying hands upon the head of the animal (v. Lev. I, 4; III, 2, 8). The dispute refers to festivals. (2) This matter was disputed by Shammai and Hillel's predecessors too; v. Ḥag. 16a. For the importance of this particular question v. Frankel, *Darke ha-Mishnah*, p. 44; Weiss, *Dor*. I, 104. (3) V. *supra* 12a, nn. a1–4; the same applies to grapes. Now, if the grapes are to be eaten, the liquid they exude whilst being gathered does not subject them to uncleanness, since their owner is displeased therewith. But when they are vintaged for wine they differ; V. *infra* 17a for the full discussion. (4) I.e., he was unable to refute his proofs and accepted Shammai's ruling. (5) Judea appears to have entered into official relations with Rome for the first time in 161 B.C.E. at the instance of Judas Maccabeus; Margolis and Marx, *Jewish History*, p. 145. But the first step which laid Judea under subjection of Rome was the quarrel of Hyrcanus II and Aristobulus II over the throne, when both brothers appealed to Pompey (c. 66 C.E.). A date midway between these two is given here (110 B.C.E.) which may be assumed as merely approximate. This corresponds roughly to the death of Hyrcanus I in 106 B.C.E.

c (1) I.e., they forsook their locale in the Chamber of Hewn Stones in the Temple. (2) A place on the Temple Mount; *Ḥannuth*, v. Sanh., 41a, n. d11. (3) E.g., the fine for seduction, Deut. XXII, 29. (4) Any court in Palestine consisting of ordained judges was competent to adjudicate in laws of fine, whatever its locale. (5) V. Krauss, op. cit., pp. 23f. (6) I.e., Hillel commenced his Patriarchate a hundred years before the destruction of the Temple, and he was followed by Simeon, Gamaliel and Simeon, his direct descendants, the four spreading over that century. V. Halevi, *Doroth*, I, 3, pp. 706 *seq*.

*שלמה גזר לקדשים ואתו אינהו וגזור אף לתרומה גופא אמר רב יהודה אמר שמואל י"ח גזרו ובי"ח נחלקו והתניא הושוו בו ביום נחלקו ולמחר הושוו גופא אמר רב הונא בג' מקומות נחלקו שמאי והלל *שמאי אומר מקב חלה והלל אומר מקביים וחכמים אומרים לא כדברי זה ולא כדברי זה אלא [א]קב ומחצה חייב בחלה משהגדילו המדות אמרו חמשת רבעים קמח חייבין בחלה ר' יוסי אומר ה' פטורין ה' ועוד חייבין ואידך *הלל אומר מלא הין מים שאובים פוסלים את המקוה *שחייב אדם לומר בלשון רבו שמאי אומר תשעה קבין וחכמים אומרים לא כדברי זה ולא כדברי זה עד שבאו ב' גרדיים משער האשפה שבירושלים והעידו משום שמעיה ואבטליון [ב]שלשה לוגין מים שאובין פוסלים את המקוה וקיימו חכמים את דבריהם ואידך *שמאי אומר כל הנשים דיין שעתן והלל אומר מפקידה לפקידה ואפילו לימים הרבה וחכמים אומרים לא כדברי זה ולא כדברי זה אלא [ג]מעת לעת ממעט ע"י מפקידה לפקידה ומפקידה לפקידה ממעט על יד מעת לעת ותו ליכא והאיכא *הלל אומר לסמוך ושמאי אומר שלא לסמוך כי קאמר רב הונא היכא דליכא פלוגתא דרבוותא בהדייהו והאיכא *הבוצר לגת שמאי אומר הוכשר והלל אומר לא הוכשר בר מיניה דההיא דהתם קא שתיק ליה הלל לשמאי: יוסי בן יועזר איש צרידה ויוסי בן יוחנן איש ירושלים גזרו טומא' על ארץ העמים ועל כלי זכוכית: והא רבנן דשמנים שנה גזור *דאמר רב כהנא כשחלה ר' ישמעאל בר' יוסי שלחו לו ר' אמור לנו ב' וג' דברים שאמרת(א) (לנו) משום אביך שלח להם כך אמר אבא ק"פ שנה עד שלא חרב הבית פשטה מלכות הרשעה על ישראל פ' שנה עד שלא חרב הבית גזרו טומאה על ארץ העמים ועל כלי זכוכית מ' שנה עד שלא חרב הבית גלתה לה סנהדרין וישבה לה בחנויות למאי הילכתא א"ר יצחק בר אבדימי לומר שלא דנו דיני קנסות ס"ד אלא אימא שלא דנו דיני נפשות וכי תימא בפ' שנה נמי אינהו הוו והתניא הלל ושמעון גמליאל ושמעון נהגו נשיאותן *(לפני) הבית מאה שנה ואילו יוסי בן יועזר איש צרידה ויוסי בן יוחנן הוו קדמי טובא

אלא

ולמחר הושוו. שחזרו בהן ב"ה: קב ומחצה. ירושלמי' שהן ז' לוגין ובילה וחומש בילה למדה מדברית והוא עומר לגלגולת עשירית האיפה שחייב בחלה כדכתיב עריסותיכם כדי עיסת מדבר והוסיפו שתות בירושלים נמלא שש מדבריות נכנסות בחמש ירושלמיות ולוג הנשאר ובילה וחומש בילה עולין ללוג ירושלמי שהלוג מדברי ששה בילים נכנסין בחמשה בילים גדולים נמלא הלוג חסר בילה גדולה תן בילה וחומש בילה תחת בילה גדולה שהחומש הוא שתות מלבר [טוסף] על הבילה נמלאו ששה בילים גדולים שהן לוג גדול הרי הן ששה לוגים ירושלמי' דהן קב ומחצה: משהגדילו המדות. היא מדת לפורי שטודפ' שתות על ירושלמית* נמלאו הו' לוגין ה': ה' רבעים. לוגין שהן רביעית הקב: חמשה ועוד חייבין. דסבר רבי יוסי מדה מדברית היו בילים גדולים משלנו והכי נמי א"ר יוסי בעירובין בפרק כילד משתתפין (דף פג:) כמה שיעור חלי פרס שני בילים שוחקות והתם מפרש האי ועוד אחד מכ' בבילה לכל בילה: הין. י"ב לוג: פוסלין. אם נפלו לתוכן קודם שנשלם אבל אם נשלם שוב אינו נפסל ואפילו המשיך לתוכן אחרי כן אלף סאה: שחייב אדם כו'. כלומר הין אינו לשון משנה אלא לשון תורה אלא כך שמעה מפי שמעיה ואבטליון ורבותי מפרשין [בלשון] משה רבינו ולבי מגמגם שהרי בכמה מקומות לא הקפיד על כך: שני גרדיים משער האשפות. במסכת עדיות* מפ' למה הוזכר שם אומנותם ושם מקומם לומר שלא ימנע אדם עלמו מבית המדרש שאין לך אומנות פחותה מגרדי שאין מעמידין ממנו לא כהן גדול ולא מלך כדאמרינן בקדושין (דף פב.) ואין שער בירושלים פחות משער האשפות והכריעו בעדותן כל חכמי ישראל: כל הנשים. הרואות דם: דיין שעתן. לטמא טהרות משעת ראייתן ואילך: מפקידה לפקידה. למפרע בדקה היום ומצאתה טהורה ובדקה לסוף שבוע ומצאתה טמאה חוששין למגעה מבדיקה ראשונה ואילך שמא עם סילוק ידיה ראתה: מעת לעת ממעט על יד מפקידה לפקידה. שני זמנים הוזכרו בה למפרע להלך אחר הקל שבהן אם מפקידה לפקידה יתר על מעת לעת הלך אחר מעת לעת ואם מעת לעת יתר על מפקידה לפקידה הלך אחר הפקידה · ממעט על יד · ממעט אחריו: לסמוך. פלוגתא היא *דב"ש וב"ה גבי מביאין נדרים ונדבות וסומכין בי"ט: כי קאמר רב הונא היכא דליכא פלוגתא דרבוותא. שלש מקומות שאמר רב הונא לא נחלקו בהן רבותיהן הראשונים אבל סמיכה כל האבות ב"ד (ב) והנשיאים מיוסי בן יועזר עד הלל נחלקו בה במסכת חגיגה: הבוצר. ענבים לדורכן בגת דאילו הבוצר לצימוקין משקה היוצא מהם אין מכשירים דלא ניחא ליה. שמאי אומר הוכשרו. ביין הנדלף מהן על גביהן ואע"ג דאזיל לאיבוד לארץ ששותת מן הסלים גזירה שמא יבצרנו בקופות מזופפות כדמפרש לקמיה (דף יז:): הא שתיק ליה הלל. ולא עמד במחלוקתו כדתניא בפרקין (שם) אותו היום היה הלל כפוף כו': המלכות. הרשעה רומי: פשטה. התחילו לכובשן: הלל ושמעון. רבן שמעון בנו של הלל היה: ורבן גמליאל. הוא רבן גמליאל הזקן: ושמעון. הוא (ג) רבי שמעון הנהרג עם הרוגי מלכות והוא היה אביו של ר"ג דלעזריה לרבי יהושע בן חנניה (ברכות פ"ד דף כז:) ושעשה מחלוקת עם ר"א בן הורקנוס (ב"מ פ"ד דף נט:): בפני הבית. בעוד הבית קיים: ק' שנה. אחרונים שלפני החורבן התחיל נשיאותו של הלל ופרנסו אלו ארבע דורות ק' שנה אלמא הלל קודם לחורבן ק' שנה: ואילו יוסי בן יועזר. קדים להלל כמה דורות במסכת אבות:

אלא שלמה גזר לקדשים. תימה דבפ"ק דפסחים (דף יט: ושם) קאמר רבי עקיבא זכינו שאין טומאת ידים במקדש ופריך ולימא שאין טומאת ידים וכלים במקדש ומשני רב יהודה ידים קודם גזירת כלים נשנית א"ל רבה והא תרוייהו בו ביום גזרו דתנן הספר והידים והכלים כו' והשתא מאי קפריך רבה והא ידים דקדש דמיירי התם שלמה גזר וכלים גזרו בי"ח דבר ויש לומר דר"ע א"ח דבר קאי שהיה מחדש וה"ק זכינו שכשעסקו בי"ח דבר בדיני ידים שלא רצו לגזור טומאת ידים במקדש ורב יהודה דשני ידים קודם גזרת כלים נשנית דהיינו בימי שלמה ולהכי לא נקט ר"ע אלא ידים משום דלעולם הוי (ד) זה זכות במקדש אפילו בימי שלמה אפילו הכי חוזר ומקשה לו רבה והא תרווייהו כו' משום דלא משמע ליה לישנא הכי:

שלמה גזר כו'. והשתא לא הוי צריך לשנויי דאינהו גזור ולא קבלו מינייהו אלא אינהו גזור לתלות כו' ואילפא קאמר דידים דגזור שלמה תחלתן לשריפה אלא משמע ליה דקאי אילפא אי"ח דבר [ת"י]:

שמאי אומר מקב לחלה הלל אומר מקביים. בירושלמי מפרש טעמא דשמאי והלל משום דאיפה י"ח קבים ועשירית מלבר היינו ב' קבין ובאותו שיעור לריך להפריש חלה להלל ומאי סבר דלריך ב' חלות לעומר שהיו עושין ממנו ב' אכילות אחת בבוקר ואחת בערב וכשיעור אכילה אחת חשיב שמאי עיסת מדבר:

רבי יוסי אומר ה' פטורין ה' ועוד חייבין. דקסבר ראשית עריסותיכם שכשיפרישו חלה שעדיין ישאר כדי עיסת מדבר ואור"ת דאין למחוק בפרק כלל גדול (לקמן דף עו.) ובפ' אלו עוברין (פסחים דף מח.) דמייתי התם חמשה רבעים ועוד חייבין בחלה דאתיא כר' יוסי*:

אלא שלא דנו דיני נפשות. תימה דוקמת ועלית אל המקום דדרשינן מיניה (סנהדרין יד: פז.) מלמד שהמקום גורם לא כתיב אלא בזקן ממרא ובזקן ממרא גופיה לא כתיב אלא בהמראתו שלריך שימרה עליהם במקומן אבל לדון יכול אע"פ שאין ב"ד הגדול בלשכת הגזית ואין נראה לומר דבעינן שיהיו במקומן בשעת עבירה כמו בזקן ממרא דהא בזקן ממרא לא על המראתו לבד מיחייב אלא עד שיחזור לעירו ועשה כהוראתו והאיא לא כתיב מקום ועוד דלא מלינו בשום מקום שהיו בודקין אם היו ב"ד בלשכת הגזית בשעת עבירה אם לאו*:

אתו

עין משפט נר מצוה

קיד א מיי' פ"ח מהלכות שאר אבות הטומאות הלכה ה

קטו ב מיי' פ"ו מהלכות בכורים הלכה טו סמג עשין קמא טור שו"ע או"ח סימן תנו סעיף א ועור שו"ע יו"ד סימן שכד סעיף א:

קטז ג מיי' פ"ד מהלכות מקואות הלכה ב סמג עשין רמח טור שו"ע יו"ד סימן רא סעיף טו:

קיז ד מיי' פ"ג מהלכות טומאת משכב ומושב הלכה ד סמג עשין רמג:

עדיות פ"א מ"ג

[ברכות מז. וש"נ]

עדיות פ"א מ"ה נדה ב.

רבינו חננאל

אמר רב יהודה אמר שמואל בג' מקומות נחלקו שמי והלל שמי אומר מקב חלה כו' וכולן מפורשים במשנתנו בתחלת עדיות והיא מסכת בחירתא: ארץ העמים יוסי בן יועזר איש צרדה ויוסי בן יוחנן איש ירושלים גזרו על

[וע"ע תוס' עירובין פג: ד"ה שבעה ותוס' פסחים מח: ד"ה חמשה]

[נ"ל בפני]

[וע"ע תוס' ע"ז ח: ד"ה מלמד כו' ותוס' סנהדרין יד: ד"ה מלמד]

רב נסים גאון

מלא הין מים שאובין פוסלין את המקוה שיעור ההין י"ב לוג והקב יש בו ד' לוגין הנה בפ' קבין ל"ו לוג ופירושן מבואר במס' עדיות ובתלמוד בפרק ערבי פסחים וקבא מנלן דארבע לוגי הויא דתניא (עדיות פ"א) הלל אומר מלא הין מים שאובין פוסלין את המקוה וכמה הין י"ב לוג שמאי אומר ט' קבין שהן ל"ו לוג אלמא קבא ארבעה לוגי הויא ולוגא מנלן דארבעה רביעתא הויא דתניא (מנחות דף פט) הין וחצי הין ושלישית ההין ורביעית ההין לוג וחצי לוג ורביעית אלמא לוג ארבעה רביעיתא הויא ובגמרא דשתי מדות אמרו (שם דף פט) והין תריסר לוגי הוי דכתיב יהיה זה בגימטריא י"ב לוגי הואי:

מסורת הש"ס

עדיות פ"א מ"ב

נמלא הו' לוגין חמש שהן ה' רביעי הקב שהקב ד' לוגין כצ"ל וכ"ה בפי' הברטנור' [אולם לפי הגה' מהרש"ל לוגין ה' הוא ס"ד כאשר לפנינו וכ"ע ובד"ה ה' רבעים צריך למחוק אות ה' וכ"ה בדפוס ישן]

חגיגה טז.

[בתוספ' פ"א]

[לק"ן יז. ע"ז לט: חולין לו:]

ע"ז ח:

הגהות הב"ח

(א) גמ' וג' דברים שאמרת משום כצ"ל ותיבת לנו נמחק: (ב) רש"י ד"ה כי קאמר וכו' האבות ב"ד עם הנשיאים וכו' במסכת חגיגה כ"ב פ' אין דורשין דט"ז סוף ע"א: (ג) ד"ה ושמעון הוא שנקרא רשב"ג הנהרג עם הרוגי: (ד) תוס' ד"ה אלא וכו' הוי זכות זה במקדש:

אלא אתו *אינהו גזור אגושא לשרוף ואאוירא ולא כלום ואתו רבנן דפ' שנה גזור אאוירא לתלות למימרא (א) דחדא גזירתא הוה לשריפה *והאמר אילפא ידים תחלת גזירתן לשריפה ידים הוא דתחלת גזירתן לשריפה הא מידי אחרינא לא אלא אתו אינהו גזור אגושא לתלות ואאוירא ולא כלום ואתו רבנן דפ' שנה גזור אגושא לשרוף ואאוירא לתלות ואכתי באושא גזור *דתנן בעל ו' ספקות שורפין את התרומה על ספק בית הפרס ועל ספק עפר הבא מארץ העמים °ועל ספק בגדי עם הארץ ועל ספק כלים הנמצאין ועל ספק הרוקין ועל ספק מי רגלי אדם שכנגד מי רגלי בהמה געל ודאי מגען *(ועל) ספק טומאתן שורפין את התרומה ר' יוסי אומר אף על ספק מגען ברה"י שורפין וחכ"א ברה"י תולין ברה"ר טהורין ואמר עולא אלו ו' ספיקות באושא התקינו אלא אתו אינהו גזור אגושא לתלות ואאוירא ולא כלום ואתו רבנן דשמנים שנה גזור אידי ואידי לתלות ואתו באושא גזור אגושא לשרוף ואאוירא כדקאי קאי: דכלי זכוכית מ"ט גזור בהו רבנן טומאה *א"ר יוחנן אמר ר"ל הואיל ותחלת ברייתן מן החול שוינהו רבנן ככלי חרס אלא מעתה הלא תהא להן טהרה במקוה אלמה תנן *ואלו וחוצצין בכלים הזפת והמור בכלי זכוכית הכא במאי עסקינן כגון שניקבו והטיף לתוכן אבר ור"מ היא דאמר *הכל הולך אחר המעמיד °דתניא *כלי זכוכית שנקבו והטיף לתוכן אבר אמר רבן שמעון ב"ג ר"מ מטמא וחכמים מטהרין אלא מעתה לא

רש"י

אתו אינהו · יוסי (ב) ויוסי: גזור אגושא לשרוף · תרומה הנוגעת בגוש העפר: ואאוירא לתלות · תרומה הנכנסת באוירא ואין דבר מפסיק בינתים כגון שידה פרועה מתחתיה: ואכתי · אגושא לשרוף באושא גזור: על ספק בית הפרס · כלומר על ספקו של בית הפרס כגון תרומה שנכנסת לבית הפרס דהוא שדה שאבד בה קבר היינו ספק דלא ידעינן אם האהילה. על הקבר אם לאו: ועל ספיקו של עפר ארץ העמים· דכל עפר ארץ העמים מספקא לן בקבר של מת: ועל ספיקו של בגדי עם הארץ· דכולהו מספקא לן שמא ישבה עליהם אשתו נדה כדתנן (חגיגה דף יח:) בגדי ע"ה מדרס לפרושים: ועל ספק כלים הנמצאים· דלא ידעינן אם טמאים הן: ספק רוקין · כל רוקין מספקא לן דדילמא דזב נינהו: ועל ספק מי רגלי אדם· הך ספק לא דמי להנך דלעיל אלא אפי' מספקא לן אם מי רגלי אדם הן אם מי רגלי בהמה הן דאיכא תרי ספיקי לקולא דאם תמצי לומר דאדם שמא טהור: שכנגד מי רגלי בהמה· רבותא אשמעינן דלא תימא מדהני דבהמה הני נמי דבהמה: ודאי מגען וספק טומאתן· יודע ודאי שנגע בהן תרומה אבל אינו יודע אם הם טמאים אם לאו כדמפרש בכולהו: שורפים·והיינו אגושא:באושא התקינו· כמה שנים אחר חורבן כדאמרינן בר"ה (פ"ד דף לא·) גבי י' מסעות נסעה שכינה: ואלו חוצצין · לגבי טבילה: הזפת והמור גרסינן: בכלי זכוכית · שהן חלקין ואין אדם מקפיד על טיט ודבר אחר הנדבק בהן לפי שנופל מאיליו והני הוא דמדבקי טובא וקפיד עלייהו ואין חוצץ אלא דבר המקפיד עליו: כגון שנקבו · וטהרו מתורת כלי חרס דכלי חרס שבירתו מטהרתו: והטיף לתוכו אבר · דחשיב ליה ככלי מתכות דכל קבלת טומאתו משום אבר המעמידו הלכך אית ליה טהרה במקוה: מטמא · ולא אמרינן בטיל ליה מתורת כלי כשאר כלי חרס הנשבר דקסבר הלך אחר המעמיד ותורת כלי מתכות עליו: אלא מעתה · הואיל ושוינהו ככלי חרס:

נתר

תוספות

אתו אינהו גזור אגושא לשרוף כו' · וקשה דמכלי זכוכית לא תירץ כלום אפי' לפי המסקנא דהא ליכא למימר דמעיקרא גזור אזכוכית לתלות ולבסוף גזור לשרוף כדמסקינן אגושא דאכלי זכוכית לא שורפים כדאמרינן לקמן דעבוד רבנן היכרא דלא לישרוף עליה תרומה וקדשים וי"ל דדוקא בטומאת גבן אמר לקמן דאין שורפין תרומה וקדשים דאינו טמא אלא משום דמדמי להו לכלי מתכות אבל שאר טומאות המטמאין מתורת כלי חרס שפיר שורפים תרומה וקדשים דהא דמו לגמרי לכלי חרס וכן בלאו הכי צריך לפרש כן לקמן ולספרים דגרסי הכא אלא מעיקרא גזור ולא קבלו מינייהו ואתו רבנן דשמונים שנה וגזרו וקבלו מינייהו למימרא דחדא גזרה הואי לשרוף והאמר אילפא כו' אתי שפיר דכלי זכוכית נמי בשינויא קמא תירץ: ואאוירא לתלות · תימה דתנן במסכת אהלות (פ"ב מ"ג) אלו מטמאין במגע ובמשא ולא באהל עצם כשעורה וארץ העמים °וי"ל דהתם מיירי כגון שהביא עפר מארץ העמים לארץ ישראל אי נמי כר' שמעון דאמר *קברי עכו"ם אין מטמאין באהל דלא החמירו בארץ העמים יותר מקבריהם ועוד תירץ דההיא משנה נשנית קודם גזירה שגזרו על אוירה אלא על גושא בלבד וכן משמע מדקאמר על גושא לתלות ועל אוירה ולא כלום ואמאי קאמר ועל אוירה ולא כלום לימא דמעיקרא גזרו על תרוייהו לתלות ולבסוף גזרו על גושא לשרוף ועל אוירה כדקאי קאי אלא משום דמוכח ממתניתין דאהלות דמתחלה כשגזרו על גושא לא גזרו על אוירה והא דבעי בנזיר בפרק כהן גדול (דף נד: ושם) ארץ העמים משום אוירה גזרו עליה או משום גושא גזרו עליה הא פשיטא דאאוירה נמי גזרו כדקאמר הכא אלא התם ה"פ משום אוירה (ג) גזרו עליה שלא יכנס באויר ארץ העמים בשום ענין אפי' ע"י שידה תיבה ומגדל או משום גושא שהוא מאהיל על הגוש אבל כשאינו מאהיל על הגוש כגון ע"י שידה תיבה ומגדל טהור*:

על ששה ספקות שורפין · אומר ר"י דאפי' איכא ספקות יותר ששורפין את התרומה עליהן כגון סככות ופרעות וכיוצא באלו הכא לא חשיב אלא הנהו דתקינו באושא:

על ספק בית הפרס · נראה לר"י דמיירי בשדה שנחרש בה קבר דטהור מדאורייתא ולא חיישינן לעצם כשעורה ולא הוי אלא מדרבנן אבל שדה שאבד בה קבר הוי ספיקא דאורייתא כדמוכח במ"ק (ד' ה:) וא"כ לחכמים אמאי קאמרי אף ספק מגע ברשות היחיד תולין והתנן בפ' ו' דטהרות דכל ספקות ברשות היחיד טמא: ועל בגדי עם הארץ · דגזרו עליהם שיהיו כזבין לכל דבריהם ואפילו רוק שלו טמא דאמר בפ' בתרא דחגיגה (ד' כג·) גזירה משום ליטורא דעם הארץ ואפילו טמא מת רוק שלו אינו טמא אלא שעשאוהו כזב לבד מהיסט ומדרס שלא גזרו עליו כדתנן במסכת טהרות (פ"ז משנה ו) דקתני התם בגנבים שנכנסו לבית אין טמא אלא מקום רגלי הגנבים ומה הן מטמאין אוכלים ומשקין אבל כלי חרס המוקף למיד פתיל ומשכבות ומושבות טהור ואם יש עמהן נכרי או אשה הכל טמא ובהניזקין (גטין דף סא: ושם) משמע נמי הכי דפריך וליחוש שמא תסיטם אשתו נדה משמע דהוא אינו מטמא בהיסט ועל ספק רוקין נמי דקאמר דחיישינן שמא של עם הארץ הן שרוקו טמא היינו כדפרישית ולא כפ"ה דפירש דבגד ע"ה טמא דחיישינן שמא ישבה עליו אשתו נדה: ועל ספק מי רגלי אדם שכנגד מי רגלי בהמה·פ"ה דספק ספיקא הוא וקשה דבפרק בנות כותים (נדה דף נג: ושם) תנן דאין שורפין עליהן תרומה מפני שטומאתן בספק ורמינהו על ו' ספקות שורפין כו' ומשני דמתני' דהתם מיירי דאיכא ספק ספיקא ומש"ה אין שורפין ולפירוש הקונטרס הא על ספק מי רגלי אדם שורפין אע"ג דהוי ספק ספיקא ונראה לר"י דנקט מי רגלי בהמה משום דכשהן זה אצל זה הן ניכרות טפי שהן של אדם וליכא אלא ספק אחד: אלמה תנן אלו חוצצין בכלים · וליכא למימר דההיא טבילה בכלים חדשים מיירי כשקונים מן הנכרים כדאמר בסוף מסכת ע"ז (דף עה:) דלריכי טבילה דהא קתני סיפא בפ"ט דמסכת מקוואות (משנה ה) על השלחן ועל הטבלא ועל הדרגש (ועל הדולבקי) חוצצין: ורבי מאיר היא דאמר הכל הולך אחר המעמיד · ובפרק במה אשה (לקמן דף נט:) דקתני שהיה רבי נחמיה אומר בטבעת הלך אחר חותמה בעול הלך אחר סמלוניו בסולם הלך אחר שליבותיו כו' וחכמים אומרים הכל הולך אחר המעמיד לא מייתי הכא דהכא קרי מעמיד זה מה שנותנין לתוכם והתם קרי מעמיד דבר המעמיד כלי עצמו כגון עמודי סולם שמחברים את השליבות: וחכמים מטהרין · ואם תאמר והיכי מוכח מהכא דרבי מאיר סבר הכל הולך כו' דילמא הא דמטמא ר' מאיר משום דחשיב סתימה מעלייתא ומטמא מדין כלי זכוכית ולא מדין כלי מתכות וחכמים לא חשבו ליה כתימה מעלייתא ולכך מטהרים לגמרי ויש לומר דמסתבר ליה דלכולי עלמא הוי כתימה מעלייתא ופליגי דר' מאיר מטמא טומאה דאורייתא מדין כלי מתכות דסבר הכל הולך אחר המעמיד וחכמים מטהרין מדאורייתא אבל מדרבנן מיהא טמא לפי שגזרו על כלי זכוכית דסתימה מעלייתא היא אבל אין לפרש דרבנן מטהרין

רבינו חננאל

· גושה שהוא קרקע עצמו כדכתיב (איוב ז) וגוש עפר לתלות כלומר טומאתה בספק לפיכך קדשים הנוגעים בה תולין לא אוכלין ולא שורפין ועל אוירן ולא כלום כלומר אם נכנסה התרומה בשידה תיבה ומגדל ולא נחה בקרקע הרצה לארץ אלא באוירה ולא כלום ורבנן דשמוני' שנה גזרו על אוירה נמי לתלות ואתו רבנן דבאושא גזרו תרומה שנגעה בגוש חוצה לארץ לשרפה ועל אוירה כדקאי [קאי] לתלות . על כלי זכוכית מ"ט גזרו יוסי בן יועזר ויוסי בן יוחנן טומאה בהן א"ר שמעון בן לקיש הואיל ותחלת ברייתן מן החול שינהו רבנן ככלי חרס ואקשינן אם ככלי חרס הן לא יטהרו במקוה אלמה תנן ואלו חוצצין בכלים הזפת והמור בכלי זכוכית (ושביק) מכלל שאם אין עליה דבר חוצץ עלתה להן טבילה תאשרו ושנינן האי בכלי זכוכית שניקבו והטיפו לתוכן אבר וסתם תנא והעמ' ומשקן טלצאת

עין משפט נר מצוה

קיח א מיי' פי"א מהל' טומאת מת הלכה א ב:

קיט ב ג מיי' פי"ג מהלכות אבות הטומאות הלכה יג:

קכ ד ה ו מיי' פ"א מהל' כלים הל' ה:

מסורת הש"ס

[לעיל יד:] · נדה נג: טהרות פ"ד מ"ה · [נ"ל שהוא וכן איתא במשנה] · [יבמות סא.] · בסו"י ליתא א"ר יוחנן · מקוואות פ"ט [משנה ה] · [לקמן ס.] · ר"ס יט. ע"ש · פ' ע הוספות גיטין ח: ד"ה דגזרו]

הגהות הב"ח

(א) גמרא למימרא דתחלה חדא גזירתא: (ב) רש"י ד"ה אתו אינהו יוסי ויוסף: (ג) תוס' ד"ה ואאוירא וכו' ה"פ משום אוירא ממש גזרו:

גליון הש"ס

גמ' ועל ספק בגדי ע"ה. עי' נדה דף לד ע"א תוד"ה והוא: שם דתני' כלי זכוכית. עיין פרק בתרא דכלים מ"ג: תוס' ד"ה ואאוירא וכו' וי"ל דהתם מיירי כגון שהביא עפר. עי' סנהדרין דף י"ב ע"א תוס' ד"ה חושין:

of Ẓeredah and Jose b. Joḥanan were much earlier![7] [15b] Rather say: They came and decreed in respect to a clod, that it be burnt,[8] but nothing at all in respect to the atmosphere;[9] while the Rabbis of the eighty years came and decreed in respect to the atmosphere that it [*terumah*] be suspended.[10] Shall we say that the original enactment was for burning? Surely Ilfa said: The original decree concerning hands was for burning. Thus, only concerning hands was the original decree for burning, but concerning nothing else?—Rather say: They came and decreed in respect to a clod, that it be suspended, and nothing at all in respect to the atmosphere; and then the Rabbis of these eighty years came and decreed in respect to a clod that it be burnt and in respect to the atmosphere that it be suspended. Yet still, that[11] was decreed in
a Usha?[1] For we learnt: *Terumah* is burnt on account of six doubtful cases [of uncleanness]:—[i] The doubt of *Beth ha-Peras;*[2] [ii] The doubt of earth which comes from the land of the heathens;[3] [iii] The doubt attached to the garments of an *'am ha-arez;*[4] [iv] the doubt of vessels which are found;[5] [v] doubtful saliva;[6] and [vi] the doubtful human urine near cattle urine.[7] On account of their certain contact, which is doubtful defilement, *terumah* is burnt.[8] R. Jose said: It is burnt even on account of their doubtful contact in a private domain.[9] But the Sages maintain: [If there is doubtful contact] in a private domain we suspend it; in public ground, it [the *terumah*] is clean. Now 'Ulla observed, These six cases of doubt were enacted at Usha![10]—Rather say: They [Jose b. Jo'ezer and Jose b. Joḥanan] came and decreed suspense in respect of a clod and nothing at all in respect of atmosphere; then the Rabbis of the eighty years came and decreed suspense in both cases; then they came at Usha and decreed burning in respect of a clod, and as to the atmosphere they left it in *statu quo*.

Why did the Rabbis impose uncleanness upon glassware?—Said R. Joḥanan in the name of Resh Laḳish, Since it is manufactured
b from[1] sand, the Rabbis declared it the same as earthenware.[2] If so, let them be incapable of purification in a *miḳweh?*[3] Why then did we learn, And the following interpose in utensils: pitch and myrrh gum in the case of glass vessels?[4]—The circumstances here[5] are e.g., they were perforated, and molten lead was poured into them, this agreeing with R. Meir, who maintained, Everything depends on the support.[6] For it was taught: If glass vessels are perforated and [molten] lead is poured into them,—said R. Simeon b. Gamaliel: R. Meir declares them

(7) V. *supra* 14b, n. b4. (8) *Sc. terumah* which came into contact with a clod of earth from the 'land of the heathens', as something definitely unclean. (9) When *terumah* enters the atmosphere of the 'land of the heathen' with nothing intervening between it and the ground. (10) On 'suspended' v. *supra* 14b, n. c2. (11) The enactment of burning in respect to a clod.

a (1) A city in Galilee, near Sepphoris and Tiberias, and the scene of an important Rabbinical synod or synods about the time of the Hadrianic persecution in the middle of the second century C.E. V. *J.E.* 'Synod of Usha'. (2) A field one square *peras* (*peras* = half the length of a furrow = fifty cubits) in area, declared unclean because a grave was ploughed in it and the crushed bones scattered over the field, so that their exact position is not known. If *terumah* enters its atmosphere it must be burnt, though it is doubtful whether it was actually over the crushed bones. (3) I.e., any earth which comes thence. (4) V. *supra* 13a, n. a1. His garments are doubtful, because his wife may have sat upon them while a menstruant; v. Ḥag. 18b. (5) And it is unknown whether they are clean or not. (6) All saliva found is suspected of uncleanness, as it may be of a *zab*; v. *supra* 14b, n. a10. (7) This is not the same as the preceding, where the substances themselves were not in doubt; e.g., the object was definitely a utensil, or saliva. Here, however, there is a double doubt; it may not be human urine at all, but cattle urine; and even if it is, it may not be a *zab*'s (only his defiles). Yet the Rabbis ruled it definitely unclean, even when found near cattle urine, so that it might be supposed that this is the same. (8) If *terumah* comes definitely into contact (or as explained in n. 2) with these, which renders it doubtfully unclean, it is burnt. (9) Cf. *supra* 6b, n. a5. (10) The difficulty arises from ii.

b (1) Lit., 'the beginning of its making'. (2) Other edd. omit 'R. Joḥanan said in the name of', reading simply Resh Laḳish. It is certainly unlikely that R. Joḥanan, who, as head of the Academy at Tiberias enjoyed a superiority over Resh Laḳish, his contemporary, would report his statement. (3) Just as earthenware. (4) Miḳ. IX, 5. When a utensil is purified in a *miḳweh*, nothing must interpose between it and the water; if it does, the immersion is ineffective: pitch and gum on the side of a glass vessel constitute an interposition. (5) In Miḳ. IX, 5. (6) The perforated glass vessel is supported by the lead, i.e., it can be used only through the lead. Hence, according to R. Meir, it is a *metal*, not a glass vessel.

unclean, while the Sages declare them clean.[7] If so,[8] [16a] let them not become unclean through their [flat or convex] backs.[9] Why did we learn, Earthen vessels and *nether* vessels[10] are alike in regard to their uncleanness: they become defiled and defile [other objects] through their air space;[11] they become unclean through their
a outside,[1] but they cannot be defiled through their backs;[2] and their breaking renders them clean.[3] Thus, only earthen and *nether* vessels are alike in regard to their uncleanness, but not other things?[4]—I will tell you: since they can be repaired when broken,[5] they were assimilated to metal utensils.[6]

If so, let them revert to their former uncleanness, like metal utensils? For we learnt: Metal vessels, both flat and hollow,[7] are subject to defilement. If broken, they become clean; if remade into utensils, they revert to their former uncleanness. Whereas in respect to glass vessels we learnt: Wooden, skin, bone and glass utensils, if flat, they are clean;[8] if hollow, they are unclean;[9] if broken, they become clean; if remade into vessels, they are liable to defilement from then onwards. [Thus] only from then onwards, but not retrospectively?—The uncleanness of glass utensils is Rabbinical, and [the resuscitation of] former uncleanness is [also] Rabbinical: now, in the case of that which is unclean by Scriptural law, the Rabbis have imposed [retrospective] uncleanness upon it, but upon that which is unclean by Rabbinical law the Rabbis have imposed no [retrospective] uncleanness.

Yet at least let their flat utensils be unclean, since flat metal utensils are [susceptible to uncleanness] by Scriptural law!—The Rabbis made a distinction in their case, so that *terumah* and sacred

(7) Rashi in R.H. 19*a* offers two explanations: (i) When an unclean vessel is perforated, it becomes clean, since it can no longer be used as a vessel. Now, if a metal utensil is thus broken and then repaired, it reverts to its former state, but not so a glass vessel (*infra* 16*a*). R. Meir maintains that a glass vessel supported by metal is treated as metal; while the Rabbis hold that it is still regarded as a glass vessel. (ii) A clean glass vessel supported by metal becomes *Biblically* unclean, according to R. Meir, as a metal utensil, while the Rabbis hold that it is Biblically clean, as a glass vessel, and is subject to defilement only on account of the Rabbinical enactment; the reasoning being the same as before. Tosaf. a.l. s.v. יהודה is inclined to agree with the second interpretation. (8) Since they are treated as earthenware vessels. (9) If an unclean object touches them on the back, which is flat or convex, they should not become unclean, in accordance with the Mishnah quoted. (10) Rashi: a kind of white earth; Jast.: a vessel made of alum crystals. (11) If an unclean object is suspended in the hollow of one of these vessels, even if it does not touch its side, it becomes unclean. Again, if a clean object is suspended in the hollow of an unclean vessel, though it does not actually touch it, it too becomes unclean.

a (1) E.g., if the base is concave, and an unclean object is suspended from the outside in the hollow. (2) Which are flat or convex. (3) If these vessels, being already unclean, are broken, they become clean; cf. *supra*, n. b7. (4) Yet glass vessels too should be the same according to Resh Lakish's reason. (5) By being melted down and refashioned, which is impossible with earthen utensils. (6) Which can be repaired in the same way. (7) Lit., 'those of them which receive'. (8) I.e., they cannot be defiled. (9) As in n. a7.

לא ליטמו מגבן אלמה תנן *כלי חרס וכלי נתר טומאתן שוה מיטמאין ומטמאין מאויריהן ומיטמאין מאחורידהן ואין מיטמאין מגביהן ושבירתן מטהרתן כלי נתר וכלי חרס הוא דטומאתן שוה אבל מידי אחרינא לא אמרי *כיון °דכי נשתברו יש להם תקנה שוינהו ככלי מתכות אלא מעתה יחזרו לטומאתן ישנה ככלי מתכות *דתנן כלי מתכות פשוטיהן ומקבליהן טמאין נשברו טהרו חזר ועשה מהן כלים חזרו לטומאתן ישנה ואילו גבי כלי זכוכית תנן *כלי עץ וכלי עור וכלי עצם וכלי זכוכית *פשוטיהן טהורין ומקבליהן טמאין נשברו טהרו חזר ועשה מהן כלים מקבלין טומאה מכאן ולהבא *מכאן ולהבא אין למפרע לא טומאת כלי זכוכית דרבנן וטומאה ישנה דרבנן בטומאה דאורייתא אחיתו בה רבנן טומאה בטומאה דרבנן לא אחיתו לה רבנן טומאה פשוטיהן מיהא ליטמא דהא פשוטי כלי מתכות דאורייתא נינהו °[ב]עבדי בהו רבנן *הבירא כי היכי דלא לשרוף עלייהו תרומה וקדשים

רב

נתר. מין אדמה לבנה: מיטמאין ומטמאין מאוירן. נתלית טומאה באוירן נטמא מן האויר חזר ותלה אוכלין באוירן מטמאין את האוכלים ואע״פ שלא נגעו טמא דכתיב כל אשר בתוכו יטמא ואפי׳ מלא חרדל שאין נוגע בדפנותיו אלא הסמוך לדפנות: ומיטמאין מאחוריהן. אם נכנס טומאה לתוך אחוריהן מבחוץ במקום חקק בית מושבם כדרך שעושין לכלי עץ: ואין מיטמאין מגבן. דכתיב אל תוכו: יש להן תקנה. להתיכן ולחזור ולעשותן כלים: לטומאתן ישנה. אם נטמאו ונקבו וטהרו וחזר ועשה מהן כלים יחזרו לטומאתן להצטרך טבילה הואיל וככלי מתכות נינהו: טהרו. דאינה כלי: חזרו לטומאתן ישנה. לקמיה מפרש טעמא: פשוטיהן טהורים. דאיתקש עץ ועור לשק דיש לו בית קבול וכלי עצם איתקש לעץ ועור בפרשת מדין (במדבר לא) כל בגד וכל כלי עור וגו׳ ואמרי׳ בהכל שוחטין (חולין דף כה:) להביא דבר הבא מן העזים מן הקרנים ומן העלמות ומן הטלפים וכלי זכוכית לקמן מפרש טעמא אמאי פשוטיהן טהורים מאחר דדמו למתכות: וטומאה ישנה. שיחזרו לה מאחר שטהרו ממנה דרבנן היא כדלקמן בהילכתא: בטומאת כלי מתכות דאורייתא. גזור טומאה ישנה אבל בכלי זכוכית דעיקר תחילת טומאתו ליתא אלא מדרבנן לא גזרו טומאה ישנה: פשוטיהן מיהא ליטמא. ככלי מתכות דהא פשוטי כלי מתכות דאוריי׳ וכיון דדכוותייהו שוינהו ליטמא דליכא לשנויי בהא כדשני׳ בטומא׳ ישנה: עבדי רבנן היכרא. בטומאת כלי זכוכית וחילקו בה מטומאה דאורייתא להודיע שהיא מדבריהם ולא ישרפו עליה תרומה וקדשים דלא שרפי תרומה משום טומאה דרבנן בר מן ו׳ ספיקות (לעיל דף טו:):

מטהרין לגמרי משום דחשיבי להו ככלי חרס דאמרי׳ בתוספתא כלי חרס שטיהר שעה אחת שוב אין לו טומאה לעולם דא״כ מנגן דרבי מאיר אזיל בתר מעמיד דילמא לאו מדין כלי מתכות מטמא ליה אלא משום דאזיל לטעמיה דאית ליה בתוספתא דכלים דכלי חרס שטיהר שוב יש לו טומאה דתניא התם שולי המחצין ושולי הפחתים וקרקרות הכלים ודופנותיהן כו׳ שיפן ועשאן כלים ממלאין בהן כו׳ ומקבלים טומאה מכאן ולהבא דברי ר׳ מאיר וחכמים אומרים כל כלי חרס שטיהר שעה אחת שוב ט׳ ורבינו שמואל גרים ור״מ היא דחשיב סתימה מעלייתא ולא גרים דאמר הכל הולך אחר המעמיד ומפרש דפליגי ר״מ ורבנן בהכי דר״מ חשיב ליה סתימה מעלייתא ורבנן לא חשיבי להו סתימה מעלייתא הלכך מטהרים לגמרי ודכ״ע אי הוה סתימה מעלייתא הוה אזלינן בתר מעמיד הלכך לר״מ יש לו טהרה במקוה*:

אלא מעתה לא ליטמאו מגבן. וה״ה דה״מ למימר וליטמאו מאוירן וכי משני דהא דמיטמאו מגבן מפני שנראה תוכן כברן לא מצי למיפרך אכתי ליטמאו מאוירן דאיכא למימר אה״נ והא דלא תני בהדי נתר וכלי חרס משום דכלי זכוכית מיטמי מגבן:

לא ליטמאו מגבן אלמה תנן כלי נתר וכלי חרס כו׳. וקשה לרשב״א דהוה ליה לאתויי ברייתא דתוספתא דכלים מחט וטבעת ושולי כלי עץ וכלי זכוכית וכלי עצם אין ממלאין בהן ואין מקדשין בהן ואין מזלין בלמיד פתיל אלמא דמיטמאין מגבן ואמאי מייתי הא דלא מצי לאוכוחי מינה אלא על ידי דיוק כלי נתר וכלי חרס הוא דטומאתן שוה כו׳ ועוד אהך דמייתי איכא למימר דלא חשיב אלא כלי נתר וכלי חרס דהוו דאורייתא דכלי נתר נפקא לן בת״כ דכתיב [וכל] כלי חרס לרבות כלי נתר: **ה״ג** רש״י מיטמאין ומטמאין מאויריהן ומיטמאין מאחוריהן *ואין מיטמאין מגביהן ופירש דמיטמאין מאחוריהן במקום חקק בית מושבן כל שכן דמטמאין אחרים כדמוכח בפ׳ העור והרוטב (חולין דף קיח:) מרובה מדת לטמא ממדת ליטמא דהשתא עיולי עיילא אפוקי מיבעיא והא דלא קתני מטמאין ומיטמאין מאחוריהן כדתנן גבי אויריהן משום דגבי אויריהן יש חידוש משניהם מה שאין כן בכלים אחרים שאינם מטמאין ולא מיטמאין מאויר אבל במה שמטמא אחרים מאחוריו אין זה חידוש דאפילו מגבן נמי מטמאין אחרים וכן כל הכלים וכ״ש אלו מאחוריהן דאיכא חקק אבל מיטמאין מאחוריהן תנא לאשמעינן דאע״ג דאין מיטמאין מגבן אפילו הכי מיטמאין מאחוריהן והכי לא עריב להו מטמאין ומיטמאין מאויריהם ומאחוריהן משום דבאויריהן הוי חידוש משניהם אבל באחוריהם אין חידוש אלא במיטמאין לחוד א״נ מטמאין מאויריהן הייתו דאוריי׳ אבל מאחוריהן לא הוי אלא מדרבנן ועוד דמיטמאין מאויריהן היינו כל הכלי אבל מיטמאין מאחוריהן מגי למימר שאין מיטמא אלא גבו לבד והא דתניא בת״כ מרובה מדת לטמא מליטמא שמטמא אחרים מאחוריו ואין מיטמא מאחוריו מצינו למימר דאחוריו דקאמר התם היינו גב ולא חקק בית מושב א״נ אינו מיטמא מאחוריו מדאוריי׳ אבל מדרבנן מיטמא א״נ אפי׳ מדאוריי׳ מיטמא מאחוריו והא דקאמר אינו מיטמא מאחוריו היינו כולו דאינו טמא כשקבל טומאה מאחוריו אלא גבו אבל תוכו לא והשתא אתי שפיר הא דאמרי׳ בפ׳ אלו מומין (בכורות דף לח: ושם) כלי חרס נטמא גבו לא נטמא תוכו משמע דגבו מיהא טמא והיינו כי נטמא מאחוריו במקום חקק וקרי ליה זימנין גבו וזמנין אחוריו ומה שכלי חרס מציל היינו אפילו ביש לו חקק שאם נטמא גבו תוכו טהור גמור והא דתניא בתוספתא דכלים כלי חרס אין לו טומאה אלא מאוירו והיסטו לא אתי למעוטי אחוריו אלא גבו וחקק הוי בכלל אוירא והקשה ה״ר אליעזר הזקן ז״ל לפ״ה דתניא בתוספתא דכלים זה הכלל כל המשמש כפוי בכלי חרס טהור ואחורים הן משתמשין כפויים ותירץ רבינו שמואל דהתם בכיסוי קדרה ואלפס דאיירי בהם התם לעיל כמו שמפורש הטעם בת״כ יכול שאני מרבה אף חפוי הכלי ת״ל אשר יעשה מלאכה בהם פרט לכיסוי הכלי שאין עושין בהן מלאכה אבל אחורים פעמים שכופין פניהם למטה ועושין בהן מלאכה בתוך אחורים ור״י מפרש דגרסי׳ הכי מטמאין מאחוריהם פירוש מאויר אחוריהן אם קבלו טומאה מתוכן ואין מיטמאין מגבן פירוש לא מקבלי טומאה אפילו בנגיעת גבן וכ״ש מאויר אחוריהן דאין מקבלין טומאה וה״ה בנגיעת אחוריו נמי לא מקבלי טומאה והא דלא נקט דאין מיטמאין מאחוריהם משום דלא נטעי לומר דהיינו אויר אחוריהן אבל בנגיעת אחוריהן טמא להכי נקטו ואין מיטמאין מגבן דאין כאן אלא נגיעה והא דלא עריב ותני להו מטמאין ואין מיטמאין מאחוריהן ומגביהן היינו משום שלא הוי מפרש רבותא בגביהן ורבותא באחוריהם אבל השתא תנן מטמאין מאחוריהן לרבותא דאפי׳ באויר אחוריהן מטמאין ואין מיטמא מגבן דאפי׳ בנגיעה לא מקבלין טומאה*:

אלא כיון דכי נשברו יש להם תקנה. ל״ג אלא דלא הדר ביה ממאי דאמר שוינהו רבנן ככלי חרס דמשום טעם דנשברו יש להם תקנה אין סברא להוריד להם טומאה אלא משום דלכלי חרס דמי לגמרי וכיון דכבר הורידו להם טומאה משום דדמו לכלי חרס משום כיון דנשברו יש להם תקנה שוינהו רבנן כמתכות לענין טומאת גבן:

בטומאה דרבנן לא אחיתו לה רבנן טומאה. וקשה לר״י דאמר במס׳ ע״ז פ׳ ר׳ ישמעאל (דף נב: ושם) ריקן כלי לע״ז מהו אמר רב המטגנא טומאה ישנה קמיבעיא להו דתנן חזר ועשה מהן כלים חזרו לטומאתן ישנה אלמא אפילו בטומאה דרבנן נמי איכא טומאה ישנה ויש° לומר אע״פ דאמר התם בטומאה דרבנן היא מ״מ הכלי מקבל טומאה מדאורייתא אבל הכא כלי זכוכית דלא מקבל שום טומאה מדאורייתא אלא מדרבנן פשיטא ליה דלא אחיתו להו רבנן טומאה:

עבדי רבנן היכרא דלא לישרוף תרומה וקדשים. במאי דאין חוזרין לטומאה ישנה לא הוי היכרא דהא כלי מתכות נמי אין חוזרין לטומאה ישנה אלא מדרבנן וליכא היכרא דהוריית׳ וקשה לר״י דילמא לעולם לכלי חרס דמו דאין מטמאין מגבן והאי דלא תני ליה בהדי כלי נתר וכלי חרס משום דהנהו מיטמאין באויר אבל כלי זכוכית לא מיטמא מאויר דעבדו רבנן היכרא דלא נישרוף וכו׳ דכה״ג אמר בפרק במה טומנין (לקמן דף מח:) דבית הפך ובית התבלין ר׳ מאיר מטמא במגע אבל לא באויר דעביד רבנן היכרא ותי׳ ר״י הבחור דע״כ כלי זכוכית מטמו מגבן מתוספתא דכלים שהבאתי לעיל שאין מזלין בלמיד פתיל ולמאי דפרישית נמי לעיל דדווקא אטומאת גב לא שורפין שאין טמא אלא משום דדמי לכלי מתכות אבל ממה שמטמא מאוירו כלי חרס שורפין אתי נמי שפיר:

קכד א מיי׳ פי״ג מהל׳ כלים הלכה י׳:
קכה ב מיי׳ פ״א מהל׳ כלים הלכה ס׳:

[וע״ע תוס׳ ר״ה יט. ד״ה יוסדס בן שמוע]

וזה דאמר בבכורות [לח.] נטמא גבו לא נטמא תוכו ה״ה דגבו נמי לא נטמא אלא אגב דקאמר נטמא תוכו נטמא גבו קאמר נמי נטמא גבו לא נטמא תוכו והא דלא מקבל טומאה מגבו נפקא לן בפ״ק דחולין [כה.] ממוקף למיד פתיל דסתור והא דדריש בפ״ב אשר יפול מהם אל תוכו מתוכו ולא מאויר אסמכתא היא דהא תוך דרשינן בפ״ק דחולין לדרשה אחריתי [תוספות ישנים]

רבינו חננאל

ור״מ הוא דאמר כיון שהטיפו לתוכן אבר ככלי מתכות דמי שהכל הולך אחר המעמיד ומטמאין ומטהרין דתניא כלי זכוכית שניקבו כו׳ ואקשינן אם ככלי מתכות הן יחזרו לטומאתן ישנה כו׳ ושנינן טומאה ישנה דרבנן וכי אחיתו להו רבנן טומאה בטומאה דאורייתא בטומאה דרבנן לא אחיתו להו טומאה ואקשינן והא פשוטיהן טומאה דאורייתא היא בכלי מתכות ובכלי זכוכית שנינו פשוטיהן טהורין ושנינן עבדו בהו רבנן היכירא ללמד כי אינן ככלי מתכות לכל מילי.

רב

כלים פ״ב מ״א
[ע״ז עה:]
ע״ז נב. כלים פי״א מ״א
כלים פ״ב מ״א

הא דלא חשיב כלי חרס בהדייהו משום דכלי חרס מטמא אפילו בלא שוליים א״נ משום דהכהו דחשיב מקבלי טומאה אפילו מגבן [תוס׳ ישנים]

הא דעביד היכירא בפשוטי כלי טפי מגבו משום דאין סברא לטהר טפי מגבו מפשוטי כלי כיון שיש לו בית קיבול מאחוריו [ת״י]

וע״כ לא אתי למעוטי אלא גבו דהא מקבל טומאה על ידו דאמר בהמפלת [כו.] אבן היוצא מן הכיר׳ ומן התנור וכו׳ והיינו אפילו להכנים כדאמר בר״פ העור והרוטב [קיח:] ומיהו יש לדחות דהתם איירי בטומאת אוכלין וכלי שטף אבל בכלי חרס לא יכנים [תוס׳ ישנים]

[וע״ע תוס׳ חולין כד: ד״ה וגבו ותוספות בכורות לח. ד״ה הרי]

גליון הש״ס

גמ׳ דכי נשתברו יש להם תקנה. עיין סנהדרין דף נ״א ע״א ברש״י ד״ה יש להם תקנה: שם עבדו בהו רבנן היכירא. לקמן דף מח ע״ב נדה דף ל ע״א:

רב אשי אמר לעולם לכלי חרס דמו ודקא קשיא לך לא ליטמו מגבן [א]הואיל ונראה תוכו כברו *שמעון בן שטח תיקן כתובה לאשה וגזר טומאה על כלי מתכות כלי מתכות דאורייתא נינהו דכתיב °אך את הזהב ואת הכסף וגו' לא נצרכה אלא לטומאה ישנה דאמר רב יהודה אמר רב מעשה בשל ציון המלכה שעשתה משתה לבנה ונטמאו כל כליה ושברתן ונתנתן לצורף וריתכן ועשה מהן כלים חדשים ואמרו חכמים יחזרו לטומאתן ישנה מ"ט משום גדר מי חטאת נגעו בה הניחא למאן דאמר לא לכל הטומאות אמרו אלא לטומאת המת בלבד אמרו שפיר אלא למאן דאמר לכל הטומאות אמרו מאי איכא למימר אמר אביי גזירה שמא לא יקבנו בכדי טהרתו רבא אמר [ב]גזירה *שמא יאמרו טבילה בת יומא עולה לה מאי בינייהו °א"ב דרצפינהו מרצף: ואידך מאי היא *[ג]דתנן המניח כלים תחת הצינור לקבל בהן מי גשמים אחד כלים גדולים ואחד כלים קטנים ואפילו כלי אבנים וכלי אדמה וכלי גללים פוסלין את המקוה אחד המניח ואחד השוכח דברי ב"ש וב"ה מטהרין בשוכח אמר ר' מאיר נמנו ורבו ב"ש על ב"ה ומודים ב"ש בשוכח בחצר שהוא טהור אמר רבי יוסי עדיין מחלוקת במקומה עומדת אמר רב משרשיא דבי רב אמרי [ד]הכל מודים כשהניחם בשעת קישור עבים טמאים בשעת פיזור עבים ד"ה טהורין לא נחלקו אלא שהניחם בשעת קישור עבים ונתפזרו וחזרו ונתקשרו מר סבר [ה]בטלה מחשבתו ומר סבר לא בטלה מחשבתו [א] ולר' יוסי דאמר מחלוקת עדיין במקומה עומדת בצרי להו א"ר נחמן בר יצחק אף *בנות כותים נדות מעריסתן בו ביום גזרו: ואידך מאי היא *דתנן כל המטלטלי' מביאין את הטומאה בעובי המרדע אמר רבי טרפון אקפח

במדבר לא

רש"י

לעולם לכלי חרס דמו. הואיל ובריתן מן החול הלכך פשוטיהן טהורין ואין בהן טומאה [ישנה]: הואיל ונראה תוכו. מבחוץ דכך דפשוטיו לא חשיב גב אלא תוך: בשל ציון. בימי שמעון בן שטח היתה: כל כליה. במת שהיתה צריכה להמתין הזאת שלישי ושביעי לפיכך שברתן למהר טהרתן לבו ביום: וריתכן. שולדי בלע"ז שמחבר כסף במקום שבר: גדר מי חטאת. כמלאו מי חטאת בטלים שאין לך אדם ממתין ז' ימים אלא שוברן ותשתכח תורת מי חטאת: למ"ד כו'. °לא ידענא היכא: אמרו. שיחזרו: בכדי טהרתו. כמוציא רמון: בת יומא. בלא הערב שמש שהרואה שנטמאו ומשתמשין בהן בו ביום ואינו יודע שנשברו סובר שהטבילום: עולה. מועלת: דרלפינהו מרלף. הריקן ושברן כולן כמו *מאכולת רצופה שמא לא יקבנו ליכא ושמא יאמרו איכא ואיכא דאמרי שמא לא יקבנו איכא שמא יאמרו כו' ליכא דהא מינכר עשייה שנתחדש כולו וזה נראה בעיני: תחת הצינור. שקבעו ולבסוף חקקו להמשיך מים למקוה דשוב אינו פוסל אבל הכלים פוסלים משום שאיבה: ואחד כלים קטנים. דלא תימא לא חשיבי: ואפילו כלי גללים. שאינם קרויין כלים לענין קבלת טומאה הוו כלים לענין שאיבה: גללים. (א)°שייש: כלי אדמה. דלאו ע"י גיבול הוא ככלי נתר וכלי חרס: מטהרין. דשוכח לא חשיבה שאיבה הואיל ולא לכך נתכוון: בחצר. שלא תחת הצינור ונתמלא מן הנוטפין ונפלו למקוה שהוא טהור דבמניח תחת הצינור וכשהניחן בשעת קישור עבים ואח"כ נתפזרו ושכחן כדמוקי לקמן הוא דפליגי ביה דגלי דעתיה שרצה שיפלו לתוכו ומשום פזור עבים לא בטלה מחשבתו ראשונה אבל במונח בחצר ואפי' בשעת קישור ונתפזרו לא מוכחא מחשבה קמייתא שפיר מעיקרא הלכך בטלה: במקומה עומדת. במניח תחת הצינור בקישור עבים לא נמנו ורבו עליה לבטל דברי בית הלל דלא חזרו בהן: הניחן. תחת הצינור בשעת קישור עבים ואיחרו גשמים לבוא ויצא למלאכתו ושכחן דברי הכל הואיל ומתחלה לכך נתכוון לא בטלה מחשבתו בשכחתו: דברי הכל טהורים. דליכא גלויי דעתא: בטלה מחשבתו. דכי נתפזרו אסח דעתיה דסבר לא ירדו גשמים עוד: בצרי להו. י"ח דבר שאין זו מן המנין דכל זמן שלא נמנו ורבו הויא הלכה כבית הלל וטהור: נדות מעריסתן. מיום שנולדה דגזרינן דילמא חזאי נדות דקטנה בת יומא מטמאה בנדה דתניא אין לי אלא אשה תינוקת בת יום אחד לנדה מנין תלמוד לומר ואשה וכותים אין דורשין מדרש זה וכי חזיין לא מפרשי לה הלכך גזור בהו רבנן: כל המטלטלין מביאין את הטומאה. משום אהל שאם אהיל ראשו אחד על המת וראשו אחד על הכלים מביאין להן טומאת אהל המת ליטמא ז' ימים ולהיות אב הטומאה כדין אהל טמא: בעובי המרדע. אפילו אין בהן פותח טפח אלא כעובי המרדע ולקמן מפרש יש בהיקפו טפח שנו טפח צריך להקיפו ואף על גב דאהל דאורייתא פחות מטפח לא הוי דהלכה למשה מסיני הוא כשאר כל השיעורין הכא גזור רבנן היקפו משום עביו: אקפח

תוספות

רב אשי אמר לעולם לכלי חרס דמו. הכא לית ליה לרב אשי טעמא הואיל וכי נשברו יש להם תקנה שויוהו כו' ומיהו לענין להצריכן טבילה כשהן חדשים אית ליה לרב אשי האי טעמא בהדיא בפרק בתרא דמסכת ע"ז (דף עה:): דאמר רב יהודה מעשה בשל ציון המלכה. ומייתי ראיה דבימי שמעון בן שטח גזרו טומאה על כלי מתכות דיחזרו לטומאתן ישנה דהוא היה בימי של ציון המלכה כדאיתא בפרק ג' דתענית (דף כג:) דאמר מעשה בימי ר"ש בן שטח *ושל ציון המלכה שהיו גשמים יורדים מע"ש לע"ש וכו': הניחא למ"ד דלא לכל הטומאות אמרו. רשב"ג סבירא ליה הכי (ג) (בתוספתא) דכלים (*פ"א) גבי ההוא דמייתי לעיל (*כלי עץ וכלי עור כו') ופליג את"ק דאמר סתמא יחזרו לטומאתן ישנה וטעמא משום דטומאת מת היא זמן מרובה ויסבר ולא ירצה להמתין: אחד כלים גדולים. שמרוב גודלן אינן מקבלים טומאה כגון כלי עץ שהן יתרים על ארבעים סאה שאינן מיטלטלים מלא וריקן אפ"ה מיקרי שאיבה ואחד כלים קטנים כדאמר במס' כלים (פ"ב מ"ב) ומייתי לה בפ' אלו טריפות (חולין דף כד:) הדקין שבכלי חרס הן וקרקרותיהן ודפנותיהם יושבין שלא מסומכים שעורן מכדי סיכת קטן ועד לוג אבל בציר מהכי טהורים: אף בנות כותים. תימה לר"י דבריש בנות כותים (נדה דל"ב: ושם) מוקי לה כר"מ דחייש למיעוטא והאי טעמא לא שייך אלא למ"ד כותים גרי אמת הן ואם ראתה טמאה מדאורייתא אבל למ"ד כותים גרי אריות הן לא שייך האי טעמא דאפי' אם ראתה טהורה מדאורייתא דעו"ג לא מטמאו בזיבה ובשמעתין מוכח דלכ"ע בנות כותים הוי מי"ח דבר ולמאן דלא חייש למיעוטא או למ"ד גרי אריות הן היכי מני לה בי"ח דבר ועוד דר' יוסי אית ליה דגרי אריות הן במנחות בפרק רבי ישמעאל (דף סו: ושם) דאית ליה תורמין משל עו"ג על של כותים ומשל כותים על של עו"ג והכא חשיב אליבי' בנות כותים בי"ח דבר וי"ל דבנות כותים אתיא לכ"ע וגזרו עליהן שיהיו נדות שלא יטמעו בהן והא דמוקי התם מתני' כר"מ משום דסיפא מוכחא דלא הוי משום טימוע דקתני הכותים מטמאין משכב התחתון כעליון מפני שהן בועלי נדות מספק ומסיים ואין שורפין עליהן את התרומה מפני שטומאתן ספק משמע דקאי אף אקטנות דאיירי בהן והא דקאמר התם רבי יוסי מעשה היה בעינבול והטבילוה קודם לאמה לאו משום דחייש למיעוט מייתי ראיה דמיעוט דשכיח הוא דהא טעמא דרבי יוסי משום טימוע אלא לכך מייתי ראיה דאי לאו דשכיח הוא לא הוי לן למיגזר שיהו נדות מעריסותיהם משום טימוע דלא ליהוי כחוכא ואיטלולא וא"ת היכי חשיב ליה לר"מ בי"ח דבר והלא בלאו הכי בכל מקום חייש ר' מאיר למיעוטא וי"ל דהכא הוצרכו לגזור משום דדמי לחזקה ורובא שלא ראתה דמסתמא עם יציאתה לעולם לא ראתה ואוקמי אחזקה וסמוך רובא לחזקה ואיתרע ליה מיעוטא ולא הוה חייש רבי מאיר אי לאו דגזרו ליה בי"ח דבר דהוה ליה מיעוטא דמיעוטא כדמוכח בריש פרק בתרא דיבמות (דף קיט.) וא"ת למ"ד בפ"ב דמסכתא ע"ז (דף לו:) גזרו על בנותיהן משום דבר אחר היינו שיהו נדות מעריסותן אמאי חשיב להו בתרתי גזרות בנותיהן ובנות כותים וי"ל דצריכי דאי גזרו בעו"ג ה"א משום דאדוקי בעבודת כוכבים טפי אבל בנות כותים לא ואי גזרו בכותים משום דרגילין ושייכי טפי גבי ישראל מעובדי כוכבים אבל עכו"ם לא: כל המטלטלין. נקט מטלטלין משום שלא גזרו טומאת אהל בעובי המרדע אלא על האדם הנושאו אבל בפותח טפח אפילו במחוברים נמי מביאין את הטומאה דדוקא זרעים וירקות לפי שאין בהן ממש קתני התם דלא מביאין ולא חוצצים דהוי כמו טיפת הברד והשלג וכפור והגליד והמלח אבל אילן המיסך על הארץ קתני התם דמביא את הטומאה:

*) אקפח את כו'. לשון שבועה הוא כלומר אקפח את בני אם אין זה דבר אמת שהלכה זו מקופחת וכענין זה מליט במקרא (בראשית מב) חי פרעה אם תצאו מזה כלומר °שלא תצאו מזה *:

*) שייך לדף יז׳

שמעו

עין משפט נר מצוה

קכו א מיי' פ"א מהל' כלים הלכה ה:

קכז ב מיי' פי"ב מהל' כלים הלכה ג:

קכח ג ד ה מיי' פ"ד מהלכות מקואות הלכה ד סמג עשין רמח טוש"ע יו"ד סימן רא סעיף מא:

[שם ליתא ושל ציון המלכה ע"ש ועי' רבה בחקותי פרשה לה]

[נ"ל כלי מתכות פשוטיהן ומקבליהן כו']

רבינו חננאל

רב אשי אמר לעולם כלי זכוכית ככלי חרס הן ודקא קשיא לך אם ככלי חרס הן לא יטמאו מגבן דהא אין כלי חרס מטמא אלא באויר ולא מגבו מה שאינכן [בשאר כלים] דגרסינן בשחיטת חולין ס"פ ראשון. ת"ר אויר כלי חרס טמא וגבו טהור אויר כל הכלים טהורין וגבן טמא ותו אמרינן וכל כלי פתוח אשר אין צמיד פתיל עליו טמא הוא איזהו כלי שטומאתו קודמת לפתחיו הוי אומ' זה כלי חרס וכי אין צמיד פתיל עליו הוא דטמא הא יש צמיד פתיל עליו טהור הא למדת שכלי חרס אם אינו צמיד פתיל [עליו] טומאה קודמת לפתחו ואפילו באויר ואם הוא צמיד פתיל אינו מטמא מגבו ושאר כל הכלים אפילו הן צמיד פתיל ונגעה בהן טומאה מגבן נטמאו ופשוטי כלי זכוכית אין מקבלין טומאה ככלי חרס דתנינן (כלים פ"ב) זה הכלל כל שאין לו תוך בכלי חרס אין לו אחוריים פי' אין מטמאין מגבן באויר שאין כלי חרס מטמא באויר מגבו אלא מתוכו שנאמר אל תוכו לפיכך מוקף צמיד פתיל טהור מפני שאינו מטמא מגבו שהן אחוריו אבל שאר הכלים ואפילו כלי זכוכית אין צמיד פתיל מציל בהן בזמן שיש לכלי זכוכית בית קבול מפני שמטמאין מגבן הכא אמר רב אשי כלי זכוכית ככלי חרס הן ובסוף ע"ז אמרינן כלי זכוכית ככלי מתכות הן ושנינן לא קשיא הכי קאמר כלי זכוכית ככלי חרס הן ולא מקבלי טומאה אא"כ יש להן תוך ככלי חרס והוא בית קבול אבל פשוטיהן טהורין וגזרו עליהן להיות מיטמאין מגבן הואיל וכלי זכוכית מראת הטומאה מגבן שהוא אחוריו כאילו בתוכו הוא. אבל לעלות מידי טומאתן כלי זכוכית ככלי מתכות הקוצרכין טבילה במ' סאה והכין קיי"ל כרב אשי דהוא בתראה: שמעון בן שטח תיקן כתובה לאשה מפורש במס' כתובות פ' האשה שנפלו לה נכסים בסופו עד שבא שמעון בן שטח [ותיקן שיהא כותב] כל נכסיי אחראין לכתובתיך. וגזר טומאה [על כלי מתכות] ואסיק' טומאה ישנה כגון שנטמאו כלי זכוכית ועמד ושיברן

כדקיי"ל נשברו טהרו וריתכן ועשאן מיד כלי גזרו עליהן לחזור לטומאתן הישנה ולא לכל טומאה גזרו גזירה זו אלא לטומאת מת בלבד ומ"ט אמר עולא משום גדר מי חטאת פי' דאי מטהרת להן אתי לאקולי במי נדה ואקשינן ולמאן דאמר דלכל הטומאות חוזרין לטומאתן ישנה ושבירתן כהאי גוונא לא טיהרתן מ"ט אמר אביי גזירה שמא לא יקבנו בכדי טהרתו כדתנן (כלים פי"ד) כלי מתכות כמה שיעורן הדלי למלאות בו כו' רבא אמר גזירה שמא יאמרו טבילה בת יומא עולה פי' הרואה כי שברו ותקנו ונטהר מידי כך יטבילוהו וישתמש בו מיד בלא הערב שמש יאמרו שבירתן מטהרתן וטבילתן מטהרתן מה שבירתו אינה צריכה הערב שמש אף טבילתו אינה צריכה הערב שמש מכדי אביי ורבא סברי תרווייהו יחזרו לטומאתן ישנה מאי בינייהו איכא בינייהו דרצפונהי מרצף פירוש כגון שפוד שנרצף שיקע כותלי הכלי בתוכן ונעשה כאלו נשברו כותליו ואביי דחייש שמא לא יקבנו בכדי טהרתו אע"ג דרצפה חייש ועדיין טומאתו ישנה עליו ולרבא פרחה טומאתו דהא רציף ולא כלי הוא: המניח את כליו תחת הצינור · כולה פשוטה היא:

מסורת הש"ס

[לעיל יד: ע"ש כתובות פב:]

[חולין קכב.]

מקוואות פ"ד מ"א

[ועי' תוס' חגיגה טז: ד"ה אקפח]

הגהות הגר"א

[א] גמ' (ולרבי יוסי דאמר כו' עד בו ביום גזרו) תא"מ (וכ"ה בח"ה וכמה ראשוני' דל"צ לה):

הגהות הב"ח

(א) רש"י ד"ה גללים שייש נ"ב בעלמא פרש"י לסיפי בקר: (ב) תוס' ד"ה הניחא וכו' סבירא ליה הכי במסכת כלים (וכן הוא בס"י) · נ"ב ע"ש בפ' י"א:

גליון הש"ס

גמ' איכא בינייהו דרלפינהו מרלף. עי' במתני' דכלים פי"א מ"ג ובתוי"ט שם ד"ה ריצ"ב: רש"י ד"ה למ"ד ל"י היכא. עיין ברכות דף כב ע"ב ברש"י ד"ה מאן שמעת ליה כו' וש"נ: רש"י ד"ה גללים שייש. עיין רש"י לקמן דף נח ע"א ד"ה כלי גללים. ועי' שו"ת תשב"ץ ח"א סימן קכא: תוס' ד"ה אקפח וכו' שלא תצאו מזה. ועי' חגיגה דף טז ע"ב תוס' ד"ה ארחה בנחמה ובכתובות דף סז ע"א:

רב נסים גאון

שמעון בן שטח תיקן כתובה לאשה תמצא דבריו מבוארין במס' כתובות בפרק האשה שנפלו לה נכסים (דף פב) תניא נמי הכי בראשונה היו כותבין לבתולה מאתים ולאלמנה מנה וכו' עד שבא שמעון בן שטח ותיקן שיהא כותב כל נכסאי אחראין לכתובתיך ועיקר זאת הברייתא בתוספ' כתובות בראש פרק י"ב והוא אחרון המסכת: הניחא למאן דאמר לא כל הטמאות אמרו תיובתא לרבו

food should not be burnt on their account.[10] [16b] R. Ashi said: After all, it is similar to earthen utensils, and as for your difficulty, 'let them not become unclean through their [flat or convex] backs', [the reply] is because its inside is as visible as
a its outside.[1]

'Simeon b. Sheṭaḥ instituted a woman's marriage settlement and imposed uncleanness upon metal utensils.' But [the uncleanness of] metal utensils is Biblical, for it is written, *howbeit the gold, and the silver* [. . . etc.]?[2]—This [the Rabbinical law] was necessary only in respect of former uncleanness.[3] For Rab Judah said in Rab's name: It once happened that Queen Shalẓion[4] made a banquet for her son and all her utensils were defiled. Thereupon she broke them and gave them to the goldsmith, who melted them down and manufactured new utensils of them. But the Sages declared, They revert to their previous uncleanness. What is the reason?—They were concerned there to provide[5] a fence against the water of separation.[6]

Now, that is well on the view that they [the Sages] did not rule thus in respect of all forms of defilement but only in respect of the defilement of the dead:[7] then it is correct. But on the view that they ruled thus for all forms of uncleanness, what can be said?—Abaye answered: As a preventive measure lest he might not perforate it to the standard of purification.[8] Raba said: As a preventive measure lest it be said that *ṭebillah*[9] of that very day is effective for it.[10] Wherein do they differ?—They differ where a smith refashioned it.[11]

b And what is another?[1] For we learnt: If one places vessels under a spout to catch rain water therein, whether they are large vessels or small, or even vessels [made] of stone, earth[2] or dung, they render the *mikweh* unfit. It is all one whether he places or forgets them [there]: that is Beth Shammai's view; but Beth Hillel declare it clean[3] if he forgets them.[4] Said R. Meir: They took a count, and Beth Shammai outnumbered Beth Hillel. Yet Beth Shammai admit that if he forgets [the utensils] in a courtyard,[5] it is clean.[6] R. Jose said: The controversy still stands in its place.[7]

R. Mesharsheya said: The scholars of Rab[8] said: All agree that, if he places them [under the spout] when clouds are massing, they[9] are unclean;[10] [if he places them there] when the clouds are dispersed, all agree that they are clean.[11] They differ only if he places them there when the clouds were massing, but they
c then dispersed, and subsequently massed together again:[1] one Master [Beth Hillel] holds that his intention was nullified,[2] while the other Master holds that his intention was not nullified.

Now, according to R. Jose, who maintained, The controversy still stands in its place, they are less [than eighteen]?[3]—Said R. Naḥman b. Isaac: On that same day they also enacted that the daughters of Cutheans[4] are *niddoth*[5] from their cradles.[6]

And what is another? For we learnt: All movable objects induce uncleanness by the thickness of an ox-goad.[7] Said R. Tarfon,

(10) For these must not be burnt when defiled by Rabbinical law, except in the six cases of doubtful uncleanness enumerated on 15*b*.

a (1) From without; hence it is all regarded as the inside. (2) Num. XXXI, 22. The text continues: *everything that may abide the fire, ye shall make go through the fire, and it shall be clean; nevertheless it shall be purified with the water of separation.* (3) V. *supra* 16*a*. (4) I.e., Salome Alexandra, wife and successor of Alexander Jannai and according to the Talmud, sister of Simeon b. Sheṭaḥ. (5) Lit., 'on account of'. (6) V. n. a2.; i.e., they were anxious to safeguard this law, which would fall into disuse if the expedient of melting and refashioning were widely adopted. (7) Only then is the former uncleanness revived.—The verse quoted in n. a2 refers to such. (8) The hole which removes its status of a utensil must be of a certain size,—large enough to permit a pomegranate to fall through. (9) V. Glos. (10) When it is purified by means of *ṭebillah* it may not be used until the evening; but making a hole and repairing it permits its immediate use. One seeing this vessel thus used on the same day may think that it underwent *ṭebillah*, and that the latter too releases it for immediate use. (11) Abaye's reason still holds good, for one may think that a small hole too would have sufficed. But Raba's reason does not operate, for it is plainly evident that this was newly remade.

b (1) Of the eighteen enactments. (2) Roughly manufactured, without being kneaded and baked. (3) I.e, the *mikweh* retains its powers of purification. (4) V. *supra* 15*a*, n. a3. The spout was fixed in the earth before it was actually a spout, and after fixing it was made hollow to act as a water duct to the *mikweh*. In that case the water that passes through it is regarded as 'living water'. When, however, the water falls from the spout into vessels, it becomes 'drawn water', which renders the *mikweh* unfit. This holds good whether they are very large vessels, too big to be susceptible to uncleanness, e.g., a tub more than forty *se'ahs* in capacity, or very small, so that I might think of disregarding them altogether; also, even if of dung, when they are not regarded as vessels at all in respect to uncleanness. If they are merely forgotten there, Beth Hillel maintain that the water is not 'drawn', since it was unintentional. (5) But not under the spout, and they are filled with the rain water which flows thence into the *mikweh*. (6) V. n. b3. Because he had no intention at all of filling it, since he did not place it under the spout. (7) I.e., they differ here too. (8) The term *debe Rab* means either the disciples of the Academy founded by Rab or scholars in general; Weiss, *Dor*, III, 158 (Ed. 1924). (9) Utensils purified in the *mikweh*. (10) Because the *mikweh* was rendered unfit, as above. For he showed that he desired the water to flow into the utensils, and though he had forgotten them by the time the rain descended, his original intention was fulfilled, and the water is regarded as drawn. (11) Since there were no clouds, his placing the utensils there was not with the intention of filling them.

c (1) And by then he has forgotten them. (2) By the dispersal of the clouds; hence the subsequent filling does not render the water drawn. (3) Since there is a controversy, the *halachah* agrees with Beth Hillel, that the *mikweh* is fit. (4) The Cutheans were the descendants of the heathens who settled in Samaria after the destruction of the Northern Kingdom. They accepted a form of Judaism, and the Rabbis' attitude towards them varied. At times they were regarded as Jews, but they were subsequently declared non-Jews. The present enactment treats them as Jews, who, however, are looked upon with disfavour. (5) Pl. of *niddah*, a menstruant woman. (6) I.e., from birth they are treated as unclean, like a *niddah*. The purpose of this enactment was to discourage intermarriage with them (Tosaf.). (7) This refers to the defilement caused by a dead person, not by contact but through the fact that both the dead person and the object defiled are under the same covering, e.g., the roof of a house or an overhead awning (cf. Num. XIX, 14f), which induces uncleanness to the object defiled. The width of the covering object must not be less than the thickness of an ox-goad, for which v. *infra* 17*a*.

[17a] May I bury my children,[8] if this is not an erroneous *halachah*, for the hearer heard [a ruling] and erred [therein]. [Viz.,] a peasant was passing with an ox-goad on his shoulder and one end thereof overshadowed a grave, and he was declared unclean in virtue of [the law of] utensils which overshadowed the dead.[9] R. Akiba said, I will rectify [it] so that the words of the Sages[10] may be fulfilled. [Viz.,] all movable objects induce uncleanness in their bearers by the thickness of an ox-goad; [and induce uncleanness] in themselves, by any thickness; and in other
a people or utensils, by the width[1] of a handbreadth. And R. Jannai observed: and the ox-goad of which they spoke is not a handbreadth in thickness but in circumference, and they enacted [this law] concerning its circumference on account of its thickness.[2] But according to R. Tarfon who said, 'May I bury my children but this *halachah* is incorrect!' they are less [than eighteen]?—Said R. Naḥman b. Isaac, That the daughters of Cutheans are *niddoth* from their cradles was also enacted on that same day; and on the other [question][3] he agrees with R. Meir.[4]

And another?—When one vintages [grapes] for the vat [i.e., to manufacture wine], Shammai maintains: It is made fit [to become unclean]; while Hillel ruled, It is not made fit.[5] Said Hillel to Shammai: Why must one vintage [grapes] in purity, yet not gather [olives] in purity?[6] If you provoke me, he replied, I will decree uncleanness in the case of olive gathering too. A sword was planted in the Beth Hamidrash and it was proclaimed, 'He who would enter, let him enter, but he who would depart, let him not depart!'[7] And on that day Hillel sat submissive before Shammai, like one of the disciples,[8] and it was as grievous to Israel[9] as the day when the [golden] calf was made. Now, Shammai and Hillel enacted [this measure], but they would not accept it from
b them; but their disciples came[1] and enacted it, and it was accepted from them.[2]

[Now,] what is the reason?[3]—Said Ze'iri in R. Ḥanina's name: For fear lest he vintage it into unclean baskets.[4] Now, that is well on the view that an unclean vessel renders fluid effective;[5] but on the view that an unclean vessel does not render fluid effective, what can be said?—Rather, said Ze'iri in R. Ḥanina's name: For fear lest he vintage it in pitch lined baskets.[6] Raba said: It is a preventive measure on account of tightly cleaving [clusters].[7] R. Naḥman said in Rabbah b. Abbuha's name: [It is a preventive measure, for] a man sometimes goes to his vineyard to see if the grapes are ready for vintaging, takes a bunch of grapes to squeeze it, and sprinkles [the juice] on the grapes, and at the time of gathering the moisture is still dripping on them.

(8) Lit., 'may I cut off my children that this *halachah* is cut off'. (9) I.e., any utensil which overshadows the dead becomes itself unclean, whatever its width, and the peasant was declared unclean for the same day till the evening because he was actually carrying and in direct contact with this ox-goad. But one of the disciples who heard this ruling erroneously imagined that he was unclean in virtue of the law stated in *16b*, n. c7 involving an uncleanness of seven days, and thus drew a false conclusion. (10) Who said that all movable objects induce uncleanness by the thickness of an ox-goad.

a (1) Lit., 'aperture'. (2) If its thickness is a handbreadth, it induces uncleanness of seven days by Biblical law, and therefore the Sages extended this to the former case too, to prevent confusion. This is one of the eighteen enactments. V. Oh. XVI, 1. (3) *Sc.* one who places vessels under a spout, v. *supra 16b*. (4) Rashba's version omits this passage, because R. Tarfon accepted R. Akiba's view; v. Halevi, *Doroth*, I, 3, p. 587-8. (5) V. *supra 12a*, nn. a1 and a4. (6) You maintain that grapes are fit to become defiled, and therefore must be vintaged into ritually clean baskets: why then do you not insist upon it when the olives are gathered too, for surely the same reasoning applies?

(7) This was the practice when a vote was taken upon any question; Halevi, *Doroth*, I, 3, p. 585 n. 18. (8) I.e., the assembly voted against him—of course the actual expression is not to be understood literally. (9) In view of the humility to which Hillel, who was the Nasi, had been subjected.

b (1) At the assembly in the house of Ḥananiah b. Hezekiah b. Garon. (2) Hence it is one of the eighteen measures. (3) Why does the exuding liquid make the grapes susceptible to uncleanness? For the logic is the reverse, seeing that this liquid is wasted and its exuding is not with its owner's desire, whereas the owner's desire is necessary for it to cause susceptibility to defilement. (4) Since the uncleanness comes simultaneously with the fluid, the latter renders the grapes fit to become unclean, even without the owner's desire. (5) Lit., 'makes the liquid count'—to qualify other objects to become unclean. (6) Since the liquid is not lost, its exuding is not contrary to the owner's desire. (7) Lit., 'the biting ones'. One must separate these by force, thus causing juice to spurt out. Since he does this himself, the juice certainly makes the grapes susceptible; then as a preventive measure the law was extended to all exuding juice, in order to obviate confusion.

מסורת הש״ס

*אקפח את בני שזו הלכה מקופחת ששמע השומע וטעה *האיכר עובר ומרדעו על כתפו ואיהל צדו אחת על הקבר טימאו אותו משום כלים המאהילים על המת א״ר עקיבא אני אתקן שיהו דברי חכמים קיימים שיהו כל המטלטלים מביאין את הטומאה על האדם שנושא אותן בעובי המרדע ועל עצמן בכל שהן ועל שאר אדם וכלים בפותח טפח וא״ר ינאי ומרדע שאמרו אין בעביו טפח ויש בהיקפו טפח וגזרו על היקפו משום עביו [א] ולר' טרפון דאמר אקפח את בני שהלכה זו מקופחת בצרו להו א״ר נחמן בר יצחק אף בנות כותים נדות מעריסתן בו ביום גזרו ובאידך ס״ל כר' מאיר: ואידך *הבוצר לגת שמאי אומר הוכשר הלל אומר לא הוכשר א״ל הלל לשמאי *מפני מה בוצרין בטהרה ואין מוסקין בטהרה א״ל אם תקניטני גוזרני טומאה אף על המסיקה נעצו חרב בבית המדרש אמרו הנכנס יכנס והיוצא אל יצא ואותו היום היה הלל כפוף ויושב לפני שמאי כאחד מן התלמידים *והיה קשה לישראל כיום שנעשה בו העגל וגזור שמאי והלל ולא קבלו מינייהו ואתו תלמידייהו גזור וקבלו מינייהו מ״ט אמר (ר') זעירי אמר ר' חנינא גזירה שמא יבצרנו בקופות טמאות הניחא למ״ד כלי טמא חושב משקין שפיר אלא למ״ד אין כלי טמא חושב משקין מאי איכא למימר אלא אמר זעירי אמר ר' חנינא גזירה שמא *יבצרנו בקופות מזופפות רבא אמר גזירה משום הנושכות (דאמר) רב נחמן אמר רבה בר אבוה פעמים שאדם הולך לכרמו לידע אם הגיעו ענבים לבצירה או לא ונוטל אשכול ענבים לסוחטו ומזלף על גבי ענבים ובשעת בצירה עדיין משקה טופח עליהם: ואידך אמר טבי

רש״י

אקפח את בני. מצטער היה על תורה המשתכחת ומקלל את עצמו: אקפח. אקברם לשון חיתוך וקיצור: ששמע השומע. כשנשאלה השאלה על ידי מעשה בבית המדרש ושמע שטמאוהו וטעה ולא ידע משום מה טמאוהו הם טמאו את המרדע משום כלים המאהילים על המת שהכלי עצמו המאהיל טמא בכל שהו דלא בעינן פותח טפח אלא לשוייה אהל להביא טומאה תחת ראשו השני להביא טומאה על אחרים אבל לגבי דידיה בכל שהו וטמאוהו לאיכר טומאת ערב משום שנגע באותו כלי שהוא אב הטומאה וזה שנגע בו ראשון והשומע טעה לומר שעשאוהו לאיכר אב הטומאה לטמא ז' ולטעון הזייה: אני אתקן שיהו דברי חכמים. שאומרים עובי המרדע מביא טומאה קיימין יש דבר שמביאין עליו טומאה ממש לטעון הזייה מדבריהם כגון על האדם הנושאו שטמא בו טומאת מגע מן התורה גזרו עליו בעובי המרדע ליטמא טומאת אהל מדבריהם גזירה היקפו משום עביו דכיון דמטמאת ליה על כרחך טומאה דאורייתא לאצרוכיה הערב שמש והוא לא נגע במת כסבור שמשום אהל אתה מטמאו ומשום שיש בהיקפו טפח וכיון דלא מטמאת ליה טומאת ז' אתי למימר באהל גמור נמי טומאת ערב אבל שאר אדם וכלים שאין נוגעין בו ואין עליך לטמאן כלל אין מביאין שום טומאה אלא בפותח טפח ר״ע מילתייהו דרבנן פריש: וא״ר ינאי גרסינן: מרדע שאמרו. דמביא את הטומאה על נושאו לטמאו שבעה מדבריהם: אין בעביו טפח. דאם כן הוי אהל דאורייתא: ולר' טרפון. דאמר לא גזרו שום גזירה אלא בדין תורה דלא טמאוהו אלא טומאת ערב משום מגע בצרי להו י״ח: בנות כותים כו': ובאידך. דמניח כלים: סבר לה. ר' טרפון כר' מאיר דחשיב ליה בי״ח דבר ואפיק הא ועייל הך דבנות כותים: מפני מה בוצרין בטהרה. מפני מה אתה מצריך לבצור בכלים טהורים דקאמרת הוכשר ואין אתה מצריך למסוק זיתים בכלים טהורים: יכנס. לבית המדרש: והיוצא אל יצא. לפי שהיו רוצין לעמוד במנין: קשה. לפי שהלל נשיא ועניותן: וגזור שמאי והלל ולא קבלו מינייהו ואתו תלמידייהו וגזור וקבלו מינייהו: מ״ט. הוכשר הא לא ניחא ליה בההיא משקה דנפיק וקאזיל לאיבוד: בקופות טמאות. דאתיא טומאת הכלי ומחשבה ליה למשקה להכשיר הוכיל וטומאתו והכשרו כאחת: הניחא למאן דאמר. *לא ידענא היכא: חושב משקה. להכשיר אוכל שבתוכו ואף על גב דלא אחשביה הוא: מזופפות. כיון דלא אזיל לאיבוד ניחא ליה ליליאתו: הנושכות. אשכולות הנושכות זו את זו וכשבא להפרידן נסחט המשקה עליהן וכיון דעבד בידים ולא אפשר בלא סחיטה מכשר:

תוספות

ששמע השומע וטעה כו' טמאוהו משום כלים המאהילים על המת. פי' בקונטרס טמאוהו לאיכר טומאת ערב משום דנגע בכלים המאהילים שהן טמאין טומאת ז' כדין הנוגע בטמא מת דטמא טומאת ערב מדאורייתא וקשה למה טעה השומע והיה סבור שטמאוהו טומאת ז' כיון דדבר פשוט הוא שאדם הנוגע בטמא מת דטמא טומאת ערב ועוד דמן התורה האיכר טמא טומאת ז' משום טומאה בחבורים דיקרב בדיקרב בחבורים טמא ז' מדאורייתא כדאמר בפ״ב דע״ז (דף לז: ושם) ואפילו בחבורים על ידי אהל טמא טומאת ז' כדמוכח בריש אהלות (פ״א מ״ג) לכך נראה שטמאוהו לאיכר טומאת ז' משום טומאה בחבורים והשומע טעה לפי שאינו פשוט כ״כ דין טומאה בחבורים והיה סבור דמשום אהל טמאוהו כיון שיש בהקיפו טפח לכך שנה כל המטלטלין מביאין טומאה לטמא כל אשר תחתיו משום אהל בעובי המרדע:

*אמר רבי עקיבא אני אתקן שיהו דברי חכמים קיימין שיהו כל המטלטלין מביאין טומאה על האדם הנושאן בעובי המרדע. משום אהל לטמאו טומאת שבעה *אפי' היכא דלא שייך טומאה בחבורים כגון שיש סודר מפסיק בין המרדע לבשרו שהסודר טמא טומאת שבעה משום חבורים דהייתו *חבורי אדם במת והאדם אינו טמא אפי' מדרבנן אלא טומאת ערב דטמא מדאורייתא כדמוכח בפ' ג' מינין (נזיר דף מב: ושם) גזרו שיהא אדם טמא טומאת ז' משום אהל שלא יטעו אותם שאין יודעים דין טומאה בחבורים ויאמרו שטמא טומאת ערב משום אהל כיון שיש בהיקפו טפח א״כ אתי למימר שאין באהל אלא טומאת ערב לכך גזרו שיהא טמא ז' כאדם המיטמא באהל שלא חלקו אפילו יהא מפסיק בינו לבין המרדע שלשה סודרים או ד' ויהא אדם רביעי או חמישי או יותר ואפי' אם המטלטלין פשוטי כלי עץ שאינן בני קבולי טומאה דלא שייכא בהם טומאה בחבורים ודוקא בעובי המרדע שיש בהיקפו טפח אבל בפחות מכן ליכא למטעי כלל שהיא משום אהל ואף על פי שלא ידעו טומאה בחבורים לא יטעו אלא ישאלו הטעם: **ועל** שאר אדם וכלים בפותח טפח. כיון דליכא בהן שום טומאה בחבורין בעי אהל חשוב כבשאר דברים וא״ת למה טמאוהו ז' משום חבורים לר' טרפון והא מרדע פשוטי כלי עץ הוא ולא מקבל טומאה דהא ע״כ איירי שאין הדרבן בתוך המרדע שאם יש דרבן בתוכו היה מטמא אפילו בכל שהוא כל מה שתחתיו דחרב הרי הוא כחלל אפי' ע״י אהל כדמוכח בריש אהלות וכל הפסוק דבחלל חרב דרשינן ליה בטומאת אהל בנזיר פ' כ״ג (דף נג:) ואור״ת דחשיב בית קבול מקום שנותנין דרבן במרדעת ולא הוי בית קיבול העשוי למלאות שאין קובעין אותו שם אלא פעמים מניחין ופעמים מסירין וכן מוכח במסכת כלים דחשיב בית קבול דתנן* המרדע יש לו אחורים ותוך והא דתנן בפ״ט דכלים (משנה ו) כוש שבלע ליטרא ומלמד שבלע דרבן כו' היו טהורים ונכנסו לאהל נטמא פי' הדרבן לבדו נגע בהן ככר של תרומה טהור משמע דמלמד חשוב פשוטי כלי עץ לכך טהור ככר של תרומה שנגע במלמד שהמלמד לא קיבל טומאה מן הדרבן ומלמד ומרדע מסתמא הכל אחד ואור״י דאיכא לאוקמי בכה״ג שא״א להוציא הדרבן אא״כ ישבר בית קבולו ולכך לא חשיב תו בית קבול: **גוזרני** טומאה אף על המסיקה. פי' הר״ר פורת דלהכי לא גזרו על המסיקה דגזירה שמא יבצרנו בקופות מזופפות *לא שייך בזיתים דמוהל היוצא מהם לא חשיב משקה והא דתנן במס' מכשירין (פ״ו מ״ה) מוהל השמן כשמן י״ל דהייתו במוהל היוצא לאחר אגילה לאחר שעמדו בכומר ב' ימים או ג' ואתיא כר' יעקב דריש חבית (לקמן קמד:) אבל מוהל היוצא ע״י מסיקה אפי' רבי יעקב מודה דטהור וכן גזירה דנושכות ופעמים שאדם יולא לכרמו לידע אם הגיעו ענביו לבצור נמי לא שייך בהן והשתא אתי שפיר דתניא לקמן בריש חבית (דף קמה· ושם) המפלע בזיתים לידע אם הגיעו זיתיו למסוק אם לאו לא הוכשר*: **הניחא** למ״ד כלי טמא חושב משקה. [בתוספתא][א] דמכשירין (פ״ד מ״ה) גבי עריבה שירד דלף לתוכה ב״ש אומר הרי זה בכי יותן כו' בד״א בטהורה אבל בטמאה הכל מודים הרי זה בכי יותן דברי רבי מאיר ר' יוסי אומר אחת טמאה ואחת טהורה ב״ש אומרים בכי יותן ובית הלל אומרים אינו בכי יותן: כיון

עין משפט נר מצוה

קכו א ב מיי' פי״ד מהלכות טומאת מת הלכה ה סמג עשין רלה:

קכז ג ד מיי' פי״א מהל' טומאת אוכלין הל' א סמג עשין רמו:

[לקמן קטז זבחים יג.]

מהרש״ל ומהר״ם כתבו דהך עם דיבור התוספות דבסמוך ד״ה ועל כו' כולם דיבור אחד עם לעיל ד״ה ששמע

חבורי אוהל כמת והאדם כו' כצ״ל מהרש״א ועי' ר״מ ורש״ל

רבינו חננאל

מרדע שאמרו אין בעביו טפח ויש בהיקפו טפח והוא לא חשיב ליה אהל עד דהוי בעביו טפח וגזרו על מי שיש בהיקפו טפח להחשב אהל אטו עוביו: **הבוצר** לגת כו' אוקימנא לעילא שתיק ליה הלל לשמי פי' מי שבצר ענבים שכוונתו להוצאת יין מהן ואמרו בזה כמה טעמים אחד גזירה שמא יבצרנו בקופות טמאות [שחושב] (שחשיבת) משקין גזרו אפילו על הטהורות: שני שמא יבצרנו בקופות מזופפות שאינן פולטות משקין וכאילו מתכוין באותן משקין ודעתו עליהן: שלישי גזירה משום הנושכות פי' יש מי שאומר כגון שיש לקופו' הללו אוננין ונושכות בהן הענבים ופולטין משקין ויש מי שאומר שנושך אדם מאשכול וטופחין ממנו משקין ורב נחמן אמר גזירה שמא יש עליהן בשעת בצירה משקין ממה שזולף עליה' בעודם מחוברין והמשקה ההוא עדיין טופח פירוש טופח שאם תטפח ידך עליו מתלחלחת היד:

רב נסים גאון

לרבן שמעון בן גמליאל דאמר לא לכל טמאות אלא לטומאת מת אלא למאן דאמר אף לכל הטמאו' אמרו מאי איכא למימר מחלוקת ·התנא קמא דפליג עליה רשב״ג והמשנה שחלקו בה התנאים היא שהזכירה במתנות פשוטיהן ומקבליהן טמאין כו' ודבריה בראש פר' י״א מן מסכת כלים: **אמר** ר' ינאי ומרדע שאמרו אין בעביו טפח כו' תמצא בתוספתא כלים פר' י״ד עובי המרדע ב' אצבעות והיקפו טפח: **הניחא** למאן דאמר כלי טמא חושב את המשקין אלא למאן דאמר אין כלי טמא חושב את המשקין מאי איכא למימר דע כי זו החלוקה נלאו למצוא אותה הרבה מהחכמים ולא תמצא אחד מן הקדמונים שפירשה וביררה ברהמי שמיא כבר יגעתי ומצאתי בתוס' מכשירין (פ״ג) עריבה שירד דלף לתוכה המים הניתזין והצפין אינן בכי יותן נסלה לשפכה בית שמאי אומרים בכי יותן ובית הלל אומרים אינן בכי יותן במה דברים אמורים בטהורה אבל בטמאה הכל מודים שהן בכי יותן דברי ר״מ ר' יוסי אומר אחת טהורה ואחת טמאה בית שמאי אומרים הרי זה בכי יותן וב״ה אומרים אינם בכי יותן סבר ר״מ כי בעריבה טמאה מודים ב״ש וב״ה שהן בכי יותן וכלי טמא חושב את המשקה ור' יוסי סבר כי לא (פרש) [כי לא יש הפרש] אצל בית הלל בין הטמאה לטהורה שאינו בכי יותן ואין כלי טמא חושב את המשקה והזהר לך בזה הפירוש כי נסתר הוא מאד

מסורת הש״ס (גליון)

ול״ד לקופץ ועוף הפורח דלא חשבינן במס' אהלות דסא רגלי האיכר נוגעים ב״רן כשהוא עוכר [ת״י]

[לעיל טו.] ע״ז לט: חולין לו:

כלומר היה לך לגזור אף במסיקה משום דאי לא הא לא קיימא הא [תוס' יבמות]

[תוספתא פ״א]

הגהות הב״ח

(א) תוס' ד״ה הניחא וכו' מס' מכשירין [illegible]

הגהות הגר״א

[א] גמ' ולר' טרפון [illegible]

[וע״ע תוס' פסחים ג: ד״ה אין ותוס' חגיגה כה. ד״ה יתננה ותוס' יבמות טו: ד״ה לריכה]

גליון הש״ס

גמ' גוזרני טומאה אף על המסיקה. עי' חגיגה דף כה ע״א תוס' ד״ה יתננה: שם הניחא למ״ד כלי טמא חושב. עי' עורי אבן חגיגה דף יט ע״א ד״ה ידיו טהורות: רש״י ד״ה הניחא. לא ידענא היכא. עי' ברכות דף כה ע״ב ברש״י ד״ה מאן שמעת ליה כו' וצ״ע: תוס' ד״ה אמר ר״ע וכו' אפי' היכא דלא שייך טומאה בחיבורין. עי' בכ״מ דף קה ע״ב תוס' ד״ה על אדם: תוס' ד״ה גוזרני טומאה וכו' לא שייך בזיתים דמוהל וכו'. עי' רפ״ט דטהרות בר״ע ובתוי״ט שם:

טבי רישבא אמר שמואל אף *גידולי תרומה תרומה בו ביום גזרו מ"ט א"ר חנינא גזירה משום תרומה טהורה ביד ישראל אמר רבא אי דחשידי להכי אפרושי נמי לא ליפרשו (אלא אמר רבא ישראל) כיון דאפשר למעבד חטה אחת *כדשמואל ולא קעביד הימוני מהימני *אלא גזירה ^אמשום תרומה טמאה ביד כהן דילמא משהי לה גביה ואתי לידי תקלה : ואידך אמר ר' חייא בר אמי משמיה דעולא אף *מי שהחשיך לו בדרך נותן כיסו לנכרי בו ביום גזרו : *ואידך אמר באלי אמר אבימי סנוותאה פתן ושמנן ויינן ובנותיהן כולן מי"ח דבר הן הניחא לרבי מאיר אלא לר' יוסי שבסרי הויין איכא הא דרב אחא בר אדא דאמר רב אחא בר אדא אמר ר' יצחק גזרו על פתן משום שמנן ועל שמנן משום יינן על פתן משום שמנן מאי אולמיה דשמן מפת אלא גזרו על ^בפתן ושמנן משום יינן ^גועל יינן משום בנותיהן ^דועל בנותיהן משום דבר אחר ועל דבר אחר משום דבר אחר מאי דבר אחר *אמר רב נחמן בר יצחק ^הגזרו על תינוק נכרי שמטמא בזיבה שלא יהא תינוק ישראל רגיל אצלו במשכב זכור אי הכי לר"מ נמי תשסרי הויין אוכלין וכלים שנטמאו במשקין בחדא חשיב להו : **מתני'** ב"ש אומרים אין שורין דיו וסמנים וכרשינין אלא כדי שישורו מבעוד יום וב"ה מתירין ב"ש אומרים אין נותנין אונין של פשתן לתוך התנור אלא כדי שיהבילו מבעוד יום ולא את הצמר ליורה אלא כדי שיקלוט העין וב"ה מתירין ב"ש אומרים אין פורסין מצודות חיה ועופות ודגים אלא כדי שיצודו מבעוד יום וב"ה מתירין ב"ש אומרים אין מוכרין לנכרי ואין טוענין עמו ואין מגביהין עליו אלא כדי שיגיע למקום קרוב ובית הלל מתירין ב"ש אומרים אין נותנין עורות לעבדן ולא כלים לכובס נכרי אלא כדי שיעשו מבעוד יום ובכולן ^ובית הלל מתירין עם השמש

רש"י

טבי · שם האיש : רישבא · פורש גשבין לצוד חיה ועוף : גידולי תרומה · אם זרעה ואפי' דבר שזרעו כלה כגון תבואה וקטנית : תרומה טהורה ביד ישראל · ועינו צרה ליתנה לכהן וזורעה לבטלה מתורת תרומה: אי דחשידי להכי אפרושי נמי לא ליפרשו · אלא חטה אחת מן הכרי כדשמואל ומדאפרשו ש"מ לא חשידי : משום תרומה טמאה ביד כהן · שאסורה באכילה ובא לזורעה וגזור שתהא בשמה הראשון והרי היא תרומה טמאה דחיישינן דילמא משהי לה עד זמן זריעה ואתי למיכל בטומאתה : נותן כיסו לנכרי ולא יטלטלו פחות פחות מד' אמות : סנוותאה · שם מקום : ובנותיהן · במס' ע"ז פרכינן בנותיהן דאורייתא נינהו : כולן מי"ח דברים הן · והא כולהו חדא היא דגזרו על פיתן משום שמנן ועל שמנן כו' כדלקמן : הניחא לר"מ · דמנו להו להא דמניח כלים תחת הצינור הוו להו י"ח ט' דפסלי תרומה ואין קורין ואין פולין הא חדסר פשו להו ז' צינור ומרדע ובנות כותים ובולר וגידולי תרומה ונותן כיסו ופיתן ושמנן חדא : איכא הא · דמוסיף רב יצחק אדאבימי על דבר אחר משום ד"א : ועל בנותיהן משום ד"א · ע"ז ועוד גזרו על ד"א שלא הוזכר כאן: שמטמא בזיבה · °ואפילו אינו זב: אוכלין וכלים שנטמאו *במשקין חדא חשיב להו : **מתני'** סמנין · לצבע : כרשינין · למאכל בהמה ביק"א בלע"ז : וב"ה מתירין · משנתן את המים מבעוד יום : אונין · אריסב"א והן אגודות של פשתן מנופץ ונותנין אותו בקדרה לתנור ומתלבן: שיהבילו · שיתחממו (א): העין · הצבע שיקלוט מבעוד יום : מתירין · לתתה מבעו"י והיא קולטת כל הלילה: ולא טוענין עמו · על החמור: ולא מגביהין עליו · משאוי על כתיפו דנראה כמסייעו להוליך בשבת : אלא כדי שיגיע למקום קרוב · כלומר שיהא המקום קרוב שיוליכנו שם מבעו"י :

עם

תוספות

כיון דאפשר למיעבד כשמואל מהימני · הקשה ריב"א תרומת מעשר דלא אפשר להו למיעבד כשמואל ליגזור ותירץ ר"י דמ"מ אמת הוא שגזרו אף על גידולי תרומה גדולה ורוצה לפרש טעם בכולן : ומהר"ם אמר דתרומת מעשר מהימני הלוים דאין נותנין מעשר אלא לחברים וריב"א תירץ דאותן שהיו חשודים לא היו מפרישין כלל כדאמ' בסוטה ודברים שהיו מפרישים מהימני [תוס ישנים] : **דילמא** משהי ליה גביה ואתי ביה לידי תקלה · פי' בקונטרס ולכך גזרו דאפי' יזרענה להוי טמאה וקשה לר"י דאמר בהדיא בפרק כל שעה (פסחים דף לד· ושם) שתילי תרומה טמאה טהורים מלטמא ואסורין מלאכול פי' לזרים כדמפרש התם אלמא לכהנים שרי וי"ל כיון דאין נאכלין לזרים משום ריוח פורתא שמטהרין לא משהי גביה והא דהכא חיישינן לתקלה ובספ"ק דפסחים (דף כ:) אמרי ב"ה תעשה זילוף איכא למימר דהכא מודו ב"ה דפעמים שצריך להשהות שנה שלימה עד זמן זריעה*: **על** פתן ושמנן משום יינן. הקשה ריב"א מ"ש שהחמירו טפי ביין לאסור בהנאה מפת ושמן ותירץ מפני שהיין משמח אלהים ואנשים והיו רגילין לנסכו אפי' שלא בפני ע"ז הואיל והוצרכו לאוסרו משום בנותיהם נהגו בו חכמים דין וחומר יין נסך ממש כיון דפעמים היו מנסכין אותו אפי' שלא בפני ע"ז : **הניחא** לר' מאיר אלא לרבי יוסי שבסרי הויין. ה"מ נמי למימר אלא לר' טרפון מאי איכא למימ' רש"י חשיב אין פולין ואין קורין בתרתי וכן משמע מדקתני בברייתא אלו מן ההלכות ולא קתני בברייתא אלא הנהו תרתי והא דלא חשיב מבחין בין בגדו לבגדי אשתו ושמש הבודק כוסות וקערות לאור הנר הנך נפקו מכלל הני תרתי שהן עיקר מיהו קשה דלא מני רש"י הך דלא יאכל הזב עם הזבה דודאי מי"ח דבר הוא דקתני לה במתניתין בהדיא ולפי זה אוכל ראשון ואוכל שני חדא חשיב להו א"כ הבא ראשו ורובו במים שאובין וטהור שנפלו כו' חשיב חדא משום דלאי לא הא לא קיימא הא כי היכי דפתן ושמנן ויינן ובנותיהן חשיב גזירה אחת והאי דלא יאכל זב פרוש עם זב עם הארץ דקתני עלה בתוספתא אלו מן ההלכות איכא למימר דהוי בכלל לא יאכל הזב עם הזבה : **ועל** בנותיהם משום דבר אחר . ואם תאמר הניחא למ"ד דמפרש בפרק ב' דמסכת ע"ז (דף לו:) דעל בנותיהם גזרו יחוד דשייך למיגזר משום ע"ז אלא למ"ד דעל בנותיהם גזרו נדות מה שייך הך גזירה לע"ז וי"ל דע"י שגזרו עליהם נדות יפרשו ממגען ולא יטמעו בהם כ"כ : **אונין** · פי' בקונ' נותנים בתנור *ומתלבן וכן משמע בפ"ב (דף כז:) דאמרי' האונין של פשתן משיתלבנו: **אין** פורסין מצודות כו'. אע"ג דבשבת נמי אם פירש מצודה אינו חייב חטאת שאינו יודע אם יצוד אם לאו מ"מ גזרו לפרוש מצודה דפעמים אתי לידי חיוב חטאת כגון שבשעת פריסתו ילכוד דהכי קתני בתוספתא הפורש מצודה לבהמה או לעוף ונכנס לתוכה חייב : **אלא** בכדי שיצודו . וא"ת מנא ידע מתי יבא החיה וי"ל דבירושלמי מוקי לה בפורש בחורשין דמצוין שם חיותא ומיירי בענין זה שלא יוכל ללכוד במצודה אלא א' או ב' דהא מה מועיל שיצודו מבעוד יום אם יכול לצוד גם משתחשכה: **אין** מוכרים לנכרי . אף על גב דאי עביד להו בשבת לא מיחייב חטאת מ"מ אחר שהנכרי מחמר או עושה בשבת בידים דבר שישראל אסור מן התורה גזרו רבנן עם חשכה כדפירש בקונטרס משום דמיחלף בשלוחו אבל בהנך דברים דרישא שאינו עושה בשבת איסור בידים לא גזרו אי לאו דמיחייב חטאת והיינו טעמא דאין נותנין עורות לעבדן : **אין** נותנין עורות לעבדן וב"ה מתירין . מכאן היה נראה לר"ת להתיר על ידי קבלנות נכרי לבנות בשבת ועוד מביא ראיה מריחים דשרי ב"ה אליבא דרב יוסף בגמ' דמתירין להניח שם חיטין מבעוד יום ויניחו כל השבת כל שכן קבלנות על ידי נכרים דשרי ואינו ראיה דידעי כ"ע שהריחים טוחנות מעצמם וידעי נמי שהחטין הושמו שם מע"ש · אבל קבלנות יאמרו שלוה להם· בשבת לעשות ועוד מביא ראיה מסוף פ"ק דע"ז (דף כא: ושם*) דאמר רשב"ג משכיר אדם שדהו לנכרי מ"ט אריס אריסותיה קעביד וה"נ קבלנותיה קעביד ואף על גב דר"ש בן אלעזר פליג עליה קיימא לן כרשב"ג דסתם מתני' כוותיה והא דאמרינן במ"ק (דף יב· ושם) מקבלי קבולת בתוך התחום אסור חוץ לתחום מותר מוקי ר"ת התם כולה שמעתיה באבל ולכך החמיר ול"נ דהתם איכא דמחמרי בחול המועד טפי מבאבל ואפילו למאן דמחמרי טפי באבל מבחול המועד מודה בשבת דחמיר טפי ונראה לר"י דהא דשרי בשמעתין עורות לעבדן היינו בתלוש דלא מפרסמא מילתא שהנכרי עושה מלאכה בביתו ולא ידעי שהוא של ישראל וכן נמי אמר במ"ק (דף יא: ושם) גבי אבל מלאכתו ביד אחרים בביתו לא יעשו בבית אחרים יעשו אבל קבלנות דמחובר דהוי ברשות ישראל דמפרסמא מלתא אסור בתוך התחום דהרואה יאמר שכירי יום ניהו והכי משמע בירושלמי דפירקין דקאמר התם אומני נכרים שהן עושים עם ישראל בתוך ביתו אסור בתוך ביתם מותר אמר ר' שמעון בן אלעזר בד"א בקבולת אבל

עין משפט נר מצוה

קכח א מיי' פ"א מהל' תרומות הלכה כח:

קכט ב מיי' פ"ז מהל' מאכלות אסורות הלכה ט יב סמג לאוין קמב טוש"ע יו"ד סימן קיב סעיף א :

קל ג מיי' פ"א שם הלכה ג סמג לאוין קמט טוש"ע יו"ד סימן קכג סעיף א :

[קידושין נח: ע"ז עג: חולין קלז:]

קלא ד מיי' פי"ב מהל' איסורי ביאה הל' ה סמג לאוין קיב טוש"ע אה"ע סי' טז סעיף א :

קלב ה מיי' פ"ד מהל' איסורי ביאה הל' ד ופ"א מהל' טומאת מת הלכה יד ופ"ב מהלכות משכב ומושב הלכה י :

[וע"ע תוס' ב"ק קטו: ד"ה אמי]

קלג ו מיי' פ"ג מהלכות שבת הלכה ב' ופ"ו שם הלכה יט סמג לאוין סה טור שו"ע או"ח סימן רמד סעיף א וסימן רנג סעיף א ב :

[ג"ז שם: ע"ש]

רבינו חננאל

גידולי תרומה תרומה' אסיק' משום תרומה טמאה ביד כהן אבל משום טהורה ביד ישראל לא פי' דאפשר למעבד כדשמואל דאמר חטה אחת פוטרת את הכרי ומפורשת הא דשמואל בסוף ע"ז. הא דאמר עולא והא דאמר באלי פשוטות הן : י"ח דברים שגזרו בו ביום אלו הן שפוסלין את התרומה האוכל אוכל ראשון או אוכל שני אע"ג דסתיין הכא כר' יהושע דאמר זה וזה שני הוא הא מיפרש בשחיטת חולין פרק השוחט (דף לד ע"א) מימרא דרבה בר בר חנה (דילן) האוכל אוכל אוכל ראשון והאוכל אוכל שני כי שנים הם והשותה משקין טמאים והבא ראשו ורובו במים שאובין וטהור שנפלו עליו על ראשו ועל רובו ג' לוגין מים שאובין והספר והידים אבל טבול יום לא דאמרינן (פוסל האוכלין) סמי מיכן טבול יום כלומר טבול יום אינה גזירה אלא מן התורה פוסל . האוכלין והכלים לר' מאיר דמחשב להו בחדא הרי ח' דברים הללו שפוסלין את התרומה גזרו בו ביום ועוד גזרו עשרה אחרים ואלו הן המניח כלים תחת הצינור וכל' הממלטלין מביאין הטומאה והבוצר לגת גדולי תרומה ומי שהחשיך ופיתן ושמנן ויינן ובנותיהן ודבר אחר הרי י"ח דברים אליבא דר' מאיר ולר' יוסי דאמר כי המניח כלים תחת הצינור לא גזרו בו אלא עדיין הוא מחלוקת פיתת זה ומחשב זה אוכלין והכלים שנטמא במשקין שניים הרי גם לר' יוסי י"ח דבר שגזרו ובנות כותים נדות מעריסתן ותינוק נכרי שיהא מטמא בזיבה כדי שלא יהא תינוק ישראל רגיל אצלו בעבירה : ירושלמי ר' אליעזר אומר בו ביום גדשו סאה לחבית מלאה אגוזים כל מה שאתה נותן לתוכה שומשמין מחזקת פי' הוסיפו גזירות לגזור גזירות ר' יהושע אומר בו ביום מחקו סאה לא הוסיפו ולא גרעו אלא התירו המותר ואסרו האיסור לחבית מלאה שמן אם יתן לתוכה מים מקיא השמן . תני רשב"י בו ביום גזרו פיתן ויינן וגבינתן וחמצן וציקן ומורייסן וכבושיהן ושלוקיהן ומלוחיהן ועל החליקה ושחיקה וטיסני ועל לשונם ועל עדותן ומתנתן ובטוריהן ובניהן שנטמאו בזיבה מבן ט' שנים ויום אחד כדי שלא יהא תינוק ישראל מצוי אצלו במשכב זכור ובנותיהן מבת ג' שנים ויום א'. פת עימעמו עליה והתירוה במקום שאין פת ישראל מצויה מפני חיי נפש. שמן רבי ובית דינו התירוהו מפני שלא פשט איסורו ברוב ישראל ופירושן במס' ע"ז [ל"ו ע"א]. רבי חייא רבה מפקד לרב אין את יכול מיכל כל שתא בטהרה אכול. ואין לא תהא אכול ז' יומין בשתא. מיכן היה ר' פנחס בן יאיר אומר זריזות מביאה [לידי נקיות נקיות מביאה] לידי טהרה טהרה מביאה לידי קדושה קדושה מביאה לידי ענוה ענוה מביאה לידי יראת חטא יראת חטא מביאה לידי רוח הקדש רוה"ק לידי חסידות חסידות לידי תחיית המתים תחיית המתים לידי אליהו ז"ל זריזות לידי נקיות שנאמר וכלה מכפר נקיות לידי טהרה שנאמר וכפר וטהר וגו'. תני בשם ר"מ כל הקבוע בא"י ואוכל חולין בטהרה ומדבר בלשון הקודש וקורא את שמע בבקר ובערב מובטח לו שהוא בן העולם הבא : **אלו** כולן ששנינו במשנתינו כגון שריית דיו ונתינת אונין של פשתן לתנור וכיוצא בהן : **הלכתא** כב"ה דמתירין עם השמש

מסורת הש"ס

[תרומות פ"ט מ"ד] פסחים לד. נדרים ס.]

רש"ע מ"ז

אלא אמר רבא כצ"ל רש"ל

לקמן קנג.

ע"א לו. ע"ש

כ"א אוכלין וכלים מטמאין משקין ע' מהרש"א

הגהות הב"ח

(א) רש"י ד"ה שיהבילו שיתחממו הס"ד ואח"כ מתחיל סדיבור שיקלוט . מבעוד יום הוא סו"ד ואח"כ מ"ה ספין הלבע :

וריב"א רצה לפרש שנותנין אותו בתנור כדי לייבשן כשמעלן מן המשרה ויש בו איסור בישול טרם שיתייבשו מתרכך מחמת הלחלוחית וכדאמר [לקמן עד:] האי מאן דשדי סיכתא לאתונא חייב משום מבשל [תוס' ישנים]

גליון הש"ס

רש"י ד"ה שמטמא בזיבה ואפי' אינו זב. עיין מהרש"א לקמן דף כא ע"ב בתוד"ה שהיה מונח

רב נסים גאון

וכבר סייעני המקום לגלותו ולבררו : **אלא** אמר רבה ישראל כיון דאפשר למיעבד כשמואל ולא קא עבדי דאמר שמואל חטה אחת פוטרת את הכרי ותמצא במס' קידושין (דף נח) בסוף האיש מקדש ובמסכת *)בכורות בפרק יש בכור לנחלה ובשחיטת חולין בפ' ראשית הגז (דף קלו). ואידך אמר באלי גיותאה משמיה דרב פיתן ושמנן ויינם ובנותיהם כולן אמורין משנה עשר דבר תמצא בפ' אין מעמידין בהמה (ע"ז דף לו) כבר הודו ואסרו בנותיהן דאורייתא היא דכתיב (דברים ז) לא תתחתן בם והזכירו בזה הענין הרבה פנים ולא נתקיימו ובירורו בסוף הדברים דאורייתא יחוד דאשת איש אתא דוד גזר אפילו יחוד דפנויה אתו אינהו גזור

*) לפנינו לא נמצא בפ' יש בכור מימרא דשמואל הלזו רק הוא בע"ז ד' עג ע"ב.

And another?—Said [17b] Ṭabi the hunter in Samuel's name: That the produce of *terumah* is *terumah* was also enacted on that day.[8] What is the reason?—R. Ḥanina said: It was a preventive measure, on account of undefiled *terumah* [being retained] in the hand of an Israelite.[9] Raba observed: If they are suspected of this, they would not separate [*terumah*] at all: [and furthermore][10] since he can render one grain of wheat [as *terumah* for the whole],
a in accordance with Samuel,[1] and does not, he is indeed trusted.[2] Rather, said Raba, it is a preventive measure on account of unclean *terumah* in the priest's hands, lest he keep it with him and be led to sin.[3]

And another?—R. Ḥiyya b. Ammi said in 'Ulla's name: That one must give his purse to a Gentile if [the Sabbath] evening falls upon him on the road was also enacted on that day.[4]

And another?—Bali said in the name of Abimi of Senawta:[5] [The interdict against] their bread, oil, wine and daughters[6]—all these are of the eighteen measures.[7]

Now, this is well according to R. Meir; but according to R. Jose, there are only seventeen?[8]—There is also that of R. Aḥa b. Adda. For R. Aḥa b. Adda said in R. Isaac's name: Their bread was forbidden on account of their oil, and their oil on account of their wine.[9] 'Their bread on account of their oil'!—wherein is [the interdict of] oil stronger than that of bread?[10] Rather [say] they decreed against their bread and oil on account of their wine, and against their wine on account of their daughters, and against their daughters on account of 'the unmentionable,'[11] and [they decreed] something else on account of some other thing. What is this 'something else?'—Said R. Naḥman b. Isaac: They decreed that a heathen child shall defile by gonorrhoea,[12] so that an Israelite child should not associate with him for
b sodomy.[1] But if so, according to R. Meir too [it is difficult, for] there are nineteen!—Food and drink which were defiled through liquid he accounts as one.

MISHNAH. BETH SHAMMAI RULE: INK, DYES AND ALKALINE PLANTS[2] MAY NOT BE STEEPED UNLESS THEY CAN BE DISSOLVED WHILE IT IS YET DAY;[3] BUT BETH HILLEL PERMIT IT. BETH SHAMMAI RULE: BUNDLES OF WET FLAX MAY NOT BE PLACED IN AN OVEN UNLESS THEY CAN BEGIN TO STEAM WHILE IT IS YET DAY, NOR WOOL IN THE DYER'S KETTLE UNLESS IT CAN ASSUME THE COLOUR [OF THE DYE]; BUT BETH HILLEL PERMIT IT. BETH SHAMMAI MAINTAIN: SNARES FOR WILD BEASTS, FOWLS, AND FISH, MAY NOT BE SPREAD UNLESS THEY CAN BE CAUGHT WHILE IT IS YET DAY; BUT BETH HILLEL PERMIT IT. BETH SHAMMAI RULE: ONE MUST NOT SELL TO A GENTILE, OR HELP HIM TO LOAD [AN ASS], OR LIFT UP [AN ARTICLE] UPON HIM UNLESS HE CAN REACH A NEAR PLACE;[4] BUT BETH HILLEL PERMIT IT. BETH SHAMMAI MAINTAIN: HIDES MUST NOT BE GIVEN TO A TANNER, NOR GARMENTS TO A GENTILE FULLER, UNLESS THEY CAN BE DONE WHILE IT IS YET DAY; BUT IN ALL THESE [CASES]

(8) By Biblical law, if *terumah* is resown its produce is *hullin* (q.v. Glos.), but the Rabbis decreed that it is *terumah* and belongs to the priest. (9) Who may resow and keep it for himself, thus depriving the priest of his dues. (10) The text is in slight disorder.

a (1) V. Ḳid. 58*b*. (2) Not to retain the *terumah*, by resowing it. (3) Whilst keeping it for resowing, he may forget that it is unclean, and eat it. Therefore it was enacted that even if resown its produce may not be eaten, though it will not be regarded as unclean (Tosaf. as explained by Maharsha). (4) *Infra* 153*a*; and not carry it along short distances of less than four cubits each. (5) In A.Z. 36*a* the reading is Niwte, i.e., the Nabatean. Senawta is probably a dialect form of the same. (6) *Sc.* of Gentiles. (7) They are counted as one. (8) V. *supra* 16*b*. This seems a repetition of the question there. (9) Actually these were ancient prohibitions, going back to the days of Daniel (cf. Dan. I, 8; Josephus, *Ant.* I, 3, 12). But in the course of time their observance grew weak, and the disciples of Shammai and Hillel renewed and strengthened the prohibition as one of their eighteen enactments. V. Halevi, *Doroth*, I, 3, pp. 591ff, *seq.*, v. also Weiss, *Dor*, I, 129. (10) For this implies that there was greater reason for prohibiting their oil than their bread. (11) Lit., 'something else', viz., idolatry. (12) Even if he is not suffering therewith.

b (1) Thus this is the eighteenth. (2) Jast. Rashi: horse beans, used for cattle. (3) These materials had to be steeped in water before they were fit for their purpose, and Beth Shammai rule that this may not be done on Friday unless there is time for the process to be completed before the Sabbath. *Yashuru* means dissolved and soaked through, and will bear the latter meaning in respect of beans, according to Rashi's translation. (4) I.e., his destination must be near enough to be reached before the Sabbath.

BETH HILLEL PERMIT [THEM] [18*a*] BEFORE SUNSET.[5] R. SIMEON B. GAMALIEL SAID: IT WAS THE PRACTICE IN MY FATHER'S HOUSE TO GIVE WHITE GARMENTS TO A GENTILE FULLER THREE DAYS BEFORE THE SABBATH.[6] AND BOTH [SCHOOLS] AGREE THAT THE BEAM OF THE [OIL] PRESS AND THE CIRCULAR WINE PRESS MAY BE LADEN.[7]

GEMARA. Which Tanna [holds that] pouring water into ink
a constitutes its steeping?[1]—Said R. Joseph, It is Rabbi. For it was taught: If one pours in flour and another water, the second is liable:[2] this is Rabbi's view.[3] R. Jose son of R. Judah said: He is not liable unless he kneads [them]. Abaye said to him, Yet perhaps R. Jose [son of R. Judah] ruled thus only in respect to flour, which is subject to kneading: but as for ink, which is not subject to kneading, I may say that he is liable?[4]—You cannot think so, for it was taught: If one pours in the ashes and another the water, the second is liable: this is Rabbi's view. R. Jose son of R. Judah said: [He is not liable] unless he kneads them.[5] Yet perhaps what is [meant by] ashes? Earth [dust],[6] which does require kneading.[7] But both ashes and earth [dust] were taught?—Were they then taught together?[8]

Our Rabbis taught: Water may be conducted into a garden on the eve of the Sabbath just before dark, and it may go on being filled the whole day; and a perfume brazier may be placed under garments which continue to absorb the perfume the whole day; and sulphur may be placed under [silver] vessels and they undergo the process of sulphuring the whole day; and an eye salve[9] may be placed on the eye and a plaster on a wound and the process of healing continues all day.[10] But wheat may not be placed in a water-mill unless it can be ground when it is still day. What is the reason? Rabbah answered, Because it makes a noise.[11] Said R. Joseph to him. Let the Master say it is on account of the resting of utensils? For it was taught: *And in all things that I have said unto*
b *you take ye heed:*[1] this includes the resting of utensils![2] Rather, said R. Joseph, it is on account of the resting of utensils.

Now that you say that according to Beth Hillel the resting of utensils is a Biblical precept,[3] why are sulphur and a perfume brazier permitted?—Because it [the vessel in which they lie] performs no action. Why are wet bundles of flax permitted?—Because it [the oven in which they lie] performs no action and is motionless. But what of the trap for wild beasts, fowl and fish, which performs an action,[4] why are they permitted?—There too [it means] with a fish hook and a trap made with little joists,[5] so that no action is performed.

Now, however, that R. Oshaia said in R. Assi's name, Which Tanna [maintains that] the resting of utensils is a Biblical precept? It is Beth Shammai: then according to Beth Shammai, whether it [the utensil] performs an action or not, it is forbidden, while in the opinion of Beth Hillel even if it performs an action it is permitted. And now that you say that according to Beth Shammai

(5) Lit., 'with the sun', i.e., while the sun is shining. (6) Because these require more time. (7) By day, though the fluid goes on oozing during the Sabbath.

a (1) The Mishnah merely discusses this, and does not speak about kneading the ingredients too. Hence the mere pouring must be regarded as a labour forbidden on the Sabbath, for otherwise there would be no controversy in respect to Friday. (2) For desecrating the Sabbath. (3) Thus he holds that the mere pouring in of water constitutes kneading, which is forbidden on the Sabbath. The making of ink is prohibited as a derivative (v. *supra* 2*b*, n. a2) of kneading. (4) For mere pouring, even according to the view of R. Jose son of R. Judah. (5) Though ashes do not require kneading. (6) In Heb. these words are very similar and sometimes interchanged. (7) For making clay. (8) In the same Baraitha? They were stated in separate Baraithas, not necessarily by the same teacher, and both may mean the same thing. (9) Heb. *kilur*, Κολλύριον, collyrium. (10) Healing on the Sabbath itself is forbidden, unless there is danger to life. (11) Which detracts from the sanctity of the Sabbath.

b (1) Ex. XXIII, 13. The preceding verse deals with the Sabbath. (2) A man is commanded to let the vessels rest as well as he himself. (3) For this Baraitha must reflect Beth Hillel's ruling, since its other clauses oppose the views of Beth Shammai as expressed in our Mishnah. (4) The spring of the trap closes and the mesh of the nets tightens as they catch their prey. (5) So arranged as to permit the animal to get in but not out. Thus they are passive instruments.

תורה אור

השמש *אמר רשב"ג נוהגין היו בית אבא שהיו נותנין כלי לבן לכובס נכרי שלשה ימים קודם לשבת ושוין אלו ואלו שטוענין קורת בית הבד ועגולי הגת: **גמ'** מאן תנא נתינת מים לדיו זו היא שרייתן אמר רב יוסף רבי היא דתניא *אחד נותן את הקמח וא' נותן (א) את המים האחרון חייב דברי רבי רבי *יוסי אומר אינו חייב עד שיגבל א"ל אביי ודילמא עד כאן לא קאמר ר' יוסי אלא בקמח דבר גיבול הוא אבל דיו דלאו בר גיבול הוא אימא ליחייב לא סלקא דעתך דתניא אחד נותן את האפר ואחד נותן את המים האחרון חייב דברי רבי ר' יוסי ברבי יהודה אומר עד שיגבל ודילמא מאי אפר [א]עפר דבר גיבול הוא והתניא אפר והתניא עפר *מידי גבי הדדי תניא: *ת"ר [ב]פותקין מים לגינה ע"ש עם חשיכה ומתמלאת והולכת כל היום כולו ומניחין מוגמר תחת הכלים *(ע"ש) ומתגמרין והולכין כל היום כולו ומניחין גפרית תחת הכלים *(ע"ש עם חשיכה) ומתגפרין והולכין כל השבת כולה ומניחין קילור ע"ג העין ואיספלנית על גבי מכה *(ע"ש עם חשיכה) ומתרפאת והולכת כל היום כולו אבל אין נותנין חטין לתוך הריחים של מים אלא בכדי שיטחנו מבעוד יום מאי טעמא אמר רבה מפני שמשמעת קול א"ל רב יוסף ולימא מר משום שביתת כלים *דתניא °ובכל אשר אמרתי אליכם תשמרו לרבות שביתת כלים שמות כג אלא אמר רב יוסף משום שביתת כלים והשתא דאמרת לב"ה אית להו שביתת כלים דאורייתא גפרית ומוגמר מאי טעמא שרו משום דלא קעביד מעשה אונין של פשתן מאי טעמא שרו משום דלא עביד מעשה ומינח נייחא מצודת חיה ועוף ודגים דקא עביד מעשה מאי טעמא שרו התם נמי בלחי *וקוקרי דלא קעביד מעשה והשתא דאמר רב אושעיא אמר רב אסי מאן תנא שביתת כלים דאורייתא ב"ש היא ולא בית הלל *לב"ש בין קעביד מעשה בין דלא קעביד מעשה אסור לבית הלל [ג]אע"ג דקעביד מעשה שרי והשתא דאמרת דלב"ש אע"ג דלא עביד מעשה אסור אי הכי מוגמר

רש"י

עם השמש · בעוד החמה זורחת: כלי לבן · שהוא קשה לכבס וצריך ג' ימים ומחמירין על עצמן כב"ש: שטוענין · את הזיתים בקורות בית הבד ואת הענבים בעיגולי הגת שלא היו עוצרין אותן בגלגל כמו שלנו אלא טוענין אותן בקורות כבדין והגי דגת קרי עיגולין שהיו דפין עבין עשוין כעיגולין ושוין שטוענין אותן מבעוד יום והמשקה הולך וזב כל השבת ובגמרא (דף יט·) פריך מאי שנא דלא פליגי ב"ש בהא ומפרש משום דאי נמי עביד להו בשבת ליכא חיוב חטאת דכי אמרי' סחיטת זיתים וענבים אב מלאכה בפ' חבית שנשברה (לקמן דף קמג:) הני מילי בזיתים וענבים שלא ריסקן מבעוד יום דהוה ליה מפרק דבר ממאו הגדל בתוכו והיא תולדה דדש אבל הכא אין נותנין קורה על גבי זיתים עד שטוחנין תחלה בריחים וכן ענבים דורכין אותן תחלה ברגל ובלאו קורה נמי משקה נפיק ממילא אלא דלא נפיק שפיר כי השתא ולא דמי לדש: **גמ'** מאי שנא בכולא כו' ל"ג לה הכא אלא לקמן במשנה ושוין שטוענין: מאן תנא נתינת מים לדיו · ואע"פ שלא גיבל הדיו זו היא שרייתן והוי לישה דידיה בהכי ומיחייב משום לש דהא מתני' ליכא גבול ואפליגו בה מבעוד יום מכלל דבשבת חייב חטאת הוא: האחרון חייב · משום לש שהוא אב מלאכה: אפר · לאו בר גיבול הוא: עפר · בר גיבול הוא לטיט של בנין: והא תניא·תרתי מתניתא חדא דאפר וחדא דעפר: מידי גבי הדדי *תניניהו· חדא תניא ר' חייא וחדא תניא רבי אושעיא וחדא מינייהו תניא לעפר בלשון אפר: פותקין · פותחין עושין נגר קטן משפת המעין לגנה: מוגמר· לבונה ומיני בשמים נותנין על האש ומעשנין הבגדים שיהא ריחן נודף: גפרית· תחת כלי כסף שמליירין בהם פרחים וצורות בחרט ומעשנן בגפרית והן משחירות וניכרות וקורין נייל"ר: קילור · תחבושת שקורין לוז"א: ואספלנית· רטייה: ברחיים של מים· וכ"ש ברחיים של יד ושל חמור דאדם מצווה על שביתת בהמתו: שיטחנו מבעוד יום · מפני שמשמעת את הקול ואוושא מילתא בשבת ואיכא זילותא: לרבות שביתת כלים·דכתיב לעיל מינה למען ינוח שורך וחמורך וגו': והשתא דאמרת בית הלל אית להו שביתת כלים · דהא על כרחיך האי מתניתא בית הלל מדשרי בהנך וקתני דרחיים אסור משום שביתת כלים: מוגמר וגפרית אמאי שרו · וה"ה לכל הנך דמתני' הרי המוגמר מונח בעדשקאות ונמצא כלי עושה מלאכה: לא קא עביד הכלי שום מעשה · אלא מונח על הארץ והן בתוכו אבל הרחיים עבדי מעשה ולב"ש כיון דמונחין בנווה הייתו מעשה דיליה: מצודות דקא עבדי מעשה· שהפח נקשר ותופס העוף וכן יקוש שפוסטים לחיות ללוכדן ברגלים כשנוגעין בו קופץ ומתחבר אליו ולוכד: בלחי · חכה שקורין איימ"א שהדג בולעו ומהדקו והכלי אינו זז ממקומו: וקוקרי · שעושין סלים פיה אחד רחב ופיה השני קצר מאד והדג (ס"א והחיה) נכנס שם ומוציא ראשו בפי הקצר ואין גופו יכול לצאת וכשבא להחזיר ראשו לפנים ראשי קרומות נכנסין לו תחת לחיו דהשתא לא עביד כלי מידי: והשתא דאמרת כו' ב"ש היא· והא דריחים ב"ש וב"ש לא שני להו בין היכא דעביד כלי מעשה בין היכא דלא עביד דהא אסרי באונין דמתני' וכיון דב"ש היא: מוגמר

היא והיכא דעביד מעשה אבל היכא דלא עביד מעשה כי הגך דמתני' טעמייהו משום גזירה ומצודות דמתני' בלחי וקוקרי:

תוספות

אבל בשכר אסור פירוש שכיר יום כד"א בתלוש אבל במחובר אסור ובעיר אחרת בין בתלוש בין במחובר מותר אמר ר"ש בר כהנא בשם רבי אחא בשבת ובאבל ובע"ז הלכה כר"ש בן אלעזר ורבינו תם נמי כשבנה את ביתו לא סמך על תשובתו ולא רצה להתיר:

ומיהו בשדה מותר כרשב"ג דבשדה רגילות לעשות באריסות ולא בשכירות יום וכשישראל אומר לנכרי לתקן מנעלים או לקנות אל יאמר תעשה למחר דא"כ הוי כשכיר יום אלא תעשה לכשתרצה ואם הביא לו נכרי כליו ויודע שכבסן בשבת אסור ללובשן בשבת דאמר לקמן (קכב·) נכרי שהדליק נר בשביל ישראל אסור להשתמש לאורה (תוספות ישנים):

אבל דיו דלאו בר גיבול הוא · והא דאמר בבמה מדליקין (לקמן דף כג· ושם) כל השמנים יפים לדיו איבעיא להו לגבל או לעשן לאו דוקא גיבול אלא האי גיבול הייט עירוב בעלמא ואם תאמר והא מורכן דאמר בפרק בתרא (דף קנה: ושם) דלאו בר גיבול הוא וקאמר התם ר' יוסי ברבי יהודה אינו חייב עד שיגבל וי"ל דהתם לגבי קמח קאמר דאינו בר גיבול אבל בר גיבול הוא טפי מדיו והכי לא מייתי מיניה הכא אדיו ומכאן קשה על המפרש ההא דאמר בבילה בפרק המביא (דף לב: ושם) קיטמא שרי הייט כשנותנין מים לתוטו לשרוק התנור סביב הואיל ולאו בר גיבול הוא והכא משמע דאדרבה דמידי דלאו בר גיבול הוא חייב טפי אלא יש לפרש קיטמא שרי בלא מים לשרוק התנור סביביו וקמ"ל דלא גזרינן שמא יגבל בי"ט:

ומתרפאת והולכת כל השבת כולה · ואם תאמר הא דאמר בפרק שמונה שרצים (לקמן דף קח:) שורין קילורין מע"ש ומניח תחת העין בשבת וא"כ בשבת נמי שרי להניח ויש לומר דלקמן מיירי באדם בריא ואינו מניח בעין לרפואה אלא תחת העין לתענוג וליכא למיחש לשחיקת סממנים והכא מניח בעין לרפואה ולא שריא אלא מערב שבת*:

אונין של פשתן מאי טעמא שרו · הא דנקיט אונין טפי מדיו וסממנין וכרשינין משום דהתם פשיטא דליכא מעשה כלל אבל באונין התנור עושה קצת מעשה כשמחממו ועוד דבהנך לא הזכיר כלי אבל גבי אונין הוזכר התנור:

ולימא מר משום שביתת כלים · ואם תאמר למאי דמסיק מאן תנא שביתת כלים דאורייתא ב"ש מאי פריך רב יוסף ולימא מר משום שביתת כלים וכי אינו יותר טוב כמו שמפרש רבה שמשמעת הקול ואתי כב"ה וי"ל דלא סבירא ליה לרב יוסף טעמא דהשמעת הקול כלל ומסתברא ליה טפי לאוקמה כב"ש משום שביתת כלים ונראה דרבה סבר דטעמא דב"ש לאו משום שביתת כלים הוא אלא סבר דטעמא דב"ש דגזרינן דילמא אתי למעבד בשבת דאי לרבה נמי טעמא דב"ש משום שביתת כלים למה היה צריך רב יוסף להביא הברייתא והא מתני' היא דאסרי בית שמאי משום שביתת כלים ועוד דאמר לקמן (דף יט·) הני דאי עביד להו בשבת חייב חטאת גזרו בית שמאי עם חשכה משמע דטעמא דבית שמאי משום גזירה ולא משום שביתת כלים ולרב יוסף לא תקשה אמאי [לא] אסרי בית שמאי טעינת קורה משום שביתת כלים דהתם אתי ממילא טפי מכל הנך דמתניתין ואם תאמר לרבה הך ברייתא דשביתת כלים אמאן תרמייה ויש לומר דרבה סבר דברייתא דשביתת כלים בית שמאי:

והשתא דאמר רב אושעיא הא מני ב"ש היא · אומר ר"ת דהלכתא כרב יוסף דמוקי ברייתא כב"ש דהא רב אושעיא קאי כוותיה ולפ"ז ריחים מותרים דלדידיה לב"ה שרי אפי' היכא דקעביד מעשה ולא חיים להשמעת קול ולי נראה דרב אושעיא לא מוקי לה.

מסורת הש"ס

[פי' תוס' ע"ז כא: ד"ה מאי טעמא]

לקמן קנה:

[נ"ל יוסי ברבי יהודה וכ"א לקמן קנה:]

[עירובין כ: וש"נ] תוספתא פ"א

[כרב אלפס וכרא"ש ליתא]

[ג"ז שם ליתא]

[ג"ז שם ליתא]

תניניהו וחד תני לתרוייהו יכיון דלאו גבי הדדי תניניהו חדא תניא כצ"ל רש"ל

[עי' בערוך ערך לח ובערך קקרי שהאריך לפרש עניינם קחנו משם]

הא מני ב"ש היא ולב"ש ס"א

הגהות הב"ח

(א) גמ' ואחד נותן לתוכו את המים וכו' ודילמא לא סיא ע"כ:

עין משפט נר מצוה

קלד א מיי' פ"ח מהל' שבת הלכה טז סמג לאוין סה:

קלה ב ג מיי' פ"ג מהל' שבת הלכה ב ופ"ז הלכה טז סמג שם טור שו"ע או"ח סימן רנב סעיף ה וסימן רש סעיף א:

[מכילתא פרשת משפטים]

א"נ התם אינו משים קילור עצמו בתחבושת אלא שורה הקילור במים ולגבי דידיה ליכא למיגזר שיודע כי לא התירו לו אלא ע"י שרייה ואחרים סבורין שלרחוץ מים הוא צריך [תוס' ישנים]

רבינו חננאל

אלו ששנינו בברייתא פתיחת מים לגינה בע"ש והנחת מוגמר תחת הכלים והנחת גפרית תחת הכלי' כולן מותרין וכן קילור על העין בע"ש ואיספלנית על המכ' ומתרפאת והולכת בשבת · ואע"ג דקיי"ל כב"ה וב"ה לית להו שביתת כלים נתינת חטים ברחיים של מים בע"ש להטחן בשבת אסור דלא אמרו משום

רב נסים גאון

אפילו יהוד דנכרית ונתבאר עוד בזה הפרק כי תינוק נכרי מטמא בזיבה בן ט' שנים ויום אחד לדבריהם אימתי ראוי לביאה בן ט' שנים ויום אחד אימתי מטמא בזיבה בן ט' שנים ויום אחד:

מוגמר ונפרית מ"ט שרו ב"ש התם מנח ארעא גיגית ונר וקדרה ושפוד מ"ט שרו ב"ש דמפקר להו אפקורי מאן תנא להא דת"ר *לא תמלא אשה קדרה עססיות ותורמסין ותניח לתוך התנור ע"ש עם חשכה ואם נתנן למוצאי שבת אסורין בכדי שיעשו כיוצא בו לא ימלא נחתום חבית של מים ויניח לתוך התנור ע"ש עם חשכה ואם עשה כן למוצאי שבת אסורין בכדי שיעשו לימא ב"ש היא ולא ב"ה אפילו תימא ב"ה גזירה שמא יחתה בגחלים א"ה מוגמר וגפרית נמי לגזור התם לא מחתי להו דאי מחתי סליק בהו קוטרא וקשי להו אונין של פשתן נמי ליגזור התם כיון דקשי להו זיקא לא מגלו ליה צמר ליורה. ליגזור אמר שמואל ביורה עקורה וניחוש שמא מגים בה בעקורה וטוחה והשתא דאמר מר גזירה שמא יחתה בגחלים האי *קדרה חייתא שרי לאנוחה ע"ש עם חשיכה בתנורא מ"ט כיון דלא חזי לאורתא אסוחי מסח דעתיה מיניה ולא אתי לחתויי גחלים ובשיל שפיר דמי בשיל ולא בשיל אסיר ואי שדא ביה גרמא חייא שפיר דמי והשתא דאמר מר כל מידי דקשי ליה זיקא לא מגלו ליה האי בשרא דגדיא ושריק שפיר דמי דברחא ולא שריק אסור דגדיא ולא שריק דברחא ושריק רב אשי שרי ורב ירמיה מדיפתי אסיר ולרב אשי דשרי *(והתניא) *אין צולין בשר בצל וביצה אלא כדי שיצולו מבעוד יום התם דברחא ולא שריק איכא דאמרי *דגדיא בין שריק בין לא שריק שפיר דמי דברחא נמי ושריק שפיר דמי כי פליגי דברחא ולא שריק דרב אשי שרי ורב ירמיה מדפתי אסיר ולרב אשי דשרי *(והתניא) אין צולין בשר בצל וביצה אלא כדי שיצולו מבעוד יום התם בבשרא אגומרי אמר רבינא האי קרא חייא שפיר דמי כיון דקשי ליה זיקא כבשרא דגדיא דמי: ב"ש אומרים אין מוכרין: ת"ר ב"ש אומרים לא ימכור אדם חפצו לנכרי ולא ישאילנו ולא ילונו ולא יתן לו במתנה אלא כדי שיגיע לביתו וב"ה אומרים כדי שיגיע לבית הסמוך לחומה רבי עקיבא אומר כדי שיצא מפתח ביתו א"ר יוסי בר' יהודה הן הן דברי רבי עקיבא הן הן דברי בית הלל לא בא רבי עקיבא אלא לפרש דברי ב"ה: ת"ר *בש"א לא ימכור אדם חמצו לנכרי אלא אם כן יודע בו שיכלה קודם הפסח דברי ב"ש ובית הלל אומרים כל זמן שמותר לאוכלו מותר למוכרו רבי יהודה אומר כותח

רש"י

מוגמר ונפרית מ"ט שרו. הא מנחי בכלים: כגון דמנחי מוגמר ונפרית בארעא. ולא בכלי: גיגית. שהשכר בתוכו ואי אפשר לשופכו לארץ והשעורין נשורין כל השבת יותר מח' ימים והשבת בכלל וכן נר הדולק בשבת וכן קדרה שעל גבי כירה שאי אפשר שלא תצטמק בשבת וכן שפוד המונח בתנור כדתנן (דף יט:) משלשלין את הפסח ולא פליגי ב"ש: בדמפקר להו. לכלים ושוב אינו מצווה על שביתתן: עססיות ותורמסין. מיני קטניות וצריכין בישול יותר: בכדי שיעשו. כדי שלא יהנה ממלאכת שבת: יחתה בגחלים. למהר בישולן: סליק בהו קוטרא. של עלים ומשחיר הבגדים ועשן העלים קשה להם וכן בגפרית: לא מגלי. משטח פי תנור וליכא למגזר שמא יחתה בגחלים: לגזור. שמא יחתה בגחלים: עקורה. מעל האור: מגים. מהפך בה ובמבושל הוי בישול: וטוחה. מכוסה בכיסוי שלה וטוחה בטיט סביב דכולי האי לא טרח ומידכר: והשתא דאמר מר. דהנחת קדרה לא אסירא אלא משום חתויה: האי קדר' חייתא שפיר דמי. להשהותה לכתחלה מבעוד יום בתנור והיא מתבשלת כל הלילה דודאי חייתא לאו אדעתא למיכלה לאורתא אנחה התם ומשום למחר לא אתי לחתויי שהרי יש לה שהות גדול ולא דמי לעססיות ותורמסין שאין כל הלילה והיום די להן: ובשיל שפיר דמי. מבושלת כל צרכה שפיר דמי להניחה דלא בעי חיתוי: שדא ביה גרמא חייא. דלאו דעתיה למיכליה לאורתא: גדיא. קשי ליה זיקא: שריק. פי התנור בטיט סביב כיסוי אינו מוכן לחתות: ברחא. איל גדול לא קשיא ליה זיקא ואתי לגלויי פי התנור ליטול כיסויו לחתות: דגדיא ולא שריק. איכא חדא לאיסורא וחדא להיתרא: בבשרא אגומרי. שאינו בתנור דאפילו כיסוי ליכא ומוכן להפוך בו ולחתות: לא ישאילנו. שאלה דבר החוזר בעין הלואה בדבר הניתן להוצאה: אלא כדי שיגיע. הנכרי לביתו מבעוד יום ולטעמייהו דבדידיה קטרח מחמירין ב"ש דמיחלף בשלוחו: בית הסמוך לחומה. של עיר אחרת שהנכרי דר שם שהרי יכול להגיעו שם: מפתח ביתו. של ישראל: הן הן דברי כו'. לא בא ר"ע לחלוק על ב"ה אלא לחלוק על תנא בן מחלוקתו שאמר אליבא דב"ה לבית הסמוך לחומה ובא ר"ע לומר לא אמרו ב"ה כן אלא כו':

כותח

תוספות

לה כב"ש אלא הש"ס הוא דקאמר הכי הא מני ב"ש היא אליבא דרב יוסף דמוקי לה משום שביתת כלים אבל לרב אושעיא מצינן למימר דמוקי לה כב"ה ואית ליה השמעת קול כרבה וכן פסק ר"ח דטעמא דריחים משום השמעת קול ואתי כב"ה ועוד דסוגיא דלקמן לא מיתוקמא אלא כרבה כדפי' וקי"ל כרב אושעיא דמאן תנא שביתת כלים בית שמאי היא ומותר להשאיל כלים לנכרי ואין לחוש במה שיעשה בו הנכרי מלאכה אבל בהמתו אסור להשאיל דשביתת בהמתו עליו דאורייתא: *ולבית שמאי אף על גב דלא קעביד מעשה וכו'. השתא דטעמא דב"ש משום שביתת כלים הנך ג' בבות קמייתא אין שורין דיו וסממנים ואונין ומצודות הוו משום שביתת כלים שהמלאכה נעשית בתוך הכלי וכמלא שהכלי עושה המלאכה אבל מוכרין לנכרי ועורות לעבדן וכלים לכובס לא הוי משום שביתת כלים דבמה שהעורות מתעבדין אין העור עושה המלאכה אלא האדם המעבד עושה המלאכה וכן בגד המתלבן האדם המלבנו עושה המלאכה אלא טעמא דאסרי בית שמאי משום דמיחלף בשלוחו ולהכי נמי מוגמר וגפרית דמוקי בסמוך דמנחי אארעא אף על גב שהכלים העליונים מתגפרים ונלבעים לא שייך שביתת כלים כדפרישי' שהכלי שאין המלאכה נעשית בו אין בהן משום שביתת כלים:

דמפקרא להו אפקורי. אע"ג דאמר בנדרים (דף מה:) דבעינן הפקר בפני ג' הכא לא בעינן דמסתמא *מפקיר להו ואין לסמוך על זה להשכיר סוס לנכרי ולהפקיר דהכא שאני משום דלא אפשר בענין אחר ועוד שאין הדבר מפורסם*: **לא** ימלא נחתום כו'. כדמסיק גזירה שמא יחתה אף ע"פ שיש שהות הרבה להתחמם חיישינן שמא יצטנן לפי שרגילים לחמם על אש רפה ויהא צריך לחתות: **גזירה** שמא יחתה. ואם תאמר מעיקרא דלא ידע האי טעמא תקשי ליה מתני' דבשר בצל וביצה וחררה. ויש לומר דהתם ידע שפיר דהוי טעמא משום שמא יחתה שאין דבר מפסיק ° בינו לגחלים: **דילמא** מגיס בה והוי צובע: **ביורה** עקור' וטוחה. ואין לחוש שמא יגלה ויגיס שאין דרך להגיס כמו לחתות ועוד דשמא מיהדק טפי: **בשיל** ולא בשיל אסור. נ"ל דלא הוי כמאכל בן דרוסאי דאי הוה כמאכל בן דרוסאי שרי להשהותו על גבי כירה אע"פ *שאינה גרופה וקטומה: **האי** בישרא דגדיא ושריק. מפרש בה"ג דמכאן ואילך איירי בגלי וכן משמע מדמייתי עלה אין צולין בשר בצל וביצה ולקמן בפרקין נמי מייתי לה אמשלשלים את הפסח ולהכי ברחא ולא שריק אסור אפי' בחייא כיון דמיירי בגלי ראוי לאוכלה בלילה ואתי לחתויי: **התם** בבשרא אגומרי. וא"ת לרב אשי דשרי ברחא ולא שריק ולא אסר אלא בשרא אגומרי תיקשי ליה מתני' דאין טומנין הפת בתוך התנור (דף יט:) ועוד משלשלין את הפסח (א) אמרי' מאי טעמא משום דבני חבורה זריזין הן *כדמפרש לקמן (דף כ:) והא בלאו הכי נמי שרי ויש לומר דמיירי שהתנור פתוח דהוי כמו בשרא אגומרי ונראה דאין הלכה כרב אשי בהאי לישנא דשרי ברחא ולא שריק דסוגיא דלעיל דקאמר כיון דקשי ליה זיקא לא מגלה לה לא אתיא כוותיה וכן סוגיא דלקמן גבי בני חבורה זריזין הם דמשני האי מנתח פי' וקשי ליה זיקא והאי לא מנתח ולרב אשי אפי' היכא דלא קשי ליה זיקא שרי: **ולא** ישאילנו כו' אלא כדי שיגיע לביתו. לא מיירי בכלים דלאסור לב"ש משום שביתת כלים דאפילו ברביעי או בחמישי נמי אלא כגון חלוק ושאר דברים וטעמא משום הולאה ונראה כשלוחו כדפ"ה:

טומנין

רבינו חננאל

שביתת כלי אלא רב יוסף אבל רבה אמר מפני שמשמעת את הקול וכותיה מסתברא וכל היכא דאיכא למיחש שמא יחתה בגחלים כגון הנחת קדרה בתנור או חבית של מים וכיוצא אפילו ב"ה אסרי והא דתניא לא ימכור אדם חפץ לנכרי ולא ילונו ולא ישאילנו כו' קיי"ל כר' עקיבא דאמר כדי שיצא מפתח ביתו כר' יוסי דאמר הן הן דברי ר"ע הן הן דברי בית הלל וכן גבי חמץ אוקימנא בפסחים (כא.) כל שעה שמותר לאכול כהן תרומה מותר למכור ישראל חמץ לנכרי

כירה בחמין ותבשיל דקדירה מספיק ואף לפי הלד איבעיא דשם דלהחזיר תנן הא מבואר שם דנ"ל תסורי מתסרלא וכו' ומה הן משהין כו' חמין ולא תבשיל דהטעם ע"כ משום חיתוי דאילו משום בישול אף אם יסבור דיש בישול אחר בישול ומשום שביתת כלי מה מהני בזה גירוף וגם אמאי חמין מותר. וכיון דמצינו לב"ש דבקדירה מפסיק חיישינן לחיתוי י"ל דגם ב"ש ס"ל הכי גם בהא דפרכינן מוגמר ונפרית נמי ליגזור הא בלא"ה כיון דאינו מפסיק כלי ניחוש לחיתוי כמו באין צולין בשר:

עין משפט נר מצוה

קלו א מיי' פ"ג מהל' שבת הלכה יב סמג לאוין סה טוש"ע או"ח סימן רנד סעיף א:

קלז ב מיי' שם טוש"ע שם סעיף ט:

קלח ג מיי' פ"ג שם הלכה יד:

קלט ד מיי' שם הלכה יז סמג שם טוש"ע או"ח סימן רנג סעיף א וסימן שיח סעיף יא:

שייך לעיל ע"א ושם הגי' דלב"ש

קמ ה מיי' שם הלכה ח סמג שם טוש"ע או"ח סימן רנג סעיף א:

קמא ו ז מיי' שם הלכה יג וסמג שם טור שו"ע או"ח סימן רנד סעיף א:

קמב ח ט מיי' שם הל' טו טור שו"ע שם סעיף ב:

קמג י מיי' פ"ו מהלכות שבת הלכה יט סמג שם טוש"ע או"ח סימן רמו סעיף ב:

קמד כ מיי' פ"ג מהל' חמץ ומצה הלכה יא סמג לאוין עו טור שו"ע או"ח סי' תמג סעיף א:

[עי' תוס' ב"מ ל: ד"ה אפקרה]

[נ"ל והתנן]

ואם השכיר או השאיל בהמתו לנכרי ועיכבה נכרי אצלו בשבת היה צריך להפקיר בפני שלשה [תוס' ישנים]

[כדלקמן ריש פ' כירה]

מסורת הש"ס

תוספתא שבת פ"ד

[עי' תוס' תענית ח. ד"ה לירחים]

[לקמן יט:]

[לקמן כ.]

[נ"ל והתנן]

פסחים כא.

הגהות הב"ח

(א) תוס' ד"ה התם וכו' את הפסח בתנור אמרינן

גליון הש"ס

גמ' האי קדירה חייתא וכו' עם חשיכה בתנור. עיין לקמן דף לח ע"א תוס' ד"ה שכח: תוס' ד"ה גזירה שאין דבר מפסיק. ק"ל הא מ"מ תיקשי ליה מתני' דר"ס

it is forbidden even if it performs no action, if so, [18*b*] why are a perfume brazier and sulphur permitted?[6]—There it lies upon the earth.[7] What of a tank [for brewing beer], a lamp, a pot and a spit—why do Beth Shammai permit [them]?[8]—Because their ownership is renounced.[9]

Who is the author of the following, which our Rabbis taught:
a A woman must not fill a pot with pounded wheat[1] and lupines and place it in the oven on the eve of the Sabbath shortly before nightfall; and if she does put them [there], they are forbidden at the conclusion of the Sabbath for as long as they take to prepare.[2] Similarly, a baker must not fill a barrel of water and place it in the oven on the eve of the Sabbath shortly before nightfall; and if he does, it [the water] is forbidden at the conclusion of the Sabbath for as long as it takes to prepare [boil]. Shall we say that this agrees with Beth Shammai, not Beth Hillel?[3]—You may even say that it is Beth Hillel: it is a preventive measure, lest he stir the coals. If so, let us decree [likewise] in respect of a perfume brazier and sulphur?—There he will not stir them, for if he does, the smoke will enter and harm them.[4] Let us decree in respect of wet bundles of flax too?—There, since a draught is injurious to them, he will not uncover it.[5] Let us decree also in respect of wool in the dye kettle?—Samuel answered: This refers to a kettle removed [from the fire]. But let us fear that he may stir within it?[6]—This refers to [a kettle] removed from [the fire] and sealed down.[7]

And now that the Master said: 'It is a preventive measure, lest one rake the coals', a raw dish[8] may be placed in an oven on the eve of Sabbath shortly before nightfall. What is the reason? Since it will not be fit for the evening,[9] he withdraws his mind from it and will not come to rake the coals.[10] Again, if it is [quite]
b boiled, it is well.[1] If partly boiled,[2] it is forbidden. Yet if a raw bone is thrown into it, it is permitted.[3]

And now that the Master said, 'Whatever may be harmed by the draught, one will not uncover it': with flesh of a kid, where it [the oven] is daubed round,[4] it is well;[5] with [flesh] of a buck, where it [the oven] is not daubed round, it is forbidden. But as to [flesh] of a kid, where it is not daubed round, or of a buck, where it is daubed round: R. Ashi permits it, while R. Jeremiah of Difti[6] forbids it. Now, according to R. Ashi, who permits it, did we not learn, Meat, onion[s] or egg[s] may not be roasted unless they can be roasted before sunset?—There the reference is to [flesh] of a buck, and where it [the oven] is not daubed round.

Others state: With [the flesh] of a kid, whether it [the oven] is daubed round or not, it is well; of a buck too, if it is daubed round, it is well. They differ in respect to [flesh] of a buck, it [the oven] not being daubed: R. Ashi permits it, while R. Jeremiah of Difti forbids it. Now, according to R. Ashi who permits it, did we not learn, Meat, onion[s] or egg[s] may not be roasted unless they can be roasted before sunset?—There the reference is to meat on the coals [direct].[7] Rabina said: As for a raw gourd, it is well:[8] since a draught is injurious to it, it is like flesh of a kid.

BETH SHAMMAI MAINTAIN: ONE MUST NOT SELL [etc.]. Our Rabbis taught: Beth Shammai maintain: A man must not sell an article to a Gentile, nor lend [it] to him nor loan him [money] nor make him a gift [on the eve of Sabbath], unless he can reach his house [before sunset]; while Beth Hillel rule: [unless] he can reach the house nearest the [city] wall.[9] R. Akiba said: [Unless] he can depart from the door of his [the Jew's] house [before the Sabbath]. Said R. Jose son of R. Judah: The words of R. Akiba are the very
c words of Beth Hillel:[1] R. Akiba comes only to explain the words of Beth Hillel.[2]

Our Rabbis taught: Beth Shammai maintain: A man must not sell his leaven to a Gentile, unless he knows that it will be consumed before Passover: this is Beth Shammai's view. But Beth Hillel say: As long as he [the Jew] may eat it, he may sell it.

(6) For on this hypothesis the Baraitha must agree with Beth Shammai, since the placing of wheat in a mill is forbidden. (7) Not in a vessel. (8) Beer brews in its tank more than eight days, thus including the Sabbath. Similarly, the lamp burns during the Sabbath, the pot stands on the heated range, causing some shrinkage of its contents, and the spit was allowed to lie in the oven with the Passover sacrifice roasting on Friday night. Thus all these utensils are employed on the Sabbath. (9) This is a legal fiction. Their owner formally renounces his ownership, and then he is under no obligation to ensure that they rest.

a (1) Or, peas. (2) So that she should not profit by having virtually prepared it on the Sabbath. (3) Since Beth Hillel do not require utensils to rest. (4) The garments or vessels. (5) The oven, to rake up the coals.—The coals burnt inside the ancient ovens. (6) *Sc.* the wool within the kettle, to make it absorb the dye more thoroughly. This too is forbidden. (7) Hence he is not likely to forget.—In this and the following cases the fear is not that he may do these things intentionally but unintentionally in a moment of forgetfulness. (8) I.e., a pot containing a raw dish. (9) The evening meal was eaten soon after nightfall, and it would not be ready by then. (10) There is ample time for it to be ready on the morrow without his stirring. But pounded wheat and lupines require very much boiling, and therefore they are forbidden.

b (1) Permitted, because the coals will not require raking. (2) Lit., 'boiled and not boiled'. (3) This serves to show that he has no intention of eating it before the morrow. (4) To seal it down. (5) Goat flesh is tender and injured by a draught. (6) V. *supra* 10*a*, n. b5. (7) Not in the oven. It is then easy to turn it and rake the coals: hence it is forbidden. (8) It may be placed in the oven even if it cannot be cooked by the Sabbath. (9) If the Gentile lives in another town, it is sufficient if he can take it to the nearest house there, even if he cannot reach his own before the Sabbath.

c (1) Their views are identical. (2) I.e., he states Beth Hillel's ruling, not an independent one, and thus differs from the first Tanna's interpretation of Beth Hillel's attitude.

R. Judah said: [19a] Babylonian *kutaḥ*[3] and any [other] kind of *kutaḥ* may not be sold thirty days before Passover.[4]

Our Rabbis taught: Food may be placed before a dog in a courtyard, [and] if it takes it and goes out, one has no duty toward it.[5] Similarly, food may be placed before a Gentile in a courtyard, [and] if he takes it and goes out, one has no duty toward him. What is the purpose of this further [dictum]; [surely] it is the same [as the first]?—You might argue, The one is incumbent upon him, whereas the other is not:[6] therefore we are informed [otherwise].[7]

Our Rabbis taught: A man must not hire his utensils to a Gentile on the eve of Sabbath; [but] on Wednesday or Thursday it is permitted.[8] Similarly, letters may not be sent by a Gentile on the eve of Sabbath, [but] on Wednesday or Thursday it is permitted. It was related of R. Jose the priest—others say, of R. Jose the Pious—that his handwriting was never found in a Gentile's hand.[9]

a Our Rabbis taught: Letters may not be sent by Gentiles on the eve of Sabbath unless a fee is stipulated.[1] Beth Shammai maintain: There must be time to reach his [the addressee's] house [before the Sabbath];[2] while Beth Hillel rule: There must be time to reach the house nearest the [city] wall.[3] But has he not stipulated?[4]—Said R. Shesheth, This is its meaning: And if he did not stipulate, Beth Shammai maintain: There must be time to reach his [the addressee's] house; while Beth Hillel rule: to reach the house nearest the [city] wall. But you said in the first clause that one must not send [at all]?[5]—There is no difficulty: in the one case a post office is permanently located in the town,[6] in the other case a post office is not permanently located in the town.[7]

Our Rabbis taught: One may not set out in a ship less than three days before the Sabbath. This was said only [if it is] for a voluntary purpose, but [if] for a good deed,[8] it is well; and he stipulates with him[9] that it is on condition that he will rest [on the Sabbath], yet he does not rest:[10] this is Rabbi's view. R. Simeon b. Gamaliel said: It is unnecessary. But from Tyre to Sidon[11] it is permitted even on the eve of Sabbath.[12]

Our Rabbis taught: Gentile cities must not be besieged less than three days before the Sabbath, yet once they commence they need not leave off. And thus did Shammai say: *until it fall*,[13] even on the Sabbath.

R. SIMEON B. GAMALIEL SAID: IT WAS THE PRACTICE IN MY FATHER'S HOUSE etc. It was taught: R. Ẓadoḳ said, This was the practice of R. Gamaliel's house, viz., they used to give white garments to the fuller three days before the Sabbath, but coloured garments even on the eve of the Sabbath. And b from their usage[1] we learn that white [garments] are more difficult to wash than coloured ones. Abaye was giving a coloured garment to a fuller and asked him, How much do you want for it? 'As for a white garment,' he answered. 'Our Rabbis have already anticipated you,' said he.[2]

Abaye said: When one gives a garment to a fuller he should deliver it to him by measure and receive it back by measure, for if it is more, he spoiled it by stretching, and if less he spoiled it by shrinking.[3]

AND BOTH AGREE THAT THE BEAM OF THE [OIL] PRESS AND THE CIRCULAR WINE PRESS MAY BE LADEN. Wherein do all [the other acts] differ that Beth Shammai forbid them, and wherein do [those relating to] the beam of the [oil] press and the circular wine press differ, that Beth Shammai do not forbid them?—Those other [acts] which, if done on the Sabbath involve a sin-offering, Beth Shammai forbade on the eve of the Sabbath just before nightfall; [but the loading of] the beam of the [oil] press and the circular wine press, which if done on the Sabbath does not involve a sin-offering, they did not forbid.[4]

Which Tanna [maintains] that everything which comes automatically is well?[5]—Said R. Jose son of R. Ḥanina, It is R. Ishmael. For we learnt: [In the case of] garlic, half-ripe grapes, and parched ears [of corn] were crushed before sunset, R. Ishmael said: One may

(3) Jast.: a preserve consisting of sour milk, bread-crusts and salt. (4) It is used as a sauce or relish and hence lasts a long time. It was customary to give popular lectures about the Festivals thirty days before them, and therefore from that time one was forbidden to sell *kutaḥ* to a Gentile. (5) To restrain it from carrying it out into the street. (6) He has a duty towards his animals which he does not owe to a stranger, and therefore I might think that in the latter case food must not be given, since it may be carried out. (7) That even so food may be placed before a Gentile. Because though one has no legal obligation, he has the duty of charity towards him, just as towards a Jew, as stated in Giṭ. 61*a* (Tosaf.). (8) Though he will use it on the Sabbath. (9) He never sent a letter by a Gentile lest he might take it to its destination on Sabbath. This was a measure of ultra stringency.

a (1) Once the fee is stipulated the Gentile works for himself, to earn it, and not for the Jew. (2) Otherwise it is forbidden even if the fee was already stipulated. (3) If the addressee lives in a different town; cf. *supra* 18*b*, n. b9. (4) In which case the first Tanna, i.e., Beth Hillel, rules that it may be carried on the Sabbath itself. (5) Other edd. more plausibly, But it was taught that they must not be sent (at all)? The reference is then to the preceding Baraitha, not this one, for this one distinctly states that if the fee was arranged it is permitted; v. marg. gloss, cur. edd. (6) Of the addressee. Then letters may be sent, even if the fee was not stipulated, providing that the messenger can reach the post office or the nearest house in that town before the Sabbath. (7) Rashi: then one must not send if the fee was not stipulated, as he may go searching for him on the Sabbath. (8) Lit., 'a matter of a precept'. (9) The Gentile owner of the ship. (10) I.e., though the condition will not be carried out. (11) Both on the Phoenician coast, about thirty miles apart. (12) Being such a short distance. (13) Deut. XX, 20. The reference is to a besieged city.

b (1) Lit., 'words'. (2) I know from them that this requires less labour. (3) And he is entitled to make a deduction. (4) On Sabbath eve before nightfall. (5) I.e., permitted, as here, the beams being laden before the Sabbath and the juice then oozing automatically on the Sabbath.

כותח הבבלי וכל מיני כותח אסור למכור ל' יום קודם הפסח: ת"ר *נותנין מזונות לפני הכלב בחצר נטלו ויצא אין נזקקין לו כיוצא בו נותנין מזונות *לפני הנכרי בחצר נטלו ויצא אין נזקקין לו הא תו למה לי היינו הך מהו דתימא האי רמי עליה והאי לא רמי עליה קמ"ל: ת"ר *לא ישכיר אדם כליו לנכרי בע"ש בד' ובה' מותר כיוצא בו אין משלחין איגרות ביד נכרי בע"ש בד' ובה' מותר אמרו עליו על ר' יוסי הכהן ואמרי לה על ר' יוסי החסיד שלא נמצא כתב ידו ביד נכרי מעולם ת"ר אין משלחין איגרת ביד נכרי ע"ש אא"כ קוצץ לו דמים ב"ש אומרים כדי שיגיע לביתו וב"ה אומרים כדי שיגיע לבית הסמוך לחומה והלא קצץ אמר רב ששת ה"ק ואם לא קצץ בית שמאי אומרים עד שיגיע לביתו ובית הלל אומרים עד שיגיע לבית הסמוך לחומה *והאמרת רישא אין משלחין לא קשיא הא דקביע בי דואר במתא והא דלא קביע בי דואר במתא: ת"ר אין מפליגין בספינה פחות מג' ימים קודם לשבת במה דברים אמורים לדבר הרשות אבל לדבר מצוה שפיר דמי ופוסק עמו על מנת לשבות ואינו שובת דברי רבי רשב"ג אומר אינו צריך ומצור לצידן אפילו בע"ש מותר: ת"ר *אין צרין על עיירות של נכרים פחות מג' ימים קודם לשבת ואם התחילו אין מפסיקין וכן היה שמאי אומר עד רדתה אפי' בשבת: אמר רבן שמעון בן גמליאל נוהגין היו וכו': תניא *א"ר צדוק כך היה מנהגו של בית רבן גמליאל שהיו נותנין כלי לבן לכובס ג' ימים קודם לשבת וצבועים אפילו בע"ש ומדבריהם למדנו שהלבנים קשים לכבסן יותר מן הצבועים אביי הוה יהיב ליה ההוא מנא דצביעא לקצרא אמר ליה כמה בעית עילויה א"ל כדחיורא אמר ליה *כבר קדמוך רבנן אמר אביי האי מאן דיהיב מנא לקצרא במשחא ניתיב ליה ובמשחא נשקול מיניה דאי טפי אפסדיה דמתחיה ואי בציר אפסדיה דכווציה: ושוין אלו ואלו שטוענין כו': מאי שנא כולהו דגזרו בהו ב"ש ומ"ש קורות בית הבד ועיגולי הגת דלא גזרו להו הנך דאי עביד להו בשבת מיחייב חטאת גזרו בהו ב"ש ע"ש עם חשכה קורות בית הבד ועיגולי הגת דאי עביד להו בשבת לא מיחייב חטאת לא גזרו מאן תנא דכל מידי דאתי ממילא שפיר דמי אמר רב יוסי *(בר) חנינא רבי ישמעאל היא דתנן *השום והבוסר והמלילות שרסקן מבעוד יום רבי ישמעאל אומר יגמור משתחשך ורבי עקיבא אומר לא

רש"י

כותח הבבלי. טחנין בו חמץ כדאמרי' באלו עוברין ואינו עשוי לאכול יחד אלא לטבול בו ואינו כלה עד זמן מרובה: שלשים יום. משמתחילין לדרוש בהלכות הפסח חלה אזהרת פסח עליו: כלב. רמי עליה לזונו: לא ישכיר אדם כליו. לעשות בהן מלאכה בע"ש דנראה שמשכירו לו לצורך השבת: שלא נמצא כתב ידו · שלא יוליכנו בשבת: אלא אם כן קצץ לו דמים. דכיון דקוצץ לו דמים בדידיה טרח וב"ש לא מודו בקצץ דאפילו בקצץ פליגי דהא לא עדיף ממוכר ומשאיל ונותן מתנה אלא מילתא דב"ה אשמעינן דבדלא קוצץ לא פליגי דאסור: לביתו. של מי שנשתלח לו: לבית הסמוך. לחומת העיר שנשתלח שם: והלא קצץ · ואמאי אסרי ב"ה הא איכהו שרו לעיל: והא אמרת רישא אין משלחין. אא"כ קצץ: דואר. שלטון העיר ולו רגילין לשלוח אגרות: שכיחא במתא. משלחין בלא קוצץ בכדי שיגיע השליח למר לבית הדואר ולמר לבית הסמוך לחומה ורישא דאין משלחין בלא קוצץ כלל דלא קביע במתא ואם לא ימצאנו יהא צריך לילך אחריו בשבת: מפליגין. מפרישין מן היבשה לים וזהו לשון [הפלגת] ספינה על שם שמפליג עצמו מן היישוב ומרבינו יעקב שמעתי בעירובין שאמצעיתו של ים נקרא פילגוס ואף בלשון לעז פילגס: ופוסק · עם הנכרי ע"מ לשבות ואין צריך לשבות: ומצור לצידן. אין אלא מהלך יום ובע"ש היה שם יום השוק כדאמרינן בפסחים במקום שנהגו [דף נ:]: ומדבריהם למדנו כו'. ונפקא מינה לשכר הכובס: לקצרא. כובס: כמה בעית עלויה. בשכר כיבוס: כבר קדמוך רבנן. שלמדונו שהלבנים קשים לכבסן יותר מן הצבועים: לימשחיה. ימדדנו בנתינתו ובחזירתו: דכווצי. ברותחין: דאתי ממילא. כגון משקין הללו שנסחטים מאליהם ובלבד שיתחיל מבעוד יום: בוסר. ענבים בתחילתן כשהן דקים מוציא מהן משקין לטבל בו בשר לפי שהוא חזק וקרוב להחמיץ: מלילות. שבולין שלא בשלו כל צרכן מרסקן וטוענן באבנים ומשקה זב מהן ומטבל בו: יגמור. מאחר שרסקן ונכבש כבודו יניחם בכלים ויצאו מעצמן ומותר לכתחלה: לא

תוספות

נותנין מזונות לנכרי בחצר. בשבת אפילו לב"ש דרגיל לאוכלו מיד ודוקא מזונות אבל שאר חפצים אסורים אפילו לב"ה דלא שרי ב"ה אלא בע"ש אבל בשבת לא וא"ת ואמאי נותנין מזונות לנכרי בשבת הא כיון דאין מזונותיהן עליך כדאמרינן הכא ובפ"ב דביצה (דף כא:) דמוציא אני את הנכרי שאין מזונותיהן עליך ליתסר כדאמרינן בפרק בתרא (דף קנה:) דאסור לטרוח בשבת להא מזונות לפני חיה משום דאין מזונותי' עליך ה"נ ה"ל למיסר בנכרי ויש לומר כיון דמפרנסים עניי נכרים עם עניי ישראל *משום דרכי שלום חשיב קצת מזונותיו עליך לענין איסור טורח שבות דרבנן אבל לענין עשיית מלאכה בי"ט דהוי איסור דאורייתא לא חשיב מזונותיו עליך:

כתוב בא"ז ספ"א חלה נכרי ושלח ליהודי א' בי"ט שישלח לו מיינו ואם לא ישלח לו ימות והנכרי היה מוחזק בעיר והתיר לשלוח לו ע"י נכרי משום דרכי שלום ושלח אל רבינו שמחה והתיר לו אבל לא ע"י ישראל וה"ר יצחק נראה דהוא הדין בשבת אם היה הענין כך שהיה דבר שצריך דרכי שלום כגון שהיה הנכרי אלם נראה שמותר לשלוח לו על ידי נכרי לדידן דלית לן השתא רשות הרבים דאורייתא [תוס' ישנים]:

לא ישכיר. אין לפרש משום שביתת כלים וכב"ש דא"כ אפי' ברביעי ובחמישי נמי אלא כב"ה היא דלית להו שביתת כלים או בחלוק וטלית וכיוצא בהן איירי דלא שייך שביתת כלים ואסור לפי שנראה כנוטל שכר שבת אף על פי שמשכירו יחד חדש או שבוע דאם משכירו ליום אפילו ברביעי ובחמישי אסור כדמשמע בסוף הזהב (ב"מ דף נח.) גבי שוכר פועלים לשמור פרה או תינוק ודוקא לשוכרו דמיחזי כנוטל שכר שבת אבל שאלה שריא:

אלא אם כן קוצץ לו דמים. מתני' נמי דנותנים כלים לכובס ועורות לעבדן איירי נמי בקוצץ והא דפריך והלא קצץ לב"ה פריך:

אין מפליגין בספינה · אפילו תוך התחום אסור משום שט כדמוכח בפ' תולין (לקמן קלט: ושם) גבי ההוא צורבא מדרבנן דאמר למינם בעינא ואזיל לאידך גיסא ושמר פירי משמע דתוך התחום היה ואפ"ה בלא הערמה אסור*:

השום והבוסר והמלילות. למאי דקאמר בפ' חבית (לקמן קמה:) מודים חכמים לר' יהודה בשאר פירות ומייתי מדתניא סוחטין בפגעין (א) ועוזרדין אבל לא ברמונים צ"ל דשום ובוסר יותר עשוין למשקין מפגעין ועוזרדין ומיהו התם מסיק דתרדין אע"ג דלאו בני סחיטה נינהו הואיל ואחשבינהו ה"ל משקין ולפ"ז הא דקתני סוחטין בפגעים לאו סחיטה גמורה קאמר אלא מיתוק בעלמא:

רבי ישמעאל אומר יגמור. פי' אינו צריך לסלק הטעינה סמוך לחשכה אלא מניחן כל השבת קשה לר"י היכי מוכח דסבר ר' ישמעאל כל דאתי ממילא אפי' עביד בשבת ליכא חיוב חטאת דילמא ר' ישמעאל סבר כב"ה דשרו אפי' בהנך דלא אתי ממילא והא דנקט ריסקן משום רבותא דר"ע ועוד תימה דר"ע דאמר *לא יגמור לא כב"ש ולא כב"ה ונראה לר"י דיגמור היינו דיגמור ויאכל בשבת ולא דמי למשקין שזבו שאסורין דגזרינן שמא יסחוט דהכא אפילו יסחוט ליכא איסור דאורייתא משום דאתי ממילא והשתא מייתי שפיר דקסבר ר' ישמעאל כל דאתי ממילא ש"ד אפי' לב"ש כיון דאי עביד ליה בשבת לא מיחייב ור"ע דאמר לא יגמור לא שצריך להסיר הקורה דסבר כב"ה אלא שלא יגמור כדי לאכול משקים היוצאים דאסורין אפי' לב"ה כשאר משקין שזבו דאסורין דהך סחיטה נמי דאורייתא אע"ג דאתי ממילא ועי"ל דיגמור בידים משתחשך דלא דמי למתני' דלא שרו ב"ה אלא טעינת קורה אבל בידים לא דהכא כשאין מחוסרין דיכה כדאמר בסמוך והשתא מייתי שפיר דכיון דשרי ר' ישמעאל לסחוט בידים ולא גזר אטו מחוסרי דיכה א"כ במחוסרי דיכה נמי סבר דלא מיחייב ובתר הכי קאמר דלרבי ישמעאל במחוסרי דיכה מיחייב ואפ"ה כשאין מחוסרין שרי בידים ולא גזר אטו מחוסרין אבל כר"ע לא אתיא כיון דאסר בשאין מחוסרין דיכה אטו מחוסרין דיכה מכלל דמחוסרין דיכה מיחייב וא"כ אסור עם חשכה לב"ש:

שמן

עין משפט נר מצוה

קמה א ב מיי' פ"ו מהל' שבת הלכה כא סמג לאוין סה טור שו"ע או"ח סימן שכה סעיף א:

קמו ג ד ה מיי' שם הלכה כ סמג שם טוש"ע או"ח סימן רמז סעיף א:

קמז ו מיי' פכ"ד מהלכות שבת הל' ו ופ"ל שם הלכה יג סמג עשין לו סמג לאוין סה טוש"ע או"ח סימן רמח סעיף א:

[גיטין סא.]

קמח ז מיי' פ"ג מהל' שבת הלכה כה ופ"ל הלכה יג ופ"ו מהל' מלכים הלכה יא טור או"ח סימן רמט:

קמט ח מיי' פכ"א מהל' שבת הלכה טז טור ושו"ע או"ח סימן רנב סעיף ה וסימן שכ סעיף ב:

[תוספתא עירובין פ"ג]

[תוספתא פ"א]

[וע"ע תוס' עירובין מג. ד"ה הלכה]

עדיות פ"ב מ"ו

מסורת הש"ס

[תוספת' פי"ד]

[ת"ל ברבי]

לא יגמור כב"ש ולא כב"ה כל"ע מהרש"א

הגהות הב"ח

(א) תוס' ד"ה השום וכו' בפגעים ופרישים ועוזרדין:

תימה דילמא רישא ה"ק אין משלחין בשאינו יכול להגיע אלא א"כ קצץ והיינו בפלוגת' דסיפא בשלא קצץ אם יכול להגיע דשרי ויש ספרים דגרסי והתניא דאין משלחין והיינו ברייתא דלעיל דכיוצא בו וכן הגיה ה"ר יהודה בספרו [ת"י]

גליון הש"ס

גמ' לפני הנכרי בחצר · עי' לעיל דף ג ע"א תוס' ד"ה בבא דרישא:

[ב"ב קטז. חולין קה.]

רבינו חננאל

והיא שעה חמישית · כרבן גמליאל דאמר חולין נאכלין כל ארבע ותרומה כל חמש: נתינת מזונות לפני נכרי בחצר או לפני כלב מותר ואם נטל ויצא אין נזקקין לו: ת"ר לא ישכיר אדם כליו לנכרי בע"ש כו' ת"ר אין משלחין אגרת ביד נכרי בע"ש כו' אוקימנא כדברי בית הלל אי לא קביעא דואר במתא פי' איש ידוע שכל כתב אליו יובל והוא המשכיר ומשלח כל אגרת למי שנשתלחה לו אין משלחין אא"כ קצץ שכר לשליח או אם יכול השליח להגיע במקום שהוא שרוי (בין) מי שהאגרת שלוחה אליו מבעוד יום ואפילו בבית הסמוך לחומה ואי קבוע דואר במתא כעניין שפירשנו למעלה אע"פ שלא קצץ שרי דהא אגרת לבי דואר שדורה ובי דואר הוא במתא בהדיה ואם קצץ שכר המשלח לשליח בין יש בי דואר בין אין שם בי דואר בין מגיע אצל מי שנשתלחה לו בין אין מגיע מותר. אמרו על יוסף הכהן החסיד שלא נמצא כתב ידו ביד נכרי מעולם. הא דתנן נתינת כלי לבן לכובס נכרי פשוטה היא. הא דתנו רבנן אין מפליגין בספינה פחות מג' ימים קודם לשבת יש מי שאומרים בזמן שגוששת ואין במים י' טפחים ומשום גזירת תחומין נגעו בה אבל למעלה מי' טפחים לא גזרו ומשום הכי נהגו להפליג בים הגדול: ת"ר אין מפליגין בספינה פחות מג' ימים קודם לשבת בד"א לדבר הרשות אבל לדבר מצוה מותר. ופוסק עמו לשבות ואינו שובת דברי רבי רשב"ג אומר אינו צריך לפסוק. והלכתא כרשב"ג דכי קיי"ל הילכתא כר' מחבירו ולא מאביו וכבר פירשנוהו למעלה בספינה גוששת שאין במים י' טפחים ומשום תחומין גזרו אבל למעלה מי' טפחים לא גזרו: ושוין ב"ש וב"ה שטוענין בקורת בית הבד כו' ודייקינן מתניתין דכל מידי דאי עביד הוא מעשה חייב עליו חטאת כגון שריית דיו ונתינת אונין של פשתן וכיוצא בהן בהני פליגי ב"ש אבל הכא דאי עביד לעצמו לא מחייב חטאת אפילו ב"ש מתירין והוא שאמרו כל מידי דאתי ממילא שפיר דמי:

אוקמה

לא יגמור ורבי אלעזר אמר רבי אלעזר היא דתנן *חלות דבש שריסקן בערב שבת ויצאו מעצמן אסור ורבי אלעזר מתיר ור' יוסי בר חנינא מ"ט לא אמר כרבי אלעזר אמר לך התם הוא °דמעיקרא אוכל ולבסוף אוכל הכא מעיקרא אוכל והשתא משקה ור' אלעזר אמר לך הא שמעינן ליה לר' אלעזר דאפילו זיתים וענבים נמי שרי דהא *כי אתא רב הושעיא מנהרדעא אתא ואייתי מתניתא בידיה זיתים וענבים שריסקן מערב שבת ויצאו מעצמן אסורין ר' אלעזר ור"ש מתירין ורבי יוסי בר חנינא *ברייתא לא שמיע ליה ור' אלעזר מ"ט לא אמר כר' יוסי בר חנינא אמר לך לאו איתמר עלה אמר רבא בר חנינא אמר רבי יוחנן *במחוסרין דיכה דכ"ע לא פליגי כי פליגי במחוסרין שחיקה והני נמי כמחוסרין דיכה דמו הורה רבי יוסי בר חנינא ג כרבי ישמעאל שמן של בדדין ומחצלות של בדדין רב אסר ד ושמואל שרי *הני כרכי דזוזי רב ה אסר ושמואל שרי א"ר נחמן עז לחלבה ורחל לגיזתה ותרנגולת לביצתה ותורי דרדיא °ותמרי דעיסקא רב אסר ושמואל אמר ו מותר וקמיפלגי בפלוגת' דר' יהודה ור' שמעון ההוא תלמידא דאורי בחרתא דארגיז כרבי שמעון שמתיה רב המנונא והא כר' שמעון סבירא לן באתריה דרב הוה לא איבעי ליה *למיעבד הכי הני תרי תלמידי חד מציל בחד מנא וחד מציל בארבע וחמש מאני וקמיפלגי בפלוגתא *דרבה בר זבדא ורב הונא:

מתני' *ז אין צולין בשר בצל וביצה אלא כדי *שיצולו מבעוד יום *א אין נותנין פת לתנור עם חשכה ולא חררה על גבי גחלים אלא כדי *שיקרמו פניה מבעוד יום רא"א כדי שיקרום התחתון שלה *משלשלין את הפסח בתנור עם חשכה ומאחיזין את האור במדורת בית המוקד ובגבולין

רש"י

לא יגמור · אסור להניחם מבעוד יום תחת טוכבן כדי לגמור משתחשך: ור' אלעזר אומר · הוא ר' אלעזר בן פדת דהוא אמורא: ר' אלעזר היא · הוא ר' אלעזר בן שמוע סתם ר' אלעזר של משנה וברייתא: חלות דבש · שהכוורת רודה ועשויין כמין חלות של שעוה והדבש בתוכן: שריסקן · כותשן: אסורין · לאותו שבת באכילה: דבש לאחר שזב מן החלות נמי אוכלא הוא הלכך ליכא למיגזר ביה שמא יסחוט משתחשך דלא שייכא ביה סחיטה הכא · זיתים וענבים דמתני' דמעיקרא אוכלא והשתא משקה איכא למיגזר שמא יסחוט משתחשך דהא ודאי סחיטה היא: ור' יוסי בר' חנינא · הך ברייתא דקתני דפליג ר' אלעזר אף בזיתים ובענבים לא הוה שמיע ליה ומההיא דחלות דבש שהיא משנה בפרק חבית שנשברה לא הוי מצי לדמויה למתני' משום פירכא דלעיל: במחוסרין דיכה כ"ע לא פליגי · דאסירי דטעינתן היא גומרת וכמלא הכל עשוי בשבת: שחיקה · יותר מדיכה לשון או דכו במדוכה (במדבר יא) ורבותי גורסין כי פליגי במחוסרין סחיטה שנידוכו יפה ואין טעינתן גומרת אלא סחיטה ולמאן דגריס שחיק' טעינתן שוחקתן והני דמתני' מחוסרין דיכה הן וטעינתן היא דיכתן היא שוחקתן היא סוחטתן ובהא ר' ישמעאל מודה לאסור: שמן של בדדין · איידי דאיירי בבית הבד נקט ליה שמן המשתייר בזוית הבד תחת הטעינה והוא ניתן לבדדין וכן מחצלות של בדדין שמכסין בהן את הזיתים: רב אסר · לטלטולי' משום מוקצה דרב סבר כר' יהודה במוקצה ושמואל סבר כר"ש דלית ליה מוקצה והכי אמרינן במי שהחשיך: כרכי דזוזי · זוג של מחצלות שמכסים בהן את פרגמטיא של ספינה וזוזי לשון זוג לפי שהן שתים ושוויות כאהל ובתשובות הגאונים מצאתי כ"כי דזיווי (א) ומפרש שהוא לשון ספינה בלשון ארמי: עז · העומדת לחלבה: וכן רחל · העומדת לגיזתה: ותורא דרדיא · העומד לחרישה: ותמרי דעיסקא · העומדין להוליכן לסחורה למקום אחר: פלוגתא דר' יהודה כו' · דלר' יהודה דאית ליה מוקצה בפרק אחרון (דף קנו:) אסור לשוחטן ביום טוב אלא אם כן הזמינן מבעוד יום ולר' שמעון שרו: חרתא · שם מקום: דארגיז · אדם אחד היה אמגושי שבנה לאותה העיר ורב המגושא דר בה ועדיין מערת קבורתו קיימת שם °כך מצאתי בתשובה: והא כר' שמעון סבירא לן · השתא כדלקמן * ואמאי שמתיה: חד מציל · אוכלין ומשקין מפני הדליקה הרבה לחצר המעורבת: בחד מנא · כדתנן מצילין סל מלא ככרות ואע"ג שיש בו מאה סעודות: וחד מציל בארבע וחמש מאני · אלא שמקפלן כולן לתוך כלי גדול ומשאן בפעם אחת: וקא מיפלגי כו' · בפרק כל כתבי הקדש*: **מתני'** חררה · עוגת רצפים (מלכים א יט) פוגאצ"ה בלע"ז: יקרמו · כמו קרום קרוסט"ן בלע"ז: התחתון · מפרש בגמרא: משלשלין את הפסח כו' · והוא צלי והולך משתחשך ואע"ג דבעלמא אין צולין כדאמרן הכא שרי דבני חבורה זריזין הן ומדכרי אהדדי ולא אתו לחתויי בגחלים: ומאחיזין את האור · מעט מעט בעצים של מדורת בית המוקד שהיתה בעזרה והיא מתבערת והולכת משתחשך ולא חיישינן שמא יהו כהנים נריכין להבעירה משתחשך כדמפרש בגמרא: בית המוקד · לשכה גדולה היא שהכהנים מתחממין שם במדורת אש הגסקת תמיד מפני שמהלכין יחפים על רצפת שיש בעזרה כדאמרי' בזבחים (פ"ב דף כד·) והויל ורצפה מקודשת דכתיב* ביום ההוא קדש המלך תוך החצר וכלי שרת מקודשין דכתיב* וימשחם ויקדש אותם מה כלי שרת לא יהא דבר חוצץ בינו לבין כלי שרת אף רצפה לא יהא דבר חוצץ בינו לבין הרצפה: ובגבולין

תוספות

שמן של בדדין · פ"ה המשתייר בזוית בית הבד וקשה לר"י דמה לו להזכיר כאן דין מוקצה ועוד דלמה יהיה השמן מוקצה *ותירץ ר"י דקאי אדלעיל דקאמר דאם טען בית הבד מבעוד יום והשמן זב והולכת כל השבת רב אסר אותו שמן משום מוקצה דהוי נולד גמור דמחמת קורות והעיגול שעליו לא היה ראוי בין השמשות לאכילה אע"ג דע"מ כן הניחו וסמך על זה שיזוב כל השבת כיון דאין משקין בעולם האי סמיכה לאו מידי היא והוי נולד גמור ולא דמי לקדרה חייתא דשרי אע"ג דבין השמשות לא חזי לאכילה דהתם כיון דהבשר בעולם מהני דע"מ כן מניחה וכן מעיינות הנובעות כבר הם בעולם °וכן לואת קטן שהיה כבר במעיו מהני בהן סמיכה ולא דמי לזיתים וענבים שריסקן מבעוד יום וכן השום והבוסר שריסקן מבערב דהתם חזו מבערב לאכילה אבל הכא דלא חזו בין השמשות לאכילה והמשקה אינו בעולם הרי נולד גמור ואסור לרב וא"ת בפ"ב לקמן (דף כט·) דאמר רב אכל תמרי ושדא קשייתא לאווזא מאי לאו בפרסייתא ולא קבלה לא בארמייתא וקבלה והשתא היכי המ"ל דהוי פרסייתא והא רב אסר נולד הכא ויש לומר דה"פ מאי לאו בפרסייתא ולא קבלה משום דלא חשיבא ליה רב נולד כיון דמעיקרא גרעין והשתא גרעין אבל הכא שמן הבלוע בזיתים כל זמן *שלא יצא הוי נולד גמור ולא הוי משקה:

ושמואל שרי · תימה דבס"פ נוטל (לקמן קמג.) אמרי' דשמואל הוה מטלטל גרעיני פרסייתא אגב ריפתא פי' בשולת כל צרכן שאין נשאר מן האוכל עליהם כלל וכיון דשרי נולד כר"ש בלא ריפתא נמי לישתרי ותירץ ר"ת דשמואל מחמיר על עצמו היה לפי שהיה אדם חשוב וכן מוכח סוגיא התם דאמר אביי אי לאו דאדם חשוב אנא: **הני** כרכי דזוזי רב אסר · לטלטל משום מוקצה תימה דבפ' מפנין (לקמן דף קכח·) אמרינן דרב במוקצה לאכילה סבר לה כר' יהודה ובמוקצה לטלטל סבר לה כר"ש והכא אוסר לטלטל לכרכי דזוזי ומפרש ר"ת דכרכי דזוזי °הן מוקצה מחמת מיאוס *כגון בגדים ומחצלות שמכסין בהם דגים ושאר דברים המלכלכין אותם והתם דקאמר רב דבמוקצה לטלטל סבר לה כר"ש במוקצה שמקצה האדם מדעתו לעיסקא לאוצר שאין בו מיאוס והא דאמר בפרק בתרא (דף קנו:) דאף רב ס"ל כר' יהודה מדכרכי דזוזי דרב אסר מפרש ר"ת דנבילה המתנבלת בשבת מוקצה מחמת איסור הוא דאף לכלבים אינו ראוי מחיים ומוקצה מחמת איסור חמור ממוקצה מחמת מיאוס והא דאמר בפ"ק דחולין (דף יד:) בשמעתא וסבין חבריא למימר מתני' ר' יהודה היא אימור דשמעת ליה לרבי יהודה במוקצה מחמת מיאוס במוקצה מחמת איסור מי שמעת ליה דיחוי בעלמא הוא ולפי המסקנא נאמר דמוקצה מחמת איסור טפי חמור תדע דהא קאמר התם אימור דשמעת ליה לר' מאיר במבשל דראוי לכוס שוחט דאינו ראוי לכוס מי שמעת ליה משמע דאית ליה לר' מאיר מוקצה מחמת איסור ובפרק כירה *משמע דלית ליה מוקצה מחמת מיאוס גבי מטלטלים נר חדש אבל לא ישן ר' מאיר אומר כל הנרות מטלטלים חוץ מן הנר שהדליקו בו באותו שבת: **וחד** מציל בארבע וחמש מאני · פי' בקונטרס ומקפלן כולן בתוך כלי אחד ונושאן בבת אחת ואין נראה לר"ת דבפ' כל כתבי (לקמן דף קכ·) לא פליגי אמוראי בהא דבעיא היא ופשיט דכבא להציל דמי ושרי לכ"ע ומפרש ר"ת דחד מציל בחד מנא אפי' מאה סעודות אבל בארבע וחמש מאני כגון להציל ולחזור ולהציל אפי' באותו חצר לא וחד מציל בד' וה' מאני לאותו חצר ובהא פליגי התם רבה בר זבדא ורב הונא:

איבעיא

עין משפט נר מצוה

בז ונראה לר"י וכ"ה בתוס' ישנים

קנ א ב מיי' פרק כ"א מהלכות שבת הלכה יג טור שו"ע או"ח סימן שכא סעיף יט:

קנא ג מיי' פכ"ו מהל' שבת הלכה יד:

קנב ד מיי' פכ"ה מהל' שבת הלכה ט:

קנג ה מיי' פכ"ו מהל' שבת הלכה יד סמג לאוין סה טוש"ע או"ח סימן שי סעיף ב:

קנד ו מיי' פ"ג מהל' שבת הלכה טו סמג שם טור שו"ע או"ח סי' רנד סעיף ב:

קנה ז מיי' שם הלכה יח טור שו"ע שם סעיף ה:

שלא יצא לא הוי משקה לזה הוי נולד גמור כצ"ל וכ"ה בתוס' ישנים

לקמן קכ.

[פי' תוס' מנחות נח: ד"ה פורסה]

עירובין קג.

בקצת כת"מ מה צריך להעמיד במוקצה מחמת מיאוס יעמיד אותו במוקצה משום ספירת אכל [פיי]

מסורת הש"ס

לקמן קמג:

שם קמה:

[לקמן סא. עירובין יט: פסחים קה: גיטין מה. ערכין ג.]

לקמן קס:

ס"א לסיטר

[לעיל יח:]

ס"א שיתבשלו

[דף לב.]

[דף קכ.]

[מלכים א ח]

[ויקרא ח]

הגהות הב"ח

(א) רש"י ד"ה כרכי דזוזי וכו' בגאונים מצאתי כרכי דזיווי. נ"ב ולי נראה דלגירסת כרכי דזיווי יותר מתיישב לפרש מלשון זוג כמו דקאי אלדים בזוזי דס"פ מפנין:

רבינו חננאל

אוקמה רבי יוסי ב"ר חנינא לר' ישמעאל ור' אלעזר בן פדת אוקמה לר' אלעזר ב"ר (שמעו,) [שמוע]. חלות שריסקן פירשנוהו בפ' חבית שנשברה כי שם מקומה. הורה ר' חנינא [כר' ישמעאל] שמן של בדדין [ומחצלות של בדדין] רב אסר ושמואל שרי פירוש שמן הנמשך מתחת קורות בית הבד וזב בשבת אסור באכילה ובשבת ומחצלות המוקצות למלאכת בית הבד אסור לישב עליהן (כרב) [לרב] פי' כרכי דוזי מחצלות סדורות שתים שתים זוגות זוגות והן עשויות לסחורה להשתלח בספינות אסור להתירן בשבת ולישב עליהן אמר רב נחמן עז לחלבה ורחל לגיזתה ותרנגולת לביצתה ותורי דרדיא ותמרי לעסקא פלוגתא דר' יהודה ור' שמעון פי' כל אלו שהעמידו לדברים הללו ולא העמידו לאכילה עכשיו אם ביקש לוכל מן התמרים הללו בשבת או העז והרחל וכיוצא בהן לשוחטן ביו"ט מותר וקי"ל הלכה כר"ש דלית ליה מוקצה אלא גרוגרות וצימוקים בלבד. הנהו תרי תלמידי חד מציל סל מלא ככרות אפילו באותה חצר בחד מנא כרב הונא

רב נסים גאון

אמר רב נחמן עז לחלבה ורחל לגיזתה כולה פלוגתא דר' יהודה ור"ש נתבאר פלוגתם במוקצה ועיקר דבריהם בפרק כירה (דף מד) דתנו רבנן מטלטלין נר חדש בשבת אבל לא ישן דברי ר' יהודה ר"ש אומר כל הנרות מטלטלין בשבת חוץ מן הנר הדולק בשבת כבתה מותר לטלטלה ובסוף הגמ' (דף קנו) מחתכין את הדילועין לפני הבהמה כו' ואמרו פליגי בה רב אחא ורבינא חד אמר בכולה שבת הלכה כר"ש לבר ממוקצה מחמת כו' ובמקומות הרבה מן התלמוד תמצא פלוגתן והנה תמצא עיקר פלוגתן לדבריהן אין מוקצה לר"ש אלא גרוגרות וצימוקין ופרישו טעמא דהא מילתא בגמ' דבני מערבא בגמ' יום טוב (פ' כמה ס"א)ובגמ' עשרות(פ"א)אמר רב שמואל בר סוטרטא מפני שמסריחות בנתים: **הנך** תרי תלמידי חד מציל בחד מאנא וחד מציל בתרי תלתי מאני קמיפלגי בפלוגתא דר' אבא בר זבדא ורב הונא פליג ר' אבא בר זבדא ורב הונא בפרק

גליון הש"ס

גמ' דמעיקרא אוכל. עי' כר"ש פ"ג מי"א דעוקצין: **שם** ותמרי דעיסקא רב אסר ושמואל כו'. ג"י כרי"ף והרא"ש ותמרי דעיסקא פלוגתא דר"י ור"ש דר"י אית ליה מוקצה ור"ש לית ליה מוקצה: **רש"י** ד"ה דארגיז וכו'. כך מצאתי בתשובה. וכ"כ רש"י בעירובין דף סג ע"א ד"ה דארגיז: **תוס'** ד"ה שמן של בדדין. וכן לואת קטן. לקמן דקמ"א ע"ב: **שם** ד"ה הני כרכי דזוזי כו' הן מוקצה מחמת מיאוס. עי' תוס' לקמן דקנ"ט ע"ב ד"ה אלא דכיחרא:

finish them at night; R. Akiba said: [19*b*] One may not finish them [at night].[6] And R. Eleazar [b. Pedath] said, It is R. Eleazar [b. Shammua']. For we learnt: If honeycombs are crushed on the
a eve of Sabbath and it [the honey] exudes spontaneously,[1] it is forbidden;[2] but R. Eleazar permits it.

Now, as to R. Jose son of R. Ḥanina, what is the reason that he did not answer as R. Eleazar?—He can tell you: it is only there [that R. Eleazar permits it], since it was originally food and still food;[3] but here[4] it was originally food and now a liquid.[5] And R. Eleazar [b. Pedath]?[6]—He can answer you: But we know R. Eleazar [b. Shammua'] to hold that even olives and grapes are also permitted. For when R. Hoshaya came from Nehardea, he came and brought a Baraitha in his hands: If olives and grapes are crushed on the eve of Sabbath and they [their juices] exude spontaneously, they are forbidden;[7] R. Eleazar and R. Simeon permit it. And R. Jose b. R. Ḥanina?—He did not know this Baraitha.[8]

And R. Eleazar! what is the reason that he did not answer as R. Jose son of R. Ḥanina?—He can tell you: was it not stated thereon:[9] Raba b. Ḥanina said in the name of R. Joḥanan: Where they lack crushing there is no controversy at all;[10] they differ only where pounding is lacking:[11] and these too[12] are similar to those that lack crushing. R. Jose son of R. Ḥanina gave a practical decision in accordance with R. Ishmael.[13]

As to the oil belonging to the pressers, and the mats of the pressers:[14] Rab forbade it,[15] and Samuel permitted it.[16] As to
b coupled mattings[1] Rab forbids them,[2] and Samuel permits [them].

R. Naḥman said: As to a goat [kept] for its milk, a ewe for its shearings, a fowl for its eggs, oxen for ploughing and dates for trading: Rab forbids, and Samuel permits [them],[3] and they differ in the controversy of R. Simeon and R. Judah.[4] A certain disciple gave a practical decision in Ḥarta of Argiz[5] in accordance with R. Simeon;[6] thereupon R. Hamnuna banned him.[7] But do we not hold as R. Simeon?—It was in the place of Rab,[8] and so he should have acted accordingly. There were two disciples: one saved [food, etc.] in one utensil, and one saved [it] in four or five utensils;[9] and they differ in the same dispute as that of Rabbah b. Zabda and R. Huna.[10]

MISHNAH. MEAT, ONION[S], AND EGG[S] MAY NOT BE ROASTED UNLESS THEY CAN BE ROASTED WHILE IT IS YET DAY. BREAD MAY NOT BE PUT INTO AN OVEN JUST BEFORE NIGHTFALL, NOR A CAKE UPON COALS, UNLESS ITS SURFACE CAN FORM A CRUST WHILE IT IS YET DAY; R. ELEAZAR SAID: THERE MUST BE TIME FOR THE BOTTOM [SURFACE] THEREOF TO FORM A CRUST. THE PASSOVER SACRIFICE MAY BE LOWERED INTO THE OVEN JUST BEFORE NIGHTFALL;[11]
c AND THE FIRE MAY BE LIGHTED WITH CHIPS[1] IN THE PILE

(6) A heavy weight was placed upon them to cause their juice to run out, and the controversy is whether this may be done (v. Tosa. a.l.) or allowed to continue on the Sabbath.

a (1) On the Sabbath. (2) To consume them on the Sabbath. (3) Honey is a food, not a drink, even after it oozes out. (4) The case of the Mishnah, where the oil exudes from the olives, etc. (5) Olives and grapes are food; oil and wine are liquid. Since it changes so much on the Sabbath, it may be that R. Eleazar forbids it. (6) Does he not admit the force of this argument? (7) For drinking on the Sabbath. (8) This may also mean: he rejects the authenticity of this Baraitha, for not all Baraithas were of equal authority. (9) On the Mishnah quoted by R. Jose b. R. Ḥanina. (10) It is certainly forbidden on all views. (11) 'Pounding' (*sheḥikah*) connotes a further stage in the process, after crushing. (12) In our Mishnah. (13) *Supra* 19*a* bottom. (14) The remnants of the oil in the corners and the oil which gathered in the mats with which the olives were covered belonged to the workers who pressed it out. (15) To be handled on the Sabbath. (16) This oil is '*mukẓeh*,' v. *infra*, n. b4, and it is disputed *infra* 44*a* *et passim* whether such may be handled on the Sabbath. Rab and Samuel differ on the same question.

b (1) *Keroke* (כרכי) connotes mattings which can be rolled up, and *zuze* means in pairs. Rashi explains: mattings used in couples to form a roof-like protection for merchandise. He also quotes a variant found in Geonic responsa: כרכי דזיוזי ship mattings. (2) To be handled on the Sabbath. (3) V. next note. (4) *Infra* 156*b* on '*mukẓeh*'. All these are '*mukẓeh*', set apart, i.e., their owner has set them apart not to be eaten but for the purposes stated, and it is disputed *infra* 156*b* whether one may change his mind and slaughter them on Festivals for food. With the exception of dates kept for trading the present controversy is in respect of Festivals, whilst that of dates refers to the Sabbath too. (5) In S. Babylon on the right arm of the Euphrates, subsequently called Hira. Obermeyer, *Landschaft*, p. 234. (6) That the above are permitted. (7) A form of excommunication. The banned person observed certain mourning rites and was shunned by his colleagues. Generally speaking it lasted for thirty days. (8) I.e., it was within his jurisdiction. (9) They saved them from being destroyed in a fire. (10) V. *infra* 120*a*. (11) And left to roast on the Sabbath. We have no fear that one may rake the coals on the Sabbath (v. *supra* 18*b*), because a whole company is present and should one man forget himself another will remind him.

c (1) *Ma'aḥizin* means to ignite logs by means of burning chips.

IN THE CHAMBER OF THE HEARTH;[2] [20a] BUT IN THE COUNTRY[3] THERE MUST BE TIME FOR THE FIRE TO TAKE HOLD OF ITS GREATER PART.[4] R. JUDAH SAID: IN THE CASE OF CHARCOAL JUST A LITTLE [SUFFICES].[5]

GEMARA. And how much?[6]—R. Eleazar said in Rab's name: That it may be roasted before sunset as the food of the son of Derusai.[7] It was stated likewise: R. Assi said in R. Johanan's name: Whatever is as the food of the son of Derusai is not subject to [the interdict of] the cooking of Gentiles.[8] It was taught: Ḥananiah said: Whatever is as the food of the son of Derusai may be kept on the stove,[9] though it is not swept [clear of the cinders] and besprinkled with ashes.[10]

BREAD MAY NOT BE PUT, etc. The scholars propounded: Does the BOTTOM [surface] mean the one by the oven, or perhaps BOTTOM means the one by the fire?[11]—Come and hear: R. Eleazar said: There must be time for the surface adhering to the oven to form a crust.

THE PASSOVER SACRIFICE MAY BE LOWERED, [etc.]. What is the reason?—Because the members of the company are extremely
a careful.[1] But otherwise, it would not [be permitted]? Yet a Master said: [With the flesh of] a kid, whether it [the oven] is daubed round or not, it is well?[2]—There it is cut up, whereas here it is not cut up.[3]

AND THE FIRE IS LIGHTED WITH CHIPS, etc. Whence do we know this?—Said R. Huna: *Ye shall kindle no fire throughout your habitations:*[4] [only] throughout your habitations you may not kindle, but you may kindle in the pile in the chamber of the Hearth. R. Ḥisda demurred: If so, even on the Sabbath too![5] Rather, said R. Ḥisda: The verse, when it comes, comes to permit [the burning of] limbs and the fat;[6] while the priests are very particular.[7]

BUT IN THE COUNTRY, THERE MUST BE TIME FOR THE FIRE TO TAKE HOLD, etc. What is meant by 'their greater part?'—Rab said: the greater part of each [log]; and Samuel said: That it should not be said, Let us bring chips to place under them.[8] R. Ḥiyya taught [a Baraitha which affords] support to Samuel: That the flame should ascend of its own accord, and not with the help of something else.[9]

As to a single log, Rab said: The greater part of its thickness;[10] while others state, The greater part of its circumference. R. Papa observed: Therefore we require the greater part of both its thickness and its circumference. This is a controversy of Tannaim: R. Ḥiyya said: That the log may be rendered unfit for an artisan's work;[11] R. Judah b. Bathyra said: That the fire should take hold
b on both sides.[1] And though there is no proof of the matter, there is a hint thereof: *the fire hath devoured both the ends of it, and the midst of it is burned; is it profitable for any work?*[2]

And there was a fire in the aḥ[3] *burning before him.*[4] What is '*aḥ?*'—Rab said, Willow-fire;[5] while Samuel said: Logs kindled by willow-fire. A certain man announced, who wants *aḥwawna?* and it was found to be willows.

R. Huna said: Canes do not require the greater part,[6] [but] if they are tied together, the greater part is required;[7] kernels [of dates] do not require the greater part; but if they are put in bales they require the greater part. R. Ḥisda demurred: On the contrary, [separate] canes may fall apart,[8] but if tied together they cannot fall apart; kernels can fall apart, but if placed in bales

(2) A room where the priests warmed themselves, as they performed the service in the Temple barefoot and became cold. The priests were very careful, and so it is sufficient if the fire just catches on, and no fear is entertained that they may forgetfully rake it into a blaze in the evening. (3) Lit., 'borders', the technical term for Palestine in contradistinction to the Temple (and generally, though not here, to Jerusalem). (4) *Sc*. of the logs. (5) Providing that the coals start burning before nightfall, even if only slightly, it is permitted. (6) Must the meat etc. be roasted before the Sabbath? (7) I.e., a third done. Rashi: he was a robber and always ate in a hurry. (8) Food cooked entirely by Gentiles is forbidden; but if a third is done by a Jew, it may be finished by a Gentile. (9) On the Sabbath; i.e., if it was a third done before. (10) V. *infra* 36b. (11) The oven or stove would appear to have been without a closed bottom, but perhaps consisted of a number of bars over the fire, and the loaves were placed thereon and pressed to the sides of the oven; v. *T.A.*, pp. 87f. The question is whether BOTTOM surface means the surface directly on the open bars facing the fire underneath, or that adhering to the side of the oven.

a (1) *V. supra* 19b, n. b11. (2) V. *supra* 18b. (3) The Passover sacrifice was roasted whole. Hence the draught would not injure it, and therefore it is permitted only on account of the reason stated. (4) Ex. XXXV, 3. (5) Let it be permitted. (6) Of animals sacrificed on Friday; these may be burnt on Friday night, the interpretation being, '*through all your habitations*', i.e., for a secular purpose, but not for a sacred purpose. (7) That is the real reason of the ruling in the Mishnah, as explained in *supra*, n. c2. (8) It should be burning strongly enough not to require such assistance. (9) V. *infra* 21a. But Rashi observes that its author there is Rami b. Ḥama, and further that it is not a Baraitha, and so he mentions that other scholars relate it immediately to this Mishnah, whereof it is an explanation. (10) The fire must take hold of the greater part of its thickness before the Sabbath. (11) I.e., the fire must take hold of the greater part of its thickness.

b (1) I.e., the greater part of its circumference. (2) Ezek. XV, 4. (3) A.V. hearth; R.V. brazier. (4) Jer. XXXVI, 22. (5) אחוונא *aḥwawna;* willow twigs used for kindling a fire. (6) It is sufficient if they are kindled before the Sabbath, even if the greater part has not caught on, because they will go on burning without further attention. (7) To be burning before the Sabbath, because the air has no access and it may otherwise require attention. (8) And fail to catch alight from each other, thus necessitating attention.

תורה אור

ובגבולין כדי שתאחוז האור ברובו ר' יהודה אומר *בפחמין כל שהוא: **גמ'** וכמה א"ר אלעזר אמר רב *כדי שיצולו מבעו"י כמאכל בן דרוסאי איתמר נמי *אמר רב אסי א"ר יוחנן *כל שהוא כמאכל בן דרוסאי אין בו משום בישולי נכרים *תניא חנניא אומר כל שהוא כמאכל בן דרוסאי מותר להשהותו ע"ג כירה ואע"פ שאין גרופה וקטומה: אין נותנין את הפת כו': איבעיא להו תחתון האיך דגבי תנור או דילמא תחתון האיך דגבי האור ת"ש ר"א אומר *כדי שיקרמו פניה המדובקין בתנור: *משלשלין את הפסח: מ"ט *משום דבני חבורה זריזין הן הא לאו הכי לא והאמר *מר גדיא בין שריק בין לא שריק שפיר דמי התם מינתח *הכא לא מינתח: *ומאחיזין את האור וכו': מנהני מילי אמר רב הונא °לא תבערו אש בכל מושבותיכם בכל מושבותיכם אי אתה מבעיר °אבל אתה מבעיר במדורת בית המוקד מתקיף לה רב חסדא אי הכי אפילו בשבת נמי אלא אמר רב חסדא קרא כי אתא למשרי אברים ופדרים הוא דאתא *וכהנים זריזין הן: ובגבולין כדי שתאחוז כו': מאי רובן אמר רב רוב כל אחד ואחד ושמואל אמר כדי שלא יאמרו הבא עצים ונניח תחתיהן תנא רב חייא לסיועיה לשמואל *כדי *שתהא שלהבת עולה מאליה ולא שתהא שלהבת עולה ע"י דבר אחר עץ יחידי רב אמר רוב עביו ואמרי לה ברוב היקפו °אמר רב פפא הלכך *בעינן רוב עביו ובעינן רוב היקפו כתנאי ר' חייא אמר (א) כדי שישחת העץ ממלאכת האומן רבי יהודה בן בתירא אומר כדי שתאחז האש משני צדדין ואע"פ שאין ראיה לדבר זכר לדבר °את שני קצותיו אכלה האש ותוכו נחר היצלח למלאכה: °והאח לפניו מבערת מאי אח אמר רב אחוונא ושמואל אמר עצים שנדלקו באחוונא ההוא דאמר להו מאן בעי אחוונא אשתכח ערבתא א"ר הונא קנים אין צריכין רוב אגדן צריכין רוב גרעינין אין צריכין רוב נתנן בחותלות צריכין רוב מתקיף לה רב חסדא אדרבה איפכא מסתברא קנים מבדרן אגדן לא מבדרן גרעינין מבדרן נתנן בחותלות לא מבדרן איתמר נמי אמר

(שמות לה) (יחזקאל טו) (ירמיה לו)

רש"י

ובגבולין · צריך להבעיר מדורתן מבעוד יום כדי שתאחוז האש ברובו : ר' יהודה אומר · אם היתה מדורת פחמין אין צריך להאחיז בהן האור אלא כל שהוא והיא דולקת והולכת דאין דרכה להיות כבה והולכת וא"צ לחתות בהן : גמ' בן דרוסאי · לסטים היה ומבשל בישולו שליש : איתמר נמי . דמאכל בן דרוסאי חשוב בישול : כל שהוא . מבושל ביד ישראל כמאכל בן דרוסאי שוב אין בגמרו משום בישולי נכרים : גרוף . מן הגחלים במגריפה שקורין וודילי: קטום· מפוזרים אפר מלמעלה כדי להפיג חומו שלא יוסיף הבל בשבת וזה תבשיל שהוא כמאכל בן דרוסאי לא חיישי' אם מתבשל והולך בשבת : דגבי תנור· שהככרות נדבקים בדופני התנור סביב הילכך מבעיא ליה הי קרי תחתון הנך פנים דגבי דופני התנור או פנים הפונים למטה לחלל התנור לצד האור : מדובקים בתנור · ותומרא היא דפנים שכלפי האור ממהרין לקרום : התם מנתח · ואם פותח פי התנור עייל ביה זיקא וקשי ליה : הכא לא מנתח · דכתיב (שמות יב) על ראשו ועל קרבו ואי מגלי ליה לא קשי ליה זיקא הלכך אי לא דזריזין הן אסור: אברים ופדרים הוא דאתא· להתיר את הקטירן כל הלילה אבל מדורת בית המוקד שאינה לורך גבוה אלא לורך כהנים לא הותרה וסמוך לחשיכה הייט טעמא דלא גזור משום דכהנים זריזין הם שכולם היו בני תורה וחרדים ונזכרים ולא אתו לחתויי משתחשך : כל אחד ואחד · כל עץ ועץ ולא תימא כיון שאחזה ברוב מנין העצים : ושמואל אמר· כדי שלא יצטרך לומר הבא עצים דקים ונניח תחתיהן להבעיר את אלו : תני ר' חייא · בפ' במה מדליקין לגבי מנורה להעלות נר תמיד שתהא שלהבת עולה מאליה אלמא בכי האי גוונא הויא הדלקה משום ר"י הלוי וקשה לי הדא דרמי בר חמא קתני לה התם ועוד דלאו מתניתא היא אלא הוא אמר לה בפירוש דמתני' אשכחתי ושאר רבותינו תנו לה לענין מדורה ואני מצאתי אותה בת"כ לגבי מנורה : עץ יחידי. כעין לוק"ש שלנו : רוב עביו · שיכנס האור בתוך עביו עד רובו : רוב היקפו · מבחוץ : כתנאי · רוב עביו או רוב היקפו : שישחת · רוב עביו: ב' לדדיו · רוב היקפו : זכר לדבר · דשוב הולך ודולק : שני קצותיו אכלה האש · בידוע שתוכו נחר והולכה לחה שלו ונעשה יבש : נחר · פסק לחה שלה ויבש כמו נחר גרוני (תהלים סט) וכן חרה מני חורב (איוב ל) : והאח · בשריפת יהויקים המגילה כתיב : אחוונא · ערבה : באחוה · כל העצים נדלקין זה מזה הקטן מדליק הגדול : אין צריכין רוב · להצית את האור ברובן מע"ש אלא מאחיז בהן אור מבעוד יום לפי שאין כבין והולכים אלא דולקים והולכים : צריכים רוב · לפי שאין שלהבת יכול ליכנס ביניהם : גרעינין · של תמרה אם עשה מהם מדורה לכשיבשו אין צריכין רוב : נתנן בחותלות · כלים שעושין מלולבין ונתן הכלי מלא במדורה צריכין רוב לפי שנצבורין יחד ואין השלהבת יכולה להכנס בהן : קנים מבדרן · לכאן ולכאן ואחת מהן היוצאה לא תמלא את חברתה לבערה הלכך כי לא אגדן צריכי רוב אבל אגדן לא מבדרן ואין צריכין רוב וכן גרעינין :

רב

תוספות

איבעיא להו תחתון האיך דגבי תנור · ולפ"ה דפי' דלגבי האור ממהר לקרום ומיבעיא ליה אם תחתון דקאמר ר' אליעזר דגבי תנור והא דקאמרי רבנן עד שיקרמו פניה אחת מפניה ואפילו בעליון סגי ואם תחתון דקאמר ר"א היינו דגבי האור אם כן הא דקאמרי רבנן עד שיקרמו פניה היינו כל פניה את שמע ר' אליעזר כו' ופשטו דר"א לחומר' ומיהו בירושלמי משמע דלהקל בא דקאמר התם ומודה ר"א בלחם הפנים שאין קרוי לחם עד שיקרמו פניו בתנור משמע דהכא סגי בקרימה כל דהו אבל בלחם הפנים בעינן קרימה מעליא · ריב"א*.

למשרי אברים ופדרים . וא"ת אי אברים ופדרים דחול כדפ"ה הא אמר בפרק [במה מדליקין] (דף כד:) עולת שבת בשבתו ולא עולת חול בשבת ואי אברים ופדרים דשבת ואשמועינן מבכל מושבותיכם דאע"ג דמלותן כל הליל' ואפשר להקטירן במוצאי שבת אפ"ה דחי שבת הא מעולת שבת נפק מדממעט עולת חול דהיינו ע"כ אברים ופדרים דחול דשחיטה וזריק' עבר זמנו בשקיעת החמה א"כ אברים ופדרים דשבת קרבים בשבת וי"ל דאתי למשרי אברים ופדרים דחול בשמשלה בהן האור מבעוד יום והא דקאמר ולא עולת אברים ופדרי' דחול בשבת היינו דוקא בשלא משלה בהן האור וכן הא דאמר בפרק טרף בקלפי (יומא דף מו· ושם) אברי *חול שנתותרו עושה להן מערכה בפני עצמן וסודרן אפי' בשבת ואפי' לרב הונא דפליג התם היינו דאמר דאין עושה להן מערכה בפני עצמן אבל ד"ה דסודרן על המערכה גדולה היינו כשמשלה בהן האור כדמוכח התם והא דקאמר התם לחד לישנא דדוקא בפסולין אי משלה בהן האור אין אי לא לא לאו משום דכשרים לא בעינן משלה בהן האור אלא ה"ק דדוקא בפסולים אצטריך לאשמעינן במשלה בהן האור אבל בכשרים לא איצטריך לאשמעי' וריב"א מסתפק בשאר קרבנות כשמשלה בהן האור אם נעשו כלחמו של מזבח למשריינהו בשבת אי לאו דדילמא דוקא בתמיד מהני האי טעמא משום דשם תמיד דוחה שבת וקשה דהתם מפיק ליה ביומא מבמועדו ואפי' בשבת והכא מפיק ליה מבמושבותיכם ונראה דעיקר דרשא מבמושבותיכם והתם נקט במועדו ואפי' בשבת אגב דבעי למנקט במועדו ואפי' בטומאה · ועוד קשה והא במושבותיכם אצטריך לשריפת בת כהן דלא דחיא שבת כדדרשי' פ"ק דיבמות (דף ו: ושם) ופרק אחד דיני ממונות (סנהדרין לה:) נאמר כאן במושבותיכם כו' אף מושבות האמור כאן כו' וי"ל דהכא מכם דריש מדכתי' מושבותיכם ולא כתיב *מושבות והא דדרשי' בפ"ק דקדושין (דף לז· ושם) מושבות דכתב רחמנא גבי שבת ל"ל וקאמר דסד"א הואיל ובענין מועדות כתיב תבעי קדוש ב"ד כמועדות קמ"ל לא מלא תבערו אש בכל מושבותיכם דריש כדפירש הקונטרס דההוא לא כתיבא בענין דמועדות ואצטריך לה נמי כדדריש הכא אלא מושבותיכם דכתי' באמור (ויקרא כג) דההוא כתיב בעניינא דמועדות*:

כדי שתהא שלהבת עולה מאליה · אלמא במקום שהקפיד הכתוב שלא יכבה סגי שתהא שלהבת עולה מאליה ואין צריך שתהא הפתילה שורפת ברובה: **עד** שישחת ממלאכת האומן · אבל למ"ד משתאחוז האור מסני לדדין אינו נשחת בהכי ממלאכת האומן ואע"ג דכתיב את שני קצותיו אכלה האש היצלח למלאכה היינו גבי עץ הגפן אבל שאר עצים אין נשחתין כ"כ במהרה ממלאכת האומן :

הדרן עלך יציאות השבת

עין משפט נר מצוה

קנו א מיי' פ"ג מהל' שבת הלכה יט טור וש"ע או"ח סי' רנג סעיף ב :

קנז ב מיי' פ"ג מהלכות שבת הלכה טו טור ש"ע או"ח סימן רנד סעיף ב :

קנח ג מיי' פי"ז מהל' מ"א טור וש"ע יו"ד סי' קיג סעיף ח:

קנט ד מיי' פ"ג מהל' שבת הלכה יח סמג לאוין סה טור ש"ע או"ח סימן רנד סעיף ה:

קס ה ו מיי' שם הלכה טו :

[ועי' תוס' מנחות מז: ד"ה ושמעינן]

קסא ז מיי' שם הל' כ :

קסב ח ט מיי' שם הל' יט סמג שם טור ש"ע או"ח סימן רנה סעיף א :

[לעיל יח:]

[שם איתא עולה ועי' ברש"י שם ד"ה הכי גרסינן]

[קמן כח.]

רבינו חננאל

וחד מציל בד' ה' מאני כב' אבא בר זבדא וחלוקת רבי אבא בר זבדא ורב הונא בפ' כל כתבי הקודש:צליית בשר וביצה אסיק' כמאכל בן דרוסאי וכל שהוא כמאכל בן דרוסאי מותר לשהותו ע"ג כירה אע"פ שאינה גרופה ולא קטומה . קרומיו של פת אוקימ' קרומת פנים המדובקים בתנור וכיון שקרמו פנים מותר לשהותה והכין מפרשא בפ' דלקמן בכירה (לז:): משלשלין את הפסח לתנור עם חשכה אוקימ' משום דבני חבורה זריזין הן הא שאר בני אדם לא ואי גדיא הוא מינתח הוא כלומר אינו שלם אלא מנותח אברים כיון דקשי ליה זיקא לא מגלי ליה הלכך לא אתי לחתויי בגחלים בין שריק התנור בין לא שריק התנור שרי . אברי דברחא שריק שרי לא שריק רב ירמיה מדפתי אסר ורב אשי שרי וקיי"ל כוותיה . בשרא אנומרי אסיר אלא א"כ נצלה כל צרכן . קרא חייא בתנור רבינא שרי. ומחיזין את האור במדורת בית המוקד משום דכהנים זריזין הם . וקרא לאברים ופדרים הוא דאתא דכתיב לא תבערו אש בכל מושבותיכם בכל מושבותיכם אינכם מבערים אבל אתם מבערים לאברים ופדרים ובגבולין כדי שיצית האור ברובו רב אמר רוב כל עץ ועץ. ושמואל אמר כדי שאין צריכין להביא אחרים תחתיהן כדי שידליקם והלכתא כשמואל דתני ר' חייא לסועיה [לשמואל] שתהא שלהבת עולה מאליה ולא על ידי דבר אחר. עץ יחידי אסיק' בעינן רוב עביו ורוב היקפו ואת

מסורת הש"ס

פ"ז נח.

לקמן לו:

[עירובין קג. פסחים סה.]

[לקמן קיד: עירובין קג. פסחים נט: סה. פס. ביצה יח. כ"ב ל. חולין קכג. זבחים לה.]

הגהות הב"ח

(א) גמ' ר' חייא אמר עד שישחת העץ ממלאכה:

גליון הש"ס

גמ' אבל אתה מבעיר במדורת בית המוקד. עי' יומא דף מו ע"ב תוס' ד"ה ואתת: שם אמר ר' פפא הלכך בעינן רוב עביו. חולין דף ע"ב וכעין זה סוטה דף מ ע"א וחולין דף סח ע"א:

[ועי' תוספות לקמן ע. ד"ה הבערה]

[וע"ע תוס' קידושין לז. ד"ה וכי שבת]

רב נסים גאון

בפ' כל כתבי הקודש (דף כ) דתנן מצילין סל מלא רכרות כו' ואמרינן אמר רב הונא לא קשיא כאן בבא להציל כאן בבא לקפל ר' אבא בר זבדא אמר רב כאן לאותה חצר כאן לחצר אחרה: סליק פירקא קמא

אמר רב כהנא [א]קנים שאגדן [א]צריכין רוב [ג]לא אגדן אין צריכין רוב גרעינין צריכין רוב נתנן בחותלות אין צריכין רוב תני רב יוסף [ב]ארבע מדורות אין צריכין רוב של זפת ושל גפרית ושל [ג] גבינה *ושל רבב במתניתא תנא [ג]אף של קש ושל גבבא א"ר יוחנן עצים של בבל אין צריכין רוב מתקיף לה רב יוסף מאי היא אילימא סילתי השתא פתילה אמר עולא *המדליק צריך שידליק ברוב היוצא סילתי מבעיא אלא אמר רב יוסף שוכא דארזא רמי בר אבא אמר *זאזא:

הדרן עלך יציאות השבת

*במה מדליקין ובמה אין מדליקין [ד]אין מדליקין לא *בלכש ולא בחוסן ולא בכלך ולא בפתילת האידן ולא בפתילת המדבר ולא בירוקה שעל פני המים *[ה]ולא בזפת ולא בשעוה ולא בשמן קיק ולא בשמן שריפה ולא באליה ולא בחלב *נחום המדי אומר מדליקין בחלב מבושל וחכ"א אחד מבושל ואחד שאינו מבושל אין מדליקין בו:

גמ' לכש שוכא דארזא שוכא דארזא עץ בעלמא הוא בעמרניתא דאית ביה: ולא בחוסן: אמר רב יוסף נעורת של פשתן אמר ליה אביי והכתיב °והיה *החסון לנעורת (מבלל דחוסן לאו נעורת הוא) אלא אמר אביי כיתנא דדייק ולא נפיץ: ולא בכלך: אמר שמואל שאלתינהו לכל נחותי ימא ואמרי (*לה) כולכא שמיה רב יצחק בר זעירא אמר גושקרא רבין ואביי הוו יתבי קמיה דרבנא נחמיה אחוה דריש גלותא חזייה דהוה לביש מטכסא א"ל רבין לאביי היינו כלך דתנן א"ל אנן שירא פרנדא קרינן ליה °מיתיבי *השיראים והכלך והסיריקין חייבין בציצית (תיובתא דרבין) *תיובתא איבעית אימא שירא לחוד ושירא פרנדא לחוד*): ולא בפתילת האידן: אחוינא: רבין ואביי הוו קאזלו בפקתא דטמרוריתא חזינהו להנהו *ארבתא אמר ליה רבין לאביי היינו אידן דתנן אמר ליה ההיא עץ בעלמא הוא קלף ואחוי ליה עמרניתא דביני ביני: ולא בפתילת המדבר: שברא: ולא בירוקה שעל כו': מאי היא אילימא אוכמתא דהריצי איפרוכי מפרכן אלא אמר רב פפא אוכמתא דארבא תנא [ו]הוסיפו עליהן של צמר ושל שער ותנא דידן צמר מבווץ כוויץ שער איחרוכי מיחרך: ולא בזפת: זפת זיפתא שעוה קירותא תנא עד כאן פסול פתילות מכאן ואילך פסול שמנים פשיטא [ז]שעוה איצטריכא ליה מהו דתימא לפתילות נמי לא חזיא קא משמע לן אמר רמי בר אבין עטרנא פסולתא דזיפתא שעוה פסולתא דדובשא למאי

*) רש"ל גורס ואב"א פירושא קא מפרש

רב כהנא אמר קנים שאגדן צריכין רוב · כרב הונא דלא עיילא בהן טרא ולאבדורי לא חיישינן דארוכין הן וכבדין: גרעינין שנתנן בחותלות אין צריכין רוב · כרב חסדא שנוחין לידלק אבל בלא חותלות מבדרי: מדורה · לשון היסק גדול: רבב · שומן ושעוה וכל דבר הניתך: גבבא · שגובבין מן השדה בל"א שטובל"א: קש · זנבות שבולין אשטריי"ש: סילתי · לאחר שעאוס עלים דקים ובבבל נוהגין כן: השתא פתילה · של בגד הטבולה בשמן ונוח לידלק: אמר עולא המדליק · נר של שבת צריך שידליק ברוב היוצא מראש הפתילה חוץ לנר: שוכא דארזא · יבש הוא ודק ויש כמין צמר בין קליפה לעץ והוא מבעירו משאחזה בו אור: זאזא · מולש"א בלעז:

הדרן עלך יציאות השבת

במה מדליקין · לעשות פתילה כל הני דמתני' מפרש בגמרא: לא בזפת ולא בשעוה · לאו לענין פתילה אלא לתת במקום שמן וכל הני מזפת ואילך פסולי שמנים הן: גמ' עץ בעלמא הוא · ופשיטא דלא חזי לפתילה אלא למדורה: עמרניתא · כמין צמר יש בין קליפתו לעצו: והיה החסון לנעורת · אלמא חסון לאו נעורת הוא: כיתנא דדייק ולא נפיץ · דכיון דלא נפיץ אין שמן נמשך אחריו נפיץ קרפר"י ונעורת מן הדק שבו והכי קאמר קרא פשתן החזק יהפך לנעורת כלומר הגבור יהיה חלש: גושקרא · פסולת של משי העשוי כבוצעים והוא בית התולעת וקורין לו פולויי"ל ונופלים אותו וטווהו ועושה ממנו בגד ואסור לעשות ממנו פתילה כדאמר בכל פסולי פתילות דמתניתין שהאור מסכסכת בהן קופלת ונפסקת ואין השלהבת עומדת במקומה: גושקרא. על שם פסולת וגם פת סובין כמו כן נקראת במסכת גיטין (דף נו:): מטכסא. לבוש העשוי מאותו כלך: שיראים. מטיל העשוי מעיקר המשי: סיריקין. עשוי מן המשי הרך המתפלל ומלוי במשי וקורין לו במקומו יד"ש: חייבין בציצית. ודלא כמאן דאמר כל בגדי צמר ופשתים דוקא חייבין בציצית מדאורייתא אי נמי מדרבנן קתני מיהא השיראים והכלך אלמא שיראין לאו היינו כלך: אחווינא. ערבה ויש כמין צמר בין קליפה לעץ: בפקתא. בקעה: עץ בעלמא הוא. והיכי ליחזי לפתילה: שברא. מין עשב ארוך וקורין אותו אורטי"א: אוכמתא דחריצי. מקום כנס מים גדל עליהם כמין ירקרוקת: איפרוכי מיפרכן. ולא מצי ליעבד פתילה מינה: אוכמתא דארבא. ספינה המתעכבת במקום אחד במים גדל ירקרוקת סביב שוליה מבחוץ: מכווץ כווץ. מפני האור ואין דולק כלל ואין שלהבת אוחזת בו ולא צריך למתנייה: עד כאן. עד ירוקה שעל פני המים פסול פתילות: מכאן ואילך פסול שמנים. שלא יתן חתיכה זפת או שעוה בנר במקום שמן: שעוה איצטריכא ליה. לפי שרגילין לעשות כמין פתילה ארוכה והפתילה לתוכה כמו שאנו עושין: מהו דתימא לפתילה נמי. קאסר לה: פסולתא דזיפתא. לאחר שיוצא הזפת מן העץ זב ממנו על ידי האור, פסולת נגול כשמן והוא עיטרן (א): למקח

במה מדליקין כו' · פעמים מפרש מאי דסליק מיניה ופעמים במה שהתחיל*: אחד מבושל כו' · הכא מזכיר שאינו פשוט תחילה וכן בכמה מקומות ומה שקשה על גירסת רש"י דסוכה [דף ז·] מפורש במקום אחר*: בעמרניתא דאית ביה · וא"ת הא מסיפא שמעינן ליה כל היוצא מן העץ אין מדליקין בו אלא פשתן וכן קשה גבי אידן ויש לומר דאין למדין מן הכללות אפילו במקום שנאמר בהן חוץ*: אנן שירא פרנדא קרינן ליה · פר"ת דכלך דמתניתין קרינן שירא פרנדא אבל מטכסא לאו היינו שירא פרנדא דלא הוה אחר חורבן כדאמר בפ' בתרא דסוטה (דף מח:) משחרב בית המקדש בטל שמיר וזכוכית לבנה ושירא פרנדא ור"י מפרש דקאי נמי אמטכסא והא דקאמר התם בטל לא לגמרי בטל אלא *שלא היה נמצא כ"כ דהא זכוכי' לבנה היתה אחר חורבן דאמרי' בפ' אין עומדין (ברכות דף לא·) תבר קמייהו זכוכית חיורתא בחופת בט*: ותנא דידן צמר מכוון כוון ושער איחרוכי מחרך · ולא איצטריך תנא דמתני' למיתני וא"ת כיון דמתני' נמי סברה דצמר ושער פסולים להדלקה א"כ מאי הוסיפו וי"ל דהוסיפו הייט טעמא מפני שאין מושכין השמן יפה ותנא דמתניתין פסיל להו משום דצמר כווץ ושער מחרך ולא איצטריך למתני: עד כאן פסול פתילות מכאן ואילך פסול שמנים · בני נרבונא אוסרין נר שעוה שלנו ומפרשי הכי מהו דתימא לפתילות נמי לא שאם שם נר שעוה בנר שמן יהא אסור קמ"ל מכאן ואילך פסול שמנים כיון שיש בו שמן כשר מותר אבל נר של שעוה בלא שמן אסור להדליק ולי נראה דאם אסור להדליק בלא שמן כי הניחה בשמן נמי אסור כדאמרינן לקמן כרך דבר שמדליקין על גבי דבר שאין מדליקין דאסור אלא ודאי כי לא הגיח בשמן נמי שרי: למאי

[ק' מסיק כש"ס נדרים כ: וכנזיר ג.]

[עי' תוס' פסחים פס. קח: ד"ה אחד ובסוכה כ. ד"ה אחת זבחים לב: ד"ה אי הכי מנחות סג: ד"ה ר"י ועי' תוספות קידושין יג. ד"ה כשם]

[כדאיתא עירובין כז·]

קסג א ב ג מיי' פ"ג מהל' שבת הלכה כא כב סמג לאוין סה טוש"ע או"ח סי' רנה ס"ג:

א ד מיי' פ"ה מהלכות שבת הלכה ה סמג שם טור או"ח סימן רסד:

ב ה מיי' שם הלכה א סמג שם טור טוש"ע שם סעיף ג:

ג ו מיי' שם הלכה ה טוש"ע שם סעיף א:

ד ז מיי' שם הלכה א טוש"ע שם סעיף ג:

[ועי' תוס' ב"מ כט: ד"ה בזכוכית ותוספות חולין סד: ד"ה בזוגיתא]

[עי' רש"י לקמן כד: ד"ה ס"ג נחום וכו']

רבינו חננאל

האח לפניו מבוערת רב אמר אחואנה. פי' עצי (מערכה) [ערבות] תני רב יוסף ארבע מדורות אין צריכות רוב של זפת ס"א של נפת ושל גפרית ושל רבב ושל גבינה. פתילה אמר עולא צריך להדליק ברוב היוצא עצים של בבל שוכא דארזא פי' זאזא נוותא יבש דרומני:

פ"ב במה מדליקין כו' לכש עמרניתא זביני ביני דארזא. חוסן כיתנא דדייק ולא נפיץ. כלך רבין אמר מיטכס' השיראים. והכלך והסיריקין חייבין בציצי' פתילת האידן ערמניתא דביני ביני ערבה. פתילת המדבר שיברא. ירושלמי אמר שמואל בר רב יצחק כתיב להעלות נר תמיד שערו לומר אין לך עושה שלהבת אלא פשתן: לא בזפת ולא בשעוה תנא ע"כ פסול פתילות

הגהות הגר"א

[א] גמ' קנים שאגדן. נ"ב אין· גירסת הרא"ש אבל הרי"ף ורמב"ם גרסי כל הא' שמעתא בהיפך מגירסת הרא"ש: [ב] שם (לא אגדן א"צ רוב גרעינין צריכין רוב נתנן בחותלות א"צ רוב) תא"מ ונ"ב הרי"ף והרא"ש לא גרסי כל זה: [ג] שם גבינה. נ"ב גירסת הרי"ף קירה:

גי' הרי"ף גפרית ושל רבב ושל קירה

לקמן כח:

ענף. של עץ [עי' ערוך]

[נדרים כ: נזיר ג.]

[גי' הערוך בלגש ע"ש]

[גי' רש"י וכן הרב מברטנורה לא בזפת וכן נכון כי זה התחלת בבא דפסול שמנים]

יש מפרשים דקרא משמע שהנעורת דולק ואין נראה דקש נמי דולק יפה ואין דומה לפתילה [פ"י]

מנחות לט:

[גיטין כח. זבחים פה.]

נ"ל ערבתא

הגהות הב"ח

(א) רש"י ד"ה פסולתא דזיפתא וכו' והוא עיטרן שקורין דוהיס בלשון כנען הס"ד:

גליון הש"ס

גמ' מיתיבי השיראים והכלך. ק"ל

אמאי פריך מהברייתא ולא פריך ממתניתין פ"ט מ"ב דכלאים: תוס' ד"ה אנן שירא כו' שלא היה נמצא כל כך. עיין בר"ש פ"ט מ"ב דכלאים:

they cannot? It was stated likewise, [20b] R. Kahana said: Canes tied together require the greater part; if not tied together, they do not require the greater part. Kernels require the greater part; if put in bales they do not.[9]

R. Joseph learned: Four fires do not require the greater part, [viz.,] of pitch, sulphur, cheese,[10] and grease.[11] In a Baraitha it was taught: straw and rakings too.[12] R. Joḥanan said: Babylonian woods do not require the greater part. R. Joseph demurred: To what does this refer? Shall we say, To chips?[13] But if [concerning] a wick 'Ulla said, He who kindles must kindle the great part of what protrudes,[14] is there a question of chips![15] Rather, said R. Joseph: [It refers to] the bark of cedar.[16] Rami b. Abba said: [It refers to] dry twigs.

CHAPTER II

MISHNAH. WHEREWITH MAY WE KINDLE [THE SABBATH LIGHTS], AND WHEREWITH MAY WE NOT KINDLE
a [THEM]?[1] WE MAY NOT KINDLE [THEM] WITH LEKESH, ḤOSEN [TOW], KALLAK, A BAST WICK, A DESERT WICK, SEAWEED, ZEFETH [PITCH], SHA'AWAH [WAX], ḲIḲ OIL, OIL OF BURNING,[2] TAIL FAT, OR TALLOW. NAHUM THE MEDE SAID: WE MAY KINDLE [THEM] WITH BOILED ḤELEB; BUT THE SAGES MAINTAIN: WHETHER BOILED OR NOT, YOU MAY NOT KINDLE THEREWITH.[3]

GEMARA. *Lekesh* is cedar bark. But cedar bark is simply wood![4]—It means the woolly substance [bast] within it.

NOR WITH ḤOSEN [TOW]. R. Joseph said: [That is,] hatcheled flax. Abaye demurred: But it is written, *And the* ḥason *shall be as* ne'oreth?[5] Rather said Abaye: It is crushed but uncombed flax.

NOR WITH KALLAK. Samuel said: I asked all seafarers about it, and they told me that it is called *kulka*.[6] R. Isaac b. Ze'ira said: *Gushkera*.[7] Rabin and Abaye were sitting before Rabana[8] Nehemiah the brother of the Resh Galutha.[9] Seeing that he was wearing *metaksa*,[10] Rabin said to Abaye, That is the *kallak* of which we learnt. We call it *peranda* silk,[11] he answered him. An objection is raised: [Garments of] silk, *kallak* and corded [silk], are liable to
b fringes.[1] This refutes it.[2] Alternatively, silk is one thing and *peranda* silk is another.

NOR WITH A BAST WICK: [I.e.,] willow-bast. Rabin and Abaye were walking in the valley of Tamruritha,[3] when they saw some willows. Said Rabin to Abaye, That is the *idan* [bast] of which we learnt. But that is simply wood, he objected. Thereupon he peeled it and showed him the wool-like substance within.

NOR WITH A DESERT WICK: Mullein.[4]

NOR WITH SEAWEED. What is this? Shall we say, The black moss of pits? But that is crumbly![5] Rather said R. Papa: it is the black fungus of ships. A Tanna taught: To these [enumerated in the Mishnah] were added [wicks] of wool and hair.[6] And our Tanna?—Wool shrinks [and] hair smoulders.[7]

NOR WITH PITCH [ZEFETH]. ZEFETH is pitch; SHA'AWAH is wax. A Tanna taught: Thus far the unfitness of wicks [is taught]; from here onwards it is the unfitness of oils.[8] But that is obvious?—It is necessary in respect to wax: you may say, It is not fit for wicks either; hence we are informed [otherwise].[9]

Rami b. Abin said: *'Iṭrona*[10] is the by-product of pitch; wax

(9) Thus he agrees with R. Huna in respect to canes, and with R. Ḥisda in respect to kernels. (10) Alfasi reads: wax. (11) I.e., any fatty substance. (12) 'Rakings' refers to small stubble collected in the field. (13) Because they burn easily. (14) Before the Sabbath. (15) Which burn less freely. (16) This was extremely dry and burnt rapidly.

a (1) I.e., of what must the wick be made? (2) Explained in the Gemara. (3) The foreign terms are discussed in the Gemara. (4) And is obviously unfit for a wick. (5) Isa. I, 31. E.V. *And the strong shall be as tow*, but Abaye identifies *ḥason* with *ḥosen* and thus deduces that *ḥosen* is not *ne'oreth* (hatcheled flax). (6) Jast.: cissaros—blossom, 'a woolly substance growing on stones at the Dead Sea, looking like gold, and being very soft; its name is כלך (κάλκη, κάλχη) and it resembles sheep wool'. (7) A cotton-like plant. (8) I.e., Rabbi. This is a Babylonian title, perhaps = Rabbenu, our teacher. (9) 'Head of the Exile', the title of the official head of Babylonian Jewry. (10) μέταξα, silk. (11) Sachs, *Beitr*. II, p. 185 refers to late Greek πράνδιοι (πράνδιον, fillet) from which he derives French *frange*, Eng. fringe (Jast.).

b (1) V. Num. XV, 38.—This shows that *kallak* is not identical with silk. (2) Rabin's observation. (3) Or perhaps, in a secluded valley. (4) A tall, woolly weed. (5) A wick cannot be made from it in any case. (6) As being unfit for use. (7) When lit; hence they are unfit in any case. (8) I.e., from PITCH. (9) A waxen wick (i.e., a wax candle) is permitted. V., however, Tosaf. a.l. (10) A sort of resin.

is the residue of honey. [21a] What is the practical bearing of this?—In respect of buying and selling.[11]

Our Rabbis taught: All those of which they ruled that you must not light [the Sabbath lamp] therewith on the Sabbath, yet a fire may be made of them, both for warming oneself and for using the light thereof, whether on the earth or on the stove;[12] and they merely prohibited the making of a wick of them for the [Sabbath] lamp.

NOR WITH ḲIḲ OIL. Samuel said: I asked all seafarers about it, and they told me that there is a certain bird in the sea towns
a called *ḳiḳ*.[1] R. Isaac son of Rab Judah said: It is cotton-seed oil; Resh Laḳish said: Oil from Jonah's *ḳiḳayon*.[2] Rabbah b. Bar Ḥanah said: I myself have seen Jonah's *ḳiḳayon*; it resembles the ricinus tree and grows in ditches. It is set up at the entrance of shops;[3] from its kernels oil is manufactured, and under its branches rest all the sick of the West [i.e., Palestine].

Rabbah said: As to the wicks which the Sages said that you must not kindle therewith for the Sabbath, [the reason] is because their flame burns unevenly.[4] The oils which the Sages said you must not kindle therewith is because they do not flow [freely] to the wick.[5] Abaye asked Rabbah: As to the oils which the Sages said you must not kindle therewith for the Sabbath, is it permissible to pour a little [good] oil into them and light [therewith]? Do we forbid it, lest one come to light therewith [the forbidden oil] in its unmixed state, or not? He answered him, You must not light [therewith]. What is the reason?—Because you must not light.[6]

He raised an objection: If one wraps a material which may be used [as a wick] for lighting around a material which may not be lit, one must not light therewith. R. Simeon b. Gamaliel said: In my father's house a wick was wound over a nut and they did light therewith. Thus he teaches that one may light![7]—He replied: Instead of refuting me by R. Simeon b. Gamaliel's view, support me by the first Tanna's [ruling]!—That is no difficulty: an act is
b [more] weighty.[1] Thus the difficulty still remains, [for] surely it was for lighting?[2]—No: for floating.[3] If for floating, what is the reason of the first Tanna?[4]—It is all R. Simeon b. Gamaliel, but there is a lacuna, and it was taught thus: If one wraps a material which may be used for lighting around a material which may not be lit, you must not light therewith. When is that said? For lighting; but for floating it is permitted, for R. Simeon b. Gamaliel said, In my father's house a wick was wound about a nut and lit.

Yet that is not so, for R. Beruna said in Rab's name: The melted tallow and the dissolved inwards of fish, one may pour a little oil and light [therewith]?[5]—These flow [freely] in their natural state, while those [in the Mishnah] do not flow [freely] in their natural state,[6] but that the Rabbis forbade melted tallow on account of unmelted tallow and the dissolved inwards of fish on account of the undissolved inwards of fish.[7] Then let us prohibit melted tallow and the dissolved inwards of fish diluted with oil on account of the same without an admixture of oil?[8]—That itself is [merely] a preventive measure, and are we to arise and enact one preventive measure to safeguard[9] another preventive measure?

Rami b. Ḥama recited: The wicks and oil which the Sages said, One must not light therewith on the Sabbath, one must [also] not light therewith in the Temple, because it is said, *to cause a lamp to burn continually*.[10] He recited and he interpreted it: the flame must ascend of itself, and not through something else.[11] We learnt: The outworn breeches and girdles of priests were
c unravelled, and with these they kindled [the lights]?[1]—The rejoicing of the Water-Drawing[2] was different.[3] Come and hear: For Rabbah b. Mattenah taught: Worn out priestly garments were unravelled, and of these wicks were made for the Temple. Surely that means [the garments] of composite materials?[4]—No: [the garments] of linen [are meant].[5]

R. Huna said: With regard to the wicks and oils which the Sages said, One must not light therewith on the Sabbath, one may not light therewith on *Ḥanukkah*,[6] either on the Sabbath or on weekdays. Raba observed, What is R. Huna's reason? He holds that if it [the *Ḥanukkah* lamp] goes out, one must attend thereto,[7] and one may make use of its light.[8] R. Ḥisda maintained: One may light therewith on weekdays, but not on the

(11) When one orders *'iṭrona* or wax, he must be supplied with the residue of pitch or honey respectively. (12) Var. lec.: in the lamp.
a (1) Jast. identifies it with the pelican. (2) V. Jonah IV, 6. E.V. *gourd*, Jast.: ricinus tree, or the sprout bearing the castor-berry. (3) To provide shade and fragrance. (4) In a notched manner, as it were (Rashi). Jast.: the flame nibbles at them, producing sputtering sparks. (5) And so one may trim the wick or tilt the lamp on the Sabbath; hence they are forbidden. Riban states the reason because the lamp may go out, thus destroying the cheerfulness of the Sabbath. (6) Rashi: you must not light it when unmixed, and therefore when mixed too it is forbidden, as a preventive measure. The 'Aruk explains; Because etc., i.e., there is a tradition to that effect. But there is also another reading: because it cannot be lit., i.e., the mixture has the same defects as the forbidden oil itself. (7) Though a nut itself is not fit.

(1) Lit., 'an act is a teacher'. Since R. Simeon b. Gamaliel relates that this was actually done, it must be presumed that this is the *halachah*, for an individual did not act upon his view in opposition to the majority (2) I.e., the wick and the nut were meant to burn together. (3) To enable the wick to float on the surface of the oil instead of sinking. (4) Why does he forbid it? (5) Though tallow itself is forbidden (*supra* 20b), which refutes Rabbah. (6) The Mishnah speaks of unmelted tallow. (7) But the prohibition went no further; hence if diluted with oil, it is permissible. (8) If the former is permitted, the latter too may be used. (9) Lit., 'for'. (10) Ex. XXVII, 21. (11) *Le-ha'aloth* (E.V. *to burn*) literally means to cause to go up.—These wicks and oils do not burn of themselves but need frequent attention. V. *supra* 20a, n. a9.

c (1) The girdles contained wool, which, as stated on 20*b*, was added to the forbidden materials enumerated in the Mishnah. The reference is to the Temple, and thus this refutes Rami b. Ḥama. (2) Lit., 'the house of drawing'. (3) At the daily morning service during the Feast of Tabernacles a libation of water, in addition to the usual libation of wine, was poured out on the altar. This was drawn from the Pool of Siloam on the night of the first day, and carried in procession to the Temple amid great rejoicing; cf. Suk. 53*a*: 'He who has not seen the rejoicing of the Water-Drawing has never seen rejoicing in his life.' The outer court of the Temple was brilliantly illuminated, and for this, not for the ordinary Temple lamp, the unravelled breeches and girdles were used. Rashi observes: because this was not a Biblical precept. Another reason may be that so much was used that it was really a fire, rather than a flame, which is permitted *supra*. V. *J.E.* XII, 476[2]. (4) Of wool and linen. I.e., the girdles; v. n. c1. (5) The breeches. (6) V. *infra* 21*b*. (7) I.e., relight it. Therefore it must be made of good oil in the first place, lest it go out and is not relit.—This, of course, can only apply to weekdays. (8) E.g., for reading. Therefore these wicks and oils are forbidden on the Sabbath as the first reason in *supra* 21*a*, n. a5 applies here too.

למאי נפקא מינה למקח וממכר: *ת"ר כל אלו שאמרו אין מדליקין בהן בשבת [א]אבל עושין מהן מדורה בין להתחמם כנגדה בין להשתמש לאורה בין ע"ג קרקע בין על גבי [א]*כירה ולא אסרו אלא לעשות מהן פתילה לנר בלבד: ולא בשמן קיק וכו': מאי שמן קיק אמר שמואל שאילתינהו לכל נחותי ימא ואמרו לי עוף אחד יש בכרכי הים וקיק שמו רב יצחק בריה דרב יהודה אמר משחא דקאזא ריש לקיש אמר קיקיון דיונה אמר רבה בר בר חנה לדידי חזי לי קיקיון דיונה *ולצלוליבא דמי ומדפשקי רבי ועל פום חנותא מדלן יתיה ומפרצידוהי עבדי משחא ובענפוהי נייחן כל *בריחי דמערבא אמר רבה [ב]פתילות שאמרו חכמים אין מדליקין בהן בשבת מפני שהאור מסכסכת בהן שמנים שאמרו חכמים אין מדליקין בהן מפני שאין נמשכין אחר הפתילה בעא מיניה אביי מרבה שמנים שאמרו חכמים אין מדליקין בהן בשבת מהו שיתן לתוכן שמן כל שהוא וידליק מי גזרינן דילמא אתי לאדלוקי בעינייהו או לא א"ל [ג]אין מדליקין מאי טעמא *לפי *שאין מדליקין איתיביה *כרך דבר שמדליקין בו ע"ג דבר שאין מדליקין בו (אמר) *רשב"ג [נ"ל רשב"ג אומר] של בית אבא היו כורכין פתילה על גבי אגוז ומדליקין קתני מיהת מדליקין א"ל אדמותבת לי מדרשב"ג סייעינהו מדתנא קמא הא לא קשיא *מעשה רב מ"מ קשיא מאי לאו להדליק לא להקפות [ד]אי להקפות מ"ט דת"ק כולה רשב"ג היא וחסורי מיחסרא והכי קתני כרך דבר שמדליקין בו ע"ג דבר שאין מדליקין בו [ה]בד"א להדליק אבל להקפות מותר שרבן שמעון בן גמליאל אומר של בית אבא היו כורכין פתילה ע"ג אגוז איני והאמר רב ברונא *אמר רב [ו]חלב מהותך וקרבי דגים שנמוחו אדם נותן לתוכו שמן כל שהוא ומדליק הני מימשכי בעינייהו והני לא מימשכי בעינייהו וגזרו רבנן על חלב מהותך משום חלב שאינו מהותך ועל קרבי דגים שנמוחו משום קרבי דגים שלא נמוחו וליגזור נמי חלב מהותך וקרבי דגים שנמוחו שנתן לתוכן שמן משום חלב מהותך וקרבי דגים שנמוחו שלא נתן לתוכן שמן*) היא גופה גזירה *ואנן ניקום וניגזור גזירה לגזירה: תני רמי בר חמא פתילות ושמנים שאמרו חכמים אין מדליקין בהן בשבת [ז]אין מדליקין בהן במקדש משום שנא' °להעלות נר תמיד הוא תני לה והוא אמר לה כדי *שתהא שלהבת עולה מאיליה ולא שתהא עולה על ידי דבר אחר תנן *מבלאי מכנסי כהנים ומהמיניהם היו מפקיעין ומהן מדליקין שמחת בית השואבה שאני ת"ש דתני רבה בר מתנה [ח]בגדי כהונה שבלו מפקיעין אותן ומהן היו עושין פתילות למקדש מאי לאו דכלאים לא [ח]דבוץ: אמר רב הונא פתילות ושמנים שאמרו חכמים אין מדליקין בהן בשבת אין מדליקין בהן בחנוכה בין בשבת בין בחול אמר רבא מאי טעמא דרב הונא קסבר כבתה זקוק לה ומותר להשתמש לאורה ורב חסדא אמר מדליקין בהן בחול אבל לא בשבת קסבר כבתה אין

תורה אור
שמות כז
[עי"ל כ.]
יומא כג: סוכה נא:

רש"י

למקח וממכר. למאן דמתני למזבן שעוה ליתיב ליה פסולתא דדובשא: אבל עושין מהן מדורה. היסק גדול שאחד מבעיר חבירו: לנר. קרויז"ל: בשמן קיק. שמן של עוף אחד נותנין בנר ודולק: משחא דקאזא. שמן שעושין מגרעיני צמר גפן שקורין קוטו"ן: קיקיון. כעין אותה של יונה: לדידי חזי לי. מין קיקיון דיונה: ומדפשקי רבי. בבלעי המים הוא גדל: ועל פום חנותא מדלן יתיה. על פום החנויות מדלין אותו לצל ולריח טוב: מפרצידוהי. מגרעיניו: נייחן. שוכבין: בריחי. חולין: מסכסכת. כמין סכין פגומה מסכסכת בבשר אגמילי"ר בלע"ז שאין אורו זקוף ונוח במקום אחד אלא נדעך וקופץ ליסנא אחריגא מסכסכת בהן אינה נכנסת תוך הפתילה אלא סביב מבחוץ כמו סיכסכה אבניו ברוטא"ש בלע"ז: שאין נמשכין. ואתי להטות: שמן כל שהוא. שמן הניתן בתוכו ממשיכו לאחר הפתילה: לפי שאין מדליקין. בעינייהו וגזרינן הא אטו הא: כרך דבר לעשות פתילה על גבי דבר שאין מדליקין בו. כגון פסול פתילות דמתני': קתני מיהא. בדר"ש מדליקין ואע"ג דאגוז לא חזי לפתילה על ידי תערובות שפיר דמי: מעשה רב. הואיל ומעיד שכך היו של בית אביו עושין הלכה היא: מאי לאו להדליק. היו כורכים שתדליק הפתילה עם האגוז: לא להקפות. לא היו מדליקין האגוז אלא סומך עליה הפתילה להציפה שלא תטבע בשמן ויצף הברזל מתרגמינן וקפא פרזלא (מלכים ב ו): חלב מהותך. פונד"ר בלע"ז: הני מימשכי בעינייהו. אחר הפתילה ובלא תערובות שמן נמי הוו אלא דגזור רבנן מהותך אטו אינו מהותך הלכך בעינייהו גופה גזירה ואנן ניקום וניגזור ע"י תערובות אטו בעינייהו: והוא אמר לה. מפרש מאי תלמודא והיכי משמע מהאי קרא: ולא שתהא עולה כו'. ולא שתהא צריכה תיקון והטייה: מבלאי מכנסי הכהנים. ממכנסי הכהנים הבלואים: היו מפקיעין. קורעין ועושין פתילות בשמחת בית השואבה שהיא בעזרת נשים: ומהמיניהם. של כלאים הם דכתיב ואת האבנט שש משזר ותכלת וארגמן וקי"ל תכלת עמרא הוא ותני' לעיל לענין שבת הוסיפו עליהן של צמר לפסול וקתני מדליקין בהן במקדש: שמחת בית השואבה שאני. דלא כתיב להעלות בה ולאו דאורייתא היא: מאי לאו דכלאים. כגון אבנט: כבתה. נר חנוכה: זקוק לה. לתקנה הלכך צריך לכתחלה לעשות יפה דילמא פשע ולא מתקן לה: ומותר להשתמש לאורה. הלכך בשבת אסור שמא יטה לצורך תשמיש: אין

תוספות

למאי כ"מ למקח וממכר. פשיטא ליה להש"ס שהיו מכירין השעוה והעטרן כדאמרינן שעוה קירותא לכך קאמר למאי כ"מ למקח וממכר שאם נדר לתת לחבירו שעוה יתן לו פסולתא דדובשא ואין יכול לכופו לתקן לו וכן עיטרן אבל לעיל דקאמר מאי לכש שוכא דארזא לא קאמר למאי כ"מ לפי שלא היו מכירין בשם לכש ומפרש שהוא שוכא דארזא: מפני שאין נמשכין כו'. שמעתי ממהר"א ז"ל שמשמע באם שיש רק נר א' כשר בבית ע"י זה יזכור ולא ישה שאר נרות שבחדר ושבמרתף ור"ש מקולי אומר דבר שיכול לעשות בלא נר כגון להוציא יין מן החבית מותר להשתמש לאור כל נר [תוספות ישנים]: חלב מהותך וקרבי דגים שנימוחו נותן לתוכן שמן כו'. קרבי דגים לאו היינו שמן דגים דשמן דגים שרי ליה מתני' בעיניה (לקמן דף כד:): שמחת בית השואבה שאני. תימה היכי שרי להדליק והא לאו צורך קרבן הוא ואמר בפ"ב דקידושין (דף נד. וסס) בגדי כהונה שבלו מועלין בהן ודוחק לומר לב ב"ד מתנה עליהן *דמה צורך יש להן להתנות בשביל זה ונראה לר"י דהואיל ולכבוד הקרבן היו עושין דכתיב ושאבתם מים בששון (ישעיה יב) צורך קרבן חשוב ליה והא דאמר (סוכה פ"ה דף נג.) בוררת אשה חטין לאור בית השואבה לא שהיתה בוררת אלא שהיתה יכולה לברור. ומיהו בירושלמי דייק מהכא דקול ומראה וריח אין בהן משום מעילה וקשה לר"י מאי פריך *ממכנסי הכהנים הלא היה בהן פשתן דכתיב תכלת וארגמן ותולעת שני ושש משזר (שמות כח) וטוב לפתילה דהוי ככרך דבר שמדליקין בו ע"ג דבר שאין מדליקין בו ובשבת הוא דאסור שמא ידליק בעיניה אבל במקדש לא שייכא הך גזירה ונראה לר"י דכיון שאין מן הפשתן אלא רביע בטל בשאר מינים והוי כאילו אין בו פשתן כלל: ומותר להשתמש לאורה. וא"ת מאי ליה לרבא דסבר רב הונא דמותר להשתמש לאורה דילמא הא דאמר אין מדליקין בשבת משום דסבר כבתה זקוק לה ואין

וא"ת אכתי הוי גזירה לגזירה מהותך אטו שאינו מהותך ושאינו מהותך שמא יטה וי"ל דהדא גזירה היא דא"א שלא יטה וריב"ן פי' דהא דאמר לעיל נמשכין אחר הפתילה לא משום שמא יטה אלא שמא יכבה וליכא שלום בית [תוס' ישנים]

ועוד דלא מצינו לב ב"ד באה דכיון דכבר קדשו בגדי כהונה לא נפקי לחולין בלא פדיון [ת"י]

עין משפט נר מצוה

ה א מיי' פ"ג מהלכות שבת הלכה יע סמג לאוין סה טור שו"ע או"ח סימן רנה סעיף א:
ו ב מיי' פ"ה מהל' שבת הלכה ה סמג שם טור שו"ע או"ח סימן רסד סעיף א ג:
ז ג מיי' שם הלכה ט טור שו"ע שם סעיף ד:
ח ד מיי' שם הלכה ו טוש"ע שם סעיף ב:
ט ה מיי' שם הלכה ט טוש"ע שם סעיף ה:
י ו מיי' פ"ג מהלכות תמידין ומוספין הלכה טו:
יא ז ח מיי' פ"ח מהלכות כלי המקדש הלכה ו:

מסורת השי"ס

תוספתא פ"ב
ס"א מנורה
ערוך פי' אילן סרק
[נ"ל כריחי פי' ערוך ערך כרח ובמתורגמן]
ז"ם א"ל לפי שאינן כו' נ"ל רש"ל [ועי' בערוך ערך לפי פי' שאין מדליקין כלומר קנבה היא כך שאין מדליקין]
[לקמן קכו: ב"ב פג. קל.] נדה סה:
[לקמן כד:]
ג"א שאינן נדלקין תוספתא פ"ב
[נ"ל מהמיני' דהיינו אבנט ועי' רש"א]

הגהות הגר"א

[א] גמ' כירה. נ"ב מנורה גירסת רי"ף וה"פ וכן בתוספתא:

רבינו חננאל

מיכן ואילך פסול שמנים: ת"ר כל אלו שאמרו חכמים אין מדליקין בהם בשבת משום פסול פתילות אבל עושה בהם מדורה בין להתחמם כנגדה בין להשתמש לאורה בין ע"ג קרקע בין ע"ג מנורה לא אסרו אלא לעשותן פתילה לנר בלבד. בשמן קיק שמואל אמר (עץ) [עוף] ושמו קיק ר"ל אמר קיקיון דיונה' אמר רבה פתילות שאמרו חכמים אין מדליקין בהן מפני שהאור מסכסכת בהן שמנים שפסלו[חכמי'] מפני שאין נמשכין אחר הפתילה. בעא מיניה אביי מרבה שמנים שאמרו חכמים להדליק בהן בשבת מהו לתת לתוכן שמן ולהדליק א"ל אסור לפי שאין מדליקין כלומר כיון שאין מדליקין בפני עצמן כשישלים השמן שתתן בתוכו שוב אין מדליקין שכבר אמרו אין נמשכין אחר הפתילה ואותיב עלה ותרצה הכי כרך דבר שמדליקין בו על גבי דבר שאין מדליקין בו אין מדליקין בו בד"א להדליק אבל להקפות מותר כדכתיב (יחזקאל כב) כהתוך כסף בתוך כור וכתיב (איוב ג) ויתכו כמים וקרבי דגים שנימוחו נותן לתוכן שמן כל שהוא ומדליק ושנינן הני ממשכי בעינייהו ואסיק' לקמן*) דשני הני משמן דגים לפיכך שמן דגים מזוקק הוא ודולק ונמשך אחר הפתילה ואין צריך תערובת. תני רמי בר חמא פתילות שאסרו חכמים להדליק בהן בשבת גם במקדש אין מדליקין בהם שנאמר להעלות נר תמיד והא דתנן מבלאי מכנסי כהנים ומהמייניהם מהן היו מפקיעין ובהן היו מדליקין והאבנט יש בו צמר הני לשמחת בית השואבה אבל למנורה אין מדליקין אלא בשל (בוץ) [פשתן] וכבר פירשנוהו היטב בראיות בפרק החליל.

פירוש להעבות ראש הפתילה להרבות אורה מותר שרשב"ג אומר של בית אבא היו כורכין כו' וקיי"ל (כרבא) [כרבה] איני והא אמר רב ברונא אמר רב חלב מהותך (מ"ש) [פי'] מלשון היתוך

*) לפנינו ליתא בגמ' הני משמן דגים ואולי דכוון למ"ש לקמן דף כ"ו ע"א איכא בינייהו דרב ברונא ומפרש כפי' ר"ת שם בתוס' ודו"ק היטב · ועי' תוס' כאן ד"ה חלב:

גליון השי"ס גמ' אין מדליקין מ"ט לפי שאין מדליקין. כעין זה עירובין דף לו ע"א נ"ז דף כו ע"ב גיטין דף ס ע"א נדה דף ס ע"א וכן בלשון התורה ויקרא כ"ב אשר יהיה בו מום לא יקרב כי כל איש אשר בו מום לא יקרב ועי' ריטב"א קידושין דף ו ע"ב ד"ה ה"ג: שם שמנים ופתילות כו' אין מדליקין בהם במקדש. ק"ל למאי נקט שמנים הא במקדש אין מדליקין רק בשמן זית זך: תוס' ד"ה חלב מהותך כו' קרבי דגים לאו היינו. ע"ל דף כו ע"א תוס' ד"ה איכא בינייהו דרב ברונא:

אין זקוק לה ומותר להשתמש לאורה א"ר זירא אמר רב מתנה ואמרי לה א"ר זירא אמר רב *פתילות ושמנים שאמרו חכמים אין מדליקין בהן בשבת מדליקין בהן בחנוכה בין בחול בין בשבת א"ר ירמיה מאי טעמא דרב קסבר ב כבתה אין זקוק לה ג ואסור להשתמש לאורה אמרוה רבנן קמיה דאביי משמיה דר' ירמיה ולא קיבלה כי אתא רבין אמרוה רבנן קמיה דאביי משמיה דר' יוחנן וקיבלה אמר אי זכאי גמירתיה לשמעתיה מעיקרא והא גמרה נפקא מינה לגירסא דינקותא וכבתה אין זקוק לה ורמינהו ד מצותה *משתשקע החמה עד שתכלה רגל מן השוק מאי לאו דאי כבתה הדר מדליק לה לא ה דאי לא אדליק מדליק וא"נ לשיעורה: עד שתכלה רגל מן השוק ועד כמה אמר רבה בר בר חנה אמר ר' יוחנן עד דכליא ריגלא דתרמודאי: ת"ר ו מצות חנוכה נר איש וביתו והמהדרין נר לכל אחד ואחד והמהדרין מן המהדרין ב"ש אומרים יום ראשון מדליק שמנה מכאן ואילך פוחת והולך וב"ה אומרים ז יום ראשון מדליק אחת מכאן ואילך מוסיף והולך אמר עולא פליגי בה תרי אמוראי במערבא ר' יוסי בר אבין ור' יוסי בר זבידא חד אמר טעמא דב"ש כנגד ימים הנכנסין וטעמא דב"ה כנגד ימים היוצאין וחד אמר טעמא דב"ש כנגד פרי החג וטעמא דבית הלל *דמעלין בקדש ואין מורידין אמר רבה בר בר חנה א"ר יוחנן שני זקנים היו בצידן אחד עשה כב"ש ואחד עשה כדברי ב"ה זה נותן טעם לדבריו כנגד פרי החג וזה נותן טעם לדבריו דמעלין בקדש ואין מורידין ת"ר *ח נר חנוכה מצוה להניחה על פתח ביתו מבחוץ אם היה דר בעלייה מניחה בחלון הסמוכה לרה"ר ובשעת הסכנה מניחה על שלחנו ודיו אמר רבא ט צריך נר אחרת [א] להשתמש לאורה ואי איכא מדורה לא צריך ואי אדם חשוב הוא אע"ג דאיכא מדורה צריך נר אחרת: מאי חנוכה דתנו רבנן י בכ"ה בכסליו יומי דחנוכה תמניא אינון דלא למספד בהון [ב] ודלא להתענות בהון שכשנכנסו יוונים להיכל טמאו °כל השמנים שבהיכל וכשגברה מלכות בית חשמונאי ונצחום בדקו ולא מצאו אלא פך אחד של שמן שהיה מונח בחותמו של כהן גדול ולא היה בו אלא להדליק יום אחד נעשה בו נס והדליקו ממנו שמונה ימים לשנה אחרת קבעום ועשאום ימים טובים בהלל והודאה *)תנן התם גץ היוצא מתחת הפטיש ויצא והזיק חייב *כ גמל שטעון פשתן והוא עובר ברשות הרבים ונכנסה פשתנו לתוך החנות ודלקה בנרו של חנוני והדליק את הבירה בעל הגמל חייב ל הניח חנוני את נרו מבחוץ חנוני חייב רבי יהודה אומר בנר חנוכה פטור *אמר רבינא *(משום דרבה) זאת אומרת מ נר חנוכה מצוה להניחה בתוך עשרה דאי ס"ד למעלה מעשרה לימא ליה היה לך להניח למעלה מגמל ורוכבו ודילמא אי מיטרחא ליה טובא אתי לאימנועי ממצוה: *אמר רב כהנא דרש רב נתן בר מניומי משמיה דרבי תנחום נר

*) ב"ק סב: ב"ב כו:

אין זקוק לה. הלכך בחול שרי: ואסור להשתמש לאורה. שיהא ניכר שהוא נר מצוה וליכא למיחש להטייה: ולא קבלה. שלא חשבו לסמוך על דבריו: אי זכאי. אילו הייתי זוכה לטמדה הייתי גורסה כששמעתיה ראשון: גירסא דינקותא. מתקיים יותר משל זקנה: לשיעורה. שיהא בה שמן כשיעור הזה ומיהו אם כבתה אין זקוק לה: רגלא דתרמודאי. שם אומה מלקטי עצים דקים ומתעכבין בשוק עד שהולכים בני השוק לבתיהם משחשכה ומבעירים בבתיהם אור וכשצריכין לעצים יוצאים וקונין מהן: נר איש וביתו. נר אחד בכל לילה ואיש וכל בני ביתו סגי להו בנר אחד: והמהדרין. אחר המצות עושין נר אחד בכל לילה לכל אחד ואחד מבני הבית: כנגד ימים הנכנסים. העתידים לבא: ימים היוצאין. שיצאו כבר וזה שהוא עומד בו נמנה עם היוצאין: פרי החג. מתמעטים והולכים בקרבנות דפרשת פנחס: מעלין בקדש ואין מורידין. מקרא ילפינן לה במנחות בפרק שתי הלחם (דף צט.): מבחוץ. משום פרסומי ניסא ולא ברה"ר אלא בחצרו שבתיהן היו פתוחין לחצר: ואם היה דר בעלייה. שאין לו מקום בחצרו להניחה שם: מניחה. מבפנים כנגד חלון הסמוך לרה"ר: הסכנה. שהיה להם לפרסיים חוק ביום אידם שלא יבעירו נר אלא בבית ע"ז שלהם כדאמרינן בגיטין (פ"ב דף יז:): נר אחרת. לעשות היכר לדבר: ואי איכא מדורה. אש לא צריך נר אחרת לפי שמשתמש לאור המדורה ויש היכרא שהנר של מצוה היא: ואי אדם חשוב הוא. שאין רגיל להשתמש לאור המדורה: צריך נר אחרת. דאי לא לא הוי היכר: מאי חנוכה. על איזה נס קבעוה: בחותמו. בהצנע וחתום בטבעתו והכיר שלא נגעו בו: ה"ג ועשאום ימים טובים בהלל והודאה. לא שאסורין במלאכה שלא נקבעו אלא לקרות הלל ולומר על הנסים בהודאה: גץ. ניצוץ אישטינציל"ש: פטיש. קורנס גדול של נפחים: בעל גמל חייב. שלא היה לו להגדיל בחבילתו שתכנס לחנות: בנר חנוכה פטור. חנוני שברשות פירסום מצוה הניחה שם: זאת אומרת. הא דקתני בנר חנוכה פטור: פסולה

ואין יכול להדליק בשבת וי"ל דא"כ לא הוה צריך ליה למימר בין בחול בין בשבת כיון דחד טעמא הוא אלא ה"ל למימר *אין מדליקין סתם מדקאמר בין בחול בין בשבת ש"מ שעוד יש טעם אחר בשבת שלא להדליק לבד מטעם חול והיינו שמא יטה וא"כ סבר דמותר להשתמש לאורה ומיהו רב דקאמר מדליקין בין בחול בין בשבת לא הוה מצי למימר מדליק סתם דה"א דוקא בחול אבל בשבת אין מדליקין שמא יטה דבשמא לא הייתי אומר ששום אדם יחמיר לאסור להשתמש. לאורה וכן הלכתא דנר חנוכה אסור להשתמש לאורה כרב וכר' יוחנן ואביי נמי קיבלה ורב יוסף נמי משמע לקמן דס"ל הכי וכבתה אין זקוק לה דכולהו סבירא להו הכי ורב הונא יחיד הוא ולית הלכתא כוותיה:

דאי לא אדליק מדליק. אבל מכאן ואילך עבר הזמן אומר הר"י פורת דיש ליזהר ולהדליק בלילה מיד שלא יאחר יותר מדאי ומ"מ אם איחר ידליק מספק דהא משני שינויי אחרינא ולר"י נראה דעתה אין לחוש מתי ידליק דאנו אין לנו היכרא אלא לבני הבית שהרי מדליקין מבפנים:

והמהדרין מן המהדרין. נראה לר"י דב"ש וב"ה לא קיימי אלא אנר איש וביתו שכן יש יותר הידור דאיכא היכרא כשמוסיף והולך או מחסר שהוא כנגד ימים הנכנסים או היוצאים אבל אם עושה נר לכל אחד אפי' יוסיף מכאן ואילך ליכא היכרא שיסברו שכך יש בני אדם בבית: מצוה להניחה על פתח ביתו מבחוץ. ומיירי דליכא חצר אלא בית עומד סמוך לרה"ר אבל אם יש חצר לפני הבית מצוה להניח על פתח חצר דאמר לקמן *חצר שיש לה ב' פתחים צריכה ב' נרות ואמרי' נמי נר שיש לה שני פיות עולה לשני בני אדם משמע לשני בתים ואם היו מניחים על פתחי בתיהם היה לזה מימין ולזה משמאל אבל אי מניחים על פתח החצר אתי שפיר: ובשעת הסכנה. נראה לר"י דהיינו מכי אתו חברי לבבל כדאמר בפ' כירה (לקמן דף מה. ושם) מהו לטלטל שרגא דחנוכתא מקמי חברי בשבתא וא"ת דעל השלחן נמי יקחו אותו כדאמר בגיטין (דף יז.) רבה בר בר חנה חלש אתא חברא שקל שרגא מקמייהו וי"ל דאין רגילות כ"כ לחפש בבתים*:

שהיה מונח בחותמו של כ"ג. אם כבר גזרו על הנכרים להיות כזבים *(נדה פ"ד דף לד.) צ"ל שהיה מונח בחותם בקרקע שלא °הסיטו הכלי:

עין משפט נר מצוה

ובהא ליכא למימר דאי הוי אמר אין מדליקין סתם ה"א דהיינו בשבת ומשום דמותר להשתמש לאורה אבל בחול מדליקין דכבתה אין זקוק לה דא"כ לא ה"ל למימר אין מדליקין בחנוכה אלא בהדיא הל"ע כ"ת מותר להשתמש לאורה [תוספות ישנים]

יב א מיי' פ"ד מהלכות חנוכה הלכה ו סמג לאוין ס ועשין ה טוש"ע או"ח סימן תרע"ג סעיף א:

יג ב מיי' שם הלכה ה טוש"ע שם סעיף ב:

יד ג מיי' שם הלכה ו טוש"ע שם סעיף א:

טו ד מיי' שם הלכה ה סמג שם טוש"ע או"ח סימן תרעב סעיף א:

טז ה מיי' שם טור שו"ע שם סעיף ב:

יז ו ז מיי' שם הלכה א סמג שם טוש"ע או"ח סימן תרעא סעיף ב:

יח ח ט מיי' שם הלכה ז ח טור שו"ע שם סעיף ה:

יט י מיי' פ"ג מהלכות חנוכה הלכה א ב סמג שם טור שו"ע או"ח סימן תרע סעיף א:

כ כ ל מיי' פי"ד מהל' נזקי ממון הלכה יג טוש"ע חו"מ סימן תיח סעיף יב:

כא מ טוש"ע או"ח סי' תרעא סעיף ו:

רבינו חננאל

אמר רב פתילו' ושמנים שאמרו חכמים אין מדליקין בהן בשבת מדליקין בהם בחנוכה בין בחול בין בשבת מ"ט קסבר כבתה אין זקוק לה ואסו' להשתמש לאורה. מיתיבי מצותה משתשקע החמה ועד שתכלה רגל מן השוק מאי לאו דאי כבתה הדר מדליק לה ושנינן לא אי לא אדליק נר של חנוכה עדיין לא יאחר כבר עבר זמנה אלא מדליק עד דכלי רינלא דתרמודאי אי נמי שיעורא דשמן דנר חנוכה כמה הוא כדי שיהא דולק משקיעת החמה עד שתכלה רגלא דתרמודאי: ת"ר מצות חנוכה נר איש וביתו והמהדרין נר לכל אחד ואחד והמהדרין מן המהדרין ב"ה אומרים יום ראשון מדליק אחד מיכן והילך מוסיף והולך. פי' המהדרין מהדרי מצות כדאמרינן (ב"ק ט ב) להדור מצוה עד שליש במצוה. ת"ר נר חנוכה מצוה להניחה על פתח ביתו מבחוץ ואם היה דר בעליה מניחה בחלון הסמוך לרה"ר ובשעת הסכנה מניחו על השלחן ודיו אמר רבא וצריך נר (אחד) [אחר] לתשמישו [ואי איכא מדורה לא צריך] ואי אדם חשוב הוא אף על גב דאית ליה מדורה צריך נר (אחד) [אחר] להשתמשו ואסיק'

מסורת הש"ס

[מס' סופרים פ"כ הלכה ד ועי' תוספות זבחים נו. ד"ה מנין ותוספות מנחות כ: ד"ה נפסל]

[ברכות כח. יומא יב: עג. מגילה ט: כח: הוריות יב: מנחו' צט: לט.]

[מס' סופרים פ"כ הלכה ה]

הגהות הגר"א

[א] גמרא (להשתמש לאורה) תא"מ: [ב] שם (ודלא להתענות בהון) תא"מ:

גליון הש"ס גמ' כל השמנים שבהיכל. עי' ברמב"ם פ"ה מהלכות בית הבחירה הלכה ח ועיין בתשובת כתי כהונה ח"א בבית ועד סימן א': תוס' ד"ה שהיה מונח וכו' שלא הסיטו. עיין לקמן דף פד ע"ב תוספות ד"ה שטהורים כאן:

Sabbath. He holds, If it goes out, [21b] it does not require attention, and one may make use of its light. R. Zera said in R. Mattenah's name—others state, R. Zera said in Rab's name—: Regarding the wicks and oils which the Sages said, One must not light therewith on the Sabbath, one may light therewith on *Ḥanukkah*, either on weekdays or on the Sabbath. Said R. Jeremiah, What is Rab's reason? He holds, If it goes out, it does not require attention, and one may not make use of its light.[9] The Rabbis stated this before Abaye in R. Jeremiah's name, a but he did not accept it. [But] when Rabin came,[1] the Rabbis stated it before Abaye in R. Joḥanan's name, whereupon he accepted it.[2] Had I, he observed, merited the great fortune,[3] I would have learnt this dictum originally. But he learnt it [now]?—The difference is in respect of the studies of one's youth.[4]

Now, if it goes out, does it not require attention? But the following contradicts it: Its observance is from sunset until there is no wayfarer in[5] the street. Does that not mean that if it goes out [within that period] it must be relit?—No: if one has not yet lit, he must light it;[6] or, in respect of the statutory period.[7]

'Until there is no wayfarer in the street.' Until when [is that]? —Rabbah b. Bar Ḥanah said in R. Joḥanan's name: Until the Palmyreans have departed.[8]

Our Rabbis taught: The precept of *Ḥanukkah* [demands] one light for a man and his household;[9] the zealous [kindle] a light for each member [of the household]; and the extremely zealous,—Beth Shammai maintain: On the first day eight lights are lit and thereafter they are gradually reduced;[10] but Beth Hillel say: On the first day one is lit and thereafter they are progressively increased.[11] 'Ulla said: In the West [Palestine] two amoraim,[12] R. Jose b. Abin and R. Jose b. Zebida, differ therein: one maintains, The reason of Beth Shammai is that it shall correspond to the days still to come,[13] and that of Beth Hillel is that it shall correspond to the days that are gone; but another maintains: Beth Shammai's reason is that it shall correspond to the bullocks b of the Festival;[1] whilst Beth Hillel's reason is that we promote in [matters of] sanctity but do not reduce.

Rabbah b. Bar Ḥana in the name of R. Joḥanan said: There were two old men[2] in Sidon:[3] one did as Beth Shammai and the other as Beth Hillel: the former gave the reason of his action that it should correspond to the bullocks of the Festival, while the latter stated his reason because we promote in [matters of] sanctity but do not reduce.

Our Rabbis taught: It is incumbent to place the *Ḥanukkah* lamp by the door of one's house on the outside;[4] if one dwells in an upper chamber, he places it at the window nearest the street. But in times of danger[5] it is sufficient to place it on the table. Raba said: Another lamp is required for its light to be used;[6] yet if there is a blazing fire it is unnecessary. But in the case of an important person,[7] even if there is a blazing fire another lamp is required.

What is [the reason of] *Ḥanukkah?* For our Rabbis taught: On the twenty-fifth of Kislew[8] [commence] the days of *Ḥanukkah*, which are eight, on which a lamentation for the dead and fasting are forbidden.[9] For when the Greeks entered the Temple, they defiled all the oils therein, and when the Hasmonean dynasty prevailed against and defeated them, they made search and found only one cruse of oil which lay with the seal of the High Priest,[10] but which contained sufficient for one day's lighting only; yet a miracle was wrought therein and they lit [the lamp] therewith for eight days. The following year these [days] were appointed c a Festival with [the recital of] Hallel[1] and thanksgiving.[2]

We learnt elsewhere: If a spark which flies from the anvil goes forth and causes damage, he [the smith] is liable. If a camel laden with flax passes through a street, and the flax overflows into a shop, catches fire at the shopkeeper's lamp, and sets the building alight, the camel owner is liable; but if the shopkeeper placed the light outside, the shopkeeper is liable.[3] R. Judah said: In the case of a *Ḥanukkah* lamp he is exempt.[4] Rabina said in Rabbah's name: This proves that the *Ḥanukkah* lamp should [in the first instance] be placed within ten.[5] For should you think, above ten, let him say to him, 'You ought to have placed it higher than a camel and his rider.' 'Yet perhaps if he is put to too much trouble, he may refrain altogether from the [observance of the] precept'.[6]

R. Kahana said, R. Nathan b. Minyomi expounded in R.

(9) To show that it was lit in celebration of *Ḥanukkah*, not merely for illumination.

a (1) V. *supra* 5a, n. b9. (2) R. Joḥanan being a greater authority than R. Jeremiah, (3) The verb denotes both to be fortunate and to merit. (4) These are more abiding. Abaye felt that he would have had a surer hold upon it had he learned it earlier. (5) Lit., 'Until the foot ceases from'. (6) Anytime within that period. (7) I.e., the lamp must contain sufficient oil to burn for that period. Nevertheless, if it goes out sooner, it need not be rekindled. (8) Lit., 'until the feet of the Tarmodians have ceased'. Tarmod or Tadmor is Palmyra, an oasis of the Syrian desert. They sold lighting materials and went about in the streets later than the general populace as their wares might be needed. (9) I.e., one light is lit every evening of the eight days (v. *infra*) for the entire household. (10) One less each day. (11) Up to eight. (12) V. Glos. (13) I.e., each evening one must kindle as many lights as the number of days of *Ḥanukkah* yet to come.

b (1) 'The Festival', without a determinate, always refers to Tabernacles (Sukkoth). Thirteen bullocks were sacrificed on the first day, twelve on the second, and so on, one less each succeeding day; v. Num. XXIX, 12 *seqq.* (2) The Heb. *zaḳen*, pl. *zekenim*, frequently means learned men, without particular reference to age (Ḳid. 32b), and may connote this here. (3) On the coast of Phoenicia. (4) To advertise the miracle. Their houses did not open directly on to the street but into a courtyard, and there the lamp was to be placed (Rashi); v., however, Tosaf. a.l. (5) When there is religious persecution. (6) Agreeing with the view *supra* that the light of the *Ḥanukkah* lamp may not be used. (7) Who is not accustomed to work at the light of a blazing fire. (8) The ninth month of the Jewish year, corresponding to about December. (9) This is an extract of the *Megillath Ta'anith*, lit., 'the scroll of fasting'. (10) Hence untouched and undefiled.

c (1) 'Praise', Ps. CXIII-CXVIII, recited on all Festivals; v. Weiss, *Dor*, I, p. 108, n. 1. (2) This lighting took place in 165 B.C.E. Exactly three years before, on the same day, Antiochus Epiphanes had a pagan altar erected in the Temple, upon which sacrifices were offered (I Macc. I, 41-64). Apart from the Talmudic reason stated here, Judas Maccabeus chose 25th of Kislew as the anniversary of the Temple's defilement, and the dedication of the new altar was celebrated with lights for eight days, similarly to the Feast of Tabernacles, which lasted eight days and was celebrated by illuminations (I Macc. IV, 36; II Macc. X, 6; *supra* 21a, n. c3). Actually the revolt was against the Syrians, of whom Antiochus Epiphanes was king, but the term 'Greeks' is used loosely, because the Seleucid Empire was part of the older Empire founded by Alexander the Great of Macedon, and because it was a reaction against the attempted Hellenization of Judea. The historic data are contained in the First Book of the Maccabees. (3) For the loss of the flax. (4) Because, as stated above, it should be placed outside; the onus then lies upon the camel driver. (5) Handbreadths from the ground. (6) Possibly the lamp may be placed at the outset higher, yet the Rabbis did not wish to make the precept too burdensome.

Tanḥum's name: [22*a*] If a *Ḥanukkah* lamp is placed above twenty cubits [from the ground] it is unfit, like *sukkah* and a cross-beam over [the entrance of] an alley.[7]

R. Kahana also said, R. Nathan b. Minyomi expounded in R. Tanḥum's name: Why is it written, *and the pit was empty, there*
a *was no water in it?*[1] From the implication of what is said, '*and the pit was empty*', do I not know that there was no water in it; what then is taught by, '*there was no water in it*'? There was no water, yet there were snakes and scorpions in it.

Rabbah said: The *Ḥanukkah* lamp should be placed within the handbreadth nearest the door.[2] And where is it placed?—R. Aḥa son of Raba said: On the right hand side: R. Samuel[3] of Difti[4] said: On the left hand side.[5] And the law is, on the left, so that the *Ḥanukkah* lamp shall be on the left and the *mezuzah*[6] on the right.

Rab Judah said in R. Assi's name:[7] One must not count money by the *Ḥanukkah* light. When I stated this before Samuel, he observed to me, Has then the lamp sanctity?[8] R. Joseph demurred: Does blood possess sanctity? For it was taught: *he shall pour out* [*the blood thereof*], *and cover it* [*with dust*]:[9] wherewith he pours out, he must cover,[10] i.e., he must not cover it with his foot,[11] so that precepts may not appear contemptible to him. So here too[12] it is that precepts may not appear contemptible to him.

R. Joshua b. Levi was asked: Is it permitted to make use of the booth decorations during the whole of the seven days?[13] He answered him [the questioner], Behold! it was said, One must not count money by the *Ḥanukkah* light.[14] God of Abraham! exclaimed R. Joseph, he makes that which was taught dependent upon what was not taught: [of] booths it was taught, whereas of *Ḥanukkah* it was not. For it was taught: If one roofs it [the booth] in accordance with its requirements, beautifies it with hangings and sheets, and suspends therein nuts, peaches, almonds, pomegranates, grape clusters, garlands of ears of corn, wines, oils and flours; he may not use them until the conclusion of the last day of
b the Feast; yet if he stipulates concerning them,[1] it is all according to his stipulation.—Rather, said R. Joseph: The basis[2] of all is [the law relating to] blood.[3]

It was stated: Rab said: One must not light from lamp to lamp;[4] but Samuel maintained, You may light from lamp to lamp. Rab said: Fringes[5] may not be detached[6] from one garment for [insertion in] another, but Samuel ruled, Fringes may be detached from garment to garment. Rab said, The *halachah* is not as R. Simeon in respect to dragging; but Samuel maintained, The *halachah* is as R. Simeon in respect to dragging. Abaye said: In all matters the Master [Rabbah] acted in accordance with Rab, except in these three, where he did as Samuel: [viz.,] one may light from lamp to lamp; one can detach [the fringes] from one garment for [insertion in] another; and the *halachah* is as R. Simeon in respect to dragging. For it was taught: R. Simeon said: One may drag a bed, seat, or bench,[7] provided that he does not intend to make a rut.

One of the Rabbis sat before R. Adda b. Ahabah and sat and said: Rab's reason[8] is on account of the cheapening of the precept. Said he to them, Do not heed him: Rab's reason is because he
c impairs the precept.[1] Wherein do they differ?—They differ where he lights from lamp to lamp:[2] on the view that it is because of the cheapening of the precept, one may light from lamp to lamp;[3] but on the view that it is because he impairs the precept, even from lamp to lamp is forbidden.

(7) A *sukkah* (q.v. Glos.) built higher than twenty cubits, or a cross-beam which permits carrying in a side street (v. *supra* 9*a*, n. a5 and 'Er. 2*a*) placed higher than twenty cubits from the ground, is unfit. Similarly a *Ḥanukkah* lamp, because it is too high to be noticed and does not advertise the miracle.

a (1) Gen. XXXVII, 24. (2) On the outside, as stated on 21*b*. But if it is placed further away, there is nothing to show that it was set there by the owner of the house. (3) In She'eltoth, *Wa-yishlaḥ*, 26 the reading is R. Jeremiah. (4) V. *supra* 10*a*, n. b5. (5) Both meaning as one enters the house. (6) V. Glos. (7) Cur. ed. adds: in Rab's name: Rosh omits it, and it appears to be absent from Rashi's text too. (8) Surely not. (9) Lev. XVII, 13. This refers to a beast or a fowl killed for food. (10) *Sc.* with his hand. (11) Kicking the dust over it. (12) Viz., the *Ḥanukkah* lamp. (13) The booths which were erected for the Feast of Tabernacles (Lev. XXIII, 42) were adorned with fruit suspended from the roofs. (14) Being dedicated to a religious observance, it must not be put to secular use. The same applies here.

b (1) The prohibition is regarded as coming into force at twilight of the first day, when they become dedicated to their religious purpose. The stipulation whereby the prohibition is lifted is: 'I will not hold aloof from them throughout the period of twilight', so that it does not become dedicated then. (2) Lit., 'the father'. (3) As stated above: things taken for religious purposes must not be treated slightingly. (4) One *Ḥanukkah* lamp must not be lit from another. Or, when a lamp with several branches is used, in accordance with the practice of the 'most zealous' (*supra* 21*b*; this too is the modern usage), one branch must not be lit from another. (5) V. Num. XV, 38. (6) Lit., 'untied'. (7) Over an earthen floor on the Sabbath. (8) For ruling that one must not kindle one lamp from another.

c (1) It looks like taking light away from one lamp and giving it to another. (2) Directly, without an intermediary chip. (3) There is nothing degrading when it directly lights another lamp for the same religious purpose.

תורה אור

נר של חנוכה שהניחה למעלה מכ' אמה פסולה כסוכה וכמבוי: ואמר רב כהנא דרש רב נתן בר מניומי משמיה דרב תנחום מאי דכתיב והבור רק אין בו מים ממשמע שנא' והבור רק איני יודע שאין בו מים אלא מה ת"ל אין בו מים מים אין בו אבל נחשים ועקרבים יש בו: אמר רבה נר חנוכה מצוה להניחה בטפח הסמוכה לפתח והיכא מנח ליה רב אחא בריה דרבא אמר מימין רב שמואל מדפתי אמר משמאל והילכתא משמאל כדי שתהא נר חנוכה משמאל ומזוזה מימין: אמר רב יהודה אמר רב אסי (אמר רב) אסור להרצות מעות כנגד נר חנוכה כי אמריתה קמיה דשמואל אמר לי וכי נר קדושה יש בה מתקיף לה רב יוסף וכי דם קדושה יש בו דתניא ושפך וכסה במה ששפך יכסה שלא יכסנו ברגל שלא יהו מצות בזויות עליו ה"נ שלא יהו מצות בזויות עליו: בעו מיניה מרבי יהושע בן לוי מהו להסתפק מנויי סוכה כל שבעה א"ל הרי אמרו אסור להרצות מעות כנגד נר חנוכה אמר רב יוסף מריה דאברהם תלי תניא בדלא תניא סוכה תניא חנוכה לא תניא דתניא סככה כהלכתה ועיטרה בקרמים ובסדינין המצויירין ותלה בה אגוזים אפרסקין שקדים ורמונים ופרכילי ענבים ועטרות של שבלים יינות (של) שמנים וסלתות אסור להסתפק מהן עד מוצאי יום טוב האחרון של חג ואם התנה עליהן הכל לפי תנאו אלא אמר רב יוסף אבוהון דכולהו דם: איתמר רב אמר אין מדליקין מנר לנר ושמואל אמר מדליקין רב אמר אין מתירין ציצית מבגד לבגד ושמואל אמר מתירין מבגד לבגד רב אמר אין הלכה כרבי שמעון בגרירה ושמואל אמר הלכה כרבי שמעון בגרירה אמר אביי כל מילי דמר עביד כרב לבר מהני תלת דעביד כשמואל מדליקין מנר לנר ומתירין מבגד לבגד והלכה כרבי שמעון בגרירה דתניא רבי שמעון אומר גורר אדם מטה כסא וספסל ובלבד שלא יתכוין לעשות חריץ יתיב ההוא מרבנן קמיה דרב אדא בר אהבה ויתיב וקאמר טעמא דרב משום ביזוי מצוה אמר להו לא תציתו ליה טעמיה דרב משום דקא מכחיש מצוה מאי בינייהו איכא בינייהו דקא מדליק משרגא לשרגא מ"ד משום ביזוי מצוה משרגא לשרגא מדליק מ"ד משום אכחושי מצוה משרגא לשרגא נמי אסור מתיב רב אויא[א] סלע של מעשר

רש"י

פסולה. דלא שלטא בה עינא למעלה מכ' אמה וליכא פרסומי ניסא: כסוכה וכמבוי. דתנן בהו בהדיא בעירובין ומסכת סוכה דפסילי: מצוה להניחה. בחצר או בר"ה בטפח הסמוך לפתח שאם ירחיקנו להלן מן הפתח אינו ניכר שבעה"ב הניחו שם: מימין. בכניסתו לביתו לימין: מזוזה. קי"ל דבימין דכתיב ביתך דרך ביאתך וכי עקר איניש כרעיה דימינא עקר ברישא: להרצות. למנות: במה ששפך. בידו ששפך בה ולא ברגלו: נויי סוכה. פירות שתולין בה לנוי: מריה דאברהם. לשון תמיה הוא: תלי. סוכה דהגיא בברייתא בהדיא כדמפרש ואזיל: בדלא תניא. בנר חנוכה דמימרא דרב אסי הוא ולאו ברייתא: ועטרה בקרמים. פארה ביריעות של צבעים שקורין אובריי"ן: התנה עליהן. במס' ביצה (דף ל:) אוקימנא באומר איני בודל מהן כל בין השמשות של קידוש יו"ט ראשון דלא חל עלייהו קדושה כלל אבל תנאי אחר אינו מועיל: אבוהון דכולהו. שילמדו כולן ממנו: דם. כיסוי הדם דנפקא לן מקרא ושפך וכסה ומפרש בה טעמא שלא יהיו מצות בזויות עליו: מנר לנר. דחנוכה כדמפרש טעמא לקמיה: מתירין. להטיל ציצית מטלית ישן לטלית חדש ובמנחות מפרש טעמא דמאן דאסר: הלכ' כר"ש. דאמר דבר שאין מתכוין מותר ואע"ג דקעביד חריץ והוי תולדה דחורש או בונה ומשום דהילכתא כרב באיסורי בכוליה הש"ס בר מהני תלת נקטינהו גבי הדדי: כל מילי דמר. רבה בר נחמני: לעשות חריץ גרסינן: טעמא דרב. מנר לנר משום ביזוי מצוה שמדליק קיסם שאינה מן המצוה מנר של מצוה וממנו מדליק האחר: אכחושי. דמיחזי כמאן דשקיל נהורא ושואב קצת מלחלוחית שמנו: משרגא לשרגא. מביא נר אצל נר ושתיהן של מצוה ולא בקיסם:

תוספות

נר חנוכה שהניחה למעלה מכ' אמה פסולה כסוכה וכמבוי. וא"ת הוה ליה למימר ימעט כמו גבי מבוי דאמר התם מבוי דרבנן תני תקנתא והיכא למימר דנקט פסולה משום דבעי למימר כסוכה שהיא מן התורה אי נמי לא רצה להצריך יכבנה וימעטנה ויחזור וידליק' דלמטה ולהניחה כמו שהיא דולקת אי אפשר כדמוכח לקמן*:

אסור להסתפק מהן עד מוצאי יו"ט האחרון. והא דשרי אתרוג ביו"ט האחרון טפי מסוכה מפרש בפרק לולב וערבה (סוכה מו:) משום דסוכה בספק שביעי ספק שמיני יתובי יתבינן ואי מתרמי ליה סעודה בין השמשות אכיל ליה התם והואיל ואיתקצי בין השמשות איתקצי כוליה יומא של ספק ח' וט' אבל האתרוג אינו ניטל בספק ז' וח' *ולא איתסר בספק שמיני (א) אלא משום דאיתקצי בין השמשות של ז' ואע"פ דבין השמשות של ח' נמי אסור משום שהוא ספק יום הואיל ולא אסור אלא משום ספק יום וספק לילה לא איתקצי בכך כולי יומא מידי דהוה אביצה שנולדה בזה דמותרת בזה אע"פ דבין השמשות אסור משום ספק יום וספק לילה:

סוכה תניא. משמע דטעמא דנויי סוכה משום ביזוי מצוה וקשה לר"י בפרק כירה (לקמן דף מה: ושם) משמע דטעמא משום מיגו דאיתקצי למצותה ותירץ דצריכי לתרווייהו דמשום דאיתקצי למצותה לא הוה אסרינן בחולו של מועד דלא שייך מוקצה אלא (בנפל) בשבת וביו"ט ומשום ביזוי מצוה לא הוה אסרינן להו היכא דנפלו אבל השתא דאמרי' דאיתקצי וביזוי מצוה אסרינן אפילו נפלו ואפי' בחוה"מ *וקשה לר"י כיון דנויי סוכה אסורין משום ביזוי א"כ מאי פריך בביצה בפ' המביא (דף ל: ושם) מנויי סוכה אעצי סוכה דקאמר וסוכת החג לא מהני בה תנאה והתני' סככה כהלכתה כו' ומאי קושיא דילמא עצי סוכה לא מהני ביה תנאה דמקרא נפקא כדדריש התם מניין לעצי סוכה שאסורין כל שבעה ת"ל חג הסוכות ז' ימים וגו' ודרשה גמורה היא כדמוכח בפ"ק דסוכה (דף ט. ושם) דב"ש פסלי מהאי קרא סוכה ישנה וב"ה מכשירין דההוא מיבעי ליה לעצי סוכה שאסורין כל שבעה אבל נויי סוכה דלא אסירי אלא משום ביזוי מהני בהו תנאה ועוד בפרק כירה (לקמן דף מה.) משמע בהדיא *דעצי סוכה לא אסור אלא משום דאיתקצאי למצותה *והשיב ר"ת דבין נויי סוכה ובין עצי סוכה היתרים על הכשר סוכה לא אסירי אלא משום ביזוי או משום הואיל והוקצה למצותו ולא אסירי מקרא אלא דווקא כדי הכשר סוכה והמקשה דפריך בביצה (דף ל:) מנויי סוכה אעצי סוכה לא ידע שיש חילוק בין יותר מכדי הכשר סוכה לכדי הכשר סוכה ומשני באומר איני בודל מהם כל בה"ש דלא חיילא קדושה על נויי סוכה וכן על עצים היתרין על הכשר סוכה מהני בה תנאה אבל עצי סוכה כדי הכשר חיילא קדושה עלייהו על כרחו דבר תורה כל שבעה ולא מהני תנאה והא דקאמר התם ואם התנה עליהן הכל לפי תנאו ופריך למימרא דמהני בה תנאה כו' ומשני סיפא אתאן לסוכה דעלמא ובתר הכי פריך וסוכת החג לא מהני בה תנאה והתניא סככה כו' לא בעי לשנויי הכל לפי תנאו על יתרות מכדי הכשר סוכה דהכל לפי תנאו משמע בכל הסוכה:

אבוהון דכולהו דם. הא דלא קאמר אבוהון דכולהו עצי סוכה דנפקי מקרא כדאמר בריש המביא בביצה (דף ל: ושם) אומר ר"י משום דמעצי סוכה לא הוה ילפינן דשאני סוכה דבמסתפק מהן איכא ביטול מצוה אבל בנויי סוכה ובהרצאת מעות לאור נר חנוכה ליכא ביטול מצוה:

רב אמר אין מתירין מבגד לבגד. לא מבעיא אי חובת טלית הוא דאסור אלא אפילו חובת גברא הוא נמי אסור כדאשכחן במזוזה דנעגש אותו שנטלה בבבא מציעא בסוף פרק השואל (דף קב.) אף על גב דחובת הדר היא ושמואל אמר מתירין אע"ג דשמואל גופי' סבר *דחובת טלית היא אפ"ה מתירין כיון שעושהו לצורך בגד אחר וגבי מזוזה שנענש שמא לא היה בדעתו להניח בבית אחר א"כ מזוזה שאני שעשויה להציל מן המזיקין ואע"ג דלכ"ע אין מתירין שלא להניח בבגד אחר אין קשה מה שנהגו להתיר ציצית מטליתות של מתים דדווקא בטלית של חי שהוא בר חיובא אין מתירין:

כל מילי דמר עביד כרב. קשיא דפ"ק דכתובות (ד' ו) שם כתובה: וכי

עין משפט נר מצוה

כב א מיי' פ"ד מהל' חנוכה הל' ז סמג עשין ה טוש"ע א"ח סי' תרעא סעיף ז:

כג ב ג מיי' שם טוש"ע שם סעיף ז:

[ועי' תוס' עירובין ב: ד"ה סוכה ותוס' סוכה ב: ד"ה דאורייתא]

כד ד מיי' שם הל' ו סמג שם טוש"ע א"ח סי' תרעג סעיף א:

כה ה מיי' פ"ו מהל' סוכה הל' טז סמג עשין מג טוש"ע א"ח סימן תרלח סעיף ב:

כו ו טוש"ע א"ח סימן תרעז סעיף ד:

ר"ל לא איתסר בה"ש של ח' וט' אלא משום דאתקצי בה"ש של ז' וח' ורש"ל גורס ולא איתסר בשמיני משום דאתקצי כו' דבה"ש של ז' נמי אסור:

כז ז מיי' פ"ד מהלכות חנוכה הל' ט סמג עשין ה טוש"ע א"ח סי' תרעד סעיף א:

כח ח מיי' פ"א מהל' ציצית הל' יג סמג עשין כו טוש"ע א"ח סי' טו סעיף א:

כט ט מיי' פ"א מהל' שבת הלכה ה סמג לאוין סה טוש"ע א"ח סי' שלז סעיף א:

אי נמי טעמא דהוקצה למצותו כ"מ דאסירי אפי' ביו"ט האחרון משום דאתקצי בה"ש דלטעמא דביזוי ליכא א"נ בכל אחד אתקצי למצותו משום ביזוי מצוה [ת"י]

*אולי צ"ל דפריך

פי' ר"ת נראה דחוק דלא ה"ל למימר באומר איני בודל כו' אלא בהדיא התם בהכשר סוכה ומיהו נראה דהאמרינן לשויי באומר איני בודל דתנאי אחר לא מהני בהו משום ביזוי מצוה אבל כשהוא אומר איני בודל לא חייל עלייהו קדושה כלל וליכא ביזוי [ת"י]

מסורת הש"ס

[יומא יא:]

[בשאלתות פ' וישלח סי' כו איתא ידמי']

[בהרא"ש ליתא וכן משמע מלשון רש"י ד"ה תני]

חולין פז.

[עירובין עה: כתובות ו: ב"ב קלד:]

לקמן מה: ביצה ל: סוכה י: [תוספ' סוכה פ"א]

מנחות מא:

שם לקמן מ: פסחים קא.

לקמן כט: מו: [פסחים קא.] ביצה כג: [מנחות מא:] [תוספתא ביצה פ"ב]

[תוספתא דמעשר שני רפ"א]

[מנחות מא:]

הגהות הב"ח

(א) תוס' ד"ה אסור וכו' ולא איתסר בספק שביעי ושמיני אלא וכו' של ז' וח' ואע"ג דבין השמשות של ח' וט' נמי אסור:

רבינו חננאל

נר חנוכה למעלה מעשרים אמה פסולה כמבוי וכסוכה

הגהות הגר"א [א] גמ' (סלע של) תא"מ:

להניחה מבחוץ בתוך י' טפחים בטפח הסמוך לפתח בצד שמאל כדי שתהא מזוזה מימין ונר חנוכה משמאל דרך ביאתו לביתו · ואסור להרצות מעות כנגד נר של חנוכה שלא יהא מצות בזויות עליו כמו הדם דאמר רחמנא ושפך וכסה שלא יכסנו ברגל וכו' וכן סככה כהלכתה כו' אמר רב יוסף אבוהון דכולהו דם פי' כל המצות מן הדם לומדות שלא יהא מצות בזויות עליו: תניא בכ"ה בכסליו חנוכה תמניא יומי דלא למספד שכשנכנסו עכו"ם להיכל טמאו כל שמן שבהקדש וכשגברו כו': אתמר רב אמר אין מתירין ציצית מבגד לבגד כלומר מזו הטלית ומטילין לטלית אחרת וכו' · אין מדליקין מנר של חנוכה נר אחר הלכה כרבי שמעון בגרירה · רבה בר נחמני לעולם היה עושה כרב בר מהני תלתי דעביד כשמואל דהוה שרי להתיר ציצית מבגד לבגד ולהדליק מנר של חנוכה נר אחר של חנוכה והלכתא כר"ש דאמר גורר אדם

גליון הש"ס גמרא אמר אביי כל מילי דמר · עיין לקמן דף מו ע"א תוספות ד"ה דנפלה ובעירובין דף נג ע"ב תוספות ד"ה לא תימא:

*מעשר שני אין שוקלין כנגדו דנרי זהב ואפילו לחלל עליו מעשר שני אחר אי אמרת בשלמא כי פליגי רב ושמואל מנר לנר אבל בקינסא אסר שמואל הא לא תהוי תיובתא אלא אי אמרת בקינסא נמי שרי הא תהוי תיובתא אמר רבה [ג]גזירה שמא לא יכוין משקלותיו וקא מפיק להו לחולין מתיב רב ששת °מחוץ לפרוכת העדות יערוך *וכי לאורה הוא צריך והלא כל ארבעים שנה שהלכו בני ישראל במדבר לא הלכו אלא לאורו אלא עדות היא לבאי עולם שהשכינה שורה בישראל מאי עדות אמר *רב זו נר מערבי שנותן בה שמן כמדת חברותיה *וממנה היה מדליק °ובה היה מסיים והא הכא כיון דקביעי נרות לא סגיא דלא משקיל ואדלוקי קשיא בין למ"ד משום בזויי מצוה ובין למ"ד משום אכחושי מצוה תרגמא ר"פ [ג]בפתילות ארוכות סוף סוף למ"ד משום אכחושי מצוה קשיא קשיא מאי הוי עלה א"ר הונא בריה דרב יהושע חזינא אי הדלקה עושה מצוה מדליקין מנר לנר ואי הנחה עושה מצוה אין מדליקין מנר לנר דאיבעיא להו הדלקה עושה מצוה או הנחה עושה מצוה ת"ש דאמר רבא [ד]היה תפוש נר חנוכה ועומד לא עשה ולא כלום שמע מינה הנחה עושה מצוה התם הרואה אומר לצורכו הוא דנקיט לה ת"ש דאמר רבא [ה]הדליקה בפנים והוציאה לא עשה כלום אא"ב הדלקה עושה מצוה הדלקה במקומו בעינן משום הכי לא עשה כלום אלא אי אמרת הנחה עושה מצוה אמאי לא עשה ולא כלום התם נמי הרואה הוא אומר לצורכו הוא דאדלקה תא שמע דאמר רבי יהושע בן לוי

עששית

תורה אור: ויקרא כד

רש"י

מעשר שני · דינרין שחילל עליהם מעשר שני אין שוקלין כנגדן דינרין של חולין לראות שיהיו שלימים : אי אמרת בשלמא כי פליגי רב ושמואל מנר לנר · ממש ולא בקיסם ובהא הוא דשרי שמואל דלא חיים לאכחושי אבל בקינסא דביזוי הוא מודה הא לאו הויא תיובתיה דהנך דינרים דחולין לא גופייהו מצוה ואע"ג דלמצוה קבעי להו לקינסא דמיא אלא אי אמרת בקינסא נמי שרי שמואל הואיל וצורך מצוה הוא הא הויא תיובתיה דאסר לשקול ואע"ג דצורך מצוה : לא יכוין משקלותיו · שמא לא ימצאם טובים או ימצאם יתירים ויחוס עליהן ולא יחלל המעשר עליהן ונמצא שביזה המעשר שלא לצורך : ומפיק להו לחולין · כלומר יניחם בחוליהן כמו שהן: נר מערבי · למ"ד במנחות *מזרח ומערב מונחין סדר הקנים קרי מערבי נר שני שבצד החיצון שהוא במזרח ולמ"ד לצפון ודרום מונחים אמצעי קרי מערבי על שם שהיה פיו כנגד מערב וכל שאר הנרות כלפי האמצעית דכתיב אל מול פני המנורה דהיינו אמצעי יאירו וגו' של צפון היו פונות לדרום ושבדרום פונות לצפון · נרות לוג"ש של זהב שנותנין לתוכן שמן ופתילה : כמדת חברותיה · חצי לוג שיערו בה ללילי תקופת טבת הגדולים ואם ידלק ביום (ובלילה) בלילות הקצרים ידלק אבל פחות לא שלא יכבה בטבת בלילה והתורה אמרה מערב עד בקר : וממנה היה מדליק · הנרות בין הערבים : ובה היה מסיים · הטבת הנרות שדלק כל היום ואינו מטיבו עד הערב ומשנה זו בת"כ שנויה וסבירא ליה דמזרח ומערב מונחין והכי תניא לעיל מיניה להעלות נר תמיד שתהא נר מערבי תמיד שממנו יהא מתחיל ובו יהא מסיים ומדלא כתיב להעלות נרות ש"מ הוקבע נר אחד להתחיל בו בכל יום וזהו נר מערבי השני של מזרח והכי תנן (תמיד לג·) נכנס ומצא נרות מזרחים דולקות מדשן המזרחי ומניח את המערבי דולק שממנו מדליק את המנורה בין הערבים מצאו שכבה כגון משמת שמעון הצדיק מדליקו ממזבח העולה ונראה בעיני דאמור רבנן קביעותא בנר שני משום דאין מעבירין על המצות וכי עייל בהיכל בקמא פגע ברישא וביה לא מצי לאתחולי דכתיב יערוך אותו לפני ה' צריך שיהא אחד חולה לו דאי לא לא קרינן ביה לפני ה' והכי אמרינן במנחות (דף נח:) דכתיב בנר מערבי לפני ה' מכלל דכולהו לאו לפני ה' כו' ובה היה מסיים ההטבה לפי שהשאר היה מטיב שחרית וזו מטיב בין הערבים ואוחז הישנה בידו או מניחה בכלי עד[א] שנותן שמן ופתילה ומדליק ממנה את השאר והא דאמרינן בסדר יומא (דף לג:) הטבת ה' נרות קודם להטבת ב' נרות משמע כולהו הוה מטיב שחרית ויליף לה מקראי היינו בשלא הי' הנס מתקיים והי' מוצאו שכבה דלא סמך קרא אניסא וכל זמן שהיו ישראל חביבין היה דולק כל היום והיינו עדותה : והא הכא כיון דקביעי נרות · במנורה ולא היה יכול לנתק נר מערבי מן המנורה להדליק בו האחרים על כרחיך הא דקתני ממנה הי' מדליק לא סגי דלאו משקל קינסא: ואדלוקי· לקינסא מנר מערבי ובההיא קינסא מדליק את השאר : בפתילות ארוכות · כל הפתילות יוצאות חוץ לנרותיהם עד שמגיעות זו לזו ומדליק ממנה הסמוכה לה והשאר זו מזו : סוף סוף למ"ד כו' · דהא לדידיה מסרגא לשרגא אסור : אי הדלקה עושה מצוה· אי המצוה של חנוכה תלויה בהדלקה מדליקין כדאשכחן במנורה: ואי הנחה עושה מצוה· ועיקר מצותה תליא בהנחה: אין מדליקין מנר לנר · דהדלקה לאו מצוה היא כולי האי : דאיבעיא להו גרסי' · כלומר דהא מילתא כבר איבעיא לן ומפשטא דההיא בעיא מיפשטא לן הך : היה תפוש נר חנוכה · בידו משהדליקה עד שכבתה : ועומד · לאו דוקא אלא כן לשון הש"ס : לצרכו · להשתמש וליכא היכר ניסא : בפנים · בבית : והוציאה לחוץ . כדאמר לעיל דצריך להניחה על פתח ביתו מבחוץ : אי אמרת בשלמא הדלקה עושה מצוה משום הכי לא עשה ולא כלום · דכיון דזו היא מצוה צריך שתעשנה במקום חובתה :

עששית

תוספות

וכי לאורה הוא צריך והלא כל אותם מ' שנה כו' · תימה אמאי נקט מ' שנה לעולם כל העולם כולו לאורו של מקום הולכין וי"מ וכי אהרן כשהיה נכנס לפנים לאורה היה צריך והלא מ' שנה היה מאיר להם עמוד ענן בכל המקומות כדאמרינן בברייתא דמלאכת המשכן היה מסתכל בטפיח *(ורואה בו) ויודע מה בתוכו בחבית ויודע מה בתוכה וכן משמע בת"כ דאכהנים קאי דגרס התם וכי צריכים לנר והלא כל אותן מ' שנה לא הוצרכו לנר שנא' כי ענן ה' על המשכן וגו' ומיהו בשלהי כל קרבנות (מנחות ד' פו: ושם) משמע דאשכינה קאי דמייתי לה גבי הא דא"ר אליעזר לא לאכילה אני צריך ולא לאורה אני צריך וקאמר נמי התם לפרוכת העדות עדות היא לכל באי עולם שהשכינה שורה בישראל וא"ת לאורה אני צריך והלא כל אותן ארבעים שנה : **ובה** היה מסיים · פירש בקונטרס ובה היה מסיים ההטבה שהשאר היה מטיב שחרית וזה היה מטיב בין הערבים ואוחז הישנה בידו או מניחה בכלי עד שנותן לתוך מערבית שמן ופתילה ומדליקה ומדליק השאר ממנה וקשה לריב"א שאם (ב) אפשר להדליק מן הישנה א"כ גם השאר ידליק ממנה ומאי פריך לרב כיון דהוציא הפתילה הישנה מן הנר תו ליכא לא משום בזיון מצוה ולא משום אכחושי מצוה אלא ודאי א"א לעשות כן וכשבא להטיב היה מטיב כל מה שבנר והפתילה היתה כבה מאליה אלא בעוד שהפתילה ישנה בנר מערבי דולקת היה מדליק ממנה השאר והיה מטיבה ונותן בה שמן ופתילה חדשה ומדליקה מן השאר ובה היה מסיים היינו ההדלקה* : **והא** הכא כיון דקביעי נרות כו' · כמ"ד בפרק ב' מדות (מנחות ד' פח:) דנר של פרקים היה דמשמע התם דמחובר הוה והיה של פרקים כדי שיוכל להטיבו יפה ואיכא מ"ד התם דלא הוה קבוע אלא היה מסלקו לגמרי בשעת הטבה ואחר כך מניחו : **מאי** הוי עלה · תימה מאי קמיבעיא ליה ומאי קאמר נמי חזינן אי הדלקה כו' הא לכאורה משמע דהלכה כשמואל דהא רבה עבד כוותיה וא"כ קינסא נמי שרי דהא ע"כ בקינסא פליגי ובביזוי מצוה דהא מאן דמפרש טעמא דרב משום אכחושי מצוה איתותב וצ"ל דאינו תופס דברי רבה עיקר ומבעיא ליה אי הנחה עושה מצוה ואסור לרב מנר לנר משום ביזוי מצוה כמו בקינסא או הדלקה עושה מצוה ושרי כמו במנורה דלא חיישינן לאכחושי מצוה ומסיק דהדלקה עושה מצוה ושרי א"כ מצאתי בשם ריב"ם דמיבעיא ליה אליבא דשמואל דהילכתא כוותיה אי שרי בקינסא אי לאו ומיבעיא ליה אי קי"ל כמו שאמר למעלה דלמ"ד משום בזויי מצוה שרי להדליק מנר לנר לרב ואם כן בקינסא פליגי ושרי שמואל בקינסא או דילמא לא קי"ל הכי ומנר לנר נמי איכא ביזוי מצוה ואסר רב (פי') דהנחה עושה מצוה ולא דמי למנורה ודוקא מנר לנר שרי שמואל אבל בקינסא אפילו שמואל מודה לאסור ומסיק חזינן דאיבעיא לן ואפשיט דהדלקה עושה מצוה ומדליק לרב מנר לנר כמו במנורה ולשמואל אפילו בקינסא שרי : **דאיבעיא** להו הדלקה עושה מצוה כו' · ונפקא מינה אם הדליקה חש"ו או הניחה :

מכבה

לא ב מיי' פ"ג מהל' מעשר שני הלכ' יט :

לא ג מיי' פ"ג מהל' תמידין הלכה יד :

לב ד ה מיי' פ"ד מהל' חנוכה הל' ט סמג עשין ה טוש"ע א"ח סי' תרעה סעיף א :

[ילקוט סוף פקודי לית']

[במנחות פו: אית' רבא וכ"א בילקוט פרשת תצוה רמז שעח]

[ועי' תוס' מנחות פו: ד"ה ממנה וכו']

רבינו חננאל

אדם מטה כסא וספסל ובלבד שלא יתכוון לעשות חריץ ואסיקנ' דטעמא דרב משום בזוי מצוה וכיון דנר של מצוה הוא [דמדליק מנר של] מצוה ליכא בזיון מצוה והדלקה היא המצוה ולא הנחת הנר בטפח הסמוך לפתח הלכך מותר להדליק נר של חנוכה מנר של חנוכה שנמצא מדליק מצוה ממצוה שהדלקת נר השני היא מצותו

מנחות פו:

[דף נח:]

תמיד לג: פ"ז מ"א

הגהות הב"ח

(א) רש"י ד"ה ובה היה מסיים וכו' מניחה בכלי עד שנותן לתוכה שמן ופתילה וכו' : (ב) תוס' ד"ה וקשה לריב"א שאם היה אפשר להדליק בישנה א"כ :

גליון הש"ס

גמרא ובה היה מסיים. עיין חגיגה כו ע"ב תוס' ד"ה מנורה :

R. Awia objected: As to a *sela'*[4] of [22b] second tithe,[5] one may not weigh by it gold *denarii*,[6] even to redeem therewith other second tithe. Now, it is well if you say that Rab and Samuel differ [over direct lighting] from lamp to lamp, yet with a chip Samuel admits that it is forbidden: then this is not a refutation.[7] But if you [on Samuel's view] say that it is permitted even with a chip, then this is a refutation?—Rabbah answered: It is a preventive measure, lest he does not find his weights exact and leaves[8] them *ḥullin*.[9]

R. Shesheth objected: *Without the vail of testimony... shall [Aaron] order it*:[10] does He then require its light: surely, during the entire forty years that the Israelites travelled in the wilderness they travelled only by His light! But it is a testimony to mankind[11] that the Divine Presence rests in Israel. What is the testimony?[12] —Said Rab: That was the western branch [of the candelabrum] in which the same quantity of oil was poured as into the rest, and yet he kindled [the others] from it and ended therewith.[13] Now here, since the branches are immovable, it is impossible other
a than that he take [a chip] and kindle [it];[1] which is a difficulty both on the view that it is because of the cheapening of the precept and on the view that it is because of the impairing of the precept? —R. Papa reconciled it [thus: it is lit] by long wicks.[2] Yet after all, on the view that it is because of the impairing of precepts there is a difficulty? That is [indeed] a difficulty.

What is our decision thereon?—R. Huna, the son of R. Joshua, said: We consider: if the lighting fulfils the precept, one may light from lamp to lamp;[3] but if the placing [of the lamp] fulfils the precept,[4] one may not light from lamp to lamp.[5] For the scholars propounded: Does the kindling or the placing constitute the precept?—Come and hear: For Raba said, If one was holding the *Ḥanukkah* lamp and thus standing, he does nothing:[6] this proves that the placing constitutes the precept!—[No:] There a spectator may think that he is holding it for his own purposes.[7] Come and hear: For Raba said: If one lights it within and then takes it outside, he does nothing. Now, it is well if you say that the kindling constitutes the precept; [for this reason] we require the kindling to be [done] in its proper place,[8] [and] therefore he does nothing. But if you say that the placing constitutes the precept, why has he done nothing?—There too an observer may think that he lit it for his own purposes.

(4) V. Glos. (5) The tenth of the produce eaten by its owner in Jerusalem. When the actual produce could not be carried, it was redeemed, and the redemption money assumed the sanctity of second tithe and was expended in Jerusalem, v. Deut. XIV, 22-26. (6) One *sela'* = four *denarii*, and the value depended on the weight. (7) For the gold *denarii* are not actually sanctified when they are weighed, though that is their purpose. Thus they are similar to the chip which may not be lit at the *Ḥanukkah* lamp because it is secular itself. (8) Lit., 'withdraws'. (9) The gold *denarii* may be deficient in weight and not be declared second tithe after all. Thus he will have used the second tithe *sela'* purely for a secular purpose. (10) Lev. XXIV, 3; v. 1-4. (11) Lit., 'those who enter the world'. (12) How was this a testimony? (13) Half a *log* of oil was poured into each branch, which was estimated to burn through the longest night. Thus by the morning they were extinguished. The following evening the priest cleaned out the old wicks, poured in fresh oil, and relit it: yet this western branch was still burning when he came to clean them out, which was done last of all. This miracle testified to the Divine Presence in Israel. On the western branch of the candelabrum v. Men. 78*b*.

a (1) In order to light the others. (2) Which reached the other branches. (3) Just as the kindling of the branches of the candlestick in the Temple from the western branch. (4) I.e., the prime observance of the *Ḥanukkah* lamp is not the kindling thereof but placing it in a conspicuous place. (5) For the lit lamp or branch is already sanctified, as it were, whilst no complete religious observance is fulfilled by the act of lighting the next, on the present hypothesis. (6) He does not fulfil the precept. (7) Whereas the essence of the *Ḥanukkah* lamp is to advertise the miracle. (8) *Sc.* outside; *supra* 21*b*.

Come and hear: For R. Joshua b. Levi said, [23a] With regard to a lantern which was burning the whole day [of the Sabbath],[1] at the conclusion of the Sabbath it is extinguished and then [re-]lit.[2] Now, it is well if you say that the kindling constitutes the precept: then it is correct. But if you say that the placing constitutes the precept, is it [merely] to be extinguished and [re-]lit: surely it should [have stated], It must be extinguished, lifted up, replaced and then relit? Moreover, since we pronounce a benediction, 'Who sanctified us by His commandments and commanded us to kindle the lamp of *Ḥanukkah*,' it proves that the kindling constitutes the precept. This proves it.

And now that we say that the kindling constitutes the precept, if a deaf-mute, idiot, or minor[3] lights it, he does nothing. But a woman may certainly light [it], for R. Joshua b. Levi said: The [precept of the] *Ḥanukkah* lamp is obligatory upon women, for they too were concerned in that miracle.[4]

R. Shesheth said: The [precept of the] *Ḥanukkah* lamp is incumbent upon a guest.[5] R. Zera said: Originally, when I was at the academy, I shared the cost[6] with mine host;[7] but after I took a wife I said, Now I certainly do not need it, because they kindle [the lamp] on my behalf at my home.[8]

R. Joshua b. Levi said: All oils are fit for the *Ḥanukkah* lamp, but olive oil is of the best. Abaye observed: At first the Master [Rabbah] used to seek poppy-seed oil, saying, The light of this is more lasting;[9] but when he heard this [dictum] of R. Joshua b. Levi, he was particular for olive oil, saying, This yields a clearer light.

b R. Joshua b. Levi also said: All oils are fit[1] for ink, and olive oil is of the best. The scholars propounded: for kneading or for smoking?[2]—Come and hear: For R. Samuel b. Zuṭra recited: All oils are fit for ink, and olive oil is of the best, both for kneading and for smoking. R. Samuel b. Zuṭra recited it thus: All soots are fit for ink: and olive oil is the best. R. Huna said: All gums are good for ink, but balsam gum is the best of all.

R. Ḥiyya b. Ashi said: He who lights the *Ḥanukkah* lamp must pronounce a blessing; while R. Jeremiah said: He who sees the *Ḥanukkah* lamp must pronounce a blessing. Rab Judah said: On the first day, he who sees must pronounce two, and he who lights must pronounce three blessings;[3] thereafter, he who lights pronounces two, and he who sees pronounces one. What is omitted?[4]—The 'season' is omitted.[5] Yet let the 'miracle' be omitted?[6]—The miracle holds good for every day.[7]

What benediction is uttered?[8]—This: Who sanctified us by His commandments and commanded us to kindle the light of *Ḥanukkah*.[9] And where did He command us?[10]—R. Awia said: [It follows] from, *thou shalt not turn aside [from the sentence which they shall shew thee]*.[11] R. Nehemiah quoted: *Ask thy father, and he will shew thee; Thine elders, and they will tell thee.*[12]

(1) Having been lit on the Sabbath eve as a *Ḥanukkah* lamp. (2) As a *Ḥanukkah* lamp for the next day. (3) These three are frequently grouped: their actions have no legal or religious validity. (4) According to the Talmud Jewish virgins were subjected to the *jus primae noctis* before the Maccabean revolt (cf. I Macc. I, 26f, which may perhaps refer to this), and were rescued from it by the 'miracle', i.e., the successful Maccabean uprising. (5) Not living in his own house but as a guest or boarder elsewhere. (6) Lit., 'the coins'—the cost of the oil for the *Ḥanukkah* lamp. (7) He did not kindle lights for himself but purchased a share in those lit by his host. (8) He continued to study away from home after marriage. (9) Rashi: this oil burned slower. Tosaf.'s reading seems to be: this gives a stronger light: on grounds of logic this would appear preferable.

(1) Ink was made of soot and oil or gum, and was a solid cake of pigment which had to be loosened before use. Cf. *supra*, Mishnah on 17*b*. (2) Is it the best for kneading with soot or for creating the smoke which produces the soot? (3) V. *P.B.* p. 274; the spectator omits the first, since he does not kindle the lights. Rashi and Asheri observe that only a spectator who has not yet kindled the lights himself, or who cannot do so, e.g., when he is in a boat, is required to pronounce these benedictions. (4) After the first day. (5) Ibid. the third blessing: '... and has enabled us to reach this season'. This is appropriate for the first evening only. (6) I.e., the second benediction: '...Who wroughtest miracles ...' (7) The cruse miraculously burned all the eight days; v. *supra* 21*b*. (8) Lit., 'he blesses'. (9) Ibid. the first blessing. The literal translation is given here, the passage being in the third person. (10) This precept is not Biblical, of course. (11) Deut. XVII, 11. (12) Ibid. XXXII, 7. Both verses teach that a Rabbinical observance has Biblical sanction, and thus roots subsequent tradition in the Bible itself. Cf. I. Abrahams, *Permanent Values of the Talmud*, pp. 79ff.

For the continuation of the English translation of this page see overleaf.

עין משפט נר מצוה

לג א ב מיי' פ"ד מהל' חנוכה הל' ט סמג עשין ה טוש"ע א"ח סי' תרעה סעיף א :
לד ג ד מיי' שם טוש"ע שם סעיף ג :
לה ה ו ז מיי' פ"ד שם הל' יא סמג שם טוש"ע א"ח סימן רסג סעיף ז וסימן תרעו סעיף א :
לו ח מיי' פ"ה מהל' שבת הל' יא סמג לאוין סה טוש"ע א"ח סי' רסד סעיף ו וסימן תרעג סעיף א :
לז ט מיי' פ"א מהל' תפילין הלכ' ד סמג עשין כה טוש"ע א"ח סי' לב סעיף ג :
לח י מיי' פ"ג מהל' חנוכה הל' ד סמג עשין ה טוש"ע א"ח סי' תרעו סעי' א ב ג :
לט כ מיי' פי"א מהל' ברכות הל' ג סמג עשין כו :
מ ל מיי' פ"ג מהלכות חנוכה הל' ה וע"ש במ"מ :
מא מ נ מיי' פ"ד מהל' חנוכה הל' י סמג עשין ה טוש"ע א"ח סי' תרעא סעיף א :
מב ס מיי' פ"ב מהל' מתנות עניים הלכה יב :

מסורת הש"ס

[פסחים קח: מגילה ד. ערכין ג:]

[מס' סופרים פ"כ הלכה ו]

[בשאלתות סי' כו ליתא רב נחמן בר יצחק] *ומברכין כיינו ברהמ"ז בג' ומזמנין בי"ולא לו ברכת המוציא פשיטא דמברכין דאסו' ליהנות מהעוה"ז בלא ברכה [ת"י] לעיל יג: כתובות כד: גיטין סא: [בילה לה: מנחות לא:]

סוכה מו.

תוספת' דפאה פ"א ת"כ פ' קדושים

גליון הש"ס

גמ' איבעיא להו לגבל. עי' לעיל דף יח ע"א תוס' ד"ה אבל דיו :

גמרא

תורה אור

עששית *שהיתה דולקת והולכת כל היום כולו למוצ"ש מכבה ומדליקה אי אמרת בשלמא הדלקה עושה מצוה שפיר אלא אי אמרת הנחה עושה מצוה האי מכבה ומדליקה מכבה ומגביהה ומניחה ומדליקה מיבעי ליה ועוד מדקא מברכינן אשר קדשנו במצותיו וצונו להדליק נר של חנוכה ש"מ הדלקה עושה מצוה ש"מ והשתא דאמרינן הדלקה עושה מצוה הדליקה חרש שוטה וקטן לא עשה ולא כלום אשה ודאי מדליקה דא"ר יהושע בן לוי נשים חייבות בנר חנוכה *שאף הן היו באותו הנס : אמר רב ששת אכסנאי חייב בנר חנוכה א"ר זירא מריש כי הוינא בי רב משתתפנא בפריטי בהדי אושפיזא בתר דנסיבי איתתא אמינא השתא ודאי לא צריכנא דקא מדליקי עלי בגו ביתאי: א"ר יהושע בן לוי כל השמנים כולן יפין לנר ושמן זית מן המובחר אמר אביי מריש הוה מהדר מר אמשחא דשומשמי אמר האי משך נהורי טפי כיון דשמע לה להא דרבי יהושע בן לוי מהדר אמשחא דזיתא אמר האי צליל נהוריה טפי ואריב"ל כל השמנים יפין לדיו ושמן זית מן המובחר איבעיא להו °לגבל או לעשן ת"ש דתני רב שמואל בר זוטרי כל השמנים יפין לדיו ושמן זית מן המובחר בין לגבל בין לעשן רב שמואל בר זוטרא מתני הכי כל העשנים יפין לדיו ושמן זית מן המובחר אמר רב הונא כל השרפין יפין לדיו ושרף קטף יפה מכולם : *א"ר חייא בר אשי אמר רב המדליק נר של חנוכה צריך לברך ורב ירמיה אמר הרואה נר של חנוכה צריך לברך אמר רב יהודה *יום ראשון הרואה מברך ב' ומדליק מברך ג' מכאן ואילך מדליק מברך שתים ורואה מברך אחת מאי ממעט ממעט זמן ונימעוט נס נס כל יומי איתיה מאי מברך מברך אשר קדשנו במצותיו וצונו להדליק נר של חנוכה* והיכן צונו רב אויא אמר °מלא תסור (דברים יז) רב *נחמיה אמר °שאל אביך ויגדך זקניך ויאמרו לך (שם לב) מתיב רב עמרם *הדמאי מערבין בו ומשתתפין בו *ומברכין עליו ומזמנין עליו ומפרישין אותו ערום ובין השמשות ואי אמרת כל מדרבנן בעי ברכה הכא כי קאי ערום היכי מברך והא בעינן °והיה מחניך (שם כג) קדוש וליכא אמר אביי ודאי דדבריהם בעי ברכה ספק דדבריהם לא בעי ברכה והא יו"ט שני דספק דבריהם הוא ובעי ברכה התם כי היכי דלא לזילזולי בה *רבא אמר רוב עמי הארץ מעשרין הן : אמר רב הונא חצר שיש לה ב' פתחים צריכה שתי נרות (*ואמר) (נ"ל אמר) רבא לא אמרן אלא משתי רוחות אבל מרוח אחת לא צריך מ"ט אילימא משום חשדא חשדא דמאן אילימא חשדא דעלמא אפילו ברוח אחת נמי ליבעי אי חשדא דבני מתא אפי' משני רוחות נמי לא ליבעי לעולם משום חשדא דבני מתא וזימנין דמחלפי בהאי ולא חלפי בהאי ואמרי כי היכי דבהאי פיתחא לא אדליק בהך פיתחא נמי לא אדליק ומנא תימרא דחיישינן לחשד *דתניא אמר רבי שמעון בשביל ארבעה דברים אמרה תורה להניח פיאה בסוף שדהו מפני גזל עניים ומפני ביטול עניים ומפני החשד ומשום °בל תכלה (ויקרא יט) מפני גזל עניים שלא יראה בעל הבית שעה פנוייה ויאמר לקרובו עני הרי זו פאה ומפני

דמאי פ"א מ"ד

רש"י

עששית · כלי גדול של זכוכית בלעז לנטרנ"א : דולקת · שהדליקה למצות חנוכה בע"ש : ומדליקה · למצות הלילה : היו באותו הנס · שגזרו יוונים על כל בתולות הנשואות להיבעל לטפסר תחלה ועל יד אשה נעשה הנס : אכסנאי · אורח : בתר דנסיבי · ופעמים שהייתי אכסנאי ללמוד תורה: עלי · בשבילי : בגו ביתאי · בביתי : משך נהוריה · אינו ממהר לכלות כשמן זית : צליל נהוריה · צלול ומאיר : לגבל · מצאתי בתשובו' הגאוני' שמעשנין כלי זכוכית בעשן שמן זית עד שמשחיר וגורר השחרורי' ונותן בו שמן קימעא ומגבל בו ומייבשו בחמה וממחה אותו לתוך הדיו : לעשן · כמו כדפרישית : שרף · גומא : קטף · פרוגיי"ל של יער כמו שאנו עושים משל שרף: הרואה · העובר בשוק ורואה באחד החצרות דולק ומצאתי בשם רבינו יצחק בן יהודה שאמר משם רבינו יעקב דלא הוזקקה ברכה זו אלא למי שלא הדליק בביתו עדיין או ליושב בספינ': הרואה מברך שתים · שעשה נסים ושהחיינו שאין עליו לברך להדליק דהא לא אדליק איהו : מאי ממעט · המדליק בשאר ימים איזו מן השלש ממעט : כל יומי איתיה · שהרי כל שמנה הדליקו מן הפך אבל זמן משהגיעו להתחלת זמן הגיעו : היכן צונו · הא לאו דאורייתא היא אלא מדבריהם: מלא תסור · מן הדבר אשר יגידו לך וגו' : מערבין בו · עירובי חצרות ותחומין : משתתפין בו · במבוי דאי בעי מפקר לנכסיה והוה עני וחזי ליה כדתנן מאכילין את העניים דמאי הלכך חשוב דידיה : ומברכין עליו · המוציא : ומזמנין עליו · ברכת הזימון : ומפריש אותו · אדם שהוא ערום כלומר דלא צריך לברוכי עליה בהפרשתו : והיה מחניך קדוש · ולא יראה בך ערות דבר אפילו דבור דהזכרת השם לא יראה בך ערות דבר: ודאי דדבריהם. כגון נר חנוכה : ספק דדבריהם · כגון דמאי שהפרשתו אינה אלא מספק : ובעי ברכה · קדוש היום : רבא אמר · ספק דדבריהם בעי ברכה ודמאי אפילו ספק לא הוי אלא חומרא בעלמא דרוב עמי הארץ מעשרין : חצר שיש לה ב' פתחים · שיש לבית ב' פתחים פתוחים לחצר צריכ' שתי נרות נר לכל פתח כדמפ' טעמא משום חשדא שהרואה יהא סבור שהבית חלוק והרי הוא של שני בני אדם ויאמרו האחד אינו מקיים מצות נר : מב' רוחות · אחד בצפון ואחד במזרח : חשדא דעלמא · בני עיר אחרת העוברין משם בשוק: אפי' מרוח אחת נמי · סבורין הן שהבית חלוק מתוכו : ואי חשדא דבני מתא · שיודעים שאין חלוק : לסוף שדהו · בגמר קצירו כדכתי' לא תכלה משמע בשעת כילוי ולא שיקצה אותה קודם לכן: מפני בטול עניים· וכולהו מפרש להו : שעה פנויה · שאין עניים אצלו ויאמר לקרובו עני מהר וטול כאן עד שלא יבאו אחרים אבל עכשיו שמניחה בגמר קציר השד' העניים רואין ובאין:

תוספות

מכבה ומגביהה ומניחה וחוזר ומדליק מיבעי ליה · וא"ת אמאי מכבה וחוזר ומדליק בהגבהה סגי כיון דהנחה עושה מצוה דאטו מי גרע דלוקה ועומדת מהדליקה חש"ו וי"ל דמיירי שהדליקה מתחלתה לצורך שבת ולכך גרע מהדליקה חש"ו דהתם שמדליקה בעתה ניכר הדבר שהוא מדליקה לשם חנוכה · ריב"א :

שמע מינה הדלקה עושה מצוה · וא"כ מותר להדליק מנר לנר ומכל מקום כיון שנהגו העולם להחמיר אין לשנות המנהג :

מריש הוה מהדר מר אמשחא דשומשמי · נראה דאנר חנוכה קאי ומשום טעמא דמסיק דנפיש נהוריה טפי אבל לנר שבת פשיטא דשמן זית מצוה מן המובחר לפי שנמשך אחר הפתילה טפי מכולהו כדמוכח במתניתין דכולהו מודו ביה דמדליקין :

כל השרפים יפים לדיו · פירש בקונטרס שרף גומא ואין נראה לר"ת דהא דיו אין זה גומא כדאמרינן בפ"ב דגיטין (דף יט. ושם) בכל כותבין בדיו בסם ובסקרא ובקומוס ומפרש בגמרא קומוס גומא ודיו נמי אין זה מי עפצים שרגילין להניח בהן גומא דהא בברייתא קתני התם כתבו במי טריא ועפצא דהיינו עפצים כשר משמע דלאו היינו דיו דקתני במתניתין ועוד דכשר משמע דיעבד ובדיו היא עיקר הכתיבה ועוד דבפרק כל היד (נדה דף כ. ושם) אמרינן פלי קורטא דדיותא ובדיק דהיינו דיו שלנו שהוא קשה ולא של עפצים ואין דרך להניח גומא לתוך דיו שלנו אלא שרף [דהכא] היינו לחלוחית של אילן כמו שאנו עושין דיו שלנו וכן יש בנדה בפ"ק (דף ט:) גבי בתולה זו שירפה מצוי וזו אין שירפה מצוי וכן בפ' כל שעה (פסחים לט. ושם) ירק מר יש לו שרף ופניו מכסיפין דע"כ ההוא שרף היינו לחלוחית ועל כן היה פוסל ר"ת ס"ת שאין כותבין בדיו שלנו דשאר לא מיקרי דיו כדפי' ואמרי' בפ' הבונה (לקמן קד:) כתבו שלא בדיו הרי אלו יגנזו ומוקמי' לה בהקומץ רבה (מנחות דף לד*) בס"ת:

הדר

[נ"ל בא"י אמ"ה שעשה נסים וכו' ושהחיינו וכו' וכ"א בסרי"ף והרא"ש]

[לפי פרש"י ד"ה והיה מחניך כו' סמיך הש"ס אסיפא דקרא כמ"ש תוס' כתובות כט: סד"ה אלו וכן כתבו בשאר דוכתא ועי' ב"מ קיד: מנין לערום שלא יתרום דכתי' ולא יראה בך ערות דבר ע"ש פרש"י]

רבינו חננאל

ובעי'(להדליק)[שידליק] מי שהי' חייב ובר מצות והנשים מדליקות עששית שהיתה דולקת כל היום כולו לערב מכבה ומדליקה ואכסנאי חייב בנר חנוכה ואי משתתף בהדי אושפיזו או אם היה נסיב תו לא צריך · כל השמנים יפין לנר ושמן זית יפה מכולם המדליק ביום ראשון מברך להדליק ושעשה נסים וזמן · מיכן והילך מברך שתים ומניח זמן· היכן צונו דמברכין אשר קדשנו במצותיו וצונו להדליק רב נחמן בר יצחק אמר שאל אביך ויגדך כו' [רב] אויא אמר לא תסור מן הדבר אשר יגידו לך הנה צונו אלהינו לשמוע דברי הכמים ואקשינן וכי מצוה מדרבנן בעי ברכה והתנן הדמאי מערבין בו ומשתתפין בו ומברכין ומזמנין עליו ומפרישין אותו ערום בין השמשות ואי אמרת דכל מצוה כדרבנן בעי ברכה היכי מברך ערום הא בעינן והיה מחניך קדוש ולא יראה בך ערות דבר וליכא ושני אביי ודאי דדבריהם כגון הנוכה וכיוצא בו בעי ברכה אבל דמאי דאפי' לרבנן ספק הוא לא בעי ברכה איני והא יו"ט שני דספק מדרבנן הוא ומברכינן ומשנינן התם הוא משום דלא ליזלזלי בה רבא אמר רוב עמי הארץ מעשרין הן לפיכך לא בעי ברכה בדמאי השתא כן רבנן דדייק ואמרי לענין נולד כשהוא מהול אע"ג דקיי"ל (כרבא) [כרבה] דאמר שמא ערלה כבושה הוא לפיכך צריך להטיף ממנו דם ברית בחול כיון שהוא ספק מדבריהם כד מהיל ליה בחול לא צריך ברכה כמו הדמאי · אמר רב הונא הצר שיש לה ב' פתחים בב' רוחות צריך ב' נרות דחיישינן לחשדא ומנלן דחיישינן דתני

Continuation of translation from previous page as indicated by ◁

R. Amram objected: *Dem'ai*[13] can be employed for an *'erub*[13]
c and for a joint ownership;[1] a benediction is pronounced over it, and grace in common is recited after it,[2] and it[3] may be separated by a naked person, and at twilight.[4] But if you say that every Rabbinical [precept] requires a benediction, here, when one stands naked, how can he pronounce a benediction: lo! we require, *therefore shall thy camp be holy [that He see no unclean thing in thee]*,[5] which is absent?—Said Abaye, A certain Rabbinical law[6] requires a benediction, whereas a doubtful Rabbinical law does not.[7] But what of the second day of Festivals, which is a Rabbinical [institution] based on doubt,[8] and yet it requires a benediction?[9]—There it [was instituted] in order that it should not be treated slightingly.[10] Raba said: The majority of the *'amme ha-arez'*[11] tithe [their produce].[12]

R. Huna said: If a courtyard has two doors, it requires two [*Ḥanukkah*] lamps. Said Raba, That was said only [if they are situated] at two [different] sides; but [if] on the same side, it
d is unnecessary. What is the reason?[1] Shall we say, because of suspicion?[2] Whose suspicion? Shall we say, that of strangers:[3] then let it be necessary even on the same side?[4] Whilst if the suspicion is of townspeople, then even [if] on two different sides it is still unnecessary?[5]—After all, it is on account of the suspicion of the townspeople, yet perchance they may pass one [door] and not the other, and say, 'just as it [the lamp] has not been lit at this door, so has it not been lit at the other.'

And whence do you know[6] that we pay regard to suspicions?—Because it was taught, R. Simeon said: On account of four considerations the Torah ordered *pe'ah*[7] to be left at the end of the field:[8] [as a precaution] against the robbing of the poor, against wasting the time of the poor, against suspicion, and against [transgressing], *thou shalt not* finish off [*the* corners *of thy field*].[9] [As a precaution] against the robbing of the poor: lest the owner see a free hour[10] and say to his poor relations, 'This

(13) V. Glos.

c (1) I.e., to link up a number of side streets in respect of carrying on the Sabbath; v. *supra* 6a, n. b7; it is the same with side streets. (2) 'Grace in common' is recited when three persons or more dine together; it is then prefaced by one of them saying, 'My masters, let us recite grace;' this man acts as leader. When only two dine together, each recites grace by himself. (3) The tithe of *dem'ai*. (4) Friday evening. The tithe of certain *ṭebel* (v. Glos.) may not be separated on the Sabbath, nor at twilight, for it is doubtful whether this belongs to the previous or to the following day. But since *dem'ai* is only a doubtful tithe, it is permitted as a double doubt; cf. *supra* 15b, n. a7. (5) Deut. XXIII, 15. (6) Lit., 'a certain (law) of their words'. (7) The kindling of light is a definite and certain observance; the tithing of *dem'ai*, however, is done through doubt. (8) Scripture ordained Festivals of one day only at the beginning and end (viz., Passover and Tabernacles, v. Lev. XXIII, 7f, 35f) or one day altogether (Pentecost and New Year; ibid. 21, 24). The exact days when these were to be observed depended upon New Moon of the month in which they fell (except Pentecost), which was originally determined by direct observation, not by calculation. By experience it was found that New Moon was always either twenty-nine or thirty days after the previous New Moon, and as soon as it was thus fixed by the Great Court in Jerusalem, envoys were dispatched to inform the communities in time for the Festival. But they could not reach the Jewish communities outside Palestine in time, and therefore they observed two days instead of one. Thus the original reason of the added second day at the beginning and the end was on account of doubt, though it was retained even when the New Moon came to be determined by calculation, which precluded doubt. (9) Viz. 'sanctification of the Festival', which was done by means of a benediction. (10) Unless the second day was formally sanctified people would not treat it as holy. (11) Pl. of *'am ha-arez*; v. *supra* 13a, n. a1. (12) So that *dem'ai* is less than an ordinary doubt, but merely a Rabbinical stringency; therefore a benediction is not required.

d (1) That two lamps are required. (2) Viz., if a person sees a door without a lamp he may suspect the owner of having neglected it altogether. (3) Lit., 'the world'—i.e., a stranger passing through the town may be unaware that a lamp is burning at another door. (4) For a stranger may think that the courtyard fronts two separate houses. (5) They know that both belong to the same house. (6) Lit., 'say'. (7) V. Glos. (8) Instead of enacting that a certain portion of the field be left for the poor, its situation to be at the owner's discretion. (9) Lev. XIX, 9. '*Thou shalt not* finish *off*' implies at the end of the field, where the harvesting is completed. (10) When no poor are about in the field.

עששית ^אשהיתה דולקת והולכת כל היום כולו למוצ"ש מכבה ומדליקה אי אמרת בשלמא הדלקה עושה מצוה שפיר אלא אי אמרת הנחה עושה מצוה האי מכבה ומדליקה מכבה ומגביהה ומניחה ומדליקה מיבעי ליה ועוד מדקא מברכינן אשר קדשנו במצותיו וצונו להדליק נר של חנוכה ^בש"מ הדלקה עושה מצוה ש"מ והשתא דאמרינן הדלקה עושה מצוה ^גהדליקה חרש שוטה וקטן לא עשה ולא כלום ^דאשה ודאי מדליקה דא"ר יהושע בן לוי נשים חייבות בנר חנוכה *שאף הן היו באותו הנס: אמר רב ששת ^האכסנאי חייב בנר חנוכה א"ר זירא ^ומריש כי הוינא בי רב משתתפנא בפריטי בהדי אושפיזא בתר דנסיבי איתתא אמינא ^זהשתא ודאי לא צריכנא דקא מדליקי עלי בגו ביתאי: א"ר יהושע בן לוי ^חכל השמנים כולן יפין לנר ושמן זית מן המובחר אמר אביי מריש הוה מהדר מר אמשחא דשומשמי אמר האי משך נהורי טפי כיון דשמע לה להא דרבי יהושע בן לוי מהדר אמשחא דזיתא אמר האי צליל נהוריה טפי ואריב"ל ^טכל השמנים יפין לדיו ושמן זית מן המובחר איבעיא להו °לגבל או לעשן ת"ש דתני רב שמואל בר זוטרי כל השמנים יפין לדיו ושמן זית מן המובחר בין לגבל בין לעשן רב שמואל בר זוטרא מתני הכי כל העשנים יפין לדיו ושמן זית מן המובחר אמר רב הונא כל השרפין יפין לדיו ושרף קטף יפה מכולם: *א"ר חייא בר אשי אמר רב המדליק נר של חנוכה צריך לברך ורב ירמיה אמר הרואה נר של חנוכה צריך לברך אמר רב יהודה *^ייום ראשון הרואה מברך ב' ומדליק מברך ג' מכאן ואילך מדליק מברך שתים ורואה מברך אחת מאי ממעט ממעט זמן ונימעוט נס נס כל יומי איתיה מאי מברך מברך אשר קדשנו במצותיו וצונו להדליק נר של חנוכה* ^כוהיכן צונו
דברים יז רב אויא אמר °מלא תסור רב *נחמיה אמר
שם לב °שאל אביך ויגדך זקניך ויאמרו לך מתיב רב עמרם *הדמאי מערבין בו ומשתתפין בו *ומברכין עליו ומזמנין עליו ומפרישין אותו ערום ובין השמשות ואי אמרת כל מדרבנן
שם כג בעי ברכה הכא כי קאי ערום היכי מברך והא בעינן *°והיה מחניך קדוש וליכא אמר אביי ^לודאי דדבריהם בעי ברכה ספק דדבריהם לא בעי ברכה והא יו"ט שני דספק דבריהם הוא ובעי ברכה התם כי היכי דלא לזילזולי בה *רבא אמר רוב עמי הארץ מעשרין הן: אמר רב הונא
צ"ל אמר ^מחצר שיש לה ב' פתחים צריכה שתי נרות (*ואמר) רבא ^נלא אמרן אלא משתי רוחות אבל מרוח אחת לא צריך מ"ט אילימא משום חשדא חשדא דמאן אילימא חשדא דעלמא אפילו ברוח אחת נמי ליבעי אי חשדא דבני מתא אפי' משני רוחות נמי לא ליבעי לעולם משום חשדא דבני מתא וזימנין דמחלפי בהאי ולא חלפי בהאי ואמרי כי היכי דבהאי פיתחא לא אדליק בהך פיתחא נמי לא אדליק ומנא תימרא דחיישינן לחשד *דתניא אמר רבי שמעון ^סבשביל ארבעה דברים אמרה תורה להניח פיאה בסוף שדהו מפני גזל
ויקרא יט עניים ומפני ביטול עניים ומפני החשד ומשום °בל תכלה מפני גזל עניים שלא יראה בעל הבית שעה פנויה ויאמר לקרובו עני הרי זו פאה ומפני

דמאי פ"א מ"ד

רש"י

עששית · כלי גדול של זכוכית בלעז לנטרנ"א: דולקת · שהדליקה למצות חנוכה בע"ש: ומדליקה · למצות הלילה: היו באותו הנס · שגזרו יוונים על כל בתולות הנשואות להיבעל לטפסר תחלה ועל יד אשה נעשה הנס: אכסנאי · אורח: בתר דנסיבי · ופעמים שהייתי אכסנאי ללמוד תורה: עלי · בשבילי: בגו ביתאי · בביתי: משך נהוריה · אינו ממהר לכלות כשמן זית: צליל נהוריה · צלול ומאיר: לגבל · מצאתי בתשוב' הגאוני' שמעשנין כלי זכוכית בעשן שמן זית עד שמשחיר וגורר השחרורי' ונותן בו שמן קימעא ומגבל בו ומייבשו בחמה וממחה אותו לתוך הדיו: לעשן · נמי כדפרישית: שרף · גומא: קטף · פרוני"ל של יער כמו שאנו עושים משל שרף: הרואה · העובר בשוק ורואה באחד החלונות דולק ומצאתי בשם רבינו יצחק בן יהודה שאמר משם רבינו יעקב דלא הוזקקה ברכה זו אלא למי שלא הדליק בביתו עדיין או ליושב בספינ': הרואה מברך שתים · שעשה נסים ושהחיינו שאין עליו לברך להדליק דהא לא אדליק איהו: מאי ממעט · המדליק בשאר ימים איזו מן השלש ממעט: כל יומי איתיה · שהרי כל שמנה הדליקו מן הפך אבל זמן משהגיעו להתחלת זמן הגיעו: היכן צונו · הא לאו דאורייתא היא אלא מדבריהם: מלא תסור · מן הדבר אשר יגידו לך וגו': מערבין בו · עירובי חצרות ותחומין: משתתפין בו · במבוי דאי בעי מפקר לנכסיה והוה עני וחזי ליה כדתנן מאכילין את העניים דמאי הלכך חשוב דידיה: ומברכין עליו · המוציא: ומזמנין עליו · ברכת הזימון: ומפרישין אותו · אדם שהוא ערום כלומר דלא צריך לברוכי עליה בהפרשתו: והיה מחניך קדוש · ולא יראה בך ערות דבר אפילו דבור דהזכרת השם לא יראה בך ערות דבר: ודאי דדבריהם · כגון נר חנוכה: ספק דדבריהם · כגון דמאי שהפרשתו אינה אלא מספק: ובעי ברכה · קדוש היום: רבא אמר · ספק דדבריהם בעי ברכה ודמאי אפילו ספק לא הוי אלא חומרא בעלמא דרוב עמי הארץ מעשרין: חצר שיש לה ב' פתחים · שיש לבית ב' פתחים פתוחים לחצר צריכ' שתי נרות נר לכל פתח כדמפ' טעמא משום חשדא שהרואה יהא סבור שהבית חלוק והרי הוא של שני בני אדם ויאמרו האחד אינו מקיים מצות נר: מב' רוחות · אחד בצפון ואחד במזרח: חשדא דעלמא · בני עיר אחרת העוברין משם בשוק: אפי' מרוח אחת נמי · סבורין הן שהבית חלוק מתוכו: ואי חשדא דבני מתא · שיודעים שאין חלוק: לסוף שדהו · בגמר קצירו כדכתי' לא תכלה משמע בשעת כילוי ולא שיקצור אותה קודם לכן: מפני בטול עניים · וכולהו מפרש להו: שעה פנויה · שאין עניים אצלו ויאמר לקרובו עני מהר וטול כאן עד שלא יבאו אחרים אבל עכשיו שמניחה בגמר קציר השד' העניים רואין ובאין:

תורה אור

תוספות

מכבה ומגביהה ומניחה וחוזר ומדליק מיבעי ליה · וא"ת אמאי מכבה וחוזר ומדליק בהגבהה סגי כיון דהנחה עושה מצוה דאטו מי גרע דלוקה ועומדת מהדליקה חש"ו וי"ל דמיירי שהדליקה מתחלתה לצורך שבת ולכך גרע. מהדליקה חש"ו דהתם שמדליקה בעתה ניכר הדבר שהיא מדליקה לשם חנוכה · ריב"א:

שמע מינה הדלקה עושה מצוה · וא"כ מותר להדליק מנר לנר ומכל מקום כיון שנהגו העולם להחמיר אין לשנות המנהג:

מריש הוה מהדר מר אמשחא דשומשמי · נראה דאנר חנוכה קאי ומשום טעמא דמסיק דנפיש נהוריה טפי אבל לנר שבת פשיטא דשמן זית מצוה מן המובחר לפי שנמשך אחר הפתילה טפי מכולהו כדמוכח במתניתין דכולהו מודו ביה דמדליקין:

כל השרפים יפים לדיו · פירש בקונטרס שרף גומא ואין נראה לר"ת דהא דיו אין זה גומא כדאמרינן בפ"ב דגיטין (דף יט. ושם) בכל כותבין בדיו בסם ובסקרא ובקומוס ומפרש בגמרא קומוס גומא ודיו נמי אין זה מי עפצים שרגילין להניח בהן גומא דהא בברייתא קתני התם כתבו במי טריא ועפצא דהיינו עפצים כשר משמע דלאו היינו דיו דקתני במתניתין ועוד דכשר משמע דיעבד ובדיו היא עיקר הכתיבה ועוד דבפרק כל היד (נדה דף כ. ושם) אמרינן פלי קורטא דדיותא ובדיק דהיינו דיו שלנו שהוא קשה ולא של עפצים ואין דרך להניח גומא לתוך דיו שלנו אלא שרף [דהכא] הייני לחלוחית של אילן כמו שאנו עושין דיו שלנו וכן יש בנדה בפ"ק (דף י:) גבי בתולה זו שירפה מצוי וזו אין שירפה מצוי וכן בפ' כל שעה (פסחים לט. ושם) ירק מר יש לו שרף ופניו מכסיפין דע"כ ההוא שרף הייני לחלוחית ועל כן היה פוסל ר"ת ס"ת שאין כותבין בדיו שלנו דשאר לא מיקרי דיו כדפי' ואמרי' בפ' הבונה (לקמן קג:) כתבו שלא בדיו הרי אלו יגנזו ומוקמי' לה בהקומץ רבה (מנחות דף לד*) בס"ת:

הדר

[צ"ל בא"י אמ"ה שעשה נסים וכו' ושהחיינו וכו' וכ"א בסרי"ף וברא"ש]

[לפי פרש"י ד"ה והיה מחניך כו' סמיך הש"ס אסיפא דקרא כמ"ש תוס' כתובות כד· סד"ה אלו וכן כתבו בשאר דוכתא ועי' ב"מ קיד: מנין לערום שלא יתרום דכתי' ולא יראה בך ערות דבר ע"ש פרש"י]

עין משפט נר מצוה

לג א ב מיי' פ"ד מהל' חנוכה הל' ט סמג עשין ה טוש"ע א"ח סי' תרעה סעיף א:

לד ג ד מיי' שם טוש"ע שם סעיף ג:

לה ה ו ז מיי' פ"ד שם הל' יא סמג שם טוש"ע א"ח סימן רסג סעיף ז וסימן תרעו סעיף א:

לו ח מיי' פ"ה מהל' שבת הל' יא סמג לאוין סה טוש"ע א"ח סי' רסד סעיף ו וסימן תרעג סעיף א:

לז ט מיי' פ"א מהל' תפילין הל' ד סמג עשין כב טוש"ע א"ח סי' לב סעיף ג:

לח י מיי' פ"ג מהל' חנוכה הל' ד סמג עשין ה טוש"ע א"ח סי' תרעו סעי' א ב ג:

לט כ מיי' פי"א מהל' ברכות הל' ג סמג עשין כו:

מ ל מיי' פ"ג מהלכות חנוכה הל' ה וע"ש במ"מ:

מא מ נ מיי' פ"ד מהל' חנוכה הל' י סמג עשין ה טוש"ע א"ח סי' תרעא סעיף א:

מב ס מיי' פ"ב מהל' מתנות עניים הלכה יב:

מסורת הש"ס

[פסחים קח: מגילה ד· ערכין ג·]

סוכה מו·

[מס' סופרים פ"כ הלכה ו]

[בשאלתות סי' כו איתא רב נחמן בר יצחק] *ומברכין כיינו ברהמ"ז בג' ומזמנין בי' דאילו ברכת המוציא פשיטא דמברכין דאסו' ליהנות מהעוה"ז בלא ברכה [ת"י] לעיל יג· כתובות כד· כו: גיטין סא· [ביצה לה:] [מנחות לא·]

תוספתא דפאה פ"א ה"כ פ' קדושים

גליון הש"ס

גמ' איבעיא להו לגבל· עי' לעיל דף יח ע"א תוס' ד"ה אבל דיו:

רבינו חננאל

ובעי' (להדליק) [שידליק] מי שהי' חייב ובר מצות והנשים מדליקות עששיות שהיתה דולקת כל היום כולו לערב מכבה ומדליקה ואכסנאי חייב בנר חנוכה ואי משתתף באושפיזו או אם היה נסיב תו לא צריך · כל השמנים יפין לנר ושמן זית יפה מכולם המדליק ביום ראשון מברך להדליק ושעשה נסים וזמן · מיכן והילך מברך שתים ומניח זמן· היכן צונו דמברכין אשר קדשנו במצותיו וצונו להדליק רב נחמן בר יצחק אמר שאל אביך ויגדך כו' [רב] אויא אמר לא תסור מן הדבר אשר יגידו לך הנה צונו אלהינו לשמוע דברי הכמים ואקשינן וכי מצוה מדרבנן בעיא ברכה והתנן הדמאי מערבין בו ומשתתפין בו ומברכין ומזמנין עליו ומפרישין אותו ערום בין השמשות ואי אמרת דכל מצוה כדרבנן בעי ברכה היכי מברך ערום הא בעינן והיה מחניך קדוש ולא יראה בך ערות דבר וליכא ושני אביי ודאי דדבריהם כגון חנוכה וכיוצא בו בעי ברכה אבל דמאי דאפי' לרבנן ספק הוא לא בעי ברכה איני והא יו"ט שני דספק מדרבנן הוא ומברכינן ומשנינן התם הוא משום דלא ליזלזולי בה רבא אמר רוב עמי הארץ מעשרין הן לפיכך לא בעי ברכה בדמאי השתא כן רבנן דדייק ואמרי לענין נולד כשהוא מהול אע"ג דקיי"ל (כרבא) [כרבה] דאמר שמא ערלה כבושה הוא לפיכך צריך להטיף ממנו דם ברית בחול כיון שהוא ספק מדבריהם כד מהיל ליה בחול לא צריך ברכה כמו הדמאי · אמר רב הונא חצר שיש לה בב' פתחים בב' רוחות צריך ב' נרות דחיישינן לחשדא ומנלן דחיישינן דתני

ומפני ביטול עניים שלא יהו עניים יושבין ומשמרין עכשיו מניח בעה"ב פאה ומפני חשד שלא יהיו עוברין ושבין אומרים תבא מארה לאדם שלא הניח פאה בשדהו ומשום °בל תכלה אטו כולהו לאו משום בל תכלה נינהו אמר רבא מפני הרמאין: אמר רב יצחק בר רדיפה א"ר הונא [א]נר שיש לה שני פיות עולה לב' בני אדם אמר רבא [ב]מילא קערה שמן והקיפה פתילות כפה עליה כלי עולה לכמה בני אדם לא כפה עליה כלי עשאה כמין מדורה ואפילו לאחד נמי אינה עולה: אמר רבא פשיטא לי [ג]נר ביתו ונר חנוכה נר ביתו עדיף משום שלום ביתו נר ביתו וקידוש היום נר ביתו עדיף משום שלום ביתו בעי רבא נר חנוכה וקידוש היום מהו קידוש היום עדיף דתדיר או דילמא נר חנוכה עדיף משום *פרסומי ניסא בתר דאבעיא הדר פשטה [ד]נר חנוכה עדיף משום פרסומי ניסא: אמר רב הונא [ה]הרגיל בנר הויין ליה בנים תלמידי חכמים הזהיר במזוזה זוכה לדירה נאה הזהיר בציצית זוכה לטלית נאה הזהיר בקידוש היום זוכה וממלא גרבי יין רב הונא הוה רגיל דהוה חליף ותני אפתחא דרבי אבין נגרא חזא דהוה רגיל בשרגי טובא אמר תרי גברי רברבי נפקי מהכא נפקי מינייהו רב אידי בר אבין ורב חייא בר אבין רב חסדא הוה רגיל דהוה חליף ותני אפיתחא דבי נשא דרב שיזבי חזא דהוה רגיל בשרגי טובא אמר גברא רבא נפק מהכא נפק מינייהו רב שיזבי דביתהו דרב יוסף הות מאחרה ומדלקת לה אמר לה רב יוסף תניא * °לא ימיש עמוד הענן יומם ועמוד האש לילה מלמד שעמוד ענן משלים לעמוד האש ועמוד האש משלים לעמוד הענן סברה לאקדומה אמר לה ההוא סבא תנינא [ו]ובלבד שלא יקדים ושלא יאחר: °אמר רבא דרחים רבנן הוו ליה בנין רבנן[א] דמוקיר רבנן הוו ליה חתנוותא רבנן[ב] דדחיל מרבנן הוא גופיה הוי צורבא מרבנן ואי לאו בר הכי הוא משתמען מיליה כצורבא מרבנן: ולא בשמן שריפה וכו': מאי שמן שריפה אמר רבה [ז]שמן של תרומה שנטמאה ואמאי קרו לה שמן שריפה הואיל ולשריפה עומד ובשבת מ"ט לא כתוך שמצוה עליו לבערו גזרה שמא יטה א"ל אביי אלא מעתה ביו"ט לישתרי אלמה תנן *אין מדליקין בשמן שריפה ביו"ט גזרה י"ט אטו שבת רב חסדא אמר לשמא יטה לא חיישינן אלא הכא ביו"ט שחל להיות ע"ש עסקינן. לפי *שאין שורפין קדשים ביו"ט והא מדקתני סיפא אין מדליקין בשמן שריפה ביו"ט מכלל דרישא לאו ביו"ט עסקי' א"ר חנינא מסורא מה טעם קאמר מה טעם אין מדליקין בשמן שריפה ביו"ט לפי שאין שורפין קדשים ביו"ט

תניא

תורה אור
ויקרא יט
שמות יג

רש"י

ומפני בטול עניים · שלא היו יודעים מתי יקצור אותם: מפני החשד · שהעוברין רואין בגמר קצירו שהוא מכלה את הכל לא ידעו שנתנה כבר: ומשום לא תכלה · דמשמע שעת כילוי: אטו כולהו · הני דאמרן לא טעמא דלא תכלה קא מפרשי מאי שנא שעת כילוי: אמר רבא מפני הרמאין · העוברין על לא תכלה ואומרים כבר הנחנוה: שתי פיות · שהנרות שלהם של חרס הן ומכוסין ועושים לו נקב בלדי כסויו להכנים בו הפתילה והוא הפה ולמעלה בכיסויו יש נקב קטן וגם חלל יש למעלה מן הכסוי וממלאו שמן והוא נכנס דרך הנקב מעט מעט אם יש בו שני נקבים משני צדדין עולה לשני בני אדם למהדרין העושין נר לכל אחד ואחד: עשאה כמדורה · שהאש מתחברת לאמצעיתה ואינו דומה לנר: נר ביתו ונר חנוכה · נר ביתו בשבת והוא עני ואין לו כדי לקנות שמן לשתי נרות: שלום ביתו · והכי אמרינן לקמן (דף כה:) ותזנח משלום נפשי זו הדלקת נר בשבת שבני ביתו מצטערין לישב בחשך: בנים תלמידי חכמים · דכתיב (משלי ו) כי נר מצוה ותורה אור על ידי נר מצוה דשבת וחנוכה בא אור דתורה: דרבי אבין נגרא · חרש עצים: בשרגא · דשבת: חליף ותני · עובר ושונה כלומר עובר תמיד: דבי נשא[א] · אביו ואיכא דאמרי חמיו: נפק מינייהו דחתנו כנגו: מאחרה ומדלקת · נר של שבת סמוך לחשכה: לא ימיש · קרא יתירא הוא להך דרשה דהא כתיב וה' הולך לפניהם יומם: עמוד הענן · של יום משלים אורו לעמוד האש שהיה עמוד האש בא קודם שישקע עמוד הענן אלמא אורח ארעא בהכי: לאקדומי · בעוד היום גדול: תנינא · שונה אני: שלא יקדים · דלא מינכרא שהיא של שבת: דרחים · אוהב: הו ליה בנין רבנן·[ב] ואהבתו עליהם כאב על בן: ואי לאו בר הכי [ג] · שאינו רגיל לעסוק בתורה: ולשריפה עומד · שאסור באכילה: שמצוה עליו לבערו · דילמא אתי ביה לידי תקלה דאכילה: שמא יטה · כדי שיתבער מהר: ביום טוב · דליכא למיחש להטייה לישתרי בערב שבת · והוא צריך להדליקה מבעוד יום כמלא שורף קדשים ביו"ט ולקמן בפרקין (דף כד:) ילפינן מקראי דאין שורפין:

בברכת

תוספות

הדר פשטה נר חנוכה עדיף משום פרסומי ניסא · ונראה לרשב"א כשחל ר"ח טבת להיות בשבת שיש להפטיר בנרות דזכריה משום פרסומי ניסא ולא בהשמים כסאי שהיא הפטרת ר"ח ועוד כיון שהמפטיר קורא בשל חנוכה יש לו להפטיר מענין שקרא ומה שמקדימים לקרות בשל ר"ח משום דבקריאת התורה כיון דמלי למיעבד תרוייהו תדיר ופרסומי ניסא עבדינן תרוייהו ותדיר קודם אבל היכא דלא אפשר למעבד תרוייהו פרסומי ניסא עדיף ועוד דבקריאת התורה אין כל כך פרסומי ניסא שאינו מזכיר בה נרות כמו בהפטרה ועוד נראה לרשב"א דעל כן הקדימו של ר"ח כדי שהמפטיר יקרא בשל חנוכה ויפטיר בנרות דזכריה:

ה"ג חזא דהוו רגילי בשרגא · פי' הבעל והאשה לכך אמר תרי גברי רברבי נפקי מהכא ולקמן אמר חזא דהוה רגילה האשה לבדה לכך קאמר דנפיק חד גברא רבא בזוגתה:

דבי נשא דרב שיזבי · אומר ר"ת דכבר נפטר אביו לכך קאמר בהאי לישנא דאי מחיים הוה ליה למימר דבי אבוה ואומר ר"ת בשם רבינו שמואל שכשכותבין כתובה אם אבי הכלה מחיים כותבין דהנעלת ליה מבי אבוה ואם כבר מת כותבין דהנעלת ליה מבי נשא ולרשב"א נרא' דאפי' מחיים אשכחן דקאמר בי נשא בפרק מי שהחשיך (לקמן דף קנו·) לוי בריה דרב הונא בר חייא אשכחיה לגבלא דבי נשא דקגביל וספי לתוריה בטש ביה אתא אבוה אשכחיה ט' ויכול לכתוב בכתובה כאשר ירצה*:

גזרה יו"ט אטו שבת · וא"ת בכל שמנים שאין מדליקין בהן בשבת נגזור יו"ט אטו שבת ובמתני' תנן אין מדליקין בשמן שריפה ביו"ט משמע דבשאר שמנים מדליקין וי"ל דבשאר שמנים דכיון דאין נמשכין אחר הפתילה כי שרי ביו"ט לא אתי למישרי בשבת דפשיטא הוא דאיכא למיגזר בהן שמא יטה אבל שמן שריפה אי שרי ביו"ט איכא למטעי ואתי למשרי בשבת כיון דנמשך אחר הפתילה לפי שאינו פשוט לעולם דטעמא דמתוך שמצוה עליו לשורפו גזרה שמא יטה הקשה ה"ר אליעזר דהכא מפרש רבה דטעמא גזרה יו"ט אטו שבת ולקמן (דף כה:) מפיק מקרא דאוא לבדו והשיב לו רבינו שמואל דע"כ לקמן הוי רבא שהוא אחר אביי והכא רבה שהרי משיב לו אביי תלמידו וגם פליג עליה רב חסדא חבירו אדקשה מאי פריך הכא אביי אלא מעתה ביו"ט לישתרי והוא גופיה מפיק לקמן דאין מדליקין בשמן שריפה מעולת שבת בשבתו ונראה לפרש דאביי ורבא לקמן לא קיימי אמאי דקאמר מ"ט אין מדליקין לפי שאין שורפין קדשים ביו"ט ולית להו האי גזרה [תרומה אטו קדשים] אלא קיימי לפרושי מנ"ל שאין שורפין קדשים ביום טוב ורשב"א מפרש הכי אלא מעתה ביום טוב לישתרי אי אמרת בשלמא דמיירי ביום טוב שחל בערב שבת וטעמא לפי שאין שורפין קדשים ביום טוב כדמוקי לה רב חסדא שפיר אלא כיון שאמרת טעמא דאין מדליקין בשבת גזירה שמא יטה השתא לא מצי לפרושי דביום טוב אין מדליקין לפי שאין שורפין קדשים ביו"ט דהא מה שייך יו"ט למיתני הכא כיון דביו"ט טעמא אחרינא הוא אלא צריך לפרש דביו"ט נמי שמא יטה ומאי יטה שייך ביו"ט ולפ"ז מתיישב לישנא אלא מעתה דמשמע שיש לפרש בענין אחר שלא יקשה ביו"ט לישתרי ולא קשה דאביי אדאביי ואם תאמר דהכא גזר רבה יו"ט אטו שבת ושבת גופיה שמא יטה א"כ סבר דגזרינן גזרה לגזרה וברים פירקין קאמר היא גופה גזרה והכן ניקום ונגזר גזרה לגזרה ולא

עין משפט נר מצוה

מג א מיי' פ"ד מהל' חנוכה הל' ד סמג עשין ה טוש"ע א"ח סי' תרעא סעיף ג:

מד ב מיי' שם טוש"ע שם סעיף ד·

מה ג ד מיי' פ"ד מהל' חנוכה הל' יד טוש"ע א"ח סי' רסג סעי' ג' וסי' רנו סעיף ה וסי' תרעח:

מו ה מיי' פ"ה מהל' שבת הל' א' סמג לאוין סה טוש"ע א"ח סי' רסג סעיף א ב:

מז ו [מיי' פ"ד מהל' חנוכה הל' ה] טוש"ע א"ח שם סעיף ד:

מח ז מיי' פי"א מהל' תרומות הלכה א:

[ועי' תוס' ב"ב קיב: ד"ה אמרה]

רבינו חננאל

דתני ר' שמעון בשביל ד' דברים אמרה תורה הנח פאה בסוף שדה מפני החשד כו' אמר רב הונא [נר] שיש לו ב' פיות עולה לב' בני א"ם אמר רב מילא קערה שמן והקיפה פתילות עולה מנין פתילות לבני אדם · אלו הן מן המהדרין שצריכין נר לכל אחד ואחד ואם לא כפה עליה כלי נעשת כמדורה ואפילו לאחד אינו עולה· אמר רבה נר ביתו עדיף מנר חנוכה ומקדוש היום משום שלום ביתו שנאמר (איוב ה) וידעת כי שלום אהלך ונר חנוכה עדיף מקדוש היום כדי לפרסומי ניסא· אמר רב הונא הרגיל בנר חנוכה הויין לו בנים ת"ח הזהיר במזוזה כו' · דביתהו דרב יוסף הוית מאחרה ומדלקה סמוך לחשיכה בע"ש · אמר רב יוסף תנינא לא ימיש עמוד הענן יומם וגו' מלמד שעמוד הענן משלים לעמוד האש כלומר בא עמוד האש ועדיין עמוד הענן קיים · סברה לאקדומי טובא תנא ליה ההוא סבא ובלבד שלא יקדים ובלבד שלא יאחר אלא בעת שקיעת החמה קודם כמעט תהיה הדלקה: ולא בשמן שרפה · יוקמה רב חסדא ביו"ט שחל להיות ע"ש עסקי' דבעי אדלוקי נר של שבת מבעוד יום ונמצא מדליקו ביו"ט ואין מדליקין שמן שרפה ביו"ט דקי"ל שאין שורפין קדשים ביו"ט ותניא

מסורת הש"ס

[ברכות יד·]

[לקמן כד:]

לקמן כה:
[מנחות מו:]

[תוספת' סוטה פ"ד]

הגהות הב"ח

(א) רש"י ד"ה דבי נשא· נ"ב ע"ל בדף קנו ע"ב מבואר דבי נשא פי' אביו: (ב) ד"ה הוו ליה בנין רבנן הואיל ואהבתו: (ג) ד"ה ואי לאו בר הכי הוא שאינו:

הגהות הגר"א

[א] גמ' דמוקיר רבנן נ"ל דדחיל מרבנן: [ב] שם דדחיל מרבנן. נ"ל דמוקיר רבנן:

גליון הש"ס

גמ' אמר רבא דרחים רבנן· עי' מכות יו"ד ע"א:

is *pe'ah;'*[11] [23*b*] and against wasting the time of the poor: that the poor should not have to sit and watch out, 'now the owner will leave *pe'ah'*; and against suspicion: that passers-by may not say, 'cursed be the man who has not left *pe'ah* in his field'; and against [transgressing] *thou shalt not finish off*: are not all these on
a account of, '*thou shalt not finish off*'?[1]—Said Raba, [It means, as a precaution] against cheats.[2]

R. Isaac b. Redifah said in R. Huna's name: A lamp with two spouts is credited to two people.[3] Raba said: If one fills a dish with oil and surrounds it with wicks, and places a vessel over it,[4] it is credited to many people; if he does not place a vessel over it, he turns it into a kind of fire,[5] and is not credited even to one.

Raba said: It is obvious to me [that if one must choose between] the house light and the *Ḥanukkah* light,[6] the former is preferable, on account [of the importance] of the peace of the home;[7] [between] the house light and [wine for] the Sanctification of the Day,[8] the house light is preferable, on account of the peace of the home. Raba propounded: What [if the choice lies between] the *Ḥanukkah* lamp and the Sanctification of the Day: is the latter more important, because it is permanent;[9] or perhaps the *Ḥanukkah* lamp is preferable, on account of advertising the miracle? After propounding, he himself solved it: The *Ḥanukkah* lamp is preferable, on account of advertising the miracle.

R. Huna said: He who habitually practises [the lighting of] the lamp will possess scholarly sons; he who is observant of [the precept of] *mezuzah*[10] will merit a beautiful dwelling; he who is observant of fringes[11] will merit a beautiful garment; he who is observant of the Sanctification of the Day will be privileged to fill barrels of wine.[12]

R. Huna was accustomed frequently to pass the door of R. Abin the carpenter.[13] Seeing that he habitually lit many lights, he remarked, Two great men will issue hence. R. Idi b. Abin and R. Ḥiyya b. Abin issued thence. R. Ḥisda was accustomed frequent-
b ly to pass the house of R. Shizbi's father.[1] Seeing that he habitually lit many lights, he remarked, A great man will issue hence. R. Shizbi issued thence.

R. Joseph's wife used to kindle [the Sabbath lights] late.[2] [Thereupon] R. Joseph said to her, It was taught: *He took not away the pillar of cloud by day, and the pillar of fire by night*:[3] this teaches that the pillar of cloud overlapped[4] the pillar of fire, and the pillar of fire overlapped the pillar of cloud. Thereupon she thought of doing it very early. Said an old man to her: It was taught: Providing that one is not too early[5] or too late.

Raba said: He who loves the Rabbis will have sons who are Rabbis; he who honours the Rabbis will have Rabbis for sons-in-law; he who stands in awe of the Rabbis will himself be a Rabbinical scholar. But if he is not fit for this, his words will be heeded like those of a Rabbinical scholar.[6]

NOR WITH OIL OF BURNING. What is OIL OF BURNING? Said Rabbah, Oil of *terumah* which was defiled; and why is it called OIL OF BURNING? Because it stands to be burnt. And why is this forbidden for the Sabbath?—Since it is one's duty to destroy it, we fear lest he tilt [the lamp].[7] Abaye objected: If so, let it be permitted for Festivals.[8] Why did we learn: One must not kindle [the lamp] on Festivals with oil of burning!—Festivals are forbidden on account of the Sabbath.[9] R. Ḥisda said: We have no fear lest he tilt [it], but here the reference is to a Festival which falls on the eve of the Sabbath, and as for the prohibition, [the reason is] because sacred food[10] must not be burnt on Festivals.[11] But since the second clause[12] states, One must not light on Festivals with oil of burning, it follows that the first clause does not refer to Festivals?—R. Ḥanina of Sura answered: This [the second clause] states, 'What is the reason': what is the reason that one must not light [the lamp] on Festivals with oil of
c burning? Because sacred food must not be burnt on Festivals.[1]

(11) But now the poor will know when the end of the field is likely to be reached.
a (1) The other three are reasons why the Torah said this. (2) Who may not leave anything and maintain that they left *pe'ah* in the middle of the field. (3) Who each fulfils his obligations, i.e., where only one light is used; *supra* 21*b*. (4) So that the whole looks like a lamp with many spouts. (5) All the flames merge into one and create one great blaze; it does not look like a lamp at all then. (6) He cannot afford both. Rashi observes that this refers to the Sabbath. (7) V. *infra* 25*b*. (8) The Sabbath and the Festivals were sanctified over wine. (9) Coming every week; by comparison *Ḥanukkah* is temporary, coming but once a year. (10) V. Glos. (11) V. Num. XV, 38. (12) I.e., he will be wealthy. (13) Many of the Rabbis were workers or tradespeople, the office of the Rabbinate being unpaid in most cases.
b (1) So translated by BaḤ. (2) Just before nightfall. (3) Ex. XIII, 22. (4) Lit., 'completed'. (5) As it is not evident that it is lit in honour of the Sabbath. (6) This dictum was possibly a reproof of the hostility sometimes shown towards the Rabbis: cf. Sanh. 99*b*. (7) To accelerate it. (8) Since making a fire on Festivals is permitted. (9) Lest it be thought that the latter too is permitted. (10) Which includes *terumah*. (11) Even when, being defiled, it is unfit for food. (12) The Mishnah on 24*b*.
c (1) [The words, 'one must not light on Festivals with oil of burning' in the second clause, is another way of stating the rule that holy food must not be burnt on Festivals].

[24a] It was taught in accordance with R. Ḥisda: All those [materials] concerning which the Rabbis ruled, One must not light therewith on Sabbath, may be used for lighting on Festivals, except oil of burning,[2] because sacred food must not be burnt on Festivals.

The scholars propounded: Is *Ḥanukkah* to be mentioned in grace after meals? Since it is a Rabbinical [institution], we do not mention it; or perhaps it is mentioned to give publicity to the miracle?—Said Raba in R. Seḥora's name in R. Huna's name: It need not be mentioned; yet if one comes to mention it, he does so in the 'Thanks' [benediction].[3] R. Huna b. Judah chanced to visit Raba's academy [and] thought to mention it [*Ḥanukkah*] in [the benediction] 'he will rebuild Jerusalem.'[4] Said R. Shesheth to them [the scholars], It is as the Prayer:[5] just as [it is inserted in] the Prayer in the [benediction of] 'Thanks,'[6] so [is it inserted in] grace after meals in the [benediction of] 'Thanks'.[7]

The scholars propounded: Is New Moon to be mentioned in grace after meals? Should you say that it is unnecessary in the case of *Ḥanukkah*, which is only Rabbinical, then on New Moon, which is Biblical,[8] it is necessary; or perhaps since the performance of work is not forbidden, it is not mentioned? Rab said: It is mentioned; R. Ḥanina said: It is not mentioned. R. Zeriḳa said: Hold fast[9] to Rab's [ruling], because R. Oshaia supports him. For R. Oshaia taught: On those days when there is an additional
a offering,[1] viz., New Moon and the weekdays of Festivals[2]—at the Evening, Morning and Afternoon [services] the Eighteen [Benedictions] are recited, and the nature of the occasion is inserted in the '*Abodah*;[3] and if one does not insert it, he is turned back;[4] and there is no Sanctification over wine,[5] and mention thereof is made in grace after meals. On those days when there is no additional offering, viz., Mondays, Thursdays,[6] Fasts,[7] and *Ma'amadoth*[8]—What business have Mondays and Thursdays [here]?[9]—Rather [say thus:] on the Mondays, Thursdays and the [following] Mondays of Fasts[10] and of *Ma'amadoth*[11]—at the Evening, Morning and Afternoon [Services] the Eighteen [Benedictions] are recited, and the nature of the occasion is inserted in 'Thou hearkenst unto Prayer';[12] yet if one does not insert it he is not made to repeat it,[13] and no reference is made on these [days] in grace after meals.[14]

The scholars propounded: Should one refer to *Ḥanukkah* in
b the Additional Services?[1] Since there is no Additional Service for [*Ḥanukkah*] itself, we do not refer to it; or perhaps it [the Sabbath and New Moon] is a day which requires four services?[2] —R. Huna and Rab Judah both maintain: It is not referred to; R. Naḥman and R. Joḥanan both maintain: It is referred to. Abaye observed to R. Joseph. This [ruling] of R. Huna and Rab Judah is [synonymous with] Rab's. For R. Gidal said in Rab's name: If New Moon falls on the Sabbath, he who reads the *hafṭarah*[3] in the prophetic lesson need not mention New Moon,[4] since but for the Sabbath there is no prophetic lesson on New Moon.[5] How compare! There, there is no prophetic lesson on New Moon at all; whereas here it [the reference to *Ḥanukkah*] is found in the Evening, Morning and Afternoon Services. Rather it is similar to the following: viz., R. Aḥadebuy said in the name of R. Mattenah in Rab's name: When a Festival falls on the Sabbath, he who reads the *hafṭarah* in the prophetic lesson at the Sabbath Afternoon Service[6] need not mention the Festival, since but for the Sabbath there is no prophetic lesson at the Afternoon Service on Festivals.

(2) [Although one may light therewith on Sabbaths, one may not do so on Festivals, v. Tosaf. a.l.]. (3) The second benediction of grace; so called because it commences with, 'we give thanks unto Thee'. (4) The third benediction of grace. (5) The 'Prayer' *par excellence* is the Eighteen Benedictions; v. *supra 9b*, n. a3. (6) The eighteenth benediction. (7) The 'mention' is an added passage which relates very briefly the story of *Ḥanukkah*. (8) Cf. Num. XXVIII, 11-15. (9) Lit., 'in your hand'.

a (1) I.e., additional to the daily burnt-offering; v. Num. XXVIII, 1, *seq*. (2) The first and seventh days of Passover, and the first and eighth of Tabernacles have the full sanctity of Festivals, and no work, except what is necessary for the preparation of food, is permitted. The intermediate days are of a semi-festive nature, other work too being permitted under certain conditions. (3) Lit., '(sacrificial) service', the name of the seventeenth Benediction. (4) To repeat the passage, because these are special occasions instituted in the Bible. (5) Lit., 'goblet'. V. *supra 23b*, n. a8. (6) On these days Reading of the Law forms part of the Service, as on the Sabbath. According to the Talmud (B.Ḳ. 82*a*) this was instituted by Ezra, so that three days should not pass without Torah. (7) Specially proclaimed for rain (Ta'an. 10*a*). (8) *Ma'amad*, pl. *ma'amadoth*, lit., 'posts': 'a division of popular representatives deputed to accompany the daily services in the Temple with prayers, and also a corresponding division in the country towns, answering to the divisions of priests and Levites' (Jast.). Each district sent its representatives on certain days; v. Ta'an. Mishnah 26*a*.

(9) This is an interjection. Why should I think that special mention must be made? The Reading of the Law is certainly insufficient cause. (10) In times of drought fasts were held on Monday, Thursday and the following Monday. (11) On these four days fasts were kept: Monday, Tuesday, Wednesday and Thursday; Ta'an. ibid. (12) The name of the sixteenth Benediction. (13) Because these are not Biblical institutions. (14) The first clause states that a reference is made on New Moon, in agreement with Rab.

b (1) Of the Sabbath and New Moon; these always occur during *Ḥanukkah*, which commences on the 25th of the month and lasts eight days. (2) The three stated above plus the Additional. Hence this Additional Service ranks as the rest, and requires a mention of *Ḥanukkah*. (3) 'Conclusion'. A passage of the Prophets, with which the Reading of the Law concludes. The passage generally had some bearing upon the portion of the Law, except on special occasions. On the origin and the development of the *hafṭarah* v. *J.E.* s.v. 'Haftarah' and 'Liturgy': Elbogen, *Der Jüdische Gottesdienst*, 174 *seq*. (4) 'Who sanctifieth the Sabbath and the New Moon', the conclusion of the last benediction after the *hafṭarah*. (5) This is the same reasoning as that which governs R. Huna's and Rab Judah's view above. (6) This is not mentioned elsewhere in the Talmud. Rashi quotes a Geonic responsum that a *hafṭarah* from the prophets was read in early times, until the practice was forbidden by the Persians. V. Elbogen, op. cit., p. 182.

תניא כוותיה דרב חסדא *כל אלו שאמרו אין מדליקין בהן בשבת מדליקין בהן ביום טוב חוץ משמן שריפה לפי שאין שורפין קדשים ביום טוב : איבעיא להו מהו להזכיר של חנוכה בברכת המזון כיון דמדרבנן הוא לא מדכרינן או דילמא משום פרסומי ניסא מדכרינן אמר רבא אמר רב סחורה אמר רב הונא אינו מזכיר ואם בא להזכיר מזכיר בהודאה רב הונא בר יהודה איקלע לבי רבא סבר לאדכורי בבונה ירושלים אמר להו רב ששת כתפלה *מה תפלה בהודאה אף ברכת המזון בהודאה : איבעיא להו מהו להזכיר ראש חודש בברכת המזון אם תימצי לומר בחנוכה דרבנן לא צריך ראש חודש דאורייתא צריך או דילמא כיון דלא אסור בעשיית מלאכה לא מזכרינן רב אמר ג מזכיר רבי חנינא אמר אינו מזכיר אמר רב זריקא נקוט דרב בידך דקאי רבי אושעיא כוותיה דתני ר' אושעיא *ד ימים שיש בהן קרבן מוסף כגון ר"ח וחוש"מ ערבית ושחרית ומנחה מתפלל שמונה עשרה ואומר מעין המאורע בעבודה ואם לא אמר מחזירין אותו ואין בהן קדושה על הכוס ויש בהן הזכרה בברכת המזון ימים שאין בהן קרבן מוסף כגון שני וחמישי (ושני) ותעניות ומעמדות מאי עבידתייהו אלא שני וה' וב' של תעניות ומעמדות ה ערבית ושחרית ומנחה מתפלל שמונה עשרה ואומר מעין המאורע בשומע תפלה ו ואם לא אמר אין מחזירין אותו *(ואין בהן קדושה על הכוס) ואין בהן הזכרה בברכת המזון : איבעיא להו מהו להזכיר של חנוכה במוספין כיון דלית ביה מוסף בדידיה לא מדכרינן או דילמא יום הוא שחייב בארבע תפלות רב הונא ורב יהודה דאמרי תרוייהו אינו מזכיר רב נחמן ורבי יוחנן דאמרי תרוייהו ז מזכיר אמר אביי לרב יוסף הא דרב הונא ורב יהודה דרב הוא דאמר רב גידל אמר רב ראש חדש שחל להיות בשבת המפטיר בנביא בשבת אינו צריך להזכיר של ראש חדש שאילמלא שבת אין נביא בראש חדש מי דמי התם נביא בדר"ח ליכא כלל הכא איתיה בערבית ושחרית ומנחה אלא להא דמיא דאמר רב אחדבוי אמר רב מתנה אמר רב יום טוב שחל להיות בשבת המפטיר בנביא במנחה בשבת א"צ להזכיר של יום טוב שאילמלא שבת אין נביא במנחה ביום טוב

ולית

בברכת המזון · בתפלה פשיטא לן שהרי להלל ולהודאה נקבעו כדאמרינן לעיל* : לא מזכרינן · לא חייבו להזכיר : אינו מזכיר· אינו צריך להזכיר : מה תפלה בברכת הודאה · דהא כולה מילתא דחנוכה עיקרה להודאה נתקנה : בהודאה · בברכת הארץ : ואומר מעין המאורע בעבודה· לבקש רחמים על ישראל ועל ירושלים להשיב עבודה למקומה לעשות קרבנות היום : שני וחמישי · משמע של כל שבתות השנה ומאי עבידתייהו לזוכרם ולחלקם משאר ימות השנה : של תעניות · שהיו גוזרים תעניות על הגשמים שני וחמישי ו[שני] במס' תענית (דף י·): ושל מעמדות · כלומר לימים של מעמדות שהיו מתענין ארבעה תעניות בשבת שני ושלישי ורביעי וחמישי ומעין המאורע דידהו תפלת תענית : ערבית · לילי כניסתן ואע"פ שאוכל ושותה כל הלילה מתפלל תפלת תענית מאחר שנכנס היום והכי נמי אמר רב הונא במסכת תענית (דף יא:) יחיד שקבל עליו תענית אף על פי שאוכל ושותה כל הלילה מתפלל תפלת תענית · ובתשו' הגאונים מצאתי ברייתא שנו רבותינו פעמים שאדם שרוי בתענית ואינו מתפלל ופעמים שאינו שרוי בתענית ומתפלל הא כיצד כאן בכניסתה כאן ביציאתה כלומר ערב תענית אע"פ שעתיד לאכול לאחר תפלה מתפלל תפלת תענית וליל מחרתו אף על פי שעודנו בתענית כשמתפלל תפלת ערבית אינו מתפלל תפלת תענית וסוף דברי הגאונים כתבו אבל אין אנו רגילים לומר ערבית ואפילו שחרית שמא יארע לו אונס חולי או בולמוס ויטעום כלום ונמצא שקרן בתפלתו : אין מחזירין אותו · דלאו דאורייתא נינהו : בברכת המזון · של ערבית בכניסתו וכ"ש ביציאתו שכבר עבר היום : של חנוכה במוספין · בתפלת מוספין דשבת ור"ח שבתוך ימי חנוכה מהו להזכיר על הניסים בהודאה : בד' תפלות · ערבית ושחרית ומוסף ומנחה וכיון שחובת תפלה זה היום אינה פחותה משאר תפלות של יום : אין נביא בר"ח · הכא נמי הואיל אלמלא ר"ח אין מוספין בחנוכה לא בעי לאזכורי : הכא איתיה (*בשחרית וערבית) ומנחה וכיון שהיום מחויב בארבע תפלות כולן כן זו : המפטיר בנביא במנחה בשבת · מצאתי בתשובת הגאונים שהיו רגילים לקרות בנביא בשבתות במנחה עשרה פסוקים ובימי פרסיים גזרו גזרה שלא לעשות וכיון שנסתלקו נסתלקו : אין נביא במנחה ביום טוב · ואף על גב דאיתיה שחרית הואיל ומנחה לאו משום יום טוב אתי לא מזכרינן :

ככל

ולא גזרי' נתן לתוך חלב מהותך שמן אטו לא נתן דבלא נתן נמי לא אסור אלא אטו שאין מהותך אע"ג דבחלב מהותך גזרינן גזרה לגזרה דגזרי' אטו שאינו מהותך ושאינו מהותך אטו שמא יטה הא לא חשיב גזרה לגזרה דכשאינו מהותך דואי יטה לפי שאינו נמשך אחר הפתילה אבל הכא משום שמלוה עליו לית לן למימר ודאי יטה ותירץ ר"י דהכא לא חשיב גזירה לגזרה דיו"ט ושבת כי הדדי נינהו כדאמרינן בפרק במה אשה (לקמן דף ס· ושם) גבי סנדל המסומר וקשה לרשב"א דהכא גזרינן יו"ט אטו שבת ובריש כל הכלים (לקמן דף קכד· ושם) מסקינן דלא גזרינן ושמא אין להשוות גזרות של חכמים זו לזו אותם שאינם במלאכה אחת : **גזירה** יו"ט אטו שבת · וקשה לרשב"א הא דתנן בפ"ג דביצה (דף כז: ושם) מעשה ושאל ר' טרפון עליה ועל החלה שנטמאת ואמרו לו לא יזוז ממקומם והשתא לרבה אמאי לא יזוזנה והא חזיא להיסק תחת תבשילו דלא שייך בה למיגזר יו"ט אטו שבת כמו בשמן ולפי טעמא דאין שורפין קדשים ביום טוב ניחא וצריך לדחוק דגזרינן חלה בשבת אטו שמן* :

תניא כוותיה דרב חסדא · וא"ת והא משמע חוץ משמן שריפה דאין מדליקין בשבת ולא ביו"ט והיינו דלא כרב חסדא דלדידי' מדליקין בשבת וי"ל דה"ק כל אלו שאמרו אין מדליקין בשבת מדליקין ביום טוב וכ"ש אותו שמדליקין בשבת מדליקין ביום טוב חוץ משמן שריפה שאף על פי שמדליקין בשבת אין מדליקין ביום טוב וכו' :

איבעיא להו מהו להזכיר של חנוכה בברכת המזון· תימה דהך מילתא הוה ליה לאסוקי לעיל גבי מילי דחנוכה :

מהו להזכיר של חנוכה בבהמ"ז · בתפלה פשיטא ליה דמזכיר משום דתפלה בצבור הוא ואיכא פרסומי ניסא אבל בבהמ"ז שבבית ליכא פרסומי ניסא כולי האי :

מזכיר בהודאה · דעל הנסים הודאה היא ולא תפלה :

בבונה ירושלים · כמו בר"ח שאומר יעלה ויבא בבונה ירושלים ומשום דיעלה ויבא היא תפלה ותחנונים תקנוה בבונה ירושלים דהיא נמי תפלה ובי"ח תיקנוה בעבודה שהיא תפלה להשב ישראל לירושלים : **או** דילמא כיון דלא אסור בעשיית מלאכה כו' · והא דאמר בפ"ג דמגילה (דף כב: ושם) כל שיש בו ביטול מלאכה לעם כגון תענית ציבור וט' באב קורין שלשה ושאין בו ביטול מלאכה לעם כגון ראש חודש וחולו של מועד קורין ד' היינו מנהג בעלמא שאין רגילין לעשות מלאכה* :

דתני ר' אושעיא (כוותיה) כו' · מהכא לא הוי בעי למיפשט לעיל דאינו מזכיר חנוכה בברכת המזון דאיכא למידחי דדוקא נקט תעניות ומעמדות אבל חנוכה ופורים אף על פי שאין בהן קרבן מוסף צריך להזכיר משום פרסומי ניסא ואיפכא ליכא למיפשט דדילמא נקיט תעניות ומעמדות משום תפלת מוסף והוא הדין דחנוכה ומיהו אף בחנוכה ופורים אם לא אמר בתפלה אין מחזירין אותו כדתניא בהדיא בתוספתא דברכות (פרק ת"ה) : **תעניות** ומעמדות ערבית שחרית ומנחה כו' · מה שפי' הגאונים שאין אנו רגילין לאומרה ערבית ואפילו שחרית שמא יארע לו אונס חולי או בולמוס ונמצא שקרן בתפלתו ומה שש"צ מתפלל שחרית היינו לפי שא"א שלא יתענה אחד מהם וקשה לר"י אם כן היאך לוה אדם תעניתו ופורע הלא ימצא שקרן בתפלתו קודם תקנת הגאונים ולעיל בפ"ק (דף יא·) דאמר ליזוף מר וליפרע הלא כבר התפלל תפלת תענית : **אלא** להא דמיא דאמר רב אחדבוי כו' · תימה תרתי מילתא דרב למה לי לאשמועינן יום טוב שחל להיות בשבת וכ"ש ראש חודש דליכא נביא כלל ותירץ ר"י דחדא מכלל חבירתה איתמר :

שאלמלא שבת אין נביא במנחה · וקשה לר"י דתנן בפרק שלישי דמגילה (דף כא· ושם ע"ש) בשני ובחמישי ובשבת במנחה קורין שלשה ואין מפטירין בנביא ותירץ ר"ת דנביא דהכא היינו כתובים שהיו מפטירין בכתובים בשבת במנחה כדאמר בפרק כל כתבי (לקמן דף קטז:) בנהרדעא פסקי סידרא בכתובים במנחתא דשבתא ובמגילה איירי בנביא ממש :

ולית

מסורת הש"ס

[דף כא:]

תוספתא פ"ב

[תוספתא ברכות פ"ג ע"ש]

פ"ח ל"ג

[נ"ל בערבית וכן שחרית]

עין משפט
נר מצוה

מט א מיי' פ"ב (מהל' תפלה הל' יג ופ"ב) מהלכות ברכות הלכה ו סמג עשין כז טוש"ע א"ח סי' תרפב סעיף א:

נ ב מיי' פ"ב מהל' ברכות הלכה ה סמג שם טוש"ע א"ח סי' תכד ·

נא ג מיי' פ"ב מהל' תפלה הלכה י סמג עשין יט טוש"ע א"ח סי' תכב סעי' א וסימן תל סעיף ב :

נב ד מיי' שם הל' יד טור וש"ע א"ח סי' תקסה סעיף א ג :

נג ה שם סעיף ב :

נד ו מיי' שם הל' יג סמג שם טוש"ע א"ח סי' תרפב סעיף ב :

עיין רש"א

רבינו חננאל

ותניא כותיה כל השמנים שאמרו חכמים אין מדליקין בהן בשבת אבל מדליקין בהן ביו"ט חוץ משמן שריפה שאין שורפין קדשים [פסולין] ביו"ט: אמר רבא מזכיר של חנוכה בברכת המזון כתפלה מה תפלה בהודאה אף ברכת המזון בהודאה אמר רב מזכיר של ר"ח בברכת המזון דתני רב הושעיא ימים שיש בהן קרבן מוסף כגון ר"ח וחוש"מ ערבית שחרית ומנחה מתפלל י"ח ואומרין מעין המאורע בעבודה ואם לא אמר מחזירין אותו ואין בהם קדושה על הכוס ויש בהן הזכרה בבהמ"ז · ימים שאין בהם קרבן מוסף כגון שני וחמישי ושל תעניות ומעמדות ערבי' ושחרית ומנחה מתפלל י"ח ואומר מעין המאורע בשומע תפלה ואם לא אמר אין מחזירין אותו ואין בהם קדושה על הכוס ולא הזכרה

[וע"ע תוספות מגילה יח: ד"ה ר"ח ותוס' ר"ה כב: ד"ה ותוס' מגילה כב: ד"ה ושאין]

ולית הילכתא ככל הני שמעתתא אלא כי הא דא"ר יהושע בן לוי *יום הכפורים שחל להיות בשבת המתפלל נעילה צריך להזכיר של שבת יום הוא שנתחייב בארבע תפלות קשיא הילכתא אהילכתא אמרת הילכתא כריב"ל וקיימא לן הילכתא כרבא דאמר רבא יו"ט שחל להיות בשבת שליח ציבור היורד לפני התיבה ערבית אינו צריך להזכיר של יום טוב שאילמלא שבת אין שליח צבור יורד ערבית ביו"ט הכי השתא התם בדין הוא דאפילו בשבת נמי לא צריך ורבנן הוא דתקוני משום סכנה אבל הכא יום הוא שנתחייב בארבע תפלות: ולא באליה כו': חכמים היינו תנא קמא איכא בינייהו *דרב ברונא אמר רב ולא מסיימי:

מתני' *אין מדליקין בשמן שריפה ביו"ט רבי ישמעאל אומר אין מדליקין בעטרן מפני כבוד השבת וחכמים מתירין בכל השמנים בשמן שומשמין בשמן אגוזים בשמן צנונות בשמן דגים בשמן פקועות בעטרן ובנפט ר' טרפון אומר אין מדליקין אלא בשמן זית בלבד:

גמ' *מ"ט לפי *שאין שורפין קדשים ביו"ט מנהני מילי אמר חזקיה וכן *תנא דבי חזקיה אמר קרא °ולא תותירו ממנו עד בקר והנותר ממנו עד בקר* שאין ת"ל עד בקר מה ת"ל עד בקר בא הכתוב ליתן לו בקר שני לשריפתו אביי אמר *אמר קרא °עולת שבת בשבתו *ולא עולת חול בשבת ולא עולת חול ביו"ט רבא אמר אמר קרא °הוא לבדו יעשה לכם הוא ולא מכשירין לבדו ולא מילה שלא בזמנה דאתיא בק"ו רב אשי אמר (שבת) °שבתון עשה

רש"י

ככל הני שמעתתא · רב הונא ורב יהודה ורב גידל ורב אחדבוי אלא כתפלה אחת כך חברתה לכל דבר היום ומזכיר: צריך להזכיר של שבת · לומר ותתן לנו את יום המנוח ואת יום הכפורים הזה וחותם מקדש השבת ויוה"כ ואע"פ שאין תפלת נעילה בשבת: יום הוא שנתחייב בד' תפלות · לאו תפלת הלילה בכלל אלא תפלות היום שחרית מוסף מנחה ונעילה: שליח ציבור היורד ערבית · המתפלל ברכת מעין שבע קונה שמים וארץ מגן אבות בדברו: משום סכנה · מזיקין שלא היו בתי כנסיות שלהן בישוב וכל שאר לילי החול היו עסוקין במלאכתן ובגמרן מלאכתן מתפללין ערבית בביתן ולא היו באין בבית הכנסת אבל לילי שבת באין בבית הכנסת וחשו שיש שאין ממהרין לבא ושוהין לאחר תפלה לכך האריכו תפלת הצבור: *הכי גרסינן נחום(א) אומר מדליקין בחלב מבושל· והוא מהותך: היינו ת"ק · דאמר ולא בחלב כל חלב במשמע: דרב ברונא · דשרי ע"י תערובת שמן כל שהוא: ולא מסיימי · אין ניכר מי אוסר ומי מתיר: מתני' שמן שריפה · שמן של תרומה טמאה ובגמ' מפרש טעמא: רבי ישמעאל אומר כו' · בשבת: עטרן · °פסולתא דזיפתא: מפני כבוד השבת · שריחו רע: שמן שומשמין כו' · מסקנא דמילתא דחכמים היא: צנונות · לנון: שמן דגים · °מקרבי דגים שנימוחו: פקועות · °דלעת מדברי: נפט · מין שמן שריחו רע כדאמרינן בסדר יומא (דף לט·) בא למדוד נפט אומרים לו מדוד לעצמך שאין אדם רוצה לסייעו: גמ' מנהני מילי · דאין שורפין דאי לא ממעט לה קרא אית לן למימר ליתי עשה דבאש תשרופו וידחה את לא תעשה כל מלאכה: שאין ת"ל עד בקר · זימנא אחריתי אלא והנותר ממנו באש תשרופו דהא כתיב עד בקר ברישא: בקר שני · שהוא חולו של מועד והכי משמע והנותר ממנו לבקר ראשון עד בקר שני המתינו ותשרפהו: עולת חול · כגון אברי תמיד של ערב יו"ט שלא הוקטרו מבעוד יום אין מעלין אותן משחשכה וכ"ש קדשים פסולים לא שרפינן: הוא לבדו · קראי יתירי נינהו דמצי למכתב אך אשר יאכל לכל נפש יעשה לכם: מכשירין · מכשירי האוכל כגון לעשות שפוד וסכין ותנור וכירים: לבדו · למעוטי מילה שלא בזמנה דלא דחיא שבת ויו"ט דאי לא מעטיה קרא אתיא בק"ו דתידחי בפ' ר' אליעזר (לקמן קלב:) דהכי תניא התם ומה צרעת שדוחה את עבודה ועבודה דוחה את השבת מילה שלא בזמנה דוחה אותה דהכי תניא התם מילה דוחה את הצרעת בין בזמנה בין שלא בזמנה ויליף לה מקראי שבת שנדחית מפני עבודה אינו דין שתהא מילה שלא בזמנה דוחה אותה אתא לבדו לאפוקי מהאי ק"ו דלא תדרוש ליה וממילא שמעינן מינה דמצוה שאין זמנה קבוע ויכול לעשותה למחר אינה דוחה יום טוב וה"ה לשריפת קדשים טמאים:

עשה

תוספות

ולית הילכתא ככל הני שמעתתא · פי' בקונטרס כרב הונא ורב יהודה ורב גידל ורב אחדבוי ואומר ר"י דלא ה"נ לו למנות דרב גידל בהדייהו דאפילו ריב"ל מודה דאין צריך להזכיר של ראש חדש בנביא כיון דנביא בר"ח ליכא כלל וכן אנו נוהגין שלא להזכיר*: איכא בינייהו דרב ברונא אמר רב ולא מסיימי · הקשה ריב"א אמאי לא מסיימי והא אמר בהמוכר פירות (ב"ב דף קנ:) דכל תנא בתרא לטפויי אתא °וי"ל דהכא דאיכא ג' תנאים איכא למימר דלא אתא לטפויי אלא אנחום המדי דאמר מדליקין בחלב מבושל בעיניה ואתו חכמים למימר אפילו במבושל אין מדליקין בעיניה אבל בנתינת שמן לתוכו מותר וטעמא דת"ק נמי איכא למימר דאסר בנתינת שמן דומיא דזפת ושעוה ולא מסיימי משום דאיכא למימר תנא בתרא לטפויי אתא: לפי שאין שורפין קדשים ביו"ט · וא"ת היכי ילפינן תרומה מקדשים דקדשים דין הוא שאין שריפתן דוחה יו"ט לפי שאין יכול ליהנות בשעת שריפה ולא אמרינן מתוך שהותרה הבערה לצורך הותר' נמי שלא לצורך אלא שלא לצורך אוכל נפש אבל צריך שיהא קצת צורך להתחמם או לשום הנאה אבל הבערה דגמרי שלא לצורך לא הותרה אלא שריפת תרומה טמאה שמותר ליהנו' בשעת שריפה למה יאסר מאי שנא משמן חולין שמותר לשורפו ולהדליקו להנאתו דאטו תרומה לפי שיש מצוה בשריפתה מיגרע גרע ואומר ריב"א דודאי גרע *דכיון שאסרה תורה כל הנאות רק הנאת שריפה אם כן הבערה זו אינה לצורך הנאתו אלא לשם מצות שריפה אלא שהתורה לא הקפידה שיהנה ממנה בשעת ביעור' והכי לא דחיא יו"ט מידי דהוה אנדרים ונדבות *דאין קרבים ביו"ט למ"ד משלחן גבוה קא זכו וכן שתי הלחם לדידיה אין אפייתן דוחה יו"ט אע"פ שיש בהן אכילת אדם משום דעיקרן לצורך גבוה ולמ"ד קריבין ביו"ט היינו משום דקסבר דעיקר שחיטתן ואפייתן נמי לצורך אדם אבל שריפת תרומה טמאה ודאי לשם מצות ביעור ולא לשם הנאה הלכך אסור ביו"ט כשאר קדשים ולר"י נראה דלא שייך בשריפת תרומה לומר משולחן גבוה קא זכו ולא דמו לשתי הלחם שהאפייה היא לצורך גבוה שהרי אחר אפייה צריך לעשות בהם תנופה וכן אחר שחיטת נדרים ונדבות עושין מהן לגבוה אבל תרומה טמאה אין עושין ממנה לגבוה כלום וליכא למימר בה משולחן גבוה קא זכו והכי מפרש ר"י לפי שאין שורפין קדשים ביו"ט פי' גזרו תרומה אטו קדשים *וא"ת ומאי איריא אטו קדשים משום דאין שורפין קדשים ביו"ט °נגזור משום תרומה שלא לצורך דאפילו שורפין קדשים ביו"ט דאתי עשה ודחי לא תעשה תרומה שלא לצורך אין שורפין דמשמע מתוך פרש"י בסמוך דאין עשה בשריפתה אלא מדרבנן וי"ל דשריפת תרומה שלא לצורך לא שכיח דשום אדם לא ישרפנה חנם כיון שיכול ליהנות בשריפתה וכדמוכח בירושלמי כלשון הזה: בקר שני לשריפתו · וא"ת אי בקר שני דוקא ואינו יכול לשורפו בליל מוצאי יו"ט היכי מוכח דאין שריפת קדשים דוחה יום טוב הא ע"כ אינו מטעם דאין שריפת קדשים דוחה יום טוב דהא בליל מוצאי יום טוב נמי אין שורפו ואם כן גזרת הכתוב הוא לשרוף בבקר שני וי"ל הא דאין שורפין בלילה היינו משום דהקפיד הכתוב שלא לשרוף הקדשים בלילה כדאשכחן בשלמים דאין נאכלין לאור שלישי ואפילו הכי אין נשרפין אלא ביום שלישי כדדריש בריש פסחים (דף ג· ושם) ביום השלישי באש ישרף ביום אתה שורפו כו': ולא עולת חול בשבת ולא עולת חול ביום טוב · תימה כיון דקרא בשבת איירי מנא ליה למדרש ולא עולת חול ביום טוב דילמא דוקא ולא חול בשבת דחמיר מיום טוב וי"ל דאביי סבר כרבי עקיבא דדריש בפרק אלו קשרים (לקמן דף קיד·) עולת שבת בשבת אחרת לימד על חלבי שבת שקריבין ביום טוב מדאיצטריך קרא למשרי עולת שבת ביום טוב אם כן עולת חול ביום טוב אסור דסבר נדרים ונדבות אין קרבין ביום טוב כדאמר התם ורבי ישמעאל פליג התם ודריש עולת שבת בשבתו לימד על חלבי שבת שקריבין בי"ה אבל שקריבין ביום טוב לא איצטריך דקסבר נדרים ונדבות קריבין ביום טוב: ולא מילה שלא בזמנה דאתיא בק"ו · פירש בקונטרס מה צרעת שדוחה את העבודה ועבודה דוחה את השבת מילה דוחה אותה שבת שנדחית כו' וקשה בפרק ר"א דמילה (לקמן דף קלב: ושם) לית ליה לרבא ה) האי קל וחומר דקסבר האי דצרעת דוחה את העבודה לאו משום דחמירא אלא משום דגברא הוא דלא חזי והר"ר יוסף פורת לא גריס דאתיא בק"ו

ה) ור"ת עשה ק"ו מאוכל נפש שלא נכרתו עליו [י"ג כריתות] ואיכא למיפרך מה לאוכל נפש שכן מצוה עוברת [ת"י]:

רבינו חננאל

בהחמ"ז ואשכחנא נמי דמזכיר של חנוכה בתפלת המוסף של שבת ושל ר"ח מכת כרבי יהושע בן לוי דאמר יוה"כ שחל להיות בשבת המתפלל תפלת נעילה צריך להזכיר של שבת יום הוא שנתחייב בד' תפלות והלכתא כרבא דאמר ש"צ היורד ערבית ביום טוב שחל להיות בשבת א"צ להזכיר של יו"ם שאלמלא שבת אין ש"צ יורד ערבית ביום טוב ומשום סכנה הוא בשבת אין ביום טוב לא אבל הא דאמר רב ר"ח שחל להיות בשבת המפטיר בנביא א"צ להזכיר של ר"ח שאלמלא שבת אין נביא בר"ח וגם זה שאמר המפטיר בנביא במנחה ביו"ם שחל להיות בשבת א"צ להזכיר של יו"ם שאלמלא שבת אין נביא במנחה ביו"ם בהני (תלת) [תרתי] לית הלכתא כוותיה דרב: ואקשינן אהא דתנן והכ"א אחד חלב מבושל ואחד שאינו מבושל אין מדליקין בו היינו ת"ק דתני לא באליה ולא בחלב ונחום פליג עלייהו ואמר מדליקין בחלב מבושל מכלל דת"ק אסר אפילו בחלב מבושל ושנינן יש לומר כן ת"ק סבר אין מדליקין בחלב מבושל בפני עצמו ואם נתן בהו שמן מותר כרב ברונא אמר רב נחום מתיר בחלב מבושל אע"פ שלא נתן בהו שמן ורבנן בתראי אסרי אפילו בשנתן בהו שמן: ומנא לן שאין שורפין קדשים ביו"ם חזקיה תני מלא תותירו אביי אמר עולת שבת בשבתו זו לבדה ולא עולת חול בשבת ולא עולת יו"ם בשבת וכן לא עולת חול ביו"ם רבא אמר כתיב הוא

רב נסים גאון

פרק ב לבדו ולא מילה שלא בזמנה הבאה מק"ו · עיקרה בפ' ר' אליעזר אומר אם לא הביא כלי מערב שבת (דף קלב) דת"ר מילה דוחה את הצרעת בין בזמנה בין שלא בזמנה יו"ט אינה דוחה אלא בזמנה ואמרי' (שם דף קלג) מנא הני מילי אמר חזקיה וכן תנא דבי חזקיה (שמות יב) לא תותירו ממנו עד בוקר וכו' והכין כתב אדוננו האיי גאון בפירושיה מילה אינה דוחה יו"ט אלא בזמנה ומי שעבר שמיני שלו אינו נימול ביו"ט ותנן (שבת דף קלז) קטן נימול לח' לט' לי' לי"א לי"ב ותני בה יו"ט אחר שבת נימול לי"א ואפי' י"ט שני אינה דוחה דקתני ב' ימים טובים של ראש השנה נימול לי"ב מנהני מילי ושמעתתא דעיקר דילה בגמ' דכיצד צולין (פסחים דף פג) דתנן העצמות והגידים והנותר כו' שאין דוחה לא את השבת ולא את יו"ט ואיתמרו בה הני ד' טעמי וקאמר רבה מילה הבאה שלא בזמנה לא דחיא יו"ט

עין משפט נר מצוה

[וע' תוספות כתובות כד. ד"ה לית]

נה א מיי' פ"ב מהל' תפלה הל' טו טוש"ע א"ח סי' רפב סעיף ג וסי' תכה סעיף ג:

נו ב מיי' פ"ב מהל' תפלה הל' ז טוש"ע א"ח סי' תרכג סעיף ג:

נז ג מיי' פ"ט מהלכות תפלה הל' יב סמג עשין יט טוש"ע א"ח סי' רסח וסי' תפז סעיף ג:

נח ד מיי' פ"ה מהל' שבת הלכה י סמג לאוין סה טוש"ע א"ח סי' רסד סעיף ג:

נט ה מיי' שם הל' יא טוש"ע שם סעיף ו:

ס ו מיי' פ"ג מהל' יו"ט הל' ח:

תוספתא פ"ב

[וע' מ"ש רש"י במשנה ביצה כו: ד"ה אלא בנשמטת וכו']

[פי' תוס' לעיל כג: ד"ה גזרה]

[ביצה יט.]

ספרי ליתא

[וע' תוס' פסחים מו: ד"ה לא מקרא ותוס' ביצה כו: ד"ה וכן]

מסורת הש"ס

[ביצה לעיל במשנה כ:]

[לעיל כא:]

[לעיל כג:]

[לעיל כג: וש"נ]

לקמן קלג. פסחים כג. תמורה ד: ע"ש

[צ"ל באש תשרופו שאין כו]

[פסחים נט:]

הגהות הב"ח

(א) רש"י ד"ה נחום המדי אומר:

גליון הש"ס

רש"י ד"ה עטרן פסולתא דזיפתא. עי' לעיל כ ע"ב ד"ה · ד"ה שמן דגים מקרבי דגים שנמוחו · עי' לקמן כו ע"א תוס' ד"ה איכא בינייהו: שם ד"ה פקועות דלעת מדברי · עיין בד"ה (מ"ב ד לש) ד"ה תוס' ד"ה איכא ביניהו דרב ברונא כו' וי"ל דהכא דאיכא שלשה תנאים · עיין כה ע"א תוס' ד"ה איכא ביניהו כתב נוספת: שם ד"ה לפי כו' נגזור משום תרומה שלא לצורך הוי רק דרבנן דמדאורייתא שרי הואיל ואי מקלעי אורחים מש"ה לא גזרי' בכך · והוי' דקושייתם ההוא דלעיל כג ע"ב ר"ת אמר כו' לפי שאין שורפין קדשים דאינו לא ס"ל הואיל גבי האופה מיום טוב לחול:

[24b] Yet the law is as none of these rulings, but as R. Joshua b. Levi's dictum: When the Day of Atonement falls on the Sabbath, he who recites the *Ne'ilah* Service[7] must refer to the
a Sabbath:[1] it is a day when four services are obligatory.[2] Then one law contradicts another! [First] you say that the law is as R. Joshua b. Levi, whereas it is an established principle that the law is as Raba. For Raba said: On a Festival that falls on the Sabbath, the Reader[3] who descends before the desk[4] at the Evening Service[5] need not make mention of the Festival,[6] since but for the Sabbath the Reader would not descend [before the desk] at the Evening Service on Festivals.[7]—How compare! There, by ritual law it is not required even on the Sabbath,[8] and it was the Rabbis who instituted it on account of danger;[9] but here it is a day when four services are a [statutory] obligation.

NOR WITH TAIL FAT etc. But the SAGES are identical with the first Tanna?[10]—They differ in respect to R. Beruna's dictum in Rab's name,[11] but it is not clearly defined.[12]

MISHNAH. ONE MAY NOT KINDLE [THE SABBATH LAMP] WITH OIL OF BURNING ON FESTIVALS.[13] R. ISHMAEL SAID:
b ONE MAY NOT LIGHT [IT] WITH 'IṬRAN,[1] FOR THE HONOUR OF THE SABBATH; BUT THE SAGES PERMIT IT WITH ALL OILS; WITH SESAME OIL, NUT OIL, RADISH OIL, FISH OIL, GOURD OIL, 'IṬRAN AND NAPHTHA. R. TARFON SAID: ONE MAY LIGHT [IT] WITH OLIVE OIL ONLY.

GEMARA. What is the reason?—Because sacred [commodities] may not be burnt on Festivals.[2] Whence do we know it?—Said Hezekiah, and the School of Hezekiah taught likewise: *And ye shall let nothing of it remain until the morning; but that which remaineth of it until the morning [ye shall burn with fire]*:[3] now [the second] '*until the morning*' need not be stated. What then is the teaching of, '*until the morning*'? Scripture comes to appoint the second morning for its burning.[4] Abaye said: Scripture saith, '*the burnt-offering of the Sabbath* [shall be burnt] *on its Sabbath*',[5] but not the burnt-offering of weekdays on the Sabbath, nor the burnt-offering of weekdays on Festivals.[6] Raba said, Scripture saith, [*no manner of work shall be done in them, save that which every man must eat,*] that only *may be done of you*:[7] '*that*', but not its preliminaries;[8] '*only*', but not circumcision out of its proper time, which might [otherwise] be inferred *a minori*.[9] R. Ashi said: [*on the first*

(7) The 'closing service'. Originally this was held daily in the Temple just before the closing of the Temple gates (cf. Ta'an. IV, 1). Outside the Temple a *Ne'ilah* service was held only on public fast days; subsequently, however, it was abolished and retained for the Day of Atonement only. Elbogen, pp. 68, 152.

a (1) 'Thou didst sanctify the Sabbath and this Day of Atonement'. (2) And the same applies to Festivals falling on the Sabbath. (3) Lit., 'the congregation messenger or representative'. (4) In Talmudic times the reading desk in Babylonian synagogues was on a lower level than the rest of the synagogue. (5) He recites the 'one benediction embodying the seven'. V. *P.B.* pp. 119f. (6) He merely concludes with 'Who sanctifiest the Sabbath'. (7) To read the benediction mentioned in n. a5. This runs counter to the view of R. Joshua b. Levi. (8) The repetition of the Eighteen Benedictions on weekdays and the 'seven benedictions' on Sabbaths and Festivals by the Reader was originally instituted on account of the uneducated, who could not pray for themselves. In the Evening Service, however, which in origin was regarded as of a voluntary character (v. Ber. 27*b*), this repetition was omitted, and the same should apply to the Sabbath too. (9) The Synagogues were situated outside the town, therefore the Rabbis prolonged the service by the addition of this passage so that latecomers might not be left alone in the synagogue and have to return home by themselves. (10) V. Mishnah on 20*b*. (11) *Supra* 21*a*. (12) Who accepts and who rejects that view. (13) V. *supra* 23*b*.

b (1) Jast.: a sort of resin used for lighting in place of oil. (2) V. *supra* 23*b*. (3) Ex. XII, 10. The reference is to the Passover sacrifice. (4) I.e., the sixteenth of the month, which was not a Festival, v. *supra* 24*a*, n. a2. This shows that its burning on the Festival is forbidden. (5) Num. XXVIII, 10. This is the literal translation of the verse; the E.V. is not so true to the original. (6) E.g., the animal sacrificed before the Sabbath or a Festival is not to be burnt the following evening. Hence sacrifices and sacred food in general, if unfit, may *a minori* not be burnt on Festivals. (7) With reference to festivals. Ex. XII, 16. (8) E.g., one may roast meat, but not construct an oven or make a spit for the roasting. (9) A child is circumcised on the Sabbath if it is the eighth day after birth (Lev. XII, 3), but not otherwise. This is deduced from '*alone*', which is a limitation. But for this one could infer *a minori* (v. *infra* 132*b*) that it is permissible. Thus we learn that when an act need not be done on a particular day, it may not be done on the Sabbath or Festivals, and the same applies to the burning of defiled sacred food.

day shall be] *a solemn rest* [Shabbathon][10] [25*a*] is an affirmative precept:[11] thus there is an affirmative and a negative precept in respect of Festivals, and an affirmative precept cannot
a supersede a negative and an affirmative precept.[1]

Thus it [the burning of defiled *terumah*] is forbidden only on Festivals, but on weekdays it is well.[2] What is the reason?—Said Rab: Just as it is obligatory to burn defiled sacred food, so it is obligatory to burn defiled *terumah*, and the Torah said, When it is burnt, you may benefit therefrom. Where did the Torah say thus?—[It follows] from R. Naḥman's [dictum]. For R. Naḥman said in Rabbah b. Abbuha's name, Scripture saith, *And I, behold, I have given thee the charge of Mine heave-offerings:*[3] the Writ refers to two *terumoth*,[4] viz., clean and unclean *terumah*, and the Divine Law said '[*I have given*] thee', [meaning], let it be thine for burning it under thy pot. Alternatively, [it follows] from R. Abbahu's [dictum]. For R. Abbahu said in R. Joḥanan's name: '*Neither have I put away* thereof, *being unclean*:'[5] '*thereof*' you may not '*put away*,'[6] but you may '*put away*' [burn] defiled oil of *terumah*. Yet [perhaps] say: '*thereof*' you may not '*put away*', but you may '*put away*' defiled oil of *ḳodesh*[7] which is defiled?—Does it [the reverse] not follow *a fortiori*: if tithe, which is light,[8] yet the Torah said, '*neither have I put away thereof, being unclean*'; then how much more so *ḳodesh*, which is more stringent? If so, in the case of *terumah* too let us say, does it [the reverse] not follow *a fortiori*?[9]—Surely '*thereof*' is written![10] And why do you prefer it thus?[11]—It is logical that I do not exclude *ḳodesh*, since it is [stringent] in
b respect of (Mnemonic: *Pa NaḲ 'aKaS*):[1] [i] *Piggul*, [ii] *Nothar*, [iii] sacrifice [*Ḳorban*], [iv] *Me'ilah*, [v] *Kareth*, and [vi] it is forbidden [*asur*] to an *onen*.[2] On the contrary, *terumah* is not to be excluded, since [it is stringent] in respect of its (mnemonic *Ma ḤPaZ*): [i]

(10) Lev. XXIII, 39. (11) For it intimates, rest therein.
a (1) The negative precept is '*no manner of work*' etc.; while the affirmative precept *to burn* what is left over is in Ex. XII, 10, quoted *supra*. Thus unfit sacred food may not be burnt on Festivals, and the same applies to unclean *terumah*. (2) One may benefit from the burning, e.g., by using it as fuel. (3) Num. XVIII, 8. Heb. *terumothai*, pl. of *terumah* with poss. suff. (4) Since it is in the plural. (5) Deut. XXVI, 14; v. whole passage. The reference is to the second tithe, and '*being unclean*' is understood as meaning whether the person or the tithe was unclean. (6) I.e., by using it as fuel. (7) V. Glos. E.g., that used in connection with the meal offerings; v. Lev. II, 1. (8) I.e., its sanctity is less than that of sacrifices. (9) For its sanctity is higher than that of tithes. (10) Implying a limitation as stated. (11) Lit., 'what (reason) do you see?'—Why exclude *terumah* by exegesis and include *ḳodesh a fortiori*? Perhaps it should be the reverse?

b (1) A mnemonic is a word or phrase made up of the initial letters of a number of other words or phrases, as an aid to the memory. (2) V. Glos. for these words. (i) *Piggul*, lit., 'abomination', is a sacrifice killed with the intention of eating it without the boundaries appointed for same; (ii) *nothar*, with the intention of eating it after its appointed time. These are the connotations of the words here, though elsewhere *piggul* has the meaning given here to *nothar* (Tosaf.). These unlawful intentions render the sacrifice an 'abomination', and it may then not be eaten even within its lawful boundaries and time on pain of *kareth*. (iii) It is designated a sacrifice (*Ḳorban*). (iv) If one puts it to secular use he is liable to a trespass-offering (*Me'ilah*). (v) *Kareth* is incurred for eating it in an unclean bodily state. *Kareth* (lit., 'cutting off') is the Divine penalty of premature death and childlessness, which is severer than 'Death at the hand of Heaven', which does not include childlessness.—Since *Ḳodesh* is so strict in all these matters, it is logical that the limitation does not apply to it.

עשה והוה ליה *יום טוב עשה ולא תעשה ואין עשה דוחה את לא תעשה ועשה ביום טוב הוא דאסיר הא בחול שפיר דמי מ"ט אמר רב כשם שמצוה לשרוף הקדשים שנטמאו *כך מצוה לשרוף את התרומה שנטמאת ואמרה תורה אבשעת ביעורה תיהני ממנה היכן אמרה תורה מדרב נחמן *דאמר רב נחמן אמר רבה בר אבוה אמר קרא °ואני הנה נתתי לך את משמרת תרומותי *בבשתי תרומות הכתוב מדבר אחת תרומה טהורה ואחת תרומה טמאה ואמר רחמנא לך שלך תהא להסיקה תחת תבשילך ואיבעית אימא מדרבי אבהו דאמר *רבי אבהו א"ר יוחנן °ולא בערתי ממנו בטמא ממנו אי אתה מבעיר אבל אתה מבעיר שמן של תרומה שנטמאת ואימא ממנו אי אתה מבעיר אבל אתה מבעיר שמן של קדש שנטמא לאו קל וחומר הוא *מה מעשר הקל אמרה תורה לא בערתי ממנו בטמא קדש חמור לא כ"ש א"ה תרומה נמי לימא ק"ו הוא הא כתיב ממנו ומה ראית מסתברא קדש לא ממעיטנא שכן סימן פנ"ק עכ"ס פיגול נותר קרבן מעילה וכרת אסור לאונן אדרבה תרומה לא ממעיטנא שכן מחפ"ז סימן מיתה חומש

ואין

תורה אור: ז"ל הניתר · במדבר יח · דברים כו

עשה הוא · דמשמע שבות בו : ואין עשה · דהוא לא תעשה ועשה ואע"ג דהדלקת נר ביו"ט מלאכה המותרת היא הואיל והבערת שאר קדשים שאין נהנין מהן נאסרין גם זו לא יצא מן הכלל : הא בחול שפיר דמי · לאיתהנויי מינה : מצוה לשרוף את התרומה שנטמאת · דדמיא לקדש ועוד משום תקלה : לא בערתי ממנו · במעשר שני כתיב : בטמא · בין שאני טמא בין שהוא טמא : קדש לא ממעיטנא · מהך חומרא : שכן · יש בו חומרי פנקעכ"ס וראוי גם לזו חייבין עליו משום פיגול שחט על מנת לאכול חוץ לזמנו ואכל אפילו בזמנו ומשום נותר חוץ לזמנו ממש ולא חשב מתחלה וקרוי קרבן ויש בו מעילה ואף על גב שקדש *(הנותר) [הניתר] לאכילת כהנים אין בהן מעילה מ"מ תורת מעילה שייכא ביה אם קדשי קדשים הן יש בהן מעילה לפני זריקה לכל הנאה מהן ואם קדשים קלים הן יש מעילה באימוריהן לאחר זריקת דמים לאפוקי תרומה דלית בה כלל : וכרת · לאוכלה בטומאת הגוף ותרומה במיתה בידי שמים ימיו נקצרים אבל אינו הולך ערירי : אסור לאונן · ק"ו ממעשר אבל תרומה מותרת לאונן ביבמות בפרק הערל (דף ע:) זר זר ב' פעמים זרות אמרתי לך ולא אנינות · אונן כל זמן שלא נקבר מתו : מחפ"ז · מיתה בידי שמים לזר האוכלה או כהן טמא וחומש לזר האוכלה בשוגג דכתיב (ויקרא כב) כי יאכל קדש בשגגה ויסף חמישיתו עליו אבל קדש מפעה שיש היתר לכהנים כתרומה ויצא מידי מעילה שוב אין חומש בשגגת אכילתו ויש דמוקמי לה בחומשין דחומשא ולא נהירא דהא רבינן ביה חומש דהקדש בפרק הזהב (בבא מציעא דף נד:) :

ואין

בק"ו דהא בלאו ק"ו נמי אתיא דאתי עשה ודחי לא תעשה ורב אשי הוא דמשני דיו"ט עשה ולא תעשה הוא ואין עשה דוחה לא תעשה ועשה וקשה לר"י דבפ"ק דבילה (דף ח: ושם) משמע *דאית ליה לרבא דיו"ט עשה ולא תעשה הוא גבי אפר כירה דפריך סוף סוף יו"ט עשה ולא תעשה הוא ואין עשה דכיסוי דוחה לא תעשה ועשה אלא אמר רבא כו' ודוחק למימר דהש"ס ניחא ליה למיפרך דיו"ט עשה ולא תעשה הוא דקי"ל כרב אשי אבל רבא אע"ג דלית ליה ליו"ט עשה ולא תעשה מ"מ אין כיסוי דוחה יו"ט מלבדו ור"י מפרש דאתיא בק"ו מנדרים ונדבות דדחו יו"ט אף על גב שלא נכרתו עליהם י"ג בריתות מילה לכ"ש וקסבר רבא דקריבין ביו"ט וליכא למיפרך מה לנדרים ונדבות שכן לצורך גבוה כדפריך בפ' ר' אליעזר דמילה (לקמן קלא:) מה לעומר ושתי הלחם שכן לצורך גבוה דהא לאו חובה נינהו ואפילו חטאות ואשמות לא מיקרו צורך גבוה כיון דאי לא חטא לא בעי לאייתינהו ואית ליה לרבא דיום טוב עשה ולא תעשה כדמוכח בבילה להכי איצטריך ק"ו דאי לאו ק"ו לא הוה צריך קרא למיסר ורבא לא קאי אשריפת קדשים אלא הש"ס מייתי משום דמיניה נמי שמעינן דאין שריפת קדשים דוחה יו"ט :

ה"ל יו"ט עשה כו' · וא"ת הנך אמוראי דלעיל דסברי דיו"ט לא תעשה גרידא נילף מהכא דלא דחי עשה את ל"ת וכי האי גוונא פריך בפ"ק דיבמות (דף ו·) ושמא מיכן לא נילף לפי שיכול לעשות אחר יו"ט [ת"י] :

הא בחול שפיר דמי מ"ט כו' · תימה מהיכא תיתי דתרומה טמאה אסורה בהנאה דבעי מ"ט אי ממעשר הקל כדמשמע בסמוך איכא למיפרך מה למעשר שכן הד"ס ט"ב כדפריך בהערל (יבמות דף עד:) וליכא למימר דהוה אסרינן ליה משום דאיקרי קדש דכתיב (ויקרא כב) ונתן לכהן את הקדש או משום דהוקשה לקדשים כדאמר במעילה בפרק הנהנה (דף יט·) דקדש אקשי רחמנא לתרומה וקדש גופיה אסור בהנאה כשניטמא אפילו אותו קדש שהיה מותר בהנאה קודם כמו שלמים נפקא לן שפיר מק"ו למעשר או מהיקשא דמעשר כדאמר בפרק כל שעה (פסחים דף כד·) דא"כ מאי פריך ומה ראית ואימא ממנו אתא למעוטי קדש ולא תרומה ואם נמעט קדש מהיכא תיתי איסור תרומה וי"ל דהוה גמרינן תרומה מדאיתקש לבכורים ובכורים למעשר כדאמרינן בהערל (יבמות דף עג:) ולקמן לא סמיך אק"ו אלא אהיקשא סמיך ומיהו קדש אתי שפיר בק"ו ממעשר כדאמרי' בפ' כל שעה (פסחים דף כד·) וליכא למיפרך שכן הד"ס ט"ב דכולהו איתנהו בקדש בר מוידוי ואר"ת דמוידוי לא שייך למיפרך דלא שייך וידוי גבי קדש אבל בתרומה שייך דהא אגב מעשר מתודה נמי אתרומה כדאמר *וגם נתתיו ללוי זו תרומה ואין לה וידוי בפני עצמה °וא"ת אכתי היכי יליף בק"ו קדש ממעשר הא איכא למיפרך מה למעשר שכן טעון כסף צורה כדפריך בפרק בתרא דמכות (דף יז:) ואור"י דלא שייך האי פירכא אלא דוקא גבי חוץ לחומה כדהתם דבעי למילף דאוכל תודה או שלמים חוץ לחומה דלוקה ממעשר ואם תאמר הכא אסרינן הסקה והדלקה באיסורי הנאה וערלה דאסורה בהנאה ושרי ליהנות בשעת ביעור כדאמר בפרק כל שעה (פסחים כז:) ולא משכח התם עלים לרבנן דאסורים אלא בשריפה וצריך לדחות ולומר דשמן ובשר ותבואה חשיבי בעין טפי בשעת היסק מעלים : **כך** אתה מצווה לשרוף את התרומה · פי' בקונטרס משום דלא ליתי בה לידי תקלה לפי טעם זה נראה דלאו דוקא שריפה אלא ה"ה שאר ביעור וכ"פ בהדיא בהלו עוברין ול"נ דבסוף תמורה (דף לג:) קתני תרומה טמאה בהדי הנשרפין וקתני התם הנשרפין לא יקברו ע"כ נראה דשריפה דוקא משום דדמיא לקדש °ומדרבנן א"נ מדאורייתא מדאיקרי קדש ואם תאמר דאמר בספ"ק דפסחים (דף כ:) גבי תרומה טמאה שתעשה זילוף הא תנן בתמורה הראוי לקבורה קבורה פירוש כגון משקין ויש לומר דלא קאי אלא אערלה וכלאי הכרם ולא אתרומה דשריא בהנאה* : **אחת** תרומה טמאה ואחת תרומה טהורה · ואף על גב דדריש רבי אליעזר (בכורות דף לד· ושם) אחת תרומה טהורה ואחת תלויה יניחנה במקום המוצנע ולא במקום התורפה דאסור לגרום לה טומאה התם דריש משמרת תרומותי משמע שתי תרומות לריכות שימור דהיינו טהורה ותלויה והכא דריש מלך : **שכן** פנקעכ"ס · תימה דמאי לאחשובי נמי דחמירי קדשים מתרומה בהא העריב שמשו אוכל בתרומה הביא כפרתו אוכל בקדשים* : **פגול** · היינו חישב לאוכלו חוץ למקומו ובכלל זה הוי אוכל חוץ לחומה דלוקה בקדשים ונותר היינו חישב לאוכלו חוץ לזמנו והוי נותר בכלל זה והוי האי פיגול ונותר כי ההוא דאם עון פיגול הוא הרי כבר נאמר לא יחשב ואם עון נותר כו' (פסחים דף טז:) ולא כמו פיגול שבכל הש"ס דקרי פיגול דחישב לאוכלו חוץ לזמנו דהיינו נותר דהכא: **כרת** · שאינו מגיע לששים שנה שהוא מיתת כל אדם כדמשמע בשילהי מ"ק (דף כח· ושם) דאמר התם רב יוסף כי הוה בר שיתין שנין עבד יומא טבא לרבנן אמר השתא נפקי לי מכרת א"ל אביי נהי דנפק מר מכרת דשני מכרת דיומי מי נפק מר פירוש כדאמר התם מת ביום א' מיתה של זעם שנים מיתה של בהלה שלשה מיתה של כרת ומיתה בידי שמים אין לה זמן קבוע אלא שמת בשביל עון זה אפי' אין בידו עון אחר ואפי' למ"ד (לקמן דף נה·) יש מיתה בלא חטא בשביל עון זה יקצרו ימיו ומיהו בירושל'* קאמר דכרת אינו מגיע לחמשים ומפיק לה מאל תכריתו את שבט הקהתי וגו' וזאת עשו להם וחיו פי' אמרה תורה עשו להם תקנה שלא ימותו בעבודתן קודם חמשים וכתיב אל תכריתו משמע כרת היינו שמת קודם חמישים ומיתה האמורה בתורה דקאמר התם היינו שמת עד ששים דכתיב במדבר הזה יתמו ושם ימותו ולא נגזרה גזירה אלא על בני עשרים שימותו קודם ארבעים וקרי לה מיתה אבל זרעו אומר ריב"א דאין בכרת אלא בהנהו דכתיב בהו ערירי ואין נראה לר"ת דהא בפרק הבא על יבמתו (יבמות דף נה·) קאמר ערירי דכתב רחמנא גבי דודתו למה לי לכדרבא כו' ואי אין זרעו נכרת אלא דוקא בהנהו דכתיב ערירי *מאי קבעי והא דלא קאמר במועד קטן (דף כח· ושם) נהי דנפק מר מכרת דשני מכרת דבני מי נפק מר התם מיירי כשאין לו בנים קטנים ודוקא קטנים נענשים בעון אביהם ולא גדולים כדמשמע בפירקין (דף לב:) ומיהו קשה דבתורת כהנים ממעט אשת אח מן האם מכרת מדכתיב אשת אחיו נדה היא מה נדה יש לה היתר אף אשת אח דיש לה היתר דהיינו מן האב דשריא כשאין לה בנים ובכולי הש"ס משמע דיש בה כרת כמו בשאר עריות דהא מני לה גבי חמש עשרה נשים פוטרות צרותיהן ולפירוש ריב"א אתי שפיר דמלינן למימר דממעט לה מערירי ואין להאריך [וע"ע תוספות יבמות נ: ד"ה אשה] :

תתן

עין משפט נר מצוה

סא א ב מיי' פ"ב מהל' תרומות הי"ד ופ"א ה"א טוש"ע י"ד סימן שלא סי"ט בהג"ה :

*ועי"כ אית ליה לרבא דיו"ט עשה ול"ת הוא דאי לא הוי אלא ל"ת גרידא אמאי מוקי קרא אמילתא דאיכא ק"ו ולוקמא בנותר או בשאר דליכא ק"ו ומיהו אכולהו ק"ו איכא למיפרך שכן נוהגים בנשים כבאנשים תאמר במילה שאינה נוהגת כ"א באנשים ואיכא למימר עולת ראיי' תוכיח דקריבה לב"ה ביו"ט · וא"ת בפרק ר' אליעזר דמילה דבעי למילף מילה שלא בזמנה דלא דחי יו"ט לחזקיה מנותר ולאביי מעולת שבת והיכא בעי למילף הא במילה איכא ק"ו [ת"י] :

רבינו חננאל

לבדו יעשה לכם הוא ולא מכשירין לבדו ולא מילה שלא בזמנה דאתיא בק"ו ומה מילה שנכרתו עליה י"ג בריתות שלא בזמנה אין דוחה יום טוב קדשים שלא נכרתו עליהן ברית אינו דין שלא ידחו יו"ט שלא בזמנם כגון קדשים שעבר זמנן שנעשו נותר וטעונין שריפה : **תרומה** טמאה ביו"ט אסור לשורפה הא בחול מותר מנלן אמר רבא כשם שמצוה לשרוף קדשים הפסולים בחול כן מצוה לשרוףהתרומה שנטמאת ואמרה תורה בשעת שרפתה תהנה ממנה שנאמר ואני נתתי לך את משמרת תרומותי בב' תרומות הכתוב מדבר אחת תרומה טהורה ואחת תרומה טמאה ואמר רחמנא בשתיהן נתתי לך שלך תהא להסקה תחת תבשילך להנות ממנה ור' יוחנן אמר מהכא לא בערתי ממנו בטמא (מן המעשר) ממנו אינו מבעיר בטמא אבל מבעיר בשמן תרומה שנטמאה : ואקשינן אמאי קא מרבית תרומה להנאה תרבה קודש שנטמא שמותר להנות ממנו ודחי' (קאי') ק"ו הוא ומה מעשר הקל (יום) [אם] נטמא אסור בהנא' קדש החמור לא כ"ש אי הכי תרומה נמי נימא ק"ו ותהיה אסורה בהנאה ודחי הא כתיב במעשר ממנו מכלל שיש אחר שמותר בהנאה כו' ומייתינן בק"ו הקדש שכן חומר מן התרומה כי הקדש יש בו חומרא שנעשה פיגול ונותר כי בשר הוא וקבוע לו זמן לאכילתו ואם עבר [הזמן] נעשה נותר והאוכל קודש וטומאתו עליו חייב כרת והנהנה מן הקדש מביא קרבן

רב נסים גאון

יו"ט מק"ו והיכי דאמי מה עצמות וגידים ונותר דפסח לא דחו ועולת חול לא דחיא יו"ט מילה שלא בזמנה לא כל שכן ושמעתי בה פירוש אחר בפנים

אחרות והכין איתמר לבדו ולא מילה שלא בזמנה הבאה בק"ו הראה כי המילה שלא בזמנה ביו"ט הייתי סבור שהיא מותרת מק"ו והיה לי לומר (א"כ) [דמה] עשיית אוכל נפש שהוא רשות כגון שחיטה ובישול ואפייה פטריה רחמנא עשייתו ביו"ט מילה שלא בזמנה שהיא מצוה לא כל שכן שתעשה ביו"ט לפיכך הוצרך לבדו להודיענו כי אוכל נפש לבדו מותר לעשותו ביו"ט ולא מילה שלא בזמנה ונדחה זה שהייתי סבור מק"ו בזה המיעוט שמיעט

מסורת הש"ס

[ביצה ח:]

תמורה לג:

בכורות לד· ע"ש יבמות עד· ע"ש

[יבמות פב: ולקמן כו.]

יבמות עג:

[פסחים כד·]

גליון הש"ס

תוס' ד"ה הא בחול וכו' וא"ת אכתי היכי יליף בק"ו · עיין זבחים קא ע"א תוס' ד"ה ומה מעשר : שם ד"ה כך אתה מצווה וכו' ומדרבנן אי נמי מדאורייי מדאיקרי קדש· עיין פסחים ס"ב ע"ב תוס' ד"ה אבל נטמא ול"ע :

[במעשר שני פ"ה מ"י]

[ועי' תוספות פסחים כ: ד"ה ראוי]

[ביבמות עג: ד"ה שכן וכו' כתבו בפשיטות מחוסר כפורים לא חשיב משום *מאי טעמא יפא נפקא לן וכו']

ב דבכורים

אע"ג דהוקשו כל עריות זה לזה דילמא אחות לאשוויה כ' כתובים הבאים כאחד. [ת"י]

ואין לה פדיון ואסורה לזרים הנך נפישן ואיבעית אימא קדש חמור שכן ענוש כרת *רב נחמן בר יצחק אמר קרא °תתן לו לו ולא לאורו מכלל דבת אורו הוא : רבי ישמעאל אומר כו': מאי טעמא אמר (א)רבא מתוך שריחו רע גזרה שמא יניחנה ויצא אמר ליה אביי ויצא אמר ליה שאני אומר *הדלקת נר בשבת חובה דאמר רב נחמן בר רב זבדא ואמרי לה אמר רב נחמן בר רבא אמר רב הדלקת נר בשבת חובה רחיצת ידים ורגלים בחמין ערבית רשות ואני אומר ג)מצוה מאי מצוה דאמר רב יהודה אמר רב כך היה מנהגו של ר' יהודה בר אלעאי ע"ש מביאים לו עריבה מלאה חמין ורוחץ פניו ידיו ורגליו ומתעטף ויושב בסדינין המצוייצין° ודומה למלאך ה' צבאות והיו תלמידיו מחבין ממנו כנפי כסותן אמר להן בני לא כך שניתי לכם *סדין בציצית בית שמאי פוטרין וב"ה מחייבין והלכה כדברי בית הלל ואינהו ג)סברי גזירה משום כסות לילה : °ותזנח משלום נפשי נשיתי טובה מאי ותזנח משלום נפשי אמר ר' אבהו זו הדלקת נר בשבת נשיתי טובה אמר רבי ירמיה זו בית המרחץ(ב)(*אמר רבי יוחנן) זו רחיצת ידים ורגלים בחמין ר' יצחק נפחא אמר זו מטה נאה וכלים נאים שעליה ר' אבא אמר זו מטה מוצעת ואשה מקושטת לתלמידי חכמים : ת"ר איזה עשיר כל שיש לו נחת רוח בעשרו דברי רבי מאיר : סימן מ"ט ק"ס : רבי טרפון אומר כל שיש לו ק' כרמים ומאה שדות וק' עבדים שעובדין בהן רבי עקיבא אומר כל שיש לו אשה נאה במעשים רבי יוסי אומר כל שיש לו בית הכסא סמוך לשולחנו *תניא רבי שמעון בן אלעזר אומר ד)אין מדליקין בצרי מאי טעמא אמר רבה מתוך שריחו נודף גזרה שמא יסתפק ממנו אמר ליה אביי לימא

דברים יח | איכה ג

רש"י

ואין לה פדיון · להוציאה לחולין אבל קדש יש קדש שנפדה כגון שהומם לפני שחיטה : ואסורה לזרים · לעולם אבל קדש יש קדש שמותר לזרים לאחר זריקה כגון מעשר בהמה ותודה ושלמים : הנך נפישין · בשם : כרת · עדיפא דאית בה תרי° חומרי ימיו נכרתין והולך ערירי : ראשית דגנך תתן לו ולא לאורו · מכאן שאין תורמין מן הטמא על הטהור דכתיב תתן לו דבר הראוי לו לאכול ולא לתת לאורו להסיק ומדאיצטריך למעוטי מכלל דבת אורו היא להסקה : ויצא · מאי איכפת לן : חובה · כבוד שבת הוא שאין סעודה חשובה אלא במקום אור כעין יממא בפרק בתרא דיומא (דף עה:) : רחיצת ידים ורגלים · ערבית ליל שבת: בסדינין המצויינין · סדינים של פשתן ובהן ציצית של תכלת כלאים אלא שמותר מן התורה דדרשינן סמוכין לא תלבש שעטנז גדילים תעשה לך (מנחות פ"ד לט·) : מחבין ממנו כנפי כסותן· שהיו להם סדינים שאינן מצויינין : בית שמאי פוטרין · ואף על גב דציצית חובה הוא בכל טליתות שיש לו לאדם ואפילו מונחים בקופסא הני דפשתן פטורין משום דכלאים לא שרא רחמנא דלא דרשי סמוכין:וב"ה מחייבין· דדרשי סמוכין: ואינהו סברי · [תלמידיו] שהיו אוסרין סבור נהי דהלכה כב"ה ג)מחייבין מדאורייתא מיהו [רבנן] גזור בהו משום כסות לילה שמא יהא לו כסות שמיוחד ללילות ויטיל בו ציצית ונמצא לובש כלאים שלא במקום מצוה דכסות לילה לא מיחייב בציצית דכתיב וראיתם אותו וביבמות *פרכינן וכי ב"ד מתנין לעקור דבר מן התורה לפטור את החייב ומשני שב ואל תעשה שאני : הדלקת נר בשבת · שלא היה לו ממה להדליק ובמקום שאין נר אין שלום שהולך ונכשל (ג)והולךבאפילה: איזהו עשיר· נפקא מיניה למטרח להדורי אמילתא: נחת רוח בעשרו · שמח בחלקו אם מעט אם רב : שעובדין בהן · בשדות עבודה הצריכה להם : שמא יסתפק ממנו · ותניא בתוספתא* הנותן שמן לנר חייב משום מבעיר והמסתפק חייב משום מכבה במסכת ביצה בגמרא דיום טוב (דף כב·) :

שהוא

תורה אור

תוספות

תתן לו ולא לאורו מכלל דבת אורו היא · ואם תאמר מידי ולא לאורו כתיב אימא תתן לו ולא דבר שאין ראוי לו כלל וי"ל דאם כן לא לכתוב אלא תתן דאין נתינה פחות משוה פרוטה° מדכתיב לו משמע לו ולא לאורו :

הדלקת נר בשבת חובה · פי' במקום סעודה דחובה היא שיסעוד במקום הנר משום עונג אבל מהדלקת נר גופיה לא הוה פריך אביי דפשיטא דחובה היא דהתנן (לקמן דף לד:) על ג' עבירות נשים כו' על שאינן זהירות בהדלקת הנר :

חובה · לגבי רחיצת (ד)ידים בחמין קרי ליה חובה דלא הוי כל כך מצוה ומים אחרונים קרי ליה חובה *משום סכנה דמלח סדומית שהרגו הנפש וחמירי טפי מנהראשוני' ויש שרוצים לומר דאין לברך אהדלקת נר מדקרי ליה חובה כדאמרינן (חולין קה·) מים אחרונים חובה ואין טעונין ברכה ואומר ר"ת דשיבוש הוא דלא דמי למים אחרונים דלא הוי אלא להצלה בעלמא אבל הדלקת נר היא חובה של מצות עונג שבת וכמה חובו' הן דטעונין ברכה ומה שאומר טעם אחר שלא לברך משום שאם היתה מודלקת ועומדת לא היה צרי' לכבותה ולחזור ולהדליקה ולא להדליק אחרת אין נראה דהא גבי כיסוי הדם (שם פז·) אם כסהו הרוח פטור מלכסותו אפ"ה כשמכסה צריך לברך וכן נולד מהול איכא למ"ד *דאין צריך להטיף ממנו דם ברית וכשמל תניא בשילהי פר' ר' אליעזר דמילה (לקמן דף קלז:) המל אומר כו' ובסדר רב עמרם יש המדליק נר בשבת מברך אשר קדשנו כו' ועוד נראה לר"ת שאם היה הנר מודלק ועומד שצריך לכבות ולחזור ולהדליק כדאמר ליה ההוא סבא ובלבד שלא יקדים ובלבד שלא יאחר (לעיל דף כג:) :

[לקמן קלה·]

מתוך שריחו רע · ואף על גב דנפט נמי ריחו רע כדאמר בפ"ק (דף יב:) הא בדמשחא והא בדנפטא ובפרק אמר להם הממונה (יומא דף לט·) בא למדוד נפט אומרים לו מדוד לעצמך אין ריחו רע כמו עטרן :

סדין בציצית ב"ש פוטרין · פירש בקונטרס ב"ש לא דרשי סמוכין והא דלא קאמר אוסרין משום דסברי בעלמא כלי קופסא חייבין בציצית והכא פטירי דלא שייך למיתני בהו אוסרין ובסיפא דהך ברייתא קתני בפ' התכלת (מנחות דף מ·) א"ר אליעזר כל המטיל תכלת בסדינו בירושלים אינו אלא מן המתמיהין אמר ר' אם כן למה אסרוה פי' *א"כ (כל אותן) שמתמיהין עליו למה עושין כן כיון דהלכה כב"ה ומשני גזרה שמא יקרע סדינו כו' ועוד מתרץ גזרה משום כסות לילה ופירש"י בתשובה אחת שלא גזרו אלא על התכלת אבל במינו חייב והא דא"ל *מלאכא לרב קטינא סדינא בקייטא סרבלא בסיתוא ציצית מה תהא עליה היינו ציצית מן המובחר מה תהא עליה אבל ציצית במינו היה עושה ובשמעתין נמי היה להם ציצית של מינו והיו מחבאים מר' יהודה לפי שהיה מחייב לעשות תכלת והיה סבור שעושין כב"ש מדאורייתא ואינהו סבור אפי' לב"ה אסור מדרבנן משום כסות לילה וקשה לר"י דבפרק התכלת (שם דף מא·) מהדר לאתויי דציצית חובת טלית הוא מחסידים הראשונים משארגו בבגד ג' היו מטילין בו ציצית ודחי לה ואמאי לא מייתי מהכא דלא קתני אוסרין ועוד דבה"ג פוסק דחובת גברא הוא מדמברכינן להתעטף בציצית ועוד דאמרינן בפ"ק דיבמות (ד' ד·) גבי כלאים בציצית דאפילו מאן דלא דריש סמוכין בעלמא במשנה תורה דריש ואיך יתכן לומר דב"ש לא דרשי סמוכין ועוד דרב עמרם גאון פוסק כב"ש בששה דברים וחשיב הך בהדייהו ועוד אמאי נקט סדין בציצית הוה ליה למנקט כלאים בציצית ונראה לר"ת דכ"ע דרשי סמוכין וב"ש פטרי מדרבנן משום כסות לילה או משום שמא יקרע ופטרי אפילו ממינו מדקתני סדין בציצית ולא קתני סדין בתכלת כדאמר ר' אליעזר בר' לדוק כל המטיל תכלת בסדינו כו' וב"ה מחייבין אפי' תכלת דלית להו הנהו גזרות דב"ש וכב"ש קי"ל כדמוכח בסיפא דהך ברייתא והשתא ניחא דרב קטינא שלא היה לו ציצית כלל וכן תלמידיו של רבי יהודה לא היה להם כלל ציצית דסברי כב"ש ואומר ר"ת דאין לעשות טליתות של פשתן ולעשות בו ציצית אפילו מינו דכב"ש קיימא לן דפטרי והמברך מברך ברכה לבטלה* :

גזרה משום כסות לילה · מדנקט סתמא דש"ס האי טעמא ולא נקט טעמא שמא יקרע משמע דקי"ל כרבי שמעון דפוטר כסות לילה בפ' התכלת (מנחות ד' מג·) וכן משמע בפ"ב דברכות (ד' יד:) דאמר במערבא לא היו אומרים פרשת ציצית בלילה אלא מתחילין דבר אל בני ישראל אמר אביי כיון דאיכהו מתחילין אנן נמי מתחילין וכיון דמתחילינן מסיימינן משמע דמודו כולהו דאין מצות ציצית בלילה ולכך נשים פטורות מן הציצית ורב יהודה ורב עמרם דהוו רמי תכלתא לפרזומא דאינשי ביתיה בהתכלת (ד' מג·) ובפרק קמא דסוכה (ד' יא· ושם) משום דסברי דהויא מצות עשה שלא הזמן גרמא לא קיימא לן כוותייהו דהא משמע שהם דווקא היו עושין ולא האחרים ובפרק קמא דקדושין (ד' לג:) תנו רבנן מצות עשה שהזמן גרמא שופר ולולב סוכה וציצית :

ולימא

סב א מיי' פ"ה מהל' שבת הלכה א' סמג לאוין סה טוש"ע א"ח סי' רסג סעיף ב :

סג ב מיי' פ"ל מהל' שבת הלכה ב' סמג עשין ל טוש"ע א"ח סי' רס סעיף א :

סד ג מיי' פ"ג מהלכו' ציצית הלכה ז סמג עשין כו טוש"ע א"ח סי' יח סעיף ב :

סה ד מיי' פ"ה מהל' שבת הלכה י סמג לאוין סה טוש"ע א"ח סי' רסד סעיף ג' :

[חולין קה:]

רבינו חננאל

מעילה ׳והוא קרבן לפיכך אסור לאונן משא"כ בתרומה כי לא תמצא מאלו כלום בתרומ' אע"פ שהתרומה יש בה מיתה שנאמר ומתו בו כי יחללוהו והנהנה ממנה משלם אותה וחומשה ואין לה פדיון ואסורה לזרים מה שאין כן בקודש כי השלמים מותרין לישראל שאין זרים ואם נפסלו*) יש להן פדיון אפ"ה חומרות דקודש נפישי : **אמרו** משמיה דרב הדלקת נר בשבת (חנוכה) [חובה] וכן אמר רבא הדלקת נר בשבת (חנוכה) [חובה] **) ורב חנן אמר אפילו רחיצת ידים ורגלים בחמין חובה ממנהג של רבי אלעזר וי"א רחיצת ידים ורגלים בחמין מצוה : **סדין** בציצית ב"ש פוטרין וב"ה מחייבין והלכה כב"ה : **ותזנח** משלום נפשי זו הדלקת הנר נשיתי טובה זו בית המרחץ רבי יוחנן אמר רחיצת ידים ורגלים

*) נ"ל אם נפסלו ע"י מום קודם שחיטה וכ"ה בפירש"י.

**) נ"ל דכן צ"ל רב חנן משמיה דרב אמר רחיצת ידים ורגלים בחמין ערבית רשות ואני אומר מצוה ממנהג של ר"י בר אלעאי.

[שם מא·]

רב נסים גאון

שמיעם בו הכתוב דהיינו לבדו ולולי הוא היה עולה על דעתנו כי מילה שלא בזמנה ביום טוב מותרת מקל וחומר: **אינהו** סבור גזירה משום כסות לילה׳ עיקר דילה במס' מנחות בפ' התכלת (דף מ) דתנו רבנן סדין בציצית בית שמאי פוטרין ובית הלל מחייבין והלכה כב"ה וכו' רב זירא אמר גזירה משום כסות לילה :

פסחים לג·

הגהות הב"ח

(א) גמ' אמר רבה מתוך שריחו:(ב) שם זו בית המרחץ רבי חייא בר אבא אמר רבי יוחנן זו רחיצת: (ג) רש"י ד"ה הדלקה וכו' ונכשל (והולך) תז"מ וכ"ב ס"א והולך: (ד) תוס' ד"ה חובה לגבי רחיצת ידים ורגלים בחמין דלא הוי (אב) כל כדמצוה קרי ליה חובה ומים אחרונים :

מנחות מ: עדיות פ"ד [מ"י]

[נ"ל ר' יוחנן אמר]

[דף ג:]

[תוספתא פ"ב]

[פ"ב]

א"כ כיון דהלכ' כב"ה למה עושין כן שמתמיהין עליו כצ"ל מהרש"א ובה"י א"י א"כ שמתמיהין עליו למה אסרו כיון דהלכה כב"ה :

[וע"ע תוספות יבמות ד: ד"ה כולהו ותוס' מנחות מ: ד"ה סדין]

גליון הש"ס גמרא ודומה למלאך ה' צבאות · עיין קדושין דף עב ע"א ברש"י ד"ה דומים למלאכי השרת : רש"י ד"ה כרת עדיפא דאית בה תרי וכו' · עיין בכרע"ב ספ"ט דסנהדרין : תוס' ד"ה תתן לו וכו' דאין נתינה פחות משוה פרוטה · עיין גיטין דף כ ע"א תוספות ד"ה דלמא :

Death [*Mithah*], [ii] a fifth [*Ḥomesh*], [25*b*], [iii] it cannot be redeemed [*Pidyon*], and [iv] it is forbidden to *Zarim?*[3] The former are more numerous. Alternatively, *ḳodesh* is more stringent, since it involves the penalty of *kareth*. R. Naḥman b. Isaac said: Scripture saith, [*The firstfruits of thy corn, of thy wine, and of thine oil . . .*] *shalt thou give* to him:[4] *to 'him'*, but not for its light;[5] hence it can be used for light [if defiled].[6]

R. ISHMAEL SAID etc. What is the reason?—Rabbah answered, Since it is malodorous, it is feared that he [the occupant of the house] will leave it and go out. Said Abaye to him, Then let him leave it! I maintain, he replied, that the kindling of the lamp on a the Sabbath is a duty,[1] for R. Naḥman b. R. Zabda—others state, R. Naḥman b. Raba—said in Rab's name: The kindling of the lamp for the Sabbath is a duty; the washing of the hands and the feet in warm water on the eve [of the Sabbath] is voluntary. Whilst I maintain that it is a *mizwah*.[2] How is it a *mizwah?* For Rab Judah said in Rab's name: This was the practice of R. Judah b. Il'ai: On the eve of the Sabbath a basin filled with hot water was brought to him, and he washed his face, hands, and feet, and he wrapped himself and sat in fringed linen robes,[3] and was like an angel of the Lord of Hosts. But his disciples hid the corners of their garments from him.[4] Said he to them, My sons! Have I not thus taught you: A linen robe, in respect to fringes—Beth Shammai exempt it, while Beth Hillel hold it liable, and the *halachah* is as Beth Hillel? But they held, It is forbidden on account of a night garment.[5]

And Thou hast removed my soul far off from peace; I forgot prosperity.[6] What is the meaning of, '*and Thou hast removed my soul far off from peace*'?—R. Abbahu said: This refers to the kindling of the light on the Sabbath.[7] *I forgot prosperity;*[8] R. Jeremiah said: This refers to the [loss of] baths. R. Joḥanan said: This means the washing of hands and feet in hot water. R. Isaac Nappaḥa[9] said: This refers to a beautiful bed and beautiful bedclothes upon it.[10] R. Abba said: This refers to a decked-out bed and an adorned wife for scholars.

Our Rabbis taught: Who is wealthy? He who has pleasure in his b wealth: this is R. Meir's view. (Mnemonic: *MaT KaS*).[1] R. Tarfon said: He who possesses a hundred vineyards, a hundred fields and a hundred slaves working in them.[2] R. Akiba said: He who has a wife comely in deeds.[3] R. Jose said: He who has a privy near his table.[4]

It was taught: R. Simeon b. Eleazar said: One may not light [the Sabbath lamp] with balsam. What is the reason?—Rabbah said: Since its smell is fragrant, there is [the need of] a preventive measure, lest one draw supplies from it.[5] Said Abaye to him,

(3) *Zar*, pl. *Zarim*, v. Glos. (i) If a *zar* or unclean priest eats *terumah*, he is liable to Death at the hand of heaven; (ii) if a *zar* eats it unwittingly, he must restore it and add a fifth; (iii) under no circumstances can *terumah* be redeemed and converted to *ḥullin*, whereas *ḳodesh* can be redeemed if it is blemished; and finally (iv), it is always forbidden to *zarim*. But certain sacrifices (*ḳodesh*) are permitted to *zarim* after the sprinkling of the blood, e.g., the thanksgiving and the peace-offerings. (4) Deut. XVIII, 4. (5) I.e., the priest must be able to use it himself, and not have to burn it for its heat or light. Hence defiled corn, etc., which may not be eaten as *terumah*, may not be separated as *terumah* for undefiled corn. (6) For otherwise, why exclude it?

a (1) I.e., the lamp must be lit where the evening repast is consumed. If the person leaves it and dines elsewhere he does not fulfil his obligation. (2) *Mizwah* denotes either a definite precept or something which while not actually commanded is meritorious. The latter is meant here. (3) The fringes were of wool. This constitutes a forbidden mixture (v. Deut. XXII, 11), and it is disputed by Tannaim whether this should be done. (4) Because they were not provided with fringes. V. next note. (5) A garment worn only at night is not subject to fringes; consequently, this forbidden mixture (v. n. a3) is then forbidden, since there is no precept of fringes to supersede it. The disciples held that Beth Hillel's ruling was Scriptural only; nevertheless it is forbidden by Rabbinical law, to avoid confusing night attire with day attire. (6) Lam. III, 17. (7) Jeremiah laments that they could not even afford this; loss of light brings loss of peace. (8) Lit., 'good'. (9) Or, the smith; *v. supra* 23*b*, n. a13. (10) Or, a beautiful couch and its appointments.

b (1) V. *supra* 25*a*, n. b1. R. *M*eir, R. *T*arfon, R. A*K*iba, and R. Jo*S*e. (2) The most famous dictum on wealth is in Ab. IV, 1: Who is wealthy? He who rejoices in his portion. Nevertheless, other Rabbis took a more material view of wealth, as here. Maharsha suggests that R. Tarfon intentionally states his case in an exaggerated form, to intimate that one who seeks wealth can never really attain it, unless he is satisfied with what he possesses. On that view R. Tarfon's statement really agrees with that in Aboth. Actually R. Tarfon was very wealthy, and Judaism is not opposed to wealth in principle. 'Despise not riches. Honour the wealthy if they are benevolent and modest. But remember that the true riches is contentment'.—Sefer *Ma'aloth Hammidoth*, quoted by M. Joseph in *Judaism as Creed and Life*, p. 388. (3) He spoke from personal experience: his wife stood out as a model of fidelity and trust, and it was she alone who enabled and encouraged him to attain his high position (Ned. 50*a*). (4) In a time when sanitary arrangements were very primitive and privies were situated in fields, this would be a sign of wealth, V. *T.A.* I, 48. (5) Which is forbidden; v. Beẓ. 22*a*.

[26a] Let the Master say, because it is volatile?[6]—He states, 'one thing and yet another.' One thing, because it is volatile; and yet another, as a preventive measure, lest he draw supplies from it.

A certain mother-in-law hated her daughter-in-law. Said she to her, 'Go and adorn yourself with balsam oil.'[7] She went and adorned herself. On her return she said to her, 'Go and light the lamp.' She went and lit the lamp: a spark flew out on her and consumed her.

But Nebuzaradan the captain of the guard left of the poorest of the land to be vinedressers [kormim] *and husbandmen* [yogbim].[8] '*Kormim:*' R. Joseph learnt: This means balsamum gatherers from En Gedi
a to Ramah. *Yogbim:* These are those which catch *ḥilazon*[1] from the promontory of Tyre as far as Haifa.[2]

Our Rabbis taught: One must not feed a lamp with unclean *ṭebel*[3] on weekdays, and all the more so on the Sabbath. Similarly, one must not light [a lamp] with white naphtha on weekdays, and all the more so on the Sabbath. As for white naphtha, that is well, [the reason being] because it is volatile. But what is the reason of unclean *ṭebel?*—Scripture saith, *And I, behold, I have given thee the charge of Mine heave-offerings* [terumothai]: [4] the Writ refers to two *terumoth*, clean and unclean *terumah:*[5] just as you enjoy nought of clean *terumah* save from its separation and onwards,[6] so also unclean *terumah*, you may enjoy nought thereof save from its separation and onwards.[7]

[To turn to] the main text: R. Simeon b. Eleazar said: One may not kindle [the Sabbath lamp] with balsam. And thus did R. Simeon b. Eleazar say: Balsam [*ẓari*] is merely the sap of resinous trees. R. Ishmael said: All that proceeds from trees, one may not light. R. Ishmael b. Beroḳah said: One may light only with the produce of fruit.[8] R. Tarfon said: One may light [the Sabbath lamp] with nought but olive oil. Thereupon R. Joḥanan b. Nuri rose to his feet and exclaimed, What shall the Babylonians do, who have only sesame oil? And what shall the Medeans do, who have only nut oil? And what shall the Alexandrians do, who have only radish oil? And what shall the people of Cappadocia[9] do, who have neither the one nor the other, save naphtha? But you have nought else but that concerning which the
b Sages said, One may not kindle [therewith].[1] And one may kindle with fish oil and '*iṭran*.[2] R. Simeon Shezuri[3] said: One may kindle with oil of gourds and with naphtha. Symmachos said: All that which comes from flesh, we may not kindle therewith, except fish oil. But Symmachos is identical with the earlier Tanna?[4]—They differ in respect to R. Beruna's dictum in Rab's name,[5] but it is not clearly defined.[6]

It was taught, R. Simeon b. Eleazar said: Whatever comes forth from trees is not subject to the law of three by three fingerbreadths,[7] and one may cover [a booth] therewith,[8] except flax.[9]

(6) Explosive and dangerous. (7) Anointing with oil is and was a common practice in the hot eastern countries; Krauss, *T.A.* I, 229 and 233. (8) Jer. LII, 16.

a (1) Purple-fish, used for dyeing *tekeleth*, a peculiar kind of blue. (2) יוגבים is derived from גוב 'to split', with reference to the splitting of the mollusc in order to extract the dye; v. *infra* 76a. (3) V. Glos. (4) Num. XVIII, 8. (5) V. *supra* 25a. (6) Clean *terumah* is used for human consumption, and before it is actually separated it is forbidden, even to the priest, i.e., he may not enjoy the produce in which it is contained. (7) Unclean *terumah* can be used only as fuel, and the analogy shows that this is permitted only when it is actually separated, but not while it is yet *ṭebel*. (8) Excluding fish and mineral oil, and oil tapped direct from the tree. (9) A district of Asia Minor.

b (1) You cannot add to the list of forbidden oils enumerated on 20b. (2) A sort of resin. (3) Of Shezor, supposed to be Sheghor, near Kefar Anan in Galilee, v. Neub., *Géogr.*, p. 278. (4) *Sc.* R. Joḥanan b. Nuri. (5) V. *supra* 11a. One holds that tallow, being flesh, may not be used at all, even if mixed with oil, thus rejecting the view expressed there, and the other maintains that the mixture is permitted. (6) Who accepts R. Beruna's dictum and who rejects it. (7) A piece of cloth three fingerbreadths square (or more) is liable to become unclean. R. Simeon b. Eleazar excepts the produce of trees, e.g., cotton cloth. (8) The booth (*sukkah*), in which one must dwell during the Feast of Tabernacles (Lev. XXIII, 42), must be covered with a material that is not liable to defilement (Suk. 12b); hence the produce of trees is fit for this purpose. (9) Even if not made up into a garment and as yet merely spun (v. *infra* 27b). Though not liable to defilement by reptiles it is subject to the uncleanness of leprosy.

תורה אור

לימא מר מפני שהוא עף חדא ועוד קאמר חדא מפני שהוא עף ועוד גזירה שמא יסתפק ממנו ההיא חמתא דהוות סניאה לה לכלתה אמרה לה זיל איקשיט במשחא דאפרסמא אזלא איקשיט כי אתת אמרה לה זיל איתלי שרגא אזלא אתלא שרגא אינפח בה נורא ואכלתה: °ומדלת הארץ השאיר נבוזראדן רב טבחים לכורמים וליוגבים (ירמיה נב) כורמים תני רב יוסף אלו מלקטי אפרסמון מעין גדי ועד רמתא יוגבים אלו ציידי חלזון מסולמות של צור ועד חיפה: ת"ר אין מדליקין בטבל טמא בחול ואצ"ל בשבת כיוצא בו אין מדליקין בנפט לבן בחול ואצ"ל בשבת בשלמא נפט לבן מפני שהוא עף אבל טבל טמא מאי טעמא אמר קרא °ואני הנה נתתי לך את משמרת תרומותי (במדבר יח) *בשתי תרומות הכתוב מדבר אחת תרומה טהורה ואחת תרומה טמאה מה תרומה טהורה אין לך בה אלא משעת הרמה ואילך אף תרומה טמאה אין לך בה אלא משעת הרמה ואילך: גופא ר"ש בן אלעזר אומר אין מדליקין בצרי וכן היה רבי שמעון בן אלעזר אומר *צרי אינו אלא שרף מעצי הקטף *ר' ישמעאל אומר כל היוצא מן העץ אין מדליקין בו ר' ישמעאל בן ברוקה אומר אין מדליקין אלא ביוצא מן הפרי ר' טרפון אומר אין מדליקין אלא בשמן זית בלבד עמד רבי יוחנן בן נורי על רגליו ואמר מה יעשו אנשי בבל שאין להם אלא שמן שומשמין ומה יעשו אנשי מדי שאין להם אלא שמן אגוזים ומה יעשו אנשי אלכסנדריא שאין להם אלא שמן צנונות ומה יעשו אנשי קפוטקיא שאין להם לא כך ולא כך אלא נפט אלא אין לך אלא מה שאמרו חכמים אין מדליקין ומדליקין בשמן דגים ובעטרן רבי שמעון שזורי אומר מדליקין בשמן פקועות ובנפט סומכוס אומר כל היוצא מן הבשר אין מדליקין בו אלא בשמן דגים סומכוס היינו ת"ק איכא בינייהו דרב ברונא אמר רב ולא מסיימי *תניא רבי שמעון בן אלעזר אומר כל היוצא מן העץ אין בו משום שלש על שלש ומסככין בו חוץ מפשתן אמר אביי

ר'

רש"י

שהוא עף · ונדבק בכותלי הבית ומדליק את הבית: חמתא · חמותה: איתלי שרגא · הדלק את הנר: עד רמתא · שם מקום: לכורמים · לשון מאספים כמו כורמים עליו את הכלים לקמן בפרק רבי עקיבא (דף פח:): וליוגבים · לשון יקבים שעוצרין ופוצעין את החלזון להוציא דמו כדאמרן בפרק כלל גדול לקמן (דף עה.) והניחם נבוזראדן ללבושי המלך: סולמא דצור · מעלה הר וקצרה המסילה וגבוהה וקורין אותה פוייאלא"ה: אין מדליקין בטבל טמא · וכ"ש בטהור ולקמיה מפרש טעמא: מה תרומה טהורה · שהיא לאכילה אין לך בה אלא משעת הרמה ואילך ומקמי הכי אסירא שהרי טבל במיתה לאוכלה אף תרומה טמאה אע"פ שאין אתה אוכלה אלא מסיקה אסור להסיקו בטבלו: אין מדליקין בצרי · כדמפרש לעיל ועוד כדקתני ואזיל דאינו בא מן הפרי אלא מן העץ שרף בעלמא והוה ליה כזפת ואינו נמשך ליסנא אחרינא וכן היה רבי שמעון בן אלעזר אומר כו' לאו טעמא למילתיה יהיב אלא הכי קאמר ועוד היה אומר דבר אחר בצרי: עצי הקטף · כך שמם: מן הפרי · לאפוקי שמן דגים ועטרן וצרי: אין לך אלא מה שאמרו חכמים אין מדליקין בהן · כגון פסולי שמנים דמתניתין: ומדליקין בשמן דגים · ואע"ג דדמי לחלב ואינו יוצא מפרי: ובעטרן · ואע"ג דמזפת קאתי: סומכוס היינו ת"ק · רבי יוחנן בן נורי דפסיל כל הנך דמתניתין וחלב אימני בהדייהו דהוא יוצא מן הבשר ואכשר בשמן דגים: איכא בינייהו דרב ברונא · דאמר צריך לתת לתוכו שמן כל שהוא אי נמי דאכשר חלב מהותך בתערובת שמן כל שהוא חד מהנך תנאי סבר לדרב ברונא דחלב ניתר בתערובת אבל שמן דגים אפילו בעיניה וחד סבר שמן דגים על ידי תערובת אבל חלב כלל וכלל לא: אין בו משום שלש על שלש · לקבל טומאה בג' אצבעות: יוצא מן העץ · כמו קנבוס וצמר גפן: ומסככים בו · סוכה הואיל ואינו מקבל טומאה דאין מסככין בדבר המקבל טומאה כדילפינן במסכ' סוכה (דף יב.) מגרנך ומיקבך: חוץ מפשתן · דילפינן לקמן דאיקרי עץ ומקבל טומאת נגעים אפילו אונין שבו כדלקמן הלכך אין מסככין באונין:

תוספות

ולימא מר מפני שהוא עף · ויבא בהול על ממונו ויבא לכבות תימה דה"ל למימר אפילו בחול נמי ליתסר כדאמר לקמן דאין מדליקין בנפט לבן אפילו בחול מפני שהוא עף:

חדא ועוד קאמר · וקשה לר"י דתניא בסמוך צרי אינו אלא שרף מעצי הקטף משמע דהטעם לפי שאינו נמשך אחר הפתילה ומה הוצרך לבדות הטעם מדעתו:

אין מדליקין בטבל טמא · פירש בקונטרס וכ"ש בטבל טהור ואין נראה דלא הוי כ"ש דמהיכא תיתי אלא ה"ה בטבל טהור דילפינן טבל טהור מטבל טמא מה טבל טמא אין לך בו שום הנאה של כילוי אלא מהרמה ואילך אף טבל טהור כן אבל הנאה שאינה של כילוי שרי דלא מצינו בשום מקום שיהא טבל אסור בהנאה ומהכא נמי ילפינן כהן ששכר פרה מישראל לא יאכילנה כרשיני תרומה (יבמות פ"ז דף סו:) דהנאה של כילוי אסורה לזרים אבל שאר הנאות שרי דתנן בפרק בכל מערבין (עירובין דף כו:) דמערבין לישראל בתרומה*:

רבי ישמעאל אומר כל היוצא מן העץ אין מדליקין בו · הא דלא קתני אלא פשתן כדקתני במתני' משום דמתניתין איירי בפסול פתילות והכא איירי בפסול שמנים קשה לרשב"א דרבי ישמעאל דתני במתני' דאין מדליקין בעטרן מפני כבוד השבת משמע שנמשך אחר הפתילה יפה אלא דגזרינן שמא יניחנו וילך כדמפרש לעיל והכא משמע כל היוצא מן העץ אינו נמשך אחר הפתילה ועטרן יוצא מן העץ הוא דהוא פסולתא דזיפתא כדאמר לעיל:

רבי שמעון שזורי אומר מדליקין בשמן פקועות ובנפט · *קשה לרשב"א מה בא לומר רבי שמעון שזורי דהא לרבי יוחנן בן נורי נמי מדליקין בהן מדקאמר אין לך אלא מה שאמרו חכמים אין מדליקין משמע דוקא הנהו אבל שמן פקועות ונפט מכשיר ועוד דנפט מכשיר בהדיא רבי יוחנן ואין לומר דרבי שמעון שזורי איירי בנפט לבן דהא אפי' בחול אמר לעיל אין מדליקין בו ואי גרסינן אין מדליקין במילתיה דרבי שמעון שזורי אתי שפיר:

איכא בינייהו דרב ברונא · פירש בקונטרס דחד מינייהו סבר דחלב מהותך שרי בתערובות אבל שמן דגים אפילו בעיניה וחד סבר שמן דגים בתערובות אבל חלב כלל וכלל לא והשתא תרוייהו לא סברי בכולה מילתא כרב ברונא ולא משמע הכי ובקונטרס דחק לפי שפירש במתניתין דשמן דגים היינו קרבי דגים שנימוחו ונראה לר"ת דשמן דגים היינו שמן שבא מעיטו של דג כדאמר בהמוכר את הספינה (ב"ב דף עג:) נגדו מגלגלתא דעינא תלת מאה גרבי מישחא ובשמן דגים מודה רב ברונא דשרי בעיניה והשתא חד מינייהו סבר לגמרי כרב ברונא:

ולא מסיימי · ולא שייך הכא תנא בתרא לטפויי אתא *דמוכח קצת דת"ק להחמיר מדקאמר אין לך אלא מה כו' ומדליקין בשמן דגים ובעטרן משמע דווקא הנך מדנחת לפרושי ולא פי' נמי דרב ברונא:

אין בו משום שלש על שלש ומסככין בו חוץ מפשתן · קשה לריב"א דמשמע דפחות משלש על שלש מסככין אפי' בשל פשתן ובפ"ק דסוכה (דף טז:) אמרינן סיככה במטלניות שאין בהן שלש על שלש פסולה ותירץ דהתם איירי דבאות מבגד גדול שכבר היו ראויות לקבל טומאה אבל הכא מיירי בהנהו שלא היה בהם מעולם שלש על שלש וקשה לרשב"א דאפי' אם לא נארג בו מעולם שלש על שלש מקבל טומאה כדאמר בפרק במה אשה (לקמן דף סג:) אריג כל שהוא טמא ואין מסככין בו וי"ל דהתם מיירי כשאין בדעתו לארוג בו יותר והכא מיירי כשיש בדעתו לארוג בו יותר הלכך אם אין בו שלש על שלש טהור:

רבי

[לעיל כה: וש"נ]

[כריתות ו׳]

תוספתא פ"ב

תוספתא שם

[פי' תוס' לעיל כה: ד"ה איכא בינייהו וכו']

[ועי"ע תוס' מנחות סז: ד"ה כדי שתהא והתוספ' פסחי' לג: ד"ה מחמין לו]

[לפי מ"ש תוס' בחולין פה: ד"ה אנא כי הא ס"ל כו' דר"ש שזורי דוקא קאמר ולא בא להוסיף אלא רק כהנך דקחשיב בלחוד מכשיר פ"ש אין מקום לקושית הרשב"א ודע עוד התם בחולין הביאו תוס' במלתא דר"ש שזורי בעטרן ובנפט]

עין משפט נר מצוה

סו א מיי' פ"ז מהלכות מעשר הל' ג טוש"ע י"ד סי' שלא סעיף קח:

סז ב מיי' פ"ה מהל' שבת הלכה י:

סח ג ד מיי' שם הלכה יא ופכ"ב מהלכות כלים הלכ' א סמג לאוין סה טוש"ע א"ח סי' רסד סעיף ו:

רבינו חננאל

בחמין: ת"ר אין מדליקין בטבל טמא בחול · ואין צ"ל בשבת מ"ט (בתרומה) [בב' תרומות דכתוב מדבר] מה תרומה טהורה אין לך בה אלא משעת הרמה ואילך אף תרומה טמאה אין לך בה אלא משעת הרמה · תניא אין מדליקין בעטרן מפני שריחו רע שמא יניח הנר ויצא · אין מדליקין בצרי מפני שריחו נודף שמא יסתפק ממנו · ועוד מפני שהוא עף · רבי [טרפון] אומר אין מדליקין אלא בשמן זית בלבד · א"ר יוחנן בן נורי מה יעשו אנשי בבל שאין להם אלא שמן שומשמין · מה יעשו אנשי מדי שאין להם אלא שמן אגוזים · ואנשי אלכסנדריא שאין להם אלא שמן צנונות · אין לך אלא השמנים שאמרו חכמים אין מדליקין בהן וכן הלכה · רבי שמעון בן אלעזר אומר כל היוצא מן העץ אין בו משום שלש על שלש · ומסככין בו חוץ מן הפשתן שבגד פשתן מקבל טומאה אפילו אין בו אלא שלש על שלש אצבעות ואין מסככין בו · ואתא אביי למימר כי

דבי

רב נסים גאון

איכא בינייהו דרב ברונא אמר רב ולא מסיימי · [והוא] שמעתתא דאיתמרא בפירקא (דף כג) חלב מהותך וקירבי דגים שנימוחו:

עין משפט
נר מצוה

סט א מיי' פי"ב מהל' טומאת צרעת הל' י ופכ"ב מהל' כלים הל' יב:

ע ב מיי' פי"ג שם הל' א סמג עשין רלח :

מסורת הש"ס

תורה אור

ר' שמעון בן אלעזר ותנא דבי ר' ישמעאל אמרו דבר אחד ר' שמעון בן אלעזר הא דאמרן תנא דבי ר' ישמעאל מאי היא *דתני דבי ר' ישמעאל הואיל ונאמרו בגדים בתורה סתם ופרט לך הכתוב באחד מהן צמר ופשתים מה להלן צמר ופשתים אף כל צמר ופשתים רבא אמר שלשה על שלשה בשאר בגדים איכא בינייהו *דר' שמעון בן אלעזר אית ליה לתנא דבי ר' ישמעאל לית ליה דכולי עלמא מיהת שלש על שלש בצמר ופשתים מיטמא בנגעים מנלן דתניא בגד אין לי אלא בגד *שלש על שלש מנין ת"ל °והבגד (ויקרא יג) ואימא לרבות שלשה על שלשה לאו ק"ו הוא השתא שתי וערב מיטמא שלשה על שלשה מיבעיא אי הכי שלש על שלש נמי ליתי בק"ו אלא שלשה על שלשה דחזו בין לעשירים בין לעניים אתי בק"ו שלש על שלש לעניים הוא דחזיין לעשירים לא חזיין לא אתי בק"ו טעמא דכתביה קרא הא לא כתביה קרא לא גמרינן בק"ו ואימא לרבות שלשה על שלשה בשאר בגדים אמר קרא °בגד צמר ופשתים (שם) בגד צמר ופשתים אין מידי אחריני לא ואימא כי אימעוט משלש על שלש אבל שלשה על שלשה מיטמא (א) תרי מיעוטי כתיבי °בגד צמר או [בבגד] פשתים (שם) חד למעוטי משלש על שלש וחד למעוטי משלשה על שלשה ולרבא דאמר שלשה על שלשה בשאר בגדים איכא בינייהו לרשב"א אית ליה לתנא דבי רבי ישמעאל לית ליה שלשה על שלשה בשאר בגדים מנא

ר' שמעון בן אלעזר ותנא דבי ר' ישמעאל אמרו דבר אחד · דמהיכא תיתי לר' שמעון למעוטי שאר בגדים מטומאה אי לאו דאית ליה הא דתנא דבי ר' ישמעאל והלכך יוצא מן העץ לאו דווקא נקט דה"ה לנוצה של עזים וכל מידי דלאו צמר ופשתים הוא ואיידי דנקט יוצא מן העץ לענין סוכה נקט לה נמי לענין טומאה : הואיל ונאמרו בגדים בתורה סתם · כגון בטומאת שרצים וטומאת מת דכתיב בטומאת שרצים או בגד או עור ובמת וכל בגד וכל כלי עור וכן בשכבת זרע וכל בגד וכל עור אשר יהיה עליו שכבת זרע וגו' ובציצית על כנפי בגדיהם : ופרט לך הכתוב באחד מהן · בטומאת נגעים כלל תחלה ואח"כ פרט והבגד כי יהיה בו נגע צרעת כלל בבגד צמר כו' פרט אף כל בגדים הסתומים ילפי' במה מליט דהוא בנין אב דאיט אלא צמר ופשתים : שלשה · טפחים : לר' שמעון אית ליה · דבהדיא תנא אין בו משום שלש על שלש אבל שלשה על שלשה דחזי אף לעשירים מיטמא ולקמן יליף מנליה בהו טומאה כלל הואיל ומנגעים יליף דאי לא יליף מנגעים מהיכא תיתי ליה לחלק בין פשתן לשאר מינין : דכולי עלמא · בין לאביי בין לרבא אליבא דהני תנאי : בגד אין לי כו' · כלומר אי הוה כתיב בנגעים בגד אין לי דמיטמא בנגעים אלא בגד שלם : לעשירים לא חזיין · אין מקפידין להצניע ובטולי מבטלי להו לא אתיין בק"ו : וטעמא דכתביה קרא כו' · מסקנא דפירושה דמילתא היא ובניחותא כלומר הלכך טעמא דכתב קרא והבגד לרבויינהו הלכך מיטמו הא לא רבינהו לא מיטמו : ואימא לרבות שלשה על שלשה בשאר בגדים · ושלש על שלש בצמר ופשתים מיטמו מק"ו והאי רבויא לשלשה על שלשה אתא ולשאר בגדים : אמר קרא בבגד צמר · פרט אחר כלל למימר דאפי' גדול דשאר מינין לא מיטמו בנגעים : ואימא כי אמעיט · שאר בגדים משלש על שלש דבצמר ופשתים אתי בק"ו משתי וערב אבל שלשה על שלשה מיטמו מריבויא דוהבגד : תרי מיעוטי כתיבי · תרי זימני כתיבי בגד צמר ופשתים זאת תורת נגע הצרעת בגד הצמר או הפשתים : מנא ליה · לרבי שמעון שום טומאה בשאר בגדים הואיל ושאר בגדים הסתומים למדין הן מן המפורש :
מאו

רבי שמעון בן אלעזר ותנא דבי ר' ישמעאל אמרו דבר אחד · וא"ת כיון דבשאר בגדים אפי' שלשה על שלשה טהור לר' שמעון בן אלעזר אמאי נקט שלש על שלש ותירץ הרב פורת דנקט שלש על שלש משום פשתן דאפי' שלש על שלש טמא ואע"ג דאמר לקמן (דף כז:) ר"ש בן אלעזר וסומכוס אמרו דבר אחד דאמר סומכוס סיככה בטווי פסולה משמע דהא דקאמר הכא חוץ מפשתן היינו טווי ולא בגד וי"ל דעיקר מילתיה איירי בבגדי פשתן ומ"מ דייק לקמן מדלא קאמר חוץ מבגד פשתן דבטווי נמי איירי וא"ת מאי דוחקיה דאביי לאוקמה דתנא שלש על שלש משום פשתן ולימא דדוקא נקט כמו שאמר רבא ואי משום דלא ליפלוג ר"ש בן אלעזר אתנא דבי ר' ישמעאל הא אביי גופיה קאמר לקמן דהאי תנא דבי ר' ישמעאל מפיק מאידך תנא דבי ר' ישמעאל וי"ל דסבירא ליה לאביי הא דמרבה לקמן תנא דבי ר' ישמעאל שאר בגדים היינו אפי' שלש על שלש וסבר דשאר בגדים או יהיה בהן טומאה כמו בצמר ופשתים או יהיו טהורים לגמרי :

השתא שתי וערב מיטמא · תימה לר"י דילמא הא דתנן בפי"א דנגעים (משנה ח) כמה יהא בפקיע ויטמא כדי לארוג בו שלש על שלש היינו בתר דקיי"ל באריג דמיטמא בשלש על שלש אבל כל כמה דלא ידעינן באריג גם שתי וערב לא יטמא אלא כשיהיה כדי לארוג בו הרבה וא"כ היכי אתי שלשה על שלשה בק"ו דשתי וערב ותירץ ר"י דנראה לו להש"ס סברא דאריג שלשה על שלשה עדיף משתי וערב אפי' כדי לארוג בו אלף על אלף ולרשב"א נראה דודאי בבגד שייך לחלק בשיעורו משום דכתב רחמנא בגד דמשמע בגד שלם אבל שתי וערב השיעור תלוי בסברא והיינו שלש על שלש דחזי אפילו לעשירים דהא חזי לאיצטרופי לבגד גדול : *אתי בק"ו · מפרש הרב פורת דהאי ק"ו לא נקט אלא להרווחא דמילתא ובלאו ק"ו נמי אין צריך ריבוי לשלשה על שלשה דכיון דחזו לעניים ולעשירים בגד חשוב הוא דמה לי שלשה על שלשה ומה לי ד' או ה' אמות כיון שגם זה ראוי כמו זה וכן מוכח מדברי רבא דאמר שלשה על שלשה בשאר בגדים מאו בגד ומנא ליה דילמא איצטריך קרא לבגד שלם אלמא משמע דאין חילוק בין בגד שלם לשלשה על שלשה וכן אביי דמוקי או בגד לשלש על שלש בצמר ופשתים דמיטמא בשרצים ולא מוקי לשלשה על שלשה משום דשלשה על שלשה הוי בכלל בגד ולא צריך ריבוי וכן משמע ממאי דפריך ואימא כי אימעוט משלש על שלש וגם אפרש ויש ליישב דאיצטריך ק"ו דאי לאו ק"ו ה"א בגד משמע בגד שלם אבל השתא דאיכא ק"ו גלי לן דבכל מקום דכתיב בגד הוי שלשה על שלשה :

ואימא לרבות שלשה על שלשה בשאר בגדים · פי' בקונטרס אבל שלש על שלש בצמר ופשתים אתי בק"ו ולא נהירא דהא אמרן כיון דלא חזי לעניים ולעשירים לא אתי בק"ו ונראה לפרש (ב) דהכי פריך ואימא לרבות שלשה על שלשה פי' שנרבה שלשה על שלשה בשאר בגדים דהא ליכא מיעוטא למעוטינהו וצמר ופשתים אתי למעוטי שאר בגדים משלש על שלש דאי לאו צמר ופשתים הוה מרבינן בכל בגדים מוהבגד שלש על שלש כיון דקרא סתמא כתיב והמתרץ לא הבין קושייתו והיה סבור שהמקשה לא ידע דצמר ופשתים כתיב ולהכי הדר פריך אימא כי אימעוט משלש על שלש הייט קושיא ראשונה אלא שמפרש היטב :

ואימא כי אימעוט משלש על שלש · מכאן נמי משמע כפי' הרב פורת דשלשה על שלשה אי בכלל בגד וק"ו להרווחא דמילתא נקט דאי שלשה על שלשה לא שמעי' מבגד אלא מק"ו א"כ מאי פריך כי אימעוט משלש על שלש מה צריך מיעוט מהיכא תיתי לרבות שלש על שלש בשאר בגדים דריבויא דוהבגד בצמר ופשתים מוקמית לה אפי' בשלש על שלש דשלשה על שלשה לא איצטריך בצמר ופשתים דהא מק"ו דשתי וערב אתי אבל בשאר בגדים דלא אתי בק"ו דהא בשתי וערב בהדיא כתיב צמר ופשתים איצטריך ריבוי מוהבגד *לשלש על שלש ומיהו שמא המקשה סבר דיש לרבות בשאר בגדים שלש על שלש כמו בצמר ופשתים כיון דקרא סתמא כתיב וחד ריבוי לכולהו :

[נ"א לשלשה על שלשה]

תרי מיעוטי כתיבי · ואם תאמר לשתוק מריבויא דוהבגד וע"כ שלש על שלש טמא בצמר ופשתים דאי לאו הכי תרי מיעוטי למה לי וי"ל *דאי לאו ריבויא דוהבגד הוה מוקמינן תרי מיעוטי לרבות שלשה בשאר בגדים דאין מיעוט אחר מיעוט אלא לרבות (ולבי מהסס דהיאך נאמר דאין מיעוט אחר מיעוט אלא לרבות שלשה על שלשה בשאר בגדים ויותר נראה לומר כיון דאיכא לאוקמי שפיר תרי מיעוטי ליכא למימר דאתי לרבות) [ת"י] ושלש על שלש בצמר ופשתים ה"א דטהור אבל השתא דכתיב ריבוי דוהבגד ע"כ הנך תרי מיעוטי אתי למעוטי ולאו לרבות דאי לרבות מוהבגד וחד מיעוט הוה ידעינן שלשה על שלשה בשאר בגדים כדפרישית לעיל וא"ת אכתי לשתוק מריבויא דוהבגד וחד מיעוטא ולא ניכתב אלא חד צמר ופשתים ואנא ידענא דשאר בגדים דלא יטמאו בנגעים דמהיכא תיתי וידעינן נמי דצמר ופשתים מיטמו בשלש על שלש דאי לאו הכי אמאי כתב רחמנא טומאה כלל בבגד צמר ופשתים דשלשה על שלשה שמעינן מק"ו דשתי וערב אלא ודאי לשלש על שלש אתיא וי"ל דהשתא דגלי לן קרא דשייכי טומאה דנגעים בבגדים ילפינן השיעור שפיר בק"ו דשתי וערב אבל אי לאו איכתיב טומאת בגדים לא הוה ילפינן מק"ו דשייך טומאה בבגד וה"א דאין שייך נגע אלא בשתי וערב אבל בבגד לא שייך נגע דשמא לא יבא בו נגע כלל :
נפקא

רבינו חננאל

רבי שמעון בן אלעזר פתנא דבי ר' ישמעאל תני הא מתניתא דיליה ודחי רבא ואמר שלשה על שלשה טפחים בשאר בגדים זולתי בגדי פשתן איכא בינייהו · ר' שמעון בן אלעזר לא מיעט שאר בגדים אלא משלש על שלש · אבל ג' על ג' טפחים אפילו דשאר בגדים מקבלי טומאה ותנא דבי רבי ישמעאל סבר לא איקרי בגד אלא צמר ופשתים · ובגדים אחרים שעושין משאר עצים לאו בגדים נינהו ולא מיטמא ג' על ג' ולא שלשה על שלשה: ושקלינן וטרינן

יבמות ד: מנחות לט:

בנ"י לר'

(א) תרי מיעוטי כתיבי בגד צמר ופשתים כצ"ל ובח"י כתבו על זה גם זה משמע כפי' ה"ר פורת דאי שלשה על שלשה אינו בכלל בגדים נוקי תרי מיעוטי חדא לשלש על שלש וחדא לשלשה על שלשה ואכתי בגד שלם בשאר בגדים דלא מטמא בנגעים מנא ליה אלא משמע כפי' ואין זה הוכחה דכמיעוט אי נתמעט גם משלשה על שלשה דשלש על שלש ושלשה על שלשה שניהם איתרבו לשאר בגדים מריבוי אחד מוהבגד אבל מ"מ קצת יש להוכיח מדלא קאמר כי אימעוט מג' על ג' ומשלשה על שלשה דמחד ריבוי נפקא תרווייהו אבל בגד שלם מטמא [ת"י] : (ב) אבל אין לפרש ואימא לרבות מוהבגד שלשה על שלשה בשאר בגדים ולא שלש על שלש בצמר ופשתים דהא מדאיצטריך ריבוי לשאר בגדים ידע דצמר ופשתים כתיב ועוד דקושיא שניה ידע דצמר ופשתים כתיב א"כ מה פריך כיון דצמר ופשתים כתיב טפי הוי לן לאוקמי ריבוי לג' על ג' בצמר ופשתים ממה שנרבה שלשה על שלשה בשאר בגדים כמו בצמר ופשתים דהא רבוי צמר ופשתים נכתב בתנס כדאמר לקמן קאי בצמר ופשתים מרבה שאר בגדים ועוד מה פריך אימא כי אימעוט מג' על ג' אבל שלשה על שלשה מטמא מנ"ל כיון דאיצטריך ריבוי לג' על ג' בצמר ופשתים וי"ל ואימא לרבות נמי שלשה על שלשה בשאר בגדים וזהו כפי' המפורש בפנים [ת"י] :

כ"ס גירסת הרש"ל שזהו דיבור בפ"ע וגרים לעיל דאריג שלש על שלש עד ף אבל בת"י גרים לשיל דאריג שלשה על שלשה כו' והך מפי' הרב פורת שייך לדיבור א' עם דלעיל וקאי אק"ו דשלשה על שלשה

מצאתי בשם ה"ר שלמה אשטרוביצ"ג זצ"ל ק"ל א"כ יהיו שוין כל הבגדים ולמה כתב ד' תיבות הללו בגד צמר בגד פשתים אלא י"ל אי לא יתורא דוהבגד ה"א אין מיעוט אחר מיעוט אלא לרבות שלש על שלש בצמר ופשתים וממילא נרבה שלש על שלש בשאר בגדים דסברא הוא שיהא שוין אם אין מיעוט כדפירש' לעיל וכך מועיל יתור של שני מיעוטים כמו והבגד אבל השתא דכתיב ריבוי דוהבגד לרבות ג' על ג' בצמר ופשתים אם כן אתי תרי מיעוטי למעט ולמעוטי זה וזה משאר בגדים דאי לרבות לישתוק מרבוי דוהבגד [ת"י] :

Abaye observed, [26b] R. Simeon b. Eleazar and the Tanna of the School of R. Ishmael[10] said the same thing. R. Simeon b. Eleazar, as stated. The Tanna of the School of R. Ishmael: what is that? For the School of R. Ishmael taught: Since garments are mentioned in the Torah unspecified, while the Writ specified wool and flax in the case of one of them: [then] just as there, wool and flax [are specified], so all [garments] are of wool and flax.[11] Raba said: They differ in respect to three [handbreadths] by three in other clothes [not wool or linen]: R. Simeon b.
a Eleazar accepts [their liability to defilement],[1] whilst the Tanna of the School of R. Ishmael rejects it.[2]

Now all at least agree that an area of three [fingerbreadths] of wool or linen is subject to the defilement of leprosy. How do we know it? Because it was taught, *A garment:*[3] I know it only of a [complete] garment; whence do I learn it of [cloth] three [fingerbreadths] square? From the verse, and *the garment.*[4] Yet say that it is to include three [handbreadths] square?[5]—Does that not follow *a minori:* if a warp and a woof become unclean,[6] is there a question of three [handbreadths] square?[7] If so, if it is three [fingerbreadths] square, let it also be deduced *a minori?*[8]—Rather, [this is the reply]: three [handbreadths] square, which is of use[9] both to the wealthy and to the poor, can be deduced *a minori;*[10] three [fingerbreadths] square, which is of use to the poor only, but not to the rich,[11] cannot be learnt *a minori:* hence it is only because Scripture wrote it; but had Scripture not written it, we could not deduce it *a minori.*

Yet say [that its purpose is] to include three [handbreadths] square of other materials?[12]—Scripture saith, *a* woollen *garment, or a* linen *garment:*[13] only a woollen or a linen garment, but not anything else. Yet say, when it is excluded it is from [the defilement of] three [fingerbreadths] square, but three [handbreadths] square can become unclean?—Two limitations are
b written: 'a woollen garment or a linen garment',[1] [hence] one is to exclude [them] from [the defilement of] three [fingerbreadths] square, and the other to exclude them from [the defilement of] three [handbreadths] square.

Now, according to Raba, who said, They differ in respect of three [handbreadths] by three in other cloths, R. Simeon b. Eleazar accepting [their liability to defilement], whilst the Tanna of the School of R. Ishmael rejects it,—how does he [R. Simeon b. Eleazar] know [the defilement of] three [handbreadths] square

(10) No particular Tanna is meant, but the collective view of that School. (11) E.g., the uncleanness of garments caused by the carcases of forbidden animals (Lev. II, 25) or reptiles (v. 32): there the garments are unspecified. On the other hand, with respect to leprosy in garments wool and flax are specified: *The garment also that the plague of leprosy is in, whether it be a* woollen *garment, or a* linen *garment.*—Lev. XIII, 47.

a (1) In his statement he employs the word *shalosh*, feminine, which must refer to fingerbreadths (*ezba'oth*, fem.). Hence they are not subject to the stricter law that even when only three fingerbreadths square they shall be liable to defilement. Whence it follows that they are subject to the next standard of liability, viz., three handbreadths (*sheloshah*, masc. agreeing with *tefahim*, handbreadths); v. *infra*. (2) For he simply rules that wherever 'garments' is stated it means wool or flax. (3) Lev. XIII, 47: referring to leprosy. (4) *We-habeged*, E.V. *The garment also*, 'And' is regarded as an extension. (5) But not the smaller standard.—*Shalosh* refers to *ezba'oth*, fingerbreadths; *sheloshah* to *tefahim*, handbreadths; v. n. a1. (6) Lev. ibid. (7) No extension is needed for that. (8) Since cloth containing a warp and a woof can be less. (9) Lit., 'fit'. (10) For it is then nearer to an actual garment. (11) A rich man would not trouble to save it for some possible service—hence it is further removed from 'garment'. (12) Lit., 'garments'. (13) Lev. XIII, 48; these are also specified in v. 47.

b (1) V. *supra* n. a13.

of other materials? [27a]—He deduces it from, or *raiment*.[2] For it was taught:[3] '*raiment*': I know [it] only of raiment, [4] how do I know [it of] three [handbreadths] square of other materials?[5] Therefore it is stated, 'or *raiment*.' And Abaye? how does he employ this or *raiment!*—He utilizes it to include three [fingerbreadths] square of wool or linen, that it becomes unclean through creeping things.[6] And Raba?[7]—The Merciful One revealed this in reference to leprosy,[8] and the same holds good of reptiles. And Abaye?[9]—It [the analogy] may be refuted: as for leprosy, [the reason is] because the warp and the woof [of wool or linen] become defiled in their case.[10] And the other?[11]—Should you think that leprosy is stricter, let the Divine Law write [it][12] with reference to reptiles,[13] and leprosy would be learnt from them. And the other?—Leprosy could not be derived from reptiles, because it may be refuted: as for reptiles, [the reason is] because they defile by the size of a lentil.[14]

Abaye said: This Tanna of the School of R. Ishmael rebuts another Tanna of the School of R. Ishmael. For the School of R. Ishmael taught: '*A garment*': I know it only of a woollen or a
a linen garment: whence do I know to include camel hair[1], rabbit wool, goat hair,[2] silk, *kallak*,[3] and *serikin*?[3] From the verse, 'or *raiment*'. Raba said: When does this Tanna of the School of R. Ishmael reject [the defilement of] other materials? [Only in respect of] three [fingerbreadths] square; but [if it is] three [handbreadths] square, he accepts it. But it was Raba who said that in respect of three [handbreadths] by three in other clothes, R. Simeon b. Eleazar accepts [their liability to defilement], while the Tanna of the School of R. Ishmael rejects it?—Raba retracted from that [view]. Alternatively, this latter [statement] was made by R. Papa.[4]

R. Papa said: 'So all [are of wool or flax],'[5] is to include *kil'ayim*.[6] But of *kil'ayim* it is explicitly stated, *Thou shalt not wear a mingled stuff, wool and linen together?*[7]—I might argue, That is only in the manner of wearing,[8] but to place it over oneself[9] any two materials [mingled] are forbidden. Now, does that not follow *a fortiori:* if of wearing, though the whole body derives benefit from *kil'ayim*,[10] you say, wool and linen alone [are forbidden] but nothing else; how much more so wrapping oneself! Hence this [dictum] of R. Papa is a fiction.[11]

(2) Lev. XI, 32, q.v. '*Or*' (Heb. או) is an extension. (3) This phrase always introduces a Baraitha, which contains the teaching of a Tanna. Since it is controverted by Abaye (v. text), Rashi deletes 'for it was taught', for it is axiomatic that an amora (Abaye was such) cannot disagree with a Tanna, and he assumes that it is a continuation of Raba's statement. Tosaf. defends it, and the style too is that of a Baraitha. (4) *Sc.* that a garment is subject to defilement. (5) Not wool or linen. (6) '*Or raiment*' is in a passage referring to these. (7) How does he know that? (8) V. *supra* 26*b*. (9) Does he not admit this? (10) I.e., the thread itself, whether warp or woof, is liable to defilement. But Scripture does not state this in reference to reptiles, and so the deduction of three fingerbreadths square may not apply to it either. (11) Raba: how does he dispose of this refutation? (12) The extention of '*and the garment*' *supra* 26*b*. (13) Instead of leprosy. (14) A piece the size of a lentil is sufficient to defile, whereas the smallest leprous eruption to defile is the size of a bean, which is larger than a lentil.

a (1) Lit., 'wool of camels'. (2) I.e., stuffs made of these. (3) V. *supra* 20 *b*, n. a6. *Sericum*, silk stuff. (4) Raba's successor; of many dicta it was not known whether they were his or Raba's; Tosaf. *infra b*. s.v. רב פפא. (5) In the first citation of the Tanna of the School of R. Ishmael, *supra* 26*b*. (6) V. Glos. I.e., only a mixture of wool or flax is forbidden, but no other. Accordingly it does not relate to defilement at all, and does not contradict the other teaching of the School of R. Ishmael.—Rashi reads at the beginning of this passage, *For* R. Papa said, since this dictum of R. Papa explains why in his opinion the two are not contradictory. (7) Deut. XXII, 11. (8) Then a mixture of wool and linen alone is forbidden. (9) E.g., as a covering or wrap. (10) When one wears a garment it comes into closer contact with the separate limbs of the body, affording them protection and warmth, than when he merely covers or wraps himself in a robe. (11) Incorrect.

מסורת הש"ס

עין משפט נר מצוה

עא א מיי' פכ"ב מהל' כלים הל' א ופכ"ג הלכה ג:

עב ב מיי' פ"א מהל' כלים הלכה יא:

עג ג מיי' פי' מהלכות כלאים הלכה א סמג לאוין רפג טוש"ע יו"ד סימן רצח סעיף א:

מנא ליה נפקא °מאו בגד דתניא בגד אין לי אלא בגד [א]שלשה על שלשה בשאר בגדים מניין ת"ל או בגד ואביי האי או בגד מאי עביד ליה מיבעי ליה לרבות שלש על שלש בצמר ופשתים דמטמא בשרצים ורבא גלי רחמנא גבי נגעים והוא הדין לשרצים ואביי איכא למיפרך מה לנגעים שכן שתי וערב מטמא בהם ואידך אי ס"ד נגעים חמירי לכתוב רחמנא גבי שרצים וליתו נגעים מינייהו ואידך נגעים משרצים לא אתו דאיכא למיפרך מה לשרצים שכן מטמא בכעדשה *אמר אביי האי תנא דבי רבי ישמעאל מפיק מאידך תנא דבי ר' ישמעאל דתני דבי רבי ישמעאל בגד אין לי אלא בגד צמר ופשתים [ב]מניין לרבות צמר גמלים וצמר ארנבים נוצה של עזים והשירין והכלך והסריקין תלמוד לומר או בגד רבא אמר כי לית ליה להך תנא דבי רבי ישמעאל בשאר בגדים שלש על שלש שלשה על שלשה אית ליה והא רבא הוא דאמר שלשה על שלשה בשאר בגדים לרשב"א אית ליה לתנא דבי רבי ישמעאל לית ליה הדר ביה רבא מההיא ואב"א *הא *רב פפא אמרה רב פפא אמר אף כל [ג]לאתויי כלאים כלאים בהדיא כתיבי ביה °לא תלבש שעטנז צמר ופשתים יחדיו ס"ד אמינא ה"מ דרך לבישה אבל בהעלאה כל תרי מיני אסור ולאו ק"ו הוא ומה לבישה דקא מיתהני כולי גופיה מכלאים אמרת צמר ופשתים אין מידי אחרינא לא העלאה לא כ"ש אלא דרב פפא *בדותא היא רב נחמן בר יצחק אמר אף כל לאתויי

מאו בגד · דכתיב בשרצים או ריבויא הוא: דתניא ל"ג דאי מתניתא היא היכי פליג עלה אביי ואמר מיבעיא ליה לשלש על שלש הא תנא תני בהדיא שלשה על שלשה בשאר בגדים מניין אלא דרשא דרבא היא: גלי רחמנא בנגעים · דרבייה מן והבגד וה"ה לשרצים דכיון דכתיב בהן בגד כי התם מיניה ילפינן בבנין אב: שרצים אין שתי וערב מטמא בהן · דבגד כתיב בהו ולא שתי ולא ערב: ואידך אי ס"ד · ורבא אמר לך על כרחיך לשלשה על שלשה בשאר בגדים אתא דאילו ג' על ג' בצמר ופשתים בשרצים מנגעים יליף דאי נגעים חמירי לכתוב רחמנא האי ריבויא בשרצים ולשתוק מריבויא דהבגד בנגעים אלא לדרשא אחריתי אתא: בכעדשה · ונגעים בעינן כגריס: מפיק מאידך · כלומר מוצא הוא מסברת אידך תנא דפליג עליה דהשכן דמרבי שאר בגדים לטומאת שרצים: של עזים · קרי נוצה על שם שאין גוזזין אותם אלא מורטין: רבא אמר כי לית ליה · לתנא דרישא בשאר בגדים בשרצים ג' על ג' דילמד סתום מן המפורש אבל שלשה על שלשה בשרצים אית ליה בהו דאיתרבו מאו בגד: הדר ביה רבא מההיא · ואמר דתנא דבי רבי ישמעאל ורשב"א אמרו דבר אחד ולאו כאביי אלא דלתרוייהו בשאר בגדים טומאת ג' על ג' ליכא שלשה על שלשה איכא: ואיבעית אימא הא · שמעתא דסיפא לאו רבא אמרה אלא רב פפא אמרה לאוקמי תרוייהו תרי תנאי דרבי ישמעאל כהדדי ולמימר דמודה תנא דרישא דיש טומאת שרצים בשאר בגדים: ה"ג דרב פפא אמר אף כל לאתויי כלאים · אף כל דתנא דרישא דקאמר אף כל בגדים סתם צמר ופשתים לאו לפרושי בגדים סתומים דטומאה קא אתי דבשאר טומאה ודאי מטמאו שאר בגדים דאיתרבו מאו בגד אלא לפרושי בגד האמור בכלאים סתם ובגד כלאים שעטנז וגו' הלכך לרב פפא *לא מפיק האי תנא מילתיה דהאי תנא והך פירוקא דסיפא איהו אמרה ולא איתמר כדאמרת ליה אליבא דרבא דמפליג בין ג' על ג' לשלשה על שלשה אלא הכי איתמר רב פפא אמר לא מפיק האי תנא מאידך תנא דאף כל לאתויי כלאים דכי הוה מוקמינן ליה כרבא הוה צריך לפלוגי דכיון דאף כל לטומאת שרצים נמי אתא על כרחיך אף כל למעוטינהו משלש על שלש כדין נגעים ואו בגד לרבויי שלשה על שלשה ואף על גב דלא מטמו שאר בגדים בנגעים דהא נתמעטו בתרי מיעוטי איתרבו בשרצים אבל לרב פפא לא מיבעי לן לפלוגי דכיון דאתרבו שאר בגדים לשרצים איתרבו לכל תורת צמר ופשתים בין לשלש בין לשלשה: בהדיא כתיבי ביה · צמר ופשתים - לא תלבש שעטנז וגו': לאתויי

נפקא ליה מאו בגד דתניא בגד ט' · פירש בקונטרס דלא גרסינן דתניא דאי ברייתא היא היכי פליג אביי ולאו פירכא היא דהא אביי מודה דלאו אתא לרבות שאר בגדים לאידך תנא דבי רבי ישמעאל כדאמר אביי גופיה בסמוך והיינו ההיא ברייתא גופיה דלקמן אלא שקיצרה רבא והא דקאמר לאביי האי או מאי עביד ליה הייני אליבא דרשב"א והיך תנא דבי רבי ישמעאל אבל לאידך תנא דבי ר' ישמעאל אתא או לרבות שאר בגדים אפי' לשלש על שלש כדפרישי' לעיל *ולרבא דאמר דאידך תנא דבי רבי ישמעאל לא מרבה שאר בגדים אלא לשלשה על שלשה לא מפיק האי תנא דבי רבי ישמעאל מאידך וה"נ דהוה מצי למיבעיא הכא ורבא האי או להך תנא דבי ר' ישמעאל מאי עביד ליה דלא פליגי אביי ורבא אלא אליבא דרשב"א וכמו שדורש אביי כן צריך למדרש רבא אליבא תנא דבי ר' ישמעאל דהכא:

תלמוד לומר או בגד · תימה דלקמן בפרק במה אשה יוצאה (דף סג:) דרשינן מאו בגד דאריג כל שהוא טמא וכי תימא שקולים הם ויבואו שניהם מ"מ כי פריך ואביי האי או בגד מאי עביד ליה לימא דאיצטריך לאריג כל שהוא ואפי' אם נמחק שם ספרים דכתוב בהן או בגד וניגרוס דיליף מאו בבגד פשתים דכתיב גבי נגעים הניחא לרבא דיליף שרצים מנגעים על ידי דגלי רחמנא וה"ה לענין אריג כל שהוא אלא לאביי מאי איכא למימר: מה לנגעים שכן שתי וערב טמא בהן · אבל בשרצים לא כדאמר בפרק במה אשה (לקמן דף סד.) יכול שאני מרבה את החבלים ואת המשיחות ת"ל שק מה שק טווי ואריג אף כל טווי ואריג: אי ס"ד נגעים חמירי · הא ודאי דנגעים חמירי אלא מפר' הר"ס דה"ק אי ס"ד כדקאמרת דאו בגד לרבות ג' על ג' בצמר ופשתים דהא נגעים חמירי:

שכן מטמא בכעדשה · ורבא אע"ג דפירכא גמורה היא לא חשיב ליה דלא הוי אלא גילוי מילתא בעלמא דגלי רחמנא בנגעים דג' על ג' קרוי בגד בצמר ופשתים והוא הדין בשרצים והקשה ה"ר יעקב מקורביי"ל הקדוש ונימא ק"ו *[הכי] מה שתי וערב דטהור בשרצים טמא בנגעים ג' על ג' שטמא בשרצים אינו דין שטמא בנגעים ויש לומר דכלים יוכיחו שמטמא בשרצים ולא בנגעים אף אני אביא ג' על ג' וכי תימא מה לכלים שכן אין מטמאין ואין נעשין אהל המת במחובר דג' על ג' נמי אין נעשה אהל כיון דלית ביה פותח טפח אי נמי שק יוכיח אי נמי בגד לבוע ובגד נכרי יוכיח שטמא בשרצים °ולא בנגעים כדאמר בת"כ וא"ת דהכא משמע דעדשה הוי פחות מכגריס ותימה לר"י בפסחים בריש אלו דברים (ד' סז:) קאמר מצורע חמור מבעל קרי שכן טעון פריעה ופרימה אדרבה בעל קרי שכן מטמא במשהו סבר ליה כרבי נתן דאמר כחתימת פי האמה משמע דחתימת פי האמה לא הוי פחות מכגריס והתם לעיל מיניה קאמר זב חמור משרץ שכן טומאה יוצאה עליו מגופו ואי כעדשה הוי פחות מגריס ומחתימת פי האמה ליפרוך *מה לשרץ שכן מטמא בכעדשה ומיהו אי לא משמעתיה מסברא אין להקשות דאיכא למימר דכעדשה שהיא עבה כדמרדד לה הוי רחבה טפי מגריס:

מנין לרבות צמר גמלים · וא"ת צמר גמלים אמאי לא הוי בכלל צמר ומה צריך ריבוי וי"ל דסתם צמר הוא של כבשים אבל של גמלים לא איקרי צמר סתם אלא צמר גמלים וכן שאר צמר והואיל דיש להם שם לווי איצטריך ריבוי כדאמר באלו טרפות (חולין דף סב:) אווז כוחלית: ונוצה של עזים · תימה מאי איצטריך ריבוי לנוצה של עזים הא כתיב שק בהדיא בקרא ושק הוי מדבר הבא מן העזים כדמוכח בפרק במה אשה (לקמן דף סד:) ותירץ ר"י דשק הוי מן השער של עזים והיא מיקרי שער ולא נוצה ומן הדק שבנוצה עושים בגדים ולא שק ועל שם שמורטין אותה כמו נוצת התרנגולין קרי ליה נוצה ואור"י דכן משמע בפרק ראשית הגז (חולין דף קלז:) דקאמר דראשית הגז אינו נוהג אלא ברחלים דאמר קרא ראשית גז לאנך ואתיא גיזה גיזה מגז כבשי יתחמם (איוב לא) ופריך התם ונילף גיזה גיזה מבכור ויהא נוהג אף בשוורים אמר קרא תתן לו ולא לשקו ופריך נוצה של עזים ליחייב אלמא נוצה לא הויא בכלל שק:

הדר ביה רבא מההיא · ומשום שלא יחלוק שהוא תנא דבי רבי ישמעאל אהך הדר ביה מההיא דלעיל ולא מהך דהכא ואית ליה לרבא אף כל לאתויי שרצים וא"ת בריש יבמות (דף ד: ושם) היכי פריך הש"ס והא תנא דבי רבי ישמעאל לית ליה דרבא ההיא דהכנף מין כנף מנא ליה דלית ליה הא רבא אית ליה דאף כל קאי אשרצים דאי לאו אף כל ה"א דנויירי גבי שרצים בכל בגדים ואו לג' על ג' אבל השתא דאמר אף כל צמר ופשתים הצטריך או לרבות שלשה על שלשה אבל שלש על שלש בשאר בגדים לא וי"ל דהתם קאמר אליבא דרב נחמן בר יצחק דאמר אף כל לאתויי ציצית דהשתא ודאי לית ליה דרבא דאיהו מחייב שאר מינים בציצית: אלא הא דרב פפא בדותא היא · תימה לר"י דבריש יבמות (גם זה שם) משמע דלתנא דבי רבי ישמעאל אף כל לאתויי כלאים כי היכי דליהוי צמר ופשתים מופנה למדרש

כ' תי' וכ"כ הרא"ש דקך ולרבא וכו' עד מאידך סוי גליון:

[עי' מעל"ד תוספות ד"ה ריש]

[עי' מ"ש על הגליון פסחים יא.]

מנחות לט:

גליון הש"ס

תוס' ד"ה שכן מטמא וכו' ולא בנגעים כדאית' בת"כ ומפורש כן במתני' רפי"א דנגעים:

[ב"ק סו: שבועות כו: בכורות כד:]

וק"ק דהא רב פפא אמרה משמע ממש מילתא דרבא דאמר כי לית ליה ג' על ג' ונראה דלרב פפא נמי לא מרבינן שאר בגדים אלא דוקא שלשה על שלשה והא דקאמר לאתויי כלאים ניחא ליה למינקט כלאים דמילתא דפסיקא דצמר ופשתים דוקא (ת"י)

וי"ל דבגלות מחות נפקא לן ... ועוד ומיהו איכא למיפרך מה להצד השוה שבהן שכן מטמא שק ושאר כלים [ת"י]

רבינו חננאל

ואסיקנא הדר ביה רבא מההיא · ואיתוקמה דאביי ואמר רב נחמן בר יצחק אהא דתנא דבי רבי ישמעאל הואיל ונאמרו בתורה בגדים סתם ופרט לך הכתוב בא' מהן צמר ופשתים אף כל צמר ופשתים לאיתויי ציצית שאינו חייב בציצית אלא צמר ופשתים ואקשינן ציצית בהדיא כתיב לא תלבש שעטנז צמר ופשתים גדילים תעשה לך · כלומר אינו חייב לעשות גדילים אלא צמר ופשתים · ושנינן איצטריך סד"א כדרבא דרבא רמי כתיב על ציצית הכנף מן כנף · כלומר האי קרא משמע תו ציצית מכנף עצמו של זה הבגד וכתוב אחרינא צמר ופשתים גדילים תעשה לך הא כיצד שאר מינין במינן פוטרין שלא במינן אין פוטרין · אבל אם תעשה ציצית מן צמר ופשתים פוטרין בין במינן בין שלא במינן קמ"ל דליתיה לדרבא ואתינן לרבויי שאר בגדים לציצית מאשר תכסה · ודחינן האי אשר תכסה לרבות כסות סומא שחייב בציצית: האי תנא דתנא אין מטמא בגדים אלא בגד צמר ופשתים מפ"ק מהאי תנא דבי רבי ישמעאל דתני רבי ישמעאל בגד צמר אין לי אלא בגד צמר מנין לרבות צמר גמלים צמר ארנבים נוצה של עזים והשיראין והכלך והסיריקין מנין ת"ל או בגד · ואמרינן

רב נסים גאון

מה לשרצים שכן מטמאין בכעדשה · עיקר דילה בתורת כהנים (ויקרא יא) כל הנוגע בהם יכול בכולם תלמוד לומר מהן אי מהן יכול במקצתן תלמוד לומר בהם הא כיצד עד שיגיע במקצתו שהוא ככולו שיערו חכמים בכעדשה שכן החומט תחילת ברייתו כעדשה ותמצא בגמרא דחגיגה (דף יא) בסוף פרק הכל חייבים בראייה ובנזירות (דף נג) בפרק כהן גדול:

°לאתויי ציצית בהדיא כתיב °לא תלבש שעטנז צמר ופשתים וכתיב °גדילים תעשה לך סד"א כדרבא *דרבא רמי כתיב °הכנף מין כנף וכתיב צמר ופשתים יחדיו הא כיצד צמר ופשתים פוטרין בין במינן בין שלא במינן שאר מינין במינן פוטרין שלא במינן אין פוטרין ס"ד כדרבא קמ"ל אמר רב אחא בריה דרבא לרב אשי לתנא דבי רבי ישמעאל מאי שנא לענין טומאה דמרבי שאר בגדים דכתיב או בגד הבא נמי לימא לרבות שאר בגדים מאשר תכסה בה ההוא לאתויי כסות סומא הוא דאתא דתניא *וראיתם אותו פרט לכסות לילה אתה אומר פרט לכסות לילה או אינו אלא פרט לכסות סומא כשהוא אומר אשר תכסה בה הרי כסות סומא אמור הא מה אני מקיים וראיתם אותו פרט לכסות לילה ומה ראית לרבות סומא ולהוציא כסות לילה מרבה אני כסות סומא שישנה בראייה אצל אחרים ומוציא אני כסות לילה שאינה בראייה אצל אחרים ואימא לרבות שאר בגדים מסתברא קאי בצמר ופשתים מרבה צמר ופשתים קאי בצמר ופשתים מרבה שאר בגדים: אמר אביי רבי שמעון בן אלעזר וסומכוס אמרו דבר אחד רשב"א הא דאמרן סומכוס דתניא סומכוס אומר סיככה בטווי פסולה מפני שמטמאה בנגעים כמאן כי האי תנא דתנן *שתי וערב מטמא בנגעים מיד *דברי רבי מאיר ורבי יהודה אומר השתי משישלה והערב מיד והאוני' של פשתן משיתלבנו: **מתני'** כל היוצא מן העץ אין מדליקין בו אלא פשתן וכל היוצא מן העץ אינו מטמא טומאת אהלים אלא פשתן: **גמ'** מנלן דפשתן איקרי עץ *אמר מר זוטרא דאמר קרא °והיא העלתם הגגה ותטמנם בפשתי העץ: והיוצא מן העץ אינו מטמא טומאת אהלים אלא פשתן: מנלן אמר רבי אלעזר *גמר אהל אהל ממשכן

תורה אור השלם: דברים כב; במדבר טו; יהושע ב

רש"י

לאתויי ציצית · דלא מחייבי בציצית אלא בגדי צמר ופשתים: גדילים תעשה לך · לאלו: סד"א כדרבא · כלומר סד"א דלא דרשינן הכי סמוכין לענין טלית למימר דטלית צמר ופשתים תעשה ציצית ולא לשאר טלית אלא לענין ציצית תדרשיה גדילים תעשה לך מצמר ופשתים ולא משאר מינין כדדריש ליה רבא: כתיב הכנף מין כנף · דהאי כנף קרא יתירא הוא דהא כתיב על כנפי בגדיהם והוה ליה למכתב ונתנו על הציצית פתיל תכלת: מין כנף · מין הטלית יהא הציצית דהכי משמע ציצית של כנף תהא ואם של משי הוא ציצית של משי פוטר בה: וכתיב צמר ופשתים · גדילים תעשה לך דמשמע כמי מהן תעשה: סד"א כדרבא · דאמר דהכנף אתא לאשמועינן דלא תדרוש סמוכין למיפטר שאר בגדים דודאי מיחייב מיהא בציצית דמינן קמ"ל אף כל דלא תדרוש הכנף הכי אלא אורחיה דקרא הוא ולאשמעינן דמצות ציצית בשני מיני לבע שני חוטין של תכלת ושני חוטין של לבן דהייטו מין כנף דסתמיה לבן: מאי שנא כו' · אליבא דרב נחמן קבעי לה דאמר אף כל לאתויי ציצית: אשר תכסה · ריבויא דקרא הוא: לכסות לילה · כסות המיוחד ללילות דלא ניחייב: שישנה בראייה אצל אחרים · וקרינן ביה וראיתם לאחרים ביום ולא אתי אשר תכסה ומפיק וראיתם: שאינה בראייה · ואי מרבינן לה מאשר תכסה קא עקרת ליה וראיתם: ואימא לרבות שאר בגדים · ולא כסות סומא: קאי בצמר ופשתים · כדאמר דסמך צמר ופשתים לגדילים מרבה כסות סומא דצמר ופשתים: מרבה שאר בגדים · בתמיה: אמרו דבר אחד · דדבר המיטמא בנגעים אין מסככין ואע"ג דאינו מטמא בטומאת מגע: הא דאמרן · חוץ מפשתן ולא קאמר חוץ מבגד פשתן משמע אע"ג דלאו בגד שלא נטוה כגון אונין או נטוה ולא נארג אין מסככין הואיל ומטמו בנגעים ואע"ג דלא מטמא בשרצים: סיככה בטווי · הואיל ומטמו בנגעים דכתיב או בשתי או בערב וה"ה נמי לאונין משיתלבנו והאי דנקט טווי לאשמעינן דטווי מטמא מיד דטווייתו הוא גמר מלאכתו ולא בעי שישלה: כמאן · אמרה סומכוס להא כר' מאיר דאמר מטמא מיד' שנטווה ל"א כמאן אמרה אביי להאי מילתא דהיא חוץ מפשתן פשתן דווקא קאמר אע"ג דלאו בגד ועל כרחיך אפי' אונין במשמע אלמא אונין מיטמא בנגעים: כי האי תנא · כר' יהודה: משישלה · שיהיו שולין אותו מן היורה ששולקין אותו בה ללבנו: משיתלבנו · בתנור: **מתני'** אין מדליקין בו · לעשות פתילה מקנבוס ובגד קנבוס ומצמר גפן: אינו מטמא טומאת אוהלים · אם עשה מהן אהל והמת תחתיו הוי כשאר בית וא"צ להטביל האהל עצמו דלא קבל טומאה אלא כלים שתחתיו: אלא פשתן · שאף אהל טמא כדכתיב והזה על האהל ובגמ' יליף דבפשתן משתעי קרא: **גמ'**

תוספות

למדרש סמוכין להתיר כלאים בציצית וי"ל דהייטו עד דלא ידע דשעטנז לאפטויי אבל במסקנא דאמר לרבנן שעטנז לאפטויי הכי נמי לתנא דבי ר' ישמעאל וצמר ופשתים לגופייהו אתו הלכך לא צריך אף כל לאתויי כלאים וא"ת לתנא דבי ר' ישמעאל צמר ופשתים גבי לבישה מ"מ ל"ל דמדכתיב ובגד כלאים שעטנז לא יעלה עליך שמעינן דכל בגדים צמר ופשתים הן וי"ל דה"א דווקא העלאה אבל בלבישה כל תרי מיני אסירי והשתא ליכא למימר לתנא דבי ר' ישמעאל דתיתי שעטנז שעטנז מהעלאה כדאמר בריש סוגיא ביבמות (דף ד: ושם) דהא השתא אילטריך שעטנז לאפטויי למדרש סמוכין ולא מופנה למדרש מיניה גזירה שוה: *רב פפא אמרה · לא בעי למימר רב נחמן בר יצחק אמרה דאמר אף כל לאתויי ציצית דאין לטעות ולהחליף דברי רבא לרב נחמן אלא ברב פפא שהיה תלמידו ומלך אחריו וכשהיה אומר דבר לא היו יודעים אם מדעתו אמרה או למדה לפני רבו *: **סד"א** כי דוקיא דרבא · ל"ג כי דוקיא דהא מגוף מילתא דרבא הוא דמפיק ובריש יבמות (ג"ז שם) הוא דגרס לה ונראה אע"ג דבפרק התכלת (מנחות ד' לט: ושם) אמר רב נחמן השיראין פטורין מן הציצית קיי"ל כרבא דבתראה הוא וחייב בציצית מדאורייתא: **מסתברא** קאי בצמר ופשתים כו' · לא שייך למיפרך אדרבה קאי ברואין מרבה רואין קאי ברואין מרבה סומין דהא עיקר המצוה היא בטלית ולא באדם שאם אין לו טלית בת ד' כנפות פטור מן הציצית: **רבי** שמעון בן אלעזר וסומכוס אמרו דבר אחד · וא"ת דר"ש בן אלעזר קאמר מסככין בו חוץ מן הפשתן. משמע אפי' לא נטוה וכדאמרינן נמי בפ"ק דסוכה (דף יב: ושם) סיככה באניצי פשתן פסולה ומשמע התם דהייטו דייק ונפיק אע"ג דלא נטוה וסומכוס קאמר דדוקא בטווי פסולה וי"ל דלרשב"א קאסר מדרבנן *וסבר בדדייק ונפיץ לפי שהוא קרוב לטווי וטווי הוא דאסור מן התורה הואיל דמטמא בנגעים והייטו אמרו דבר אחד דהא דקאמר סומכוס סיככה בטווי פסולה הייטו דבר תורה מדאמר מפני שמטמא בנגעים דמדרבנן אין סברא לאוסרו אי מדאורייתא שרי לסכך בטומאת נגעים גזירה משום טומאת מת וכיון דבטווי אסור מדאוריית' א"כ באניצי פשתן יאסור מדרבנן מפני שהוא קרוב לטווי כדפרישית: **אונין** של פשתן · פי' בקונטרס שלא נטוה ודחק לפרש כן מפני דכבר תנא שתי וערב וקשה לריב"א דמנלן לטמאותו בנגעים הא שתי וערב כתיב ונראה לר"י דאונין הייטו נטווה וכן פי' בערוך* ושתי וערב דקאמר הייטו למר לפי שבצמר ניכר בין שתי לערב דהשתי הוא מן הלשונות של צמר הגדול וטווי כלאחר יד ולא כמו שטווים הערב ודרך היה לשולקו אע"פ שעכשיו אין רגילין ואונין של פשתן שהוא הטווי לא הוזכר לא שתי ולא ערב לפי שלא ניכר איזה של שתי ואיזה של ערב כדאמר בפ"ק דמס' ע"ז (ד' יז:) אייתו ליה תרי קיבורי אמרו ליה הי דשתיא והי דערבא איתרחיש ליה ניסא אתא זיבורא *(למיתב) על דערבא כו' אלמא לא מיכּכר בפשתן*: **כל** היוצא מן העץ אין מדליקין · פי' בקונטרס לעיל כגון בקנבוס וצמר גפן ואין נראה לר"ת דא"כ יהא אסור להדליק בו ומעשים בכל יום שמדליקין בצמר גפן וגם טוב מאד לפתילה ואור"י ודאי מותר להדליק בקנבוס וצמר גפן דאיכא יוצאים מן העץ אלא זרע הוא כדאמרי' במנחות קנבוס ולוף אסרה תורה שאר זרעים כו' ופשתן נמי מין זרע כמו קנבוס אלא דאילטריך במתני' למשרי פשתן משום דאיקרי עץ כדכתיב ותטמנם בפשתי העץ וכמו עץ הדעת *למ"ד חטה היתה וקרי לה עץ אע"פ שאינה עץ ועוד דאמר בכילד מברכין (ברכות דף מ: ושם) כל היכא דאי שקלת לפירא ולא הדר אילנא ומפיק לא מברכין עליה בורא פרי העץ ופשתן וקנבוס וצמר גפן אי שקלת לפירא הייטו הזרע לא הדר אילנא ומפיק הלכך לאו יוצא מן העץ ניכהו: **ואין** מטמא טומאת אהלים אלא פשתן · והא דאמר לעיל בפ"ק (דף יז·) ועל עצמן בכל שהן משמע דכל הכלים נעשה אהל לקבל טומאה מחמת אהל הכא איירי בדבר הקבוע שחיברו לקרקע אע"ג שמתחילה היה בגד כיון שחיברו לאהל בטלו מתורת בגד ואין מיטמא אלא פשתן אע"פ שהוא מחובר כדכתיב והזה על האהל כו' וקשה לר"י דתנן באהלות (פ"ח מ"א) אלו מביאין וחוצצין השידה והתיבה כו' והסדינים שהם עשוים אהלים ואיך חוצצין סדינין של פשתן בפני הטומאה והא כל דבר המקבל טומאה אינו חוצץ בפני הטומאה וי"ל דמיירי בסדינין של משי וקבועין שאינן מטמאים ורשב"א פירש במשניות בע"א:

ויפרוש

עין משפט נר מצוה

עד א מיי' פ"ג מהל' ציצית הלכה א סמג עשין כו טוש"ע א"ח סי' ט סעיף א:
עה ב מיי' שם הלכה ה טוש"ע שם סע"ב:
עו ג מיי' שם טוש"ע שם סעיף ג:
עז ד ה מיי' שם הל' ז סמג שם טוש"ע א"ח סי' יז סעיף א וסי' יח סעיף א:
עח ו מיי' פ"ה מהלכות סוכה הלכה ד סמג עשין מג טוש"ע א"ח סי' תרכט סעיף ד:
שייך לעיל ע"א
עט ז מיי' פי"ג מהל' טומאת צרעת ה"ח:
פ ח מיי' פ"ה מהל' שבת הל' ה סמג לאוין סה טוש"ע א"ח סימן רסד סעיף א:
[וע"ע תוס' שבועות כו· ותוס' בכורות נד: ד"ה חדא ותוס' ב"ק סו: ד"ה רבא]
פא ט מיי' פ"ה מהל' טומאת מת הל' יב:

מסורת הש"ס

מנחות לט: יבמות ד: נזיר נח: ע"ש
זבחים יח: מנחות מג.
נגעי' פי"א מ"ח ת"כ פ' תזריע [במשנה דנגעים לא נזכר דברי ר' מאיר ומעטם זה כתבו תוס' בסוכה י"ב: ד"ה באניצי וכו' לייש"ב דלא קאמר הכא רשב"א וסומכוס ורבי מאיר אמרו דבר אחד וגם דלא אמר כמאן כר' מאיר ע"ש ודע דגם בת"כ ליתא דברי רבי מאיר]
ר"ה מסכרא
[סוכה כא·]
[ערך תוי' ע"ש]
[צ"ל ויתיב]
[וע"ע תוספות סוכה יב: ד"ה באניצי]
[ברכות מ:]

גליון הש"ס

גמ' אמר מר זוטרא דאמר קרא · ורבות מ"ג ע"ב:

רבינו חננאל

ואמרינן אינן מטמא בנ' על נ' אלא צמר ופשתים והאי דתני דמיטמאין בנגעים שאר בגדי' בשלשה על שלשה' אמרנו בתחלת הפרק השיראין והכלך והסיריקין חייבין בציצית' ואמרינן בתחלת יבמות אמר רחמנא עביד ציצית פתיל תכלת ותכלת עמרא הוא · וממאי דתכלת עמרא הוא ואמרינן מדשש כיתנא דכתיב שש ברקמה ממצרים כו' · כמו שנתפרש ביומא · מדשש כיתנא תכלת עמרא הוא שמעינן מינא דעמרא הוא דמיקריא פתיל תכלת הילכך ליכא ציצית אלא עמרא · תנינא שתי וערב מטמאין בנגעים מיד דברי רבי מאיר רבי יהודה אומר השתי משישלה והערב מיד · והאונין של פשתן משיתלבנו: מתני' כל היוצא מן העץ אין מדליקין בו אלא פשתן [כו': גמרא מנלן דפשתן] איקרי עץ שנאמר ותטמנם בפשתי העץ: כל היוצא מן העץ אינו מטמא טומאת אוהלים אלא פשתן מנהני מילי אמר רבי אלעזר יליף אהל אהל ממשכן

a R. Naḥman b. Isaac said: 'So all etc.' [27b] is to include fringes.[1] [But] of fringes it is explicitly stated, '*Thou shalt not wear a mingled stuff, wool and linen together*'; and then it is written, *Thou shalt make thee fringes?*[2] I might argue, it is as Raba. For Raba opposed [two verses]: it is written, [*and that they put upon the fringe of*] *each border,*[3] [which indicates] of the same kind of [material as the] border; but it is also written, '[*Thou shalt not wear a mingled stuff,*] *wool and linen together*'?[4] How is this [to be reconciled]? Wool and linen fulfil [the precept][5] both in their own kind and not in their own kind;[6] other kinds [of materials] discharge [the obligation] in their own kind, but not in a different kind. [Thus,] you might argue, it is as Raba:[7] therefore we are informed [otherwise].[8]

R. Aḥa son of Raba asked R. Ashi: According to the Tanna of the School of R. Ishmael, why is uncleanness different that we include other garments? Because '*or raiment*' is written! Then here too[9] let us say that other garments are included from [the verse] *wherewith thou coverest thyself?*[10]—That comes to include a blind person's garment. For it was taught: *That ye may look upon it:*[11] this excludes a night garment. You say, this excludes a night garment; yet perhaps it is not so, but rather it excludes a blind man's garment? When it is said, '*wherewith thou coverest thyself*', b lo! a blind man's garment is stated. How then do I interpret[1] '*that ye may look upon it*'? As excluding a night garment. And what [reason] do you see to include a blind man's [garment] and to exclude a night garment? I include a blind man's garment, which can be seen by others,[2] while I exclude night garments, which are not seen by others. Yet say [rather] that it[3] is to include other garments?[4] It is logical that when one treats of wool and linen he includes [a particular garment of] wool and linen; but when one treats of wool and linen, shall he include other garments?[5]

Abaye said: R. Simeon b. Eleazar and Symmachos said the same thing. R. Simeon b. Eleazar, as stated.[6] Symmachos, for it was taught: Symmachos said: If one covers it [the booth] with spun [flax], it is unfit, because it may be defiled by leprosy. With whom [does that agree]? With this Tanna. For we learnt: The warp and the woof are defiled by leprosy immediately:[7] this is R. Meir's ruling. But R. Judah maintained: The warp, when it is removed;[8] the woof, immediately; and bundles of [wet] flax,[9] after bleaching.[10]

MISHNAH. WHATEVER COMES FORTH FROM A TREE ['EẒ] YOU MAY NOT LIGHT [THE SABBATH LAMP] THEREWITH,[11] SAVE FLAX; AND WHATEVER COMES FORTH FROM A TREE CANNOT BE DEFILED WITH THE UNCLEANNESS OF TENTS,[12] EXCEPT LINEN.[13]

GEMARA. How do we know that flax is designated tree ['*eẓ*]?—Said Mar Zuṭra, Because Scripture saith, *But she had brought them* c *up to the roof, and hid them with the stalks* ['*eẓ*] *of the flax*.[1]

AND WHATEVER COMES FORTH FROM A TREE CANNOT BE DEFILED WITH THE UNCLEANNESS OF TENTS, EXCEPT LINEN. How do we know it?—Said R. Eleazar, [The meaning of]

a (1) Num. XV, 38; i.e., only wool and linen garments are liable thereto. (2) And the juxtaposition shows that they are required only in garments of wool or linen. It may be observed that the Talmud regards the deduction from this juxtaposition as an explicit statement, and not merely as something derived by exegesis. (3) Num. ibid. '*Border*' is superfluous, since the first half of the verse reads, *and bid them that they make them fringes in the borders of their garments*. Hence it is thus interpreted. (4) Since this is immediately followed by the precept of fringes, we translate: though a mixture of wool and linen are forbidden, yet '*thou shalt make thee fringes*', i.e., wool fringes are permitted in a linen garment and *vice versa*, which contradicts the implication of the other verse. (5) Lit., 'acquit' (the garment of its obligation). (6) Whatever the material, wool or linen fringes may be inserted. (7) That the juxtaposition illumines the nature of the fringes, but does not teach that the garment itself must be of wool or linen. For in fact, according to Raba, there is an obligation whatever the material. (8) V. Yeb., 4b and notes. (9) In reference to fringes. (10) Ibid. This too is superfluous and indicates extension. (11) *Sc.* the fringed garment.—Num. XV, 39.

b (1) Lit., 'fulfil'. (2) Lit., 'which is subject to looking in respect to others'. (3) *Sc.* '*wherewith thou coverest thyself*'. (4) Not of wool or linen. (5) Surely not. (6) *Supra*, 26a bottom, and note a.l. (7) After spinning, though given no further treatment. (8) From the kettle in which it is boiled. Maim. Neg. XI, 8 appears to read: when it has been boiled. (9) Jast. Rashi: unspun flax; Tosaf.: spun flax. (10) Thus Symmachos, who rules that it is liable to leprous defilement immediately it is spun (this being the reason that it may not be used as a covering of the booth, v. *supra* 26a, n. b8), agrees with R. Meir. (11) Using it as a wick. (12) If a tent or awning of such material overshadows a dead body, it does not become unclean, just as the roof of a house which contains a dead body is not unclean, though all utensils under the same roof or covering are defiled. (13) If the tent is of linen, that itself is defiled.

c (1) Josh. II, 6.

tent [*ohel*] is learnt [28*a*] from the Tabernacle. Here it is written, *This is the law when a man dieth in a* tent [*ohel*];[2] and there it is written, *and he spread the* tent [*ohel*] *over the Tabernacle:*[3] just as there [the covering] of linen is designated tent, so here too, [a covering] of linen is designated tent.[4] If so, just as there it was twisted and the thread was doubled sixfold,[5] so here too it must be twisted and its thread doubled sixfold?[6]—The repetition of *tent*[7] is an extension.[8] If the repetition of tent is an extension, then everything else[9] too should be included?—If so, what avails the *gezerah shawah?*[10] Yet [perhaps] say, just as there [the Tabernacle was of] boards, so here too [a tent of] boards [is meant]?—Scripture saith, *And thou shalt make boards* for *the tabernacle:*[11] the tabernacle[12] is called tabernacle, but the boards are not designated tabernacle. If so, [when it is stated,] *and thou shalt make a covering*[13] *for the tent* [ohel],[14] is the covering indeed not designated tent [*ohel*]? But when R. Eleazar propounded: Can the skin of an unclean animal[15] be defiled by overshadowing[16] the dead?—[What doubt was there] seeing that the skin of a clean animal cannot be defiled,[17] is there a question of the skin of an unclean animal![18]—There it is different,
a because Scripture restored it,[1] as it is written, *they shall bear the curtains of the tabernacle, and the tent of meeting, its covering and the covering of sealskin that is above it:*[2] thus the upper [covering][3] is assimilated to the lower:[4] just as the lower is designated tent,[5] so is the upper designated tent.

[To revert to] the main text: 'R. Eleazar propounded: Can the skin[6] of an unclean animal be defiled with the defilement of tents?'[7] What is his problem?[8]—Said R. Adda b. Ahabah: His question relates to the *taḥash* which was in the days of Moses,[9]—was it unclean or clean? R. Joseph observed, What question is this to him? We learnt it! For the sacred work none but the skin of a clean animal was declared fit.

R. Abba objected: R. Judah said: There were two coverings, one of dyed rams' skins, and one of *taḥash* skins. R. Nehemiah said: There was one covering[10] and it was like a squirrel['s].[11] But the squirrel is unclean!—This is its meaning: like a squirrel['s], which has many colours, yet not [actually] the squirrel, for that is unclean, whilst here a clean [animal is meant]. Said R. Joseph: That being so, that is why we translate it *sasgawna* [meaning] that it rejoices in many colours.[12]

Raba said: That the skin of an unclean animal is defiled by
b overshadowing[1] the dead [is inferred] from the following. For it was taught: [Scripture could state] *skin;* [by stating] *or in skin*[2] it extends [the law to] the skin of an unclean animal and to one which was smitten [with leprosy] in the priest's hand.[3] If one cuts off [pieces] of all these[4] and makes one [piece] out of them, how do we know [it]?[5] From the verse, '*or in any thing* [meleketh] *made of skin*'.[6] But this [Raba's statement] can be refuted: as for leprosy, [the reason[7] is] because the warp and the woof is defiled in their case?[8] Rather it is learnt from reptiles. For it was taught: *Skin:*[9] I know it only of the skin of a clean animal; how do I know it of the skin of an unclean animal? Therefore it is stated, *or skin.*[10] But this may be refuted: as for reptiles, [the reason is] because they defile by the size of a lentil.[11] Let leprosy prove it.[12] And thus the argument revolves: the characteristic of one is not that of the other, and *vice versa:* the feature common to both is that skin is unclean in their case, and the skin of an unclean animal was assimilated to that of a clean animal: so also do I adduce the tent of the dead, that skin is unclean in its case,[13] and the skin of an unclean animal is assimilated to that of a clean animal.

Raba of Barnesh[14] observed to R. Ashi: But this can be refuted: as for the feature common to both, it is that they defile others
c in less than the size of an olive:[1] will you say [the same] of the dead, which defiles only by the size of an olive? Rather,

(2) Num. XIX, 14. (3) Ex. XL, 19. (4) The only covering of vegetable growth of the Tabernacle was linen. (5) Deduced in Yoma 71*b*. (6) Otherwise it should not be defiled. (7) Lit., 'tent, tent': 'tent' is mentioned three times in Num. XIX, 14 in reference to defilement. (8) Extending the law to a linen tent even if not made in the same way as the covering of the Tabernacle. (9) Any other material. (10) V. Glos. (11) Ex. XXVI, 15. (12) I.e., the ten joined strips passing over the boards and forming the roof. (13) Of animal skins. (14) Ibid. 14. (15) I.e., which is not fit for food. (16) Lit., 'by the uncleanness of tents'. (17) On the present hypothesis that the covering, which included ramskins (Ex. XXVI, 14; the ram is a clean animal), is not a tent, hence excluded from Num. XIX, 14. (18) For this is less likely to suffer such defilement, as is shown below, where a superfluous word is necessary to include it, and also in the Sifra, *Thazria'*.

a (1) To be included in the term 'tent' (*ohel*). (2) Num. IV, 25. (3) The covering of animal skins. (4) Viz., the eleven curtains of goats' hair, v. Ex. XXVI, 7. (5) The '*tent of meeting*' is understood to refer not to the Tabernacle as a whole but to these curtains. (6) As it is designated in verse 7. (7) The wording is not exactly as above, but the sense is. (8) How can he think that it is subject to such defilement, seeing that he learns the definition of 'tent' from the Tabernacle (*supra* 27*b* bottom), where the skins of clean animals alone were used? (9) A.V. badger; R.V. seal, Levy, *Wörterbuch:* marter, others: badges, sea-dog, seal, cf. Lewysohn, *Zool. d. Tal.* I, 95f. *Taḥash* skins formed one of the coverings of the Tabernacle; verse quoted *supra et passim.* (10) Consisting half of rams' skin and half of *taḥash* skins.—I.e., apart from the coverings of linen, etc. and of goats' hair. (11) Jast., lit., 'hanging on the tree'. It is doubtful, however, whether a squirrel is meant, as the context shows that a striped (or speckled) animal of many colours is referred to. (12) *Sas*, it rejoices, *be-gawwanim*, in colours. R. Joseph was an expert in the Targumim (Aramaic translations of the Bible), and given to quoting them.

b (1) Lit., 'by the tent of a dead'. (2) Lev. XIII, 48. (3) In Heb. ב is an extension (Rashi). Even if the skin was not leprous when the priest was sent for, but became affected whilst he was examining it (or after), it is unclean. By analogy, the skin of an unclean animal too is defiled by overshadowing the dead. (4) Materials mentioned in the verse, q.v. (5) That it is liable to defilement. (6) *Meleketh, melakah*, work, suggests a manufactured article, and is therefore applied to a combination of materials. (7) *Sc.* the defilement of the skin of an unclean animal. (8) Which is not the case with corpse defilement, v. *infra* 64*a*. (9) Ibid. XI, 32. This refers to the materials liable to defilement by reptiles. (10) *Or* is an extension. By analogy the same applies to the defilement of the dead. (11) V. *supra* 27*a*, n. b14. But the minimum portion of a human corpse is the size of an olive, which is larger than a lentil. Since the defilement of reptiles is stricter in that respect, it may also be stricter in respect of the skin of an unclean animal. (12) The minimum for leprosy is the size of a bean. (13) I.e., if it forms a tent. (14) In Babylon on the canal of the same name, near the town of Meḥasia, and some three *parasangs* from a synagogue named after Daniel; Obermeyer, *Landschaft*, p. 302.

c (1) A bean too is less.

ממשכן *כתיב הכא °זאת התורה אדם כי ימות באהל וכתיב התם °ויפרוש את האהל על המשכן מה להלן של פשתן קרוי אהל אף כאן של פשתן קרוי אהל אי מה להלן שזורין וחוטן כפול ו' אף כאן שזורין וחוטן כפול ו' ת"ל *אהל אהל ריבה אי אהל אהל ריבה אפילו כל מילי נמי אם כן גזירה שוה מאי אהני ליה ואימא מה להלן קרשים אף כאן קרשים אמר קרא °ועשית קרשים למשכן ^ב^משכן קרוי משכן ואין קרשים קרויין משכן אלא מעתה ועשית מכסה לאהל הכי נמי מכסה לא איקרי אהל אלא הא דבעי רבי אלעזר עור בהמה טמאה מהו שיטמא באהל המת השתא עור בהמה טהורה לא מטמא עור בהמה טמאה מיבעיא שאני התם דהדר אהדריה קרא דכתיב °ונשאו את יריעות המשכן ואת אהל מועד מכסהו ומכסה התחש אשר עליו מקיש עליון לתחתון מה תחתון קרוי אהל אף עליון קרוי אהל: גופא בעי רבי אלעזר ^ג^עור בהמה טמאה מהו שיטמא טומאת אהלין מאי קמיבעיא ליה אמר רב אדא בר אהבה תחש שהיה בימי משה קמיבעיא ליה טמא היה או טהור היה אמר רב יוסף מאי תיבעי ליה תנינא לא הוכשרו למלאכת שמים אלא עור בהמה טהורה בלבד מתיב רבי אבא רבי יהודה אומר שני מכסאות היו אחד של עורות אילים מאדמים ואחד של עורות תחשים רבי נחמיה אומר מכסה אחד היה ודומה כמין תלא אילן והא תלא אילן טמא הוא ה"ק כמין תלא אילן הוא שיש בו גוונין הרבה ולא תלא אילן דאילו התם טמא והכא טהור °א"ר יוסף א"ה היינו דמתרגמינן ססגונא ששש בגוונין הרבה רבא אמר עור בהמה טמאה דמטמא באהל המת מהכא דתניא עור או בעור ריבה *עור בהמה טמאה ^ד^ושלקה ביד כהן *)^ה^קצץ מכולן ועשה אחת מהן מנין תלמוד לומר °או בכל מלאכת עור ואיכא למיפרך מה לנגעים שכן שתי וערב טמא בהן אלא גמר משרצים דתניא עור אין לי אלא עור בהמה טהורה עור בהמה טמאה מנין תלמוד לומר או עור ואיכא למיפרך מה לשרצים שכן מטמאין בכעדשה נגעים יוכיחו וחזר הדין לא ראי זה כראי זה ולא ראי זה כראי זה הצד השוה שבהן שעור טמא בהן ועשה עור בהמה טמאה כעור בהמה טהורה אף אני אביא אהל המת שעור טמא בו ונעשה בו עור בהמה טמאה כעור בהמה טהורה אמר ליה רבא מברניש לרב אשי איכא למיפרך מה להצד השוה שבהן שכן מטמאין בפחות מכזית תאמר במת שאינו מטמא אלא בכזית אלא אמר רבא מברניש אתיא

*) מעילה יח. ע"ש

תורה אור: במדבר יט; שמות מ; שם כו; במדבר ד; ויקרא יג. נ"ל אלעזר. [יומא עב.] [סוכה כח.]

רש"י

ממשכן. דלא הוה ביה שום יוצא מן העץ אלא פשתן כדכתיב עשר יריעות שש משזר: שזורין. דטור"ש בלע"ז דכתיב משזר: וחוטן כפול ששה. כדאמרינן בפ' בא לו בסדר יומא (דף עא:) דברים שנאמר בהן שש חוטן כפול ששה ואי קשיא כיון דיליף ממשכן כלים ואדם שתחת גג הבית וכל שאר אהלים דלא דמו למשכן מנלן דמטמו בספרי תניא מנין לעשות שאר המאהילים כאהל אמרת מה מצורע סקל עשה בו כל המאהיל כו': אף כאן קרשים. ואימא דעץ נמי איקרי אהל: משכן קרוי משכן. כגון עשר יריעות שש משזר ומשכן איקרי אהל דכתיב (שמות לט) את משכן אהל מועד: הכי נמי. דמכסה עורות לאו אהל ולענין טומאה נמי לא מקבל: השתא עור בהמה טהורה. כגון אילים מאדמים: מה תחתון. עשתי עשרה יריעות עזים לאהל על המשכן דמשכן היינו עשר יריעות המחוברות בקרסי זהב מלמעלה מהן אהל יריעות עזים ולמעלה מהן מכסה העורות: מאי קמיבעי ליה. הא ממשכן גמר לה ר' (*אליעזר) לעיל ברים שמעתין והתם טהורה היא דהוי למלאכת משכן: מכסה אחד היה. חציו של אילים וחציו של תחשים ולמעלה דקרא אתרוייהו כתיב דבין אילים בין תחשים היה מכסה אחד מלמעלה לאהל יריעות העזים: תלא אילן. חיה טמאה היא ומנומרת בגוונין: אי הכי. סייעתא היא: ששש. ששמח ביופיו בגוונין: עור או בעור. גבי נגעים כתיב או בעור והוה מצי למכתב או עור: ושלקה ביד כהן. משהראהו ביד כהן נעשה נגע ומתחלה לא היה נגע: קצץ מכולן. מכל האמורים בפסוק וחיברן יחד: שרצים מטמאין בכעדשה ומת בכזית ונגעים בכגרים והוא פחות מכזית: אף אני אביא אהל המת שעור טמא בו. כדאמר לעיל מקיש עליון לתחתון דקרוי אהל: *שאינה מטמאה בנגעים. דהא צמר ופשתים כתיב:

מטמא

תוספות

ויפרוש את האהל וגו'. תימה לר"י מנא ליה דהאי אהל היינו שש משזר אימא היינו יריעות עזים דאשכחנא בהדיא דאיקרי אהל כדכתיב ועשית יריעות עזים לאהל על המשכן וכן משמע פשטיה דקרא ויפרוש את האהל דהיינו יריעות עזים על המשכן *דהיינו שש משזר כדכתיב ואת המשכן תעשה עשר יריעות שש משזר ויש לומר דדייק משום דקרא כתיב בהקמת המשכן וחשיב לעיל בסדר הקמתן דמתחלה נתן אדנים (ואח"כ עמודים)(א) ואחר כך הקרשים וכתיב אחר הקרשים ויפרוש את האהל משמע היינו יריעות התחתונות שהם שש משזר דהם תחלת הפרשה ותימה דאמאי לא יליף מהא דמשכן היינו יריעות שש משזר כדכתיב ואת המשכן תעשה וגו' ומשכן איקרי אהל דכתיב את משכן אהל מועד ושמא אהאי קרא סמיך: אם כן ג"ש מאי אהני ליה. והא דאמר כל פותח טפח מביא את הטומאה היינו מק"ו ממצורע כדיליף בספרי וכדפיר' בקונטרס וא"ת והיכי יליף נימא דיו כמצורע שלא יטמא אלא טומאת ערב ודווקא בעומד או ביושב ולא עובר כדתניא במסכת נגעים ומייתי לה *ובפ"ק דקדושין (ד' לג:) טמא יושב תחת האילן וטהור עובר טמא כו' וי"ל דאינו אלא גילוי מילתא בעלמא מק"ו דמצורע דלית לן למילף אהל אהל ממשכן לענין למעט הבאת טומאה בשאר אהלים דלאו פשתן ולא ילפינן ממשכן אלא לטומאת עצמו אפילו מחובר דדוקא פשתן ולא שאר יוצא מן העץ ולענין אהל שאינו עשוי בידי אדם לרבי יהודה בפ"ב דסוכה (דף כא. ושם) דלא מצינן למילף ממצורע ולא אשכחן ביה קרא לא למעט ולא לרבות(ב) *אהל שאינו עשוי בידי אדם: אי מה להלן קרשים כו'. פירש בקונטרס דאף עץ יהא קרוי אהל וקשה לריב"א דהא דפנות אינקרויות אהל אלא המכס' שמלמעלה הוא קרוי אהל ומפ' דה"ק אי מה להלן קרשים בהדי פשתן אף כאן בטומאת אהל קרשים בהדי פשתן ואע"ג דאהל אהל ריבה לענין דלא בעינן שזורים ולכפול ששה וכן לענין דלא בעינן צמר ופשתים יחד כי התם אלא אפילו פשתים ולא צמר מ"מ פריך דליהוי קרשים בהדי פשתים דהתם אהל קרוי עם הכיסוי ועם הדפנות: ואין קרשים קרויים משכן. וקשה לר"י הא כתיב יהיה סרוח על לדי המשכן מזה ומזה לכסותו ואמר לקמן בהזורק (דף צח:) לכסות אמה של קרשים ואיכא למ"ד אמה של אדנים אלמא דקרשים איקרי משכן ויש לומר דלדי המשכן איקרי ולא משכן: ריבה עור בהמה טמאה. פירש רבינו שמואל דלהכי איצטריך לרבויי עור בהמה טמאה כדקתני בת"כ (פ' תזריע) למר אין לי אלא מין בהמה דקה ונאכל כו' דומיא דלמר שהוא דוקא של כבשים מנין לרבות עור בהמה דקה ואין נאכלת בהמה גסה נאכלת ואין נאכלת עד שתהא מרבה עורות שרצים תלמוד לומר *בעור בעור ונראה דהא דנקט בהמה גסה נאכלת אגב אחריני נקט דאיהי לא בעיא קרא דהא בשמעתין ילפינן לענין טומאת אהל כל מין טהורה מאילים: ושלקה ביד כהן. מפרש נמי רבינו שמואל דאיצטריך לרבויי משום דכתיב והבגד כי יהיה בו נגע צרעת וגו' והראה אל הכהן דמשמע דהם לא היתה בו נגע קודם שהראהו לכהן טהור: שכן שתי וערב טמא בהן. מה שאין כן במת כדנפקא לן בפרק במה אשה (לקמן דף סד.): אלא גמר משרצים דתניא עור אין לי אלא עור של בהמה טהורה. וא"ת מנלן דאיירי קרא בעור בהמה טהורה ויש לומר כמו בנגעים דהכא כתיב שק וה"א מה שק מין בהמה דקה ונאכל כדמוכח בת"כ ולקמן דשק הוי דבר הבא מן העזים אף עור מין בהמה דקה ונאכל אע"ג דבת"כ מרבה אף שק הבא מחזיר שהוא דבר טמא אפ"ה הוה אמינא דלא הוקשה עור אלא למשמעות דשק דהיינו של עזים ולא הוקש למאי דמרבי בשק לכך איצטריך ריבוי · הרב פורת: מה לשרצים. וליכא למיפרך שיטמא מת בכעדשה מק"ו דהא כל שיעורים הם הלכה למשה מסיני וקשה לר"י וניליף מת משרצים בגזירה שוה דבגד ועור כדאמר לקמן בפרק במה אשה (ג"ז שם) ואומר ר"י משום דג"ש דאהל אהל ממשכן סתרה לה לכך איצטריך ריבוי ועוד י"ל דג"ש לא איירי בטומאת אהל[המת] עצמו המחובר:

אהיא

עין משפט נר מצוה

פב א ב ג מיי' פ"ה מהלכות טומאת מת הלכה יב:

פג ד מיי' פי"ג מהלכות טומאת צרעת הל"ו:

דאי על האהל הוי יריעות שש משזר ועל המשכן היינו על הקרשים הא אין הקרשים קרויים משכן [תוס' ישנים]

פד ה מיי' שם פי"ב הלכה יב:

רבינו חננאל

ממשכן כתיב זאת התור' אדם כי ימות באהל וכתיב ויפרוש את האהל על המשכן מה להלן שש ותכלת והן צמר ופשתי' אף הכא צמר ופשתים. כיון דיליף אהל דטומאה מאהל המשכן. בעי ר' אלעזר עור בהמה טמאה מהו שיטמא באהל המת. ומיבעיא ליה תחש שהיה בימי משה טהור היה או טמא היה. ומפרש רב יוסף תנינא לא הוכשרו למלאכת שמים אלא עור בהמה טהורה בלבד. איני והא"ר נחמיה דומה כמין תלא אילן ותלא אילן טמא הוא. ושנינן דומה לו שיש לו גוונין הרבה כמותו. אבל טהור הוא. רבה אמר עור בהמה טמאה דמטמאה באהל המת. אתי בק"ו מנגעים. דתניא היה לו לומר עור למה כתב בעור לרבו' עור בהמה טמאה. ושלקה ביד כהן שמטמאה בנגעים קיצץ מכולן. פי' כגון שנטל מזה העור רצועה ומזה רצועה ודיבקן ועשאן אחד. מנין שמטמא בנגעים ת"ל או בכל מלאכת עור. פי' שלקה ביד כהן כגון שהחזיק הכהן בעור לבודקו ועודנו בידו לקה בצרעת לאלתר. איכא למיפרך מה לנגעים שכן מטמאין שתי וערב כו' מה להצד השוה שבהן שכן מטמאין פחות מכזית. הבגדי' מטמאין בכגרים. והשרץ כעדשה אלא

רב נסים גאון

אי מה להלן שזורין וחוטן כפול ו' אף כאן שזורין וחוטן כפול ו'. ותמצא עור עיקרו במס' יומא בפרק בא לו כהן גדול (דף ע"א) ת"ר בגדים שנאמר בהן שש חוטן כפול ו' וכו' ואמרו קראי כמה הוו שיתא חד לגופיה דכיתנא ניהו וחד שיהו שזורין וחד לחוטן שיהא כפול ו' ומהנה יודע לנו כי כל בגד שכתב בהן שש העשויים במשכן היו שזורים וחוטן כפול ו': תאמר במת שאינו מטמא אלא בכזית עיקר דילה בספרי הנוגע במת יכול כל שהוא וכו' אחר שרבה הכתוב מיעט אמרו כזית מן המת טמא שכן היא תחלת ברייתו ובמשנה במס' אהלות בפרק ב' אלו מטמאין באהל המת וכזית מן המת ולא היה ביניהם הפרש והוא כבר פירושו בפרק ג' כזית מן המת פתחו בטפח והמת פתחו בד' טפחים ובתוספ' בראש סדר טהרות דומר בכזית (מזה) [מן] המת שכזית פתחו בטפח ומת פתחו בד' טפחים ובתוספתא דמגילה בפרק א' אין בין כזית מן המת למת אלא שכזית מן המת פתחו בטפח והמת פתחו

בד'

הגהות הב"ח

(א) תוס' ד"ה ויפרוש וכו' דמתחלה נתן אדנים ואח"כ קרשים ואח"כ עמודים וכתיב אחר העמודים ויפרוש את האהל:
(ב) ד"ה א"כ וכו' לא למעט ולא לרבות סס"ד והשאר נמחק:

מסורת הש"ס (הערות)

הקשה מהר"מ מה צריך אהל אהל ריבה ליליף מק"ו מנוגה של עזים דלא מטמא בנגעים מטמא באהל המת שאין חוטן כפול ששה דמטמא בנגעי' לא כ"ש ותי' דהכא קיימינן אליבא דר"א דלית ליה ק"ו מדבעי בסמוך עור בהמה טמאה מהו וכי דאית להו ק"ו דרשי אהל אהל לדרשה אחריתא [ת"י]

[שייך לע"ב]

נראה קצת דכל כלי עור דכתיב במת ושכבת זרע דאתי לדרשה אחרינא ולא לעור בהמה טמאה דא"כ תקשי אמאי איצטריך למיכתבינהו דליתי בג"ש דבגד ועור שרצים [ת"י]

ס"א או בעור

גליון הש"ס

גמ' אמר רב יוסף א"ה היינו דמתרגמינן. עי' קדושין דף מו ע"א תוס' ד"ה א"ר:

גמרא

אתיא בק"ו מנוצה של עזים שאין מטמא בנגעים מטמא באהל המת עור בהמה טמאה שמטמאה בנגעים אינו דין שמטמאה באהל המת ואלא הא דתני רב יוסף לא הוכשרו במלאכת שמים אלא עור בהמה טהורה בלבד למאי הלכתא [א]לתפילין תפילין בהדיא כתיב בהו °למען תהיה תורת ה' בפיך (שמות יג) *מן המותר בפיך אלא [ב]לעורן °והאמר אביי [ג]שי"ן של תפילין *הל"מ אלא לכורכן בשערן ולתופרן בגידן הא נמי הל"מ הוא *דתניא [ד]תפילין מרובעות הל"מ *[ה]נכרכות בשערן [ו]ונתפרות בגידן [לקמן קח.] אלא [ז]לרצועות' והא"ר יצחק [ח]רצועות שחורות הל"מ נהי דגמירי שחורות טהורות מי גמירי מאי הוי עלה דתחש שהיה בימי משה א"ר אלעא אמר רשב"ל אומר היה ר"מ תחש שהיה בימי משה בריה בפני עצמה היה ולא הכריעו בה חכמים אם מין חיה הוא אם מין בהמה הוא וקרן אחת היתה לו במצחו ולפי שעה נזדמן לו למשה ועשה ממנו משכן ונגנז *מדקאמר קרן אחת היתה לו במצחו ש"מ טהור היה *דא"ר יהודה שור שהקריב אדם הראשון קרן אחת היתה לו במצחו שנאמר °ותיטב לה' משור פר מקרין מפריס (תהלים סט) מקרין תרתי משמע אמר ר"נ בר יצחק מקרן כתיב וליפשוט מיניה דמין בהמה הוא כיון [ט]דאיכא קרש דמין חיה הוא ולית ליה אלא חדא קרן איכא למימר מין חיה הוא:

מתני' פתילת הבגד שקיפלה ולא הבהבה ר"א אומר טמאה היא ואין מדליקין בה רע"א טהורה היא ומדליקין בה:

גמ' בשלמא לענין טומאה בהא פליגי דר"א סבר קיפול אינו מועיל ובמילתיה קמייתא קיימא ור"ע סבר קיפול מועיל ובטולי בטיל אלא לענין הדלק' במאי פליגי א"ר אלעזר א"ר אושעיא וכן א"ר אדא בר אהבה הכא בג' על ג' מצומצמות עסקינן ובי"ט שחל להיות ע"ש עסקינן דכ"ע אית להו דר' יהודה *דאמר מסיקין בכלים ואין מסיקין בשברי כלים ודכ"ע אית להו דעולא דאמר עולא *[י]המדליק צריך שידליק ברוב היוצא ר"א סבר קיפול אינו מועיל וכיון דאדליק ביה פורתא הויא ליה שבר כלי וכי קא מדליק בשבר כלי קמדליק ור"ע סבר קיפול מועיל ואין תורת כלי עליו וכי קמדליק בעץ בעלמא קמדליק °אמר רב יוסף היינו דתנינא ג' על ג' מצומצמות ולא ידענא למאי הלכתא ומדקא מתרץ רב אדא בר אהבה אליבא דר' יהודה ש"מ כר"י ס"ל ומי א"ר אדא בר אהבה הכי והא"ר אדא בר אהבה נכרי

רש"י

מטמאה באהל המת. אם עשאו אהל דהא ממשכן גמר ליה ועיקר אהל דכתיב במשכן יריעות עזים כתיב הא דכתיב בספרים כל מעשה עזים לא"ג ליה דמהכא לא נפקא לן אהל דבכלים הוא דכתיב וכדאמר בעלמא להביא דבר הבא מן העזים מן הקרנים ומן הטלפים: אלא הא דתני רב יוסף כו'. כיון דרבינן עור בהמה טמאה לאהל המת הא דתני רב יוסף למאי הלכתא מאי דהוה הוה אי לאו למילף מיניה לטומאה: לתפילין. איתמר דהיא נמי מלאכת שמים: לעורן. עור דפוס שלהן שהכתבים של פרשיות מונחים בו דהאי לא מלמען תהיה נפקא דהא גלאו תורה כתיבא ביה: שי"ן של תפילין. שיהא העור נקמט מבחוץ ג' קמטין ודומה לשי"ן והרצועה נקשרת כמין דלית *ויש רצועה כפופה כמין י' דהיינו שדי וכיון דאות השם נכתב בקמטין שלו מותר בפיך בעינן ומקרא נפיק: אלא לנכרכות בשערן. תניא להאי דרב יוסף שצריך לקשור איגרות הפרשיות בשער עור בהמה טהורה ולתופרן בגיד בהמה טהורה: בשערן. בשער *מן הקלף כלומר בשל טהורה: לרצועותיהן. שיהיו מעור בהמה טהורה: הל"מ. וכיון דהלכתא רצועות מסיני טהורות נמי הל"מ ומתניתא דרב יוסף לאו הל"מ קאמר: מאי הוי עלה דתחש. הואיל ולרב יוסף לאו לענין מלאכה דמשכן איתמר לא איפשיט בעיין: מקרין תרתי משמע. דסתם מקרין כל קרניו:

מתני' שקיפלה. כמו שגודלין פתילות: הבהבה. על השלהבת כדי שתהא מחורכת ותדליק יפה: טמאה היא. דבגד כלי הוא ומקבל טומאה אם היה שלש על שלש דקפול אין מבטלה מתורת בגד הואיל ולא הבהבה: ואין מדליקין בה. כדמפרש טעמא בגמ':

גמ' קפול מועיל. לבטולה מתורת בגד: מצומצמות. דאי הוה טפי פורתא לכולי עלמא מדליקין: ובי"ט שחל להיות בע"ש. דשייך ביה איסור מוקצה עסקינן: ואין מסיקין בשברי כלים. שנשברו בו ביום דהוו להו נולד אבל בכלים מסיקין דהא חזו לטלטלן: ודכולי עלמא אית להו. צריך המדליק להדליק בידים קודם סילוק ידיו רוב היוצא מן הפתילה חוץ לנר הלכך על כרחך צריך לעסוק בו לאחר שנפחת משלש הלכך טעמא דר"א דאסר קסבר קיפול אינו מועיל והוה ליה כלי שנשבר בי"ט וכי קמדליק ביה פורתא כיון דמצומצמות היו הוו שברי כלי דפחות משלש לאו כלי הוא והוה ליה כלי שנשבר בי"ט וכי קמדליק בידים להשלים רוב היוצא בשבר כלי קמדליק והא דאמרינן מסיקין בכלים דוקא שלא יגע בו אחר שנפחת אלא אם כן ריבה עליו עצים מוכנים כדלקמן (דף כט:): קיפול מועיל. ועל כרחך מעי"ט קיפלה דאין גודלין פתילה בי"ט כדתניא בהמביא (ביצה לב:) וככר נתבטל הכלי מבע"י ואין כאן שבר כלי: היינו דתניא. שהייתי שונה מרבותי משנה ג' על ג' מצומצמות ולא הוה ידענא למאי הלכתא איתמר דאי לענין טמויי כל שכן דאי איכא טפי דמטמא: ומדקא מתרץ כו'. מילתא באפי נפשיה היא בתמיה למירמי דרב אדא אדרב אדא מדקא מתרץ למתניתין ואוקי דכולי עלמא אית להו אין מסיקין בשברים דהיינו אליבא דר"י דאית ליה נולד ש"מ כו':

בההק

תוספות

אתיא בק"ו מנולה של עזים. וא"ת נימא שתי וערב יוכיח שמטמא בנגעים ואינו מטמא במת אף אני אביא עור בהמה טמאה כו' ועוד קשה אמאי איצטריך קרא בשרצים לעור בהמה טמאה ליתי בק"ו מנולה של עזים שאין מיטמא בנגעים מיטמא בשרצים וי"ל דאי לא הוה כתיב קרא בשרצים ליכא למילף עור בהמה טמאה בק"ו מנגעים לא בשרצים ולא באהל המת דאיכא למימר שתי וערב יוכיח אבל השתא דכתיב טומאה בשרצים ילפינן שפיר בק"ו מנגעים שיטמא באהל המת וליכא למימר שתי וערב יוכיח דמה לשתי וערב שכן אינו מטמא בשרצי' תאמר בעור בהמה טמאה שמטמא בשרצים הכי נמי יטמא באהל המת:

ור"י אומר דליכא למימר שתי וערב יוכיח דהכי עביד ק"ו ומה נולה של עזים שאין מטמא בנגעים מטמא באהל המת ככלי העשוי מנולה של עזים עור בהמה טמאה שטמא בנגעים אינו דין שיטמא באהל המת ככליו דהשתא לא שייך למימר שתי וערב יוכיח שמטמא בנגעים ולא באהל המת דשתי וערב אין שייך בו כלי ואין לומר דכל היוצא מן העץ ועלם יוכיח שמטמא בנגעים ואינו מטמא במת דמה שמטמא בנגעים אינו מחמת עצמו אלא מחמת הבית דהא בית שסיככו בזרעים אמר בשור והרוטב דמטמא בנגעים אבל נולה והעור מטמא מחמת עלמו. ומהר"ם כתב דליכא למימר שתי וערב יוכיח דמה לשתי וערב שכן אין מטמאין לא במת ולא בש"ז תאמר בעור בהמה טמאה דמטמא דהא כתיב במת ובש"ז כל בגד וכל כלי עור. ולעיל כי פריך מה לשרצים ליכא למימר נגיעת מת וש"ז יוכיח דמה לכולהו שכן פחות מכזית דנגיעת מת בכשעורה וש"ז במשא או בחתימת פי האמה (והוא תי' דאיצטריך קרא בשרצים לאפוקי מהיקש דשק) וזה אין נראה דע"כ דגם לענין אהל הוי שיעורו בכזית להביא טומאה על כל הכלים ועל עלמן אפי' יוצא מן העץ דזהו תלוש קיי"ל דמביא. ונ"ל דלא שייך כלל למימר אהל תלוש יוכיח כיון דלא אתינא למילף אלא לענין אהל המחובר דלא מטמא אלא מאי דילפי' ממשכן וכי האי גוונא איכא בפ"ק דמנחות גבי טריפה שהיתה לה שעת הכושר דלא ילפינן מטריפה שלא היתה לה שעת הכושר אפי' במה הלד [ת"י]:

והקשה השר מקולי מאי בעי בסמוך מאי הוי עלה דתחש תיפוק ליה דטהור היה מדאיצטריך קרא בשרלי' לטמא עור בהמה טמאה דאי טמא היה לשתוק קרא בשרלים ותיתי בק"ו מנגעים דהשתא ליכא למימר שתי וערב יוכיח דמה לשתי וערב שכן אין מטמאין באהל המת תאמר בעור בהמה טמאה דמיטמא באהל המת כיון דתחש טמא היה וי"ל דמהכא ליכא למיפשט דטהור היה דאפילו טמא היה כתיב בשרלים דמילתא דאתיא בק"ו טרח וכתב לה קרא ועוד אומר רש"י דשרלים לא אתו מק"ו מנגעים דאיכא למיפרך פשוטי כלי עור יוכיח דמטמא בנגעים ולא בשרלים:

למאי הלכתא לא בעי למימר לאשמעינן דתחש טהור היה דמשמע דאתא לאשמעינן שום צורך הוראה: תפילין בהדיא כתיב בהו למען תהיה וגו'. תימה לר"י וכי אין לברייתא לשנות מה שדורש מן הפסוק וכל הנך דמייתי בסמוך וכי לית ליה לרב יוסף לשנות הברייתא לפי שזה אמרו אמורא אחד או ברייתא ואומר רבינו יצחק דהכי פריך תפילין בהדיא כתיב בהו ואי הא הוה אתי לאשמעי' הוה ליה לאתויי קרא אע"כ מילתא אחריתי אתא לאשמעי' ודרשה דמן המותר בפיך היתה פשוטה ולא איצטריך לאשמעי' וקאמר אלא לעורן והאמר אביי שין של תפילין ט' ובזה הלשון הוה ליה לרב יוסף למימר והוה ידעינן שפיר דבעי עור בהמה טהורה דדרשה דמן המותר בפיך היא פשוטה אלא לכורכן בשערן לריך בהמה טהורה הא נמי הל"מ דתניא כו' מדלא קתני רב יוסף בהאי לישנא ונכרכות בשערן ש"מ דמילתא אחריתא אתא לאשמעינן אלא לרצועותיהן והא"ר יצחק רצועות שחורות הל"מ וכיון דמצריך שיהו הרצועות שחורות כמו הקציצה כל שכן דבעינן שיהו טהורות כמו הקציצה דסברא הוא להקפיד על הטהרה מעל השחרות ואי הא אתא רב יוסף לאשמעי' לישמעינן שיהו שחורות דהוה שמעינן מינה תרתי שחורות וטהורות ומשני נהי דגמירי שחורות טהורות מי גמירי דמשחורות ליכא למיגמר טהורות: **לא** צריכא אלא לכורכן בשערן. קשה לרשב"א אי הא אתא לאשמעי' אמאי נקט עור במילתיה:

רבא

עין משפט נר מצוה

פה א מיי' פ"א מהלכות תפילין הלכה י ופ"י מהלכות ס"ת הלכה א סמג עשין כב כה טוש"ע א"ח סימן לב סעיף יב טור שו"ע יו"ד סימן רעא סעיף א:

פו ב מיי' פ"ג מהלכות תפילין הלכה טו סמג עשין כב טור שו"ע א"ח סי' לב סעיף לז:

פז ג מיי' שם הלכה א טוש"ע שם סעיף מב:

פח ד מיי' שם הלכ' ד טוש"ע שם סעיף לט:

פט ה מיי' שם טוש"ע שם סעיף מד

צ ו מיי' שם הל' ט טור שו"ע שם סעיף מט:

לקמן סב. מנחות לה.

מנחות שם מגילה כד:

צא ז ח מיי' שם הלכה יד טו סמג שם טור שו"ע א"ח סימן לג סעיף ג:

צב ט מיי' פ"א מהל' מאכלות אסורות הלכה יב טור שו"ע יו"ד סימן פ סעיף ד:

צג י טוש"ע א"ח סימן רסד סעיף ט:

צד כ מיי' פ"ה מהלכות שבת הלכה ה סמג לאוין סה טור שו"ע שם סעיף ח:

[עי' תוספות חולין נט: ד"ה וקרש]

פ"ז ת. ע"ש חולין פ:

רבינו חננאל

אתיא בק"ו מנוצה של עזים. ומה נוצה של עזים שאינה מטמאה בנגעים (בג' על ג') מטמא באהלים דילפינן אהל אהל ממשכן. עור בהמה טמאה שמטמא בנגעים אינו דין שיטמא באהלים ואלא הא דתני רב יוסף לא הוכשרו למלאכת שמים אלא עור בהמה טהורה למאי הלכתא ואסיקנא לרצועות של תפילין. שיהו מבהמה טהורה. אבל תפילין עצמן בהדיא כתיב בהו למען תהיה תורת ה' בפיך. ודרשינן מן המותר בפיך. וגם שי"ן של תפילין. וכי נכרכות בשערן ונתפרות בגידן ורצועותיהן שחורות הלכה למשה מסיני הן. ואסיק' נמי תחש בריה בפ"ע היא ולא הכריעו חכמים אי מין חיה הוא [או מין בהמה] וקרן היה לו וטהור היה: פיסקא פתילת הבגד שקפלה ולא הבהבה כו'. א"ר אלעזר מתניתין בג' על ג' מצומצמות הוא ובי"ט שחל להיות בע"ש. וכולי עלמא אית להו דר' יהודה דאמר מסיקין בכלים ואין מסיקין בשברי כלים. וכולי עלמא אית להו דעולא דאמר צריך להדליק ברוב היוצא. ר' אלעזר סבר קיפול אינו מועיל וכיון דאדליק בה פורתא הוה ליה שבר כלי. וכי קא מדליק בשבר כלי קא מדליק. ולפיכך אסור. ור"ע סבר קיפול מועיל וכיון דקפליה בטליה וכי קא מדליק בעץ בעלמא

רב נסים גאון

בד' ספחים: אתיא בק"ו מנוצה של עזים שאין מטמא טומאת נגעים. תמצא עיקר דילי' בתורת כהנים והבגד יכול השיראין והסיריקון והכלך וצמר גפן וצמר גמלים וצמר ארנבאין ונוצה של עזים ת"ל בבגד צמר או בבגד פשתים אין לי אלא צמר ופשתים המיוחדין: כיון דאיכא קרש דמין חיה הוא ולית ליה אלא קרן אחד · במס' שחיטת חולין בפרק אלו טריפות (דף ס) אמרו וקרש אע"פ שאין

מסורת הש"ס

לקמן קח. [מכות יא.]

[עי' פרש"י מנחות לה: ובתוס' שם ד"ה אלו תפילין שבגולה וכו' שהשיגו על פירש"י מסוגי' דהכא דמסיק אלא לרצועות וכו' ועי' רש"י ותוס' לקמן סב. ד"ה שי"ן של תפילין ועי' תוס' מגילה כד: ד"ה תפלה מרובעת וכו' ותוס' עירובין צז. ד"ה קשר ותוס' כתובות ד"ה אלו]

לקמן קכד: ביצה לב. וש"נ

לעיל כ:

גליון הש"ס

גמ' והאמר אביי שי"ן של תפילין. עי' חולין דף ט. תוס' ד"ה ושל תפלה יד וש"נ: גמ' אמר רב יוסף היינו דתנינא על שלש כו'. עיין יבמות דף עו ע"ב ודף פ ע"א

said Raba of Barnesh, [28b] it is inferred *a minori* from goats' hair, which is not defiled by leprosy, yet is defiled by overshadowing the dead; then the skin of an unclean animal, which is defiled by leprosy, is surely defiled by overshadowing the dead.

Then when R. Joseph recited, 'For the sacred work none but the skin of a clean animal was considered fit,' for what practical law [did he say it]?[2]—In respect of phylacteries.[3] Of phylacteries it is explicitly stated, *that the law of the Lord may be in thy mouth*,[4] [meaning] of that which is permitted in thy mouth?[5] Rather in respect of their hide.[6] But Abaye said, The skin of phylacteries is a law of Moses from Sinai?[7]—Rather, it is in respect of tying it with its hair and sewing it with its tendons.[8] But that is a law of Moses from Sinai. For it was taught: Rectangular phylacteries[9] are a law of Moses from Sinai: they must be tied with their hair and sewn with their tendons.[10]—Rather it is in respect of
a their straps.[1] But R. Isaac said, Black straps are a law of Moses from Sinai? Granted that black is traditional, is clean traditional?[2]

What is our conclusion with respect to the *taḥash* which existed in Moses' days?—Said R. Elai in the name of R. Simeon b. Laḳish, R. Meir used to maintain, The *taḥash* of Moses' day was a separate species, and the Sages could not decide whether it belonged to the genus of wild beasts or to the genus of domestic animals; and it had one horn in its forehead, and it came to Moses' hand [providentially] just for the occasion,[3] and he made the [covering of the] Tabernacle, and then it was hidden. Now, since he says that it had one horn in its forehead, it follows that it was clean. For R. Judah said, The ox which Adam the first [man] sacrificed had one horn in its forehead, for it is said, *and it shall please the Lord better than an ox, or a bullock that hath a horn* [sic] *and hoofs*.[4] But *maḳrin*[5] implies two?—Said R. Naḥman b. Isaac: *Mi-ḳeren*[6] is written.[7] Then let us solve thence that it was a genus of domestic animal?[8]—Since there is the *ḳeresh*,[9] which is a species of beast, and it has only one horn, one can say that it [the *taḥash*] is a kind of wild beast.

MISHNAH. A WICK [MADE] OF A CLOTH WHICH WAS TWISTED BUT NOT SINGED,—R. ELIEZER SAID: IT IS UNCLEAN, AND ONE MAY NOT LIGHT [THE SABBATH LAMP] THEREWITH; R. AKIBA MAINTAINED: IT IS CLEAN, AND ONE MAY LIGHT THEREWITH.[10]

GEMARA. As for the matter of uncleanness, it is well, [for] they differ in this: R. Eliezer holds that twisting is of no effect,
b and it remains in its previous condition;[1] while R. Akiba holds that twisting is effective, and it [its previous condition] is indeed annulled. But with reference to lighting, wherein do they differ?—R. Eleazar said in R. Oshaia's name, and R. Adda b. Ahabah said likewise: The reference here is to [a rag] exactly three [fingerbreadths] square;[2] and also to a Festival falling on the eve of the Sabbath. Now, all agree with R. Judah, who maintained, One may fire [an oven, etc.,] with [whole] utensils, but not with broken utensils.[3] Further, all agree with 'Ulla's dictum, viz.: He who lights must light the greater part [of the wick] which protrudes. R. Eliezer holds that twisting is of no avail, and immediately one kindles it slightly it becomes a broken utensil,[4] and when he goes on kindling it,[5] he kindles a broken utensil. But R. Akiba holds that twisting is effective, and it does not bear the character of a utensil, and therefore when he kindles, he kindles a mere piece of wood.[6] R. Joseph observed: This is what I learnt, exactly three [fingerbreadths] square, but did not know in reference to what law.

Now, since R. Adda b. Ahabah explains it in accordance with R. Judah,[7] it follows that he himself holds as R. Judah. Yet did R. Adda b. Ahabah say thus? Surely R. Adda b. Ahabah said:

(2) As a mere historical fact it is of no importance. Hence what is its purpose, seeing that it does not teach that the skin of an unclean animal is not defiled by overshadowing the dead, as one wished to deduce *supra* 28a? (3) That the parchment of these must be made of the skin of a clean animal. (4) Ex. XIII, 9; the reference is to *tefillin* (v. Glos.). (5) Cf. *supra* 27b, n. a2 (on explicitness). (6) The leather of the capsules in which the parchment is placed. This cannot be deduced from the verse quoted, for '*the law of the Lord*' was not written upon them. (7) The letter *shin* (ש) is stamped out of the leather itself at the side of the capsule. This is part of the Name *Shaddai* (שדי), and therefore comes within the meaning of '*the law of the Lord*'.—With respect to the meaning of 'a law of Moses from Sinai', some take it literally: this was handed down direct from Moses; others understand it in a more figurative sense: it is traditional, but its exact origin is unknown, and hence ascribed to Moses, who in general is the source of Jewish law. V. Weiss, *Dor*, I, 71 *seq*. (8) The parchment within the phylacteries, on which Biblical passages are written, is rolled up and tied round with animal hair. The receptacles themselves are sewn together with the tendons of animals. Both must be from clean animals. (9) I.e., the faces of the capsules must be rectangular in shape, the whole forming a cube. (10) 'Their' meaning of the same animal or species which furnishes the parchment and the leather. Thus they must be all of a clean animal, and this is a traditional law.

a (1) These must be of the skin of a clean animal. (2) I.e., is there a tradition that they must be of the skin of a clean animal? Surely not! Hence R. Joseph's teaching is necessary. (3) Lit., 'garment'. (4) Ps. LXIX, 32. (5) E.V. '*that hath horns*.' (6) Than a horn. (7) I.e., מקרן, which is normally punctuated מִקֶּרֶן (*mi-ḳeren*), but here מַקְרִין *maḳrin*. On the identification of this ox with that sacrificed by Adam v. A.Z. 8a. (8) Viz., an ox or bullock. (9) Jast.: a kind of antelope, unicorn. (10) The reasons are discussed in the Gemara.

b (1) A rag, being part of a garment, is liable to become unclean, a wick does not become unclean. R. Eliezer holds that mere twisting without singeing—this was done to facilitate the lighting—does not make it a wick, and therefore it is still subject to uncleanness. (2) This is the smallest size liable to defilement (*supra* 26b); in that sense it is regarded as a whole garment (or utensil). (3) On Festivals. A whole utensil may be handled on Festivals, and therefore it may be taken for burning. But if a utensil is broken on the Festival so that it can now be used as fuel only, it is regarded as a thing newly-created (*nolad* v. Glos.)—i.e., a new use for it has just been created—and such may not be handled on Festivals. (4) Since it was the minimum size originally. (5) Until the greater part is alight. (6) I.e., this twisted rag is just like a piece of wood. (7) That *nolad* (v. n. b3) is forbidden.

[29a] If a Gentile hollows out a *ḳab*[8] in a log, an Israelite may heat [the oven] therewith on a Festival.[9] Yet why? Is it not *nolad!*—He states [it] according to the views of R. Eliezer and R. Akiba, but does not hold thus himself.

Raba said, This is R. Eliezer's reason: Because one must not light [the Sabbath lamp] with an unsinged wick or unsinged
a rags.[1] Then when R. Joseph recited, Exactly three [fingerbreadths] square, in respect of what law [was it]?—In respect of uncleanness. For we learnt, The three [fingerbreadths] square of which they [the Sages] spoke is exclusive of the hem: this is R. Simeon's view. But the Sages say: Exactly three [fingerbreadths] square.[2]

Rab Judah said in Rab's name: One may fire [an oven, etc.,] with [whole] utensils, but not with broken utensils: this is R. Judah's opinion; but R. Simeon permits it.[3] One may fire [it] with dates;[4] but if they are eaten, one may not fire [it] with their stones:[5] that is R. Judah's opinion; but R. Simeon permits it. One may heat with nuts: if they are eaten, one must not heat with their shells: this is R. Judah's ruling; but R. Simeon permits it.

Now, they are [all] necessary. For if we were told the first, R. Judah rules [thus] in that case, because it was a utensil before but only a fragment of a utensil now, and so it is *nolad*, hence forbidden; but as for dates, since they were stones originally and are stones now, I might argue that it is well [permitted]. And if we were informed [this] of dates, I might say, [the reason is] because they [the stones] were originally concealed but are now revealed; but as for nutshells, which were uncovered originally and are uncovered still, I might argue that it is well [permitted]. Thus they are necessary.[6]

Now, this [ruling] of Rab was stated not explicitly but by implication. For Rab ate dates and threw the stones into a pan;[7] whereupon R. Ḥiyya said to him, 'Son of great ancestors![8] A similar act on Festivals is forbidden.' Did he accept [this ruling] from him or not?—Come and hear: For when Rab came to
b Babylon,[1] he ate dates[2] and threw the stones to animals. Surely this means Persian [dates]?[3] No: this means Syrian [dates], since they are fit [for handling] on account of their flesh.[4]

R. Samuel b. Bar Ḥanah said to R. Joseph: According to R. Judah who ruled, One may fire [an oven] with utensils, but not with broken utensils,—immediately one lights with it a little it becomes a broken utensil, and when he stirs [the fuel] he is stirring something that is forbidden?—He acts in accordance with R. Mattenah: For R. Mattenah said in Rab's name: If wood falls from a palm tree into a stove on a Festival, one adds more prepared wood and lights them.[5]

R. Hamnuna said: The reference here [in our Mishnah] is to [a rag] less than three [handbreadths] square,[6] and they taught here some of the leniencies [relating to the law] of rags, both R. Eliezer and R. Akiba following their views. For we learnt: If [material] less than three [handbreadths] square is set aside for stopping a bath, pouring from a pot,[7] or cleaning a mill therewith, whether it is of prepared [material] or not,[8] it is unclean:[9] that is R. Eliezer's view; R. Joshua maintained: Whether it is of prepared [material] or not, it is clean; R. Akiba ruled: If of prepared [material], it is unclean; if of unprepared, it is clean. Now 'Ulla—others state, Rabbah b. Bar Ḥanah in R. Joḥanan's name—said: All admit that if it was thrown away on the refuse

(8) A measure; or, a kind of artificial leg. (9) Though it is *nolad*.
a (1) These do not burn well. Thus R. Eliezer refers to all Sabbaths. (2) V. Kelim. XXVIII, 7. (3) He permits *nolad*. (4) Since they may be handled as food, they may be handled as fuel. (5) This and the following are similar to the first, the stones of dates and the shells of nuts being like fragments of utensils. (6) Reversing the argument, all cases are necessary for R. Simeon's view. (7) A kind of coal brazier.—This was done on weekdays. (8) V. *supra* 3b.
b (1) Rab was a Babylonian who went to study in Palestine and then returned. (2) On Festivals. (3) These become very ripe, so that the whole of the fruit can be removed from the stones. Since he threw them to animals, he evidently held that they might be handled, and could also have used them for fuel. Hence he must have rejected R. Ḥiyya's view. (4) The fruit cannot be entirely separated from the stone. (5) The timber that falls may not be handled by itself, since it was not destined for this before the Festival. Hence a greater quantity of wood set aside for fuel must be added, and both may be handled together. The same must be done here. (6) He holds that if it is three handbreadths square, it retains the character of a garment and is liable to defilement on all views. (7) Using this material as a holder. (8) The meaning is discussed below. (9) I.e., liable to uncleanness as a garment (*beged*), which connotes any material that may be put to a useful purpose.

נכרי שחקק קב בבקעת ישראל מסיקה *ביו"ט ואמאי נולד הוא לדבריהם דר"א ור"ע קאמר ליה וליה לא סבירא ליה רבא אמר היינו טעמא דרבי אליעזר לפי שאין מדליקין בפתילה שאינה מחורכת ולא בסמרטוטין שאינן מחורכין אלא הא דתני רב יוסף ג' על ג' מצומצמות למאי הלכתא לענין טומאה *דתנן ג' על ג' שאמרו חוץ מן המלל דברי ר"ש וחכ"א ג' על ג' מכוונות: אמר רב יהודה אמר רב *מסיקין בכלים ואין מסיקין בשברי כלים דברי רבי יהודה ור"ש מתיר מסיקין בתמרין אכלן אין מסיקין בגרעיניהן דברי רבי יהודה ור"ש מתיר מסיקין באגוזים אכלן אין מסיקין בקליפותיהן דברי רבי יהודה ורבי שמעון מתיר וצריכא דאי אשמעינן קמייתא בההיא קאמר רבי יהודה משום דמעיקרא כלי והשתא שבר כלי והוה ליה נולד ואסור אבל תמרים דמעיקרא גרעינין והשתא גרעינין אימא שפיר דמי ואי אשמעינן גרעינין הוה אמינא דמעיקרא מכסיין והשתא מיגליין אבל קליפי אגוזין דמעיקרא מיגלו והשתא מיגלו אימא שפיר דמי צריכא והא דרב *לאו בפירוש איתמר אלא מכללא איתמר דרב אכל תמרי ושדא קשייתא *לבוכיא אמר ליה רבי חייא *בר פחתי כנגדו ביו"ט אסור קיבלה מיניה או לא קיבלה מיניה ת"ש דכי אתא רב לבבל אכל תמרי ושדא קשייתא לחיותא מאי לאו בפרסייאתא ולא קיבלה לא *בארמיאתא הואיל וחזי אגב אימייהו א"ל ר' שמואל בר בר חנה לרב יוסף לרבי יהודה דאמר מסיקין בכלים ואין מסיקין בשברי כלים כיון דאדליק בהו פורתא הוה ליה שברי כלים וכי קא מהפך באיסורא קא מהפך דעבד כדרב מתנה *דאמר רב מתנה אמר רב עצים שנשרו מן הדקל לתנור ביו"ט מרבה עצים מוכנין ומסיקן רב המנונא אמר הכא בפחות משלשה על שלשה עסקינן *ומקולי מטלניות שנו כאן ואזדא ר' אליעזר לטעמיה ור"ע לטעמיה *דתנן פחות משלשה על שלשה שהתקינו לפקק בו את המרחץ ולנער בו את הקדירה ולקנח בו את הרחיים בין מן המוכן ובין שאין מן המוכן טמא דברי רבי אליעזר ורבי יהושע אומר בין מן המוכן ובין שלא מן המוכן טהור ר"ע אומר מן המוכן טמא ושלא מן המוכן טהור ואמר עולא ואיתימא רבה בר בר חנה א"ר יוחנן הכל מודים זרקו באשפה דברי הכל טהור

הניחו

רש"י

שחקק קב · בי"ט דהוה ליה נולד: לדבריהם דר' אליעזר ור' עקיבא קאמר · האי דאוקי' לאו רב אדא אליבא דר' יהודה דהא פלוגתייהו דלא מיתוקמא אלא אליבא דר' יהודה ומיהו איהו לא סבירא ליה אלא כר' שמעון: טעמא דרבי אליעזר · בהדלקה משום דאין מדליקין בו שאין דולקין יפה ובכל שבתות השנה אסור ולאו משום נולד: חוץ מן המלל · דרך תופרי בגדים למלול מן הבגדים לכופלן מעט סביב התפירה ואח"כ תופר וג' על ג' סופו לתפור לטלאי בבגד עני לכן אחשבוה להיות כלי הלכך צריך להיות בו יותר משיעור המלל כדי שיהא הטלאי שלש על שלש: מכוונות · מצומצמות ובהכי אחשבוה ואע"ג דכשיתפור לא הוה שלש והיינו הך דרב יוסף ולאו משום דאי הוה טפי לא מיטמא *(דכל שכן) אלא לאפוקי מדתנא קמא: מסיקין בתמרים · דאגב דמטלטל להו לאכילה חזו נמי להסקה: אכלן · ביו"ט אין מסיקין בגרעינין ביו"ט דהוה להו נולד: והשתא מגליין · הלכך נולד הוה: והא דרב · דאמר כר' יהודה אין מסיקין בגרעינין לאו בפירוש איתמר: אכל תמרי · בחול: לבוכיא · כירה של רעפים שקורין טיול"ש והיא חלולה וספרים שכתוב בהן לבי תפי היינו נמי כירה והוא תרגום של בית ספיתת שתי קדרות: קשייתא · גרעינין: בר פחתי · בן גדולים: אכל תמרי · ביום טוב: פרסייתא · תמרים טובים ומתבשלים יפה וכל אוכל שלהם נפרש מעל גרעיניהן ואין הגרעינין ראוין לטלטל ואפ"ה שרי לטלטלן למישדינהו לחיותא אלמא לא קיבלה מיניה: בארמיתא · דאין מתבשלות יפה ואין האוכל נפרש מהן ומשתייר בגרעיניהן וחזו לאדם: אגב אימייהו · שיש עוד אוכל עליהן: מרבה · עליהן ומבטלן ברוב: רב המנונא אמר · מתניתין בפחות משלשה טפחים על שלשה טפחים פליגי לענין טומאה: ומקולי מטלניות · מטלניות הקלות בעיניו דומיא דמתוקנות לפקוק מרחץ דמידי דלא חשיב הוא וקיפול דנקט במתניתין משום הבהוב דנקט דוקא ולפלוגתא דהדלקה תנא קיפול: פחות משלשה כו' · דאילו שלשה על שלשה חשיבי ולא בטלי ואע"ג דקילי כגון סמרטוטין: שהתקינו לכך · שהקצו לכך: לפקוק המרחץ · נקבים שהמים באים דרך שם למרחץ: ולנער בו את הקדרה · לאחוז בהן שולי הקדרה ולנערה לתוך התמחוי: בין מן המוכן · לקמיה מפרש:

תוספות

רבא אמר היינו טעמא דר' אליעזר · משמע דרבא לענין טומאה אית ליה שיטיא דרב אדא בר אהבה ולקמן משמע דאית ליה שיטיא דרב המנונא דאמר מקולי מטלניות שנו כאן דקאמר והדר ביה ר' עקיבא לגבי ר' יהושע על כן נראה דהכא גרס רבה ולקמן רבא וכ"ל דבהגס נהגו אנשים להדליק הפתילה ולכבותה כדי שתהא מהובהבת דהא אין הלכה כרבי אליעזר דשמותי הוא ועוד אמרינן לקמן הכא בפתילה שצריך להבהבה עסקינן משמע דיכול להדליק אע"פ שאינה מהובהבת:

ולא בסמרטוטין שאינן מחורכין · קשה כיון דתנא דאפילו בפתילה שאינה מחורכת אין מדליקין כ"ש בסמרטוטין שאינם מחורכין ומיהו בתוספתא גרס ולא בסמרטוטין אפי' מחורכין:

אכלן אין מסיקין בגרעיניהן · תימה לר"י דבפרק נוטל (לקמן דף קמב:) אמר למימרא דרבא כרבי יהודה סבירא ליה פירוש דאסר נבלה שנתנבלה בשבת והא"ל לשמעי' טווי לי בר אווזא ושדי מיעיה לשונרא ומשני התם כיון דמסרח דעתיה עילויה מאתמול אלמא כיון דדעתו מאתמול לתת לשונרא כשיסריח למחר שרי אע"ג דכל זמן שלא הסריח חזי לאדם *משום דחשיב כאילו הכינו מבעוד יום לשונרא ה"נ מאתמול דעתיה עילויה להסיר הגרעינין כשיאכל התמרים למחר ואמאי חשיב ליה טפי נולד ממיעיה דבר אווזא וי"ל דהתם בר אווזא נשחט מעי"ט ואין המעיים צריכים לאווז וכיון דמבעוד יום דעתיה למיתביה לשונרא אם יסריחו חשיבה הכנה מעלייתא אבל הכא הגרעינין צריכין לאוכל וחשיבי כאוכל עצמו עד שיאכל התמרים לכך חשיב להו נולד ולא מהני מה שדעתו עליהם מאתמול:

והא דרב לאו בפירוש איתמר כו' · הא פשיטא דרב אסר נולד כרבי יהודה מכרכי דזוזי (לעיל דף יט:) אלא מייתי ראיה דאף בגרעינין דאיכא למימר מעיקרא גרעינין והשתא גרעינין אסר רבי יהודה וא"ת ובאגוזים דמעיקרא מגלו והשתא מגלו מנלן דאסר וי"ל דאע"ג דמטעם זה עושה צריכותא מ"מ מטעם זה לפי האמת אין נראה לו לחלק ביניהם:

בין מן המוכן כו' · פירש בקונטרס מוכן דרבי אליעזר קופסא שאינו מוכן תלאו במגוד והניחו אחורי הדלת ומוכן דר' יהושע תלאו במגוד והניחו אחורי הדלת *ושאינו מוכן זרקו לאשפה ורבי עקיבא מוכן תלאו במגוד ושאינו מוכן הניחו אחורי הדלת וקשה לר"י דהשתא מוכן ושאינו מוכן דהאי תנא לא הוי כאידך ועוד מה להם להזכיר בדבריהם קופסא ואשפה דלא פליגי בה ועוד דבפרק כירה (לקמן דף לט: ושם) קרי לרבי עקיבא מכריע ואמאי והלא לא גילו בדבריהם רבי אליעזר ורבי יהושע שיש לחלק בין תלאו במגוד להניחו אחורי הדלת וגראה לר"י דמוכן דכולהו היינו תלאו במגוד ושאינו מוכן היינו הניחו אחורי הדלת והאי דקאמר אמאי קרי ליה שלא מן המוכן פירש רבי אליעזר אמאי קרי להניחו אחורי הדלת שלא מן המוכן הואיל והוא טמא ומשני משום דלגבי קופסא לאו מוכן הוא ולא בעי למימר משום דלגבי מגוד לאו מוכן הוא דלא חשיב כולי האי תלאו במגוד מאחורי הדלת דהוה קרי ליה לגביה שלא מן המוכן וכן לר' יהושע קא בעי אמאי חשיב לתלאו במגוד מן המוכן הואיל והוא טהור ומשני דלגבי אשפה מוכן הוא והא דלא קאמר דלגבי אחורי הדלת מוכן הוא משום דלא גריע כולי האי טפי ממגוד דליהוי אינו מוכן לגביה:

גזירה

עין משפט נר מצוה

צה א מיי' פכ"ב מהל' כלים הלכה א:

צו ב מיי' פ"ב מהל' יו"ט הלכה יב סמג לאוין סה טוש"ע א"ח סי' תקא סעיף ו:

צז ג מיי' שם טוש"ע שם סעיף ז:

צח ד שם סעיף ו בהג"ה:

צט ה מיי' שם הלכה יא סמג שם טוש"ע א"ח סי' תקו סעיף ב:

מסורת הש"ס

[ברכות ס: וש"נ]

[גי' הערוך לבוביא]

[פי' תמרי ארמיתא גרעינייהו רכין ונאכלין עם התמרים ערוך ערך ארס]

כלים ד:

[לקמן לט:]

כלים פכ"ח מ"ב

[ביצה לג: וש"נ ע"ש]

ורש"י פי' לקמן משום דאין דרך לאכול מעיים ביו"ט ולא נהירא דמשום זה לא הוי אסור לטלטלו כמו בשר מלוח דמותר לטלטלו [תו"י]

[לעיל ג: וש"נ]

גם בירושלמי פירש כן

רבינו חננאל

מדליק רבא אמר טעמא דר' אליעזר לפי שאין מדליקין לא בסמרטוטין ולא בפתילה שאינה מחורכת · ורבי עקיבא מתיר: ירושלמי מהו מכורכין מפספסין דכתי' (דניאל ג') ושער ראשיהון לא התחרך · ג' על ג' מצומצמות שאמרו חוץ מן המלל דברי ר' שמעון וחכ"א ג' על ג' מכוונות:

אמר רב יהודה אמר רב מסיקין בכלים ואין מסיקין בשברי כלים · מסיקין בתמרים · אכלן אין מסיקין בגרעיניהן · מסיקין באגוזים · אכלן אין מסיקין בקליפיהן דברי רבי יהודה · ורבי שמעון מתיר בכולן · יצריכא דאי אשמעינן וכו' ופשוטה היא · עד אבל קליפי אגוזים דמעיקרא מיגלו אימא קא שרי ר' יהודה צריכא · והא דרב מכללן איתמר דרב אכל תמרי ושדא קשייתא לבוכיא א"ל ר' חייא בר פחתי כנגדו ביו"ט אסור ואסיקנא קיבלה מיניה והא כי אתא רב לבבל אכל תמרי ושדא קשייתא לחייתא · ואוקימנא בתמרי ארמייתא שגרעיניהן רכים · והואיל וראוין להיאכל בכלל התמרים כאוכל הן ולפיכך מלטלם · אבל שדו גרעינין דלא חזי אגב אימייהו אסור כר' חייא אליבא דרבי יהודה · קסבר הלכה כר' יהודה ביו"ט הואיל וסתם לן כותיה ביו"ט · ומדמתרץ להו דר' יהודה כרב מתנה שמע מינה הלכתא כוותיה · דאמר רב מתנה עצים שנשרו מן הדקל לתנור ביו"ט מרבה עליהם עצים מוכנים ומסיקן · ואוקמה רב המנונא למתני' במטלניות פחות מג' אצבעות והא דסייתי ראיה ממטלת פחותה מג' על ג' מקולי מטלניות שנו כו' · דתנן בכלים בפ' כ"ח פחות מג' על ג' שהתקינו לפקק את המרחץ ולנער בו הקדירה ולקנח בו הריחיים בין מוכן בין שאינו מוכן טמא דברי ר' אליעזר · ר' יהושע אומר בין מוכן בין שאינו מוכן טהור · רע"א

רב נסים גאון

מאי לאו בפריסאתא ולא קבלה לא בארמיאתא הואיל וחזיאן אגב אימיהו' תמצא פירושיה בסוף פ' נוטל אדם את בנו (דף קמג) הני גרעיני דתמרי ארמיאתא שרי לטלטולינהו בשבתא הואיל וחזיאן אגב אימן כי התמרים יבשים תאכל אותם הבהמה ודפריסאתא אסור לפי שהרוטב של תמרים לא תאכל הבהמה אלא גרעינא בלבד לא חזיין אגב אימן:

ק א מיי' פכ"ב מהל' כלים הלכה כב :
קא ב מיי' פ"ה מהל' שבת הל' יב טוש"ע א"ח סי' רסה סעיף א :
קב ג מיי' שם טוש"ע שם סעיף ב :
קג ד מיי' שם טוש"ע שם סעיף א :
קד ה מיי' פ"י מהל' כלאים הל' טו סמג לאוין רפג טוש"ע י"ד סי' שא סעיף ו :
קה ו מיי' פי"א מהל' שבת הלכה ה סמג לאוין סה טוש"ע א"ח סי' שלו סעיף א :
קו ז ח מיי' פ"א שם הלכה ז ופי"ב הלכה ג סמג שם טוש"ע א"ח סימן רעח :

גזירה עיליתא דשישא אטו עיליתא דעלמא · והא דקאמר בסוף המצניע (לקמן דף צה· ושם) אמימר שרא זילחא במחוזא ומפרש דטעמא מאי אמור רבנן דילמא אתי לאשויי גומות הכא ליכא גומות ומפרש בקונטרס דכולה מחוזא רצפה היתה התם אין לגזור מחוזא אטו שאר עיירות אבל בעיר אחת גזרינן עלייה זו *אטו עלייה אחרת : **ה"ג** מחלוקת בקטנים אבל בגדולים ד"ה מותר · ול"ג ד"ה אסור דבפרק כל שעה (פסחים דף כה: ושם) משמע דטפי שרי היכא דלא אפשר מהיכא דאפשר :

ובלבד שלא יתכוין בחמה מפני החמה וכו' · ובענין דלא הוי פסיק רישיה כגון שהוא לבוש מלבושים אחרים להגין עליו מפני החמה ומפני הצינה :

שהמ"ו

הניחו בקופסא דברי הכל טמא לא נחלקו אלא שתלאו במגוד או שהניחו לאחורי הדלת ר' אליעזר סבר *מדלא זרקו באשפה דעתיה עילויה ומאי(א) קרי ליה שלא מן המוכן דלגבי קופסא לאו מוכן הוא ור' יהושע סבר מדלא הניחו בקופסא בטולי בטליה ומאי קרי ליה מוכן דלגבי אשפה מוכן הוא ור' עקיבא בתלאו במגוד סבר כרבי אליעזר בהניחו אחורי הדלת סבר לה כרבי יהושע *והדר ביה ר"ע לגביה דר' יהושע ממאי אמר רבא מדקתני פתילת הבגד מאי איריא דתני פתילת הבגד ליתני פתילה של בגד מאי פתילת הבגד דעדיין בגד הוא :

מתני' [ג]לא *יקוב אדם שפופרת של ביצה וימלאנה שמן ויתננה על פי הנר בשביל שתהא מנטפת ואפילו היא של חרס ורבי יהודה מתיר אבל אם חברה היוצר מתחלה מותר מפני שהוא כלי אחד [ד]לא ימלא אדם קערה של שמן ויתננה בצד הנר ויתן ראש הפתילה בתוכה בשביל שתהא שואבת ורבי יהודה מתיר :

גמ' וצריכא דאי אשמעינן שפופרת של ביצה בהא קאמרי רבנן דכיון דלא מאיסא אתי לאסתפוקי מינה אבל של חרס דמאיסא אימא מודו ליה לרבי יהודה ואי אשמעינן של חרס בהא קאמר רבי יהודה אבל בההיא אימא מודי להו לרבנן ואי אשמעינן הנך תרתי בהני קאמר רבי יהודה משום דלא מיפסק אבל קערה דמיפסקא אימא מודי להו לרבנן ואי אשמעינן בההיא בההיא קאמרי רבנן אבל בהני תרתי אימא מודו לרבי יהודה צריכא : ואם חברה היוצר מתחלה מותר וכו' : תנא אם [ה]חברה בסיד ובחרסית מותר והאנן יוצר תנן מאי יוצר כעין יוצר : *תניא א"ר יהודה פעם אחת שבתינו בעליית בית נתזה בלוד והביאו לנו שפופרת של ביצה ומלאנוה שמן ונקבנוה והנחנוה על פי הנר והיה שם ר"ט וזקנים ולא אמרו לנו דבר אמרו לו *משם ראיה שאני בית נתזה דזריזין הן אבין ציפוראה גרר ספסלא בעיליתא דשישא לעילא מרבי יצחק בן אלעזר א"ל אי שתוקי לך כדשתיקו ליה חבריא לר' יהודה נפיק מיניה חורבא °גזירה עיליתא דשישא אטו עליתא דעלמא ריש כנישתא דבצרה גרר ספסלא לעילא מר' ירמיה רבה א"ל כמאן *כר"ש אימר דאמר ר"ש בגדולים דלא אפשר בקטנים מי אמר ופליגא דעולא דאמר עולא מחלוקת בקטנים אבל בגדולים ד"ה מותר מתיב רב יוסף *ר"ש אומר גורר אדם מטה כסא וספסל ובלבד שלא יתכוין לעשות חריץ קתני גדולים וקתני קטנים קשיא לתרווייהו עולא מתריץ לטעמיה ור' ירמיה רבה מתריץ לטעמיה עולא מתריץ לטעמיה מטה דומיא דכסא ור' ירמיה רבה מתריץ לטעמי' כסא דומיא דמטה מתיב רבה *מוכרי [ו]כסות מוכרין כדרכן ובלבד שלא יתכוין בחמה מפני החמה ובגשמים מפני הגשמים והצנועין מפשילין במקל לאחוריהן והא הכא דאפשר למיעבד כצנועין דכי קטנים דמי וכי [ז]לא מתכוין שרי ר"ש לכתחלה תיובתא דר"י רבה *תיובתא :

מתני' [ח]המכבה את הנר מפני שהוא מתירא מפני נכרים ומפני ליסטי' מפני רוח רעה מפני החולה שיישן פטור כחס על הנר כחס על השמן כחס על הפתילה חייב [ט]רבי יוסי *פוטר בכולן חוץ מן הפתילה מפני שהוא עושה פחם :

גמ'

הניחו בקופסא · גלי דעתיה דחשיב ליה : במגוד · קבילא דגרע מקופסא ועדיף מאחורי הדלת ואחורי הדלת עדיף מזרקו לאשפה ומוכן דר' אליעזר הייט קופסא ושלא מן המוכן מגוד ואחורי הדלת : ומאי (ג) קרי ליה שלא מן המוכן · הואיל ולרבי אליעזר חשיב לקבולי טומאה דלגבי קופסא לאו מוכן הוא : ורבי יהושע סבר כו' · ומוכן דרבי יהושע מגוד ואחורי הדלת ושלא מן המוכן זרקו לאשפה : ומאי(ג) קרי ליה · למגוד מוכן הואיל ולר' יהושע בטל דלגבי אשפה דאיירי בה רבי יהושע מוכן הוא ורבי עקיבא תלאו במגוד קרי מוכן ואחורי הדלת שלא מן המוכן : והדר ביה ר' עקיבא לגבי רבי יהושע · ומטהר אף במוכן : מדקתני · במתניתין פתילת הבגד דמשמע שעדיין בגד הוא קצת וחשבו בעיניו ואפ"ה קאמר רבי עקיבא במתני' טהורה היא אלמא הדר ביה : של בגד · משמע שקפלה מבגד הבגד משמע שקפל הבגד עצמו שלם ולענין הדלקה כדאוקימנא לעיל טעמא דרבי אליעזר דבעי פתילה מחורכת שתדלק יפה : **מתני'** שתהא מנטפת · ויתקיים הנר שתהא השמן מטפטף כל שעה לתוך הנר וטעמא משום גזרה שמא יסתפק הימנו וכיון שהקלהו לנר חייב משום מכבה ואפי' אותה שפופרת של חרס דמאיסא ליה גזרינן : אבל אם חיברה · ליכא למיחש דמשום איסור שבת בדיל מיניה : ויתן ראש הפתילה · השני שהוא יוצא דרך הנקב האחר שבנר לשאוב שמן נמשך דרך הפתילה לראש הדולק : ורבי יהודה מתיר · דלא גזר : **גמ'** דלא מיפסק · מידי שהוא מונח בתוך חלל הנר למעלה מכיסוי : דמפסקא · שהרי אצל הנר מונחת ויש כאן הפסק וליכא למימר גופיה הוא אימא מודה דנגזור : תנא אם חיברה · בעה"ב עצמו מבעוד יום בסיד או בחרסית מותר : כעין יוצר · שחברה ספיר : דשישא · רצפה של שיש דלא עביד בה חריץ : לעילא מרבי יצחק · לפניו : כדשתיקו ליה חבריא · רבי טרפון וזקנים שמפני שלא אמרו לו דבר דימה והעיד דמותר : נפק מיניה חורבה · וינהגו היתר בדבר ור' יצחק סבירא ליה כרבי יהודה דדבר שאין מתכוין אסור ואע"ג דבשיש לא עביד חריץ גזר אטו עיליתא דעלמא : ריש כנישתא · מפטיר כנסיות המכניס ומוציא ומיישב תלמידים ותינוקות : דבצרה · שם מקום כי זבח לה' בבצרה (ישעיה לד) : כר' שמעון · דאמר גורר אדם : דלא אפשר · אלא בגרירה שאין יכול ליטלן בידו : מחלוקת בקטנים · ואע"ג דאפשר בטלטול שרי רבי שמעון הואיל ואין מתכוין לחריץ ורבי יהודה סבר כיון דאפשר אסור : קתני גדולים · מטה : וקתני קטנים · כסא ורבי יהודה פליג עליה דתנן במסכת ביצה רבי יהודה אומר כל הכלים אין נגררים דאי לאו משום פלוגתייהו למה לי למיתני גדולים השתא קטנים שרי רבי שמעון גדולים מיבעיא אלא תנא קטנים משום ר' שמעון ותנא גדולים משום רבי יהודה : דומיא דכסא · קטנים ובהא הוא דאסר רבי יהודה אבל בגדולים שרי : כסא דומיא דמטה · גדולים ובהא הוא דשרי רבי שמעון אבל בקטנים אסר : מוכרין כדרכן · כסות של כלאים לובשו בשוק כדי להראותו למוכרו דלא אסרה תורה אלא לבישה שהיא להתחמם כדרך כל הלובשים והעלאה דומיא דלבישה כמי דמיתהני בה : ובלבד שלא יתכוין כו' · ור' שמעון הוא דאזיל בתר כוונה : והצנועים · כשרים שמרחיקין עצמן מכל לזות שפתים : והא הכא דאפשר · לכל אדם למעבד שלא על ידי איסור ואפילו הכי שרי : **מתני'** מפני נכרים · כגון פרסיים שהיה להם יום חג שאין מניחין אור אלא בבית עבודת אלילים שלהם : ומפני הלסטין · שלא יראו שיש שם אדם ויבאו עליו : ומפני רוח רעה · *) הבאה עליו וכשאינו רואה נוח לו : פטור · ובגמרא מפרש לכולה : כחס על הנר · שרואהו שמתקלקל וחס עליו וכבה את הפתילה : הנר . קרוויז"ל : חייב · ובגמרא מפרש לה : פוטר בכולן · מפרש בגמרא (דף לא:) : שהוא עושה פחם · בכיבוי זה והוי מלאכה הצריכה לגופה כדאמר בגמרא :

*) ס"א מרה שחורה

אע"ג דר' יוסי אית ליה דהבערה ללאו יצאת בפיגור מודה דחייב אף בפני עצמו כדתנן בפרק כלל גדול · ושוב אמר מהר"מ דמהר"ל אמר דבפ' ספק אכל בהדיא פוטר רבי יוסי בהבערה ומחייב בכיבוי [תי"]

[לקמן מ.] · פסחים יח. · תוספתא פ"ב ע"ש · [לקמן מה: וש"נ] · לעיל כב. לקמן מו: ביצה כג: [תוספ' ביצה פ"ב] פסחים קא. מנחות מא: · כלאים פ"ט מ"ה לקמן מו: פסחים כו: · [לקמן סב: ברכות יט: עירובין יג: מו: סו. ר"ה כד: סוכה כ: יד: כח. לח: לו: לז: מגילה כז: יבמות כב. קד: ב"מ פב: ב"ב קטו: ע"ז כד. חולין מג. מד. סנהדרין יב. מנחות כח: בכורות כח: חולין כז: ערכין לד: מ"ס כג: סא.] · [עיין תוספות פסחים כה: סד"ה לא אפשר]

הגהות הב"ח

(א) גמ' ואמאי קרי ליה שלא מן המוכן : (ב) רש"י ד"ה ומאי קרי ליה מוכן : (ג) ד"ה ואמאי קרי ליה למגוד :

גליון הש"ס

גמ' גזירה עיליתא דשישא · עיין לקמן דף קנא ע"ב : תוס' ד"ה גזרה וכו' אטו עלייה אחרת · ועיין לקמן דף קנא ע"ב בתוס' ד"ה קקטע :

רבינו חננאל

[רע"א מן המוכן טמא שלא מן המוכן טהור] ואוקימנא בשזרקו לאשפה דברי הכל טהור הניחו בקופסא דברי הכל טמא · כי פליגי בשתחבו בבגדו או בשהניחו אחורי הדלת · רבי אליעזר סבר מדלא זרקו לאשפה דעתיה עילויה לפיכך הוא טמא ואמאי קרי ליה אינו מוכן דלגבי קופסא לאו מוכן הוא · ורבי יהושע סבר כיון שלא הניחו בקופסא בטליה הלכך טהור הוא · ואמאי קרי ליה מוכן דאחורי הדלת או תחוב בבגדו לגבי אשפה מוכן הוא · ור' עקיבא (סבר מספקא ליה) בתחבו בבגדו סבר לה כר' אליעזר שהוא טמא בהניחו אחורי הדלת סבר לה כר' יהושע והדר ביה ר' עקיבא לגבי ר' יהושע ואמר אפי' התחובה בבגדו טהור טמאי מדקתני במתני' פתילת הבגד ולא קתני פתילה של בגד ש"מ דעדיין בגד הוא ותני ר' עקיבא אומר טהורה ומדליקין בה · ומאן דחזא רב המנונא דאייתי ראיה מג' על ג' מוקים לה לפתילה דקתני במתני' פתילה שיש בה פחות מג' [טפחים] והא דרויה היא דהכי קתני ר' עקיבא אומר טהורה ומשנה שלימה שנינו מפני שאמרו ג' על ג' שנתמעטה טהורה אבל שלשה על שלשה שנתמעטה אע"פ שטהר מן המדרס טמא בכל הטומאות אלא פחות משלש הוא (וכן) [וכיון] דאוקימנא רב אדא בג' אוקימנא רב המנונא בפחות משלש והאי (דקתני) [דקאמר] שלשה דהכנת מטליות בהדיא [בפחות] משלשה קתני לה והוא הדין לפחות מג' *) והלכה כר"ע דקאי ר' יהושע כוותיה דהא הדר ביה ר' עקיבא לגבי דר' יהושע וכן מפורש בברייתא: **מתני'** לא יקוב אדם שפופרת של ביצה כו' · ופשוטה היא · זו השפופרת של חרס · תנא אם חיברה זו השפופרת של חרס בסיד ובגפסים כעין היוצר מותר · ומלאנוה שמן ונקבנוה והנחנוה ע"פ הנר · והיה שם ר' טרפון והזקנים ולא אמרו לנו דבר אמרו לו משם ראיה מפני כי [בית] נתזה (זהיר) [זריז] הוה: **תנא** (תוספתא פ"ב) נותנין פים או חרסית תחת [הנר] או גרגיר מלח או גרים של טול ע"ש מבעוד יום ע"פ הנר להיות שוהה. אבין ציפוראה גרר ספסלא בעיליתא דשישא לעילא מר' יצחק בן אלעזר אמר ליה [אי] שתוקי לך כי האי דשתקו ליה חבריא לר' יהודה בשפופרת של ביצה ונפיק מינה חורבה דהוראה להיתר לאו שפיר עבדת בגרירת ספסלא גזירה עיליתא דשישא דלית בה חריץ אטו עיליתא דעלמא · ריש כנישתא דבצרה גרר ספסלא לעילא מר' ירמיה רבה א"ל כמאן כר' שמעון [illegible] **מתני'** המכבה את הנר מפני שהוא מתירא כו' . [illegible]

*) ע' ברי"ף שמחנו אוקימנא

רב נסים גאון

מותיב רבא מוכרי כסות מוכרין כדרכן ובלבד שלא יתכוין בחמה מפני החמה ובגשמים מפני הגשמים· זו המשנה שנויה בפרק ט' דמסכת כלאים בסוף המסכת לפי שאסרו קודם לכן און עראי לכלאים כו' הוצרכו להתיר לאלו דברים שהם תולים בהם ובלבד שלא יתכוונו בהם החמה חוק להרחיק בעת החום וחוק הגשמים בעתם וכמותו התירו לתופרים כמו ששנינו תופרי כסות תופרין כדרכן כו' כלומר

heap,[10] it is universally agreed that it is clean;[11] [29b] if one placed
a it in a chest, all agree that it is unclean.[1] They differ only where he hung it on a frame or placed it behind the door: R. Eliezer holds: Since he did not throw it on the refuse heap, he had his mind upon it; why then does he call it 'unprepared'?[2] Because relatively to [placing it in] a chest it is not prepared.[3] While R. Joshua maintains: Since he did not place it in a chest, he has indeed accounted it as nought;[4] and why then does he call it 'prepared'? Because relatively to [throwing it on] a refuse heap it is prepared. But R. Akiba agrees with R. Eliezer where he hangs it on a clothes frame, and with R. Joshua, where he puts it behind the door. Yet R. Akiba retracted in favour of R. Joshua ['s view]. Whence [is this deduced]?—Said Raba, Since it is stated, A WICK [MADE] OF A CLOTH: why choose to teach A WICK [MADE] OF A CLOTH, teach A WICK OF CLOTH; why A WICK [MADE] OF A CLOTH? [To show] that it is still a cloth.[5]

MISHNAH. A MAN MAY NOT PIERCE AN EGG SHELL, FILL IT WITH OIL, AND PLACE IT OVER THE MOUTH OF A LAMP, IN ORDER THAT IT SHOULD DRIP, AND EVEN IF IT IS OF POT;[6] BUT R. JUDAH PERMITS IT. BUT IF THE POTTER JOINS IT BEFOREHAND, IT IS PERMITTED, BECAUSE IT IS ONE UTENSIL. A MAN MUST NOT FILL A DISH OF OIL, PLACE IT AT THE SIDE OF A LAMP, AND PUT THE WICK END THEREIN IN ORDER THAT IT SHOULD DRAW; BUT R. JUDAH PERMITS IT.

GEMARA. Now, they are [all] necessary. For if we were told about an eggshell; there the Rabbis say [that it is forbidden]
b because since it is not loathsome[1] he will come to take supplies therefrom;[2] but as for an earthen [shell], which is loathsome,[3] I might argue that they agree with R. Judah.[4] While if we were told of an earthen [shell]: [only] there does R. Judah rule thus, but in the other case I might say that he agrees with the Rabbis.[5] And if we were told of these two: R. Judah rules [thus] of these because nothing interposes;[6] but as for a dish, which interposes,[7] I would say that he agrees with the Rabbis. While if we were told of that: [only] there do the Rabbis rule [thus], but in the first two I would say that they agree with R. Judah. Thus they are necessary.

BUT IF THE POTTER JOINS IT BEFOREHAND, IT IS PERMITTED, etc. A Tanna taught: If he joins it with plaster or potter's clay, it is permitted. But we learnt, THE POTTER?[8]—What is

(10) And then salved for one of these purposes. (11) Since it is less than three handbreadths square, and was also thrown away as worthless, it is certainly not a 'garment', even when salved.

a (1) He showed that he attributed value to it, hence it is a 'garment'. (2) Since he intends to use it, it is 'prepared', i.e., designated for use. (3) When he places it in a chest he certainly intends using it; but here he merely ensures that he will have it in case he wants it. (4) Not assigning any real worth to it. (5) The suggested reading פתילה של בגד implies that a portion of a *beged* (cloth) is taken, viz., such as itself is not a cloth (in the sense stated in *supra* 29a, n. b9). The actual reading פתילת הבגד implies that a cloth itself is turned into a wick. Since R. Akiba maintains in the Mishnah that it is not liable to uncleanness, he evidently agrees with R. Judah that it is not 'prepared'. (6) I.e., even a pot shell may not be used thus.

b (1) The oil in the eggshell is clean. (2) On the Sabbath. This is forbidden on account of extinguishing the light. [Though it is not actually extinguished when he removes some oil, it subsequently goes out sooner than it would otherwise have done.] (3) The oil in it becomes soiled and unclean. (4) There is no fear that one may draw supplies from it. (5) Inverting the reasoning. (6) Between the lamp and the shell, which is directly over its mouth: hence R. Judah regards it all as one, even when not actually joined. (7) Between the lamp and the oil. (8) Which implies that it must be professionally done, whereas 'he joins it' denotes an amateur job by the owner.

◁ *For the continuation of the English translation of this page see overleaf.*

הניחו בקופסא דברי הכל טמא לא נחלקו אלא שתלאו במגוד או שהניחו לאחורי הדלת ר' אליעזר סבר *מדלא זרקו באשפה דעתיה עילויה ומאי(א) קרי ליה שלא מן המוכן דלגבי קופסא לאו מוכן הוא ור' יהושע סבר מדלא הניחו בקופסא בטולי בטליה ומאי קרי ליה מוכן דלגבי אשפה מוכן הוא ור' עקיבא בתלאו במגוד סבר כרבי אליעזר בהניחו אחורי הדלת סבר לה כרבי יהושע *והדר ביה ר"ע לגביה דר' יהושע ממאי אמר רבא מדקתני פתילת הבגד מאי איריא דתני פתילת הבגד ליתני פתילה של בגד מאי פתילת הבגד דעדיין בגד הוא:

מתני' ״לא *יקוב אדם שפופרת של ביצה וימלאנה שמן ויתננה על פי הנר בשביל שתהא מנטפת ואפילו היא של חרס ורבי יהודה מתיר אבל אם חברה היוצר מתחלה מותר מפני שהוא כלי אחד ״לא ימלא אדם קערה של שמן ויתננה בצד הנר ויתן ראש הפתילה בתוכה בשביל שתהא שואבת ורבי יהודה מתיר:

גמ' וצריכא דאי אשמעינן שפופרת של ביצה בהא קאמרי רבנן דכיון דלא מאיסא אתי לאסתפוקי מינה אבל של חרס דמאיסא אימא מודו ליה לרבי יהודה ואי אשמעינן של חרס בהא קאמר רבי יהודה אבל בההיא אימא מודי להו לרבנן ואי אשמעינן הנך תרתי בהני קאמר רבי יהודה משום דלא מיפסק אבל קערה דמיפסקא אימא מודי להו לרבנן ואי אשמעינן בההיא בההיא קאמרי רבנן אבל בהני תרתי אימא מודו לרבי יהודה צריכא:

ואם חברה היוצר מתחלה מותר וכו': תנא אם ״חברה בסיד ובחרסית מותר והאנן יוצר תנן מאי יוצר כעין יוצר: *תניא א"ר יהודה פעם אחת שבתינו בעליית בית נתזה בלוד והביאו לנו שפופרת של ביצה ומלאנוה שמן ונקבנוה והנחנוה על פי הנר והיה שם ר"ט וזקנים ולא אמרו לנו דבר אמרו לו *משם ראיה שאני בית נתזה דזריזין הן אבין ציפוראה גרר ספסלא בעיליתא דשישא לעילא מרבי יצחק בן אלעזר א"ל אי שתוקי לך כדשתיקו ליה חבריא לר' יהודה נפיק מיניה חורבא °גזירה עליתא דשישא אטו עליתא דעלמא ריש כנישתא דבצרה גרר ספסלא לעילא מר' ירמיה רבה א"ל כמאן *כר"ש אימר דאמר ר"ש בגדולים דלא אפשר בקטנים מי אמר ופליגא דעולא דאמר עולא מחלוקת בקטנים אבל בגדולים ד"ה מותר מתיב רב יוסף *ר"ש אומר גורר אדם מטה כסא וספסל ובלבד שלא יתכוין לעשות חריץ קתני גדולים וקתני קטנים קשיא לתרווייהו עולא מתרץ לטעמיה ור' ירמיה רבה מתרץ לטעמיה עולא מתרץ לטעמיה מטה דומיא דכסא ור' ירמיה רבה מתרץ לטעמי' כסא דומיא דמטה מתיב רבה *מוכרי ״כסות מוכרין כדרכן ובלבד שלא יתכוין בחמה מפני החמה ובגשמים מפני הגשמים והצנועין מפשילין במקל לאחוריהן והא הכא דאפשר למיעבד בצנועין דכי קטנים דמי וכי ״לא מתכוין שרי ר"ש לכתחלה תיובתא דר"י רבה *תיובתא:

מתני' ״המכבה את הנר מפני שהוא מתירא מפני נכרים ומפני ליסטי' מפני רוח רעה מפני החולה שיישן פטור כחס על הנר כחס על השמן כחס על הפתילה חייב ״רבי יוסי *פוטר בכולן חוץ מן הפתילה מפני שהוא עושה פחם:

גמ'

הניחו בקופסא · גלי דעתיה דחשיב ליה: במגוד · קס"ל דגרע מקופסא ועדיף מאחורי הדלת ואחורי הדלת עדיף מזרקו לאשפה ומוכן דר' אליעזר היינו קופסא ושלא מן המוכן מגוד ואחורי הדלת: ומאי (ג) קרי ליה שלא מן המוכן · הואיל ולרבי אליעזר חשיב לקבולי טומאה דלגבי קופסא לאו מוכן הוא: ורבי יהושע סבר כו'. ומוכן דרבי יהושע מגוד ואחורי הדלת ושלא מן המוכן זרקו לאשפה: ומאי(ג) קרי ליה' למגוד מוכן הואיל ולר' יהושע בטל דלגבי אשפה דאיירי בה רבי יהושע מוכן הוא ורבי עקיבא תלאו במגוד קרי מוכן ואחורי הדלת שלא מן המוכן: והדר ביה ר' עקיבא לגבי רבי יהושע · ומטהר אף במוכן: מדקתני · במתניתין פתילת הבגד דמשמע שעדיין בגד הוא קצת וחשבו בעיניו ואפ"ה קאמר רבי עקיבא במתני' טהורה היא אלמא הדר ביה: של בגד · משמע שקפלה מבגד הבגד משמע שקפל הבגד עצמו שלם ולענין הדלקה כדאוקימנא לעיל טעמא דרבי אליעזר דבעי פתילה מחורכת שתדלק יפה: **מתני'** שתהא מנטפת · ויתקיים הנר שתהא השמן מטפטף כל שעה לתוך הנר וטעמא משום גזרה שמא יסתפק הימנו וכיון שהקלהו לנר חייב משום מכבה ואפי' אותה שפופרת של חרס דמאיסא ליה גזרינן: אבל אם חיברה · ליכא למיחש דמשום איסור שבת בדיל מיניה: ויתן ראש הפתילה · השני שהוא יוצא דרך הנקב האחר שבנר לשאוב ושמן נמשך דרך הפתילה לראש הדולק: ורבי יהודה מתיר · דלא גזר: **גמ'** דלא מיפסק · מידי שהוא מונח בתוך חלל הנר למעלה מכיסוי: דמפסקא · שהרי אצל הנר מונחת ויש כאן הפסק וליכא למימר גופיה הוא אימא מודה דנגזור: תנא אם חיברה · בעה"ב עצמו מבעוד יום בסיד או בחרסית מותר: כעין יוצר · שחברה שפיר: דשישא · רצפה של שיש דלא עביד בה חריץ: לעילא מרבי יצחק · לפניו: כדשתיקו ליה חבריא · רבי טרפון וזקנים שמפני שלא אמרו לו דבר דימה והעיד דמותר: נפק מיניה חורבה · וינהגו היתר בדבר ור' יצחק סבירא ליה כרבי יהודה דדבר שאין מתכוין אסור ואע"ג דבשיש לא עביד חריץ גזר אטו עיליתא דעלמא: ריש כניסתא · מפטיר כנסיות המכניס ומוציא ומיישב תלמידים ותינוקות: דבצרה · שם מקום כי זבח לה' בבצרה (ישעיה לד): כר' שמעון · דאמר גורר אדם: דלא אפשר · אלא בגרירה שאין יכול ליטלן בידו: מחלוקת בקטנים · ואע"ג דאפשר בטלטול שרי רבי שמעון הואיל ואין מתכוין לחריץ ורבי יהודה סבר כיון דאפשר אסור: קתני גדולים · מטה: וקתני קטנים · כסא ורבי יהודה פליג עליה דתנן במסכת ביצה רבי יהודה אומר כל הכלים אין נגררים דאי לאו משום פלוגתייהו למה לי למיתני גדולים השתא קטנים שרי רבי שמעון גדולים מיבעיא אלא תנא קטנים משום ר' שמעון ותנא גדולים משום רבי יהודה: דומיא דכסא · קטנים ובהא הוא דאסר רבי יהודה אבל בגדולים שרי: כסא דומיא דמטה · גדולים ובהא הוא דשרי רבי שמעון אבל בקטנים אסר: מוכרין כדרכן · כסות של כלאים לובשו בשוק כדי להראותו למוכרו דלא אסרה תורה אלא לבישה שהיא להתחמם כדרך כל הלובשים והעלאה דומיא דלבישה כמי דמיתהני בה: ובלבד שלא יתכוין כו' · ור' שמעון הוא דאזיל בתר כוונה: והצנועים · כשרים שמרחיקין עצמן מכל לזות שפתים: והא הכא דאפשר · לכל אדם למעבד שלא על ידי איסור ואפילו הכי שרי: **מתני'** מפני נכרים · כגון פרסיים שהיה להם יום חג שאין מניחין אור אלא בבית עבודת אלילים שלהם: ומפני הלסטין · שלא יראו שיש שם אדם ויבאו עליו: ומפני רוח רעה · *) הבאה עליו וכשאינו רואה נוח לו: פטור · ובגמרא מפרש לכולה: כחס על הנר · שראוהו שמתקלקל וחס עליו וכבה את הפתילה: הנר . קרוייז"ל: חייב · ובגמרא מפרש לה: פוטר בכולן · מפרש בגמרא (דף לא:): שהוא עושה פחם · בכיבוי זה והוי מלאכה הצריכה לגופה כדאמר בגמרא:

*) ס"א מרה שחורה

גמ'

גזירה עיליתא דשישא אטו עיליתא דעלמא · והא דקאמר בסוף המצניע (לקמן דף צה· ושם) אמימר שרא זילחא במחוזא ומפרש דטעמא מאי אמור רבנן דילמא אתי לאשויי גומות הכא ליכא גומות ומפרש בקונטרס דכולה מחוזא רצפה היתה התם אין לגזור מחוזא אטו שאר עיירות אבל בעיר אחת גזרינן עלייה זו °אטו עלייה אחרת: **ה"ג** מחלוקת בקטנים אבל בגדולים ד"ה מותר · ול"ג ד"ה אסור דבפרק כל שעה (פסחים דף כה: ושם) משמע דטפי שרי היכא דלא אפשר מהיכא דאפשר:

ובלבד שלא יתכוין בחמה מפני החמה וכו' · ובענין דלא הוי פסיק רישיה כגון שהוא לבוש מלבושים אחרים להגין עליו מפני החמה ומפני הצינה:

[עיין תוספות פסחים כה: סד"ה לא אפשר]

אע"ג דר' יוסי אית ליה דהבערה ללאו יצאת מודה אף בכבוי עצמו כדתנן בפרק כלל גדול · ושוב אמר מהר"מ דמהר"א אמר דבפ' ספק אכל בהדיא פוטר רבי יוסי בהבערה ומחייב בכיבוי [ת"י]

עין משפט נר מצוה

ק א מיי' פכ"ב מהל' כלים הלכה כב:

קא ב מיי' פ"ה מהל' שבת הל' יב טוש"ע א"ח סי' רסה סעיף א:

קב ג מיי' שם טוש"ע שם סעיף ב:

קג ד מיי' שם טוש"ע שם סעיף א:

קד ה מיי' פ"י מהל' כלאים הל' טז סמג לאוין רפג טוש"ע י"ד סי' שא סעיף ו:

קה ו מיי' פ"א מהל' שבת הלכה ה סמג לאוין סה טוש"ע א"ח סי' שלז סעיף א:

קו ז ח מיי' פ"א שם הלכה ז ופי"ב הלכה ב סמג שם טוש"ע א"ח סימן רעח:

מסורת הש"ס

[לקמן מ.]

פסחים יח.

[לקמן פב: ברכות יט: עירובין יג: מה: פו. ר"ה כד: סוכה כד: יד: כז. לו: לז. מגילה כו: יבמות כב: קד: ב"מ סג: כד. קב. כד. מד. סנהדרין יב. מנחות כה: בכורות מה: חולין נו: ערכין לא: נדה כ: סא.]

הגהות הב"ח

(א) גמ' ומאי קרי ליה שלא וכו' ומאי קרי ליה מוכן: (ב) רש"י ד"ה ומאי קרי ליה שלא: (ג) ד"ה ומאי קרי ליה למגוד:

גליון הש"ס

גמ' גזירה עיליתא דשישא · עיין לקמן דף קנא ע"ב: תוס' ד"ה גזרה וכו' אטו עלייה אחרת · ועיי' לקמן דף קנא ע"ב ברש"י ד"ה קרקע:

תוספתא פ"ב ע"ש

[לקמן מח: וש"נ]

לעיל כב. לקמן מו: ביצה כג: [תוספ' ביצה פ"ב] פסחים קא. מנחות מא:

כלאים פ"ט מ"ה לקמן מו: פסחים כו:

רבינו חננאל

[רע"א מן המוכן טמא שלא מן המוכן טהור] ואוקימנא בשזרקו לאשפה דברי הכל טהור הניחו בקופסא דברי הכל טמא · כי פליגי בשתחבו בבגדו או בשהניחו אחורי הדלת · רבי אליעזר סבר מדלא זרקו לאשפה דעתיה עילויה לפיכך הוא טמא ואמאי קרי ליה אינו מוכן דלגבי קופסא לאו מוכן הוא · ורבי יהושע סבר כיון שלא הניחו בקופסא בטליה הלכך טהור הוא · ואמאי קרי ליה מוכן דאחורי הדלת או תחוב בבגדו לגבי אשפה מוכן הוא · ור' עקיבא (סבר מספקא ליה) בתחבו בבגדו סבר לה כר' אליעזר שהוא טמא בהניחו אחורי הדלת סבר לה כר' יהושע והדר ביה ר' עקיבא לגבי ר' יהושע ואמר אפי' התחובה בבגדו טהור ממאי מדקתני במתני' פתילת הבגד ולא קתני פתילה של בגד ש"מ דעדיין בגד הוא ותני ר' עקיבא אומר טהורה ומדליקין בה · ומאן דחזא רב המנונא דאייתי ראיה מג' על ג' מוקים לה לפתילה דקתני במתני' פתילה שיש בה פחות מג' [טפחים] והא דחויה היא דהכי קתני ר' עקיבא אומר טהורה ומשנה שלימה שנינו מפני שאמרו ג' על ג' שנתמעטה טהורה אבל שלשה על שלשה שנתמעטה אע"פ שטהר מן המדרס טמא בכל הטומאות אלא פחות משלש הוא (וכן) [וכיון] דאוקימנא רב אדא בג' אוקימנא רב המנונא בפחות משלש והאי (דקתני) [דקאמר] שלשה דהכנת מטליות בהדיא [בפחות] משלשה קתני לה והוא הדין לפחות מג' *) והלכה כר"ע דקאי ר' יהושע כוותיה דהא הדר ביה ר' עקיבא לגבי דר' יהושע וכן מפורש בכירה: **מתני'** לא יקוב אדם שפופרת של ביצה כו' · ופשוטה היא זו השפופרת של חרס · תנא אם חיברה זו השפופרת של חרס בסיד ובגפסים כעין היוצר מותר· ומלאנוה שמן ונקבנוה והנחנוה ע"פ הנר· והיה שם ר' טרפון והזקנים ולא אמרו לנו דבר אמרו לו משם ראיה מפני כי [בית] נתזה (זהיר) [זריז] הוה: **תנא** (תוספתא פ"ב) נותנין טיט או חרסית תחת [הנר] או גרגיר מלח או גרים של פול ע"ש מבעוד יום ע"פ הנר להיות שוהה. אבין ציפוראה גרר ספסלא בעיליתא דשישא לעילא מר' יצחק בן אלעזר אמר ליה [אי] שתוקי לך כי האי דשתקו ליה חבריא לר' יהודה בשפופרת של ביצה ונפיק מינה חורבה דהוראה להיתר לאו שפיר עבדת בגרירת ספסילא גזירה עיליתא דשישא דלית בה חריץ אטו עיליתא דעלמא · ריש כנישתא דבצרה גרר ספסילא לעילא מר' ירמיה רבה א"ל כמאן כר' שמעון אימור דשרי ר' שמעון בגדולים דלא אפשר להגביהן בקטנים דאפשר להגביהן מי אמר · עולא אמר מחלוקת בקטנים אבל בגדולים דברי הכל מותר ומותבינן לתרווייהו מהאי ר' שמעון אומר גורר אדם מטה כסא וספסל ובלבד שלא יתכוין לעשות חריץ הנה קתני מטה דהיא גדולה וקתני כסא וספסל שהן קטנים מכלל דפליגי בקטנים ובגדולים קשיא לתרווייהו ופרק' ר' ירמיה רבה כסא וספסל גדולים הן דומיא דמטה· עולא מפרק לטעמיה מטה קטנה שיכול להגביהה דומיא דכסא וספסל · מתיב רבא מוכרי כסות של כלאים מוכרין כדרכן ובלבד שלא יתכוין בחמה מפני החמה ובגשמים מפני הגשמים · שאם יתכוין נמצא נהנה מן הכלאים ואסור והצנועין מפשילין במקל לאחוריהן כדי שלא יהא כלאים עולה על גופן כלל · והא הכא דאפשר למעבד כצנועים כי היכי דאפשר להגביה כלים · וכי לא מכוין קא שרי רבי שמעון בהעלאה עליהן · תיובתא דרבי ירמיה רבה תיובתא: **מתני'** המכבה את הנר מפני שהוא מתירא כו'

*) עי' בכי"ף שסתרו ·

אוקימנא

רב נסים גאון

מותיב רבא מוכרי כסות מוכרין כדרכן ובלבד שלא יתכוין בחמה מפני החמה ובגשמים מפני הגשמים' זו המשנה שנויה בפרק ט' דמסכת כלאים בסוף המסכת לפי שאמרו קודם לכן אין עראי לכלאים כו' הוצרכו להתיר לאלו דברים שהם רגילים בהם ובלבד שלא יתכוונו בהם להרחיק הזק החמה בעת החום והזק הגשמים בעתם וכמותו התירו לתופרים כמו ששנינו תופרי כסות תופרין כדרכן כו'

כלומר

Continuation of translation from previous page as indicated by ◁

meant by POTTER? After the manner of a potter.[9]

It was taught, R. Judah said: We were once spending the Sabbath in the upper chamber of Nithzeh's house in Lydda, when an eggshell was brought, which we filled with oil, perforated, and placed over the mouth of the lamp; and though R. Tarfon and the elders were present, they said nothing to us.[10] Said they [the Sages] to him, Thence [you adduce] proof? The house of Nithzeh is different, because they were most heedful.[11]

Abin of Sepphoris dragged a bench in a stone-paved upper chamber in the presence of R. Isaac b. Eleazar. Said he to him, If I let this pass in silence,[12] as his companions kept silent before R. Judah, harm will ensue: a stone-paved chamber is forbidden
c on account of an ordinary chamber.[1] The synagogue overseer[2] of Bazrah[3] dragged a bench in front of R. Jeremiah Rabbah. Said he to him, In accordance with whom?[4] [Presumably] R. Simeon![5] Assume that R. Simeon ruled [thus] in the case of larger ones, since it is impossible otherwise;[6] did he say thus of small ones?[7] Now, he disagrees with 'Ulla, who said: They differ [only] in respect of small ones, but as for large, all agree that it is permitted.

R. Joseph objected: R. Simeon said, A man may drag a couch, chair, or bench, providing that he does not intend making a rut. Thus both large and small [articles] are taught,[8] which is a difficulty on both views.[9]—'Ulla reconciles it according to his view, and R. Jeremiah Rabbah reconciles it according to his. 'Ulla reconciles it according to his view: the couch is like the chair.[10] While R. Jeremiah Rabbah reconciles it according to his: the chair is like the couch.[11]

Rabbah objected: Clothes merchants sell in their normal fashion, providing that one does not intend [to gain protection] from the sun in hot weather[12] or from the rain when it is raining;[13] but the strictly religious[14] sling them on a staff behind their back.[15] Now here that it is possible to do as the strictly religious, it is the same as small [articles of furniture], yet when one has no intention R. Simeon permits it at the outset? This refutation of R. Jeremiah Rabbah is indeed a refutation.

MISHNAH. IF ONE EXTINGUISHES THE LAMP BECAUSE
d HE IS AFRAID OF GENTILES, ROBBERS, OR AN EVIL SPIRIT, OR FOR THE SAKE OF AN INVALID, THAT HE SHOULD SLEEP HE IS NOT CULPABLE.[2] IF [BECAUSE] HE WOULD SPARE THE LAMP, THE OIL, OR THE WICK, HE IS CULPABLE. R. JOSE EXEMPTS HIM IN ALL CASES, EXCEPT IN RESPECT OF THE WICK, BECAUSE HE MAKES CHARCOAL.[3]

(9) I.e., firmly. (10) To forbid it. (11) And there was no fear of their drawing off oil. (12) Lit., 'if I am silent for you'.

c (1) Which is earth-paved; dragging there is prohibited because it forms a rut. (2) Rashi: the man who conducts worshippers (assemblies) in and out of the synagogue and supervises the seating of pupils. (3) An Idumean town; cf. Isa. XXXIV, 6; LXIII, 1. (4) Do you act thus. (5) *Supra* 22a. (6) A large bench, table, etc., cannot be lifted but must be dragged. (7) Here it was a small one. (8) A couch is large; a chair is small. (9) For R. Judah forbids both. (10) I.e., a small couch is meant. (11) A large, heavy chair is meant. (12) Lit., 'in the sun'. (13) The reference is to garments containing the forbidden mixture of wool and linen (v. Deut. XXII, 11) sold to Gentiles. Merchants slung their wares across their shoulders for display, and though some protection is afforded thereby and it is like wearing them, it is permitted. (14) [צנועים 'modest', 'humble', hence punctilious in carrying out religious duties. V. Büchler, *Types* p. 60ff]. (15) So that they do not actually lie upon them.

d (1) V. *MGWJ*. 11 (1927) pp. 162-165. (2) For desecrating the Sabbath. (3) By extinguishing the light he makes kindling material, i.e., prepares the wick for easier lighting.

GEMARA. [30*a*] Since the second clause teaches, HE IS CULPABLE, it may be inferred that it is R. Judah.[4] Then to what does the first clause refer? If to an invalid dangerously ill, [the Tanna] should have stated, 'It is permitted'?[5] While if to an invalid who is not in danger, he should have stated, He is liable to a sin-offering?[6]—After all, [it refers] to an invalid dangerously sick, and logically he should teach, it is permitted; but because he wishes to teach 'HE IS CULPABLE' in the second clause, he also teaches 'HE IS NOT CULPABLE' in the first. And as for what R. Oshaia taught: If it is for the sake of a sick person, that he should sleep, he must not extinguish it; but if he extinguishes it, he is not liable, though it is forbidden—that refers to one who is not dangerously ill, and agrees with R. Simeon.[7]

This question was asked before R. Tanḥum of Neway:[8] What about extinguishing a burning lamp for a sick man on the Sabbath?—Thereupon he commenced and spake:[9] Thou, Solomon, where is thy wisdom and where is thine understanding? It is not enough for thee that thy words contradict the words of thy father David, but that they are self-contradictory! Thy father David said, *The dead praise not the Lord;*[1] whilst thou saidest, *Wherefore I praised the dead which are already dead,*[2] but yet again thou saidest, *for a living dog is better than a dead lion.*[3] Yet there is no difficulty. As to what David said: '*The dead praise not the Lord*', this is what he meant: Let a man always engage in Torah and good deeds before he dies, for as soon as he dies he is restrained from [the practice of] Torah and good deeds, and the Holy One, blessed be He, finds nought to praise in him. And thus R. Joḥanan said, What is meant by the verse, *Among the dead* [*I am*] *free?*[4] Once a man dies, he becomes free of the Torah and good deeds. And as to what Solomon said, '*Wherefore I praised the dead that are already dead*'—for when Israel sinned in the wilderness, Moses stood before the Holy One, blessed be He, and uttered many prayers and supplications before Him, but he was not answered. Yet when he exclaimed, '*Remember Abraham, Isaac, and Israel, Thy servants!*'[5] he was immediately answered. Did not then Solomon well say, '*wherefore I praised the dead that are already dead*'? Another interpretation: In worldly affairs, when a prince of flesh and blood issues a decree, it is doubtful whether it will be obeyed or not; and even if you say that it is obeyed, it is obeyed during his lifetime but not after his death. Whereas Moses our Teacher decreed many decrees and enacted numerous enactments, and they endure for ever and unto all eternity. Did then not Solomon well say, '*wherefore I praise the dead, etc.*' Another interpretation [of] '*wherefore I praise, etc.*' is in accordance with Rab Judah's dictum in Rab's name, viz., What is meant by, *Shew me a token for good, that they which hate me may see it, and be ashamed?*[6] David prayed before the Holy One, blessed be He, 'Sovereign of the Universe! Forgive me for that sin!'[7] 'It is forgiven thee,' replied He. 'Shew me a token in my lifetime,' he entreated. 'In thy lifetime I will not make it known,' He answered, 'but I will make it known in the lifetime of thy son Solomon.' For when Solomon built the Temple, he desired to take the Ark into the Holy of Holies, whereupon the
b gates clave to each other. Solomon uttered twenty-four prayers,[1] yet he was not answered. He opened [his mouth] and exclaimed, '*Lift up your heads, O ye gates; and be ye lifted up, ye everlasting doors: And the King of glory shall come in.*'[2] They rushed upon him to swallow him up, crying, '*Who is the king of glory*'? '*The Lord, strong and mighty,*'[3] answered he. Then he repeated, '*Lift up your heads, O ye gates; Yea, lift them up, ye everlasting doors: and the King of glory shall come in. Who is this King of glory? The Lord of hosts, He is the King of glory. Selah*';[4] yet he was not answered. But as soon as he prayed, '*O Lord God, turn not away the face of Thine anointed: remember the good deeds of David Thy servant,*'[5] he was immediately answered. In that hour the faces of all David's enemies turned [black] like the bottom of a pot, and all Israel knew that the Holy One, blessed be He, had forgiven him that sin. Did then not Solomon well say, '*wherefore I praised the dead which are already dead*'? And thus it is written, *On the eighth day he sent the people away, and they blessed the king, and went unto their tents joyful and glad of heart for all the goodness that the Lord had shewed unto David His servant, and to Israel His people.*[6] '*And they went unto their tents*' [means] that they found their wives clean; '*joyful*', because they had enjoyed the lustre of the Divine Presence; '*and glad of heart*', because their wives conceived and each one bore a male child; '*for all the goodness that the Lord had shewed unto David His servant*', that He had forgiven him that sin; '*and to Israel His people*', for He had forgiven them the sin of the Day of Atonement.[7]

And as to what Solomon said, '*for a living dog is better than a dead lion*',—that is as Rab Judah said in Rab's name, viz.; what is meant by the verse, *Lord, make me to know mine end, and the measure of my days, what it is; let me know how frail I am.*[8] David said before the Holy One, blessed be He, 'Sovereign of the Universe! *Lord, make me to know mine end.*' 'It is a decree before Me,' replied He, 'that
c the end of a mortal[1] is not made known.' '*And the measure of my days, what it is*'—'it is a decree before Me that a person's span [of life] is not made known.' '*Let me know how frail* [ḥadel] *I am.*'[2] Said He to him, 'Thou wilt die on the Sabbath.' 'Let me die on the first day of the week!'[3] 'The reign of thy son Solomon shall already have become due, and one reign may not overlap another even by a hairbreadth.' 'Then let me die on the eve of the Sabbath!' Said He, '*For a day in thy courts is better than a thousand*':[4] better is to Me the one day that thou sittest and engagest in learning than the thousand burnt-offerings which thy son Solomon is destined to sacrifice before Me on the

(4) The work of extinguishing is not needed *per se* but merely to effect something else, e.g., to spare the oil, and it is R. Judah who maintains that such work involves liability. (5) 'He is exempt' implies that it is actually forbidden. (6) Since there is no danger of life, it is prohibited like any other work. (7) That no liability is incurred on account of a labour not required for itself; v. n. 4 and *infra* 93*b*. (8) A district in North Palestine (Jast.). MS.M. reads: Nineweh. V. Ta'an., 14*b*, n. 5. (9) This formula generally introduces a popular sermon, which preceded the answering of the question. Such follows here.

(1) Ps. CXV, 17. (2) Eccl. IV, 2. (3) Ibid. IX, 4. (4) Ps. LXXXVIII, 6 (E.V. 5: *Cast off among the dead*). (5) Ex. XXXII, 13. (6) Ps. LXXXVI, 17. (7) *Sc.* of Bathsheba.

b (1) Heb. רננות, songs. In Solomon's prayer (I Kings VIII, 23-53) expressions of entreaty (רנה, song; תפלה, prayer; and תחינה, supplication) occur twenty-four times. (2) Ps. XXIV, 7. (3) Ibid. 8. (4) Ibid. 9f. (5) II Chron. VI, 42. (6) I Kings VIII, 66. (7) Which they had kept as a Feast instead of a Fast. V. vv. 2 and 65: the fourteen days must have included the tenth of the seventh month, which is the Day of Atonement; v. M.Ḳ. 9*a*. (8) Ps. XXXIX, 5 (E.V. 4).

c (1) Lit., 'flesh and blood'. (2) Translating: Let me know when I will cease (to be), fr. *ḥadal*, to cease. (3) The following day, so that the usual offices for the dead may be performed, some of which are forbidden on the Sabbath. (4) Ps. LXXXIV, 11 (E.V. 10).

מסורת הש"ס

עין משפט נר מצוה

גמ' מדקתני סיפא חייב ש"מ ר' יהודה היא רישא במאי עסיקנא אי בחולה שיש בו סכנה מותר מיבעי ליה ואי בחולה שאין בו סכנה חייב חטאת מיבעי ליה לעולם בחולה שיש בו סכנה °ובדין הוא דליתני מותר ואיידי *דבעי למתני סיפא חייב תנא נמי רישא פטור והדתני רבי אושעיא אם בשביל החולה שיישן לא יכבה ואם כבה פטור אבל אסור ההיא בחולה שאין בו סכנה ורבי שמעון היא: שאול °שאילה זו לעילא מר' תנחום דמן נוי מהו לכבות בוצינא דנורא מקמי באישא בשבתא פתח ואמר אנת שלמה אן חכמתך אן *סוכלתנותך לא דייך שדבריך סותרין דברי דוד אביך אלא שדבריך סותרין זה את זה דוד אביך אמר °לא המתים יהללו יה ואת אמרת °ושבח אני את המתים שכבר מתו וחזרת ואמרת °כי לכלב חי הוא טוב מן האריה המת לא קשיא הא דקאמר דוד לא המתים יהללו יה הכי קאמר לעולם יעסוק אדם בתורה ובמצות קודם שימות שכיון שמת בטל מן התורה ומן המצות ואין להקב"ה שבח בו והיינו דאמר ר' יוחנן *מאי דכתיב °במתים חפשי כיון שמת אדם נעשה חפשי מן התורה ומן המצות ודקאמר שלמה ושבח אני את המתים שכבר מתו שכשחטאו ישראל במדבר עמד משה לפני הקב"ה ואמר כמה תפלות ותחנונים לפניו ולא נענה וכשאמר °זכור לאברהם ליצחק ולישראל עבדיך מיד נענה ולא יפה אמר שלמה ושבח אני את המתים שכבר מתו דבר אחר מנהגו של עולם שר ב"ו גוזר גזרה ספק מקיימין אותה ספק אין מקיימין אותה ואם תמצי לומר מקיימין אותה בחייו מקיימין אותה במותו אין מקיימין אותה ואילו משה רבינו גזר כמה גזירות ותיקן כמה תקנות וקיימות הם לעולם ולעולמי עולמים ולא יפה אמר שלמה ושבח אני את המתים וגו' ד"א ושבח אני וגו' כדרב יהודה אמר רב דאמר רב יהודה אמר רב מאי דכתיב °עשה עמי אות לטובה ויראו שונאי ויבושו אמר דוד לפני הקב"ה *רבונו של עולם מחול לי על אותו עון אמר לו מחול לך אמר לו עשה עמי אות בחיי אמר לו בחייך איני מודיע בחיי שלמה בנך אני מודיע *כשבנה שלמה את בית המקדש ביקש להכנים ארון לבית קדשי הקדשים דבקו שערים זה בזה אמר שלמה עשרים וארבעה רננות ולא נענה פתח ואמר °שאו שערים ראשיכם והנשאו פתחי עולם ויבא מלך הכבוד רהטו בתריה למיבלעיה אמרו מי הוא זה מלך הכבוד אמר להו ה' עזוז וגבור חזר ואמר °שאו שערים ראשיכם ושאו פתחי עולם ויבא מלך הכבוד מי הוא זה מלך הכבוד ה' צבאות הוא מלך הכבוד סלה ולא נענה כיון שאמר °ה' אלהים אל תשב פני משיחך זכרה לחסדי דוד עבדך מיד נענה באותה שעה נהפכו פני כל שונאי דוד כשולי קדירה וידעו כל העם וכל ישראל שמחל לו הקב"ה על אותו עון ולא יפה אמר שלמה ושבח אני את המתים שכבר מתו* והיינו דכתי' °ביום השמיני שלח את העם ויברכו את המלך וילכו לאהליהם שמחים וטובי לב על כל הטובה אשר עשה ה' לדוד עבדו ולישראל עמו וילכו לאהליהם שמצאו נשותיהן בטהרה שמחים שנהנו מזיו השכינה וטובי לב שנתעברו נשותיהן של כל אחד ואחד וילדה זכר על כל הטובה אשר עשה ה' לדוד עבדו (ולישראל עמו׳ לדוד עבדו) שמחל לו על אותו עון ולישראל עמו דאחיל להו עון דיום הכפורים ודקאמר שלמה כי לכלב חי הוא טוב מן האריה המת כדרב יהודה אמר רב דאמר רב יהודה אמר רב מאי דכתיב °הודיעני ה' קצי ומדת ימי מה היא אדעה מה חדל אני אמר דוד לפני הקדוש ברוך הוא רבונו של עולם הודיעני ה' קצי אמר לו גזרה היא מלפני שאין מודיעין קצו של בשר ודם ומדת ימי מה היא גזרה היא מלפני שאין מודיעין מדת ימיו של אדם ואדעה מה חדל אני אמר לו *בשבת תמות אמות באחד בשבת אמר לו כבר הגיע מלכות שלמה בנך *ואין מלכות נוגעת בחברתה אפי' כמלא נימא אמות בערב שבת *אמר לו °כי טוב יום בחצריך מאלף °טוב לי יום אחד שאתה יושב ועוסק בתורה מאלף עולות שעתיד שלמה בנך להקריב לפני על גבי המזבח כל

תורה אור: תהלים קטו · קהלת ד · שם ט · תהלים פח · שמות לב · תהלים פו · תהלים כד · שם · דה"ב ו · מלכים א ח · תהלים לט · תהלים פד

גמ' מדקתני סיפא · כאם על הנר כו' חייב חטאת אם שגג בשבת ששכח שהוא שבת או סבר שכיבוי מותר בשבת: ש"מ ר' יהודה היא · דאמר *מלאכה שאינה צריכה לגופה חייב עליה דכיבוי זה אין צריך לגופו אלא לצורך דבר אחר שלא תדלק הפתילה או שלא יפקע הנר ואין לך כיבוי הצריך לגופו אלא כיבוי של פחמין כשעושין אותו וכיבוי של הבהוב פתילה שהכיבוי נעשה להאחיז בו האור מהר כשידליקו וכיון דרבי יהודה היא רישא דפטר משום חולה וה"ה לשאר פטורי דמתניתין: אי · דאית בהו סכנת נפשות ומשום פקוח נפש שרי להו ליתני מותר לכתחלה: חייב מיבעי ליה · הואיל ורבי יהודה היא דלא פטר ליה משום דאינה צריכה לגופה: והא דתני רבי אושעיא · בההיא אבל אסור: ור' שמעון היא* · דפטר ליה משום אינה צריכה לגופה: שאול שאילתא · שאלו שאלה: לעילא מר' תנחום · לפניו וכן לשון הש"ס (א) והמקרא שרפים עומדים ממעל לו (ישעיה ו') ועל שם שיראים להתקרב לפניו עומדין מרחוק: דמן נוי · מקום: באישא · חולה תרגום של רעה בישתא: פתח ואמר · כך היו רגילין לפתוח באגדה תחילה והוא דומה לשאלה ודרש: כי לכלב חי · כלומר גדולים החיים ופקוח נפש: אן היא · אנה הלכה: וחזרת ואמרת · לסתור דברי עצמך: לא קשיא · איהו גופיה הוה מפרש להו: דאמר ר' יוחנן · קרא קא דריש במתים חפשי: ושבח אני את המתים · שעסקו בחייהם בתורה ומצות ומתו ראויים לשבחם אפילו מצדיקים חיים שגדולים הן במיתתן מבחייהן: עמד משה · ואין לך צדיק ממנו ולא נענה בזכותו: ד"א ושבח אני את המתים · הראשונים מן החיים של עכשיו שהראשונים טובים מאלה תדע שמתקיימות גזרותיו של משה ואין מתקיימות גזירות שרים של עכשיו: ותקן כמה תקנות · כי ההיא דתני במגילה (דף ד' ולב:) משה תיקן להם לישראל שיהו שואלין ודורשין בענייט של יום: על אותו עון · דבת שבע: דבקו שערים · של בית קדשי הקדשים: כ"ד רננות · רנה תפלה תחינה כתובים בתפלת שלמה עד כ"ד ויש אומרים כ"ד ברכות דתענית ולא נהירא *): רהטו שערים בתריה למבלעיה · סברי דעל עצמו אמר מלך הכבוד א"ע שערים מי הוא זה מלך הכבוד אמר איהו ה' עזוז וגבור (תהלים כד): שונאי דוד · משפחת שאול שמעי וכיוצא בו: דיום הכפורים · שאכלו ושתו בחנוכת הבית כדכתיב את החג שבעת ימים ושבעת ימים כדאמרינן במועד קטן (דף ט·): ודקאמר שלמה כי לכלב חי הוא טוב מאריה המת · לאו לענין חשיבותא אמרו אלא לענין הלכות שבת וי"ט: קיצי · העתידות לבא עלי: *מדת ימי · כמה ימי חיי: מה חדל אני · באיזה יום אני חדל ובטל מן העולם: אמות באחד בשבת · שיוכלו להתעסק בי ובהספדי: כי טוב יום בחצריך · כלומר כבר אמרת לפני טוב יום שאתה עומד בחצרי ועוסק בתורה מאלף עולות שעתיד בנך שלמה להעלות כדכתיב (מלכים א ג) אלף עולות יעלה שלמה וגו':

*) משום דבברכות דכ"ט ע"א איתא להיפך. כ"כ בכתנות אור פ' שמיני

[עי' תוספות לקמן נד: ד"ה את הסמת]

[לקמן צג:]

[עירובין מז. פסחים ז: יבמות לח: קב: כתובות ל. נדרים כח: עב: נזיר כח: ב"ק מט: לד: ב"מ סב: סנהדרין נז. זבחים לח: חולין סח. קס: בכורות מו:]

[תרגום אונקלוס של בחכמה ובתבונה בחוכמתא ובסוכלתנו בפ' תשא]

[לקמן קנא: ע"ש ולא תשכיל ותבין פרש"י דשכא ד"ה דאמר רבי יוחנן וכו' נדה סא:]

[מ"ק ט.]

[עי' תוספות חגיגה יז: ד"ה לא עלתה כו' תהלים סד]

סנהד' קז: ע"ש מ"ק ט·

[ברכות מח: מ"ק כח. יומא לה. תענית ה:]

*[מכות י.]

קו א ב מיי' פ"ב מהל' שבת הלכה ב טוש"ע א"ח סימן רעח:

הגהות הב"ח

(א) רש"י ד"ה לעילא מר' תנחום וכו' הש"ס והמקרא · נ"ב ע"ל בפי' ר"ע דף פ"ח ע"א פי' בדרך אחר:

גליון הש"ס

גמ' טוב לי יום אחד שאתה יושב ועוסק בתורה · וביר' פ"ז דברכות איתא חביבי עלי משפט ולדקה שאתה עושה יותר מקרבנות:

נ"א קצי מנין שנותי מדת ימי באיזה יום בשנה לדעת מנין ימי שאני מתקיים בשנה אחרונה כצ"ל

רבינו חננאל

אוקימנא למתני' כרבי יהודה ובחולה שיש בו סכנה שאם יראה אור הנר ימות והוא הדין לכל הזכורין במשנתנו °ובדין הוא דליתני מותר ואיידי דתני סיפא בפחם חייב תני רישא פטור דמשמע פטור אבל אסור ואינו אלא פטור ומותר והא דתני רבי אושעיא אם בשביל שיישן חולה לא יכבה ואם כבה פטור אבל אסור ההוא בחולה שאין בו סכנה ואליבא דרבי שמעון דאמר דבר שאין מתכוין פטור*) נשאלה שאלה זו לפני ר' תנחום דמן נ͏ֿוֹי שם מקום מן

*) עי' בכריתות כ' ב' ובתוספות שם ·

רב נסים גאון

[שם ר' יהודה היא]' כלומר הדבר שנא' לדעת ר' יהודה שהיה סובר מלאכה שאינה צריכה לגופה חייב עליה וכבר הקדמנו פירושו בפרק הראשון [רישא] במאי עסקי' אי בחולה שיש בו סכנה מותר מיבעי ליה והעיקר דיליה הוא דאמר הכתוב (ויקרא יח) אשר יעשה אותם האדם וחי בהם ובפרק יום הכפורים (יומא דף פה) אמרו וכבר היה רבי ישמעאל ורבי עקיבא ורבי אלעזר בן עזריה מהלכין בדרך ולוי הסדר וישמעאל בנו של רבי אלעזר בן עזריה מהלכין אחריהם נשאלה שאילה זו לפניהם מנין לפיקוח נפש שדוחה את השבת נענה רבי ישמעאל ואמר (שמות כב) אם במחתרת ימצא הגנב ולאחר דבריו אמר רב יהודה אמר שמואל אי הואי התם הוה אמינא מילתא דעדיפא מכולהו וחי בהם ולא שימות בהם אמר רבא לכולהו אית להו פירכא לבר מדשמואל דלית ליה פירכא וכו' וכבר אמרו קודם (שם דף פג) שאין לך דבר שעומד בפני פיקוח נפש חוץ מע"ז וגילוי עריות ושפיכות דמים ובפרק מפנין (דף קכט) אמרו מר זוטרא מתני לקולא טעמא דאמרה אין צריכה הא סתמא מחללין עליה את השבת אמר ליה רבינא (למרי) [למרימר] הילכתא כמאן אמר ליה כמר זוטרא שספק נפשות להקל ואמרו (שם) אמר רב יהודה אמר שמואל עושין מדורה לחיה בשבת סבור מינה לחיה אין לחולה לא בימות הגשמים אין בימות החמה לא איתמר אמר ר' חייא בר אבין אמר שמואל הקיז דם ונצטנן עושין לו מדורה אפילו בתקופת תמוז ושנו במשנה (פרק ר"א דמילה דף קלד) רבי אליעזר בן עזריה אומר מרחיצין את הקטן ביום השלישי שחל להיות בשבת שנאמר ויהי ביום השלישי בהיותם כואבים ואמרו בתלמוד כי אתא רב דימא אמר רבי אלעזר הלכה כרבי אלעזר בן עזריה הוו בה במערבא הרחצת כל גופו או הרחצת מילה עצמה אמר להו ההוא מרבנן ורבי (עקיבא) [יעקב] שמיה מסתברא דהרחצת כל גופו דאי סלקא דעתך הרחצת מילה עצמה מי נרע מחמין שעל גבי מכה בשבת דאמר רב אין מונעין חמין ושמן מעל גבי מכה בשבת מתקיף לה רב יוסף ולא שני לך בין חמין שהוחמו בשבת לחמין שהוחמו מערב שבת מתקיף לה רב דימי וממאי דהכא בחמין שהוחמו בשבת פליגי דילמא בחמין שהוחמו מערב שבת פליגי אמר אביי אנא בעאי דאישני ליה וקדים ושני ליה רב יוסף מפני שסכנה היא לו כי אתא רבין אמר ר' אבא אמר רבי אלעזר ואמרי לה אמר רבי אבהו אמר רבי יוחנן הלכה כרבי אלעזר בן עזריה בין בחמין שהוחמו בשבת ובין בחמין שהוחמו מערב שבת בין בהרחצת כל גופו ובין בהרחצת מילה מפני שסכנה היא לו ואלו העיקרים אמרו ובחולה שיש בו סכנה מותר מיבעיא ליה ובמסכת ע"ז תמצא כמו אלו העיקרים רבים: ואילו משה רבינו גזר כמה גזירות ותיקן כמה תקנות מעצמו לישראל והרי אנו מזכירין מהן מה שיזדמן לנו במסכת דיבמות אמרינן בפרק הערל (דף עט) אמרו ונתינים דוד גזר עליהם משה גזר עליהם מחוטב עציך עד שואב מימיך ובמסכת ברכות בפרק שלשה שאכלו כאחת (דף מח) אמר רב נחמן משה תיקן להם לישראל ברכת הזן בשעה שירד להן המן ובמסכת מגילה בפרק בני העיר (דף לג) תנו רבנן משה תיקן להן לישראל שיהו קורין ודורשין בעניינו של יום ובפ' יוה"כ (יומא עה) משה תיקן להם זמן סעודה (ובפ') [ובמסכת] תעניות (דף כז) [בפרק] בג' פרקים בשנה משה תיקן להם לישראל שמונה משמרות ארבעה מאלעזר וארבעה מאיתמר: בשלבא לדוד עבדו שמחל לו הקב"ה על אותו עון אלא לישראל עמו מאי היא שמחל להם עון יום הכפורים תמצא פירו' בפרק משקין בית השלחין (מו"ק דף ט) אמר

קח א מיי' פכ"א מהל' שבת הלכה יח סמג לאוין סה טוש"ע א"ח סימן שכד סעיף ז :

קט ב מיי' פכ"ו מהל' שבת הלכה כא סמג שם טוש"ע א"ח סי' שיא סעיף א :

קי ג מיי' פ"ח מהלכות לולב הלכה טו :

קיא ד מיי' פ"ז מהל' יסודי התורה הלכה ד [ברא"ש פ"ה דברכות סימן ב:]

קיב ה מיי' פ"ב מהל' דעות הלכה ג :

לקמן קנו:

תורה אור

כל יומא דשבתא הוה יתיב וגריס כולי יומא ההוא יומא דבעי למינח נפשיה קם מלאך המות קמיה ולא יכיל ליה דלא הוה פסק פומיה מגירסא אמר מאי אעביד ליה הוה ליה בוסתנא אחורי ביתיה אתא מלאך המות סליק ובחיש באילני נפק למיחזי הוה סליק בדרגא איפחית דרגא מתותיה אישתיק ונח נפשיה שלח שלמה לבי מדרשא אבא מת ומוטל בחמה וכלבים של בית אבא רעבים מה אעשה שלחו ליה *חתוך *נבלה והנח לפני הכלבים ואביך *הנח [ב]עליו ככר או תינוק וטלטלו ולא יפה אמר שלמה °כי לכלב חי הוא טוב מן האריה המת ולענין שאילה דשאילנא קדמיכון נר קרויה נר ונשמתו של אדם קרויה נר מוטב תכבה נר של בשר ודם מפני נרו של הקב"ה : אמר רב יהודה בריה דרב. שמואל בר שילת משמיה דרב בקשו חכמים לגנוז ספר קהלת מפני שדבריו סותרין זה את זה ומפני מה לא גנזוהו מפני שתחילתו דברי תורה וסופו דברי תורה תחילתו דברי תורה דכתיב °מה יתרון לאדם בכל עמלו שיעמול תחת השמש ואמרי דבי ר' ינאי תחת השמש הוא דאין לו קודם שמש יש לו סופו דברי תורה דכתיב °סוף דבר הכל נשמע את האלהים ירא ואת מצותיו שמור כי זה כל האדם *מאי כי זה כל האדם אמר רבי *(אליעזר) כל העולם כולו לא נברא אלא בשביל זה ר' אבא בר כהנא אמר שקול זה כנגד כל העולם כולו שמעון בן עזאי אומר ואמרי לה שמעון בן זומא אומר לא נברא כל העולם כולו אלא לצוות לזה ומאי דבריו סותרין זה את זה כתיב °טוב כעס משחוק וכתיב °לשחוק אמרתי מהלל כתיב °ושבחתי אני את השמחה וכתיב °ולשמחה מה זה עושה לא קשיא טוב כעס משחוק טוב כעס שכועס הקב"ה על הצדיקים בעוה"ז משחוק שמשחק הקב"ה על הרשעים בעולם הזה ולשחוק אמרתי מהלל זה שחוק שמשחק הקב"ה עם הצדיקים בעולם הבא ושבחתי אני את השמחה [ג]שמחה של מצוה ולשמחה מה זה עושה זו שמחה שאינה של מצוה *ללמדך [ד]שאין שכינה שורה לא מתוך עצבות ולא מתוך עצלות ולא מתוך שחוק ולא מתוך קלות ראש ולא מתוך *שיחה ולא מתוך דברים בטלים אלא מתוך דבר שמחה של מצוה שנאמר °ועתה קחו לי מנגן והיה כנגן המנגן ותהי עליו יד ה' אמר רב יהודה וכן לדבר הלכה אמר רבא וכן לחלום טוב איני והאמר רב גידל אמר רב *כל תלמיד חכם שיושב לפני רבו ואין שפתותיו נוטפות מר תכוינה שנאמר °שפתותיו שושנים נוטפות מור עובר אל תקרי מור עובר אלא מר עובר *אל תקרי שושנים אלא ששונים לא קשיא הא ברבה והא בתלמיד ואיבעית אימא הא והא ברבה ולא קשיא הא מקמי דלפתח הא לבתר דפתח כי הא דרבה מקמי דפתח להו לרבנן אמר מילתא דבדיחותא ובדחי רבנן לסוף יתיב באימתא ופתח בשמעתא ואף ספר משלי בקשו לגנוז שהיו דבריו סותרין זה את זה ומפני מה לא גנזוהו אמרי ספר קהלת לאו עיינינן ואשכחינן טעמא הכא נמי ליעיינן ומאי דבריו סותרים זה את זה כתיב °אל תען כסיל כאולתו וכתיב °ענה כסיל כאולתו לא קשיא הא בדברי תורה הא במילי דעלמא כי הא דההוא דאתא לקמיה דרבי אמר ליה אשתך אשתי ובניך בני אמר ליה רצונך שתשתה כוס של יין שתה ופקע ההוא דאתא לקמיה דרבי חייא אמר ליה אמך אשתי ואתה בני אמר ליה רצונך שתשתה כוס של יין שתה ופקע אמר רבי חייא אהניא ליה צלותיה לרבי דלא לשוייה בני ממזירי דרבי כי הוה מצלי אמר *יהי רצון מלפניך ה' אלהינו שתצילני היום מעזי פנים ומעזות פנים בדברי תורה מאי היא כי הא דיתיב רבן גמליאל וקא דריש עתידה אשה *שתלד בכל יום שנאמר °הרה ויולדת יחדיו ליגלג עליו אותו תלמיד אמר אין כל חדש תחת השמש א"ל בא ואראך דוגמתן בעוה"ז נפק אחוי ליה תרנגולת ותו יתיב רבן גמליאל וקא דריש עתידים אילנות שמוציאין פירות בכל יום שנאמר °ונשא ענף ועשה פרי מה ענף בכל יום אף פרי בכל יום ליגלג עליו אותו תלמיד אמר והכתיב אין כל חדש תחת השמש א"ל בא ואראך דוגמתם בעולם הזה נפק אחוי ליה צלף ותו יתיב רבן גמליאל וקא דריש *עתידה ארץ ישראל שתוציא גלוסקאות וכלי מילת שנאמר °יהי פסת בר בארץ ליגלג עליו אותו תלמיד ואמר אין כל חדש תחת השמש אמר ליה בא ואראך דוגמתן בעולם הזה נפק אחוי ליה כמיהין ופטריות ואבלי מילת נברא בר קורא : *ת"ר [ה]לעולם יהא אדם ענותן כהלל ואל יהא קפדן כשמאי מעשה בשני בני אדם שהמרו

כל יומא דשבתא · של כל שבתות השנים : הוה יתיב וגריס · שלא יקרב מלאך המות אליו שהתורה מגינה ממות כדאמרינן בסוטה (דף כא·) : סליק ובחיש באילני · מנענע המלאך באילנות להשמיע קול תימה : וכלבים של בית אבא רעבים · לשתי שאלות הללו הוצרך : ולא יפה אמר כו' · שלתקנת הכלבים לא הצריכוהו לשנות טלטול נבילה ואת האריה המת הסרו לטלטל אלא על ידי ככר או תינוק ל"א שהקדימוהו תשובת הכלב לתשובת האריה לשון רבותי : ולענין שאילתא · דמהו לכבות : דשאילנא קדמיכון · דרך ענוה אמר דהוה ליה למימר דשאילתון קדמי : קרויה נר · נר *אלהים נשמת אדם (משלי כ) : מוטב תכבה נרו כו' · לאו מהכא יליף חלול שבת דפיקוח נפש נפקא לן *מוחי בהם ולא שימות בהם אלא להטעימן הדבר באגדה המושכת את הלב לפי שהיו באים לשמוע הדרשה נשים ועמי הארץ והיו צריכין הדרשנין למשוך את לבבם : תחלתו וסופו · וכ"ש שיש עוד בינתיים : קודם השמש · אם יעמול בתורה שקדמה לשמש *יש יתרון : לצוות · צוותא שולא"ש : מהולל · משובח : משחוק שמשחק עם הרשעים · שנותן להם שעה משחקת כדי להאכילן חלקן ולטורדן מן העולם הבא : שמחה של מצוה · כגון הכנסת כלה : שחוק · שחוק ממש שאין דעת שוחק מיושבת עליו ואפילו אינו של לצון מ"מ אין בו יישוב : קלות ראש · לצון : קחו לי מנגן · מצוה היא להשרות עליו שכינה : לדבר הלכה · צריך לפתוח במילי דבדיחותא ברישא : לחלום טוב · אם בא לישן מתוך שמחה מראין לו חלום טוב : נוטפות מר · מרירות מחמת אימה : ובדחי רבנן · נפתח לבם מחמת השמחה : מעזי פנים · שלא יזיקוני : ומעזות פנים · שלא ילא עלי שם ממזרות דהוא עז פנים : בדברי תורה · מותר לענות כאולתו : הרה ויולדת יחדיו · ביום שהרה זה יולדת ולד אחר כמו תרנגולת וכיון שמשמשת בכל יום נמצאת יולדת בכל יום דהכי משמע קרא בכל עת שהיא מתעברת יולדת שממהרת לגמור צורת הולד לזמן מועט : בא ואראך · טרח לענותו כאולתו כדי להעמיד דברי תורה על מכונו : ליגלג · זו אוולת : צלף · מין אילן הטוען ג' מיני פירות אביונות וקפריסין ולולבין וכי איתיה להאי ליתיה להאי כדאמר בריש חזקת הבתים* : פיסת בר · משמע גלוסקאות שרחבות כמין פס יד ומשמע כלי מילת כמו כתונת פסים : בר · כמו לשבור בר (בראשית מב) ולענין כלי מילת בר נקי כמו ברה כחמה (שיר ו) : כמהין ופטריות · שיוצאין כמות שהן בלילה אחד ורחבין ועגולין כגלוסקאות : נברא בר קורא · סיב כמין לבוש מצוייר גדל סביבות הקור של דקל כשהוא רך קור ענף האילן כשהוא רך יוצא בכל שנה קודם שיתקשה קרוי קור :

[נ"ל ס'] · [יומא פה:] · [כדאי' פסחים כד. נדרים לט:] · לקמן מ"ב קמב: · קהלת ט · שם א · [דף כח:] · שם יב · ברכות ו: · [נ"ל אלעזר] · שם ז · שם ב · שם ח שם ב · פסחים קיז. ע"ש · ס"א שמחה · מלכים ב ג · פיין בערוך ערך סף · שיר השירים ה · [לקמן פח: פסחים קיז:] · משלי כו · משלי כו · [ברכות טז: ושם איתא שתצילנו וכו' וכן לאוי להיות] · ירמיה לא · [עי' תוספות ע"ז ה: ד"ה אין בן דוד] · יחזקאל יז · כתובות קיא: · תהלים עב · [אבות דר"נ פט"ו ע"ש שינויים רבים]

רב נסים גאון

אמר רבי פרנך אמר רבי יוחנן אותה שנה לא עשו ישראל צום הכפורים כו' : ואביך הנח עליו ככר או תינוק וטלטלו · תמצא עיקר המעשה בפרק כירה (דף מג) איתמר מת המוטל בחמה רב יהודה אמר שמואל הופכו ממטה למטה ורבי חיננא משמיה דרב אמר מניח עליו ככר או תינוק ומטלטלו ובפ"ק נוטל אדם את בנו (דף קמב) אמרו לא אמרו ככר או תינוק אלא למת בלבד מיכן נלמוד כי אותם שמניחין פת על המטה שהוליכו את הנר עליה כדי שיסירו המנורה ממקומה עוברין הן על המצות ואסור לעשות כן שלא התירו חכמים להניח ככר אלא למת בלבד ולא לדבר אחר :

פליט

רבינו חננאל

העיירות : מהו לכבות בוצינא דנהורא מקמי באישא בשבתא · פי' באישא שכיב מרע : פתח ואמר שלמה אן הוא חכמתנותך וסכלתנותך לא דייך שדבריך סותרין דברי אביך כו' ולענין שאילתא דשאילנא ת"ש נשמתו של אדם היא נרו של הקב"ה שנאמר נר ה' נשמת אדם · מוטב תכבה נרו של ב"ו מפני נרו של הקב"ה · כלומר אם הוא חולה שיש בו סכנה שרי : אין השכינה שורה אלא מתוך שמחה שנאמר והיה כנגן המנגן ותהי עליו רוח אלהים · וכן לדבר הלכה והני מילי ברבה אבל בתלמיד לא שכל תלמיד שאין שפתותיו נוטפות מר תכוינה : תנו רבנן לעולם יהא אדם ענוותן כהלל ואל יהא קפדן כשמיי מעשה בב'

altar.'[5] [30b] Now, every Sabbath day he would sit and study all day.[6] On the day that his soul was to be at rest,[7] the Angel of death stood before him but could not prevail against him, because learning did not cease from his mouth. 'What shall I do to him?' said he. Now, there was a garden before his house; so the Angel of death went, ascended and soughed in the trees. He [David] went out to see: as he was ascending the ladder, it broke under him. Thereupon he became silent [from his studies] and his soul had repose. Then Solomon sent to Beth Hamidrash: My father is dead and lying in the sun; and the dogs of my father's house are hungry; what shall I do? They sent back, Cut up a carcase and place it before the dogs; and as for thy father, put a loaf of bread or a child upon him and carry him away.[8] Did then not Solomon well say, *for a living dog is better than a dead lion?*[9] And
a as for the question which I asked before you,[1]—a lamp is designated lamp, and the soul of man is called a lamp:[2] better it is that the lamp of flesh and blood be extinguished before the lamp of the Holy One, blessed be He.[3]

Rab Judah son of R. Samuel b. Shilath said in Rab's name: The Sages wished to hide the Book of Ecclesiastes,[4] because its words are self-contradictory; yet why did they not hide it? Because its beginning is religious teaching[5] and its end is religious teaching. Its beginning is religious teaching, as it is written, *What profit hath man of all his labour wherein he laboureth under the sun?*[6] And the School of R. Jannai commented: Under the sun he has none, but he has it [*sc.* profit] before the sun.[7] The end thereof is religious teaching, as it is written, *Let us hear the conclusion of the matter, fear God, and keep His commandments: for this is the whole of man.*[8] What is meant by, *'for this is the whole of man'?*—Said R. Eleazar, The entire world was created only for the sake of this [type of] man. R. Abba b. Kahana said: This man is equal in value to the whole world. Simeon b. 'Azzai—others state, Simeon b. Zoma—said: The entire world was created only to be a companion to this man.

And how are its words self-contradictory?—It is written, *anger is better than play;*[9] but it is written, *I said of laughter, It is to be praised.*[10] It is written, *Then I commended joy;*[11] but it is written, *and of joy [I said] What doeth it?*[12] There is no difficulty: *'anger is better than laughter'*: the anger which the Holy One, blessed be He, displays to the righteous in this world is better than the laughter which the Holy One, blessed be He, laughs with the wicked in
b this world.[1] *'And I said of laughter, it is to be praised'*: that refers to the laughter which the Holy One, blessed be He, laughs with the righteous in the world to come. *'Then I commended joy'*: this refers to the joy of a precept.[2] *'And of joy [I said], what doeth it'*: this refers to joy [which is] not in connection with a precept.[3] This teaches you that the Divine Presence rests [upon] man] neither through gloom,[4] nor through sloth, nor through frivolity, nor through levity, nor through talk, nor through idle chatter,[5] save through a matter of joy in connection with a precept, as it is said, *But now bring me a minstrel. And it came to pass, when the minstrel played, that the hand of the Lord came upon him.*[6]

(5) Thus your life is too precious for a single day to be renounced.—Study itself is regarded in Judaism as an act of worship—indeed, the greatest, though only when it leads to piety; cf. Pe'ah I, 1. (6) The angel of death cannot approach one who is studying the Torah; Soṭ. 21*a*. (7) A euphemism for death. (8) V. *infra* 156*b*. (9) For the sake of the living dogs it was permitted to handle the carcase without further ado, yet the great king David might not be handled thus! Or, the answer concerning the dogs was given precedence over that concerning David.

a (1) *Supra a*. This was said in a spirit of humility, instead of 'which you asked before me.' (2) Prov. XX, 27: *the soul of man is the lamp of the Lord*. (3) Where life is endangered, the lamp may certainly be extinguished. (4) V. *supra* 13*b*, n. b2. Weiss, *Dor*, I, p. 212 conjectures that this was at the time of the Synod in the upper chamber of Ḥanania b. Hezekiah b. Garon (v. *supra* 13*b*, n. a1), when it was desired to 'hide' Ezekiel too. This activity was occasioned by the spread of books of Hellenistic tendencies, in consequence of which existing material was closely scrutinized as to its fitness. (5) Lit., 'words of the Torah'. (6) Eccl. I, 3. (7) I.e., one profits if he toils in the Torah, which existed before the sun; Pes. 54*a*; Ned. 39*b*. (8) Ibid. XII, 13. (9) Ibid. VII, 3. (10) Ibid. II, 2. (11) Ibid. VIII, 15. (12) Ibid. II, 2.

b (1) The latter is an idiom for prosperity and well being: the sufferings inflicted upon the righteous are preferable to the prosperity conferred upon the wicked. (2) The celebrations of such, e.g., a marriage. (3) The Rabbis frowned upon this. But in all probability this does not apply to a simple and harmless gathering, but to attendance at theatres and circuses, at which the Jewish authorities looked askance, perhaps because they originated in idolatry and also because images of royalty were placed there.—Lev. R. XXXIV. The early Christians too were opposed to this, Tertullian (*De Spectaculis*, X) describing the theatre as a place of sexual immorality. (4) Judaism does not encourage asceticism; cf. Ned. 10*a*. (5) Or, vain pursuits. (6) II Kings III, 15. Maharsha observes

◁ *For the continuation of the English translation of this page see overleaf.*

עין משפט
נר מצוה

קח א מיי' פכ"ה מהל' שבת הלכה יח סמג לאוין סה טוש"ע א"ח סימן שכד סעיף ז:

קט ב מיי' פכ"ו מהל' שבת הלכה כא סמג שם טוש"ע א"ח סי' שיא סעיף א:

קי ג מיי' פ"ח מהלכות גזלה הלכה טו:

קיא ד מיי' פ"ז מהל' יסודי התורה הלכה ד [ברא"ש פ"ב דברכות סימן ב:]

קיב ה מיי' פ"ב מהל' דעות הלכה ג:

תורה אור

כל יומא דשבתא הוה יתיב וגריס כולי יומא ההוא יומא דבעי למינח נפשיה קם מלאך המות קמיה ולא יכיל ליה דלא הוה פסק פומיה מגירסא אמר מאי אעביד ליה הוה ליה בוסתנא אחורי ביתיה אתא מלאך המות סליק ובחיש באילני נפק למיחזי הוה סליק בדרגא איפחית דרגא מתותיה אישתיק ונח נפשיה שלח שלמה לבי מדרשא אבא מת ומוטל בחמה וכלבים של בית אבא רעבים מה אעשה שלחו ליה *חתוך ^ג נבלה והנח לפני הכלבים ואביך *הנח ^ב עליו ככר או תינוק וטלטלו ולא יפה אמר שלמה °כי לכלב חי הוא טוב מן האריה המת ולענין שאילה דשאילנא קדמיכון נר קרויה נר ונשמתו של אדם קרויה נר מוטב תכבה ^ד נר של בשר ודם מפני נרו של הקב"ה: אמר רב יהודה בריה דרב שמואל בר שילת משמיה דרב בקשו חכמים לגנוז ספר קהלת מפני שדבריו סותרין זה את זה ומפני מה לא גנזוהו מפני שתחילתו דברי תורה וסופו דברי תורה תחילתו דברי תורה דכתיב °מה יתרון לאדם בכל עמלו שיעמול תחת השמש ואמרי דבי ר' ינאי תחת השמש הוא דאין לו קודם שמש יש לו סופו דברי תורה דכתיב °סוף דבר הכל נשמע את האלהים ירא ואת מצותיו שמור כי זה כל האדם *מאי כי זה כל האדם אמר רבי *(אליעזר) כל העולם כולו לא נברא אלא בשביל זה ר' אבא בר כהנא אמר שקול זה כנגד כל העולם כולו שמעון בן עזאי אומר ואמרי לה שמעון בן זומא אומר לא נברא כל העולם כולו אלא לצוות לזה ומאי דבריו סותרין זה את זה כתיב °טוב כעס משחוק וכתיב °לשחוק אמרתי מהולל כתיב °ושבחתי אני את השמחה וכתיב °ולשמחה מה זה עושה לא קשיא טוב כעס משחוק טוב כעס שכועס הקב"ה על הצדיקים בעוה"ז משחוק שמשחק הקב"ה על הרשעים בעולם הזה ולשחוק אמרתי מהולל זה שחוק שמשחק הקב"ה עם הצדיקים בעולם הבא ושבחתי אני את השמחה ^ה שמחה של מצוה ולשמחה מה זה עושה זו שמחה שאינה של מצוה *ללמדך ^ו שאין שכינה שורה לא מתוך עצבות ולא מתוך עצלות ולא מתוך שחוק ולא מתוך קלות ראש ולא מתוך *שיחה ולא מתוך דברים בטלים אלא מתוך דבר שמחה של מצוה שנאמר °ועתה קחו לי מנגן והיה כנגן המנגן ותהי עליו יד ה' אמר רב יהודה וכן לדבר הלכה אמר רבא וכן לחלום טוב איני והאמר רב גידל אמר רב *כל תלמיד חכם שיושב לפני רבו ואין שפתותיו נוטפות מר תכוינה שנאמר °שפתותיו שושנים נוטפות מור עובר אל תקרי מור עובר אלא מר עובר *אל תקרי שושנים אלא ששונים לא קשיא הא ברבה והא בתלמיד ואיבעית אימא הא והא ברבה ולא קשיא הא מקמי דלפתח הא לבתר דפתח כי הא דרבה מקמי דפתח להו לרבנן אמר מילתא דבדיחותא ובדחי רבנן לסוף יתיב באימתא ופתח בשמעתא ואף ספר משלי בקשו לגנוז שהיו דבריו סותרין זה את זה ומפני מה לא גנזוהו אמרי ספר קהלת לאו עיינינן ואשכחינן טעמא הכא נמי ליעיינן ומאי דבריו סותרים זה את זה כתיב °אל תען כסיל כאולתו וכתיב °ענה כסיל כאולתו לא קשיא הא בדברי תורה הא במילי דעלמא כי הא דההוא דאתא לקמיה דרבי אמר ליה אשתך אשתי ובניך בני אמר ליה רצונך שתשתה כוס של יין שתה ופקע ההוא דאתא לקמיה דרבי חייא אמר ליה אמך אשתי ואתה בני אמר ליה רצונך שתשתה כוס של יין שתה ופקע אמר רבי חייא אהניא ליה צלותיה לרבי דלא לשוייה בני ממזירי דרבי כי הוה מצלי אמר *יהי רצון מלפניך ה' אלהינו שתצילני היום מעזי פנים ומעזות פנים בדברי תורה מאי היא כי הא דיתיב רבן גמליאל וקא דריש עתידה אשה *שתלד בכל יום שנאמר °הרה ויולדת יחדיו ליגלג עליו אותו תלמיד אמר אין כל חדש תחת השמש א"ל בא ואראך דוגמתן בעוה"ז נפק אחוי ליה תרנגולת ותו יתיב רבן גמליאל וקא דריש עתידים אילנות שמוציאין פירות בכל יום שנאמר °ונשא ענף ועשה פרי מה ענף בכל יום אף פרי בכל יום ליגלג עליו אותו תלמיד אמר והכתיב אין כל חדש תחת השמש א"ל בא ואראך דוגמתם בעולם הזה נפק אחוי ליה צלף ותו יתיב רבן גמליאל וקא דריש *עתידה ארץ ישראל שתוציא גלוסקאות וכלי מילת שנאמר °יהי פסת בר בארץ ליגלג עליו אותו תלמיד ואמר אין כל חדש תחת השמש אמר ליה בא ואראך דוגמתן בעולם הזה נפק אחוי ליה כמיהין ופטריות ואבלי מילת נברא בר קורא: *ת"ר ^י לעולם יהא אדם ענותן כהלל ואל יהא קפדן כשמאי מעשה בשני בני אדם
שהמרו

כל יומא דשבתא. של כל שבתות השנים: הוה יתיב וגריס. שלא יקרב מלאך המות אליו שהתורה מגינה ממות כדאמרינן בסוטה (דף כא.): סליק ובחיש באילני. מנענע המלאך באילנות להשמיע קול תימה: וכלבים של בית אבא רעבים. לשתי שאלות הללו הוצרך: ולא יפה אמר כו'. שלאתקנת הכלבים לא הצריכוה לשנות טלטול נבילה ולא האריה המת אסרו לטלטל אלא על ידי ככר או תינוק ל"א שהקדימוהו תשובת הכלב לתשובת האריה לשון רבותי: ולענין שאילתא. דמהו לכבות: דשאילנא קדמיכון. דרך ענוה אמר דהוה ליה למימר דשאילתון קדמי: קרויה נר. נר *אלהים נשמת אדם (משלי כ): מוטב תכבה נרו כו'. לאו מהכא יליף חלול שבת דפיקוח נפש נפקא לן *מוחי בהם ולא שימות בהם אלא להטעימן הדבר באגדה המושכת את הלב לפי שהיו באים לשמוע הדרשה נשים ועמי הארץ והיו צריכין הדרשנין למשוך את לבבם: תחלתו וסופו. וכ"ש שיש עוד בינתיים: קודם השמש. אם יעמול בתורה שקדמה לשמש *יש יתרון: לצוות. צוותא שותא"ש: מהולל. משובח: משחוק שמשחק עם הרשעים. שנותן להם שעה משחקת כדי להאכילן חלקן ולטורדן מן העולם הבא: שמחה של מצוה. כגון הכנסת כלה: שחוק. שחוק ממש שאין דעת שוחק מיושבת עליו ואפילו אינו של לצון מ"מ אין בו יישוב: קלות ראש. לצון: קחו לי מנגן. מצוה היא להשרות עליו שכינה: לדבר הלכה. צריך לפתוח במילי דבדיחותא ברישא: לחלום טוב. אם בא לישן מתוך שמחה מראין לו חלום טוב: נוטפות מר. מרירות מחמת אימה: ובדחי רבנן. נפתח לבם מחמת השמחה: מעזי פנים. שלא יזיקוני: ומעזות פנים. שלא יצא עלי שם ממזרות דהוא עז פנים: בדברי תורה. מותר לענות כאולתו: הרה ויולדת יחדיו. ביום שהרה זה יולדת ולד אחר כמו תרנגולת וכיון שמשמשת בכל יום נמצאת יולדת בכל יום דהכי משמע קרא בכל עת שהיא מתעברת יולדת שממהרת לגמור צורת הולד לזמן מועט: בא ואראך. פרח לענותו כאולתו כדי להעמיד דברי תורה על מכונ: ליגלג. זו אוולת: צלף. מין אילן הטוען ג' מיני פירות אביונות וקפריסין ולולבין וכי איתיה להאי ליתיה להאי כדאמר בריש חזקת הבתים*: פיסת בר. משמע גלוסקאות שרחבות כמין פס יד ומשמע כלי מילת כמו כתונת פסים: בר. כמו לשבור בר (בראשית מב) ולענין כלי מילת בר נקי כמו ברה כחמה (שיר ו): כמהין ופטריות. שיוצאין כמות שהן בלילה אחד ורחבין ועגולין כגלוסקאות: נברא בר קורא. סיב כמין לבוש מצוייר גדל סביבות הקור של דקל כשהוא רך קור ענף האילן כשהוא רך יוצא בכל שנה קודם שיתקשה קרוי קור:
שהמרו

מסורת הש"ס

[ת"ל ס'] [יומא פה:] [כדאי' פסחים סח. נדרים לט:] לקמן ס"ב קמב: [דף כח:] [לקמן ס"ב] [ת"ל אלעזר] ברכות ו: לקמן קנו: [ברכות טז: ושם איתא שתצילנו וכו' וכן הלוי בזיות] [עי' תוספות ע"ז כ: ד"ה אין בן דוד] כתובות קיא: [אבות דר"נ פט"ו ע"ש שינויים רב']

רב נסים גאון

אמר רבי פתך אמר רבי יוחנן אותה שנה לא עשו ישראל צום הכפורים כו': ואביך הנח עליו ככר או תינוק וטלטלו · תמצא עיקר המעשה בפרק כירה (דף מג) איתמר מת המוטל בחמה רב יהודה אמר שמואל הופכו ממטה למטה ורבי חיננא משמיה דרב אמר מניח עליו ככר או תינוק ומטלטלו ובפ"ק נוטל אדם את בנו (דף קמב) אמרו לא אמרו ככר או תינוק אלא למת בלבד מיכן נלמוד כי אותם שמניחין פת על המטה שהוליכו את הנר עליה כדי שיסירו המנורה ממקומה עוברין יב על המצות ואסור לעשות כן שלא התירו חכמים להניח ככר אלא למת בלבד ולא לדבר אחר:

רבינו חננאל

העיירות: מהו לכבות בוצינא דנהורא מקמי באישא בשבתא · פי' באישא שכיב מרע: פתח ואמר א שלמה אן הוא חכמתנותך ושכלתנותך לא דייך שדבריך סותרין דברי אביך כו' ולענין שאילתא דשאיל ת"ש נשמתו של אדם היא נרו של הקב"ה שנאמר נר ה' נשמת אדם · מוטב תכבה נרו של ב"ו מ נרו של הקב"ה · כלומר אם הוא חולה שיש בו סכנה שרי: אין השכינה שורה אלא מתוך שמחה שנא והיה כנגן המנגן ותהי עליו רוח אלהים · וכן לדבר הלכה והני מילי ברבה אבל בתלמיד לא שכל תלו שאין שפתותיו נוטפות מר תכוינה: תנו רבנן לעולם יהא אדם ענותן כהלל ואל יהא קפדן כשמיי מע בנ'

Continuation of translation from previous page as indicated by ◁

Rab Judah said: And it is likewise thus for a matter of *halachah*.[7] Raba said: And it is likewise thus for a good dream.[8] But that is not so, for R. Giddal said in Rab's name: If any scholar sits before his teacher and his lips do not drip bitterness,[9] they shall be burnt, for it is said, *his lips are as lilies* [shoshanim], *dropping liquid myrrh* [mor 'ober]:[10] read not *mor 'ober*, but *mar 'ober* [dropping bitterness]; read not *shoshanim* but *sheshonim* [that study]?[11]—There is no difficulty: the former applies to the teacher; the latter to the disciple. Alternatively, both refer to the teacher, yet there is no difficulty: the one means before he commences; the other, after he commences. Even as Rabbah before he commenced [his discourse] before the scholars used to say something humorous, and the scholars were cheered; after that he sat in awe and began the discourse.

The Book of Proverbs too they desired to hide, because its statements are self-contradictory. Yet why did they not hide it? They said, Did we not examine the Book of Ecclesiastes and find a reconciliation? So here too let us make search. And how are its statements self-contradictory?—It is written, *Answer not a fool*
c *according to his folly;*[1] yet it is also written, *Answer a fool according to his folly?*[2] There is no difficulty: the one refers to matters of learning;[3] the other to general matters. Even as a certain person came before Rabbi and said to him, 'Your wife is my wife and your children are mine.'[4] 'Would you like to drink a glass of wine?' asked he. He drank and burst.

A certain man came before R. Ḥiyya and said to him, 'Your mother is my wife and you are my son!' 'Would you like to drink a glass of wine?' asked he. He drank and burst.

R. Ḥiyya observed: Rabbi's prayer was in-so-far effective that his sons were not made illegitimate.[5] For when Rabbi prayed he used to say, May it be Thy will, O Lord our God, to save me this day from the impudent and from impudence.[6]

'Matters of learning'—what is that?—As R. Gamaliel sat and lectured, Woman is destined to bear every day, for it is said,
d *the woman conceiveth and beareth simultaneously.*[1] But a certain disciple scoffed at him, quoting, *'there is no new thing under the sun.'*[2] Come, and I will show you its equal in this world,[3] he replied. He went forth and showed him a fowl. On another occasion R. Gamaliel sat and lectured, Trees are destined to yield fruit every day, for it is said, *and it shall bring forth boughs and bear fruit:*[4] just as the boughs [exist] every day, so shall there be fruit every day. But a certain disciple scoffed at him, saying, but it is written, *'there is no new thing under the sun!'* Come, and I will show you its equal in this world, replied he. He went forth and showed him the caper bush.[5] On another occasion R. Gamaliel sat and expounded, Palestine is destined to bring forth cakes and wool robes, for it is said, *There shall be an handful of corn in the land.*[6] But a certain disciple scoffed at him, quoting, *'there is no new thing under the sun!'* 'Come, and I will show you their equal in this world,' replied he. He went forth and showed him morels and truffles;[7] and for silk robes [he showed him] the bark of a young palm-shoot.[8]

Our Rabbis taught: A man should always be gentle like Hillel, and not impatient like Shammai. It once happened

that the verse is quoted merely to show that the Divine Presence does not rest on a man plunged in gloom, Elisha requiring the minstrel to dissipate the gloom occasioned by Jehoram's visit. (7) Serious study must be preceded by some light-hearted conversation. (8) If one goes to sleep in good spirits, he has happy dreams. (9) Caused by his awe and reverence. (10) Cant. V, 13. (11) Translating: the lips of those who study drop bitterness.—This shows that one must not study light-heartedly.

c (1) Prov. XXVI, 4. (2) Ibid. 5. (3) Then he may be answered. (4) Thus accusing his wife of adultery and his children of illegitimacy. (5) The man's miraculous death proved his accusation unfounded. [The text is not clear. Var. lec.: that he was not made (accused to be) illegitimate unlike R. Ḥiyya, who was declared by the man to be his son; only the character of Rabbi's son was impugned but not of Rabbi himself]. (6) Private prayers were added after the Eighteen Benedictions (v. *supra 9b*, n. a3); Elbogen, *Der Jüdische Gottesdienst*, p. 75. This prayer has become incorporated in the daily liturgy. Weiss, *Dor*, II, 192 conjectures, though on insufficient grounds, that it was occasioned by the opposition he met with among the Rabbis.

d (1) Jer. XXXI, 7. (E.V. 8: *the woman with child and her that travaileth with child together*). (2) Eccl. I, 9. (3) 'This world' is here contrasted with the destined future of change, while generally it is contrasted with the 'world to come'. Whether these two are synonymous it is difficult to say; v. Sanh. 90*a*, n. d3. But perhaps the phrase here means, 'the world under present conditions.' (4) Ezek. XVII, 23. (5) Jast: of which the various products are eaten successively; v. B.B. 28*b*. (6) Ps. LXXII, 16. Rashi: 'this implies, corn as wide as a handbreadth, i.e., cakes as wide. The Hebrew *pissath bar* may also be translated pure wool (or, silken) garments'. (7) Which resemble cakes. (8) This has a downy, silk-like substance on the inside.

that two men [31a] made a wager with each other, saying, He who goes and makes Hillel angry shall receive four hundred *zuz*. Said one, 'I will go and incense him.' That day was the Sabbath eve, and Hillel was washing his head. He went, passed by the door of his house, and called out, 'Is Hillel here, is Hillel here?'[9] Thereupon he robed and went out to him, saying, 'My son, what do you require?' 'I have a question to ask,' said he. 'Ask, my son,' he prompted. Thereupon he asked: 'Why are the heads of the Babylonians round?'[1] 'My son, you have asked a great question,' replied he: 'because they have no skilful midwives.' He departed, tarried a while, returned, and called out, 'Is Hillel here; is Hillel here?' He robed and went out to him, saying, 'My son, what do you require?' 'I have a question to ask,' said he. 'Ask, my son,' he prompted. Thereupon he asked: 'Why are the eyes of the Palmyreans[2] bleared?' 'My son, you have asked a great question,' replied he: 'because they live in sandy places.' He departed, tarried a while, returned, and called out, 'Is Hillel here; is Hillel here?' He robed and went out to him, saying, 'My son, what do you require?' 'I have a question to ask,' said he. 'Ask, my son,' he prompted. He asked, 'Why are the feet of the Africans [negroes] wide?' 'My son, you have asked a great question,' said he; 'because they live in watery marshes.'[3] 'I have many questions to ask,' said he, 'but fear that you may become angry.' Thereupon he robed, sat before him and said, 'Ask all the questions you have to ask,' 'Are you the Hillel who is called the nasi[4] of Israel?' 'Yes,' he replied. 'If that is you,' he retorted, 'may there not be many like you in Israel.' 'Why, my son?' queried he. 'Because I have lost four hundred *zuz* through you,' complained he. 'Be careful of your moods,' he answered. 'Hillel is worth it that you should lose four hundred *zuz* and yet another four hundred *zuz* through him, yet Hillel shall not lose his temper.'

Our Rabbis taught: A certain heathen once came before Shammai and asked him, 'How many *Toroth*[5] have you?' 'Two,' he replied: 'the Written Torah and the Oral Torah.'[6] 'I believe you with respect to the Written, but not with respect to the Oral Torah; make me a proselyte on condition that you teach me the Written Torah [only].' [But] he scolded and repulsed him in anger. When he went before Hillel, he accepted him as
b a proselyte. On the first day[1] he taught him, *Alef, beth, gimmel, daleth*;[2] the following day he reversed [them] to him. 'But yesterday you did not teach them to me thus,' he protested. 'Must you then not rely upon me?[3] Then rely upon me with respect to the Oral [Torah] too.'[4]

On another occasion it happened that a certain heathen came before Shammai and said to him, 'Make me a proselyte, on condition that you teach me the whole Torah while I stand on one foot.' Thereupon he repulsed him with the builder's cubit which was in his hand.[5] When he went before Hillel, he said to him, 'What is hateful to you, do not to your neighbour:[6] that is the whole Torah, while the rest is the commentary thereof; go and learn it.'

(9) Insolently, without the courtesy of a title.
(1) Hillel himself was a Babylonian. (2) V. *supra* 21b, n. a8. (3) Hence their feet must be wide to enable them to walk there, just as ducks' feet are webbed. (4) Patriarch, the religious head of the people. (5) Torah, pl. Toroth, is generally, though incorrectly, translated 'law'. It means rather a system of teaching; v. R.T. Herford, *The Pharisees*, pp. 53ff. (6) The Written Torah is the Pentateuch; the Oral Torah is the whole body of Rabbinical and traditional teaching thereon. This was originally not committed to writing (for the reasons v. Weiss, *Dor*, 111, 24b; and Kaplan, *Redaction of the Talmud*, ch. XIX), and hence designated the Oral Torah. Weiss, op. cit. I, p. 1, n. 1. observes that Hillel was the first man to whom the use of the term תורה שבעל פה 'Oral Law' is found ascribed.
b (1) Of teaching him. (2) The first four letters of the Hebrew alphabet. (3) As to what the letters are. (4) There must be a certain reliance upon authority before anything can be learnt at all. Cf. M. Farbridge, *Judaism and the Modern Mind*, chs. VII and VIII. (5) Rashi: a cubit to measure off the amount of work done by a builder. (6) The golden Rule; cf. Lev. XIX, 18: *but thou shalt love thy neighbour as thyself*. V. Hertz, *Leviticus*, pp. 220-223, and cf. R. T. Herford, *Talmud and Apocrypha*, p. 148.

For the continuation of the English translation of this page see overleaf.

מסורת הש"ס

[סוטה מז. סנהדרין קז: בכורות מד.]

גליון הש"ס

גמרא הלל גייריה · עי' יבמות דף כד ע"ב תוס' ד"ה לא בימי ודף קט ע"ב תוס' ד"ה רעה :

[ברכות לג: וש"נ]

ישעיה לג

שם

ה' פייך לדיני מכירה

עין משפט נר מצוה

קיג א טור וש"ע א"ח סי' קנו :

קיד ב מיי' פ"א מהל' ת"ת הלכה א טור וש"ע א"ח סימן קנה סעיף א :

רבינו חננאל

בג' בני אדם שהמרו זה את זה · כל מי שיקנים הלל יטול [ד' מאות] זוז כו' אמר ר"ל והיה אמונת. עתיך וגו' אמונת זה סדר זרעים · עתיך זה סדר מועד · חוסן זה סדר נשים · ישועות זה סדר נזיקין · חכמת זה סדר קדשים · ודעת זה סדר טהרות · ואף על פי [כן] יראת ה' היא אוצרו · אי איכא יראת ה' אין ואי לא לא : רבא אמר בשעה שמכניסין את האדם לדין אומרים לו נשאת ונתת באמונה · קבעת עתים לתורה · עסקת בפריה ורביה · צפית לישועה · פלפלת בהכמה · הבנת דבר מתוך דבר · אע"פ שיש בידך כל אלו אי איכא יראת שמים אין ואם לא לא · פי' הומטין חול מערבין בתבואה · ואינו בא בה סלמנטון · והיא רצינתא· ומפורש בסוף המוכר את הספינה: כל ת"ח שיש בו תורה ואין בו

שהמרו · נתערבו כמו שממרין את היונים דסנהדרין (דף כה:) : מי כאן הלל · כלום כאן הלל ולשון גנאי לנשיא ישראל : מפני מה ראשן של בבליים סגלגלות · בילוצ"ה בלעז שאינו עגול לישנא אחרינא ראשן של בבליים סגלגל עגול : תרוטות · רכות : שדרים בין החולות · והרוח נושבת ונכנס בתוך עיניהם ובמקום אחר *מפרש תרוטות לשון עגולות בית מושב שלהן ואף כאן אני אומר כן ומפני שדרים בין החולות שינה אותם המקום שלא יהא סדק של עיניהם ארוך כשלא ויכנס בו החול וכן רגליהם של אפרקיים רחבות שלא יטבעו בבצעי המים וטיטיט מפרשים שדרים בין בצעי המים והולכין יחפין ומתפשטין רגליהן לפי שהמנעל דוחק הרגל ומעמידו על דפוס שלו: כדי הוא הלל · ראוי לכך : הוציאו בנזיפה · דתניא הבא לקבל דברי חברות חוץ מדבר אחד וכן גר הבא להתגייר וקבל עליו דברי תורה חוץ מדבר אחד אין מקבלין אותו במסכת בכורות (דף ל:) : גייריה · וסמך על חכמתו שסופו שירגילנו לקבל עליו דלא דמיא הא לחוץ מדבר אחד שלא היה כופר בתורה שבעל פה אלא שלא היה מאמין שהיא מפי הגבורה והלל הובטח שאחר שילמדנו יסמוך עליו : אפיך ליה · כגון תשר"ק: לאו עלי קא סמכת · מנין אתה יודע שזו אלף וזו בית אלא שלמדתיך וסמכת עלי דעל פה נמי סמוך על דברי : אמת הבנין · מקל שהוא אמת אורך ומודדים בו אורך הבנין שהיו קוצצין עם האומנין כך וכך אמות בכך וכך דמים : דעלך סני לחברך לא תעביד · ריעך וריע אביך אל תעזוב (משלי כז) זה הקב"ה אל תעבור על דבריו שהרי עליך שנאוי שיעבור חבירך על דבריך ל"א חבירך ממש כגון גזלה גנבה ניאוף ורוב המצות : ואידך · שאר דברי תורה : פירושה · דהא מילתא הוא לדעת איזה דבר שנאוי זיל גמור ותדע : סופר · מלמד תינוקות : טכסיסי · תיקוני נרכי המלך לפי הכבוד : שלשתן · הגרים הללו : סדר זרעים · שבעל אמונת האדם סומך להפריש מעשרותיו כראוי : חוסן · לשון יורשין ועל ידי אשה וולדו יורשין: סדר נזיקין · מושיען מזהיר לפרוש מהיזק ומהתחייב ממון : דעת · עדיף מחכמה: היא אוצרו · הוא עיקר החשוב בעיניו לאצור ולעשות סגולה לזכרון : קבעת עתים · לפי שאדם צריך להתעסק בדרך ארץ שאם אין דרך ארץ אין תורה הוצרך לקבוע עתים לתורה דבר קצוב שלא ימשך כל היום לדרך ארץ : בפריה ורביה · היינו חוסן : צפית לישועה · לדברי הנביאים : הבנת דבר מתוך דבר · היינו דעת : קב חומטין · ארץ מלחה ומשמרת את הפירות מהתליע : ואינו חושש · למוכרה בדמי חטין דלאו אונאה היא שהרי שמירתן בכך :

יראת

תורה אור

שהמרו זה את זה · דיני אסמכתא מפורש במקום אחר (בבא מציעא דף עד· וסס) : אמונת זה סדר זרעים · מפרש בירושלמי שמאמין בחי העולמים וזורע : וסותר

שהמרו זה את זה אמרו כל מי שילך ויקניט את הלל יטול ד' מאות זוז אמר אחד מהם אני אקניטנו אותו היום ע"ש היה והלל חפף את ראשו הלך ועבר על פתח ביתו אמר מי כאן הלל מי כאן הלל נתעטף ויצא לקראתו אמר לו בני מה אתה מבקש א"ל שאלה יש לי לשאול א"ל שאל בני שאל מפני מה ראשיהן של בבליים סגלגלות א"ל בני שאלה גדולה שאלת מפני שאין להם חיות פקחות הלך והמתין שעה אחת חזר ואמר מי כאן הלל מי כאן הלל נתעטף ויצא לקראתו אמר לו בני מה אתה מבקש א"ל שאלה יש לי לשאול א"ל שאל בני שאל מפני מה עיניהן של תרמודיין תרוטות אמר לו בני שאלה גדולה שאלת מפני שדרין בין החולות הלך והמתין שעה אחת חזר ואמר מי כאן הלל מי כאן הלל נתעטף ויצא לקראתו א"ל בני מה אתה מבקש א"ל שאלה יש לי לשאול א"ל שאל בני שאל מפני מה רגליהם של אפרקיים רחבות א"ל בני שאלה גדולה שאלת מפני שדרין בין בצעי המים אמר לו שאלות הרבה יש לי לשאול ומתירא אני שמא תכעוס נתעטף וישב לפניו א"ל כל שאלות שיש לך לשאול שאל א"ל אתה הוא הלל שקורין אותך נשיא ישראל א"ל הן א"ל אם אתה הוא לא ירבו כמותך בישראל א"ל בני מפני מה א"ל מפני שאבדתי על ידך ד' מאות זוז א"ל הוי זהיר ברוחך כדי הוא הלל שתאבד על ידו ד' מאות זוז וד' מאות זוז והלל לא יקפיד : ת"ר מעשה בנכרי אחד שבא לפני שמאי אמר לו כמה תורות יש לכם אמר לו שתים תורה שבכתב ותורה שבעל פה א"ל שבכתב אני מאמינך ושבעל פה איני מאמינך גיירני ע"מ שתלמדני תורה שבכתב גער בו והוציאו בנזיפה בא לפני הלל גייריה יומא קמא א"ל א"ב ג"ד למחר אפיך ליה א"ל והא אתמול לא אמרת לי הכי א"ל לאו עלי דידי קא סמכת דעל פה נמי סמוך עלי : שוב מעשה בנכרי אחד שבא לפני שמאי א"ל גיירני ע"מ שתלמדני כל התורה כולה כשאני עומד על רגל אחת דחפו באמת הבנין שבידו בא לפני °הלל *גייריה אמר לו דעלך סני לחברך לא תעביד זו היא כל התורה כולה ואידך פירושה הוא זיל גמור : שוב מעשה בנכרי אחד שהיה עובר אחורי בית המדרש ושמע קול סופר שהיה אומר °ואלה הבגדים אשר יעשו חושן ואפוד אמר הללו למי אמרו לו לכהן גדול אמר אותו נכרי בעצמו אלך ואתגייר בשביל שישימוני כהן גדול בא לפני שמאי אמר ליה גיירני על מנת שתשימני כהן גדול דחפו באמת הבנין שבידו בא לפני הלל גייריה א"ל כלום מעמידין מלך אלא מי שיודע טכסיסי מלכות לך למוד טכסיסי מלכות הלך וקרא כיון שהגיע °והזר הקרב יומת אמר ליה מקרא זה על מי נאמר א"ל אפי' על דוד מלך ישראל נשא אותו גר קל וחומר בעצמו ומה ישראל שנקראו בנים למקום ומתוך אהבה שאהבם קרא להם °בני בכורי ישראל כתיב עליהם והזר הקרב יומת גר הקל שבא במקלו ובתרמילו על אחת כמה וכמה בא לפני שמאי א"ל כלום ראוי אני להיות כהן גדול והלא כתיב בתורה והזר הקרב יומת בא לפני הלל א"ל ענוותן הלל *ינוחו לך ברכות על ראשך שהקרבתני תחת כנפי השכינה לימים נזדווגו שלשתן למקום אחד אמרו קפדנותו של שמאי בקשה לטורדנו מן העולם ענוותנותו של הלל קרבנו תחת כנפי השכינה : אמר ר"ל מאי דכתיב °והיה אמונת עתיך חוסן ישועות חכמת ודעת וגו' אמונת זה סדר זרעים עתיך זה סדר מועד חוסן זה סדר נשים ישועות זה סדר נזיקין חכמת זה סדר קדשים ודעת זה סדר טהרות ואפ"ה °יראת ה' היא אוצרו אמר רבא בשעה שמכניסין אדם לדין אומרים לו *נשאת *ונתת באמונה [ג]קבעת עתים לתורה עסקת בפו"ר צפית לישועה פלפלת בחכמה הבנת דבר מתוך דבר ואפ"ה אי יראת ה' היא אוצרו אין אי לא לא משל לאדם שאמר לשלוחו העלה לי כור חיטין לעלייה הלך והעלה לו א"ל עירבת לי בהן קב חומטון א"ל לאו א"ל מוטב אם לא העליתה : תנא דבי ר"י *מערב אדם קב חומטון בכור של תבואה ואינו חושש : אמר רבה בר רב הונא כל אדם שיש בו תורה ואין בו

יראת

שמות כח

במדבר א

שמות ד

[עי' תוס' יבמות קט: ד"ה רעה וכו']

[עי' תוס' סנהדרין ד ד"ה אלא ותוס' קדושין צ: ד"ה אין]

Continuation of translation from previous page as indicated by ◁

On another occasion it happened that a certain heathen was passing behind a Beth Hamidrash, when he heard the voice of a teacher[7] reciting, *And these are the garments which they shall make; a breastplate, and an ephod.*[8] Said he, 'For whom are these?' 'For the High Priest,' he was told. Then said that heathen to himself, 'I will go and become a proselyte, that I may be appointed a High Priest.' So he went before Shammai and said to him, 'Make me a proselyte on condition that you appoint me a High Priest.' But he repulsed him with the builder's cubit which was in his hand. He then went before Hillel, who made him a proselyte. Said he to him, 'Can any man be made a king but he who knows the arts of government? Do you go and study the arts of govern-
c ment!'[1] He went and read. When he came to, *and the stranger that cometh nigh shall be put to death*,[2] he asked him, 'To whom does this verse apply?' 'Even to David King of Israel,' was the answer. Thereupon that proselyte reasoned within himself *a fortiori:* if Israel, who are called sons of the Omnipresent,[3] and who in His love for them He designated them, *Israel is my son, my firstborn*,[4] yet it is written of them, *'and the stranger that cometh nigh shall be put to death'*: how much more so a mere proselyte, who comes with his staff and wallet! Then he went before Shammai and said to him. 'Am I then eligible to be a High Priest; is it not written in the Torah, *'and the stranger that cometh nigh shall be put to death?'* He went before Hillel and said to him, 'O gentle Hillel; blessings rest on thy head for bringing me under the wings of the *Shechinah!*'[5] Some time later the three met in one place; said they, Shammai's impatience sought to drive us from the world, but Hillel's gentleness brought us under the wings of the *Shechinah*.[6]

Resh Laḳish said, What is meant by the verse, *and there shall be faith in thy times, strength, salvation, wisdom and knowledge?*[7] *'Faith'* refers to the Order of Seeds; *thy times*, the Order of Festivals; *strength*, the Order of Women; *salvation*, the Order of Neziḳin;[8] *wisdom*, the Order of Sacrifices; *and knowledge*, to the Order of Purity.[9] Yet even so *the fear of the Lord is his treasure*.[10]

Raba said, When man is led in for judgment[11] he is asked, Did you deal faithfully [i.e., with integrity], did you fix times for learning, did you engage in procreation, did you hope for salvation, did you engage in the dialectics of wisdom, did you under-
d stand one thing from another.[1] Yet even so, if *'the fear of the Lord is his treasure,'* it is well: if not, [it is] not [well]. This may be compared to a man who instructed his agent, 'Take me up a *kor* of wheat in the loft,' and he went and did so. 'Did you mix in a *ḳab* of *ḥumton?*'[2] he asked him, 'No,' replied he. 'Then it were better that you had not carried it up,' he retorted. The School of R. Ishmael taught: A man may mix a *ḳab* of *ḥumton* in a *kor* of grain, and have no fear.[3]

Rabbah b. R. Huna said: Every man who possesses learning

(7) Lit., 'a scribe'. (8) Ex. XXVIII, 4.

c (1) The laws appertaining to the functions of a High Priest. (2) Num. I, 51. (3) Deut. XIV, 1. (4) Ex. IV, 22. (5) V. Glos. (6) From these stories it would appear that proselytes were eagerly accepted by Hillel; v. Ḳid., 62b, n. 3. (7) Isa. XXXIII, 6. (8) V. n. 9. (9) These are the six orders into which the Talmud is divided. Faith is applied to Seeds, because it requires faith in the Almighty to sow with the assurance of a crop (J.T.); 'times' as meaning Festivals is self-explanatory; *ḥosen*, here translated 'strength', is derived by Rashi from a root meaning to inherit, and thus identified with the Order of Women, because heirs are created through women; *Neziḳin* treats of civil law, knowledge of which saves man (i.e., brings him 'salvation') from encroaching upon his neighbour's rights or allowing his own to be filched away; the last two Orders are very intricate and require deep understanding, and are therefore identified with wisdom and knowledge. (10) Ibid. Learning without piety is valueless. (11) In the next world.

d (1) That is Raba's interpretation of the verse; he too translates *'ḥosen'* as inheritance, and thus applies it to procreation (v. preceding note), and understands 'knowledge' as the process of inferring the unknown from the known. (2) Jast.: a sandy soil containing salty substances and used for the preservation of wheat. (3) Of dishonesty, when he sells the whole as grain, because that proportion is necessary for its preservation. One *kab* = one hundred and eightieth of a *kor*.

שהמרו זה את זה אמרו כל מי שילך ויקניט את הלל יטול ד' מאות זוז אמר אחד מהם אני אקניטנו אותו היום ע"ש היה והלל חפף את ראשו הלך ועבר על פתח ביתו אמר מי כאן הלל מי כאן הלל נתעטף ויצא לקראתו אמר לו בני מה אתה מבקש א"ל שאלה יש לי לשאול א"ל שאל בני שאל מפני מה ראשיהן של בבליים סגלגלות א"ל בני שאלה גדולה שאלת מפני שאין להם חיות פקחות הלך והמתין שעה אחת חזר ואמר מי כאן הלל מי כאן הלל נתעטף ויצא לקראתו אמר לו בני מה אתה מבקש א"ל שאלה יש לי לשאול א"ל שאל בני שאל מפני מה עיניהן של תרמודיין תרוטות אמר לו בני שאלה גדולה שאלת מפני שדרין בין החולות הלך והמתין שעה אחת חזר ואמר מי כאן הלל מי כאן הלל נתעטף ויצא לקראתו א"ל בני מה אתה מבקש א"ל שאלה יש לי לשאול א"ל שאל בני שאל מפני מה רגליהם של אפרקיים רחבות א"ל בני שאלה גדולה שאלת מפני שדרין בין בצעי המים אמר לו שאלות הרבה יש לי לשאול ומתירא אני שמא תכעוס נתעטף וישב לפניו א"ל כל שאלות שיש לך לשאול שאל א"ל אתה הוא הלל שקורין אותך נשיא ישראל א"ל הן א"ל אם אתה הוא לא ירבו כמותך בישראל א"ל בני מפני מה א"ל מפני שאבדתי על ידך ד' מאות זוז א"ל הוי זהיר ברוחך כדי הוא הלל שתאבד על ידו ד' מאות זוז וד' מאות זוז והלל לא יקפיד: ת"ר מעשה בנכרי אחד שבא לפני שמאי אמר לו כמה תורות יש לכם אמר לו שתים תורה שבכתב ותורה שבעל פה א"ל שבכתב אני מאמינך ושבעל פה איני מאמינך גיירני ע"מ שתלמדני תורה שבכתב גער בו והוציאו בנזיפה בא לפני הלל גייריה יומא קמא א"ל א"ב ג"ד למחר אפיך ליה א"ל והא אתמול לא אמרת לי הכי א"ל לאו עלי דידי קא סמכת דעל פה נמי סמוך עלי: שוב מעשה בנכרי אחד שבא לפני שמאי א"ל גיירני ע"מ שתלמדני כל התורה כולה כשאני עומד על רגל אחת דחפו באמת הבנין שבידו בא לפני °הלל *גייריה אמר לו דעלך סני לחברך לא תעביד זו היא כל התורה כולה ואידך פירושה הוא זיל גמור: שוב מעשה בנכרי אחד שהיה עובר אחורי בית המדרש ושמע קול סופר שהיה אומר °ואלה הבגדים אשר יעשו חושן ואפוד אמר הללו למי אמרו לו לכהן גדול אמר אותו נכרי בעצמו אלך ואתגייר בשביל שישימוני כהן גדול בא לפני שמאי אמר ליה גיירני על מנת שתשימני כהן גדול דחפו באמת הבנין שבידו בא לפני הלל גייריה א"ל כלום מעמידין מלך אלא מי שיודע טכסיסי מלכות לך למוד טכסיסי מלכות הלך וקרא כיון שהגיע °והזר הקרב יומת אמר ליה מקרא זה על מי נאמר א"ל אפי' על דוד מלך ישראל נשא אותו גר קל וחומר בעצמו ומה ישראל שנקראו בנים למקום ומתוך אהבה שאהבם קרא להם °בני בכורי ישראל כתיב עליהם והזר הקרב יומת גר הקל שבא במקלו ובתרמילו על אחת כמה וכמה בא לפני שמאי א"ל כלום ראוי אני להיות כהן גדול והלא כתיב בתורה והזר הקרב יומת בא לפני הלל א"ל ענוותן הלל *ינוחו לך ברכות על ראשך שהקרבתני תחת כנפי השכינה לימים נזדווגו שלשתן למקום אחד אמרו קפדנותו של שמאי בקשה לטורדנו מן העולם ענוותנותו של הלל קרבנו תחת כנפי השכינה: אמר ר"ל מאי דכתיב °והיה אמונת עתיך חוסן ישועות חכמת ודעת וגו' אמונת זה סדר זרעים עתיך זה סדר מועד חוסן זה סדר נשים ישועות זה סדר נזיקין חכמת זה סדר קדשים ודעת זה סדר טהרות ואפ"ה °יראת ה' היא אוצרו אמר רבא בשעה שמכניסין אדם לדין אומרים לו *נשאת *ונתת באמונה *קבעת עתים לתורה עסקת בפו"ר צפית לישועה פלפלת בחכמה הבנת דבר מתוך דבר ואפ"ה אי יראת ה' היא אוצרו אין אי לא לא משל לאדם שאמר לשלוחו העלה לי כור חיטין לעלייה הלך והעלה לו א"ל עירבת לי בהן קב חומטון א"ל לאו א"ל מוטב אם לא העליתה: תנא דבי ר"י *מערב אדם קב חומטון בכור של תבואה ואינו חושש: אמר רבה בר רב הונא כל אדם שיש בו תורה ואין בו

יראת

שהמרו · נתערבו כמו שממרין את היוניס דסנהדרין (דף כה:): מי כאן הלל · כלוס כאן הלל ולשון גנאי לנשיא ישראל: מפני מה ראשן של בבליים סגלגלות · בילונ"ה בלעז שאינו עגול לישנא אחרינא ראשן של בבליים סגלגל עגול: תרוטות · רכות: שדרים בין החולות · והרוח נושבת ונכנס בתוך עיניהם ובמקום אחר *מפרש תרוטות לשון עגולות בית מושב שלהן ואף כאן אני אומר כן ומפני שדרים בין החולות שיהא אותם המקום שלא יהא סדק של עיניהם ארוך כשלט ויכנס בו החול וכן רגליהם של אפרקיים רחבות שלא יטבעו בבצעי המים ופטוטיט מפרשים שדרים בין בצעי המים והולכין יחפין ומתפשטין רגליהן לפי שהמנעל דוחק הרגל ומעמידו על דפוס שלו: כדי הוא הלל · ראוי לכך: הוציאו בנזיפה · דתניא הבא לקבל דברי חברות חוץ מדבר אחד וכן גר הבא להתגייר וקבל עליו דברי תורה חוץ מדבר אחד אין מקבלין אותו במסכת בכורות (דף ל:): גייריה · וסמך על חכמתו שסופו שירגילנו לקבל עליו דלא דמיא הא לחוץ מדבר אחד שלא היה כופר בתורה שבעל פה אלא שלא היה מאמין שהיא מפי הגבורה והלל הובטח שאחר שילמדנו יסמוך עליו: אפיך ליה · כגון תשר"ק: לאו עלי קא סמכת · מנין אתה יודע שזו אלף וזו בית אלא שלמדתיך וסמכת עלי דעל פה נמי סמוך על דברי: אמת הבנין · מקל שהוא אמת אורך ומודדים בו אורך הבנין שהיו קוצצין עם האומנין כך וכך אמות בכך וכך דמים: דעלך סני לחברך לא תעביד · ריעך וריע אביך אל תעזוב (משלי כז) זה הקב"ה אל תעבור על דבריו שהרי עליך סנאוי שיעבור חבירך על דבריך ל"א חבירך ממש כגון גזלה גנבה ניאוף ורוב המצות: אידך · שאר דברי תורה: פירושה · דהא מילתא הוא לדעת איזה דבר שנאוי זיל גמור ותדע: סופר · מלמד תינוקות: טכסיסי · תיקוני דרכי המלך לפי הכבוד: שלשתן · הגרים הללו: סדר זרעים · שבעל אמונת האדם סומך להפריש מעשרותיו כראוי: חוסן · לשון יורשין ועל ידי אשה טולדו יורשין: סדר נזיקין · מושיען מזהיר לפרוש מהיזק ומהתחייב ממון: דעת · עדיף מחכמה: היא אוצרו · הוא עיקר החשוב בעיניו לאצור ולעשות סגולה לזכרון: קבעת עתים · לפי שאדם צריך להתעסק בדרך ארץ שאם אין דרך ארץ אין תורה הוצרך לקבוע עתים לתורה דבר קבוע שלא ימשך כל היום לדרך ארץ: בפריה ורביה · היינו חוסן: צפית לישועה · לדברי הנביאים: הבנת דבר מתוך דבר · היינו דעת: קב חומטין · ארץ מלחה ומשמרת את הפירות מהתליע: ואינו חושש · למוכרה בדמי חטין דלאו אונאה היא שהרי שמירתן בכך:

ירא[ת]

שהמרו זה את זה · דיני אסמכתא מפורש במקום אחר (בבא מציעא דף עד· ושם): אמונת זה סדר זרעים · מפרש בירושלמי שמאמין בחי העולמים וזורע: וסותר

עין משפט נר מצוה

קיג א טור וש"ע א"ח סי' קנו:

קיד ב מיי' פ"א מהל' ת"ת הלכה ח טור וש"ע א"ח סימן קנה סעיף א:

רבינו חננאל

בג' בני אדם שהמרו זה את זה · כל מי שיקנים הלל יטול [ד' מאות] זוז כו' אמר ר"ל והיה אמונת. עתיך וגו' אמונת זה סדר זרעים · עתיך זה סדר מועד · חוסן זה סדר נשים · ישועות זה סדר נזיקין · חכמת זה סדר קדשים · ודעת זה סדר טהרות · ואף על פי [כן] יראת ה' היא אוצרו · אי איכא יראת ה' אין ואי לא לא: רבא אמר בשעה שמכניסין את האדם לדין אומרים לו נשאת ונתת באמונה · קבעת עתים לתורה · עסקת בפריה ורביה · צפית לישועה · פלפלת בחכמה · הבנת דבר מתוך דבר· אע"פ שיש בידך כל אלו אי איכא יראת שמים אין ואם לא לא · פי' הומטון חול מערבין בתבואה · ואינו בא בה סלמנטון · והיא רצינתא' ומפורש בסוף המוכר את הספינה: כל ת"ח שיש בו תורה ואין בו

[עי' תוס' יבמות קט. ד"ה רעה וכו']

[עי' תוס' סנהדרין ד ד"ה אלא ותוס' קדושין ב: ד"ה אין]

מסורת הש"ס

[סוטה מח. סנהדרין קז: בכורות מב.]

[ברכות לג: וש"נ]

ע"ז לדיני מגילה

גליון הש"ס

גמרא הלל גייריה · עי' יבמות דף כד ע"ב תוס' ד"ה לא בימי ודף קט ע"ב תוס' ד"ה רעה:

תורה אור

שמות כח · במדבר א · שמות ד · ישעיה לג · שם

תורה אור

יראת שמים דומה לגזבר שמסרו לו מפתחות הפנימיות ומפתחות החיצונות לא מסרו לו בהי עייל *מכריז רבי ינאי חבל על דלית ליה דרתא ותרעא לדרתא עביד אמר רב יהודה לא ברא הקב"ה את עולמו אלא כדי שייראו מלפניו שנאמר °והאלהים עשה שייראו מלפניו *ר' סימון ור' אלעזר הוו יתבי חליף ואזיל ר' יעקב בר אחא א"ל חד לחבריה ניקו מקמיה דגבר דחיל חטאין הוא א"ל אידך ניקו מקמיה דגבר *בר אוריין הוא א"ל אמינא לך אנא דגבר דחיל חטאין הוא ואמרת לי את בר אוריין הוא תסתיים דרבי אלעזר הוא דאמר דגבר דחיל חטאין הוא דא"ר יוחנן משום ר' *אלעזר °אין לו להקב"ה בעולמו אלא יראת שמים בלבד שנאמר °ועתה ישראל מה ה' אלהיך שואל מעמך כי אם ליראה וגו' וכתיב °ויאמר לאדם הן יראת ה' היא חכמה וגו' *שכן בלשון יוני קורין לאחת הן *תסתיים: דרש רב עולא מאי דכתיב °אל תרשע הרבה וגו' הרבה הוא דלא לירשע הא מעט לירשע אלא מי שאכל שום וריחו נודף יחזור ויאכל שום אחר ויהא ריחו נודף דרש רבא בר רב עולא מאי דכתיב °כי אין חרצובות למותם ובריא אולם אמר הקב"ה לא דיין לרשעים שאינן חרדין ועצבין מיום המיתה אלא שלבם בריא להן כאולם והיינו דאמר רבה מאי דכתיב °זה דרכם כסל למו יודעין רשעים שדרכם למיתה ויש להם חלב על כסלם שמא תאמר שכחה היא מהן ת"ל ואחריהם בפיהם ירצו סלה: כחס על הנר כו': ר' יוסי כמאן ס"ל *אי כר' יהודה ס"ל אפילו בהנך נמי ליחייב ואי כר"ש ס"ל פתילה נמי ליפטר אמר עולא *לעולם כר' יהודה ס"ל וקסבר ר' יוסי [ב]סותר על מנת לבנות במקומו הוי סותר על מנת לבנות שלא במקומו לא הוי סותר א"ל רבה מכדי *כל מלאכות ילפינן להו ממשכן והתם סותר ע"מ לבנות שלא במקומו הוא א"ל שאני התם כיון דכתיב °על פי ה' יחנו כסותר ע"מ לבנות במקומו דמי ור' יוחנן אמר לעולם כר"ש ס"ל ומאי שנא פתילה כדאמר רב המנונא ואיתימא רב אדא בר אהבה הכא בפתילה שצריך להבהבה עסקינן דבההיא אפילו ר"ש מודי דקא מתקן מנא אמר רבא דיקא נמי דקתני שהוא עושה פחם ולא קתני מפני שנעשית פחם ש"מ: **מתני'** על שלש עבירות נשים מתות בשעת לידתן על שאינן זהירות בנדה בחלה [ג]ובהדלקת הנר: **גמ'** נדה מ"ט א"ר יצחק היא קלקלה בחדרי בטנה לפיכך תלקה בחדרי בטנה תינח נדה חלה והדלקת הנר מאי איכא למימר כדדרש ההוא גלילאה עליה דרב חסדא אמר הקב"ה *רביעית דם נתתי בכם על עסקי דם הזהרתי אתכם ראשית

רש"י

יראת שמים דומה · לפתחים חיצונים שדרך להם נכנסים לפנימיים כך אם יראת שמים הוא נעשה חרד לשמור ולעשות ואם לאו אינו חש לתורתו: בהי עייל · באיזה פתח נכנס לפתוח את הפנימים: (א)(*ואנא) אמינא לך · כלומר אתה מיעטת בשבחו: הן יראת ה' · יחידה היא היראה בעולם: מי שאכל שום וריחו נודף כו' · פירוקא הוא כלומר הכי קאמר קרא אם רשעת מעט אל תוסף על רשעך דמי שאכל שום וריחו נודף כבר לחבריו כלום יחזור ויאכל עוד אחר ויהיה נודף יותר לזמן ארוך: חרדין ועצבין · נוטריקון דחרצובות: כאולם · שפתחו פתוח ורחב: זה דרכם · לעיל מיניה כתיב קרבם בתימו לעולם דהיינו קבורה והדר כתיב זה דרכם כסל למו כלומר יודעין הם שזו דרכם אבל כסל למו כליותיהם מתופין בחלבם מהשיב (ב)כליותיהם מחשבת סופם ושמא תאמר מחמת החלב שכחו והרי הם שוגגין ת"ל ואחריהם את העתיד לבא לנפשם אחרי אובדם בפיהם ירצו ויספרו תמיד ואעפ"כ אינן חוזרין: אפי' בפתילה נמי ליפטר · דחס על הפתילה נמי אינה צריכה המלאכה לגופה דמלאכה היינו כיבוי וכיבוי עצמו אינו צריך לו דאם לא הובערה מעולם הוה ניחא ליה אם מתחלה הובהבה הואיל וחס עליה כי אית בה טפי הוה ניחא ליה בה: לעולם כר' יהודה סבירא ליה · דמשום אין צריכה לגופה לא מיפטר הואיל וצריכה לדבר אחר מלאכת מחשבת הוא וכי מכבה לה משום חייסא דשמן ונר היינו טעמא דפטור קסבר דסותר ע"מ לבנות במקומו הוי סותר כל מקלקל דשבת הוי פטור דלאו היינו מלאכת מחשבת וסותר דתנן *באבות מלאכות דמיחייב סותר ע"מ לבנות הוא ואינו יכול לבנות אלא אם כן סותרו והשתא לאו קלקול הוא ור"י סבר דאם במקומו חוזר ובונה הוא דמחייב אסתירה ואי לא לא ומכבה דומיא דסותר הוא וכן קורע דומיא דסותר ולהכי תנן הקורע ע"מ לתפור וכן מוחק תנן ע"מ לכתוב דכולם סותר ניהו הלכך על הפתילה חייסא דידיה איכא אלא להדליק הלכך מכבה על מנת להדליק היינו במקומו אבל כי חס על הנר או על השמן ועל הפתילה אינו חס ואינו חושש אם משליכה אפי' צריך לשמן להדליק בו פתילה אחרת לאחר זמן בתוך נר זה אין זה סותר ע"מ לבנות במקומו שאין הכיבוי וההבערה לא בשמן ולא בנר אלא בפתילה הלכך לא שייכא סתירה ובנין אלא בפתילה וכיון דאין מחשבת סופו לחזור ולהדליק פתילה זו אין כאן עוד בנין במקום סתירה ודקתני שהוא עושה פחם כלומר מפני שהם עושין פחם מתחלתה ועומדת לחזור ולהאחיז בה אור ואיכא בנין במקום סתירה ורבותינו מפרשין נר ושמן איכא למימר מיבעי ליה למידי אחריני ולא להדליק ולי נראה שאין צריכין אנו לדוחק זה דמשום דאיכא למימר לית לן למיפטריה שהרי הוא יודע למה חס עליהן והם נר אינו אלא להדליק בו פתילה: ומשכן סותר על מנת לבנות שלא במקומו הוא · שהיו סותרין אותו בחנייה זו ונוסעים למקום אחר וחונים וחוזרים ומקימין אותו: כר' שמעון · דפטר ליה משום דאין צריכין לגופה וכחס על הפתילה היינו טעמא דמחייב כגון שצריך להבהבה שלא הובהבה מבעוד יום דכיבוי זה צריך לגופו שיהא הלהב נוח לאחוז בה כשיבא להדליקה: שהוא עושה פחם · שהוא °מתכוין ממש לעשותה כמין פחם עכשיו אלמא בכבוי הצריך לגופו מיירי ולא קתני שנעשית פחם מתחלתו שהובהבה דנמי למימר טעמא משום דבת בנין היא דאיכא בנין במקום סתירה מה שאין כן בשמן ונר דלא שייך בהו בנין וסתירה: **מתני'** בשעת לידתן · בגמרא מפרש מאי שנא שעת לידתן: **גמ'** הכי גרסינן בנדה מאי טעמא: בחדרי בטנה · מקור דמה: קלקלה · מרדה: רביעית דם · חיי אדם תלויין בה:

ראשית

תוספות

וסותר על מנת לבנות במקומו · ור"ש פוטר אפי' בסותר על מנת לבנות במקומו אלא במקום שע"י סתירה יש תיקון (בבנין אחרון) יותר משלא היה בנין ראשון מעולם שם כגון בפתילה שצריך להבהבה דמחייב ר' שמעון כדאמר בסמוך ואם תאמר לר' שמעון הא דתנן בפרק כלל גדול (לקמן דף עג·) המכבה והסותר בשלמא מכבה משכחת לה דמתקן כדפירש כגון לעשות פחמין אלא סותר לא משכחת שיהא מתקן בסתירה זו יותר משלא היה בנוי שם מעולם ואמאי חייב לר' שמעון וי"ל דכולהו ממשכן ילפינן לה ולא היה כיבוי במשכן כ"א לעשות פחמין ולהכי לא מחייב ר"ש אלא בכה"ג אבל סותר אשכחן במשכן שאין מתקן בסתירה זו יותר משלא היה בנוי שם מעולם ולהכי מחייב שם אפי' ר"ש וא"ת כיון דסותר ומכבה בעינן ע"מ לבנות ולהבעיר א"כ בפרק כלל גדול (שם) דתנן המכבה והסותר הוי ליה למיתני המכבה ע"מ להבעיר והסותר ע"מ לבנות כי היכי דקתני המוחק ע"מ לכתוב שתי אותיות והקורע ע"מ לתפור שתי תפירות וי"ל דהתם נמי לא קתני ליה אלא משום דבעי למיתני שיעורא דשתי אותיות ושתי תפירות אבל במכבה וסותר על מנת להבעיר ולבנות כל שהוא מיחייב לא איצטריך למיתנייה:

עין משפט נר מצוה

קטו א מיי' פ"א מהל' שבת הל' ז ופי"ב הל' ב סמג לאוין סה טור א"ח סימן רסח:

קטז ב מיי' פ"י מהל' שבת הלכה טו:

קיז ג מיי' פ"ה מהל' שבת הל' ג טוש"ע א"ח סי' רסג סעיף ג:

[בילקוט פרשת עקב רמז תתנה איתא רבי ור' אלעזר בר' שמעון הוו יתבי וכו' וע"ע ילקוט קהלת ג' רמז תתקסט]

[מ"ק כח· סנהדרין צט: ע"ש]

רבינו חננאל

יראת שמים דומה לגזבר שמסרו לו מפתחות הפנימיות והחיצוניות לא מסרו לו בהי עייל מכריז ר' יוחנן חבל על דלית[ליה]דירתא ותרעא לדירתה עביד · אמר להו [רבא] לרבנן במטו מינייכו רבנן לא תירתון תרתי ניהגם *): א"ר יוחנן אין להקב"ה אלא יראת שמים בלבד שנא' ויאמר לאדם הן יראת ה' היא חכמה וסור מרע בינה: פיס' כחס על הנר כחס על השמן וכו' · אוקימנא למתני' כולה המכבה את הנר כחס על הנר כחס על השמן כחס על הפתילה כו' לר' יהודה דסבר דבר שאין מתכוין אסור והלק עליו רבי יוסי בכולהו והודה לו בפתילה · ואוקמה עולא דרבי יוסי נמי כרבי יהודה סבירא ליה דדבר שאין מתכוין אסור · מיהו אמר לך לא מחייב אלא היכא דקא מתעבדא מלאכה וסותר ע"מ לבנות במקומו כגון פתילה שכבה ע"מ להדליק במקום שכבה בראש הפתילה הוי סותר ונגמרה מלאכה לפיכך חייב · אבל מכבה הפתילה ליטול השמן או הנר נמצא סותר בפתילה ובונה בנר או בשמן כי האי גוונא לא הוי סותר ואין שם מלאכה כלל לפיכך פטור . ואקשינן מכדי מלאכות דשבת ילפינן להו [ממשכן] ובמשכן סותר מזה המקום שנוסעין ממנו לבנות במקום אחר הוא והנה סותר שלא לבנות במקומו הוי סותר ושנינן כיון דכתיב על פי ה' יחנו ועל פי ה' יסעו · ויתכן שיאמר להם שובו חנו במקום שסרתם כסותר ע"מ לבנות [במקומו] דמי רבי יוחנן אמר לעולם רבי יוסי כרבי שמעון ס... ומתני' בפתילה שצריך להבהבה עסקי' · דבהא אפילו רבי שמעון מודה דקא מתקן מנא דחירוכי משויא ליה מנא ודייקא נמי מתני' הכי דקתני מפני שהוא עושה פחם כלומר מתכוין לעשותה פחם הוא ולא ק... שנעשה פחם בלא כוונתו ש"מ · נתברר כי ההבהוב הוא חירוך כדכתיב (דניאל ג) ושער ראשיהון לא התחרך והחירוך הוא עשיה כמין פחם: מתני' על שלש עבירות נשים וכו' · אסיקנא כי הא דדו... גלילאה

*) לפנינו ליתא כאן מימרא דרבא אלא ביומא ד' עב ע"ב:

מסורת הש"ס

ז"ל ואנא · יומא עב: · [בגיטין סב· פרש"י בנותרה] · [בילקוט פרשת עקב הג"ל איתא ר' אלעזר בר' שמעון] · [במגילה כ... פרש"י ד"ה תסתיים יש סימן] · לעיל יב: לקמן עג: וש"נ · [לקמן מט:] · [סוטה ה' ע... רש"י ותוס' ד"ה אדם]

הגהות הב"ח

(א) רש"י ד"ה בהי וכו' הפנימיים הס"ד ואח"כ מ"ה אמינא לך כלומר: (ב) ד"ה דרכם וכו' מהשיב אל כליותיהם ירצו סלה ויספרו:

גליון הש"ס

גמרא אין לו להקב"ה בעולמו · עיין ברכות דף לג ע"ב: **רש"י** ד"ה מפני שהוא עושה פחם · שהוא מתכוין ממש · וק"ל הא בפשוטו י"ל דחוץ מן הפתילה היינו ... על הפתילה חייב דמיירי בלא הובהבה מבעו"י וכיון דרצונו לחזור ולהדליק הפתילה וניחא ליה בפחם מיקרי צריכה לגופה דאפילו באינו מתכוין אלא דהוי פ"ר היכא ... מקרי צריכה לגופה כדלקמן קג ע"א בהולש עולשין בארעא לידיה · ומכוות יותר דבפתילה שצריך להבהבה עסקינן היינו דהוא אינו מתכוין לכך אלא דממילא ניחא ליה:

without [31b] the fear of Heaven is like a treasurer who is entrusted with the inner keys but not with the outer: how is he to enter? R. Jannai proclaimed: Woe to him who has no courtyard yet makes a gate for same![4] Rab Judah said, The Holy One, blessed be He, created His world only that men should fear Him,[5] for it is said, *and God hath done it, that men should fear before Him.*[6]

R. Simon and R. Eleazar[7] were sitting, when R. Jacob b. Aḥa came walking past. Said one to his companion, 'Let us arise before him, because he is a sin-fearing man.' Said the other, 'Let us arise before him, because he is a man of learning.' 'I tell you that he is a sin-fearing man, and you tell me that he is a man of learning!' retorted he.[8] It may be proved that it was R. Eleazar who observed that he was a sin-fearing man. For R. Joḥanan said in R. Eleazar's
a name:[1] The Holy One, blessed be He, has nought else in His world but[2] the fear of Heaven alone, for it is said, *And now, Israel, what doth the Lord thy God require of thee, but to fear the Lord thy God?*[3] and it is written, *And unto man he said, Behold* [hen], *the fear of the Lord, that is wisdom,* and in Greek one is *hen*.[4] That proves it.[5]

R. 'Ulla expounded: Why is it written, *Be not much wicked?*[6] must one not be much wicked, yet he may be a little wicked! But if one has eaten garlic and his breath smells, shall he eat some more garlic that his breath may [continue to] smell?[7]

Raba son of R. 'Ulla expounded: What is meant by, *For there are no pangs* [ḥarẓuboth] *in their death: but their strength is firm* [bari ulam]?[8] The Holy One, blessed be He, said, It is not enough for the wicked that they do not tremble and are not grief-stricken before the day of death, but their hearts are as firm as an edifice.[9] And that is what Rabbah said, What is meant by, *This their way is their confidence* [kesel]?[10] The wicked know that their way is to death, but they have fat on their loins [*kislam*].[11] But lest you think that it is their forgetfulness, therefore it is stated, *and they approve their end with their own mouths.*[10]

IF HE WOULD SPARE THE LAMP, etc. With whom does R. Jose agree? If with R. Judah,[12] then one should be liable for the others too; and if with R. Simeon,[13] he should be exempt even for [sparing] the wick?—Said 'Ulla, After all, he agrees with R. Judah; yet R. Jose holds that demolishing in order to rebuild on the same site is destroying, but if it is in order to rebuild elsewhere, it is not
b destroying.[1] Said Rabbah to him, Consider; all forms of labour are derived from the Tabernacle,[2] yet there it was taking down in order to rebuild elsewhere?[3] It was different there, answered he; for since it is written, *At the commandment of the Lord they encamped,* [*and at the commandment of the Lord they journeyed*],[4] it was like demolishing in order to rebuild on the same site.

But R. Joḥanan maintained: After all, he agrees with R. Simeon, yet why is the case of a wick different? As R. Hamnuna—others state, R. Adda b. Ahabah—said: This refers to a wick which needs singeing,[5] and in such a case even R. Simeon agrees since he renders an object fit.[6] Raba said, This may be inferred too, for it is stated, BECAUSE HE MAKES CHARCOAL, and not, because a charcoal is formed.[7] This proves it.

MISHNAH. FOR THREE SINS WOMEN DIE IN CHILDBIRTH: BECAUSE THEY ARE NOT OBSERVANT OF [THE LAWS OF] NIDDAH, ḤALLAH,[8] AND THE KINDLING OF THE [SABBATH] LIGHTS.[9]

GEMARA. What is the reason of *niddah?*—Said R. Isaac: She transgressed through the chambers of her womb, therefore she is punished through the chambers of her womb. That is right of *niddah*, but what can be said of *ḥallah* and the kindling of lights?—As a certain Galilean lectured before R. Ḥisda: The Holy One,
c blessed be He, said: I put a *rebi'ith* of blood in you;[1] therefore I

(4) Learning is a gate whereby one enters the court of piety. Woe to him who prepares the entry without the court itself! (5) By 'fear' not dread but awe and reverence is to be understood, proceeding out of man's realization of God's essential perfection. This reverence, and the attempt to attain something of that perfection which it inculcates, is man's highest aim in life, and that is probably the meaning of this dictum; cf. Maim. *Guide*, III, 52. (6) Eccl. III, 14. (7) In the *Yalkuṭ*, *'Ekeb*, 855 the reading is: Rabbi and R. Eleazar b. R. Simeon. (8) The former is a greater attribute.

a (1) This would be R. Eleazar b. Pedath, R. Joḥanan's younger contemporary; he is hardly likely to have quoted him. Hence the *Yalkuṭ's* version given in *supra* n. d7 is preferable, and the reading is: R. Joḥanan in the name of R. Eleazar b. R. Simeon. (2) I.e., cherishes nothing so highly. (3) Deut. X, 12. (4) Thus translating: the fear of the Lord is one, unique (in God's affections). (5) Sc. R. Eleazar's (or, R. Eleazar b. R. Simeon's) view. (6) Eccl. VII, 17. (7) I.e., having sinned a little, do not think that you must go on sinning. (8) Ps. LXXIII, 4. (9) Regarding *ḥarẓuboth* as a combination of *ḥared* (trembling) and *'aẓeb* (griefstricken) and translating *ulam*, a hall, edifice. (10) Ps. XLIX, 14. (11) Which close their understanding. The loins (reins) were regarded as the seat of understanding. (12) That one is liable for work not needed in itself: v. *supra* 30a, n. d4. (13) V. *supra* 12a.

b (1) One is not liable for desecrating the Sabbath when his work is destructive; but if he demolishes a house in order to rebuild, it is regarded as constructive. Now, extinguishing a wick, thereby destroying its light, is the equivalent of demolishing a house; if the purpose is to save the wick to be used again later, it is analogous to demolishing a house to build on the same site, since it is the wick which is extinguished and the wick which is to be relit. But if the purpose is to save the oil or the lamp, it is analogous to demolishing a house in order to rebuild elsewhere, for whereas the wick is extinguished, it is the oil or lamp that is saved for subsequent use. (2) *Infra* 49b. (3) The Tabernacle was only taken down when they had to journey onwards, and it was re-erected on their new camping pitch. (4) Num. IX, 23. (5) In order to burn clearer. (6) For its purpose, and thus it is a labour needed for itself, which involves liability. (7) The text implies that by extinguishing it he *intends* making charcoal, i.e., to make it more ready for relighting, and thus must apply to a wick which needs singeing. (8) On the terms v. Glos. (9) [In time before Sabbath sets in, v. Strashun].

c (1) *Rebi'ith* = one *log* = one fourth of a *ḳab*, and was held to be the smallest quantity of blood within a human being on which life can be supported.

commanded you concerning blood.[2] [32a] I designated you the first;[3] wherefore I commanded you concerning the first.[4] The soul which I placed in you is called a lamp, wherefore I commanded you concerning the lamp.[5] If ye fulfil them, 'tis well; but if not, I will take your souls.

And why particularly in childbirth?—Rabbah said, When the ox is fallen, sharpen the knife. Abaye said, Let the bondmaid increase her rebellion: it will all be punished by the same rod. R. Ḥisda said, Leave the drunkard alone: he will fall of himself. Mar 'Uḳba said, When the shepherd is lame, and the goats are fleet, at the gate of the fold are words, and in the fold there is the account. R. Papa said, At the gate of the shop there are many brothers and friends; at the gate of loss[6] there are neither brothers nor friends.[7]

And when are men examined?—Said Resh Laḳish: When they pass over a bridge.[8] A bridge and nothing else?—Say, that which is similar to a bridge. Rab would not cross a bridge where a heathen was sitting; said he, Lest judgment be visited upon him, and I be seized together with him. Samuel would cross a bridge only when a heathen was upon it, saying, Satan has no power over two nations [simultaneously]. R. Jannai examined [the bridge] and then crossed over. R. Jannai [acted] upon his views, for he said, A man should never stand in a place of danger and say that a miracle will be wrought for him, lest it is not. And if a miracle is wrought for him, it is deducted from his merits.[1] R. Ḥanin said, Which verse [teaches this]? *I am become diminished*[2] *by reason of all the deeds of kindness and all the truth.*[3] R. Zera would not go out among the palm-trees on a day of the strong south wind.[4]

R. Isaac the son of Rab Judah said: Let one always pray for mercy not to fall sick; for if he falls sick he is told, Show thy merits [rights] and be quit.[5] Said Mar 'Uḳba, Which verse [teaches this]? *If any man fall* mimmenu;[6] it is from him [*mimmenu*] that proof must be brought.[7] The School of R. Ishmael taught: '*If any man* [hanofel] *fall from thence*': this man was predestined to fall since the six days of Creation, for lo! he has not [yet] fallen, and the Writ [already] calls him *nofel* [a faller].[8] But reward [*zekuth*] is brought about through a person of merit [*zakkai*], and punishment [*ḥobah*] through a person of guilt.[9]

Our Rabbis taught: If one falls sick and his life is in danger,[10] he is told, Make confession, for all who are sentenced to death make confession. When a man goes out into the street, let him imagine that he is given in charge of an officer;[11] when he has a headache, let him imagine that he is put in irons; when he takes to bed, let him imagine that he ascended the scaffold to be punished; for whoever ascends the scaffold to be punished, if he has great advocates he is saved, but if not he is not saved. And these are man's advocates: repentance and good deeds. And even if nine hundred and ninety-nine argue for his guilt, while one argues in his favour, he is saved, for it is said, *If there be with him an angel, an advocate, one among a thousand, To shew unto man what is right for him; Then he is gracious unto him, and saith, Deliver him from going down to the pit*, etc.[1] R. Eliezer the son of R. Jose the Galilean said: Even if nine hundred and ninety-nine parts of that angel are in his disfavour and one part is in his favour, he is saved, for it is said, '*an advocate, one part in a thousand*'.

Our Rabbis taught: For three sins women die in childbirth. R. Eleazar said: women die young.[2] R. Aḥa said, As a punishment for washing their children's napkins[3] on the Sabbath. Others say, Because they call the holy ark a chest.

It was taught: R. Ishmael b. Eleazar said: On account of two sins '*amme ha-areẓ*[4] die: because they call the holy ark a chest, and because they call a synagogue *beth-'am*.[5]

It was taught: R. Jose said: Three death scrutineers were created in woman; others state: Three causes[6] of death: *niddah*, *ḥallah*, and the kindling of the [Sabbath] lights. One agrees with R. Eleazar, and the other with the Rabbis.[7]

It was taught: R. Simeon b. Gamaliel said: The laws of *heḳdesh*, *terumoth*[8] and tithes are indeed essential parts of the law, [32b]

(2) Not to shed it; Gen. IX, 5f. (3) Jer. II, 3: *Israel was holiness unto the Lord, the firstfruits of his increase.* (4) *Sc.* the first portion of the dough, which is *ḥallah*; Num. XV, 20. (5) *Sc.* the Sabbath lights. (6) Rashi. Levi, *Wörterbuch* s.v. זִיְנָא conjectures that בי זיינא should be read instead of אבב בזיונא: he translates as Rashi: where there is loss. Jast.: at the prison gate. Krauss in *T.A.* II, p. 699, n. 435 appears to translate: at the toll-gate, and this is a reference to the severity with which tolls were exacted. (7) These are a series of proverbs, the general tenor of which is that when danger is near, one's faults are remembered and punished. Childbirth is dangerous, and that is when a woman is punished for her transgressions.—Mar 'Uḳba's proverb means: the shepherd waits until the goats are by the gate of the fold or pen, and then rebukes and punishes them. (8) That involves danger, and then they are liable to be punished for their misdeeds.

a (1) The miracle is a reward for some of his merits, and so he has now less to his credit. (2) I.e., I have less merit to my credit. (3) Gen. XXXII, 10. (4) *'Aruch*: east wind. (5) I.e., he must prove by what merit he is entitled to regain his health. (6) Deut. XXII, 8. (7) Of merit, that he is entitled to recover from his injuries. (8) The lit. translation of the verse is: if the faller falls. But before he starts falling he should not be designated the faller. (9) And this man who builds a house without a parapet is guilty therein, and he is used as the Divine instrument for fulfilling the other man's destiny to fall as a punishment. (10) Lit., 'inclines to death'. (11) To be brought to trial.

b (1) Job. XXXIII, 23f. (2) For these three sins. The variants involve but a change of vocalization in the Hebrew text. (3) Lit., 'excrement'. (4) Pl. of *'am ha-areẓ*, q.v. Glos. (5) Lit., 'house of the people'—a contemptuous designation. (6) Cf. n. b2. (7) 'Death scrutineers' connotes sins which scrutinize a woman when she is in danger, *sc.* at childbirth; thus this agrees with the Rabbis. 'Causes' implies avenues to premature death, thus agreeing with R. Eleazar's dictum, 'women die young'—The translation of the first follows Rashi. Jast.: breaches through which death enters, i.e., sins for which one is visited with death. (8) V. Glos.

ראשית קראתי אתכם על עסקי ראשית הזהרתי אתכם נשמה שנתתי בכם קרויה נר *על עסקי נר הזהרתי אתכם אם אתם מקיימים אותם מוטב ואם לאו הריני נוטל נשמתכם ומ"ש בשעת לידתן אמר *רבא נפל תורא הדד לסכינא אביי אמר תפיש תירוס אמתא בחד מחטרא ליהוי רב חסדא אמר שבקיה לרויא דמנפשיה נפיל מר עוקבא אמר רעיא חגרא ועיזי ריהטן אבב חוטרא מילי ואבי דרי חושבנא רב פפא אמר אבב חנואתא נפישי אחי ומרחמי אבב בזיוני לא אחי ולא מרחמי וגברי היכא מיבדקי אמר ריש לקיש בשעה שעוברים על הגשר גשר ותו לא אימא כעין גשר רב לא עבר במברא דיתיב ביה עכו"ם אמר דילמא מיפקיד ליה דינא עליה ומתפיסנא בהדיה שמואל לא עבר אלא במברא דאית ביה עכו"ם אמר שטנא בתרי אומי לא שליט ר' ינאי בדיק ועבר ר' ינאי לטעמיה *דאמר לעולם אל יעמוד אדם במקום סכנה לומר שעושין לו נס שמא אין עושין לו נס ואם עושין לו נס מנכין לו מזכיותיו אמר רבי חנין מאי קראה °קטנתי מכל החסדים ומכל האמת רבי זירא ביומא דשותא לא נפיק לביני דיקלא אמר ר' יצחק בריה דרב יהודה לעולם יבקש אדם רחמים שלא יחלה שאם יחלה אומרים לו הבא זכות והפטר אמר מר עוקבא מאי קראה °כי יפול הנופל ממנו ממנו להביא ראיה תנא דבי רבי ישמעאל כי יפול הנופל ממנו (ממנו) ראוי זה ליפול מששת ימי בראשית שהרי לא נפל והכתוב קראו נופל אלא *שמגלגלין זכות על ידי זכאי וחובה על ידי חייב: ת"ר [ב]מי שחלה ונטה למות אומרים לו התודה שכן כל המומתין מתודין אדם יוצא לשוק יהי דומה בעיניו כמי שנמסר לסרדיוט חש בראשו יהי דומה בעיניו כמי שנתנוהו בקולר עלה למטה ונפל יהי דומה בעיניו כמו שהעלוהו לגרדום לידון שכל העולה לגרדום לידון אם יש לו פרקליטין גדולים ניצול ואם לאו אינו ניצול ואלו הן פרקליטין של אדם תשובה ומעשים טובים ואפי' תשע מאות ותשעים ותשעה מלמדים עליו חובה ואחד מלמד עליו זכות ניצול שנאמר °אם יש עליו מלאך מליץ אחד מני אלף להגיד לאדם ישרו ויחננו ויאמר פדעהו מרדת שחת וגו': ר' אליעזר בנו של ר' יוסי הגלילי אומר אפילו תשע מאות ותשעים ותשעה באותו מלאך לחובה ואחד לזכות ניצול שנאמר מליץ אחד מני אלף: תנו רבנן על שלש עבירות נשים מתות יולדות רבי אלעזר אומר נשים מתות ילדות ר' אחא אומר בעון שמכבסות צואת בניהם בשבת וי"א על שקורין לארון הקודש ארנא: תניא ר' ישמעאל בן אלעזר אומר בעון שני דברים עמי הארצות מתים על שקורין לארון הקודש ארנא ועל שקורין לבית הכנסת בית עם תניא ר' יוסי אומר *שלשה בדקי מיתה נבראו באשה ואמרי לה שלשה דבקי מיתה נדה וחלה והדלקת הנר חדא כר' אלעזר וחדא כרבנן *תניא רשב"ג אומר הלכות הקדש תרומות ומעשרות הן הן גופי תורה ונמסרו

°ירמיה ב · °תהלים לג · °דברים כב · °איוב לג

רש"י

ראשית קראתי אתכם · ראשית תבואתה (ירמיה ב): עסקי ראשית · ראשית עריסותיכם (במדבר טו): הריני נוטל נשמתכם · ותאבד רביעית דמכם ויכבה נרכם ויבטל שם ראשיתכם ונשים נלכוו על כך כדאמרינן בבראשית רבה היא איבדה חלתו של עולם שעל ידה נטרד אדה"ר שנתרם כחלה וכבתה נרו של עולם ושפכה דמו ועוד שארכי הבית תלוין בה: נפל תורא · לארץ שהוא עומד לשחיטה הכל אומרים חדדו לסכינא עד שלא יקום ויהא טורח להשליכו כך הואיל ואיתרע מזלה מזומנת פורענותה לבא: תפיש תירוס אמתא · תרבה פשעים השפחה וכולן תלקה בחבטה אחת: תפיש · תרבה: תירוס · פשע והתרסה: מחטרא · בטדו"ר בלע"ז כלומר אשה עומדת ליסורי לידה על עונשה של חוה ומצרפין לה עונשין הרבה לאותו מלקות: שבקיה לרויא · לשיכור אינך צריך להפילו שהוא יפול מאליו כך האשה עומדת לילד משנתעברה והיא צריכה לבקש להקב"ה לפתוח רחמה והוא נמנע והיא מתה מאליה כל הני משל הדיוט נינהו: רעיא חגרא ועיזי רהיטין · קלים לרוץ ואינו יכול להגיען ולהלקותן על סרחונן: אבב חוטרא מילי · כשהיא באה לפני גדרות הצאן שם הוא מדבר עמה להלקותה על פשעה ואבי דרי לבית הדיר של צאן באין לחשבון · גדרות צאן מתרגמינן חוטרין דען (במדבר לב) כלומר האשה כשהיא בבריאות פעמים שזכיותיה תולין ואין כח במקטרג להזכיר עונה אבל משהגיעה לפתח הסכנה וצריכה לנסים שם מזכירין עונותיה ומעשיה אם ראויה היא לנס אם לאו: אבב חנואתא נפישי אחי ומרחמי · לפתח החנות שמחלקים בו מזונות ויש שם עושר הרבה אחים והרבה אוהבים יש הכל נעשים אוהבים: מרחמי · אוהבים: אבב בזיוני · במקום שיש הפסד ועוני לא אחי ולא מרחמי כך בשעת הסכנה הורע מזלה וחשיבותה וחדלו פרקליטין שלה: וגברי היכא מיבדקי · מעשים שלהם להזכיר עונם וזכותם: כעין גשר · כל מקום סכנה כגון קיר נטוי ויוצא לדרך: דילמא מיפקיד · נכרי דינא על חטאיו ומתפיסנא בהדיה: מברא · ספינה שעוברין בה את הנהר: בדיק · הספינה שלא יהא בה נקב: מנכין · פוחתין: קטנתי מכל החסדים · הוקטנו ונתמעטו זכיותי בשביל החסדים אשר עשית וגו': יומא דשותא · שמנשבת בו הרוח דרומית חזקה המפלת חומות ועוקרת אילנות: לביני דקלי · שלא יפיל הרוח דקל עליו: ממנו להביא ראיה · מאחר שהוא נופל צריך למצוא ממנו וממעשיו ראיה לזכות: מששת ימי בראשית · דכתיב קורא הדורות מראש (ישעיה מא) שנגלו לפניו הדורות ומעשיהם *וקנס פורענותם: שהרי · כשניתנה תורה עדיין לא נפל זה והכתוב קראו נופל: על ידי חייב · בע"ה זה שלא קיים מצות מעקה: אומרים · העומדין שם: שכן דרך כל המומתים מתודין · כדתנן בסנהדרין שכל המתודה יש לו חלק כו' שכן מצינו בעכן שאמר לו יהושע כו' בפ' נגמר הדין (סנהדרין דף מג:): לשוק · מצויים שם מריבות ובעלי דינים נכרים וישראלים: דומה כמו שנמסר לסרדיוט · להוליכו לפני השופט: חש בראשו · חששא בעלמא מיחוש קל: נתנוהו בקולר · הוי טפי משנמסר לסרדיוט וגרוע מעולה לגרדום שאין דנין שם אלא להריגה ועל סרחון חמור וצריך פרקליטין גדולים: עלה למטה · שחלה הרבה שצריך לעלות וליפול למשכב: ואלו הן פרקליטין · [א]שעושה למטה[ג] רצוי לב"ד של מעלה תשובה ומעשים טובים: באותו מלאך · שמליץ עליו זכות והוא אחד מני אלף ואפילו הוא עצמו מעיד עליו חובה ניצול באחת של זכות שנאמר מליץ אחד מני אלף במליצתו של מלאך אין אלא אחת מאלף להגיד ישרו ומשמע כמי שהמלאך המליץ הוי אחד מני אלף דהא מלאך כתיב מכלל דהשאר מגידים עליו חובה אלא מדלא כתיב אם יש עליו מליץ מלאך אחד מני אלף היכא למידרשיה אמלאך ואמליצה: יולדות · בשעת לידתן: שלש עבירות · הנך דמתניתין: ילדות · בחורות ואפילו שלא בשעת לידה: רבי אחא אומר · הילדות מתות על עון שמכבסות: ארנא · כך היו קורין מגדלות שלהם פריט"ש ובלשונינו משטי"ר: בית עם · לשון ביזוי שמתקבלין בו הכל: ולארון הקדש ארנא · אין קורין אותו ארון הקדש: בדקי[ג] · עונות שבודקין אותן בהן בשעת סכנה כרבנן דאמרי יולדות: דבקי · שמדבקין ומקרבין מיתה לפני זמנה כר' אלעזר דתני ילדות: ונמסרו

תוספות

על שקורין לארון הקדש ארנא · לא ארון שעשה בצלאל קאמר דמסתמא לא היו מזכירים ארון שהיה לפני כמה שנים שנגנז בבית הראשון אלא לארון שבבית הכנסת אע"ג דבכל דוכתי קרי ליה תיבה כדתנן העובר לפני התיבה היורד לפני התיבה (ברכות פ"ה דף לד.) אור"י אשכחן נמי דקרי ליה ארון כדאמר תשעה וארון מצטרפין (שם פ"ז דף מז:): מקרא

עין משפט נר מצוה

קיח א מיי' פי"ב מהל' רוצח ושמירת נפש הל' ו סמג עשין עט ש"ע י"ד סי' קיו סעיף ס בהג"ה:

קיט ב מיי' פ"א מהל' תשובה הל' ה סמג עשין יג טוש"ע קנז סי' שלא סעיף א:

מסורת הש"ס

[בדכתיב נר ה' נשמת אדם תנחומא ריש פ' נח] [נ"ל רבה]

תענית כ:

[סנהדרין מ. ב"ב קיט: תוספתא יומא פ"ד]

ברכות לא. תוספתא פ"ב

תוספתא פ"ב

ר"א וזמן

הגהות הב"ח

(א) רש"י ד"ה ואלו הן פרקליטין (שעושה למטה) תא"מ ונ"ב פ"א אין זה: (ב) בא"ד שבכן רצוי לב"ד: (ג) ד"ה בדקי מיתה עונות:

רבינו חננאל

גלילאה רביעית דם נתתי בכם על עסקי דם הזהרתי אתכם ראשית קראתי אתכם על עסקי ראשית הזהרתי [אתכם] כגון החלה והתרומה נשמה שקרויה נר נתתי בכם על עסקי נר הזהרתי אתכם אם אתם מקיימין אותן מוטב ואם לאו הריני נוטל נשמתכם · ולמה בשעת לידה אמר רבה נפל תורא חדד סכינא תיפוש תירוס אמתא חד מחבטא ניהוי פי' תרבה להתרומם השפחה על אדונתה אחת הכאה תהיה עליה · כלומר פעמים רבות מכעסת אדונתה ומקבעת אדונתה את הכל בלבה והיא משלמת לה בהכאה אחת הכל · וכן רעיא מהגרא ועיזא רהיטתא אבב חוטרא ואבי [דרי] חושבנא · *) פי' רועה פסח שאין יכול לרוץ · ועז בורחת ורצה בשדות כשמגיע בשער גדרות הצאן כדמתרגמינן חוטרין דען ובבית הדיר (בו) כדתנן הכונס צאן לדיר שם מעלה חשבון הבריחות שברחה ושם מכה אותה · בחנות של יין הכל (אי הכין) [אוהביו] באין שם ושואלין בשלום בעל החנות כדי שישתו עמו אבל אם רואין שנתפס אדם בבית המכס או בבית המושל להיענש כל אוהביו בורחין אין אחד מהן פונה אליו: לא יעמוד אדם במקום סכנה ויאמר עושין לי נס [שמא] אין עושין לו נס · ואם עושין לו מנכין לו מזכיותיו שנא' קטנתי מכל החסדים וגו': לעולם יבקש אדם רחמים שלא יחלה שאם יחלה אומרים לו הבא זכיות והפטר: ת"ר חלה ונטה למות אומרים לו התודה שכן דרך כל המומתים מתודים אדם יוצא לשוק יהיה דומה כמי [שנמסר] לסרדיוט חש בראשו דומה כמי שנתנוהו בקולר עלה למטה דומה כמי שהעלוהו לגרדום לידון אם יש לו פרקליטין המלמדין עליו זכות נצול אם לאו לא נצול תשובה ומעשים טובים הן פרקליטין של אדם · אפי' תתקצ"ט מלמדין עליו חובה ואחד מלמד עליו זכות נצול שנאמר אם יש עליו מלאך מליץ אחד מני אלף להגיד ישרו ויחננו ויאמר פדעהו מרדת שחת מצאתי כופר: שלשה בדקי מיתה · כרבנן דאמרי מתות יולדות [ואמרי לה ג' דבקי מיתה כר"א דאמר מתות ילדות] כלומר דבקה בהו מיתה שלא בעתה · פי'

*) ע' ערוך ערך כב.

קב א מיי' פ"ג מהל' ציצית הל' יב סמג עשין כו טור או"ח סימן כד:

[כדאיתא בקדושין כט:]

ונמסרו לעמי הארץ תניא רבי נתן אומר בעון
נדרים מתה אשה של אדם שנאמר °אם אין (משלי כב)
לך לשלם למה יקח משכבך מתחתיך רבי
אומר *בעון נדרים בנים מתים כשהן קטנים
°שנאמר °אל תתן את פיך לחטיא את בשרך (קהלת ה)
ואל תאמר לפני המלאך כי שגגה היא למה
יקצוף האלהים על קולך וחבל את מעשה
ידיך. איזה הן מעשה ידיו של אדם הוי אומר
בניו ובנותיו של אדם ת"ר בעון נדרים בנים
מתים דברי ר"א בר"ש ר' יהודה הנשיא אומר
בעון ביטול תורה בשלמא למאן דאמר בעון
נדרים כדאמרן אלא למ"ד °בעון ביטול
תורה מאי קראה דכתיב °לשוא הכיתי את (ירמיה ב)
בניכם מוסר לא לקחו ר"נ בר יצחק אמר
למ"ד בעון נדרים נמי מהכא לשוא הכיתי
את בניכם על עסקי שוא מכדי *ר' יהודה
הנשיא היינו רבי ורבי בעון נדרים קאמר בתר
דשמעה מר"א בר' שמעון פליגי בה ר' חייא
בר אבא °ור' יוסי חד אמר בעון מזוזה וחד
אמר בעון ביטול תורה למ"ד בעון מזוזה
מקרא נדרש לפניו ולא לפני פניו ולמ"ד בעון
ביטול תורה *מקרא נדרש לפניו ולפני פניו:
פליגי בה ר"מ ור' יהודה חד אמר בעון מזוזה
וחד אמר בעון ציצית בשלמא למ"ד בעון
מזוזה דכתיב °וכתבתם על מזוזות ביתך (דברים יא)
וכתיב בתריה למען ירבו ימיכם וימי בניכם אלא למ"ד בעון ציצית מ"ט
א"ר כהנא ואיתימא שילא מרי דכתיב °גם בכנפיך נמצאו דם נפשות אביונים (ירמיה ב)
נקיים ר"נ בר יצחק אמר למ"ד בעון מזוזה נמי מהכא דכתיב °לא במחתרת (שם)
מצאתים שעשו פתחים כמחתרת אמר ר"ל *כל הזהיר בציצית זוכה ומשמשין
לו ב' אלפים וח' מאות עבדים שנא' °כה אמר ה' [צבאות] בימים ההמה אשר (זכריה ח)
יחזיקו עשרה אנשים מכל לשונות הגוים [והחזיקו] בכנף איש יהודי לאמר נלכה
עמכם וגו': סימן שנא חלה תרומה נגזלת דינא שבועה שיפכתא גילויא
ונבלותא: תניא ר' נחמיה אומר בעון שנאת חנם מריבה רבה בתוך ביתו
של אדם ואשתו מפלת נפלים ובניו ובנותיו של אדם מתים כשהן קטנים:
ר' אלעזר בר' יהודה אומר בעון חלה אין ברכה במכונס ומארה משתלחת
בשערים וזורעין זרעים ואחרים אוכלין שנאמר °אף אני אעשה זאת לכם (ויקרא כו)
והפקדתי עליכם בהלה את השחפת ואת הקדחת מכלות עינים ומדיבות נפש
וזרעתם לריק זרעכם ואכלוהו אויביכם אל תקרי בהלה אלא בחלה ואם נותנין
מתברכין שנאמר °[ו]ראשית עריסותיכם תתנו לכהן להניח ברכה אל ביתך: (יחזקאל מד)
בעון ביטול תרומות ומעשרות שמים נעצרין מלהוריד טל ומטר והיוקר הוה
והשכר אבד ובני אדם רצין אחר פרנסתן ואין מגיעין שנאמר °ציה גם חום (איוב כד)
יגזלו מימי שלג שאול חטאו מאי משמע *תנא דבי רבי ישמעאל בשביל דברים
שצויתי אתכם בימות החמה ולא עשיתם יגזלו מכם מימי שלג בימות הגשמים
ואם נותנין מתברכין שנאמר °הביאו את כל המעשר אל בית האוצר ויהי טרף (מלאכי ג)
בביתי ובחנוני נא בזאת אמר ה' צבאות אם לא אפתח לכם את ארובות השמים
והריקותי לכם ברכה עד בלי די *מאי עד בלי די אמר רמי בר (*רב) א"ר עד
שיבלו שפתותיכם מלומר די: בעון גזל הגובאי עולה והרעב הווה ובני אדם
אוכלים בשר בניהן ובנותיהן שנאמר °שמעו הדבר הזה פרות הבשן אשר בהר (עמוס ד)
שומרון העושקות דלים הרוצצות אביונים אמר רבא כגון* הני נשי דמחוזא
דאכלן

תוספות

מקרא נדרש לפניו ולפני פניו · תימה לר"י דבפ"ק דקדושין (דף לד· ושם) דאמר כל מצות עשה כו' ופריך ונקיש מזוזה לתלמוד תורה פי' וליפטרי נשים ממזוזה כי היכי דפטירי מתלמוד תורה ומשני לא ס"ד דכתיב למען ירבו ימיכם וגו' אטו גברי בעו חיי נשי לא בעו חיי והשתא הא קאי נמי אתלמוד תורה כדמשמע הכא אע"פ שאין הנשים חייבות וי"ל דבת"ת הוה מחייבינן נמי מהאי טעמא אי לא מיעט קרא בהדיא *דכתיב ולמדתם אותם את בניכם ולא את בנותיכם אבל במזוזה דליכא מיעוט אלא היקשא מהאי טעמא אית לן למימר דאין להקיש: **רבי** יהודה הנשיא היינו רבי ורבי בעון נדרים קאמר · והכא לא משני דאף בעון ביטול תורה קאמר כדמשני לקמן (דף לג:) גבי אף על לשון הרע דהתם שייך למימר דאף קאמר דבברייתא שניה שמביא אחריה קאי נמי אתנא קמא דקאמר על לשון הרע וקאמר איהו אף שאוכלים דברים שאינם מתוקנים אבל. הכא אי אף קאמר א"כ ברייתא דלעיל דלא קאי את"ק הוה ליה למינקט נמי בעון ביטול תורה:

בעון ציצית כו' · דוקא בימיהם שהיו מלבושיהם כך בארבע כנפות היו נענשים מי שלא היה להם ציצית כדמוכח (מנחות מא.) גבי א"ל מלאכא לרב קטינא כו' אבל השתא שאין העולם רגילים במלבושים כאלו אין צריך לקנות · אך טוב לקנות טלית ולברך עליו בכל יום כדאמר בסוף פרק קמא דסוטה (דף יד·) וכי לאכול מפריה היה רוצה משה אלא אמר משה מצוה שאוכל לקיים יתקיים על ידי [ת"י]:

ה"ג

רש"י

ונמסרו לעמי הארץ · שלא מסרו לב"ד למנות שומרין לדבר והאמינה תורה את כל אדם עליהן והן הן גופי תורה שחברים אוכלין פתן וסומכין שניטל ממנו חלה ותרומה ומעשרות והקדש נמי מסור לכל אדם להקדיש וחל הקדש ע"פ כל אדם והן גופי תורה שהיינו צריכים לחוש במטלטלין שמא הקדישו וחזר בו ואע"ג דתקון רבנן · דמאי מ"מ תורה האמינתו ורבותי מפרשים הלכות הקדש כגון יין לנסכים כדמפרש בחומר בקדש (חגיגה דף כו:) שעמי הארץ נאמנים עליו וקשיא לי אי מדרבנן קאמר דחשיב מאי דהימנוהו רבנן לא הוה ליה למיתני תרומות ומעשרות דרבנן לא הימנוהו: אם אין לך לשלם · עולות והקדשות שתדור: משכבך · אשתך: אל תתן את פיך(א) · בנדר לחטיא את בשרך לחייב את בניך: לפני המלאך · גזבר של הקדש: כי שגגה · בשוגג קפלתי לנדור ולא אשלם: על קולך · בשביל קול נדריך: לשוא הכיתי · בתמיה וכי בחנם הכיתים איני אלא בשביל המוסר דהיינו תורה לא לקחו לא למדו לשון לקח: על עסקי שוא · ששקרו בנדריהם דדמי לשבועה: והא בעון נדרים אמר בברייתא קמייתא ומשני ההיא קמייתא בתר הך איתמר דמעיקרא אמר בעון ביטול תורה ובתר דשמע מר' אלעזר דשמע מר' שמעון אבוה דהוה רביה דרבי בעון נדרים אמר איהו נמי הכי: מקרא נדרש · למען ירבו ימיכם וימי בניכם נדרש לפניו קאי אקרא דלקמיה דמשתעי במזוזה ולא לפני פניו ולמדתם אותם את בניכם: ולפני פניו · ואף בעון בטול תורה קאמר: גם בכנפיך · בשביל כנפיך שבטלת מוטם נמלאו עליך חובת דם נפשות אביונים נקיים בנים קטנים שלא חטאו: כמחתרת · שאין לה פלימין הכי אמר קרא לא במחתרת *פתחיהן מלאתים שלמים במלותי כי על כל אלה הכיתי דהאי קרא בתר לשוא הכיתי את בניכם כתיב: בכנף איש יהודי · בשכר הכנף יחזיקו בכנף עשרה אנשים מכל לשון הרי שבע מאות לשבעים לשון ולארבע כנפות יש לו הרי אלפים ושמנה מאות: שנאת חנם · שלא ראה בו דבר עבירה שיהא מותר לשנאותו ושונאו: מריבה רבה · מדה כנגד מדה: ובניו קטנים מתים · אהבתו ניטלת ממנו היינו נמי במדה: במכונס · באולרות יין ושמן ומתוך כך באה מארה בשערים שמוכרים ביוקר: בחלה · בעון חלה: והפקדתי · כמו לא נפקד ממנו איש (במדבר לא) אמעט את מה שעליכם שכנסתם כבר: השמים נעצרים · ומתוך שאין גשמים היוקר הוה: ושכר אבד · שכר ריוח: ציה גם חום · ציה כמו צוי דברים שצויתי אתכם בשעת החום היינו תרומות ומעשרות:

דאכלן

כתובות עב. ע"ש

[יבמות סג: קדושין מ.]

[ר"ה טז: קדושין טו: ב"מ לה: זבחים כב: מנחות יט: חולין קיח:]

ס"א פתחיהן

[תענית ז:]

[צ"ל חטאו]

[פסחים כ:]

הגהות הב"ח

(א) רש"י ד"ה אל תתן את. פיך. נ"ב עי' בתוספות ר"ה סד"ה ולאין כשרך:

רבינו חננאל

פי' מקרא נדרש לפניו שנאמר למען ירבו ימיכם וימי בניכם וגו' ולפני זה הפסוק כתיב וכתבתם על מזוזות ביתך וגו' · ונדרש בזכות שתעשה מזוזות ירבו ימי בניכם ורבי יהודה הנשיא אמר לפני פניו כתיב ולמדתם אותם את בניכם לדבר והן התורה ומקרא זה למען ירבו ימיכם וימי בניכם נדרש לפניו שהוא המזוזה ולפני פניו בטול תורה: **תניא** רשב"א הלכות קודש ותרומה ומעשרות הן הן גופי תורה · וכולן נמסרו לעמי הארץ: **ירושלמי** תני רשב"ג הלכות. קודש חטאת והבכורות הן הן גופי הלכות ושלשתן נמסרו לעמי הארץ (הלכך הקודש) [וכמו דתנינן בחגיגה כד] אם אמר הפרשתי לתוכה רביעית קודש (שמו) [נאמן] וכו' ושאר כל השמועה כולה ופשוטה היא:

מכות כג: תענית ט: [כב: ע"ש]

גליון הש"ס גמ' שנאמר אל תתן · עי' שבועות דף לט ע"א תוס' ד"ה ואין כשרך: שם בעון ביטול תורה מאי קראה · במסכת כלה איתא רבי יהושע אומר בעון ביטול תורה בנים קטנים מתים דכתיב ותשכח תורת אלהיך אשכח בניך גם אני: שם רבי חייא בר אבא ורבי יוסי · צ"ל ור' אסי או ר' אמי · סדר הדורות בהקדמה אות ד':

רב נסים גאון

פליגי בה ר' אבא(חייה) [חייא] בר אבא ור' יוסי חד אמר בעון מזוזה וחד אמר בעון ביטול תורה · פי' הוא שאמר הקב"ה לישראל (דברים יא) ולמדתם אותם את בניכם לדבר בם וכתיב וכתבתם על מזוזות ביתך ובשעריך ואמר שכרה כנגדה: למען ירבו ימיכם וימי בניכם והך דאמר בעון מזוזה הבנים מתים קסבר מקרא נדרש לפניו ולא לפני פניו כלומר כי תתן שכרו של מי שקיים מצות מזוזה שיאריכו חיי בניו וחילופה שאם יעזוב עשייתה ויהיו דברי הכתוב למען ירבו חוזרין על הפסוק שלפניו שהוא וכתבתם על מזוזות ביתך והך דאמר בעון ביטול תורה הבנים מתים קסבר מקרא נדרש לפניו ולפני פניו וכי זו ההבטחה ומתן השכר הכתוב בפסוק שהוא למען ירבו ימיכם שלא הבטיח הקב"ה אלא למי שמלמד את בנו תורה כמו שאמר בפסוק שהוא לפני פניו ולמדתם אותם יהיה עכשיו זה שכתוב למען ירבו ימיכם וימי בניכם חוזר על הפסוק שכתב ולמדתם אותם הלכך כל מי שמלמד תורה לבניו זוכין לאריכות ימים וחילופה כי אם אינו מלמדם תורה לא תהיה להם אריכות ימים כי הם מתים בעון ביטול תורה: **כל** הזהיר במצות ציצית זוכה ומשמשין אותו שני אלפים ושמונה מאות עבדים שנא' (זכריה ח) כה אמר ה' [צבאות] בימים ההמה אשר יחזיקו עשרה אנשים מכל לשונות הגוים והחזיקו בכנף איש יהודי כבר ידעת כל לשונות הגוים הם שבעים לשון ואם יהיו י' אנשים מכל לשון לע' לשון יהיו הכל שבע מאות הרי אלו יחזיקו בכנף אחד והטלית של ישראל יש לה ד' כנפים שנאמר (דברים כב) על ארבע כנפות כסותך הרי אם יהיו שבע מאות מחזיקים בכנף אחד יהיו כל המחזיקים בד' כנפים אלפים ושמונה מאות:

אמר

and they were entrusted to the ignorant.[9]

It was taught: R. Nathan said: A man's wife dies in punishment for [his unfulfilled] vows, for it is said, *If thou hast not wherewith to pay* [thy vows], *why should he take away thy bed* [i.e., wife]
a *from under thee?*[1] Rabbi said, For the sin of [unfulfilled] vows one's children die young, for it is said, *Suffer not thy mouth to cause thy flesh to sin, neither say thou before the angel, that it was an error: wherefore should God be angry at thy voice, and destroy the work of thine hands?*[2] What is the work of a man's hands? Say, it is a man's sons and daughters.

Our Rabbis taught: Children die as a punishment for [unfulfilled] vows: this is the view of R. Eleazar b. R. Simeon. R. Judah the Nasi said: For the sin of neglect of Torah [study]. As for the view that it is for the sin of vows, it is well, even as we have said. But on the view that it is for the sin of neglect of Torah, what verse [teaches this]?—For it is written, *Have I smitten your children for nought? They received no instruction!*[3] R. Naḥman b. Isaac said: The view that it is for the sin of vows is also [deduced] from this: *For vain* [*utterance*] *have I smitten your children*, i.e., on account of vain [neglected] vows.[4] Consider: R. Judah the Nasi is identical with Rabbi, whereas Rabbi said that it is for the sin of vows. —He said that after he had heard it from R. Eleazar son of R. Simeon.[5]

R. Ḥiyya b. Abba and R. Jose[6] differ therein: one maintained: It is for the sin of [neglect of] *mezuzah;*[7] while the other held that it is for the sin of neglect of Torah. On the view that it is for the sin of *mezuzah:* a verse is interpreted with its precedent, but not with its ante-precedent verse. While on the view that it is for the sin of neglect of Torah: a verse is interpreted with its precedent and its ante-precedent.[8]

R. Meir and R. Judah differ therein: One maintains, It is for the neglect of *mezuzah*, while the other holds that it is for the neglect
b of fringes.[1] Now, as for the view that it is for the neglect of *mezuzah*, it is well, for it is written, '*and thou shalt write them upon the door posts* [mezuzoth] *of thine house*', which is followed by, '*that your days may be multiplied, and the days of your children*'. But what is the reason of the view that it is for the neglect of fringes?—Said R. Kahana—others state, Shila Mari: Because it is written, *Also in thy skirts is found the blood of the souls of the innocent poor.*[2] R. Naḥman b. Isaac said, The view that it is for the neglect of *mezuzah* is also [learnt] from this: *did I not find them like caves?*[3] [which means] that they made their entrances like caves.[4]

Resh Lakish said: He who is observant of fringes will be privileged to be served by two thousand eight hundred slaves, for it is said, *Thus saith the Lord of hosts: In those days it shall come to pass, that ten men shall take hold, out of all the languages of the nations, shall even take hold of the skirt of him that is a Jew, saying, We will go with you*, etc.[5]

(Mnemonic: Hate, *Ḥallah*, *Terumah*, Robbed, Law, Oath, Shedding, Uncovering, Folly.)[6] It was taught: R. Nehemiah said: As a punishment for causeless hate strife multiplies in a man's house, his wife miscarries, and his sons and daughters die young.

R. Eleazar b. R. Judah said: Because of the neglect of *ḥallah* there is no blessing in what is stored, a curse is sent upon prices,[7] and seed is sown and others consume it, for it is said, *I also will do this unto you: I will visit you with terror* [behalah], *even consumption and fever, that shall consume the eyes, and make the soul to pine away:*
c *and ye shall sow your seed in vain, for your enemies shall eat it:*[1] read not *behalah* but *be-ḥallah*.[2] But if they give it, they are blessed, for it is said, *ye shall also give unto the priest the first of your dough, to cause a blessing to rest on thine house.*[3]

As a punishment for the neglect of *terumoth* and tithes the heavens are shut up from pouring down dew and rain, high prices are prevalent, wages are lost, and people pursue a livelihood but cannot attain it,[4] for it is written: *Drought* [ẓiyyah] *and heat* [ḥom] *consume the snow waters: So doth the grave those which have sinned.*[5] How does this imply it?—The School of R. Ishmael taught: On account of the things which I commanded you in summer[6] but ye did them not, the snowy waters shall rob you in winter.[7] But if they render them, they are blessed, for it is said, *Bring ye the whole tithe into the storehouse, that there may be meat in Mine house, and prove Me now herewith, saith the Lord of Hosts, if I will not open you the windows of heaven, and pour you out a blessing, that there shall not be room enough to receive it* ['ad beli day].[8] What is meant by '*ad beli day?*—Said Rami b. Ḥama: Until your lips are exhausted[9] through saying, '*Enough!*' [*day*].

For the crime of robbery locusts make invasion, famine is prevalent, and people eat the flesh of their sons and daughters, for it is said, *Hear this word, ye kine of Bashan, that are in the mountain of Samaria, which oppress the poor, which crush the needy.*[10] (Said Raba,

(9) No supervisors were appointed to ensure that the ignorant observe them. Rashi: *ḥaberim* (q.v. Glos.) eat the bread of the ignorant and assume that the priestly dues have been rendered. Likewise, they use their moveables without fearing that they may have dedicated them as *hekdesh* and rendered them forbidden for secular use.

a (1) Prov. XXII, 27. (2) Eccl. V, 5. (3) Jer. II, 30. (4) The Heb. is *la-shaw*, which bears this meaning too. Cf. Deut. V, 11: *Thou shalt not take the name of the Lord thy God in vain* (la-shaw). (5) But the compiler of this Baraitha quoted his former view. (6) Wilna Gaon emends this to R. Ammi or R. Assi. (7) V. Glos. (8) V. Deut. XI, 19-21: *And ye shall teach them your children ... and thou shalt write them upon the door posts of thine house* (mezuzoth) ... *that your days may be multiplied, and the days of your children*. One maintains: the promise '*and the days of your children*' is made conditional upon the immediately preceding command, *and thou shalt write them* (*sc.* mezuzah); the other holds that it refers to the previous verse too, viz., *and ye shall teach them your children*.

b (1) Num. XV, 38. (2) Jer. II, 34: '*in thy skirts*'—i.e., in the neglect of fringes, which are inserted in the skirts of one's garment: '*the innocent poor*,' i.e., the children who die guiltlessly. (3) E.V.: *I have not found it at the place of breaking in.* (4) Without *mezuzoth*. (5) Zech. VIII, 23. '*Skirt*' is regarded as referring to the fringe (cf. n. b2). There are four fringes, and traditionally there are seventy languages: we thus have $70 \times 10 \times 4 = 2800$. (6) Catchwords of the themes that follow, as an aid to memory. (7) What is stored—grain, wine, oil, etc.—does not keep, with the result that prices rise.

c (1) Lev. XXVI, 16. (2) On account of (the neglect of) *ḥallah*. (3) Ezek. XLIV, 30. (4) Cf. Ab. V, 8. (5) Job. XXIV, 19. (6) Viz., the rendering of *terumoth* and tithes. (7) I.e., there will be no rain, etc. *Ẓiyyah* (E.V. *drought*) is thus connected with *ẓiwah* (he commanded), and *ḥom* (E.V. *heat*) with summer. (8) Mal. III, 10. (9) *Yibelu*, connected here with *beli*. (10) Amos. IV, 1. The proof lies in the sequel, quoted below.

E.g., these women of Maḥoza,[11] [33a] who eat without working).[12] And it is [further] written, *I have smitten you with blasting and mildew: the multitude of your gardens and your vineyards and your fig*
a *trees and your olive trees hath the palmerworm devoured:*[1] and it is also written, *That which the palmerworm hath left hath the locust eaten; and that which the locust hath left hath the cankerworm eaten; and that which the cankerworm hath left hath the caterpillar eaten;*[2] and it is written, *And one shall snatch on the right hand, and be hungry, and he shall eat on the left hand, and they shall not be satisfied; they shall eat every man the flesh of his own arm.*[3] Read not, *the flesh of his own arm* [zero'o], but, *the flesh of his own* seed [*zar'o*].

As a punishment for delay of judgment,[4] perversion of judgment,[5] spoiling of judgment,[6] and neglect of Torah, sword and spoil increase, pestilence and famine come, people eat and are not satisfied, and eat their bread by weight, for it is written, *and I will bring a sword upon you, that shall execute the vengeance of the covenant:*[7] now *'covenant'* means nothing else but Torah, as it is written. *But for My covenant of day and night* [*I had not appointed the ordinances of heaven and earth*];[8] and it is written, *When I break your staff of bread, ten women shall bake your bread in one oven, and they shall deliver your bread again by weight;*[9] and it is written, *because, even because they rejected My judgments.*[10]

For the crime of vain oaths, false oaths,[11] profanation of the Divine Name,[12] and the desecration of the Sabbath, wild beasts multiply, [domestic] animals cease, the population decreases, and the roads become desolate, for it is said, *And if by these things* [be-eleh] *ye will not be reformed unto Me;*[13] read not *be-eleh* but *be-alah;*[14]
b and it is written, *and I will send the beast of the field among you*, etc.[1] Now, in respect to false oaths it is written, *And ye shall not swear by My name falsely, so that you profane* [we-ḥillalta] *the name of thy God;*[2] and of the profanation of the Name it is written, *and that they profane not* [ye-ḥallelu] *My holy name;*[3] and of the profanation of the Sabbath it is written, *every one that profaneth it* [meḥallelehah] *shall surely be put to death:*[4] and [the punishment for] profanation is learnt[5] from a false oath.[6]

Through the crime of bloodshed the Temple was destroyed and the *Shechinah* departed from Israel, as it is written, *So ye shall not pollute the land wherein ye are; for blood, it polluteth the land ... And thou shalt not defile the land which ye inhabit, in the midst of which I dwell:*[7] hence, if ye do defile it, ye will not inhabit it and I will not dwell in its midst.[8]

As a punishment for incest,[9] idolatry, and non-observance of the years of release and jubilee[10] exile comes to the world, they [the Jews] are exiled, and others come and dwell in their place, for it is said, *for all these abominations have the men of the land done*, etc.;[11] and it is written, *and the land is defiled; therefore do I visit the*

(11) The famous town on the Tigris not far from Ktesifon, where Raba possibly founded the academy (Weiss, *Dor*, III, 202) with himself as head, which was recognized as one of the foremost in Babylon; Obermeyer, p. 166. (12) Thus they rob their husbands; or, demanding food and producing nothing in return, they may force their husbands to robbery.—Women were expected to do a certain amount of labour, e.g., spinning; Keth. 59*b*, cf. Prov. XXXI, 13, 19. It would appear that Raba was not very popular in Maḥoza (cf. Sanh. 99*b*); such sentiments may be either partially the cause, or Raba's reaction.

a (1) Amos IV, 9. (2) Joel I, 4. (3) Isa. IX, 19. (4) Lit., 'affliction of judgment'—through unnecessary delay in executing judgment. (5) Intentionally, through bias or partiality. (6) Giving erroneous verdicts through carelessness and insufficient deliberation; cf. Aboth, I, 2. (7) Lev. XXVI, 25. (8) Jer. XXXIII, 25. *'The covenant of day and night'* is understood to refer to the Torah, which should be studied day and night; v. Ned. 32*a*. (9) Lev. XXVI, 26. (10) Ibid. 43. (11) Rashi: the first is swearing what is obviously untrue; the second is an ordinary false oath which can deceive. Cf. Aboth, Chap. IV, Mish. 7, n. 11. (12) Any unworthy action which reflects discredit upon Judaism—since Judaism is blamed for it—is regarded as profanation of the Divine Name. Cf. Aboth, V, 9, and IV, 4. (13) Lev. XXVI, 23. (14) The consonants are the same. The verse then reads: and if ye will not be reformed unto me in the matter of (false) oaths.

b (1) Lev. XXVI, 22. (2) Ibid. XIX, 12. (3) Ibid. XXII, 2. (4) Ex. XXXI, 14. (5) Lit., 'and profanation, profanation is learnt'. I.e., the statement made in respect to one profanation holds good for the others too. (6) Just as this is punished by the sending of wild beasts, etc. (Lev. XXVI, 22), so are the others. (7) Num. XXXV, 33f. (8) It may be remarked that the destruction of the Temple is regarded here as synonymous with exile from the country. (9) Which includes adultery. (10) V. Lev. XXV, 1ff. (11) Ibid. XVIII, 27; *'abominations'* refers to incest, of which the whole passage treats.

◁ *For the continuation of the English translation of this page see overleaf.*

דאכלן ולא עבדן · ונמלא שגזולות את בעליהן ועוד מתוך שמלומדות במאכל ובמשתה גורמות לבעלים לגזול : וכתיב · בההיא פרשה בנבואת עמוס הכיתי אתכם בשדפון וסיפיה דקרא כרמיכם(ב) וזיתיכם יאכל הגזם וכתיב ביואל יתר הגזם דמשמע שהגזם אינו אלא תחלת מכה ואחריה באים ארבה וחסיל אלמא גובאי עולה בעון גזל וכיון דמיני גובאי עולין רעב הוה וכיון דהרעב הוה כתיב בישעיה ויגזור על ימין ורעב וגו' וסיפיה דקרא איש בשר זרועו יאכלו : עינוי הדין · שמאחרין הדיינין לדון ולא לשם שמים אלא לאחר שהוברר להן הדין משהין אותו : עוות הדין · שמעוותין אותו מזידין : קלקול הדין · שלא היו מתכוין בו לעיין כל צרכן ונתקלקל מאליו : חרב וביזה רבה כו' · דכתיב נקם ברית ואין ברית אלא תורה דכתיב אם לא בריתי יומם ולילה והגית בו יומם ולילה וכתיב חרב ועל ידי חרב דהיינו משלחת גירוי מלחמה הביזה באה וכתיב ושלחתי דבר הרי דבר וכתיב בשברי לכם מטה לחם הרי בצורת וכתיב בסוף כל הקללות יען וביען במשפטי מאסו הרי עינוי ועיוות וקלקול בכלל : שבועות שוא · כל המשנה את הידוע כגון על האיש שהוא אשה שבועת שקר שאין בדאותו ניכרת ומאמין שקר לבריות : והדרכים משתוממין · מאין עובר : אלא באלה · ויש במשמע בין שוא בין שקר וכתיב בשבועת שקר וחללת ובשבת ובחילול השם כתיב חילול וגמרינן משבועה : חילול השם · אדם גדול שבני אדם למדים הימנו ואינו נזהר במעשיו נמצאו הקטנים מזלזלין בתורה על ידו ואומרים זהו מבין שאין ממש בתורה ובמצות ונמצא השם מתחלל נעשה דבריו חולין : אין אני שוכן · חורבן הבית במשמע שאין משכני (ג) בתוכם : כי את כל התועבות · בפרשת עריות כתיב : ונתתי את פגריכם על פגרי גלוליכם · דהיינו ע"ז וכתיב בתריה ואתכם אזרה בגוים וכתיב ושממו עליה אויביכם היושבים בה הרי שהם גולין ואויביהם יושבין במקומן : שבתותיה · שמיטין : ואתם בארץ אויביכם · ולעיל מיניה כתיב ושממו עליה אויביכם : לא ישמח · הרי צרות וגזירות ואת יתומיו ואת אלמנותיו לא ירחם הרי צועקין ואינם נענין בעון מה כי כלו חנף ומרע וכל פה דובר נבלה ועוד ידו נטויה לשון ועד כל שנותיו של אדם שהן ע' שנה יד הדין נטויה עליו לבטל זכיותיו בעון זה : הכל יודעין כו' · ולא הוצרך לאדם לפרש למה נכנסה והמנבל פיו בכך אפילו כו' : שוחה עמוקה · מוכנת לפי זרות למי שפיו זרה : זעום ה' יפול שם · זעם של הקב"ה הוא שורה שם אצל פי זרות היושב אצלו ושומע קרוי זעומו של הקב"ה : המתמרק עצמו · מפנה לבו לכך ממרק עצמו משאר עסקים להתעסק בעבירות : תמרוק ברע · הממרק ברע : הדרוקן · חולי הוא : של עבירה עבה · הבאה בשביל עבירה עבה בשרו מתקשה ועב ונפוח בעובי : תפוח · שייפ"ס נפוח עורו על בשרו ומים בינתיים ונראה כזכוכית ורך מתוכו : דק · בשרו דק וכחוש : מי מפים · מי מטיל גורל להבחין ולהודיע שאינו של עבירה עכשיו יאמרו עלי שעברתי על דת ואין הכל יודעין בג' סימנים שאמרנו ופעמים שמשתנין : ידענא ביה · שמחמת רעב בא לו ואין צריך לחשדו : והא רבא דאמר · כלומר למה חש בו והא לא הרעיב את עצמו מדקאמר ידענא ביה בנחמני מכלל דהמרעיב עצמו רע בעיניו ואי משום שהיה משהה נקביו ואמרינן בבכורות (דף מד:) נוטה רבה הדרוקן רבה שבעל שהיית נקבים הוא בא : הא איהו אמר נפישי קטילי קדר · רבים הרוגי נקבים ממותי הדרוקן של רעב קדר לשון קדרה על שם ששופך כקדרה : דאנסי ליה רבנן בעידניה · התלמידים הקבועים להם עת לפניו אונסין אותו להשהות נקביו : סימן לגסות הרוח עניות · בפרק האיש מקדש (קדושין דף מט:) מפרש מאי עניות עניות דתורה : אסכרה · חולי המתחיל במעיים וגומר בגרון הנקרא בונמלא"ן :

תורה אור

דאכלן ולא עבדן וכתיב °הכיתי אתכם בשדפון ובירקון הרבות גנותיכם וכרמיכם ותאניכם וזיתיכם יאכל הגזם וכתיב °יתר הגזם אכל הארבה ויתר הארבה אכל הילק ויתר הילק אכל החסיל וכתי' °ויגזור על ימין ורעב ויאכל על שמאל ולא שבעו איש בשר זרועו יאכלו אל תקרי בשר זרועו אלא בשר זרעו: בעון עינוי הדין ועיוות הדין וקלקול הדין וביטול תורה חרב וביזה רבה ודבר ובצורת בא ובני אדם אוכלין ואינן שבעין ואוכלין לחמם במשקל דכתיב °והבאתי עליכם חרב נוקמת נקם ברית וגו' ואין ברית אלא תורה *שנאמר °אם לא בריתי יומם ולילה וגו' וכתיב °בשברי לכם מטה לחם ואפו עשר נשים וגו' וכתיב °יען וביען במשפטי מאסו : בעון שבועת שוא ושבועת שקר וחילול השם וחילול שבת חיה רעה רבה ובהמה כלה ובני אדם מתמעטין והדרכים משתוממין שנא' °ואם באלה לא תוסרו לי אל תקרי באלה אלא באלה וכתיב °והשלחתי בכם את חית השדה וגו' וכתיב בשבועת שקר °ולא תשבעו בשמי לשקר וחללת את שם אלהיך ובחלול השם כתיב °ולא תחללו את שם קדשי ובחלול שבת כתיב °מחלליה מות יומת ויליף חילול חילול משבועת שקר : בעון *שפיכות דמים בית המקדש חרב ושכינה מסתלקת מישראל שנאמר °ולא תחניפו וגו' ולא תטמא את הארץ אשר אתם יושבים בה אשר אני שוכן בתוכה הא אתם מטמאים אותה אינכם יושבים בה ואיני שוכן בתוכה : בעון גלוי עריות ועבודת כוכבים והשמטת שמיטין ויובלות גלות בא לעולם ומגלין אותן ובאין אחרים ויושבין במקומן שנאמר °כי את כל התועבות האל עשו אנשי הארץ וגו' וכתיב ותטמא הארץ ואפקוד עונה עליה וגו' וכתיב °ולא תקיא הארץ אתכם בטמאכם אותה ובעבודת כוכבים כתיב °ונתתי את פגריכם וגו' וכתיב והשמותי את מקדשיכם וגו' ואתכם אזרה בגוים בשמיטין וביובלות כתיב °אז תרצה הארץ את שבתותיה כל ימי השמה ואתם בארץ אויביכם וגו' וכתיב °כל ימי השמה תשבות : בעון נבלות פה צרות רבות וגזירות קשות מתחדשות ובחורי שונאי ישראל מתים יתומים ואלמנות צועקין ואינן נענין שנא' °על כן על בחוריו לא ישמח ה' ואת יתומיו [ואת](ו) אלמנותיו לא ירחם כי כלו חנף ומרע וכל פה דובר נבלה בכל זאת לא שב אפו ועוד ידו נטויה מאי *ועוד ידו נטויה א"ר חנן בר רבא הכל יודעין כלה למה נכנסה לחופה אלא כל המנבל פיו אפי' חותמין עליו גזר דין של שבעים שנה לטובה הופכין עליו לרעה אמר רבה בר שילא אמר רב חסדא כל המנבל את פיו מעמיקין לו גיהנם שנאמר °שוחה עמוקה פי זרות רב נחמן בר יצחק אמר אף שומע ושותק שנאמר °זעום ה' יפול שם אמר רב אושעיא כל הממרק עצמו לעבירה חבורות ופצעין יוצאין בו שנאמר °חבורות פצע תמרוק ברע ולא עוד אלא שנדון בהדרוקן(א) שנאמר °ומכות חדרי בטן אמר רב נחמן בר יצחק *סימן לעבירה הדרוקן ת"ר ג' מיני הדרוקן הן של עבירה עבה ושל רעב תפוח ושל כשפים דק שמואל הקטן חש ביה אמר רבש"ע מי מפיס איתסי אביי חש ביה אמר רבא ידענא ביה *בנחמני דמכפין נפשיה רבא חש ביה והא רבא הוא דאמר נפישי קטילי קדר מנפיחי כפן שאני רבא דאנסי ליה רבנן בעידניה בעל כורחיה ת"ר ד' סימנין הן סימן לעבירה הדרוקן סימן לשנאת חנם ירקון סימן *לגסות הרוח עניות סימן ללה"ר אסכרה ת"ר אסכרה באה לעולם על

עמוס ד · יואל א · ישעיה ט · ויקרא כו · ירמיה לג · ויקרא כו · שם · שם · שם · שם כב · שמות לא · במדבר לה · ויקרא יח · שם · שם · שם · שם · ישעיה ט · משלי כב · שם · שם כ · שם

[מגילה ג.] · [יומא פה. ע"ש] · [כתובות ח:] · [שבת מ: ע"ש] · [קדושין מט:]

הגהות הב"ח
(א) גמ' שנידון בהדרוקן כ"כ עי' בעירובין דף מא ע"ב : (ב) רש"י ד"ה וכתיב וכו' כרמיכם ותאניכם וזיתיכם : (ג) ד"ה אין אני וכו' משכני (בתוכם) תו"מ ונ"ב ס"א בתוכה :

[עי' רש"י גטין לה: ד"ה והלכתא והר"ן נדרים כד: ד"ה איתמר טעם דיקרא נחמני]

Continuation of translation from previous page as indicated by ◁

iniquity thereof upon it;[12] and it is written, *that the land vomit not you out also, when ye defile it.*[13] Again, with respect to idolatry it is written, *and I will cast your carcases [upon the carcases of your idols]*;[14] and it is written, *And I will make your cities a waste, and will bring your sanctuaries into desolation etc. . . .*[15] *and you will I scatter among the nations.*[16] [Further], in reference to release and jubilee years it is written, *Then shall the land enjoy her sabbaths, as long as it lieth*
c *desolate, and ye be in your enemies' land*, etc.;[1] and it is written, *As long as it lieth desolate it shall have rest.*[2]

As a punishment for obscenity,[3] troubles multiply, cruel decrees are proclaimed afresh, the youth of Israel's enemies[4] die, and the fatherless and widows cry out and are not answered; for it is said, *Therefore shall the Lord not rejoice over their young men, neither shall he have compassion over their fatherless and their widows: for every one is profane and an evil-doer, and every mouth speaketh folly. For all this his anger is not turned away, but his hand is stretched out still.*[5] What is meant by, *'but his hand is stretched out still'?*—Said R. Ḥanan b. Raba: All know for what purpose a bride enters the bridal canopy, yet against whomsoever who speaks obscenely [thereof], even if a sentence of seventy years' happiness had been sealed for him,[6] it is reversed for evil.

Rabbah b. Shila said in R. Ḥisda's name: He who puts his mouth to folly,[7] Gehenna is made deep for him, as it is said, *A deep pit is for the mouth [that speaketh] perversity.*[8] R. Naḥman b. Isaac said, Also [for] one who hears and is silent,[9] for it is said, *he that is abhorred of the Lord*[10] *shall fall therein.*[11]

R. Oshaia said: He who devotes himself[12] to sin, wounds and bruises break out over him, as it is said, *Stripes and wounds are for him that devoteth himself to evil.*[13] Moreover, he is punished by dropsy, for it is said, *and strokes reach the innermost parts of the belly.*[14] R. Naḥman b. Isaac said: Dropsy is a sign of sin.

Our Rabbis taught: There are three kinds of dropsy: that [which is a punishment] of sin is thick; that caused by hunger is
d swollen; and what is caused by magic is thin.[1] Samuel the Little[2] suffered through it. 'Sovereign of the Universe!' he cried out, 'who will cast lots?'[3] [Thereupon] he recovered. Abaye suffered from it. Said Raba, I know of Naḥmani[4] that he practises hunger.[5] Raba suffered from it. But was it not Raba himself who said, More numerous are those slain by delayed calls of nature[6] than the victims[7] of starvation?[8]—Raba was different, because the scholars compelled him [to practise restraint] at the set times [for lectures].

Our Rabbis taught: There are four signs:—[i] Dropsy is a sign of sin; [ii] jaundice is a sign of causeless hatred; [iii] poverty is a sign of conceit;[9] croup[10] is a sign of slander.[11]

(12) Ibid. 25. (13) Ibid. 28. (14) Ibid. XXVI, 30. (15) Ibid. 31. (16) Ibid. 33.
c (1) Lev. XXVI, 34. (2) Ibid. 35. (3) Lit., 'folly of the mouth'. (4) A euphemism for the youth of Israel. It was held inauspicious even merely to express a possible mishap, on the score of 'open not thy mouth to Satan'. (5) Isa. IX, 16. (6) This derives from the idea that there is a book of Life, in which man's destiny is recorded; cf. Ned., 22*a*, n. 7. (7) Speaks lewdly. (8) Prov. XXII, 14. Lit., 'strange (things)'.—Gehenna, as an equivalent of hell, takes its name from the place where children were once sacrificed to Moloch, viz., *ge ben hinnom*, the valley of the son of Hinnom, to the south of Jerusalem. (Josh. XV, 8; II Kings XXIII, 10; Jer. II, 23; VII, 31-32; XIX, 6). (9) Does not protest. (10) Viz., who hears it without protesting. (11) Prov. XXII, 14. (12) Either: makes himself empty—from all other purposes; or, polishes himself up, i.e., prepares himself. (13) Ibid. XX, 30. (14) Ibid.
d (1) Jewish magic is mentioned in Deut. XVIII, 10-11, in a passage forbidding its practice. But its potency was generally recognized. V. *J.E.* Arts, 'Magic', and 'Demonology'. (2) A Tanna, contemporary of R. Gamaliel I. (3) To see from what cause I am suffering—I will be accused of sin. (4) A nickname of Abaye, who was brought up in the house of Rabbah b. Naḥmani. (5) This may indicate that Abaye was an ascetic. Judaism generally was opposed to asceticism (cf. Ned. 10*a*: he who deprives himself of what he may legitimately enjoy is called a sinner); nevertheless, in times of stress or for particular reasons Rabbis resorted to fasting (B.M. 85*a*), and private fasts were practised from early times: Judith VIII, 6; I Macc. III, 47. (6) Lit., 'pot'. (7) Lit., 'swollen'. (8) Now, Raba evidently disapproved of Abaye's fasting; also, he himself warned against trifling with nature's calls. How then did he come to dropsy—sin being ruled out?—Presumably its symptoms precluded the assumption that he was a victim of witchcraft. (9) In Ḳid. 49*b* it is explained that this refers to poverty of knowledge, which results when one is too conceited to learn from others. (10) אסכרה, or perhaps 'Diphtheria'. (11) Each is the punishment for the other.

מסורת הש"ס

דאכלן ולא עבדן וכתיב °הכיתי אתכם בשדפון ובירקון הרבות גנותיכם
וכרמיכם ותאניכם וזיתיכם יאכל הגזם וכתיב °יתר הגזם אכל הארבה ויתר
הארבה אכל הילק ויתר הילק אכל החסיל וכתי' °ויגזור על ימין ורעב ויאכל על
שמאל ולא שבעו איש בשר זרועו יאכלו אל תקרי בשר זרועו אלא בשר זרעו:
בעון עינוי הדין ועיוות הדין וקלקול הדין וביטול תורה חרב וביזה רבה ודבר
ובצורת בא ובני אדם אוכלין ואינן שבעין ואוכלין לחמם במשקל דכתיב
°והבאתי עליכם חרב נוקמת נקם ברית וגו' ואין ברית אלא תורה *שנאמר
°אם לא בריתי יומם ולילה וגו' וכתיב °בשברי לכם מטה לחם ואפו עשר נשים
וגו' וכתיב °יען וביען במשפטי מאסו: בעון שבועת שוא ושבועת שקר וחילול
השם וחילול שבת חיה רעה רבה ובהמה כלה ובני אדם מתמעטין והדרכים
משתוממין שנא' °ואם באלה לא תוסרו לי אל תקרי באלה אלא באלה וכתיב
°והשלחתי בכם את חית השדה וגו' וכתיב בשבועת שקר °ולא תשבעו בשמי
לשקר וחללת את שם אלהיך ובחלול השם כתיב °ולא תחללו את שם קדשי
ובחלול שבת כתיב °מחלליה מות יומת ויליף חילול חילול משבועת שקר:
בעון *שפיכות דמים בית המקדש חרב ושכינה מסתלקת מישראל שנאמר
°ולא תחניפו וגו' ולא תטמא את הארץ אשר אתם יושבים בה אשר אני שוכן
בתוכה הא אתם מטמאים אותה אינכם יושבים בה ואיני שוכן בתוכה: בעון
גלוי עריות ועבודת כוכבים והשמטת שמיטין ויובלות גלות בא לעולם
ומגלין אותן ובאין אחרים ויושבין במקומן שנאמר °כי את כל התועבות האל
עשו אנשי הארץ וגו' וכתיב ותטמא הארץ ואפקוד עונה עליה וגו' וכתיב
°ולא תקיא הארץ אתכם בטמאכם אותה ובעבודת כוכבים כתיב °ונתתי את
פגריכם וגו' וכתיב והשמותי את מקדשיכם וגו' ואתכם אזרה בגוים בשמיטין
וביובלות כתיב °אז תרצה הארץ את שבתותיה כל ימי השמה ואתם בארץ
אויביכם וגו' וכתיב °כל ימי השמה תשבות: בעון נבלות פה צרות רבות
וגזירות קשות מתחדשות ובחורי שונאי ישראל מתים יתומים ואלמנות צועקין
ואינן נענין שנא' °על כן על בחוריו לא ישמח ה' ואת יתומיו [ואת](ו) אלמנותיו
לא ירחם כי כלו חנף ומרע וכל פה דובר נבלה בכל זאת לא שב אפו ועוד ידו
נטויה מאי *ועוד ידו נטויה א"ר חנן בר רבא הכל יודעין כלה למה נכנסה
לחופה אלא כל המנבל פיו אפי' חותמין עליו גזר דין של שבעים שנה לטובה
הופכין עליו לרעה אמר רבה בר שילא אמר רב חסדא כל המנבל את פיו
מעמיקין לו גיהנם שנאמר °שוחה עמוקה פי זרות רב נחמן בר יצחק אמר אף
שומע ושותק שנאמר °זעום ה' יפול שם אמר רב אושעיא כל הממרק עצמו
לעבירה חבורות ופצעין יוצאין בו שנאמר °חבורות פצע תמרוק ברע ולא
עוד אלא שנדון בהדרוקן(א) שנאמר °ומכות חדרי בטן אמר רב נחמן בר יצחק
*סימן לעבירה הדרוקן ת"ר ג' מיני הדרוקן הן של עבירה עבה ושל רעב תפוח
ושל כשפים דק שמואל הקטן חש ביה אמר רבש"ע מי מפיס איתסי אביי חש
ביה אמר רבא ידענא ביה *בנחמני דמכפין נפשיה רבא חש ביה והא
רבא הוא דאמר נפישי קטילי קדר מנפיחי כפן שאני רבא דאנסי ליה רבנן
בעידניה בעל כורחיה ת"ר ד' סימנין הן סימן לעבירה הדרוקן סימן לשנאת
חנם ירקון סימן *לגסות הרוח עניות סימן ללה"ר אסכרה ת"ר אסכרה באה לעולם
על

תורה אור: עמוס ד · יואל א · ישעיה ט · ויקרא כו · ירמיה לג · ויקרא כו · שם · שם · ויקרא יט · שמות לא · במדבר לה · ויקרא יח · שם · שם · שם · ישעיה ט · משלי כב · שם · שם כ · שם

רש"י

דאכלן ולא עבדן · ונמלא שגזולות את בעליהן ועוד מתוך שמלומדות במאכל ובמשתה גורמות לבעלים לגזול: וכתיב · בההיא פרשה בנבואת עמוס הכיתי אתכם בשדפון וסיפיה דקרא כרמיכם(ג) וזיתיכם יאכל הגזם וכתיב ביואל יתר הגזם דמשמע שהגזם אינו אלא תחלת מכה ואחריה באים ארבה וחסיל אלמא גובאי עולה בעון גזל וכיון דמיני גובאי עולין רעב הוה וכיון דהרעב הוה כתיב בישעיה ויגזור על ימין ורעב וגו' וסיפיה דקרא איש בשר זרועו יאכלו: עינוי הדין · שמאחרין הדיינין לדונו ולא לגמור אלא לאחר שהוברר להן הדין מצערין אותו: עוות הדין · שמעוותין אותו מזידין: קלקול הדין · שלא היו מתונין בו לעיין כל צרכו ונתקלקל מאליו: חרב וביזה רבה כו' · דכתיב נקם ברית ואין ברית אלא תורה דכתיב אם לא בריתי יומם ולילה והגית בו יומם ולילה וכתיב חרב ועל ידי חרב דהיינו משלחת גירוי מלחמה הביזה באה וכתיב ושלחתי דבר הרי דבר וכתיב בשברי לכם מטה לחם הרי בצורת וכתיב בסוף כל הקללות יען וביען במשפטי מאסו הרי עינוי ועיוות וקלקול בכלל: שבועות שוא · כל המשנה את הידוע כגון על האיש שהוא אשה שבועת שקר שאין בדאותו ניכרת ומאמין שקר לבריות: והדרכים משתוממין · מאין עובר: אלא באלה · ויש במשמע בין שוא בין שקר וכתיב בשבועת שקר וחללת ובשבת ובחילול השם כתיב חילול וגמרינן משבועה: חילול השם · אדם גדול שבני אדם למדים הימנו ואינו נזהר במעשיו נמצאו הקטנים מזלזלין בתורה על ידו ואומרים זהו מבין שאין ממש בתורה ובמצות ונמצא השם מתחלל נעשה דבריו חולין: אין אני שוכן · חורבן הבית במשמע שאין משכני (ג) בתוכם: כי את כל התועבות · בפרשת עריות כתיב: ונתתי את פגריכם על פגרי גלוליכם · דהיינו ע"ז וכתיב בתריה ואתכם אזרה בגוים וכתיב ושממו עליה אויביכם היושבים בה הרי שהם גולין ואויביהם יושבין במקומן: שבתותיה · שמיטין: ואתם בארץ אויביכם · ולעיל מיניה כתיב ושממו עליה אויביכם: לא ישמח · הרי צרות וגזירות ואת יתומיו ואת אלמנותיו לא ירחם הרי צועקין ואינם נענין בעון מה כי כלו חנף ומרע וכל פה דובר נבלה ועוד ידו נטויה לשון ועד כל שנותיו של אדם שהן ע' שנה יד הדין נטויה עליו לבטל זכיותיו בעון זה: הכל יודעין כו' · ולא הוצרך לאדם לפרש למה נכנסה והמנבל פיו בכך אפילו כו': שוחה עמוקה · מוכנת לפי זרות למי שפיו זרה: זעום ה' יפול שם · זעום של הקב"ה הוא שורה שם אצל פי זרות היושב אצלו ושומע קרוי זעומו של הקב"ה: הממרק עצמו · מפנה לבו לכך ממרק עצמו מאחר עסקים להתעסק בעבירות: תמרוק ברע · הממרק ברע: הדרוקן · חולי הוא: של עבירה עבה · הבאה בשביל עבירה עבה בשרו מתקשה ועב ונפוח בעובי: תפוח · שייפ"ס נפוח עורו על בשרו ומים בינתיים ונראה כזכוכית ורך מתוכו: דק · בשרו דק וכחוש: מי מפיס · מי מטיל גורל להבחין ולהודיע שאינו של עבירה עכשיו יאמרו עלי שעברתי על דת ואין הכל יודעין בג' סימנים שאמרו ופעמים שמשתנין: ידענא ביה · שמחמת רעב בא לו ואין צריך לחשדו: והא רבא דאמר · כלומר למה חש בו והא לא הרעיב את עצמו מדקאמר ידענא ביה בנחמני מכלל דהמרעיב עצמו רע בעיניו ואי משום שהיה משהה נקביו ואמרינן בבכורות (דף מד:) נוחה רבה הדרוקן רבה שעל שהיית נקבים הוא בא: הא איהו אמר נפישי קטילי קדר · רבים הרוגי נקבים ממותי הדרוקן של רעב קדר לשון קדרה על שם ששופך כקדרה: דאנסי ליה רבנן בעידניה · התלמידים הקבועים להם עת לפניו אונסין אותו להשהות נקביו: סימן לגסות הרוח עניות · בפרק האיש מקדש (קדושין דף מט:) מפרש מאי עניות עניות דתורה: אסכרה · חולי המתחיל במעיים וגומר בגרון הנקרא בונמלא"ן:

[מו"ק כג.] · [יומא פה. ע"ש] · [כתובות ח:] · [יבמות ס: ע"ש] · [קדושין מט:]

הגהות הב"ח
(א) גמ' שנידון בהדרוקן נ"ב עי' בעירובין דף מא ע"ב: (ב) רש"י ד"ה וכתיב וכו' כרמיכם ותאניכם וזיתיכם: (ג) ד"ה אין אני וכו' משכני (בתוכם) תז"מ וכ"כ ס"א בתוכה:

[עי' רש"י גטין לד: ד"ה והלכתא והר"ן נדרים נד: ד"ה איתמר טעם דנקרא נחמני]

עין משפט
נר מצוה

קבא א מיי' פ"ז מהל' דעות הלכה ה :

מסורת
הש"ס

על המעשר ר' אלעזר בר' יוסי אומר על לשון הרע אמר רבא ואיתימא ריב"ל מאי קראה °והמלך ישמח באלהים יתהלל כל הנשבע בו כי יסכר פי דוברי שקר איבעיא להו רבי אלעזר ברבי יוסי על לשון הרע קאמר או דילמא אף על לשון הרע נמי קאמר ת"ש כשנכנסו רבותינו לכרם ביבנה היה שם רבי יהודה ור' אלעזר בר' יוסי ור"ש נשאלה שאלה זו בפניהם מכה זו מפני מה מתחלת בבני מעיים וגומרת בפה נענה רבי יהודה ברבי אלעאי *ראש המדברים בכל מקום ואמר אע"פ *שכליות יועצות ולב מבין ולשון מחתך פה גומר נענה רבי אלעזר ברבי יוסי ואמר מפני שאוכלין בה דברים טמאין דברים טמאים סלקא דעתך אלא שאוכלין בה דברים שאינן מתוקנים נענה ר' שמעון ואמר בעון ביטול תורה אמרו לו נשים יוכיחו שמבטלות את בעליהן נכרים יוכיחו שמבטלין את ישראל תינוקות יוכיחו שמבטלין את אביהן תינוקות של בית רבן יוכיחו התם כדרבי גוריון דאמר רבי גוריון ואיתימא רב יוסף ברבי שמעיה בזמן שהצדיקים בדור צדיקים נתפסים על הדור *אין צדיקים בדור תינוקות של בית רבן נתפסים על הדור א"ר יצחק בר זעירי ואמרי לה א"ר שמעון בן נזירא מאי קראה °אם לא תדעי לך היפה בנשים צאי לך בעקבי הצאן וגו' ואמרינן גדיים הממושכנין על הרועים ש"מ אף על לשון הרע נמי קאמר ש"מ ואמאי קרו ליה ראש המדברים בכל מקום דיתבי רבי יהודה ורבי יוסי ורבי שמעון ויתיב יהודה בן גרים גבייהו פתח ר' יהודה ואמר כמה נאים מעשיהן של אומה זו תקנו שווקים תקנו גשרים תקנו מרחצאות ר' יוסי שתק נענה רשב"י ואמר כל מה שתקנו לא *תקנו אלא לצורך עצמן תקנו שווקין להושיב בהן זונות מרחצאות לעדן בהן עצמן גשרים ליטול מהן מכס הלך יהודה בן גרים °וסיפר דבריהם ונשמעו למלכות אמרו יהודה שעילה יתעלה יוסי ששתק יגלה לציפורי שמעון שגינה יהרג אזל הוא ובריה טשו בי מדרשא כל יומא הוה מייתי להו דביתהו ריפתא וכוזא דמיא וכרכי כי תקיף גזירתא °א"ל לבריה *נשים דעתן קלה עליהן דילמא מצערי לה ומגליא לן אזלו טשו במערתא איתרחיש ניסא איברי להו חרובא ועינא דמיא והוו *משלחי מנייהו והוו יתבי עד צואריהו בחלא כולי יומא גרסי °בעידן צלויי לבשו מיכסו *ומצלו והדר משלחי מנייהו כי היכי דלא ליבלו איתבו תריסר שני °במערתא אתא אליהו וקם אפיתחא דמערתא אמר מאן לודעיה לבר יוחי דמית קיסר ובטיל גזירתיה נפקו חזו אינשי דקא כרבי וזרעי אמר *מניחין חיי עולם ועוסקין בחיי שעה כל מקום שנותנין עיניהן מיד נשרף יצתה בת קול ואמרה להם להחריב עולמי יצאתם חיזרו למערתכם הדור אזול איתיבו תריסר ירחי שתא אמרי *משפט רשעים בגיהנם י"ב חדש יצתה בת קול ואמרה צאו ממערתכם נפקו כל היכא דהוה מחי ר' אלעזר הוה מסי ר"ש אמר לו בני די לעולם אני ואתה בהדי פניא דמעלי שבתא חזו ההוא סבא דהוה נקיט תרי *מדאני אסא ורהיט בין השמשות אמרו ליה הני למה לך אמר להו לכבוד שבת ותיסגי לך בחד חד כנגד °זכור וחד כנגד °שמור א"ל לבריה חזי כמה חביבין מצות על ישראל יתיב דעתייהו שמע ר' פנחס בן יאיר חתניה ונפק לאפיה עייליה לבי בניה הוה קא *אריך ליה לבישריה חזי דהוה ביה פילי בגופיה הוה קא בכי וקא נתרו דמעת עיניה וקמצוחא ליה א"ל אוי לי שראיתיך בכך א"ל אשריך שראיתני בכך שאילמלא לא ראיתני בכך לא מצאת בי כך דמעיקרא כי הוה מקשי ר"ש בן יוחי קושיא הוה מפרק ליה ר' פנחס בן יאיר תריסר פירוקי לסוף כי הוה מקשי ר"פ בן יאיר קושיא הוה מפרק ליה רשב"י עשרין וארבעה פירוקי אמר הואיל ואיתרחיש ניסא איזיל אתקין מילתא דכתיב °ויבא יעקב שלם ואמר רב שלם בגופו שלם בממונו שלם בתורתו °ויחן את פני העיר אמר רב מטבע תיקן להם ושמואל אמר שווקים תיקן להם ור' יוחנן אמר מרחצאות תיקן להם אמר איכא מילתא דבעי לתקוני אמרו ליה איכא דוכתא דאית ביה ספק טומאה ואית

תהלים סג · שיר א · שמות כ · בראשית לג שם

תוספות

ה"ג ר"ת הלך רבי יהודה בן גרים וסיפר דברים ונשמעו למלכות ויש ספרים שכתב בהן יהודה ואין נראה לרבינו תם דאמרינן בפרק קמא דמועד קטן (דף ט·) כי הוו מיפטרי ר' יהודה בן גרים ור"ש בן חלפתא מר' שמעון בן יוחי אמר ליה לבריה אנשים הללו אנשי צורה הם זיל גבייהו דליברכוך מכלל דגברא רבה היה ובסוף שמעתא ל"ג גל של עצמות בלשון גנאי אלא נח נפשיה עבד

רש"י

על המעשר · האוכל פירותיו טבלים והוא במיתה בידי שמים וזוהי מיתתו מדה במדה דדרך גרוט נכנס במעיו : יסכר · אסכרה : לכרם · זה בית המדרש שיושבין שורות שורות ככרם כך מפורש בירושלמי בברכות : מכה זו · אסכרה : ראש המדברים · במלות המלך שגזה עליו לדבר תחלה בכל מקום כדלקמן : פה גומר · לשון הרע והוא בא על כך לפיכך מתחיל במעיים ומסיים בפה שהלב מבין לספר לשון הרע וגודה הדברים מלבו : פה גומר · הכל יוצא מן הגרון : דברים טמאים סלקא דעתך · וכי עונשה מיתה דבשלמא לשון הרע עונשה מיתה דכתיב (תהלים קא) מלשני בסתר רעהו אותו אצמית : מתוקנין · מעושרים שהטבל במיתה בידי שמים כדיליף בחלא הן הגשרפים (סנהדרין דף פג·) : בעון בטול תורה · דעשו נמי מיתה כדאמרן מקרא נדרש לפני פניו למען ירבו ימיכם הא אם לא תלמדו יתמעטו : נשים יוכיחו · שאינן מצוות על דברי תורה דכתיב ולמדתם אותם את בניכם ולא בנותיכם ומתות באסכרה אמר להן אף הן מבטלות את בעליהן: תינוקות יוכיחו · שאינן בני לימוד אמר להן אף הן בעון שמבטלים את אביהם להוליכן לחמה ולטנן ולפייסן באגוזים : של בית רבן · לא בטלין ולא מבטלין : אם לא תדעי לך · לשמור מצותי לאי לך ובקשי רחמים בזכות עקבי הצאן אבות הראשונים שהיו רגלי הצאן והחזקם ורעי בזכותן את גדיותיך תינוקות שלך שלא יתפשו על משכנות הרועים רועי הדור ופרנסיו : ש"מ אף על לשון הרע · ולא פליג אמעשר דהא קאמר הכא שהם אוכלין דברים שאינן מתוקנין : בן גרים · בן גר וגיורת היה : של אומה זו · רומיים : שווקין · סדר מושב שווקי עיירות וחוצותיהן : וסיפר דבריהם · לתלמידיו או לאביו ואמו ולא להשמיען למלכות ונשמעו על ידו למלכות : יתעלה · להיות ראש המדברים : איברי להו חרובא · לאכול פירותיו ועינא דמיא לשתות : בחלא · בחול שהיו פושטין בגדיהם שלא יבלו ומכסין ערותן בחול : כרבי · חורשים : ועוסקין בחיי שעה · דאפשר על ידי נכרים והקב"ה מחלק מזון וריוח לעושי רצונו : משפט רשעים בגיהנם י"ב חדש · שנאמר (ישעיה סו) והיה מדי חדש בחדשו ומדי שבת בשבתו יבא כל בשר אף הגדולים בו במשמע מה שבתות למיני שלהם אף חדשים למיני שלהן והאי ודאי בפושעי גיהנם משתעי דכתיב לעיל מיניה ויצאו וראו בפגרי האנשים הפושעים בי הכי תני לה בסדר עולם (פ"ו) : די לעולם · בעוסקי תורה אני ואתה : תרי מדאני · חבילות של הדס להריח בשבת : מדאני · כמו מעדנות כימה (איוב לח) : אריך · מתקן ומחליק : פילי · בקעים סדקים מחמת החול : וקמצוותו ליה · לר' שמעון שהדמעות מלוחין ומכאיבין את המכה בתחלתן : אתקין מילתא · כדרך שעשה יעקב כשניצול מיד עשו : שלם בגופו · שנתרפא מצלעתו : שלם בתורתו · שלא שכח תלמודו מפני טורח הדרך : תיקן להם · דברי חן ונויה ולי נראה מויקן את חלקת השדה לשון תיקון : ואית

גליון הש"ס

שם א"ל לבריה נשים דעתן קלה עליהן · עי' מג"א סס"י קנ"ו : שם בעידן צלויי לבשו · עיין לעיל דף יא ע"א תוס' ד"ה כגון רשב"י : גמ' במערתא אתא אליהו · בירושלמי פ"ט דשביעית הוא בענין אחר ועוד שם ענינים נפלאים מרשב"י :

[ברכות סא.]

[תרגום של ויפשיטו ויפלתו ועי' רש"י כתובות סב: ד"ה כאי תנא וכו' ורש"י סוטה מ: ד"ה בכגי אית לה]

[נ"י' הערוך מדני פי' פתן פיין מובלט וכוא מע"ן כדכ ז"ב מעדנות כימה איוב ל"ח ע"ל ועי' סוכה יג: וברש"י שם ד"ה ראשי מעדנים וכו' ולכאורה טוב לגרוס הכא בגמרא וברש"י מעדני אסא]

[ברכות סג: מנחות קג:]

[שנאמר וממקדשי תחלו (יחזקאל ט) כך כתב רש"י כתובות ח: ד"ה תשיב אף]

ע"ז ב

[קידושין פ:]

[עי' תוספות לעיל יא. ד"ה כגון ר"ש]

[לעיל י· ביצה טו· תענית כא·]

[עדיות פ"ב מי' ר"ה יז·]

[כלומר שורך בשר גופו ומתקנו שרוך ע"ש בערך א]

Our Rabbis taught: Croup comes to the world [33b] on account of [neglect of] tithes.[12] R. Eleazar b. R. Jose said: On account of slander. Said Raba—others maintain, R. Joshua b. Levi—what verse [teaches this]? *But the king shall rejoice in God: Everyone that sweareth by Him shall glory; For the mouth of them that speak lies shall be stopped* [yissaker].[13]

The scholars propounded: Does R. Eleazar son of R. Jose say, [Only] on account of slander, or perhaps on account of slander too?—Come and hear: For when our Rabbis entered the 'vineyard' a in Yabneh,[1] R. Judah, R. Eleazar son of R. Jose and R. Simeon were present, and this question was raised before them: why does this affliction commence in the bowels and end in the throat? Thereupon R. Judah son of R. Ila'i, the first speaker on all occasions[2] answered and said: Though the kidneys counsel, the heart gives understanding,[3] and the tongue gives form,[4] yet the mouth completes it. R. Eleazar son of R. Jose answered: Because they eat unclean food therewith. 'Unclean food!' can you think so?[5] Rather [say] because they eat unfit food.[6] R. Simeon answered and said, As a punishment for the neglect of study.[7] Said they to him. Let women prove it![8]—That is because they restrain their husbands [from study]. Let Gentiles prove it![9]—That is because they restrain Israel. Let children prove it!—That is because they make their fathers to neglect [study].[10] Then let school-children prove it!—There it is as R. Gorion. For R. Gorion—others state, R. Joseph son of R. Shemaiah—said: When there are righteous men in the generation, the righteous are seized [by death] for the [sins of the] generation; when there are no righteous in a generation, school-children are seized for the generation.[11] R. Isaac b. Ze'iri—others state, R. Simeon b. Nezira—said: Which verse [teaches this]? *If thou know not, O thou fairest among women, Go thy way forth* b *by the footsteps of the flock*, etc.,[1] and we interpret this as [referring to] the goats which are taken in pledge for the [debts of the] shepherds. Thus this proves that he said on account of slander *too*. This proves it.

Now, why is he [R. Judah son of R. Ila'i] called the first speaker on all occasions?—For R. Judah, R. Jose, and R. Simeon were sitting, and Judah, a son of proselytes, was sitting near them. R. Judah commenced [the discussion] by observing, 'How fine are the works of this people![2] They have made streets, they have built bridges, they have erected baths.' R. Jose was silent. R. Simeon b. Yoḥai answered and said, 'All that they made they made for themselves; they built market-places, to set harlots in them; baths, to rejuvenate themselves; bridges, to levy tolls for them.' Now, Judah the son of proselytes went and related their talk,[3] which reached[4] the government. They decreed: Judah, who exalted [us], shall be exalted;[5] Jose, who was silent, shall be exiled to Sepphoris;[6] Simeon, who censured, let him be executed.

He and his son went and hid themselves in the Beth Hamidrash, [and] his wife brought him bread and a jug of water and they

(12) Rashi: one who eats untithed food (*tebel*) is liable to death by a divine visitation, which takes the form of croup. Having sinned through his throat (eating), he is punished through his throat. (13) Ps. LXIII, 12. *Yissaker* is connected here with *askera*, croup.

a (1) The famous town north west of Jerusalem, the seat of the Sanhedrin and R. Joḥanan b. Zakkai's academy after the destruction of the Temple. Sittings were held in a 'vineyard', i.e., members sat in rows similar to vines in a vineyard. (2) The reason is given below. (3) 'Counsel' and 'understanding' were ascribed to these two organs respectively. Rashi in Ber. 61a s.v. וחלב quotes: Ps. XVI, 7: *yea, my kidney* (E.V. *reins*) *admonish me in the night seasons*, and Isa. VI, 10: *and he understands with his heart*. (4) To the words. Lit., 'cuts'. (5) That does not merit so heavy a punishment, particularly as only *terumah* and sacred food are forbidden when defiled. (6) I.e., untithed. (7) Which is likewise performed with the mouth. (8) Who are not bidden to study (Ḳid. 29b), and yet suffer from croup. (cf. Soṭ. III, 4). (9) Who are not bidden to study the Torah, and are yet subject to it. (10) By childish demands on their time;—a harsh doctrine, but it is abandoned. (11) This is not to be confused with the doctrine of vicarious atonement, which is rejected by Judaism.

b (1) Cant. I, 8. The Midrash and the Targum interpret the whole of this poem as a dialogue between God and Israel. This verse is explained: If you do not understand how to keep God's commandments, go and learn them for the sake of the flocks, *sc.* your children, who otherwise may die on your account. (2) The Romans. (3) Rashi: to his parents, without evil intent. (4) Lit., 'and they were heard by'. (5) With the privilege of being the first to speak on all occasions. (6) In Upper Galilee.

◁ *For the continuation of the English translation of this page see overleaf.*

עין משפט
נר מצוה

קבא א מיי׳ פ״ז מהל׳ דעות הלכה ס:

על המעשר ר׳ אלעזר בר׳ יוסי אומר על לשון הרע אמר רבא ואיתימא ריב״ל מאי קראה °והמלך ישמח באלהים יתהלל כל הנשבע בו כי יסכר פי דוברי שקר איבעיא להו רבי אלעזר ברבי יוסי על לשון הרע קאמר או דילמא אף על לשון הרע נמי קאמר ת״ש כשנכנסו רבותינו לכרם ביבנה היה שם רבי יהודה ור׳ אלעזר בר׳ יוסי ור״ש נשאלה שאלה זו בפניהם מכה זו מפני מה מתחלת בבני מעיים וגומרת בפה נענה רבי יהודה ברבי אלעאי *ראש המדברים בכל מקום ואמר אע״פ *שכליות יועצות ולב מבין ולשון מחתך פה גומר נענה רבי אלעזר ברבי יוסי ואמר מפני שאוכלין בה דברים טמאין דברים טמאים סלקא דעתך אלא שאוכלין בה דברים שאינן מתוקנים נענה ר׳ שמעון ואמר בעון ביטול תורה אמרו לו נשים יוכיחו שמבטלות את בעליהן נכרים יוכיחו שמבטלין את ישראל תינוקות יוכיחו שמבטלין את אביהן תינוקות של בית רבן יוכיחו התם כדרבי גוריון דאמר רבי גוריון ואיתימא רב יוסף ברבי שמעיה בזמן שהצדיקים בדור צדיקים נתפסים על הדור *אין צדיקים בדור תינוקות של בית רבן נתפסים על הדור א״ר יצחק בר זעירי ואמרי לה א״ר שמעון בן נזירא מאי קראה °אם לא תדעי לך היפה בנשים צאי לך בעקבי הצאן וגו׳ ואמרינן גדיים הממושכנין על הרועים ש״מ אף על לשון הרע נמי קאמר ש״מ ואמאי קרו ליה ראש המדברים בכל מקום דיתבי רבי יהודה ורבי יוסי ורבי שמעון ויתיב יהודה בן גרים גבייהו פתח ר׳ יהודה ואמר כמה נאים מעשיהן של אומה זו תקנו שווקים תקנו גשרים תקנו מרחצאות ר׳ יוסי שתק נענה רשב״י ואמר כל מה שתקנו לא *תקנו אלא לצורך עצמן תקנו שווקין להושיב בהן זונות מרחצאות לעדן בהן עצמן גשרים ליטול מהן מכס הלך יהודה בן גרים °וסיפר דבריהם ונשמעו למלכות אמרו יהודה שעילה יתעלה יוסי ששתק יגלה לציפורי שמעון שגינה יהרג אזל הוא ובריה טשו בי מדרשא כל יומא הוה מייתי להו דביתהו ריפתא וכוזא דמיא וכרכי כי תקיף גזירתא °א״ל לבריה *נשים דעתן קלה עליהן דילמא מצערי לה ומגליא לן אזלו טשו במערתא איתרחיש ניסא איברי להו חרובא ועינא דמיא והוו *משלחי מנייהו והוו יתבי עד צוארייהו בחלא כולי יומא גרסי °בעידן צלויי לבשו מיכסו *ומצלו והדר משלחי מנייהו כי היכי דלא ליבלו איתבו תריסר שני °במערתא אתא אליהו וקם אפיתחא דמערתא אמר מאן לודעיה לבר יוחי דמית קיסר ובטיל גזירתיה נפקו חזו אינשי דקא כרבי וזרעי אמר *מניחין חיי עולם ועוסקין בחיי שעה כל מקום שנותנין עיניהן מיד נשרף יצתה בת קול ואמרה להם להחריב עולמי יצאתם חיזרו למערתכם הדור אזול איתיבו תריסר ירחי שתא אמרי *משפט רשעים בגיהנם י״ב חדש יצתה בת קול ואמרה צאו ממערתכם נפקו כל היכא דהוה מחי ר׳ אלעזר הוה מסי ר״ש אמר לו בני די לעולם אני ואתה בהדי פניא דמעלי שבתא חזו ההוא סבא דהוה נקיט תרי *מדאני אסא ורהיט בין השמשות אמרו ליה הני למה לך אמר להו לכבוד שבת ותיסגי לך בחד חד כנגד °זכור וחד כנגד °שמור א״ל לבריה חזי כמה חביבין מצות על ישראל יתיב דעתייהו שמע ר׳ פנחס בן יאיר חתניה ונפק לאפיה עייליה לבי בניה הוה קא *אריך ליה לבישריה חזי דהוה ביה פילי בגופיה הוה קא בכי וקא נתרו דמעת עיניה וקמצוחא ליה א״ל אוי לי שראיתיך בכך א״ל אשריך שראיתני בכך שאילמלא לא ראיתני בכך לא מצאת בי כך דמעיקרא כי הוה מקשי ר״ש בן יוחי קושיא הוה מפרק ליה ר׳ פנחס בן יאיר תריסר פירוקי לסוף כי הוה מקשי ר״פ בן יאיר קושיא הוה מפרק ליה רשב״י עשרין וארבעה פירוקי אמר הואיל ואיתרחיש ניסא איזיל אתקין מילתא דכתיב °ויבא יעקב שלם ואמר רב שלם בגופו שלם בממונו שלם בתורתו °ויחן את פני העיר אמר רב מטבע תיקן להם ושמואל אמר שווקים תיקן להם ור׳ יוחנן אמר מרחצאות תיקן להם אמר איכא מילתא דבעי לתקוני אמרו ליה איכא דוכתא דאית ביה ספק טומאה ואית

תוספות

ה״ג ר״ת הלך רבי יהודה בן גרים וסיפר דברים ונשמעו למלכות ויש ספרים שכתב בהן יהודה ואין נראה לרבינו תם דאמרינן בפרק קמא דמועד קטן (דף ט.) כי הוו מיפטרי ר׳ יהודה בן גרים ור״ש בן חלפתא מר׳ שמעון בן יוחי אמר ליה לבריה אנשים הללו אנשי צורה הם זיל גבייהו דליברכוך מכלל דגברא רבה היה ובסוף שמעתא ל״ג גל של עצמות בלשון גנאי אלא נח נפשיה:

רש״י

על המעשר · האוכל פירותיו טבלים והוא במיתה בידי שמים וזוהי מיתתו מדה במדה דדרך גרוט נכנס במעיו : יסכר · אסכרה : לכרם · זה בית המדרש שיושבין שורות שורות ככרם כך מפורש בירושלמי בברכות : מכה זו · אסכרה : ראש המדברים · במלות המלך שלוה עליו לדבר תחלה בכל מקום כדלקמן : פה גומר · לשון הרע והוא בא על כך לפיכך מתחיל במעיים ומסיים בפה שהלב מבין לספר לשון הרע ובודה הדברים מלבו : פה גומר · הכל יוצא מן הגרון : דברים טמאים סלקא דעתך · וכי עונשה מיתה דבשלמא לשון הרע עונשה מיתה דכתיב (תהלים קא) מלשני בסתר רעהו אותו אצמית : מתוקנין · מעושרים שהטבל במיתה בידי שמים כדיליף באלו הן הנשרפים (סנהדרין דף פג׳) : בעון בטול תורה · דעונש נמי מיתה כדאמרן מקרא נדרש לפני פניו למען ירבו ימיכם הא אם לא תלמדו יתמעטו : נשים יוכיחו · שאינן מצוות על דברי תורה דכתיב ולמדתם אותם את בניכם ולא בנותיכם ומתות באסכרה אמר לכן אף הן מבטלות את בעליהן: תינוקות יוכיחו · שאינן בני לימוד אמר לכן אף הן בעון שמבטלים את אביהם להוליכן לחמה ולצונן ולפייסן באגוזים : של בית רבן · לא בטלין ולא מבטלין : אם לא תדעי לך · לשמור מצותי לאי לך ובקשי רחמים בזכות עקבי הצאן אבות הראשונים שהיו רגלי הצאן וחזוקם ורעי בזכותן את גדיותיך תינוקות שלך שלא יתפשו על משכנות הרועים רועי הדור ופרנסיו : ש״מ אף על לשון הרע · ולא פליג אמעשר דהא קאמר הכא שהם אוכלין דברים שאינן מתוקנין : בן גרים · בן גר וגיורת היה : של אומה זו · רומיים : שווקין · סדר מושב שווקי עיירות וחוצותיהן : וסיפר דבריהם · לתלמידיו או לאביו ואמו ולא להשמיען למלכות ונשמעו על ידו למלכות : יתעלה · להיות ראש המדברים : איברי להו חרובא · לאכול פירותיו ועינא דמיא לשתות : בחלא · בחול שהיו פושטין בגדיהם שלא יבלו ומכסין ערותן בחול : כרבי · חורשים : ועוסקין בחיי שעה · דאפשר על ידי נכרים והקב״ה מחלק מזון וריוח לעושי רצונו : משפט רשעים בגיהנם י״ב חדש · שנאמר (ישעיה סו) ואשם לא תכבה והיה מדי חדש בחדשו ומדי שבת בשבתו יבא כל בשר אף הנדונים בו במשמע מה שבתות למיני שלהם אף חדשים למיני שלהן והאי ודאי בפושעי גיהנם משתעי דכתיב לעיל מיניה ויצאו וראו בפגרי האנשים הפושעים בי הכי תני לה בסדר עולם (פ״ו) : די לעולם · בעוסקי תורה אני ואתה : תרי מדאני · חבילות של הדס להריח בשבת : מדאני · כמו מעדנות כימה (איוב לח) : אריך · מתקן ומחליק : פילי · בקעים סדקים מחמת החול : וקמצווחו ליה · לר׳ שמעון שהדמעות מלוחין ומכאיבין את המכה בתחלתן : אתקין מילתא · כדרך שעשה יעקב כשניצול מיד עשו : שלם בגופו · שנתרפא מצלעתו : שלם בתורתו · שלא שכח תלמודו מפני טורח הדרך : תיקן להם · דברי חן ונוי ולי נראה מויקן את חלקת השדה לשון תיקון :
ואית

תורה אור
תהלים פג
שיר א
שמות כ
בראשית לג
שם

גליון הש״ס
שם א״ל לבריה נשים דעתן קלה עליהן · עי׳ מג״א סס״י קנ״ו :
שם בעידן צלויי לבשו · עיין לעיל דף יא ע״א תוס׳ ד״ה כגון רשב״י :
גמ׳ במערתא אתא אליהו · בירושלמי פ״ט דשביעית הוא בענין אחר ועוד שם ענינים נפלאים מרשב״י :

[ברכות סא.]
[תרגום שני ויפשיטו וישלחו ועי׳ רש״י כתובות סב: ד״ה האי תנא וכו׳ ורש״י סוטה ח: ד״ה בכגי אית לה]
[גיר׳ הערוך מדני פי׳ מין עירן מובלע והוא מענין כדכ ג״כ מעדנות כימה איוב ל״ח ע״כ ועי׳ סוכה יג: וברש״י שם ד״ה ראשי מעדנים וכו׳ ולכאורה טוב לגרוס ככה בגמרא וברש״י מעדני אסא]

מסורת הש״ס
[ברכות סג: מנחות קג:]
[שנאמר וממקדשי תחלו (יחזקאל ט) כך כתב רש״י כתובות ח: ד״ה תשיב אח]
ע״ז ב
[קידושין פ:]
[עי׳ תוספות לעיל יא· ד״ה כגון ר״ש]
[לעיל י· ביצה טו: תענ׳ כא·]
[עדיות פ״ב מ״י ר״ה יז·]
דברים ה
[כלומר פורך בשר גופו ומתקנו ערוך ע״ש בערך א]

Continuation of translation from previous page as indicated by ◁

dined.[7] [But] when the decree became more severe he said to his son, Women are of unstable temperament: she[8] may be put to the torture and expose us.'[9] So they went and hid in a cave. A miracle occurred and a carob-tree and a water well were created for them. They would strip their garments and sit up to their necks in sand. The whole day they studied; when it was time for prayers they robed, covered themselves, prayed, and then put off their garments again, so that they should not wear out.
c Thus they dwelt twelve years in the cave.[1] Then Elijah came and stood at the entrance to the cave and exclaimed, Who will inform the son of Yoḥai that the emperor is dead and his decree annulled?[2] So they emerged. Seeing a man ploughing and sowing, they exclaimed, 'They forsake life eternal and engage in life temporal!' Whatever they cast their eyes upon was immediately burnt up. Thereupon a Heavenly Echo came forth and cried out, 'Have ye emerged to destroy My world: Return to your cave!'[3] So they returned and dwelt there twelve months, saying, 'The punishment[4] of the wicked in Gehenna is [limited to] twelve months.'[5] A Heavenly Echo then came forth and said, 'Go forth from your cave!' Thus they issued: wherever R. Eleazar wounded,[6] R. Simeon healed. Said he to him, 'My son! You and I are sufficient for the world.'[7] On the eve of the Sabbath before sunset they saw an old man holding two bundles of myrtle and running at twilight. What are these for?' they asked him. 'They are in honour of the Sabbath,' he replied.[8] 'But one should suffice you'?—One is for *'Remember'* and one for *'Observe.'*[9] Said he to his son, 'See how precious are the commandments to Israel.' Thereat their minds were set at ease.

R. Phinehas b. Ya'ir his son-in-law heard [thereof] and went
d out to meet him. He took him into the baths and massaged[1] his flesh. Seeing the clefts in his body[2] he wept and the tears streamed from his eyes, causing him additional pain. 'Woe to me that I see you in such a state!' he cried out. 'Happy are you that you see me thus,' he retorted, 'for if you did not see me in such a state you would not find me thus [learned].'[3] For originally, when R. Simeon b. Yoḥai raised a difficulty, R. Phinehas b. Ya'ir would give him twelve answers, whereas subsequently when R. Phinehas b. Ya'ir raised a difficulty, R. Simeon b. Yoḥai would give him twenty-four answers.

Since a miracle has occurred, said he, let me go and amend something, for it is written, *and Jacob came whole*[4] *[to the city of Shechem]*,[5] which Rab interpreted: bodily whole [sound], financially whole, and whole in his learning. *And he was gracious to the city:*[6] Rab said: He instituted coinage for them.[7] Samuel said: He instituted markets for them; R. Joḥanan said: He instituted baths for them. Is there ought that requires amending? he[8] asked. There is a place of doubtful uncleanness,[9] he was

(7) Lit., 'they wrapped (bread)'; a term derived from the custom of eating bread with a relish wrapped in it. (8) His wife. (9) The context shows that he was not censuring women for constitutional instability, but feared their weakness.

c (1) Notwithstanding its miraculous elements this story is substantially true. R. Simeon b. Yoḥai was persecuted very much by the Roman authorities; this explains his anti-Gentile (i.e., Roman) utterances, which are not illustrative of the Talmud as a whole. (2) Elijah the Prophet was believed to appear frequently to men; cf. *supra* 13*b*. (3) This story is a protest against super piety and an assertion that practical work is necessary for the world. Their return to the cave is thus depicted as a punishment, not a meritorious deed. (4) Lit., 'judgment'. (5) On 'Gehenna' v. *supra* 33*a*, n. c8. Judaism rejects on the whole the idea of eternal punishment, for punishment is regenerative, not vindictive, and therefore must terminate; v. M. Joseph, *Judaism as Creed and Life*, p. 145. (6) With a glance of his eyes. (7) Not to be taken literally. (8) Their fragrance is to beautify the Sabbath and lend cheer to it.—Contrary to the opinion of many, the Sabbath, in spite of its prohibitions, is and has been 'a day of delight' and spiritual nourishment to millions of observant Jews, not a day of gloom; v. Shechter, *Studies in Judaism*, p. 296. (9) Ex. XX, 8. *Remember the Sabbath day;* Deut. V, 12: *Observe the Sabbath day.*

d (1) Lit., 'dressed'. (2) Caused by the sand. (3) He felt that all his sufferings were compensated for by the knowledge he had gained. R. Simeon b. Yoḥai was one of the few Rabbis who devoted himself entirely to learning, 'his study being his profession' (*supra* 11*a*) not interrupting it even for prayer. (4) E.V. '*in peace*'. (5) Gen. XXXIII, 18. (6) Ibid.; *wa-yiḥan* is thus derived from *ḥanan*, to be gracious. E.V.: *and he encamped before the city.* (7) In place of barter. (8) R. Simeon b. Yoḥai. (9) A grave of human bones having been lost there.

informed, [34a] and priests have the trouble of going round it. Said he: Does any man know that there was a presumption of cleanness here?[10] A certain old man replied, Here [R. Johanan] b. Zakkai cut down lupines of *terumah*.[11] So he did likewise. Wherever it [the ground] was hard he declared it clean, while wherever it was loose he marked it out.[12] Said a certain old man. The son of Yoḥai has purified a cemetery![13] Said he, Had you not been with
a us, or even if you have been with us but did not vote,[1] you might have said well. But now that you were with us and voted with us,[2] it will be said, [Even] whores paint one another; how much more so scholars![3] He cast his eye upon him, and he died. Then he went out into the street and saw Judah, the son of proselytes. 'That man is still in the world!' he exclaimed. He cast his eyes upon him and he became[4] a heap of bones.

MISHNAH. ON THE EVE OF THE SABBATH JUST BEFORE NIGHT[5] A MAN MUST SAY THREE THINGS IN HIS HOUSE: HAVE YE RENDERED TITHES?[6] HAVE YE PREPARED THE 'ERUB?[7] KINDLE THE [SABBATH] LAMP. WHEN IT IS DOUBTFUL WHETHER IT IS NIGHT[8] OR NOT,[9] THAT WHICH IS CERTAINLY [UNTITHED] MAY NOT BE TITHED, UTENSILS MAY NOT BE IMMERSED,[10] AND THE LIGHTS MAY NOT BE KINDLED. BUT DEM'AI[11] MAY BE TITHED,[12] AN 'ERUB MAY BE PREPARED, AND HOT FOOD MAY BE STORED AWAY.[13]

GEMARA. Whence do we know it?—Said R. Joshua b. Levi, Scripture saith, *And thou shalt know that thy tent is in peace; and thou shalt visit thy habitation, and shalt not err.*[14]

Rabbah son of R. Huna said: Although the Rabbis said, A MAN MUST SAY THREE THINGS, etc., yet they must be said with sweet reasonableness, so that they may be accepted from him. R. Ashi observed: I had not heard this [statement] of Rabbah
b b. R. Huna, but inferred[1] it by logic.

This is self contradictory. You say, ON THE EVE OF THE SABBATH JUST BEFORE NIGHT A MAN MUST SAY THREE THINGS IN HIS HOUSE: only just before night, but not when it is doubtful whether it is night or not;[2] then you teach, WHEN IT IS DOUBTFUL WHETHER IT IS NIGHT OR NOT ... AN 'ERUB MAY BE PREPARED? (Mnemonic: Self, Pruning, Bird, Cord, Silk.)[3]—Said R. Abba in the name of R. Ḥiyya b. Ashi in Rab's name: There is no difficulty: the one refers to *'erub* of boundaries; the other to the *'erub* of courtyards.[4] Now Raba said: If two men said to one person, 'Go forth and place an *'erub* for us', and he placed an *'erub* for one while it is yet day, and for the other he made the *'erub* at twilight, and the *'erub* of him for whom he placed it by day was eaten at twilight, and the *'erub* of him for whom he placed it at twilight was eaten after nightfall, both acquire [their] *'erub*.[5] What will you: if twilight is day, the second should acquire, but not the first; while if twilight is night, the first should acquire,
c but not the second?—Twilight is doubtful,[1] and a doubt in respect to a Rabbinical law is judged leniently.[2]

Raba said: Why was it said, One must not store [food] after nightfall [even] in a substance that does not add heat?[3] For fear lest he make it boil.[4] Said Abaye to him: If so, let us forbid it at twilight too?—The average pot is at the boil, he replied.[5]

(10) Before the doubt arose, was there a time when this place was assumed to be clean, so that it enjoyed the status of cleanness? (11) I.e., he planted them while *terumah* and cut them down after they had grown. (12) As unclean. In the Pesiḳta and J. Shab. VII it is stated that a miracle happened and the dead floated upwards (v. Rashi). (13) Derisively.
a (1) Lit., 'you were not counted'.—R. Simeon b. Yoḥai had acted in accordance with the decision of the majority of the Rabbis. (2) In favour of this. (3) Surely they should pay regard to each other's honour. (4) Lit., 'he made him'. (5) Lit., with darkness (setting in). (6) Of the food we are to eat on the Sabbath. (7) V. Glos. The *'erub* referred to is for courtyards; v. *supra* 6a, n. b7. (8) Lit., 'dark'. (9) I.e., at twilight. (10) Made fit for use by means of *ṭebillah* (immersion) in a ritual bath (*miḳweh*). Both these acts render objects fit for use, which is forbidden at twilight. (11) V. Glos. (12) Because the probability is that tithes have already been rendered, and thus this tithing does not really make it fit. (13) To retain its heat. (14) Job V. 24. She'eltoth 63 explains: If an *'erub* has not been prepared, so that the carrying of utensils is forbidden, or if the lights have not been kindled, or the tithes rendered, so that the food may not be eaten, the resultant inconvenience and lack of cheer are inimical to the peace of the household.
b (1) Lit., 'adduced'. V. Marginal Gloss. (2) Which implies that there is no purpose in his saying it then, since an *'erub* may not be prepared then. (3) These indicate statements made in the Tractate by R. Abba in the name of R. Ḥiyya on Rab's authority. Doubt arose as to the authorship of some of these, and so this mnemonic was given. 'Self' indicates the present passage, 'This is self contradictory'. For the others v. *infra* 73b (pruning); 107a (bird), 113a (cord) and 124b (silk).—Maharsha. (4) V. *supra* 6a, n. b7. The limitation of boundaries was held to be either Biblical or partaking of the nature of a Scriptural law; therefore the *'erub*, whereby that limitation is extended, really makes the territory beyond these boundaries accessible on the Sabbath, and consequently its preparation is forbidden at twilight, when the Sabbath may have commenced, although where it was prepared at twilight, it is effective. But the prohibition of carrying between houses and courtyards was merely a measure of stringency; hence the *'erub* permits only what might have been permitted in any case, and so it may be prepared at twilight. (5) 'Acquire their *'erub*' means that the *'erub* confers upon them the rights for which it is set. Now, an *'erub* must be prepared by day and be still in existence when the Sabbath commences, otherwise it is invalid. Now, in respect of the first, whose *'erub* was placed by day and eaten at twilight, twilight is regarded as night, i.e., the commencement of the Sabbath, when the *'erub* was still in existence. Whilst in respect of the second twilight is regarded as day, so that it was placed by day.—Rashi: the reference is to the *'erub* of boundaries which, though it may not be set at the outset at twilight, is nevertheless effective. Tosaf.: the *'erub* of courtyards is meant.
c (1) Whether it is day or night. (2) The law of *'erub* is Rabbinical, as stated above. (3) The Mishnah states that storing away food is permitted at twilight, whence it follows that it is forbidden after nightfall. And the reference must be to a substance which does not add heat, for if it does, food may not be stored in it even by day (*infra* 47b). (4) When he comes to put it away, he may find it cold and heat it up first, which is the equivalent of cooking on the Sabbath. (5) At twilight, because it has only just been removed from the fire.

מסורת הש"ס

עין משפט נר מצוה

ואית להו צערא לכהנים לאקופי אמר איכא איניש דידע דאיתחזק הכא טהרה א"ל ההוא סבא כאן קיצץ *בן זכאי תורמסי תרומה עבד איהו נמי הכי כל היכא דהוה קשי טהריה וכל היכא דהוה רפי צייניה °אמר ההוא סבא °טיהר בן יוחי בית הקברות א"ל אילמלי *(לא) היית עמנו ואפי' היית עמנו ולא נמנית עמנו יפה אתה אומר עכשיו שהיית עמנו ונמנית עמנו יאמרו זונות מפרכסות זו את זו תלמידי חכמים לא כל שכן יהב ביה עיניה ונח נפשיה נפק לשוקא חזייה לידהודה בן גרים אמר עדיין יש לזה בעולם *נתן בו עיניו ועשהו גל של עצמות:

מתני' *ג' דברים צריך אדם לומר בתוך ביתו ערב שבת עם חשכה עשרתם ערבתם הדליקו את הנר °ספק חשכה ספק אינו חשכה אין מעשרין את הודאי ואין מטבילין את הכלים ואין מדליקין את הנרות °אבל *מעשרין את הדמאי ומערבין וטומנין את החמין:

גמ' מנא הני מילי א"ר יהושע בן לוי אמר קרא °וידעת כי שלום אהלך ופקדת נוך ולא *תחטא אמר רבה בר רב הונא *אע"ג דאמור רבנן שלשה דברים צריך אדם לומר וכו' צריך למימרינהו בניחותא כי היכי דליקבלינהו מיניה אמר רב אשי אנא לא שמיע לי הא דרבה בר רב הונא וקיימתי מסברא הא גופא קשיא אמרת שלשה דברים צריך אדם לומר בתוך ביתו ערב שבת עם חשכה עם חשכה אין ספק חשכה ספק אינו חשכה לא והדר תני ספק חשכה ספק אינו חשכה מערב: *סימן °*בגופיא *זימרא *ציפרא *בחבלא *דמילתא: א"ר אבא אמר רב חייא בר אשי אמר רב לא קשיא כאן בעירובי תחומין כאן בעירובי חצרות *ואמר *רבא אמרו לו שנים צא וערב עלינו לאחד עירב עליו מבעוד יום ולאחד עירב עליו בין השמשות זה שעירב עליו מבעוד יום נאכל עירובו בין השמשות וזה שעירב עליו בין השמשות נאכל עירובו משחשכה שניהם קנה עירוב מה נפשך אי בין השמשות יממא הוא בתרא ליקני קמא לא ליקני ואי בין השמשות ליליא הוא קמא ליקני בתרא לא ליקני בין השמשות ספקא הוא *וספקא דרבנן לקולא: *(ואמר) רבא מפני מה אמרו *אין טומנין בדבר שאינו מוסיף הבל משחשכה גזרה שמא ירתיח אמר ליה אביי אי הכי בין השמשות נמי ניגזר א"ל סתם קדירות רותחות הן ואמר רבא מפני

*[נ"ל אמר]

תורה אור

רש"י

ואית להו צערא לאקופי · שהיה אותו שוק שהספק בו מקום מעבר העיר לרבים והכהנים לא היו יכולין ליכנס שם מפני טומאה וצריך להקיף דרך אחר ארוך: איכא דידע דאיתחזק טהרה · בהאי שוק מימיו שלא היה בית הקברות גמור ולא ניתן לפנותו: כאן קיצץ בן זכאי · שתלן ועקרן לאחר גידולן: תורמסי תרומה · הצריכות לשמרן בטהרה וגם הוא היה כהן כדאמרינן [*בתוספתא דפרה] (פ"ג) אם מה שעשו ידי שכחתי: עבד איהו נמי הכי · היה מקלן תורמסין ומשליכן שם ונעשה נס ולף המת במקום שהוא שם וציינו למקום הקבר הכי מפרש בפסיקתא דפרשת העומר ובסדר זרעים ירושלמי*): היית · במעמד: ונמנית · הסכמת לדעתנו להיות מן המנין: מפרכסות זו את זו · את שער חברתה להיות נאה: גל מעצמות · כמת שנרקב בשרו ונפל מזמן הרבה:

מתני' עם חשכה · שאם ימהר להזכירם מבעוד יום יפשעו ויאמרו עדיין יש שהות: עשרתם · פירות האילן לסעודת שבת שאף אכילת עראי של שבת קובעת למעשר כדאמרינן במסכת ביצה (דף לד:) דשבת עונג איקרי מכל שהוא הוי עונג: ערבתם · ערובי *תחומין וחצירות והני תרי שייכי למימרינהו בלשון שאלה דשמא כבר עשו אבל בנר לא שייך הדלקתם דדבר הנראה לעין הוא: ספק חשכה · כגון בין השמשות אין מעשרין את הודאי דתיקון מעליא הוא אע"ג דשבות בעלמא היא קסבר גזרו על השבות אף על בהש"מ: ואין מטבילין את הכלים · דהוי נמי שבות כדאמרינן במסכת ביצה (דף יח·) דנראה כמתקן כלי: ואין מדליקין את הנרות · כ"ש דספיקא דאורייתא היא וזו ואין צריך לומר זו קתני: אבל מעשרין את הדמאי · דלא דמי למתקן דרוב ע"ה מעשרין הן: ומערבין · עירוב ובגמרא פריך הא תנן לעיל עם חשכה ערבתם מקמי דליהוי ספק: וטומנין את החמין · נותנן בקופה של מוכין להיות חומם משתמר בהן אבל משחשכה ודאי אין טומנין בהן כדמפרש בגמ':

גמ' עם חשכה · מבעוד יום הוא ויש שהות לעשר ולערב(א): בעירובי תחומין · תיקון מעליא דאסמכוה רבנן תחומין אקראי ואפי' למאן דאמר תחומין דרבנן כדאמרינן בעירובין (דף נא·) ילפינן מקום ממקום ומקום מניסה כו' אבל עירובי חצרות חומרא בעלמא הוא ולא מיקרי שביתה מעלייתא וספקא דבין השמשות שפיר דמי: בין השמשות קונה עירוב · שהוא תחילת קדושת היום: נאכל · שאכלו כלב או אדם: שעירב עליו מבעוד יום · הניח עירוב לסוף התחום מבעוד יום ולא הספיק להחשיך ממש עד שנאכל בין השמשות: שניהם קנו עירוב · דלגבי האי שנאכל בין השמשות משוינן ליה ליליא ואמרינן כבר קדש היום בעוד העירוב קיים וקנה עירוב דהלכה כר' יוסי דאמר בעירובין (דף לה·) ספק עירוב כשר ולגבי דהאי שהונח עליו בין השמשות ונתקיים עד שחשכה משוינן לבין השמשות יממא ועדיין לא קדש היום כשהונח ונמצא שהיה שם כבר בשעת קניית עירוב: בתרא ליקני · זה שהונח עליו בין השמשות: קמא לא ליקני · שהרי נאכל מבעוד יום: ה"ג ספקא דרבנן היא · כלומר הא מילתא דמספקא לן אי בין השמשות יממא או ליליא במילתא דרבנן איתרע לן בעירובי תחומין דרבנן וכל ספקא דרבנן לקולא: ה"ג אמר רבא מפני מה אמרו אין טומנין בדבר שאינו מוסיף הבל · כגון צמר ומוכין: משחשכה · כדתנן במתניתין וטומנין את החמין טעמא דספק חשכה הא ודאי חשכה אין טומנין וסתם הטמנה בדבר שאינו מוסיף הבל דאילו בדבר המוסיף הבל אפי' מבעוד יום אסור כדתנן בפ"ד (דף מז:) אין טומנין לא בגפת כו': גזירה שמא ימצא קדרתו שנצטננה כשירצה להטמינה וירתיחנה תחילה ונמצא מבשל בשבת: אי הכא בין השמשות נמי ניגזר · דהא שבות מעלייתא היא דהא איכא גזירת איסור דאורייתא ותנא דמתניתין אית ליה דגזרו על השבות ביה"ש דקתני אין מעשרין את הודאי: רותחות הן · שסמוך לביה"ש הוא מעבירם מעל האור וליכא למיחש לשמא נצטננה וירתיחנה:

תוספות

עבד איהו נמי הכי · מפר"ת כמו יעקב אבינו ותיקן מילתא:

כל היכא דהוה קשי טהריה · כדאיתא בנדה בפרק האשה (דף סא· ושם) דתניא אמר רבי יוסי בן שאול מעשה בסלע שהיו מחזיקין בה טומאה כו' אמר להו הביאו לי סדינין הביאו לו ושראן במים ופרסו עליו מקום טומאה לח מקום טהרה נגוב:

לא קשיא כאן בעירובי תחומין כו' · נראה לר"ת כפירוש הקונטרס דבעירובי תחומין מחמרינן משום דאית להו סמך מן המקרא וכן פר"ח וכן יש בירושלמי וכן משמע בפרק מי שהוציאוהו (עירובין דף מו: ושם) גבי הא דקאמר הלכה כדברי המיקל בעירוב רב פפא אמר אילטריך סד"א ה"מ עירובי חצרות אבל בעירובי תחומין אימא לא ומעיקרא היה מפרש ר"ת דעירובי חצרות חמירי טפי דאין מערבין אלא בפת כדמשמע בפרק הדר (שם דף עא:) ובחלון (שם דף פא· ושם) אבל בעירובי תחומין מערבין בכל דבר חוץ ממים ומלח *ואין נראה דהא ר"מ ס"ל דתחומין דאורייתא בפרק בכל מערבין (שם לה·) ואפ"ה אית ליה בהדר* דעירובי חצרות בפת ובעירובי תחומין מערבין בכל דבר דלא אשכחן דפליג ר"מ אהתם משנה דבכל מערבין וטעמא דמקילי בתחומים דלא בעי פת משום *דאין מערבין אלא לדבר מצוה:

נאכל עירובו משחשכה · לאו דווקא וה"ה לא נאכל:

שניהם קנו עירוב · פירש בקונטרס דרבא איירי בעירובי תחומין וכן משמע לשון לא וערב ולע"פ דספק חשכה אין מערבין עירובי תחומין ה"מ לכתחילה אבל בדיעבד כשר כר' יוסי דאמר (עירובין פ"ג דף לה·) ספק עירוב כשר וקשה לרשב"א דר' יוסי לית ליה התם גבי נפל עליו גל או נשרף או תרומה ונטמאה ספק עירוב [כשר] אלא · משום חזקה כדתניא התם בהדיא (דף לו·) כיצד אמר רבי יוסי ספק עירוב כשר כו' אבל בספק כי הכא שהניחו בין השמשות או נאכל בין השמשות לא מכשר ומפר"ת דהכא מיירי בעירובי חצרות וכן פר"ח וכן מוכח בסוף הדר (שם דף עו·) ולא אשכחן נמי דלאו חוץ לעיר קאמר כמו לא ושכור לנו פועלים (ב"מ דף פג·)*: ורבי

רבינו חננאל

מתניתין ג' דברים צריך אדם לומר בתוך כו' · ואסיקנא צריך ליימרינהו בנידותא כי היכי דנקבלו אינשי ביתיה מיניה מנא לן דצריך הדלקת נר בשבת שנאמר וידעת כי שלום אהלך וגו' ואין שלום אלא באור שנא' וירא אלהים את האור כי טוב ואוקמינן הא דתנן הכא ערבתם עם השכה הן עירובי תהומין והא דתני בסיפא בספק חשיכה ומערבין וטומנין את החמין ערובי חצרות אמר רבא אמר (לשנים צאו ועירבו עלי)[אמרו לו שנים צא וערב עלינו] פי' ערובי חצרות (אחד) [לאחד] עירב עליו מבע"י (ואחד) [ולאחד] עירב עליו בין השמשות זה שעירב עליו מבע"י נאכל ערובו בין השמשות וזה שעירב עליו בין השמשות נאכל עירובו משחשיכה שניהם קנו עירוב. מה נפשך וכו' ואסיקנא בין השמשות ספק מן היום הוא ספק מן הלילה הוא ועירובי חצירות דרבנן וספק דבריהם להקל: **ירושלמי** הדא דתימר בעירובי חצרות אבל בעירובי תחומין דבר תורה **וטומנין** החמין אמר רבא מפני מה אמרו אין טומנין בדבר המוסיף ואפילו מבע"י גזרה שמא ירתיח *) בין השמשות ומפני מה אמרו אין טומנין אפילו בדבר שאינו מוסיף משחשיכה גזרה שמא יטמין

*) נראה דחסר כאן כדברי רבינו וצ"ל וכבין השמשות לא גזרינן דבביה"ש סתם קדרות רותחות הן:

רב נסים גאון

אמר רבא מפני מה אין טומנין אפילו בדבר שאינו מוסיף הבל משחשכה (מה שחשכה) דבר המוסיף הוא הנזכר בבמה טומנין (לקמן מז) גפת וזבל ומלח וסיד וחול ודבר שאינו מוסיף תבן וזגין ומוכין ...ין בזמן שהן יבשים ומה שהתירה המשנה מהטמנה מבעוד יום אבל בשבת לא כמו שאמרה ספק חשיכה ספק אינה חשיכה טומנין את החמין אבל ודאי חשיכה אין טומנין כלל ואפילו בדבר שאינו מוסיף ופירוש דילה בתוספתא (פרק רביעי) אין טומנין את החמין בתחילה ובסוף פרק במה טומנין (דף נא) תנו רבנן אע"פ שאמרו אין טומנין בדבר שאינו מוסיף כו' ולפי שהיתה הטמנת החמין בשבת אסורה מכל צד למדנו ראיה מזה על דבר המשנה שאמרה אבל טומנין בהן יבשין אינן אלא מבעוד יום ערב שבת ואפילו הכי הרי אמרו אין טומנין כו' לא בגפת ולא בזבל כולה ובפ' כירה אמרו (דף לט) אמר רב חסדא מטעשה שעשו אנשי טבריא ואסרו להן רבנן בטלה הטמנה בדבר המוסיף ואפילו מבעוד יום ועמד לנו מדבר זה כי הגפת והזבל וכל דבר שהוא מוסיף הבל לא נכשר ההטמנה בהם ואפילו מבעוד יום ואו

מסורת הש"ס (margin notes)

[עי' תוספות מנחות כה: ד"ה שהכהנים סופרים ואמרו ועיין בספרי ר"פ חקת]

[עיין תוספות מגילה כח· ד"ה אילמלא]

ברכות נח. [ב"ב עה. סנהדרין ק.]

[ועיין פרש"י גיטין ו:]

[כאלפס ... עוד ... סימן ...]

עירובין פו· [ושם אי' רבה וכו' הגיה רבא וכן כבל מ"מ כרמב"ם שם שזה מימרא דרבא]

עין משפט נר מצוה

קכב א מיי' פ"ט מהל' שבת הל' ג סמג עשין לא טוש"ע א"ח סי' רס סעיף א:

קכג ב מיי' פ"ד מהל' שבת הל' ד ופ"ה מהל' ... הלכה טו סמג עשין ... טוש"ע א"ח סי' רסא סעיף א:

[עי' בערוך ערך עבד נוספתות שונות ונכנס בן עזאי]

קכד ג טוש"ע א"ח סי' רס סעיף ג:

קכה ד מיי' פ"א מהל' עירובין הלכה כא סמג עשין א טוש"ע א"ח סימן רסא סעיף א וסי' שצג סעיף ב וסי' תטו סעיף ב:

קכו ה מיי' פ"א מהל' עירובין הלכה יג טוש"ע א"ח סימן שצג סעיף ג:

[ועי' תוספות גיטין ה: ד"ה ערבתם]

קכז ו מיי' פ"ד מהל' שבת הלכה ג סמג לאוין סה טוש"ע א"ח סי' רנז סעיף א:

[עירובין לה. סג.]

קכח ז טוש"ע א"ח סי' שיח סעיף ד:

גיטין ו: ע"ש

סימן להלכות שאמר כאן ... במסכת זו [רש"א]

[נ"ל ר' אבא וכ"כ תוס' דף מז. ד"ה סימנין דוק ... והמלה ... ואמר רבא ...]

[לקמן נח.]

[וע"ע תוס' עירובין עו. ד"ה שניהם]

הגהות הב"ח

(א) רש"י ד"ה עם חשכה וגו' ולערב הס"ד ואח"כ מ"ה בעירובי תחומין תיקון מעליא הוא דאסמכוה:

גליון הש"ס

גמ' אמר סבא · עי' חולין דף ... ע"א תוס' ד"ה אסכתיה: שם טיהר בן יוחי · עי' תוס' ...

... יומא דף עה ע"א: **מתני'** ספק חשיכה · עי' ר"ה דף ט ע"א תוס' ד"ה ור"ע: **שם** אבל מעשרין · עי' חולין דף ז ע"א תוס' ד"ה ודילמא וגיטין דף לא ע"א תוס' ד"ה כמחשבה: גמ' סימן בגופיא · מבואר במהרש"א · וה"מ למתשב עוד הסימן דלקמן דף כ ע"ב:

מפני מה אמרו "אין טומנין בדבר המוסיף הבל ואפילו מבעוד יום גזירה שמא יטמין ברמץ שיש בה גחלת אמר ליה אביי ויטמין גזירה שמא יחתה בגחלים : ת"ר ביה"ש ספק מן היום ומן הלילה ספק כולו מן היום ספק כולו מן הלילה מטילין אותו לחומר שני ימים ואיזהו בין השמשות משתשקע החמה כ"ז שפני מזרח מאדימין הכסיף התחתון ולא הכסיף העליון בין השמשות הכסיף העליון והשוה לתחתון זהו לילה דברי רבי יהודה ר' נחמיה אומר כדי שיהלך אדם משתשקע החמה חצי מיל *רבי יוסי אומר בין השמשות כהרף עין *זה נכנס וזה יוצא (א)ואי אפשר לעמוד עליו אמר מר מטילין אותו לחומר שני ימים למאי הלכתא אמר רב הונא בריה דרב יהושע לענין טומאה *כדתנן "ראה שני ימים בין השמשות ספק לטומאה ולקרבן ראה יום אחד בין השמשות ספק לטומאה הא גופה קשיא אמרת איזהו ביה"ש משתשקע החמה כ"ז שפני מזרח מאדימין הא הכסיף התחתון ולא הכסיף העליון לילה הוא והדר תנא הכסיף התחתון ולא הכסיף העליון בין השמשות אמר רבה אמר רב יהודה אמר שמואל כרוך ותני "איזהו ביה"ש משתשקע החמה כל זמן שפני מזרח מאדימין והכסיף התחתון ולא הכסיף העליון נמי בין השמשות הכסיף העליון והשוה לתחתון לילה ורב יוסף אמר רב יהודה אמר שמואל הכי קתני משתשקע החמה כ"ז שפני מזרח מאדימין יום הכסיף התחתון ולא הכסיף העליון ביה"ש הכסיף העליון והשוה לתחתון לילה ואזדו לטעמייהו דאיתמר שיעור ביה"ש בכמה אמר רבה אמר רב יהודה אמר שמואל שלשה חלקי מיל מאי ג' חלקי מיל אילימא תלתא פלגי מילא נימא מיל ומחצה אלא תלתא תילתי מילא נימא מיל °אלא "תלתא ריבעי מילא ורב יוסף אמר רב יהודה אמר שמואל שני חלקי מיל מאי שני חלקי מיל אילימא תרי פלגי מילא לימא מיל ואלא תרי רבעי מילא לימא חצי מיל אלא תרי

רש"י

מפני מה אמרו אין טומנין בדבר המוסיף הבל ואפילו מבעוד יום. כדתנן לקמן *לא בגפת ולא בזבל ואף על גב דסתם הטמנה מבעוד יום הוא דהא אסרינן משחשכה : ברמץ · אפר המעורב בגחלים : ויטמין · דהא מבעוד יום הוא : גזירה שמא יחתה בגחלים · משחשכה שבא לבשל הקדרה שלא בשלה כל צרכה וגזרו אף בבישלה כל צרכה עד שיגרוף או שיקטום והכי מסקינן בפרק כירה (דף לז:) דאמר *רבי קטמה והובערה משהין עליה חמין שהוחמו מבעוד יום כל צרכן ותבשיל שבישל כל צרכו וכן אמר רבי יוחנן* : מן היום ומן הלילה · כלומר ספק(ב) יש בו משניהם : ספק כולו מן היום ספק כולו מן הלילה · הרי ג' ספיקות לפיכך מטילין עליו חומר שני הימים ולקמן מפרש למאי הילכתא שייך לומר שמא יש בו משניהם : מאדימין · שנראה אדמומית חמה בעבים : הכסיף · השחיר : התחתון · תחתון של כיפת הרקיע הסמוכה לארץ : עליון · גובהה של כפה אינה ממהרת להכסיף ולקמן פריך מאי קאמר דקשיא סיפא ארישא : חצי מיל · זהו שיעור אורך בין השמשות ולאחר חצי מיל הוי לילה : כהרף עין · כשיעור קריצת עין ברפיון ולא בחוזקה : זה נכנס · הלילה נכנס והיום יוצא יציאת זה עם כניסת זה כשהם מתפרשין קרי בין השמשות וכל דמקמי הכי הוי יום מעליא : למאי הילכתא · יטילו עליו ספק שמא משניהם יש בו בשלמא ספק כולו מן היום איכא למימר לענין מוצאי שבת להביא אשם תלוי ספק כולו מן הלילה לענין לילי שבת אלא חומר שניהם למאי הילכתא : ראה שני ביה"ש · זיבה דזב מטמא בימים ובראיות בין שראה שתים ביום אחד בין שראה שתים בשני ימים רצופים בין שראה אחת בשני ימים כגון בין השמשות חשיב ליה כשתי ראיות משום ימים דילפינן מזוכר ונקבה מה נקבה בימים אף זכר בימים וראיות בגופיה מיפרשא כדתניא במגילה (דף ח·) מנה הכתוב שתים וקראו טמא כו' : ספק לטומאה ולקרבן · ספק טמא ספק טהור ספק חייב קרבן עם הטומאה ספק אינו חייב קרבן אבל טמא שבעה דזב בעל שתי ראיות או שני ימים כל תורת טומאת זבין עליו ושלישי מביאתו לידי קרבן וזה שראה שני בין השמשות ספק יום אחד הוא וטמא בשני ראיות או שני ימים רצופין הן וטמא נמי בתורת ימים ספק ב' ימים שאין רצופים הן וטהור מטומאת שבעה אלא כבעל קרי בעלמא דלאו שתי ראיות ביום אחד איכא ולא שני ימים רצופין איכא ספק שהן ג' ימים רצופין דזב גמור הוא אף לקרבן כיצד שמא בין השמשות הראשון כולו מן היום וביה"ש השני כולו מן הלילה ונמצא יום אחד הפסק בינתיים וטהור או שניהם מן היום דהוו להו שני ימים רצופין וכן אם שניהם מן הלילה הוו להו נמי שני ימים רצופין או שמא אם הראשון מן הלילה והשני מן היום הוו להו נמי שתי ראיות ביום אחד וטמא שבעה בכל אלו ואין כאן קרבן או שמא שתיהן הראיות היו מקצתן ביום ומקצתן בלילה ויש כאן שלשה רצופים וכן אם הראשונה מקצתה ביום ומקצתה בלילה והשניה כולה מן הלילה או הראשונה כולה מן היום והשניה מקצתה ביום ומקצתה בלילה הוו להו ג' ימים רצופין וטעון קרבן הלכך ספק אף לקרבן ומביא חטאת העוף הבאה על הספק ואין נאכלת דשמא לאו בר קרבן הוא ומליקת חולין נבלה : ראה אחת ביה"ש ספק לטומאה · שמא מקצתה ביום ומקצתה בלילה והיינו חומר ב' ימים וטמא ז' או שמא כולה או מן היום או מן הלילה ואין כאן אלא אחת : פני מזרח מאדימים · עדיין לא הכסיף אפי' תחתון : כרוך ותני · שני הדברים בכרך אחד בתורה אחת : ואזדו לטעמייהו · דרבה סבר שיעור ביה"ש נפיש ורב יוסף סבר זוטר :

פלגא

תוספות

רבי יוסי אומר בין השמשות כהרף עין · פירש רשב"א דאין להסתפק בו אלא כשהוא כהרף עין ולא בזמן גדול כמו שמסתפק בו תנא קמא אבל אין לפרש רבי יוסי אין מסתפק בבין השמשות כלל והכי קאמר כהרף עין אני מכיר ובקי בו מתי זה נכנס וזה יוצא ויודע אני מתי הוא יום מתי הוא לילה דהא בתוספתא דמסכת זבים בפ"ק קתני וכן היה ר' יוסי אומר ראה אחד בין השמשות ואחד ודאי ספק לטומאה ולקרבן פירוש שראה במוצאי שבת ביה"ש וביום שני ראה ביום ספק לטומאה דשמא בין השמשות כולו מן היום והוי יום מפסיק וטהור או שמא כולו מן הלילה והוו שני ימים רצופין וטמא ושמא מן היום ומן הלילה ואיכא שלשה ימים רצופין וחייב קרבן אלמא דר' יוסי נמי מספקא ליה בההוא כהרף עין : ספק לטומאה ולקרבן · פירש בקונטרס דשמא בין השמשות ראשון כולו מן היום ושני כולו מן הלילה ול"נ דאי ראשון כולו מן היום שני נמי כולו מן היום ותו דאמר לקמן במשנתין (דף לה:) העושה מלאכה בשני בין השמשות חייב חטאת ממה נפשך ולפירוש הקונטרס הא איכא למימר שמא בין השמשות דע"ש כולו יום ומוצאי שבת כולו לילה ולא יתחייב חטאת אלא אשם ומפרש רשב"ם ספק לטומאה ולקרבן שראה בין השמשות במוצאי שבת וביה"ש דמוצאי יום שני דשמא בין השמשות שניהם כולו מן היום או כולו מן הלילה מפסיק יום אחד בינתים ואין כאן טומאה או שמא חציו מן היום וחציו מן הלילה והוו רצופין וטמא טומאת שבעה ומתחייב קרבן וקשה לפירושו חדא דשני ימים בין השמשות משמע רצופין ועוד דלפי זה לא משכחת טומאת ז' בלא קרבן ולישנא משמע ספק טומאה לחוד ולקרבן לחוד ועוד קשה לר"י דאם מיירי כשראה כל בין השמשות כמו העושה מלאכה שני בין השמשות כדמפרש רשב"ם א"כ בראיה אחת חייב קרבן דהא ביה"ש הוי לכל הפחות חצי מיל דהוו אלף אמה דשיעור מיל הוי אלפים אמה כדפי' רש"י בפרק שני שעירים (יומא דף סז· וסם) ואמר בפרק ד' מיתות (סנהדרין דף סג.) ראה אחת מרובה כג' שהיא כמגדיון לשילה שהם שתי טבילות ושני סיפוגין הרי זה זב גמור ובתוספתא בריש מסכת זבין משמע היינו שיעור ק' אמה לכך מפרש ר"ת דמיירי שלא ראה כל בין השמשות אלא שעה אחת מועטת דבין השמשות זה ושעה אחרת בין השמשות אחר ובכל שהוא שבין השמשות יש להסתפק שמא כולו מן היום או כולו מן הלילה או חציו יום וחציו לילה והשתא אתי שפיר דספק לטומאה דשמא הראשון כולו מן היום והשני כולו מן הלילה ומפסיק יום בינתים או שמא תרווייהו יום או תרווייהו לילה ואיכא ב' ימים רצופין וספק לקרבן שמא הראשון מן היום ומן הלילה והשני לילה או הא' יום והב' חציו יום וחציו לילה ואיכא ג' רצופין והאי

דהעושה

עין משפט נר מצוה

קכט א מיי' פ"ד מהל' שבת הלכה ב סמג לאוין סה טוש"ע א"ח סימן רנז סעיף א :

קל ב מיי' פ"ב מהל' מחוסרי כפרה הל' י ג יד :

קלא ג ד מיי' פ"ה מהל' שבת הל' ד סמג עשין לב טוש"ע א"ח סימן רסא סעיף ב :

רבינו חננאל

יטמין ברמץ ויבא לחתוי בגחלים : ת"ר בין השמשות [ספק] מן היום ומן הלילה ספק כולו מן היום ספק כולו מן הלילה מטילין אותו לחומר ב' ימים ואמרינן למאי הלכתא לטומאה כדתנן במסכת זבין פרק א' ראה ב' ימים בין השמשות ספק לטומאה ולקרבן פי' האיש מטמא בראות והאשה בג' ימים · עכשיו איש שראה ביום שבת בין השמשות אם תאמר בין השמשות כולו (א') יום הוא הנה [ראה] ראיה אחת בשבת עוד ראה ביום ראשון בין השמשות הנה ראה ראיה שניה ביום ראשון וא"ת בין השמשות של יום ראשון חציו מליל יום ב' הוא נמצא שראה ג' ימים (בג') [בב'] ראיות בשבת וביום א' ויום שני וקיי"ל ב' לטומאה וג' לקרבן ראה אחד ביה"ש ספק לטומאה יש לומר כולו מן היום ובעל קרי הוא ואינו טמא אלא יומו ויש לומר בין השמשות חציו יום (ותצטרף) (לג') [וג'] ימים או (לג') [ג'] לילות הרי זה זב גמור ותניא בתוספתא (פ"א דזבים) ומודה ר' יוסי שאם ראה אחת בין השמשות אף על פי שאין כאן כדי טבילה וסיפוג יש בו ב' ראיות שב' ימים חולקין אותה וכן היה ר' יוסי אומר ראה אחת בין השמשות ספק לטומאה ופטור מן הקרבן ראה שתים בין השמשות ספק לטומאה ולקרבן אחת ודאי ושתים בין השמשות או אחת בין השמשות [ושתים ודאי] ודאי לטומאה וספק לקרבן שתים ודאי ואחת בין השמשות [או שתים בין השמשות ואחת ודאי] ודאי לטומאה ולקרבן סוף הברייתא ואיזהו בין השמשות משתשקע החמה וכ"ז שפני מזרח מאדים הכסיף התחתון ולא הכסיף העליון (והוה יום) [ביה"ש] הכסיף העליון והשוה לתחתון והו לילה דברי רבי יהודה ור' נחמיה אומר בה"ש משתשקע החמה עד כדי הילוך חצי מיל רבי יוסי אומר ביה"ש כהרף עין הלילה נכנס והיום יוצא ואי אפשר לעמוד עליו ואמרי על הא דר' יהודה · הא גופה קשיא ומתרץ רבה כרוך ותני איזהו בה"ש משתשקע החמה וכ"ז שפני מערב מאדימין את המזרח וסימנך

כוותא · פי' אם יהיה נר דולק בבית ובו חלון פתוח למערב מתראה אור הנר כנגד פתח החלון במזרח וגם הכסיף התחתון ולא הכסיף העליון עדיין ביה"ש הוא · הכסיף העליון והשוה לתחתון זהו לילה · ורב יוסף תני לה הכי איזהו ביה"ש משתשקע החמה וכ"ז שפני מערב מאדימין למזרח עדיין הוא יום הכסיף התחתון ולא הכסיף העליון ביה"ש הכסיף העליון והשוה לתחתון לילה ואזדו לטעמייהו דאתמר שיעור בין השמשות בכמה רבה אמר כדי הילוך ג' רבעי מיל [ור"י אמר ב' שלישי מיל] נתננו סימן זה לדבר שיהא *(נום) לתלמיד בהין של תורה שהוא י"ב לוגין רביעית ג' לוגין ושליש ד' לוגין נמצאו ג' רביעית ט' לוגין ונמצאו שני שלישי הין ח' לוגין הרי יש בין ג' רביעיות ובין ב' שלישים לוג א' שהוא חצי שתות כמוהו חשבון המיל ששיערו בו רבה ורב יוסף נמצא שיעור רבה יתר על השיעור דרב יוסף כדי הילוך חצי יו"ת מיל ש"מ שלא נתנו סימן לשיעור אלא לדבר שנחלקו בו שהוא משתשקע החמה וכ"ז שפני מזרח מאדימין והיינו חצי שתות מיל (משיכסיף עליון עד שישוה לתחתון)[משתשקע החמה עד שיכסיף התחתון]

*) אולי צ"ל נוח

מסורת הש"ס

[דף מז:]

שם איתא רבי יצחק בר נחמני א"ר אושעיא

[לקמן לז:]

ברכות ב:

[נ"ט נג.] [עי' תוספות פסחים ב: ב"ק ס: ד"ה לעולם יכנס]

זבים פ"א מ"ו

הגהות הב"ח

(א) גמ' וזה יוצא (ואי אפשר לעמוד עליו) תא"מ וכ"ב בתוספות משמע דלא גרסי' ול"א לעמוד עליו גם בהאשרי ל"ג ליה הכל בהלכות גרס ליה : (ב) רש"י ד"ה מן היום וכו' ספק א"י יש בו :

גליון הש"ס

גמ' אלא תלתא רבעי · עיין פירש"י ברכות דף ב ע"ב ד"ה והלא כהנים ובנדה דף נג ע"א ברש"י ד"ה ביה"ש וצ"ע :

רב נסים גאון

ואן אל תבן אל יאבס וכל דבר (שמוסיף)[שאינו מוסיף]הבל פי' אלחרארה אנמא אבאה אל הטמנה בהם מבעוד יום אבל משחשיכה אסור*) הרי מכאן אמר רבא מפני מה אמרו אין טומנין בדבר המוסיף ואפילו מבעוד יום ואין טומנין בדבר שאינו מוסיף משחשיכה כי העת שאסרו בו ההטמנה בגפת ובזבל בו בעת עצמו אמרו אבל טומנין בהם יבשים ואי אפשר להיות משחשיכה מפני שאמרו אין טומנין בתחלה בשבת ולא יתכן להיות אלא מבעוד יום ואעפ"כ אסרו דבר שהוא מוסיף ולא התירו אלא דבר שאינו מוסיף ואם היה דבר שאינו מוסיף מבעוד יום הוא שמותר מכלל שמחשיכה אסור : ראה ב' ימים בין השמשות ספק לקרבן ראה יום אחד בין השמשות ספק לטומאה. כבר ידענו כי הזב אפילו ראה ג' ראיות מופסקין ביום אחד הרי הוא זב גמור כדתניא (ב"ק פרק כיצד הרגל דף כד) תלה הכתוב את הזב בראיות ואת הזבה בימים וכן אם לא יהיו מופסקין אלא מחוברין ויש בהן שיעור שיטבול אדם ב' טבילות ויסתפג ב' סיפוגין הרי (זה) [זב] גמור כדתנן (מס' זבים פ"א משנה ה) ראה אחת מרובה כשלש שהיא (כמי גדיון) [כמין גד יון] לשילוח שהן כדי שתי [טבילות] וכשני סיפוגין הרי זה זב גמור וכן נמי אם ראה בסוף היום ראיה אחת מחוברת שלא פסקה עד שנכנס הלילה הרי דינה כדין ב' ראיות כי יציאת היום וכניסת הלילה מחלקין הראיה ומפסיקין אותה שאמרה המשנה ראה אחת ביום ואחת בין השמשות אחת בין השמשות ואחת למחר אם ידוע שמקצת הראיה מהיום ומקצתה למחר ודאי לטומאה ולקרבן ואם ספק שמקצתה היום ומקצתה למחר ודאי לטומאה וספק לקרבן אבל אם ראה בין השמשות הואיל ובין השמשות הוא סוף היום שעבר ותחילת יום שאחריו ואנו מסתפקים בו יהיה דין זה האיש ספק לטומאה

*) פי' הדברים אמנם התבן היבש וכל דבר שאינו מוסיף הבל אינו אסור הטמנה בהם מבעוד יום אבל משחשיכה אסור וכן הוא במשנה אבל טומנין בהן כשהן יבשין :

כי

Raba also said: [34b] Why was it said that one must not put away [food] in a substance which adds heat, even by day? For fear lest he put it away in hot ashes containing a burning coal. Said Abaye to him, Then let him put it away![6]—[That is forbidden] for fear lest he rake the coals.[7]

Our Rabbis taught: As to twilight [period] it is doubtful whether it is partly day and partly night, or the whole of it [belongs to the] day, or the whole of it night: [therefore] it is cast upon the stringencies of both days.[8] And what is twilight? From sunset as long as the face of the east has a reddish glow: when the lower [horizon] is pale[9] but not the upper, it is twilight; [but] when the upper [horizon] is pale and the same as the lower, it is night: this is the opinion of R. Judah. R. Nehemiah said: For as long as it takes a man to walk half a *mil*[10] from sunset. R. Jose said: Twilight is as the twinkling of an eye, one entering and the other departing,[11] and it is impossible to determine it.

The Master said: 'One applies to it the stringencies of both days.' In respect of what [point of] law?—Said R. Huna son of R. Joshua, In respect of uncleanness. Even as we learnt: If he saw [discharges] on two days at twilight, he is doubtful in respect of uncleanness and sacrifice: if he sees [a discharge] one day at twilight,
a he is doubtful in respect of uncleanness.[1]

This is self-contradictory. You say, 'What is twilight? From sunset as long as the face of the east has a reddish glow.' Hence, if the lower horizon is pale but not the upper, it is night.[2] Then it is taught, 'When the lower [horizon] is pale but not the upper, it is twilight'?—Rabbah answered in the name of Rab Judah in Samuel's name: Combine [them] and learn: What is twilight? From sunset as long as the face of the east has a reddish glow. And if the lower [horizon] is pale but not the upper, that too is twilight. But when the upper horizon is pale and the same as the lower, it is night. While R. Joseph answered in the name of Rab Judah in Samuel's name, This is what he teaches: From sunset as long as the face of the east has a reddish glow, it is day; if the lower [horizon] is pale but not the upper, it is twilight; when the upper is pale and the same as the lower, it is night.

Now, they follow their views. For it was stated: How long is the period of twilight?—Rabbah said in the name of Rab Judah
b in Samuel's name. Three parts of a *mil*.[1] What is meant by, 'three parts of a *mil*'? Shall we say, three half *mils*? Then let him say, 'A *mil* and a half'? While if it is three thirds of a *mil*, let him say, 'One *mil*'? Hence it must mean three quarters of a *mil*. While R. Joseph said in the name of Rab Judah in Rab's name: Two parts of a *mil*. What is 'two parts of a *mil*'? Shall we say, two halves: let him say, 'One *mil*'? while if it means two quarters of

(6) Even in such, since it is yet day. (7) In the evening. (8) This is explained *infra*. (9) I.e., dark, no longer red. (10) = Two thousand cubits = 112,037·316 cm, i.e., about three fourths of an English mile; v. *J.E.* XII, 487. (11) Night enters and day departs in the twinkling of an eye.

a (1) If a *zab* (q.v. Glos.) has two discharges on one day or on two consecutive days, or one discharge spread over parts of two days, e.g., the end of one and the beginning of the next, which likewise counts as two discharges, he becomes unclean for seven days, as a *zab*. If he has three discharges (taking into account that one discharge spread over two days ranks as two), he incurs a sacrifice in addition. Now, if he has discharges for a short period at twilight on Sunday and Monday there are the following possibilities:—(i) The twilight of both were either day or night, so that he had two discharges on two consecutive days, viz., Sunday and Monday or Monday and Tuesday, the night belonging to the following day, which render him unclean, but not liable to a sacrifice; (ii) the first twilight period was day, while the second was night, so that his two discharges were on Sunday and Tuesday, and he is not unclean for seven days, because the discharges were not on consecutive days; and (iii) the first twilight period was day (Sunday) and the second embraced the end of one day (Monday) and the beginning of the night (Tuesday), so that he had three discharges on three consecutive days, and therefore incurs a sacrifice.—On account of these doubts he is unclean for seven days and must bring a sacrifice, which, however, may not be eaten. Similarly, if he has one discharge at twilight, it is doubtful whether it counts as one or two. (2) For 'the face of the east' includes the lower horizon.

b (1) As long as it takes to walk this.

a *mil;* let him say, 'half a *mil*'. Hence [35a] it must mean two thirds of a *mil*. What is the difference between them?—One half of a sixth.[2]

Now, it is the reverse in respect of a bee-hive.[3] For Rabbah said: A bee-hive of two *kors* capacity[4] may be moved; of three *kors* capacity, may not be moved. But R. Joseph said: Three *kors* capacity also is permitted; four *kors* is forbidden.[5]

Abaye said: I asked it of Mar[6] at the time of action,[7] and he did not permit one [to move] even a two-*kors* size. With whom [does that agree]?—With the following Tanna. For we learnt: A receptacle of stubble, or of staves, and the cistern of an Alexandrian boat, though they have rims and contain forty *se'ahs* in liquid measure which is two *kors* in dry measure,[8] are clean.[9] Abaye observed: This proves that the heap [in dry measures] is a third.
a Abaye saw Raba gazing at the West.[1] Said he to him, But it was taught, 'As long as the face of the east has a reddish glow?' Do you think that the face of the east is meant literally? he replied. No, it means the face which casts a red glow upon the east.[2] Some say: Raba saw Abaye gazing at the west. Said he to him: Do you think the face of the east is meant literally? [It means] the face which *casts* a red glow upon the east, and your token is a window.[3]

'R. Nehemiah said: For as long as it takes a man to walk half a *mil* from sunset.' R. Ḥanina said: One who wishes to know R. Nehemiah's period should leave the sun on the top of the Carmel,[4] descend, dip in the sea, and reascend, and this is R. Nehemiah's period. R. Ḥiyya said: One who wishes to see Miriam's well should ascend to the top of the Carmel and gaze, when he will observe a kind of sieve in the sea, and that is Miriam's well. Rab said: A moveable well is clean,[5] and that is Miriam's well.[6]

Rab Judah said in Samuel's name: At twilight, as defined by R. Judah, unclean priests may perform *ṭebillah*.[7] According to whom? Shall we say, according to R. Judah [himself]? but it is doubtful![8] But if it means twilight, as defined by R. Judah, according to R. Jose; [why state] priests may perform *ṭebillah* then—it is obvious![9]—I might think that twilight, as defined by R. Jose, is a continuation of R. Judah's; [therefore] we are told that R. Judah's twilight ends and then R. Jose's commences.

Rabbah b. Bar Ḥanah said in R. Joḥanan's name: The *halachah* is as R. Judah in respect to the Sabbath, and the *halachah* is as R. Jose in respect to *terumah*. Now, as for the *halachah* being as R. Judah in respect to the Sabbath, it is well: this is in the direction
b of stringency.[1] But in respect of *terumah*, what is it? Shall we say,

(2) Rabbah's period is one twelfth of a *mil* longer than R. Joseph's; above too Rabbah gives a longer period than R. Joseph.—In the East night comes more quickly than in the West. (3) Rashi. Jast.: a loose wicker-work used for making bee-hives, etc. (4) One *kor* = thirty *se'ahs* = 395,533·2 cu.cent; *J.E.* XII, 489 (Table). (5) A utensil may be moved on the Sabbath. Rabbah maintains that if it is more than two *kors* in capacity it ceases to be a utensil, while R. Joseph holds that it is a utensil up to three *kors*. Thus R. Joseph's standard here is larger than Rabbah's, while in respect to twilight it is smaller. (6) The Master—i.e., Rabbah. (7) When I actually wished to move it. (8) Two *kors* = sixty *se'ahs*. A utensil held more in dry measure, because it could be heaped up. (9) These are too large to rank as utensils, and only utensils are liable to uncleanness; v. 'Er., 14*b* notes.
a (1) To see whether the reddish glow was still discernible. (2) By reflection—hence the west. (3) Through which light enters and irradiates the opposite wall. (4) I.e., when the sun is going down and its dying rays illumine the top of the mountain. (5) Its waters cannot become unclean and it is fit for ritual purification (*ṭebillah*). (6) According to the Rabbis the well miraculously followed Israel for Miriam's sake; Ta'an. 9*a*. (7) V. Glos. Its purpose was to cleanse them and permit them to eat sacred food. Sunset had to follow the *ṭebillah* before they might do so, but Rab Judah holds that twilight, as defined by R. Judah, is day, and therefore sunset does follow it. (8) Whether it is day or night. It may be night already, in which case the *ṭebillah* is not followed by sunset. (9) R. Judah's twilight period is certainly earlier than that of R. Jose which is but the twinkling of an eye.
b (1) All those things which are forbidden Friday at twilight are forbidden at the earlier time stated by R. Judah.

עין משפט
נר מצוה

קלב א מיי' פכ"ה מהל' שבת הל' ו [וע"ע כמ"מ] סמג לאוין סה טוש"ע א"ח סימן שח סעיף ב:
קלג ב מיי' פ"ג מהל' כלים הלכה ·

[עירובין יד: קאמר אביי הך מלתא אקרא דש"מ האי גודשא וכו' ולע"ע]

מסורת הש"ס

עירובין יד: כלים פט"ו מ"א אהלות פ"ח מ"א

[פי' תוספות עירובין יד: ד"ה ש"מ וכו' דנ"מ לענין מקח וממכר]

הגהות הגר"א
[א] גמרא (אע"פ) תא"מ:

תרי תילתי מיל מאי בינייהו איכא בינייהו פלגא דדנקא וחילופה בחלתא דאמר רבה *חלתא בת תרי כורי שרי לטלטולה ובת תלתא כורי אסור לטלטולה ורב יוסף אמר בת תלתא כורי נמי שרי בת ארבעה כורי אסור אמר אביי בעי מיניה דמר בשעת מעשה ואפילו בת תרי כורי לא שרא לי כמאן כהאי תנא דתנן * [ב]כוורת הקש וכוורת הקנים ובור ספינה אלכסנדרית אע"פ[א] שיש להם שולים והן מחזיקות מ' סאה בלח שהן כוריים ביבש טהורים *אמר אביי שמע מינה *האי גודשא תילתא הוי אביי חזייה לרבא דקא דאוי למערב א"ל והתניא כל זמן שפני מזרח מאדימין א"ל מי סברת פני מזרח ממש לא פנים המאדימין את המזרח א"ד רבא חזייה לאביי דקא דאוי למזרח א"ל מי סברת פני מזרח ממש פנים המאדימין את המזרח וסימניך כוותא: ר' נחמיה אומר כדי שיהלך אדם משתשקע החמה חצי מיל: א"ר חנינא הרוצה לידע שיעורו של ר' נחמיה יניח חמה בראש הכרמל וירד ויטבול בים ויעלה וזהו שיעורו של ר' נחמיה א"ר חייא הרוצה לראות בארה של מרים יעלה לראש הכרמל ויצפה ויראה כמין כברה בים וזו היא בארה של מרים אמר רב מעין המיטלטל טהור וזהו בארה של מרים: אמר רב יהודה אמר שמואל ביה"ש דר' יהודה כהנים טובלין בו למאן אילימא לר' יהודה ספקא הוא אלא ביה"ש דר' יהודה לר' יוסי כהנים טובלין בו פשיטא מהו דתימא בין השמשות דר' יוסי מישך שייך בדר' יהודה קא משמע לן דשלים בין השמשות דר' יהודה והדר מתחיל בין השמשות דר' יוסי אמר רבה בר בר חנה א"ר יוחנן הלכה כר' יהודה לענין שבת והלכה כר' יוסי לענין תרומה בשלמא הלכה כר' יהודה לענין שבת לחומרא אבל לענין תרומה מאי היא אילימא לטבילה ספקא היא
אלא

פלגא דדנקא · אחד מי"ב במיל דשיעורא דרבה תלת ריבעי מילא הייני תשעה פלגי דנקא ושיעורא דרב יוסף שמונה פלגי דנקא · דנקא שתות: וחילופה · איפליגו רבה ורב יוסף בחלתא דהתם שיעורא דרב יוסף נפיש מדרבה רבה דאמר הכא תלתא אמר התם תרי ורב יוסף דאמר הכא תרי אמר התם תלתא: חלתא · כוורת: שרי לטלטולה · דתורת כלי עליה: בת תלתא · גדולה יותר מדאי ואין תורת כלי עליה: בעי מיניה דמר · רבה: בשעת מעשה · שהייתי צריך לדבר: כמאן · הא דאפי' בתרתי כורי לא שרא: קש · זנבות שבולין אשטריי"ם: ובור ספינה אלכסנדרית · ספינה גדולה שפורשים בה לים הגדול ומי הים מלוחין ועושין כלי גדול כמין בור ונותנין לתוכו מים יפים: לא · אין בו גודש: שהן כוריים · שהים סאה ביבש שהגודש מחזיק שליש בכלים שלהם שהיו עשויין כים שעשה שלמה גובהן כאלו רחבן והם עגולים: טהורין · דאיתקש כלי עץ לשק דמיטלטל מלא וריקן וזהו אינו מיטלטל מלא דגדול יותר מדאי ואם יטלטלוהו ישבר בידיהם: דאוי · מביט ערב שבת לראות אם יש שם אדמומית חמה: פנים המאדימים את המזרח · לערב חמה שוקעת במערב וזהרורי החמה מאדימין את המזרח כחלון דכשהחמה נכנסת בה מאדמת כותל שכנגדה: וסימנך כוותא · חלון כמו שפירשתי: כרמל · הר שעל שפת הים וחמה סמוך לשקיעתה נראית על ראשי ההרים ובכדי שירד ויטבול ויעלה הוי לילה: כמין כברה · סלע עגול ועשוי ככברה: זהו בארה של מרים · שהיה מתגלגל עם ישראל במדבר בזכותה של מרים דכתיב (במדבר כ) ותמת שם מרים וסמיך ליה ולא היה מים לעדה: טהור · מלקבל טומאה וטובלין בו דלאו ככלי דמי להיות המים הנובעין ממנו כשאובין ואין לך מעין מיטלטל אלא בארה של מרים: כהנים טובלין בו · ואע"פ שצריכין הערב שמש אחר טבילה לאכול בתרומתן קסבר יממא הוא ויש שהות אחריו לשקיעת החמה: ספק הוא · לדידיה הואיל וקרי ליה בין השמשות כוליה ספקא הוא ושמא טבלו בלילה ואין כאן הערב שמש: אלא בין השמשות דרבי יוסי לרבי יהודה לא גרסינן דהא בהדיא אמר שמואל בין השמשות דר' יהודה כהנים טובלין בו ומאן דגריס ליה מפרש הכי אלא בין השמשות דר' יוסי לרבי יהודה והכי אתמר בין השמשות דר' יוסי לרבי יהודה כהנים טובלין בו ואשמעינן שמואל דבין השמשות דר' יוסי קדים לדר' יהודה ותחילת בין השמשות דר' יהודה לר' יוסי ליליא הוא ודר' יוסי לר' יהודה יממא הוא והא בעי הערב שמש נהי דלר' יהודה יממא הוא מיהו היכי טביל הא בין השמשות דר' יהודה ספק לילה הוא וכיון דבין השמשות דר' יוסי כהרף עין מקמי דסליק מטבילה שלים ועייל בין השמשות דר' יהודה וספק לילה הוא ואין כאן הערב שמש ולאו מילתא היא דליכא למימר דר' יוסי קדים מדקאמר בסיפא אלא דרבי יהודה לר' יוסי ופרכינן פשיטא ואי הוה לן לספוקי דדילמא דר' יוסי קדים מאי פשיטותא טובא אשמעינן שמואל דאשמעינן דבין השמשות דר' יהודה קדים: פשיטא · דלר' יוסי כהנים טובלים בו בדר' יהודה דהא ספקא דר' יוסי כהרף עין וכל למעלה הימנו יממא הוא ושיעוריה דר' יהודה נפיש טובא ומעריב שמשיה: *בין השמשות דר' יוסי מישך שייך בדר' יהודה · בסופו הוא נכלל וכי שלים דר' יהודה ליליא הוא אפי' לר' יוסי וכי טביל בסוף בין השמשות דר' יהודה תו ליכא הערב שמש קא משמע לן שמואל דכל בין השמשות דר' יהודה לר' יוסי יממא הוא וכשר לטבילה והדר מתחיל דר' יוסי והוא הערב שמש: בשלמא הלכה כר' יהודה לענין שבת לחומרא · כלומר מדקאמר ר' יוחנן הלכה כר' יהודה להכי והלכה כר' יוסי להכי ש"מ מספקא ליה הלכך על כרחך לחומרא בעי למיזל ובשלמא כי אמר הלכה כר' יהודה לענין שבת איכא למימר דלחומרא אמרה ובע"ש שמר שאם עשה בו מלאכה מביא אשם תלוי אבל במוצ"ש לא עבדינן כוותיה למימרא דביה"ש דידיה ליליא הוא: אילימא לטבילה · דס"ל דכהנים טובלין בדר' יהודה כדקאמר ר' יוסי והא לר' יוחנן דר' יהודה ספיקא הוא מדלענין שבת קאי כוותיה לחומרא:
אלא

[רש]"י לא גרס [צר]יך תיבות בין [ה]שמשות אך [גו]רס ומעריב [ש]משיה דר"י סוף דיבור [ו]אח"כ מתחיל דיבור מישך [ש]ייך והוא נכון

דהעושה מלאכה בשני בין השמשות הייט שעשה כל בין השמשות או שעשה בשניהם בתחילת בין השמשות וכן הא דתניא בתוספתא דמסכת זבים בפ"ק דשני בין השמשות ודאי לטומאה וספק לקרבן מיירי נמי דידעינן כגון שראה בשניהם בתחילת בין השמשות ועוד י"ל דמיירי כשראה כל בין השמשות דר' יוסי תני לה דאמר בין השמשות כהרף עין וליכא ביה שיעור שלשה ראיות: תרי תילתי מיל · קשה דהכא משמע דמשקיעת החמה עד הלילה ליכא אלא תלתא ריבעי מיל ור' יהודה גופיה בפסחים בפרק מי שהיה טמא (דף צד. ושם) סבר דמשקיעת החמה עד צאת הכוכבים ארבע מילין וצאת הכוכבים לילה הוא כדאמרינן בריש פ"ק דפסחים (דף ב: ושם) וכדמוכח קרא (נחמיה ד) ואנחנו עושים במלאכה וגו' דמייתי מפיק בפ"ב דמגילה (דף כ:) דמעלות השחר יממא הוא ואומר ר"ת דהתם מיירי בתחילת שקיעה והכא משתשקע מסוף שקיעה אחר שנכנסה חמה בעובי הרקיע אבל תימה לר"י דבמאי פליגי דהא ודאי משעת צאת הכוכבים הוי לילה כדפי' וי"ל דאמרינן לקמן לא גדולים הנראים ביום ולא קטנים כו' אלא בינונים והשתא פליגי דלר' יהודה מספקא ליה בכל כוכבים הנראים משקיעת החמה עד שהכסיף העליון אם הם בינונים אם לאו וע"ק דניחזי אנן באדם בינוני שילך מתחילת שקיעת החמה ד' מילין כדאמר בפסחים וי"ל דמספקא להו מהו אדם בינוני: ואפילו בת תרי כורי לא שרא לי · לית הילכתא הכי שיתבטל ממנו תורת כלי משום טובדו דאמר בפ"ב דעירובין (דף קני· *ושם) ההיא שריתא דהוה בי רבי פדת דהוי שקלי לה עשרה ושדי לה אדשא אמר תורת כלי עליה אפילו אביי גופיה לא קיבלה כדאמרינן בפרק כירה (לקמן דף מה:) מנרתא שאני שאדם קובע לה מקום א"ל אביי והרי כילת חתנים דאדם קובע לה מקום ומותר לנטותה ולפורקה בשבת אלא אמר אביי כו' והא דאמרינן בשילהי כל כתבי (לקמן קכה:) פמוטות של בית רבי מותר לטלטלן בשבת א"ל ר' זירא בניטלין בידו אחת או בשתי ידים אמר ליה כאותן של בית אביך פירוש שהן גדולות ולא כר"ח ורש"י שפירשו כאותן של בית אביך שהם קטנות דהא מוכח בהדיא בפ' כירה (לקמן מו.) דמנורות דלית להו חדקי דכולי עלמא שרי דהייט פמוטות גדולות: וירד ויטבול ויעלה · פי' בקונטרס ובתוך כדי שירד ויעלה הוי לילה וקשה דלא ה"ל למינקט סימנא דטבילה אי לאו דאתא לאשמעינן דטבילה מעליא היא ובירוש' משמע בפ' (ב') [א'] דברכות דמשיעלה מתחיל בין השמשות והשתא קמ"ל דשפיר טבל ועלה לו הערב שמש *וה"ה דלפי זה הוה ליה למינקט הרוצה לידע בין השמשות דרבי יהודה אלא שמא סבר כרב יוסף דבין השמשות דרבי יהודה אינו מתחיל משתשקע החמה אלא משהכסיף התחתון:
אלא

גיר' רש"ל וקשה לרשב"א דלפי זה לא היה לו להזכיר עלייה אלא כשירד ויטבול ותו לא

רבינו חננאל

התחתון] כדי הילוך חצי שתות מיל (וכיון שפירשנו רבה) [וע"ז שפירשנו דרבה] אמר ג' רביעי מיל ורב יוסף אמר ב' שלישי מיל · אמרו וחלופה בחלתא רבה נותן בה מדה ב' כור ורב יוסף נותן בה מדה ג' כור (ביותר) [יותר] אסור נמצא רב יוסף מוסיף על שיעורו של רבה ותרווייהו סבירא להו דכהאי שיעורא מטלטלא מליאה וריקנית ומנא היא והלכך שריא לטלטולה · אמר אביי בעי מיניה דמר הלכה למעשה ואפילו חלתא בת ארבעים סאה שהוא כור ושליש כור לא התיר לי כי האי דתנן בכלים פרק (י"ד) [ט"ו] כוורת הקש וכוורת הקנים ובור ספינה אלכסנדרית אף על פי שיש להם שולים ומחזיקות מ' סאה בלח שהן כוריים ביבש טהורים כלומר אינה כלי לפיכך אינה מקבלת טומאה והלכתא כרבה: רבי נחמיא אומר משתשקע החמה עד שיעור כדי הילוך חצי מיל וזהו בין השמשות אמר רבי (נחמי') [חנינא] הרוצה לידע שיעורו של ר' נחמיה יניח חמה בראש הכרמל וירד ויטבול בימא של טבריא ויעלה וזהו שיעור של ר' נחמיה א"ר

רב נסים גאון

כי בחליפת זה היום וכניסת יום אחר נתחלף הראיה ויהיה על זה האיש דין הטומאה כאילו ראה ב' ראיות ותמצא ברור זה הדבר בפרק ראשון מתוספתא זבין ומודה רבי יוסי [א]ם ראה אחת בין השמשות אע"פ שאין בה כדי טבילה וספוג ויש בידו ב' ראיות מפני שב' ימים הולקין אותו ומטילין אותו להוטרי ב' ימים וספק לטומאה ולדאלך *) אמרו מטילין להוטרי ב' ימים:
[א]מר אביי ש"מ מי' גדאשא תילתא הוי דייק לה אביי מדברי המשנה והן מחזיקות ארבעים סאה בלח שהן כורים ביבש כי הכור ל' סאין כמו שתמצא בפרק המוכר את הספינה (ב"ב דף סו) כור בל' סאה [ו]סלע אני מוכר לך והואיל והכלי שיכיל מן היבש כורים שהן ס' סאה לא יכיל מן הלח יותר מס' סאה והם ב' שלישי הס' מכלל שהשליש הנשאר לא יכילנו הכלי עצמו שלא יהיה גדוש על פי הסדיא והראיל וכו'

*) ולדאלך פירושו בלשון ערבי ולכן:

אלא לאכילת תרומה דלא אכלי כהנים תרומה עד דשלים בין השמשות דר' יוסי א"ר יהודה אמר שמואל *כוכב אחד יום שנים בין השמשות שלשה לילה תנ"ה כוכב אחד יום שנים בין השמשות שלשה לילה א"ר יוסי(א) לא כוכבים גדולים הנראין ביום ולא כוכבים קטנים שאין נראין אלא בלילה אלא בינונים א"ר יוסי בר' זבידא העושה מלאכה בשני בין השמשות חייב חטאת ממה נפשך א"ל רבא לשמעיה אתון דלא קים לכו בשיעורא דרבנן אדשימשא אריש דיקלי אתלו שרגא ביום המעונן מאי במתא חזי תרנגולא בדברא עורבי אי נמי אדאני : ת"ר שש תקיעות תוקעין ערב שבת ראשונה להבטיל את העם ממלאכה שבשדות שניה להבטיל עיר וחנויות שלישית להדליק את הנר דברי ר' נתן ר' יהודה הנשיא אומר שלישית לחלוץ תפילין ושוהה כדי צליית דג קטן או כדי להדביק פת בתנור ותוקע ומריע ותוקע ושובת אמר רשב"ג מה נעשה להם לבבליים שתוקעין ומריעין ושובתין מתוך מריעין תוקעין ומריעין הוו להו חמשה אלא שתוקעין וחוזרין ותוקעין ומריעין ושובתין מתוך מריעין מנהג אבותיהן בידיהן מתני ליה רב יהודה לרב יצחק בריה שניה להדליק את הנר כמאן לא כר' נתן ולא כר' יהודה הנשיא אלא שלישית להדליק את הנר כמאן כרבי נתן תנא דבי רבי ישמעאל שש תקיעות תוקעין ע"ש התחיל לתקוע תקיעה ראשונה נמנעו העומדים בשדה מלעדור ומלחרוש ומלעשות כל מלאכה שבשדות ואין הקרובין רשאין ליכנס עד שיבואו רחוקין ויכנסו כולם כאחד ועדיין חנויות פתוחות ותריסין מונחין התחיל לתקוע תקיעה שניה נסתלקו התריסין וננעלו החנויות ועדיין חמין מונחין על גבי כירה וקדירות מונחות על גבי כירה התחיל לתקוע תקיעה שלישית סילק המסלק והטמין המטמין והדליק המדליק ושוהה כדי צליית דג קטן או כדי להדביק פת בתנור ותוקע ומריע ותוקע ושובת א"ר יוסי *(בר) חנינא שמעתי שאם בא להדליק אחר שש תקיעות מדליק שהרי נתנו חכמים שיעור לחזן הכנסת להוליך שופרו לביתו אמר לו *אם כן נתת דבריך לשיעורין אלא מקום צנוע יש לו לחזן הכנסת בראש גגו ששם מניח שופרו לפי שאין מטלטלין לא את השופר ולא את החצוצרות והתניא שופר מיטלטל והצוצרות אינם מיטלטלין אמר רב (*יוסי) לא קשיא כאן ביחיד כאן בצבור א"ל אביי וביחיד למאי חזי הואיל וראוי לגמע בו מים לתינוק

רש"י

אלא לאכילה · וכולה מילתא דר' יוחנן לחומרא דלא תימא כי שלים בין השמשות דר' יהודה ליליא הוא וניכול וממילא נמי לענין מולאי שבת לא אמרינן כר' יהודה דנימא דר' יוסי ליליא הוא ושרי : בשני בין השמשות · ערב שבת ומולאי שבת בהעלם אחד אין כאן עוד אשם תלוי אלא חטאת : ממה נפשך · אי ליליא הוא חייב על ערב שבת ושל מולאי שבת איהו כלום ואי יממא הוא חייב על מולאי שבת ואין של ערב שבת כלום וכגון דעבד ליה כל בין השמשות דליכא לספוקי להאי בתחילתו ולהאי בסופו : בשיעורי דרבנן · בין השמשות : אתלו · הדליקו את הנר מבעוד יום : חזו תרנגולין · היושבים על הקורות מבעוד יום וכן העורבים בשדה : אדאני · עשב הקרוי מלווא ועלין שלו נוטין לנגד החמה שחרית כפופין למזרח ובחצי היום זקופין ולערב כפופים מאד למערב : שש תקיעות · אף התרועות במנין דסדר שלהן תקיעה תרועה ותקיעה: להבטיל ממלאכה שבשדות · ויבא להן שהות ליכנס לעיר : להבטיל העיר · ממלאכה : והחנויות · ממקח וממכר : לחלוץ תפילין · והדלקת נר ברביעית : להדביק פת בתנור · ועדיין יש שהות כדי שיקרמו פניה שהיו ממהרים התקיעות כדי להוסיף מחול על הקדש : ותוקע ומריע ותוקע · הרי שש : ושובת · חל שבת עליו : מלעדור · מלחפור : ויכנסו כולם כאחד · שלא יחשדו הנכנסים באחרונה לומר שעסקו במלאכתן אחר ששמעו קול השופר שאין הכל מכירין מי קרובים ומי רחוקים : תריסין · הן דלתות *החנויות ומסלקין אותן ומניחן ע"ג יתדות ומוכרין עליהן תבלין ושאר דברים ולערב מחזירין אותן לפתחים: חמין · מים חמין למזוג בהן יין לשתות: סילק המסלק · קדרות העשויות להסתלק למאכל הלילה : והטמין המטמין · את הראויות למחרת : חזן הכנסת · שמש הציבור : להוליך שופרו לביתו · שהיה גג מיוחד בגובה העיר ואמלעיתה לתקוע שם ומשם מוליכו לביתו אלמא אכתי לא נקיט קדושת שבת עלייהו : לשיעורין · פעמים שביתו קרוב פעמים שביתו רחוק : בראש גגו · שתקע שם : שאין מטלטלין · אפילו ברשות היחיד : והתניא שופר מיטלטל · לפי שכפוף ראשו וראוי לשאוב בו מים ולשתות התינוק : חצוצרות · פשוטה ואינה ראויה אלא לתקוע והוי דבר שמלאכתו לאיסור ואסור משום מוקצה : לתיוק

תוספות

אלא לענין אכילה · קשה דמשום שיעורא פורתא דהוי כהרף עין לא הוי ליה למיפסק כר' יוסי וליכא למימר דכהרף עין דר' יוסי אינו מיד אחר בין השמשות דר' יהודה ומתאחר הרבה אחריו א"כ(ב) הא דאמר רב יהודה כו' בין השמשות דר' יהודה לרבי יוסי כהנים טובלים בו מאי איריא בין השמשות אחר בין השמשות דר' יהודה נמי כהנים טובלים לר' יוסי וי"ל דאינו מתאחר כל כך שיהא שיעור טבילה בינתיים א"נ ספק היה להם אם היה מתחיל מיד אחר דר' יהודה או מתאחר הרבה ולהכי אילטריך למיפסק דלא אכלי כהנים תרומה עד דודאי שלים בין השמשות דרבי יוסי :

הקשה ה"ר פורת דבשבת גופיה הוה מצי למינקט הלכה כר' יהודה בע"ש וכר' יוסי במולאי שבת וכן לענין תרומה הוה מצי למימר הלכה כר' יהודה לענין טבילה וכר' יוסי לענין אכילה ונראה לר"י דניחא ליה לאשמועינן רבותא דאפי' בשבת דחמיר מיקל ר' יוסי ושרי לעשות מלאכה בבין השמשות דר' יהודה ואפי' בתרומה דקיל משבת או בתרומה דרבנן מחמיר ר' יוסי דלא אכלי כהנים עד דשלים בין השמשות דידיה :

רבי יהודה הנשיא אומר שלישית לחלוץ כו' · פירש"י ורביעית להדליק את הנר וכן משמע דלא פליג אתרתי קמייתא ועוד דאמר בסמוך שניה להדליק את הנר כמאן לא כר' נתן ולא כר' יהודה הנשיא וליכא למימר כמי דאף לחלוץ תפילין קאמר ומדליק נמי בשלישית מדקאמר אלא ג' להדליק את הנר כמאן כר' נתן משמע ולא כר' יהודה הנשיא וקשה דבס"פ ד' מיתות (סנהדרין דף סח· ושם) גבי שחלה ר"א ואותו היום ע"ש היה ונכנס הורקנוס בנו לחלוץ תפילין גער בו אביו ויצא בנזיפה א"ל היאך מניחין איסור סקילה ועוסקין באיסור שבות אלמא הדלקת נר קודם לחליצת תפילין וי"ל דשאני התם דמשום חוליו איחרו מלהדליק את הנר לפי שהיו טרודין בו עד שהיה סמוך לחשכה ולכך אמר יעסוק באיסור סקילה קודם ואדרבה משם יש ראיה דחליצת תפילין קודמת מדרצה הורקנוס לחלוץ תפילין קודם הדלקה ומסתמא היה יודע שכך היו רגילין לעשות :

שש תקיעות · כמו שפירש בקונטרס שהיו תוקעין תקיעה תרועה תקיעה אע"ג דקא משמע לקמן דשלש ראשונות תקיעות הן דקתני התחיל לתקוע תקיעה שניה לאו דווקא נקט תקיעה וכן מוכיח בפרק החליל (סוכה דף נג: ושם) דתנן אין פוחתין מכ"א תקיעות במקדש ואין מוסיפין על מ"ח תקיעות וחשיב בהותן מ"ח שלש להבטיל את העם ממלאכה ואמר בגמרא מתניתין דלא כר' יהודה דתניא רבי יהודה אומר הפוחת אל יפחות משבע והמוסיף אל יוסיף על ט"ז ומפרש במאי פליגי ר' יהודה סבר תקיעה תרועה תקיעה אחת היא ואם ג' להבטיל את העם ממלאכה כולן תקיעות למה היה ר' יהודה מחשיבם כאחת :

והתניא שופר מטלטלין כו' · תימה לר"י הא ע"כ האי דשרי לטלטל שופר היינו לצורך גופו או לצורך מקומו דמחמה לצל אפי' ר' שמעון אסר כמו שאפרש בסמוך דשופר מלאכתו לאיסור הוא ובריתא דלעיל דאסר להצניעו היינו מחמה לצל והוי כמו מרא שלא יגנב בפרק כל הכלים (לקמן דף קכד:) דהיינו טלטול שלא לצורך ואומר ר"י דמשמע ליה דאסר בברייתא דלעיל אפי' לצורך גופו ומקומו מדקתני לפי שאין מטלטלין ולא קתני לפי שאין מצניעין וא"ת וכיון דאיירי הכא הא דמטלטל שופר היינו לצורך גופו א"כ חצוצרות אמאי אין מטלטלין וי"ל דחצוצרות מוקצה יותר משופר כמו שאפרש בסמוך ומיהו מתוך פירוש הקונטרס משמע דשופר הוי מלאכתו להיתר : הא

עין משפט נר מצוה

קלד א ב מיי' פ"ט מהל' שבת הלכה ד ופ"ז מהל' תרומות הל' ב טוש"ע א"ח סי' רלה סעיף א :

קלה ג מיי' פ"ה מהל' שבת הלכה ד :

קלו ד טוש"ע א"ח סי' רסא סעיף ג :

קלז ה מיי' פ"ה מהל' שבת הלכה יח יט סמג עשין ל טוש"ע א"ח סימן רנו :

רבינו חננאל

חייא הרוצה לראות בארה של מרים יעלה בראש הכרמל ויצפה ויראה כמין כברה בים וזהו בארה של מרים אמר רב יהודה אמר רב מעין המטלטל מטהר זה היא בארה של מרים : ואסיק' בתר דשלים ביה"ש דרבי יהודה מתחיל ביה"ש דר' יוסי הלכך לר' יוסי בבין השמשות דרבי יהודה טובלין הכהנים בו דהא עדיין לא העריב השמש ולכשיעריב השמש לר' יוסי נטהרו· א"ר יוחנן הלכתא כרבי יהודה לענין שבת דאמר משתשקע החמה קידש היום והלכתא כר' יוסי דאין כהנים טבולי יום אוכלין בתרומה עד שלים ביה"ש דר' יוסי אמר רב יהודה אמר שמואל תניא נמי הכי ר' יוסי אומר כוכב א' יום ב' ביה"ש ג' לילה ולא כוכבים גדולים הנראים ביום ולא כוכבים קטנים שאין נראין אלא בלילה אלא בינונים : ירושלמי בתחלת ברכות כמה כוכבים יצאו ויהיה לילה ר' פינחס בשם ר' אבא בר אבא כוכב א' ודאי יום שנים ספק ג' לילה · ואסיק' הדא דתימר באילין דלית אורחיהן למיחמי בימא ברם באילין דאורחיהן למיתחמי בימא לא משערינן בהו א"ר יוסי בר אבין ובלחוד דתיחמון תלתא כוכבים בר מן*) הד כוכבתא · אמר להו רבא לבני מחוזא**) אתון דלא קים לכו בשיעורא דרבנן אדאיכא שמשא בריש דיקלא אתלו [שרגא] . פירוש אדליקו שרגא . ביום המעונן במתא חזי תרנגולא אימתי עיילי בקינייהו בדברא חזי עורבי אימתי עיילו בקינייהו א"נ אדוני פי' ירקות השדה הן ידועין העלין שלהן בבוקר מתפתחין ומתפשטין ומבין השמשות מתכווצין ונראין כסתומין : העושה מלאכה בשני בין השמשות בע"ש ובשבת חייב חטאת · ממה נפשך אי ביה"ש יום הוא הנה נתחייב במלאכה שעשה בשבת אם לילה הוא נתחייב במלאכה שעשה בע"ש : ת"ר ו' תקיעות תוקעין בע"ש תקיעה אחת להבטיל המלאכה שבשדות שניה להבטיל מלאכה שבעיר ושבחנויות שלישית להדליק נר דברי ר' נתן ר' יהודה הנשיא אומר שלישית לחלוץ את התפילין כו' תנא דבי שמואל ו' תקיעות תוקעין ע"ש התחילו לתקוע ראשונה נמנעו הכל מלחרוש ומלעדור ומלזרוע ואין הקרובים נכנסין עד שיגיעו רחוקים הגיעו רחוקים נכנסו הכל ועדיין חנויות פתוחות ותריסין מונחים . תקע שניה נסתלקו התריסין וננעלו החנויות ועדיין החמין והקדירות מונחין ע"ג הכירה תקע שלישית סילק המסלק

*) לפנינו סגי' שם בירושלמי מן סלא כוכביא וכ"ה בחדושי הרשב"א כתי' ועי' בהגהות מיי' פ"ה מהל' שבת עוד גי' אחרת בירושלמי . **) וכן בספר דברי יוסף מביא ג"כ נוסחא זו בשם ש"ס כ"י .

מסורת הש"ס

[חלונות עי' בילה רש"י ד"ה תריסין]

[נ"ל ברבי]

[מגילה יח: גיטין יד. ב"ב כט. חולין ס. נב:]

[נ"ל יוסף]

הגהות הב"ח

(א) גמ' אמר רבי יוסי בר אבין לא כוכבים : (ב) תוס' ד"ה אלא וכו' דא"כ הא דאמר :

גליון הש"ס

גמרא ושוהה כדי צליית דג. עי' בר"ן בפירקין בהל' חנוכה דף י ע"ב :

רב נסים גאון

ובזמן שהוא גדוש יכיל ס' אע"פ שמן הלח לא יכיל אלא ארבעים נפקא לן מינה הא דאביי שהגדוש על פי הסדה הוא שליש מה שתכילנו כלל הסדה : במאי קמיפלגי **) בפלוגתא דר' אלעזר והורקנוס בנו · תמצא פירוש דבריהם במסכת סנהדרין בסוף פרק ד' מיתות (דף סח) תניא כשחלה ר' אליעזר נכנסו חכמי ישראל אצלו והוא יושב בקינוף שלו והן יושבין בטריקלין שלו ואותו היום ערב שבת היה ונכנס הורקנוס בנו לחלוץ תפיליו גער בו אביו ויצא בנזיפה אמר להן חבריו של אבא כמדומה שדעתו של אבא נטרפה אמר לו דעתך ודעת אמך נטרפה היאך מניחין איסור סקילה ועוסקים באיסור שבות סבר ר' אליעזר הדלקת הנר שהוא איסור סקילה קודמת לחליצת תפילין שהיא איסור שבות וצריך להקדים הדלקת הנר ואחר כן יחלוץ והורקנוס בנו סבר חליצת תפילין קודמת להדלקת הנר ותמצא בפרק במה מדליקין דבני מערבא מעשה בר' אליעזר שהיה גוסס בערב שבת עם חשיכה ונכנס הורקנוס בנו לחלוץ תפיליו אמר לו בני הנחת מצות הנר שהוא שבות וחייבין עליה כרת

**) נראה דחסר כאן בדעת הגאון וצריך לציין על הברייתא דשלישית להדליק את הנר ר"י הנשיא אומר שלישית לחלוץ תפילין וע"ז אמר דקמפליגי בפלוגתא דר"א והורקנוס בנו וכו' ועי' תוס' ד"ה ר"י .

for *ṭebillah?*[2] it is doubtful![3] [35*b*]—Rather it is in respect of the eating of *terumah*, viz., the priests may not eat *terumah* until twilight, as defined by R. Jose, ends.[4]

Rab Judah said in Samuel's name: When [only] one star [is visible], it is day; when two [appear], it is twilight; three, it is night. It was taught likewise: When one star [is visible], it is day; when two [appear], it is twilight; three, it is night. R. Jose b. Abin[5] said: Not the large stars, which are visible by day, nor the small ones, visible only at night, but the medium sized.

R. Jose son of R. Zebida said: If one performs work at two twilights,[6] he incurs a sin-offering, whatever view you take.[7]

Raba said to his attendant: You, who are not clear in the Rabbinical standards, light the lamp when the sun is at the top of the palm trees.[8] How is it on a cloudy day?—In town, observe the fowls; in the field, observe the ravens or *arone*.[9]

Our Rabbis taught: Six blasts were blown on the eve of the Sabbath. The first, for people to cease work in the fields, the second, for the city and shops to cease [work]; the third, for the lights to be kindled: that is R. Nathan's view. R. Judah the Nasi said: The third is for the *tefillin* to be removed.[10] Then there was an interval for as long as it takes to bake a small fish,
a or to put a loaf in the oven,[1] and then a *teḳi'ah*, *teru'ah*, and a *teḳi'ah* were blown,[2] and one commenced the Sabbath. Said R. Simeon b. Gamaliel, What shall we do to the Babylonians who blow a *teḳi'ah* and a *teru'ah*, and commence the Sabbath in the midst of the *teru'ah?*[3] (They blow a *teḳi'ah* and a *teru'ah* [only]: but then there are five?—Rather they blow a *teḳi'ah*, repeat the *teḳi'ah*, and then blow a *teru'ah* and commence the Sabbath in the midst of the *teru'ah*.)—They retain their fathers' practice.[4]

Rab Judah recited to R. Isaac, his son: The second is for the kindling of the lights. As which [Tanna]? Neither as R. Nathan nor as R. Judah the Nasi!—Rather [read] 'the third is for the kindling of the lights'. As which [Tanna]?—As R. Nathan.

The School of R. Ishmael taught: Six blasts were blown on the eve of the Sabbath. When the first was begun, those who stood in the fields ceased to hoe, plough, or do any work in the fields, and those who were near [to town] were not permitted to enter [it] until the more distant ones arrived, so that they should all enter simultaneously.[5] But the shops were still open and the shutters were lying.[6] When the second blast began, the shutters were removed and the shops closed. Yet hot [water] and pots still stood on the range. When the third blast was begun, what was to be removed[7] was removed, and what was to be stored away[8] was stored away, and the lamp was lit.[9] Then there was an interval for as long as it takes to bake a small fish or to place a loaf in the oven; then a *teḳi'ah*, *teru'ah* and a *teḳi'ah* were sounded, and one commenced the Sabbath. R. Jose b. R. Ḥanina said: I have heard that if one comes to light after the six blasts
b he may do so, since the Sages gave the *ḥazzan* of the community[1] time to carry his *shofar*[2] home.[3] Said they to him, If so, your rule depends on [variable] standards.[4] Rather the *ḥazzan* of the community had a hidden place on the top of his roof, where he placed his *shofar*, because neither a *shofar* nor a trumpet may be handled [on the Sabbath].[5] But it was taught: A *shofar* may be handled, but not a trumpet?[6]—Said R. Joseph: There is no difficulty: The one refers to an individual['s]; the other to a community['s]. Said Abaye to him, And in the case of an individual's, what is it fit for?—It is possible to give a child a drink therewith?

(2) That priests may perform *ṭebillah* during twilight as defined by R. Judah, because the *halachah* is as R. Jose that it is still day then. (3) Since he rules that the *halachah* is as R. Judah in respect to the Sabbath, he must regard R. Judah's view as possibly correct. (4) Only then is it evening for certain, but not at the end of R. Judah's period. (5) So the text as amended by BaḤ. (6) Of Friday and Saturday. It means either during the whole of both twilights or at exactly the same point in each (Tosaf. 34*b* s.v. ספק). (7) Whether twilight is day or night, he has worked on the Sabbath. (8) I.e., by day. (9) Fowls and ravens retire to roost at night: hence the lamp should be lit before. *Arone* is a plant whose leaves turn eastward by day and westward by night (Rashi). MS.M. reads: in marsh-land observe *arone* (Jast.: name of certain plants growing in marshes which close their leaves at nightfall). (10) In Talmudic times they were worn all day; but they are not worn on the Sabbath.
a (1) The word literally means to cause it to cleave, because the loaf was pressed to the side of the oven. (2) *Teḳi'ah* is a long blast; *teru'ah*, a series of very short blasts, all counted as one. These three were blown in rapid succession. (3) I.e., hard on the heels of (or, immediately they hear) the *teru'ah*. (4) This was a very ancient custom; v. Neh. XIII, 19 and Halevi, *Doroth*, I, 3, pp. 336f. (5) To protect the more distant ones from the suspicion of continuing their work after the first blast. (6) The shutters were placed on trestles during the day to serve as stalls. (7) For the evening meal. (8) For the next day. (9) Lit., 'and the lighter lit'.
b (1) V. *supra* 11*a*, n. b7. (2) The ram's horn, on which these blasts were produced. (3) The *shofar* was blown on the top of a high roof, and R. Jose b. Ḥanina assumed that the *ḥazzan* then took it home. (4) The commencement of the Sabbath will depend on the distance of that roof from his house. (5) A *shofar* was curved, whereas a trumpet was straight. (6) The *shofar*, being curved could be used for taking up a drink of water; this being permitted, its handling too (even without that use) is permitted.

[36a] Then in the case of a community['s] too, it is fit for giving a drink to a poor child?[7] Moreover, as to what was taught: 'Just as a *shofar* may be moved, so may a trumpet be moved': with whom does that agree?—Rather [reply thus]; there is no difficulty: one agrees with R. Judah, one with R. Simeon, and one with R. Nehemiah;[8] and what indeed is meant by '*shofar*', a trumpet,[9] in accordance with R. Ḥisda. For R. Ḥisda said: The following three things reversed their designations after the destruction of the Temple: [i] trumpet [changed to] *shofar*, and *shofar* to trumpet. What is the practical bearing thereof? In respect of the *shofar* [blown] on New Year.[1] [ii] '*Arabah* [willow] [changed to] *ẓafẓafah* and *ẓafẓafah* to '*Arabah*. What is the practical bearing thereof?—In respect of the *lulab*.[2] [iii] *Pathora*[3] [changed to] *pathorta*[4] and *pathorta* to *Pathora*. What is the practical bearing thereof?—In respect of buying and selling.[5] Abaye observed: We too can state: *Hoblila* [changed to] *be kasse* and *be kasse* to *hoblila*.[6] What is the practical bearing thereof? In respect of a needle which is found in the thickness of the *beth hakosoth*,[7] which if [found] on one side, it [the animal] is fit [for food]; if through both sides,[8] it [the animal] is *ṭerefah*.[9] R. Ashi said, We too will state: Babylon [changed to] Borsif and Borsif

(7) The community has to look after him, and therefore the community's *shofar* may be used for this purpose. (8) (i) R. Judah holds that a *shofar* may be moved, since it can be put to a permitted use, but not a trumpet. This can be used only in a way that is forbidden on the Sabbath, *sc.* drawing a blast, and is therefore *mukẓeh* (q.v. Glos.), the handling of which R. Judah prohibits on the Sabbath. (ii) R. Simeon holds that *mukẓeh* may be handled, hence both may be moved. (iii) R. Nehemiah holds that a utensil may be handled only for its *normal* use: hence both are forbidden. (9) In the first Baraitha, once it is stated that a *shofar* may not be moved, though it can be put to a permitted use, a trumpet need not be mentioned. Hence it is stated that the language changed in the course of time, '*shofar*' and 'trumpet' reversing their meaning. Thus the first Baraitha first states that a trumpet may not be handled, and then adds that the same applies even to a *shofar*.

a (1) V. Lev. XXIII, 24; Num. XXIX, 1. This must be blown on what is popularly called a trumpet, which is really a *shofar* (ram's horn). (2) The palm-branch; v. Lev. XXIII, 40. For the willow (Heb. '*arabah*), what is now called *ẓafẓafah* must be taken. (3) A small money-changer's table, counter. (4) A large table. (5) If one orders a *pathora* it now means a large table. (6) *Hoblila* is the second stomach in ruminants; *be kasse* the first. But nowadays the terms have reversed their meanings. (7) I.e., the *be kasse*. (8) I.e., penetrating both sides of the wall. (9) Unfit for food. Abaye states that this law applies only to what is now called *hoblila*.

מסורת הש"ס

עין משפט
נר מצוה

קלח א מיי' פכ"ב מהל' שבת הל' ג סמג לאוין סה טוש"ע א"ח סי' שח סעיף ג ד:

לתינוק בציבור נמי חזי לגמע לתינוק עני ותו הא דתניא כשם שמטלטלין את השופר כך מטלטלין את חצוצרות מני אלא לא קשיא הא ר' יהודה הא *ר' שמעון הא *ר' נחמיה ומאי שופר נמי חצוצרות כדרב חסדא דא"ר חסדא *הני תלת מילי אישתני שמייהו מכי חרב בית המקדש חצוצרתא שופרא שופרא חצוצרתא למאי נפקא מינה לשופר של ראש השנה ערבה צפצפה צפצפה ערבה למאי נ"מ ללולב פתורה פתורתא פתורתא פתורה למאי נ"מ למקח וממכר אמר אביי אף אנו נאמר הובלילא בי כסי בי כסי הובלילא למאי נפקא מינה *למחט שנמצאת בעובי בית הכוסות דמצד אחד כשירה ומשני צדדים טריפה אמר רב אשי *אף אנו נאמר בבל *בורסיף בורסיף בבל למאי

נתינוק עני · שעל הציבור לפרנסו : הא ר' יהודה · שופר מיטלטל וחצוצרות אין מיטלטלין דמוקצה הגא אבל שופר חזות כלי עליו כדאמרן לעיל : הא · דקתני תרווייהו מטלטלין ר' שמעון היא דלית ליה מוקצה : הא · דקתני אף שופר אין מטלטלין ר' נחמיה דאמר *אפי' תרווד אפי' טלית אין ניטלין אלא לצורך תשמישו המיוחד ועיקר שופר לאו לגמוע מים קאי : ומאי שופר · דקתני בההיא דר' נחמיה דאקדמית בה לחצוצרות לאיסורא וכיון דתני אין מטלטלין את השופר תו לא צריך למתני חצוצרות דכ"ש היא הואיל ואינו ראוי לגמע בו תינוק אלא שופר דתנא רישא הוא חצוצרות וחצוצרות דתנא בסיפא הוא שופר דאישתנו שמייהו כדרב חסדא : לשופר של ראש השנה · אין תוקעין אלא באותו שעם הארץ קורין חצוצרות והוא שופר או אם בא עם הארץ לשאול במה יתקע אומרים לו בחצוצרות : צפצפה · פסולה ללולב ועלה שלה עגול וקנה שלה לבן כדאמרן בסוכה : פתורה · מתחילה היו קורין לגדול פתורה ולקטנה פתורתא ועכשיו נשתנו : אף אנו נאמר · אף אנו יכולים להוסיף אדרב חסדא לומר שגם זה נשתנה : הובלילא · מתחילה היו קורין להמסס הובלילא ולבית הכוסות בי כסי ועכשיו נשתנו: המסס · הוא הסמוך לבית הכוסות עשוי סגלגל כמין כדור ובתוכו קליפות קליפות הרבה כגלגל של ריחים וקורין ליכפי"ל ודופנו דק מאד : בית הכוסות · סוף הכרס שקורין פאנצ"א ויש בו עובי שקורין דובלון ותוכו עשוי כמין כוס עובי בית הכוסות דופן כפולה ודבוקין הכפלים זה בזה בשומן : מצד א' · שלא ניקב אלא א' מן הכפלים כשרה שחבירו סותמו : מב' צדדין · שניקבו שניהם טריפה ובבית הכוסות הוא דאיכא לפלוגי בין צד א' לשני צדדין אבל בהמסס אפי' מצד א' שלא נראה הנקב לחוץ אין זו סתימה לפי שהדופן דק מאד:
לגיטי

[לקמן קמו.] [לקמן קכג· קכד. קמו. עירובין לה. ביצה לג.] [כתובות עו: חולין מח: נ:] [סוכה לד. ע"ש]

הא ר' יהודה · לר' יהודה מטלטלין שופר אע"ג דמלאכתו לאיסור שרי לטלטלו לצורך גופו ומקומו כדמוכח בפרק כל הכלים (לקמן קכד:) דאמר רב מכבדות של מילתא מותר לטלטל בשבת ושל תמרה אסור פירוש לפי שמלאכתו לאיסור ור' אלעזר אמר אף של תמרה במאי עסקינן אילימא לצורך גופו ומקומו בהא לימא רב של תמרה לא והא רב כרבא ס"ל דשרי דבר שמלאכתו לאיסור לצורך גופו ומקומו ואי ר' יהודה אסר והא רב סבר כר' יהודה דאית ליה מוקצה ובפרק תולין (לקמן דף קמא: ושם) גבי הא דפריך לאביי [ורבא] ממגעל שעל גב האימום משמע בהדיא דשרי ר"י בדבר שמלאכתו לאיסור לצורך גופו ומקומו ותניא נמי בפרק כירה (לקמן דף מד·) ר' יהודה אומר כל הנרות של מתכת מטלטלין חוץ מן הנר שהדליקו בו בשבת אבל בחצוצרות אסר משום דכיון דלא חזי למלאכת היתר אלא מעט מקצה ליה לגמרי ממלאכת היתר והוי כמטה שיחדה למעות והניח עליה מעות דאמר רב יהודה א"ר (לקמן דף מד:) דאסור לטלטלה °ומוקי לה כר' יהודה וכמו קינה של תרנגולים דמשמע לקמן (דף מה:) °דאסור לר' יהודה אפי' לצורך גופו ומקומו : **הא** ר' שמעון · דלית ליה מוקצה אלא מוקצה מחמת חסרון כיס ודוקא לצורך גופו או מקומו הוא דשרי אבל מחמה לצל מודה ר"ש דאסור דתנן בפרק כל הכלים (לקמן דף קכב:) נוטל אדם את הקורנס לפצע בו את האגוזים קורדום לחתוך בו דבילה אבל מחמה לצל אסור וכר' שמעון היא מדקתני סיפא מחט של יד ליטול בו את הקוץ ובהנחנקין (סנהדרין דף פד:) מוקי לה כר' שמעון ובשילהי הורג (לקמן קז·) נמי מוכח מינה דמפיס מורסא מותר לכתחילה וההיא דמפיס מורסא מוקמא כר"ש בריש פ' ח' שרצים (לקמן דף קז:) ובפ' בתרא (לקמן קכז·) נמי פשיטא לן דמתניתין דכל הכלים אתיא כר"ש דקאמר דבמוקצה מחמת חסרון כיס מודה ר"ש דתנן כל הכלים ניטלין בשבת חוץ ממסר הגדול ויתד של מחרישה וגבי מכבדות של תמרה (דף קכד:) דפריך אלא מחמה לצל בהא לימא ר' אלעזר אף של תמרה ואי שרי ר"ש אף מחמה לצל מאי קושיא דילמא ר' אלעזר כר"ש ס"ל :

הא ר' נחמיה ·· ההיא דאסרה שופר וחצוצרות דתניא בפרק חבית (לקמן דף קכג·) אפי' תרווד אפי' טלית סכין אין נוטלין אלא לצורך תשמישן ופי' בקונטרס תשמישן המיוחד להם ומשמע לפי' דכלי שמלאכתו לאיסור אסור לטלטלו לשום צורך דהא מיוחד למלאכת היסור והכן בעינן שיהא מיוחד לצורך אותו דבר שנוטלו בשבת וקשה לר"ת דאמר בפרק חבית (ג"ז שם) חותלות של תמרים ושל גרוגרות מתיר אבל לא מפקיע ולא חותך ומוקי לה כר' נחמיה וכן בפרק בכל מערבין (עירובין דף לה· ושם) הכא במגעול דקטיר במיתנא ובעי סכינא למיפסקיה ומוקי כר' נחמיה ואמאי אסר בסכין כיון שהוא עומד ומיוחד להתיכה והר"ר שמעון הזקן הקשה לפירוש הקונטרס דהיכי קאמר רבא בפרק כל הכלים (לקמן דף קכד·) והתא ר' נחמיה למימר דאפי' כלי שמלאכתו להיתר לצורך גופו או לצורך מקומו אין מחמה לצל לא היכי שרי לצורך מקומו והלא אין זה תשמיש המיוחד לו *ודוחק ר"ת לומר לפי' הקונטרס דקערות אחר שאכלו בהן דדרך להסיקן כל שעה חשיב צורך מקומו תשמיש המיוחד לו ונראה לר"ת דלא שרי ר' נחמיה אלא תשמיש הרגיל לעשות בו בחול אפי' אינו תשמיש המיוחד לו ואפי' דבר שמלאכתו לאיסור שרי כיון שדרך אותו תשמיש לעשות ממנו בחול כגון קורנס לפצע בו את האגוזים וקורדום לחתוך בו את הדבילה והיינו לצורך תשמישו דקאמר כלומר מה שרגיל לעשות בו בחול ולא אתא לאפוקי אלא מחמה לצל וכגון תשמיש שאינו רגיל לחתוך כגון חותלות של תמרים בסכין או מגעול דקטיר במיתנא ושופר נמי אין דרך בחול לגמע בו מים לתינוק והסקה בכלים דתניא בפרק כל הכלים (לקמן דף קכד: *) אין מסיקין בכלים כו' ומוקי לה כר' נחמיה ומביא ר"ת ראיה מפרק כל הכלים (ג"ז שם) דתנן כל הכלים ניטלין לצורך ושלא לצורך ר' נחמיה אומר אין ניטלין אלא לצורך ומפרש רבה בגמרא דבר שמלאכתו להיתר לצורך גופו ולצורך מקומו דבר שמלאכתו לאיסור לצורך גופו אין לצורך מקומו לא והשתא מה לו להזכיר דבר שמלאכתו לאיסור כיון דמתניתין לא איירי אלא במלאכתו להיתר אלא ודאי משום ר' נחמיה נקטיה דבעי למימר והתא ר' נחמיה למימר דאפי' דבר שמלאכתו להיתר כו' ומשום דמשוה ר' נחמיה מלאכתו להיתר למלאכתו לאיסור נקט מלאכתו לאיסור דלר' נחמיה תרווייהו לצורך גופו שרי ולצורך מקומו לא ולרבנן תרווייהו לצורך גופו ומקומו שרי מחמה לצל לא ולשון אפי' משמע נמי הכי :

למחט שנמצאת · דתניא באלו טרפות (חולין דף נ· ושם) ובהמדיר (כתובות דף עו:) מצד אחד כשירה מב' צדדין טרפה ופי' בקונטרס בעובי בית הכוסות הוא דאיכא לפלוגי הכי אבל בהמסס אפי' מצד אחד שלא נראה הנקב לחוץ טרפה דאין זו סתימה והקשה ה"ר אליעזר ממי"ץ דהא תנן *המסס ובית הכוסות שניקבו לחוץ משמע דבהמסס נמי לא מיטרפה אלא בנקב מפולש ואור"י דהאי לחוץ לא לגמרי לחוץ אלא כלומר נגד חוץ לאפוקי ניקבו זה לתוך זה דכשירה כדקתני בתר הכי וקמ"ל דמצד אחד כשירה אע"ג דניקב עור אחד שלם אבל הא דקתני מב' צדדין טרפה אין חידוש אי נמי מב' צדדין טרפה נמי אין חידוש הוא דקמ"ל אע"פ ששוכב על המסס וס"ד שמגין כמו חלחולת שנקבה וירכים מעמידין אותה דכשירה קמ"ל דהכא טרפה ור"ת אומר דבהמסס נמי מצד אחד כשירה ופשיטא דלא הויא טרפה אא"כ ניקב נקב מפולש לחוץ דאין סברא שיהיה טרפה בשום מקום אלא בנקב מפולש והא דנקט בברייתא בית הכוסות לאשמועינן מצד אחד כשירה אע"ג דניקב עור שלם ונפקא מינה הא דשמעינן דאישתני שמייהו אע"ג דדינם שוה דאי לא אשמעינן ה"א דהאי דקתני מחט שנמצאת בעובי בית הכוסות היינו דקרו השתא בי כסי שאין לו אלא עור אחד והוה אתי למימר דדוקא בההוא מצד אחד כשירה אבל במאי דקרו הובלילא אפי' מצד אחד טרפה כיון שניקב עור אחד שלם להכי אשמעינן דאישתני שמייהו דאפי' בהובלילא מצד אחד כשירה ועוד אור"י דמצינו למימר כפי' רש"י דבהמסס אפי' מצד אחד טרפה דחיישינן שמא ניקב לחוץ וחזר והבריא כמו ישב לו קוץ בוושט* דהכי הלכתא התם דחיישינן שמא הבריא וחוששין לספק דרוסה ואפי' למאן דלא חייש התם בקוץ שמא במחט שהוא דק חייש והא דבעי באלו טרפות ניקבו לחוץ הייט כגון דידעינן דשוב לא הבריא כגון שאכלה מחט בפניו ושחטוה מיד :
נפקא

סוכה לד. ע"ש

[עי' בערוך ערך הגגרא ובסנהדרין קט' מאי בורסיף וכו']

[ושם] [חולין מג.] חולין מג:

גליון הש"ס
תוס' ד"ה הא ר' יהודה וכו' ומוקי לה כר' יהודה · וע"ש ע"ב תוס' ד"ה הא אין עליה : **בא"ד** דאסור לר' יהודה · עי' פירש"י שם ד"ה אלא לתרנגולין :

רבינו חננאל

והטמין המטמין והדליק המדליק ושוהה כדי לצלות דג קטן או כדי להדביק פת בתנור והוקע ומריע והוקע ושובת וכו' ואסיק' מקום צנוע יש בראש גגו ששם מניח את השופר שאין מטלטלין לא את השופר ולא את חצוצרות ותניא מטלטלין שופר והצוצרות ותניא מטלטלין שופר ולא הצוצרות ואוקימנא להו הא ר' יהודה הא ר' שמעון והא ר' נחמיה :

הדרן עלך
במה מדליקין

ועוד קשה הא דה"ל אביי (שם) לרבה אליבא דר"נ קערות היכי מטלטלים להו ולרבה דידיה מי ניחא הא לא מטלטלי אלא לתשמיש המיוחד לו ודוחק ר"ת כו' [ת"י]

רב נסים גאון

ובאת לחלוץ תפילין שהן רשות ואינן אלא מצוה : למאי נפקא מינה למחט שנמצאת בעובי בית הכוסות תגד אצל דלך*) בפרק אלו טריפות (דף נ) ובכתובות בפ' המדיר (דף עו) :
*) פירושו בעברי תמצא עיקר זה :

נפקא מינה לגיטי נשים · מה שפי' בקונטרס לענין שינה שם עירו ושם עירה אין נראה לרשב"א דבבל הוא שם מדינה ולא שם העיר כדאמר בפרק עשרה יוחסין (קדושין דף עא·) כל הארצות עיסה לארץ ישראל וארץ ישראל עיסה לבבל וקאמר נמי התם *עד היכן היא בבל ולא אשכחן שום דוכתא עיר ששמה בבל אלא מדינה היא ואין כותבין שם מדינה בגט:

[דף עא:]

לגיטי נשים: דקיימא לן בני בבל בקיאין שצריך לכתוב גם לשמה והמביא גט משם אין צריך לומר בפני נכתב ובפני נחתם ובני שאר ארצות אין בקיאין וצריך ועכשיו בני בורסיף היא בבל ובבל של עכשיו היא בורסיף והן עמי הארץ כדאמרינן בעלמא (סנהדרין דף קט·) בור שאפי' שנטלו מימיו ואני אומר נפקא מינה לגיטי נשים לענין שינה שמו ושמה ושם עירו ועירה פסול וצריך לכתוב שם של עכשיו:

למאי נפקא מינה לגיטי נשים:

הדרן עלך במה מדליקין

כירה שהסיקוה בקש ובגבבא נותנים עליה תבשיל בגפת ובעצים לא יתן עד שיגרוף או עד שיתן את האפר בית שמאי אומרים חמין אבל לא תבשיל ובית הלל אומרים חמין ותבשיל בית שמאי אומרים נוטלין אבל לא מחזירין ובית הלל אומרים אף מחזירין: **גמ'** איבעיא להו האי לא יתן לא יחזיר הוא אבל לשהות משהין אף על פי שאינו גרוף ואינו קטום ומני חנניה היא דתניא *חנניה אומר כל שהוא כמאכל בן דרוסאי מותר לשהותו על גבי כירה אע"פ שאינו גרוף ואינו קטום או דילמא לשהות תנן ואי גרוף וקטום אין אי לא לא וכל שכן להחזיר ת"ש מדקתני תרי בבי במתני' ב"ש אומרים חמין אבל לא תבשיל ובית הלל אומרים חמין ותבשיל ב"ש אומרים נוטלין אבל לא מחזירין וב"ה אומרים אף מחזירין אי אמרת בשלמא לשהות תנן הכי קתני כירה שהסיקוה בקש ובגבבא משהין עליה תבשיל בגפת ובעצים לא ישהא עד שיגרוף או עד שיתן אפר ומה הן משהין בית שמאי אומרים חמין אבל לא תבשיל וב"ה אומרים חמין ותבשיל וכי היכי דפליגי בלשהות פליגי נמי בלהחזיר שבית שמאי אומרים נוטלין אבל לא מחזירין ובית הלל אומרים אף מחזירין אלא אי אמרת להחזיר תנן הכי קתני כירה שהסיקוה בקש ובגבבא מחזירין עליה תבשיל בגפת ובעצים לא יחזיר עד שיגרוף או עד שיתן אפר ומה הן מחזירין בית שמאי אומרים חמין אבל לא תבשיל ובית הלל אומרים חמין ותבשיל בית שמאי אומרים נוטלין אבל לא מחזירין ובית הלל אומרים אף מחזירין הא *תו למה לי לעולם

הדרן עלך במה מדליקין

כירה שהסיקוה בקש ובגבבא · נראה לר"י דקש הייט זנבות השבולים שנשאר בשדה הנקרא אשטובל"א בלעז ותבן הוא הנקצר עם השבולת דהכי משמע לקמן בפרק שואל (לקמן דף קנ:) דקאמר בשלמא קש משכחת לה במחובר אלא תבן היכי משכחת לה ומסיק בתבנא סריא והא דאמר בריש המקבל (בבא מציעא דף קג·) גבי מקום שנהגו לקצור אינו רשאי לעקור משום דאמר ניחא לי דתיתבן ארעאי הוה ליה למימר דתיתקש דהנשאר בקרקע נקרא קש כדפירש רש"י אלא משום דתיתבן משמע טפי לשון זיבול נקט ליה*: **לא** יתן עד שיגרוף · פירש בקונטרס משום תוספת הבל ואין נראה לר"י דאפילו גרופה וקטומה היא מוספת הבל יותר מכמה דברים השטיין בבמה טומנין ועוד דחנניה שרי להשהות אף כשאינה גרופה ולא אסרו מוסיף הבל אלא דוקא בהטמנה אבל להשהות שרי וכשאינה גרופה אסרי רבנן דחנניה משום דילמא אתי לאחתויי:

[ועי' תוס' ב"מ קג· ד"ה המקבל]

חמין ותבשיל · נראה לר"י דסתם חמין ותבשיל הייט אפי' לא בשיל כל צרכו אלא כמאכל בן דרוסאי דהא כי מוקי מתניתין להחזיר תנן הוי מתניתין כחנניה דשרי חמין ותבשיל להשהות על גבי כירה אפילו בשאינה גרופה אפילו לא בשיל כל צרכו ולא כרבנן ואמאי ודילמא מתניתין אפילו כרבנן ומתני' בחמין ותבשיל שנתבשלו כל צרכן דמודו רבנן דמשהין ע"ג כירה שאינה גרופה וקטומה אלא ודאי משום דסתם חמין ותבשיל כמאכל בן דרוסאי כמי משמע ומיהו סתם חמין ותבשיל הוי כמי בשיל כל צרכו כדמוכח בסוף שמעתין (דף לח·) גבי קשיא דרבי מאיר אדרבי מאיר אע"פ שיש לדחות ושם אפרש בע"ה ואפילו אי סתם חמין ותבשיל לא הוה בשיל כל צרכו צריך לומר הא דאסרי בית שמאי להחזיר היינו אפילו חמין שהוחמו כל צרכן וכן לבית הלל בשאינה גרופה מדקאמר בגמרא (דף לח:) ואף רבי אושעיא סבר מחזירין אפילו בשבת דאמר רבי אושעיא פעם אחת כו' והעלנו לו קומקומוס של חמין ומזגנו לו את הכוס והחזרנוהו למקומו ואי לא אסיר בהוחמו כל צרכן מנא ליה דמחזירין אפילו בשבת דילמא הוחם כל צרכו הוה ואם תאמר ואם סתם חמין ותבשיל הוי בין בשיל כל צרכו בין לא בשיל אם כן סברי בית שמאי מצטמק ויפה לו אסור כיון דאסיר תבשיל שבישל כל צרכו ואם כן היכי שרי חמין שלא הוחמו כל צרכן והא יפה לו הוא ואור"י דודאי תבשיל אסרי בית שמאי משום דלעולם יפה לו אע"ג דנתבשל כל צרכו אבל חמין שאין יפה להם אלא עד כדי צרכן אבל מכאן ואילך רע להן כדמוכח לקמן לא אסרי בית שמאי דליכא למיגזר שמא יחתה דבלא חיתוי יוחמו כל צרכן: **וב"ה** אומרים אף מחזירין · אפילו בשבת מחזירין *כדאמר בגמרא ולשון נוטלין נמי משמע דבשבת מיירי דבחול לא הוה צריך למיתני נוטלין ולמאן דאסר להחזיר אסר אפילו בחול לבית הלל כשאינה גרופה ולבית שמאי אפי' בגרופה מדקאמר בגמרא לדברי האומר מחזירין מחזירין אפילו בשבת משמע דעיקר פלוגתא הוי בחול ועוד מדקדק ר"ת מדקאמר לא יתן עד שיגרוף ואי לא יתן לא יחזיר בשבת הוא היך יגרוף או יקטום בשבת °והוה ליה למימר אלא אם כן גרף וקטם אלא בחול נמי אסור להחזיר וא"ת מה שיעור הוא נותן לאסור בע"ש דהיכא דסלקו בהשכמה פשיטא דשרי להחזיר ואומר ר"י דמשעה שלא יוכלו להרתיחו מבעוד יום אסור להחזיר ומיהו בשבת אפילו רותח אסור להחזיר למאן דאסר דאי לאו הכי מנא ליה דרבי אושעיא סבר מחזירין אפילו בשבת דילמא קומקמוס של חמין רותח הוה ועוד אומר ר"י דמליט למימר דבערב שבת נמי אסור להחזיר אפילו רותח משפה שאם היה קר לא היה יכול להרתיח מבע"י וקשה לרשב"א היכי שרי להחזיר קדרה על גבי כירה בשבת והא אמר בפרק המביא כדי יין (ביצה דף לג: ושם) דבילים וקדרה וחביתא ופוריא מלמטה למעלה אסור משום אהל ואור"י דכי אסרו חכמים אהל עראי ה"מ כשעושה הדפנות תחלה ואח"כ הכיסוי אבל הכא שדופני הכירה כבר עשויות מאיליהן לא אחמור רבנן לאסור ליתן קדרה על גבה ומיהו הא דאמר בהמוצא תפילין (עירובין דף קב·) גבי דיכרי דרב הונא דאמר ליה כרוך בודיא ושייר בה טפח למחר מוסיף על אוהל עראי הוא משמע דבלא שיור אסור אע"ג דהדפנות כבר עשויות אור"י התם משום דדמי אהל טפי אסור אפי' בלא עשיית דפנות אבל קדרה דלא דמי אהל כולי האי לא אסרו חכמים בלא עשיית דפנות:

[דף לד·]

לעיל כ·

כירה· עשויה כעין קדירה וטתנין קדירה לתוכה: קש · זנבות השבולין: גבבא · הנגבב מן השדה אישטובל"א: גפת · פסולת של שומשמין שהוציא שומנן: עד שיגרוף · הגחלים משום דמוסיף הבל וטעמא פרישנא בפרק דלעיל* שמא יחתה בגחלים: או עד שיתן אפר · על גבי גחלים לכסותם ולכנסם: בית שמאי אומרים · טתנין עליה חמין אחר שגרפה דלא צריכי לבשולי דליכא למגזר שמא יחתה: אבל לא תבשיל · דניחא ליה בישוליה ואתי לאחתויי א"נ נתקיימה מחשבתו ומיחזי כמבשל(א): לא מחזירין · בשבת דמיחזי כמבשל: אף מחזירין · הואיל וגרוף: **גמ'** קטום · הייט נתן אפר על הגחלים דאפר מתרגמינן קיטמא: תרי בבי · בית שמאי אומרים חמין וכו' ותו תנא בבא אחריתי טטלין ולא מחזירין: ומה הן משהין · בגרוף וקטום: פליגי נמי בלהחזיר · את המותר לשהות כגון חמין לבית שמאי וחמין ותבשיל לב"ה: אלא אי אמרת להחזיר תנן הכי קתני · כלומר ע"כ הכי מפרשא: ב"ש אומרים טטלין ולא מחזירין · ע"כ אתבשיל קיימי דהא שרו בחמין: הא תו למה לי · הא תנא ליה רישא אבל לא תבשיל:

לעולם

א א ב ג מיי' פ"ג מהל' שבת הלכה ד ה סמג לאוין סה טוש"ע א"ח סי' רנג סעיף א:

הגהות הב"ח

(א) רש"י ד"ה אבל לא תבשיל וכו' כמבשל. הס"ד ואח"כ מ"ה אבל לא:

גליון הש"ס

תוס' ד"ה וב"ה אומרים וכו' וכו"ל א"כ גרף. לענ"ד הא מלינו כזה במ"ק דף ע"ב עד שיעמיק ט' כגון שהעמיק:

ולא רצה לומר דתנא רישא דאפילו בחול אין מחזירין לב"ש כדמשמע עד שיגרוף וסיפא קתני דאפילו בשבת מחזירין לב"ה כדמשמע נוטלין דבלאו תרי בבא סברא הוא דבתרווייהו פליגי דהא אי להשהות תנן ליכא אלא חד בבא בהחזרה ומהר"מ אומר דאי משום ב"ה הני סיפא לא ה"ל למיתני דברי בית שמאי [פ"י]

ומיהו רש"י פי' בגמרא מחזירין אפילו בשבת למחרת דנראה דאין דעתו להחזיר ובטלה הטמנה אבל בלילה אין נראה כן [ת"י]

רבינו חננאל

פ"ג כירה שהסיקוה בקש ובגבבא וכו' כירה זו היא מקום שפיתת ב' קדרות. איבעיא להו הא דתנינן לא יתן עד שיגרוף או עד שיתן האפר על גבי גחלים נתינה זו בע"ש וקס"ל דאסור לשהות ע"ג כירה אא"כ גרופה וקטומה או דילמא נתינה זו החזרת הקדירה היא בשבת וקס"ל דאסור להחזיר אלא ע"ג כירה קטומה או גרופה אבל לשהות מותר · ומתני' מני חנניה היא דתניא כל שהוא כמאכל בן דרוסאי מותר לשהותו על גבי כירה אע"פ שאינה גרופה ולא קטומה ·

רב נסים גאון

נפקא מינה לגיטי נשים · כלומר בראלך*) המביא גט מבבל או מבורסיף אין צריך לומר בפני נכתב ובפני נחתם לדבריהם שאמרו במסכת גיטין בפר' א' (דף ו) בבל רב אמר כארץ ישראל לגיטין מכי אתא רב לבבל ובפרק עשרה יוחסין (דף עב) היכא חביל ימא אמר רב פפא סבא משמיה דרב זו פרת בורסיף ובבראשית דר' אושעיא (פרשה לח) חד תלמיד ר' יוחנן הוה יתיב קדמוי הוה מסבר ליה ולא סבר אמר ליה מה דין לית את סבר אמר ליה דאנא גלי מן אתראי אמר ליה מן הדין אתר את אמר ליה מן בורסיף אמר ליה לא תאמר כן אלא בולסיף שנאמר (בראשית יא) כי שם בלל ה' שפת כל הארץ ובגמרא דכל ישראל יש להן חלק (סנהדרין דף קט) אמרו אמר רב יוסף בבל בורסיף סימן רע לתורה מאי בורסיף אמר רב אסי בור ספת ואדוננו האיי ז"ל אמר בבל בורסיף ובורסיף בבל כוונת דבר זה לאותה ששנינו במשנה שינה שמו ושמה שם עירו ושם עירה פסול הרי נודע כי בבל ובורסיף עיר אחת הן והגט כשר: סליק פרק במה מדליקין

*) פירושו כזה

to Babylon.[10] [36b] What is the practical difference?—In respect of women's bills of divorce.[11]

CHAPTER III

a *MISHNAH.* WHEN A [DOUBLE][1] STOVE IS HEATED WITH STUBBLE OR RAKINGS, A POT MAY BE PLACED THEREON;[2] WITH PEAT OR WOOD, ONE MAY NOT PLACE [A POT THERE] UNTIL HE SWEEPS IT[3] OR COVERS IT WITH ASHES.[4] BETH SHAMMAI MAINTAIN: HOT WATER, BUT NOT A DISH;[5] BUT BETH HILLEL RULE: BOTH HOT WATER AND A DISH. BETH SHAMMAI MAINTAIN: ONE MAY REMOVE [IT], BUT NOT PUT [IT] BACK; BUT BETH HILLEL RULE: ONE MAY PUT [IT] BACK TOO.

GEMARA. The scholars propounded: Does this, ONE MAY NOT PLACE, mean one must not put [it] back,[6] yet it is permitted to keep [it there],[7] even if it [the stove] is neither swept nor covered with ashes: and who is the authority thereof? Ḥananiah. For it was taught, Ḥananiah said: 'Whatever is as the food of the son of Derusai[8] may be kept on the stove, even if it is neither swept nor covered with ashes'.[9] Or perhaps we learnt about keeping [it there], and that is [permitted] only if it is swept or covered with ashes, but not otherwise: how much more so with respect to putting it back!—Come and hear! For two clauses are taught in our Mishnah: BETH SHAMMAI MAINTAIN: HOT WATER, BUT NOT A DISH; BUT BETH HILLEL RULE: BOTH HOT WATER AND A DISH. BETH SHAMMAI MAINTAIN: ONE MAY REMOVE [IT], BUT NOT PUT [IT] BACK; BUT BETH HILLEL RULE: ONE MAY PUT [IT] BACK TOO. Now, if you say that we learnt about keeping [it there], it is well, for this is what he [the Tanna] teaches: IF A STOVE IS HEATED WITH STUBBLE OR RAKINGS, a pot may be kept thereon; WITH PEAT OR WOOD, one may not keep [a pot] there UNTIL HE SWEEPS IT OR COVERS IT WITH ASHES. And what may be kept there? BETH SHAMMAI MAINTAIN: HOT WATER, BUT NOT A DISH; BUT BETH HILLEL RULE: BOTH HOT WATER AND A DISH. And just as they differ in respect to keeping it there, so do they differ in respect to putting it back, where BETH SHAMMAI MAINTAIN: ONE MAY REMOVE [IT], BUT NOT PUT [IT] BACK; BUT BETH HILLEL RULE: ONE MAY PUT [IT] BACK TOO. But if you say that we learnt about putting it back, then this is what he teaches: IF A STOVE IS HEATED WITH STUBBLE OR RAKINGS, A POT MAY BE PUT BACK THEREON; WITH PEAT OR WOOD, one must not put it back UNTIL HE SWEEPS IT OR COVERS IT WITH ASHES. And what may be put back? BETH SHAMMAI MAINTAIN: HOT WATER, BUT NOT A DISH; BUT BETH HILLEL RULE: BOTH HOT WATER AND A DISH. BETH SHAMMAI MAINTAIN: ONE MAY REMOVE [IT],
b BUT NOT PUT [IT] BACK;[1] BUT BETH HILLEL RULE: ONE MAY PUT [IT] BACK TOO. Then what is the purpose of this addition?[2]

(10) The town Babylon is on the Euphrates, and Borsipha is on an arm of the Euphrates. V. Obermeyer, p. 314 and map. (11) The name of the towns in which the husband and wife are residing must be written in divorces. With respect to Babylon and Borsipha, the names as after the change must be written.

a (1) A stove which held two pots. (2) On the eve of the Sabbath, the reference being to a cooked dish. (3) Clear of burning pieces. (4) Otherwise it adds heat, which is forbidden; v. *supra* 34a. (5) Only the former may be placed there after it is swept; but not the latter, because he may wish it to boil more, forget himself, and rake the coals or logs. (6) After the commencement of the Sabbath. (7) From the eve of the Sabbath. (8) A third cooked. (9) V. *supra* 20a, q.v. notes.

b (1) Presumably referring to a dish, since Beth Shammai permit the replacing of hot water. (2) It has already been stated in the previous clause, 'BUT NOT A DISH'.

—[37a] After all, I can tell you that we learnt about replacing it, but the text is defective, and this is what he [the Tanna] teaches: IF A STOVE IS HEATED WITH STUBBLE OR RAKINGS, A POT may be replaced thereon; WITH PEAT OR WOOD, one must not replace it UNTIL HE SWEEPS IT OR COVERS IT WITH ASHES; but as for keeping it there, that is permitted even if it is neither swept nor covered with ashes. Yet what may be kept there? BETH SHAMMAI MAINTAIN; HOT WATER, BUT NOT A DISH; WHILE BETH HILLEL RULE: BOTH HOT WATER AND A DISH. And as to this replacing, of which I tell you,[3] it is not an agreed ruling, but [the subject of] a controversy between Beth Shammai and Beth Hillel. For BETH SHAMMAI MAINTAIN: WE MAY REMOVE [IT], BUT NOT REPLACE [IT]; BUT BETH HILLEL RULE: WE MAY REPLACE [IT] TOO.

Come and hear: For R. Ḥelbo said in the name of R. Ḥama b. Goria in Rab's name: We learnt this only of the top [of the stove]; but within it is forbidden. Now, if you say that we learnt about replacing it, it is well: hence there is a difference between the a inside and the top.[1] But if you say that we learnt about keeping it there, what does it matter whether it is within or on top?—Do you think that R. Ḥelbo refers to the first clause? He refers to the last: BUT BETH HILLEL RULE: WE MAY REPLACE [IT] TOO. Whereon R. Ḥelbo said in the name of R. Ḥama b. Goria in Rab's name: We learnt this only of the top; but within it is forbidden.

Come and hear: If two stoves that are joined, one being swept or covered with ashes, whilst the other is not, we may keep [aught] upon the one that is swept or covered with ashes[2] but not upon the one that is not swept or covered with ashes. And what may be kept there? Beth Shammai maintain: Nothing at all; while Beth Hillel rule: Hot water, but not a dish. If one removes it, all agree that he must not replace it: that is R. Meir's view. R. Judah said: Beth Shammai maintain: Hot water, but not a dish; while Beth Hillel rule: Both hot water and a dish. Beth Shammai maintain: We may remove, but not replace it; while Beth Hillel rule: We may replace it too. Now, if you say that we learnt about keeping [it] there, it is well; with whom does our Mishnah agree? R. Judah. But if you say that we learnt about replacing, who is the authority of our Mishnah? neither R. Judah nor R. Meir! [For] if R. Meir, there is a difficulty on Beth Shammai's view in one respect,[3] and on Hillel's in two?[4] If R. Judah, [the case of a b stove that is] swept or covered with ashes is difficult![1]—After all, I can tell you that we learnt about replacing it, but our Tanna agrees with R. Judah in one respect and disagrees with him in another. He agrees with R. Judah in one respect, viz., in respect to hot water, and a dish, and removing and replacing [them]. But he disagrees with him in another. For whereas our Tanna holds that keeping them [there is permitted] even if it is neither swept nor covered with ashes, R. Judah maintains that even keeping [them there] is [permitted] only if it is swept or covered with ashes, but not otherwise.

The scholars propounded: May one lean [a pot] against it?[2] On the inside and top thereof it is forbidden, but leaning against it may be permitted; or perhaps, there is no difference?—Come and hear: If two stoves are joined, one being swept and covered with ashes, whilst the other is neither swept nor covered with ashes: we may keep [aught] upon the one that is swept or covered with ashes, but not upon the one that is not swept or covered with ashes, though the heat reaches it from the other.[3] Perhaps there it is different, because since it is elevated, the air affects it.[4]

Come and hear: For R. Safra said in R. Ḥiyya's name: If it [the stove] was covered with ashes, yet blazed up again, one may lean [a pot] against it, keep [a pot] upon it, remove [it] thence and replace [it]. This proves that even leaning is [permitted] only when it is covered with ashes, but not otherwise. Yet according to your reasoning, when he states, 'one may remove [it] thence,'—[does this imply] only if covered with ashes, but not otherwise?[5] But [you must answer,] removing is mentioned on account of c replacing; so here too, leaning is stated on account of keeping.[1] How compare! There, since removing and replacing refer to the same place, removing is stated on account of replacing; but here, the leaning is in one place whereas the keeping is in another!

What is our decision thereon?—Come and hear: If a stove is heated with peat or wood, one may lean [a pot] against it, but must not keep [it there] unless it is swept or covered with ashes. If the coals have died down,[2] or thoroughly beaten flax is placed upon it, it is as though covered with ashes.[3]

R. Isaac b. Naḥmani said in R. Oshaia's name: If one covered it with ashes yet it blazed up again, one may keep upon it hot water that has [previously] been heated as much as is required, or a

(3) That it is permissible provided the stove is swept.

a (1) It is intelligible that a pot may not be replaced within the oven, even after it is swept or covered with ashes, since the heat there is naturally greater than on top (Ri in Tosaf.). (2) Though heat reaches it from the second stove. (3) In our Mishnah they permit hot water to be kept there even if it is not swept or covered with ashes, whilst here they permit nothing. (4) In the Mishnah they permit hot water and a dish to be kept there even if it is *unswept*, etc., whilst here it is stated that if it is *swept* hot water only may be kept there, and nothing at all if it is unswept. Again, in the Mishnah they state that it may be replaced if it is swept, whereas here it is taught that all agree that it may not be replaced.

b (1) Here it is stated that nothing at all may be kept there, while in the Mishnah either hot water alone or a dish too may be kept there according to Beth Shammai and Beth Hillel respectively. (2) *Sc.* a stove that is unswept etc. (3) Our problem is similar, and this shows that it is permitted. (4) The pot stands on the stove and is surrounded by air, which cools it, and therefore the heat from the other stove is disregarded. But leaning against an unswept stove, without air interposing, may be forbidden. (5) Surely not!

c (1) Yet covering with ashes may not be required for leaning. (2) Not being entirely extinguished, but burning dully and feebly. (3) Thus for leaning it need not be swept, etc.

לעולם אימא לך להחזיר תנן וחסורי מיחסרא והכי קתני כירה שהסיקוה בקש ובגבבא מחזירין עליה תבשיל בגפת ובעצים לא יחזיר עד שיגרוף או עד שיתן את האפר אבל לשהות משהין אע"פ שאינו גרוף ואינו קטום ומה הן משהין בית שמאי אומרים חמין אבל לא תבשיל ובית הלל אומרים חמין ותבשיל והך חזרה דאמרי לך לאו דברי הכל היא אלא מחלוקת בית שמאי ובית הלל שבית שמאי אומרים נוטלין ולא מחזירין ובית הלל אומרים אף מחזירין ת"ש דאמר ר' חלבו א"ר חמא בר גוריא אמר רב לא שנו אלא על גבה אבל לתוכה אסור אי אמרת בשלמא להחזיר תנן היינו דשני בין תוכה לעל גבה אלא אי אמרת לשהות תנן מה לי תוכה מה לי על גבה מי סברת ר' חלבו ארישא קאי אסיפא קאי ובית הלל אומרים אף מחזירין ואמר ר' חלבו אמר רב חמא בר גוריא אמר רב לא שנו אלא על גבה אבל תוכה אסור *תא שמע ב' כירות המתאימות אחת גרופה וקטומה ואחת שאינה גרופה ואינה קטומה משהין על גבי גרופה וקטומה ואין משהין על שאינה גרופה ואינה קטומה ומה הן משהין בית שמאי אומרים ולא כלום ובית הלל אומרים חמין אבל לא תבשיל עקר דברי הכל לא יחזיר דברי רבי מאיר רבי יהודה אומר בית שמאי אומרים חמין אבל לא תבשיל ובית הלל אומרים חמין ותבשיל בית שמאי אומרים נוטלין אבל לא מחזירין ובית הלל אומרים אף מחזירין אי אמרת בשלמא לשהות תנן מתני' מני רבי יהודה היא אלא אי אמרת להחזיר תנן מתניתין מני לא רבי יהודה ולא ר' מאיר אי רבי מאיר קשיא לב"ש בחדא ולבית הלל בתרתי אי רבי יהודה קשיא גרופה וקטומה לעולם אימא לך להחזיר תנן ותנא דידן סבר לה כרבי יהודה בחדא ופליג עליה בחדא סבר לה כרבי יהודה בחדא בחמין ותבשיל ונוטלין ומחזירין ופליג עליה בחדא דאילו תנא דידן סבר לשהות ואף על פי שאינו גרוף וקטום ורבי יהודה סבר בלשהות נמי גרוף וקטום אין אי לא לא איבעיא להו מהו לסמוך בה תוכה וגבה אסור אבל לסמוך בה שפיר דמי או דילמא לא שנא תא שמע שתי כירות המתאימות אחת גרופה וקטומה ואחת שאינה גרופה וקטומה משהין על גבי גרופה וקטומה ואף על גב דקא סליק ליה הבלא מאידך דילמא שאני התם דכיון דמידליא שליט בה אוירא תא שמע דאמר רב ספרא אמר רב חייא קטמה ונתלבתה סומכין לה ומקיימין עליה ונוטלין ממנה ומחזירין לה שמע מינה לסמוך נמי קטמה אין לא קטמה לא ולטעמיך נוטלין ממנה דקתני קטמה אין לא קטמה לא אלא תנא נוטלין משום מחזירין הכא נמי תנא סומכין משום מקיימין הכי השתא התם נוטלין ומחזירין בחד מקום הוא תנא נוטלין משום מחזירין אלא הכא סומכין בחד מקום הוא ומקיימין בחד מקום הוא מאי הוי עלה ת"ש *כירה שהסיקוה בגפת ובעצים סומכין לה ואין מקיימין אא"כ גרופה וקטומה גחלים שעממו או שנתן עליה נעורת של פשתן דקה הרי היא כקטומה אמר ר' יצחק בר נחמני א"ר אושעיא קטמה והובערה משהין עליה חמין שהוחמו כל צורכן ותבשיל שבישל כל צורכו

לעולם אימא לך להחזיר תנן · ואילו לשהות אע"פ שאינו גרוף שרי: והך חזרה דאמרי לך · לא יחזיר עד שיגרוף דכי גרוף מיהא שרי: לאו דברי הכל היא · ולבית שמאי לא סבירא להו: לא שנו · שריותא דמתני' אלא על גבה דלא נפיש הבלא כולי האי אבל תוכה אסור: אי אמרת בשלמא להחזיר תנן · אבל לשהות משהין אפילו בשאין גרופה כדמחסרינן ליה חסורי ורבי חלבו אשריותא דלשהות על שאינה גרופה קאי: הייט דשני בין תוכה לעל גבה · דכי משהי לתוכה דשאינה גרופה מטמין ממש ברמץ: אלא אי אמרת לשהות תנן · דאפילו לשהות בעי גרופה כיון דגרופה ומבעוד יום הוא נותנו לתוכה מה לי תוכה מה לי על גבה: ארישא · עד שיגרוף: אסיפא קאי · דאיירי בחזרה אבל רישא לשהות הוא ובין תוכה ובין גבה שרי: שתי כירות המתאימות · מחוברות יחד וקיר של חרס מפסקת ביניהם: משהין על גבי גרופה וקטומה · דלא חיישינן משום דסליק לה הבלא מאידך: ומה הן משהין · על הגרופה: לא יחזיר · בשבת: אא"ב · רישא דמתניתין לשהות קאמר דבעי גרופה ובלשהות פליגי בחמין ובתבשיל ובגרוף וסיפא פליגי בחזרה מתני' ר' יהודה היא אלא אי אמרת להחזיר תנן דבעי גרופה אבל לשהות לא בעי גרופה ופלוגתא דחמין ותבשיל כשאינו גרוף כדקמחסרת ומתרצת לה: קשיא לב"ש בחדא · דקאמרי ב"ש במתני' משהין חמין אף בשאינו גרוף והכא קאמר רבי מאיר לב"ש דאפילו גרוף ולא כלום וכ"ש כשאינו גרוף והא כולה חדא פירכא היא דבית שמאי לא שני להו בין גרוף לשאינו גרוף: ולב"ה בתרתי · דבמתניתין שרי בית הלל להשהות חמין ותבשיל אף בשאינו גרוף והכא קתני דבגרוף חמין אין תבשיל לא ובשאינה גרוף אין משהין כלל ולענין חזרה בגרוף תנן במתניתין נב"ה מחזירין והכא קתני עקר דברי הכל לא יחזיר: ואי ר' יהודה · דאמר כמי כי מתניתין מ"מ גרופה וקטומה קשיא דמתניתין תרלת דפלוגתא קמייתא בשאינו גרוף ושרו ב"ש חמין ובית הלל חמין ותבשיל והכא קתני אין משהין על גבי שאינה גרופה ואינה קטומה כלל ופלוגתא דלשהות בגרופה וקטומה: בחמין ותבשיל ונוטלים ומחזירין · דמוקי פלוגתא דב"ש וב"ה בשהיית חמין ותבשיל דבית שמאי שרו חמין ותבשיל לא וב"ה חמין ותבשיל ולא כר' מאיר דאמר לב"ש לא כלום: מהו לסמוך · קדרה אצל דופן הכירה בלא גרופה שהכירה מטלטלת היא ומושיבים אותה על גבי קרקע: גבה · עובי שפתה או כסוי שעל חללה: דמדלי · הקדרה על גבי הכירה: ונתלבתה · חזרה והובערה: התם נוטלין ומחזירין בחד מקום · ולא שייך למתני מחזירין עד דתני נוטלין: נעורת · ארישט"ש: שהוחמו כל צרכן · דליכא למיחש לחיתויי:
מצטמק

לעולם אימא לך להחזיר תנן וחסורי מיחסרא כו' · משום דקיי"ל כחנניה כמו שאפרש בע"ה דחיק לאוקמא מתני' כוותיה:
אא"ב להחזיר תנן הייט דשני בין תוכה לעל גבה · פי' בקונטרס משום דאי להחזיר תנן(א) א"כ לשהות משהין אפילו באינה גרופה להכי שני בין תוכה דהוי מטמין ממש ברמץ לעל גבה וקשה להר"ח דלחנניה אפילו תוכה משהין אפי' באינה גרופה דהא תנן (לעיל דף יט:) ולא חררה על גבי גחלים אלא עד שיקרמו פניה הא קרמו פניה שרי אע"ג דחררה בתוכה היא ובלאו הכי אור"י דבחנם דחק רש"י לפרש כן דאיכא למימר שפיר הייט דשני לן בין תוכה לעל גבה מהא דשרי להחזיר בגרופה ובהשהאה דוקא לא ניחא ליה לחלק אבל בהחזרה ניחא ליה שפיר לחלק קדמוכח במאי דמשני מי סברת ארישא קאי אסיפא קאי כו' קשה לר"י *היכי בעי למימר אליבא דרב למתניתין להחזיר תנן אם כן אתיא מתניתין כחנניה ורב דלא כחנניה דהא חנניה שרי במצטמק ויפה לו דהא דתנן (שם) אין צולין בשר ובילה אלא כדי שיצולו מבעוד יום אתיא כחנניה ובילה אמרינן לקמן דמצטמק ויפה לו הוא ורב אסר לקמן *דמצטמק ויפה לו וי"ל דבלאו הכי לא סבר לה רב כשום תנא דהא ר"מ ור' יהודה אסרי באינה גרופה אפילו במצטמק ורע לו ורב שרי במצטמק ורע לו אפילו באינה גרופה דבגרופה לא אשכחן שום אמורא דאסר אפילו יפה לו ועוד דרב קאי אמילתיה דרבי יוחנן דאיירי באינה גרופה וכן רבי יוחנן דשרי לקמן חמין ותבשיל שבישל כל צרכו באינה גרופה אבל לא בישל כל צרכו אסור לא אשכחן תנא דסבר הכי:
מהו לסמוך · באינה גרופה קבעי ואי מתניתין להשהות תנן קא בעי להשהות ולהחזיר ואי להחזיר תנן ושרי להשהות אפי' תוכה וגבה בעי להחזיר ולהשהות היכא שאינו מבושל כמאכל בן דרוסאי:
תא שמע כירה שהסיקוה כו' · ומסיק דשרי לסמוך ומכל מקום אין ללמוד מכאן לסמוך אצל האש דשאני הכא דדופני כירה מפסיקין בינו ולאש:
שמע

ב א מיי' פ"ג מהל' שבת הלכה י' סמג לאוין סה טוש"ע א"ח סי' רנג סעיף ב:
ג ב שם סעיף א בהג"ה:
ד ג מיי' שם הלכה ז טוש"ע שם סעיף א:
ה ד מיי' שם הלכה ד:

ולפסק דרב מוקי מתני' בלהחזיר אבל לשהות אפילו אינה גרופה שרי מצטמק ורע לו ולרבי יוחנן אפי' מצטמק ויפה לו [ת"י]

תוספתא פ"ג
הגהות הב"ח
(א) תוס' ד"ה אא"ב וכו' דאי להחזיר תנן אבל לשהות:
גליון הש"ס
תוס' ד"ה לעולם וכו' משום דקיי"ל כחנניה · כעין זה בתוספות מגילה דף יט ע"ב ד"ה ודילמא:
תוספתא [פ"ג]

רבינו חננאל

ושקלינן וטרינן ותריצנן כירה שהסיקוה בגפת או בעצים אסור להחזיר אבל לשהות משהין בה אע"פ שאינה גרופה ולא קטומה בין תבשיל בין חמין כחנניה:ואע"ג דעמדה אמרינן תוב תא שמע ב' כירות המתאימות אחת גרופה וקטומה ואחת שאינה גרופה ולא קטומה כו' לר' מאיר אליבא דבית הלל משהין ע"ג גרופה וקטומה חמין אבל לא תבשיל ולב"ש לא כלום לר' יהודה אליבא דב"ש משהין חמין אבל לאו תבשיל · וב"ה חמין ותבשיל ב"ש אומרים נוטלין חמין אבל לא (ת ב ש י ל) מחזירין · וב"ה [אומרים] נוטלין אף מחזירין בשלמא אי אמרת מתני' לשהות [נמי בעינן] ע"ג גרופה וקטומה מתני' ר' יהודה היא · אלא אי אמרת להחזיר היא אבל לשהות בש"א משהין חמין ובה"א חמין ותבשיל אף על פי שאינה גרופה ולא קטומה · מני מתני' אי ר' מאיר קשיא לב"ש (בהו) [בחדא] במתני' דקתני בש"א חמין אבל לא תבשיל · ודרבי מאיר קתני לבית שמאי ולא כלום · ולבית הלל בתרתי דר' מאיר קתני לב"ה משהין חמין אבל לא תבשיל· ומתני' קתני לב"ה חמין ותבשיל · ותוב דרבי מאיר קתני דברי הכל לא יחזיר ומתני' קתני לב"ה אף מחזירין · אי לרבי יהודה קשיא גרופה וקטומה דכי קתני משהין לב"ש חמין לב"ה חמין ותבשיל בגרופה וקטומה קתני ומתני' אע"פ שאינה גרופה וקטומה · ושנינן לעולם אימא לך להחזיר תנן · ותנא דידן סבר לה כרבי יהודה בחדא ופשוטה היא ועמדה [הסוגיא] דמתני' להחזיר תנן. עכשיו יש מי שאומר כיון דלא איפשיטא בהדיא להחזיר אשנויי לא סמכינן [ומוקמי] מתני' לשהות · ויש מי שאומר הלכה להחזיר תנן ומסייעא ליה הא דא"ר יוחנן כירה שהסיקוה בגפת ובעצים משהין עליה חמין שלא הוחמו כל צרכן ותבשיל שלא בישל כל צרכו עקר לא יחזיר וקסבר מתני' להחזיר תנן כו' · ועוד מדאמר רבא תרוייהו תננהי ואמרינן מכדי תרוייהו תנהי ר' יוחנן מאי אתא לאשמעינן ואמר דינקא דמתני' קמ"ל ש"מ דרבי יוחנן סבר דוקא דמתני' להחזיר הוא*) ושידה זה אינה הטמנה אלא כגון כסא של בחל והקדירה יושבת עליה והיא תלויה (או) באבנים [או] כיוצא בה · אבל הטמנה ע"ג גחלים דברי הכל אסור · דקי"ל הטמנה בדבר המוסיף אסור ואפילו מבעוד יום : איבעיא להו מהו לסמוך לה · תוכה וגבה אסור · אבל לסמוך שרי או דילמא לא

*) עי' בבעל המאור :

שמע מינה מצטמק ויפה לו מותר שאני הכא דקטמה אי הכי מאי למימרא הובערה איצטריכא ליה מהו דתימא כיון דהובערה הדרא לה למילתא קמייתא קמשמע לן אמר רבה בר בר חנה אמר רבי יוחנן קטמה והובערה משהין עליה חמין שהוחמו כל צורכן ותבשיל שבישל כל צורכו ואפי' גחלים של רותם ש"מ מצטמק ויפה לו מותר שאני הכא דקטמה אי הכי מאי למימרא הובערה אצטריכא ליה היינו הך גחלים של רותם אצטריכא ליה אמר רב ששת אמר ר' יוחנן כירה שהסיקוה בגפת ובעצים משהין עליה חמין שלא הוחמו כל צורכן ותבשיל שלא בישל כל צורכו עקר לא יחזיר עד שיגרוף או עד שיתן אפר קסבר מתניתין להחזיר תנן אבל לשהות משהין אע"פ שאינו גרוף ואינו קטום אמר רבא תרווייהו תנגהי לשהות תנינא *אין נותנין את הפת בתוך התנור עם חשיכה ולא חררה על גבי גחלים אלא כדי שיקרמו פניה הא קרמו פניה שרי להחזיר נמי תנינא בית הלל אומרים אף מחזירין ועד כאן לא קשרו בית הלל אלא בגרופה וקטומה אבל בשאינה גרופה וקטומה לא ורב ששת נמי דיוקא דמתני' קמ"ל אמר רב שמואל בר יהודה אמר רבי יוחנן *כירה שהסיקוה בגפת ובעצים משהין(א) עליה תבשיל שבישל כל צורכו וחמין שהוחמו כל צורכן ואפי' מצטמק ויפה לו אמר ליה ההוא מדרבנן לרב שמואל בר יהודה הא רב ושמואל דאמרי תרווייהו מצטמק ויפה לו אסור אמר ליה אטו לית אנא ידע דאמר רב יוסף אמר רב יהודה אמר שמואל מצטמק ויפה לו אסור כי קאמינא לך לרבי יוחנן קאמינא אמר ליה רב עוקבא ממישן לרב אשי אתון דמקרביתו לרב ושמואל עבידו כרב ושמואל אנן נעביד כרבי יוחנן אמר ליה אביי לרב יוסף מהו לשהות אמר ליה הא רב יהודה משהו ליה ואכיל א"ל בר מיניה דרב יהודה דכיון דמסוכן הוא אפילו בשבת נמי שרי למעבד ליה לי ולך מאי אמר ליה בסורא משהו דהא רב נחמן בר יצחק *מרי דעובדא הוה ומשהו ליה ואכיל אמר רב אשי קאימנא קמיה דרב הונא ושהין ליה כסא דהרסנא ואכל ולא ידענא אי משום דקסבר מצטמק ויפה לו מותר אי משום דכיון דאית ביה מיחא מצטמק ורע לו הוא אמר רב *נחמן מצטמק ויפה לו אסור מצטמק ורע לו מותר כללא דמלתא כל דאית ביה מיחא מצטמק ורע לו לבר מתבשיל דליפתא דאף על גב דאית ביה מיחא מצטמק ויפה לו הוא והני מילי דאית ביה בשרא אבל לית ביה בשרא מצטמק ורע לו הוא וכי אית ביה בשרא נמי לא אמרן אלא דלא קבעי לה לאורחין אבל קבעי לה לאורחין מצטמק ורע לו לפרא דייסא ותמרי מצטמק ורע להן בעו מיניה מרבי חייא בר אבא

שבח

רש"י

מצטמק · מתמעט וסין רעיי"ש לשון שדים צומקין (הושע ט) כמו שאתה אומר בלשון עוי נצטוה ובלשון צדק נצטדק וכן כל תיבה שראשה יסודה צד"י כשהיא מתפעלת נותן ט' אחר צד"י : מותר · להשהותן בכירה דאי לא במצטמק ויפה לו קאמר מאי אתא לאשמעינן אלא ע"כ במצטמק ויפה לו קאמר ואפילו הכי לא גזרו משום חיתוי הואיל ונתבשל כל צרכו ותנא חמין לאשמעינן דבעינן שהוחמו כל צרכן מבעוד יום : שאני הכא דקטמה · וגלי דעתיה דלא ניחא ליה בצמוקי : גחלים של רותם · חמין יותר משאר גחלים ואינם ממהרין לכבות כדאמרינן בהמוכר את הספינה (ב"ב דף עד:) : משהין עליה · ואע"פ שלא קטמה ואמוראי נינהו אליבא דר' יוחנן : מתניתין · דקתני עד שיגרוף : להחזיר תנן · דלא שרו בית הלל להחזיר עד שיגרוף ופירוקא דמתניתין כדאמרינן לעיל חסורי מיחסרא הלכך עקר לא יחזיר הואיל ואינה גרופה : תרווייהו תנינהו · בין לשהות בשאינה גרופה תנינא בהדיא סתם משנה דמותר ועקר לא יחזיר נמי תנינא ולמה ליה לרבי יוחנן לאשמעינן : הא קרמו פניה שרי · והיינו לא בישל כל צרכו ותנור לאו גרוף וקטום הוא ואי נמי גרוף בתנור לא מהניא גריפה כדתנן במתניתין וכ"ש פת דאדעתא לבשולי יהביה בגוויה : ועד כאן · לא שרו כו' · דמתניתין אלאחר שיגרוף קאי דקתני לא יתן עד שיגרוף ובין למאן דאמר לא ישהה ובין למ"ד לא יחזיר מ"מ חזרה דסיפא אגרוף וקטום מהדר : ורב ששת נמי דיוקא דמתני' קמ"ל · משום דלא מתני לה בהדיא הא קרמו שרי ואנן דמשהינן קדירה על גבי כירה שאינה גרופה אדתנניה סמכינן הואיל ותנן סתם מתניתין כוותיה כדאמר הא קרמו שרי ואע"ג דלא בישל כל צרכו ואמר רב ששת משמיה דרבי יוחנן כוותיה דמתניתין דפרקין משום חזרה הוא דבעי גרופה אבל לשהות לא וכל הני אמוראי דאסרי סברי מתניתין לשהות תנן : מהו לשהות · בשאינה גרופה : מסוכן הוא · רגיל לאוחזו בולמוס וצריך לאכול מאכל מתוק וטוב : מרי דעובדא · מדקדק במעשיו : מיחא · קמח : כסא דהרסנא · דגים המבושלים בשמן בקמח : דאית ביה בשרא · מצטמק ויפה לו שומן הבשר משבר כח הלפת כדאמר בברכות (דף מד:) : לאורחין · צריך חתיכות חשובות לשום לפניהם ואין דרך כבוד בתבשיל המצטמק שאין הבשר ניכר בו : לפדא · מאכל שעושה מתאנים : תמרי · מאכל תמרים :

שכח

תוספות

שמע מינה מצטמק ויפה לו מותר · פירש בקונטרס דאי האי תבשיל במצטמק ורע לו מאי אתא לאשמעינן וקשה לר"י הא איצטריך לאפוקי מדרבי מאיר ורבי יהודה דאסרי בשאינה גרופה אפילו חמין דמצטמק ורע להם ועוד קשה כיון דהשתא ס"ד דמשום דהובערה הדרא למילתא קמייתא כי משני שאני הכא דקטמה מאי פריך מאי למימרא הא איצטריך טובא לאפוקי ממאי דס"ד מעיקרא ונראה לר"י דהשתא ס"ד דלא חשיבא קטומה כלל משום דהובערה ואשמעינן דהדרא למילתא קמייתא דאי חשיבא קטומה אמאי נקט בישל כל צרכו אפי' לא בישל כל צרכו שרי דאפילו רבי מאיר דמחמיר מכולהו תנאי שרי בחמין שלא הוחמו כל צרכן כדפירשנו לעיל דסתם חמין ותבשיל הוי שלא הוחמו כל צורכן ופריך שמע מינה מצטמק ויפה לו מותר דהא סתם תבשיל אמר לקמן דמצטמק ויפה לו הוא ומשני שאני הכא דקטמה פירוש וחשיבא לגמרי קטומה וה"ה אפילו לא בישל כל צרכו שרי והא דנקט בישל כל צרכו לאשמעינן דאי לאו קטומה אפילו בישל כל צרכו אסור משום דמצטמק ויפה לו הוא ופריך אי הכי מאי למימרא אף על גב דאשמעינן דאי לא קטמה אסור מ"מ מדנקט למילתיה בלשון היתר משמע דהתירא אתי לאורויי לן ואף על גב דאשמעינן דלא הדרא למילתא קמייתא נראה לו דהא לא איצטריך לאשמעינן דסברא הוא דלא הדרא למילתא קמייתא ואף על גב דמעיקרא הוה בעי למימר דהדרא למילתא קמייתא לאו משום דסברא הוא לומר כן אלא משום דנקט במלתיה בישל כל צרכו היה ר"ל כן כדפרישית ומשני דמכל מקום אצטריך דמהו דתימא כו' ועוד יש לומר שאני הכא דקטמה דלאו לגמרי מהניא קטימה אלא דוקא משום דבישל כל צרכו אבל לא בישל כל צרכו אסור משום דהובערה והשתא אתי שפיר הא דנקט הכא קטמה והובערה ולעיל נקט ונתלבתה דנתלבתה הוי פחות מהובערה והויא לגמרי כקטומה ופריך א"ה מאי למימרא דהא בלאו מילתיה מסברא ה"א דלא הדרא למלתא קמייתא כמו בנתלבתה ושרי ואפי' לא בישל כל צרכו ובלשון איסור ה"ל לאשמעינן ולא בלשון היתר ומשני הובערה איצטריך ליה ואי לאו מילתיה לא היה פשוט היתר אלא הוה ס"ד למימרא דהדרא למילתא קמייתא :

אמר רב ששת אמר ר' יוחנן כירה שהסיקוה בגפת ובעצים משהין עליה תבשיל שלא בישל כל צרכו כו' · פסק ר"ח דהלכה כרב ששת אמר ר' יוחנן דרבא דאמר תרווייהו תנינהו סבירא ליה כוותיה וכן פסק רש"י דסתם מתניתין דפרק קמא (דף יט:) כחנניה ומותר להשהות אפי' באינה גרופה אבל להחזיר ודאי אסור אא"כ גרוף וקטום ואפי' *בישל כל צרכו כדפי' לעיל: דיוקא דמתני' קמ"ל · פי' רש"י דקמ"ל דקרמו פניה שפיר דמי ואין נראה דדיוק פשוט הוא דהא כיון דתנא עד שיקרמו פניה ממילא שמעינן דקרמו פניה שרי ונראה לפרש דדיוקא דמתניתין דכירה אתא לאשמעי' דלהחזיר תנן וחסורי מחסרא והכי קתני : מהו להשהות · באינה גרופה ולא בישל כל צרכו קבעי או במצטמק ויפה לו :

מיהו אמאי אסור להחזיר מ"ש מדאמר לקמן [דף מ:] נותן אדם קיתון של מים כנגד המדורה שהפיג צינתן ושמן איכא מאן דשרי אפילו יד סולדת בו ואם כן אמאי אסור תבשיל שבישל כל צרכו להחזיר הא לא שייך ביה בישול ולעיל [דף לד.] נמי דאסור להטמין משחשיכה אפילו באין מוסיף הבל גזרה שמא ירתיח הא לא שייך ביה בישול וצ"ל דודאי בשמן לא שייך בישול אבל בתבשיל אפילו במבושל מבעוד יום שייך בישול והא דברינן קיתון של מים סיינו ליתן במקום שאפי' תהיה שם כל היום לא תהיה יד סולדת בו [ת"י]

עין משפט נר מצוה

ו א ב (מיי' פ"ג מהל' שבת הל' ד') סמג לאוין סה טוש"ע א"ח סימן רנג סעיף א :

רבינו חננאל

לא שנא ופשטנא מהא דתניא כירה שהסיקוה בגפת ובעצים סומכין ואין מקיימין עליה אלא אם כן גרופה וקטומה עממו הגחלים או שנתן לתוכה נעורת של פשתן דקה הרי כקטומה (דבי) [אמר רב] (שמעון) [שמואל] בר יהודה א"ר יוחנן כירה שהסיקוה בגפת ובעצים משהין עליה חמין שהוחמו כל צרכן ותבשיל שבישל כל צרכו ודוקא כירה שהיא שפיתת ב' קדרות אבל אם אין בה אלא שפיתת קדרה אחת אסור ואפי' מצטמק ויפה לו מותר ואע"ג דרב ושמואל פליגי הא קי"ל דרבי יוחנן לגבי רב ושמואל הלכתא כר' יוחנן ומה שאמר רב (עקיבא) [עוקבא] ממישן לרב אשי אתון דמקרביתון לרב ושמואל עבידו כרב ושמואל לאו משום דהלכתא כוותייהו אלא לעולם הלכתא כר' יוחנן דשרי אבל אתון דנהיגתון איסורא כרב ושמואל הוו להו דברים המותרין ואחרים נהגו בהן איסור אי אתה רשאי להתירן בפניהם והא דאמר רב יהודה מסוכן בשבת שרי למיעבד ליה פשוטה הוא : הא דאמר רב נחמן בר יצחק מצטמק ויפה לו אסור מצטמק ורע לו מותר · כללא דמילתא כל דאית ליה מיחא מצטמק ורע לו הוא בר מתבשילא דליפתא דאע"ג דאית ליה מיחא מצטמק ויפה לו הוא כו' · האי כללא (לגברי) [לגבי] רב ושמואל אמרה ולית הלכתא אלא כר' יוחנן דהא סייעיה ר' עקיבא ממישן לרב אשי · לפדא דייסא ותמרי מצטמק ורע לו מותר

מסורת הש"ס

לעיל יט:

[ביצה כט: חולין קי.]

הגהות הב"ח

(א) גמ' אמר רב שמואל בר יהודה א"ר יוחנן כירה וכו' משהין עליה חמין שהוחמו כל צורכן ותבשיל שבישל כל צורכו ואפי' מצטמק

לספרי' דגרסי הכא רבנ"י ז"ל דאליבא דרב ושמואל קאמר דהא איהו גופיה משני ליה ואכיל [ת"י]

dish which has been boiled all it needs. [37b] Then this proves that when it shrinks[4] and is improved thereby, it is permitted?[5]—[No.] There it is different, because he covered it with ashes. If so, why state it?—It is necessary [to state it, because] it blazed up again. You might argue, since it blazed up again, it reverts to its original state;[6] hence he informs us [that it is not so].[7]

Rabbah b. Bar Ḥanah said in R. Joḥanan's name: If one covered it with ashes, yet it blazed up again, one may keep upon it hot water, if that has been heated all it needs, or a dish which has been boiled all it needs, even if they are coals of broom.[8] Then this proves that when it shrinks and is improved thereby it is permitted?—[No.] Here it is different, because he covered it with ashes. If so, why state it? It is necessary [to state it where] it blazed up again. Then it is identical with the first [dictum]?—It is necessary [to state it] of coals of broom.

R. Shesheth said in R. Joḥanan's name: If a stove is fired with peat or wood, hot water insufficiently heated, and a dish insufficiently cooked, may be kept upon it. But if he [the owner] removed [them], he must not replace [them] before he sweeps or covers [it] with ashes. Thus he holds that we learnt our Mishnah with respect to replacing, but keeping is permitted even if it is not swept
a or covered with ashes.[1] Said Raba: We learnt both: We learnt with respect to keeping: 'Bread may not be set in an oven before nightfall, nor a cake set upon coals, unless its surface can form a crust [while it is yet day]'.[2] Hence if its surface formed a crust, it is permitted.[3] With respect to replacing we also learnt: BETH HILLEL RULE: WE MAY REPLACE TOO. Now Beth Hillel permit it only when it is swept or covered with ashes, but not if it is neither swept nor covered with ashes.[4]—R. Shesheth indeed informs us of the deduction of the Mishnah.[5]

R. Samuel b. Judah said in R. Joḥanan's name: If a stove is fired with peat or wood, one may keep upon it a dish sufficiently cooked or hot water which is sufficiently heated, even if it [the dish] shrinks and is improved thereby. Said one of the Rabbis to R. Samuel b. Judah, But Rab and Samuel both maintain: If it shrinks and is improved thereby it is forbidden?[6]—He answered him: Do I then not know that R. Joseph said in Rab Judah's name in Samuel's name: If it shrinks and is improved thereby it is forbidden? I tell it to you[7] according to R. Joḥanan. R. 'Uḳba of Mesene[8] said to R. Ashi: You, who are near to Rab and Samuel, do act as Rab and Samuel; but we will act according to R. Joḥanan.[9]

Abaye asked R. Joseph, What about keeping [a pot on the
b stove]?[1]—He answered him, It is indeed kept for Rab Judah, and he eats thereof! Put Rab Judah aside, said he, for since he is in danger,[2] it may be done for him even on the Sabbath. What about keeping it for me and you?—In Sura,[3] he replied, they do keep it. For R. Naḥman b. Isaac is most particular,[4] and yet they keep it for him and he eats.

R. Ashi said: I was standing before R. Huna, when he ate a fish pie which they had kept [on the stove] for him. And I do not know whether it is because he holds that if it shrinks and is improved thereby it is permitted, or because since it contains flour paste it deteriorates in shrinking. R. Naḥman said: If it shrinks and is improved thereby, it is forbidden;[5] if it shrinks and deteriorates, it is permitted. This is the general rule of the matter: whatever contains flour paste, shrinks and deteriorates, except a stew of turnips, which though containing flour paste shrinks and improves. Yet that is only if it contains meat; but if it contains no meat, it shrinks and deteriorates. And even if it contains meat, we say thus only if it is not intended for guests; but if it is intended for guests, it deteriorates in the shrinking.[6] Pap of dates, *daysa*,[7] and a dish of dates shrink and deteriorate.

(4) Through cooking. (5) Rashi: the reference must be to a dish which improves the longer it is kept on the stove, for if it deteriorates, it may obviously be kept there, as we certainly need not fear that the owner may rake up the coals, and the dictum is superfluous. Ri: the reference is presumably to the average dish, which improves with shrinking. (6) And the dish may not be kept there. (7) For by covering it with ashes he showed that he did not desire any further shrinkage. (8) *Rothem* is a species of broom growing in the desert (Jast.), which retains its heat longer than other coals and is slower to go out.

a (1) V. *supra* 37a. (2) V. *supra* 19b. (3) To keep it there, though the oven is not swept, etc. (4) What need then of R. Joḥanan's dictum? (5) This is the answer: R. Shesheth informs us that the Mishnah refers to replacing (v. Tosaf. a.l.). Though Raba takes that for granted, the matter was in doubt (*supra* 36b). (6) To keep it on the stove. (7) That it is permitted. (8) In Babylon: it is the island formed by the Euphrates, the Tigris, and the Royal Canal. (9) Though they too were much nearer to the academies of Rab and Samuel than to R. Joḥanan's, the communities of Mesene preferred the authority of Palestine; v. Obermeyer, p. 204.

b (1) If the stove is unswept. (2) He suffered from bulimy, and had to eat hot food. (3) A town on the Euphrates, where Rab founded his famous academy. (4) Rashi. Or perhaps, a master of practice (Jast.), i.e., thoroughly versed in correct practice. (5) To keep it on the stove. (6) When intended for personal consumption it is cut up into small pieces before being placed in the pot, and so the fat pervades the whole and prevents deterioration. But when intended for guests it is cut up in large chunks; since the fat cannot pervade the whole the shrinking causes it to deteriorate. (7) A dish of pounded grain.

R. Ḥiyya b. Abba was asked: [38a] What[8] if one forgot a pot on the stove and [thus] cooked it on the Sabbath? He was silent and said nothing to them [his questioners]. On the morrow he went out and lectured to them: If one cooks [food] on the Sabbath unwittingly, he may eat [it]; if deliberately, he may not eat [it];[9] and there is no difference. What is meant by, 'and there is no difference'?—Rabbah and R. Joseph both explain it permissively: only he who cooked it, thus performing an action, may not eat a if it was deliberate; but this one[1] who did no action may eat even if it was deliberate. R. Naḥman b. Isaac explained it restrictively: only one who cooks may eat if it was done unwittingly, because he will not [thereby] come to dissemble;[2] but this one, who may come to dissemble,[3] may not even eat if it was unwitting.

An objection is raised: If one forgot a pot on the stove and [thus] cooked it on the Sabbath: unwittingly, he may eat [thereof]; if deliberately, he may not eat. When is that said? In the case of hot water insufficiently heated or a dish insufficiently cooked; but as for hot water sufficiently heated or a dish sufficiently cooked, whether unwitting or deliberate, he may eat [thereof]: thus said R. Meir. R. Judah said: Hot water sufficiently heated is permitted, because it boils away[4] and is thus harmed;[5] a dish sufficiently cooked is forbidden, because it shrinks and is thereby improved, and whatever shrinks and is thereby improved, e.g., cabbage, beans, and mincemeat, is forbidden; but whatever shrinks and thereby deteriorates, is permitted. At all events, a dish insufficiently cooked is mentioned.[6] As for R. Naḥman b. Isaac, it is well, there is no difficulty: here[7] it is before [the enactment of] the preventive measure;[8] there[9] it is after the preventive measure.[10] But [on the view of] Rabbah and R. Joseph who b explain it permissively, if before the preventive measure,[1] 'deliberate' is a difficulty;[2] if after the preventive measure, even 'unwitting' too is a difficulty.[3] That is [indeed] a difficulty.

What was the preventive measure?—For R. Judah b. Samuel said in the name of R. Abba in the name of R. Kahana in Rab's name: At first it was ruled: One who cooks [food] on the Sabbath unwittingly, he may eat [thereof], if deliberately, he may not eat; and the same applies to one who forgets.[4] But when those who intentionally left [it there] grew numerous, and they pleaded, We had forgotten [it on the stove], they [the Sages] retracted and penalized him who forgot.

Now, R. Meir is self-contradictory, and R. Judah is [likewise] self-contradictory?[5]—R. Meir is not self-contradictory: the one means at the outset; the other, if done.[6] R. Judah too is not self-contradictory: there it means that it [the stove] was swept or covered with ashes;[7] here, that it was not swept or covered with ashes.

The scholars propounded: What if one transgressed and deliberately left it? Did the Rabbis penalize him or not?—Come and hear: For Samuel b. Nathan said in R. Ḥanina's name: When R. Jose went to Sepphoris, he found hot water which had been left on the stove, and did not forbid it to them; [he also found] shrunken eggs,[8] and forbade them to them. Surely it means for that Sabbath?[9]—No: for the following Sabbath.[10]

Now, this implies that shrunken eggs go on shrinking and are thereby improved?—Yes. For R. Ḥama b. Ḥanina said: My Master and I were once guests in a certain place, and eggs shrunk to the size of crab-apples were brought before us, and we ate many of them.

BETH HILLEL RULE: ONE MAY REPLACE [IT] TOO. R.

(8) On the view forbidding the keeping of food on an unswept stove. (9) This is a Mishnah. 'And there is no difference' is R. Ḥiyya b. Abba's addition in answer to the question.

a (1) *Sc.* who left the pot on the stove. 'If one cooks' means by placing it on the stove. (2) I.e., cook deliberately and pretend that it was unwitting. Since cooking is Biblically forbidden, one is not suspected of evading the prohibition. (3) If it may be eaten when it is inadvertently left on the stove and cooked, he may leave it there deliberately and pretend forgetfulness, for the prohibition of leaving a pot on the stove is only Rabbinical. (4) Lit., 'shrinks'. (5) By the loss. Hence there is no fear of raking up the coals to make it boil more.—'Sufficiently heated' means to boiling point. (6) And a distinction is drawn between inadvertence and a deliberate act. This contradicts both views *supra*. (7) In the Baraitha quoted. (8) Stated *infra*. (9) R. Naḥman's interpretation of R. Ḥiyya b. Abba's ruling. (10) The prohibition stated by R. Naḥman is only a preventive measure of the Rabbis, and the Baraitha states the law prior thereto.

b (1) I.e., if R. Ḥiyya b. Abba's ruling was stated before the preventive measure was enacted. (2) The Baraitha states that it is forbidden, whilst he ruled that it is permitted. (3) Because the Baraitha which states that it is permitted in that case was taught before the preventive measure. (4) A dish on the stove, and it is cooked. (5) V. *supra* 37a. There R. Meir forbids a dish, even if sufficiently cooked, whilst here he permits it. On the other hand, R. Judah permits there a dish if sufficiently cooked, whilst here he forbids it.—The views they both give there of Beth Hillel's ruling must be regarded as their own too, since the *halachah* is always as Beth Hillel. (6) On 37a the question is what may be done at the outset; there R. Meir rules that one must not leave a dish on the stove, even if it was sufficiently cooked before the Sabbath. But here he rules that if it was so left it is permitted. (7) Then the dish is permitted. (8) Eggs boiled or roasted down to a small size. (9) He forbade them to eat the eggs on that Sabbath. This answers the question. (10) He told them not to leave the eggs on the stove for the future.

שכח קדירה על גבי כירה ובישלה בשבת מהו אישתיק ולא א"ל ולא מידי למחר נפק דרש להו *המבשל *בשבת *בשוגג יאכל במזיד לא יאכל ולא שנא מאי ול"ש רבה ורב יוסף דאמרי תרווייהו להיתירא מבשל הוא דקא עביד מעשה במזיד לא יאכל אבל האי דלא קא עביד מעשה במזיד נמי יאכל רב נחמן בר יצחק אמר ג לאיסורא מבשל הוא דלא אתי לאיערומי בשוגג יאכל אבל האי דאתי לאיערומי בשוגג נמי לא יאכל מיתיבי *שכח קדירה על גבי כירה ובישלה בשבת בשוגג יאכל במזיד לא יאכל בד"א בחמין שלא הוחמו כל צורכן ותבשיל שלא בישל כל צורכו אבל חמין שהוחמו כל צורכן ותבשיל שבישל כל צורכו בין בשוגג בין במזיד יאכל דברי ר"מ ר' יהודה אומר חמין שהוחמו כל צורכן מותרין מפני שמצטמק ורע לו ותבשיל שבישל כל צורכו אסור מפני שמצטמק ויפה לו וכל המצטמק ויפה לו כגון כרוב ופולים ובשר *טרוף אסור וכל המצטמק ורע לו מותר קתני מיהא תבשיל שלא בישל כל צורכו בשלמא לרב נחמן בר יצחק לא קשיא כאן קודם גזרה כאן לאחר גזרה אלא רבה ורב יוסף דאמרי להיתירא אי קודם גזרה קשיא מזיד אי לאחר גזרה קשיא נמי שוגג קשיא מאי גזירתא דאמר רב יהודה בר שמואל א"ר אבא אמר רב כהנא אמר רב בתחילה היו אומרים המבשל בשבת בשוגג יאכל במזיד לא יאכל וה"ה לשוכח משרבו משהין במזיד ואומרים שכחים אנו חזרו וקנסו על השוכח קשיא דר' מאיר אדר' מאיר קשיא דר' יהודה אדר' יהודה דר' מאיר אדר"מ לא קשיא הא לכתחילה הא דיעבד דר' יהודה אדר' יהודה נמי לא קשיא כאן בגרופה וקטומה כאן בשאינה גרופה וקטומה איבעיא להו עבר ושהה מאי מי קנסוהו רבנן או לא ת"ש דאמר שמואל בר נתן א"ר חנינא כשהלך רבי יוסי לציפורי מצא חמין שנשתהו על גבי כירה ולא אסר להן ביצים מצומקות שנשתהו על גבי כירה ואסר להן מאי לאו לאותו שבת לא ד לשבת הבאה מכלל דביצים מצומקות מצטמקות ויפה להן נינהו אין דאמר רב חמא בר חנינא פעם אחת נתארחתי אני ורבי למקום ·אחד והביאו לפנינו ביצים מצומקות כעוזרדין ואכלנו מהן הרבה: ב"ה אומרים אף מחזירין: אמר רב ששת לדברי האומר מחזירין

מחזירין

רש"י

שכח קדרה· אליבא מאן דאסר: המבשל בשבת· משנה היא: ולא שנא. אבל האי דשכח קדרה לא שנא בין שוגג למזיד והכי דרש להו סתמא ולא פירש אי השוגג מדמה לה ומותר לאוכלה אי אמזיד מדמה לה ואסור: במזיד נמי· אם השהה על גבי כירה מבעוד יום יאכל: דלא אתי לאיערומי· ולעשות מזיד ולומר שוגג הייתי דלא נחשדו ישראל על השבתות: דאתי לאיערומי· דאיסור דרבנן הוא וקילא ליה ואתי לשהויי מזיד ויאמר שכחתי: מיתיבי שכח קדרה כו' בשוגג· כגון האי דשכח יאכל בשבת: במזיד· דלא שכח אלא הניח לא יאכל: ובשר טרוף· דגלי דעתיה דלא לאורחים קבעי לה: וכל המצטמק ויפה לו· כלומר וכן כל שאר המצטמק ויפה להם אסור לאוכלן אם השהן מזיד: קתני מיהת· בשלא בישל כל צרכו דיש חילוק בין שוגג למזיד במשהה קשיא בין לרבה ורב יוסף דשרו מזיד בין לרב נחמן דאסר שוגג: בשלמא לרב נחמן· מצי לתרוצי כי תניא ההיא דשוגג יאכל לפני גזירה דאמרינן לקמן דגזרו על השוכחין וכי איתמר דר' חייא בר אבא דתריצנא אליביה דשוגג אסור לאחר גזירה: אלא לרבה ורב יוסף· דאמרי אליבא דר' חייא בר אבא להתירא אף במזיד: אי קודם גזירה· אתמר דר' חייא: קשיא מיהא מזיד· דהכא תניא במזיד לא יאכל: ואי לאחר גזירה קשיא נמי שוגג· דאפי' שוגג ה"ל למיסר דאילו מתני' קודם גזירה נשנית: המבשל בשבת· בידים דאיכא חיובא דאורייתא: וה"ה לשוכח· דהמשהה נמי מבעוד יום אם שכח בשוגג יאכל ואם במזיד המשהה לא יאכל כאילו בשלה בידים בשבת: קשיא דר' מאיר אדר' מאיר· דתנן לעיל בריש פירקין לר' מאיר אליבא דב"ה חמין אבל לא תבשיל והכא שרי חמין ותבשיל שבישל כל צרכו: וקשיא דר' יהודה אדר' יהודה· דהתם א"ר יהודה חמין ותבשיל והכא אסר תבשיל שבישל כל צרכו: הא לכתחלה· משנה קמייתא לשהות לכתחלה קמיירי והך בהשהה כבר קאמר דמותר לאוכלה: כאן בגרופה וקטומה· ההיא דלעיל איירי בגרופה וקטומה כדקתני בה משהין על גבי גרופה וקטומה ואין משהין על שאינה גרופה ומה הן משהין על הגרופה שהתרנו לשהות ר"מ אומר כו' הלכך אפי' לכתחלה שרי ר' יהודה והכא בשאינה גרופה הלכך דיעבד אסר: עבר ושהה במזיד מאי· מותר לאוכלה או לא: חמין לא אסר· דמצטמק ורע לו: ביצים אסר· דמצטמק ויפה לו: מאי לאו לאותו שבת· אסרן עליהן באכילה: לא לשבת הבאה· אסר להן עכשיו שלא לעשות כן לשבת הבאה אבל באכילה שרו: מכלל דביצים מצומקות כו'· בעיא היא: והביאו לפניו· בחול: כעוזרדין· שנצטמקו עד שנעשו דקות כעוזרדין קורמ"ש בלע"ז ומדאמר ואכלנו הרבה מכלל דיפה להן:

תוספות

שכח קדרה על גבי כירה ובישלה בשבת מהו· אע"ג דקיי"ל כחנניא הכא בעי בדלא בשיל כמאכל בן דרוסאי דמודה ביה חנניא אי נמי בעי אפי' בקידרא חייתא והא דשרינן בפ"ק (דף יח: ושם) קידרא חייתא היינו דוקא בתנור שחומו רב דבלא חיתוי יתבשל עד למחר אבל כירה דשליט בה אוירא אסור דאיכא למיחש שמא יחתה:

אבל האי דלא קעביד מעשה במזיד נמי יאכל· תימה דהא אמר בפ"ק (שם) לא תמלא אשה קדרה עססיות כו' ואם נתנה למוצאי שבת אסורין בכדי שיעשו וי"ל דבלאו הכי פריך שפיר מברייתא דמייתי:

בשלמא לרב נחמן בר יצחק כאן קודם גזירה כו'· תימה לר"י *לימא תרווייהו קודם גזירה והא דשרי בברייתא שוגג היינו בבשיל כמאכל בן דרוסאי ורב נחמן איירי בדלא בשיל כמאכל בן דרוסאי כדפי' ותירץ ר"ת דבישלה בשבת משמע שלא היתה קודם לכן כלל מבושלת ולא בעי למימר נמי דרב נחמן סבר כר' יהודה דאסר תבשיל אפי' בישל כל צרכו וכ"ש לא בישל משום דדילמא ר' יהודה לא איירי אלא במזיד אבל בשוגג מודה לר"מ דשרי אפי' לא בישל כל צרכו:

קשיא דר' מאיר אדר' מאיר· כאן משמע דסתם חמין ותבשיל הוי נמי מבושל כל צרכו דאי לאו הכי לא הוה פריך מידי ורשב"א אומר דאפי' אי סתם חמין ותבשיל הוי בלא בשיל כל צרכו פריך שפיר דהא בשאינה גרופה משמע בברייתא דלעיל דאין משהין כלל אפי' בישל כל צרכו דאי הוה שרי בישל כל צרכו ה"ל לפרש מה הן משהין בשאינה גרופה כדמפרש אגרופה והכא שרי ר"מ בישל כל צרכו אפי' בשאינה גרופה מ"מ נראה דסתם חמין ותבשיל הוי נמי בבשיל כל צרכו מדפשיטא ליה לתלמודא דמאן דאסר להחזיר אסר אפי' בישל כל צרכו כדמוכח גבי ואף ר' אושעיא סבר כו':

הא לכתחלה הא דיעבד· לא סגי בהאי שינויא דהא לעיל שרי ר' מאיר סתם חמין דהויא אפי' לא הוחמו כל צורכן אפי' לכתחלה והכא אסר חמין שלא הוחמו כל צורכן אפי' דיעבד אלא צריך לשנויי כדמשני אקשיא דר' יהודה אדר' יהודה הא בגרופה וקטומה הא בשאינה גרופה ואדרבי יהודה נמי צריך לשנויא (דהכא) דהא לכתחלה הא דיעבד דהא בשאינה גרופה אסר לעיל אפי' חמין שנתבשל כל צרכו והכא שרי אלא דאיכא לשנויי הא לכתחלה הא דיעבד:

עבר ושהה מאי· בדלא בשיל כמאכל בן דרוסאי ליכא לאוקמי דהא כבר פשט לעיל לאיסורא כרב נחמן בר יצחק ונראה לר"י דמבעיא ליה בבשיל ובשוגג ואליבא דר' יהודה אע"ג דאין הלכה כר' יהודה אי אסר מצטמק ויפה לו דוקא במזיד או דילמא אפי' בשוגג ומייתי ראיה ממעשה דר' יוסי דאסר ומשמע ליה דאפי' בשוגג היה מדקאמר ונשתהו ולא קאמר ושיהו ומיהו לשון עבר ושהה משמע במזיד כמו עברה ולשה דפסחים (דף מב·) ואומר רשב"א דקודם גזירה בעו דאחר גזירה פשיטא דאסור בשוגג כמו מזיד:

לא לשבת הבאה· כולה סוגיא בשאינה גרופה דבגרופה ליכא שום אמורא דאסר כדפרישית לעיל והיינו כרב דאסר לעיל מצטמק ויפה לו: אפי'

עין משפט נר מצוה

ז א מיי' פ"ג מהל' שבת הלכה ד ופ"ו הל' כג סמג לאוין סה טור וש"ע א"ח סימן שיח סעיף א

ח ב ג מיי' פ"ג מהל' שבת הלכה ט סמג לאוין סה טוש"ע א"ח סימן רנג סעיף א:

[עי' תוספות ע"ז סו: ד"ה אמר רבא]

ושמא לתלמודא לא נראה לחלק כיון דר"מ אוסר אפילו תבשיל

מסורת הש"ס

תוספתא פ"ג ב"ק עא. חולין טו. גיטין נג: ביצה יז: [תרומות פ"ב מ"ג] כתובות לד.

תוספתא פ"ג

[פי' שמחתכין אותו חתיכות קטנות ומרסקין אותו עד שנטרף במקפה או בעיסוי שכל זמן שמצטמק יותר טפי ומתערב עם התבשיל ערוך ערך ג]

רבינו חננאל

הא דבעו מר' חייא בר אבא שכח קדירה ע"ג כירה ובישלה בשבת ודרש להו המבשל בשבת בשוגג יאכל במזיד לא יאכל ולא שנא כלומר במבשל יש להפריש בין שוגג למזיד אבל בשוכח השוגג והמזיד שוין: רבה ורב יוסף אמרי שוכח בין שוגג ובין מזיד מותר לא קנסו רבנן אפילו במזיד רב נחמן בר יצחק אמר שניהן אסורין וקי"ל כוותיה ואותבינא עליה שכח קדירה על גבי כירה ובישלה בשבת בשוגג יאכל במזיד לא יאכל כו'· ועלתה לרבה ורב יוסף בקושיא ואקשינן הכא א"ר מאיר חמין שהוחמו כל צרכן ותבשיל שבישל כל צרכו בין בשוגג בין במזיד מותר ובתחלת הפרק אמר ומה הן משהין בש"א ולא כלום ובה"א חמין אבל לא תבשיל [ושנינן התם] לכתחילה דרבי יהודה אדרבי יהודה לא קשיא הא דקתני רבי יהודה הכא תבשיל שבישל כל צרכו אסור כירה שאינה גרופה ולא קטומה ולפיכך אסור והאי דקתני התם משהין ע"ג כירה לב"ה חמין ותבשיל בגרופה וקטומה וכיון שנתקשה רבה ורב יוסף נתקיימו דברי רב נחמן בר יצחק וקי"ל כוותיה כל השוכח קדירה ובישלה קודם גזירה הוה שרי ובתר גזירה קנסו רבנן אפילו שוגג ומאי גזירה דבתחלה היו אומרים המבשל בשבת בשוגג יאכל במזיד לא יאכל וה"ה לשוכח ומשרבו משהי קדירה במזיד ואומרים שוכחים אנן גזרו אף על השוכח· וכיון דסלקי דמצטמק ויפה לו אסור איבעיא לן עבר ושהה מאי ואתינן למפשטא מהא דתניא דאסיר רבי יוסי בצפורי ביצים מצומקים שנשתהו על גבי כירה (שמא) [ש"מ] שי"ר ושהה קנסו רבנן ודחינן לא אסר להו לעשות

רב נסים גאון

פרק כירה אמר רבי חנינא כשהלך רבי יוסי לציפורי· הדבר שגרם לו לילך לציפורי הוא שמפורש בבמה מדליקין (דף לג) יוסי ששתק יגלה לציפורי:

מחזירין אפילו בשבת ואף ר' אושעיא סבר אף מחזירין אפי' בשבת דא"ר אושעיא פעם אחת היינו עומדים לעילא מר' חייא רבה והעלנו לו קומקמוס של חמין מדיוטא התחתונה לדיוטא העליונה ומזגנו לו את הכוס והחזרנוהו למקומו ולא אמר לנו דבר א"ר זריקא א"ר אבא א"ר תדאי לא שנו אלא שעודן בידו אבל הניחן ע"ג קרקע אסור א"ר אמי ר' תדאי *דעבד לגרמיה הוא דעבד אלא הכי א"ר חייא א"ר יוחנן אפילו הניחה על גבי קרקע מותר פליגי בה רב דימי ורב שמואל בר יהודה ותרווייהו משמיה דרבי אלעזר אמרי חד אמר עודן בידו מותר ע"ג קרקע אסור וחד אמר הניחן על גבי קרקע נמי מותר אמר חזקיה משמיה דאביי הא דאמרת עודן בידו מותר לא אמרן אלא שדעתו להחזיר אבל אין דעתו להחזיר אסור מכלל דעל גבי קרקע אע"פ שדעתו להחזיר אסור איכא דאמרי אמר חזקיה משמיה דאביי הא דאמרת על גבי קרקע אסור לא אמרן אלא שאין דעתו להחזיר אבל דעתו להחזיר מותר מכלל שבעודן בידו אע"פ שאין דעתו להחזיר מותר בעי ר' ירמיה תלאן במקל מהו הניחן על גבי מטה מהו בעי רב אשי פינן ממיחם למיחם מהו תיקו: **מתני'** תנור שהסיקוהו בקש ובגבבא לא יתן בין מתוכו בין מעל גביו כופח שהסיקוהו בקש ובגבבא ה"ז ככיריים בגפת ובעצים הרי הוא כתנור: **גמ'** תנור שהסיקוהו סבר רב יוסף למימר תוכו תוכו ממש על גביו על גביו ממש אבל לסמוך שפיר דמי איתיביה אביי כופח שהסיקוהו בקש ובגבבא הרי הוא ככיריים בגפת ובעצים הרי הוא כתנור ואסור הא ככירה שרי במאי עסקינן אילימא על גביו ובמאי אילימא כשאינו גרוף וקטום אלא כירה כי אינה גרופה וקטומה על גביו מי שרי אלא לאו לסמוך וקתני הרי הוא כתנור ואסיר אמר רב אדא בר אהבה הכא בכופח גרוף וקטום ותנור גרופה· וקטומה עסקינן הרי הוא כתנור דאע"ג דגרוף וקטום על גביו אסור דאי ככירה כי גרופה וקטומה שפיר דמי: תניא כוותיה דאביי תנור שהסיקוהו בקש ובגבבא אין סומכין לו ואין צריך לומר על גביו ואין צריך לומר לתוכו ואין צריך לומר בגפת ובעצים כופח שהסיקוהו בקש ובגבבא· סומכין לו [א] ואין נותנין על גביו בגפת ובעצים אין סומכין לו אמר ליה רב אחא בריה דרבא לרב אשי האי כופח היכי דמי אי ככירה דמי אפילו בגפת ובעצים נמי אי כתנור דמי אפילו בקש ובגבבא נמי לא אמר ליה נפיש הבליה מדכירה וזוטר הבליה מדתנור היכי דמי כופח היכי דמי כירה א"ר יוסי בר חנינא כופח מקום שפיתת קדרה אחת כירה מקום שפיתת שתי קדרות אמר אביי ואיתימא רבי ירמיה אף אנן נמי תנינא *כירה שנחלקה לאורכה טהורה לרחבה טמאה כופח בין לאורכו בין לרוחבו טהור: **מתני'** אין נותנין ביצה בצד המיחם בשביל שתתגלגל ולא יפקיענה בסודרין ור' יוסי מתיר ולא יטמיננה בחול ובאבק דרכים בשביל שתצלה מעשה שעשו אנשי טבריא והביאו סילון של צונן לתוך אמה של חמין אמרו להם חכמים אם בשבת כחמין שהוחמו בשבת ואסורין ברחיצה ובשתיה אם ביום טוב כחמין שהוחמו ביום טוב ואסורין ברחיצה ומותרין בשתיה: **גמ'** איבעיא להו גלגל מאי אמר רב יוסף [ב] גלגל חייב חטאת אמר מר בריה דרבינא אף אנן נמי תנינא כל

רש"י

מחזירין אפילו בשבת · ביום המחרת ולא תימא פלוגתייהו משחשכה והתם הוא דשרו משום דמוכחא מילתא דאדעתא דאהדורי לצורך מחר שקיל ליה אבל ביום לא מוכח דשקיל ליה אדעתא דאהדורי ובטלה לה הטמנה וה"ל כמטמין לכתחלה : קומקמוס · יורה קטנה : דיוטא · עלייה : למקומו · לכירה : אבל הניח על גבי קרקע אסור · להחזיר דבטלי לה הטמנה דאתמול והוי כמטמין לכתחלה : לגרמיה · יחיד הוא בדבר ואין הלכה כמותו : תלאן במקל מהו · כעודן בידו דמי או כהניחן ע"ג קרקע דמי : פינן ממיחם למיחם מהו · מי הוי כמטמין לכתחלה ואסור להחזירן לכירה או לא : מיחם · קומקמוס שמחמם בו חמין : מתני' תנור · מתוך שקצר למעלה ורחב למטה נקלט חומו לתוכו טפי מכירה: כופח · בגמרא מפרש לה עשוי חלל ככירה אבל ארכו כרחבו ואין בו אלא שיעור שפיתת קדירה אחת וכירה יש בה שפיתת שתי קדירות : גמ' על גביו · על שפתו : אבל לסמוך · אצל דופנו : הא ככירה שרי · כלומר מדקתני הרי הוא כתנור מכלל דאי הוה מדמי ליה לכירה הוה שרי ושמעינן מינה דכירה שהוסק בגפת ובעצים שרי : ובמאי קאי · קס"ד בשאינה גרופה ואי על גבה מי שרי : תניא כוותיה דאביי · דאסור לסמוך אתנור : אפי' בגפת ועצים · לשתרי בגרופה וקטומה : שנחלקה לאורכה · הרי בטלו שתי שפיתותיה שנחלקת רחבה לשתים הלכך טהרה מטומאתה שהרי ניתלה : נחלקה לרחבה . נמצאו שתי השפיתות קיימות זו לבדה וזו לבדה : כופח בין לאורכה בין לרחבה טהורה · שהרי ארכה כרחבה וכולה מקום שפיתה אחת : מתני' אין טומנין ביצה בצד המיחם · קומקמוס של נחשת : בשביל שתתגלגל · שתצלה קצת עד שתהא מגולגלת : ולא יפקיענה בסודרין · לא ישברנה על סודר שהוחם בחמה כדי שתצלה מחומו של סודר : בחול ובאבק דרכים · שהוחמו מכח חמה ובגמרא מפרש אמאי לא פליג רבי יוסי בהא : והביאו סילון · מבעוד יום : של צונן · כדי לחממן דהמים נמשכין ובאין כל השבת : לתוך אמה · של חמי טבריא : אם בשבת · אותן שבאו בשבת : ה"ג כחמין שהוחמו :

תוספות

אפילו בשבת · פירש בקונטרס בשבת ביום המחרת ולפ"ז ה"ל למינקט אפי' ביום השבת ולמאי דפרישית דעיקר פלוגתייהו בחול אתי שפיר : **פינה** ממיחם למיחם מהו · וא"ת דבפרק במה טומנין (לקמן דף נא.) תניא וקניה רשב"ג אומר לא אסרו אלא בתוכו מיחם אבל פינה ממיחם למיחם מותר אלמא במיחם אחר שרי טפי והכי משמע איפכא ואור"ת דהכא גבי השהה ע"ג כירה כשהוא בתוכו מיחם שהוא חם לא אתי לחתויי אבל במיחם אחר שהוא קר אתי לחתויי אבל גבי הטמנה שרי טפי כשהוא קר דבחיתוי מועט לא יועיל: ורשב"א מפרש בשם ר"י דהתם בהטמנה דהוי לצורך מחר ליכא למיחש לחיתויי דבלא חיתוי יתחמם הרבה אבל הכא דבעי לה בלילה איכא למיחש לחיתויי ומיהו קצת משמע התם דמיירי במטמין בלילה (ת"י) :

תנור שהסיקוהו בקש ובגבבא לא יתן כו' · אי להחזיר תנן הכא נמי האי לא יתן לא יחזיר אבל להשהות משהה אפילו בתנור שאינו גרוף וקטום כדמשמע בפ"ק (דף יח:) *דשריקן קידרא חייתא ובשיל כמאכל בן דרוסאי אפילו באינו גרוף וקטום ומשמע התם דבתנור איירי דקאי אהא דקתני התם לעיל לא תמלא אשה קדרה *עססיות כו' :

אילימא בשאינה גרופה · האי לישנא לאו דוקא דאביי סבר דלא מיתוקמה בגרופה דבגרופה לא מסתבר ליה שיהא חילוק בין גפת ועצים לקש וגבבא דאי הוה מצי אביי לאוקמה בגרופה כדמוקי לה רב אדא לא הוה מצי למפשט מידי ורב אדא דמוקי לה בגרופה סבר דיש לעולם יותר חום כשהסיקוה בגפת ובעצים אע"ג דגרופה מבקש ובגבבא :

תניא כוותיה דאביי כו' · יש דגרסי בסיפא כופח שהסיקוהו בגפת ובעצים *אין סומכין לה דאי גרס סומכין לה לא אתא כוותיה דאביי דאית ליה דבכופח נמי אין סומכין כדאמרינן לעיל וי"ל דאי גרסינן סומכין איכא לאוקמה בגרופה ונקט גפת ועצים לרבותא דאפילו הכי סומכין לה :

לא יטמיננה בחול · אע"ג דאמר בלא יחפור (ב"ב דף יט. ושם) דחול דקריר מקרר דחמים מחים והכא ביצה היא קרה הכא מיירי בחול שהוחם בחמה דומיא דאבק דרכים :

מעשה והביאו סילון של צונן לתוך אמה של חמין כו' · מבעוד יום הביאוהו כדפירש בקונטרס ואין שום איסור כלל בהבאה כדתניא בפרק קמא (דף יח.) פותקין מים לגינה ומתמלאת והולכת כל השבת כולה ואסרו ברחיצה גזירה שמא יערבס בשבת ולערבס בשבת אסור משום תולדות האור וחשיבא כחדא גזירה *ואם היינו מפרשים דבסילון היו בו נקבים וכשהיו רוחצים בשבת היו פותחים הנקבים ומתערבין הצוננין בחמין הוה אתי שפיר טפי דהשתא ליכא אלא חדא גזירה אטו חמי האור אך בגמרא מדמי לה להטמנה מבעוד יום ויליף מינה לאסור להטמין

ואי מתני' להשהות תנן בתנור נמי אסור להשהות אע"ג דקידרא חייתא לעיל שרי הואיל כחנניה ומתני' אי להשהות תנן אתיא דלא כחנניה [ת"י]

ולפ"ז צריך למגרס בתר הכי ואצ"ל ע"ג ואצ"ל בתוכה ואי גרסי' סומכין גרסי' ונותנין אפילו ע"ג ואפילו בתוכה [ת"י]

והא דחשיב לה כחמין שהוחמו בשבת משמע טפי כפי' ראשון [ת"י]

עין משפט נר מצוה

ט א ב ג ד ה ו ז מיי' פ"ג מהל' שבת הלכה ב ז י סמג לאוין סה טוש"ע א"ח סימן רנג סעיף ב :

י ח מיי' פט"ז מהל' כלים הלכה יג :

יא ט י מיי' פ"ט מהל' שבת הל' ב ג טוש"ע א"ח סי' שיח סעיף ג :

יב כ מיי' פכ"ב מהל' שבת הלכה ג סמג שם טוש"ע א"ח סימן שכו סעיף ג וסימן רנז סעיף ה ו וסעיף א :

[יב] ב [מיי' פ"ט מהל' שבת הלכה ב] :

מסורת הש"ס

[ברכות מח: וש"נ]

כלים פ"ו מ"ג

הגהות הגר"א

[א] גמ' סומכין לו ואין נותנין · נ"ב נ"ל סומכין לו ונותנין כו' :

גליון הש"ס

תוס' ד"ה תנור כו' דשריקן קידרא חייתא ובשיל כמאכל בן דרוסאי · ק"ל הא שם לא נזכר מן מאב"ד אלא שהם ובשיל שפיר דמי אלא דאו' כתבו שם דהיינו כמאב"ד דהא קיימא לן כחנניה וא"כ איך עשו כאן סוככה מזה דלמא באמת תנור חמיר דכמאב"ד אסור ודאמרי' ובשיל ש"ד היינו כפשוטו ובשיל לגמרי גם אמאי לא הוכיחו כפשוטו דהא קתני ולא תרדה על גבי גחלים אלא כדי שיקרמו פניה תררה היינו בתנור כמ"ש תוס' לעיל דף לז ע"א ד"ה אא"כ וכו' אף על גב דתררה בתוכה היא · והיינו ע"כ משום דתררי אופין בתנור עכ"ם לא ייסם מפי' תמוה מאד :

רבינו חננאל

כן אלא לשבת הבאה וכן סוגיא דשמעתא : פיס' בה"א אף מחזירין אוקימנא הא דקתני מחזירין בשבת הוא ואפי' כמה פעמים ודוקא בכירה גרופה וקטומה והני מילי שלא הניחם ע"ג קרקע כלל אלא מחזיקם בידו ודעתו עליהם להחזירם הוא ששנינו אף מחזירין אבל אם הניחם ע"ג קרקע אע"פ שהיה בדעתו להחזירם לכירה אסור ואסיקנא לשמעתא בתרי לשני · וקי"ל כל כי האי גוונא בדאורייתא עבדינן לחומרא · ושבת איסורא דאורייתא היא : תלאם במקל או הניחם ע"ג המטה או הניחם בכרעי המטה או פינם ממיחם למיחם הני כולהו איבעיא ולא אפשיטו ועלו בתיקו · וקי"ל כל תיקו דאיסורא לחומרא : מתני' תנור שהסיקו בקש ובגבבא כו' אוקמא אביי לא יסמוך · תניא כוותיה תנור שהסיקו בקש ובגבבא אין סומכין לו ואין צ"ל על גביו · ואין צ"ל שהסיקו בגפת או בעצים · כופח שהסיקוה בקש ובגבבא הרי הוא ככירה · בגפת ובעצים הרי הוא כתנור ואסור · ואע"פ שהוא גרוף וקטום · ואסיק' כופח מקום שפיתת קדירה אחת · כירה מקום שפיתת ב' קדירות · ודייקינן לה מהא דתנן כירה שנחלקה לארכה טהור לרחבה טמא פי' עדיין תורת כלי עליה דהא יכול לשפות קדירה אחת כופח בין לארכה בין לרחבה טהורה · והאי כופח נפיש הבליה מדכירה וזוטר הבליה מדתנור וקי"ל מתני' בתנור של נחתומין · מפורש בלא יחפור (ב"ב כ:) אבל תנור [דידן] ככירה של נחתומין היא : פיס' אין נותנין ביצה בצד המיחם בשביל שתתגלגל גלגל

Shesheth said: On the view of him who maintains [38b] that one
a may replace it, [it is permitted] even on the Sabbath.[1] And R. Oshaia too holds that ONE MAY REPLACE IT TOO means even on the Sabbath. For R. Oshaia said: We were once standing before R. Ḥiyya Rabbah, and we brought up a kettle of hot water for him from the lower to the upper storey, mixed the cup for him,[2] and then replaced it, and he said not a word to us. R. Zeriḳa said in the name of R. Abba in R. Taddai's name: We learnt this only if they[3] are still in his hand: but if he set them down on the ground, it is forbidden.[4] R. Ammi observed: R. Taddai who acted [thus] acted for himself [only].[5] But thus did R. Ḥiyya say in R. Joḥanan's name: Even if he set them down on the ground, it is permitted.

R. Dimi and R. Samuel b. Judah differ therein, and both [state their views] in R. Eleazar's name: One says: If they are still in his hand, it is permitted; on the ground, it is forbidden. While the other maintains: Even if he placed them on the ground, it is still permitted. Hezekiah[6] observed in Abaye's name: As to what you say that if it is still in his hand it is permitted—that was said only where it was his [original] intention to replace them; but if it was not his intention to replace them, it is forbidden. Hence it follows that [if they are] on the ground, even if it was his intention to replace them, it is forbidden. Others state: Hezekiah observed in Abaye's name: As to what you say that if they are on the ground it is forbidden, that was said only if it was not his [original] intention to replace them; but if it was his intention to replace them, it is permitted. Hence it follows that [if they are] in his hand, even if it was not his intention to replace them, it is permitted.

R. Jeremiah propounded: What if he hung them on a staff
b or placed them on a couch?[1] R. Ashi propounded: What if he emptied them from one kettle to another? The questions stand over.

MISHNAH. IF AN OVEN WAS HEATED WITH STUBBLE OR RAKINGS, ONE MUST NOT PLACE [A POT, ETC.,] EITHER INSIDE OR ON TOP.[2] IF A KUPPAḤ[3] WAS HEATED WITH STUBBLE OR RAKINGS, IT IS LIKE A DOUBLE STOVE;[4] WITH PEAT OR TIMBER, IT IS LIKE AN OVEN.

GEMARA. IF AN OVEN WAS HEATED: R. Joseph thought to explain INSIDE AND ON TOP literally, but as for leaning [a pot against it], that is well. Abaye objected to him: IF A KUPPAḤ WAS HEATED WITH STUBBLE OR RAKINGS, IT IS LIKE A DOUBLE STOVE; WITH PEAT OR TIMBER, IT IS LIKE AN OVEN, and is forbidden. Hence if it were like a [double] stove, it would be permitted. To what is the reference: Shall we say, on its top? Then under what circumstance? Shall we say that it is not swept or covered with ashes? Is the top of a stove permitted when it is not swept or covered with ashes? Hence it must surely mean to lean against it; yet it is taught, IT IS LIKE AN OVEN, and forbidden?—Said R. Adda b. Ahabah: Here the reference is to a *kuppaḥ* that is swept or covered with ashes, and an oven that is swept or covered with ashes: IT IS LIKE AN OVEN, in that though it is swept or covered with ashes, the top is forbidden; for if it were like a [double] stove, if swept or covered with ashes,
c it would be well.[1]

It was taught in accordance with Abaye: If an oven is heated with stubble or rakings, one may not lean [a pot, etc.,] against it, and [placing on] the top goes without saying,[2] and in the inside goes without saying; and it goes without saying [when it is heated] with peat or wood. If a *kuppaḥ* is heated with stubble or rakings, one may lean [a pot] against it, but not place [it] on top;[3] [but if it is heated] with peat or wood, one must not lean [a pot] against it.

R. Aḥa son of Raba asked R. Ashi: How is this *kuppaḥ* regarded? If like a [double] stove, even with peat or wood too?[4] If like an oven, neither with stubble or rakings?[5] He answered: Its heat is greater than a [double] stove's but less than an oven's.[6]

What is a *kuppaḥ* and what is a [double] stove [*kirah*]?—Said R. Jose b. Ḥanina: A *kuppaḥ* has room for placing one pot; a [double] stove [*kirah*] has room for placing two pots. Abaye—others state, R. Jeremiah—said: We learnt likewise: If a [double] stove [*kirah*] is divided along its length, it is clean; along its breadth, it is unclean; [if] a *kuppaḥ* [is divided], whether along its length or along its breadth, it is clean.[7]

MISHNAH. ONE MUST NOT PLACE AN EGG AT THE SIDE OF A BOILER FOR IT TO BE ROASTED,[8] AND ONE MUST NOT BREAK IT INTO A [HOT] CLOTH;[9] BUT R. JOSE PERMITS IT. AND ONE MAY NOT PUT IT AWAY IN [HOT] SAND OR ROAD DUST FOR IT TO BE ROASTED. IT ONCE HAPPENED THAT THE PEOPLE OF TIBERIAS DID THUS: THEY CONDUCTED A PIPE
d OF COLD WATER THROUGH AN ARM OF THE HOT SPRINGS.[1] SAID THE SAGES TO THEM: IF ON THE SABBATH,[2] IT IS LIKE HOT WATER HEATED ON THE SABBATH, AND IS FORBIDDEN BOTH FOR WASHING AND FOR DRINKING; IF ON A FESTIVAL, IT IS LIKE WATER HEATED ON A FESTIVAL, WHICH IS FORBIDDEN FOR WASHING BUT PERMITTED FOR DRINKING.

GEMARA. The scholars propounded: What if one does roast[3] it?—Said R. Joseph: If one roasts it, he is liable to a sin-offering. Mar son of Rabina said, We learnt likewise: [39a]

a (1) Rashi: not only Friday evening, but on the morrow too. (2) Wine was not drunk neat but diluted. (3) The pot or hot water. (4) To replace them on the stove. (5) Being stricter than necessary. (6) Var. lec.: Rab Hezekiah.

b (1) That is intermediate between retaining them in his hand and placing them on the ground. (2) The oven (*tannur*) had a broad base and narrowed at the top. It thereby retained more heat than a stove (*kirah*); hence the prohibition even if it is heated with stubble or rakings only. (3) Jast.: a small stove or brazier. (4) I.e., the ordinary stove which held two pots; v. 38b.

c (1) I.e., permitted. (2) That it is forbidden. (3) Wilna Gaon emends: *and* may place (it) on top. (4) It should be permitted, if it is swept or covered with ashes. (5) Should it be permitted. (6) Hence it occupies an intermediate position. (7) When the *kirah* is divided along its length it cannot be used at all, hence it ceases to be a utensil and is clean (cf. *supra* 35a; n. b9); but when divided along its breadth, each portion can be used for one pot, and it is therefore subject to uncleanness. Since a *kuppaḥ* has room for only one pot, whichever way it is divided it ceases to be a utensil and is clean. (8) Lit., 'that it should be rolled'. (9) To be roasted thus (Rashi). Others: he must not cause it to crack by wrapping it in a hot cloth and rolling it; v. Tosaf. Yom. Ṭob. a.l.

d (1) Tiberias possesses thermal springs. This was done before the Sabbath. (2) I.e., the water which is drawn from the pipe on the Sabbath. (3) Lit., 'roll'.

That which came into hot water before the Sabbath[4] may be steeped in hot water on the Sabbath;[5] but whatever did not come into hot water before the Sabbath, may be rinsed with hot water on the Sabbath,[6] except old salted [pickled] fish and the colias of the Spaniards,[7] because their rinsing completes their preparation.[8] This proves it.

AND HE MUST NOT BREAK IT INTO A [HOT] CLOTH. Now, as to what we learnt: 'A dish may be placed in a pit, in order that it should be guarded, and wholesome water into noisome water,[9] for it to be cooled, or cold water in the sun, for it to be heated',[10] shall we say that that agrees with R. Jose, but not with the Rabbis?—Said R. Naḥman: In the sun, all agree that it is permitted;[11] in a fire-heated object,[12] all agree that it is forbidden.[13] Where do
a they differ? Concerning a sun-heated object.[1] One Master holds that we forbid a sun-heated object on account of a fire-heated object; whilst the other Master holds that we do not forbid it.

AND ONE MAY NOT PUT IT AWAY IN [HOT] SAND. Now, let R. Jose differ here too?—Rabbah said: It is a preventive measure, lest one come to hide it in hot ashes.[2] R. Jose said: Because he may move earth [sand] from its place.[3] Wherein do they differ?—In respect of crushed earth.[4]

An objection is raised: R. Simeon b. Gamaliel said: An egg may be rolled [roasted] on a hot roof[5] but not on boiling lime.[6] As for the view that it is forbidden lest he hide it in hot ashes, it is well: there is nought to fear [here].[7] But on the view that it is because he may move earth from its place, let us forbid it?—The average roof has no earth.

Come and hear: IT ONCE HAPPENED THAT THE PEOPLE OF TIBERIAS DID THUS: THEY CONDUCTED A PIPE OF COLD WATER THROUGH AN ARM OF THE HOT SPRINGS etc. On the view that it is forbidden lest he hide it in hot ashes, it is well: hence this is similar to hiding.[8] But on the view that it is because he may move earth from its place, what can be said?[9]—Do you think that the incident of Tiberias refers to the second clause?[10] It refers to the first clause: ONE MUST NOT BREAK IT INTO A [HOT] CLOTH; BUT R. JOSE PERMITS IT; and the Rabbis argued thus with R. Jose: but in the incident of the people of Tiberias, it was a sun-heated object,[11] yet the Rabbis forbade it? That was a product of fire, he retorted, because they[12] pass over the entrance to Gehenna.[13]

(4) I.e., anything which was boiled before the Sabbath. (5) To soften it. It is not regarded as preparing the food in any way, since it was already prepared before the Sabbath. (6) But not steeped. (7) Jast.: A species of tunny fish. (8) The phrase implies that it is 'work' in the full sense of the term, involving the doer in a sin-offering. The same applies to an egg placed at the side of a boiler and roasted. (9) A vessel of hot water may be placed in a pool of stagnant cold water. (10) V. *infra* 146b. (11) Because it is unusual to cook thus, and there is no fear that it will lead to cooking by fire. (12) *Sc.* a cloth. (13) Because it can be confused with the fire itself, and if that is permitted, people will roast directly on the fire.

a (1) A cloth heated by the sun. (2) Which is definitely forbidden as cooking; hence R. Jose admits the interdict here. (3) He may have insufficient sand, and scoop out more, which itself is forbidden; therefore R. Jose agrees.—The Mishnah treats of sand scooped out before the Sabbath, and even then it is forbidden. (4) In a large quantity. R. Joseph's reason does not operate, hence it will be permitted; but Rabbah's reason still holds good. (5) Heated by the sun. (6) Heated by the fire. (7) In the case of a hot roof, since the egg is not hidden in anything. (8) The cold water is kept in the pot. (9) That does not apply here; why did they forbid it? (10) The prohibition of putting an egg in hot sand, etc. (11) They thought that the thermal springs were hot through the sun. (12) The springs. (13) And are heated by the fires of hell!—On Gehenna v. *supra* 33a, n. c8. [Maim. Mishnah Commentary *Nega'im* IX, 1: It is said that the springs (of Tiberias) are hot because they pass a sulphur source.]

כל *שבא בחמין מלפני השבת שורין אותו בחמין בשבת וכל שלא בא בחמין מלפני השבת מדיחין אותו בחמין בשבת חוץ מן המליח ישן וקולייס האיספנין שהדחתן זו היא גמר מלאכתן ש"מ: ולא יפקיענה בסודרין: והא דתנן *נותנין תבשיל לתוך הבור בשביל שיהא שמור ואת המים היפים ברעים בשביל שיצננו ואת הצונן בחמה בשביל שיחמו לימא רבי יוסי היא ולא רבנן אמר רב נחמן *בחמה דכ"ע לא פליגי דשרי בתולדות האור כ"ע לא פליגי דאסיר כי פליגי בתולדות החמה מר סבר גזרינן 'תולדות החמה אטו תולדות האור ומר סבר לא גזרינן: ולא יטמיננה בחול: וליפלוג נמי ר' יוסי בהא רבה אמר גזרה שמא יטמין ברמץ רב יוסף אמר מפני שמזיז עפר ממקומו מאי בינייהו איכא בינייהו עפר תיחוח מיתיבי רשב"ג אומר מגלגלין ביצה על גבי גג רותח ואין מגלגלין ביצה על גבי סיד רותח בשלמא למאן דאמר גזרה שמא יטמין ברמץ ליכא למיגזר אלא למאן דאמר מפני שמזיז עפר ממקומו ליגזר סתם גג לית ביה עפר ת"ש מעשה שעשו אנשי טבריא והביאו סילון של צונן לתוך אמה של חמין וכו' בשלמא למאן דאמר גזרה שמא יטמין ברמץ היינו דדמיא להטמנה אלא למאן דאמר מפני שמזיז עפר ממקומו מאי איכא למימר מי סברת מעשה טבריא אסיפא קאי ארישא קאי לא יפקיענה בסודרין ור' יוסי מתיר והכי קאמרי ליה רבנן לר' יוסי הא מעשה דאנשי טבריא דתולדות חמה הוא ואסרי להו רבנן אמר להו ההוא תולדות אור הוא °דחלפי אפיתחא דגיהנם אמר רב חסדא ממעשה

רש"י

גמ' כל שבא בחמין · כל מלוח שבא בחמין מע"ש חוזרין ושורין אותו בחמין בשבת ואין בו משום תיקון שהרי נתקן כבר: מדיחין · שאין זה גמר מלאכתו אבל לא שורין: חוץ מדג מלוח ישן או קוליים האיספנין · דג שקורין טוניי"א: שהדחתו זהו גמר מלאכתו · מדקרי ליה גמר מלאכתו ש"מ זהו בישולו וחייב: והא דתנן · בפרק חבית טתנין כו' המים לונן: בחמה · בשמש: דשרי · דאין דרך בישולו בכך וחמה באור לא מיחלפא דליגזר הא אטו הא: בתולדות האור · כגון אם הוחם הסודר הזה באור מתחילה: דאסיר · דהוי בישול: תולדות חמה · שהוחם הסודר בחמה: אטו תולדות האור · דמאן דחזי סבר דתולדות האור נינהו: שמא יטמין ברמץ · דמאן דחזי סבר מכדי האי לבשולי והאי לבשולי ותרוייהו דרך הטמנה מה לי רמץ מה לי חול ומשום הכי מודה ר' יוסי: שמא יזיז עפר · שמא לא יהא שם חול עקור לכל הצורך ואתי לאזוזי עפר הדבוק והוי חופר גומא: עפר תיחוח · כלומר תיחוח בעומק דליכא למיחש למזיז: גג רותח · שרתחו חמה: ואין מגלגלין בסיד רותח · דהוא תולדות האור: ליכא למיגזר · בגג רותח דהא לא מטמין ליה: אלא · לשמא יזיז עפר ויכסה בו ליגזר: לתוך אמה של חמין · וחמי טבריא לאו תולדות האור נינהו ואפ"ה אסרו להו ומודה בהא ר' יוסי: דדמיא להטמנה · שמטמין מים במים: מי סברת מעשה (א) אסיפא קאי · לסייעתא דחול ואבק ולאורויי דתולדות חמה כי האי גוונא אסירי לדברי הכל: ארישא קאי · אפלוגתא ורבנן הוא דאמרי לה אבל לר' יוסי כה"ג לא מיתסר אלא משום דהכי תולדות האור נינהו: והא מעשה · דחמי טבריא דתולדות חמה נינהו ודמי לאפקעתא דסודרין דליכא למגזר לשמא יזיז ואסרי להו: בטלה

תוספות

להטמין מבעוד יום בדבר המוסיף הבל גזירה שמא יטמין ברמץ *ושמא יחתה ולר"י נראה דמה שהיו מתערבין צונן בחמין לא הוה דמי להטמנה וליכא למילף מינה דאיכא למימר דאסרי להו מפני שמבשל המים צוננין ונראה לו דסילון לא היה מתערב בחמין כי היה מוקף מחיצות מכל לד והיו מתחממין המים צוננים שבסילון מחמת חמי טבריא ולא היו רוחצות בחמי טבריא עצמן לפי שריחן רע והשתא דמיא להטמנה שמים צוננין היו נטמנין בתוך החמין להתחמם:

כל שבא בחמין מלפני השבת · פירוש שנתבשל לגמרי כדמפרש לקמן בפרק חבית (דף קמה:) כגון תרנגולת דרבי אבא שורין אותו בחמין אפילו בכלי ראשון וכל שלא בא כו' מדיחין אותו לפירוש רשב"א דמפרש דעירוי ככלי שני אתי שפיר הכא דאין שורין אותו בכלי ראשון אבל מדיחין אותו מכלי ראשון דרך עירוי אבל לפר"ת דמפרש דעירוי הוי ככלי ראשון ע"כ מדיחין אותו מכלי שני קאמר וא"כ מאי איריא מדיחין אפילו שורין נמי ואומר ר"י דאפילו בכלי שני אין שורין דהואיל דהמים חמין נויחזי כמבשל ואע"ג דתנן לקמן (דף מב:) אבל נותן לתוך הקערה או לתוך התמחוי הייטו דוקא תבלין שהן עשויין למתק את הקדירה ולא מיחזי כמבשל א"נ ה"ה שורין אותו כיון דאיירי בכלי שני והא דנקט מדיחין לאשמעינן דאפילו הדחה הויא גמר מלאכה במליח הישן וקולייס האיספנין:

שמא יטמין ברמץ · אבל הפקעת סודרין לא גזרו אטו שמא יטמין ברמץ דסודרין לא דמו לרמץ ואטו סודרין שנתחממו באור לא בעי ר' יוסי למיגזר דאין דרך לחממן כל כך שלא יהיו נשרפין:

מפני שמזיז עפר ממקומו · פי' בקונטרס מתוך שלא יהיה לו חול עקור כל הצורך לכסות אתי לאזוזי עפר הדבוק והוי חופר גומא וקשה לריב"א דהא ליכא איסורא דאורייתא בחופר גומא ואינו צריך אלא לעפרה לרבי שמעון דאמר מלאכה שאינה צריכה לגופה פטור עליה וצריך לומר לפי פירוש הקונטרס גזירה שמא יחפור הגומא לטמון הבילה בתוכה ור"ת *הקשה לפירוש הקונטרס דמאי דמשני בסמוך סתם גג לית ביה עפר אדרבה הא סתם גג יש בו מעזיבה וכיון דגזרינן שמא יחפור לגזור שמא יחפור במעזיבה ויכסה ועוד שמלא בספרים ישנים מפני שמזיז עפר ממקומו ולפירוש הקונטרס צריך לגרוס שמא יזיז ומפרש ר"ת שמזיז עפר שהוא מוקצה ממקומו כשתוחב הבילה בתוך העפר וסבר רב יוסף דטלטול מן הצד שמיה טלטול ואיכא בינייהו עפר תיחוח הייט שהוא תיחוח כל כך כשמניח הבילה מידו ליפול נטמנת מעצמה בתוך העפר ואינו מזיז עפר ממקומו בידים והשתא אתי שפיר דסתם גג לית ביה עפר כל כך שיוכל להטמין בתוכו דלחפירת מעזיבה לא חיישינן ולפירוש זה הוה מצי למימר איכא בינייהו עפר מוכן ובלאו הכי איכא בינייהו טובא כגון גג דאית ביה עפר שמא יטמין ליכא למימר ושמא יזיז איכא וכגון מעשה דאנשי טבריא דשייך יטמין ולא שייך יזיז אבל קשה לרשב"א דקאמר בסמוך אלא למ"ד שמא יזיז עפר לגזור ולהאי פירוש לא שייך למימר לגזור אלא הוה ליה למימר ליתסר ויש ליישב דמשום דכל איסורי דרבנן הם גזירה אטו דאורייתא נקט האי לישנא ועוד פירש רבינו תם בספר הישר שמזיז עפר ממקומו והוי חופר שהוא תולדה דחורש אפילו בעפר תיחוח כגון חול ואבק דרכים כדמוכח בבילה (דף ה׳ ושם) דקאמר והא קעביד כתישה בעפר תיחוח והא קעביד גומא אלמא בעפר תיחוח שייך נמי גומא והא דקאמר הכא איכא בינייהו עפר תיחוח הייט כל כך תיחוח כשמניח בילה עליו נשקעת מאליה דבההוא ודאי לא שייך חורש וקשה לפי' דהאמאי פליג רבה אדרב יוסף ולא חייש למה שמזיז עפר מדקאמר אלא למאן דאמר שמזיז כו' משמע דלרבה ניחא ויש לומר דרבה סבר דלא שייך גומא אלא כשנוטל בידו מן העפר ונשאר מקום מן הגומא אבל בנעילת בילה לא שייכא גומא לפי שאינה ניכרת:

איכא בינייהו עפר תיחוח · פירש בקונטרס דבעפר תיחוח לא שייכא גומא והא דמשמע בבילה (שם) דבעפר תיחוח נמי שייך גומא צריך לומר לפי' דהתם איירי שיש מעט עפר תיחוח וסביבו קרקע קשה דכשמסיר עפר תיחוח תשאר הגומא קיימת אבל הכא כשיש עפר תיחוח הרבה כשיעשה גומא אינה מתקיימת כי דופני הגומא יפלו ולא יוכלו להתקיים לפי שאין הקרקע קשה:

ואין מגלגלין בילה על גבי סיד רותח · קשה אדמפליג בין תולדות חמה לתולדות האור לפלוג בתולדות חמה גופייהו בין גג רותח לחול ואבק דרכים וגג דאית ביה עפר ולמ"ד דשמא יטמין ברמץ אתי שפיר דמפליג בין גג רותח לסיד רותח שלא כדרך הטמנה אבל בתולדות חמה גופייהו לא מצי למיפלג אלא בין דרך הטמנה לשלא כדרך הטמנה דבחול נמי אם אינו מטמיט בו אלא מגלגלו על גביו שרי:

אלא למ"ד שמא יזיז וכו' · וא"ת לרב יוסף אטו מי לית ליה גזירה שמא יטמין ברמץ והא מהאי טעמא אסרינן להטמין בדבר המוסיף הבל ויש לומר דמבעוד יום איכא למיגזר שמא יטמין ברמץ ושמא יחתה אבל הכא לא שייך למיגזר דאטו אי שרינן לבשל בחמי חמה ניחוש דילמא אתי לבשל בחמי אור בשבת וא"ת הא אסרינן משחשיכה להטמין אף כשאין מוסיף הבל גזירה שמא ירתיח ויש לומר דהני מילי בדבר המבושל איכא למיחש שמא ירתיח אבל בישול גמור כי הכא לא טעו אינשי אטו תולדות חמה: ממעשה

עין משפט נר מצוה

וביו"ט נמי אסרי שמא יחתה דאף ביו"ט אסור לחתות לצורך רחילה [ת"י]

יג א ב מיי' פ"ט מהל' שבת הלכה ג ופכ"ב הלכה ט סמג לאוין סה טוש"ע א"ח סימן שיח סעיף ג:

רבינו חננאל

גלגל מאי · אמר רב יוסף גלגל חייב חטאת כענין מליח ישן וקוליס האיספנין שהדחתן היא גמר מלאכתן: ולא יפקיענה בסודרין · ור' יוסי מתיר · ואוקמה רב נחמן [בחמה כ"ע לא פליגי דשרי] בתולדות האור כולי עלמא לא פליגי [דאסור] כי פליגי בתולדות חמה ת"ק סבר גזרינן תולדות חמה אטו תולדות אור · ור' יוסי סבר לא גזרינן ואמרו ליה רבנן לרבי יוסי והא מעשה שעשו אנשי טבריא תולדות חמה הוא ואסרי להו רבנן לאנשי טבריא [אע"ג דדחי ר' יוסי ואמר תולדות אור הן]

מסורת הש"ס

לקמן קמה:

שם קמו:

הגהות הב"ח

(א) רש"י ד"ה מי סברת מעשה טבריא אסיפא:

גליון הש"ס

גמרא דחלפי אפיתחא דגיהנם · עיין חולין דף ח ע"א תוס' ד"ה כחמי טבריא:

ואין נראה כ"כ קושיא דלא חיישינן שמא יחפור במעזיב' אלא בחול דוקא חיישינן ובשאין לו כל צורכו וחסר לו מעט [ת"י]

ממעשה שעשו אנשי טבריא ואסרי להו רבנן בטלה *הטמנה בדבר המוסיף הבל ואפילו מבעוד יום אמר עולא הלכה כאנשי טבריא א"ל רב נחמן כבר תברינהו אנשי טבריא לסילונייהו: מעשה שעשו אנשי טבריא: מאי רחיצה אילימא רחיצת כל גופו אלא חמין שהוחמו בשבת הוא דאסורין הא חמין שהוחמו מע"ש מותרין והתניא *חמין שהוחמו מע"ש למחר רוחץ בהן פניו ידיו ורגליו אבל לא כל גופו אלא פניו ידיו ורגליו אימא סיפא *בי"ט כחמין שהוחמו בי"ט ואסורין ברחיצה ומותרין בשתיה לימא תנן סתמא כבית שמאי דתנן *בית שמאי אומרים לא יחם אדם חמין לרגליו אא"כ ראויין לשתיה וב"ה מתירין א"ר איקא בר חנניא להשתטף בהן כל גופו עסקינן והאי תנא הוא דתניא *לא ישתטף אדם כל גופו בין בחמין ובין בצונן דברי ר"מ ר"ש מתיר ר' יהודה אומר בחמין אסור בצונן מותר אמר רב חסדא מחלוקת בכלי אבל בקרקע דברי הכל מותר והא מעשה דאנשי טבריא בקרקע הוה ואסרי להו רבנן אלא אי איתמר °הכי איתמר מחלוקת בקרקע אבל בכלי דברי הכל אסור אמר רבה בר בר חנה אמר רבי יוחנן הלכה כרבי יהודה א"ל רב יוסף *בפירוש שמיע לך או מכללא שמיע לך מאי כללא דאמר רב תנחום א"ר יוחנן א"ר ינאי אמר *(רב) כל מקום שאתה מוצא שנים חלוקין ואחד מכריע הלכה כדברי המכריע חוץ *מקולי מטלניות שאף על פי שרבי אליעזר מחמיר ורבי יהושע מיקל ור' עקיבא מכריע אין הלכה כדברי המכריע חדא דרבי עקיבא תלמיד הוא ועוד הא הדר

רש"י

בטלה הטמנה · נאסרה הטמנה בדבר המוסיף הבל דהא מבע"י נתנו שם הסילון ומפני שהצוננין מתחממין בכך ואע"ג דממילא אסור: לסילונייהו · לסילונין שלהן שחזרו בהן: ראוין לשתיה · דמחים להו לשתייה ואי בעי רוחץ בהן פניו: להשתטף · שנותן על גופו ומשתטף: והאי תנא · ר' שמעון היא דמתיר להשתטף כל גופו בשבת בחמין שהוחמו מע"ש והיינו דקאמר כחמין שהוחמו בשבת אסור (א) הא שהוחמו מאתמול שרי ואי בי"ט כחמין שהוחמו בי"ט ואסור ברחיצה דאפי' בית הלל לא שרי להחם בי"ט אלא לפניו ידיו ורגליו אבל לשיטוף כל גופו לא: לא ישתטף · בשבת: בין בחמין · ואפי' הוחמו בחול: בכלי · דהרואה אומר היום הוחמו ומוכחא מילתא דתולדות האור נינהו ואתי להחם בשבת כגון נותן צונן בחמין: אבל בקרקע · כגון אמבטאות של מרחצאות והן חמי האור: מותר · דבטלי להו מתורת חמין: והא מעשה דאנשי טבריא כו' · אלמא במילתייהו קיימי:

הדר

תוספות

ממעשה שעשו אנשי טבריא ואסרו להם בטלה הטמנה מבע"י בדבר המוסיף הבל · וא"ת מה צריך למילף ממעשה דאנשי טבריא הא מתני' היא דאין טומנין בדבר המוסיף הבל בפרק במה טומנין (לקמן ד' מז: ושם) ומבע"י איירי דמשחשיכה אפי' בדבר שאינו מוסיף הבל אסור כדאמרינן בפ"ב (לעיל דף לד·) ואומר ר"י דמתניתין דלקמן איכא לאוקמא בבין השמשות אבל מבעוד יום ה"א דשרי וא"ת והא קתני טומנין בגיזי צמר ואין מטלטלין אותן ואי בין השמשות איך טומנין בהן והא אסור לטלטלן וי"ל דהוה מוקמינן כר' דאמר (לעיל ד' לה:) כל דבר שהוא משום שבות לא גזרו עליו בין השמשות וא"ת אי כר' אתיא אי מבעוד יום שרי להטמין ביה"ש נמי שרי דכל דבר שהוא משום שבות כו' וי"ל דה"א בהטמנה החמירו וה"ר שמואל מוורדין מפרש ממעשה אנשי טבריא בטלה הטמנה דאסור אפי' לאכול כדקתני ואסורין בשתיה וה"ר יונה מפרש ·בטלה אפי' בקדירה חייתא והיינו דקאמר בטלה משמע לגמרי מכל דבר: אלא פניו ידיו ורגליו כו' · הכל היה יכול לדקדק מסיפא דקתני בי"ט כחמין שהוחמו בי"ט אילימא רחיצת כל גופו הא הוחמו מעי"ט שרי והא לקמן אסר רחיצה בי"ט דקאמר למחר נכנס ומזיע אבל רוחץ לא ודוקא שטיפה שרי בבית החיצון אלא דרך הש"ס *מה שיכול לדקדק מרישא מדקדק ומיהו קשה לרשב"א דמגופה דמתניתין הוי מצי למידק בלא הך ברייתא דמייתי מדקתני ואסורין בשתיה, כ"ש פניו ידיו ורגליו דאסירי: אלא אם כן ראוין לשתיה · נראה לר"י ·דווקא שמחמם אותם לצורך שתיה אבל לצורך רחיצה אע"ג דראוין לשתיה אסרי ב"ש °דהא לית להו מתוך (ביצה ד' יב· ושם) ובפ"ב דביצה (ד' כא: ושם) אסרי ב"ש מדורה להתחמם כנגדה ואע"ג דראויה היא לבשל ולאפות ועוד אומר ר"י דמהכא נמי יש לדקדק דאי שרו ב"ש לצורך רחיצה משום דראוין לשתיה א"כ לא אתיא מתני' אפי' כב"ש דקתני ואסורין ברחיצה ומותרין בשתיה ומדקתני ומותרין בשתיה מכלל דראוין לשתיה ואפ"ה קתני דאסורין ברחיצה אלא ודאי לא שרו ב"ש אלא כשעושה לצורך שתיה ונראה לר"י דיכול לחמם אפי' ביותר מכדי שתיה כדאמר בפרק הדר (עירובין ד' סה·) °נשיילה לאימיה אי צריכה נחימו אגב אימיה ודוקא בכדי שיעור לרגליו אבל לצורך כל גופו לא והיינו טעמא שהבלנים חשודים דפעמים שיחממו עיקרן לרחיצה:

ובה"ה מתירין · משמע דוקא לרגליו אבל לצורך כל גופו לא וכן משמע בכולה שמעתין דמחמירין בחמין שהוחמו בי"ט כחמין שהוחמו בשבת וגזרו על הזיעה ביו"ט כמו בשבת כדאמר בביצה בהמביא ולקמן (דף מ· ושם) א"כ משמע שאסור לעשות הבערה משום רחיצה שאם לא כן לא היו גוזרים על הזיעה ותימה דמ"ש הבערה דרחיצה מהבערה דזיעה דשרי מדאורייתא כדמוכח התם ואומר ר"י בשם ריב"א דרחיצה אינה אלא לתענוג ואסורה כמו מוגמר דאסור בפ"ק דכתובות (ד' ז· ושם) משום דאין שוה לכל נפש וכן משמע בירושלמי דהיינו טעמא דרחיצה אבל זיעה שוה היא לכל נפש דאינה תענוג אלא לבריאות והא דתניא לקמן (ד' מ·) מרחץ שפקקו נקביו מעי"ט למחר נכנס ומזיע ה"ה אפי' הוחם בו ביום אלא נקט מעי"ט דלפ"ה דוקא מזיע אבל רוחץ לא:

בין בחמין בין בצונן · נראה לר"י דהיינו אפי' חמין שהוחמו מע"ש דהא אוסר אפי' צונן ומסתמא בהנך חמין אסיר ר' יהודה ועוד דמסתמא לא מיירי בדעבדי איסורא והאי תנא הוא דקאמר היינו ר"ש ועוד אומר ר"י דיש להוכיח דבחמין שהוחמו מע"ש פליגי דאמר בפרק חבית (לקמן ד' קמז· ושם) מה חמי טבריא חמין אף מי מערה חמין הרוחץ דיעבד אין לכתחילה לא מכלל דלהשתטף אפי' לכתחילה מני ר"ש היא דתניא לא ישתטף כו' ואי בשהוחמו בשבת פליגי אבל מערב שבת שרי ר' יהודה אמאי צריך לאוקמה כר"ש לוקמה כר' יהודה ובהוחמו מע"ש דהא דומיא דחמי טבריא קתני: והא מעשה דאנשי טבריא בקרקע הוה ואסרי להו · הקשה ה"ר אליעזר ממי"ץ מאי פריך התם הוחמו בשבת כדקתני כחמין שהוחמו בשבת משמע דבהוחמו מע"ש שרי והכא *בהוחמו מע"ש פליגי כדפרישית ומפרש הר"ר יוסף דס"ל להש"ס מדמחמיר ר"מ כ"כ דאוסר אפי' צונן מחמיר נמי לאסור ע"ש אטו שבת ולהכי פריך והא מעשה דאנשי טבריא בקרקע הוה ואסרי להו בהוחמו בשבת ורב חסדא קאמר אבל בקרקע ד"ה מותר אפי' בהוחמו בשבת דהא לר"מ אי הוה אוסר להו בהוחמו בשבת בהוחמו מע"ש נמי הוה אוסר וקשה דר"מ אוסר להשתטף בצונן אפי' בקרקע כדמסיק דבקרקע פליגי ובפרק שמונה שרצים (לקמן דף קט· ושם) משמע דשרי דקאמר התם רוחצין במי גרר ובמי חמתן ובמי עסיא ובמי טבריא אבל לא בים הגדול ורמינהו רוחצין במי טבריא ובים הגדול כו' ומוקים בתרייתא כר' מאיר וי"ל דבקרקע דהכא דאסר היינו דומיא דכלי דדמי לרוחץ בחמין והתם בנהר התירו שנראה כמיקר בנהר ואפי' בחמי טבריא לא דמי לאדם רוחץ בחמין:

אמר רבה בר בר חנה *) הלכה כר' יהודה · אע"ג דר' יוחנן אית ליה הלכה כסתם משנה הכא משום דר' יהודה מכריע הוא אין הלכה כסתם וקשה דבפרק קמא דפסחים (דף יג· ודף כא· ושם) פריך ונימא מר הלכה כר' מאיר דסתם לן תנא כוותיה אע"ג דסבר דרבן גמליאל מכריע הוא דפריך בתר הכי ונימא מר הלכה כרבן גמליאל דהוה ליה מכריע וי"ל דסתם דהכא גריע מההוא סתם דהכא סתם במתני' ומחלוקת בברייתא והלכה כמכריע ומיהו אי לאו הכרעה הוה הלכה כסתם מתני' אע"ג דמחלוקת בברייתא: (לעיל) הא חמין שהוחמו מבעוד יום מותרים והתניא חמין שהוחמו כו' · תימה לוקי ההיא ברייתא דאסרה בכלי משום דהרואה אומר היום הוחמו ומתניתין בקרקע כמשמעה כדמפליג בסמוך בין כלי לקרקע וי"ל דדוקא בשיטוף דקיל איכא לפלוגי אבל ברחיצה דחמירא לא מסתברא לפלוגי בהכי:

*) [אמר ר' יוחנן הלכה כו']

דילמא

עין משפט נר מצוה

יד א ב מיי' פ"א מהל' יו"ט הלכה טז סמג לאוין עה טוש"ע או"ח סימן תקיא סעיף ב:

הא דלא מייתי בעבר ובהא מהכא דלאסור דשאני הטמנה דיש להחמיר [ת"י]

טו ג ד מיי' פכ"ב מהל' שבת הלכה ג סמג לאוין סה טוש"ע או"ח סימן שכו סעיף א:

ביצה כא:

[וכ"כ תוספות עירובין סז· ד"ה אימא ובכתובות נא· ד"ה מני ודף סט. ד"ה ש"מ וב"ב כז: ד"ה הא ועי' תוס' לקמן מו: ד"ה ככתה ותוס' ברכות מב· ד"ה הסבו ותוספות ב"מ יג: ד"ה הא מכני וע"ע רש"י ב"מ כג: ד"ה הא של ב"ב]

מסורת הש"ס

[לקמן מ·] ואם תאמר ולימא דמתני' קודם גזירה וי"ל דמסתמא אחר גזירה דגזירה קדמוני' סיתם [ת"י]

לקמן קמו: ע"ש תוספתא פ"ד

[ברכות פי' וש"נ]

[נ"ל רבי]

[לעיל כט.]

הגהות הב"ח

(א) רש"י ד"ה והאי תנא וכו' שהוחמו בשבת אסור ברחיצה הא שהוחמו:

ומהר"מ מפרש דחמין שהוחמו מע"ש היינו שנסתלקו מעל האור מבע"י ושהוחמו בשבת היינו נמי שהוחמו מבע"י כל צורכן אך מתחממים והולכין גם בשבת דומיא דאנשי טבריא ובהכנו פליגי ר"מ ור"י ור"ש וצונן קרי שהיו חמין כבר ולצננו אבל בנסתלקו מבע"י אפילו ר"מ מודה דשרי להשתטף ולא לרחוץ והאי תנא הוא ר"מ ור"י דאסרי חמין שמתחממין והולכין גם בשבת והשתא פריך שפיר והא מעשה דאנשי טבריא בקרקע הוי ויתיישב נמי סוגיא דפ' שמנה שרצים דשרי ר"מ לרחוץ בקרקע וכן בפרק חבית דמוקי כר"ש [ת"י]

רבינו חננאל

ק"ל כת"ק אמר רב חסדא מדאסרו להו רבנן] שמע מיניה דבטלה הטמנה בדבר המוסיף ואפילו מבעוד יום · אסיקנא דכופח מקום שפיתת קדירה אחת הוא · ואם הוסק בגפת או בעצים הרי הוא ·כתנור ואסור לסמוך בו · וכ"ש בתוכו או על גבו · וכן לשהות בו אע"פ שהוא גרוף וקטום אסור · נמצא האסור שני פנים · צונן שלא הוחמו כל עיקר · ותבשיל שהתחיל להתבשל ולא הגיע למאכל בן דרוסאי · ומותר שני פנים· חמין שהוחמו ולא בשלו כל עיקר ושבשלו כמאכל בן דרוסאי · ואפילו [לא] בשלו כל צרכן מותר · ומאי דקשי ליה [זיקא] מסקנא כלישנא בהראה דרב אשי דבין דגריא ובין [דברחא] בין שריק ובין שלא שריק שרי · ולא יטמיננה בחול ובאבק דרכים בשביל שתצלה דברי הכל אסור : מעשה שעשו אנשי טבריא הביאו סילון של צונן כו' אין הלכה כאנשי טבריא דהא תברינהו לסילונייהו אוקימנא הא דתנן אסור ברחיצה להשתטף בהן כל גופו ור' שמעון הוא דשרי בחמין שהוחמו מע"ש להשתטף דתניא אסור להשתטף בין בחמין בין בצונן דברי רבי מאיר ורבי שמעון מתיר רבי יהודה אומר בחמין אסור בצונן מותר · אמר רבה בר בר חנה אמר רבי יוחנן הלכה כר' יהודה : הא דקאמר שמואל חמין שהוחמו מע"ש אינו רוחץ בהן בשבת אלא פניו ידיו ורגליו תניא כוותיה וקי"ל כוותיה דשמואל בהא : א"ל לרבה בר בר חנה בפירוש שמיע לך מיניה דר' יוחנן דהלכתא כר' יהודה דבצונן מותר להשתטף אבל בחמין אסור · או מכללא · מאי כללא דא"ר יוחנן א"ר ינאי כל מקום ששנים חולקין ואחד מכריע הלכה כדברי המכריע חוץ מקולי מטליות שפירשנום בפרק של מעלה · והוא זה ששנינו בכלים בפרק כ"ח פחות משלשה על שלשה שהתקינה לפקק בה את המרחץ כו' · אף על פי שרבי אליעזר מחמיר ורבי יהושע מיקל ורבי עקיבא מכריע שאין הלכה כרבי עקיבא · חדא דתלמיד הוא ואין תלמיד מכריע על רבו ·

רב נסים גאון

חדא דר' עקיבא לגבי רבי אליעזר ורבי יהושע תלמיד הוא · פירוש שלו תמצאנו בנדרים בפרק הנודר מן המבושל (דף נ) ר' עקיבא אקדשא ליה ברתיה דבר כלבא שבוע כו' אמרה ליה זיל הוי בבי רב אזל הוה י"ב שנין קמיה רבי אליעזר ורבי יהושע ובהרבה מקומות תמצאנו כשהוא מדבר עם אחד מהן אומר ר' תרשני לומר לפניך דבר אחד ממה שלימדתני תנד דאלך (פירושו, תמלא זה) בר"ה (כה) בשעה ששיגר רבן גמליאל לר' יהושע גוזר אני עליך שתבוא אצלי במקלך כו' דתניא הלך ר"ע לר' יהושע מיצר א"ל ר"ע ר' תרשני לומר לפניך דבר אחד שלימדתני ובסנהדרין (פ' ד' מיתות דף סח) ר"ע אומר משום ר' יהושע שנים מלקטין קישואין כו' ובתלמוד אמרו גמרה מר' אליעזר ולא סברה הדר גמרה מר' יהושע ואסברה ניהליה · ועוד הא הדר ביה רבי עקיבא לגבי ר' יהושע מפורש זה בפרק במה מדליקין (דף כט) :

גליון הש"ס

גמ' הכי איתמר מחלוקת בקרקע· עי' מ"ק דף יט ע"ב תוס' ד"ה לאסור וכו' בטלה אפילו בקדירה חייתא · עי' לקמן דף מז ע"ב תוס' ד"ה במה טומנין : ד"ה אא"כ וכו' נראה לר"י דוקא שמחמם · עי' לקמן דף מו ע"א תוס' ד"ה הואיל וראוין : בא"ד דהא לית להו מתוך · דבריהם צ"ע דלענין מתוך מה הפרש בין ראויים או אינן ראויים · וראיתי ברשב"א שהוסיף ומאן דלית ליה מתוך לית ליה הואיל ויסוד זה נסתר מפירכת הגמ' פסחים דף מז ע"ב וכמ"ש התוס' שם ד"ה אהבערה לא ליחייב ועע"ג ובתשובה וגם בדרשות הארכתי בזה בעה"י : בא"ד כדאמרינן פרק הדר נשיילה ק"ל למאי צורכו לדאיס זו דאפשר לצורך מילה עדיף · הא להדיא איתא ברייתא ערוכה בביצה ממלא נחתום חבית מים אע"פ שא"צ אלא לקיתון אחד :

R. Ḥisda said: [39*b*] On account of the incident of what the people of Tiberias did and the Rabbis forbade them, [the practice of] putting away [aught] in anything that adds heat, even by
a day,[1] has no sanction.[2] 'Ulla said: The *halachah* agrees with the inhabitants of Tiberias.[3] Said R. Naḥman to him, The Tiberians have broken their pipe long ago![4]

IT ONCE HAPPENED THAT THE PEOPLE OF TIBERIAS DID THUS: [etc.] Which washing [is meant]? Shall we say, of the whole body; is only hot water heated on the Sabbath forbidden, whereas hot water heated on the eve of the Sabbath is permitted? Surely it was taught: As to hot water which was heated on the eve of the Sabbath, on the morrow [Sabbath day] one may wash his face, hands, and feet in it, but not his whole body. Hence [it must refer to] his face, hands, and feet. Then consider the second clause: IF ON A FESTIVAL, IT IS LIKE WATER HEATED ON A FESTIVAL, WHICH IS FORBIDDEN FOR WASHING BUT PERMITTED FOR DRINKING. Shall we say that we learnt an anonymous [Mishnah] in accordance with Beth Shammai? For we learnt, Beth Shammai maintain: A man must not heat water for [washing his] feet, unless it is fit for drinking; but Beth Hillel permit it![5]—Said R. Iḳa b. Ḥanina: The reference is to the sousing[6] of the whole body, and it agrees with the following Tanna. For it was taught: A man must not souse the whole of his body, whether with hot or with cold water:[7] this is R. Meir's view; but R. Simeon permits it. R. Judah said: It is forbidden with hot water, but permitted with cold.

R. Ḥisda said: They differ only in respect to a vessel;[8] but if
b [the water is] in the earth,[1] all agree that it is permitted. But the case of the people of Tiberias was in respect to the earth,[2] yet the Rabbis forbade them?—Rather if stated, it was thus stated: They differ only in respect to earth [-heated water]; but as for a vessel, all agree that it is prohibited.

Rabbah b. Bar Ḥanah said in R. Joḥanan's name: The *halachah* is as R. Judah. Said R. Joseph to him, Did you hear this explicitly, or [learn it] by deduction? What is the deduction? For R. Tanḥum said in the name of R. Joḥanan in the name of R. Jannai in Rabbi's name: Wherever you find two disputing and a third compromising, the *halachah* is as the words of the compromiser, except in the case of the leniencies relating to rags,[3] where though R. Eliezer is stringent and R. Joshua is lenient and R. Akiba makes a compromise, the *halachah* is not as the words of the compromiser. Firstly, because R. Akiba was a disciple;[4] moreover, R. Akiba indeed

a (1) I.e., before the Sabbath. (2) Lit., 'has ceased'. (3) Their action is permitted. (4) They themselves retracted. Thus all agree now that it is forbidden. (5) The reference is to Festivals.—Thus our Mishnah would appear to agree with Beth Shammai, whereas it is a principle throughout the Talmud that Beth Hillel's view is always *halachah*, and no anonymous Mishnah is taught according to the former. (6) Not washing—sousing is more lenient. (7) On the Sabbath. 'Hot water' means even if it was heated before the Sabbath. (8) I.e., if the water is in a vessel. Obviously it was heated by fire, and one seeing it may think that it was heated on the Sabbath. Hence it was forbidden.

b (1) E.g., a spring. (2) The water was heated by being passed through a natural hot-water spring. (3) V. *supra* 29*a*. (4) His principal teacher was R. Eliezer, but he studied under R. Joshua too (Ab. R.N.; Ned. 50*a*).—From Raba (fourth century) and onwards the *halachah* is always as the *later* view, hence, generally speaking as the disciple; but before that it was always as the teacher. V. Asheri: 'Er. I, 4.

[40a] retracted in favour of R. Joshua.[5] Yet what if it is by deduction?—Perhaps that[6] is only in the Mishnah, but not in a Baraitha?—I heard it explicitly, said he to him.

It was stated: If hot water is heated on the eve of the Sabbath,—Rab said: On the morrow one may wash his whole body in it, limb by limb; while Samuel ruled: They [the Sages] permitted one to wash his face, hands, and feet only.

An objection is raised: If hot water is heated on the eve of the Sabbath, on the morrow one may wash his face, hands, and feet therein, but not his whole body. This refutes Rab?—Rab can answer you: Not his whole body at once, but limb by limb. But he [the Tanna] states, his face, hands, and feet?—[It means] similar to the face, hands, and feet.[7] Come and hear: It was permitted to wash only one's face, hands, and feet [on the Sabbath] in water heated on the eve of the Sabbath?—Here too [it means] similar to the face, hands, and feet.

It was taught in accordance with Samuel: If hot water is heated on the eve of the Sabbath, on the morrow [the Sabbath day] one may wash his face, hands, and feet therein, but not his whole body limb by limb; and with water heated on a Festival
a it goes without saying.[1] Rabbah recited this ruling of Rab in the following version: If hot water is heated on the eve of the Sabbath,—Rab said, On the morrow one may wash his whole body in it,[2] but must omit one limb. He raised against him all the [above] objections. He is [indeed] refuted.[3]

R. Joseph asked Abaye, Did Rabbah act in accordance with Rab's ruling? I do not know, he replied. What question is this? It is obvious that he did not act, for he was refuted! He did not hear them.[4] But if he had not heard them he certainly acted [thus]! For Abaye said: In all matters the Master [*sc.* Rabbah] acted in accordance with Rab, except in these three where he did as Samuel: [viz.,] one can detach [the fringes] from one garment for [insertion in] another, one may light from lamp to lamp, and the *halachah* is as R. Simeon in respect to dragging.[5]—He followed Rab's restrictions, but not his leniencies.

Our Rabbis taught: If the holes of a bath-house are plugged[6] on the eve of the Sabbath, one may bathe therein immediately after the conclusion of the Sabbath; if on the eve of a Festival, one may enter on the morrow,[7] sweat, and go out and have a souse bath[8] in the outer chamber.[9] Rab Judah said: It once happen-
b ed at the baths of Bene Berak[1] that the holes were plugged on the eve of a Festival: on the morrow R. Eleazar b. 'Azariah and R. Akiba entered, sweated therein, went out, and had a souse bath in the outer chamber, but the warm water was covered over with boards.[2] When the matter came before the Sages, they said: Even if the warm water is not covered with boards.[3] But when transgressors grew in number, they began forbidding it.[4] One may stroll through the baths of large cities and need have no fear.[5]

What is [this reference to] transgressors? For R. Simeon b. Pazzi said in the name of R. Joshua b. Levi on the authority of Bar Ḳappara: At first people used to wash in hot water heated on the eve of the Sabbath; then bath attendants began to heat the water on the Sabbath, maintaining that it was done on the eve of the Sabbath. So [the use of] hot water was forbidden, but sweating was permitted. Yet still they used to bathe in hot water and maintain, We were perspiring. So sweating was forbidden, yet the thermal springs of Tiberias were permitted. Yet they bathed in water heated by fire and maintained, We bathed in the thermal springs of Tiberias. So they forbade the hot springs of Tiberias but permitted cold water. But when they saw that this [series of restriction] could not stand,[6] they permitted the hot springs of Tiberias, whilst sweating remained in *statu quo*.[7]

Raba said: He who violates [even] a Rabbinical enactment, may be stigmatized a transgressor.[8] According to whom?

(5) *Supra* 29b. (6) *Sc.* Joḥanan's rule on compromise. (7) I.e., limb by limb.
a (1) One may certainly not wash his whole body therein on the Festival. (2) This, in view of the reservation that follows, must mean simultaneously (Rashi). (3) As the answer given previously that it means similar to the face, etc., does not apply to his version in which he permits the wholy body simultaneously, v. n. 2. (4) Rabbah did not know of these refutations. Or possibly, he did not accept them; cf. Kaplan, *Redaction of the Talmud*, p. 138. (5) V. *supra* 22a, q.v. notes. (6) So that its steam should not be lost. (7) I.e., the Festival day. (8) Of cold water, or water warmed on Sabbath eve, v. *supra* 39b. (9) But not in the inner chamber where people wash, lest it be said that he washed his whole body, which is forbidden.
b (1) Near Jaffa, the seat of R. Akiba's academy: v. Josh. XIX, 45. (2) I.e., and they had no fear that the water in which they soused might have been heated by the heat of the baths. (Rashi). [*Aliter:* they took a souse in cold water, and the hot water in the bath house was covered to prevent the shower-bath water getting warm, v. Tosaf. a.l.] (3) It is permitted. (4) A steam bath on Sabbath. (5) He may stroll through, not to sweat, and need not fear that he will be suspected of an unlawful purpose. (6) They could not be enforced, being regarded as too onerous for the masses. (7) Forbidden.—It is not clear whether these subterfuges were resorted to because the Rabbis might punish non-observance, or because public opinion condemned the open desecration of the Sabbath, even in respect of Rabbinical enactments. (8) Without fear of proceedings for libel.

[פי' ברכות יט: במשנתינו קאמרינן והא בריי' סיא]

[ועי' תוס' מנחות לה: ד"ה מי קאמר וכו' תירצו בלשון אחר]

טז א מיי' פכ"ב מהלכות שבת הלכה ב סמג לאוין סה טוש"ע או"ח סימן שכו סעיף א:

יז ב שם סעיף יא:

יח ג מיי' פ"א מהלכות י"ט הלכה טז סמג לאוין עה טור שו"ע או"ח סימן תקיא סעיף ב:

שם איתא תבל

תבל

יט ד מיי' פכ"ב מהלכות שבת הלכה ב סמג לאוין סה טוש"ע או"ח סימן שכו סעיף א:

כ ה מיי' שם טוש"ע שם סעיף יב:

לעיל כב. פסחים קח. מנחות מח:

תוספתא שבת פ"ד

[ועי' יתר אריכות בתוס' ב"ק קטו: ד"ה הכרעה]

רבינו חננאל

הדר ביה ר"ע לגבי דר' יהושע. ואסיקנא דאי מכללא מאי הוי ר' יהודה מכריע הוא והלכתא כדברי המכריע ובין [בפי' ובין] מכללא חדא הוא. ואמרינן דילמא הני מילי אם תהיה מחלוקתם במשנה אבל חלוקתם בברייתא לא. אמר ליה בפירוש שמיעא לי. והא דאמר אביי כל מילי דמר עביד כרב בר מהני תלת. אסיקנ' רבה כחומרי דרב הוה עביד. כקולי דרב לא הוה עביד: ת"ר מרחץ שפקקו. פי' פקקו סתמו נקביו מע"ש למוצאי שבת רוחץ בה מיד. פקקו נקביו מערב יום טוב למחר נכנס ומזיע ויוצא ומשתטף בבית החיצון. וכן עשו ר' אלעזר בן עזריה ור"ע במרחץ של בני ברק. משרבו עוברי עבירה התחילו לאסור שהיו מחמין בשבת ואומרים מע"ש החמנו. אסרו להן חמין והתירו הזיעה כו'. ואסיקנא אסרו להן אפילו חמין שהוחמו מע"ש ואפילו חמי טבריא וכ"ש חמי האור. ואפילו זיעה אסרו להן

תוספות

דילמא ה"מ במתני' אבל בברייתא לא *אע"ג דלא קאמר במשנתינו *הכא משמע דאין הלכה כמותו משום דסתם מתני' דלא כוותיה*: **הלכה** כדברי המכריע. הכרעה כגון קולי מטלניות שר"א ור"י הזכירו בפירוש בדבריהם מוכן ושאינו מוכן דהיינו תלאו במגוד והניחו אחורי הדלת שגילו בדבריהם שיש סברא לחלק ביניהם אלא שנראה להם דסוף סוף אין לחלק ביניהם לכך הוי ר' עקיבא שמחלק ביניהם מכריע וכן ר' יהודה הוי מכריע דר' שמעון ור"מ הזכירו בדבריהם חמין וצונן והכרעה שלישית דלא הויא הכרעה הוי כי ההיא דפ"ק דפסחים (דף כא.) חבית של יין של תרומה שנטמאה ב"ש אומרים תשפך *הכל וב"ה אומר תעשה זילוף אמר ר' ישמעאל בר' יוסי אני אכריע בשדה תשפך *הכל ובבית תעשה זילוף אמרו לו אין הכרעה שלישית מכרעת משום דלא הזכירו ב"ש וב"ה בדבריהם בית ושדה ולא גילו שיש סברא לחלק בין בית לשדה חשיב לה הכרעה שלישית ולא כפירוש הקונטרס דפירש התם דטעמייהו דב"ש לא משום תקל' אלא מטעם אחר כמו משום ריחא אלא משום דלא הזכירו בדבריהם בית ושדה כדפי' וה"ה דהוה מצי למימר ליה דאין הכרעת תלמיד הכרעה כדאמר הכא אלא רבותא אמרו דאפי' לא היה תלמיד אינה הכרעה והא דתנן בברכות (דף מג:) ב"ש אומרים מברך על השמן ואח"כ מברך על ההדס וב"ה אומרים מברך על ההדס ואח"כ על השמן א"ר גמליאל אני אכריע שמן זכינו לריחו וזכינו לסיכתו הדס לריחו זכינו לסיכתו לא זכינו וא"ר יוחנן הלכה כדברי המכריע פר"ת התם דהויא כהכרעה שבכל הש"ס ולא נהירא דלא הויא הכרעה אלא כדפי' והתם אינו אלא מפרש טעמא דבית שמאי ור"ח פי' אין הכרע' שלישית מכרעת היינו הכרע' דור שלישי כמו ר' ישמעאל בר' יוסי שהיה דור שלישי לב"ש וב"ה ולאו דוקא דור שלישי אלא ה"ה שני ובכל מקום נקט הכרעה שלישית משום ברייתא דפסחים*:

למוצאי שבת רוחץ מיד. דוקא לרחוץ אבל להזיע נכנס אפי' בשבת ומזיע כמו בי"ט כדאמר בסמוך דאפי' בשבת הוי זיעה שריא עד הגזירה ולאחר גזירה אפילו בי"ט אסרו דאיום טוב קתני משרבו עוברי עבירה התחילו לאסור והוה מצי לערוביהו וליתניהו מרחץ שפקקו נקביו מערב שבת או מערב יום טוב למחר נכנס ומזיע ולמוצאי שבת ויום טוב רוחץ מיד אלא אי עריב ותני להו הוה אמינא דדוקא בשבת אסרו הזיעה ולא ביום טוב דעובדא דמייתי בשבת הוה להכי מפליג להו השתא משרבו עוברי עבירה קאי איום טוב אבל לא אשבת דזיעה לא הוזכרה גבי שבת: **אלא** שחמין שלו מחופין בנסרים. פי' בקונטרס שלא היו צריכין לחוש שהוחמו בשבת מחום המרחץ משמע שסובר שנשתטפו בחמין שהוחמו מע"ש ולעיל אסר רבי יהודה גופיה ושמא יחלק בין שבת ליום טוב ומיהו בתוספתא גרסינן ונשתטפו בצונן אלא שחמין שלו מחופים ולא יסברו העולם שרחצו בחמין: מפני

גמרא

*הדר ביה ר"ע לגבי דרבי יהושע *ואי מכללא מאי דילמא ה"מ במתניתין אבל בברייתא לא א"ל אנא בפירוש שמיע לי [תוספתא יח: ע"ש] אתמר חמין שהוחמו מע"ש רב אמר למחר רוחץ בהן כל גופו אבר אבר ושמואל אמר לא התירו לרחוץ אלא פניו ידיו ורגליו מיתיבי חמין שהוחמו מע"ש למחר רוחץ בהן פניו ידיו ורגליו אבל לא כל גופו תיובתא דרב אמר לך רב לא כל גופו בבת אחת אלא אבר אבר והא פניו ידיו ורגליו קתני כעין פניו ידיו ורגליו תא שמע לא התירו לרחוץ בחמין שהוחמו מע"ש אלא פניו ידיו ורגליו ה"נ כעין פניו ידיו ורגליו תניא כוותיה דשמואל* חמין שהוחמו מע"ש למחר רוחץ בהן פניו ידיו ורגליו אבל לא כל גופו אבר אבר ואצ"ל חמין שהוחמו בי"ט רבה מתני לה להא שמעתא דרב בהאי לישנא חמין שהוחמו מע"ש למחר אמר רב רוחץ בהן כל גופו ומשייר אבר אחד איתיביה כל הני תיובתא תיובתא א"ל רב יוסף לאביי רבה מי קא עביד כשמעתיה דרב א"ל לא ידענא מאי תיבעי ליה פשיטא דלא עביד דהא איתותב (*דילמא) לא שמיעא ליה ואי לא שמיעא ליה ודאי עביד *דאמר אביי כל מילי דמר עביד כרב בר מהני תלת דעביד כשמואל (*) מטילין מבגד לבגד ומדליקין מנר לנר והלכה כר"ש בגרירה כחומרי דרב עביד כקולי דרב לא עביד *ת"ר מרחץ שפקקו נקביו מע"ש למוצ"ש רוחץ בו מיד פקקו נקביו מעי"ט למחר נכנס ומזיע ויוצא ומשתטף בבית החיצון אמר רב יהודה מעשה במרחץ של בני ברק שפקקו נקביו מעי"ט למחר נכנס ראב"ע ור"ע והזיעו בו ויצאו ונשתטפו בבית החיצון אלא שחמין שלו מחופין בנסרים כשבא הדבר לפני חכמים אמרו אף על פי שאין חמין שלו מחופין בנסרין ומשרבו עוברי עבירה התחילו לאסור אמבטיאות של כרכין מטייל בהן ואינו חושש מאי עוברי עבירה דא"ר שמעון בן פזי אמר ריב"ל משום בר קפרא בתחלה היו רוחצין בחמין שהוחמו מע"ש התחילו הבלנים להחם בשבת ואומרים מערב שבת הוחמו אסרו את החמין והתירו את הזיעה ועדיין היו רוחצין בחמין ואומרים מזיעין אנחנו אסרו להן את הזיעה והתירו חמי טבריה ועדיין היו רוחצין בחמי האור ואומרים בחמי טבריה רחצנו אסרו להן חמי טבריה והתירו להן את הצונן ראו שאין הדבר עומד להן התירו להן חמי טבריה וזיעה במקומה עומדת אמר רבא האי מאן דעבר אדרבנן שרי למיקרי ליה עבריינא כמאן כי

(*) בכל המקומות איתא מתירין

רש"י

הדר ביה רבי עקיבא. כדאמרינן בפירקין דלעיל (דף כט:) לשון מכריע מכביד מטה כף מאזנים ומכריע את שכנגדו כגון הכא בחמין אסור השתא הוה ליה ר' שמעון דמתיר בחמין יחיד במקום שנים כמאן ר' יהודה מכביד את כף המשקולת שהרי ר' יהודה עם רבי מאיר שוים לאיסור ובצונן מותר הוי ליה ר' מאיר בצונן יחיד במקום שנים כמאן ר' יהודה מכביד את כף המשקולת: ה"מ. דא"ר יוחנן הלכה כדברי המכריע במכריע במשנה כי ההיא דמטלניות: כעין פניו. כלומר כל אבר בפני עצמו: רוחץ בהן כל גופו. ביחד אלא שמשייר אבר אחד: איתיביה כל הני. וליכא לשנויי כעין פניו ידיו ורגליו דהא כל גופו יחד קאמר חוץ מאבר אחד: א"ל רב יוסף לאביי. משום דגדל אביי בבית רבה בר נחמני שהיה ראש קודם לרב יוסף ומת היה שואלו רב יוסף איך היה רואהו נוהג: מי עביד כשמעתי' דרב. בהא מילתא דרחילה: מאי תבעי ליה. שיטה דהש"ס פרכא ליה: לא שמיע ליה. *לרבה הא תיובתא משום הכי מספקא ליה לרב יוסף ברבה דדילמא עביד כרב: ואי לא שמיעא ליה. אמאי מספקא ליה לרב יוסף: הא ודאי עביד. רבה בכל מילי כרב: כחומרי דרב הוה עביד. בר מהני תלת חומרי אבל כקולי דרב איכא דלא עביד והא קולא היא ודילמא לא עביד: שפקקו נקביו. שלא יצא חמימותו: רוחץ בו מיד. ואין צריך להמתין בכדי שיעשה ל"א שפקקו נקביו אותן נקבים שמרחץ מתחמם על ידיהן שאור ניסקת מבחוץ מתחתיו *לוי"ה ועיקר רוחץ בו מיד שהרי לא נתחמם בשבת אבל בשבת לא שהרי גזרו על הרחילה: ומשתטף בבית החיצון. שלפני המרחץ ולא בתוך המרחץ שלא יאמרו רוחץ הוא כדאמרן דאסרו את הרחילה אבל הזיעה התירו והיאך היא זיעה עומד או יושב בבית המרחץ ואינו נותן מים עליו והוא מתחמם ומזיע: מחופין בנסרים. ולא היו צריכין לחוש שמא נתחממו בשבת מחומו של מרחץ: התחילו לאסור. את הזיעה: אמבטאות. בתי מרחץ גדולים: מטייל בהן. מהלך בתוכן לפי דרכו ולא להזיע: ואינו חושש. שמא יאמרו מזיע הוא ואע"ג דאסרו את הזיעה: מאי עוברי עבירה. דקאמר לעיל שאסרו זיעה על ידיהן: אסרו להן את החמין. לגמרי: ועדיין היו רוחצין בחמין. שהוחמו מבע"י: שאין הדבר עומד. שלא היו ציבור יכולין לקבל מתוך שאסרו להם את הכל: במקומה עומדת. לאיסור:

כי

[לעיל כט:]

[לעיל לט:]

מאן דגרס בגמ' דילמא גרס הכא לא שמיע ליה לר' יוסף

[הש"ל מ"ז]

פירוש לוי"ה רמז לרבינו יהודה הלוי

גליון הש"ס

תוס' ד"ה דילמא ה"מ במתניתין וכו' אע"ג דלא קאמר במשנתינו. עי' משנה למלך ריש הלכות בית הבחירה:

כי האי תנא אמבטיאות של כרכים מטייל בהן ואינו חושש אמר רבא דוקא כרכין אבל דכפרים לא מ"ט כיון דזוטרין נפיש הבלייהו ת"ר מתחמם אדם כנגד המדורה ויוצא ומשתטף בצונן ובלבד שלא ישתטף בצונן ויתחמם כנגד המדורה מפני שמפשיר מים שעליו *ת"ר מיחם אדם אלונטית ומניחה על בני מעים בשבת ובלבד שלא יביא קומקומוס של מים חמין ויניחנו על בני מעים בשבת ודבר זה אפי' בחול אסור מפני הסכנה *ת"ר מביא אדם קיתון מים ומניחו כנגד המדורה לא בשביל שיחמו אלא בשביל שתפיג צינתן ר' יהודה אומר מביאה אשה פך של שמן ומניחתו כנגד המדורה לא בשביל שיבשל אלא בשביל שיפשר רשב"ג אומר אשה סכה ידה שמן ומחממתה כנגד המדורה וסכה לבנה קטן ואינה חוששת איבעיא להו שמן מה הוא לתנא קמא רבה ורב יוסף דאמרי תרוייהו להתירא רב נחמן בר יצחק אמר לאיסורא רבה ורב יוסף דאמרי תרוייהו להתירא שמן אע"פ שהיד סולדת בו מותר קסבר ת"ק שמן אין בו משום בשול ואתא רבי יהודה למימר שמן יש בו משום בשול והפשרו לא זה הוא בשולו ואתא ר' שמעון בן גמליאל למימר שמן יש בו משום בשול והפשרו זהו בשולו רב נחמן בר יצחק אמר לאיסורא שמן אע"פ שאין היד סולדת בו אסור קסבר שמן יש בו משום בשול והפשרו זהו בשולו ואתא ר' יהודה למימר הפשרו לא זהו בשולו ואתא רשב"ג למימר שמן יש בו משום בשול והפשרו זהו בשולו רשב"ג היינו ת"ק איכא בינייהו כלאחר יד א"ר יהודה אמר שמואל אחד שמן ואחד מים יד סולדת בו אסור אין יד סולדת בו מותר והיכי דמי יד סולדת בו אמר רחבא כל שכריסו של תינוק נכוית א"ר יצחק בר אבדימי פעם אחת נכנסתי אחר רבי לבית המרחץ ובקשתי להניח לו פך של שמן באמבטי ואמר לי טול בכלי שני ותן שמע מינה תלת שמע מינה שמן יש בו משום בשול וש"מ כלי שני אינו מבשל וש"מ הפשרו זהו בשולו היכי עביד הכי והאמר רבה בר בר חנה א"ר יוחנן *בכל מקום מותר להרהר חוץ מבית המרחץ ובית הכסא וכ"ת בלשון חול א"ל והאמר אביי דברים של חול מותר לאומרן בלשון קודש של קודש אסור לאומרן בלשון חול אפרושי מאיסורא שאני תדע דאמר *רב יהודה אמר שמואל מעשה *בתלמידו של ר' מאיר שנכנס אחריו לבית המרחץ ובקש להדיח קרקע ואמר לו אין מדיחין לסוך לו קרקע אמר לו אין סבין אלמא אפרושי מאיסורא שאני הכא נמי לאפרושי מאיסורא שאני אמר רבינא שמע מינה המבשל בחמי טבריה בשבת חייב דהא מעשה דר' לאחר גזירה הוה ואמר ליה טול בכלי שני ותן איני *והאמר רב חסדא המבשל בחמי טבריה בשבת פטור מאי חייב נמי דקאמר *מכת מרדות א"ר זירא אנא חזיתיה לר' אבהו דשט באמבטי ולא ידענא אי עקר אי לא עקר פשיטא דלא עקר דתניא לא ישוט אדם בבריכה מלאה מים ואפי' עומדת בחצר לא קשיא הא
דלית

מפני שמפשיר מים שעליו. בכולה שמעתא ובמתניתין גבי מיחם שפיכהו משמע דלהפשיר מים לצורך שתייה מותר דהפשרן לא זהו בישולן. והכא דאסורין מפרש ריב"א דדומה כרוחץ במים חמין ויבא להחם חמין לרחוץ גופו:

ובלבד שלא יביא קומקומוס כו'. פירוש כל זמן שהאלונטית שם שמא יפלו המים על האלונטית ואתי לידי סחיטה אי נמי לא יביא משום רפואה וגזרו אטו שחיקת סממנים טפי מבאלונטית דלא מיחזי כרפואה כ"כ:

ושמע מינה כלי שני אינו מבשל. תימה מאי שנא כלי שני מכלי ראשון דאי יד סולדת אפי' כלי שני נמי ואי אין יד סולדת אפילו כלי ראשון נמי אינו מבשל ויש לומר לפי שכלי ראשון מתוך שעמד על האור דופנותיו חמין ומחזיק חומו זמן מרובה ולכך נתנו בו שיעור דכל זמן *שהיד סולדת בו אסור אבל כלי שני אף על גב דיד סולדת בו מותר שאין דופנותיו חמין והולך ומתקרר: **ורבי** תימא בלשון חול קאמר ליה. ואע"ג דאסור להרהר נימא דאין אסור להרהר אלא בלשון קדש והוא הרהר בלשון חול:
פשיטא

כי האי תנא. דאמר לעיל משהתחילו עוברי עבירה התחילו לאסור הזיעה והרי לא נאסרה אלא ע"י הרוחצין בחמין מאתמול ואומרים מזיעין אנחנו ואין כאן אלא עבירת דבריהם שאסרו את החמין: כפיש הבלייהו. ומזיע: מפשיר. מחמם לשון פושרין: מיחם אדם. מחמם: אלונטית. טוואי"לא ונראה לי בגד שמסתפגין בו דבבל דוכתא קרי ליה אלונטית: על גבי מעיים. כשהוא חש במעיו מחממין לו כלי או בגד ומניחו שם ומועיל: ובלבד שלא יביא קומקומוס כו'. שמא ישפכו עליו ונמצא רוחץ בשבת בחמין: מפני סכנה. פעמים שהן רותחין: לא שיחמו. לא שיניחם שם עד שיחמו: אלא שתפיג צינתן. במקצתן שתפיג שתתחלף כמו וריחו לא נמר (ירמיה מח) מתרגמינן וריחיה לא פג: לא בשביל שיבשל. שלא תניחנו שם כדי בישול שתהא היד סולדת בו: סכה ידה. אבל להפשירו בפך כדרך שעושה בחול לא ופליג אדרבי יהודה: להתירא. מאי דאסר רבי יהודה בשמן בישול שרי ת"ק ומים דוקא נקט ולא שיחמו דיש בהן בישול אבל שמן אע"פ שהיד סולדת דהיינו בישול דר' יהודה שרי לת"ק: סולדת. נמשכת לאחוריה מדאגה שלא תכוה וזהו לשון ואסלדה בחילה (איוב ו) ואדאג ברעדה ואמשך מתלונתי מדאגת יום הדין אם הייתי יודע שמיתתי קרובה ולא יחמול: שמן יש בו משום בישול. הלכך לא כדי שיבשל אלא כדי שיפשר שרי דהפשרו אין זה בישולו: ואתא רבי שמעון למימר דהפשירו זהו בישולו. הלכך כדעבדין בחול לא ליעביד אלא כלאחר יד על ידי שינוי: לאיסורא. אמרה תנא קמא לשמן דמיא הוא דשרי להפשיר אבל שמן הפשרו זהו בישולו: איכא בינייהו כלאחר יד. דלתנא קמא אפי' ע"י שינוי אסור: והיכי דמי. סלוד יש שסולד מרתיחה מועטת ויש שאינו סולד: נכנסתי. בשבת ובחמי טבריא הוה שלא נאסרו כדאמר לעיל התירו להם חמי טבריא: באמבטי. כגון בריכה עשויה בקרקע שהמים נכנסים שם ונאספין: ובקשתי להניח שם פך שמן. להפשיר לסוך הימנו קודם הרחיצה: טול. מן המים: בכלי שני. שיטלנו מעט דכלי שני אינו מבשל ואח"כ תן הפך לתוך אותו כלי שני דהך אמבטי שהחמין נמשכין לה מן המעיין חשיב לה ככלי ראשון שנרתחו בו שאע"פ שהעבירו מעל האור מבשל כדתנן לקמן (ד' מב:) האילפס והקדירה שהעבירן מרותחין לא יתן לתוכן תבלין: וש"מ הפשרו. במקום הראוי לבישול: זהו בישולו. דהא להפשיר בעלמא הוא דקבעי ואסר ליה:

והיכי עביד הכי. להורות הוראה שהוא דבר תורה בבית המרחץ: להרהר. בדברי תורה: דברים של קדש. דברי תורה: אסור לאומרן. במקום הטנופת ואפי' בלשון חול: אין מדיחין. דלמא אתי לאשויי גומות: דהא מעשה דרבי אחר גזירה הוה. שגזרו על הזיעה ועל כרחין בחמי טבריא הוא דהוי ורבי יהושע (א) דאמר לעיל בימי רבי הוה אלמא בימי רבי כבר נגזרה: וקאמר ליה טול בכלי שני. אבל ראשון לא אלמא יש בהן משום בישול: מרדות. רדוי: שט. צף: דשט באמבטי. בשבת: ולא ידענא אי עקר. רגליו מן הארץ דקסבר כי תנן אין שטין על פני המים במשילין פירות *בנהר גדול תנן דאיכא למגזר שמא יעשה חבית של שייטין כדאמרינן התם אבל באמבטי לא: אי לא עקר. רגליו: לא ישוט. דאע"ג דליכא למיגזר אסור: ואפילו עומדת בחצר. דליכא למיגזר שמא יתיז מים ברגליו חוץ לארבע אמות: הא. דאסיר:
דלית

עין משפט
נר מצוה

כא א מיי' פכ"ב מהל' שבת הלכה ג סמג לאוין סה טוש"ע או"ח סימן שכו סעיף ד:
כב ב מיי' שם הלכה ד טוש"ע שם סעיף ו:
כג ג ד מיי' וסמג שם טוש"ע או"ח סימן שיח סעיף יד:
כד ה ו מיי' פכ"ב שם הלכה ה ו טור שו"ע כס סעיף יג וטוש"ע יו"ד סימן קה סעיף ב:
כה ז ח ט מיי' פ"ג מהלכות ק"ש הלכה ד ה טוש"ע או"ח סימן פה סעיף ב:
כו י מיי' פכ"א מהלכות שבת הלכה ג טוש"ע או"ח סימן שלו סעיף ג:
כז כ מיי' פ"ט מהלכות שבת הלכה ג:

והכא באמבטי במקום שרגלה להניח הפך היתה יד סולדת בו והא דלא א"ל תן במקום שאין היד סולדת דהיינו במקום שרחק ודאי לא היה היד סולדת ושמא שם לא היה יכול להפשיר א"נ פעמים החמירו בכלי ראשון אף אם אין היד סולדת בו וכן החמירו חכמים אפי' בכלי שני לקמן (מב:) גבי ספל ה"ה באמבטי [תו"י]

כח ל מ מיי' פכ"ג מהל' שבת הלכה ה טור שו"ע או"ח סימן שלט סעיף ב:

[לקמן קנא:]
[עי' תוס' לקמן קמז: ד"ה דתניא]

רבינו חננאל

להן אלא צונן בלבד. ראו שאין הדבר עומד חזרו והתירו להן חמי טבריא בלבד. וזיעה במקומה עומדת באיסור אמר רבא מאן דעבר על דברי חכמי' שרי למיקריי' עבריינא. כי האי תנא דתנא משרבו עוברי עבירה: **תנא** אמבטאות של כרכין מטייל בהן ואינו חושש. והני מילי דכרכין אבל דכפרין כיון דזוטרן נפיש הבליהון: **ת"ר** מתחמם אדם כנגד המדורה ויוצא (ומשתטף בצונן) [ובלבד שלא ישתטף בצונן] ויתחמם כנגד המדורה מפני שנפשרו המים שעליו: **ת"ר** מיחם אדם אלונטית ומניחה ע"ג מעיו בשבת ובלבד (ישתטף בצונן ויתחמם כנגד המדורה מפני שתפשר המים) שלא יביא קומקומוס של חמין ויניחנו על גבי מעיו בשבת. ודבר זה אפילו בחול [אסור] מפני הסכנה שלא יכוה: **ת"ר** מניח אדם קיתון של מים כנגד המדורה לא שיחמו אלא כדי שתפוג צינתן. ר' יהודה אמר מנחת אשה פך שמן כנגד המדורה לא שיתבשל אלא כדי שתפשר. רשב"א אשה סכה ידה שמן כנגד המדורה. וסכה לבנה קטן ואינה חוששת: **איבעיא** להו שמן מה לי בו אמר ת"ק. ואסיק' אמר רב אמר שמואל אחד שמן ואחד מים אם נתחמם כשעור שהיד סולדת בו אסור אין היד סולדת בו מותר. ושיעור שהיד סולדת בו. פי' (פירוש) [בירושל'] שהיד * שולטת בו סולדת היא שולטת והוא כל שכריסו של תינוק נכוית הימנו. הא מעשה דר' שבקשו לו פך של שמן באמבטי ואמר להן טלו בכלי שני ותנו. שמעינן מינה תלת. ש"מ שמן יש בו משום בישול. ולפיכך בכלי ראשון אסור. שנמצא מבשל שמן בשבת. וש"מ מדשרי בכלי שני דכלי שני אינו מבשל. וש"מ הפשרו לא זהו בישולו: **אמר** רבינא ש"מ המבשל בחמי טבריא הוא"ל וגזרו רבנן עלייהו חייבין מכת מרדות מדרבנן. ואקשינן דר' היאך מורה הוראה במרחץ ואמר טלו בכלי שני כלומר זהו מותר וזהו אסור. והא"ר יוחנן כל מקום מותר להרהר חוץ מבית המרחץ ובית הכסא. ולא דאקשינן מדברי ר' יוחנן לר' דר' יוחנן לגבי דר' תלמיד קטן הוא. (ולא) [אלא] הא דר' יוחנן דברי הכל קבלה הוא

*) ט"ס יש כאן ולשון הירושלמי הובא ברא"ש.

מסורת הש"ס

תוספתא שבת פ"ד
[תוספתא שם]

הגהות הב"ח
(א) רש"י ד"ה דהא מעשה וכו' ור' יהושע בן לוי דאמר:

ברכות כד: (לעיל י.) לקמן קנ. זבחים קב: ע"ז מד: קדושין לג.
פסחים מא.
[יבמות כב. כתובות מה: נזיר כג. נח: חולין קמא:]
[דף נו:]

[40b] According to this Tanna.[9]

'One may stroll through the baths of large cities, and need have no fear.' Raba said: Only in large cities, but not in villages. What
a is the reason? Since they are small, their heat is great.[1]

Our Rabbis taught: A man may warm himself at a big fire, go out, and have a souse in cold water; providing that he does not have a souse in cold water [first] and then warm himself at the fire, because he warms the water upon him.

Our Rabbis taught: A man may heat a cloth on the Sabbath to place it on his stomach, but must not bring a hot water bottle[2] and place it on his stomach on the Sabbath;[3] and this is forbidden even on weekdays, because of its danger.[4]

Our Rabbis taught: A man may bring a jug of water and stand it in front of a fire; not for it to become warm, but for its coldness to be tempered. R. Judah said: A woman may bring a cruse of oil and place it in front of the fire; not for it to boil, but to become lukewarm. R. Simeon b. Gamaliel said: A woman may smear her hand with oil, warm it at a fire, and massage her infant son without fear.[5]

The scholars propounded: What is the first Tanna's view on oil?—Rabbah and R. Joseph both interpret it permissively; R. Naḥman b. Isaac interprets it restrictively. Rabbah and R. Joseph both interpret it permissively: Oil, even if the hand shrinks from it,[6] is permitted, the first Tanna holding that oil is not subject to [the prohibition of] cooking. Then R. Judah comes to say that oil is subject to cooking, but making it lukewarm is not cooking [boiling] it; whereupon R. Simeon b. Gamaliel comes to say that oil is subject to cooking, and making it lukewarm is tantamount to cooking in its case. R. Naḥman b. Isaac interprets it restrictively: oil, even if the hand does not shrink from it, is forbidden, the first Tanna holding that oil is subject to [the prohibition of] cooking, and making it lukewarm is cooking it; then R. Judah comes to say that oil is subject to cooking, but making it lukewarm is not boiling it; whereupon R. Simeon b. Gamaliel comes to say: Oil is subject to boiling, and making it lukewarm is tantamount to
b boiling it.[1] Then R. Simeon b. Gamaliel is identical with the first Tanna?—They differ in respect to a back-handed manner.[2]

Rab Judah said in Samuel's name: Both in the case of oil and water, if the hand shrinks from it,[3] it is forbidden;[4] if the hand does not shrink from it, it is permitted. And how is 'the hand shrinking from it' defined?—Said Raḥaba: If an infant's belly is scalded [by it].

R. Isaac b. Abdimi said: I once followed Rabbi into the baths, and wished to place a cruse of oil for him in the bath.[5] Whereupon he said to me, Take [some water] in a second vessel[6] and put [the cruse of oil in it]. Three things are inferred from this: [i] Oil is subject to [the prohibition of] boiling; [ii] a second vessel cannot boil; [iii] making it lukewarm is boiling it.[7] But how might he [Rabbi] act thus? Did not Rabbah b. Bar Ḥanah say in R. Johanan's name: One may meditate [on the words of the Torah]
c everywhere, except at the baths or a privy?[1] And should you answer, He said it to him in secular language,[2]—surely Abaye said: Secular matters may be uttered in the Holy language, whereas sacred matters must not be uttered in secular language.—Restraining one from transgression is different. The proof is: Rab Judah said in Samuel's name: It once happened that a disciple of R. Meir followed him into the baths and wished to swill the ground for him, but he said to him, One may not swill;[3] [then he wished] to oil the ground for him, but he said to him, One may not oil. This proves that restraining one from transgression is different; so here too, restraining one from transgression is different.

Rabina said: This proves that if one cooks in the hot waters of Tiberias on the Sabbath, he is liable. For the incident of Rabbi happened after the decree,[4] yet he said to him, Take [some water] in a second vessel and put [the cruse of oil in it].[5] But that is not so? For R. Ḥisda said: If one cooks in the hot springs of Tiberias on the Sabbath, he is exempt?—By 'liable' he too meant flagellation for disobedience.[6]

R. Zera said: I saw R. Abbahu swimming in a bath, but I do not know whether he lifted [his feet] or not.[7] Is it not obvious that he did not 'lift' [his feet]? For it was taught: One must not swim in a pool full of water, even if it stands in a courtyard.[8]—

(9) Who refers to the above as transgressors for evading Rabbinical enactments.

a (1) And even a stroll through them causes sweating. (2) *Ḳumḳumos* is a kind of kettle; obviously something in the nature of an open hot water bottle is meant here. (3) Rashi: in case it spills, and so he will have bathed on the Sabbath. (4) Of scalding.—Needless self-endangering of life is forbidden. (5) Of desecrating the Sabbath. (6) I.e., even if it becomes so hot that one involuntarily withdraws his hand when he touches it.—In respect to Sabbath prohibitions, as also in respect to certain laws concerning the mixing of forbidden with permitted commodities, this is recognized as the last stage before boiling.

b (1) Since a higher temperature is not required. Hence he permits it only when the oil is smeared on one's hand, which is an unusual way of heating it, but it may not be put in front of the fire in a cruse. (2) An idiom for doing anything in an unusual way. R. Simeon permits it, while the first Tanna forbids it. (3) I.e., the hand put in it is spontaneously withdrawn. (4) They may not be placed in front of a fire to reach that temperature. (5) This was in the hot springs of Tiberias, which was finally permitted; *supra a.*—He wished to warm the oil before use. (6) A vessel into which a boiling mass has been poured, opposed to כלי ראשון, a first vessel, containing the mass direct from the fire. The water was drawn direct from the spring into the bath (it was a bath naturally constructed in the ground), which is regarded as a first vessel. It is a Talmudic principle that a first vessel, if the mass in it is still seething, can cook or boil something placed in it, but a second vessel, even if very hot, cannot do this. He therefore told him to pour water out of the bath into a second vessel, and then place the oil in it, to avoid boiling. (7) For he did not intend more than this, and yet Rabbi forbade him to place it in the bath itself. In the second vessel it would not even become lukewarm, but merely have its coldness tempered.

c (1) Hence Rabbi should not have thought of the religious aspect of the act in the bath. (2) Probably: in a phraseology not usually associated with learning. This might indicate that the language of learning as incorporated in the Mishnah was an artificial one; scholars, however, are opposed to that view; v. Segal, *Mishnaic Hebrew Grammar*, Introduction; S. D. Luzatto in *'Orient. Lit.'* 1846, col. 829; 1847, cols. 1 *et seq.* (3) Lest the water form ruts, which is forbidden. (4) Forbidding sweating in ordinary (artificially heated) baths. Hence this must have happened in the natural thermal baths of Tiberias. (5) But he forbade him to put it directly in the first vessel (v. *supra* n. b6), which proves that boiling even in naturally hot water involves liability. (6) Punishment decreed by the Rabbis, as opposed to stripes, ordained by Biblical law. (7) I.e., he did not know whether he was actually swimming or merely bathing. (8) Where there is no fear of splashing water for a distance of four cubits in public ground.

There is no difficulty: in the one case [41a] it [the pool] has no
a embankments; in the other case it has.[1]

R. Zera also said: I saw R. Abbahu put his hand near his buttocks,[2] but do not know whether he touched them or not. It is obvious that he did not touch them, for it was taught, R. Eliezer said: He who holds his membrum and passes water is as though he brought a flood upon the world?[3]—Said Abaye: It was accounted as [analogous to] a marauding band. For we learnt: If a marauding band enters a town[4] in peace-time, open barrels [of wine] are forbidden,[5] closed barrels are permitted; in war time, both are permitted, because they have no time to make *nesek*.[6] Thus we see, since they are afraid,[7] they do not make *nesek;* so here too, since he is in fear, he will not come to meditate [impure thoughts]. And what fear is there here?—The fear of the river.

But that is not so? For R. Abba said in the name of R. Huna in Rab's name: He who puts his hand near his buttocks is as though he denied the covenant of Abraham?[8] There is no difficulty: the one means when he descends [into the river];[9] the other refers to when he ascends.[10] Just as Raba used to bend over; R. Zera would stand upright. The scholars of the college of R. Ashi,—when they descended, they stood upright, [but] when they ascended they bent over.

R. Zera was evading Rab Judah. For he [R. Zera] desired to emigrate[11] to Palestine, whereas Rab Judah said, He who emigrates from Babylon to Palestine violates a positive command, for it is said, *They shall be carried to Babylon, and there they*
b *shall be.*[1] Said he, I will go, hear a teaching from him, return and emigrate. He went and found him standing at the baths and saying to his attendant, Bring me natron,[2] bring me a comb,[3] open your mouths and expel the heat,[4] and drink of the water of the baths. Said he, Had I come to hear nought but this, it would suffice me. As for 'bring me natron, bring me a comb,' it is well: he informs us that secular matters may be said in the Holy Tongue. 'Open your mouths and expel the heat' too is as Samuel. For Samuel said: Heat expels heat.[5] But 'drink the water of the baths'—what is the virtue of that?—For it was taught: If one eats without drinking, his eating is blood,[6] and that is the beginning of stomach trouble. If one eats without walking four cubits [after it], his food rots,[7] and that is the beginning of a foul smell.[8] One who has a call of nature yet eats is like an oven which is heated up on top of its ashes,[9] and that is the beginning of perspiration odour. If one bathes in hot water and drinks none, he is like an oven heated without but not within. If one bathes in hot water and does not have a cold shower bath, he is like iron put into fire but not into cold water.[10] If one bathes without anointing,[11] he is like water [poured] over a barrel.[12]

MISHNAH. IF A MILIARUM IS CLEARED [OF ITS] COALS,[13] ONE MAY DRINK FROM IT ON THE SABBATH. BUT AS TO AN
c ANTIKI,[1] EVEN IF ITS COALS HAVE BEEN CLEARED ONE MAY NOT DRINK FROM IT.[2]

GEMARA. What is meant by 'IF A MILIARUM IS CLEARED [OF ITS] COALS'?—A Tanna taught: the water is within and the coals are without.[3] *Antiki:* Rabbah said: [It means a vessel suspended] between fire places [heated bricks]; R. Naḥman b. Isaac said: [It means a vessel suspended] within a cauldron-like vessel.[4] He who defines it [as a vessel suspended] within a cauldron-like vessel, all the more so a vessel between fire places;[5] whereas he who defines it as [a vessel] between fire places,—but not one within a cauldron-like vessel.[6] It was taught in accordance with R. Naḥman: From an *antiki,* even when cleared of coals and covered with ashes, one may not drink, because its copper heats it.[7]

MISHNAH. IF A BOILER IS REMOVED, ONE MAY NOT POUR COLD WATER THEREIN TO HEAT IT, BUT ONE MAY POUR IT [WATER] THEREIN [THE BOILER] OR INTO A GOBLET IN ORDER TO TEMPER IT.[8]

GEMARA. What does this mean?—Said R. Adda b. Mattenah, This is its meaning: In the case of a boiler from which the hot water is removed, one must not pour into it a little [cold] water in order to heat it, but he may pour in a large quantity of [cold]

a (1) Rashi: in the former case it is like a river; hence forbidden (the prohibition in Beẓ. 36b refers to a river); in the latter case it is like a large utensil, hence permitted. (2) When bathing in the river; this was a gesture of decency. (3) Because lust is inflamed. (4) And they may have touched or moved open barrels of wine, thus rendering them forbidden. (5) V. preceding note. (6) Lit., 'make a libation'. That is the reason of the interdict mentioned in n. 4, because the heathen is suspected of having dedicated the wine to his deity. (7) To put their minds to such things. (8) As though he were ashamed of being circumcised. (9) As his face is towards the river, a gesture of decency is not needed. (10) His face is towards the people, and so he can cover his circumcision in modesty. (11) Lit., 'ascend'.

b (1) Jer. XXVII, 22.—Weiss, *Dor,* III, p. 188, maintains that R. Zera's desire to emigrate was occasioned by dissatisfaction with Rab Judah's method of study; this is vigorously combatted by Halevi, *Doroth,* II pp. 421 *et seq.* The sequel of this story, as also of the similar one in Ber. 24b, shows that he prized Rab Judah's teaching very highly indeed; Rab Judah's prohibition of emigration was merely a reflex of his great love for Babylon, though his love for Palestine too was extraordinarily great: v. Ber. 43a. (2) For cleansing. (3) These were said in pure Hebrew. (4) Rashi: let the heat of the baths enter and the heat of perspiration be driven out. (5) V. n. b4. (6) I.e., harmful. (7) Is not properly digested. (8) Issuing from the mouth. (9) New fuel being added without the ashes of the old being cleared out. (10) To temper it. (11) Anointing with oil is and was practised in hot countries; *T.A.* I, 229 and 233. (12) Which is poured all over the barrel, but does not enter it. (13) Lit., 'a cauldron that is swept out'—before the Sabbath.

c (1) The Gemara discusses what this is. (2) The *antiki* retains its heat more effectively than the *miliarum* and therefore adds heat on Sabbath to the water it contains, which makes it forbidden. (3) This explains מוליאר (*miliarum*). It is a large vessel on the outside of which a receptacle for coals is attached. Thus it would be something like the old-type Russian samowar. (4) The vacant space beneath being filled with coals.—Jast. (5) The ruling of the Mishnah will certainly apply to the latter too. (6) The ruling of the Mishnah will not apply to the latter, which in his opinion is the same as a *miliarium.* (7) Thus it adds heat, which is forbidden. (8) This is discussed in the Gemara.

דלית ליה גידודי הא דאית ליה גידודי: וא"ר זירא אנא חזיתיה לר' אבהו שהניח ידיו כנגד פניו של מטה ולא ידענא אי נגע אי לא נגע פשיטא דלא נגע דתניא *ר' אליעזר אומר *כל האוחז באמה ומשתין כאילו מביא מבול לעולם אמר אביי עשאוה כבולשת דתנן *בולשת שנכנסה לעיר בשעת שלום חביות פתוחות אסורות סתומות מותרות בשעת מלחמה אלו ואלו מותרות לפי שאין פנאי לנסך אלמא כיון דבעיתי לא מנסכי ה"נ כיון דבעית לא אתי להרהורי והכא מאי ביעתותא ביעתותא דנהרא איני והאמר ר' אבא אמר רב הונא אמר רב כל המניח ידיו כנגד פניו של מטה כאילו כופר בבריתו של אברהם אבינו לא קשיא הא כי נחית הא כי סליק כי הא דרבא שחי ר' זירא זקיף רבנן דבי רב אשי כי קא נחתי זקפי כי קא סלקי שחי *ר' זירא הוה קא משתמיט מדרב יהודה דבעי למיסק לארעא דישראל דאמר רב יהודה [ב]כל העולה מבבל לא"י עובר בעשה שנאמר °בבלה יובאו ושמה יהיו [ירמיה כז] אמר איזיל ואשמע מיניה מילתא ואיתי ואיסק אזל אשכחיה דקאי בי באני וקאמר ליה לשמעיה הביאו לי נתר הביאו לי מסרק פתחו פומייכו ואפיקו הבלא ואשתו ממיא דבי באני אמר אילמלא *(לא) באתי אלא לשמוע דבר זה דיי בשלמא הביאו נתר הביאו מסרק קמ"ל דברים של חול מותר לאומרם בלשון קדש פתחו פומייכו ואפיקו הבלא נמי כדשמואל דאמר שמואל הבלא מפיק הבלא אלא אשתו מיא דבי באני מאי מעליותא דתניא [ג]אכל ולא שתה אכילתו דם וזהו תחילת חולי מעיים *אכל ולא הלך ד' אמות אכילתו מרקבת וזהו תחילת ריח רע הנצרך *לנקביו ואבל דומה לתנור שהסיקוהו ע"ג אפרו וזהו תחילת ריח זוהמא רחץ בחמין ולא שתה מהן דומה לתנור שהסיקוהו מבחוץ ולא הסיקוהו מבפנים רחץ בחמין ולא נשתטף בצונן דומה לברזל שהכניסוהו לאור ולא הכניסוהו לצונן רחץ ולא סך דומה למים ע"ג חבית: **מתני'** מוליאר הגרוף שותין הימנו בשבת אנטיכי אע"פ שגרופה אין שותין הימנה: **גמ'** היכי דמי מוליאר הגרוף תנא מים מבפנים וגחלים מבחוץ אנטיכי רבה אמר בי כירי רב נחמן בר יצחק אמר בי דודי מאן דאמר בי דודי כ"ש בי כירי ומאן דאמר בי כירי אבל בי דודי לא תניא כוותיה דרב נחמן אנטיכי אע"פ שגרופה וקטומה אין שותין הימנה מפני שנחושתה מחממתה: **מתני'** המיחם שפינהו לא יתן לתוכו צונן בשביל שיחמו אבל נותן הוא לתוכו או לתוך הכוס כדי להפשירן: **גמ'** מאי קאמר אמר רב אדא בר מתנא הכי קאמר [ד]המיחם שפינה ממנו מים חמין לא יתן לתוכן מים מועטים כדי שיחמו אבל נותן לתוכו מים מרובים כדי להפשירן והלא

רש"י

דלית ליה גידודי. שאין שפתה גבוהה שיהיו המים עמוקים אצל שפתה כמו באמצע דכיון שאין עמוקים שם כי מטי סמוך לשפתה נועץ רגליו בקרקע וחופר וממחה העפר לתוך המים ודמי למגבל ולי נראה דאית ליה גידודי שרי דלא דמי לנהר אלא לכלי דלית ליה גידודי דמיא לנהר ואסור: שהניח ידיו. כשהיה רוחץ משום צניעות: אי נגע. באמה: כאילו מביא מבול לעולם. שמתחמם ובא לידי קרי וזה קלקולו של דור המבול מוציאים שכבת זרע לבטלה דכתיב כי השחית כל בשר וגו' (בראשית ו): כבולשת. עשאוה להא דר' אבהו בולשת חיילות גיים הבא לעיר על שם שמחפשין ובולשים את העיר קרי לה בולשת: בשעת שלום. כגון שהוא של אותה מלכות: כאילו כופר. דנראה שהוא בוש בדבר: כי נחית. לנהר פניו כלפי הנהר ואין כאן משום צניעות אסור לכסותו: כי סליק. ופניו כלפי העם מותר משום צניעות: ר' זירא זקיף. דחייש לדרב שלא יראה ככופר: משתמיט. היה ירא לראות לו משום דהוה בעי רבי זירא למיסק לארעא דישראל ורב יהודה לא סבירא ליה וירא פן יגזור עליו מליך: בבלה יובאו ושמה יהיו עד יום פקדי וגו'. ור' זירא אמר לך ההוא קרא בכלי שרת כתיב כדאמרינן בשני דייני גזירות (כתובות קיא.): הביאו לי נתר. לחוף את ראשי וקאמר להו בלשון הקודש: פתחו פומייכו. ויכנס הבל בית המרחץ לתוך הגוף ויוציא הבל של זיעה: ואשתו. מן מים חמין ואפי' לא הוחמו אלא לרחיצה: מותר לאומרן. בבית המרחץ ואפי' בלשון קודש: הבלא. דמרחץ הנכנס דרך הפה: מפיק הבלא. דזיעה: ולא הלך ד' אמות. קודם שישן: מרקבת. אינה מתעכלת לעשות זבל: ריח רע. ריח הפה: ריח זוהמא. כל גופו מזוהם בזיעה תמיד: ולא הסיקוהו מבפנים. שאינו מטיב לכלום: ולא הכניסוהו לצונן. שהן מחזקין את הברזל: למים ע"ג חבית. על שוליו ולדדיו שאינם נכנסים לתוכו: **מתני'** מוליאר הגרוף. מן הגחלים מבע"י: שותין. ממימיו בשבת ואע"פ שהוחמו קצת מחמת הכלי לפי שאינו מוסיף הבל אלא משמר ומקיים חום שלהם שלא יצטננו בגמרא מפרש מוליאר מים מבפנים וגחלים מבחוץ כלי שיש בו בית קיבול קטן אצל דופנו מבחוץ מחובר לו ונותן שם גחלים והמים בקיבולו הגדול ורבותינו מפרשים מוליאר שני שולים ואנטיכי בי דודי מחיצה בינתיים ולי נראה להפך דאם כן ה"ל למיתני מים מלמעלה וגחלים מלמטה ועוד דבמשנה דתני באנטיכי לשון שולים הן והן אומרים לשון נחושת ושאני נחשת מחרס: אנטיכי. מפרש בגמרא: **גמ'** בי כירי. חלל יש בכירה אצל חלליה שהגחלים בו ומים נתונים בחללה השני ואע"ג דדמי למוליאר מיהו כירה דופנה עב והאור תדיר בתוכה כל ימות החול ודופנה חם מאד ומוסיף הבל במים אע"פ שגרופה מן הגחלים: בי דודי. יורה גדולה עושין לה שתי שוליים ונותנין גחלים בין שניהם והמים על העליונים: וכל שכן. דבי כירי אסור כדפרישית שמתוך שהאור תדיר בו ודופנו עב מרתיח: אבל בי דודי לא. שהרי הוא כמוליאר: שנחושתה. נחושת שלה אלמא ביורה של נחשת קאי ונחשת משמר רתיחתו ולי אומר לשון נחושתה לשון שולים כדכתיב (יחזקאל טז) יען השפך נחשתך ולשון של המשנה נחשתו של תנור במסכת כלים (פ"ה מ"ג) ושאני אנטיכי ממוליאר דמתוך שהשולים מכוסים חומם משתמר ואע"ג שגרפו גחלים: **מתני'** המיחם. קומקמוס של חמין: שפינהו. מפרש בגמרא: **גמ'** מאי קאמר. מאי פינהו ומאי לא יתן ומאי הדר אמר אבל נותן והלא

תוספות

פשיטא דלא נגע דתניא ר' אליעזר אומר כו'. ואע"ג דרבנן פליגי עליה ושרו בפרק כל היד (נדה יג. ושם) לא שרי אלא משום ממזרות שלא יראה ככרות שפכה ויוציאו לעז על בניו שהן ממזרים*: **רחץ** ולא סך. ול"ג מעיקרא דהא בכולי הש"ס רחיצה קודם סיכה כדאמר בפ"ק דקידושין (דף כב:) רחצו סכו וקרא כתיב ורחצת וסכת (רות ג) מיהו קרא איכא לאוקמי בסיכה שהיתה מתקשטת עצמה לריח טוב לכך לא היתה סכה בתחלה שעל ידי רחיצה היתה מעברת הסיכה מעליה:

מוליאר הגרוף שותין ממנו בשבת. פי' בקונטרס לפי שאין מוסיף הבל אלא משמר ומקיים חום שלהן ואנטיכי אפי' גרופה אין שותין הימנה לפי שמוספת הבל ואין נראה דלא שייך למיגזר במוסיף הבל אלא בהטמנה גזירה שמא יטמין ברמץ ועוד דדוחק לומר דמתני' איירי כשעשה האיסור ועוד דאנטיכי אוסר בכל ענין לשתות הימנו אפילו בהשהאה ואי להחזיר תנן משהין אפילו באינו גרוף ועוד אי משום תוספת הבל אסרה ליה מתני' בשתיה תקשה לרבה ורב יוסף דשרו לעיל (דף לח.) בשכח קדרה ע"ג כירה ובשלה בשבת אע"ג דלא נתבשלה כמאכל בן דרוסאי ואפי' במזיד ונראה כפי' ה"ר פורת מוליאר הגרוף שותין הימנו בשבת שמוזגין המים חמין ביין לפי שהמים אינן כ"כ חמין במוליאר שיתבשל היין מן המים שמוזגין לתוכו אבל אנטיכי אע"פ שגרופה אין שותין הימנה לפי שאנטיכי יש בה הבל יותר ומתבשל היין מן המים בשעת מזיגה וכ"מ בירושלמי: והלא

רבינו חננאל

הוא ומשום דשמעיה מר' יוחנן הוכיח בעל השמועה. ושנינן לאפרושי מאיסורי שרי כמעשה דתלמידו של ר' מאיר: תניא לא ישוט אדם בבריכה מליאה מים ואפילו עומדת בחצר א"ר זירא חזיתיה לר' אבהו שהניח ידיו כנגד פניו של מטה וכו' פי' ר' אבהו היה יורד בנהר לטבול ואפילו (לא) נגע לא חיישינן (לה) [והא] דתניא ר' אליעזר אומר כל האוחז באמה ומשתין מביא מבול לעולם כלומ' מתחמם ומוציא ש"ז ונמצא משחית זרעו על הארץ. הני מילי היכא דלא מיבעית אבל היכא דמיבעית כגון ר' אבהו דהוה מבעית מעליית הנהר אין לו פנאי להתחמם כמו שאין פנאי לבלשת לנסך. הלכך אפילו נגע לא חיישינן ליה והני מילי דשרי להניח ידיו כנגד פניו של מטה כשעולה מן הנהר אבל כשיורד בנהר לא כרב דאמר כל המניח ידיו כנגד פניו של מטה כאילו כופר בבריתו של אברהם אבינו וכרבנן דבי רב אשי דכי נחתי זקפו כי סלקי שחו: אמר רב יהודה כל העולה מבבל לא"י עובר בעשה שנאמר בבלה יובאו ושמה [יהיו] עד יום פקדי אותם נאם ה'. הלך ר' אבא ומצא לר' יהודה במרחץ והי' אומר לשמשיו בלה"ק הביאו לי נתר הביאו לי מסרק פתחו פומייכו והסיקו הבלא ואשתו מיא דבי באני למדנו ממנו כי דברים של חול מותר לאומרן במרחץ בלה"ק. אמר אילו לא [באתי] אלא לשמוע דבר זה דיי: מתני' מוליאר תנא מים מבפנים וגחלים מבחוץ והוא של חרס ואם גרף גחלים שרי. אנטיכי א"ר נחמן בי דודי ושל נחושת הוא ותניא כרב נחמן אנטיכי אע"פ שגרופה אין שותין הימנה בשבת מפני והלא

עין משפט נר מצוה

[וע"ע תוספות יומא ל. ד"ה מנוס]

כט א מיי' פכ"א מהל' איסורי ביאה הלכה כג טוש"ע או"ח סימן ג סעיף יד וטוש"ע אה"ע סימן כג סעיף ד:

ל ב מיי' פ"ה מהלכות מלכים הלכה יב:

לא ג מיי' פ"ד מהלכות דעות הלכה ג:

לב ד מיי' פ"ג מהל' שבת הלכה א ופכ"ב הלכה ו סמג לאוין סה טוש"ע או"ח סימן שיח סעיף יב:

מסורת הש"ס

נדה יג. מג.

ע"ז ע: כתובות כז. [נדה יג.]

כתובות קי. ברכות כד:

[פי' תוספות מגילה כח. ד"ה אלמלא]

[עי' ב"מ קיג:]

[לקמן פב. ע"ש]

מחממתה: ירושלמי מוליאר שאינו גרוף אסור מפני שהגחלים נוגעות בגופו ר' חנניא בר הלל אמר מפני שהרוחה נכנסת לתוכו והגחלים בוערות. ר' יוסי בר אבון אמר מפני שעשוי פרקין פרקין ומתיירא שמא נתאכל דיבוקו ומוסיף מים. אנטיכי בשם ר' יוחנן אמרי מפני שמתחממת מכתליה: פיסקא מיחם שפינהו לא יתן לתוכו צונן

מסורת הש"ס

והלא מצרף ר' שמעון היא דאמר *דבר שאין מתכוין מותר מתקיף לה אביי מידי מיחם שפינה ממנו מים קתני מיחם שפינהו קתני אלא אמר אביי הכי קאמר המיחם שפינהו ויש בו מים חמין לא יתן לתוכו מים מועטין בשביל שיחומו אבל נותן לתוכו מים מרובים כדי להפשירן ומיחם שפינה ממנו מים לא יתן לתוכו מים *כל עיקר מפני שמצרף ור' יהודה היא דאמר דבר שאין מתכוין אסור אמר רב ל"ש אלא להפשיר אבל לצרף אסור ושמואל אמר אפי' לצרף נמי מותר לצרף לכתחילה מי שרי אלא אי איתמר הכי איתמר אמר רב לא שנו אלא שיעור להפשיר אבל שיעור לצרף אסור ושמואל אמר אפי' שיעור לצרף מותר

רש"י

והלא מצרף. כשכלי מתכות חם ונותן לתוכו צונן מחזקים את הכלי וזו היא גמר מלאכת הצורפין שרתיחת האור מפעפעתו וקרוב להשבר והמים מצרפין פעפועיו שולדי"ר בלע"ז: שפינהו. משמע שפינהו לעצמו מעל האור: אבל מיחם שפינה ממנו. שפינהו ממנו החמין: הכי איתמר לא שנו. דפינהו שרי לתת לתוכו צונן: אלא שיעור להפשיר. ולא לצרף כגון שלא מלאהו כולו ורב משמע ליה פינהו כרב אדא שפינה ממנו חמין: אפילו שיעור לצרף. שמלאהו כולו: מותר

תוספות

והלא מצרף. וליכא לשנויי בשלא הגיע לצירוף כדמשני בפרק אמר להם הממונה (יומא דף לד: ושם) דהתם מיחם הגיע לצירוף הוא:

מידי מיחם שפינה הימנו מים קתני המיחם שפינהו קתני. תימה והכתיב ופנו את הבית (ויקרא יד) ואנכי פניתי הבית (בראשית כד) סולו פנו דרך (ישעיה נז) וכן בש"ס *פנו מקום לבר ליואי שאינו מפנה אלא מה שבתוכם וי"ל כיון דבכמה מקומות הוזכר פינוי על הדבר המפנין כגון *המפנה תפליו מזוית לזוית *) מפנין ד' וה' קופות (*) פנו כלים (מבית) הטומאה *(תנן) ועתיד לפנותו לא הוה ליה למנקט פינהו אלא פנה ממנו מים כיון דליכא למיעטי:

מיחם שפינה ממנו מים לא יתן לתוכו מים כל עיקר מפני שמצרף ורבי יהודה היא. אבל לר"ש שרי אע"פ שמצרף כיון דאינו מבשל כגון שיש בו מים הרבה שאין המיחם מספיק לבשל רוב המים שבתוכו כדאשכחן בפרק אמר להם הממונה (יומא דף לד: ושם) שאין מבשל ומצרף דקאמר רבי יהודה מביאין עששיות של ברזל ומטילין לתוך המים שתפיג צינתן ואם היה מבשל היה אסור ואפ"ה פריך והלא מצרף ואע"ג דאביי סבר כר"ש דהא אמר לעיל *כל מילי דמר עביד כרב לבר מהני תלת דעביד כשמואל וחד מינייהו הלכה כר"ש בגרירה ומסתמא אביי כרבה רביה סבירא ליה מ"מ מוקי מתניתין כרבי יהודה משום דקשיא ליה מידי מיחם שפינה ממנו מים קתני ורב אדא לא חייש לקושיית אביי ומוקי לה כהלכתא כר"ש ול"ג לעיל אמר רב אדא בר מתנא אמר רב דרב סבר *כר' יהודה בגרירה ועוד דבהדיא מוקי בסמוך מתני' כר' יהודה וצ"ל דלא הוי פסיק רישיה שיכול להיות שלא יצרף דבפסיק רישיה מודה ר"ש והא דפריך והלא מצרף ה"ק והלא שמא מצרף קשה דהכא משמע דבצירוף אסר ר' יהודה נמי דבר שאין מתכוין ובפרק אמר להם הממונה גריס רש"י ה"מ דאורייתא אבל הכא צירוף דרבנן ול"ג אין שבות במקדש ומפרש דדוקא בדבר שהוא מן התורה אית ליה לר' יהודה דבר שאין מתכוין אסור אבל בצירוף שהוא דרבנן לא ומיהו בלאו הכי קשה לפי' דהא ר' יהודה אסר בגרירה במתניתין דבילה דפרק י"ט (דף כג:) דתנן ואינה נגררת אלא ע"ג כלים דמשמע אבל ע"ג קרקע לא ומוקמינא כר' יהודה דאסר באין מתכוין אע"ג דבגרירה ליכא איסורא דאורייתא אפי' במתכוין כדמשמע בסוף פירקין דהוי חורש כלאחר יד ועוד דשמעתא דהתם קשה דמשני אביי אפי' תימא כשהגיע לצירוף דבר שאינו מתכוין מותר ופריך ומי אמר אביי הכי והתניא ימול בשר ערלתו אפי' במקום בהרת יקוץ דברי רבי אושעיא והוינן בה קרא ל"ל ואמר אביי לא נצרכה אלא לר' יהודה דאמר דבר שאין מתכוין אסור והשתא אמאי לא מייתי ההיא דבילה דהיא משנה שלמה דאסר ר' יהודה דבר שאין מתכוין ומייתי מילתיה דאביי ועוד מוחק הספר דגרס ואין שבות במקדש לכך נראה לפרש התם אביי אמר אפילו כו' דבר שאין מתכוין מותר פי' מותר לר' יהודה ולא אסר °ליה ר' יהודה דבר שאין מתכוין אלא מדרבנן ופריך מימול בשר ערלתו דמוקי אביי דאיצטריך לר' יהודה קרא א"כ ש"מ דאסר ר' יהודה אין מתכוין מן התורה ומשני וה"ג ה"מ בכל התורה כולה פי' בכל התורה כולה חוץ משבת אסור מן התורה אבל צירוף דגבי שבת לא אסור אין מתכוין אלא מדרבנן דכיון דאין מתכוין לא הויא מלאכת מחשבת ושרי דאין שבות במקדש והשתא א"ש הכא וסוגיא דהתם וקשה דבפרק ספק אכל (כריתות דף כ: *ושם) א"ר אשי כגון שנתכוין לכבות העליונות והובערו התחתונות מאליהן ת"ק סבר לה כר"י דאמר דבר שאין מתכוין אסור ולכך קאמר דחייב חטאת ומאן דפטר כר"ש דאמר דבר שאין מתכוין מותר אלמא משמע דדבר שאין מתכוין אסור לר"י אפי' בשבת מן התורה וי"ל דהתם הוי פסיק רישיה שאי אפשר כלל לכבות העליונות אם לא יובערו התחתונות וחשיב מלאכת מחשבת ואע"ג דהוי פסיק רישיה פטר ר"ש משום דהויא מלאכה שאינה צריכה לגופה דאינו צריך להבערת התחתונות והא דנקט לישנא מתכוין ושאין מתכוין ולא נקט ת"ק כר"י דאמר מלאכה שאינה צריכה כו' משום רבותא דר"י נקט דלא תימא דלא מחייב ר"י מלאכה שאינה צריכה לגופה אלא במקום שמתכוין לעשות המלאכה כגון מכבה גחלת של עץ שלא יוזקו רבים שמתכוין לכיבוי אבל התם שאינו מתכוין להבעיר התחתונות לא קמ"ל כיון דהוי פסיק רישיה חייב ובההיא דהחותה גחלים להתחמם והובערו מאליהן נקט הא ר"י דאמר מלאכה שאינה צריכה לגופה חייב הא ר"ש כו' אע"ג דאין כוונתו להבעיר מדפטר ר"ש דאי כוונתו להבעיר הויא צריכה לגופה מ"מ כיון דניחא ליה בהך הבערה לא קרינן ביה שאינו מתכוין והכי לא נקט לישנא דאין מתכוין אבל בנתכוין לכבות העליונות לא ניחא ליה בהבערת התחתונות כלל שהרי בא לכבות שייך לישנא דאין מתכוין אע"ג דהוי פסיק רישיה ור"ש שרי בחותה גחלים להתחמם אע"ג דבפרק הבונה (לקמן קג: ושם) משמע דהתולש לאכילה או לבהמה בארעא דידיה חייב חטאת בכל שהוא אע"ג דאין מתכוין ליפות הקרקע לא דמי לכל מלאכה שאינה צריכה לגופה כגון חותה להתחמם דהתם אע"פ שאין מתכוין ליפות אנן סהדי דניחא ליה אבל בחותה אינו נהנה בהבערה זו דבלא הבערה זו יתחמם וכיון שאינו נהנה (א) בברור לא נתכוון להבעיר והויא מלאכה שאינה צריכה לו*:

לא שנו אלא להפשיר. מתוך פי' הקונט' משמע דמפרש הסוגיא כן לא שנו אלא בדבר שאין שייך צירוף אלא פישור כגון מיחם שפינהו אבל לצרף פי' בדבר ששייך צירוף כגון מיחם שפינו ממנו מים אסור ושמואל אמר אף לצרף כלומר אף בדבר ששייך צירוף מותר ומשמע אפי' במתכוין והכי פריך ולצרף לכתחילה מי שרי אלא אי איתמר הכי איתמר לא שנו דפינה ממנו מים שרי לתת לתוכו צונן אלא שיעור להפשיר ולא לצרף כגון שלא מלאהו כולו דליכא צירוף עד שימלאנו על כל גדותיו ורב מפרש פינהו כרב אדא והא דפריך לעיל והא מצרף משום דמשמע ליה הא דקאמר אבל נותן לתוכו מים מרובין שיש שיעור לצרף מדקאמר מרובים אבל כשפינהו והמים בתוכו א"א להיות צירוף ודוחק ור"י מפרש בענין אחר דפינהו נמי איכא צירוף כשמילאהו ובפינה ממנו מים כל שהוא יש בו שיעור לצרף מדפריך לעיל והלא מצרף ולא משני שאין בו שיעור לצרף ועוד מדקאמר אביי אבל מיחם שפינה ממנו מים אסור מפני שמצרף משמע דהתם פשיטא ליה שמצרף ולא שייך לפלוגי ביה דבכל שהוא מצרף וה"פ לא שנו אלא להפשיר פי' שמתכוין להפשיר השתא סבירא ליה דמיירי רב אפי' בשיעור לצרף אבל לצרף שמתכוין לצרף אסור כר"ש ומפרש פינהו שפינה ממנו מים כרב אדא אי נמי פינהו עם המים כאביי ומיירי כשיש בו שיעור לצרף כגון שממלאו כולו מים צוננין דאע"ג דהמים חמין שבתוכו לא נסתלקו יש שיעור לצרף ומחלק בין אין מתכוין למתכוין כר"ש ולא כאביי דמוקי לה באין בו שיעור לצרף וכר' יהודה וכי פריך אליבא דשמואל ולצרף לכתחילה מי שרי ה"ה דהוה מצי למיפרך אליבא דרב כיון דסבר דהלכה כרבי יהודה בגרירה דהיינו בדבר שאינו מתכוין מאי דוחקיה לאוקמי מתני' כשיש בו שיעור לצרף וכר"ש לוקמה כשאין בו שיעור לצרף כאביי וכרבי יהודה דסבירא ליה כוותיה אלא אדשמואל קפריך דעדיפא ליה אלא אי איתמר הכי איתמר השתא מפרש מתניתין כאביי לגמרי שפינהו עם המים וה"פ לא שנו אלא שיעור להפשיר שאינו ממלא המיחם על כל גדותיו אבל שיעור לצרף אע"פ שאינו מתכוין אלא להפשיר אסור כרבי יהודה דסבר כוותיה אבל פינה ממנו מים לעולם אסור דבכל ענין יש שיעור לצרף כדפי' וכי קאמר אביי אבל מיחם שפינה ממנו מים כו' ה"ה דמצי למימר בד"א בשיעור להפשיר אבל שיעור לצרף אסור אלא ניחא ליה למינקט האי לישנא משום דמלשון פינהו דייק דאתיא כר' יהודה שמואל אומר אף שיעור לצרף מותר כר"ש וא"ת מדקאמר שמואל אף שיעור לצרף אם כן מוקי מתני' כאביי דדייק שפינהו דלרב אדא דמפרש שפינה ממנו מים לעולם יש שיעור לצרף ומאי אף שיעור לצרף דקאמר שמואל וכיון דמפרש כאביי אם כן נידוק דווקא פינהו הא פינה ממנו אסור כר"י וי"ל דשמואל קאי אמילתיה דרב וקאמר אף שיעור לצרף שרי דהכא סבירא לי כר"ש מוקמי' מתני' כוותיה דרב אדא כשפינה ממנו מים ויש לעולם שיעור לצרף:

לא שנו אלא להפשיר. פ"ה דרב משמע ליה מתני' פינהו כרב אדא שפינה ממנו המים ושיעור להפשיר כשלא מלאהו ושיעור לצרף כשמילאהו וקשה כי פריך לעיל והלא מצרף לימא כשלא מילאהו ועוד מדקאמר אביי אבל מיחם שפינה ממנו מים לא יתן לתוכו כל עיקר מפני שהוא מצרף משמע בכל ענין הוא מצרף אפי' לא מילאהו וי"ל דמשמע ליה פינהו כאביי וקאמר לא שנו אלא שיעור להפשיר שלא נתן בו מים כ"כ שיצטנן החמין אבל נתן בו מים כ"כ שיצטננו החמין אסור ואע"פ שאינו מתכוין לצרף מיתסר (תו"י בשם מהר"ש ממירזבורג):

אפילו

[כתובות עז:]

[עפר ועתיד לפנותו עירובין עט.]

לסברת התוס' אליבא דרש"י דאינו מצרף אלא כשהוא מלא ממש צריך למחוק תיבות כל עיקר [תו"י]

[לעיל כב.]

הגהות הב"ח

(א) תוס' סוף ד"ה מיחם וכו' וכיון שאינו נהנה: כ"ב ע"ל פ' כלל גדול דף עה בד"ה ספי ניחא:

[וע"ע תוספות בסמוך ד"ה ל"ש ותוס' לקמן מב. ד"ה אפי' ותוס' לקמן קג. ד"ה לא צריכא ותוס' לקמן קיא. ד"ה האי ותוספות יומא לד: ד"ה ה"מ ותוספות סוכה לג: ד"ה מודה ותוספות כתובות ה: ד"ה את"ל ועוד שם ו. ד"ה האי ותוס' כריתות כ: ד"ה סבירא]

גליון הש"ס

תום' ד"ה מיחם שפינה וכו' ליה ר"י דבר שאינו מתכוין אלא מדרבנן. וכ"כ רש"י לקמן קלא ע"ב ד"ה לפי תומו. ועיין לקמן דף לה ע"א תוס' ד"ה סמכבד:

*[ערוב' כו:] *)[לק' קכו:] (*) [פנו כלים מפני הטומאה ברכות כה:]

[לעיל כט: ביצה כג: כתובות ס: פסחים כה: נזיר מב. לקמן ל. כריתות כ:]

רבינו חננאל

אוקמא מיחם שפינהו מע"ג הכירה ויש בו מים חמין לא יתן לתוכו מים מועטין בשביל שיחמו אבל נותן לתוכו מים מרובין כדי לפשר. פינה ממנה החמין לא יתן לתוכו מים כל עיקר מפני (הוא) שמצרף. ור' יהודה הוא דאמר דבר שאין מתכוון אסור אמר רב לא שנו אלא מים מועטין שיעור להפשיר אבל מים מרובין שיעור לצרף אסור. פי' צירוף הכלי בעת שיתחמם נעשה כגחלת וכשמביאו בשעת גמר מלאכתו בצונן מחזקתו ולוטש פניו ונמצא לו כמו צירוף רב אמר שיעור לצרף אסור ושמואל אמר אפילו שיעור לצרף נמי מותר *) ואוקמה שמואל כר"ש ורב אדא בר מתנה כר' שמעון ודאביי נמי בבא דרישא (נמי) קאי כשמואל וסוגינא כשמואל אליבא דר"ש [ור' אדא] ואקשינן

*) מן ואוקמה עד קאי כשמואל הובא גם ברמב"ן במלחמה בשם ר"ח:

[ע"ש]

רב נסים גאון

ר"ש היא דאמר דבר שאינו מתכוין מותר וזה העיקר בפרק במה מדליקין (דף כט) דתניא ר"ש אומר גורר אדם מטה כסא וספסל ובלבד שלא יתכוין לעשות חריץ. ור' יהודה דאמר דבר שאין מתכוין אסור עיקר דברי ר' יהודה במשנה במס' יו"ט בפ' יום טוב שחל להיות ערב שבת (דף כג) דתנן ר' יהודה אומר אין מקרדין ביו"ט מפני שהוא עושה חבורה ובגמ' גרסי ר' יהודה סבר דבר שאין מתכוין אסור ובמס' בכורות בפ' כל פסולי המוקדשין (דף לג) שנינו בכור שאחזו דם אפילו מת אין מקיזין לו את הדם דברי ר' יהודה כו' ר' שמעון אומר יקיז אע"פ שהוא עושה מום הרי מיכן תדע שר' יהודה סבר דבר שאין מתכוין אסור ור"ש [סבר] דבר שאין מתכוין מותר:

water to temper it. [41*b*] But does he not harden it?[9]—This agrees with R. Simeon, who ruled: That which is unintentional
a is permitted.[1] Abaye demurred to this: Is it then stated, A BOILER from which the water IS REMOVED: Surely it is stated, IF A BOILER IS REMOVED? Rather said Abaye, this is the meaning: If a boiler is removed [from the fire] and it contains hot water, one must not pour therein a little water to heat it [the added water], but he may pour a large quantity of [cold] water therein to temper it.[2] But if the water is removed from a boiler, no water at all may be poured therein, because that hardens it; this agreeing with R. Judah, who maintains: [Even] that which is unintentional is forbidden.

Rab said: They taught [that it is permitted] only to temper [the water]; but if it is to harden [the metal], it is forbidden. Whereas Samuel ruled: Even if to harden it, it is still permitted. If the primary purpose is to harden it, can it be permitted![3] Rather if stated, it was thus stated: Rab said: They taught this only where there is [merely] a sufficient quantity to temper it; but if there is enough to harden it, it is forbidden.[4] Whereas Samuel maintained: Even if there is a sufficient quantity to harden it, [42*a*] it is permitted.[5]

(9) *Sc.* the metal of the boiler, by pouring cold water into it while it is hot. This itself is forbidden on the Sabbath.

a (1) *Supra* 22*a*, 29*b*. (2) I.e., reduce its heat. (3) Surely not. (4) Rashi: Rab explains the Mishnah as R. Adda b. Mattenah, viz., that the water was removed from the boiler. Thereon Rab observes: though a large quantity of water may be poured into it, it must nevertheless be insufficient to harden it, but merely enough to temper the water, i.e., it must not be completely filled with cold water, for that hardens the metal. Ri maintains that if the hot water is first emptied, even a small quantity of cold water poured into it immediately afterwards will harden it. Hence he interprets it thus: Rab explains the Mishnah as Abaye, as meaning that the boiler was removed with its hot water. Nevertheless, it must not be filled up with cold water, for that hardens it, as before. (5) Since that is not his intention.

Shall we say that Samuel agrees with R. Simeon?[6] But surely Samuel said: One may extinguish a lump of fiery metal in the street, that it should not harm the public,[7] but not a burning
a piece[1] of wood.[2] Now if you think that he agrees with R. Simeon, even that of wood too [should be permitted]?[3]—In respect to what is unintentional he holds with R. Simeon; but in the matter of work which is not needed *per se*, he agrees with R. Judah.[4] Rabina said: As a corollary, a thorn in public ground may be carried away in stages of less than four cubits;[5] whilst in a *karmelith*[6] even a great distance too [is permitted].

BUT ONE MAY POUR, etc. Our Rabbis taught: A man may pour hot water into cold, but not cold water into hot; this is the view of Beth Shammai;[7] while Beth Hillel maintain: Both hot into cold and cold into hot are permitted. This applies only to a cup,[8] but in the case of a bath, hot into cold [is permitted], but not cold into hot.[9] But R. Simeon b. Menassia forbids it.[10] R. Naḥman said: The *halachah* is as R. Simeon b. Menassia.

R. Joseph thought to rule: A basin is as a bath. Said Abaye to him, R. Ḥiyya taught: A basin is not as a bath. Now, on the original supposition that it is as a bath, while R. Naḥman ruled, The *halachah* is as R. Simeon, can there be no washing in hot water
b on the Sabbath?[1]—Do you think that R. Simeon refers to the second clause? He refers to the first clause: 'While Beth Hillel maintain: Both hot into cold and cold into hot are permitted';[2] but R. Simeon b. Menassia forbids even cold into hot. Shall we say that R. Simeon b. Menassia rules as Beth Shammai?[3]—He says thus: Beth Shammai and Beth Hillel did not differ in this matter.[4]

R. Huna son of R. Joshua said: I saw that Raba was not particular about vessels,[5] since R. Ḥiyya taught: A person may pour a jug of water into a basin of water, hot into cold or cold into hot.[6] Said R. Huna to R. Ashi: Perhaps it is different there, because the vessel intervenes?[7]—It is stated that he pours it, was his answer.[8] [Thus:] A person may pour a jug of water into a basin of water, both hot into cold and cold into hot.

MISHNAH. IF A STEW POT OR A BOILING POT[9] IS REMOVED SEETHING [FROM THE FIRE],[10] ONE MUST NOT PUT

(6) That whatever is unintentional is permitted. (7) Metal does not really burn, but throws off fiery sparks when red-hot. The prohibition of extinguishing does not apply in this case by Biblical law at all, save by Rabbinical law; hence where general damage may ensue the Rabbis waived their prohibition.

a (1) Lit., 'coal'. (2) For that is Biblically forbidden. (3) For R. Simeon rules that if work is not needed *per se* (v. *infra* 105*b*, n. b3) it imposes no liability, and every case of extinguishing, except the extinguishing of a wick to make it easier for subsequent relighting (v. *supra* 29*b* bottom), falls within this category. Hence it is only Rabbinically forbidden, and therefore the same as metal. (4) That it is interdicted. (5) The least distance which is Biblically forbidden is four cubits in a single passage, without an interval. A thorn too may cause harm to the public; hence the Rabbinical interdict is waived. (6) V. Glos. and *supra* 6*a*. (7) Rashi: they hold that the lower prevails against the upper. Hence in the former case the hot water is tempered by the cold, which is permitted; but in the latter the cold is heated by the hot, which is forbidden. R. Tam: 'hot water into cold' implies that the cold water exceeds the hot, and therefore cools it, hence it is permitted. 'Cold water into hot' implies that there is more hot water, which heats the cold; consequently, it is forbidden. According to this interpretation this is independent of the question whether the lower prevails against the upper or the reverse, which refers to equal quantities; cf. ערוך השלחן; Yoreh De'ah XCI, 12. (8) The water being required for drinking, one does not wish it to become very hot. Moreover, a cup is a 'second vessel' (v. *supra* 40*b*, n. b6), i.e., the water is not actually heated therein, and the contents of a second vessel cannot cause anything that comes into contact therewith to boil. (9) The water is needed for washing, and must be very hot. Therefore if the latter case is permitted, we fear that one will come intentionally to heat water in a forbidden manner. The reference is to a bath which is a 'second vessel', and yet it is forbidden for this reason. (10) Even hot into cold.

b (1) Rashi: even if heated on the eve of the Sabbath, cold water must be added to temper its heat, which according to R. Simeon b. Menassia is forbidden. (2) The reference being to a cup, not a bath, as stated. (3) Surely not, for it is axiomatic that the *halachah* is always as Beth Hillel. (4) Both agreeing that it is forbidden. (5) Pouring hot water into cold and *vice versa*. Asheri omits 'about vessels.' (6) Tosaf. suggests that this may be the identical Baraitha cited above, but that there it was quoted in brief. (7) He assumed that the water is poured on to the inner side of the basin first, which somewhat cools it. (8) I.e., directly into the water. (9) The first means a tightly covered pot. (10) At twilight on Friday.

מותר למימרא דשמואל כרבי שמעון סבירא ליה *והאמר שמואל [ב]מכבין גחלת של מתכת ברה"ר בשביל שלא יוזקו בה רבים [ג]אבל לא גחלת של עץ ואי ס"ד סבר לה כרבי שמעון אפילו של עץ נמי *בדבר שאין מתכוין סבר לה כרבי שמעון במלאכה שאינה צריכה לגופה סבר לה כרבי יהודה אמר רבינא [ג]הלכך *קוץ ברשות הרבים מוליכו פחות פחות מד' אמות ובכרמלית אפילו טובא: אבל נותן כו': ת"ר נותן אדם חמין לתוך הצונן ולא הצונן לתוך החמין דברי בית שמאי ובית הלל אומרים [ד]בין חמין לתוך הצונן ובין צונן לתוך החמין מותר בד"א בכוס אבל באמבטי חמין לתוך הצונן ולא צונן לתוך החמין ורבי שמעון בן מנסיא אוסר אמר רב נחמן הלכה כר"ש בן מנסיא סבר רב יוסף למימר ספל הרי הוא כאמבטי א"ל אביי תני ר' חייא ספל אינו כאמבטי ולמאי דסליק אדעתא מעיקרא דספל הרי הוא כאמבטי ואמר רב נחמן הלכה כרבי שמעון בן מנסיא אלא בשבת רהיצה בחמין ליכא מי סברת רבי שמעון אסיפא קאי ארישא קאי ובית הלל מתירין בין חמין לתוך צונן ובין צונן לתוך החמין ורבי שמעון בן מנסיא אוסר צונן לתוך חמין לימא רבי שמעון בן מנסיא דאמר כב"ש הכי קאמר *לא נחלקו ב"ש וב"ה בדבר זה אמר רב הונא בריה דרב יהושע חזינא ליה לרבא דלא קפיד *אמנא מדתני רבי חייא נותן אדם קיתון של מים לתוך ספל של מים בין חמין לתוך צונן ובין צונן לתוך חמין אמר ליה רב הונא לרב אשי דילמא שאני התם דמיפסק כלי אמר ליה מערה איתמר [ה]מערה אדם קיתון של מים לתוך ספל של מים בין חמין לתוך צונן בין צונן לתוך חמין: **מתני'** *[ו]האילפס והקדרה שהעבירן מרותחין לא יתן לתוכן תבלין אבל

רש"י

מותר. שאין מתכוין לכך: גחלת של מתכת. שמשליכין לחוץ פסולת של ברזל דלא שייך כבוי בהכי מדאורייתא ומדרבנן אסורה והיכא דאיכא נזקא לרבים לא גזרו על השבות: אבל לא של עץ. דאיסורא דאורייתא היא וחייב סקילה: אפילו של עץ נמי. דהא לרבי שמעון מלאכה שאינה צריכה לגופה פטור עליה וכל כיבוי אינו צריך לגופו הוץ מעושי פחמין או מהבהבי פתילה: הלכך. כיון דאמרת לא גזרו שבות דכיבוי מתכת במקום נזקא דרבים: קוץ ברשות הרבים מוליכו פחות פחות מד' אמות. עד שיסלקנו לצידי רשות הרבים דאיסורא דרבנן הוא: ובכרמלית. דטלטול דידיה דרבנן: אפילו טובא. יעבירנו בעקירה אחת: חמין לתוך צונן. דקסבר תתאה גבר ואין החמין מרתיחין את הצונן אלא מפשירין: ולא צונן לתוך חמין. שהתחתונים מרתיחים את העליונים דתתאה גבר: בכוס. דלשתיה קבעי להו ולא ניחא ליה שיחומו הרבה ועוד דכלי שני הוא: אוסר. אפילו חמין לתוך צונן: ספל הרי הוא כאמבטי. ואף על גב דכלי שני הוא הואיל ולאו לשתיה אלא לרחיצה אסירי דניחא ליה שיחמו הרבה וגזרינן: אלא בשבת רחיצה בחמין ליכא. בתמיה דהא לרבי שמעון אפילו חמין לתוך צונן אסור לא משכחת חמין שהוחמו ואפילו מע"ש שלא יהיו צריכין להפיג רתיחתן ואם כן לא ירחוץ אפילו פניו ידיו ורגליו בחמין: מי סברת ר' שמעון אסיפא קאי. דלא שרי ת"ק אלא חמין לתוך צונן ואתא איהו ואסר אף חמין לתוך צונן: ארישא קאי. לשתיה וצונן לתוך חמין דקשרו ב"ה קאסר: **מתני'** שהעבירן. מן האור: מרותחין. בין השמשות: לא יתן לתוכן תבלין. משתחשך דכלי ראשון כל זמן שרותח מבשל:
אבל

תוספות

אפילו של עץ נמי. ואם תאמר ומאי ס"ד דמקשה וכי משום דסבר שמואל כרבי שמעון בדאין מתכוין יסבור כמותו במלאכה שאינו צריך לגופה וי"ל דס"ד דמקשה דודאי הא בהא תליא משום דסבר רבי יהודה דמלאכה שאינו צריך לגופה חייב עליה היכא דמתכוין בשאין מתכוין נמי החמירו חכמים אבל לרבי שמעון דפטור עליה מן התורה אף במתכוין לא תם לאסור מדרבנן כשאין מתכוין כיון דמתכוין עצמו ליכא אלא איסורא דרבנן ומיהו לפי האמת לאו הא בהא תליא דשמואל אע"ג דבמלאכה שאינה צריכה לגופה סבר כרבי יהודה דחייב [מתיר] באין מתכוין ולרבי יהודה נמי אסור אין מתכוין אפילו בגרירה דמתכוין עצמו לא אסיר אלא מדרבנן כדאמרי' לקמן ובשילהי כל התדיר (זבחים דף צא: ושם*) דאמר שמואל המתנדב יין מביאו ומזלפו ע"ג האשים ופריך והא קא מכבה ומשני דסבר דבר שאין מתכוין מותר ופריך כי הכא דאמר שמואל מכבין גחלת של מתכת אבל לא של עץ והשתא אומר רשב"א דפריך מכ"ש דכיון דסבר שמואל דמלאכה שאינה צריכה לגופה חייב א"כ סבירא ליה נמי בשבת דבר שאין מתכוין אסור דסבר המקשה דהתם דהא בהא תליא כמו מקשה דהכא וכיון דבשבת אסור אין מתכוין כ"ש בעלמא אך הקשה דמשמע דאי הוי סבר שמואל מלאכה שאינה צריכה לו פטור עליה הוה אתי שפיר ואמאי והא מלאכה שאינה צריכה לגופה בשאר איסורים דלאו שבת חייב עליה וכיון דסבירא ליה דהא בהא תליא א"כ אמאי קאמר התם דבר שאין מתכוין מותר:

נותן אדם חמין לתוך צונן. *אפי' בכלי ראשון דחמין לתוך צונן אינו מבשל כמו שאפרש. ולא צונן לתוך חמין אפילו בכלי שני דגזרי ב"ש כלי שני אטו כלי ראשון וב"ה דפליגי ושרו צונן לתוך חמין היינו דוקא בכלי שני כדקתני בד"א בכוס משמע דבכלי ראשון מודו ב"ה ולא משום דסברה הך ברייתא דתתאה גבר כדפירש בקונטרס דאם כן יקשה מהכא למ"ד *עילאה גבר ולמאן דאמר תתאה גבר נמי הא מבשל כדי קליפה כמו שאפרש לקמן בע"ה אלא נראה כמו שאומר ר"ת דחמין לתוך צונן משמע שהצוננין של מטה מרובים שהדרך ליתן המועט במרובה ולכך אין מבשלים החמין המועטים כלל לפי שמתערבין בצוננין המרובין ומתבטל חמימותן ולא צונן לתוך חמין שהחמין של מטה מרובין ומתערבין בהן הצוננין המועטין ומתבשלין: **אבל** באמבטי כו'. נראה דהאי אמבטי איירי כגון שהוא כלי שני ולא הוי כההוא אמבטי דלעיל *דקאמר בקשתי להגיה כך באמבטי מדקאמר ספל אינו כאמבטי והאי ספל ע"כ כלי שני דאי כלי ראשון אמאי אינו כאמבטי ודעותיה אמבטי הוי כלי שני ועוד דאי באמבטי שהוא כלי ראשון איירי לא הוה ליה למינקט אמבטי אלא מיחם שהוא לשתיה דומיא דכוס ומדנקט אמבטי משמע דבכלי שני איירי ואתא לפלוגי בכלי שני בין כוס שהוא לשתיה לאמבטי לפי שחמין הרבה ואיכא למיגזר דהרואה אותן חמין כל כך סבור דכלי ראשון הוא ובמתני' דנקט במיחם שהוא ראשון לא יתן לתוכו מים הוה מצי למימר באמבטי שהוא שני לא יתן לתוכו מים אלא דמתני' מיירי בשתיה ומפליג בין מיחם לכוס: **מי** סברת ר"ש בן מנסיא אסיפא קאי ארישא קאי. היינו דוקא למאי דס"ד לרב יוסף מעיקרא אבל למאי דמסקי' דספל אינו כאמבטי קאי אסיפא בכוס וסבר שפיר ר"ש בן מנסיא כב"ה דאפילו צונן לתוך חמין מותר ואתיא מתני' דשריא לתוך הכוס אליבא דהלכתא כר"ש בן מנסיא וא"ת למאי דסלקא דעתך דארישא קאי ואסר בכוס צונן לתוך חמין מאי קמ"ל רב יוסף דספל הרי הוא כאמבטי כוס נמי הרי הוא כאמבטי לר"ש בן מנסיא דהלכתא כוותיה וי"ל דרב יוסף לב"ה אתא לאשמעינן דשרו בכוס: **נותן** אדם קיתון של מים. וא"ת ואמאי לא מייתי ברייתא דלעיל דספל אינו כאמבטי ואמאי איצטריך כמי רבי חייא למיתני תרוייהו וי"ל דהשתא קמ"ל בין חמין לתוך צונן בין צונן לתוך חמין דההיא דספל אינו כאמבטי ה"א דקאי אר"ש בן מנסיא דאסר באמבטי אפי' חמין לתוך צונן ועליה קאמר דספל אינו כאמבטי ושרי חמין לתוך צונן אבל צונן לתוך חמין ה"א דאסור ואפשר דההיא דלעיל הייתו הך דהכא אלא שקיצרה ונקט לישנא דרב יוסף דמייתי עלה: **שאני** התם דמפסיק כלי. וא"ת דאמר לעיל (דף מ:) טול בכלי שני ותן אבל בכלי ראשון לא אע"ג דמפסיק מנא וי"ל דהתם בכלי ראשון והכא דבכלי שני שאני:
אבל

שבת כט: | [שם נב.] | [ביצה כח:] | [וזם נב.] | [לקמן קלה. יבמות כח. ב"ק לב. סוכה טו.] [בכה"ש ליתא ועי' ברב אלפס] | פסחים מ: | [דף מ:]

עוד נוכל לומר דחמין לתוך צונן כב"ש [כלי] שני ב"ש אבל בכלי ראשון אסור אפי' צונן לתוך חמין [תו"י]

עין משפט נר מצוה

לג א ב מיי' פ"א מהל' שבת הלכה ז ופי"ב הלכה ב טוש"ע או"ח סי' שלד סעיף כז:

לד ג מיי' שם פ"א הל' ז טוש"ע או"ח סי' שח סעיף יח:

לה ד ה מיי' פכ"ב מהל' שבת הלכה ו טוש"ע או"ח סימן שיח סעיף יב:

לו ו מיי' שם טור שו"ע שם סעיף ט:

רבינו חננאל

למימרא דשמואל כר' שמעון (ורב אדא) והאמר שמואל מכבין גחלת של מתכת ברה"ר בשביל שלא יוזקו בה רבים אבל גחלת של עץ לא ואילו ר"ש סבר אפילו של עץ מותר לפי שאין מתכוון לכבות אלא כדי שלא יוזק וכי האי גוונא פטר ר' שמעון ואסיק' לעולם כר' יהוד' סבירא לי' דאמר מלאכה שאינה צריכה לגופה חייב עליה *) מיהו דבר שיש בו היזק לרבים כגון צידת נחש וכבוי גחלת של מתכת בזמן שהיא חמה והיא שחורה והרואה אותה חומה שהיא צוננת לפי שאין בה אדמומית כגחלת לוחשת ונמצאו בני אדם ניזוקין בו לפיכך מותר אבל הגחלת של עץ אם תסיר אדמומיתה נכבת כבר ואינה מזקת ואם אדמומיתה בה כל הרואה אותה מתרחק ממנה ומכל פנים אין אדם ניזוק שהשחורה כבר כבתה והארומה מתרחקין ממנה לפיכך המכבה אותה חייב ולפיכך היה שמואל אוסר בגחלת של עץ. (ומדוקיה) אמר רבינא קוץ ברה"ר מוליכו פחות פחות מד' אמות ואע"ג דרב ושמואל הלכה כרב באיסורי בהא קיי"ל כשמואל דאמר במלאכה שאינה צריכה לגופה סבר לה כר' יהודה בדבר שאין מתכוין סבר לה כר"ש ומדרב אחא ורבינא שמע מינייהו דהלכתא כר' שמעון: פיסקא אבל נותן הוא לתוכו או לתוך הכוס כדי להפשירן. ת"ר לא יתן אדם חמין לתוך צונן [ולא צונן] לתוך חמין וב"ה מתירין כו'. ואוקימנא להא דר"ש בן מנסיא שאוסר כלומר לא נחלקו ב"ש וב"ה אלא אפילו ב"ה אוסרין ואע"ג דאמר רב נחמן הלכתא כר' שמעון בן מנסיא כיון דאמר רב הונא חזינא לרבא דלא קפיד זימנין עביד כמר וזמנין עביד כמר מדתני ר' חייא דתני ר' חייא נותן אדם קיתון של מים לתוך ספל כו' ורב אשי מתרץ לה לרב הונא ואמר ליה מערה תניא כלומר מערה אדם קיתון של מים לתוך ספל של מים בין חמין לתוך צונן בין צונן לתוך חמין קיי"ל כוותייהו דאינון בתראי ומעשה רב ולא רמו ספל לאמבטי וכוס למיחם דאוקימנא ליה שאסור לתת בתוכו צונן מועטין בהיות המים בו כדי שיחמו אלא מרובין כדי להפשיר כי המיחם הוא עצמו מייחם אבל ספל ואמבטי וכוס מתחממין בכלי אחד ומערין
בתוך

*) עי' ביאור דברי רבינו ז"ל בחידושי הרשב"א ז"ל ד"ה גחלת של מתכות ע"ש סיפב.

עין משפט
נר מצוה

לז א מיי' פכ"ב מהל' שבת הלכה ו טוש"ע או"ח סימן שיח סעיף ט:

לח ב מיי' פכ"ה מהלכות שבת הלכה כג ופ"ה הלכה יג סמג לאוין סה טור שו"ע או"ח סימן רסה סעיף ג:

לט ג מיי' פכ"ה שם סמג שם טור ושו"ע או"ח סימן שי סעיף ו וסימן שכב סעיף א וסי' תקיג סעיף ד:

אבל נותן הוא לתוך הקערה או לתוך התמחוי רבי יהודה אומר *לכל הוא נותן חוץ מדבר שיש בו חומץ וציר: גמ' איבעיא להו רבי יהודה ארישא קאי ולקולא או דילמא אסיפא קאי ולחומרא ת"ש דתניא רבי יהודה אומר לכל אילפסין הוא נותן לכל הקדירות רותחות הוא נותן חוץ מדבר שיש בו חומץ וציר סבר רב יוסף למימר מלח הרי הוא כתבלין דבכלי ראשון בשלה ובכלי שני לא בשלה א"ל אביי תני רבי חייא מלח אינה כתבלין דבכלי שני נמי בשלה ופליגא דרב נחמן דאמר רב נחמן צריכא מילחא בישולא כבישרא דתורא ואיכא דאמרי סבר רב יוסף למימר מלח הרי הוא כתבלין דבכלי ראשון בשלה בכלי שני לא בשלה א"ל אביי תני ר' חייא מלח אינה כתבלין דבכלי ראשון נמי לא בשלה והיינו דאמר רב נחמן צריכא מילחא בישולא כבישרא דתורא: מתני' אין נותנין כלי תחת הנר לקבל בו את השמן ואם נתנוה מבעוד יום מותר ואין ניאותין ממנו לפי שאינו מן המוכן: גמ' אמר רב חסדא אע"פ שאמרו אין נותנין כלי תחת תרנגולת לקבל ביצתה אבל כופה עליה כלי שלא תשבר אמר רבה מ"ט דרב חסדא קסבר תרנגולת עשויה להטיל ביצתה באשפה ואינה עשויה להטיל ביצתה במקום מדרון והצלה מצויה התירו והצלה שאינה מצויה לא התירו איתיבי' אביי והצלה שאינה מצויה לא התירו והתניא *נשברה לו חבית של טבל בראש גגו מביא כלי ומניח תחתיה בגולפי חדתי דשביחי דפקעי איתיביה *נותנין כלי תחת הנר לקבל ניצוצות נמי שכיחי איתיביה

אבל נותן הוא לתוך הקערה. דכלי שני אינו מבשל: תמחוי. כעין קערה גדולה שמערה כל האילפס לתוכה ומשם מערה לקערות: ר' יהודה אומר לכל וכו'. בגמ' מפרש אהי קאי אכלי ראשון או אכלי שני: חוץ מדבר שיש בו חומץ או ציר. שהן מבשלין את התבלין כשהן רותחין: ציר. הנוטף מן הדגים כשכובשים אותן במכבש: גמ' ארישא קאי. אאילפס דקא אסר ת"ק וקאמר ר' יהודה לכל אילפסין הוא נותן דכלי ראשון לא מבשל: או דילמא אסיפא קאי. אקערה ותמחוי דקא שרי ת"ק וקא אמר ליה רבי יהודה בכל קערות ותמחויין מודינא לך חוץ מדבר שיש בו חומץ ואפילו כלי שני נמי לא: דבכלי ראשון נמי לא בשלה. ומותר ליתן ואפילו בכלי ראשון משהעבירו מן האור: מתני' אין נותנין. בשבת: כלי תחת הנר. לקבל בו שמן המטפטף משום דשמן מוקצה הוא וקסבר אין כלי ניטל בשבת אלא לצורך דבר הניטל אי נמי קסבר אסור לבטל כלי מהיכנו להושיב כלי במקום שלא יוכל עוד ליטלו *(משום) דהוי כקובע לו מקום ומחברו בטיט ודמי למלאכה וכלי זה משיפול בו השמן המוקצה יהא אסור לטלטלו: מותר. להניחה שם: ואין ניאותין. נהנין: גמ' אע"פ שאמרו אין נותנין כלי תחת תרנגולת לקבל ביצתה. כשהיא מטילתה במקום מדרון שמא תתגלגל ותשבר ומדיוקא דמתניתין שמעינן לה דדמי לנותן כלי תחת הנר לקבל בו שמן: אבל כופה עליה כלי. ולא תימא אין כלי ניטל אלא לצורך דבר הניטל: באשפה. ויש לחוש שמא תשבר ברגלי אדם וכופה עליה כלי: והצלה מצויה התירו. לטלטל כלי לצרכה ואף על פי שהבילה דבר שאינו ניטל בשבת: שאינה מצויה. כגון מדרון וטיפטוף דשמן דמתני': נשברה לו חבית של טבל גרסינן: מביא כלי. ואף על גב דטבל דבר שאינו ניטל הוא וחבית לא שכיחא דפקעה: גולפי. חביות: נותנין כלי. מתניתין היא ומותיב ליה מינה: ניצוצות. שלהבת הנוטפת מן הנר כדי שלא ידלק מה שתחתיה ואע"ג דניצוצות לא מיטלטלי ולא שכיחי: איתיביה

אבל נותן הוא לתוך הקערה כו'. מהכא ליכא למידק דעירוי ככלי שני מדקתני לא יתן לתוכה תבלין ולא אשמעינן רבותא אפילו שלא יערה על הקערה שתבלין בתוכה דאדרבה דוק מסיפא דקתני אבל נותן הוא לתוך הקערה ולא קתני מערה על הקערה שתבלין בתוכה ורבינו שמואל מביא ראיה דעירוי ככלי שני מהא דקי"ל תתאה גבר ולר"י נראה דעירוי ככלי ראשון ומביא ראיה דבזבחים בפרק דם חטאת (דף צה: ושם) ת"ר אשר תבושל בו אין לי אלא שבישל בו עירה לתוכו רותח מניין תלמוד לומר [אשר תבושל] בו ישבר אלמא דעירוי חשיב מבשל ובירושלמי בפרק כירה בעי מהו ליתן תבלין מלמטה ולערות עליהן מלמעלה ר' יונה אמר אסור דעירוי ככלי ראשון חיליה דר' יונה מן הדא אחד שבישל בו ואחד שעירה לתוכו רותח ודחי ר' יוסי תמן כלי חרס בולע תבלין אינו מתבשל השיב רבי יוסי בר בון והתניא מניין שבכלי נחשת כן תלמוד לומר ואם בכלי נחשת בשלה אית לן למימר כלי נחשת בלע בתמיה פי' ע"י עירוי אם אינו מבשל לא בלע אלמא דמסיק דעירוי ככלי ראשון ונראה דעירוי לא הוי ככלי ראשון ולא ככלי שני אלא מבשל כדי קליפה דהא קי"ל כשמואל דאמר תתאה גבר דתניא כוותיה בכילד צולין (פסחים עו.) ומ"מ מבשל כדי קליפה דאמר התם תניא כוותיה דשמואל חם לתוך צונן או צונן לתוך צונן מדיח ופריך חם לתוך צונן אדמיקר ליה בלע אלא אימא חם לתוך צונן קולף צונן לתוך צונן מדיח וכן משמע בשילהי מסכת ע"ז (דף עו.) דאמר מר *עוקבא זבן יורה מעכו"ם אהדר ליה גדנפא ומסיק כבולעו כך פולטו מה בולעו בניצוצות אף פולטו בניצוצות ואי עירוי ככלי ראשון °מאי איריא משום דבלע בניצוצות אפילו בלע בליעה גמורה פלט בניצוצות שהוא עירוי אלא ודאי לא מבשל אלא כדי קליפה ואם עירו רותחים על התרנגולת צריכה קליפה וכלי שתשמישו ע"י עירוי כגון קערות יכול להגעילן ע"י עירוי דכבולעו כך פולטו אבל כלי שנתבשל בו איסור לא סגי להגעילו על ידי עירוי והא דאמר בפרק בתרא דע"ז (דף עה:) דרש רבא נעוה ארתחיה דהתם מסתמא ע"י עירוי שאני התם דלותה נעוה לא בלעה ע"י רותח**: לכל קדרות רותחות הוא נותן. נראה דדוקא בתבלין פליג אבל בשאר דברים מודה דכלי ראשון מבשל אף כשהעבירו מעל האור: והיינו דר"נ. נראה דאף לפי' הקונטרס שפי' *)דבכל מקום דאיכא לישני דפליגי בשל תורה הלך אחר המחמיר ובשל סופרים הלך אחר אחרון ולר"ת בשל סופרים הלך אחר המיקל וכן לריב"א שפירש שבכל מקום איכא דאמרי טפל לגבי לשון ראשון שהוא עיקר הכא הלכה כלישנא בתרא דללישנא קמא פליג ברייתא דרבי חייא אדרב נחמן וללישנא בתרא הייטו דרב נחמן ומתוך כך פסק רבינו שמואל שמותר לתת מלח בתבשיל בשבת אפילו בכלי ראשון שהעבירו מן האור והמחמיר כלישנא קמא שלא ליתן מלח בקערה כל זמן שהיד סולדת בו תבא עליו ברכה: ואם נתנוהו מבעוד יום מותר. הלשון דחוק דהוה ליה למימר אבל מבעוד יום נותנין: ואין נאותין ממנו לפי שאינו מן המוכן. איכא לאוקמה כר"ש *דמתיר מותר השמן שבנר ואין ניאותין דקתני הכא היינו כל זמן שדולק °דבמוקצה מחמת מצוה מודה ר"ש כדאמר בגמ' לקמן (דף מה.) אין מוקצה לר"ש אלא שמן שבנר בשעה שהוא דולק הואיל והוקצה למצותו הוקצה לאיסורו ולא שבנר ממש קאמר דההיא אסור בלאו הכי משום מכבה כדאמר בביצה פ"ב (דף כב. ושם) המסתפק ממנו חייב משום מכבה אלא כלומר שמן המטפטף מן הנר והטלטול דנר עצמו אין לאסור מטעם דהוקצה למצותו ולא אסור לטלטלו אלא משום דנעשה בסיס לדבר האסור כדאמרינן בסוף פירקין (דף מז.) הגה לנר שמן ופתילה הואיל ונעשה בסיס לדבר האסור אבל מטעם דהוקצה למצותו לא היה אסור לטלטלו שאין ביטול מצוה במה שמטלטלו: אע"פ שאמרו חכמים אין נותנין כו'. אין נותנין כלי תחת הנר לקבל בו את השמן ה"ל למימר דתנן במתניתין וכלי לקבל ביצה לא שמעינן אלא מדיוקא דמתני' אלא משום דבעי למימר אבל כופה עליה כלי נקט ביצה: הצלה שאינה מצויה לא התירו. פי' בקונטרס לדבר שאינו ניטל וגרס בההוא דפריך אביי מינה בסמוך נשברה לו חבית של טבל בראש גגו דטבל אינו ניטל וקשה לריב"א דאי גרס בה טבל אמאי פריך לרב יוסף מברייתא אחרת מהך דהכא הוה ליה לאקשויי ועוד דבפרק כל כתבי (לקמן דף קיז: ושם) משמע בהדיא דלא גרסי' בברייתא דהכא טבל דלא בשל טבל מיירי דקתני סיפא נזדמנו לו אורחין מביא כלי אחר כו' ונראה לו לפרש דהצלה שאינה מצויה לא התירו לטרוח בכל דבר אפילו בדבר הניטל משום טירחא: שאינה מצויה לא התירו. והא דאין נותנין כלי תחת הנר לקבל שמן חשיב הצלה שאינה מצויה לפי שרגילים לעולם לתת כלי תחת הנר מבעוד יום וניצוצות אע"ג דקאמר בסמוך דשכיחי לא שכיחי כולי האי שיחושו לתת שם כלי מבעוד יום ולהכי חשיב לה הצלה מצויה:

דמבטל

מסורת הש"ס
[כצאי גוולא במעשרות פ"א מ"ז]
[צ"ל משם]
לקמן קיז: ע"ש
לקמן מג. מה:
[וע' תוספות זבחים לה: ד"ה עירה כו']
*) [עי' תוס' ע"ז ז. ד"ה בשל תורה]
[לקמן מד.]

יש ספרים שגורסין כאן בתוס' רב עקביא כמו שכתב הגאון מהרי"פ בע"ש שם בהגהותיו. ואולי יצאה גירסא מר עוקבא מסוגיא דב"מ ע. הכוא דולא דבני מר עוקבא כמו שהעיר בסה"ד

א"נ ארתחי' שיעשה האש למטה והיא של חרס דכפ' כל שעה איכא למ"ד זה וזה לפטור המעסה והחלוט ומוגלשין ואיירי בפיש למלוס כשיעור חלה ולהכי בין תתאה גבר בין עילאה גבר מבשל כדי קליפה ובצר ליה משיעור חלה [תו"י]

גליון הש"ס
תום' ד"ה אבל. מאי איריא משום דבלע בניצוצות. ק"ל דלטעמיך אף אם עירוי לא הוי ככ"ר היינו בעירוי על צונן אבל הכא דהעירוי על גופם שכלי שהוא חם. אף אם הוי העירוי מצונן להם הוי חם דתתאי גבר מכ"ש בעירוי מכ"ר על כ"ר וה' יאיר עיני: שם ד"ה ואין נאותין דבמוקצה מחמת מצוה מודה ר"ש. וכיון דאינו ראוי לאכלו ממש באותה שעה הוי מוקצה בעצמותו כדין כל מאכל שאינו חזי לכלום. עי' מג"א ריש סימן תקט"ו ורק בטלטול הנר בשעה שהוא דולק להאיר זהו מדינא מותר אלולי טעמא דבסיס ולק"מ קושית המהרש"א:

רבינו חננאל
בתוך חללו לפיכך מותר שנמצאו כלי שני וקיי"ל כלי שני מותר: ר' יהודה אומר לכל הוא נותן כו' אסיק' ר' יהודה ארישא דקתני האלפס והקדירה שהעבירן מרותחין לא יתן בתוכן תבלין התם פליג ומקיל הוא דתניא ר"י אומר לכל אלפסין רותחין [הוא נותן] לכל קדרות רותחין הוא נותן חוץ מדבר שיש בו חומץ וציר מלח כתבלין הוא אי לא ואסיק' כדתני ר' חייא מלח אינו כתבלין דכלי ראשון נמי לא בשלה והיינו דרב נחמן דאמר צריכה מילחא בשולי כבשרא דתורא ש"מ כי נותן מלח בתבשיל בשבת ואפילו בכלי ראשון אינו בישול: מתניתין אין נותנין כלי תחת הנר לקבל בו את השמן כו' אמר רב חסדא אע"פ שאמרו אין נותנין נר תחת התרנגולת כו' כלומר אפילו אם עומדת במקום מדרון ורואין כיון שתלד תפול הביצה במקום מדרון ותשבר לא התירו לו להטיל תחתיה כלי לקבלה לביצה כדי שלא תשבר שזה לילד התרנגולת במקום מדרון דבר שאינו מצוי הוא ומשום אחת שנזדמנה לה כך לא חיישינן לה. אבל כיון שדרך רוב התרנגולת להטיל ביציהן לאשפה התירו לכפות על נותה ביצה כלי בשביל שלא תשבר וזהו פירוש הצלה מצויה התירו הצלה שאינה מצויה לא התירו ואקשינן והצלה שאינה מצויה לא התירו והא חבית שנשברה בראש גגו כו' ושנינן בגולפי חדתי פי' קנקנים חדשים

SPICES THEREIN,[11] [42b] BUT ONE MAY PUT [SPICES] INTO A DISH OR A TUREEN.[12] R. JUDAH SAID: HE MAY PUT [SPICES] INTO ANYTHING EXCEPT WHAT CONTAINS VINEGAR OR BRINE.[13]

GEMARA. The scholars propounded: Does R. Judah refer to
a the first clause, and [he rules] in the direction of leniency;[1] or perhaps he refers to the second clause, [inclining] to stringency?[2] —Come and hear: R. Judah said: One may put [spices] into all stew pots and into all boiling pots that are seething, except aught that contains vinegar or brine.[3]

R. Joseph thought to rule that salt is like spices, [viz.,] that it boils in a 'first vessel' but not in a 'second vessel'. Said Abaye to him, R. Ḥiyya taught: Salt is not like spices, for it boils even in a 'second vessel'. Now, he differs from R. Naḥman, who said: Salt requires as much boiling as ox flesh. Others state, R. Joseph thought to rule: Salt is like spices, [viz.,] that it boils in a 'first vessel' but not in a 'second vessel'. Said Abaye to him, R. Ḥiyya taught: Salt is not like spices, for it does not boil even in a 'first vessel'. And this is identical with R. Naḥman's dictum: Salt requires as much boiling as ox flesh.[4]

MISHNAH. ONE MAY NOT PLACE A VESSEL UNDER A LAMP TO CATCH THE OIL.[5] BUT IF IT IS PLACED THERE BEFORE SUNSET,[6] IT IS PERMITTED. YET ONE MAY NOT BENEFIT FROM IT,[7] BECAUSE IT IS NOT OF MUKAN.[8]

GEMARA. R. Ḥisda said: Though they [the Sages] ruled, A
b vessel may not be placed under a fowl to receive its eggs,[1] yet a vessel may be overturned upon it [the egg] that it should not be broken. Said Rabbah, What is R. Hisda's reason?—He holds that it is usual for a fowl to lay her eggs in a dung heap, but not on sloping ground; now, they [the Sages] permitted[2] in a common [case of] saving,[3] but in an uncommon [case of] saving they did not permit.[4] Abaye raised an objection: Now, did they [the Sages] not permit in an uncommon [case of] saving? Surely it was taught: If a person's barrel of *ṭebel*[5] burst on the top of his roof, he may bring a vessel and place it beneath it.[6]—The reference is to new jars, which frequently burst.

He raised an objection: A vessel may be placed under a lamp

(11) After nightfall. The pot is a 'first vessel' (v. *supra* 40b, n. b6) and its contents, as long as they are seething, cause any other commodity put therein to boil likewise. (12) Containing a hot stew. The dish or tureen is a 'second vessel', which cannot make the spices boil. (13) Being sharp, they cause the spices to boil.

a (1) I.e., the first Tanna, having stated that spices may not be put into a 'first vessel', R. Judah permits it, save where it contains vinegar or brine. (2) The first Tanna permits spices to be put into a 'second vessel', no matter what its contents, whereas R. Judah makes an exception. (3) Thus he refers to a 'first vessel'. (4) Hence it does not boil unless actually on the fire. (5) On the Sabbath. Rashi offers two reasons: (i) The oil, having been set apart for fuel, is *mukẓeh*, i.e., it must not be used in any other manner, nor may it be handled, and this Tanna holds that a utensil can be moved only for the sake of an object which may itself be handled. (ii) At present the vessel may be handled for a number of purposes. Once oil drops into it, it may not be moved, because the oil is *mukẓeh*, and in the opinion of this Tanna one may not cause a vessel to become immovable, for it is as though he joins it to the lamp on the Sabbath. (6) Lit., 'while it is yet day.' (7) I.e., use the oil which drops therein. (8) V. Glos.

b (1) When she lays them on sloping ground; the vessel is to prevent them from rolling down the incline and breaking. (2) To move a vessel for the sake of an object that may not be handled, as the egg in question. (3) Viz., to save the eggs from being trampled upon while they lay on the dung heap. People walked over dung (manure) heaps; cf. B.Ḳ. 30a. (4) Viz., to save them from rolling down the slope. (5) V. Glos. The reference is to oil or wine. (6) Though *ṭebel* itself may not be handled, while such a case of saving is uncommon, as it is rare for a barrel to burst. The same assumption is made in the other attempted refutations, that the savings permitted are in an uncommon case.

to catch the sparks?—Sparks too are common. [43a] He raised an objection: A dish may be overturned above a lamp, that the beams should not catch [fire]?—This refers to houses with low ceilings, for it is a common thing for them to catch fire. [He raised a further objection:] And likewise, if a beam is broken, it may be supported by a bench or bed staves?[7]—This refers to new planks, for it is a common thing for them to split. [Another objection:] A utensil may be placed under a leak [in the roof] on the Sabbath?—This refers to new houses, where leaking is common.

R. Joseph said: This is R. Ḥisda's reason, [viz.,] because he deprives the vessel of its readiness [for use].[8] Abaye objected to him: If a barrel [of *ṭebel*] is broken, another vessel may be brought and placed under it?[9]—*Ṭebel* is ready [for use] in respect to the
a Sabbath, replied he, for if he transgresses and prepares it,[1] it is prepared. [Another objection:] A vessel may be placed under a lamp to catch the sparks?—Said R. Huna son of R. Joshua: Sparks are intangible.[2] [Another objection:] And likewise, if a beam is broken, it may be supported by a bench or bed-staves?[3]—That means that it is loose,[4] so that, if he desires, he can remove it. [Another objection:] A vessel may be placed under drippings on the Sabbath?[5]—The reference is to drippings that are fit [for use]. [Another objection:] A basket may be overturned before fledglings, for them to ascend or descend?[6]—He holds that it [the basket] may [still] be moved. But it was taught, It may not be moved?—That is [only] while they [the fledglings] are yet upon it. But it was taught, Though they are not still upon it, it is forbidden?—Said R. Abbahu: That means that they were upon it throughout the period of twilight; since it was forbidden to handle[7] at twilight, it remains so forbidden for the whole day.[8]

R. Isaac said: Just as a vessel may not be placed under a fowl to receive her eggs, so may a vessel not be overturned upon it [the egg] that it should not be broken. He holds that a vessel may be handled only for the sake of that which itself may be handled on the Sabbath.[9] All the foregoing objections were raised;[10] and he answered, It means that its place is required.[11]

Come and hear: An egg laid on the Sabbath or an egg laid on
b a Festival may not be moved, neither for covering a vessel[1] nor for supporting the legs of a bed therewith;[2] but a vessel may be turned over it, that it [the egg] should not be broken?—Here too it means that its place is required.

Come and hear: Mats may be spread over stones on the Sabbath?[3]—The reference is to smoothly rounded stones, which are fit [for use] in a privy.

Come and hear: Mats may be spread on the Sabbath upon bricks which were left over from a building?—That is because they are fit for reclining [thereon].

Come and hear: One may spread mats over bee-hives on the Sabbath: in the sun on account of the sun and in the rain on account of the rain, providing he has no intention of capturing [the bees]?[4]—The circumstances are that they contain honey. Said R. 'Uḳba of Mesene[5] to R. Ashi: That is correct of summer, [43b]

(7) I.e., the long-sides of bedsteads. (8) V. *supra* 42b, n. b6. (9) *Ṭebel* may not be made fit for food on the Sabbath by rendering its dues. Hence neither it nor the vessel which receives it may be handled. Thus that too loses its general fitness, and yet it is permitted.

a (1) On the Sabbath, by separating the tithes. (2) Consequently the vessel into which they fall may be handled. (3) Though it is then impossible to remove them for general use. (4) The bench, etc., is not planted there firmly. (5) He assumed that the drippings consisted of dirty water, unfit for use, as a result of which one may not handle the vessel which receives them. (6) Into or from the hen-coop. (7) I.e., *muḳẓeh*, q.v. Glos. (8) This is a principle often met with. But if the basket is placed there after nightfall, so that it was fit for handling at twilight, it may be moved when the birds are not upon it. (9) Which excludes an egg laid on the Sabbath. (10) In every case there the article itself for which the utensil is taken may not be handled. (11) A utensil may be moved when its place is required, and when so moved it may be utilized for the purposes enumerated above.

b (1) E.g., the neck of a bottle. (2) The egg did not actually support the bed, but was placed near it for magical purposes; v. A. Marmorstein, *MGWJ*. 72, 1928, pp. 391-395. (3) Stones, being unfit for use, may not be handled. (4) Though the hives themselves may not be handled. (5) The region to the south of Babylon bounded by the Tigris, the Euphrates and the Royal Canal, and differentiated from Babylon proper in respect to marriage; v. Ḳid. 71b, Obermeyer, pp. 90 *seqq*.

איתיביה *כופין קערה על הנר שלא יאחז בקורה בבתי גחיני דשכיח בהו דליקה *וכן קורה שנשברה סומכין אותה בספסל ובארוכות המטה בכשורי חדתי דעבידי דפקעי *נותנין כלי תחת הדלף בשבת בבתי חדתי דשכיחי דדלפי רב יוסף אמר היינו טעמא דרב חסדא [א]משום *דקא מבטל כלי מהיכנו איתיביה אביי *[ג]חבית של טבל שנשברה מביא כלי אחר ומניח תחתיה א"ל *טבל מוכן הוא אצל שבת שאם עבר ותקנו מתוקן *נותנין כלי תחת הנר לקבל ניצוצות א"ר הונא בריה דרב יהושע ניצוצות אין בהן ממש *[ג]וכן קורה שנשברה סומכין אותה בספסל או בארוכות המטה דרפי דאי בעי שקיל ליה *נותנין כלי [ד]תחת הדלף בשבת בדלף הראוי *כופין [ה]את הסל לפני האפרוחין שיעלו וירדו קסבר מותר לטלטלו והתניא *אסור לטלטלו [ו]בעודן עליו והתניא אע"פ שאין עודן עליו אסור א"ר אבהו בעודן עליו כל בין השמשות מיגו דאיתקצאי לבין השמשות איתקצאי לכולי יומא א"ר יצחק כשם שאין נותנין כלי תחת תרנגולת לקבל ביצתה כך אין כופין עליה כלי בשביל שלא תשבר *קסבר אין כלי ניטל אלא לדבר הניטל בשבת מיתיבי כל הני תיובתא ושני בצריך למקומו תא שמע *אחת ביצה שנולדה בשבת ואחת ביצה שנולדה ביום טוב אין מטלטלין .לא לכסות בה את הכלי ולסמוך בה כרעי המטה אבל כופה עליה כלי בשביל שלא תשבר הכא נמי בצריך למקומו *ת"ש פורסין מחצלות על גבי אבנים בשבת באבנים מקורזלות דחזיין לבית הכסא ת"ש *פורסין מחצלות על גבי לבנים בשבת דאישתיור· מבנינא דחזיין למיזגא עלייהו ת"ש [ז]פורסין מחצלת על גבי כוורת דבורים בשבת בחמה מפני החמה ובגשמים מפני הגשמים ובלבד שלא יתכוין לצוד הכא במאי עסקינן דאיכא דבש א"ל רב עוקבא ממישן לרב אשי תינח בימות החמה דאיכא

רש"י

איתיביה כופין קערה. של חרס על גבי הנר כו': גחיני. נמוכין: וכן קורה שנשברה כו'. משנה היא לקמן: שנשברה. בשבת: ארוכות המטה. לימוני"ש: בספסל. דכלי הוא ומותר לטלטלו: בכשורי חדתי. שלא נבדקו עדיין וכשמכביד משא הבית עליהן שהיו טחין על גגותיהן בטיט שכיחי דפקעי: תחת הדלף. לקבלו: טעמא דרב חסדא. דאין נותנין כלי תחת התרנגולת: מפני שמבטל כלי מהיכנו. שהיה מוכן מתחלה לטלטלו ועכשיו עושהו מוקצה: מוכן הוא. שאין בו מוקצה אלא איסורו ואם בא אחד ועבר על דברי חכמים שאסרו לתרום בשבת ותיקנו מתוקן ומותר לטלטלו ולאוכלו הלכך לאו מבטל כלי מהיכנו חשיב ליה: אין בהן ממש. ומותר ליטלן אחר שנפלו לתוכו: וכן קורה כו'. קס"ד שמהדקו שם ואינו יכול שוב ליטלו: הראוי. לשתיה כל אלו משניות הן: כל בין השמשות. אבל כתנו שם משתשיכה מותר ליטלו אם אין האפרוחים עליו: בצריך למקומו. להשתמש במקום הכלי ומתוך שיכול ליטלו לצורך מקומו מוליכו למקום שירצה: לכסות בה את הכלי. לסתום פי צלוחית: על גבי אבנים. מפני הגשמים שלא ימחו או לא יקבלו סיד מאחר שרויות במים: מקורזלות. ראשן חד וראויות לקינוח דהוי דבר הניטל: למיזגא. להשען שכל הסבתן כך היתה יושב קצת ונשען קצת על שמאלו: דהיכא

תוספות

דמבטל כלי מהיכנו · בפרק בתרא *פירש בקונטרס דאסור משום דמתחזי כסותר וכאן פירש דחשיב כאלו מחברו שם בטיט: טבל מוכן הוא אצל שבת. אף על פי שאסור לטלטלו כדתנן בפרק מפנין (לקמן קכו:) מ"מ לא חשיב מבטל כלי מהיכנו כיון דאם עבר ותיקנו מתוקן ק' לרשב"א דתנן במסכת תרומות בפ"ב (משנה ג) ומייתי לה בהניזקין (גיטין נד·) המעשר בשבת בשוגג יאכל במזיד לא יאכל ולישנא דקאמר הכא אם עבר ותיקנו משמע במזיד מדלא קאמר *שאם שגג ותיקנו ונראה דנקט עבר כגון דלית ליה פירי אחריני דאמר בבילה בפרק י"ט (דף יז:) דאפילו במזיד יאכל עוד הקשה דבפרק בתרא (דף קנד:) תניא היתה בהמתו טעונה טבל ועששית מתיר את החבלים והשקים נופלים ואע"פ שמשתברין משמע דאסור להניח תחתיהן כרים וכסתות אלמא טבל לאו מוכן הוא ואור"י דאף על פי שמשתברין לא קאי אטבל אלא אעששית ועוד הקשה כי היכי דאמר דאם עבר ותיקנו מתוקן ה"נ כשמניח כלי תחת תרנגולת לקבל ביצתה נימא שאם עבר והסיר הבילה מותר הכלי לטלטל ואם כן ביטלת תורת ביטול כלי מהיכנו ולאו פירכא היא דהא כמו שהכלי עם הבילה אין לה היתר אבל טבל יש לו היתר על ידי תיקון ועוד הקשה היכא דאית ליה פירי אחריני בשוגג אמאי יאכל נימא מגו דאיתקצאי לבין השמשות איתקצאי לכולי יומא ועוד מ"ש בהכא אמר דאם עבר ותיקנו מתוקן ובבילה בפ' אין צדין (דף כו: ושם) גבי בכור לר"ש דאמר אין רואין מומין בי"ט אמר שאם עבר וביקרו אינו מבוקר ואדא בר אוכמי דאמר בשוגג מבוקר אמרינן התם דליתא דמשבש ותני*: כופין את הסל. לעיל לא מצי פריך מינה דהאלה מטיה היא: בעודן עליו. אבל אחר שירדו מותר לטלטלו נראה לר"י דקסבר דאין מוקצה לחצי שבת דלמ"ד בפ' אין צדין (ביצה כו: ושם) דיש מוקצה אסור לטלטלו אף אחר שירדו וקשה לרשב"א למ"ד יש מוקצה לחצי שבת אמאי כופין את הסל לפני האפרוחים והא מבטל כלי מהיכנו וקי"ל דאסור לבטלו דבסוף פירקין *פריך סתמא דהש"ס והא קא מבטל כלי מהיכנו וכן בפ' מפנין (לקמן קכח:) ובפ' בתרא (דף קנד:) פריך אליבא דרב הונא אע"ג דלא מליט שהיה סובר כן משמע דלכ"ע אסור לבטל כלי מהיכנו וכן אפרש בסמוך וי"ל דלמ"ד יש מוקצה לחצי שבת הך דכופין את הסל מוקי כר"ש דלדידיה ודאי שרי לטלטל הסל כשירדו דאפי' מיגו דאיתקצאי לבין השמשות איתקצאי לכולי יומא לית ליה דהא מתיר להסתפק מן הנר שכבה *א"נ הא דיש מוקצה לחצי שבת הייט לאכילה ולא לטלטול וא"ת רב יוסף דמפרש מתני' משום דאסור לבטל כלי מהיכנו לא אתיא מתני' כר"ש דלדידיה לא מבטל כלי מהיכנו כיון דשרי לאחר שכבה כי היכי דלא תשבינן הכא כפיית הסל ביטול כלי משום דשרי אחר שירדו וי"ל דלא דמי דהכא ודאי לא חשיב ביטול כלי כי מיד כשבאו על הסל בידו להפריחם ולהבריחם משם: בעודן עליו כל בין השמשות. תימה הא כיון דבידו להפריחם למטה הוי גמרו בידי אדם ולית לן למימר מיגו דאיתקצאי לבין השמשות כדמוכח בפ' אין צדין (ביצה כו:) דפריך ר' זירא למ"ד יש מוקצה לחצי שבת והא פולין ועדשים דמבשלים בי"ט דמעיקרא חזו לכוס כי שדינהו בקדרה חייתא [א]אידחו להו גמר בישולייהו אישתרו להו א"ל אביי ולטעמיך תקשי לך קדירות דעלמא דהא קדירות דשבתא בין השמשות רותחות הן ולאורתא קא אכלינן מינייהו אלא גמרו בידי אדם לא קמבעיא ליה כי קא מיבעיא ליה גמרו בידי שמים וי"ל דשאני קדירות אם הוה צריך להו בין השמשות היה מקררן וכן פולין ועדשים רצונו שיתבשלו בלא שום דיחוי אבל הכא רצונו היה שיעלו האפרוחין על הסל שלכך כפאו והרי שעה אחת הקצה אותו לצרכן ומיגו דאיתקצאי לבין השמשות איתקצאי לכולי יומא: ושני ליה בצריך למקומו. ההיא דנותנין כלי תחת הדלף איכא נמי לשנויי בדלף הראוי כדשני לעיל ובפרק משילין (ביצה לו· ושם) משני ליה הכי לרבי יצחק תימה לר"י מ"ש דגבי שמן תנא אין נותנין וגבי ניצוצות נותנין בתרוייהו הוה מצי למתני נותנין בצריך למקומו או בתרוייהו אין נותנין באין צריך למקומו ונראה לר"י דמעיקרא אשמעינן דאין כלי ניטל אלא לדבר הניטל בשבת וגבי ניצוצות דבתר הכי אשמעינן דבצריך למקומו שרי אי נמי ר' יצחק אית ליה נמי דאסור לבטל כלי מהיכנו ולהכי גבי שמן אין נותנין אפילו בצריך למקומו ולרב הונא נפרש בסמוך דאית ליה נמי תרוייהו אין כלי ניטל אלא לדבר הניטל ואסור לבטל כלי מהיכנו ואם נאמר לרב יוסף לא אתיא מתניתין כר"ש דכיון דלדידיה מותר לאחר שכבה לא חשיב ביטול כלי אם כן מלין למימר דאפילו רבה אית ליה דאסור לבטל כלי מהיכנו ואיצטריך למימר דהגלה שאינה מטיה לא התירו כדי לאוקמה מתניתין כר"ש וא"ת מאי צריך בכל הני משניות לאשמעינן דבצריך למקומו שרי ויש לומר דלגבי ניצוצות איצטריך לאשמעינן· דלא תימא אפילו בצריך למקומו אסור משום דילמא אתי לכבויי וכן ההיא דכופין קערה שלא תאחוז כו' וההיא דקורה שנשברה נראה לרשב"א דאיצטריך לאשמעינן דלא חיישינן שמא יעלה את הקורה דאסור להעלות כדתנן בפ' שואל (לקמן קנא:) וכן קורה שנשברה סומכין אותה כו' לא שתעלה אלא שלא תוסיף: כופה עליה כלי שלא תשבר כו'. כל הנהו דמייתי ידע המקשה דמצי לשנויי בצריך למקומו אלא שרוצה לידע אם יש לתרץ בענין אחר: דאייתור מבניינא. כדאמר לקמן בפ'·כל הכלים (דף קכד:) הני לבני דאייתרי מבניינא שרי לטלטולינהו: דחשיב

וזה אין להקשות דלר"ש אמאי חשיב מתניתין ביטל כלי מהיכנו הא עבר וכיבה מותר כמו גבי טבל שאם עבר כו' וי"ל שאיסור דכיבוי איסורא דאורייתא ולא אמר ביה שאם עבר כו' [תוספות ישנים]

רבינו חננאל

חדשים שהן מצוין להפקיע. וניצוצות תחת הנר נמי מילתא דשכיחא היא ובבתי גחיני כלומר בתים נמוכים להיאחז בהן דליקה מילתא דשכיחא היא וכן כולם. פירק רבא לדבריו דהאלה מצויה התירו הצלה שאינה מצויה לא התירו אליבא דרב חסדא . רב יוסף אמר ט"ם דרב חסדא משום דאי שרית ליה לקבל הביצה בכלי במקום מדרון כבר ביטל אותו הכלי היום שאסור לטלטלו והביצה בתוכו . כשם שאסור לטלטל הביצה . אבל כפיית הכלי על הביצה אינו ביטול שאם הוצרך הכלי מותר לו לטלטלו שהרי אין בכלי כלום ולא מבטל כלי מהיכנו . איתיביה אביי (טלטל) [חבית של טבל] כו' והא טבל אסור לטלטלו ושני ליה טבל מוכן הוא שאם עבר ותיקנו מתוקן הוא . ושני בניצוצות . ניצוצות אין בהם ממש והכלי שמקבל בו הניצוצות לא מיבטיל ומותר להשתמש בה . וספסל שסמוך בה הקורה רפויה היא שיכול ליטלה ולהשתמש בה . והכלי שמקבל בו הדלף בדלף הראוי לשתיה שהמים מותרים וכ"ש הכלי . וכן הסל שכופין שיעלו וירדו בו האפרוחים אוקמה בעודן האפרוחים עומדין על הסל [או שהיו עומדין על הסל] בין השמשות אסור לטלטל אותו הסל שנעשה מוקצה ואם לאו מותר . ור' יצחק חולק על רב חסדא ואומר אפי' כלי לכוף עליה בשביל שלא תישבר ביצה בשבת אסור . קסבר אין כלי ניטל [אלא] לדבר הניטל בשבת . ואותיבנא עליה כל הני תיובתא . ומשני בצריך למקומו. ת"ש אחת ביצה [שנולדה] בשבת ואחת ביצה שנולדה ביו"ט אין מטלטלין אותה לא לכסות בה את הכלי ולא לסמוך בה כרעי המטה. אבל כופה עליה כלי כו' ומשני הכא נמי בצריך לאותו מקום · פי' לאותו מקום של כלי ולא למקום הביצה.

רב נסים גאון

באבנים מקורזלות של בית הכסא תמצא פירושו בפרק המוציא יין (דף פא) ונין על לבי מדרשא אמר להו רבותיי שיעור אבנים מקורזלות בכמה אמרו לו כזית וכאגוז וכביצה תנו רבנן בשבת ג' אבנים מקורזלות מותר להכניסן לבית הכסא כו': בליבני דאייתור מבניינא דחזיין למיזגא עלייהו עיקרם בפרק כל הכלים ניטלין בשבת (דף קכד) אמר רב נחמן הני ליבני דאשתיור מבניינא שרי לטלטולינהו בשבתא משום דחזו למיזגא עלייהו וכמס' יום .טוב (דף לא) בפרק המביא כדי יין מסקם למקום . אמר ליה לא נצרכה אלא לאותן ב' חלות מנהג הוא בעת תתיכת הדבש מן הכוורת להניח ב' חלות לעסק הדבורים ותישתכח עיקר דיליה בבבא [בתרא] בפרק המוכר את הספינה (דף פ) הלות דבש מניח שתי חלות היצונות :

עין משפט נר מצוה

[דף קכד: וכ"כ רש"י לקמן קכח: ד"ה וסא]

מ א מיי' פכ"ה מהלכות שבת הלכה פג סמג לאוין סה טור שו"ע או"ח סימן שי סעיף ו:

מא ב מיי' שם הל' כה:

מב ג מיי' שם טוש"ע או"ח סימן שיג סעיף ז:

מג ד מיי' שם הלכה כד טוש"ע או"ח סימן שלח סעיף ה וסימן תקכא סעיף ג:

מד ה ו מיי' שם הלכה כה סמג שם טוש"ע או"ח סימן שח סעיף לט:

מה ז מיי' וסמג שם טוש"ע או"ח סימן שט"ז סעיף ד:

מסורת הש"ס

[לקמן קכ. קכא.] [לקמן קכח:] ביצה לו: [לקמן מז:] [לקמן קכד:] [תוספתא פי"ד] [ביצה לד: לה.] לעיל מב: לקמן מז: לקמן קכח: [תוספ' פט"ז] [תוספתא שם] [ביצה לו.] ביצה ג: [שם לו. כל הסוגיא ע"ש כמה שינויים] שם לו. [דף מד:]

הגהות הב"ח

(א) תוס' ד"ה בעודן וכו' כי שדינהו בקדר' אידחו כצ"ל ותיבת חייתא נמחק:

גליון הש"ס

תוס' ד"ה טבל מוכן. שאם שגג. עי' לעיל לח ע"א תוס' ד"ה עבר ובפסחים דף מב ע"א ברש"י ד"ה היכא דאתמר וברא"ש שם: תוס' ד"ה בעודן עליו. א"נ הא דיש מוקצה. עיין לקמן דף מד ע"ב תוס' ד"ה יש עליה מעות:

עין משפט
נר מצוה

כו א מיי' פכ"ה מהלכו' שבת הלכה ו ופכ"ו הלכה כב סמג לאוין סה טוש"ע או"ח סימן שיא סעיף ו:

מז ב ג מיי' שם פכ"ו הלכה כה טור שו"ע או"ח שם סעיף א:

מה"ר שכנא הגיה והלא משמע דאע"ג דאינו כו'

מסורת הש"ס

דאיכא דבש בימות הגשמים דליכא דבש מאי איכא למימר לא נצרכא אלא לאותן שתי חלות והא מוקצות נינהו דחשיב עלייהו הא לא חשיב עלייהו מאי אסור אי הכי הא דתני ובלבד שלא יתכוין לצוד לפלוג ולתני בדידה בד"א כשחישב עליהן אבל לא חישב עליהן אסור הא קמ"ל אע"פ שחישב עליהן ובלבד שלא יתכוין לצוד מני אי ר"ש *לית לי' מוקצה אי ר' יהודה כי לא מתכוין מאי הוי הא דבר שאין מתכוין אסור לעולם ר' יהודה מאי ובלבד שלא יתכוין לצוד שלא יעשנה כמצודה דלישבוק להו רווחא כי היכי דלא ליתצדו ממילא רב אשי אמר מי קתני בימות החמה ובימות הגשמים בחמה מפני החמה ובגשמים מפני הגשמים קתני ביומי ניסן וביומי תשרי דאיכא חמה (ואיכא צינה) ואיכא גשמים ואיכא דבש אמר להו רב ששת פוקו ואמרו ליה לר' יצחק כבר תרגמא רב הונא לשמעתיך בבבל דא"ר הונא עושין מחיצה למת בשביל חי ואין עושין מחיצה למת בשביל מת מאי היא דא"ר שמואל בר יהודה וכן תנא שילא מרי *מת המוטל בחמה באים שני בני אדם ויושבין בצדו חם להם מלמטה זה מביא מטה ויושב עליה וזה מביא מטה ויושב עליה חם להם מלמעלה מביאים מחצלת ופורסין עליהן זה זוקף מטתו ונשמט והולך לו וזה זוקף מטתו ונשמט והולך לו ונמצאת מחיצה עשויה מאליה איתמר מת המוטל בחמה רב יהודה אמר שמואל *הופכו ממטה למטה רב חנינא בר שלמיא משמיה דרב אמר *מניח עליו ככר או תינוק ומטלטלו היכא דאיכא ככר או תינוק כולי עלמא לא פליגי דשרי °כי פליגי דלית ליה מ"ס *טלטול מן הצד שמיה טלטול ומ"ס לא שמיה טלטול לימא כתנאי *אין מצילין את המת מפני הדליקה אמר ר' יהודה בן לקיש שמעתי שמצילין את המת מפני הדליקה היכי דמי אי דאיכא ככר או תינוק מ"ט דתנא קמא אי דליכא מ"ט דר' יהודה בן לקיש אלא לאו בטלטול מן הצד פליגי דמר סבר טלטול מן הצד שמיה טלטול ומ"ס לא שמיה טלטול לא *דכ"ע טלטול מן הצד שמיה טלטול והיינו טעמא דר' יהודה בן לקיש *דמתוך שאדם בהול על מתו אי

רש"י

דאיכא דבש. דבר הניטל: שתי חלות. כל הכוורת עושין אותה הדבורים חלות חלות של לפיחית דבש ושעוה וכשרודים אותן מניחין בה שתים שיתפרנסו מהן הדבורים כל ימות הגשמים כדתנן בהמוכר את הספינה (ב"ב פ:) הלוקח חלות כוורתו של חבירו מניח שתי חלות דסתמא לא מכרן: מוקצות נינהו. לדבורים הדר הוה ליה דבר שאינו ניטל ואפ"ה מטלטלין מחצלת להצלתן: דחשיב עלייהו. מאתמול לאכילה: ומני. היא שהצרכת לתרוצה כשחישב וקתני דדבר שאין מתכוין מותר כר"ש: אי ר"ש. אמר °למה לי לאוקמיה בשחישב: שלא יעשנו כמצודה. שלא יכסנה כולה אלא דנשבוק רווחא שיוכלו לצאת כי היכי דלא ליתצדו בהאי כיסוי ממילא ואע"ג דלא מיכוין למיצד אסור: רב אשי אמר. לעולם דאיכא דבש טובא ודקשיא לך ימות הגשמים מי קתני בה ימות הגשמים: לשמעתיך. דאין כלי ניטל אלא לדבר הניטל: מת המוטל בחמה. ויש לחוש שמא ימהר להסריח: ויושבין בצדו. ע"ג הקרקע כדי שיצטערו מחום הקרקע ויצטרכו להביא מטות לישב עליהן והמטות יהיו למחיצה כדמסיים ואזיל: חם להם למטה. מן הקרקע שרתחו חמה: ופורסין. על ראשן צל: זה זוקף מטתו. שתהא המחצלת מונחת עליה וכן זה נמצאת מחיצה עשויה מאליה ולכשירצו נשמטין והולכין להם ודוקא נקט חם להם מלמטה ברישא שיביאו המטות לישיבה ברישא והדר מחצלת לפרוש עליהן צל ואוחזין אותה בידיהן עד לאחר שעה שיזקפום וישמטום דהוה ליה כי ההוא דאמרינן (עירובין דף קב.) האי מדורתא מלמעלה למטה שרי אבל לאתויי מעיקרא מטות לצורך האהל לא דהוה ליה מלמטה למעלה כדרך בנין וקי"ל אין עושין אהל עראי בתחילה בשבת: הופכו ממטה למטה. עד שמגיע לצל: מן הצד. כלאחר יד: אי דליכא. והאי מצילין דקאמר ר' יהודה בן לקיש דמטלטל ליה להדיא הוא: מאי טעמא דר' יהודה. אלא לאו מן הצד הוא דקשרי: אי

תוספות

דחשיב עלייהו. וא"ת והא אסור לרדותם כדתניא בסוף פרק המצניע (לקמן צה. ושם) הרודה חלות דבש בשוגג חייב חטאת דברי ר"א ורבנן שבות מיהא איכא והוי דבר שאינו ניטל וי"ל דמיירי ברדויות ומונחות שם בכוורת אי נמי רגילות שיש דבש צף ע"ג חלות ואותו אינו צריך רדייה:

שלא יעשנו כעין מצודה. וא"ת מאי קמ"ל פשיטא דאי עביד כעין מצודה דאסור *והא לא משמע מברייתא דאע"ג דאינו מתכוין אסור וי"ל דאתא כפ' משילין (ביצה לו: ושם) דקמ"ל דס"ד במינו ניצוד אסור שאין במינו ניצוד מותר:

רב אשי אמר כו'. מסתמא רב אשי השיב מיד כן לרב עוקבא כששאלו אלא שסידר הש"ס תירוץ שלו תחילה ורשב"א אומר דשניהם השיב רב אשי דבמסכת ביצה גרס א"ל לא נצרכה אלא לאותן שתי חלות ובשיטה דהכא גרס ואב"א מי קתני בימות החמה כו':

כבר תירגמ' רב הונא לשמעתיך. בפרק בתרא (דף קכד:) משמע דאית ליה נמי לרב הונא דאסור לבטל כלי מהיכנו דפריך אמילתיה דקאמר התם רב הונא היתה בהמתו טעונה כלי זכוכית מביא כרים וכסתות ומניח תחתיהן והא קמבטל כלי מהיכנו ומשני בשליפי זוטרי וא"ת אכתי תקשה ליה התם דהא רב הונא סבר הכא דאין כלי ניטל אלא לדבר הניטל וי"ל דמיירי בצריך למקומו וא"ת וכי פריך ליה התם מהיא דהיתה בהמתו טעונה טבל ועששית לימא דמיירי באין צריך למקומו וי"ל דהוה מצי לשנויי הכי דה"נ הוה מצי לשנויי בשליפי רברבי ור"י מתרץ דאיסור דאין כלי ניטל אלא לדבר הניטל שרי *היכא דאיכא הפסד מרובה וכן משמע דקאמר התם מהו דתימא כי היכי דלהפסד מרובה חששו כו' משמע חששו והתירו לטלטל אף לדבר שאינו ניטל דמה חששו *להתיר אם לא זה האיסור:

חם להם מלמטה. תימה בלא שום חום מאי איסור איכא שיביאו כל אחד מטה לישב עליה ותו אמאי מייתי ברישא מטה והדר מחצלת ימתינו עד שיחם להם גם מלמעלה ויביאו מטות ומחצלות יחד ונראה דלאחמור רבנן למיעבד היכרא שהוא לצורך חי כל כמה דאיפשר למיעבד:

ופורסין עליהן זה זוקף כו'. דוקא בכה"ג כמו שפי' רש"י אבל ממטה למעלה אסור משום אהל כדאמרי' בהמביא כדי יין (ביצה לב: ושם) אמר רב יהודה מדורתא מלמעלה למטה שרי מלמטה למעלה אסור וכן ביעתא וכן קידרא וכן חביתא ופוריא דהא דאמרי' בהמוצא תפילין (עירובין קב.) גבי דיכרי דרב הונא אתא לקמיה דרב א"ל זיל כרוך בודיא ושייר בה טפח למחר פשטוה מוסיף על אהל עראי הוא ושפיר דמי אבל בלא שיור אסור היינו משום שהמחיצות התחתונות היו כבר עשויות ואם היה פורש עליהן היה עושה אהל כדרך לעשות אהל ואע"ג דרב הונא אית ליה הכא דאין כלי ניטל אלא לדבר הניטל °מה שהיה מוסיף למחר לא חשיב טלטול או שמא היו מושיבין שם אדם א"נ משום הפסד מרובה שרי כדפירש לעיל:

זה זוקף מטתו. תימה לר"י (*) דרבא לא שרי אלא בשביל חי ובפ' מי שהוציאוהו (שם מד. ושם) תניא זוקף את המטה פורס עליה סדין שלא תפול החמה על המת ועל האוכלין והתם מוקי לה במחיצה רביעית שסוכה כשירה בלאו הכי ולא הוי אלא תוספת אהל אבל מ"מ (אין) ניטל הכלי בשביל מת ויש לומר דהתם נמי לא שרי אלא בענין שאומר כאן שעושה בשביל חי אי נמי שיש אוכלין עם המת:

ונשמט והולך לו. ואין צריך לישאר שם תחת האהל כדי שיהא נראה שנעשה בשביל חי כיון דבשעת עשייה היה נראה שעושה בשביל חי:

דכ"ע טלטול מן הצד שמיה טלטול. נראה לר"י דכן הלכה מדלא קאמר דכ"ע לא שמיה טלטול וכגון דליכא ככר ותינוק ואין לו אלא מטה אחת וטעם דרבי יהודה בן לקיש מתוך שאדם בהול כו'. אלא משום דהלכתא דשמיה טלטול נקט הכי וקשה לר"י דבריש כל הכלים (לקמן קכג.) פסיק רב נחמן כר' אלעזר בן תדאי דקסבר לא שמיה טלטול וע"ק דרב אדרב דהכא סבר שמיה טלטול ובסוף פ' תולין (שם קמא.) אמרי בי רב טלטול מן הצד לא שמיה טלטול °ובדוכתא אחריתי פריך מדרב אאמרי בי רב ובפרק השואל (ב"מ קב:) ובפרק בית כור (ב"ב קה:) מצריך מילתיה דרב ודאמרי בי רב ועוד אמאי אסר רב

(*) נ"ל דהכא

ולעיל מיניה ס"מ לשנויי דשרי משום הפסד אלא דמשני שינויא חדא לכולהו בצריך למקומו [תו"י]

ומיהו דוחק כרשב"א דחששו להתיר טורח (דהמלאכה) [דהא רבה] דמפרש טעמא משום הלכה שאינה מצויה ולית ליה דביטול כלי ולא טעמא דאין כלי ניטל (אלא) [הלא] תיקשי ליה ברייתא דאסרי' בפ' בתרא דף קכד: להביא תחתיו כרים וכסתות אלא ודאי משום טורח [תו"י]

ומשמע ליה שיש שם חלות הרבה דלא הוי מוקצה מחמת חסרון כיס [תוס' ישנים]

[לעיל ל: לקמן קמג:]

[לקמן קכו. קמא.]

[תוספ' פי"ד] יומא פה.

יומא שם

רבינו חננאל

וכיון שמותר לפנותו מאותו מקום ולטלטלו מטלטלו למקום הביצה (כו') וכופהו על הביצה וכן כולם *) ולא יתכן לישב ע"ג הביצה כדי שלא יטנפו בגדיו. לפיכך כופה עליה [כלי] ויושב עליו וכל התיובתות פשוטות הן. ושנינו על הכוורת באותן ב' חלות ששנינו בפ' המוכר את הספינה בענין המוכר חלת דבש טורתו לחבירו שחייב הקונה להניח לו שתי חלות דבש כדי שיהו מזון לדבורים שלא יברחו. ולפיכך אמרנו אותן ב' חלות מוקצות ממאכל אדם הן (לא השאילו) דשאולין לדבורים. ושנינן כגון (שחייב) [שחשב] עליהן בפירוש למאכל אדם. ואקשינן אי הכי אדתני ומזהיר בפריסת ע"ג הכוורת ובלבד שלא יתכוין לצוד. ליפלוג עליה כו'. ואסיקנא לעולם ר' יהודה [היא] והאי דקתני ובלבד שלא יתכוין לצוד. שלא ישלשל המחצלת וידחקנה בכותלי הכוורת שנמצא הדבורין כתומין בכוורת אלא ירויח כמעט המחצלת מן הנקב של כוורת שהוא פתח לצאת ולכנוס בו הדבורים כו'. אמר רב ששת כבר תירגם רב הונא לשמעתיה דר' יצחק בבבל דאמר עושין מחיצה למת בשביל החי ואין עושין מחיצה למת בשביל המת כיצד מת מוטל בחמה באין ב' בני אדם ויושבין בצידו. חם להם מלמטה [זה] מביא מטה ויושב עליה וזה מביא מטה ויושב עליה כו'. איתמר מת המוטל בחמה רב יהודה אמר שמואל הופכו ממטה למטה. ומשמיה דרב אמרו מניח עליו ככר או תינוק ומטלטלו. ואסקינן בשיש ככר או תינוק כ"ע לא פליגי שמניח עליו ככר או תינוק ומטלטלו (וכ"ע) [כי פליגי היכא דל"ל מ"ס] טלטול מן הצד שמיה טלטול. [ומ"ס לא שמיה טלטול]. ואתינן ואוקמינן בתנאי. אין מצילין [את המת] מפני הדליקה. אמר ר' יהודה בן לקיש שמעתי שמצילין את המת מפני הדליקה. ואמרינן כ"ע טלטול מן הצד שמיה טלטול. היינו טעמא דר' יהודה בן לקיש מתוך שאדם בהול על מתו אי

*) ט"ס כאן ופי' אחר הוא צריך למקום הביצה לישב.

גליון הש"ס

רש"י ד"ה אי ר"ש לית לי' בחשיב. משמע דמכ"ע צריכים לשיטתו דליכא ב' חלות דס"ל לר"ש ליכא לדיוק ד"ס ולר"ש דמיקל במוקצה ולר"ש רק בכ"ב וכלל לר"ש

באמת דפירכת הש"ס דלר"ש ל"ל כלל לתרץ דאיכא ב' חלות מבואר דס"ל לרש"י שם (דלר"ש ליכא לד... ולדברי רש"י אלו כוונת הרז"ה פ' מי שהחשיך שכתב דריו"ן הוא רק לר"י וכתב עלה שכ"כ רש"י... פליגי דלית ליה. ק"ל אמאי לא הוי המטה עצמה במקום ככר או תינוק ועי' מג"א סי' ש"ח ס"ק כ... שבת. ומזה לא הערו כלום וצע"ג: תוס' ד"ה ופורסין וכו' מה שהיה מוסיף למחר. עי' לקמן... תוס' ד"ה מהו ליתן: שם ד"ה דכו"ע וכו' ובדוכתא אחריתי. עי' בכורות דף כז ע"ב

when there is honey; but what can be said of winter, when it does not contain honey?[6]—It is in respect of two loaves.[7]—But they are *mukzeh?*[8]—It means that he designated them.[9] Then what if he did not designate them? It is forbidden! If so, instead of teaching, 'providing he has no intention of capturing [the bees],' let a distinction be drawn and taught in that itself: [thus:] when is that said? When he designated them; but if he did not designate them, it is forbidden?—He [the Tanna] teaches us this: even if he designated them, yet there is the proviso that he must not intend to capture [the bees]. With whom does this
a agree?[1] If R. Simeon, surely he rejects [the prohibition of] *mukzeh!* If R. Judah, then what matters if one does not intend [to capture the bees],—[surely he holds that] an unintentional act is forbidden?[2]—In truth this agrees with R. Judah; and what is meant by, 'providing he has no intention of capturing [the bees]?' That he must not arrange it like a net, namely, he must leave an opening[3] so that they [the bees] should not be automatically caught.

R. Ashi said:[4] Is it then taught, 'in summer' and 'in winter'? Surely, it is stated, 'in the sun because of the sun and in the rain because of the rain.' [That means,] in the days of Nisan and Tishri,[5] when there is sun, rain, and honey.

R. Shesheth said to them [his disciples], 'Go forth and tell R. Isaac, R. Huna has already stated your ruling in Babylon. For R. Huna said: A screen may be made for the dead for the sake of the living, but not for the sake of the dead. What does this mean? As R. Samuel b. Judah said, and Shila Mari recited likewise: If a dead man is lying in the sun, two men come and sit down at his side. If they feel hot underneath,[6] each brings a couch and sits upon it.[7] If they feel hot above, they can bring a hanging and spread it above them: then each sets up his couch, slips away and departs, and thus the screen [for the dead] is found to have been made automatically.[8]

It was stated: If a corpse is lying in the sun,—Rab Judah maintained in Samuel's name: It may be changed over from bier to bier.[9] R. Ḥanina said on Rab's authority: A loaf or a child is placed upon it,[10] and it is moved away. Now, if a loaf or a child is available, all agree that that is permitted. When do they differ?—When they are not available: one Master holds, Sidelong moving is
b designated moving;[1] while the other Master holds, Sidelong moving is not designated moving.

Shall we say this is dependent on Tannaim? [For it was taught]: A corpse may not be saved from a fire.[2] R. Judah b. Laḳish said: I have heard that a corpse may be rescued from a fire. What are the circumstances? If a loaf or a child is available, what is the reason of the first Tanna? If it is not,[3] what is the reason of R. Judah b. Laḳish? Hence they surely differ in respect to sidelong moving, one Master holding that such is designated moving, while the other Master holds that it is not?—No. All agree that sidelong moving is designated moving, but this is the reason of R.

(6) The questioner assumes 'in the sun' and 'in the rain' to mean 'in the days of the sun' and 'in the days of rain' respectively, i.e., in summer and in winter. (7) Of honey, left in the honeycomb for the bees themselves. (8) V. Glos. Having been set apart for the bees, they may not be handled. (9) For food, before the Sabbath.
a (1) Assuming that the reference is to one who designated the two loaves, who is the author of this Baraitha? (2) Since the covering blocks the bees' exit, he does in fact capture them, notwithstanding his lack of intention. (3) Lit., 'space'. (4) In reply to the objecton from the last cited Baraitha. (5) The first and seventh months of the Jewish year, corresponding roughly to mid-March-April and mid-September-October. (6) The sun having heated the pavement. (7) The prohibitions of carrying from domain to domain (v. *supra* 2a, 6a) must of course not be violated. (8) Thus the awning is not made for the dead, but for the sake of the living. This is a legal fiction. (9) Until it reaches the shade. (10) Cf. *supra* 30b; *infra* 142b.
b (1) Moving indirectly, by changing over from bier to bier, is nevertheless moving, and forbidden. (2) On the Sabbath, because it must not be handled. (3) And consequently the point at issue is whether the dead may be rescued directly.

Judah b. Laḳish: since a man is agitated over his dead, [44a] if you do not permit [it] to him, he will come to extinguish [the fire].[4] R. Judah b. Shila said in the name of R. Assi in R. Joḥanan's name: The *halachah* is as R. Judah b. Laḳish in the matter of the corpse.

YET ONE MAY NOT BENEFIT FROM IT, BECAUSE IT IS NOT OF MUKAN. Our Rabbis taught: The residue of oil in the lamp or in the dish is forbidden; but R. Simeon permits [it].

MISHNAH. A NEW LAMP[5] MAY BE HANDLED, BUT NOT AN OLD ONE.[6] R. SIMEON MAINTAINED: ALL LAMPS MAY BE HANDLED, EXCEPT A LAMP [ACTUALLY] BURNING ON THE SABBATH.

GEMARA. Our Rabbis taught: A new lamp[7] may be moved, but not an old one: this is R. Judah's opinion. R. Meir ruled: All lamps may be moved, except a lamp which was lit on the Sabbath;[1] R. Simeon said: Except a lamp burning on the Sabbath; if it is extinguished, it may be moved; but a cup, dish or glass lantern[2] may not be stirred from its place. R. Eliezer son of R. Simeon said: One may take supplies from an extinguished lamp or from dripping oil, even while the lamp is burning.

Abaye observed: R. Eliezer son of R. Simeon agrees with his father on one [point] and disagrees with him on another. He agrees with his father on one [point] in rejecting [the prohibition of] *mukẓeh*. Yet he disagrees with him on another: for whereas his father holds, Only if it is extinguished [is it permitted], but not otherwise; he holds, Even if it is not extinguished. 'But a cup, dish, or glass lantern may not be stirred from its place'. Wherein do these differ? —Said 'Ulla: This last clause follows R. Judah. Mar Zuṭra demurred to this: If so, why 'but'?—Rather, said Mar Zuṭra: In truth, it follows R. Simeon; yet R. Simeon permits [handling] only in the case of a small lamp, because one's mind is set upon it;[3] but not [in the case of] these, which are large. But it was taught: The residue of oil in a lamp or in a dish is forbidden; while R. Simeon permits [it]?—There the dish is similar to the lamp:[4] here the dish is similar to the cup.[5]

R. Zera said: A shaft[6] in which [a lamp] was lit on [that] Sabbath,[7] in the view of him who permits [an earthen lamp],[8] this is prohibited;[9] in the view of him who forbids [an earthen lamp],[10] this is permitted.[11]

Shall we say that R. Judah accepts [the prohibition of] *mukẓeh* on account of repulsiveness, but rejects [that of] *mukẓeh* on account of an interdict? But it was taught, R. Judah said: All metal lamps
b may be handled, except a lamp which was lit on the Sabbath?[1] But if stated, it was thus stated: R. Zera said: A shaft on which a lamp was lit[2] on the Sabbath, all agree that it is forbidden [to handle it]; if a lamp was not lit therein, all agree that it is permitted.

Rab Judah said in Rab's name: If a bed is designated for money, it may not be moved.[3] R. Naḥman b. Isaac objected: A NEW LAMP

(4) Yet he may not permit it when the corpse is lying in the sun. (5) I.e., one which has never been used. (6) Once used it is *mukẓeh* (q. v. Glos.) on account of its repulsiveness, which this Tanna holds is forbidden. (7) The reference is to an earthenware lamp.

(1) Var. lec.: on that Sabbath. (2) The three used as lamps. For the various types of lamps and their descriptions v. *T.A.* 1, 68 *seq*. (3) Thinking, the oil will not last long, and when it goes out I will use the lamp. (4) I.e., small. (5) Large. (6) פמוט: 'a shaft with a receptacle for a lamp, a plain candlestick', Jast. Rashi: a metal candlestick. (7) Jast. reads: a shaft on which a lamp was lit etc. V. also *T.A.* I, p. 70 and n. 234. (8) R. Meir. (9) Because it burnt on that Sabbath. This is known as *mukẓeh* on account of an interdict, i.e., the lamp was employed on that Sabbath for burning, and one may not light a lamp on the Sabbath itself. (10) R. Judah: the reference is to an old lamp, which is *mukẓeh* on account of repulsiveness. (11) Because R. Judah rejects the prohibition of *mukẓeh* on account of an interdict.—Being of metal, the lamp is not regarded as repulsive, even when it has been used.

b (1) Var. lec.: on that Sabbath. (2) V. *supra* n. a7. Here this is the reading of cur. edd. (3) Mere designation renders it forbidden, even if money was not actually placed there.

אי. לא שרית ליה אתי לכבויי א"ר יהודה בן שילא א"ר אסי א"ר יוחנן *הלכה כר' יהודה בן לקיש במת: אין ניאותין הימנו לפי שאינו מן המוכן: תנו רבנן *מותר השמן שבנר ושבקערה אסור ורבי שמעון מתיר:

מתני' *מטלטלין נר חדש אבל לא ישן רבי שמעון אומר כל הנרות מטלטלין חוץ מן הנר הדולק בשבת:

גמ' *ת"ר מטלטלין נר חדש אבל לא ישן דברי רבי יהודה ר"מ אומר כל הנרות מטלטלין חוץ מן הנר שהדליקו בו *בשבת ר' שמעון אומר חוץ מן הנר הדולק בשבת כבתה מותר לטלטלה אבל כוס וקערה ועששית לא יזיזם ממקומם ור' אליעזר בר' שמעון אומר מסתפק מן הנר הכבה ומן השמן המטפטף ואפי' בשעה שהנר דולק אמר אביי רבי אליעזר ברבי שמעון סבר לה כאבוה בחדא ופליג עליה בחדא סבר לה כאבוה בחדא דלית ליה מוקצה ופליג עליה בחדא דאילו אבוה סבר כבה אין לא כבה לא ואיהו סבר אע"ג דלא כבה אבל כוס וקערה ועששית לא יזיזם ממקומם מאי שנא הני אמר עולא סיפא אתאן לר' יהודה מתקיף לה מר זוטרא אי הכי מאי אבל אלא אמר מר זוטרא לעולם רבי שמעון וכי קשרי רבי שמעון בנר זוטא דדעתיה עלויה אבל הני דנפישי לא והתניא מותר השמן שבנר ושבקערה אסור ורבי שמעון מתיר התם קערה דומיא דנר הכא קערה דומיא דכוס א"ר זירא פמוט שהדליקו בו בשבת לדברי המתיר אסור לדברי האוסר מותר למימרא דרבי יהודה מוקצה מחמת מיאוס אית ליה מוקצה מחמת איסור לית ליה והתניא *ר' יהודה אומר כל הנרות של מתכת מטלטלין חוץ מן הנר שהדליקו בו *בשבת אלא אי איתמר הכי איתמר א"ר זירא פמוט שהדליקו עליו בשבת ד"ה אסור לא הדליקו עליו ד"ה מותר: אמר *רב יהודה א"ר מטה שיחדה למעות אסור לטלטלה מיתיבי' רב נחמן בר יצחק מטלטלין נר חדש אבל לא ישן ומה

רש"י

אי לא שרית ליה וכו'. אבל במוטל לחמה לא שרי: **מתני'** מטלטלין נר חדש. שאינו מאוס וחזי לאשתמושי (א) להדיא שלא דלק בו נר מעולם: אבל לא ישן. דמוקצה מחמת מיאוס הוא: **גמ'** חוץ מן הנר שהדליקו. ואף על גב שכבה אסור דאית ליה לרבי מאיר מוקצה מחמת איסור ולית ליה מוקצה מחמת מיאוס: *חוץ מן הנר הדולק בשבת. בעוד שהוא דולק אסור שמא יכבה הנר: עששית. כוס גדול של זכוכית שקורין לנפ"א: לא יזיזם ממקומן. ואפי' כבה הנר ולקמן מפרש טעמא: מן הנר הכבה. דכיון דכבה והולך לא מחייב תו משום מכבה: כבה אין לא כבה לא. דלא שמעינן ליה לרבי שמעון דשרי במתני' אלא מותר שמן שבנר ושבקערה דמשמע לאחר שכבה: מאי אבל. מדקאמר אבל מכלל דבנר מותר: בזוטא. דדעתי' עליה מבע"י סבר שיכלה השמן מהר ואשתמש בנר לכשיכבה: אבל הני. לא אסיק אדעתיה שיכבו כל היום: ור' שמעון מתיר וקערה כפישא קשיא קערה אקערה: דומיא דנר. קתני לה דזוטרא: פמוט. מנורה של מתכת ואינה מאוסה: לדברי המתיר. ר' מאיר המתיר בנר ישן: אוסר. בהאי דמוקצה מחמת איסור כדקתני לעיל חוץ מן הנר שהדליקו בו בשבת: לדברי האוסר. רבי יהודה האוסר בנר ישן של חרס התם הוא דמאיס אבל הכא שרי ולית ליה מוקצה מחמת איסור: נר של מתכת. לא מאיס כגון של נחשת דלא. בלע: שיחדה למעות. מיתסרא בהזמנה בעלמא ואע"פ שלא הניח עליה מעולם: מטלטלין נר חדש. והא רבי יהודה קאמר לה דאית ליה מוקצה אלמא לא מיתסר בהזמנה מדקאמר אבל לא ישן ולא קתני אבל לא המיוחד לכך: הניח

תוספות

רב הונא טלטול מן הצד הא תנן בפ' נוטל (לקמן קמב:) מעות שע"ג הכר מנער את הכר והן נופלות ואבן שעל פי החבית מטה על צדה וכו' ומוקי לה רב התם בשוכח אבל במניח נעשה בסיס לדבר האסור והכא (ג)(חשיב) בשוכח מדשרי שמואל וכל דבר שדעתו ליטלו בשבת ולא להניחו כל השבת *אפילו מניח חשיב כשוכח כי ההיא דמנער את הכיסוי והם נופלות אע"פ שבמתכוין כיסה בדבר שאינו ניטל ואפי' רבנן דרבי אלעזר בן תדאי שרו בכי האי גוונא דהכא דהא שרו פגה שהטמינה בתבן וחררה שהטמינה בגחלים אם מגולה מקצתה ובמכוסה כולה פליגי דרבי אלעזר שרי אפי' מכוסה כולה דתוחב בכוש או בכרכר ואומר ר"י דיש לחלק *דהכא עיקר הטלטול לצורך מת ולא דמי לכל הנהו שעושה עיקר הטלטול לצורך כר וחבית ולא לצורך מעות ואבן *ולהכי לא מייתי הכא פלוגתא דר' אלעזר בן תדאי ורבנן וע"ק לר"י דאפי' בטלטול דמת שיש לאסור יותר. משאר טלטול מן הצד כדפי' שרי שמואל ובסוף במה טומנין (לקמן דף נ:) אמר שמואל האי סכינא דביני אורבי דלא שלפה והדר דלא שרי ואי לא אסיר ופירש בקונט' לקמן דאסור משום טלטול מן הצד וכן קשה דרב הונא אמר התם האי סליקוסתא דלא שלפה והדר דלא שרי ואי לאו אסור א"כ אסר טלטול מן הצד ובסוף תולין אמרי בי רב טלטול מן הצד לא שמיה טלטול ואמרי בי רב הייעו רב הונא כמו שמפרש ר"ת בספ"ק דסנהדרין*(דף יז: ושם) ונראה לר"י דרב הונא ושמואל לא אסרי התם משום טלטול מן הצד אלא משום שמסיר עפר ומרחיב הגומא ואיידי דאיירי לעיל מיניה בגומא נקטה ומותיב מהטומן לפת וצנונות דהתם לפת וצנונות לאו דלה ושלפה ולהכי השיב הש"ס תיובתא ור"ה ושמואל *הוו ידעי לה דמתני' היא בסדר זרעים אלא דדחקי לאוקמה בדלה ושלפה והש"ס לא ניחא ליה לאוקמה הכי ועומדת בתיובתא:

*מתוך שאדם בהול על מתו אי לא שרית לי' אתי לכבויי. ואע"ג דגבי ממון אמרינן *איפכא אי שרית ליה אתי נכבויי הייעו משום שאין מצטער על ממונו כמו על מתו ואי שרית ליה מתוך שיהא טרוד להציל ישכח שהיום שבת ויבא לכבות בשוגג אבל על מתו מצטער ביותר ואי לא שרית ליה אתי לכבויי במזיד:

שבנר ושבקערה אסור ור' שמעון מתיר. ואחר השבת מותר אפי' לר' יהודה וה"נ תניא לקמן גבי נויי סוכה אסור להסתפק מהן עד מוצאי י"ט האחרון אבל בתר הכי שרי וקשה לר"י דמ"ש מנר חנוכה דתניא *כבה ליל ראשון מוסיף עליו בליל ב' ומדליק בו כבה ליל ח' עושה לו מדורה בפני עצמו מפני שהוקצה למצותו ואומר ר"י דנר חנוכה עיקרו לא להנאתו בא אלא לפרסומי ניסא ומשום חביבותא דנס אינו מצפה שיכבה אלא מקצה לגמרי למצוה אבל נר שבת להנאתו בא יושב ומצפה שיכבה ולכך מותר ואח"ת ומ"ש נר שכבה דאסור לטלטל לר' יהודה מסוכה רעועה דעלמא דמהני בה תנאי כדאמר לקמן בשמעתין ואם התנה עליה הכל לפי תנאו ומוקי לה במסכת ביצה (דף ל:) בסוכה דעלמא ורעועה דאתמול דעתיה עילויה שתפול ונר נמי דעתיה עילויה שיכבה ואמאי אין מועיל תנאי להסתפק ממותר השמן ולר"ש נמי יועיל תנאי להסתפק מן השמן המטפטף בשעה שהנר דולק וי"ל דהתם סוכה דעלמא היתה עשויה מזמן גדול ועתה ביה"ש אינו בודל ממנה ויושב ומצפה מתי תפול אבל נר עיקר הקצאתו הוא ביה"ש ודחייה בידי' לצורך שבת וחמיר טפי ולא מהני ביה תנאי*:

לדברי המתיר אסור. פי' בקונטרס לדברי ר' מאיר וא"ת מאי קמ"ל הא בהדיא קאסר ר' מאיר נר שהדליקו בה באותו שבת וי"ל דה"א ה"מ בנר של חרס דאית ביה תרתי מוקצה מחמת מיאוס ומחמת איסור קמ"ל דאפי' בשל מתכת דלא מאיס ולית ביה אלא מוקצה מחמת איסור אסר ר' מאיר ואין נראה לר"ת דלפי זה הא דמסיק דברי הכל אסור לא הוי אלא ר' מאיר ור' יהודה דקאי עלייהו ולא ר"ש ומפרש וכן פר"ח לדברי המתיר הייעו ר' שמעון אסר כאן בפמוט דהא פמוט גדול הוא ככוס וקערה ועששית כמו פמוטות של בית ר' דשילהי כל כתבי (לקמן קכא:) לדברי האוסר הייעו ר' מאיר ור' יהודה דאסרי בנר חרס שהדליקו בו באותו שבת וה"מ בנר של חרס דאיכא תרתי מוקצה מחמת מיאוס ומחמת איסור אבל בנר מתכת שרו ומסיק דאפי' בשל מתכת אסר ר' מאיר וה"נ אמרי' בפ"ק דחולין (דף טו.) ע"כ לא שרי רבי מאיר אלא במבשל דראוי לכוס אבל בשוחט לא*:

מטה שיחדה למעות אסור לטלטלה. נראה דאפי' לצורך גופה או לצורך מקומה אסור דכיון שיחדה למעות שוב אין עושין ממנה שום תשמיש *והויא כאבנים כמו לקבורות. דאסור לטלטלה לרבי יהודה אפילו לצורך גופה ומקומה ולרבי שמעון שום מוקצה לא אסור לצורך גופו ומקומו אלא מוקצה מחמת חסרון כיס:

דהתם אפי' ר"ש מודי' אף על גב דשרי בנתגלגלה בשבת התם אינו מעלה על לבו שישתמש בהם אדם בשבת והוי כמו דיש במינו במחובר דפרש"י דבילה [דף כד:] דאפילו ר"ש אסר כגרוגרות וצימוקין מדלא לקטן מאתמול אקצינהו [תוספות ישנים]

עין משפט נר מצוה

מח א מיי' פכ"ו מהל' שבת הלכה כא סמג לאוין סה טוש"ע או"ח סימן שיא סעיף א:

מט ב מיי' פ"ה מהל' שבת הלכה יב ופרק כו הלכה יד סמג לאוין סה טוש"ע או"ח סימן רסה סעיף ג וסימן רעט סעיף א:

נ ג מיי' פכ"ה מהלכות שבת הלכה י יא טוש"ע או"ח סימן רעט סעיף א:

מסורת הש"ס

[דבור זה שייך לעיל במשנה] | [לקמן מו: ביצה ל:] | חולין יד: | תוספתא שבת פ"ד | י"ג באותה שבת | חולין טו. | בכ"י באותה שבת | [לפמ"ש תוס' יבמות קח: ד"ה אמר וכו' מוכח דכי' גרסתי' רב הונא ע"ש] | [לקמן קיז:] | נתנו ד"ה אלא | שייך לעמוד הקודם | [בש"ס לא נמצא מקומו אלא בשאלתות פ' ויגלא הביאו הרא"ש פרק במה מדליקין רס"ט ובטור וב"י סימן תרעג]

ורשב"א מפרש דאפילו למאי דס"ד אתי הכיא דחולין שפיר דבמוקצה מחמת איסור

הגהות הב"ח

(א) רש"י ד"ה מטלטלין וכו' לאשתמושי ביה להדיא: (ג) תוס' ד"ה דכ"ע טלטול וכו' אבל במניח נעשה בסיס לדבר האסור והכא חשיב בשכח מדשרי שמואל דאפילו מניח דבר שדעתו ליטלו בשבת ולא להניחו כל השבת חשוב כשכח כי ההיא דמנער:

רבינו חננאל

[אי לא] שרית ליה לטלטולי אתי לכבויי ולמעבד איסורא דאורייי' א"ר יהודה בר שילא א"ר אסי א"ר יוחנן הלכה כר' יהודה בן לקיש במת: ואין נאותין ממנו לפי שאינו מן המוכן: ת"ר מותר השמן שבנר ושבקערה אסור להסתפק ממנו. ור"ש מתיר (מטלטלין נר חדש אבל לא ישן) אע"ג דקיי"ל דהלכתא כר' שמעון בכולה שבת בהא לית הלכתא כוותיה. דתנא דידן קתני דברי ר' יהודה סתמא במתניתין [מטלטלין נר חדש אבל לא ישן]. ובברייתא מפרש דברי ר' יהודה מטלטלין נר חדש אבל לא ישן. ר' מאיר [אומר] כל הנרות מטלטלין חוץ מן הנר שהדליקו בה באותה שבת. נמצא ר' מאיר ור' יהודה שניהן אוסרין בנר שהדליקו בו באותה שבת. ור"ש מתיר ואין הלכתא כוותיה. דהוא יחיד במקום רבים ואע"פ דא"ר יוחנן אנו אין לנו אלא בנר כר' שמעון [לר' שמעון] אמרו וליה [לר'] יוחנן לא סבירא ליה טעמא דר"ש. ואפילו ר"ש לא שרי לטלטולי בשבת בנר שכבה אלא בנר קטן דכיון דהוא נר קטן ושמנו מעט דעתו עליו מאתמול לכשיכבה יטלטלנו ואינו מוקצה. אבל נר גדול כגון כוס וקערה ועששית שיתכן שידליקו היום כולו לא אמרינן דחשיב עלייהו מאתמול לכשיכבו יטלטלם. אלא אמרינן ודאי כיון דגדולים הן נתייאשו מלטלטלן ומוקצין הן. לפיכך קתני סיפא אבל כוס וקערה ועששית לא יזיזם ממקומן וכן כיוצא בהן. פעמים שיש קערה ועששית קטנה דומיא דנר קטן ודינם כדין נר קטן ופעמים שיש נר גדול דומיא דקערה ועששית ודינו כדינם. והא דא"ר אלעזר [בר"ש] מסתפק אדם מנר הכבה ומשמן המטפטף אע"פ שהנר דולק*) א"ר זירא פמוט שהדליקו עליו לדברי המתיר בנר אסר בפמוט. כלומר לר' שמעון דמתיר בנר קטן בפמוט שהוא גדול אוסר. ולדברי ר' מאיר ור' יהודה שאוסרין בנר של חרש מפני שהוא מטנף. והוא צאו כלי. ולפיכך הוקצהו מאתמול בפמוט שהוא של מתכת ואינו מטנף מתיר: ירושל' נר מאוס. פמוט אינו מאוס. תני נר המונח על הדלת פותח ונועל בשבת ובלבד שלא יתכוין לכבות. רב ושמואל פותרין לה בשוכח ומקללין למאן דעבד כן [יכרת] ה' לאיש אשר יעשנה וגו'. ואקשי' ולר' יהודה מוקצה מחמת מיאוס אית ליה מוקצה מחמת איסור שהדליקו בה באותה שבת לא. והתניא ר' יהודה אומר כל הנרות של מתכת מטלטלין חוץ מן הנר שהדליקו בה באותה שבת. ואסיקנ' הכי לדברי

*) עי' ברשב"א וברמב"ן

רב נסים גאון

אמר ר' זירא פמוט שהדליקו עליו באותה שבת לדברי המתיר אוסר לדברי האוסר מתיר פמוט מין מנורה ויש לה קנה אחד ובמנחות בפרק הקומץ את המנחה (דף כח) כשאמרו על דרך קושיא ואימא נמי באה

גליון הש"ס תוס' ד"ה דכ"ע כו' אפילו מניח חשיב כשוכח כי ההיא דמנער. עי' לקמן דף נה ע"א תוס' ד"ה או שטמן: **בא"ד** דהכא עיקר. עי' לעיל דף נט ע"א תוס' ד"ה מפני שמזיז: **בא"ד** הוו ידעי לה דמתני' היא. עי' מנחות דף ט ע"א תוס' ד"ה הכר הלוג. ומו"ק דף ה ע"א תוס' ד"ה להוויי: **תוס'** ד"ה מטה שיחדה כו' והויא כאצוצרות. לעיל דף לו ע"א:

ומה נר דלהכי עבידא כי לא הדליק בה שרי לטלטולה מטה דלאו להכי עבידא לא כ"ש אלא אי איתמר הכי איתמר אמר רב יהודה אמר רב *מטה שיחדה למעות הניח עליה מעות אסור לטלטלה לא הניח עליה מעות מותר לטלטלה לא יחדה למעות יש עליה מעות אסור לטלטלה אין עליה מעות מותר לטלטלה והוא שלא היו עליה בין השמשות אמר עולא מתיב ר' *אליעזר *מוכני שלה °בזמן שהיא נשמטת אין חיבור לה ואין נמדדת עמה ואין מצלת עמה באהל המת ואין גוררין אותה בשבת בזמן שיש עליה מעות הא אין עליה מעות שריא אף על גב דהוו עליה ביה"ש ההיא ר' שמעון היא דלית ליה מוקצה ורב כרבי יהודה סבירא ליה הכי

רש"י

הניח עליה מעות. אפילו בחול הרי הוקצה לאיסור ואסור לטלטלה ואפילו נסתלקו המעות מבעוד יום ולא דמי לנר של מתכת דשרי רבי יהודה דהתם בלא יחדו: לא יחדה למעות. אין עליה מעות בשבת: מותר לטלטלה. ואע"ג דהניח עליה מעות בחול: והוא שנסתלקו מבעוד יום. שלא היו עליה כל בין השמשות אבל היו עליה כל בין השמשות איתקצאי לכולי יומא: מוכני שלה. גבי שידה תנן במסכת כלים והיא עגלה של עץ מוקפת מחיצות למרכב אנשים ונשים. מוכני אופן: בזמן שהיא נשמטת. כעין אופני עגלה שלנו שאדם יכול לסלקו מן העגלה: אינו חיבור לה. דחשובה היא כלי לעצמה דאי שידה בת קבולי טומאה היא כגון שאינה מחזקת מ' סאה בלח ונטמאה השידה לא נטמא המוכני ואי לאו בת קבולי טומאה היא ונגעה טומאה במוכני המוכני טמאה לעצמה דלא חשיבה משידה והיא מטלטלה מלאה וריקנית דיש לה בית קיבול: ואינה נמדדת עמה. לענין טומאה כדפרישית דכלי עץ המחזיק מ' סאה בלח שהן כוריים ביבש טהור כדאמרי' בבמה מדליקין (דף לה.) דכלי עץ איתקש לשק שיהא מיטלטל מלא וריקן וזו אינו מיטלטל מלא ותנן במסכת כלים* ומייתינן בגמ' דמנחות *השידה ב"ה אומרים נמדדת מבחוץ דרואין אותה כאילו היא עומדת בתוך כלי גדול ואם מחזיק אותו כלי מ' סאה טהורה השידה ואע"פ שהיא אינה מחזקת מ' סאה דקסבר אף עוביה נמדד עמה והמוכני אינו נמדד עמה להשלים דרואין כאילו ניטל המוכני ואח"כ תנתן השידה לתוך הכלי: ואינה מצלת עמה באהל המת. דאם השידה מחזקת מ' [סאה] דאינה מקבלת טומאה מצלת באהל המת והוי אהל לעצמה ולא שנכנסה לבית שהמת בו דא"כ אין כאן הצלה שהרי הגג מאהיל על הטהרות מלמעלה אלא כגון שנכנסה לבית הקברות כדאמרינן בעירובין* ר' יהודה אומר אף בבה"ק מפני שיכול לחוץ בשידה תיבה ומגדל בפ' בכל מערבין* דקסבר אהל זרוק כלומר אהל המיטלטל שמיה אהל ומפסיק (א)כלפי הטומאה והמוכני אם הוא גבוה מדופני השידה וכלים [בולטים] מלמעלה מדופני השידה וגובה המוכני מגין עליהם אינו מגין דמוכני כלי הוא לעצמו ומקבל טומאה ואינו חוצץ בפני הטומאה ורבותי דוחקין ומפרשין אותה באהל המת ממש ובשל חרס המוקפת צמיד פתיל והרבה תשובות יש חדא דנמדדת לא שייך בשל חרס דלא איתקש לשק ובין מיטלטל ובין אינו מיטלטל טמא ועוד אם המוכני מוקף· צמיד פתיל יציל בפני עצמו כלים שבתוכו ועוד בפירוש נשנית במסכת כלים בהלכות כלי עץ והלכות כלי חרס נשנו לבדן והלכות כלי עץ נשנו לבדן: ההיא ר' שמעון היא. ומיהו מעות לא חזו מידי ומודה רבי שמעון דעודן עליו אסור: מניחין

תוספות

ומה נר דלהכי עבידא כו'. פי' בקונטרס דדייק מדקתני אבל לא ישן משמע דוקא ישן אבל חדש אפילו יחדו וקשה לר"י דלמאי דמסיק נמי מטה שיחדה והניח עליה מעות כו' תקשה ליה מנר של מתכת דשרי ר' יהודה אפילו יחדו לעיל מדקתני חוץ מן הנר שהדליקו בה באותה שבת אבל לא הדליקו בה באותה שבת אע"פ שיחדה והדליקו בה בחול שרי ונראה לר"י דלא דייק כלל מדקתני אבל לא ישן אלא דוקא בנר של חרס הוא דקאמ' דלהכי עבידא שתחלת עשייתה היא להדלקה והוי כמו יחוד שמיד שמדליקין בה פעם אחת נמאסת ואין ראויה לתשמיש אחר ולכך תחלת עשייתה אינה אלא להדלקה אע"פ שראויה לתשמיש אחר בין עשייה להדלקה מ"מ אין עושין אותה לכך שאין זה אלא זמן מועט אבל בנר מתכת אין עשייתה להדלקה לבד דראויה כל שעה לתשמיש אחר:

לא הניח עליה מעות מותר לטלטלה. ואצטרוכות דאסר ר' יהודה לעיל (דף לו.) נראה לר"י דאסר אפי' לא תקע בה דחצוצרות לא חזיא אלא לתקיעה ואין לחלק בין תקע ללא תקע אבל מטה ונר חזי לתשמיש אחרינא: יש עליה מעות אסור לטלטלה. ע"כ במניח איירי *דבשבת תנן פרק טטל (לקמן קמב:) מנער הכר והן נופלות ובמניח בשבת איירי דהניח מבעוד יום והיו עליה בין השמשות אפילו אין עליה מעות אסור לטלטלה כדקאמר בסיפא דמילתיה וקשה דהיך יכול להיות שמניח לדעת בשבת וי"ל כגון שהניח נכרי או תינוק לדעת ישראל וא"ת אמאי לא מוכח מהכא בפ' אין לדין (ביצה כו:) דאין מוקצה לחצי שבת וי"ל דאיכא לאוקמא כגון שהניחם לדעת ישראל כדי להסירם אחר שעה והוו כגמרו בידי אדם ולמאי דפרישית לעיל דהא דיש מוקצה לחצי שבת הייט באיסור אכילה ולא בטלטול א"ש: מוכני שלה. פי' בקונטרס דגבי שידה תנן לה במסכת כלים (פי"ח מ"א) והיא עשויה למרכבת אנשים ונשים *ואין נראה לר"י דאי חזיא למדרס לא שייך בה מדידה דלא איתקש לשק ולא בעינן מיטלטל מלא וריקן כדמוכח בפרק אלו מומין (בכורות לח. ושם) דפריך ושאין לו תוך בכלי שטף מקבל טומאה הוא והא דומיא דשק בעינן ומשני בהנך דחזו למדרסות לכך נראה דאינה עשויה אלא לכלים והא דאמר לקמן בפרק רבי עקיבא (דף פד. ושם) שלש תיבות הן תיבה שפתחה מלדה טמאה מדרס מלמעלה טמאה מת פי' אבל מדרס לא לפי שאומרים עמוד ונעשה מלאכתנו והבאה במדה טהורה מכלום פי' שיש לה מ' סאה אור"י דצריך לומר דלא קאי אפתחה מלדה דכיון דחזיא למדרס אפילו באה במדה טמאה כדפי'*): ואין מצלת עמה באהל המת. פי' בקונט' בבית הקברות (ב)שהכלים על דופני השידה וקשה דמי יביא טומא' על הכלים ומפרש ריב"א דמיירי שפיר דקיימא השידה באהל המת ומוקפת צמיד פתיל ואע"ג דכלי עץ אינו מציל בצמיד פתיל היכא דמקבל ארבעים סאה מציל כיון דלא מקבל טומאה כדתנן במסכת כלים ואלו מצילין בצמיד פתיל כלי גללים כו' וכלי עץ הטהורים ואין צ"ל דמוכני יש לו בית קיבול אלא פשוטי כלי עץ הוא ויש נקב בשידה בלדה והכלים בתוך השידה והמוכני חופפת שם וממעטת אותו נקב עד שאין נשאר פותח טפח וקאמר כיון דנשמטת אינו ממעט דדוקא כי מבטלו שם ממעט בחלון כדמוכח בלא יחפור (ב"ב כ: ושם) דפריך אהא דקתני דכלי חרס ממעט בחלון הא קחזי ליה פי' ולא מבטל התם והיכי ממעט ומשני דמטוקף ומיירי שאינו סותם כל הנקב דאם סותם כל הנקב אפי' אינו מבטלו שם סותם כדאמר בפ' בתרא (דף קנז.) בימי אבא שאול בן בטנית פקקו את המאור בטפיח והתם לא בטלוהו שאם ביטלוהו בשבת היה חייב משום בונה דהא מוסיפים על הבנין אלא ודאי בלא ביטול איירי ואפ"ה סותם ובכלי עץ אמרינן נמי בפ' בתרא דמגילה (דף כו:) ההיא בי כנישתא דרומאי דהות פתיחה להאי אנדרונא דהוו מחתי בה מיתי בעו כהני למיזל לצלויי התם אמרו ליה לרבא אמר להו זילו דלו תיבותא ואותבוהו אבבא דה"ל כלי עץ העשוי לנחת ומסתמא לא היו מבטלין אותו שם שהרי ס"ת מניחין בתוכו ומיהו תבן וגרוגרות אין להם דין כלים דאפי' סותמין כל החלון צריכין ביטול כדמוכח בפרק לא יחפור (ב"ב יט:) ולר"ת אין נראה לפרש דמוכני הוי אופן דאין דרך להניח מעות על האופן דקתני ואין גוררין אותה בשבת בזמן שיש עליה מעות ומפרש דמוכני הייטו כן של שידה כמו את הכיור ואת כנו (שמות ל) וכמו מכונות במלכים (א ז) פי' בסיס שהשידה מונחת עליו ויש בשידה נקב מתחתיה כנגד המוכני והיא בבה"ק והטומאה נכנסת דרך נקב בשידה ואין המוכני מצלת כיון שהיא נשמטת ואין מבטלין אותה שם ומיירי נמי שאין סותמת כל הנקב אלא ממעטת אותו מפותח טפח כדפי' לעיל וצ"ל דמיירי שאין הטומאה כנגד הנקב דכשהטומאה כנגד הנקב אפילו אין בו פותח טפח בוקעת ועולה כדאמר בפ"ק דסוכה (דף יח: ושם) ארובה בבית ואין בה פותח טפח טומאה כנגד ארובה כל הבית טהור לפי שבוקעת ועולה וכן במסכת אהלות* ומייתי לה בהעור והרוטב (חולין קכה:) חבילי המטה וסריגי חלונות כו' פירסן על המת באויר הנוגע כנגד הנקב טמא שלא כנגד הנקב טהור והתם אין בנקבים פותח טפח דקתני רישא דמפסיק בין בית לעלייה: אין גוררין אותה בשבת בזמן שיש עליה מעות. מפרש ר"י דכשהיא נשמטת היא כלי בפני עצמה אבל כשאינה נשמטת מותר לגוררה אע"פ שיש עליה מעות דכיון שאינם ע"ג השידה שהיא עיקר הכלי שרי: הא אין עליה מעות שריא אע"ג דהוו עליה כל בין השמשות. קשה לרשב"א דמאי פריך לוקמא בשבת ולהכי אין עליה מעות אע"ג דהוו עליה כל בין השמשות שריא כדאמר בפרק טטל (לקמן קמב:) ובזמן שיש עליה מעות אסור לגוררה אפי' בשבת שהוא טלטול גמור וקמ"ל דבאינה נשמטת שרי לגוררה טלטול גמור ומתרץ דע"כ במניח איירי דהא אין גוררין אותה משמע אפי' לצורך מקומה ואי בשבת הא אמרי' בפרק טטל (ג"ז שם) לא שנו אלא לצורך גופו אבל לצורך מקומו מטלטלו ועודן עליו (*ומיהו מטה שיחדה והניח עליה מעות °איכא למימר דמודה ר"ש דמקפיד עליה מיחד לה מקום כדאמרי' בריש כל הכלים (שם קכג: ושם) הכל מודים כיון דקפיד עליה מיחד לה מקום ופר"ת דהכל מודים אפי' ר"ש והא דפריך לעיל מנר הייטו משום שאין לחלק בין מטה לשאר דברים אלא כשהניח עליה מעות ולפ"ז לא קשה לעיל אפי' הקונטרס שפי' דדייק מדקתני אבל לא ישן):

*) [ועי' תוס' מנחות לח. ד"ה שידה]

עין משפט נר מצוה

נא א מיי' פכ"ה מהל' שבת הלכה י טוש"ע א"ח סימן שי סעיף ז:

וכמותם [מא:] דקאמר גבי מגריפות וכו' ע"ש משמע דדוקא ע"י אפ' אבל ת"ח לא היו עושין אף על גב דבייתוסין לא הניחו לדעתם לא חשיב כשכח א"נ לא היו יכולין לנערם בלא טלטול קצת אע"ג דקאמר וטמטום [תו"י]

גרס"א פירש במשניות דכיון דאין נכנסין לה אלא מאליה בשלמא לא הוי כבר מיוחד למדרס שארי ספינה עשוים לישב בם בני אדם ואפ"ה כמחזקת מ' סאה טהורה [תוספות ישנים]

רבינו חננאל

הכל פמוט שהוא מנורה שאין לה אלא קנה אחד ואין על ראשה אלא בף אחת הדליקו עליו באותה שבת דברי הכל (אחר) [אסור]. לא הדליקו עליו דברי הכל מותר. הא דאמר רב מטה שיחדה למעות והניח עליה מעות *) והיו עליה המעות כל בין השמשות. אע"פ שנטלו המעות עכשיו ואינם במטה אסור לטלטלה. אסיקנא דרב כר' יהודה אמרה לשמעתיה. מתיב ר' אליעזר הא דתנן בכלים פ' י"ח מוכני שלה בזמן שהיא נשמטת אינה חבור ואינה נמדדת עמה ואינה נצלת באהל המת. פי' [כאן] [כן] של שידה בזמן שהיא נשמטת אינה כמו השידה ואינה נשלפת עמה ולא נצלת עמה מפני שהשידה כלי וזו אינה כלי **) מכללא לפיכך אמרו אין גוררין

*) ע"ס כאן. **) ע"ס כאן ועי' בכתבי' ובכנ"א.

רב נסים גאון

זהב באה קנים אינה באה זהב אינה באה קנים השיבו ההוא פמוט מיתקרי והפמוט שהזכיר ר' זירא בשמועה זו נחשת היא וחדש ואינו נמאס ואם הדליקו עליו נר באותו שבת הרי הוא מוקצה מחמת איסור ולפי שהוא מנוקה מלכלוך לא הוי מוקצה מחמת מיאוס ועל דעת ר' מאיר שהיה מתיר טלטול הפמוט אם לא הדליקו עליו באותה שבת זה הפמוט אע"פ שהוא כחדש שאינו נמאס אסור לטלטלו לפי שנהיה מוקצה מחמת איסורו מפני הנר שהדליקו עליו באותו יום ועל דעת ר' יהודה שהיה אוסר טלטול [נר ישן] (חדש) [של חרש] הרי הפמוט מותר לטלטלו לפי שנראה נר חדש ואינו מאוס ולפיכך באה הקושיא מידי למימרא דר' יהודה מוקצה מחמת מיאוס אית ליה מוקצה מחמת איסורו לית ליה והתניא ובגמ' דבני מערב' גרסי מעשה היה וטילטלו פמוט מתחת הנר בשבת מה אנן קיימין אי כר' מאיר אפילו פמוט יהא אסור כמו שאר כל הנרות מטלטלין חוץ מן הנר שהדליקו בה באותה שבת והוה הפמוט הדליקו בו באותה שבת והרי הוא לר' מאיר אסור ואי כר"ש אפילו נר עצמו יהא מותר וכל שכן הפמוט שיהא מותר ואין אנו צריכים להודיענו זה ההיתר בפמוט על דעת ר' שמעון שהיה סובר נר עצמו מותר לטלטלו וכ"ש פמוט מתחתיו אלא כן אנן כר' יהודה דר' יהודה אומר נר מאוס פמוט אינו מאוס וזה סיוע הפירוש שפירשנו אבל בארתי זה הטעם כי ראיתי מי שפירש אותו בטעם אחר וסבר שר' שמעון שהוא

מסורת הש"ס

[לקמן קנו: כלים פי"ח מ"ב]

פי"ח מ"ח

[דף לח.]

[דף ל:]

[שם]

[סוף תוספתא דאהלות פ"ט]

רש"ל מ"ז ומהרש"א כתב שזהו שייך לסוף דיבור שאח"ז (ועי' מהרש"א):

הגהות הב"ח

(א) רש"י ד"ה ואינה מצלת וכו' ומפסיק כלפי הטומאה: (ב) תוס' ד"ה ואין מצלת וכו' בבית הקברות והכלים מעל דופני השידה:

גליון הש"ס

גמ' בזמן שהיא נשמטת. עי' לקמן דף מח ע"ב תוס' ד"ה דבר תורה: תוס' ד"ה אין וכו'. איכא למימר דמודה ר"ש. עי' לעיל דף לו ע"א תוס' ד"ה הא לן יסודה:

MAY BE HANDLED, BUT NOT AN OLD ONE. [44b] Now if a lamp, though made for that purpose, may be handled if it was not lit, how much more so a bed, which was not made for that purpose! Rather if stated, it was thus stated: Rab Judah said in Rab's name: In the case of a bed which was designated for money, if money was placed upon it,[4] it may not be handled; if money was not placed upon it, it may be handled. But if it was not designated for money, then if money is lying upon it [now], it may not be handled; if money is not lying upon it, it may be handled, provided that there was none upon it at twilight.[5]

Said 'Ulla, R. Eleazar objected: Its wheel-work, if detachable, has no connection therewith, is not measured with it, does not protect together with it in [the matter of] a covering above the dead, and it may not be rolled on the Sabbath if there is money upon it.[6] Hence if there is no money upon it [now] it is permitted, though it was there at twilight?—That is according to R. Simeon, who
a rejects [the law of] *mukzeh*,[1] whereas Rab agrees with R. Judah.

(4) Even on weekdays, and it was removed before the Sabbath. Yet it has thereby been set apart and employed for something (*sc.* money) that may not be handled on the Sabbath, and therefore may not be handled itself either. (5) Before the commencement of the Sabbath. For if there was money upon it at twilight, it could not be handled then, and being interdicted then it remains so for the whole Sabbath. (6) Kel. XVIII, 2. The reference is to the wheel-work of a carriage. It has no connection with the body of the carriage: if either the wheel-work or the carriage comes into contact with an unclean object, the other remains unaffected. Now, a utensil can become unclean only if its capacity is less than forty *se'ahs*, which Beth Hillel defines as referring to its *displacement*. Thus, not only is the hollow of the vessel reckoned, but also its sides, etc. Consequently, if the wheel-work were not detachable, its own volume too would be measured in conjunction with the body itself; but being detachable, it is not. Again, if any object or a human being is stationed directly above a corpse, e.g., it is suspended above a grave, even without touching it, it becomes unclean; but if an object of forty *se'ahs* capacity, e.g., a large box or the body of a carriage, intervenes, it is saved from uncleanliness. Now, if the body of this carriage, which is of forty *se'ahs* capacity, is piled up with articles, some of which protrude and overflow its sides, while the detachable wheel-work too is higher than the body, and thus the wheel-work interposes between these articles and the grave, it does not save them from uncleanness. For the body itself does not intervene, while the wheel-work has not a capacity of forty *se'ahs*, and it is not counted as part of the whole. The object which becomes unclean is technically called a tent or covering (*ohel*) of the dead. With respect to the last clause Ri explains: if it is not detachable it may be rolled even if money is lying upon it, because the wheel-work is then only part of the carriage, whilst there is no money upon the body thereof, which is the chief portion.

a (1) Nevertheless, since money may not be handled for any purpose whatsoever, he admits that the wheel may not be rolled when there is actually money upon it now.

[45a] Logic too avers that Rab agrees with R. Judah. For Rab said: A lamp may be placed on a palm tree for the Sabbath,[2] but not on a Festival.[3] Now, it is well if you admit that Rab holds as R. Judah: hence he draws a distinction between the Sabbath and Festivals.[4] But if you say that he holds as R. Simeon, what is the difference between the Sabbath and Festivals?[5]

But does Rab hold as R. Judah? Surely Rab was asked: Is it permitted to move the *Ḥanukkah* lamp[6] on account of the Guebres
a on the Sabbath?[1] and he answered them, It is well.[2]—A time of emergency is different. For R. Kahana and R. Ashi asked Rab: Is that the law? Whereat he answered them, R. Simeon is sufficient to be relied upon in an emergency.

Resh Lakish asked R. Johanan: What of wheat sown in the earth or eggs under a fowl?[3] When does R. Simeon reject [the prohibition of] ***mukẓeh?*** Where one has not rejected it [an object] with his [own] hands; but where one rejects it with his own hands,[4] he accepts [the interdict of] ***mukẓeh:*** or perhaps there is no difference?—He answered him: R. Simeon accepts ***mukẓeh*** only in respect of the oil in the [Sabbath] lamp while it is burning: since it was set apart for its precept,[5] and set apart on account of its prohibition.[6] But does he not accept it where it [only] was set apart for its precept?[7] Surely it was taught: If one roofs it [the booth] in accordance with its requirements, beautifies it with hangings and sheets, and suspends therein nuts, peaches, almonds, pomegranates, grape clusters, garlands of ears of corn, wines, oil, and flours, he may not use them until the conclusion of the last Festival day of the Feast; yet if he stipulates concerning them, it is all according to his stipulation.[8] And how do you know that this is R. Simeon's view? Because R. Ḥiyya b. Joseph recited before R. Joḥanan: Wood must not be taken from a hut on a Festival,[9] save from what is near it;[10] but R. Simeon
b permits it.[1] Yet both agree in respect to the ***sukkah*** of the Festival[2] that it is forbidden on the Festival;[3] yet if he [the owner] stipulated concerning it, it all depends on his stipulation![4]—We mean, similar to the oil in the lamp: since it was set apart for its precept, it was set apart for its interdict.[5] It was stated likewise: R. Ḥiyya b. Abba said in R. Joḥanan's name: R. Simeon rejects ***mukẓeh*** save in a case similar to the oil in the lamp while it is burning: since it was set apart for its precept, it was set apart for its interdict.

Rab Judah said in Samuel's name: In R. Simeon's view ***mukẓeh*** applies only to drying figs and grapes.[6] But [does it apply] to nothing else? Surely it was taught: If one was eating figs, left [some] over, and took them up to the roof to make dried figs; or grapes, and left [some] over and took them up to the roof to make raisins: he may not eat [of them] unless he designates them.[7] And you must say the same of peaches, quinces, and other kinds of fruit.[8] Which Tanna is this? Shall we say, R. Judah: seeing that he maintains [the prohibition of] ***mukẓeh*** even where one does not reject it with his own hands, how much more so where he does reject it with his own hands![9] Hence it must
c surely be R. Simeon?[1]—After all, it is R. Judah, yet the case of eating is necessary: I might argue, since he was engaged in eating, no designation is required; hence we are informed that since he took them up to the roof, he withdrew his thoughts thence.

(2) I.e., before the Sabbath, that it should burn during the Sabbath. There is no fear that he will take and use it if it goes out, thereby technically making use of what is attached to the soil. For since it was ***mukẓeh*** at twilight it may not be used for the whole of the Sabbath. (3) For then one may remove it from the tree, replace it, and so on, thus making use of the tree itself, which is prohibited. (4) He will not remove it from the tree on the Sabbath, because of the interdict of ***mukẓeh***, which in this respect does not operate on Festivals. (5) None at all. Hence he must hold as R. Judah. (6) After it has been extinguished.

(1) The Parsees, being fire worshippers, forbade the Jews to have fire in their houses during their (the Parsees') festivities. Consequently the *Ḥanukkah* lamp, which was lit near the street (*supra* 21*b*), would have to be hidden on the approach of a Parsee. (2) This does not agree with R. Judah. (3) May they be removed on the Sabbath for use, before the wheat has taken root or the egg become addled? (4) As here. When one sows wheat in the soil or places an egg under a fowl, he rejects it for the time being. (5) I.e., for the Sabbath lamp. (6) *Sc.* the prohibition of extinguishing a light on the Sabbath renders this oil inaccessible while the lamp is burning. The text follows an old Tosaf. (v. Marginal gloss). Curr. edd.: since it was set apart for its precept, it was set apart (i.e., rendered ***mukẓeh*** and forbidden) for its interdict. But the general context shows that the amended version is preferable. (7) Viz., that that *alone* suffices to render it forbidden. (8) V. *supra* 22*a* for notes. Thus we see that mere setting apart for the fulfilment of a precept casts an interdict. (9) The reference is not to a ***sukkah*** (q.v. Glos.) but to an ordinary booth or hut. Even if it collapses during a Festival, one must not take the timber for use, because had it not collapsed it might not be pulled down on the Festival, and this renders it ***mukẓeh***. (10) Or, supporting it. If a bundle of wood was laid against the wall of the hut, in a measure serving as a support, it may be used on the Festival, because that must have been the owner's intention before the Festival, and so it is not ***mukẓeh***. Again, its removal will not cause the hut to collapse.

b (1) Because he rejects the prohibition of ***mukẓeh***. (2) 'The Festival' without a determinant always means Tabernacles. (3) If the ***sukkah*** collapses, its wood must not be used during the whole seven days of the Festival, as it had been set aside for the precept. (4) Thus we see that the previous Baraitha does agree with R. Simeon! (5) I.e., the former alone imposes the interdict. (6) When they are spread out to dry they cease to be fit for food until fully dried. Hence they are certainly rejected as food, and so even R. Simeon admits the prohibition. (7) He may not eat them on a Festival, because he has rendered them ***mukẓeh***, unless he designates them as food before the Festival, thereby annulling their character of ***mukẓeh***. (8) Though they are fit during the process of drying. (9) Hence it is unnecessary to state it where he puts fruit aside for drying. Even if he merely stores it, it is forbidden, according to R. Judah.

c (1) Proving that he admits ***mukẓeh*** in other cases too.

גמרא

הכי נמי מיסתברא דרב כר' יהודה סבירא ליה דאמר רב *מניחין נר על גבי דקל בשבת ואין מניחין נר ע"ג דקל בי"ט אי אמרת בשלמא דרב כרבי יהודה סבירא ליה היינו דשני בין שבת לי"ט אלא אי אמרת כרבי שמעון סבירא ליה מה לי שבת ומה לי י"ט ורב כרבי יהודה ס"ל והא בעו מיניה דרב מהו לטלטולי שרגא דחנוכתא מקמי חברי בשבתא ואמר להו שפיר דמי שעת הדחק שאני דהא א"ל רב כהנא ורב אשי לרב הכי הלכתא אמר להו *כדי הוא ר' שמעון לסמוך עליו בשעת הדחק בעא מיניה ריש לקיש מר' יוחנן חטים שזרען בקרקע וביצים שתחת תרנגולת מהו כי לית ליה לר' שמעון מוקצה היכא דלא דחייה בידים היכא דדחייה בידים אית ליה מוקצה או דילמא [ג]לא שנא א"ל אין מוקצה לרבי שמעון אלא שמן שבנר בשעה שהוא דולק הואיל והוקצה למצותו *הוקצה לאיסורו ולית ליה הוקצה למצותו *והתניא סיככה כהלכתה ועיטרה בקרמים ובסדינין המצויירין ותלה בה אגוזין אפרסקין שקדים ורמונין ואפרכלי של ענבים ועטרות של שבולין יינות שמנים וסלתות אסור להסתפק מהן עד מוצאי י"ט האחרון ואם התנה עליהן הכל לפי תנאו וממאי דר' שמעון היא דתני *ר' חייא בר יוסף קמיה דר' יוחנן אין נוטלין עצים מן הסוכה בי"ט אלא מן הסמוך לה ור' שמעון מתיר ושוין בסוכת החג בחג שהיא אסורה ואם התנה עליה הכל לפי תנאו כעין שמן שבנר קאמרינן הואיל והוקצה למצותו הוקצה לאיסורו איתמר נמי א"ר חייא בר אבא א"ר יוחנן אין מוקצה לרבי שמעון אלא כעין שמן שבנר בשעה שהוא דולק הואיל והוקצה למצותו הוקצה לאיסורו אמר רב יהודה אמר שמואל אין מוקצה לר' שמעון אלא גרוגרות וצימוקים בלבד ומידי אחרינא לא והתניא *היה אוכל בתאנים והותיר והעלן לגג לעשות מהן גרוגרות בענבים והותיר והעלן לגג לעשות מהן צימוקין לא יאכל עד שיזמין וכן אתה אומר באפרסקין וחבושין ובשאר כל מיני פירות מני אילימא רבי יהודה ומה היכא דלא דחייה בידים אית ליה מוקצה היכא דדחייה בידים לא כל שכן אלא לאו ר' שמעון היא לעולם רבי יהודה ואוכל אצטריכא ליה סד"א כיון דקאכיל ואזיל לא ליבעי הזמנה קמ"ל כיון דהעלן לגג אסוחי אסחי לדעתיה מינייהו *בעא מיניה רבי שמעון בר רבי מרבי פצעילי

רש"י

מניחין נר. מבעוד יום: ע"ג דקל. וידלק שם בשבת דליכא למיחש לכשיכבה ליסקליה מיניה וגמלא משתמש במחובר דכיון דאקצייה לדבר האסור בין השמשות איתקצי לכולי יומא: ואין מניחין כו' בי"ט. דשקיל ומנח ליה ומשתמש באילן: מה לי שבת כו'. בשבת נמי שקיל ליה לכשיכבה: שרגא דחנוכתא. אחר שכבה: מקמי חברי. שלא יראוהו בחצר כדאמרינן בפרקין דלעיל (דף כא:) דנותנו בטפח הסמוך לרשות הרבים וידעו שהדליקו בו נר והם גזרו שלא להדליק אי נמי ביום חגם אין מניחין לדלוק אור אלא בבית ע"ז: חברי. שם אומה שהיתה עם פרסיים: הכי הילכתא. בתמיה: בשעת הדחק. סכנה אלמא שלא בשעת הדחק אסור: שזרען בקרקע. ועדיין לא השרישו מהו ללקוט ולאכול: אין מוקצה לר' שמעון בדבר הראוי. אלא בשמן שבנר בשעה שהוא דולק כדתניא לעיל: הואיל והוקצה למצותו. לשבת: הוקצה לאיסורו. איסור כיבוי: והוקצה למצותו לית ליה. בתמיה דקס"ד שמן שבנר דוקא קאמר דאיכא תרתי מוקצה למצוה ומוקצה של שעת דליקתו משום איסור כיבוי אבל מוקצה למצוה גרידא לא אסר ואפילו בשעת המצוה: והתניא סיככה. לסוכה כו': קרמים. בגדי צבעונים שקורין אובריי"א: אפרסקין. פירסיק"י בלע"ז: יינות שמנים. בכלי זכוכית: עד מוצאי י"ט האחרון. והכא מוקצה למצוה איכא מוקצה דאיסור ליכא דאי משום סתירת אהל כי מטא חולו של מועד לסתרי דומיא דנר שכבה: והא ממאי דר' שמעון היא. דמותיבנא לך מיניה: דתני ר' חייא כו' אין נוטלין עצים. בפסח ועצרת מסוכה העשויה לצל ואפילו נפלו משום מוקצה דאיתקצאי מחמת סתירת אהל בי"ט: אלא מן הסמוך לה. אם סמך חבילות עצים אצל דופנה ליכא איסור מוקצה דדעתיה עילויה מאתמול למישקלינהו למחר דלא סתר בהו אהלא ומהך דתני ר' חייא בר יוסף הוי מצי לאותבי ברישא אלא ניחא ליה לאותבי ממתניתא דר' חייא ור' אושעיא כדאמרינן בעלמא (חולין דף קמא.) כל מתניתא דלא מיתניא בי ר' חייא כו': ור' שמעון מתיר. אם נפלה דלית ליה מוקצה והכי מוקמינן ליה במסכת ביצה: ושוין בסוכת החג בחג. שהוקצה למצותה דמצותה כל שבעה אלמא כל שעת מצותה נוהג מוקצה שלה ואע"ג דליכא איסור סתירה: כעין שמן קאמינא. ולא משום איסור אלא משום מצוה דהואיל דהוקצה למצותו דשבת הוקצה לכל זמן איסור דליקתו ולא יותר דאין מצותו אלא בשעת דליקתו ומשכבה אין בו מצוה אבל בסוכת החג מצותה כל שבעה והקצאתה כל זמן מצותה: אלא גרוגרות וצמוקין. גרוגרות תאנים שמעלה לגג ליבשן ומשנשתהו שם מעט אין ראוים לאכילה עד שיתייבשו וכן צימוקים דענבים: היה אוכל בתאנים. רבותא אשמעי' (א)דהוה אכיל ואזיל מכיון דאסקינהו אסח דעתיה ואקצן: חבושין. קויינ"ץ: וכן אתה אומר כו'. ואע"ג דהני חזי כל שעתא ואפי' כשתהו לא נתקלקלו מיהו הואיל ואקצינהו אסירי: אי נימא ר"י. למה לי האך דנקט דדחינהו בידים אפי' הכניסן נמי לאוצר בעו הזמנה: פצעילי

תוספות

הכי נמי מסתברא דרב כר' יהודה ס"ל. בכמה מקומות אשכחן דרב סבר כר' יהודה דאסר מטה שייחדה למעות והניח עליה מעות ואילו לר' שמעון שרי דהא שרי חצוצרות אפי' תקע בה כמה זימני ודכרכי דזוזי (לעיל דף יט:) אלא דבעי לאוכוחי דסבר כר' יהודה במיגו דאיתקצאי בין השמשות כו': מקמי חברי בשבתא. שביום חג שלהם לא היו מניחין נר אלא בבית ע"ז ומאי דקמבעיא ליה בנר חנוכה טפי מבנר שבת משום דלצורך אכילה היו מניחים להם ואע"ג דבשעת הסכנה אמרינן בבמה מדליקין (לעיל דף כא:) דמניחה על שולחנו ודיו הכא מיירי אם יארע שלא הניחה על שולחנו א"נ אומר ר"י דשעת הסכנה דלעיל לאו סכנת חברים קאמר אלא סכנת גזירה שגזרו שלא להדליק נר חנוכה: היכא דדחייה בידים אית ליה. ואף על גב דנר שכבה שרי ר' שמעון אף על גב דדחייה בידים דהתם שאני כיון שכבר פסק דיחוי שלה אבל הכא לעולם הן דחויין כל זמן שמונחין שם: אלא שמן שבנר. לאו דווקא שבנר דההוא אסור משום מכבה כדאמר בפ"ב דביצה (דף כב.) המסתפק ממנו חייב משום מכבה אלא המטפטף מנר ומשום דמוקצה למצותו לא אסור *נר הדולק לטלטל כדפרישית לעיל אלא כדאמר בסוף פירקין משום דהוי בסיס לדבר האסור תימה לר"י דאמאי נקט שמן שבנר טפי ה"ל למינקט אין מוקצה לר' שמעון אלא גרוגרות וצימוקין דדמו טפי לחיטין שזרען דלא איתקצאי לא מחמת מצוה ולא מחמת איסור וליכא למימר דסבר ר' יוחנן דלר' שמעון אין מוקצה בגרוגרות וצימוקין דהא רבי קאמר בסמוך דאית ליה לרבי שמעון מוקצה בגרוגרות וצימוקין ומסתמא לא פליג: עד מוצאי י"ט האחרון של חג. הקשה ר"ת ביום טוב האחרון דלא אסר אלא מטעם מיגו דאיתקצאי בין השמשות מחמת יום שעבר והא רבי שמעון שרי מותר השמן שבנר אף על גב דהוקצה בין השמשות למצותו משום יום הבא ונראה לר"י דבמה שאוסרת הברייתא יום טוב האחרון לא אתיא כר' שמעון: ולא מן הסמוך לה. בפרק המביא כדי יין (ביצה ל: ושם) גרס במשנה אלא מן הסמוך לה ופריך בגמ' והא קסתר אוהלא ומשני מאי מן הסמוך לה סמוך לדפנות והשתא אי גרס בברייתא דהכא אלא מן הסמוך לה אי בסמוך לדפנות ואי גרס ולא מן הסמוך לה מיירי במה שעל הסכך וטעמא משום דסתר אוהלא כדאמר התם: ואם התנה הכל לפי תנאו. בריש המביא (ג"ז שם) פריך עלה והא קא סתר אוהלא ומוקי לה בסוכה נפולה וברעועה דמאתמול דעתיה עלה: אלא בגרוגרות וצימוקין. בירושלמי מפ' שמסריחין בינתיים כיון שמתקלקלין כל כך אין דעתו לקחתם עד שיתקנו היטב: וכן אתה אומר באפרסקין. אף על פי שאין מתקלקלין כל כך מקצה אותם מדעתו: היכא דלא דחייה בידים אית ליה מוקצה. כגון הא דתנן בפרק מפנין (לקמן קכו:) ולא את האוצר ותנן נמי בפרק בתרא (דף קנו:) רבי יהודה אומר אם לא היתה נבלה מע"ש אסורה כו': ואוכל איצטריכא ליה. מדנקט אוכל במוקצה דדחייה בידים נראה דאזיל ואכיל שרי ליה לר"י במוקצה דלא דחייה בידים כגון גבי אוצר: לדבריו

עין משפט נר מצוה

נב א מיי' פ"ס מהלכות שבת הלכה יז ופ"ד מהלכות י"ט הלכה ס סמג לאוין סה טור שו"ע או"ח סימן רעז סעיף ד וסימן תקי"ד סעיף ו:

נג ב מיי' פכ"ו מהלכות שבת הלכה יד סמג לאוין סה טוש"ע או"ח סימן שי סעיף ג:

רבינו חננאל

אותה בשבת. בזמן שיש עליה מעות. פי' מוכני כן. מלשון את הכיור ואת כנו. נמדלת מלשון שילוף. כדתנן המידל בנפנים. וגרסינן במשקין (מ"ק ג) מאי מדלי שלופי. נמצלת מלשון צל. קתני מיהת אין גוררין אותה בשבת בזמן שיש עליה מעות הא אין עליה מעות שרי'. ואע"ג דהוו עליה בין השמשות. ושנינן משנה זו לר' שמעון היא. ורב דאמר כרבי יהודה. דהא רב הוא דאמר מניחין נר ע"ג דקל בשבת [ואין מניחין נר ע"ג דקל ביום טוב]. מכלל דרב כר' יהודה סבר ליה דאסר הנר שהדליקו בו בשבת אין מטלטלין אותו. אבל ביו"ט שמטלטלין אותו ונמצא משתמש במחובר לקרקע אסור. (ואין מניחין נר ע"ג דקל ביו"ט) ואוקימנא אליבא דר' יהודה דשני ליה בין שבת ליו"ט. אבל ר' שמעון לא שני ליה בטלטול הנר בין שבת ליו"ט. איני דרב כר' יהודה עביד ליה. והא רב התיר לטלטל נר מפני חבארי בשבת. ושנינן הא אמר רב כדאי הוא ר"ש לסמוך עליו בשעת הדחק מכלל דרב סבר לית הלכתא כר' שמעון. והא דא"ר יוחנן אין מוקצה לר"ש אלא מידי דאיתקצאי לאיסורא כגון שמן שבנר בשעה שדולק או כגון עיטורי סכה וכיוצא בהן הואיל והוקצו למצוה פשוטה היא

רב נסים גאון

שהוא מתיר בנר אומר בפמום ולדבריהם בתלמוד ארץ ישראל או כר' שמעון אפילו נר עצמו יהא מותר נתבאר כבר שר' שמעון מתיר הנר עצמו וכ"ש הפמוט: מהו לטלטולי שרגא דחנוכה מיקמי חבארא בשבתא. שמענו כי בימי החברים פרסיי' היו חברים מחזרין בכל בתי ישראל ומכבין את הנרות ולוקחין מכל בית נר והיה צער גדול לישר' מזה המעשה מפני שהיו מוליכין את נרותיהם לע"ז ואשכחנן בפרק ב' (דגיטין דף טז) רבה בר בר חנה חלש על ר' יהודה ורבנן לשיולי ביה בעו מיניה שנים שהביאו גט ממדינת הים צריכים שיאמרו בפנינו נכתב בפנינו נחתם או אין צריכין אמר להו אין צריכין ומה אילו אמרו בפנינו גירשה מי לא מהימני אדהכי אתא ההוא חברא שקלא לשרגא מיקמייהו

…רחמנא או בטולך או בטולא דבר עשו למימרא דרומאי מעלו מפרסאי והא תני ר' חייא מאי דכתיב (איוב לח) אלהים הבין דרכה והוא ידע את מקומה ידע הקב"ה בישראל שאין יכולים לקבל גזירות של … הרשע לפיכך הגלה אותם לבבל ובמס' יבמות בפרק הבא על יבמתו (דף סג) אמרו מאי דכתיב בגוי נבל אכעיסם ר' יוחנן אמר אלו חברים אמרו ליה לר' יוחנן אתו חבארי לבבל (שאג) [שגא] ונפל [א"ל] מקבלי … דא תריץ ויתיב גזרו על שלש מפני שלש על בשר מפני המתנות על מרחצאות מפני טבילה קא מחטטי שכבי מפני ששמחים ביום אידם ובשאלתות דרב אחא מן שבהא כך פי' בפרשת וארא אל אברהם ובמלכות … ים היו חברים שבהן מחזרין על בתי ישראל ומכבין את הנרות וחותין את הגחלים ומוליכין אותן לבית האור שלהן שהיא ע"ז ולא היו עובדים לא אש ולא גחלים שלינו בלילה חוץ מע"ז שלהן שהיא בית … א: כדי הוא ר' שמעון בן יוחי לסמוך עליו בשעת הדחק. הוא ר' שמעון שאמר הנר שכבתה מותר לטלטלה דלית ליה מוקצה וכל ר' שמעון סתם במשנה ובברייתא הוא ר"ש בן יוחאי וכל ר' יהודה סתם הוא ר' יהודה בר' אלעאי ובמס' מנחות בפרק הקומץ (דף יח) אמרו מפני שר' יהודה בנו של ר' אלעאי ור' אלעאי תלמידו של ר' אליעזר שנה לך משנת ר' אליעזר:

מסורת הש"ס

[ברכות ט. עירובין מו.] גיטין יט. נדה ז. ע:

נ"ל הוקצה [תוס' ישנים]

לעיל כב. סוכה י. [תוספתא סוכה פ"א]

ביצה ל:

ביצה כו:

[ביצה מ.]

הגהות הב"ח

(א) רש"י ד"ה היה אוכל וכו' אתא אשמעי' … יכוס:

גליון הש"ס

תוס' ד"ה שמן וכו' נר הדולק לטלטל כדפי' לעיל דף מב תוס' ד"ה נאותין:

פצעילי *תמרה לרבי שמעון מהו א"ל *[א]אין מוקצה לר"ש אלא גרוגרות וצימוקין בלבד ורבי לית ליה מוקצה והתנן *[ב]אין משקין ושוחטין את המדבריות אבל משקין ושוחטין את הבייתות ותניא *[ג]אלו הן מדבריות כל שיוצאות בפסח ונכנסות ברביעה בייתות כל שיוצאות ורועות חוץ לתחום ובאות ולנות בתוך התחום ר' אומר אלו ואלו בייתות הן ואלו הן מדבריות כל שרועות באפר ואין נכנסות לישוב לא בימות החמה ולא בימות הגשמים איבעית אימא הני נמי כגרוגרות וצימוקין דמיין ואי בעית אימא לדבריו דר"ש קאמר ליה וליה לא סבירא ליה ואיבעית אימא לדבריהם דרבנן קאמר להו לדידי לית לי מוקצה כלל לדידכו אודו לי מיהת דהיכא דיוצאות בפסח ונכנסות ברביעה דבייתות נינהו ורבנן אמרו ליה לא מדבריות נינהו אמר רבה בר בר חנה אמר ר' יוחנן אמרו הלכה כרבי שמעון ומי א"ר יוחנן הכי והא בעא מיניה ההוא סבא קרויא ואמרי לה סרויא מר' יוחנן קינה של תרנגולת מהו לטלטולי בשבת אמר ליה כלום עשוי אלא לתרנגולין הכא במאי עסקינן דאית ביה אפרוח מת הניחא למר בר אמימר משמיה *(דרב) *דאמר מודה היה ר' שמעון בבעלי חיים שמתו שאסורין אלא למר בריה דרב יוסף משמיה דרבא דאמר חלוק היה רבי שמעון [אפי'] בבעלי חיים שמתו שהן מותרין מאי איכא למימר הכא במאי עסקינן בדאית ביה ביצה והאמר *רב נחמן מאן דאית ליה מוקצה אית ליה נולד דלית ליה מוקצה לית ליה נולד דאית ביה ביצת אפרוח כי אתא רב יצחק בר' יוסף א"ר יוחנן הלכה כר' יהודה ור' יהושע בן לוי אמר הלכה כרבי שמעון אמר רב יוסף היינו דאמר רבה בר בר חנה א"ר יוחנן אמרו הלכה כרבי שמעון אמרו וליה לא סבירא ליה א"ל אביי לרב יוסף ואת לא תסברא דר' יוחנן כר' יהודה הא ר' אבא ורבי אסי איקלעו לבי ר' אבא דמן חיפא ונפל מנרתא על גלימיה דר' אסי ולא טילטלה מאי טעמא לאו משום דרבי אסי תלמידיה דר' יוחנן הוה ור' יוחנן כרבי יהודה ס"ל דאית ליה מוקצה א"ל מנרתא קאמרת מנרתא שאני דא"ר אחא בר חנינא א"ר אסי הורה ריש לקיש בצידן מנורה הניטלת בידו אחת מותר לטלטלה בשתי ידיו אסור לטלטלה ור' יוחנן אמר אנו אין לנו אלא בנר כרבי שמעון אבל מנורה בין ניטלה בידו אחת בין ניטלה בשתי ידיו אסור לטלטלה וטעמא מאי רבה ורב יוסף דאמרי תרווייהו הואיל ואדם קובע לה מקום אמר ליה אביי לרב יוסף והרי כילת חתנים דאדם קובע לו מקום ואמר שמואל משום רבי חייא *כילת חתנים מותר

רש"י

פצעילי תמרה. [א]) תמרים הגלקטים קודם בישולן וכונסין אותם בסלים שעושין מלולבין והן מתבשלות מאליהן מהו לאכול מהן קודם בישולן מי מודה בהן דמוקצות הן כגרוגרות וצימוקין או לא: אלא בגרוגרות וצימוקין. דאיכא תרתי דדחינהו בידים ולא חזו: ור' לית ליה מוקצה. דקס"ד מדבעי מיניה אליבא דרבי שמעון אלמא הוה שמיע ליה מאבוה דכרבי שמעון סבירא ליה: משקין. דרך להשקות בהמה לפני שחיטה שתהא נוחה להפשיט: המדבריות. הבייתות: ברביעה. במרחשון: ואלו מדבריות כל שרועות באפר. והני מיהא אסירי אלמא אית ליה מוקצה: איבעית אימא הני. מדבריות נמי כגרוגרות דמי דדחינהו בידים ויש טורח לילך ולהביאם: ואיבעית אימא. ההיא דפצעילי תמרה לדבריו דרבי שמעון קאמר ולר' לא ס"ל: ה"ג אמר רבה בר בר חנה א"ר יוחנן אמרו הלכה כר' שמעון: אמרו. בני הישיבה: סרויא קרויא. על שם מקומו: כלום עשוי. לשום תשמיש: אלא לתרנגולין. הלכך ה"ל מלאכתו לאיסור ואסור אלמא אית ליה מוקצה: דאית ביה אפרוח מת. דלא חזי למיכל ולכלבים נמי לא חזי ואף על גב דא"ר שמעון מחתכין את הנבלה לפני הכלבים הני מילי במסוכנת אבל בריאה לא דלא הוה דעתיה מאתמול לכלבים והאי אפרוח שמת בשבת נמי לא הוה דעתיה מאתמול לכלבים: הניחא למר כו' דאמר מודה היה ר"ש. דאע"ג דאמר מחתכין הנבלה לפני הכלבים ה"מ במסוכנת דדעתיה עליה מאתמול לכלבים אבל מודה הוא בבעלי חיים כלומר בבריאים שמתו שאסורין שפיר קתנלת דלרבי שמעון גופיה לא חזי לכלבים: מאי איכא למימר. הא חזי לכלבים: דאית בה ביצה. שנולדה היום ומודה ר' שמעון בנולד: והא אמר רב נחמן כו'. בשמעתא קמייתא דביצה: דאית בה בילת אפרוח. וכלב לא אכיל לה משום *קליפה: וליה לא סבירא ליה. לר' יוחנן לא סבירא דתיהוי הלכה כר' שמעון והיינו דרב יצחק: ואת לא תסברא. ומקמי דשמעת ליה לדרב יצחק לא הוה ידעת דר' יוחנן כר' יהודה: בשתי ידים אסור לטלטלה. כדמפרש טעמא לקמיה דלאו לטלטולי עבידא דאדם קובע לה מקום: ור' יוחנן אמר אנו אין לנו. שום היתר בהלכות טלטול נרות: אלא בנר. ישן כרבי שמעון דמתיר אבל מנורה כו' הלכך אי לאו נודרב יצחק לא הוה ידענא ליה אבל השתא ידענא דכר' יהודה סבירא ליה בכולהו בר ממוקצה מחמת מיאוס דנר ישן:

תוספות

לדבריו דר' שמעון קאמר ליה וליה לא סבירא ליה. משמע דמספקא ליה אי ר' סבר לה כר' שמעון ותימה אמאי לא מוכח מהיא דלקמן דסבר כר"ש דאמר פעם אחת הלך ר' כו' והורה במנורה כר"ש בנר וכן מברייתא דמייתי באין ·לדין* בכור תם שנפל לבור ר' יהודה הנשיא אומר ירד מי שבקי במומין ויראה אם יש בו מום יעלה וישחוט כו' ומיהו במאי דמתיר לראות במומין לא אתי כר"ש אלא במאי דלית ליה מוקצה ומיהו רש"י לא גרים בכור תם אלא בכור שנפל לבור והשתא מצי אתי כר' יהודה ויראה אם היה בו מום זה מעי"ט*:

הכא במאי עסקינן דאית ביה אפרוח מת. פירש הר"ר יוסף דלא נקט אפרוח חי משום דחי חזי לשחק בו תינוק כסבורה ואין נראה דהא בההיא דכופין את הסל לפני האפרוחין (לעיל דף מג·) משמע דאסור לטלטל ועוד אי מחיים שרי אמאי קאמר בסמוך דמודה ר"ש בבעלי חיים שמתו שאסורין אלא ודאי בעלי חיים *מוקצין הם כגרוגרות וצימוקין ומקצה אותם גם מכלבים ולא דמי לבשר תפל שמותר לר"ש מדפריך בפרק מפנין (לקמן קכח·) על רב הונא דשרי והא תלמיד דרב הוה ורב כר' יהודה סבירא ליה אבל לר' שמעון משמע דשרי משום דאינו מקצהו מכלבים כמו בעלי חיים:

דאית ביה ביצה. דאסור משום נולד ל"ע דר' יוחנן גופיה *מפרש טעמא דביצה משום משקין שזבו ואפשר דמשום הכי לא הוה אסר ר"ש לטלטלה אלא לאכילה:

דאית ביה בילת אפרוח. נראה לר"י דאסור לר' שמעון משום דכיון דאית ביה אפרוח הוי *כמו גרוגרות וצימוקין וקא מיבעיא ליה לסבא קירוייא אי שרי לטלטולי על ידי שינער משם הבילה אי חשיב כמו מניח או כשכח והשיב לו רבי יוחנן כלום עשוי אלא לתרנגולין ואין זה כשכח אלא כמניח ואסור:

אמר ליה מנרתא שאני. וא"ת אמאי לא מוכח מהא דא"ר יוחנן בפ' לולב וערבה (סוכה מו:) דסוכה אפי' בשמיני אסורה אלמא אית ליה מיגו דאיתקצאי כו' כר' יהודה ותירץ ר"י דנר אינו מוקצה למצותו מטלטול שאין ביטול מצוה בטלטול ולא דמי לסוכה דאיתקצאי ביה"ש מחמת מצוה ולהכי אינו יכול להוכיח מסוכה אנר: לעיל לאו משום דר' אסי תלמידו דר' יוחנן כו'. וא"ת דילמא ר' אסי כרב רביה סבירא ליה כדאמר לעיל גבי שרגא דחנוכה אמרו ליה רב כהנא ורב אסי לרב הילכתא הכי ונראה דרב אסי דלעיל לאו היינו ר' אסי דהכא דההוא דלעיל חבירו של רב כהנא והכא ר' אסי חבירו של ר' אמי*: אין לנו אלא בנר כר' שמעון. פי' במוקצה מחמת מיאוס דהיינו נר ישן שלא הדליקו בה באותה שבת ולעיל דפסיק כרבי יהודה היינו בהדליקו בה באותה שבת דהוי מוקצה מחמת איסור והא דפסיק בפרק בתרא* כר"ש בנבלה לפני הכלבים אף על גב דנבלה מוקצה מחמת איסור היא כדפר"ת (לעיל יט: ד"ה ושמואל) התם *לא דחייה בידים אבל הכא דדחייה בידים סבר כר' יהודה ולפי זה לא קיימי ר' יוחנן וריב"ל דפסקי כר' שמעון אהדא ברייתא דר' יוחנן קאי אברייתא דכל הנרות של מתכת מטלטלין כו' אבל במאי דקאמר ר' יהודה בברייתא דלעיל מטלטלין נר חדש אבל לא ישן לא סבר רבי יוחנן כוותיה וריב"ל אברייתא דמטלטלין נר חדש קאי דבההיא ברייתא שרי רבי

א) אין נראה לר"י פירוש זה דל"ד לגרוגרות וצימוקין דלא דחיה בידים ונ"ל כפירוש הערוך שפירש פצעילי תמרה לשון מפצע שמפצעין תמרים כדי להתבשל ולהתייבש ובעת הפציעה מתקלקלת מאליהם ואחר זמן משתבחות ודמי לגרוגרות וצימוקין אף שגרוגרות וצימוקין מתקלקלות יותר מהם. [תוספות ישנים]:

רבינו חננאל

וכן הא דאמר ליה [ר'] לר' שמעון בריה אין מוקצה לר' שמעון אלא גרוגרות וצמוקין בלבד פשוטה היא: אמר רבה בר בר חנה א"ר יוחנן אמרו הלכה כר"ש איני והא בעא מיניה ההוא סבא קרוייה קינה של תרנגולין מהו לטלטלה בשבת ואמר ליה אסור כלום עשוי אלא לתרנגולים מכלל דר' יוחנן כר' יהודה סבירא ליה דאית ליה מוקצה. ושנינן בדאית ליה בהאי קינה אפרוח מת ומשום הכי אסורה לטלטלה הניחא למ"ד בעלי חיים שמתו בשבת דברי הכל אסור לטלטלן בשבת הא אפילו לר' שמעון ואלא למ"ד ר"ש מתיר בבעלי חיים שמתו שמותר לטלטלן אע"ג דאית בהאי קינה אפרוח שמת בשבת ר"ש מתי אמאי קא אסר ר' יוחנן והא איהו הלכתא כר' שמעון סבירא ליה. ואסיקנא בדאית בהאי קינה ביצה שיש בה אפרוח דלדברי הכל אסורה. ואעפ"כ לא נתברר כי ר' יוחנן כר' שמעון סבירא ליה. וכי אתא רב יצחק בר' יוסף א"ר יוחנן הלכתא כר' יהודה וריב"ל אמר הלכה כר"ש. אמר רב יוסף היינו דאמר רבה בר בר חנה א"ר יוחנן אמרו הלכה כר"ש וליה לא סבירא ליה. ודייק נמי אביי מדר' אסי נפלה מנרה על גלימיה [בבי] ר' אבא ולא טלטלה. ואמר (משמיה) [משום] דר' אסי תלמיד דר' יוחנן הוא. ור' יוחנן במוקצה סבר לה כר' יהודה. ודחינן להא דאביי. ואמרינן לא אפילו תימא ר' יוחנן כר' שמעון מנרה שני

עין משפט נר מצוה

נד א מיי' פכ"ו מהל' שבת הלכה יד סמג לאוין סה טוש"ע או"ח סימן שי סעיף ב:

[דף כו.]

נה ב ג מיי' פ"ב מהל' יו"ט הלכה ב סמג לאוין עה טור שו"ע או"ח סימן תצז סעיף ב וסימן תצח סעיף ג:

[וע"ע תוספות ביצה כו. ד"ה ת"ר]

והא דלא בעי באפרוח חי אם מותר לטלטל הקינה משום דאפשר להפריחו [תוספות ישנים]:

[ביצה ג.]

א"נ הוי מוקצה מחמת חסרון כיס [תו"י]

[ועי' תוספות חולין יט. ד"ה אמר רב הונא]

מסורת הש"ס

ביצה מ.

שם:[לקמן קנו.]

[ביצה שם]

[נ"ע דרבא]

ביצה כו:

שם ב.

קשה דאפשר להסיר הקליפה ויאכלנה ככלב [תוס' ישנים]

עירובין קב. לקמן קלח:

[דף קנו.]

הסוגיא מתחלת ולפ"ז וכו' הגרסא בס"א נמצא בדף מ ע"א כי שם מקומו

R. Simeon b. Rabbi asked Rabbi: [45*b*] What of unripe dates[2] according to R. Simeon? Said he to him: R. Simeon holds that ***mukzeh*** applies only to drying figs and raisins.

But does not Rabbi accept ***mukzeh?***[3] Surely we learnt: Pasture animals may not be watered and killed,[4] but home animals may be watered and killed. And it was taught: These are pasture animals: those that go out on Passover and re-enter [the town limits] at the rainfall;[5] home animals: those that go out and graze beyond the ***tehum*** and re-enter and spend the night within the ***tehum.***[6] Rabbi said: Both of these are home animals; but the following are pasture animals: those that graze in the meadow[7] and do not enter the town limits[8] either in summer or in winter.[9]—If you wish I can answer: these too are like drying figs and raisins. Alternatively, he[10] answered according to R. Simeon's view, which he himself does not accept. Another alternative: he[11] speaks according to the view of the Rabbis. As for me, I do not accept ***mukzeh*** at all;[12] but even on your view, you must at least agree with me that if they go out on Passover and return at the rainfall they are home animals? But the Rabbis answered him: No! they
a are pasture animals.[1]

Rabbah b. Bar Hanah said in R. Johanan's name: They[2] ruled: The ***halachah*** is as R. Simeon. But did R. Johanan say thus? Surely a certain old man of Kirwaya—others say, of Sirvaya—asked R. Johanan: May a fowl-nest be handled on the Sabbath? He answered him: Is it made for aught but fowls?[3]—Here the circumstances are that it contains a dead bird.[4] That is well according to Mar b. Amemar in Raba's name, who said: R. Simeon admits that if living creatures die, they are forbidden;[5] but on the view of Mar son of R. Joseph in Raba's name, who maintained: R. Simeon differed even in respect of living creatures that died, [ruling] that they are permitted, what can be said?—The reference here is to one [*sc.* a hen coop] that contains an egg.[6] But R. Nahman said: He who accepts [the prohibition of] ***mukzeh*** accepts [that of] ***nolad;*** he who rejects ***mukzeh***, rejects ***nolad?***—That is when it contains the egg of a fledgling.[7]

When R. Isaac son of R. Joseph came,[8] he said in the name of R. Johanan The ***halachah*** is as R. Judah: while R. Joshua b. Levi said: The ***halachah*** is as R. Simeon. R. Joseph observed: Hence Rabbah b. Bar Hanah said in R. Johanan's name, They said, The ***halachah*** is as R. Simeon: ***they*** said, but he himself [R. Johanan] did not rule thus. Said Abaye to R. Joseph: And do you yourself not hold that R. Johanan [rules] as R. Judah?[9] Surely R. Abba and R.
b Assi visited R. Abba of Haifa,[1] when a candelabrum fell on R. Assi's robe, but he did not remove it. What is the reason? Surely because R. Assi was R. Johanan's disciple, and R. Johanan held as R. Judah, who maintained [the prohibition of] ***mukzeh?***—You speak of a candelabrum? he replied. A candelabrum is different, for R. Aha b. Hanina said in R. Assi's name: Resh Lakish gave a practical ruling in Zidon: A candelabrum which can be lifted with one hand may be moved; that which requires two hands may not be moved. But R. Johanan said: In the matter of a lamp we accept no other view but R. Simeon's; but as for a candelabrum, whether it can be lifted by one hand or by two, it may not be moved.[2] And what is the reason?[3]—Rabbah and R. Joseph both say: Because one appoints a place for it. Said Abaye to R. Joseph, But what of a bridal couch[4] for which [too] one appoints a place, yet Samuel said on R. Hiyya's authority: A

(2) Lit., 'burst dates', i.e., unripe dates that fell off from the tree and were placed in the sun to ripen (Jast.). Others: dates that are split and placed in the sun to ripen. Whilst they are ripening and drying they suffer discoloration and are unfit, yet not so unfit as drying figs and raisins. (3) It is now assumed that Rabbi was asked about R. Simeon's view because it is his own too. (4) On Festivals. The animals were first watered, to make it easier to flay them. (5) Which takes place in Marheshwan: thus they spend about eight months in the commons beyond the town limits. (6) V. Glos. (7) Outside the town limits. (8) Lit., 'inhabited territory'. (9) Pasture animals may not be slaughtered on Festivals because they are ***mukzeh***, i.e., their owner has altogether put them out of mind.—Animals were frequently watered before slaughter, in order to facilitate the flaying of their skin. (10) Rabbi, in his reply to his son Simeon. (11) Rabbi, in the last cited Baraitha. (12) So that pasture animals, however defined, are permitted.

a (1) On this passage see Bezah, 40*a* and notes. (2) The scholars of the Academy. (3) I.e., it is ***mukzeh***, and forbidden. Thus he does not rule as R. Simeon. (4) Hence it may not be handled, even according to R. Simeon. (5) They may not even be cut up for dogs. That is if they were in good health at twilight, so that one's thoughts were completely turned away from it. If the animal was dying at twilight and perished after nightfall, R. Simeon maintains that it can be cut up for dogs, because the owner must have thought of it. (6) Laid that day. It is then *nolad* (newly created), which R. Simeon admits is forbidden. (7) I.e., upon which the fowl is brooding. This is quite unfit and the nest may not be handled on all views. (8) From Palestine to Babylon. He was a Palestinean amora, the disciple of R. Abbahu and R. Johanan, and transmitted teachings in the latter's name; he travelled to Babylon (Hul. 101*a*) and acted as an intermediary between the two countries on religious questions. (9) Even before you heard it from R. Isaac.

b (1) A harbour of the Mediterranean sea on the coast of Palestine. (2) Hence, but for the dictum of R. Isaac, R. Joseph would not have known R. Johanan's view. But now he knows that in all cases R. Johanan ruled as R. Judah, that ***mukzeh*** is forbidden, save in the matter of an old lamp, which he holds may be handled, agreeing there with R. Simeon. (3) That a candelabrum which requires both hands for lifting may not be moved. (4) Without an overhead awning. V. also *T.A.* III, 42f, § 122.

bridal couch [46*a*] may be set up and dismantled on the Sabbath?[5] Rather, said Abaye: [it refers to a candelabrum] of [movable] joints.[6] If so, what is the reason of R. Simeon b. Lakish, who permits it? What is meant by 'joints'? Similar to joints, viz., it has grooves.[7] Hence, [if it is of real] joints, whether large or small it may not be handled; also, a large one which has grooves is forbidden on account of a large jointed one;[8] where do they differ? In respect to a small grooved one: one Master holds, a We forbid it as a preventive measure;[1] while the other Master holds, We do not forbid it thus.[2]

But did R. Johanan rule thus?[3] Surely R. Johanan said: The ***halachah*** is [always] as an anonymous Mishnah,[4] and we learnt: As for its wheel-work, if detachable, it has no connection therewith, is not measured with it, and does not protect together with it in [the matter of] a covering over the dead, and it may not be rolled on the Sabbath if there is money upon it.[5] Hence if there is no money upon it, it is permitted, though it was upon it at twilight?[6]—Said R. Zera: Interpret our Mishnah as meaning[7] that there was no money upon it during the whole of twilight, so as not to overthrow[8] R. Johanan's words.

R. Joshua b. Levi said: Rabbi once went to Diospera[9] and gave a practical ruling in respect to a candelabrum as R. Simeon's view in respect to a lamp.[10]—The scholars asked: Did he give a practical ruling in respect to a candelabrum as R. Simeon's view in respect to a lamp, i.e., permissively; or perhaps he gave a restrictive ruling in respect to a candelabrum, and as R. Simeon in respect to a lamp, i.e., permissively?[11] The question stands over.

R. Malkia visited R. Simlai's home and moved a lamp,[12] to which R. Simlai took exception. R. Jose of Galilee visited the town of R. Jose son of R. Ḥanina; he moved a lamp, to which R. Jose son of R. Ḥanina took exception. When R. Abbahu visited R. Joshua b. Levi's town he would move a lamp: when he visited R. Johanan's town he would not move a lamp. What will you: if he holds as R. Judah, let him act accordingly; while if he holds as R. Simeon, let him act accordingly?—In truth, he agreed with R. Simeon, but did not act [thus] out of respect to R. Johanan.

b R. Judah said: An oil lamp may be handled;[1] a naphtha lamp may not be handled:[2] Rabbah and R. Joseph both maintain: A naphtha [lamp] too may be handled.[3]

R. Awia visited Raba's home. Now, his boots were muddied with clay, [yet] he sat down on a bed before Raba. [Thereupon] Raba was annoyed and wished to vex him. Said he to him: What is the reason that Rabbah and R. Joseph both maintain that a naphtha lamp too may be handled?—Because it is fit for covering a utensil, replied he. If so, all chips of the yard may be handled, since they are fit to cover a utensil?—The one [a naphtha lamp] bears the character of a utensil; the others do not bear the

(5) The ordinary bed had an overhead awning. Hence when it was set up or dismantled, technically speaking it constituted the erecting or the taking down of a tent, which is forbidden. But that prohibition does not hold good here, since there is no overhead awning. (6) It may not be handled lest it fall to pieces and be put together again, which is tantamount to making a utensil. (7) It is all fastened in one piece, but by means of grooves it looks like being moveably jointed. (8) Since a large one is generally jointed, even if it is only an imitation, it is still forbidden, lest they be confused with each other.

a (1) Likewise lest it be confused with a jointed candelabrum. (2) Since a small one is not generally jointed. (3) That the *halachah* is as R. Judah. (4) If a Mishnah bears no name it represents the final decision of Rabbi and his colleagues. (5) V. *supra* 44*b*. n. b6. (6) Which renders it *mukzeh*, (7) Lit., 'let our Mishnah be.' I.e., the Mishnah, Kel. XVIII, 2. (8) Lit., 'break'. (9) Probably Diosopolis = Lydda (Jast.). (10) *Menorah* is a branched candlestick; *ner* a single lamp. (11) The exact version of R. Joshua's statement is in doubt. (12) That had gone out.

b (1) Because it is not repulsive. (2) Even R. Simeon agrees, because of its unpleasant odour it cannot be used for anything save its purpose. (3) Its unpleasant odour does not make it repulsive, whilst at the same time it is fit for covering a utensil.

מותר לנטותה ומותר לפרקה בשבת אלא אמר אביי בשל חוליות אי הכי מ״ט דר״ש בן לקיש דשרי מאי חוליות כעין חוליות דאית בה חידקי הלכך ״חוליות בין גדולה בין קטנה אסורה לטלטלה גדולה נמי דאית בה חידקי גזירה אטו גדולה דחוליות כי פליגי בקטנה דאית בה חידקי ״מר סבר גזרינן ומר סבר לא גזרינן ומי א״ר יוחנן הכי והאמר ר׳ יוחנן *הלכה כסתם משנה ותנן *מוכני שלה בזמן שהיא נשמטת אין חיבור לה ואין נמדדת עמה ואין מצלת עמה באהל המת ואין גוררין אותה בשבת בזמן שיש עליה מעות הא אין עליה מעות שריא ואע״ג דהוו עליה ביה״ש א״ר זירא תהא משנתינו שלא היו עליה מעות כל ביה״ש שלא לשבור דבריו של ר׳ יוחנן א״ר יהושע בן לוי פעם אחת הלך רבי לדיוספרא והורה במנורה כר׳ שמעון בנר איבעיא להו הורה במנורה כר שמעון בנר להיתרא או דילמא הורה במנורה לאיסורא וכר׳ שמעון בנר להיתרא תיקו רב מלכיא איקלע לבי רבי שמלאי וטילטל שרגא ואיקפד ר׳ שמלאי ר׳ יוסי גלילאה איקלע לאתריה דר׳ יוסי ברבי חנינא טילטל שרגא ואיקפד ר׳ יוסי בר׳ חנינא *ר׳ אבהו כי איקלע לאתריה דר׳ יהושע בן לוי הוה מטלטל שרגא כי איקלע לאתריה דר׳ יוחנן *לא הוה מטלטל שרגא מה נפשך אי כרבי יהודה סבירא ליה ליעבד כרבי יהודה אי כר׳ שמעון סבירא ליה ליעבד כר׳ שמעון לעולם כר׳ שמעון ס״ל ומשום כבודו דר׳ יוחנן הוא דלא הוה עביד °א״ר יהודה שרגא דמשחא שרי לטלטולה דנפטא אסור לטלטולה רבה ורב יוסף דאמרי תרוייהו דנפטא נמי שרי לטלטולה (דהואיל וחזי לכסות ביה מנא) רב אויא איקלע לבי רבא הוה מאיסן בי כרעיה בטינא אתיבי אפוריא קמיה דרבא איקפד רבא בעא לצעוריה א״ל מ״ט רבה ורב יוסף דאמרי תרוייהו שרגא דנפטא נמי שרי לטלטוליה א״ל הואיל וחזיא לכסויי בה מנא אלא מעתה כל צרורות שבחצר מטלטלין הואיל וחזיא לכסויי בהו מנא א״ל הא איכא תורת כלי עליה הני ליכא תורת כלי עליה מי לא תניא

רש״י

מותר לנטותה. דסתם כילת חתנים אין לה גג טפח שנקליטין יולאין לשני ראשי המטה באמצעה אחד לכאן ואחד לכאן ונותן כלונס׳ מזה לזה ומשליך האהל עליה והוא שופע לכאן ולכאן וכיון שאינו רחב טפח אינו אהל ואין בו לא בנין ולא סתירה: בשל חוליות. במנורה של פרקים שמא תפול ותתפרק ויחזירנה ונמלא עושה כלי: חידקי. חיתוכין סביב לה קרונ״ש ודומה לפרקים ומאן דחזי סבר של פרקים הוא: גדולה. הואיל ודרכה לעשותה של חוליות כי אית ביה חידקי סברי דחוליות הן ואסור אפילו לריש לקיש כדאמר לעיל ניטלת בשתי ידים אסור לטלטלה: כי פליגי בקטנה דאית בה חידקי. דכולי עלמא ידעי דלאו חוליות נינהו: גזרינן. אטו חוליות: ומי אמר רבי יוחנן הכי. הלכה כר׳ יהודה: תהא משנתינו. דמוכני דקתני הא אין עליה מעות שריא כגון שלא היו עליה בין השמשות והכי תידוק מינה טעמא דיש עליה מעות כשקדש היום הא אין עליה כשקדש היום שריא: לדיוספרא. מקום: איבעיא להו. חדא הוראה הואי והכי קאמר הורה במנורה להיתרא כדרך שהיה ר׳ שמעון מתיר בנר ישן או דילמא שתי הוראות הוה הורה במנורה לאיסור כדאמרן בדחידקי וגזרינן אטו חוליות וכר״ש הורה בנר להיתר: וטלטל שרגא. נר שכבה: לעולם כרבי שמעון סבירא ליה. דאי סבירא ליה דאסור לא הוה מטלטל ליה לכבוד ר׳ יהושע בן לוי דליעבד איסורא: שרגא דמשחא. שדלק בו של שמן: שרי לטלטולה. אחר שכבה כר׳ שמעון דלא מאיס: אבל בנפטא. דמסרח אפילו רבי שמעון מודה דלא חזי אלא למלאכתו: איקפד רבא. משום טינוף המטה: ובעא לצעוריה. בשאלות קשיות:

תוספות

רבי שמעון נר שהדליקו באותה שבת והא דלא פסיק רבי יוחנן כרבי מאיר דהא סבר לגמרי כוותיה דשרי מוקצה מחמת מיאוס ואסר מוקצה מחמת איסור נקט רבי יהודה משום דבכל מקום הוזכר גבי מוקצה ועוד דלא מליט דאית ליה לרבי מאיר מוקצה מחמת איסור גרידא אלא בנר ישן דאיכא תרתי מחמת מיאוס ומחמת איסור אך לפי זה קשה לרשב״א דמשמע דנקט במנורה אין לנו כרבי שמעון אבל רבי שמעון מיהא שרי במנורה ולמאי דמפרש טעמא דמנורה משום דאדם קובע לו מקום היכי שרי רבי שמעון הא אמרי׳ בריש כל הכלים (לקמן דף קכג.) הכל מודים בסיכי וזירי ומזורי כיון דקפיד עלייהו מיחד להו מקום ונראה לפרש דרבי יוחנן פסק כרבי יהודה במוקצה מחמת מיאוס וכ״ש במוקצה מחמת איסור *כדמוכח בפרק בתרא (דף קנז.) דקאמר בכולי שבת הלכה כרבי שמעון בר ממוקצה מחמת מיאוס וחד אמר במוקצה מחמת מיאוס נמי הלכה כרבי שמעון בר ממוקצה מחמת איסור דהיינו שהדליקו בה באותה שבת והא דקאמר אנו אין לנו אלא בנר כרבי שמעון לאו משום דסבר כוותיה בנר אלא כלומר אין לנו שיתיר אפי׳ רבי שמעון דמיקל אלא בנר אבל במנורה אסר והשתא קיימי תרוייהו אחד ברייתא ולא מצי נמי למינקט רבי מאיר:

והא כילת חתנים דאדם קובע לה מקום. פי׳ רשב״א דאדם קובע לה מקום כמו למנורה ואפ״ה שרי שמואל אלא ודאי לא חשיב קביעות שלה ושל מנורה קביעות אלא היכא דקבע מקום לגמרי כדאמר בפ׳ כל הכלים (לקמן קכג. ושם):

דחוליות בין גדולה בין קטנה אסורה. קשה לר״י דבפ״ב דביצה (דף כב:) תנן ג׳ דברים ר״ג מחמיר כב״ש וחשיב אין זוקפין את המנורה ומשמע דב״ה שרי ומפרש התם בגמרא *הכא במנורה של חוליות עסקינן משום דמיחזי כבונה דב״ש סברי יש בנין בכלים ויש סתירה בכלים וב״ה סברי אין בנין כו׳ אלמא שרי ב״ה מנורה של חוליות להחזיר ומאן דשרי בסוף פירקא להחזיר מטה של חוליות ברפוי איכא לאוקמא ה״נ ברפוי אבל למאן דאסר קשה ותירץ ר״י דהתם מיירי כגון שהחוליות מחוברין יחד ואינם מתפרקין ופעמים מטין אותן ופעמים זוקפין אותן *: הורה במנורה להיתרא וכר״ש בנר נמי להיתרא או דילמא במנורה הורה לאיסורא וכר״ש בנר להיתרא. וא״ת אמאי לא קאמר נמי או דילמא הורה במנורה להיתרא כרבי שמעון בנר וכרבי שמעון בנר לא סבירא ליה דכה״ג איתא בהאו טריפות (חולין דף נג: ושם) הורו בטרפחת כרבי בזפק איבעיא להו הורו בטרפחת לאיסורא וכרבי בזפק להיתרא או דילמא הורו בטרפחת להיתרא כרבי בזפק וכרבי בזפק לא סבירא להו וי״ל דהכא לא שייך למיתני מנורה בנר כדתני טרפחת בזפק דהכא אין טעם אחד לשניהם דנר משום מוקצה ומנורה משום בנין ועוד דלא בעי למימר דר׳ לא סבר בנר כר״ש משום דריב״ל פסיק לעיל כר״ש ואם תאמר ובההיא דהנו טריפות אמאי לא קאמר נמי תרוייהו להיתרא כדאמר הכא או דילמא הורו בטרפחת להיתרא וכר׳ בזפק נמי להיתרא ומיהו בלאו הכי מגיהין שם הספרים ול״ג הורו בטרפחת לאיסורא דהא כ״ע שרו לה דתניא התם *היא האם היא טרפחת היא שלחופית וביטל האם *הוה עובדא והאכילה רבי טרפון לכלבים ואמר הלכה חמורך טרפון ואמר ליה רבי עקיבא טועה בדבר משנה אתה וגרס התם הורו בטרפחת להיתרא וכרבי בזפק להיתרא כו׳ ורש״י פי׳ הורה במנורה להיתרא כר״ש בנר וחדא הוראה הוי ואין נראה דאין לתלות מנורה בנר ועוד דהכתי הוי ליה למיבעיא או דילמא תרוייהו להיתרא: דנפטא אסור לטלטלה. פי׳ בקונט׳ אפילו לר״ש וכן משמע דהא שרגא דמשחא דשרי לטלטולה הייט לר׳ שמעון ועוד מדפריך רבא בסמוך לרבה ורב יוסף מ״ש מצרורות שבחצר ואי שרי ר׳ שמעון דנפטא תיקש׳ ליה לכ״ע אליבא דרבי שמעון לכך פי׳ בקונט׳ דהכא אליבא דר׳ שמעון קאי ואע״ג דרב אית ליה מוקצה *גבי מטה שיחדה למעות °ורבה נמי אית ליה כדאמר אביי *כל מילי דמר עביד כרב ורב יוסף נמי משמע דאית ליה מוקצה בפ׳ נוטל (לקמן קמב:) דקאמר כמה חריפא שמעתא דרדקי אימור דאמור בשכח לכתחילה מי אמור הכא אליבא דר״ש קאמר וליה לא ס״ל ומיהו נראה לפרש דהכא מיירי נמי אליבא דרבי יהודה ולא מיירי בהדליקו בו באותה שבת וה״ק שרגא דמשחא של מתכת שרי לטלטולה ואפילו לרבי יהודה כדתניא לעיל (ד׳ מד.) כל הנרות של מתכת מטלטלין דנפטא אסור אפי׳ לרבי שמעון דמאיס טפי מנר ישן ורבה ורב יוסף שרו אפי׳ לרבי יהודה דלא מאיס אלא שריחו רע וחזי לכסויי ביה מנא אבל נר ישן מקלה ליה לגמרי משום דמאיס ואפילו מכיסוי מנא: [ועי׳ תוס׳ מנחות מא: ד״ה כל מילי]:

עין משפט נר מצוה

נו א ב מיי׳ פכ״ו מהל׳ שבת הלכה יא טוש״ע או״ח סי׳ רעט סעיף ז:

[לעיל מד: כליס פי״ח מ״ב]

ולפי זה תמור מוקצה מחמת מיאוס ממוקצה מחמת איסור לר׳ יוחנן דלא דחייה בידים כמו נבילה דפסק כר״ש ורב סבר איפכא דקאמר בפ״ק דחולין [דף טו.] ע״כ לא שרי ר״מ כו׳ אבל שוחט דאין ראוי לכוס לא ור״מ לית ליה בפרקין [לעיל מד.] מוקצה מחמת מיאוס להכי אמר בפרק בתרא דרב סבר כר״י מדכרכי דוזי אסור דהוי מוקצה מחמת מיאוס כדפי׳ ר״ת בפ״ק מוכח׳ מכ״ש דלדידים מחמת איסור חמיר טפי. [תוס׳ ישנים]:

מסורת הש״ס

[לקמן פה.] [ביצה כב:] [לקמן קמח:] עירובין לג. כליס פ״ח מ״ב כליס פ״ח מ״ב. יבמות יח. [כתובות מב:] גיטין פא: ב״ק נה. [כליס פ״ח] סא: [כתובות] [נדה ט:]

[יבמות יד. ע״ש]

[פי׳ תוספות יבמות יד. ד״ה לא הוס]

[צ״ל מותק זכ]

[פי׳ תוספות ולא כ. ד״ה וכ״ש]

[חולין נה:] [סנהדרין לג.]

[לעיל מד:] [לעיל כב.]

רבינו חננאל

שני דא״ר יוחנן אנו אין לנו כר״ש אלא בנר. אבל מנורה בין ניטלת בידו אחת בין ניטלת בב׳ ידים אסור לטלטלה ופשטא מאי ואוקמה רחבה במנורה דאית בה חידקי חידקי שהן כעין חוליו׳ שנראה המעמידה או המטלטלה כבונה. הילכך דחוליות בין גדולה בין קטנה אסורה. לית בה חוליות ואית בה חידקי חידקי גדולה אסורה דמיחלפא בגדול׳ של חוליות. כי פליגי במנורה קטנה דאית בה חידקי חידקי. ר׳ יוחנן סבר גזרינן קטנה דאית בה חידקי אטו גדולה דאית בה חידקי. וריש לקיש סבר לא גזרינן. איני דגזר ר׳ יוחנן והא איהו דאמר הלכה כסתם משנה. ותנן סתמא בכלים פ׳ י״ח במוכני של שידה ואין גוררין אותה בשבת בזמן שיש עליה מעות. ודייקינן מינה. הא אין עליה מעות אסור כשיש עליה מעות. שלא לשבור דברי ר׳ יוחנן. [בדיוספרא] עלתה בתיקו. [אמר רב יהודה] שרגא דמשחא ... וחזו לכסויי בהו מנא דנפטא. שני

גליון הש״ס

גמ׳ אמר ר׳ יהודה שרגא דמשחא. עי׳ ...

הגהות

ע״ב תוס׳ ד״ה רחת: תוס׳ ד״ה דנפטא וכו׳ ורבה נמי אית ליה. עי׳ מנחות דף מא ע״ב תוס׳ ד״ה כל מילי. ובעירובין דף לג ע״ב תוס׳ ד״ה לא תימא:

מעות שריא. ואע״ג דהוו עליה כל בין השמשות ולא גוררין כשאין עליה מעות אלא כשיש עליה מעות. וא״ר זירא תהא משנתנו בשלא היו עליה מעות כל בין השמשות (גורי׳) שלא לשבור דברי ר׳ יוחנן. כלומר לא תקשי לך דר׳ יוחנן אדר׳ יוחנן. והא דהורה ר׳ (זירא ספרא) [בדיוספרא] עלתה בתיקו.

... לחומרא ומוקמינן לה הורה ר׳ במנורה לאיסורא וכר׳ שמעון בנר להיתרא: ר׳ אבהו מטלטל ליה שרגא כר״ש. ובאתריה דר׳ יוחנן לא הוה מטלטל ליה משום כבודו דר׳ יוחנן (רב) [אמר רב יהודה] שרגא דמשחא ... לה. אבל שרגא דנפטא (הוה) אסיר ורבה ורב יוסף שרו אפילו שרגא דנפטא. ואסיק׳ משום דחזו לכסויי בהו מני דנפטא. ואם תאמר אי הכי כל צרורות שבחצר יטלטלו הואיל וחזו לכסויי בהו מנא דנפטא.

א) *השירים והנזמים והטבעות הרי הן ככל הכלים הנטלים בחצר °ואמר עולא מה טעם הואיל ואיכא תורת כלי עליה הכא נמי הואיל ואיכא תורת כלי עליה א"ר נחמן בר יצחק בריך רחמנא דלא כסיפיה רבא לרב אויא רמי ליה אביי לרבה תניא *מותר השמן שבנר ושבקערה אסור ורבי שמעון מתיר אלמא לר' שמעון לית ליה מוקצה ורמינהו *רבי שמעון אומר כל שאין מומו ניכר מעי"ט אין זה מן המוכן הכי השתא התם אדם יושב ומצפה אימתי תכבה נרו הכא אדם יושב ומצפה מתי יפול בו מום מימר אמר מי יימר דנפיל ביה מומא ואת"ל דנפיל ביה מומא מי יימר דנפיל ביה מום קבוע ואם תמצי לומר דנפל ביה מום קבוע מי יימר דמזדקק ליה חכם מתיב רמי בר חמא *מפירין נדרים בשבת [ונשאלין לנדרים שהן] לצורך השבת ואמאי לימא מי יימר דמיזדקק לה בעל התם כדרב פנחס משמיה דרבא *דאמר רב פנחס משמיה דרבא כל הנודרת על דעת בעלה היא נודרת ת"ש *) נשאלין לנדרים של צורך השבת בשבת ואמאי לימא מי יימר דמזדקק ליה חכם התם אי לא מיזדקק ליה חכם סגיא ליה בג' הדיוטות הכא מי יימר דמיזדקק ליה חכם רמי ליה אביי לרב יוסף מי אמר ר' שמעון כבתה מותר לטלטלה כבתה אין לא כבתה לא מאי טעמא דילמא בהדי דנקיט לה כבתה הא שמעינן ליה לר' שמעון דאמר דבר שאין מתכוין מותר דתניא *ר' שמעון אומר גורר אדם כסא מטה וספסל ובלבד שלא יתכוין לעשות חריץ כל היכא דכי מיכוין איכא איסורא דאורייתא כי לא מיכוין גזר ר"ש מדרבנן כל היכא דכי מיכוין איכא איסורא דרבנן כי לא מיכוין שרי ר"ש לכתחילה מתיב רבא *מוכרי כסות מוכרין כדרכן ובלבד שלא יתכוין בחמה מפני החמה ובגשמים מפני הגשמים והצנועין מפשילין במקל לאחוריהן והא הכא דכי מיכוין איסורא דאורייתא איכא כי לא מיכוין שרי רבי שמעון לכתחילה אלא אמר רבא הנח

*) לקמן קנז. נדרים עז:

רש"י

השירים. אצעדות: הרי הן ככל הכלים. אע"פ שאסור לצאת בהן לרה"ר כדאמרי' בפרק במה אשה יוצאה (לקמן נט:) גזירה דילמא שלפא ומחויא מיהו תורת כלי עליהן ומותר לטלטלן שלא כדרך מלבוש: מומו ניכר. גבי בכור קאי: מי יימר דמזדקק ליה חכם. שימלא חכם שיזקק לו ביו"ט לראות אם מום קבוע הוא או לא: מפירין נדרים. בעל לאשתו: ונשאלין לנדרים. לחכם להתירן: שהן לצורך שבת. כגון נדר שלא יאכל היום: ולמאי. מותרת לאכול ואי' שרי לה בעל ליתסר לה משום מוקצה דהא אסחה דעתה ואמרה מי יימר דמזדקק לה בעל: על דעת בעלה. ע"מ אם ירצה הבעל וסמכה עליה דמזדקק לה ביום שמעו: הכא מי יימר כו'. והדיוטות לא מצו למישרייה לבכור אלא במום הידוע לכל כגון מחוסר אבר: איסורא דאורייתא. כיבוי אב מלאכה הוא חריץ ליכא איסור דאורייתא דחופר כלאחר יד הוא דחופר דאמר לקמן תולדה דחורש וחייב ה"מ חופר כדרכו במרא וקרדום: מוכרין כדרכן. ואפי' של כלאים לובשו להראותו בשוק: ובלבד שלא יתכוין. להנאת חימום והא ר"ש היא מדאזיל בתר כוונה: לדבר

תוספות

ואמר עולא מה טעם. להכי איצטריך לפרושי האי טעמא משום דמשמע ליה דסבר האי תנא כמאן דאסר לקמן להתקשט בהן בחצר מדקתני הרי הן ככל הכלים הניטלין בחצר פירוש ככל הכלים שמלאכתן לאיסור דשרי לצורך גופן ומקומן ולהכי מפרש עולא דאיכא תורת כלי עליה וקשה לר"י דאמר בפ' מי שהפך (מ"ק יב: ושם) ר' יהודה נשיאה נפק בחומרתא דמדושא [עי' פי' רש"י שם] שמע ר' אמי ואיקפיד אמר רב יוסף מ"ט איקפיד והתניא השירים והנזמים כו' ומאי פריך מינה אדרבה מינה משמע דאסור לצאת בהן כדפי' והתם קאמר נפק דמשמע דרך מלבוש ונראה לר"י דחומרתא דמדושא הייט טבעת של עץ כמו שמפרשים רבותיו של רש"י ולא של אלמוג כמו שהוא מפרש דאלמוגין מפרש בראש השנה (דף כג.) כסיתא והכא קאמר דמדושא אלא של עץ אחר הוא ששמו מדושא ואין שם תכשיט עליו וכשיוצאים בו דרך מלבוש לא הוי קישוט אלא טלטול בעלמא ולהכי ידע רב יוסף. דר' אמי לא איקפד אלא משום טלטול והשתא מייתי שפיר מהך ברייתא דשרי לטלטל לצורך גופו או לצורך מקומו כשאר כלי' שמלאכתן לאיסור דניטלין לצורך גופו או לצורך מקומו ונפק לחצר קאמר אבל לרה"ר אסור כדאמרי' בפ' הדר (עירובין סט. ושם) ההוא גברא דנפיק בחומרתא דמדושא חזייה לר' יהודה נשיאה כסייה אמר כגון זה מבטל רשות לר' יהודה: **והתנן** ר"ש אומר כל שאין מומו ניכר מעי"ט אין זה מן המוכן. קשה לר"י מאי קא פריך הא ע"כ טעמא דר"ש לאו משום מוקצה אלא משום דסבר דאין רואין מומין ביו"ט דהא ר' יהודה דאית ליה טפי מוקצה שרי התם בריש אין צדין (ביצה כה: ושם) בכור שנפל לבור ירד מומחה ויראה אם יש בו מום יעלה וישחוט ואם לאו לא ישחוט וי"ל דדייק מדלא קתני ר"ש אוסר לפי שאין רואין מומין בי"ט דהוה משמע לכתחילה אסור אבל בדיעבד מבוקר ומדקתני אין זה מן המוכן משמע דהוי מוקצה ואפי' בקרו אינו מבוקר ובהכי פליגי דר' יהודה סבר רואין מומין בי"ט הלכך לא הוי מוקצה דמיירי בנפל בו מום מעי"ט כדמוקי לה התם ור"ש סבר אין רואין ולכך אפי' ביקרו אינו מבוקר משום מוקצה וא"ת דבביצה משמע דאביי סבר כאדא בר אוכמי דאמר לר"ש היכא דנפל בו מום מעי"ט אם בקרו מבוקר דאמר אביי התם כוותיה דרבה בר רב הונא מסתברא מדקתני תלת בבי בברייתא*(ומוקמא הכא ברייתא כאדא בר אוכמי) וע"כ הא דשני ליה בין נפל בו מום קבוע מעי"ט לנפל בו מום בי"ט משום דבנפל בו בי"ט ב) איכא תלתא מי יימר כדקאמר בסמוך ובנפל בו מעי"ט ליכא אלא חד מי יימר דמיזדקק ליה חכם מאי קשיא מנר שכבה דליכא כל הני מי יימר וי"ל דחזר בו אביי ולית ליה *(דאדא בר אוכמי) משמע מתני' דרב אושעיא דאדא בר אוכמי משבש ותני דמתני' דהתם נמי דיקא כרב אושעיא כדמפרש התם: **מי** יימר דנפל ביה מומא. נראה דכל הני מי יימר דקאמר רבה לאו דוקא דהא ר"ש אסר אפי' בנפל בו מום קבוע מעי"ט דהשתא ליכא אלא חד מי יימר דמיזדקק ליה חכם דהא קאי אר' יהודה דלא שרי אלא כשהיה בו מום קבוע מעי"ט דהא פריך אהא דקאמר ר' יהודה ואם לאו לא ישחוט פשיטא ומשני לא צריכא דנפל ביה מאתמול מום עובר והשתא הוה ליה מום קבוע מהו דתימא כיון דדעתיה עילויה נשחטיה קמ"ל א"כ הא דקאמר אם יש בו מום יעלה וישחוט הייט ע"כ מום קבוע מעי"ט ואפי' לאדא בר אוכמי דשרי ר"ש בדיעבד בחד מי יימר מ"מ בנפל בו מום עובר מעי"ט דאיכא תרתי מי יימר לכאורה משמע התם דאסר לכך נראה דלאו דוקא הן דאפי' בחד מי יימר סגי וכן מוכחא מאתקפתא דרמי בר חמא דפריך מחד מי יימר: **מי** יימר דמיזדקק לה בעל. ואע"ג דפירות שנדרה מהם אינם מוקצין לענין טלטול °דהא חזו לשאר בני אדם מ"מ אית לן למימר מיגו דאיתקצאי לכולי יומא אי נמי מיירי בפירות שלה ואסרתן לכל אדם: **מי** יימר דמיזדקק לה בעל. תימה מי דמי התם ודאי לא מיזדקיק ליה חכם דאין רואין מומין בי"ט אבל הכא דאין לך איסור בדבר מיזדקק לה בעל ולית לן למימר מי יימר דהא לר' יהודה דקסבר רואין מומין בי"ט לא אמרי' מי יימר *וי"ל דבעל נמי לא ניחא להזדקק דזימנין דשרי נדרים שנדרה לדבר מצוה: **התם** אי לא מיזדקיק ליה חכם סגי ליה בג' הדיוטות אבל הכא כו'. ואע"ג דבפ"ק דחולין (דף יח:) אמר רב יהודה אמר ר' ירמיה ספק משמיה דשמואל ג' מתירין את הבכור במקום שאין מומחה הייט דוקא במומין מובהקין לגון ניסמת עינו נקטעה ידו נשברה רגלו כדאמרינן בשילהי כל פסולי המוקדשין (בכורות לו:) וה"נ דהוה מצי למימר מי יימר דמזדקקי ליה ג' הדיוטות דודאי לא מיזדקקי ליה משום דאין רואין בי"ט והא דנקט דמיזדקק ליה חכם משום דחכם שרי בכל מומין: ולפ"ז א"ש נמי מבל דאמר אם עבר ותיקנו מתוקן דדוקא חכם אמר הכא לא מיזדקיק אבל בג' הדיוטות לא אמר מי יימר ומיהו לפי מ"ש בפנים ה"ג המ"ל כו' לא א"ש מבל כדפי' לעיל ולהכי נקט חכם משום דמתיר בכל מומין ועיקר טעמא משום דהכא איכא איסורא והתם ליכא והא דנקט התם אם לא מיזדקיק ליה חכם סגיא בג' הדיוטות אע"ג דשרי חשיב מוקצה אי לא סגיא ליה בג' הדיוטות [ת"י]:

כבתה אין לא כבתה לא. כן דרך הש"ס דאע"ג דהוה מצי לאתויי רישא דקתני בהדיא חוץ מן הנר הדולק בשבת מייתי סיפא ודייק מינה*: **דכל** היכא דקמכוין איכא איסורא דאורייתא. וא"ת דהכא בכיבוי ליכא איסורא דאורייתא לר"ש דמלאכה שאינה צריכה לגופה היא וי"ל דה"ק דכי מיכוין איכא איסורא דאורייתא כגון בפתילה וצריך להבהבה °אע"פ שזה התירוץ דחוק הוא הא בלאו הכי פריך ליה שפיר הרב פור"ת:

הנח

א) הא דלא מייתי מתניתין דכל הכלים נוטל אדם קורנס לפצוע בו אגוז י' משום דהתם נמי מיוחד להיתר לפצוע בו אגוזים אבל השירים כו' אין עושין כ"א ללבוש וכיון דאסור להתקשט בהן ה"ל לאסרן לטלטל אפי' כיון דאיכא תורת כלי עליה שרי והכא נמי ל"ש [תו"י]: ב) וליכא למימר דאע"ג דנפל מום מעי"ט איכא ג' מי יימר דהבעלים לא היו יודעים כלל שהיה בו מום לא היא דהתם מפ' כל שאין מומו ניכר להכם משמע הא בעלים יודעים ולאדא בר אוכמי צ"ל דאע"ג דר"ש איירי דנפל ביה מום מעי"ט מדקאי על ר"י ת"מ מיירי נמי בנפל בו מום בי"ט או מום עובר מעי"ט מדקתני אין זה מן המוכן דמשמע דאפילו ביקרו אינו מבוקר [תו"י]

רבינו חננאל

שני צרורו' הואיל ואינה תורת כלי עליהן כמו (ש"מ עולה)[שא' עולא] בשירים ונזמים וטבעות הואיל [תורת] כלי עליהן: **תנא** מותר שמן שבנר ושבקערה אסור להסתפק ממנו. ור"ש מתיר. אלמא לר"ש לית ליה מוקצה. איני והא לענין בכור שנפל בו מום ביו"ט אמר ר"ש אין זה מן המוכן. ושנינן שני זה מזה. אדם מצפה מתי תכבה נרו ויסתפק מן השמן ומכין ליה. אבל לגבי מום ליכא למימר הכי. דאמר מי יימר דנפיל ביה מומא. ואי נפל מי יימר דמזדקיק ליה חכם ומותבינן מהא דתנן מפירין °נדרים בשבת *) לצורך השבת ושנינן כל הנודרת על דעת בעלה היא נודרת ומבתחלה כך נדרה בחזקת שיפר לה בעלה והא [דתנן] נשאלין נדרים לצורך השבת נימא מי יימר דמיזדקיק ליה חכם. ושנינן שני התם דסגיא בג' הדיוטות: **רמי** אביי ומי אמר ר' שמעון כבה הנר מותר לטלטלו. מכלל דאי לא כבה הייש. דילמא כי מטלטל ליה שמא יכבה והא איהו דאמר גורר אדם מטה כסא וספסל ובלבד שלא יתכוין לעשות חריץ הנה דאע"ג דנעשה חריץ כיון דבלא כוונה נעשה לא חייש ר' שמעון. ושני כל היכא דכי מכוין אתי למנגע באיסורא דאורייתא כגון כביית הנר וכיוצא בו חייש ר"ש וגזר מדרבנן. וכל היכא דכי מכוין איסורא [דרבנן] היא. כי לא מכוין שרי ר"ש לכתחלה איני והא מוכרי כסות כו' וכלאים איסורא דאורייתא היא. וכי לא מיכוין שרי ר"ש לכתחלה. ומשני רבא

*) עי' בחלופי גרסאות

רב נסים גאון

התם אי לא מזדקק ליה חכם סגיא בג' הדיוטות. משתכח עיקר דילה במסכתא דנדרים בפרק נערה מאורסה (דף עח) אהרן ובניו וכל ישראל בפרשת נדרים למאי הילכתא אמר רב אחא בר יעקב להכשיר ג' הדיוטות וכותיה גרסי' בפרק יש נוחלין (בבא בתרא דף קכ):

גליון הש"ס

גמ' ואמר עולא. עי' לקמן דף נט ע"ב תוס' ד"ה מאן דרכה: תוס' ד"ה מי יימר דמזדקק לה בעל ואע"ג וכו' דהא חזי לשאר ב"א. עי' לקמן דף קכז ע"ב תוס' ד"ה כיון דתניא: שם ד"ה דכל היכא וכו' אע"פ שזה התירוץ דחוק. עי' בבכורות דף כה ע"א תוס' ד"ה דהוי ליה:

מסורת הש"ס

מו"ק יב. • [לעיל מד. ביצה ל:] • ביצה כו. • לקמן קנז. נדרים עז: • יבמות כט: גיטין פג: נדרים עג: נדה מו: • [תוספתא ביצה פ"ב] [לעיל כב. כט: ביצה כג: פסחים קא: מנחות מא:] כלאים פ"ט מ"ה [לעיל כט:] פסחים כו: • רש"ל מ"ז • רש"ל מ"ז • והר"ס תירן דהכא בנדרים דדחיא בידים הי' לנו לאסרן כי התם דלא דחיא בידים [תוס' יבמות] • [עי' תוס' לעיל כט: ד"ה אי פניו וע' הר"מ]

character of a utensil. Was it not taught: [46b] Bracelets, ear-rings and [finger]rings are like all utensils which may be handled in a yard.[4] And 'Ulla said: What is the reason? Since they bear the character of a utensil. So here too, since it bears the character of a utensil [it may be handled]. R. Naḥman b. Isaac observed: Praised be the All Merciful, that Raba did not put R. Awia to shame.

Abaye pointed out a contradiction to Rabbah: It was taught: The residue of the oil in the lamp or in the dish is forbidden; but R. Simeon permits [it]. Thus we see that R. Simeon rejects *mukẓeh*. But the following opposes it: R. Simeon said: Wherever the blemish was not perceptible from the eve of the Festival, it is not *mukan!*[5]—How compare! There, a man sits and hopes, When will his lamp go out![6] But here, does a man sit and hope, When will it receive a blemish?[7] [For] he argues: Who can say that it will receive a blemish? And even if you say that it will, who can
a say that it will be a permanent blemish?[1] And even if you say that it will be a permanent blemish, who can say that a scholar will oblige him?[2]

Rami b. Ḥama objected: [We have learnt:] Vows can be annulled on the Sabbath,[3] and one may apply[4] for absolution from vows where such is necessary for the Sabbath. Yet why: let us argue, Who can say that her husband will oblige her?[5]—There it is as R. Phinehas in Raba's name. For R. Phinehas said in Raba's name: Whoever vows does so conditional upon her husband's consent.[6]

Come and hear: One may apply for absolution from vows on the Sabbath where it is necessary for the Sabbath. Yet why? let us argue, Who can say that a Sage will oblige him?—There, if a Sage will not oblige, three laymen suffice; but here,[7] who can say that a Sage will oblige him?[8]

Abaye raised a difficulty before R. Joseph: Did then R. Simeon rule, If it [the lamp] is extinguished, it may be handled: thus, only if it is extinguished, but not if it is not extinguished. What is the reason? [Presumably] lest through his handling it, it goes out?[9] But we know R. Simeon to rule that whatever is unintentional is permitted. For it was taught, R. Simeon said: One may drag a bed, seat, or bench, providing that he does not intend to make a rut!—Wherever there is a Scriptural interdict if it is intentional,[10] R. Simeon forbids it by Rabbinical law even if unintentional; but wherever there is [only] a Rabbinical interdict
b even if it is intentional,[1] R. Simeon permits it at the outset if unintentional.

Raba objected: Clothes' merchants may sell in their normal fashion, providing that one does not intend [to gain protection] from the sun in hot weather or from the rain when it is raining; but the strictly religious sling them on a staff behind their back.[2] Now here, though it is Scripturally forbidden if intentional, yet if unintentional R. Simeon permits it at the outset?—Rather said Raba,

(4) Though a woman may not wear them in the street; v. *infra* 59b and M.Ḳ. 12b. (5) V. Beẓ. 27a. A firstling may not be slaughtered and consumed unless it has a blemish: R. Simeon said that it may not be slaughtered on a Festival unless its blemish was already known on the eve thereof. Otherwise the animal was not *mukan*, i.e., prepared for the Festival. Thus he accepts the interdict of *mukẓeh*. (6) To save the oil. Hence R. Simeon holds that it is not really *mukẓeh*. (7) Surely not! In fact, he does hope, but without expecting it, whereas one does expect a lamp to go out.

a (1) For a temporary blemish does not permit the animal to be slaughtered. (2) A scholar had to examine the blemish and declare it permanent. Could he be sure that he would obtain a scholar for this on the Festival? (3) A husband can annul his wife's vows, or a father his daughter's. (4) To a scholar. (5) When a woman forswears benefit from anything, she thrusts it away from herself, and it becomes like *mukẓeh*. Even if her husband annuls her vow, she could not have anticipated it, and so it should remain *mukẓeh*. (6) Hence she relies that her husband will annul it as soon as he is cognizant of it and the object was never *mukẓeh*. (7) In the case of the blemish of a firstling. (8) Absolution can be granted by a Sage or three laymen; but only a Sage can declare a blemish permanent, unless it is obvious, e.g., when a limb is missing. (9) By lifting it up he may create a draught. (10) Extinguishing a light is Scripturally forbidden.

b (1) E.g., indirectly making a rut by dragging a heavy article over the floor. (2) V. *supra* 29b.

[47a] leave the lamp, oil, and wicks alone,[3] because they become a base for a forbidden thing.[4]

R. Zera said in R. Assi's name in R. Johanan's name in R. Hanina's name in the name of R. Romanus: Rabbi permitted me to handle a pan with its ashes.[5] Said R. Zera to R. Assi: Did R. Johanan say thus? But we learnt: A man may take up his son while he is holding a stone, or a basket containing a stone. Whereon Rabbah b. Bar Hanah said in R. Johanan's name: The reference is to a basket filled with fruit. Thus, only because it contains fruit; but if it does not contain fruit, it is not so?[6] *'He was astonied for a while,'*[7] then answered, Here too it means that it [the pan] contains [also] some grains [of spice]. Abaye objected: Did grains have any value in Rabbi's house?[8] And should you answer, They were fit for the poor,—surely it was taught: 'The garments of the poor for the poor, and the garments of the wealthy for the wealthy'.[9] But those of the poor are not [deemed fit] for the purpose of the
a wealthy?[1] But, said Abaye, it is analogous to a chamber pot.[2] Raba observed: There are two refutations to this. Firstly, a chamber pot is repulsive, while this is not repulsive.[3] And secondly, a chamber pot is uncovered, whereas this is covered![4] Rather, said Raba, when we were at R. Nahman's we would handle a brazier on account of its ashes,[5] even if broken pieces of wood were lying upon it.[6]

An objection is raised: And both[7] agree that if it [a lamp] contains fragments of a wick, it may not be handled.[8] Said Abaye: They learnt this of Galilee.[9]

Levi b. Samuel met R. Abba and R. Huna b. Hiyya standing at the door of R. Huna's college. Said he to them: Is it permissible to re-assemble a weaver's frame on the Sabbath?[10]—It is well, answered they. Then he went before Rab Judah, who said: Surely Rab and Samuel both rule: If one re-assembles a weaver's frame on the Sabbath, he is liable to a sin-offering.[11]

An objection is raised: If one puts back the branch of a candelabrum on the Sabbath, he is liable to a sin-offering; as for the joint of a whitewasher's pole,[12] it must not be re-inserted, yet if
b one does re-insert it, he is exempt, but it is forbidden.[1] R. Simai said: For a circular horn, one is liable; for a straight horn, one is exempt![2]—They[3] ruled as this Tanna. For it was taught: The sockets of a bed,[4] the legs of a bed, and the archer's tablets,[5] may not be re-inserted, yet if one does re-insert [them], he

(3) They cannot be compared with others. (4) *Sc.* the flame. Whilst the lamp is alight everything may be regarded as subsidiary to the flame: R. Simeon admits that such *mukzeh* is forbidden. (5) Used for fumigating. This is the meaning as first supposed. Ashes are *mukzeh*, and it is assumed that he was permitted to move the ashes on account of the pan, which is a utensil. (6) And the pan is analogous. (7) Dan. IV, 16. (8) Surely not! Hence the pan with the ashes may not be handled on their account. (9) The reference is to the minimum size of material which is liable to defilement as a 'garment'. The smallest size which has any value to a wealthy person is three handbreadths square; if it is less, he throws it away. A poor man, however, endeavours to find a use for it even if it is only three fingerbreadths square, and that accordingly is his minimum (cf. *supra 26b seq.*). These are the minima for the wealthy and the poor respectively which are technically called 'garments.'

a (1) They do not rank as 'garments' when in a wealthy man's possession. The same principle applies here. (2) Which may be carried away with the excrements, and similarly the pan and ashes. (3) Hence the former must be removed. (4) Their shovels or coal pans were covered with a lid or top. (5) I.e., when the ashes were needed for covering anything. These ashes were counted upon for this from before the Sabbath, and hence the whole might be handled. So here too, R. Romanus states that Rabbi permitted him to handle a fumigating pan on account of the ashes. (6) The latter might not be handled, and therefore the utensil which contained it likewise, save that it also contained ashes. (7) R. Judah and R. Simeon. (8) The same applies to pieces of wood on a brazier. For the lamp also contains oil, just as the brazier contains ashes too. (9) Owing to the abundance of oil in Galilee the residue of oil in the lamp would be of no value to its owner, and therefore the lamp with the fragments of wick may not be handled on account of its oil (Tosaf. and R. Nissim Gaon). (10) The frame or loom consisted of jointed parts, which fitted into each other. (11) If done in ignorance. (12) The handle of the painter's brush was jointed, to allow of different lengths according to requirements.

b (1) A candelabrum is not taken to pieces frequently, and therefore when one inserts its branches he finishes its manufacture; hence he is liable to a sin-offering, it being a general rule that this is incurred for the completion of any utensil. But a painter's brush is continually taken to pieces; therefore the insertion of one of its parts is only temporary and does not complete it. (2) These are musical instruments into which reeds were inserted to give various notes; v. *T.A.* III, 96. The putting together of the former was skilled work; hence liability is incurred. But the latter was assembled amateurishly, being frequently taken to pieces; hence no liability is incurred.—The difficulty is presented by the branch of a candelabrum, whose principle is the same as a weaver's frame. (3) R. Abba and R. Huna b. Hiyya. (4) Into which the legs of a bed fitted, to prevent them from being rotted by the damp earth. (5) Rashi: a small wooden plaque inserted in the bow upon which the arrow presses before it is released. Jast. translates: 'the boards on which the straw rests', but does not make it clear what fitting or joining is required there.

הנח לנר שמן ופתילה הואיל (א) דנעשה בסיס לדבר האסור א"ר זירא א"ר אסי א"ר יוחנן אמר ר' חנינא אמר רבי רומנוס לי התיר רבי לטלטל מחתה באפרה א"ל רבי זירא לרבי אסי מי אמר רבי יוחנן הכי והתנן *נוטל אדם בנו והאבן בידו או כלכלה והאבן בתוכה ואמר רבה בר בר חנה א"ר יוחנן בכלכלה מלאה פירות עסקינן טעמא דאית בה פירי הא לית בה פירי לא *°אישתומם כשעה חדא ואמר הכא נמי דאית בה קרטין אמר אביי קרטין בי רבי מי חשיבי וכי תימא חזו לעניים והתניא *בגדי עניים לעניים בגדי עשירים לעשירים *אבל דעניים לעשירים לא אלא אמר אביי מידי דהוה אגרף של ריעי אמר רבא שתי תשובות בדבר חדא גרף של ריעי מאים והאי לא מאים ועוד גרף של ריעי מיגלי והאי מיכסי אלא אמר רבא כי הוינן בי רב נחמן [א]הוה *מטלטלינן כנונא אגב קיטמא ואע"ג דאיכא עליה שברי עצים מיתיבי ושוין שאם יש בה שברי פתילה שאסור לטלטל *אמר אביי [ב]בגלילא שנו לוי בר שמואל אשכחינהו לרבי אבא ולרב הונא בר חייא דהוו קיימי אפיתחא דבי רב הונא אמר להו מהו להחזיר מטה של טרסיים בשבת אמרו ליה [ג]שפיר דמי אתא לקמיה דרב יהודה אמר הא רב ושמואל דאמרי תרוייהו המחזיר מטה של טרסיים בשבת חייב חטאת מיתיבי *המחזיר קנה מנורה בשבת חייב חטאת קנה סיידין לא יחזיר ואם החזיר פטור אבל אסור רבי סימאי אומר °קרן עגולה חייב קרן פשוטה פטור אינהו דאמור כי האי תנא דתניא מלבנות המטה וכרעות המטה ולווחים של סקיבס [ד]לא יחזיר ואם החזיר פטור אבל

דניאל ד

[לעיל כט:]

לדבר האסור. לשלהבת דבכי האי מוקצה מודה ר"ש שהכלי טפל לשלהבת בעודה בו ולאו משום דחייש לכבייה: בסיס. מושב את כנו מתרגמינן בסיסיה: א"ר רומנוס לי התיר רבי לטלטל מחתה. של לבונה באפרה קס"ד באפרה עם אפרה קאמר שהאפר מוקצה ולא הא צריכין לו ואשמעינן דאגב מחתה דאיכא תורת כלי עליה טלטלה עם אפרה: נוטל אדם. הכלכלה בשבת והאבן בתוכה: הא ליכא פרי לא. דכלי נעשה בסיס לאבן וטפלה לו ובטל תורת כלי דידיה והכי נמי נעשית מחתה בסיס לאפר ורבי יוחנן שמעי' ליה לעיל דכר' יהודה סבירא ליה: דאית ביה קרטין. שנשתיירו מן האור ולבונה דחזיא להריח ואגב לבונה מטלטל למחתה עם אפרה דומיא דכלכלה מלאה פירות והאבן בתוכה: קרטין. של שיור לבונה: בי רבי. דנשיא ועשיר הוא מי חשיבי: בגדי עניים. שלש על שלש הוא. שחוטן עבה הוו בגדים לעניים לענין טומאה: בגדי עשירים. שלשה על שלשה הוו בגדים לעשירים וכל שכן לעניים אבל בגדי עניים לעשירים לא הוה בגד גבייהו ולא מקבלי טומאה הכא נמי בי רבי (ג) בטלי קרטין: אלא אמר אביי. הא דשרי ליה לטלטל מחתה באפרה משום דאפרה מאיס עליה לראותו והוי כגרף של רעי דתניא במסכת ביצה (דף לו:) מותר להוציאו לאשפה שבחצר: גרף. כלי חרס המוכן לכך: מיכסי. כל מחתות מכוסות הן ויש בהן נקבים להוציא הריח: כנונא. כלי נחשת שמביאין בו האור לפני שרים להתחמם: אגב קטמיה. שהיו צריכין לאפרו לכסות רוק או צואה וא"ת מה צד איסור יש כאן היינו רבותא דאע"ג דאיכא עליה שברי עצים והא דר' רומנוס נמי האי מחתה באפרה דקאמר מחתה בשביל אפרה שהיה צריך לו ודעתייהו עליה מאתמול ורבותא אשמעינן (כיון) אע"ג דאיכא עליה שברי עצים דהוי ככלכלה של פירות והאבן בתוכה: ושוין. ר' יהודה ור"ש שנחלקו בנר ישן: בגלילא שנו. שחשובות להן שברי פתילה שאין בגדים של פשתן מצויין להם הלכך לא בטלי ונעשה נר בסיס להן: טרסיים. צורפי נחשת או גרדיים והולכין מעיר לעיר למלאכתן ונושאין עמהן מטות של פרקים: חייב חטאת. הוא תחלתו וגמרו ונמצא עושה כלי וחייב משום מכה בפטיש אב לכל גומרי מלאכה ולא משום בנין דאין בנין בכלים: קנה מנורה. שעושין ממנה קנים לנרות הרבה ונוטלין הימנה ובשעת הצורך מחזירין אותו: קנה של סיידין. הטחין ומלבנין הבית בסיד יש להן קנים של פרקים ונותן מטלית בראשה ושורין בסיד המחוי וטח את הבית וכשהוא טח מלמטה אי אפשר לו אלא בקנה קצר וכשהוא הולך ומגביה מוסיף קנה על קנה ומאריכו: פטור. שאין זה גמרו שהרי צריך לחזור ולפרקו תמיד: קרן עגולה וקרן פשוטה. שניהם מין כלי זמר והוא עשוי נקבים נקבים ככברה ומכניס בהן חלילים ומוציאין קולות הרבה קרן עגולה מעשה אומן הוא וצריך לתקוע בנקבים בחוזק והויא מלאכה ובקרן פשוט מכניסו בריוח ודרכן לפרקם תמיד ופטור קתני מיהת בקני מנורה דחייב והוא הדין למטה של טרסיים: אינהו. רבי אבא ורב הונא בר חייא: דאמור כי האי תנא. כרבי שמעון דמתיר לכתחלה: מלבנות המטה. כעין רגלים קטנים יש להן בית קיבול ומכניס לתוכן ראשי כרעי המטה שלא ירקבו בארץ: לווחים של סקיבס. עץ קטן כמין דף שתוקעין בקשת שקורין ארבלסטר"א שעליו מושך החץ:

יתקע

הנח לנר שמן ופתילה הואיל ונעשה בסיס לדבר האסור. אילטריך למימר בשמן דנעשה בסיס לדבר האסור דאי לאו הכי לא היה הנר אסור לטלטל דהוי בסיס לדבר האסור ולדבר המותר ושרי כדאמר בסמוך כי הוינן בי רב נחמן הוה מטלטלינן כנונא אגב קיטמא אע"ג דאיכא עליה שברי עצים ואם תאמר פתילה אמאי קאמר דהויא בסיס לדבר האסור היא עצמה הויא דבר האסור כדאמר לקמן ושוין שאם יש בה שברי פתילות שאסור לטלטלה וי"ל דשברי פתילה הוי שברי כלים ודמי לצרורות אבל פתילה שלימה שהיא כלי הוה שרי אי לאו דנעשה בסיס לדבר האסור: לי התיר רבי לטלטל מחתה באפרה. השתא ס"ד דאפר מחתה מוקצה הוא: ואמר רבה ב"ב חנה א"ר יוחנן כו'. תימה אמאי לא פריך בלאו מילתיה דרבי יוחנן ממתני' דפ' נוטל (לקמן דף קמב:) דתנן מעות שע"ג הכר מנער את הכר והן נופלות וכן אבן שעל פי החבית מטה על צדה והיא נופלת אבל טלטול גמור אסור ואור"י דה"א דשאני מעות דחשיבי ולא בטלי ואבן שע"פ החבית ה"א דמיירי שהוא מתוקן לסתום פי החבית והחבית צריכה לה ולכך לא בטלה: בגדי עניים לעניים. אומר ר"ת דדוקא בטומאת מדרס דבייחוד תליא מלתא אבל בשאר טומאות לא תליא מלתא בייחוד דאפי' היה מוטל באשפה מרביץ *מוהבגד דשלש על שלש מיטמא בין לעניים בין לעשירים דבקרא לא מפליג מידי ומייתי ר"ת ראיה דתנן במסכת כלים (פרק כ"ז מ"ב) דבגד מטמא משום שלשה על שלשה למדרס משום שלש על שלש לטמא מת וע"כ בעשירים מיירי דבפכ"ח תנן התם בגדי עניים אע"פ שאין בהם שלשה על שלשה טמאין מדרס וא"ת הכא דפריך מברייתא אמאי לא פריך ממתני' דפכ"ח דכלים שהבאתי ואור"י דאי ממתני' ה"א דבגדי עניים היינו כעין שק שעיקרו עשוי לעניים ואפי' ביד עשירים אינו צריך שלשה על שלשה אבל שאר בגדים בעי שלשה על שלשה שאינו עומד אלא לעשירים להכי מייתי ברייתא דלא שייך לפרשה הכי: הוה מטלטלינן כנונא אגב קיטמא. פי' כנונא מחתה והיינו מחתה באפרה דלעיל פי' אגב אפרה שהוסק מע"ש ומוכן הוא דחזי לכסות בה רוק או צואה וקשה דמשמע דוקא אגב קיטמא שרי הא לאו הכי נעשה בסיס לדבר האסור ואילו בפ"ב דביצה (כא: ושם) אמר גבי אין מזמנין נכרי בשבת משום שיורי כוסות פריך וניטלטליניהו אגב כסא מי לא אמר רבא כי הוינן בי רב נחמן הוה מטלטלינן כנונא אגב קיטמא אף על גב דאיכא עליה שברי עצים ומאי פריך שאני כנונא דאגב קטמא מטלטל לה אבל בכוס ליכא אלא דבר האסור ואור"י דשיורי כוסות לא חשיבי למיהוי כוס בטל לגבייהו אף על גב שאין היתר עמהן בכוס טפי גרעי משברי עצים שעם הקיטמא בכנונא: אע"ג דאיכא עליה שברי עצים. נראה לרבינו תם דשברי עצים חשיבי טפי מאבן שבכלכלה דאם לא כן מאי קמ"ל ואדמקשי ליה מברייתא דשוין כו' ליסייעיה ממתני' דכלכלה והאבן בתוכה אלא שברי עצים חשיבי טפי ויש לדמות שברי עצים לגבי אפר כשברי פתילה לגבי שמן: בגלילא שנו. פי' בקונט' שחשובות להן שברי פתילה שאין בגדי פשתן מצויין להם ואין נראה לר"ת דהא אמרי' בשילהי ב"ק (דף קיח:) לוקחין מן הנשים כלי צמר ביהודה וכלי פשתן בגליל משמע שמצוי פשתן הרבה שם ומפרש ר"ת בגלילא שנו שהיה להם רוב שמן ולהכי לא בטלי שברי פתילה אגב שמן וכן משמע בפ"ק דסנהדרין (דף יא:) גבי טול איגרת וכתוב לאחנא בני גלילא עילאה ותתאה כו' דזמן ביעורא מטא לאפרושא מעשרא ממעטני זיתא ואמר בנזיר בפרק בית שמאי (דף לא:) בגלילא שנו דחמרא עדיף ממשחא ויין היה מצוי להם הרבה כדאמר בהמוציא יין (לקמן עז.) גבי מים כדי לשוף בהן את הקילור וקאמר בגלילא שנו *דרפואת מים שכיח טפי משתיה שהיה להן רוב יין והיו שותין הכל יין ואפילו הכי חמרא עדיף להו ממשחא כי השמן היה להם בזול יותר ורש"י פי' נמי בהמוציא (שם) שמחמת עניותא היו עושין רפואה מן המים ואין עושין מן היין רק שתייה ולפיכך היתה רפואת מים שכיחא ואין נראה דכיון שלא היה להם יין לשיפות הקילור א"כ שכיחא שתיית מים טובא ואמרי' בעלמא *אף ערב יוה"כ בגליל שהיו מרבים בסעודה משמע שעשירים היו [וע"ע תוספות חגיגה כה: ד"ה בגלילא]:

*[חולין פג:]

רשב"ג

נז א ב מיי' פכ"ו מהל' שבת הלכה יג טור שו"ע או"ח סימן שי סעיף ח:

נח ג ד מיי' פכ"ב מהל' שבת הלכה כו כח סמג לאוין סה טור שו"ע או"ח סימן שיג סעיף ו:

רבינו חננאל

הנח לנר ופתילה ושמן דלא גזר ר"ש אלא הואיל ונעשה כל אחד בסיס לדבר האסור. ופשוטה היא: אמר רבא כי הוינו בי רב נחמן היינו מטלטלי כנונא אגב קיטומה אף על גב דאיכא עליה שברי עצים. מיתיבי ושוין שאם יש בה שברי פתילה שאסור לטלטלה. ופריק אביי בגלילא שנו. פירוש בגליל שנו שדרכם להדליק בשברי פתילות. וכיון שדרכם להדליק בשברי פתילות נעשו מוקצות בשבת לפיכך אסור לטלטל אפילו הנרות שיש בהן שברי פתילות. אבל שברי עצים דכנונא לא חשיבי ובטלי: לוי בר שמואל בעא מר' אבא ומרב הונא בר חייא מהו להחזי' מטה של(פרסים) [טרסיים] בשבת אמרו ליה שרי. אמר להו רב יהודה רב ושמואל דאמרי תרווייהו המחזיר מטה של (פרסים) [טרסיים] בשבת חייב חטאת. מיתיבי המחזיר קנה מנורה בשבת חייב הטאת קנה של ציירין לא יחזיר ואם החזיר פטור אבל אסור. ר' סימאי א' קרן [עגולה חייב קרן] פשוטה פטור. קתני מיהת המחזיר קנה מנורה בשבת חייב הטאת. קשיא לר' אבא ולרב הונא דשרי. ושני' אינהו דאמור כי האי תנא דתניא אם היה רפוי מותר. דתניא מלבנות המטה וכרעי המטה [ולווחין] של סקיבס לא יחזיר. ואם החזיר פטור אבל

רב נסים גאון

אלא אמר אביי מידי דהוה אגרף של רעי. משתכח בפס' יום טוב בפרק משילין פירות (דף לו) אמר שמואל גרף של רעי ועביט של מימי רגלים מותר להוציאו לאשפה ובפרק נוטל אדם את בנו (דף קמב) אמרו הני גרעיני דתמרי כו' רב הונא בריה דרב יהושע עביד להו גרף של רעי וכן אמימר עביד להו גרף של רעי: אמר אביי בגלילא שנו. כבר פרשו בזה השינוי ששנה אביי הרבה מן החכמים ולא שמעתי מהם כלום ולא מצאתי בו לאחד מן הגאונים פירוש אבל טרחתי על שינויו ומצאתי במס' נזירות בפ' בית שמאי אומרים הקדש טעות הקדש (דף לא) והא שמן עדיף מיין אי משום הא לא קשיא בגלילא שנו דחמרא עדיף ממשחא זה מודיע שהשמן היה אצלם מצוי הרבה וכי מה שרושם בנר ויש בו שברי פתילה אין לו חשיבות אצלם ואינן משתמשין בו לצרכם והרי הוא כדין המוקצה שאסור לטלטלו ולכך שנו חכמים כי בגליל אסור לטלטל נר שיש בו שברי פתילה לפי שהשמן הנותר בנר לא חשיב להו וכבר זה הפירוש הודעתי באלו הימים לתלמידנו ופירשנו להם בזה הענין ואפשר להיאמר בו פירוש אחר שאנשי גליל לפי שלא היו מקפידין על לשונם ולא דייקי לישנא ולא גמיר מחד רבה ולא גלו מסכתא למסכתא כמו שהוא מפורש במסכת עירובין בפרק כיצד מעברין (דף נג) ולא היה תלמודם מקויים בידם אסרו עליהם החכמים טלטול נר שיש בתוכו שברי פתילה *) עלי דרך האיסורים ואל תרבם ואל תסייג ויקוי דאלך איצא קולהום פי ערה (מוצאע) [מוצאע] מן אל תלמוד מתל הדא אל קול עלי פריק אל תנקיץ להם

*) פירושם בערבי על דרך האיסורים והגדר והסייג ונמצא סיוע לזה במקומות הרבה מהתלמוד משל זה כמאמר על דרך הגירעון להם נזכיר מזה מה שנמצא בס' תומר בקודש.

לקמן קמא:

[מו"ק ג: קידושין לט: סוכה מד. חולין כח.]

[ערכין כט:]

[ע' תוספות לקמן קכז: ד"ה כיון וכו']

ביצה לו: ע"ש

[לקמן עח.]

[תוספ' פי"ג]

הגהות הב"ח

(א) גמ' ופתילה הואיל ונעשה בסיס: (ב) רש"י ד"ה בגדי עשירים וכו' בי רבי חשיבי קרטין ובטלי בסיד:

גליון הש"ס

גמ' קרן עגולה חייב. עי' כלים פי"א מ"ז:

ורבינו מאיר פי' כי מרוב שתיית יין הי' להם הכלים גיעים ושכיחי רפואת מים טובה [תוי"ט]

עין משפט נר מצוה

נט א מיי' פכ"ב מהל' שבת הלכה ו וסמג שם טוש"ע שם סעיף ו וסעיף ט :
ס ב מיי' שם טור שו"ע שם סעיף ו :
סא ג מיי' שם פ"ה הלכה יג סמג שם טוש"ע או"ח סימן רסה סעיף ד :
א ד ה מיי' פ"ד מהלכות שבת הלכה א טוש"ע או"ח סימן רנז סעיף ג :

אבל אסור ^א ולא יתקע ואם תקע חייב חטאת רשב"ג אומר ^ב אם היה רפוי מותר בי רב חמא הוה מטה גללניתא הוה מהדרי לה ביומא טבא א"ל ההוא מדרבנן לרבא מאי דעתיך בנין מן הצד הוא נהי דאיסורא דאורייתא ליכא איסורא דרבנן מיהא איכא אמר ליה אנא כרשב"ג סבירא לי דאמר אם היה רפוי מותר : **מתני'** * ^ג נותנין כלי תחת הנר לקבל ניצוצות ולא יתן לתוכו מים מפני שהוא מכבה : **גמ'** והא * קמבטל כלי מהיכנו אמר רב הונא בריה דרב יהושע ניצוצות אין בהן ממש : ולא יתן לתוכו מים מפני שהוא מכבה : לימא תנן סתמא כרבי יוסי * דאמר גורם לכיבוי אסור ותסברא אימור דאמר ר' יוסי בשבת בערב שבת מי אמר וכי תימא הכא נמי בשבת והתניא נותנין כלי תחת הנר לקבל ניצוצות בשבת ואין צריך לומר בע"ש ולא יתן לתוכו מים מפני שהוא מכבה מע"ש ואין צריך לומר בשבת אלא אמר רב אשי אפילו תימא רבנן שאני הכא מפני שמקרב את כיבויו :

הדרן עלך כירה

במה * ^ד טומנין ובמה אין טומנין אין טומנין לא בגפת ולא בזבל לא במלח ולא בסיד ולא בחול בין לחין בין יבשין ולא בתבן ולא בזגין ולא במוכין ולא בעשבין בזמן שהן לחין אבל טומנין בהן כשהן יבשין : **גמ'** איבעיא להו גפת של זיתים תנן אבל דשומשמין שפיר דמי או דילמא דשומשמין תנן וכל שכן דזיתים ת"ש דאמר ר' זירא משום חד דבי ר' ינאי קופה שטמן בה אסור להניחה על גפת של זיתים ש"מ של זיתים תנן לעולם אימא לך ^ה לענין הטמנה דשומשמין נמי אסור לענין אסוקי

רש"י

יתקע. בחוזק על ידי יתדות שקורין קויי"ש : מטה גללניתא. טירנדי"ן והוא כעין של טרסיים* : מן הצד. מפני שאינה תקועה ומהדקה בחוזק קרי לה מן הצד כלומר ע"י שינוי : **גמ'** והא קא מבטל כלי מהיכנו. דלא יוכל ליטלו משם כל היום דנעשה בסיס לניצוצות לימא תהוי תיובתיה דרב חסדא דאסר בפירקין (דף מג.) : אין בהן ממש. משכבו ומותר ליטלן : כרבי יוסי. בכל כתבי הקדש דקתני עושה מחיצה בכל הכלים בין מלאין בין ריקנין כדי שלא תעבור הדליקה רבי יוסי אוסר בכלי חרס חדשים מלאים מים שאין יכולין לקבל האור והן מתבקעים ומכבין את הדליקה : בערב שבת. כגון זה שנותן המים מבעוד יום בכלי תחת הנר : וכי תימא הכא נמי. אין נותנין לתוכו מים בשבת קאמר ור' יוסי היא : והתניא. אפילו בע"ש אסור ואי נגרס כיבוי מדמית לה אפילו כרבי יוסי לא מיתוקמה דבע"ש לא אמר רבי יוסי : אלא אמר רב אשי. מתניתין אפילו לרבנן דלא דמי לגרם כיבוי דהתם כי מטי דליקה לכלים דליקה הוא דפקע להו וגרמא בעלמא הוא אבל זה שנתן המים ממש תחת הנר מכבה ממש הוא וגזירה מבעוד יום אטו משחשכה : שמקרב את כיבויו. זימן כיבוי להדיא והוה ליה מכבה ממש אי הוה יהיב ליה בשבת :

הדרן עלך כירה

במה טומנין. הבא לסלק קדירה מעל גבי כירה ולטומנה בדבר אחר ואמרו חכמים *אין טומנין בדבר המוסיף הבל אלא בדבר המעמיד הבל מי הוא המוסיף ואסור : גפת. פסולת של בית הבד של שמן שהוא כנוס יחד וחם מאד : לחין. יש בהן הבל הרבה יותר מיבשין : זגין. פסולת של יקב יין : מוכין. כל דבר רך קרוי מוכין כגון צמר גפן ותלישי צמר רך של בהמה וגרירת בגדים בלויים : **גמ'** קופה שטמן בה. שנותן בה מוכין וטומן בה קדירה : לענין הטמנה. לטומנו בתוכה : אסוקי

תוספות

רבן שמעון בן גמליאל אומר אם היה רפוי מותר. ולעיל נמי מיירי ברפוי °וקשה קצת דהיכי פליגי טולי האי דמר מחייב חטאת ומר שרי אפי' לכתחלה ועוד הא אין בנין וסתירה בכלים ועוד תקשה לרב יהודה הך ברייתא דליכא תנא דמחייב חטאת ויש לומר דהכי קאמר לעיל הא רב ושמואל דאמרי תרווייהו המחזיר מטה של טרסיים בשבת חייב חטאת כשאינו רפוי ואם כן ברפוי אין סברא להתיר לכתחלה :

לימא תנן סתמא כרבי יוסי דאמר גורם לכיבוי אסור. הוה מצי למימר וליטעמיך הא רבי יוסי גופיה לא אמרה אלא בדליקה משום דאדם בהול על ממונו אי שרינא ליה אתי לכבויי והכי מפרש בכל כתבי (לקמן קכ:) אבל הכא ליכא למגזר דהא יש כלי תחת הנר ואינו בהול ובכמה מקומות בהש"ס יכול לומר וליטעמיך ואינו אומר :

מפני שמקרב את כבויו. פירוש דגזרינן ע"ש אטו שבת ובשבת יכול לבא לידי כיבוי אם יגביה הכלי בשעת נפילת הניצוצות ואם תאמר מאי שנא שריית דיו וסממנים ופריסת מצודה דשרינן בפ"ק (דף יז:) עם השמש והכא אסרינן מע"ש שלא יבא לעשות בשבת ותירץ הרב פור"ת דהתם ליכא למיחש שמא יעשה כן בשבת דהא אב מלאכה הן אבל הכא איכא למיחש דלא דמי איסור כל כך במה שמניח כלי תחת הניצוצות ואיכא למיחש שמא יבא לידי כיבוי שיתחיל ליתן המים קודם נפילת הניצוצות וקודם גמר הנתינה יפלו ומכבה בידים או שיגביה הכלי עם המים כנגד הניצוצות כדפרישית ואף על גב דבאותו כיבוי אין בו חיוב חטאת לר' שמעון דמלאכה שאינה צריכה לגופה היא החמירו אטו כיבוי דחיוב חטאת ואע"ג דהוי גזירה לגזירה קים להו לרבנן דהכא שייך למגזר טפי ורש"י דפי' דהוה מכבה ממש לאו דוקא אלא כלומר שיוכל לבא לידי כיבוי ור"ת גרים כפירוש ר"ח מפני שמקרב כיבוי דהתם הוא דשרי לעשות מחיצה מכלים שיש בתוכן מים שאינו מכבה כלום עד שיתבקעו הכלים אבל הכא אין הפסק בין מים לניצוצות ומיד נכבות כשנופלות בכלי והוי כמחילת מים דאסירא כגון מחילת שלג וברד וקשה לפירושו דבירושלמי מוקי מתני' כר' יוסי אבל לרבנן אפי' מחילות של מים מותר ובפ' כל כתבי (לקמן קכ:) נמי שרו רבנן דר' יוסי בטלית שאחז בו האור מצד אחד ליתן עליו מים מצד אחר ואם כבתה כבתה ונראה דלפי הש"ס שלנו יש לחלק דבמחילה של מים אע"ג דאין דבר מפסיק מ"מ שרי שאין האש טפלת לתוך המים להדיא כי הכא שהמים תחת הניצוצות ומקרב כיבוין טפי ועוד דאיכא למימר דהש"ס שלנו אוסר במחילות של מים לרבנן ומשום הכי מוקי מתניתין כרבנן ופליג אירושלמי ולא דמי לטלית שאחז בו האור מצד אחד שאינו אלא שלא תתפשט האור ומה שרגילים לתת מים בזכוכית שקורין לאמפ"א ונותנין עליה שמן בע"ש אין זה קרוי קירוב כיבוי דכיון שאין מתכוין לכיבוי כלל אלא להגביה את השמן לא שייך למגזר מידי שמא יעשה בשבת ושרי אפי' לר' יוסי וכ"ש לרבנן דאל"כ אפי' בלא מים אסור שהניצוצות נופלות בשמן : ועוד איכא למימר דתלמוד שלנו אסר מחילה של מים לרבנן ומש"ה מוקי מתני' כר' יוסי ופליג אירושלמי ול"ד לטלית שאחז בו האור מצד אחד שאינו אלא שלא תתפשט האור [ת"י] :

הדרן עלך כירה

במה טומנין וכו' אין טומנין לא בגפת. פירש הר"ר יוסף בשם רבינו שמואל דמיירי בבשיל ולא בשיל °אבל קדרא חייתא ובשיל שרינן בפ"ק (דף יח:) ואין נראה לר"ת דהא אית לן לאוקמא מתניתין בסתם קדרות שהן מבושלים בין השמשות ועוד דמסתמא איירי מתני' דומיא דמתני' דכירה דמיירי בבשיל כמאכל בן דרוסאי ונראה לר"ת שיש לחלק בין השהאה להטמנה דודאי להשהות מותר כשהוא מאכל בן דרוסאי שאין חיתוי מעט מועיל לו שהרי מגולה הוא ושליט ביה אוירא אבל הטמנה שעושין לצורך מחר והוא מוטמן יש לחוש שמא יחתה שמעט חיתוי מועיל לו ליתפס חומו וגזרו להטמין בכל דבר המוסיף הבל גזירה שמא יטמין ברמץ ויחתה :

רבינו חננאל

אסור. לא יתקע ואם תקע חייב חטאת רבן שמעון בן גמליאל אומר אם היה רפוי מותר המחזיר קני מנורה חייב חטאת כמשמעו מפני שמתקן כלי כבנין · קנה של ציידין דרכם לתת קנה דק דק בתוך ראש קנה עבה כדי שיהא (נכוה) [גבוה] ולא יהא נשבר וזהו פטור אבל אסור. קרן עגולה חייב פשוטה פטור. אלו הן כלי שיר. והן של חליות · ויש מהן קרן עגולה וקרן פשוטה כדכתיב (דניאל ג) קל קרנא משרוקיתא. וזה שהיא עגולה היא כלי יש בו מלאכה להחזירה לפיכך חייב חטאת אבל פשוטה אין בה עסק כלום כדתנן בכלים פ' י"א. הכוש והאימא והמקל וסומפאניא וחליל של מתכת טמאין והמצופין טהורין וסמפאניא שיש בה בית קיבול כנפים בין כך ובין כך טמאה. קרן עגולה טמאה וכו' טמאין יבשעת חבורן הכל טמאה בי רב חמא הוה ליה מיטה גליתא והוו מהדרי ליה בי"ט א"ל לרב חמא מאי דעתיך בנין מן הצד הוא נהי דאיסורא דאוריי' ליכא דרבנן מיהא איכא. א"ל רב חמא אנא כרבן שמעון בן גמליאל סבירא לי אם היה רפוי מותר. נמצא רב חמא כר' אבא ורב הונא דשרו. ומסתברא מטה של טורסיים הוא כגון מטה גליתא : נותנין כלי תחת הנר לקבל בו ניצוצות. והא קא מבטל כלי מהיכנו. אמר רב הונא בריה דרב יהושע ניצוצות אין בהן ממש ומותר להשתמש באותו כלי ולא יתן בתוכו מים חפני שהוא מכבה. לימא תנן סתמא כר' יוסי דאמר גרם כבוי אסור דתנן ר' יוסי אוסר לעשות מחיצה שלא תעבור הדליקה בכלי חרש חדשים מלאים מים שאין יכולין לקבל את האור והן מתבקעין ומכבין הדליק' ודחי אימור דאסר ר' יוסי בשבת. בע"ש מי אסר. וכי תימא הכא נמי כי תנן אסור בשבת אבל בע"ש שרי. והא תניא נותנין כלי תחת הנר לקבל ניצוצות בשבת ואין צורך לומר בע"ש. ולא יתן לתוכו מים בע"ש מפני שהוא מכבה ואין צריך לומר בשבת. ואוקמה רב אשי אפילו לרבנן דפליגי עליה דר' יוסי הכא אסרי מפני שמקרב כיבויו פי' כיון שנופלין הניצוצות במים מיד נכבין ובכלים עד שיתבקעו. וקי"ל דהלכתא כר"ש דאפי' במוקצה מחמת מיאוס שרי : ואין הלכה כר"ש במוקצה מחמת איסור כגון במנורה ומפני שהדליקו עליהן באותה שבת וכיוצא בהן וכגון מטה שיחדה למעות ונכרי שהביא דורון לישראל דבר המחובר לקרקע וכיוצא בהן דמוקצה מחמת איסור הן. וגרסי' במי שהחשיך בדרך פליגי בה רב אחא ורבינא חד אמר בכולה שבת הלכתא כר"ש בר ממוקצה מחמת מיאוס וחד אמר אפילו במוקצה מחמת מיאוס נמי הלכתא כר"ש בר ממוקצה מחמת איסור בלבד וקי"ל דבכל התורה רב אחא לחומרא ורבינא לקולא והלכתא כרבינא לקולא בר מהני תלת אומצא כו' ואע"ג דעולא ולוי ורב אמרו הלכה כר' יהודה הא שמואל וזעירי ור' יוחנן אמרו הלכתא כר' שמעון. ורבינא דהוא בתראה פסק הלכתא כר' שמעון כדאמרן. לפיכך כל מוקצה מותר לבר ממוקצה מחמת איסור כמו שפירשנו. ומוקצה מחמת חסרון כיס מודה ר' שמעון ונרונרות וצמוקין כדאמרן : הדרן עלך כירה

פרק רביעי במה טומנין ובמה אין טומנין כו' אין טומנין בגפת. אוקימנא בגפת של שומשין וכל שכן בגפת של זיתים דמסיק נמי הבלא אסיק' אמר רבא אנוחי

מסורת הש"ס

עי' לקמן קלט. רש"י ד"ה וכסא גלגין

[לעיל מב: מג.]

[לעיל מג: וש"נ]

לקמן קכ.

בבא בתרא יט. [נדרים נ:] מו"ק ב.]

לעיל לה:

גליון הש"ס

תוס' ד"ה רשב"ג וכו' וקשה קצת. עי' לקמן דף קלח ע"א : שם ד"ה במה טומנין וכו' אבל קדרא חייתא. עי' לעיל דף לט ע"ב תוספות ד"ה ממעשה :

רב נסים גאון

נדבר מן דאלך מא יחצרנא בפרק הומר בקודש (דף כה) אמרו אמר רב יוסף בגלילא שנו מינו דלא מהימני אקודש לא מהימני אתרומה נמי בנדרים בפרק *) ואלו נדרים ובגליל אסורין שאין אנשי גליל מכירין את חרמי כהנים ובפרק המוציא יין (דף עח) ובפרק מקום שנהגו (דף נה) בפסחים עוד ובגמרא ירושלמי שבת פרק כל כתבי הלכה ח) גרסי אמר עולא י"ח שנין עבד רבן יוחנן בן זכאי יתיב בהדה ערב ולא אתא קימוי אלא אילין תרתין עובדיה אמר גליל גליל שנאת את התורה סופך להעשות כמציקין וכל דין סיוע לפירושנו : **לימא** תנן סתמא כר' יוסי דאמר גרם כיבוי אסור. עיקר דיליה במשנה בפרק כל כתבי הקודש (דף קכ) דתנן ר' יוסי אוסר בכלי חרש הדשים מלאים מים שאין יכולין לקבל את האור והן מתבקעין ומכבין את הדליקה ובגמ' גרסי ר' יוסי סבר גרם כיבוי אסור : סליק פרק כירה

*) נ"ל ואלו מותרין דף יח במשנה.

is not liable [to a sin-offering]. [47*b*] but it is forbidden; nor must they be [tightly] fixed in, and if one does so, he is liable to a sin-offering. R. Simeon b. Gamaliel said: If it is loose, it is permitted.[6]

At R. Ḥama's home there was a folding bed, which they used to put up on Festivals. Said one of the Rabbis to Raba: What is your view, that it is building from the side:[7] granted that there is no Scriptural prohibition, yet it is Rabbinically forbidden?—Said he to him, I agree with R. Simeon b. Gamaliel, who ruled: If it is loose, it is permitted.

MISHNAH. A VESSEL MAY BE PLACED UNDER A LAMP TO CATCH THE SPARKS, BUT ONE MUST NOT POUR WATER THEREIN, BECAUSE HE EXTINGUISHES [THEM].

a *GEMARA.* But he deprives the vessel of its readiness?[1]—Said R. Huna the son of R. Joshua: Sparks are intangible.[2]

BUT ONE MUST NOT POUR WATER THEREIN, BECAUSE HE EXTINGUISHES [THEM]. Shall we say that we learnt anonymously as R. Jose, who maintained: That which is a cause of extinguishing is forbidden?[3] Now, is that logical: granted that R. Jose ruled thus for the Sabbath: did he rule thus for the eve of the Sabbath? And should you say, Here also it refers to the eve of the Sabbath,—surely it was taught: A vessel may be placed under a lamp on the Sabbath to catch the sparks, and on the eve of the Sabbath goes without saying; but one must not pour water therein on the eve of the Sabbath, because he extinguishes [them], and the Sabbath goes without saying?—Rather, said R. Ashi, you may say that it agrees even with the Rabbis: here it is different, because one brings the extinguisher near.[4]

CHAPTER IV

MISHNAH. WHEREIN MAY WE STORE [FOOD], AND WHEREIN MAY WE NOT STORE [IT]?[1] WE MAY NOT STORE [IT] IN PEAT,[2] FOLIAGE,[3] SALT, LIME, OR SAND, WHETHER MOIST OR DRY; NOR IN STRAW, GRAPE-SKINS, SOFT FLOCKING[4] OR HERBAGE, WHEN THEY ARE MOIST; BUT WE MAY STORE [FOOD] IN THEM WHEN THEY ARE DRY.

b

GEMARA. The scholars propounded: Did we learn, peat of olives, whereas peat of poppy seed is well; or perhaps we learnt peat of poppy seed, and how much more so of olives?—Come and hear: For R. Zera said on the authority of one of the disciples of the School of R. Jannai: A basket in which one put away [food][5] may not be placed on peat of olives. This proves that we learnt peat of olives!—[No.] After all I may tell you that in respect of storing [peat] of poppy seed too is forbidden; [but] as for [48*a*]

(6) I.e., if it is so constructed that it need be only loosely joined, it is permitted even at the very outset. R. Abba and R. Huna b. Ḥiyya likewise refer to branches that sit lightly in their sockets. (7) The technical term for work not done in a professional and usual way.—I.e., do you think that because it is loosely fitted it does not constitute building?

a (1) V. *supra* 42*b*, n. a5. (2) V. *supra* 43*a*, n. a2. (3) Even if one does not directly extinguish; v. *infra* 120*a*. (4) By pouring water into the vessel, and therefore as a preventive measure it is forbidden, also on the eve of Sabbath. But in the case below, q.v., it is indirect extinguishing, because the heat must first cause the jars to burst before the water is released.

b (1) When a pot is removed from the fire on the eve of the Sabbath, it may be stored in anything that preserves heat, but not in something that adds heat (*supra* 34*b*). (2) I.e., a pressed, hard mass. The Gemara discusses which mass is meant. (3) *Zebel* is foliage piled up for forming manure. (4) E.g., rags, wool, etc. (5) For the Sabbath, to preserve its heat.

causing heat to ascend,[6] [peat] of olives causes heat to ascend, but not [peat] of poppy seed.

Rabbah and R. Zera visited the Resh Galutha,[7] and saw a slave place a pitcher of water on the mouth of a kettle.[8] Thereupon Rabbah rebuked him. Said R. Zera to him: Wherein does it differ from a boiler [placed] upon a boiler?[9]—There he [merely]
a preserves [the heat],[1] he replied, whereas here he creates it.[2] Then he saw him spread a turban over the mouth of a cask and place a cup[3] upon it. Thereupon Rabbah rebuked him. Said R. Zera to him: Why? You will soon see,[4] said he. Subsequently he saw him [the servant] wringing it out.[5] Wherein does this differ from [covering a cask with] a rag?[6] he asked him. There one is not particular about it;[7] here he is particular about it.[8]

[NOR WITH] STRAW. R. Adda b. Mattenah asked Abaye: Is it permissible to handle flocking in which one stored [food]?[9]—Said he to him: Because he lacks a bundle of straw, does he arise and renounce a bundle of soft flocking?[10] Shall we say that the following supports him: We may store [food] in wool clip, hatchelled wool, strips of purple [wool],[11] and flocking, but they may not be handled?—As for that, it is no proof: this may be its meaning: if one did not store [food] in them, they may not be handled. If so, why state it?[12]—You might say, They are fit for reclining:[13] hence we are told [otherwise].

R. Ḥisda permitted stuffing to be replaced in a pillow on the Sabbath. R. Ḥanan b. Ḥisda objected to R. Ḥisda: [We have learnt:] The neck [of a shirt] may be undone on the Sabbath,[14] but may not
b be opened;[1] nor may flocking be put into a pillow or a bolster on a Festival, and on the Sabbath it goes without saying?—There is no difficulty: one refers to new ones, the other to old ones.[2] It was taught likewise: Flocking may not be put into a pillow or a bolster on the Festival, and on the Sabbath it need not be stated; if it falls out, it may be replaced [even] on the Sabbath, while on Festivals it goes without saying.

Rab Judah said in Rab's name: One who opens the neck [of a shirt] on the Sabbath incurs a sin-offering.[3] R. Kahana objected:

(6) As here, the food is stored in a substance which does not add heat, but heat may mount up from the peat and penetrate the basket. (7) Head of the Exile, Exilarch, official title of the head of Babylonian and Persian Jewry, whose authority was recognized and sustained by the State. V. *J.E.* V, p. 228, s.v. Exilarch. (8) The pitcher contained cold water, and the kettle was hot. (9) Which is permissible; 51*b*.

a (1) For the upper boiler too is filled with hot water. (2) The kettle below heats the cold water in the pitcher. (3) *Naṭla* is a ladle or a small vessel for taking liquid out of a large vessel. (4) Lit., 'you see now'. (5) This is forbidden on the Sabbath. (6) Which is permitted, and we do not fear that the owner will wring it dry. And though the servant did so here, yet on what grounds did Rabbah rebuke him at the outset? (7) He does not mind if the rag remains wet. (8) Hence he is likely to wring it. (9) Normally they may not be handled; the question is whether this use converts it into a 'utensil' which may be handled on the Sabbath. (10) Where possible straw is used, because it is cheaper. When one must use rags, he does not on that account renounce them, i.e., declare that they have no value in his eyes save for that purpose, but they remain independent, as it were, just as before they were so used: hence they may not be handled. (11) ארגמן is translated purple in E.V. (Ex. XXV, 4). But this was an extremely costly dye, and its proposed use here for storing food shows that such is not meant. It is rather a scarlet red dye, more brilliant than purple but not so enduring; v. *T.A.* I, 146f. (12) In their present state they cannot be used, hence they certainly do not rank as 'utensils'. (13) So that they are utensils. (14) When it is returned by the launderer, who generally tied the neck up.

b (1) The first time after it is sewn. This opening makes it fit for wear and thus finishes its work. (2) A pillow etc., must not be stuffed for the first time, as that is part of its manufacture; but if the stuffing falls out, it may be replaced. (3) V. n. b1.

אסוקי הבלא דזיתים מסקי הבלא דשומשמין לא מסקי הבלא רבה ורבי זירא איקלעו לבי ריש גלותא חזיוה להההוא עבדא דאנח כוזא דמיא אפומא דקומקומא *נזהיה רבה א"ל ר' זירא מאי שנא ממיחם על גבי מיחם א"ל התם אוקומי קא מוקים הכא אולודי קא מוליד הדר חזייה דפרס דסתודר אפומיה דכובא ואנח נטלא עילויה [ג]נזהיה רבה א"ל ר' זירא אמאי אמר ליה השתא חזית לסוף חזייה דקא מעצר ליה א"ל מאי שנא מפרונקא א"ל התם לא קפיד עילויה הכא קפיד עילויה: ולא בתבן: בעא מיניה רב אדא בר מתנה מאביי מוכין שטמן בהן מהו לטלטלן בשבת א"ל [ד]וכי מפני שאין לו קופה של תבן עומד ומפקיר קופה של מוכין לימא מסייע ליה *טומנין בגיזי צמר ובציפי צמר ובלשונות של ארגמן ובמוכין ואין מטלטלין אותן אי משום הא לא איריא הכי קאמר אם לא טמן בהן אין מטלטלין אותן אי הכי מאי למימרא מהו דתימא חזי למזגא עלייהו קמ"ל: רב חסדא [ה]שרא לאהדורי *אודרא לבי סדיא בשבתא איתיביה רב חנן בר חסדא לרב חסדא מתירין בית הצואר בשבת אבל לא פותחין ואין נותנין את המוכין לא לתוך הכר ולא לתוך הכסת ביו"ט ואין צריך לומר בשבת לא קשיא הא בחדתי הא בעתיקי תניא נמי הכי אין נותנין את המוכין לא לתוך הכר ולא לתוך הכסת בי"ט ואין צריך לומר בשבת נשרו מחזירין אותן בשבת ואין צריך לומר ביום טוב אמר רב יהודה [ו]אמר רב *[ו]הפותח בית הצואר בשבת חייב חטאת מתקיף לה רב כהנא

מה

רש"י

אסוקי הבלא. כגון זה שהטמין בדבר אחר והניח קופה על הגפת דליכא אלא שהגפת מעלה הבל למעלה ומרתיח קדרה שבקופה: אפומא דקומקומא. מיחם של חמין והכוזא היתה מלאה צונן: נזהיה. גער בו: מאי שנא ממיחם על גבי מיחם. דתניא בברייתא בסוף פרקין דשרי: התם אוקומי מוקים. שהמיחם העליון גם בו יש מים חמין והתחתון אינו אלא מעמיד חומו שלא יפיג: דסתודר. סודר של ראש: כובא. קנקן: נטלא. כלי ששואבין יין מן הכובא: דקא עצר. שהיה סוחטו מן המים שנבלעו בו: מאי שנא מפרונקא. בגד העשוי לפרוס על הגיגית שפורסין אותו בשבת: לא קפיד עליה. אם שרוי במים שהרי לכך עשוי ולא אתי לידי סחיטה: מוכין. אינן אלא לעשות מהן לבדין שקורין פלט"ר ומוקצין הן למלאכה ואסור לטלטלן ואלו שטמן בהן מי אמרינן יחדן להטמנה ואיכא תורת כלי עליהן ומותר לטלטלן בשבת או לא: עומד ומפקיר לכך. קופה של מוכין שדמיה יקרין אין דרך בכך ולא בטלי להטמנה: גיזי של צמר. כמות שנגזזו: ציפי צמר. לאחר שנפצוה ושטחוה כמין מחללות משטיחין: לשונות. לאחר שלבנן וסורקין אותן כעין לשונות ארוכין לטוותן: ואין מטלטלין אותן. קס"ד דהכי קאמר ואע"פ שטמן בהן אין מטלטלין אותן: אם לא טמן בהן כו'. ומילי מילי קתני ברישא אשמועינן דטומנין בהן דלא מוספי הבלא ואשמועינן סיפא דסתם מוכין מוקצות נינהו אבל הני דטמן בהן הוי כמי שיחדן לכך: למזגא. להיסב עליהן: לאהדורי אודרא לבי סדיא. להחזיר מוכין שנפלו מן הכר לתוכן: מתירין בית הצואר. שדרך הכובסים לקושרן: אבל לא פותחין. לכתחילה דהשתא עביד ליה מנא: בחדתי. שלא היו מעולם לתוכו אסור דהשתא עביד ליה מנא: בעתיקי. להחזירו לכר זה שנפלו ממנו: הפותח בית הצואר. של חלוק לכתחילה: חייב חטאת. דהשתא קמשוי ליה מנא וחייב משום מכה בפטיש והיינו גמר מלאכה:

מה

תוספות

דזיתים מסקי הבלא. מכאן יש לאסור להניח גחלים תחת הקדרה אפי' יתן עליהן אפר אין להטמין קדרה עליהם שהרי הגחלים מעלין הבל למעלה כמו גפת של זיתים ויש תימה היאך אנו מטמינין על כירות שלנו שקורין אשטר"א ואע"פ שגורפין אותו הוא מוסיף הבל כמו גפת של זיתים ואומר ר"י שיש ליתן טעם לקיים המנהג דגבי גפת איכא למיחש שמא יטמין כולה בתוכה אבל בכירות שלנו לא שייך למיחש הכי ועוד יש שעושין חפירה גדולה ועושין בה בנין לבנים סביב מכל צד ומלמטה ומחממין אותה היטב וגורפין אותה ומטמינין בה את הקדרה ולא דמיא למטמין בדבר המוסיף הבל דלא אסרו אלא כשמטמין ומדביק סביב הקדרה דומיא דרמץ אבל תנור או חפירה שיש אויר בין הדפנות לקדרה אין לאסור יותר מהשהאה אף על פי שכל הקדרה בתוך התנור ורבינו ברוך פי' שיש לחלק בין תוספת הבל דגפת לתוספת הבל דכירה שלנו לפי שהכירה אין הומה אלא מחמת האש ולעולם מתקרר והולך אבל הגפת מוסיף הבל מעצמו אומר רבינו שמואל דמותר לשום תפוחים אצל האש סמוך לחשכה אע"פ שלא יוכלו. ללגות מבע"י דנאכלין טפי כמו שהן חיין מתבשיל שנתבשל כמאכל בן דרוסאי דשרי ואע"ג דבפ"ק (ד' יט:) תנן אין צולין בשר בצל וביצה אלא כדי שיצולו מבע"י אע"פ שפעמים אוכלים בצל חי מ"מ אינו ראוי לאכול חי כמו תפוחים ורוצה להפיג חריפותן ולמתקן בבישולו ואם הטמין תפוחים עם הקדרה אסור להחזיר כרים וכסתות על הקדרה שעמהן או להוסיף על אותן כרים אע"ג דאם אין שם תפוחים מותר להחזיר כדתנן בפירקין (ד' נא:) כסהו ונתגלה מותר לכסותו ולהוסיף כמו אמרינן בגמרא (שם.) אם בא להוסיף מוסיף כשיש עם הקדרה תפוחים אסור דאם מחזיר קודם שנתבשלו נמצא מבשל בשבת ומה שנהגו להסיר הקדרה מעל הכירה ומניחין על הקרקע עד שיגרפו הכירה שמא סבירא לן כהך לישנא דריש כירה (לעיל דף לח:) דשרי חזקיה משמיה דאביי הניחו על גבי קרקע אם דעתו להחזיר:

מאי שנא ממיחם ע"ג מיחם. קשה לר"י דבברייתא גופה דשרי מיחם ע"ג מיחם בסוף פרקין קתני בהדיא ולא בשביל שיחמו אלא בשביל שיהו משומרין ואומר ר"י דברייתא לא שמיע ליה ולא מכח ברייתא פריך אלא ממעשים בכל יום שנותנין מיחם על גבי מיחם תימה דהיכי דמי אי יד סולדת בו היכי הוה בעי למישרי אע"פ שמבשל מי לא ידע דתולדות האור כאור דתנן (לעיל דף לט.) אין נותנין ביצה בצד המיחם ואמר אם גלגל חייב חטאת ותנן נמי (דף מא.) המיחם שפינהו לא יתן לתוכו צונן ואי להפשיר היכי מסיק דאסור והא תניא בפ' כירה (דף מ:) נותן אדם קיתון של מים כנגד המדורה לא בשביל שיחמו אלא בשביל שתפוג צינתן והיינו הפשר כדמוכח סוגיא דהתם ורב יהודה נמי קאמר התם אחד מים ואחד שמן יד סולדת בו אסור אין יד סולדת בו מותר ואין לחלק דגבי מדורה יזהר שלא יבשל כיון שהוא אצל האש אבל הכא אפילו אין יד סולדת בו אסור דשמא יבא לטעות ויניח עד שיתבשל דהא גבי מיחם שרינן לתת לתוכו מים מרובין כדי להפשירן ולא גזרינן אטו מים מועטין אע"פ שאינו אצל האש ונראה לרשב"א דהא דשרינן לתת קיתון של מים כנגד המדורה היינו ברחוק מן המדורה שלעולם לא יוכל לבא לידי בשול אבל בקרוב אסור אפי' להפשיר דילמא משתלי ואתי להניחן שם עד שיתבשל והכי מסיק הכא דאסור ולא בשביל שיחמו דקתני התם היינו כלומר במקום שיכול לבא לידי שיחמו והלשון דחוק קצת: **מאי** שנא מפרונקא. פר"ח דאמר רבה בפרק תולין (לקמן קלט:) האי פרונקא אפלגא דכובא שרי דלא הוי אהל ולא חיישינן שמא יסחוט: **התם** לא קפיד. פר"ת בפ"ק דכתובות (דף ו.*): **וכי** מפני שאין לו קופה של תבן כו'. וא"ת מאי קבעי הא תנן במתניתין טומנין בגיזי צמר ואין מטלטלין אותן והיינו אפילו טמן דהא קתני בהדיא כיצד עושה מנער את הכיסוי והן נופלות וכי מייתי מברייתא דמסייע ליה לייתי ממתניתין דלא מצי למדחי ממתניתין כדדחי ברייתא וליכא למימר דמתני' איכא לאוקומי בשל הפתק כדמוקי לקמן רבינא ע"כ סוגיא דהכא לא סבירא כרבינא מדלא מוקי ברייתא דמייתי בשל הפתק ותירץ ר"י דגיזי צמר חשיבי טפי ממוכין ואסורים לטלטל יותר ואע"ג דרבא קאמר לקמן דאפילו גיזי צמר טמן בהן מטלטלין אין לחוש אי פליגא אאביי דהכא כיון דלא קיימא לקמן מילתיה דרבא ולמאי דמשני רבינא מילתיה דרבא ומוקי מתניתין בשל הפתק ודרבא בשאין של הפתק אומר רשב"א דה"נ מיירי במוכין. של הפתק ולא פליגא דרבא אדאביי אך ק"ק דמאי משני בסמוך מהו דתימא חזי למזגא עלייהו כיון דמיירי בשל הפתק היכי ס"ד דשרי לטלטל משום דחזי למזגא עלייהו:

ה"ק אם לא טמן אין מטלטלין אותן. אמוכין קאי ולא אגיזי צמר דגיזי צמר אפי' טמן אין מטלטלין: **הא** בחדתי הא בעתיקי. אומר ר"י שאם נתקו תוטי הסרבל אם הנקב רחב ויכול להכניס בלא טורח שרי כיון דעתיקי ובלבד שיתכס בענין זה שלא יהא לחוש שמא יתקע דבענין שהוא רגילות לתקוע ולקשור נראה דאסורין להחזיר כדאסרינן בריש כל הכלים (דף קכב:) החזרת שידה תיבה ומגדל גזירה שמא יתקע:

וכי

מסורת הש"ס

ב"ב יט.

[ג"י הערוך אודרא פי' הגוצה]

מכות ג:

ד"ה סלי

עין משפט נר מצוה

ב א טוש"ע או"ח סימן רנ"ח סעיף יז:

ג ב מיי' פכ"ב מהלכות שבת הלכה טו טור ושו"ע או"ח סימן שכ סעיף טו:

ד ג מיי' פכ"ו מהלכות שבת הלכה יג טוש"ע או"ח סימן רנט סעיף א.

ה ד מיי' פכ"ב מהלכות שבת הלכה כג טור ושו"ע או"ח סימן ש"מ סעיף ח:

ו ה מיי' פי' מהלכות שבת הלכה י טוש"ע או"ח סימן שיז סעיף ג:

רבינו חננאל

כוזא דמיא אפומא דקומקומא משום דמיא צונן ומוליד חימום. ואסר נמי למפרס סודרא אפומא דכובא ולאנוחי נטלא אגביה דסודרא משום (דשארי) [דשיורי] הכוס מתחזין בסודרא וקפיד בנשירא דסודרא וסחיט ליה ולא דמי לפרונקא שהיא מטלית קשורה בפומא דכובא כדגרסי' בפ' דר' אליעזר אומר תולין(ד' קלט:)אמר רבא האי פרונקא אפלגי דכובא שרי ולא חייש דניחזי כמו מסננת אפומא דכולא כובא אסיר דהא עביד (אבל) אהל כמסננת. ואמאי שרי רבא התם אפלגי דכובא לירוש שמא יסחום המטלית. ושנינו מטלית לא קפיד בנשירותא מלשון (לקמן קמו:) מי שנשרו כליו בדרך שוטחן בחמה אבל לא כנגד העם סודר קפיד בנשירותא הילכך האי אסור והאי שרי: פי' מוכין סמרטוטין. בגדים מקוצצין כדתנן בנגעים פרק י"א בגד מוסגר שנתערב באחרים כולן טהורין קיצצו ועשאו מוכין טהור. מוכין אסיקנא כי הא דתניא אין נותנין מוכין לא לתוך הכר ולא לתוך הכסת בי"ט ואין צריך לומר בשבת נשרו מחזירין אותן בשבת [ואין צריך לומ' ביו"ט]. אמר רב הפותח בבגד בית הצואר בשבת חייב

רב נסים גאון

פ"ד אמר ליה ר' זירא מאי שנא ממיחם על גבי מיחם. בסוף הפרק (דף נא) בברייתא גרסי ומניחין מיחם על גבי מיחם ומאי שנא מפורנקא. עיקר דיליה בפרק ר' אליעזר אומר תולין את המשמרת ביו"ט (דף קלט) אמר רבא האי פורנקא אפלגא דפומא דכובא שרי וכו' ואיכא דאמרי מאי שנא מפורנקיה דמר לפי שר' זירא עם רבא הוה מפליג והוא

עין משפט
נר מצוה

ז א מיי' פי"ב מהלכות פרה הלכה ו:
ח ב מיי' פ"כ מהלכות כלים הלכה יג:
ט ג מיי' פי"ז מהלכות כלים הלכה ה:
י ד מיי' פי"ב מהלכות פרה הלכה ד:

[עוקצין פ"ב מ"ו ע"ש]

מה בין זו למגופת חבית א"ל רבא ·זה חיבור וזה אינו חיבור רמי ליה ר' ירמיה לרבי זירא *תנן *°שלל של כובסין ושלשלת של מפתחו' והבגד שהוא תפור בכלאים חיבור לטומאה עד שיתחיל להתיר אלמא שלא בשעת מלאכה נמי חיבור ורמינהו *מקל [ב]שעשה (א) יד לקורדום חיבור לטומאה בשעת מלאכה בשעת מלאכה אין שלא בשעת מלאכה לא א"ל התם שלא בשעת מלאכה אדם עשוי לזורקו לבין העצים הכא שלא בשעת מלאכה נמי ניחא ליה דאי מיטנפו הדר מחוור להו בסורא מתנו לה להא שמעתא משמיה דרב חסדא בפומבדיתא מתנו משמי דרב כהנא ואמרי לה משמיה דרבא מאן תנא הא מלתא דאמור רבנן כל המחובר לו הרי הוא כמוהו א"ר יהודה אמר רב ר"מ היא דתנן *[ג]בית הפך ובית התבלין ובית הנר שבכירה מטמאין במגע ואין מטמאין באויר דברי ר' מאיר ור"ש מטהר בשלמא לר"ש קסבר לאו ככירה דמו אלא לר' מאיר אי ככירה דמו אפילו באויר נמי ליטמו אי לאו ככירה דמו אפילו במגע נמי לא ליטמו לעולם לאו ככירה דמו ורבנן הוא דגזרו בהו אי גזרו בהו אפילו באויר נמי ליטמו °עבדו בהו רבנן היכרא כי היכי דלא אתי למשרף עליה תרומה וקדשים *תנו רבנן [ד]מספורת של פרקים ואיזמל של רהיטני חיבור לטומאה ואין חיבור להזאה מה נפשך אי חיבור הוא אפילו להזאה נמי אי לאו חיבור הוא °אפילו לטומאה נמי לא אמר רבא דבר תורה בשעת מלאכה חיבור בין לטומאה בין להזאה ושלא בשעת מלאכה אינו חיבור לא לטומאה ולא להזאה
וגזרו

כלים פ"כ מ"ג

רש"י

מה בין זו למגופת חבית. דתניא בפרק חבית שנשברה (לקמן דף קמו.) מביא אדם חבית ומתיז את ראשה בסייף ומניחה לפני האורחים: מגופה. אינה מן החבית עצמו ואע"פ שדבוקה בו אינו חשוב חיבור שהרי ליטל עומדת אבל הבגד כשנארג כולו חבור: שלל של כובסים. דרכם לשלול הבגדים זה עם זה קטנים עם הגדולים כדי שלא יאבדו*: ובגד שתפרו בכלאים. והן שתי חתיכות של בגד צמר שתפרו בחוט של פשתן דודאי סופו ליקרע ולהפרד זה מזה משום איסור כלאים וכן שלל של כובסין סופן להפרד אפ"ה חיבור לטומאה ואם נטמא ·זה נטמא זה: עד שיתחיל להתיר. דמעשה מוציא מיד מעשה וכיון שהתחיל להתיר גלי על ידי מעשה דלאו חד בגד הוא: שלא בשעת מלאכה. כגון שלל של כובסין שלא הוצרך לשוללו אלא משום שעת כיבוס ואפילו הכי חשיב ליה חיבור אחר כיבוס: מקל. של עצים בעלמא: שעשאו יד לקורדום. שלא קבעו לתוכו: חיבור בשעת מלאכה. ואע"פ דבאנפי נפשיה פשוטי כלי עץ לא מקבלי טומאה הכא בית יד הוא ונתרבו ידות לכל תורת כלי או האוכל בפ' העור והרוטב (חולין קיח.): לזורקו. למקל ומלניע הקורדום לבדו: ניחא להו. שיהו שלולין: דאי מיטנפי הדר מחוור להו. ע"י השלל הזה: להא שמעתין. דלקמיה מאן תנא להא כו'. כל המחובר לו כגון שלל של כובסין דאמרן לעיל חיבור ונטמא אף זה שלא נגעה בו הטומאה ואי לאו דחיבור הוא הוי טהור ואע"ג דנגע בהאי דאין כלי מקבל טומאה אלא מאב הטומאה: בית הפך ובית התבלין ובית הנר שבכירה. כירה זו מיטלטלת היא ומחוברין לה כלי חרס קטנים · בית הפך שמושיבין בתוכן שמן להפשיר: מטמאין במגע. אם נפלה טומאה באוירן או לאויר הכירה ונגעה הטומאה לשולי הכירה נטמאו גם אלו או נגעה טומאה לשוליהם של אלו נטמאת הכירה: ואין מטמאין.. בטומאת הכירה כלומר בטומאת האויר. שאם נפל שרץ באויר הכירה ולא נגעה הטומאה בדופניה היא טמאה דכלי חרס מטמא באויר והן טהורין שאינן חיבור לה אלא לענין מגע כדמפרש טעמא לקמיה: ור' שמעון מטהר. במגע את מי שלא נגעה בו הטומאה דכל חד כלי באנפי נפשיה הוא אלמא לרבי מאיר חיבור ופליגי עליה: אפי' באויר ליטמו. מחמת כירה אם נטמאת כירה מאוירה בלא נגיעה: דגזרו בהו. דליהוו חיבור מדרבנן: עבוד בהו רבנן היכרא. דלא עבדו להו ככירה ממש ליטמא באויר כי היכי דלידעו שחיבור מדבריהם ולא לשרוף על טומאתן תרומה וקדשים: אוזמל של רהיטני. פלייג"א שממחקים בה את התריסין ונותנין הברזל לתוך דפוס של עץ המתוקן לו ולאחר מלאכתו נוטלו הימנו: חיבור לטומאה. נטמא זה נטמא זה: ואין חיבור להזאה. וצריך להזות על שניהם:
וגזרו

תוספות

וכי מה בין זה למגופת חבית. פי' בקונטרס דתניא לקמן בפרק חבית (דף קמו. ושם) רשב"ג אומר מתיזה בסייף ומניחה לפני האורחין ואין נראה לר"י דא"כ מאי משני זה חיבור וזה אינו חיבור התם נמי חיבור הוא דרשב"ג שרי להתיז אפילו גוף החבית עם המגופה כדמוכח התם דבעו מיניה מרב ששת מהו למיברז חביתא בבורטיא כו' · אמר להו לפתחא קא מכוין ואסור ופריך מהא דשרי רשב"ג להתיז ראשה בסייף ומשני התם ודאי לעין יפה קא מכוין אבל הכא אי לעין יפה קא מכוין ליפתחיה מיפתח והא דאסר למיברז חביתא היינו בגוף החבית דחביתא חבית גופא משמע ועוד דמגופה שרי דתנן במתני' אין טוקבין מגופה של חבית דברי רבי יהודה וחכמים מתירין משמע דשרי רשב"ג אפי' בגוף החבית דלעין יפה קא מיכוין והכי הוה ליה לשנויי בשמעתין הכא לפתחא מכוין התם לעין יפה מכוין ופיר"ת וכי מה בין זה לנקיבת מגופת חבית דתנן בפ' חבית (גם זה שם) אין טוקבין מגופת חבית דברי ר' יהודה וחכמים מתירין וא"ת [התם] לכ"ע לא מיחייב חטאת כדאמר התם בגמ' דבר תורה כל פתח שאינו · עשוי להכניס ולהוציא אינו פתח אבל הכא פתח בית הצואר עשוי הוא להכניס ולהוציא ואם כן מאי קשיא ליה ויש לומר דהכי פריך כיון דמחייבת חטאת בפותח בית הצואר משום דעשוי להכניס ולהוציא א"כ נמי גבי מגופה אם עשוי להכניס ולהוציא היה חייב חטאת הלכך השתא נמי שאינו עשוי אלא להוציא היה לאסור מדרבנן ומשני זה חיבור וזה אינו חיבור שהמגופה אינה מן החבית ואפילו אם היה עשוי נקב שבמגופה להכניס ולהוציא לא היה חייב חטאת לכך שרו רבנן: **חיבור** עד שיתחיל להתיר. האי חיבור היינו לטומאה ולא להזאה כדתנן במסכת פרה (פי"ב מ"ט) וא"ת ואמאי לא מייתי מתני' דמסכת פרה וי"ל משום דלא קתני בה עד שיתחיל להתיר ולא הוה מצי לאוכוחי מינה דשלא בשעת מלאכה נמי חיבור: **אמר** רב יהודה אמר רב רבי מאיר היא. אההיא דשלל של כובסים קאי וכן פירש בקונטרס דבההוא דמקל שמא אפי' רבי שמעון מודה דכיון שצריך הקרדום למקל הוי חיבור: **עבדו** רבנן היכרא כו'. וגבי שלל של כובסין איכא נמי היכרא מה שאינו חיבור להזאה והכא גבי כירה לא שייך הך היכרא דלית ביה הזאה: **אי** חיבור הוא אפי' להזאה נמי כו'. קשה לר"י דבשלל של כובסין נמי תקשה לן הכי אי חיבור הוא אפילו להזאה נמי אי לאו חיבור הוא לטומאה נמי לא ורבא נמי דקאמר דבר תורה בשעת מלאכה חיבור בין לטומאה בין להזאה אמאי לא קאמר דבין בשעת מלאכה בין שלא בשעת מלאכה גזרו בה רבנן טומאה כי ההיא דשלל של כובסין ותירץ ר"י דשלל של כובסין ודאי לא הוי חיבור אלא מדרבנן אפילו בשעת מלאכה שאינם צריכים זה לזה והכי מדמה לה לבית הפך ולבית התבלין שכל אחד הוא תשמיש בפני עצמו ולהכי אינו חיבור להזאה כיון דמדאורייתא אינו חיבור אבל מספורת של פרקים פשיטא ליה דבשעת מלאכה הוי חיבור דבר תורה כיון שמשמשין שניהם תשמיש א' °וצריכים זה לזה בשעת מלאכה מה שאין כן בשלל של כובסים שאין תשמיש בגד זה צריך לזה כלל והא דפריך אי לאו חיבור הוא אפילו לטומאה נמי לא לאו דוקא ועיקר קושיתו הוא דאמאי אינו חיבור להזאה ורשב"א מפרש דגבי שלל של כובסין אתי ליה שפיר אע"ג דאינו חיבור להזאה משום דלא הוי חיבור מן התורה גזרו רבנן שיהא חיבור לטומאה כיון שכל בגד טמא בפני עצמו מן התורה אבל גבי מספורת פריך שפיר אי לאו חיבור הוא מדאורייתא אם כן אמאי גזרו חכמים טומאה כלל דהא כל פרק בפני עצמו טהור מדאורייתא לרבנן דתנן במס' כלים בפי"ג (מ"א) מספורת שנחלקה לשנים רבי יהודה מטמא וחכמים מטהרים אף על גב דאיכא למימר דהתם מיירי כשאינה של פרקים ולפי זה הא דאמר השחור והזוג של מספרים אף על פי שנחלקו טמאים אתי כרבי יהודה ודוחק והא דאמר דגזרו על הזאה שבשעת מלאכה משום הזאה שלא בשעת מלאכה אף על גב דשלא בשעת מלאכה טהור גמור הוא ואין צריך הזאה כלל מ"מ כשחוזרים ועושים בו מלאכה חוזר לטומאתו ישנה והחמירו חכמים בטומאה ישנה שלא תועיל לו הזאה שלא בשעת מלאכה כיון שאינו חיבור דבר תורה וגזרו על הזאה שבשעת מלאכה אטו הזאה שלא בשעת מלאכה · רשב"א: **דבר** תורה בשעת מלאכה חיבור. תימה מאי שנא ממוכני דאמר (לעיל דף מד:) בזמן שהיא נשמטת דאינו חיבור וצריך לחלק:
ועל

רבינו חננאל

חטאת מפני שהוא מחובר בבגד אבל מגופת החבית שאינה מן החבית עצמה מותר לפתחה בשבת. רמי ליה (ר' יוחנן) ר' ירמי' לר"ז שלל הכובסין כו' עד המקל שעשאו יד לקורדום כו' פירוש הכובסין שוללין יריעות זו עם זו כדי שיהו נוחין לכביסה ואינה תפירה אלא שלילה מלשון (מו"ק כב:) על המתים כולן שולל לאחר שבעה ומשני ליה ר' זירא מקל שעשאו יד לקורדום כיון שמשלים מלאכתו זורק אותו מקל לבין העצים אבל שלל של כובסין אע"פ ששלמה כביסתם רוצה בשלילותן שמא יטנפו יחזור ויחוורום: מאן תנא כל המחובר לו הרי הוא כמוהו אמר רב ר"מ היא ונדחה ופשוטה היא: ת"ר מספורת של פרקין פי' שמתפרק זה מזה וכן איזמל של רהיטי. חיבור לטומאה ואם נטמא אחד נטמא האחר ואינן חיבור להזאה. פרשה רבא דבר תורה בשעת מלאכה. כלומר בשעה שעוזו בהן חיבור הן לטומאה ולהזאה. שלא בשעת מלאכה אינן חיבור לא לטומאה ולא

רב נסים גאון

בעל השמועה: אי ככירה דמו אפילו באויר נמי ליטמו. עיקר דילה משתכח בתורת כהנים וכל כלי חרש אשר יפול מהם אל תוכו מתוכו הוא מיטמא ואינו מטמא מאחוריו כו' יכול אף הכלים יהו מיטמאין באויר כלי חרש תלמוד לומר [וכו'] אוכלין מיטמאין באויר כלי חרס ואין הכלים מיטמאין באויר כלי חרס ובפרק ב' מן מס' כלים שנינו כלי חרס וכלי נתר טומאתן שוה ומטמאין באויר ותמצא בפרק יציאות השבת (דף טז) והמשנה והתוס' מליאה מענין זה ובתלמוד בפ' ראשון מן שחיטת חולין (דף כד) שנו במשנה הטהור בכל הכלים טמא בכלי חרס ובברייתא גרסינן ת"ר אויר כלי חרס טמא וגבו טהור:

מסורת הש"ס

וככלים ז. פיר"י בעק"א בלע"ז ע"ש
[ג"י הערוך בערך שלל תנן שלל הכובסין והבגד שהוא תפור בכלאים חיבור לטומאה וכו']
כלים פ"ט מ"ג
לקמן נח: [שתי ברייתות הן בתוספתא דכלים ב"מ פ"ג]

הגהות הב"ח

(א) גמ' מקל שעשאו יד:

גליון הש"ס

גמ' עבדו בהו רבנן היכרא. לעיל דף טז ע"א נדה דף לד ע"א: תוס' ד"ה אי חיבור וכו' וצריכים זה לזה בשעת מלאכה. עי' ביצה דף כב ע"ב תוס' ד"ה משום שלשה כלים:

[48b] What is the difference between this and the bung of a barrel?[4]—Said Raba to him: The one is an integral part thereof, whereas the other is not.

R. Jeremiah pointed out a contradiction to R. Zera. We learnt: The fuller's loosely stitched bundle,[5] or a bunch of keys, or a garment stitched together with *kil'ayim* thread[6] are counted as connected in respect of uncleanness,[7] until one begins to undo them. This proves that they are [regarded as] joined even not at the time of work.[8] But the following is opposed thereto: If a stick is improvised to serve as a handle for an axe, it is counted as connected in respect of uncleanness at the time of work. [Thus,] only at the time of work, but not otherwise?—There, he replied, a man is wont to throw it [the handle] among the timber when it is not being used. Here, a man prefers [that pieces remain together][9] even not at the time of work, so that if they are soiled he can rewash them.[10]

In Sura the following discussion was recited in R. Ḥisda's name. In Pumbeditha it was recited in R. Kahana's name—others state, in Raba's name. Who is the Tanna responsible for the statement of the Rabbis: Whatever is joined to an article is counted as the article itself?—Said Rab Judah in Rab's name, It is R. Meir. For we learnt: The receptacles on a stove for the oil-flask, spice-pot, and the lamp are defiled through contact, but not through air space: this is R. Meir's opinion. But R. Simeon declares them a clean.[1] Now, as for R. Simeon, it is well: he holds that they are not as the stove. But according to R. Meir,—if they are as the stove, let them be defiled even through air space; if they are not as the stove, let them not be defiled even through contact?—In truth, they are not as the stove, but the Rabbis decreed [uncleanness] in their case. If they decreed it, let them be defiled even through air space too?—The Rabbis made a distinction, so that people might not come to burn *terumah* and holy food on account of them.[2]

Our Rabbis taught: A shears of separate blades[3] and the cutter of a [carpenter's] plane are [counted as] connected in respect of uncleanness,[4] but not in respect of sprinkling.[5] What will you: if they are both [counted as] connected, [they are so] even in respect of sprinkling too; if [they do] not [count as] connected, [they are not so] even in respect of defilement?—Said Raba: By Scriptural law, when in use they are [counted as] connected in respect of both defilement and sprinkling; when not in use, they are [counted as] connected in respect of neither

(4) Which according to the Rabbis *infra* 146a, may be pierced on the Sabbath. (5) Of linen; they used to sew articles of washing loosely together, to prevent loss. (6) V. Glos. (7) If one part becomes unclean, the others are likewise, though they are sure to be untied at a later stage. (8) E.g., the fuller's bundle need be sewn together only at the actual washing, yet the single pieces are regarded as one even afterwards, so long as one has not commenced to untie them. (9) That the pieces remain together until required. (10) Without having to search for the pieces.

a (1) Separate receptacles for a flask of oil, spices, and a lamp were attached to earthen stoves. These stoves are defiled in two ways: (i) when an unclean object actually touches them on the inside; (ii) if an unclean object is suspended within their cavity, i.e., their air space. R. Meir holds that in the first case the attached receptacles too are defiled, as part of the stove, but not in the second; while R. Simeon maintains that they remain clean in both cases. (2) If these receptacles, having been defiled through the stove, came into contact with *terumah* and holy food, they are unclean in their turn, but only by Rabbinical law, whereas they must be unclean by Scriptural law before they may be burnt. Hence the Rabbis limited their defilement, that it might be fully understood that it is merely Rabbinical. (3) Lit., 'joints'. (4) If one part becomes unclean the other is too. (5) If a utensil is defiled through a corpse, it needs sprinkling of water mixed with the ashes of the red heifer to render it clean (v. Num. XIX). If the mixture is sprinkled on one part but not on the other the latter is not cleansed.

defilement nor sprinkling. [49a] But the Rabbis imposed a preventive measure in respect of defilement, when they are not a in use,[1] on account of defilement when they are in use;[2] and in respect of sprinkling, when they are in use,[3] on account of when they are not in use.

WHEN THEY ARE MOIST. The Scholars propounded: Naturally moist, or artificially moist?[4]—Come and hear: [WE MAY NOT STORE ...] IN STRAW, GRAPE-SKINS, FLOCKING OR HERBAGE WHEN THEY ARE MOIST. Now, if you say [that it means] artificially moistened, it is well; but if you say, naturally moist, how can flocking be naturally moist?—[It is possible] in the case of wool plucked from between the flanks.[5] And as to what R. Oshaia taught: We may store [food] in a dry cloth[6] and in dry produce, but not in a damp cloth or moist produce,—how is naturally damp cloth possible?—In the case of wool plucked from between the flanks.

MISHNAH. WE MAY STORE [FOOD] IN GARMENTS, PRODUCE,[7] DOVES' WINGS, CARPENTERS' SAWDUST[8] AND THOROUGHLY BEATEN HATCHELLED FLAX. R. JUDAH FORBIDS [STORING] IN FINE, BUT PERMITS [IT] IN COARSE [BEATEN FLAX].

GEMARA. R. Jannai said: *Tefillin*[9] demand a pure body, like Elisha, the man of wings. What does this mean?—Abaye said: That one must not pass wind while wearing them; Raba said: That one must not sleep in them.[10] And why is he called 'the man of wings'? Because the wicked Roman government once proclaimed a decree against Israel that whoever donned *tefillin* b should have his brains pierced through;[1] yet Elisha put them on and went out into the streets. [When] a quaestor saw him, he fled before him, whereupon he gave pursuit. As he overtook him he [Elisha] removed them from his head and held them in his hand. 'What is that in your hand?' he demanded. 'The wings of a dove,' was his reply. He stretched out his hand and lo! they were the wings of a dove. Therefore he is called 'Elisha the man of the wings'. And why the wings of a dove rather than that of other birds? Because the Congregation of Israel is likened to a dove, as it is said, *as the wings of a dove covered with silver*:[2] just as a dove is protected by its wings, so is Israel protected by the precepts.[3]

IN CARPENTERS' SAWDUST, etc. The scholars propounded: Does R. Judah refer to carpenters' sawdust or to hatchelled flax?—Come and hear: R. Judah said: Fine hatchelled flax is like foliage.[4] This proves that he refers to hatchelled flax. This proves it.

MISHNAH. WE MAY STORE [FOOD] IN FRESH HIDES, AND THEY MAY BE HANDLED;[5] IN WOOL SHEARINGS, BUT THEY MAY NOT BE HANDLED.[6] WHAT THEN IS DONE? THE LID [OF THE POT] IS LIFTED, AND THEY [THE SHEARINGS] FALL OFF OF THEIR OWN ACCORD. R. ELEAZAR B. 'AZARIAH SAID: THE BASKET[7] IS TILTED ON ONE SIDE AND [THE FOOD] IS REMOVED, LEST ONE LIFT [THE POT] AND BE UNABLE TO REPLACE IT.[8] BUT THE SAGES SAY: ONE MAY TAKE AND REPLACE [IT].[9]

GEMARA. R. Jonathan b. Akinai and R. Jonathan b. Eleazar were sitting, and R. Ḥanina b. Ḥama sat with them and it was asked: Did we learn, FRESH HIDES belonging to a private indi- c vidual, but those of an artisan, since he is particular about them,[1] may not be handled; or perhaps, we learnt about those of an artisan, and all the more so those of a private individual?—Said R. Jonathan b. Eleazar to them: It stands to reason that we learnt about those belonging to a private individual, but as for those of an artisan, he is particular about them. Thereupon R. Ḥanina b. Ḥama observed to them: Thus did R. Ishmael b. R. Jose say:

a (1) That both limbs should count as one. (2) To prevent laxity in the latter case. (3) That they should not count as one. (4) Lit., 'through themselves or through something else'. The former throws out more heat. (5) Of a living animal: this contains its own moisture. (6) Lit., 'raiment'. (7) E.g., corn or pulse. (8) Or, shavings. (9) V. Glos. (10) Phylacteries used to be worn all day.

b (1) V. *infra* 130a. (2) Ps. LXVIII, 14. (3) In Gen. R. XXXIX, 8 the point of comparison is stated thus: all birds fly with both wings, and when exhausted they rest on a crag or rock; but the dove, when tired, rests on one wing and flies with the other. So Israel, when driven from one country, finds refuge and rest in another; v. also note a.l. in Sonc. ed. (4) Which may not be used; *supra* 47b. (5) Whether food was put away in them or not. They are fit for reclining upon, and therefore rank as utensils, which may be handled. (6) Because they are *mukẓeh*, being set aside to be woven and spun. (7) Containing the pot and the shearings. (8) If the pot is bodily lifted out, the shearings may all collapse, and since they must not be handled, they cannot be parted in order to replace the pot. (9) This is discussed in the Gemara.

c (1) He has to sell, and is therefore particular not to spoil them. This may render them *mukẓeh*.

וגזרו רבנן על טומאה שלא בשעת מלאכה משום טומאה שבשעת מלאכה ועל הזאה שבשעת מלאכה משום הזאה שלא בשעת מלאכה: בזמן שהן לחין: איבעיא להו לחין מחמת עצמן או דילמא לחין מחמת דבר אחר ת"ש לא בתבן ולא בזגים ולא במוכין ולא בעשבים בזמן שהן לחין אי אמרת בשלמא לחין מחמת דבר אחר שפיר אלא אי אמרת לחין מחמת עצמן מוכין לחין מחמת עצמן היכי משכחת לה ממרטא דביני אטמי והא דתני רבי אושעיא טומנין בכסות יבשה ובפירות יבשין אבל לא בכסות לחה ולא בפירות לחין כסות לחה מחמת עצמה היכי משכחת לה ממרטא דביני אטמי: **מתני'** טומנין בכסות ובפירות בכנפי יונה ובנסורת של חרשים ובנעורת של פשתן *דקה רבי יהודה אוסר בדקה ומתיר בגסה: **גמ'** *א"ר ינאי תפילין צריכין גוף נקי *כאלישע בעל כנפים מאי היא אביי אמר שלא יפיח בהן רבא אמר שלא יישן בהן ואמאי קרי ליה בעל כנפים שפעם אחת גזרה מלכות רומי הרשעה גזירה על ישראל שכל המניח תפילין ינקרו את מוחו והיה אלישע מניחם ויוצא לשוק ראהו קסדור אחד רץ מפניו ורץ אחריו וכיון שהגיע אצלו נטלן מראשו ואחזן בידו אמר לו מה זה בידך אמר לו כנפי יונה פשט את ידו ונמצאו כנפי יונה לפיכך קורין אותו אלישע בעל כנפים *ומאי שנא כנפי יונה משאר עופות משום דאמתיל כנסת ישראל ליונה שנאמר °כנפי יונה נחפה בכסף וגו' מה יונה כנפיה מגינות עליה אף ישראל מצות מגינות עליהן: בנסורת של חרשין וכו': איבעיא להו רבי יהודה אנסורת של חרשין קאי או אנעורת של פשתן קאי ת"ש דתניא *רבי יהודה אומר נעורת של פשתן דקה הרי הוא כזבל ש"מ אנעורת של פשתן קאי ש"מ: **מתני'** טומנין בשלחין ומטלטלין אותן בגיזי צמר ואין מטלטלין אותן כיצד הוא עושה נוטל את הכסוי והן נופלות ר"א בן עזריה אומר קופה מטה על צדה ונוטל שמא יטול ואינו יכול להחזיר וחכ"א נוטל ומחזיר: **גמ'** יתיב ר' יונתן בן עכינאי ורבי יונתן בן אלעזר ויתיב ר' חנינא בר חמא גבייהו וקא מיבעיא להו שלחין של בעה"ב תנן אבל של אומן כיון דקפיד עלייהו לא מטלטלינן להו או דילמא של אומן תנן וכ"ש של בעה"ב אמר להו ר' יונתן בן אלעזר מסתברא של בעה"ב תנן אבל של אומן קפיד עלייהו אמר להו ר' חנינא בר חמא כך אמר ר' ישמעאל בר' יוסי אבא

רש"י

וגזרו על הטומאה שלא בשעת מלאכה. שיהא חיבור: ועל הזאה שבשעת מלאכה. שלא יהא חיבור הלכך חיבור לטומאה לעולם ואין חיבור להזאה כלל: לחין מחמת עצמן. מחממות טפי מלחין מחמת משקין שטופלין עליהן מסיבתו: ה"ג מוכין לחין מחמת עצמן היכי משכחת לה: ממרטא דביני אטמי. מלמר הנמרט מבין ירכותיה של בהמה שהוא מלא זיעה והוא לח מעלמו להכי קרי ליה מרטא דלאו בר גיזה הוא: **מתני'** נעורת. דק דק שנוערין מן הפשתן וקורין ארישט"ש: נסורת. שמנסרים הנגרים מן העצים: ובפירות. כגון חטין וקטניות: כנפי יונה. נוצה: **גמ'** שלא יפיח. שיכול להעמיד עצמו בשעת הרוח: שלא יישן בהן. שמא יפיח או יראה קרי אבל אם יכול להזהר שלא יישן בהן כל הגופים נקיים בהפחה שיכולין להעמיד עצמן: ינקרו את מוחו. שהוא תחת התפילין ינקרו לשון ניקור עינים: קסדור. מניסטרא"ל שהיה ממונה על כך: כנפי יונה. כדמפרש לקמיה מפני שהם מצות והם מגינין לישראל והויא להם ככנפים ליונה שהיא נמשלת ליונה והמצות ככנפים: כנפיה מגינות עליה. מן הצנה ומכל עוף ואדם הבא עליה היא נלחמת ומכה בראש גפה מה שאין כן בשאר עופות: הרי הוא כזבל. דמוסיף הבל: **מתני'** שלחין. עורות כמו והפשיט תרגום ושלח: ומטלטלין אותן. בין שטמן בהן בין שלא טמן בהן דחזו למזגא עלייהו: ואין מטלטלין אותן. דמוקצות הן לטוות ולארוג: כיצד הוא עושה. זה שטמן בהן כיצד יטול קדרתו הואיל ואסור לטלטלן שהרי היא טמונה כולה בהן: נוטל כיסוי. של קדרה שיש תורת כלי עליה ואף על גב שהן עליה לא איכפת לן דלא נעשית בסיס להן שאין עשוי אלא לכסות קדרה: רבי אלעזר בן עזריה אומר קופה מטה על לדה ונוטל. כשבא ליטול הקדרה מטה הקופה על לדה: שמא יטול. הקדרה ויפלו הגיזין שמכאן ומכאן לתוך גומא שישבה בהן ואם יצטרך לחזור ולהטמינה לא יוכל לטלטל גיזין לכאן ולכאן ולעשות גומא להחזירה בתוכה: נוטל ומחזיר. בגמרא מפרש לה: **גמ'** שלחין של בעה"ב תנן. דמותר לטלטלן שאין עומדין לימכר ולא קפיד עלייהו כי מטנפי וחזי למזגא עלייהו: אבל של אומן. שעומדות למוכרן קפיד עלייהו הלכך לא למזגא קיימי ואין מטלטלין אותן: שלחה

תוספות

ועל הזאה שבשעת מלאכה משום הזאה שלא בשעת מלאכה. תימה דהא גבי מקל שעשאו יד לקורדם קאמר דהוי חיבור לטומאה משמע אבל לא להזאה ואמאי והא לא שייך למגזר התם אטו שלא בשעת מלאכה כדאמר לעיל דאדם עשוי לזורקו בין העצים וי"ל דהתם לא הוי חיבור להזאה משום דאפילו בשעת מלאכה לא הוי חיבור דבר תורה דלא חשיב כלל בית יד בשום פעם כיון שהוא עשוי לזורקו כל שעה:

אבל לא בכסות לחה כו'. נראה דרבי אושעיא פליג אמתני':

כאלישע בעל כנפים. להכי נקט אלישע דמסתמא כיון שנעשה לו נס בתפילין היה זהיר בהן והיה לו גוף נקי ומזה הטעם אין אנו יכולין ליפטר שהרי בזה אנו יכולין להזהר ואין תימה על מה שמצוה זאת רפויה בידינו שגם בימי חכמים היתה רפויה כדתניא בפרק ר' אליעזר דמילה (לקמן קל.) ר"ש בן אלעזר אומר כל מצוה שלא מסרו עצמן ישראל עליה בשעת גזירת המלכות כגון תפילין עדיין היא רפויה בידם והא דאמרינן בפ"ק דראש השנה (דף יז.) פושעי ישראל בגופן קרקפתא דלא מנח תפילין אומר ר"ת דמיירי באותן שעושין מחמת מרד ומבזין המצות ושוחקין ברלועה שבידם ובראשם כדאמר ביומא (דף לו:) פשעים אלו המרדין והא דאמר במדרש תפילין מפני מה לא החזיקו בהן מפני הרמאים אין נראה לר"י דמשום רמאין נמנעו מלעשות מצוה אלא ה"פ מפני מה לא החזיקו נאמנות באדם המניח תפילין *וקאמר מפני הרמאין שהיו מניחין תפילין לרמות בני אדם כדמפרש התם מעשה בתלמיד אחד שהפקיד מעותיו אצל אחד שהיה מניח תפילין כשתבע בו אמר להד"ם אמר ליה אותו תלמיד לא לך הפקדתי אלא לתפילין שעל ראשך וע"ע שם:

אביי אמר שלא יפיח בהן. שיוכל לשמור עצמו מלהפיח עד שיסיר תפילין כדפירש בקונט' אבל לא חייש שמא יישן דאע"ג דפעמים יוכל ליזהר משינה ורבא מצריך גם שיוכל להעמיד עצמו בשעה שתאחזנו השינה שלא ישן פתאום ומיהו אביי נמי מודה דאסור לישן בהן כדתניא בפרק הישן (סוכה כו. ושם) דאסור לישן בתפילין בין שינת קבע בין שינת עראי:

שלא יישן בהן. משום שלא יפיח בהן בשעת שינה או משום היסח הדעת אבל משום קרי אין לחוש כדאמר בפ' הישן (ג"ז שם:) דא"ר יוסי ילדים לעולם הוללין מפני שרגילין בטומאה ופריך לימא קסבר ר' יוסי בעל קרי אסור להניח תפילין ומשני הכא בילדים ונשותיהם עמהם עסקינן שמא יבאו לידי הרגל דבר. אבל משום קרי לא בעי למיסר:

נטלם מראשו. ואף על גב דאמר בסנהדרין (דף עד: ושם) בשעת גזרת המלכות אפי' על מצוה קלה יהרג ואל יעבור ואפילו לשנויי ערקתא דמסאנא אסור הייט משום דבשינוי ערקתא מתנהג כעובד כוכבים ודומה שמוציא עצמו מכלל ישראל. אבל הכא היט עושה כלום אלא שאין לו תפילין בראשו שעה אחת והרבה ישראל שאין להם תפילין כמותו:

כנפיה מגינות עליה. אור"י דאמרינן במדרש* כל העופות כשהן יגעין ניטחין ע"ג סלע והיונה בשעה שהיא יגעה פורחת באחת וניטחת באחת:

טומנין בשלחין ומטלטלין אותן. הא דאמר בפ"ק דבילה (ד' יא.) נותנין העור לפני הדורסן דהתירו סופן משום תחילתן פי' כדי שישחוט לצורך יו"ט אבל עור דמערב יו"ט משמע התם דאסור לטלטל ובפרק כל כתבי (לקמן קטז:) קאמר אם מטלטלין תיק הספר עם הספר לא נטלטל עור אגב בשר משמע דעור בלא בשר אסור פירש"י בפרק כל כתבי (ג"ז שם*) דהכא מיירי בעור בהמה גסה והתם בעור בהמה דקה דלא חזי למזגא כולי האי ולפירושו האי דבילה נמי מיירי בעור בהמה דקה והא דתנן בפ' כל כתבי (דף קכ.) פורסין עור גדי על גבי התבה ט' צריך לומר לפי' דמיירי כשיחדו לישיבה °ור"ת מפרש דהכא מיירי ביבשין דחזי למזגא עלייהו והתם בלחין: אבא

רבינו חננאל

להזאה וגזרו שאם נטמא הא' שלא בשעת מלאכה נטמא גם האחר בכל מקו' שהוא. ודוק' אם הוא (מחברן) מחובר עדיין משום טומאה שבשעת מלאכה. וגזרו נמי על הזאה שאם יזה על הא' אפילו בשעת מלאכה לא נטהר האחר אע"פ שהוא מחובר עמו משו' הזאה שלא בשעת מלאכה. פי' אם יראה שהזה בשעת מלאכה על האחד ונטהר גם האחר יטהר הוא כשיזה על האחד אפילו השני שלא בשעת מלאכה: פי' מירטא דביני אטמא העמר שבין הירכות של בהמה כיון שתמיד השתנתה שותת בין ירכותיה יש בו לחלוחית לעולם ואינו מתנגב לעולם ואפילו עושה מאותו צמר כסות יש בו לחלוחית: תפלין צריכין גוף נקי. קיי"ל כרבא דאמר שלא יישן בהן: ר' יהודה אוסר. אוקימנא בנעורת: טומנין בשלחין ומטלטלין אותן. פירוש שלחין עורות גלשין שנגזז (כצמר) [הצמר] ועדיין לא נעבדו: אבא שלהא פירש

עין משפט נר מצוה

יא א מיי' פ"ד מהלכות שבת הלכה א:
יב ב מיי' פ"ד מהלכות שבת הלכה א טוש"ע או"ח סימן רנז סעיף ג:
יג ג מיי' פ"ד מהלכות תפילין הלכה טו סמג עשין כב טוש"ע או"ח סימן לז סעיף ב ג:
יד ד מיי' פ"ד מהלכות שבת הלכה א:
טו ה מיי' פ"ד מהלכות שבת שם ופכ"ו הל' יב סמג לאוין סה טור שו"ע או"ח סימן רנט סעיף א:

[ברי"ף וברא"ש ליתא]

[ועי' ירושלמי פרק הים קורא הלכה ד]

מסורת הש"ס

לקמן קל.
[עי' תוספות בבא בתרא י: ד"ה אלא]
[ברכות נג: ע"ש גיטין מה. סנהדרין לה. לקמן קל.]
[לקמן נח:]
[בב"ר סדר לך לך פרשה לט]
בר"ס נתרתי פליגי

תהלים סח

גליון הש"ס

תום' ד"ה טומנין בשלחין וכו' ור"ת מפרש. עי' זבחים דף לג ע"ב תוס' ד"ה מגע בכס"ד:

עין משפט נר מצוה

טז א מיי' פכ"ו מהלכות שבת הלכה יב סמג לאוין סה טוש"ע או"ח סימן שח סעיף כה:

יז ב שם סעיף כו:

יח ג מיי' פכ"ו מהלכות שבת שם סמג שם טור שו"ע או"ח סימן רנט סעיף א:

אבא שלחא הוה *ואמר הביאו שלחין ונשב עליהן מיתיבי נסרין של בעה"ב מטלטלין אותן ושל אומן אין מטלטלין אותן ואם חישב לתת עליהן פת לאורחין בין כך ובין כך מטלטלין שאני נסרים דקפיד עלייהו ת"ש עורות בין עבודין ובין שאין עבודין מותר לטלטלן בשבת לא אמרו עבודין אלא לענין טומאה בלבד מאי לאו לא שנא של בעל הבית ולא שנא של אומן לא של בעה"ב אבל של אומן מאי אין מטלטלין אי הכי הא דתני ולא אמרו עבודין אלא לענין טומאה בלבד לפלוג וליתני בדידה בד"א בשל בעה"ב אבל בשל אומן לא כולה בבעל הבית קמיירי כתנאי עורות של בעה"ב מטלטלין אותן ושל אומן אין מטלטלין אותן ר' יוסי אומר אחד זה ואחד זה מטלטלין אותן:

הדור יתבי וקמיבעיא להו הא *דתנן אבות מלאכות ארבעים חסר אחת כנגד מי אמר להו ר' חנינא בר חמא כנגד עבודות המשכן אמר להו ר' יונתן בר' אלעזר כך אמר רבי שמעון ברבי יוסי בן לקוניא כנגד *מלאכה מלאכתו ומלאכת שבתורה ארבעים חסר אחת בעי רב יוסף ויבא הביתה לעשות מלאכתו ממנינא הוא או לא א"ל אביי וליתי ספר תורה ולימני מי לא *אמר רבה בר בר חנה א"ר יוחנן לא זזו משם עד שהביאו ספר תורה ומנאום אמר ליה כי קא מספקא לי משום דכתיב והמלאכה היתה דים ממנינא הוא והא כמאן דאמר* לעשות צרכיו נכנס או דילמא ויבא הביתה לעשות מלאכתו ממנינא הוא והאי והמלאכה היתה דים הכי קאמר דשלים ליה עבידתא תיקו תניא כמאן דאמר כנגד עבודות המשכן דתניא אין חייבין אלא על מלאכה שכיוצא בה היתה במשכן הם זרעו ואתם לא תזרעו הם קצרו ואתם לא תקצרו הם העלו את הקרשים מקרקע לעגלה ואתם לא תכניסו מרה"ר לרה"י הם הורידו את הקרשים מעגלה לקרקע ואתם לא תוציאו מרה"י לרה"ר הם הוציאו מעגלה לעגלה ואתם לא תוציאו מרה"י לרשות היחיד מאי קא עביד אביי ורבא דאמרי תרווייהו ואיתימא רב אדא בר אהבה מרשות היחיד לרה"י דרך רשות הרבים: בגיזי צמר ואין מטלטלין: אמר רבא לא שנו אלא שלא טמן בהן אבל טמן בהן מטלטלין אותן איתיביה ההוא מרבנן בר יומיה לרבא טומנין בגיזי צמר ואין מטלטלין אותן כיצד הוא עושה נוטל

תורה אור: בראשית לט; שמות לו

רש"י

שלחא הוה. אומן לעבד עורות: ואמר. בחול: הביאו שלחין ונשב עליהן. אלמא לא קפיד: דקפיד עלייהו. שמא יתקלקלו: ולא אמרו עבודין. לא הוזכרו לחלק בין עבודין לשאין עבודין אלא לענין טומאה. דעבודין מקבלין טומאה ולא שאין עבודין: לפלוג בדידה. בטלטול גופיה איכא לפלוגי בשל אומן בין עבודין לשאין עבודין דעבודין קפיד עלייהו: בד"א. דעבודין מותר לטלטלן בשל בעה"ב אבל של אומן מאחר שעבדן קפיד עלייהו: כולה בבעה"ב איירי. ומהדר ליפלוגי בבעה"ב דאיירי ביה ולא אשכח לפלוגי אלא לענין טומאה ואי שבקיה לבעה"ב דאיירי ביה ונקט אומן *מפסקא למילתיה טפי מדהשתא: הדור יתבי. הנך רבנן דלעיל: כנגד עבודות המשכן. אותן המנויות שם בפרק כלל גדול היו צריכין למשכן ופרשת שבת נסמכה לפרשת מלאכת המשכן ללמוד הימנה: שבתורה. שכתובים בכל התורה והכי קאמר קרא (שמות כ) לא תעשה כל מלאכה כמנין כל מלאכה שבתורה: לא זזו משם. °לא ידענא היכא איתמר ומיהו [אפשר] לענין וי"ו דגחון אתמר מדפרכינן לה נמי בקדושין *גבי וי"ו דגחון ומתרצינן אינהו הוו בקיאי בחסרות ויתרות ש"מ לענין אותיות איתמר והכא ליכא לשנויי הכי: משום דכתיב והמלאכה היתה דים. ואי מנינן לתרווייהו הוו ארבעים ומדתנן אבות מלאכות ארבעים חסר אחת איכא חד דלא ממנינא ובהני תרי דאיכא למימר דלא מלאכה נינהו ולא ידענא הי מינייהו נפיק והכי קא מיבעיא ליה והמלאכה היתה דים ממנינא היא ומלאכה ממש קאמר והכי קאמר המלאכה שהיו עושין היו עושין די לא פחות מן הצורך ולא יותר מן הצורך כגון רידודי טסין לציפוי הקרשים לדי היו מרדדין אותם וכן בטווי של יריעות והאי לעשות מלאכתו הוא דמפיק ומסייע למאן דאמר במסכת סוטה לעשות צרכיו נכנס לשכב עמה אלא שנראתה לו דמות דיוקנו של אביו ואמר לו עתידין אחיך ליכתב על אבני אפוד רצונך שימחה שמך מביניהם כו' או דילמא האי לעשות מלאכתו מלאכה ממש הוא ומסייע לה לאידך: והאי והמלאכה היתה דים. לאו מלאכה היא אלא כדמשמע קרא בהבאת נדבה וכמאן דאמר שלימא ליה עבידתא מלאכת ההבאה שלא היו צריכין עוד וכל מידי דרמי עליה דאיניש קרי ליה עבידתא כדאמרינן במסכת סוטה (דף לג.) בטילת עבידתא דאמר סנאה לאייתואה להיכלא ואינו אלא צבא מלחמה להחריב: הם זרעו וקצרו סמנין. לצבוע תכלת ועורות אילים וטחנו ולשו נמי סמנין לצבוע ואופה דקתני במתני' באבות מלאכות הוא בישול סמנין אלא דנקט סידורא דפת והכי מפרש בפרק כלל גדול (לקמן דף עד:): קרקע. רשות הרבים: עגלה. רשות היחיד שגבוהה י' ורחבה ד': דרך רשות הרבים. דאויר שבין העגלות רשות הרבים: אבל טמן בהן מטלטלין אותן. קס"ד השתא דמילי מילי קתני מתניתין ולאו אהנך דטמן בהן קאי: ההוא מרבנן בר יומיה. אותו היום בא לבית מדרשו תחלה*:

[פי' אחר רב אידי הוה דסוס קרי לי' בר בי רב דחד יומא בחגיגה ה: ערוך]

תוספות

אבא שלחא. פר"ח ואמר הביאו לי שלחין בשבת והלכה כר' יוסי דקי"ל מעשה רב וכן נראה דלאו בחול מיירי כדפי' בקונט' ולא מייתי ראיה אלא דאומן נמי לא קפיד טפי הוה ליה לאתויי דר' יוסי אבוה דשרי לקמן בהדיא של אומן: לא אמרו עבודין אלא לענין טומאה בלבד. פרש"י שאין עור מקבל טומאה עד לאחר עיבוד ואם תאמר והא אמר בזבחים בפ' דם חטאת (דף צג: ושם) מניין לרבות עור משהופשט תלמוד לומר אשר יזה עליה תכבס יכול אף עור שלא הופשט תלמוד לומר בגד מה בגד מקבל טומאה אף כל דבר המקבל טומאה משמע דעור משהופשט מקבל טומאה ויש לומר דהתם כשיחדו לישיבה והכא כשלא יחדו ואפ"ה מותר לטלטלו בשבת והא דאמר רבא בריש כל הכלים (לקמן קכג.) מדלענין טומאה לאו מנא הוא לענין שבת נמי לאו מנא הוא גבי מחט שניטל חורה או עוקצה ה"פ מדלענין טומאה לאו מנא הוא אפי' ע"י יחוד דניטל חורה או עוקצה טהורה ולא מהני בה יחוד והא דתנן במסכת כלים בפרק י"ג (משנה ה) מחט שניטל חורה או עוקצה טהורה ואם התקינה למיתוח טמאה אומר ר"י דהתם מיירי כשעשה בה שום שינוי ותיקון למיתוח אבל ביחוד בעלמא למיתוח אינה טמאה אבל היכא דהוי מנא לענין טומאה ע"י יחוד לגבי שבת הוי מנא בלא יחוד וכן משמע התם דקאמר תרגמא אביי אליבא דרבא בגלמי דזמינן דממליך עלייהו ומשוי להו מנא להכי מותר לטלטלה אע"ג דאכתי לא אימליך עלה והיא טהורה: ארבעים אבות מלאכות חסר אחת כנגד מי. הרבה מלאכות יש דדמיין להדדי והוה לן למחשביניהו כולן כאחת כדפריך בפרק כלל גדול (לקמן עג:) היינו זורה היינו בורר היינו מרקד ומשום חילוק מועט שביניהם לא הוה מחלקינן להו אי לאו דקים להו דל"ט מלאכות הן כנגד שום דבר לכך בעי כנגד מי: כנגד כל מלאכה שבתורה. לכאורה נראה דיליף נמי ממשכן שהרי לכך נסמכה פרשת שבת לפרשת משכן ועוד דאי לא יליף ממשכן א"כ היכי ידעינן לדידיה הי ניהו אבות מלאכות והי תולדות דאין סברא לומר שמדעתם בירכו מלאכות החשובות ועשאום אבות ועוד דבהדיא תנן לקמן בהזורק* המושיט חייב שכך [דף צו:] היתה עבודת הלוים אלא לפי שיש מלאכות דומות זו לזו ואנו עושין שתיהן אבות כגון מרקד ובורר לכך חלקום חכמים להשלים מנין מלאכות שבתורה הואיל וחלוקות קצת זו מזו ואי אפשר לומר כן דלא פליג מדקאמר בסמוך תניא כמ"ד כנגד עבודות המשכן משמע דפליגי ועוד למאן דלית ליה דרשא דמלאכת ומלאכה מנא ליה דחשיב זורה ובורר בשתים ועוד לקמן משמע דמטעם דכנגד עבודות המשכן לא אית לן לאחשוביניהו בתרתי דקאמר אביי ורבא בפרק כלל גדול (לקמן עג:) כל מילתא דהואי במשכן אע"ג דאיכא דדמיא לה חשיב לה: הם העלו קרשים כו'. אפילו רבנן דפליגי ארבי יוסי ברבי יהודה גבי *) נעץ קנה ברשות הרבים ובראשו טרסקל ולית להו גוד אחית מודו בעגלה שהיא רשות היחיד כיון דעגלה גופה יש אורך בזקיפה עשרה ורוחב ארבעה אע"פ שתחתיה רשות הרבים ובריש כל גגות (עירובין פט.) [ד"ה במחיצות] הארכתי יותר: ואתם אל תכניסו. ואפ"ה לא הויא אב כדפרישית לעיל (דף ב.) [ד"ה פשט]:

*) [לעיל ה. לקמן קא.]

מסורת הש"ס

פ"א מספקא

ב"ק ב. לק עג. וש"נ

[דף ל.]

[ועי' תוי"ט שבת פ"ז מ"ב סד"ה אבות ועי' חידושי רמב"ן ורשב"א בשם פיר"ח]

קידושין ל. ע"ש

סוטה לו:

גליון הש"ס

רש"י ד"ה לא זזו לא ידענא כו'. עיין ברכות דף כה ע"ב רש"י ד"ה מאן שמעת ליה וש"נ:

רבינו חננאל

פשט עורות היה וקבלנו מרבותינו דהלכתא כר' יוסי דקיי"ל מעשה רב ואמר ר' ישמעאל בר' יוסי אבא שלחא הוה ואמר הביאו שלחין ונשב עליהן. נמצא כי עשה מעשה כשמועתו דתניא עורות של בעל הבית מטלטלין אותן. של אומן אין מטלטלין אותן. ר' יוסי אומר זה וזה מטלטלין הלכך עורו. של אומן הואיל וראויין לישב עליהן ואין נפסדין אינו מקפיד עליהן ומותר לטלטלן. אבל נסרין של אומן הואיל ואם ישב עליהן נפגמין הלכך קפיד עליהן ואסור לטלטלן: אמר ר' חנינה הא דתנן אבות מלאכות ארבעים חסר אחת כנגד עבודות המשכן. ותניא כוותיה אין חייבין אלא על מלאכה שכיוצא בה היתה במשכן כיצד הן זרעו וקצרו והעלו קרשים מקרקע לעגלה אתם לא תזרעו ולא תקצרו כו' הא דתנן אבות מלאכות ארבעים חסר אחת כו'. וא"ר יונתן בן אלעזר כנגד מלאכת ומלאכה שבתורה *) והן ס"א. לשתוציא ג' מלאכות הכתובין בויכולו השמים וד' שכתוב בהן ועשית ויעשה ותעשה ולרגל המלאכה וי"ג שכתב כל מלאכת עבודה הרי כ"א נשארו מ' ובכללם ששת ימים וכו' לא תעשה מלאכה. ולמה (כה:) כי בפירוש אמרו בתלמוד א"י שבא וח הכתוב להשלים ל"ט מלאכות בתורה ויש מי שמוציא מכלל אלו מ' ויבא יוסף הביתה לעשות מלאכתו ונשארו ל"ט ויש מי שמוציא והמלאכה היתה דים ולדברי הכל נשארים ל"ט מלאכות: פיס' בגיזי צמר ואין מטלטלין אותן' וקיי"ל

*) עי' רהכ"ן סימן ש"נ שמבאר היטב דברי הר"ח כמ"ש כאן וברמב"ן ורשב"א ע"ש:

רב נסים גאון

ולא אמרו עבודין אלא לענין טומאה בלבד. עיקר דיליה משתכח במסכת חולין בפ' העור והרוטב (דף קכב) וכולן שעיבדן או שהילך בהן כדי עבודה טהורין ובתוספתא וכולן שעיבדן ושהילך בהן כדי עבודה טהורין משום עור: אותיביה ההוא מרבנן בר יומיה לרבא זה התלמיד אמרו עליו באותו היום נכנס לבית המדרש על כן קרו ליה בר יומיה וכיוצא בו אמרנו בשחיטת קדשים (זבחים פ"ה דף נז) היה שם תלמיד אחד שבא לשמש לבית המדרש ור' יוסי הגלילי שמו וכבר היה רב אידי אבוה דר' יעקב בר אידי הוו קרי ליה בר בי רב דחד יומא כמו שאמרו (חגיגה דף ה) רב אידי אבוה דר' יעקב בר אידי הוה רגיל דהוה אתי תלתא ירחין באורחא והוה קאי חד יומא בבי רב והדר אזיל תלתא ירחין באורחא הוה קאי חד יומא באושפיזיה והדר אתי הוה קא קרו ליה בר בי רב דחד יומא חלש דעתיה קרי אנפשיה (איוב יב) שחוק לרעהו אהיה אמר ליה ר' יוחנן במטותא מינך לא תעניש רבנן נפק ר' יוחנן ודרש (ישעיה נח) ואותי יום יום ידרושון וכי ביום דורשין אותו ובלילה אין דורשין אותו אלא לומר לך כל העוסק בתורה אפילו יום אחד בשנה מעלה עליו הכתוב כאילו עוסק כל השנה כולה:

[49*b*] My father was a hide worker, and he would say: Fetch hides so that we may sit on them.[2]

An objection is raised: Boards belonging to a householder may be handled; those of an artisan may not be handled;[3] but if one intended to place bread upon them for guests, in both cases they may be handled?—Boards are different, for one is [certainly] particular about them.

Come and hear: Hides, whether tanned or not, may be handled on the Sabbath, 'tanned' being specified only in respect to uncleanness.[4] Now surely, no distinction is drawn whether they belong to a householder or an artisan?—No: [it means those] of a householder. But what of those of an artisan? They may not be handled? If so, when it is taught, '"tanned" being specified only in respect to uncleanness,' let a distinction be drawn and taught in that itself: [viz.,] when is that said? [Only] of those belonging to a householder, but not concerning those of an artisan?—The whole deals with those of a householder.[5]

This is dependent on Tannaim: Hides of a private individual may be handled, but those of an artisan may not: R. Jose maintained: Either the one or the other may be handled.

a Again they[1] sat and pondered: Regarding what we learnt, The principal categories of labour[2] are forty less one,—to what do they correspond?[3]—Said R. Ḥanina b. Ḥama to them: To the forms of labour in the Tabernacle.[4] R. Jonathan son of R. Eleazar said to them, Thus did R. Simeon b. R. Jose b. Laḳonia say: They correspond to [the words] *'work'* [melakah], *'his work'* [melakto], and *'the work of'* [meleketh], which are [written] thirty-nine times in the Torah.[5] R. Joseph asked: Is *'and he went into the house to do his work'*[6] included in this number, or not?—Said Abaye to him, Then let a Scroll of the Torah be brought and we will count! Did not Rabbah b. Bar Ḥanah say in R. Joḥanan's name: They did not stir thence until they brought a Scroll of the Torah and counted them?[7] The reason that I am doubtful, replied he, is because it is written, *for the work*[8] *they had was sufficient:*[9] is that of the number, while this[10] is [to be interpreted] in accordance with the view that he entered to perform his business;[11] or perhaps *'and he went into the house to do his work'* is of the number, while this *'for the work they had was sufficient'* is meant thus: their business was completed?[12] The question stands over.

It was taught as the opinion that it corresponds to the forms of labour in the Tabernacle. For it was taught: Liability is incurred only for work of which the same was performed in the Tabernacle. They sowed, hence ye must not sow; they reaped, hence ye must
b not reap;[1] they lifted up the boards from the ground to the waggon,[2] hence ye must not carry in from a public to a private domain; they lowered the boards from the waggon to the ground, hence ye must not carry out from a private to a public domain; they transported [boards, etc.,] from waggon to waggon, hence ye must not carry from one private to another private domain. 'From one private to another private domain'—what [wrong] is done? Abaye and Raba both explained—others say, R. Adda b. Ahabah: It means from one private to another private domain via public ground.

IN WOOL SHEARINGS, BUT THEY MAY NOT BE HANDLED. Raba said: They learnt this only where one had not stored [food] in them; but if one had stored food in them [on that Sabbath], they may be handled. A certain student of one day's standing[3] refuted Raba: WE MAY STORE [FOOD] . . . IN WOOL SHEARINGS, BUT THEY MAY NOT BE HANDLED. WHAT THEN IS DONE?

(2) This shows that he was not particular. (3) This shows that an artisan is particular. (4) Tanned hides are subject to the laws of defilement; untanned hides are not. (5) In whose case no distinction can be drawn between tanned and untanned skins save in respect of defilement.

a (1) The Rabbis mentioned above. (2) Forbidden on the Sabbath; for *aboth*, lit., 'fathers', v. *supra* 2*b*. (3) On what basis are they selected? (4) Every form of labour necessary in the Tabernacle was regarded as a principal category of work forbidden on the Sabbath. This is learnt from the juxtaposition of the commands concerning the Sabbath and the erection of the Tabernacle, Ex. XXXV, 1-3; 4 *seq*. (5) Lit., 'forty times minus one' (6) Gen. XXXIX, 11. (7) Rashi conjectures that the reference may be to the waw (ו) of *gaḥown* (גחון); v. Ḳid. 30*a*. (8) E.V. *'stuff'*. (9) Ex. XXXVI, 7. (10) *'And he went into the house to do his work'*. (11) A euphemism for adultery; v. Soṭ. 36*b*. In that case *melakto* (*his work*) does not connote actual work, and is not included. (12) They had brought all the materials required. On this supposition the verse is translated as in the E.V.

b (1) Certain vegetables had to be sown and reaped to provide dyes for the hangings. (2) The ground was a public domain, while the waggon was a private domain. (3) I.e., who had come to the college for the first time that day. V. Ḥag. 5*b*.

[50a] THE LID [OF THE POT] IS LIFTED, AND THEY [THE SHEARINGS] FALL OFF OF THEIR OWN ACCORD.[4] Rather if stated, it was thus stated: Raba said: They learnt this only when one had not designated them for storing, but if he had, they may be handled. It was stated likewise: When Rabin came,[5] he said in the name of R. Jacob in the name of R. Assi b. Saul in Rabbi's name: They learnt this only where one had not designated them for [constant][6] storing; but if he had designated them for [constant] storing, they may be handled. Rabina said: They [the Sages of the Mishnah] learnt in reference to the [merchant's] shelves.[7] It was taught likewise: Wool shearings of the shelves may not be handled; but if a private individual prepared them for use, they may be handled.

Rabbah b. Bar Ḥanah recited before Rab: If one cuts down dried branches of a palm tree for fuel and then changes his mind,
a [intending them] for a seat, he must tie [them] together;[1] R. Simeon b. Gamaliel said: He need not tie them together. He recited it and he stated it: The *halachah* is as R. Simeon b. Gamaliel.

It was stated: Rab said: He must tie [them] together; Samuel maintained: He must intend [to sit upon them]; while R. Assi ruled: If he sits upon them,[2] though he had neither tied nor intended them [for sitting, it is well].[3] As for Rab, it is well: he rules as the first Tanna: and Samuel too [is not refuted, for he] rules as R. Simeon b. Gamaliel. But according to whom does R. Assi rule?—He rules as the following Tanna. For it was taught: One may go out [into the street] with a wool tuft or a flake of wool,[4] if he had dipped them [in oil][5] and tied them with a cord. If he did not dip them [in oil] and tie them with a cord, he may not go out with them; yet if he had gone out with them for one moment[6] before nightfall,[7] even if he had not dipped or tied them with a cord, he may go out with them [on the Sabbath].[8]

R. Ashi said, We too have learnt [so]: One must not move straw [lying] upon a bed with his hand, yet he may move it with his body;[9] but if it is fodder for animals, or a pillow or a sheet
b was upon it before nightfall,[1] he may move it with his hand.[2] This proves it.

And which Tanna disagrees with R. Simeon b. Gamaliel?—R. Ḥanina b. Akiba. For when R. Dimi came,[3] he said in the name of Ze'iri in R. Ḥanina's name: R. Ḥanina b. Akiba once went to a certain place and found dried branches of a palm tree cut down for [fire] wood, and he said to his disciples, 'Go and declare your intention[4] so that we may sit upon them tomorrow And I do not know whether it was a house of feasting or a house of mourning.[5] Since he says, '[I do not know] whether it was a house of feasting or a house of mourning', [it implies] only there, because they are occupied;[6] but elsewhere it must be tied together; but if not, it is not [permitted].

Rab Judah said: A man may bring a sack full of earth [into the house] and use it for his general needs.[7] Mar Zuṭra lectured in the name of Mar Zuṭra Rabbah: Providing that he allotted a certain corner to it.[8] Said the students before R. Papa: With whom [does this agree]: R. Simeon b. Gamaliel? For if with the Rabbis,—an act is required![9]—R. Papa answered: You may even say, with the Rabbis. The Rabbis ruled that an act is required only where an act is possible,[10] but not where it is impossible.[11]

Shall we say that this is disputed by Tannaim? Utensils may be cleaned[12] with anything,[13] save silver vessels with white earth.[14] This [implies] that natron[15] and sand are permitted. But surely it was taught, Natron and sand are forbidden? Surely they differ in this:
c one Master holds that an act is required,[1] while the other Master holds that no act is required? No. All agree that no act is required, yet there is no difficulty: one is according to R. Judah, who maintains, What is unintentional is forbidden; the other is according to R. Simeon, who rules, What is unintentional is permitted.[2] How have you explained the view that it is permitted? As agreeing with R. Simeon! Then consider the last clause: But one must not cleanse his hair with them.[3] Rather if it is R. Simeon, surely he

(4) This proves that even when food was stored in the shearings on that day, they may not be handled. (5) V. *supra* 5a, n. b9. (6) So Rashi. (7) Wool shearings stored in the merchant's shelves are certainly not designated for storing, and even if thus employed they will eventually be replaced in the shelves. Hence they may not be handled even if used for storing. But Raba referred to ordinary shorn wool: when one employs them for such a purpose, it is as though he designated them for storing, and therefore they may be handled. Thus Rabina justifies the first version of Raba's statement.

a (1) Before the Sabbath, thus indicating their purpose. Otherwise they are regarded as fuel and may not be handled on the Sabbath, a change of mind without corresponding action being of no account.—'Intended' means that this was verbally stated, and not mental. (2) Before the Sabbath. (3) He may handle and use them as a seat on the Sabbath. (4) Both used as a dressing for a wound. Tosaf. translates a wig. (5) So Rashi. He thereby shows that his purpose is to prevent his garments from chafing the wound. Rashal deletes 'in oil', and translates: if he had dyed them, thus rendering them an adornment. Otherwise, on both translations, they are a burden and may not be taken out into the street. (6) Lit., 'one hour'. (7) Lit., 'while yet daytime'—i.e., before the Sabbath. (8) The principle is the same as in R. Assi's ruling. (9) Generally speaking, straw is meant for fuel or brickmaking, and is therefore *mukzeh*. Therefore if straw is lying on a bed, not having been designated for a mattress, one must not move it with his hand to straighten it and make the bed more comfortable, but he may do so with his body, because that is an unusual manner (v. *supra* 43b, n. b1 and 47b, n. b7.)

b (1) Lit., 'by day'—i.e., if one had lain upon it before the Sabbath, though he had neither put aside the straw nor declared his intention to use it as a mattress. (2) Here too the principle is the same as in R. Assi's ruling. (3) V. *supra* 5a, n. b9. (4) To sit upon them on the Sabbath. (5) This is Ze'iri's comment. (6) Lit., 'troubled'. For that reason mere intention was sufficient. (7) On the Sabbath or Festivals. This must be done before the Sabbath or Festivals. (8) Which renders it prepared (*mukan*) for these purposes. (9) The equivalent of tying the branches. (10) Lit., 'for something that can be the subject of an act'. (11) Nothing can be done to the earth to show that it is meant for a particular purpose. (12) Lit., 'rubbed'. (13) On the Sabbath. (14) A kind of chalk. Rashi: אלום i.e., the tartar deposited in wine vessels; *'Aruch*: pulverized resin.—These do more than cleanse, but actually smooth the silver, which is forbidden work. (15) V. Sanh., 49b, n. a5.

c (1) To show its purpose, and since such is impossible, they are forbidden, but not because there is anything objectionable in them *per se*. (2) *Supra* 22a, 29b. Natron and sand sometimes smooth the silver too, in addition to cleansing it, but that smoothing is unintentional. But white chalk always smooths: hence all rule it out. (3) Because it pulls hair out.

נוטל את הכיסוי והן נופלות אלא אי איתמר הכי איתמר אמר רבא לא שנו אלא שלא יחדן להטמנה אבל יחדן להטמנה מטלטלין אותן איתמר נמי כי אתא רבין א"ר יעקב א"ר אסי בן שאול אמר רבי לא שנו אלא שלא יחדן להטמנה אבל יחדן להטמנה מטלטלין אותן רבינא אומר ^א^בשל הפתק שנו תניא נמי הכי *גיזי צמר של הפתק אין מטלטלין אותן ואם התקינן בעל הבית להשתמש בהן מטלטלין אותן תנא רבה בר בר חנה קמיה דרב *חריות של דקל שגדרן לעצים ונמלך עליהן לישיבה צריך לקשר רשב"ג ^ב^אומר אין צריך לקשר הוא תני לה והוא אמר לה הלכה כרשב"ג איתמר רב אמר קושר ושמואל אמר חושב *ורב אסי אמר ^ג^יושב אע"פ שלא קישר ואע"פ שלא חישב בשלמא רב הוא דאמר כת"ק ושמואל נמי הוא דאמר כרשב"ג אלא רב אסי דאמר כמאן הוא דאמר כי האי תנא דתניא *^ד^יוצאין בפקורין ובציפא בזמן שצבען (בשמן) וכרכן במשיחה לא צבען (בשמן) ולא כרכן במשיחה אין יוצאין בהם ואם יצא בהן שעה אחת מבעוד יום אע"פ שלא צבע ולא כרכן במשיחה מותר לצאת בהן אמר רב אשי אף אנן נמי תנינא *הקש שעל גבי המטה לא ינענעו בידו אבל מנענעו בגופו אבל אם היה (עליו) מאכל בהמה או שהיה עליו כר או סדין מבעוד יום מנענעו בידו ש"מ ומאן תנא דפליג עליה דרשב"ג רבי חנינא בן עקיבא דכי אתא רב דימי אמר זעירי א"ר חנינא פעם אחת הלך רבי חנינא בן עקיבא למקום אחד ומצא חריות של דקל שגדרום לשום עצים ואמר להם לתלמידיו צאו וחשבו כדי שנשב עליהן למחר ולא ידענא אי בית המשתה הוה אי בית האבל הוה מדקאמר אי בית המשתה הוה אי בית האבל הוה דוקא בית האבל או בית המשתה דטרידי אבל הבא קשר אין לא קשר לא *אמר רב יהודה ^ה^מכנים אדם מלא קופתו עפר ועושה בה כל צרכו דרש מר זוטרא משמיה דמר זוטרא רבה ^ו^והוא שיחד לו קרן זוית אמרו רבנן קמיה דרב פפא כמאן כרבן שמעון בן גמליאל דאי כרבנן האמרי בעינן מעשה אמר להו רב פפא אפילו תימא רבנן עד כאן לא קאמרי רבנן דבעינן מעשה אלא מידי דבר עבידא ביה מעשה אבל מידי דלא בר מיעבדא ביה מעשה לא נימא כתנאי בכל ^ז^חפין את הכלים חוץ מכלי כסף בגרתקון *הא נתר וחול מותר והתניא *נתר וחול אסור מאי לאו בהא קמיפלגי דמר סבר בעינן מעשה ומר סבר לא בעינן מעשה לא דכולי עלמא לא בעינן מעשה ולא קשיא (הא רבי יהודה הא ר' שמעון) הא *רבי יהודה דאמר דבר שאין מתכוין אסור הא ר' שמעון דאמר *דבר שאין מתכוין מותר במאי אוקימתא להא דשרי כר"ש אימא סיפא אבל לא יחוף בהם שערו ואי ר"ש משרא קשרי דתנן

נזיר

רש"י

נוטל את הכיסוי. אלמא בהנך דטמן נמי קאסר לטלטולי אלא על ידי כיסוי: יחדן להטמנה. לעולם: רבינא אומר. לעולם כדקאמר רבא אם טמן בהן מותר לטלטל דכמאן דיחדן להכי דמו ורבא נמי אמתניתין קאי דמתניתין בגיזין של הפתק דודאי עתיד להחזירן משם ולא יחדן לכך: הפתק. מערכה גדולה שעורכין ומושיבין להקצותן לסחורה שקורין ט"ש בין של בגדים בין של צמר בין של חגבים ובשר מלוח: חריות. ענפים קשים כעץ משהוקשו שדראות של לולבין ונפלו עלין שלהן קרי להן חריות: שגדרן. כל (לקיטת) [קצילת] תמרים קרי גדירה: צריך לקשר. לקשרם יחד מבעוד יום להוכיח שלישיבה עומדים ואם לא קשרם יחד אסור לטלטלן למחר דלא הוי יחוד במחשבה: ורב אסי אמר ישב. עליהן מבעוד יום: ואע"פ שלא חישב. עליהן לישב למחר גלי דעתיה דלישיבה קיימי: פקורין. פשתן סרוק שנותנין על המכה: בציפא. צמר מנופץ הניתן על המכה: בזמן שצבען בשמן. גלי דעתיה דלמכה קיימי להניחן עליה בשבת דלאו לרפואה ניהו אלא שלא ישרטו מלבושיו את מכתו והוה ליה כמלבוש דעלמא אבל לא צבען בשמן דלאו מלבוש ניהו הוה ליה משאוי ואין יוצאין בו לר"ה: ואם יצא בהן כו'. הייני כרב אסי דאמר ישב אע"פ שלא קשר ולא חישב: אף אנן נמי תנינא. כרב אסי: קש. סתמיה לטינא קאי ללבנים או להסקה ומוקצה הוא ואם היה נתון על המטה ולא לשכב עליו ובא בשבת לשכב עליו והוצרך לנענעו ולשוטחו לשכיבה שלא יהא צבור וקשה: לא ינענעו בידו. שאסור לטלטלו: אבל מנענעו בגופו. כלאחר יד: או שהיה עליו כר או סדין. ששכב עליו מבעוד יום ואע"פ שלא יחדו לכך ולא חישב עליו דהיינו כרב אסי: ומאן תנא. דלעיל דאמר צריך לקשור ופליג אדרבן שמעון: ולא ידענא. זעירי קאמר לה: דטרידי. ולא יכלו לקשור מבעוד יום והתם הוא דשרי בלא קישור אבל בעלמא לא: מכנים מלא קופתו עפר. לכסות בו צואה ורוק ומערה העפר בביתו לארץ ונוטלו תמיד לכל צרכיו: והוא שייחד לו קרן זוית. דהוי כמוכן ועומד לכך אבל נתנו באמצע ביתו למדרס רגלים הרי הוא בטל לגבי קרקעית הבית ומוקצה ואסור: כרבן שמעון. דשרי במחשבה בעלמא שאין מעשה מוכיח שעומד לעשות צרכיו: דבר מעביד מעשה. שכן מעשה הוא שיכול לעשות בו מעשה הוכחה: לימא כתנאי. הא דרב יהודה במידי דלאו בר מעשה: חפין. משפשפין את הכלים בשבת לנאותן: חוץ מכלי כסף בגרתקון. כמין עפר שגדל בחבית של יין וקורין לו אלו"ם והוא עיקר תקון כלי כסף וגורר אותו שהכסף רך והוא ממחק שהוא אב מלאכה: אבל נתר וחול מותר. דלא גריר ליה לכסף: מאי לאו. הא דתניא אסור לאו משום דגריר ליה אלא משום מוקצה קאסר ליה ותנא דשרי כגון שהכניס מלא קופתו לכך ועירה על גבי קרקע ומאן דאסר קסבר בעינן מעשה וזה לא יכול: לא דכולי עלמא. במידי דלאו בר מעשה לא בעינן מעשה דחית להו הא דרב יהודה וטעמא מאן דאסר דזימנין דגריר ואף על גב דלא מיכוין נגזור אסור כרבי יהודה דאמר דבר שאין מתכוין אסור ומאן דשרי כר"ש ומיהו גרתקון אסור דודאי גריר ומודה ר"ש בפסיק רישיה ולא ימות: לא יחוף בהן. בנתר וחול שערו בשבת מפני שמשירו:

נזיר

תוספות

אלא אי איתמר כו'. אין גירסא זו נכונה דלכאורה משמע שלרבא עצמו היה מקשה ועפי הוי ניחא אי הוה גרס אלא אמר רבא אבל לפי זה הוה צריך לומר דרבינא לפלוגי אתא:

רבינא אומר בשל הפתק שנו. ונוילתא דרבא כדקאמר מעיקרא ובשאינה של הפתק ותימה דרבא קאמר לא שנו משמע דאמתניתין קאי והא מתניתין איירי בשל הפתק וי"ל דרישא איירי בכל גיזי צמר בין של הפתק בין שאינם של הפתק דאין מטלטלים אותן וקאמר רבא לא שנו בהגהו שאינה של הפתק אלא שלא טמן בהן אבל טמן בהן מטלטלים אותן והא דקתני סיפא כיצד הוא עושה כו' בשל הפתק קאמר ואע"פ שטמן בהן אין מטלטלין כיון שלא הזמינן:

ורב אסי אמר ישב אע"פ שלא קשר ושלא חישב. רבינו שמשון הזקן פסק כרב אסי מדקאמר בסמוך רב אשי שהוא בתרא מתני' נמי דיקא ור"ת פוסק כרב מכח קושיא כמו שמפורש בפרק כל הכלים (לקמן דף קכו: בד"ה ר"י אומר ושם):

בפקורין ובציפא. פר"ח ציפה שיש בה שער ונותנין אותה בראש הקרח, ונראה שהוא שער ראשו:

אבל לא צבען בשמן אין יוצאין בהן. לאו דוקא אין יוצאין דאפילו לטלטלם אסור לפי שאינם מוכנים אלא נקט אין יוצאין אגב רישא ובסמוך נמי דקאמר אבל יצא בהן שעה אחת מבעוד יום לאו דוקא יצא דהוא הדין ישב בהן בביתו:

ואם יצא בהן שעה אחת כו'. אע"פ *שלא צבע ולא חישב הייני כרב אסי דאמר ישב אע"פ שלא חישב ולא קישר קשה לר"י רישא דקתני יוצאין בהן בזמן שצבען מאי אריא צבען אפילו חישב נמי דהא כיון דמתיר יצא אע"פ שלא צבע ולא חישב כל שכן חישב ולא צבע דלכאורה ישיבה גריעא ממחשבה וכן נמי יציאה ותירץ דהאי דקאמר צבען לא לצאת בהן בשבת אלא כדי לצאת בהן מבעוד יום ואחר כך נמלך ואפ"ה יכול לצאת בהן בשבת:

ולא ידענא אי בית האבל הוה. פי' אי משום בית האבל הוה אי משום בית המשתה:

רבי

עין משפט נר מצוה

יט א (מיי' פכ"ה מהל' שבת) סמג לאוין סה טוש"ע או"ח סימן רנט סעיף א:

כ ב ג מיי' פכ"ה מהל' שבת הלכה כא טור שו"ע או"ח סימן שח סעיף כ:

כא ד מיי' פי"ט מהל' שבת הלכה טז טור שו"ע שם סעיף כד [וסי' שא סעיף ג]:

כב ה ו מיי' פכ"ה מהל' שבת הלכה כב סמג שם טוש"ע שם סעיף לח וסימן תנא סעיף יז:

כג ז מיי' פכ"ג מהלכות שבת הלכה ז סמג שם טוש"ע או"ח סימן שכג סעיף ט:

שלא צבען ולא כרכן במשיחה והיינו כרב אסי כצ"ל

רבינו חננאל

כרבא דאמר לא שנו אלא שלא יחדן להטמנה אבל יחדן להטמנה מטלטלין אותן דהא ר' נמי תני כוותיה · ורבינא דהוא בתראה אוקמה למשנתנו בשל הפתק *). פי' הפתק לשון יוני הוא · כגון אוצר המוטל לסחורה: כדתנן בע"ז (ל"ט:) החגבים הבאים מן הסלילה אסורין ומן ההפתק מותרין ותני' (שם מ:) חגבין והקפלוטאות הבאים מן ההפתק ומן האוצר ומן הספינה מותרין · כדתנינן גיזי צמר של הפתק אין מטלטלין אותן אם התקינן בעל הבית להשתמש בהן מותר: חריות של דקל שגדרן לעצים ונמלך עליהן לישיבה · אוקימנא ר' חנינא בן עקיבא אומר צריך לקשר. ר' שמעון בן גמליאל אומר אין צריך לקשר · אמר רבה בר בר חנה הלכתא כרשב"ג ואע"ג דאמר רב יקשור הא אמר שמואל יחשוב כרבה בר בר חנה · ודר' אסי נמי דאמר כי האי תנא דתני יוצאין בפיקרין ובציפא כו' פי' פאה נכרית והוא שיער שעושה בקפח והקרח נותנן בראשו ונראה כי אותו שיער שבקפח שיער ראשו הוא ואם יצא בהן שעה אחת מבעוד יום דיו והא דאמר רב אסי עריפא מדשמואל · ונמצא רב לגבייהו יחיד ויחיד ורבים הלכה כרבים: הא דאמר רב יהודה מכנים אדם מלא קופתו עפר כבר פרשתי' בפס' י"ט ולא (אכרע בהא מילתא) [בר מיעברא

*) עיין ערוך ערך אפתק ·

מסורת הש"ס

[תוספתא פ"ד] · [לקמן קכו:] · [עי' תוס' לקמן קכה: סד"ה ואדו] · [תוספתא פ"ו] · רש"ל מ"ז עי"ש · לקמן קמא. · ביצה ת. · ב"ה אבל · [תוספתא ביצה פ"ד] · [לעיל מא:] · [שם וש"נ]

*נזיר חופף *ומפספס אבל לא סורק אלא הא והא ר' יהודה היא ותרי תנאי אליבא דר' יהודה האי תנא אליבא דר' יהודה סבר גריר והאי תנא אליבא דר' יהודה סבר לא גריר במאי אוקימתא כר' יהודה אימא סיפא אבל פניו ידיו ורגליו מותר הא מעבר שיער איבעית אימא בקטן ואיבעית אימא באשה ואיבעית אימא בסריס אמר רב יהודה *עפר לבינתא שרי אמר רב יוסף *כוספא דיסמין שרי אמר רבא עפר פלפלי שרי אמר רב ששת ברדא שרי מאי ברדא אמר רב יוסף תילתא אהלא ותילתא אסא ותילתא סיגלי אמר רב נחמיה בר יוסף *כל היכא דליכא רובא אהלא שפיר דמי בעו מיניה מרב ששת מהו לפצוע זיתים בשבת אמר להו וכי בחול מי התירו קסבר משום הפסד אוכלין לימא פליגא דשמואל דאמר שמואל *עושה אדם כל צורכו בפת אמרי פת לא מאיסא הני מאיסי אמימר ומר זוטרא ורב אשי הוו יתבי אייתו לקמייהו ברדא אמימר ורב אשי משו מר זוטרא לא משא אמרו ליה לא סבר לה מר להא דאמר רב ששת ברדא שרי אמר להו רב מרדכי בר מיניה דמר דאפילו בחול נמי לא ס"ל סבר לה כי הא דתניא מגרר אדם גלדי צואה וגלדי מכה שעל בשרו בשביל צערו אם בשביל ליפות אסור ואינהו כמאן סברוה כי הא דתניא *רוחץ אדם פניו ידיו ורגליו בכל יום בשביל קונו משום שנאמר °כל פעל ה' למענהו: רבי אלעזר בן עזריה אומר קופה מטה על צדה ונוטל שמא יטול וכו': אמר רבי אבא אמר רבי חייא בר אשי *(אמר רב) *הכל מודים שאם נתקלקלה הגומא שאסור להחזיר תנן וחכמים אומרים נוטל ומחזיר היכי דמי אי דלא נתקלקלה הגומא *שפיר קא אמרי רבנן אלא לאו אף על פי דנתקלקלה הגומא לא לעולם דלא נתקלקלה והכא בחוששין קמיפלגי מר סבר חוששין שמא נתקלקלה הגומא ומר סבר *אין חוששין אמר רב הונא *האי סליקוסתא *דצה שלפה והדר דצה שריא ואי לאו אסיר אמר שמואל האי *סכינא דביני אורבי דצה שלפה והדר דצה שרי ואי לאו אסיר מר זוטרא ואיתימא רב אשי אמר בגורדיתא דקני שפיר דמי אמר ליה רב מרדכי לרבא מתיב רב קטינא תיובתא *הטומן לפת וצנונות תחת הגפן אם היה מקצת עליו מגולים אינו חושש

לא

רש"י

נזיר. בחול ככל אדם בשבת: חופף. שערו בנתר וחול*: ומפספס. מנפץ שערו דכיון דאינו מתכוין מותר ועל כרחיך ר"ש קא אמר לה אלמא נתר וחול זימנין דאינו משיר ולא דמי לפסיק רישיה ולא ימות: אבל לא סורק. במסרק דודאי משיר: אלא הא והא. הנך תרתי מתני' דלעיל דפליגי בנתר וחול ר' יהודה ומאן דאסר סבר זימנין דגריר ור' יהודה האמר דבר שאין מתכוין אסור ומאן דשרי סבר לא גריר כלל ואין כאן משום ממחק: במאי אוקימתא כר' יהודה ה"ג. ול"ג להא דתניא אסור דהא תרוייהו כר' יהודה אוקימנא להו ועוד הך סיפא דפריך אבל פניו ידיו ורגליו מותר להו סיפא דההיא דתניא אסור הוא אלא סיפא דההיא דתניא מותר דהכי תני בה לא יחוף בהן שערו אבל פניו ידיו ורגליו מותר והא מלתא גבי הך דתני מותר פריכנא ליה לעיל: בקטן אשה וסריס. דלית להו זקן: עפר לבינתא. כתישת לבינה: שרי. לחוף פניו ואפי' מי שיש לו זקן: כוספא דיסמין. פסולת שומשמין: עפר פילפלי. שחיקת פלפלין: ברדא שרי. לרחוץ פניו: אהלא. שורש עשב ששמו אהל: אסא. הדס: סגלי. עשב שקורין ויאו"ל ויש בו שלשה עלין: כל היכא דליכא רובא אהלא שפיר דמי. ואפי' הוי טפי מתלתא אהלא ופליג אדרב יוסף דרב יוסף תלתא אהלא דווקא קאמר שהאהל עשוי ללבן ולאחא כבורית ומשיר שיער: לפצוע זיתים. בליל"א בלע"ז על הסלע למתק מרירותו: כל צרכו. בין תשמיש בין לפרר אותה ולמהתה בתבשיל רותח: משום ליפות את עצמו אסור. משום לא ילבש גבר שמלת אשה (דברים כב): בשביל קונהו. לכבוד קונהו דכתיב (בראשית ט) כי בצלם אלהים עשה וגו' ועוד דהרואה בריות נאות אומר ברוך שככה לו בעולמו: כל פעל ה' למענהו. הכל ברא לכבודו: שאם נתקלקלה הגומא. שנפלו הגיזין למקום מושב הקדרה: שאסור להחזיר. לפי שמזיז הגיזין לכאן ולכאן: שפיר קאמרי רבנן. ומאי טעמא דר' אלעזר: חוששין. אי שרית ליה ליטול לכתחילה בקופה זקופה פעמים שנתקלקלה ואתי נמי להחזירה הלכך תקון ליה רבנן להטות קופה על לדה: סליקוסתא. עשב שהוא נאה למראה ולהריח וממלאין כד עפר לח ותוחבין אותו לתוכו ונותנו לפני שרים וכשהוא רולה נוטלו ומריח בו ומחזירו למקומו ואי מבעוד יום דלה לתוך העפר ושלפה והדר דלה שפיר דמי ליטלה למחר ולהחזירה שהרי הורחב מקום מושבה והוחלק מבעוד יום ואינו מזיז עפר: סכינא דביני אורבי. שנועלין סכין בין שורות הלבנים שבבנין להשתמר: בגורדיתא דקני. קנים הדקלים(א) שיולאין הרבה בגזע אחד ותכופין זה בזה שפיר דמי לנעוץ בתוכן סכין לשמרו ואין חוששין שמא יגרור הקליפה וחייב משום מוחק: מתיב רב קטינא תיובתא. להנך רבנן דאמרי דאי לא דלה ושלפה אסור: הטומן לפת. להשתמר בקרקע שכן דרכו הא דנקט מקצת עליו מגולין משום ניטלין בשבת נקט לה ולאו משום מידי אחריני דאי אין מקצת עליו מגולין אין לו במה לאוחזה אא"כ מזיז העפר בידים:

לא

תוספות

*רבי שמעון אומר נזיר חופף ומפספס כו'. ומיירי בנתר וחול דתנן בתר הכי בפ' ג' מינין (נזיר דף מב.) ר' ישמעאל אומר נזיר לא יחוף ראשו באדמה לפי שמשיר את השער: אבל לא סורק. התם מפרש טעמא משום דלהשרת נימין המדולדלות מתכוין:

במאי אוקימתא כר' יהודה אימא סיפא כו'. בשלמא אי כר"ש אתיא שפיר דאיכא למימר דשערות פניו ידיו ורגליו אינם נושרות מהר ולא הוי פסיק רישיה ושרי אבל בראשו אסור דהוי פסיק רישיה אבל השתא דאוקימתא כר' יהודה אע"ג דלא הוה פסיק רישיה הוה לן למיסר:

מהו לפצוע זיתים בשבת. פירש בקונט' להכותם על הסלע למתק מרירותן ומיבעיא ליה אי אסיר בשבת משום שווי אוכלא ותיקוני אוכלא ופריך ובחול מי התירו דאיכא הפסד אוכלין שנפסד המשקה הזב מהן: וקשה לפ"ז דבפ' חבית גבי דיני סחיטה ה"ל למיתני ועוד מה הפסד אוכלין יש כיון שעושה לתקנם ומפרש ר"י מהו לפצוע לחוף פניו ידיו ורגליו כי ההוא דלעיל ודרך מי זיתים להעביר וללבן כדאמר במסכת ע"ז חולטן ברותחין או מולגן במי זיתים ופריך ובחול מי התירו דאיכא הפסד, דנמאסין לאכילה. (ת"י)

בשביל צערו. ואם אין לו צער אחר אלא שמתבייש לילך בין בני אדם שרי דאין לך צער גדול מזה:

הכל מודים שאם נתקלקלה הגומא שאסורה להחזיר. ואפי' לר"א בן תדאי דאמר בפרק כל הכלים (לקמן קכג.) תוחב בכוש או בכרכר והן ננערות מאליהן דטלטול מן הצד לא שמיה טלטול וכן קי"ל הכא עדיף טפי מטלטול מן הצד שצריך לטלטל אילך ואילך כשרולין להטמין: אי לא נתקלקלה הגומא פשיטא. טפי הוה ליה למפרך מ"ט דמאן דאסר:

גורדיתא דקני. מין אילן כפירוש הקונטרס כדמשמע בעושין פסין (עירובין יט:) ומיירי למטה מג' דליכא איסור משתמש במחובר כדאמר בפרק כל הכלים (לקמן קכה:) ובפרק בתרא דעירובין (דף ק.):

הטומן לפת ולנועות כו'. ע"כ בשלא השרישו מיירי דבהשרישו לא היו ניטלין בשבת ואם תאמר בשלמא כלאים ושביעית איצטריך לאשמעינן דלא גזרינן כשמתכוין להטמין אטו דילמא אתי לנוטעה אבל מעשר אמאי נקטיה דאפי' השרישו לא שייך מעשר כיון דליכא תוספת ואי נקטיה דשרי לעשר מן התלוש ממקום אחר עליו או לעשותו מעשר על התלוש ולא חיישי' דילמא אתי לעשר מן התלוש על המחובר או להפך א"כ הוה ליה למינקט תרומה דבכל דוכתא רגיל להזכיר תרומה על זה כדאמר (תרומות פ"א מ"ה) אין תורמין מן התלוש על המחובר *פירות ערוגה זו תלושין יהיו תרומה על פירות ערוגה זו מחוברין ואומר ר"י דרגילות הוא שמתוספין מחמת ליחלוחית הקרקע כמו שאנו רואין שומין ובצלים שמתוספין אפי' כשמונחין בחלון ועל אותו תוספת קאמר דלא בעי לעשורי ודוקא נקט הטומן אבל במתכוין לנטיעה חושש משום כולן:

מקצת עליו מגולים. משום דבעי למתני וניטלין בשבת נקט מקצת עליו מגולים כדפירש בקונטרס ובערוך* משמע דמשום כולהו נקט דפירש בשם רב האי גאון דגרס אם היו מקצתם מגולים שאם האמהות טמונים בקרקע והעלים מגולים הרי זו זריעה מעולה אלא דוקא מקצתן מגולים אינו חושש משום כלאים ושביעית דלאו זריעה היא ומה שהקשה והלא זריעה מעולה היא לאו פירכא היא דבלא השרישו איירי כדפרישית ולפירושו קשה דבפרק חלון (עירובין דף עז. ושם) קאמר רב יחיאל כפה ספל ממעט ופריך והא ניטלת בשבת הוא [ערך לפת]

עין משפט נר מצוה

[בלא תיבות הללו ר"ש אומר צריך תיקון וא"א לומר דהגי' כך כי' לפניהם שהרי לבדיא אמרינן בנזיר מב. עלה דהך משנה דתנן נזיר חופף וכו' וחופף ומפספס מני ר"ש היא דאמר דבר שאין מתכוין וכו' ע"ש]

כד א מיי' פ"ה מהלכות נזירות הלכה יד סמג לאוין כד:

כה ב ג מיי' פכ"ב מהל' שבת הלכה יג סמג לאוין סה טוש"ע או"ח סימן שכו סעיף ט:

כו ד טוש"ע או"ח סימן קעא סעיף א:

כז ה ו מ"י' פ"ד ופכ"ו מהלכות שבת [דין זה ליתא בהרמב"ם ועיין בכ"י] סמג שם טוש"ע או"ח סימן רנט סעיף ג:

כח ז מיי' פכ"ה מהל' שבת הלכה טו טור שו"ע או"ח סימן שלו סעיף ו:

כט ח שו"ע או"ח סי' שי"ד ס"א:

בהל"ש ליתא

ס"א פשיטא

לקמן קיג. עירובין עז. כלאים פרק א מ"ט [עי' תוספות מנחות ע. ד"ה חסר וכו' מה שהניחו בתימה ועיין תוס' לעיל מג: סד"ה דכו"ע טלטול וכו' ויתישב התימה]

מסורת הש"ס

עי' רש"י ברכות ו. ד"ה מתוסיף

לקמן פא: נזיר מב.

[פי' פסולת שומשמין שכובשין אותו בורד של יסמין ומייבשין אותו ושוחקין אותו ורוחצין בהן ידים מזוהמות ערוך בערך כספן ועיין רש"י שקיר בזה כמ"ד]

ברכות נ: לקמן קמג. ביצה כא:

[תוספ' ברכות פ"ד ע"ש]

מִשְׁלֵי טז

הגהות הב"ח

(א) רש"י ד"ה בגורדיתא דקני (קנים הדקלים) תא"מ וכ"ב ס"א קנים סדוקים:

[כמו דעלה הלא שמכלים סעי' ומקלא את לשון כ"ב רש"י ויצא למ"ד פ"ח]

גליון הש"ס

גמ' האי סליקוסתא. עי' לעיל דף מג ע"ב תוס' ד"ה דכ"ע טלטול:

רבינו חננאל

מיעבדא ביה מעשה]: נימא כתנאי בכל חפין את הכלים כו' מלשון אשה הופפת וסורקת כו' ברחיצת ידים דקא אמרי' אבל רוחץ פניו ידיו ורגליו הא תנא דסבר משום השרת נימין מדולדלות · אליבא דר' יהודא מוקים לה בקטן וסרים ואשה דלית להון שיער אבל הלכה כר' שמעון דאפי' גברי בעלי שיער שרו וכן עפר לבינתה שרי למימשא ביה ידיה · ויש מי שמפרש לבינתה מלשון (ש"ה ג) מור ולבונה וכן כוספא דיסמין · וכן בראדא דהיא תילתא אהלא · תילתא סיגלי · תילתא אסא הני כולהו לענין רחיצת ידים בהן · וקיי"ל דבכולהי הני שרי אבל רובא אהלא רב נחמיה לא הוה שרי וכ"ש כולה (אוכלין וכ"ש בשבת) לפצוע זיתים וכיוצא בהן לרחוץ בהן ידיו בחול אסור משום הפסד אוכלין · וכ"ש בשבת שאסור · וזה שאמר שמואל עושה אדם כל צורכיו בפת לית הלכתא כוותיה והאוסר ידיו לרחוץ (כרב אדא) [בבררא] סבר ליה כי האי תנא דתניא מגרר אדם גלדי צואה וגלדי מכה שעל בשרו בשביל צערו · ואם לייפות עצמו אסור · והמתיר סבר לה כר' שמעון בן גמליאל דאמר רוחץ אדם פניו ידיו ורגליו בשביל כבוד קונו משום שנאמר כל פעל ה' למענהו: מתני' ר' אלעזר בן עזריה אומר קופה מטה על צדה ונוטל כו' · אסיקנא הכל מודים שאם נתקלקלה הגומא שאסור להחזיר סליקוסתא שהיא אגודה של חבצלת וכיוצא בה אמר רב הונא דעצה בחול או בטיט וחלצת והרויח בטיט מע"ש כדי שתהא נכנסת ויוצא בגומא מותרת (כולה) [לטלטלה] בשבת וכן אמר שמואל בסכינא דנעיצא ביני אורבי כמו שאמר בסליקוסתא ומותבינן עליה הטומן לפת וצנונות תחת הגפן אם היו מקצתן מגולין

permits it? For we learnt: [50b] A nazirite may cleanse [his hair][4] and part it,[5] but he must not comb it.[6] Rather both are according to R. Judah, yet two Tannaim differ as to R. Judah's view: one Tanna holds that in R. Judah's view they [natron and sand] smooth,[7] while the other Tanna holds that in R. Judah's view they do not smooth. How have you explained them? As agreeing with R. Judah! Then consider the second clause: 'But the face, hands, and feet are permitted';[8] but surely it removes the hair?—If you wish, I can answer that it refers to a child; alternatively, to a woman; another alternative, to a eunuch [by nature].[9]

Rab Judah said: Powdered brick is permitted.[10] R. Joseph said: Poppy pomace [scented] with jasmine is permitted.[11] Raba said: Crushed pepper is permitted. R. Shesheth said: *Barda* is permitted. What is *barda?*—Said R. Joseph: [A compound consisting of] a third aloes, a third myrtle, and a third violets. R. Nehemiah b. Joseph said: Providing that there is not a greater quantity of
a aloes, it is well.[1]

R. Shesheth was asked: Is it permissible to bruise olives on the Sabbath?[2] He answered them: Who permitted it then on weekdays? (He holds [that it is forbidden] on account of the destruction of food).[3] Shall we say that he disagrees with Samuel; for Samuel said: One may do whatever he desires with bread?—I will tell you: A loaf [crumbled] is not repulsive, but these are.

Amemar, Mar Zuṭra, and R. Ashi were sitting, when *barda* was brought before them.[4] Amemar and R. Ashi washed [their hands therewith]; Mar Zuṭra did not. Said they to him, Do you not accept R. Shesheth's ruling that *barda* is permitted? R. Mordecai answered them: Exclude the Master [Mar Zuṭra], who does not hold it [permitted] even on weekdays. His view is as what was taught: One may scrape off the dirt scabs and wound scabs that are on his flesh because of the pain;[5] [but] if in order to beautify himself, it is forbidden.[6] And whose view do they adopt?—As what was taught: One must wash his face, hands, and feet daily in his Maker's honour, for it is said, *The Lord hath made every thing for his own purpose.*[7]

R. ELEAZAR B. 'AZARIAH SAID: THE BASKET IS TILTED ON ONE SIDE AND [THE FOOD] IS REMOVED, LEST ONE LIFT [THE POT], etc. R. Abba said in R. Ḥiyya b. Ashi's name: All agree that if the cavity becomes disordered,[8] we may not replace [the pot].[9] We learnt: BUT THE SAGES SAY: ONE MAY TAKE AND REPLACE [IT]. What are the circumstances? If the
b cavity is not disordered, the Rabbis [surely] say well?[1] Hence it must mean even if the cavity becomes disordered!—No. In truth, it means that [the cavity] was not disordered, but here they differ as to whether we fear. One Master holds: We fear lest the cavity become disordered;[2] while the other Master holds: We do not fear.

R. Huna said: With respect to *seliḳustha*,[3] if one put it in, drew it out, and put it in again,[4] it is permitted;[5] if not, it is forbidden.

Samuel said: As regards the knife between the rows of bricks,[6]—if one inserted it, withdrew it, and re-inserted it,[7] it is permitted; if not, it is forbidden. Mar Zuṭra—others state R. Ashi—said: Yet it is well [to insert a knife] between the branches of a reed hedge.[8] R. Mordecai said to Raba, R. Kaṭṭina raised an objection: If one stores turnips or radishes under a vine, provided some of their leaves are uncovered, he need have no fear [51a]

(4) By rubbing it (*hafaf* denotes to rub) with sand or natron. (5) With his fingers (Jast.). Rashi: he may beat out his hair. (6) With a comb. A *nazirite* may not cut his hair (v. Num. VI, 5); a comb is *certain* to pull some hair out (v. *T.A.* I, 197 and note a.l.), and therefore it is forbidden as cutting. Now the first clause permits sand or natron: it can only agree with R. Simeon, who holds that what is unintentional is permitted, and it must be assumed therefore that sand or natron is not bound to pull out the hair. But that being so, R. Simeon will permit it on the Sabbath too. (7) Lit., 'scrape'. (8) This follows the prohibition of cleansing the hair with natron or sand. (9) None of these three have hair on the face or body. (10) For cleaning the face, even to one who has a beard. (11) To be used as lotion.

a (1) He permits even more than a third of aloes, but there must not be more of aloes than of the other ingredients combined, because aloes act as a depilatory. (2) May olives be bruised on a stone, which improves their taste? (Rashi). Ri: May one rub his face with olives, using them as a detergent? (3) He regarded it as wanton waste. (4) On Sabbath. (5) Which their presence causes him. (6) Rashi: on account of, *neither shall a man put on a woman's garment* (Deut. XXII, 5), which he interprets as a general injunction against aping femininity. Self adornment for its own sake is a woman's prerogative! (7) Prov. XVI, 4. (8) Its walls collapsing. (9) Because we thereby move the shearings.

b (1) There can be no reason for prohibiting its return. (2) If one is permitted to remove the pot without tilting the basket on one side, we fear that he might replace it even if the walls of the cavity happened to collapse. (3) A fragrant plant used after meals in place of burnt spices (Jast.). It was removed from its pot earth, its fragrance inhaled, and then put back. (4) Before the Sabbath, thus loosening the earth around it. (5) To remove it from the pot and replace it on the Sabbath. (6) Where it was inserted for safety (Rashi). (7) Cf. n. b4. (8) The branches spreading from a common stem (Jast.). We do not fear that in removing it he may scrape off the peel of the reeds, which is forbidden.

on account of *kil'ayim*,[9] or the seventh year,[10] or tithes,[11] and they may be removed on the Sabbath.[12] This is indeed a refutation.[13]

MISHNAH. IF IT [A POT] WAS NOT COVERED[14] WHILE IT
a WAS YET DAY, IT MAY NOT BE COVERED AFTER NIGHTFALL.[1] IF IT WAS COVERED BUT BECAME UNCOVERED, IT MAY BE RECOVERED. A CRUSE MAY BE FILLED WITH [COLD] WATER AND PLACED UNDER A PILLOW OR BOLSTER.[2]

GEMARA. Rab Judah said in Samuel's name: Cold [water, food, etc.] may be hidden.[3] Said R. Joseph, What does he inform us? We learnt: A CRUSE MAY BE FILLED WITH [COLD] WATER AND PLACED UNDER A PILLOW OR A BOLSTER. Abaye answered him: He tells us much. For if [we learnt] from the Mishnah [alone], I might argue: That applies only to an object which it is not customary to store away,[4] but not to an object which it is customary to store away.[5] Therefore he informs us [that it is not so].

R. Huna said on Rabbi's authority: Cold [water, food, etc.] may not be hidden.[6] But it was taught: Rabbi permitted cold [water, etc.] to be hidden?—There is no difficulty: the one [ruling was given] before he heard it from R. Ishmael son of R. Jose; the other after he heard it [from him]. For Rabbi sat and declared: Cold [water, etc.] may not be hidden. Said R. Ishmael son of R. Jose to him, My father permitted cold [water] to be hidden. Then the Elder[7] has already given a ruling, answered he.[8] R. Papa observed: Come and see how much they loved each other! For were R. Jose alive, he would have sat submissively before Rabbi, since R. Ishmael son of R. Jose, who occupied his father's place,[9] sat submissively before Rabbi,[10] yet he [Rabbi] said, Then the Elder has already given a ruling.[11]

R. Naḥman said to his slave Daru: Put away cold water for me,[12] and bring me water heated by a Gentile[13] cook.[14] When R. Ammi heard thereof, he objected. Said R. Joseph: Why should he have objected? He acted in accordance with his teachers, one [act] being according to Rab, and the other according to Samuel. According to Samuel, for Rab Judah said in Samuel's name: Cold [water, etc.] may be hidden. According to Rab, for R. Samuel son of R. Isaac said in Rab's name: Whatever can be
b eaten in its natural state,[1] raw, is not subject to [the interdict against] the cooking of Gentiles. But he [R. Ammi] held that an important man is different.[2]

Our Rabbis taught: Though it was said, One may not store [food] after nightfall even in a substance which does not add heat, yet if one comes to add,[3] he may add. How does he do it? R. Simeon b. Gamaliel said: He may remove the sheets[4] and replace them with blankets, or remove the blankets and replace them with sheets.[5] And thus did R. Simeon b. Gamaliel say: Only the self-same boiler was forbidden;[6] but if it [the food] was emptied from that boiler into another, it is permitted: seeing that he cools it,[7] will he indeed heat it up![8] If one stored [food] in something [that may be handled on the Sabbath] and covered [it] with a substance that may be handled on the Sabbath, or if he stored [it] in something that may not be handled on the Sabbath, but covered [it] with something that may be handled on the Sabbath, he may remove [the covering] and replace it.[9] If one stored [food] in something [that may not be handled on the Sabbath] and covered [it] with a substance that may not be handled on the Sabbath, or if he stored [it] in something that may be handled on the Sabbath, but covered it with something that may not be handled on the Sabbath, provided it was partly uncovered, he may take it [out] and re-

(9) V. Glos. This does not constitute the planting of diverse seeds. (10) If these are from the sixth year and are placed in the earth in the seventh, they are not subject to the laws of seventh year produce. (11) Having been tithed before they were placed in the earth they are not to be retithed on removal, as though this were a new harvest. (12) On this account the proviso is made that some of the leaves must be uncovered, for otherwise it would be necessary to remove the earth, which may not be done. But the other statements hold good even if they are entirely covered (Rashi and Tosaf.). (13) For it is not stated that the earth must be loosened before the Sabbath. (14) I.e., put away in something to retain its heat.

a (1) V. *supra* 34*a*. (2) To prevent the sun from reaching and warming it. (3) V. preceding note. (4) To heat it, as for instance cold water; therefore it may be hidden in order to keep it cold. (5) For if permission is given to hide it in order to keep it cold, the reverse too may be regarded as permitted. (6) To keep it cool. (7) The Sage, referring to R. Jose. (8) And I retract. (9) I.e. he was as great as his father (Rashi). (10) As a disciple before his master. (11) Thus showing deference to his views. (12) On the Sabbath. (13) Lit., 'Syrian'. (14) On weekdays. Food cooked by Gentiles is forbidden. R. Naḥman showed that this interdict does not apply to boiled water.

b (1) Lit., 'as it is, raw'. (2) He should be more stringent for himself. (3) Another covering. (4) In which the pot is wrapped. (5) According as he desires more or less heat. (6) I.e., food may not be stored after nightfall in the same pot in which it was cooked. (7) By emptying it from one pot into another. (8) Surely there is no fear of this, which is the reason for the usual prohibition (*supra* 34*a*); hence it is permitted. (9) Since the cover can be removed, one can take hold of the pot.

לא משום כלאים ולא משום שביעית ולא משום מעשר וניטלין בשבת תיובתא : **מתני'** לא כסהו מבעוד יום לא יכסנו משתחשך [א]כסהו ונתגלה מותר לכסותו ממלא את הקיתון ונותן לתחת הכר או תחת הכסת : **גמ'** אמר רב יהודה אמר שמואל [ב]מותר להטמין את הצונן אמר רב יוסף מאי קמ"ל תנינא ממלא אדם קיתון ונותן תחת הכר או תחת הכסת אמר ליה אביי טובא קמ"ל דאי ממתני' הוה אמינא ה"מ דבר שאין דרכו להטמין אבל דבר שדרכו להטמין לא קמ"ל אמר רב הונא *(אמר רב) אסור להטמין את הצונן והתניא רבי התיר להטמין את הצונן לא קשיא הא מקמיה (א)דלישמעיה מר' ישמעאל ברבי יוסי הא לבתר דלישמעי' *כי הא דיתיב רבי ואמר אסור להטמין את הצונן אמר לפניו רבי ישמעאל ברבי יוסי אבא התיר להטמין את הצונן אמר *כבר הורה זקן אמר רב פפא *בא וראה כמה מחבבין זה את זה שאילו ר' יוסי קיים היה כפוף ויושב לפני רבי דהא רבי ישמעאל ברבי יוסי דממלא מקום אבותיו הוה וכפוף ויושב לפני רבי וקאמר כבר הורה זקן אמר ליה רב נחמן לדרו עבדיה אטמין לי צונן ואייתי לי מיא דאחים קפילא ארמאה *שמע רבי אמי ואיקפד אמר רב יוסף מ"ט איקפד כרבוותיה עביד חדא כרב וחדא כשמואל כשמואל דאמר רב יהודה אמר שמואל מותר להטמין את הצונן כרב *דאמר רב שמואל בר רב יצחק אמר רב [ג]כל שהוא נאכל כמות שהוא חי אין בו משום בשולי נכרים (*הוא) סבר *אדם חשוב שאני : *ת"ר [ד]אע"פ שאמרו* אין טומנין אפילו בדבר [לעיל לד.] שאינו מוסיף הבל משחשכה אם בא להוסיף מוסיף כיצד הוא עושה רשב"ג אומר נוטל את הסדינין ומניח את הגלופקרין או נוטל את הגלופקרין ומניח את הסדינין וכן היה רשב"ג אומר [ה]לא אסרו אלא אותו מיחם אבל פינה ממיחם למיחם מותר השתא אקורי קא מקיר לה ארתוחי קא מירתח לה *[ו]טמן וכיסה בדבר הניטל בשבת או טמן בדבר שאינו ניטל בשבת וכיסה בדבר הניטל בשבת הרי זה נוטל ומחזיר [ז]טמן וכיסה בדבר שאינו ניטל בשבת או שטמן בדבר הניטל בשבת וכיסה בדבר שאינו ניטל בשבת אם היה מגולה מקצתו נוטל ומחזיר ואם לאו אינו

רש"י

לא משום כלאים. דאין זו שתילה : ולא משום מעשר דנימא בעלה לה אגב קרקע והרי הוא כלוקטה מתחלה ויהא צריך לעשר על הנוסף שמא ניתוסף : וניטלין בשבת. שאוחזה במקלת עליה המגולין ולא חייש אם העפר ניזוז מאליו וה"ה לסליקוסתא : **מתני'** לא יכסנו משתחשך. הא פרישנא טעמא בפ"ב (דף לד:) מפני מה אמרו אין טומנין בדבר שאינו מוסיף הבל משחשיכה גזירה שמא ירתיח : ממלא הקיתון. של צונן : ונותן לתוך הכר. שלא יחמו בחום הקיץ והחמה כגון כר וכסת של צבדין שאינו מחמם : **גמ'** מותר להטמין את הצונן. מפני החמה שלא יחמו ולא גזרינן אטו הטמנה כדי שיחמו : אי ממתני' הוה אמינא הני מילי. כגון מים צוננין שאין דרכן להטמין תחת כר וכסת לחממן שאין מתחממין בכך הלכך ליכא למיגזר : אבל דבר שדרכו להטמין. לחמם כגון תבשיל אימא לא יטמיננו מפני החמה : התיר להטמין את הצונן. מפני החום : זקן. ר' יוסי : ממלא מקום אבותיו. גדול כאביו : היה כפוף ויושב לפני רבי. מפני כבוד הנשיאות ולא היה מורה לפניו אע"פ שגדול הימנו : כבר הורה זקן. גדלו ונשאו עליו : אטמין לי צונן. בשבת : ואייתי לי מיא דאחים קפילא ארמאה. שהחמן נחתום נכרי ובחול ולאשמועינן דאין בהן משום בשולי נכרים : כרבוותיה. כרבותיו : אדם חשוב שאני. שהרואה אותו שהוא מיקל עומד ומיקל יותר : אין טומנין את החמין משחשכה ואפילו בדבר שאינו מוסיף הבל. וכדאמרן שמא ימצא קדרתו צוננת כשרוצה להטמינה וירתיחנה בשבת אבל אם בא להוסיף כיסוי על כיסוי משחשיכה מוסיף : גלופקרא. קו"ט ויש בו הבל יותר מן הסדינין ונוטל את הגלופקרא בימות החמה אם ירא שמא יקדיח תבשילו מחמת רוב כיסוי : וכן היה רשב"ג. מיקל קולא אחריתי בהטמנה : לא אסרו. להטמין משחשיכה אלא במיחם שהוחמו בו דהתם הוא דאיכא למיגזר שמא ירתיח : אבל מפנה הוא ממיחם למיחם אחר ומטמין זהו לשון התוספתא והיינו נמי פינהו ממיחם למיחם מותר דהשתא ליכא למיגזר שמא ירתיח דהשתא אקורי קא מיקר להו במתכוין ארתוחי מרתח להו בתמיה : טמן. הקדרה בדבר הניטל מה שנתן סביבותיה הוי דבר מוכן : וכיסה. על פיה נמי דבר המוכן כגון כלי:או שטמן בדבר שאינו ניטל. וכיסה בדבר הניטל : הרי זה נוטל ומחזיר. דהואיל והכיסוי ניטל מגלה הקדרה ואוחזה אבל טמן וכיסה בדבר שאינו ניטל או אפי' טמן בדבר הניטל וכיסה בדבר שאינו ניטל אם אין מקצת פיה מגולה לא יטול דאין לו במה יאחזנה ואם תאמר יפנה סביבותיה הואיל ודבר הניטל הוא ויאחזנה בדופניה(ג) ויטנה על צדה ויפול הכיסוי כי ההיא דתנן לקמן (פרק נוטל דף קמב:) האבן שעל פי החבית מטה על צדה והיא נופלת ואם היתה בין החביות מגביהה ומטה על צדה והיא נופלת הא אוקימנא התם בשכח אבל במניח נעשה בסיס לדבר האסור והיכא דמגולה מקצתו אין זה טלטול שמלדדו והכיסוי נופל מאליו : הרי

תוספות

הוא ואמאי ממעט ומשני דאית לה אוגנים וחבריה בארעא ופריך וכי יש לו מאי הוי והתנן הטומן לפת כו' ואי גרס מקצת מגולים מאי פריך הא לא דמי לכפל שיש לו אוגנים ואומר ר"י דיש לומר דבנטיעה איכא קרקע קשה ודבוק ביותר ומדמה ליה לכפל שיש לו אוגנים ואין להקשות לפירוש הערוך דמאי פריך מינה לשמואל לימא דהך משנה סבר טלטול מן הצד לא שמיה טלטול(ג) כאלעזר בן תדאי ומקצת מגולין נקט משום אחריני ולא משום שבת ושמואל סבר כרבנן דהיכא למימר דמשמע ליה דמשום שבת נמי נקט לה מדלא תנא בהדיא וניטלין בשבת אפילו מכוסין ש"מ דמכוסין אסורין כרבנן ואפ"ה מקצתן מגולין שרי : **כסהו** ונתגלה מותר לכסותו. נראה לר"י דה"ה דמותר לגלותו בידים ולחזור ולכסותו כמו שמותר ליטול הקדרה ולהחזירה והא דנקט כסהו ונתגלה משום דנתגלה מבעוד יום איירי דומיא דרישא לא כסהו מבעוד יום וקאמר דמותר לכסותו משתחשך אבל אם גילהו בידים מבעוד יום כדי לכסותו משתחשך אסור לכסותו משתחשך דדמיא לתחלת הטמנה :

אילו היה ר' יוסי קיים היה כפוף כו'. פי' רבינו שלמה מחמת נשיאותו דהא ר"י היה גדול מרבי כדמוכח בפ"ב דנדה (דף יד: ושם) דאמר ליה רבי ישמעאל ברבי יוסי לר' חמא בר ביסנא כדברי רבי אומר לך או כדברי אבא אמר ליה כדברי רבי המור לי אמר ליה זהו שאומרים עליו דאדם גדול הוא שמניח דברי הרב ושומע דברי התלמיד ור"ת מפרש דודאי מתחלה היה רבי תלמידו של רבי יוסי אבל אח"כ נתחכם רבי כדקאמ' התם ור' חמא סבר רבי ריש מתיבתא שכיחי רבנן גביה ומחדדן שמעתתיה : **כיצד** הוא עושה רשב"ג אומר נוטל את הסדינין כו'. נראה לר"י ולה"ר פור"ת דל"ג כיצד הוא עושה דרשב"ג פליג את"ק דלא שרי אלא להוסיף אבל להחליף אסור ורשב"ג שרי אף להחליף וכ"ש ליטול ולהחזיר אותו דבר דלא הוי כל כך תחלת הטמנה והיינו דקאמר וכן היה רשב"ג אומר כלומר שהיה מיקל קולא אחריתי גבי הטמנה :

אבל פינה ממיחם למיחם מותר. ול"ד להואל דכירה דבעי בפרק כירה (לעיל לח:) פינה ממיחם למיחם מהו דהתם רולה בחמימותן לכך יש לאסור כשהוא לונן אבל הכא גבי הטמנה כל כמה שהוא לונן טפי שפיר דמי כדאמר לעיל רבי התיר להטמין את הלונן וא"ת ורבי לא ידע לעיל דמותר להטמין את הלונן וכי לא ידע דשמיע ליה מאבוה הכא דשרי וי"ל דהכא דוקא דמוכח מילתא שנתכוין ללנן שפינהו ממיחם למיחם אבל קיתון של מים דלא מוכח מידי יהא אסור להטמין : מתוספות רבינו יהודה (ת"י) :

או שטמן בדבר הניטל וכיסה בדבר שאינו ניטל. הקשה בקונט' יפנה סביבה ויאחזנה בדופניה ויגביהנה ויטנה על לדה כדתנן בפרק נוטל (לקמן קמב:) היתה בין החביות מגביהה כו' ומתרץ דהא אוקמינן התם בשכח אבל במניח נעשה בסיס לדבר האסור וקשה דאי חשיב הכא כמניח אם כן במגולה מקלתה היאך נוטל ומחזיר מה בין זה לאבן שעל פי החבית דאסרי' במניח אפי' להטותה על לדה ועוד קשה לר"ת דהא תנן נוער את הכיסוי והן נופלות אפי' אינן מגולות מקלתן ועל כן אומר ר"ת דלא חשיב כמניח °כיון שדעתו ליטלו בשבת וכפ' נוטל (שם דף קמג.) כמי תנן בית שמאי אומרים מגביהין מעל גבי השלחן עלמות וקליפים וב"ה אומרים מסלק את הטבלא ומנערה ולא חשיב לב"ה כמניח והכא מיירי בכיסוי כעין כלי חרס שנותנים על הקדרה שהקדרה בלועה בתוכה ואי אפשר לנער הכיסוי אלא.אם כן יגביהו קלת ור"י מפרש כגון שטמן הקדרה בקופה בדבר הניטל ולמעלה מן הקדרה מילא כל הקופה בדבר שאינו ניטל שאי אפשר לו להגיע לקדרה אם לא יטלטל דבר שאינו ניטל בידים* : אינו

עין משפט נר מצוה

כט א מיי' פ"ד מהל' שבת הלכה ד סמג לאוין סה טוש"ע או"ח סימן רנז סעיף ד :
ל ב מיי' שם טוש"ע שם סעיף ו :
לא ג מיי' פי"ז מהלכות מאכלות אסורות הל' יד סמג לאוין קמב טור שו"ע יו"ד סימן קיג סעיף א :
לב ד מיי' פ"ד מהלכות שבת הלכה ד סמג לאוין סה טוש"ע או"ח סימן רנז סעיף ד :
לג ה מיי' שם הלכה ה טוש"ע שם סעיף ה :
לד ו (מיי') סמג שם טוש"ע או"ח סימן רנט סעיף ד :
לה ז שם סעיף ה :

[לקמן קמב: ברכות יט. פסחים קי. מו"ק יא: יב. מגילה כב: כתובות נב: סו. ב"מ עג. ע"ז ח: כח. מח: חולין קלד:]

רבינו חננאל

מגולין אין חושש משום כלאים דלא ירק באילן הוא ולאו משום שביעית דלאו זריעה היא וכן משום מעשר ונטלין בשבת דלאו מחובר לקרקע אינון . ועלתה בתיובתא לשמואל · וקיי"ל כי הא מתניתא דמותבינא מינה ש"מ דסליקוסתא אע"ג דלא ארווח בגומא שרי וכ"ש סכין דנעיצה בין הנדבך ובין הקנים . וזו הלפת טומנה לתתרכך כגון טמינת פגא בתבן : **ממלא** קיתון כו' ואסיק' מותר להטמין את הצונן אפי' בדבר שדרכו להטמין [כי] הא דאמר רב נחמן לדראי עבדיה אטמין לי את הצונן ואייתי לי חמין דאחים קפילא ארמאה · ואסי' אע"ג דקיי"ל דשרי להטמין

גליון הש"ס

תוס' ד"ה או שטמן וכו' כיון שדעתו ליטלו בשבת. עי' לעיל דף מג ע"ב תוס' ד"ה דכו"ע טלטול ·

מסורת הש"ס

[נ"ל אמר רבי]
סנהדרין כד.
שם ודף כט:]
[שם כד.]
[מו"ק יב:]
מו"ק יב: יבמות מו. פ"ז לח. נט.
[נ"ל והוא]
תוספתא פ"ד
[תוספתא שם כל הענין עד סוף הפרק]
[ועי' תוספות לקמן קכב. ד"ה הלי סוגלא]

הגהות הב"ח

(א) גמ' מקמי' דלשמעיה מר' ישמעאל וכו' לבתר דלשמעיה כו': (ב) רש"י ד"ה או שטמן וכו' ויאחזנה בדופניה ויגביהנה ויטנה : (ג) תוס' ד"ה מקלת וכו' טלטול כרבי אלעזר בן תדאי :

אינו נוטל ומחזיר *רבי יהודה אומר נעורת של פשתן דקה הרי היא כזבל *מניחין מיחם על גבי מיחם וקדרה על גבי קדרה *אבל לא קדרה על גבי מיחם ומיחם על גבי קדרה וטח את פיה בבצק ולא בשביל שיחמו אלא בשביל שיהיו משומרים וכשם שאין טומנין את החמין כך אין טומנין את הצונן רבי התיר להטמין את הצונן *ואין מרזקין לא את השלג ולא את הברד בשבת בשביל שיזובו מימיו אבל נותן הוא לתוך הכוס או לתוך הקערה ואינו חושש:

הדרן עלך במה טומנין

*במה בהמה יוצאה ובמה אינה יוצאה יוצא הגמל *באפסר ונאקה בחטם ולובדקים בפרומביא וסוס בשיר וכל בעלי השיר יוצאין בשיר ונמשכין בשיר *ומזין עליהן(א) *וטובלן במקומן: **גמ'** מאי נאקה בחטם אמר רבה בר בר חנה *נאקתא חיורתי בזממא דפרזלא: ולובדקים בפרומביא: אמר רב הונא חמרא לובא *בפגי דפרזלא לוי שדר זוזי לבי חוזאי למיזבן ליה חמרא לובא צרו שדרו ליה שערי למימר דניגרי דחמרא שערי אמר רב יהודה אמר שמואל מחליפין לפני רבי של זו בזו מהו נאקה באפסר לא תיבעי לך כיון דלא מינטרא ביה משאוי הוא כי תיבעי לך גמל בחטם מאי כיון דסגי ליה באפסר משאוי הוא או דילמא נטירותא יתירתא לא אמרי' משאוי הוא אמר לפניו ר' ישמעאל ברבי יוסי כך אמר אבא ארבע בהמות יוצאות באפסר הסוס והפרד והגמל והחמור למעוטי מאי לאו למעוטי גמל בחטם לא למעוטי נאקה באפסר במתניתא תנא לובדקים וגמל יוצאין באפסר כתנאי אין חיה יוצאה בסוגר חנניה אומר יוצאה בסוגר ובכל דבר המשתמר במאי עסקינן אילימא בחיה גדולה מי סגי לה סוגר ואלא בחיה קטנה מי לא סגי לה סוגר אלא לאו חתול איכא בינייהו תנא קמא סבר כיון דסגי לה במיתנא בעלמא משאוי הוא וחנניה סבר כל נטירותא יתירתא לא אמרינן משאוי הוא אמר רב הונא בר חייא אמר שמואל הלכה כחנניה לוי בריה דרב הונא בר חייא ורבה בר רב הונא הוו קאזלי באורחא קדמיה חמרא דלוי לחמרא דרבה בר רב הונא חלש דעתיה דרבה בר רב הונא אמר איזמא ליה מילתא כי היכי דאיתותב

תוספות

אינו נוטל ומחזיר. נראה לרשב"א דהיינו כרשב"ג דאמר בפרק נוטל כל היכא דאיכא איסורא והיתרא בהיתרא טרחינן באיסורא לא טרחינן אבל לרבנן דפליגי עליה שרו במכוסות לגמרי ליטול בידים דבר שאינו ניטל דבפרק נוטל (לקמן קמב:) מתני' דהיתה בין החביות מגביהה ומטה על צדה מוקי לה כרשב"ג משמע דרבנן דרשב"ג שרו לטלטל את האבן עצמו:

אין מרסקין לא את השלג ולא את הברד. מכאן יש ליזהר שלא ירחוץ ידיו בשלג וברד בשבת *ופעמים שמתקרשים ויש ברד מעורב בהם אין לרחוץ בהן דאי אפשר שלא ירסק הברד וכל הזהיר בו תבא עליו ברכה:

הדרן עלך במה טומנין

במה בהמה יוצאה. דאדם מוזהר על שביתת בהמתו דכתיב למען ינוח וגו' ומיהו לאו דלא תעשה מלאכה אתה ובהמתך ליכא אלא במחמר אחר בהמתו כדמוכח בריש מי שהחשיך (לקמן קנג:) ובריש נדרים (דף ב:) דייק בהך דהכא ובכל הני דלעיל דאיכא דוכתא דתנא ברישא הא דסליק מיניה ואיכא דוכתא דתני ברישא הא דפתח ביה:

חמרא לובא. אומר ר"ת דלובא היינו מצרים דכתיב (נחום ג) פוט ולובים היו בעזרתך ואמרינן בירושלמי גרים הבאים מלוב מהו להמתין להם שלשה דורות ומייתי עלה דהדא עלם מצראה דלווחין ליה לוב*: **או** דילמא כל נטירותא יתירתא לאו משוי היא. וא"ת תפשוט ממתניתין דתנן ולובדקים בפרומביא אע"ג דסגי לה באפסר כדאמר בסמוך תנא לובדקים וגמל יוצאים באפסר ופרומביא עדיפא מאפסר דאמר לקמן חמור שעסקיו רעים כגון זה מהו לצאת בפרומביא בשבת אלמא משמע דעדיף מאפסר וי"ל דלא הוי נטירותא יתירתא ואורחיה נמי בהכי ולא חשיב משוי:

קדמיה חמרא דלוי. משמע שמכבדין בדרכים ובפ' אמר להם הממונה (יומא כז:) נמי אמרינן שלשה שהיו מהלכין בדרך הרב באמצע גדול מימינו וקטן משמאלו וכן מצינו במלאכי השרת שבאו אצל אברהם וכו' והקשה ר"ת דבפ' שלשה שאכלו (ברכות מז:) מסיק דאין מכבדין אלא בפתח הראוי למזוזה ותירץ רבינו תם דהתם כשאין הולכים בחבורה אחת אלא כל אחד הולך לצורך עצמו אבל כשהולכים בחבורה אחת מכבדים בכל מקום:

רש"י

הרי זה כזבל. דמוסיף הבלא ואין טומנין בה אפילו מבעוד יום: מיחם. של נחשת: קדרה. מעל חרס יש ספרים שכתוב בהן אבל לא מיחם על גבי קדירה ומפרשים טעמא מפני שהקדירה מרבה חמימות ומוספת הבלא למיחם אבל בתוספתא גרסינן ומיחם על גבי קדירה: וטח את פיה (ב) בבצק. הגילוש מבעו"י כל הנך מניחין נמי בשבת: ולא שיחמו. שיהא העליון לוקח ונתנו כדי שיחום מחומו של תחתון: אלא שיהו משומרין. שהיו שניהן חמין ונתנו על גביו של זה כדי שיהא חומו משתמר בהן: ואין מרזקין. כמו מרסקין משברין לחתיכות דקות ברד גלצ"א בלע"ז כדי שיזובו מימיו. משום דקא מוליד בשבת ודמי למלאכה שבורא המים הללו: אבל נותן לתוך הכוס. של יין בימות החמה כדי לצנן ואע"פ שנימוח מאליו ואינו חושש:

הדרן עלך במה טומנין

במה בהמה יוצאה כו'. לפי שאדם מצווה על שביתת בהמתו בשבת ומידי דמינטרא ביה בהמה הוי תכשיט ואורחא ולא הוי משוי ומידי דלא מינטרא ביה הוי משוי: אפסר. קבישט"א: נאקה. דרומי"ל: בחטם. מפרש בגמרא: ולובדקים בפרומביא. מפרש בגמ': בשיר. כמו אצעדה סביב צוארו וטבעת קבוע בה ומכניסין בו רצועה או חבל ומושכין הבהמה: וכל בעלי השיר. כגון כלבים [של] ציידים וחיות קטנות שנותנין שיר לצוארם לנוי: יוצאין ונמשכין. מפרש בגמ': ומזין עליהם במקומן. כמו שהם בצואר הבהמה אם נטמאו: וטובלן במקומן. מכניסין בהמה למים להטביל את השיר: **גמ'** מאי נאקה. ומאי חטם: חיורתי. שהיא קשה להשתמר מפני שבורחת: בזממא דפרזלא. מוזי"ל בלע"ז נוקב את חוטמו ומכניסו בתוכו והוא כמין טבעת: חמרא לובא. חמור הבא ממדינת לוב כמו הכושים והלובים דאסא בדברי הימים (ב טז): בפגי דפרזלא. פריי' כעין שלנו פגי כמו זה קנה חמור ובית פגי (ב"מ ד' פ:) קיבליי"ל בית ראשה ולחייה: צרו שדרו ליה שערי. צרו מעותיו ושלחו לו שעורים בצרור מעותיו ולא רצו לקנות לו חמור מפני שהוא רחוק מבבל מהלך חצי שנה כדאמר בהגוזל (ב"ק ד' קיב:) והשיאוהו עצה לקנות חמור במקומו ויאכילנו שעורים תמיד ונמצא חמורו טוב ומשובח: ניגרי דחמרא שערי. פסיעותיו של חמור לפי שעורים שהוא אוכל: מחליפין. שאילתם נאקה באפסר וגמל בחטם מהו משוי הוא ואסור: לאו למעוטי גמל בחטם. והכי קאמר ארבע בהמות הללו משתמרים באפסר ואסורות לצאת בחטם: לא למעוטי נאקה באפסר. דהואיל ולא מינטרא ביה משאוי הוא אבל נטירותא יתירתא כגון חטם לגמל לאו משאוי הוא: יוצאין באפסר. דלובדקי נמי מינטרא ביה: ה"ג כתנאי אין חיה יוצאה בסוגר: כתנאי. נטירותא יתירתא אי משוי הוא או לא: בסוגר. קולא"ר של חבל כדמתרגמינן ויתנהו בסוגר בקולרין (יחזקאל יט): בחיה גדולה. כגון דוב: קטנה. כגון נמייה וחולדה: חתול. לא בעי נטירותא אפילו כחיה קטנה שאינו תאב לברוח כל כך: במיתנא. חבל קטן: הלכה כחנניה. ונטירותא יתירתא לאו משאוי הוא: חלשא דעתיה דרבה בר רב הונא. שהיה גדול וכסבור שעשה מדעת דאיתותב

עין משפט נר מצוה

לו א מיי' פ"ד מהלכות שבת הלכה ו סמג לאוין סה טוש"ע או"ח סימן רנח וסימן שיח סעיף ו:

לז ב מיי' פכ"ה מהלכות שבת הלכה יג סמג לאוין סה טוש"ע או"ח סימן שכ סעיף טו וסי' שיח סעיף טז:

א ג מיי' פ"כ מהלכות שבת הלכה ח סמג לאוין סה טוש"ע או"ח סימן שה סעיף א:

נ"ל ומים שמתקרשים רש"א

[בתוספתא פ"ד איתא מרסקין בסמ"ך וכ"א בפירש"י הכא על נכון יכן בערוך וכי"ף ולא"ש ובב"י סי' שיח מרסקין]

ב ד מיי' שם טור ש"ע שם סעיף ס:

ג ה מיי' שם טור ש"ע שם סעיף ג:

ד ו מיי' שם טור ש"ע שם סעיף א:

[עי' תוס' שם ד"ה וטובלין]

[ועי' תוס' בכורות ס: ד"ה הטעים וכו']

מסורת הש"ס

[לעיל מט.]

קך אבל לא הוא טעות וצ"ל וקדירה ע"ג וכו' ואע"ג דרש"י גרס אבל לא היינו במיחם ע"ג קדירה אבל בקדירה ע"ג מיחם ליכא מאן דפליג עי' בב"י באו"ח סימן רנח

[נדרים כ: נזיר ב.]

[עי' תוס' נב: ד"ה מזין]

גמלא נקיבה גדולה ערוך

פי' רסן שבלחי

הגהות הב"ח

(א) במשנה ומזין עליהן במקומן וטובלין:

(ב) רש"י ד"ה וטח את פיה בבצק:

רבינו חננאל

את הצונן וכל הנאכל כמות שהוא חי אין בו משום בשולי נכרים · אדם חשוב לא איבעי ליה למיעבד הכי · ת"ר אע"פ שאמרו אין טומנין בדבר שאינו מוסיף [הבל] אבל אם בא להוסיף מוסיף כיצד ר"ש ב"ג אומר נוטל הסדינין ומניח [את] הגלופקרין כו' פשוטה היא · ר' יהודה אומר נעורת של פשתן דקה הרי הוא כזבל ומניחין מיחם ע"ג מיחם וקדירה על גבי קדירה מיחם ומיחם על גבי קדירה וטח פיהן בבצק ולא כדי שיחמו אלא כדי שישתמרו כו' רבי התיר להטמין את הצונן כו':

הדרן עלך במה טומנין

פ"ה במה בהמה יוצאה ובמה אינה יוצאה · יוצאה הגמל באפסר כו' ונאקה בחטם נקתא חורתי בזממא דפרזלא · לובדקים בפרומביא · חמרא לובא בפגי דפרזלא לבדקם לובא חמור לוב · מקום ששמו לוב כדכתיב (דניאל י"א) לובים וכוש במצעדיו · כדגרסי' בירושלמי גרים הבאים מלוב מהו להמתין להו ג' דורות וקיי"ל כר' יוסי דאמר ארבע בהמות יוצאות באפסר בשבת הסוס והפרד והחמור והגמל: ירושלמי אמר חזקיה וסטניך וכן תהיה מגפת הסוס וגו' למעוטי גמל בחטם שלא יצא · רב אמר הלכה כר' יוסי · ולית הלכתא כחנניה דתני כל נטירותא יתירתא לאו (משום) [משוי] הוא ושפיר דמי ואע"ג דאמר שמואל הילכתא כחנניה פליג רב עליה

place [it];[10] but if not, [51b] it may not be removed and replaced.
a R. Judah said: Thoroughly beaten flax is the same as foliage.[1] A boiler may be placed upon a boiler, and a pot upon a pot,[2] but not a pot upon a boiler,[3] or a boiler upon a pot;[4] and the mouth [thereof][5] may [also] be daubed over with dough:[6] not in order to make them[7] hotter, but that [their heat] may be retained. And just as hot [food] may not be hidden, so may cold [food] not be hidden. Rabbi permitted cold [food] to be hidden. And neither snow nor hail may be broken up on the Sabbath in order that the water should flow, but they may be placed in a goblet or dish, without fear.[8]

CHAPTER V

b *MISHNAH.* WHEREWITH MAY AN ANIMAL[1] GO OUT [ON THE SABBATH], AND WHEREWITH MAY IT NOT GO OUT? A CAMEL MAY GO FORTH WITH A BIT, A DROMEDARY [NE'AḲAH] WITH ITS NOSE-RING [ḤOṬEM], A LYBIAN ASS WITH A HALTER, A HORSE WITH ITS CHAIN, AND ALL CHAINWEARING ANIMALS MAY GO OUT WITH THEIR CHAINS AND BE LED BY THEIR CHAINS, AND [WATER OF LUSTRATION] MAY BE SPRINKLED UPON THEM, AND THEY MAY BE IMMERSED IN THEIR PLACE.[2]

GEMARA. What is meant by a NE'AḲAH WITH A ḤOṬEM?—Said Rabbah b. Bar Ḥanah: A white [female] camel with its iron nose-ring.

A LYBIAN ASS WITH A HALTER. R. Huna said: That means a Lybian ass with an iron halter.[3] Levi sent money to Be Ḥozae[4] for a Lybian ass to be bought for him. [But] they parcelled up some barley and sent it to him, to intimate to him that an ass's steps depend on barley.[5]

Rab Judah said in Samuel's name: They [the scholars] transposed them[6] [in their questions] before Rabbi: What about one animal going forth with [the accoutrement] of the other? As for a dromedary [*ne'aḳah*] with a bit, there is no question; since it is
c not guarded thereby, it is a burden.[1] The problem is in respect of a camel with a nose-ring. How is it: Since a bit is sufficient, this [the nose-ring] is a burden; or perhaps an additional guard is not called a burden? Said R. Ishmael son of R. Jose before him, Thus did my father rule: Four animals may go out with a bit: a horse, mule, camel and ass. What does this exclude? Surely it excludes a camel [from being led out] with a nose-ring?—No: it excludes a dromedary [*ne'aḳah*] with a bit. In a Baraitha it was taught: A Lybian ass and a camel may go out with a bit.

This is dependent on Tannaim: A beast may not go forth with a muzzle;[2] Ḥananiah said: It may go forth with a muzzle and with anything whereby it is guarded. To what is the reference? Shall we say, to a large beast? Is a muzzle sufficient! But if a small beast is meant, is a muzzle insufficient?[3] Hence they must surely differ in respect to a cat: the first Tanna holds: since a mere cord is sufficient, it [a muzzle] is a burden;[4] while Ḥananiah holds, Whatever is an additional guard is not called a burden. R. Huna b. Ḥiyya said in Samuel's name: The *halachah* is as Ḥananiah.

Levi son of R. Huna b. Ḥiyya and Rabbah b. R. Huna were travelling on a road, when Levi's ass went ahead of Rabbah b. R. Huna's, whereupon Rabbah b. R. Huna felt aggrieved.[5] Said

(10) Since there is something by which he can grasp it.
a (1) It adds heat, and therefore food may not be put away in it even before the Sabbath. (2) A boiler is of copper, and a pot is of earthenware. (3) That is the corrected text. (4) Var. lec.: and a pot upon a boiler, but not a boiler upon a pot. [The reason for the distinction is not clear and Rashi explains because a pot being of earthenware retains more effective heat which it communicates to the boiler of copper. Tosef. Shab. VI, however reads: and a pot upon a boiler and a boiler upon a pot. V. Asheri and Alfasi]. (5) [I.e., of the lower vessel, v. R. Ḥananel]. (6) Kneaded before the Sabbath. (7) [I.e.. the contents of the upper vessel]. (8) Of desecrating the Sabbath, though they may melt there.
b (1) To whom the law of Sabbath rest applies. V. Ex. XX, 10; Deut. V, 14. (2) If the chain becomes ritually unclean, the ceremony of sprinkling (v. Num. XIX, 14 *seq.*) and immersion (*tebillah*) may be performed while they are on the animal. (3) The words used in the Mishnah had become unfamiliar to the Babylonian Amoraim and needed explaining. (4) A district on the caravan route along the Tigris and its canals. The modern Khuzistan, a province of S.W. Persia, Obermeyer, *Landschaft*, pp. 204ff. (5) I.e., barley is the proper food for asses.—Rashi: they returned the money, not wishing to send an ass so far. (6) I.e., the appurtenances mentioned in the Mishnah.
c (1) And must certainly not be led out with it. (2) Or, collar. (3) It is a complete guard in itself, and there can be no reason for prohibiting it. (4) Therefore it is forbidden. (5) He thought that Levi had acted intentionally, which was disrespectful, for Rabbah b. R. Huna was a greater scholar.

[Levi], I will say something to him, so that [52a] his mind may appeased. Said he: An ass of evil habits, such as this one, may go forth wearing a halter on the Sabbath?—Thus did your father y in Samuel's name, he answered him, The *halachah* is as ananiah.[6]

The School of Manasseh taught: If grooves are made between goat's horns, it may be led out with a bit on the Sabbath.[7] R. seph asked: What if one fastened it through its beard:[8] since is painful [to the goat] to tug at it,[1] it will not come to do so;[2] perhaps it may chance to loosen and fall, and he will come to rry it four cubits in the street? The question stands over.

We learnt elsewhere: Nor with the strap between its horns.[3] . Jeremiah b. Abba said: Rab and Samuel differ therein: One aintains: Whether as an ornament or as a guard, it is forbidden; hile the other rules: As an ornament it is forbidden; as a guard is permitted. R. Joseph observed: It may be proved that it as Samuel who maintained: As an ornament it is forbidden; as guard it is permitted. For R. Huna b. Ḥiyya said in Samuel's me: The *halachah* is as Ḥananiah.[4] Said Abaye to him, On e contrary, It may be proved that it was Samuel who maintined: Whether as an ornament or as a guard it is forbidden. For ab Judah said in Samuel's name: They transposed them [in their jestions] before Rabbi: What about one animal going forth with he accoutrement] of the other? Said R. Ishmael b. R. Jose before m, Thus did my father rule: Four animals may go out with a t: A horse, mule, camel and ass. What does it exclude?[5] Surely excludes a camel [from being led out] with a nose-ring?[6]—elete the latter on account of the former.[7] And what [reason] you see to delete the latter on account of the former? Delete e former on account of the latter!—[Because] we find that it as Samuel who ruled: As an ornament it is forbidden; as a ıard it is permitted. [For] it was stated:[8] R. Ḥiyya b. Ashi id in Rab's name: Whether as an ornament or as a guard it is rbidden; while R. Ḥiyya b. Abin said in Samuel's name: As ornament it is forbidden; as a guard it is permitted.

An objection is raised: If the owners tied it [the red heifer] up y a cord,[9] it is fit.[10] Now if you say that it is a burden, rely Scripture saith, *Upon which never came yoke?*[1]—Abaye answered: This is when it is led from one town to another.[2] Raba said: The red heifer is different, because its value is high. Rabina said: This refers to an intractable [animal].[3]

A HORSE WITH ITS CHAIN, etc. What is GO OUT and what is LED?—R. Huna said: [It means,] They may either go out [with the chain] wound round them,[4] or led [by the chain]; while Samuel maintained: [It means,] They may go out led [by the chain], but they may not go out [with the chain] wound round them. In a Baraitha it was taught: They may go out [with the chain] wound round them [ready] to be led.[5]

R. Joseph said: I saw the calves of R. Huna's house go forth with their cords[6] wound about them on the Sabbath. When R. Dimi came,[7] he related in R. Ḥanina's name: The mules of Rabbi's house went forth with their reins on the Sabbath. The scholars propounded: 'Wound about them', or 'led'?—Come and hear: When R. Samuel b. Judah came, he related in R. Ḥanina's name: The mules of Rabbi's house went forth on the Sabbath with their reins wound about them. Said the Rabbis before R. Assi, This [dictum] of R. Samuel b. Judah is unnecessary, [because] it may be deduced from R. Dimi's [statement]. For should you think that R. Dimi meant 'led', it would follow from Rab Judah's [statement] in Samuel's name. For Rab Judah said in Samuel's name: They [the scholars] transposed them [in their questions] before Rabbi: What about one animal going forth with [the accoutrement] of the other? Said R. Ishmael son of R. Jose before him, Thus did my father rule: Four animals may go out with a bit: a horse, mule, camel, and ass![8]—Said R. Assi to them, This [R. Samuel b. Judah's statement] is necessary. For if it were derived from Rab Judah's [dictum], I could argue: He [R. Ishmael son of R. Jose] stated it before him, but he did not accept it. Hence R. Dimi's statement informs us [that he did]. And if there were R. Dimi's [alone], I could argue: It means 'led', but not merely 'wound round'; hence R. Samuel b. Judah's [statement] informs us [otherwise].

AND [WATER OF LUSTRATION] MAY BE SPRINKLED UPON THEM, AND THEY MAY BE IMMERSED IN THEIR PLACE. Are we to say that they can contract uncleanness? But we learnt: A
c man's ring is unclean,[1] but the rings of animals and utensils and

(6) Hence 'en if it is an extra guard it is permitted. (7) Which is fastened to the ooves. But otherwise it is forbidden, because it can easily slip off the head, hich is very narrow, and its owner may carry it in the street. (8) Making a rcle of the beard and inserting the bit through it.

(1) On account of the beard. (2) Hence we may assume that it is safe there, d is permitted. (3) V. *infra* 54b. (4) Hence he holds that an extra guard is ermitted, and this includes the strap between a cow's horns. (5) V. *supra* b. (6) That being forbidden because it is an extra guard. Since Samuel ıotes it with evident approval, it is his view too. (7) Because these two atements of Samuel are contradictory. (8) Other edd. omit the bracketed passage, and substitute: What is our decision on the matter?—It was stated: (9) Or, the reins. (10) For its purpose; v. Num. XIX, 2 *seq*.

b (1) Num. XIX, 2. A burden is a yoke. (2) The cord or reins are then required as an ordinary, not an additional, guard. (3) According to both answers, what would be an extra guard elsewhere is only an ordinary one here. (4) Even that is permitted. (5) I.e., either that it must be wound round it loosely, so that one can insert his hand between the animal's neck and the chain and grasp it; or that a portion of the cord must be left free, whereby the animal may be led. (6) Lit., 'bit'. (7) V. *supra* 5a, n. b9. (8) V. *supra* 51b.

c (1) I.e., it is liable to uncleanness.

דאיתותב דעתיה א"ל חמור שעסקיו רעים כגון זה מהו לצאת בפרומביא בשבת א"ל הכי אמר אבוך משמיה דשמואל הלכה כחנניא תנא דבי מנשיא *עז שחקק לה בין קרניה יוצאה באפסר בשבת בעי רב יוסף תחב לה בזקנה מהו כיון דאי מנתח לה כאיב לה לא אתיא לנתוחה או דילמא זימנין דרפי ונפיל ואתי לאתויי ד"א ברה"ר תיקו *תנן התם ולא ברצועה שבין קרניה אמר (ליה) ר' ירמיה בר אבא פליגי בה רב ושמואל חד אמר בין לנוי בין לשמר אסור וח"א לנוי אסור ולשמר מותר אמר רב יוסף תסתיים דשמואל הוא דאמר לנוי אסור לשמר מותר דאמר רב הונא בר חייא אמר שמואל הלכה כחנניא א"ל אביי אדרבה תסתיים דשמואל הוא דאמר בין לנוי בין לשמר אסור דאמר רב יהודה אמר שמואל מחליפין לפני רבי של זו בזו מהו אמר לפניו *ר' ישמעאל בר' יוסי כך אמר אבא ד' בהמות יוצאות באפסר הסוס הפרד והגמל והחמור לאו למעוטי גמל בחטם סמי הא מקמי הא ומאי חזית דמסמית הא מקמי הא סמי הא מקמי הא (דאשכחן שמואל הוא דאמר לנוי אסור לשמר מותר דאתמר) רב חייא בר אשי *אמר רב בין לנוי בין לשמר אסור ורב חייא בר אבין *אמר שמואל לנוי אסור לשמר מותר מיתיבי קשרה בעליה במוסרה כשרה ואי ס"ד משאוי הוא °אשר לא עלה עליה עול אמר רחמנא אמר אביי במוליכה מעיר לעיר רבא אמר שאני פרה דדמיה יקרין רבינא אמר במורד': הסוס בשיר וכו': מאי יוצאין ומאי נמשכין אמר רב הונא או יוצאין כרוכין או נמשכין ושמואל אמר יוצאין נמשכין ואין יוצאין כרוכין במתניתא תנא יוצאין כרוכין לימשך אמר רב יוסף הזינא להו לעיגלי דבי רב הונא יוצאין באפסריהן כרוכין בשבת כי אתא רב דימי אמר ר' חנינא מולאות של בית רבי יוצאות באפסריהן בשבת איבעיא להו כרוכין או נמשכין ת"ש כי אתא רב שמואל בר יהודה א"ר חנינא מולאות של בית רבי יוצאות באפסריהן כרוכים בשבת אמרוה רבנן קמיה דרב אסי הא דרב שמואל בר יהודה לא צריכא מדרב דימי נפקא דאי ס"ד דרב דימי נמשכין קאמר מדרב יהודה אמר שמואל נפקא דאמר רב יהודה אמר שמואל מחליפין היו לפני רבי של זו בזו מהו אמר לפניו ר' ישמעאל בר' יוסי כך אמר אבא ארבע בהמות יוצאת באפסר הסוס והפרד והגמל והחמור אמר להו רב אסי איצטריך להו דאי מדרב יהודה נפקא הוה אמינא אמר לפניו ולא קיבלה מיניה קמ"ל דרב דימי ואי דרב דימי הוה אמינא ה"מ נמשכין אבל כרוכין לא קמ"ל דרב שמואל בר (רב) יהודה: ומזין עליהן וטובלין במקומן: למימרא דבני קבולי טומאה נינהו והתנן *טבעת אדם טמאה וטבעת בהמה וכלים ושאר כל הטבעות טהורות

רש"י

דאיתותב דעתיה · להודיעו שלא נתכוונתי: בפרומביא · מי הוי נטירותא יתירתא לגביה או לא: הלכה כחנניא · ולא איכפת לן אי הוי נטירותא יתירתא: יוצאה באפסר · אם תחבו בחקיקת קרן אבל בקשירה בעלמא לא דילמא שלפא מרישה מתוך שראשה דק והיא מתנתקת לכאן ולכאן כשמושכין אותה ואתי לאתויי ארבע אמות ברשות הרבים: תחב לה בזקנה · שקשר שער זקנה כמין נקב ותחב האפסר לתוכו: מנתחא · מתנתקת וקופלת אנה ואנה לברוח מידו: כאיב לה · הזקן שנתלש השער ומכאיבה: תנן התם · בסוף פרקין ולא פרה ברצועה שבין קרניה: לנוי · שצובעה וקולעה לנוי בין קרניה כמין קליעה מקרן לקרן ואינו אוחזה בה: לשמר · שאוחזה בה: אסור · דפרה מינטרא בלא אחיזה אלא מוליכה לפניו וקסבר נטירותא יתירתא משוי הוא: ולשמר מותר · קסבר נטירותא יתירתא לאו משוי הוא: ארבע בהמות. וקס"ד דהכי קאמר באפסר יוצאו' ולא בחטם אלמא נטירותא יתירתא משוי הוא: ומאי חזית. דמסמית האי דשמואל מקמיה ההיא סמי ההיא מקמי הא: דאיתמר · בהדיא דשמואל הוא דשרי והוא דמחליפין כדאוקימנא דלא (א) למעוטינהו מחטם אלא למעוטי נאקה מאפסר דלא מינטרא ביה: קשרה בעליה · לפרה אדומה: במוסרה · אפסר: במוליכה מעיר לעיר · וסתם פרה פונה למקום מרבץ שלה וצריך לאוחזה כשמוליכה לעיר אחרת ולאו נטירותא יתירתא הוא אלא אורחא היא: שאני פרה · אדומה: דדמיה יקרים · ובעי נטירותא יתירתא משמרה: במורדת · שאינה מקבלת מרות: יוצאין כרוכין · הרצועה סביב צוארן ואע"פ שאינו אוחזה לאו משוי הוא דלנוי כמי אורחייהו הוא: נמשכין · שמושכה ברצועה הקבועה בטבעת השיר: יוצאין נמשכים · דנטירותא אורחא הוא: ואין יוצאין כרוכים · דלנוי לאו אורחא הוא: כרוכין לימשך · כרוכים בריוח שיכול להכניס ידו בין הכרך לצואר או יניח מעט מן החבל שאם באת לברוח ימהר ויאחזנה: מולאות · פרדות: דאי ס"ד רב דימי נמשכין לחוד קאמר · אבל כרוכין לא ולא אתא לאשמועינן אלא דמולאות משתמרות באפסר ולא הוי משוי להו: מדרב יהודה אמר שמואל נפקא · דקס"ד דקיבלה רבי מיניה דרבי ישמעאל ברבי יוסי: טבעת אדם · שנותן באצבע לנוי: טמאה · דתכשיט הוא וממדין ילפינן דמנה בהן תכשיטין אצעדה וצמיד וגו' ואכולהו קאי תתחטאו אתם ושביכם (במדבר לא): טבעת בהמה · כגון שיר: טבעת כלים · כעין שעושין בראש ידות הכלים: ושאר כל הטבעות. כגון העשויות לדלת: טהורות

תוספות

אמר שמואל הלכה כחנניא · פר"ח דהלכה כרב דאמר בין לנוי בין לשמר אסור מדמשני אביי ורבא ורבינא דהוו בתראי אליביה ההיא דקשרה בעליה במוסרה ועוד דקיי"ל *דהלכתא כרב באיסורי הלכך אומר הרב פור"ת דכל נטירותא יתירתא אסור כגון פרה באפסר ובכל טוי בהמה אסור לצאת ומיהו עגלים יוצאות באפסר כדאמר בסמוך ויוצא סוס ברסן דאורחיה בהכי או באפסר אבל בשניהם ברסן ובאפסר אסור ומותר להשים הרסן או האפסר בראש הסוס בשבת ואין בו איסור טלטול דמוכן הוא לבהמה ואדם המנהיג סוס ברשות הרבים יזהר שלא יוציא ראש החבל מתחת ידו טפח ומה שבין ידו לסוס יגביה מן הקרקע טפח דהכי אמרינן לקמן בפרקין(ג) ומותר לכרוך חבל האפסר סביב צואר הבהמה ולצאת דהא עגלי דרב הונא ומולאות של בית רבי יוצאים כרוכין:

אדרבה תסתיים דשמואל הוא דאמר כו' · תימה לרשב"א מה ראייה מייתי מדאמר שמואל מחליפין לפני רבי כו' דלכאורה משמע דהא דקאמר לעיל לא למעוטי נאקה באפסר דכל זה מדברי שמואל:

קשרה בעליה במוסרה. הוה מצי לשנויי הא מני חנניא היא והא דמשמע בריש הכונס (ב"ק נה:) דמוסרה שמירה פחותה היא היינו דוקא בשור:

אין יוצאין כרוכין · פי' בקונט' דמכוין לנוי וכן פירש במתניתין וקשה לרשב"א ולהרב פור"ת דלעיל משמע דלנוי לכ"ע אסור ותירץ הרב פור"ת דבהא פליגי דרב הונא סבר דנטירותא נמי איכא בכרוכין שאם רוצה הבהמה לברוח יתפסנה בכריכת האפסר ולא הוי משוי ושמואל סבר כרוכין לא הוי נטירותא:

במתניתא תנא כרוכין לימשך · רב הונא מתרץ כרוכים לימשך שיש חלל בין אפסר לצואר שהוא נוח לימשך כשירצה ושמואל סבר לימשך דוקא שיש חבל תלוי באפסר:

*בבאין מנוי אדם לנוי בהמה · פירש"י ובעודו לאדם נטמא ובחנם פירש כך דאפילו אחר שיחדו לבהמה מקבל טומאה שאינו עולה מלקבל טומאה מכאן ואילך אלא בשינוי מעשה כדמוכח בפ"ק דסוכה (דף יג:) גבי קוצר להבילה ונמלך לסיכוך ורש"י בעצמו פירש כן בריש במה אשה (לקמן נה:) °וכופת שאור שיחדו לישיבה דאמר טהור אור"י דמיירי כשיש שינוי מעשה:

*ומזין עליהם במקומן · אצטריך לאשמעינן במקומן דלא חיישינן שמא תפול הזאה על הבהמה ויפסלו דתנן במסכת פרה (פי"ב מ"ג) נתכוון להזות על האדם והזה על הבהמה אם יש בחזוב [לא] ישנה:

וטובלין במקומן · הקשה הר"ר אליעזר אמאי לא מקשה הכא טבילה מאן דכר שמיה כדפריך בריש במה אשה (דף נז.) אמאי דתנן ולא תטבול עד שתרפס ותירץ ר"ת דהכא לא פריך משום דמתני' מיירי בדין כלים שמחלק בין כלי לכלי ואיזה מותר לצאת בו ואיזה אסור ואגב אורחיה אשמעינן שאר דיני כלים ומזין עליהם וטובלן במקומן דכן דרך התנא כי ההוא (לקמן דף סו.) דקיטע יוצא בקב שלו ואם יש בו בית קבול כתותין טמא אבל בריש במה אשה דמיירי בדיני כלים ואשמעינן דין טבילת אשה פריך שפיר טבילה מאן דכר שמיה:

והא

עין משפט נר מצוה

ה א ב מיי' פ"כ מהל' שבת הלכה יא:

[בכורות מה:]

ו ג מיי' שם סמג לאוין סה טוש"ע או"ח סי' שה סעיף יז:

ז ד מיי' שם ופ"א מהל' פרה אדומה הלכה ז' סמג עשין רלב טוש"ע א"ח סי' שה סעיף ד:

ח ה (מיימ' פ"כ מהל' שבת הל' ח') טור וש"ע שם סעיף ה:

ט ו מיי' פ"ח מהל' כלים הלכה ו:

י ז שם הלכה ז:

יא ח שם הלכה ט:

רבינו חננאל

רב עליה. ואמר בין לנוי בין לשמר אסור. ושמואל אמר לנוי אסור לשמר מותר. ומותבנן לרב קשרה לפרה ארומה בעליה במוסרה כשרה. קשיא לרב דאמר לשמור בשבת אסור שנמצאת מוסרה בפרה (מחוי) [משוי]. והמשאוי פוסל בפרה אמאי קתני כשרה. ופריק אביי ורבא ורבינא דאיהו בתרא לעולם לשמר כמשאוי והכא בפרה מורדת ומשום הכי לא היה מוסרה משאוי עליה. אבל כולי עלמא משאוי היא כרב ומדמשני רבינא לאוקמה כרב שמע מינה הלכתא כוותיה דרב: יוצאין כרוכין. שהיו אפסריהן כרוכין על צואריהן. ואסיקנא דיוצאין כרוכין וכ"ש נמשכין. מולאות פי' פרדות של בית רבי היו יוצאות באפסריהן כרוכין בשבת. יוצאין בשיר ונמשכין בשיר ומזין עליהן וטובלין במקומן. פי' שיר כעין צמידין. כדמתרגמינן שירין. ואקשינן וכי טבעות של בהמה בני קיבולי טומאה נינהו. והתנן בכלים פ' י"ב טבעת אדם טמאה. טבעת בהמה וכלים ושאר כל

רב נסים גאון

פ"ה שאני פרה דדמיה יקרין. במס' ע"ז בפרק אין מעמידין בהמה (דף כ"ד) דברו עלה *) פי דאלך למא קאל ר"א אומר ישראל היו משמרין אותה משעה שנוצרה הסב מאנא אל תירוץ קאלו עלי טריק אל סואל מנא ידעינן וג' אל גואב אמר רב כהנא כוס אדום מעבירין לפניה בשעה שעולה עליה זכר אי הכי אמאי דמיה יקרין הואיל ושתי שערות פוסלות בה:

*) כוונת הדברים כן הוא. כי דברו בזה הענין למה שאמר רבי אליעזר לפי מה שבא התירוץ אמרו בדרך שאלה מנא ידעינן ובאה התשובה אמר רב כהנא וכו'.

מסורת הש"ס

לקמן ה:

[תוספ' פ"ה]

ב"מ אינו וה"ג מאי הוה עלה אתבר וכו' [לקמן נד:]

[שם]

כלים פי"ב מ"א

הגהות הב"ח

(א) רש"י ד"ה דאתמר וכו' דלאו למעוטי גמל מחטם אלא: (ב) תום' ד"ה אמר וכו' לקמן בפירקין. נ"ב ד' נד ע"ב:

גליון הש"ס

תום' ד"ה בבאין וכו' וכופת שאור שיחדו לישיבה דאמר טהור. חולין קכט ע"א ועי' ב"ב יט ע"ב תוס' ד"ה מיפוק ליה:

עין משפט
נר מצוה

יב א מיי' פ"ח מהל' כלים הלכה י:
יג ב ג שם הלכה ט:
יד ד מיי' פ"ג מהל' מקוואות הלכה טו:
טו ה מיי' פ"ח מהל' כלים הלכה י:
טז ו שם הלכה ט:
יז ז מיי' פ"ד מהל' כלים הלכה ו:
יח ח מיי' פי"ח מהל' כלים הלכה יד:
יט ט שם הלכה טו:
כ י מיי' פי"כ מהל' שבת הלכה י סמג לאוין סה טוש"ע א"ח סי' שח סעיף ז:

[ועי' תוס' סוכה יב: ד"ה מהו דתימא ומה שנכתב שם על הגליון ויש ליישב קצת]

מסורת הש"ס

טהורות א"ר יצחק (נפחא) *בבאין מנוי אדם לנוי בהמה ורב יוסף אמר הואיל ואדם מושך בהם את הבהמה מי לא תניא מקל של בהמה של מתכת מקבל טומאה מה טעם הואיל ואדם רודה בהן ה"נ הואיל ואדם מושך בהן: וטובלן במקומן: והאיכא חציצה א"ר אמי בשריתכן לימא ר' אמי כרב יוסף סבירא ליה דאי כר' יצחק (*נפחא) דאמר בבאין מנוי אדם לנוי בהמה כיון דריתכן עבד בהו מעשה ופרחה לה טומאה מינייהו דתנן*) כל הכלים יורדין לידי טומאתן במחשבה ואין עולין מטומאתן אלא בשינוי מעשה סבר לה כרבי יהודה דאמר מעשה לתקן לאו מעשה הוא דתניא ר' יהודה אומר לא אמר שינוי מעשה לתקן אלא לקלקל במתניתא תני במחוללין *שאל תלמיד אחד מגליל העליון את ר"א שמעתי שחולקין בין טבעת לטבעת אמר לו שמא לא שמעת אלא לענין שבת דאי לענין טומאה דא ודא חדא היא ולענין טומאה דא ודא אחת היא *והתנן טבעת אדם טמאה וטבעת בהמה וכלים ושאר כל הטבעות טהורות כי קאמר ליה איהו נמי דאדם קאמר ליה ודאדם דא ודא אחת היא והתניא* טבעת שהתקינה לחגור בה מתניו ולקשר בה בין כתפיו טהורה ולא אמרו טמאה אלא של אצבע בלבד כי קאמר ליה איהו נמי דאצבע קאמר ליה ודאצבע דא ודא אחת היא והתנן *טבעת של מתכת וחותמה של אלמוג טמאה היא של אלמוג וחותמה של מתכת טהורה כי קאמר ליה איהו נמי כולה של מתכת קאמר ליה ועוד שאל שמעתי שחולקין בין מחט למחט אמר ליה שמא לא שמעת אלא לענין שבת דאי לענין טומאה דא ודא אחת היא ולענין טומאה דא ודא אחת היא *והתנן מחט שניטל חורה או עוקצה טהורה כי קאמר ליה בשלימה ובשלימה דא ודא אחת היא *והתנן מחט שהעלתה חלודה אם מעכב את התפירה טהורה ואם לאו טמאה ואמרי דבי ר' ינאי והוא שרישומה ניכר כי קאמר ליה בשיפא קאמר לי' ובשיפא דא ודא אחת היא והתניא *מחט בין נקובה בין אינה נקובה מותר לטלטלה בשבת ולא *אמרינן נקובה אלא לענין טומאה בלבד הא *תרגמא אביי אליבא דרבא בגלמי: **מתני'** חמור יוצא במרדעת בזמן שהיא קשורה בו זכרים יוצאין לבובין רחלות יוצאות שחוזות כבולות וכבונות העזים יוצאות צרורות רבי יוסי אוסר בכולן חוץ מן הרחלין הכבונות רבי יהודה אומר עזים יוצאות צרורות ליבש אבל לא לחלב:

גמ'

*) כלים פכ"ה מ"ט לקמן נה: סוכה יג: קדושין נט. [מנחות סט:]

נפ"י ליתא

ל"ל אמרו

תוספות

והא איכא חלילה · פירש בקונטרס שטבעת תקוע בשיר בחוזק ואין המים נכנסים שם ואומר ר"י דלריך לומר שפעמים מסירים אותן ועושים מהן מלאכה בפני עלמן שאם כל שעה היו קבועים בלואר הבהמה היה הכל חשיב כלי אחד ולא הוי חלילה וה"ר פור"ת פירש והא איכא חלילה לפי שהוא דבוק בלואר הבהמה:

בשריתכן · להכי לא מוקי לה במחוללין דאין דרך השיר להיות כן:

טבעת שהתקינה לחגור בה מתניו · נראה לר"י דהיינו לחגור מלבושיו שהן רחבים ואוגדם כנגד מתניו בטבעת כעין שפי' בקונטרס לקשור בה את כתפיו:

היא של אלמוג וחותמה של מתכת · וא"ת והא יש בה בית קיבול מקום מושב החותם וי"ל דאין זה בית קיבול דאמרינן בית קיבול העשוי למלאות °לא שמיה בית קבול*:

והתניא מחט בין נקובה בין אינה נקוב' · נראה לר"י דלא פריך אליב' דאביי דאיהו הוה מפרש שאינה נקובה היינו שניטל חורה או עוקצה אלא אליב' דרבא פריך דלדידיה לא מצינן לפרש הכי כדמוכח בריש כל הכלים (לקמן קכג·) ותימה לר"י דכיון דלא ידע המקשה דמיירי בגלמי א"כ בלאו הכי תקשה ליה לרבא כדפריך בריש כל הכלים (ג"ז שם):

והוא

רש"י

טהורות · דלאו משום תכשיט מיטמאו דאין תכשיט לכלי וכלי נמי לא הוו אלא תכשיט כלי ומיהו בעודן מחוברות לכלי מיטמו עם הכלי דהוי יד לכלי דכל המחובר לו הרי הוא כמוהו: בבאין מנוי אדם לנוי בהמה · מתני' כגון שנעשה שיר זה לתכשיט אדם ובעודו לאדם נטמא ולאחר טומאתו נתנו לבהמה וצריך להטבילו מטומאתו ראשונה שלא יגע בטהרות: הואיל ואדם מושך בהן את הבהמה · חשיב ליה כלי תשמיש דאדם: מקל של בהמה · שרודין בו את הגמל או את האנקה *אי נמי כעין שעושין להנהיג את הדוב: של מתכת · דאילו של עץ פשוטי כלי עץ לא מקבל טומאה: מאי טעם · הרי לורך בהמה: רודה · מכה ומייסרה: והאיכא חלילה · שטבעת הקבוע בשיר קבוע בו בחוזק ואין המים נכנסין שם: בשריתכן · הכה בפטיש עד שנתפשט ונתרחק הנקב סביב סביב: כרב יוסף סבירא ליה · דאמר כשהן של בהמה נמי מקבלי טומאה הואיל ואדם מושך בהן הלכך כי ריתכן לאחר טומאה אכתי במילתייהו קיימי ולא פרחה טומאתן דאכתי חזו לבהמה: דאי כרבי יצחק · דאמר לא מקבל טומאה אלא בעודן לאדם טומאה זו שקבלו בעודן לאדם כיון דריתכן ושוב אין נאים לאדם בטלי להו מתורת תכשיט וטהרו מטומאתן: יורדין לידי טומאתן במחשבה · מאחר שחישב עליו שיניחנו כמות שהוא עכשיו ולא יוסיף תיקון אחר הוא גמר מלאכתן ומקבל טומאה: ואין עולין מטומאתן · מאחר שחישב על העור לעשות שטיח ירד לידי טומאה ואם חזר וחישב עליו לרצועו' וסנדלים לא בטל מתורת כלי *ולא טהר בכך עד שיתן בו אזמל דהוי שינוי מעשה הא בשינוי מעשה מיהא עולה מטומאתו: לתקן · וזו היא תקונו לצורך בהמה: לאו מעשה הוא · לבטל מתורת כלי: במחוללין · מתחלה נעשו חלולין רחבים שיש חלל בדביקתן שנתן טבעת בתוך טבעת כמות שהוא רחב: שחולקין · יש חילוק בהלכותיהן ואיני יודע מהו חילוקן: אלא לענין שבת · לענין הוצאת שבת יש חילוק בין יש עליה חותם לשאין עליה חותם כדאמר לקמן בפ' במה אשה (דף נט·):דא ודא אחת היא · כל טבעות דין אחד להן: שהתקינה לחגור בה מתניו · שקבעה בראש רצועה ועשאה כמין בוקלא שעושין לסרגין של סוסים: ולקשור בה בין כתפיו · בתי זרועותיו ברא"ייר"א: טהורה · דהדר הויא לה כטבעת כלים ולא דמיא לאדם מושך בהם שאינו משתמש בה כלום אלא מונחת ועומדת לרצועה ומיהו עם הרצועה מקבלת טומאה אבל אם היא נוטלה ומחזירה אינה מקבלת טומאה לעצמה: כי קאמר ליה איהו נמי · דא ודא אחת היא: דאצבע קאמר ליה · ולענין שבת יש חילוק: אלמוג · עצי אלמוגים והוא נאה: טמאה · דבתר טבעת אזלינן ותשמיש כלי מתכות טמאים: היא של אלמוג טהורה · דפשוטי כלי עץ הוא: אלא לענין שבת · לענין הוצאת שבת יש חילוק בין נקובה לשאינו נקובה דנקובה קתני חייב חטאת ובשאינה נקובה כגון אישפיגל"א שהיא תכשיט קתני אינו חייב חטאת בפרק במה אשה (דף נז:): חורה · חור שלה: עוקצה · פונטא: חלודה · רואיילר"ה: והוא שרישומה של מחט ניכר דהוי כלי וטמאה · ל"א שרישומה של חלודה ניכר בבגד היינו עיכוב תפירה וטהורה: בשיפא · נישופת בשופינא שקורין לימ"א שאין בה חלודה: מותר לטלטלה בשבת · בתמר דהא חזיא ליטול את הקוץ ותורת כלי עליה: ולא אמרו נקובה · חלוקה להלכותיה אלא לענין טומאה בלבד דנקובה מקבלת טומאה ושאינה נקובה לא: הא תרגמא אביי · בפרק כל הכלים: בגלמי · שהוא גולם שנקללה מן החוטן ועומדת ליקב התם הוא דכל זמן שלא נקבה אינה מקבלת טומאה דהא לא נגמרה מלאכתה ולענין טומאה כלי מעשה כתיב (במדבר לא) שנגמר כל מעשהו ומיהו לענין שבת שריא דזימנין דממליך עלה ומנח לה הכי ומשוי לה מנא לנטילת קוץ אבל מחט שנגמרה מלאכתה כגון אישפיגל"א שאינה עומדת ליקב דא ודא אחת היא לטומאה: **מתני'** מרדעת · בשטי"ל ומניחין אותו כל היום על החמור לחממו דאמרי אינשי חמרא אפילו בתקופת תמוז קריר ליה: שהיא קשורה בו · בגמ' מפרש: זכרים · אילים: לבובים שחוזות כבולות וכבונות · מפרש בגמרא: צרורות · דדיקן צרורות פעמים ליבש שמהדקן כדי שלא יחלבו עוד ויתעברו או יהו שמנות לאכול ופעמים לחלב לשמור חלבן שלא יטפטף לארץ וקושרין להם כיס בדדיהן: ר' יוסי אוסר בכולן · דמשוי הוא: חוץ מן הרחלים הכבונות · שהוא שמירת למרן שלא יטנף והוי להו תכשיט: יוצאות צרורות ליבש · ר' יהודה סבירא ליה כתנא קמא דלאו משוי הוא ומיהו ליבש דמיהדק שפיר וליכא למיחש דילמא נפיל ואתי לאיתויי אבל ליחלב דלא מיהדק שפיר חיישינן:

גמרא

אלמוג וכו' לא שמיה בית קבול. עי' לעיל ד' יז ע"א תוס' ד"ה ועל שאר. סוכה דף יב ע"ב תד"ה מהו דתימא:

רש"ל כ' דהאי א"נ שייך אחר דיבור רודה ואינו דרש"י כא להשמיענו ענינו של מקל אבל ודאי דמה שפירודה מכה ומיסרה אינו אלא לפי' אחד של רש"י ולא"נ פי' של רודה שמכה בו את הבהמה

תוספתא דכלים (ב"מ) פ"ד

כלים פי"ב מ"א

תוספתא שם

לקמן נט: כלים פי"ג מ"ו

לטהר בכרכל"א

לקמן קכג. כלים שם מ"ה

כלים שם

לקמן קכג. [תוספתא שם]

[לקמן קכג. קטו: קכג. עירובין פח: פסחים יב: סוכה יט. כתובות קי. ב"מ כב. כריתות נט. קטו. ועי' סוכה כ' וכתוס' שם ד"ה סיכן]

גליון הש"ס

גמ' ושאר כל הטבעות. עי' כלים פי"א מ"ג בר"ש ד"ה למעלה מן הנחשב: שם דאי לענין טומאה דא ודא אחת היא. עי' לקמן ס ע"א תוס' ד"ה למאי חזיא: שם בשלימה. עי' לקמן ס ע"א תוס' ד"ה הואיל ואדם אוגדת: תוס' ד"ה היא של

רבינו חננאל

הטבעות טהורות. ואוקמה ר' יצחק נפחא בבאין מנוי אדם. כלומר טבעת אדם היתה ונעשה עתה שיר לבהמה. ואוקמה רב יוסף הואיל ואדם מושך בהן. פי' פעמים שמכניס אדם אצבעו באותו השיר ומושך בו הבהמה שנמצאת טבעת העשויי לאצבעו של אדם. כמו מקל בהמה של מתכת טמאה מפני שמחזיקה אדם ורודה בה כו'. וטובלן במקומה והא עביד חציצה. כלומר כיון שהשירים הללו נושכין זה לזה הרי מקום הנשיכה סתום ואין המים באין בהם. ופריק ר' אמי בשריתכן. כלומר ריתכן באור והטבילן במים בעודן השירין כמו גחלים לוחשות שהמים באין אליהם מכל צד. ואמרינן האי פירוקא דר' אמי דלא כר' יצחק נפחא היא. דאי אליבא דר' יצחק נפחא טבעת של בהמה יורד לקבל טומאה. אפי' אם יחשב עליה להיות טבעת של אדם. וטבעת של אדם אינה עולה מידי טומאה להבטל מעליה תורת כלי אלא בשינוי מעשה כדתנן כל הכלים יורדין לידי טומאתן כו' ואי בשריתכן הנה עשה בהן מעשה ונסתלקה תורת כלי מעליהן. ואין צריכין לא הזאה ולא טבילה. (כי בעינן) [ושנינן] מעשה לסלק תורת כלי מעליהו מעש' לקלקל כגון שבירה וכיוצא בה. אבל ריתוך שהוא תיקון וחיזוק לכלי מתכת כי האי גוונא אינו מעשה לטהר ולא מבטל הטומאה מעל הטבעת. במתניתא תנא במחוללין. כלומר חלולין הן מלשון נבובים אלו השירין. והמים באין בהם מכל צד. ואין שם חציצה: **תנא** (תוספתא פ"ה) ומכנים חבילין לתוך ידו. ובלבד שלא יכרוך לתוך ידו. ובלבד שלא יכרוך ע"ג ידו ולא ישלשל חבלים מידו יותר מטפח: **שאל** תלמיד את ר' אלעזר שמעתי חלוקה בין טבעת לטבעת. א"ל לענין שבת בין טבעת שיש עליה חותם. לטבעת שאין עליה חותם. אבל לענין טומאה כל טבעות דינם אחד. ואסיקנא טבעת של אדם של אצבע של מתכת הכל דינם אחד לענין טומאה. וכן נמי מחט שלימה שיפא [נקובה ושאינה] נקובה הכל דינם אחד לענין טומאה. ואם היא ניטל חרירה או עוקצה או העלת חלודה ומעכבת התפירה (או נקובה) טהורה היא. ואקשינן ולענין (שבת אנה) [טומאה אינה] היא חלוקה בין מחט למחט. והתניא מחט בין נקובה בין שאינה נקובה מותר לטלטלה בשבת. [ולא אמרו כו'] ושנינן הא תרגמה אביי זו הברייתא אליבא דרבא דאמר מחט שניטל עוקצה או חרירה מדלענין טומאה לאו כלי הוא וטהורה היא. לענין שבת נמי לאו כלי ואסור לטלטלה. מתניתא דקתני בין נקובה בין שאינה נקובה מותר לטלטלה בגלומי כלי מתכת היא. כלומר עדיין גולם הוא חוט של ברזל ועדיין הוא צריך לנקבו ולחדר לו עוקם לעשותה מחט. ועכשיו אין לה לא נקב ולא עוקם. ואמרינן זמנין דמימליך עליה דהאי גולם ומשוי ליה מנא כמות שהיא. אבל מחט שניטל חרירה שלה או עוקצה לבין גרוטאות זריק לה: [מתני'] חמור יוצא במרדעת בזמן שהיא קשורה לו כו'. אוקמה שמואל בשקשורה לו מע"ש. וקיי"ל כוותיה. ומתניתא מסייעא ליה. נתינת מרדעת ע"ג חמור דברי הכל

רב נסים גאון

והא איכא חציצה. בראש מס' (עירובין דף ד) אמרו חציצין דאורייתא נינהו דכתיב (ויקרא טו) ורחץ במים את כל בשרו שלא יהא דבר חוצץ בין מים לבשרו ועיקר דילה במס' (סוכה דף ו) בפרק א' במס' מקוואות בפ' ט': **הא** תירגמא אביי בגלומי. ותמצא עיקר דיבור זה בפ' כל הכלים (ד' קכג) הציפלין בשבת ואני אבאר לך פירושו כי ראיתי פירוש להרבה מן החכמים מחט נקובה שנגמרה מלאכתה אם ניטל עוקצה טהורה עוקצה התתנבא שלה שהוא פי המחט או חרידה הוא מקום הנקב כבר אין לה תקנה ויצאה מתורת כלי ונתיאשו הבעלים ממנה ולפיכך שנינו בה טהורה כי מעת שניטל עוקצה או

all other rings [52b] are clean![2]—Said R. Isaac: It [our Mishnah] refers to such as pass from [being] men's ornaments to [become] animals' ornaments;[3] while R. Joseph said: [They[4] become unclean] because a man leads the animal by them. [For] was it not taught: An animal's staff[5] of metal[6] is susceptible to uncleanness? What is the reason? Since a man beats [the animal] with it. So here too; [they are unclean,] because a man leads [the animals] by them.

AND THEY MAY BE IMMERSED IN THEIR PLACE. But there is an intervention?[7]—Said R. Ammi: It means that he beat them out.[8] Shall we say that R. Ammi holds as R. Joseph? For if as R. Isaac, who maintained that it refers to such as pass from [being] men's ornaments to [become] animals' ornaments, since he beat them out, he has performed an act, and their uncleanness vanishes. For we learnt: All utensils enter upon their uncleanness by intention, but are relieved from their uncleanness only by a change-effecting act![9]—He holds as R. Judah, who maintained, An act to adapt
a [an object] is not [considered] an act.[1] For it was taught: R. Judah said: A change-effecting act was not mentioned[2] where it adapts [the object], save where it spoils it. In a Baraitha it was taught: It [our Mishnah] refers to [chains] with movable links.[3]

A certain disciple from Upper Galilee asked R. Eleazar: I have heard that a distinction is drawn between one ring and another?[4] Perhaps you heard it only in reference to the Sabbath;[5] for if in connection with uncleanness, they are all alike.[6] Now, in connection with uncleanness, are they all alike? Surely we learnt: A man's ring is unclean, but the rings of animals and utensils and all other rings are clean.[7]—He[8] too was referring to men's [rings]. And are all men's [rings] alike? Surely it was taught: A ring made to gird one's loins therewith or to fasten [the clothes about] the shoulders is clean, and only a finger [ring] was declared to be unclean!—He too was referring to finger rings. And are all finger rings alike? Surely we learnt: If the ring is of metal and its signet is of coral,[9] it is unclean; if it is of coral while the signet is of metal, it is clean.[10]—He too referred to [rings] wholly of metal.

He asked him further: I have heard that we distinguish between one needle and another? Perhaps you heard it only in respect to the Sabbath,[11] for if in the matter of uncleanness, they are all alike. Now, in the matter of uncleanness, are they all alike? Surely we learnt: If the eyehole or the point of a needle is removed, it is clean!—He referred to a whole [needle]. And are all whole [needles] alike? Surely we learnt: If a needle gathers rust and it hinders the sewing, it is clean; if not, it is unclean. And the
b School of R. Jannai said: Providing that its mark is perceptible.[1]—He referred to a bright [needle]. But are all bright [needles] alike? Surely it was taught; A needle, whether containing an eyehole or not, may be handled on the Sabbath;[2] while a needle with an eyehole was specified only in respect to uncleanness.[3]—Surely Abaye interpreted it according to Raba as referring to unfinished utensils![4]

MISHNAH. AN ASS MAY GO OUT WITH ITS CUSHION IF IT IS TIED TO IT.[5] RAMS MAY GO OUT COUPLED [LEBUBIN]. EWES MAY GO OUT [WITH THEIR POSTERIORS] EXPOSED [SHEḤUZOTH], TIED [KEBULOTH], AND COVERED [KEBUNOTH]; GOATS MAY GO OUT [WITH THEIR UDDERS] TIED UP. R. JOSE FORBIDS IN ALL THESE CASES, SAVE EWES THAT ARE COVERED. R. JUDAH SAID: GOATS MAY GO OUT [WITH THEIR UDDERS] TIED IN ORDER TO DRY UP,[6] BUT NOT TO SAVE THEIR MILK.[7]

(2) Because they do not rank either as utensils or ornaments, v. Kel. XIII. (3) And they had become unclean as human ornaments. But when they are animals' ornaments they cannot become unclean, though they retain the defilement contracted before. (4) The appurtenance mentioned in our Mishnah. (5) With which it is beaten. (6) Flat wooden implements are not susceptible to defilement. (7) Nothing must come between the object that is immersed and the water; but here the neck of the animal intervenes. (8) *Sc.* the rings, halters, etc., were beaten thin, so that they fit loosely about the animal and leave room for the water to touch it on all sides. (9) Utensils become unclean only from when they are quite finished for use; if they still require smoothing, scraping, etc., they are not liable to uncleanness, unless their owner declares his intention to use them as they are. On the other hand, having done so, it is not enough that he subsequently declares that he will not use them, in order to relieve them from their susceptibility to defilement, unless he actually begins smoothing them. Or, if the utensils are unclean, it is insufficient for their owner to state that he will not use them any more, so that they should lose the status of utensils and become clean, but must render them unfit for use by an act, e.g., break or make a hole in them.

a (1) To annul the status of a utensil. Hence he can agree with R. Isaac in the explanation of the Mishnah. (2) In this connection (3) Loosely joined and fitting roomily round the animal's neck, so that the water can enter. (4) In respect to what is that drawn? (5) Where a distinction is made between a signet ring and an ordinary one; v. *infra* 59a. (6) Lit., 'this and this are one'. (7) V. *supra* 52b. (8) R. Eleazar. (9) Probably a species of cedar-tree. (10) Only a metal ring becomes unclean, the matter being determined by the ring itself, not the signet. This shows that a distinction is drawn also in connection with uncleanness between finger ring and finger ring. (11) For carrying a needle with an eye in it from public or private ground or *vice versa* one is liable to a sin-offering, but not if it has no eye.

b (1) I.e., providing it is recognizable as a needle—only then is it unclean. Others: providing that the mark of the rust is perceptible when one sews with it—that is regarded as hindering the sewing and makes it clean. (2) Like any other utensil. (3) This shows that there is a distinction in connection with defilement between needle and needle also. (4) I.e., if it is unfinished and a hole is still to be punched therein, it is not liable to defilement. But if it is thus finished off without an eye, e.g., as a kind of bodkin, it is a utensil and liable to uncleanness, no distinction being drawn in connection with defilement between needle and needle. In connection with Sabbath, however, even the former may be handled, for one may decide to use it in its unfinished state, e.g., as a toothpick or for removing splinters from the flesh, and so it ranks as a utensil. (5) The cushion is to protect it from the cold. (6) To cease giving milk. (7) A pouch is sometimes loosely tied round the udder to prevent the milk from dripping; hence it may fall off and therefore R. Judah forbids it (v. 53a). But in the second case it is tied very tightly.

GEMARA. [53*a*] Samuel said: Providing it was tied thereto since the eve of the Sabbath. R. Naḥman observed, Our Mishnah too proves it, as it states: An ass may not go out with its b cushion if it is not tied thereto.[1] How is this meant? Shall we say that it is not tied thereto at all,—then it is obvious, lest it fall off and he come to carry it? Hence it must mean that it was not tied to it since the eve of the Sabbath, whence it follows that the first clause[2] means that it was tied thereto since the eve of the Sabbath. This proves it.

It was taught likewise: An ass may go out with its cushion when it was tied thereto on the eve of the Sabbath, but not with its saddle, even if tied thereto on the eve of the Sabbath. R. Simeon b. Gamaliel said: With its saddle too, if it was tied to it since the eve of the Sabbath,[3] providing, however, that he does not tie its band thereto,[4] and providing that he does not pass the strap under its tail.[5]

R. Assi b. Nathan asked R. Ḥiyya b. R. Ashi: May the cushion be placed on an ass on the Sabbath?[6] It is permitted, replied he. Said he to him, Yet wherein does this differ from a saddle? He remained silent. Thereupon he refuted him:[7] One must not move by hand the saddle upon an ass, but must lead it [the ass] up and down in the courtyard until it [the saddle] falls off of its own accord. Seeing that you say that it must not [even] be moved, can there be a question about placing it [on the ass]?[8]—Said R. Zera to him, Leave him alone: he agrees with his teacher. For R. Ḥiyya b. Ashi said in Rab's name: A fodder-bag may be hung around [the neck of] an animal on the Sabbath, and how much more so [may] a cushion [be placed on its back]: for if it is permitted there for [the animal's] pleasure, how much more so here, that it is [to save the animal] suffering![1] Samuel said: A cushion is permitted, a fodder-bag is forbidden.[2] R. Ḥiyya b. Joseph went and related Rab's ruling before Samuel. To which he said: If Abba[3] said thus, then he knows nothing whatsoever on matters pertaining to the Sabbath.

When R. Zera went up [to Palestine], he found R. Benjamin b. Jephet sitting and saying in R. Joḥanan's name: A cushion may be placed on an ass on the Sabbath. Said he to him, 'Well spoken! and thus did Arioch teach it in Babylon too.' Now, who is Arioch? Samuel![4] But Rab too ruled thus?—Rather he had heard him conclude: Yet a fodder-bag may not be hung [around the animal's neck] on the Sabbath. Thereupon he exclaimed, 'Well spoken! And thus did Arioch teach it in Babylon.'[5]

At all events, it is generally agreed that a cushion is permitted: wherein does it differ from a saddle?—There it is different, as it may possibly fall off of its own accord.[6] R. Papa said: The former[7] is to warm it [the ass]; the latter[8] is in order to cool it.[9] Where it needs warming it suffers; but where it needs cooling it does not. And thus people say: An ass feels cold even in the summer solstice.[10]

An objection is raised: A horse must not be led out with a fox's tail,[11] nor with a crimson strap between its eyes.[12] A *zab* must not go out with his pouch,[13] nor goats with the pouch attached to c their udders,[1] nor a cow with a muzzle on its mouth,[2] nor may foals [be led out] into the streets with fodder-bags around their mouths; nor an animal with shoes on its feet, nor with an amulet, though it is proven;[3] and this is a greater stringency in the case of an animal than in that of a human being.[4] But he may go out with a bandage on a wound or with splints on a fracture; and [an animal may be led out] with the after-birth hanging down;[5] and the bell at the neck must be stopped up,[6] and it may then amble about with it in the courtyard.[7] At all events it is stated, 'nor may foals [be led out] into the street with fodder-bags around their mouths': thus only into the street is it forbidden, but in a courtyard it is well [permitted]. Now, does this not refer to large [foals], its purpose being [the animals' greater] pleasure?[8]—No: it refers to small ones, the purpose being [to obviate] suffering.[9]

(1) V. *infra* 54*b*. (2) *Sc*. the present Mishnah. (3) The saddle too affords some warmth. (4) The band with which the saddle is fastened around the ass's belly. Rashi: lest it appear that he intends placing a burden upon it. (5) Which is generally placed there to prevent the saddle and burden from slipping forward or backward. (6) Not to be led out with it, but to warm it. (7) Thinking that his silence meant that no answer was necessary, the difference being too obvious. (8) Surely not!

(1) Suffering from cold. (2) The animal of course must be fed, but the fodder can be placed on the ground, and it is a mere luxury to hang the nose-bag around its neck. (3) An affectionate and reverential name for Rab—'father'. Others maintain that his name was Abba Arika, while Rab was a title—the teacher *par excellence*—, the equivalent of Rabbi as the title of R. Judah ha-nasi. (4) V. Ḳid., 39*a*, n. b11. (5) Whereas Rab permitted it. (6) And the owner might carry it, which, of course, is forbidden; *supra*. (7) *Sc*. the cushion. (8) *Sc*. the removing of the saddle. (9) When it becomes overheated through its burden. But in any case an ass cools very rapidly. (10) Tammuz is the fourth month of the Jewish year, generally corresponding to mid June-July. (11) Rashi: it was suspended between its eyes to ward off the evil eye; cf. Sanh., 93*a*, n. b2. Animals too were regarded as subject thereto. (12) Suspended as an ornament. (13) V. *supra* 11*b*.

c (1) Either to catch the milk that may ooze out, or to protect the udders from thorns, etc. (2) It was muzzled until it came to its own fields, so that it should not browse in other peoples' land. (3) I.e., three animals had been healed thereby. Generally speaking, Judaism is opposed to superstitious practices (v. Sanh. 65*b*, 66*a*; M. Joseph, *Judaism as Creed and Life*, pp. 79-81; 384); nevertheless, the Rabbis were children of their time and recognized the efficacy of such practices and took steps to regulate them. (4) This is now assumed to refer to an amulet; a human being may wear a proven amulet; *infra* 61*a*. (5) Not having been removed yet. (6) With cotton, wool, etc., to prevent if from ringing, which is forbidden on the Sabbath. (7) But not in the street, v. *infra* 54*b*. (8) Though they can stretch their necks and eat from the ground. This contradicts Samuel. (9) It is difficult for very young foals to eat from the ground.

גמ' מתניתין נמי דיקא· לקמן בהאי פירקא: אף באוכף · דאיהו נמי מהני לחממה : ובלבד שלא יקשור לו מסריכן · פוטרא"ל דמיחזי כמי שרוצה להטעינו משוי : רצועה תחת זנבו · פושל"א שנותנים שם שלא תרד האוכף והמשוי על צוארה כשהיא יורדת לעמק והמסרך שלא תרד על זנבה כשהיא עולה על ההרים : מהו ליתן מרדעת · ולא לצאת לרה"ר אלא בחצר ומפני הצינה : ה"ג אמר ליה מותר א"ל וכי מה בין זה לאוכף אישתיק : איתיביה כו' · כסבור הא דאישתיק משום דלא אשגח ביה דסבר אוכף נמי שרי ואותיביה מברייתא דאסר ליטלה והשתא ליטול אמרת לא להניח מיבעי' דדמי כאילו צריך להטעינה משוי : כרביה · רב : טרסקל · כלי מלא שעורים תולין לה בצוארה ופיה נתון לתוכו ואוכלת ותענוג בעלמא הוא שלא תטרח לשוח צוארה לארץ : צער · של צינה : מרדעת מותר · דלצערא היא הלכך אורחה בהכי ולאו משוי הוא : לשמעתא דרב · דשרי בטרסקל : אבא · *חברי כמו אברך אבא למלכא (בראשית מא) : שמואל קרי אריוך על שם שהיה בקי בדינין ושופט כמלך השופט על הארץ לשון ריכא *מלך (ב"ב דף ד·) : והא רב נמי אמרה · דכיון דשרי בטרסקל כ"ש מרדעת : מאי שנא מאוכף · שאסור ליטול וכ"ש להניחו : דנפיל ממילא · כדקתני מוליכו ומביאו לחצר והוא נופל מאליו : כאן לחממה · מרדעת צריך לחממה ומותר משום צער דצינה אבל נטילת אוכף אינו אלא שילטנן שנתחממה ע"י משאוי שנשאה מבעוד יום ואי לא שקיל ליה לא איכפת לן שהרי הוא ילטנן מאליו דאמרי אינשי וכו' : בזנב שועל · שתולין לו בין עיניו שלא ישלוט בו עין : זהרורית · לנוי : בכיס שלו · שתולין לו באמתו לקבל זוב ולבדוק מנין ראיותיו שאינו תכשיט לו : בכיס שבדדיהן · לקבל חלב הנוטף אי נמי שלא ישרטו דדיהן על הקוצים שהיו דדיהן גסין : בחסום שבפיה · שחוסמין אותה שלא תרעה בשדות אחרים וכשמגיעין למקום מרעיתם נוטלין אותה הימנה:בסנדל שברגליה· שעושין לה סנדל של מתכת שלא יזיקוה האבנים : קמיע· כתב לרפואת חולי : מומחה · שריפא כבר ג' פעמים : וזה חומר בבהמה מבאדם· קס"ד השתא דאקמיע קאי דאמרינן לקמן בפרק במה אשה יוצאה (ד' סא·) שהאדם יוצא בקמיע מומחה וכל הני דקתני לא תצא הנך דלאו שמירת גופה הוא אלא משאוי וסנדל משום דדילמא מישתליף ואתי לאתויי : אגד שעל גבי המכה · ליכא למימר אתי לאתויי : קשישין שעל השבר · בהמה שנשבר בה עצם עושין לה דפין מכאן ומכאן וקושרים אותן שם והן מעמידין העצם שלא יזוד אנה ואנה עד שמתחבר : ובשליא המדולדלת בה · שיליתה מקלתה : ופוקקין לה זוג · אבל כשאינו פקוק אפי' בחצר לא תצא מפני שהעינבל שבתוכה מקשקש ומוליד קול לכך פוקק בצמר או במוכין שלא יקשקש העינבל שבתוכה : זוג · אישקלי"ט : עינבל · בטדי"ל: ומטיילת· באותו זוג בחצר אבל לא תצא בו לרה"ר כדמפרש לקמן בפרקין (דף נד:) דמיחזי כמאן דאזיל לחינגא: מאי לאו · בסייחים גדולים קאמר דצוארן ארוך ואין להם צער לשוח ולאכול מע"ג הקרקע ותולה להן טרסקל לתענוג וקשיא לשמואל : קטנים · ארכובותיהן גבוהין וצוארן קטן ויש להם צער לשוח ע"ג הקרקע ולאכול :

גמ' אמר שמואל *והוא שקשורה לו מע"ש אמר רב נחמן מתני' נמי דיקא דקתני *אין החמור יוצא במרדעת בזמן שאינה קשורה לו היכי דמי אילימא שאינה קשורה לו כלל פשיטא דילמא נפלה ליה ואתי לאתויי אלא לאו שאינה קשורה מע"ש מכלל דרישא שקשורה לו מע"ש ש"מ תניא נמי הכי *חמור יוצא במרדעת בזמן שקשורה לו מע"ש ולא באוכף אע"פ שקשורה לו מע"ש רבן שמעון בן גמליאל אומר אף באוכף בזמן שקשורה לו מע"ש ובלבד שלא יקשור לו מסריכן ובלבד שלא יפשול לו רצועה תחת זנבו בעא מיניה רב אסי בר נתן מר' חייא בר רב אשי מהו ליתן מרדעת על גבי חמור בשבת אמר ליה מותר א"ל וכי מה בין זה לאוכף אישתיק איתיביה *אוכף שעל גבי חמור לא יטלטלנה בידו אלא מוליכה ומביאה בחצר והוא נופל מאיליו השתא ליטול אמרת לא להניח מיבעיא אמר ליה ר' זירא שבקיה כרביה סבירא ליה דאמר רב חייא בר אשי אמר רב תולין *טרסקל לבהמה בשבת וקל וחומר למרדעת ומה התם דמשום תענוג שרי הכא דמשום צער לא כל שכן שמואל אמר מרדעת מותר טרסקל אסור אזל ר' חייא בר יוסף אמרה לשמעתא דרב קמיה דשמואל א"ל אי הכי אמר אבא לא ידע במילי דשבתא ולא כלום כי סליק ר' זירא אשכחיה לר' בנימין בר יפת דיתיב וקאמר ליה משמיה דר' יוחנן נותנין מרדעת על גבי חמור בשבת א"ל *יישר וכן תרגמה אריוך בבבל *אריוך מנו שמואל והא רב נמי אמרה אלא שמעיה דהוה מסיים ביה ואין תולין טרסקל בשבת א"ל יישר וכן תרגמה אריוך בבבל דכולי עלמא מיהת מרדעת מותר מאי שנא מאוכף שאני התם דאפשר דנפיל ממילא רב פפא אמר כאן לחממה כאן לצננה לחממה אית לה צערא לצננה לית לה צערא והיינו דאמרי אינשי חמרא אפי' בתקופת תמוז קרירא לה מיתיבי *לא יצא הסוס בזנב שועל ולא *בזהרורית שבין עיניו *לא יצא הזב בכיס שלו ולא עזים בכיס שבדדיהן ולא פרה בחסום שבפיה ולא סייחים בטרסקלין שבפיהם לרה"ר ולא בהמה בסנדל שברגליה ולא בקמיע אע"פ שהוא מומחה וזו חומר בבהמה מבאדם אבל יוצא הוא באגד שעל גבי המכה *ובקשישין שעל גבי השבר ובשליא המדולדלת בה *ופוקקין לה זוג בצוארה ומטיילת עמו בחצר קתני מיהת ולא סייחין בטרסקלים שבפיהם לרה"ר לרה"ר הוא דלא הא בחצר שפיר דמי מאי לאו בגדולים ומשום תענוג לא בקטנים ומשום צער דיקא נמי דקתני דומיא

והוא שקשורה לו מע"ש · רש"י פי' לקמן דבקשורה מע"ש הוי מלבוש החמור אבל באינה קשורה מע"ש הוי משאוי ועוד יש לפרש דבאינה קשורה מע"ש מיחזי כמתכוין להוליא המרדעת וה"ר פור"ת פירש דמיחזי כאילו מתכוין להוליך הבהמה למקום רחוק :

אילימא שאינה קשורה לו כלל פשיטא · ולא בעי למפרך דמרישא שמעינן לה דקתני בזמן שהיא קשורה הא אינה קשורה לא דדרך משניות כן במסכת ע"ז (דף לה:) אלו דברים אסורין באכילה כבשים שדרכן לתת לתוכן יין כו' ובכיפא (שם דף לט:) קתני ואלו מותרים באכילה כו' וכבשים שאין דרכן לתת כו' ובפרק אלו טרפות (חולין דף נד·) קתני אלו כשרות אע"ג דאיכא מינייהו דשמעי' מרישא *וא"ת ונפשוט מרישא דבקשורה מערב שבת איירי מדאיצטריך למיתני בזמן שהיא קשורה דבלאו הכי הוה ידעי' דאיירי בקשורה דאי באינה קשורה פשיטא דאסור דילמא נפלה ואתי לאתויי כדקאמר הכא אילימא כו' אלא ודאי בזמן שקשורה מע"ש קאמר וי"ל דמרישא לא תפשוט דאדרבה ה"א דלהכי תנא בזמן שהיא קשורה לאשמעי' דאפי' קשורה בשבת דאי לא תנא ליה ה"א דוקא בקשורה לו מע"ש אבל בקשורה בשבת לא קמ"ל להכי דייק מסיפא :

מהו ליתן המרדעת ע"ג חמור בשבת · ואין לאסור משום דאין כלי ניטל אלא לדבר הניטל דבהמה חשיבא כדבר הניטל כיון דיכול למושכה ולהוליכה בכל מקום ורב אסי בר נתן דבעי אם אסור אין לפרש משום דמיחזי כרוצה להוליך הבהמה למקום רחוק דא"כ היכי דייק דמאן דשרי טרסקל כ"ש מרדעת · ואין לפרש נמי דבעי למיסר בחצר אטו רה"ר כדאמר גבי אשה בפ' במה אשה (לקמן דף סד:) דגבי בהמה לא גזרו כדתניא בסמוך גבי זוג ומטיילת עמו בחצר אלא נראה לר"י דטעמא משום טרחא דשבת ואע"ג דשריא קרצוף בפ"ב דביצה (דף כג·) התם יש לה צער ביותר א"נ לא שרי אלא בי"ט אבל בשבת אסור :

אוכף שע"ג החמור · וא"ת ויתיר האוכף ויִנער ויפול כדאמר *בפ' כל כתבי גבי היתה בהמתו טעונה טבל כו' וי"ל דהתם מיירי בשקין שתוכל הבהמה להתקלקל אבל מחמת האוכף לא תוכל הבהמה להתקלקל לכך לא התירו :

תולין טרסקל · וא"ת ותאסר משום דמשתמש בבע"ח כי היכי דאסור להניח נר על גבי דקל בשבת משום דמשתמש במחובר וי"ל דהתם מנענע הענפים אבל הכא אינו מנענע הבהמה בכך ורב אסי ברבי נתן דבעי למיסר *אפשר משום דילמא אתי להשתמש בבע"ח (ת"י) :

אריוך · שם מלך כדכתיב אריוך מלך אלסר (בראשית יד) ונקטי' טפי משאר מלכים לפי שמובלע בו לשון ארי :

דשמעיה דקא מסיים בה כו' · אע"ג דקיי"ל *כרב באיסורי היינו לגבי שמואל לחודיה אבל הכא ר' יוחנן דקי"ל כוותיה לגבי רב קאי כשמואל וברייתא דאוכף נמי קיימא כשמואל למאי דמשני כאן לחממה כאן לצננה ומתני' דאין סכין ומפרכסין לבהמה דמייתי לקמן נמי פליגא אדרב כדפירש בקונטרס :

מאי לאו בגדולים ומשום תענוג · וא"ת ומאי קושיא דילמא הכא מיירי בטרסקל שנתלה מע"ש אבל לתלות בשבת אפי' בחצר אסור ותירץ דדייק מדנקט רה"ר גבי טרסקל טפי משאר דכולהו נמי ברה"ר איירי אלא נקט רה"ר דבחצר מותר בכל ענין :

כגון

עין משפט נר מצוה

כא א ב מיי' פ"כ מהל' שבת הל' י סמג לאוין סה טוש"ע א"ח סי' שה סעיף ז :
כב ג מיי' שם הל' יג טוש"ע שם סעי' ח :
כג ד מיי' שם טוש"ע שם סעיף ט :
כד ה מיי' שם טוש"ע שם סעיף י :
כה ו מיי' שם טוש"ע שם סעיף יא :
כו ז שם סעיף י :

[חולין מ"ב. ועי"ש בתוס' ד"ה ניקב ותוס' נד. ד"ה ואלו כשרות כולהו צריכי וקצ"ע]

[גי' הערוך קרסטל וכן איתא בר"ף]

[חולין שו:]

רבינו חננאל

מותר לדחות צער בהמה לתלות(קרצטל)[טרסקל] בפיה משום תענוג הוא. ור' יוחנן ושמואל אסרי וכן הלכה והני מילי בבהמות גדולות ומשום תענוג. אבל קטנים דמשום צערא הוא ברה"ר אסורים לצאת הסייחין (בקרצטלין) [בטרסקלין] שבפיהם אבל בחצר שרי. מטרטו פי' חגורו: תניא יוצא אדם באגד שעל גבי (בהמה) [המכה].

רב נסים גאון

או חרירא אדם וזורקה לבין הגרוטאות ונתיאש ממנה מלעשותה כלי וטהורה היא ואם היתה מחט שאינה נקובה ויש לה עוקץ וכבר שיפה אותה ומירקה ואע"פ שעדיין לא נקבה מפני שהיא ראויה ליטול בה את הקוץ הרי היא כתורת כלי וטמאה כמו הנקובה לפי שהנקובה ראויה לתפירה והיא ראויה להוציא בה את הקוץ וזו וזו שוין בתורת טומאה כמו שאמרו אבל לענין טומאה דא ודא אחת היא ובכדומה לו אמרו בתוספתא (דכ"מ דכלים פי"ה) ואם מתחילה עשאו לכן אפי' פחות מיכן טמא ובנסטרא אמרו (מס' כלים פ"ד מ"ג) אי זו היא נסטרא כל שניטלו אזניה ואמרו בתוספתא (ב"ק דכלים פ"ג) ואם פתחלה עשאה בלא אזנים נידונית כחבית ואשר אמרו בין נקובה ובין שאינה נקובה מותר לטלטלה בשבת ולא אמרו נקובה אלא לענין טומאה בלבד הוא דתירגם אביי אליבא דרבה בגלומי והוא ברזל חתוך שראויה להעשות מחט והואיל ויש לומר שאם ירצה בעלה לעשותה כלי יכול הוא לעשות כמו שאמרו זימנין דמימליך עלה ומשוי לה כלי מותר לטלטלה בשבת ונחשב אותה לענין טלטול כמו הכלים והיא כמו מחט נקובה לענין שבת אבל לענין טומאה לא והרי היא בחזקת טהורה עד שיגמור מלאכתה ותהיה כלי כמו שאמרו בתוספתא בסוף בבא קמא דכלים גולמי כלי מתכות הרי הן ככל הכלים אלא שהן טהורין :

אמר

לקמן סד:

[תוספ' פ"ה]

פי' ברש"י חולין מה:

[וכתולין עו: פרש"י על שם אריוך מלך אלסר כמ"ש תוס' כאן ובמנחות לה: פרש"י כמו גור אריה יהודה ולהכי קרי לשמואל אריוך דקי"ל הלכתא כשמואל בדינא וקדקדין לט. ולתפרש"י בלום]

[תוספתא פ"ה]

[פי' לבון של זהורית שתולין לסוס משום עין]

[גי' הערוך בערוך קס ובקשקשין]

לקמן סד:

עין משפט
נר מצוה

כז א מיי' פ"כ מהל' שבת הלכה יג טוש"ע א"ח סי' שה סעי' יח בהג"ה:

כח ב ג מיי' פכ"א מהל' שבת הל' ל' סמג לאוין סה טוש"ע א"ח סי' שכח סעיף כב וסי' של"ב סעיף ב:

כט ד מיי' וסמג שם טוש"ע א"ח סי' של"ב סעיף ג וסעיף ד:

ל ה ו ז מיי' פ"כ מהל' שבת הל' יב סמג שם טוש"ע א"ח סי' שה סעיף ו:

כגון שהיה תחום שלה מובלע כו' · ומ"מ לא התירו אלא דרך קריאה אבל ליגך מעבר לבהמה ולרודפה לעיר לא:

תנאי היא · רב יהודה ידע שפיר דתנאי היא אלא דניחא ליה לאוקמי תרי סתמי דברייתא אליבא דחד תנא:

כאן ליבש כאן ליחלב · פי' בקונט' ליחלב שיקבלו בכיס את החלב וקשה דהא ודאי משוי הוא ולכ"ע חייב דהויא מלאכה הצריכה לגופה ופי' ה"ר פור"ת ליחלב לשמור החלב בדדיהן שלא יזוב לארץ ושרי ת"ק דהוי כמו רחלים כבונות דחשבי' ליה מלבוש אף על פי שאינו עשוי לצורך עצמן אלא לשמור הצמר ור"י פירש דבין ליבש ובין ליחלב תרווייהו עבדי להו כדי שלא יסרטו דדיהן כדאמרינן בסמוך וליבש בזמן שאינו חפץ בחלב שרי לפי שמהדקו וליכא למיחש דילמא נפיל ואתי לאתויי אבל ליחלב שאינו רוצה שיתייבשו אינו מיהדק איכא למימר דילמא נפיל ואתי לאתויי:

שקושרין להן כנגד זכרותן כו' · ולשון לבובין הוי שלא לקרב כמו ובכל תבואתי תשרש (איוב לא) וכמוהו הרבה:

ממאי מדקתני סיפא · טפי הוי ליה לאתויי כבולות דהוי ממש כעין זה אלא משום דשחוזות הוי ברישא:

תורה אור

דומיא דקמיע ש"מ: אמר מר ולא בקמיע אע"פ שהוא מומחה והא אנן תנן *ולא בקמיע שאינו מומחה הא מומחה שפיר דמי ה"נ אשאינו מומחה והא אע"פ שהוא מומחה קתני מומחה לאדם ואינו מומחה לבהמה ומי איכא מומחה לאדם ולא הוי מומחה לבהמה אין אדם *דאית ליה מזלא מסייע ליה בהמה דלית לה מזלא לא מסייע לה אי הכי מאי זה חומר בבהמה מבאדם מי סברת אקמיע קאי אסנדל קאי ת"ש בסכין *ומפרכסין לאדם ואין סכין ומפרכסין לבהמה מאי לאו דאיכא מכה ומשום צער לא גדגמר מכה ומשום תענוג ת"ש בהמה שאחזה דם אין מעמידין אותה במים בשביל שתצטנן אדם שאחזו דם מעמידין אותו במים בשביל שיצטנן אמר עולא גזירה משום שחיקת סממנין אי הכי *אדם נמי נראה כמיקר א"ה בהמה נמי נראה כמיקר אין מיקר לבהמה °ולבהמה מי גזרינן והתניא *היתה עומדת חוץ לתחום קורא לה והיא באה ולא גזרינן דילמא אתי לאתויי אמר רבינא כגון שהיה תחום שלה מובלע בתוך תחום שלו ר"נ בר יצחק אמר שחיקת סממנין גופה תנאי היא דתני' בהמה שאכלה כרשינין לא יריצנה בחצר בשביל שתתרפה ורבי *דאושעיא מתיר דרש רבא הלכה כרבי *אושעיא: אמר מר לא יצא הזב בכיס שלו ולא עזים בכיס שבדדיהן והתניא יוצאות עזים בכיס שבדדיהן אמר רב יהודה לא קשיא הא דמיהדק הא דלא מיהדק רב יוסף אמר *תנאי שקלת מעלמא תנאי היא דתנן העזים יוצאות צרורות רבי יוסי אוסר בכלן חוץ מן הרחלות הכבונות ר' יהודה אומר עזים יוצאות צרורות ליבש אבל לא ליחלב ואיבעית אימא הא והא ר' יהודה ולא קשיא הכאן ליבש כאן ליחלב תניא אמר ר' יהודה מעשה בעזים בית אנטוכיא שהיו דדיהן גסין ועשו להן כיסין כדי שלא יסרטו דדיהן: ת"ר מעשה באחד שמתה אשתו והניחה בן לינק ולא היה לו שכר מניקה ליתן ונעשה לו נס ונפתחו לו דדין כשני דדי אשה והניק את בנו אמר רב יוסף בא וראה כמה גדול אדם זה שנעשה לו נס כזה א"ל אביי אדרבה כמה *גרוע אדם זה שנשתנו לו סדרי בראשית אמר רב יהודה בא וראה כמה קשים מזונותיו של אדם שנשתנו עליו סדרי בראשית אמר רב נחמן תדע דמתרחיש ניסא ולא אברו מזוני: ת"ר מעשה באדם אחד שנשא אשה גידמת ולא הכיר בה עד יום מותה אמר *רב בא וראה כמה צנועה אשה זו שלא הכיר בה בעלה אמר לו רבי חייא זו דרכה בכך אלא כמה צנוע אדם זה שלא הכיר באשתו: וזכרים יוצאין לבובין: מאי לבובין אמר רב הונא תותרי מאי משמע דהאי לבובין לישנא דקרובי הוא דכתיב °לבבתני אחותי כלה (שיר ד) עולא אמר עור שקושרין להם כנגד לבם כדי שלא יפלו עליהן זאבים זאבים אזכרים נפלי אנקיבות לא נפלי משום דמסגו בריש עדרא וזאבין בריש עדרא נפלי בסוף עדרא לא נפלי אלא משום דשמני ובנקבות ליכא שמני ותו מי ידעי בין הני להני אלא משום דזקפי חוטמייהו ומסגו כי דוו רב נחמן בר יצחק אמר עור שקושרין להן תחת זכרותן כדי שלא יעלו על הנקבות ממאי מדקתני סיפא והרחלים יוצאות שחוזות מאי שחוזות שאוחזין האליה שלהן למעלה כדי שיעלו עליהן זכרים רישא כדי שלא יעלו על הנקבות וסיפא כדי שיעלו עליהן זכרים מאי משמע דהאי שחוזות לישנא דגלויי הוא דכתיב °והנה אשה לקראתו (משלי ז) שית

דומיא דקמיע · משום חולי: והא אנן תנן · גבי אדם לקמן בפ' במה אשה (דף ס:): הא מומחה שפיר דמי · מאי שנא בהמה מאדם: מזליה · מלאך שלו ומליץ עליו: אי הכי · דבהמה נמי נפקא בקמיע המומחה לבהמה: מאי זה חומר · אדם נמי לא נפיק אלא בקמיע מומחה לאדם: אסנדל קאי · וזה חומר דקתני ולא בהמה בסנדל שברגליה: סכין · שמן: ומפרכסין · גלדי מכה: ומשום צער · [ואפילו] הכי לבהמה לא וקשיא בין לרב בין לשמואל דשרי במרדעת: לא דגמר מכה · שנתרפאה המכה וסיכה ופירכוס משום תענוג ולרב ודאי קשיא וההיא מתניתא קמייתא דאוכף נמי קשיא ליה דנהי נמי דלדידיה ליכא צער תענוג מיהא הוא אלא רב תנא הוא ופליג: שאחזה דם · אנפודור"א: אין מעמידין כו' · אלמא אפילו צער נמי אסור: גזירה משום שחיקת סממנים · במידי דרפואה גזור רבנן דאי שרית שום רפואה אתי למישרי שחיקת סממנים והוא איסורא דאורייתא דהוי טוחן: אין מיקר לבהמה · אין דרך להקר בהמה הלכך כולי עלמא ידעי דלרפואה קמיכוין ואתי למישרי שחיקת סממנים: ומי גזרינן · במקום פסידא כי האי גוונא: חוץ לתחום · קס"ד חוץ לתחום שלו היתה עומדת בהמה: שהיה תחום שלה מובלעת בתוך תחום שלו · דחוץ לתחום דקתני חוץ לתחום שלה שהבהמה המסורה לרועה המיוחד הרי היא כרגלי הרועה וזה הקורא לה בעליה ויכול לילך כגון שהוא שבת קרוב לאותו מקום ואפילו הכי לא יביאנה ממש בידיו הואיל והיא יוצאה חוץ לתחומה אין לה אלא ד' אמות ומיהו קורא לה והיא באה דלא הוזהר הוא על תחום בהמתו ובלבד שלא יביאנה ממש בידיו: תנאי היא · דאיכא דלא גזר שאר רפואות אטו שחיקת סממנין: שאכלה כרשינין · הרבה ועל ידי אכילה מרובה אחזה חולי שקורין מיניזונ"א וצריכה להשתלשל ולהוציא רעי ומרילה כדי שתתרפה · גרסינן הכא לשון ריפוי שיהיו מעיה רפויים בשילשול ומוליאה רעי: לא יריצנה · גזירה בכל רפואה אטו שחיקת סממנין: דמיהדק · דליכא למיחש דילמא נפיל ואתי לאתויי: תנאי שקלת מעלמא · איבדת כולם שאין אתה מוצא תנאים שנחלקו בכך דתוקי הנך תרתי מתניית' חדא כמר וחדא כמר: תנאי היא · במתניתין ר"מ שרי ר' יוסי אסר: ליבש · מיהדק שפיר ולענין משוי נמי לא הוי משוי דצורך גופה היא דחלבה מכחישה: ליחלב · הוי משוי שטוענת את החלב בכיס: גסין · גדולין ונגררין על הקוצין ומסרטין דדיהן: שנשתנו עליו כו' · ולא זכה ליפתח לו שערי שכר: תדע · דקשין דמרחשי ניסא · מן השמים לכמה הצלות לנפשות אדם: ולא איברו מזוני · ואין נס זה רגיל שיברא מזונות לצדיקים בביתם שימצאו חטין גדלין באוצרותיהן: גידמת · ידה קטועה: זו דרכה בכך · לכסות כל אשה עצמה וכ"ש זו שהיתה צריכה לכך: תותרי · קופל"א שמחברין אותם בקשר שנים שנים שלא יברחו: לבבתני · קרבתני אצלך מחמת נוי מעשיך: דרך זאבים לאחוז בהמה בלבה: אנקבות לא נפלי · בתמיה: דמסגי · מהלכין: בסוף עדרא לא נפלי · בתמיה: כי דוו · מביטין כאן וכאן לפיכך מתקנאין בהם כסבורים שרוצים להלחם בהם: אליה · זנב שלהן קושרים כלפי גבן שלא יכסה ערותן:

שית

[לקמן ס.]

[כ"ק כ:]

[גירי' הערוך ומפרכין פי' מגרדין]

[בילה יח.]

[לקמן קנג. ותוספ' פי"ח]

[נ"ל יאשיה וכ"א בר"א והרא"ש וכן הטעתיקו תוס' מ"ק י: ד"ה ואין]

ובבראשית רבה על פסוק ויהי אומן את הדסה שנפתחו למרדכי שני דדים כדדי אשה ליכא למיפרך הכי דהכי קאמר כשתנו דלא הי' שכר מניקה ומרדכי כ"ל שכר אך לא הי' מוצא מניקה [ת"י]

[נ"ל יאשיה]

[עירובין לו: פסחים מה: ביצה יט. סנהדרין סח.]

[נ"ל רבי]

גליון הש"ס

גמ' ולבהמה מי גזרינן והתניא. ק"ל דלמא משום שחיקת סממני' דאורייתא גזרי' אבל בתחומין דרבנן לא:

רבינו חננאל

ובקששין: תניא אדם שאחזו דם מעמידין אותו במים בשביל לרפאותו. ט"ט משום דנראה כמיקר. אבל בהמה שאחזה דם אין מעמידין אותה במים כו'. אמר עולא בהמה גזירה משום שחיקת סמנים. ושחיקת סמנים תנאי היא. דתניא בהמה שאכלה כרשינין הרבה אין מריצין אותה בחצר בשביל לרפאותה. ור' יאשיה מיקל. והלכתא כוותיה דדרש רבא הלכתא כר' יאשיה. והא דר' יאשיה מסייעא לשמואל. מעשה שנעשה נס ונפתחו שני דדין כשני דדי אשה כו' וזו שהיתה גידמת כו'. פשוטות הן: פי' תותרי. סמרטוטין של רקמה ושל משי שעושין על הבהמה ליפותה. עולא אמר עור שמעמידין להן כנגד לבן שלא יפלו עליהן זאבים. משום דמסגו כי דוו. ומסתברא כוותיה דתנן (ע"ז דף כט:) באיסורי הנאה ועורות לבובין. ות"ר (שם דף לב.) איזהו עור לבוב. כל שהוא יקרוע כנגד הלב. (וקרודה) [וקדורה] כמו ארובה כו'. שחוזות מלשון שית זונה:

This may be proved too, because it is taught [53*b*] analogous to an amulet.[10] This proves it.

The Master said: 'Nor with an amulet, though it is proven'. But we learnt: 'Nor with an amulet that is not proven'; hence if it is proven, it is permitted?—Here also it refers [to an amulet] that is not proven. But it says, 'though it is proven'!—That means proven in respect of human beings but not in respect of animals. But can they be proven in respect of human beings yet not in respect of animals?—Yes: for it may help man, who is under planetary influence, but not animals, who are not under planetary influence.[11] If so, how is this 'a greater stringency in the case of an animal than in the case of a human
a being'?[1]—Do you think that that refers to amulets? It refers to the shoe.[2]

Come and hear: One may anoint [a sore] and scrape [a scab] off for a human being, but not for an animal. Surely that means that there is [still] a sore, the purpose being [to obviate] pain?—No. It means that the sore has healed,[3] the purpose being pleasure.[4]

Come and hear: If an animal has an attack of congestion, it may not be made to stand in water to be cooled; if a human being has an attack of congestion, he may be made to stand in water to be cooled?[5]—'Ulla answered: It is a preventive measure, on account of the crushing of [medical] ingredients.[6] If so, the same should also apply to man?—A man may appear to be cooling himself.[7] If so, an animal too may appear to be cooling itself?—There is no [mere] cooling for an animal.[8] Now, do we enact a preventive measure in the case of animal? But it was taught: 'If it [an animal] is standing without the *tehum*,[9] one calls it and it comes',[10] and we do not forbid this lest he [thereby] come to fetch it?—Said Rabina: It means, e.g., that *its tehum* fell[11] within *his tehum*.[12] R. Nahman
b b. Isaac said: The crushing of ingredients itself[1] is dependent on Tannaim. For it was taught: If an animal ate [an abundance of] vetch,[2] one must not cause it to run about in the courtyard to be cured; but R. Josiah[3] permits it.[4] Raba lectured: The *halachah* is as R. Josiah.

The Master said: 'A *zab* may not go out with his pouch, nor goats with the pouch attached to their udders.' But it was taught: Goats may go out with the pouch attached to their udders?—Said Rab Judah, There is no difficulty: Here it means that it is tightly fastened;[5] there it is not tightly fastened. R. Joseph answered: You quote Tannaim at random![6] This is a controversy of

(10) The purpose of which is not pleasure but the avoidance of sickness. (11) The planetary influence was regarded as in the nature of a protecting angel; v. Sanh., 94*a*, n. 10.

a (1) For a man too may go out only with an amulet proven for humans. (2) With which an animal may not be led out, though that is permitted for men. (3) Lit., 'is finished'. (4) To mollify the slight rawness which remains; that rawness, however, does not really cause suffering. (5) On the Sabbath. This proves that in the case of an animal, even to obviate its sufferings, it is forbidden. (6) This is forbidden on the Sabbath, save where life is in danger. If cooling in water is permitted, it will be thought that crushing ingredients is likewise permitted. (7) Not for medical purposes. (8) It is not customary to take an animal for cooling save for medical purposes. (9) V. Glos. (10) V. *infra* 151*a*. (11) Lit., 'was swallowed up'. (12) When an animal is entrusted to a cowherd, its *tehum* is that of the cowherd, i.e., it may go only where the cowherd may go. Here the owner's *tehum* stretched beyond that of the cowherd; hence he may call the animal that strayed beyond its own *tehum*, for even if he forgets himself and goes for it, he is still within his own boundaries. Nevertheless he may not actually go for it, because when one (a man or a beast) goes beyond his *tehum*, he becomes tied to that spot and may only move within a radius of four cubits from it; hence the owner must not actually lead the animal away, but may only call it. (One can extend his *tehum* by placing some food at any spot within the two thousand cubits, whereupon he may then walk a further two thousand cubits from that spot. Here the owner had extended his *tehum*, but not the cowherd).

b (1) I.e., whether any other form of healing is forbidden as a preventive measure, lest one come to crush ingredients too. (2) Which made it constipated. (3) V. marginal gloss cur. edd. R. Oshaia. (4) The first Tanna forbids it as a preventive against the crushing of ingredients, while R. Josiah declares this preventive measure unnecessary. (5) And there is no fear of its falling off, so that the owner may carry it. (6) *Aliter*: have you removed Tannaim from the world, v. Rashi.

◁ *For the continuation of the English translation of this page see overleaf.*

תורה אור

דומיא דקמיע ש"מ: אמר מר ולא בקמיע אע"פ שהוא מומחה והא אנן תנן *ולא בקמיע שאינו מומחה הא מומחה שפיר דמי ה"נ ^א^שאינו מומחה והא אע"פ שהוא מומחה קתני מומחה לאדם ואינו מומחה לבהמה ומי איכא מומחה לאדם ולא הוי מומחה לבהמה אין אדם *דאית ליה מזלא מסייע ליה בהמה דלית לה מזלא לא מסייע לה אי הכי מאי זה חומר בבהמה מבאדם מי סברת אקמיע קאי אסנדל קאי ת"ש ^ב^סכין *ומפרכסין לאדם ואין סכין ומפרכסין לבהמה מאי לאו דאיכא מכה ומשום צער לא ^ג^דגמר מכה ומשום תענוג ת"ש בהמה שאחזה דם אין מעמידין אותה במים בשביל שתצטנן אדם שאחזו דם מעמידין אותו במים בשביל שיצטנן אמר עולא גזירה משום שחיקת סממנין אי הכי *אדם נמי אדם נראה כמיקר א"ה בהמה נמי נראה כמיקר אין מיקר לבהמה °ולבהמה מי גזרינן והתניא *היתה עומדת חוץ לתחום קורא לה והיא באה ולא גזרינן דילמא אתי לאתויי אמר רבינא כגון שהיה תחום שלה מובלע בתוך תחום שלו ר"נ בר יצחק אמר שחיקת סממנין גופה תנאי היא דתני' בהמה שאכלה כרשינין לא יריצנה בחצר בשביל שתתרפה ורבי *^ד^אושעיא מתיר דרש רבא הלכה כרבי *אושעיא: אמר מר לא יצא הזב בכיס שלו ולא עזים בכיס שבדדיהן והתניא יוצאות עזים בכיס שבדדיהן אמר רב יהודה לא קשיא הא דמיהדק הא דלא מיהדק רב יוסף אמר *תנאי שקלת מעלמא תנאי היא דתנן העזים יוצאות צרורות רבי יוסי אוסר בכלן חוץ מן הרחילות הכבונות ר' יהודה אומר עזים יוצאות צרורות ליבש אבל לא ליחלב ואיבעית אימא הא והא ר' יהודה ולא קשיא ^ה^כאן ליבש כאן ליחלב תניא אמר ר' יהודה מעשה בעזים בית אנטוכיא שהיו דדיהן גסין ועשו להן כיסין כדי שלא יסרטו דדיהן: ת"ר מעשה באחד שמתה אשתו והניחה בן לינק ולא היה לו שכר מניקה ליתן ונעשה לו נס ונפתחו לו דדין כשני דדי אשה והניק את בנו אמר רב יוסף בא וראה כמה גדול אדם זה שנעשה לו נס כזה א"ל אביי אדרבה כמה *גרוע אדם זה שנשתנו לו סדרי בראשית אמר רב יהודה בא וראה כמה קשים מזונותיו של אדם שנשתנו עליו סדרי בראשית אמר רב נחמן תדע דמתרחיש ניסא ולא אברו מזוני: ת"ר מעשה באדם אחד שנשא אשה גידמת ולא הכיר בה עד יום מותה אמר *רב בא וראה כמה צנועה אשה זו שלא הכיר בה בעלה אמר לו רבי חייא זו דרכה בכך אלא כמה צנוע אדם זה שלא הכיר באשתו: ^ו^זכרים יוצאין לבובין: מאי לבובין אמר רב הונא תותרי מאי משמע דהאי לבובין לישנא דקרובי הוא דכתיב °לבבתני אחותי כלה [שיר ד] עולא אמר עור שקושרין להם כנגד לבם כדי שלא יפלו עליהן זאבים זאבים אזכרים נפלי אנקיבות לא נפלי משום דמסגו בריש עדרא וזאבין בריש עדרא נפלי בסוף עדרא לא נפלי אלא משום דשמני ובנקבות ליכא שמני ותו מי ידעי בין הני להני אלא משום דזקפי חוטמיהו ומסגו כי דוו רב נחמן בר יצחק אמר עור שקושרין להן תחת זכרותן כדי שלא יעלו על הנקבות ממאי מדקתני סיפא ^ז^והרחלים יוצאות שחוזות מאי שחוזות שאוחזין האליה שלהן למעלה כדי שיעלו עליהן זכרים רישא כדי שלא יעלו על הנקבות וסיפא כדי שיעלו עליהן זכרים מאי משמע דהאי שחוזות לישנא דגלויי הוא דכתיב °והנה אשה לקראתו [משלי ז] שית

[נ"י יאשיה] [עירובין לז: פסחים מה: ביצה יט. סנהדרין סא.] [נ"ל רבי]

רש"י

דומיא דקמיע · משום חולי : והא אנן תנן · גבי אדם לקמן בפ' במה אשה (דף ס·): הא מומחה שפיר דמי· מאי שנא בהמה מאדם: מזליה· מלאך שלו ומליץ עליו : אי הכי · דבהמה נמי נפקא בקמיע המומחה לבהמה : מאי זה חומר · אדם נמי לא נפיק אלא בקמיע מומחה לאדם: אסנדל קאי· וזה חומר דקתני ולא בהמה בסנדל שברגליה : סכין · שמן : ומפרכסין · גלדי מכה : ומשום צער · [ואפילו] הכי לבהמה לא וקשיא בין לרב בין לשמואל דשרי במרדעת : לא דגמר מכה· שנתרפאה המכה וסיכה ופירכוס משום תענוג ולרב ודאי קשיא וההיא מתניתא קמייתא דאוכף נמי קשיא ליה דנהי נמי דלצינה ליכא לצער תענוג מיהא הוא אלא רב תנא הוא ופליג : שאחזה דם · אנפודור"א : אין מעמידין כו' · אלמא אפילו צער נמי אסור : גזירה משום שחיקת סממנים · במידי דרפואה גזור רבנן דאי שרית שום רפואה אתי למישרי שחיקת סממנים והוא איסורא דאורייתא דהוי טוחן : אין מיקר לבהמה . אין דרך להקר בהמה הלכך כולי עלמא ידעי דלרפואה קמיכוין ואתי למישרי שחיקת סממנים : ומי גזרינן · במקום פסידא כי האי גוונא : חוץ לתחום · קס"ד חוץ לתחום שלו היתה עומדת בהמה : שהיה תחום שלה מובלעת בתוך התחום שלו · דחוץ לתחום דקתני חוץ לתחום שלה שהבהמה המסורה לרועה המיוחד הרי היא כרגלי הרועה וזה הקורא לה בעליה ויכול לילך כגון שהוא שבת קרוב לאותו מקום ואפילו הכי לא יביאנה ממש בידיו הואיל והיא יוצאה חוץ לתחומה אין לה אלא ד' אמות ומיהו קורא לה והיא בהה דלא הוזהר הוא על תחום בהמתו ובלבד שלא יביאנה ממש בידיו : תנאי היא · דאיכא דלא גזר שאר רפואות אטו שחיקת סממנין: שאכלה כרשינין· הרבה ועל ידי אכילה מרובה אחזה חולי שקורין מינייזונ"א וצריכה להשתלשל ולהוציא רעי ומרילה : כדי שתתרפה · גרסינן הכא לשון ריפוי שיהיו מעיה רפויים בשילשול ומוליאה רעי : לא יריצנה · גזירה בכל רפואה אטו שחיקת סממנין : דמיהדק · דליכא למיחש דילמא נפיל ואתי לאתויי : תנאי שקלת מעלמא · איבדת כולם שאין אתה מוצא תנאים שנחלקו בכך דתוקי הנך תרתי מתניית' חדא כמר וחדא כמר : תנאי היא · במתניתין ר"מ שרי ר' יוסי אסר : ליבש · מיהדק שפיר ולענין משוי נמי לא הוי משוי דלורך גופה היא דחלבה מכחישה: ליחלב · הוי משוי שטוענת את החלב בכיס : גסין · גדולין ונגררין על הקוצין ומסרטין דדיהן : שנשתנו עליו כו' · ולא זכה ליפתח לו שערי שכר : תדע · דקשין : דמרחשי ניסא · מן השמים לכמה הצלות לנפשות אדם : ולא איברו מזוני · ואין נס זה רגיל שיבראו מזונות לצדיקים בביתם שימצאו חיטין גדלין באוצרותיהן : גידמת · ידה קטועה : זו דרכה בכך · לכסות כל אשה עצמה וכ"ש זו שהיתה צריכה לכך : תותרי · קופל"א שמחברין אותם בקשר שנים שנים שלא יברחו : לבבתני · קרבתני אצלך מחמת נוי מעשיך : דרך זאבים לאחוז בהמה בלבה : אנקבות לא נפלי · בתמיה : דמסגי · מהלכין : בסוף עדרא לא נפלי . בתמיה : כי דוו · מביטין כאן וכאן לפיכך מתקנאין בהם כסבורים שרוצים להלחם בהם : אליה · זנב שלהן קושרים כלפי גבן שלא יכסה ערותן :

שית

תוספות

כגון שהיה תחום שלה מובלע כו' · ומ"מ לא התירו אלא דרך קריאה אבל לילך מעבר לבהמה ולרודפה לעיר לא :

תנאי היא · רב יהודה ידע שפיר דתנאי היא אלא דניחא ליה לאוקמי תרי סתמי דברייתא אליבא דחד תנא :

כאן ליבש כאן ליחלב · פי' בקונט' ליחלב שיקבלו בכיס את החלב וקשה דהא ודאי משוי הוא ולכ"ע חייב דהויא מלאכה הצריכה לגופה ופי' ה"ר פור"ת ליחלב לשמור החלב בדדיהן שלא יזוב לארץ ושרי ת"ק דהוי כמו רחלים כבונות דחשבי' ליה מלבוש אף על פי שאינו עשוי לצורך עצמן אלא לשמור הצמר ור"י פירש דבין ליבש ובין ליחלב תרווייהו עבדי להו כדי שלא יסרטו דדיהן כדאמרינן בסמוך וליבש בזמן שאינו חפץ בחלב שרי לפי שמהדקו וליכא למיחש דילמא נפיל ואתי לאתויי אבל ליחלב שאינו רוצה שיתייבשו אינו מיהדק איכא למימר דילמא נפיל ואתי לאתויי :

שקושרין להן כנגד זכרותן כו' · ולשון לבובין הוי שלא לקרב כמו ובכל תבואתי תשרש (איוב לא) וכמוהו הרבה :

ממאי מדקתני סיפא · טפי הוי ליה לאתויי כבולות דהוי ממש כעין זה אלא משום דשחוזות הוי ברישא :

עד

עין משפט נר מצוה

כז א מיי' פ"כ מהל' שבת הלכה יג טוש"ע א"ח סי' שה ספי' יח בהג"ה :

כח ב ג מיי' פכ"א מהל' שבת הל' ל' סמג לאוין סה טוש"ע א"ח סי' שפח סעיף כב וסי' שלב סעיף ב :

כט ד מיי' וסמג שם טוש"ע א"ח סי' שלב סעיף ג וסעיף ד :

ל ה ו ז מיי' פ"כ מהל' שבת הל' יב סמג שם טוש"ע א"ח סי' שה סעיף ו :

מסורת הש"ס

[לקמן ס.] [ב"ק כ:] [גירי' הערוך ומפרכסין פי' מגרדין] [ביצה יח:] [לקמן קנא. ותוספ' פי"ח] [נ"א יאשיה וכ"א בר"ה והרא"ש וכן סעתיקו תוס' מ"ק י: ד"ה ואין] [ובבראשית רבה על פסוק ויהי אומן את הדסה שנפתחו למרדכי שני דדים כדדי אשה ליכא למיפרך הכי דהכי קאמר נשתנו דלא היה שכר מניקה ומרדכי כ"ל שכר אך לא היה מוצא מניקה] [תי']

גליון הש"ס

גמ' ולבהמה מי גזרינן והתניא. ק"ל דלא משום שחיקת סממני' דאורייתא' גזרי' אבל בתחומין דרבנן לא :

רבינו חננאל

ובקששין: תניא אדם שאחזו דם מעמידין אותו במים בשביל לרפאותו . מ"ט משום דנראה כמיקר . אבל בהמה שאחזה דם אין מעמידין אותה במים כו' , אמר עולא בהמה גזירה משום שחיקת סמנים . ושחיקת סמנים תנאי היא . דתניא בהמה שאכלה כרשינין הרבה אין מריצין אותה בחצר בשביל לרפאותה . ור' יאשיה מיקל . והלכתא כוותיה דדרש רבא הלכתא כר' יאשיה. והא דר' יאשיה מסייעא לשמואל. מעשה שנעשה נס ונפתחו שני דדין כשני דדי אשה כו' וזו שהיתה גידמת כו' . פשוטות הן : פי' תותרי . סמרטוטין של רקמה ושל משי שעושין על הבהמה ליפותה . עולא אמר עור שמעמידין להן כנגד לבן שלא יפלו עליהן זאבים . משום דמסגו כי דוו . ומסתברא כוותיה דתנן (בע"ז דף כט:) באיסורי הנאה ועורות לבובין . ות"ר (שם דף לב.) איזהו עור לבוב . כל שהוא יקרוע כנגד הלב . (וקרודה) [וקדורה] כמו ארובה כו'. שחוזות מלשון שית זונה:

Continuation of translation from previous page as indicated by ◁

Tannaim. For we learnt: GOATS MAY BE LED OUT [WITH THEIR UDDERS] TIED UP. R. JOSE FORBIDS IN ALL THESE CASES, SAVE EWES THAT ARE COVERED. R. JUDAH SAID: GOATS MAY BE LED OUT [WITH THEIR UDDERS] TIED UP IN ORDER TO GO DRY, BUT NOT IN ORDER TO SAVE THEIR MILK.[7] Alternatively, both are according to R. Judah: in the one case it is in order that they may go dry; in the other it is for milking.[8] It was taught: R. Judah said: It once happened that goats in a household of Antioch[9] had large udders, and pouches were made for them that their udders should not be lacerated.

Our Rabbis taught: It once happened that a man's wife died and left a child to be suckled, and he could not afford to pay a wet-nurse, whereupon a miracle was performed for him and his teats opened like the two teats of a woman and he suckled his son. R. Joseph observed, Come and see how great was this man, that such a miracle was performed on his account! Said Abaye to him, On the contrary: how lowly was this man, that the order
c of the Creation[1] was changed on his account![2] Rab Judah observed, Come and see how difficult are men's wants [of being satisfied], that the order of the Creation had to be altered for him! R. Naḥman said: The proof is that miracles do [frequently] occur, whereas food is [rarely] created[3] miraculously.

Our Rabbis taught: It once happened that a man married a woman with a stumped hand, yet he did not perceive it in her until the day of her death. Rabbi observed: How modest this woman must have been, that her husband did not know her! Said R. Ḥiyya to him, For her it was natural;[4] but how modest was this man, that he did not scrutinize his wife!

RAMS MAY GO OUT COUPLED [LEBUBIN]. What is *lebubin?* R. Huna said: coupled. How is it indicated that LEBUBIN implies nearness? For it is written, *Thou hast drawn me near,*[5] *my sister, my bride.*[6] 'Ulla said: It refers to the hide which is tied over their hearts[7] that wolves should not attack them.[8] Do then wolves attack rams only but not ewes?—[Yes,] because they [the rams] travel at the head of the flock. And do wolves attack the head of the flock and not the rear?—Rather [they attack rams] because they are fat. But are there no fat ones among ewes? Moreover, can they distinguish between them?—Rather it is because their noses are elevated and they march along as though looking out [for the wolf].[9]

R. Naḥman b. Isaac said, It means the skin which is tied under their genitals, to restrain them from copulating with the females. Whence [is this interpretation derived]? Because the following clause states: AND EWES MAY GO OUT SHEḤUZOTH. What
d is SHEḤUZOTH? With their tails tied back[1] upwards, for the males to copulate with them: thus in the first clause it is that they should not copulate with the females, whilst in the second it is for the males to copulate with them. Where is it implied that SHEḤUZOTH denotes exposed? In the verse, *And behold, there*

(7) Thus this is disputed in our Mishnah, and so possibly in the Baraithas too. (8) Rashi: to preserve the milk in its pouch. Ri: both are to protect the udders from being scratched by thorns, but in the one case it is desired that the goats shall go dry; then it is permitted, since it is tied very tightly; but in the other it is desired that the goats shall remain milkers; then it is forbidden, because it is lightly tied. (9) The capital of Syria.

c (1) Lit., 'the beginning'; i.e., nature. (2) In Ber. 20*a* Abaye himself regards miracles wrought for people as testifying to their greatness and merit. Rashi observes that his lowliness lay in the fact that a means of earning money was not opened to him. (3) So Rashi. (4) It is natural for a woman to cover herself, particularly when it is in her own interest. (5) Heb. *libabtini* (E.V. *Thou hast ravished my heart*). (6) Cant. IV, 9. (7) Heb. *leb*, which 'Ulla takes to be the root of *lebubin*. (8) Thus he translates: RAMS MAY GO OUT with their hides over their hearts. Wolves usually seize beasts at the heart (Rashi). (9) Which rouses its ire, Var. lec.: *ke-dubin*, like bears, i.e., proudly and fiercely. V. *D.S.*

d (1) Heb. *she'oḥazin*, lit., 'we catch up'.

met him a woman [54*a*] *exposed*[2] *and wily of heart.*[3]

EWES MAY GO OUT TIED [KEBULOTH]. What is KEBULOTH?—With their tails tied downwards, to restrain the males from copulating with them. How is it implied that *kabul*[4] denotes non-productively?—Because it is written, *What cities are these which thou hast given me, my brother? And he called them the land of Cabul, unto this day.*[5] What is 'the land of Cabul'?—Said R. Huna: It contained inhabitants who were smothered [*mekubbolin*] with silver and gold. Said Raba to him, If so, is that why it is written, *and they pleased him not?*[6] because they were smothered with silver and gold they pleased him not!—Even so, he replied; being wealthy and soft-living, they would do no work. R. Naḥman b. Isaac said, It was a sandy region,[7] and why was it called Cabul? Because the leg sinks into it up to the ankle, and people designate it an ankle-bound land which produces no fruit.

[AND COVERED] KEBUNOTH. What is KEBUNOTH?—It means that they [the sheep] are covered for the sake of the fine wool.[8] As we learnt: [The hue of] a rising is like white wool.[9] What is white wool?—Said R. Bibi b. Abaye: Like pure wool [from a sheep] which is covered from birth[10] in order to produce fine wool.

AND GOATS MAY BE LED OUT [WITH THEIR UDDERS] TIED UP. It was stated: Rab said: The *halachah* is as R. Judah; while Samuel said: The *halachah* is as R. Jose. Others learn this controversy independently. Rab said: If it is in order to go dry, it is permitted, but if it is for milking it is forbidden; while Samuel said: Both are forbidden. Others learn it in reference to the following: Goats may go out [with their udders] tied up in order to go dry, but not for milking. On the authority of R. Judah b. Bathyra it was said: That is the *halachah;* but who can vouch[1] which is for going dry and which is for milking? And since we cannot distinguish [between them], both are forbidden. Said Samuel,—others say, Rab Judah said in Samuel's name: The *halachah* is as R. Judah b. Bathyra. When Rabin came,[2] he said in the name of R. Joḥanan: The *halachah* is as the first Tanna.[3]

MISHNAH. AND WHEREWITH MAY IT NOT GO OUT? A CAMEL MAY NOT GO OUT WITH A PAD [TIED TO ITS TAIL] OR AKUD OR RAGUL;[4] AND SIMILARLY OTHER ANIMALS. ONE MUST NOT TIE CAMELS TOGETHER AND PULL [ONE OF THEM], BUT HE MAY TAKE[5] THE CORDS IN HIS HAND AND PULL [THEM], PROVIDING HE DOES NOT TWINE THEM TOGETHER.

GEMARA. It was taught: A camel must not go out with a pad tied to its tail, but it may go out with a pad tied to its tail and its hump.[6] Rabbah son of R. Huna said: A camel may be led out with a pad tied to its after-birth.[7]

OR 'AKUD OR RAGUL. Rab Judah said: 'AKUD means the tying of hand and foot[8] together, like Isaac the son of Abraham; RAGUL means that the forefoot must not be bent back on to the shoulder and tied. An objection is raised: '*Akud* refers to the two forefeet or the two hindfeet [tied together]; *ragul* means that the forefoot must not be bent back on to the shoulder and tied?—He interprets as the following Tanna. For it was taught: '*Akud* means the tying together of the forefoot and the hindfoot, or of the two forefeet or the two hindfeet; *ragul* means that the forefoot must not be bent back on to the shoulder and tied. Yet it is still not the same: as for the first and the last clauses,
b it is well; but the middle one is difficult?[1]—Rather [he maintains] as the following Tanna. For it was taught: '*Akud* means the tying of hand and foot, like Isaac the son of Abraham; *ragul* means that the forefoot must not be bent back on to the shoulder and tied.

ONE MUST NOT TIE CAMELS TOGETHER. What is the reason?—Said R. Ashi: Because it looks as if he is going to the fair.

BUT HE MAY TAKE [etc.]. R. Ashi said: This was taught only in respect to *kil'ayim.*[2] *Kil'ayim* of what? Shall we say, *kil'ayim* of man?[3] Surely we learnt: A man is permitted to plough and pull with all of them.[4] But if it means *kil'ayim* of the cords,[5]—surely we learnt: If one fastens [two pieces together] with one fastening,[6] it is not a connection?[7]—After all, it means *kil'ayim* of the cords, but this is its teaching: providing that he does not twine *and knot* [them together].[8]

Samuel said: Providing that a handbreadth of a cord does not hang out of his hand.[9] But the School of R. Ishmael taught, Two handbreadths?—Said Abaye, Now that Samuel said one handbreadth, while the School of R. Ishmael taught two handbreadths,
c Samuels comes to inform us the *halachah* in actual practice.[1] [54*b*]

(2) Heb. *Shith zonah*, which is regarded as connected with SHEḤUZOTH. E.V.: *With the attire of a harlot*. (3) Prov. VII, 10. (4) Sing. masc. of *kebuloth*. (5) I Kings IX, 13. (6) Ibid. 12. (7) Jast.: the land of Humton, a district of northern Palestine. (8) That the wool should be of a fine, silky texture. (9) The reference is to Lev. XIII, 2. (10) Lit., 'its first day'.

(1) Lit., 'cast lots'. (2) V. *supra* 5*a*, n. b9. (3) In our Mishnah that both are permitted. (4) This is explained in the Gemara. (5) Lit., 'insert'. (6) In the first case it can slide off (v. *supra* 53*a* top), but not in the second. (7) The camel refrains from pulling at it, because it is painful; hence it will not fall off. (8) In the case of an animal, the forefoot and the hindfoot.

(1) For this Tanna includes the tying together of the two forefeet or the two hindfeet in the term '*akud*, whereas according to Rab Judah, who gives the analogy of Isaac, only the tying of the forefoot to the hindfoot is thus designated. (2) V. Glos. The prohibition of twining them together cannot refer to the Sabbath. (3) When he winds the cords round his hand, he may pull at something simultaneously with the camels; thus they act in unison, and this may be regarded as two different species working together, which is forbidden, v. Deut. XXII, 10. On this supposition the Mishnah must be translated: providing he does not wind them (round his hand). (4) *Sc.* various animals, and this does not constitute *kil'ayim.* (5) In case some are of wool, while others are of flax; when twined together they become *kil'ayim*, and as he holds them they warm his hands, which is the equivalent of 'wearing' (v. Deut. XII, 11). (6) I.e., if he joins two pieces of cloth, one of wool and the other of linen, with a single stitch or knot. (7) Hence when he twines the cords together they are not *kil'ayim.* (8) This is a double fastening, which renders the combination *kil'ayim.* (9) For then it looks like a separate cord which he is carrying.

c (1) I.e., to be on the safe side we rule one handbreadth, yet no prohibition is violated for less than two.

שית זונה ונצורת לב: הרחלים יוצאות כבולות: מאי כבולות "שמכבלין אליה שלהן למטה כדי שלא יעלו עליהן הזכרים מאי משמע דהאי כבול לישנא דלא עביד פירי הוא דכתיב °מה הערים [האלה] אשר נתת לי אחי ויקרא (להן) ארץ כבול עד היום הזה מאי ארץ כבול א"ר הונא שהיו בה בני אדם שמכובלין בכסף ובזהב אמר ליה רבא אי הכי היינו דכתיב (°*כי לא) ישרו בעיניו מפני שמכובלין בכסף ובזהב לא ישרו בעיניו אמר ליה אין כיון דעתירי ומפנקי לא עבדי עבידתא רב נחמן בר יצחק אמר ארץ חומטון היתה ואמאי קרי לה כבול דמשתרגא בה כרעא עד כבלא ואמרי אינשי ארעא מכבלא דלא עבד פירי: כבונות: מאי כבונות "שמכבנין אותו למילת *כדתנן שאת כצמר לבן *מאי צמר לבן אמר רב ביבי בר אביי כצמר נקי בן יומו שמכבנין אותו למילת: והעזים יוצאות צרורות: איתמר רב אמר "הלכה כר' יהודה ושמואל אמר הלכה כר' יוסי ואיכא דמתני להא שמעתא באפי נפשיה רב אמר ליבש מותר ולא לחלב ושמואל אמר אחד זה ואחד זה אסור ואיכא דמתני לה אהא עזים יוצאות צרורות ליבש אבל לא לחלב משום ר' יהודה בן בתירא אמרו כך הלכה אבל מי מפים איזו ליבש ואיזו לחלב ומתוך שאין מכירים אחד זה ואחד זה אסור אמר שמואל ואמרי לה אמר רב יהודה אמר שמואל הלכה כר' יהודה בן בתירא כי אתא רבין אמר ר"י הלכה כת"ק: **מתני'** ובמה אינה יוצאה לא יצא גמל במטולטלת לא עקוד ולא רגול וכן שאר כל הבהמות "לא יקשור גמלים זה בזה וימשוך אבל מכניס חבלים לתוך ידו וימשוך ובלבד שלא יכרוך: **גמ'** תנא "לא יצא הגמל במטולטלת הקשורה לו בזנבו אבל יוצא הוא במטולטלת הקשורה בזנבו ובחוטרתו אמר רבה בר רב הונא יוצא הגמל במטולטלת הקשורה לה בשילייתה: לא 'עקוד ולא רגול: א"ר יהודה *עקוד עקידת יד ורגל כיצחק בן אברהם רגול שלא יכוף ידו על גבי זרועו ויקשור מיתיבי עקוד שתי ידים ושתי רגלים רגול שלא יכוף ידו על גבי זרועו ויקשור הוא דאמר כי האי תנא דתניא עקוד עקידת יד ורגל או שתי ידים ושתי רגלים רגול שלא יכוף ידו ע"ג זרועו ויקשור ואכתי לא דמי בשלמא רישא וסיפא ניחא מציעתא קשיא אלא הוא דאמר כי האי תנא עקוד עקידת יד ורגל כיצחק בן אברהם רגול שלא יכוף ידו על גבי זרועו ויקשור: ולא יקשור גמלים: מאי טעמא אמר רב אשי משום דמיחזי *כמאן דאזיל לחינגא: אבל מכנים: אמר רב אשי לא שנו אלא לענין כלאים דמאי אילימא כלאים דאדם והתנן *אדם 'מותר עם כולם לחרוש ולמשוך אלא כלאים דחבלים *והתניא *התוכף "תכיפה אחת אינה חיבור לעולם כלאים דחבלים והכי קאמר ובלבד שלא יכרוך ויקשור אמר שמואל °ובלבד שלא יצא [חבל] מתחת ידו טפח והא תנא דבי שמואל טפחיים אמר אביי השתא דאמר שמואל טפח ותנא דבי שמואל *טפחיים שמואל *הלכה למעשה אתא לאשמעינן

והתניא

רש"י

שית זונה · נוטריקון דשחוות: שית · בית הבשת: שכבולין · לשון כבלי ברזל קשורה: ויקרא להם · בעשרים ושתים עיר שנתן שלמה לחירם משתעי קרא: מכובלין · מעוטפין ומקושרין: עבידתא · אנגריא של מלך: חומטון · מלחה ומתבקעת: דמשתרגא בה כרעא · שוקעת בה הרגל: עד כבלא · פרק התחתון שקורין קויל"ה: שמכבנין · קושרין בגד סביבו °כיום שנולד שצמרו נקי ומשמר צמרו שלא יטנף: למילת · לעשות מצמרו כלי מילת*: מכבנין · על שעושין כמין קרסי מתכת לחבר הבגד כמו תנתן כבינתי לבתי (גיטין דף כו·) נוסק"א בלע"ז: באנפי נפשה · ולא אפלוגתא דמתני': ואיכא דמתני · להא דשמואל אהא: כך הלכה · דליבש מותר ולחלב אסור: אבל מי מפים · מי מטיל גורל ומבחין איזו ליבש ואיזו לחלב והרואה אותם צרורות ליבש אומר דלחלב הוא ואתי למישרי תרווייהו: כת"ק · דמתני' דשרי בתרווייהו: **מתני'** מטולטלת · י"מ פושלא שתחת זנבו וי"מ מרדעת והאחרון נראה בעיני דאי רצועה שתחת הזנב קשורה ומחוברת לסרגא ואיך תפול וטעמא דמתני' משום שמא תפול ומייתי לה הוא: לא עקוד ולא רגול · מפרשינן בגמ' שעוקדים ידיהם עם רגליהם בכבלים שלא יברחו: ולא יקשור גמלים זו לזו וימשוך · האחד כדמפרש בגמרא: ובלבד שלא יכרוך · החבלים בכרך אחד ובגמרא מפרש טעמא: **גמ'** בזנבו ובחוטרתו · דכיון דקשורה בשניהם לא נפלה: חוטרתו · חלדרוב"א שיש לכל גמלים על גביהם: בשלייתה · דכיון דכחיש לא מנתחא לי' ול"נ מטולטלת כר קטן מלא מוכין נותנין לו תחת הזנב כדי שלא תשחית הרצועה הבשר לפי שהמשוי שעל גבה כשהגמל יורד מכביד ויורד כלפי צוארה אלא שהרצועה מעכבתו: יד ורגל · אחד מן הידים ואחד מן הרגלים כובל ביחד: יד על גב זרועו · אחד מידיו כופף כלפי מעלה וקושר כדי שלא יהו לו אלא ג' רגלים לברוח: שתי ידים · כאחד או שתי רגלים כאחד: ואכתי לא דמי · האי תנא לדרב יהודה: רישא וסיפא ניחא · כדרב יהודה אבל מציעתא דקתני או שתי ידים או שתי רגלים קשיא לדרב יהודה דלא קרי עקוד אלא יד ורגל כיצחק בן אברהם דכתיב (בראשית כב) ויעקד כפף ידיו ורגליו לאחוריו וקשר יד ורגל יחד ונפשט צוארו לאחוריו: לחינגא · לשוק למוכרם חינגא ע"ש שסובבין את השוק מחולות מחולות עגולות של בני אדם: לענין כלאים שנוי. האי שלא יכרוך דמתני' לא שייך ביה איסור שבת אלא משום כלאים אסר ליה כדמפרש ואזיל: כלאים דחבלים · שיש בהן חבלי למר וחבלי פשתן וכי כריך להו הוו כלאים וידו מתחממת באחיזתן וקסבר °דבר שאין מתכוין אסור: אי נימא כלאים דאדם · דכי כריך להן סביבות ידו נמצא קשור עם הגמלים ופעמים שהן מושכין שום דבר ונמצא אדם וגמל מנהיגין יחד: והתנן אדם מותר עם כולם · עם כל הבהמות לחרוש ולמשוך שלא אסרה תורה אלא שני מיני בהמה יחד כעין שור וחמור ומשנה זו במסכת כלאים: התוכף · בגדי למר ופשתים: בתכיפה אחת · כגון ע"י מחט פעם אחת או שקשר קשר אחד: אינו חיבור · דכתיב (דברים כב) למר ופשתים יחדו לא אסרה התורה אלא חבור יפה המתקיים: כריכה וקשירה · בשתי תכיפות: שלא יצא חבל · ראש החבל לא יצא מתחת ידו טפח למטה דדמי כמי שנושאה בידו ולא מתחזיא שהיא מאפסר הגמלים: שמואל · דאמר טפח לאורויי הלכה למעשה אתא לאשמעינן דהבא לימלך לפנינו אמרינן ליה טפח שלא להקל באיסורין ומיהו עד טפחיים ליכא איסור:

והתניא

תוספות

עד כבלא · מפרש ר"י עד השוק כדאמר בפ' במה אשה (לקמן דף סג:) בירית באחת כבלים בשתים שמניחין הכבלים בשוק:

רב אמר ליבש מותר כו' · וא"ת לימא מר הלכה כמר וי"ל משום °דאיכא דמפכי להו לתנאי*:

הלכה כר' יהודה בן בתירא · הא דנקט ר' יהודה בן בתירה ולא נקט ר' יוסי משום דבמקום שאין עושין כלל אלא כדי ליבש שרי ר' יהודה בן בתירא דלא שייך התם מי מפים ור' יוסי אוסר משום דילמא נפיל: ר"ת גרים

אמר רב הלכה כת"ק ושמואל אמר כו' וכן כי אתא רבין א"ר יוחנן הלכה כתנא קמא ואתי שפיר איכא דמתני לה לדרב ושמואל דלעיל אהא:

והתנן אדם מותר עם כולם לחרוש ולמשוך · וא"ת אפי' יהא אדם נמי אסור תקשה דמאי כלאים שייך הכא כיון שאינו מושך בעגלה ובקרון דהא בשבת איירי ואין לומר דאסור להנהיג בכלאים אפי' לא ימשוך שום דבר דא"כ כן יהא אסור להוליך ולהזיז ממקומו שור פסולי המוקדשין דחשיב כשני מינים כדאמרי' בפרק בתרא דמכות (דף כב·) המנהיג בשור פסולי המוקדשין לוקה גוף אחד הוא ועשאו הכתוב שני גופים וי"ל דה"ק אילימא כלאים דאדם והא דקתני ובלבד שלא יכרוך בחול קאמר כדאוקימנא לעיל (פ"ב דף כג:) ולא בשמן שריפה דאיירי ביו"ט ומיירי שמושכין שום דבר אי נמי י"ל דחשיב משיכה מה שנושאים שניהם את החבלים:

מ"ס

עין משפט נר מצוה

לא א ב ג מיי' פ"כ מהל' שבת הלכה יב סמג לאוין סה טוש"ע א"ח סי' שה סעיף ו:

[וע' תוספות מנחות לט: ד"ה ולימא]

לב ד מיי' שם הלכה ט טוש"ע שם סעי' טו:

לג ה מיי' שם הלכה י טוש"ע שם סעיף יג:

לד ו מיי' שם טוש"ע שם סעיף יד:

לה ז מיי' פ"ט מהל' כלאים הלכה יו"ד סמג לאוין רפ"ב טוש"ע י"ד סי' רצז סעיף טו:

לו ח מיי' פ"י מהל' כלאים הלכה כד סמג לאוין רפג טוש"ע י"ד סי' ש' סעיף ב:

לז ט מיי' פ"כ מהל' שבת הלכה ט סמג לאוין סה טוש"ע א"ח סי' ש"ה סעיף טו:

כלאים פ"ח מ"י [יבמות ה': מנחות לט.]

מסורת הש"ס

[פי' רש"י יחזקאל כז יח ולמד לחר]

[צ"ל להם]

[צ"ל ולא]

שבועות כה: נגעים פ"א מ"א [שבועות ו:]

[תמיד לא:]

[ביצה לג.]

כלאים פ"ח מ"ו [ב"ק נד:] [צ"ל והתנן]

[ביצה כט:]

[ברכות כד. ושם נסמן]

גליון הש"ס

רש"י ד"ה שמכבנין וכו' כיום שנולד. עי' רש"י יחזקאל כז יח: שם ד"ה כלאים דחבלים וכו' דבר שאין מתכוין אסור. עי' לקמן קמ ע"א ברש"י ד"ה אבל מוטל: תוס' ד"ה רב אמר וכו' דאיכא דמפכי להו לתנאי. כעין זה מגילה לב ע"א

רבינו חננאל

כבולות מלשון כבלים כדכתיב ארץ כבול וגו' ופי' [דמשתקעא] כרעא בגוה · כי כבלא שהיא עפרא וחול וזו היא חומטון. כבונות. מכבנין עור הטלה מיום לידתו עד ח' ימים וזהו צמר רך הנקרא (מילא) [מילת]. ר' יהודה אומר עזים יוצאות צרורות ליבש אבל לא לחלב כיון דאשתכח' ת"ק דברייתא כר' יהודה דמתניתין ורב אמר הלכתא כוותייהו הלכה כמותם ואפי' ר' יהודה לא חלק אלא אמר כך הלכה. לצרור דדי הבהמה לצמקן כדי שתתעבר הבהמה מותר. אבל מי מפים כלומר מי המבחין בין קשירת דד ליבש לקשירת דד לחלב וקי"ל הלכתא כרב באיסורי וכן הלכתא ואע"פ שר' יוסי חולק: לא יצא הגמל במטולטלת כו' תנא [לא] יצא הגמל במטולטלת בחטרתא שתכנס בו הרוח אבל יוצא בזנבו הקשורה בדמרתו שלא תכנס בו הרוח. לא עקוד ולא רגול. אוקמה רב יהודה עקוד יד ורגל כעקידת יצחק בן אברהם. רגול שלא יכוף על זרועו ויקשור. ותניא כוותיה ולא יקשור גמלים זה בזה וימשוך: ירושלמי שלא יהו אומרים פלוני יוצא לעשות מלאכתו בשבת. פי' הינגא שוקי מלשון חגאיד חגינת נכרים. אבל מכנים הוא חבלים לתוך ידו ובלבד שלא יכרוך·אתינו למימר הא דתנן ובלבד שלא יכרוך משום דנראה כאלו מושך האדם עם הבהמה ומשום כלאים. והתנן בכלאים בסוף פרק ח' אדם מותר עם כולם לחרוש ולמשוך אלא משום כלאים דחבלין חיישינן דלמא חבל אחד צמר ואחד פשתים וכיון שיכרוך עובר משום כלאים והתנן התוכף תכיפה אחת אינה חבור הנה תכיפה שהיא כגון תפירה אחת אינה חיבור וכ"ש כריכה שאינה חיבור. ושנינן מתניתין לא יכרוך ויקשור שנמצאת כריכה ותפירה כעין שתי תכיפות. אמר שמואל ובלבד שלא יהא אפסר יוצא מתחת ידו טפח ואסיק' הלכה למעשה שלא יהא אפסר יוצא מתחת ידו טפח כלומר אינו משולשל האפסר מתחת ידו כדי כריכה וכן לא יהא אפסר הניתן בראש הבהמה וראש

והתניא ובלבד שיגביה מן הקרקע טפח כי תניא ההיא בחבלא דביני ביני : **מתני'** *אין *חמור יוצא במרדעת בזמן שאינה קשורה לו *ולא בזוג אף על פי שהוא פקוק ולא בסולם שבצוארו ולא ברצועה שברגלו ואין התרנגולים יוצאין בחוטין ולא ברצועה שברגליהם ואין הזכרים יוצאין בעגלה שתחת האליה שלהן ואין הרחלים יוצאות חנונות ואין העגל יוצא בגימון ולא פרה בעור *הקופר ולא *ברצועה שבין קרניה *פרתו של רבי אלעזר בן עזריה היתה יוצאה ברצועה שבין קרניה שלא ברצון חכמים : **גמ'** מאי טעמא *כדאמרן : ולא בזוג אע"פ שהוא פקוק : משום *דמיחזי כמאן דאזיל לחינגא : ולא בסולם שבצוארו : א"ר הונא בי לועא למאי עבדי ליה להיכא דאית ליה מכה דלא הדר חייך ביה : ולא ברצועה שברגלו : דעבדי ליה לגיזרא : ואין התרנגולין יוצאין בחוטין : דעבדי ליה סימנא כי היכי דלא ליחלפו : ולא ברצועה : דעבדי ליה כי היכי דלא ליתברו מאני : ואין הזכרים יוצאין בעגלה : כי היכי דלא לחמטן אלייתיה : ואין הרחלים יוצאות חנונות : יתיב רב אחא בר עולא קמיה דרב חסדא ויתיב וקאמר משעה שגוזזין אותה טומנין לה עזק בשמן ומניחין לה על פדחתה כדי שלא תצטנן אמר ליה רב חסדא א"כ עשית' מר עוקבא אלא יתיב רב פפא בר שמואל קמיה דרב *חסדא ויתיב וקאמר בשעה שכורעת לילד טומנין לה שני עזקין של שמן ומניחין לה אחד על פדחתה ואחד על הרחם כדי שתתחמם א"ל רב נחמן אם כן עשיתה ילתא אלא א"ר הונא עץ אחד יש בכרכי הים וחנון שמו ומביאין קיסם ומניחין לה בחוטמה כדי שתתעטש ויפלו דרני ראשה אי הכי זכרים נמי כיון דמנגחי זכרים בהדדי ממילא נפלן שמעון נזירא אמר קיסמא דריתמא בשלמא דרב הונא היינו דקתני חנונות אלא לרבנן מאי חנונות דעבדינן להו מילתא דמרחמינן עלייהו : ואין העגל יוצא בגימון : מאי עגל בגימון א"ר הונא בר נירא אמר ר' אלעזר מאי משמע דהאי גימון לישנא דמיכף דכתיב °הלכוף כאגמון ראשו : ולא פרה בעור הקופר : דעבדי לה כי היכי דלא למציוה יאלי : ולא ברצועה שבין קרניה : אי לרב (דאמר) *בין לנוי בין לשמר אסור אי לשמואל (דאמר) לנוי אסור לשמר מותר : פרתו של רבי אלעזר בן עזריה : *וחדא פרה הויא ליה והא אמר רב ואמרי לה אמר רב יהודה אמר רב תריסר אלפי עגלי הוה מעשר רבי אלעזר בן עזריה מעדריה כל שתא ושתא תנא לא שלו היתה אלא של שכינתו היתה ומתוך שלא מיחה בה נקראת על שמו *רב ורבי חנינא ור' יוחנן ורב חביבא מתנו בכוליה דסדר מועד כל כי האי זוגא חלופי רבי יוחנן ומעייל רבי יונתן כל מי שאפשר למחות לאנשי ביתו ולא מיחה נתפס על אנשי ביתו באנשי עירו נתפס על אנשי עירו בכל העולם כולו נתפס על כל העולם כולו אמר רב פפא והני דבי ריש גלותא נתפסו על כולי עלמא כי הא דאמר רבי חנינא מאי דכתיב °ה' במשפט יבא עם זקני עמו ושריו אם שרים חטאו

זקנים

תורה אור

והתניא ובלבד שיגביה מן הקרקע טפח · אבל כל כמה דבעי ניפוק מתותיה ידיה : בחבלא דביני ביני · שבין ידו לגמל בההוא קאמר כמה דבעי נהוי ובלבד שיגביהנו מן הקרקע טפח כדי שתהא נראה הבהמה נמשכת בו דאי לא לא מיתחזי נטירותא דבהמה אלא כמשאוי בעלמא שאין נראה שאוחז ראשה בידו : **מתני'** בזוג · איסקליטא : אע"פ · שחללו פקוק במוכין שאין העינבל שלו מקשקש להשמיע קול ובגמ' מפרש טעמא : סולם ורצועה וכל הנך דמתניתין מפרש בגמרא וכולהו משום דקיים עלייהו ואי נפלי אתי לאיתויי : עגלה · כגון קרון קטן שעושין לו תחת זנבו שראש זנב אותן האילים רחב כמין כר קטן ואין בו עצם אלא שומן ועב וכבד וכשנגרר לארץ נשרט ונשחת ועושים לו עגלה מתגלגלת אחריו כשהוא הולך והזנב קשור עליה : קופר · שרץ הוא שנימיו חדין כמחט וקורין לו הריצו"ן וקושרין עורו בדדי הפרה שלא יניקוה שרצים : ולא ברצועה שבין קרניה · דמשאוי הוא לה כדמפרש בגמרא : **גמ'** כדאמרן · שאינה קשורה בו מע"ש דלא גלי מאתמול שיהא צריכה לכך שיהא לה למלבוש : פקוק · סתום : לחינגא · לשוק למכור ותולין לו זוג להנאותו : בי לועא · שקושרין אצל הלחי : דלא הדר חייך לה · שלא יוכל להחזיר צוארו לצד המכה לחככה בשיניו וקושרין בצוארו ותשובים הן יותר מקשישין שעל גבי השבר ואי נפלו חיים עלייהו ומייתי להו בשגגה : לגיזרא · אנטורטליי"ר בלע"ז בהמ' שפסיעותיה קצרים ומכה רגליה זה בזה עושין לה כמין טבעת של עקלים או רצועות עבות וקושרין אותה למעלה מפרסות הרגל מקום שמנקשין זו בזו : דלא ליחלפו · בתרנגולי חבריהם : דלא ליתברו מאני · שקושרין שני רגליה יחד ברצועה קצרה שלא תוכל להריס רגליה ולהתיז : דלא ליחמטן · שלא ילקו בסלעים וטרשים בלניי"ר בלע"ז : לאחר שגוזזין אותה טומנים לה עזק בשמן · עד שיגדל למרה : עזק · למר גפן או כל דבר רך : פדחתה · מצחה : עשיתה מר עוקבא · ניהגת ברחל זו חשיבותו של מר עוקבא שהיה עשיר ואב בית דין וכי דרך חשיבותה לכך : ילתא · אשתו של רב נחמן : דרני · תולעים : קיסמא דריתמא · קיסם של רותם שמניחין לה בחוטמה : בר נירא · עול קטן שמניחין* לעגל בצוארו שיהיה למוד לכוף ראשו לכשיגדל : דלא למציוה יאלי · שלא ינקוה עלוקה שקורין שנשוא"ש : בין לנוי בין לשמר אסור · דכל נטירותא יתירתא אמרי' משאוי הוא : (מתנו) בכולי סדר מועד כל כי האי זוגא · ארבעתן יחד : חלופי ר' יוחנן · יש מחליפין ר' יוחנן ומעיילי ר' יונתן : נתפס · נענש על עבירות שבידן : בכל העולם כולו · בכל ישראל כגון מלך ונשיא שאפשר לו למחות שיראין מפניו ומקיימין דבריו :

זקנים

מאי טעמא דילמא נפיל ואתי לאתויי · אע"ג דאוקימנא לעיל דאיירי בקשורה הכא מפרש לפום משמעות דיסכא דמתני' ומשום שהאריך לעיל לא חש להאריך הכא ומתוך פי' הקונט' משמע דל"ג דילמא נפיל ואתי לאתויי : **משום** דמיחזי כמאן דאזיל לחינגא · אבל משוי אינו שבטל אגב אפסר ומשום דילמא נפיל נמי ליכא למיחש כדחיש גבי זוג בריש במה אשה (לקמן דף נח: ושם) דהכא מיירי באריג ואמר התם כל שהוא אריג לא גזרו : **דלא** למציוה יאלי · פירש"י שאנשוא"ש דהיינו עלוקה ואין נראה דאין מוצצות אלא דם ועוד דהוה ליה למימר עלוקות ולא אשכחן דקרי להו יאלי בשום מקום ונראה דיאלי היינו נמי קופר דמתני' כדאמר בריש בבא בתרא (דף ד·) גבי הורדוס אהדר ליה כלילא דיאלי ונקרינהו לעיניה והאנקה מתרגמינן יאלי (ויקרא יא) והוא שקורין הירצו"ן : **הוה** מעשר ר' אלעזר בן עזריה כל שתא ושתא · הקשה ר"ת דאמר בפ' בתרא דבכורות (דף נג: ושם) דאין מעשר בהמה נוהג אחר החורבן מפני התקלה א"כ בזמן הבית הוה מעשר ומסתמא בן י"ג שנה היה כשעישר וא"כ מאי קאמר דהוה מעשר כל שתא ושתא דע"כ לא היה בשעת חורבן הבית לכל היותר כי אם בן י"ד או ט"ו שהרי רבי יוחנן בן זכאי משך נשיאותו אחר החורבן שנה או שנתים דכמה תקנות תקן אחר החורבן כדתנן* משחרב בהמ"ק התקין רבי יוחנן בן זכאי ואחריו ר"ג היה נשיא שנתים או ג' קודם שמינו רבי אלעזר בן עזריה כדאמר בפרק תפלת השחר (דף כז:) אשתקד לצעריה *לרבי צדוק וקודם לכן לצעריה לרבי יהושע על תקנת המועדות וכשהעמידוהו נשיא היה בן י"ח שנה כדאמר התם הרי בשעת החורבן היה בן י"ד או ט"ו לכל היותר וי"ל דקודם גזרה הוה מעשר אי נמי אפוטרופוס הוה מעשר בקטנותו °והר"ר אלחנן מפרש הוה מעשר אחר חורבן בהמת ארנונא למלך* : **רב** ור' חנינא ור' יוחנן ורב חביבא מתני · פירוש מתני הך שמעתא דאמר בסמוך והשתא פסק הש"ס למילתיה וקאמר בכולי *(הש"ס) (א) כל כה"ג זוגא מיחלפא רבי יוחנן כו' ולא קאי מתני אחילוף כך קבל רבינו שמואל בשם רבינו שלמה ששמע מרבי אליעזר רבו :

ותוס

עין משפט
נר מצוה

לח א ב מיי' פ"כ מהל' שבת הלכה י יא סמג לאוין סה טוש"ע א"ח סי' שה סעיף יז [ורב אלפס כ"מ עז.]

לט ג מיי' פ"ו מהל' דיעות הלכה ז סמג עשין יא :

רבינו חננאל

וראש האפסר (בין) [ביד] המושך הבהמה אותו וביני ביני יגביהנו שלא יהא קרוב לקרקע טפח . וכן הלכה . פי' סמוקלת צפיחה . פי' דלא נחמטה שלא יעלה כעין עיפוש באליה . חנונות עץ ושמו עץ וחנון . ומניחין קיסם ממנו בחוטמו כדי שתתעטש ויפלו דרני ראשה . שמעון נזירא אומר כו' . גמון עץ קטן כמו עול . לא פרה בעור הקופר ברצועה שבין קרניה אי לרב בין כך ובין כך אסור אי לשמואל לשמר מותר לנוי אסור וזה היתה לנוי : כל מי שיש בידו ספק למחות ואינו מוחה נתפס עליו כו' . ה' במשפט יבא עם זקני עמו ושריו אם שרים חטאו זקנים מה חטאו אלא על שלא מיחו :

[במעשה דרבי צדוק כצ"ל]

[ועי' תוספות בכורות נג. ד"ה אלא ותו' שם דחו פי' זה וגם לתי' דאפוטרופוס ע"ש אבל בביצה כג. ד"ה תליסר וכו' כתבו כמו הכא וע"ע תוס' ע"ז יג. ותוס' יומא סו. ד"ה אין מקדישין]

רב נסים גאון

אמר ליה רב נחמן אם כן עשיתה ילתא ילתא היא אשתו של רב נחמן ותנד דאלך*) בסוף פרק שלשה שאכלו כאחת (ברכות דף נא) עולא בר רב איקלע לבי רב נחמן בריך וכו' שמעא ילתא ואיקפדה ובעשרה יוחסין (קדושין דף ע) אמר רב נחמן לרב יהודה נישדר מר שלמא לילתא :

*) הוצאתו והגהה זכ'

מסורת
הש"ס

[לעיל נג.]

[לקמן סד:]

[לעיל נב. עדיו' פ"ג מי"ב ביצה דף כג.]

לעיל נג.

[לעיל ע"א וביצה כג.]

הגהות
הב"ח

(א) תוס' ד"ה רב וכו' בכולי סדר מועד כל כי האי זוגא מיחלפא :

גירס' רש"ל רב נחמן

גליון
הש"ס

תוס' ד"ה הוה מעשר וכו' והר"ר אלחנן מפרש ע' מ"ל רפ"ז מהלכות בכורות :

בד"א שמניחין

[לעיל נב:]

ביצה כג.

סוכה ד: מגילה

ישעיה נח

ישעיה ג

But it was taught: Providing that he lifts it a handbreadth from the ground?[2]—That was taught of the cord between.[3]

MISHNAH. AN ASS MAY NOT GO OUT WITH A CUSHION, WHEN IT IS NOT TIED TO IT, OR WITH A BELL, EVEN IF IT IS PLUGGED, OR WITH A LADDER[-SHAPED YOKE] AROUND ITS NECK, OR WITH A THONG AROUND ITS FOOT. FOWLS MAY NOT GO OUT WITH RIBBONS, OR WITH A STRAP ON THEIR LEGS; RAMS MAY NOT GO OUT WITH A WAGGONETTE UNDER THEIR TAILS,[4] EWES MAY NOT GO OUT PROTECTED [ḤANUNOTH],[5] OR A CALF WITH A GIMON,[6] OR A COW WITH THE SKIN OF A HEDGEHOG,[7] OR WITH THE STRAP BETWEEN ITS HORNS. R. ELEAZAR B. 'AZARIAH'S COW USED TO GO OUT WITH A THONG BETWEEN ITS HORNS, [BUT] NOT WITH THE CONSENT OF THE RABBIS.

GEMARA. What is the reason?[8]—As we have said.[9]

OR WITH A BELL, EVEN IF IT IS PLUGGED UP. Because it looks like going to the fair.

OR WITH A LADDER[-SHAPED YOKE] AROUND ITS NECK. R. Huna said: That is a jaw bar.[10] For what purpose is it made?—For where it has a bruise, lest it chafe it afresh.[11]

OR WITH A STRAP ON THEIR LEGS. It is put on him [the ass] as a guard.[12]

FOWLS MAY NOT GO OUT WITH RIBBONS. Which are put on them for a sign, that they should not be exchanged.

OR WITH A STRAP. Which is fastened on them to restrain
a them from breaking utensils.[1]

RAMS MAY NOT GO OUT WITH A WAGGONETTE. [Its purpose is] that their tails may not knock [against rocks, etc.].

EWES MAY NOT GO OUT PROTECTED [ḤANUNOTH]. R. Aḥa b. 'Ulla sat before R. Ḥisda, and he sat and said: When it is sheared, a compress is saturated[2] in oil and placed on its forehead that it should not catch cold. Said R. Ḥisda to him: If so, you treat it like Mar 'Ukba![3] But R. Papa b. Samuel sat before R. Ḥisda,[4] and he sat and said: When she kneels for lambing two oily compresses are made for her, and one is placed on her forehead and the other on her womb, that she may be warmed. Said R. Naḥman to him, If so, you would treat her like Yaltha![5] But, said R. Huna, there is a certain wood in the sea towns called *ḥanun*, whereof a chip is brought and placed in her nostril to make her sneeze, so that the worms in her head should fall out. If so, the same [is required] for males?—Since the males butt each other, they fall out in any case. Simeon the Nazirite said: A chip of the juniper tree [is placed in its nostril]. As for R. Huna, it is well: hence ḤANUNOTH is mentioned. But according to the Rabbis, what is the meaning of ḤANUNOTH?—That an act of kindness is done for it.[6]

NOR MAY A CALF GO OUT WITH A GIMON. What is the meaning of A CALF WITH A GIMON?—Said R. Huna: A little yoke.[7] Said R. Eleazar: Where is it implied that 'GIMON' connotes bending?[8]—In the verse, *Is it to bow down his head as a rush* [ke-agmon]?[9]

NOR A COW WITH THE SKIN OF A HEDGEHOG. It is placed upon it to prevent hedgehogs[10] from sucking it.

NOR WITH THE STRAP BETWEEN IT HORNS. On Rab's view, whether as an ornament or as a protection, it is forbidden; on Samuel's view, as an ornament it is forbidden, as a protection it
b is permitted.[1]

R. ELEAZAR B. 'AZARIAH'S COW. Did he have [but] one cow? Surely Rab—others state, Rab Judah in Rab's name—said: The tithe of R. Eleazar b. 'Azariah's flocks amounted to thirteen thousand calves annually?—It was taught: This was not his,[2] but a female neighbour of his; yet since he did not protest thereat, it was designated his.[3]

Rab and R. Ḥanina, R. Joḥanan and R. Ḥabiba taught [the following] (In the whole of the Order *Mo'ed*[4] whenever this pair[5] occur some substitute R. Jonathan for R. Joḥanan)[6]—Whoever can forbid his household [to commit a sin] but does not, is seized[7] for [the sins of] his household; [if he can forbid] his fellow citizens, he is seized for [the sins of] his fellow citizens; if the whole world, he is seized for [the sins of] the whole world. R. Papa observed, And the members of the Resh Galutha's [household][8] are seized for the whole world. Even as R. Ḥanina said, Why is it written, *The Lord will enter into judgement with the elders of His people, and the princes thereof:*[9] if the princes sinned, [55a]

(2) Implying that there is no limit to the length that may hang out of his hand. (3) Between the man and the camel. If it trails nearer to the ground, it looks as though he is carrying a cord. (4) This refers to a species of ram whose tail was very fat, to preserve which it was yoked to a waggonette. (5) V. Gemara. (6) Discussed in the Gemara. (7) Tied round its udder. (8) For the prohibition relating to the cushion. (9) *Supra* 53a. (10) Jast.: a bandage or bar under the jaw. (11) I.e., it should let it heal. (12) To prevent the legs from knocking each other.
a (1) The two legs were tied together; hence it could not run about and cause damage. (2) Lit., 'hid' (3) The head of the Beth din.—A sheep will not be treated with such care. (4) Rashal reads: R. Naḥman. (5) His wife. (6) Deriving ḤANUNOTH from *ḥanan*, to be gracious, kind. (7) To accustom it to bend its head under the yoke when it grows up. (8) V. preceding note. (9) Isa. LVIII, 5. (10) 'Believed to suck and injure the udders of cattle' (Jast).
b (1) V. *supra* 52a. (2) *Sc.* the cow referred to in the Mishnah. (3) Lit., 'it was called by his name'. (4) V. Introduction to this Order, in this volume. (5) I.e., these four names. (6) This is a parenthetic observation by the Talmud (Tosaf.). (7) Just as a pledge is seized for non-payment of debt. I.e., he is punished. (8) V. *supra* 48a, n. b7. (9) Isa. III, 14.

Novellae of Hagaon Rabbi Moshe Feinstein o.b.m.
Tractate Shabbath

55a. **אמרו The ministering angels asked...'But Moses and Aaron fulfilled the whole Torah,' they pursued, 'yet they died.' 'There is one event etc.' He replied.** It appears difficult how this *baraitha* can differ with R. Simeon b. Eleazar. The Torah states explicitly, *Because ye believed not in Me,* meaning that they died because of their sins. It seems to me that this *baraitha* holds that the sin of the water of Meribah was not what made them liable to death. They would have died in any case because there is death without sin. They would have died later, however. Since they committed a sin, although a minor infraction, they died early. The difficulty is, however, that R. Simeon b. Eleazar also states only, 'had you believed in Me, your time had not yet come to depart from the world.' What then is the indication that the *baraitha* of the ministering angels differs with him? Perhaps he, too, holds that the sin of the water of Meribah was instrumental only in their early demise, not in the death itself. It appears that the only evidence of their difference is R. Simeon's expression, 'Moses and Aaron too died through their sin.' This indicates that their sin was the reason for their death. Although he states, 'your time had not come to depart from the world,' R. Amni does not interpret this literally, but that they would never have died had they not sinned. This expression applies somewhat in that sense, meaning that, had they not sinned, their time would never arrive to depart from the world, although this could be forever. According to the conclusion of the Gemara, however, R. Simeon b. Eleazar also holds that there is death without sin. Accordingly, we explain his language literally, viz. that their time had not yet arrived, for had they not sinned, their sin would arrive sometime later. The controversy between R. Simeon b. Eleazar and the *baraitha,* according to the conclusion, is that R. Simeon b. Eleazar holds that only four died through the serpent's machination, whereas the *baraitha* holds that Moses and Aaron, too, are included in that category. We must say that this difference is based on the question of whether bringing about an early death is considered the same as a death sentence. In fact, we find that, as regards saving one's life, we violate the Sabbath even to enable one to live a short time. Accordingly, we see that as far as the halachah is concerned, the verse, *he shall live* how did the elders sin? But say, [He will bring punishment] upon the elders because they do not forbid the princes.

Rab Judah was sitting before Samuel, [when] a woman came and cried before him,[10] but he ignored her. Said he to him, Does not the Master agree [that] *'whoso stoppeth his ears at the cry of the poor, he also shall cry, but shall not be heard'?*[11] 'O keen scholar!'[12] he replied, 'Your superior [will be punished] with cold [water], but your superior's superior [will be punished] with hot.[13] Surely
a Mar 'Ukba, the Ab-Beth-din[1] is sitting!' For it is written, *O house of David, thus saith the Lord. Execute judgement in the morning, and deliver the spoiled out of the hand of the oppressor, lest My fury go forth like fire, and burn that none can quench it, because of the evil of your doings*, etc.[2]

R. Zera said to R. Simeon, Let the Master rebuke the members of the Resh Galutha's suite. They will not accept it from me, was his reply. Though they will not accept it, returned he, yet you should rebuke them. For R. Aha b. R. Hanina said: Never did a favourable word[3] go forth from the mouth of the Holy One, blessed be He, of which He retracted for evil, save the following, where it is written, *And the Lord said unto him, Go through the midst of the city, through the midst of Jerusalem, and set a mark* [taw] *upon the foreheads of the men that sigh and that cry for all the abominations that be done in the midst thereof*, etc.[4] The Holy One, blessed be He, said to Gabriel,[5] Go and set a *taw*[6] of ink upon the foreheads of the righteous, that the destroying angels may have no power over them; and a *taw* of blood upon the foreheads of the wicked, that the destroying angels may have power over them. Said the Attribute of Justice[7] before the Holy One, blessed be He, 'Sovereign of the Universe! Wherein are these different from those?' 'Those are completely righteous men, while these are completely wicked,' replied He. 'Sovereign of the Universe!' it continued, 'they had the power to protest but did not.' 'It was fully known[8] to Me that had they protested they would not have heeded them.'[9] 'Sovereign of the Universe!' said he, 'If it was revealed to Thee, was it revealed to them?' Hence it is written, [*Slay utterly*] *the old man, the young and the maiden, and little children and women; but come not near any man upon whom is the mark; and begin at My Sanctuary* [mikdashi]. *Then they began at the elders which were before*
b *the house.*[1] R. Joseph recited: Read not *mikdashi* but *mekuddashay* [My sanctified ones]: this refers to the people who fulfilled the Torah from *alef* to *taw*.[2] And straightway, *And behold, six men came from the way of the upper gate, which lieth toward the north, every man with his slaughter weapon in his hand; and one man in the midst of them clothed in linen, with a writer's inkhorn by his side. And they went in, and stood beside the brazen altar.*[3] Was then the brazen altar [still] in existence?[4]—The Holy One, blessed be He, spake thus to them; Commence [destruction] from the place where song is uttered before Me.[5] And who were the six men?—Said R. Hisda: Indignation [*Kezef*], Anger [*Af*], Wrath [*Hemah*], Destroyer [*Mashhith*], Breaker [*Meshabber*] and Annihilator [*Mekaleh*]. And why a *taw?*—Said Rab: *Taw* [stands for] *tihyeh* [thou shalt live], *taw* [stands for] *tamuth* [thou shalt die]. Samuel said: The *taw* denotes, the merit of the Patriarchs is exhausted [*tamah*].[6] R. Johanan said: The merit of the Patriarchs will confer grace [*tahon*].[7] While Resh Lakish said: *Taw* is the end of the seal of the Holy One, blessed be He. For R. Hanina said: The seal of the Holy One, blessed be He, is *emeth* [truth]. R. Samuel b. Nahmani said: It denotes the people who fulfilled the Torah from *alef* to *taw*.[8]

And since when has the merit of the Patriarchs been exhausted?—Rab said, Since the days of Hosea the son of Beeri, for it is written, [*And now*] *will I discover her lewdness in the sight of her lovers, and none shall deliver her out of Mine hand.*[9] Samuel said, Since the days of Hazael, for it is said, *And Hazael king of Syria*
c *oppressed Israel all the days of Jehoahaz;*[1] and it is written, *But the Lord was gracious unto them, and had compassion upon them, and had respect unto them, because of the covenant with Abraham, Isaac, and Jacob, and would not destroy them, neither cast He them from His presence* until now.[2] R. Joshua b. Levi said: Since the days of Elijah, for it is said, *And it came to pass at the time of the offering of the evening oblation, that Elijah the prophet came near, and said, O Lord, the God of Abraham, of Isaac, and of Israel, let it be known* this day *that Thou art God in Israel, and that I am Thy servant, and that I have done all these things at Thy word.*[3] R. Johanan said: Since the days of Hezekiah, for it is said, *Of the increase of his government and of peace there shall be no end, upon the throne of David, and upon his kingdom, to establish it, and to uphold it with judgement and with righteousness from henceforth even for ever. The zeal of the Lord of hosts shall perform this.*[4]

R. Ammi said: There is no death without sin,[5] and there is no suffering without iniquity. There is no death without sin, for it is written, *The soul that sinneth, it shall die: the son shall not bear the iniquity of the father, neither shall the father bear the iniquity of the son, the righteousness of the righteous shall be upon him, and the wickedness of the wicked shall be upon him*, etc.,[6] There is no suffering without iniquity, for it is written, *Then will I visit their transgression with the rod, and their iniquity with stripes.*[7]

(10) About a wrong done to her. (11) Prov. XXI, 13. (12) Or, man of long teeth. (13) I.e., I, your superior, will go unscathed, because there is a higher court than mine, viz., Mar 'Ukba's, which should really take the matter up.

a (1) The father, i.e., the head of the Beth din. (2) Jer. XXI, 12. From this Samuel deduced that only the head, with whom lay the real power, would be punished. (3) Lit., 'a good attribute'. (4) Ezek. IX, 4. (5) Gabriel, 'man of God', is mentioned in the Book of Daniel VIII, 16-26; IX, 21-27. He was regarded as God's messenger, who executes His will on earth. (6) The last letter of the Hebrew alphabet. (7) Justice was often hypostasized as an independent being. (8) Lit., 'it was revealed and known'. (9) Lit., 'accepted (it) from them'.

b (1) Ezek. IX, 6. (2) The first and the last letters of the alphabet—as we say from '*Alpha* to *Omega*'. Nevertheless they were included, because they had failed to protest. Thus the Almighty retracted from His original intention, the change being for evil. (3) Ibid. 2. (4) According to tradition Solomon hid it and substituted an earthen altar for it; v. I Kings VIII, 64 and Zeb. 59*b*. (5) I.e., start with the Levites, who utter song to the accompaniment of musical instruments of brass. (6) The merit of the Patriarchs, which acted as a shield for the wicked, is at an end. (7) Samuel explains the *taw* on the wicked; R. Johanan that on the righteous. (8) V. n. b2. (9) Hos. II, 12; '*and none*', i.e., their merit has no longer the power to save.

c (1) II Kings XIII, 22. (2) Ibid. 23. '*Until now*' implies, but no longer. (3) I Kings XVIII, 36. Here too *this day* implies a limitation. (4) Isa. IX, 6. '*The zeal*, etc.' implies, but not the merit of the Patriarchs, this being exhausted by now. (5) One's sins cause his death. (6) Ezek. XVIII, 20. (7) Ps. LXXXIX, 33.

Novellae of Hagaon Rabbi Moshe Feinstein o.b.m.
Tractate Shabbath

by them (Lev. xviii. 5) is interpreted to mean that even a short life is accounted the same a long life. Therefore, if the sin of the water of Meribah could not bring about their death, it could not cause them to die earlier. Accordingly, R. Simeon b. Eleazar reasons that they died because of their sin, because the sin of the water of Meribah could possibly bring about their death itself judging by the fact that it brought about their early death, although only that is stated in the verse. The Tanna of the *baraitha* of the ministering angels holds that bringing about an early death is not the same as the death sentence itself. Therefore, we must perforce conclude that Moses and Aaron died because of the serpent's machination, without which they would not have died because of their sin of the water of Meribah. That sin was only serious enough to cause them to die earlier, not to sentence them to death. This is not analogous to the law of saving a life, because the expression, *he shall live by them* means even a short life, but as regards punishment, bringing about an early death is a lighter punishment than the death penalty itself.

זקנים מה חטאו אלא אימא על זקנים שלא מיחו בשרים °רב יהודה הוה יתיב קמיה דשמואל אתאי ההיא איתתא קא צווחה קמיה ולא הוה משגח בה א"ל לא סבר ליה מר °אוטם אזנו מזעקת דל גם הוא יקרא ולא יענה א"ל *שיננא ריישך בקרירי רישא דרישך בחמימי הא יתיב מר עוקבא אב ב"ד דכתיב °בית דוד כה אמר ה' דינו לבקר משפט והצילו גזול מיד עושק פן תצא כאש חמתי ובערה ואין מכבה מפני רוע מעלליהם וגו' °א"ל ר' זירא לר' סימון לוכחינהו מר להני דבי ריש גלותא א"ל לא מקבלי מינאי א"ל אע"ג דלא מקבלי לוכחינהו מר דא"ר אחא בר' חנינא מעולם לא יצתה מדה טובה מפי הקב"ה וחזר בה לרעה חוץ מדבר זה דכתיב °ויאמר ה' אליו עבור בתוך העיר בתוך ירושלים והתוית תיו על מצחות האנשים הנאנחים והנאנקים על כל התועבות הנעשות בתוכה וגו' א"ל הקב"ה לגבריאל לך ורשום על מצחן של צדיקים תיו של דיו שלא ישלטו בהם מלאכי חבלה ועל מצחם של רשעים תיו של דם כדי שישלטו בהן מלאכי חבלה אמרה מדת הדין לפני הקב"ה רבש"ע מה נשתנו אלו מאלו אמר לה הללו צדיקים גמורים והללו רשעים גמורים אמרה לפניו רבש"ע היה בידם למחות ולא מיחו אמר לה גלוי וידוע לפני שאם מיחו בהם לא יקבלו מהם (*אמר) לפניו רבש"ע אם לפניך גלוי להם מי גלוי והיינו דכתיב °זקן בחור ובתולה טף ונשים תהרגו למשחית ועל כל איש אשר עליו התיו אל תגשו וממקדשי תחלו וכתיב ויחלו באנשים הזקנים אשר לפני הבית *תני רב יוסף אל תקרי מקדשי אלא מקודשי אלו בני אדם שקיימו את התורה כולה מאלף ועד תיו ומיד °והנה ששה אנשים באים מדרך שער העליון אשר מפנה צפונה ואיש כלי מפצו בידו ואיש אחד בתוכם לבוש הבדים וקסת הסופר במתניו ויבאו ויעמדו אצל מזבח הנחושת מי הוה אמר להו הקב"ה התחילו ממקום שאומרים שירה לפני ומאן נינהו ששה אנשים א"ר חסדא קצף אף וחימה ומשחית ומשבר ומכלה ומ"ש תיו אמר רב תיו תחיה תיו תמות ושמואל אמר תמה זכות אבות ורבי יוחנן אמר תחון זכות אבות ור"ל אמר תיו סוף חותמו של הקב"ה *דאמר רבי חנינא חותמו של הקב"ה אמת (אמר) ר' שמואל בר נחמני *אלו בני אדם שקיימו את התור' כולה מאלף ועד תיו מאימתי תמה זכות אבות °אמר רב מימות הושע בן בארי שנא' °אגלה את נבלתה לעיני מאהביה ואיש לא יצילנה מידי ושמואל אמר מימי חזאל שנאמר °וחזאל מלך ארם לחץ את ישראל כל ימי יהואחז וכתיב ויחן ה' אותם וירחמם ויפן אליהם למען בריתו את אברהם יצחק ויעקב ולא אבה השחיתם ולא השליכם מעל פניו עד עתה ר' יהושע בן לוי אמר מימי אליהו שנאמר °ויהי בעלות המנחה ויגש אליהו הנביא ויאמר ה' אלהי אברהם יצחק וישראל היום יודע כי אתה אלהים בישראל ואני עבדך ובדברך עשיתי [את] כל הדברים האלה וגו' ורבי יוחנן אמר מימי חזקיהו שנאמר °למרבה המשרה ולשלום אין קץ על כסא דוד ועל ממלכתו להכין אותה ולסעדה במשפט ובצדקה מעתה ועד עולם קנאת ה' צבאות תעשה זאת וגו': אמר רב אמי אין מיתה בלא חטא ואין יסורין בלא עון אין מיתה בלא חטא דכתיב °הנפש החוטאת היא תמות בן לא ישא בעון האב ואב לא ישא בעון הבן צדקת הצדיק עליו תהיה ורשעת הרשע עליו תהיה וגו' אין יסורין בלא עון דכתיב °ופקדתי בשבט פשעם ובנגעים עונם מיתיבי

זקנים · סנהדרין: ריישך בקרירי · אני שאני רבך איני נכוה אבל מר עוקבא שהוא ראש לי ולך ואב ב"ד יכווה בחמין: דכתיב בית דוד וגו' · לא ענש אלא מי שבידו לשפוט: חוץ מדבר זה · שנא' במקרא זה שהוציא דבור לטובה ומפני עונש תוכחה חזר בו: והתוית תיו על מצחות האנשים הנאנחים והנאנקים תורה אור על כל התועבות הנעשות בתוכה · אלו צדיקים: שלא ישלטו בהם מלאכי חבלה · שאני רוצה לשלוח בעיר: היינו דכתיב · מעיקרא ועל כל איש אשר עליו התיו אל תגשו ולבסוף וממקדשי תחלו: ממקודשי · שהודה למקטרג מדת הדין וחזר מן הטוב: מי הוה מזבח הנחשת · בימי יחזקאל והלא שלמה גנזו ועשה מזבח אבנים של ל"ב אמה דכתיב (מלכים א ה) כי מזבח הנחשת אשר לפני ה' קטן מהכיל *כאדם האומר לחבירו ננס פלוני ופסול לעבודה: ממקום שאומרים שירה · מן הלוים שאומרים שיר בכלי נחשת: תיו תמות · לרשעים: חותמו של הקב"ה אמת · אמצעית להותיות וראשון ואחרון על שם אני ראשון ואני אחרון ואני הוא: אלו בני אדם שקיימו התורה כולה · התיו סימן להם שקיימו התורה מראש עד סוף: ואיש לא יצילנה · שאין עוד זכות לאבות שתצלוה: ויפן אליהם למען בריתו את אברהם וגו' ולא השליכם מעל פניו עד עתה · אבל מכאן ואילך השליכם ולא פנה אל ברית אבות: ה' אלהי אברהם ואלהי יצחק וישראל היום יודע · שאתה זוכר ברית אברהם יצחק וישראל מדקאמר היום יודע ותו לא מכלל דתמה ועל ידי רחמים הוזכרה להם בימי חזאל: בימי חזקיהו · דכתיב מעתה ועד עולם קנאת ה' צבאות תעשה זאת ולא זכות אבות: בלא חטא · וחטאו של אדם גורם לו מיתה: בשבט ובנגעים · היינו יסורים וקאמר שאין באין אלא משום פקידת עון: בעטיו

ואע"ג דלא מקבלי לוכחינהו מר · הייט היכא דספק אי מקבלי כדאמר בסמוך לפניהם מי גלוי אבל היכא דודאי לא מקבלי הנח להם מוטב שיהו שוגגין ואל יהיו מזידין כדאמרינן בהמביא כדי יין (ביצה דף ל. ושם) ובפרק שואל (לקמן דף קמח:) גבי תוספת יוה"כ*:

ועל הרשעים תי"ו של דם · לא מקרא קאמר הכי אלא מסבר' דהא דכתיב והתוית תיו על מצחות האנשים הנאנחים והנאנקים על כל התועבות הנעשות בתוכה היינו בצדיקים גמורים:

מזבח נחשת בימי שלמה מי הוה · כדכתיב ששלמה הסירו כי היה קטן מהכיל וא"ת והא כתיב בדברי הימים (ב ד) ויעש שלמה את מזבח הנחשת וי"ל דדרשינן ליה כי הכא מזבח שאומרים לפניו °שירה בכלי נחשת:

קצף אף וחימה · קשה לרשב"א דאמר בפ"ק דמסכת ע"ג (דף ד· ושם) כתיב חימה אין לי וכתיב נוקם ה' ובעל חימה ומשני כאן לישראל כאן לנכרים אלמא דאין להקב"ה חימה על ישראל והההיא דמס' ע"ג קשה דבס"פ ארבעה נדרים (דף לב·) אמר חימה משה הרגו דכתיב חימה אין לי ופריך והא כתיב כי יגורתי מפני האף והחימה ומשני תרי חימה הוו:

ושמואל אמר תמה זכות אבות ורבי יוחנן אמר תחון זכות אבות · אומר רבינו תם דזכות אבות תמה אבל ברית אבות לא תמה דהא כתיב (ויקרא כו) וזכרתי את בריתי יעקוב אף לאחר גלות ולכן אין אנו מזכירין זכות אבות אלא הברית °ומפרש דשמואל דאמר מימי חזאל דייק מדכתיב למען בריתו ולא למען זכותו ואומר ר"י דבויקרא רבה (פ' לו) דייק מעד עתה כדפי' בקונטרס ולר"י נראה דלא פליגי שמואל ור"י אלא שמואל קאמר דלרשעים תמה אבל לצדיקים לא תמה ובצדיקים איירי ר"י תדע דהא ר"י אמר בסמוך דמימי חזקי' תמה זכות אבות והכא קאמר דאף בשעת חורבן דבתר הכי תחון זכות אבות ועל זה אנו סומכין להזכיר זכות אבות ובשלהי ויקרא רבה רבי אחא אומר לעולם זכות אבות קיימת ולעולם אנו מזכירים אותם וכן הוא אומר כי אל רחום וגו' ולא ישכח את ברית אבותיך וגו':

אין מיתה בלא חטא · פי' (מיתה) לפי שהגזרה באה אף על השגגה ואין יסורים בלא עון של מזיד כדאמר ביומא (דף לו:) חטאים אלו השגגות עונות אלו הזדונות ואף על גב דאמר (שבועות דף ה:) גבי שעיר של יה"כ להגין עליו מן היסורים משמע דיסורים באים על שוגג הכא מיירי ביסורי נגעים שהן מטעדים כדמייתי קרא: ארבעה

[וע"ע תוס' ב"ב ס: ד"ה מוטב ובתוס' ע"ז ד. ד"ה שהיה בידם]:

רבינו חננאל

ד' סתו בעטיו של נחש כבר פירשנוהו:

רב נסים גאון

דאמר ר' חנינא חותמו של הקב"ה אמת· תמצא עיקר דברי ר' חנינא בפרק בא לו כהן גדול (דף סט) במס' יומא ובפ' ד' מיתות (דף סד) במס' סנהדרין ובתלמוד ארץ ישראל במסכת סנהדרין (כראש פ"א) אמרו בדבר זה טעם נאה ביותר ונראה לי לכתבה הנה והכי אמרו מהו חותמו של הקב"ה רב ביבי בשם ר' ראובן אמר אמת מהו אמת אמר ר' אבין שהוא אלהים חיים ומלך עולם אמר ר' שמעון בן לקיש אלף ראשה דאלפא ביתא מם באמצעיתה תיו בסופ' לומר (ישעי' מד) אני ה' ראשון שלא קבלתי מלכותי מאחר ומבלעדי אין אלהים שאין לי שותף ואת אחרונים אני הוא שאין אני עתיד למוסרה לאחר ואיתא נמי בבראשית [רבה] דר' אושעיא (פרשה פא):

גליון הש"ס

גמ' ר"י הוה יתיב. עי' ב"ב דף י ע"ב תוס' ד"ה עליונים: שם א"ל ר"ז לר' סימון לוכחינהו. עי' מדרש רבה איכה שני ד"ה ולא זכר הדום רגליו: שם אמר רב מימות הושע בן בארי · ירושלמי פרק חלק ושם איתא הך לימוד בשם שמואל: תוס' ד"ה מזבח נחושת וכו' שירה בכלי נחושת. עי' זבחים דף ס ע"א תוס' ד"ה ה"ק: שם ד"ה ושמואל וכו' ומפרש דשמואל דאמר מימי חזאל· אולם בירושלמי פ' חלק מסיים עד עתה עד אותה שעה הזכות קיימת והיינו כפי' רש"י:

מסורת הש"ס

משלי כא · ירמיה כא · [לקמן קנב. וש"נ ועי' מ"ש בתוס' חגיגה טו: על הגליון] · [זבחים נט:] · יחזקאל ט · [צ"ל אמרה] · שם · [ע"ז ד. ע"ב] · [שם] · יומא סט: סנהדרין סד. [צ"ל אמר אלו וכו'] · הושע ב · מלכים ב יג · מלכים א יח · ישעיה ט · יחזקאל יח · תהלים פט

מסורת הש"ס

מיתיבי אמרו מלאכי השרת לפני הקב"ה רבונו של עולם מפני מה קנסת מיתה על אדם הראשון אמר להם מצוה קלה צויתיו ועבר עליה א"ל והלא משה ואהרן שקיימו כל התורה כולה ומתו א"ל °מקרה אחד לצדיק ולרשע לטוב וגו' הוא דאמר כי האי תנא דתניא ר"ש בן אלעזר אומר אף משה ואהרן בחטאם מתו שנא' °יען לא האמנתם בי *הא האמנתם בי עדיין לא הגיע זמנכם ליפטר מן העולם מיתיבי °*ארבעה מתו בעטיו של נחש ואלו הן בנימין בן יעקב ועמרם אבי משה וישי אבי דוד וכלאב בן דוד וכולהו גמרא לבר מישי אבי דוד דמפרש ביה קרא דכתיב °ואת עמשא שם אבשלום תחת יואב (*שר) הצבא ועמשא בן איש ושמו יתרא הישראלי אשר בא אל אביגיל בת נחש אחות צרויה אם יואב וכי בת נחש הואי והלא בת ישי הואי דכתיב °ואחיותיהן צרויה ואביגיל אלא בת מי שמת בעטיו של נחש מני אילימא תנא דמלאכי השרת והא איכא משה ואהרן אלא לאו ר"ש בן אלעזר היא וש"מ יש מיתה בלא חטא ויש יסורין בלא עון ותיובתא דרב אמי °תיובתא: א"ר שמואל בר נחמני א"ר יונתן כל האומר ראובן חטא אינו אלא טועה שנאמר °ויהיו בני יעקב שנים עשר מלמד שכולן שקולים כאחת אלא מה אני מקיים °וישכב את בלהה פילגש אביו מלמד שבלבל מצעו של אביו ומעלה עליו הכתוב כאילו שכב עמה תניא ר"ש בן אלעזר אומר מוצל אותו צדיק מאותו עון ולא בא מעשה זה לידו אפשר עתיד זרעו לעמוד על הר עיבל ולומר °ארור שוכב עם אשת אביו ויבא חטא זה לידו אלא מה אני מקיים וישכב את בלהה פילגש אביו עלבון אמו תבע אמר אם אחות אמי היתה צרה לאמי שפחת אחות אמי תהא צרה לאמי עמד ובלבל את מצעה אחרים אומרים שתי מצעות בלבל אחת של שכינה ואחת של אביו והיינו דכתיב °אז חללת יצועי עלה (אל תקרי יצועי אלא יצועיי) כתנאי פחז כמים אל תותר ר' אליעזר אומר פזתה חבתה זלתה ר' יהושע אומר פסעתה על דת חטאת זנית ר"ג אומר פיללתה חלתה זרחה תפלתך אמר ר"ג עדיין צריכין אנו למודעי ר' אלעזר המודעי אומר הפוך את התיבה ודורשה *זעזעתה הרתעתה פרחה חטא ממך רבא אמר ואמרי לה ר' ירמיה בר אבא זכרת עונשו של דבר חלית עצמך חולי גדול פירשת מלחטוא: ראובן בני עלי שמואל דוד ושלמה ויואש* סימן: *אמר ר' שמואל בר נחמני א"ר יונתן כל האומר בני עלי חטאו אינו אלא טועה שנאמר °ושם שני בני עלי (עם ארון ברית האלהים) חפני ופנחס כהנים לה' סבר לה כרב דאמר רב פנחס לא חטא מקיש חפני לפנחס מה פנחס לא חטא אף חפני לא חטא אלא מה אני מקיים אשר ישכבון את הנשים מתוך ששהו את קיניהן שלא הלכו אצל בעליהן מעלה עליהן הכתוב כאילו שכבום גופא אמר רב פנחס לא חטא שנאמר °ואחיה בן אחיטוב אחי אי כבוד בן פנחס בן עלי כהן ה' וגו' אפשר חטא בא לידו והכתוב מייחסו והלא כבר נאמר °יכרת ה' לאיש אשר יעשנה ער ועונה מאהלי יעקב ומגיש מנחה לה' צבאות *אם ישראל הוא לא יהיה לו ער בחכמים ולא עונה בתלמידים ואם כהן הוא לא יהיה לו בן מגיש מנחה אלא לאו שמע מינה פנחס לא חטא אלא הא כתיב °אשר ישכבון *ישכבן כתיב והכתיב °אל בני כי לא טובה השמועה א"ר נחמן בר יצחק בני כתיב והכתיב מעבירים א"ר הונא בריה דרב יהושע מעבירם כתיב והכתיב בני בליעל מתוך שהיה לו לפנחס למחות לחפני ולא מיחה מעלה עליו הכתוב כאילו חטא א"ר שמואל בר נחמני א"ר יונתן כל האומר

בני

ארבעה מתו בעטיו של נחש · והא דכתיב (קהלת ז) כי אדם אין צדיק בארץ וגו' ברוב בני אדם קאמר: ש"מ יש מיתה בלא חטא ויש יסורים בלא עון · ואע"ג דבמאי דקאמר אין יסורין בלא עון לא איתותב: כל האומר בני עלי חטאו אינו אלא טועה · פירוש במאי דכתיב אשר ישכבון לא חטאו אלא מבזים קדשים היו כדכתיב (שמואל א ב) בטרם יקטירון החלב וגו': מעבירם כתיב · הש"ס שלנו חולק על ספרים שלנו שכתוב בהם (*מעבירים) וכן מצינו בירושלמי בשמשון והוא שפט את ישראל ארבעים שנה מלמד שהיו פלשתים יראים ממנו כ' שנה אחר מותו כמו בחייו °ובכל ספרים שלנו כתיב כ' שנה (שופטים טז): מתוך שהיה לו לפנחס למחות · ופליג אר"י יונתן דאמר שניהם לא חטאו:

שהיה

בעטיו של נחש · בעלתו של נחש שהשיא לחוה ולא בחטא אחר שלא חטאו · בעטיו כמו עטא וטעם (דניאל ב): ואחיותיהם · בבני ישי משתעי: אלא לאו ר"ש בן אלעזר · דאמר משה ואהרן בחטאם מתו ומודה בהני: כל האומר ראובן חטא · במעשה בלהה: דכתיב בההוא קרא: ויהיו בני יעקב וגו' · להוציא מלבך שלא תחשדו: ויבא חטא זה לידו · ויגזור הקב"ה שיהיו מן המקללים: אחת של שכינה · כך היה יעקב עושה בארבעה אהלי נשיו מעמיד מטה לשכינה ובאותו אהל שהוא רואה בו השכינה הוא בא ולן אותו הלילה: חללת · אותו שם שעלה על יצועי דהיינו שכינה מדלא כתיב יצועי עלית טעם אחר עד שלא נבנה אהל מועד היתה שכינה מצויה באהלי צדיקים: פחז · נוטריקון הוא: פזתה · לשון עמא פזיזא (לקמן דף פח·)· פזתה מיהרת בעצמך וחטאת: זלתה · זלזלת: פיללת · להגלל מן החטא: חלתה · *ויחל משה (שמות לב): זעזעת · יראת לחטוא לר' אליעזר ור' יהושע חטא ולרבן גמליאל ולמודעי בקש לחטוא ולא חטא: חלית · חולי גדול להתאפק לכבוש יצרך: כל האומר בני עלי חטאו · באשת איש אינו אלא טועה ומיהו בבזיון קדשים חטאו: דאמר רב · לקמן בשמעתין פנחס לא חטא ויליף לה מקרא ור' יונתן יליף לה לחפני מהאי קרא דמקיש חפני לפנחס: ששהו את קיניהן · שהיו מסרבין להקריב שום קרבן אלא בקושי כדכתיב (שמואל א ב) גם בטרם יקטירון את החלב וגו' וכשהיו זבות ויולדות באות ממקום אחר לשילה להקריב את קיניהן והן היו משהין מלהקריבם והנשים לא היו יכולין לסמוך עליהם שיקריבו והיו שוהות שם ולא היו חוזרות אצל בעליהן עד שראו קיניהן קרבין והיו טהורות לקדשים וליכנס לעזרה לפיכך מעלה עליהם כאילו שכבום שהיו מונעים אותן מפריה ורביה: פנחס לא חטא · באשת איש דאשר ישכבון את הנשים אינו אלא חפני לבדו: ואחיה בן אחיטוב וגו' כהן ה' · בשילה נושא אפוד הרי שמיחסו לשבח ומזכיר עליו שם פנחס אבי אביו: אפשר בא חטא לידו והכתוב מייחסו · לשבח ואת בן בנו מייחסו אחריו והכתיב גבי עבירה דטופפים יכרת ה' לאיש וגו' והאי קרא בבא על הנכרית ועל הזונה משתעי כדדרשינן ליה באלו הן הנשרפין *דכתיב לעיל מיניה כי חלל יהודה קדש ה' אשר אהב ובעל בת אל נכר ודרשינן כי חלל יהודה קדש זו זונה וכן הוא אומר לא תהיה קדשה וגו': ער · חריף להבין ולהורות בין החכמים כדאמרי' בעירובין (דף נג:) אהרנית ערנית: ואם כהן הוא ט' · וכאן מייחס כהן מגיש מנחה אחר פנחס: והכתיב אל בני כי לא טובה השמועה אשר אנכי שומע מעבירים עם ה' אביהם היה מוכיחם: והא כתיב מעבירים אמר *רב הונא בריה דרב יהושע מעבירם כתיב · קשה בעיני שם החכם הנזכר כאן כי תומר אני · שטעות גדול הוא ול"נ לה להא מילתא שהרי בספרים מוגהים כתיב מעבירים וגם במסורה הגדולה במקום שמעיין שם כל התיבות דלא כתיב בהן יו"ד וקורין ולא נמנה זה והם מעיין ע"פ החשבון וזו אינה קשיא דהאי מעבירים לאו לשון עבירה הוא אלא לשון ויעבירו קול במחנה (שמות לו) וה"ק להו לא טובה השמועה אשר אנכי שומע את עם ה' מעבירים ומכריזין וקובלים עליכם והאי מעבירים לשון רבים הוא ואעם ה' קאי ולאו אבני עלי שהרי הם היו עוברים ולא היו מעבירים את אחרים:

בני

תורה אור: קהלת ט · במדבר כ · שמואל ב יז · ד"ה א ב · בראשית לה · שם · דברים כז · בראשית מט · ש"א ב · ש"א יד · מלאכי ב · ש"א ב · שם

[נ"ל מעברים] · [יומא סו.] · ב"ב יז. · [נ"ל כמו ויחל משה] · [נ"ל על] · רש"ל מ"ז ועי' רש"י · לשון רמה · נ"ל ויאשרו · יומא ט. · סנהדרין פב. [פג.] · [עי' תוספות סנהדרין ד. ד"ה ולכן] · מהרש"א גורס רבנא

גליון הש"ס

גמ' ד' מתו בעטיו של נחש כו' · בזוה"ק פ' בראשית ועל דא יהושע לא מת אלא בעטיו דנחש וכו' ובזוה"ק פ' בראשית בפסוק וינחם ה' תלתא דאיסתלקו בגין ההוא עטיא דנחש עמרם לוי בנימין ואית דאמרי אף ישי: שם תיובתא · עי' ברא"מ פ' וישלח ד"ה אומרא וכפ' שופטים ד"ה ריה"ג: תום' ד"ה מעבירם כתיב וכו' ובכל ספרים שלנו . וכן מצינו בנדה דף לג ע"א תוס' ד"ה והנושא שכתבו דהמסורת שלנו מחולק עם הש"ס . ובמגילה דף כב ע"א כתבו תוס' דויחל הוא ג' פסוקים סמוך לפרשה שלפניו וכן והקרבתם ובס"ת שלנו ויחל הוא ד' פסוקים מהפרשה וכן והקרבתם ג"פ וכמ"ש מהרש"א שם ובפסחים דף קיז ע"א בתוס' ד"ה שעומדים כתבו שלא יתכן שיהיה מזמור ב' פסוקים ואלו בספרים שלנו מזמור קיז הוא ב' פסוקים . ע' מהרש"א שם ע"א ובסנהדרין דף ד ע"א פירש"י שם דבכבשה דיחיד כתיב קרנות מלא ובס"ת שלנו כתיב חסר . ובדף ד ע"א כ' רש"י דבפרשה והיה כי יביאך כתיב לטטפת חסר ובפ' והיה אם שמע כתיב מלא . ובס"ת שלנו גם בפ' והיה כי יביאך כתיב מלא . ובדף כ ע"א כתי' להכרית וקרי להכרו' ובספרים שלנו גם הכתיב להכרות . עוד שם דף קא ע"א . ויעתר לו ויעתר לו מיבעיא ליה . ובספרים שלנו כתיב ויעתר. ובב"ב דף ט ע"א שלא פרוש בשין ובספרים שלנו כתיב בסין . ועי' במ"א שם במהרש"א . ובקדושין דף ל ע"א . והתגלח תליין של פסוקי' ובתיקונים בפ' ט בפסוק ויאפוד לו בו ליין דשם חצי התורה בפסוקים . ובירושלמי שהביא תוס' בכתובות דף ז ע"ב דבמקהלת ברכו אלהים חסר . ובספרים שלנו כתיב מלא . ובפרש"י בחומש פ' תרומה ואת כל אשר אצוה שוה ו"ו יתירה ולפנינו כתיב את בלא ו'. עי' ברא"ם שם· ובמדרש רבה שיר השירים בפסוק אחזו לנו שועלים שעלים א"ר ברכיה קדמאה מלא תניינא חסר . ובמסורה אינו כן אלא תרוייהו חסר . ובברכות דף ז ע"ב כתי' לבלותו ובספרי' שלנו כד"ה א יז כתיב לבלותו . (ובפסחים דף ג ע"א ו' דטהור . ובספרים שלנו כתיב טהר חסר ו') . ובנדרים דף לז ע"ב את דהוגד הוגד קרי ולא כתיב . ובספרים שלנו הוא קרי וכתיב כמ"ש הר"ן שם ; ובפסוק אני ה' אלהיך אשר הוצאתיך איתא בירושלמי פ"ס דסוכה דחסר י' . ובספרים שלפנינו הוא מלא יו"ד . ובמדרש ויקרא רבה פ' ט' ושם דרך . א"ר ינאי ושם כתיב ובספרים שלנו כתיב בסין . ובפירש"י בחומש בראשית כ"ד כפילגשים חסר כתיב ובכל הספרים איתא מלא . ובמדרש בראשית רבה פרשה ע"ו ר"ל אמר הנתרת כתיב ובכל הספרים שלנו כתיב הנותרת . ובערוכין דף לב ע"א בתוספת ד"ה אשר דרש"י כ' דהכתיב ויקרא כ"ה אשר לוא חומה והם כתבו דהכתיב אשר לו וקרי לא ובספרים שלנו שכתיב לא באל"ף והקרי לו כמ"ש התי"ט שם:

[55*b*] An objection is raised: The ministering angels asked the Holy One, blessed be He: 'Sovereign of the Universe! Why didst Thou impose the penalty of death upon Adam?' Said He to them, I gave him an easy command, yet he violated it.' 'But Moses and Aaron fulfilled the whole Torah,' they pursued, 'yet they died'. '*There is one event to the righteous and to the wicked; to the good*, etc.,[8] He replied.[9]—He maintains as the following Tanna. For it was taught: R. Simeon b. Eleazar said: Moses and Aaron too died through their sin, for it is said, *Because ye believed not in Me* [... *therefore ye shall not bring this assembly into the land which I have given*
a *them*]:[1] hence, had ye believed in Me, your time had not yet come to depart from the world.[2]

An objection is raised: Four died through the serpent's machinations,[3] viz., Benjamin the son of Jacob, Amram the father of Moses, Jesse the father of David, and Caleb the son of David. Now, all are known by tradition, save Jesse the father of David, in whose case the Writ gives an explicit intimation. For it is written, *And Absalom set Amasa over the host instead of Joab. Now Amasa was the son of a man whose name was Ithra the Israelite, that went in to Abigail the daughter of Nahash, sister to Zeruiah Joab's mother.*[4] Now, was she the daughter of Nahash? Surely she was the daughter of Jesse, for it is written, *and their sisters were Zeruiah and Abigail?*[5] Hence it must mean, the daughter of one who died through the machinations of the *naḥash* [serpent].[6] Who is [the author of this]? Shall we say, the Tanna [who taught] about the ministering angels?—Surely there were Moses and Aaron too! Hence it must surely be R. Simeon b. Eleazar, which proves that there is death without sin and suffering without iniquity. Thus the refutation of R. Ammi is [indeed] a refutation.

R. Samuel b. Naḥman said in R. Jonathan's name: Whoever maintains that Reuben sinned is merely making an error, for it is said, *Now the sons of Jacob were twelve*,[7] teaching that they were all equal.[8] Then how do I interpret, *and he lay with Bilhah his father's concubine?*[9] This teaches that he transposed his father's couch,[10] and the Writ imputes [blame] to him as though he had lain with her. It was taught, R. Simeon b. Eleazar said: That righteous man
b was saved from that sin and that deed did not come to his hand.[1] Is it possible that his seed was destined to stand on Mount Ebal and proclaim, *Cursed be he that lieth with his father's wife*,[2] yet this sin should come to his hand? But how do I interpret, '*and he lay with Bilhah his father's concubine*'? He resented his mother's humiliation. Said he, If my mother's sister was a rival to my mother, shall the bondmaid of my mother's sister be a rival to my mother? [Thereupon] he arose and transposed her couch. Others say, He transposed two couches, one of the *Shechinah* and the other of his father.[3] Thus it is written, *Then thou defiledst*, my couch on which [the *Shechinah*] went up.[4]

This is dependent on Tannaim. *Unstable* [PaḤaZ] *as water, thou shalt not excel:*[5] R. Eliezer interpreted: Thou wast hasty [*Paztah*], thou wast guilty [*Ḥabtah*], thou didst disgrace [*Zaltah*]. R. Joshua interpreted: Thou didst overstep [*Pasatah*] the law, thou didst sin [*Ḥaṭatha*], thou didst fornicate [*Zanitha*]. R. Gamaliel interpreted: Thou didst meditate [*Pillaltah*],[6] thou didst supplicate [*Ḥaltah*], thy prayer shone forth [*Zarḥah*]. Said R. Gamaliel, We still need [the interpretation of] the Modiite. R. Eleazar the Modiite[7] said, Reverse the word and interpret it: Thou didst tremble [*Zi'az'atha*], thou didst recoil [*Hirt'atah*], thy sin fled [*Parḥah*] from thee.[8] Raba—others state, R. Jeremiah b. Abba—interpreted: Thou didst remember [*Zakarta*] the penalty of the crime, thou wast [grievously] sick [*Ḥalitha*],[9] thou heldest aloof [*Pirashta*] from sinning.

(Mnemonic: Reuben, the sons of Eli, the sons of Samuel, David,
c Solomon, and Josiah.)[1] R. Samuel b. Naḥmani said in R. Jonathan's name: Whoever maintains that the sons of Eli sinned is merely making an error, for it is said, *And the two sons of Eli, Hophni and Phinehas, priests unto the Lord, were there.*[2] Now he agrees with Rab, who said, Phinehas did not sin. [Hence] Hophni is likened to Phinehas: just as Phinehas did not sin, so did Hophni not sin. Then how do I interpret, *and how that they* [*sc.* Eli's sons] *lay with the women?*[3] Because they delayed their bird-offerings[4] so that they did not go to their husbands,[5] the Writ stigmatizes them as though they had lain with them.

It was stated above, 'Rab said, Phinehas did not sin,' for it is said, *and Ahijah, the son of Ahitub, Ichabod's brother, the son of Phinehas, the son of Eli, the priest of the Lord*, etc.[6] Now, is it possible that sin had come to his hand, yet the Writ states his descent? Surely it is said, *The Lord will cut off to the man that doeth this, him that waketh* ['er] *and him that answereth, out of the tents of Jacob, and him that offereth an offering unto the Lord of hosts:*[7] [this means:] if an Israelite,[8] he shall have none awakening [i.e., teaching] among the Sages and none responding among the disciples; if a priest, he shall have no son to offer an offering? Hence it follows that Phinehas did not sin. But it is written, '*how that they lay* [etc.']?—'He *lay*' is written.[9] But it is written, *Nay, my sons*; *for it is no good report that I hear?*[10]—Said R. Naḥman b. Isaac: *My son* is written.[11] But it is written, ye *make* [*the Lord's people*] *to transgress?*[12]—Said R. Huna son of R. Joshua, It is written, he *causes them to transgess.*[13] But it is written, sons *of Belial?*[14]—Because Phinehas should have protested to Hophni but did not, the Writ regards him as though he [too] sinned.

R. Samuel b. Naḥmani said in R. Jonathan's name: Whoever

(8) Eccl. IX, 2. (9) Showing that death may come without sin.
a (1) Num. XX, 12. (2) On the view that they died sinless, this deduction is made: but had ye believed, you would have led the assembly into the land, etc. The punishment therefore was that they would not lead, not that they should die, which would have been disproportionate to their fault (Maharsha). (3) I.e., because the serpent caused Adam and Eve to sin, but not on account of their own sin.—This is not to be confused with the doctrine of Original sin, which is rejected by Judaism, v. B.B., 17*a*, n. a11. (4) II Sam. XVII, 25. (5) I Chron. II, 16. 'Their sisters' refers to the sons of Jesse; v. preceding verse. (6) It may be observed that the Talmud calls this an explicit intimation. (7) Gen. XXXV, 22. (8) Lit., 'balanced as one'—they were all equal in righteousness. (9) Ibid. (10) Placing it in Leah's tent; v. *infra*.
b (1) He did not even have the opportunity. (2) Deut. XXVII; 20; v. 13. (3) Rashi: Jacob set a couch for the *Shechinah* in the tents of each of his wives, and where the *Shechinah* came to rest, there he spent the night. (4) Gen. XLIX, 4. This translation is based on the change of person from second (*defiledst*) to third (*went*), which implies a different subject for '*went*'. (5) Ibid. (6) To be saved from sin. (7) Of Modim, some fifteen miles north of Jerusalem. (8) All treat the word *PaḤaZ* (E.V. *unstable*) as a mnemonic, each letter indicating a word. Thus R. Eliezer and R. Joshua maintain that he sinned, while the others hold that his nobler feelings triumphed. (9) Through defying his lust.
c (1) V. *supra* 32*b*, n. b6. (2) I Sam. I, 3. (3) Ibid. II, 22. (4) After childbirth; v. Lev. XII, 6-8. (5) They had to wait in Shiloh until their birds were sacrificed. (6) Ibid. XIV, 3. (7) Mal. II, 12. (8) I.e., not a priest. (9) [ישכבן, defectively, and to be treated as 3rd. person singular; cf. Arabic ending in *ăn*]. (10) I Sam. II, 24. (11) The sing. and the plural are the same in Heb. He must mean that the earlier traditional reading was *my son*. (12) Ibid. (13) [מעבירם: M.T. has מעבירים, but in a number of places the Talmud version differs from ours. V. Tosaf. and Marginal Gloss]. (14) Ibid. 12.

maintains [56*a*] that Samuel's sons sinned is merely erring. For it is said, *And it came to pass when Samuel was old . . . that his sons* a *walked not in his ways:*[1] thus, they [merely] walked not in his ways, yet they did not sin either. Then how do I fulfil, '*they turned aside for lucre*'?[2] That means that they did not act like their father. For Samuel the righteous used to travel to all the places of Israel and judge them in their towns, as it is said, *And he went from year to year in circuit to Beth-el, and Gilgal, and Mizpah; and he judged Israel.*[3] But they did not act thus, but sat in their own towns, in order to increase the fees of their beadles[4] and scribes.[5]

This is a controversy of Tannaim: '*They turned aside for lucre*': R. Meir said, [That means,] They openly demanded their portions.[6] R. Judah said: They forced[7] goods on private people. R. Akiba said: They took an extra basket of tithes by force. R. Jose said: They took the gifts by force.[8]

R. Samuel b. Naḥmani said in R. Jonathan's name: Whoever says that David sinned is merely erring, for it is said, *And David behaved himself wisely in all his ways: and the Lord was with him.*[9] Is it possible that sin came to his hand, yet the Divine Presence was with him? Then how do I interpret, *Wherefore hast thou despised the word of the Lord, to do that which is evil in His sight?*[10] He wished to do [evil], but did not. Rab observed: Rabbi, who is descended from David, seeks to defend him, and expounds [the verse] in David's favour. [Thus:] The '*evil*' [mentioned] here is unlike every other '*evil*' [mentioned] elsewhere in the Torah. For of every other *evil* [mentioned] in the Torah it is written, '*and he did,*' whereas here it is written, '*to do*': [this means] that he desired to do, b but did not. *Thou hast smitten Uriah the Hittite with the sword:*[1] thou shouldst have had him tried by the Sanhedrin,[2] but didst not. *And hast taken his wife to be thy wife:* thou hast marriage rights in her.[3] For R. Samuel b. Naḥmani said in R. Jonathan's name: Every one who went out in the wars of the house of David wrote a bill of divorcement for his wife, for it is said, *and bring these ten cheeses unto the captain of their thousand, and look how thy brethren fare, and take their pledge* ['arubatham].[4] What is meant by '*arubatham?*' R. Joseph learned: The things which pledge man and woman [to one another].[5] *And thou hast slain him with the sword of the children of Ammon:*[1] just as thou art not [to be] punished for the sword of the Ammonites, so art thou not [to be] punished for [the death of] Uriah the Hittite. What is the reason? He was rebellious against royal authority, saying to him, *and my lord Joab, and the servants of my lord, are encamped in the open field* [etc].[6]

Rab said: When you examine [the life of] David, you find nought but '*save only in the matter of Uriah the Hittite.*'[7] Abaye the Elder pointed out a contradiction in Rab['s dicta]: Did Rab say thus? Surely Rab said, David paid heed to slander? The difficulty remains.

[To revert to] the main text: 'Rab said, David paid heed to slander,' for it is written, *And the king said unto him, where is he? And Ziba said unto the king, Behold, he is in the house of Machir the son of* c *Ammiel,* belo dabar [*in Lo-debar*].[1] And it is written, *Then David sent, and fetched him out of the house of Machir the son of Ammiel,* millo dabar [*from Lo-debar*].[2] Now consider: he [David] saw that he [Ziba] was a liar; then when he slandered him a second time, why did he pay heed thereto? For it is written, *And the king said, And where is thy master's son? And Ziba said unto the king, Behold, he abideth at Jerusalem* [*: for he said, To-day shall the house of Israel restore me the kingdom of my father*].[3] And how do we know that he accepted it [the slander] from him? Because it is written, *Then said the king to Ziba, Behold, thine is all that pertaineth unto Mephibosheth. And Ziba said, I do obeisance; let me find favour in thy sight, my lord, O king.*[4]

But Samuel maintained: David did not pay heed to slander, [for] he saw self-evident things in him,[5] For it is written, *And Mephibosheth the son of Saul came down to meet the king; and he had neither dressed his feet, nor trimmed his beard, nor washed his clothes,* etc.[6] While it is written, *And it came to pass, when he was come to Jerusalem to meet the king, that the king said unto him, Wherefore wentest thou not with me, Mephibosheth? And he answered, my lord, O king, my servant deceived me: for thy servant said, I will saddle me an ass, that I may ride thereon, and go with the king, because thy servant is lame,*

a (1) I Sam. VIII, 1, 3. (2) Ibid. (3) Ibid. VII, 16. (4) Who are sent to summon the litigants. On *ḥazzan* v. *supra* 11*a*, n. b7. (5) Who record the pleas, arguments, verdicts, etc. (6) They were Levites, and personally demanded the tithes. Owing to their exalted position their demands were acceded to, while the humbler Levites might starve. But they did not actually pervert judgment. —R. Meir's interpretation may have been called forth by the troublous times before the overthrow of the Jewish state, when many High Priests abused their positions by such extortion; v. Halevi, *Doroth* I, 5, pp. 4 *seq*. (7) They compelled people to be their business agents. (8) Either the priestly dues, viz., the shoulder, cheeks, and maw of animals, though they were not priests; or the Levitical dues, *sc.* the first tithes, their sin being that they used force. (9) Ibid. XVIII, 14. (10) II Sam. XII, 9.

b (1) II Sam. XII, 9. (2) The great court; v. Sanh. 2*a*. (3) *Lakaḥ*, the verb employed here, denotes marriage; cf. Deut. XXIV, 1. (4) I Sam. XVII, 18. (5) Lit., 'him and her', *sc.* the marriage. I.e., take away their marriage—cancel it by means of a divorce.—The divorce was conditional, in the sense that it became retrospectively valid if the husband died. Thus, since Uriah died, she was a free woman from the time he went out, and was not married when David took her. (6) II Sam. XI, 11. Thus he disobeyed David's order to go home. (7) I Kings XV, 5. Rashi: his only sin lay in encompassing Uriah's death, but not in taking Bathsheba (as explained above). From the context, however, it appears that Rab does not exculpate him from adultery with Bathsheba, but means that David was guilty of no other sin save that in connection with Uriah, which naturally includes his behaviour with Bathsheba. On that view Rab rejects Rabbi's exegesis (That too appears from Rab's prefacing remark: 'Rabbi who is descended, etc.').

c (1) II Sam. IX, 4. (2) Ibid. 5. Maharsha: *belo dabar* is translated: He (Mephibosheth son of Jonathan and grandson of Saul) has words, i.e., makes unloyal accusations against you. But David found that he was *millo dabar*, i.e., he had not made such accusations. Thus Ziba's charges were unfounded. This explains the Gemara that follows. (3) Ibid. XVI, 3. (4) Ibid. 4. (5) Which substantiated Ziba's charges. Thus it was not a mere acceptance of slander. (6) Ibid. XIX, 24.

תורה אור

בני שמואל חטאו אינו אלא טועה שנאמר °ויהי (*כי זקן שמואל ובניו לא הלכו) בדרכיו בדרכיו הוא דלא הלכו מיחטא נמי לא חטאו אלא מה אני מקיים °ויטו אחרי הבצע שלא עשו כמעשה אביהם שהיה שמואל הצדיק מחזר בכל מקומות ישראל ודן אותם בעריהם שנאמר °והלך מדי שנה בשנה וסבב בית אל והגלגל והמצפה ושפט את ישראל והם לא עשו כן אלא ישבו בעריהם *כדי להרבות שכר לחזניהן ולסופריהן כתנאי *ויטו אחרי הבצע ר' מאיר אומר חלקם שאלו בפיהם רבי יהודה אומר מלאי הטילו על בעלי בתים ר' עקיבא אומר קופה יתירה של מעשר נטלו בזרוע ר' יוסי אומר מתנות נטלו בזרוע: א"ר שמואל בר נחמני אמר ר' יונתן כל האומר דוד חטא אינו אלא טועה שנאמר °ויהי דוד לכל דרכיו משכיל וה' עמו וגו' אפשר חטא בא לידו ושכינה עמו אלא מה אני מקיים °מדוע בזית את דבר ה' לעשות הרע שביקש לעשות ולא עשה אמר רב רבי דאתי מדוד מהפך ודריש בזכותיה דדוד מדוע בזית את דבר ה' לעשות הרע רבי אומר משונה רעה זו מכל רעות שבתורה שכל רעות שבתורה כתיב בהו ויעש וכאן כתיב לעשות שביקש לעשות ולא עשה °את אוריה החתי הכית בחרב °שהיה לך לדונו בסנהדרין ולא דנת ואת אשתו לקחת לך לאשה ליקוחין יש לך בה *דא"ר שמואל בר נחמני א"ר יונתן כל היוצא למלחמת בית דוד כותב גט כריתות לאשתו שנאמר °ואת עשרת חריצי החלב האלה תביא לשר האלף ואת אחיך תפקוד לשלום ואת ערובתם תקח מאי ערובתם תני רב יוסף דברים המעורבים בינו לבינה °ואותו הרגת בחרב בני עמון *מה חרב בני עמון אי אתה נענש עליו אף אוריה החתי אי אתה נענש עליו מאי טעמא מורד במלכות הוה דאמר ליה °ואדוני יואב ועבדי אדוני על פני השדה חונים אמר רב כי מעיינת ביה בדוד לא משכחת ביה בר מדאוריה דכתיב (א) °רק בדבר אוריה החתי אביי קשישא רמי דרב אדרב מי אמר רב הכי *והאמר רב קיבל דוד לשון הרע קשיא גופא רב אמר קיבל דוד לשון הרע דכתיב °ויאמר לו המלך איפוא הוא ויאמר ציבא אל המלך הנה הוא בית מכיר בן עמיאל *(בלא) דבר וכתיב וישלח המלך ויקחהו מבית מכיר בן עמיאל *(מלא) דבר מכדי חזייה דשקרא הוא כי הדר אלשין עילויה מ"ט קיבלה מיניה דכתיב °ויאמר המלך *(אל ציבא איה) בן אדוניך ויאמר ציבא אל המלך הנה (הוא) יושב בירושלים וגו' ומנא לן דקיבל מיניה דכתיב °ויאמר המלך הנה לך כל אשר למפיבשת ויאמר ציבא השתחויתי אמצא חן *(בעיני) המלך ושמואל אמר לא קיבל דוד לשון הרע דברים הניכרים חזא ביה דכתיב °ומפיבשת בן שאול ירד *(לפני) המלך לא עשה רגליו ולא עשה שפמו ואת בגדיו לא כיבס וגו' וכתיב ויהי כי בא ירושלים לקראת המלך ויאמר לו המלך למה לא הלכת עמי מפיבשת ויאמר אדוני המלך עבדי רמני כי אמר עבדך אחבשה לי החמור וארכב עליה ואלך את המלך כי פסח עבדך

רש"י

בני שמואל חטאו. במקח שוחד והטיית דין: לחזניהם. שמשיהם שסוכרין אותן לילך ולהזמין את הנקראים לדין: ולסופריהם. לשטרי בירורין ולאגרות שום: מלאי הטילו על בעלי בתים. עותנים להן פרגמטיא לעסוק בה ולתת להם השכר ומתוך כך היה נמשך לבם להטות דין כשבאין לפניהם לדון והיינו חטאם: חלקם שאלו בפיהם. מעשר ראשון הראוי להם שלוים היו שאלו בפיהם מתוך שהיו גדולי הדור ושופטים לא היו מונעים מהם ובאר לוים עניים מלטערים ולר' מאיר לא חטאו בהטיית משפט: קופה יתירה. יותר מן הראוי: מתנות. זרוע לחיים וקיבה והם לא היו כהנים ל"א מתנות לויה כגון מעשר וקרא כתיב ונתן לכהן ודרשינן ולא שיטול מעצמו בשחיטת חולין בפ' הזרוע (דף קלג.) וה"ה לכל מתנות כהונה ולויה: דוד חטא. בבת שבע קודם שקבלה גט: שבקש. לשכב עמה קודם שקבלה גט שהיה בעלה שולח לה מן המלחמה שאם ימות לא תיזקק ליבום או שמא יהרג ואין מעיד עליו ותתעגן אשתו או שמא יהא שבוי כדאמרינן לקמן כל היוצא למלחמת בית דוד כו': משונה רעה זו. בכתיבתה ובלשונה: שהיה לך לדונו. על שמורד במלכות כדלקמן: ליקוחין יש לך בה. קדושין תופסין בה שאינה אשת איש כדשמואל כו': גט כריתות. על תנאי שאם ימות תהא מגורשת מעכשיו ופעמים שהוא טרוד באשתו ושולחו מן המלחמה: ואת ערובתם תקח. במלחמת שאול כתיב: דברים המעורבים ביניהם. הייתו קדושין תקח תבטל ע"י גט שתביא להם מן המלחמה: בחרב בני עמון. כאותן שהורגים בני עמון שלא מדעתך: ואדוני יואב. לאו אורח ארעא לקבל עליו מרות אחרים בפני המלך: רק בדבר אוריה. מקרא כתיב כך בדבר אוריה שגרם לו שיהרג אבל בבת שבע לא חטא: לשון הרע. לקמיה מפרש: בלא דבר. אינו חכם בתורה והוא מלאו מלא דבר וחכם בתורה: חזייה דשקרא הוה. מתחילה מלאו שקרן בכך: כי הדר אלשין עליה. ליבא על מפיבשת כשהיה דוד בורח מפני אבשלום מאי טעמא קביל מיניה: איה בן אדוניך ויאמר הנה יושב בירושלים. כי אמר היום ישיבו לי את ממלכת אבי: דברים הניכרים חזא ביה. במפיבשת כשנהרג אבשלום וחזר דוד למלכותו ובא לפניו לא עשה רגליו ולא עשה שפמו כסבור דוד שניכרים דברי ליבא שנלטער על שחזר דוד ולא קישט עצמו *ועוד היה מלפה שכשיושיבוהו במלכות יתגאה ויתכפר לכך לא קבל דבריו ואמר לו אתה וליבא תחלקו השדה והוא השיבו קשה אין לי לצעוק אלא על מי שהביאך בשלום הנה שמלטער על שובו והם לא שראה בו דברים הניכרים היה חוזר ממה שאמר הנה לך כל אשר למפיבשת ואע"פ שמיהר ואמר לו מתחלה הנה לך כל אשר למפיבשת אין זו קבלה כי כל זמן שלא היה דוד שב למלכותו יודע היה שאין מתנתו מתנה ולא אמר לו אלא על תנאי אם יראה אמת בדבריו:

תוספות

שהיה לך לדונו בסנהדרין. קשה לר"י דפ"ק דמגילה (דף יד: ושם) אמרינן גבי נבל דמורד במלכות לא בעי למדייניה ואוריה מורד במלכות הוה כדאמר בסמוך ויש לומר דודאי לריך לדונו ולידע אם הוא מורד במלכות אבל לעיין בדינו ולעשות הלנת דין ולהמתין עד למחר אין לריך וכן משמע דבסנהדרין (דף לו. ושם) אמר שדן דוד את נבל בסנהדרין מויחגרו איש חרבו וגו':

ליקוחין יש לך בה. אף על גב דאפילו אשת כמי יש לו בה ליקוחין דהא אנוסה היתה ושריא לבעל וה"ה לבועל מ"מ ליקוחין יש לך בה משמע לא היה לך בה עבירה:

גט כריתות כותב לאשתו. פרש"י על תנאי שאם ימות במלחמה תהא מגורשת מעכשיו ולריך לומר לפירושו דאף על גב דאוריה בא מן המלחמה התנאי היה שאם לא ישוב בסוף המלחמה שיהא גט אך קשה דתנן במי שאחזו (גיטין דף עג. ושם) מה היא באותן הימים רבי יהודה אומר הרי היא כאשת איש לכל דבריה והם כן לר' יהודה היתה אשת איש גמורה ונראה לר"ת שהיה מגרשה לגמרי בלא שום תנאי והא דאמרינן בהזהב (ב"מ דף נט. ושם) מוטב שיבעול אדם ספק אשת איש ואל ילבין פני חבירו ברבים מנלן מדוד קרי לה ספק אשת איש לפי שהיו מגרשים בלנעה והעולם סבורים שהיא אשת איש:

דאמר ליה ואדוני יואב. פרש"י דמורד במלכות הוה משום דקאמר ואדוני יואב °ואין נראה דאין זה מורד שלא היה בלבו להמליכו ולקרותו מלך אלא כמו שפירש רבינו מאיר דהוי מורד משום דבסיפא דקרא כתיב ואני אבא אל ביתי לאכול ולשתות ולשכב עם אשתי וגו' שדוד אמר לו לעשות ולא רצה לעשות:

רק בדבר אוריה החתי. קשה דהא איכא מעשה דהסתה בריש פ"ב דיומא (דף כב:) וי"ל דלא חשיב ליה דלא הוי כל כך עון גדול וגם שגג: אלא

על

עין משפט נר מצוה
מ א מיי' פכ"ג מהל' סנהדרין הלכה ג סמג לאוין רח טוש"ע ח"מ סי' ט סעיף ד:
מא ב מיי' פ"ג מהל' מלכים הלכה ח:

גליון הש"ס
גמ' שהיה לך לדונו בסנהדרין עי' מגילה דף יד ע"ב תוס' ד"ה מורד במלכות: תוס' ד"ה דאמר ליה וכו' ואין נראה. עיין יומא דף סו ע"ב תוס' ד"ה מהו לסגיל:

[נ"ל מלו וע' במהרש"א]
[נ"ל בעיניך אדוני]
[נ"ל לקראת]

מסורת הש"ס
[צ"ל כאשר זקן שמואל ולא הלכו בניו]
[חולין קלג. הוספ' סוטה פי"ד]
כתובות ט:
קידושין מג.
יומא כב:
[צ"ל בלו]
[צ"ל ואיה]
רש"י מפ' דעת אמיתית של מפיבושת דהא דלא קישט היינו משום שעוד היה מלפה שכשיושיבו לדוד במלכות יתגאה [כ"מ] ורש"ל גרס ועד עתה הי' מלפה:

הגהות הב"ח
(א) גמ' לא משכחת ביה רק בדבר אוריה כצ"ל ותיבת בר מדאורי' דכתי' נמחק:

עבדך וירגל בעבדך אל ארוני המלך ואדוני המלך כמלאך האלהים ועשה הטוב בעיניך ויאמר לו המלך למה תדבר עוד דבריך אמרתי אתה וציבא תחלקו את השדה ויאמר מפיבשת אל המלך גם את הכל יקח אחרי אשר בא אדוני המלך בשלום אל ביתו אמר לו אני אמרתי מתי תבא בשלום ואתה עושה לי כך לא עליך יש לי הרעומות אלא על מי שהביאך בשלום היינו דכתיב °ובן יהונתן מריב בעל וכי מריב בעל שמו והלא מפיבשת שמו אלא מתוך שעשה מריבה עם בעליו יצתה בת קול ואמרה לו נצא בר נצא נצא הא דאמרן בר נצא דכתיב °ויבא שאול עד עיר עמלק וירב בנחל אמר רבי מני על עסקי נחל *אמר רב יהודה אמר רב בשעה שאמר דוד למפיבשת אתה וציבא תחלקו את השדה יצתה בת קול ואמרה לו רחבעם וירבעם יחלקו את המלוכה אמר רב יהודה אמר רב אילמלי *לא קיבל דוד לשון הרע לא נחלקה מלכות בית דוד ולא עבדו ישראל ע"ז ולא גלינו מארצנו: אמר ר' שמואל בר נחמני א"ר יונתן כל האומר שלמה חטא אינו אלא טועה שנאמר °ולא היה לבבו שלם עם ה' אלהיו כלבב דוד אביו כלבב דוד אביו הוא דלא הוה מיחטא נמי לא חטא אלא מה אני מקיים °ויהי לעת זקנת שלמה נשיו הטו את לבבו ההיא כרבי נתן דר' נתן רמי כתיב ויהי לעת זקנת שלמה נשיו הטו את לבבו והכתיב כלבב דוד אביו כלבב דוד אביו הוא דלא הוה מיחטא נמי לא חטא הכי קאמר ויהי לעת זקנת שלמה נשיו הטו את לבבו ללכת אחרי אלהים אחרים ולא הלך והכתיב °אז יבנה שלמה במה לכמוש שקוץ מואב שבקש לבנות ולא בנה אלא מעתה °אז יבנה יהושע מזבח לה' שבקש לבנות ולא בנה אלא דבנה הכא נמי דבנה אלא כדתניא רבי יוסי אומר °ואת הבמות אשר על פני ירושלים אשר מימין להר *המשחה אשר בנה שלמה מלך ישראל לעשתרות שקוץ צדונים וגו' *אפשר בא אסא ולא ביערם יהושפט ולא ביערם עד שבא יאשיה וביערם והלא כל ע"ז שבארץ ישראל אסא ויהושפט ביערום אלא מקיש ראשונים לאחרונים מה אחרונים לא עשו ותלה בהן לשבח אף ראשונים לא עשו ותלה בהן לגנאי והכתיב °ויעש שלמה הרע בעיני ה' אלא מפני שהיה לו למחות בנשיו ולא מיחה מעלה עליו הכתוב כאילו חטא אמר רב יהודה אמר שמואל נוח לו לאותו צדיק שיהא שמש לדבר אחר ואל יכתב בו ויעש הרע בעיני ה' *אמר רב יהודה אמר שמואל בשעה שנשא שלמה את בת פרעה הכניסה לו אלף מיני זמר ואמרה לו כך עושין לעבודה זרה פלונית וכך עושים לע"ז פלונית ולא מיחה בה *אמר רב יהודה אמר שמואל בשעה שנשא שלמה את בת פרעה ירד גבריאל ונעץ קנה בים ועלה בו שירטון ועליו נבנה כרך גדול [של רומי] במתניתא תנא אותו היום שהכניס ירבעם שני עגלי זהב אחד בבית אל ואחד בדן נבנה צריף אחד וזהו איטליאה של יון: א"ר שמואל בר נחמני א"ר יונתן כל האומר יאשיהו חטא אינו אלא טועה שנאמר °ויעש הישר בעיני ה' וילך בכל דרך דוד אביו אלא מה אני מקיים °וכמוהו לא היה לפניו מלך אשר שב וגו' *שכל דין שדן מבן שמנה עד שמנה עשרה החזירן להן שמא תאמר נטל מזה ונתן לזה תלמוד לומר בכל מאודו שנתן להם משלו ופליגא דרב דאמר רב אין לך גדול בבעלי תשובה יותר מיאשיהו בדורו ואחד בדורנו ומנו אבא אבוה דרבי ירמיה *בר אבא ואמרי לה אחא אחוה דאבא אבוה דרב ירמיה בר אבא דאמר מר רבי אבא ואחא אחי הוו אמר רב יוסף ועוד אחד בדורנו ומנו עוקבן בר נחמיה ריש גלותא והיינו *נתן דצוציתא אמר רב יוסף הוה יתיבנא בפירקא והוה קא מנמנם וחזאי בחלמא דקא פשט ידיה וקבליה:

הדרן עלך במה בהמה

רש"י

על עסקי נחל. ומה על נפש אחת אמרה תורה הבא עגלה ערופה בנחל נפשות הללו על אחת כמה וכמה אם גדולים חטאו קטנים מה חטאו*: ולא עבדו ישראל עבודה זרה. שעל ידי שנחלקה המלכות העמיד ירבעם העגלים שלא יעלו ישראל ירושלים לממשלתו של רחבעם: שלמה חטא. בע"ז: כדר' נתן. דשני קרא הטו ללכת והוא לא הלך: הכא נמי דבנה. קשיא היא: אלא. מהכא תילף דלא בנה כדתניא רבי יוסי אומר כו': להר המשחה. לשון שמן דמתרגמינן משחא והוא הר הזיתים: מקיש ראשונים. מקיש את בניינו של שלמה לביעורו של יאשיהו מה יאשיהו לא עשה ביעור זה ותלו בו מן השמים לשבח הואיל וביער השאר שנעשה משמת יהושפט אף שלמה לא עשה בנין זה ותלו בו לגנות מתוך שלא מיחה בנשיו: שמש. לחטוב עצים ולשאוב מים בשכר לע"ז: ואל יכתב בו דבר זה. ללמדך שקשה התוכחה במי שבידו למחות: מיני זמר. כלי שיר: נעץ קנה. ושרטון מדבק בו עד שנוסף והולך וגדל שרטון חול ורפש וטיט שהים גורש: כרך גדול של רומי. שהוא מיצר לישראל והוא (איטליא) של יון במסכת מגילה (דף ו:): ביום שהעמיד ירבעם את העגלים נבנה צריף אחד. באותו שרטון שגדל שם בימי שלמה צריף כוך קטן מליידין שעושין מן קנים ומן ערבה ומאז נתוספו בתים על בתים: איטליאה. שם העיר והיא ממדינת יון וכשנטלה רומי מלכות יוונים לכדוהו והפקלהם: יאשיהו חטא. דכתיב שב אל ה' משמע דחטא מעיקרא: מבן ח'. שישב על כסא מלכותו דכתיב בן ח' שנה וגו': עד בן י"ח. שמצא חלקיה את הספר ועיין ודקדק בתורה ובדיניה בכתב ובעל פה והבין שמא טעה בדינא: נטל מזה. ממי שנתן לו תחילה: ה"ג ואמרי לה אחא אחוה דאבא אבוה דרב ירמיה בר אבא: נתן דצוציתא. על שם ניצוצין דנורא שהמלאך פשט את ידו וקיבל תשובתו לישנא אחרינא על שאחזו המלאך בציצית ראשו:

הדרן עלך במה בהמה

תוספות

אלא מעתה אז יבנה יהושע כו'. הקשה הר"ר אלחנן דבחלק (סנהדרין דף נח:) מפקינן מדכתיב אז יבנה יהושע ולא כתב אז בנה מכאן לתחיית המתים מן התורה אם כן אתא לדרשה ה"נ אתא לדרשה דהכא ואומר ר"י דמ"מ פריך מדלא כתיב שבקש לבנות אלא יבנה ש"מ שרוצה לומר שבנה כההוא דיהושע דודאי בנה:

מה אחרונים לא עשו ותלה בהן כו'. לא שייך למימר הכא מקום הניחו לו אבותיו להתגדר בו כדאמר בפ"ק דחולין (דף ו ושם:) גבי נחש נחשת שביער חזקיה דהתם לא ביערוהו אבותיו שהיו יראים לבערו לפי שעשאו משה על פי הדבור אבל הכא למה היו מניחים מלבערם:

דצוציתא. אומר ר"ת דאמר במדרש שהיה נר דולק °על ראשו:

הדרן עלך במה בהמה

עין משפט נר מצוה

מב א טוש"ע ח"מ סי' ז' סעיף ג:

רב נסים גאון

נצא בר נצא [נצא] הא דאמרן בר נצא דכתיב (ש"א טו) ויבא שאול עד עיר(שלמה)[עמלק]וירב בנחל אמר ר' מני על עסקי נחל בשעה שאמר הקב"ה לשאול ועתה לך והכיתה את עמלק נשא שאול קל וחומר בעצמו ואמר ומה על נפש אחת אמרה תורה הבא עגלה ערופה בנחל המאבד נפשות הרבה על אחת כמה וכמה ועוד אם אדם חטא בהמה מה חטאת אם גדולים חטאו קטנים מה חטאו:

סליק פרק במה בהמה

מסורת הש"ס

[כדמפרש ביומא כב:]

יומא כב:

[עי' תוספת מגילה כא.]

[חולין ו: ועי' תוס' שם ז. ד"ה אלא]

בכ"י הגי' ואמר וכן לקמן

סנהדרין כא: ע"ש

מלכים ב כג

שם כג

ע' ברכת הזבח כריתות כב:

[ועמ"ש רש"י סנהדרין לח: ד"ה לחיו וכו' שהיה מר עוקבא בעל תשובה שנתן עינו וכו' וכשהוא יוצא לשוק היה נר דולק בראשו מן השמים ועל שם כך קרא ליה רבי נתן צוציתא ופי']

גליון הש"ס

תוס' ד"ה דצוציתא וכו' על ראשו. ע' סנהדרין דף לח ע"ב ברש"י ד"ה לחיו ליה:

[בקרא כתיב המשחית וגם בע"י איתא כך ועי' פירש"י במלכים שכתב הוא הר המשחה וכיון שהזכיר את שמו ע"י ע"ז שינו שמו לגנאי עכ"ל]

Verse references: שמואל ב ט; דה"א ח; ש"א טו; מ"א יא; שם; שם; יהושע ח; מ"ב כג; שם; שם א יא

[56b] *And he hath slandered thy servant unto my lord the king; but my lord the king is as an angel of God: do therefore what is good in thine eyes. For all my father's house were but dead men before my lord the king: yet didst thou set thy servant among them that did eat at thine own table. What right therefore have I yet that I should cry any more unto the king? And the king said unto him, Why speakest thou any more of thy matters? I say, Thou and Ziba divide the land. And Mephibosheth said unto the king, Yea, let him take all, forasmuch as my lord the king is come in peace* a *unto his own house.*[1] He said [thus] to him: I prayed,[2] when wilt thou return in peace? Yet thou treatest me so. Not against thee have I resentment, but against Him who restored thee in peace![3] Hence it is written, *And the son of Jonathan was Merib-baal:*[4] was then his name Merib-baal? Surely it was Mephibosheth? But because he raised a quarrel [*meribah*] with his Master,[5] a Heavenly Echo went forth and rebuked him, Thou man of strife, [and] the son of a man of strife! Man of strife, as we have stated. Son of a man of strife, for it is written, *And Saul came to the city of Amalek, and strove in the valley.*[6] R. Manni said: [That means,] concerning the matter of the valley.[7]

Rab Judah said in Rab's name: When David said to Mephibosheth, '*Thou and Ziba divide the land,*' a Heavenly Echo came forth and declared to him, Rehoboam and Jeroboam shall divide the kingdom.[8] Rab Judah said in Rab's name: Had not David paid heed to slander, the kingdom of the House of David would not have been divided, Israel had not engaged in idolatry,[9] and we would not have been exiled from our country.[10]

R. Samuel b. Naḥmani said in R. Jonathan's name: Whoever maintains that Solomon sinned is merely making an error, for it is said, *and his heart was not perfect with the Lord his God, as was the heart of David his father:*[11] it was [merely] not as the heart of David his father, but neither did he sin. Then how do I interpret, *For it came to pass, when Solomon was old, that his wives turned away his heart?*[12] That is [to be explained] as R. Nathan. For R. Nathan opposed [two verses]: It is written, *For it came to pass, when Solomon was old, that his wives turned away his heart;* whereas it is [also] written, *and his heart was not perfect with the Lord his God, as was the heart of David his father,* [implying that] it was [merely] not as the heart of David his father, but neither did he sin? This is its meaning: his wives b turned away his heart to go after other gods, but he did not go.[1] But it is written, *Then would*[2] *Solomon build a high place for Chemosh the abomination of Moab?*[3]—That means, he desired to build, but did not.[4] If so, *Then Joshua built* [yibneh] *an altar unto the Lord,*[5] [does this too mean,] he desired to build but did not! Hence it [surely means] that he [actually] built; so here too it means that he built?—Rather it[6] is as was taught: R. Jose said, *and the high places that were before Jerusalem, which were on the right hand of the mount of corruption, which Solomon the king of Israel had builded for Ashtoreth the abomination of Moab.*[7] Now, is it possible that Assa came and did not destroy them, then Jehoshaphat, and he did not destroy them, until Josiah came and destroyed them! But surely Assa and Jehoshaphat destroyed all the idolatrous cults in Palestine? Hence [the explanation is that] the earlier are assimilated to the later: just as the later did not do, yet it was ascribed to them, to their glory, so the earlier ones too did not do, yet it was ascribed to them, to their shame.[8] But it is written, *And Solomon did that which was evil in the sight of the Lord?*[9]—But because he should have restrained his wives, but did not, the Writ regards him as though he sinned.

Rab Judah said in Samuel's name: Better had it been for that righteous man to be an acolyte to the unmentionable,[10] only that it should not be written of him, '*and he did that which was evil in the sight of the Lord*'.

Rab Judah said in Samuel's name: When Solomon married Pharaoh's daughter, she brought him a thousand musical in- c struments and said to him, Thus we play[1] in honour of that idol, thus in honour of that idol, yet he did not forbid her.

Rab Judah said in Samuel's name: When Solomon married Pharaoh's daughter, Gabriel descended and planted a reed in the sea, and it gathered a bank around it, on which the great city of Rome was built.[2] In a Baraitha it was taught: On the day that Jeroboam brought the two golden calves, one into Bethel and the other into Dan, a hut was built,[3] and this developed into Greek Italy.[4]

R. Samuel b. Naḥmani said in R. Jonathan's name: Whoever maintains that Josiah sinned is merely making an error, for it is said, *And he did that which was right in the eyes of the Lord, and walked in all the ways of David his father.*[5] Then how do I interpret, *and like unto him there was no king before him, that returned* [shab] *to the Lord with all his heart* etc.?[6] [This teaches] that he revised every judgment which he had pronounced between the ages of eight and eighteen.[7] You might say that he took from one and gave to another:[8] therefore it is taught, '*with all* me'odo [*his might*]', [teaching] that he gave of his own.[9] Now, he disagrees with Rab. For Rab said: There was no greater penitent than Josiah in his generation and a certain person in ours; and who is that? Abba the father of R. Jeremiah b. Abba, and some say Aḥa the brother of Abba the father of Jeremiah b. Abba. (For a Master said: R. Abba and Aḥa were brothers). R. Joseph said: And there is yet another in our generation. And who is he? 'Uḳban b. Nehemiah d the Resh Galutha.[1] And he is 'Nathan with the ray of light.'[2] R. Joseph said: I was sitting at the session and dozing, and saw in a dream how one [an angel] stretched out his hand and received him.

a (1) II Sam. XIX, 25-30. (2) Lit., 'said'. (3) Thus he confirmed Ziba's accusation. For David regarded Mephibosheth's unkempt appearance too as a sign that he grieved over his return. (4) I Chron. VIII, 34; IX, 40. (5) *Be'alaw* fr. *ba'al*. (6) I Sam. XV, 5. (7) Saul argued: If the Torah decreed that a heifer should have its neck broken in the valley on account of a single murdered man (Deut. XXI, 1-9), how much greater is the sin of slaying all these Amalekites! (v. Yoma 22*b*). Thus he strove against God's command. (8) This agrees with Rab's view (*supra* 56*a*) that David paid heed to slander and acted unjustly. Hence this punishment. (9) The first step to idolatry was Jeroboam's setting up of the golden calves in order to maintain the independence of his kingdom (v. I Kings XII, 26 *seq.*). (10) As a punishment for idolatry. (11) I Kings XI, 4. (12) Ibid.

b (1) His wives attempted to seduce him, but failed. (2) E.V. '*did*'. (3) I Kings XI, 7. (4) *Yibneh* is imperfect, denoting uncompleted action; v. Driver's *Hebrew Tenses*, ch. III, §§ 21 *seq.* (5) Josh. VIII, 30. (6) The statement that Solomon did not sin. (7) II Kings XXIII, 13. This refers to the religious reformations of Josiah. (8) Josiah merely removed the idols that were reintroduced after the deaths of the former two kings, but not *all* idols, since they had already been destroyed, yet it is all attributed to him. So Solomon too was not responsible for the building of the idolatrous high places; nevertheless, since he did not veto them, they are ascribed to him. (9) I Kings XI, 6. (10) Lit., 'something else'—i.e., to an idol, receiving pay for drawing water and hewing wood in its service, etc., though not believing in it.

c (1) Lit., 'do'. (2) This, of course, is an allegory. Solomon's unfaithfulness laid the seeds for the dissolution of the Jewish State. (3) On the site of Rome. (4) This term was particularly applied to the southern portion of Italy, called Magna Graecia, Cf. Meg. 6*b* in the ed. Ven. (omitted in later ed.): Greek Italy, that means the great city of Rome, v. Meg., 6*b*, nn. 5-6. (5) II Kings XXII, 2. (6) Ibid. XXIII, 25. *Shab* really means that he repented, and thus implies that he first sinned. (7) I.e., from his accession until the finding of the Book of the Law, i.e., the Torah (v. XXII, 1-8). He revised his judgments in the light of the Torah, and *shab* is translated accordingly. (8) In the course of this revision. (9) *Me'odo* < *me'od* is translated money, wealth, in the Talmud. Cf. Sanh. 74*a* on Deut. VI, 5.

d (1) V. p. *supra* 48*a*, n. 7. (2) Jast.: a repentant sinner with a halo; others: whom an angel seized by his forelock (accepting his repentance and bringing him to God).

CHAPTER VI

MISHNAH. [57a] WHEREWITH MAY A WOMAN GO OUT,
a AND WHEREWITH MAY SHE NOT GO OUT?[1] A WOMAN MAY NOT GO OUT WITH RIBBONS OF WOOL, LINEN RIBBONS, OR FILLETS ROUND HER HEAD;[2] NOR MAY SHE PERFORM RITUAL IMMERSION WHILST WEARING THEM, UNLESS SHE LOOSENS THEM. [SHE MAY NOT GO OUT] WITH FRONTLETS,[3] GARLANDS [SARBIṬIN], IF THEY ARE NOT SEWN,[4] OR WITH A HAIR-NET [KABUL][5] INTO THE STREET,[6] OR WITH A GOLDEN CITY,[7] OR WITH A NECKLACE [ḲAṬLA], OR WITH EAR-RINGS, OR WITH A FINGER-RING WHICH HAS NO SIGNET, OR WITH A NEEDLE WHICH IS UNPIERCED. YET IF SHE GOES OUT [WITH THESE], SHE IS NOT LIABLE TO A SIN-OFFERING.[8]

GEMARA. Who mentioned anything about ritual immersion?[9] —Said R. Naḥman b. Isaac in Rabbah b. Abbuha's name: He [the Tanna] states what is the reason. [Thus:] what is the reason that A WOMAN MAY NOT GO OUT WITH WOOL RIBBONS OR LINEN RIBBONS? Because the Sages ruled, SHE MAY NOT PERFORM RITUAL IMMERSION WHILST WEARING THEM, UNLESS SHE LOOSENS THEM. And since she may not perform ritual immersion on weekdays while wearing them, she may not go out [with them] on the Sabbath, lest she happen to need immersion
b by ritual law[1] and she untie them, and so come to carry them four cubits in the street.

R. Kahana asked Rab: What of openwork bands?[2]—Said he to him, You speak of something woven:[3] whatever is woven, no prohibition was enacted [in respect thereof].[4] It was stated likewise: R. Huna son of R. Joshua said: Whatever is woven, no prohibition was enacted [in respect thereof]. Others state, R. Huna son of R. Joshua said: I saw that my sisters are not particular about them.[5] What is the difference between the latter version and the former?—There is a difference where they are soiled. On the version that no prohibition was enacted for anything that is woven, these too are woven. But according to the version which bases it on [not] being particular; since they are soiled, one does indeed object to them.[6]

We learnt elsewhere: And the following constitute interpositions in the case of human beings: Wool ribbons, linen ribbons, and the fillet round maidens' heads.[7] R. Judah said: [Ribbons] of wool or of hair do not interpose, because the water enters through them.[8] R. Huna observed: And we learnt all with reference to maidens' heads.[9] R. Joseph demurred: What does this exclude? Shall we say it excludes [ribbons] of the neck,—and of what [material]? Shall we say, it excludes wool: [The question can
c be raised] if soft [material] on hard[1] forms an interposition, is there a question of soft upon soft?[2] Again, if it excludes linen ribbons, [one might ask] if hard upon hard constitutes an interposition, is there a question of hard upon soft?[3] Rather, said R. Joseph, this is R. Huna's reason, because a woman does not strangle herself.[4]

Abaye refuted him: Maidens may go out with the threads through their ears,[5] but not with fillets round their necks. Now if you say that a woman will not strangle herself, why not with

a (1) On the Sabbath. The general rule is that a woman may wear superfluous garments which are ornamental, save some which the Rabbis prohibited for fear that she might remove them for a friend's inspection and admiration, carrying them meanwhile in the street. Those which are not considered ornamental constitute a burden, and are always forbidden. (2) 'Her head' applies to all three. These are for tying the hair. (3) Ornaments worn on the forehead. (4) To the wig which was generally worn. (5) The Gemara discusses these. V. also *T.A.* I, 188 and note a.l. (6) But she may wear it in a courtyard, whereas all the others are forbidden even in a courtyard, lest she forget herself and go out into the street; v. *infra* 64*b*. (7) An ornament which contained a picture of Jerusalem. (8) Because all these are ornaments, hence only Rabbinically prohibited; v. n. a1. (9) The reference to immersion is apparently irrelevant.

b (1) I.e., if the first evening, when she is permitted to take a ritual bath after menstruation to enable her to cohabit with her husband, falls on the Sabbath. (2) Chains or cords formed in network fashion. These cannot be tied very tightly; hence the question is whether they need be loosened before a ritual bath and by corollary, must not be worn on the Sabbath, or not. (3) I.e., a network. (4) In connection with Sabbath, since they need not be removed for immersion. (5) To remove them before bathing. This shows that they know that the water enters through the network. Consequently it is unnecessary to remove them before a ritual bath, and they may be worn on the Sabbath. (6) And is particular to remove them. (7) When one takes a ritual bath, nothing must interpose between the water and his body. If one of these is worn it does interpose, rendering the bath invalid. (8) And reaches the skin. (9) I.e., the wool and linen ribbons also mean those that are used for tying the hair.

c (1) *Sc.* the hair, which is hard in comparison with the skin of the neck. (2) Surely not, for it is more clinging, making it more difficult for the water to enter. (3) Linen ribbon is regarded as hard in comparison with wool. (4) Though ribbons cling more closely to flesh than to hair when tied with equal strength, they are always worn more loosely around the neck, for the reason stated. (5) They are inserted there after the ear is pierced for ear-rings to prevent the hole from closing up.

Novellae of Hagaon Rabbi Moshe Feinstein o.b.m.

Shabbath

56b. הקשו The Tosafists ask in the name of R. Elhanan that in *Heleq* we derive that since Scripture states, *Az yibneh,* rather than *Az banah,* there is biblical basis for the resurrection of the dead. If so, this verse is written for a *derash* (and it is not analogous to the verse written about Solomon). It appears to me that the word *yibneh,* although grammatically in the future tense, can be interpreted as the present when it can mean that he constantly builds and rebuilds. For a one-time building, however, the future tense cannot be employed to mean the present. Therefore, concerning Joshua, although Scripture refers to the altar that he built at that time, we must perforce conclude that he will build another altar in the future. Since he built and will build again, it is appropriate to employ the future form for the present, thereby furnishing us with a biblical basis for the doctrine of the resurrection. Concerning Solomon, however, when Scripture writes, *Az yibneh,* we can very easily explain this expression is its very simple sense, viz. that he built many times, because the verse mentions the altars of many pagan deities. Hence, there is no proof from the expression of *yibneh* that he desired to build but did not, because for such a present tense, that he built many times, the future tense can be employed. Perhaps this is the meaning of R. Isaac's solution to this question, which is apparently incomprehensible.

*במה *אשה יוצאה ובמה אינה יוצאה לא תצא אשה לא בחוטי צמר ולא בחוטי פשתן ולא ברצועות שבראשה ולא תטבול בהן עד שתרפם ולא בטוטפת ולא בסרביטין בזמן שאינן תפורים ולא בכבול לרה"ר ולא *בעיר של זהב ולא בקטלא ולא בנזמים ולא בטבעת שאין עליה חותם ולא במחט שאינה נקובה ואם יצאת אינה חייבת חטאת: **גמ'** טבילה מאן דכר שמה אמר רב נחמן בר יצחק אמר רבה בר אבוה מה טעם קאמר מה טעם לא תצא אשה לא בחוטי צמר ולא בחוטי פשתן מפני שאמרו חכמים בחול לא תטבול בהן עד שתרפם וכיון דבחול לא תטבול בהן עד שתרפם בשבת לא תצא דילמא מיתרמי לה טבילה של מצוה ושריא להו ואתי לאתויינהו ד' אמות ברה"ר בעא מיניה רב כהנא מרב תיכי חלילתא מאי א"ל אריג קאמרת כל שהוא אריג לא גזרו איתמר נמי *אמר רב הונא בריה דרב יהושע 'כל שהוא אריג לא גזרו ואיכא דאמרי אמר רב הונא בריה דרב יהושע חזינא לאחוותי דלא קפדן עלייהו מאי איכא בין הך לישנא ובין הך לישנא איכא בינייהו דטניפן להך לישנא דאמר כל שהוא אריג לא גזרו הני נמי ארוג ולהך לישנא דאמרת משום קפידא 'כיון דטניפא מקפד קפדא עלייהו *תנן התם ואלו חוצצין באדם חוטי צמר וחוטי פשתן והרצועות שבראשי הבנות ר' יהודה אומר של צמר ושל שער אין חוצצין מפני שהמים באין בהן אמר רב הונא וכולן בראשי הבנות שנינו מתקיף לה רב יוסף למעוטי מאי אילימא למעוטי דצואר ודמאי אילימא למעוטי דצמר השתא רך על גבי קשה חוצץ רך על גבי רך מיבעיא ואלא למעוטי דחוטי פשתן השתא קשה על גבי קשה חוצץ קשה על גבי רך מיבעיא אלא אמר רב יוסף היינו טעמא דרב הונא 'לפי שאין אשה חונקת את עצמה איתיביה אביי הבנות יוצאות בחוטין שבאזניהן אבל לא בחבקין שבצואריהן ואי אמרת אין אשה חונקת עצמה חבקין שבצואריהן אמאי לא 'אמר רבינא הבא

במה אשה יוצאה. דהוי תכשיט ולא משוי והיכא דהוי תכשיט וגזור ביה רבנן דילמא שלפא ומחויא לחברתה חשיבותו ודילמא אתי לאיתויי ד' אמות: לא בחוטי צמר ופשתן ורצועה שבראשה. שקולעת בהן שערה: שבראשה. אכולהו קאי ובגמ' מפרש טעמא: ולא תטבול בהן. משום חלילה: עד שתרפם. שתתירם קצת שיהיו רפויין ויכנסו המים ביניהם לשער: טוטפת וסרביטין. מפרש בגמרא וחשובין הן וחיישינן דילמא שלפא ומחויא לחברתה: בזמן שאין תפורין. עם השבכה שקורין שקופיי"א אבל תפורין ליכא למיחש לאחוויי שאינה נוטלת השבכה מראשה ברה"ר שתגלה כל שערה: כבול. מפרש בגמ': לרה"ר. אבל לחצר שרי וכל הנזכרים למעלה אסורים אף לחצר שמא תרגילם ברה"ר וחדא גזירה היא דגזור בהם שלא תתקשט בהם בשבת כלל ובכבול התירו כדמפרש לקמן בפרקין (דף סד:) שלא לאסור את כל תכשיטיה ותתגנה על בעלה: עיר של זהב. כמין נושקא ומציירין בה כמין עיר: קטלא. מפרש בגמרא (לקמן דף נט:): חותם. צורה לחתום בה איגרת או כל דבר סגור: שאינה נקובה. כגון אישפיגל"א: ואם יצאת אינה חייבת חטאת. דכולהו תכשיטין נינהו ורבנן הוא דגזור בהו דילמא שלפא ומחויא: **גמ'** טבילה מאן דכר שמה. מה ענין טבילה אצל הלכות שבת: ושריא להו. ומותרת אותם לטבול בשבת שעל הטבילה לא גזרו כדאמרינן במסכת ביצה (דף יח.) אדם נראה כמיקר ואין נראה כמתקן עצמו: תיכי חלילתא. שרשרות של חוטין חלולות ועגולות: מהו. לקלוע בהן שערה ולצאת בשבת שאינה יכולה למותחן ולדוחקן על השער בחוזקה והמים נכנסין בה ומיבעיא ליה מי הוי חלילה ולא תצא בהן בשבת משום גזירת טבילת מצוה או לא הוי חלילה: כל שהוא אריג לא גזרו. לצאת בו בשבת דלענין חלילה לא חיין דלא מצי להדוקי שפיר: לאחוותי דלא קפדן עלייהו. ליטלן מראשן כשהן רוחצות בחמין אלמא עיילי בהו מיא שפיר אפילו להנאת רחיצה וכיון שכן לענין טבילה נמי לא צריכין להתירן ומותר לצאת בהן בשבת דהא אי מתרמי טבילה לא שרו להו לא משום חלילה ולא משום קפידא: דמיטנפי. שנטנפו הנך תיכי בטיט: הא נמי אריג הוא. והא קאמר לא גזרו כלל לצאת ולהאי לישנא דלא קפדי משמע דאי קפדי לטלנן מראשן כשהן רוחצות אסור לצאת בהן בשבת ואע"ג דלענין איהדוקי לא חייצי ומותרות לטבול בהן הלכך הני כיון דמיטנפי מקפד קפדן שלא להיות בראשן בשעת טבילתן מפני שהמים ממחין את הטיט ומלכלך בשרן בעלייתן מן הטבילה ואע"ג דחלילה לא הוי דהא עיילי בהו מיא מיהו כיון דשקלי לה משום טינוף אתי לאיתויינהו ואסור לצאת בהן וללישנא קמא לא גזרו אלא במידי דהיין לטבילה ורבותי מפרשין הך קפידא לענין חלילה כדקי"ל רובו ומקפיד עליו חוצץ (עירובין דף ד:) וקשיא לי בגוה טובא חדא דכי איתמר ההוא במידי דמיהדק איתמר ואשמעינן דאע"ג דלא עיילי ביה מיא כיון דלא קפיד עליה חשיב כגופיה ובטל לגבי שערו אבל במידי דלא מיהדק ועיילי ביה מיא מאי חוצץ איכא למימר הא לאו חוצץ הוא ואי אתית למימר דההוא חוצץ דהתם לא דק בלישניה ומיהו כל מידי דקפיד עלייהו אסור היכי אמרינן הכא האי נמי אריג הוא ומותר כיון דפשיטא לן דהיכא דמיטנפי מקפד קפדן על כרחיך חיין דהא רב הונא בריה דרב יהושע אהלכה למשה מסיני לא אתא לאיפלוגי: ואלו חוצצין באדם. משום דתני התם אלו חוצצין בכלים תני לענין טבילת אדם ואלו חוצצין באדם: של צמר ושל שער אין חוצצין. דלא מיהדק על גבי שער: הבנות קטנות. אורחא דמילתא נקט: וכולן בראשי הבנות שנינו. לא תימא שבראשי הבנות ארצועות לחודייהו קאי אלא אחוטין נמי קאי: למעוטי מאי. אשמעינן רב הונא דהוטין נמי בראשי הבנות שנינו: אילימא למעוטי חוטין הקשורין בצוארן דלא חייצי: ודמאי הי חוטין אתא למעוטי דלא חייצי בצואר: צמר קרוי רך לגבי פשתן ולגבי שער: על גבי קשה. שער: ע"ג רך. בשר: מיבעיא. בתמיה הא ודאי על גבי רך טפי מיהדק: לפי שאין אשה חונקת עצמה. להדק חוטין בצוארה וקושרתן בריוח שיהו רפין: בחוטין שבאזניהם. שנותנין שם שלא יסתם הנקב: חבקין. ענקי רצועות שאינן מוזהבות רחבות דלאו תכשיט עבידן דומיא דחוטין שבאזניהן: חבקין. לשון קילקלי וחבק (לקמן דף סד.) כיעג"א לאסור. בו סוס: בקטלא

במה אשה כו' לא בחוטי צמר. מפרש בגמ' משום דילמא מיתרמי לה טבילה של מצוה ושרי להו ואתי לאתויינהו ארבע אמות ברה"ר אומר ר"י דהיינו דוקא בחוטין שאינן נתונין בקליעת השער אבל חוטין הנתונין בקליעת השער יוצאה בהן דבהנהו ליכא למיגזר דילמא שריא להו כדתנן בהמצניע (לקמן דף צד:) דאיכא לכל הפחות איסור שבות בגודלת וסברא הוא דכי היכי דיש איסור בעשיית קליעה ה"נ יש איסור בסתירת קליעה וא"ת מהאי טעמא תהא אשה אסורה לצאת בטלית דהא ודאי שריא לה בשעת טבילה וניחוש דילמא אתי לאתויי וי"ל דבדברים שהם עיקר מלבוש ליכא למיגזר דאפילו בחול אין דרך ללכת כלל ממקומו עד שילבישם אלא דוקא בדברים קטנים יש לחוש שאין מקפיד אם אינם עליו ורגילות הוא בחול כשמתירין פעמים נושאן בידו עד ביתו ונראה לר"י דדוקא בדברים שרגילות להסירן כדי להראותן או משום חלילה או משום קפידא גזרו שלא לצאת דשמא כשיסיר ישכח שהוא שבת ואתי לאתויי אבל דברים שמותר לצאת בהן שאין רגילות להסירן מותר לקשור ולהתיר ברה"ר דליכא למיחש למידי דאם יהא זכור שבת בשעת התרה לא אתי לאתויי ואם לא יהיה זכור שבת אפילו נאסר להתיר ולהסיר לא יועיל וכ"מ לקמן (דף סו.) דקתני בברייתא וקושר ומתיר קמיע אפילו ברה"ר והא דאיצטריך התם לאשמעי' דשרי אע"פ שכל דבר מותר להסיר כדפרישית איצטריך לאשמעינן דלא אסרינן משום דמיחזי דקושרו עליו שלא לרפואה ומתכוין להוציא כי היכי דאסור בפילפל וגרגיר מלח לכתחילה לתת בפיה בשבת או להחזיר אלא כמלבוש גמור חשיב מחמת הרפואה: **השתא** רך על גבי קשה חוצץ כו'. וא"ת דילמא רב הונא נקט וכולן בראשי הבנות לרבותא דאפילו בראשי הבנות דהוי רך ע"ג קשה חוצץ ואור"י דבלאו רב הונא הוה ידעינן דבכל מקום חוצצין אפילו בראש אלא ודאי למעוטי שום דבר אתא: **השתא** קשה ע"ג קשה חוצץ. סבר הש"ס דקשה ע"ג רך חייץ טפי מקשה ע"ג קשה ורך ע"ג קשה לא חייץ כקשה ע"ג קשה דהא לר' יהודה חוטי צמר אין חוצצין דהוי רך על גבי קשה וחוטי פשתן דהוי קשה ע"ג קשה חוצצין וחוטי שיער דהוי נמי קשה על גבי קשה לכ"ע אין חוצצין אף על פי שחוטי פשתן חוצצין לכולי עלמא: **אלא** א"ר יוסף. לפי שרב יוסף בעצמו מקשה שייך לומר אלא: הכא

עין משפט נר מצוה

א א מיי' פי"ט מהל' שבת הל' ו' ומיי' פ"ב מהל' מקואות הל' ה סמג לאוין סה וסמג עשין רמח טוש"ע א"ח סי' שג סעיף א וטוש"ע י"ד סי' קצח סעיף ג:

ב ב מיי' פי"ט מהל' שבת הלכה ד' טוש"ע א"ח סי' שג סעיף י וסעיף יח:

ג ג ד מיי' שם הלכה ט טוש"ע א"ח סי' שג סעיף א וטוש"ע י"ד סי' קצח סעיף ג:

ד ה ו מיי' שם הלכה ז י טוש"ע א"ח שם סעיף ג וטוש"ע י"ד שם סעיף ג:

רבינו חננאל

במה אשה יוצאה ובמה אינה יוצאה. לא תצא אשה בחוטי כו'. איקמה רב נחמן גזירה שמא תזדמן לה טבילה של מצוה ומשום שחוצצת מתרתן ומהלכת בהן ד' אמות ברה"ר. אבל תיכי הלילתא לא גזו בהו רבנן דהא אחוותיה דרב הונא בריה דר' יהושע הוו טבלי בדמחת הני תיכי הלילתא בראשיהן ולא הוו קפדי וכיון דלא הוו קפדי שרו. וה"מ תיכי הלילתא אבל תיכי טמיתא לא דחוצצות ואסיק' דחוטי שיער אינן חוצצין ואפילו הן קשורין בראש הבנות ואע"פ שהראש קשה הוא המים נכנסין בשיער ואין חוצצין אבל חוטי צמר וחוטי פשתן בראש הבנות חוצצין וכ"ש אם הן קשורין בצואר שמשתקעין בבשר ואין המים באין תחתיהן. ולפיכך חוצצין. כיוצא בהן החבקין שבצוארי הבנות ואוקימנא

מסורת הש"ס: [נדרים כ: נזיר ג.] | [ע' תוס' לקמן נט. ד"ה ולא] | לקמן נח. | מקואות פ"ט מ"ח

גליון הש"ס

גמ' תיכי חלילתא מאי. עי' זבחים דף לד ע"א תוס' ד"ה מקנחת:

עין משפט נר מצוה

ה א מיי' פ"ב מהל' מקואות הלכה ה סמג עשין רמח טור וש"ע יו"ד סי' קלח סעיף ד:

ו ב (מיי' פי"ט מהל' שבת הל' י"ד) טוש"ע א"ח סי' שג סעיף טו:

ז ג מיי' פי"ט מהל' שבת הלכה י"ד סמג לאוין סה טור וש"ע א"ח סי' שג סעיף טו:

ח ד מיי' שם הלכה ו' טוש"ע שם סעיף ג:

ט ה מיי' פ"י מהל' כלאים הלכה כ סמג לאוין רפג טור וש"ע י"ד סי' שא סעיף יד:

י ו מיי' פי"ג מהל' טומאת צרעת הלכה א:

גמרא

הבא בקטלא עסקינן °דאשה חונקת את עצמה דניחא לה שתראה כבעלת בשר: ר' יהודה אומר של צמר ושל שער אין חוצצין מפני שהמים באין בהן: אמר רב יוסף אמר רב יהודה אמר שמואל הלכה כרבי יהודה בחוטי שער *א"ל אביי הלכה מכלל דפליגי וכי תימא אי לאו דשמעינן מתנא קמא דאיירי בחוטי שער איהו נמי לא הוה מיירי ודילמא כשם קאמר להו כי היכי דמודיתו לי בחוטי שער אודו לי נמי בחוטי צמר *איתמר אמר רב נחמן אמר שמואל ^אמודים חכמים לרבי יהודה בחוטי שער תניא נמי הכי חוטי צמר חוצצין חוטי שער אין חוצצין ר' יהודה אומר של צמר ושל שער אין חוצצין אמר רב נחמן בר יצחק מתניתין נמי דיקא *דקתני יוצאה אשה בחוטי שער בין משל חברתה מני אילימא רבי יהודה אפילו חוטי צמר נמי אלא לאו רבנן היא וש"מ בחוטי שער לא פליגי ש"מ: לא בטוטפת: מאי טוטפת א"ר יוסף חומרתא דקטיפתא א"ל אביי ^בתהוי כקמיע מומחה ותשתרי אלא אמר רב יהודה משמיה דאביי *אפוזיינו תניא נמי הכי ^גיוצאה אשה בסבכה המוזהבת ובטוטפת ובסרביטין הקבועין בה איזו טוטפת ואיזו סרביטין א"ר אבהו טוטפת המוקפת לה מאזן לאזן סרביטין המגיעין לה עד לחייה אמר רב הונא עניות עושין אותן של מיני צבעונין עשירות עושין אותן של כסף ושל זהב: ולא בכבול: אמר רבי ינאי כבול זה איני יודע מהו אי כבלא דעבדא תנן אבל כיפה של צמר שפיר דמי או דילמא כיפה של צמר תנן וכ"ש כבלא דעבדא *אמר רבי אבהו מסתברא כמ"ד ^דכיפה של צמר תנן ותניא נמי הכי יוצאה אשה בכבול ובאיסטמא לחצר ר"ש בן אלעזר אומר *אף בכבול לרה"ר כלל °אמר רשב"א כל שהוא למטה מן השבכה יוצאין בו כל שהוא למעלה מן השבכה אין יוצאין בו מאי איסטמא א"ר אבהו ביזיוני מאי ביזיוני אמר אביי אמר רב כליא פרוחי ת"ר *ג' דברים נאמרו באיסטמא ^האין בה משום כלאים ^ואינה מטמאה בנגעים ואין יוצאין בה לרה"ר משום ר"ש אמרו אף אין

[דף סד:] [ע' תוס' ב"ב כ. ד"ה כבול] [פ"ט מ"ט דכלאים]

רש"י

בקטלא עסקינן. בגד חשוב לתלות בצוארה כנגד לבה שלא ישול מה שהיא אוכלת על בגדיה ויש לו מקום שנים כעין שעושים למכנסים ותוחב בו רצועה רחבה ומוללתו סביב הרצועה שהבגד רחב הרבה וקושרת הרצועה סביב צוארה וחונקת עצמה בחוזק כדי שתהא בשרה בולטת ותראה בעלת בשר ומתוך שהרצועה חלקה ורחבה אינה מזיקתה: מכלל דפליגי. בתמיה והא ת"ק לא איירי בשערה שמע מינה בשער מודה דלא מיהדק על גבי שער: דילמא. האי דאדכר שער: כשם קאמר להו. כשם שאתם מודים לי בחוטי שער אודו לי בחוטי צמר (א): חומרתא דקטיפתא. קשר שעושין לרפואות קיטוף עין רע שלא תשלוט: ותיהוי כקמיע מומחה. דקתני מתני' ולא בקמיע בזמן שאינו מן המומחה הא מומחה שפיר דמי: אפוזייני. פרונטי"ל של זהב: שבכה. קופיי"ה דאי שלפא ליה מיגליא ראשה: המקפת. את הפדחת מאוזן לאוזן: המגיעים עד לחייה. על ראשה כורכתו ותולה לה על לחייה מכאן ומכאן: אי כבלא דעבדא תנן. חותם שעושין לעבד בכסותו לסימן הוכחה שהוא עבד ובההוא קתני מתני' דשפחה לא תצא בו: אבל כיפה של צמר. כובע שתחת השבכה דמקרי נמי כבול ומתקשטת בו: שפיר דמי. דכיון דמיגליא שערה לא שלפא ומחויא: או דילמא כיפה תנן. דלא תצא דחיישינן דילמא שלפא ומחויא מתחת השבכה ואינה מגלה וכל שכן כבלא דעבדא: בכבול ובאיסטמא. לקמיה מפרש מאי איסטמא ומדקתני כל שהוא למטה מן השבכה ש"מ כיפה תנן: כליא פרוחי. מגנפת קטנה לאחר קישוריה שקולעת ראשה וכסתה יש שערות קטנות שיוצאין חוץ לקישוריה והן נקראין פרוחי על שמפריחין ויוצאין לחוץ ואוגדתן לתחת קישוריה ע"י מגנפת קטנה: כליא. מונעת אותן שערות מלצאת: אין בה משום כלאים. שעשויה כמין לבד שקורין פולטר"א ואינה טוויה: ואינה מטמאה בנגעים. מהאי טעמא גופיה דגבי נגעים כתיב נמי בגד ויליף מכלאים שוע וטווי:

תוספות

הבא בקטלא עסקינן. תימה דמשמע דקטלא טעמא משום חציצה וא"כ אמאי תני (ג) במתניתין בסיפא בהדי חוטי לאמר ברישא הוה ליה למיתנייה ואומר רשב"א דקטלא נמי דבר של נוי הוא ויש לחוש דילמא שליף ומחויא ומיירי מתני' ברפוי דליכא חציצה ולכך אין לאוסרו אלא משום תכשיט אבל ברייתא דהכא איירי במיהדק דליכא למיחש דילמא שלפא שאינה מסירה לפי שלא תראה בעלת בשר וא"ת ומאי דוחקיה לאוקמא ברייתא משום חציצה לוקמא ברפוי ומשום משלפא כמתני' וי"ל דברייתא משמע ליה דטעמא משום חציצה דומיא דרישא דקתני הבנות יוצאות בחוטין שבאזניהם דלא איצטריך דליכא למיחש דילמא שלפא ומחויא דפשיטא הוא דמאי נוי שייך בחוטין אלא איצטריך לאשמעינן דאין בו חציצה ואינה מסירתן בשעת טבילה וה"נ סיפא טעמא משום חציצה: תניא נמי הכי כו'. מדתני (ג) וסרביטין הקבועים בה ודרך לקבוע אפזייני בסבכה אבל חומרתא דקטיפתא אין קובעין:

אי כבלא דעבדא תנן. תימה אי כבלא דעבדא תנן אמאי קתני טפי גבי אשה וי"ל דבעי למיתני בסיפא דמתני' יוצאה בכבול ובפאה נכרית לחצר ופאה נכרית לא שייכא אלא באשה °וא"ת אמאי לא תני נמי ברישא פאה נכרית בהדי כבול דאין יוצאין בה לרה"ר ויש לומר דמילתא דפשיטא היא דאסור לצאת בה לרה"ר דודאי משלפה משום דמחכו עלה וא"ת אי כבלא דעבדא תנן אמאי שרי בחצר טפי משאר דברים אבל אי כיפה של צמר תנן ניחא דשרי בחצר שלא תתגנה על בעלה כדמפרש עולא לקמן (דף סד:) וי"ל דכבלא דעבדא שרי כדי לעשות בו קורת רוח לרבו שאם היה כל היום בלא כבול אפילו בחצר בדבר מועט שיעשה העבד כנגד רבו סבור רבו שדעתו למרוד בו ואתי לידי קטטה ולקמן *דפירש"י דבסיפא מודו כ"ע דכבול כיפה של צמר היא קשה לר"י דהא משמע הכא למ"ד כבלא דעבדא תנן שרי כיפה של צמר אף לרה"ר:

אין בה משום כלאים. פרש"י משום שאינה טווי וריב"א אומר דמשום הכי אין להתיר דהתנן *הלבדים אסורין מפני שהן שועין אלא משום דאיסטמא דבר קשה הוא ובדבר קשה לא אסרו רבנן משום כלאים כדאמר בפרק קמא דביצה (דף טו: ושם) א"ר הונא בריה דרב יהושע האי נמטא גמדא דנרש שריא אע"ג דשאר לבדים אסורין האי שריא לפי שהיא קשה וכן משמע ביומא פרק בא לו (דף סט.) רב אשי אמר בגדי כהונה קשין הן ולכך שרי להציע תחתיהם כי הא דאמר רב הונא בריה דרב יהושע האי נמטא גמדא דנרש שריא וקשה לר"ת דאמרינן בפ"ק דערכין (דף ג:) הכל חייבים בציצית כהנים לוים וישראלים ופריך פשיטא ומשני כהנים איצטריך ליה סד"א הואיל ואישתרי כלאים לגבייהו כו' לא ליחייבי והשתא היכי אישתרי להו והא בגדי כהונה קשין הן וכה"ג לישראל נמי שרי ואומר ר"ת דדבר שהוא שוע טווי ונוז [ובדרך מלבוש והעלאה] דאסור מן התורה אין חילוק בין רך לקשה דבכל ענין אסור מן התורה אבל בכלאים דרבנן כגון לבדים שאינם אלא שוע שרי בקשין אפילו ללבוש כיון דאין בהו כלאים אלא מדרבנן ובגדי כהונה נמי כיון דשרי מדאורייתא *להציע תחתיהן כדתניא לא יעלה עליך אבל אתה מותר להציעו תחתיך אבל אמרו חכמים אסור לעשות כן כו' שרי אפילו מדרבנן כיון דקשין הן דבקשין לא גזרו רבנן כלל ובדבר רך נמי היכא דלא שכיח כריכה מותר להציעו תחתיך כגון מרדעת החמור וכרים וכסתות ומילי אחריני דחשיב במס' כלאים ועל אותן קוטש פורפונטש הסיב ר' יצחק שאם יש בתוכן בלאי בגדים של צמר ושל פשתן ונתחב בהן המחט שתי תפירות דאסורין בהעלאה אפילו חוט התפירה של קנבוס או של משי שלא התירו כרים וכסתות אלא בהצעה אבל בהעלאה לא אבל אם אין בתוכן רק גיזי צמר יכול להיות דמותר אף בהעלאה שאין חוט התפירה מחברן לבגד כלל אלא שמחבר ומקרב שני הבגדים של פשתן שהן כסוי הקוטש משני צדדין ומתוך כך מתהדק הצמר שבינתים ואין זה חיבור כחיבור אריג או תפירה או קשירת חבלים דבמה בהמה: ואינה מטמאה בנגעים. קשה לר"י מאי איריא בנגעים אפי' במת ושרץ לא מטמא דבעינן טווי ואריג כדאמר לקמן (דף סד.) ואומר ר"י דמטמאה במת ושרצים מק"ו דפכין קטנים שטהורין בזב ומטמאים במת ושרץ איסטמא שטמא בזב דשייך בה מדרס כמו בכפה דאמר (כלים פרק כ"ח משנה ה) כפה שנתנתו לס"ת טהור מן המדרס אינו דין שיטמא במת ושרץ ובערוך פי' איסטמא חתיכה של בגד מוזהב וקובעין בה אבנים טובות ומרגליות ולפ"ז ניחא דמטמאה במת ושרצים כשאר תכשיט אבל בנגעים לא שאין הבגד עיקר כ"א הזהב והאבנים טובות ומהאי טעמא נמי אין בה משום כלאים: והאמר

רבינו חננאל

בקטלא ומשום דאשה חונקת עצמה כדי שתראה בעלת בשר. פירש רב יוסף טוטפת חומרתא דקטיפתא יש מי שאומרים כי הוא ממיני מוצליות שתולות הנשים בצואריהן משום עין רעה. ונדחו דבריו. ואיתוקמא מאי טוטפת אבזייני כלומר אב שיש בו מינין הרבה. כי מינין תרגם זני דכתיב (דניאל ג) זני זמרא פירוש כל מיני זמר והיא נקראת טוטפת מפני שנותנת למעלה מן המצח במקום הטוטפת כדתניא יוצאה אשה בסבכה המוזהבת ובטוטפת ובסרביטין ואוקמה ר' אבהו טוטפת המוקפת מאזן לאזן סרבוטין המגיעין לה עד לחייה: ולא בכבול איקמה ר' אבהו כיפה של צמר דתניא יוצאה אשה בכבול ובאיצטמא לחצר ר'. שמעון בן אלעזר אומר בכבול אף לרה"ר כו' דייקינן דכבול דומיא דאיצטמא מה איצטמא כיפה אף כבול כיפה. וכדגרסינן (חולין קלח ע"א) כיפה של צמר היה מונח בראש כ"ג ועליו הציץ שנאמר ושמת אותו על פתיל תכלת. והן חוטין גדילין מעשה עבות רחבין בשתים ושלש אצבעות כגון אבנט ולית הלכתא כשמואל דאמר כבלא דעבדא דאין עושין ברבר של תורה להקל מספקא אלא הכבול שאסרה משנתנו היא כיפה של צמר וכ"ש כבלא דעבדא שאסור. איצטמא היא ביזני. כלומר חוטין הרבה ממיני צבעונין ותולין אותן בפני הכלה שלא יצערוה הזבובין שמתביישת להסיר הזבובין מעליה ותולין זה בפניה ונקראת כליא דיבי והוא כגון אותה ששנינו (מדות פ"ד מ"ו) אמה כולה עורב. לפי שבמקדש [ראשון] שהיתה קדושתו בכל הקהל והיתה השכינה שרויה בו לא היו עופות פורחות עליו אבל במקדש שני פחדו שמא אין קדושתו כקדושת ראשון ושמא יפרחו העופות על המקדש וישליכו שם דבר טומאה ועשו צורה להבריח העופות מגגי ההיכל וקראו אותה כולה עורב כלומר זו מונעת העורבים מלפרוח בגג ההיכל וזו צורה כדרך שעושין עכשיו שומרי הזרעים: ת"ר שלשה דברים נאמרו באצטמא אין יוצאין בה לרה"ר לפי שאינה כליו כשאר חשוב ואין בה משום כלאים דלא אריג הוא ואינה מטמאה בנגעים שאין בר הזות

מסורת הש"ס

[לקמן קי: וסס נסמן]

ס"א אלא מדרי' א"ר אמר רב יוסף אמר ר"י אמר שמואל

לקמן סד:

פי' ליין [ונערוך ערך אב פי' אב זיינא]

ס"א איתמר רב אמר כיפה של צמר תנן ושמואל אמר כבלא דעבדא תנן אבל כיפה של צמר שפיר דמי

[תוספ' פ"ה]

להציע כלאים תחתיהן כ"ל

הגהות הב"ח

(א) רש"י ד"ה כשם שאתם מודים וכו' לאמר. נ"ב ואח"כ לאמר הס"ד ואח"כ מ"ה אלא מודים לימאר כו' כ"ג בספר הס"ד וכ"ל שהוא ס"א:

(ג) תוס' ד"ה הבא וכו' אמאי תני לקטלא במתניתין: (ג) ד"ה תניא וכו' מדתני ובטוטפת ובסרביטין

רב נסים גאון

פ"ו תנו רבנן שלשה דברים נאמרו באיסטמא וכו' לדברי תנא קמא אין בה משום עטרת חתנים ולדברי ר' שמעון בן אלעזר אין בה משום עטרות כלות הוא מחמת הטעם שאמרו במס' סוטה בפרק האחרון (דף מט) בפולמוס של אספסינוס גזרו על עטרות חתנים בפולמוס של טיטוס גזרו על עטרות כלות ובפ' א' מן גיטין (דף ז) אמרו אמר ליה ריש גלותא לרב הונא כלילא מנלן דאסיר אמר ליה מדרבנן דתנן בפולמוס של אספסינוס קיסר גזרו על עטרות חתנים ועל האירוס אדהכי קם רב הונא לאיפנויי אמר ליה רב חסדא קרא כתיב (יחזקאל כא) כה אמר ה' הסר המצנפת וכי מה מצנפת אצל העטרה לומר לך בזמן שהמצנפת בראש כהן גדול תהא עטרה בראש חתנים נסתלקה מצנפת מראש כהן גדול תסתלק העטרה מראש כל אדם אדהכי אתא רב הונא אשכחינהו דהוו יתבי וקאמרי להא שמעתא אמר להו האלהים מדרבנן הוא דאסור:

fillets round their necks?[6]—Said Rabina: [57*b*] The reference here is to a broad band[7] which a woman ties very tightly,[8] as she is pleased to have a fleshy appearance.[9]

'R. Judah said: [Ribbons] of wool or of hair do not interpose, because the water enters through them.' R. Joseph said in the name of Rab Judah in Samuel's name: The *halachah* is as R. Judah in respect of ribbons of hair. Said Abaye to him: 'The *halachah* [is thus]' implies that they differ thereon?[10] And should you say, Had he not known the first Tanna to treat of ribbons of hair [too], he would not have treated thereof either: but perhaps he argued with them from analogy:[11] just as you agree with me in the matter of ribbons of hair, so should you agree with me in respect of wool ribbons? It was stated: R. Naḥman said in Samuel's name: The Sages agree with R. Judah in respect to ribbons of hair. It was taught likewise: Ribbons of wool interpose; ribbons of hair do not interpose. R. Judah maintained: [Ribbons] of wool or of hair do not interpose. R. Naḥman b. Isaac said: Our Mishnah too proves this. For it teaches: A woman may go out with ribbons
a of hair, whether of her own [hair] or of her companion's.[1] Who is the authority [for this]? Shall we say, R. Judah—even ribbons of wool too [are permitted]? Hence it must surely be the Rabbis, which proves that they do not disagree in respect of ribbons of hair. This proves it.

[SHE MAY] NOT [GO OUT] WITH FRONTLETS [ṬOṬEFETH]. What is ṬOṬEFETH?—Said R. Joseph: A charm containing balsam.[2] Said Abaye to him: Let it be [regarded] as an approved amulet, and hence permitted? Rather said Rab Judah on Abaye's authority: It is an ornament of beads.[3] It was taught likewise: A woman may go out with a gilded hair-net,[4] a *ṭoṭefeth*, and with *sarbiṭin* that are fastened to her. What is *ṭoṭefeth* and what is *sarbiṭin?*—Said R. Abbahu: A *ṭoṭefeth* encompasses her [head] from ear to ear; *sarbiṭin* reach to her cheeks. R. Huna said: Poor women make them of various dyed materials; wealthy women make them of gold and silver.

NOR WITH A HAIR-NET [KABUL]. R. Jannai said: I do not know what is this [*kabul*]: whether we learnt of a slave's chain, but a wool hair-net[5] is permitted; or perhaps we learnt of a wool hair-net and how much more so a slave's neckchain?[6]—Said R. Abbahu: Reason supports the view that we learnt of a wool hair-net. And it was taught likewise: A woman may go out into a courtyard with a *kabul* and a clasp [*istema*].[7] R. Simeon b. Eleazar said: [She may go out] with a *kabul* into the street too. R. Simeon b. Eleazar stated a general rule: Whatever is [worn] beneath the net, one may go out therewith: whatever is [worn] above the net, one may not go out with it.[8]

What is *istema?*—Said R. Abbahu: *Bizyune*. What is *bizyune?*—Said Abaye in Rab's name: That which imprisons the flying
b [locks].[1] Our Rabbis taught: Three things were said of an *istema:* It is not subject to [the interdict of] *kil'ayim*,[2] it is not defiled by leprosy,[3] and one may not go out with it into the street. On the authority of R. Simeon it was said: It is also not subject to [the interdict against] [58*a*] bridal crowns.[4]

(6) For they need not be removed before a ritual bath, being loose; v. *supra* 57*a*, n. b5. (7) Rashi. (8) Lit., 'chokes or strangles herself'. (9) In eastern countries that constitutes beauty. Being broad, the band does not injure her. (10) But the first Tanna says nothing about this! (11) Lit., 'he said to them, "just as".'

a (1) V. *infra* 64*b*. (2) Rashi: to ward off the evil eye. (3) Jast.: obsidian beads. (4) For if she removes it, her hair is uncovered; hence she is unlikely to remove it. (5) Or wig. (6) The term *Kabul* bears both meanings. (7) To keep the hair in order under the net or wig. (8) Thus he refers to the *kabul* as something above the hair band. Hence it can only mean the hair-net.

b (1) I.e., a clasp or buckle. (2) V. Glos. This may contain diverse materials. Rashi: because it is not spun; Riba: because it is hard, in which case the Rabbis did not impose a prohibition. (3) I.e., if leprosy breaks out in the *istema*. The reason is that it is not technically a garment. (4) The wearing of bridal crowns was forbidden as a sign of mourning for the destruction of the Temple; v. Soṭ. 49*a*.

But Samuel maintained: We learnt of a slave's neck-chain. Now, did Samuel say thus? Surely Samuel said: A slave may go out with a seal round his neck,[5] but not with a seal on his garments?—There is no difficulty: in the one case [the reference is] where his master set it upon him; in the other where he set it upon himself.[6] How have you explained this latter [dictum] of Samuel? that his master set it upon him! Then why [may he] not [go out] with the seal on his garment?—Lest it break off, and he be afraid and fold it [the garment] and put it over his shoulder.[7] This is as R. Isaac b. Joseph, who said in R. Johanan's name: If one goes out on the Sabbath with a folded garment slung over his shoulder, he incurs a sin-offering. And [this is] as Samuel said to R. Ḥinena b. Shila: No scholar of the house of the Resh Galutha[8] may go out with a cloak bearing a seal, except you, because the house of the Resh Galutha is not particular about you.[9]

It was stated above: 'Samuel said: A slave may go out with a seal around his neck, but not with the seal on his garments.' It was taught likewise: A slave may go out with a seal around his neck, but not with the seal on his garments. But the following contradicts this: A slave may not go out with the seal around his neck, nor with the seal on his garments; and neither are suscepti-
a ble to defilement.[1] [He may] not [go out] with the bell around his neck, but he may go out with the bell on his garments, and both are susceptible to defilement.[2] An animal may not go out with a seal around its neck nor with a seal on its covering, nor with the bell on its covering nor with the bell around its neck,[3] and none of these are susceptible to defilement.[4] Shall we say that in the one case his master had set it upon him, while in the other he had set it upon himself?[5]—No. In both cases his master had set it upon him, but one refers to a metal [seal] while the other refers to a clay [seal].[6] And [this is] as R. Naḥman said in Rabbah b. Abbuha's name: That about which the master is particular,[7] one [a slave] may not go out with it; that about which the master is not particular, one may go out with it. Reason too supports this, since it is stated: 'none of these are susceptible to defilement'. Now, if you say [that the reference is to] metal [seals], it is well; [hence] only these are not susceptible to defilement, but their utensils[8] are. But if you say that we learnt of clay [seals], [it might be asked] are only these not susceptible to defilement, whereas their utensils[9] are? Surely it was taught: Utensils of stone, dung, or earth do not contract uncleanness either by Biblical or by Rabbinical law.[10] Hence it follows that the reference is to metal [seals]. This proves it.

The Master said: '[He may] not [go out] with the bell around his neck, but he may go out with the bell on his garment.' Why not with the bell around his neck; [presumably] lest it snap off and he come to carry it: then also in the case of the bell on his garment let us fear that it may snap off and he come to carry it?—The reference here is to one that was woven [sewn] into it. And [this is] in agreement with R. Huna the son of R. Joshua, who said: Concerning whatever is woven they enacted
b no prohibition.[1]

The Master said: 'An animal may not go out with a seal around its neck, nor with a seal on its covering, nor with a bell around its neck, nor with a bell on its coat, and none of these are susceptible to defilement.' Now, does not an animal's bell contract uncleanness? But the following contradicts it: An animal's bell is unclean,[2] [58b]

(5) This is the slave's neck-chain. (6) In the former case he fears to remove it; hence he may wear it. But he is not afraid to remove it in the latter case, and possibly will. (7) He may fold the garment to hide the absence of the signet, fearing that his master may accuse him of having purposely removed it in order to pass as a free man. (8) V. *supra*, 48*a*, n. b7. (9) From this it appears that some scholars wore a badge to indicate that they belonged to the retinue of the exilarch, and were possibly in the position of his clients. He was also evidently very particular about this, so that if the seal fell off one might fold up the garment to hide its absence.

a (1) Because they are neither ornaments nor useful utensils, but merely badges of shame. (2) These are ornamental. (3) V. *supra* 54*b* for the reason. (4) They are not ornamental for the animal. (5) V. *supra* n. b6. (6) It is shown below that this must refer to a metal seal; hence even if his master set it upon him he may not go out with it, for should it accidentally snap off the slave would be afraid to leave it in the street on account of its value, but would bring it home, which is forbidden. But the value of a clay seal is negligible, whilst if his master set it upon him he is certainly afraid to remove it; hence he may go out with it. Consequently, the prohibition in the Mishnah, which treats of a clay seal, must refer to one that he set upon himself. (7) On account of its value. (8) I.e., the general appointments of an animal, its accoutrement and equipment, which rank as utensils. (9) Of clay. (10) Lit., 'the words of the scribes; v. Ḳid., 17*b*, n. b7. These clay seals were not glazed or burnt in a kiln, to be regarded as pottery, which can be defiled. Thus there is no point in teaching that they are free thereof, for no utensil of similar make is susceptible.

b (1) I.e., if something is woven into a garment, it may be worn on the Sabbath without fear of its falling off. V. *supra* 57*b*. (2) I.e., liable to uncleanness.

אין בה משום עטרות כלות ושמואל אמר כבלא דעבדא תנן ומי אמר שמואל הכי והאמר שמואל יוצא העבד בחותם שבצוארו אבל לא בחותם שבכסותו לא קשיא *הא דעבד ליה רביה הא דעבד איהו לנפשיה במאי אוקימתא להא דשמואל דעבד ליה רביה בחותם שבכסותו אמאי לא דילמא מיפסק ומירתת ומיקפל ליה ומחית ליה אכתפיה כדרב יצחק בר יוסף דא"ר יצחק בר יוסף א"ר יוחנן *היוצא בטלית מקופלת ומונחת לו על כתפיו בשבת חייב חטאת וכי הא דא"ל שמואל לרב חיננא בר שילא כולהו רבנן דבי ריש גלותא לא ליפקו בסרבלי חתימי לבר מינך דלא קפדי עליך דבי ריש גלותא: גופא אמר שמואל יוצא העבד בחותם שבצוארו אבל לא בחותם שבכסותו תניא נמי הכי [ב]יוצא העבד בחותם שבצוארו אבל לא בחותם שבכסותו ורמינהו לא יצא העבד בחותם שבצוארו ולא בחותם שבכסותו [ג]זה וזה אין מקבלין טומאה ולא בזוג שבצוארו אבל יוצא הוא בזוג שבכסותו [ד]זה וזה מקבלין טומאה [ה]ולא תצא בהמה לא בחותם שבצוארה ולא בחותם שבכסותה ולא בזוג שבכסותה ולא בזוג שבצוארה זה וזה אין מקבלין טומאה לימא הא דעבד ליה רביה הא דעבד איהו לנפשיה לא אידי ואידי דעבד ליה רביה וכאן [ו]בשל מתכת וכאן בשל טיט וכדרב נחמן אמר רבה בר אבוה דבר המקפיד עליו רבו אין יוצאין בו דבר שאין מקפיד עליו יוצאין בו ה"נ מסתברא מדקתני זה וזה אין מקבלין טומאה אי אמרת בשלמא של מתכת הני הוא דלא מקבלי טומאה הא כלים דידהו מקבלי טומאה אלא אי אמרת בשל טיט תנן הני הוא דלא מקבלי טומאה הא כלים דידהו מקבלי טומאה והא *תניא [ז]כלי אבנים כלי גללים וכלי אדמה אין מקבלין טומאה לא מדברי תורה ולא מדברי סופרים אלא ש"מ של מתכת ש"מ: אמר מר ולא בזוג שבצוארו אבל יוצא הוא בזוג שבכסותו *זוג שבצוארו אמאי לא דילמא מיפסיק ואתא לאיתויי זוג שבכסותו נמי ליחוש דילמא מיפסיק ואתי לאיתויי הבא במאי עסקינן דמיחא ביה מומחא וכדרב הונא בריה דרב יהושע דאמר *רב הונא בריה דרב יהושע כל שהוא ארוג לא גזרו: אמר מר לא תצא בהמה לא בחותם שבצוארה ולא בחותם שבכסותה ולא בזוג שבצוארה ולא בזוג שבכסותה זה וזה אין מקבלין טומאה וזוג דבהמה אין מקבלין טומאה ורמינהו זוג של בהמה טמאה ושל

רש"י

אין בה משום עטרות כלות · דגזרו עליהן שלא תלא בהן מחורבן ואילך משום צער במס' סוטה (דף מט.): ושמואל אמר · כבול דמתני' כבלא דעבדא ופליג אדר' אבהו: חותם שבצוארו · הוא כבלא דעבדא והיו עושין אותו משל טיט: דעביד ליה רביה · אית ליה אימתא ולא שקיל ליה מצוארו להוליכו בידו: מיפסק · החותם ונשבר ומירתת מרבו שלא יאמר שהוא נטלו להראות בשוק שהוא בן חורין: ומקפל ליה · הטלית על כתפיו כדי שלא יראה מקום החותם ולא יביטו שנפל ודמי הטלית על כתפו כמשוי: חייב חטאת · דאינו תכשיט אלא בזמן שלובשו דרך מלבוש: כולהו רבנן לא ליפקו בסרבלי חתימי · היו עושין חותמות לטליתות שלהן כעין עבדים להראות שהן כפופין לריש גלותא לא ליפקו דאי מפסקי מרתתי ומקפלי להו: דלא קפדי עלך · אם תלך בלא חותם: יוצא העבד בחותם שבצוארו · ובשל טיט דלא קפיד עליה לאתויי ואי משום דמירתת מאי חורבא נפקא מינה משום אימתא דרביה. לא מייתי ליה בידיה דהא לאו הוכחה היא דעבדות אלא כשישנו על צוארו או בכסותו: וזה וזה אין מקבלין טומאה · דלאו לנוי עביד שיהא טמא משום תכשיט ואע"ג דבשל מתכת מוקמינן לה להא לקמן מיהו לאו לנוי דיליה הוא אלא לגנאי וכלי תשמיש נמי לא הוי: זוג · לנוי עביד: ולא בזוג שבצוארו אבל יוצא הוא בזוג שבכסותו · לקמיה מפרש טעמא: מקבלין טומאה · שתכשיט הוא: שבכסותה · עושים לסוסים מעילין שלא יטנפו: לא תצא · כדאמרינן באידך פרקין (ד' נד:) דמתחזי כמאן דאזיל לחינגא: אין מקבלין טומאה · דאין תכשיט לבהמה: לא אידי ואידי דעבד ליה רביה · דאע"ג דכבול דמתניתין אוקימנא בדעבד איהו לנפשיה התם הוא דאיכא לאוקמיה בסתם חותמות של טיט דאי מיתבר אין מקפיד עליו להביא שבריו לבית אדונו הלכך ליכא לאוקמיה בדעבד ליה רביה דאי עבד ליה רביה לא הוה מיתסר דכל זמן שלא נפסק לא שקיל ליה מצוארו משום אימתא דרביה ואי מיפסק לא קפיד עליה בעליו משום פסידא דליכא פסידא הלכך לא מייתי ליה אבל הך לא איכא לאוקמא בשל טיט כדמסתברא לקמן מסיפא הלכך אפילו עבד ליה רביה נמי אסור דאי מיפסק קפיד עליה משום פסידא ומירתת עבד ומייתי ליה בידיה: דבר המקפיד עליו רבו · אם יאבד לא יצא דאי מפסיק מייתי ליה: מסתברא · דבשל מתכת קאי מדאיצטריך למיתני אין מקבלין טומאה וטעמא משום דלאו לנוי עבידא: הני הוא דלא מקבלין טומאה · משום דלאו כלים נינהו הא שאר כלי מתכות מקבלין: כלים דידהו · דמתכות: אלא אי אמרת · כלים דידהו כלי העשוי מטיט כזה שאינו מצרפו בכבשן מעשה ידי יוצר דניהוי קרוי כלי חרס אלא כלי אדמה מי מקבל טומאה בתמיה: כלי גללים · °לפיעי בקר שעשה מהן כלי: דמיחא מומחא · שארגו בבגד ותו לא מיפסיק: לא גזרו · לצאת בו ודרב הונא לענין אריג כי האי גוונא נמי איתמר דאשמעינן דלא חיישינן תו לדלמא מיפסק: ושל

תוספות

והאמר שמואל יוצא העבד בחותם כו' · ולא בעי לאוקמי מתניתין בחותם שבכסותו דניחא ליה לאוקמה בדעבד איהו לנפשיה ואיירי מתני' בכל חותמות: הא דעבד איהו לנפשיה · קשה לרשב"א אמאי שריא מתני' בדעבד איהו לנפשיה בחצר כיון דליכא קפידא דרבו וי"ל דאיכא קצת קפידא אבל לא כל כך כמו בעבד ליה רביה: במאי אוקימתא להא דשמואל בדעבד ליה רביה כו' · אבל אי מיירי בדעבד איהו לנפשיה אתי שפיר דבצוארו ליכא למיחש דלמא פסיק ליה בידים כדי שלא יביטו הרואין שהוא עבד אבל בכסותו איכא למיחש דלמא מקפל טליתו לכסות החותם ולא ידע דיש בזה חיוב חטאת אבל בדעבד ליה רביה משום אימתא דרביה ירא לקפל והשתא נמי ידע הש"ס לדרב יצחק אלא דלא ידע שיש לחוש דילמא מיפסיק ובתר דמשני מייתי דרב יצחק ונחת לפרושי שיש חיוב חטאת בקיפול: דילמא מיפסק ומרתת ומקפל ליה · דניחא ליה טפי שיהיה מקופל משיראה רבו שנפסק לגמרי ויסבור שבמזיד פסקו למרוד בו: לא תצא בהמה כו' · דמיחזי כמאן דאזיל לחינגא כדפי' בקונ' דלא מצינן למימר משום דילמא מיפסיק ואתי לאתויי דהא לעיל (דף נד:) מפרש דזוג אסור משום דמיחזי כמאן דאזיל לחינגא ולא קאמר דלמא מיפסק דומיא דחותם: מאי שנא זוג שבצוארו דלמא מיפסיק ואתי לאתויי · והא דתנן לקמן (דף סו:) בני מלכים יוצאין בזוגין וכל אדם אלא שדברו חכמים בהווה אומר ר"י דמיירי בזוגין יקרים שיוצאין בהן בני מלכים כגון של כסף ושל זהב דליכא למיחש בהו דילמא מיפסיק דמסתמא תקועין הן יפה בשלשלאות של כסף והכא מיירי בזוג דעלמא דומיא דזוג של בהמה ולמאי דמוקי לה בגמרא באריג בכסותו אתי נמי שפיר: הב"ע דמחי · וא"ת כי היכי דזוג איירי במחי הכי נמי איירי חותם שבכסותו במחי ואם כן אמאי אסור וי"ל דזוג מותר לפי שדרך לאורגו בבגד שאין שום בגד שלא יהא ראוי לנוי ותכשיט כזה ולא הטריחוהו לפוסקו מכלי בגדים ולגנות הבגד אבל חותם אין דרך לעשותו בכל הבגדים שאינו יפוי הבגד ולכך גזרו חכמים אפילו באריג בכסותו שיהא צריך לפוסקו אטו היכא שאין אריג וא"ת אדמפליג בין זוג שבצוארו לזוג שבכסותו ליפלוג בזוג שבכסותו גופיה בין מחי ללא מחי ויש לומר דניחא ליה לאשמעינן דזוג שבצוארו אסור אפילו בחתיכת הבגד שסביב צוארו ואינה יכולה ליפול אלא ע"י חתיכה: כדרב הונא כו' · ואע"ג דמילתא דרב הונא אייתי לעיל (דף נז.) גבי חלילה מדקאמר כל שהוא אריג משמע דה"ק בין לענין חלילה בין לענין דלמא מיפסיק לא חיישינן באריג: *אע"פ שחברו בדלת וקבעו במסמרים טמא · והא דאמר בהקומץ רבה (מנחות דף כט.) סדין שעשאו וילון טהור מן המדרס לאו משום קביעות גרידא טהור אלא מיירי שעשה שום שינוי מעשה · והא דאמר בנגמר הדין (סנהדרין דף מח:) כפה שנתנו לספר טהור מן המדרס אף על פי שלא עשה שום שינוי מעשה כיון דנאסר בגאה ע"י כן חשוב כשינוי מעשה: אין

רבינו חננאל

שתי וערב. [אמר] רב הונא טוטפת עניות עושות של מיני צבעונין עשירות עושות אותן של כסף ושל זהב: הא דאמר שמואל יוצא העבד בשבת בחותם שבצוארו אבל לא בחותם שבכסותו הא והא בחותם דעבד ליה רביה ובחותם שבכסותו אמאי לא נפיק חיישינן דלמא מיפסק ומירתת מרביה ומכפל לכסותיה ומנח ליה אכתפיה וכר' יוחנן דאמר היוצא בטלית מקופלת ומונחת לו על כתיפו בשבת חייב חטאת וכדאמרו ליה לרב חנניא בר שילא רבנן כולהו לא ליפקו בסרבלא חתימה פי' דת המלך היתה באותה העת כל הקונה סרבלא מייתי לה גבי מוכס ויהיב ליה מיכסיה וחתים עליה במטבע של אינך כדי לידע שנטל מיכסא וכל טלית שנמצאת בלא חותם אינך נתפש לובשה כגנב המכס הלכך מתיירא כל אדם לצאת בטלית שתלוי עליה חותם זה חיישינן שמא יפסק החותם ומפני פחדו מן המוכס יסירה מעליה ויקפלה וישאנה על כתיפו כמשא לפיכך אסורה לכל אדם לצאת בטלית שיש עליה חותם אבל רב חנינה בר שילא שיש לו נשיאות פנים ואינו חושש מן המוכס מותר לו לצאת בטלית שיש בה חותם שאם יחתך החותם אינו חושש שאינו מתיירא מן המוכס ולא מזולתו ומפני זה הטעם אסר שמואל לצאת העבד בחותם שעשה לו רבו בכסותו. תנ"ה יוצא העבד בחותם שבצוארו אבל לא בחותם שבכסותו איני והא תנינן לא יצא העבד לא בחותם שבצוארו ולא בחותם שבכסותו וזה וזה אין מקבלין טומאה כו' ושנינן הא והא דעביד ליה רביה. ולא קשיא*) הא דתני

*) נראה דחסר כאן וכצ"ל ולא קשיא כאן בשל מתכת וכאן בשל טיט אמר מר לא תצא בהמה וכו' זה וזה אין מקבלין טומאה ורמינהו זוג של בהמה טמאה לא קשיא וכו'.

עין משפט נר מצוה

יא א ב מיי' פי"ט מהל' שבת הל' יח [ועיין במ"מ] סמג לאוין סה טוש"ע א"ח סי' דש סעיף א' בהג"ה:

יב ג מיי' פ"ח מהל' כלים הלכה ט:

יג ד שם הלכה ח:

יד ה מיי' פ"כ מהל' שבת הלכה י סמג לאוין סה טוש"ע א"ח סי' שה סעיף יב:

טו ו מיי' פי"ט מהל' שבת הלכה יח סמג שם טוש"ע א"ח סי' דש סעיף א בהג"ה:

טז ז מיי' פ"א מהל' כלים הלכה ו:

מסורת הש"ס

לקמן סו.

[כלים פ"י מ"א ע"ש] מנחות סט: [ושם איתא דבר זה בשם דאמר מר כלי אבנים]

מ"ש זות שבצנארו דלא דילמא כו' כצ"ל רש"ל

[לעיל ס.]

גליון הש"ס

רש"י ד"ה כלי גללים לפיעי בקר. ע"ל דף סז ע"ב ברש"י ד"ה גללים. ועי' מנחות סט ע"ב תד"ה כלי גללים:

עין משפט נר מצוה

יז א מיי' פ"ח מהל' כלים הלכה יב :

יח ב מיי' פ"ח מהל' כלים הלכה ז :

יט ג מיי' פ' יב מהל' פרה הלכה ט :

תורה אור

ושל דלת טהורה *של דלת ועשאו לבהמה טמאה של בהמה ועשאו לדלת אף על פי שחיברו לדלת וקבעו במסמרים טמא שכל הכלים *יורדין לידי טומאתן במחשבה ואין עולין מידי טומאתן אלא בשינוי מעשה לא קשיא הא דאית ליה עינבל הא דלית ליה עינבל מה נפשך אי מנא הוא אע"פ דלית ליה עינבל אי לאו מנא הוא עינבל משוי ליה מנא אין כדר' שמואל בר נחמני א"ר יונתן *דאמר ר' שמואל בר נחמני אמר ר' יונתן מנין למשמיע קול בכלי מתכות שהוא טמא שנאמר °כל דבר אשר יבא באש תעבירו באש אפי' דיבור יבא באש [במדבר לא] במאי אוקימתא בדלית ליה עינבל אימא מציעתא ולא בזוג שבצוארו אבל יוצא הוא בזוג שבכסותו וזה וזה מקבלין טומאה אי דלית ליה עינבל מי מקבלי טומאה ורמינהו *[ג]העושה זגין למכתשת ולעריסה ולמטפחות ספרים ולמטפחות תינוקות יש להם עינבל טמאין אין להם עינבל טהורין ניטלו עינבליהן עדיין טומאתן עליהם ה"מ בתינוק דלקלא עבידי ליה אבל גדול תכשיט הוא ליה אע"ג דלית ליה עינבל : אמר מר ניטלו עינבליהן עדיין טומאתן עליהן למאי חזו אמר אביי הואיל שההדיוט יכול להחזירו מתיב רבא *[ג]הזוג והעינבל חיבור וכי תימא הכי קאמר אע"ג דלא מחבר כמאן דמחבר דמי והתניא *מספורת של פרקים ואיזמל של רהיטני חיבור לטומאה ואין חיבור להזאה ואמרינן מה נפשך אי חיבור הוא אפילו להזאה (א) ואי לא חיבור הוא אפילו לטומאה נמי לא ואמר רבה דבר תורה בשעת מלאכה חיבור בין לטומאה בין להזאה שלא בשעת מלאכה אינו חיבור לא לטומאה ולא להזאה וגזרו על טומאה שלא בשעת מלאכה משום טומאה שהיא בשעת מלאכה ועל הזאה שהיא בשעת מלאכה משום הזאה שלא בשעת מלאכה אלא אמר רבא

הואיל

רש"י

ושל דלת טהור · דלת מחובר לבית הוא שהוא חבור לקרקע ואינו כלי לקבל טומאה וזוג העשוי לו בטיל לגביה כדאמרי' בריש פרקין דלעיל* כל המחובר לו הרי הוא כמוהו : של דלת ועשאו לבהמה טמא· מכאן ולהבא ואע"פ דלא עבד ביה מעשה אלא שחישב עליו ותלאו ותלייה לאו מעשה היא שכל הכלים יורדים לידי תורת טומאה במחשבה שלו : של בהמה ועשאו לדלת טמא · ואפי' מכאן להבא יקבל טומאה שאין חיבורו מעשה עד שישנהו מכמות שהיה : שאין עולין מטומאתן . מתורת טומאה שירדה להן ואע"פ שעדיין לא נטמאו משנמלך עליהן אין עולין מלקבל טומאה אלא בשינוי מעשה : עינבל · בטדי"ל שעשוי בתוכו להשמיע קול : אי מנא הוא · דתכשיט חשיב ליה : עינבל משוי ליה מנא · בתמיה משום העינבל מי הוי תכשיט : אין · עינבל משוי ליה מנא ולא משום תכשיט אלא משום כלי : כל דבר שיבא באש· בכלי מתכות משתעי במעשה מדין : אימא מציעתא · זוג דאדם : מי מקבל טומאה · אפי' דאדם : העושה זגין למכתשת · שמפטמין בה סממנין להקטיר לריח דקיי"ל בכריתות (פ"א ד' ו) שהקול יפה לבשמים: ולעריסה · שהתינוק שוכב בתוכה שקורין בירל"ה ותולה בו זגין לקשקש כדי שישמע התינוק ויַשן : ולמטפחות ספרים · כשנושאין אותן לבית הכנסת שהתינוקות של בית רבן קורין שם מקשקשין הזגין והתינוקות שומעין ובאין : ולמטפחות תינוקות · שתולין בצוארן : ניטלו עינבליהם כו' · (אם ניטלו קודם שנטמאו תורת טומאה עליהם ומקבלין טומאה כדמפרש טעמא לקמיה מעיקרא כי אין להם עינבל דקתני טהורין (ב) דעדיין לא נגמרה מלאכתן אבל משירדה להם תורת טומאה לא בטל שם כלי מעליהם בנטילת העינבל) ואם ניטל לאחר שנטמאו עדיין טומאתן עליהן דלא הוי ככלי שנשבר ובטל מתורת כלי ליטהר מטומאתו : הדיוט · שאין צריך אומן : הזוג והעינבל חיבור · כשהן יחד הרי הן כלי אחד נטמא זה נטמא זה הזה על זה טהור זה וכיון דקרי ליה חיבור שמע מינה דכי נתפרדו הוי כלי שניטל מקלתו ואף על גב דהדיוט יכול להחזירו כל כמה דלא אהדריה לאו שלם הוא : וכי תימא · דהאי חיבור דקאמר הכי קאמר אפי' מפורדים קרינן ליה חיבור ואתא לאשמעי' דאם נתפרדו משנטמאו לא עלו מטומאתן : הא תניא · גבי ההיא : מספורת של פרקים · שעשוי סכינים שלה מתפרדין : ואיזמל של רהיטני · פליינה של אומנים תריסים שנותנים האיזמל לתוך בין שני עצים העשוין לכך ולאחר מלאכתו נוטלו ומצניעו : חיבור לטומאה · ואם נטמא זה נטמא זה : שלא בשעת מלאכה הואיל ואין צריכין להיות מחוברין הוו להו כשני כלים ואין חיבור ואף על פי שמחוברין דע"כ שלא בשעת מלאכה דומיא דשעת מלאכה קאמר ובשעת מלאכה מחוברין הן אלמא במחוברין עסקינן וגזרו לחומרא על הטומאה דליהוי חיבור ועל הזאה דלא ליהוי חיבור ומשום הכי קתני חיבור לטומאה לעולם ואין חיבור להזאה לעולם : אלא אמר רבא . לא תימא הואיל והדיוט יכול להחזיר דודאי (ג) חד מנא הוא כדקתני בברייתא הזוג והעינבל חיבור וכי מיפרדי הוי כלי שניטל מקלתו *ואינו מקבל טומאה העינבל לעצמו אבל הזוג טמא לעצמו דלא בטל ליה מתורת כלי :

הואיל

תוספות

אין כדר' שמואל כו' · דחשיב ליה כלי תשמיש לאדם משום דבעי ליה לקלא דע"י הזוג ששומע יודע היכן בהמתו עומדת ומולאה ע"י כך °והוי כמקל של בהמה של מתכת דטמאה הואיל ואדם רודה בה וכ"מ לקמן גבי בירית טהורה דמשמיע [קול] בכלי מתכות אינו טמא אלא היכא דבעי ליה לקלא והא דמשני הא דאית ביה עינבל הא דלית ביה עינבל ולא מחלק באית ביה עינבל בין בעי ליה לקלא בין לא בעי אומר ר"י דלא שכיח שיעשו עינבל אלא אם כן בעי ליה לקלא :

כל דבר אשר יבא · ואע"ג דהאי קרא לא לגבי טומאה כתיב אלא לגבי הגעלה מסתברא דהתם אין דיבור מעלה ומוריד ואם אינו ענין להגעלה תנהו לענין טומאה :

מתיב רבא הזוג והעינבל חיבור · פי' בקונטרס מדקרי ליה חיבור ש"מ דכי נתפרדו הוי כלי שניטל מקלתו ואע"ג דהדיוט יכול להחזיר כל כמה דלא אהדרי' לאו שלם הוא וקשה לר"י דהא מעיקרא נמי הוי ידעינא דהוי כלי שניטל מקלתו ולהכי פריך למאי חזו ומשני דודאי באפי נפשה לא חזו לא זוג ולא עינבל אלא משום דהדיוט יכול להחזירו ומה שפירש נמי והתניא כו' גבי ההיא מספורת של פרקים לא עיין דההוא דזוג ועינבל משנה היא במסכת פרה (פי"ב משנה ח) וההיא דמספורת בתוספתא דכלים ומפרש הרב פור"ת בשם ר' שמואל הואיל והדיוט יכול להחזירם ואע"ג דהשתא בלא עינבל לא חזי מידי כיון דהדיוט יכול בקל להחזירה כמאן דמיחברי דמי ואם נטמא העינבל נטמא גם הזוג כאילו הן מחוברין נפקא מינה דלכשיתחברו יטמא הזוג את הנוגע בו ומיהו בלא חיבור לא יטמא כי אם העינבל לבדו שנגע בטומאה והכי משמע לישנא דקאמר וכי תימא ה"ק אע"ג דלא מיחברי כמאן דמיחברי דמי משמע דאביי הכי סבירא ליה דמדתלי טעמא בחזרת הדיוט משמע דסבר דלא חזי השתא למידי ואי לאו כמחובר חשיב ליה היאך יקבל טומאה אחר דלא חזי מידי בלא חזרה: *מתיב רבא הזוג והעינבל חיבור · שאם נטמא זה נטמא זה וה"מ כשמחוברים אבל שלא בשעת חיבור אם נטמא זה לא נטמא זה ולא חיישינן להדיוט יכול להחזיר דהשתא מיהא לאו מחוברין ניהו וממשנה זו אין לנו להוכיח דמיירי בשעת חיבור כדקאמר וכי תימא כו' אבל מכח ברייתא מוכיח דבשעת חיבור מיירי ומברייתא גרידתא הוה מצי רבא לאותוביה לאביי אלא דניחא ליה לאקשויי מהך דמיירי בזוג ועינבל בהדיא לאביי דאיירי נמי בזוג ועינבל : ([illegible] תימא כו') והתניא מספורת של פרקים ואיזמל של רהיטני. שתי ברייתות הן במסכת כלים* כל אחד בפני עצמה ובריישא קתני בהדיא דכשאינן מחוברין מקבל כל א' טומאה בפני עצמו וגזרו על טומאה שלא בשעת מלאכה שיהא חיבור לטומאה ליטמא זה כשניטמא זה משום דדמי לשעת מלאכה אבל שלא בחיבורין משמע דאפי' גזירה דרבנן ליכא ואם נטמא זה לא נטמא זה דלא חיים למה שהדיוט יכול להחזירו : (אלא) אמר רבא הואיל ויכול להקישו · פי' מקבל טומאה הזוג אבל עינבל דאין ראוי להקישו לא ומספורת ואיזמל נמי בלא חיבור ראויין למעין מלאכה ראשונה ומקבלי טומאה כל אחד בפני עצמו כדתני בתוספתא : אלא אמר רבא כו' · פירש בקונטרס דטומאה לא פרח הימנו כשנפרד משקיבל הואיל וראוי להקישו והוה ליה ככלי (עין) שניקב בפחות ממוליא רמון דלא טהר מטומאה ומשמע שרוצה לומר דמכאן ואילך לא מקבל טומאה וקשה לר"י דלמה לא יקבל טומאה כיון דנפחת פחות מכשיעור דהאי כאילו שלם לגמרי ונראה לר"י דודאי גם מקבל טומאה מכאן ולהבא ולקונטרס דחק לפרש כן משום דכשלא היה להם עינבל טהורין ולא מקבלי טומאה אף על גב דראוי להקישו ואינו דומה דכשלא היה בו עינבל מעולם ודאי טהור דכיון שעומד ליתן בו עינבל דהא עביד לקלא והוי גולמי כלי מתכות אבל משנגמר שהיה בו עינבל אף על פי שניטל מקבל טומאה שלא בטל מתורת כלי שהיה עליו קודם לכן והר"ס הביא ראיה מחמת שתפרה ושייר פחות ממוליא רמון דטהורה (חולין קלה·) אע"ג דאמת שלם שנקרע

פחות

רבינו חננאל

אין מקבלין טומאה בדלית ליה עינבל והא דתני טמא בזוג שיש לו עינבל פי' עינבל הברזל שבתוך הזוג המקיש בדופני הזוג ומשמיע הקול וכי הא דאמר כו' מנין למשמיע קול בכלי מתכות שטמא שנאמר כל דבר אשר יבא באש אפילו דבור במשמע ואקשינן במאי אוקימנא להא דתני בזוג בהמה אין מקבלין טומאה בדלית לה עינבל אימ' מציעתא אין העבד יוצא בזוג שבצוארו אבל יוצא בזוג שבכסותו וזה וזה מקבלין טומאה ואי לית ליה עינבל מי מקבלי טומאה והתנן העושה זגין למכתשת ו[ל ע ר י ס ה] ולמטפחות ספרים ולמטפחת תינוקו' כולן יש להן עינבליהן טמאין אין להן עינבליהן טהורין כו' . ושנינן הא בתינוק דלקלא עבידי אבל גדול כגון העבד דלתכשיט עביד ליה רביה אע"ג דלית ליה עינבל מקבל טומאה ואקשינן ניטלו עינבליהן עדיין טומאתן עליהן אי נטלו עינבליהן למאי חזו ושנינן בזה דכיון דהדיוט יכול להחזיר אע"פ שעדיין לא החזירו כמוחזר דמי . איני והא תנינן מספורת של פרקים ואיזמל של רהיטני כו' וכבר פירשנו למעלה (מח:) ומשני

רב נסים גאון

הזוג והעינבל חיבור . ראוי לידע כי זה הזוג אלתי הזוג הנאמר גבי נזיר ותמצא פי' דבר זה במסכת נזירות בפ' ג' מינין (דף לד) תרצנים אלו החיצונים הזגין אלו הפנימיים דברי ר' יהודה ר' יוסי אומר שלא תטעה בזוג של בהמה החיצון זוג והפנימי

רש"ל ומהר"מ כתבו דכל הגהדיבורי תוס' הם דיבו' אחד מן מתיב רבא עד סוף ד"ה אלא וכו' כדתני בתוספתא

ר"מ מ"ז [נס"ג דבבא מליעא]

מסורת הש"ס

דף נב:

כלים פכ"ה מ"ט סוכה יג: לעיל נב: קדושין נט. [מנחות סט.]

לקמן סג:

תוספ' דכלים ב"מ פ"א

רש"ל מוחק כ"ז

פרה פי"ב מ"ח

לעיל מח: [תוספ' כלים ב"מ פ"ג]

הגהות הב"ח

(א) גמ' ואפי' להזאה נמי ולאו חיבור : (ב) רש"י ד"ה ניטלו עינבליהם וכו' ומעיקרא כי אין להם עינבל דקתני טהורין משום דעדיין : (ג) ד"ה אלא אמר וכו' דודאי לאו חד מנא :

גליון הש"ס

תוס' ד"ה אין וכו' כמקל של בהמה לעיל נ"ב ע"ב

ואינו מקבל טומאה הזוג לעצמו אבל לענין טומאה לא פרחה מיניה משקבלה כבר והשאר נמחק רש"ל

but a door bell is clean.[3] A door [bell] appointed for an animal['s use] is unclean; an animal [bell] appointed for [fixing] to a door, even if attached to the door and fastened with nails, is unclean; for all utensils enter upon their uncleanness by intention, but are relieved from their uncleanness only by a change-effecting act?[4]—There is no difficulty: in the one case [the reference is] where it has a clapper: in the other where it has no clapper.[5] What will you: if it is a utensil, then even if it has no clapper [it is unclean]; if it is not a utensil, does the clapper make it one?—Yes, as R. Samuel b. Naḥmani said in R. Joḥanan's name, Viz.: How do we know that a metal object which causes sound is unclean?[6] Because it is said, *Everything* [dabar] *that may abide the*
a *fire, ye shall make go through the fire:*[1] even speech [*dibbur*—i.e., sound] must pass through the fire.[2]

How have you interpreted it? as referring to [a bell] without a clapper! Then consider the middle clause: 'Nor with a bell around his neck, but he may go out with a bell on his garments, and both can contract uncleanness.' But if it has no clapper, can it become defiled? Surely the following contradicts this: If one makes bells for the mortar,[3] for a cradle,[4] for the mantles of Scrolls,[5] or for children's mantles, then if they have a clapper, they are unclean; if they have no clapper,[6] they are clean. If their clappers are removed,[7] they still retain their uncleanness.[8]—That is only in the case of a child, where its purpose is [to produce] sound.[9] But in the case of an adult, it is an ornament for him even without a clapper.

The Master said: 'If their clappers are removed, they still retain their uncleanness.' What are they fit for?[10] Said Abaye: [They are still utensils,] because an unskilled person can put it back. Raba objected: A bell and its clapper are [counted as] connected.[11] And should you answer, This is its meaning: Even when they are not connected, they are [counted as] connected,[12]—surely it was taught: A shears of separate blades[13] and the cutter of a [carpenter's] plane are [counted as] connected in respect of uncleanness, but not in respect of sprinkling. Now we objected, What will you: if they are [counted as] connected, [they should be so] even in respect of sprinkling too; [if they count] not as connected, they should not [be so] even in respect of defilement either? And Rabbah answered: By Scriptural law, when in use they are [counted as] connected in respect of both defilement and sprinkling; when not in use, they are [counted as] connected in respect of neither defilement nor sprinkling. But they [the Rabbis] enacted a preventive measure in respect of defilement when they are not in use on account of defilement when they are in use; and in respect of sprinkling, when they are in use, on account of when

(3) The door being part of the house, it is not a utensil, and hence cannot become unclean; the bell, in turn, is part of the door. (4) V. *supra* 52b, n. c9. Here too the bells were left unchanged. (5) If it has a clapper it is susceptible to defilement as a utensil. .(6) I.e., it ranks as a utensil.

a (1) Num. XXXI, 23. (2) In order to cleanse it, which shows that it is liable to defilement. This connects *dabar* (E.V. *thing*) with *dibbur*, speech, i.e., a sound-producing object is a utensil. (3) In which the spices are pounded for use as frankincense in the Temple. Sound was thought to add to the efficacy of crushing; v. Ker. 6b. (4) To amuse the baby or lull it to sleep. (5) Of the Torah. It was customary to adorn these with bells. (6) From the very outset. (7) After the bells were defiled. (8) Because they do not lose the status of utensils and become as broken utensils through the removal of the clapper. (9) Hence without a clapper its purpose is not fulfilled, and it is not a utensil. (10) That they are not regarded as broken utensils. (11) And rank as a single utensil, so that if one becomes unclean the other is too. (This is, of course, when they are together.) Similarly, if one is besprinkled (v. Num. XIX, 18f), the other becomes clean. This shows that when they are separated, each is but a fragment of a utensil, though an unskilled person can replace it, and should therefore be clean. (12) Exactly as the sense in Abaye's explanation. (13) Lit., 'joints'.

a they are not in use![1]—Rather, said Raba, [59a] [The reason is] because they[2] are fit for beating on an earthen utensil.[3] It was stated likewise: R. Jose son of R. Ḥanina said: [The reason is] because they are fit for beating on an earthen utensil. R. Joḥanan said: Because they are fit for giving a child a drink of water therein.

Now, does not R. Joḥanan require [that it shall be fit for] a usage of its original nature?[4] Surely it was taught: *And everything whereon he sitteth* [*shall be unclean*];[5] I might think that if he [the *zab*] overturns a *se'ah*[6] and sits upon it, or a *tarkab*[7] and sits upon it, it is unclean: hence it is stated, '*whereon he sitteth*', teaching, [only] that which is appointed for sitting, excluding this, where we say to him, 'Get up, that we may do our business!'[8]
b R. Eleazar said: In cases of *midras*[1] we say, 'Get up, that we may do our business'; but we do not say in the case of the defilement of the dead, 'Get up, that we may do our business!'[2] But R. Joḥanan maintained: In the case of defilement through the dead too we say, 'Get up, that we may do our business!'[3]—Reverse the former.[4] But what [reason] do you see to reverse the former; reverse the latter?[5]—Because we know R. Joḥanan to require [fitness for] usage of its original nature. For we learnt: An animal's shoe, [if] of metal, is unclean.[6] For what is it fit?—Rab said: It is fit for drinking water therein in battle.[7] R. Ḥanina said: It is fit for anointing oneself with oil from it in battle.[8] R. Joḥanan said: When one is fleeing from the field of battle, he places this [shoe] on his [own] feet and runs over briars and thorns.[9] Wherein do Rab and R. Ḥanina differ?—Where it is repulsive.[10] R. Joḥanan and R. Ḥanina differ where it is [too] heavy.[11]

NOR WITH A GOLDEN CITY, what is meant by, WITH A GOLDEN CITY?—Rabbah b. Bar Ḥanah said in R. Joḥanan's name: A

a (1) For notes v. *supra* 48b and 49a. Now, obviously this must all refer to where the parts are joined, since we compare these utensils when not in use to same when in use. Hence it is implied that when not actually together they do not become defiled even by Rabbinical law, because each is regarded as a fragment, though an unskilled person can join them. (2) The bells that had their clappers removed. (3) Then they produce a bell-like sound just as when they have a clapper. Hence it is a utensil like before, and so remains unclean. But when the parts of a shears of or a plane are separated, they cannot be used at all. (4) Where a utensil is damaged or divided, does not R. Joḥanan hold that in order to remain unclean or susceptible to defilement it must still be fit for the same usage as before, it being insufficient that it shall merely be fit for some purpose? (5) Lev. XV, 6. The reference is to a *zab*, q.v. Glos. (6) A measure of capacity. V. Glos. (7) Half a *se'ah*. (8) I.e., the *zab* would be told that the measure is needed for its main purpose; hence it is not unclean. This shows that as a general principle every article is regarded from the point of view of its original and primary function.

b (1) Lit., 'treading'. The uncleanness caused by a *zab*'s treading, leaning against, or weighing down upon an article, even if he does not actually touch it with his body. This includes sitting. (2) I.e., in respect of an article's defilement through a corpse, or by a person who was himself defiled by a corpse, we do not say that in order to become unclean or remain unclean it shall be fit for its main purpose, but even if one has to say to the person using it, 'Get up, that we may do our business' it is still subject to the laws of uncleanness. (3) Thus he insists that it shall be fit for its original function. Rashi maintains that this can refer only to a utensil which is broken or divided after becoming defiled; it does not remain unclean unless fit for a usage of its original nature. R. Ḥan. holds that it refers to its defilement from the very outset. (4) Transpose the reasons given by R. Jose b. Ḥanina and R. Joḥanan. (5) Transpose the views of R. Joḥanan and R. Eleazar. (6) I.e., liable to become unclean. (7) On a field of battle where no other utensils may be available, one can take up water in the cavity of the shoe into which the animal's foot fits. (8) This is a necessary part of one's toilet in the hot eastern countries; v. *T.A.*, I, 229, 233. The shoe might serve as an improvised oil pot. (9) Thus R. Joḥanan justifies its uncleanness only because it is still fit for a usage of the original nature. (10) For drinking. Hence, on Rab's view it is not subject to defilement, but on R. Ḥanina's it is. Rab disregards its possible use as an oil container, holding that soldiers dispense with oil on a field of battle. (11) For running. According to R. Ḥanina it is nevertheless susceptible to defilement, but not according to R. Joḥanan.

הואיל וראוי להקישו על גבי חרס איתמר נמי אמר ר' יוסי בר' חנינא הואיל וראוי להקישו על גבי חרס ר' יוחנן אמר הואיל וראוי לגמע בו מים לתינוק ור' יוחנן לא בעי מעין מלאכה ראשונה *והתניא °וכל כלי אשר ישב עליו וגו' *יכול כפה סאה וישב עליה כפה תרקב וישב עליה יהא טמא תלמוד לומר (א) אשר ישב עליו הזב מי שמיוחד לישיבה יצא זה שאומרים לו עמוד ונעשה מלאכתנו ר' אלעזר אומר במדרסות אומרים עמוד ונעשה מלאכתנו ואין אומרים בטמא מת עמוד ונעשה מלאכתנו ור' יוחנן אמר אף אומר בטמא מת עמוד ונעשה מלאכתנו איפוך קמייתא ומאי חזית דאפכת קמייתא איפוך בתרייתא הא שמעינן ליה לרבי יוחנן דבעי מעין מלאכה ראשונה (*דתניא) *סנדל של בהמה של מתכת טמא למאי חזי אמר רב ראוי לשתות בו מים במלחמה ור' חנינא אמר ראוי לסוך בו שמן במלחמה ור' יוחנן אמר בשעה שבורח מן הקרב מניחו ברגליו ורץ על קוצין ועל הברקנים מאי בין רב לר' חנינא איכא בינייהו דמאים בין ר' יוחנן לר' חנינא איכא בינייהו דיקיר: ולא בעיר של זהב: מאי בעיר של זהב רבה בר בר חנה א"ר יוחנן ירושלים דדהבא כדעבד

הואיל וראוי להקישו ע"ג חרס · ומשמיע קול כבתחלה ולא בטל ליה ממלאכה ראשונה והוה ליה ככלי שניקב בפחות ממוציא רימון דקי"ל דלא טיהר מטומאתו משום דראוי למלאכתו והשתא איתרצו כולהו דבהמה טהורה בלא עינבל כדקתני במתני' קמייתא דלאו מנא הוא ובעינבל טמא כדאוקימנא בבתרייתא דעינבל משוי לה מנא ודאדם גדול אף בלא עינבל טמא דלתכשיט הוא ולא בעי עינבל והיינו דקתני בקמייתא דמקבלין טומאה ודקטנים דלקלא עביד קבולי הוא דלא קביל בלא עינבל כדקתני אין להם עינבל טהורים בשלא היה לו עינבל מעולם דלא נגמרה מלאכתן *נטלו עינבלין בין לפני טומאה בין לאחר טומאה טמאים דלא נשתברו כשיעור: ה"ג לה בת"כ וכל הכלי אשר ישב עליו · רישיה דקרא וכל המשכב וגו' יכול כל כלי במשמע ואפי' אין עשוי לישיבה: תרקב · חצי סאה פי' תרי וקב: ת"ל אשר ישב מדלא כתיב גבי משכב אשר שכב וגבי מושב אשר ישב וכתיב ישכב ישב משמע שישכב עליו תמיד וישב עליו תמיד במיוחד לשכיבה ולישיבה וגבי משכב נמי דריש ליה התם הכי ובכל הספרים כתיב והיושב על הכלי אשר ישב עליו וקרא אחר הוא ומפרשים אותו התלמידים מדכתיב היושב על הכלי אשר ישב עליו שתי ישיבות ריבה הכתוב ללמדך דבמיוחד לישיבה קאמר ולא היא דשתי ישיבות דקאמר טובא צריכי כדמפרש התם יושב אע"פ שלא נגע אלא ישב או נתלה ולא נגע טמא דאיצטריך למיכתב גבי זב שטימא כלי בישיבתו ואע"פ שלא נגע ואיצטריך גבי טהור נמי שנטמא גם הוא ביושבו עליו אע"פ שלא נגע ועוד בת"כ לאו אההוא קרא קתני לה: ר' אלעזר אומר במדרסות כו' · בין בתחלת טומאה לענין שאמרו דאינו מטמא מדרס למיהוי אב הטומאה בין בסוף טומאה כגון ג' על ג' שנטמא מדרס למיהוי אב הטומאה ונחלקו טהור מן המדרס דאמרינן בו עמוד ונעשה מלאכתנו הראשונה שהיה ראוי לישיבה והרי עתה אינו ראוי לכך הלכך טהור מן המדרס ואע"ג דאית בכל חד שלש על שלש והוי כלי לקבל טומאה מיהו מתורת אב הטומאה טיהר לו: ואין אומרים · לענין אב הטומאה של טומאת מת עמוד ונעשה מלאכתנו כלומר אם נטמא ונשבר ועודהו ראוי למלאכה בעלמא שאין מעין מלאכה ראשונה טמא ולא אמרי' עמוד ונעשה מלאכתנו ראשונה וכיון דלא חזי להכי יהא טהור וכ"ש דבתחלת טומאה אין אומרים עמוד ונעשה מלאכתנו ראשונה דנימא אם אינו מיוחד למת לא יקבל טומאת מת דהא כלי מעשה כתיב: אומר כו' · דאי לא עביד מעין מלאכה ראשונה טהור ועל כרחיך לא איתמר דר' יוחנן אלא לענין שנשבר ולטהרו כדפרישית דליכא לפרושא כי ההיא דמדרסות ולמימרא דכלי שאינו עשוי למת לא יטמא במת דהא כתיב (במדבר יט) והזה על האהל ועל כל הכלים: איפוך קמייתא · דר' יוסי בר' חנינא לר' יוחנן: סנדל של בהמה · שלא ליזוק בפרסותיה באבנים: למאי חזי · אי משום בהמה אין תכשיט לבהמה: מניחו ברגליו · הוא בעצמו אלמא הואיל ולשם סנדל עשאו אי לאו דראוי לנעילה לא הוה מטמא ליה ר' יוחנן: איכא בינייהו דמאים · לרב לא מטמא דאין ראוי לשתות ורב חנינא לית ליה קסבר אין מוליכין שמן למלחמה לסוך וה"ה בין רב (בין) לר' יוחנן נמי איכא בינייהו דמאים: בין ר' חנינא וכו' איכא בינייהו דיקיר · כבד ואין ראוי בו לברוח:

כדעבד

פחות ממוציא רימון מקבל טומאה ועוד קשה לר"י לפי' הקונטרס דלטומאה שהיתה עליה שלא תפרח מהני שפיר טעמא דהדיוט יכול להחזירו בלא טעמא דראוי להקישו כדאשכחן בפ' שלשה שאכלו (ברכות נ:) גבי מטה דאפי' מפורקת לא פרחה טומאה מינה אא"כ נגנבה או שאבדה חציה או שחלקוה אחים או שותפים שאין סופן לחברה ולא איצטריך כלל לטעמא דהקשה אלא לענין לקבל טומאה מכאן ולהבא דהאי טעמא הואיל והדיוט יכול להחזירו לא מהני לקבל בה טומאה כדקתני התם החזירוה מקבלת טומאה מכאן ולהבא ולאביי נמי הוה בעי למימר דמשום דהדיוט יכול להחזירו מקבלין שניהן זוג והעינבל טומאה מכאן ולהבא וריצב"א הביא ראיה לפי' הקונט' דתניא בתוספתא דמסכת כלים בפ' רשב"ג העושה זוג למכתשת ולעריסה ולמטפחות תינוקות ניטלו עינבליהן טהורין משמע דזגין טהורין ולפירוש הקונט' ניחא דטהורין דלא מקבלי טומאה מכאן ולהבא אבל לפר"י קשה אמאי טהורין ור"י השיב דכמה ברייתות יש בתוספתא דפליגי אש"ס שלנו: **ורבי** יוחנן אמר הואיל וראוי לגמע בו מים לתינוק · קשה לרשב"א דע"כ בלא ייחדו מיירי מדקאמר הואיל וראוי משמע בראוי בעלמא אפי' בלא ייחוד ועוד דביחדו לכך לא הוה פליג ר' יוסי בר' חנינא ועוד דביחדו אפי' לא היה לו עינבל מעולם נמי מקבל טומאה ועוד אי ביחדו מיירי מאי פריך דר' יוחנן אדר' יוחנן הא התם ע"כ איירי בלא ייחדו דביחדו אפי' במדרסות נמי אין אומרים עמוד ונעשה מלאכתנו ולקמן בס"פ המצניע (דף צה: ושם) גבי ניקב כמוציא זית טהור מלקבל בו זיתים ועדיין כלי הוא לקבל בו רימונים ופי' בקונטרס אם ייחדו לרימונים ואי לאו פי' הקונט' דהתם הוה ניחא וי"ל דאפי' לפירוש הקונטרס הכא חזי טפי ע"י גימוע משום דהואיל דמעיקרא הוה כלי גמור וגם עתה הדיוט יכול להחזירו אית לן למימר דע"י דבר מועט שעדיין ראוי לגמוע בו מים חשיב כלי אפי' בלא ייחוד ולמ"ד נמי הואיל וראוי להקישו דבעי מעין מלאכה ראשונה אתי שפיר בכל ענין דאפי' לא בעינן בעלמא ייחוד הכא אתי שפיר דלא מהני גמוע מים משום שעומד עדיין למלאכתו ראשונה להחזיר בו העינבל ואומר לו עמוד ונעשה מלאכתנו וכ"ש דאי בעינן בעלמא ייחוד דאתי טפי שפיר: **ואין** אומרים בטמא מת עמוד ונעשה מלאכתנו · לפירוש הקונט' קשה לר"י למה ליה לאתויי ברייתא דתרקב כיון דלא שייכא למילתיה דר' אלעזר ור' יוחנן אלא נראה לר' יצחק כפירוש ריב"א אומרים במדרסות עמוד מעל תרקב זה ונעשה מלאכתנו שאינו יכול להיות טמא מדרס ע"י שאתה יושב עליו הואיל ואינו מיוחד לכך כדקתני בברייתא ואין אומרים בטמא מת עמוד מגמוע מים בזה הזוג או בזה הסנדל של בהמה ונעשה מלאכתנו ליתן בו העינבל כדי להשמיע הקול וליתן סנדל ברגלי הבהמה אלא טמא טומאת מת על ידי הגימוע אע"פ שאינו מיוחד לכך והוי בר קבולי טומאה דחשיב כלי ע"י גימוע מים ור' יוחנן אמר אף אומר כו' דבעינן שיהא ראוי למלאכתו ראשונה ולא מהני ליה מידי לקבולי טומאה מה שראוי למלאכה אחרת אבל הקשת זוג ע"ג החרס והנחת סנדל של בהמה ברגלו כשבורח מן הקרב הוי מעין מלאכה ראשונה ולהכי הוי בר קבולי טומאה ולא שייך למימר ביה עמוד ונעשה מלאכתנו דהיינו נמי מלאכתו: **סנדל** של בהמה של מתכת · ושל עץ אינו ראוי לכל הני דברים דמפרש בסמוך דדרך הבהמה לקלקלו ורבינו שמואל גריס סנדל של בהמה ושל מתכת ומיירי בסנדל של סיידין דלקמן (ס.): **הואיל** וראוי לשתות בו מים במלחמה. וא"ת והא בזוג שלא היה בו עינבל מעולם לא מטמינן משום דחזי לגמוע והכא חשוב כמו זוג שלא היה בו עינבל מעולם דכיון דנעשה לצורך בהמה אינו מקבל טומאה וי"ל דתחלתו נמי עשוי לשתות בו מים במלחמה או לסוך אלא שעיקרו עומד לבהמה ואומר לו עמוד ונעשה מלאכתנו למאן דבעי מעין במלאכה ראשונה: **בשעה** שבורח מן הקרב מניחו ברגליו. תימה א"כ יטמא מדרס ותניא בתוספתא דכלים פרק ג' סנדלים הם של אדם טמא מדרס של מתכת ושל בהמה טמא טומאת מת משמע אבל מן המדרס טהור: *ולא בעיר של זהב. אור"ת דלאו היינו עטרה כדפי' בקונט' דהא אמרי' בפרק בתרא דסוטה (דף מט:) מאי עטרות כלות עיר של זהב משמע דעשוי הוא כעין עטרה ואע"ג דאמרי' התם בפולמוס של טיטוס גזרו על עטרות חתנים וכלות והכא לא אסרו אלא בשבת אור"ת דדוקא לחתנים וכלות גזרו ולא לשאר בני אדם*):

מאן

*) [מפני שיש לכן שמחה בכן ועי' תוס' גיטין ז. ד"ה עטרות]

מסורת הש"ס

חגיגה כג: נדה מט:

נטלו עינבלין אחרי טומאתן טמאין דלא כצ"ל רש"ל

[צ"ל דתנן]

הגהות הב"ח

(א) גמ' תלמוד לומר וכל הכלי אשר ישב:

[עיין במשנה לעיל נז.]

כ א מיי' פ"ו מהל' משכב ומושב הלכה ה:

כא ב מיי' פי"ט מהל' שבת הלכה ו סמג לאוין סה טור וש"ע א"ח סי' שג סעיף ד:

[כלים פי"ד מ"ס]

רבינו חננאל

רבא הואיל וראוי להקישו התינוק ע"ג חרס ולהשמיע קול. ר' יוחנן אמר הואיל וראוי לגמע בו מים לתינוק עדיין תורת כלי עליהן ילפיכך עדיין טומאתו עליהן ואקשינן וכי ר' יוחנן לא בעי (שישא) [שיהא] בכלי המשמש מעין מלאכתו [והתניא] והיושב על הכלי אשר ישב עליו הזב יטמא יכול כפה סאה וישב עליה כפה כו' עד ור' יוחנן אמר בטומאת מת עמוד ויעשה מלאכתנו הנה בפי' ר' יוחנן אמר כי אין הכלי מקבל טומאה אלא אם הוא ראוי למלאכתו שנעשה בו ואפיך קמייתא ואימא ר' יוחנן אמר· הואיל וראוי להקישו ע"ג חרס משום דשמעינן ליה לר' יוחנן בהדיא דבעי מעין מלאכתו ראשונה דתניא סנדל של מתכת של בהמה טמא ואמרינן למאי חזית [רב] אמר חזי לשתות מים. ר' חנינא אמר ראוי לסוך בו שמן ר' יוחנן [אמר] ראוי להניחו ברגליו כשבורח ורץ על הקוצי' ועל הברקנים הנה שמענו לר' יוחנן דבעי מעין מלאכתו ראשונה כשם שמתחלה למנעל הרגל כך באחרונה: מתניתין ולא תצא אשה בעיר של זהב. מאי עיר של זהב. ירושלים דדהבא

רב נסים גאון

עינבל: מאי עיר של זהב אמר רבה בר בר חנה אמר ר' יוחנן ירושלים דדהבא כי דעביד לה (ר' יוחנן) [ר"ע] לדביתהו תמצא במס' נדרים בפרק הנודר מן המבושל (ד' נ) ר' עקיבא איקדשא ליה ברתיה ד כלבא שבוע שמע אבוהא אדרא הנאה מכל נכסיה אזלא ואיתנסיבא ליה בסיתוא הוה גנו בי תיבנא הוה מנקיט לה תיבנא מן מזייה אמר לה אי הואי לי רמינא ליך ירושלם דדהבא והזכירו אחר כך שהצ"ע

כב א ב מיי' פי"ט מהל' שבת הלכה י' טוש"ע א"ח סי' שג סעיף ה:
כג ג מיי' שם הל' כ' סמג לאוין סה:
כד ד טוש"ע א"ח סי' שא סעיף לו:
כה ה טוש"ע א"ח סי' שג סעיף ו:
כו ו מיי' שם הלכה ז טוש"ע שם סעיף ח:

תורה אור

כדעבד ליה רבי עקיבא לדביתהו *ת"ר לא תצא אשה בעיר של זהב ואם יצתה חייבת חטאת דברי רבי מאיר וחכמים אומרים לא תצא ואם יצתה פטורה *רבי אליעזר אומר יוצאה אשה בעיר של זהב לכתחלה במאי קמיפלגי ר"מ סבר משוי הוא ורבנן סברי תכשיט הוא דילמא שלפא ומחויא ליה ואתיא לאתויי ור"א סבר מאן דרכה למיפק בעיר של זהב אשה חשובה ואשה חשובה לא משלפא ומחויא כלילא רב אסר ושמואל [א]שרי דאניסכא כולי עלמא לא פליגי דאסור כי פליגי דארוקתא מר סבר אניסכא עיקר ומר סבר ארוקתא עיקר רב אשי מתני לקולא [ב]דארוקתא דכולי עלמא לא פליגי דשרי כי פליגי דאניסכא מר סבר דילמא שלפא ומחויא ואתי לאתויי ומר סבר מאן דרכה למיפק בכלילא אשה חשובה ואשה חשובה לא שלפא ומחויא °א"ל רב שמואל בר בר חנה לרב יוסף בפירוש אמרת לן משמיה דרב כלילא שרי *אמרו ליה לרב אתא גברא רבה אריכא לנהרדעא ומטלע ודרש כלילא שרי אמר מאן גברא רבה אריכא [דאיטלע] לוי ש"מ נח נפשיה דרבי אפס ויתיב ר' חנינא ברישא ולא הוה ליה איניש ללוי למיתב גביה (א) וקאתי להכא ודילמא נח נפשיה דרבי חנינא ור' אפס כדקאי קאי ולא הוה ליה איניש ללוי למיתב גביה וקאתי להכא אם איתא דרבי חנינא שכיב לוי לר' אפס מיכף הוה כייף ליה ותו דרבי חנינא לא סגי דלא מליך דכי הוה קא ניחא נפשיה דרבי אמר חנינא בר' חמא יתיב בראש וכתיב בהו בצדיקים °ותגזר אומר ויקם לך וגו' דרש לוי בנהרדעא כלילא שרי נפיק עשרין וארבע כלילי מכולה נהרדעא דרש רבה בר אבוה במחוזא כלילא שרי ונפקו תמני סרי כלילי מחדא מבואה אמר רב יהודה אמר רב שמואל קמרא שרי איכא דאמרי דארוקתא ואמר רב ספרא מידי דהוה אטלית מוזהבת ואיכא דאמרי [ג]דאניסכא ואמר רב ספרא מידי דהוה אאבנט של מלכים א"ל רבינא לרב אשי קמרא עילוי המיינא מאי א"ל [ד]תרי המייני קאמרת אמר רב אשי [ה]האי רסוקא אי אית ליה מפרחייתא שרי ואי לא אסיר: ולא בקטלא: מאי קטלא מנקטא פארי: נזמים: [ו]נזמי האף: ולא בטבעת שאין עליה חותם: הא יש עליה חותם חייבת אלמא לאו תכשיט הוא ורמינהו *תכשיטי נשים טמאים ואלו הן תכשיטי נשים קטלאות נזמים וטבעות וטבעת בין שיש עליה חותם בין שאין עליה חותם ונזמי האף ואמר רבי זירא לא קשיא הא ר' נחמיה הא רבנן *)דתניא *היא של מתכת ותותמה של אלמוג טמאה היא של אלמוג ותותמה של מתכת טהורה ורבי נחמיה מטמא שהיה ר' נחמיה אומר בטבעת הלך אחר חותמה בעול הלך אחר סמלוניו בקולב

*) [בכלים פי"ג מ"ו לא נזכר פלוגתא דר' נחמי' הלכך שפיר גרסי דתניא]

איוב כב

רש"י

כדעבד ליה ר' עקיבא לדביתהו · במסכת נדרים (דף נ·): כלילא · על פדחתה היא קושרתו מאזן לאזן יש שכולו טס זהב שקורין לימ"א ויש שעושין ממשי טווי עם הזהב שקורין פריז"ש: דניסכא · טס העשוי כולו מניסכא דהיינו זהב או כסף דבר הניתך: דאסיר · מגו דחשיב גזירה דילמא שלפא ומחוייא: דארוקתא · רצועה שמצויירת בזהב ובאבנים טובות: אניסכא · דאית ביה עיקר ומחויא ליה ומר סבר ארוקתא הוא עיקר דידיה ולא חשיב ליה ולא מחויא ליה: כולי עלמא לא פליגי דשרי · דארוקתא עיקר: בפירוש אמרת לן משמיה דרב · לפני חלייך קודם ששכחת תלמודך: כלילא שרי · אלמא דרב אסי עיקר דמוקי פלוגתא בדניסכא אבל בארוקתא מודה רב ואיכא לאוקמי לדידיה בארוקתא: גברא רבה אריכא ומטלע · לוי איטלע לאחוי קידה קמיה דרבי*: נח נפשיה דרבי אפס · במסכת כתובות בהנושא (קג:) אמרינן דכי שכיב רבי אמר רבי חנינא בר חמא ישב בראש ולא קיבל עליו רבי חנינא שהיה רבי אפס גדול ממנו שתי שנים (ב) ויתיב רבי אפס ברישא ומתוך שהיה רבי חנינא חשוב לא נכנס לבית מדרשו והיה יושב בחוץ ומשום כבודו ישב לו לוי אצלו: וקאתי להכא · שלא היה רבי חנינא גדול הימנו לא בתורה ולא בשנים ולא ניכף ליה לוי ובא לכאן: לוי לרבי אפס מיכף הוה כייף ליה · שהרי זקן ממנו: קמרא · אבנט חשוב יש שעושין אותו טס של זהב ויש שעושין אותו רצועה משבצות זהב ואבנים קבועות בו: מידי דהוה אטלית מוזהבת · דהוי תכשיט ושריא ולמישלף ואחויי כמי לא חיישינן שאין דרך להתיר אזורו בשוק ויפלו בגדיו: אאבנט של מלכים · שעשוי כולו דניסכא °וכל ישראל בני מלכים ראוים לו: תרי המייני קאמרת · הא ודאי משאוי הוא ואסור לשון תלמידי רבינו יצחק (ג) כ"ע [ובתלמידי] רבינו הלוי מצאתי מותר והראשון נראה לי משום דגבי הללת דליקה מנינן לר' יוסי שמנה עשר כלים והתם חד חגור הוא דמנינן בכל כתבי הקדש (לקמן דף קכ·) ואי שני חגורות שרי לכתחילה נימני התם תרי: רסוקי · חתיכת מעיל רחבה: אי אית ליה מפרחייתא · רצועות קצרות תלויות בה לקושרה בהם ולהדקה סביבותיו: שרי · דמיהדק שפיר וליכא למיחש דילמא משתרי קטרי ונפיל ואתי לאיתויי: מפרחייתא · פינדל"א בלע"ז: מנקטא פארי (ד) · מוסטניל"א והוא בגד שיש לו שנצים כעין מכנסים ומכנסת בו רצועה רחבה וקושרת סביב צוארה והבגד תלוי על לבה והוא חשוב ומצוייר בזהב וי"מ כמין חלי עגול עשוי כמין כלבוס* (ה) אוחזת בו מפתחי חלוקה והפגם בולע צוארה והיא של זהב לוי"ה: נזמי האף · אבל נזמי האזן מותרין לכתחלה דטריחא לה מילתא למישלף ואחויי מפני שאזניה מכוסות בקישורין: ולא בטבעת שאין עליה חותם · קתני מתניתין דאם יצאת פטורה דתכשיט הוא לה ומשום דילמא משלפא ומחויא הוא דמיתסר: הא יש עליה חותם חייבת חטאת · דלאו תכשיט הוא והוי משאוי: נזמים · נזמי האזן: וטבעת בין שיש כו' · כלומר וטבעת שאמרנו בין שיש עליה כו': הא רבי נחמיה · דאמר עיקר טבעת לדעתא דחותם הוא חייבת חטאת דחותם לאשה לאו תכשיט הוא דאין דרך לאשה לחתום ולשלוח שלוחים שאין חותם עשוי אלא לאדם גדול וממונה והא דקתני תכשיט הוא רבנן דאמרי גופה של טבעת עיקר ולדעתא דטבעת נפקא ביה וטבעת ודאי תכשיט הוא: טמאה · דטבעת עיקר והוה ליה פשוטי כלי מתכות: היא של אלמוג ותותמה של מתכת טהורה · דהוה ליה פשוטי כלי עץ: הלך אחר סמלוניו · ואם של מתכות הם טמא: סמלוניו · העול שלהם לא היה פגום כשלנו אלא חלק ונוקבים בו שני נקבים וביניהם כעובי עורף השור ותוחבין בהן שתי יתדות והם סימלונין: בקולב

תוספות

מאן דרכה למיפק בכלילא אשה חשובה · אומר ר"י דדוקא בכלילא שרי שמואל הכא וכן רבי אליעזר דוקא בעיר של זהב שאין כל הנשים רגילות בהן אלא אשה חשובה אבל שאר תכשיטי נשים אסירי אפי' לאשה חשובה דאין לחלק בין הנשים והביא ראיה מס"פ כירה (לעיל דף מו:) דקאמר עולא מה טעם הואיל ואיכא תורת כלי עליהן ומה דחק לומר כן כיון דחזי לנשים חשובות דאפי' לרבנן דאסרי בעיר של זהב לאשה חשובה מודו בשאר תכשיטים איכא דשמואל דשרי כלילא אפילו לרבנן:

אאבנט של מלכים · שמלבושם הוא ואין להם אבנט אחר ה"נ שרי האי קמרא לאיתתא דמלבושה היא ולא משלפא ומחויא:

תרי המייני קאמרת · לשון אחד פי' בקונטרס לאיסור ואע"ג דחשיב בפ' כל כתבי (לקמן דף קכ:) בי"ח כלים פונדא וחגור ופי' התם בקונט' דפונדא הוא אזור היינו כגון שיש בגד מפסיק בינתים אבל תרי המייני זה על גב זה אסור ולא דמי לכמה מלבושים שאדם לובש בשביל הקור אבל תרי המייני מה הנאה יש ואין דרך לחגור ומשוי הוא:

מנקטא פארי · פירורי הפת ותכשיט הוא:

נזמי האף · ונזמי האוזן שרו כדפי' בקונטרס ואע"ג דאמר לקמן [דף סה.] *הבנות יוצאות בחוטין שבאזניהן ואמר בגמ' דשל מיני צבעונים אסירי דילמא משלפי הואיל ותכשיט נינהו התם יותר קל °ליטלם מנזמי האוזן:

הא יש עליה חותם חייבת חטאת · אסיפא סמיך *דקתני בהדיא [לקמן סד.] דחייבת חטאת:

רבי נחמיה מטמא · נראה לר"י דבריתא מטהר דלא בעי למימר הלך אף אחר חותמה אלא דוקא אחר חותמה שהוא עיקר וכן משמע בהדיא בתוספתא דמסכת [פי"ג דכלים מציעא] כלים *דתניא טבעת של מתכת וחותמה של אלמוג רבי נחמיה מטהר שהיה רבי נחמיה אומר בטבעת הלך אחר חותמה:

וכל ישראל בני מלכים. עיין לקמן דף קיא ע"א: תוס' ד"ה נזמי האף וכו' ליטלם מנזמי האזן. עיין תשו' ב"ח החדשות סי' מ"ח

רבינו חננאל

כדעבד ר' עקיבא לדביתהו. ת"ר לא תצא אשה בעיר של זהב ואם יצא חייבת חטאת דברי ר' מאיר וחכ"א לא תצא ואם יצאת פטורה. ר' אליעזר אומר יוצאה אשה בעיר של זהב לכתחלה: כלילא רב אסר ושמואל שרי. פי' נסכא חוטין מלשון המסכת (כלים פכ"ח). רוקתא מטלית. וקיי"ל כרב אשי דהוא בתראה דאמר ארוקתא כו' כ"ע לא פליגי דשרי כי פליגא כלילא דאניסכא רב אסר ושמואל שרי וקיי"ל כרב באיסורי ואע"ג דאיכא למימר מעשה רב והא דדרש [לוי] כלילא [שרי] ונפקו כ"ד כלילי מנהרדעא וכן הא דדרש רבה בר אבוה במחוזא כלילא שרי כלילא דאניסכא דרשו דשרי. כיון דלא איתמר א בהדיא לא שרינן לה דדלמא לא שרי אלא דארוקתא: אמר רב ששת קמרא שרי הוא חגור שבמתנים כגון אבנט רחב מדבעא רבינא מרב אשי קמרא עילוי המיינא מאי ואמר ליה תרי המייני קאמרת ש"מ דקמרא המיינא הוא והא דרב אשי אתמר בה תרי לישני ולישנא בתראה אניסכא שרי פי' כלילא וקמרא. חתיכות חתיכות של זהב נקובות ובהן מרגלית ומעמידין בחוטין שמכניסין עקבין. נמצא דאניסכא כגון מלאכת אבנט של מלכים כי כן מלאכתן היעשות בחוטין. רוקתא מטלית. שנמצא בין כלילא בין קמרא חתיכות של זהב נקובות ומרגלית קבועו' במטלי' שנמצאת מלאכתן כגון מלאכת טלית מוזהבת. אמר רב אשי ריסוקא. פי' חגור של עור אי אית ביה מפרחייתא שרי ותכשיט הוא ואי לא אסור פי' אם יש לו מפרחייתא חתיכות יוצאות ועודפות ממנו לימינו ולשמאלו תכשיט הוא ואי לא אינו מלאכת תכשיט ואסור לצאת בו בשבת כי אינו כלי. קטלא תכשיט בצואר. כגון ענק והיא בלשון ערבי מכנקא. נזמים יש נזמי האף ונזמים שבאזנים: ולא בטבעת שאין עליה חותם הא יש עליה חותם משאוי ואם תצא בו חייבת חטאת. אלמא לאו תכשיט הוא איני והתניא תכשיטי נשים עיר של זהב קטלאות נזמים וטבעות אחת טבעת שיש עליה חותם ואחת טבעת שאין עליה חותם ונזמי האף [טמאים] ומשני ר' זירא בטבעת של אלמוג וחותמה של מתכת ומתניתין [כרבנן] בכלים פרק י"ג דאמרי טהורה. [וכיון] לענין טומאה לאו כלי הוא לענין שבת נמי לאו כלי הוא. ומשוי הוא. הא ברייתא ר' נחמיה היא דמשוי ליה לענין [טומאה] מנא לענין שבת נמי תכשיט הוא דתנינן טבעת של מתכת וחותמה של אלמוג [טמאה היא של אלמוג] וחותמה של מתכת טהורה. ור' נחמיה מטמא: סימלוניו פי' רצועות שהן בעול דתנינן בתורת כהנים מיד בא ושיבר העול וקיצץ סימלונין כדכתיב

רב נסים גאון

שהגיע לעושר גדול כמו שאמרו מן ו' מילי איעתר ר' עקיבא ולאחר שהגיעה ידו שילם לה נדרו ועשה לה ירושלם דדהבא ובגמ' דהדין פירקא דבני מערבא אמרי מעשה ברבי עקיבא שעשה לאשתו עיר של זהב חמתה איתתיה דרבן גמליאל וקניאת בה אתת ואמרה קמי בעלה אמר לה מה הוית עבדא לי כמה דהוות עבדא ליה דהות מזבנא מן קלעיתה דשערה ויהיבא ליה והוא לעי באורייתא: גברא רבא אריכא אתא לנהרדעאי ומטלע פירוש והוא צולע על ירכו כדמתרגמינן והוא מטלע והדבר שגרם לו זה מפורש בפ' ג' דתענית (דף כה) לוי גזר תעניתא בעא רחמי ולא אתא מיטרא אמר לפניו רבונו של עולם עלית וישבת למעלה במרום ואי אתה משגיח על בניך ואתא מיטרא ואיטלע אמר ר' אלעזר אל יטיח אדם דברים כלפי למעלה שהרי אדם גדול הטיח דברים כלפי למעלה ואטלע ובמסכת סוכה (דף נג) בפ' החליל קאמרי לוי אחוי קידה קמיה דר' ואטלע ואמרו בפירוקה הא והא גרמא ליה אבל מעשה דר' אפס בר חמא ומה דאמר רבנו הקדוש בצוויו חנינא בר חמא ישב בראש כו' (מעשה כמפורש) [מפורש] בפרק הנ"שא

מסורת הש"ס

[לקמן קלח. תוספ' פ"ה]
עדיות פ"ב מ"ו
[סוכה נג.]
כתובות קג:
[כלים פי"א מ"ח ע"ש]
לעיל נב: תוספתא דכלים ב"מ פ"ב כלים פי"ג מ"ו
כום

הגהות הב"ח

(א) גמ' למיתב גביה וקאתי להכא: (ב) רש"י ד"ה נח נפשיה וכו' שתי שנים ומתוך שהיה: (ג) ד"ה תרי וכו' ר' יצחק בר יהודה כ"ע: (ד) ד"ה מנקטא פארי כ"ב כדף מ"ו ע"ב במה שכתבתי: (ה) בא"ד כמין כלבוס כזה

גליון הש"ס

גמ' א"ל רב שמואל בר בר חנה לרב יוסף. לקמן קמו ע"ב: רש"י ד"ה לאבנט וכו'

a golden Jerusalem,[1] [59b] such as R. Akiba made for his wife.[2]

Our Rabbis taught: A woman must not go out with a golden city, and if she does, she incurs a sin-offering: this is R. Meir's view. The Sages maintain: She may not go out [therewith], but if she does, she is not liable. R. Eliezer ruled: A woman may go out with a golden city at the very outset. Wherein do they differ?—R. Meir holds that it is a burden; while the Rabbis hold that it is an ornament, [and it is forbidden only] lest she remove it to show [to a friend], and thus come to carry it [in the street];[3] but R. Eliezer reasons: Whose practice is it to go out with a golden city? [That of] a woman of rank; and such will not remove it for display.

As for a coronet,[4] Rab forbids it;[5] Samuel permits it. Where it is made of cast metal, all agree that it is forbidden;[6] they differ about an embroidered stuff:[7] one Master holds that the cast metal [sewn on to it] is the chief part;[8] while the other Master holds that the embroidered stuff is the chief part.[9] R. Ashi learnt it in the direction of leniency. As for an embroidered stuff, all agree that it is permitted. They differ only about what is made of cast metal: one Master holds [that it is forbidden] lest she remove it in order to show, and [thus] come to carry it; while the other Master holds: Whose practice is it to go out with a coronet? That of a woman of rank; and such will not remove it for display.

R. Samuel b. Bar Ḥanah said to R. Joseph: You explicitly told
b us in Rab's name that a coronet is permitted.[1]

Rab was told: A great, tall, and lame man has come to Nehardea, and has lectured: A coronet is permitted. Said he: Who is a great tall man who is lame? Levi. This proves that R. Afes is dead[2] and R. Ḥanina [now] sits at the head [of the Academy], so that Levi has none for a companion,[3] and therefore he has come hither.[4] But perhaps R. Ḥanina had died, R. Afes remaining as before, and since Levi [now] had no companion he had come hither?—Had R. Ḥanina died, Levi would indeed have subordinated himself to R. Afes.[5] Moreover, it could not be that R. Ḥanina should not rule.[6] For when Rabbi was dying he ordered, 'Let Ḥanina son of R. Ḥama sit at the head.' And of the righteous men it is written, *Thou shalt also decree a thing, and it shall be established unto thee.*[7]

Levi lectured in Nehardea: A coronet is permitted; [whereupon] there went forth twenty-four coronets from the whole of Nehardea. Rabbah b. Abbuha lectured in Maḥoza:[8] A coronet is permitted: [whereupon] there went forth eighteen coronets from a single alley.[9]

c Rab Judah said in the name of R. Samuel:[1] A girdle [*ḳamra*] is permitted.[2] Some say, That means of embroidered stuff,[3] and R. Safra said: It may be compared to a robe shot through with gold.[4] Others say, It means of cast metal; whereon R. Safra observed: It may be compared to a royal girdle.[5] Rabina asked R. Ashi: What about wearing a *ḳamra* over a [plain] girdle [*hemyana*]?—You ask about two girdles! he replied.[6] R. Ashi said: As for a piece of a garment, if it has fringes, it is permitted;[7] if not, it is forbidden.

NOR WITH A ḲAṬLA. What is a ḲAṬLA?—A trinket holder.[8]

NEZAMIM. [That is] ear-rings.

NOR WITH A FINGER-RING THAT HAS NO SIGNET. This [implies that] if it has a signet, she is liable;[9] hence it proves that it is not an ornament. But the following contradicts this: Women's ornaments are unclean.[10] And these are women's ornaments: Necklaces, ear-rings and finger-rings, and a finger-ring, whether it has a signet or has no signet, and nose-rings?—Said R. Zera, There is no difficulty: one agrees with R. Nehemiah; the other with the Rabbis. For it was taught: If it [the ring] is of metal and its signet is of coral, it is unclean; if it is of coral while the signet is of metal, it is clean.[11] But R. Nehemiah declares it unclean. For R. Nehemiah maintained: In the case of a ring, follow its signet; in the case of a yoke, go by its carved ends;[12]

a (1) An ornament with the picture or the engraving of Jerusalem; v. *T.A.*, I, p. 662, n. 961. (2) V. Ned. 50*a*. (3) Thus it is only Rabbinically forbidden, and involves no sacrifice. (4) A wreath or chaplet worn on the forehead. Some were entirely of gold or silver; others of silk shot through with gold or silver. (5) To be worn by a woman in the street on the Sabbath. (6) This being very costly, a woman is more likely to remove it to show to her friends. (7) I.e., where the chaplet or coronet is of a stuff with gold or silver embroidery, which would contain pieces of cast metal too. (8) And therefore a woman may be tempted to remove and show it. (9) And that is not worth showing. The translation follows what seems to be Rashi's interpretation. Jast.: they differ in respect of what is made of beaten, wrought metal, opp. to cast metal. One Master holds that what is made of cast metal is original (or perhaps, reading מיקר, v. MS.M., more precious), while the other holds the reverse.

b (1) Hence R. Ashi's version must be correct, for on the other version there is no case where Rab permits it. (2) Lit., 'his soul has gone to rest'. (3) Lit., 'to be by his side'. On R. Afes' accession as head of the Academy R. Ḥanina, who would not recognize him as his superior, pursued his studies outside, where he was joined by Levi; v. Keth. 103*b*. (4) Levi being in no way inferior to R. Ḥanina, he could not accept him as a head, and so he has come hither. Zuri, I. S. *Toledoth*, First Series, Bk. 2 pp. 137-139 observes that Levi was probably born in Babylon, whither he was now returning to resettle. (5) Who was his senior. (6) As head of the academy. Lit., 'there is no way or path that R. Ḥanina' etc.: i.e., it is impossible. (7) Job XXII, 28. (8) The famous town on the Tigris where Raba had his great academy; v. Obermeyer, pp. 161-186. (9) V. I. S. Zuri, op. cit., Part I, Bk. 3, pp. 19-27 on the significance of numbers. He maintains that eighteen is often used symbolically to denote a large number.—Maḥoza was a very wealthy town, owing to its central position and the great caravan and shipping trade that passed through it; this is reflected in the present statement. Obermeyer, p. 173.

c (1) Var. lec.: Mar Judah in the name of R. Shesheth, v. *D.S.* (2) *Ḳamra* was a costly girdle, made either of solid gold or of cloth adorned with gold and precious stones (Rashi). (3) V. *supra* n. a7. (4) There is no fear of either being removed. (5) Which was likewise made of beaten gold. Rashi: all Israel are princes, and worthy to wear such belts. (6) Rashi: That is certainly forbidden, for one is superfluous and a burden. Rashi quotes another interpretation to the effect that it is permitted, but prefers the first. (7) For by their means it can be firmly tied to the wearer, so that it will not fall off and necessitate its being carried in the street. (8) A band or necklace on which beads, trinkets, etc., are suspended. (9) The deduction is from the end of the Mishnah. (10) I.e., susceptible to defilement. (11) V. *supra* 52*b* for notes. (12) Jast. Rashi: Two rods fitted into the yoke the breadth of an ox's shoulder apart. Jast.: if they are broken off, the yoke ceases to be susceptible to defilement. Rashi: if they are of metal, the yoke is susceptible to defilement. The yoke itself is a straight piece of wood, and wood utensils are not subject to uncleanness unless they possess a cavity which, e.g., can hold water.

a [60a] in the case of a rack,[1] go after its nails;[2] in the case of a ladder, go after its rungs; in the case of a weighing machine, go after its chains.[3] But the Sages maintain: Everything depends on the support.[4]

Raba said: It is taught disjunctively:[5] if it has a signet, it is a man's ornament; if it has no signet, it is a woman's ornament. R. Naḥman b. Isaac answered: Do you oppose uncleanness to the Sabbath![6] [In respect to] uncleanness, the Divine Law said, *utensils [fit] for work*,[7] and this [a signet ring] is a utensil. But the Sabbath [interdiction] was imposed by the Divine Law on account of the burden: if it has no signet, it is an ornament; if it has a signet, it is a burden.

NOR WITH A NEEDLE WHICH IS UNPIERCED. What is it fit for?[8]—Said R. Joseph: Since a woman tidies[9] her hair with it [it is therefore ornamental]. Said Abaye to him: Let it be as a garter, which is clean, and hence permitted?[10] But R. Adda of Naresh[11] interpreted it before R. Joseph: Since a woman parts her hair with it, [it is ornamental]. What is it fit for on the Sab-
b bath?[1]—Said Raba: It has a golden plaque at the end thereof:[2] on weekdays she parts her hair therewith, [while] on the Sabbath she lets it lie against her forehead.[3]

MISHNAH. A MAN MAY NOT GO OUT WITH A NAIL-STUDDED SANDAL, NOR WITH A SINGLE [SANDAL], IF HE HAS NO WOUND ON HIS FOOT;[4] NOR WITH TEFILLIN, NOR WITH AN AMULET, IF IT IS NOT FROM AN EXPERT, NOR WITH A COAT OF MAIL [SHIRYON], NOR WITH A CASQUE [ḲASDA], NOR WITH GREAVES [MEGAFAYYIM]. YET IF HE GOES OUT, HE DOES NOT INCUR A SIN-OFFERING.[5]

GEMARA. A NAIL-STUDDED SANDAL: What is the reason?—Said Samuel: It was at the end of the period of persecution,[6] and they [some fugitives] were hiding in a cave. They proclaimed, 'He who would enter, let him enter,[7] but he who would go out, let him not go out.'[8] Now, the sandal of one of them became reversed, so that they thought that one of them had gone out and been seen by the enemies, who would now fall upon them. Thereupon they pressed against each other,[9] and they killed of each other more than their enemies slew of them. R. Ila'i b. Eleazar said: They were stationed in a cave when they heard a sound [proceeding] from above the cave. Thinking that the enemy was coming upon them, they pressed against each other and slew amongst themselves more than the enemy had slain of them. Rami b. Ezekiel said: They were stationed in a synagogue, when they heard a sound from behind the synagogue. Thinking that the enemy was coming upon them, they pressed against each other and slew amongst themselves more than the enemy had slain of them. In that hour it was enacted: A man must not go out
c with a nail-studded sandal.[1] If so, it should be forbidden on weekdays too?—The incident happened on the Sabbath.[2] Then let

a (1) Placed outside a shop and fitted with nails and hooks for exhibiting goods. (2) If they are of metal, the whole is susceptible to uncleanness. (3) The machine itself was of wood. (4) E.g., the ladder depends on its frame, not on the rungs, etc.—Hence, according to R. Nehemiah the signet is the chief part of the ring, and since a signet is not ornamental, a sin-offering is incurred. But the Rabbis hold that the ring itself is the chief part, and that is an ornament. (5) Lit., 'to (separate) sides'. The clause 'and a ring whether it has a signet etc.' is not included in the definition of 'women's ornaments'. (6) He likewise treats the clause 'and a ring etc.' as independent of the preceding but as referring to the general laws of uncleanness. (7) Num. XXXI, 51; i.e., which have a definite function. (8) How can it be regarded as an ornament? V. *supra* 57a, n. a1. (9) Lit., 'gathers up': if some wisps of hair stray out from under her wig, they are wound about this needle or bodkin and pushed back (Rashi). Tosaf.: the needle is thrust through the wig to keep the hair in order and prevent it from straying out. 'Aruch reads: *ogedeth*, she fastens. (10) V. *infra* 63a. So here too, since the bodkin is required to keep the hair in order, and uncovered hair is considered disgraceful (v. Sanh. 58b), a woman will certainly not remove it for display. (11) Identical with Nahras or Nahr-sar, on the canal of the same name, which was a tributary falling into the Euphrates on its eastern bank; Obermeyer, pp. 307 *seq*.

b (1) When parting the hair is forbidden. (2) One end was needle-like while the other was flattened and broadened into a plaque. (3) She thrusts the needle end into her wig, letting the other end come over her forehead as an ornament. (4) Either because he may be suspected of carrying the other sandal under his garments (T.J.), or because he may evoke ridicule, which will cause him to remove and carry it. But when one foot is wounded, there is no fear of this. V. Rashi. (5) Because these are garments in war, hence do not rank as burdens. (6) So Jast. Rashi: There were fugitives from persecution. [The reference is generally held to be to the Syrian persecutions under Antiochus Epiphanes; v. Berliner, *Hoffmann Magazin* XX, p. 123]. (7) As he could see beforehand whether the enemies' spies were on the watch. (8) For fear of spies, lest their whereabouts be disclosed. (9) Panic stricken, in order to flee.

c (1) According to Samuel, because this had led them astray. According to R. Ila'i b. Eleazar and Rami b. Ezekiel, because the carnage had been wrought by their nail-studded sandals. (2) The interdict was felt to be in memory of the disaster rather than through actual fear of its repetition, and therefore confined to the Sabbath.

בקולב: הלך אחר מסמרותיו בסולם הלך אחר שליבותיו בערסי הלך אחר שלשלותיו וחכמים אומרים *הכל הולך אחר המעמיד רבא אמר לצדדים קתני יש עליה חותם תכשיט דאיש אין עליה חותם תכשיט דאשה רב נחמן בר יצחק אמר *טומאה אשבת קרמית טומאה °כלי מעשה אמר רחמנא (במדבר לא) וכלי הוא שבת משום משוי אמר רחמנא אין עליה חותם תכשיט יש עליה חותם משוי: ולא במחט שאינה נקובה: *למאי חזיא אמר רב יוסף הואיל ואשה *אוגרת בה שערה א"ל אביי ותהוי כבירית טהורה ותשתרי אלא תרגמא רב אדא נרשאה קמיה דרב יוסף הואיל ואשה חולקת בה שערה בשבת למאי חזיא אמר רבא טס של זהב יש לה על ראשה בחול חולקת בה שערה בשבת מניחתה כנגד פדחתה: **מתני'** [ב]לא יצא האיש בסנדל המסומר ולא [ג]ביחיד בזמן שאין ברגלו מכה ולא בתפילין *ולא בקמיע בזמן שאינו מן המומחה °ולא בשריון ולא בקסדא ולא במגפיים ואם יצא אינו חייב חטאת: **גמ'** סנדל המסומר מאי טעמא אמר שמואל שלפי הגזרה היו והיו נחבאין במערה ואמרו הנכנס יכנס והיוצא אל יצא נהפך סנדלו של אחד מהן כסבורין הם אחד מהן יצא וראוהו אויבים ועכשיו באין עליהן דחקו זה בזה והרגו זה את זה יותר ממה שהרגו בהם אויבים רבי אילעאי בן אלעזר אומר במערה היו יושבין ושמעו קול מעל גבי המערה כסבורין היו שבאו עליהם אויבים דחקו זה בזה והרגו זה את זה יותר ממה שהרגו בהן אויבים רמי בר יחזקאל אמר בבהכ"נ היו יושבין ושמעו קול מאחורי בהכ"נ כסבורין היו שבאו עליהם אויבים דחקו זה בזה והרגו זה את זה יותר ממה שהרגו בהן אויבים באותה שעה אמרו אל יצא אדם בסנדל המסומר אי הכי בחול נמי ליתסר מעשה כי הוה בשבת הוה ביום טוב לישתרי אלמה תנן משלחין

רש"י

בקולב. הוא כמין עמוד רחב מלמטה ודק מלמעלה ומיטלטל והחנוני מעמידו לפני חלון חנותו ומסמרין תחובין בו ותולין בהן אבנטים ורצועות למכור: בערסה. איסתרייד"א בלע"ז והן מאזנים גדולות לשקול למר ושעוה ונחשת והן של עץ: הלך אחר שלשלותיו. שתלוי בהן ואם של מתכת הן טמאות: המעמיד. גוף הטבעת מעמיד החותם והעול מעמיד את סמלוניו והקולב את מסמרותיו והסולם את שליבותיו שהרי בהם קבועים והערסה הוא עץ (א) ארוך שהקנה שקורין ייש"א והלשון תחוב בו והשלשלות קבועות בקנה וכולן העץ ארוך מעמידן שהוא פליי"ל ששתי כפות המאזנים תלויות בב' ראשין: רבא אמר. ברייתא דקתני וטבעת הוי תכשיט בין שיש עליה חותם בין שאין עליה חותם לאו אדישא דאיירי בתכשיטי נשים קיימי תרוייהו אלא חד תכשיט דאיש וחד תכשיט דאשה ולצדדין קתני: טומאה אשבת קרמית. הא דקתני וטבעת בין שיש עליה כו' לאו אדישא קאי דקרי ליה תכשיט נשים אלא הכי קאמר וטבעת שאמרו שנטמאת בין שיש עליה חותם דלאו תכשיט הוא מיהו כלי מעשה הוא בין שאין עליה חותם דהוי תכשיט וכי קתני רישא תכשיטי נשים אשאין עליה חותם: למאי חזיא. לתכשיט דקתני אינה חייבת חטאת: אוגרת בה שערה. היוצא חוץ לקישוריה כורכתו סביב המחט ותוחבת המחט בשבכה מתחתיה שלא יראה שערה: ותיהוי כבירית. דתנא מתניתין (לקמן דף סג.) בירית טהורה מלטמא ויוצאין בה והיא כמין אצעדה שעושה לשוקיה מעל בתי שוקיה להדקן שלא יפלו על רגלה: טהורה. דלאו תכשיט היא אלא תשמיש לבתי שוקיה והוי (ב) כטבעת הכלים דאמרן טהורות בפרקין דלעיל ויוצאין בה שצריך לה עם בתי שוקיה ולא הוי משאוי ויוצאין דכיון דלצניעותא היא לא שלפא ומחוי והאי מחט כמי לצניעות דשער באשה ערוה ולא מחויא ואמאי לא תנא לכתחילה: חולקת. לכאן ולכאן באמצע ראשה שקורין גריוו"א בלע"ז: ובשבת למאי חזיא. הרי בשבת אינה חולקת שערה: טס של זהב יש לה על ראשה. האחד והשני עוקץ הוי: בחול חולקת שערה. בעוקץ: ובשבת. תוחבת העוקץ בשבכה והטס שבראשה השני מונח על פדחתה: **מתני'** סנדל המסומר. של עץ הוא ותוחבין מסמרות (ג) למעלה לחזק התחתון עם העליון *(העץ עם העור שלמעלה הימנו ויש לו שתי פיות ותוחב רגלו בו) ובגמרא מפרש מאי טעמא גזרו ביה: ולא ביחיד. ולא בסנדל יחיד: בזמן שאין ברגלו מכה. בש"ס ירושלמי מפרש דלא ליחשדיה דטעין ליה לחבריה תותי כנפיה ולשון רבותי דילמא מחייכי עליה ושקיל דשליף ליה וממטי ליה בידי' בשכחת שבת ומיהו בזמן שיש ברגלו מכה שרי עגמרא בעי בהי מינייהו יהיב ליה: ולא בתפילין. כדמפרש טעמא בגמרא (לקמן דף סא.): ולא בקמיע. שכותבין וטוענין לרפואה: שאינו מן המומחה. אבל בקמיע מומחה שרי דתכשיט הוא לחולה כאחד ממלבושיו: שריון קסדא ומגפיים. מפרש בגמרא: אינו חייב חטאת. דכולהו מין מלבושין נינהו בחול למלחמה: **גמ'** שלפי הגזירה היו. בני אדם השמטים מן הגזירה היו: הנכנס יכנס. הרוצה ליכנס יכנס שהנכנס יראה תחלה שאין אדם רואה: והיוצא אל יצא. שמא יש אויבים מבחוץ והוא לא ידע ויראוהו ויביטו שאנו כאן: נהפך סנדלו. שיש לו שתי פיות ויכול לנועלו מב' צדדין אבל ניכר מי הוא לפנים ומי הוא לאחור וכשנועלו זה הפוך נראה הנכנס כאילו הוא יוצא וניכר מקומו בקרקע: והרגו זה את זה. בדחיקתן שהיו סנדליהן מסומרין כעין אותם שעושין לרגלי הסוסים ראשיהן עבים: אל יצא. האיש בשבת כדמפרש לקמיה דבשבת היה מעשה ומעין המאורע אסרו: אלמה תנן. במסכת ביצה: משלחין

תוספות

רב נחמן בר יצחק אמר טומאה אשבת קא רמית. דאפילו בלאו טעמא דהוי תכשיט לאיש היא טמאה מכל כלי מעשה והשתא בין לרבא בין לרב נחמן בר יצחק מוקמי תרוייהו כרבי נחמיה ולא מטמא מטעם תכשיט דאשה אלא מטעם תכשיט דאיש או מטעם דהוי כלי מעשה ולצדדין קתני בין לרבא בין לרב נחמן בר יצחק:

למאי חזיא. פי' בקונטרס למאי חזיא והא משוי הוא וקשה לר"י דאם כן מאי משני הואיל ואשה חולקת בה שערה אטו משום הכי לא הוי משוי והא אינו לא מלבוש ולא תכשיט אלא נראה לפרש למאי חזיא למה היא רגילה לצאת בה בחול אמר רב יוסף כו' ובתר הכי פריך ובשבת למאי חזיא כהי שרגילה לנושאה בשביל שצריכה לחלק בה שערה בשבת תיהוי משוי כיון דאינו לא מלבוש ולא תכשיט ובקונטרס פי' בסמוך בשבת למאי חזיא והלא בשבת אינה חולקת שערה וקשה לר"י חדא דהא מנא ליה דאסור לחלק בה שיער בשבת ועוד דאמאי פריך והא אסור אפילו יהא מותר תקשה והא משוי הוא:

הואיל ואשה אוגרת בה שערה. נראה לר"י שתוחבת המחט בתוך השבכה ודוחקת את השבכה כדי שלא יפלו שערותיה חוץ לקישוריה והשתא אתי שפיר דהויא כעין בירית שאוחזת בתי שוקיה שלא יפלו ולא כפירוש הקונטרס:

ותיהוי כבירית טהורה ותשתרי. פירש בקונטרס דכי היכי דהתם לא חיישי לדילמא משלפא ומחויא הואיל ולצניעותא עבידא ה"נ לא ניחוש למישלף ואחוויי מהאי טעמא וקשה לר"י דהא כבלים אין יוצאין בהן בשבת דחיישינן דילמא משלפא להו משום דהוי תכשיט כמו שאפרש אע"ג דלצניעותא עבידא כמו בירית דהכל ענין אחד אלא שבירית באחת וכבלים בשתים כדאמרינן לקמן (דף סג:) ועוד דלמה לו להזכיר כאן טהרת בירית הוה ליה למימר ותיהוי כבירית ותשתרי ונראה לר"י דה"פ ותהוי כבירית שיוצאין בה לפי שהיא טהורה משום שאינה תכשיט דאינה טי לאשה כיון דאינה כ"א באחת והויא כטבעת הכלים דאינה כ"א לצורך בתי שוקים ה"נ האי מחט שהיא טהורה לפי שאינה אלא כטבעת הכלים תשתרי דאינה תכשיט וא"ת אמאי לא משני השתא כמין טס של זהב יש לה בראשה כדמשני לאידך שינויא דבסמוך וי"ל דאם היתה אוגרת בה שערה לא היתה מניחתה לעולם כנגד פדחתה ואינה חשובה תכשיט אלא טס וקשה לרשב"א לפירוש זה דכיון דמחט שאוגרת בה שערה היא טהורה היכי קאמר לעיל (דף נב:) אבל לענין טומאה דא ודא אחת היא הרי יש חילוק אפילו בשלימה דאותה שאינה אוגרת בה טמאה ואותה שאוגרת בה טהורה וצריך לומר דאטומאה נמי פריך ותיהוי טהורה כבירית שהיא טהורה גם תשתרי לצאת בה:

ומניחתה כנגד פדחתה. השתא לא היה צריך לומר שחולקת בה שערה כלל אלא האמת מפרש: **ושמעו** קול מעל גבי המערה: קול של סנדל המסומר: (סייך לע"ב) **לא** *בסנדל המסומר ולא *במנעל שאינו תפור. תימה לר"י והא קתני סיפא זה הכלל כל שניאותין בו משלחין אותו ביו"ט ומפרש בגמ' דכל שנאותין בו בחול קאמר וסנדל המסומר ניאותין בו בחול ואמאי אין משלחין אותו בי"ט וי"ל דהחמירו בו לפי שבא תקלה על ידו כי היכי דאסר ליה במעתין ר' אלעזר בר' שמעון לטלטלו לכסות בו את הכלי או לסמוך בו כרעי המטה אע"פ *שאר כלים שמלאכתן לאיסור שרי לטלטלן לצורך גופן ומקומן וזה הכלל דקתני התם לא קאי אלא אמנעל שאינו תפור ונראה לר"י דאפי' לרבנן דר' אלעזר דשרי לטלטל לצורך גופו ומקומו אסור לשלחו בי"ט אע"ג דשילוח משום שמחת י"ט חשיב כמו לצורך גופו מדשרי' לשלוח דברים שמלאכתן לאיסור כיון שבאת תקלה על ידו ליכא שמחת י"ט:

אין

עין משפט נר מצוה

כז א מיי' פי"ט מהל' שבת הלכה ה סמג לאוין סה טוש"ע א"ח סי' שג סעיף ט:

כח ב מיי' פי"ט מהל' שבת הלכה ג:

כט ג מיי' שם הלכה טו סמג שם טוש"ע א"ח סי' שא סעיף ו:

רבינו חננאל

ה' צדיק קצץ עבות רשעים. קולב. יש מי שאומרים ממיני תכשיט הוא להשמיע קול כדורך בנת ומחזקו במסמרים: שליבות ושלשלאות פשוטות הן. רבא אמר הא מתניתא לצדדין קתני אין עליה חותם תכשיט דאשה יש עליה חותם תכשיט דאיש והדין כך הוא. שיהא האיש מותר לצאת בטבעת שיש עליה חותם והאשה בטבעת שאין עליה חותם. מפני שתכשיט הוא להן וכל תכשיט שרי אלא משום גזירה *) דרבא כדבעינן למימר לקמן (סב.) דאמר פעמים שהאשה נותנת לבעלה טבעת שאין עליה חותם להוליכה אצל האומן ומניחה באצבעו עד שמגיע אל האומן. ופעמים שהאיש נותן לאשתו טבעת שיש עליה חותם להניחה בקופסא ומניחתה באצבעתה עד שמגעת לקופסא. לפיכך אסרו אחד האיש ואחד האשה לצאת בין בטבעת שיש עליה חותם בין בטבעת שאין עליה חותם. רב נחמן בר יצחק אמר טומאה אשבת קרמית כו'. ולא במחט שאינה נקובה אוקימנא כדתניא כמין טס של זהב יש לה על ראשה. בחול חולקת בה שערה בשבת מנחת על פדחתה. ונוי הוא לה: לא יצא בסנדל מסומר כו'. מ"ט שלפי השמד כו' פשוטה היא.

*) עי' נרשב"א שתמה ע"ד רבינו בזה.

מסורת הש"ס

[לעיל טו:]

לקמן קכג.

[גי' הערוך בערך אגד אגודת]

[לעיל נג:]

הגהות הב"ח

(א) רש"י ד"ה המעמיד וכו' והערסה הוא עץ ארוך שהקנה שקורין: (ב) ד"ה טהורה וכו' וזכרי הוא כטבעת: (ג) ד"ה סנדל וכו' מסמרות לחזק כצ"ל ותיבת למעלה נמחק:

גליון הש"ס

מתני' ולא בשריון. עי' לקמן סד ע"ב תוס' ד"ה כל שאסרו:

רש"ל מוחק זה

[נ"ל סנדל]

[נ"ל מנעל]

[לקמן קמב:]

עין משפט
נר מצוה

לא טוש"ע א"ח סי' הקטו סעיף ג:
לא ב ג מיי' פ' יט מהל' שבת הלכה כ:

רבינו חננאל

ואסיקנא בסנדל מסומר אחד שבת ואחד יו"ט אסיר דיו"ט ושבת כי הדדי ניהו: הא דר' חנינא בן עקיבא דאמר לא אסרו אלא בירדן ובספינה. וכמעשה שהיה מפורש ביבמות פרק האשה שהלכה היא ובעלה למדינת הים. מעשה באחד שהיה מעביר מי חטאת ואפר חטאת בירדן ובספינה ונמצאת כזית מת תחוב בקרקעיתה של ספינה. באותה שעה אמרו לא ישא אדם מי חטאת ואפר חטאת ויעבירם בירדן ובספינה [וצריך לעיין] התם כדי שיתברר לו השמועה היטב: קי"ל סנדל המסומר לחזק אסיר לנוי מותר כרב יהודה אמר שמואל דהא דייק אשמעתיה לאוקימה דאמרינן וכמה לנוי דשרי ר' יוחנן אמר ב' מכאן וב' מכאן וא' בתרסיותיו ר' חנינא אמר ג' מיכן ג' מכאן וא' בתרסיותיו וכר' חנינא קיי"ל דר' יוחנן לגבי ר' חנינא תלמיד הוא. והא דאמר ליה איפה לרבה בר בר חנה אתון תלמידי דר' יוחנן (אתון) עבידו כר' יוחנן לאו משום דהלכה כר' יוחנן אלא משום דבאתריה דר' יוחנן ביותר מחשש נהגו בו איסור. ודברים המותרים ואחרים נהגו בהן איסור אי אתה רשאי להתירן בפניהם. *) ור' אמי נמי קם ליה כר' חנינא דשבע מותר והא דקתני ר' מתיר עד י"ג בנוטה הוא. כגון שניטל עקיבו ולדברי הכל. ור' חייא מתיר בה הרבה. בסורא אמרו כ"ב בפומבדיתא אמרי כ"ד. תפרו לסנדל מבפנים שרי משום דהוי ליה מנעל ואסנדל גזרו רבנן אמנעל לא גזרו. כמין כלבוס מותר. אמר רב ששת חיפהו כולו במסמרים כדי שלא יהא קרקע אוכל ממנו מותר תניא כוותיה דרב ששת לא יצא האיש בסנדל מסומר ולא יטייל בו מבית לבית כו': ולא ביחיד בזמן שאין ברגלו מכה. ירושלמי אמר ר' אבא מפני חשד שלא יאמרו איש פלוני נפסק סנדלו ותלאו בבית שחיו:

*) מדברי רבינו נראה שהיה גורס כעי מיניה רב הונא מרב אמי וכו'.

תוספות

אין בין יו"ט לשבת כו'. והע"פ דבפ' משילין (ביצה דף לז. ושם) ולקמן בפ' כל הכלים (דף קכד. ושם) מוקמינן לה כב"ש דאי כב"ה הא אמרי מתוך שהותרה הבערה לצורך הותרה נמי שלא לצורך מ"מ דמי טפי יו"ט לשבת הואיל ולא שריא שאר דברים אלא מטעם שהותרה לצורך אוכל נפש:

השתא חמש שרינן כו'. בפרק קמא דסוכה (ד' ב: ושם) גבי רבי יהודה מכשיר עד ארבעים וחמשים אמה לא פריך השתא חמשים כו' וכן בריש אע"פ (כתובות דף נז. ושם) גבי אבל חכמים אומרים משהה אדם עם אשתו אפילו שתים ושלש שנים בלא כתובה ונראה לר"י דכל היכא דפשיטא ליה דבעי למימר אפי' טובא לא פריך אבל הכא ליכא לפרושי ד' וה' אפילו טובא דא"כ התירה סנדל המסומר וכן בפרק בנות כותים (נדה דף לז: ושם) פריך [גבי] וכמה היא קישוייה ר' מאיר אומר אפילו מ' וכ' יום דליכא למימר אפילו טובא דאין סברא שיחשב דם קישוי מיום תחילת עיבורה ומשמע ליה בכל הני דשיעורא בתרא דוקא ולהכי פריך דלימא שיעורא בתרא ולא לימא שיעורא קמא ולקמן בפרק מפנין ד' וה' קופות (דף קכו:) פריך נמי השתא חמש שרי ד' כו' משמע ליה דטפי לא שרינן משום טורח שבת ומשני רב חסדא ד' מאוצר קטן חמש מאוצר גדול ושמואל משני ד' וה' אפילו טובא כדאמרי אינשי דסבר אפילו טובא מצי לפנות ובלבד שלא יגמור את האוצר פי' קרקעית האוצר משום אשווי גומות וכדאמרן התם וא"ת דבפרק אע"פ (כתובות דף ס. ושם) אמרינן תינוק יונק והולך אפילו ד' וה' שנים ולא פריך אף על גב דהוי דוקא מדפריך התם מחבילתו על כתפו ומשני אידי ואידי חד שיעורא וי"ל הא בכחוש הא בבריא והא דאמרינן בפרק הזרוע (חולין דף קלב:) כהן טבח שתים וג' שבתות פטור מן המתנות מכאן ואילך חייב במתנות אומר ר"י דנקט שתים לרבי דאית ליה בהבא על יבמתו (יבמות דף סד:) דבתרי זימני הויא חזקה וג' לרשב"ג*):

דעבר

*(משלחין *כלים בי"ט בין תפורין בין שאינן תפורין) אבל לא סנדל המסומר ולא מנעל שאינו תפור (*בי"ט) בשבת מ"ט דאיכא כינופיא בי"ט נמי איכא כינופיא תענית צבור איכא כינופיא ליתסר מעשה כי הוה בכינופיא דאיסורא הבא כינופיא דהתירא הוה ואפילו לר' *חנינא בן עקיבא *דאמר לא אסרו אלא בירדן ובספינה וכמעשה שהיה הני מילי ירדן דשאני משאר נהרות אבל י"ט ושבת כי הדדי נינהו *דתנן אין בין י"ט לשבת אלא אוכל נפש בלבד א"ר יהודה אמר שמואל לא שנו אלא לחזק אבל לנוי מותר וכמה לנוי ר' יוחנן אמר חמש בזה וחמש בזה ור' חנינא אמר שבע בזה ושבע בזה א"ל ר' יוחנן לרב שמן בר אבא אסברא לך לדידי שתים מכאן ושתים מכאן ואחת בתרסיותיו לר' חנינא ג' מכאן וג' מכאן ואחת בתרסיותיו מיתיבי סנדל הנוטה עושה לו שבע דברי רבי נתן ורבי מתיר בי"ג בשלמא לרבי חנינא הוא דאמר כרבי נתן אלא רבי יוחנן דאמר כמאן הוא דאמר כר' נהוראי דתניא ר' נהוראי אומר ה' מותר ושבע אסור א"ל איפה לרבה בר בר חנה אתון תלמידי רבי יוחנן עבידו כר' יוחנן אנן נעביד כרבי חנינא בעא מיניה רב הונא מרב אשי חמש מהו א"ל אפילו ז' מותר ט' מאי א"ל אפילו ח' אסור בעא מיניה ההוא רצענא מרבי אמי תפרו מבפנים מהו א"ל מותר ולא ידענא מ"ט אמר (א) רב אשי ולאידע מר מ"ט כיון דתפרו מבפנים הוי ליה מנעל בסנדל גזרו ביה רבנן במנעל לא גזרו ביה רבנן בעא מיניה ר' אבא בר זבדא מר' אבא בר אבינא עשאו כמין *כלבוס מהו א"ל מותר איתמר נמי אמר רבי יוסי בר' חנינא עשאו כמין כלבוס מותר א"ר ששת חיפהו כולו במסמרות כדי שלא תהא קרקע אוכלתו מותר תניא כוותיה דרב ששת *לא יצא האיש בסנדל המסומר ולא יטייל מבית לבית אפילו ממטה למטה אבל מטלטלין אותו לכסות בו את הכלי ולסמוך בו כרעי המטה ור' אלעזר בר' שמעון אוסר נשרו רוב ממסמרותיו ונשתייר בו ד' או ה' מותר ורבי מתיר עד שבע *חיפהו בעור מלמטה וקבע לו מסמרות מלמעלה מותר עשאו (ב) כמין כלבוס או כמין טס או כמין יתד או שחיפהו כולו במסמרות כדי שלא תהא קרקע אוכלתו מותר הא גופה קשיא אמרת נשרו רוב מסמרותיו אע"ג דנשתיירו ביה טובא והדר תני ארבע או חמש אין טפי לא א"ר ששת לא קשיא כאן שנגממו כאן שנעקרו: ארבע או חמש מותר: השתא חמש שרי ארבע מיבעיא א"ר חסדא ארבע מסנדל קטן וחמש מסנדל גדול: ורבי מתיר עד שבע: והתניא רבי מתיר עד שלש עשרה נוטה שאני השתא דאתית להכי לרבי יוחנן נמי לא קשיא נוטה שאני אמר רב מתנה ואמרי לה אמר רב אחדבוי בר מתנה אמר רב מתנה אין הלכה כר' אלעזר בר' שמעון פשיטא *יחיד ורבים הלכה כרבים מהו דתימא מסתברא טעמא דרבי אלעזר ברבי שמעון בהא קמ"ל אמר רבי חייא אי לאו דקרו לי בבלאי שרי איסורי שרינא ביה טובא וכמה בפומבדיתא אמרין עשרין וארבע בסורא אמרין עשרין ותרתין אמר רב נחמן בר יצחק וסימניך עד דאתא מפומבדיתא לסורא חסר תרתי: ולא ביחיד בזמן שאין ברגלו מכה:

*)[ועי' תוס' עירובין ג. ד"ה עד ותוס' יומא כג. ד"ה שתים ותוס' סוכה ב: ד"ה עד ותוס' כתובות נז. ד"ה שתים ודף ס. ד"ה רבי יהושע ותוס' ב"מ ע"ס: ד"ה השתא ותוס' נדה לז: ד"ה ארבעים]

רש"י

משלחין כלים ביו"ט בין תפורין בין שאינן תפורין אבל לא סנדל המסומר. אלמא לאו בר מנעלי' ביו"ט היא דהא קתני התם כל שנאותין בו ביו"ט משלחין אותו: איכא כינופיא. שאין עושין מלאכה ונקבצין לבתי כנסיות ולבתי מדרשות כי ההיא מעשה דהוה כינופיא דאיסורא. בעשיית מלאכה: ואפילו לרבי חנינא בן עקיבא. בפרק חומר בקדש גבי טשא מי חטאת ואפר חטאת בירדן ובספינה שנמצא כזית מן המת תחוב בקרקעית' של ספינה °ונטמאו וקאמרי רבנן דגזרו שלא יעביר אדם מי חטאת בספינה ולא על הגשר ולא ישוט על פני המים אחד ירדן ואחד שאר נהרות ופליג ר' חנינא ואמר לא אסרו אלא בירדן ובספינה ולא גשר ושאר נהרות דגזירה שגזרו מחמת מאורע אין להם לגזור אלא מעין המאורע: דשאני משאר נהרות. ברוחב או בעומק: אלא לחזק. שמסמרותיו נעשו לחזק העקב שקורין סול"א עם הפנתא שקורין אינפייל"א אבל לנוי מותר דלא גזרו אלא מעין המאורע והנהו לחזק היו כשהם מסמרים דסנדל: שתים מכאן. לצד חילון אחד בראשו לצד האצבעות ואחד לצד עקיבו ושתים מכאן לצד פנימי לעבר בין הרגלים: תרסיותיו. רצועותיו: סנדל הנוטה. שתחתון שלו אינו שוה שעב מצד זה ודק מצד זה וכשדורס נוטה לצד הדק וצריך להגביהו שיהא שוה לצד שכנגדו: איפה. שם חכם ובנו של ר' רחבה דפומבדיתא הוה*: תפרו מבפנים. שנתן מנעל של עור לפנים מן הסנדל תפרו פורדרי"ן בלע"ז: מותר. שמעתי מרבי יוחנן וטעמא לא ידענא: מותר. לקבוע בו מסמרים מבחוץ: עשאו. למסמר כמין כלבוס בלע"ז טינפיילו"ן שני ראשין חדין וכפופין ונועץ שני ראשים בעץ כדאמרי' בסוטה (יג:) כלבוס של ברזל מטילין לה לתוך פיה: מותר. הואיל ונשתנה. משאר מסמרים דלא גזרו אלא מעין המאורע: חיפהו. מלמטה: אבל מטלטלין אותו. דתורת כלי עליו: אוסר. דילמא אתי לנועלו: נשרו רוב מסמרותיו כו'. לקמן מפרש לה: מותר. הואיל ונשתנה מכמו שהיה דמעין המאורע גזרו: עשאו. לראש מסמר רחב כמין טס או שעשאו חד כמין יתד: אע"ג דישתאר טובא. ובלבד שיהיו מעוט: שנגממו. מלמעלה ורשומו ניכר בתוך העץ אפילו טובא דהא מינכר שאינו כברייתו: שנעקרו. לגמרי שאין ניכר שהיה בו יותר ד' או ה' [אין] טפי לא לוי"ה ולשון חבירו איפכא: נוטה שאני. שכולן צריכין לו להשוותו ואין אחד מהן לחזק: השתא דאתית להכי. לחלק בין נוטה לשאין נוטה: לרבי יוחנן נמי. דקפרכת לעיל מינה ואמרי דאמר כמאן איכא נמי לתרוצי לעולם כרבי נתן ונוטה שאני דהתם מתיר עד שבע אבל אין נוטה ה' ותו לא: מסתברא טעמא. דאסור לטלטל שמא ינעלנו: בבלאי שרי איסורי. דר' חייא מבבל הוה כדאמרינן בסוכה* עלו ר' חייא ובניו ויסדוה: עד דאתא רבי חייא. כשעלה מבבל לארץ ישראל ובא דרך סוריא מפומבדיתא: חסר תלתי. כפלו שתים ממסמרותיו בדרך: לסורא חסר. (תרתי) דומה אל דומה:

הא

מסורת הש"ס

ביצה יד:
[כמשנה ליתא]
[תוספ' פרס פ"ח] יבמות קטז: חגיגה כג.
לקמן קכד: קלז: מגילה ז: ביצה כח. לז:
[תוספ' דמגילה פ"א]
[סנהדרין יז:]
[תוספ' פ"ט ותוספ' יומא פ"ד]
[שם פ"ט]
[ברכות ס. וש"נ]
[דף כ.]

הגהות הב"ח

(א) גמ' אמר ליה רב אשי ולא: (ב) שם מלמעלה מותר עשאו כמין טס כצ"ל ותיבות כמין כלבוס או נמחק:

גליון הש"ס

רש"י ד"ה ואפי' לר"ח בן עקביא וכו' ונטמאו. עי' זבחים כג ע"א תוס' ד"ה מי חטאת:

כוס

רב נסים גאון

הנושא את האשה בכתובות (קג): ואפי' לר' חנניא בר עקיבא דאמר לא אסרו אלא בירדן וספינה וכמעשה שהיה. זה המעשה עיקרו במשנה חגיגה בפ' חומר בקידש (דף כג) וביבמות בפרק האשה [שהלכה] היא ובעלה למדינת הים שלום בינה לבינה (קטז) מאי מעשה שהיה דאמר רב יהודה אמר רב מעשה באדם אחד שהיה מעביר מי חטאת ואפר חטאת בירדן ובספינה ונמצא כזית מת תחוב בקרקעית' של ספינה באותה שעה אמרו לא ישא אדם מי חטאת ואפר חטאת ויעבירם בירדן ובספינה: ולא ביחיד בזמן שאין ברגלו מכה גרסי. דבני מערבא אמר ר' אבא

it be permitted on Festivals! Why did we learn: [60b] But one may not [send] a nail-studded sandal or an unsewn shoe [on Festivals]?[3] — What is the reason of the Sabbath?[4] Because there is a gathering [of people]. So on Festivals too there is a gathering. But there is a gathering on a public fast day:[5] let it be forbidden [then too]? — The incident happened on a day of assembly when there is an interdict [against work]; but here it is [a day of] assembly when it is permitted [to work]. And even according to R. Ḥanina b. Akiba who maintained, They enacted a prohibition only in respect of the Jordan and a ship, just as the incident that occurred:[6] that applies only to the Jordan, which differs from other rivers;[7] but Festivals and the Sabbath are alike, for we learnt: There is no difference between Festivals and the Sabbath save in respect of food consumption.[8]

Rab Judah said in Samuel's name: They learnt this only [where the nails are] to strengthen [the sandal], but where they are orna-
a mental, it is permitted.[1] And how many [nails] constitute an ornament? — R. Joḥanan said: Five on each; R. Ḥanina maintained: Seven on each[2]. Said R. Joḥanan to R. Shaman b. Abba: I shall explain it to you; in my view there are two according to each side and one on [each of] the straps; according to R. Ḥanina, there are three on each side[3] and one in the strapping.

An objection is raised: For an inclining sandal[4] one inserts seven [nails]; this is R. Nathan's view. But Rabbi permits thirteen.[5] As for R. Ḥanina, it is well: he rules as R. Nathan. But whose view does R. Joḥanan state? — He rules as R. Nehorai. For it was taught, R. Nehorai said: Five are permitted, but seven are forbidden. Efah said to Rabbah b. Bar Ḥanah: You, as disciples of R. Joḥanan, should act as R. Joḥanan; but we will act as R. Ḥanina.

R. Huna asked R. Ashi: What of five [nails]? — Even seven are permitted, he answered him. What of nine? Even eight are forbidden, was his reply. A certain shoe-maker asked R. Ammi: What if it is sewn from within?[6] It is permitted, replied he, but I do not know what is the reason.[7] Said R. Ashi, And does not the Master know what is the reason?[8] Since it was sewn from within, it becomes a shoe:[9] the Rabbis enacted a decree in respect to a sandal, but in respect of a shoe they did not enact any decree.

R. Abba b. Zabda asked R. Abba b. Abina: What if he arranged
b them [the nails] zigzag-shape?[1] — It is permitted, he answered him. It was stated likewise: R. Jose b. R. Ḥanina said: If they are arranged zigzag-shape, it is permitted.

R. Shesheth said: If the whole of it [the sole] is covered with nails [underneath] so that the ground should not wear it away, it is permitted. It was taught in accordance with R. Shesheth: A man may not go out wearing a nail-studded sandal, nor may he stroll [in it] from house to house,[2] and even from bed to bed. But it may be handled in order to cover a utensil or support the legs of a bed therewith;[3] but R. Eleazar b. R. Simeon forbids this.[4] If most of its nails are fallen out, but four or five are left, it is permitted; while Rabbi permits it up to seven. If one covers it with leather underneath and drives nails into it on top, it is permitted.[5] If one arranges them [the nails] zigzag-fashion,[6] or flattens [them] out, or points [them],[7] or covers the whole of it with nails so that the ground should not wear it out, it is permitted. Now, this is self-contradictory: You say, if most of the nails are fallen out, [implying], even if many are left [it may be worn]; then it is taught, only four or five, but not more? — Said R. Shesheth, There is no difficulty: in the one case they are smoothed out; in the other they are pulled out.[8]

'[If] four or five [are left], it is permitted.' Seeing that it is permitted [with] five, need four be stated? — Said R. Ḥisda: [It means] four in a small sandal and five in a large sandal.

'While Rabbi permits it up to seven.' But it was taught: Rabbi
c permits it up to thirteen? An inclining [sandal] is different.[1] Now that you have arrived at this [distinction], on R. Joḥanan's view too there is no difficulty: an inclining [sandal] is different.[2]

R. Mattenah — others state, R. Aḥadboi b. Mattenah in R. Mattenah's name — said: The *halachah* is not as R. Eleazar son of R. Simeon. But that is obvious: [where] one disagrees with many, the *halachah* is as the majority? — You might argue, R. Eleazar son of R. Simeon's view is logical here;[3] hence we are informed [that we do not follow him].

R. Ḥiyya said: But that I would be dubbed a Babylonian who permits forbidden things,[4] I would permit more. And how many? — In Pumbeditha they say, Twenty-four; in Sura, twenty-two. R. Naḥman b. Isaac said: And your sign [to remember this is]: by the time he [R. Ḥiyya] travelled from Pumbeditha to Sura[5] two [nails] were missing [from his sandals].

NOR WITH A SINGLE [SANDAL], IF HE HAS NO WOUND [or

(3) V. Beẓ. 14*b*. These may not be sent because they cannot be used for the Festival. — A sandal (סנדל) consists only of a sole and straps, while a shoe (מנעל) has uppers in addition, Levi, *Wörterbuch*, s.v. סנדל. (4) Why was it forbidden then? (5) V. Ta'an. 15*a*. (6) V. Ḥag. 23*a*. It once happened that the purification water (v. Num. XIX, 9 *seq.*) was carried in a boat over the Jordan, when a portion of a corpse was found in the bottom of the boat, whereby the water itself was defiled. The Rabbis maintain that it was then enacted that the water of lustration must not be carried over *any* river, whether in a boat or over a bridge. But R. Ḥanina disputes this, as quoted. It might therefore be thought that in the matter under discussion he maintains that there was no prohibition in respect to Festivals. (7) In breadth, depth, current, etc. (8) Lit., 'food for a person', which may be prepared on Festivals (Ex. XII, 16) but not on the Sabbath.

a (1) To go out wearing the sandal on the Sabbath. Nails are normally put in to strengthen the sandal, and such must have been worn on the occasion of the tragedy; hence the decree was only in respect of same. (2) But if there are more, their purpose is to strengthen, not ornamental. (3) Of the sandal, one at the heel and the other at the toe. (4) The sole of which is thicker at one side than at the other. It is levelled by nails inserted at the thin end. (5) These too are ornamental, not for strength. But if there are more, the sandal may not be worn on the Sabbath, as above. (6) Rashi. i.e., a leather shoe was placed inside a sandal and sewn thereto. (7) He had heard this ruling, but did not know why. (8) [MS.M. omits 'but I do not know' and 'does not the Master . . . reason'. This reading is preferable as R. Ashi and R. Ammi were not contemporaries]. (9) A sandal (סנדל) is merely a sole, while a shoe (מנעול) has uppers too.

b (1) *Kalbus* is a tongs or pinchers, which presumably opened X-wise. (2) Probably from room to room in the same house, where each room has a separate occupant. (3) Because it ranks as a utensil: v. *supra* 46*a*. (4) Lest he put it on. (5) Because the sandal is not exactly similar to that which caused the disaster. (6) BaḤ deletes this. (7) These refer to the tops of the nails (Rashi). (8) If they are levelled down, leaving marks of nails on the sole, then even if more than four or five are left it is permissible, since the sandal was obviously not made like this originally. But if they are clean pulled out, leaving no mark on the wood of the sole, the sandal may appear to have been originally manufactured thus, and therefore not more than five are permitted. Others reverse the translation, but the sense remains the same.

c (1) All are necessary to level it up, and none are for strength. (2) V. *supra*. (3) V. *supra* n. b4. (4) He was a Babylonian who went to study in Palestine; Suk. 20*a*. This may indicate that the Palestinians on the whole were stricter. (5) On his way to Palestine.

BRUISE] ON HIS FOOT. [61a] Hence if he has a wound on his foot, he may go out. With which of them does he go out?[6]—R. Huna said: With that [worn on the foot] which has the wound. This proves that he holds that the purpose of the sandal is [to save him] pain. Ḥiyya b. Rab said: With that [worn] where there is no wound. This proves that he holds that it is employed as a luxury, while this [foot] that has a wound, its wound is evidence for it.[7] Now, R. Joḥanan too holds as R. Huna. For R. Joḥanan said to R. Shamen b. Abba: Give me my sandals. When he gave him the right one, he [R. Joḥanan] observed, You treat it as though it had a wound.[8] [No]. Perhaps he agrees with Ḥiyya b. Rab, and he meant thus: You treat the *left* [foot] as though it had a wound? Now, R. Joḥanan [here] follows his general view. For R. Joḥanan said: Like *tefillin*, so are shoes: just as *tefillin* [are donned] on the left [hand], so are shoes [put on] the left [foot first]. An objection is raised: When one puts on his shoes, he must put on the right first and then the left?—Said R. Joseph: Now that it was taught thus, while R. Joḥanan said the reverse, he who acts in either way
a acts [well].[1] Said Abaye to him: But perhaps R. Joḥanan did not hear this Baraitha, but if he had heard it, he would have retracted? Or perhaps he heard it and held that the *halachah* is not as that Mishnah?[2] R. Naḥman b. Isaac said: A God-fearing person satisfies both views. And who is that? Mar, the son of Rabina. What did he do? He put on the right foot [sandal] but did not tie it. Then he put on the left, tied it, and then tied the right [sandal]. R. Ashi said: I saw that R. Kahana was not particular.

Our Rabbis taught: When one puts on his shoes, he must put on the right [first] and then the left; when he removes [them], he must remove the left [first] and then the right.[3] When one washes, he must [first] wash the right [hand, foot] and then the left. When one anoints [himself] with oil,[4] he must [first] anoint the right and then the left. But one who desires to anoint his whole body must anoint his head first, because it is the king of all the limbs.[5]

NOR WITH TEFILLIN. R. Safra said: Do not think that this is [only] according to the view that the Sabbath is not a time for *tefillin;* but even on the view that the Sabbath is a time for *tefillin,*[6] one must not go out [with them], lest he come to carry them [four cubits] in the street.[7] Others learn this in reference to the last clause: YET IF HE GOES OUT, HE DOES NOT INCUR A SIN-OFFERING: Said R. Safra: Do not think that this is [only] according to the view that the Sabbath is a time for *tefillin;* but even on the view that the Sabbath is not a time for *tefillin,* he is [nevertheless] not liable to a sin-offering. What is the reason? He
b treats it as a garment.[1]

NOR WITH AN AMULET, IF IT IS NOT FROM AN EXPERT. R. Papa said: Do not think that both the man [issuing it] and the amulet must be approved; but as long as the man is approved, even if the amulet is not approved.[2] This may be proved too, for it is stated, NOR WITH AN AMULET, IF IT IS NOT FROM AN EXPERT; but it is not stated, if it is not approved.[3] This proves it.

Our Rabbis taught: What is an approved amulet? One that has healed [once], a second time and a third time; whether it is an amulet in writing or an amulet of roots, whether it is for an invalid whose life is endangered or for an invalid whose life is not endangered. [It is permitted] not [only] for a person who has [already] had an epileptic fit, but even [merely] to ward it off.[4] And one may tie and untie it even in the street, providing that

(6) Wearing the sandal on which foot? (7) For the sandal is obviously being worn merely as a luxury, and no one will suspect him of carrying the other (v. *supra* 60a, n. b4) which he is not wearing, because he cannot put it on on account of the wound. (8) R. Joḥanan holds that the *left* sandal must be put on first (*infra*). Hence if he put on the right, the other foot would have to be left unshod, and people would think that his right foot was wounded. Thus he holds with R. Huna that the sandal is donned on the wounded foot as a protection.

a (1) [It is left to each individual to decide for himself whether to assign pride of place to the right or left since each enjoys in some respects distinction over the other. V. Tosaf.]. (2) It is really a Baraitha, not a Mishnah. (3) The right half of the body being stronger, more honour must be shown to it. Removing the left first is likewise a mark of honour to the right, for the right shoe remains longer on the foot. (4) V. *supra* 59a, n. b8. (5) I.e., the most important. (6) V. 'Er. 95b. (7) In his hand, in case of need.

b (1) By donning it in the usual manner. (2) It may be worn on the Sabbath. (3) Heb. *mumḥeh* describes both the practitioner who issues it and the charm itself. The Mishnah, however, refers only to the former. (4) Even if the wearer has not actually suffered but fears an attack of epilepsy.

הא יש ברגלו מכה נפיק בהי מינייהו נפיק אמר רב הונא באותה שיש בה מכה אלמא קסבר סנדל לשום צער עביד וחייא בר רב אמר *באותה שאין בה מכה אלמא קסבר לשום תענוג עביד וזו שיש בה מכה מכתה מוכחת עליה ואף רבי יוחנן סבר לה להא דרב הונא דאמר ליה ר' יוחנן לרב שמן בר אבא הב לי מסנאי יהב ליה דימין אמר ליה עשיתו מכה ודילמא כחייא בר רב ס"ל והכי קאמר עשית של שמאל מכה ואזדא רבי יוחנן לטעמיה דאמר ר' יוחנן כתפילין כך מנעלין מה תפילין בשמאל אף מנעלין בשמאל מיתיבי כשהוא נועל נועל של ימין ואחר כך נועל של שמאל אמר רב יוסף השתא דתניא הכי ואמר רבי יוחנן הכי דעבד הכי עבד ודעבד הכי עבד אמר ליה אביי דילמא רבי יוחנן הא מתני' *לא הוה שמיע ליה ואי הוה שמיע ליה הוה הדר ביה ואי נמי שמיע ליה וקסבר אין הלכה כאותה משנה *אמר רב נחמן בר יצחק ירא שמים יוצא ידי שתיהן ומנו מר בריה דרבנא היכי עביד סיים דימיניה ולא קטר וסיים דשמאליה וקטר והדר קטר דימיניה אמר רב אשי חזינא לרב כהנא דלא קפיד תנו רבנן *כשהוא נועל נועל של ימין ואחר כך נועל של שמאל כשהוא חולץ חולץ של שמאל ואח"כ חולץ של ימין כשהוא רוחץ רוחץ של ימין ואח"כ רוחץ של שמאל כשהוא סך סך של ימין ואח"כ של שמאל והרוצה לסוך כל גופו סך ראשו תחילה מפני שהוא מלך על כל איבריו: ולא בתפילין: אמר רב ספרא לא תימא אליבא דמ"ד *שבת לאו זמן תפילין הוא אלא אפילו למ"ד שבת זמן תפילין הוא לא יצא דילמא אתי לאיתויי ברה"ר ואיכא דמתני לה אסיפא ואם יצא אינו חייב חטאת אמר רב ספרא לא תימא אליבא דמ"ד *שבת זמן תפילין הוא אלא אפילו למ"ד שבת לאו זמן תפילין הוא אינו חייב חטאת מ"ט דרך מלבוש עבידא: ולא בקמיע בזמן שאינו מן המומחה: אמר רב פפא לא תימא עד דמומחה גברא ומומחה קמיע אלא כיון דמומחה גברא אף על גב דלא מומחה קמיע דיקא נמי דקתני ולא בקמיע בזמן שאינו מן המומחה ולא קתני בזמן שאינו מומחה ש"מ: ת"ר *איזהו קמיע מומחה כל שריפא ושנה ושלש אחד קמיע של כתב ואחד קמיע של עיקרין אחד חולה שיש בו סכנה ואחד חולה שאין בו סכנה לא שנכפה אלא שלא יכפה וקושר ומתיר אפילו ברה"ר ובלבד שלא יקשרנו

בשיר

רש"י

הא יש ברגלו מכה. איכא למידק דנפיק ביחיד והשתא בעי תלמודא בהי מרגליו נפיק: סנדל לשם צער עביד. שלא יגנף ביתדות הדרכים וילטער הילכך כשרואין אותו נועל ויודעין שיש ברגליו מכה אין חושדין אותו שטוען את השני בידו אלא מכירין בו לפי מעשיו שפרסותיו קשות ואינו מצטער ביתדות הדרכים ולא נעלו אלא משום מכה ודיו בזה לבדו וללשון רבותי אי נמי מחכו עלה דלא חזו למכה לא שליף לה דמצטער ביתדות הדרכים מחמת המכה: לשום תענוג עביד. אדם איסטניס ורך ומכירין מתוך מעשיו שנעל נעלו אחת שהוא איסטניס וזו מכתה מוכחת עלה ומבינין שהמכה מונעתו מלנעול ולא חשדי ליה ולענין אחוכי נמי לא מחייכי עליה: עשיתו מכה. ורבי יוחנן סבירא ליה דהנועל סנדלים נועל של שמאל תחילה ואח"כ של ימין וקס"ד דהכי קאמר ליה א"כ שאנעול זה שוב לא אנעול של שמאל אחריו והנני יוצא ביחיד ועשית את זו של ימין כאילו היתה בה מכה אלמא קסבר באותה שיש בה מכה נועל: ודילמא כר' חייא סבירא ליה. דאמר באותה שאין בה מכה נועל והכי קאמר ליה א"כ הריני יוצא ביחיד בזו של ימין ועשית את רגלי של שמאל כאילו יש בה מכה דאלא ביחיד באותה שאין בה מכה: ואזדא ר' יוחנן. דאמר עשית מכה דשמעינן מינה דאי הוה נעיל דימין ברישא תו לא הוה נעיל דשמאל בתריה לטעמיה דאמר דשמאל חשיבא: תפילין בשמאל. כדילפינן במנחות (דף לז.) מעל ידכה מלא יד כהה דהיינו שמאל שהיא כהה לענין תשמיש: הוה הדר ביה. ולא עבדינן כר' יוחנן: אין הלכה. וכרבי יוחנן בעינן למעבד: יוצא ידי שניהם. עביד כתרוייהו: וסיים דשמאליה וקטר. נמצא נעילת ימין קודמת לשמאל כי מתניתא וקשירת שמאל לשל ימין כר' יוחנן: חולץ של שמאל. דזהו כבודו של ימין בכולהו גרסינן של ימין ברישא חוץ מחולץ: לא תימא כו'. בפרק בתרא דעירובין (ד' צה:) מייתינן פלוגתייהו בגמרא: דילמא. שקיל להו מרישא אם בא לפנות וממטי להו ד' אמות: דמומחה גברא ומומחה קמיע. שעשה אדם זה קמיע זו לג' אנשים דנעשה אדם זה מומחה שריפא ג' אנשים והקמיע מומחה שריפא כתב זה ג' אנשים א"נ שכתב אדם זה ג' מיני קמיעים של ג' מיני חלאים לג' אנשים היינו איתמחי גברא בכל קמיעים שיעשה לעולם ומומחה קמיעה שנעשית [קמיע זו] לג' אנשים מחולי זה בין שכתבה רופא זה בין שכתבה רופא אחר נעשה הקמיע מומחה: אלא כיון דאיתמחי גברא. בג' מיני קמיעות לג' בני אדם אע"ג דלא איתמחי קמיע שלא ריפא קמיע זה אדם מעולם: מן המומחה. משמע מאדם מומחה: ולא קתני בזמן שאינו מומחה. דליהוו משמע דקפיד אמומחה קמיע עצמו קמיע אינו אלא לשון קשר ודעיקרין של שרשי סממנין נמי קרויין קמיע: ולא שנכפה. כלומר לא תימא דלא יצא אלא מי שבא עליו החולי כבר פעם אחת: נכפה. היינו חולי שאדם נופל מחמתו לארץ ומכהו בראשו במוחו ומפילו: אלא שלא יכפה. שבא ממשפחת נכפין ודואג שלא יכפה:

בשיר

תוספות

דעבד הכי עבד. פירוש דברייתא לא פליגא ארבי יוחנן ולא ר' יוחנן אברייתא וה"פ כתפילין אע"ג דימין חשובה לענין בהן יד ובהן רגל וכן לענין חליצה יכול לנעול של שמאל תחילה ברייתא נמי קמ"ל דאע"ג דשמאל חשובה לתפילין יכול לנעול של ימין תחילה וא"ת א"כ אמאי הקפיד רבי יוחנן על רב שמן שנתן לו של ימין כיון דיכול לנעול איזה שירצה תחילה ונראה לר"י דה"פ דעבד הכי עבד מי שרוצה לחבב של שמאל משום מצות תפילין הרשות בידו ומי שרוצה לחבב של ימין יותר משום חשיבות של ימין הרשות בידו ורבי יוחנן היה דרכו לחבב כל שעה של שמאל יותר ורב שמן בר אבא (לא) היה יודע מנהגו: וסיים דשמאליה וקטר. אומר ריב"א דדוקא לענין קשירה הוא דחשיבא של שמאל טפי משום דחשיבות תפילין הוא בקשירה אבל איפכא לא ולהאי טעמא יש לנעול של ימין תחלה במנעלים שאין בהן קשירה: דילמא מיפסקי ואתי לאתוייהו ד' אמות ברה"ר. קשה לר"י דאפילו לא חיישינן דילמא מיפסקו אסור משום דזימנין דאיצטריך לבה"כ ואתי לאתוייהו ד"א ברה"ר דהכי אמר לקמן גבי קמיע ומתוך פי' הקונטרס משמע דלא גרס דילמא מיפסקו ופי' דילמא שקיל להו מראשו אם בא ליפנות והקדוש מקורבי"ל אומר דגרסינן לה שפיר ואיצטריך טעמא דמיפסקו לתפילין של יד דאין צריך לחלוץ כשצריך °לבה"כ אלא של ראש משום שי"ן: עד דמימחי גברא ומימחי קמיע. נראה לר"י שאם כתב לחש אחד בשלש איגרות וריפאו שלשתן ג' בני אדם כל אחד אדם אחד היינו מומחי גברי וכאשר רפאו שלשתן אדם אחד בעיא היא בסמוך אי מימחי גברא או לא ודוקא לאותו לחש הוא מומחה אבל לשאר לחשים לא ודוקא שכתבם הוא אבל אחר לא ואם כל אחת מאיגרות ריפא שלש פעמים אפילו אדם אחד מומחות שלשתן ואין הלחש מומחה כל מקום שהוא אלא דווקא איגרת לבדה שהומחת והיינו מומחה גברא ומומחה קמיע שקמיע זה הומחה שריפא שלש פעמים וכתבו אדם מומחה שכתב שלשה קמיעין והועילו שלשתן: אע"ג דלא מימחי קמיע. נראה דכל שכן מימחי קמיע ולא גברא שהמחאת קמיע עדיפא מהמחאת הרופא כדמוכח לקמן דבהמחאת קמיע פשיטא ליה דאיתמחי אפילו בחד גברא ובאיתמחי גברא מספקא ליה אי איתמחי בתלת קמיע לחד גברא אי לא: אע"ג דלא מימחי קמיע. קשה לרשב"א היכי משכחת לה דאתמחי גברא ולא קמיע כיון שהאיש מומחה לכתוב לחש זה א"כ אגרת זו שכתב ודאי תועיל ואומר ר"י דכ"מ שאסבדה מחאתו שכתב ג' קמיעים ולא הועילו אם הומחה הקמיע מועיל אפילו אבד אדם מחאתו: ולא קתני בזמן שאינו מומחה. קשה לרשב"א דילמא לעולם בעינן תרוייהו ואי הוה תני הכי הוה משמע מומחה קמיע ולא גברא וי"ל דאינו מומחה משמע שפיר בין אגברא בין אקמיע דהא לקמן תניא איזהו קמיע מומחה כו' ומוקמינן לה לאמחויי גברא:

כל

מסורת הש"ס

[לעיל יט: וש"נ] [ברכות לט:] [מס' ד"א פ"י] [עירובין צה: מנחות לו:] [שם ולקמן סב.] [תוספתא פ"ה]

עין משפט נר מצוה

לב א מיי' פי"ט מהל' שבת הלכה טו סמג לאוין סה טוש"ע א"ח סי' שא סעיף ז:

לג ב טוש"ע א"ח סי' ב סעיף ד:

לד ג שם סעיף ה:

לה ד טוש"ע א"ח סי' ד סעיף י:

לו ה מיי' פי"ט מהל' שבת הלכה יד סמג לאוין סה טוש"ע א"ח סי' שא סעיף ז:

לז ו ז ח מיי' וסמג שם טוש"ע א"ח שם סעיף כה:

רבינו חננאל

סוגיא כחייא בר רב דאמר נועל הרגל (עראי) [שאין] בה הכאה. כיהרגל שיש בה הכאה המכה מוכחת עליה. *דר' יוחנן קאי כוותיה הלא תראה כיון שהביא לו רב שמן בר אבא הסנדל של ימין והיה ראוי לו [להביא] של שמאל שהדין לנעול השמאל תחלה אמר לו עשיתה השמאל מכה ואמרת בדעתך כיון שהשמאל מוכה אין לה נעילת סנדל לפיכך הבאתה לי של ימין ש"מ דסבר ר' יוחנן כי מי שאין עליה מכה היא שיש בה נעילת סנדל. ומי שיש בה המכה היא נשארת יחיפה. ואזדא ר' יוחנן לטעמיה דאמר כתפילין מה תפילין בשמאל אף מנעל בשמאל. ואסקא רב אשי דזמנין חזינא לרב פהנא דנועל של שמאל תחלה ואח"כ של ימין וזמנין חזינא דנועל של ימין תחלה ואח"כ של שמאל. ולא קפיד וקיי"ל כוותיה דרב אשי דהוא בתרא: ולא בתפילין ואם יצא אינו חייב חטאת. אסיקא לישנא בתרא. אמר רב ספרא לא תימא מתניתין דקתני אם יצא אינו חייב חטאת אליבא דמאן דאמר שבת זמן תפילין היא אלא אפילו למ"ד שבת לאו זמן תפילין הוא חיוב חטאת ליכא מ"מ דרך מלבוש עבידן. והוצאה דרך מלבוש אינו חייב ומפורש בפרק אחרון דעירובין: ולא בקמיע בזמן שאינו מן המומחה. אוקמה רב פפא אי אתמחי גברא אע"ג דלא אתמחי קמיעא שרי למיפק ביה בשבת ודייק ממתניתין דקתני בזמן שאינו מן המומחה ולא קתני בזמן שאינו (מן המומחה) [מומחה] הקמיע עצמו.

* נראה מזה כי רבינו סי' לו גי' אחרת בסוגיא דר"י ע"כ ס"ל כחייא בר רב וצ"ע.

רב נסים גאון

אבא מפני החשד שלא יהו אומרים איש פלוני נפסק סנדלו ותלאו בבית שחיו: אמר רב ספרא לא תימא אליבא דמאן דאמר שבת לאו זמן תפילין הוא וכו'. משתכח עיקר דילה במס' עירובין בפרק המוצא תפילין (דף צו) דתניא ושמרת את החקה הזאת למועדה מימים ימימה ימים ולא לילות מימים ולא כל הימים פרט לשבתות ולימים טובים דברי ר' יוסי הגלילי ור' עקיבא כר' יוסי הגלילי סבירא ליה דאמר שבת לאו זמן תפילין הוא כמו שאמרה הברייתא דתניא ר' עקיבא אומר יכול יניח אדם תפילין בשבתות וימים טובים ת"ל והיה לך לאות על ידך מי שצריכין אות יצאו שבתות וימים טובים שהן גופן אות וחקרו בתלמוד לידע איזה תנא דקסבר שבת לאו זמן תפילין ונשאו ונתנו בדבר זה הרבה עד שקיימו כי הוא ר' מאיר כדאמרינן בסיפא אלא האי תנא הוא דתניא המוצא תפילין מכניסן זוג זוג אחד איש ואחד אשה כו' עד כאן לא פליגי אלא בחדשות ובישנות אבל באשה לא פליגי דקסברי תפילין מצות עשה שלא הזמן גרמא הוא ונשים חייבות ומכלל דבריהם למדנו שר' מאיר ור' יהודה סברי שבת זמן תפילין הוא ועל דעת מי שסבר שבת לאו זמן תפילין הוא הויא לה מצות עשה שהזמן גרמא לפי שהיא נוהגת בחול בלבד ואלו שחייבו הנשים בה סברו כי חובתה נוהגת בכל עת ואינה מיוחדת בזמן ידוע ובפ' האשה נקנית (קידושין לה) אמרו מאן שמעת ליה דאמר תפילין מצות עשה שלא הזמן גרמא ר' מאיר היא ואמרו עוד ולר' יהודה דאמר ב' כתובין הבאין כאחד מלמדין ותפילין מצות עשה שלא הזמן גרמא מאי איכא למימר זה הברייתא דפליגו בה ר' יוסי הגלילי ור' עקיבא עם הברייתא בתראה דהיא דברי ר' עקיבא אשכחן במס' דמנחות בפ' הקומץ את המנחה (לו) ואשכחן עוד בגמ' דלא תצא אשה במחט נקובה (לקמן סב) אקשייה אביי לרב יוסף מדברי הברייתא ואותביה רב יוסף התם קסבר ר"מ לילה זמן תפילין ושבת זמן תפילין:

מותיב

גליון הש"ס

תוס' ד"ה דילמא מיפסקי וכו' אלא של ראש משום שי"ן. עי' מנחות לה צ"ב תוס' ד"ה אלו תפילין:

בשיר ובטבעת ויצא בו ברשות הרבים משום מראית העין והתניא איזהו קמיע מומחה כל שריפא ג׳ בני אדם כאחד לא קשיא הא למחויי גברא הא למחויי קמיעא אמר רב פפא פשיטא לי תלת קמיע לתלת גברי תלתא תלתא זימני איתמחי גברא *ואתמחי קמיע תלתא קמיע לתלתא גברי חד חד זימנא גברא איתמחי קמיעא לא איתמחי חד קמיע לתלתא גברי קמיעא איתמחי גברא לא איתמחי בעי רב פפא תלתא קמיע לחד גברא מאי קמיעא ודאי לא איתמחי גברא איתמחי או לא איתמחי מי אמרינן הא אסי ליה או דילמא *מזלא דהאי גברא הוא דקא מקבל כתבא תיקו: איבעיא להו קמיעין יש בהן משום קדושה או דילמא אין בהן משום קדושה למאי הילכתא אילימא לאצולינהו מפני הדליקה ת״ש *הברכות והקמיעין אע״פ שיש בהן אותיות ומענינות הרבה שבתורה אין מצילין אותן מפני הדליקה ונשרפים במקומן אלא לענין גניזה *ת״ש היה כתוב על ידות הכלים ועל כרעי המטה *יגוד ויגנזו אלא ליכנס בהן בבית הכסא מאי יש בהן קדושה ואסיר או דילמא אין בהן קדושה ושרי ת״ש ולא בקמיע בזמן שאינו מן המומחה הא מן המומחה נפיק ואי אמרת קמיעין יש בהן משום קדושה זמנין דמיצטריך לבית הכסא ואתי לאיתויינהו ד׳ אמות ברה״ר הכא במאי עסקינן בקמיע של עיקרין והתניא אחד קמיע של כתב ואחד קמיע של עיקרין אלא הכא במאי עסקינן בחולה שיש בו סכנה והתניא אחד חולה שיש בו סכנה ואחד חולה שאין בו סכנה אלא כיון דמסי אף על גב דנקיט ליה בידיה נמי שפיר דמי

והתניא

כל שריפא שלשה בני אדם כאחד. נראה לר״י דגרסינן כאחד והכי פירושו מדקתני כאחד אלמא משמע דבג׳ קמיעים איירי ולעיל קתני כל שריפא ושנה ושילש משמע קמיע אחד ומשני דההוא דלעיל לאתמחויי קמיע והך לאתמחויי גברא וה״ה אפילו לא נתרפאו יחד אלא הא דנקט כאחד לאשמעינן דבג׳ קמיעין איירי ולאתמחויי גברא: **תלתא** קמיעין לג׳ גברי תלת תלת זימני. פירוש שכתב לחש אחד בג׳ איגרות וכל אחת הועילה לג׳ אנשים או לאחד שלש פעמים קשה לרשב״א קמיע ג׳ היכי איתמחי הלא מיד כשנתרפא האדם שלישי בקמיע ג׳ [פעם א׳] איתמחי גברא וכיון דאתמחי גברא ודאי שאותה האיגרת תועיל מכאן ואילך וי״ל כגון דשני קמיעין הללו ריפאו תלת זימני לתרי גברי וקמיע שלישי לחד מהנך תרי גברי תרי זימני והשתא מימחו כבר תרי קמיעי וגברא וקמיע שלישי אכתי לא איתמחי וחזר וריפא קמיע שלישי אדם שלישי דהשתא בא בבת אחת המחאת גברא והמחאת קמיע: **תלת** תלת זימני. הוה מצי למימר חד תלת זימני והיינו חד זימנא אלא בעי למימר שיהיו שלשה קמיעין מומחין: **חד** קמיע לתלת גברי. נראה לר״י דה״ה לחד גברא תלת זימני דודאי לגבי המחאת גברא הוא דמבעיא ליה בסמוך אי אתמחי בחד גברא מתלת קמיעי אבל לענין המחאת קמיע דעדיף לא קא מיבעיא ליה דפשיטא דתלינן בהמחאת קמיע ולא אמרינן מזליה דהאי גברא הוא דמקבל כתבא והאי דנקט לתלתא גברי משום רבותא דאפילו הכי גברא לא אתמחי: **תלת** קמיע לחד גברא מאי. תימה תיפשוט ליה מדתני לעיל איזהו קמיע מומחה כל שריפא שלשה בני אדם ומוקמינן לה לאתמחויי גברא משמע חקא תלת גברי אבל חד גברא לא מדלא קתני כל שריפא אדם א׳ בג׳ קמיעין ובקונטרס פי׳ בפי׳ א׳ מימחי גברא מימחי קמיע שעשה אדם זה קמיע לשלשה אנשים דנעשה אדם זה מומחה שריפא שלשה אנשים והקמיע מומחה שריפא כתב זה ג׳ אנשים ולהאי פירושא נמי לא אימחי גברא אלא דוקא לאותו לחש וקשה לר״י לפירוש זה דהא אמרינן לקמן חד קמיע לתלתא גברי קמיע איתמחי *גברא לא איתמחי ויש ליישב לשון הקונטרס דה״ק שעשה אדם זה לחש זה בשלשה איגרות לג׳ אנשים דנעשה אדם זה מומחה שריפא לג׳ אנשים והלחש מומחה שריפא לחש זה ג׳ אנשים וגם זה אין נראה לר״י דאם בענין זה נמי קרוי חד קמיע לתלתא גברא הדרא קושיא לדוכתיה ואם הוא קרוי בענין זה תלתא קמיע לתלתא גברי חד חד זימנא הא אמרינן לקמן דגברא איתמחי ולא קמיע לכך נראה לר״י כדפירש וכן פירוש אחר שפי׳ בקונטרס מיושב מן הראשון: *הא לאתמחויי קמיע. פירש בקונטרס דנעשה הקמיע לבדו מומחה ע״י אדם זה תימה דהוא עצמו פירש בסמוך גבי תלת תלת זימני דכל לחש שריפא ג׳ פעמים נעשו ג׳ קמיעות הללו מומחים מיד כל אדם אע״פ שרוצה לומר הקונטרס שרופא אחד* כתבם מדפירש ואין לומר שמזל הרופא גרם וכן נראה ודאי עיקר דלא ע״י אדם זה לבד נעשה הקמיע מומחה אלא אף מיד כל אדם דהא אמרינן בסמוך תלתא קמיע לתלתא גברי תלת תלת זימני איתמחי גברא ואיתמחי קמיע והאי תלתא קמיעי לתלתא גברי דקאמר איירי שרופא אחד עשאם דבענין אחר לא איתמחי גברא וא״כ האי דקאמר נמי תלת תלת זימני איירי נמי ברופא אחד כמו רישא וקאמר דאיתמחי קמיע והיינו ע״כ מיד כל אדם דאי מיד רופא זה הא בלאו הכי הוא מומחה בכל קמיעין שבעולם וממה שפירש נמי גבי תלת תלת זימני כל לחש ריפא ג׳ פעמים ואפילו אדם אחד חזר בו מזה דפירש איתמחי קמיע ואין לומר מזל החולה גרם שמתרפא ע״י קמיעתא שהרי בשלשה אנשים הוחזק משמע דלא אמרינן איתמחי קמיע אלא א״כ ריפא ג׳ אנשים: **איתמחי** קמיע. פירש הקונטרס ואין לומר מזל הרופא גרס דאין הדבר תלוי במזל הרופא אלא בחכמתו משמע שרוצה ליתן טעם אמאי איתמחי קמיע במזל הרופא היה לנו לתלות שכבר הומחה שריפא ג׳ אנשים בג׳ מיני קמיעים ולא היה לנו להטות בקמיע ולא ידע רשב״א מה טעם טוען על זה דהא לא איתמחו שאר קמיעין של שאר חולאים אע״ג דהרופא איתמחי בכל קמיעין שבעולם ה״נ אלו ג׳ קמיעים נמי לתלות ברופא אלא צריך לתרץ כמו שפירשתי ללשון ר״י בענין שיבא המחאת קמיע והמחאת גברא בבת אחת:

בשיר. אלעדה: מפני מראית העין. דלא מיחזי כמאן דבעי ליה לרפואה אלא לתכשיט ולאו תכשיט הוא אלא מחמת דאגת חולי: והתניא כל שריפא ג׳ בני אדם. ולעיל קתני כל שריפא ושנה ושילש ואפילו אדם אחד: הא לאמחויי גברא כו׳. הא דקתני ג׳ בני אדם משום דכתם ג׳ בני אדם שלשה מיני חלאים ואיירי בג׳ מיני קמיעין שאינן דומין זה לזה ולאמחויי גברא שנעשה מומחה בכל קמיעים שיעשה לעולם כדאמרינן בב״ק (דף לז׳) נגח שור וחמור וגמל נעשה מועד לכל אבל הקמיע אינו מומחה אם יכתוב רופא אחר אחד מהן: והא. דקתני כל שריפא ושנה ושילש איירי בחולי אחד וכתבו זה הלחש וריפא ג׳ פעמים או לאדם אחד או לשלשה ולאיתמחויי קמיעא איירי דנעשה הקמיע לבדו מומחה על יד אדם זה או אם כתבום שלשה רופאים נעשה קמיע של לחש זה מומחה מיד כל אדם: תלתא קמיעי. ג׳ מיני לחש: תלתא תלתא זימני. כל לחש ריפא שלשה פעמים ואפילו אדם אחד: אתמחי גברא. בכל קמיעות לעולם שהרי הומחה בשלשה מיני קמיעים: ואתמחי קמיע. שלשה קמיעין הללו נעשים מומחים מיד כל אדם שהרי ריפא כל אחד ג״פ ואין לומר מזל הרופא גורם דאין הדבר תלוי במזל הרופא אלא בחכמתו ואין לומר נמי (א) החולה גרם שמתרפא על ידי קמיעין שהרי בשלשה אנשים הוחזק: קמיעא לא אתמחי. לבא מיד רופא אחר: חד קמיע לתלתא גברי. לחולי אחד: קמיעא איתמחי. מיד כל אדם: גברא לא איתמחי. לקמיע אחר שאינו של לחש [זה] ושל חולי זה: תלתא קמיעי. של שלש מיני חולי: קמיעא ודאי לא איתמחי. מיד אדם אחר שהרי לא ריפא אלא פעם אחת: מזליה דהאי גברא. מלאכו של חולי זה דמקבל קמיעא וא״ת ממתני׳ דלעיל שמעינן לה דתני כל שריפא ושנה ושילש דמשמע לאדם אחד ואוקימנא דאיתמחי קמיעא ולא אמרינן מזליה הוא לא דמי התם חד קמיעא הוא וליכא למיתלייה במזלא דגברא אלא בקמיע הכי ודאי בגברא תלוי או ברופא או במתרפא הלכך מיבעיא לן במאי ניתליה: לאצולינהו. בשבת °לחצר *המעורבת כשאר כתבי הקדש: הברכות. שתקנו חכמים כגון תשעה של ר״ה שיש בהן מלכיות וזכרונות ושופרות: מעניינות. מפרשיות הרבה שכותבין בהן אף מקראות של רפואה: היה כתוב שם יגוד. *יקוץ מקום השם ויגנזו: שתם בית הכסא שלהן בשדות: שיש בו סכנה. אי שקיל ליה מיניה דשרי למיעל בהן לבית הכסא משום פקוח נפש: אף על גב דנקיט ליה בידיה. תכשיטו הוא הלכך אי נמי מייתי ליה ד׳ אמות בידים לא מחייב:

שלא

עין משפט נר מצוה

לח א מיי׳ וסמג שם טוש״ע א״ח סי׳ שא סעיף כה:

לט ב מיי׳ פ״ו מהל׳ יסודי התורה הלכה ו סמג לאוין ג:

ק״ק דאכתי לא משכחת שיתמחי הקמיע הג׳ את״ל דגברא אתמחי אפילו בג׳ קמיעין לחד גברא והיכי קאמר פשיטא לי דמשמע נמי דקאי אקמיע שלישית מדקאמר תלת זימני משמע דהומחו שלשתן וי״ל אע״ג דכבר אתמחי גברא כי ריפא כל אחד ג״פ יש לנו לתלות גם בקמיע דעדיף כל מה שאנו יכולין למימחי קמיע ולא גברא כגון שכתב זה ריפא תלתא זימנא חד גברא ואתמחי גברא ולא קמיע כגון שריפא בג׳ אגרות לג׳ אנשים [ת״י]:

רבינו חננאל

וכדתניא איזהו קמיע מומחה כל שריפא ג׳ בני אדם כאחד. בעי רב פפא תלתא גווני קמיע רפאו לאחד ג׳ מיני חלאים כל קמיע ריפא חולי מאי קמיעא ודאי לא אתמחאי גברא מאי מי אמרינן הא מסי ליה ג׳ זמני אי דלמא מולא דהאי גברא דמקבל קמיעא ועלתה בתיקו. ולא אתמחי לא גברא ולא קמיעא. ירושלמי נאמן אדם לומר קמיעא זו ריפאתי בו ב׳ וג׳ פעמים. קמיעין יש בהן משום קדושה ואסור למיעל בהו לבית הכסא אי לא [לגניזה] לא קא מיבעי לן דלא גרעי הקמיעין מן הכלים שאם היה שם כתוב עליהן תנינן הרי זה יגור ויגנז[כי] קא מיבעיא לן למיעל בהו לבהכ״ס.

גברא לא איתמחי ולהאי פי׳ היינו דלא איתמחי אפילו ללחש זה כצ״ל [ת״י]

שייך לעיל קודם ד״ה תלתא

מסורת הש״ס

לקמן קטו: וש״נ

ערכין ו. [מס׳ סופרים פ״ה ה״ג] [גיר׳ הערוך יגור]

הגהות הב״ח

(א) רש״י ד״ה ואיתמחי כו׳ נמי מזל החולה גרם:

לחצר שאינה מעורבת כצ״ל וכ״ה ברש״י שבאלפס

וגי׳ הערוך יגור בכ״י ש״ פי׳ יגור אותו במגירה רש״ל

גליון הש״ס

רש״י ד״ה לאצולינהו בשבת לחצר המעורבת. עי׳ לקמן קטו ע״א ברש״י ד״ה מצילין אותן וצ״ע:

he does not secure it [61*b*] with a ring or a bracelet and go out therewith into the street, for appearances' sake.[5] But it was taught: What is an approved amulet? One that has healed three men simultaneously?[6]—There is no difficulty: the one is to approve the man; the other is to approve the amulet.[7]

a R. Papa said: It is obvious to me that if three amulets[1] [are successful for] three people, each [being efficacious] three times,[2] both the practitioner[3] and the amulets are [henceforth] approved. If three amulets [are successful for] three people, each [being efficacious] once, the practitioner is [henceforth] approved, but not the amulets. If one amulet [is efficacious] for three men, the amulet is approved but not the practitioner. [But] R. Papa propounded: What if three amulets [are efficacious] for one person?[4] The amulets are certainly not rendered approved: but does the practitioner become approved or not? Do we say, Surely, he has healed him! Or perhaps, it is this man's fate[5] to be susceptible to writings?[6] The question stands over.

The scholars propounded: Have amulets sanctity or not? In respect of what law? Shall we say, in respect of saving them from a fire?[7] Then come and hear: Benedictions[8] and amulets, though they contain the [divine] letters and many passages from the Torah, may not be saved from a fire, but are burnt where they are. Again, if in respect to hiding,[9]—Come and hear: If it [the Divine Name] was written on the handles of utensils or on the legs of a bed,[10] it must be cut out and hidden.[11] Rather [the problem is] what about entering a privy with them? Have they sanctity, and it is forbidden; or perhaps they have no sanctity, and it is permitted? —Come and hear: NOR WITH AN AMULET, IF IT IS NOT FROM AN EXPERT. This [implies that] if it is from an expert, one may go out [with it]; now if you say that amulets possess sanctity, it may happen that one needs a privy, and so come to carry it four cubits
b in the street?[1] The reference here is to an amulet of roots.[2] But it was taught, Both a written amulet and an amulet of roots?—The reference here is to an invalid whose life is endangered.[3] But it was taught: 'Both an invalid whose life is endangered and one whose life is not endangered'?—Rather [this is the reply]: since it

(5) If secured with a ring or a bracelet it looks like being worn as an ornament, which it is not, and it would be forbidden to wear it as such. (6) 'Simultaneously' is absent from Rashi's version, but present in cur. edd. and Tosaf., which explains that it refers to three amulets (presumably of exactly the same pattern) worn by three men. Whereas by the previous definition it is sufficient if it has healed three times, even the same person. (7) In order that the practitioner may rank as an expert, he must have healed three different men with three different amulets; these three men would be suffering from three different maladies, and the amulets likewise would be different, i.e., contain different charms. Whatever amulet he subsequently issues is approved. The second Baraitha must now accordingly be translated thus: What is an amulet of an approved person? (An amulet issued by) one who has healed three persons. But the first Baraitha refers to the approving of the amulet itself; once it has healed three times, whether the same person or three different persons suffering from the same complaint, it is now approved for all men. Or, the same charm can now be written by any man, and it is approved.

a (1) Each with a different charm and all written or prepared by the same man. (2) Even for the same person. (3) Who prepared them. (4) V. *supra* n. 7. (5) Lit., 'planetary destiny', v. *infra* 156*a*, *b*. (6) *Sc.* written amulets. But the practitioner might not be successful for another. (7) That if a fire breaks out in a house, it shall be permitted to carry these into a courtyard which is not formally joined to the house by means of an '*erub* (v. Glos.). Nothing may be taken out of a house into this courtyard, except sacred writings, to save them from fire; *infra* 115*a*. (8) In writing. (9) When sacred writings are worn out and not fit for use, they may not be thrown away or burnt, but must be 'hidden', i.e., buried; Meg. 26*b*. (10) For magical purposes; v. A. Marmorstein in *MGWJ*. (1928), pp. 391 *seq*. (11) Thus whatever contains the Divine Name must be treated as sacred in this respect.

b (1) He may have to remove it in order to deposit it somewhere and carry it thither. (2) This certainly does not possess sanctity, since the Divine Name is not there. (3) If the amulet is removed. He may take it into a privy even if it possesses sanctity.

heals even when he holds it in his hand, it is well.[4] [62a] But it was taught: R. Oshaia said: Providing one does not hold it in his hand and carry it four cubits in the street? But the reference here is to [an amulet that is] covered with leather.[5] But *tefillin* are leather-covered,[6] yet it was taught: When one enters a privy, he must remove his *tefillin* at a distance of four cubits and then enter?—There it is on account of the [letter] *shin*, for Abaye said: The *shin* of *tefillin* is a *halachah* of Moses at Sinai.[7] Abaye also said: The *daleth* of *tefillin* is a *halachah* of Moses at Sinai. Abaye also said: The *yod* of *tefillin* is a *halachah* of Moses at Sinai.[8]

NOR WITH A SHIRYON, NOR WITH A ḲASDA, NOR WITH MEGAFAYYIM. SHIRYON is a coat of mail. ḲASDA,—Rab said: It is a polished metal helmet.[9] MEGAFAYYIM,—Rab said: These are greaves.

MISHNAH. A WOMAN MAY NOT GO OUT WITH A NEEDLE THAT IS PIERCED, NOR WITH A RING BEARING A SIGNET, NOR WITH A KOKLIAR,[1] NOR WITH A KOBELETH,[2] NOR WITH A BALSAM PHIAL; AND IF SHE DOES GO OUT, SHE IS LIABLE TO A SIN-OFFERING; THIS IS R. MEIR'S VIEW.[3] BUT THE SAGES RULE THAT SHE IS NOT CULPABLE IN THE CASE OF A KOBELETH AND A BALSAM PHIAL.

GEMARA. 'Ulla said: And it is the reverse in the case of a man.[4] Thus we see that 'Ulla holds that whatever is fit for a man is not fit for a woman, and whatever is fit for a woman is not fit for a man.[5] R. Joseph objected: Shepherds may go out [on the Sabbath] with sackcloths;[6] and not only of shepherds did they [the Sages] say [thus], but of all men, but that it is the practice of shepherds to go out with sacks.[7] Rather said R. Joseph, 'Ulla holds that women are a separate [independent] people.

Abaye put an objection to him: If one finds *tefillin*,[8] he must bring them in[9] pair by pair;[10] [this applies to] both a man and a woman. Now if you say that women are a separate people, surely it is[11] a positive command limited in time, and from all such women are exempt?[12]—There R. Meir holds that night is a time for *tefillin*, and the Sabbath [too] is a time for *tefillin*: thus it is a positive precept not limited by time, and all such are incumbent upon women.

b But it is carrying out in a 'backhanded' manner?[1]—Said R. Jeremiah: The reference is to a woman who is a charity overseer.[2] Raba said [to him]: You have answered the case of a woman; but what can be said of a man?[3] Said Raba, [This is the answer:] sometimes a man gives a signet-ring to his wife to take it to a chest, and she places it on her hand[4] until she comes to the chest. And sometimes a woman gives a non-signet ring to her husband to take it to an artisan to be repaired, and he places it on his hand until he comes to the artisan.[5]

NOR WITH A KOKLIAR, NOR WITH A KOBELETH. What is a KOKLIAR?—Said Rab: A brooch.[6] KOBELETH?—Said Rab: A charm [bead] containing phyllon; and thus did R. Assi explain it: A charm containing phyllon.

Our Rabbis taught: She may not go out with a *kobeleth*, and if she does, she incurs a sin-offering, this is R. Meir's view; while the Sages maintain: She may not go out, but if she does, she is not culpable. R. Eliezer ruled: A woman may go out with a *kobeleth* at the very outset. Wherein do they differ? R. Meir holds that it is a burden, whereas the Rabbis hold that it is an ornament, and [she hence may not wear it at the outset] lest she remove it for display, and so come to carry it. But R. Eliezer argues: Whose practice is it to wear this? A woman with an unpleasant odour;[7] and such a woman will not remove it for display, and so will not come to carry it four cubits in the street. But it was taught: R. Eliezer declares [her] non culpable on account of a *kobeleth* and a flask of spikenard oil?[1]—There is no difficulty: the one [ruling] is in reference to R. Meir; the other, in reference to the Rabbis. [Thus:] when referring to R. Meir, who maintained that she is liable to a sin-offering, he [R. Eliezer] said to him that she is not culpable. When treating of the Rabbis who maintained that there is no culpability, yet it is forbidden, he ruled that it is permitted at the outset.

(4) Permitted as a kind of cure. For even if one does carry it in the street in his hands, it is not a culpable act. (5) Or, skin. This may be taken into a privy. (6) I.e., the strips of parchment bearing the Biblical passages are encased in leather capsules. (7) V. *supra* 28b, n. 7c. Thus part of the Divine Name itself is uncovered; therefore one may not enter a privy with it. (8) The strap of the head-phylactery is knotted at the back of the head in the shape of a *daleth* (ד); that of the hand-phylactery forms a noose and is knotted near the capsule in the shape of a *yod* (י). Cf. Heilprin, *Seder ha-Doroth*, I, p. 208 ed. Maskileison. Warsaw, 1897. Thus the three together make up the word שדי = Almighty. Tosaf., however, s.v. שין, deletes Abaye's last two statements on the *daleth* and *yod*. (9) Jast. Rashi: a leather helmet worn under the metal helmet. (1) A pin of the shape of a cochlea, which is a part of the inner ear. (2) 'Aruch reads: *kokeleth*, a perfume charm. (3) He regards these as burdens, not ornaments. (4) This refers to a ring. If it bears a signet he is not culpable; if not, he is. (5) So that what is an ornament for one is a burden for the other. (6) As a protection from the rain. (7) This shows that even when people are not in the habit of wearing it, yet since it is an ornament for one it is the same for the other. (8) In the street on the Sabbath. (9) To a safe place, where they will not be exposed to misuse. (10) I.e., he dons one pair on the hand and the head as they are usually worn, and walks with them as with an ordinary article of attire to his destination; then he returns and does the same with the second pair, and so on. This is R. Meir's view: 'Erub. 96b. (11) The precept of donning *tefillin*. (12) V. Ḳid. 29a. The difficulty is based on the assumption that *tefillin* are not to be worn on the Sabbath, nor at night. Since women are exempt, and at the same time they rank as a separate people, *tefillin* can surely not be accounted for them an article of attire?

b (1) V. *supra* 40b, n. b2. This raises a difficulty on the Mishnah. Why is a woman culpable for going out wearing a signet ring, seeing that this is not the usual manner of carrying out an object? [Liability is incurred only when the work done is performed in the usual manner.] (2) Lit., 'treasurer'. She impresses the seal of her signet ring upon her orders for charity disbursements. Thus she usually wears the ring on her finger, and that is her way of carrying it out into the street. Yet since women do not generally wear such rings, this cannot be regarded as an ornament.—It is interesting to observe a woman occupying this position. (3) 'Ulla states that a man is culpable for wearing a non-signet ring; but that too is a backhanded manner? (4) I.e., on her finger. (5) Thus in both cases this becomes the *usual* manner of carriage. Hence the reference in the Mishnah is to any woman, not particularly a treasurer. (6) V. note on Mishnah. (7) Which the *kobeleth* counteracts.

c (1) This implies that they may nevertheless not be worn.

מסורת הש"ס

עין משפט נר מצוה

והתניא רבי אושעיא אומר ובלבד שלא יאחזנו בידו ויעבירנו ארבע אמות ברשות הרבים [אלא] *הכא במאי עסקינן במחופה עור והרי תפילין דמחופה עור ותניא *[ב]הנכנס לבית הכסא חולץ תפילין ברחוק ארבע אמות ונכנס התם משום שי"ן דאמר אביי [ג]*שי"ן של תפילין הלכה למשה מסיני ואמר אביי ד' של תפילין הלכה למשה מסיני ואמר אביי יו"ד של תפילין הלכה למשה מסיני: ולא בשריון ולא בקסדא ולא במגפיים: שריון *זרדא קסדא אמר רב סנוארתא מגפיים אמר רב פומקי: **מתני'** [ג]לא תצא אשה במחט הנקובה ולא בטבעת שיש עליה חותם ולא בכוליאר ולא *בכובלת ולא בצלוחית של פלייטון °ואם יצתה חייבת חטאת דברי ר' מאיר וחכמים פוטרין בכובלת ובצלוחית של פלייטון: **גמ'** [ד]אמר עולא וחילופיהן באיש אלמא קסבר עולא כל מידי דחזי לאיש לא חזי לאשה ומידי דחזי לאשה לא חזי לאיש מתיב רב יוסף *הרועים יוצאין בשקין ולא הרועים בלבד אמרו [ד]אלא כל אדם אלא שדרכן של הרועים לצאת בשקין [אלא] אמר רב יוסף קסבר עולא נשים עם בפני עצמן הן איתיביה אביי [ה]*המוצא תפילין מכניסן זוג זוג אחד האיש ואחד האשה ואי אמרת נשים עם בפני עצמן הן והא מצות עשה שהזמן גרמא הוא *וכל מצות עשה שהזמן גרמא נשים פטורות התם קסבר ר"מ לילה זמן תפילין הוא *ושבת זמן תפילין הוא הוה ליה מצות עשה שלא הזמן גרמא וכל מצות עשה שלא הזמן גרמא נשים חייבות והא הוצאה כלאחר יד היא אמר רבי ירמיה באשה גזברית עסקינן אמר *רבה (בר בר חנה אמר רבי יוחנן) תרצת אשה איש מאי איכא למימר אלא אמר רבא [ו]פעמים שאדם נותן לאשתו טבעת שיש עליה חותם להוליכה לקופסא ומניחתה בידה עד שמגעת לקופסא ופעמים שהאשה נותנת לבעלה טבעת שאין עליה חותם להוליכה אצל אומן לתקן ומניחה בידו עד שמגיע אצל אומן: [ז]ולא בכוליאר ולא בכובלת: מאי כוליאר א"ר *מכבנתא כובלת אמר רב חומרתא דפילון וכן אמר רב אסי חומרתא *דפילון ת"ר לא תצא בכובלת ואם יצתה חייבת חטאת דברי ר"מ וחכמים אומרים [ח]לא תצא ואם יצתה פטורה רבי אליעזר אומר יוצאה אשה בכובלת לכתחלה במאי קמיפלגי רבי מאיר סבר משאוי הוא ורבנן סברי תכשיט הוא ודילמא שלפא ומחויא ואתיא לאיתויה ורבי אליעזר סבר מאן דרכה למירמיה אשה שריחה רע ואשה שריחה רע לא שלפא ומחויא ולא אתיא לאתויה ארבע אמות ברשות הרבים °והתניא *ר' אליעזר פוטר בכובלת ובצלוחית של פלייטון לא קשיא הא *כי קאי אדרבי מאיר הא כי קאי אדרבנן כי קאי אדרבי מאיר דאמר חייב חטאת אמר ליה פטור כי קאי אדרבנן דאמרי פטור אבל אסור אמר איהו מותר לכתחלה

ומאי

רש"י

שלא יאחזו . דלא הוי תכשיט שלו אלא דרך מלבוש : במכוסה עור . דליכא גנותא אי מעייל לבית הכסא ולא בעי למיסקליה : חולץ תפילין. ואע"ג דמכוסה עור שהארבע אגרות שהפרשיות כתובות בהן תחובות בדפוסן של עור : התם משום שי"ן · שעשויה מעור החילון עצמו קומט בו ג' קמטין כעין שי"ן משדי והדלי"ת והיו"ד עשויין בקשר שקושר הרצועה (א) אחת לצפון ואחת למזרח כמין ד' ורצועה קטנה אחד תלויה בה ואין בה אלא כפיפה כמין יו"ד וכופאה בעוד העור לח והיא כפופה לעולם : זרדא . ברוני"א : סגוארתא . כובע עור תחת כובע המתכת : פומקי . אנפלייאות של ברזל במלחמה : **מתני'** בכוליאר · מפרש בגמרא וכן כובלת : פלייטון . בלשו"א משחא דאפרסמא : חייבת חטאת . קסבר לאו תכשיט נינהו : **גמ'** אמר עולא וחילופיהן באיש. אטבעת קאי דטבעת שיש עליו חותם אם יצא פטור ואם אין עליו חותם ויצא חייב חטאת : בשקין . שמתכסין בהן מפני הגשמים שקין מלבוש שק : אלא כל אדם . אלמא אע"ג דלא רגילי ביה מגו דלגבי האי תכשיט לגבי האי נמי תכשיט הוא : המוצא תפילין . בשבת בשוק או בדרך : מכניסן. לעיר דרך מלבוש : זוג זוג . כדרך שהוא לובש בחול אחד בראש ואחד בזרוע וחולצן וחוזר ומניח זוג אחר ומכניסן וכן כולן : ואחד האשה . ואע"ג דלאו תכשיט דאשה נינהו מגו דהוו תכשיט לאיש שרי אף לאשה: לילה זמן תפילין הוא וכן שבת. הלכך לעולם זמנם הוא ואין להם זמן קבוע שתהא מצותן מצות עשה שהזמן גרמא להפטר נשים מהן הלכך נקט לילה ושבת משום דפלוגתא בתרווייהו ואי הוי סבירא ליה לרבי מאיר בחד מינייהו דלאו זמן תפילין הוא כמלא זמן קבוע לתפילין והוו להו נשים פטורות : נשים חייבות . הלכך תכשיטין הן לה : והא הוצאה כלאחר יד הוא. אמתני' קאי יהוצאת טבעת שמוציאתה דרך מלבוש באצבע וזה שאינו תכשיט לה אמאי חייבת חטאת הרי לא הוציאה כדרך כל המוציאין שכל המוציא דבר שאינו תכשיט לו מוציאין אותו בידים ולא דרך מלבוש : גזברית . שעולתת חותמות תמיד לממונין תחתיה לאמר תנו כך וכך מעות לפלוני והרי חותמה בידה הלכך רגילה היא להניחה באצבעה ומיהו תכשיט לא הוי לדידה דאין דרך נשים בכך ומיהו דרך הוצאתה של זו בכך : איש מאי איכא למימר. דקאמר עולא וחילופיהם באיש דמחייב אטבעת שאין עליה חותם והא הוצאה כלאחר יד הוא שאין דרכו להוציא בזו דרך מלבוש : לקופסא . אישקריינ"ה בלע"ז כדי להגניעה שם וי"מ שהקופסא חתומה בו וכשפותחה חוזרה וחותמת בה ולא נהירא דאם כן מנחתה באצבעה עד שמחזירתה לבעלה מיבעי ליה : אצל אומן לתקנה ומניחה באצבעו . אלמא דרך הוצאה היא : מכבנתא . טסקא"ה *ע"ש שמכבנת וקושרת מפתחי החלוק : חומרתא דפילון . קשר שקשור בו °סם ששמו פילון וריחו ערב ובלע"ז בלסמ"ו ואשה שריחה רע טוענתו עליה : ורבנן סברי תכשיט הוא . הלכך אם יצאת פטורה ומיהו לכתחלה לא תצא דילמא שלפא ומחויא : למרמיה . להניח בצוארה כמו שקיל ורמי : ה"ג ואשה שריחה רע לא שלפא ומחויא . שגנות הוא לה : והתניא ר' אליעזר פוטר . והכא שרי לכתחלה : הא. דקתני פוטר: כי קאי אר' מאיר . בההיא מתנית' לא איירו רבנן אלא ר"מ לחודיה וגבי חיוב דר"מ שייך למיתני רבי אליעזר פוטר ואע"פ שהוא מתיר לכתחלה: הא כי קאי ארבנן . במתנית' דלעיל דאיירו רבנן בה ואמרו פטור פריש ר' אליעזר בהדיא למילתיה לאיפלוגי עלייהו ואמר יוצאה לכתחלה :

ומאי

תוספות

והתניא ר' אושעיא אומר ובלבד כו' . תימה לר"י דילמא משום מראית העין דוקא הוא אסור מדרבנן כמו קושר בשיר ובטבעת דהשתא ליכא למיגזר דאפילו מייתי לה ליכא איסורא מדאורייתא ואומר ר"י דשלא יאחזו בידו משמע אפילו בקומצו דליכא מראית העין אלא איסורא דאורייתא איכא ואפילו למ"ד כל דבר שאסרו חכמים משום מראית העין אפילו בחדרי חדרים אסור הכא לא שייך למיגזר דאפילו עומד בשוק ושאן בקומצו אין כאן מראית העין :

שי"ן של תפילין . ול"ג דלי"ת ויו"ד של תפילין כו' כדמוכח בפ' במה מדליקין (לעיל כח:) גבי הא דתני רב יוסף לא הוכשרו למלאכת שמים כו' ומוקי לה לרצועותיהן ולא פריך דלי"ת של תפילין הלכה למשה מסיני כדפריך גבי שי"ן* :

וחילופיהן באיש . °אור"ת דאחיוב חטאת קאי:

וכל מצות עשה שהזמן גרמא נשים פטורות . פירוש דהוי משוי וליתסר וא"ת והא הוצאה כלאחר יד היא ושריא משום בזיון תפילין וי"ל כיון דמשוי הוא ויכול לבא לידי חיוב חטאת היכא דמוציא בלא שינוי משום בזיון לא שרינן ליה :

אין

עין משפט נר מצוה

מ א מיי' פי"א מהל' ש"ת הלכה ס טוש"ע י"ד סי' רפב סעיף ו :

מא ב מיי' פ"ד מהל' תפילין הלכה יז : סמג עשין כב טוש"ע א"ח סי' מג סעיף ה :

[מא] [ב] [מיי' שם פ"ג הלכה א' טוש"ע א"ח סי' לב סעיף מב נב]

מב ג ד מיי' פי"ט מהל' שבת הלכה ד ה סמג לאוין סה טור א"ח סי' שג סעיף ט י וסי' שא סעיף ח ט :

מג ה מיי' שם הלכה יז טוש"ע א"ח סי' שא סעיף כא :

[וע"ע תוס' ברכות ו. ד"ה אלו וכו']

[מג] [ה] [מיי' פי"ט מהל' שבת הלכה כג טוש"ע א"ח סי' שא סעיף מג] :

מד ו מיי' פי"ט שם הלכה ג :

מה ז ח מיי' פי"ט שם הלכה ז סמג שם טוש"ע א"ח סי' שג סעיף יא ·

[קידושין כט. ושם נסמן]

נ"ל רבא

[רב אלפס פי' מלשון בלולה בשמן מתרגמין דפילא במשח וכ"ה בהרא"ש]

[פי' תוס' לעיל ג. ד"ה בר מהני]

מסורת הש"ס

ברכות כג.

לעיל כח: מנחות לה.

פירוש שריון משבצות קטנו'

[גיר' הערוך בכובלת]

[תוספתא פ"ו נדרים נה:]

עירובין צו: תוס' דעירובין פ"ח ביצה טו.

[לעיל סא. וש"נ]

הגהות הב"ח

(א) רש"י ד"ה התם וכו' הרצועה שבראש אחת לצפון :

[עתוס' ב"ב קנו: ד"ה כבינתי]

[לקמן סה. תוספתא פ"ה ע"ש]

ע' רש"י יומא כה. ד"ה בכוליאר

רבינו חננאל

ופשטינא אם מחופין עור (כיון) שפיר דמי והא דתניא לא יכנס אדם בתפילין לבית הכסא קבע אפי' להשתין מים התם משום שי"ן דאמר אביי שי"ן של תפילין הל"מ . ת"ר איזהו קמיע מומחה כל שריפא ושנה ושלש אחד קמיע של כתב ואחד קמיע של עקרין אחד חולה שיש בו סכנה ואחד חולה שאין בו סכנה [ולא] שנכפה אלא שלא יכפה וקושר ומתיר . ואפילו ברה"ר ובלבד שלא יקשרנו בשיר או בטבעת ויוצא בו לרה"ר מפני מראית העין : שירין זרדא : לא תצא אשה במחט נקובה . ולא בטבעת שיש עליה חותם . אמר עולא חילופיהן באיש כלומר האיש אסור בטבעת שאין עליה חותם ופטור בטבעת שיש עליה חותם . וכי קאמר עולא וחילופיהן באיש בטבעת בלבד קאמר מותבינן אמאי חייב חטאת והא הוצאה כלאחר יד היא כלומר באצבעה היא מוציאה ואין דרך המוציאין דבר להוציאה דרך מלבוש . ומוקים לה ר' ירמיה באשה גזברית עסקינן שכן דרכה להיות הטבעת באצבעה כדי שתהא חותמת בו כיסים ובתים . הוצאה בכוונה היא לחתום בו ולאו משום תכשיט הוא ודחינן תרצת אשה איש בטבעת שאין עליה חותם אמאי חייב חטאת . ואוקמה רבא לעולם באשה שאינה גזברית ומשום הכי חייבת חטאת דפעמים אדם [נותן] טבעת שיש עליה חותם לאשתו להוליכה לקופסא ומנחתה באצבעה עד שמגעת לקופסא שנמצאת הוצאה בכוונה כדרכה . והאשה נמי פעמים שנותנת כו' וקיי"ל טבעת שיש עליה חותם תכשיט לאיש ולא לאשה ושאין עליה חותם תכשיט לאשה ולא לאיש . ובדין הוא להיות כל אחד ואחד מותר במה שהוא תכשיט לו אלא גזרו משום דרבא שכבר פרשנוהו למעלה (ס.) : בכולייר . תכשיט שמסבב הראש כולה כדגרסינן ביומא (כה.) הכהנים היו מוקפין ועומדין ככולייר . כובלת חומרתא דפילון . פי' בשמים בלולין כדמתרגם בלולה דפילא . צלוחית של פלייטון

ראשית

גליון הש"ס מתני' ואם יצתה חייבת חטאת . עי' לעיל דף יא ע"ב תוס' ד"ה ואם יצא : גמ' והתניא ר"א פוטר . עיין לעיל דף ג ע"א תוס' ד"ה בר מהני : רש"י ד"ה חומרתי דפילון וכו' סם ששמו פילון . עיין סוטה דף טו ע"א תוס' ד"ה כמין חומר : תום' ד"ה וחילופיהן באיש . אור"ת דאחיוב חטאת קאי . עיין עירובין דף סט ע"א תוס' ד"ה כיון דחזיא :

ומאי ר' מאיר דתניא *לא תצא אשה במפתח שבידה ואם יצאת חייבת חטאת דברי רבי מאיר רבי אליעזר פוטר *בכובלת ובצלוחית של פלייטון כובלת מאן דכר שמה חסורי מחסרא והכי קתני וכן בכובלת וכן בצלוחית של פלייטון לא תצא ואם יצאה חייבת חטאת דברי רבי מאיר רבי אליעזר פוטר בכובלת ובצלוחית של פלייטון *במה דברים אמורים כשיש בהם בושם אבל אין בהם בושם חייבת אמר רב אדא בר אהבה זאת אומרת המוציא אוכלין פחות מכשיעור בכלי חייב דהא אין בה בושם כפחות מכשיעור בכלי דמי וקתני חייבת רב אשי אמר בעלמא אימא לך פטור ושאני הכא דליתיה לממשא כלל: °וראשית שמנים ימשחו אמר רב יהודה אמר שמואל זה פלייטון מתיב רב יוסף *אף על פלייטון גזר רבי יהודה בן בבא ולא הודו לו ואי אמרת משום תענוג אמאי לא הודו לו אמר ליה אביי ולטעמיך הא דכתיב °השותים במזרקי יין ר' אמי ור' אסי חד אמר קנישקנין וחד אמר שמזרקין כוסותיהן זה לזה הכא נמי דאסיר והא *רבה בר רב הונא איקלע לבי ריש גלותא ושתה בקנישקנין ולא אמר ליה ולא מידי אלא כל מידי דאית ביה תענוג ואית ביה שמחה גזרו רבנן אבל מידי דאית ביה תענוג ולית ביה שמחה לא גזרו רבנן: °השוכבים על מטות שן וסרוחים על ערשותם *אמר רבי יוסי ברבי חנינא מלמד שהיו משתינין מים בפני מטותיהן ערומים מגדף בה ר' אבהו אי הכי היינו דכתיב °לכן עתה יגלו בראש גולים משום דמשתינין מים בפני מטותיהם ערומים יגלו בראש גולים אלא א"ר אבהו אלו בני אדם שהיו אוכלים ושותים זה עם זה ודובקין מטותיהן זו בזו ומחליפין נשותיהן זה עם זה ומסריחין ערסותם בשכבת זרע שאינו שלהן א"ר אבהו ואמרי לה במתניתא תנא ג' דברים מביאין את האדם לידי עניות ואלו הן *המשתין מים בפני מטתו ערום °ומזלזל בנטילת ידים ושאשתו מקללתו בפניו *המשתין מים בפני מטתו ערום אמר רבא לא אמרן אלא דמהדר אפיה לפורייה אבל לבראי לית לן בה ומהדר אפיה לפורייה נמי לא אמרן אלא לארעא אבל במנא לית לן בה °ומזלזל בנטילת ידים אמר רבא לא אמרן אלא דלא משא ידיה כלל אבל משא ולא משא לית לן בה ולאו מלתא היא דאמר רב חסדא °אנא משאי מלא חפני מיא ויהבו לי מלא חפני טיבותא ושאשתו מקללתו בפניו אמר רבא על עסקי תכשיטיה וה"מ הוא דאית ליה ולא עביד: דרש רבא בריה דרב עילאי מאי *דכתיב °ויאמר ה' יען כי גבהו בנות ציון שהיו מהלכות בקומה זקופה ותלכנה נטויות גרון שהיו מהלכות עקב בצד גודל ומשקרות עינים דהוה מלאן כוחלא לעינייהו ומרמזן הלוך וטפוף שהיו מהלכות ארוכה בצד קצרה °וברגליהן תעכסנה אמר רב יצחק דבי ר' אמי °מלמד שמטילות מור ואפרסמון במנעליהן ומהלכות בשוקי ירושלים וכיון שמגיעות אצל בחורי ישראל בועטות בקרקע ומתיזות עליהם ומכניסות בהן יצר הרע כארס *בבעוס מאי פורענותיהם כדדריש רבה בר עולא °והיה תחת בושם מק יהיה מקום שהיו מתבשמות בו נעשה נמקים °ותחת חגורה נקפה מקום שהיו חגורות בצלצול נעשה נקפים °ותחת מעשה מקשה קרחה מקום שהיו מתקשטות בו נעשה קרחים קרחים °ותחת פתיגיל מחגורת שק פתחים המביאין לידי גילה יהיו למחגורת שק °כי תחת יופי אמר רבא היינו דאמרי אינשי חלופי שופרא כיבא °*(וספח) ה' קדקוד בנות ציון אמר רבי יוסי ברבי חנינא מלמד שפרחה בהן צרעת כתיב הכא ושפח וכתיב התם °לשאת ולספחת וה' פתהן יערה רב ושמואל חד אמר שנשפכו כקיתון וחד אמר שנעשו פתחיהן כיער אמר רב יהודה אמר רב אנשי ירושלים אנשי שחץ היו אדם אומר לחברו במה סעדת היום בפת עמילה או בפת שאינה עמילה ביין גורדלי או ביין

רש"י

ומאי רבי מאיר. היכא אשכחן דאיירי בה רבי מאיר בלא רבנן ופליג רבי אליעזר עליה: בד"א. דרבי אליעזר פוטר והאי פוטר היינו מותר לכתחלה כדאוקימנא: כשיש בה בושם. פלייטון יש בההוא חומרתא העשויה כקמיע דכיון דיש בה בושם תכשיט היא לזו שריחה רע ולמשלף ואיתויי נמי לא חייש כדאמרן דגנות הוא לה: אבל אין בה בושם. חומרתא לחודא לאו תכשיט הוא וחייבת: זאת אומרת. הא דקתני אין בה בושם חייבת אלמא דקסבר רבי אליעזר המוציא אוכלין בשבת בכלי פחות מכשיעור דלא מיחייב על הוצאת אוכלין פחות מגרוגרת כדלקמן (דף עו:) חייב מיהא על הכלי ולא אמרינן הכלי טפל להן ולא מיחייב עליה שלא נתכוין להוציא אלא משום אוכלין ופלוגתא היא על סתם משנה השנויה בפרק המצניע (לקמן דף צג:) דקתני פטור אף על הכלי: דהא אין בו בושם כפחות מכשיעור דמי. שהכלי קלט את הריח ושיעור הוצאת בשמים בכל שהוא וכיון שאינו כל שהוא הוי ריחה פחות מכשיעור (הוא) וקתני חייבת ולא אמרינן נעשה כלי טפל לריח שבתוכו והריחא לא מיחייב דפחות מכשיעור הוא: ושאני הכא. ליכא למימר נעשה כלי טפל לריח שאין בו שום ממש ואפילו פחות מכשיעור לא מיקרי אבל פחות מכשיעור בדבר שיש בו ממש נעשה כלי טפל לו ופטור: ראשית שמנים. מובחר שבשמנים: גזר. משום לער חורבן: ואי אמרת. זה פלייטון והאי קרא בתענוג משתעי שלא היו נותנים לב לדברי הנביאים הניבאים על הפורענות ועסוקים בתענוגים: ולטעמיך הא דכתיב. בהאי ענינא השותים במזרקי יין ורבי אמי ורבי אסי פירשו °זהו קנישקנין כלי זכוכית ארוך ולו שני פיות ויין נזרק מזה לזה: שמזרקין. על ידי אומנות כדאמר בהחליל (סוכה דף נג.) מטייל בתמני כסי: הכי נמי דאסור. למשתי השתא בקנישקנין: משתינין. דדייק מסרוחים: לידי עניות דאמרינן בע"פ (פסחים דף קיא:) שרא דעניותא נביל שמיה ונביל קרי ליה והוהב מקום מיאוס ומשתין מים לפני מטתו היינו מיאוס: ערום. אורחא דמילתא נקט מתוך שהוא ערום אינו יוצא לחוץ להשתין דטורח הוא לו ללבוש ולצאת: אבל לבראי לית לן בה. שהקילוח ארוך וניתז למרחוק: משא ולא משא. שאינו רוחץ ומשפשף יפה אלא מעט מים כגון רביעית מצומצם: על עסקי תכשיטיה. שאינו רוצה לקנות לה: גבהו. היינו קומה זקופה: ותלכנה נטויות גרון. שהיו הולכות עקב בצד גודל למעט בהילוכם שהיו מסתכלין בה והיא שוהה בפסיעותיה ודרך נוטין גרון לילך בנחת לפי שאינו רואה לרגליו: ומשקרות עינים דמליין כוחלא. לשון סיקרא: ומרמזן. את הבחורים: סיקור. לשון הבטה: הלוך וטפוף שהו מהלכות ארוכה בצד קצרה. שתראה נפה על ראש חברתה והוא נוי לה וגשואות היו לפיכך מספר בגעתן: וטפוף. כמו על דאטפת אטפוך (אבות פ"ב מ"ו): תעכסנה. כמו וכעכס אל מוסר אויל (משלי ז) והוא ארס של נחש וקרי ליה עכס על שם שאינו מטילו אלא על ידי כעס: בכעוס. נחש כעוסה: נמקים. כמו המק בשרו (זכריה יד): צלצול. בגדי"ל נאה: נקפים. חבורות לשון המנקף רגלו וניקף סבכי היער (ישעיה י): מתקשטות. היינו שער שסורקות ומפרכסות: מתקשטות. דומה למקשה כעין טוטריקון: פתיגיל. נוטריקון פתח גילה אותו מקום: כי תחת יופי. כי כל אלה יבא לך תחת יפייך: כיבא. קיוטור"א ליחה כמו שיחנא וכיבי דקודשין דפלימו (דף פא:): פתהן. כמו פתחיהן: שנשפכו כקיתון. שופכות דם זיבה: יערה. כמו ותער כדה (בראשית כד): כיער. נתמלאו שער ונמאסות לתשמיש: אנשי שחץ. מדברים בלשון גאוה ולעגי שפה: סעדת. תשמיש: פת עמילה. בעולה: בתולה: שאינה עמילה. ברייאו"ה בלע"ז: גורדלי. לבן היה:

ייין

עין משפט נר מצוה

מו א טוש"ע א"ח סי' רמא:

מז ב ג מיי' פ"ז מהל' ברכות הלכה יט טוש"ע א"ח סי' קנח סעיף ט:

מח ד מיי' פכ"א מהל' איסורי ביאה הלכה ... טוש"ע אה"ע סי' כא סעיף א:

רבינו חננאל

ראשית שמנים כמשמעו ואפילו מאן דפטר לא פטר אלא בשיש בה בושם. אבל אין בה בושם חייבת. קנישקנין כוס שיש בה שתי פיות ושותין ממנה שנים בבת אחת. משקרות עינים. דהוו מליין כוחלא רמזא. ארס בכעוס. פי' החיה כשתכעוס גוררת ומשלכת. ארס קשה. פי' פת עמילה. אשה בעולה ופת שאינה עמילה בתולה. וכולן על זה הענין: צלצול חגור. כדגרסינן בסוף מנחות (דף קט:):

רב נסים גאון

מותיב רב יוסף אף על פליאטון גזר ר' יהודה בן בבא. עיקר זאת הברייתא בתוספ' סוטה בסוף המסכת בפולמוס האחרון גזרו על חופת חתנים אלו זהוריות המוזהבות כו' אף על פליאטון גזר ר' יהודה בן בבא ולא הודו לו:

מסורת הש"ס

[תוס' פ"ס ע"ב] [לקמן סס.]

[תוספתא שם ע"ש]

[תוספ' דסוטה ספט"ו]

[פ"ז עב: ע"ש]

קדושין עב.

נדה יז.

[יומא עז: ע"ש]

[עי' ערוך ערך ארס]

גליון הש"ס

גמ' ומזלזל בנט"י. עי' סוטה ד ע"ב תוס' ד"ה נעקר: רש"י ד"ה ולטעמיך וכו' זהו קנישקנק. פי' ע"ז דף עב ע"ב ברש"י ד"ה קנישקנין:

[62b] And what is [this reference to] R. Meir?[2]—As it was taught: A woman may not go out with a key in her hand, and if she does, she incurs a sin-offering; this is R. Meir's view. R. Eliezer holds her non-culpable in the case of a *kobeleth* and a flask of spikenard oil. Who mentioned a *kobeleth?*[3]—There is a lacuna, and it was thus taught: And she may likewise not go out with a *kobeleth* or a flask of spikenard oil; and if she does, she incurs a sin-offering: this is R. Meir's view. R. Eliezer holds her non-culpable in the case of a *kobeleth* and a flask of spikenard oil. When is that said? When they contain perfume;[4] but if they do not contain perfume, she is culpable.[5] R. Adda b. Ahabah said: This implies that if one carries out less than the statutory quantity of food in a utensil, he is culpable. For when it [the flask] does not contain perfume, it is analogous to less than the statutory quantity [of food carried out] in a utensil, and yet it is taught that she is culpable.[6] R. Ashi said: In general I may hold that there is no liability, but here it is different, because there is nothing concrete at all.[7]

a *And anoint themselves with the chief ointments:*[1] Rab Judah said in Samuel's name: This refers to spikenard oil. R. Joseph objected: R. Judah b. Baba forbade spikenard oil too, but they [the Sages] did not agree with him.[2] Now if you say [that the prophet's objection] is on account of its being a luxury,[3] why did they not agree with him? Said Abaye to him, Then on your view, when it is written, *that drink in bowls of* [mizreke] *wine*,[4] where R. Ammi and R. Assi dispute—one interpreting it [as meaning] *kenishkanim*,[5] while the other said, It means that they threw [*mezarkim*] their goblets to each other[6]—is that too forbidden? Surely Rabbah son of R. Huna visited the house of the Resh Galutha,[7] who drank from a *kenishkanim*, yet he said nothing to him![8] But whatever provides both enjoyment and rejoicings, the Rabbis forbade; but that which is a luxury but not associated with rejoicing, the Rabbis did not forbid.

That lie upon beds of ivory, and stretch themselves [seruhim] *upon their couches.*[9] R. Jose son of R. Hanina said: This refers to people who urinate before their beds naked.[10] R. Abbahu derided this: If so, is that why it is written: *Therefore shall they now go captive with the first that go captive:*[11] because they urinate before their beds naked they shall go captive with the first that go captive! Rather said R. Abbahu: This refers to people who eat and drink together, join their couches, exchange their wives, and make their couches foul [*maserihim*] with semen that is not theirs.

R. Abbahu said—others say, In a Baraitha it was taught: Three things bring man to poverty, viz., urinating in front of one's bed naked, treating the washing of the hands with disrespect,[12] and being cursed by one's wife in his presence. 'Urinating in front of one's bed naked': Raba said, This was said only when his face is turned to the bed: but if it is turned in the opposite direction, we have nought against it. And even when his face is turned to the

b bed, this was said only when it is on to the ground;[1] but if it is into a vessel, we have nought against it. 'And the treating of the washing of the hands with disrespect': Raba said, This was said only when one does not wash his hands at all; but if he washes them inadequately,[2] we have nought against it. (But this is not so, for R. Hisda said: I washed with full handfuls of water and was granted full handfuls of prosperity).[3] 'And being cursed by one's wife in his presence': Said Raba: [That is when she curses him] on account of her adornments.[4] But that is only when he has the means but does not provide them.[5]

Raba son of R. Ilai lectured: What is meant by, *Moreover the Lord said, Because the daughters of Zion are haughty?*[6] That means that they walked with haughty bearing.[7] *And walk with outstretched necks*[8]—they walked heel by toe.[9] *And wanton* [mesakroth] *eyes:*[10] they filled their eyes with stibium and beckoned.[11] *Walking and mincing:* they walked, a tall woman by the side of a short one. *And making a tinkling* [te'akasnah] *with their feet:* R. Isaac of the School of R. Ammi said: This teaches that they placed myrrh and balsam in their shoes and walked through the market-places of Jerusalem, and on coming near to the young men of Israel, they kicked their feet and spurted it on them, thus instilling them with passionate desire like with serpent's poison.[12]

And what is their punishment?—As Rabbah b. 'Ulla lectured: *And it shall come to pass, that instead of sweet spices* [bosem] *there shall be rottenness:*[13] the place where they perfumed themselves [*mithbasmoth*] shall be decaying sores. *And instead of a girdle a rope* [nikpeh]: the place where they were girded with a girdle shall become full of bruises [*nekafim*]. *And instead of well-set hair baldness:* the place where they adorned themselves shall be filled with bald patches. *And instead of a stomacher* [pethigil] *a girding of sackcloth:* the openings

c that lead to [sensual] joy[1] shall be for a girding of sackcloth. *Branding* [ki] *instead of beauty:* Said Raba, Thus men say, Ulcers instead of beauty.

Therefore the Lord will smite with a scab [wesipah] *the crown of the head of the daughters of Zion.*[2] R. Jose son of R. Hanina said: This teaches that leprosy broke out in them: here is written *wesipah;* whilst elsewhere it is written, [*This is the law for all manner of plagues of leprosy . . .*] *and for a rising and for a scab* [sapahath].[3] *And the Lord will lay bare* [ye'areh] *their secret parts:*[4] Rab and Samuel—one maintained: This means that they were poured out like a cruse;[5] while the other said: Their openings became like a forest.

Rab Judah said in Rab's name: The men of Jerusalem were vulgar. One would say to his neighbour, On what did you dine to-day: on well-kneaded bread or on bread that is not well kneaded;[6]

(2) Where is R. Meir's view found without that of the Rabbis that R. Eliezer should refer exclusively to his ruling? (3) R. Eliezer's ruling does not bear upon R. Meir's statement. (4) Then they are ornaments. (5) Because they are burdens. (6) V. 76b; also 93b for an opposing view. Liability is incurred for carrying out *any* quantity of perfume, no matter how little. Now even a flask without any perfume at all contains its fragrance: this fragrance may be regarded as less than the minimum quantity of food which imposes liability, and R. Eliezer rules that when it is together with the utensil it does involve culpability.—The opposing view on 93b is that the utensil is merely subordinate in purpose to the food, and since the food does not impose liability, the utensil does not either. (7) Mere fragrance is not a concrete object; hence the utensil cannot be subordinate to it, but is an independent article, for which liability is incurred. But even a very small quantity of food may render the utensil subordinate to it.

a (1) Amos VI, 6. (2) This was during the Hadrianic persecutions, when luxuries were proscribed. (3) The people, by setting their minds on such things, disregarded the essentials, viz., the teachings of the prophets. (4) Ibid. (5) A cup with spouts, enabling several persons to drink from it; v. *T.A.* II, pp. 280 and 641 (n. 237). (6) Both derive *mizreke* from *zarak*, to throw, the first holds that the wine was 'thrown', i.e., passed from one spout to the other.—Thus the prophet criticizes this too as an unnecessary luxury. (7) V. *supra* 48a, n. 7. (8) In reproof. (9) Ibid. 4. (10) Translating *seruhim* that act indecently. (11) Ibid. 7. (12) Eating without washing the hands.

b (1) Their floors were of earth. (2) Lit., 'he washes and does not wash',—i.e., he uses the barest minimum. (3) Lit., 'goodness'. This shows that water must be used generously. (4) Because he refuses them. (5) Cf. this with Raba's statement *supra* 32b, 33a. (6) Isa. III, 16. (7) Lit., 'erect stature'. (8) Ibid. (9) I.e., with short mincing steps. One who walks with outstretched neck must take short steps, because he cannot see his feet (Rashi). (10) Ibid. (11) To the men. (12) Reading *'akus* (serpent) and connecting *te'akasnah* with it by a play on words. (13) Ibid. 24.

c (1) Reading *pethigil* as an abbreviation for *pethahim* (openings) of *gilah* (joy). (2) Isa. III, 17. (3) Lev. XIV, 56. (4) Isa. III, 17. (5) I.e., they discharged an abundance of matter. *Ye'areh* (E.V. *lay bare*) is translated, will empty; cf. Gen. XXIV, 20: *and she emptied* (wate'ar) *her pitcher*. (6) The whole is a vulgar metaphor for the satisfaction of one's lust.

on white wine[7] or [63a] on dark [i.e., mustard-coloured] wine; on a broad couch or on a narrow couch; with a good companion or with a poor companion? R. Ḥisda observed: And all these are in reference to immorality.

Rahabah said in R. Judah's name: The [fuel] logs of Jerusalem were of the cinnamon tree, and when lit their fragrance pervaded the whole of Eretz Israel. But when Jerusalem was destroyed they were hidden, only as much as a barley grain being left, which is to be found in the queen's collections of rarities.[8]

MISHNAH. A MAN MUST NOT GO OUT WITH A SWORD, BOW, SHIELD, LANCE [ALLAH], OR SPEAR; AND IF HE DOES GO OUT, HE INCURS A SIN-OFFERING. R. ELIEZER SAID: THEY ARE ORNAMENTS FOR HIM. BUT THE SAGES MAINTAIN, THEY ARE MERELY SHAMEFUL, FOR IT IS SAID, AND THEY SHALL BEAT THEIR SWORDS INTO PLOWSHARES, AND THEIR SPEARS INTO PRUNINGHOOKS: NATION SHALL NOT LIFT UP SWORD AGAINST NATION, NEITHER SHALL
a THEY LEARN WAR ANY MORE.[1] A KNEE-BAND [BERITH] IS CLEAN, AND ONE MAY GO OUT WITH IT ON THE SABBATH; ANKLE-CHAINS [KEBALIM] ARE UNCLEAN,[2] AND ONE MAY NOT GO OUT WITH THEM ON THE SABBATH.

GEMARA. What is, WITH AN ALLAH?—A lance.

R. ELIEZER SAID: THEY ARE ORNAMENTS FOR HIM. It was taught: Said they [the Sages] to R. Eliezer: Since they are ornaments for him, why should they cease in the days of the Messiah? Because they will not be required, he answered, as it is said, ***nation shall not lift up sword against nation***. Yet let them exist merely as ornaments?—Said Abaye, It may be compared to a candle at noon.[3]

Now this disagrees with Samuel.[4] For Samuel said, This world differs from the Messianic era only in respect to servitude of the exiled, for it is said, *For the poor shall never cease out of the land*.[5] This supports R. Ḥiyya b. Abba,[6] who said, All the prophets prophesied only for the Messianic age, but as for the world to come, ***the eye hath not seen, O Lord, beside Thee*** [***what he hath prepared for him that waiteth for Him***].[7]

Some there are who state: Said they [the Sages] to R. Eliezer: Since they are ornaments for him, why should they cease in the days of the Messiah? In the days of the Messiah too they shall not cease, he answered. This is Samuel's view, and it disagrees with R. Ḥiyya b. Abba's.

Abaye asked R. Dimi—others state, R. Awia,—others again state, R. Joseph [asked] R. Dimi—and others state, R. Awia—whilst others state, Abaye [asked] R. Joseph: What is R. Eliezer's reason for maintaining that they are ornaments for him?—Because it is written, *Gird thy sword upon thy thigh, O mighty one, Thy glory*
b *and thy majesty*.[1] R. Kahana objected to Mar son of R. Huna: But this refers to the words of the Torah?[2]—A verse cannot depart from its plain meaning, he replied.[3] R. Kahana said: By the time I was eighteen years old I had studied the whole *Shas*,[4] yet I did not know that a verse cannot depart from its plain meaning,[5] until to-day. What does he inform us?—That a man should study and subsequently understand.[6]

(Mnemonic: *ZaRuTH*.)[7] R. Jeremiah said in R. Eleazar's name: When two scholars sharpen each other in *halachah*,[8] the Holy One, blessed be He, gives them success, for it is said, ***and in thy majesty*** [wa-hadareka] ***be successful***:[9] read not *wa-hadareka* but *wa-ḥadadeka*

(7) *Gurdeli* fr. *garad*, to scrape, means scraper, a nickname for an inferior white wine. (8) Jast. Rashi: of Queen Zimzemai.

a (1) Isa. II, 4. (2) 'Clean' and 'unclean' mean not susceptible and susceptible to uncleanness respectively. (3) Being unnecessary then, it is not beautiful either. Thus, when war will be abolished, the instruments of war will not be adornments. Now, however, that they may be needed, they are also ornamental. (4) *Sc.* the view that they will cease to be in the days of the Messiah. (5) Deut. XV, 11. This implies that poverty will continue in the Messianic era. Hence the prophets' tidings of a new state of affairs cannot refer to the Messianic era, which will be the same as the present, save in this matter. (6) *Sc.* the Baraitha which states that weapons of war will cease to exist in the Messianic age. (7) Isa. LXIV, 3.—The conception of the future world is rather vague in the Talmud. In general, it is the opposite of עולם הזה, this world. In Ber. I, 5, 'this world' is opposed to the days of the Messiah, and this in turn is differentiated here from the future world. The following quotation from G. Moore, '*Judaism*' (Vol. 2, p. 389) is apposite: 'Any attempt to systematize the Jewish notions of the hereafter imposes upon them an order and consistency which does not exist in them'.

b (1) Ps. XLV, 4. (2) '*Thy sword*' is metaphorical for learning, which is Israel's weapon. It is indicative of the peace-loving spirit of the Rabbis and their exaltation of Torah that they regarded it as axiomatic that such a verse could not be taken literally. (3) Granted that it is metaphorical, yet the Torah would not have been likened to the sword, unless the latter were ornamental. (4) An abbreviation of *shishah sedarim*, the six orders into which the Talmud is divided: v. *supra* 31a. [MS.M. Talmud, *Shas* being a correction by the censor]. (5) [In the narrative and poetical passages v. Chayyes, Z. H. Glosses]. (6) Even when one does not understand all he learns he should nevertheless study, and understanding will come eventually. (7) V. *supra* 25a, n. b1. For the explanation of this Mnemonic v. Hyman, *Toledoth*, p. 18. (8) By means of debating, etc. (9) Ibid.5

◁ *For the continuation of the English translation of this page see overleaf.*

עין משפט נר מצוה

מט א מיי' פי"ט מהל' שבת הלכה א סמג לאוין סה טוש"ע א"ח סי' ש"א סעיף ז:

נ ב מיי' פי"ב מהל' מלכים הלכה ב:

נא ג מיי' פ"ח מהל' תשובה הלכה ז:

[ועי' תוס' תענית יג: ד"ה מאי שייר ותוס' מגילה ח: ד"ה אין בין ומ"ש שם על הגליון]

נב ד מיי' פ"י מהל' מ"ע הלכה ח טוש"ע י"ד סי' רמט סעיף ו:

נג ה מיי' פ"ו מהל' דעות הלכה א ב:

[פי' שבט שמכין בו ורא"ו עב]

[במיכה כתיב ישאו] חולין ס:

נד ו מיי' פי"א מהל' רוצח הלכה ד:

[יבמות יא: כד.]

גליון הש"ס

גמ' אלא שעבוד גליות. עי' פסחים נ ע"ב

[פי' תוס' פ"ו כב: ד"ה רגלא וכו' אסירום רש"י דהכא]

[נ"ל וא"ר]

[נ"ל וא"ר]

מסורת הש"ס

פי' מגן

נ"ל לא

[גי' הערוך מאי אלה קופל פי' דומה למקל וכו' וראשו עגול כמו כדור וכו' ע"ש]

ברכות לד: לקמן קנא: פסחים סח. סנהדרין צט.

י"ג דרבינא

הגהות הב"ח

(א) רש"י ד"ה ותורך ותלמדך כס"ד ואח"כ מ"ה עושר וכבוד וכו' עושר וכבוד הס"ד ואח"כ מ"ה למיימינין בה שמפשפשין כצ"ל ותיבת של תורה נמחק ונ"ב ע"ל בדף סח ע"ב:

מכות י.

ברכות ו. קדושין מ. ע"ש

[מ"ק טז: ב"מ פה.]

[עתו' ע"ז שם]

פסחים נג:

[נ"ל ר' שמעון בן לקיש]

בין חרדלי. שחור כלומר לבנה או שחורה: במסב רחב. מיסב מטה שמיסב עליה בשעת אכילה ולענין ניאוף אשה שמנה: קצר. כחושה: חבר טוב. אשה טובת מראה: דצימצמאי מלכתא. כך שמה: מתני' באלה. מפרש בגמ' קולפא מנוק"ה בלע"ז: וכתתו חרבותם. ואי תכשיטין נינהו לא יהו בטלין לעתיד: בירית. בגמרא מפרש: טהורה. אינה מקבלת טומאה: ויוצאין בה. דלא שלפא ומחויא שלא ירא השוקה: כבלין טמאין. בגמ' מפרש לה: גמ' שרגא בטיהרא. נר בצהרים מתוך שאינו צריך אינו נאה אבל בזמן הזה שהוא עת מלחמה תכשיטין הן: ופליגא. הא דקתני בטלין לימות המשיח פליגא דשמואל דלשמואל אין בטלין לימות המשיח: לא יחדל. משמע לעולם אלמא יש עניות ועשירות ש"מ נחמות שנתנבאו הנביאים ולא יהיה כנעני עוד (זכריה יד) לא לימות המשיח נתנבאו שהן מן העולם הזה דאם כן חדל לך אביון: מסייע ליה. ברייתא דקתני בטלין לימות המשיח לרבי חייא בר אבא: לא נתנבאו. דברי נחמות שלהן: עין לא ראתה. עין של נביאים לא שלטה לראותו: בדברי תורה כתיב. הוי זהיר לחזור על משנתך שתהא מזומנת לך בשעת הדין להביא ראיה כחרב על ירך גבור לנצח במלחמה והוא הודך והדרך: דליגמר איניש. לגרוס שמעתא מרביה ואף על גב דלא ידע לכולהו טעמיה והדר ליסבר. טעמיה דהא קשה ליה לרב כהנא ולא הוה ידע להאי טעמא ותלמודיה הוה קים ליה מדהוה בר תמני סרי: המחדדין. שואלין ומשיבין ולא נקפח אלא להתחדד: והדרך. כמו וחדדך: ותורך. ותלמדך (א): למיימינין. של תורה שמפשפשין טעמיהן בדקדוק וגוררין כימין המיומנת למלאכה: עושר וכבוד ליכא. בתמיה כיון דאיכא אורך ימים כ"ש עושר וכבוד: למשמאילין בה. שאין יגעים בה כל צרכן אי נמי מיימינין בה עוסקין לשמה משמאילים שלא לשמה: הנוחין זה לזה. נושאין ונותנין בה בנחת רוח מתעסקין כדי שילמדו זה מזה: ידבר עמים תחתינו. ישפיל וכל שפלות בנחת ל"א הנוחין מנהיגין זה את זה להבנתה של הלכה כמו לך נחה (שמות לב) ידבר תרגום של ינהג: ומי יאמר לו מה תעשה. שומר מצות יוכל לומר לו: המקשיבין. מלמדים זה את זה ומבינים זה מזה ולישנא דקרא נקט: בגנים. בתי מדרשות: חבירים מקשיבים. זה לזה להם אני אומר שישמיעוני קולם ואענם: ברח דודי. בתריה כתיב: המדגילים. מאספין זה את זה ואומרים בא ונלמוד ונבין בין שניהם הואיל ואין לנו רב ללמדנו: צורתא. שורש הדבר קלא למדו מרבם: גדול המלוה. לפי שאין העני בוש בדבר: ומטיל בכיס. מעות ומלאי להשתכר בהן למחצית שכר ואיידי דאיירי רבי אבא אמר ריש לקיש נקט כל הני מילי דאגדתא דאמר להו ר' אבא משמיה: חוגרו. הדבק בו שסופך ליהנות מתלמודו: אל תדור בשכונתו. שאינו יודע בדקדוקי מצות ואין חסידותו שלם וסופך ללמוד ממנו: מונע חסד. שאינו מניח העניים לבא לפתחו: למס. דהיינו כלב מרעהו

תורה אור

בין חרדלי במסב רחב או במסב קצר בחבר טוב או בחבר רע א"ר חסדא וכולן לזנות אמר רחבה אמר רבי יהודה עצי ירושלים של קינמון היו ובשעה שהיו מסיקין מהן ריחן נודף בכל ארץ ישראל ומשחרבה ירושלים נגנזו ולא נשתייר אלא כשעורה ומשתכח בגזאי דצימצמאי מלכתא:

מתני' לא יצא האיש לא בסייף ולא בקשת ולא *בתרים ולא באלה ולא ברומח ואם יצא חייב חטאת רבי אליעזר אומר תכשיטין הן לו וחכ"א אינן אלא לגנאי שנאמר °וכתתו חרבותם לאתים וחניתותיהם למזמרות *ולא ישא גוי אל גוי חרב ולא ילמדו עוד מלחמה בירית טהורה ויוצאין בה בשבת כבלים טמאים ואין יוצאין בהן בשבת:

גמ' *מאי באלה *קולפא: ר' אליעזר אומר תכשיטין הן לו: תניא אמרו לו לרבי אליעזר וכי מאחר דתכשיטין הן לו מפני מה הן בטלין לימות המשיח אמר להן לפי שאינן צריכין שנאמר °לא *ישא גוי אל גוי חרב ותהוי לנוי בעלמא אמר אביי מידי דהוה *אשרגא בטיהרא ופליגא דשמואל דאמר שמואל *אין בין העולם הזה לימות המשיח אלא שיעבוד גליות בלבד שנאמר °כי לא יחדל אביון מקרב הארץ מסייע ליה לרבי חייא בר אבא דא"ר חייא בר אבא כל הנביאים לא נתנבאו אלא לימות המשיח אבל לעולם הבא °עין לא ראתה אלהים זולתך ואיכא דאמרי אמרו לו לר' אליעזר וכי מאחר דתכשיטין הן לו מפני מה הן בטלין לימות המשיח אמר להן אף לימות המשיח אינן בטלין היינו דשמואל ופליגא דר' חייא בר אבא א"ל אביי לרב דימי ואמרי לה לרב אויא ואמרי לה רב יוסף לרב דימי ואמרי לה לרב אויא ואמרי לה אביי לרב יוסף מ"ט דר"א דאמר תכשיטין הן לו דכתיב °חגור חרבך על ירך גבור הודך והדרך א"ל רב כהנא למר בריה *דרב הונא האי בדברי תורה כתיב א"ל *אין מקרא יוצא מידי פשוטו א"ר כהנא כד הוינא בר תמני סרי שנין והוה גמירנא ליה לכוליה הש"ס ולא הוה ידענא דאין מקרא יוצא מידי פשוטו עד השתא מאי קמ"ל דליגמר איניש והדר ליסבר: סימן זרות: א"ר ירמיה א"ר אלעזר שני תלמידי חכמים המחדדין זה לזה בהלכה הקב"ה מצליח להם שנאמר °והדרך צלח אל תקרי והדרך אלא וחדדך ולא עוד אלא שעולין לגדולה שנאמר °צלח רכב יכול אפילו שלא לשמה תלמוד לומר °על דבר אמת יכול אם הגיס דעתו ת"ל °וענוה צדק ואם עושין כן זוכין לתורה שניתנה בימין שנאמר °ותורך נוראות ימינך רב נחמן בר יצחק אמר זוכין לדברים שנאמרו בימינה של תורה דאמר רבא בר רב שילא ואמרי לה אמר רב יוסף בר חמא א"ר ששת מאי דכתיב °אורך ימים בימינה בשמאלה עושר וכבוד אלא בימינה אורך ימים איכא עושר וכבוד ליכא אלא למיימינין בה אורך ימים איכא וכ"ש עושר וכבוד למשמאילים בה עושר וכבוד איכא אורך ימים ליכא א"ר ירמיה אמר ר' שמעון בן לקיש שני תלמידי חכמים הנוחין זה לזה בהלכה הקדוש ברוך הוא מקשיב להן שנאמר °אז נדברו יראי ה' וגו' *אין דיבור אלא נחת שנאמר °ידבר עמים תחתינו *מאי ולחושבי שמו א"ר אמי אפילו חישב לעשות מצוה ונאנס ולא עשאה מעלה עליו הכתוב כאילו עשאה א"ר חיננא בר אידי כל העושה מצוה כמאמרה אין מבשרין אותו בשורות רעות שנאמר °שומר מצוה לא ידע דבר רע א"ר אסי ואיתימא ר' חנינא אפילו הקב"ה *גוזר גזירה הוא מבטלה שנאמר °באשר דבר מלך שלטון ומי יאמר לו מה תעשה וסמיך ליה שומר מצוה לא ידע דבר רע אמר רבי אבא אמר רבי שמעון בן לקיש שני תלמידי חכמים המקשיבים זה לזה בהלכה הקדוש ב"ה שומע לקולן שנאמר °היושבת בגנים חברים מקשיבים לקולך השמיעני ואם אין עושין כן גורמין לשכינה שמסתלקת מישראל שנאמר °ברח דודי ודמה וגו' אמר רבי אבא א"ר שמעון בן לקיש שני ת"ח *המדגילים זה לזה בהלכה הקדוש ברוך הוא אוהבן שנאמר °ודגלו עלי אהבה אמר רבא והוא דידעי צורתא דשמעתא *והוא דלית להו רבה במתא למיגמר מיניה (*א"ר) אבא א"ר שמעון בן לקיש גדול המלוה יותר מן העושה צדקה *ומטיל בכיס יותר מכולן (*א"ר) אבא אמר ר' שמעון בן לקיש אם תלמיד חכם נוקם ונוטר כנחש הוא חגריהו על מתניך אם עם הארץ הוא חסיד אל תדור בשכונתו אמר רב כהנא אמר רבי שמעון בן לקיש ואמרי לה אמר רב אסי אמר (*ריש לקיש) ואמרי לה אמר רבי אבא אמר רבי שמעון בן לקיש כל המגדל כלב רע בתוך ביתו מונע חסד מתוך ביתו שנאמר °למס מרעהו

אין בין העוה"ז לימות המשיח. אע"ג דהשתא אין ירושלים ואין בהמ"ק ואילו לימות המשיח יהיה הכל בנוי נ"ל דהאי אין בין לאו דוקא*: ואילו

Continuation of translation from previous page as indicated by ◁

[thy sharpening]. Moreover, they ascend to greatness, as it is said, *'ride on prosperously'* [successfully]. One might think [that this is so] even if it is not for its own sake, therefore it is taught, *'In behalf of truth'*. I might think [that this is so] even if he becomes conceited; therefore it is taught, *'and meekness of right-*
c *eousness'*. But if they do thus, they are privileged to acquire[1] the Torah, which was given by the right Hand,[2] as it is said, *and thy right hand shall teach thee awe-inspiring things.*[3] R. Naḥman b. Isaac said: They will obtain the things which were promised at the right hand of the Torah. For Raba b. R. Shila said—others state, R. Joseph b. Ḥama—said in R. Shesheth's name: What is meant by the verse, *Length of days is in her right hand, In her left hand are riches and honour:*[4] is there in her right hand length of days only, but not riches and honour? But to those who go to the right hand thereof there is length of days, and riches and honour *a fortiori;* but for those that go to the left hand thereof there is riches and honour, but not length of days.[5]

R. Jeremiah said in the name of R. Simeon b. Laḳish:[6] When two scholars are amiable to each other in [their discussions in] *halachah*, the Holy One, blessed be He, gives heed to them, for it is said, *Then they that feared the Lord spake* [nidberu] *one with another: and the Lord hearkened, and heard;*[7] now speech [*dibbur*] can only mean [with] gentleness, for it is said, *He shall subdue* [yadber] *the peoples under us.*[8] What is meant by, *and that thought upon his name?*[9]—Said R. Ammi: Even if one thinks of doing a good deed but is forcibly prevented and does not do it, the Writ ascribes it to him as though he did it.

R. Ḥinena b. Idi said: Whoever fulfils a precept as it is commanded,[10] no evil tidings are told to him, for it is said, *Whoso*
d *keepeth the commandment shall know no evil thing.*[1] R. Assi—others state, R. Ḥanina—said: Even if the Holy One, blessed be He, makes a decree, He annuls it,[2] for it is said, *Because the king's word hath power; and who may say unto him, what doest thou;*[3] in proximity to which [is written,] *Whoso keepeth the commandment shall know no evil thing.*[4]

R. Abba said in the name of R. Simeon b. Laḳish: When two scholars pay heed to each other in *halachah*, the Holy One, blessed be He, listens to their voice, as it is said, *Thou that dwellest in the gardens, The companions hearken to thy voice: Cause me to hear it.*[5] But if they do not do thus, they cause the *Shechinah* to depart from Israel, as it is said, *Flee, my beloved, and be thou like*, etc.[6]

R. Abba said in the name of R. Simeon b. Laḳish: When two disciples form an assembly[7] in *halachah*,[8] the Holy One, blessed be He, loves them, as it is said, *and his banner over me was love.*[9] Said Raba: Providing they know the features of a subject;[10] providing also that there is no greater [scholar] in the town from whom to learn.

R. Abba also said in the name of R. Simeon b. Laḳish: He who lends [money] is greater than he who performs charity;[11] and he who forms a partnership[12] is greater than all.

R. Abba also said in the name of R. Simeon b. Laḳish: [Even]
e if a scholar is vengeful and bears malice like a serpent,[1] gird him on thy loins;[2] [whereas even] if an *'am ha-areẓ* is pious, do not dwell in his vicinity.[3]

R. Kahana said in the name of R. Simeon b. Laḳish—others state, R. Assi said in the name of R. Simeon b. Laḳish—others state, R. Abba said in the name of R. Simeon b. Laḳish: He who breeds a wild dog in his house keeps lovingkindness away from his house,[4] as it is said, *To him that is ready to faint* [lamos] [63*b*]

c (1) *Zakah* implies to acquire through one's merit. (2) V. Deut. XXXIII, 2. (3) Ps. XLV, 5. (4) Prov. III, 16. (5) Rashi: '... to the right hand' means that they study the Torah profoundly and intensively, just as the right hand is the stronger for work; alternatively, it refers to those who study the Torah for its own sake. '... to the left hand' implies the opposite of these. (6) Otherwise known as Resh Laḳish. (7) Mal. III, 16. (8) Ps. XLVII, 3. Subdue implies lowliness, which in turn implies gentleness. (9) Mal. III, 16. (10) In the proper spirit.

d (1) Eccl. VIII, 5. (2) 'He' may refer either to God or to the observer of the precept, who is given power to annul God's decree—a daring thought. The former interpretation is indicated in the parallel passage in B.M. 85*a*; the latter in M.Ḳ. 16*b*; but v. Weiss, *Dor*, I, p. 145. (3) Ibid. 4. (4) I.e., in spite of the king's word, viz., God's decree, *whoso keepeth*, etc. (5) Cant. VIII, 13. The Song of Songs was allegorically interpreted as a dialogue between God and Israel. 'In the gardens' thus means in the academies, and when one scholar hearkens to another's voice, God says, *'Cause me to hear it'*. (6) Ibid. 14. (7) Rashi, deriving the word from *degel*, a flag, i.e., who come under one flag. Tosaf. in A.Z. 22*b*, s.v. רנלא, interprets: even when two students outwit each other by sophistries, without seeking the real truth, yet God loves them. (8) In the absence of a teacher. (9) Ibid. II, 4. (10) I.e., they have a general understanding of the subjects to be studied, so that a teacher is not indispensable. (11) Rashi: because the poor man is not ashamed to borrow. Also perhaps because one generally lends a larger sum than one would give as charity, and that may suffice to make the poor man independent. (12) With a poor man, providing the capital for him to trade with on agreed terms. Lit., 'who throws (money) into a (common) purse'.

e (1) The serpent was probably given that character on account of its part in the sin of Adam and Eve; cf. also Ta'an., 8*a*, Yoma 23*a*. (2) Cleave to him, for you will benefit by his scholarship. (3) His piety is tainted by his ignorance, which may influence his neighbour too. (Cf. Ab. II, 6, n.5). (4) The poor are afraid to call. Thus he can show no lovingkindness to them, nor can he earn the love of God.

מסורת הש"ס

עין משפט נר מצוה

בוין חרדלי. שחור כלומר לבנה או שחורה: במסב רחב. מיסב מטה שמיסב עליה בשעת אכילה ולענין כיאוף אשה שמנה: קצר. כחושה: חבר טוב. אשה טובת מראה: דצימצמאי מלכתא. כך שמה: מתני' באלה. מפרש בגמ' קולפא מנוק"ה בלע"ז: וכתתו חרבותם. ואי תכשיטין נינהו לא יהו בטלין לעתיד: בירית. בגמרא מפרש: טהורה. אינה מקבלת טומאה: ויוצאין בה. דלא שלפא ומחויא שלא ירארה שוקה: כבלין טמאין. בגמ' מפרש לה: גמ' סרגא בטיהרא. נר בצהרים מתוך שאינו צריך אינו נאה אבל בזמן הזה שהוא עת מלחמה תכשיטין הן: ופליגא. הא דקתני תורה אור בטלין לימות המשיח פליגא דשמואל דלשמואל אין בטלין לימות המשיח: לא יחדל. משמע לעולם אלמא יש עניות ועשירות ש"מ נחמות שנתנבאו הנביאים ולא יהיה כנעני עוד (זכריה יד) לא לימות המשיח נתנבאו שהן מן העולם הזה דאם כן חדל לך אביון: מסייע ליה. ברייתא דקתני בטלין לימות המשיח לרבי חייא בר אבא: לא נתנבאו. דברי נחמות שלהן: עין לא ראתה. עין של נביאים לא שלטה לראותו: בדברי תורה כתיב. האי זהיר לחזר על משנתך שתהא מזומנת לך בשעת הדין להביא ראיה כחרב על ירך גבור לנצח במלחמה והוא הודך והדרך: דליגמר איניש. לגרוס שמעתא מרביה ואף על גב דלא ידע לכולהו טעמיה: והדר ליסבר. טעמיה דהא קשה ליה לרב כהנא ולא הוה ידע להאי טעמא ותלמודיה הוה קים ליה מדהוה בר תמני סרי: המחדדין. שואלין ומשיבין ולא לקפח אלא להתחדד: והדרך. כמו וחדדך: ותורך. ותלמדך (א): למיימינין. של תורה שמפשפשין טעמיהן בדקדוק וטורחין כימין המיומנת למלאכה: עושר וכבוד ליכא. בתמיה כיון דאיכא אורך ימים כ"ש עושר וכבוד: למשמאילין בה. שאין יגעים בה כל צרכן אי נמי מיימינין בה עוסקין לשמה משמאילים שלא לשמה: הנוחין זה לזה. נושאין ונותנין בה בנחת רוח מתעסקין כדי שילמדו זה מזה: ידבר עמים תחתינו. ישפיל וכל שפלות בנחת ל"א הנוחין מנהיגין זה את זה להבנתה של הלכה כמו לך נחה (שמות לב) ידבר תרגום של ינהג: ומי יאמר לו מה תעשה. שומר מצות יוכל לומר לו: המקשיבין. מלמדים זה את זה ומבינים זה מזה ולישנא דקרא נקט: בגנים. בתי מדרשות: חברים מקשיבים. זה לזה להם אני אומר שישמיעוני קולם ואענם: ברח דודי. בתריה כתיב: המדגילים. מאספין זה את זה ואומרים בא ונלמוד ונבין בין שניהו הואיל ואין לנו רב ללמדנו: צורתא. שורש הדבר קצת למדו מרבם: גדול המלוה. לפי שאין העני בוש בדבר: ומטיל בכיס. מעות ומלאי להשתכר בהן למחצית שכר ואיידי דאיירי רבי אבא אמר ריש לקיש נקט כל הני מילי דאגדתא דאמר להו ר' אבא משמיה: חוגרו. הדבק בו שסופך ליהנות מתלמודו: אל תדור בשכונתו. שאינו יודע בדקדוקי מצות ואין חסידותו שלם וסופך ללמוד ממנו: מונע חסד. שאינו מניח העניים לבא לפתחו: למס. דהיינו כלב: מרעהו

אין בין העוה"ז לימות המשיח. אע"ג דהשתא אין ירושלים ואין בהמ"ק ואילו לימות המשיח יהיה הכל בנוי צ"ל דהאי אין בין לאו דוקא*: ואילו

ביין הרדלי במסב רחב או במסב קצר בחבר טוב או בחבר רע א"ר חסדא וכולן לזנות אמר רחבה אמר רבי יהודה עצי ירושלים של קינמון היו ובשעה שהיו מסיקין מהן ריחן נודף בכל ארץ ישראל ומשחרבה ירושלים נגנזו ולא נשתייר אלא כשעורה ומשתכח בגנזאי דצימצמאי מלכתא:

מתני' לא יצא האיש לא בסייף ולא בקשת ולא *בתריס ולא באלה ולא ברומח ואם יצא חייב חטאת רבי אליעזר אומר תכשיטין הן לו וחכ"א אינן אלא לגנאי שנאמר °וכתתו חרבותם לאתים וחניתותיהם למזמרות *ולא ישא גוי אל גוי חרב ולא ילמדו עוד מלחמה בירית טהורה ויוצאין בה בשבת כבלים טמאים ואין יוצאין בהן בשבת: **גמ'** *מאי באלה *קולפא: ר' אליעזר אומר תכשיטין הן לו: תניא אמרו לו לרבי אליעזר וכי מאחר דתכשיטין הן לו מפני מה הן בטלין לימות המשיח אמר להן לפי שאינן צריכין שנאמר °לא *ישא גוי אל גוי חרב ותהוי לנוי בעלמא אמר אביי מידי דהוה *אשרגא בטיהרא ופליגא דשמואל דאמר שמואל *אין בין העולם הזה לימות המשיח אלא שיעבוד גליות בלבד שנאמר °כי לא יחדל אביון מקרב הארץ מסייע ליה לרבי חייא בר אבא דא"ר חייא בר אבא כל הנביאים לא נתנבאו אלא לימות המשיח אבל לעולם הבא °עין לא ראתה אלהים זולתך ואיכא דאמרי אמרו לו לר' אליעזר וכי מאחר דתכשיטין הן לו מפני מה הן בטלין לימות המשיח אמר להן אף לימות המשיח אינן בטלין היינו דשמואל ופליגא דר' חייא בר אבא א"ל אביי לרב דימי ואמרי לה לרב אויא ואמרי לה רב יוסף לרב דימי ואמרי לה לרב אויא ואמרי לה אביי לרב יוסף מ"ט דר"א דאמר תכשיטין הן לו דכתיב °חגור חרבך על ירך גבור הודך והדרך א"ל רב כהנא למר בריה *דרב הונא האי בדברי תורה כתיב א"ל *אין מקרא יוצא מידי פשוטו א"ר כהנא כד הוינא בר תמני סרי שנין והוה גמירנא ליה לכוליה הש"ס ולא הוה ידענא דאין מקרא יוצא מידי פשוטו עד השתא מאי קמ"ל דליגמר איניש והדר ליסבר: סימן זרות: א"ר ירמיה א"ר אלעזר שני תלמידי חכמים המחדדין זה לזה בהלכה הקב"ה מצליח להם שנאמר °והדרך צלח אל תקרי והדרך אלא וחדדך ולא עוד אלא שעולין לגדולה שנאמר °צלח רכב יכול אפילו שלא לשמה תלמוד לומר °על דבר אמת יכול אם הגיס דעתו ת"ל °וענוה צדק ואם עושין כן זוכין לתורה שניתנה בימין שנאמר °ותורך נוראות ימינך רב נחמן בר יצחק אמר זוכין לדברים שנאמרו בימינה של תורה דאמר רבא בר רב שילא ואמרי לה אמר רב יוסף בר חמא א"ר ששת מאי דכתיב °אורך ימים בימינה בשמאלה עושר וכבוד אלא בימינה אורך ימים איכא עושר וכבוד ליכא אלא למיימינין בה אורך ימים איכא וכ"ש עושר וכבוד למשמאילים בה עושר וכבוד איכא אורך ימים ליכא א"ר ירמיה אמר ר' שמעון בן לקיש שני תלמידי חכמים הנוחין זה לזה בהלכה הקדוש ברוך הוא מקשיב להן שנאמר °אז נדברו יראי ה' וגו' *אין דיבור אלא נחת שנאמר °ידבר עמים תחתינו *מאי ולחושבי שמו א"ר אמי אפילו חישב לעשות מצוה ונאנס ולא עשאה מעלה עליו הכתוב כאילו עשאה א"ר חיננא בר אידי כל העושה מצוה כמאמרה אין מבשרין אותו בשורות רעות שנאמר °שומר מצוה לא ידע דבר רע א"ר אסי ואיתימא ר' חנינא אפילו הקב"ה *גוזר גזירה הוא מבטלה שנאמר °באשר דבר מלך שלטון ומי יאמר לו מה תעשה וסמיך ליה שומר מצוה לא ידע דבר רע אמר רבי אבא אמר רבי שמעון בן לקיש שני תלמידי חכמים המקשיבים זה לזה בהלכה הקדוש ב"ה שומע לקולן שנאמר °היושבת בגנים חברים מקשיבים לקולך השמיעני ואם אין עושין כן גורמין לשכינה שמסתלקת מישראל שנאמר °ברח דודי ודמה וגו' אמר רבי אבא א"ר שמעון בן לקיש שני ת"ח *המדגילים זה לזה בהלכה הקדוש ברוך הוא אוהבן שנאמר °ודגלו עלי אהבה אמר רבא והוא דידעי צורתא דשמעתא *והוא דלית להו רבה במתא למיגמר מיניה (*א"ר) אבא א"ר שמעון בן לקיש גדול המלוה יותר מן העושה צדקה *ומטיל בכיס יותר מכולן (*א"ר) אבא אמר ר' שמעון בן לקיש אם תלמיד חכם נוקם ונוטר כנחש הוא חגריהו על מתניך אם עם הארץ הוא חסיד אל תדור בשכונתו אמר רב כהנא אמר רבי שמעון בן לקיש ואמרי לה אמר רב אסי אמר (*ריש לקיש) ואמרי לה אמר רבי אבא אמר רבי שמעון בן לקיש כל המגדל כלב רע בתוך ביתו מונע חסד מתוך ביתו שנאמר °למס מרעהו

מט א מיי' פי"ט מהל' שבת הלכה א סמג לאוין סה טוש"ע א"ח סי' ש"א סעיף ז:

נ ב מיי' פי"ב מהל' מלכים הלכה ב:

נא ג מיי' פ"ח מהל' תשובה הלכה ז:

[ועי' תוס' תענית יג: ד"ה מאי שייר ותוס' מגילה ח: ד"ה אין בין ומ"ש שם על הגליון]

נב ד מיי' פ"י מהל' מ"ע הלכה ח טוש"ע י"ד סי' רמט סעיף ו:

נג ה מיי' פ"ו מהל' דעות הלכה א ב:

[פי' שבט שמכין בו וראשו עב]

[במיכה כתיב ישאו] חולין ס:

נד ו מיי' פי"א מהל' רוצח הלכה ד:

[יבמות יא: כד.]

גליון הש"ס

גמ' אלא שעבוד גליות. עי' פסחים נ ע"ב.

[עי' תוס' ע"ז כב: ד"ה רגלא וכו' שהביאו אפירוש רש"י דהכא]

[נ"ל וא"ר]

[נ"ל וא"ר]

איוב ו

פי' מגן

נ"ל לא

[גי' הערוך מאי אלה קופל פי' דומה למקל וכו' וראשו עגול כמו כדור וכו' ע"ש]

ברכות לד: לקמן קנא: פסחים סח. סנהדרין צט.

י"ל דרבינא

הגהות הב"ח

(א) רש"י ד"ה ותורך ותלמדך כס"ד ואח"כ מ"ה עושר וכבוד וכו' עושר וכבוד הס"ד ואח"כ מ"ה למיימינין בה שמפשפשין כצ"ל ותיבת של תורה נמחק ונ"ב ע"ל בדף פח ע"ב:

מכות יא.

ברכות ו. קדושין מ. ע"ש

[מ"ק טז: ב"מ פה.]

[עתו' ע"ז שם]

פסחים נג:

[נ"ל ר' שמעון בן לקיש]

מרעהו חסד °שכן בלשון יונית קורין לכלב למס רב נחמן בר יצחק אמר אף פורק ממנו יראת שמים שנאמר °ויראת שדי יעזוב ההיא *איתתא דעיילא להו‍א ביתא למיפא נבח בה כלבא איתעקר ולדה אמר לה מרי דביתא לא תידחלי דשקילי ניביה ושקילין טופריה אמרה ליה *שקולא טיבותיך ושדיא אחיזרי כבר נד ולד אמר רב הונא מאי דכתיב °שמח בחור בילדותך ויטיבך לבך בימי בחורותיך והלך בדרכי לבך ובמראה עיניך ודע כי על כל אלה יביאך האלהים במשפט עד כאן דברי יצר הרע מכאן ואילך דברי יצר טוב ריש לקיש אמר °עד כאן לדברי תורה מכאן ואילך למעשים טובים: *בירית טהורה: אמר רב יהודה בירית זו אצעדה מתיב רב יוסף בירית טהורה ויוצא בה בשבת ואילו אצעדה טמאה היא ה"ק בירית תחת אצעדה עומדת יתיב רבין ורב הונא °קמיה דרב ירמיה ויתיב רב ירמיה וקא מנמנם ויתיב רבין וקאמר בירית באחת כבלים בשתים א"ל רב הונא אלו ואלו בשתים ומטילין שלשלת ביניהן. ונעשו כבלים ושלשלת שבו משויא ליה מנא וכ"ת כרבי שמואל בר נחמני *דאמר רבי שמואל בר נחמני א"ר *יוחנן מניין למשמיע קול בכלי מתכות שהוא טמא שנאמר °כל דבר אשר יבא באש אפילו דיבור במשמע בשלמא התם קא בעו לה לקלא וקעביד מעשה הכא מאי מעשה קעביד הכא נמי קא עביד מעשה דאמר רבה בר בר חנה א"ר יוחנן משפחה אחת היתה בירושלים שהיו פסיעותיהן גסות והיו בתולותיהן נושרות עשו להן כבלים והטילו שלשלת ביניהן שלא יהיו פסיעותיהן גסות ולא היו בתולותיהן נושרות איתער בהו ר' ירמיה אמר להו *יישר וכן א"ר יוחנן כי אתא רב דימי א"ר יוחנן מניין לאריג כל שהוא שהוא טמא מציץ א"ל אביי וציץ אריג הוא והתניא *ציץ [ב]כמין טס של זהב ורוחב שתי אצבעות ומוקף מאוזן לאוזן וכתוב עליו בב' שיטין יו"ד ה"א למעלה וקודש למ"ד למטה ואמר ר' אליעזר בר' יוסי אני ראיתיו בעיר רומי וכתוב קדש לה' בשיטה אחת כי סליק רב דימי לנהרדעא שלח להו *דברים שאמרתי לכם טעות הם בידי ברם כך אמרו משום רבי יוחנן מניין לתכשיט כ"ש שהוא טמא מציץ ומניין לאריג כ"ש שהוא טמא °מאו בגד תנו רבנן [ג]אריג כ"ש טמא ותכשיט כ"ש טמא אריג ותכשיט כ"ש טמא מוסף שק על הבגד שטמא משום אריג אמר רבא אריג כל שהוא טמא מאו בגד תכשיט כל שהוא טמא מציץ אריג ותכשיט כל שהוא טמא °מכל כלי מעשה א"ל ההוא מרבנן לרבא ההוא במדין כתיב א"ל גמר כלי כלי

איוב ו | קהלת יא | במדבר לא | ויקרא יא | במדבר לא

תורה אור

מרעהו. מונע חסד ואע"ג דלא כתיב מונע ממילא משמע שכל תיבה שראשה מ"ם משמשת נטילה יהא כמו ויקח מידם (שמות לב) אבדו גוים מארצו (תהלים י): למיפא. לאפות עיסה שהשאיל בעה"ב תנורו: שקילי ניבי. נטולות ד' שיניו שהוא נושך בהן אותן שיניים קרי ניבין כדאמרינן באלו טרפות (חולין דף נט.) גמל ניבי אית ליה: שקילי טופריה. נטולות לפרניו מלסרוט: שקולא. נטולה טובתך ומוטלת על הקוצים: טיבותיך. טובת הנאת נחמתך כמו מחזיק טוב הגרי"א בלע"ז: עד כאן. עד ודע כי על כל אלה וגו': עד כאן לתורה. שמח בתלמודך למוד משמחה ומטוב לב והלך בדרכי לבך להבין מה בלבך לפי ראות עיניך: מכאן ואילך למעשים טובים. ודע כי על כל אלה על כל מה שלמדת סופך ליתן את הדין אם לא תקיים: אצעדה. של זרוע: ואילו אצעדה טמאה היא. דכתיב (במדבר לא) במעשה מדין אצעדה וצמיד וגו' וכתיב תתחטאו אתם ושביכם: תחת אצעדה. שבזרוע עומדת בשוק להחזיק בתי שוקיה שלא יפלו ויראו שוקיה הלכך טהורה דלאו לנוי היא וכלי תשמיש נמי לא הוי אלא כלי המשמש כלי דומיא דטבעות הכלים דאמרינן בפרקין דלעיל דטהורין ויוצאין בהם דצורך לבישה היא ומישלף ואחויי נמי ליכא למיחש דלא מיגליא לשוקה: בירית באחת. משוקיה: ושלשלת משוי להו מנא. בתמיה דקתני כבלים טמאים: וכי תימא כדר' שמואל כו': משמיע קול בכלי מתכות. בריש פרקין: ועשו להן שלשלת כו'. הלכך שלשלת תשמיש אדם הוא ולאו תשמיש כלי דלא תקבל טומאה ואין יוצאין בהן דילמא שלפא לשלשלת שהיא של זהב ומחויא דכי שקלה לשלשלת לא מיגליא שוקה שהרי בירית במקומה עומדת: יישר וכן אמר ר' יוחנן. יפה אמרת וכן שמעתי מר' יוחנן: מנין. שהוא דבר מועט ומנאו עם תכשיטי כהן: יו"ד ה"א מלמעלה קדש למ"ד מלמטה. כלומר השם שלם בשיטה עליונה וקדש למ"ד בשיטה תחתונה שלא להקדים שאר אותיות למעלה מן השם מאחר ששני שיטין היו ורבינו הלוי שונה *קודש לה' מלמטה והיא היא: אני ראיתיו ברומי. שנכנס לאוצר המלך ליטול מה שירצה במס' מעילה (דף יז:) במעשה בן תלמיון: כי סליק רב דימי לנהרדעא. חזר בו ממה שאמר ציץ אריג הוא: מאו בגד. דכתיב גבי שרצים או בגד או עור או ריבוי הוא: אריג ותכשיט כל שהוא. אליו אריג ואליו תכשיט שאינו אריג וכולו הוי כל שהוא כלומר דבר קטן: מוסיף שק על הבגד. בדבר זה שהשק טמא משום אריג ולקמיה מפרש ליה: ההוא במדין כתיב. גבי טומאת מת ושרץ ממת לא יליף להחמיר דמה למת שכן טומאתו חמורה: כלי

ואילו אצעדה טמאה היא. פ"ה דכתיב במעשה מדין אצעדה וצמיד וגו' וכתיב תתחטאו אתם ושביכם ולא נהירא דע"כ תתחטאו לא אכל השבי קאי דהא בהמות נמי הוו בשבי ולאו בני קבולי טומאה נינהו לכן נ"ל משום דכתיב אצעדה וצמיד וכתיב בתריה ויקח *(מהם) כל כלי מעשה דקאי אכל הכלים שנלקחו ויליפינן לקמן כלי כלי משרצים:

בירית תחת אצעדה עומדת. פי' בקונטרס (א) בשוק להחזיק בתי שוקיה שלא יפלו ויראו שוקיה וקשה לפי' זה דא"כ בכבלים אמאי אין יוצאין למאי דס"ד השתא דאין חילוק בין בירית לכבלים אלא שזה באחת וזה בשתים לכן נ"ל דאפשר ליטלן בלא גילוי שוקים ומש"ה כבלים אין יוצאין בהן דילמא שלפא ומחויא דתכשיט לנוי הם אבל בירית שהיא באחת לא שלפא ומחויא דאין זה תכשיט דכיון שאין לה אלא באחת גנאי היא לה ומש"ה ניחא דבירית טהורה דלאו תכשיט לנוי הוא וכלי תשמיש נמי לא הוי אלא כלי המשמש כלי דומיא דטבעת הכלי דאמר לעיל דטהור וכן פירש הקונטרס וטעמא דכבלים טמאים משום דתכשיט הם לנוי כדפי': וכתוב עליו בשני שיטין יו"ד ה"א מלמעלה וקדש למ"ד למטה. נראה לר"ת שהיה כתוב יו"ד ה"א בסוף שיטה ראשונה וקדש ל' בתחלת שיטה שניה והשתא נקרא יפה ואין לפרש כמשמעו דא"כ אינו נקרא כהלכתו: מניין לאריג כל שהוא שהוא טמא ת"ל או בגד. וא"ת והא לעיל בפרק במה מדליקין (דף כו: ושם) לא מרבינן אלא ג' על ג' וי"ל דהתם איירי בבא מבגד גדול אבל הכא איירי באריג כל שהוא דמתחלה לא היה דעתו להוסיף עליו ותרוייהו שמעינן מאו בגד דשקולים הם דחשיב כל שהוא אריג מתחלה כמו ג' על ג' מבגד גדול*וא"ת ואכתי בגד כל שהוא למה הוא טמא והא בעינן שיטלטל מלא וריקן דומיא דשק וי"ל *דראוי הוא לכוף ולקפל וליקח בו מרגלית או מחט ואם תאמר א"כ פשוטי כלי עור אמאי טהורין הרי ראויין הם לקפל בו שום דבר כמו הכא וי"ל דמיירי בעור שלוק שהוא קשה: מניין לתכשיט כל שהוא טמא. ואם תאמר תיפוק ליה דתכשיט כל שהוא טמא מדכתיב בכלי מדין טבעת ויש לומר דאפשר שהטבעת היא עבה וגדולה מאד ולא הוי כל שהוא: אריג ותכשיט. פי' חציו אריג וחציו תכשיט טמא מכאן משמע דמ"מ בעינן שיעור קצת דאל"כ חציו דכ"ש מאי הוי: ההוא במדין כתיב. פ"ה ובמדין הויא טומאת מת ושרץ ממת לא יליף להחמיר דמה למת שכן טומאה חמורה ומשני גמר כלי כלי משרץ פירוש מה כלי האמור בשרץ מטמא בשרץ אף כלי האמור כאן מטמא בשרץ וקשה דא"כ הוה ליה למיפרך ההוא בטומאת מת כתיב ועוד כי משני גמר כלי כלי הוה ליה לשויי גמר בגד ועור לג"ש לכן נ"ל דההוא במדין כתיב בשלל מדין ולא מיירי הך פרשה בטומאה כלל והיכי יליף דאריג ותכשיט כל שהוא טמא מכל כלי מעשה ומשני גמר כלי כלי פי' כי היכי דלכי דכתיב גבי שרצים מיירי לענין טומאה הכי נמי כלי דכתיב גבי מדין לענין טומאה: מניין

עין משפט נר מצוה

נה א מיי' פ"ט מהל' שבת הלכה ה ומיי' פ"ט מהל' כלים הלכה ד סמג לאוין סה טוש"ע א"ח סי' שג סעיף טו: [צ"ל מאתם]

נו ב מיי' פ"ט מהל' כלי המקדש הלכה א סמג עשין קעג:

נז ג מיי' פ"א מהל' כלים הלכה יא ופכ"ב הלכה א:

רבינו חננאל

בירית זו אצעדה. אוקימנא בשתי ירכות בלא שלשלת נקראת בירית. ואם יש בהן שלשלת נקרא כבלים. הא דתניא ציץ דומה כמין טס של זהב רחב ב' אצבעות ומוקף מאוזן לאוזן וכתוב עליו בב' שיטין יו"ד ה"א מלמעלה קדש למ"ד מלמטה. א"ר אלעזר בר' יוסי אני ראיתיו ברומי כו':

לעיל נז:

[פי' תוס' לעיל כו. ד"ה אין בו וכו']

[לעיל נג. ברכות מב: עירובין לג: פסחים נג: ב"מ נה. סנהדרין ק. שבועות מ. מה: חולין יז: עה: עו:]

סוכה ה.

[ברכות לו: עירובין טו: קד. יבמות כ: טו. ב"ב קכו. קלא. סנהדרין סא. מכות ח: זבחים לד. מנחות יב: לג. חולין ט. נדה סח.]

רב נסים גאון

אמר ר' אלעזר בר' יוסי אני ראיתיו ברומי וכתוב עליו קודש לה' בשיטה אחת. ותניא כוותיה במס' יומא בפ' הוציאו לו את הכף (דף מ) אמר ר' אלעזר בר' יוסי אני ראיתיה ברומי והיו עליה כמה טיפי דמים והדבר שגרם לו לצאת לרומי מפורש במס' מעילה בפ' קדשי מזבח (דף יז) שאל ר' מתיה בן חרש את ר' שמעון בן יוחי ברומי מניין לדם שרצים שהוא טמא אמר ליה דאמר קרא וזה לכם הטמא אמרו לו תלמידיו (גזר עליו) [חכים ליה] רשב"י אמר להם תלמוד ערוך הוא מפיו של ר' אלעזר בר' יוסי פעם אחת גזרה מלכות הרשעה גזרה על ישראל שלא ישמרו את השבת ושלא ימולו בניהם ושיבעלו נשותיהם כשהן נדות הלך ר' ראובן בן איצטרובולי וספר קומוי והלך וישב עמהם אמר להם מי שיש לו אויב רוצה שיעשיר או שיעני אמרו לו יעני אמר להן אם כן לא יעשו מלאכה בשבת כדי שיענו אמרו לו טבות אמר ובטלוה חזר ואמר להן מי שיש לו אויב יכחיש או יבריא אמרו לו יכחיש אמר אם כן ימלו בניהם לח' ימים כדי שיכחישו אמרו טבות אמר ובטלוה חזר ואמר מי שיש לו אויב ירבה או ימעיט אמרו ימעיט אמר להם (לא) אם כן לא יבעלו נשותיהם כשהן נדות ובטלוה הכירו בו שהוא יהודי החזירום אמרו מי ילך ויבטל את הגזירה ילך ר' שמעון בן יוחי שהוא מלומד בנסים וילך עמו ר' אלעזר בר' יוסי וכו' על לבי גזא אשכחוה להוא אגרתא שקלוה וקרעוה והיינו דאמר ר' אלעזר אני ראיתיה ברומי והיו עליה כמה טיפי דמים ובתוספ' מקואות (פרק ד) אמר ר' אלעזר בר' יוסי הלכה זו הוריתי ברומי לטהרה וכשבאתי אצל חברי אמרו לי יפה הוריתה ובמס' נדה בפ' הרואה כתם (דף נח) תניא כוותיה אמר ר' אלעזר בר' יוסי הלכה זו כו':

הציונא

מסורת הש"ס

ב"ק סג.

[כילה כט: כתובות נג. בבא קמא סג. ב"מ סג:]

[עם אי' יונתן]

קודש מלמטה לה' מלמעלה כצ"ל וכ"כ הרמב"ם בפ"ט מהל' כה"מ וגם בי' ירושלמי פי' ורף יקוהי נוטה כך

הגהות הב"ח

(א) תוס' ד"ה בירית וכו' פי' בקונט' עומדת פסוק:

גליון הש"ס

גמ' שכן בל' יונית. וכן סוטה לה ע"ב וסנהדרין ע"ב טס בכתפי שמים וכו': שם עד לדברי תורה. עי' ערכין יא ע"א תוס' ד"ה ממשה: שם קמיה דר' ירמיה ויתיב ר"י וקא מנמנם. גיטין יא ע"ב ונדרים כט ע"ב: תוס' ד"ה מנין לאריג. דראוי הוא לכוף. ק"ל ממתני' פ' כ"ו מ"ב דכלים לצור המרגלית ועי' ברמב"ם ור"ש שם והכי מ"מ הוא בכלל אפשר לקפל ולהניח בו מעות כמקדש. ולע"ג:

kindness should be shewed from his friend;[5] and in Greek a dog is called *lamos.*[6] R. Naḥman b. Isaac said: He also casts off the fear of Heaven from himself, as it is said, *and he forsaketh the fear of the Almighty.*[7]

A certain woman entered a house to bake. The dog barked at her, [whereupon] her child[8] moved [from its place]. Said the householder to her, 'Fear not: his fangs and claws have been extracted.' 'Take your favours and throw them on the thorns,' she retorted, 'the child has already moved.'

R. Huna said: What is meant by the verse, *Rejoice, O young man, in thy youth; and let thy heart cheer thee in the days of thy youth, and walk in the ways of thine heart, and in the sight of thine eyes: but know thou, that for all these things God will bring thee into judgement?*[9] Thus far are the words of Evil Desire; thereafter are the words of Good Desire.[10] Resh Lakish said: Thus far the reference is to study;[11] thereafter, to good deeds.[12]

a A BERITH IS CLEAN. Rab Judah said: A *berith* is a bracelet.[1] R. Joseph objected: A BERITH IS CLEAN, AND ONE MAY GO OUT WITH IT ON THE SABBATH; but a bracelet is [liable to become] unclean?—He meant this: A *berith* stands in the place of a bracelet.[2]

Rabin and R. Huna were sitting before R. Jeremiah, and R. Jeremiah was dozing. Now Rabin sat and said: A *berith* is on one [leg]; whilst *kebalim* [ankle-chain] is on two.[3] Said R. Huna to him, Both are on two, but a chain is placed between them and they become *kebalim* [anklets]. Does then the chain turn it into a utensil?[4] And should you answer, This is in accordance with R. Samuel b. Naḥmani, for R. Samuel b. Naḥmani said in R. Jonathan's name: How do we know that a metal object which causes sound is unclean? Because it is said: *Everything* [dabar] *that may abide the fire,* [*ye shall make go through the fire:*][5] even speech [*dibbur*—i.e., sound] is implied;[6]—As for there, it is well: it [the utensil] is needed for sound[7] and it performs an action;[8] but here, what action does it perform?[9]—Here too it performs an action, for Rabbah b. Bar Ḥanah said in R. Joḥanan's name: There was a certain family in Jerusalem that had large steps, whereby their virginity was destroyed. So they made them leg-suspenders and placed a chain between them, that their steps should not be large, and then their virginity was not destroyed. R. Jeremiah awoke at that and exclaimed to them, Well spoken![10] and thus did R. Joḥanan say [too].

When R. Dimi came,[11] he said in the name of R. Joḥanan: How do we know that woven [material] of whatever size is [liable to
b become] unclean? From the *ẓiẓ.*[1] Said Abaye to him, Was then the *ẓiẓ* woven? But it was taught: The *ẓiẓ* was a kind of golden plate two fingerbreadths broad, and it stretched round [the forehead] from ear to ear, and upon it was written in two lines '*yod he*' above and 'Holy *lamed*' below.[2] But R. Eliezer son of R. Jose said: I saw it in the city of Rome,[3] and 'Holy unto the Lord' was written in one line.[4] When R. Dimi went up to Nehardea, he sent word: The things that I told you were erroneous. But in truth it was thus said on R. Joḥanan's authority: How do we know that an ornament of whatever size is [liable to become] unclean? From the headplate. And how do we know that woven material of whatever size is unclean? From [the phrase] *or raiment.*[5]

Our Rabbis taught: Woven stuff of whatever size is unclean, and an ornament of whatever size is unclean. [An object partly] woven and [partly] an ornament of whatever size is unclean.[6] A sack goes beyond a garment, in that it is unclean as woven material.[7] Raba said: Woven stuff of whatever size is unclean: this is [deduced] from, '*or raiment*'. An ornament of whatever size is unclean: [this is learnt] from the headplate. [An object partly] woven and [partly] an ornament of whatever size is unclean: this is [deduced] from, *every serviceable utensil.*[8] Said one of the Rabbis to Raba, But that is written in reference to Midian?[9]

(5) Job. VI, 14. (6) Perhaps from the Gk. λαιμός. Thus he translates: on account of a (wild) dog, love is kept back from one's neighbour. (7) Ibid. (8) She was pregnant. (9) Eccl. XI, 9. (10) From '*Rejoice*' to '*thine eyes*' is spoken by the Tempter (sin personified), urging man to sin; 'but know thou, etc.' is the warning of Good Desire, man's better nature (Rashi). Maharsha explains it differently. (11) Lit., 'the words of the Torah'. (12) Rejoice in your youth, when you can study, and apply your heart and eyes, i.e., your full understanding, to same. But know that you will be judged for nonfulfilment of the precepts learned by you in your studies.

a (1) For the hand. (2) It corresponds to a bracelet, i.e., the bracelet encircles the arm while the *berith* encircles the foot. (3) V. Krauss, *T.A.* I, pp. 205 and 665 (n. 977) on these terms. (4) That it is susceptible to uncleanness, as taught in the Mishnah. Surely not! (5) Num. XXXI, 23. (6) V. *supra* 58*b* for notes. (7) E.g., a bell. (8) Viz., it makes a sound. (9) Though, of course, it holds up the stockings, that does not make it a utensil, which must serve an independent function, whereas this is merely an adjunct, as it were, to the stockings. (10) Lit., (with כח understood) 'thy strength be well.' (11) V. *supra* 5*a*, n. b9.

b (1) The headplate worn by the High Priest, v. Ex. XXVIII, 36ff. Though quite small, it was counted among the High Priest's adornments, and was therefore susceptible to uncleanness. (2) I.e., the Divine Name on the upper line and 'Holy unto' on the lower line. (3) Whither it was taken after the destruction of the Temple. (4) From this Baraitha we see that the *ẓiẓ* was not of woven material. (5) Lev. XI, 32. '*Or*' is an extension. (6) Tosaf. observes that this implies that nevertheless some minimum is required in the size of woven material and ornaments. (7) This is explained below. (8) Num. XXXI, 51 (E.V.: *all wrought jewels*). (9) Which treats of defilement through the dead. Such is graver than uncleanness through dead reptiles (*sheraẓim*), which it is sought to prove here.

Novellae of Hagaon Rabbi Moshe Feinstein o.b.m.

Shabbath

63b. בתוה"ה **Tos. s.v. [An object partly] woven and [partly] an ornament. From here, it appears that a certain small amount is required; otherwise, what is half of 'whatever size'?** This reasoning does not appear conclusive, because a woven fabric of whatever size is (susceptible to uncleanness) only when it is a whole garment. If it is not a whole garment, we require an area of three fingerbreadths by three fingerbreadths, as stated in *Tos.* s.v. מנין , that a woven object of whatever size is susceptible to uncleanness only if he does not intend to add to it. The same is found in *Rambam, Hilkoth Kelim,* 22:1. Therefore, a whole garment that was not made entirely of woven fabric, only half of it, and it was not entirely an ornament, only half of it, (should not be susceptible to uncleanness) for the derivation of the ornament is from *ziz,* which was a complete object. Accordingly, because of the woven fabric, alone, it would not be susceptible to uncleanness since it does not measure three fingerbreadths by three fingerbreadths, and because of the ornament alone, it would not be susceptible to uncleanness, since it was not made into a complete object. We, therefore, require a third verse to teach us that it is regarded as a complete object through a combination of both together, that if half is woven and half is an ornament, it is susceptible to uncleanness. This appears to be the only explanation of the Gemara. Hence, the evidence brought by the Tosafists is inconclusive, because even if there is no measure at all for the woven fabric and the ornament, that is only if there is a complete object. Therefore, we need a verse to declare unclean an object that is partly woven and partly an ornament if the object is not complete with the weaving along or with the ornament alone, only with the combination of both, that this also is susceptible to uncleanness. In summation, this statement of Tosafoth requires much deliberation.

We learn [64*a*] the meaning of '*utensil*' [here] from [the employment of] '*utensil*' there, answered he.[10]

'A sack goes beyond a garment, in that it is unclean as woven material.' Is then a garment not woven material?—This is its meaning: A sack goes beyond a garment, for though it is not of
a woven material, yet it is unclean.[1] For what is it fit?—Said R. Joḥanan: A poor man plaits three threads [of goats' hair][2] and suspends it from his daughter's neck.

Our Rabbis taught: [*And upon whatsoever any of them ... doth fall, it shall be unclean; whether it be any vessel of wood ... or*] *sack:*[3] I know it only of a sack:[4] how do we know to include a horse cover and the saddle band?[5] Therefore it is said, '*or sack*'.[6] I might think that I can include ropes and cords;[7] therefore '*sack*' is stated: just as a sack is spun and woven, so must everything be spun and woven.[8] Now, concerning the dead it is stated, *and all that is made of skin, and all work of goats' hair ... ye shall purify yourselves:*[9] this is to include a horse cover and the saddle band.[10] I might think that I can include ropes and cords. (But it [the reverse] is logical:[11] [the Divine Law] teaches defilement by a dead reptile, and it teaches defilement by the dead: just as when it teaches defilement by a reptile, it declares unclean only that which is spun and woven; so when it teaches defilement by the dead, it declares unclean only that which is spun and woven. How so! If it is lenient in respect
b to defilement through a reptile, which is lighter, shall we be lenient[1] in respect to defilement by the dead, which is graver?)[2] Therefore '*raiment and skin*' is stated twice, to provide a *gezerah shawah.*[3] Thus: *raiment and skin* are mentioned in connection with reptiles,[4] and also in connection with the dead:[5] just as the '*raiment and skin*' which are mentioned in connection with reptiles, it [Scripture] declares unclean only that which is spun and woven, so the '*raiment and skin*' which are stated in connection with the dead, it declares unclean only that which is spun and woven;[6] and just as '*raiment and skin*' which are stated in connection with the dead, anything made of goats' hair is unclean, so '*raiment and skin*' which are stated in connection with reptiles, anything made of goats' hair is unclean.[7] Now, I know it only of that which comes from goats: how do I know to include what is produced from the tail of a horse or a cow? Therefore it is stated, '*or sack*'.[8] (But you have utilized it in respect of a horse cover and saddle bands?—That was only before the *gezerah shawah* was adduced; but now that we have the *gezerah shawah*, it [*sc.* the '*or*'] is superfluous.)[9] And I know this only in the case of a reptile: how do we know it in respect to defilement by the dead? But it is logical:[10] [Scripture] declares uncleanness through the dead, and also declares uncleanness through reptiles: just as when it declares uncleanness through the dead, it treats that which is produced from the tail of a horse or cow as that which is made of goats' hair, so when it declares uncleanness through the dead, it treats that which

(10) Concerning defilement by dead reptiles it is written, *every* utensil *wherewith any* work *is done* (Lev. XI, 32), and the meaning of '*utensil*' is learnt from '*utensil*' mentioned in connection with the dead, where ornaments are referred to. Tosaf. explains the passage differently: But that.. Midian, i.e., it treats of the spoil of Midian and has no bearing upon uncleanness at all? To which Raba replied that as 'utensil' in Lev. XI, 32 refers to uncleanness, so 'utensil' in Num. XXXI, 51 provides a teaching on uncleanness, notwithstanding that this does not appear so from the context.

a (1) The words are explained: ... it is unclean as woven material though it is not woven.—By 'sack' a few plaited strands of goats' hair is meant. (2) Which are first spun. (3) Lev. XI, 32.—The reference is to defilement by dead reptiles (*sheraẓim*). (4) Which is usually worn by shepherds. (5) The band with which the saddle or housing of a horse is fastened to its belly. Others: the housing itself. It was made of goats' hair spun and woven. (6) '*Or*' is an extension. (7) Used for measuring. These were of unspun plaited goats' hair. (8) Before it is susceptible to uncleanness. (9) Num. XXXI, 20. These become unclean through contact with the dead. (10) '*All*' is an extension. (11) This is a parenthesis. A verse will be quoted to show that they are not included, but before that it is parenthetically argued that it is logical *not* to include them, so that no verse for their exclusion is required. But it is shown that logic does not suffice to exclude them, so that a verse is required.

b (1) I.e., shall we deduce a lenient ruling by analogy? (2) Surely not! Hence logic does *not* prove the exclusion of cords and ropes, and therefore a verse is necessary. (3) V. Glos. (4) Lev. XI, 32. (5) Num. XXXI, 51. E.V. *garment.* (6) Though an analogy between the two cannot be drawn, as shown, because the uncleanness of one is graver than that of the other, yet one can deduce *equality* of law through the *gezerah shawah.* (7) Providing it is spun and woven. (8) '*Or*' being an extension. (9) For the susceptibility of a horse cover and a saddle band to uncleanness follows from the *gezerah shawah*, on the same lines as before. (10) V. *supra* n. a11; the same applies here.

◁ *For the continuation of the English translation of this page see overleaf.*

תורה אור

כלי כלי מהתם: מוסף *שק על הבגד שטמא משום אריג: אטו בגד לאו אריג הוא הכי קאמר מוסף שק על הבגד אף על פי שאינו אריג טמא למאי הוי אמר רבי יוחנן שבן עני קולע שלש נימין ותולה בצואר בתו (ויקרא יא) *תנו רבנן °שק אין לי אלא שק [ב]מניין לרבות את הקילקלי ואת החבק ת"ל או שק [ג]יכול שאני מרבה את החבלים ואת המשיחות ת"ל שק מה שק טווי ואריג אף כל טווי (במדבר לא) ואריג הרי הוא אומר במת °וכל כלי עור וכל מעשה עזים וגו' תתחטאו לרבות הקילקלי ואת החבק יכול שאני מרבה את החבלים ואת המשיחות ודין הוא טימא בשרץ וטימא במת מה כשטימא בשרץ לא טימא אלא טווי ואריג אף כשטימא במת לא טימא אלא טווי ואריג הן אם היקל בטמא שרץ שהיא קלה נקיל בטומאת המת שהיא חמורה תלמוד לומר בגד ועור בגד ועור לגזירה (ויקרא יא) שוה נאמר °בגד ועור בשרץ ונאמר (במדבר לא) °בגד ועור במת מה בגד ועור האמור בשרץ לא טימא. אלא טווי ואריג אף בגד ועור האמור במת לא טימא אלא טווי ואריג ומה בגד ועור האמור במת טמא כל מעשה עזים אף בגד ועור האמור בשרץ טמא כל מעשה עזים אין לי אלא דבר הבא מן העזים [ד]מניין לרבות דבר הבא מזנב הסוס ומזנב הפרה תלמוד לומר או שק והא אפיקתיה לקילקלי וחבק הני מילי מקמי דליתיה ג"ש השתא דאתי גזירה שוה אייתור ליה ואין לי אלא בשרץ בטומאת מת מניין ודין הוא טימא במת וטימא בשרץ מה כשטימא בשרץ עשה דבר הבא מזנב הסוס ומזנב הפרה כמעשה עזים אף כשטימא במת עשה דבר הבא מזנב הסוס ומזנב הפרה כמעשה עזים הן אם הרבה בטומאת ערב שהיא מרובה נרבה בטומאת שבעה שהיא מועטת תלמוד לומר בגד ועור בגד ועור לגזירה שוה נאמר בגד ועור בשרץ ונאמר בגד ועור במת מה בגד ועור האמור בשרץ עשה דבר הבא מזנב הסוס ומזנב הפרה כמעשה עזים אף בגד ועור האמור במת עשה דבר הבא מזנב הסוס ומזנב הפרה כמעשה עזים ומופנה דאי לאו מופנה איכא למיפרך מה לשרץ שכן מטמא בבעדשה *לאי אפנויי מופני *)מכדי שרץ איתקש (ויקרא כב) לשכבת זרע דכתיב °איש אשר תצא ממנו שכבת זרע וסמיך ליה איש אשר יגע בכל שרץ וכתיב ביה בשכבת זרע וכל בגד וכל עור אשר יהיה עליו שכבת זרע בגד ועור דכתב רחמנא בשרץ למה לי שמע מינה לאפנויי ואכתי מופנה מצד אחד הוא הניחא למאן דאמר *מופנה מצד אחד למידין ואין משיבין אלא למאן דאמר *למידין ומשיבין מאי איכא למימר דמת (שם) נמי אפנויי מופנה מכדי מת אתקש לשכבת זרע דכתיב °והנוגע בכל טמא נפש או איש אשר תצא ממנו שכבת זרע וכתיב בשכבת זרע וכל בגד וכל (במדבר לא) עור בגד ועור דכתב רחמנא במת למה לי ש"מ לאפנויי: °ונקרב את קרבן ה' איש אשר מצא כלי זהב אצעדה וצמיד טבעת עגיל וכומז א"ר אלעזר *עגיל זה דפוס של דדין כומז זה דפוס של בית הרחם אמר רב יוסף אי הכי היינו דמתרגמינן מחוך דבר המביא לידי גיחוך אמר ליה רבה מגופיה (שם) דקרא ש"מ כומז כאן מקום זימה: °ויקצוף משה על פקודי החיל אמר רב נחמן אמר רבה בר אבוה אמר להן משה לישראל שמא חזרתם לקלקולכם הראשון אמרו לו לא נפקד ממנו איש אמר להן אם כן כפרה למה אמרו לו אם מידי עבירה יצאנו מידי הרהור לא יצאנו מיד ונקרב את קרבן ה' תנא דבי רבי ישמעאל מפני מה הוצרכו ישראל שבאותו הדור כפרה מפני שזנו

*) [ב"ק כה:]

כלי כלי. בשרלים כתיב כל כלי אשר יעשה מלאכה וגו' ומגופיה דקרא דשרלים לא מצי יליף דאשר יעשה מלאכה לאו כלי תכשיט משמע: שק. הוא עשוי מנולה של עזים שאף על פי שאינו אריג אלא קלע קטן עשה מנולה של עזים להלות בו בתי נפש לנואר בתו טמא שדרכו בכך ותכשיט הוא וה"ק שהוא טמא משום אריג ואע"פ שאינו אריג: קולע ג' נימין כו'. ג' חוטין של מטוה של נולה של עזים לבועה: ותולה בלואר בתו. וקליעתה זו היא אריגתו מאחר שהוא טווי כדאמרן גבי תיכי חלילתא בריש פירקין דקרי להו אריג והא דקאמר אע"פ שאינו אריג כלומר לאו אריג ממש: אין לי אלא שק. העשוי ללבוש רועים: קילקלי. משרך של סוס שקורין פייטרא"ל: חבק. ליגולא של סרגא ואוכף ועושין אותה מנולה של עזים טווי ואריג: יכול שאני מרבה החבלים והמשיחות. נ"ל שעושין למדוד וקולעין מן הנולה כמו שנתלשה ואינו טווי ולא דמי לקולע שלש נימין דלעיל דהתם טווי הוא וזו היא אריגתו: יכול שאני מרבה כו'. הואיל וכתיב כל: ודין הוא שלא נרבה. ולא לריך קרא למעוטי: הן. תמיה הוא וכי דברים כוונים הם: אם היקל בטומאת שרץ שהיא קלה. כלומר אם היקל מלטמא חבלים ומשיחות היקל לך בשרץ שטומאתו קלה טומאת ערב: נקל. גם אנחנו בבנין אב זה במת שטומאתו חמורה טומאת ז': השתא דהתיא גזירה שוה. וכי היכי דיליף מת משרץ למעוטי חבלים ומשיחות יליף נמי שרץ ממת לכל מעשה עזים לרבות קילקלי וחבק: אין לי אלא בשרץ. דאו שק התם כתיב: אם ריבה. לטמא דבר הבא מזנב הסוס בטומאת ערב הוא דריבה: שהיא מרובה. שכל המגעות טומאת ערב הן בין דשרץ ונבילה ושכבת זרע מגע הזב ומגע טמא מת: נרבה אנו בטומאת ז' שכן מועטת היא. שאינה בכל המגעות אלא במגע המת בלבד: מופנה. לריך שתהא גזירה שוה זו מב' תיבות דבגד ועור מופנין למדרש זה שלא יהו לריכין לגופן ומאחר שמופנין ללמוד גזירה שוה ה"ל כמאן דכתיב דרשא בקרא בהדיא ואין משיבין עליה: דאי לאו מופנה. אמרינן לגופן באו ולא ילפינן להא מילתא מינייהו: דאיכא למיפרך כו'. וה"ה דמלי למימר הכי אגזירה שוה קמייתא ומיהו אסקי לכולה ברייתא ברישא ופריך אהא דסליק מינה ובשינויא דמשנינן בהא מיתרלה נמי קמייתא: לאי. באמת: וכתיב ביה בשכבת זרע. דבגד ועור טמאים הם בו: מלד אחד. הכתובין בשרץ מופנים כדאמרן אבל הכתובין במת אין מופנין: הניחא למ"ד כו'. פלוגתא דרבי ישמעאל ורבנן היא במסכת נדה בהמפלת (דף כב:): אלא למאן דאמר למידין. אם אין תשובה: ומשיבין. אם יש להשיב: מאי איכא למימר. הרי יש להשיב שכן מטמא בכעדשה: והנוגע בכל טמא נפש או איש אשר תלא ממנו שכבת זרע: דפוס של דדין. שמונחות בו: גיחוך. ליצנות: לקלקולכם. של מעשה שטים לזנות את בנות מואב שמא כך עשיתם במדין לכך אתם לריכין קרבן: לא נפקד. לא נחסר מדת יהודית:

מניין לרבות את הקילקלי והחבק. ואם תאמר והא לא מיטלטל מלא וריקן ואי משום דאפשר לקפלה אם אינו עשוי לכך לאו כלום הוא כדאמר לקמן גבי קב הקיטע דאע"ג דיש לו בית קיבול לראש שוקו אם אינו עשוי לקבל טהור וי"ל דהכי נמי לשם כל צורכן הן עשוין מתחלה אך קשה דלעיל פ' במה מדליקין (דף כז: ושם) מפיק דבר הבא מן העזים דמטמא בשרלים מאו בגד וקילקלי וחבק באין מן העזים ומפיק להן הכא מאו שק וע"ק דהתם מרבה לנולה של עזים לג' על ג' ואילו שק שיעורו בד' ואומר ר"י דתרי גווני נולה של עזים הוו והתם מיירי [בדקה] שעושים ממנה בגדים חשובים והלכך איתרבו לשלשה על שלשה כמו שאר בגדים והכא מיירי בנולה גסה שממנה עושין קילקלי וחבק וחבלים ומשיחות ושק: שמע מינה לאפנויי. הקשה ה"ר אליעזר ממיץ כיון דאיתקש שרץ ומת לשכבת זרע א"כ ג"ש דבגד ועור ל"ל דכל מה שיהיה במת ניתן בשכבת זרע וכל מה שיהיה בשכבת זרע ניתן בשרץ וכן להפך דהא קי"ל *דבר הבא מן ההיקש חוזר ומלמד בהיקש חוץ מן הקדשים: מידי הרהור מי יצאנו. וא"ת והא אפילו (א) יפת תואר הותרה להם וי"ל דמכל מקום שייך בה איסור כדאמרינן (קדושין דף כב.) וחשקת בה ולא בחברתה: ובמוך

[זבחים מט:]

פ"כ פ' שמיני

הגהות הב"ח
(א) תוס' ד"ה מידי וכו' אפי' ליקח יפת תואר

[בערוך איתא לאיי ומפרש דלשון יון הוא ע"ש]

[נדה כב:]

[קמן קלב. יבמות ע: עד. נדה כב:]

[מס' מלה]

נח א ב ג ד מיי' פ"א מהל' כלים הלכה יב:

רבינו חננאל

קילקלי. מלשון יון הוא והוא עשוי בגד [(גלוין)] משיער של עזים והוא קשה עשוי להצניע תחת הכרים והכסתות. חבקים כסוי הכסאות (ת"ל) או בגד או עור או שק אין לי אלא] שק בלבד מנין לרבות הקילקלי וחבק ת"ל או שק פי' מרבינן להו מאי כלומר הוה ליה למימר שק. או דכתב רחמנא למה לי לרבויי קילקלי והבק. יכול שאני מרבה חבלים ומשיחין שיטמאו ת"ל שק מה שק טווי ואריג אף כל טווי ואריג הרי הוא אומר במת כל מעשה עזים יכול שאני מרבה חבלים ומשיחים דין הוא טימא בשרץ טימא במת כו'. והדינן ואם היקל בטומאת שרץ שהיא קלה פי' טומאה שרץ קלה היא שהיא טומאת ערב אבל טומאת מת חמורה היא שהיא טומאת שבעה לא נתרבה ת"ל (או) בגד ועור בגד ועור לג"ש נאמר בגד ועור בשרץ ונאמר בגד ועור במת. פי' דין ג"ש ב' פסוקים וכל פסוק ופסוק כתוב מלין שאינן צריכין לפסוק ואין מילין פטין לא נכתבו אלא בתיך פסוקים אלו אלא להון מהם ג"ש להיות כל דין שמפירש באחד מהן שיהא גם השני כמותו וזהו שכתוב בעניננו בגד ועור בשרץ בגד ועור במת וצריכין להיות אלו בגד ועור מופנים בשני הפסוקים. שאם הן בפסוק אחד יתירין כגון שלמדו טומאת בגד ועור בשרץ משכבת זרע ונמצא בגד ועור האמור בשרץ מופנה כגון זה למידין ואם יש פירכא משיבין ופורכין ואם הן אלו פסוקים בגד ועור יתירין בשרץ ובמת למידין במת מן השרץ זהו שמאין במת דבר הבא מזנב הסוס מזנב הפרה כשם שמטמאין בשרץ ואין משיבין ואע"ג דאיכא למפרך ואם ריבה בטומאת שרץ שהיא מרובה. פי' טומאת שרץ (נותנת) [נוהגת] בשמנה שרצים. נרבה טומאת מת שהיא מועטת שאינה אלא במת בלבד ואוקימנא כיון שהן מופנה משני צדדין למידין ואין משיבין. ואלו הדברים הל"מ להדרש בענין הזה מסורת בידי חכמים:

רב נסים גאון

הניחא למאן [דאמר] מופנה מצד א' למדין ואין משיבין אלא למאן דאמר למידין ומשיבין מאי איכא למימר. מחלוקת בין ר' ישמעאל ורבנן ועיקר דילה במס' נדה בפרק המפלת (דף כב) אמר רב יהודה אמר שמואל משום ר' כל גזירה שוה שאינה מופנה כל עיקר אין למידין ממנה מופנה מצד אחד לר' ישמעאל למידין ואין משיבין לרבנן למידין ומשיבין: אמר להם משה לישראל שמא חזרתם לקלקולכם הראשון אמרו לו לא נפקד ממנו איש. במס' יבמות בפרק הבא על יבמתו (דף סא) אמרו ור' שמעון לא נפקד ממנו איש לעבירה ולדבר זה נתכוונו בהם בתשובה זו:

קסבר

Continuation of translation from previous page as indicated by ◁

is produced from the tail of a horse or a cow as that which is made of goats' hair. How so! If it [Scripture] includes [this] in defilement until evening, which is extensive, shall *we* include [it] in
c seven days' defilement, which is limited?[1] Therefore *'raiment and skin'* are stated twice, to provide a *gezerah shawah*. *'Raiment and skin'* are stated in connection with reptiles, and *'raiment and skin'* are stated also in connection with the dead; just as *'raiment and skin'* which are stated in connection with reptiles, that which comes from the tail of a horse or cow is treated as that which is made of goats' hair, so *'raiment and skin'* which are stated in connection with the dead, that which is produced from the tail of a horse or cow is treated as that which is made of goats' hair. And this must be redundant.[2] For if it is not redundant, one can refute [the deduction]: as for a reptile, that is because it defiles by the size of a lentil.[3] In truth, it is redundant. For consider: a reptile is likened to semen, for it is written, *a man whose seed goeth from him,*[4] in proximity to which it is written, *or whosoever toucheth any creeping thing;*[5] while in respect to semen it is written, *and every garment and every skin, whereon is*
d *the seed of copulation;*[1] then what is the purpose of *'raiment and skin'* written by the Divine Law in connection with reptiles? Infer from this that its purpose is to leave it redundant.[2] Yet it is still redundant [only] on one side:[3] this is well on the view that where it is redundant on one side we can learn [identity of law] and cannot refute [the deduction]; but on the view that we can learn, but also refute,[4] what can be said?—That [stated] in connection with the dead is also redundant. For consider: the dead is likened to semen, for it is written, *'and whoso toucheth anything that is unclean by the dead, or a man whose seed goeth from him'*; while in respect to semen it is written, *'and every garment and every skin, whereon shall be the seed of copulation'*. What then is the purpose of *'raiment and skin'* written by the Divine Law in connection with the dead? Infer from this that its purpose is to leave it redundant.

And we have brought the Lord's oblation, what every man hath gotten, of jewels of gold, ankle chains, and bracelets, signet-rings, ear-rings, and armlets.[5] R. Eleazar said: *'Agil* is a cast of female breasts; *kumaz* is a cast of the womb. R. Joseph observed: Thus it is that we translate it[6] *maḥok*, [meaning] the place that leads to obscenity [*giḥuk*]. Said Rabbah to him, It is implied in the very Writ itself: *KuMaZ*= here [*Ka'an*] is the place [*Meḳom*] of unchastity [*Zimmah*].[7]

And Moses was wroth with the officers of the host.[8] R. Naḥman said in Rabbah b. Abbuha's name: Moses said to Israel: 'Maybe ye have returned to your first lapse [sin]?'[9] *'There lacketh not one man of us,'*[10] they replied. 'If so,' he queried, 'Why an atonement?' 'Though we escaped from sin,' said they, 'yet we did not escape from meditating upon sin.' Straightway, *'and we have brought the Lord's offering.'*[11] The School of R. Ishmael taught: Why were the

c (1) Uncleanness through a reptile ceases on the evening after the defiled object is subjected to ritual immersion, but uncleanness caused by the dead lasts seven days (v. Lev. XI, 32; Num. XIX, 11 *seq.*). Now, defilement until evening is extensive, in that it can be caused by many agencies, e.g., reptiles, the carcase of an animal (*nebelah*), semen, the touch of a *zab* and the touch of one who is himself unclean through the dead. Therefore it is logical that many objects too shall be susceptible to such uncleanness. But seven days' defilement is limited to the direct action of a corpse; hence it is probable that it does not extend to many objects either. Therefore the fact that what is made from the tail of a horse or cow is subject to defilement by reptiles is no warrant that it is also liable to defilement through the dead. (2) In a *gezerah shawah* the word used as a basis of deduction must be redundant (*mufneh*). Otherwise the deduction may be refuted if a point of known dissimilarity is found between the two subjects which are linked by the *gezerah shawah*. On this redundancy there are two views: (i) the redundancy is required in one passage only; (ii) the redundancy is necessary in both subjects.—There is a third view, that of R. Akiba, that no redundancy at all is required in order to make the deduction conclusive and incapable of being refuted. (3) Whereas the smallest portion of corpse to defile must be the size of an olive. In this matter defilement by a reptile is more stringent, and thus it may also be more stringent in the matter under discussion. (4) Lev. XXII, 4. (5) Ibid. 5. Proximity indicates likeness in law.

d (1) Lev. XV, 17. Thus raiment and skin are defiled by semen, and therefore by reptiles too. (2) For the *gezerah shawah*. (3) I.e., in one of the two passages. (4) V. *infra* 131a, n. b2. (5) Num. XXXI, 50. (6) *Metargeminan*, i.e., in the *Targum*, the Aramaic version of the Scriptures. The citation given here by R. Joseph is from the *Targum* ascribed to Onḳelos the proselyte. (7) Treating *KuMaZ* as an abbreviation. (8) Ibid. 14. (9) When they sinned with the daughters of Moab; v. Num. XXV. (10) Ibid. 49. (11) V. 50, to make atonement for their impure thoughts.

כלי כלי מהתם : מוסף א שק על הבגד שמטמא משום אריג : אטו בגד לאו אריג הוא הכי קאמר מוסף שק על הבגד אף על פי שאינו אריג טמא למאי חזי אמר רבי יוחנן שכן עני קולע שליש נימין ותולה בצואר בתו *תנו רבנן °שק אין לי אלא שק ב מניין לרבות את הקילקלי ואת החבק ת"ל או שק ג יכול שאני מרבה את החבלים ואת המשיחות ת"ל שק מה שק טווי ואריג אף כל טווי ואריג הרי הוא אומר במת °וכל כלי עור וכל מעשה עזים וגו' תתחטאו לרבות הקילקלי ואת החבק יכול שאני מרבה את החבלים ואת המשיחות ודין הוא טימא בשרץ וטימא במת מה כשטימא בשרץ לא טימא אלא טווי ואריג אף כשטימא במת לא טימא אלא טווי ואריג הן אם היקל בטמא שרץ שהיא קלה נקיל בטומאת המת שהיא חמורה תלמוד לומר בגד ועור בגד ועור לגזירה שוה נאמר °בגד ועור בשרץ ונאמר °בגד ועור במת מה בגד ועור האמור בשרץ לא טימא אלא טווי ואריג אף בגד ועור האמור במת לא טימא אלא טווי ואריג ומה בגד ועור האמור במת טמא כל מעשה עזים אף בגד ועור האמור בשרץ טמא כל מעשה עזים אין לי אלא דבר הבא מן העזים ד מניין לרבות דבר הבא מזנב הסוס ומזנב הפרה תלמוד לומר או שק והא אפיקתיה לקילקלי וחבק הני מילי מקמי דליתיה ג"ש השתא דאתי גזירה שוה אייתור ליה ואין לי אלא בשרץ בטומאת מת מניין ודין הוא טימא במת וטימא בשרץ מה כשטימא בשרץ עשה דבר הבא מזנב הסוס ומזנב הפרה כמעשה עזים אף כשטימא במת עשה דבר הבא מזנב הסוס ומזנב הפרה כמעשה עזים הן אם הרבה בטומאת ערב שהיא מרובה נרבה בטומאת שבעה שהיא מועטת תלמוד לומר בגד ועור בגד ועור לגזירה שוה נאמר בגד ועור בשרץ ונאמר בגד ועור במת מה בגד ועור האמור בשרץ עשה דבר הבא מזנב הסוס ומזנב הפרה כמעשה עזים אף בגד ועור האמור במת עשה דבר הבא מזנב הסוס ומזנב הפרה כמעשה עזים ומופנה דאי לאו מופנה איכא למיפרך מה לשרץ שכן מטמא בכעדשה *לאי אפנויי מופני *)מכדי שרץ איתקש לשכבת זרע דכתיב °איש אשר תצא ממנו שכבת זרע וסמיך ליה איש אשר יגע בכל שרץ וכתיב ביה בשכבת זרע וכל בגד וכל עור אשר יהיה עליו שכבת זרע בגד ועור דכתב רחמנא בשרץ למה לי שמע מינה לאפנויי ואכתי מופנה מצד אחד הוא הניחא למאן דאמר *מופנה מצד אחד למידין ואין משיבין אלא למאן דאמר *למידין ומשיבין מאי איכא למימר דמת נמי אפנויי מופנה מכדי מת אתקש לשכבת זרע דכתיב °והנוגע בכל טמא נפש או איש אשר תצא ממנו שכבת זרע וכתיב בשכבת זרע וכל בגד וכל עור בגד ועור דכתב רחמנא במת למה לי ש"מ לאפנויי : °ונקרב את קרבן ה' איש אשר מצא כלי זהב אצעדה וצמיד טבעת עגיל וכומז א"ר אלעזר *עגיל זה דפוס של דדין כומז זה דפוס של בית הרחם אמר רב יוסף אי הכי היינו דמתרגמינן מחוך דבר המביא לידי גיחוך אמר ליה רבה מגופיה דקרא ש"מ כומז כאן מקום זימה : °ויקצוף משה על פקודי החיל אמר רב נחמן אמר רבה בר אבוה אמר להן משה לישראל שמא חזרתם לקלקולכם הראשון אמרו לו לא נפקד ממנו איש אמר להן אם כן כפרה למה אמרו לו אם מידי עבירה יצאנו מידי הרהור לא יצאנו מיד ונקרב את קרבן ה' תנא דבי רבי ישמעאל מפני מה הוצרכו ישראל שבאותו הדור כפרה מפני

*) [כ"ק כה:]

שזנו

ויקרא יא · במדבר לא · ויקרא יא · במדבר לא · ויקרא כב · שם · במדבר לא · שם

רש"י

כלי כלי. בשרצים כתיב כל כלי אשר יעשה מלאכה וגו' ומגופיה דקרא דשרצים לא מצי יליף דאשר יעשה מלאכה לאו כלי תכשיט משמע : שק. הוא עשוי מנוצה של עזים שאף על פי שאינו אריג אלא קלע קטן עשה מנוצה של עזים לתלות בו בתי נפש לצואר בתו טמא שדרכו בכך ותכשיט הוא וה"ק שהוא טמא משום אריג ואע"פ שאינו אריג : קולע ג' נימין כו'. ג' חוטין של מטוה של נוצה של עזים צבועה : ותולה בצואר בתו. וקליעתה זו היא אריגתו מאחר שהוא טווי כדאמרן גבי תיכי חלילתא בריש פירקין דקרי להו אריג והא דקאמר אע"פ שאינו אריג כלומר לאו אריג ממש : אין לי אלא שק. העשוי ללבוש רועים : קילקלי. מסרך של סוס שקורין פייטרא"ל : חבק. ליגגלא של סרגא ואוכף ועושין אותה מנוצה של עזים טווי ואריג : יכול שאני מרבה החבלים והמשיחות. לניא"ל שעושין למדוד וקולעין מן הנוצה כמו שנתלשה ואינו טווי ולא דמי לקולע שלש נימין דלעיל דהתם טווי הוא וזו היא אריגתו : יכול שאני מרבה כו'. הואיל וכתיב כל : ודין הוא שלא נרבה. ולא צריך קרא למעוטי : הן. תמיה הוא וכי דברים כונים הם : אם היקל בטומאת שרץ שהיא קלה. כלומר אם היקל מלטמא חבלים ומשיחות היקל לך בשרץ שטומאתו קלה טומאת ערב : נקל. גם אנחנו בבנין אב זה במת שטומאתו חמורה טומאת ז' : השתא דאתיא גזירה שוה. וכי היכי דיליף מת משרץ למעוטי חבלים ומשיחות יליף נמי שרץ ממת לכל מעשה עזים לרבות קילקלי וחבק : אין לי אלא בשרץ. דהא שק התם כתיב : אם ריבה. לטמא דבר הבא מזנב הסוס בטומאת ערב הוא דריבה : שהיא מרובה. שכל המגעות טומאת ערב הן בין דשרץ ונבילה ושכבת זרע מגע הזב ומגע טמא מת : נרבה אנו בטומאת ז' שכן מועטת היא. שאינה בכל המגעות אלא במגע המת בלבד : מופנה. צריך שתהא גזירה שוה זו מב' תיבות דבגד ועור מופנין למדרש זה שלא יהו צריכין לגופן ומאחר שמופנין ללמוד גזירה שוה ה"ל כמאן דכתיב דרשא בקרא בהדיא ואין משיבין עליה : דאי לאו מופנה. אמרינן לגופן באו ולא ילפינן להא מילתא מינייהו : דאיכא למיפרך כו'. וה"ה דמצי למימר הכי אגזירה שוה קמייתא ומיהו אסקי לכולה ברייתא ברישא ופריך אהא דסליק מינה ובשינויא דמשנינן בהא מיתרצה נמי קמייתא : לאי. באמת : וכתיב ביה בשכבת זרע. דבגד ועור טמאים הם בו : מצד אחד. הכתובין בשרץ מופנים כדאמרן אבל הכתובין במת אין מופנין : הניחא למ"ד כו'. פלוגתא דרבי ישמעאל ורבנן היא במסכת נדה בהמפלת (דף כב:) : אלא למאן דאמר למידין. אם אין תשובה : ומשיבין. אם יש להשיב : מאי איכא למימר. הרי יש להשיב שכן מטמא בכעדשה : והנוגע בכל טמא נפש או איש אשר תצא ממנו שכבת זרע : דפוס של דדין. שמונחות בו : גיחוך. ליצנות : לקלקולכם. של מעשה שטים לזנות את בנות מואב שמא כך עשיתם במדין לכך אתם צריכין קרבן : לא נפקד. לא נחסר מדת יהודית :

שזנו

תוספות

מניין לרבות את הקילקלי והחבק. ואם תאמר והא לא מיטלטל מלא וריקן ואי משום דאפשר לקפלה אם אינו עשוי לכך לאו כלום הוא כדאמר לקמן גבי קב הקיטע דאע"ג דיש לו בית קיבול לראש שוקו אם אינו עשוי לקבל טהור וי"ל דהכי נמי לשם כל צורכן הן עשוין מתחלה אך קשה דלעיל פ' במה מדליקין (דף כז: ושם) מפיק דבר הבא מן העזים דמטמא בשרצים מאו בגד וקילקלי וחבק באין מן העזים ומפיק להן הכא מאו שק וע"ק דהתם מרבה לנוצה של עזים לג' על ג' ואילו שק שיעורו בד' ואומר ר"י דתרי גווני נוצה של עזים הוו והתם מיירי [בדקה] שעושים ממנה בגדים חשובים והלכך איתרבו לשלשה על שלשה כמו שאר בגדים והכא מיירי בנוצה גסה שממנה עושין קילקלי וחבק וחבלים ומשיחות ושק : שמע מינה לאפנויי. הקשה ה"ר אליעזר ממיץ כיון דאיתקש שרץ ומת לשכבת זרע א"כ ג"ש דבגד ועור ל"ל דכל מה שיש במת ניתן בשכבת זרע וכל מה שיש בשכבת זרע ניתן בשרץ וכן להפך דהא קי"ל *דבר הבא מן ההיקש חוזר ומלמד בהיקש חוץ מן הקדשים : [זבחים מט:] מידי הרהור מי יצאנו. וא"ת והא אפילו (א) יפת תואר הותרה להם וי"ל דמכל מקום שייך בה איסור כדאמרינן (קדושין דף כב.) ותשקת בה ולא בחברתה :

ובמוך

עין משפט נר מצוה

נח א ב ג ד מיי' פ"א מהל' כלים הלכה יב :

רבינו חננאל

קילקלי. מלשון יון הוא והוא עשוי בגד [(גלוין)] משיער של עזים והוא קשה עשוי להצניעו תחת הכרים והכסתות. חבקים כסוי הכסאות (ת"ל) או בגד או עור או שק אין לי אלא] שק בלבד מנין לרבות הקילקלי וחבק ת"ל או שק פי' מרבינן להו מאו כלומר הוה ליה למימר שק. או דכתב רחמנא למה לי לרבויי קילקלי וחבק. יכול שאני מרבה חבלים ומשיחין שיטמאו ת"ל שק מה שק טווי ואריג אף כל טווי ואריג הרי הוא אמר במת כל מעשה עזים יכול שאני מרבה חבלים ומשיחים דין הוא טימא בשרץ טימא במת כו'. והחינן ואם היקל בטומאת שרץ שהיא קלה פי' טומאת שרץ קלה היא שהיא טומאת ערב אבל טומאת מת חמורה היא שהיא טומאת שבעה לא נתרבה ת"ל (או) בגד ועור בגד ועור לג"ש נאמר בגד ועור בשרץ ונאמר בגד ועור במת. פי' דין ג"ש ב' פסוקים וכל פסוק ופסוק כתוב מלין שאינן צריכין לפסוק ואין מילין פטין לא נכתבו אלא בתיך פסוקים אלו אלא לדון מהם ג"ש להיות כל דין שמפורש באחד מהן שיהא גם השני כמותו וזהו שכתוב בענינו בגד ועור בשרץ בגד ועור במת וצריכין להיות אלו בגד ועור מופנים בשני הפסוקים. שאם הן בפסוק אחד יתירין כגון שלמדו טומאת בגד ועור בשרץ משכבת זרע ונמצא בגד ועור האמור בשרץ מופנה כגון זה למידין ואם יש פירכא משיבין ופורכין ואם הן אלו פסוקים בגד ועור יתירין בשרץ ובמת למידין במת מן השרץ זהו שמאין במת דבר הבא מזנב הסוס מזנב הפרה כשם שמטמאין בשרץ ואין משיבין ואע"ג דאיכא למפרך ואם ריבה בטומאת שרץ שהיא מרובה. פי' טומאת שרץ (נותנת) [נוהגת] בשמנה שרצים. נרבה טומאת מת שהיא מועטת שאינה אלא במת בלבד ואוקימנא כיון שהן מופנה משני צדדין למידין ואין משיבין. ואלו הדברים הל"מ להדרש בענין הזה מסורות בידי חכמים :

רב נסים גאון

הניחא למאן [דאמר] מופנה מצד א' למדין ואין משיבין אלא למאן דאמר למידין ומשיבין מאי איכא למימר. מחלוקת בין ר' ישמעאל ורבנן ועיקר דילה במס' נדה בפרק המפלת (דף כב) אמר רב יהודה אמר שמעאל משום ר' כל גזירה שוה שאינה מופנה כל עיקר אין למידין ממנה מופנה מצד אחד לר' ישמעאל למידין ואין משיבין לרבנן למידין ומשיבין : אמר להם משה לישראל שמא חזרתם לקלקולכם הראשון אמרו לו לא נפקד ממנו איש. במס' יבמות בפרק הבא על יבמתו (דף סא) אמרו ור' שמעון לא נפקד ממנו איש לעבירה ולדבר זה נתכוונו בהם בתשובה זו :

קסבר

מסורת הש"ס

פ"ג פ' שמיני

[במלוך איתא לאיי ומפרש דלשון יון הוא ע"ש]

[נדה כב:]

[לקמן קלא. יבמות ע: עד. נדה כב:]

[מס' כלה]

הגהות הב"ח

(א) תוס' ד"ה מידי וכו' אפי' יפת תואר

עין משפט
נר מצוה

נט א מיי' פכ"א מהל' איסורי ביאה הלכה ב סמג לאוין קכו טוש"ע אה"ע סי' כא סעיף א :

ס ב מיי' פי"ט מהל' שבת הלכה ט סמג לאוין סה טוש"ע א"ח סי' שג סעיף יד :

סא ג מיי' שם הלכה יב טוש"ע שם סעיף טו :

סב ד מיי' שם הלכה ט טוש"ע שם סעיף יד:

סג ה מיי' שם הלכה ח טוש"ע שם סעיף יח :

סד ו מיי' פי"א מהל' איסורי ביאה הלכה יט סמג לאוין קיא טוש"ע י"ד סימן קצה סעיף ט :

סה ז מיי' פ"ד שם הלכה ג ופי"א הלכה טז סמג שם טוש"ע שם סעי' א וסי' קנז סעי' א:

רבינו חננאל

מתני' יוצאה אשה בחוטי שיער כו' . אמר [רב] כל שאסרו חכמים לצאת בו לרה"ר אסור לצאת בו אפילו לחצר חוץ מכבול ופאה נכרית כדי שלא תתגנה על בעלה. והלכתא כותיה דרב ואע"ג דאמרינן ר' ישמעאל ב"ר יוסי תנא הוא ופליג לית הלכתא כוותיה. אמר רב יהודה אמר רב כל מקום שאסרו חכמים מפני מראית העין אפי' בחדרי חדרים אסור . ואקשינן עליה תנן בפרקין דקמי דין תנן לא בזוג אע"פ שהוא פקיק ותניא פוקקין לה זוג ומטיילתא בחצר . ומשני תנאי היא דתניא מי שנשרו כליו

שזנו עיניהם מן הערוה אמר רב ששת **מפני מה מנה הכתוב תכשיטין שבחוץ עם תכשיטין שבפנים לומר לך כל המסתכל באצבע קטנה של אשה כאילו מסתכל במקום התורפה: **מתני'** *יוצאה אשה בחוטי שער בין משלה בין משל חבירתה בין משל בהמה ובטוטפת ובסרביטין בזמן שהן תפורין בכבול ובפאה נכרית לחצר במוך שבאזנה ובמוך שבסנדלה ובמוך שהתקינה לנדתה בפילפל *ובגלגל מלח וכל דבר שניתן לתוך פיה ובלבד שלא תתן לכתחלה בשבת ואם נפל לא תחזיר שן תותבת שן של זהב רבי מתיר וחכמים אוסרים: **גמ'** וצריכא דאי אשמעינן דידה משום דלא מאים אבל חבירתה דמאים אימא לא ואי אשמעינן דחבירתה דבת מינה הוא אבל דבהמה לאו בר מינה הוא אימא לא צריכא תנא ובלבד שלא תצא ילדה בשל זקנה וזקנה בשל ילדה בשלמא זקנה בשל ילדה שבח הוא לה* אלא ילדה בשל זקנה אמאי גנאי הוא לה איידי דתנא זקנה בשל ילדה תנא נמי ילדה בשל זקנה: בכבול ובפאה נכרית לחצר: אמר רב כל שאסרו חכמים לצאת בו לרה"ר אסור לצאת בו לחצר *חוץ מכבול ופאה נכרית רבי ענני בר ששון משמיה *דר' ישמעאל אמר הכל ככבול תנן בכבול ובפאה נכרית לחצר בשלמא לרב ניחא אלא לרבי ענני בר ששון קשיא רבי ענני בר ששון משמיה דמאן קאמר ליה משמיה דר' ישמעאל בר יוסי רבי ישמעאל בר יוסי תנא הוא ופליג ורב מאי שנא הני אמר עולא כדי שלא תתגנה על בעלה כדתניא °והדוה בנדתה זקנים הראשונים אמרו שלא תכחול ולא תפקוס ולא תתקשט בבגדי צבעונין עד שבא ר"ע ולימד אם כן אתה מגנה על בעלה ונמצא בעלה מגרשה אלא מה ת"ל והדוה בנדתה בנדתה תהא עד שתבא במים *אמר רב יהודה אמר רב כל מקום שאסרו חכמים מפני מראית העין אפילו בחדרי חדרים אסור *תנן ולא בזוג אע"פ שפקוק ותניא *אידך *פוקק לה זוג בצוארה ומטייל עמה בחצר תנאי היא דתניא

שוטחן

[נ"ל דר' ישמעאל בר' יוסי]

ויקרא טו

[תוספתא פ"ה]

תורה אור

ובמוך שהתקינה לנדתה . פ"ה באותו מקום שיבלע בו הדם ולא יטנפו בגדיה ול"נ דא"כ אצולי טינוף הוא ומשוי הוא כדאמר בפ"ק (דף יא:) דכל אצולי טינוף לא חשיב ומשוי הוא לכן נ"ל שלא יפול על בשרה ותייבש עליה ונמצא מצטערה :

ובלבד שלא תתן לכתחלה בשבת . פירש הר"ר פורת גזירה משום שחיקת סממנים כיון דלרפואה הוא ול"נ דאם כן אם נפל אמאי לא תחזיר האמר בפרק בתרא דעירובין (דף קב: ושם) מחזירין רטיה במקדש אבל לא במדינה וע"כ לא אסרינן להחזיר הרטיה אלא משום שמא ימרח והכא לא שייך מירוח דאין שייך מירוח אלא בדבר לח כגון רטיה אבל בפלפלין ובגלגלא לא שייך מירוח לכן נ"ל ובלבד שלא תתן לכתחלה מפני שנראה כמערמת להוציאה ולפירוש זה כל הנך דלעיל מוך שבאזנה ושבסנדלה אסורין לתת לכתחלה וא"ת א"כ היכי שרו לקמן פורפת על האבן או על האגוז והא נראה כמערמת וי"ל דהתם ניכר הדבר והכל יודעין דלכך צריכה וליכא שום חששא אבל בדבר שהיא נותנת בתוך פיה אינם יודעין למה היא נותנת:

ובלבד שלא תצא זקנה בשל ילדה וילדה בשל זקנה . כך היא עיקר הגירסא והשתא פריך שפיר בשלמא זקנה בשל ילדה שבח הוא לה פירוש ומשום הכי איצטריך לאשמעינן שלא תצא דאפילו הכי מחכו עלה אלא ילדה בשל זקנה אמאי גנאי הוא לה פירוש אמאי איצטריך לאשמעינן דלא תצא פשיטא דכיון דגנאי הוא לה ודאי מחכו עלה ושקלה להו וכיון דתנא זקנה בשל ילדה אסור כל שכן ילדה בשל זקנה ודוחק הוא לומר זו ואצ"ל לומר זו קתני ואית דגרסי איפכא ובלבד שלא תצא ילדה בשל זקנה וזקנה בשל ילדה ואינו מיושב דא"כ אמאי פריך ילדה בשל זקנה אמאי שהרי כך הוא דרך הש"ס לשנות הפשוט תחלה והרב פורת מיישב גירסא זו וה"פ אלא ילדה בשל זקנה אמאי איצטריך גנאי הוא לה דלעולם לא תצא בהן אפילו בחול :

רבי ענני ברבי ששון אמר הכל ככבול . ונראה דהלכה כרבי ענני *מדאמר מילתיה משמיה דרבי ישמעאל בר' יוסי ור' ישמעאל תנא הוא ופליג ועוד דבשל סופרים הלך אחר המיקל ור' ענני דמתיר בחצר היינו אפילו בחצר שאינה מעורבת דבחצר מעורבת ליכא שום חדוש אם כן נשים מותרות להתקשט בבית ובחצר בטבעות ובתכשיטין ואנו שאין לנו רה"ר גמור דכל רה"ר שלנו כרמלית היא שהרי אין מבואות שלנו רחבות י"ו אמה ולא ס' ריבוא בוקעים בו הרי הוא כחצר שאינה מעורבת ומותרות נשים שלנו להתקשט בטבעות ובתכשיטים כפר"ת והקשה ר"י דאפילו אי רה"ר שלנו חשיב ככרמלית היכי שרו כמו חצר והאמר לקמן פרק כל כתבי (דף קכ.) גבי דליקה דמותר להציל בחצר שאינה מעורבת ולא בכרמלית ואומר רבינו ברוך כיון דלדידהו הוו להו רה"ר גמורה לא מדמו כרמלית לחצר שאינה מעורבת ואסרינן כרמלית משום רה"ר אבל אנו שאין לנו רה"ר כלל °אין להחמיר בכרמלית כ"כ וה"ר שמשון מלא כתוב בספרים של שלום דדבר שהוא רגילות להראות זו לזו אסור וכשאינם רגילות מותרות ונשי דידן אינן מראות תכשיטיהן וטבעותיהן ומש"ה מותרות לצאת בהן וסוף דבר אמרו הקדמונים דמותרות לצאת בהן דמוטב יהו שוגגות ואל יהו מזידות:

אמר

שזנו . לשון מזון שנהנו במראית העין : תכשיטין שבחוץ . טבעת : תכשיטין שבפנים . כומז : לומר לך המסתכל באצבע . שהיא מקום טבעת כמסתכל במקום כומז שהרי כפרה זו על שנסתכלו בה : **מתני'** בחוטי שער . שקולעת בהן שערה : בין משלה . תלושין : בין משל בהמה . כגון של סוס : שהן תפורין . לסבכה דתו לא שלפא להו לאחוויי: לחצר . אכבול ופיאה נכרית קאי דאסרו לעיל למיפק בה לרה"ר ואיצטריך לאשמעינן דלחצר מותר וכבול דסיפא דמתני' לא איפלגו בה אמוראי דלכולי עלמא כיפה של צמר : פיאה נכרית . קליעת שער תלושה וקושרתה על שערה עם קליעתה שתראה בעלת שער : במוך שבאזנה . שנותנת לבלוע ליחה של צואת האוזן : שבסנדלה . לתענוג : לנדתה . באותו מקום שיבלע בו הדם ולא יטנף בגדיה : פלפל . פלפל ארוך נותנת אשה בפיה שריחה רע : גלגל מלח . כמו גרגיר מלח לרפואת חולי שינים : שנתנה לתוך פיה . מכעוד יום : שן תותבת . שנתנת בלחייה ממקום אחר והיא של זהב : רבי מתיר . לצאת בה : וחכמים אוסרין . דכיון דמשונה משאר השינים דילמא מיחייכי עלה ושקלה לה מהתם וממטי לה בידה ובגמרא אמרינן דשל זהב נקט דווקא ל"א שן תותבת שן של אדם היתה והאיסורא דלעיל קאי ולאו אפלוגתא דרבי ורבנן והכי קאמר בפלפל ובגלגל מלח ושן תותבת שן של זהב רבי מתיר כו' : **גמ'** דלא מאיס . וליכא למימר דמשלפא ליה משום דמחכו עלה וממטי ליה בידיה : דבת מינה הוא . ולא מינכר ולא מחייכי עלה : ובלבד שלא תצא זקנה . בחוטי שער של ילדה וילדה בשל זקנה דלבנות על שחורות או שחורות על לבנות מאים ואתי למישלף : כל שאסרו חכמים . בריש פרקין חוטי צמר ופשתן טוטפת ושאר השטיים במשנה שאסור ללכת בהן לרה"ר : אסור לצאת לחצר . ואף על גב דשרי לטלטולינהו דתורת כלי עליהן כדאמרן הרי הן ככל הכלים הניטלים בחצר מיהו דרך מלבוש אסור דמרגלא ליה ונפקא ביה לרה"ר : חוץ מכבול ופיאה . שמותר לחצר כדתנן במתניתין וטעמא מפרש לקמיה : הכל ככבול . כל האסורים לא נאסרו אלא לרה"ר אבל לחצר מותרים ככבול : בשלמא לרב ניחא . מדנקט הני ושבקינהו לאינך דמיתני בהדייא לאיסורא ברישא דמתניתין מכלל דכולהו אף לחצר באיסורייהו קיימי : כדי שלא תתגנה . התירו לה קצת קישוטים הנאים : כדתניא . דחשו רבנן להכי : בנדתה . היו דורשין הראשונים כמשמעו כדבר המנודה ומרחיקה מבעלה : שלא תכחול . עיניה : ולא תפקוס .*שרק על פניה טינפאנ"ל בלע"ז והוא אדום : תהא בנדתה . בטומאתה : עד שתבא במים . לטבול ואע"פ שעברו ז' שלה ופסק מעיינה : כל שאסרו חכמים משום מראית העין . שלא יחשדוהו באיסור כגון שריון וקסדא ומגפיים או לא יקשור גמלים זה בזה דמיחזי כאזיל לחינגא : ולא בזוג אע"פ שהוא פקוק . ואינו מוליד קול לא תצא בהמה בו וטעמא פרישנא בפ' במה בהמה (לעיל דף נד:) משום דמיחזי כאזיל לחינגא : ותניא . בברייתא דבחצר דליכא מראית העין מותר :

שוטחן

מסורת הש"ס

נדרים כד.

[לעיל מ:]

[גיר' הערוך ובנרגר וכן איתא במשנה שבמשניות]

כס"י הגיר' ואתיא לאחוויי

[עי' תוס' מנחות לו: ד"ה אי קסבר]

לקמן קמו: ביצה ס. ע"ז יב.

לעיל מד:

לעיל נג:

עי' לקמן נה: רש"י ד"ה וכן הספוקסת ובפ"ק ס: תוס' ד"ה פוקסת

[עי' תוס' במנחות לו: ד"ה אי]

גליון הש"ס

תום' ד"ה ר' ענני כו' אין להחמיר בכרמלית . עי' כתובות דף ז ע"א תוס' ד"ה מתוך :

Israelites of that generation in need of atonement? Because [64b] they gratified their eyes with lewdness. R. Shesheth said: Why
a does the Writ enumerate the outward ornaments with the inner?[1] To teach you: Whoever looks upon a woman's little finger is as though he gazed upon the pudenda.[2]

MISHNAH. A WOMAN MAY GO OUT WITH RIBBONS MADE OF HAIR,[3] WHETHER THEY ARE OF HER OWN [HAIR] OR OF HER COMPANIONS, OR OF AN ANIMAL, AND WITH FRONTLETS AND WITH SARBIṬIN[4] THAT ARE FASTENED TO HER. [SHE MAY GO OUT] WITH A HAIR-NET [KABUL] AND WITH A WIG[5] INTO A COURTYARD; WITH WADDING IN HER EAR, WITH WADDING IN HER SANDALS,[6] AND WITH THE CLOTH PREPARED FOR HER MENSTRUATION; WITH A PEPPERCORN, WITH A GLOBULE OF SALT AND ANYTHING THAT IS PLACED IN HER MOUTH,[7] PROVIDING THAT SHE DOES NOT PUT IT IN HER MOUTH IN THE FIRST PLACE ON THE SABBATH, AND IF IT FALLS OUT,[8] SHE MAY NOT PUT IT BACK. AS FOR AN ARTIFICIAL TOOTH, [OR] A GOLD TOOTH,[9]—RABBI PERMITS BUT THE SAGES FORBID IT.

GEMARA. And it is necessary [to state all the cases].[10] For if we were told about her own [hair], that might be because it is not ugly; but as for her companions', which is unbecoming,[11] I might say [that it is] not [permitted].[12] While if we were informed about her companions', that might be because she is of her own kind; but an animal's, that is not of her own kind, I
b might say [that it is] not [permitted].[1] Thus they are necessary.

It was taught: Providing that a young woman does not go out with an old woman's [hair], or an old woman with a young woman's.[2] As for an old woman [not going out] with a young woman's hair, that is well, because it is an improvement for her; but [that] a young woman [may not go out] with an old woman's [hair], why [state it], seeing that it is unsuitable for her?[3]—Because he teaches of an old woman's [going out] with a young woman's [hair], he also teaches of a young woman's [going out] with an old woman's hair.

WITH A HAIR-NET AND A WIG INTO A COURTYARD. Rab said: Whatever the Sages forbade to go out therewith into the street, one may not go out therewith into a courtyard,[4] except a hair-net and a wig. R. 'Anani b. Sason said on the authority of R. Ishmael son of R. Jose: It is all like a hair-net. We learnt: WITH A HAIR-NET AND A WIG INTO A COURTYARD. As for Rab, it is well; but according to R. 'Anani b. Sason it is a difficulty?—On whose authority does R. 'Anani b. Sason say this? On that of R. Ishmael son of R. Jose! R. Ishmael son of R. Jose is a Tanna, and can disagree.[5]

Now, according to Rab, why do these differ?—Said 'Ulla, [They are permitted] lest she become repulsive to her husband.[6] As it was taught: *And she that is sick shall be in her impurity:*[7] the early Sages[8] ruled: That means that she must not rouge nor paint nor adorn herself in dyed garments; until R. Akiba came and taught: If so, you make her repulsive to her husband, with the result that he will divorce her! But what [then] is taught by, '*and she that is sick shall be in her impurity*'? She shall remain in her
c impurity until she enters into water.[1]

Rab Judah said in Rab's name: Wherever the Sages forbade [aught] for appearances' sake, it is forbidden even in one's innermost chambers.[2]

We learnt: Nor with a bell, even if it is plugged.[3] And it was elsewhere taught,[4] One may plug the bell around its [the animal's] neck and saunter with it in the courtyard?[5]—It is

a (1) In this verse, according to the translation given above of *'agil* and *kumaz*. (2) The first is where the finger-ring is worn, and since it is enumerated, it follows that even for looking upon that they needed atonement. (3) With which she dresses her hair. (4) V. *supra* 57*b*. (5) Lit., 'strange (false) curls'. (6) I.e., any soft substance to ease the foot. (7) Before the commencement of the Sabbath. (8) On the Sabbath. (9) Rashi regards these as one: an artificial tooth of gold. (10) Referring to ribbons of hair. (11) I.e., ribbons made of another woman's hair may not match her own. (12) She may be ridiculed and thereby tempted to remove it, and thus carry it in the street.

b (1) For there the disharmony is even more striking. (2) Young hair on old—e.g. black on grey—or *vice versa* is ugly, and so the wearer might remove it in the street. (3) No young woman would dream of wearing ribbons made from an old woman's hair.—The translation follows one interpretation given in Tosaf. Tosaf. offers another, which is based on a reversed order of the text. (4) Lest she forget herself and go out into the street too. (5) It is axiomatic that an amora cannot disagree with a Tanna, but another Tanna of course can. The Mishnah certainly disagrees with R. 'Anani b. Sason, but it does not matter, as he is supported by another Tanna. (6) Hence some ornaments must be permitted. (7) Lev. XV, 33. The reference is to a menstruant. (8) Lit., 'elders'.

c (1) I.e., until she has a ritual bath. (2) E.g., one must not lead on Sabbath a number of animals tied together, lest he be suspected of going to market with them (*supra* 54*a*). Accordingly he may not do so even in the utmost privacy. (3) V. *supra* 54*b* Mishnah. (4) Var. lec.: and it was taught thereon. (5) This refutes Rab, for though it may not be done publicly in the street, it may be done privately in one's courtyard.

[a controversy of] Tannaim. For it was taught: [65a] He may spread them out in the sun, but not in the sight of people; R. Eleazar and R. Simeon forbid it.[6]

AND WITH THE WADDING IN HER EAR. Rami b. Ezekiel learnt: Providing it is tied to her ear.

AND WITH THE WADDING IN HER SANDALS. Rami b. Ezekiel learnt: Providing it is tied to her sandal.

AND WITH THE CLOTH SHE PREPARED FOR HER MENSTRUATION. Rami b. Ezekiel thought to say, Providing it is fastened between her thighs. Said Raba, Even if it is not tied to her: since it is repulsive, she will not come to carry it.[7] R. Jeremiah asked R. Abba: What if she made a handle for it?[8]—It is permitted, replied he.[9] It was stated likewise: R. Naḥman b. Oshaia said in R. Joḥanan's name: [Even] if she made a handle for it, it is permitted.

R. Joḥanan used to go out with them[10] to the Beth Hamidrash,
a but his companions disagreed with him.[1] R. Jannai would go out with it into a *karmelith*,[2] but all his contemporaries disagreed with him. But Rami b. Ezekiel learnt: Providing it is tied to her ear?[3]—There is no difficulty: in the one case it is firmly placed;[4] in the other it was not.[5]

WITH A PEPPERCORN, AND WITH A GLOBULE OF SALT. A peppercorn is for [counteracting] the [evil] breath of the mouth; a globule of salt is for the gums [6]

AND WITH ANYTHING THAT SHE PLACES[7] IN HER MOUTH. [*Sc.*] ginger, or cinnamon.

AN ARTIFICIAL TOOTH, [OR] A GOLD TOOTH,—RABBI PERMITS BUT THE SAGES FORBID IT. R. Zera said: They taught this only of a gold [tooth], but as for a silver one, all agree that it is permitted.[8] It was taught likewise: Abaye said: Rabbi, R. Eliezer, and R. Simeon b. Eleazar all hold that whatever detracts from a person['s appearance], one will not come to display it. Rabbi, as stated.[9] R. Eliezer, for it was taught: R. Eliezer declares [her] non-culpable on account of a *kobeleth* and a flask of spikenard oil.[10] R. Simeon b. Eleazar, for it was taught: R. Simeon b. Eleazar stated a general rule: Whatever is [worn] beneath the net, one may go out therewith; whatever is [worn] above the net, one may not go out with it.[11]

MISHNAH. SHE MAY GO FORTH WITH THE SELA'[12] ON
b A ẒINITH [CALLUS]. YOUNG GIRLS[1] MAY GO OUT WITH THREADS, AND EVEN WITH CHIPS IN THEIR EARS.[2] ARABIAN WOMEN MAY GO FORTH VEILED, AND MEDIAN WOMEN MAY GO FORTH WITH THEIR CLOAKS THROWN OVER THEIR SHOULDERS.[3] INDEED, ALL PEOPLE [MAY DO LIKEWISE], BUT THAT THE SAGES SPOKE OF NORMAL USAGE.[4] A WOMAN MAY WEIGHT [HER CLOAK] WITH A STONE, NUT, OR COIN, PROVIDING THAT SHE DOES NOT ATTACH THE WEIGHT IN THE FIRST PLACE ON THE SABBATH.

GEMARA. What is ẒINITH? A growth caused by the soil.[5] And why particularly a *sela'*? Shall we say that anything hard is beneficial thereto? Then let a shard be prepared for it? Again, if it is on account of the corrosion,[6] let a metal foil be used? But if it is on account of the figure,[7] let him use any circular plate?[8] Said Abaye: This proves that all [these things] are beneficial for it.[9]

YOUNG GIRLS MAY GO OUT WITH THREADS. Samuel's father did not permit his daughters to go out with threads, nor to sleep together; and he made *miḳwa'oth*[10] for them in the days of Nisan, and had mats placed in the days of Tishri.[11] 'He did not permit them to go out with threads'. But we learnt, YOUNG GIRLS MAY GO OUT WITH THREADS!—The daughters of Samuel's father
c had coloured ones.[1] 'He did not permit them to sleep together'. Shall we say that this supports R. Huna? For R. Huna said: Women that commit lewdness with one another are unfit for the

(6) This refers to one whose garments are accidentally wetted on the Sabbath. The first Tanna forbids them to be spread out in the sight of the people, lest they suspect him of having washed them on the Sabbath, yet he permits it to be done privately, thus agreeing with the Baraitha just quoted. While R. Eleazar and R. Simeon forbid it even in private, which agrees with Rab. (7) If it drops out. (8) Sewing on to it a piece that she could hold in her hand. This is not repulsive, and so she may carry it. (9) It is repulsive none the less. (10) *Sc.* the wadding in his ear, because he had a copious discharge of pus, and with wadding in his sandals. This must be the explanation according to cur. edd. which reads 'with them'; this appears to be Alfasi's version too (v. *Ḳorban Nethanel* on Asheri a.l.). Rashi reads: with it, and refers it to the first mentioned.

a (1) Rashi: because he did not have it tied to his ear. (2) V. Glos. and *supra 6a.* (3) Whereas R. Johanan did not have it tied to his ear. (4) In which case tying to the ear is not necessary. Hence the practice of R. Joḥanan. (5) Rami b. Ezekiel refers to the latter case. (6) Jast. Rashi: toothache. (7) *Sic.* The reading in the Mishnah is slightly different. (8) Rashi: a gold tooth being valuable, the woman may take it out of her mouth for display, and meanwhile carry it in the street; but this does not apply to a silver tooth. (9) As for a silver one, all agree it is permitted; a golden one Rabbi permits, but the Sages forbid it. (10) V. *supra 62a.* (11) V. *supra 57b.* (12) A coin.

b (1) Lit., 'daughters'. (2) To prevent the hole pierced for ear-rings from closing up. (3) *Parap,* p.p. *parup,* f.p. *perupoth,* means to fasten a garment over the shoulder by attaching a weight to its overhanging corner (Jast.). (4) Arabian and Median women affect these fashions. (5) The pressure or chafing of the ground on the foot causing a wound or a bunion. (6) Of the metal, which softens the callus. (7) Stamped on the coin, which may protect the growth. (8) Rashi: of wood, upon which a figure is impressed. (9) Viz., the hardness, corrosion, and the figure, and only a coin possesses all three. (10) *Miḳweh,* pl. *miḳwa'oth,* ritual bath. (11) A *miḳweh* made of collected rain water is efficacious only if its water is still, not running or flowing. But a well or spring, with its waters gushing forth from its source, is efficacious even when they flow onward. Now, during the whole year the river may contain more rain water or melted snow (which is the same) than its own natural waters; consequently it is all considered as rain water, which does not cleanse when in a running state. But in Tishri when the rains have ceased, nor is there any melted snow in the river, it is like a well or spring, and even though running its waters are efficacious.—According to this the river's rise is caused mainly by rain.—Hence in Nisan he did not permit them to take their ritual bath in the river, but made special enclosed baths for them. But in Tishri they could perform their ablutions in the river. Yet since the bed of the river is miry, and should the feet sink into it, the water cannot reach the soles, thus rendering the immersion invalid, he placed mats on the river bed for them to stand on (Rashi). R. Tam a.l. and Rab in Ned. 40b explain: he hung up mats on the shore, to serve as a screen.

c (1) Which they might remove and show.

*שוטחן בחמה אבל לא כנגד העם רבי *אליעזר ורבי שמעון אוסרין : [צ"ל אלא] *ובמוך שבאזנה : תני רמי בר יחזקאל והוא שקשור באזנה : ובמוך שבסנדלה : תני רמי בר יחזקאל והוא שקשור לה בסנדלה: ובמוך שהתקינה לה לנדתה : סבר רמי בר חמא למימר והוא שקשורה לה בין ירכותיה אמר רבא אע"פ שאינו קשור לה כיון דמאיס לא אתיא לאיתויי בעא מיניה רבי ירמיה מרבי אבא עשתה לה בית יד מהו א"ל מותר איתמר [נמי] אמר רב נחמן בר אושעיא א"ר יוחנן עשתה לה בית יד מותר רבי יוחנן נפיק בהו לבי מדרשא וחלוקין עליו חבריו רבי ינאי נפיק בהו לכרמלית וחלוקין עליו כל דורו והתני רמי בר יחזקאל והוא שקשור לה באזנה לא קשיא הא דמיהדק הא דלא מיהדק : בפלפל ובגלגל מלח : פלפל לריח הפה גלגל מלח *לדורשיני : וכל דבר שנותנת לתוך פיה : זנגבילא אי נמי דרצונא : שן תותבת שן של זהב רבי מתיר וחכמים אוסרין : א"ר זירא לא שנו אלא של זהב אבל בשל כסף דברי הכל מותר תניא נמי הכי בשל כסף ד"ה מותר של זהב רבי מתיר וחכמים אוסרין אמר אביי רבי ור' אליעזר ור' שמעון בן אלעזר כולהו סבירא להו דכל מידי דמיגניא ביה לא אתיא לאחויי רבי הא דאמרן ר' אליעזר *דתניא ר' אליעזר פוטר בכובלת ובצלוחית של פלייטון ר' שמעון בן אלעזר דתניא *כלל אמר רבי שמעון בן אלעזר כל שהוא למטה מן הסבכה יוצאה בו למעלה מן הסבכה אינה יוצאה בו :

מתני' יוצאה בסלע שעל הצינית הבנות קטנות יוצאות בחוטין ואפי' בקיסמין שבאזניהם ערביות יוצאות רעולות ומדיות פרופות וכל אדם אלא שדברו חכמים בהווה פורפת על האבן ועל האגוז ועל המטבע ובלבד שלא תפרוף לכתחלה בשבת : **גמ'** מאי צינית בת ארעא ומאי שנא סלע אילימא כל מידי דאקושא מעלי לה ליעבד לה חספא אלא משום שוכתא ליעבד לה טסא אלא משום צורתא ליעבד לה פולסא אמר אביי שמע מינה כולהו מעלין לה : הבנות יוצאות בחוטין : אבוה דשמואל לא שביק להו לבנתיה דנפקי בחוטין ולא שביק להו גניאן גבי הדדי *ועביד להו מקואות ביומי ניסן ומפצי ביומי תשרי לא שביק להו יוצאות בחוטין והאנן תנן הבנות יוצאות בחוטין בנתיה דאבוה דשמואל דצבעונין הוו לא שביק להו גניאן גבי הדדי לימא מסייע ליה לרב הונא *דאמר ר"ה נשים המסוללות זו בזו

פסולות

רש"י

שוטחן בחמה · מי שנשרו כליו בדרך *במי גשמים : אבל לא כנגד העם · שלא יאמרו כבסן בשבת האי תנא סבר דמידי דמשום מראית העין מותר בחדרים : אוסרין · כרב : עשתה לו בית יד · למוך שבאזנו מקום מהו למיסריה דילמא שקלה וממטא לה בידים דלא מאים לאוחזה בבית יד שלה : עשתה לה בית יד מותר · דלא אמרינן לא מאים אלא אפילו בבית יד מאים : רבי יוחנן נפיק ביה לבי מדרשא · במוך שבאזנו שהיה זקן והיתה לו צואת האוזן מרובה : וחלוקין עליו חבריו · מפני שלא היה קשור באזנו והוא יוצא בו לרה"ר : הא דמיהדק · דר' יוחנן היה תוחב באזנו יפה ומהדק ולא בעי קשירה ודרמי בר יחזקאל בדלא מיהדק ל"א מתלמידי רבינו הלוי דרבי יוחנן קשור הוה ובית מדרשו סמוך לביתו הוה ולא היתה רה"ר מפסקת : והא תני רמי והוא שקשור כו' · וכי קשור מיהא אפילו לרה"ר מותר ואמאי קאמר לבי מדרשו ולא קאמר לרשות הרבים ומשני דר' יוחנן קשור ולא מיהדק הקשר ולשון ראשון מיושב מזה : לדורשיני · לחולי השינים : זנגבילא · גינזירו : דרצונא · קנמון : לא שנו · דחכמים אוסרין אלא של זהב שמשונה במראה משאר שינים ודילמא מבזו לה ושקלה לה בידה וממטיא : אבל של כסף · שדומה לשאר השינים דברי הכל מותר לשון רבותי ולי נראה טעמא דשל זהב משום דחשיבא ואתי' לאחויי לכך אסור אבל של כסף לא חשיבא ולא אתי' לאחויי וללשון רבותי קשיא לי הא דאמר אביי רבי ור"ש בן אלעזר כו' ואי טעמא דרבנן משום דחייכי עלה הוא מאי שנא רבי (א) דקשיב ליה רבנן נמי להו לאחויי חיישי ויש לתרץ דרבנן מיסר קאסרי מכל מקום ורבי מתיר דקסבר לא חייכו עלה ולא שלפא להו ומיהו ה"ל למיחש דלמא שלפא לה משום אחויי אלא לא שלפא משום דלאי מחוי לה גנותא היא : רבי הא דאמרן · דלא חייש דילמא שלפא · פוטר בכובלת · ואוקימנא דהאי פוטר מותר לכתחילה הוא ואמר טעמא מאן דרכה למיפק בכובלת אשה שריחה רע ולא שלפא ומחויא גנותה: למטה מן הסבכה · כגון כיפה של צמר : יוצאה בה · דלא חיישינן דילמא שלפא ומחויא דמיגלי שערה ומגניא בה שהסבכה נוי הוא לשער : **מתני'** סלע · מטבע הוא : צינית · מפרש בגמ' : הבנות קטנות · שמנקבות אזניהם ואין עושין נזמים עד שיגדלו ונותנין חוטין או קסמים באזניהם שלא יסתמו אזניהם לוי"ה : ואפילו · רבותא קאמר דאע"ג דלאו תכשיט נוי הוא אורחא בהכי ולא משאוי הוא ויש מפרשין חוטין שקולעת בהן שערה דאסרינן לגדולה בריש פרקין התם משום דשכיחא בהו טבילה אבל קטנות דלא שכיחא בהו טבילה שרי ולשון ראשון הגון מזה חדא דקטנות נמי צריכות טבילה לטומאת מגע משום טהרות ואף נדות נמי שכיחות בהו כדתניא (נדה דף לב:) מעשה שהיה והטבילוה קודם לאמה ועוד מדקתני אפי' בקסמין איכא למישמע דחוטין נמי אאזנים קיימי דאי חוטי הראש לא שייך למיתני אפי' בקסמין : ערביות · נשים ישראליות שבערב : יוצאות רעולות · דרך ערביות להיות מעוטפות ראשן ופניהם חוץ מן העינים וקרי לה בלשון ערבי רעולות היינו הרעלות דכתיב גבי תכשיטי נשים בספר ישעיה (ג) : מדיות · נשים ישראליות שבמדי : פרופות · שמעטפות בטלית ותולה הרצועה בשפתה האחת כנגד צוארה ובשפתה השנית כורכת אבן או אגוז וקושרת הרצועה בכרך ואין הטלית נופל מעליה : פורפת · כמו קרסים דמתרגמינן פורפין כל המחבר בגד לחבירו קרי פריפה : ובלבד שלא תפרוף לכתחלה בשבת · ובגמ' פריך והאמרת רישא פורפת : **גמ'** בת ארעא · מכה שהיא תחת פרסת הרגל וקושר בה סלע לרפואה : דאקושא · שהיא קשה ומגינה על המכה מקוצים ויתדות דרכים : שוכתא · ליאלוחית היוצא מן הכסף ובלע"ז רוי"ל ויפה למכה שוכתא כמו דשתך טפי דאלו מציאות (ב"מ דף כו·) ומשתכין כנחשת דתענית (דף ה·) : ליעבד טסא · דכספא טיבעא למה לי אלא משום צורתא דטיבעא מעליא למכה ולאו שוכתא : ליעבד פולסא · עגול של עץ ויצור עליו : אמר אביי ש"מ · ממתני' דנקט סלע : כולהו בהדדי מעלו לה · ולהכי נקט סלע דאיתנהו לכולהו אקושא ושוכתא וצורתא : לא שביק להו לבנתיה כו' · מפרש לקמן טעמא דכולהו : גניאן גבי הדדי · לישן זו אצל זו בעודן בתולות : מקואות ביומי ניסן · של מים מכונסין או סמוך לנהר וממשיך לתוכן מי הנהר וטובלות שם : ומפצי ביומי תשרי · שטובלות בפרת ומפני הטיט שלא יהא אגילה נותנות המפץ תחת רגליהן : דצבעונין · וחיש למישלף ואחויי : המסוללות · מתחככות משום תאות תשמיש :

תוספות

אמר רב כל מקום שאסרו חכמים כו' · י"מ דאין הלכה כרב *מדתני בחולין (דף מא·) אין שוחטין לתוך גומא ברשות הרבים שלא יחקה האפיקורסים ובחצר מותר ומיהו אין זה ראיה דבחצר מותר דאף הרואה אותו אומר לנקר חצרו הוא צריך אבל בעלמא בהם יראה אדם הרואה יחשדנו אפילו בחדרי חדרים אסור :

ליעבד לה פולסא · פ"ה חתיכה של עץ ויצור עליה צורה ולפירושו (ג) ניחא מה שמקשים דבעלמא אמר* מאי הסימון פולסא ופ"ה התם היינו דבר שאין עליו צורה וקשה דהכא משמע דפולסא הוא דבר שיש עליו צורה ולפירש"י ניחא דפירש ליעבד פולסא בלא צורה ויצור עליו הצורה אבל לפיר"ת קשה דפירש הסימון הוי של מתכת ויש עליו צורה אבל אינה חשובה ואינה יוצאה אם כן הכא מאי איריא סלע אפילו אסימון ושמא י"ל דצורת סלע צריך :

ומפצי ביומי תשרי · פ"ה מפני הטיט שלא יהיה אגילה ונותנות המפץ תחת רגליהן ורבינו תם פירש שהיו נותנות מפצי זקופות שלא יראו אותן העולם ויתביישו מהם ולא יטבלו היטב* :

פסולות

עין משפט נר מצוה

סו א ב ג ד מיי' פי"ט מהל' שבת הלכה יא סמג לאוין סה טוש"ע א"ח סי' שג סעיף טו :

סז ה ו מיי' שם הל' ז טוש"ע שם סעי' יב:

ביצה ט: [לקמן קמו:]

סח ז מיי' שם הלכה יג סמג שם טוש"ע א"ח סימן שא סעיף כח :

[ב"מ מז:]

סט ח מיי' שם הלכה יב סמג שם טוש"ע א"ח סימן שג סעיף כ :

ע ט מיי' שם טוש"ע שם סעיף כא :

עא י מיי' פ"א מהל' מקואות הלכה יא טוש"ע י"ד סימן קצא סעיף לג לד :

עב כ מיי' פי"ט מהל' שבת הל' י' סמג לאוין סה טוש"ע א"ח סימן שג סעיף כ :

עג ל מיי' פכ"א מהל' איסורי ביאה הלכה ח סמג לאוין קכו טוש"ע אה"ע סי' כ סעיף ב :

[וע"ע תוס' נדה סו: ד"ה אשה]

[לעיל נז:]

מסורת הש"ס

[עיין תוספות לקמן קמו: ד"ה מי שנשרו ותוספות ביצה ט: ד"ה מי · שהשיגו על פרש"י דהכא אבל לקמן קמו: במשנה וביצה ט: עולה פירושו כפירוש תוספות וביצה ט' פרש"י כדהכא]

[גיר' הערוך ערך דר ה' לדור שיני ע"ש]

[לעיל סב: תוספתא פ"ה ע"ש]

[נדרים מ: בכורות מה: נדה סז.]

יבמות עו.

רבינו חננאל

שוטחן בחמה אבל לא כנגד העם ור' אלעזר ורבי שמעון אוסרין ואיתו דאמר כר' אלעזר ורבי שמעון : במוך שבאזנה תני רמי [בר יחזקאל] והוא שקשור באזנה · ובמוך שבסנדלה והוא שקשור בעקבה·במוך שהתקינה לנדתה והוא שקשור בירכותיה ורבא אמר אע"פ שאינו קשור כיון דמאים לה לא אתיא לאחווייה · אמר רבא עשתה לה בית יד מותר · פי' בית יד שעושה לידה שתכסה אותה כדי שתבדוק מוך לנדתה ולא תגע בו ולא תטנף בו . והא דאמר במוך שבאזנה ותני רמי בר יחזקאל והוא שקשור באזנה אוקמה במהדק ואי לא מהדק אסור : ושן תותבת של כסףדברי הכל מותר: ר' שמתיר בשל זהב ור' אלעזר שמתיר בצלוחית של פלייטון ור' שמעון בן אלעזר שמתיר בכל שהוא למטה מן הסבכה אלו כולן סבירא להו כל מידי דגנאי הוא לא אתא לאחווייה והני שיטה נינהו ולית הלכתא כחד מינייהו : **מתני'** יוצאין בסלע שעל הצינית סילעיא שיש עליה צורת מטבע ומעלא לצינית שהוא מכה תחת הרגל · ציניתא בת ארעא · הבנות יוצאות בחוטין אפילו בקסמים שבאזניהן · בנתיה דאבוה דשמואל תלתא גווני צבעונים הוו חוטי דידהו ולא שביק להו למיפק בהו סבר דילמא שלפא ומחויא להברתה

הגהות הב"ח

(א) רש"י ד"ה אבל של כסף וכו' ומאי שנא רבי דקא שרי ליה משום דלא אתיא לאחווי רבנן נמי :

(ב) תוס' ד"ה ליעביד וכו' ולפירושו· נ"ב ובתוס' פ' בכל מערכין דף לא ע"ב כתבו בענין אחר ע"ש בד"ה שפדאו :

גליון הש"ס תוס' ד"ה אמר רב וכו' מדתני בחולין · ראיה זו כתבו תוספות בחולין בשם ירושלמי :

פסולות לכהונה לא סבר כי היכי דלא לילפן גופא נוכראה *ועביד להו מקוה ביומי ניסן מסייע ליה לרב דאמר רב *מטרא במערבא סהדא רבה פרת [ב]סבר שלא ירבו הנוטפין על הזוחלין ופליגא דשמואל דאמר שמואל נהרא מכיפיה מיברך ופליגא דידיה אדידיה דאמר שמואל אין המים מטהרין בזוחלין אלא פרת ביומי תשרי בלבד: [ג]פורפת על האבן כו': והאמרת רישא פורפת אמר אביי [ד]סיפא אתאן למטבע בעי אביי [ה]אשה מהו שתערים ותפרוף על האגוז להוציא לבנה קטן בשבת תיבעי למ"ד [*] (א) מערימין תיבעי למאן דאמר אין מערימין תיבעי למאן דאמר מערימין בדליקה התם הוא דאי לא שרית ליה אתי לכבויי אבל הכא אי לא שרית ליה לא אתי לאפוקי או דלמא אפילו למאן דאמר אין מערימין בדליקה התם דרך הוצאה בכך אבל הכא אין דרך הוצאה בכך אימא שפיר דמי תיקו:

מתני' *הקיטע יוצא בקב שלו דברי ר' מאיר ורבי

רש"י

פסולות לכהונה · לכהן גדול דלא הויא בתולה שלימה, דאע"ג דכהן גדול ביומיה לא הוה הואיל ודרך זנות חשיב ליה לאו אורח ארעא: דלא לילפן גופא נוכראה · ויתאוו לשכב עם איש: מטרא במערבא · בארץ ישראל: סהדא רבה פרת · פרת מעיד בדבר שהוא יורד מארץ ישראל לבבל וגדל ממי הגשמים ויודעין בני בבל שירדו גשמים בהרי ארץ ישראל ושמחים על אחיהם ואבוה דשמואל נמי כרב סבירא ליה דאמר פרת גדל ומימיו מתברכין ע"י גשמים: וסבר שמא ירבו נוטפים · היינו גשמים על הזוחלין הנובעין ותנן במסכת מקואות (פ"ה מ"ה) הזוחלין כמעיין והנוטפין כמקוה ושנינו בת"כ אך מעין ובור מקוה מים יכול מילא על כתפו ועשה מקוה בתחילה יהא טהור ת"ל מעיין מה מעיין בידי שמים אף מקוה בידי שמים אי מה מעיין מטהר בזוחלין אף מקוה מטהר בזוחלין תלמוד לומר אך מעיין המעיין מטהר בזוחלין ומקוה מטהר באשבורן ומהו אשבורן דקוו וקיימי לאפוקי שאם הטביל בו כלים דרך זחילתו כשהן נמשכין ויורדים למקוה לא עלתה להם טבילה דבור ומקוה כתיב דקוו וקיימי אבל נובעין מטהרין כמו שהן זוחלין ומושכין מגבוה לנמוך כדרך כל הנהרות הלכך ביומי ניסן שהנהרות גדילים ממי הגשמים של ימי החורף ומהפשרת השלגים חייש שמא ירבו הנוטפין על הזוחלין שניתוספו בנהר(ב) מן הגשמים על הזוחלים החיים ובטלו הזוחלין החיים בנוטפים ואין תורת מעיין עליהן לטהר בזוחלין אלא באשבורן ועביד להו מקוואות דקוו וקיימי ואני קבלתי מרבינו הלוי משום דספק זיבות נינהו וזבה טעונה מים חיים ואי אפשר להעמיד שמועתו משום דאמרינן* חומר בזב מבזבה שהזב טעון מים חיים וזבה אינה טעונה מים חיים וחזרתי ובדקתי לפרשה וכן נראה בעיני כמו שפירשתי ורובא דעלמא מפרשים טטפין כשאובין ולאו מילתא היא דתנן הנוטפין כמקוה: דהוו להו שאובין ל"ג: מכיפיה מיברך · משפתו וממקורו ומסלעו סלע מתרגמינן כיפה מכיפיה מיברך ולא ממי הגשמים: ופליגא דידיה אדידיה · דשמואל אשמואל: אין המים מטהרין בזוחלין · אין מטהרין אדם וכלים הטובלין בהן דרך זחילה וצריך להמשיכן למקוה ולטבול במקוה: אלא פרת ביומי תשרי · שחדלו הגשמים ורבו הזוחלין עליהם ויש תורת מעיין על נהרות המושכין אלמא סבירא ליה שגדילין ממי הגשמים ואני שמעתי בבכורות מטהרין בזוחלין שהטטפין שבתוכן מטהרין בריבוי הזוחלין ויתבטלו הנוטפין בהן להיות זב וזבה טובלין בהן בשביל הזוחלין: והא אמרת רישא פורפת · והיא ודאי לכתחלה קאמר בשבת דאי מבעוד יום ולאשמועינן דיוצאה בו בשבת הא תנא רישא מדיות פרופות: סיפא · דקתני לא תפרוף: אתאן למטבע · דלאו בר טלטול הוא אבל אבן שהקצה לכך ראוי לטלטול: להוציא לבנה הקטן · לאוכלו: תיבעי למאן דאמר · פלוגתא בכל כתבי הקדש (לקמן דף קכ:) לובש כל מה שיכול ללבוש דברי רבי מאיר ואפילו עשרה חלוקים זה על זה רבי יוסי אומר שמונה עשרה כלים כדרך שהוא לובש בחול: דרך הוצאה בכך · כגון מוכרי כסות מוליכין אותו דרך מלבוש:

מתני' הקיטע · שנקטעה רגלו*: יוצא בקב שלו · דמנעל דידיה הוא: ורבי

תוספות

פסולות לכהונה · פי' לכהונה גדולה דלאו בתולה שלימה היא ואע"ג דכהן גדול בימי *שמואל לא הוה היה מחמיר וי"מ משום זונה ופסולות אף לכהן הדיוט וכן משמע בפ' הערל (יבמות עו·) דקאמר התם לית הלכתא [לא כרבא ולא] כאבא (עד דקאמר)[וקאמר] ואפילו לרבי אלעזר דאמר פנוי הבא על הפנויה שלא לשם אישות עשאה זונה כו' משמע דטעמא משום זונה:

סהדא רבה פרת · פי' הקונטרס פרת מעיד (ג) שהוא יורד מא"י לבבל וגדל ממי גשמים ולא נהירא שהרי בבל במזרח א"י קאי וכל הנהרות יורדים ממזרח למערב לכך פר"ת שהיו מכירים שירדו הגשמים לא"י ע"י שחוזר פרת לאחוריו על ידי גדילתו בא"י מתוך הגשמים:

שמא ירבו הנוטפים · פירוש מי גשמים על מי נהרות שהיו זוחלין והוו להו מקוה ואמרינן דאין מקוה מטהר בזוחלין כ"א באשבורן דתנן במסכת מקוואות (פ"ה מ"ה) הזוחלין כמעיין והנוטפין כמקוה ותניא בת"כ יכול מילא מים על כתיפו ועשאו מקוה בתחילה יהא טהור תלמוד לומר מעיין מה מעיין בידי שמים אף מקוה בידי שמים אי מה מעיין מטהר בזוחלין אף מקוה מטהר בזוחלין פי' אף בזוחלין וכ"ש באשבורן תלמוד לומר אך מעיין מטהר בזוחלין ומקוה באשבורן ומהו אשבורן דקוו וקיימי ויש מפרשים שלא היה רוצה להטבילן בהן משום דהוו להו ספק זבות וזב וזבה טעונים מים חיים ושמא ירבו הנוטפין והוו להו מכונסין ולא נהירא חדא דמ"מ עביד להו מקוואות והא בעינן מים חיים ועוד (דבת"כ) [דבתוספתא פ"ג דזבים] קאמר חומר בזב מבזבה שהזב טעון מים חיים והזבה אינה טעונה מים חיים וא"ת ולשמואל דאמר אין המים מטהרין בזוחלין אלא פרת ביומי תשרי זב דבעי מים חיים איך יטבול ביומי ניסן וי"ל במעיין מכוסה שאין מי גשמים יורדין בתוכו וא"ת אמאי חיישינן שמא ירבו הנוטפים לימא קמא קמא בטיל כדאמר בפ"ה דמסכת ע"ז (דף עג.) המערה יין נסך לבור אפילו כל היום כולו כשר דאמרינן קמא קמא בטיל וי"ל דלא מהני טעמא דקמא קמא בטיל כיון שהאיסור רבה מכשיעור והיא דיין נסך דקאמר קמא קמא בטיל היינו קודם שרבה האיסור עד כדי נתינת טעם בהיתר:

דאמר שמואל נהרא מכיפיה מיתבריך · פי' ממקומו ומסלעו סלע מתרגם כיפיה מגביעתו מיתבריך ולא ממי גשמים וא"ת והא קא חזינן שמחמת הגשמים הם גדילים וי"ל כדאמר במסכת תענית (דף כה:) שאין לך טפח יורד מלמעלה שאין טפחיים עולים כנגדו מלמטה ואור"ת דהילכתא כוותיה דשמואל ומייתי ראיה מפרק בתרא דבכורות (דף נה:) דתניא רבי מאיר אומר לא פרת שמו אלא יובל שמו ולמה נקרא שמו פרת שמימיו פרין ורבין ולאו דוקא נקט פרת דה"ה לכל נהרות והא דנקט פרת משום שהוא גדול מכל נהרות ולפי שהוא מא"י וקאמר התם מסייע ליה לשמואל דאמר נהרא מכיפיה מיתבריך ועל זה אנו סומכין לטבול בנהרות אפילו אם גדלו מאד:

הקיטע יוצא בקב שלו · פ"ה קיטע שנקטעה רגלו עושה כמין דפוס רגל וחוקק בו מעט לשום ראש שוקו בתוכו ואינו [ס"א והוא] נסמך עליו ומש"ה יוצא בקב שלו דמנעל דידיה הוא ור' יוסי אוסר דלאו תכשיט הוא ואינו מנעל והוי משוי והקשה רבינו תם דבמסכת יומא (דף עח: וסם) משמע דלכ"ע מנעל הוא ואסור לנעול בו ביוה"כ ולענין שבת בהא הוא דפליגי דרבי יוסי גזר דילמא מיפסיק ואתי לאתויי ורבי מאיר לא גזר וי"ל דה"ע בהא פליגי דטעמא דר' יוסי דכיון דלא הוי של עור לא מיהדק ואיכא למיחש דילמא מיפסיק ואתי לאתויי אך קשה מהא דאמר בגמרא הלכה בסנדל כו' חליצתו כשרה ואמר שמואל ר"מ הוא משמע דלר' יוסי חליצתו פסולה ואמאי כיון דמנעל הוא וי"ל דהאי כמי בהא תליא דכיון דלענין שבת גזר דילמא מיפסיק אינו ראוי להלך בו ודמי לקטן שחלץ במנעל גדול דחליצתו פסולה כדאיתא בפ' מצות חליצה (יבמות קג:) משום דנעלו כתיב נעלו הראוי לו וא"ת היכי גזרי דילמא נפיל ואתי לאתויי הלא אין לו אלא רגל אחד ואי נפיל לא יזוז ממקומו ואומר ר"י דמיירי שנושא בידו מקל ועיקר הליכתו היא בסמיכת המקל והשתא אי נמי מיפסיק יוכל להלך מכאן יש להתיר למי שכווצו גידי שוקיו ללכת במקלו בשבת והרב פור"ת פי' דקיטע יש לו סמך שקושר בכרעו ומגיע לארץ והשוק כפופה לאחוריה וברגל השוק במקום הרגל עושה לו קב(ד) להראות כמו שיש לו רגל ובהא פליגי ר' יוסי סבר כיון שאינו נסמך עליו אלא תלוי באויר חיישינן דילמא נפיל ור"מ לא חייש ולפי זה אין ראיה להתיר לקיטע ללכת במקלו אמנם יש להתיר מסיפא דמתניתין דאינו אוסר אלא סמוכות שלו לפי ששוקיו תלויין באויר ודילמא נפיל ואתי לאתויי (אבל הכסא) והספסלים שבידו אינו אוסר ואיכא הוו דומיא דמקל וק"ק לפי זה אמאי מטמא ליה רבא משום מדרס כיון שאינו נסמך עליו ושמא כשהוא יושב פעמים הוא נסמך עליו ולכך עושה לו בית קבול כתיתין שלא יוזק בקשר העץ שהוא יושב:

סנדל

עין משפט נר מצוה

[נ"ל אבוה דשמואל]

עד א ב מיי' פ"ט מהל' מקואות הלכה יג סמג עשין רמח טוש"ע י"ד סי' רא סעיף ב:

עה ג ד מיי' פי"ט מהל' שבת הלכה יב סמג לאוין סה טוש"ע א"ח סי' שג סעיף כב:

עו ה מיי' שם טוש"ע שם סעיף כג:

[*] למאי דפסק כר"י סימן שלד וכר"ן הכתם מיירי לגבי המשכבות קשה לפרש כן סוגיא זו · ואין ענין כלל לכך דהכא ולפלעיך דכוונת למאי דפליגי בתוספתא פי"ד מצילין מפני הדליקה כו' ועיין וכו' יעי"ל כו' ואין מערימין בכך ר"ל בנ"ש · מהרב סג' ר' בנימין קארנגאלד ז"ל

מסורת הש"ס

מדיס פי: בכורות נה: ע"ש

יומא עח: [יבמות קג:]

[בתוספתא מגילה פ"א ותוספתא דזבים פ"ג]

[פי' רש"י ברכות נח: ד"ה קטען]

הגהות הב"ח

(א) גמ' תיבעי למ"ד מערימין בדליקה תיבעי למ"ד אין מערימין בדליקה תיבעי: (ב) רש"י ד"ה וסבר שמא וכו' שניתוספו בנהר מי הגשמים: (ג) תוספות ד"ה סהדא וכו' מעיד בדבר שהוא: (ד) תוס' ד"ה הקיטע וכו' עושה לו קב כמין סמוך להראות כמו שיש:

רבינו חננאל

להברתה ולא הוה שביק להו דגנייו גבי הדדי סבר דלא לילפו גופא נוכראה (ואמר רב הונא נשים המסוללות זו בזו פסולות לכהונה) והוה עביד לבנתי' מקוה (ביום) [ביומי] ניסן ולא היה מניחן לטבול בפרת מפני שרוב מי פרת בניסן מי מטר הן כרב דאמר מטרא במערבא שהדא רבה פרת · כלומר כיון שתראה כי רבו מי פרת עדות היא שהוגשמה ארץ המערב וסבר אבוה דשמואל שמא ירבו נוטפין שהן מי גשמים הנוטפין מן הגגות ונעשו שאובין על מי הפרת שהן זוחלין כדתני במקוואות בפ' ה' הזוחלין כמעין והנוטפין כמקוה העיד ר' (יצחק) [צדוק] על הזוחלין שרבו על הנוטפין שטכשירין ושאמר שמואל נהרא מכיפיה מתברך כלומר הנהר הגדול מן הסלע שיוצא ממנו משום נרבת מליאתו ולא ממי המטר פליגא על אבוה דשמואל ועל רב ועוד דברי שמואל סותרין זה את זה בכאן אמר כי מי המטר אינם ממלאים הנהר אלא מכיפיה מיבריך ועוד אמר אין המים מטהרין בזוחלין אלא פרת ביומי תשרי בלבד מכלל דבשאר החדשים זולתי תשרי נוטפין הם דגשמים יבו עליהן ומפני ביומי תשרי היה מסתירו לבטחתיו במפני מפני בני אדם שעל הנהר ושובלת בפרת כי דברי הכל בתשרי זוחלין הן ולמה במפני דלית לדו שהרה במקוה: פורפת על האבן ועל האגוז ועל המטבע מע"ש · פי' נותנת אבן או אגוז או מטבע בקצה הסדין כמין קרס בלולאות שלא ישמט הסדין מעליה כדי שתהא מתעטפת באותו סדין ונותנת זה שעשאתו כמין קרס · נשים מדיות מנהגן לצאת בענין הזה פרופות · ובלבד שלא תפרוף בתחלה בשבת על המטבע · והנשים הערביות מנהגן לצאת רעלות ופי' רעלות בירושלמי בליבריאה והן כמו כסוי פנים כדכתיב (ישעיה ג) השרות והרעלות · וי"א זוג ללמדך שבמקושות הללו כך היה מנהגם ומותר להם וכל אדם מותר בכך אלא שדברו חכמים בהווה: בעי אביי אשה מהו שתערים ותפרוף באגוז להוציא לבנה קטן בשבת ועלתה בתיקו: [מתני'] הקיטע יוצא בקב שלו דברי רבי מאיר ורבי

רב נסים גאון

קסבר שמא ירבו הנוטפין על הזוחלין · עיקר דילה בתורת כהנים אי מה מעין מטהר בזוחלין אף מקוה מטהר בזוחלין תלמוד לומר אך המעין מטהר בזוחלין והמקוה מטהר באשבורן ובמסכת מקואות (פרק ה משנה ה) הזוחלין כמעין והנוטפין כמקוה העיד רבי צדוק על הזוחלין שרבו על הנוטפין שהן כשרים ותישתכח בפרק ז' דעדיות הנוטפין שרבו על הזוחלין אינן כשרים:

תיבעי למאן דאמר (סדליקין) [מערימין] בדליקה תיבעי למאן דאמר אין מערימין · עיקר דיליה בפרק כל כתבי הקודש (דף קכ) דתנן לובש כל שהוא יכול ללבוש ועוטף כל מה שהוא יכול להתעטף רבי יוסי אומר י"ח כלי מכלל דתנא קמא סבר מותר ללבוש ולהציל אפילו יתר מי"ח כלי ואף על פי שהוא מערים בכך:

priesthood.[2]—[65b] No: it was in order that they should not become accustomed to a foreign body. 'And he made a *mikweh* for them in the days of Nisan'. This supports Rab, for Rab said: Rain in the West [Palestine] is strongly testified to by the Euphrates;[3] and he [Samuel's father] feared that the rainwater might exceed the running water.[4] Now, he differs from Samuel, who said: A river increases in volume from its beds.[5] But this conflicts with another [statement] of his. For Samuel said: No water purifies when flowing, save the Euphrates in the days of Tishri alone.[6]

A WOMAN MAY WEIGHT [HER CLOAK] WITH A STONE, etc. But you say in the first clause, that she may weight it?[7]—Said Abaye: The second clause refers to a coin.[8]

Abaye asked: May a woman evade [the Sabbath prohibition] by weighting [her cloak] with a nut in order to carry it out to her infant child on the Sabbath? This is a problem on the view of both him who maintains that an artifice may be used and him
a who holds that an artifice may not be used.[1] It is a problem on the view that an artifice may be used in the case of a conflagration: that is only there, because if you do not permit it to him, he will come to extinguish it; but here, if you do not permit it, one will not come to carry it [*sc.* the nut] out.[2] Or perhaps, even on the view that an artifice may not be used; there that is a normal way of carrying [clothes] out;[3] but here this is not a usual way of carrying it, and therefore I might say that it is well.[4] The question stands over.

MISHNAH. A STUMP-LEGGED PERSON MAY GO FORTH WITH HIS WOODEN STUMP:[5] THIS IS R. MEIR'S VIEW; [66a]

(2) *Sc.* to marry a High Priest, who must marry none but a virgin (Lev. XXI, 13), for their lewdness destroys their virginity. Though there were no High Priests in his days, he nevertheless objected to this on grounds of decency, and therefore may have taken steps to prevent it.—V. Weiss, *Dor*, II, 23. (3) Rashi: for when it rains in Palestine the water flows down to Babylon and causes the swelling of the Euphrates. Obermeyer, p. 45 and n. 2 rejects this on hydrographical grounds, and explains that in most cases the rains in northern Mesopotamia in the Taurus range, where the Euphrates has its source, are the precursors of rain in Palestine. —Thus Rab too holds that the swelling of a river is caused chiefly through rain. (4) I.e., the added rain water might exceed the normal volume of the river, in which case it is all regarded as rain water; v. *supra* 65a, n. b11. (5) Lit., 'rock'. Though it seems to swell through the rains, actually more water gushes upward from the river bed than is added by the rain. (6) Which is in accordance with his father and with Rab. (7) Which certainly means that she may do so in the first place on the Sabbath, since the preceding clause has already taught that she may wear a weighted cloak. (8) Which may not be handled on the Sabbath.

a (1) V. *infra* 120a. (2) Hence it is possibly forbidden. (3) E.g., clothes; merchants wear the clothes they have to sell (Rashi). (4) Since the first is the normal way of carrying, when one puts on more than he requires the excess is a mere burden, carried out in the normal manner; hence it is forbidden. But in the case under discussion, even if a person intentionally carries a nut out thus, without any subterfuge, he does not transgress by Biblical law and is not liable to a sin-offering, which is incurred only for doing a thing in its normal fashion. Hence a subterfuge may be permitted even by Rabbinical law (R. Jacob Emden, *Novellae*). (5) A log of wood hollowed out to receive the stump.

WHILE R. JOSE FORBIDS IT. AND IF IT HAS A RECEPTACLE FOR PADS,[6] IT IS UNCLEAN.[7] HIS SUPPORTS[8] ARE UNCLEAN THROUGH MIDRAS,[9] AND ONE MAY GO OUT THEREWITH
a ON THE SABBATH,[1] AND ENTER THE TEMPLE COURT WHILST WEARING THEM.[2] HIS STOOL AND SUPPORTS[3] ARE UNCLEAN AS MIDRAS, AND ONE MAY NOT GO OUT WITH THEM ON THE SABBATH,[4] AND ONE MAY NOT ENTER THE TEMPLE COURT WITH THEM.[5] AN ARTIFICIAL ARM [LUKIṬMIN][6] IS CLEAN, BUT ONE MAY NOT GO OUT THEREWITH.[7]

GEMARA. Raba asked R. Naḥman, How do we learn [this]?[8]—I do not know, replied he. What is the law? I do not know, was his answer. It was stated: Samuel said: A stump-legged person may not, [etc.]; and R. Huna said likewise: A stump-legged person may not, [etc.].[9] R. Joseph observed: Since Samuel said: A stump-legged person may not [etc.], and R. Huna [also] said: A stump-legged person may not [etc.], then we too should learn, A stump-legged person may not. Rabbah b. Shila demurred: Did they not hear what R. Ḥanan b. Raba recited to Ḥiyya b. Rab before Rab in a little room of Rab's academy: A stump-legged person may not go out with his wooden stump: this is R. Meir's view; but R. Jose permits it; whereupon Rab signalled to them that it was the reverse? R. Naḥman b. Isaac observed: And your token is
b *samek samek*.[1]

Now, Samuel too retracted.[2] For we learnt: If she performs *ḥaliẓah*[3] with a shoe that is not his,[4] with a wooden shoe, or with a left-footed [shoe] placed on the right foot, the *ḥaliẓah* is valid. Now we observed, Which Tanna [rules thus]?[5] Said Samuel, R. Meir: For we learnt: A STUMP-LEGGED PERSON MAY GO OUT WITH HIS WOODEN STUMP: THIS IS R. MEIR'S VIEW; WHILE R. JOSE FORBIDS IT.[6]

Now, R. Huna too retracted. For it was taught: A lime burner's shoe[7] is unclean as *midras*, a woman may perform *ḥaliẓah* therewith, and one may go out with it on the Sabbath: this is R. Akiba's view; but they [the Sages] did not agree with him. But it was taught:[8] They agree with him?—Said R. Huna, Who agreed with him? R. Meir.[9] And who did not agree with him? R. Jose.[10] R. Joseph said: Who did not agree with him? R. Joḥanan b. Nuri. For we learnt: A hive of straw and a tube of canes:[11] R. Akiba declares it unclean; while R. Joḥanan b. Nuri declares it clean.[12]

The Master said: 'A lime-burner's shoe is unclean as *midras*'. But
c it is not made for walking?[1]—Said R. Aḥa son of R. 'Ulla: That is because the lime-burner walks in it until he comes home.

AND IF IT HAS A RECEPTACLE FOR PADS, IT IS UNCLEAN. Abaye said: It has the uncleanness of a corpse, but not *midras*; Raba said: It is unclean even as *midras*.[2] Said Raba: Whence do I know it? For we learnt: A child's waggonette[3] is unclean as *midras*. But Abaye said: There he [the child] leans upon it, but here he [the stump-legged person] does not lean upon it. Abaye said: How do I know it? Because it was taught: A staff of old men

(6) Upon which the stump rests. (7) 'Unclean' and 'clean' in this and similar passages means susceptible and not susceptible to uncleanness respectively. A wooden article is unclean only when it has a receptacle for objects to be carried therein. If the log is merely hollowed out for the stump, it is not a receptacle in this sense. (8) Leather supports for one who is stumped in both legs. (9) If he is a *zab*, q.v. Glos. *Midras*, lit., 'treading' is the technical term for the uncleanness occasioned by a *zab* through bringing his weight to bear upon an object, e.g., by treading, sitting, or leaning, even if he does not actually touch it with his body. The degree of defilement imposed thereby is called 'the principal degree of uncleanness' (Heb. *ab*, father), and is only one grade less than that of a corpse: cf. *supra* 13*b*, n. b6.

a (1) They rank as ornaments. (2) Though one may not enter wearing his shoes (Ber. 54*a*), these are not accounted as such. (3) This refers to one who is unable to walk upon supports alone, the muscles of his foreleg being atrophied or paralysed. A stool is made for him, and also supports for his stumps, and he propels himself along with his hands and just a little with his feet too. R. Israel Lipshitz in his commentary זרע ישראל on the Mishnah seems to translate סמוכות here as referring to the *hand* supports used by the cripple in propelling himself along, and not to the foot supports, which meaning it bears in the earlier clause. (4) Rashi: as he does not actually walk upon them, they dangle in the air and may fall off, which will cause him to carry them in the street. (5) There seems no adequate reason for this, and most commentators are silent upon the matter. Tosaf. Yom Ṭob states that 'ONE MAY NOT ... SABBATH' refers only to the 'SUPPORTS' mentioned in the first clause, not to the 'STOOL AND ITS SUPPORTS' (he appears to agree with R. Israel Lipshitz in his interpretation), which are mentioned only to teach that they are unclean as *midras*. (6) Jast. s.v. אנקטמין: for carrying burdens. Rashi: a kind of mask for frightening children. The actual meaning of the word is discussed in the Gemara. (7) Jast.: because it is intended for carrying burdens. Rashi: because it is neither useful nor ornamental. (8) The text seems to have been doubtful, and it was not clear whether R. Meir gave a lenient ruling and R. Jose a stringent one or the reverse. V. Weiss, *Dor*, II, 213 *seqq*. on doubtful and corrupt readings in the Mishnah. (9) This was their text in the Mishnah; thus it differed from ours.

b (1) *Samek* (ס) is a letter of the Hebrew alphabet. Thus R. Jose (יוסי) forbids (אוסר), the *samek* occurring in the name and in the ruling. (2) 'Too' in the sense that he too subsequently held as Rab. (3) V. Glos. (4) *Sc*. her brother-in-law's. (5) That a wooden shoe comes within the term *'and she shall loose his shoe'* (Deut. XXV, 9). (6) R. Meir regards even a hollowed-out log as a shoe, though it is unusual, and the same applies here, though wood is an unusual material for a shoe. Thus Samuel quotes Rab's version of the Mishnah. (7) Rashi states two views: (i) that it was of wood; (ii) that it was of straw. Rashi and Tosaf. incline to the latter view. (8) Wilna Gaon emends: but we learnt, since the citation is from a Mishnah. (9) V. n. 6; the same argument applies here. (10) Thus he accepts our version of the Mishnah. (11) Or reeds. Wilna Gaon emends: A straw mat and a tube of straw. (12) The former holds that straw is the same as wood, which is susceptible to uncleanness, while the latter regards it as a different material.

c (1) It was put on over the ordinary leather shoe to protect the latter from the burning action of the lime. In order to be subject to *midras* uncleanness an object must be used for walking, sitting, or lying upon. (2) 'The uncleanness of a corpse' is mentioned merely as an example of any ordinary defilement, where the uncleanness of the object defiled is one degree less than that of the object which defiles it, and which requires either actual contact or that the object be under the same covering as the corpse. Thus Abaye holds that it attains even a primary degree of uncleanness (*ab haṭum'ah*) through a corpse, which itself possesses a supra-primary degree of uncleanness, but not through the *midras* of a *zab*. Abaye holds that the wooden stump is not made primarily for leaning upon. (3) Rashi: on which it is carried, thus a perambulator. Tosaf: with which a child learns to walk, by holding on to it.

ורבי יוסי אוסר ואם יש לו בית קיבול כתיתין טמא סמוכות שלו טמאין מדרס ויוצאין בהן בשבת ונכנסין בהן בעזרה כסא וסמוכות שלו טמאין מדרס ואין יוצאין בהן בשבת ואין נכנסין בהן בעזרה *לוקטמין טהורין ואין יוצאין בהן: **גמ'** אמר ליה רבא לרב נחמן *היכי תנן אמר ליה לא ידענא *הילכתא מאי אמר ליה לא ידענא איתמר אמר שמואל אין הקיטע וכן אמר רב הונא אין הקיטע אמר רב יוסף הואיל ואמר שמואל אין הקיטע ואמר רב הונא אין הקיטע אנן נמי ניתני אין הקיטע מתקיף לה רבא בר שירא לא שמיע להו הא דמתני ליה רב חנן בר רבא לחייא בר רב קמיה דרב בקיטונא דבי רב אין הקיטע יוצא בקב שלו דברי ר' מאיר ור' יוסי מתיר ומחוי ליה רב איפוך אמר רב נחמן בר יצחק וסימנא סמך סמך(א) ואף שמואל הדר ביה דתנן *חליצה בסנדל שאינו שלו בסנדל של עץ או של שמאל בימין חליצה כשרה ואמרינן מאן תנא אמר שמואל ר"מ היא דתנן הקיטע יוצא בקב שלו דברי ר"מ ר' יוסי אוסר ואף רב הונא הדר ביה דתניא *סנדל של סיידין טמא מדרס ואשה חולצת בו ויוצאין בו בשבת דברי ר"ע ולא הודו לו [א]והתניא הודו לו אמר רב הונא מאן הודו לו ר' מאיר ומאן לא הודו לו ר' יוסי (*אמר רב יוסף) מאן לא הודו לו ר' יוחנן בן נורי *דתנן [ב]*כוורת של קש ושפופרת של קנים ר"ע מטמא ור' יוחנן בן נורי מטהר אמר מר סנדל של סיידין טמא מדרס הא לאו להילוכא עבדי אמר רב אחא בר רב עולא שכן הסייד מטייל בו עד שמגיע לביתו: ואם יש לו בית קיבול כתיתין טמא: אמר אביי טמא טומאת מת ואין טמא מדרס רבא אמר אף טמא מדרס אמר רבא מנא אמינא לה *דתנן עגלה של קטן טמאה מדרס ואביי אמר התם סמיך עילויה הכא לא סמיך עילויה אמר אביי מנא אמינא לה דתניא מקל של זקנים טהור מכלום ורבא התם לתרוצי

רש"י

ור' יוסי אוסר · דלאו תכשיט הוא: ואם יש לו בית קבול כתיתין · שנחקק בו כדי קיבול כתיתין של בגדים רכין ומוכין להניח ראש שוקו עליהן: טמא · מקבל טומאת מגע אבל אם אין לו אלא בית קבול ראש שוקו ואינו מניח שם כתיתין לאו בית קבול לטומאה(ב) והוה ליה כפשוטי כלי עץ ודומיא דשק בעינן שקבול שלו עשוי לטלטל על ידו מה שנותנין לתוכו אבל שוקו אינו מיטלטל ע"ג הכלי: סמוכות שלו · סמוכות של קיטע יש קיטע בשתי רגליו מהלך על שוקיו ועל ארכובותיו ועושה סמוכות של עור לשוקיו: טמאין מדרס · אם זב הוא דהא לסמיכת גופו עביד ומדרס הזב עושה אב הטומאה: ויוצאין בהן בשבת · דתכשיט דידיה הוא: ונכנסין בהן לעזרה · דאע"ג דתנן (ברכות דף נד·) לא יכנס אדם להר הבית במנעלו הני לאו מנעל נינהו דלאו בראש רגלו הן: כסא · יש קיטע שיבשו וכווצו גידי שוקיו ואפי' על ארכובותיו אינו יכול לילך ועושין כמין כסא נמוך ויושב עליו וכשהוא מהלך נסמך על ידיו בספסלים קטנים ועוקר גופו מן הארץ ונדחף לפניו וחוזר ונח על אחוריו והכסא קשור לו מאחוריו: סמוכות · של אותו קיטע עושה לה סמוכות של עור או של עץ לראשי שוקיו או רגליו התלויין וכשהוא נשען על ידיו ועוקר עצמו נשען גם על רגליו קצת: ואין יוצאין בהן בשבת · רבותינו אומרים מפני שאינם צריכין לו כל כך ולא נהירא לי טעמא ואיכא למימר דאיידי דתלו ולא מנחי אארעא זימנין דמשתלפי: ואין נכנסין בהן בעזרה · דמנעל נינהו: לוקטמין · טלמשק"א נעשין לשחוק להבעית תיוקות: טהורים · מלקבל טומאה דאינו לא כלי תשמיש ולא תכשיט: **גמ'** היכי תנן · הקיטע יוצא ורבי יוסי אוסר או אין הקיטע יוצא ורבי יוסי מתיר: בר שירא: קיטונא · חדר קטן של בית המדרש: סמך סמך · ר' יוסי אוסר שתי תיבות שיש בהן סמך סמך זו אצל זו: או של שמאל בימין · סנדל של שמאל נעל בימין וחלצה דחליצה בימין הוא דגמר רגל רגל ממצורע: מאן תנא · דסנדל של עץ חשיב נעלו: סנדל של סיידין · מוכרי סיד וכשמתעסקין בו נועלין אותו ושל עץ הוא מפני שהסיד שורף את העור: ואמר רב הונא גרסי': מאן הודו לו ר' מאיר · דאמר הקיטע יוצא בקב שלו: ור' יוחנן בן נורי מטהר · דלאו אורחא לעשות מקש אלא מקנים ומנעל נמי לאו אורחיה מעץ אלא מעור זה לשון רבותי ולי נראה סנדל של סיידין של קש הוא ור' יוחנן בן נורי מטהר בכלי קש דלאו עץ נינהו ור' עקיבא כעץ חשיב להו דקשין הן: קש · זנבות השבלים: ואין טמא מדרס · דלא מסתמיך עליה הא דנקט טומאת מת ה"ה לכל טומאת מגע אלא משום דאמר אין טמא מדרס שהוא אב הטומאה נקט נמי טומאת מת והכי קאמר נעשה אב הטומאה ע"י מת דכלי עץ שיש לו בית קבול הוא ומקבל כל טומאת מגע ואהל ועל ידי כל הטומאות הוא נעשה ראשון ועל ידי מת שהוא אבי אבות הטומאה נעשה אב הטומאה ואין נעשה אב הטומאה ע"י מדרס דקסבר לאו לסמיכה עבידי אלא לתכשיט ואומרים לו עמוד ונעשה מלאכתנו: עגלה של קטן · לנחק בה ולטלטלו עליה: טמאה מדרס · הואיל ופעמים שיושב עליה והאי נמי זימנין דמסתמיך עליה: טהור מכלום · לא מדרס ולא שאר טומאה לא מטמא מדרס משום דלאו לסמיכה עביד שעל רגלו מהלך ואע"ג דמיסתמיך עליה לפרקים ושאר טומאה נמי לא דפשוטי כלי עץ הוא אלמא אע"ג דזימנין דמסתמיך עליה הואיל ועיקר עשייתה אינה לכך אינה טמאה מדרס ואין לומר משום דפשוט הוא יהא טהור ממדרס דלא הוזכרה טהרת פשוטי כלי עץ אלא לטומאת מגע ואהל דטעמא משום דאיתקש לשק הוא וגבי מת ושרצים הויא היקישא:

תוספות

סנדל של סיידין · פ"ה מוכרי הסיד וכשמתעסקין בסיד נועלין אותו ושל עץ הוא מפני שהסיד שורף את העור זה לשון רבותי ול"נ סנדל סיידין של קש הוא וכפי' זה נראה דהכי תניא בתוספתא סנדל של קש ר' עקיבא מטמא כו':

טמא מדרס ולא הודו לו · וא"ת ואמאי לא הודו לו ומי גרע מכופת שאור שיחדו לישיבה דקי"ל* דטמא מדרס דגבי מדרס לא בעינן דומיא דשק דכל דבר המיוחד למדרס טמא מדרס וי"ל דללשון שפירש רש"י של קש הוא ניחא דכיון דלאו בר קיימא הוא אינו טמא ולא דמי לכופת שאור שהוא בר קיימא והכי אשכחן במשניות* דקתני גבי האלון והאגוז ורימון שחקקום תינוקות למוד בהן עפר שמקבלין טומאה ואילו גבי לפת ואתרוג שחקקו קתני שאינן מקבלין טומאה לפי שאינן מתקיימין וללשון שפירש שסנדל הוי של עץ קשה שהרי ראוי הוא להתקיים כיון שהוא של עץ ושמא י"ל דהיינו טעמא דמטהר סנדל דלא חשיב עביד להילוכא מה שמטייל בו הואיל ואין רגילות לעשות מנעל להילוך כמותו דכוותה בשפופרת כיון שאין רגילות לעשותה מקנים לא חשיבה כלי ולא דמי לכופה שרגילות לעשות לישיבה כמותה: **כוורת** הקש ושפופרת של קנים ר"ע מטמא · ואם תאמר והיכי מטמא (*לענין טמא מת) כיון דלא חזי לישיבה לא מטמא מדרס ולענין טומאת מת הא לא כתיב בפרשה אלא כלי עץ ועור ובגד ושק וי"ל דקש נמי חשיב של עץ כדאמר (ברכות דף מ·) פרי שאכל אדם הראשון חטה היתה אי נמי הך טומאה דרבנן היא: **ורבי** יוחנן מטהר · לפירוש אחרון שפי' בקונטרס דסנדל של קש הוא מדמי שפיר כוורת לסנדל של סיידין ולאידך פירושא שפי' דסנדל של עץ הוא צ"ל דמייתי הכי דכי היכי דר' יוחנן מטהר בכוורת של קש לפי שאין רגילות לעשותה מקש הכי נמי במנעל של סיידין לפי שאין רגילות לעשות מנעל של עץ מטהר: **והא** לאו להילוכא עביד · הקשה הר"ר אליעזר ממיץ לרשב"א מאי פריך והלא משעת מלאכתו הוא מהלך בו ולכך הוא נעשה ותירץ לו דסנדל של סיידין לאו לנעול עשוי אלא אחד מכלי אומנתו של סיידין הוא ועשוי כעין סנדל ויכול לתת רגלו בתוכו לנועלו אך אין עשוי רק לטוח בו את הבית ופעמים שנועל בו ומטייל בו עד שיגיע לביתו ולהכי פריך והא לאו להילוכא כו' ור"י פירש הואיל ואין עשוי כלל לנעילה רק לשמור מנעליו שלא ישרפו בסיד לאו להילוכא עביד ומכל מקום משני לו שכן הסייד כו': **רבא** אמר אף טמא טומאת מדרס · פי' הרב פור"ת הא דלא קתני ברישא דמתניתין ואם יש לו בית קיבול כתיתין טמא מדרס כדקתני בסיפא משום דהוה משמע אבל אם אין לו בית קיבול טהור מן המדרס אבל טמא טומאת מת ולא היא דהא פשוטי כלי עץ הוא ולהכי תנא טמא סתמא דבכה"ג טמא הא אין לו בית קיבול כתיתין טהור לגמרי וא"ת למה לי בית קיבול כתיתין תיפוק ליה דכל הטמא מדרס טמא טומאת מת* וי"ל דבית קיבול כתיתין עושין אותו ראוי למדרס: **עגלה** של קטן · פ"ה עגלה שהקטן יושב עליה ול"נ דא"כ מאי קמ"ל פשיטא דאין לך מיוחד למדרס גדול מזה לכך נ"ל דהיינו עגלה שעושין לקטן להתלמד להלך טמאה מדרס דנשען עליה: קישורי

עין משפט נר מצוה

עז א מיי' פי"ט מהל' שבת הלכה טז סמג לאוין סה טוש"ע א"ח סימן שא סעיף טו:

עח ב שם סעיף טז:

עט ג מיי' פכ"ה מהל' כלים הלכה יח:

[חולין קכט·]

פ ד ה שם הלכה יט:

פא ו שם הלכה טז:

פב ז שם הלכה יז:

[כלים פי"ז מט"ו]

יבמות קא.

בס"י ליתא

[בפי"ז דכלים מי"ז תנן מחצלת הקש ושפופרת הקש ר"ע מטמא ור"י בן נורי מטהר וע"ש בפי' הר"ש ד"ה ר"ע ולכאורה נראה שצ"ל דתניא כוורת וכו']

רבינו חננאל

ורבי יוסי אוסר וכדאוקמוה*) ומחתי בה סימנא סמך סמך כלומר ר' יוסי אוסר (סבר) [דר"ע סברי] הקב של קיטע (אינו) חשוב כסנדל ואסור לצאת בו ביוה"כ והיינו טעמא דר' יוסי דאסר בשבת גזרה דלמא משתמיט ואתי לאתויי ד' אמות ברה"ר (כו') ושמואל נמי ורב יוסף (לפניו הגי' רב הונא) הדרו ואוקמוה למתני' הקטע יוצא דברי ר"מ: סנדל של סיידין · פי' הסייד כשהוא סד קרקעית הבית בסיד נועל סנדלו של עץ ברגלו כדי שלא יהא הסיד אוכל ברגלו· בית קבול כתיתין · פי' חקוק בתוך הקב חקיקה להיות

*) הוצא בא"ז בשם רבינו

רב נסים גאון

סמיכות שלו אין נכנסין בהן לעזרה· מהות מה שנאמרה בפ' הרואה מקום במסכת ברכות (דף נד) ולא יכנס בה לחר הבית במקל

מסורת הש"ס

[במשנה שבמשניות לית' אנקטמין ובערוך כתב כדה כא]

עדיות פ"ב מ"ח תוספתא דכלים ב"ב פ"ד [ע"ש]

נ"ל רב יוסף אמר] שם

ביצה כג: תוספתא דכלים ב"ב פ"ד

הגהות הב"ח

(א) גמרא וסימנא סמך סמך· נ"ב עי' בפ' ח' שרצים דף קי ע"א במ"ש התוספו' בד"ה סיסאני: (ב) רש"י ד"ה טמא מקבל וכו' לטומאה הוא והוה וכו' דדומיא דשק:

הגהות הגר"א

[א] גמ' והתניא· נ"ב והתנן · מתני' בעדיות: [ב] שם (כוורת) של קש ושפופרת של (קנים) תא"מ נ"ב מחלת הקש ושפופרת הקש ועיין בפי"ז דכלים:

גליון הש"ס

גמ' אמר רב יוסף מאן לא הודו לו· ברמב"ן במלחמות פ"ח דיומא רס כאן רבה אמר: רש"י ד"ה טמא וכו' אבל שוקו אינו מיטלטל· עיין לקמן דף פא ע"א תוס' ד"ה אפי' פותחות:

עין משפט
נר מצוה

פג א ב ג מיי' פי"ט מהל' שבת הלכה טו סמג לאוין סה טוש"ע א"ח סימן שא סעיף כ :
פד ד מיי' פכ"א מהל' שבת הל' לא סמג לאוין סה טוש"ע א"ח סי' שכח סעיף מ וסעי' מג :
פה ה מיי' שם הל' כג טוש"ע שם סעי' מא :
[ערך אנקטמין]
פו ו ז מיי' פכ"א שם הלכה לא :
[וע"ע תוספות מנחות לא: תד"ה שידה]
[פרמאי פי' חתיכה של בגד שקושרין לזקנים על פיהם למען ירים מפני ששפתותיהן מתרפטות ערוך ערך אנקטמין וע"ע בערוך ערך פרמא]
פז ח ט מיי' פי"ט שם הלכה יד סמג שם טוש"ע א"ח סימן שג סעיף כד :

לתרוצי סוגיא · לתקן פסיעותיו ולזקוף קומה מפני שרגליו ושוקיו רותתות ולא לסמיכת כל גופו : אני שונה אשה חולצת בהן · אלמא נעל קרינא ביה : חמרא דאכפא · חמור הגישא בכתפיים הליצנים עושין אותו ונראה כמי שרוכב עליו ובמקומנו נקרא אודפיס"א : קישורי · אשקלי"ש שמהלכין בהם במקום טיט וקשיא לי הני דטהורין מטומאת מגע דפשוטי כלי עץ נינהו אבל מן המדרס למה טהורין : פרמי · טלמושא הנקשרת על הפרצוף להבעית הבנים קטנים : מתני' בקשרים · מפרש בגמרא : בזגין · איסקליט"ש של זהב לנוי : גמ' אדא מרי · כך שמו : קשרי פואה · גרנצ"א קושרים בקשרים ותולין בצואר לרפואה ולא ידעתי לאיזה חולי : מוקמי · מעמידין החולי שלא יגדל : ה' · קשרים : מסו · מתרפאין : נגרי · פסיעות : נפל פותא בבירא · נפל רפואת הפואה בבור דאין אדם נזהר בכל אלו : מאי איריא בנים · לרב יהודה פריך אי קישורין דמתני' לרפואת חולי נינהו מאי איריא בנים : געגועין · ברמור"ט מגעגע עליו ואינו יכול ליפרד ממנו ורפואה זו לא שייכא בנקבות שאין האב מחבבן כל כך מתחילתן שיהו מגעגעין עליו : תפילין · שיד ימינו קושרתו לשמאלו זהו סימן לגירסא : סכנתא · שמגעגע יותר מדאי : סחופי כסא · כוס שיש בו הבל כגון שעירו ממנו מים חמין וכופהו על הטיבור למי שחש במעיו ואוחז הכוס את הבשר ומושך אליו את המעיים ומושיבן במקומן : לסוך · בכפות ידיו ורגליו : דרב הונא מבי רב · שהיה בא מבי רב שהוא רבו וכן רב מבי ר' חייא ור' חייא מבי רבי : מבסמי · שכורין שהיו משקין את התלמידים ואנו מפני שחשובין הן היו עושין להן דבר להפג את יינן : לגוייתא דידייהו · תוכי ידיהם דהיינו כף : דלייל · שהולך ונעשה לנול כל שעה מחום הבשר : שיעא דדנא · מגופת החבית : דליל האי שיעא · מחמת המים : ליחנק · מי שנפרקה חוליא של מפרקת צוארו(ג) וטפלת בגרונו תולין אותו בראשו שיהא צוארו נפשט ודומה לחניקה : לפופי · לכורכו בבגדים וקושרו בחגורה רחבה ומתיישבין פרקי אבריו שהן רכין ונשמטין בחבלי הלידה וקורין אנמלטוויי"ר בלע"ז : מתני בנים · שתי שמועות דאיירי בקטנים היה שונה בשם רבי (*אבא) בר הונא משמיה דרב חמא בר גוריא : בן · חדא שמעתא דאיירי בקטן מתני בשמיה : תרוייהו · געגועין ולפופי : כל מנייני · כל לחשות ומפני שכופלין אותן יש ג' פעמים ויש יותר קרי להו מנייני : בשמא דאמא · פלוני בן פלונית : דמיפרשי · כל לחשים שמפורש מניין כמה פעמים שיאמרו ויכפלו אותו : כדמפרשי · כופלין אותו כפי מניינו ודלא מיפרשי בהם סתם כופלין ארבעין וחד זימנין : אבן תקומה · אבן שנשאות אותה נשים עוברות שלא יפילו וקורין לה קוטאנ"א בלע"ז : במשקל · שום דבר ששקלוהו כנגדה :

*לתרוצי סוגיא עבידא הכא לסמוך עילויה הוא דעבידא וסמיך עליה(א) : טמאין מדרס ואין יוצאין בהן בשבת ואין נכנסין בהן לעזרה : תני תנא קמיה דר' יוחנן נכנסין בהן לעזרה א"ל אני שונה אשה חולצת בו ואת אמרת נכנסין תני אין נכנסין בהן לעזרה : לוקטמין טהורה : מאי לוקטמין אמר ר' אבהו *חמרא דאכפא *רבא בר פפא אמר קישורי רבא בר רב הונא אמר *פרמי : **מתני'** הבנים יוצאין בקשרים ובני מלכים בזוגין וכל אדם אלא שדברו חכמים בהווה : **גמ'** מאי קשרים אמר אדא מרי אמר רב נחמן בר ברוך אמר רב אשי בר אבין אמר רב יהודה קשורי פואה אמר אביי *אמרה לי אם תלתא מוקמי חמשה מסו שבעה אפילו לכשפים מעלי אמר רב אחא בר יעקב והוא דלא חזי ליה שמשא וסיהרא ולא חזי מיטרא ולא שמיע ליה קול ברזלא וקל תרנגולתא וקל ניגרי אמר רב נחמן בר יצחק *נפל פותא בבירא מאי איריא בנים אפי' בנות נמי מאי איריא קטנים אפי' גדולים נמי אלא מאי קשרים כי הא דאמר אבין בר הונא א"ר חמא בר גוריא בן שיש (ב) געגועין על אביו נוטל רצועה ממנעל של ימין וקושר לו בשמאלו אמר רב נחמן בר יצחק וסימניך תפילין והילופא סכנתא אמר אבין בר הונא אמר רב חמא בר גוריא סחופי כסא אטיבורי בשבתא שפיר דמי ואמר אבין בר הונא אמר רב חמא בר גוריא מותר לסוך שמן ומלח בשבת כי הא דרב הונא מבי רב ורב מבי ר' חייא ור' חייא מבי רבי כי הוו מיבסמי מייתי משחא ומילחא ושייפי להו לגוייתא דידייהו וגוייתא דכרעייהו ואמרי כי היכי דציל הא מישחא ליציל חמריה דפלניא בר פלניתא ואי לא מייתי שיעא דדנא ושרי ליה במיא ואמר כי היכי דליציל האי שיעא ליציל חמריה דפלניא בר פלניתא ואמר אבין בר הונא אמר רב חמא בר גוריא מותר לחנק בשבת ואמר אבין בר הונא אמר רב חמא בר גוריא *לפופי ינוקא בשבתא שפיר דמי רב פפא מתני בנים רב זביד מתני בן רב פפא מתני בנים ותרוייהו מתני להו באבין בר הונא רב זביד מתני בן קמייתא מתני באבין בר הונא והאי מתני לה ברבה בר בר חנה דאמר *רבה בר בר חנה לפופי ינוקא בשבתא שפיר דמי אמר אביי אמרה לי אם כל מנייני בשמא דאימא וכל קטרי בשמאלא ואמר אביי אמרה לי אם כל מנייני דמפרשי כדמפרשי ודלא מפרשי ארבעין וחד זימני ת"ר יוצאין באבן תקומה בשבת משום ר"מ אמרו אף במשקל אבן תקומה ולא שהפילה אלא שמא תפיל ולא שעיברה אלא שמא תתעבר ותפיל אמר רב יימר בר שלמיא משמיה דאביי והוא דאיכוון ואיתקל בעי אביי משקל דמשקל מאי תיקו ואמר אביי אמרה לי אם לאשתא בת יומא לישקול זוזא חיוורא וליזיל למלחתא וליתקול מתקליה מילחא ולצייריה בחללא דבי צואר בנירא ברקא ואי לא ליתוב אפרשת דרכים וכי חזי שומשמנא גמלא דדרי מידי לישקליה ולישדייה בגובתא דנחשא וליסתמיא באברא וליחתמי בשיתין גושפנקי ולברזוליה ולידריה ולימא ליה טעונך עלי וטעונאי עלך אמר ליה רב אחא בריה דרב הונא לרב אשי ודילמא איניש אשכחיה ואיפסק ביה אלא לימא ליה טעונאי וטעונך עלך ואי לא לישקול כוזא חדתא וליזיל לנהרא ולימא ליה נהרא נהרא אוזפן כוזא דמיא לאורחא דאיקלע לי ולהדר שב זימני על רישיה ולשדיין לאחוריה ולימא ליה נהרא נהרא שקול מיא דיהבת לי דאורחא דאיקלע לי ביומיה אתא וביומיה אזל אמר רב הונא לאשתא

קישורי · פי' הקונטרס אשקל"ש והקשה בקונטרס ור"י תירץ דכיון שאינם עשויים אלא ללכת דרך העברה בטיט *אינו טמא מדרס ובערוך* פירש דקישורי הייגו אשקל"ש שעושין הליצני והן גבוהין מאד ואינן אלא לרקד עליהן ולא להילוך עבידי* :

בני

ולא שהפילה · ולא תאמר שלא התירו לצאת בה אלא לאשה שעלולה להפיל עוברה שהפילה כבר עובר אחר : ולא שעיברה · שידוע לה שהיא מעוברת : והוא דאיכוון ותקל · שנמלא החפץ מאליו למשקל האבן ולא שחיסרו ממנו או הוסיפו עליו לכוונו : בת יומא · שאחזתו בכל יום : זוזא חיוורא · צרוף וחדש : למלהתא · למקום שריפת המים שעושין נגרים על שפת הים להמשיך מים לבריכות רחבות העשויות לכך וכשנתמלאו סותם החריצין והשמש שורף את המים שמלוחין הן ונעשה מלח : בחללא דבי צואריה · תחת גרונו כנגד מפתחי חלוקו לשון רבינו הלוי : נירא ברקא · לילא של שער : פרשת דרכים · מקום ששני דרכים מתפרשים : שומשמנא גמלא · נמלה גדולה* : דדרי מידי · שטוען כלום : לישקליה · לשומשמנא : בגובתא דנחשא · כמין קנה של נחשת : ולסתמייה באברא · יסתום פיה בעופרת : גושפנקי · חותמות ולאו דוקא שיתן נקט ולאו דוקא חותמות של צורה אלא סתימות הרבה זו על זו שטוח על העופרת וטוח זפת וטוח טיט : ולברזוליה · ינענענו : ולידריה · ישאנו : ולימא ליה · לשומשמנא : טעונך עלי · מה שהיית נושא אשאנו : וטעונאי · החולי שלי : איניש אשכחיה ואיפסיק ביה · חולי כזה שזה עושה וכי אמר ליה טעונך עלי זהו חולי של חברו : כוזא חדתא · כלי חרס קטן חדש : אוזפן · הלוני : וליהדריה ז' זימני ארישיה · יקיפנו סביבות ראשו : לאשתא

מסורת הש"ס

[תרגום של וכמישור ובתרגומא ועי' בערוך ערך אכן]
בד' ספד"ע רפרם וכ"ס בר"ף
[קדושין לא: וש"נ]
[כרתות ט.]
[לקמן קמו: ע"ש]
[נ"ל אבין]
[פי' שמתכרכין איבריו כמו ויתכר תרגומו ולפוף ערוך]

הגהות הב"ח

(א) גמ' כסא וסמוכות שלו טמאין מדרס : (ב) שם בן שיש לו געגועין : (ג) רש"י ד"ה ליחנק וכו' צוארו נ"ב ס"א או נפלה לו ערלת הגרון וטפל בגרונו וכו' :

גליון הש"ס

תוס' ד"ה קישורי וכו' אינו טמא מדרס · עיין מנחות דף לא ע"א תוספות ד"ה שידה :

בלשון ארמית אומר לכל דבר גדול גמלא הרמב"ם בפי' המשנה כלאים פ"ט מ"ב

רבינו חננאל

הכתיתין ומוגלא הזבה מרגלו זבין מתקבצין באותה החקיקה ולא יהו מצערין אותו בארכובותיו אמר אביי טמא טומאת מת מפני שיש בו בית קבול והוי כלי · רבא אמר אף טמא מדרס כמו עגלה של קטן יוצאין בהן בשבת כי אולם (משא וכלים הם) [משתמשים] תני תנא קמיה דרבי יוחנן נכנסין בהן לעזרה כלומר אינם סנדל כי אסור אדם ליכנס בסנדל בעזרה כדתנן (ברכות נד') לא יכנס אדם להר הבית במקל ובמנעלו כו' א"ל אני שונה אשה חולצת בסנדל של עץ ואתה שונה נכנסין תני אין נכנסין : לוקטמין חמרא דאכפי · גידם מי שידיו קצוצות עושין לו יד של עץ ונקרא חמרא דאכפי : פרמי פי' פרמו יש מי שאומרים חתיכה של בגד שקושרין לזקנים*) ששפתותיהן מתרפטות: קשרים קשרי פואה משום רפואה · בן שיש לו געגועין על אביו יש מי שאומרים כי כשיגדל עצב הבן במיתת אביו נוטל רצועה ממנעל אביו הימין וקושרה בשמאל הבן ואומרים שמשקים לבו ואם יחליף אומרים שהוא סכנה וסימניך תפילין והן שעל היד השמאל : סחופי כסא אטיבורא · פי' אם בולם טיבורו של אדם ברוק ממעיו או אם ניקב מניחין שם [כוס] קטן על טיבורו כדי שלא יבלום ויתבקע ומניחין אותו עד שיתרפא הא דשרו לבסימא לסוך מלח ושמן לכרעייהו פשוטה היא פי' לחנק פי' לפופי ינוקא · אבן תקומה פי' אומרים כי יש אבן ידועה כשהיא תלויה על אשה הרה אינה מפלת וגם המשקל שכנגד אותו האבן מועלת ומותר לצאת בהן בשבת אבל

*) עי' בגליון בשכ הערוך וכ"ה בא"ז בשם רבינו ·

רב נסים גאון

ובמנעלו : **רב** פפא מתני בנים תרווייהו · כלומר שהיה שונה הראשונה בן שיש לו געגועין על אביו וזו האחרת לפופי משום אבון בר הונא אמר רב חמא בר גוריא והיה רב זביד שוה עמו בשמועה ראשונה בן שיש לו געגועין על אביו וחלוק עליו בשמועה שניה לפופי ינוקא והיה רב זביד אומרה משם רבה בר בר חנה אמר רבי יוחנן ולפי שהיתה השמועה הראשונה, בן שיש לו געגועין על אביו והשניה לפופי ינוקא ואמר על שניהם מתני בנים זה הוא פירושם והוזקקתי לכותבו הנה מפני שראיתיו קשה לתלמידים וביארתיו כדי שיתגלה לכל : סליק פרק במה אשה

is completely clean.[4] And Raba?[5]—There [66b] it is made to facilitate his steps;[6] whereas here it is made to lean on, and he does so.[7]

HIS STOOL AND SUPPORTS ARE UNCLEAN AS MIDRAS, AND ONE MAY NOT GO OUT WITH THEM ON THE SABBATH, AND ONE MAY NOT ENTER THE TEMPLE COURT WITH THEM. A tanna recited before R. Joḥanan: One may enter the Temple court with them. Said he to him, I learn, A woman can perform *ḥaliẓah* therewith,[8] yet you say [that] they may enter! Learn, One may not enter the Temple court with them.

AN ARTIFICIAL ARM [LUḲIṬMIN] IS CLEAN. What is *luḳiṭ-* a *min?*—Said R. Abbahu: A pulley for loads.[1] Raba b. Papa said: Stilts. Raba son of R. Huna said: A mask.

MISHNAH. BOYS MAY GO OUT WITH GARLANDS [ḲESHARIM], AND ROYAL CHILDREN MAY GO OUT WITH BELLS, AND ALL PEOPLE [MAY DO LIKEWISE], BUT THAT THE SAGES SPOKE OF THE USUAL PRACTICE.

GEMARA. What is ḲESHARIM?—Said Adda Mari in the name of R. Naḥman b. Baruch in the name of R. Ashi b. Abin in Rab Judah's name: Garlands of *pu'ah*.[2] (Abaye said, Mother[3] told me: Three[4] arrest [illness], five cure [it], seven are efficacious even against witchcraft. R. Aḥa b. Jacob observed: Providing that neither the sun nor the moon see it, and that it does not see rain nor hear the sound of iron, or the cry of a fowl or the sound of steps. R. Naḥman b. Isaac said: The *pu'ah* has fallen into a pit!)[5] Why [then] particularly BOYS; even girls too [may go out therewith]? And why particularly children; even adults too?[6]—But [then] what is meant by ḲESHARIM? As Abin b. Huna said in the name of R. Ḥama b. Guria: If a son yearns for his father [the father] takes a strap from his right shoe and ties it to his left [hand].[7] R. Naḥman b. Isaac said: And your token is phylacteries.[8] But if the reverse there is danger.[9]

Abin b. Huna said in the name of R. Ḥama b. Guria: The placing of a [hot] cup upon the navel on Sabbath[10] is permitted. Abin b. Huna also said in the name of R. Ḥama b. Guria: One may b rub in oil and salt on the Sabbath.[1] Like R. Huna at Rab's college, and Rab at R. Ḥiyya's, and R. Ḥiyya at Rabbi's,[2] when they felt the effect of the wine they would bring oil and salt and rub into the palms of their hands and the instep of their feet and say, 'Just as this oil is becoming clear,[3] so let So-and-so's wine become clear.'[4] And if [this was] not [possible], they would bring the sealing clay of a wine vessel and soak it in water and say, 'Just as this clay becomes clear, so let So-and-so's wine become clear.'[5]

Abin b. Huna also said in the name of R. Ḥama b. Guria: One may reset [a laryngeal muscle][6] on the Sabbath. Abin b. Huna also said in the name of R. Ḥama b. Guria: To swaddle a babe on the Sabbath is in order.[7] R. Papa recited [two dicta about] children, [while] R. Zebid recited [one dictum] about a child.[8] R. Papa recited [the two dicta about] children,[9] and both in the name of Abin b. Huna. While R. Zebid recited a dictum about a child [in his name]; for the first he recited in the name of Abin b. Huna, but this [latter one] he recited in the name of Rabbah b. Bar Ḥanah, for Rabbah b. Bar Ḥanah said: To swaddle a babe on the Sabbath is in order.

Abaye said: Mother told me, All [incantations] which are repeated several times must contain the name of the patient's mother, and all knots[10] must be on the left [hand?]. Abaye also said: Mother told me, Of all [incantations], the number of times they are to be repeated, is as stated; and where the number is not stated, it is forty-one times.

Our Rabbis taught: One may go out with a preserving stone[11] on the Sabbath. On the authority of R. Meir it was said: Even c with the counterweight of a preserving stone.[1] And not only when one has miscarried,[2] but even [for fear] lest she miscarry; and not only when she is [already] pregnant, but even lest she become pregnant and miscarry. R. Yemar b. Shalmia said on Abaye's authority: Provided that it was found to be its natural counterweight.[3] Abaye asked: What about the counterweight of the counterweight? The question stands over.

Abaye also said: Mother told me, For a daily fever[4] one must take a white *zuz*,[5] go to a salt deposit,[6] take its weight in salt, and tie it up in the nape of the neck with a white twisted cord. But if this is not [possible], let one sit at the cross-roads, and when he sees a large ant carrying something, let him take and throw it into a brass tube and close it with lead, and seal it with sixty seals.[7] Let him shake it, lift it up and say to it, 'Thy burden be upon me and my burden be upon thee.' Said R. Aḥa son of R. Huna to R. Ashi: But perhaps [another] man had [previously] found it and cast [his illness] upon it?[8] Rather let him say to it, 'My burden and thy burden be upon thee.' But if this is impossible, let him take a new pitcher, go to the river and say to it, 'O river, O river, lend me a pitcher of water for a journey that had chanced to me.' Let him then turn it seven times about his head, throw it behind his back, and say to it, 'O river, O river, take back the water thou gavest me, for the journey that chanced to me came in its day and departed in its day!'

(4) I.e., it is susceptible neither to *midras* nor to any other form of defilement. It is not susceptible to *midras* because it is not made for leaning, since one walks on his feet. This shows that though one does lean on it occasionally, yet since that is not its main purpose, it is not defiled as *midras*, and the same applies here.—It is not susceptible to other forms of defilement because it is a wooden utensil without a cavity (p. *supra* 52*b*, n. c6). (5) How does he rebut this proof? (6) But not that his whole body should lean upon it. (7) I.e., its purpose is to bear the weight of his whole body. (8) Which shows that they count as shoes, in which one may not enter the Temple court.

a (1) So Jast. Rashi: a wooden donkey's head worn by mummers. (2) A vegetable; dyer's madder; a prophylactic. (3) She was really his foster-mother, v. Ḳid. 31*a*. (4) Garlands; or, plants. (5) It is useless as a remedy to-day, as none take all these precautions—probably a sarcastic remark showing his disbelief in these remedies. (6) This is an objection to Rab Judah's explanation. If the Mishnah means garlands used as prophylactics, they are surely not confined to young boys! (7) This cures him so that he is able to bear his father's absence. (8) The right hand winds the strap on the left hand. (9) If the strap of his left is tied to the son's right. (10) To alleviate stomach ache.

b (1) Into the skin. (2) I.e., when they were at these colleges. (3) The heat of the flesh would clarify it. (4) Let the fumes depart! (5) This is an instance of sympathetic magic. (6) Lit., 'strangle'. An operation performed in cases of abdominal affection by squeezing the jugular veins. Rashi and *'Aruk* reads: one may have the laryngeal muscle reset. (7) In order to set its limbs. (8) I.e., R. Papa recited two separate dicta about children, both in the name of Abin b. Huna, as explained below, while R. Zebid recited a single law about children in his name. (9) The one referring to the child that yearns for his father and the other relating to swaddling. (10) For magical purposes of healing. (11) As a safeguard against abortion. [The *aetit* (or Eagle stone). For the belief in the efficacy of this stone against abortion among the ancients v. Preuss, *Medizin*, p. 446].

c (1) Anything that was weighed against it. (2) To protect her from a repetition. (3) Without anything having been added or taken away. (4) A quotidian whose paroxysms recur every day. (5) I.e., new and clean. (6) In a cavity in which sea-water was allowed to evaporate. (7) The number is not exact, but simply means many e.g., sealing wax over the lead, then pitch above that, then clay, etc. (Rashi). (8) And the second would now take it over.

R. Huna said: [67a] [As a remedy] for a tertian fever one should procure seven prickles from seven palm trees, seven chips from seven beams, seven pegs from seven bridges, seven [heaps of] ashes from seven ovens, seven [mounds of] earth from under seven door-sockets, seven specimens of pitch from seven ships, seven handfuls of cummin, and seven hairs from the beard of an old dog, and tie them in the nape of the neck with a white twisted a thread.[1]

R. Joḥanan said: For an inflammatory fever let one take an all-iron knife, go whither thorn-hedges[2] are to be found, and tie a white twisted thread thereto.[3] On the first day he must slightly notch it, and say, *'and the angel of the Lord appeared unto him,* etc.'[4] On the following day he [again] makes a small notch and says, *'And Moses said, I will turn aside now, and see,* etc.' The next day he makes [another] small notch and says, *'And when the Lord saw that he turned aside* [sar] *to see.'*[5] R. Aḥa son of Raba said to R. Ashi, Then let him say, *'Draw not nigh hither?'*[6] Rather on the first day he should say, *'And the angel of the Lord appeared unto him,* etc. . . . *And Moses said, I will,* etc.'; the next day he says, *'And when the Lord saw that he turned aside to see'*; on the third, *'And He said, Draw not nigh.'* And when he has recited his verses he pulls it down [*sc.* the bush] and says thus: 'O thorn, O thorn, not because thou art higher than all other trees did the Holy One, blessed be He, cause His *Shechinah* to rest upon thee, but because thou art lower than all other trees did He cause His *Shechinah* to rest upon thee. And even as thou sawest the fire [kindled] for Hananiah, Mishael and Azariah and didst flee from before them, so look upon the fire [i.e., fever,] of So-and-so[7] and flee from him.'

For an abscess one should say thus: 'Let it indeed be cut down, let it indeed be healed, let it indeed be overthrown; Sharlai and b Amarlai are those angels who were sent from the land of Sodom[1] to heal boils and aches: *bazak, bazik, bizbazik, mismasik, kamun kamik,*[2] thy colour [be confined] within thee, thy colour [be confined] within thee,[3] thy seat be within thee,[4] thy seed be like a *ḳaluṭ*[5] and like a mule that is not fruitful and does not increase; so be thou not fruitful nor increase in the body of So-and-so.'[6] Against ulcers[7] one should say thus: 'A drawn sword and a prepared sling, its name is not Joheb, sickness and pains.' Against a demon one should say thus: 'Thou wast closed up; closed up wast thou. Cursed, broken, and destroyed be Bar Ṭiṭ, Bar Ṭame, Bar Ṭina[8] as Shamgez, Mezigaz and Isṭamai.' For a demon of the privy one should say thus: 'On the head of a lion and on the snout of a lioness did we find the demon Bar Shirika Panda; with a bed of leeks I hurled him down, [and] with the jawbone of an ass I smote him.'

AND ROYAL CHILDREN MAY GO OUT WITH BELLS. Who is the authority [for this ruling]?—Said R. Oshaia: It is R. Simeon, who maintained: All Israel are royal children. Raba said: It means that it is woven [sewn] into his garment; thus it agrees with all.

MISHNAH. ONE MAY GO OUT WITH A ḤARGOL'S EGG,[9] A FOX'S TOOTH, AND A NAIL FROM [THE GALLOWS OF] AN IMPALED CONVICT AS A PROPHYLACTIC: THIS IS R. MEIR'S VIEW; BUT THE SAGES FORBID THIS EVEN ON WEEKDAYS ON ACCOUNT OF 'THE WAYS OF THE AMORITE.'[10]

GEMARA. ONE MAY GO OUT WITH A ḤARGOL'S EGG, which is carried for ear-ache; AND WITH A FOX'S TOOTH, which is worn on account of sleep: a living [fox's] for one who sleeps [too much], a dead [fox's] for him who cannot sleep.

AND A NAIL FROM [THE GALLOWS OF] AN IMPALED CONVICT. It is applied to an inflammation.

AS A PROPHYLACTIC: THIS IS R. MEIR'S VIEW. Abaye and Raba both maintain: Whatever is used as a remedy is not [for- c bidden] on account of the ways of the Amorite.[1] Then if it is not an [obvious] remedy, is it forbidden on account of the ways of the Amorite? But surely it was taught: If a tree casts its fruit, one paints it with *sikra*[2] and loads it with stones. Now, as for loading it with stones, that is in order to lessen its strength.[3] But when he paints it with *sikra*, what remedy does he effect?[4] —That is in order that people may see and pray for it. Even as it was taught: *And he* [the leper] *shall cry, 'Unclean, unclean'*:[5] he must make his grief publicly known, so that the public may pray for him. Rabina observed: In accordance with whom do we suspend a cluster of dates on a [sterile] date tree? In accordance with this Tanna.

A tanna recited the chapter of Amorite practices[6] before R. Ḥiyya b. Abin. Said he to him: All these are forbidden as Amorite practices, save the following: If one has a bone in his throat, he may bring of that kind, place it on his head, and say thus: 'One by one go down, swallow, swallow, go down one by one': this is not considered the ways of the Amorite. For a fish bone he should say thus: 'Thou art stuck in like a pin, thou art locked up as [within] a cuirass; go down, go down.'

a (1) Magical properties were ascribed to the number seven, which was regarded as the most sacred number. Various factors were responsible for this: it is a combination of three and four, themselves held to be sacred; there are seven days in the week; the seventh day is holy.—The Rabbis, though opposed to superstitious practices in general (v. *supra* 53a, n. c3), were nevertheless children of their age, and recognized their efficacy. (2) Or, wild rose bushes. (3) The knife, or the thorn bush? (4) Ex. III, 2. (5) Ibid. 4. *Sar* also means to depart, and it is applied magically to the fever. The belief in the efficacy of sacred books or verses to effect cures, etc., was widespread in ancient times both among pagans and believers in God. V. *J.E.* art. Bibliomancy. (6) Ibid. 5; this may appropriately be referred to the illness. (7) Mentioning the mother's name.

b (1) Rashi: this is the incantation formula, but they were not actually sent thence. (2) Unintelligible words forming part of the incantation. (3) Let it not change to a deeper red. (4) Let it not spread. (5) An animal with uncloven hoofs (the sign of uncleanness) born of a clean animal. Rashi: one whose semen is locked up, so that he cannot reproduce. (6) Mentioning the mother's name. (7) Others: epilepsy. (8) Lit., 'the son of clay, son of defilement, son of filth' —names for the demon. (9) *Ḥargol* is a species of locust. (10) These are forms of heathen magic, forbidden in *neither shall ye walk in their statutes*, Lev. XVIII, 3.

c (1) I.e., where its remedial character is obvious, in contrast to magic. (2) A red paint. (3) It casts its fruit because they grow too heavy, owing to the tree's super-vitality. (4) Surely it is only magic? (5) Lev. XIII, 45. (6) Chapters seven and eight of the Tosefta on Shabbath, which deals with these.

לאשתא תילתא לייתי שבעה סילוי משבעה דיקלי ושבעה *ציבי משבעה כשורי ושבעה סיכי משבעה גשורי ושבעה קטימי משבעה תנורי ושבעה עפרי משבעה *סנרי ושבעה כופרי משבעה ארבי ושבעה בוני כמוני ושבעה ביני מדיקנא דכלבא סבא ולציירינהו בחללא דבי צוארא בנירא ברקא א"ר יוחנן לאשתא צמירתא לישקל סכינא דכולא פרזלא וליזל להיכא דאיכא וורדינא וליקטר ביה נירא ברקא יומא קמא ליחרוק ביה פורתא °ולימא °וירא מלאך ה' אליו וגו' למחר ליחרוק ביה פורתא ולימא °ויאמר משה אסורה נא ואראה למחר ליחרוק ביה פורתא *ולימא° וירא ה' כי סר לראות וגו' א"ל רב אחא בריה דרבא לרב אשי ולימא °ויאמר אל תקרב הלום וגו' אלא ליומא קמא לימא וירא מלאך ה' אליו וגו' ויאמר משה וגו' ולמחר לימא וירא ה' כי סר לראות ולמחר ויאמר (ה') אל תקרב הלום וכי פסק ליה ליתתיה ולפסקי ולימא הכי הסנה הסנה לאו משום דגביהת מכל אילני אשרי הקב"ה שכינתיה עלך אלא משום דמיכת מכל אילני אשרי קודשא בריך הוא שכינתיה עלך וכי היכי דחמיתיה אשתא לחנניה מישאל ועזריה ועריקת מן קדמוהי כן תחמיניה אשתא לפלוני בר פלונית ותיערוק מקדמוהי לסימטא לימא הכי בז בזייה מס מסייא כס כסייה שרלאי ואמרלאי אלין מלאכי דאישתלחו מארעא דסדום ולאסאה שחינא כאיבין בזך בזיך בזבזיך מסמסיך כמון כמיך עיניך ביך עינך ביך אתריך בך זרעיך כקלוט וכפרדה דלא פרה ולא רביא כך לא תפרה ולא תרבה בגופיה דפלוני בר פלונית *לכיפה לימא הכי חרב שלופה וקלע נטושה לא שמיה יוכב חולין מכאובין לשידא לימא הכי הוית דפקיק דפקיק הוית ליטא תבור ומשומת בר טיט בר טמא בר טינא כשמגז מריגז ואיסטמאי לשידא דבית הכסא לימא הכי אקרקפי דארי ואאוסי דגורייתא אשכחתון לשידאי בר שיריקא פנדא במישרא דכרתי חבטיה בלועא דחמרא חטרתיה: ובני מלכים בזגין: מאן תנא א"ר אושעיא רבי שמעון היא דאמר *כל ישראל בני מלכים הם רבא אמר *באריג בכסותו ודברי הכל:

מתני' [ב]יוצאין בביצת החרגול ובשן שועל ובמסמר מן הצלוב משום רפואה *דברי ר"מ וחכמים אוסרין אף בחול משום דרכי האמורי: **גמ'** יוצאין בביצת החרגול דעבדי לשיחלא ובשן של שועל דעבדי לשינתא דחייא למאן דניים דמיתא למאן דלא ניים: ובמסמר מן הצלוב: דעבדי לזירפא: משום רפואה דברי רבי מאיר: *אביי ורבא דאמרי תרווייהו °[ג]כל דבר שיש בו משום רפואה אין בו משום דרכי האמורי *הא אין בו משום רפואה יש בו משום דרכי האמורי והתניא אילן שמשיר פירותיו סוקרו (וצובע אותו) בסיקרא וטוענו באבנים בשלמא טוענו באבנים כי היכי דליכחוש חיליה אלא סוקרו בסיקרא מאי רפואה קעביד כי היכי דליחזייה אינשי וליבעו עליה רחמי כדתניא °וטמא טמא יקרא *[ד]צריך להודיע צערו לרבים ורבים יבקשו עליו רחמים אמר רבינא כמאן תלינן כובסי בדיקלא כי האי תנא תני תנא בפרק *אמוראי קמיה דר' חייא בר אבין א"ל °כולהו אית בהו משום דרכי האמורי לבר מהני מי שיש לו עצם בגרונו מביא מאותו המין ומניח ליה על קדקדו ולימא הכי חד חד נחית בלע בלע נחית חד חד אין בו משום דרכי האמורי *לאדרא לימא הכי ננעצתא כמחט ננעלתא כתרים *שייא שייא האומר

לאשתא תילתא · שחפת שלישית שבאה מג' ימים לג' ימים: סילוי · ענבים(א) קטנים: ושבעה ליבי · קסמים: כשורי · קורות: ושבעה סיכי · יתידות קייבל"ש בלע"ז: משבעה גשורי · גשרים: ז' סיכרי · לטר הדלת חור האסקופה שציר הדלת סובב בו: כופרי · זפת שזופתין הספינות: ארבי · ספינות: ושבעה בוני(ב) כמוני · גרעיני כמון ל"א בוני כמון גרסי' מלא אגרוף: ושבעה ביני מדיקנא דכלבא סבא · שבעה נימי מזקן כלב זקן: אשתא צמירתא · חולי שמחממת וקודחת את הגוף: וורדינא · סנה: ליחרוק · אישקרני"ר כמו דמיבלע חירקייהו דאלו טריפות (חולין דף נט:): ויאמר משה · משום סיפיה מדוע לא יבער הסנה: כי סר · שיסור החולי: אל תקרב הלום · שלא יקרב זה החולי אליו: ליתתיה ולפסקיה · סמוך לקרקע ליתתיה ישפיל: דמייכת · שאתה שפילה: דחמיתא אשתא · שראית האש: לסימטא · שחין קרו"ג בלע"ז: בזבזיה מסמסייה כסכסייה · שמות המלאכים על שם שקורעים וממסמסים ומכסכסים אותו בו לשון בזעה: מארעא דסדום · כך הוא הלחש ולא מסדום באו: בזך בזיך · אין לו משמעות אלא כך הוא הלחש: עיניך ביך · מראיך בך שלא תאדים יותר: אתריך ביך · שלא תרחיב: כקלוט · שנקלט זרעו בשריר בטנו שלא יוליד: לכיפה · אונפול"ש אבעבועות כך לשון רבי יצחק ברבי מנחם נ"ע ולשון רבותי לכיפה למי שכופהו שד: לימא הכי · לחש בעלמא הוא: הוית דפקיק דפקיק הוית · לחש הוא: ליט תבר ומשומת · מקולל ונשבר ומשומת יהא שד זה ששמו בר טיט בר טינא: לשידא דבית הכסא · אם הזיק לימא לחש זה: אקרקפי דארי · בראש הארי זכר: ואאוסי דגורייתא · ובחוטם לביאה נקבה: אשכחתא לשידאי בר שריקאי פנדאי · כך שמו: במישרא דכרתי חבטיה · בערוגת כרשין הפלתיו: בלועא דחמרא חטרתיה · בלחי החמור הלקיתיו: מאן תנא · דקתני וכל אדם ואפילו עני שבישראל: רבי שמעון · בפרק שמונה שרצים: בני מלכים · הלכך לעני נמי חזיא ולא גנותא דידיה דליתחזיא כיוהרא ושליף אי נמי דמגו דחידוש הוא שליף ומחוי: באריג בכסותו · דלא שליף ליה ומחוי: **מתני'** דרכי האמורי · ניחוש הוא וכתיב ובחוקותיהם לא תלכו (ויקרא יח): **גמ'** לשיחלא · לכאב האוזן ותולין באזנו: לשינתא · יש שעשאו כדי שיישן ויש כדי שלא יישן: דחייא · של שן שועל חי: לזירפא · נפח מכה דכל פרזלא זריף והאי מסי לזירפא: שיש בו משום רפואה · שנראית רפואתו כגון שתיית כוס ותחבושת מכה ופרכינן הא אין בו כו' כגון לחש שאין ניכר שיהא מרפא יש בו משום דרכי האמורי בתמיה: דליכחוש חיליה · שעל ידי שהוא שמן וכחו רב פירותיו נושרין: דליחזיוה אינשי · ולסימנא עבדי ליה לאודעי דמשיר פירותיו: טמא טמא · הוא עצמו אומר טמא רחקו מעלי: כובסי · אשכול תמרים וסימן הוא שמשיר פירותיו: בפרק אמוראי · בפרק אחד* ששנוי בתוספתא דמסכת שבת בהלכות דרכי האמורי: א"ל · רבי חייא לתנא: כולהו אית בהו · כל השנויות שם אל תטעה לומר באחד מהן אין בו משום דרכי האמורי אלא בכולן אתה שונה יש בו לבר מהני ב' אלו שאפרש לך: מי שיש לו עצם וכו' ולחש דנעלתה כמחט אלו ב' לבדם אין בהם: חד חד נחית · לחש הוא: לאדרא · עצם של דג שישב לאדם בושט: שייא שייא · לחש הוא רד רד: האומר

בני מלכים יוצאין בזגין מאן תנא ר"ש היא כו' · פי' הקונטרס וליכא למיחש דילמא מחייכי בהו ואתו לאתויי וא"ת מכל מקום ליחוש דילמא איפסיק ואתי לאתויי כדאמרינן לעיל גבי עבד דלא יצא בחותם שבצוארו וי"ל דהכא מיירי בתלוים בשלשלת דלא מיפסקי וריב"א פירש דבירושלמי מוקי לה בקטנים דאפילו אי פסיק, ומייתי לה ליכא איסור והכי איתא בירושלמי ר' זעירא אומר בזוג שבצוארו ומהו כל אדם דקתני במתניתין בין קטנים עשירים בין קטנים עניים מתניתין פליגא עליה דרבי זעירא ולא בזוג שבצוארו כאן בגדולים כאן בקטנים פירוש ההוא דלא יצא בזוג שבצוארו בגדולים דלמא מיפסיק ואתי לאתויי והא דשרי הכא בקטנים דליכא למיחש כדפי' מ"מ יש לדקדק אמאי נקט בני מלכים כיון דליכא חששא אי מייתי להו קטן בידים וי"ל דאי לאו בני מלכים הוו מחייכו עליה בני מלכים כל שעה ואי אפשר שלא ישמע אביו מעולם ויטלם אביו בידו ואתו לאתויי אבל אי בני מלכים לא מחייכי אם כן אפילו אי מיפסיק ליכא למיחש דילמא מייתי להו אבוה דלא שכיח שיהא אביו אצלו בשעה שיפסוק:

הדרן עלך במה אשה

פח א מיי' פי"ט מהל' שבת הלכה יח סמג לאוין סה טוש"ע א"ח סימן שא סעיף כג:

פט ב ג מיי' שם הלכה יג טוש"ע שם סעיף כז:

צ ד מיי' פי' מהלכות טומאת צרעת הלכה ח וסמג עשין רלה:

רבינו חננאל

אבל משקל דמשקל עלתה בתיקו · וכל [תיקו] דאיסורא [לחומרא] ואין יוצאין בה בשבת בני מלכים בזוגים אוקמה (רב) [רבא] בזוג ארוג בכסות ולדברי הכל כי האי גוונא שרי פר' שיח לא פצע האוזן פי' זירפא [ענביתא] (עביבתא) אביי ורבא דאמרי תרווייהו כל שהוא משום רפואה אין בו משום דרכי האמורי: ירושלמי רבי אבהו בשם רבי יוחנן כל שמרפא אין בו משום דרכי האמורי

[מלת הא ליתא בחולין ומשמע שם דהכל מהכרי אביי ורבא ועי' בפירש"י דהכא ד"ה שיש וכו' ופרכינן הא אין בו וכו']

עי' בערוך ערך אמרי

[גירס' הערוך שה שה פי' כמס המס]

פ"ז ופ"ח

מסורת הש"ס

[בערוך גרס שיבי פי' חתיכה קטנה]

[גירס' הערוך סוכרי פי' קנרים ע"ש בערך סכר א']

שמות ג

שם

שם

שם

[עי' תוספות שבועות טו: ד"ה אסור]

הגהות הב"ח

(א) רש"י ד"ה סילוי ענבים קטנים: (ב) ד"ה ושבעה מיני כמונא גרעיני:

[גיר' הערוך לביבא בערך כב ג]

לקמן קיא: קכח. [ב"מ קיג:]

[גירס' ירושל' דברי רבי יוסי ר' מאיר אוסר אף בחול]

חולין עז:

ויקרא יג

מו"ק ה. [סוטה לב:] חולין עח. נדה סו.

[גירסת הערוך לאדרא]

גליון הש"ס

גמרא ולימא וירא מלאך · עיין שבועות דף טו ע"ב תוספות ד"ה אסור ופסחים דף קיא ע"א תוספות ד"ה נפתח: שם אביי ורבא דאמרי תרווייהו כל דבר שיש בו משום רפואה · עיין בב"מ דף כז ע"ב תוספות ד"ה כיס ואנקי: שם כולהו אית בהו משום דרכי האמורי · עיין תשובת רשב"א סימן תי"ג בארוכה:

האומר גד גדי וסנוק לא אשכי ובושכי יש בו משום דרכי האמורי ר' יהודה אומר גד אינו אלא לשון ע"ז שנאמר °העורכים לגד שלחן (ישעיה סה) הוא בשמה והיא בשמו יש בו משום דרכי האמורי *דונו דני יש בו משום דרכי האמורי ר' יהודה אומר אין דן אלא לשון ע"ז שנאמר °הנשבעים באשמת שומרון ואמרו חי אלהיך דן (עמוס ח) האומר *לעורב צרח ולעורבתא שריקי והחזירי לי זנביך לטובה יש בו משום דרכי האמורי *האומר שחטו תרנגול זה שקרא ערבית ותרנגולת שקראה גברית יש בו משום דרכי האמורי אשתה ואותיר אשתה ואותיר יש בו משום דרכי האמורי *המבקעת ביצים בכותל (והטח) בפני האפרוחים יש בו משום דרכי האמורי והמגים בפני אפרוחים יש בו משום דרכי האמורי המרקדת והמונה שבעים ואחד אפרוחין בשביל שלא ימותו יש בו משום דרכי האמורי המרקדת לכותח והמשתקת לעדשים והמצווחת לגריסין יש בו משום דרכי האמורי המשתנת בפני קדירתה בשביל שתתבשל מהרה יש בו משום דרכי האמורי אבל נותנין קיסם של תות ושברי זכוכית בקדירה בשביל שתתבשל מהרה וחכמים אוסרין(א) בשברי זכוכית מפני הסכנה תנו רבנן *נותנין בול של מלח לתוך הנר בשביל שתאיר ותדליק ונותנין טיט וחרסית תחת הנר בשביל שתמתין ותדליק אמר רב זוטרא האי מאן דמיכסי שרגא דמשחא ומגלי נפטא קעבר משום בל תשחית חמרא וחיי לפום רבנן אין בו משום דרכי האמורי מעשה ברבי עקיבא שעשה משתה לבנו ועל כל כוס וכוס שהביא אמר חמרא וחיי לפום רבנן חיי וחמרא לפום רבנן ולפום תלמידיהון:

הדרן עלך במה אשה

כלל *גדול אמרו בשבת [א]כל השוכח עיקר שבת ועשה מלאכות הרבה בשבתות הרבה אינו חייב אלא חטאת אחת היודע עיקר שבת ועשה מלאכות הרבה בשבתות הרבה חייב על כל שבת ושבת [ב]היודע שהוא שבת ועשה מלאכות הרבה בשבתות הרבה חייב על כל

אב

רש"י

האומר גד גדי · התמזל מזלי: וסטק לא · עיף אל תהי*: אשכי ובושכי · יום ולילה: יש בו משום דרכי האמורי · וכן בכולן עד סוף פירקא גרסינן הרי זה מדרכי האמורי וה"ג בתוספ': הוא בשמה והיא בשמו · הוא ואשתו מחליפין שמותיהן זה בזה בלילה משום ניחוש: דוני דני · התחזקו חביותי: דן · אינו חק האמורי אלא ע"ז ממש וחייב משום קורא בשם עבודת גלולים: האומר לעורב צרח · כשהוא קורא אומר לו כן מפני שהוא מבשר בשורות ונותן לו לחש זה: שקרא ערבית · אחר יותר משאר חביריו ול"נ שקרא כעורב: שקראה גברית · כתרנגול כמו קרא גברא (יומא דף כ:): אשתה ואותיר · כדי שתהא ברכה מצויה בייתו: המבקעת בילים בכותל · ולית דגרסי בילים (ב)מקבעת לאחר שילאו האפרוחים מחזרת(ג) הקליפות במקל וקובעתן בכותל לפניהם וזהו לנחש שלא ימותו: המרקדת לכותח · כשעושה כותח מרקדת לפניו והוא ניחוש שיתחזק: המשתקת לעדשים · כשנותנת בקדרה משתקת את כל העומדים כדי שיתבשלו ולגריסין מצווחת: ה"ג אבל נותנין קיסם של תות · מוריי"ר וחזק הוא כחומץ ומועיל לבשל ואין זה לנחש: ה"ג אבל אסרו חכמים בשברי זכוכית · אע"פ שמשום דרכי האמורי אין בו אסרו חכמים מפני הסכנה שלא יבלעו: בול של מלח · מלא אגרוף מלח בשביל שתאיר ותדליק שאין זה ניחוש אלא מסייע ממש שהמלח גולל את השמן וימשך אחר הפתילה: טיט וחרסית · מצננין את השמן ואינו דולק מהר: דמכסי שרגא דמשחא · שעושה לו כיסוי למעלה ממהר לידלק: נפטא · כשמגלין אותו האור הולך ונמשך אליו ומבעיר: חמרא וחיי · כשמוזגין ונותנין כוס אומר כן לברכה בעלמא:

הדרן עלך במה אשה

כלל גדול · בגמרא מפרש אמאי קרי ליה גדול: השוכח עיקר שבת · כסבור אין שבת בתורה: אינו חייב אלא חטאת אחת · בגמרא (לקמן דף סט:) יליף לה שמירה אחת לשבתות הרבה ושמירה לכל שבת ושבת ומסתברא דכי כתיב שמירה אחת לשבתות הרבה כי האי גוונא כתיב דכולא חדא שגגה היא וקרבן אשוגג קאתי: היודע עיקר שבת · שיש שבת בתורה ונאסרו בה מלאכות: ועשה מלאכות הרבה בשבתות הרבה · על ידי שגגת שבת ששכח שבת היום מדקתני סיפא היודע שהוא שבת מכלל דרישא בדאין יודע שהוא שבת ועשה מלאכות הרבה בשבתות הרבה בענין זה ולא נודע לו בינתים שחטא: חייב על כל שבת ושבת · חטאת אחת לכל שבת ואע"פ שלא נודע לו בינתים והעלם אחד הוא אמרינן ימים שבינתים הויין ידיעה לחלק שא"א שלא שמע בינתים שאותו היום הויא שבת אלא שלא נזכר לו במלאכות שנעשו בו ושגגה קמייתא משום שבת הוא דהואי והא אתיידע ליה ביני ביני הלכך כל חדא שבת חדא שגגה היא ומיהו על הרבה מלאכות שבכל שבת לא מיחייב אלא חדא דכולה שבת חדא שגגה דהא לא שגג אמלאכות דיודע הוא שהמלאכות אסורות אלא אשבת הוא דשגג: היודע שהוא שבת ועשה מלאכות הרבה · שלא ידע שהמלאכות הללו אסורות ועשאם כמה פעמים בכמה שבתות חייב על כל אב מלאכה חטאת אחת ואף על פי שחזר וכפלה בכמה שבתות כולה חדא שגגה היא דהא לא נודע לו בינתים ולענין שגגת שבת הוא דאיכא למימר ימים שבינתים הויין ידיעה לחלק אבל לענין שגגת מלאכות לא אמרו הכי דמשום הפסק ימים אין לו לדעת אלא אם כן ישב ועסק לפני חכמים בהלכות שבת ומיהו בחטאת אחת לא מיפטר על כל שבת דשגגה לאו בשבת הויא אלא במלאכות ושגגות טובא הוו לשבת אחת ובגמרא (לקמן דף ע·) יליף פעמים שהוא חייב על כל אחת ואחת ופעמים שאינו חייב אלא אחת על כל שבת ומסתברא דחיובא בזדון שבת ושגגת מלאכות דאיכא שגגות טובא ופטורא בשגגת שבת וזדון מלאכות דחדא שגגה היא:

אב

תוספות

כלל גדול · כל היודע עיקר שבת חייב על כל שבת ושבת כו' · פי' בקונטרס אע"פ שלא נודע לו בינתים אמרינן ימים שבינתים הויין ידיעה לחלק שאי אפשר שלא שמע בינתים שאותו יום שבת היה אלא שלא נזכר במלאכות וקשה לה"ר אליעזר דאמר בגמרא (לקמן דף עא·) קצר וטחן כגרוגרת בשגגת שבת וזדון מלאכות וחזר וקצר וטחן כגרוגרת בזדון שבת ושגגת מלאכות קצירה גוררת קצירה וטחינה גוררת טחינה פירוש ואינו חייב אלא אחת ובשבת אחת איירי דבשתי שבתות היה חייב שתים דימים שבינתים הויין ידיעה לחלק אלמא אע"פ שנודע לו קודם קצירה אחרונה שאותו יום שבת הוא דהא בזדון שבת קצר וטחן אפי' הכי לא הויא ידיעה ותשיב העלם אחד כיון שלא נודע לו שחטא שהרי סבור שהמלאכה מותר' וטעמא משום דכתיב או הודע אליו חטאתו שיהיה לו ידיעת חטא ועוד הקשה ריב"ם דבגמרא מפקינן לה מקרא ואי כדפי' בקונטרס שאי אפשר שלא נודע לו למה לן קרא ועוד קשה לר"י דתנן בפרק אמרו לו (כריתות דף טז·) א"ר עקיבא שאלתי את ר' אליעזר העושה מלאכות הרבה בשבתות הרבה מעין מלאכה כו' אמר ליה חייב על כל אחת ואחת ק"ו מנדה כו' ופליגי התם אמוראי בגמרא היכי בעי מיניה וקאמר בסוף שמעתא ולרב חסדא דאמר שגגת שבת וזדון מלאכות הוא דבעא מיניה אי ימים שבינתים הויין ידיעה לחלק או לא נדה מאי ימים שבינתים איכא ומשני שבא עליה וטבלה וראתה וחזר ובא עליה והתם אפילו איחרה כמה שנים ולא טבלה חשיב הכל העלם אחד אלא כשטבלה ימי היתר שבינתים אע"פ דלא ידע כמי שידע דמי ה"נ גבי שבת אע"פ שלא שמע ימי היתר שבינתים הויין ידיעה לחלק דגזרת הכתוב היא שתהא שמירה לכל שבת ותימה דהתם יליף רבי אליעזר שבת מנדה ואדרבה בשבת כתיב קרא ובנדה לא כתיב ונראה לר"י דהא דנפקא לן מקרא בגמרא הייני כרבי אליעזר ברבי שמעון דהתם דאמר לא כך שאלו רבי עקיבא לרבי אליעזר אלא הבא על הנדה והשיב לו רבי אליעזר דחייב על כל אחת ואחת ק"ו משבת:

וגבי

גא א מיי' פי"א מהל' ע"ז הלכה ד סמג לאוין נא טוש"ע י"ד סימן קעט סעיף ג:

א ב מיי' פ"ז מהלכות שגגות הלכה ג:

ב ג שם הלכה ג:

רבינו חננאל

(כפסא) ת"ר נותנין בול של מלח לתוך הנר כדי שתאיר ותדליק · טיט וחרסית תחת הנר כדי שתמתין ותדליק · חמרא חייא לפום רבנן ותלמידיהון:

הדרן עלך במה אשה יוצאה

כלל גדול אמרו בשבתי אסיקנא

פסחים נג

[תוספתא פ"ז]

[שם פ"ו]

[בערוך ערך קבע איתא מקבעת ופי' כדאיתא כרש"י]

[תוספתא פי"ב]

כריתות טז:

הגהות הב"ח

(א) גמרא שתתבשל מהרה אבל אסרו חכמים בשברי זכוכית: (ב) רש"י ד"ה המבקעת וכו' ולית דגרסי מקבעת כצ"ל ותיבת בילים נמחק: (ג) בא"ד שהאפרוחים מחזרת הקליפות:

[67b] He who says, 'Be lucky, my luck [*gad gedi*] and tire not by day or night,'[7] is guilty of Amorite practices. R. Judah said: *Gad* is none other but an idolatrous term, for it is said,
a *ye that prepare a table for Gad.*[1] If husband and wife exchange their names,[2] they are guilty of Amorite practices. [To say], 'Be strong, O ye Barrels'! is [forbidden] as the ways of the Amorite. R. Judah said: Dan [Barrel] is none other but the designation of an idol, for it is said, *They that swear by the sin of Samaria, and say, As thy god Dan liveth.*[3] He who says to a raven, 'Scream,' and to a she-raven, 'Screech, and return me thy tuft for [my] good,' is guilty of Amorite practices. He who says, 'Kill this cock, because it crowed in the evening,'[4] or, 'this fowl, because it crowed like a cock,' is guilty of Amorite practices. He who says, 'I will drink and leave over, I will drink and leave over,'[5] is guilty of the ways of the Amorite. He who breaks eggs on a wall in front of fledglings, is guilty of Amorite practices. He who stirs [eggs?] before fledglings is guilty of Amorite practices. He who dances and counts seventy-one fledglings in order that they should not die, is guilty of Amorite practices. He who dances for *kutaḥ*,[6] or imposes silence for lentils, or cries for beans,[7] is guilty of Amorite practices. She who urinates before her pot in order that it should be quickly cooked is guilty of Amorite practices. Yet one may place a chip of a mulberry tree and broken pieces of glass in a pot in order that it should boil quickly.[8] But the Sages forbade broken pieces of glass [to be employed thus] on account of danger.

Our Rabbis taught: A lump of salt may be placed in a lamp in order that it should burn brightly;[9] and mud and clay may be placed under a lamp in order that it should burn slowly.[10]

R. Zuṭra said: He who covers an oil lamp or uncovers a naphtha [lamp] infringes the prohibition of wasteful destruction.[11] 'Wine
b and health to the mouth of our teachers!'[1] is not considered the ways of the Amorite. It once happened that R. Akiba made a banquet for his son and over every glass [of liquor] that he brought he exclaimed, 'Wine and health to the mouth of our teachers; health and wine to the mouths of our teachers and their disciples!'

CHAPTER VII

MISHNAH. A GREAT PRINCIPLE WAS STATED WITH RESPECT TO THE SABBATH: HE WHO FORGETS THE FUN-
c DAMENTAL LAW OF THE SABBATH[1] AND PERFORMS MANY LABOURS ON MANY SABBATHS, INCURS ONE SIN-OFFERING ONLY. HE WHO KNOWS THE FUNDAMENTAL LAW OF THE SABBATH AND PERFORMS MANY LABOURS ON MANY SABBATHS,[2] INCURS A SIN-OFFERING ON ACCOUNT OF EACH SABBATH. HE WHO KNOWS THAT IT IS THE SABBATH AND PERFORMS MANY LABOURS ON MANY SABBATHS, IS LIABLE

(7) This is the conjectured translation.
a (1) Isa. LXV, 11. Hence this statement is an invocation to an idol. (2) Lit., 'he by her name and she by his name'—probably done to ward off evil. (3) Amos. VIII, 14. This translation differs from that of the E.V. q.v. (4) Later than usual. Others: it crowed like a raven. (5) That the rest may be blessed. (6) V. Glos. (7) That they should be well prepared.—Sound (or silence in some cases) was thought to benefit certain food preparations; cf. Ker. 6b. (8) This is not enchantment. (9) The salt clarifies the oil. (10) These cool the oil and retard its flow. (11) Derived from Deut. XX, 19, q.v. Because these cause the lamp to burn with unnecessary speed.
b (1) A drinking toast.
c (1) Not knowing at all that there exists a law of the Sabbath. (2) Forgetting on each occasion that it was the Sabbath.

FOR EVERY [68a] PRIMARY LABOUR.[3] HE WHO PERFORMS MANY LABOURS BELONGING TO THE SAME CATEGORY OF WORK[4] IS LIABLE TO ONE SIN-OFFERING ONLY.

GEMARA. Why does he [the Tanna] state, A GREAT PRINCIPLE? Shall we say that because he wishes to teach 'another principle',[5] he [therefore] states here, A GREAT PRINCIPLE?[6] And in respect to *shebi'ith*[7] too, because he wishes to teach another principle, he states, This is a great principle?[8] But what of tithes, though 'another principle' is taught, he nevertheless does
a not teach [elsewhere] 'a great principle'?[1]—Said R. Jose b. Abin: As for the Sabbath and *shebi'ith*, since they possess both primaries and derivatives,[2] he teaches GREAT; but in respect to tithes, since there are no primaries and derivatives, he does not teach 'great'. Then according to Bar Ḳappara, who did learn 'A great principle' in respect to tithes,[3] what primaries and what derivatives are there? But surely this must be the reason:[4] The penal scope of the Sabbath is 'greater' than that of *shebi'ith*, for whereas [the restriction of] the Sabbath is found in respect of both detached and growing [produce], [the prohibitions of] *shebi'ith* do not operate in respect of detached, but only in respect of growing [produce].[5] Again, the penal scope of the seventh year is 'greater' than that of tithes: for whereas [the law of] *shebi'ith* applies to both human food and animal fodder, [the law of] tithes operates in the case of human food, but not of animal fodder.[6] And according to Bar Ḳappara who learned 'a great principle' in connection with tithes,—the penal scope of tithes is greater than that of *pe'ah*:[7] for whereas [the law of] tithes operates in figs and vegetables [too], *pe'ah* does not operate in figs and vegetables.[8] For we learnt: A general principle was stated in respect to *pe'ah*: whatever is a foodstuff, is guarded, grows from the earth, is [all] gathered simultaneously,[9] and is collected for storage,[10] is
b liable to *pe'ah*. 'Foodstuff' excludes the aftergrowth of woad[1] and madder;[2] 'is guarded' excludes *hefker*;[3] 'grows from the earth' excludes mushrooms and truffles;[4] 'is [all] gathered simultaneously' excludes the fig-tree;[5] 'and is taken in to be stored' excludes vegetables.[6] Whereas in respect to tithes we learnt: A general principle was stated in respect to tithes: Whatever is a foodstuff, is guarded, and grows from the earth is subject to tithes; but we did not learn, 'is gathered simultaneously and is collected for storage.'

Rab and Samuel both maintain: Our Mishnah treats of a child who was taken captive among Gentiles, or a proselyte who became converted in the midst of Gentiles.[7] But if one knew and subsequently forgot, he is liable [to a sin-offering] for every Sabbath.[8] We learnt: HE WHO FORGETS THE ESSENTIAL LAW OF THE SABBATH: surely that implies that he knew [it] originally?—No: what is meant by HE WHO FORGETS THE ESSENTIAL LAW OF THE SABBATH? That the very existence of the Sabbath was unknown[9] to him. But what if he knew and subsequently forgot; he is liable for every Sabbath? Then instead of teaching, HE WHO KNOWS THE ESSENTIAL LAW OF THE SABBATH AND PERFORMS MANY LABOURS ON MANY SABBATHS, INCURS A SIN-OFFERING ON ACCOUNT OF EACH SABBATH: let him teach, He who knew and subsequently forgot, and how much more so this one?—What is meant by, HE WHO KNOWS THE ESSENTIAL LAW OF THE SABBATH? That he who knew the essen-

(3) The general principle is this: a sin-offering in connection with the Sabbath is incurred for every *unwitting* transgression. The number of transgressions is determined by the number of unknown facts. Thus, when a man is ignorant of the Sabbath law altogether, he is unaware of a single fact, and incurs one sin-offering only. If he forgets a number of Sabbaths, each is a separate fact; hence he is liable for each. If he knows that it is the Sabbath but forgets that certain labours are forbidden, each labour is a separate fact, and he is liable for each separately.—For primary (Heb. *ab*, lit., 'father') labours v. *supra* 2b, n. a2. (4) I.e., all derivatives (*toledoth*) of the same primary labour (*ab*). (5) *Infra* 75b. (6) By contrast, this being wider in scope. (7) V. Glos. It is also the name of a Tractate dealing with the laws thereof. (8) V. Sheb. V, 5 and VII, 1.

a (1) V. Ma'as. I, 1, and II, 7. (2) V. *infra* 73a *seq*. Agricultural labour forbidden during the seventh year is likewise divided into primaries and derivatives: sowing, harvesting, reaping and fruit gathering are primaries, other forms of labour in a field or vineyard are derivatives; v. M.Ḳ. 3a. (3) In his collection of Baraithas. These are collections of Tannaitic teachings not incorporated by R. Judah ha-Nasi in the Mishnah; there were several such collections, the most authoritative being those of R. Ḥiyya and R. Oshaia. (4) Why GREAT is stated in connection with Sabbath. (5) Thus: one must do no work on growing (lit., 'attached') produce on the Sabbath, e.g., sow, reap, etc., nor on detached produce, e.g., grind corn. But only the former is forbidden in the seventh year, not the latter. (6) Thus the scope of both the Sabbath and *shebi'ith* is greater than that of tithes, and for that reason 'great' is employed in connection with the first two. (7) V. Glos. (8) 'Penal scope', Heb. *'onesh*, is employed here in the sense that the violation of these laws is punishable. (9) I.e., the whole of the crop ripens about the same time. (10) Lit., 'is brought in to be kept'. This applies to cereals in general, which are stored in granaries over long periods.

b (1) ἰσάτις, *isatis tinctoria*, a plant producing a deep blue dye. (2) Both being used as dyes. (3) V. Glos. (4) Though these grow in the earth, they were held to draw their sustenance mainly from the air. (5) Whose fruits do not all ripen at the same time. The same holds good of many other trees, which are likewise excluded. (6) Which must be consumed whilst fresh. (7) So that they never knew the laws of the Sabbath. (8) He is regarded as knowing the sanctity of the Sabbath but forgetting on each occasion that it is the Sabbath. (9) Lit., 'forgotten'.

אב מלאכה ומלאכה* "העושה מלאכות הרבה מעין מלאכה אחת אינו חייב אלא חטאת אחת : **גמ'** מ"ט תנא כלל גדול אילימא משום דקבעי למיתני עוד כלל אחר תנא כלל גדול וגבי שביעית נמי משום דקבעי למיתני עוד כלל אחר תנא כלל גדול והא גבי מעשר דקתני(א) כלל אחר ולא תני כלל גדול א"ר יוסי בר אבין שבת ושביעית דאית בהו אבות ותולדות תנא גדול מעשר דלית בה אבות ותולדות לא תנא כלל גדול ולבר קפרא דתני כלל גדול במעשר מאי אבות ומאי תולדות איכא אלא לאו היינו טעמא גדול עונשו של שבת יותר משל שביעית דאילו שבת איתא בין בתלוש בין במחובר ואילו שביעית בתלוש ליתא במחובר איתא וגדול עונשה של שביעית יותר מן המעשר דאילו שביעית איתא בין במאכל אדם בין במאכל בהמה ואילו מעשר במאכל אדם איתא במאכל בהמה ליתא ולבר קפרא דתני כלל גדול במעשר גדול עונשו של מעשר יותר משל פיאה דאילו מעשר איתא בתאנה וירק ואילו פיאה ליתא בתאנה וירק *דתנן כלל אמרו בפיאה כל שהוא אוכל ונשמר וגידולו מן הארץ ולקיטתו כאחת ומכניסו לקיום חייב בפיאה אוכל למעוטי ספיחי סטים וקוצה ונשמר למעוטי הפקר וגידולו מן הארץ למעוטי כמיהין ופטריות ולקיטתו כאחת °למעוטי תאנה ומכניסו לקיום למעוטי ירק ואילו גבי מעשר תנן* כלל אמרו במעשר כל שהוא אוכל ונשמר וגידולו מן הארץ חייב במעשר ואילו לקיטתו כאחת ומכניסו לקיום לא תנן : רב ושמואל דאמרי תרוייהו מתניתין בתינוק שנשבה לבין הנכרים וגר שנתגייר לבין הנכרים אבל הכיר ולבסוף שכח חייב על כל שבת ושבת תנן השוכח עיקר שבת לאו מכלל דהויא ליה ידיעה מעיקרא לא מאי כל השוכח עיקר שבת דהיתה שכוח ממנו עיקרה של שבת אבל הכיר ולבסוף שכח מאי חייב על כל שבת ושבת אדתני היודע עיקר שבת ועשה מלאכות הרבה בשבתות הרבה חייב על כל שבת ושבת ליתני הכיר ולבסוף שכח וכ"ש הא מאי היודע עיקר שבת מי שהיה יודע עיקרה של שבת ושכחה
אבל

רש"י

אב מלאכה דנקט לאו למעוטי תולדות דה"ה לתולדות ובלבד שיהו תולדות דשני אבות אלא למעוטי היכא דהוו ב' תולדות דאב אחד או אב ותולדה שלו דאינו חייב אלא אחת כדקתני סיפא העושה מלאכות הרבה מעין מלאכה אחת שתי תולדות של אב אחד אינו חייב אלא חטאת אחת דהרי הוא כעושה וחוזר ועושה בהעלם אחד ואין חילוק חטאות בהעלם אחד אלא בגופי עבירה שאינן דומין או בחילוק שבתות לענין שגגת שבת : **גמ'** עוד כלל אחר · לקמן בפירקין (דף עה:) ולא כלל בו אלא ב' דברים כל הכשר להצניע וכל שאינו כשר להצניע וכאן כלל יותר ומשום הכי קרי להו גדול : וגבי שביעית · בפרק *(בנות שוח) : גבי מעשר · בפ"ק דמסכת מעשרות : אית ביה אבות · ארבעים חסר אחת שהוצרכו למשכן ותולדות הדומות לכל אחת הויא תולדות דידיה אבות דשביעית זריעה וקצירה וזמירה ובצירה דכתיבן תולדות שאר עבודות שבשדה וכרם כדאמרינן במועד קטן בפ"ק (דף ג.) : ולבר קפרא דתנא · בתוספתא דידיה במעשר מאי אבות כו' : אלא לאו היינו טעמא · משום אבות ואולדות אלא דבר שנאמר בו כלל ועונשו גדול מדבר אחר שנאמר בו כלל תני ביה כלל גדול : שבת איתא · לאיסור דידה בין בדבר שהיה תלוש מבעוד יום כגון טוחן ולש בין בדבר שמחובר משקדש היום : ואילו שביעית · בדבר שהיה מחובר משקדש שביעית איתא אבל בדבר שהיה תלוש לפני שביעית ליתא : שביעית · נמי איתיה במאכל בהמה דכתיב ולבהמתך ולחיה וגו' (ויקרא כה) מעשר ליתיה במאכל בהמה דמדאורייתא דגן תירוש ויצהר כתיב ורבנן תקון פירות האילן וירק דמאכל אדם כדקתני כל שהוא אוכל כו' : איתיה בתאנה וירק · מדרבנן : כל שהוא אוכל כו' · דגבי פיאה קציר כתיב מה קציר מיוחד שיש בו כל אלו : למעוטי ספיחי סטים וקוצה · שעומדים לצבע להכי נקט ספיחים דאין דרך ללוקטן בשנה שנזרעים אלא לסוף ד' וה' שנים שהשרשין מתפשטין בארץ ומשביחין ושורש שלהן עיקר והא דנקט הני ולא נקט שאר מינים שאינן ראוין לאכילה משום דאיידי דגבי שביעית תני להו דיש להן שביעית נקט הכא דבפיאה ומעשר ליתנהו לשון רבינו הלוי · סטים וויסד"א קוצ' וורנצ"א : ומכניסו לקיום למעוטי ירק · כגון לפת וקפלוטות : ואילו מכניסו לקיום ולקיטתו כאחד לא תנן · דכי תקון רבנן אדידהו לא פלוג בפירות האילן ובירק בין מין למין : מתניתין · דפטר בחד חטאת : בתינוק שנשבה · ולא ידע שבת מעולם : אבל הכיר ולבסוף שכח · הוה ליה כשוכח שהיום שבת ויודע עיקר שבת וחייב על כל שבת ושבת : שהיתה שכוחה ממנו · מעולם : לתני הכיר ולבסוף שכח · דחייב ואע"ג דליכא למימר ימים שבינתים הווין ידיעה לחלק וכ"ש הא דאיכא למימר שימים שבינתים הווין ליה ידיעה לחלק:
אבל

תוספות

וגבי שביעית נמי כו' · הכי תנן בשביעית (פ"ז מ"א) כלל גדול אמרו כל שהוא מאכל אדם ומאכל בהמה וממין הצובעין ואינו מתקיים בארץ פירוש שכלה לחיה יש לו שביעית ולדמיו שביעית יש לו ביעור ולדמיו ביעור ועוד כלל אחר אמרו דקתני כל שאינו מאכל אדם ומאכל בהמה וכו' ומתקיים בארץ יש לו שביעית ולדמיו שביעית ואין לו ולדמיו ביעור דכלל הראשון גדול דיש לו ביעור ואחרון אין לו ביעור ואע"ג דקתני התם בבבא אחריתא כלל גדול אמרו בשביעית ולא קתני בתריה כלל אחר כיון דקתני כלל קטן קמיה שייך למתני בתריה כלל גדול : **והא** גבי מעשר דקתני עוד כלל אחר אמרו כו' · תימה למה ישנה בראשון כלל גדול כיון דאינו גדול מן השני וצ"ע :

דאית ביה אבות ותולדות · ואפילו לרבא דאמר במועד קטן (דף ב:) גבי שביעית אבות אסר רחמנא תולדות לא אסר רחמנא מ"מ מדרבנן מיהא אית ביה אבות ותולדות וא"ת במעשר איכא נמי אבות ותולדות דמדאורייתא דגן ותירוש ויצהר ומדרבנן כל מילי וי"ל דלא שייך להזכיר אבות ותולדות במילי דלית ביה איסור מלאכות וא"ת ובכלל אחר דשבת ושביעית ליתני נמי כלל גדול מהאי טעמא ויש לומר דלא צריך למיתני דאכלל גדול קמא קאי וה"ק עוד כלל גדול אחר אמרו :

גדול עונשו של שבת משל שביעית · לפירוש הקונטרס דמפרש בתלוש שנתלש קודם שבת וקודם שביעית משמע שרוצה לפרש שביעית במחובר איתא היינו במחובר ערב שביעית ונתלש בשביעית ומיירי באיסור פירות שביעית לאכילה וקשה לר"י דלפי' לא הוה ליה למימר אלא גדול עונשו של שבת ושביעית משל מעשר דאיתנהו במאכל בהמה מה שאין כן במעשר ולמה ליה למימר כלל גדול עונשה של שבת משל שביעית אלא נראה לר"י דבמידי דאכילה דלא שייכא לענין שבת לא שייך למימר גדול שבת לא משביעית ולא ממעשר ולהכי לא קאמר גדול שבת ושביעית ממעשר אלא קאמר גדול שבת משביעית דאיסור מלאכות איתנהו בין בתלוש בין במחובר ואילו איסור מלאכות דשביעית במחובר איתא בתלוש ליתא וכן משמע בירושלמי דקתני שהשבת חלה על הכל ושביעית לא חלה אלא על עבודת הארץ בלבד:

ולבר קפרא דתני כלל גדול במעשר כו' · נראה לרשב"א דאחרים לא שנו כלל גדול במעשר לפי שאינו גדול מפאה אלא מדרבנן אבל כלל גדול דשבת גדול משביעית מדאורייתא וכן של שביעית משל מעשר : **ואילן** פאה ליתא בתאנה וירק · לאו דוקא תאנה דהא רוב אילנות אין לקיטתן כאחד ואינן רק ה' אילנות דחשיב בפ"ק דפאה (מ"ה) דחייב בפאה אלא נקט תאנה משום דנלקטת כמה פעמים כדאמרינן בחזקת הבתים (ב"ב דף כח:) אכל ג' פירי בחד יומא כגון תאנה כו' ואומר ר"ת דמדאורייתא לא מיחייב בפאה אלא בדגן ותירוש ויצהר דסתם קציר דכתיב גבי פאה הוא דגן וכתיב כי תחבוט זיתך כי תבצור כרמך והא דדריש בת"כ יכול שאני מרבה קישואין ודלועין שיהיו חייבים בפאה ת"ל ובקוצרכם את קציר ארצכם מה קציר שהוא אוכל ונשמר כו' אסמכתא היא דהתם נמי דריש מעשר ירק מקרא אע"ג דהוי מדרבנן ומה שלא תקנו פאה בירק ובתאנה ודדמי לה כמו שתקנו מעשר מהן אומר ר"ת משום דאין לקיטתן כאחד דבר מועט הוא פאה דידיה ויש הפסד לעניים בה יותר מן הריוח שמתבטלין לפי שאין יודעים זמן לקיטתן ודבר שאין מכניסו לקיום נמי לא חשיב ויפסידו יותר ממה שירויחו במקום אחר : **ספיחי** סטים וקוצה · הא דלא קאמר סתם למעוטי מידי דלאו אוכל אלא נקט הני אומר ר"י משום דקלא הם ראויים לאכילה וקמ"ל דאפילו הכי אין פאה נוהגת בהן וכן מלא רשב"ם בתשובת רש"י והא דנקט ספיחים משום דשמא סטים וקולה עצמם אינם ראוים כלל לאכילת אדם ולא הוה חידוש או שמא הן אוכל גמור ולא ממעטינן :

גר שנתגייר בין הנכרים · בפני ג' ולא הודיעוהו מצות שבת דאי נתגייר ביני לבין עצמו לא הוי גר כדאמרינן בהחולץ (יבמות דף מז:) :
אבל

עין משפט נר מצוה

ג א מיי' שם הלכה ז ופ"ז מהלכות שבת הלכה ט :

רבינו חננאל

תנא כלל גדול הכא משום חומרא דשבת גדולה מכלל שביעית דאילו איסורא דשבת חלה בין בתלוש ובין במחובר ואיסורא דשביעית אינה אלא מן המחובר לקרקע והוב איסורא דשביעית גדולה מאיסורא דמעשר שהשביעית חלה באוכלי אדם ובאוכלי בהמה והמעשר אינו חל [אלא] על אוכלי אדם בלבד לפיכך קתני כלל גדול בשביעית ולבר קפרא משום דעונש של מעשרות גדול מעונשה של פאה לפיכך תני כלל גדול במעשר · ותנא דידן שבת ושביעית דחומרא דאורייתא תני כלל גדול · אבל מעשר כגון ירק וכיוצא בו דחומרא דרבנן הוא לא קתני כלל גדול :

רב נסים גאון

פרק ז אמרו גדול עונשה של שבת יותר משל שביעית דאילו שבת איתא בי' בתלוש ובין במחובר · ודבר זה מפורסם וברור כי אפילו המוציא מרשות לרשות בשבת חייב חטאת והרבה מן המלאכות שאינן במחובר והן ידועות ואין אנו צריכין למנותן ואילו שביעית במחובר איתא בתלוש ליתא ועיקר דילה בתורת כהנים הזרע והזומר בכלל היו ולמה יצאו להקיש אליהן מה זרע וזמר מיוחדין שהן עבודה בארץ ובאילן אף אין לי אלא דבר שהיא עבודה בארץ ובאילן ועיקר דילה בפרק משקין בית השלחין (מועד קטן דף ג) וגדול עונשה של שביעית יותר משל מעשר דאילו שביעית איתא בין במאכל אדם בין במאכל בהמה ועיקרה בתורה דכתיב (ויקרא כה) ולבהמתך ולחיה אשר בארצך ובמשנה (שביעית פ' ז') כלל גדול אמרו בשביעית כל שהוא מאוכל אדם ומאוכל בהמה וממין הצובעים ואינו מתקיים בארץ יש לו שביעית ולדמיו שביעית: **ואילו** מעשר במאכל אדם איתיה במאכל בהמה ליתיה · עיקר דבר זה הוא כתוב בתורת (דברים יד) עשר תעשר את כל תבואת זרעך וסמיך ליה ואכלת דבר שהוא אוכל ובמשנת (מעשרות פרק א) כל שהוא אוכל :

מסורת הש"ס

[כריתות טז:]

[צ"ל שביעי]

פאה פ"א מ"ד פסחים נו: נדה נ·

מעשרות פ"א מ"א נדה נ·

הגהות הב"ח

(א) גמ' מעשר דקתני עוד כלל אחר :

גליון הש"ס

גמ' למעוטי תאנה · עיין ר"ס דף טו ע"ב תוס' ד"ה נטעו טעם :

עין משפט נר מצוה

ד א מיי' פ"ב מהלכות שגגות הלכה ו ופ"ז הלכה ב סמג עשין ריג:

מסורת הש"ס

ונוקי אחת שהיא הנה בין שגגת שבת וזדון מלאכה בין בזדון שבת ושגגת מלאכה כפי' רב נחמן לרב חייא והנה שהיא אחת בהכיר ולבסוף שכח [ת"י]

יבמות ס: סוכיות ח:

תורה אור

אבל לא שכחה מאי *חייב על כל מלאכה ומלאכה אדתני היודע שהוא שבת ועשה מלאכות הרבה בשבתות הרבה חייב על כל מלאכה ומלאכה ליתני היודע עיקר שבת וכל שכן הא אלא מתניתין כשהכיר ולבסוף שכח ודרב ושמואל נמי כהכיר ולבסוף שכח דמי והכי איתמר רב ושמואל דאמרי תרוייהו °אפילו תינוק שנשבה בין הנכרים וגר שנתגייר לבין הנכרים כהכיר ולבסוף שכח דמי וחייב ורבי יוחנן ורבי שמעון בן לקיש דאמרי תרוייהו דוקא הכיר ולבסוף שכח אבל תינוק שנשבה בין הנכרים וגר שנתגייר לבין הנכרים פטור מיתיבי כלל גדול אמרו בשבת כל השוכח עיקר שבת ועשה מלאכות הרבה בשבתות הרבה אינו חייב אלא אחת כיצד תינוק שנשבה לבין הנכרים וגר שנתגייר בין הנכרים ועשה מלאכות הרבה בשבתות הרבה אינו חייב אלא חטאת אחת וחייב על הדם אחת ועל החלב אחת ועל ע"ז אחת ומונבז פוטר וכך היה מונבז דן לפני רבי עקיבא הואיל ומזיד קרוי חוטא ושוגג קרוי חוטא מה מזיד שהיתה לו ידיעה אף שוגג שהיתה לו ידיעה אמר לו ר' עקיבא הריני מוסיף על דבריך אי מה מזיד שהיתה הידיעה בשעת מעשה אף שוגג שהיתה לו ידיעה בשעת מעשה אמר לו הן וכל שכן שהוספת אמר לו לדבריך אין זה קרוי שוגג אלא מזיד קתני מיהא כיצד תינוק בשלמא לרב ושמואל ניחא אלא לרבי יוחנן ולרבי שמעון בן לקיש קשיא אמרי לך רבי יוחנן וריש לקיש לא מי איכא מונבז דפטר אנן דאמרינן כמונבז מאי טעמא דמונבז דכתיב °תורה אחת יהיה לכם לעושה בשגגה וסמיך ליה והנפש אשר תעשה ביד רמה הקיש שוגג למזיד מה מזיד שהיתה לו ידיעה אף שוגג שהיתה לו ידיעה ורבנן האי תורה אחת מאי עבדי ליה מיבעי להו *לכדמקרי ליה ר' יהושע בן לוי לבריה תורה אחת יהיה לכם לעושה בשגגה וכתיב וכי

במדבר טו

אבל לא שכחה· לעיקר שבת אלא ששכח שהיום שבת מאי: חייב על כל אב מלאכה· דע"כ אי הוה סבירא ליה דאינו חייב אלא אחת לכל שבת ושבת הוה ליה(א) למיכרך ולמיתני הכי מי שידע עיקר שבת ושכחה וכן היודע עיקר שבת ועשה מלאכות הרבה בשבתות הרבה חייב על כל שבת ושבת: ליתני היודע עיקר שבת· דהוה שגגת שבת וזדון מלאכות הרבה חייב על כל מלאכה אע"ג דבכל שבת ליכא אלא חדא שגגה וכ"ש שגגת מלאכות וזדון שבת דאיכא שגגות הרבה: כהכיר ולבסוף שכח דמי· ומתניתין איצטריך למינקט הכיר ולבסוף שכח דלא תימא חייב על כל שבת ושבת: פטור· דקסברי רבי יוחנן ור"ל אומר מותר אנוס הוא ולא שגגה היא: וחייב על הדם· שאכל כל ימיו אחת וכן על כל דבר כרת שבתורה: מזיד קרוי חוטא· דכתיב (ויקרא ה) בשבועת העדות נפש כי תחטא ושמעה וגומר ולא כתיב ביה ונעלם: הריני מוסיף על דבריך· כלומר אם כך באת לדרוש ג"ש ללמד שוגג ממזיד בא ואוסיף גם אני על דבריך עוד ובה תראה אם יעמדו דבריך: אף שוגג שהיתה לו ידיעה בשעת מעשה· תחייבהו גם בזו חטאת: כ"ש שהוספת· על דברי והרי אתה מסייעני וגם בזו אני אומר שהוא חייב ולקמן מפרש במאי שגג: קתני מיהא· רישא תינוק שנשבה לבין הנכרים חייב: בשלמא לרב ושמואל ניחא· דאינהו נמי מחייבי ואיכא לאוקמי דהוא הדין להכיר ולבסוף שכח כי מתניתין ובריית' דקתני תינוק היא גופא איצטריך לאשמעינן פלוגתא דמונבז ורבנן: מאי טעמא דמונבז· הבין אב ודאי לא סמיך למיעבד שוגג דומיא דמזיד דהאי שוגג חילוף דמזיד וליכא לדמוייהו דהאי חייב והאי פטור: מקיש שוגג· לענין חטאת למזיד לענין כרת ואף על גב דלא דמי ע"כ הקישן הכתוב: ורבנן· הך הקישא בעיא לכדרבי יהושע ב"ל: תורה אחת יהיה לכם· גבי קרבן ע"ז כתיב בפרשת שלח לך אנשים: וכי

הגהות הב"ח

(א) רש"י ד"ה חייב על וכו' ה"ל למיתני כצ"ל ותיבת למיכרך נמחק: (ב) תוס' ד"ה אבל תינוק וכו' דהא בפירקין· נ"ב בסוף דף ע"ב:

אבל לא שכחה מאי חייב על כל מלאכה ומלאכה· תימה לר"י מנא ליה למידק הכי אימא דלא שכחה נמי אינו חייב על כל מלאכה ומלאכה אלא על כל שבת ושבת כמו בהכיר ולבסוף שכח ותנא הכיר ולבסוף שכח וכ"ש הא כדפרי' ומה שפי' בקונטרס דדייק דחייב על כל מלאכה ומלאכה מדלא כייל להו אהדדי מי שידע עיקר שבת ושכחה והיודע עיקר שבת חייב על כל שבת ושבת דהוה משמע דוקא על כל שבת ושבת ולא על כל מלאכה אין נראה לר"י דא"כ היכי פריך לעיל לתני הכיר ולבסוף שכח וכל שכן הא דמשמע דהא לא איצטריך למיתני והא נמי איצטריך לאשמעינן דאינו חייב על כל מלאכה ומלאכה ונראה לר"י דלעיל דקאמר ליתני הכיר ולבסוף שכח וכ"ש הא לא בעי למימר דלא ליתני' כלל במשנה אלא ה"פ מדקתני חייב על כל שבת ושבת ולא קתני אינו חייב אלא על כל שבת דהוה משמע ולא על כל מלאכה ומלאכה משמע דעיקר מתניתין חיובא אתא לאשמעינן דחייב על כל שבת ושבת ולא פטורא דאינו חייב על כל מלאכה ואם כן ליתני הכיר ולבסוף שכח דהוי רבותא טפי וכ"ש האי דחייב על כל שבת ולא הוה צריך למתנייה בהאי בבא אלא ה"ל למיתני בתר הכי בבבא אחריתי היודע עיקר שבת אינו חייב אלא על כל שבת ושבת לאשמעינן דאינו חייב על כל מלאכה והשתא דייק שפיר אבל לא שכחה מאי חייב על כל מלאכה ומלאכה מדלא תני בבבא אחריתי דאינו חייב אלא על כל שבת ושבת*:

ליתני היודע עיקר שבת וכ"ש הא· תימה לר"י לרבא דאמר בכריתות בסוף פרק אמרו לו (דף טז:) דבזדון שבת ושגגת מלאכות לא מיחייב אלא אכל שבת ושבת ודייק ממתניתין דהכא דלא קתני חייב על כל אב מלאכה ומלאכה של כל שבת ושבת ולדידיה היכי פריך הכא ליתני היודע עיקר שבת הא לא מצי למיתני הכי דאם כן הוה משמע דלא מיחייב היודע עיקר שבת אלא אכל שבת ושבת ותירץ דהכי פריך דליתני היודע עיקר שבת דחייב אכל אב מלאכה של כל שבת ושבת ורשב"א מפרש דאי הוה תני בהדיא היודע עיקר שבת חייב על כל אב מלאכה ליכא למידק דלא מיחייב אכל שבת מדלא קתני חייב על כל אב מלאכה של כל שבת דלא צריך למיתני' דמרישא שמעינן ליה דקתני בהכיר ולבסוף שכח דחייב על כל שבת ושבת כ"ש יודע עיקר שבת כדאמר לעיל: וכ"ש האי· ה"נ לא בעי למימר דלא לתני' כלל במשנה דאם כן הוה אמינא דחייב נמי על כל שבת ושבת ואינו כן לרבה דכריתות אלא ליתני בבא אחריתי היודע שהוא שבת אינו חייב על כל שבת:

כי הכיר ולבסוף שכח דמי· פירש בקונטרס דלהכי לא תנא במתניתין שכח מעיקרו דהיינו תינוק שנשבה דלא תימא דהכיר ולבסוף שכח חייב על כל שבת וקשה לר"י דמ"מ ליתנייה וליתני נמי בתר הכי הכיר ולבסוף שכח אינו חייב אלא אחת דהכ"ג פריך לעיל ליתני הכיר ולבסוף שכח וכ"ש הא כדפרישית ונראה לר"י דודאי אי הוה תני חייב חטאת דהוה אתי לאשמעינן חיובא הוה שייך למיפרך דליתני תינוק שנשבה דהוי רבותא טפי אבל השתא דקתני אינו חייב אלא אחת דפטורא אתא לאשמעינן נקט הכיר ולבסוף שכח דהוי רבותא טפי ומיהו קשה לר"י דמ"מ ליתני תינוק שנשבה דלא נטעה לומר דפטור כרבי יוחנן וריש לקיש והדר ליתני הכיר ולבסוף שכח:

אבל תינוק שנשבה פטור· פירש בקונטרס דקסברי אומר מותר אנוס הוא ואין נראה דטעמייהו כמונבז כדאמר בסמוך וטעמא דמונבז מפרש לקמן דיליף מקרא והא דאמר בפ"ב דמכות (דף ז:) גבי גלות בשגגה פרט למזיד ומפרש (אביי) [נ"ל רבא] פרט לאומר מותר ופריך ליה (רבא) [נ"ל אביי] אומר מותר אנוס הוא לאו דוקא קאמר אנוס דבכל מקום מחייבין ליה אלא לגבי גלות דוקא ממעט (אביי) [נ"ל רבא] אומר מותר משום דטובא בשגגה כתיב התם דהא בפירקין(ב) מחייבי אומר מותר בע"ז ובחלב אע"ג דכתיב בהן בשגגה (ורבא) [נ"ל ואביי] פריך ליה אומר מותר אנוס הוא ולא הוה ליה למיתני בברייתא בשגגה פרט למזיד אלא פרט לאנוס דיותר דמי וקרוב לאנוס מלמזיד:

וחייב על הדם אחת· אע"ג דמילתא דפשיטא היא דאכל מה שאכל דם אינו חייב אלא אחת כיון שאין בדם חילוק איסור כמו שיש בשבת חילוק מלאכות וכל אדם נמי בלא תינוק שנשבה אכל דם ודם אינו חייב אלא אחת אלא אומר ר"י דמיירי דאפי' אכלן בכמה תמחויין דלר"י (לקמן דף עא·) אדם אחר חייב על כל תמחוי אפי' בהעלם אחד ובתינוק שנשבה אינו חייב אלא אחד אך קשה לרשב"א דמאי איצטריך תו לאשמעינן ולמתני ועל החלב אחד:

כל שכן שהוספת· כדפירש בקונטרס דאף בזו מחייב ומחייב נמי כי ליכא ידיעה בשעת מעשה דהא רבי יוחנן וריש לקיש סברי כמונבז ומחייבי הכיר ולבסוף שכח ותניא נמי לקמן שגג בזה ובזה זהו שוגג האמור בתורה ומוקמינן לה כמונבז והיינו טעמא משום דסברא הוא דלא איתקש שוגג למזיד לאפוקי ליה ממשמעות שגגה דאדרבה שוגג משמע דלית ליה ידיעה בשעת מעשה ולא אתא היקשא אלא לחייב נמי כי אית ליה ידיעה בשעת מעשה ומיהו קשה לר"י דהא פטרי מהיקשא תינוק שנשבה מהאי טעמא נמי יפטור הכיר ולבסוף שכח:

מה

רבינו חננאל

מתני' לדברי הכל בהכיר ולבסוף שכח אינו חייב אלא חטאת אחת ורב ושמואל הוסיפו אפילו קטן שנשבה לבין עו"ג כהכיר ולבסוף שכח דמי וחייב חטאת ורבי יוחנן וריש לקיש אמרי קטן שנשבה בין עו"ג פטור ואותיבנא עלייהו מהא דתניא השוכח עיקר שבת ועשה מלאכות הרבה בשבתות הרבה אינו חייב אלא חטאת אחת וחייב על ע"ז אחת· פירש אם עבד ע"ז הרבה דינו כדין שבת וכן כל מצוה ומצוה אינו חייב אלא בכל מצוה אחת ומונבז פוטר בכל ומשני רבי יוחנן וריש לקיש אנן דאמרינן כמונבז דסבר כיון דלא הויא ידיעה ליה בתחלה בעיקר שבת אף על גב דבתר דעביד מלאכות הרבה בשבתות הרבה אתידע ליה איסורא דשבת לא מחייב וכי אמרו רבי יוחנן ור"ל דאנן כמונבז סבירא לן בהאי לחוד דפטר קטן שנשבה בין הנכרים אבל בהאי דבעי ידיעה למונבז בשעת מעשה שידע

לר"י דפי' דדייק מדלא קתני לה בבא אחריתי ולא פירש אינו חייב על כל מלאכה לא נתיישב לי דהא לא איצטריך למיתני בבא אחריתא דמסיפא שמעינן מדקתני היודע שהוא שבת חייב על כל מלאכה ומשמע הא שכחה אינו חייב על כל מלאכה ועוד מאי פריך בסמוך ליתני היודע עיקר שבת וכ"ש הא אמאי הוי צריך למיתני היודע עיקר שבת שהוא חייב על כל מלאכה והא שמעינן לה מדלא תני בבא אחריתי כדפרי' והיה נ"ל דלעיל פריך ליתני הכיר ולבסוף שכח בהדיא וכ"ש היודע עיקר שבת ולא הוי צריך כלל למיתני דחייב על כל שבת דשמעינן מכ"ש דהכיר ולבסוף שכח שאינו חייב על כל מלאכה מדנקט בסיפא היודע שהוא שבת כו' משמע דהיודע עיקר שבת ושבת אינו חייב על כל מלאכה אבל השתא דתני דיודע עיקר שבת היינו הכיר ולבסוף שכח פריך שפיר אבל לא שכחה מאי חייב על כל מלאכה דאי אינו חייב כמו בשכחה א"כ אמאי נקט היודע עיקר שבת דמשמע טפי דאיירי בלא שכחה ה"ל למיתני בהדיא הכיר ולבסוף שכח דהוי משמע רבותא טפי אלא ודאי בשלא שכחה חייב על כל מלאכה והוי' בכלל בבא דסיפא להכי ליכא למיטעי במאי דנקט האי לישנא דהיודע עיקר שבת ולא נקט הכיר ולבסוף שכח בהדיא אימא סיפא היודע שהוא שבת וכו' בשלמא אי הוי תני בהדיא היודע עיקר שבת ולא שכחה בסיפא הוי ידעינן ליה מכ"ש דסיפא א"ש כדפרישית אבל השתא דהיודע עיקר שבת ולא שכחה לא שמעינן מסיפא אלא אדרבה משמע דוקא יודע שהוא שבת חייב על כל מלאכה אם כן מציעתא משמע דמיירי ביודע עיקר שבת ולא שכחה כדמשמע לישנא ומשמע דוקא לא שכחה אבל שכחה אינו חייב על כל שבת דאי חייב ליתני הכיר ולבסוף שכחה בהדיא וכל שכן שיודע עיקר שבת ולא שכחה כדפרי' לעיל [תוספות ישנים]:

רב נסים גאון

ורבנן כדמקרי ליה ר' יהושע בן לוי לבריה תורה אחת יהיה לכם לעושה בשגגה והנפש אשר תעשה ביד רמה הוקשה כל התורה כולה לע"ז דע שפרשת (במדבר טו) וכי תשגו ולא תעשו ואם נפש אחת תחטא בשגגה שסמנה אלו הפסוקים אמרו רבותינו ז"ל כי היא מיוחדת בע"ז ותמצא פירוש זה בספרי בע"ז הכתוב מדבר אתה אומר בע"ז או אינו אלא באחת מן המצות האמורות בתורה ת"ל והיה אם מעיני העדה נעשתה ייחד הכתוב מצוה זו בפני עצמה ואיזו זו ע"ז וכו' ובמסכת הוריות בפ' הורה כהן משיח (דף ח) אמרו דכולי עלמא הני קראי בע"ז הוא דכתיבי מנא לן אמר רבא ואיתימא ר' יהושע בן לוי ואמרי לה כדי וכי תשגו ולא תעשו את כל המצות האלה איזו היא מצוה שהיא שקולה כנגד כל המצות כולן הוי אומר זו ע"ז דבית ר' תנא אמר קרא*) את כל אשר דבר ה' אליכם ביד משה איזו היא מצוה

*) אשר דבר ה' אל משה את כל אשר צוה ה' אליכם ביד משה כצ"ל

tial law of the Sabbath and forgot it. [68b] What if he did not forget it?[10] He is liable for each labour? Then instead of teaching, HE WHO KNOWS THAT IT IS THE SABBATH AND PERFORMS MANY LABOURS ON MANY SABBATHS, IS LIABLE FOR EVERY LABOUR, let him teach, He who knows the essential law of the Sabbath, and how much more so this case? Rather our Mishnah refers to one who knew but subsequently forgot, and Rab and Samuel's [ruling] too is similar to the case of one who knew but subsequently forgot, and it was thus stated: Rab and Samuel both maintain: Even a child who was taken captive among Gentiles or a proselyte who became converted in the midst of Gentiles is as one who knew but subsequently forgot, and so he is liable. But R. Joḥanan and Resh Lakish maintain: Only one who knew but subsequently forgot [is liable], but a child who was taken captive among Gentiles, or a proselyte who became converted in the midst of Gentiles, is not culpable.

An objection is raised: A great principle is stated in respect to Sabbath: He who forgets the essential law of Sabbath and performs many labours on many Sabbaths, incurs one sin-offering only. E.g., if a child is taken captive among Gentiles or a proselyte is converted in the midst of Gentiles and performs many labours on many Sabbaths, he is liable to one sin-offering only. And he is liable to one [sin-offering] on account of blood,
a one on account of *ḥeleb*,[1] and one on account of idolatry.[2] But Monabaz exempts him. And thus did Monabaz argue before R. Akiba: Since a wilful transgressor is designated a sinner, and an unwitting transgressor [too] is designated a sinner;[3] then just as wilful transgression implied that he had knowledge,[4] so when unwittingly transgressing he must have had the knowledge.[5] Said R. Akiba to him, Behold, I will add to your words. If so, just as wilful transgression involves that he shall have had knowledge at the time of his deed, so in unwitting transgression he must
b have had knowledge at the time of his deed.[1] Even so, he replied, and all the more so since you have added [this argument]. As you define it,[2] such is not designated unwitting, but wilful transgression, he retorted. Now after all it is stated, 'E.g., if a child' [etc.]: as for Rab and Samuel, it is well.[3] But according to R. Joḥanan and Resh Lakish it presents a difficulty?—R. Joḥanan and Resh Lakish can answer you: Is there not Monabaz who declares him non-culpable? We rule as Monabaz.

What is Monabaz's reason?[4] Because it is written, *Ye shall have one law for him that doeth unwittingly;*[5] and in proximity thereto [it is written], *And the soul that doeth aught with a high hand:*[6] hence unwitting is assimilated to wilful transgression:[7] just as wilful transgression involves that he shall have had knowledge, so unwitting transgression implies that he shall have had knowledge.[8] And the Rabbis: how do they employ this [verse], *Ye shall have one law,* [etc.]?—They employ it even as R. Joshua b. Levi taught his son: *Ye shall have one law for him that doeth unwittingly;* and it is

(10) *Sc.* the essential law of the Sabbath, but merely that that particular day was the Sabbath.

a (1) V. Glos. (2) I.e., for the violation of each law, which if deliberately infringed, carries with it the penalty of *kareth*, he incurs one sin-offering only, no matter how many times he actually infringes it. The consumption of blood and *ḥeleb* and the worshipping of idols are given as examples. (3) For a wilful trangressor v. Lev. V, 1: *And if any one sin*, etc. That refers to wilful transgression, since Scripture does not maintain that *his sin be hidden from him*, i.e., committed in ignorance. For unwitting transgression v. Lev. IV, 2 *et passim*. (4) Of the forbidden nature of his action. (5) Formerly, though at the time of sinning he had forgotten it.

b (1) Which is absurd! (2) Lit., 'according to your words'. (3) For they too maintain that he is liable. Now, they can argue that the same holds good even if one originally knew the law but subsequently forgot it, just as they explain the Mishnah, while the particular illustration is given because of Monabaz's dissent in this case. (4) The analogy on mere grounds of logic is insufficient, since wilful and unwitting transgression are obviously dissimilar. (5) Num. XV, 29. (6) Ibid. 30; this obviously applies to deliberate transgression. (7) I.e., Scripture itself intimates by this proximity that the two are similar. (8) Before a sin-offering is incurred.

written, [69a] ***and when ye shall err, and not observe all these commandments;***[9] and it is written, ***And the soul that doeth aught with a high hand . . .*** [***that soul shall be cut off***]: thus they are all assimilated to idolatry: just as there it is something for the wilful transgression of which *kareth*[10] is incurred, and for the unwitting transgression a sin-offering is incurred,[11] so for everything the wilful transgression of which involves *kareth*, its unwitting transgression involves a sin-offering.[12]

But according to Monabaz, wherein lies his non-wilfulness?[1]—E.g., if he was ignorant in respect of the sacrifice.[2] But the Rabbis hold that ignorance in respect of the sacrifice does not constitute ignorance.

Now according to the Rabbis, in respect to what is ignorance [required]? R. Johanan said: As long as one errs in respect to *kareth*, even if he wilfully sins in respect of the negative command;[3] while Resh Lakish maintained: He must offend unwittingly in respect of the negative injunction and *kareth*. Raba said, What is R. Simeon b. Lakish's reason? Scripture saith, [***And if any one of the common people sin unwittingly, in doing any of the things which the Lord hath commanded***] ***not to be done, and be guilty:***[4] hence he must err both as to the negative injunction and its attendant *kareth*.[5] And R. Johanan: how does he employ this verse adduced by R. Simeon b. Lakish?—He utilizes it for what was taught: [***And if any one***] ***of the common people:*** this excludes a *mumar*.[6] R. Simeon b. Eleazar said on the authority of R. Simeon:[7] [. . . ***sin unwittingly in doing any of the things which the Lord hath commanded***] ***not to be done, and be guilty:*** he who would refrain[8] on account of his knowledge, brings a sacrifice for his unwitting offence; but he who would not refrain on account of his knowledge cannot bring a sacrifice for his unwitting offence.[9]

We learnt: The primary forms of labour are forty less one.[10] Now we pondered thereon, Why state the number?[1] And R. Johanan replied: [To teach] that if one performs all of them in a single state of unawareness,[2] he is liable [to a sin-offering] for each. Now, how is this possible? [Surely only] where he is aware of the Sabbath but unconscious of [the forbidden nature of] his labours.[3] As for R. Johanan, who maintained that since he is ignorant in respect of *kareth*, though fully aware of the negative injunction, [his offence is unwitting], it is well: it is conceivable, e.g. where he knew [that labour is forbidden on] the Sabbath by a negative injunction. But according to R. Simeon b. Lakish, who maintained that he must be unaware of the negative injunction and of *kareth*, wherein did he know of the Sabbath?[4]—He knew of [the law of] boundaries,[5] this being in accordance with R. Akiba.[6]

Who is the authority for the following which was taught by the Rabbis: If one is unaware of both,[7] he is the erring sinner mentioned in the Torah;[8] if one wilfully transgresses in respect of both, he is the presumptuous offender mentioned in the Torah. If one is unaware of the Sabbath but conscious of [the forbidden character of] his labours or the reverse, or if he declares, 'I knew that this labour is forbidden, but not whether it entails a sacrifice or not,' he is culpable? With whom does this agree? With Monabaz.[9]

Abaye said: All agree in respect to an 'oath of utterance'[10] that a sacrifice is not incurred on account thereof unless one is unaware
c of its interdict.[1] 'All agree': who is that? R. Johanan?[2] But that is obvious! When did R. Johanan say [otherwise], where there is [the penalty of] *kareth*; but here [in the case of an 'oath of utterance'] that there is no [penalty of] *kareth*, he did not state [his ruling]?—One might argue: Since liability to a sacrifice [here] is an anomaly,[3] for we do not find in the whole Torah that for a [mere] negative injunction[4] one must bring a sacrifice, whilst here it is brought; hence even if he is unaware of the [liability to a]

(9) Ibid. 22; in Hor. 8a it is deduced that this refers to idolatry. (10) I.e., cutting off. (11) V. v. 27. (12) But where wilful transgression involves a lesser penalty than *kareth*, an unwitting offence does not involve a sin-offering.

(1) When the offender has knowledge at the time of his action. (2) He knew that the wilful offence involved *kareth*, but not that the unwitting transgression involved a sin-offering. (3) I.e., he knows that it is forbidden by a negative injunction but not that its penalty is *kareth*. This constitutes sinning in ignorance, and involves a sin-offering. (4) Lev. IV, 27. (5) '*Not to be done*' after '*sin unwittingly*' implies that he is ignorant that it is forbidden at all. (6) One who is professedly antagonistic to Jewish law. If he sins unwittingly, he cannot offer a sacrifice, even if he desires. This is deduced from the partitive *of the common people*, expressed in the original by the letter *mem* (מ), which is regarded as a limitation. (7) I.e., R. Simeon b. Yohai. (8) Lit., 'turn back'. (9) For the verse implies that he acted solely through his ignorance; only then can he atone with a sacrifice. R. Simeon too teaches the exclusion of a *mumar*, but deduces it differently. (10) *Infra* 73a.

(1) Since they are enumerated by name. (2) Of their forbidden nature. (3) For in the reverse case he incurs only one sin-offering (v. Mishnah 67b). Now awareness of the Sabbath implies that he knows at least one of the labours forbidden, for otherwise the Sabbath is the same to him as any other day, and he cannot be said to be aware thereof. But in the present passage he appears to have known none at all: how then can we regard him as being aware of the Sabbath? This the Talmud proceeds to discuss. (4) Seeing that he was ignorant of all the forbidden labours. (5) That one may not go on the Sabbath more than a certain distance beyond the town limits. Infringement of this law does not entail a sacrifice. (6) Who maintains that the limitation of boundaries is Biblical. The Rabbis dispute this. (7) I.e., of the Sabbath and that this labour is forbidden on the Sabbath. (8) He certainly falls within this category. (9) *Supra*. (10) E.g., 'I swear that I will eat', or, 'I swear that I will not eat', and then broken, cf. Lev. V, 4.

c (1) I.e., the offender must have forgotten his oath at the time of breaking it, so that he is unaware that his action is interdicted by his oath. A sacrifice for a broken oath is decreed in Lev. V, 4 *seq*. (2) For Abaye cannot mean by 'all' that even Monabaz agrees that it is insufficient that he shall merely be ignorant that a vain oath entails a sacrifice. For how can this be maintained? On the contrary, the reverse follows *a fortiori*: if Monabaz regards unawareness of the liability to a sin-offering elsewhere as true unawareness, though such liability is in accordance with the general principle that where *kareth* is incurred for a wilful offence a sin-offering is incurred for an unwitting transgression, how much more so here, seeing that the very liability to a sacrifice is an anomaly unexpected, for the deliberate breaking of an oath does not entail *kareth*. Hence Abaye must refer to R. Johanan's view on the ruling of the Rabbis. (3) Lit., 'a new thing'—something outside the general rule. (4) Which does not entail *kareth*.

מסורת הש"ס

עין משפט נר מצוה

ה א מיי' פ"א מהלכות שגגות הלכה ב :

ו ב ג מיי' פ"ב מהלכות שגגות הלכה ב סמג עשין רג :

ז ד מיי' שם ופ"ז ס"ג:

תורה אור

(במדבר טו) וכי תשגו ולא תעשו את כל המצות האלה וכתיב (שם) °והנפש אשר תעשה ביד רמה *הוקשו כולם לע"ז °מה להלן דבר שחייבים על זדונו כרת ושגגתו חטאת אף כל דבר שחייבין על זדונו כרת ועל שגגתו חטאת ואלא מונבז שגגה במאי כגון ששגג בקרבן ורבנן °שגגת קרבן לא שמה שגגה ורבנן שגגה במאי רבי יוחנן אמר °כיון ששגג בכרת אף על פי שהזיד בלאו וריש לקיש אמר עד שישגוג בלאו וכרת אמר רבא (ויקרא ד) מאי טעמא דרשב"ל אמר קרא °אשר לא תעשינה (בשגגה) ואשם עד שישגוג בלאו וכרת שבה ורבי יוחנן האי קרא דרשב"ל (שם) מאי עביד ליה מיבעי ליה *לכדתניא °מעם הארץ פרט למומר רבי שמעון בן אלעזר אומר משום רבי שמעון אשר לא תעשינה (בשגגה) ואשם *השב מידיעתו מביא קרבן על שגגתו לא שב מידיעתו אינו מביא קרבן על שגגתו: תנן *אבות מלאכות ארבעים חסר אחת והוינן בה *מנינא למה לי ואמר ר' יוחנן °שאם עשאן כולן בהעלם אחד חייב על כל אחת ואחת היכי משכחת לה בזדון שבת ושגגת מלאכות בשלמא לרבי יוחנן דאמר כיון ששגג בכרת אע"פ שהזיד בלאו משכחת לה כגון דידע לה לשבת בלאו אלא לר"ש ב"ל דאמר עד שישגוג בלאו ובכרת דידע ליה לשבת במאי *דידעה *)בתחומין [כריתות ג.] *ואליבא דר"ע [*סוטה כז:] מאן תנא להא דתנו רבנן שגג בזה ובזה זהו שוגג האמור בתורה הזיד בזה ובזה זו היא מזיד האמור בתורה שגג בשבת והזיד במלאכות או ששגג במלאכות והזיד בשבת או שאמר יודע אני שמלאכה זו אסורה אבל איני יודע שחייבין עליה קרבן או לא חייב כמאן כמונבז אמר אביי הכל מודים בשבועת ביטוי שאין חייבין עליה קרבן עד שישגוג בלאו שבה הכל מודים מאן ר' יוחנן פשיטא כי קא"ר יוחנן היכא דאיכא כרת אבל הכא דליכא כרת לא סד"א *הואיל וחייב קרבן חידוש הוא דבכל התורה כולה לא אשכחן לאו דמייתי עליה קרבן והכא מייתי כי שגג בקרבן נמי ליחייב קמ"ל

*) [לקמן ע: עג· קנג: סנהדרין סו·]

רש"י

וכי תשגו ולא תעשו את כל המצות האלה · וילפינן בהוריות (דף ח·) זו ע"ז שהיא שקולה ככל המצות וכתיב תורה אחת כל התורה במשמע: הוקשו · קרבנות של שגגות של כל עבירות לשל ע"ז מה ע"ז קרבן שלה אינו בא אלא על עבירה גמורה שחייב על זדונו כרת דסמיך ליה והנפש אשר תעשה ביד רמה ונכרתה: אף כל התורה · אין מביאין חטאת אלא על דבר שזדונו כרת: ואלא מונבז · דאמר לעיל דמי שהיתה לו ידיעה בשעת מעשה חייב חטאת: דשגג במאי · הא גבי חטאת שגגה כתיב: דשגג בקרבן · דיודע שחייב על זדונו כרת אבל אינו יודע שחייב עליה חטאת: לא שמה שגגה. עד ששגג בעבירה עצמה: ורבנן · דבעו שגגה בעבירה עצמה שגגה במאי קאמרי שגגה בכולה מילתא בלאו וכרת או בכרת לחודיה: כיון ששגג בכרת אע"ג שהזיד בלאו · שאין הקרבן על הכרת הוא בא כדאמרן לעושה בשגגה וסמיך ליה והנפש אשר תעשה וגו': לא תעשינה · היינו לאו: מנינא למה לי · ליתני אבות מלאכות הזורע והחורש כו' למה לי למיתנא ארבעים חסר אחת ליתניוהו ואנן ידעינן דמ' חסר אחת איכא: שאם עשאן כולן כו' · וסימנא בעלמא אשמעינן לידע כמה חטאות חייב על חילול שבת אחת: היכי משכחת לה · דמיחייב ע"כ לא משכחת לה אלא בזדון שבת דיודע שהוא שבת ושגגת מלאכות דאינו יודע שהמלאכות הללו אסורות דאי בזדון מלאכות ושגגת שבת דיודע שהן אסורות בשבת אבל שכח שהיום שבת הא תנן דאינו חייב אלא אחת לכל שבת וזדון שבת לא הוי אא"כ יודע אחת מהלכותיה דאי לא ידע בחדא מינייהו אין שבת חלוק לו משאר ימים וזה ששגג בכולן אין כאן זדון שבת: בשלמא לר' יוחנן · דאמר שגגת כרת שמה שגגה: משכחת לה · זדון שבת בלאוין ושגגת מלאכות בכריתות דיודע לה לשבת שהוזהר על הלאוין או של כולן או של אחת מהן: דידע לה לשבת במאי · הלא בכולן שגג כסבור שכל ל"ט מלאכות מותרות: בתחומין · דאין בקרבן: ואליבא דר' עקיבא · דאמר במסכת סוטה (א) תחומין דאורייתא נינהו דתנן בו ביום דרש רבי עקיבא ומדותם מחוץ לעיר כו': זהו שוגג האמור בתורה · כלומר היכא דשגג בשבת ובמלאכות אין כאן לא דין ולא דיין לקנתר ואין לך שוגג כזה: הזיד בזה ובזה · אין לך מזיד כזה: שגג באחת מהן · אף זה שוגג וחייבים עליה קרבן: שבועת ביטוי · שאוכל ולא אוכל שאכלתי ולא אכלתי חייב עליה קרבן וכתיב ביה ונעלם דהיינו שוגג הכל מודים בשוגג שלה דאם נשבע שלא אוכל ואכל אינו חייב אלא אם כן שכח שבועתו כשאכל דהשתא שגג בלאו שבה: הכל מודים מאן רבי יוחנן · כלומר על כרחין אביי לאו אפלוגתא דמונבז ורבנן קאי דלישמעינן דמודה מונבז בהא (דהא) *שגגת קרבן לא הויא שגגה דמהיכא תיתי והא ק"ו היא השתא בכל התורה כולה דליכא חידוש בקרבן דידהו אמר מונבז דמיחייב בשגגת קרבן הכא דחידוש הוא דאין בה כרת ומביא קרבן עליה לא כ"ש אלא לרבנן קאמר ואפלוגתא דר"י ור"ל קאי ומאן הכל מודים ר"י דאף על גב דבעלמא קאמר אף על פי שהזיד בלאו הכא בעינן שישגוג בלאו: פשיטא · כיון דאליבא דרבנן איפליג דאמרי שגגת קרבן לאו שגגה היא אי בלאו שלה הזיד במאי שגג דע"כ לא קאמר ר"י בעלמא אלא במקום כרת דשגג בכרת: סלקא דעתך אמינא · בשבועת ביטוי נמי קאי רבי יוחנן במילתיה דאף על פי שהזיד בלאו ודקשיא לך במאי שגג שגג בקרבן דהואיל וחידוש מודו ביה רבנן:

קמ"ל

תוספות

מה ע"ז שחייבים על זדונו כרת. וא"ת מ"מ הקישא דשוגג למזיד למה לי דאפילו לא הוי כתיב התם קרא דוהנפש אשר תעשה ביד רמה ילפינן שפיר מע"ז שחייב על זדונה כרת כו' וי"ל דלית לן לאקושה לע"ז אלא במאי דכתיב בההיא פרשה כדמשמע מתוך פירוש הקונטרס ולהכי אצטריך לאתויי הכא והנפש אשר תעשה תדע דהא לא ילפינן מע"ז דניבעי על זדונו סקילה כע"ז משום דלא כתיב סקילה בההיא פרשה אלא כרת והא דממעטינן בריש פרק בתרא דמכות (דף יג:) פסח ומילה מקרבן אע"פ שיש בהן כרת משום דמה ע"ז דאמר רחמנא לא תעביד והני קום עשה נינהו הייט נמי משום דכתיב והנפש אשר תעשה ביד רמה °דמשמע מה שצויתי שלא לעשות וא"ת רבנן דהכא כר' עקיבא ור' עקיבא אית ליה בפ"ק דכריתות (דף ז:) דהאי קרא דמגדף במברך את השם כתיב וי"ל דלישנא דנקט הכא הוקשה כל התורה כולה לע"ז נקט אליבא דרבנן דרבי עקיבא אבל לר"ע אית לן למימר דהוקשה כל. התורה כולה למברך את השם וא"ת ולמונבז האי דרשא דר' יהושע בן לוי מנא ליה ואומר ר"י דנפקא ליה כדדריש רבי בפ"ק דיבמות (דף ט·) ובפ"ב דהוריות (דף ח·) נאמר כאן ונודעה החטאת אשר חטאו עליה ונאמ' ואשה אל אחותה לא תקח לצרור לגלות ערותה עליה: **אלא** למונבז שגגה במאי. לא מצי למימר ששגג בלאו והזיד בקרבן דאין סברא לחייב בהזיד בקרבן דלא שב מידיעתו הוא וליכא נמי למימר שגג בלאו וקרבן דסברא הוא דכיון דמקיש למזיד אפי' מזיד בכל דבר ושוגג רק בדבר אחד דהיינו בקרבן יש לנו לחייבו(א) ומיהו היכא דאיכא סקילה בעינן שיהא שוגג גם בסקילה דאי הוה מזיד בסקילה אין לחייבו בקרבן דכיון דאינו שב מסקילה פשיטא שאפילו היה יודע שחייב גם קרבן שלא היה שב ולא שב מידיעתו הוא ואע"ג דבהזיד בכרת חשיב ליה שב מידיעתו לקרבן היינו משום דכרת אפשר בתשובה וקרבן לא אפשר בתשובה ועוד דגבי כרת שייך שפיר למימר אם היה יודע שחייב כרת עם הקרבן היה שב: **כגון** ששגג בכרת אע"פ שהזיד בלאו · וטעמא דר' יוחנן משום דלא כתיב לאו בהיקשא דר' יהושע ולא כתיב אלא כרת בההיא ענינא ולהכי בעי מ"ט דריש לקיש ולא בעי מ"ט דר' יוחנן וצ"ל דרבי יוחנן מיירי אליבא דרבנן דאית להו היקשא דרבי יהושע בן לוי °אבל לרבי דנפקא ליה מג"ש דעליה מודה רבי יוחנן דבעי עד שישגוג בלאו וכרת דהא כתיב לאו בההוא קרא ואשה אל אחותה לא תקח וגו': **אמר** קרא אשר לא תעשינה בשגגה · קשה לר"י מנא ליה לריש לקיש דרבנן דרשי הכי ובעו שגגת לאו וליכא למימר דמשמע ליה למדרש קרא הכי דהא ע"כ סבירא ליה דאין סברא לדרוש כן דהא איהו סבר כמונבז כדאמר לעיל ומונבז לא בעי שגגת לאו אלא שגגת קרבן גרידא דבהדיא תניא לקמן או שאמר יודע אני שמלאכה זו אסורה אבל איני יודע אם חייבים עליה קרבן אם לאו חייב ולא קאמר קרבן ומלקות אם לאו: **דידע** לה בתחומין(ג) · לא מצי למימר דידע לה בדאיסי דבההוא נמי חייב חטאת כדפירשתי בפרק קמא (דף ו: בד"ה הא קמ"ל) תימה לר"י דאמאי לא קאמר דידע לה לשבת בעשה דכתיב וביום השביעי תשבות וגו' (שמות כג) וכתיב נמי ושמרתם את השבת (כס לא) : **עד** שישגוג בלאו שבה · כגון נשבע שלא יאכל ואכל ובשעת אכילה שכח איסור שבועה וקרינן ביה האדם דבשעת שבועה שנשבע היה יודע היטב איסור שבועה אלא שבשעת אכילה היה סבור דמותר לעבור על שבועתו ורש"י פירש דבשעת אכילה שכח שנשבע ואין נראה דאין זה קרוי שגג בלאו שבה במה שאינו זוכר שנשבע: הא

רבינו חננאל

שהיא מעשה שבת וידע שהעושה מלאכה זו חייב עליה לאו וכרת וכי לא שגג אלא בקרבן בלבד וסבר כל כי האי גוונא הוא דחייב חטאת וזולתי כן פטור · וכדתניא אמר אני יודע שמלאכה זו אסורה אבל איני יודע אם חייבין עליה קרבן אם לאו חייב דאוקימנא כמונבז. בהאי סברא בתרא דמונבז רבי יוחנן ור"ל לא סבירא להו כוותיה · וקא מפרש ר' יוחנן כטעמא דרבנן כיון ששגג בכרת אע"פ שהזיד בלאו חייב חטאת · ור"ל אמר אינו חייב חטאת עד שישגוג בלאו וכרת ומותבינן על ר"ל הא דתנן אבות מלאכות ארבעים חסר אחת והוינן בה מנינא למה לי ואמר ר' יוחנן אם עשאן כולם בהעלם אחד חייב על כל אחת ואחת ואוקימנא בזדון שבת ושגגת מלאכות בשלמא לר' יוחנן כגון שהזיד בלאו פי' ידע שהיא היום שבת וידע שהעושה מלאכה (חייב כרת) [עובר בלאו] אמרי' כיון ששגג [בכרת] אף על פי שהזיד בלאו שגגה היא וחייב חטאת אלא לריש לקיש דאמר עד שישגוג בלאו וכרת זדון שבת היכי משכחת ליה ומשני כגון דידע לשבת בתחומין אמרת אין השבת אסור אלא בתחומין כדכתיב אל יצא איש ממקומו וגו' וכרבי עקיבא דסבר תחומין דאורייתא כדמפרש בסוטה פ' ה' ואף על גב דדחי התם ואמרינן (עירובין ס:*) לית דחש להא דרבי עקיבא: **אמר** אביי הכל מודים בשבועת ביטוי שאין חייבין עליה קרבן עד שישגוג בלאו שבה · מאן הכל מודים רבי יוחנן דסבר עד שישגוג בכרת והאי כיון דלית בה כרת בעי שגגה בלאו ואמרינן פשיטא מהו דתימא הואיל וחדוש הוא דלא אשכחן בכל התורה לאו שאין בה כרת שמייתי קרבן והכא בשבועת ביטוי מייתי קרבן אע"פ שאין בה כרת הוה אמינא כי שגג בקרבן (נמי) בלבד [נמי] מחייב קמ"ל דלא מחייב רבי יוחנן עד שישגוג בלאו שבה . קיי"ל דכל לאו שבתורה שחייבין עליו מלקות בלבד ואין בו כרת אינו חייב עליו חטאת וכי אינו חייב חטאת אלא על דבר

* ע"ש דלא מיירי כלל מדין תחומין דאורייתא · אכן מ"מ יש ללמוד מהתם דגם כדין תחומין דאורייי' לא קיי"ל כר"ע ועיין תוס' שם ד"ה לית ודו"ק.

רב נסים גאון

מצוה שהיא בדברו של הקב"ה וצוה על ידי משה הוי אומר זו ע"ז : **דידע** להו בתחומים ואליבא דרבי עקיבא כמה דאמר ר' עקיבא במסכת סוטה בפ' כשם שהמים בודקין אותה (דף כז) בו ביום דרש רבי עקיבא ומדותם מחוץ לעיר ומקרא אחד אומר מקיר העיר וחוצה אלף אמה אי אפשר לומר אלף אמה שכבר נאמר אלפים אמה ואי אפשר לומר אלפים שכבר נאמר אלף ולמה נאמר אלפים אלא אלף אמה מגרש ואלפים אמה תחום שבת ר' אלעזר בנו של ר' יוסי הגלילי אומר אלף אמה מגרש ואלפים שדות וכרמים ואסרו בגמרא במאי

מסורת הש"ס

[לקמן קנג: ע"א]

יומא פ. הוריות ב. ח. ע"ש חולין ה:

שבועות כו: וש"נ

לקמן עג· [לו:] [לעיל ו:]

לעיל ו: לקמן ע: עג· לו: כריתות ב:

[עי' תוספות חגיגה יז: ד"ה דכתיב ותוס' לעיל ו: ד"ה הא קמ"ל]

הואיל והידוש הוא כצ"ל רש"ל

הגהות הב"ח

(א) רש"י ד"ה ואליבא דרבי עקיבא דאמר במסכת סוטה· נכתב בלדו דף כו ע"ב ודף ל ע"ב:

נ"ל דשגגת רש"ל

גליון הש"ס

תוס' ד"ה מה ע"ז וכו' דמשמע מה שצויתי שלא לעשות · עיין בב"ק דף קה ע"ב תוס' ד"ה מאי לאו : שם ד"ה כגון ששגג וכו' אבל לרבי דנפקא ליה מגז"ש · עיין בחידושי הר"ן שבועות דף ה ע"א ובחי' הרמב"ן שם :

א) דהא ודאי ליכא למימר דשגג בכרת דא"כ היינו רבנן ועוד כיון דמקיש שוגג למזיד בכרת אית לן למימר דמכרת אית ליה ידיעה בשעת מעשה ועוד דשגגת לאו אפילו לרבנן לא חיישינן (תוספות ישנים) :
ב) לא מצי למימר דידע לי' בלאו דמחמר למ"ד בפר' בתרא דאין בו חטאת דכיון דסבור דעצמו מותר בכל המלאכות כ"ש שסבור שאינו מוזהר על בהמתו ולא מצי למימר דידע ליה בהבערה אליבא דרבי יוסי דהא קתני ליה במתניתין ול"א למימר דידע לה בתולדה דכיון דלא ידע אבות כ"ש תולדות וליכא למימר דידע לה בסקילה דאם כן לא שב מידיעתו הוא ואין סברא לומר כגון שטעה בשיעורין כגון דסבר דלא מיחייב אלא בהעביר ס' אמות ברשות הרבים או בתופר ג' תפירות וכותב ג' אותיות דלא שכיח בישכא ויאמר מדעהו שיעור שאינו (ת"י) :

קמ״ל מיתיבי ״איזהו *שגגת שבועת ביטוי לשעבר שאם אמר יודע אני ששבועה זו אסורה אבל איני יודע אם חייבין עליה קרבן או לא חייב הא מני מונבז היא (לישנא אחרינא מני אילימא מונבז פשיטא השתא בכל התורה דלאו חידוש הוא אמר(א) שגגת קרבן שמה שגגה הכא דחידוש הוא לא כ״ש אלא לאו רבנן היא ותיובתא דאביי תיובתא): ואמר אביי הכל מודים בתרומה שאין חייבין עליה חומש עד שישגוג בלאו שבה הכל מודים מאן רבי יוחנן פשיטא כי אמר רבי יוחנן היכא דאיכא כרת היכא דליכא כרת לא מהו דתימא מיתה במקום כרת עומדת וכי שגג במיתה נמי ליחייב קמ״ל רבא אמר ״מיתה במקום כרת עומדת וחומש במקום קרבן קאי: אמר רב הונא ״היה מהלך *(בדרך או) במדבר ואינו יודע אימתי שבת מונה ששה ימים ומשמר יום אחד חייא בר רב אומר משמר יום אחד ומונה ששה במאי קמיפלגי מר סבר כברייתו של עולם ומר סבר כאדם הראשון מיתיבי היה מהלך בדרך ואינו יודע אימתי שבת משמר יום אחד לששה מאי לאו מונה ששה ומשמר יום אחד לא משמר יום אחד ומונה ששה אי הכי משמר יום אחד לששה משמר יום אחד ומונה ששה מיבעי ליה ועוד תניא היה מהלך בדרך או במדבר ואינו יודע אימתי שבת מונה ששה ומשמר יום אחד תיובתא *(דר׳ חייא) בר רב תיובתא אמר רבא בכל יום ויום עושה לו כדי פרנסתו [בר מההוא יומא] וההוא יומא לימות *דעביד מאתמול שתי פרנסות ודילמא מאתמול שבת הואי אלא ״כל יום ויום עושה לו פרנסתו אפילו ההוא יומא וההוא יומא במאי מינכר ליה בקידושא ואבדלתא אמר רבא ״אם היה מכיר *מקצת היום שיצא בו עושה מלאכה כל היום כולו פשיטא מהו דתימא כיון דשבת לא נפיק במעלי שבתא [נמי] לא נפיק והאי אי נמי בחמשה בשבתא נפיק לישתרי ליה למיעבד מלאכה תרי יומי קא משמע לן זימנין דמשכח שיירתא ומקרי ונפיק: היודע עיקר שבת: מנהני מילי אמר רב נחמן אמר רבה בר אבוה תרי קראי כתיבי °)ושמרו בני ישראל את השבת וכתי׳ °ואת שבתותי תשמורו הא כיצד ושמרו בני ישראל את השבת שמירה אחת לשבתות הרבה ואת שבתותי תשמורו שמירה אחת לכל שבת ושבת מתקיף לה רב נחמן בר יצחק אדרבה איפכא מסתברא ושמרו בני ישראל את השבת שמירה אחת לכל שבת ושבת ואת שבתותי תשמורו שמירה אחת לשבתות הרבה: היודע שהוא שבת: מאי

ויקרא יט · °) שמות לא

תוספות

הא מני מונבז היא · פירש בקונטרס אבל לרבנן דפליגי אמונבז לא אשכחן שגגת שבועת ביטוי לשעבר וסברי כרבי ישמעאל דאמר בשבועות דאינו חייב אלא על העתיד לבא והקשה ה״ר אליעזר לרבינו שמואל דהא רבנן דמונבז רבי עקיבא ור״ע מחייב בהדיא על לשעבר בשבועות *[פ״ג וכלשון אחר שפי׳ בקונטרס מוכח בשבועות] בפ״ג (דף כו:) דאמר בעא מיניה רבא מרב נחמן איזהו שגגת ביטוי לשעבר אמר ליה כגון דאמר יודע אני ששבועה זו אסורה אבל איני יודע אם חייבין עליה קרבן אם לאו ופריך ליה כמאן כמונבז ומשני אפילו תימא רבנן אע״ג דבכל התורה כולה לית להו שגגה בקרבן כו׳ ומה שהקשה בקונטרס מאי פשיטא הא קמ״ל אף על גב דבעלמא (ג)הוי שגגה הכא לאו שגגה היא משום דהאדם בשבועה בעינן לאו פירכא היא דאי משום הא איצטריך ליתני בהדיא האדם בשבועה פרט לאנוס אלא משמע דשגגת קרבן אתא לאשמעינן שמה שגגה ומיהו קשה דבלאו הך ברייתא הוה מצי למיפרך לאביי ממתניתין דשבועות דמחייב ר״ע שבועת ביטוי לשעבר ולא משכחת לה אלא אם כן הזיד בלאו על כן נראה כפירוש רבינו שמואל שהשיב(ד) לרבנן דשגגת קרבן לאו שמה שגגה משכחת שגגת שבועת ביטוי לשעבר כגון שיודע ששבועה זו אסורה אבל אינו יודע שיש בה לאו אבל סבור שיש בה איסור עשה וחשיב שפיר האדם בשבועה בענין זה וכן מוכח בשבועות (שם) דמהאדם בשבועה לא ממעט אלא כסבור בשעת שבועה שבאמת נשבע כגון תלמידי דרב דמר משתבע דהכי אמר רב כו׳ הלכך הא מני מונבז הוא דלרבנן הוה ליה למיתני ואינו יודע אם חייבין עליה לאו והואי דשבועות דבעא מיניה רבא מרב נחמן פליגא אדאביי: **עושה** כדי פרנסתו · אבל להלך יכול כל מה שירצה רק ביום שמשמר דאי לאו הכי לא יגיע לעולם ליישוב והא דקאמר במאי מינכר משום דאין זה היכר שבת במה שיושב ואינו הולך אי נמי אפי׳ ביום שמשמר הולך כמו שרוצה והשתא לא מינכר אלא בקידושא · הרב פור״ת: אם

רש״י

קמ״ל · אביי דמודה רבי יוחנן בה דבעינן שגגת לאו דאי הזיד בלאו תו ליכא שגגה דבהא נמי פליגי רבנן אמונבז ואמרי דאין שגגת קרבן שגגה: איזהו שבועת ביטוי לשעבר · בשלמא להבא כגון שלא אוכל משכחת לה כגון שנתעלמה השבועה ואכל אלא לשעבר כגון שאכלתי והוא לא אכל אין כאן שוגג דאי כסבור שאכל בשעה שנשבע אינו חייב קרבן דתניא בשבועות (פ״ג דף כו·) האדם בשבועה פרט לאנוס כלומר האדם בשבועה שיהא אדם בשעת שבועה שתהא דעתו עליו בשעת שבועה ופרשינן לה התם לאפוקי כי האי גוונא ומהשתא לא משכחת שגגה אלא בקרבן: אמר יודע אני שאני נשבע לשקר · ונזהרתי על כך: אבל איני יודע כו׳ · דאי בנתעלמה ממנו אזהרת שבועה אין לך אונס בשעת שבועה כזה: חייב · אלמא מודו ביה רבנן דמיחייב אשגגת קרבן: הא מני מונבז היא · דאמר נמי בעלמא שמה שגגה אבל לרבנן דפליגי עליה לית להו ביטוי לשעבר דסברי כר׳ ישמעאל דאמר בשבועות אינו חייב אלא על העתיד לבא (שם דף כה·) יש גורסין הא מני(ב) מונבז פשיטא השתא בכל התורה אמר מונבז שגגת קרבן שמה שגגה הכא דחידוש הוא לא כ״ש אלא לאו רבנן תיובתא דאביי תיובתא ולא נהירא לי דמאי פשיטותא הא איצטריך לאשמעינן דחלוקה שגגה זו משאר שגגות דאילו בכל התורה למונבז בין שגג בקרבן בין שגג בלאו וכרת שמה שגגה וכאן בלשעבר אם שגג בלאו שבה לאו שגגה היא דכתיב האדם בשבועה: הכל מודים בתרומה · זר שאכל תרומה בשוגג משלם חומש על שגגתו דכתיב (ויקרא כב) ואיש כי יאכל קדש בשגגה אבל מזיד אין מוסיף חומש וחייב מיתה בידי שמים דכתיב (שם) ומתו בו כי יחללוהו וסמיך ליה וכל זר לא יאכל קדש: בלאו שבה · כסבור חולין ואין כאן לאו: מיתה · דכתיב בתרומה: במקום כרת · דשאר עבירות: וחומש · דשגגת תרומה במקום קרבן דשגגת שאר עבירות ולרבי יוחנן מיחייב חומש אשגגת מיתה: מונה ו׳ · מיום שטעה אל לבו שכחתו ומשמר השביעי: משמר יום אחד ומונה ו׳ · וכל יום שטעה אל לבו אינו משמר דשמא עשה מלאכה אבל יום המחרת משמר ולקמן מפרש דההך דאינו משמר לא עביד נמי מלאכה אלא כדי פרנסת היום: כברייתו של עולם · ימי חול נמנו תחלה: כאדם הראשון · שנברא בע״ש ויום ראשון למניינו שבת היה: יום אחד לששה · משמע לו׳ שעברו: ההוא יומא לימות · בתמיה: ודלמא אתמול שבת הוה · ונמצא מחלל שבת שלא לפקוח נפש: בקידושא ואבדלתא · לזכרון בעלמא שיהא לו שם יום חלוק משאר ימים ולא תשתכח שבת ממנו: אם היה מכיר מקצת יום שיצא בו · לא שזכר איזה יום בשבת היה אלא זכור שהיום יום שלישי ליציאתו או רביעי ליציאתו ומתוך כך ידע שמונה ליציאתו עושה מלאכה כל יום ח׳ וכן לעולם ודאי זהו יום שיצא בו וקים ליה דבשבת לא יצא שהרי בישוב לא שכח את השבת: במעלי שבתא נמי לא נפיק · דאין דרך לצאת מפני כבוד השבת ועל כן כל יום ח׳ וט׳ ליציאתו לישתרו דליכא לספוקינהו בשבת: מנא הני מילי · שיש מחלל בשבתות הרבה וחייב אחת על כולן ויש מחללן וחייב על כל שבת: הכי גרסינן הא כיצד ושמרו בני ישראל את השבת שמירה אחת לשבתות הרבה ואת שבתותי תשמורו שמירה לכל שבת ושבת · דקרא קמא חדא שבת הוא דחשיב משמע שאינו מקפיד אלא על האחת והכא כתיב את שבתותי אכולהו קפיד ולא מסרן אלא לחכמים להודיען מסברא הלי בשכח עיקר שבת דחדא שגגה היא והאי בשוכח שהיום שבת אבל יודע עיקר שבת דאיכא למימר ימים שבינתים [הוין] ידיעה לחלק: איפכא מסתברא · ושמרו בני ישראל את השבת משמע שמירה אחת לשבת אחת ואת שבתותי תשמורו ב׳ שבתות ואינו מזהיר אלא על שמירה אחת ובין רב נחמן ובין רב נחמן בר יצחק לא פליגי אלא במשמעותא מאי דיליף מר מהאי קרא יליף מר מאידך: מאי

רבינו חננאל

שזדונו חייב כרת בשגגתו חייב חטאת זולתי המביאין על הזדון כשגגה ומותבינן עליה דר׳ יוחנן איזהו שבועת ביטוי לשעבר אמר אני יודע ששבועה זו אסורה אבל איני יודע אם חייבין עליה קרבן או לאו חייב והדר ר׳ יוחנן הא למונבז היא ואנא דאמרי כרבנן מיהא שמעינן דרבי יוחנן פליג עליה דמונבז בהא תו אמר אביי הכל מודים והוא ר׳ יוחנן בזר שאכל תרומה שאין חייבין עליה חומש עד שישגוג [בלאו] שבה מ״ט כיון דתרומה יש בה מיתה שנאמר ומתו בו כי יחללוהו אבל כרת לית בה עד שישגוג בלאו שבה דקיי״ל שגגת דכרת היא שגגה וכל מאן דלית ליה כרת בעינן שגגה בלאו שבה ואע״ג דתרומה עון מיתה היא שגגת דמיתה אינה חשובה כשגגה דכרת אלא בעינן שגגה בלאו שבה ודחה רבא להא דאביי ואמר לעולם מיתה במקום כרת עומדת וכשם שבשאר מצות אם שגג בכרת אע״פ שהזיד בלאו לר׳ יוחנן מביא קרבן הכי נמי לענין תרומה אם שגג במיתה אע״פ שהזיד בלאו מוסיף חומש שחומש במקום קרבן הוא וקיי״ל כרבא. וקמייתא נמי דאמר אביי בשבועת ביטוי עד שישגוג בלאו שבה אבל שגגת קרבן לאו שמה שגגה לרבנן [אוקמינה] להא מתניתא בשבועות פר׳ ב׳ אפילו תימא רבנן בשגגת קרבן בשבועת ביטוי מחייבי דעד כאן לא פליגי רבנן עליה דמונבז אלא בעלמא אבל בשבועת ביטוי דהוא חידוש דלא אשכחן מזיד קאי בלאו בשוגג מייתי קרבן והכא בשבועת ביטוי

מזיד קאי בלאו ושוגג מייתי קרבן שגגה דקרבן נמי הוא שגגה וחייב חטאת: הא דאמר רב הונא היה מהלך במדבר ואינו יודע מתי שבת כו׳ *) קיי״ל כרבא דאמר חושש בכל יום שמא היום שבת הוא ואעפ״כ עושה כדי פרנסתו בכל יום · ומונה ו׳ ימים ומשמר שביעי ואם אין לו מאין יתפרנס עושה גם בו ביום כדי פרנסתו ומינכר ליה בקידושא ובאבדלתא כלומר בו ביום מקדש ומבדיל לעשות היכר בין זה היום לשאר ששת ימים ואם מכיר סכום הימים שיצא כל יום שמיני מותר לעשות מלאכה כל היום (דלא מנפקא ליה) דודאי יום שבת לא יצא וכל יום שמיני ליציאתו הוא יום יציאתו · ואם ברי לו שלא יצא בע״ש עושה יום ... ויום תשיעי בלא ספק אבל אי לא ידע בבירור חיישינן דלמא אזדמן ליה שירא ונפק בע״ש: היודע עיקר שבת ונעלם ממנו שהיום שבת הוא ועשה מלאכות הרבה בשבתות הרבה אינו חייב אלא אחת בכל שבת ושבת ושמעינן ליה מדכתיב ושמרתם את השבת וכתיב את שבתותי תשמורו ופשוטה היא לרבה בר אבוה כטעמיה · ולרב נחמן בר יצחק כטעמיה זה סובר [ושמרו ב״י את השבת שמירה אחת לשבתות הרבה כנגד השוכח עיקר שבת את שבתותי תשמורו שמירה לכל שבת ושבת כנגד היודע עיקר שבת וזה סובר] ושמרו בני ישראל את השבת שמירה לכל שבת ושבת כנגד היודע עיקר שבת את שבתותי תשמורו שמירה אחת לשבתות הרבה כנגד (היודע) [השוכח] עיקר שבת: היודע שהוא שבת והזיד בה ושגג במלאכות ועשה מלאכות הרבה בשבתות הרבה חייב על כל מלאכה ומלאכה מאי

*) מן קיי״ל ככהא עד סוף הענין הוכא הא״ז בשם רבינו.

רב נסים גאון

במאי קמיפלגי מר סבר תחומין דאורייתא ומר סבר תחומין דרבנן: **אמר** אביי הכל מודים בתרומה שאין חייבין עליה חומש כו׳ · עיקר דבר זה הוא כתוב בתורה (ויקרא כב) ואיש כי יאכל קדש בשגגה ויסף חמישיתו עליו וכמו כן עוד חיוב המיתה הוא כתוב בתורה (שם) ומתו בו כי יחללוהו וכמה ששנינו במסכת ביכורים בפ׳ ... התרומה והביכורים חייבין עליהן מיתה וחומש ופי׳ אל*) בריתא במסכת זבחים בפרק רבי אומר [בתוספתא דזבחים פ׳ י״ג] הפרש בין השוחט בפנים ובמסכת כריתות בפ׳ א׳ אלו שהן במיתה האוכל את הטבל והכהן טמא שאכל תרומה טהורה וזר שאכל את התרומה ותמצאנו בתלמוד בפ׳ ... (סנ) בפ׳ אלו הן הנשרפין: הבא

*) ופי׳ בכריתות.

עין משפט נר מצוה

ח א מיי׳ פ״ג מהלכות שבועות הלכה ז:

ט ב מיי׳ פ״י מהלכות תרומות הלכה א:

רפ״ל ורב״א ומהרש״א וכ״ה בתי׳

י ג ד מיי׳ פ״ב מהלכות שבת הלכה כב טוש״ע א״ח סי׳ שדמ סעיף א:

יא ה מיי׳ שם טוש״ע שם סעיף ב:

[שתי תיבות אלו ליתא בכה״י והרא״ש וכרמב״ם ובטור וש״ע]

מסורת הש״ס

שבועות כו: [ע״ש היטב]

[צ״ל דחייא]

ס״א לעביד

נ״א סכום

הגהות הב״ח

(א) גמ׳ אמר מונבז שגגת קרבן: (ב) רש״י ד״ה הא מני וכו׳ יש גורסין הא מני אילימא מונבז פשיטא השתא בכל התורה דלאו חידוש הוא אמר מונבז: (ג) תוס׳ ד״ה הא מני וכו׳ אע״ג דבעלמא שגגת לאו נמי הויא שגגה: (ד) בא״ד רבינו שמואל שהשיב להר״א דלרבנן דשגגת:

גליון הש״ס

גמרא רבא אמר מיתה במקום כרת. עי׳ כר״ש רפ״ב דתרומות:

sacrifice, he is culpable:[5] [69b] hence he [Abaye] informs us [otherwise].

An objection is raised: What is an unwitting offence in respect of an 'oath of utterance' relating to the past?[6] Where one says, 'I know that this oath is forbidden,[7] but I do not know whether it entails a sacrifice or not,' he is culpable?[8]—This agrees with Monabaz. (Another version: Who is the authority for this? Shall we say, Monabaz? But then it is obvious! seeing that in the whole Torah, where it [liability to a sacrifice] is not an anomaly, Monabaz rules that unawareness of the sacrifice constitutes unawareness, how much more so here that it is an anomaly![9] Hence it must surely be the Rabbis, and this refutation of Abaye is indeed a refutation.)[10]

Abaye also said: All agree in respect to *terumah* that one is not liable to [the addition of] a fifth unless he is unaware of its inter-
a dict.[1] 'All agree': who is that? R. Joḥanan: But that is obvious: when did R. Joḥanan say [otherwise], where there is the penalty of *kareth*, but here that there is no penalty of *kareth*, he did not state [his ruling]?—You might argue: death stands in the place of *kareth*,[2] and therefore if one is ignorant of [this penalty of] death, he is culpable; hence he informs us [otherwise]. Raba said: Death stands in the place of *kareth*, and the fifth stands in the place of a sacrifice.[3]

R. Huna said: If one is travelling on a road or[4] in the wilderness and does not know when it is the Sabbath, he must count six days and observe one.[5] Ḥiyya b. Rab said: He must observe one[6] and count six [weekdays]. Wherein do they differ? One Master holds that it is as the world's Creation;[7] the other Master holds that it is like [the case of] Adam.[8]

An objection is raised: If one is travelling on a road and does not know when it is the Sabbath, he must observe one day for six. Surely that means that he counts six days and observes one?—No: he keeps one day and counts six. If so, [instead of] 'he must observe one day for six,' he should state, 'he must observe one day and count six'? Moreover, it was taught: If one is travelling on a road or in a wilderness and does not know when it is the Sabbath, he must count six and observe one day.' This refutation of Ḥiyya b. Rab is indeed a refutation.

Raba said: Every day he does sufficient for his requirements
b [only],[1] except on that day. And on that day he is to die?—He prepared double his requirements on the previous day. But perhaps the previous day was the Sabbath? But every day he does sufficient for his requirements, and even on that day. Then wherein may that day be recognized? By *ḳiddush* and *habdalah*.[2]

Raba said: If he recognizes the relationship to the day of his departure,[3] he may do work the whole of that day.[4] But that is obvious?—You might say, Since he did not set out on the Sabbath, he did not set out on the eve of the Sabbath either;[5] hence this man, even if he set out on Thursday, it shall be permitted him to do work on two days. Hence he informs us that sometimes one may come across a company and chance to set out [on a Friday].

HE WHO KNOWS THE ESSENTIAL LAW OF THE SABBATH. How do we know it?—Said R. Naḥman in the name of Rabbah b. Abbuha, Two texts are written: *Wherefore the children of Israel shall keep the Sabbath*,[6] and it is written, *and ye shall keep My Sabbaths*.[7] How is this to be explained?[8] '*Wherefore the children of Israel shall keep the Sabbath*' [implies] one observance for many Sabbaths;[9] [whereas] '*and ye shall keep My Sabbaths*' [implies] one observance
c for each separate Sabbath.[1] R. Naḥman b. Isaac demurred: On the contrary, the logic is the reverse: *Wherefore the children of Israel shall keep the Sabbath* [implies] one observance for each separate Sabbath; [whereas] '*and ye shall keep My Sabbaths*' [implies] one observance for many Sabbaths.[2]

(5) Even on the views of the Rabbis. (6) I.e., where one falsely swears that he has eaten. (7) Knowing that he is swearing to an untruth. (8) This contradicts Abaye. (9) V. 69a, n. c2. (10) The passage 'Another ... refutation' is bracketed in the edd., and Rashi deletes it. For in fact the ruling is necessary according to Monabaz too. For whereas elsewhere ignorance is constituted by unawareness either of the forbidden nature of the act or of the sacrifice it entails, here the former does not constitute ignorance, and there must be unawareness of the liability to a sacrifice. This does not follow from Monabaz's other ruling and so must be stated.

a (1) If a non-priest eats *terumah* unwittingly, he must indemnify the priest for its value and add a fifth (Lev. XXII, 14). Abaye states that he must have been unaware of its forbidden nature, i.e., thinking it to be ordinary food. (2) If *terumah* is knowingly eaten by a non-priest, he is liable to death inflicted by Heaven. (3) Death and the addition of a fifth for the conscious and unconscious eating of *terumah* respectively are the equivalent of *kareth* and a sacrifice in the case of other transgressions. Hence according to R. Joḥanan on the basis of the ruling of the Rabbis one is liable to the addition of a fifth if he eats *terumah* in ignorance that the conscious offence is punishable by death at the hands of Heaven. (4) Alfasi, Asheri, Maim., Tur Y.D. omit 'on a road or'. (5) From the day that he discovers that he has forgotten when it is the Sabbath. (6) The first after his discovery. (7) Where the Sabbath followed six working days. (8) He was created on the sixth day; thus his first complete day was the Sabbath.

b (1) But no unnecessary work, since each day may be the Sabbath. (2) *Ḳiddush* = sanctification; *habdalah* = distinction. The former is a prayer recited at the beginning of the Sabbath; the latter is recited at the end thereof, and thanks God for making a distinction between the sanctity of the Sabbath and the secular nature of the other days of the week. (3) On the day that he discovers that he has forgotten when it is the Sabbath, he nevertheless remembers how many days it is since he set out. The passage may also possibly be translated: if he recognizes a part, viz., the day on which he set out. (4) Viz., on the seventh after he set out, without any restrictions, since he certainly did not commence his journey on the Sabbath. (5) As it is unusual. (6) Ex. XXXI, 16. (7) Lev. XIX, 3. (8) *Sc.* the employment of the sing. in one verse and the plural in the other. (9) In the sense that if one desecrates many Sabbaths he fails in a single observance and is liable to one sin-offering only.

c (1) Viz., that the desecration of each Sabbath entails a separate sacrifice. It then rests with the Rabbis to decide where each shall apply. (2) R. Naḥman b. Isaac agrees that the distinctions of the Mishnah follow from these texts, but he reverses their significance.

HE WHO KNOWS THAT IT IS THE SABBATH. [70a] Wherein does the first clause differ from the second?—Said R. Safra: Here he would refrain on account of the knowledge that it is the Sabbath: whilst there he would refrain through the knowledge of the [forbidden] labour[s]. Said R. Naḥman to him: Does one refrain from [action on] the Sabbath [for any other reason] save that the labours [are forbidden]; and does one refrain from labours for aught save because of the Sabbath?[3] But said R. Naḥman: for what does the Divine Law impose a sacrifice? For ignorance. There there is one fact of ignorance; here there are many facts of ignorance.[4]

HE IS LIABLE FOR EVERY SEPARATE LABOUR. Whence do we know the division of labours?[5]—Said Samuel: Scripture saith, *every one that profaneth it shall surely be put to death:*[6] the Torah decreed many deaths for one desecration. But this refers to wilful [desecration]?—Seeing that it is irrelevant in connection with wilful transgression, for it is written, *whosoever doeth any work therein shall be put to death,*[7] apply it to an unwitting offender;[8] then what
a is meant by, *shall be put to death?* He shall be amerced[1] in money.[2]

But let the division of labours be deduced whence R. Nathan derives it? For it was taught, R. Nathan said: *Ye shall kindle no fire throughout your habitations on the Sabbath day:*[3] why is this stated?[4] Because it is said, *And Moses assembled all the congregation of the children of Israel, and said unto them, These are the words which the Lord hath commanded ... Six days shall work be done:*[5] '*words*' [debarim], '*the words*' [ha-debarim], '*these* [eleh] *are the words*': this indicates the thirty-nine labours taught to Moses at Sinai.[6] I might think that if one performs all of them in a single state of unawareness,[7] he incurs only one [sin-offering]: therefore it is stated, *from ploughing and from harvesting thou shalt rest.*[8] Yet I might still argue, For ploughing and for harvesting one incurs two sacrifices, but for all others [together] there is but a single liability: therefore it is stated, '*Ye shall kindle no fire*'. Now kindling is included in the general law: why is it singled out? That analogy therewith may be drawn, teaching: just as kindling is a principal labour and it entails a separate liability,[9] so for every principal labour a separate liability is incurred.[10]—Samuel holds as R. Jose, who maintained: Kindling is singled out to teach that it is [merely the object of] a negative precept.[11] For it was taught: Kindling is singled out to teach that it is [merely the object of] a negative precept: this is R. Jose's view. R. Nathan said: It is particularly specified to in-
b dicate division.[1]

Now, let division of labours be derived, whence it is learnt by R. Jose? For it was taught: R. Jose said: [*If a soul shall sin through ignorance against any one of the commandments of the Lord, concerning things which ought not to be done,*] *and shall do of one of them:*[2] sometimes one sacrifice is incurred for all of them, whilst at others one is liable for each separately. Said R. Jose son of R. Ḥanina, What is R. Jose's reason?[3] [*Of one of them* teaches that liability is incurred for] one [complete act]; [for one which is but part] of one; for performing labours forbidden in themselves [i.e., '*them*'], and [for labours whose prohibition is derived] from others [i.e., '*of them*']; [further,] 'one transgression may involve liability for a number of sacrifices [i.e., '*one*' = '*them*',] while many offences may involve but one sacrifice [i.e., '*them*' = '*one*'].[4] [Thus:] one [complete act]: [the writing of] Simeon; [one which is but part] of one,—[70b]

(3) If the matter is determined by what one would refrain from, the Sabbath and its forbidden labours are tantamount to the same thing, and there would be one law for both forms of ignorance. (4) V. notes on the Mishnah 67b. (5) That a sacrifice is incurred for every separate labour, though they are all performed in one state of unawareness. (6) Ex. XXXI, 14. '*Surely*' is expressed in Hebrew by the doubling of the verb, which according to Talmudic exegesis signifies extension. (7) Ex. XXXV, 2. Here the verb is not doubled. (8) This is one of the methods of Talmudic exegesis: a text or its deduction which is irrelevant or incorrect in reference to its own case is applied to another case.

a (1) Lit., 'put to death'. (2) I.e., a sacrifice. Hence the verse teaches that many sacrifices may be incurred for the desecration of one Sabbath. (3) Ex. XXXV, 3. (4) It is apparently superfluous, being included in the general prohibition of labour. (5) Ibid. 1f. (6) '*Words*' implies at least two; '*the*' (Heb. ה) is regarded as an extension, whereby two is extended to three; '*these*' (Heb. אלה) is given its numerical value, which is thirty-six, thus totalling thirty-nine in all. (Hebrew letters are also numbers.)—The existence of a large body of oral law, stated verbally to Moses or generally known, was assumed. V. Weiss, *Dor*, I, and *supra* 28b, n. c7. (7) Without being informed in between that some of these labours are forbidden, but remaining in ignorance from the first labour to the last. (8) Ibid. XXXIV, 21. Since these are specified individually, it follows that each entails a separate sacrifice. (9) Since it is stated separately. (10) Hence the difficulty, why does Samuel quote different verses to learn this? (11) Whereas other labours, wilfully performed, are punishable by death or *kareth*, this is punished by flagellation, like the violation of any negative precept.

b (1) As above. (2) Lev. IV, 2. (3) How does he deduce this from the verse? (4) 'Of one of them', Heb. מאחת מהנה, is a peculiar construction. Scripture should have written, '*and shall do one*' (not of one) '*of them*', or, '*and do of them*' (*one* being understood), or, '*and shall do one*' (*of them* being understood). Instead of which a partitive preposition is used before each. Hence each part of the pronoun is to be interpreted separately, teaching that he is liable for the transgression of '*one*' precept, and for part of one (i.e., '*of one*'); for '*them*' (explained as referring to the primary labours); and for the derivatives '*of them*' (*toledoth*—labours forbidden because they partake of the same nature as the fundamentally prohibited labours). Also, each pronoun reacts upon the other, as explained in the text.

מאי שנא רישא ומאי שנא סיפא אמר רב ספרא כאן מידיעת שבת הוא פורש וכאן מידיעת מלאכה הוא פורש א״ל רב נחמן כלום פריש משבת אלא משום מלאכות וכלום פריש ממלאכות אלא משום שבת אלא אמר רב נחמן קרבן דחייב רחמנא אמאי אשגגה התם חדא שגגה הכא טובא שגגות הויין: חייב על כל מלאכה ומלאכה: חילוק מלאכות מנלן אמר שמואל אמר קרא °מחלליה מות יומת התורה רבתה מיתות הרבה על חילול (שמות לא) אחד האי במזיד כתיב אם אינו ענין למזיד דכתיב °כל העושה (א) מלאכה יומת תנהו (שם לה) ענין לשוגג ומאי יומת יומת בממון ותיפוק ליה חילוק מלאכות מהיכא דנפקא ליה לר׳ נתן דתניא ר׳ נתן אומר °לא תבערו אש בכל (שם) מושבותיכם ביום השבת מה ת״ל לפי שנאמר °ויקהל משה את כל עדת בני ישראל אלה (שם) הדברים וגו׳ ששת ימים תעשה מלאכה *דברים הדברים אלה הדברים אלו שלשים ותשע מלאכות שנאמרו למשה בסיני יכול עשאן כולן בהעלם אחד אינו חייב אלא אחת ת״ל °בחריש ובקציר תשבות ועדיין אני (שם לד) אומר *על חרישה ועל הקצירה חייב שתים ועל כולן אינו חייב אלא אחת ת״ל לא תבערו אש הבערה בכלל היתה ולמה יצאת להקיש אליה ולומר לך מה הבערה שהיא אב מלאכה וחייבין עליה בפני עצמה אף כל שהוא אב מלאכה חייבין עליה בפני עצמה שמואל סבר לה כרבי יוסי דאמר הבערה ללאו יצאת *דתניא הבערה ללאו יצאת דברי רבי יוסי ר׳ נתן אומר *לחלק יצאת ותיפוק ליה לחלוק מלאכות [פסחים ה:] מהיכא דנפקא ליה לר׳ יוסי *דתניא רבי יוסי אומר °ועשה מאחת מהנה פעמים (ויקרא ד) שחייבים אחת על כולן ופעמים שחייבין על כל אחת ואחת אמר ר׳ יוסי בר׳ חנינא מ״ט דר׳ יוסי אחת מאחת הנה מהנה אחת שהיא הנה הנה שהיא אחת שמעון מאחת

שם

תורה אור

רש״י

מאי שנא רישא. דשגגת שבת וזדון מלאכות לא מיחייב אלא אחת לכל שבת וסיפא דזדון שבת ושגגת מלאכות חייב על כל מלאכה ומלאכה: כאן מידיעת שבת הוא פורש. רישא כי אמרו ליה שבת הוא פורש מן המלאכה ומכיר שחטא ועל כך הוא מביא קרבן הלכך שגגת שבת היא ועל השבת הוא צריך להביא: כאן מידיעת מלאכות הוא פורש. כי אמרי ליה שבת הוא לא פריש דהא נמי ידע וכי אמרי ליה מלאכה חשובה היא זו פריש הלכך על מנין המלאכות יביא: כלום פריש משבת אלא משום. דכי אודעיה שבת הוא הכיר שחטא על המלאכות וכלום פריש ממלאכה כלומר ע״י ידיעת המלאכות אלא משום שבת דכי אמרו ליה מלאכות הן הכיר שחילל שבת: חילוק מלאכות. שגופי מלאכות מתחלקים לחטאות ואע״פ שבהעלם אחד: מות יומת. מיתות הרבה: בממון. לאפושי קרבנות: מה ת״ל. והלא כבר נאמר לא תעשה כל מלאכה: דברים. משמע תרי ה׳ לרבות חד הרי שלשה אלה בגמטריא ל״ו הרי ל״ט: ת״ל בחריש ובקציר תשבות. כלומר בלאו לא תבערו הוה לן למילף מהאי אם לא שיש להשיב: ועדיין אני אומר על חריש וקציר חייב שתים. אם עשאן בהעלם אחד שהרי הוציאם מן הכלל לחלקן לשתים ומשמע אזהרה לקציר לעצמה ואזהרה לחריש לעצמה: ועל כולן אחת. דאחדא מלאכה כייליניהו וחד להו ובדבר שהיה בכלל ויצא מן הכלל ללמד לא ללמד כו׳ לא דיינינן ליה דהוי ליה כלל בלא תעשה ופרט בעשה ואין דנין אותו בכלל ופרט אי נמי הוי חריש וקציר שני כתובין הבאין כאחד ואין מלמדין דהוה ליה למיכתב חד: ת״ל לא תבערו כו׳. וחריש וקציר לדרשה אחרינא אי כר׳ עקיבא דדריש ליה בעלמא (ר״ה דף ט.) לענין תוספת שביעית אי כרבי ישמעאל לענין שבת מה חריש רשות אף קציר רשות ללמד על קציר העומר שדוחה שבת: בכלל היתה. דלא תעשה כל מלאכה: להקיש אליה. כל שאר המלאכות שנכללו עמה בכלל שזו מדה בתורה כל דבר שהיה בכלל ויצא מן הכלל ללמד לא ללמוד על עצמו יצא כו׳: ללאו. שאין חייבין עליה כרת וסקילה כשאר מלאכות אלא מה שאמור בה: לחלק. כדאמרן מה הבערה מיוחדת: ועשה מאחת מהנה. האמור לענין חטאות הוה ליה למכתב ועשה אחת ולישתוק אייתר ליה שאר׳ מ״ם דמאחת וכל תיבת מהנה לדרשה ודרוש הכי פעמים שכל מעשה עבירותיו חשוב אחת ופעמים שהוא קרוי הנה לשון רבים: וא״ר יוסי ברבי חנינא מ״ט דרבי יוסי. כלומר מאי דריש ביה דהכתי מ׳ דמהנה ומ׳ דמאחת למאי אתא: אחת מאחת. אחת הוה ליה למכתב וכתיב מאחת ובנמי הנה ה״ל למכתב (הנה) [למדרש פעמים שהוא הנה] וכתב מהנה ודרוש אחת והנה בלא מ״ם הכי פעמים אחת שהוא הנה שבת [אחת] לבדו הוא מחלל ויש כאן חטאות הרבה דאזלי בתר מלאכות ופעמים הנה שהיא אחת מלאכות הרבה עשה ואינו חייב אלא אחת דבהנך תרי גווני איכא למשמע ועשה אחת וחייב הנה ואיכא למימר נמי הכי ועשה אחת הנה *עשייתו הוי אחת אע״פ שהן הנה [ואתיב א׳] ומ״ם יתירה [דרוש הכי] לרבות שהכותב שם משמעון דאע״ג שנתכוון לעשות תיבה גדולה הואיל ושתי אותיות הראשונות שם במקום אחר הן חייב והיינו מאחת מקצת המלאכה ולא כולה יביא חטאת:

מהנה

תוספות

אם אינו ענין למזיד דהא כתיב כו׳. ואם תאמר ולימא אם אינו ענין למזיד משום דלאו בתרי קטלא קטלת ליה וי״ל דאי לאו קרא אחרינא דמייתי הוה מוקמינן ליה להאי קרא במזיד ומות יומת דברה תורה כלשון בני אדם אבל השתא דלא איצטריך למזיד מוקמי ליה ע״כ בשוגג ולחייב קרבן על כל א׳: יכול שאם עשאן כולם בהעלם אחד כו׳. תימה א״כ מניינא דקרא דברים הדברים אלה הדברים למה לי כיון דלא אתא לחלק ויש לומר דצריך למניינא לפי שיש מלאכות שאינן חשובות ואיצטריך מניינא לאשמעינן דכולהו הויין מלאכות להתחייב עליהן ומיהו ממתניתין דמ׳ מלאכות דייק שפיר דבהעלם אחד חייב על כל אחת דלא הוה צריך למניינא כיון דמני כולהו בהדיא ומיהו קשה לר״י דלקמן בהזורק (דף צז:) משמע דהאי מניינא אתיא לחלק דאמר התם למימרא דמחייב רבי אתולדה במקום אב והתניא רבי אומר דברים הדברים אלה הדברים כו׳ ופי׳ בקונטרס התם דהכי פריך הואיל ומניינא לא אתא אלא לחילוק חטאות ואי ס״ד דמחייב אתולדה במקום אב טובא ה״ל למיתני ולפי מה שפירשנו דמניינא לא אתא אלא לאשמעינן דכולהו חשובות מלאכות להתחייב עליהם לא הוה פריך מידי ונראה לר״י דגרס הכא כמו במכילתא דתניא התם רבי נתן אומר לא תבערו אש למה נאמר לפי שנאמר ויקהל משה שומע אני שלא יהא חייב עד שיעבור ל״ט מלאכות תלמוד לומר בחריש ובקציר וכו׳ והשתא אי לאו לא תבערו ה״א דמניינא אתא למימר שאינו חייב על אחת או שתים עד שיעבור כל ל״ט וכיון דכתיב לא תבערו דילפינן מיניה דחייב על כל אחת בפני עצמה אם כן מניינא אתא למימר דהל״ט דווקא הוא דחייב על כל אחת ואחת אבל אתולדה במקום אב לא והשתא ניחא שפיר בהזורק דרבי לא מחייב אתולדה במקום אב ואתי נמי שפיר להאי גירסא דקתני לפי שנאמר דברים הדברים וגו׳ יכול ס׳ דמשמע דמתוך קרא דהדברים הוא דמשמע ליה דאינו חייב עד שיעבור כולן וכן בפ״ק דפסחים (דף ה:) לפי שנאמר לא יראה לך יכול יטמין ויקבל פקדונות מן הנכרים אבל לגירסת הספרים נוהי קאמר לפי שנאמר בלאו קרא נמי הוה אמרינן הכי כל כמה דלא נפקא לן חילוק מלאכות משום מקום: על חרישה וקצירה חייב שתים. וא״ת מנא ליה דחייב שתים נימא דלא מיחייב אתרווייהו אלא אחת וי״ל משום דכתיב בחריש ובקציר דמשמע תרי מילי מדלא כתב בחריש וקציר: ועל כולן אינו חייב אלא אחת. פירש בקונט׳ משום דהוי ליה כלל בלא תעשה ופרט בעשה וקשה דכללא נמי כתיב בעשה וביום השביעי תשבות ועוד דגבי כלל ופרט דוקא הוא דאמרינן בפרק קמא דמו״ק (דף ג.) דלא דיינינן כשאין הכלל בלשון הפרט אבל לגבי דבר שהוא יצא מן הכלל לא אשכחן בשום מקום ועוד דבמועד קטן איכא למ״ד דנין ונראה כפי׳ אחרון שפי׳ בקונט׳ דלא ילפינן מחריש וקציר משום דהוו שני כתובים הבאים כאחד וכה״ג אמרינן בפרק ד׳ מיתות (סנהדרין סז:) אוב וידעוני בכלל כל המכשפים היו כו׳ ופריך וליהוי אוב וידעוני שני כתובים הבאין כא׳ ואם תאמר והיכי יליף מלא תבערו כל שכן דהוי ג׳ כתובים הבאין כאחד ואין מלמדין לכ״ע וכ״ת דחריש וקציר אתא לכדדרשינן בריש מו״ק (ד׳ ד.) מה חריש רשות כו׳ אם כן היכי הוה בעי למילף מיניה מעיקרא הא לא אתי להכי ואומר ר״י דלא הוו ג׳ כתובים מדלא כתביניהו או כולהו בלאו או כולהו בעשה ולהכי ילפינן מהבערה ומהשתא אייתר ליה חריש וקציר לכדדרשינן במו״ק: הבערה ללאו יצאת. וא״ת *והא איצטריך למיכתב לא תבערו משום סיפיה דקרא דכתיב בכל מושבותיכם דדרשינן מיניה ביבמות (דף ו:) ובסנהדרין (דף לה:) דאין רציחה דוחה שבת וי״ל דהוה מצי למיכתב בלישנא אחריתי ולא לכתוב לא תבערו ומשום דדרש בפ״ק (דף כ.) אבל אתה מבעיר כו׳ לא הוה צריך למיכתב לא תבערו: מאי טעמא דר׳ יוסי. פי׳ בקונט׳ כלומר דהכתי מ״ס דמאחת ומהנה למה לי ולשון מאי טעמא אינו משמע כן ונראה לר״י דה״פ מ״ט דר׳ יוסי הא איצטריך קרא לשם משמעון ולאבות ולתולדות ומנא ליה דחייב על כל אחת ואחת ומפרש דמאחת נמי משמעון מהנה לאבות ותולדות ומ״מ מדסמכינהו להדדי דרשינן אחת שהיא הנה והנה שהיא אחת:

שם

רבינו חננאל

מאי שנא בהיודע עיקר שבת דחייב על כל שבת ושבת וביודע שהיא שבת דחייב על כל מלאכה ומלאכה ופריק רב חסדא כאן מידיעת שבתות הוא פורש כו׳. פי׳ היודע עיקר שבת ואינו יודע שהיום שבת הוא כיון שאמרו לו היום שבת היא מיד פורש נמצאת שגגתו על השבת לפי׳ אינו חייב אלא אחת על כל שבת ושבת אבל היודע שהיא שבת ושגג ועשה מלאכות הרבה וכיון שאומרים לו הלא מלאכה היא זו מיד פורש נמצאת שגגתו על המלאכות לפיכך חייב על כל מלאכה ומלאכה ודחה רב נחמן ואמר כלום פורש מן השבת אלא משום מלאכות כו׳ אלא אמר רב נחמן קרבן [דחייב רחמנא] אמאי אשגגה הוא השתא כיון דכי אמרו ליה שבת היא היום מיד פורש מכל מלאכה נמצאת בידו שגגה אחת שהיא שגגת שבת לפיכך אינו חייב אלא חטאת אחת אבל המזיד בשבת ושגג במלאכות אם מודיעים לו שהיא מלאכה פורש ממנה ועושה מלאכה אחרת ועוד מודיעין אותו ופורש ממנה ומתעסק באחרת הלכך כיון שצריך להודיעו על כל מלאכה ומלאכה נמצאו שגגותיו מרובים לפיכך חייב כנגד שגגותיו: העושה מלאכו׳ הרבה בשבת אחת בשגגה מנלן דחייב על כל מלאכה ומלאכה ופשט שמואל מדכתיב כל העושה בו מלאכה יומת דילפינן מיניה קטלא למזיד וכתיב קרא אחרינא מחלליה מות יומת דלא צריך ליה לקטלא דהא ילפינן ליה פשטנא לשוגג וכתיב מות יומת מיתות הרבה נמצאו בחילול שבת אחת מיתות הרבה ומאי נינהו הטאות והכי קאמר יומת בממון כלומר יתן הטאות הרבה ור׳ נתן פשט ליה מלא תבערו אש הבערה בכלל היתה למה יצאת להלק ולומר כשם שחייבין על ההבערה בפני עצמה כך חייבין בכל אחת ואחת בפני עצמה אחר שפירש בחריש ובקציר שביהה וכתב רחמנא אלה הדברים מדהוה למכתב (דאמר אלה) [ויאמר אליהם] הדברים אשר צוה ה׳ לעשות וכת׳ והוסיף אלה הדברים אלה בגימטריא ל״ו ועוד מדהוה למכתב דברים אלה שהן אלה ל״ו ודברים תרי הרי ל״ח והוסיף ה׳ בהדברים למדנו. ממנו עוד אחת הרי ארבעים חסר אחת. ור׳ יוסי מדכתיב ועשה מאחת מהנה דריש ועשה מאחת פעמים שהוא חייב אחת על כולן וזהו היודע עיקר שבת. מהנה פעמים שחייב על כל אחת ואחת. כיצד זדון שבת ושגגת מלאכות ושמואל הא דר׳ נתן סבר לה

[כך קושיא מאי קאי גם למ״ד הבערה לחלק יצאת ועי׳ תוס׳ יבמות ו: ד״ה טעמא וכו׳ ובסנהדרין לה: ד״ה מושבות וכו׳ מבואר דבריהם היטב. ועי״ע תוס׳ לעיל כ. ד״ה למפרי והוספות לקמן קו. ד״ה מה לי ותוס׳ מנחות נה: ד״ה אם כן]

מסורת הש״ס

לקמן צז: וש״נ

מכילתא פרשת ויקהל

יבמות ו: לג: סנהדרין לה: ולד סב. [כריתות כ:]

לקמן קג: סנהדרין סב. [כריתות ג.]

הגהות הב״ח

(א) גמ׳ כל העושה בו מלאכה:

עשייתו הנה ומ״ס יתירה לרבות [illegible] צ״ל רש״י [illegible] הפסוק ועשה אחת הנה [illegible] לפניו ועיין לקמן קג: משמע גם כן כמ״ש לפנינו

עין משפט נר מצוה

יב א מיי' פ"ז מהלכות שגגות הלכה ד

[עי' לקמן ק. ד"ה מה לי לבצל כו' כתב דשמואל כר"ש ע"ש]

מסורת הש"ס

שם משמעון הנה אבות מהנה תולדות אחת שהיא הנה זדון שבת ושגגת מלאכות הנה שהיא אחת שגגת שבת וזדון מלאכות ושמואל אחת שהיא הנה והנה שהיא אחת לא משמע ליה: בעא מיניה רבא מרב נחמן *העלם זה וזה בידו מהו א"ל הרי העלם שבת בידו ואינו חייב אלא אחת אדרבה הרי העלם מלאכות בידו וחייב על כל אחת ואחת אלא אמר רב אשי חזינן אי משום שבת קא פריש הרי העלם שבת בידו ואינו חייב אלא אחת ואי משום מלאכה קפריש הרי העלם מלאכות בידו וחייב על כל אחת ואחת א"ל רבינא לרב אשי כלום פריש משבת אלא משום מלאכות כלום פריש ממלאכות אלא משום שבת *אלא לא שנא תנן *אבות מלאכות ארבעים חסר אחת והוינן בה מנינא למה לי ואמר ר' יוחנן שאם עשאן כולן בהעלם אחד חייב על כל אחת ואחת אי אמרת בשלמא העלם זה וזה בידו חייב על כל אחת ואחת שפיר אלא אי אמרת העלם שבת בידו אינו חייב אלא אחת היכי משכחת לה בזדון שבת ושגגת מלאכות הניחא אי סבר ליה כרבי יוחנן דאמר כיון ששגג בכרת אע"פ שהזיד בלאו משכחת לה דידע ליה שבת בלאו אלא אי סבר לה כרבי שמעון בן לקיש דאמר עד שישגוג בלאו וכרת דידע ליה שבת במאי *דידע לה בתחומין ואליבא דרבי עקיבא: *אמר רבא קצר וטחן כגרוגרת בשגגת שבת וזדון מלאכות וחזר וקצר וטחן כגרוגרת בזדון שבת ושגגת מלאכות ונודע לו על קצירה וטחינה של שגגת שבת וזדון מלאכות וחזר ונודע לו על קצירה ועל טחינה של זדון שבת ושגגת מלאכות קצירה

שם משמעון. הכי לישנא לא הוה צריך למימר כיון דאליבא דר' יוסי קאי דסבר בפ' הבונה (לקמן ד' קג:) דאפי' שריטה אחת על שני נסרים או שני שריטות על נסר אחד חייב אלא ניחא ליה למנקט לישנא דמתני' דהבונה (שם·) א"ר יהודה מליט שם קטן משם גדול שם משמעון: לא משמע ליה. שמואל דלא כר' נתן ודלא כר' יוסי וצ"ל דמקבלה קים ליה לשמואל הכי*: העלם זה וזה בידו מהו. אומר ר"י דאפי' לא ידע לשבת בשום מלאכה חשיב ליה העלם זה וזה כדמוכח בסמוך דקאמר ר"י אי אמרת בשלמא העלם זה וזה בידו חייב כו' אלמא אע"ג דלא ידע לשבת במידי חשוב העלם זה וזה וצריך לחלק בין זה לשוכח עיקר שבת דהכא אינו שכוח כל כך דכי מדכרו ליה מדכר אבל שכח עיקר שבת היינו כעין תינוק שנשבה לבין הנכרים: אמר ליה הרי העלם שבת בידו כו'. בשבועות בפ"ב (ד' יט·) בעא מיניה רבא מרב נחמן העלם זה וזה בידו מהו א"ל הרי העלם טומאה בידו וחייב והתם בפ"ג (דף כו.) נמי השיבו הרי העלם שבועה בידו וחייב התם שפיר דמהדר ליה לחומרא והא דמהדר ליה הכא לפוטרו משום דקסבר שגגת שבת עיקר דעיקר המצוה היא משום שבת: חזינן אי משום שבת קא פריש כו'. פי' בקונטרס שאמרו לו שבת היום ופירש וקשה דשמא כי הוו אמרי ליה נמי מלאכה היא היה פורש אפי' לא יזכירוהו שבת אלא נראה לר"י דה"פ אי משום שבת קא פריש שאומר בעצמו דאי הוו מודעי ליה אשבת לבד היה פורש ואי הוו מודעי ליה אמלאכות לא היה פורש א"כ העלם שבת עיקר שהוא היה שכוח יותר ואי משום מלאכות פריש דשיילינן ליה ואמר דאי הוו מודעי ליה אמלאכות לא הוה צריך לאודועיה אשבת ואי הוו מודעי ליה אשבת הוה צריך לאודועיה אמלאכות הרי העלם מלאכות עיקר וחייב על כל אחת ואחת אבל כששניהם שכוחות בשוה מזה לא פשט כלום ולא בא רב אשי אלא לפשוט מקצת הבעיא כלומר לפעמים נוכל להבחין איזו העלמה עיקר ול"ג מה שכתוב בספרים ואי כי מודעי ליה אשבת אכתי צריך לאודועיה אמלאכות העלם מלאכות בידו כו' דלפי מה שפי' ר"י אכתי הוה צריך לפרושי וכי מודעת ליה אמלאכות לא הוה צריך לאודועיה אשבת אלא גרסי' ואי משום מלאכות קא פריש כו' וקאמר רבינא כלום פריש משבת אלא משום מלאכות כו' כלומר כיון ששניהם שכוחים במה שזה שכוח יותר מזה לא נפקא מיניה מידי אלא לא שנא ותרווייהו תבעי ורשב"א מקיים גירסת הספרים ומפרש דרב אשי בא לפשוט דהעלם זה וזה (א) חייב אי משום שבת קפריש שהשבת שכוחה יותר העלם שבת בידו ואי כי מודעת ליה אשבת אכתי צריך לאודועי אמלאכות אפילו אי כי נמי מודעת ליה אמלאכות צריך לאודועיה אשבת דהוי העלם זה וזה חשיב כהעלם מלאכות וחייב וכן מוכח מדנקט לעיל אי משום שבת קא פריש והכא נקט אי כי מודעת ליה אשבת כו' והא דקאמר כלום פריש ממלאכות אלא משום שבת ה"פ אלא משום שבת ותהא שגגת שבת עיקר ולא מיחייב אלא חדא דבעינן אחר לא הוה פריך מידי כיון דבשניהן שוה חייב על כל אחת:

מהנה לרבות תולדות. כלומר היוצאות מהן מן האבות: אחת שהיא הנה. דאמרן פעמים שחייב על כל אחת ואחת מאי היא כגון שעשאן בזדון שבת ושגגת מלאכות דאיכא שגגות טובא והנה שהיא אחת דאמרן פעמים שחייב אחת על כולן מאי היא כגון שגגת שבת וזדון מלאכות דיודע שהמלאכות אסורות בשבת אבל שכח ששבת היום: לא משמע ליה. דמיבעיא ליה כוליה לשם משמעון ולתולדות: זה וזה. שבת ומלאכות: מהו. חייב אחת על כולן או על כל אחת ואחת וקמבעיא ליה הא דתני לעיל (דף סט·) שגג בזה ובזה זהו שוגג האמור בתורה מהו לחיובי חדא או לאחיובי אכולהו וממתני' דהשוכח עיקר שבת דאינו חייב אלא אחת לא שמעינן ליה דהשוכח עיקר שבת חדא שגגה היא וכי מיבעיא לן ביודע עיקר שבת אבל מלאכות הללו אינו יודע שאסורות ועוד נעלם ממנו שהיום שבת דאיכא למיתלי שגגה אכל מלאכה ומלאכה הואיל ויודע עיקר שבת ואיכא למתלי אהעלם שבת וחדא שגגה היא: אי משום שבת קא פריש. זה שפירש מן העבירה ובא להתכפר אי משום שבת היתה שאמרו לו שבת היום ופירש אישתכח דמשום העלם שבת היה עושה: ה"ג ואי משום מלאכות הללו קא פריש שאמרו לו מלאכה היא זו ופירש הרי העלם מלאכה בידו וזיל בתר מלאכות: כלום פריש משבת אלא משום מלאכות. כשאמרו לו שבת היום הבין שהמלאכות הללו אסורות דאי לא אסורות למה הוזקקו לומר שבת היום: אלא לא שנא. ואינו חייב אלא אחת: עשאן לכולן. היינו העלם זה וזה בידו דהא לא ידע שבת במידי כיון דכל הלכותיה נעלמות ממנו אין חילוק היום משאר ימים: אא"א כו' היכי משכחת לה. דניחייב איניש אכל חדא ע"כ בזדון שבת ושגגת מלאכות הוא דמשכחת לה והכא מאי זדון שבת איכא: הניחא לר' יוחנן כו'. משכחת ליה שלא נעלמו ממנו אלא הכריתות ויודע הלאוין והיינו זדון שבת: כגרוגרת. שיעור הוא לכל איסורי מלאכות של שבת באוכלים: קצר. כגרוגרת וטחן כגרוגרת בשגגת שבת וזדון מלאכות דלא מיחייב אלא חדא: וחזר וקצר. כגרוגרת וטחן כגרוגרת בזדון שבת ושגגת מלאכות דמיחייב תרתי ולא נודע לו בינתים שחטא: ונודע לו. אחרי כן על הקצירה ועל הטחינה כלומר או על זו או על זו וכ"ש על שתיהן: (*על) שגגת שבת וזדון מלאכות. והפריש חטאת וחטאת זו מכפרת על שתיהן דהא חדא הוא דמיחייב עליה: קצירה

נודע לו על הקצירה ועל הטחינה של שגגת שבת וזדון מלאכות. פי' רבינו שמואל שנודע לו והפריש קרבן וקודם שנתכפר חזר ונודע לו על הקצירה וטחינה של שגגת מלאכות אבל אם לא נודע לו עד אחר הכפרה אין גוררין וצריכין שתי חטאות דלכ"ע כפרה מחלקת ודווקא הפריש קרבן אבל אם לא הפריש קרבן וחזר ונודע לו על קצירה וטחינה של *שגגת מלאכות יביא איזה שירצה דבו תליא מילתא אם ירצה יפריש חטאת אחת על שגגת שבת וגוררין של שגגת מלאכות עמה או אם ירצה יפריש ב' קרבנות על הקצירה וטחינה של שגגת מלאכות ויגררו עמהן של שגגת שבת כדאמר רבא בסמוך אכל שני זיתי חלב בהעלם אחד ונודע לו על אחד מהן כו' הביא קרבן על הראשון כו' אלמא אע"ג דנודע לו על הראשון תחלה הואיל ועדיין לא הפריש קרבן עליו אינו גורר האמצעי עמו כדי להתחייב קרבן על השלישי אלא אם ירצה יביא קרבן על האמצעי ויתכפרו כולן וא"ת דהשתא משמע דסבר רבא דאין הפרשות מחלקות מדנגררות של שגגת מלאכות עם של שגגת שבת והיינו כריש לקיש ורבא גופיה לא פסיק כוותיה בהחולץ (יבמות לו·) אלא בג' מקומות ומיהו מתוך פי' ר"ח שפירש דהלכתא כרבה רבו של אביי משמע דגרס רבה וכן משמע שמזכירו לפני אביי וכן בסמוך דקאמר מילתא דפשיטא לה לרבא ואביי ואפי' גרסי' רבא י"ל דלא איירי ביבמות אלא בדברים הנוהגים בזמן הזה מיהו תימה לר"י לקמן דמיבעיא לן אי פליגי בהפרשות מחלקות או לא תפשוט דבהפרשות פליגי דאי בידיעות פליגי אבל הפרשות מחלקות לכ"ע א"כ רבה ואביי דסברי הכא דאין הפרשות מחלקות כמאן וי"ל דאיכא למדחי דהכא מיירי שלא הפריש עד אחר שחזר ונודע לו גם על שגגת מלאכות והא דנקט ונודע לו על שגגת שבת היינו כלומר שלבסוף הפריש על שגגת שבת: גרירה

רבינו חננאל

כר' יוסי דאמר הבערה ללאו יצאת ולא לחלק ודרשה דר' יוסי אחת שהיא הנה והנה שהיא אחת לא משמע ליה: בעא מיניה (רבה) [רבא] מר' נחמן העלם שגגת שבת ושגגת מלאכות כשגגת שבת דיינינן ליה וחייב אחת על כל שבת ושבת או כשגגת מלאכות דיינינן ליה וחייב על כל מלאכה ומלאכה בכריתות תנן המחלל את השבת שהיא אחת מל"ו כריתות ואקשינן חדא *מחייב מ' חסר אחת הוין חיובי שבת ואוקמה ר' יוחנן בשגגת שבת וזדון מלאכות (מהדא לא פליג) דלא מחייב אלא חדא. ומקשינן וליתני זדון שבת ושגגת מלאכות דחייב על כל אחת ואחת ושנינן הא קמ"ל דאפי' שגגת שבת וזדון מלאכ' מחדא לא פליט' ופשט ליה רב נחמן לרבא · [הרי העלם שבת בידו ואינו חייב אלא אחת וא"ל אדרבה] הרי העלם מלאכה בידו וחייב על כל מלאכה ואתא רב אשי ואמר הדא מלתא בעא בידוך אי משום שבת לא מחייב אלא חדא כרב נחמן ואי כי מודעת כי שבת הוא היום עדיין צריך לאודועי הכי החורש הוא חייב. ושביק ליה לחרישה והדר לוריעה. תוב צריך לאודיעה. כי גם הזריעה חייב עליה. וכן הקוצר ושאר מלאכות כל אחת ואחת חייב עליה על כל אחת ואחת בפני עצמה ובכל אחת ואחת צריך ידיעה בפני עצמה. הרי שגגת (שבת) [מלאכות] וחייב על כל מלאכה ולא אמרינן מפני שנוספה על שגגת מלאכות שגגת שבת פקעה לה שגגת מלאכות א' לא' במקומה עומדת. ואי לא מסתברא דודאי זדון מלאכות ושגגת שבת הוא כרבא עבדין דאיסורא דספיקא דאורייתא היא. וכל איסורא דספיקא דאורייתא לחומרא עבדינן ואתא רבינא דחייא להא דרב אשי ואמר כלום פריש משבת(א' לא') [אלא] משום מלאכות כו' ומסתברא דרבינא כר"נ והכי קיימא בזדון שבת ושגגת מלאכות כגון שמכיר כי היום הוא שבת וגם היה יודע שהמלאכות אסורות ונעלם ממנו איסור מלאכות עכשיו או שידע איסור מלאכות בלאו ונעלם ממנו איסורא דכרת. שנמצאת ידיעת שבת בידו והעלם על כל מלאכה ומלאכה זהו שחייב על כל מלאכה ומלאכה אבל השוכח עיקר שבת ועיקר איסור מלאכות ולא מהניא לך כהודעת ליה עיקר שבת ועדיין צריכת לאודועיה איסור מלאכות דאי לא מודעת ליה איסור מלאכות מי ידע דאסירן דלפרוש הלכך ידיעת שבת תליא בידיעת איסור מלאכות ואיסור מלאכות תליין משום שבת וכיון שאפשר שתודיעו (א' לא') איסור שבת ואיסור מלאכות כאחת נמצאת כאילו שגגה אחת היא ואינו חייב אלא אחת כרב נחמן וקשינן על רב נחמן מדר' יוחנן דאמר אם עשאן כולם בהעלם אחת חייב על כל אחת ואחת. בשלמא אי אמרת העלם זה וזה בידו חייב על כל אחת ואחת היינו דמשכחת לה הכי אלא אי אמרת כל כי האי גוונא לא מחייב אלא חדא היכי משכחת לה דחייב על כל אחת ואחת ואם תאמר בזדון שבת ושגגת מלאכות הניחא אליבא דר' יוחנן משכחת לה זדון שבת [כו'] ומשני ר' נחמן דידע לה שהוא אסור בתחומין ואליבא דר' עקיבא כדאמרינן לעיל (סט.) שנמצאת זדון בתחומין וכי הדין בעיא דרבא העלם זה וזה בידו. גרסינן בשבועות (יט.) בענין ידיעות הטומאה ואסיקנא להו כהא: אמר (רבא) [רבה] קצר וטחן כגרוגרת בשגגת שבת וזדון מלאכות דאע"ג דשני אבות נינהו לא מחייב אלא חדא דהא

[עמ"ש לקמן עב: על הגליון]

[סנהדרין סב. שבועות יט.כו. כריתות ג:]

[לקמן עב. וש"נ]

[לעיל סט. וש"נ]

הגהות הב"ח

(א) תוס' ד"ה חזינן וכו' לפשוט דהעלם זה וזה בידו חייב:

[צ"ל על]

צ"ל שגגת שבת ופי' דקאי אסיפא אאבל נודע לו קצירה של זדון שבת [ר"ש] וע"ש

[the writing of] Shem as part of Simeon.[5] Labours forbidden in themselves' [i.e., *'them'*]—the primary labours; [labours whose prohibition is derived] from others' [i.e., *'of them'*]—derivatives; 'one transgression may involve liability for a number of sacrifices [i.e., *'one'* = *'them'*]—awareness of the Sabbath coupled with a unawareness of [the forbidden nature of his] labours.[1] Many offences may involve but one sacrifice [i.e., *'them'* = *'one'*]—unawareness of the Sabbath coupled with awareness of [the forbidden nature of his] labours.[2]—Samuel does not accept the interpretation that *'one'* [transgression] may involve liability for a number of sacrifices, while many offences may involve but one sacrifice.[3]

Raba asked R. Naḥman: What if one forgot both?[4]—Said he, Surely he is unaware of the Sabbath; hence he incurs only one [sacrifice].[5] On the contrary, he has forgotten the labours; hence he is liable for each?[6] But said R. Ashi: We see: if he would desist [from these labours] on account of the Sabbath,[7] his unawareness is of the Sabbath, and he incurs only one sacrifice. While if he would desist on account of the labours,[8] his unawareness is [chiefly] of the labours, and he is liable for each. Said Rabina to R. Ashi: Would he then desist on account of the Sabbath save because of the [forbidden nature of his] labours; and would he desist on account of [the forbidden nature of his] labours save because of the Sabbath?[9] Hence there is no difference.[10]

We learnt: The primary labours are forty less one. Now we pondered thereon, Why state the number? And R. Joḥanan answered: [It is to teach] that if one performs all of them in one state of unawareness he is liable for each separately. Now, it is well if you say that if one is unaware of both he is liable for each b separately; then it is correct.[1] But if you maintain that this is [mainly] an unawareness of the Sabbath [and] entails only one sacrifice, then how is this possible?[2] [Presumably] by awareness of the Sabbath and ignorance of the [forbidden] labours. Now, that is well if he[3] agrees with R. Joḥanan, who ruled: As long as one is unaware of *kareth*, even if he deliberately offends in respect of the negative command:[4] then it is conceivable where he knows that the Sabbath is the object of a negative injunction. But if he agrees with R. Simeon b. Lakish, who maintained: He must offend unwittingly in respect of both the negative injunction and *kareth*, then wherein does he know that it is the Sabbath?[5]—He knew of boundaries, this being in accordance with R. Akiba.[6]

Raba said: If one reaped and ground [corn] of the size of a dried fig[7] in unawareness of the Sabbath but awareness in respect of the labours,[8] and then he again reaped and ground [corn] of the size of a dried fig in awareness of the Sabbath but unawareness in respect of the labours,[9] and then he was apprised of the reaping and/or grinding [performed] in unawareness of the Sabbath but awareness of the labours,[10] then he was apprised of the reaping and/or grinding [performed] in awareness of the Sabbath but unawareness in respect of the labours: [71a] then [atonement for]

(5) A sin-offering is incurred only when a complete action is performed. The writing of a complete word—Simeon—is given as an example. Now, if one commences the word Simeon, שמעון SHiMeoN in Hebrew, but writes only the first two letters thereof, viz., SHeM שם, he is also liable, though his intention is only partly fulfilled, because SHeM is a complete word in itself. This is called one labour which is part of another (i.e., *'of them'*). If, however, the part he writes is not complete in itself, e.g., the first two letters of Reuben, in Hebrew, there is no liability.

a (1) Hence though he violates only one injunction, viz. the sacredness of the Sabbath, yet since he is ignorant of each of these acts, he is regarded as having committed a number of separate inadvertent transgressions, for each of which a sacrifice is due. (2) Since all his actions are the result of being unaware of one single fact, viz., that it is the Sabbath, only one sacrifice is due.—Hence the same difficulty, why does Samuel not learn from these verses? (The notes on this passage follow Rashi's explanation in Sanh. 62*a*; v. notes a.l.) (3) He does not agree to their implication of the verse, holding that it is all required in respect of primary and derivative labours. (4) Lit., 'if there is the forgetfulness of both in his hand'.—I.e., he was unaware that it was the Sabbath and that his acts are forbidden on the Sabbath. (5) As in n. a2. (6) As in n. a1. (7) I.e., on being informed that it is the Sabbath. (8) When informed that these labours are forbidden on the Sabbath. (9) When he is reminded of one, he naturally understands that the other is meant too, and desists on account of both. (10) Hence the problem remains in both cases; therefore only one sacrifice is brought, since a sin-offering may not be offered unless one is definitely liable thereto (Rashi as elaborated by Maharsha).

b (1) For if he is ignorant of *all* the forbidden labours of the Sabbath, the Sabbath is exactly the same as any other day to him, and he may be regarded as unaware of both. (2) That he should be liable for every single labour. (3) R. Naḥman. Rashi reads: That is well in the view of R. Joḥanan etc., v. *supra* 69*a*. (4) V. *supra* 69*a*, n. a3. (5) Seeing that he does not know of a single forbidden labour: v. n. b1. (6) V. *supra* 69*a* for notes. (7) That is the minimum for which one is culpable. (8) So that he is liable to one sacrifice only. (9) Having been apprised of the Sabbath, whilst he forgot that these are prohibited labours. In this case he is separately culpable on account of each. In the interval between his first labours and his second he did not learn of his offence. (10) Whereupon he set aside one sacrifice on account of both labours—this being before he learnt of his second series of offences.

the [first] reaping involves [atonement for] the [second] reaping and [atonement for] the [first] grinding involves [atonement for] a the [second] grinding.[1] But if he was [first] apprised of his reaping [performed] in awareness of the Sabbath but unawareness in respect of labours: then [atonement for] this [second] reaping involves [atonement for] the [first] reaping and its accompanying grinding;[2] but the corresponding [second] grinding remains in its place.[3] Abaye maintained: [Atonement for the first] grinding involves atonement for the second grinding too: the designation of grinding is the same.[4]

Now, does then Raba hold the theory of involvement?[5] But it was stated: If one eats two olive-sized pieces of *ḥeleb*[6] in one state of unawareness,[7] is apprised of one of them, and then eats another olive-sized piece whilst still unaware of the second—Raba said: If he offers a sacrifice for the first, the first and second are expiated,[8] but the third is not. If he brings a sacrifice for the third, the third and second are expiated, but not the first. If he offers a sacrifice for the middle one, all are atoned for.[9] Abaye maintained: Even if he offers a sacrifice for the first, all are expiated!—After hearing from Abaye he adopted it. If so, let grinding too be carried along with grinding?[10]—He accepts the theory of [direct], but not that of indirect involvement.[11]

b The matter that is clear to Abaye and Raba[1] was a problem to R. Zera: For R. Zera asked R. Assi—others state, R. Jeremiah asked R. Zera: What if one reaped or[2] ground [corn] of the quantity of half a dried fig in unawareness of the Sabbath but awareness in respect of the labours, then he again reaped or ground [corn] of the quantity of half a dried fig in awareness of the Sabbath but unawareness in respect of the labours; can they be combined?[3]—Said he to him: They are distinct in respect of sin-offerings,[4] therefore they do not combine.[5]

Now, wherever [acts] are distinct in respect of sin-offerings, do they not combine? Surely we learnt: If one eats *ḥeleb* and [then again] *ḥeleb* in one state of unawareness, he is culpable for only one [sin-offering]. If one eats *ḥeleb*, blood, *nothar*, and *piggul*[6] in one state of unawareness, he is culpable for each separately: in this many kinds [of forbidden food] are more stringent then one kind. But in the following one kind is more stringent than many kinds: viz., if one eats half the size of an olive and then eats half the size of an olive of the same kind of [commodity],[7] he is culpable; of two different commodities, he is not culpable. Now we questioned this: 'of the same commodity, he is culpable': need this be stated?[8] And Resh Laḳish said on the authority of Bar Tuṭani: The reference c here is to one e.g., who ate [them] from two tureens,[1] this being according to R. Joshua, who ruled: Tureens divide.[2] You might say that R. Joshua rules [thus] whether it leads to leniency or to stringency: hence we are informed that he did not rule thus leniently, but only stringently.[3] Thus here, though distinct in respect of sin-offerings, yet they combine?—Said he to him: You learn this in reference to the first clause: hence it presents a difficulty to you.[4] But we learn it in reference to the second clause, and it presents no difficulty to us. [Thus:] 'Of two kinds of [commodities], he is not culpable': need this be said? And Resh Laḳish answered on the authority of Bar Tuṭani: After all, it means of the same kind of [commodity]. Yet why is it designated two kinds of [commodities]? Because he ate them out of two tureens, this agreeing with R. Joshua, who maintained: Tureens divide, and we are informed this: that R. Joshua ruled [thus] both leniently and stringently. Now, since the second clause refers to one kind

a (1) In respect to expiation. The sacrifice for his first two acts of reaping and grinding is an atonement for his second two acts, since all were performed in one state of unawareness, without any apprisement in the interval, notwithstanding that his first unawareness differed in kind from his second unawareness. (2) When he makes atonement for his second reaping he automatically makes atonement for the first too, and since his first reaping *and* grinding only necessitate one sacrifice, his first grinding too is atoned for thereby. (3) Unatoned for, until another sacrifice is brought. (4) I.e., all acts of grinding made in one state of unawareness are covered by this sacrifice, though it is not primarily offered on account of grinding at all. (5) That atonement for one involves atonement for the other, as above. (6) This is the minimum quantity of forbidden food the eating of which entails a sacrifice. (7) Not being apprised in between that he had eaten *ḥeleb*. (8) Since they were eaten in one state of unawareness. (9) Since both the first and the third were eaten in the state of unawareness of the second.—The first two rulings show that he rejects the theory of involvement. (10) As Abaye rules above. (11) Lit., 'involvement of involvement'. Thus the first act of grinding is atoned for only because it is involved in the atonement for reaping; hence this in turn cannot involve the second act of grinding.

b (1) Viz., that awareness of the Sabbath and ignorance of the forbidden nature of one's labours followed by the reverse constitute a single state of unawareness, though the first differs in kind from the second, and the two states or periods are not separate in respect to sacrifice, but sacrifice for one makes atonement for the other. (2) The context shows that the *waw* is disjunctive here, and it is thus translated by Rashi. (3) Viz., the two reapings or the two acts of grinding. Is it all regarded as a single state of unawareness, so that they do combine, or as two states of unawareness, since they differ in kind and they do not combine? Thus he was doubtful of what was clear to Abaye and Raba. (4) Had each reaping been sufficient to entail a sin-offering, a sacrifice for one would not make atonement for the other. He thus differs from Abaye and Raba. (5) Hence there is no liability. (6) V. Glos. (7) The overall time being less than is required for the eating of half an average meal. It is then regarded as one act of eating. (8) It is obvious.

c (1) I.e., the two pieces of *ḥeleb* were differently prepared. (2) If one eats two pieces, each the size of an olive, out of different tureens, in one state of unawareness, they are treated as two separate acts, and he must make atonement on account of each. (3) Therefore the two half-olive sized pieces combine, though they are of two tureens. (4) Since it must be explained as treating of two tureens.

קצירה גוררת קצירה וטחינה גוררת טחינה אבל נודע לו על קצירה של זדון שבת ושגגת מלאכות קצירה גוררת קצירה וטחינה שעמה וטחינה שכנגדה במקומה עומדת אביי אמר טחינה נמי גוררת טחינה שם טחינה אחת היא ומי אית ליה לרבא גרירה והא איתמר אבל שני זיתי חלב בהעלם אחד ונודע לו על אחת מהן וחזר ואכל כזית בהעלמו של שני אמר רבא *הביא קרבן על ראשון ראשון ושני מתכפרין ג' אינו מתכפר הביא קרבן על השלישי שלישי ושני מתכפרין ראשון אינו מתכפר הביא קרבן על האמצעי נתכפרו כולן אביי אמר אפילו הביא קרבן על אחד מהן נתכפרו כולן בתר דשמעה מאביי סברה אי הכי טחינה נמי תגרר לטחינה גרירה איות ליה גרירה דגרירה לית ליה מילתא דפשיטא להו לאביי ורבא (א)מבעיא לר' זירא דבעי רבי זירא מרבי אסי ואמרי לה בעא מיניה רבי ירמיה מרבי זירא קצר וטחן חצי גרוגרת בשגגת שבת וזדון מלאכות וחזר וקצר וטחן חצי גרוגרת בזדון שבת ושגגת מלאכות מהו שיצטרפו אמר ליה חלוקין לחטאות ולא מצטרפין וכל היכא דחלוקין לחטאות לא מצטרפי *והתנן אכל חלב וחלב בהעלם אחד אינו חייב אלא אחת אכל חלב ודם ונותר ופגול בהעלם אחד חייב על כל אחת ואחת זו הומר במינין הרבה ממין אחד וזו הומר במין אחד ממינין הרבה שאם אכל חצי זית וחזר ואכל חצי זית ממין אחד חייב משני מינין פטור *והוינן בה ממין אחד חייב צריכא למימר ואמר ריש לקיש משום בר תוטני הבא במאי עסקינן כגון שאכלו בשני תמחויין ורבי יהושע היא *דאמר תמחויין מחלקין מהו דתימא אמר רבי יהושע בין לקולא בין להומרא קא משמע לן דלקולא לא אמר להומרא קאמר והא הכא דחלוקין לחטאות וקא מצטרפי אמר ליה מר ארישא מתני לה וקשיא ליה אנן אסיפא מתנינן לה ולא קשיא למשני מינין פטור צריכה למימר ואמר ריש לקיש משום בר תוטני לעולם ממין אחד ואמאי קרי ליה שני מינין שאכלו בשני תמחויין ור' יהושע היא דאמר תמחויין מחלקין והא קא משמע לן דאמר רבי יהושע בין לקולא בין לחומרא מדסיפא מין אחד ושני תמחויין

מכלל

רש"י

קצירה גוררת קצירה. שניה בכפרתה וטחינה גוררת את הטחינה השניה ונתכפרו כולן דקיימא לן אכל שני זיתי חלב בהעלם אחד אינו חייב אלא אחת וזה שעשה שתי קצירות בהעלם אחד שלא נודע לו בין קצירה לקצירה שחטא ואע"פ שהעלמה של שניה חלוק קצת משל ראשונה סוף סוף העלם אחד הוא דלא נודע לו חטאו בינתים וידיעות [חטא] הוא דמחלקת הלכך חטאת זו שבאה על הקצירה וטחינה ראשונה אתרווייהו קיימא ונתכפרו עם הקצירה כל קצירות שעליו שנעשו בהעלם אחד ועם הטחינה נתכפרו כל הטחינות שעליו כשעשאן בהעלם אחד: אבל נודע לו על הקצירה. אחרונה שבזדון שבת ושגגת מלאכות והפריש עליה קרבן הואיל וקרבן זה לא בייתא טחינה שעמה דהא אכל חדא מיחייב אי הוה מתידעי ליה תרווייהו: קצירה גוררת קצירה. ראשונה: וטחינה שעמה. של ראשונה: וטחינה. אחרונה. שכנגדה של ראשונה: במקומה עומדת. וכי מתידע ליה מיחייב עלה: קצירה גוררת קצירה. כמשפט דשני זיתי חלב בהעלם אחד הן וטחינה שעם קצירה ראשונה היינו משום גרירה דאף על גב דעיקר קרבן לאו משום קצירה דבהדה אתא הואיל ואיכפר ליה בהדי קצירה בתרייתא גררה לטחינה שעמה בהדה שהרי שתיהן היו תלויות בקרבן אחד ואין כפרה לזו בלא זו: וטחינה שכנגדה עומדת במקומה. דגרירה לגרירה לא אמרינן לאיכפורי טחינה אחרונה עם טחינה ראשונה משום שני זיתי חלב בהעלם אחד דהא קמייתא גופה בגרירה היא דמיכפרה: שם טחינה אחת היא. ואע"ג דקמייתא גופא בגרירה אתיא אמרינן גרירה לגרירה: ומי אית ליה לרבא גרירה. אטחינה שעמה קפריך דמגררה עם הקצירה ואע"ג דקרבן לאו אההיא קצירה איפריש דאיכך כולהו לאו גרירה איכא דקצירה וקצירה בהעלם אחד לאו גרירה היא דכל שם עבירה הנכפל כמה פעמים בהעלם אחד אין בו אלא חטאת אחת: ראשון ושני מתכפרין. שהרי בהעלמו היה: שלישי אין מתכפר. ולא אמרינן הואיל והשני מתכפר עם הראשון שבהעלמו ליגרריה לשלישי עמו בכפרתו ואע"ג דלא שייך בהדי ראשון: הביא קרבן כו'. שכשהפרישו הזכיר בו שם אותו זית: הביא קרבן על האמצעי נתכפרו כולם. ואין זה גרירה אלא כולם בהעלם של זה היו: אביי אמר כו'. דאית ליה גרירה: בתר דשמעיה. רבא מאביי דאמר אפילו הביא קרבן על אחד מהם נתכפרו כולם דאית ליה גרירה הדר ביה איהו ואמר להאיך דלעיל דמיכפרה טחינה שעמה בגרירה: אי הכי. דכאביי סבירא ליה דאמר גרירה: טחינה. שעמה דאיכפרה בגרירה תגרור נמי לטחינה שכנגדה משום שני זיתי חלב בהעלם אחד: גרירה דגרירה. כי הך דטחינה קמייתא לא איכפרה אלא בגרירה דלא עליה ולא על קצירה שעמה בא הקרבן אלא דאגריר בהדי קצירה הלכך לא הדרה גרירה לבתרייתא משום שם טחינה: מילתא דפשיטא להו. דזדון שבת ושגגת מלאכות וזדון מלאכות ושגגת שבת אין חלוקין לחטאות כדקאמרי דזה מתכפר בקרבנו של זה ולא אמרינן כשני העלמות נינהו וניחייב חד אזדון שבת ושגגת מלאכות וחד אשגגת שבת וזדון מלאכות ואע"ג דחד גופה דעבירה היא מספקא ליה כו': קצר וטחן. קצר או טחן: חזר וקצר כו'. ולא נודע לו בינתים על חטאו: מהו שיצטרפו. קצירה וקצירה לכשיעור ויתחייב מי הוי העלם אחד ומצטרפי או דילמא כשני העלמות נינהו ולא מצטרפין: חלוקין לחטאות. אי הוי כשיעור לכל חד אין אחד מהן מתכפר בקרבן הבא על חברו הלכך לא מצטרפי: הכי גרסינן וכל היכא דחלוקין לחטאות לא מצטרפי והא תנן כו': חלב וחלב. שני זיתים והפסיק ביניהם יותר מכדי אכילת פרס דהוו להו שתי אכילות: שאם אכל חצי זית וחזר ואכל חצי זית. בחותו העלם וכגון שלא שהה מתחילתו של ראשון עד סוף גמר אכילת אחרון יותר מכדי אכילת פרס ממין אחד מצטרפין: צריכא למימר. הא חדא אכילה היא דבשתי אכילות ליכא למאן דאמר חייב: תוטני. שם מקום: שני תמחויין. שני מיני תבשיל אחד צלי ואחד שלוק: ורבי יהושע היא. בכריתות דאמר תמחויין מחלקין לאוכל שני זיתים בהעלם אחד בשני תמחויין לחייבו שתי חטאות ואיצטריכא לאשמעינן דלענין חצי שיעור מצטרפי דמהו דתימא בין לקולא כי הכא בין לחומרא כגון שיעור שלם אמר רבי יהושע דחלוקין הן וגבי שני חצאי שיעור פטור והיינו קולא וגבי שני זיתים שלימים חייב שתים והיינו חומרא: ארישא מתני. להא דריש לקיש: אסיפא מתנינן לה. ולא איתמר הכי:

מכלל

תוספות

גרירה דגרירה לית ליה. ומה שגוררת קצירה וטחינה (ג) שעמה לא חשיב גרירה דגרירה כלפי' בקונט' דמה שגוררת קצירה לקצירה לא חשיב גרירה כיון דהוי בהעלם אחד אבל טחינה (ג) שכנגדה חשיבא גרירה משום דקצירה של זדון שבת אינה גוררת טחינה של שגגת שבת אלא על ידי הקצירה שעמה היא גוררת *שעיקר קרבן אינה בשבילה ולר"י נראה דקצירה חשיבא גרירה מדקאמר קצירה גוררת קצירה אבל ההיא דטחינה לא חשיבא גרירה דגרירה שאינו יכול לכפר על הקצירה אא"כ תתכפר הטחינה עמה ואע"ג דשני זיתי חלב בהעלם אחד לא חשיבא גרירה מ"מ קצירה וקצירה שאני שהאחת בשגגת שבת והאחת בזדון שבת וטעמא דמאן דאמר בסמוך דקצירה וקצירה אין מצטרפין היינו משום דלית ליה גרירה וקשה לרשב"א לפי זה הוה מצי למצוא פלוגתייהו דאביי ורבא אפילו בשלשה קצירות כגון שקצר בשגגת שבת וזדון מלאכות וחזר וקצר בזדון שבת ושגגת מלאכות ונודע לו הראשונה וחזר וקצר בשגגת שבת וזדון מלאכות דלרבא הביא קרבן על הראשון שני נתכפר שלישי לא נתכפר ולאביי גם שלישי נתכפר: ממין אחד חייב פשיטא. הוה מצי לשנויי הא מני רבן גמליאל היא כדאמרינן בסמוך: אנן אסיפא מתנינן לה. אפילו ארישא הוה מצי לשנויי כגון שאכלו בשני תמחויין ולאפוקי מרבי יהושע דאמר תמחויין מחלקין אפילו לקולא אלא דניחא ליה לאוקמי כר' יהושע: משני מינין פשיטא. אף על גב דלענין מלקות מצטרפין כדאמרינן בפרק בתרא דמס' ע"ז (דף סו.) ובמס' מעילה (דף יז:) לענין קרבן פשיטא ליה דאין מצטרפין:

מכלל

עין משפט נר מצוה

יג א מיי' פ"ז מהל' שגגות הלכה י:
יד ב מיי' פ"ז מהלכות שגגות הלכה יא:
טו ג מיי' פ"ז מהלכות שגגות הלכה י:
טז ד מיי' פ"ו מהלכות שגגות הלכה א סמג עשין ריג:
יז ה מיי' שם הלכה ד:
יח ו שם הלכה ז ופי"ד מהלכות מאכלות אסורות הלכה טז סמג שם:
יט ז מיי' פ"ו מהלכות שגגות הלכה א:

רבינו חננאל

דהא תרווייהו בשגגת שבת וחזר וקצר וטחן כגרוגרת בזדון שבת ושגגת מלאכות דחייב על כל אחת ואחת ונודע לו על קצירה של שגגת שבת וזדון מלאכות דלא מחייב עלה ואטחינה דבהדה אלא חדא. קצירה [הראשונה] גוררת (הראשונה) קצירה וכיון שמביא חטאת על קציר' של שגגת (חטאת) [שבת] נתכפר לו קצירה שהיא בזדון שבת. וכן כיון שנתכפרה הטחינה הראשונה שהיא מכלל הקצירה שבשתיהן חטאת אחת הוא חייב. גררה נמי הטחינה הראשונה את הטחינה השניה ונתכפר בשלה. אבל אם נודע לו בקצירה שהיא בזדון שבת ושגגת מלאכות שהוא חייב בקצירה חטאת אחת ובטחינה חטאת אחרת (מביא) [והביא] בקצירה זו שנודע לו בה. קצירה זו גוררת הקצירה הראשונ' ששתיהן קצירה ומעין מלאכה אחת הן והטחינה הראשונה נגררת בכלל הקצירה הראשונה שהקצירה הראשונה והטחינה הראשונה אינו חייב בהן אלא אחת. וכיון שנתכפר מקצתה נתכפר כולה. נמצא שנתכפר בקצירה וטחינה שהיא בשגגת שבת וזדון מלאכות בקרבן שהביא על הקצירה שהיא בזדון שבת ושגגת מלאכות והטחינה שעמה עומדת במקומה. לכשתודע לו מביא עליה חטאת. (אמר) אביי [אמר] גם הטחינה הראשונ' גוררת הטחינ' השני' שהטחינ' אחת היא. ומקשי' ומי אית ליה לרבה גרירה. והא אתמר אכל שני זיתי חלב בהעלם אחת ונודע לו על אחת וחזר (ונודע לו על אחת וחזר) ואכל (שני זיתי) כזית א' בהעלמו של שני. אמר רבא הביא קרבן על הראשון ראשון ושני מתכפרין שהרי הם בהעלם אחת שלישי אינו מתכפר שהרי לא היה בהעלמו של ראשון ואע"פ שהיה בהעלמו של שני ואין השני גוררו לכפרה. וכן אם הפריש קרבן על השלישי שלישי ושני מתכפרין. ראשון אין מתכפר שהרי לא היה בהעלמו של שלישי. הביא קרבן על האמצעי נתכפרו כולן שהרי כולן היו בהעלמו של אמצעי אבל גרירה לא אית ליה. ושנינן רבא כי אמר לה להא שמעתא לא (הוא') [אית] ליה גרירה. כיון דשמע להא דאמר אביי אפילו הפריש קרבן על אחד מהן כולן מתכפרין מ"מ כולהן בני בקתא דהדדי נינהו ונררי להדדי סברה ואמר איהו נמי גרירה ואקשינן אי הכי (דרבא) [דרבה] כאביי סבירא ליה טחינה נמי דשגגת שבת תגררה לטחינה דזדון שבת ושנינן קסבר רבה טחינה דשגגת שבת כיון דהיא עצמה גרירא היא לכפרה לא נגררה אחריתא וקיי"ל כרבה ואביי תלמידיה הוא והלכתא כרבה. והא שמעתא דפשיטא ליה לרבה ולאביי דקצירה דזדון שבת מצטרפת ונגררת עם קצירה דשגגת שבת דאע"פ שחלוקין לחטאות מיבעיא ליה לר' זירא. דבעי ר' זירא קצר וטחן חצי גרוגרת בשגגת שבת וזדון מלאכות ששתיהן חטאת הן וחזר וטחן חצי גרוגרת בזדון שבת ושגגת מלאכות שחייב שתים. מהו שיצטרפו שני חצאי גרוגרות והנה קצר וטחן כגרוגרות להתחייב חטאת אי לא · ואמרו ליה חלוקין לחטאת הן דזדון מלאכות ושגגת שבת חייב אחת על כולן · וזדון שבת ושגגת מלאכות חייב על כל אחת ואחת וכיון שחלוקין לחטאות שהעושה מלאכות הרבה אינו חייב אלא אחת וזה חייב על כל מלאכה ומלאכה חטאת לא מצטרפי דהא שגגת שבת וזדון מלאכות פטור הוא דהא אינו חייב אלא אחת בכולן · ואקשינן איני והא תנן בכריתות פרק ג' אכל חלב וחלב בהעלם אחת אינו חייב אלא אחת אכל חלב ודם (מותר) [ונותר] כו' · והוינן בה ממין אחד צריכא למימר ואמר ר"ל משום בר (תיטיני) [תוטיני] הבא במאי עסקינן כגון שאכלו בב' תמחוין ור' יהושע היא דאמר תמחויין מחלקין · כלומר אם אכל חלב וחלב בב' תמחוין חייב ב' חטאות ולא תימא דר' יהושע סבר (דאפי') [דאכל] חלב כשני חצאי זיתים בהעלם אחד בב' תמחוין · תמחויין מחלקין ופטור לקולא לא אמרינן · והוא כגון דאכל כזית בב' תמחוין לפוטרו לא והנה אכל ב' זיתי חלב בתמחוי אחד בהעלם אחד חייב אחת כשגגת שבת וזדון מלאכות בב' תמחוין חייב שתים כזדון שבת ושגגת מלאכות ר' יהושע מאי היא דתנן בכריתות בפ' ג' א"ר יהושע שמעתי שהאוכל מזבח אחד בה' תמחויין בהעלם אחת חייב על כל אחת משום מעילה ואמרינן התם היכי דמי בה' תמחוין ואמר שמואל (טעמא) *)

*) הסר כאן וצ"ל ולמר במולג כלותה בגינו המבה דכריס בעולה מצטרפין הכבר והחלב והיין והסולת והשמן.

רב נסים גאון

הבא כגון שאכלו בשני תמחויין מחלקין אצל קול*) ר' יהושע במס' כריתות בפרק אמרו לו אכלת חלב (דף טו) אמר ר' יהושע שמעתי באוכל מזבח אחד בחמשה תמחויין בהעלם אחד שהוא חייב על כל

*) פירושו בערבי מאמר

מסורת הש"ס / הגהות הב"ח / גליון הש"ס

[עי' לקמן עב: על הגליון]

כריתות יא:

שם יב:

שם טו:

הגהות הב"ח
(א) גמרא דפשיטא להו לרבה ולאביי וכו' ודבעי מיניה ר' זירא מר' אסי: (ב) תוס' ד"ה גרירה וכו' ומה שגוררת קצירה טחינה שעמה: (ג) בא"ד אבל טחינה שעמה שגגה:

גליון הש"ס
גמ' אמר רבא הביא קרבן על הראשון. עי' מנחות דף פ ע"ב ובתוספות ד"ה כולהו מצטרפין: שם מילתא דפשיטא להו לאביי ולרבא. עי' שבועות ד' יח ע"א תוס' ד"ה ר"א: שם אכל חלב ודם. עי' לקמן דף עב ע"ב תוס' ד"ה אמרו

כ א מיי' פ"ו מהלכות שגגות הלכה ט:
כא ב שם הלכה י:
כב ג מיי' פ"ח מהלכות שגגות הלכה א ופ"ו הלכה א והלכה ט סמג עשין ריג:

מכלל דרישא מין אחד ותמחוי אחד מין אחד ותמחוי אחד צריכא למימר אמר רב הונא הכא במאי עסקינן כגון שהיתה לו ידיעה בינתיים ורבן גמליאל היא *דאמר אין ידיעה לחצי שיעור: איתמר אכל שני זיתי חלב בהעלם אחד ונודע לו על הראשון וחזר ונודע לו על השני ר' יוחנן אמר "חייב שתים וריש לקיש אמר אינו חייב אלא אחת *רבי יוחנן אמר חייב °על חטאתו והביא *וריש לקיש אמר פטור °מחטאתו ונסלח לו וריש לקיש הכתיב על חטאתו והביא ההוא לאחר כפרה ולרבי יוחנן נמי הכתיב מחטאתו ונסלח לו הכא במאי עסקינן [ב]כגון שאכל כזית ומחצה ונודע לו על כזית וחזר ואכל כחצי זית אחר בהעלמו של שני מהו דתימא ליצטרפו קמ"ל א"ל רבינא לרב אשי דאיתידע ליה קודם הפרשה פליגי ובהא פליגי דמר סבר [ג]ידיעות מחלקות ומר סבר הפרשות מחלקות אבל לאחר הפרשה מודי ליה ריש לקיש לר' יוחנן דחייב שתים או דילמא דאיתידע ליה לאחר הפרשה פליגי ובהא פליגי דמר סבר הפרשות מחלקות ומר סבר כפרות מחלקות אבל קודם הפרשה מודי ליה ר' יוחנן לריש לקיש דאינו חייב אלא אחת או דילמא בין בזו ובין בזו מחלוקת א"ל מסתברא בין בזו ובין בזו מחלוקת דאי סלקא דעתך קודם הפרשה פליגי אבל לאחר הפרשה מודה ליה ריש לקיש לר' יוחנן דחייב שתים אדמוקים ליה קרא לאחר כפרה לוקמיה לאחר הפרשה ואי אחר הפרשה פליגי אבל קודם הפרשה מודה ליה רבי יוחנן לריש לקיש דאינו חייב אלא אחת אדמוקי ליה קרא בכזית ומחצה לוקמיה קודם הפרשה ודילמא ספוקי מספקא ליה (א) ואם תימצי לומר קאמר אם תימצי לומר קודם הפרשה פליגי בה רבי יוחנן היכי מוקי ליה לקרא בכזית ומחצה ואם תימצי לומר לאחר הפרשה פליגי ריש לקיש היכי מוקי ליה לקרא בלאחר כפרה: אמר עולא למאן דאמר אשם ודאי לא בעיא ידיעה בתחילה

בעל

ויקרא ד
שם

רש"י

מכלל דרישא. דאמר חייב: מין אחד ותמחוי אחד. בתמיה: שהיתה לו ידיעה. בין שני חצאי שיעור ואיצטריך לאשמעינן דליצטרפו דס"ד אמינא הואיל ובשיעורין שלמים חלוקין לחטאות הכא נמי לא ליצטרפו קמ"ל דהתם הוה ידיעה אבל ידיעת חצי שיעור לאו ידיעה היא: רבן גמליאל היא דאמר. לקמן בפרק הבונה אין ידיעה לחצי שיעור: וחזר ונודע לו. לקמן בעי ליה אי קודם שהפריש קרבן על ידיעה ראשונה וקסבר ידיעות מחלקות לחטאות ואע"פ שלא היתה ידיעה בין אכילה לאכילה או לאחר הפרשה וקסבר הפרשות מחלקות והא דאביי ורבא דאמרי לעיל ונודע לו על אחת מהן וחזר ואכל כו' אלמא דחדא הוא דמיחייב אי סבירא להו פלוגתא דר' יוחנן וריש לקיש בקודם הפרשה אינהו דאמור כריש לקיש אי נמי סבירא להו דלאחר הפרשה פליגי ואינהו דאמור קודם הפרשה נודע על השני ודברי הכל אין חלוקין לחטאות: על חטאתו והביא. והביא קרבנו שעירת עזים תמימה נקבה על חטאתו אשר חטא (ויקרא ד) משמע על כל חטאת וחטאת יביא: מחטאתו ונסלח לו. אפי' לא הביא אלא על מקצת חטאתו ונסלח לו כולו: קמ"ל. כיון(ג) דהאי חצי זית עם זית קמא שייך בתר ידיעה קמייתא [ו]הוה כאילו נודע לו על הכל דהא אי הוה מייתי קרבן הוה מיכפר בהדיה [דזית] בלא שום ידיעה דפחות מכשיעור לא חשיב אבל כזית לא מיכפר בלא ידיעה הלכך כי לא איתידע ליה בהדיה אלא זה אחר זה הוו ידיעות מחלקות: דאיתידע ליה. על השני קודם שהפריש קרבן על ידיעה הראשונה פליגי: אדמוקים לאחר כפרה. כי פרכינן לעיל לריש לקיש הא כתיב על חטאתו והביא ואוקימנא שיטתיה דתלמודא בלאחר כפרה לוקמא בלאחר הפרשה אבל השתא דאוקימנא בלאחר כפרה ש"מ דפשיטא לבני הישיבה שסדרו הגמ' דלאחר הפרשה נמי פטר ריש לקיש: הכי גרסינן בספרים ישנים ודילמא ספוקי מספקא להו ואת"ל קאמר אם תמצא לומר קודם הפרשה פליגי רבי יוחנן היכי מוקי ליה לקרא בכזית ומחצה את"ל אחר הפרשה פליגי ר"ל היכי מוקי ליה לקרא בלאחר כפרה. והכי פירושא ודילמא לבני תלמודא נמי מספקא להו פלוגתא דר"י ור"ל במאי כי היכי דמספקא ליה לדידי אי בקודם אי בלאחר אי בתרווייהו וכי פריך בעל התלמוד לרבי יוחנן נמי והא כתיב מחטאתו ונסלח לו ומשני ליה בכזית ומחצה בלשון את"ל פריך ליה ומשני ליה והכי קאמר אי הוה פשיטא לן דלאחר הפרשה הוא דמחייב [ר"י תרתי] אבל בקודם הפרשה מודה [לר"ל] לא הוה קשיא לן מידי דאוקימנא מחטאתו ונסלח לו בקודם הפרשה אבל השתא קשיא לן את"ל בהך בעיא דרבינא דבקודם הפרשה נמי פליגי וא"ר יוחנן חייב שתים ר' יוחנן היכי מוקי לקרא דמחטאתו ונסלח לו ושני ליה בכזית ומחצה והכי קמשני אפי' את"ל דקודם הפרשה לחודא פליגי אי נמי בתרווייהו פליגי איכא לאוקמא בכזית ומחצה ולר"ל נמי כי פריך ליה תלמודא הכתיב על חטאתו והביא ושני ליה בעל התלמוד בלאחר כפרה לעולם ספוקי מספקא ליה במאי פליגי כלדידי ובאת"ל פריך ומשני והכי קאמר את"ל בלאחר הפרשה נמי פליגי דבלאחר הפרשה פטר ליה בחד קרבן דהשתא ליכא לאוקמא לקרא דמחייב בלאחר הפרשה ר"ל היאך מוקי ליה להאי קרא כלומר במאי מוקי ליה ושני ליה אפילו אם תמצא לומר בלאחר הפרשה פליגי איכא לאוקמי בלאחר כפרה. ורוב התלמידים שגו בשיטה זו ודימו דהאי דהיכי מוקי לה לקרא בכזית ומחצה וחברו היכי מוקי ליה לקרא בלאחר כפרה לשון קושיא הוא ולפרושי כמו מ"ט והוצרכו לשבש את הספרים ולמחוק הוי"ו ואת"ל (ג) קמא ולהגיה קאמרינן ולהגיה על קודם לאחר ועל לאחר קודם ואין שיטת התלמוד כפי סוגייתם: למ"ד אשם ודאי לא בעי ידיעה. פלוגתא דר"ט ור"ע היא בכריתות בפ' דם שחיטה (דף כב:) ר"ע מחייב על ספק מעילות אשם תלוי ופי' היו לפניו שתי חתיכות א' של קדש וא' של חולין ואכל אחת מהן ואינו יודע איזו אכל מביא אשם תלוי ומודה ר"ע שאינו מביא את מעילתו כלומר אינו משלם קרן וחומש עד שיודע לו ויביא עמה אשם מעילות ודאי כי היכי דאשם תלוי דשאר עבירות דספק כרת אינו מכפר כפרה גמורה וכשיודע לו דודאי חטא מביא חטאת אף זה כשיודע לו יחזור ויביא אשם ודאי ר"ט אומר מה לזה מביא שתי אשמות ולא דמי לאשם תלוי דספק חטאת °דהתם ספיקו איל ודאי נקבה הלכך כי מתידע ליה בעי לאתויי נקבה אבל זה ששניהם מין אחד כדאמר התם שממין שמביא על הודע מביא על לא הודע שזה איל וזה איל יביא קרן וחומש ויביא איל ויאמר אם ודאי מעלתי זו מעילתי וזו אשמי ואם ספק שלא עתיד ספיקי להודע לי אשם זה יהיה אשם תלוי והקדש זה לנדבה ולכי מתיידע ליה לא בעי לאתויי אשם אחרינא אלמא לא בעי ידיעה בתחילה באשם ודאי קודם הבאת כפרתו דהא לא איתידע ליה כי אתיי' ומכפר עליה: אשם ודאי. כל אשמות קרוין אשם ודאי חוץ מאשם תלוי שהוא בא על לא הודע והן שלשה הבאין על חטא אשם מעילות אשם גזילות אשם שפחה חרופה:

בעל

תוספות

מכלל דרישא מין אחד ותמחוי אחד כו'. לעיל לא בעי למיפרך מכלל דסיפא משני מינין ושני תמחויין צריכא למימר שלא חש להאריך כיון דלא קאי הכי: מאן דאמר אשם ודאי לא בעי ידיעה בתחלה. פי' בקונטרס דאיכא פלוגתא דר' עקיבא ורבי טרפון בפרק דם שחיטה בכריתות (דף כב:) וליתא דהא תנן התם דדוקא במעילה מרובה קאמר ר"ע שמביא שתי אשמות משום דטוב לו שיביא שתי אשמות משיביא אשם אחד ויתנה שאם לא יוודע לו תהא מעילתו נדבה אבל במעילה מועטת מודה ר"ע שמביא אשם אחד ויתנה ונוח לו שיתן מעילה מועטת על הספק משיביא שתי אשמות וקאמרינן בגמ' מדברי שניהם נלמד [א] אשם ודאי לא בעי ידיעה בתחלה ואם תאמר רבי טרפון דקאמר מה לזה מביא שתי אשמות משמע דעלה טובה קמ"ל אדרבה כיון דבמעילה מרובה פליגי אם כן טוב לו שיביא שתי אשמות כדאמר ר' עקיבא משיביא אשם אחד ומעילתו ויתנה כדפרישית יש לומר דר' טרפון לאו עלה טובה קאמר אלא לעולם אינו יוצא מידי עבירה בשתי אשמות אלא שיביא אשם ומעילתו ויתנה ואם תאמר ולרבי עקיבא אמאי מביא שתי אשמות במרובה ובמועטה אשם ומעילה יביא לעולם אשם אחד ויתנה וכשיודע אז יביא מעילתו ויש לומר משום דאמר *המביא אשמו עד שלא הביא מעילתו לא יצא: [ב"ק קיא.]

בעל

רבינו חננאל

והזקיה אמר בחמשה אברים וריש לקיש אמר אפי' באבר א' [משכחת לה] בכתף · ור' יוחנן אמר בחמשה מיני קדירות · ור' יצחק נפחא [אמר] בה' טעמים · והדרי הוא כיון שהוא שני חצאי זית בב' תמחויין כמי שאינו שם חיוב חטאת היא וקתני מצטרפין והחייב חטאת · גם זה אע"פ שחלוקין הלחטאות הן מצטרפי' ושנינן מי סברת הא דריש לקיש משום בר תוספי' ארישא היא דקתני שאם אכל כחצי זית וחזר ואכל כחצי זית ממין אחד חייב בגלעת חלוקין לחטאות מוקמי ליה כר' יהושע וכגון שאכלו בב' תמחויין לא אסיפא היא דקתני סיפא אם אכל כחצי זית וחזר ואכל כחצי זית אחד משני מינין פטור עלה אמרי ר"ל משום [בר] תוספי' לעולם ממין אחד ואמאי (תני) [קרי] לה בב' מינין כגון שאכלן בב' תמחויין ור' יהושע היא דאמר מחלוקין בין לקולא בין לחומרא ונמצא גם זו בדברים שאין חלוקין לחטאות ואקשינן אי הכי מדסיפא בב' חצאי מין אחד בב' תמחויין וקתני פטור רישא משום שהוא מין אחד בתמחוי אחד לפיכך חייב אמאי איצטריך למתניא לא פשיטא ומשני רבינא כגון שהיו ב' זיתי חלב בתמחוי אחד וכגון שאכל חצי זית אחד מהן ונודע לו וחזר ושכח ואכל חצי זית האחר · ומתניתין רבן גמליאל היא דאמר [אין] ידיעה לחצי שיעור דתנן הכותב ב' אותיות בב' העלמות אחת בשחרית ואחת בין הערבים רבן גמליאל מחייב וחכמים פוטרין ואמרינן במאי פליגי רבן גמליאל סבר אין ידיעה לחצי שיעור ורבנן סברי יש ידיעה לחצי שיעור וכיון דרבן גמליאל סבר דאין ידיעה לחצי שיעור כאלו אינם ידיעה בתים והבהעלם אחת כולן לפיכך חייב: אתמר אכל ב' זיתי חלב בהעלם אחד ונודע לו על הראשון וחזר ונודע לו על השני ר' יוחנן אמר חייב שתים ור"ל אמר אינו חייב אלא אחת ר' יוחנן אומר ידיעה מחלקת לפיכך חייב שתים · ר"ל אומר אין ידיעה מחלקת ואין חייב אלא חטאת אחת ר' יוחנן דריש על חטאתו והביא כיון שנודעה לו חטאתו נתחייב בה וכשיתודע לו השניה עוד מתחייב בה דאין אדם פורע חובו במה שכבר נתחייב בו ור"ל דריש מחטאתו ונסלח כל שהוא בהעלם אחד חטאת אחד הוא ומחטאתו ונסלח קרינן ביה · ור' יוחנן האי קרא דר"ל דריש ביה הכי מניין אם אכל כזית ומחצה ונודע לו על כזית ולא נודע לו על מחצה · וחזר ואכל זית אחד בהעלמו של שני מהו דתימא לצטרף עם חצי זית הראשון ויתחייב קמ"ל מחטאתו אם כבר נתכפר מקצת מחטאתו פטור בנשאר ור"ל האי והביא מיבעי ליה כשנודע לו על כזית אחד וכפר עליו · ולאחר שנתכפר לו [נודע לו] על כזית השני כגון זה מודה ר"ל דצריך קרבן והא דרב [אשי] ודרבינא לא מוכחא בהדיא במאי פליגי דשמעתא לדברי הכל לאחר כפרה דראשון נודע לו השני צריך חטאת שניה והא סברא דרבה ואביי בגרירה פליגא אתרווייהו דהא אוקימנא דלתרווייהו לר' יוחנן ולר"ל כשנודע לו לאחר שנתכפר צריך חטאת שניה ורבה אמר אכל ב' זיתי חלב בהעלם אחד ונודע לו על אחד מהן וחזר ואכל כזית אחר בהעלמו של שני תביא קרבן על הראשון ראשון ושני מתכפר (הוה) [אלמא] ודאי אם נודע אחר שנתכפר על הראשון אינו חייב על השני קרבן אחר שכבר נתכפר בגרירה עם הראשון ודאביי עדיפא מדרבא וקיי"ל כוותיהו דאינון בתראי: אמר עולא לדברי האומר אשם ודאי לא בעי ידיעה

הגהות הב"ח

(א) גמ' ספוקי מספקא להו ואם תימצי וכו' כפרשה פליגי ר' יוחנן כצ"ל ותיבת בה נמחק: (ב) רש"י ד"ה קא משמע לן דהאי כצ"ל ותיבת כיון נמחק: (ג) ד"ה הכי גרסינן וכו' ולמחוק הוי"ו דאם תמצי לומר קאמר ולהגיה:

הגהות הגר"א

[א] תוס' ד"ה מאן. מדברי שניהם נלמד כו'. נ"ב אבל הוא דבר רבי יוסי (וכ"כ הר"ש והרמב"ן בחידושיו דלא כהרמב"ם) דבעי ידיעה בתחלה כמ"ש [כריתות] ד' ב' מודה ר"ע במתכפר כו' מ"ע התם בעי גברא ידיעה וכו' וכמו מחולק שם ר"ש ור"ש:

גליון הש"ס

רש"י ד"ה למ"ד אשם ודאי וכו' דהתם ספיקו איל. עיין מג"א סימן תל"ט ס"ק יא:

לקמן קה. [קה. ושם]
[לקמן עד.]
[שם]

רב נסים גאון

אחד ואחד ובגמרא גרסי היכי דמי ה' תמחויין אמר שמואל כאותה ששנינו חמשה דברים בעולה מצטרפין הבשר והחלב והיין והסולת והשמן חזקיה אמר כגון שאכל מה' אברים ר"ל אמר אפילו תימא באבר אחד משכחת לה בכתף ר' יצחק אמר כגון שאכל בה' מיני קדירה ר' יוחנן אמר כגון שאכלה בה' טעמים: ורבן גמליאל הוא דאמר אין ידיעה לחצי שיעור. בפרק הבונה (לקמן דף קה) הכותב ב' אותיות בב' העלמות אחת בשחרית ואחת בין הערבים רבן גמליאל מחייב וחכמים פוטרים ובגמ' גרסי במאי קא מיפלגי רבן גמליאל סבר אין ידיעה לחצי שיעור: אמר עולא למאן דאמר אשם ודאי לא בעי ידיעה בתחלה: משכחת לה במס' כריתות בפרק דם שחיטה (דף כב) אמר ר' טרפון ומה לזה מביא ב' אשמות אמר לו ר' עקיבא נראין דבריך במעילה כו' ובגמ' גרסי אמר רבא מדברי שניהם נלמוד אשם ודאי לא בעי ידיעה בתחלה ומכלל זו המימרא נלמוד כי מי שחולק על ר"ע ור' טרפון בדבר הזה סובר שאשם ודאי בעי ידיעה בתחלה וזה האשם נידון כחטאת מה חטאת בעינן ידיעה בתחלה אף אשם ודאי נמי בעי ידיעה בתחלה:

ואלא

of [commodity] and two tureens, [71b] it follows that the first clause treats of one kind of [commodity] and one tureen. But if it is one kind of [commodity] and one tureen, need it be stated?[5]—Said R. Huna: The circumstances here dealt with are e.g., that he was aware in between,[6] this agreeing with Rabban[7] Gamaliel, who maintained: Knowledge of half the standard quantity is of no consequence.[8]

It was stated: If one eats two olive-sized pieces of *heleb* in one state of unawareness, is apprised of the first and subsequently of the second,—R. Johanan maintains: He is liable to two [sin-offerings]; while Resh Lakish rules: He is liable to one only. R. Johanan maintains: He is liable [for the second], [deducing] *for*
a *his sin . . . he shall bring* [a sacrifice].[1] While Resh Lakish rules, He is not liable [for the second], [interpreting,] *of his sin . . . and he shall be forgiven.*[2] But according to Resh Lakish too, surely it is written, '*for his sin . . . he shall bring?*'—That holds good after atonement.[3] But according to R. Johanan too, surely it is written, '*of his sin . . . and he shall be forgiven*'?—That refers to one e.g., who ate an olive and a half [of *heleb*],[4] was apprised concerning the size of an olive,[5] and then ate again as much as half an olive in the unawareness of the second [half].[6] Now you might say, let these combine; therefore it[7] informs us [otherwise].[8]

Rabina asked R. Ashi: Do they disagree where it [the eating of the second piece] became known to him before setting apart [a sacrifice] for the first, and they differ in this: one Master holds, Apprisements divide,[9] whilst the other Master holds, [Only] separations [of sacrifices] divide;[10] but if [he learnt of the second piece] after setting apart [a sacrifice for the first], Resh Lakish concedes to R. Johanan that he is liable to two. Or perhaps they disagree where it became known to him after the act of setting apart, and they differ in this: One Master holds, Separations [of sacrifices] divide, while the other Master holds, [Only] acts of atonement divide;[11] but if [he learnt of the second piece] before setting apart [a sacrifice for the first], R. Johanan concedes to Resh Lakish that he is liable only to one [sacrifice]. Or perhaps they differ in both cases?—Said he to him: It is logical that they differ in both cases. For should you think that they differ before the setting apart of a sacrifice, whereas after 'setting apart' Resh Lakish concedes to R. Johanan that he is liable to two sacrifices,—then instead of interpreting the verse as referring to after atone-
b ment, let him interpret it as referring to after 'setting apart'.[1] Whilst if they differ after 'setting apart', whereas before separation R. Johanan agrees with Resh Lakish that he is liable only to one [sacrifice];—instead of interpreting the verse as referring to [one who ate] as much as an olive and a half, let him relate it to [apprisement of the second] before 'setting apart'? But perhaps that itself is in doubt, and it is hypothetically stated.[2] [Thus:] if you assume that they differ before 'setting apart', how can R. Johanan interpret the verse? As referring to [one who ate] the quantity of an olive and a half. And if you assume that they differ after separation, how can Resh Lakish interpret the verse? As referring to after atonement.

'Ulla said: On the view that a certain guilt-offering does not

(5) Surely his culpability is obvious! (6) That he had eaten *heleb*. (7) A higher title than 'Rabbi'. (8) I.e., it does not separate two acts of eating, when in each case only half the standard quantity to create liability is consumed.

a (1) Lev. IV, 28, q.v. I.e., for each sin a separate sacrifice is required. (2) Ibid. 35. 'Of' (Heb. מ) is interpreted partitively: i.e., even if he offers a sacrifice for part of his sin only, he is forgiven for the whole. (3) If he offends a second time *after* having atoned for the first, he must make atonement again. (4) At once, though the *heleb* was not in one piece. (5) That that amount of the fat was *heleb*. (6) Which was eaten the first time. (7) The verse quoted by Resh Lakish. (8) As in n. a2. (9) I.e., the knowledge first obtained concerning one piece separates this piece from the second, and necessitates a sacrifice for each. (10) And since a sacrifice was not set apart—i.e., separated—until he learnt of the second piece, it atones for both. (11) V. n. a3.

b (1) Even before it was actually sacrificed. (2) Lit., 'and he says, "should you say".'

require previous knowledge:[3] [72a] if one cohabits five times with a betrothed bondmaid,[4] he is liable to one [guilt-offering] only.[5] R. Hamnuna objected: If so, if one cohabits, sets aside a sacrifice,
a and states, 'Wait for me until I cohabit again,'[1] is he then liable to only one?[2]—Said he to him, You speak of an act after separation [of the sacrifice]: in such a case I did not state [my ruling].[3]

When R. Dimi came,[4] he said: On the view that a certain guilt-offering requires previous knowledge: If one cohabits five times with a betrothed maiden, he is liable for each [act]. Said Abaye to him, But in the case of a sin-offering [definite] knowledge is required beforehand,[5] yet R. Johanan and Resh Lakish differ [therein]?[6] He remained silent. Said he to him, Perhaps you refer to an act after separation [of the sacrifice], and as R. Hamnuna?[7] Even so, he replied.

When Rabin came,[4] he said: All agree about a betrothed bondmaid [in one respect], and all agree about a betrothed bondmaid [in another respect], and there is disagreement about a betrothed bondmaid [in a third respect].[8] [Thus:] All agree in the case of [coition with] a betrothed bondmaid, that one is liable only to one [sacrifice], as 'Ulla. All agree in the case of [coition with] a betrothed bondmaid, that one is liable for each, as R. Hamnuna. And there is disagreement about a betrothed bondmaid: on the view that a certain guilt-offering requires previous knowledge, there is disagreement between R. Johanan and Resh Lakish.[9]

(3) There are two classes of guilt-offerings (Heb. *asham*, pl. *ashamoth*): (i) A guilt-offering of doubt. This is due when one is doubtful if he has committed a sin which, when certainly committed, entails a sin-offering. (ii) A certain guilt-offering. This is due for the undoubted commission of certain offences, viz., (*a*) robbery (after restoration is made, v. Lev. V, 25); (*b*) misappropriation of sacred property to secular uses (Lev. V, 16); (*c*) coition with a bondmaid betrothed to another (Lev. XIX, 21); (*d*) a nazirite's interrupting of the days of his purity by permitting himself to be ritually defiled (Num. VI, 12); and (*e*) a leper's guilt-offering (Lev. XIV, 12). Now with respect to *b*, the Rabbis hold that no guilt-offering is incurred for doubtful misappropriation, whilst R. Akiba and R. Tarfon hold that one can bring a guilt-offering conditionally, stating: 'If I learn at some future date that I was definitely guilty, let this be accounted now as a certain guilt-offering. But if I am destined to remain in doubt, let this be a guilt-offering of doubt'. Thus on the first hypothesis a certain guilt-offering is brought, though at the time one has no knowledge whether he has actually sinned.—This follows Tosaf. Rashi holds that R. Akiba and R. Tarfon differ in this very question. (4) Unwittingly. Between each act of coition he learnt of his previous offence. (5) Since knowledge of guilt is not required, the knowledge that he does possess is insufficient to separate his actions and necessitate a sacrifice for each. But on the view that previous knowledge is essential for a guilt-offering, this matter will be disputed by R. Johanan and Resh Lakish, as on 71*b*.—Though we do not find a *doubtful* guilt-offering for doubtful coition, and so it would appear that here at least knowledge is essential, for otherwise how does he know that he sinned at all, a sacrifice is nevertheless conceivable without previous knowledge. Thus: when in doubt one might bring a conditional sacrifice and stipulate: 'If I have sinned, let this be a certain guilt-offering; if not, let this be a peace-offering' (Tosaf.).

a (1) So that this sacrifice may atone for both.—Even conscious coition with a betrothed bondmaid necessitates a sacrifice, though in all other cases only an *unwitting* offence entails an offering. (2) Surely not! (3) For this certainly divides the offences, and a sacrifice is required for each. (4) V. *supra* 5*a*, n. b9. (5) That an offence was committed. If one brings a sin-offering before he knows that he has sinned, and then learns that he has sinned, the sacrifice is invalid for atonement. (6) And the same principle applies here. How then can you make a general statement? (7) Whereas R. Johanan and Resh Lakish differ where all his actions were committed before the separation of an animal for a sacrifice. (8) 'All' and 'there is disagreement' refer to the views of R. Johanan and Resh Lakish. (9) V. *supra* n. b5.

בעל חמש בעילות בשפחה חרופה *אינו חייב אלא אחת מתקיף לה רב המנונא אלא מעתה בעל (א) וחזר ובעל והפריש קרבן ואמר המתינו לי עד שאבעול הכי נמי דאינו חייב אלא אחת א"ל מעשה דלאחר הפרשה קאמרת [א]מעשה דלאחר הפרשה לא קאמינא כי אתא רב דימי אמר למאן דאמר אשם ודאי בעי ידיעה בתחלה [ב]בעל חמש בעילות בשפחה חרופה חייב על כל אחת ואחת אמר ליה אביי הרי חטאת דבעינן ידיעה בתחלה ופליגי ר' יוחנן ורבי שמעון בן לקיש אישתיק אמר ליה דלמא [ג]במעשה דלאחר הפרשה קאמרת וכדרב המנונא א"ל אין כי אתא רבין אמר הכל מודים בשפחה חרופה והכל מודים בשפחה חרופה ומחלוקת בשפחה חרופה הכל מודים בשפחה חרופה דאינו חייב אלא אחת כדעולא והכל מודים בשפחה חרופה דחייב על כל אחת ואחת כרב המנונא ומחלוקת בשפחה חרופה למ"ד אשם ודאי בעי ידיעה בתחלה מחלוקת דרבי יוחנן ורבי שמעון בן לקיש: איתמר

נתכוון

בעל ה' בעילות בשפחה חרופה. בשוגג ונודע לו בין כל אחת ואחת אינו חייב אלא אחת להכי נקט שפחה חרופה משום דמביא קרבן אחד על עבירות הרבה כדתנן בכריתות (דף ט) ה' מביאין קרבן אחד על עבירות הרבה הבא על השפחה ביאות הרבה וכו' וכי תנן מתני' דנפטר בקרבן אחד הני מילי במזיד שהוא מן המביאים על המזיד כשוגג דכתיב (ויקרא יט) בקורת תהיה ומלקות בשוגג ליכא וגבי מזיד רבי קרא דנפטר בקרבן אחד על ביאות הרבה כדיליף התם וכ"ש על ביאות שוגג הרבה בהעלם אחד אבל שוגג ונודע לו בין ביאה לביאה למאן דבעי ידיעה בתחלה באשם ודאי חשיב הוא לחלק לאשמות כהבאת כפרה המחלקת לעושה מזיד וצריך להביא על כל אחת ואחת אליבא דר' יוחנן דאמר לעיל באוכל שני זיתי חלב בהעלם אחד ונודע לו בשתי ידיעות שמביא חטאת על כל אחת ואחת דחשיבא ליה חילוק ידיעה כאילו הביא קרבן בין ידיעה לידיעה הכא נמי חשיב חילוק ידיעה כאילו הביא קרבן בין ביאה לביאה ואשמעינן עולא דלמאן דלא בעי ידיעה באשם בתחלה אינה חשובה לחלק בינתים ואינו חייב אלא אחת דכיון דלא חשיבא ליה ידיעה לא מחלקת והא מילתא דעולא נקט לה הכא משום דרב דימי דאיירי עלה ופרכינן עלה מפלוגתא דרבי יוחנן ור"ש לקיש: המתינו. שלא תקריבוהו עד שאבעול עוד: כי אתא רב דימי. לא פליג אדעולא אלא מר אמר חדא ומר אמר חדא: חייב על כל אחת ואחת. קס"ד השתא לרב דימי הא דתנן הבא על השפחה ביאות הרבה אינו חייב אלא אחת הני מילי מזיד אי נמי שוגג בהעלם אחד אבל שוגג ונודע לו בינתים למאן דחשיבא ליה ידיעה באשם מחלקת ואפילו לריש לקיש: והרי חטאת דבעי ידיעה בתחלה. שאם הביא חטאתו קודם שנודע לו החטא אינה מכפרת דכתיב (ויקרא ד) או הודע אליו והביא: ופליגי ר' יוחנן וריש לקיש. וקאמר ריש לקיש דאין ידיעות מחלקות להתחייב בשתים על שני זיתי חלב בהעלם אחד אלמא לא חשיבא ליה חילוק ידיעה כחילוק כפרה וגבי שפחה חרופה בידיעות שבין ביאה לביאה לאו כהבאת קרבן חשיבי לחלק וכי היכי דבמזיד דידיה מביא אחת על כולן הכא נמי מביא אחת על כולן ולא דמי לידיעות שבין אכילת חלב לאכילת חלב שמחלקות לדברי הכל דהתם חיובי אשגגות הוא וכיון שיש ידיעה בינתים הויין ליה שתי שגגות: אמר ליה אביי דילמא. הא דפשטת דלמאן דבעי ידיעה חייב ואפילו לריש לקיש: במעשה דלאחר הפרשה קאמרת. וכאתקפתא דרב המנונא דלעיל אבל בידיעה דקודם אפילו לר"ע פלוגתא דרבי יוחנן וריש לקיש היא לרבי יוחנן דחשיבא ליה ידיעה לחלק באכילת חלב אפילו שתי אכילות שנאכלו בהעלם אחד ה"נ מחלקת וריש לקיש דאמר התם לא מחלקת ה"נ אפי' דבין ביאה לביאה לא מחלקת דבין ביאה לביאה דהכא כשתי אכילות דחלב בהעלם אחד ונודע לו על כל אחד ואחד לבדו דמיא: הכל מודים. ר' יוחנן וריש לקיש בשפחה חרופה דיש חילוק: והכל מודים. בה דאין חילוק: ומחלוקת. שניהם בה דלר' יוחנן יש חילוק ולריש לקיש אין חילוק וכולהו מפרש להו: כדעולא. למאן דלא בעי ידיעה בתחלה דאפי' ר' יוחנן מודה דלר' טרפון לא חשיבא ידיעה לחלק וכי א"ר יוחנן ידיעות מחלקות ואפילו בין שתים הנעשות בהעלם אחד ה"מ בחטאת דחשיב ידיעה דילה: והכל מודים. ואפילו ר"ל דיש חילוק ואפילו לרבי טרפון כגון בביאה שלאחר הפרשה כדרב המנונא: ומחלוקת. דרבי יוחנן ור"ל בשפחה חרופה ואליבא למאן דחשיבא ליה ידיעה דאשם לר' יוחנן דאמר ידיעת חטאת הואיל וחשיבא היא מחלקת אפי' חטאת דהעלם אחד הכא נמי מחלקת בין דהעלם אחד בין דשתי העלמות ולר"ל דאמר ידיעה דחטאת אף על גב דחשיבא לא מחלקת עבירות דהעלם אחד הכא אפילו דשתי העלמות לא מחלקת וכדפרישית:

נתכוון

בעל חמש בעילות בשפחה חרופה אינו חייב אלא אחת. אבל למאן דבעי ידיעה בתחלה הוי פלוגתא דרבי יוחנן ור"ל דלר' יוחנן כיון שהיא ידיעה (ב) שהיא גורמת כפרה מחלקת אפילו ידיעות של אחר הבעילות כ"ש ידיעות שבין ביאה לביאה דמחלקות ור"ל דסבר דידיעות לא מחלקות הכא בשפחה חרופה אפילו ידיעות שבין ביאה לביאה אין מחלקות אע"ג דגבי חלב מודה ר"ל דידיעות שבין אכילה לאכילה מחלקות לא דמי דהתם בשגגה תלה רחמנא וידיעות מחלקות השגגות אבל בשפחה חרופה שמביא על הזדון כשגגה אין הידיעה חשובה לחלק אבל למאן דלא בעי ידיעה בתחלה אפילו רבי יוחנן מודה כיון שאין הידיעה גורמת כפרה דלא חשיבא לחלק אפי' בין ביאה לביאה כל שכן אחר כל המעשים וא"ת הניחא אי איכא אשם תלוי בשפחה חרופה אתי שפיר למאן דלא בעי ידיעה דאינו חייב אלא אחת שאין הידיעה גורמת כפרה שיכול להביא אשם ולהתנות כמו במעילה אבל אי לית בה אשם תלוי דהא לא אשכחן בשום מקום בשפחה חרופה אשם תלוי אמאי אינו חייב אלא אחת ליחייב שתים דהא צריך ידיעה אחת לכל הפחות דאם לא נודע לו לא היה יכול להביא שום קרבן והרי הותה ידיעה גורמת כפרה ויש לומר דאפי' אין אשם תלוי בשפחה חרופה יכול להביא אשם על תנאי ולהתנות בשלמים ואפילו למאן דאמר אין מביאין קדשים לבית הפסול דהשתא ממעט ליה מאכילתו מ"מ לא חשיב גורם כפרה כיון דאם עבר והתנה מה שעשה עשוי והא דנקט עולא שפחה חרופה ולא נקט מילתיה במעילה דגבי מעילה הוא דתנן דהאשם ודאי לא בעי ידיעה משום דאתא לאשמעינן דאפי' בין מעשה למעשה לא חשיבא ידיעה לחלק אבל במעילה פשיטא דמחלקת כמו בחטאת °וכן משמע בפרק ד' מחוסרי כפרה (כריתות דף ט.) דאמר בעא מיניה ר' חייא טירנאה מר' יוחנן הבא על ה' שפחות בהעלם אחד מהו א"ל חייב על כל אחת ואחת ומ"ש מה' העלמות בשפחה אחת אמר ליה התם אין גופים מוחלקין הכא גופים מוחלקין והיינו למאן דלא בעי ידיעה אלמא דלא מחלקות אפי' ידיעות שבין ביאה לביאה ואית ספרים דגרסי במילתיה דעולא ונודע לו בין כל אחת ואחת והיינו כדפרישית וא"ת תפשוט מדעולא דלר' יוחנן ידיעות מחלקות וי"ל דעולא אליבא דר"ל קאמר:

מתקיף לה רב המנונא אלא מעתה בעל והפריש קרבן כו'. תימה מאי פריך רב המנונא דאי קסבר דהפרשה מחלקת בין ביאה לביאה כשבעל במזיד בשוגג נמי יש לחלק והיכי מדמה ליה לידיעה שאין מחלקת במזיד ואי קסבר דאין הפרשה מחלקת במזיד הכי נמי דלא מחלקת בשוגג ונראה לר"י דהכי פריך כיון דלא מחלקת בין ידיעות שבין מעשים לידיעות שלאחר מעשים אלא מעתה הפרשות נמי דאין מחלקות לר"ל לאחר כל המעשים אע"ג דבהפרשות פליגי ואפי' לר' יוחנן איכא למימר דהכא מודה דאין הפרשות מחלקות דדוקא גבי חטאת קאמר דמחלקות משום דאיכא נמי בהדי הפרשות ידיעות חשובות שגורמות כפרה אבל הכא דליכא אלא הפרשה לחודא אפי' רבי יוחנן מודה דלא מחלקת אחר כל המעשים ה"נ דלא מחלקת בין ביאה לביאה והא ודאי סברא היא דמחלקת ואין מתכפר בקרבן שכבר הפריש עבירה שאחר הפרשה אמר ליה מעשה דלאחר הפרשה לא קאמינא פי' איני משוה בין מעשה למעשה לאחר כל המעשים: כי אתא רב דימי אמר למ"ד בעי ידיעה כו'. השתא ס"ד דמיירי בידיעה וקאמר דאפי' לריש לקיש מחלקת כיון דגורמת כפרה ואפילו לאחר כל המעשים ולהכי פריך והרי חטאת כו' ומסיק דלאחר הפרשה קאמר ואומר ר"י דרב דימי פליג אדעולא מדנקט למ"ד בעי ידיעה משמע אבל למאן דלא בעי ידיעה לא משוה אותו להפרשה דלאחר כל המעשים ואין לתמוה על סברא דרב דימי דה"נ עולה מכפרת אעשה דלאחר הפרשה אף על גב דבעיא היא בפרק קמא דזבחים (דף ו:) ולא איפשיט דדחי ליה הש"ס בסוף הסוגיא דהויא בעלמא הוא א"נ התם בעי אליבא דעולא דאמר הכא דאין קרבן מכפר אעבירה דלאחר הפרשה דילמא עולה דדורון היא מכפרת א"נ אין רוצה לפשוט התם מדברי האמוראים אלא ממשנה או מברייתא כדאשכחן בפרק [אין בין המודר (נדרים דף לה:)*] ורשב"א מפרש דהא דנקט למאן דבעי ידיעה רבותא נקט דאפי' לדידיה לא מיחייב לר"ל על כל אחת אלא במעשה דלאחר הפרשה ולא פליג אעולא:

רבינו חננאל

בעל ה' בעילות שפחה חרופה אינו חייב אלא אחת עיקר זה בברייתא במשנה פרק ד' מחוסרי כפרה (כריתות ט) אלו מביאין קרבן על עבירות הרבה ועל הזדון כשגגה וחד מינייהו הבא על שפחה חרופה ואמרינן עלה תני תנא קמיה דר' אלעזר וכפר עליו הכהן באיל האשם מלמד שמביא קרבן אחד על עבירות הרבה באיל האשם ונסלח לו מלמד שמביא על הזדון כשגגה ואקשינן והא עיקר קרבן במזיד כתיב · דכתיב בקרת תהיה פי' מלקות ואין מלקות אלא במזיד ובמקום שהיא חייבת מלקות הוא חייב קרבן ושנינן אימא מלמד שמביא קרבן על השגגה כזדון והתם פליגי אית דאמר דכד בעיל שפחה חרופה בשגגה בעי ידיעה בתחלה כרבעי לענין חטאת דעלמא וכדמפרשינן השוכח עיקר שבת מכלל דהוי ליה ידיעה ואית מאן דאמר כיון דמזיד ושוגג כי הדדי מייתי· שוגג שלא היתה לו ידיעה בתחלה מייתי אשם וקאמר עולא למ"ד לא בעי ידיעה בתחלה סבר דהא לא דמיא הא שגגה לשגגת חטאת דעלמא וכשם שבזדון מביא קרבן אחד על בעילות הרבה הכי נמי שוגג אם בעל כמה בעילות בכמה העלמות או שוגג בזדון ושכן בשגגה אינו מביא אלא קרבן אחד · ואתקיף עליה רב המנונא אלא מעתה בעל ונודע לו וכיון שנודע לו עמד והפריש קרבן ואמר המתינו לא תקריבוהו עד שאבעול ובעל הכי נמי דאינו חייב בבעילה אחרונה קרבן אחר ודחי עולא ואמר מעשה דלאחר הפרשה קאמרת כלומר בעילה דלאחר הפרשה לא קאמינא שמתכפר בקרבן ראשון. כי אתא רב דימי אמר לדברי האומר אשם ודאי בעי ידיעה בתחלה וכי כמו חטאת דעלמא (אינו) [אילו] בעל הני חמש בעילות בשפחה כגון שבעל בשפחה חרופה שוגג ה' בעילות ונודע לו על הראשונה והפריש קרבן וחזר ונודע לו על השניה ואח"כ על השלישית ואח"כ על הרביעית ועדיין לא הקריבו ונודע לו ה' פעמים כי האי גוונא חייב ה' אשמות ולא תימא כיון דשוגג ומזיד בשפחה חרופה דינם שוה ידיעתו בכל אחת ואחת לא מהניא דהא אילו היו אלו ה' בעילות כולן במזיד מתחלה עד סוף אינו חייב בהן [אלא אחת] אלא כשם דמהניא ידיעה לגבי חטאת לחייב על כל ידיעה וידיעה הכי [נמי] מהניא גבי אשמות אמר ליה אביי והא חטאות דלדברי הכל בעינן ידיעה בתחלה וכשעשה כמה עבירות בהעלם א' שהוא חייב על כל אחת ואחת · דלמא (בידיעה ולאחר) [במעשה דלאחר] הפרשה קאמרת כדרב המנונא דאוקימנא בבעילה דלאחר הפרשה א"ל רב דימי אין כי אתא רבין אמר הכל מודין בשפחה חרופה שאינו חייב אלא אחת כדעולא · פי' הכל מודין הוא ר' יוחנן דמחייב על כל ידיעה חטאת בשפחה חרופה מודה דכיון דשוגג כמזיד הוא לא דמיא ידיעתו כידיעת חטאת והכל מודין בשפחה חרופה דחייב על כל אחת פי' אפילו ריש לקיש מודה שאם בעל והפריש קרבן ובעל שאינו מתכפר בקרבן שהפריש על הראשונה אלא חייב קרבן אחר וכ"ש ר' יוחנן ואם לא נמרינן הפרשה לאחר מעשה מקמי ידיעה הפרשה דקמי מעשה דאיכא למימר מעשה מודה ר"ל דהא בהפרשה דמקמי עבירה וקרבן לא הוה עליה זיקת עבירה אחרת · והאי קרבן הוה לו לאותה עבירה בלבד לפיכך אם אח"כ עבר עבירה אחרת חייב עליה אבל האי דהוו עליה ה' עבירות בהעלם אחד · ואילו נודע לו על כולן כאחד אין חייב אלא קרבן אחד כך אפילו אם נודע לו על אחת מהן והפריש עליה קרבן ואח"כ נודע לו על שאר כיון שעדיין לא נקרבה החטאת שהפריש מתכפרין כולן בה החטאת שהפריש מ"מ כולהו בני בקתא נינהו דהדדי וכולהו אית להו דרב המנונא ומחלוקת בשפחה חרופה למ"ד אשם ודאי בעי ידיעה ובפלוגתא

עין משפט נר מצוה

כג א ב ג מיי' פ"ט מהלכות שגגות הלכה ו:

מסורת הש"ס

ס"ל ונודע לו בין כל אחת ואחת

עי' תוספות ...מה דף יט: ד"ה מי איכא קדושין כב:

הגהות הב"ח

(א) גמ' אלא מעתה בעל והפריש כצ"ל ותיבות וחזר ובעל נמחק: (ב) תוס' ד"ה בעל וכו' שהיא ידיעה חשובה שהיא גורמת:

גליון הש"ס

תוס' ד"ה בעל. וכ"מ בפ"ד מחוסרי כפרה והכי מוכח מסוגיין דמיירי ע"כ בנודע בין ביאה לביאה דאלו אחר כל הביאות אין ס"ד לומר דידיעות מחלקות הא כיון דלא בעי ידיעה תחלה אפילו כיפר קודם שנודע לו על הבעילות ממילא כולם מתכפרים עמה כיון דמכפר בלא ידיעה וא"כ ממילא לא מצי למנקט בבעילות דממ"נ בין מעשה למעשה ודאי מחלקת כיון דאינו לאחר כל המעשים פשוט דלא ניחא נימא לר"ל דהא מחלקת הקרבן מכפר מיד על כולם כיון דלר"ל ידיעה תחלה ומה"ט י"ל על דאיך שייך בה"ח לא בעי ידיעה תחלה דרי"ל דסוגיין אם כבעל חמש בעילות ואח"כ כיפר על א' קודם שנודע לו על אינך כולם מתכפרין דלא בעי ידיעה תחלה ודו"ק:

ד"ה דלאמר וב"ק פו: ד"ה כיישו וב"מ דף יז: ד"ה מן

עין משפט
נר מצוה

כד א מיי' פ"ג מהלכות שגגות הלכה ז:
כה ב מיי' פ"א מהלכו' שבת הלכה ח ופ"ז מהלכות שגגות הל' יא:

*נתכוין ״להגביה את התלוש וחתך את המחובר פטור לחתוך את התלוש וחתך את המחובר *רבא אמר ׳פטור אביי אמר חייב רבא אמר פטור דהא לא נתכוון לחתיכה דאיסורא אביי אמר חייב דהא קמיכוין לחתיכה בעלמא אמר רבא מנא אמינא לה *דתניא חומר שבת משאר מצות וחומר שאר מצות משבת חומר שבת משאר מצות שהשבת עשה שתים בהעלם אחד חייב על כל אחת ואחת מה שאין כן בשאר מצות וחומר שאר מצות משבת שבשאר מצות שגג בלא מתכוין חייב מה שאין כן בשבת: אמר מר חומר שבת משאר מצות שהשבת עשה שתים בהעלם אחד חייב על כל אחת ואחת מה שאין כן בשאר מצות היכי דמי אילימא דעבד קצירה וטחינה דכוותה גבי שאר מצות אכל חלב ודם הכא תרתי מיחייב והכא תרתי מיחייב אלא שאר מצות דלא מיחייב אלא חדא היכי דמי דאכל חלב וחלב דכוותה גבי שבת דעבד קצירה וקצירה הכא חדא מיחייב והכא חדא מיחייב לעולם דעבד קצירה וטחינה ומאי מה שאין כן בשאר מצות אע"ז וכדרבי אמי *דא"ר אמי זיבח וקיטר וניסך בהעלמה אחת אינו חייב אלא אחת במאי אוקימתא בע"ז אימא סיפא חומר בשאר מצות שבשאר מצות שגג בלא מתכוין חייב מה שאין כן בשבת *האי שגג בלא מתכוין דע"ז היכי דמי אילימא כסבור בית הכנסת הוא והשתחוה לה הרי לבו לשמים ואלא °דחזי אנדרטא וסגיד לה היכי דמי אי דקבלה עליה באלוה מזיד הוא ואי דלא קבלה עליה באלוה לאו כלום הוא אלא מאהבה ומיראה הניחא לאביי *דאמר חייב אלא לרבא דאמר פטור מאי איכא למימר אלא באומר מותר משא"כ בשבת דפטור לגמרי ע"כ לא בעא מיני' רבא מרב נחמן אלא אי לחובי חדא אי לחובי תרתי אבל מפטרי לגמרי לא אלא

רש"י

נתכוין להגביה את התלוש. כגון דנפל סכין בערוגת הירק ונתכוין להגביהו: וחתך את המחובר פטור. דכתיב אשר חטא בה ודרשינן בכריתות פרט למתעסק בדבר אחר ועשה דבר זה ושוגג היכי דמי כגון שנתכוין לכך אבל שגג דסבר שאין היום שבת או סבר שמלאכה זו מותרת וזה מתעסק בהגבהה היה ולא בחתיכה: דהא לא איכוין אחתיכה דאיסורא· בשגגת שבת או בשגגת מלאכות אלא מתעסק בחתיכת היתר הוה שיודע שהוא שבת ויודע שחתיכת מחובר אסור: משא"כ בשאר מצות. כולה מפרש לה ואזיל: שגג בלא מתכוין. לקמן מפרש לה: חלב ודם. דומיא דטחינה וקצירה שהן שני גופין: אלא גבי שאר מצות היכי דמי. דפטור: כגון חלב וחלב. בהעלם אחד: דרבי אמי. במסכת סנהדרין בפרק ד' מיתות יליף למילתיה מקרא דאין חילוק חטאות לעכו"ם: והשתחוה לה. והיינו שגג שהיא ע"ז בלא מתכוין שלא נתכוון להשתחוות לע"ז: הרי לבו לשמים. ומה חיוב יש כאן אפי' ידע שהוא בית ע"ז והשתחוה בו לשמים אין חיוב כאן: אנדרטא. צורת המלך שעושין לכבוד המלך והשתחוה לה ולא לשם אלהות: מאהבה ומיראה. מאהבת אדם או מיראת אדם השתחוה לע"ז וקרי ליה שוגג בלא מתכוין כלומר שגג בהכי דסבור כיון דאין מתכוין לבו לאלהות מותר: אלא באומר מותר. כגון גר שנתגייר בין הנכרים כסבור שאין ע"ז בתורה וקרי ליה שגג בלא מתכוין: דפטור לגמרי. בתמיה: עד כאן לא קבעי מיניה רבא מרב נחמן. העלם זה וזה בידו מהו לעיל בפירקין (דף ע:) דהיינו אומר מותר דאמר אין שבת בתורה היינו העלם זה וזה: דסבור

תוספות

נתכוין להגביה את התלוש. פירש בקונטרס כגון סכין מוטל בערוגת ירק ונתכוין להגביה וחתך את המחובר א"כ הא דפליגי בנתכוין לחתוך את התלוש וחתך את המחובר היינו לחתוך תלוש(א) וחתך מחובר אחר אבל לחתוך מחובר זה וחתך מחובר אחר משמע דחייב לכ"ע וקשה לר"ת דבסוף פ' ספק אכל (כריתות יט:) אמר שמואל המתעסק בחלבים ועריות חייב שכן נהנה בשבת פטור דמלאכת מחשבת אסרה תורה ומוכח התם דאפילו בנתכוין ללקוט תאנה זו וליקט תאנה אחרת פטר שמואל ולקמן בפרק הזורק (דף צז:) פטר *(ב)רבא נתכוין לזרוק ארבע וזרק שמנה כי לא אמר כל מקום שתרצה תנוח וכל שכן בנתכוין לזרוק בצד זה וזרק בצד אחר דלא נעשה כלל רצונו או נתכוין לחתוך מחובר זה וחתך מחובר אחר דפטור ונראה לר"ת דהכא מיירי בנתכוין לחתוך תלוש ונמצא שהוא מחובר וחותך מה שהיה מתכוין אלא שלא היה יודע שהיה מחובר ופליגי אביי ורבא בקרא דאשר חטא בה דמוקי ליה רבי אליעזר בפרק ספק אכל (שם יט:) פרט למתעסק והכי איתא התם בהדיא דקאמר עלה לרבא משכחת לה שנתכוין לחתוך את התלוש וחתך את המחובר לאביי שנתכוין להגביה את התלוש כו' ושמואל דפטר מטעם מלאכת מחשבת היינו בנתכוין לחתוך מחובר זה וחתך מחובר אחר דלא נעשה מחשבתו והשתא אתי שפיר דקאמר(ג) לקמן דמפרש שגג בלא מתכוין דשאר מצות היכי דמי כגון דסבור שומן הוא ואכלו דהיינו ממש דומיא דשבת לפר"ת:

הניחא לאביי דאמר חייב. פי' הניחא לאביי בהא דמשכחת גבי ע"ז שגג בלא מתכוין אבל מ"מ גם לאביי לא מיתוקמא ברייתא שפיר בהכי דהא אם חלל שבת מאהבה ומיראה נמי חייב ולהכי איצטריך בסמוך לאוקמא אליבא דאביי שגג בלא מתכוין ה"ד דסבור רוק הוא ובלעו:

עד כאן לא בעא מיניה רבא מרב נחמן כו'. וא"ת אמאי לא מייתי מתני' דהשוכח עיקר שבת דאינו חייב אלא אחת ולא הוי פטור לגמרי וי"ל דניחא ליה לאתויי מרבא דמספקא ליה בהעלם זה וזה דדילמא אפי' תרתי מיחייב דכי אוקי הכא באומר מותר היינו בנתעלמה ממנו לפי שעה דהיינו דומיא דהעלם זה וזה בידו כדפי' לעיל דאם לא נודע לו מעולם איסור ע"ז אינו ישראל כלל כיון שמודה בע"ז דדוחק להעמיד בתינוק שנשבה לבין העכו"ם:

רבא אמר פטור. ואם תאמר והא אמר בפרק בן סורר ומורה (סנהדרין דף עד.) דע"ז וגילוי עריות ושפיכות דמים יהרג ואל יעבור אם כן אפילו לא מקבל ליה חייב ואין לומר דרבא לטעמיה דאמר במס' ע"ז בפרק ר' ישמעאל (דף נד.) דאפילו בע"ז בצינעא וחי בהם ולא שימות בהם והא דקאמר רבא בפ"ב דכתובות (דף יט.) גבי עדים שאמרו להם חתמו שקר כו' שאין לך דבר שעומד בפני פיקוח נפש אלא ע"ז וגילוי עריות ושפיכות דמים ה"פ אפילו מאן דמחמיר לא מחמיר אלא בע"ז ג"ע ושפיכות דמים דאם כן לטעמא דרבא דפטר הוי משום הכי מאי מייתי אביי בפ' ד' מיתות (סנהדרין סא:) מכמה ברייתות לימא דאתיא כמ"ד בפרק בן סורר (שם עד.) יהרג ואל יעבור דפלוגתא דתנאי היא וי"ל דסבר רבא דאפי' למ"ד דחייב למסור את עצמו אם לא מסר עצמו לא מיחייב מיתה בבית דין וקשה לרשב"א דאמר רבא במסכת ע"ז* הכל היו בכלל לא תעבדם כשפרט לך הכתוב וחי בהם יצא אונס משמע דלא מפיק אלא אונס מיתה אבל שאר אונסין הוו בכלל לא תעבדם וחייב *)והכא פטור אפי' מאהבה דליכא אונס מיתה וי"מ דההיא דאמר יהרג ואל יעבור היינו בסתם אע"ג דלא מקבל עליה לאלוה אבל הכא במפרש דקעביד מאהבה ומיראה אי נמי אפילו בסתם ובע"ז שהכל אין עובדין אותה אלא מאהבה ומיראה דומיא דהמן דמייתי עלה התם להם אי אתה משתחוה אבל אתה משתחוה לאדם כמותך יכול אפי' נעבד כהמן ת"ל לא תעבדם [וקאמר רבא כהמן ולא כהמן דאינו התם מיראה והכא לאו מיראה] ומההיא גופא נמי יש לדקדק דחייב אע"ג דלא קבל עליה באלוה דמשמע דאסר נעבד כהמן דומיא דאדם שכמותך דשרי והיינו בלא קיבלו עליו באלוה ועוד דאמר בפרק ד' מיתות (סנהדרין דף ס:) הפוער עצמו לפעור זו היא עבודתו אע"ג דקא מכוין לבזוייה הזורק אבן למרקולים זו היא עבודתו אע"ג דקא מכוין למירגמיה אלמא דחייב אע"פ שאין מקבל עליו באלוה ומיהו יש לפרש אע"ג דקא מכוין לבזוייה מכוין לעובדה דרך בזיון ורגימה זו והא דלא דחי ראיות דאביי בעובד מאהבה ומיראה סתם משום דסתם עובד כמדעתו דמי וא"ת ולמאי דפטר רבא אמאי לא השתחוה מרדכי להמן וי"ל כדאמרינן במדרש ששתי צורות היו על לבו ועוד משום קידוש השם כדאשכחן בירושלמי במסכת שביעית בפ"ד כגון פפוס ולוליינוס אחיו שנתנו להם מים בזכוכית צבועה ולא קבלו מהם*:

באומר מותר. והא דממעטינן בפ"ב דמכות (דף ז: ושם) בשגגה פרט לאומר מותר שאני גבי גלות דטובא בשגגה כתיבי התם ולהכי נמי אמר בסוף פ"ב דב"ק (דף כו: ושם) היתה אבן מונחת לו בחיקו ולא הכיר בה מעולם לענין גלות פטור מבשגגה לענין שבת פטור משום דבעינן מלאכת מחשבת והשתא תיפוק ליה דגבי שבת נמי כתיב בשגגה אלא ודאי דוקא גבי גלות ממעטינן משום דכתיבי בשגגה טובא: אלא

*) וי"א דבאומר אלי אתה מודה רבא דחייב אפילו מאהבה ומיראה דהיינו קבל עליו באלוה כיון דקאמר אלי אתה אע"פ שאומר באונס ס"פ במס' ע"ז הא בכלל לא תעבדם כשאמר אלי אתה אבל מקטיר דאונס לא הוי בכלל לא תעבדם ומיהו בהנהו דמייתי אביי ה"מ לאוקמי באלי אתה והר"א ממיץ מפרש דע"ז שכבר עבדוהו פ"א לשם ע"ז חייב בה אפי' מאהבה ומיראה [ת"י]

רבינו חננאל

ובפלוגתא דר' יוחנן ור"ל פשוטה היא: **אתמר** נתכוין להגביה את התלוש וחתך את המחובר לכולי עלמא לא מחייב קרבן דהא לא אתכוין למלתא דאית בה איסורא אלא להגביה בעולם נתכוין אע"פ שחותך את המחובר לא קרינן ביה נפש כי תחטא בשגגה ולא הוי חוטא בשגגה אלא מתכוין למעשה מביא לידי חטא. והוא אינו יודע שהוא חוטא · אבל אם נתכוון לחתוך את התלוש שהוא מותר ונזדמן לו מחובר וחתכו רבה אמר פטור דס"ל שאינו קורא ביה נפש כי תחטא בשגגה אלא בזמן שמתכוון לדבר אסור כשיקרא שוגג באיסורו וזה לא נתכוון אלא לחתיכת תלוש אביי אמר חייב דהוא מכוון לחתיכה בעלמא ויש בחתיכה איסור · וסבר אביי שאין צריך להתכוון במעשיו לדבר שהוא באיסורו אלא כל מעשה שיש במינו איסור אף על פי שלא נתכוון לדבר שיש בה איסור כיון שנזדמן לו דבר איסור הריני קורא בו כי תחטא בשגגה · וכך לענין נתכוון לזרוק שתים וזרק ד' לרבה פטור דהא לא נתכוון לדבר האיסור בשגגת איסורו אע"פ שמתכוון למקצתו דסבר ליה צריך להתכוון לכל האיסור בשגגת איסורו ולאביי חייב דהא נתכוון לזריקה ונזדמנה לו זריקה אסורה. אמ' (רבא) [רבה] מנא אמינא לה דפטור דתניא חומר בשבת משאר מצות שהשבת עושה שתים בהעלם אחת חייב שתים מה שאין כן בשאר מצות · חומר בשאר מצות ששאר מצות שגג בלא מתכוון חייב משא"כ בשבת ואוקימנא דשגג בלא מתכוין בשבת דפטור [בכה"ג דנתכוין לחתוך את התלוש וכו'] ודוק' הא מתניתא כרבה דאמר נתכוון לחתוך את התלוש וחתך את המחובר פטור דהא לא נתכוון לחתיכה (דאיסור דא)[לאיסורא]. ושקלו וטרו בהא דתנן עשה בהעלם אחד שתים בשבת חייב שתים ובשאר מצות כי האי גוונא אינו חייב אלא אחת. היכי דמי [אילימא] קצר וטחן בשבת כיוצא בו בשאר מצות אכל חלב ודם הכא שתים מחייב והכא שתים מחייב · אלא קצר וחזר וקצר בהעלם אחד כיוצא בו בשאר מצות אכל חלב וחזר ואכל חלב בהעלם אחד הכא חדא מחייב והכא חדא מחייב ודחינן מאי שאר מצות דקתני ע"ז · והכי קתני חומר בשבת שאם קצר וטחן בהעלם אחד בזדון שבת ושגגת מלאכות חייב שתים מה שאין כן בע"ז כי(אם) בע"ז אם זיבח וקיטר וניסך בהעלם אחד אינו חייב אלא אחת וכדר' (יוסי) [אמי] ודחינן לא מיתוקמא מתניתין בע"ז דקתני סיפא שגג בלא מתכוון בשאר מצות חייב משא"כ בשבת · שגג בלא מתכוון בע"ז היכי משכחת לה אי נימא דחזא ע"ז וסבר כי היא בית הכנסת והשתחוה [לה] כי האי גוונא פטור הוא דהא לבו לשמים · ואלא דחזא אנדרטא וסגיד לה · אי דקבלה עילויה באלוה מזיד הוא ולאו בר קרבן הוא ואי לא קבלה עילויה באלוה כיון דבשוגג השתחוה כנגד האי אנדרטא לא מחייב דהא לא עביד מידי אלא כגון שהשתחוה לע"ז מאהבה · שראה צורת ע"ז ואהבה או אדם שהעמיד עצמו ע"ז כהמן והשתחוה לו מאהבה בשגגת אלהים אחרים פי' שנעלם ממנו שמשתחוה לע"ז ואהבה חייב או שנעלם ממנו כי אלו העבירות בע"ז מחייב · וזה פי' מאהבה או מיראה נמי כגון מי שנתיירא מן הע"ז והשתחוה לו בשגגת אלהים אחרים או בשגגת עבירות דלא הוה ידע כי האי גוונא חייב אי אסרת כי האי גוונא שגג בלא מתכוין בע"ז חייב ניחא לאביי דמחייב דגרסינן בסנהדרין פרק ארבע מיתות דאתמר העובד ע"ז מאהבה ומיראה כגון המשתחוה מאהבתו לו או מיראתו ממנו לאדם הנעבד כהמן בשוגג שלא היה יודע כי העובד מאהבה או מיראה חייב [אביי אמר חייב] דהא פלחא לע"ז רבא אמר פטור דהא לא קבלה עליו באלוה · הניחא לאביי אלא לרבא

מסורת הש"ס

כריתות יט:

[לפמ"ש תוס' לעיל סג: ד"ה גזרה וכ"כ עוד לעיל ע: ד"ה נודע ולמ"ש הרא"ש פרק הזהב סי' יט שלא מצינו בכל הגמ' שמקדים רבא לאביי כי אביי מלך קודם רבא ע"ש וכ"כ עוד בשאר דוכתי א"כ יש לגרוס הכא אביי אמר וכו' או דצ"ל רבה אמר פטור וכו' אמר רבה מנא אמינא לה וכו' ועי' מ"ש פסחים מח. על הגליון]

סנהדרין סב. [וע"ש שצ"ל רבי זכאי]

שם סא: [כריתות ג.]

שם

הגהות הב"ח

(א) תוס' ד"ה נתכוין וכו' לחתוך תלוש זה וחתך: (ב) בא"ד בפ' הזורק פטר רב אשי נתכוין וכו': (ג) בא"ד והשתא אתי שפיר לקמן כצ"ל ותיבת דקאמר נמחק:

[דף מד.]

גליון הש"ס

גמ' דחזי אנדרטא. עי' מס' ע"ז דף מ ע"ב תוד"ה ובאנדרטי:

[ועי' תוספות סנהדרין סא: ד"ה רבא אמר]

רב נסים גאון

ואלא מאהבה ומיראה הניחא לאביי דאמר חייב אלא למאן דאמר פטור מאי איכא למימר · ופלוגתא דאביי ורבא משכחת במס' סנהדרין בפרק ד' מיתות (דף סא) איתמר העובד ע"ז מאהבה ומיראה אביי אמר חייב ורבא אמר פטור אביי אמר חייב דהא פלחה רבא אמר פטור דלא קבלה עליה באלוה אי קיבלה עליה אין ואי לא לא :

It was stated: [72b] If one intended to lift up something de-
a tached, but cut off something attached [to the soil],[1] he is not culpable. [If he intended] to cut something detached, but cut something attached [instead],[2] Raba ruled: He is not culpable; Abaye maintained: He is culpable.[3] Raba ruled, He is not culpable, since he had no intention of a prohibited cutting.[4] Abaye maintained: He is culpable, since he had the intention of cutting in general.[5]

Raba said, How do I know it? Because it was taught: [In one respect] the Sabbath is more stringent than other precepts; [in another respect] other precepts are more stringent than the Sabbath. The Sabbath is more stringent than other precepts in that if one performs two [labours] in one state of unawareness, he is culpable on account of each separately; this is not so in the case of other precepts. Other precepts are more stringent than the Sabbath, for in their case if an injunction is unwittingly and unintentionally violated, atonement must be made: this is not so with respect to the Sabbath.

The Master said: 'The Sabbath is more stringent than other precepts in that if one performs two [labours] in one state of unawareness, he is culpable on account of each separately: this is not so in the case of other precepts.' How is this meant? Shall we say, that he performed reaping and grinding? Then an analogous violation of other precepts would be the partaking of *heleb* and blood—then in both cases two [penalties] are incurred! But how is it possible in the case of other precepts that only one liability is
b incurred? If one ate *heleb* twice;[1] then by analogy, with respect to the Sabbath [it means] that he performed reaping twice—then in each case only one liability is incurred?—After all, it means that he performed reaping and grinding, and what is meant by 'this is not so in the case of other precepts'? This refers to idolatry, and is in accordance with R. Ammi, who said: If one sacrificed, burnt incense, and made libations [to an idol] in one state of unawareness, he is only liable to one [sacrifice].[2] How have you explained it: as referring to idolatry? Then consider the second clause: Other precepts are more stringent [than the Sabbath], for in their case if an injunction is unwittingly and unintentionally violated, atonement must be made: this is not so with respect to the Sabbath. Now, how is an unwitting and unintentional transgression of idolatry possible? Shall we say that one thought it [*sc.* an idolatrous shrine] to be a synagogue and bowed down to it—then his heart was to Heaven! But if he saw a royal statue and bowed down to it—what are the circumstances? If he accepted it as a god, he is a wilful sinner; while if he did not accept it as a god, he has not committed idolatry at all![3] Hence it must mean [that he worshipped it idolatrously] through love or fear:[4] now this agrees with Abaye's view that a penalty is incurred;[5] but on Raba's view that there is no culpability, what can you say? Rather it must refer to one who thinks that it [*sc.* idolatry] is permitted.[6] Then 'this is not so in the case of the Sabbath' means that there is no liability at all! Yet when Raba questioned R. Nahman,[7] it was only whether one is liable to one [sacrifice] or to two, but certainly not to exempt him

a (1) The latter is a forbidden act on the Sabbath. Rashi: e.g., if a knife fell down amidst growing corn, and whilst intending to lift it up one cut the corn. (2) R. Tam: e.g., he thought it was a detached bundle of corn, but after cutting it he discovered that it had been attached. (3) Throughout the Talmud Abaye's view is always quoted before Raba's. Hence it is suggested that either the order should be reversed here, or Rabbah (Abaye's teacher) should be read instead of Raba, v. Marginal Gloss. (4) Whereas in order to be culpable he must have intended to do what he did, save that his offence was unintentional either because he did not know that it was the Sabbath or that that action is forbidden on the Sabbath. (5) Whereas to avoid culpability he must have had no intention of cutting at all.

b (1) In one state of unawareness, not being reminded in between that *heleb* is forbidden. (2) Though he performed a number of services. (3) Lit., 'it is nothing'. (4) And this is called unwitting and unintentional, for it was unwitting in so far as he thought this permissible. (5) V. Sanh. 61*b*. (6) E.g., if he was brought up among heathens. Since he has never known of any prohibition, it is regarded not only as unwitting but as unintentional too. (7) About such a case, v. *supra* 70*b*. Where one forgets both the Sabbath and the forbidden labours it is tantamount to ignorance of the Sabbath altogether, and is thus analogous to the belief that idolatry is permitted.

completely! [73a] Surely then the first clause [dealing with the greater severity of the Sabbath] refers to idolatry, whilst the second treats of other precepts; and how is unwitting and unintentional transgression possible? When one thought that it
a [*ḥeleb*] was permitted fat, and ate it.[1] [While] 'this is not so with respect to the Sabbath,' viz., that he is not culpable, for if [by analogy] one intended cutting something detached but cut something attached [instead], he is not culpable.[2] But Abaye [maintains:] how is an unwitting and unintentional offence meant? When one thinks that it [*ḥeleb*] is spittle and swallows it.[3] [While] 'which is not so in the case of the Sabbath,' where he is exempt, for if [by analogy] one intends *lifting* something detached but cuts something attached [to the soil], he is not culpable. But if he intends to *cut* something detached and cuts something attached, he is liable.

It was stated: If one intends to throw [an object] two [cubits], but throws it four,[4] Raba said: He is not culpable; Abaye ruled: He is culpable.[5] Raba said: He is not culpable, since he had no intention of a four [cubits'] throw. Abaye ruled, He is culpable, since he intended throwing in general. If he thinks it private ground but it is learnt to be public ground, Raba ruled: He is not culpable; Abaye said: He is culpable. Raba ruled, He is not culpable, since he had no intention of a forbidden throw. While Abaye ruled that he is culpable, since he intended throwing in general.

Now, it is necessary.[6] For if we were informed of the first, [it might be argued] there [only] does Raba rule thus, since he did not intend [to perform] a prohibited cutting, but if he intended throwing [an object] two [cubits] but throws it four, since four can-
b not be thrown without two,[1] I would say that he agrees with Abaye. And if we were informed of this, [it might be argued] here [only] does Raba rule thus, since he did not intend a four [cubits'] throw; but if he thought it private ground but it was discovered to be public ground, seeing that he intended a four [cubits'] throw, I would say that he agrees with Abaye. Thus they are [all] necessary.

We learnt: The primary labours are forty less one. Now we questioned this, Why state the number? And R. Joḥanan answered: [To teach] that if one performs all of them in one state of unawareness, he is liable [to a sacrifice] on account of each separately. Now, as for Abaye who ruled that in such a case one is liable, this is well: for this is conceivable where one knows the interdict of the Sabbath and the interdicts of labours, but errs in respect of the standards.[2] But according to Raba who maintained that one is not culpable [for this], how is this conceivable? [Presumably] [only] where he was conscious of the Sabbath but unaware of [the forbidden character of his] labours. Now that is well if he agrees with R. Joḥanan who ruled, Since he was ignorant of *kareth*, even if he was conscious of the negative injunction, [he is liable]:[3] then it is possible where he knew [that his labours are prohibited on] Sabbath by a negative injunction. But if he holds with R. Simeon b. Laḳish, who maintained, He must offend unwittingly in respect of both the negative injunction and *kareth*, then wherein did he know of the Sabbath?[4]—He knew it by the law of boundaries, this being in accordance with R. Akiba.[5]

MISHNAH. THE PRIMARY LABOURS ARE FORTY LESS ONE, [VIZ.:] SOWING,[6] PLOUGHING, REAPING, BINDING
c SHEAVES, THRESHING, WINNOWING, SELECTING,[1] GRINDING, SIFTING, KNEADING, BAKING, SHEARING WOOL, BLEACHING, HACKLING, DYEING, SPINNING, STRETCHING THE THREADS,[2] THE MAKING OF TWO MESHES, WEAVING TWO THREADS, DIVIDING TWO THREADS,[3] TYING [KNOTTING] AND UNTYING, SEWING TWO STITCHES, TEARING IN ORDER TO SEW TWO STITCHES,[4] CAPTURING A DEER, SLAUGHTERING, OR FLAYING, OR SALTING IT,[5] CURING ITS HIDE, SCRAPING IT [OF ITS HAIR], CUTTING IT UP, WRITING TWO LETTERS, ERASING IN ORDER TO WRITE TWO LETTERS [OVER THE ERASURE], BUILDING, PULLING DOWN, EXTINGUISHING, KINDLING, STRIKING WITH A HAMMER,[6] [AND] CARRYING OUT FROM ONE DOMAIN TO ANOTHER: THESE ARE THE FORTY PRIMARY LABOURS LESS ONE.

a (1) Thus it was unwitting, because he thought it permitted fat, and unintentional, since he had no intention of eating *ḥeleb*. On the present hypothesis it is regarded as unwitting but intentional only when he knows that it is *ḥeleb* and eats it as such, thinking, however, that *ḥeleb* is permitted. (2) Thus on this interpretation the Baraitha supports Raba. (3) It is unwitting, because he thinks it spittle, and unintentional, because he has no intention of eating at all, swallowing not being eating. But the case posited by Raba is not unintentional in Abaye's view, since he did intend to eat. (4) Four cubits in the street is the minimum distance for culpability. (5) On Raba and Abaye v. *supra* 72b, n. a3. (6) For the three controversies—i.e., these two and that on 72b top—to be stated, though apparently two are superfluous, since the same principle underlies all.

b (1) I.e., in throwing it four cubits he did fulfil his intention. (2) In each case he intended performing less than the standard for which liability is incurred, but actually performed the full standard. (3) V. *supra* 69a, n. a3. (4) V. *supra* 69a, n. 4. (5) V. *supra* 69a, nn. b5-6. (6) Lit., 'he who sows', and similarly with the others that follow.

c (1) By hand, the unfit food from the fit. (2) On the loom. (3) I.e., dividing the ends of the web. (4) Where it is inconvenient to sew unless one tears the cloth first, that tearing is a primary labour. (5) *Sc.* its skin. (6) I.e., giving the finishing blow with the hammer.

אלא לאו רישא בעכו"ם וסיפא בשאר מצות ושגג בלא מתכוון בשאר מצות ה"ד דסבור דשומן הוא ואכלו משא"כ בשבת דפטור דנתכוון לחתוך את התלוש והתך את המחובר פטור ואביי שגג בלא מתכוון ה"ד *דסבור רוק הוא ובלעו משא"כ בשבת דפטור דנתכוון להגביה את התלוש וחתך את המחובר פטור אבל נתכוון לחתוך את התלוש וחתך את המחובר חייב: איתמר *נתכוון לזרוק שתים וזרק ארבע *רבא אמר פטור אביי אמר חייב רבא אמר פטור (א)דלא קמיכוין לזריקה דארבע אביי אמר חייב דהא קמיכוין לזריקה בעלמא כסבור רשות היחיד ונמצאת רשות הרבים רבא אמר ב פטור ואביי אמר חייב רבא אמר פטור דהא לא מיכוין לזריקה דאיסורא ואביי אמר חייב דהא קא מיכוין לזריקה בעלמא וצריכא דאי אשמעינן קמייתא בההוא קאמר רבא דהא לא קמיכוין לחתיכה דאיסורא אבל נתכוון לזרוק שתים וזרק ארבע דארבע בלא תרתי לא(ב) מיזרקא ליה אימא מודה ליה לאביי ואי אשמעינן בהא בהא קאמר רבא דהא לא קמיכוין לזריקה דארבע אבל כסבור רה"י ונמצא רה"ר דמכוין לזריקה דארבע אימא מודי ליה לאביי צריכא *תנן אבות מלאכות ארבעים חסר אחת והוינן בה מנינא למה לי וא"ר יוחנן שאם עשאן כולם בהעלם אחד חייב על כל אחת ואחת בשלמא לאביי דאמר כי האי גוונא חייב משכחת לה דידע דאסורא(ג) שבת וידע לה איסור מלאכות וקא טעה בשיעורין אלא לרבא דאמר פטור היכי משכחת לה בזדון שבת ושגגת מלאכות הניחא אי סבר לה כר' יוחנן דאמר כיון ששגג בכרת אע"פ שהזיד בלאו משכחת לה דידע לה לשבת בלאו אלא אי סבר לה כרשב"ל דאמר עד שישגוג בלאו וכרת דידע לה לשבת במאי *דידע לה בתחומין ואליבא דר"ע:

מתני' (א) אבות *ג מלאכות ארבעים חסר אחת הזורע והחורש והקוצר והמעמר והדש והזורה הבורר הטוחן והמרקד והלש והאופה הגוזז את הצמר המלבנו והמנפצו והצובעו והטווה *והמיסך והעושה שתי בתי נירין והאורג שני חוטין והפוצע שני חוטין הקושר והמתיר *והתופר שתי תפירות הקורע על מנת לתפור [שתי תפירות] הצד צבי השוחטו והמפשיטו המולחו והמעבד את עורו והממחקו והמחתכו הכותב שתי אותיות והמוחק על מנת לכתוב שתי אותיות הבונה והסותר המכבה והמבעיר המכה בפטיש *המוציא מרשות לרשות הרי אלו אבות מלאכות ארבעים חסר אחת:

גמ'

א) ס"א אלו אבות

[עמ"ש לעיל עב: על הגליון]

רש"י

דסבור שומן הוא ואכלו. והייט דשגג דסבור שומן הוא ולא נתכוון לאכול חלב וחייב ואף על פי דמתעסק הוא לרבא דהא לא מתכוון לאכילת איסור חייב דאמר שמואל בכריתות (פ"ד דף יט:) בחלבי' ועריות מתעסק חייב שכן נהנה אבל בשבת פטור דלא נהנה והייט סייעתא לדידיה דאמר נתכוון לחתוך את התלוש וחתך את המחובר פטור: ואביי. אמר לך לעולם כי האי גוונא אף בשבת חייב דלאו מתעסק הוא והיכי דמי מתעסק דשאר מצות חייב קסבר רוק הוא שהיה חלב נימוח ובלעו דלא איכוון לאכילה דרוק לאו בר אכילה הוא אלא בליעה דכתיב (איוב ז) עד בלעי רוקי ועלתה בידו אכילה דהא לא איכוון לאכילה ודכוותייהו דשבת דפטור נתכוון להגביה ועלתה בידו חתיכה: דהא לא איכוון לזריקה דאיסור. ויהא שוגג בשבת או במלאכה אבל זה אינו שוגג לא בשבת ולא במלאכות אלא מתעסק בדבר אחד של היתר ועלתה בידו איסור: וצריכא. לאיפלוגי בכולהו אף על גב דדמי להדדי: דארבע בלא תרתי לא מזדריק. וזה שנתכוון לשתים וזרק ארבע נעשית מחשבתו דהא יש בכלל ד' שתים הלכך לאו מתעסק הוא: דלא איכוון לזריקה דארבע. ובציר מהני לא שם זריקה עלה: אבל כסבור רה"י הוא וכו'. דנתכוון לזריקה גמורה: משכחת לה. להאי שנשתכחה תורת כל הלכות שבת ממנו ואפילו הכי חשיבא ליה כזדון שבת ושגגת מלאכות לחיוביה אכל חדא כגון דידע ליה לשבת באיסורין וטעה בשיעורין שנתכוון לפחות מכשיעור ועשה כשיעור דלכולן יש שיעור: אלא לרבא דאמר פטור היכי משכחת לה. דמיחייב שום אדם על כל מלאכה ומלאכה שבהעלם אחד על כרחך בזדון שבת ושגגת מלאכות הוא דבעית לאשכוחיה והכא דאיעלימו כולהו מיניה מאי זדון שבת איכא במה ניכר לו שבת מאשר ימים:

מתני' הזורה. ברחת לרוח: הבורר. פסולת בידיו: המרקד. בנפה ובגמ' פריך הני כולהו חדא היא דלהפריש פסולת מתוך אוכל נעשות שלשתן: האופה. לא הוה במשכן דלא שייך אלא בפת ופת לא שייכא במלאכת המשכן אבל כולהו קמייתא הואי בסממנין של צבע תכלת וארגמן ותולעת שני ובגמרא פריך דשביק תנא מבשל דהוי בסממנים ונקט אופה ושיעורן של אלו כגרוגרת חוץ מחורש דבכל שהוא לקמן בפרק הבונה (דף קג.): הגוזז צמר. וכל שאר מלאכות שייכי בצמר של מלאכת המשכן: המלבנו. מכבסו בנהר: המנפצו. קרפי"ר בלע"ז: המיסך. אורדי"ר: בתי נירין. ליי"ש שנתן שני חוטין בתוך הבית ניר ובגוזז ובמלבן וכולהו איכא מפרש שיעורן לקמן בפרק האורג: הפוצע. מנתק פעמים שיש בשני חוטין יותר מדאי ומנתק מהן ומקליפן לצורך והני כולהו ממיסך ואילך עד קושר ומתיר שייכי ביריעות ולקמן מפרש מאי קושר ומאי מתיר איכא: ותופר וקורע. ביריעות הוא: על מנת לתפור. פעמים שהנקב עגול ואינו יכול לתופרו יפה אא"כ קורעו כדמפרש בגמרא אבל קורע שלא לתפור לא הוי במשכן: הצד את הצבי. וכל מלאכת עורו טהגת בתחשים למשכן בעורותיהן: המולחו. לעור: ממחקו. מגרר שערו: מחתכו. מקצעו ומחתכו לרצועות וסנדלים: כותב ומוחק. לקמן (דף קג:) מפרש למאי מיבעיא למשכן שכן רושמין על קרשי המשכן לידע איזה בן זוגו וכותב אות בזו ואות בזו ומוחק פעמים שטעה: מכבה ומבעיר. באש שתחת הדוד של סממנין: מכה בפטיש. הוא גמר כל מלאכה שכן אומן מכה בקורנס על הסדן להחליקו בגמר מלאכה ומתניתין נמי לא מיחייב ליה אלא בגמר מלאכה:

גמרא

תוספות

אלא לאו רישא בע"ז וסיפא בשאר מצות. תימה לר"י דלוקמא כולה בשאר מצות ומאי מה שאין כן בשאר מצות כגון שחט וזרק. בתוך דאינו חייב אלא אחת כדאמר אביי בפרק אחד דיני ממונות (סנהדרין לד:) שם תעשה עשאן הכתוב עשיה אחת ור' אבהו נמי דפליג מודה דלרבי ישמעאל בשחיטה וזריקה ולר' עקיבא בהעלאה וזריקה דאינו חייב אלא אחת דמחד קרא נפקי ושגג בלא מתכוון כגון שנתכוון לשחוט בהמת חולין והיה צריך לשל חולין ונמצאת(ד) של קדשים דכוותה בשבת נתכוון לחתוך תלוש ונמצא מחובר ולא היה צריך אלא לתלוש דפטור דמלאכת מחשבת בעינן וי"ל דלא מצינן לפרושי הכי דמשמע דפטור בשבת לפי ששגג בלא מתכוון דכה"ג אפילו נתכוון למחובר זה ונמצא מחובר אחר פטור דאין זה מלאכת מחשבת וליכא לאוקמי נמי דמיירי כשנעשה מחשבתו כגון שהיה צריך לחתוך מה שחתך אלא שהיה סבור שהוא תלוש ונמצא שהוא מחובר הא ליכא למימר דכה"ג אם פטור לענין שבת מאשר חטא בה פטור נמי לענין חוץ ומיהו עוד קשה דלוקמא כולה בשאר מצות כגון(ה) כרבע לזכר ורבע את הזכר והבא על הבהמה והביא בהמה עליו דבין לאביי ובין לר' אבהו לר' עקיבא אינו חייב אלא אחת והשתא שגג בלא מתכוון מיתוקם שפיר דמיפטר בשבת מאשר חטא בה וכגון שנעשית מחשבתו וגבי עריות לא מיפטר שכן נהנה:

העושה שני בתי נירין. צריך לפרש למה פירש כאן ובאורג* ובפוצע ובתופר ובכותב שיעור טפי מבשאר:

הקושר והמתיר. ל"ע אי מיחייב במתיר שלא על מנת לקשור אי לא ומדלא תני ליה כדתני מוחק ע"מ לכתוב אין לדקדק דהכי נמי לא קתני סותר ע"מ לבנות ובפ' במה מדליקין (לעיל לא:) אמרינן בהדיא דבעינן סותר ע"מ לבנות ולפי מה שפירש רש"י בגמרא (דף עד:) דאי מתרמי ליה תרי קיטרי בהדי הדדי בשני חוטין זה אצל זה שרי חד ומניח חד משמע דמיחייב בלא על מנת לקשור ולשון קטר לא משמע כפירושו אבל ר"ח פירש וכן משמע בירושלמי כשנפסק חוט בשני מקומות ונקשר מתירין ב' הקשרים ומשליכין לחוץ האמצעי וחוזרין וקושרין שתי הראשים זה בזה ואין בו אלא קשר א' ולפי זה משמע דבעי מתיר ע"מ לקשור והא דלא תני ליה במתיר ובסותר פירשתי בפרק ב' (דף לא:) ד"ה וסותר:

מכדי

עין משפט נר מצוה

כו א מיי' פ"ב מהלכות שגגות הלכה ז:

כז ב מיי' פ"א מהלכות שבת הלכה ח:

כח ג מיי' פ"ז מהלכות שבת הלכה א סמג לאוין סה:

רבינו חננאל

דאמר פטור מאי איכא למימר ואמרינן לא משכחת שגג בלא מתכוין לע"ז אלא באומר מותר. פי' כגון מי שנעלם ממנו עבודת אלהים אחרים ששכח הכל לגמרי שנמצא בידו העלם אלהים אחרים והעלם עבירות ואומר שמותר. וכי האי גוונא בע"ז (אחרינא) חייב בשבת פטור לגמרי ואקשי' ומי איכא למימר דפטור לגמרי דהא עד כאן לא בעא מיניה רבא מרב נחמן העלם זה וזה בידו. פי' העלם שבת והעלם מלאכות בידו מהו אלא לחיובי חדא או תרתי אבל למפטריה לגמרי לא וחזרנו לפרק פירוק אחר משום דקשיא דלא מיתוקמא סיפא דהא מתניתין בע"ז אוקמי הכי רישא בע"ז דקתני עשה שתים בהעלם א' בשבת חייב ב' משא"כ בע"ז שאם זיבח וקיטר וניסך בהעלם א' אינו חייב אלא אחת כר' אמי אבל סיפא דקתני בשאר מצות שגג בלא מתכוין חייב משא"כ בשבת דפטור. בשאר מצות דלאו ע"ז היא והיכי דמי כגון שהי' סבור שהוא שומן ואכלו ונמצא חלב. כגון זה בשאר מצות הוא דחייב. אבל בשבת כי האי גוונא נתכוון לחתוך בתלוש וחתכו ונמצא דמחובר לקרקע פטור ודחי אביי ואמר לא כי האי גוונא (לע"ז) לעולם אימא לך חייב והיכי דמי שגג בלא מתכוין דבשאר מצות חייב ובשבת פטור. כגון שנתכוין בבליעה דרוק ובלעה ונמצא חלב שאע"פ שלא נתכוין לאכילה דחייב בשאר מצות ובשבת כה"ג דנתכוין להגביה דבר תלוש והגביהו ונמצא שחתכו מן המחובר [פטור] אבל אם נתכוין לחתיכה בעלמא חייב. (כגון) [וכ"ש] בשאר מצות אם נתכוין לאכילה בעלמא [חייב] וכדר' נחמן דאמר המתעסק בחלבין ובעריות אע"פ שלא נתכוון חייב שכבר נהנה. והמתעסק בשבת פטור. מלאכת מחשבת אסרה תורה. ור' יוחנן התם בפרק ארבע מיתות כדתני תנא הדרא מתניתין קמיה דחאה ואמר ליה פוק תני לברא. דכל מתניתין דלא מיתוקמא רישא וסיפא בחד טעמא לאו מתנית' תרצתא היא. ר' יוחנן לטעמיה דאמר בסוף פרק המפקיד מאן דמתרגם לי חבית אליבא דחד תנא מובילנא מאניה בתריה לבי מסותא: נתכוון לזרוק ב' וזרק ד' אמות (רבא) [רבה] אמר (חייב) [פטור] אביי אמר (פטור) [חייב] פשוט' היא ומקשינן (לרבא) [לרבה] מתנית' דקתני ארבעים חסר אחת ואמר ר' יוחנן עלה שאם עשאן כולם בהעלם אחד חייב על כל אחת ואחת ולא משכחת כהאי גוונא דחייב בכולן אלא בזדון שבת ושגגת מלאכות בשלמא לאביי דאמר כי האי גוונא חייב [כו'] [וקא טעה] בשיעורין כגון זריקת ב' אמות וזריקת ד' וכיוצא בהן אלא (לרבא) [לרבה] דאמר כל כה"ג פטור היכי משכחת [לה] בזדון [שבת] ושגגת מלאכה הניחא אליבא דר' יוחנן דאמר כיון ששגג בכרת אע"פ שהזיד בלאו משכחת לה דידע דאיסור השבת בלאו אלא לר"ל דאמר עד שישגג בלאו וכרת היכי משכחת לה ושנינן דידע לה בתחומין ואליבא דר' עקיבא כמו שאמרנו למעלה. דאביי אליבא דר' יוחנן פשוטה היא אלא אפילו לריש לקיש כיון דסבר אביי כשנתכוון למקצת האיסור בשגגת איסורו ונזדמן לו כל האיסור חייב כגון המתכוון לזרוק ב' אמות שהן מקצת איסורו כי האיסור ד' אמות ונתכוון לזרוק שתים מתוך ארבע (וניזורק) [ונזדמן] לו שורק ד' חייב. מוקים לה אליבא דר"ל במכיר את השבת באיסור מלאכות ויודע (בשיעורן) [בכולן] ושוגג בלאו שבשיעור: אבות מלאכות ארבעים חסר אחת למה

מסורת הש"ס

[ב"ק כו: ע"ש]

[לעיל סט. ע:]

לעיל ו: מט: סע. ע: לקמן לו: ב"ק ב. [כריתות ב:]

[פי' מותח חוטי השתי]

[לקמן קה.]

לעיל ב: [שבועות ה:]

הגהות הב"ח

(א) גמ' רבא אמר פטור דהא לא קמיכוין: (ב) שם תרתי לא מיזדרקא ליה: (ג) שם משכח' לה דידע לאיסורא דשבת וידע לה לאיסור מלאכות: (ד) תוס' ד"ה אלא וכו' לשל חולין ונמצאת אחרת והיא של קדשים וכו' תלוש זה ונמצא מחובר אחר ולא: (ה) בא"ד בשאר מצות כגון הבא על הזכור והביא עליו זכור והבא על הבהמה. נ"ב עי' פרק ד' מיתות דנ"ד:

גמ' מנינא למה לי *א"ר יוחנן *שאם עשאן כולם בהעלם אחד חייב על כל אחת ואחת: הזורע והחורש: מכדי מכרב כרבי ברישא ליתני חורש והדר ליתני זורע *תנא בארץ ישראל קאי דזרעי ברישא והדר כרבי תנא הזורע והזומר והנוטע והמבריך והמרכיב כולן מלאכה אחת הן מאי קמ"ל *[הא קמ"ל] העושה מלאכות הרבה מעין מלאכה אחת אינו חייב אלא אחת א"ר *אחא א"ר חייא בר אשי א"ר אמי זומר חייב משום נוטע והנוטע והמבריך והמרכיב חייב משום זורע משום זורע אין משום נוטע לא אימא אף משום זורע אמר *רב כהנא זומר וצריך לעצים חייב שתים אחת משום קוצר ואחת משום נוטע א"ר יוסף האי מאן דקטל אספסתא חייב שתים אחת משום קוצר ואחת משום נוטע אמר אביי האי מאן דקניב סילקא חייב שתים אחת משום קוצר ואחת משום (א) זורע: והחורש: תנא החורש והחופר והחורץ כולן מלאכה אחת הן אמר רב ששת היתה לו גבשושית ונטלה בבית חייב משום בונה בשדה חייב משום חורש *אמר רבא היתה לו גומא וטממה בבית חייב משום בונה בשדה(ב) משום חורש *אמר רבי אבא החופר גומא בשבת ואינו צריך אלא לעפרה פטור עליה ואפילו לרבי יהודה דאמר *מלאכה שאינה צריכה לגופה חייב עליה ה"מ מתקן האי מקלקל הוא: והקוצר: תנא הקוצר הבוצר *והגודר והמסיק והאורה כולן מלאכה אחת אמר רב פפא האי מאן דשדא פיסא לדיקלא ואתר תמרי חייב שתים אחת משום תולש ואחת משום מפרק רב אשי אמר אין דרך תלישה בכך ואין דרך פריקה בכך: והמעמר: אמר *רבא האי מאן דכניף מילחא ממלחתא חייב משום מעמר אביי אמר אין עימור אלא בגידולי קרקע: והדש: תנא הדש והמנפץ *והמנפט כולן מלאכה אחת הן: הזורה הבורר והטוחן והמרקד: היינו זורה היינו בורר היינו מרקד אביי ורבא דאמרי תרוייהו כל מילתא דהויא במשכן

אע"ג

גמ' מנינא למה לי. ליתני הבות מלאכות הזורע והחורש כו' ולגא חזינא לי ארבעין *ניניהו: שאם עשאן כו'. ובא להודיעך שאם נתעלמו כל הלכות שבת ממנו(ג) חייב כמה חטאות עליו: מכרב כרבי. חורשין: בה"י. קשה היא ואין יכול לכסות בלא חרישה ואשמעינן דהא נמי חרישה היא כולן מלאכה אחת הן. דזומר נמי לצמוחי אילנא הוא ונפקא מינה דאי עבד ליה כולן בהדי זורע לא מיחייב אלא חדא דהעושה מלאכות הרבה כו' זורע אב מלאכה ונוטע נמי אב מלאכה הוא דהיינו זורע אלא שזה בזרעים וזה באילנות וכן מבריך ומרכיב אבל זומר תולדה: זומר חייב. משום תולדת נוטע דלצמוחי עביד: ונוטע. גופיה וכן מבריך ומרכיב: חייב משום זורע. כלומר אינהו נמי זורע הן זה אב בזרעים וזה אב באילנות: משום נוטע לא. אמבריך ומרכיב קאי: אימא אף משום זורע. דהך זריעה באילנות ואי עביד ליה בהדי זורע מיחייב חדא ותו לא: זומר. להצמיח הגפן: וצריך לעצים. להסקה משום דצריך להם הויא תולדה דקוצר דצריך נמי לקצור: דקטל אספסתא. שחת וקוצרין אותו ג' פעמים בחדש וחוזר וצומח: דקניב סילקא. חותך תרדין מן המחובר וחוזרין וגדלין: החורץ. עושה חריצין בקרקע: מלאכה אחת הן. אינו חייב אלא אחת דכולהו לרפויי ארעא עבידי: גבשושית. תל קטן: בבית. שייך בנין שמתכוין להשוות קרקעיתו: משום חורש. דמרפי ארעא: גומא וטממה. בעפר היינו חורש שהעפר שמילאה בו הוי רפוי וטוב לזריעה והשוה לקרקע להיות נזרע עם השדה: אלא לעפרה. לכסות צואה: פטור עליה. ואין כאן משום בנין בבית דקלקול הוא ולזריעה נמי לא חזיא אבל אם היה צריך לה חייב משום בונה: לרבי יהודה. בפרק המצניע (לקמן צג:) גבי מוציא את המת במטה: מתקן. כמו מוציא את המת לקוברו אינו צריך לגופה דהוצאה ולא לגוף אלא לפנות ביתו והוצאה הצריכה לגופה כגון שהוא צריך לחפץ זה במקום אחר: מקלקל הוא. את ביתו: גודר. בתמרים: ומוסק. בזיתים: אורה. בתאנים: דשדא פיסא לדיקלא. זרק פיסת רגבים לדקל: ואתר תמרי. השיר התמרים: תולש. תולדה דקוצר: מפרק. תולדה דדש שמפרק תבואה משבליה לשון פורק מן החמור דיסקארגיי"ר בלע"ז רבינו לוי וגם בתשובת רבינו משולם הגאון מצאתי כן ואף זה מפרק התמרים מן המכבדות: אין דרך תלישה ופריקה בכך. על ידי זריקה אלא או ביד או בכלי ותולש כלאחר יד הוא ופטור: דכניף מלחא ממלחתא. שצבר מלח ממשרפות מים דמתרגמינן חרילי ימא (יהושע יא) שממשיך לתוכו מים מן הים והחמה שורפתן והן נעשין מלח ואותו חריץ קרי מילחתא: משום מעמר. שאף הוא כמאסף בשבלין הוא: המנפץ. פשתן בגבעולין: והמנפט. נמר גפן בקשת כדרך האומנין ולמר גפן גידולי קרקע הוא להכי קרי ניפוט דיליה תולדה דדש שמפרק גרעינין ממנו ולא קרי ליה תולדת מנפץ דלמר: ה"ג היינו זורה היינו בורר היינו מרקד. היינו. כמו הי ניהו כלומר דמפליג להו תנא דמתניתין לתלת והלא כולן מלאכה אחת הן דמפרים אוכל מן הפסולת:

אע"ג

מכדי מכרב כרבי ברישא והדר כו'. לא שייך למידק הכי בהא דקתני המכבה ברישא והדר המבעיר דהכא כל סידורא דפת נקט כסדר לבד מחרישה: משום זורע. אין להוכיח מכאן דצריך להתרות אתולדה משום אב דהא לא קאמר שצריך להתרותו משום זורע אלא דאם התרה בו משום זורע דחייב אבל בריש פרק תולין (לקמן קלח.) משמע קצת דצריך להתרות אתולדה משום אב דקאמר משמר משום מאי מתרינן ביה (שיהא חייב) רבה אמר משום בורר רבי זירא אמר משום מרקד וגם זה יש לדחות דהכי פירושו משום מאי מתרינן ביה שיהא חייב רבה אמר משום בורר אבל אם התרו בו משום מרקד פטור כיון דמתרהו משום דבר שאינו דומה לו הוא סבר שהוא מלעיג בו ופטור אבל אם התרה בו סתם אל תאמר חייב ונראה שגם ר"ח רוצה לפרש כן ועוד ראיה דבריש בבא קמא (דף ב.) קאמר ולר' אליעזר דמחייב אתולדה במקום אב אמאי קרי ליה אב ואמאי קרי ליה תולדה ולא משני דלהכי קרי ליה אב דצריך להתרות אתולדה [משום] אב*:

זומר וצריך לעצים חייב שתים. והא דאמר בפ' זה בורר (סנהדרין דף כו.) תו חזיוה להאי גברא דהוה קא כסח אמר להן כהן וחמור אמרו ליה יכול לומר לעקל בית הבד אני צריך אף על גב דהכא אמר חייב משום נוטע התם מיירי בכה"ג שאין האילן מיתקן בכך אלא מתקלקל:

וצריך לעצים. נראה דאפילו לר' יהודה דמחייב מלאכה שאינה צריכה לגופה בעינן צריך לעצים דלא מיקרי בעצים קוצר אלא בענין זה *מידי דהוה אקורע על מנת לתפור ומוחק על מנת לכתוב וכדאמר רבי יוחנן לקמן בפ' חבית (דף קמה.) אחד כבשים ואחד שלקות שסחטן לגופן מותר למימיהן חייב חטאת ואמאי שרי לגופן ליהוי כמלאכה שאינה צריכה לגופה אלא טעמא לפי שאין דרך דישה בכך:

ואחת משום מפרק. אין נראה לר"י כמו שמפרש רש"י שמפרק האילן ממשאו מן הפירות שעליו אלא כמו שפירש רבינו שמואל שיש על התמרים קליפה העליונה וכשהוא מכה בתמרים מפרק את הקליפה מן התמרים והוי כמו דש שמפרק את התבואה מן השבולת:

מפרק. פירש"י דהוה תולדה דדש וקשה לר"ת דבשילהי המצניע (לקמן צה.) אמר דהולב חייב משום מפרק ואי הוה תולדה דדש הא אמר לקמן* גבי הפוצע חלזון דלרבנן אין דישה אלא בגידולי קרקע ואין לומר דדוקא חלזון שהוא דג פטרי רבנן דלא הוי גידולי קרקע אבל בחולב מחייבי דבהמה חשיבא גידולי קרקע כדמוכח בריש בכל מערבין (עירובין דף כז:) דהא [ע"כ טעמא דרבנן משום] דילפינן להו מסממנין שבמשכן דאין דישה אלא בגידולי קרקע *לגבי דבר הגדל ממש מן הקרקע לא חשיבא בהמה גידולי קרקע כדאמרינן בהשוכר את הפועלים (ב"מ פט:) מה דיש מיוחד שהוא גידולי קרקע ופועל אוכל בו אף כל כו' יצא החולב והמגבן כו' ודוחק לומר דברייתא דהמצניע אתיא כר"י דפליג לקמן אדרבנן ונראה לר"ת דמפרק חייב משום ממחק דכשהולב ממחק את הדד ומחליקו ואין נראה לר"י דבפרק חבית (לקמן קמד:) אמרינן חולב אדם לתוך הקדרה אבל לא לתוך הקערה ולר"ת מה לי לתוך הקדרה מה לי לתוך הקערה ולפירוש הקונטרס א"ש דמעיקרא כשהיה בדדין חשיב אוכל וכשחולב לתוך הקדרה (דהשתא) כמי הוי אוכל ולא דמי לדש שנשתנה ונראה דלפירוש הקונטרס הלכה כרבי יהודה דהאמר בפרק אע"פ (כתובות ס.) *)אמר רבי מריטום גונח יונק חלב בשבת מ"ט מפרק כלאחר יד הוא ובמקום צער לא גזרו רבנן ופסיק התם רב יוסף הלכתא כרבי מריטום ואין נראה לומר דאף לרבנן אסור מדרבנן דמיחזי כמפרק ואף על גב דלא אסירא אלא מדרבנן לא שרי אלא משום דאיכא תרתי כלאחר יד ובמקום צער: [ועי' תוס' כתובות ס. ד"ה מפרק ותוס' יבמות קיד. ד"ה וקבבר]

*) נ"ל תני

כט א מיי' פ"ז מהלכות שבת הלכה ח ופ"ו מהלכות שגגות הלכה ג:
ל ב מיי' פ"ז מהל' שבת הלכה ג והלכה ט:
לא ג מיי' פ"ח מהלכות שבת הלכה ג:
לב ד שם הלכה ד:
לג ה מיי' פ"ז מהלכות שבת הלכה ג:
לד ו מיי' פ"ח מהלכות שבת הלכה ה:
לה ז מיי' פ"ח מהלכות שבת הלכה יז:
לו ח מיי' פ"ח מהלכות שבת הלכה ד סמג לאוין סה:
לז ט מיי' פ"ח שם הל' ... סמג שם טוש"ע או"ח סימן ש"מ סעיף ט:
לח י מיי' פ"ח מהלכות שבת הלכה ... סמג שם:

[ועי' תוס' לקמן צו: ד"ה זר"א דמחייב ותוס' ב"ק ב. ד"ה ולר"א]

רבינו חננאל

למה לי למיתנא מנינא [ס"ל] חסר אחת אמו עד האידנא מי לא ידעינן מניינו ומשני ר' יוחנן שאם עשאן כולם בהעלם אחד חייב על כל אחת ואחת. (ת"ש) [תנא] הזורע והזומר והנוטע והמבריך והמרכיב כולן מלאכה אחת הן (ק"ד) [קמ"ל] כי העושה מלאכות הרבה מעין מלאכה אחת אינו חייב אלא אחת. שמעי' מינה שאלו השנויים במשנתנו חשובין אבות והשאר הן תולדות וכל העושה אב ותולדתו אינו חייב אלא אחת. והעושה ב' אבות תולדות דלאו אב אהד [חייב] שתים. ומיפרשא בגמ' דהזורק דר' אלעזר מחייב אתולדה במקום אב דידיה תרתי ולית הלכתא כוותיה. ואסיק' מדוקיא דמתני' דאמר דעביד כל מלאכות שבעולם ואפילו אלף מלאכות אינו חייב יותר מארבעים חסר אחת המאות שהכל נכללים בכלל אבות ותולדותיהן הללו: ירושלמי כל דבר שהוא משביח הפרי חייב משום זורע. המבריך. המרכיב. והמקרסם. הזורד. המפסל. המזהם. המפרק. המעשן. המתליע. המקטף. הסך. המשקה. המנקב. והעושה בתים. חייב משום זורע. אמרינן משמיה דרב הזומר חייב משום נוטע והנוטע והמבריך והמרכיב חייב משום זורע. שמעינן מינה מדוקים המבריך והמרכיב משום נוטע ואף משום זורע דיש תולדה לתולדה. וכולן נכללין בכלל אב אהד. הנוטע וולד הוא של זורע. כי הנוטע נועץ יחור של אילן בארץ ומתגדל כגון המפיל הזרע לארץ וצומח והזומר המקום שזומר באילן מתגדל המקום ההוא ומוסיף פירות ונמצא כנוטע לפיכך אמרינ' בזומר חייב (שתים) משום נוטע ואם הוא זומר וצריך לעצים ונמצא כשזומר חייב משום נוטע כמו שאמרנו ובנטילתו העצים נמצא כקוצר. לפיכך בזומר וצריך לעצים חייב שתים. משום נוטע ומשום קוצר וכן מאן דקטיל אספסתא ומאן דקניב סילקא כולן דרך אחת הן וחייב שתים. בזמן שיש שיעור קצירה ושיעור זריעה. פי' המבריך החופר בארץ ומבריך הייחור וטומנו לעפר ומוציא ראש הייחור במקום רחוק. ההורש' החורץ. החופר כולן מלאכה אחת הן. אסיקנא כל אלו משום חרישה. כל שהיא ליפות הקרקע בשדה חייב משום חורש וכל שהן בבית להשוות חייב משום בונה. אבל להשוות קרקע השדה חייב משום חורש. כדכתיב הלא אם שוה פניה. והוא כגון המדייר והמעדר והמכבד שהוא משוה גומות והמפעפע עפר. המזבל. המכלא בקוצים שתחת הזרע. העושה נקבים לקנים. המבריך בארץ. הקנים ובאנם תמרים. ואמת המים המכשרת צדדים לזריעה. וכל דבר שהוא להנאת קרקע השדה חייב משום חורש. ...

רב נסים גאון

ואפילו לר' יהודה דאמר מלאכה שאינה צריכה לגופה חייב עליה הני מילי מתקן והאי מקלקל הוא כבר פירשנו בפרק א' עיקר דבריו של ר' יהודה אבל מקלקל הוא והוא שנינו במשנה בפרק ר' אליעזר אומר האורג (לקמן דף קה) וכל המקלקלין פטורין:

[נ"ל חסר אחת ניינהו]
[לעיל סט. וש"נ כריתות ג:]
[גיטין סה: ב"ב יט.]
גי' רש"ל
[נ"ל אבא עי' רש"ל בסוגיא דלעיל לב. ד"ה גמלא סימן וכו']
[מו"ק ב:]
[לקמן צד: פ"ג]
[לעיל יב. לא: לקמן קה. קז. קכא: חגיגה י.]
[לעיל יב. לא. לקמן קה. קכא: עי' תוס' לקמן לה. ד"ה את המת וחגיגה י.]
[גי' הרמב"ם והרא"ש והר"ן רבה וכן מוכח ממ"ש לעיל עה: על הגליון]
[נ"ל המנפס פי' גאון המנפס הוא המכה מן עפרורית את חיי משום דש וכן המנפס בכולים ע"כ ל' הערוך ערך נפס]

הגהות הב"ח

(א) גמ' דקניב סילקא וכו' ואחת משום נוטע והחורש:
(ב) שם בשדה חייב משום חורש:
(ג) רש"י ד"ה שאם עשאן וכו' כל הלכות שבת ממנו כמה חטאות חייב עליו:

גליון הש"ס

תוס' ד"ה וצריך וכו' מידי דהוי ע"מ להפור. מבואר דס"ל דלזמא כדילא ... זה ... דלקמן דף קז ע"ב ... דלריך לאיזה דבר מ"מ פטור ואפילו לר"י דס"ל שאינו ע"מ להפור לא מקרי מלאכה המובה וכ"כ מדברי הכ"מ פ"י הלכה י מהלכות שבת וק"ל מסוגיא דלקמן דף קד ע"ב גם במ"ש תוספות דלפי' לר"י דמשמע פשיטא דניחא ק"ל הא פשיטא דניחא ליה בעלים להשתמש בהם אלא דעתו אינו עושה כן בבלי מ"מ מיקרי צריכה לגופה כהיה דלקמן דף קג בתולש עולשין בארעא דלאו דיליה: לגבי דבר הגדל ממש. עי' ברה"ש בפרשת וישלח בפסוק ויהי לי שור וחמור: תוס' ד"ה מפרק וכו'

GEMARA. [73*b*] Why state the number?—Said R. Joḥanan: [To teach] that if one performs them all in one state of unawareness, he is liable on account of each separately.

SOWING AND PLOUGHING. Let us see: ploughing is done first, then let him [the Tanna] state PLOUGHING first and then SOWING?—The Tanna treats of[7] Palestine, where they first sow and then plough.

A Tanna taught: Sowing, pruning, planting, bending,[8] and grafting are all one labour.[9] What does this inform us?—This: that if one performs many labours of the same nature, he is liable only to one [sacrifice]. R. Abba[10] said in the name of R. Ḥiyya b. Ashi in R. Ammi's name: He who prunes is culpable on account of planting, while he who plants, bends [the vine], or grafts is culpable on account of sowing. On account of sowing only but
a not on account of planting?[1]—Say: on account of planting too.[2]

R. Kahana said: If one prunes and needs the wood [too], he is liable to two [penalties],[3] one on account of reaping[4] and one on account of planting.[5] R. Joseph said: He who cuts hay is liable to two [penalties], one on account of reaping and the other on account of planting.[6] Abaye said: He who trims beets [in the ground] is liable to two [penalties], one on account of reaping[7] and one on account of planting.[8]

PLOUGHING. A Tanna taught: Ploughing, digging, and trenching are all one [form of] work.[9] R. Shesheth said: If one has a mound [of earth] and removes it, in the house, he is liable on the score of building;[10] if in the field, he is liable on the score of ploughing. Raba said: If one has a depression and fills it up: if in the house, he is liable on account of building; if in the field, he is liable on account of ploughing.[11]

R. Abba said: If one digs a pit on the Sabbath, needing only the earth thereof,[12] he is not culpable on its account. And even according to R. Judah, who ruled: One is liable on account of a labour which is not required on its own account:[13] that is only when he effects an improvement, but this man causes damage.[14]

REAPING: A Tanna taught: Reaping, vintaging, gathering [dates], collecting [olives], and gathering [figs] are all one [form of] labour. R. Papa said: He who throws a clod of earth at a palm tree and dislodges dates is liable to two [penalties], one on account of
b detaching[1] and one on account of stripping.[2] R. Ashi said: This is not the mode of detaching, nor is it the mode of stripping.[3]

BINDING SHEAVES. Raba[4] said: He who collects salt out of a salina[5] is liable on the score of binding sheaves.[6] Abaye said: Binding sheaves applies only to products of the soil.

THRESHING. It was taught: Threshing, beating [flax in their stalks], and beating [cotton] are all the same form of work.

WINNOWING, SELECTING, GRINDING AND SIFTING. But winnowing, selecting, and sifting are identical?[7]—Abaye and Raba both said: Whatever was performed in [connection with

(7) Lit., 'stands in'—all the Tannaim, of course, were Palestinians. (8) Bending a vine for drawing it into the ground and making it grow as an independent plant (Jast.). (9) Involving only one liability if performed at the same time. (10) So text as amended.

a (1) Surely bending and grafting are forms of planting?—Planting and sowing are identical, the former applying to trees and the latter to cereals. (2) Hence if he grafts and sows, he is only liable to one penalty. (3) I.e., sin-offerings, if done unwittingly. (4) Cutting wood from a tree for its use is a derivative of reaping. (5) Pruning is done to enable what is left to grow more freely, and thus it is a derivative of planting. (6) The hay is cut so that new grass can grow, and thus it is a derivative of planting (i.e., sowing) too. (7) Because the beets he cuts constitute a harvest. (8) As in n. a5. (9) Involving only one liability if performed at the same time. (10) For he thereby levels the floor, which is part of building. (11) For he thereby prepares the ground for sowing. (12) But not the pit itself. (13) V. *supra* 12*a*, 31*b*. (14) He spoils the ground by the pit.

b (1) That which is attached to the soil, the clod being taken up from the soil. (2) Rashi: the tree of a burden, *sc.* the dates. Ri: the dates of their outer skin. In both cases this is a derivative of threshing, which separates the grain from the chaff. (3) Hence he is not liable on either score. (4) Maim. and Asheri read: Rabbah. (5) A salt deposit, formed by causing sea water to flow into a trench; the water evaporates through the heat of the sun, leaving the salt. Raba refers to this action of directing the water into the trench. (6) It partakes of the same nature, and ranks as a derivative thereof. (7) All consist of separating fit from unfit food.

the erection of] the Tabernacle, [74*a*] even if there are [labours] similar thereto, is counted [separately].[8] Then let him also enumerate pounding [wheat]?[9]—Said Abaye: Because a poor man eats his bread without pounding.[10] Raba said: This agrees with Rabbi, who said: The primary labours are forty less one; but if pounding were enumerated, there would be forty.[11] Then let one of these be omitted and pounding be inserted? Hence it is clear [that it must be explained] as Abaye [does].

Our Rabbis taught: If various kinds of food lie before one, he may select and eat, select and put aside; but he must not select, and if he does, he incurs a sin-offering. What does this mean? —Said 'Ulla, This is its meaning: He may select to eat on the same day, and he may select and put aside for the same day; but he must not select for [use on] the morrow, and if he does, he incurs a sin-offering. R. Ḥisda demurred: Is it then permitted to bake for [use on] the same day, or is it permitted to cook for the same day?[1] Rather said R. Ḥisda: He may select and eat less than the standard quantity, and he may select and put aside less than the standard quantity;[2] but he must not select as much as the standard quantity, and if he does, he incurs a sin-offering. R. Joseph demurred: Is it then permitted to bake less than the standard quantity?[3] Rather said R. Joseph: He may select by hand and eat, or select by hand and put aside; but he may not select with a reed-basket or a dish; and if he does, he is not culpable, nevertheless it is forbidden.[4] He may not select with a sieve or a basket-sieve, and if he does he incurs a sin-offering.[5] R. Hamnuna demurred: Are then a reed-basket and a dish mentioned?—Rather said R. Hamnuna: He may select and eat, [taking the] eatable from the non-eatable, and he may select and put aside, [taking] the eatable from the non-eatable. But he must not select the non-eatable out of the eatable, and if he does, he incurs a sin-offering.[6] Abaye demurred: Is it then taught, 'the eatable from the non-eatable'? Rather said Abaye: He may select and eat immediately, and he may select and put aside for immediate use;[7] but he may not select for [later consumption on] the same day, and if he does, it is regarded as though he were selecting for [making] a store, and he incurs
b a sin-offering.[1] The Rabbis reported this to Raba. Said he to them, Naḥmani[2] has said well.

If two kinds of food lie before a person, and he selects and eats or selects and puts aside,[3]—R. Ashi learnt: He is not culpable: R. Jeremiah of Difti[4] learnt: He is culpable. 'R. Ashi learnt: He is not culpable'! but it was taught:[5] 'He is culpable'?—There is no difficulty: the one treats of a reed-basket and a plate;[6] the other refers to a sieve and a basket-sieve.

When R. Dimi came,[7] he related: It was R. Bibi's Sabbath,[8] and R. Ammi and R. Assi chanced to be there. He cast a basket of fruit before them,[9] and I do not know whether it was because he held that it is forbidden to pick out the eatable from the non-eatable, or whether he wished to be generous.[10]

Hezekiah said: One who picks lupines [after boiling] out of their husks[11] is culpable. Shall we say that Hezekiah holds that it is forbidden to select the eatable from the non-eatable?

(8) What constitutes primary labours is learnt from the Tabernacle (v. 49*b*). All these labours were needed for the Tabernacle in the wilderness; hence they are counted separately. (9) In a mortar, to remove the husk. Drugs were pounded in connection with the Tabernacle for dyes. (10) Hence it is omitted, for the Tanna evidently follows the general order of making bread, and bread for the poor is prepared with the husk of the wheat. But it is certainly a primary labour forbidden on the Sabbath. (11) Rabbi deduces even the number of labours from Scripture (v. *infra* 97*b*).

(1) Surely not! And since you say that selecting for use on the *next* day entails a sin-offering, it is a forbidden labour in the full sense of the term, and hence prohibited even if required for the *same* day. (2) For which a penalty is incurred, viz., as much as a dried fig. (3) Granted that there is no penalty, it is nevertheless forbidden, and the same applies here. (4) There is no liability, because this is not the proper mode of selecting; nevertheless it is forbidden, because it is somewhat similar to selecting by means of a sieve. (5) Because this is the usual mode of sifting, and it is therefore a primary labour, as stated in the Mishnah. For a description of the *nafah* v. Aboth, Chap. V, Mish. 15. (6) The former is not the ordinary mode of sifting, while the latter is. (7) I.e., immediately he finishes putting aside he will consume what is eatable.

b (1) But the former does not constitute sifting and is entirely permissible. (2) A familiar name of Abaye, because he was brought up in the house of Rabbah b. Naḥmani. V. however, Git., 34*b*, n. 6. (3) For another to eat. The two kinds were mixed up, and he selected the kind he desired. (4) V. *supra* 10*a*, n. b5. (5) *Supra*. (6) When the selecting is done by these, he is not culpable. (7) V. *supra* 5*a*, n. b9. (8) It was his turn that Sabbath to wait on the scholars. (9) שדא denotes to put down with some violence. He did this instead of first separating the leaves from the fruit, as they would fall away automatically through the force of his setting it down. (10) Hence placed a large quantity before them. (11) Lit., 'refuse'.

אע"ג דאיכא דדמיא לה חשיב לה וליחשב נמי כותש אמר אביי שכן עני אוכל פתו בלא כתישה רבא אמר הא מני רבי היא דאמר אבות מלאכות ארבעים חסר אחת ואי חשיב כותש הויא ליה ארבעים וליפוק חדא מהנך ולעייל כותש אלא מחוורתא כדאביי: ת"ר היו לפניו מיני אוכלין בורר ואוכל בורר ומניח ולא יברור ואם בירר חייב חטאת מאי קאמר אמר עולא הכי קאמר בורר ואוכל לבו ביום ובורר ומניח לבו ביום ולמחר לא יברור ואם בירר חייב חטאת מתקיף לה רב חסדא וכי מותר לאפות לבו ביום וכי מותר לבשל לבו ביום אלא אמר רב חסדא בורר ואוכל פחות מכשיעור בורר ומניח פחות מכשיעור וכשיעור לא יברור ואם בירר חייב חטאת מתקיף לה רב יוסף וכי מותר לאפות פחות מכשיעור אלא אמר רב יוסף א) בורר ואוכל ביד בורר ומניח ביד בקנון ובתמחוי לא יברור ואם בירר פטור אבל אסור ובנפה ובכברה לא יברור ואם בירר חייב חטאת מתקיף לה רב המנונא מידי קנון ותמחוי קתני אלא אמר רב המנונא ב) בורר ואוכל אוכל מתוך הפסולת בורר ומניח אוכל מתוך הפסולת ג) פסולת מתוך אוכל לא יברור ואם בירר חייב חטאת מתקיף לה אביי מידי אוכל מתוך פסולת קתני אלא אמר אביי ד) בורר ואוכל לאלתר ובורר ומניח לאלתר ולבו ביום לא יברור ואם בירר נעשה כבורר לאוצר וחייב חטאת אמרוה רבנן קמיה דרבא אמר להו *שפיר אמר נחמני ה) היו לפניו שני מיני אוכלין ובירר ואכל ובירר והניח רב אשי מתני פטור רבי ירמיה מדיפתי מתני חייב רב אשי מתני פטור והא תני חייב לא קשיא הא בקנון ותמחוי הא בנפה וכברה כי אתא רב דימי אמר שבתא דרב ביבי הואי ואיקלעו רבי אמי ור' אסי שדא קמייהו כלכלה דפירי ולא ידענא אי משום דסבר אוכל מתוך פסולת אסור אי משום עין יפה הוא דמכוין חזקיה אמר ו) הבורר תורמוסים מתוך פסולת שלהן חייב לימא קסבר חזקיה אוכל מתוך פסולת אסור שאני תורמוסים דשלקי

אע"ג דאיכא. אחריתי בהדה דדמיא לה חשבינהו לתרווייהו כאבות ואע"ג דחדא נינהו: וליחשב נמי כותש. חטין במכתשת להסיר קליפתן דהואי במקדש בסממנין אלא לאו משום דדמיא לדש לא חשיב לה דהא נמי מיפרקה מלבוש היא: שכן עני אוכל פתו בלא כתישה. לכך אע"ג דהואי במקדש ואב מלאכה היא כיון דתנא ליה דש לא תנא לה וזורה ובורר ומרקד סידורא דפת נינהו וכיון דהוו במקדש והכא אתחיל בסידורא דפת תנינהו כדאמרינן גבי אופה דה"ל למתני מבשל ולא אופה דלא הוה במקדש אלא משום סדורא דפת נקט ואתא הואיל ואופה בפת כמבשל בסממנין אבל כתישה עשירים הוא דלתתי וכתשי לעשות סלת נקיה אבל עניים לא טרחי הלכך לא תנא לה ומיהו ודאי אב מלאכה היא ובכלל דש היא: רבי היא. דיליף לקמן בפרק הזורק (דף צז:) דברים הדברים אלה הדברים למנייגא: וליפוק חדא מהנך. או זורה או בורר או מרקד דהוו חדא ליפוק מינייהו חדא וליתני הך דהכי עדיף למיתני תרתי מהא ותרתי מהא מלמיתני ולמיכפל תלתא זימני בחדא ואיכא חדא דלא כפיל ביה מידי: היו לפניו מיני אוכלין גרסי' ול"ג שני: ולא יברור. לקמיה פריך מאי קאמר ברישא תנא בורר והדר תנא לא יברור: ולמחר. לצורך מחר: וכי מותר לאפות ולבשל לבו ביום. וה"נ אב מלאכה היא כיון דאמרת ולמחר חייב חטאת: פחות מכשיעור. פחות מכגרוגרת: וכי מותר לאפות פחות מכשיעור. נהי דחיוב חטאת ליכא איסורא מיהא איכא דקיימא לן חצי שיעור אסור מן התורה בפרק בתרא דיומא (דף עד.) והיכי קתני בורר לכתחלה: בקנון. כלי עץ שעושין כעין ליצור רחב מלאחריו וקצר מלפניו ובעלי מטבע עושים אותו והבורר בו קטנית נותן קטנית במקום הרחב ומנענעו והקטנית מפני שהוא סגלגל מתגלגל ויורד דרך פיו הקצר והפסולת נשאר בכלי: פטור אבל אסור. מותר לכתחלה לא הוי דדמי לברירה וחייב חטאת לא הוי דכלאחר יד הוא דעיקר ברירה בנפה וכברה אבל ביד לא דמי לבורר כלל: מידי קנון ותמחוי קתני. ה"ה נמי דפריך מידי נפה וכברה קתני אלא חדא מינייהו נקט: אוכל מתוך הפסולת. לא דרך ברירה היא: ובורר ומניח לאלתר. לאכול לאלתר שאין זה דרך בוררין: לאוצר. להצניע: נחמני. אביי: והתניא. לעיל חייב ואי בבורר ומניח לאלתר מותר לכתחלה הויא ופטור אבל אסור ליכא: שבתא דרב ביבי הואי. הגיע יומו להיות עומד ומשמש על התלמידים: ושדא קמייהו. ולא רצה לברור האוכל מתוך העלין ולתת לפני כל אחד ואחד אלא שטחן והם נוטלים ואוכלים ובשטוח זה נפרש האוכל מאליו: הבורר תורמוסין. לאחר ששלקן הוא בורר אוכל מתוך הקליפה: דשלקי

אע"ג דאיכא דדמיא לה חשיב (א). והא דלא חשיב שובט ומדקדק לפי שהם לגמרי בכלל מיסך ואורג ולא חשיב נמי מנפץ אע"ג שבמשכן היו מנפצין פשתן לעשות יריעות ושאר דברים משום דהייט דש ממש אלא שזה בתבואה וזה בפשתן אבל זורה ובורר ומרקד הם שלשה דברים:

שכן עני אוכל פתו בלא כתישה. וא"ת מ"מ ליחשיב כתישת סממנין דהוה במשכן ואע"ג דעני אוכל פתו בלא כתישה לענין סממנים מלאכה חשובה היא ואומר ר"י דלאו דוקא אוכל פתו אלא ה"ה דעני צובע בסממנים בלא כתישה וא"ת מרקד נמי לא ליתני שכן עני אוכל פתו בעיסה בלוסה כדאמר בסוף פרקין ויש לומר דרוב עניים אין אוכלין בלא הרקדה אלא שלענין חלה מצטרפין הסובין דקרינן ביה מלחם הארץ כיון דיש עניים שאוכלים בעיסה בלוסה ור"ת פירש בע"א ולא נתיישב לר"י:

היו לפניו שני מיני אוכלין גרסי'. וכן פירש ר"ח דבאוכל מתוך אוכל שייכא ברירה שבורר אותו שאינו חפץ לאכול מתוך אותו שרוצה לאכול דאותו שאינו חפץ בו חשיב פסולת לגבי אותו שחפץ לאכול וכן משמע בירושלמי דגרס הבורר אוכלים מתוך אוכלים חזקיה אמר כו':

בורר ומניח. פי' לצורך אחרים:

וכי מותר לאפות פחות מכשיעור. והמתרץ ס"ד דפחות מכשיעור הוי דרך אכילה:

מתקיף לה רב המנונא מידי קטן ותמחוי קתני. פי' הקונט' דה"נ הוה מצי למיפרך מידי נפה וכברה קתני וקשה לר"י מאי קמשני רב המנונא לדידיה נמי תקשה מידי [אוכל] מתוך פסולת קתני ועוד בסמוך פירש הקונטרס והתניא חייב דהייטו הך דהכא ומשני דבנפה וכברה מיירי והיכי משני הכא מידי נפה וכברה קתני ונראה לרביט יצחק דדוקא מקטן ותמחוי פריך וה"פ מידי קטן ותמחוי קתני כיון דנחת לפרושי דיני ברירה דביד מותר ובנפה וכברה חייב חטאת לא היה לו להניח מלשנות קטן ותמחוי דפטור אבל אסור:

בורר ואוכל אוכל מתוך פסולת. משמע דאוכל מתוך פסולת אין דרך ברירה בכך וקשה דבריש פרק תולין (לקמן קלח.) אמרי' מה דרכו (ב) של בורר בורר אוכל מתוך פסולת וי"ל דהתם בפסולת מרובה על האוכל הוי אוכל מתוך פסולת דרך ברירה דהתם במשמר איירי וקשה לרשב"א דתנן בפ"ק דביצה (דף יד:) הבורר קטניות בי"ט ב"ש אומרים בורר אוכל ואוכל וב"ה אומרים בורר כדרכו ואמר בגמרא בד"א כשהאוכל מרובה על הפסולת אבל פסולת מרובה על האוכל ד"ה נוטל את האוכל ומניח את הפסולת ואי בפסולת מרובה על האוכל הוי אוכל מתוך פסולת דרך ברירה היכי שרי לב"ש הא אינהו אסרי לברר כדרכו וצ"ע שם:

והתניא חייב. פי' בקונטרס דהייטו ברייתא דלעיל וקשה לר"י דלמאי דמוקמינן לה בנפה וכברה משמע דוקא לבו ביום אסור אבל לאלתר אפי' בנפה וכברה שרי ובפ"ק דביצה (גם זה שם.) משמע דבנפה וכברה אסור בכל ענין דתנן ב"ה אומרים בורר כדרכו בקטן ובתמחוי אבל לא בנפה ובכברה ולא מפליג בין לאלתר לבו ביום ועוד לכאורה לעולא דלעיל הוי בורר לבו ביום כמו לאלתר לאביי וא"כ שרי לעולא בנפה ובכברה אפי' לבו ביום ובמתני' דביצה אסר לכל הפחות לבו ביום ונראה לר"י דברייתא דלעיל איירי בבורר ביד והכא דמוקמי לה בנפה וכברה ברייתא אחריתי היא ואפי' לאלתר חייב חטאת וכן משמע מתוך פירוש ר"ח דפירש שיש ג' דינין בבורר לאלתר דביד מותר לכתחלה בקנון ובתמחוי פטור אבל אסור בנפה וכברה חייב חטאת:

ולא ידענא אי משום דקסבר אוכל מתוך פסולת אסור. פי' לא ידענא מה שלא בירר תחלה קודם שהביאם לפניהן אבל אין לפרש מה שלא בירר בשעה שהניח לפניהם דא"כ מאי קאמר אי משום דקסבר אוכל מתוך פסולת אסור דהא לכ"ע שרינן אוכל מתוך פסולת לאלתר:

הא

רבינו חננאל

חייב משום בונה ובשדה משום חורש וקיי"ל בהני כולה כרבה. (א"ר אבא החופר גומא ואין צריך). פי' גבשושית תל של עפר שהיתה לו ונטלה בבית חייב משום בונה כו'. [אמר ר' אבא החופר גומא ואין צריך] לחפור הפירה אלא לעפר בעלמא בלבד הוא צריך. נטילת העפר אינה מלאכה משום חפירה אינו חייב שהרי לא נתכוין לחפירה. ואפילו לר' יהודה דאמר מלאכה שאינה צריכה לגופה חייב עליה ה"מ במתקן אבל האי דחפר מקלקל הוא בין בבית א) בין בשדה. וכי האי מילתא אמרו בהכל הייבין בראיה (חגיגה י') שהן כהררי' התלויין בשערה. מקרא מעט והלכות מרובות: ת"ר הקוצר הבוצר הגודר האורה כולן מלאכה אחת הן. פי' פיסה צרור של אדמה ולענין הלכה כאן דשרא פיסא לדיקלא ואתר תמרי קיי"ל כרב אשי דאמר אין דרך תלישה ולא דרך פריקה בכך. הא דאמר רבה מאן דכניף מילחא ממלחתא חייב משום מעמר קי"ל כאביי דאמר אין עימור אלא בגידולי קרקע ואינו חייב אלא (כשמעמר) [כשמעביר] ד' אמות ברה"ר. הדש (תנא) [הוא] המפרק הפסולת המחוברת באוכל ומכינתו לברירה או כברת [בזרייה] או בהרקדה. המנפץ נופץ עפרורית מן האוכל וכן המנפס מולל שבלים נמצא זורה והבורר והמרקד כולן מעבירין פסולת המעורבות באוכל ואינה מחוברת (ואינה) כגון קליפה שצריכה פירוק או כגון עפרורית שצריך ניפוץ אלא מעורבת בלבד. וכן אם נטל בידו אדם תבוא' בתיבנא ובפסולת שיש בהו ניפחה בה ברוח פיו ובירר חשוב הוא כזורה. פי' בורר נוטל פסולת מבין האוכל ומשליכ' או נוטל האוכל ומניח הפסולת. מרקד שמטיל את האוכל והפסולת בכברה ונשארת האוכל ואם האוכל דק והפסולת עבה כמין תבן יוצא האוכל ונשארת הפסולת בכברה. וכיון דאסיק' כי הזורה והבורר והמרקד כולן מעין מלאכה אחת הן מפריש הפסולת מן האוכל ומשום דהוו במשכן הוו להו תלתא וחייב על כל אחת ואחת. ואקשינן ונחשוב נמי כותש שהוא מסיר

קליפת החיטין מעליהן לטחון אותם להוציא סולת כגון כותש לעשות דייסא או טיסני והנה גם זה מפריש פסולת מן האוכל הוא ומשני אביי שכן עני אוכל פתו בלא כתישה כלומר כל בני אדם טוחנין בחיטין שלהן סלת הנה דרך העניים לברור ולטחון ולעשות עיסה בלוסה ואין אוכלין סלת לפיכך אין צריכין כתישה ואע"פ דכתישה מלאכה היא דהא לגבי יו"ט גרסי' (ביצה יד.) אין כותשין במכתשת אע"פ שמותר ביו"ט אוכל נפש וכ"ש בשבת אמר אביי האי דלא חשיב לה בהדי אבות משום דלא חשיבא שלא כל אדם אוכל בכתישה כמו שאמרנו לפיכך אינה אלא כתולדות דמיא רבא אמר אמאי לא חשיב לכותש בהדייהו משום דמתניתין ר' (חייא) [היא] דאמר קבלה היא בידינו אבות מלאכות [ארבעים] חסר אחת כנגד ב) עבודת המשכן ור' מ' חסר אחת שנה וכבר פירשנו להא דר' בבמה סומכין (מט:) כי המלאכות הללו מן המשכן למדתן ואי חשיב כותש בהדייהו הוי להו מ' שלמות ור' מ' חסר אחת שנה לפי' לא תנא כותש בהדייהו ואקשינן וליפוק חדא מינייהו וניעול כותש ואסיק' אלא מחוורתא כדאביי: ת"ר היו לפניו ב' מיני אוכלין בורר ואוכל בורר ומניח ולא יברר ואם בירר חייב חטאת ומת' מאי קאמר [א'] עולא הכי קאמר בורר ואוכל בו ביום כו' ודחאה רב חסדא ואמר וכי מותר לאפות ולבשל בו ביום כו' ופרשה אביי בורר ואוכל לאלתר בורר ומניח לאלתר ג) שלא לאלתר לא יברור ואם בירר נעשה כבירר לאוצר וחייב חטאת וקיי"ל כוותיה דאמר רבה שפיר אמר נחמני לאלתר דאמר אביי כל זמן שיושב על השולחן ואוכל דגרסינן בתלמוד דא"י ברר אוכלין מתוך אוכלין חזקיה אמר חייב ר' יוחנן אמר פטור מתניתא פליגא על חזקיה דאמר בורר ואוכל בורר ומניח על השלחן רבין בר חייא אמר תפתר כשהיו אורחין אוכלין ראשונה ראשונה היו לפניו ב' מיני אוכלין בורר ואוכל בורר ומניח רב אשי [מתני פטור ר"מ] מתני חייב ואוקימנא להא דרב אשי בבורר בנפה או בכברה חייב חטאת בקנון ובתמחוי פטור וכל פטורי דשבת פטור אבל אסור נינהו וקיי"ל כרב אשי דבתראה הוא והא דאמר חזקיה הבורר תורמוסין מתוך פסולת שלהן חייב הלכתא היא דהא מקשינן

א) עי' תוס' פסחים מ"ז ע"ב ד"ה כתישה. ב) עי' בגמ' כאן ולעיל מ"ט ע"ב בתוס' וצ"ע. ג) מכאן ועד סוף הענין הובא בא"ז בשם רבינו.

עין משפט נר מצוה

לט א ב מיי' פ"ח מהל' שבת הלכה יב סמג לאוין סה טוש"ע א"ח סימן שיט סעיף א:
מ ג מיי' שם הלכה יג טוש"ע שם סעיף ד:
מא ד מיי' שם הלכה יב טוש"ע שם סעיף א ב:
מב ה מיי' שם הלכה יג טוש"ע שם סעיף ג:
מג ו מיי' שם טוש"ע שם סעיף ה:

מסורת הש"ס

[נדרים כד: וע"ש בר"ן טעם דקרי לאביי נחמני וע"ש פירש"י בגיטין לד:]

הגהות הב"ח

(א) תוס' ד"ה אע"ג וכו' חשיב לה והא דלא חשיב. נ"ב עיין לקמן בפ' הזורק דף צו ומכאן לעיל: (ב) ד"ה בורר וכו' דרכו של בורר נוטל אוכל ומניח פסולת:

גליון הש"ס

תוס' ד"ה אע"ג וכו' לפי שהם לגמרי בכלל מיסך. עי' לקמן דף עה ע"ב ברש"י ד"ה שוטה:

דשלקי ליה שבעא זימני ואי לא שקלי (א) ליה מסרח וכפסולת מתוך אוכל דמי: והטוחן: א"ר פפא *האי מאן דפרים סילקא חייב משום טוחן אמר רב מנשה האי מאן דסלית סילתי חייב משום טוחן אמר רב אשי אי קפיד אמשחתא חייב משום מחתך: והלש והאופה: אמר רב פפא שבק תנא דידן בישול סממנין דהוה במשכן ונקט אופה תנא דידן סידורא דפת נקט אמר רב אחא בר רב עוירא *האי מאן דשדא סיכתא לאתונא חייב משום מבשל פשיטא מהו דתימא לשרורי מנא קא מיכוין קמ"ל דמירפא רפי והדר קמיט אמר רבה בר רב הונא האי מאן דארתח כופרא חייב משום מבשל פשיטא מהו דתימא כיון דהדר ואיקושא אימא לא קמ"ל אמר רבא האי מאן דעבד חביתא חייב משום שבע חטאות תנורא חייב משום שמונה חטאות אמר אביי האי מאן דעבד *חלתא חייב אחת עשרה חטאות ואי חייטיה לפומיה חייב שלש עשרה חטאות: הגוזז את הצמר והמלבנו: אמר רבה בר בר חנה א"ר יוחנן הטווה צמר שעל גבי בהמה בשבת חייב שלש חטאות אחת משום גוזז ואחת משום מנפץ ואחת משום טווה רב כהנא אמר אין דרך גזיזה בכך ואין דרך מנפץ בכך ואין דרך טווי בכך ולא והתניא משמיה דרבי נחמיה *שטוף בעזים וטוו בעזים אלמא טויה על גבי בהמה שמה טויה חכמה יתירה שאני תנו רבנן *התולש את הכנף והקוטמו והמורטו חייב שלש חטאות (*וא"ר) שמעון בן לקיש תולש חייב משום גוזז קוטם חייב משום מחתך ממרט חייב משום ממחק: הקושר והמתיר: קשירה במשכן היכא הואי אמר רבא (ב) שכן קושרין ביתדות אהלים *(קושרים) ההוא קושר על מנת להתיר הוא אלא אמר אביי שכן אורגי יריעות שנפסקה להן נימא קושרים אותה א"ל רבא תרצת קושר מתיר מאי איכא למימר וכי תימא דאי מתרמי ליה תרי (ג) חוטי קיטרי בהדי הדדי שרי חד וקטר חד *השתא לפני מלך בשר ודם אין עושין כן לפני ממ"ה הקב"ה עושין אלא אמר רבא ואיתימא רבי עילאי שכן צדי חלזון קושרין ומתירין: והתופר שתי תפירות: והא לא קיימא אמר רבה בר בר חנה א"ר יוחנן והוא שקשרן: הקורע על מנת לתפור: קריעה במשכן מי הוה רבה ורבי זירא דאמרי תרווייהו שכן

רש"י

דשלקי ליה שבעה זימנין. למתקן: ואי לא שקלי ליה לאוכל מתוך הפסולת מתוך שהוא רך ונימוק ע"י שנשלק הרבה: מסרח. והלכך אוכל נמי כל זמן שמעורב בו הוי כפסולת ומיהו אוכל הוא ומחמירין עליה למיהוי ההוא דשקיל כפסולת מתוך אוכל ול"ג הבורר תורמוסין מתוך פסולת שלהן משלקן פעם אחת ממרקין ומערין אותן המים ובורר המתולעות שלהן כמו שעושין לפולין וכן בכל פעם ופעם וזה בורר האוכל ומניח הפסולת ואי לא שלקי ליה מסרח גרסינן הלכך משלקוס פעמים ושלש חשיב ליה פסולת הואיל ואי שביק להו הכי דלא הדר שליק להו מסרחי וכשהוא נוטלן מתוך שאר מינין גרועין המעורבין בהן כפסולת מתוך אוכל דמי דהנהו שאר מינין לא מסרחי דגמר להו בישולייהו פעם ראשונה ושניה ורבינו הלוי גריס ואי שקלי ליה מסרח כשנוטלו נימוח בין אצבעותיו ונמאס הלכך ההוא דשקיל הוי כפסולת והנשאר הוי אוכל עד שחוזר ונוטלו: דפריס סילקא. במ"ם גרסינן ולא בסמ"ך כדפירש בהעור והרוטב (חולין דף קכ.) מאי קיפה פירמא מינצי"ר בלע"ז מחתכו הדק: דסלית סילתי. עצים דקים להבעיר אש: ואי קפיד אמשחתא. לחותכן במדה: מחתך. העור מקצצו במדה: ונקט אופה. דלא שייך במלאכת המשכן כלל: סדורא דפת. שהתחיל בו נקט ואופה במקום בשול דסממנין הוא דהוא בישול דפת: דשדא סיכתא. שהשליך יתד לח לתנור חם ליבשו שיתקשה: לשרורי. לחזק ואין כאן בישול: דמרפי רפי. ע"י חום האור והמים שבתוכו יוצאין ולאחר שיצאו מימיו קמיט מתקשה וכי רפי ברישא הוי בישולו: דארתח כופרא. שהתיך זפת: דהדר אקושי. חוזר ומתקשה: חביתא. של חרס: שבע חטאות. טוחן הרגבים ושוחקן הדק הוי טוחן ובורר הצרורות הגסות מתוכן הרי שתים ומרקדן בנפה ומגבל הטיט דהיינו לש וממרח הטיט כשעושה הגולם שיהא חלק הרי ממחק ומבעיר את האור בכבשן ומצרפו בתוכו הרי מבשל חיובא דזורה ליכא דהיינו צריך אלא לעפרה: תנור חייב שמנה. דלאחר שצרפו בכבשן הוא טח עליו טפילה שיהא עב וחומו מתקיים והוא גמר מלאכתו ואמרינן לקמן (דף עה:) כל מידי דהוי גמר מלאכה חייב משום מכה בפטיש אבל גבי חבית ליכא משום מכה בפטיש דמאליה נגמרה מלאכתו בתנור: חלתא. כוורת של קנים: חייב י"א. זומר הקנים והוא צריך להם חייב משום קוצר ומשום נוטע אספס יחד הרי זה מעמר בירר יפות הרי זה בורר הצליקן הרי זה ממחק עשאן דקות מאחת שתים או שלש הרי זה טוחן התכן במדה הרי זה מחתך הסיך השתי הרי זה מיסך ארג אחת למעלה ואחת למטה כדי להעמידו הרי עושה שתי בתי נירין(ד) ארג הרי זה אורג חתך לאחר אריגתה כדי להשוותם הרי זה מכה בפטיש כדאמרינן לקמן [עה:] האי מאן דשקיל אקופי מגלימי חייב משום מכה בפטיש הרי י"א: ואי חייטיה לפומיה. לעשות לה שפה הוסיף כאן תופר וקושר שצריך לקשור לאחר התפירה ומשום בונה ליכא לחיוביה לא בחבית ולא בתנור ולא בכוורת דאין בנין בכלים מפשיט ליכא למימר בקנים דאין הפשטה אלא בעור וי"מ שקודח נקבים בעץ שתוחבין בו ראשי הקנים של שתי ומחייב ליה משום טוחן ולא נהירא לי דההיא טחינה מלאכה שאינה צריכה לגופה היא וטוב לי לפרש שעושה אותן דקות והוי כמאן דסלית סילתי: שטוף בעזים וטוו בעזים. קרא קדריש טוו את העזים (שמות לה) בגופן של עזים משמע: חכמה יתירה. כדכתיב וכל אשה חכמת לב אבל להדיוט אין דרכו בכך והוי כלאחר יד: התולש את הכנף. נוצה גדולה מן כנף העוף: והקוטמו. לאחר שתלשו חותך ראשו שהוא דק וראוי להניחו בכר וכסת: והמורטו. לצד זנבו שהוא קשה מורט שערו מכאן ומכאן ומשליך הקנה ונותן השיער בכר וכסת: משום מחתך. דקפיד להתוך עד מקום שהוא ראוי וגם מן הקנה אורג סובעים ועושה כובעים מכנפי עוף בלא שיער: משום ממחק. דתנן גבי עור הממחקו: ביתדות אהלים. טועלים יתידות בקרקע כדכתיב יתדות המשכן וקושרין היריעות בהן במיתריהם: קושר ע"מ להתיר הוא. וכי האי גוונא פטרינן ליה לקמן דתנן כל קשר שאינו של קיימא אין חייבין עליו: בהדי הדדי. בשני חוטין זה אצל זה: שרי חד. לאחר אריגתן מתיר האחד מפני שבולטין ונראין: וקטר חד. כלומר מניח כמו שהוא: השתא כו' (ה) אין עושין. שכשמתירו נראה הנקב ביריעה שחוטיה היו כפולין שנה והיו גסין ומתחלה היו זריזין בכך וכי מתרמו להו תרי קיטרי קושרין האחד ונותקין החוט השני מלמטה ולמעלה ומספקן בחוט אחר וקושרין למעלה ולמטה ואין שם שנים קשרים סמוכין: צדי חלזון. לצבוע התכלת בדמו והוא כמין דג קטן ועולה אחת לשבעים שנה: קושרין ומתירין. שכל רשתות עשויות קשרים קשרים והן קשרי קיימא ופעמים שצריך ליטול חוטין מרשת זו ולהוסיף על זו מתיר מכאן וקושר מכאן: והא לא קיימא. הכי וכיון דלא קיימא לאו מלאכה היא: שקשרן. שקשר שני ראשי החוט:

דרגא

תוספות

האי מאן דפריס סילקא. דוקא בסילקא שייך טחינה אבל שאר אוכלין שרי*: מהו דתימא לשרורי מנא קא מכוין. ה"פ ואין בו בשול כלל קמ"ל דנהי דלשרורי מנא קא מכוין בשול מיהא יש בו דמירפא רפי והדר קמיט וחייב אבל אין לפרש קמ"ל דלא אמרי' לשרורי מנא קא מכוין דבפרק אין מעמידין (ע"ז לח.) אמרי' גבי האי ככרי דשדא סיכתא לאתונא אי קבר בה ישראל קרא מעיקרא שפיר דמי ופריך פשיטא ומשני מהו דתימא לבשולי מנא קא מכוין קמ"ל לשרורי מנא קא מכוין: חביתא ותנורא וחלתא. פי' רש"י דמשום בונה לא מיחייב דאין בנין בכלים ואין נראה דדוקא במחזיר מטה ומטות של חוליות אמרי' *דאין בנין בכלים אבל כשעושה לגמרי כל הכלי מיחייב משום בונה דאמרינן בריש הבונה (לקמן ד' קב:) האי מאן דעייל שופתא בקופינא דמרא חייב משום בונה וצ"ע דלא ליחייב מנפח בכלי זכוכית דסוף פרקין*: חכמה יתירה שאני. והעושים אותם בטלה דעתם אצל כל אדם כדאמרינן בהמצניע (לקמן ד' צב:) גבי הגשי הולל: שכן צדי חלזון כו'. בריש אלו קשרים (לקמן קיא:) פירש בקונט' קושרין ומתירין פעמים קושרין את המכמורת ופעמים מתירין אותם:

עין משפט נר מצוה

[ועי' בתוס' לקמן קיד: ד"ה אלא לקינבא ירק כו' ע"ש]

מד א מיי' פ"ח מהלכות שבת הלכה ס ופ"ח הלכה טו ופכ"א הלכה יח סמג לאוין סה טוש"ע או"ח סי' שכא סעיף יב:

מה ב מיי' שם פ"ח הלכה טו:

מו ג ד מיי' פ"ט מהל' שבת הלכה ו סמג שם:

מז ה מיי' פי"ז מהלכות שבת הלכה יג:

מח ו ז מיי' פ"ט מהל' שבת הלכה ז:

[לעיל מו. עי' תוס' שם ד"ה דתוליות]

מט ח מיי' פי"א מהל' שבת הלכה ו:

נ ט שם הלכה ז:

נא י מיי' פ"י שם הל' א סמג שם טוש"ע או"ח סימן שיז סעיף א:

נב כ מיי' שם הל"ט:

נג ל מיי' שם הלכה י:

[פי' בערוך ע"ז בארוכות תמצא בערך חלתא ע"ש דקחשיב חייב משום בונה ולא קחשיב זה פי' רש"י הכא בד"ה חייב משום ממחק עיי"ש ונזה בנין דעת וכברת תוס' ד"ה חביתא]

רבינו חננאל

מקשינן ופרקינן לפרושי שמעתין דאמרינן לימא קסבר חזקיה אוכל מתוך פסולת אסור · ושנינן שאני תורמסין דשלקי להו ז' זמני כו'. שמעינן מינה דאוכל מתוך הפסולת זולתי תורמסין שרי וכדאביי דשרי לאלתר כי היכי דלא תקשי חדא אחברתא וכבר פירשנוהו השמועה סלקא כאביי וכרב אשי וכחזקיה שמעינן מדברי שלשתן כי בורר ואוכל בורר ומניח ביד שרי ולא כל היכא דבעי שרי אלא בבירת אוכל מתוך פסולת אבל פסולת מתוך אוכל לא · ואוכל מתוך פסולת דשרי [היינו] לברור ולאכול או לברור ולהניח כדי לאכלו לאלתר על השלחן כמו שפירשנו אבל להניח שלא לאלתר לא וזה שאמרנו כי מותר לברור ולאכול ולברור ולהניח ולאכלו לאלתר בקנון ובתמחוי לא ואם בירר בנפה ובכברה דברי הכל אסור ואם בירר נעשה כמי שבירר לאוצר בשוגג חייב חטאת ואע"פ דגרסינן (גיטין כו כח) לענין מי שאבד לו גט אם מצאו לאלתר כשר ואמרינן היכי דמי לאלתר י"א כל שלא עבר [אדם] שם ואחרים אומרים כל שלא שהה אדם שם הכא כיון דאשכחינן מפורש בתלמוד א"י כוותיה עבדינן ופסקינן לשמעתיה שיעור מה שמיסב על השולחן באותה סעודה בלבד וכענין הזה גרסינן בגמרא ביו"ט פרק א' (ביצה יג:) תנן התם המקלף שעורין מקלף אחת אחת על יד ואוכל. ואם קילף ונתן לתוך חיקו חייב. א"ר אלעזר וכן לשבת. והא רב מקלפי ליה כסי כסי ור' חייא מקלפי ליה כסי כסי אלא אי אתמר אסיפא איתמר המולל מלילות של חיטין (למחר) מנפח על יד על יד ואוכל ואם נפח ונתן לתוך ידו חייב · א"ר אלעזר וכן לשבת · מ"ט דמלאכת מחשבת אסרה תורה והאי לאו מלאכת מחשבת היא · דלא קא מכוון במלאכה אלא לאכילה בלבד ולפי' א' כיצד מנפח ואסיק' א"ר אלעזר מנפח בידו אחת ובכל כחו · הטוחן אמר רב פפא האי מאן דפריס סילקא · פי' כעין כתישה ולא כעין חיתוך חייב משום טוחן וכן מאן דסלית סילתי פי' עצי דקלים שעומדין שיבי שיבי כעין נימין וכשמפרק הנימין הללו יוצא בינית כמין קסת דק לפי' (המפץ) חייב משום טוחן ואי קפיד אמשחתא כלומר אם מתכוין לחתוך אלו סילתי זרת זרת אורך כל אחד ואחד חייב משום מחתך · הלש והאופה אמר רב פפא שבק בישול סממנים ונקיט אפיה ולא פירש בהדיא האי מלתא *) ואשכחן בירושלמי דאמר הכי את המי אפיה תולדת בישול הוא ואת אמרת הכן אלא כיון דתני סדר עיסה תניתא בהדייהו: ההוא דשחק [מלח] הסף (מלא) [פלפלין] חייב משום טוחן דבגל גירגבסן עפר קילורין מלוגמא סממנין חייב משום לש. כאן דשדא סיכתא לאתונא חייב משום מבשל פי' הנותן יתידות לחים בכבשן כדי לייבשן לנעצם בספינות וכיוצא בהן. פי' לשרורי לחזק ויש מי שמפרש סיכתא הן גלל בהמה דקיקין אם הטילם לכבשן מה שחייב משום מבעיר הרי חייב. ועוד חייב משום מבשל. וזה שנצרך לומר כן דלא תימא אין המפחר כלי חרס מבשל מפני שמחזיק הכלי. אשמעי' דמירפא

*) לפנינו בגמ' מפרש בהדיא הטעם משום דסידורא דפת נקיט וכמש"כ בירושלמי ואולי דלפני רבינו לא היה זה בנוסחת הגמ'

מסורת הש"ס

ע"ז לח.

לקמן צט.

בכורות כה. [תוספתא פ"י] [פ"ל אבר]

א"ל אביי כלי'

[פסחים עה: יומא מה.]

הגהות הב"ח

(א) גמ' שבעא זמני ואי (לא) שקלי: תא"מ ונ"ב ס"א לא שקלי ואי שקלי: (ב) שם אמר רבא שכן קושרים ביתדו' אהלים הוא כצ"ל ותיבת קושרים נמחק: (ג) שם דאי מיתרמו ליה תרי קיטרי כצ"ל ותיבת חוטי נמחק: (ד) רש"י ד"ה חייב וכו' עושה שתי בתי נירין כו' (ה) ד"ה השתא כו' נראה כו' ותיבת אין עושין נמחק:

רב נסים גאון

שכן צדי חלזון קושרין ומתירין. וזה חלזון היו צובעין בדמו תכלת ומשכחת לה במנחות בפרק התכלת (דף מד) תנו רבנן חלזון זה גופו דומה לים ובריאתו דומה לדג ועולה פעם אחת לע' שנה ובדמו צובעין תכלת לפיכך דמיו יקרים ואמרו עוד (שם מב) אמר ליה אביי לרב שמואל בר יהודה הא תכלתא היכא צבעיתו אמר ליה מייתינן דם חלזון וסמנין כו':

גליון הש"ס

גמ' האי מאן דפריס סילקא חייב. עי' לקמן דף קמה ע"א ברש"י ד"ה שלא יקטום: שם תולש חייב משום גוזז. עי' לקמן דף קו ע"ב ובתוס' רבב"א שם: שם דאי מתרמי ליה תרי חוטי עי' לעיל דף עג ע"א תוס' ד"ה הקושר: שם השתא לפני מלך וכו'. פסחים דף עה ע"ב יומא דף מז ע"א:

[No.] Lupines are different, [74b] because they are boiled seven times, and if one does not remove it [the edible portion], it goes rancid, hence it is like [picking] the non-edible out of the edible.[12]

GRINDING. R. Papa said: He who cuts up beets very fine is liable on account of grinding. R. Manasseh said: He who cuts chips [for fuel] is liable on account of grinding. Said R. Ashi: If he is particular about their size, he is liable on account of cutting.[13]

KNEADING AND BAKING. R. Papa said: Our Tanna omits the boiling of ingredients [for dyes],[14] which took place in [con-
a nection with] the Tabernacle, and treats of baking![1]—Our Tanna takes the order of [making] bread.[2]

R. Aha son of R. Awira said: He who throws a tent peg into a stove[3] is liable on account of cooking. But that is obvious?—You might say, His intention is to strengthen [harden] the article,[4] therefore we are informed that it [first] softens and then hardens.[5]

Rabbah son of R. Huna said: He who boils pitch is liable on account of cooking. But that is obvious?—You might argue, Since it hardens again, I might say [that he is] not [liable]. Hence he informs us [otherwise].

Raba said: He who makes an [earthenware] barrel is culpable on account of seven sin-offerings.[6] [He who makes] an oven is liable on account of eight sin-offerings.[7] Abaye said: He who makes a wicker work is liable to eleven sin-offerings,[8] and if he sews
b round the mouth thereof, he is liable to thirteen sin-offerings.[1]

SHEARING WOOL AND BLEACHING. Rabbah b. Bar Hanah said in R. Johanan's name: He who spins wool from off the animal's back on the Sabbath incurs three sin-offerings, one on account of shearing, another on account of hackling, and the third on account of spinning.[2] R. Kahana said: Neither shearing, hackling, nor spinning is [done] in this manner.[3] But is it not so? Surely it was taught in the name of R. Nehemiah: It was washed [direct] on the goats and spun on the goats:[4] which proves that spinning direct from the animal is designated spinning?—Superior skill is different.[5]

Our Rabbis taught: He who plucks the wing [of a bird], trims it [the feather], and plucks it [the down], is liable to three sin-offerings. Said R. Simeon b. Lakish: For plucking [the wing] one is liable on account of shearing; for trimming [the feather] he is liable on the score of cutting; and for plucking [the down] he is liable under the head of smoothing.

TYING AND UNTYING. Where was there tying in the Tabernacle?[6]—Said Raba: The tent-pegs were tied. But that was tying with the intention of [subsequent] untying?[7] But said Abaye: The weavers of the curtains, when a thread broke, tied it up. Said Raba to him: You have explained tying; but what can be said about untying? And should you answer that when two knots [in the material] chanced to come together, one untied one and left the other knotted:[8] [it may be asked], seeing that one would not do thus before a king of flesh and blood, how much more so before the Supreme King of kings, the Holy One, blessed be
c He?[1] Rather said Raba—others state, R. Elai: Those who caught the *hillazon*[2] tied and untied.[3]

SEWING TWO STITCHES. But it cannot endure?[4]—Said Rabbah b. Bar Hanah in R. Johanan's name: Providing that he knots them.[5]

TEARING IN ORDER TO SEW TWO STITCHES. Was there any tearing in the Tabernacle?—Rabbah and R. Zera both say: [75a]

(12) Which is forbidden.
(13) Sc. Hides to measure; v. Mishnah on capturing a deer... cutting it up.
(14) E.g., for the hangings and curtains, v. Rashi 73a, s.v. האופה.

a (1) Which has nothing to do with the Tabernacle (Rashi). (2) I.e., he takes bread as an example and enumerates the various principal labours connected with it. (3) To dry it. (4) Whereas cooking softens. (5) The fire heats the moisture in the wood, which softens it, and it is only after it evaporates that the wood hardens. This prior softening partakes of the nature of cooking. (6) So MS.M., deleting 'on account of' in cur. edd. (i) The clods of earth are first crushed and powdered—this constitutes grinding; (ii) the thicker balls which do not powder well are removed—selecting (iii) it is then sifted; (iv) the powder is mixed with water—kneading; (v) the resultant clay is smoothed when the cast of the vessel is made—smoothing; (vi) the fire is lit in the kiln; and (vii) the vessel is hardened in the kiln—boiling. (7) The seven foregoing, which are also needed here, and an additional one. For after it is hardened in the kiln, a layer of loam or plaster is daubed on the inside, to enable it to preserve heat. This completes it, and it is stated *infra* 75b that every special act needed to complete an article falls within the term 'striking with the hammer' (v. Mishnah, 73a). But a barrel needs no special labour to complete it. (8) It entails this number of labours: (i and ii) cutting the reeds is a two-fold labour: (a) reaping, (b) planting, since it leaves more room for the others to grow (v. *supra* 73b); (iii) collecting them—binding sheaves, (iv) selecting the best; (v) smoothing them; (vi) splitting them lengthwise into thinner rods—grinding; (vii) cutting them to measure; (viii) stretching the lengthwise rods; (ix) drawing one cane through these, threading it above and below the lengthwise rods—this is the equivalent of 'the making of two meshes'; (x) plaiting the canes—weaving; and finally (xi) cutting it round after plaiting in order to finish it off,—'striking with a hammer' (v. n. a7).

b (1) The additional two are sewing and then tying up (presumably the unattached lengths of the thread or twine used for same). (2) Spinning direct from the animal embraces these three labours. (3) Hence he is not liable at all, for one is liable only when he performs a labour in the usual manner. (4) The reference is to Ex. XXXV, 26, q.v., which R. Nehemiah translates literally, without adding 'hair' as in E.V., and so he deduces that it was spun directly from the animal. (5) Scripture emphasizes there the skill that this demanded (v. 25), which shows that normal spinning is different. (6) V. *supra* 49b, n. a4. (7) When they struck camp. Such is not Biblically forbidden and is not the tying referred to in the Mishnah. (8) The two knots together would spoil the evenness of the fabric.

c (1) The untying of a knot in the fabric would leave an ugly gap, particularly as the threads were six-stranded. Hence the utmost care would be taken to prevent the thread from knotting in the first place. (2) A kind of snail or purple-fish whose blood was used for dyeing the tents of the Tabernacle. (3) The nets. (4) Two stitches alone will slip out of the cloth. Thus the work is not permanent and entails no punishment. (5) After sewing, so that they will remain.

A curtain which was attacked by a moth was torn [round the moth hole] and resewn.

R. Zuṭra b. Ṭobiah said in Rab's name: He who pulls the thread of a seam[6] on the Sabbath is liable to a sin-offering; and he who learns a single thing from a magian[7] is worthy of death;[8] and he who is able to calculate the cycles[9] and planetary courses but does not, one may hold no conversation with him.[10]

As to magianism, Rab and Samuel [differ thereon]: one maintains that it is sorcery; the other, blasphemy. It may be proved that it is Rab who maintains that it is blasphemy. For R. Zuṭra b. Ṭobiah said in Rab's name: He who learns a single thing from a magian is worthy of death. Now should you think that it is a sorcerer, surely it is written, *thou shalt not learn to do [after the abominations of those nations]*,[11] [implying], but you may learn in order to understand and instruct! This proves it.

R. Simeon b. Pazzi said in the name of R. Joshua b. Levi on the authority of Bar Ḳappara: He who knows how to calculate the cycles and planetary courses, but does not, of him Scripture saith, *but they regard not the work of the Lord, neither have they con-*
a *sidered the operation of his hands.*[1] R. Samuel b. Naḥmani said in R. Joḥanan's name: How do we know that it is one's duty to calculate the cycles and planetary courses? Because it is written, *for this is your wisdom and understanding in the sight of the peoples:*[2] what wisdom and understanding is in the sight of the peoples?[3] Say, that it is the science of cycles and planets.

CAPTURING A DEER, etc. Our Rabbis taught: He who captures a purple-fish[4] and crushes it is liable to one [sin-offering];[5] R. Judah said: He is liable to two, for R. Judah maintained: Crushing comes under the head of threshing. Said they to him: Crushing does not come under the head of threshing. Raba observed: What is the Rabbis' reason? They hold that threshing is applicable only to produce from the soil. But let him be culpable too on the score of taking life?—Said R. Joḥanan: This means that he crushed it when [already] dead.[6] Raba said: You may even explain that he crushed it whilst alive: in respect to the taking of life he is but incidentally occupied.[7] But Abaye and Raba both maintain: R. Simeon admits in a case of 'cut off his head but let him not die!'[8] Here it is different, because he is more pleased that it should be alive, so that the dye should be clearer.[9]

AND SLAUGHTERING IT. As for him who slaughters, on what score is he culpable?—Rab said: On the score of dyeing;[10] while Samuel said: On the score of taking life. [75b] On the score of dyeing

(6) If the seam gapes, and he pulls the thread to draw the pieces together. This constitutes sewing. (7) One of the priestcraft of Ancient Persia. (8) This is an idiom expressing strong abhorrence, cf. similar expressions in Sanh. 58*b* and 59*a*. The Magi were hostile to Jews, and caused them much suffering in various ways; cf. Sanh., 74*b*, n. a6 and 98*a*: Yeb. 63*b*; Git. 17*a*. This evoked the present remark. (9) Sc. of the seasons. (10) The science of astronomy was necessary for the fixing of the calendar, upon which Jewish Festivals depended. In early times this was done by observation, but gradually calculation took its place. Hence Rab's indignation at one who fails to employ such knowledge. (11) Deut. XVIII, 9.

a (1) Isa. V, 12. (2) Deut. IV, 6. (3) I.e., which testifies to itself. (4) *Ḥillazon*, v. *supra* 74*b*, n. c2. (5) Crushing not being a culpable offence. (6) In order to make the blood exude. (7) I.e., the taking of life is not his main purpose, but merely follows incidentally; such does not entail culpability. (8) R. Simeon holds that a labour performed unintentionally in the course of doing something that is permitted is itself permitted, unless it follows *inevitably* from the latter, when it is the same as any other forbidden labour. Here too it must inevitably die when crushed. (9) Hence its death is more than unintentional, but actually contrary to his desire. (10) The blood that gushes forth from its cut throat stains and dyes the flesh.

תורה אור

שבן יריעה שנפל בה דרנא קורעין בה ותופרין אותה אמר רב זוטרא בר טוביה אמר רב *המותח חוט של תפירה בשבת חייב חטאת ^ב^והלומד דבר אחד מן המגוש חייב מיתה והיודע לחשב תקופות ומזלות ואינו חושב אסור לספר הימנו *מגושתא רב ושמואל חד אמר חרשי וחד אמר גדופי תסתיים דרב דאמר גדופי דאמר רב זוטרא בר טוביה אמר רב הלומד דבר אחד מן המגוש חייב מיתה דאי ס"ד חרשי הכתיב *°לא תלמד לעשות אבל אתה למד להבין ולהורות (דברים יח) תסתיים אר"ש בן פזי א"ר יהושע בן לוי משום בר קפרא כל היודע לחשב בתקופות ומזלות ואינו חושב עליו הכתוב אומר °ואת פועל ה' לא יביטו ומעשה ידיו לא ראו (ישעיה ה) א"ר שמואל בר נחמני א"ר *יוחנן ^ג^מנין שמצוה על האדם לחשב תקופות ומזלות שנאמר °ושמרתם ועשיתם כי היא חכמתכם ובינתכם לעיני העמים (דברים ד) איזו חכמה ובינה שהיא לעיני העמים הוי אומר זה חישוב תקופות ומזלות: ^ד^הצד צבי וכו': ת"ר *הצד חלזון והפוצעו אינו חייב אלא אחת רבי יהודה אומר חייב שתים שהיה ר' יהודה אומר ^ה^פציעה בכלל דישה אמרו לו אין פציעה בכלל דישה אמר רבא מ"ט דרבנן קסברי ^ו^אין דישה אלא לגדולי קרקע וליחייב נמי משום נטילת נשמה אמר רבי יוחנן שפצעו מת רבא אמר אפילו תימא שפצעו חי מתעסק הוא אצל נטילת נשמה והא אביי ורבא דאמרי תרוויהו ^ז^מודה *ר"ש בפסיק רישא ולא ימות (א) שאני הכא דכמה דאית ביה נשמה טפי ניחא ליה כי היכי *)דליציל ציבעיה: ^ח^והשוחטו: שוחט משום מאי חייב רב אמר משום צובע ושמואל אמר משום ^ט^נטילת נשמה

משום

רש"י

דרנא. תולעת ומנקב בו נקב קטן ועגול וצריך לקרוע למטה ולמעלה את הנקב שלא תהא התפירה עשויה קמטין קמטין: המותח חוט של תפירה. בגד התפור ועומד והניח החוט לתוך ונתפרדו שתי חתיכות הבגד זו מזו במקצת וחוטי התפירות נמשכין ומותח את ראשי החוט להדק ולחבר זו היא תפירתו וחייב: והלומד דבר אחד מן המגוש. מין הממשיכו לע"ז אפי' דבר תורה אסור ללמוד ממנו: והיודע כו'. הני תלת שמעתתא שמעינהו (*מר) זוטרא מרב כי הדדי וגרסינהו: אמגושא. דאמרינן בכל דוכתא רב ושמואל פליגי ביה: חד אמר חרשי. מכשף: וחד אמר גדופי. מין האדוק בע"ז ומגדף תמיד את השם ומסית הנשים לע"ז: דאי סלקא דעתך חרשי. וטעמא משום דכתיב לא ימצא בך וגו' וקא חשיב מכשף: והא כתיב. לעיל מיניה לא תלמד לעשות כדי שתעשה: להבין. שתוכל לעמוד בהן ואם יעשה נביא שקר לפניך שתבין שהוא מכשף: תסתיים דגדופי הוא. הלכך כל דבריו דברי ע"ז והסתלק מעליו שלא ישיאך: לעיני העמים. שחכמה הניכרת היא שמראה להם סימן לדבריו בהילוך החמה והמזלו' שמעידין כדבריו שאומר שנה זו גשומה והיא כן שנה זו שחונה והיא כן שכל העיתים לפי מהלך החמה במזלותיה ומולדותיה במזל תלוי הכל לפי השעה המתחלת לשמש בכניסת החמה למזל: הפוצעו. דוחקו בידיו שיצא דמו: אינו חייב אלא אחת. משום צידה אבל אפציעה ליכא חיוב: בכלל דישה. שמפרק דמו הימנו כמפרק תבואה מקשין שלה: מתעסק הוא אצל נטילת נשמה. כלומר לגבי נטילת נשמה הוי מתעסק בדבר אחר ולא הויא מלאכת מחשבת שאינו מתכוין שימות: טפי ניחא ליה. שדם החי טוב מדם המת וכיון דכל עצמו מתכוין וטורח לשומרו שלא ימות בידו אפי' מת אין כאן אלא מתעסק וכי מודה ר' שמעון במידי דלא איכפת ליה אי מיתרמי ומיהו איכווני לא מיכוון: דליציל ליבעיה גרסינן. שיהא מראית צבעו צלולה: שוחט משום מאי מחייב. שחיטה במלאכת המשכן היכא ומאי עבידת' אי מעורות אילים מאדמים למה לי בהו שחיטה בחניקה נמי סגי: משום

תוספות

שבן יריעה שנפל בה דרנא כו'. תימה לר"י דבריש האורג אמרי' קורע על מנת לתפור שתי תפירות היכי משכחת לה ומשני דעבידא ככיסתא ואומר ר"י דבמשכן היו אומנים ביותר והיו נזהרים שלא היו עושים ככיסתא והתם לא קאמר שנפל בה דרנא דנקט דשכיח טפי ועוד דהתם בעי לאשכוחי קורע על מנת לתפור שתי תפירות ותו לא ויריעה שנפל בה דרנא צריך לקורעה מתחלתה ועד סופה ויש בה כמה תפירות ואע"ג דהשתא לא משכח' במשכן על מנת לתפור שתי תפירות ותו לא סברא הוא דבשתי תפירות הוי דבר חשוב: אמגושא. פי' בערוך דפליגי בהא דאמר רב פפא באלו מגלחין (מו"ק יח.) פרעה אמגושי היה דכתיב הנה יוצא המימה חד אמר לעשות כשפים היה יוצא וחד אמר גדופי שהיה עושה עצמו ע"ז שהיה אומר לי יאורי ואני עשיתני ואין נראה לר"י דפליגי רב ושמואל במאי דאמר רב פפא אלא פליגי אאמגושא שנזכר בשום מקום במשנה או בברייתא: הצד חלזון. למאן דמוקי לה בשפצעו חי אתי שפיר הא דנקט הצד חלזון דדרך לפוצעו מיד אחר צידה כל זמן שהוא חי וקמ"ל דאע"פ שפצעו חי לא מיחייב משום נטילת נשמה ואפילו למאן דמוקי לה כשפצעו מת קמ"ל דלא מיחייב בצידה שלו משום נטילת נשמה דאף על גב דאמרי' בפרק שמונה שרצים (לקמן דף קז:) השולה דג מן הים כיון שיבש בו כו' הכא שאני חלזון דדרכו לפרכס ולקרב מיתתו ול"ע דבירושלמי משמע דצד חלזון לא מיחייב משום צידה: וליחייב נמי משום נטילת נשמה. ואפי' לרבי יהודה דאמר מקלקל בחבורה פטור פריך שפיר דהיכא דאיכא תקון קצת חייב כדאמרי' בפסחים (דף עג.) בסוף אלו דברים והכא נמי במה שממיתו יש תקון קצת שאינו מפרכס לכאן ולכאן ונוח ליטול ממנו הדם ולמאי דמסיק דכמה דאית ביה נשמה טפי ניחא ליה אתי שפיר נמי לרבי יהודה דהשתא ליכא תיקון כלל ומיהו במתניתין אתיא אפי' לר"ש דמחייב מקלקל בחבורה מדמשני מתעסק הוא אצל נטילת נשמה ולא קאמר מקלקל הוא: מתעסק הוא אצל נטילת נשמה. האי מתעסק לאו דוקא דהא מתעסק בחבורה חייב לר"ש דאמר בס"פ ספק אכל (כריתות יט:) הגה לתינוקות הוליד ומקלקל בחבורה חייב מתעסק נמי חייב וטעמא כדיליף בהאורג (לקמן קו.) מדאיצטריך למישרי מילה מכלל דמקלקל בחבורה חייב ולא חיישינן למלאכת מחשבת דמקלקל דעלמא לא מיפטר אלא משום מלאכת מחשבת כדאמר בספ"ק דחגיגה (דף י:) ומתעסק דהכא היינו דבר שאין מתכוין כיון דאין מתכוין כלל למלאכה מותר אפי' בחבורה אע"פ דלא בעי מלאכת מחשבת כמו כל איסורים שבתורה דלא שייך בהו מלאכת מחשבת ושרו אין מתכוין כדאמר מוכרי כסות מוכרין כדרכן ובלבד שלא יתכוין בחמה מפני החמה כו' (כלאים פ"ט משנה ה) וכן מוכח בפ"ק דכתובות (ד' ה:) דאמר את"ל דם חבורי מיחבר לדם הוא צריך או להנאת עצמו הוא צריך ואת"ל להנאת עצמו הוא צריך הלכה כרבי יהודה או הלכה כר"ש פירוש בדבר שאין מתכוין ואת"ל הלכה כר' יהודה בדבר שאין מתכוין במקלקל הלכה כמאן משמע דאי הלכה כר"ש בדבר שאין מתכוין תו ליכא לספוקי במקלקל דאפי' מקלקל בחבורה חייב כיון דאין מתכוין מותר: טפי ניחא ליה כי היכי דליציל ליבעי'. פי' אע"ג דהוי פסיק רישיה דמודה ר"ש הכא מיפטר משום דהוי מלאכה שאינה צריכה לגופה דאפי' במקלקל פטר ר"ש במלאכה שאינה צריכה לגופה כדאמר בפרק הנחנקין (סנהדרין פד:) מאן שמעת ליה דאמר מקלקל בחבורה חייב ר"ש הא אמר מלאכה שאינה צריכה לגופה פטור עליה וכי מודה ר"ש בפסיק רישיה ה"מ במידי דניחא ליה אי מתרמי דהוי צריכה לגופה אבל במידי דלא איכפת ליה לא מודה ורש"י פי' דהא דמודה ר"ש בפסיק רישיה היינו במאי דלא איכפת ליה אי מתרמי וליתא דהא מגרר זרדין בארעא דחבריה פטר ר"ש בפ' הבונה (לקמן קג.) והתם לא איכפת ליה אי מתרמי אלא כדפי' ותימה דבספ"ק דחגיגה (דף י:) משמע דהא דפטר ר"ש מלאכה שאינה צריכה לגופה היינו משום דבעי מלאכת מחשבת וא"כ בחבורה דלא בעי מלאכת מחשבת ליחייב בה מלאכה שאינה צריכה לגופה: כי היכי דליציל ליבעיה. קשה לר"י דמ"מ על נטילת הדם ליחייב משום נטילת נשמה ונראה כלשון אחר שפי' בקונט' בריש שמונה שרצים (לקמן קז.) דחובל בהן חייב משום דהוי תולדה דשוחט וחייב משום נטילת נשמה ונטילת הדם היינו נטילת נשמה כדכתיב כי הדם הוא הנפש ולכך ח' שרצים שיש להם עור חייב בנצרר הדם אע"פ שלא יצא דכיון שנצרר סופו לצאת אלא שעתה העור מעכבו ושאר שרצים שאין להם עור אינו חייב עד שיצא מהם דם אבל בנצרר הדם ולא יצא לא מיחייב דכיון שלא יצא סופו לחזור דאם היה סופו לצאת היה יוצא מיד שאין העור מעכבו והשיב לו ר"ת דדם חלזון הראוי לצביעה מיפקד פקיד ולא מיחייב על אותו הדם משום נטילת נשמה ועל דם אחר היוצא עמו נמי לא מיחייב דלא ניחא ליה כי היכי דליציל ליבעיה אבל אין לפרש דנטילת נשמה היינו במחליש אותו דבר שחובל בו דגבי דם בתולים מה צריך להחלישה האשה וגבי מילה מה צריך להחלישות התינוק אלא לנטילת הדם קרי נטילת נשמה כדפי': שוחט משום מאי מחייב. לאו אשוחט דמתני' קאי דההוא פשיטא דלא הוי אלא משום נטילת נשמה דלצובע תנן בהדיא במתני' אלא אשוחט דעלמא קאי:

אין

*) [נ"ל דליצלה פי' דלא ניחא ליה דתיפוק נשמה דכל כמה דאית ביה נשמה טפי מצלה לצביעה שצבעו מתעלה יפה ויהא צבעו יפה וברור כי הוא תליא. ערוך]

עין משפט נר מצוה

נד א מיי' שם הלכה פ סמג שם טור שו"ע או"ח סימן ש"מ סעיף ו:
נה ב שו"ע יו"ד סימן קעט סעיף יט:
נו ג סמג עשין מז:
נז ד מיי' פי"ז מהלכות שבת הלכה יט סמג לאוין סה טוש"ע או"ח סימן שטו סעיף ה:
נח ה מיי' פ"ח מהלכות שבת הלכה ז ופי"א הלכה יב:
נט ו מיי' שם פ"ח הלכה ז:
ס ז מיי' פ"א מהלכות שבת הלכה ו טוש"ע או"ח סימן שלז סעיף א:
סא ח מיי' פי"א מהל' שבת הלכה א:

רבינו חננאל

רפה' כשהן חיים ומתבשלין ואחר כך מתחזקין כשיצטרפו (מתחפרו) [ויתפהרו] · וכן מאן דארתח כופרא' אף על גב דהדר אקיש כבשל הוא · אמר רבה מאן דעבד חביתא חייב ז' חטאות פי' כגון שהיתה לו גבשושית ונטלה וייפה הקרקע חייב משום חורש · שחק חייב משום טוחן ניקהו מן הצרורות חייב משום בורר וכשמהתך (ממנו) [היינו] מחתך · ועיקר מלאכה א) (בנין מלאכה) וגמר מלאכה והשואתה חייב משום מכה בפטיש הרי שבע ב) בתנור עוד מוסיף אחד שצריך להחליק את תוכו ולשוף איתו נהלים וחייב משום ממחק · מאן דעבד חלתא חייב י"א חטאות. חתך קנה נעשה זומר וצריך לעצים חייב משום קוצר ומשום נוטע כינס הקנים חייב משום מעמר דקדק הקנים חייב משום טוחן · חתכם כשיעור כגון אמה אמה חייב משום מחתך · קילפם חייב משום דש · השליך קליפיהן וקנין שאין ראויין למלאכה חייב משום בורר. הטיל שתיו חייב משום מיסך וכשמטיל הערב עושה שתי בתי נירין וכשמכה אותן כדי לקרבן זה לזה (ולהדחיק אריג ג) זה כל זמן שעושה (ארבעת) [ארעי'] הכוורת וכשכופף הקנים למעלה לאריגה [והן] קירותיה בונה הוא וגמר מלאכה שישבר קרומיות היוצאת משום מכה בפטיש הרי אלו י"א מלאכות ואם כפף פיה למטה ותפרה (כשיבינו החיים) [כשמותח החוט] חייב משום תופר כרב דאמר המותח חוט של תפירה בשבת חייב (משום) חטאת וכשתופר חייב משום תופר הרי אלו י"ג חטאות: **ירושלמי** ההיא איתתא כד משתייא בקיבה משום מיסכת כד יהבה קירומה משום עושה בתין · כד מקימה לון משום בונה' כד מחיי' משום אורגת כד מקטעא בנימא משום מחתכת · כד גמרה מלאכתה משום מכה בפטיש · אונים של דיסקיא [קושר ומתיר] נעשה כנועל ופותח וכן חותלות של תמרים קושר ומתיר · א"ר יוחנן השוה צמר מעל גבי בהמה בשבת חייב ג' חטאות משום גוזז ומנפץ וטווה · ודהה רב כהנא ואמר אין דרך גזיזה ולא דרך ניפוץ ולא דרך טוויה בכך · ואקשינן על רב כהנא והתניא משום נחמיה שטוף בעזים · אלמא שטפוהו בעזים וטוות מעליהן בלא גזיזה ופריק' חכמה יתירה שאני דכתיב וכל הנשים אשר נשא לבן אותנה בחכמה טוו את העזים · ואע"ג דרב כהנא לגבי רב תלמיד הוה כיון (דיש) דאשכחן בתלמוד א"י דקיימי כוותיה דגרסינן התולש כנף מן העוף חייב משום גוזז המורטו חייב משום מוחק הקוטמה חייב משום מכה בפטיש ודחינן לא דמיא תולש כנף עוף לתולש שער בהמה דעוף שאין לו גזיזה תלישתה היא גזיזתה ברם בהמה אינו חייב עד שיגזז תדע שהוא כן דתני תלש מן המתה חייב תלישתה זו היא גזיזתה מן החיה פטור ותו מדתנן (לקמן צד:) הנוטל צפרניו זו בזו או בשיניו וכן שערו וכן שפמו וכן זקנו ר' אליעזר מחייב חטאת וחכמים אוסרים משום שבות כלומר אין דרך נטילת שיער בשיניים וכיון דקיימי חכמים כרב כהנא קיי"ל כוותיה: אמגושתא · פי' בלשון ערבי זמזמה. מגוש בלשון יון מכשף · גידופי כופר בעיקר: **הצד** צבי השוחטו כו' · ת"ר הצד חלזון והפוצעו אינו חייב אלא אחת ר' יהודה אומר חייב שתים פציעה בכלל דישה ורבנן סברי אין דישה אלא בגידולי קרקע ואקשינן לרבנן ליחייב משום צידה ומשום נטילת נשמה ופריק ר' יוחנן שפצעו מת · רבא אמר אפילו תימא שפצעו חי · מתעסק אצל נטילת נשמה וקיי"ל המתעסק [בחלבים ובעריות] חייב משום דנהנה המתעסק בשבת פטור מלאכת מחשבת אסרה תורה דלא קא ניחא לנטילת נשמה דניחא

א) אולי צ"ל ועל עיקר מלאכת החבית חייב משום בונה וגמר מלאכה וכו'. ב) לפי מה דחשיב רבינו אין כאן רק שש חטאות ואולי דחסר בדברי רבינו וצ"ל וכשמצרף את"כ בכבשן חייב משום מבשל וכ"ה ברש"י ג) אולי צ"ל חייב משום אורג וזה כל זמן וכו'.

רב נסים גאון שבן קרש שנפל בו דרנא. פי' דרנא תולעת ובסוף פרק אלו טריפות (חולין דף סז) משכחת ואת נבלתם תשקצו לרבות את הדרנין של בהמה: **רבא** אמר אפילו תימא שפצעו חי מתעסק הוא אצל נטילת

הגהות הב"ח

(א) גמ' שאני הכא. נ"ב עמ"ש דף קג:

מסורת הש"ס

[נ"ל רב]
ס"א אמגושא
[ר"ה כה: ע"ז ח. מג: סנהד' סח.]
[נ"ל יוחנן]
[תוספתא פ"ט ע"ש]
לקמן קו. קיא: קז. קכ: קלג. קמג. [ביצה לו.] כתובות ו: כתובות כה. סוכה לג:

משום צובע אין משום נטילת נשמה לא אימא אף משום צובע אמר רב מילתא דאמרי אימא בה מילתא דלא ליתו דרי בתראי וליחכו עלי צובע במאי ניחא ליה ניחא דליתווס בית השחיטה דמא כי היכי דליחזוה אינשי וליתו ליזבנו מיניה : והמולחו והמעבדו : [א]היינו מולח והיינו מעבד ר' יוחנן ור"ל דאמרי תרוייהו אפיק חד מינייהו ועייל [א] שירטוט אמר רבה בר רב הונא האי מאן דמלח בישרא חייב משום מעבד [ב]רבא אמר אין עיבוד באוכלין אמר רב אשי ואפילו רבה בר רב הונא לא אמר אלא דקא בעי ליה לאורחא אבל לביתא לא משוי איניש מיכליה עץ: [ג]והממחקו והמחתכו: אמר רבי אחא בר חנינא[ג]השף בין העמודים בשבת חייב משום ממחק אמר רבי חייא בר אבא ג' דברים סח לי רב *אשי משמיה דרבי יהושע בן לוי [ד]המגרר ראשי כלונסות בשבת חייב משום מחתך [ה]הממרח רטיה בשבת חייב משום ממחק [ו]והמסתת את האבן בשבת חייב משום מכה בפטיש אמר ר' שמעון(א) בן קיסמא אמר רבי שמעון בן לקיש [ז]הצר צורה בכלי והמנפח בכלי זכוכית חייב משום מכה בפטיש א"ר יהודה [ח]האי מאן דשקיל אקופי מגלימי חייב משום מכה בפטיש והני מילי דקפיד עלייהו : [ט]והכותב שתי אותיות : ת"ר *[י]כתב אות אחת גדולה ויש במקומה לכתוב שתים פטור מחק אות גדולה ויש במקומה לכתוב שתים חייב אמר רבי מנחם בר' יוסי וזה חומר במוחק מבכותב : הבונה והסותר המכבה והמבעיר והמכה בפטיש : רבה ור' זירא דאמרי תרוייהו [כ]כל מידי דאית ביה גמר מלאכה חייב משום מכה בפטיש : אלו אבות מלאכות : *אלו [ל]לאפוקי מדר"א דמחייב על תולדה במקום אב : חסר אחת : לאפוקי מדר' יהודה *דתניא ר' יהודה מוסיף את השובט והמדקדק אמרו לו [ל]שובט הרי הוא בכלל מיסך מדקדק הרי הוא בכלל אורג : **מתני'** ועוד כלל אחר אמרו [מ]כל הכשר להצניע ומצניעין כמוהו והוציאו בשבת חייב חטאת עליו וכל שאינו כשר להצניע ואין מצניעין כמוהו והוציאו בשבת אינו חייב אלא המצניעו : **גמ'** כל הכשר להצניע לאפוקי מאי רב פפא אמר [נ]לאפוקי דם נדה מר עוקבא אמר לאפוקי עצי אשרה מאן דאמר דם נדה כ"ש עצי אשרה מאן דאמר עצי אשרה אבל דם נדה מצנע ליה לשונרא ואידך כיון דחלשא לא מצנע ליה אמר רבי יוסי בר חנינא האי דלא כר"ש דאי כר"ש האמר *לא אמרו כל השיעורין הללו אלא למצניעיהן : וכל שאינו כשר להצניע :
אמר

משום צובע. שצובע את הבשר של בית השחיטה ולקמן מפרש אמאי מיכוין לצובעו וצביעה הואי במשכן אב מלאכה : משום נטילת נשמה. דנטילת נשמה הואי במשכן באילים מאדמים ותחש וחלזון* : אף משום צביעה. ונפקא מינה לחיוביה תרתי : מילתא דאמרי אימא כו'. דבר תימה אמרתי להזכיר צביעה בשחיטה צריך אני לומר בו דבר טעם דלא ליתו דרי בתראי השומעים וליחכו עלי : צובע בשר במאי ניחא ליה. להאי שוחט בצביעת הבשר הייט חוכא ואני אומר בו טעם: ניחא ליה דלתווס בית השחיטה בדמא. שיהא צבוע בדם : כי היכי דניחזייה אינשי. שנשחטה היום וניתו וכזבנו : היינו מולח היינו מעבד. אמו מליחה לאו צורך עיבוד הוא : ועייל שירטוט. לפי שדרך הרצענין כשהוא בא לחתכו משרטטו תחלה כפי מה שהוא רוצה להאריך ולהרחיב ולקצר החיתוך ואחר כך מעביר הסכין דרך השירטוט וכן בעורות המשכן כשחתכום : דקבעי ליה לאורחא. שמולחה הרבה : השף בין העמודים. כגון עמודי אכסדראות שעשוים חלונות חלונות ונסמכין בחלונות בין עמוד לעמוד והשף שם בקרקעית הבנין שנשענין עליו כדי שיהא חלק חייב משום ממחק : המגרר ראשי כלונסות. שיהו ראשיהן שוין וחדין : ממרח רטיה. מחליק תחבושת על המכה : מסתת את האבן. לאחר שנעקרה מן ההר ונחצבה מחליקה : משום מכה בפטיש. שהוא גמר מלאכה : הצר (ב) בכלי צורה. בכלי שעומד לכך לנאותו : מנפח בכלי זכוכית. כשהותך נעשה על ידי נפוח: דשקיל אקופי. ראשי חוטין התלויין ביריעה במקום קשורין כשניתק בה חוט וקשרוהו וכן קשין וקסמים דקין שנארגו בה בלא מתכוין ונוטלין אותם ממנה לאחר אריגה גמר מלאכה הוא וחייב משום מכה בפטיש : כתב אות אחת גדולה כו' פטור. שבקרשי המשכן שתים היו כותבים אחת בזו ואחת בזו כדי לזווגן כשסותרים אותן : מחק אות אחת כו' חייב. שאין מלאכת מחיקה חשובה אלא ע"מ לכתוב והרי יש מקום לשתי אותיות : אמר רבי מנחם ברבי יוסי. הא קמ"ל מאן תנא קמא ר' מנחם ברבי יוסי : לאפוקי מדרבי אליעזר. דהא אמרן דלא נמנו כאן אלא להודיענו מנין חטאות של העלם אחד ותנא הרי אלו למעוטי שאם עשה תולדותיהם עמהן דאינו מביא עליהן חטאת ודלא כרבי אליעזר דמחייב אתולדה עם האב בכריתות : שובט. משוה השתי בכרכר שקורין ריו"ל : מדקדק. כשמותח חוט הערב מכה בכרכר עליו במקומות מקומות ליישבו שלא יהא מתוח יותר מדאי שהמתיחה מעכבתו מהתחבר יפה עם הארג : שובט הרי הוא בכלל מיסך. דהייט מיסך ממש שמסדר חוטי השתי : הרי הוא אורג. דהייט אורג ממש ולא דמי לזורר ובורר ומרקד דזה בקשין וזה בצרורות וזה בקמח : **מתני'** כל הכשר להצניע. שהוא מין העשוי לצורך האדם : ומצניעין כמוהו. כמות זה כלומר שיש בו שיעור הראוי להצניעו : אין חייב אלא למצניעו. אם נעשה חביב לאדם א' והצניעו חייב על הוצאתו אם חזר והוציאו אבל אדם אחר אינו חייב עליו דלגביה לאו מלאכה הוא : **גמ'** מ"ד דם נדה. אינו כשר להצניע כ"ש עצי אשרה דאיסורי הנאה נינהו ומאיסי וצריך לאבדן : כיון דחלשא. המאכיל דם האדם לחתול נעשה חלש אותו אדם : הא. דתנא כל הכשר להצניע ויש בו שיעור שרוב ב"א עשויין להצניע כשיעור הזה חייב כל אדם על הוצאתו ואפילו אדם עשיר שאין שיעור זה חשוב לו : דלא כר' שמעון. לקמן בהמוציא :
אמר

אין עיבוד באוכלין. אין להתיר מכאן מליחת אוכלין דאסור מדרבנן מליחה בפרק שמונה שרצים (לקמן דף קח:) ואפילו בי"ט אסור בפ"ק דביצה (דף יא·) : **השף** בין העמודים בשבת חייב. פירש ר"ח *דשף העור על העמוד כדי להחליקו וכן משמע בירושלמי ורש"י פירש ששף קרקעית שבין עמודי חלונות ולא נהירא : **והמסתת** את האבן כו' חייב משום מכה בפטיש. אבל משום מחתך וממחק לא מיחייב דמיירי שכבר היא מרובעת ומתוקנת אלא שמייפה אותה ועושה בה שירטוטין ויפוי כעין שעושין עכשיו מסתתי האבנים. ר"י וכן ריב"א : **הרי** אלו לאפוקי מדרבי אליעזר דמחייב אתולדה במקום אב. וא"ת מרישא שמעינן לה דתנן העושה מלאכות הרבה מעין מלאכה אחת אינו חייב אלא אחת וי"מ דה"ק מעין מלאכה אחת היינו שתי תולדות מאב א' אבל האב ותולדה דידיה מיחייב תרתי קמ"ל: **חסר** אחת לאפוקי מדר' יהודה. תימה דממילא דרישא שמעינן לה וליכא למימר תנא ושייר °דהא אלו קתני ומיהו הא ליכא לאקשויי דהא מאלו דרישא שמעינן לאפוקי מדר' אליעזר דליכא למימר דנקט ברישא אלו אבות משום דקאי אדקתני לעיל חייב על כל אב מלאכה וי"ל דממילא דרישא לא שמעינן לאפוקי מדרבי יהודה דאיכא למימר דלא חשיב אלא מלאכות חשובות אבל שובט ומדקדק אע"ג דמלאכות הן לא קתני להו משום דאינם מבוררות כל כך וכה"ג משני בפ"ק דקדושין (דף טז:) גבי אלו מעניקין להן דבר שיש לו קצבה קתני דבר שאין לו קצבה לא קתני* : **לאפוקי** עצי אשרה. דלא כרבי יהודה דאמר בפרק רבי עקיבא (לקמן דף צ.) אף המוציא משמשי ע"ז כל שהוא חייב אלא כת"ק דפליג עליה כן פירש בקונט' התם וקשה לרשב"א הא דקאמר הכא מ"ד דם נדה כ"ש עצי אשרה מנא ליה דילמא סבר כרבי יהודה ומחייב בעצי אשרה שמצניעין אותן לשריפה : **הא** דלא כר' שמעון. פירש בקונטרס הא דתנן כל הכשר כו' שרוב בני אדם עשויים להצניע כשיעור הזה חייב כל אדם על הוצאתו אפילו אדם עשיר שאין שיעור זה חשוב לו משמע מדבריו דלא מחייב ר' שמעון אלא בסתם בני אדם שרגילין להצניעו שאותו שיעור חשוב להן ואפילו לא הצניעו הוא ולקמן פי' לא נאמרו שיעורים שבמשנה אלא למצניעין אותו קודם לכן וחזר המצניע והוציאו משמע דוקא בהצניעו חייב ואומר ר"י דיש ליישב פירושו דמה שמצריך

סב א ב ג מיי' פי"א מהלכות שבת הלכה ה סמג לאוין סה טוש"ע א"ח סימן שכא סעיף ה:
[ועי' בערוך ערך שף]
סג [א] [מיי' פ"י מהל' שבת הלכה ה ופי"א הלכה יז] :
סד [ג] [מיי' פי"א שם הלכה ו] :
סה ד מיי' שם הלכה ז :
סו ה מיי' שם הלכה ו ופכ"ג הלכה יח טוש"ע או"ח סימן שכב סעיף ג :
סז ו מיי' פי"א מהלכות שבת הלכה יח :
סח ז מיי' שם הלכה טז :
סט ח מיי' שם הלכה יח טוש"ע או"ח סימן שמ סעיף ג :
ע ט מיי' פי"א מהל' שבת הלכה ט סמג שם טוש"ע או"ח סימן שמ סעיף ג :
ע י מיי' שם הלכה עו ופכ"ג הלכה ד סמג שם :
ע ל מיי' פ"ז שם הל"ז ופ"ט מהל' שגגות הלכה ה :
ע [ל] [מיי' שם פ"ט הלכה יח ויט] :
עא מ נ מיי' פי"ח מהל' שבת הלכה כב :

רבינו חננאל

ליה דנהוי חי כי היכי דליצלח צבעיה דכל כמה דהוא חי מצלח ציבעיה׳ שוחט משום מאי מחייב רב אמר משום צובע אמאי ניחא ליה כי היכי דנתווס בית שחיטה דידיה דמא׳ כי היכי דידעי אינשי דחי הוה וכי היכי (דניחה) [דנחזיה] אינשי דנשחט הוא וקאתי למזבן מיניה ולא יימרו של נבילה הוא׳ והא דאמר רב משום צובע הכי קאמר חדא משום נטילת נשמה דהא בהדיא תנן באבות מלאכות השוחט׳ וסבר רב השוחט בשבת חייב שתים אחת משום נטילת נשמה ואחת משום צובע והוא אב (אחר) [אחר]׳ והמולחו והמעבדו׳ אקשינן דמולח היינו מעבד כדאמרינן (לקמן עט:) לענין היפה מליח וקמיח שנמצאת מליחתו עבודו ופרקין ר' יוחנן ור"ל דהמולח והמעבד תרווייהו מלאכת עיבוד נינהו ותני חדא והוא הדין לאחרינא׳ אי הכי בצרי להו עייל שירטוט ושני במתני' המולחו והמשרטטו: ירושלמי מה עיבוד היה במשכן שהיו משרטטין בעורות מהו משרטטין מסרגלין. מליחת בשר חי בשבת׳ אם כוונתו לצאת בו לדרך או לאוכלו אחר כמה ימים חייב משום מעבד אבל לאוכלו ביומו לא ולית הלכתא כדרבה בר רב הונא (דרבה בר רב הונא) [דרבא] דחי לה ואמר אין עיבוד באוכלין : השף בין העמודים.׳ פי' מחליק חייב משום מוחק והוא כמו ממרח את הרטיה : ירושלמי הממחק׳. מה מחיקה היתה במשכן (פי')שהיו שפין העורות ע"ג העמוד׳ השף את העור ע"ג העמוד חייב משום (מוחק) [ממחק]. המחרה איספלנית חייב משום מוחק׳ הגורד ראשי כלונסות חייב משום מחתך׳ הממרח רטיה חייב משום מוחק׳ וכן הצר בכלי צורה כל שהוא חייב משום מכה בפטיש. ואע"ג דפליג ר' ישמעאל (לקמן קג:) ואמר עד שיצור כל הצורה יחידאה היא ואי ההיא צורה אית בה אותיות דמיקרו חייב משום כותב ואי לאו חייב משום מכה בפטיש וכן המנפח בכלי זכוכית הוא גמר מלאכתו שמלאכת זכוכית בניפוח הוא׳ פי' אקופי כגון נימין הניתקין מן האריגה דנתלין בבגד או חתיכות עצים קטנים המסבכין בצמרן של בגדים חדשים וכשמשלים האומן מלאכתו כל ראשי נימין התלויים בין קיסם וקליפה שנסתבכו בבגד נוטלן׳ ונקראין אקופי׳

ע"כ שייך לעיל

[צ"ל אסור]

הגהות הב"ח
(א) גמ' אמר ר"ש בר קיסמא אמר ר"ש בן לקיש הצר: (ב) רש"י ד"ה הצר צורה כצ"ל ותיבת בכלי נמחק:

[תוספ' פי"ב]

לקמן צז: כריתות טז:

לקמן צז:

גליון הש"ס
תוס' ד"ה חסר אחת וכו' דהא אלו קתני. כדאי' קדושין דף טז ע"ב:

לקמן עט:

[ועי' תוס' יבמות פח: ד"ה אלא]

רב נסים גאון

נטילת נשמה קיי"ל שהמתעסק לענין שבת פטור . ומשכחת עיקר דילה במסכת כריתות בפרק ספק אכל חלב (דף יט) אמר רב נחמן אמר שמואל [המתעסק] בחלבים ובעריות (בחלבים פטור ובעריות) חייב שכבר נהנה מתעסק בשבת פטור מלאכת מחשבת אסרה תורה ומשכחת לה בסנהדרין בפ' ד' מיתות (דף סב) ובגמרא דהזורק דבני מערבא (הלכה ו) גרסי הזורק בשבת פטור היאך עבידא אמר הריני קוצר חצי גרוגרת וקצר כגרוגרת פטור בגמ' דכל שעה בפסחים (דף לג) גרסי לה אם אמרת בשאר מצות שכן לא חייב בהן שאין מתעסק כמתעסק שאם נתכוין להגביה את התלוש והתך המחובר פטור וכגון זה כל מלאכה שהיא באה חילוף מה שנתכוון העושה אותה מתעסק מיקרי שהרי לא נעשית מחשבתו :

אלו לאפוקי מדר' אליעזר דמחייב על תולדה במקום אב. ואשכחנן דברי ר' אליעזר בכריתות בפרק אמרו לו אכלת חלב (דף טז) אמר ר' עקיבא שאלתי את ר' אליעזר העושה מלאכות הרבה בשבתות הרבה מעין מלאכה אחת בהעלם אחד מהו חייב על כל אחת ואחת או חייב אחת על כולן אמר לי חייב על כל אחת ואחת מקל וחומר ואמרו בתלמוד בעי מיניה ולדי מלאכות אי כמלאכות דמיין אי לא ופשט ליה דולדי מלאכות כמלאכות דמיין : דאי ר' שמעון הא אמר לא נאמרו כל השיעורין האלו אלא למצניעיהן . בפירקא דלקמן המוציא יין (דף עו) משכחת להא דר' שמעון :
סליק פרק כלל גדול

a but not on the score of taking life![1] Say, on the score of dyeing too. Rab said: As to this dictum of mine, I will make an observation thereon so that later generations should not come and deride me. Wherein is one pleased with the dyeing? One is pleased that the throat should be stained with blood, so that people may see it[2] and come and buy from him.

SALTING AND CURING IT. But salting and tanning are identical?[3]—R. Joḥanan and Resh Laḳish both said: Omit one of these and insert the tracing of lines.[4] Rabbah son of R. Huna said: He who salts meat is liable on account of tanning [dressing]. Raba said: Curing does not apply to foodstuffs. R. Ashi observed: And even Rabbah son of R. Huna ruled thus only when he requires it for a journey;[5] but [when he needs it] for his house, one does not turn his food into wood.

SCRAPING AND CUTTING IT UP. R. Aḥa b. Ḥanina said: He who rubs [smooths skins] between columns[6] on the Sabbath is liable on the score of scraping. R. Ḥiyya b. Abba said, R. Ammi told me three things in the name of R. Joshua b. Levi: He who planes the tops of beams[7] on the Sabbath is culpable on account of cutting.[8] He who spreads a poultice [evenly over a sore] on the Sabbath is culpable on the grounds of scraping. And he who chisels round a stone on the Sabbath[9] is liable on the score of striking with the hammer.[10] R. Simeon b. Bisna said in the name of R. Simeon b. Laḳish: He who describes a figure on a utensil, and he who blows in glassware,[11] is liable on the score of striking with a hammer. Rab Judah said: He who removes threads[12] from garments on the Sabbath is liable on the score of striking with the hammer;[13] but that is only when he objects to them.[14]

WRITING TWO LETTERS. Our Rabbis taught: If one writes one large letter in the place of which there is room for writing two, he is not culpable. If he erases one large letter and there is room in its place for writing two, he is culpable. Said R. Menaḥem son of R. Jose: And this is the greater stringency of erasing over writing.

BUILDING, PULLING DOWN, EXTINGUISHING, KINDLING, AND STRIKING WITH A HAMMER. Rabbah and R. Zera both say: Whatever comprises the finishing of the work imposes liability
b on the score of striking with a hammer.[1]

THESE ARE THE PRIMARY LABOURS. THESE is to reject R. Eleazar's view, who imposes liability on account of a derivative labour [when performed concurrently] with a primary labour.[2]

LESS ONE. This is to reject R. Judah's view. For it was taught: R. Judah adds the closing up of the web and the beating of the woof.[3] Said they to him: Closing up of the web is included in stretching the threads, and beating [the woof] is included in weaving.

MISHNAH. THEY ALSO STATED ANOTHER GENERAL PRINCIPLE: WHATEVER IS FIT TO PUT AWAY[4] AND SUCH IS [GENERALLY] PUT AWAY,[5] AND ONE CARRIES IT OUT ON THE SABBATH, HE IS LIABLE TO A SIN-OFFERING ON ITS ACCOUNT. BUT WHATEVER IS NOT FIT TO PUT AWAY AND SUCH IS NOT [GENERALLY] PUT AWAY, AND ONE CARRIES IT OUT ON THE SABBATH, ONLY HE THAT PUT IT AWAY IS LIABLE.[6]

GEMARA. 'WHATEVER IS FIT TO PUT AWAY': What does this exclude?—R. Papa said: It excludes the blood of menstruation. Mar 'Uḳba said: It excludes the wood of an *Asherah*.[7] He who says the blood of menstruation, certainly [excludes] the wood of an *Asherah*. But he who says the wood of an *Asherah*; the blood of menstruation, however, is put away for a cat. But the other
c [argues]: since she would sicken,[1] one would not put it away [for that purpose].

R. Jose b. Ḥanina said: This does not agree with R. Simeon. For if it were as R. Simeon, surely he maintained: All these standards were stated only in respect of those who put away.[2]

a (1) Surely not! (2) That it is freshly killed. (3) Salting the hide being the first step in the tanning process. (4) Before cutting. (5) It is then salted very much and is thus akin to tanning. (6) Tosaf. and Jast. Rashi: he who smooths the ground between the columns. (7) To make them all of the same level. (8) To measure. (9) Giving it its final touches. (10) V. *infra*. (11) Where the blowing shapes it. (12) I.e., anything sticking out of the web, as thread, knots, splinters, etc., which was accidentally woven into the material. (13) As this completes their labour. (14) And would not wear the garments otherwise.

b (1) Cf. *supra*, 74*b*, n. a7. (2) Hence it is possible to incur more than thirty-nine sin-offerings, whereas the number stated is to exclude this possibility. (3) In order to even it. (4) For later use. (5) It is large enough to be put away for later use. (6) If he carries it out, since by putting it away he showed that he attaches a value to it. But for others it is of no account; hence if they carry it out there is no liability. (7) A tree, or perhaps a post, devoted to idolatry; v. Deut. XVI, 21. It is forbidden to benefit thereof.

c (1) It was thought that if an animal consumed blood drawn from any person, that person would lose strength. (2) V. *infra* Mishnah VIII, 1. Thus a wealthy man is not liable for carrying out something which he personally would not put away, though most people would. But according to our Mishnah general practice is the decisive factor for all, and the exceptions are ignored.

AND THAT WHICH IS NOT FIT TO PUT AWAY. [76a] R. Eleazar said: This does not agree with R. Simeon b. Eleazar. For it was taught: R. Simeon b. Eleazar stated a general rule: That which is not fit to put away, and such is not [generally] put away, yet it did become fit to a certain person[3] and he did put it away; then another came and carried it out, the latter is rendered liable through the former's intention.

MISHNAH. HE WHO CARRIES OUT A COW'S MOUTHFUL OF STRAW, A CAMEL'S MOUTHFUL OF PEA-STALKS ['EZAH], A LAMB'S MOUTHFUL OF EARS OF CORN, A GOAT'S MOUTHFUL OF HERBS, MOIST GARLIC OR ONION LEAVES TO THE SIZE OF A DRIED FIG, [OR] A GOAT'S MOUTHFUL OF DRY [LEAVES], [IS CULPABLE].[4] AND THEY DO NOT COMBINE WITH EACH OTHER,[5] BECAUSE THEY ARE NOT ALIKE IN THEIRSTANDARDS.

GEMARA. What is 'EZAH?—Said Rab Judah: The stalks of certain kinds of peas.

a When R. Dimi came,[1] he stated: If one carries out a cow's mouthful of straw for a camel,—R. Johanan maintained: He is culpable: R. Simeon b. Lakish said: He is not culpable. In the evening R. Johanan ruled thus, [but] in the morning he retracted. R. Joseph observed: He did well to retract, since it is not sufficient[2] for a camel. Said Abaye to him: On the contrary, logic supports his original view, since it is sufficient for a cow.[3] But when Rabin came,[4] he said: If one carries out a cow's mouthful of straw for a camel, all agree that he is culpable. Where do they differ: if one carries out a cow's mouthful of pea-stalks for a cow,[5] and the reverse was stated: R. Johanan maintained: He is not culpable; Resh Lakish maintained: He is culpable. R. Johanan maintained; He is not culpable: eating through pressing need is not designated eating. Resh Lakish maintained, He is culpable: eating through pressing need is designated eating.

A LAMB'S MOUTHFUL OF EARS OF CORN. But it was taught: As much as a dried fig?—Both standards are identical.

MOIST GARLIC OR ONION LEAVES TO THE SIZE OF A DRIED FIG, [OR] A GOAT'S MOUTHFUL OF DRY LEAVES. AND THEY DO NOT COMBINE WITH EACH OTHER, BECAUSE THEY ARE NOT ALIKE IN THEIR STANDARDS. R. Jose b. Hanina said: They do not combine for the more stringent, but they do combine for the more lenient [standard].[6] Yet can anything combine when their standards are not alike?[7] But surely we learnt: A garment[8] three [handbreadths] square, a sack[9] four square, a hide five square, and [reed] matting six square [are susceptible to uncleanness as *midras*].[10] Now it was taught thereon: A garment, sacking, a hide,
b and matting combine with each other.[1] And R. Simeon observed: What is the reason? Because they are liable to the uncleanness of sitting.[2] Thus the reason is that they are liable to the uncleanness of sitting;[3] but whatever is not liable to the uncleanness of sitting

(3) He found a use for it. (4) These are the respective minima to which value is assigned, and for which a penalty is incurred. Each is the minimum which will satisfy the animal whose food it is. Moist garlic or onion leaves are fit for human consumption, hence the standard of a dried fig, which is the minimum for all human food. (5) To make up the minimum.

a (1) V. *supra* 5a, n. b9. (2) Lit., 'fit'. (3) And since it is cow's fodder, that is the determining factor, notwithstanding that he carries it out for a camel. (4) V. *supra* 5a, n. b9. (5) This is not a cow's usual food, and it eats it only when nothing else is obtainable. (6) The commodity whose standard is greater does not combine with that whose standard is lesser to make up that lesser quantity, but the latter does combine with the former to make up the greater quantity. That which requires a lesser quantity is naturally more stringent. (7) Even for the more lenient? (8) I.e., a piece of cloth. (9) A rough material, as of goat's hair. (10) V. *supra* 66a, n. a9.

b (1) When joined to make up the requisite minimum, they are susceptible to *midras*. (2) I.e., the uncleanness caused by a *zab*'s (q.v. Glos.) sitting upon them when pieced together. That is because one may employ them thus for patching up a saddle. (3) And having that in common, they can naturally combine.

עין משפט נר מצוה

עב א ב מיי' פי"ח מהל' שבת הל' ג:

[עב] [ג] [מיי' שם]:

א"ר אלעזר הא דלא כר"ש בן אלעזר *דתניא כלל אמר ר' שמעון בן אלעזר כל שאינו כשר להצניע ואין מצניעין כמוהו והוכשר לזה והצניעו ובא אחר והוציאו נתחייב זה במחשבה של זה: **מתני'** *המוציא תבן כמלא פי פרה עצה כמלא פי גמל עמיר כמלא פי טלה עשבים כמלא פי גדי עלי שום ועלי בצלים לחים כגרוגרת יבשים כמלא פי גדי ואין מצטרפין זה עם זה מפני שלא שוו בשיעוריהן: **גמ'** מאי עצה אמר רב יהודה תבן של מיני קטנית כי אתא רב דימי אמר המוציא תבן כמלא פי פרה לגמל ר' יוחנן אמר חייב ר"ש בן לקיש אמר פטור באורתא א"ר יוחנן הכי לצפרא הדר ביה אמר רב יוסף שפיר עבד דהדר דהא לא חזי לגמל א"ל אביי אדרבה כדמעיקרא מסתברא דהא חזי לפרה אלא כי אתא רבין אמר המוציא תבן כמלא פי פרה לגמל דכולי עלמא לא פליגי דחייב כי פליגי במוציא עצה כמלא פי פרה לפרה °ואיפכא איתמר ר' יוחנן אמר פטור °ריש לקיש אמר חייב ר' יוחנן אמר פטור אכילה על ידי הדחק לא שמה אכילה *ריש לקיש אמר [ב]חייב אכילה *ע"י הדחק שמה אכילה: עמיר כמלא פי טלה: והתניא כגרוגרת אידי ואידי חד שיעורא הוא: עלי שום ועלי בצלים לחים כגרוגרת ויבשים כמלא פי הגדי ואין מצטרפין זה עם זה מפני שלא שוו בשיעוריהן: אמר ר' יוסי בר חנינא [ג]אין מצטרפין לחמור שבהן אבל מצטרפין לקל שבהן וכל דלא שוו בשיעורייהו מי מצטרפין והתנן *הבגד ג' על ג' והשק ד' על ד' והעור ה' על ה' מפץ ו' על ו' *ותני עלה הבגד והשק והעור העור והמפץ מצטרפין זה עם זה ואמר ר"ש מה טעם מפני שראויין ליטמא מושב טעמא דראויין ליטמא מושב אבל אין ראוי ליטמא מושב לא אמר רבא הבא

(בשוליים: ב"ק דף יט: ועי' בב"ק קב.)

רש"י

א"ר אלעזר הא. דקתני מתניתין דאינו כשר. להצניע והצניעו *אחר הוא מתחייב על הוצאתו וכל אדם פטורין דלא כר' שמעון בן אלעזר: **מתני'** עצה. מפרש בגמרא: כמלא פי גמל. נפיש שיעורא מפי פרה אבל כמלא פי פרה לא מיחייב דהא לא חזו לפרה: עמיר. קשין של שבלין: פי טלה. נפיש מפי גדי הלכך עמיר דלא חזי לגדי לא מיחייב כמלא פי גדי עד דאיכא מלא פי טלה אבל עשבים הואיל וחזו בין לטלה בין לגדי מיחייב אפי' כמלא פי גדי: לחין. הראויין לאדם כגרוגרת דזה שיעור לכל מאכל אדם לשבת אבל כמלא פי גדי לא דלחים לא חזו לגדי: **גמ'** המוציא תבן כמלא פי פרה. והוציאו להאכילו לגמל שפי גמל גדול מפי פרה: דהא חזי לפי פרה. הלכך שיעור חשוב הוא ולכל מי שיוציאנו לא פקע שיעוריה בהכי: דחייב. דהאיכא שיעורא דחזי לפרה הלכך כשר להצניע הוא ומצניעין כמוהו: עצה. לא חזיא לפרה אלא ע"י הדחק אלא לגמל הוא דחזי וזה הוציאו לפרה: רבי יוחנן אמר פטור. דהא לגמל דחזי ליה ליכא שיעורא ואי משום דלצורך פרה הוציאו ולגבה איכא שיעור אכילה ע"י הדחק לאו אכילה היא הלכך לא משערי' ליה בפרה: אין מצטרפין לחמור שבהם. מי ששיעורו גדול הוי קל ואינו מצטרף להשלים שיעורו של חמור דהא לא חשיב כי ההוא אבל החשוב משלים את הקל לכשיעור תבן מצטרף עם עצה להשלי' פי גמל ועצה אין מצטרף עם התבן להשלים מלא פי פרה: מי מצטרפין. אפילו להשלים חמור את הקל: ג' על ג'. לטומאת מדרס הזב ליעשות אב הטומאה: הבגד והשק מצטרפין. שהבגד משלים שיעור השק שק עשוי מנוצה של עזים: ואמר ר' שמעון מה טעם. מצטרפין: הואיל וראוין ליטמא מושב. אם לירף משנים יחד לטלאי מרדעת של חמור כשיעורו לענין מושב הזב אם קלע משנים מהן ותקןטפח על טפח לישב עליו מיטמא ליה אב הטומאה במושב הזב דתניא(א) המקלע מכולן טפח על טפח טמא מושב ואמרינן טעמא בפ"ק דסוכה הואיל וראוי לטלות על גבי חמור שאינו מקפיד אם הוא משני מינין: חמור לקל כגון תבן לעצה למלא פי גמל ואפי' לא יהא תבן ראוי לגמל שמא אגב העצה הוא ראוי:

תוספות

הכא

שמצריך לקמן הצנעה היינו לאדם עשיר שאין דרכו להצניע ומכל מקום פירוש מילתיה דר"ש צריך לפרש כמו שפירש כאן דאי מיירי במצניעין לאותו דבר עצמו שמפורש במשנה כמו שפירש התם אם כן כולהו הוה מצי למימר בכל שהוא בכדי שיפת קילור כדתנן בפ' המצניע (לקמן צ:) דלרפואה בכל שהוא ואתיא כר"ש מדלא קאמר התם בגמ' הא דלא כר"ש כי היכי דקאמר (דף צא.) הא דלא כר"ש בן אלעזר ומהתם נמי יש לדקדק דלר' שמעון סתם בני אדם שרגילין להצניעו מיחייבי אפי' לא הצניעו מדקתני המצניע לזרע כו' וכל אדם אין חייבין עליו אלא כשיעורו משמע בלא הצנעה וכר"ש נמי אתיא כדפי' ואין לפרש דבעשיר שאין דרכו להצניע לא מיחייב לר"ש אפי' בהצניעו דהא אמר בהמוציא יין בד"א במוציא אבל במצניע כל שהוא ר"ש אומר בד"א במצניע כו' ומפרש מצניע דרבנן בתלמיד שאמר לו כו' דבר שאינו חשוב לכל אי אצנעיה רביה אין אי לא לא ודומיא דהכי נראה דהוי מצניע דר"ש דתליא מילתא באותו שהצניעו היינו בעשיר קשה לרשב"א דמהאי טעמא דקאמר הכא מתני' דלא כר"ש משום דמתני' סתמא קתני דחייב משמע שכל בני אדם חייבין עליו אפי' אותן שאין חשוב להן שיעור זה מהאי טעמא נמי הוה ליה למימר בההיא דפרק המצניע דהויא דלא כר"ש ושמא י"ל דהכא דנקט לפרושי הוה ליה לפרושי טפי:

אכילה ע"י הדחק לא שמה אכילה. והא דאמר בפ' כילד הרגל (ב"ק דף יט.) אכילה ע"י הדחק שמה אכילה ה"מ לענין ניזקין דלא חשבינן ליה משונה אבל לאחשובה לענין שבת לא חשיבא אכילה:

אידי ואידי חד שיעורא הוא. והא דנקט במתני' כמלא פי טלה ולא נקט כגרוגרת לאשמעי' דמשום אכילת טלה נתנו בו חכמים שיעור זה דאי נקט כגרוגרת לא הוה ידעינן למה נתנו בו חכמים שיעור זה:

מפני שלא שוו בשיעוריהם. אבל אותם ששוו כגון עמיר ועלי שום ועלי בצלים לחים מצטרפין וכן **הבגד** והשק השק והעור כו'. דוקא בכה"ג הבגד והשק השק והעור אבל הבגד והעור והשק והמפץ אין מצטרפין שאין ראויין להתחבר יחד והמחברן בטלה דעתו ואין טמאים מדרס. ר"י:

ואמר ר"ש מה טעם כו'. תימה לר"י דמה צריך להאי טעמא דהא כיון דמצטרפין זה עם זה א"כ ראוי לחברן וחזו למדרס וכיון דחזו למדרס פשיטא דמצטרפין לטומאת מדרס דהא אפי' כופת שאור שיחדה לישיבה טמאה מדרס כדאמרינן בהעור והרוטב (חולין קכט.) והכא בטומאת מדרס איירי מדקאמר הבגד שלשה על שלשה דלענין טומאת מת אפי' ג' על ג' כדפרישית לעיל ואור"י דודאי הא דקתני הבגד שלשה על שלשה לא מיירי אלא למדרס אבל סיפא דשק ועור ומפץ מיירי נמי בטומאת מת והכי איתא במס' כלים בפכ"ז הבגד שלשה על שלשה [למדרס ומשום ג' על ג'] לטומאת מת השק ד' על ד' העור ה' על ה' המפץ ו' על ו' שוו בין למדרס בין לטמא מת אלא שהש"ס מביאה בקוצר כמו שרגיל בכמה מקומות ועל טומאת מת קאמר מה טעם מצטרפין בשלא יחדו למדרס ולא צריך האי טעמא אצירוף דעור ומפץ °דמפץ לא מטמא במת אלא כשטמא בזב דהיינו כשיחדו למדרס ומק"ו דפכין קטנים כדאמרינן בפ' ר' עקיבא (לקמן פד:):

הואיל וראוין ליטמא מושב. פי' בקונטרס אם קילע משנים ולירף יחד לטלאי מרדעת החמור והיא דהמקלע מכולם טפח על טפח דמעילה היינו שבין כולם יש טפח ואין נראה לר"י דמה צריך להביא ראיה שראויין להצטרף בלאו טעמא דמושב נמי שמעינן ממתני' דהכא שראויין להצטרף יחד באותו סדר כמו שמטייס בגד לשק ושק לעור ועור למפץ דדוקא נקט לפי שאלו ראויין להצטרף יחד ונראה לר"י כמו שפי' ריב"א דהואיל וראויין ליטמא מושב היינו הואיל ושוו שיעוריהן לענין מושב וכמו שפירש בקונטרס בפ"ק דסוכה (דף יז:) דהמקלע מכולן היינו מאיזה מהן שיקלע יהא טמא ואע"ג שכאן אין שיעורן שוה מצטרפין הואיל ולענין מושב שיעורן שוה והא דקאמר ה"נ חזו לדוגמא היינו נמי דשיעורן שוה לדוגמא כדתנן בפרק המצניע דלדוגמא כל שהוא הלכך מצטרפין אפי' לענין דבר דלא שוו שיעורייהו וה"ה דהוי מצי למינקט הכא ולזרע ולרפואה דהוו נמי בכל שהוא אלא דלא כל דברים שייך בהו זרע ורפואה אבל דוגמא שייכא בכל דבר והא דקאמר בסוכה המקלע מכולן כו' הואיל וראוי לטלות על גבי חמורו לשון הואיל וראוי לאו דווקא דדווקא אם עשה מהן טלאי ויחדן לכך טמא בטפח על טפח וכן מצינו לקמן בפ' א"ר עקיבא (דף צ:) הואיל וראויין למתק הקדרה דהוה ליה למימר הואיל וממתקין דהא מיירי שנפלו לתוך הקדרה: ר"י: **תוספתא*** המקלע למשכב אין פחות משלשה על שלשה למושב טפח ולמעמד כל שהוא:

חמשת

רבינו חננאל

ומנקה הבגד ודומה למנקב· דתנינן בכמה מקומות ואם נשארו כגון אלו בבגד ובעל הבגד קפיד עלייהו ושקיל להו בשבת חייב משום מכה בפטיש· פי' כל דבר שהוא גמר מלאכה נקרא מכה בפטיש: **המוחק** אות אחת גדולה שיש במקומה שיעור לכתוב ב' אותיות חייב והכותב אות אחת גדולה שיש במקומה שיעור לכתוב ב' אותיות פטור· זה חומר במוחק מבכותב. אלו אבות מלאכות לאפוקי מדר' אלעזר דמחייב אתולדה במקום אב כמו שכבר פרשנוהו למעלה (דף עג:) דמאן דעבד ב' אבות או ב' תולדות משני אבות או אב ותולדה דאב (אחד) [אחר] בהעלם אחד חייב בזה אחד ובזה אחד· ואי עביד אב ותולדתו לא מיחייב אלא חדא· ועוד חזר ושנה מ' חסר אחת לאפוקי מר' יהודה דאמר שובט ומדקדק מאבות מלאכות הן· אמרו לו שובט הרי הוא בכלל מיסך· מדקדק בכלל אורג· *פי' יש לארונין עץ או עצם שראשו חד ונקרא כדבר ודומה למחט של סקאין· וכך שמו בלשון יון כדבר. מעבירו על השתי כשהוא מותח לפניו לארינה ושובט בו החוטין ומקרב המבדילין בין ב' החוטין העליונים והתחתונים ומדנחים להתפרק העליונים מן התחתונים ונפתח נפש המסכת לידות בתוכם חוט הערב ואין לה אב אלא הרי הוא בכלל מיסך והמדקדק הוא המדקדק על חוט הערב כדי להדחק ולהלחץ עם חבירו וזהו בכלל אריגה: **ועוד** כלל אחר אמרו כל הכשר להצניע ומצניעין כמוהו והוציאו בשבת חייב עליו חטאת· כל הכשר להצניע רב מתנה אמר למעוטי דם נדה שאין חייבין בהוצאתו· וכ"ש איסורי הנאה· ועצי אשרה שאין חייבין בהוצאתו· מר עוקבא אמר לאפוקי עצי אשרה אבל דם נדה חייב כו' וזה ששנינו ומצניעין כמוהו א"ר יוסי ב"ר חנינא דלא כר' שמעון דאי ר' שמעון האמר דברים הללו לא נאמרו אלא למצניעיהן. והכין סבירא ליה לר' שמעון לענין המוציא יין כדי מזיגת הכוס חלב כדי גמיעה כו' דכולן שיעורן ברביעית ושיעורין הללו כדי גמיעה וכדי ליתן על הכתית כו'· לא נאמרו אלא למצניעיהן כלומר אם הצניע בחול [פחות] משיעורין הללו אע"פ שהוציאו בשבת פטור ורבנן סבירא להו אם הצניעו אדם בחול כל שהוא אע"פ שאין כשר להצניע והוציאו בשבת חייב דהא (אשביח)

[אהשביה] בהצנעתו· וזה ששנינו כל שאין כשר להצניע ואין מצניעין כמוהו והוציאו בשבת אין חייב אלא המצניעו אבל מי לא שהצניע בחול אם הוציאו בשיעורין הללו חייב· ואם לא פטור· וזהו כמו דתנן המצניע לזרע לדוגמא ולרפואה והוציאו בשבת חייב עליו כל שהוא· ושאר כל אדם אין חייבין עליו אלא כשיעורו נמצא ר' שמעון מיקל מדברי חכמים ור' שמעון בן אלעזר מחמיר מדבריהם· דקאמר כל שאינו כשר להצניע ואין מצניעין כמוהו והוכשר לזה והצניעו ובא אחר והוציאו נתחייב המוציאו ממחשבת המצניעו ואע"פ שאינו כשר להצניעו ואין מצניעין כמוהו חייב עליו· ורבנן אמרי אינו חייב בפחות מכשיעור אלא המצניעו· תמו הכללות· ובאנו לפרש שיעורי ההוצאה: **המוציא** תבן כמלוא פי פרה. עצה תבן הקטנית וקשה ממנו שיעורו כמלוא פי גמל· עמיר כמלוא פי טלה· עשבים כמלוא פי גדי ולענין המוציא תבן כמלוא פי פרה לגמל (הלכה) כר"ע לא פליגי דחייב שזה הוא שיעור הוצאתו ולא אכפת לן [אי] לגמל נתכוון להוציאו או לפרה אלא כי פליגי ר' יוחנן ור' אושעי' במוציא עצה כמלוא פי פרה לפרה· ועיקר הדבר שאין העצה מאכל פרה ואין שיעור כמלוא פי פרה אלא כמלוא פי גמל שהוא יותר ממלוא פי פרה· ועכשיו שנתכוון לפרה איפלגו ר' אושעי' סבר אכילה ע"י הדחק שמה אכילה אע"פ שאין פרה אוכלת אותו כדרכה אלא כיון שאוכלת אותו ע"י הדחק וישנו מלא פיה והוציאו לה חייב עליו(ור') [ור"י] סבר אכילה שע"י הדחק לאו שמה אכילה (וזה)ופטור:לענין הא דתנן אין מצטרפין זה עם זה מפני שלא שוו בשיעוריהן א"ר יוסי ב"ר חנינא אין מצטרפין לחמור שבהן אבל מצטרפין לקל שבהן אם הוציא עמיר ועשבים אם יש בין שניהם כמלוא פי טלה מצטרפין כי החמור משלים לקל והחייב אבל אם אין בהם כמלוא פי טלה· אע"פ שיש בהן כמלוא פי הגדי פטור שאין מצטרפין כי אין הקל משלים לחמור וכן עשבים משלימין לתבן ואין התבן משלים לעשבים וטקשינן היאך תאמר בהני דלא שוו בשיעוריהן להדדי דמצטרפין והלא הבגד והשק והעור לענין טומאה שלא שוו בשיעוריהן אע"ג דתנן הבגד והשק והעור מצטרפין והשק והעור והמפץ מצטרפין דקתני סיפא· א"ר שמעון מה טעם הואיל וראויין ליטמא מושב דראויין ליטמא מושב הא אי לא הוו ראויין ליטמא מושב לא הוו מצטרפין משום שלא שוו בשיעוריהן להדדי· וא"כ היכי קאמר ר' יוסי בר' חנינא מצטרפין לקל שבהן והכין הוה ראוי שלא יצטרפו כל עיקר· ופריק רבא לר' יוסי ב"ר חנינא ואמר הכי נמי ראויין לדוגמא כשם שהבגד והשק אף על פי שאין בזה כשיעור ולא בזה כשיעור כיון שאלו מתחברין יש בעיניהם כשיעור השק שהוא הקל ואפשר לחברן זה בזה ולישב עליהן וראויין ליטמא מושב· כן התבן והעצה אפשר להוציא מזה כמעט ומזה כמעט להראותן דוגמא לקונה לומר מאלו אני סיבי ולהבין השובין בחיבורין ויש צורך להוציאו כסדר הזה משום כן מצטרפין לקל שבהן אבל אוכלין שיעורן כולן כגרוגרת לפיכך מצטרפין זע"ז אבל קליפיהן ועוקציהן וסובן ומורסנן אין מצטרפין עמהן

*) עי' ערוך ערך שבט א' וע' דוך:

מסורת הש"ס

נ"ל אחד

לקמן צא. זבחים מז.

לקמן עט. מעילה יח. סוכה יז: כלים פכ"ז מ"ב

כלים פ"ב ס"ב

הגהות הב"ח

(א) רש"י ד"ה הואיל וכו' דתניא. נ"ב במעילה פ"ק קדשי' במזבח דף יח:

[הכסף משנה העתיק רבי אושעיא אמר חייב וכו' ופסק הרמב"ם כרבי אושעיא שהלכ' כמותו לגבי ר' יוחנן עכ"ל]

גליון הש"ס

גמ' ואיפכא איתמר. כעין זה נדה דף לג ע"א: שם ר"ל אמר חייב. בכסף משנה פי"ח הלכה ג מהלכות שבת הגירסא ר' אושעיא: תוס' ד"ה ואמר ר"ש וכו' דמפץ לא מטמא במת. עי' פכ"ד מי"ד דכלים וברע"ב שם:

חמשת רבעים קמח ועוד גרסי' כדפרי' בפ"ק (דף טו.) :

הדרן עלך כלל גדול

ה"נ חזיא לדוגמא : מתני' *המוציא אוכלים כגרוגרת חייב ומצטרפין זה עם זה מפני ששוו בשיעוריהן חוץ מקליפתן וגרעיניהן ועוקציהן וסובן ומורסנן ר' יהודה אומר חוץ מקליפי עדשין שמתבשלות עמהן : גמ' וסובן ומורסנן לא מצטרפין והתנן[*] *חמשת רבעים קמח ועוד חייבין בחלה הן וסובן ומורסנן אמר אביי שכן עני אוכל פתו בעיסה בלוסה: רבי יהודה אומר חוץ מקליפי עדשים המתבשלות עמהן : עדשים אין פולין לא והתניא ר' יהודה אומר חוץ מקליפי פולין ועדשים לא קשיא הא בחדתי הא בעתיקי עתיקי מ"ט לא אמר ר' אבהו מפני שנראין כזובובין בקערה :

הדרן עלך כלל גדול

*המוציא [ב]יין כדי מזיגת הכוס חלב כדי *גמיעה דבש כדי ליתן על הכתית °שמן כדי לסוך אבר קטן מים כדי לשוף בהם את הקילור *ושאר כל המשקין ברביעית וכל השופכין ברביעית ר"ש אומר כולן ברביעית ולא *נאמרו *כל השיעורין הללו אלא למצניעיהן : גמ' תנא *כדי מזיגת כוס יפה ומאי כוס יפה כוס של ברכה [ג]אמר רב נחמן אמר רבה בר אבוה כוס של ברכה צריך שיהא בו רובע רביעית כדי שימזגנו ויעמוד על רביעית אמר רבא אף אנן נמי תנינא

הכא נמי חזי . ביחד : לדוגמא . מי שיש לו למכור צובר מכולן ונותן לפני חלונו להראות שיש לו למכור מכולן וניחא ליה שיהו מחוברין יחד דאיידי דזוטרי כל חד וחד הרוח מפזרתו: מתני' אוכלים כו'. למאכל אדם : ומצטרפין . כל אוכלי אדם זה עם זה : חוץ מקליפיהן . שאינן אוכל ואין משלימין השיעור : ועוקציהן. זנב הפרי דהוא עץ בעלמא: וסובן . קליפת חטין הנושרת מחמת כתישה : ומורסנן. הנשאר בנפה : ר' יהודה אומר. כל הקליפין אין מצטרפין כדאמרן חוץ מקליפי עדשים שמצרפות אותן : שמתבשלות עמהן. לאפוקי קליפה חיצונה שהן גדלות בתוכה הנושרות בגורן: גמ' בלוסה. מעורבת בסובנה ובמורסנה הלכך לחם הארץ קרינן ביה ומיהו לענין שבת מידי דחשיב בעינן וסתמייהו דהני לאו אוכל נינהו : פולין חדתי · קליפתן מצטרפין : כזובובין . לפי שהן שחורות :

הדרן עלך כלל גדול

המוציא יין . חי : כדי מזיגת הכוס. כשיעור שנותנין יין חי לתוך כוס להוסיף עליו מים כהלכתו ולמזוג אותו בהן ובגמרא מפרש באיזה כוס משערו : כתית . שבגבי הסוסים והגמלים מחמת המשאות רדוי"ש בלע"ז והכי אמר בהמפקיד בבבא מציעא (דף לח.) דבש והדבים למאי חזי לכתותא דגמלי אבל רבותי פירשו כתית מכה שעל גב היד ושע"ג הרגל: לשוף. לשפשף ולהמחות בהן : קילור . שנותנין על העין לודיי"א בלע"ז : ברביעית . בילה ומחצה רביעית הלוג : שופכים . מים סרוחים ובגמרא מפרש למאי חזו : כולן ברביעית . אף היין והחלב והדבש : ולא נאמרו . שיעורין שבמשנה אלא למצניעיהן לבד וחזר המצניע והוציאו חייב אבל שאר כל אדם שהוציאו אינו חייב וסבירא לי' לר"ש דמצניע עצמו בעי שיעורא זוטא ובציר מהא שיעורא לא מיחייב כדאמרינן בפרקין דלעיל (דף עה:) דלית ליה לר"ש כל שאין כשר להצניע ואין מצניעים כמוהו שיתחייב עליו מצניעו : גמ' תנא.בתוספתא המוציא יין כדי מזיגת כוס יפה פירוש לכוס דמתני' : כוס של ברכה . ברכת המזון שהצריכו חכמים ליפותו כדאמרי' בברכות (דף נא·) עיטור ועיטוף הדחה ושטיפה חי ומלא : אמר רב נחמן גרסי' ולא גרסי' דאמר : שיעור כוס של ברכה צריך שיהא בו . יין חי רובע של רביעית הלוג: כדי שימזגנו.במים שלשה חלקים מים ואחד יין : ויעמוד על רביעי'.הלוג: תנינא

המוציא יין . חלב כדי גמיעה · הקשה רבינו אפריס דתניא בשילהי המצניע (לקמן צה.) החולב והמחבץ והמגבן כגרוגרת ואין חילוק בין מוציא לחולב דהא לקמן בפירקין *אמרי' דהמעבד עור שיעורו כמוציא עור ותירץ ר"י דסתם חלב לגמיאה דכפיס מגרוגרת והתם מיירי בחולב לגבינה דאחשוביה אחשביה וכן מוכח דכדי גמיאה כפיש מגרוגרת דבפ' בתרא דיומא(פ.) גבי שותה ביוה"כ איכא דמחייב ברביעית ואיכא למ"ד בכדי גמיאה ובעירובין (דף פב:) משמע דתשע סעודות יש בקב ובפרק חלון (שם פ:) משמע שיש י"ח גרוגרות בשתי סעודות ואי כדי גמיאה פחות מגרוגרת א"כ הוו יותר מדאי חלוקים זה מזה ומיהו(ג)כגרוגרת דהמצניע (לקמן צה.)איירי ביבש אפשר שבתחלה היה יותר מכדי גמיאה ולפי זה צריך לפרש דסתם חלב הוי לגבינה והא דמיחייב הכא בכדי גמיאה היינו במפרש בהדיא לשתיה אבל אי סתם חלב הוי לאכול ולשתות ולא לגבינה אפי' היה מפרש בהדיא לגבינה היה חייב אכדי גמיאה דזוטרא הואיל וסתמו לכך כדאמרינן לעיל המוציא תבן כמלא פי פרה לגמל חייב דהא חזי לפרה וי"מ דכשחלב ככר בעין מיחייב בכדי גמיאה אבל חולב לא מיחייב אלא כגרוגרת דאין אדם טורח לחלוב בפחות מגרוגרת דכה"ג אמרי' לקמן (דף עט.) דאין אדם טורח לגבל טיט לעשות פי כור ומיהו אומר ר"י דלא דמי דהתם אין המים חשובין מחמת שראוי לגבל בהן את הטיט כמו הטיט עצמו שהוא מגובל כבר אבל הכא כשחולב להוציא מן הדד בכדי גמיאה יש לו להיות חשוב כמו במקום אחר* : כדי גמיעה . פי' הר"ר פור"ת מלא לוגמא ולא משמע כן במסכת יומא בפרק בתרא (דף פ.) :

צריך שיהא בו רובע רביעית. רביעית דהכא הייט רביעית הלוג כדפי' הקונט' ועוד יש לדקדק דהייט רביעית דפרק ג' מינין (נזיר לח.) הם רביעית הלוג מדפריך ותו ליכא והאיכא רביעית נוטלין לידים ובמסכת ידים (פ"א מ"א) משמע בהדיא דהוי רביעית הלוג ועוד דבערבי פסחים (פסחים קט:) משמע דכוס הוי רביעית של תורה ומתוך חשבון דמקוה משמע דהייט רביעית הלוג והא דקאמר התם.קיסתא דמורייסא הות בציפורי והות כמין לוגא דמקדשא ובה משערין רביעית של פסח לאו בכולה משערין דהייט כל הלוג אלא כלומר ברובע של אותה מדה משערין רביעית של פסח: כדי שימזגט ויעמוד על רביעית . משמע דכוס של ברכה טעון מזיגה וכן בפ' שלשה שאכלו (ברכות נ:) אר"י בר חנינא מודים חכמים לר"א בכוס של ברכה שאין מברכין עליו עד שיתן לתוכו מים ותימה דבסוף פר' שלשה שאכלו (שם דף נא.) אמרו עשרה דברים נאמרו בכוס של ברכה הדחה ושטיפה חי ומלא אלמא חי בעינן ומיהו התם פירש בקונטרס דלא שיהא חי כשמברכין עליו אלא דנותט חי בכוס שמברכין בו לאפוקי שלא ימזגנו ויתננו בכוס של ברכה ור"ת מפרש דחי דקאמר הייט מזיג ולא מזיג דמיקרי חי כדאמרי' בפ' בן סורר (סנהדרין ע.) עד שיאכל תרטימר בשר וישתה יין חי ומוקי לה התם במזיג ולא מזיג ובברכת הארץ מוסיף מים עד שיהא מזוג כראוי כדאמר בפ' שלשה שאכלו(ברכות נא.)שמוסיף בברכת הארץ ולא כמו שפירש שם בקונטרס שמוסיף יין בברכת הארץ ובני נרבונא מפרשים דחי קאי אכוס שצריך שיהא שלם ואתי שפיר דכל אותן דברים דחשיב התם הוו כולהו בכוס ולא ביין וכה"ג בפרק בתרא דמכות (דף טז:) ריסק ט' נמלים ואחד חי דהייט שלם דאפי' מת חשיב בריה כדאמר בסוף פ' גיד הנשה (חולין דף קב:)*: ויעמוד על רביעית . ואע"ג דאמרינן בערבי פסחים (דף קז.) המקדש אם טעם מלא לוגמא יצא ומלא לוגמא הוי טפי מרביעית כדמוכח בפ' בתרא דיומא (דף פ.) יש לומר דמלא לוגמא דהתם לאו דוקא אלא כדי שיסלקו לצד אחד ויראה כמלא לוגמא כדמפרש ביומא אהגהו דהתם ועוד יש לומר דדוקא מקדש :

אף אנן נמי תנינא . דכוס של ברכה טעון רביעית דמסתמא יין שיעורו לכשימזגנו ויעמוד על רביעית כמו שאר משקין דקתני סיפא דהוו ברביעית וקתני כדי מזיגת כוס יפה משמע דכוס של ברכה לכשימזוג בעינן שיהא רביעית כמו בהולאה אבל הא דבעינן יין רובע רביעית לא שמעינן ממתני' אלא ממילא ידעינן דהא מזיגה הויא על חד תלת והא דלא נקט במתני' כדי מזיגת רביעית מילתא אגב אורחיה קמ"ל דכוס של ברכה ברביעית ועוד משום דמהאי טעמא דחזי לכוס של ברכה חשיב ומיחייב בפחות מרביעית לפי שיכול להוסיף עליו מים ושאר משקין לא מיחייב בפחות מרביעית אע"פ שיכול להוסיף עליהן כדמסיק ודקאמרת מים בכד ומצטרפין לגבי שבת מידי דחשיב בעינן :

דלאמר

רבינו חננאל

ר' יהודה אומר חוץ מקליפי עדשים שהן מתבשלין עמהן ולפיכך מצטרפות · והא דתנן חוץ מקליפיהן ר' יהודה אומר חוץ מקליפי עדשים חוץ מחוץ ונמצא מיעוט ממיעוט ולרבות הוא כמה שפירשנו למעלה: ושניא חלה דסובן ומורסנן הין מצטרפין לקמח להוציא מכולן חלה · שכן עני אוכל פתו מעיסה בלוסה שיש בה סובין ומורסן וזו היא עיסתו ואמר רחמנא ראשית עריסותיכ' אבל להוצאת שבת אין סובן ומורסנן מצטרפין וכן פולים אם חדשים הן הרי מנהג לבשל בקליפיהן. וקאמר ר' יהודה בברייתא שאף הן מצטרפות עם הפולין·אבל אם הם ישני' ונישתחרו נראין כזובובים בקערה ורגילין בני אדם לקלפן קודם בישול והלכך אין קליפיהן מצטרפות עמהן :

הדרן עלך כלל גדול

פ"ח המוציא יין כדי מזיגת הכוס · תנא כדי מזיגת הכוס יפה · ומאי כוס יפה כוס של ברכה · והתם אמרינן אמר רב יהודה אמר שמואל כוסות הללו צריך שיהא בהן כדי מזיגת כוס יפה · ומותבינן ד' כוסות הללו צריך שיהא בהן כדי רביעית ופרקינן אידי ואידי חד שיעורא הוא והאי דקאמר צריך שיהא בארבעתן רביעית *) בכל אחת רובע רביעית כדאמרינן הכא · אמר רב נחמן אמר רבה בר אבוה כוס של ברכה צריך שיהא בו רובע רביעית כדי שימזגנו ויעמוד על רביעית · ואמר רבה אף אנן נמי

*) נראה דחסר איזה תיבות וצ"ל שיהא בהן כדי רביעית היינו שיהא בארבעתן וכו'

רב נסים גאון

פ"ח המוציא יין. אמר : נחמן אמר רבה בר אבוה כוס של ברכה צריך שיהא בו רובע רביעית כדי שימזגנו ויעמוד על רביעית · משתכח פירושיה בפרק ערבי פסחים (דף קח) אמר רב יהודה אמר שמואל ד' כוסות הללו צריך שיהא בהן כדי מזיגת כוס יפה ואותבי' לשמואל מברייתא דקתני בה ד' כוסות הללו צריך שיהא בהן כדי רביעית ופרקינן מאי כדי מזיגת כוס יפה דאמר שמואל בהאי שיעורא ואמרו עוד (שם דף קט) אמר רב יצחק קיסטא דמוריסא דהוות בטבריא היא הוות כמין דמקדשא ובה משערין רביעית של פסח ומיכן את למד כוס של ברכה רביעית במסכת נזיריות בפרק ג' מינים אסורין (דף לח) אמרו אמר ר' אלעזר עשר רביעיות נקים רב כהנא בידיה ה' סומקאתא וה' חיורתא ה' סומקאתא נזיר ועושה פסח שהורו לטקדש ומתים סימן נזיר רביעית יין לנזיר עושה פסח דאמר רב יהודה אמר שמואל ד' כוסות הללו צריך שיהא בהן כדי רביעית שהורו השותה רביעית יין אל יורה במקדש שהשותה רביעית יין ונכנס למקדש חייב מתים דתניא מניין לרביעית דם היוצאה משני מתים שהיא מטמאה באהל שנא' (ויקרא כא) ועל כל נפשות מת לא יבא וחמש חיורתא חלה נזיר מצורע (שנפלו) [שנפסלו] בשבת סימן חלה רביעית שמן לחלה נזיר רביעית שמן לנזיר מצורע רביעית שמן לנזיר מצורע ושנפסלו דתנן ושאר כל משקין טמאין את הגויה לרביעית שבת דתנן ושאר כל המשקין ברביעית וכל השופכין ברביעית :

עין משפט נר מצוה

עג א מיי' פי"ח מהל' שבת הלכה א :

עג [א] מיי' פ"ו מהל' בכורים הלכה טו והלכה יח טוש"ע יו"ד סימן שכד סעיף א ג :

א ב ג מיי' פי"ח מהל' שבת הלכה ב :

[דף עט.]

[ג"י הערוך ערך גם ד' גמיאה]

רש"י ליתא אמרו

[ועי' תוס' פסחים סה. ד"ה כחולב]

מסורת הש"ס

חלה פ"ב מ"ו ע"ש פסחי' מח: עדיות פ"א מ"ב

[עירובין כט:]

[נזיר לח.]

[לעיל פה:]

[עירובין כט:]

[וע' תוספות ברכות נ: ד"ה מודים]

הגהות הב"ח

(א) תוס' ד"ה המוציא וכו' ומיהו אי כגרוגרות דהמצניע :

גליון הש"ס

מתני' שמן כדי לסוך. עי' פ"ב מ"ב דכלים בר"ש שם :

is not so?—Said Raba: [76b] Here too they are fit for patterns.[4]

MISHNAH. HE WHO CARRIES OUT [HUMAN] FOODSTUFFS TO THE SIZE OF A DRIED FIG IS LIABLE, AND THEY COMBINE WITH EACH OTHER, BECAUSE THEY ARE EQUAL IN THEIR STANDARDS, EXCEPT THEIR SHELLS, KERNELS, STALKS, HUSKS[5] AND COARSE BRAN.[6] R. JUDAH SAID: EXCLUDING THE SHELLS OF LENTILS, BECAUSE THEY ARE BOILED TOGETHER WITH THEM.[7]

GEMARA. Now, do not husks and coarse bran combine [with the grain or flour]? But we learnt: Just over five quarters of flour are liable to *hallah*,[8] [including] that itself [*sc*. the flour], the husks and the bran?[9]—Said Abaye: That is because a poor man eats his bread [baked] of unsifted dough.[10]

R. JUDAH SAID: EXCLUDING THE SHELLS OF LENTILS, BECAUSE THEY ARE BOILED TOGETHER WITH THEM. Only lentils, but not beans? But it was taught, R. Judah said: Excluding the shells of beans and lentils.—There is no difficulty: The one refers to new [beans],[11] the other to old. Why not old ones?—Said R. Abbahu: Because they look like flies in the dish.[12]

CHAPTER VIII

MISHNAH. WHOSOEVER CARRIES OUT [RAW] WINE, [THE STANDARD IS THAT IT BE] ENOUGH FOR THE MIXING
a OF A CUP;[1] MILK, AS MUCH AS IS QUAFFED AT A TIME; HONEY, SUFFICIENT TO PLACE ON A SCAB;[2] OIL, AS MUCH AS IS REQUIRED TO RUB IN A SMALL LIMB; WATER, ENOUGH FOR RUBBING COLLYRIUM;[3] AND ALL OTHER LIQUIDS, [THE STANDARD IS] A REBI'ITH;[4] AND ALL WASTE WATER,[5] A REBI'ITH. R. SIMEON SAID: [THE STANDARD FOR] ALL THESE IS A REBI'ITH, ALL THESE MEASURES HAVING BEEN STATED ONLY IN RESPECT OF THOSE WHO PUT THEM AWAY.[6]

GEMARA. A Tanna taught: Enough for the mixing of a full-measured[7] cup. And what is a full-measured cup? The cup of benediction.[8] R. Nahman said in Rabbah b. Abbuha's name: The cup of benediction must contain a quarter of a *rebi'ith* [of raw wine], so that it may be mixed and amount to a *rebi'ith*.

(4) These can be pieced together to serve as a commercial pattern or sample of one's ware. (5) Or, thin bran (Levy, *Wörterbuch*). (6) These are not eaten, and consequently do not combine with the edible foodstuffs. (7) Hence they count as foodstuffs too, and are excluded from the exception. (8) V. *supra* 15a for notes. (9) Thus they do combine. (10) But with respect to the Sabbath bread of better quality is required before liability is incurred. (11) Their shells combine. (12) The peel of old beans goes black and when in the dish looks like flies.

a (1) Wine had to be mixed with water before it could be drunk. (2) Rashi offers two interpretations: (i) the sore spot on the backs of horses or camels, caused by the chafing of the saddle; (ii) a bruise on the hand or foot. (3) An eye-salve. Rashi: to rub it over and cause it to dissolve.—So that it can be applied to the eye in liquid form. (4) V. Glos. (5) Any dirty liquid that must be poured out. (6) V. *supra* 75b, n. b6. Here Rashi explains: These measures are less than a *rebi'ith*, and only one who actually put away that quantity and then carries it out is liable to a sin-offering. Tosaf. on 75b s.v. הא accepts Rashi's explanation a.l. and rejects the present one. (7) Lit., 'fair'. (8) Grace after meals. It is sometimes recited over a cup of wine, which must be a full-measured *rebi'ith*, i.e., full to the very brim.

Said Raba, We too [77a] learnt likewise: HE WHO CARRIES OUT [RAW] WINE, [THE STANDARD IS THAT THERE BE] ENOUGH FOR THE MIXING OF A CUP, whereon it was taught, Enough for the mixing of a full-measured cup; while the subsequent clause states; AND ALL OTHER LIQUIDS, [THE STANDARD IS] A REBI'ITH.[1] Now Raba is consistent with his view [expressed elsewhere]. For Raba said: Wine which does not carry three parts of water to one [of itself] is not wine. Abaye observed: There are two refutations to this. Firstly, because we learnt, And as for mixed [wine], that means two parts of water and one of wine, [namely] of Sharon wine.[2] Secondly, the water is in the jug and it is to combine![3] Said Raba to him, As to what you quote, 'and as for mixed [wine], that means two parts of water and one of wine, [namely] of Sharon wine'—Sharon wine stands apart, being [exceptionally] weak. Alternatively, there it is on account of appearance,[4] but for taste more [water] is required. Whilst as for your objection, The water is in the jug and it is to combine!—in the matter of the Sabbath we require something that is of account, and this too is of account.[5]

A Tanna taught: As for congealed[6] [wine], the standard is the size of an olive:[7] this is R. Nathan's view. R. Joseph said: R. Nathan and R. Jose son of R. Judah both said the same thing. R. Nathan, as stated. R. Jose son of R. Judah, for it was taught: R. Judah said: Six things [were stated as being] of the lenient rulings of Beth Shammai and the stricter rulings of Beth Hillel.[8] The blood of a *nebelah*,[9] Beth Shammai declare it clean;[10] while Beth Hillel rule it unclean. Said R. Jose son of R. Judah: Even when Beth Hillel declared it unclean, they did so only in respect of a *rebi'ith* of blood in measure, since it can congeal to the size of an
b olive.[1] Said Abaye, Perhaps that is not so. R. Nathan states that it [*sc.* a congealed piece the size of an olive] requires a *rebi'ith* [of liquid] only here in the case of wine, which is thin; but in the case of blood, which is thick, the size of an olive [when congealed] does not require a *rebi'ith* [in liquid form]. Alternatively, R. Jose b. R. Judah states that for the size of an olive [when congealed] a *rebi'ith* [in liquid form] is sufficient only there in the case of blood, which is thick; but as for wine, which is thin, the size of an olive represents more than a *rebi'ith*, so that if one carries out [even] less than the size of an olive, he is liable.

MILK, AS MUCH AS IS QUAFFED AT A TIME. The scholars asked: As much as GEM'IAH or GEM'IAH?[2] R. Naḥman b. Isaac cited, *Give me to drink* [hagmi'ini], *I pray thee, a little water of*

(1) This shows that the lowest standard of potable liquids is a *rebi'ith;* hence the first clause must mean as much as is required for mixing to produce a cup of a *rebi'ith*. (2) Sharon is the plain along the Mediterranean coast from Japho to Carmel. Thus a proportion of two to one is stated here. (3) If the reason of our Mishnah is because with the addition of water it amounts to a *rebi'ith*, which is the average drink, but that by itself it is insufficient, are we to assume the addition of water that is elsewhere, as though he had carried it all out! Surely not. (4) The reference there is to the colours of blood which are unclean. If it is of the colour of a two to one mixture, it is unclean; but a three to one mixture is paler, and blood of that colour is clean. (5) Though it does not contain the water yet, since it can bear the addition of so much water. (6) Lit., 'dry'. (7) Because that represents a *rebi'ith* of liquid wine. (8) In the many controversies between these two schools Beth Shammai generally adopt the stricter attitude. Hence particular attention is drawn to the cases where it is the reverse. (9) V. Glos. (10) It does not defile food by its contact.

b (1) Which is the minimum quantity of flesh of *nebelah* which defiles. (2) The question is about the spelling, whether it is with an *alef* or an *'ayin*. The following questions are the same.

תנינא המוציא יין כדי מזיגת כוס ותני עלה כדי מזיגת כוס יפה וקתני סיפא ושאר כל המשקין ברביעית ורבא לטעמיה *דאמר רבא כל חמרא דלא דרי על חד תלת מיא לאו חמרא הוא אמר אביי שתי תשובות בדבר חדא דתנן *והמזוג שני חלקי מים ואחד יין מן היין השירוני ועוד מים בבד ומצטרפין א"ל רבא הא דקאמרת שני חלקי מים ואחד יין מן היין השירוני יין השירוני להוד דרפי א"נ התם משום חזותא אבל לטעמא בעי טפי ודקאמרת מים בבד ומצטרפין לענין שבת מידי דחשיב בעינן והא נמי הא חשיב תנא *[א]יבש בכזית דברי רבי נתן אמר רב יוסף רבי נתן ורבי יוסי ברבי יהודה אמרו דבר אחד רבי נתן הא דאמרן ורבי יוסי ברבי יהודה *דתניא רבי יהודה אומר *ששה דברים מקולי בית שמאי ומחומרי ב"ה דם נבלה ב"ש [*] מטהרין וב"ה מטמאין א"ר יוסי ברבי יהודה אף כשטמאו ב"ה לא טמאו אלא בדם שיש בו רביעית הואיל ויכול לקרוש ולעמוד על כזית אמר אביי דילמא לא היא עד כאן לא קאמר רבי נתן הכא דבעי רביעית אלא ביין דקליש אבל בדם דסמיך כזית לא בעי רביעית אי נמי עד כאן לא קאמר רבי יוסי בר' יהודה התם דכזית סגי ליה ברביעי' אלא בדם דסמיך אבל יין דקליש כזית הוי יותר מרביעית וכי מפיק פחות מכזית ליחייב: חלב כדי גמיעה: איבעיא להו כדי גמיאה או כדי גמיעה א"ר נחמן בר יצחק °הגמיאיני נא מעט מים מכדך איבעי' להו גראינין

מנחות קד. עדיות פ"ה מ"א
ראשית כד

תנינא. ממתניתין נמי שמעינן דזהו שיעורו מדתני בשאר משקין רביעית שמעינן מיניה דאין הוצאה במשקה הראוי לשתייה בפחות מרביעית הלכך על כרחיך כי שיערו ביין כדי מזיגת כוס של ברכה שיעור הראויה לשתיית רביעית נקט והיינו רובע רביעית דכי יהיב על חד תלת מיא כדרך המזיגות תורה אור הראויות לשתייה יעמוד על רביעית יש טועים בשמועה זו לומר [רובע] רביעית רובע הלוג ויעמוד על רביעית על לוג שהוא רביעית הקב וטעות הוא בידם ורבותינו לא אמרו כן וראי' יש לדבר במס' נזיר (דף לח.) י' רביעיות הן חמש סומקתא כלומר שנאמרו ביין ודם וה' חיוורתא שנאמרו בשאר משקין וחשיב להא הוצאת שבת דשאר משקין גבי חיורתא ועל כרחיך הנהו כולהו ברביעית הלוג נינהו דקא חשיב בהדייהו רביעית שמן לנזיר דהוא חצי שיעורה של שמן התודה במנחות וחצי לוג שמן לתודה ילפינן במנחות (דף פט.): שתי תשובות בדבר. דלא מצי למילף ממתניתין: חדא. דחמרא לא דרי מיא אלא על חד תרין במס' נדה (פ"ב דף יט.) חמשה מראה דמי' טמאין הן וחד מינייהו כמזוג ומפרש במשנה וכמזוג שאמרתי לך בשני חלקי מים ואחד יין: מן היין השירוני. שגדל בשרון שם מדינה הוא: ועוד מים בבד ומצטרפין. אי טעמא דמתני' יין משום דלכי מזיג ליה ויראה לשתייה יהא בו רביעית השתא מיהא כי מפיק ליה עדיין לא נמזג ואין כאן שיעור מים שעודן בבד היאך מצטרפין לחייבו אלא על כרחך טעמא לאו משום דליתחזי לשתייה לרביעית כשאר משקין הוא אלא הכי שיעוריה ואע"ג דכי מזיג ליה לא הוי רביעית: דרפי. רך: א"נ התם משום חזותא. נקט ליה ונהי נמי דדרי על חד תלת בטעמא מראית דם לא הוי אלא בשני חלקים מים ואחד יין ואי יהיב ביה טפי דם הדומה לו כדם ירוק הוא וטהור: הא חשיב. דחזי לגרופי ביה מיא: יבש. יין קרוש: בכזית. דמעיקרא הוה ביה רביעית ובקרוש רביעית שלימה בעינן דלאו בר מזיגה: ר' יהודה אומר ו' דברים מקולי כו'. לאו דאיכא הני ותו לא דאכתי טובא איכא אלא כשנכנסו לכרם ביבנה והעידו כל אחד ואחד על אותו שבידו במס' עדיות העיד ר' יהודה על אלו: ב"ש מטהרין. דאינו כבשר לטמא בנבלה בכזית ולא תורת משקין לטומאה קלה. לי נראה דהאי דב"ש מטהרין מטומאת נבלות לחודא קאמר שלא יטמא אדם אבל טומאה קלה יש בו: על כזית. שהוא שיעור נבלה לטמא אדם והיינו אמרו דבר אחד שכזית היבש כשנימוח הוי רביעית: עד כאן לא קאמר ר' נתן הכא. דכזית יבש בעי רביעית דלא ובליר מרביעית לא ליכא כזית יבש כדקאמר דכזית קרוש הויא ביה רביעית: אלא ביין דקליש. וכשהוא לח רב נפחו וכשמתייבש נמוק לשיעור קטן: אבל דם. כשהוא לח הוי סמיך עב וקרוב להיות קרוש וכשיבש אינו נמוק לשיעור קטן אלא מעט וכזית יבש לא בעי רביעית לח ודם נבילות מטמא בפחות מרביעית: גרסינן

[רב לז: עירובין כט:]
נדה יט.
[תוספתא פ"ט]
[רק דר"י בר' יהודה ליתא במשנה דעדיות ולכך שפיר גרסינן דתניא]

דאמר רבא כל חמרא דלא דרי על חד תלת מיא כו'. והא דאמרי' בפ' אחד דיני ממונות (סנהדרין לז.) גבי סנהדרין אל יחסר המזג אם הולרך אחד מהם לצאת אם יש כ"ג יולא כו' דהיינו שליש מסנהדרין משמע דמזיגה על חד תרין אומר ריב"א דרבא דוקא הי' מוזג כמשפט המזיגה על חד תלת כדאמר בהזהב (ב"מ ס.) אמר רבא מזיגה דידי מידע ידיעא ובכילד מעברין (עירובין נד.) דמי האי מזיגה למזיגה דרבא בריה דרב יוסף בר חמא אבל שאר העולם האוהבים יין חזק אין מוזגין אלא על חד תרין ואין נראה לר"י דא"כ מאי פריך אביי לוקי מתני' דנדה במזיגת שאר בני אדם אלא נראה לר"י דקרא דאל יחסר המזג ביין השירוני משום דליכא לאוקמי לקרא בסתם מזיגה דהוי רביע דרביע סנהדרין למאי חזו אבל שליש חזו לדיני נפשות ומיהו להוא ליגנא דהתם משום חזותא דלא מחלק בין יין השירוני קשה ויש לפרש משום חזותא כדי שלא יפסיד המראה דרך למוזגו על חד תרין ולא יותר*: חדא דתנן והמזוג שני חלקי מים. וא"ת לאביי דסתם מזוג על חד תרין אדרבה תקשה אמאי איצטריך לפרש שני חלקי מים הוה ליה למימר כמזוג סתם וי"ל דס"ד דאגב אורחיה קמ"ל דהכי הוי כל מזוג: ועוד מים בבד ומצטרפין. אע"כ טעמא לאו משום דלכי מזיג ליה הוה רביעית וחזי לשתייה כשאר משקין אלא הכי שיעורא אע"ג דלכי מזיג ליה לא הוי רביעית כדפירש בקונטרס אלא משום דיין חשוב הוא וראוי להצניעו לכוס של ברכה ואע"פ שאינו ראוי לכוס של ברכה בלא מים מ"מ הוי כמו מים שמצניען לשוף בהן את הקילור אע"פ שאינן ראויין בלא קילור ואביי לא פליג אלא בהא דלא מצריך רביעית מזוג אבל רובע רביעית יין חי צריך לכוס של ברכה כדמשמע בערבי פסחים (דף קח:) דאמר רב יהודה אמר שמואל ד' כוסות הללו צריך שיהא בהן כדי מזיגת כוס יפה מיתיבי ד' כוסות הללו צריך שיהא בהם כדי רביעית אידי ואידי חד שיעורא הוא כדי מזיגת כוס יפה לכל אחד ואחד היינו כדי רביעית משמע דרביעית דברייתא היינו לכל ארבע כוסות דהוי לכל חד רובע רביעית שהוא מזיגת כוס יפה והא דקתני התם בסיפא דברייתא אחד חי ואחד מזוג ה"פ אחד ישתה אותו רובע רביעית כמו שהוא חי ואחד ימזגנו וישתה ומיהו קשה לר"י דבסמוך קאמר אביי ע"כ לא קאמר ר' נתן הכא דכזית בעי רביעי' כו' משמע דסבירא ליה לאביי דכוס של ברכה בעי רביעית יין חי ולפי מה שפירש בקונטרס בסמוך דיין קרוש בעי רביעית משום דאינו ראוי למזיגת כוס מצינן למימר דלעולם סבר אביי דאפי' ביין מזוג לא בעי רביעית אבל קשה לר"י לפי' הקונטרס דאי כזית יבש לא חזי למזיגה למה חשוב מטעם שהיה בו רביעית מתחלה מאי שנא מגרוגרת שלמקה דריש המצניע (לקמן צא.) ונראה לר"י דרב יוסף ואביי סבירא להו דכוס של ברכה בעי רביעית יין חי כדמשמע בסמוך ובברייתא דערבי פסחים דקתני שיהא בהן כדי רביעית היינו לכל אחד ומה ששנה במתניתין יין באנפיה נפשיה אע"ג דהוי ברביעית כשאר משקין היינו משום דלא נטעה בדרבא לומר דחשיב בכדי שראוי למזוג ולעמוד על רביעית והא דלא תנא בהדיא המוציא יין חי ברביעית משום דניחא ליה למינקט כדי מזיגת הכוס דמשום ההוא טעמיה דראוי להצניעו לכוס של ברכה הוא דמיחייב בהוצאת רביעית אבל אי מיפסל מכוס של ברכה על ידי פגימה או שנגע בו נכרי לא מיחייב ברביעית משום דראוי לשתיית ישראל או נכרי משום דלא מנכעי ליה כשיעור זוטר כולי האי הואיל ולא חזי אלא ע"י מזיגה ובעיא תקון ולא חשיב כשאר משקין שראויין בלא מים ולגיבול טיט נמי לא מנכעי ליה כמו קלף דלא חשיב כשיעור קשר מוכסין אע"פ שחשוב יותר מנייר משום דלא מנכעי ליה להכי: הואיל ויכול לקרוש ולעמוד על כזית. משמע דדם חשיב כבשר ותימה א"כ אמאי לריך קרא בפ' בהמה המקשה (חולין עב.) ובריש סנהדרין (דף ד.) לרביעית דם מת דמטמא באהל תיפוק ליה דהוי כבשר משום שיכול לקרוש ואומר ר"י דגבי מת בעי קרא לרביעית דם משום דבריש דם הנדה (נדה נה:) אמרינן דבטומאת מת בעינן אין גזעו מחליף דומיא דעלם ואפילו בשר הוה מטהרינן אי לאו דאין גזעו מחליף דנעשה במקומו ללקת ודם גזעו מחליף הוא ועוד י"ל דהאי תנא דהכא לא מטמא דם נבלות משום שיכול לקרוש אלא אית ליה שום דרשה דדם נבילות טמא והאי טעמא דיכול לקרוש איצטריך שלא יטמא הדם אלא ברביעית ולא בפחות שאז יש בו שיעור בשר אבל בלאו קרא מודו כ"ע דלא הוי כבשר ולהכי איכא תנא בפרק המנחות והנסכים [מנחות קג: וע"ש קד: ד"ה הואיל] דאמר שהעידו על דם נבלות שהוא טהור וכן משמע בכל מקום דדם לא הוי בכלל בשר נבלה דבפרק כל שעה (פסחים ד' כב.) מפיק דגיד וחלב מותר בהנאה משום דכשהותר' נבלה היא וחלבה וגידה הותרו וכי פריך התם והרי דם כו' לא משני כשהותרה נבלה היא ודמה הותרה ובמעילה (דף יז:) נמי בפרק קדשי מזבח מפיק דם השרץ מוזה לכם הטמא משום דלא הויא בכלל שרץ:

דרבי

ב א מיי' פי"ח מהלכות שבת הלכה ב:
ב [א] מיי' פ"א מהלכות שאר אבות הטומאה הלכה ד]:

[וע"ע תוס' עירובין כט: ד"ה כל ותוס' ב"מ ס. ד"ה רבא ותוס' ב"ב לו: ד"ה כל ותוספות סנהדרין יד: ד"ה אל יחסר]

רבינו חננאל

תנינא המוציא יין כדי מזיגת הכוס. וקתני סיפא ושאר כל המשקין ברביעית. רבא לטעמי' דאמר כל חמרא דלא דרי על חד תלתא מיא לאו חמרא הוא. שמשיל לכוס רובע רביעית יין ושלשה רבעי רביעית שאם ימזגנו כראוי לו יהיה רביעית חייב. דדמי כמאן דאפיק רביעית. ואקשינן אמר אביי שתי תשובות בדבר חדא דתנן במס' נדה במזג ב' חלקי מים ואחד יין מן היין השירוני דאלמא כום מזוג שהוא רביעית צריך שיהא בו שליש רביעית יין. ועוד בין כך ובין כך אי מחייבת ליה למוציא [רובע] רביעית משום שאם ימזגן יהא רביעית היאך יצטרפו לו המים והרי הן בבד ואין בו מהן כלום. א"ל רבא דקא מקשת ב' חלקי מים ואחד יין ההוא הא מפרש מן היין השירוני דרפי חמריה. ועוד. איכא למימר לאו משום דהכין הוי שיעור מזיגה אלא התם בעינן מראית דמים טמאים משום חזותא הוא. ואי לא נפיש חמריה פסקה סומק. אע"ג דדארי מיא טפי. ודקא מתמהת ואמרת מים בבד ומצטרפין לא מצטרפינן בהדי יין מים*) אלא מאי דחשיב למימוני ממים שבבד אפילו למהר ועומד. אם מוצו כום ההוא כדי מזיגת כום יפה וחייבין עליו שכשר להצניעו ומצניעין כמותו: תנא יין יבש בכזית דברי ר' נתן פי' והאי יין יבש כההיא דתניא (נזיר דף מט) ר' אלעזר ב"ר צדוק אומר לול קטן היה בין כבש למזבח למערבו של כבש. אחד לשבעים שנה פרחי כהונה יורדין לשם ומלקטין משם יין קרוש שהוא דומה לעיגולי דבילה. ובאין ושורפין אותו בקדושה שנאמר הסך נסך שכר לה'. וקסבר ר' נתן יין יבש

אם מוציא ממנו כזית חייב. אמר רב יוסף ר' נתן ור' יוסי ב"ר יהודה אמרי דבר אחד. ר' נתן הא דאמרן. ר' יוסי ב"ר יהודה מאי היא. דתניא ר' יהודה אומר ששה דברים מקולי ב"ש ומחומרי ב"ה. דם הנבילות ב"ש מטהרין. וב"ה מטמאין. אמר ר' יוסי ב"ר יהודה אף כשטמאו ב"ה לא טימאו אלא בדם שיש בו רביעית הואיל ויכול לקרוש ולעמוד על כזית. וקאמר רב יוסף דקסבר ר' נתן דכזית יין יבש לא הוי אלא מרביעית ורביעית יין לכשיקרוש יהא בו כזית. ואתיא דר"נ כר' שמעון. ובני א"י מתנו בהדי' [בירושלמי בפירקין ה"א] רבנן דקיסרין ר' יוסי ב"ר אבין בש"ר יוחנן אתיא דר' נתן כר' שמעון והכין סבר ר' יוסי ב"ר יהודה [דמתניתן דכולן ברביעית] דרביעית דם לכשיקרוש יהא בו כזית וכפשוטו של דברים. והא מילתא מיפרשא בנס' דהמנחות והנסכין. דא' רב ביבי אריב"ל מעשה בפרדה של בית רבי שמחה ושיעור הכמים דמה ברביעית וכן הלכה. דקא עבדין בה מעשה. ואע"ג דמותיב ר' יצחק בר ביסנא העיד ר' יהושע ור' יהושע בן בתירה על דם שהוא טהור וא"ר יהושע בן בתירה מעשה והיו נוהרין עדות לאריות בסרסיא של מלך והיו עולי רגלים בוקעין עד רטבותיהן בדם ולא אמרו להן דבר. אישתיק. ומאן דטהריה לדם נבילות סבר הדם משקה ניהו ולאו נבילה הוא. ומאן דטמא סבר כיון דהדר הוי כנבילה. הא אמרינן עלה מאי הוי עלה. אמר רב יוסף מוריאנא דבי נשיאה מני ר' יהודה שאורי להו כשמעתיה דב"ה מטמאין. וא"ר יוסי ב"ר יהודה כשטימאו ב"ה לא טימאו אלא ברביעית הואיל ויכולה לקרוש ולעמוד על כזית. א"ל אביי לרב יוסף אמאי תיבא דר' נתן ור' יוסי ב"ר יהודה אמרו דבר אחד. דילמא עד כאן לא קאמר ר' נתן הכא דכזית יין מרביעית יין אלא ביין דקליש שאם תקרש רביעית יהא

*) סלשון מגומגם ונראה דצ"ל אלא מאן דעומד למימוני ממים שבבד אפילו למחר חשיב לענין שבת והלכך אם מוציא כוס שיש כדי מזיגת כוס יפה חייבין עליו וכו'.

עין משפט נר מצוה

ג א ב ג מיי' פי"ח מהל' שבת הלכה ב :

רש"י

גרעינין. מתניתין דפרקין דלעיל חוץ מקליפתן וגרעיניהן : ונגרע. והגרעינין זורקין ונגרעין מתוך האוכל: אוממות. גבי גחלים מייתינן ליה בכילד צולין (ה) גחלים יכול עוממות ת"ל אש אי אש יכול שלהבת כו': עממוהו. לא החשיכו מראיתו להיות הם נאים ממנו: מאמצין. לקמן גבי עינים של מת בפ' שואל (דף קנא:) : במשיפה של קילור. שרגילין לשופו בחלב של אשה : כדי לשוף במים. לשני עינים : כדי שיפה או כדי אחיזה ושיפה. מה שנדבק באצבעותיו לבד מה שנותן בעיניו : אפומא דכולה כתית. וכל מכה קרויה פה : מורשא קמא. עליון של מכה : שבלול. לימצ"א (ו) : לכתית. מניחה (לכתית) עליו: זבוב לצירעה. למי שעקצו צירעה כותש זבוב ומניחה עליו : לחפפית. מין שחין: סממית. איראניא"ה בלע"ז : לעקרב. עקיצת עקרב כותש סממית ומניחה עליו : ושייף. ומושח : מפגיע. חיה קטנה וקולה גדול ושומע וירא שהאה בריה גדולה ובורח : יתוש. נכנס לפיל בחוטמו וכן סממית לעקרב נכנס לו באזנו : סנונית. ארונדיי"א נכנסת תחת כנפי הנשר ומעכבו מפרישת כנפיו : כילבית. שרץ קטן ונכנס לדג גדול באזנו* : המבליג שוד על עז. המחזיק שדוד על הגבור : כל חללי עלמא. פירוש דברים הנעשים בכל חלל העולם : מסגיין בריש עדרא. מהלכות בראש העדר : ברישא חשוכא. שתם עזים שחורות שתם רחלות לבנות : מכסיין. בזנב : והני מגליין. שעזים אין להם אליה : הני דמכסינן מינייהו. רחלים שאנחנו מתכסין מצמרן גם הן מכוסות : דאכלה כיסי. קוצים לפיכך זנבו קצר כדי שלא ידבקו בה הקוצים : ובעי לכרכושי בקי. להבריח היתושין : קמצא. ארבה ול"נ קמצא [נמלה] : חילפי. ערבה : ואי קשיא נדיא ומתעוורא. ואם היתה קשה תנוד ותעקר כשתכה בעלים : ומתעוורא. יסתמו עיניה שמראות עיניה תלויה בה כדשמואל : תימרא דתרנגולא מידליא לעילא. ריס של עין התחתון כשעולם עיניו עולה למעלה מן העליון ובשאר כל בריה העליון שוכב על התחתון : משום דדייר אדפי. שעולה בלילות על הקרשים והקורות צריך שיעלה התחתון על העליון מפני העשן שלא יכנס בעיניו : מתכוליתא. דבר שמטבילין בו כגון כותח או שאר ליפתן : מתי תכלה דא. לכשיכלה מה נאכל ול"נ מתי תכלה דא לפי שאינו כלה עד זמן ארוך שאינו נאכל אלא מעט מעט : ביתא בא ואיתיב. שדרך לישב בבית: בקתא. בית צר וקטן : בי עקתא. בית צר : כופתא. מכתשת ל"א מדה לחטין ול"נ כמין גולם עץ עשוי לישיבה כמו כופת שאור שיחדה לישיבה דתניא בפסחים (דף מה:): כוף תיב. כפוף אותו ושב עליו: לבני לבני בני. מתקיים לדורות הרבה: הולא. גדר קוצים או נולבים : חצילה. אינו דבר קיימא אלא חצילה בעלמא : כוזא. כלי חרס קטן : כזה. כלומר דבר מועט וקל כמו זהו מהו חשוב למלאותו לי מייך במתנה : שוטיתא. בד של הדס שמרקדין בו לפני כלה : שטותא. נראה המרקד כשוטה : משיכלא. ספל גדול שהכל רוחצים ידיהם ורגליהם ממנו : משו כולא. רוחץ את הכל : משכילתא. ספל קטן ונאה : משיא כלתא. מיוחד לחשובים כמו כלה ואשה חשובה לרחוץ ממנו : אסיתא. מורטיי"ר : חסירתא. שחסר החקיקה מבפנים : בוכנא. עלי שכותשין בו : לבושא. חלוק עליון שקורין שרוק : לא בושה. למנוע הבושה שמכסה כל החלוקים התחתונים הקרועים ורעים : כגולם. שאין לו חיתוך אברים : גולתא. מקטורין נאה : גלי ותיב. כשהוא יושב מגלה עצמו שלא ישב עליו שלא ילכלכנו ולא ישופנו בקרקע וישיר שערו ויקרע ויבלה : בור זינקא. בור שיבשו מימיו קורין כן : נקי. חסר מימיו : סודרא. דרך תלמידי חכמים לעטוף סודר : אפדנא. טרקלין של מלכים : אפתחא. אל פתח זה יבאו הכל אם למשפט אם לשרת המלך : אבר קטן. אחד מפרקי אצבע קטנה : דגדול. של אדם גדול והאי קטן דאבר קאי אי נמי אבר גדול של קטן והאי קטן אגברא קאי ולא אאבר : לא אבר קטן. וקטן אכולא מילתא קאי אבר קטן של גוף קטן : דרבי שמעון כו'. והכי קאמר כדי לסוך בו אבר קטן וקטן יהא הגוף בן יומו ורבי נתן סבר חד קטן אמרינן או האבר או הגוף אבל תרי קוטני לא: ה"ג דכולי עלמא אבר קטן של קטן בן יומו לא: וליתא

תוספות

דרבי שמעון בן אלעזר סבר אבר קטן של קטן בן יומו כו'. תימה דאדרבה איפכא מסתברא דר' נתן דקאמר אבר קטן משמע טפי של קטן בן יומו מרשב"א דאמר אבר קטן וקטן בן יומו דהא לעיל פריך אדרבי ינאי דמפרש אבר קטן דמתניתין אבר קטן של קטן בן יומו דהוי כלישנא דר' נתן מברייתא דקתני בה כלישנא דרשב"א ויש לומר דלמאי דמשני הוי סברא איפכא ונקט הכא כדמסיק לעיל ואית ספרים דגרסי איפכא ואין נראה דהא מסיק דלרשב"א אבר קטן של קטן בן יומו ולמאי דגרס איפכא לא הוי כמשקנא לא לפי דמייתי השתא ולא לפי מה שדוחה לא דכולי עלמא כו' :

גמרא

גראינין או גרעינין אמר רבא בר עולא °ונגרע מערכך איבעיא להו *אוממות או עוממות אמר רב יצחק בר אבדימי °ארזים לא עממוהו בגן אלהים איבעיא להו *מאמצין תנן או מעמצין א"ר חייא בר אבא אמר רבי יוחנן °ועוצם עיניו מראות ברע ת"ר *המוציא חלב של בהמה כדי גמיאה חלב של אשה ולובן של ביצה כדי ליתן במשיפא(א) של קילור [קילור] כדי לשוף במים בעי רב אשי כדי שיפה או כדי אחיזה ושיפה תיקו : דבש כדי ליתן על הכתית : תנא כדי ליתן על פי כתית בעי רב אשי על כתית אפומא דכולה כתית או דילמא ב אמורשא קמא דכתית לאפוקי (ב) הודרנא דלא תיקו : אמר רב יהודה אמר רב כל מה שברא הקב"ה בעולמו לא ברא דבר אחד לבטלה ברא שבלול לכתית ברא זבוב לצירעה יתוש לנחש ונחש לחפפית וסממית לעקרב (ג)היכי עביד ליה מייתי חדא אוכמא וחדא חיורא ושלקי להו ושייפי ליה ת"ר חמשה אימות הן אימת חלש על גבור אימת מפגיע על ארי אימת יתוש על הפיל אימת סממית על העקרב אימת סנונית על הנשר אימת *כילבית על לויתן א"ר יהודה אמר רב מאי קרא °המבליג שוד על עז : (ד) רבי זירא אשכח לרב יהודה דהוה קאי אפיתחא דבי חמוה וחזייה דהוה בדיחא דעתיה ואי בעי מיניה כל חללי עלמא הוה אמר ליה א"ל מ"ט עיזי מסגן ברישא והדר אימרי א"ל כברייתו של עולם דברישא חשוכא והדר נהורא מ"ט הני מכסיין והני מגליין הני דמכסינן מינייהו מכסיין והני דלא מכסינן מינייהו מגליין מ"ט גמלא זוטר גנובתיה משום דאכל *כיסי מ"ט תורא אריכא גנובתיה משום דדייר באגמי ובעי לכרכושי בקי מ"ט קרנא דקמצא רכיכא משום דדיירא בחילפי ואי קשיא נדיא ומתעוורא דאמר שמואל האי מאן דבעי דליסמיה לקמצא לשלופינהו לקרני' מ"ט האי תימרא דתרנגולתא מדלי לעילא דדיירי אדפי ואי עייל קטרא מתעוורא *דשא דרך שם דרגא דרך גג מתכוליתא מתי תכלה דא ביתא בא ואיתיב בה ביקתא בי עקתא כופתא כוף ותיב לבני לבני בני הוצא חציצה חצבא שחוצב מים מן הנהר כוזה כזה שוטיתא שטותא משיכלא מאשי כולה משכילתא °משיא כלתא *אסיתא חסירתא בוכנה בוא ואבנה לבושה לא בושה גלימא שנעשה בו כגלם גולתא גלי ואיתיב פוריא שפרין ורבין עליה בור זינקא בור זה נקי סודרא סוד ה' ליראיו אפדנא אפיתחא דין ת"ר *שלשה כל זמן שמזקינין מוסיפין גבורה ואלו הן דג ונחש וחזיר : שמן כדי לסוך אבר קטן : אמרי דבי ר' ינאי שמן כדי לסוך אבר קטן של קטן בן יומו מיתיבי שמן כדי לסוך אבר קטן וקטן בן יומו מאי לאו אבר קטן דגדול ואבר גדול של קטן בן יומו אמרי לך דבי ר' ינאי לא יה"ק שמן כדי לסוך אבר קטן של קטן בן יומו לימא כתנאי שמן כדי לסוך אבר קטן וקטן בן יומו דברי ר' שמעון בן אלעזר ר' נתן אומר כדי לסוך אבר קטן מאי לאו בהא קמיפלגי דר"ש בן אלעזר סבר אבר קטן של קטן ור' נתן סבר אבר קטן דגדול או אבר גדול דקטן אבל אבר קטן של קטן בן יומו לא לא דכולי עלמא אבר קטן דקטן בן יומו לא וליתא

תורה אור: ויקרא כו · יחזק' לא · ישעיה לג · עמוס ה

מסורת הש"ס

פסחים עה: ע"ש ברכות נג: ע"ש · [לקמן קנא: ע"ש] · עי' ברשב"ם ב"ב עג: ד"ה באוסייה · [גי' הערוך כלבית ועי' חולין לז. כילבית באילפס ופירש"י כמו הכא ועי' משנה בע"ז לה: ובברייתא שם לט: מ. איתא כילבית] · כתובות י: ע"ש · פי' מדוכה · ע"ז ל: · [גי' הערוך ערך גס כ' כיסי פי' עשבים שיש בהן קוצים כיוצא]

הגהות הב"ח

(א) גמ' ולובן של ביצה כדי ליתן במשיפא קילור כדי כצ"ל ותיב' של נמחק: (ב) שם דכתית לאפוקי סדר הודרנא : (ג) שם וסממית לעקרב וכתש לחפפית היכי עביד : (ד) שם שוד על עז אמר ר' זירא אשכחיה לרב יהודה : (ה) רש"י ד"ה אוממות וכו' בכילד צולין ולקח מלא המחתה גחלי אש גחלים יכול עוממות : (ו) ד"ה שבלול לימצא · נ"ב שקורין שנעק בל"א :

רבינו חננאל

יהא בה כזית . אבל דם דסמיך שהוא עבה כשיקרוש רביעית יהא בה[יותר מכזית].אי נמי עד כאן לא קאמר ר' יוסי ב"ר יהודה שרביעי' דם לכשתקרוש יהא בה רביעית. אלא בדם דסמיך . אבל יין דקליש אין כזית יבש בא אלא מהרבה רביעיות . והלכך לר' יוסי ב"ר יהודה אם הוציא פחות מכזית יבש חייב דאפשר הוי כוס רביעית : כתית הוא הנקרא בלשון ישמעאל דומל . ולא נודע לנו על הכתית טולה להוציא סביבין . או על פיו להוציא מורשא שלו שהיו נבהן כולן והוא נופו . שבלול אמרו הוא דביש שנקרא הבלילו . חפיפית בל' ישמעאל וקובה והוא דבר שמתכנס על העיר מן הטינוף . מפגיע חיה קטנה שהיא מהלכת בין רגלי הארי וצועקת בקול גדול ומבהלת הארי ונקראת אל פרת אך . סנונית שנקרא בלשון שמעאל אלכם נאפ'ים'ם רחלות מיכסיאן באליה ועיזי מיגליאן . א"ל רחלות נוזות צמר ואנן מכסין מהן אבל עזים לא מכסין · כסי קוצים קוצים · דרגא סולם · מסיכלא . ספל קטן של סים · שמן כדי לסוך אבר קטן של תינוק בן יומו . והא דתניא כדי לסוך אבר קטן וקטן בן יומו לא פירושא ב' סיטות אבר קטן וקטן נמי בן יומו . אלא אבר קטן . והקטן ההוא בן יומו :

רב נסים גאון

(שייך לקמן דף עח ע"ב) אסור לשהות שטר פרוע א"ב · משכחת לה במסכתא דכתובות בפ' האשה שנתארמלה (דף יט) אמר ר' יהושע בן לוי אסור לאדם שישהה שטר פרוע בתוך ביתו שנא' (איוב יא) ואל תשכן באהליך עולה וכן עוד תמצא בזה הפר' עיקר הדברים במודה בשטר שכתבו אמר רב הונא אמר רב מודה שכתבו אינו צריך לקיימו אמר ליה רב נחמן גנבא גנבי למה לך אי סבירא לך כר' מאיר אימא כר' מאיר אמר ליה ומר היכי סבירא ליה אמר ליה כי אתו לקמן אמרי' להו קיימו שטרייכו ונחותו לדינא והלכתא כרב נחמן שצריך לקיימו. בכותבין שובר קמיפלגי משכחת לה בפרק גט פשוט (בבא בתרא דף קעא) דקעביד ר' חנינא בר (פאסי) [פפי] כר' יוחנן וריש לקיש דקאמרי כותבין שובר וכן כי אתא רבין אמר ר' אלעא כותבין שובר וכן הלכה ומישתכח עוד בפרק האשה שנתאלמנה (כתובות דף עז) אמר ר' אבהו כותבין שובר ובפרק הכותב (נט) לאשתו (שם דף פט) אמרו במקום דלא אפשר ודאי כותבין שובר :

גליון הש"ס גמ' משיא כלתא. עי' רש"י ע"ז דף נח ע"ב ד"ה דמסיפא ·

thy pitcher.[3] The scholars asked: [77b] *Gar'inin* or *gar'inin?*[4]—Raba b. 'Ulla cited: *and an abatement shall be made* [we-nigra'] *from thy estimation.*[5] The scholars asked: *Ommemoth or 'ommemoth?*[6]—R. Isaac b. Adbimi cited: *The cedars in the garden of God could not obscure him.*[7] The scholars asked: Did we learn *me'amẓin* or *me'amẓin?*[8]—R. Ḥiyya b. Abba cited: *and shutteth* ['oẓem] *his eyes from looking upon evil.*[9]

Our Rabbis taught: When one carries out cow's milk, [the standard is] as much as one quaffs at a time; woman's milk or the white of an egg, as much as is required for putting in an embrocation; collyrium, as much as is dissolved in water.[10] R. Ashi asked: [Does that mean] as much as is required for dissolving, or as
a much as is required for holding and dissolving?[1] The question stands over.

HONEY, SUFFICIENT TO PLACE ON A SCAB. A Tanna taught: As much as is required for putting on the opening of a scab. R. Ashi asked: 'On a scab': [does that mean] on the whole opening of the scab,[2] or perhaps [it means] on the top of the scab,[3] thus excluding [sufficient for] going all round the sore, which is not required?[4] The question stands over.

Rab Judah said in Rab's name: Of all that the Holy One, blessed be He, created in His world, He did not create a single thing without purpose. [Thus] He created the snail as a remedy for a scab; the fly as an antidote to the hornet['s sting];[5] the mosquito [crushed] for a serpent['s bite]; a serpent as a remedy for an eruption, and a [crushed] spider as a remedy for a scorpion['s bite]. 'A serpent as a remedy for an eruption':[6] what is the treatment? One black and one white [serpent] are brought, boiled [to a pulp] and rubbed in.

Our Rabbis taught: There are five instances of fear [cast] by the weak over the strong: the fear of the *mafgia'*[7] over the lion; the fear of the mosquito upon the elephant;[8] the fear of the spider upon the scorpion;[9] the fear of the swallow upon the eagle;[10] the fear of the *kilbith*[11] over the Leviathan.[12] Rab Judah said in Rab's name: What verse [alludes to these]? *That strengtheneth the despoiled* [i.e., weak] *over the strong.*[13]

R. Zera met Rab Judah standing by the door of his father-in-law's house and saw that he was in a cheerful mood, and if he would ask him all the secrets of the universe he would disclose [them] to him. He [accordingly] asked him: Why do goats march at the head [of the flock], and then sheep?—Said he to him: It is as the
b world's creation, darkness preceding and then light.[1] Why are the latter covered, while the former are uncovered?[2]—Those with whose [material] we cover ourselves are themselves covered, whilst those wherewith we do not cover ourselves are uncovered. Why is a camel's tail short?—Because it eats thorns.[3] Why is an

(3) Gen. XXIV, 17; the word there is spelled with an *alef*. (4) Kernels: with an *alef* or *'ayin*? (The word occurs in the Mishnah *supra* 76b.) (5) Lev. XXVII, 18. *We-nigra'* is with an *'ayin*, and Raba b. 'Ulla connects *gar'inin* with this, as the kernels are thrown away and so are an abatement of the edible portion. (6) Dim, i.e., dying, coals. (7) Ezek. XXXI, 8; *'ammamuhu*, with an *'ayin*—lit., 'keep him dim'. (8) In the Mishnah *infra* 151b. *Me'amẓin*, we close (the eyes). (9) Isa. XXXIII, 15; *'oẓem*, with an *'ayin*. (10) To paint both eyes.

a (1) It is dissolved by being crushed in the water. Part remains on the fingers, and R. Ashi asked whether that must be allowed for or not. (2) The entire surface being referred to as the opening. (3) Lit., 'the first projecting point'. (4) Before a penalty is incurred. (5) A crushed fly applied to the affected part is a remedy. (6) This phrase is added in the text by BaḤ. (7) Lit., 'plague'. The Ethiopian gnat (Lewysohn, *Zoöl. d. Talmud*, p. 316). Rashi: a small animal that terrifies the lion with its loud cry. (8) Caused by entering its trunk. (9) In whose ear it lodges. (10) Rashi: it creeps under its wings and hinders it from spreading them. (11) A small fish, supposed to be the stickleback. (12) Likewise caused by entering its ear. (13) Amos V, 9 (E.V. '*that bringeth sudden destruction upon the strong*').

b (1) Goats are dark coloured, while sheep are white! (2) Sheep have thick tails, which cover their hind parts; but goats have a thin tail. (3) A long tail would

◁ *For the continuation of the English translation of this page see overleaf.*

ג א ב ג מיי' פי"ח מהל' שבת הלכה כ :

גראינין. מתניתין דפרקין דלעיל חוץ מקליפתן וגרעיניהן : ונגרע . והגרעינין זורקין ונגרעין מתוך האוכל: אוממות . גבי גחלים מייתינן ליה בכילד צולין (ה) גחלים יכול עוממות ת"ל אש אי אש יכול שלהבת כו': עממוהו. לא החשיכו מראיתו להיות הם נאים ממנו: מאמצין . לקמן גבי עינים של מת בפ' שואל (דף קנא:) : במשיפה של קילור . שרגילין לשופו בחלב של אשה : כדי לשוף במים . לשני עינים : כדי שיפה או כדי אחיזה ושיפה . מה שנדבק באצבעותיו לבד מה שנותן בעיניו : אפומא דכולה כתית. וכל מכה קרויה פה : מורשא קמא . עליון של מכה : שבלול . לימצ"א (ו) : לכתית .

תורה אור

דרבי שמעון בן אלעזר סבר אבר קטן של קטן בן יומו כו'. תימה דאדרבה איפכא מסתברא דר' נתן דקאמר אבר קטן משמע טפי של קטן בן יומו מרשב"א דאמר אבר קטן וקטן בן יומו דהא לעיל פריך אדבי ינאי דמפרש אבר קטן דמתניתין אבר קטן של קטן בן יומו דהוי כלישנא דר' נתן מברייתא דקתני בה כלישנא דרשב"א ויש לומר דלמאי דמשני הוי סברא איפכא ונקט הכא כדמסיק לעיל ואית ספרים דגרסי איפכא ואין נראה דהא מסיק דלרשב"א אבר קטן של קטן בן יומו ולמאי דגרס איפכא לא הוי כנ"ל שקנא לא לפי דמייתי השתא ולא כפי מה שדוחה לא דכולי עלמא כו' :

גראינין או גרעינין אמר רבא בר עולא °ונגרע מערכך איבעיא להו *אוממות או עוממות אמר רב יצחק בר אבדימי °ארזים לא עממוהו בגן אלהים איבעיא להו *מאמצין תנן או מעמצין א"ר חייא בר אבא אמר רבי יוחנן °ועוצם עיניו מראות ברע ת"ר *המוציא חלב של בהמה כדי גמיאה חלב של אשה ולובן של ביצה כדי ליתן במשיפא (א) של קילור [קילור] כדי לשוף במים בעי רב אשי כדי שיפה או כדי אחיזה ושיפה תיקו : דבש כדי ליתן על הכתית : תנא כדי ליתן על פי כתית בעי רב אשי על כתית אפומא דכולה כתית או דילמא ב אמורשא קמא דכתית לאפוקי (ב) הודרנא דלא תיקו : אמר רב יהודה אמר רב כל מה שברא הקב"ה בעולמו לא ברא דבר אחד לבטלה ברא שבלול לכתית ברא זבוב לצירעה יתוש לנחש ונחש לחפפית וסממית לעקרב (ג) היכי עביד ליה מייתי חדא אוכמא וחדא חיורא ושלקי להו ושייפי ליה ת"ר חמשה אימות הן אימת חלש על גבור אימת מפגיע על ארי אימת יתוש על הפיל אימת סממית על העקרב אימת סנונית על הנשר אימת *כילבית על לויתן א"ר יהודה אמר רב מאי קרא °המבליג שוד על עז : (ד) רבי זירא אשכח לרב יהודה דהוה קאי אפיתחא דבי חמוה וחזייה דהוה בדיחא דעתיה ואי בעי מיניה כל חללי עלמא הוה אמר ליה א"ל מ"ט עיזי מסגן ברישא והדר אימרי א"ל כברייתו של עולם דברישא חשוכא והדר נהורא מ"ט הני מכסיין והני מגליין הני דמכסינן מינייהו מכסיין והני דלא מכסינן מינייהו מגליין מ"ט גמלא זוטר גנובתיה משום דאכל *כיסי מ"ט תורא אריכא גנובתיה משום דדייר באגמי ובעי לכרכושי בקי מ"ט קרנא דקמצא רכיכא משום דדיירא בחילפי ואי קשיא נדיא ומתעוורא דאמר שמואל האי מאן דבעי דליסמיה לקמצא לשלופינהו לקרני' מ"ט האי תימרא דתרנגולתא מדלי לעילא דדיירי אדפי ואי עייל קטרא מתעוורא *דשא דרך שם דרגא דרך גג מתבוליתא מתי תכלה דא ביתא בא ואיתיב בה ביקתא בי עקתא כופתא כוף ותיב לבני בני הוצא חציצה חצבא שחוצב מים מן הנהר כוזה כזה שוטיתא שטותא משיכלא מאשי כולה משכילתא °משיא כלתא *אסיתא חסירתא בוכנה בוא ואכנה לבושה לא בושה גלימא שנעשה בו כגלם גולתא גלי ואיתיב פוריא שפרין ורבין עליה בור זינקא בור זה נקי סודרא סוד ה' ליראיו אפדנא אפיתחא דין ת"ר *שלשה כל זמן שמזקינין מוסיפין גבורה ואלו הן דג ונחש וחזיר : שמן כדי לסוך אבר קטן : אמרי דבי ר' ינאי שמן כדי לסוך אבר קטן של קטן בן יומו מיתיבי שמן כדי לסוך אבר קטן וקטן בן יומו מאי לאו אבר קטן דגדול ואבר גדול של קטן בן יומו אמרי לך דבי ר' ינאי לא ג ה"ק שמן כדי לסוך אבר קטן של קטן בן יומו לימא כתנאי שמן כדי לסוך אבר קטן וקטן בן יומו דברי ר' שמעון בן אלעזר ר' נתן אומר כדי לסוך אבר קטן מאי לאו בהא קמיפלגי דר"ש בן אלעזר סבר אבר קטן של קטן ור' נתן סבר אבר קטן דגדול או אבר גדול דקטן אבל אבר קטן של קטן בן יומו לא לא דכולי עלמא אבר קטן דקטן בן יומו לא וליתא

מנחה (לכתית) עליו: זבוב לצירעה. למי שעקצו צירעה כותש זבוב ומניחה עליו : לחפפית . מין שרץ: סממית. איירא"ניא"ה בלע"ז : לעקרב. עקיצת עקרב כותש סממית ומניחה עליו : ושייף . ומושח : מפגיע . חיה קטנה וקולה גדול ושומע ויירא שהיא בריה גדולה ובורח : יתוש . נכנס לפיל בחוטמו וכן סממית לעקרב נכנס לו באזנו : סנונית . ארונדייל"א נכנסת תחת כנפי הנשר ומעכבו מפרישת כנפיו : כילבית. שרץ קטן ונכנס לדג גדול באזנו* : המבליג שוד על עז . המחזיק שדוד על הגבור : כל חללי עלמא . פירוש דברים הנעשים בכל חלל העולם : מסגיין ברישא . מהלכות בראש העדר : ברישא חשוכא . שתם עזים שחורות שתם רחלות לבנות : מכסיין. בזנב : והני מגליין . העזים אין להם אליה : הני דמכסינן מינייהו . רחלים שאנחנו מתכסין מצמרן גם הן מכוסות : דאכלה כיסי . קוצים לפיכך זנבו קצר כדי שלא ידבקו בה הקוצים : ובעי לכרכושי בקי . להבריח היתושין : קמצא . ארבה ול"נ קמצא [נמלה] : חילפי . ערבה : ואי קשיא נדיא ומתעוורא . ואם היתה קשה תנוד ותעקר כשתכה בעלים : ומתעוורא. יסתמו עיניה שמראות עיניה תלויה בה כדשמואל : תימרא דתרנגולא מידליא לעילא . ריס של עין התחתון כשעולם עיניו עולה למעלה מן העליון ובשאר כל בריה העליון שוכב על התחתון : משום דדייר אדפי . שעולה בלילות על הקרשים והקורות צריך שיעלה התחתון על העליון מפני העשן שלא יכנס בעיניו : מתבוליתא . דבר שמטבילין בו כגון כותח או שאר ליפתן : מתי תכלה דא . לכשיכלה מה נאכל ול"נ מתי תכלה דא לפי שאינו כלה עד זמן ארוך שאינו נאכל אלא מעט מעט : ביתא בא ואיתיב. שדרך לישב בבית: ביקתא . בית צר וקטן : בי עקתא . בית צר : כופתא . מכתשת ל"א מדה לחטין ול"נ כמין גולם עץ עשוי לישיבה כמו כופת שאור שיחדה לישיבה דתניא בפסחים (דף מה:): כוף תיב. כפוף אותו ושב עליו: לבני לבני בני . מתקיים לדורות הרבה: הוצא . גדר קוצים או נולבים : חצילה . אינו דבר קיימא אלא חצילה בעלמא : כוזא . כלי חרס קטן : כזה . כלומר דבר מועט וקל כמו זהו מהו חשוב למלאותו לי מייך במהנה : שוטיתא . בד של הדס שמרקדין בו לפני כלה : שטותא . נראה המרקד כשוטה : משיכלא . ספל גדול שהכל רוחצים ידיהם ורגליהם ממנו : משו כולא . רוחץ את הכל : משכילתא . ספל קטן ונאה : משיא כלתא . מיוחד לחשובים כמו כלה ואשה חשובה לרחוץ ממנו : אסיתא . מורטיי"ר : חסירתא . שחסר החקיקה מבפנים : בוכנא . עלי שכותשין בו : לבושא . חלוק עליון שקורין שרוק : לא בושה . למנוע הבושה שמכסה כל החלוקים התחתונים הקרועים ורעים : כגולם . שאין לו חיתוך אברים : גולתא . מקטורין נאה : גלי ותיב . כשהוא יושב מגלה עצמו שלא ישב עליו שלא ילכלכנו ולא ישופנו בקרקע ויגיר שערו ויקרע ויבלה : בור זינקא . בור שיבשו מימיו קורין כן : נקי . חסר מימיו : סודרא . דרך תלמידי חכמים לעטוף סודר : אפדנא . טרקלין של מלכים : אפתחא . אל פתח זה יבאו הכל אם למשפט אם לשרת המלך : אבר קטן . אחד מפרקי אצבע קטנה : דגדול . של אדם גדול והאי קטן אאבר קאי אי נמי אבר גדול של קטן והאי קטן אגברא קאי ולא אאבר : לא אבר קטן . וקטן אכולא מילתא קאי אבר קטן של גוף קטן : דרבי שמעון כו' . והכי קאמר כדי לסוך בו אבר קטן וקטן יהא הגוף בן יומו ורבי נתן סבר חד קטן אמרינן או האבר או הגוף אבל תרי קוטני לא : ה"ג דכולי עלמא אבר קטן של קטן בן יומו לא : וליתא

רבינו חננאל

יהא בה כזית . אבל דם דסמיך שהוא עבה כשיקרוש רביעית יהא בה [יותר מכזית]. אי נמי עד כאן לא קאמר ר' יוסי ב"ר יהודה שרביעי' דם לכשתקרוש יהא בה רביעית. אלא בדם דסמיך . אבל יין דקליש אין כזית יבש בא אלא מהרבה רביעיות . והלכך לר' יוסי ב"ר יהודה אם הוציא פחות מכזית יבש חייב דאפשר הוי כוס רביעית : **כתית** הוא הנקרא בלשון ישמעאל דומל . ולא נודע לנו על הכתית כולה להוציא סביבין . או על פיו להוציא מורשא שלו שהיו גבהן כולן והוא גופו . שבלול אמרו הוא דביש שנקרא חבלילו . חפיפית בל' ישמעאל וקובה והוא דבר שמתכנס על העיר מן הטינוף . מפגיע חיה קטנה שהיא מהלכת בין רגלי הארי וצועקת בקול גדול ומבהלת הארי ונקראת אל פרת אך . סנונית שנקרא בלשון ישמעאל אלכט נאף ימ"ש רחלות מיכסיאן באליה ועיזי מיגליאן . א"ל רחלות גוזזות צמר ואנן מכסין מהן אבל עזים לא מכסין · כסי קוצים קוצים · דרגא סולם · מסיכלא . ספל קטן של מים · שמן כדי לסוך אבר קטן של תינוק בן יומו . והא דתניא כדי לסוך **אבר** קטן וקטן בן יומו לא פירושא ב' סיטות אבר קטן וקטן נמי בן יומו . אלא אבר קטן . והקטן ההוא בן יומו :

פסחים עה: ע"ש ברכות נג: ע"ש

[לקמן קנח: ע"ש]

[גי' הערוך כלבית וע"י חולין נז. כילבית באלפס ופירש"י כמו הכא וע"י מכות בם לה: ובכריתות שם נגו: מ. איתא כילבית]

ע"ז ל:

[גי' הערוך ערך כס ב' כיסי פי' עשבים שיש בהן קוצים כיוצר]

הגהות הב"ח

(א) גמ' ולובן של ביצה כדי ליתן במשיפת קילור כדי כצ"ל ותיב' של נמחק: (ב) שם דכתית לאפוקי הדר הודרנא : (ג) שם וסממית לעקרב ונחש לחפפית היכי עביד : (ד) שם שוד על עז אמר ר' זירא אשכחיה לרב יהודה : (ה) רש"י ד"ה אוממות וכו' בכילד צולין ולקח מלא המחתה גחלי אש גחלים יכול עוממות : (ו) ד"ה שבלול לימצא · נ"ב שקורין שנעק בל"א :

רב נסים גאון

(שייך לקמן דף עח ע"ב) **אסור** לשהות שטר פרוע א"ב · משכחת לה במסכתא דכתובות בפ' האשה שנתארמלה (דף יט) אמר ר' יהושע בן לוי אסור לאדם שישהה שטר פרוע בתוך ביתו שנא' (איוב יא) ואל תשכן באהליך עולה וכן עוד תמצא בזה הפר' עיקר הדברים במודה בשטר שכתבו אמר רב הונא אמר רב מודה שכתבו אינו צריך לקיימו אמר ליה רב נחמן גנבא גנובי למה לך אי סבירא לך כר' מאיר אימא כר' מאיר אמר ליה ומר היכי סבירא ליה אמר ליה כי אתו לקמן אמרי' להו קיימו שטרייכו ונחותו לדינא והלכתא כרב נחמן שצריך לקיימו. בכותבין שובר קמיפלגי משכחת לה בפרק גט פשוט (בבא בתרא דף קעא) דקעביד ר' חנינא בר (פאסי) [פפי] כר' יוחנן וריש לקיש דקאמרי כותבין שובר וכן כי אתא רבין אמר ר' אלעא כותבין שובר וכן הלכה ומישתכח עוד בפרק האשה שנתאלמנה (כתובות דף טז) אמר ר' אבהו כותבין שובר ובפרק הכותב (שם) לאשתו (שם דף פט) אמרו במקום דלא אפשר ודאי כותבין שובר :

גליון הש"ס גמ' משיא כלתא . עי' רש"י ע"ז דף נא ע"ב ד"ה דסחיפא ·

Continuation of translation from previous page as indicated by ◁

ox's tail long?—Because it grazes in meadows and must beat off the gnats [with its tail]. Why is the proboscis of a locust soft [flexible]? Because it dwells among willows, and if it were hard [non-flexible] it [the proboscis] would be dislocated and it [the locust] would go blind. For Samuel said: If one wishes to blind a locust, let him extract its proboscis. Why is a fowl's [lower] eyelid bent upwards?[4]—Because it dwells among the rafters, and if dust entered [its eyes] it would go blind.[5]

[The word] *DaSHsha* [entrance] [implies] *Derek SHam* [there is the way];[6] *DarGa* [stairs, ladder]; *Derek Gag* [a way to the roof]; *mathkulitha* [a relish]; *mathay thikleh da* [when will this end]?[7] *BeTHa* [a house] [implies] *Bo we-eTHib* [come and sit therein]; *BiKetha* [a small house]: *Be aKetha* [a confined narrow house].[8] *KufTHa* [an inverted vessel, a low seat]: *Kof we-THab* [invert it and sit down]; *libne* [bricks]: *libene bene* [unto children's children];[9] *huẓa* [prickly shrubbery, hedge]: *haẓiẓa* [barrier]. *Ḥazba* [pitcher] [is so called] because *ḥozeb* [it draws][10] water from the river; *kuzah* [small jug]: *kazeh* [like this];[11] *shoṭitha* [myrtle branch]: c *sheṭutha* [folly];[1] *meshikla* [wash basin]: *mashe kulah* [washing everybody]; *mashkiltha* [wash-basin];[2] *mashya kalatha* [washing brides];[3] *asitha* [mortar]: *ḥasirtha* [missing];[4] *bukana* [a club used as a pestle]: *bo we-akkenah* ['come, and I will strike it']; *lebushah* [upper garment]: *lo bushah* [no shame]. *Gelima* [a cloak] [is so called] because one looks in it like a shapeless mass [*golem*].[5] *GoliTHa* [a long woollen cloak] [implies] *Galle weTHib* [roll it up and sit down]; *puria* [bed] is so called because it leads to procreation [*parin we-rabin*]; *Bur ZiNḳa* [a leaping well];[6] *Bor Zeh naḲi* [this well is empty;[7] *sudra* [turban]: *sod adonai lire'aw* [the secret of the Lord is revealed to those that fear him];[8] *ApaDna* [palace]; *Apithḥa Din* [at the door is judgment].[9]

Our Rabbis taught: Three wax stronger as they grow older, viz., a fish, a serpent, and a swine.

OIL, AS MUCH AS IS REQUIRED TO RUB IN A SMALL LIMB. The School of R. Jannai said: Oil, as much as is required to rub in a small limb of an infant one day old. An objection is raised: Oil, as much as is required to rub in a small limb[10] and [a limb of] a day-old infant. Surely this means, a small limb of an adult, and a large limb of a day-old infant?—The School of R. Jannai can reply: No. This is its meaning: Oil, as much as is required to rub in a small limb of a day-old infant.[11]

Shall we say that this is dependent on Tannaim? Oil, as much as is required to rub in a small limb and [a limb of] a day-old infant: this is the view of R. Simeon b. Eleazar. R. Nathan said: As much as is required to rub in a small limb. Now surely they differ in this, R. Simeon b. Eleazar holding a small limb of an infant, while R. Nathan holds a small limb of an adult or a large limb of an infant, but a small limb of a day-old infant [does] not [impose liability]?—No. All agree that the small limb of a day-old infant is

become entangled in the thorns. (4) Rashi: When its eyes are closed the lower eyelid turns upwards and lies upon the upper. (5) Hence this arrangement affords it the most protection. (6) Reading *DaSHsha* as an abbreviation. The following words are similarly treated. These may be regarded either as examples of popular etymology or merely as *jeux d'esprit*, not being meant seriously. (7) Relishes being used sparingly and lasting a long time. (8) Rashi. Jast. s.v. בקתא q.v. translates rather differently. (9) I.e., lasting many generations. (10) Lit., 'hews out'. (11) 'Give us a glass of this size to drink'.

c (1) People danced therewith at weddings, and looked fools in doing so! (2) V. next note. (3) A fancy-shaped, probably expensive basin, used by distinguished persons only. (4) I.e., carved out. (5) The cut of the arms being covered up. (6) A well which springs forth periodically only to disappear again (Jast.). (7) Lit., 'clean'. (8) The turban being worn by Rabbinical scholars; cf. Ḳid. 8*a*; Pes. 111*b*. (9) I.e., all come—for justice to the King's palace. (10) *Eber Ḳaṭan*. This phrase, used both there and in the Mishnah, may mean either a small limb or a limb of a child (or, infant). (11) 'And a day-old infant' is thus taken in the explanative sense, 'even a limb of a day-old infant'.

not [sufficient], [78a] R. Jannai's dictum being incorrect. But here they differ in this: R. Simeon b. Eleazar holds: an adult's small limb and a day-old infant's large limb are identical [in size]. While R. Nathan holds: Only an adult's small limb [creates cul-
a pability], but not the large limb of a day-old infant.[1] What is our decision thereon?—Come and hear: For it was taught, R. Simeon b. Eleazar said: Oil, as much as is required to rub in a small limb of a day-old infant.[2]

WATER, ENOUGH FOR RUBBING COLLYRIUM. Abaye said, Consider: Whatever has a common use and an uncommon use, the Rabbis followed the common use, [even] in the direction of leniency; where it has two common uses, the Rabbis followed the common use [which leads to] stringency. [Thus,] in the case of wine the drinking thereof is common, whilst its employment as a remedy is uncommon; hence the Rabbis followed its drinking use in the direction of leniency.[3] In the case of milk, the drinking[4] thereof is common, whilst its employment as a remedy[5] is uncommon: hence the Rabbis followed its drinking use in the direction of leniency. As for honey, both the eating thereof and its use as a remedy are common, [so] the Rabbis followed its use as a remedy in the direction of stringency.[6] But in the case of water—consider: its drinking is common, whereas its use for healing is uncommon: why then did the Rabbis follow its use for healing in the direction of stringency?—Said Abaye: They learnt this with reference to Galilee.[7] Raba said: You may even say that this refers to other places, thus agreeing
b with Samuel. For Samuel said: All liquids[1] heal [eye sickness] but dim [the eyesight], save water, which heals without dimming.[2]

AND ALL OTHER LIQUIDS, A REBI'ITH. Our Rabbis taught; As for blood, and all [other] kinds of liquids, [the standard is] a *rebi'ith*. R. Simeon b. Eleazar said: Blood, as much as is required for painting one eye, because a cataract [of the eye] is painted [with blood]. And which [blood] is that? The blood of a wildfowl. R. Simeon b. Gamaliel said: Blood, as much as is required for painting one eye, because a white spot in the eye is painted [with blood]. And with what is that? with the blood of bats.[3] And your token is: within for within, without for without.[4] Now this applies only to him who carries it out; but if one puts it away, no matter how little, he is liable.[5] R. Simeon said: This applies only to one who puts it away, but he who carries it out is culpable only when there is a *rebi'ith*. And the Sages agree with R. Simeon that if one carries out waste water into the street, the standard thereof is a *rebi'ith*.

The Master said: 'Now this applies only to him who carries it out; but if one puts it away, no matter how little, [he is liable].' And he who puts it away, does he not carry it out?[6] Said Abaye: The reference here is to an apprentice to whom his master said, 'Go, and clear me a place for a meal.' Now, if he goes and clears out [into the street] something that is valued by all, he is guilty on its account; something that is not valued by all: if his master had put it away,[7] he is guilty on its account; if not, he is not guilty.[8]

The Master said: 'And the Sages agree with R. Simeon that if one carries out waste water into the street, the standard thereof is a *rebi'ith*.' For what is waste water fit?[9] Said R. Jeremiah: To knead clay therewith. But it was taught: Clay, [the standard is]
c as much as is required for making the hole of a smelting pot?[1]—There is no difficulty: in the latter case it is kneaded, but in the former it is not [already] kneaded, because no man troubles to knead clay [only] for making the hole of a smelting pot.

MISHNAH. HE WHO CARRIES OUT CORD, [THE STANDARD IS] AS MUCH AS IS REQUIRED FOR MAKING A HANDLE FOR A BASKET; A REED CORD, AS MUCH AS IS REQUIRED FOR MAKING A HANGER FOR A SIEVE OR A BASKET-SIEVE. R. JUDAH SAID: AS MUCH AS IS REQUIRED FOR TAKING THE MEASURE OF A CHILD'S SHOE. PAPER, LARGE ENOUGH TO WRITE A TAX-COLLECTOR'S RECEIPT ON IT.[2] (AND HE WHO CARRIES OUT

a (1) And the phrasing of the controversy must be interpreted accordingly. (2) Hence this must be his meaning in the controversy quoted, while R. Nathan disagrees, as suggested in the first explanation. (3) Teaching that the minimum which creates liability for carrying out is the average drink, though a lesser quantity is used for remedial purposes.—The others are explained similarly. (4) Lit., 'eating'. (5) By external application. (6) As in the Mishnah, though for consumption the size of a dried fig—a greater standard—would be required. (7) Rashi: whose inhabitants are poor. They would never use wine or milk for dissolving collyrium, but only water, and so this use for water is as common as its drinking use.

b (1) Used for dissolving collyrium. (2) Hence this use too is common. (3) The word denotes with large eyeballs—a species of bats. (4) The white spot is within the eye, and the bat is generally found within human settlements; whereas a cataract protrudes on the outside of the eye, and the wildfowl too dwells without human settlements. (5) This is explained below. (6) Surely this alone is his sin. (7) For use, thus showing that he did value it. (8) This is consistent with R. Simeon's view (*supra* 76a) that one is guilty through another's intention. (9) No penalty is incurred for carrying out something that is entirely useless.

c (1) The hole through which the bellows are inserted. This requires less clay than is made with a *rebi'ith* of water, and since the waste water is regarded as being for the purpose of making clay, the standard should be only as much as is required for kneading this smaller quantity. (2) Lit., 'knot'. Rashi: the receipt was indicated by two letters above normal size.

עין משפט נר מצוה

ד א ב מיי' פי"ח מהל' שבת הלכה ג:
ה ג שם הלכה יג:

גמרא

וליתא דרבי ינאי והכא בהא קמיפלגי ר"ש בן אלעזר סבר אבר קטן דגדול ואבר גדול דקטן בן יומו כי הדדי נינהו ורבי נתן סבר אבר קטן דגדול אין אבר גדול דקטן בן יומו לא מאי הוי עלה תא שמע דתניא רבי שמעון בן אלעזר אומר שמן כדי לסוך אבר קטן של קטן בן יומו: מים כדי לשוף בהן את הקילור: אמר אביי מכדי כל מילתא דשכיחא ולא שכיחא אזול רבנן בתר דשכיחא לקולא שכיחא ושכיחא אזול רבנן בתר דשכיחא לחומרא יין שתייתו שכיחא רפואתו לא שכיחא אזול רבנן בתר שתייתו דשכיחא לקולא חלב אכילתו שכיחא רפואתו לא שכיחא אזול רבנן בתר אכילתו לקולא דבש אכילתו שכיחא רפואתו שכיחא אזול רבנן בתר רפואתו לחומרא אלא מים מכדי שתייתו שכיחא רפואתו לא שכיחא מאי טעמא אזול רבנן בתר רפואתו לחומרא *אמר אביי *בגלילא שנו רבא אמר אפי' תימא בשאר מקומות כדשמואל דאמר שמואל כל שקייני מסו ומטללי לבר ממיא דמסו ולא מטללי: ושאר כל המשקין ברביעית: תנו רבנן **דם וכל מיני משקין ברביעית רבי שמעון בן אלעזר אומר דם כדי לכחול בעין אחת °שבן כוחלין לברקית ומאי נינהו דמא דתרנגולת ברא רשב"ג אומר דם כדי לכחול בו עין אחת שבן כוחלין *) ליארוד ומאי נידו דמא דכרושתינא וסימניך גוא לגוא ברא לברא בד"א במוציא אבל במצניע כל שהוא חייב רבי שמעון אומר בד"א במצניע אבל במוציא אינו חייב אלא ברביעית *ומודים חכמים לר"ש במוציא שופכין לרה"ר ששיעורן ברביעית: אמר מר בד"א במוציא אבל במצניע כל שהוא אטו מצניע לאו מוציא הוא אמר אביי הכא במאי עסקינן בתלמיד שאמר לו רבו לך ופנה לי המקום לסעודה הלך ופנה לו דבר חשוב לכל חייב עילויה דבר שאינו חשוב לכל אי אצנעי' רביה מיחייב עילויה ואי לא לא מיחייב: אמר מר מודים חכמים לר"ש [ב]במוציא שופכין לרה"ר ששיעורן ברביעית: שופכין למאי חזו אמר רבי ירמיה לגבל בהן את הטיט והתניא *טיט כדי לעשות בהן פי כור לא קשיא הא דמיגבל הא דלא מיגבל לפי שאין אדם טורח לגבל טיט לעשות פי כור: **מתני'** [ג]המוציא חבל כדי לעשות אזן לקופה גמי כדי לעשות תלאי לנפה ולכברה רבי יהודה אומר *כדי ליטול ממנו מדת מנעל לקטן נייר כדי לכתוב עליו קשר מוכסין והמוציא קשר מוכסין חייב

נייר

*) [גי' הערוך ליירוד פי' שעלה קרמיתו על גב עינו]

רש"י

וליתא לדרבי ינאי. ור' שמעון בן אלעזר או או קתני או אבר קטן של גדול או להפך וכולה חד שיעורא הוא: ת"ש כו'. ודרבי ינאי תנאי היא: מכדי כל מילתא דשכיחא ולא שכיחא. כל ששיערו חכמים לענין שבת והוא ראוי לשני דברים חדא שכיחא וחדא לא שכיחא אזול רבנן בשיעורן בתר דשכיחא ואפילו היא קולא ששיעורה גדול אמרינן סתמיה להא עביד ולא אמרי' הואיל וחזי נמי למילתא אחריתי ששיעורה קטן ניזיל בתרה לחומרא ואע"פ דלא שכיחא: שכיחא ושכיחא. והיכא דשכיחי תרוייהו אזלינן לחומרא ומשערינן בשיעורא זוטא: רפואתו לא שכיחא. כגון לשוף בו קילור ואע"ג דחזי לה דאיכא דעביד בחלב אשה ואיכא דעביד במיא וחסין על היין שדמיו יקרים הלכך אזול בתר שתייתו ושיערוהו בכדי מזיגת כוס ואע"ג דקולא שיש כאן שיעור גדול וכן חלב נמי חזי לאכילה ולשוף קילור ומיהו לא שכיחא שהרי אף המים ראויין לכך ויש עושין ממים הלכך אזול רבנן בתר אכילתו ושיערו בכדי גמיאה ואע"ג דקולא היא: דבש רפואתו נמי שכיחא. שאין משקה אחר ראוי לכתית: לחומרא. הואיל ותרוייהו שכיחן לחומרא בעינן לשעוריה: רפואתו לא שכיחא. שהרי שאר משקין ראויין לכך ויש שפין קילור בשאר משקין ושתייתו שכיחא שרוב שתיית מים הם שאין אדם שותה יין לכל צמאו כי אם לסעודתו: בגלילא שנו. שהן עניים ומקפידין בדבר מועט וחסין על יין וחלב לשוף (א) קילור ואין שפין אלא במים והלכך רפואתו נמי שכיחא ובעינן למיזל לחומרא: כל שקייני. כל משקין ששפין בהן קילור: מסו. החולי: ומטללי. מסככין על העין ומוכעין מראיתו עד שיכלה מראיתו לגמרי מפני שהן עבין ונגלדין כמין דבק שקורין גלוזייר: בר ממיא. דעדיפי מכולהו דמסו ולא מטללי שנבלעין מיד או ניגבין מהר ולא נגלדין על גב העין: שכן כוחלין לברקית. מיילא שבולטת בעין: ומאי ניהו. מאיזה דם כוחלין אותו: ליארוד. תבלול ובתוספתא ראיתי לחורור וכן טיפות דקות של לובן הטולדות בעין כדתנן בבכורות גבי מומין (דף לח:): דמא דכרושתינא. עטלף שקורין טלפא: גוא. כרושתינא מצוי בתוך היישוב שהוא ליארוד שהוא שוקע בתוך העין: לברא. דמא דתרנגולת ברא לברקית שהיא בולטת: בד"א. דבעינן שיעורא במוציא לר"ה: אבל המלניע. והוציאו חייב בכל שהוא לקמיה פריך אטו מלניע לאו מוציא הוא: ר' שמעון אומר בד"א. דמיחייב בשיעורא זוטא כי האי: במלניע. בשיעור הזה וחזר והוציאו: אבל במוציא. אדם שלא הלניעו והוציאו אינו חייב אלא ברביעית: במוציא שופכין. אדם שלא הלניען אינו חייב אלא ברביעית דבליר מהכי לא חזו כדלקמן לגבל טיט: אטו מלניע לאו מוציא הוא. הלא אין מתחייב אלא על ידי הוצאה: אמר אביי הכא בתלמיד. כגון שולי דנגרי שאומר לו רבו לך ופנה לי המקום: דבר שחשוב לכל מיחייב עליה. ואף על גב דלא אלנעיה רביה לצרכו: דבר שאינו חשוב לכל כו'. והכי קאמרי בד"א דבעינן שעורא דחשיב במוציא כלומר בדבר שאין לך לילך בו אלא אחר הולאתו של זה שהמחשבה תלויה בזה שהוליא אבל במלניע בדבר שיש לך לילך אחר מחשבה של מלניע כגון המלניע כל שהוא חייב זה המוליאו ורשב"א אמרה ואזיל לטעמיה דאמר בפרקין דלעיל דבדבר שאין מלניעין כמוהו והוכשר לזה והלניעו נתחייב זה במחשבתו של זה וה"ה דמלי לאוקמי במלניע גופיה ולמימר הכי בד"א במוליא בדבר שלא הולנע ואין לך לילך בו אלא אחר הולאתו של זה אבל אם היה זה מלניע דבר זה מתחילה וחזר והוליאו חייב אלא משום דשמעי' לי' דאמר נתחייב זה במחשבה של זה אוקמא אביי אפי' באחר שהוליאו וכ"ש אם הוליאו הוא עלמו: פי כור. נקב שנותנין בו המפוח ושיעורא זוטא הוא ומרביעית חזי לגבל טובא וכיון דהולאת טיט חשיבא בכדי פי כור בעינן נמי לשעוריה בהכך (ג)דעבדי לטיט בכדי גיבול פי כור: דמיגבל. כבר חשוב בכדי פי כור אבל זה שעדיין לא נגבל אינו נשער בכך לפי שאין אדם טורח לגבל שיעור מועט כזה ואם בא לגבל מגבל יותר ועושה בו דברים אחרים: **מתני'** אזן לקופה. לאוחזה בה: תלאי. לתלותו בו: מדת מנעל. להראותו לאומן כמדה זו אני צריך: נייר. מעשבים עושים אותו: קשר של מוכסין. יש לך אדם שנותן המכס לראש הנהר במקום אחד או מוחל לו במתנה והוא מוסר לו חותם להראות למוכס שמחל לו המכס ודרכו לכתוב בו שתי אותיות והן גדולות משתי אותיות שלנו:

נייר

תוספות

שבן כוחלין ליארוד. אין נראה לר"י לפרש דהיינו תבלול דבתוספת' קתני בהך מילתא גופא שכוחלים לחורור ובבכורות (דף לח:) חשיב תבלול וחורור אלמא תבלול לאו היינו חורור: דם וכל מיני משקין ברביעית. בתוספתא גרס ושאר מיני משקין וכן נראה דהא כל מיני משקין אינן ברביעית דיין ושמן ודבש ומים שיעורן כדתנן במתני': אטו מלניע לאו מוליא הוא. פירש בקונט' דהוה מלי למימר הב"ע כשהלניעו והוליאו אלא דניחא ליה לישנויי בשלא הוליאו המלניע עלמו משום דאתיא כרשב"א וקשה דמלכן דאתיא כרשב"א אדרבה כרשב"ג אתיא דמיירי לבסוף ועוד דלמאי נקט בתלמיד שא"ל רבו אפילו אדם בעלמא נמי ודוחק לומר דלא מחייב רבי שמעון במחשבתו של זה אלא תלמיד במחשבתו של רבו לכך נראה דה"פ אטו מלניע לאו מוליא הוא דמדלא קתני אבל המלניע בכל שהוא דהוה משמע דהמלניע הוא המוליא כדדייק לעיל אינו חייב אלא המלניעו מתניתין דלא כרשב"א אלא קתני במלניע משמע אפילו אחר הלניעו חייב המוליא ולהכי קשיא ליה אטו מלניע לאו מוליא הוא דהא שום תנא לא מחייב אא"כ הוליאו המלניע אלא רשב"א לבדו ומתניתין דכלל גדול (לעיל עה:) דהמלניע דלא כוותיה ומשני בתלמיד שאמר לו רבו דכה"ג כ"ע מודו שהתלמיד עושה הכל לדעת רבו: **שופכין** למאי חזו. דוקא אברייתא קא בעי וכן משמע לקמן (דף עט:) דלאמר והא טיט דמקמי דליגבליה תנא מודים חכמים לרבי שמעון במוליא שופכין כו' והוינן בה שופכין למאי חזו משמע דבמתני' אתי שפיר ונרא' לר"י דהיינו טעמא משום דשופכין דמתניתין איכא למימר דחזו לכמה דברים לרחוץ בהם כוסות וקערות דלא מאיסי כולי האי אלא שאינן ראויין לשתיה אבל הכא דומיא דדם קתני דמאיסי טובא ולכך בעי למאי חזו:

רבב

רבינו חננאל

אמר אביי מכדי לענין שיעור הוצאה כל דבר שיש בו ב' צדדים. ב' מדות' אחת מצויה ואחת שאינה מצויה הלכו חכמים בשיעור הוצאתו אחר ההנאה המצויה. אע"ג שהיא מרובה מן האחרת ימצאת לקולא ואם שתיהן מצויות הלכו להחמיר. חלב שתייתו שכיחא ורפואתו לא שכיחא אזול רבנן בתר שתייתו לקולא. יין שתייתו שכיח' ורפואתו לא שכיחא אזול רבנן נמי בתר שתייתו לקולא. דבש אכילתו שכיחא ורפואתו שכיחא אזול רבנן אחר רפואתו לחומרא. ושאלו את אביי מים מכדי שתייתו שכיחא ורפואתו לא שכיחא מ"ט אזול רבנן בתר רפואתו ואמרו כדי לשוף בהן את הקילור. ואהדר אביי בדגלילא שנו. כלומר מי גליל שהן ידועין שמועילין לעין בקילור שהן כמי דקלים שהן ידועין שמועילין לירוקה. אבל מים דעלמא ברביעית. רבא אמר אפי' תימא מים שבשאר מקומו' שיעורן כדי לשוף בהן את הקילור כדשמואל דאמר שמואל כולהו שקייני מעלו וסעדי בר מן מיא דמעלו ונרדי. וכן תורף הדברים שאין המים סועדין כמיני מאכל. אלא עיקר שתייתן כעין רפואה היא. לפיכך שיעורן כרפואה: דם ברביעית ודם של דוכיפת דא תרנגולא ברא. או של עטלף כדי לכחול עין אחת ברקית. כאותה ששנינו השוכר את החמו' והבריק'.[ליארוד] חורור שמלבין שחור שבעין כרושתינא. תרנגולא דביתא וי"א אלכפאש ודמה מועיל לכאב שבתוך עין. ודם דוכיפת מועיל לכאב שמחוץ לעין: תנא כמ' דברים אמורים במוציא שהוציא דבר שלא קדם והצניעו. שהוא צריך לשיעורין הללו. אבל הצניע דבר בחול לצורכו והוציאו בשבת חייב עליו בכל שהוא. ר"ש אומר כל השיעורין הללו לא נאמרו אלא למצניעיהן שאם הצניע בטול בשיעורין הללו והוציאו בשבת חייב. אבל אם הוציא כלום מן כל אלו בין יין בין חלב בין דבש ובין מים שלא קדם והצניעו אינו חייב אלא על רביעית. ואקשי' אמר מר ר' שמעון אומר בד"א במצניע. אבל במוציא אינו חייב אלא ברביעי'. ואמרינן וכי מאחר שהצניעו לצרכו היאך אינו חייב אלא על הוצאתו*). פי' בכל שהוא. והיאך צריך שיעור. פי' המוציא יין כו'. ואוקימנא לדר' שמעון בתלמיד שאמר לו רבו לך ופנה לי מקום לסעודה והלך ופינה כל מה שהיה יעו ובא רבו בשבת והוציא כל מה שהצניע לו תלמידו. אם הוציא הרב דבר שהוא חשוב לכל כשיעורין הללו הרי הוא חייב. ואם הוציא הרב דבר שאינו חשוב לכל ופיחת מן השיעורין הללו בעצמו הצניען חייב עליו בכל שהוא. אבל תלמידו הצניעו ופיחת הוא מן השיעורין הללו מוציאו פטור ואם הוציא מן המשקין מה שלא הוצנע אינו חייב אלא ברביעית שנמצאו דברי ר"ש שאמר לא השיעורין הללו אלא למצניעיהן למי שהצניעם לו. (שמשו) ויש שמפרשין שמועה זו פי' אחר דהכין קאמר ר"ש לא נאמרו כל השיעורין הללו אלא לענין הצנעה. ולא סלקא. ויש שגורסין שיטה זו רישא דברייתא. בד"א במוציא אבל במצניע כל שהוא. ומקשי' הכי אטו מוציא לאו מצניע הוא. ומפרקי' פירוק דאביי ואנחנא לא קא סלקא לנא הכי וכלישנא דפרישנא דווקא. פי כוש קורין אותו בל' פילכא ובלשון ישמעאל פלכה. שעושין על פי הכוש כמו כדור אצל הצינורה כדי שיכבד הכוש ויסוב ויש עושים אותו מן העצם ויש עושים אותו מן העץ. ויש שעושין אותו מן הטיט. ומקשי' כי מכדי מים כדי לעשות פי כוש למה הוצרכו שיעור שופכין רביעית כדי לגבל בה את הטיט. והלא טיט של פי כוש מתגבל בפחות מרביעית. והשבנו אם הטיט מגובל ועומד סגי בזה השיעור. ואם צריך לגבל אין אדם טורח לגבל טיט לעשות פי כוש: **מתני'** נייר כדי לכתוב עליו קשר מוכסין [כו'].

*) ונראה דצ"ל הוצאתו כו' בכל שהוא יהא חייב והאיך צריך שיעור המפורש במשנה המוציא יין וכו'.

מסורת הש"ס

[גי' הערוך בדגלילא שנו פי' מי גליל שהן ידועין כי מועילין לעין בקילור כמו מי דקלים (לקמן דף קי.) שהם ידועים שמועילין לירקה בערך גליל ועי' תוס' לעיל מז. ד"ה בגלילא. וכן בתוס' חגיגה כה. ד"ה בגלילא]

[לקמן עט. ס:]

[לקמן פ.]

הגהות הב"ח

(א) רש"י ד"ה בגלילא שנו וכו' לשוף בו קילור כ"ב ע"ג כדף מז במ"ש התוס' בד"ה בגלילא:
(ג) ד"ה פי כור וכו' בהכך מיא דעבדי לטיט:

גליון הש"ס

גמ' שכן כוחלין לברקית. עי' בכורות דף לח ע"ב תוס' ד"ה וסימנך:

נייר מחוק כדי לכרוך על צלוחית קטנה של פלייטון עור כדי לעשות קמיע* (דוכסוסטוס כדי לכתוב מזוזה) קלף כדי לכתוב עליו *פרשה קטנה שבתפילין שהיא שמע ישראל דיו כדי לכתוב ב' אותיות כחול כדי לכחול עין אחת דבק כדי ליתן בראש השפשף זפת וגפרית כדי לעשות נקב שעוה כדי ליתן על פי נקב קטן חרסית כדי לעשות פי כור של צורפי זהב רבי יהודה אומר כדי לעשות פיטפוט סובין כדי ליתן על פי כור של צורפי זהב סיד כדי לסוד קטנה שבבנות *ר' יהודה אומר כדי לעשות כלכל רבי נחמיה אומר כדי לסוד אונדפי: **גמ'** חבל נמי ליחייב כדי לעשות תלאי לנפה ולכברה כיון דחריק במנא לא עבדי אינשי תנו רבנן הוצין כדי לעשות אוזן לסל כפיפה מצרית סיב אחרים אומרים כדי ליתן על פי משפך קטן לסנן את היין [א]רבב כדי לסוך תחת *אספגין קטנה וכמה שיעורה כסלע והתניא כגרוגרת אידי ואידי חד שיעורא הוא מוכין כדי לעשות כדור קטנה וכמה שיעורו כאגוז: נייר כדי לכתוב עליו קשר מוכסין: תנא *כמה קשר מוכסין [ב]שתי אותיות (של קשר מוכסין) ורמינהו המוציא נייר חלק אם יש בו כדי לכתוב שתי אותיות חייב ואם לאו פטור אמר רב ששת מאי שתי אותיות שתי אותיות של קשר מוכסין רבא אמר שתי אותיות דידן ובית אחיזה דהיינו קשר מוכסין מיתיבי [ג]המוציא נייר מחוק *ושטר פרוע אם יש בלובן שלו כדי לכתוב שתי אותיות או בכולו כדי לכרוך ע"פ צלוחית קטנה של פלייטון חייב ואם לאו פטור בשלמא לרב ששת דאמר מאי שתי אותיות שתי אותיות של קשר מוכסין שפיר אלא לרבא דאמר שתי אותיות דידן ובית אחיזה דהיינו קשר מוכסין הכא בית אחיזה לא צריך קשיא תנו רבנן *המוציא קשר מוכסין עד שלא הראהו למוכס חייב משהראהו למוכס פטור רבי יהודה אומר [ד]אף משהראהו למוכס חייב מפני שצריך לו מאי בינייהו אמר אביי איכא בינייהו רהיטי מוכסא רבא אמר מוכס גדול ומוכס קטן איכא בינייהו רב אשי אמר חד מוכס איכא בינייהו מפני שצריך לו להראות למוכס שני דא"ל חזי גברא דמוכס אנא: ת"ר המוציא שטר חוב עד שלא פרעו חייב משפרעו פטור רבי יהודה אומר אף משפרעו חייב מפני שצריך לו מאי בינייהו אמר רב יוסף *אסור לשהות שטר פרוע איכא בינייהו [ה]רבנן סברי אסור לשהות שטר פרוע ורבי יהודה סבר מותר לשהות שטר פרוע אביי אמר דכולי עלמא אסור לשהות שטר פרוע והכא *במודה בשטר שכתבו שצריך לקיימו קמיפלגי תנא קמא סבר מודה בשטר שכתבו צריך לקיימו ורבי יהודה סבר מודה בשטר שכתבו אין צריך לקיימו ומאי עד שלא פרעו ומשפרעו

עד

רש"י

נייר מחוק. שוב אינו ראוי לכתוב לפיכך צריך שיעור גדול לכרוך ע"פ צלוחית: קלף כדי לכתוב פרשה קטנה. דאיידי דדמיו יקרים לא עבדי מיניה קשרי מוכסין אלא תפילין ומזוזות ולא מיחייב בשיעורא זוטא: דיו לכתוב שתי אותיות. לרושם על שתי חוליות של כלי או על קרשים לזווגן: כדי לכחול עין אחת. לקמן פריך עין אחת הא לא כחלי: דבק. גליד: כדי ליתן בראש השפשף. בגמרא מפרש לה: כדי לעשות נקב קטן. כלי שנותנין בו כסף חי סותם פיו בזפת או בגפרית ונוקב בתוך הסתימה נקב דק להוציא בו: חרסית. לבינה כתושה: לעשות פי כור. שהמפוח נכנס בו: פטפוט. רגל למקום מושב הכור שהיו מושיבין על כן העשוי לכך כגון טרפייד לשפות הקדירה: סובין כדי ליתן ע"פ כור של צורפי זהב. במקום שאין פחמין צורפין זהב באש של סובין: לסוד קטנה שבבנות. טופלות סיד להסיר את השיער: **גמ'** חבל נמי ליחייב. בשיעורא זוטא דחזי נמי לתלאי דנפה וכברה: דחריק. כעין חרקי מתוך שהוא קשה פוגם את העץ: הוצא. של לולבי דקל: כפיפה מצרית. של העשוי מצורי דקל: סיב. ודילי"ת שגדל סביב הדקל כעין מלבוש ונכרך סביבותיו ועולה: על פי משפך. אונטודיי"ר: לסנן את היין. שמעכב הפסולת והקמחים מליכנס לפי הכלי: רבב. שומן או שמן: אספוגין. רקיק שנותנין בתנור וטחין תחתיו אליה: וכמה שיעורא. של אספוגין: כדור. פלוט"א: נייר חלק. שלא נכתב בו מעולם: שתי אותיות. קס"ד שתי אותיות דידן דזוטרן: קשר של מוכסין. לא בעי גליון לבית אחיזה שאוחזו כולו בכפו פשוט ורואה: בלובן. גליון: הכא בית אחיזה לא צריך. שיכול לאוחזו במקום המחק והשטר במקום הכתב: משהראהו למוכס. ורואה שמחל לו ראש הנהר את המכס שוב אין צריך לו ולא חזי למידי: מאי בינייהו. כלומר במאי פליגי ולמאי קאמר רבי יהודה דצריך לו: רהיטי מוכסא. קורצו"ש שרצין אחר העוברים להעליל עליהם שלא נתנו המכס וטורח לעוברים לחזור למוכס ומצניע החותם להראות לאלו ולת"ק לא מצנע ליה להכי דכי רהטי בתריה הדר לגבי מוכס: מוכס קטן. פעמים שיש מוכס גדול שטורח לו לעמוד על הגשר כל היום וממנה מוכס קטן וזה מתחלה אינו מראה החותם של מלך אלא לגדול ולרבי יהודה צריך לו שהרי הקטן ימנענו מלעבור ולת"ק אין צריך לו שהגדול מוסר לו סימן דברים ואומר לקטן ועובר: למוכס שני של מעבר אחר ולא לפוטרו מן המכס אלא להראות שהוא נאמן וחשוב ואינו מבריח עצמו מן המכס כדי שלא יעליל עליו לאחר זמן: משפרעו. (לוה) פטור לקמיה מפרש להו: מאי בינייהו. כלומר מאי פלוגתייהו ומה טעם נותנין לדבריהם: אסור לשהות שטר פרוע. משום שנא' (איוב יא) אל תשכן באהליך עולה הלכך מלוה לא מצי ליה לצור ע"פ צלוחיתו משום איסור ולוה נמי לא מצי ליה שמא יבא לידי מלוה ויחזור ויתבענו: מותר. הלכך כי הוציאו מלוה חייב דצריך לו לכרוך ע"פ צלוחית: במודה בשטר שכתבו. הלוה מודה שכתבו צריך לקיימו ולומר לא פרעתי וכל כמה דלא אמר הכי לאו שטרא הוא אי לאו משכח סהדי להכיר החתימה דמאן קא משוי ליה שטרא לוה דאמר כתבתיו לוה נמי הא קאמר פרעתי הפה שאסר הוא הפה שהתיר הלכך משפרעו כלומר משיאמר פרעתי פטור דלא צריך ליה ור' יהודה סבר אין צריך לקיימו דכיון דמודה שכתבו ולוה בו הרי הוא כאלו קיימוהו חותמיו וגובה בו כ"ז שמוציאו:

עד

תוספות

רבב. פירש בקונטרס שומן או שמן וע"כ אינו שמן דשמן נתנו בו חכמים שיעור אחר במתני': **תחת** אספוגין קטנה. ואע"ג דבפ' כל שעה (פסחים ל:) אמרינן אין טשין את התנור באליה ואם טש כל הפת כולה אסורה הא אמר התם בההיא פרקא *דכעין תורא שרי: ***והמוציא** קשר מוכסין חייב. אצטריך לאשמועינן אפילו כתב על הקלף אע"ג דקתני בסמוך דשיעור קלף כדי לכתוב עליו פרשה קטנה שבתפילין: **ובית** אחיזה. בשעת כתיבה צריך בית אחיזה וקשר מוכסין נ"ל דיכול לכותבו בלא אחיזה ובקונטרס פי' בשעה שרואה בו (*) בעי אחיזה: **ת"ק** סבר מודה בשטר שכתבו צריך לקיימו. ומשום הכי כי אמר לוה פרעתי פטור דאין השטר ראוי לגבות בו ומיירי שיודע שלא יוכל כלל למצוא עדי קיום וא"ת כי לא פרע נמי אמאי חייב מה תועלת יש בשטר כיון שאינו יכול לקיימו שאם יטעון הלוה פרעתי או מזוייף יפטור ואם יודה זה אינו מכח השטר וי"ל דמועיל לו השטר דמתוך כך נזכר הלוה שלוה ממנו אי נמי (א) לטרוף ממשעבדי אם יודה הלוה שאינו מזוייף וא"ת ומשפרעו אמאי פטור המוציא נהי דלא חזי לגבות חובו הא ראוי הוא לצור ע"פ צלוחיתו ואע"ג דאסור להשהות שטר פרוע הכא היאך נוציאנו מידו כיון שהוא עומד ולווה שאינו פרוע (ב) וי"ל דמיירי כגון שאמר אין לי עדים ואין לי ראיה ולא אמצא קיום ואפילו מצא אחרי כן אינו מועיל ולכך אסור להשהותו שמא לבסוף יקיימנו ויגבה בו שלא כדין ואי לא הוה טענינן ללקוחות וליתומין מזוייף הוה אתי שפיר דאסור להשהותו אך פירשתי בבבא קמא ובבבא מציעא ובגיטין דטענינן ללקוחות וליתומין פרוע ומזוייף ושם האכרתי ואם תאמר ואמאי לא קאמר איפכא דת"ק סבר אין צריך לקיימו ומשפרעו הוי כמשמעו שפרעו ממש ולכך פטור דאסור להשהות שטר פרוע שמא יגבה בו פעם אחרת שכשיטעון הלוה אמת שפרעו לא יהא המלוה צריך לקיימו ויגבה שנית ור' יהודה סבר צריך לקיימו ואף משפרעו חייב דצריך הוא לצור על פי צלוחיתו ואין אסור להשהותו דמיירי כגון בידוע שלא ימצא עדי קיום ולא יוכל לגבות שנית דכשיטעון הלוה אמת שפרע יצטרך המלוה לקיימו ויש לומר דאף לר' יהודה הוה אסור להשהותו שמא יקיימנו באקראי בעלמא ויגבה בו שלא כדין: **רש"י** גריס דכולי עלמא מודה בשטר שכתבו צריך לקיימו. וכן נראה דהכי קי"ל דאית ליה לרב נחמן הכי בפרק שני דכתובות (דף יט.) וקיימא לן כוותיה בדיני:

ת"ק

עין משפט נר מצוה

ו א מיי' פי"ח מהלכות שבת הלכה י:

[דף ל. ע"ש]

[ב"ק לע"ל משנה]

ז ב ג ד שם הלכה טו:

[עי' תוס' סוטה יז. ד"ה אינו כותב]

רבינו חננאל

ותנא כמה קשר מוכסין ב' אותיות לא שנו אלא באותו קשר [מוכסין] שהן מכירין אותו באותו פרק שכותבין בו ב' אותיות בכתב יווני שהן גדולות מאותיות שלנו אם יש בנייר החלק שיעור ב' אותיות הללו חייב עליו ואם לאו פטור. ורמינהי המוציא נייר חלק אם יש בו כדי לכתוב ב' אותיות חייב ואם לאו פטור. מדקאמר ב' אותיות סתם אסיקנן אדעתין ב' אותיות דילן דזוטרן מן ב' אותיות של קשר מוכסין וקא מחייב עליה. ומן ההיא קמייתא פטור. אמר רב ששת ב' אותיו' דתנינא בהא ברייתא שנייה נמי דקשר מוכסין. רבא אמר ב' אותיות דילן ובית אחיזה. הכי אמר רבא לא תימא אם מכיל הנייר ב' אותיות חייב עליו אלא איתא הכי אם אפשר לכתוב עליו ב' אותיות ואי אפשר עד שיהא בו בית אחיזה כדי לכתוב למעלה הימנו ונמצא מקום ב' אותיות ובית אחיזה כשיעור קשר מוכסין: מיתיבי המוציא נייר מחוק ושטר פרוע אם יש בלובן שלו כדי לכתוב ב' אותיות או בכולן כדי לכרוך על פי צלוחית קטנה של פלייטון חייב ואם לאו פטור. לרב ששת דאמר בב' אותיות של קשר מוכסין שפיר דהוה ליה כמתנית' ופירושה אלא לרבא דאמר צריך שיהא הנייר החלק כולו כשיעור ב' אותיות של קשר מוכסין והוא שיעור ב' אותיות דילן ובית אחיזה. והא הכא דשטר גדול הוא שיש בו לבן ויש בו בית אחיזה ומקום הלובן שלו ב' אותיות שלנו. ולא צריך מקום ב' אותיות של קשר מוכסין. קשיא: הא דתנן המוציא קשר מוכסין חייב. אוקימנא בברייתא עד שלא הראהו למוכס מפני שהוא צריך לו. אבל אם הראהו למוכס ואינו צריך לו פטור. ור' יהודה פליג ואמר אף משהראהו למוכס חייב מפני שהוא צריך לו. ובעינן למידע במאי פלוגתיהו ומאי בינייהו אמר אביי (דאטו) [רהיטי] מוכסא איכא בינייהו בזמן שיש כמה רצין לפני המוכס מחפשין מי נתן המכס ונטל הקשר ומי שלא נתן קאמר ר' יהודה חושש הוא שמא ישיגוהו רצי המכס בזמן שאין עמו קשר לפיכך צריך לו לדחותם. אע"פ שהראהו לגדול. אבל היכא דליכא רהטי מכסא קאמר אביי אפילו ר' יהודה מודי דפטור. רבא אמר מוכס גדול ומוכס קטן איכא בינייהו ומימריה קרוב למימרא דאביי. וסבירא ליה שאם אין שם מוכס קטן משהראהו למוכס לא פליג ר' יהודה דפטור. רב אשי אמר לעולם פליגי ולא מילתא איכא בינייהו אלא לב' אפי' היכא דליכא רהטי אלא שני מוכסין צריך ליה לקשר דכד אתי מוכסא שני מחווי ליה למוכס דקדים מוכס שני וא"ל חזי דגברא דמכס אנא ורגילנא לשלוטי מכסא שיהא לו פנים אצלו. או דמאחר ליה ולא דחיק ליה: **המוציא** שטר חוב שהוא עליו עד שלא פרעו כגון שגנבו מן המלוה או שנפל מן המלוה ומצאו המלוה בשבת עד שלא פרעו והעבירו ד' אמות ברה"ר כו' לא פליגי שהוא חייב. כי פליגי כגון שהוציא לוה אחר שפרעו. רבנן סברי פטור משום דלית ליה צורך ביה. ור' יהודה סבר עדיין צריך לו ואע"ג שפרעו וחייב. מאי בינייהו דפליגי ביה. אמר רב יוסף לשהות שטר פרוע איכא בינייהו. ת"ק סבר אסור. וכיון שהמלוה אסור לשהותו אין הלוה צריך לשטר ואם הוציאו פטור. דהוה ליה כמתעסק. ור' יהודה סבר מותר לאדם לשהות שטר פרוע בתוך ביתו. והרי הלוה חושש מן השטר ויש לו צורך בהוצאתו וחייב. אביי אמר דכולי עלמא אסור לשהות שטר פרוע. והכא במודה בשטר שכתבו קא מיפלגי. ת"ק סבר צריך לקיימו. ור' יהודה סבר אין צריך לקיימו. ועיקר דהא שמעתתא בהאשה שנתארמלה ובכמה דוכתי:

מסורת הש"ס

[מהרש"ל מוחק זה וכן משמע לקמן בגמ' עט:]

[נזיר ג.]

[רקיקי מצות מתרגמינן אספוגין פטירין ערוך וכן ברב אלפס]

[גי' הערוך ערך שתי תנא כמה קשר מוכסין שתי אותיות בכתב יווני שהן גדולות מאותיות שלנו]

[תוספתא פ"ט]

[כתובות יט.]

[שם כ"ח ז. שבת ב"ב קנד. קע.]

הגהות הב"ח

(א) תוס' ד"ה ת"ק סבר וכו' א"נ לטרוף ממשעבדי כ"ב דלא חיישינן לקנוניא אלא היכא דליתרע שטרא דהיינו שנכתב ומלוה: (ב) בא"ד עומד ולוות שאינו פרוע ואי לא הוה טענינן ללקוחות וליתומים מזוייף ופרעתי הוה אתי שפיר וכו' ושם האכרתי וי"ל דמיירי כגון שאמר אין לי וכו' שלא כדין ואם תאמר ואמאי לא קאמר כצ"ל:

גליון הש"ס

גמ' רבנן סברי אסור לשהות. ק"ל הא חזי ליה למחוק השטר ויהיה מותר להשהותו לצור ע"פ צלוחיתו וצ"ע:

A TAX-COLLECTOR'S RECEIPT IS LIABLE.) [78b] ERASED PAPER,[3] AS MUCH AS IS REQUIRED TO WRAP ROUND A SMALL PHIAL OF SPIKENARD OIL; SKIN, FOR MAKING AN AMULET; PARCHMENT, FOR WRITING THEREON THE SHORTEST PASSAGE OF THE TEFILLIN, WHICH IS 'HEAR O ISRAEL,':[4] INK, FOR WRITING TWO LETTERS; STIBIUM,[5] FOR PAINTING ONE EYE; PASTE, FOR PUTTING ON THE TOP OF A LIME BOARD [SHAFSHAF];[6] PITCH AND SULPHUR, FOR MAKING A PERFORATION [THEREIN];[7] WAX, FOR PUTTING OVER A SMALL HOLE;[8] CLAY, FOR MAKING A HOLE IN A GOLD REFINER'S POT.[9] R. JUDAH SAID: FOR MAKING A [TRIPOD'S] PEG.[10] BRAN, FOR PUTTING ON THE MOUTH OF A GOLD REFINER'S POT;
a LIME,[1] FOR SMEARING THE SMALLEST OF GIRLS.[2] R. JUDAH SAID: ENOUGH TO PRODUCE A HAIR-CROWN [ḲALḲAL].[3] R. NEHEMIAH SAID: ENOUGH FOR MAKING SIDE-CURLS [ONDAFE].[4]

GEMARA. For a cord too, let one be culpable on account of as much as is required to make a hanger for a sieve or a basket-sieve?—Since it chafes the utensil, people do not make it [thus].[5]

Our Rabbis taught: As for palm leaves, the standard is as much as is required for making a handle for a basket, an Egyptian basket. As for bast; Others say:[6] as much as is required for putting on the opening of a small funnel for straining wine. Fat; as much as is required for greasing under a small cake. And what size is that?—As [large as] a *sela'*. But it was taught, As [large as] a dried fig?—Both are the same standard. Soft rags, as much as is required for making a small ball. And what size is that?—As [large as] a nut.

PAPER, LARGE ENOUGH TO WRITE A TAX-COLLECTOR'S RECEIPT ON IT. It was taught: How much is a tax-collector's receipt? Two letters.[7] But the following contradicts this: If one carries out smooth [blank] paper, if large enough for writing two letters thereon, he is culpable; if not, he is not culpable?[8]—Said R. Shesheth: What is meant by 'two letters'? Two letters of a tax-collector's receipt. Raba said: [It means] two letters of ours, together with a margin for holding, which is the equivalent of a tax-collector's receipt.

An objection is raised: If one carries out erased paper or a receipted note; if its blank portion is large enough for two letters to be written thereon, or if the whole is sufficient for wrapping round the mouth of a small phial of spikenard oil, he is culpable; but if not, he is not culpable. As for R. Shesheth, who explained, What is meant by 'two letters'? two letters of a tax-collector's receipt,
b it is well.[1] But according to Raba, who said that it means two letters of ours together with a margin for holding, which is the equivalent of a tax-collector's receipt—surely here no margin for holding is required?[2] This is a difficulty.

Our Rabbis taught: If one carries out a tax-collector's receipt before having shown it to the collector, he is culpable;[3] after having shewn it to the collector, he is not culpable.[4] R. Judah said: Even after showing it to the collector, he is culpable, because he still needs it. Wherein do they differ? Abaye said: They differ in respect to collectors' runners.[5] Raba said: They differ in respect to the higher and the lesser collectors.[6] R. Ashi said: They [even] differ in respect of one tax-collector, because he needs it [the document] for showing to the second, so that he can say to him, 'See, I am a man [exempted] by the collector.'[7]

Our Rabbis taught: If one carries out a note of debt, if before it has been settled, he is culpable; if after it has been settled, he is not culpable. R. Judah said: Even after settlement he is culpable, because he needs it. Wherein do they differ? R. Joseph said: They differ as to whether it is forbidden to keep a settled note. The Rabbis maintain: It is forbidden to keep a settled note;[8] while R. Judah holds: One may keep a settled note.[9] Abaye said: All hold that a settled note may not be kept; but here they differ as to whether a note requires confirmation [even] when he [the debtor] admits that it was [validly] written. The first Tanna holds: Even when [the debtor] admits that a note [was validly] written, it
c must be confirmed.[1] R. Judah holds: When [the debtor] admits that a note was [validly] written, it need not be confirmed. And what is the meaning of 'if before it has been settled' and 'if after it

(3) Palimpsest paper from which writing has been erased, and which cannot be written upon again. (4) Deut. VI, 4-9. The *Tefillin* (v. Glos.) contain four Biblical passages. (5) Used for painting the eyes. (6) For catching birds; v. *infra* 80a. (7) Rashi: The phial in which mercury is kept is closed with a perforated stopper of pitch or sulphur. (8) As a plug. (9) Through which he inserts his bellows. (10) A leg of the tripod which supports the refiner's pot.

a (1) Used as a depilatory. (2) V. Gemara. (3) Formed by the depilation of the undergrowth of hair. (4) Var. lec. Andife, v. Gemara. (5) Culpability is incurred only when the article transported can be used in its normal manner. (6) 'Others' frequently refers to R. Meir, Hor. 13a. (7) *'Aruk* reads: two Greek letters—which are larger than Hebrew letters. (8) 'Two letters' implies of normal size, which is smaller than tax-collector's letters: v. also preceding note.

b (1) The same explanation holds good here too. (2) It can be held by the erased or the written portion. (3) Since he still needs it. (4) The receipt or tax-exemption was issued by a higher authority and then shown to the actual collector. Once shown, he has no further use for it, and is therefore not liable for carrying it out. (5) The police, who stop people and demand toll. R. Judah argues that the receipt must be shown to these; while the Rabbis hold that the person stopped could refer him to the collector or superintendent. (6) Cf. n. 4. R. Judah maintains that for this reason the document is always required, while the Rabbis hold that a secret password was used as a proof of exemption. (7) E.g., if the exemption is in respect of a toll-bridge. Even if there is always one man only on duty at one end, the document may be required for the man at the other end. V. *T.A.* II, p. 375. (8) Therefore it is of no value either to the creditor or to the debtor; consequently no culpability is entailed in carrying it out.—The reason of the prohibition is that one may demand payment afresh. (9) Hence the paper itself is of value.

c (1) By its signatories attesting their signatures (Rashi in Keth. 19a, B.M. 7a and 72b). Otherwise the debtor can plead that it has been settled. For without the confirmation of the signatories he could successfully plead that it is a forgery, hence he is also believed in his plea of repayment, since the validity of the note rests on his word. Consequently if the debtor pleads that he has repaid the loan—this is now the meaning of 'if after it has been settled'—the note is valueless.

has been settled'? [79a] If the debtor pleads that it has been settled or not settled [respectively].[2] Raba said: All agree that [even] when [the debtor] admits that a note was [validly] written, it must [still] be confirmed. But here they differ as to whether we write a quittance.[3] The first Tanna holds: We write a quittance;[4] while R. Judah holds: A quittance[5] is not written. R. Ashi said: [R. Judah's reason is] because he [the debtor] needs it to show to a second creditor, as he can say to him, 'See, I am a man who repays.'

SKIN, FOR MAKING AN AMULET. Raba asked R. Naḥman: If one carries out skin, what is the standard [to involve a penalty], Even as we learnt, he replied: SKIN, FOR MAKING AN AMULET. If one dresses it, what is the standard?—There is no difference, he replied. When it needs dressing,[6] what is the standard?—There is no difference, replied he. And whence do you say thus?—As we learnt: If one bleaches [wool], hatchels, dyes, or spins it, the standard is a full double span.[7] And if one weaves two threads together, the standard is a full span.[8] This shows that since
a it stands to be spun,[1] the standard is as though it were spun. So here too, since it [the skin] stands to be dressed, its standard is as though it were [already] dressed. And if it is not to be dressed [at all], what is the standard? There is no difference, said he to him.

But, is there no difference between dressed and undressed [hide]? He raised an objection to him: If one carries out dissolved dyes,[2] [the standard is] as much as is required for dyeing a sample of wool.[3] Whereas of undissolved dyes we learnt: [In the case of] nutshells,[4] pomegranate shells, woad, and madder,[5] [the standard is] as much as is required for dyeing the small piece of cloth at the opening [top] of a network?[6]—Surely it was stated thereon, R. Naḥman observed in Rabbah b. Abbuha's name: That is because one does not trouble to steep dyes [merely] for dyeing a sample of wool. Yet what of the seeds of a vegetable garden, whereof, before they are sown, we learnt: [If one carries out] garden seeds, [the standard is] less than the size of a dried fig; R. Judah b. Bathyra ruled: 'Five', yet after they are sown we learnt: As for manure, or thin sand, [the standard is] as much as is required for fertilizing a cabbage stalk; this is R. Akiba's view. But the Sages maintain: For fertilizing one leek plant?'[7] Surely it was stated thereon, R. Papa said: In the one case it refers to where it is sown, in the other where it is not sown, because one does not trouble to carry out a single seed for sowing.[8]

Yet what of clay, whereof, before it is kneaded, it was taught: 'The Sages agree with R. Simeon, that if one carries out waste water into the street, the standard is a *rebi'ith*'. And we debated thereon. For what is waste water fit? And R. Jeremiah said: For kneading clay therewith. And yet after it is mixed, it was taught: As for clay, [the standard is] as much as is required for making
b the hole of a smelting pot?[1]—There too it is as we stated, because no man troubles to knead clay [only] for making the hole of a smelting pot.

Come and hear: For R. Ḥiyya b. Ammi said on 'Ulla's authority: There are three [kinds of] hide: *maẓẓah, ḥippa,* and *diftera. Maẓẓah*[2] is as its name implies, neither salted nor treated with flour or gall-nut. And what is its standard? R. Samuel b. Rab Judah recited: As much as is required for wrapping a small weight therein. And how much is that? Said Abaye: A quarter of a Pumbedithan quarter.[3] *Ḥippa* is a skin that is salted but not treated with flour and gall-nut. And what is its standard? Even as we learnt: SKIN, AS MUCH AS IS REQUIRED FOR MAKING AN AMULET. *Diftera* is skin that has been dressed with salt and flour but not treated with gall-nut. And what is its standard? As much as is required for writing a divorce.[4] Now incidentally it is stated, As much as is required for wrapping a weight therein, which Abaye explained [as meaning] a quarter of a Pumbedithan quarter?[5]—There it treats of a steaming hide.[6] But we learnt: A garment three [handbreadths] square is susceptible to *midras*;[7] sacking four square, a hide five square and reed matting six square[8] are susceptible to [the uncleanness of] both *midras* and the dead. Now it was taught thereon: As for a garment, sacking and hide, as their standard is for uncleanness, so it is for carrying out![9]—That refers to a leather spread.[10]

(2) V. preceding note. (3) V. B.B. 170b. (4) Therefore the debtor does not require the original note, since he holds a receipt, and so if he carries it out he is not culpable (R. Ḥan. Rashi explains differently, referring this to the creditor). (5) But the creditor has to return the note to the debtor, who in turn must take care not to lose it, lest it fall into the hands of the creditor, enabling him to claim payment a second time. (6) And one carries it out—at this stage it cannot be used for an amulet. (7) Of the thumb and the forefinger. (8) The text adds 'double', but it is bracketed and is absent from the Mishnah *infra* 105b.
a (1) Bleaching, etc., are antecedent to spinning. (2) Ready for use. (3) Jast. V. also *supra* 11b. (4) These were quite commonly used in ancient days for dyes; v. *T.A.* I, p. 552, n. 222. (5) All these, including the two former, used as dyes. (6) Or, hair-net. V. also *T.A.* I, pp. 187 and 636, n. 776. This is a larger standard than the preceding and a similar distinction should be made between undressed and dressed hides. (7) Thus here too there is a different standard after sowing. (8) V. *infra* 90b.
b (1) V. notes *supra* 78a. (2) Lit., 'unleavened'. (3) Of a *liṭra*. V. *J.E.* XII, p. 48b s.v. *Liṭra*, though it is not clear whether what is stated there applies to a Pumbedithan *liṭra* too—probably not. Weights were wrapped in hide to prevent their being rubbed away; hence this standard. (4) V. Giṭ. 22a. (5) Which is a larger standard than the others. (6) I.e., immediately after it is flayed and before it has had time to dry. It is not yet fit for tanning, and hence a different standard is applied to it (Rashi). (7) V. *supra* 59a, n. b1. (8) V. notes *supra* 76a. (9) That size carried out on the Sabbath involves a penalty. Hence the standard for hide is five square, which is not the same as that given in the Mishnah. Presumably the difficulty must be answered by drawing a distinction between tanned and untanned hide, and this contradicts R. Nahman. (10) The hide being so treated that it can only be used as a leather cover on couches, etc., but not for writing thereon. Hence there is a different standard.

עד שיאמר לוה פרעתי: ולא פרעתי רבא אמר דכולי עלמא מודה בשטר שכתבו שצריך לקיימו והכא בכותבין שובר קמיפלגי תנא קמא סבר כותבין שובר *ורבי יהודה סבר אין כותבין שובר רב אשי אמר מפני שצריך להראותו לבעל חוב שני דאמר ליה חזי גברא דפרע אנא: עור כדי לעשות כו': בעא מיניה רבא מרב נחמן המוציא עור בכמה א"ל כדתנן עור כדי לעשות קמיע [*המעבדו בכמה א"ל לא שנא] לעבדו בכמה א"ל לא שנא ומנא תימרא כדתנן *המלבן והמנפץ והצובע והטווה שיעורו כמלא רוחב הסיט כפול והאורג ב' חוטין שיעורו כמלא רוחב הסיט (כפול) אלמא כיון דלטוייה קאי שיעורא כטווי ה"נ כיון דלעבדו קאי שיעורו כמעובד ושלא לעבדו בכמה אמר ליה לא שנא ולא שני בין מעובד לשאינו מעובד איתיביה המוציא *סמנין שרוין כדי לצבוע בהן דוגמא לאירא ואילו בסמנין שאינן שרוין תנן *קליפי אגוזים וקליפי רמונין סטים ופואה כדי לצבוע בהן בגד קטן [לפי] סבכה הא איתמר עלה *אמר רב נחמן אמר רבה בר אבוה לפי שאין אדם טורח לשרות סמנין לצבוע בהן דוגמא לאירא והרי זרעוני גינה דמקמי דזרעינהו תנן *זרעוני גינה פחות מכגרוגרת רבי יהודה בן בתירא אומר חמשה ואילו בתר דזרעינהו תנן *זבל וחול הדק כדי לזבל בו קלח של כרוב דברי רבי עקיבא וחכמים אומרים כדי לזבל כרישא הא איתמר עלה *אמר רב פפא הא דזריע הא דלא זריע לפי שאין אדם טורח להוציא נימא אחת לזריעה והרי טיט דמקמי דליגבליה תניא *מודים חכמים לרבי שמעון במוציא שופכין לרה"ר ששיעורן ברביעית והוינן [בה] שופכין למאי חזו וא"ר ירמיה לגבל בהן את הטיט ואילו בתר דגבליה תניא *טיט כדי לעשות בהן פי כור התם נמי כדאמרן לפי שאין אדם טורח (א) (בהן) לגבל את הטיט לעשות בו פי כור ת"ש *דאמר רבי חייא בר אמי משמיה דעולא [ב]שלשה עורות הן מצה וחיפה ודיפתרא מצה כמשמעו דלא מליח ודלא קמיח ודלא עפיץ וכמה שיעורו תני רב שמואל בר רב יהודה °כדי לצור בו משקולת קטנה וכמה אמר אביי ריבעא דריבעא דפומבדיתא חיפה דמליח ולא קמיח ולא עפיץ וכמה שיעורו כדתנן עור כדי לעשות קמיע דיפתרא דמליח וקמיח ולא עפיץ וכמה שיעורו כדי לכתוב עליו את הגט קתני מיהת כדי לצור בו משקולת קטנה ואמר אביי ריבעא דריבעא דפומבדיתא התם בבישולא והתנן *הבגד שלשה על שלשה למדרס השק ד' על ד' העור ה' על ה' מפץ ו' על ו' בין למדרס בין למת ותאני עלה [י]הבגד והשק והעור כשיעור לטומאה כך שיעור להוצאה ההוא [י]בקורטובלא:

קלף

קלף

דוכסוסטוס

עד שיאמר פרעתי ולא פרעתי. כלומר עד שלא אמר פרעתי חייב משאמר פרעתי פטור דבטל ליה: דכולי עלמא צריך לקיימו. והכא בפרעו ולא פרעו ממש קאמר ובשטר מקויים ודכולי עלמא אסור לשהות שטר פרוע: והכא בכותבין שובר קא מיפלגי. יש גורסין ת"ק סבר אין כותבין שובר על שטר פרוע שאתה מצריכו לשמור שוברו מן העכברים אלא מחזיר לו ושורפו ואסור להשהותו ורבי יהודה סבר כותבין שובר ועל ידי שובר מותר לשהות שטר פרוע לצור ע"פ צלוחיתו ולא היא חדא דכיון דאסור לשהות שטר פרוע אפי' על ידי שובר נמי אסור להשהותו שמא יאבד השובר וזה חוזר וגובה בו ועוד לרבי יהודה אין כותבין שובר שמעינן ליה בבבא בתרא (דף קע:) דתנן מי שפרע מקצת חובו ר' יהודה אומר יחליף רבי יוסי אומר יכתוב שובר וה"ג ת"ק סבר כותבים שובר והכי קאמר משפרעו לוה והוציאו מלוה בשבת פטור שאינו צריך לו ואי אמרת כיון דראוי לצור ע"פ צלוחיתו הוא דבעי אהדורי ללוה לא משהי ליה שמא יבא לידי מלוה ויחזור ויתבענו ואי נמי לא מהדר ליה מלוה לא איכפת ליה ללוה דמלוה כתב ליה ללוה שובר עילויה ורבי יהודה סבר אין כותבין שובר הלכך צריך הוא המלוה דבעי אהדורי (ג) ואי לא מהדר ליה חוזר ותובעו לו מה שפרעו דלא סגי ליה בשובר דצריך לשומרו מן העכברים: רב אשי אמר. פלוגתייהו כשהוציאו לוה הוא ומה הוא צריך לו דקאמר ודאי לא לצור דמשום סתימת פי צלוחית לא משהי ליה שמא יבא ליד המלוה אלא משהי ליה להראותו לשאר בעלי חובות ולהתהלל שהוא פורע חובותיו: המוציא עור בכמה. משום דבעי למיבעי מיניה הנך בעיי אחרייתא בעא מיניה הא ואף על גב דמתני' היא: לעבד. עור העומד לעבדו ועדיין לא עבדו בכמה שיעור הוצאתו: המלבן. למר: סיט. כדי הפרש אצבע מהאמה: כפול. שני סיטין: אלמא. כיון דמנפץ ומלבן לטוייה קאי שיעוריה כטוויה: שלא לעבדו. אינו עומד לעבד: דוגמא. כלומר מעט כעין שמראין לדוגמא לומר רוצה אתה בזה:לאירא. והוא כשיעור הצריך לאירא של גרדי לסתום פי קנה שפקעית הערב נתונה בו: קליפי אגוזים. קליפה לחה שעל קליפי האגוז: סטים. ויסודא: פואה. וורנצ"א: פי סבכה. קופ"א נותנין בגד באמצעיתה והאי שיעורא נפיש: שאין אדם טורח כו'. ואם בא לשרותה שורה כדי פי סבכה אבל עור טורח אדם לעבד כדי קמיע ומעובד נמי פחות מכדי קמיע לא חשיב: חמשה. גרעינין: ואילו בתר דזרעינהו תנן. דקלח אחד חשוב: כרישא. קפלוט: הא איתמר עלה. לקמן בפרק רבי עקיבא מתרץ לה רב פפא הכי: נימא. גרעינין: מלה כמשמעו. שאין לה שום תיקון: קמיח. משהין אותו בקמח ומים: עפיץ. מתקנין אותו בשחיקת עפצים כמו שעושין כאן בשחיקת קליפת ארז שקורין טנ"א: וכמה שיעורו. להוצאת שבת: רבעא דרבעא דפומבדיתא. רובע ליטרא של פומבדיתא דרך הסוחרים לצור משקולת של עופרת כדי שלא תפחת לפי שהמתכת נשחקת תמיד ונפחת מאליו: קמיע. בציר שיעוריה מכדי לצור משקולת: לכתוב גט. ותנן (גיטין דף פה:) גופו של גט הרי את מותרת לכל אדם ושמו ושמה והעדים והזמן ושיעור זה קטן מכולן: וקתני מיהת כו'. אלמא שיעור דאין מעובד נפיש: בבישולא. לא כמו שהופשט קרי בשולא לשון בשול שהוא לח דהכתי לא חזי לעיבוד אבל יבש חזי לעיבוד וכיון דחזי לעיבוד הוי כמעובד: שלשה על שלשה לטומאת מדרס. אבל למגע שלש על שלש והן אצבעות: כך שיעור להוצאת שבת. אלמא שאין מעובד חמשה טפחים בעינן ומתניתין מוקי במעובד: בקורטבלא. מבשלו ברותחין ומתקשה לישב עליו ולכסות דלובקאות שקורין פושדטוויי"ל ומטות ולעשותו שולחן:

ת"ק סבר כותבין שובר. ומיירי שכבר יש לו שובר ולכך משפרע פטור דאין זקוק להחזיר השטר ומתוך פירוש הקונטרס משמע שעדיין לא נכתב השובר וקשה דהרי צריך להחזירו ללוה שלא יצטרך לכתוב שובר: חזי דגברא דפרע אנא. כרב אשי תניא בתוספתא דמכילתין *ר' יהודה אומר אף המוציא שטר פרוע כל שהוא חייב מפני שמשמרו לבעל חוב ולשאר אמוראי קשה לרשב"א: אלמא כיון דלטוויה קאי. הוה ליה למינקט כיון דלאריגה קאי (ג) שהוא רחוק יותר אלא שמא לאו כולהו קיימי לאריגה: כדי לכתוב עליו את הגט. סבירא ליה כרבי אליעזר דאמר עדי מסירה כרתי דלר' מאיר אין כותבין על הדפתרא דתנן בגטין (דף כא:) אין כותבין על נייר מחוק ועל הדפתרא וחכמים מכשירין ואמר בגמ' מאן חכמים ר' אליעזר ובחנם פי' בקונטרס דשיעור גט קטן מכולן דהא אשכחן דקלף כדי לכתוב עליו פרשה קטנה שבתפילין ונייר דגרע טפי שיעורו לכתוב עליו קשר מוכסין וטעמא דקלף שהוא חשוב אין מצניעין אותו לקשר מוכסין וכן יש לפרש כאן: וקתני מיהא כדי לצור ואמר אביי. קשה לר"י דלא הוה ליה לאתויי מילתא דאביי הכא:

עין משפט
נר מצוה

ח א מיי' פי"ח מהלכות שבת הלכה ה:
ט ב מיי' פי"ח מהלכות שבת הלכה יד:
י ג שם הלכה יג:
[פ"ט]
יא ד שם הלכה יד:

רבינו חננאל

דוכתי נמי איכא. והכין הוא ראובן שתבע את שמעון במנה והוציא עליו שטר. אמר שמעון שטר זה כתבתיו לו על עצמי אלא שפרעתיו אם יכול ראובן המלוה לקיים את השטר בחותמיו כולי עלמא לא פליגי שחייב שמעון בממון דאמר רב פפא האי מאן דמפיק שטרא אחבריה וא"ל שטרא פריעא הוא לאו כל כמיניה. אבל אם אין ראובן המלוה יכול לקיימו בחותמיו ואין נודע כי נכתב באמת אלא מדברי שמעון. מר סבר אם מודה לוה בשטר שכתבו צריך המלוה לקיימו בו ואם לא יקימנו ואמר לוה כתבתיו ופרעתיו. חפה שאסר הוא הפה שהתיר ומר סבר כיון שהודה לוה שכתבו הרי נתקיים בכך ואין המלוה צריך לקיימו. ואם יאמר לוה כתבתיו ופרעתיו אומרי' לו הבא ראיה או תן זה הממון והילכך צריך לקיימו עכשיווקאמ' אביי ת"ק סבר מודה בשטר שכתבו צריך לקיימו ולא איכפת ליה ללוה אע"ג דשטרא ביד מלוה וצריך מלוה לקיימו. והילכך לוה פטור על הוצאתו דמתעסק הוא. ור' יהודה סבר מודה בשטר שכתבו אין צריך לקיימו. וצריך ליה לוה וחייב על הוצאתו: רבא אמר דכ"ע מודו בשטר שכתבו צריך לקיימו. והכא בכותבין שובר קא מיפלגי. ועיקרא הא בגמ' דגט פשוט במתני' מי שפרע מקצת חובו ר' יהודה אומר יחליף ר' יוסי אומר יכתוב שובר ואמרינן עלה אמר רב הונא אמר רב אין הלכה לא כר' יהודה ולא כר' יוסי אלא ב"ד מקרעין את השטר וכותבין לו שטר אחר מזמן ראשון. ודבר זה בין בפריעת מקצת בין בפריעת השטר כולו אם אמר המלוה אבד שמרי דקאמרינן (שם) אמר ר"ח בריה דרב יהושע אפי' למ"ד כותבין שובר ה"מ אפלגא אבל אכוליה שטרא לא כתבינן. ולא היא אפי' אכולי שטרא נמי כתבינן. ופלוגתא היא דרב ושמואל אמרי אין כותבין שובר. ור' יוחנן ור"ל אמרי כותבין שובר והלכתא כותבין שובר. השתא הכא לענין לוה שהוציא את השטר בשבת אחר שפרעו קאמר רבא בכותבין שובר פלוגתייהו. ת"ק דסבר פטור קסבר כותבין שובר דאסיק אדעתי' [שמא יאמר] שלא פרעו אלא [מבקש ממנו] שובר. וכיון שיש בידו שובר לא צריך ליה. ור' יהודה סבר אין כותבין שובר והאי פרע ליה ועדיין שטר שעליו קיים. והלכך צריך ליה *)ולא עליה מיניה חורבא. וכולהו הני סבארי אידחו במימרא דרב אשי וקאמר כ"ע כותבין שובר והכא צריך ליה לוה לשטרא דאיבעי לטיוף מן איניש אחרינא מחוי ליה וא"ל חזי דגברא דפרע אנא. ומהכא מחייב ליה ר' יהודה: בעא מיניה רבא מרב נחמן עור שיעורו בכמה א"ל תנינא עור כדי לעשות בו קמיע ולא שנא מעובד (שלא לעבדו) שראוי לקמיע. ולא שנא שלא מעובד לעבדו ול"ש שאינו מעובד שלא לעבדו. ומנא תימרא דלא שנא לן בין מעובד בין שאינו מעובד דקאי לעבוד דהא המלבן והמנפס שהוא עומד לטויה שיעורו כשיעור טויה. ואיתיביה רבא תלת תיובתא לרב נחמן דאמר לא שנא לן בין מעובד לשאינו מעובד. ראשונה מסמנין שהרי השרויין שיעורן כדי לצבוע בהן (דאמא לאמא) [דוגמא לאירא]. ושאינן שרויין שיעורן גדול מזה. כדי לצבוע בהן בגד קטן פי סבכא דאלמא טובא איכא בין שרויין בין שאינן שרויין ופריק רב נחמן התם שני בין שרויין ובין שאינן שרויין. דהא איתמר עלה. אמר רב' נחמן אמר רבה בר אבוה לפי שאין אדם טורח לשרות סממנים לצבוע בהן (רינמא לאינא) [דוגמא לאירא]. והילכך אין דרך המוציא להוציא סממנין לשרות לצבוע. אבל שרויין מוציא אדם שיעור זה. אבל הכא עור מעובד ושאינו מעובד כצמר מנופץ וכטויה דמי. שנית איתיביה זרעוני גינה בזמן שאינן זרועין שיעור הוצאתו שנים ובזמן שהן זרועין שיעור המוציא להן זבל כדי לזבל כרישה אחת דאלמא שני בין זרועין לשאינן זרועין. ופריק בהא נמי שאני זרעוני גינה דאמר רב פפא לפי שאין אדם טורח להוציא נימא אחת לזריעה ושרח הוא לזבל כרישה אחת אבל עור לא שני לן בין מעובד לשאינו מעובד. שלישית שופכין ששיעורן ברביעית כדי לגבל טיט. אבל טיט מגובל כדי לעשות פי כרש. ופרקי' חהיא שניא בדאמיד בה שאין אדם טורח. אבל טיט [שיעורו] לעשות פי כרש. אבל הכא בעור לא שנא. תא שמע דאמר רב חייא בר אמי משמיה דעולא ג' עורות הן וקא יהיב תלתא שיעורי וחד מנהון מצה דלא מליח ודלא קמיח ודלא נפיץ. והוו שאינו מעובד. ושיעורו ריבעא דריבעא דפומבדיתא. והוא כדי לצור משקולת קטנה. (בני) [פי'] רבינו האי גאון זצ"ל צוררין משקל של אבן כדי שלא יחסר. דאלמא פליג על רב נחמן דאמר לא שנא בין מעובד לשאינו מעובד. ופרקי' בישלה שאני. ופירושה בישלה העור שנתעבד כמה שהוא בלא מלח ובישל ונפסד כשמלבישין אותו על משקל או על זולתו יבש וקשה מאד (והו שהכנת) [ודרך חנוני] לצרור משקלת ולעשות ממנו כלים לשמן שנקראין בכל אחד לאביי ושיעור קטן שלו הוא המפורש. וקא מפרקינן לרב נחמן שאם לא בישל העור ולא נפסד. ועדיין ראוי הוא לעיבוד שיעורו כמעובד כדי לעשות קמיע. אבל מליח וקמיח סגי בפחות מן הלין. תרי שיעורי בין לצור משקולת ובין עשיית קמיע. והכין נמי הא דתנן העור המליח חמשה על

מסורת הש"ס

[ב"ב קע:]

לקמן פט:

[לקמן צ.]

שם

לקמן פ: צ:

[לקמן צ.]

לעיל עח.

שם לקמן פ: גיטין כב. ע"ש

לעיל עו. ע"ש סוכה יז: כלים פכ"ז מ"ב

הגהות הב"ח

(א) גמ' אדם טורח לגבל כצ"ל ותיבת בהן נמחק: (ב) רש"י ד"ה והכא בכותבין שובר וכו' דבעי אהדורי דאי לא מהדר ליה חוזר ותובעו לוה מה שפרעו: (ג) תוס' ד"ה אלמא וכו' דלאריגה קאי ר"ב נ"ל דהתוס' היו גורסים והאורג וכו' רוחב הסיט כפול:

גליון הש"ס

גמ' כדי לצור בו משקולת קטנה. עיין ב"ב פט ע"א תוס' ד"ה ולא בלל:

*) אולי צ"ל ולא ישליכנו למקום הסכר דנפיק מיניה חורבא.

קלף כדי לכתוב עליו פרשה קטנה: ורמינהו קלף ודוכסוסטוס כדי לכתוב עליו מזוזה מאי מזוזה מזוזה שבתפילין וקרי להו לתפילין מזוזה אין והתניא *רצועות תפילין עם התפילין מטמאות את הידים בפני עצמן אין מטמאות את הידים רבי שמעון בן יהודה אומר משום ר"ש *הנוגע ברצועה טהור עד שיגע בקציצה רבי זכאי משמו אומר טהור עד שיגע במזוזה עצמה והא מדקתני סיפא קלף כדי לכתוב עליו פרשה קטנה שבתפילין שהיא שמע ישראל מכלל דרישא במזוזה עצמה עסקינן *הכי קתני קלף ודוכסוסטוס שיעורן בכמה [א]דוכסוסטוס כדי לכתוב עליו מזוזה קלף כדי לכתוב עליו פרשה קטנה שבתפילין שהיא שמע ישראל: אמר רב דוכסוסטוס הרי היא כקלף מה קלף כותבין עליו תפילין אף דוכסוסטוס כותבין עליו תפילין תנן קלף כדי לכתוב (א) פרשה קטנה שבתפילין שהיא שמע ישראל (קלף אין דוכסוסטוס לא) למצוה ת"ש *[ב]הלכה למשה מסיני תפילין על הקלף ומזוזה על דוכסוסטוס קלף במקום בשר דוכסוסטוס במקום שיער למצו' והתניא שינה פסול אמזוזה והתניא שינה בזה ובזה פסול אידי ואידי אמזוזה והא דכתבינהו אקלף במקום שיער אי נמי אדוכסוסטוס במקום בשר ואיבעית אימא שינה בזה ובזה תנאי היא דתניא [ג]שינה בזה ובזה פסול רבי אחא מכשיר משום רבי אחי בר חנינא ואמרי לה משום רבי יעקב בר' חנינא רב פפא אמר רב דאמר כתנא דבי מנשה דתנא דבי מנשה כתבה על הנייר ועל המטלית פסולה על הקלף ועל הגויל ועל דוכסוסטוס כשרה כתבה מאי אילימא מזוזה מזוזה אקלף מי כתבינן אלא לאו תפילין ולטעמיך תפילין אגויל מי כתבינן [אלא] כי תניא ההיא [ד]בס"ת לימא מסייע ליה [ה]כיוצא בו *תפילין שבלו וספר תורה שבלה אין עושין מהן מזוזה לפי שאין מורידין מקדושה חמורה לקדושה קלה טעמא דאין מורידין הא מורידין עושין דכתיבא אמאי לאו דכתיבא אדוכסוסטוס לא דכתיבא על הקלף ומזוזה אקלף מי כתבינן אין והתניא כתבה על הקלף על הנייר ועל המטלית פסולה *אמר רבי שמעון בן אלעזר רבי מאיר היה כותבה על הקלף מפני שמשתמרת השתא דאתית להכי לרב נמי לא תימא דוכסוסטוס הרי הוא כקלף [ו]אלא אימא קלף הרי הוא כדוכסוסטוס מה דוכסוסטוס כותבין עליו מזוזה אף קלף כותבין עליו מזוזה: דיו כדי לכתוב:

תנא

רש"י

דוכסוסטוס. קלף שניטלה קליפתו העליונה: מזוזה. שמע והיה אם שמוע: שבתפילין. דהתם ד' אגרות לד' פרשיות ושיעור בחד מינייהו דהיינו שמע קטנה שבהם: מטמאות את הידים. לענין תרומה כדאמרן בי"ח דבר בפ"ק (דף יד:): קציצה. הוא הדפוס של עור שחתוך לד' בתים כמין בית יד של עור והאיגרות בתוכן: במזוזה. הן האיגרות שהן בתוך הבתים: והא מדקתני סיפא. דההיא דלעיל קלף כדי לכתוב כו' מכלל דרישא כו' וקשיא רישא אסיפא: שיעורן. של כל אחד בכמה: כדי לכתוב עליו מזוזה. אדוכסוסטוס קאי דלא חזי לתפילין וסיפא פריש קלף כדי לכתוב פרשה קטנה שבתפילין: קלף אין דוכסוסטוס לא. הוי בשיעורא זוטא כי האי אלא בכדי לכתוב ב' פרשיות דמזוזה ואי דוכסוסטוס חזי לתפילין הוה ליה לשעוריה כשיעור זוטא דתפילין: למצוה. מצוה מן המובחר קלף בעינן וסתמא דכל איניש מצוה מעלייתא עביד הלכך לא מצנע דוכסוסטוס לתפילין וה"ל אין מצניעין כמוהו: למזוזה. אם כתבה על הקלף: הא דכתב אקלף אפי' במקום שיער. וכ"ש במקום בשר דהילכתא מזוזה במקום שיער והא דכתבה אדוכסוסטוס במקום בשר: רבי אחי מכשיר. ורב מוקי לדר' אחי אתפילין דכתבן על דוכסוסטוס ואמר כוותיה: נייר. של עשבים: גויל. מעובד בעפצים: מסייע ליה. לרב: כיוצא בו. רישא דברייתא תפילין של יד עושין אותן של ראש ואותן של ראש אין עושין אותן של יד לפי שאין מורידין כו': ס"ת שבלה. אין מחתכין ממנה יריעה שפרשיות שמע והיה אם שמוע בתוכה לקובען במזוזה: דכתיבי. הנך תפילין אמאי: לאו דכתיבי אדוכסוסטוס. שהוא כשר למזוזה הלכך הא מורידין עושין: השתא דאתית להכי. דמזוזה אקלף כשרה: לא תימא. במילתיה דרב דוכסוסטוס הרי הוא כו':

תוספות

קלף ודוכסוסטוס כו'. גויל הוא עור שלם אלא שהסירו השיער והיינו דאמר בריש בבא בתרא (דף ג.) גויל אבני דלא משפיין אלמא שאינו מתוקן קרי גויל וכשחולקין אותו לשנים אותו שכלפי שיער קרוי קלף וכלפי בשר הוא דוכסוסטוס ואומר ר"ת דבלשון *יון קורין לבשר סוסטוס ודוך פי' מקום כמו דוך פלן לכך קרי ליה דוכסוסטוס כלומר מקום בשר וקלפים שלנו יש להן דין קלף וכותבין עליהן ס"ת תפילין ומזוזות לצד בשר ודלא כאומר שקלפים שלנו הם דוכסוסטוס לפי שמגררין האומנין המתקנים אותן קליפתן העליונה ונשאר הדוכסוסטוס דא"כ היאך כותבין עליהם תפילין דמסקינן הכא דתפילין דוקא על הקלף וי"מ דקלף ודוכסוסטוס אינם מעופצים וקשה דא"כ פסול לכתוב עליהן ס"ת (ג)ותפילין ומזוזות דבעינן ספר ולהכי פסיל במסכת מגילה (דף יט: ושם) לכתוב מגילה על הדפתרא משום דנקראת ספר ולקמן משמע דכשרין וא"ת קלפים שלנו דלא עפיצן היכי מיתכשרי ואומר ר"ת דתיקון שלנו חשיב כעיפוץ וכן משמע בהקומץ רבה (מנחות לה:) דקאמר קרע הבא בב' (ג)יתפור בג' אל יתפור ותניא אידך בשלש יתפור בד' אל יתפור ולא פליגי הא דעפיצן הא דלא עפיצן אלמא ס"ת כשר בלא עפיץ והיינו בתיקון טוב כשלנו ובפ"ק דגיטין (דף יא.) גבי שטר והא בעינן דבר שאינו יכול להזדייף ומשני דעפיצן משמע דאי לא עפיצן יכול להזדייף ופסול והנך סהדי דשלנו אינו יכול להזדייף אלמא חשוב כעפיץ: והא מדקתני סיפא כו'. הוה מצי למיפרך ברייתא גופא רישא לסיפא ומשמע דאמתני' מהדר לפרוכי ואומר ר"י דכן מצינו בהמפקיד (ב"מ דף לז.) גבי ורמי גזל אגזל כו' דברי רבי טרפון ממאי דמתני' ר' טרפון היא מדקתני עלה דההיא כו' והוה מצי למיפרך הנהו תרתי אהדדי ופריך אמתניתין דהמפקיד: תנן קלף כדי לכתוב עליו כו'. אין לפרש דהכי פריך מדנקט קלף מכלל דדוכסוסטוס לא דא"כ לעיל דמשני מאי מזוזה מזוזה שבתפילין אכתי תקשה ליה מתניתין דקתני קלף ומשמע ולא דוכסוסטוס וברייתא נותנת שיעור לדוכסוסטוס כקלף אלא הכא סמך אברייתא דלעיל: אידי ואידי אמזוזה הא דכתבה כו'. וא"ת אמאי לא קאמר אידי ואידי אתפילין קלף במקום שיער ודוכסוסטוס במקום בשר ויש לומר דניחא ליה לקומי לשינויא קמא דשני אמזוזה וה"ה דה"מ למימר אידי ואידי אתפילין: ורבי אחאי מכשיר. וא"ת ואי סבר רב כרבי אחאי לימא נמי קלף הרי הוא כדוכסוסטוס וי"ל רב מפרש דרבי אחאי לא מפרשה אלא אתפילין: אלא לאו אתפילין. והא דקתני כתבה לשון נקבה היינו מזוזה שבתפילין: תפילין אגויל מי כתבינן. וא"ת הא דתנן בפ"ק דמגילה (ד' ח:) אין בין ספרים לתפילין ומזוזות אלא שהספרים נכתבים בכל לשון ותפילין ומזוזות אין נכתבות אלא בלשון אשורית אמאי לא קתני נמי שתפילין ומזוזות אין נכתבין על הגויל ואומר ר"י דלא קתני לה משום דלא מיפסלי בגויל מחד טעמא אלא משום שזה דינו בקלף וזה בדוכסוסטוס אבל הא דנכתבים אשורית הוי מחד טעמא כדדרשינן התם בגמרא והיו בהווייתן יהו ועוד דאפי' עצמן אינן שוין שזה על הקלף וזה על הדוכסוסטוס ומיהו קשה דהוה מצי למיתני שהספרים נכתבים על הנייר שאינו מחוק דדוקא על נייר מחוק פסול ס"ת במסכת סופרים אבל תפילין אין נכתבים אלא על העור כדמוכח בריש פרק שמונה שרצים (לקמן קח.) ול"ע בירושלמי בפ"ק דמגילה ואם תאמר נייר שאינו מחוק נמי ליפסיל בספר תורה כדפסלינן מגילה דסוטה *משום דכתיב בספר ונראה דנייר נמי דקתני במגילה [דסוטה] היינו במחוק ואף על גב דלא פריש כדאשכחן הכא גבי ספר תורה דקתני נייר סתם ומיירי במחוק כדאמרינן במסכת סופרים: הא מורידין עושין. אע"ג דפרשת והיה אם שמוע רחוק מפרשת שמע עושין דקאמר היינו שאם פרשת שמע כתובה בסוף העמוד יכתוב אחריה והיה אם שמוע בגליון או אם היה פרשת והיה אם שמוע בראש העמוד יכתוב למעלה בגליון פרשת שמע: השתא דאתית להכי כו'. אומר ר"י דמילתיה דרב סתמא נשנית בבית המדרש דקלף ודוכסוסטוס שוים והיה סבור בתחילה דלענין תפילין קאמר ולא מצי קאי עד דמסיק השתא דלענין מזוזה קאמר והא דתניא לעיל שינה בזה ובזה פסול אידי ואידי אתפילין וסוגיא דהקומץ אזלא כפי מסקנא דשמעתין:

הוא

עין משפט נר מצוה

יב א מיי' פי"ח מהלכות שבת הלכה טו:

[בכ"י יד. ד"ס בגויל כתבו דבלשון מדי קורין וכו']

יג ב ג מיי' פ"א מהלכות תפילין הלכה ח סמג עשין כב טור שו"ע או"ח סימן לב סעיף ז:

יד ד מיי' שם הלכה ט סמג עשין כח טוש"ע יו"ד סימן רעא סעיף ג:

טו ה מיי' פ"ה מהלכות תפילין הלכה א סמג שם טוש"ע יו"ד סי' רל:

טז ו מיי' פ"א שם הלכה ט סמג עשין כג טור שו"ע יו"ד סימן רפח סעיף ו:

רבינו חננאל

על חמשה. ותניא אידך העור כשיעורו לטומאה כך שיעורו להוצאה. דאמרי צריך שיעור גדול. ופריק התם בקורטובלא. והוא בלשון ישמעאל ספארה: קלף כדי לכתוב עליו פרשה קטנה שבתפילין שהיא שמע ישראל. ורמינהי קלף ודוכסוסטו' כדי לכתוב עליו מזוזה. דאלמא בענין זו בעינן שיעור ב' פרשיות. ופרקי' מאי מזוזה דאמר הכא מזוזה שבתפילין דקארי לה לתפילין מזוזה וסיעתא ר' זכאי אומר משמו אף עם הקציצה טהור עד שיגיע למזוזה עצמה. ומקשי' הא מדקתני סיפא קלף כדי לכתוב עליו פרשה קטנה שבתפילין. דאלמא רישא לאו בתפילין ומתרצינן לה: אמר רב דוכסוסטוס הרי הוא כקלף. מה קלף כותבין עליו תפילין אף דוכסוסטוס כותבין עליו תפילין. מנהגא מייתי מגילתא דמעבדא בתמרי וקמחא דשערי ומתח ליה עד דיביש וקליפליה עד דהוי תרין פיסקי ויזהר שלא ינקב וקאי קלף לחודי' ומעבר ליה לקלף דהוא אפא דמגילתא מכלפי בשר. תוב בעפצא לשמה וכות' פרשיות על מקום בשר*) מנהגא הכין הוא וקאמר רב כי היכי דכותבין תפלין על הקלף דהוא אפא דמגילתא הכין נמי כותבין תפלין על דוכסוסטוס דאי קליף מקלף אם כתב על זה כשר ואם כתב על זה כשר. ומותבינן ליה הל"מ תפילין על קלף. מזוזה על דוכסוסטוס. קלף במקום בשר. דוכסוסטוס במקום שיער. ומפרק רב שאם כתב על דוכסוסטוס יצא. מיהא על הקלף מצוה. ומותבי' שינה בזה ובזה פסל ופרקי' בשבת לענין מזוזה ובמנחות לענין תפילין. ואפא דמגילתא דהוא גיסא דמיקרי קלף הוא מקום שיער בודאי. ומן נואי דיליה כתבינן מזוזה דאמרי' במזוזה כותבין על דוכסוסטוס במקום שיער לאו במקום [שער] ממש. דאי ס"ד אפא דמגילתא היא הרי זה בהדיא הל"מ תפילין על הקלף והרי יצא מקום השיער גופו בכלל קלף. אלא ש"מ מאי מקום שיער הוא מקום שנקלף הקלף משום שנמצא כנגד מקום שיער. נמצא קלף עומד לבדו ומקום שיער העיקר בו אין כותב שם כלום לתפילין אלא מן אפיה אחרנייתא ודוכסוסטוס עומד לבדו והמקום שהיה דבוק על בשר הבהמה בו אין כותב עליו מזוזה מאותן הפנים אלא מן הפנים האחרות. והא שמעתא דרב דקאמר דוכסוסטוס הרי הוא כקלף וקא מפרשא לאכשורי תפילין על הדוכסוסטוס דקא מותבינן ליה לרב שינה בזה ובזה פסל. וקא מיפרקא חד פירוקא אידי ואידי במזוזה. ועוד מיפרקא שינה בזה ובזה פסל תנאי היא וקא קאי רב כיחידאה. ורב פפא קא מוקי ליה לרב כתנא דבי מנשה. דתניא כתבה על הנייר ועל המטלית ועל הקלף ועל הגויל ועל דוכסוסטוס כשרה. וליכא לאוקמה במזוזה שאין מזוזה נכתבה על הקלף והילכך כתפילין היא. ואי משום דאית בה גויל ותפילין לא מכתבן על גויל כי קתני גויל לענין ס"ת. ואתינן נמי לסיועיה דרב דאמר כותבין תפילין על דוכסוסטוס. מדתניא תפילין שבלו אין עושין מהן מזוזה. לפי שאין מורידין מקדושה חמורה לקדושה קלה. ודייקי' מדקא יהיב טעמא לפי שאין מורידין דאלמא אי לאו הכי היו עושין מן התפילין. ואמרינן דכיון דמזוזה אין נכתבת על הקלף שמעינן דהני תפילין אדוכסוסטוס הוה כתבין. [ואי לאו] קדושה המורה היו נעשות מזוזה. והדר פרכינן דלא הויא הא סיעתא לרב. דהא ר"מ היה כותב מזוזה על הקלף ותפילין שבלו על הקלף היו. אי לאו קדושה חמורה הוה מעבדן מזוזה. השתא דאייתית להכי ההוא דאוקמה רב פפא נמי לרב לתנא דבי מנשה. ואוקימנא בתפילין משום דמזוזה אין נכתבת על הקלף. והרי היא נכתבת על הקלף. לרב נמי עיקר שמעתיה הרצה הכין דוכסוסטוס וקלף לענין מזוזה שוין נכתבת על זה ועל זה. אבל תפילין אין נכתבים על דוכסוסטוס וכן הלכה. וכן מנהג: דיו כדי לכתוב

כ'

*) עיין ערוך ערך דכסוסטוס

גליון

תוספתא דידים פרק ב

[שם]

ס"א אלא

מנחות לב.

מנחות לב:

[עי' תוס' מנחות לה: ד"ה רבנ"א]

[סוטה יז:]

הגהות הב"ח

(א) גמ' תנן קלף כדי לכתוב עליו פרשה וכו' שמע ישראל (קלף אין דוכסוסטוס לא) תא"מ ונ"ב זו הוא גירסת רש"י ובס"א ליתא וכדמוכח בתוספות: (ב) תוס' ד"ה קלף כו' לכתוב עליהן ס"ת דבעינן ספר כצ"ל ותיבת ותפילין ומזוזה נמחק: (ג) בא"ד בהקומץ רבה דקאמר קרע הבא בב' שיעין יתפור:

[*79b*] PARCHMENT, AS MUCH AS IS REQUIRED FOR WRITING THE SHORTEST PASSAGE, [etc.]. But the following contradicts
a this: Parchment [*kelaf*] and *duksustos*,[1] as much as is required for the writing of a *mezuzah?*[2]—What is meant by *mezuzah?* A parchment slip of the *tefillin*.[3] Are then *tefillin* designated *mezuzah?*—Yes, and it was taught [likewise]: *tefillin* straps, when together with the *tefillin*, defile the hands;[4] when apart, they do not defile the hands. R. Simeon b. Judah said on the authority of R. Simeon,[5] He who touches the strap is clean, unless he touches the capsule [of the *tefillin*]. R. Zakkai said in his name: He is clean, unless he touches the *mezuzah* itself.[6] But since the second clause teaches, PARCHMENT, AS MUCH AS IS REQUIRED FOR WRITING THE SHORTEST PASSAGE OF THE TEFILLIN, WHICH IS 'HEAR O ISRAEL,' it follows that the first clause refers to the *mezuzah* itself?—This is its meaning: Parchment and *duksustos*, what are their standards? *Duksustos*, as much as is required for writing a *mezuzah*;[7] parchment, for writing the shortest passage of the *tefillin*, which is *'Hear O Israel'*.

Rab said: *Duksustos* is as parchment: just as *tefillin* may be written upon parchment, so may they be written upon *duksustos*. We learnt: PARCHMENT, FOR WRITING THEREON THE SHORTEST PASSAGE OF THE TEFILLIN, WHICH IS 'HEAR O ISRAEL' [Thus, only parchment, but not *duksustos?*][8]—That is for the [most preferable observance of the] precept.[9]

b Come and hear: It is a *halachah* of Moses from Sinai[1] that *tefillin* [should be written] upon parchment, and a *mezuzah* upon *duksustos;* parchment is [the skin] on the side[2] of the flesh, and *duksustos* is [that] on the side of the hair?[3]—That is for the [most preferable observance of the] precept. But it was taught: If one does otherwise, it is unfit?—That refers to the *mezuzah*. But it was taught: If one does otherwise, in either it is unfit?—Both refer to *mezuzah*, one meaning that he wrote it on parchment [*kelaf*] facing the hair; the other, on *duksustos* facing the flesh.[4] An alternative answer is: [The ruling], If one does otherwise in either, it is unfit, is dependent on Tannaim. For it was taught: If one does otherwise, it is unfit. R. Aḥa declares it fit on the authority of R. Aḥi b. Ḥanina—others state, on the authority of R. Jacob b. R. Ḥanina. R. Papa said: Rab's ruling is as the teaching of the School of Manasseh. For the School of Manasseh taught: If one writes it on paper[5] or on a cloth strip, it is unfit; on parchment, *gewil*,[6] or *duksustos*, it is fit. 'If one writes it'—what? Shall we say, a *mezuzah;* can then a *mezuzah* be written upon *kelaf?* Hence it surely means *tefillin*. Yet [even] on your reasoning, can *tefillin* be written upon *gewil?*[7] But that was taught of a Torah Scroll.[8]

Shall we say that the following supports him: When *tefillin* or a Torah Scroll wear out, a *mezuzah* may not be made of them,[9] because we may not debase [anything] from a higher[10] sanctity to a lower sanctity. Thus there is the reason that we may not debase, but if we might debase, we could make [a *mezuzah*]: now, whereon is it written? Surely it means that it is written on *duksustos?*[11]—No: it is written upon parchment [*kelaf*].—But may a *mezuzah* be written upon *kelaf?*—Yes. And it was taught [likewise]: If one writes it on *kelaf*, on paper, or on a cloth strip, it is unfit. R. Simeon b. Eleazar said: R. Meir used to
c write it[1] upon *kelaf*, because it keeps [better]. Now that you have arrived at this [conclusion],[2] according to Rab too, do not say, *Duksustos* is as *kelaf*, but say, *kelaf* is as *duksustos:* just as a *mezuzah* may be written upon *duksustos*, so may it be written upon *kelaf*.

a (1) An inferior kind of parchment, v. *infra*. (2) V. Glos. This contains *two* passages, viz., Deut. VI, 4-9, and XI, 13-21. (3) In the head *tefillin* each of the four passages is written on a separate slip. Since the particular slip is unspecified, it is assumed that it is the one required for the shortest passage. (4) In respect of *terumah;* v. *supra* 14*a*. (5) I.e., R. Simeon b. Yoḥai. (6) Thus *mezuzah* is used of the parchment slip containing the writing. (7) Literally; that is because it is not fit for *tefillin*. (8) This passage is bracketed in the edd. It was present in Rashi's text, but absent from other versions.—But if *tefillin* might be written upon *duksustos*, the same standard would apply to that too. (9) *Kelaf* being superior, phylacteries are normally written thereon, and not upon *duksustos*, though it is permissible. Hence one would not keep *duksustos* for that purpose and consequently it does not involve a penalty; cf. *supra* 75*b* Mishnah.

b (1) V. p. *supra* 28*b*, n. c7. (2) Lit., 'place'. (3) When the hide is split in two, the portion facing the flesh is called *kelaf* (parchment), whilst that toward the hair is called *duksustos*. Tosaf. s.v. קלף reverses the reading. (4) I.e., the parchment and the *duksustos* were manufactured from the wrong portions of the hide. (5) נייר, papyrus. (6) A certain kind of parchment. Rashi: that which has been dressed with gall-nut. Tosaf.: the undivided skin (v. n. b3) with the hair removed. V. also *T.A.* II, p. 263 and notes a.l. (7) Surely not! (8) Thus it has no bearing on Rab's dictum. (9) E.g., if the margin is in good condition and fit for use. (10) Lit., 'from a graver .... lighter'. (11) Which supports Rab.

c (1) R. Meir was an expert calligraphist—a much esteemed talent before the invention of printing. (2) That a *mezuzah* may be written upon *kelaf*.

INK, FOR WRITING [TWO LETTERS]. [80a] It was taught: Two letters in ink, two letters on a pen, or two letters in an inkstand [involve culpability].[3] Raba asked: What [if one carries out sufficient for] one letter [in the form of] dry ink, one letter on the pen, and one letter in an inkstand?[4] The question stands over.

Raba said: If one carries out [ink sufficient for writing] two letters, and writes them whilst walking, he is culpable: the writing is tantamount to depositing.[5] Raba also said: If one carries out [ink sufficient for writing] one letter [only] and writes it down, and then again carries out [sufficient for] one letter, and writes it down,[6] he is not culpable. What is the reason? By the time he carries out the second, the standard of the first is defective.[7]

Raba also said: If one carries out half a dried fig and deposits it,[8] and then carries out another half of a dried fig and deposits it,[9] the first is regarded as though caught by a dog or burnt, and he is not culpable. But why so: surely it is lying there!—He means this: But if one anticipates and takes up the first before the depositing of the second, the first is regarded as though caught
a up by a dog or burnt,[1] and he is not culpable. Raba also said: If one carries out half of a dried fig and deposits it and then carries out another half of a dried fig over the same route as the first,[2] he is liable. But why: surely it does not rest [in the street]?—E.g., if he carries it within three [handbreadths].[3] But Raba said: [An article brought] within three [handbreadths] must, according to the Rabbis, be deposited upon something of small size [at least]?[4]—There is no difficulty. The latter reference is to throwing;[5] the former is to carrying.[6]

Our Rabbis taught: If one carries out half a dried fig, and then carries out another half of a dried fig in one state of unawareness, he is culpable; in two states of unawareness, he is not culpable. R. Jose said: In one state of unawareness [and] into the same ground, he is culpable; into two [different] grounds,[7] he is not culpable. Rabbah said: Providing that there lies between them a domain involving liability to a sin-offering;[8] but a *karmelith*[9] does not [effect a separation].[10] Abaye said: Even a *karmelith* [separates them], but not a board.[11] But Raba maintained: Even a board [separates them]. Now Raba is consistent with his ruling [elsewhere]; for Raba said: [The law of] domains in respect to the Sabbath is the same as domains in respect to divorces.[12]

STIBIUM, FOR PAINTING ONE EYE: But one eye [alone] is not painted?—Said R. Huna: Because modest women paint [only]
b one eye.[1] An objection is raised: R. Simeon b. Eleazar said: As for stibium, if [carried out] for medicinal use, [the standard is] as much as is required for painting one eye;[2] if for adornment, [the standard is] two eyes?—Hillel son of R. Samuel b. Naḥmani explained it: That was taught in reference to small-towners.[3]

PASTE, FOR PUTTING ON THE TOP OF A LIME BOARD. A Tanna taught: As much as is required for putting on the top of a lime board of a hunter's rod.[4]

WAX, FOR PUTTING OVER A SMALL HOLE. It was taught: As much as is required for putting over a small wine hole.[5]

CLAY, FOR MAKING A HOLE IN A GOLD-REFINER'S POT, etc.[6] Shall we say that R. Judah's standard is larger? But we know the Rabbis' standard to be larger, for we learnt: R. JUDAH SAID: AS MUCH AS IS REQUIRED FOR TAKING THE MEASURE OF A CHILD'S SHOE?[7]—Say, as much as is required for plastering [the splits in] the tripod leg of a small stove.[8]

(3) Ink, Heb. *dyo*, is the solid pigment which was dissolved before use (cf. *supra* 17*b* and note a.l.). The Baraitha teaches that whether one carries out dry pigment in his hand or the liquid on a pen or in an inkstand, in each case sufficient for writing two letters, he is culpable. (4) Do they combine to involve liability or not? The pen and inkstand do not cause culpability, since they are subsidiary to their contents, which in themselves do not separately cause liability; v. *infra* 93*b*. (5) Culpability for carrying from one domain to another is incurred only when the article transported is actually deposited in the second domain; v. *supra* 2*a*. (6) Both in the same state of unawareness, so that normally they should rank as one act. (7) The first ink has dried and is now insufficient for the writing of one letter. (8) One fig is the minimum involving liability. (9) V. n. 6.
a (1) Since the whole fig does not lie in the street. (2) The second actually passing above the first. (3) Of the ground. It is then regarded as actually lying thereon; cf. *supra* 5*a*. (4) Though not necessarily upon a place four handbreadths square; v. *infra* 100*a* for the general explanation of the passage. (5) Then it must actually come to rest. (6) In the hand. The article itself is then at rest, and if the hand moreover comes within three handbreadths of the ground, it is as though deposited thereon. (7) Both public, but separated from each other. (8) I.e., private ground. Transport between private and public ground imposes liability; hence the private ground here completely separates the two public grounds, and they do not rank as one. (9) V. Glos. and *supra* 6*a*. (10) Since by Biblical law one may carry between a *karmelith* and public (or private) ground, it is insufficient to separate the two. (11) Placed right across the street and thus dividing it. (12) And there a board is sufficient to create separate domains; v. Giṭ. 77*b*.
b (1) They go veiled, leaving only one eye visible. (2) Since only one eye may need it. (3) Or, villagers. Temptation not being so great there, it is safe even for modest women to paint both eyes. (4) The paste being to entrap the birds that alight thereon. (5) I.e., a hole through which wine is poured; this is smaller than one made for oil or honey. (6) The translation of these three passages, from PASTE, etc., follows the text as emended by BaḤ. (7) Which is less than the standard of the Rabbis which precedes it; v. Mishnah *supra* 78*a*. (8) This is a smaller standard.

עין משפט נר מצוה

תנא ב' אותיות בדיו (*ושתי) אותיות בקולמוס שתי אותיות בקלמרין בעי רבא אות אחת בדיו אות אחת בקולמוס אות אחת בקלמרין מהו תיקו אמר רבא הוציא שתי אותיות וכתבן כשהוא מהלך חייב כתיבתן זו היא הנחתן ואמר רבא הוציא אות אחת וכתבה וחזר והוציא אות אחת וכתבה פטור מאי טעמא בעידנא דאפקא לבתרייתא חסר ליה לשיעורא דקמייתא ואמר רבא הוציא חצי גרוגרת אחת והניחה וחזר והוציא חצי גרוגרת אחת והניחה ראשונה נעשה כמי שקלטה [כלב] או שנשרפה ופטור ואמאי הא מנחה הכי קאמר ואם קדם והגביה ראשונה קודם הנחת שנייה נעשית ראשונה כמי שנקלטה(א) או שנשרפה ופטור ואמר רבא הוציא חצי גרוגרת והניחה וחזר והוציא חצי גרוגרת והעבירה דרך עליה חייב ואמאי הא לא נח כגון שהעבירה תוך שלשה *והאמר רבא תוך שלשה לרבנן צריך הנחה על גבי משהו לא קשיא כאן בזורק כאן במעביר *תנו רבנן הוציא חצי גרוגרת וחזר והוציא חצי גרוגרת בהעלם אחד חייב בשתי העלמות פטור רבי יוסי אומר בהעלם אחד לרשות אחד חייב לשתי רשויות (ג) פטור *אמר רבה והוא שיש חיוב חטאת ביניהם אבל כרמלית לא אביי אמר אפילו כרמלית אבל פיסלא לא ורבא אמר אפילו פיסלא ואזדא רבא לטעמיה דאמר רבא רשות שבת כרשות גיטין דמיא: כחול כדי לכחול עין אחת: עין אחת הא לא כחלי אמר רב הונא שכן צנועות כוחלות עין אחת מיתיבי רבי שמעון בן אלעזר אומר כחול אם לרפואה כדי לכחול עין אחת אם לקשט בב' עינים תרגמא הילל בריה דר' שמואל בר נחמני כי תניא ההוא (ג) בעירניות: (שעוה כדי ליתן ע"פ נקב קטן: תנא כדי ליתן ע"פ נקב קטן של יין): דבק כדי ליתן בראש השפשף: תנא כדי ליתן בראש שפשף שבראש קנה של ציידין: זפת וגפרית כדי לעשות כו': תנא כדי לעשות נקב קטן: חרסית כדי לעשות פי כור כו': למימרא דשיעורא דרבי יהודה נפיש *הא קיי"ל דשיעורא דרבנן נפיש דתנן *רבי יהודה אומר כדי ליטול הימנו מדת מנעל לקטן אימא כדי לסוד פיטפוט כירה קטנה: (סובין כדי ליתן על פי כור של צורפי זהב):

רש"י

ב' אותיות בדיו · דיו יבש: שתי אותיות בקולמוס · כלומר כל היכא דמפיק ליה שיעורו כשתי אותיות: קלמרין · קסת הסופר: אות אחת בדיו אות אחת בקולמוס · מי מצטרפי או לא ואי אמרת תיפוק ליה משום קולמוס לא מחייב עליה משום שהוא טפל לפחות מכשיעור דתנן לקמן (דף צג:) המוציא אוכלין פחות מכשיעור בכלי פטור אף על הכלי מפני שהכלי טפילה לו: כשהוא מהלך · שלא עמד לפוש דתהוי הנחת גופו הנחה (ד) אפילו הכי חייב דעיקר הנחת דיו על הכתב הוא: וחזר והוציא · בהעלם אחד: חסר (ה) שיעור דקמייתא · כשמתייבשה נחסר השיעור ולכי גמרה הוצאה דבעינן לצרופה אין כאן שיעור ב' אותיות: ואמאי הא מנחה · וכיון דבהעלם אחד (ו) מצטרפי לכי גמרה הוצאה: כמי שקלטה כלב · דתנן לקמן (דף קב·) הזורק וקלטה כלב פטור דלא הויא הנחה מכחו והכא נמי כי גמרה הוצאה בטלה להנחה קמייתא והויא כמאן דליתא: לרבנן · דפליגי לקמן בהזורק* ולית להו קלוטה כמה שהונחה אפילו עברה סמוך לקרקע לא מיחייב עד שתנוח על גבי משהו מקום כל שהוא ולא בעינן מקום ד' הואיל ובתוך ג' הוא מ"מ הנחה כל דהו בעינן: מעביר · לא צריך הנחה דהא מנחה בידו דידו סמוכה לקרקע: לשתי רשויות · שתיקן ר"ה אלא שיש הפסק ביניהם: והוא שיש חיוב חטאת ביניהם · שמופסקות ברה"י אבל אם היה כרמלית מפסיק °כגון קרפף יותר מבית סאתים או בקעה וב' בתים פתוחים אחד לרה"ר זה ואחד לזה והוציא חצי גרוגרת מבית זה לרשות זה וחצי גרוגרת מבית זה לרשות זה שהיא פתוחה לה חייב דכיון דלא מפסיק לה רה"י חדא רשותא הוא: פיסלא · עץ שוכב לרחבו של רה"ר וממלא כל רחבו והוציא חצי גרוגרת מביתו מכאן וחצי גרוגרת מכאן: כרשות גיטין דמי · ולענין גיטין פיסלא רשות לנפשיה הוא כדאמרן בהזורק (גיטין דף עז:) ההוא גברא דזרק גיטא לדביתהו בחצירו איגנדר גיטא ונפל בפיסלא ואוקי התם שהשאיל לה מקום בחצירו חד מקום מושלי איכשי תרי מקומות לא מושלי איכשי:

בית
רה"ר
רה"י
או כרמלית
או פיסלא
רה"ר
בית

הא לא כחלי · אלא שתי עינים: צנועות · שהולכות מעוטפות ואין מגלות אלא עין אחד לראות וכוחלות אותו: בעירניות · בנות כפרים* אינן צריכות צניעות כל כך שאין שחוק וקלות ראש מצוי שם וצניעה מועטין ואינן מכסין פניהם וכוחלות ב' עיניהם: שפשף שבראש קנה של ציידין · מושיבין קנה קטן בראש קנה ונותנין עליו דבק והעוף יושב עליה ונדבק בו וצריך ליתן שם הרבה כדי שיהא העוף נדבק בו: של יין · למעוטי שמן ודבש שהיין זב דרך נקב קטן יותר משמן ודבש: לסוד · לטוח בקטים שבו: שיער

תוספות

אות אחת בקולמוס ואות אחת בקלמרין · אע"פ ששני קולמוסים מצטרפי כה"ג שמא לא מצטרפי: והעבירה דרך עליה · מפרש הרב פורת דה"ה אפי' שלא דרך עליה אם העבירה תוך שלשה לקרקע מצטרף דהא אמרינן בסמוך בהעלם אחד חייב אפילו לשתי רשויות ואפילו רבי יוסי לא בעי אלא רשות אחת אבל עליה לא בעי ונקט דרך עליה דאפי' גבוה מן הקרקע ג' טפחים חייב כיון דהוי תוך ג' לחצי גרוגרת המונחת ע"ג קרקע*: והא אמר רבא תוך שלשה לרבנן צריך הנחה ע"ג משהו · תימה לר"י דתנן לקמן בריש הזורק (דף צז·) הזורק מרה"י לרה"י ורה"ר באמצע ר' עקיבא מחייב וחכמים פוטרין ותני עלה בגמרא [צז·] תוך ג' לד"ה חייב אלמא לכ"ע לא בעינן הנחה ע"ג משהו תוך ג' ותירץ דרבא סבר כרבי יהודה דהמוצא תפילין (עירובין צז:) גבי היה קורא על ראש הגג כו' רבי יהודה אומר אפילו אינו מסולק מן הארץ אלא מלא החוט גוללו אצלו וטעמא דאפילו אין אגודו בידו ליכא איסור אם מביאו אצלו דבעי הנחה ע"ג משהו כדאמר התם בגמרא וא"ת ומאי פריך התם לימא רבא כתנאי אמרה לשמעתיה דע"כ כתנאי אמרה דתנא דברייתא דהזורק לא סבר כוותיה וי"ל דהכי פריך לימא כתנאי דמתניתין דהתם אמרה לשמעתיה דבהא לא קפיד אם תנא דברייתא פליג עליה אלא דלא ליפלגו עליה רבנן דמתניתין דהתם מיהו תימה לר"י דלקמן בהזורק (דף צז:) תנא מרה"י לרשות הרבים ועבר ד' אמות ברה"ר ר' יהודה מחייב וחכמים פוטרין ומוקי לעולם רבי יהודה חדא הוא דמחייב וחכמים פוטרין לגמרי ומשכחת לה דאמר עד דנפקא לרה"ר תנוח דרבי יהודה סבר אמרי' קלוטה כמי שהונחה דמיא אלמא לא בעינן לרבי יהודה הנחה ע"ג משהו ונראה לר"י דהתם מיירי במתגלגל ברה"ר ועדיף מבאר קלוטה באויר והוי כמונח לרבי יהודה והא דקשה ממתני' דהתם* דקתני זרק לתוך ארבע אמות ונתגלגל חוץ לארבע כו' שם [בד"ה אחזהו] נפרש בעז"ה: בהעלם אחד לרשות אחד חייב · הקשה רבינו תם דאמר בהבונה (לקמן קה:) כתב אות אחת בטבריא ואות אחת בציפורי חייב ונראה לו כגירסת ר"ח מרשות אחת חייב מב' רשויות פטור דבעי' עקירה ממקום אחד ור"י אומר דודאי גבי כתיבה אית לן למימר מחוסר קריבה לאו כמחוסר מעשה דמי אבל הוצאה לא הויא עד דמייתי תרוייהו לרשות אחד: אבל פיסלא לא · בגיטין בפרק הזורק (דף עז:) משמע דאית ביה ד' אמות על ד' אמות ואינו גבוה י' א"נ גבוה י' ואינו רחב ד' ואומר ריב"א דללישנא קמא צריך לפרש הכא שהוא רשות הרבים כגון שרבים מכתפין עליו דאי כרמלית האמר אביי אפילו כרמלית ורבא דאמר אפילו פיסלא סבר אף על פי שהוא רשות הרבים כיון דלענין גיטין חשוב מקום בפני עצמו הכי נמי מחלק רשויות ולר"י נראה אפילו פיסלא שהוא כרמלית ושני ליה לאביי בין כרמלית המיטלטלת לשאינה מיטלטלת: מיתיבי רשב"א אומר · לרב הונא פריך דאי לאו רב הונא הוה מוקמי מתני' לרפואה: אם לרפואה · פי' רבינו שמואל אם לרפואה הצניעו זה חייבין עליו כל העולם כדי לכחול עין אחת דלרשב"א אית ליה* דנתחייב זה במחשבתו של זה ואם לקשט כלומר אם לא הצניעו לרפואה אלא לקשט כדי שתי עינים דסתמו עומד לקישוט ואין נראה לר"י דלעיל תנא דם כדי לכחול עין אחת בד"א במוציא אבל במצניע בכל שהוא אלמא במצניע חייב בפחות מלכחול בו עין אחת ונראה לר"י דה"פ אם לרפואה שאותו כחול ראוי לרפואה שיעורו כדי לכחול עין אחת אפי' לא הצניעו לכך אי נמי אם לרפואה שבאותו מקום עושין אותו לרפואה ואם לקשט שעושין אותו לקישוט ואין רגילין לעשות ממנו רפואה כדי לכחול שתי עינים: חרסית כדי לעשות פי כור · אע"ג דאמר לעיל (דף עח.) אין אדם טורח לגבל טיט כדי לעשות בו פי כור של צורפי זהב אי נמי הכא מיירי במגובל:

המוציא

[וע"ע תוס' פסחים פה: ד"ה בגגרין]

רבינו חננאל

ב' אותיות דיו הוא שכותבין בו. ועוד הכלי שמניחין בו את הדיו גם הוא נקרא דיו. דתנא ב' אותיות שאמרו ב' אותיות בקלף ב' אותיות בקולמוס · ב' אותיות בקלמרין ואיכא למידק אי דאיכא בקולמוס בכדי ב' אותיו' מכוונות סגיא אבל אי איתיה לדיו בכלי בין בי דיותא ובין קלמרין צריך למיהוי יותר מב' אותיות. דיכול למיכתב מינייהו ב' אותיות משו' שא"א שיצאכולןבקולמו' שהדיו [נשאר] בדיו שהוא כלי או בקולמוס או בקלמרין ומ"מ צריך שיעור בדיו שכותבין בה. וליחייב על הדיו שהוא בית הדיו. או על הקולמוס. או על הקלמרין. ותשובה כיון שלהוציא דיו לכתוב בו הוא מתכוין עליו הוא חייב. ואינו חייב על הכלי שהוא בו מפני שהכלי טפילה לו. דתנן המוציא אוכלין פחות מכשיעור בכלי פטור אף על הכלי שהכלי טפילה לו. ותניא עליה המוציא אוכלין כשיעור בכלי פטור על הכלי וחייב על האוכלין קלמרין אשר כך היא ששנינו בסדר טהרות. קלמרין ופירושו [בלשון ישמעאל] מחברא. ותנן קלמרין של יוסף הכהן היתה נקובה מצידה: כתיבתן הנחתן. אע"ג דבעיא בהוצאה עקירה מרשות זה והנחה ברשות אחרת ע"ג מקום ד' כי היכי דהתם אמרינן ידו של אדם חשובה לו כד' [על ד'] הכי נמי הכא כתיבתו הנחתו. והיכא דהוציא חצי גרוגרת שהוא חצי שיעור הוצאה והניחה וחזר והוציא חצי גרוגרת אחרת אם הניח את החצי השני קרוב לראשון או שהעבירו דרך עליו של ראשון בקרוב ג' טפחים חייב. וזו היא שמעתא דרבא משום דהאי חצי גרוגרת וההיא חצי גרוגרת מצטרפין להיותו. ואף על פי שלא הגידו דהתם דצריך לנוח בזורק. אבל הכא במעביר אין צריך הנחה. אבל אם קדים והגביה את החצי הראשון קודם הנחת החצי השני ודוקא ברחוק יותר מג' מן ההיא חצי ראשון כדי שלא יהא מעביר עליו. נעשה הראשון כמו שנקלט או שנשרף ופטור: ת"ר הוציא חצי גרוגרת והניח ברה"ר וחזר והוציא חצי גרוגרת בהעלם אחד חייב. ב' העלמות פטור. ר' יוסי אמר בהעלם א' מרשות אחד חייב. מב' רשויות פטור. ואיכא דטעו (בנידמא)[בגירסא] דהא בריתא וגרסי ברשות אחד חייב בב' רשויות פטור. ומסתמא לפום כן שמעתא. (ואי איכא דשביק וא' ב' לרשות אחת לב' רשויות*) טעות גדולה היא. דילמא הכי קסברי אם הכניס מרה"ר לרשות אחת חייב. לב' רשויות פטור. והכי קאמר אי אפיק מרה"י בהעלם חצי שיעור לרה"ר וחזר והוציא באותו העלם חצי שיעור אחר לרה"ר. אם מחדא רשותא אפקינן לתרווייהו מצטרפין וחייב. ואם מן ב' רשויות אפקינן פטור. אמר (רבא) [רבה] והוא שיש חיוב חטאת ביניהם. אבל כרמלית לא כי פרשינן בפרק יציאות השבת שמוציא מרה"י לרה"ר חייב. אבל המוציא מכרמלית לרה"ר פטור. וקאמר רבה אי הנך ב' רשויות היחיד שהוציא חצי שיעור מזו וחצי שיעור מזו מרחקין מן הדדי ויש ביניהם רה"ר. והמוציא והמכניס מזו לזו יש בו חיוב חטאת. הרי נחלקו ועליהם קאמר ר' יוסי מב' רשויות פטור. אבל יש ביניהם כרמלית דלית בה חיוב חטאת כחדא רשותא דמיין. ואם הוציא מזו חצי שיעור וחזר והוציאו מזו חצי שיעור חייב: אביי אמר אפילו יש ביניהן כרמלית דאע"ג דלית בה חיוב חטאת אסור להוציא מזו לזו שמרשות [לרשות] הן. ואם הוציא מזו חצי שיעור ומזו חצי שיעור פטור. אבל אם יש ביניהן פיסלא דלא חשיב למיהוה כרמלית אלא מקום פטור הוא הרי הוא כרשות אחת. ואם הוציא מזו חצי שיעור ומזו חצי שיעור חייב רבא אמר אפילו איכא פיסלא ביניהן. כיון שהוא חולק רשות לעצמו אע"ג דלא כרמלית הוא דכרשות הוא קאי כיון שאסור להוציא אליו כלום מרה"י כב' רשויות דמיין. ואם הוציא מזו חצי

*) לשון זה משולל הבנה וצריך תיקון

רב נסים גאון

ואזדא רבא למעמיה דאמר רבא רשות שבת כרשות גיטין דמיא · ותמצא עיקר דילה במס' גיטין בפרק הזורק (דף עז) אמר רב חסדא רשויות חלוקות בגיטין ומיקמי הכי (שם דף עז) אמרו ההוא גברא דזרק לה

עין משפט נר מצוה

כב א ב ג מיי' שם הלכה יא:

כג ד ה מיי' שם הלכה ז ופ"ע הלכה ה:

מסורת הש"ס

תורה אור

ת"ר *המוציא שיעור כדי לגבל בו את הטיט [*טיט] לעשות פי כור של צורפי זהב: סיד כדי לסוד: תנא כדי לסוד אצבע קטנה שבבנות אמר רב יהודה אמר רב *בנות ישראל שהגיעו לפירקן ולא הגיעו [לשנים] בנות עניים טופלות אותן בסיד בנות עשירים טופלות אותן בסולת בנות מלכים טופלות אותן בשמן המור שנאמר °ששה חדשים בשמן המור *מאי שמן המור רב הונא בר חייא אמר *סטכת רב ירמיה בר אבא אמר שמן זית שלא הביאה שליש תניא רבי יהודה אומר אנפיקנון שמן זית שלא הביאה שליש ולמה סכין אותו שמשיר את השיער ומעדן הבשר *רב ביבי הויא ליה ברתא טפלה אבר אבר שקל בה ד' מאות זוזי הוה ההוא נכרי בשבבותיה הויא ליה ברתא טפלה בחד זימנא ומתה אמר קטל *רב ביבי לברתי אמר רב נחמן רב ביבי דשתי שיכרא בעיין בנתיה טפלא אנן דלא שתינן שיכרא לא בעיין בנתן טפלא: ר' יהודה אומר כדי לסוד כלכול: מאי כלכול ומאי אנדיפי *אמר רב צידעא ובת צידעא למימרא דשיעורא דר' יהודה נפיש *הא קיי"ל דשיעורא דרבנן נפיש זוטא מדרבנן ונפיש מדרבי נחמיה מיתיבי *א"ר נראין דברי רבי יהודה בחבוט ודברי רבי נחמיה בביצת (*הסיד ואי ס"ד צידעא ובת צידעא אידי ואידי חבוט אלא אמר רבי יצחק אמרי דבי רבי אמי אאנדיפא מתקיף לה רב כהנא וכי אדם עושה מעותיו אנפרות אלא אמר רב כהנא שנתות כדתנן *שנתות היו בהין עד כאן לפר עד כאן לאיל עד כאן לכבש ואיבעית אימא מאי אנדיפא אפותא וכי הא דההוא בר גליל [דאיקלע לבבל] דאמרו ליה קום דרוש לנו במעשה מרכבה (א)אמר להו אדרוש לכו כדדרש רבי נחמיה לחבריה ונפקא ערעיתא מן כותל ומחתיה באנדיפי ומית ואמרו ליה מן דיליה דא ליה: **מתני'** אדמה כחותם המרצופין דברי רבי עקיבא וחכמים אומרים כחותם האיגרות *זבל וחול הדק כדי לזבל קלח של כרוב דברי רבי עקיבא וחכ"א כדי לזבל כרישא °חול הגס כדי ליתן על מלא כף סיד *קנה כדי לעשות קולמוס ואם היה עבה או מרוסס כדי לבשל בו ביצה קלה שבביצים טרופה ונתונה באילפס: **גמ'** על מלא כף סיד תנא כדי ליתן על פי כף של סיידין מאן תנא דחול מעלי ליה לסיד אמר רב חסדא רבי יהודה היא *דתניא לא יסוד אדם את ביתו בסיד אא"כ עירב בו תבן או חול ר"י אומר תבן מותר חול אסור מפני שהוא טרכסיד רבא אמר אפילו תימא רבנן קילקולו זהו תיקונו: קנה כדי לעשות קולמוס: תנא *קולמוס המגיע לקשרי אצבעותיו בעי רב אשי קשר העליון או קשר התחתון תיקו: ואם היה עבה כו': תנא טרופה בשמן ונתונה באילפס אמר ליה מר בריה דרבינא לבריה מי שמיע לך ביצה קלה מאי היא אמר ליה ביעתא *דצילצלא מאי טעמא משום דזוטרא אימא דציפרתא אישתיק אמר ליה מידי שמיע לך בהא *[אמר ליה הכי] אמר רב ששת ביצת תרנגולת (ב) ומאי קרו לה ביצה קלה שיערו חכמים אין לך ביצה קלה לבשל יותר מביצת תרנגולת ומאי שנא כל שיעורי שבת כגרוגרת והכא כביצה אמר ליה הכי אמר רב נחמן כגרוגרת מביצה קלה: מתני'

*) [גי' הערוך הגיר פירוש שהוא עב כאבני גיר וע"ש בערך גר י"ב]

רש"י

שיער · יפה לטיט: ה"ג טיט כדי לעשות פי כור של צורפי זהב · אצבע קטנה · דרכן לסוד את כל הגוף להאדים: שהגיעו לפרקן ולא הגיעו · שהביאו שתי שערות ולא באו לכלל שנים הראויות לכך ומתביישות בדבר: טופלות · מושחות: אנפיקנון · דתנן במנחות (דף פה:) אין מביאין אנפיקנון הוא שמן זית שלא הביא שליש: ולמה סכין אותו · היינו שמן המור: טפלה · בסיד: שקל בה ד' מאות זוזי · שנתייפה וקפצו עליה המהוגנין לה ונתנו *(לה) ממון: השכר משחיר ומרבה שיער: כלכול צידעא · טינפל"א וסדין אותה להשכיב השיער: בת צידעא · למטה הימנה להסיר שיער דק והוא אנדיפי: למימרא דשיעורא דר' יהודה נפיש · בתמיה והא קיימא לן גבי גמי דשיעורא דרבי יהודה זוטא ומחמיר בשיעורי שבת: ומשני נפיש מדר' נחמיה וזוטר מדרבנן · דאמרי לסוד אצבע קטנה: בחבוט · סיד הנימוח במים הרבה דהוא עשוי לסוד כלכול: ודברי רבי נחמיה בביצת הסיד · הנגבל במים ועשוי בילים בילים מוטל"ש בלע"ז הוא עשוי לסוד אנדיפי: ואי ס"ד אנדיפי נמי *שיעור הוא כגון בת צידעא: אידי ואידי · כלכול ואנדיפי תרווייהו בסיד חבוט וכמוח סדין אותו: אנדיפא · כלי חרס ולו שני דדין אחת למעלה ואחת למטה וכשרוצה למלאותו סותם את הדד התחתון ולשון אנדיפי שתי פיות כדתניא (עירובין דף קד·) מעלין בדיופי ובתוספתא גרס באנדיפי: אנפרות · הפסד לשום יין בכלי סתום בסיד והיין ממחה הסיד ויוצא: שנתות · סימנים כלי חרס גדול ויש בו בליטות בליטות כמין אגוזים קטנים עד כאן לסאה עד כאן לסאתים וסדין אותו בסיד כדי שיהיו לבנות ונכרות: כדתנן · במנחות שנתות היו בהין: עד כאן לפר · חצי ההין: עד כאן לאיל · שלישית ההין: עד כאן לכבש · רביעית ההין דכתיב חצי ההין יהיה לפר וגו' כן לשון מורי הזקן מפי אביו ששמע מר' שמעון ורבותי מפרשים אנדיפא כל הגוף ומתוך שאינו עשוי להשכיב השיער אלא להאדים בעי סיד עב: אנפרות · שאינו סד בו בתו לאחר שקנאו *דחיים שמא תמות כי ברתיה דההוא נכרי: שנתות · כלומר אבר אבר יטפלנה ואי אפשר בלשון זה ולא נאמר שיטת הש"ס כן להזכיר אבר אבר בלשון שנתות ויצטרך להביא פירוש לפירושו שנתות היו בהין: אפותא · פדחת שלא במקום שיער ולהאדים: ערעיתא · לירעה: באנדיפי · פדחתו: מן דיליה דא ליה · מידו היתה זאת לו שלא היה לו לדרוש במרכבה: מתני' אדמה · ארזיל"א: מרצופין · שקין העשוין מקליפת עץ גדול שנושאין בהן פרקמטיא בספינות וחותמין אותם: כחותם האיגרות · שחותמין אותם שלא *יקרב איש בהן אלא מי שנשתלחו לו ושיעורא דרבנן זוטר: כרישא · קפלוט ושיעוריה זוטר משל כרוב: על מלא כף סיד · בגמרא מפרש כף של סיידין טרואי"ל בלע"ז: מרוסס · סדוק סדקין הרבה כמו והכה הבית הגדול רסיסים (עמוס ו): ביצה קלה · בגמרא מפרש לה: **גמ'** לא יסוד אדם את ביתו בסיד · לאחר חורבן משום אבילות של ירושלים: תבן או חול · שלא יהא לבן כל צרכו: טרכסיד · סיד חזק ומתקשה יותר משאם לא עירב בו: קילקולו זהו תיקונו · דאי לאו דמקלקל ליה ומשחירו לא היה מישתרי הלכך ע"כ הא דקשיא ליה מעליותא היא לגביה ורבותי מפרשין קילקולו לובן זה תיקונו לענין חוזק ולא נהירא לי דקילקולו זהו תיקונו משמע דשם הקלקול מתקנו ולהאי לישנא אין שם הקלקול מתקנו ולמה הוזכר הקילקול כאן הכי הוי [ליה] למימר נמי דאשחורי משחור אחזוקי מחזיק: קשר עליון · קשר התחתון של אמצע היד או קשר של אמצע האצבע: טרופה בשמן · שממהרת לבשלה: דצילצלא · עוף קטן: כל שיעורי שבת · באוכלין וכל הוצאתן וקלירתן וטוחנין כגרוגרת: כגרוגרת · מביצת תרנגולת שהיא ממהרת לבשל ולא כביצה שלימה שיעורו: מתני'

תוספות

המוציא שיער כדי לגבל בו את הטיט טיט כדי לעשות פי כור כן גרס בתוספתא וכן גרס רש"י ולהך גירסא שיער כדי לגבל בו את הטיט כשיעור טיט הנעשה מרביעית שופכין אבל לספרים דגרסי שיער כדי לגבל בו טיט לעשות פי כור של צורפי זהב קשה דאמר לעיל אין אדם טורח לגבל טיט כדי לעשות פי כור ויש לפרש דמיירי בטיט שהוא מגובל כבר ואחר הגיבול טחנין בו שיער כדי לתקנו:

שהגיעו לפירקן ולא הגיעו · פירוש בסמוך לפירקן שקרובות להנשא ועושות כדי ליפות וללבן עצמן כדאמרינן בפרק אע"פ (כתובות דף נט:) הרוצה ללבן את בתו ישקנה חלב ויאכילנה אפרוחין סמוך לפירקה: עיין לקמן פא·

למימרא דשיעורא דר' יהודה נפיש · ואע"ג דאשכחן תרווד שהוא גדול הרבה כדאמר בנזיר בפרק כ"ג (דף נ:) גבי מלא תרווד רקב כמה שיעורו חזקיה אמר מלא פיסת יד ור' יוחנן אמר מלא חפניו התם ודאי מיירי בתרווד גדול כדתנן במסכת כלים בפ' י"ז (משנה יב) שאמר מידה גסה מלא תרווד רקב כמלא תרווד גדול של רופאים אבל הכא להוצאת שבת מידי דחשיב בעינן ותרווד קטן חשוב הוא הרבה (א"נ) *חף סלקא דעתך שהוא חף גל שהוא גדול ומשני בחפי פותחת שהן קטנים: חפי

רבינו חננאל

שיעור ומזו הצי שיעור פטור. רבא לטעמיה דאמר רבא רשות שבת כרשות הגיטין. ועיקר הא שמעתא בגיטין בהזורק התוא נברא דזרק לגיטא לדביתהו הוה קיימא בחצר ואזל גיטא ונח בפיסלא. אמר רב יוסף אי הואי ארבע אמות על ארבע אמות פלוג ליה רשותא לנפשי' ואי לא חדא רשותא היא. וקסבר רבא חדא רשותא בשבת מיפלגא בפיסלא כי היכי דמפלגא לענין גיטין. ופי' פיסלא מקום כגון עמוד גבוה עשרה ורחב ד': **כחול** כדי לכחול עין אחת וא"ר הונא שכן צנועות כוחלות עין אחת. הכין פירושא שכוחלת עין אחת ומכסה את העין האחרת ויוצאה לשוק ותראה באחת מעיניה. ורב הונא הוא דמתנינן לאו רב הונא וההיא דר' שמעון בן אלעזר אם לתכשיט ב' עינים. אוקימנא בעניות שאינן רגילות לצאת. (רגילות לצאת) לשוק (ואם שם שוק לצאת אליו): **חרסית** כדי לעשות פי כור של צורפי זהב ר' יהודה אומר כדי לעשות פיטפוט פירוש פיטפוט גבשוש. או בנין בארץ ששופתין עליו את הקדירה. וג' פיטפוטין הן. ויש שסומכין פטפוט לכותל ומניחין עליו את הקדיר' וסומכין אותו לכותל. ומקשי' כי מכדי בשיעור' דשבת קא חזינן דר' יהודה קא מחייב וממעט מן שיעורי דרבנן דהא לענין נמי לרבנן לא מחייב אלא בכדי לעשות תלאי לנפה ולכברה. ור' יהודה מחייב אפילו על מה שנוטלין ממנו. מדת סנעל לקטן. ומוקמינן לה להא פטפוט לכירה קטנה קאמר והוא בציר מן פי הכור של צורפי זהב: **אמר** רב יהודה אמר רב בנות שהגיעו לפרקן ולא הגיעו [לשנים]. שהגיעו לשנים שהאשה בוגרת ולא בגרה ולא גדלה בשר מה עושין להן. עניות טופלין אותן בסיד. טפילה זו בלשון ישמעאל טלא. ומה צורך לכך כדי שיפתחו נקבים קטנים ויכנס הבל לפנים ויחם קרבה ותתבגר ותגדל בשר. ואם בת עשירים היא טופלין אותה בסולת. והמלכים יש להם סממנים אחרי' כגון שמן המור. וכיוצא בו. מפית. קורין אותו סמכת. ויש שקורין אותו סטכת. והוא בלשון ארמית. ובל' ישמעאל לבן אל נאמן. וריחו טוב. וי"א מן הרמונים הוא אלא כך נקרא ובסמוך שרף הוא והוא הנקרא עור בל' ארמית.

[תוספתא פ"ט] [לעיל עח. עט:] פסחים מג. מו"ק ט: [פסחים שם ע"ש ובמו"ק ע"ש] מנחות פו. מגילה יג. ע"ש [מו"ק ט: ע"ש] [ג"א שיעור] [לעיל עח. לקמן פא.] [תוספתא פ"ט] מנחות פז. ב"ב סו: [לעיל עט. לקמן צ:] שם פפ: ב"ב ס: [תוס' סוטה מט:] והוצאה את מעותיו לבטלה [תוספתא פ"ט] [גי' הערוך דציצלתא ופי' ב"ב עג. וסנהדרין ק: דגרס כביעתא דצילצלא] [צ"ל יקרב]

הגהות הב"ח

(א) גמ' כמעשה מרכבה דרש להו ואמר להו: (ב) שם ביצת תרנגולת ואמאי:

גליון הש"ס

מתני' חול הגס כדי ליתן. עי' לקמן דף צ ע"א תוס' ד"ה כורי:

רב נסים גאון

ניפא לדביתהו הוה קיימא בחצר ואזל גיטא ונח בפיסלא אמר רב יוסף...

[80b] Our Rabbis taught: If one carries out hair, [the standard is] as much as is required for the kneading of clay;[9] [if one carries out] clay, [the standard is] for making a hole in a gold-refiner's pot.

LIME, TO SMEAR [THE SMALLEST OF GIRLS]. A Tanna taught: As much as is required to smear the little finger of girls.[10] Rab Judah said in Rab's name: When maidens of Israel attain puberty before the proper age:[11] poor maidens plaster it [the unwanted hair] with lime; rich maidens plaster it with fine flour; whilst royal princesses plaster it with oil of myrrh, as it is said, *six months*
a *with oil of myrrh.*[1] What is oil of myrrh?—R. Huna b. Ḥiyya said: *Satkath.*[2] R. Jeremiah b. Abba said: Oil of olives less than a third grown.

It was taught: R. Judah said: *Anpakkinon* is oil of olives less than a third grown, and why does one anoint herself therewith? Because it removes the hair and smoothes the skin.

R. Bibi had a daughter. He treated her limb by limb [with a depilatory] and took four hundred *zuz* for her.[3] Now, a certain heathen lived in the vicinity. He [too] had a daughter, and he plastered her [whole body] all at once, whereupon she died. 'R. Bibi has killed my daughter!' he exclaimed. R. Naḥman observed: As for R. Bibi who drank strong liquor, his daughter required pasting over; [but] as for us, who do not drink strong liquor, our daughters do not require such treatment.[4]

R. JUDAH SAID: ENOUGH TO PLASTER[5] A ḲILḲUL.[6] What is ḲILḲUL and what is ANDIFE? Rab said: The [upper] temple and the lower temple. Shall we say that R. Judah's standard is larger? But we know the standard of the Rabbis to be larger![7]—It is smaller than the Rabbis', but larger than R. Nehemiah's.

An objection is raised: Rabbi said: I approve R. Judah's view in respect of loosely dissolved lime, and R. Nehemiah's view in respect of chalky lime.[8] But if you maintain that they mean the [upper] temple and the lower temple,—[surely] both require loose lime?[9] Rather, said R. Isaac, The School of R. Ammi recited *andifa* [in the Mishnah].[10] R. Kahana demurred: Does one destroy [break
b up] his wealth?[1] Rather, said R. Kahana: It means the teeth-like marks [of a vessel];[2] even as we learnt: The *hin*-measure had teeth-like marks, [to indicate] so far [must it be filled with wine] for a bullock, so far for a ram, so far for a sheep.[3] Alternatively, what is *andifa?* The lock on the forehead.[4] Even as a certain Galilean chanced to visit Babylon and was requested to lecture on the chariot passage;[5] Said he to them, 'I will lecture to you as R. Nehemiah lectured to his companions.' Thereupon a wasp came out of the wall and stung him on the *andifa* [forehead] and he died. Said they, 'This [befell] him through his own [fault].'[6]

MISHNAH. [IF ONE CARRIES OUT] EARTH [A KIND OF CLAY], [THE STANDARD IS] AS MUCH AS IS REQUIRED FOR A SEAL ON PACKING BAGS;[7] THIS IS R. AKIBA'S VIEW. BUT THE SAGES SAY; AS MUCH AS IS REQUIRED FOR THE SEAL ON LETTERS.[8] [FOR] MANURE, OR THIN SAND, [THE STANDARD IS] AS MUCH AS IS REQUIRED FOR FERTILIZING A CABBAGE STALK; THIS IS R. AKIBA'S VIEW. BUT THE SAGES MAINTAIN: FOR FERTILIZING ONE LEEK PLANT. THICK SAND, AS MUCH AS IS REQUIRED FOR PUTTING ON A FULL PLASTER TROWEL. A REED, AS MUCH AS IS REQUIRED FOR MAKING A PEN. BUT IF IT IS THICK OR CRUSHED,[9] [THE STANDARD IS] AS MUCH AS IS REQUIRED FOR BOILING THE LIGHTEST OF EGGS BEATEN UP AND PLACED IN A STEW POT.

GEMARA. ON A FULL PLASTER TROWEL. A Tanna taught: As much as is required for putting on the top of a plasterer's trowel. Which Tanna holds that sand improves plaster?—Said R. Ḥisda: R. Judah. For it was taught: One must not plaster his house with
c lime unless he mixed it with straw or sand.[1] R. Judah said: Straw is permitted, but sand is forbidden, because it becomes cement.[2] Raba said, You may say that it agrees even with the Rabbis: The spoiling thereof makes it fit.[3]

A REED, AS MUCH AS IS REQUIRED FOR MAKING A PEN. It was taught: A pen which reaches one's finger joints. R. Ashi asked: The upper joint or the lower? The question stands over.

BUT IF IT IS THICK, etc. A Tanna taught: Beaten up with oil and placed in a stew pot. Mar, son of Rabina, said to his son: Have you heard what a light egg is?—He replied: An egg of a turtle dove. What is the reason? Because it is small! Then say [the egg of a *zipparta?*[4] He was silent. Have you then heard anything on this? he[5] asked him. Said he to him, Thus did R. Shesheth say: It is a fowl's egg, and why is it called a light egg? The Sages estimated, You have no egg quicker [lighter] to boil than a fowl's egg. And wherefore [he[5] asked] are all the [food-]standards of the Sabbath the size of a dried fig, whereas here it is an egg?—Said he to him, Thus did R. Naḥman say: [It means] as much as [is required to boil the size of] a dried fig of a light egg.

(9) *Sc.* as much clay as is made with a quarter *log* of waste water (Tosaf.). Hair too was used in the kneading. (10) To redden it (Rashi). קטנה שבבנות may be rendered either the smallest of girls, or the little (finger) of girls. (11) Lit., 'and do not attain their years'—i.e., they have the hairy growth, which is the evidence of puberty, before time, and wish to remove it.

a (1) Esth. II, 12 q.v. (2) Jast.: oil of myrrh or cinnamon (a corruption of στοχτή) (3) As a dowry. This would appear to be a reversion to the very ancient practice of giving a dowry for a bride. Cf. Jacob giving his labour as a dowry for Rachel, and Shechem offering a dowry for Dinah (Gen. XXIX, 18; XXXIV, 12). (4) Their skin being white and smooth in any case—a strong argument in favour of teetotalism! (5) *Sic.* The reading in the Mishnah is, produce, make. (6) Mishnah: ḲALḲAL. (7) V. Mishnah 78a. (8) I.e., thick lime. (9) Then why this distinction? (10) Instead of *andife.* Rashi: *andifa* is an earthen vessel with two spouts, one above and one below. When one wishes to fill it with wine he closes the lower spout with lime, and it is to this that R. Nehemiah refers in the Mishnah. Jast. translates quite differently.

b (1) By keeping wine in such a vessel. The wine will gradually dissolve the lime and then run out. (2) A vessel for measuring. Notches were made to indicate the measure, e.g., *log*, *hin*, etc., and these were plastered over with lime. To this R. Nehemiah refers. (3) Sacrifices were accompanied by libations of wine, the measure of which depended upon the animal sacrificed, v. Num. XXVIII, 14. (4) Jast. Rashi: The forehead where hair does not grow. This was reddened with lime. (5) Ezek. ch. 1, which treats of the Heavenly Chariot. (6) Through wishing to lecture publicly on the Chariot. This was regarded as esoteric learning, and was to be confined to the initiated only; cf. Ḥag. 11b, 13a and 14b. (7) Large bags in which ships' cargoes were carried. (8) This is a smaller standard. (9) And unfit for a pen.

c (1) To darken it as a sign of mourning. This was after the destruction of the Temple, v. B.B. 60b. (2) And is an improvement. (3) Rashi: since it may not be used without darkening, this spoiling makes it fit for use, and hence is adopted as a standard. Others (with whom Rashi disagrees): the spoiling of the colour is nevertheless an improvement, for the sand strengthens it. (4) Jast.: a small bird, supposed to be the humming bird. (5) The son.

MISHNAH. [81*a*] [IF ONE CARRIES OUT] BONE, [THE STANDARD IS] AS MUCH AS IS REQUIRED FOR MAKING A SPOON;[6] R. JUDAH MAINTAINED: FOR MAKING THEREOF A ḤAF;[7] GLASS, LARGE ENOUGH FOR SCRAPING THE TOP OF THE WHORL [OF A SPINDLE]; A CHIP OR A STONE, LARGE ENOUGH TO THROW AT A BIRD; R. ELEAZAR B. JACOB SAID:
a LARGE ENOUGH TO THROW AT AN ANIMAL.[1]

GEMARA. Shall we say that R. Judah's standard is larger: but we know the standard of the Rabbis to be larger?[2]—Said 'Ulla: [It means] the wards of a lock.[3]

Our Rabbis taught: The wards of a lock are clean;[4] [but] when one fits them into the lock, they are [liable to become] unclean.[5] But if it [the lock] is of a revolving door,[6] even when it is fixed on the door and nailed on with nails, they [the wards] are clean, because whatever is joined to the soil is as the soil.[7]

GLASS, LARGE ENOUGH FOR SCRAPING [etc.]. A Tanna taught: Glass,[8] large enough to break across two threads simultaneously.

A CHIP, OR A STONE, LARGE ENOUGH TO THROW AT A BIRD: R. ELEAZAR [etc.]. R. Jacob said in R. Joḥanan's name: Providing that it can feel it. And what size is that? It was taught, R. Eleazar b. Jacob said: Ten *zuz* in weight.[9]

Zonin entered the Beth Hamidrash [and] said to them [the students]: My masters, what is the standard of the stones of a privy?[10] Said they to him: [One] the size of an olive, [a second] the size of a nut, and [a third] the size of an egg.[11] Shall one take [them] in a [gold] balance! he objected.[12] [Thereupon] they voted and decided: A handful.[13] It was taught; R. Jose said: [One] the size of an olive, [another] the size of a nut, and [a third] the size of an egg: R. Simeon b. Jose said on his father's authority: A handful.

Our Rabbis taught: One may carry three smoothly rounded
b stones[1] into a privy. And what is their size? R. Meir said: As [large as] a nut; R. Judah maintained: As [large as] an egg. Rafram b. Papa observed in R. Ḥisda's name: Even as they differ here, so do they differ in respect to an *ethrog*.[2] But there it is a Mishnah, whereas here it is [only] a Baraitha?[3] Rather [say:] Just as they differ in respect to an *ethrog*, so do they differ here.

Rab Judah said: But not brittle stone [*payas*].[4] What is *payas?* —Said R. Zera: Babylonian pebbles.[5]

Raba said: One may not use a chip on the Sabbath [as a suppository] in the same way as one uses it on weekdays. Mar Zuṭra demurred: Shall one then endanger [his health]?—[It may be done] in a back-handed manner.[6]

R. Jannai said: If there is a fixed place for the privy,[7] [one may carry in] a handful [of stones];[8] if not, [only] the size of the leg of a small spice mortar [is permitted].[9] R. Shesheth said: If there is evidence upon it,[10] it is permitted.[11] An objection is raised: Ten things lead to hemorrhoids in a man, and these are they: [i] eating the leaves of reeds; [ii] the leaves of vines; [iii] sprouts of grape-wine; [iv] the rough flesh[12] of an animal without salt; [v] the spine of a fish; [vi] a salted fish insufficiently cooked; [vii] drinking the lees of wine; [viii] wiping oneself with lime, [ix] with clay, [x] [and]
c with a chip which one's neighbour has [already] used thus.[1] And some say, Suspending oneself in a privy too.[2]—There is no difficulty; the one refers to a damp [stone];[3] the other to a dry one. Alternatively, here the reference is to the same side [of the stone];[4] there, to the other side. Another alternative: the one refers to his own;[5] the other, to his neighbour's. Abaye asked R. Joseph: What if rain fell on it and it [the stain] was washed away?—If the mark thereof is perceptible, he replied, it is permitted.

(6) Jast.: pointed on top and curved at the end. (7) This is first assumed in the Gemara to mean a lock, which gives a greater standard than that of the Rabbis, but is subsequently translated ward of a lock.

a (1) But one does not trouble to throw anything at a bird, which is frightened away with the voice. (2) V. *supra* 80*a*, n. b7. (3) V. note on Mishnah (4) I.e., they are not susceptible to uncleanness, being unfit for use by themselves (Rashi). Rashi also maintains that the reference is to wards made of bones; Tosaf., to wards made of metal. (5) For they are now parts of utensils. (6) It is not the lock of a box or chest, but of something fixed to soil, e.g., the door of a house. (7) Which cannot become unclean. (8) *Sekukith* is a rarer form of the more usual *zekukith*. (9) One *zuz* = 3.585 grammes (*J.E., 'Weights and Measures'*, Vol. XII, p. 489 Table 1). (10) Used for cleansing. (11) These three together constitute the standard, as they are all required. (12) For weighing them accurately. (13) Of stones, no matter what their number.

b (1) Jast. Rashi (as emended by Rashal): sharpened stones. (2) A citron, which is one of the fruits to be taken on the Feast of Tabernacles (v. Lev. XXIII, 40). R. Meir holds that its minimum size must be that of a nut, while R. Judah holds that it must be at least as large as an egg. (3) And the Mishnah being better known, he surely should have taken that as the point of comparison. (4) This being unsuited for this purpose, it may not be handled on the Sabbath. (5) Which are cloddy and brittle. (6) V. *supra* 40*b*, n. b2. (7) Their privies were in the fields. Some were permanent, others were not. (8) I.e., over a distance of less than four cubits. V., however, R. Ḥan. For those that are left over in the evening may be used in the morning. (9) This translation follows R. Ḥan and Tosaf. (10) I.e., a stain of excrements. (11) To handle it, even if larger than the standard size normally allowed on the Sabbath, since it has already been used for that purpose before. (12) Rashi. Jast.: the palate.

c (1) This contradicts R. Shesheth. (2) Instead of sitting. (3) From former use; that is unfit. (4) That is injurious. (5) I.e., a stone which he himself has used before; that is permitted.

מתני' עצם כדי לעשות תרווד רבי יהודה אומר כדי לעשות ממנו חף זכוכית כדי לגרור בו ראש *הכרכר צרור או אבן כדי לזרוק בעוף רבי אלעזר בר יעקב אומר כדי לזרוק בבהמה: **גמ'** למימרא דשיעורא דר' יהודה נפיש הא קיימא לן *דשיעורא דרבנן נפיש אמר עולא חפי פותחת: תנו רבנן חפי פותחת טהורין קבען בפותחת טמאין ושל גל אף על פי שחיברן בדלת וקבען במסמרים טהורין שכל המחובר לקרקע הרי הוא כקרקע: זכוכית כדי לגרור בו: תנא *סכוכית כדי לפצוע בה שני נימין באחת: צרור או אבן כדי לזרוק בעוף רבי אלעזר כו': אמר רבי יעקב אמר רבי יוחנן והוא שמרגשת בה וכמה שיעורו תניא רבי אלעזר בן יעקב אומר משקל עשרה זוז: זונין על לבי מדרשא אמר להו רבותי אבנים של בית הכסא שיעורן בכמה אמרו לו כזית כאגוז וכביצה אמר להו וכי טורטני יכנים נמנו וגמרו מלא היד תניא *רבי יוסי אומר כזית כאגוז וכביצה (* ר"ש ברבי יוסי אומר משום אביו מלא היד: ת"ר (בשבת) *ג' אבנים מקורזלות מותר להכנים לבית הכסא וכמה שיעורן ר"מ אומר כאגוז רבי יהודה אומר כביצה *אמר רפרם בר פפא אמר רב חסדא כמחלוקת כאן כך מחלוקת באתרוג התם מתני' הכא ברייתא אלא כמחלוקת באתרוג כך מחלוקת כאן אמר רב יהודה אבל לא את הפאיים מאי פאיים אמר רבי זירא כרשיני בבלייתא *אמר רבא אסור למשמש בצרור בשבת כדרך שממשמש בחול מתקיף לה מר זוטרא ליסתכן כלאחר יד אמר רבי ינאי אם יש מקום קבוע לבית הכסא מלא היד אם לאו כהכרע מדוכה קטנה של בשמים אמר רב ששת אם יש עליה עד מותר מיתיבי *עשרה דברים מביאין את האדם לידי תחתוניות ואלו הן האוכל עלי קנים ועלי גפנים ולולבי גפנים ומוריגי בהמה בלא מלח ושדרו של דג ודג מליח שלא בישל כל צורכו והשותה שמרי יין והמקנח בסיד ובחרסית (*בצרור שקינח בו חברו ויש אומרים אף התולה עצמו בבית הכסא* לא קשיא הא בלח הא ביבש ואיבעית אימא כאן מצד אחד וכאן מב' צדדין ואיבעית אימא הא דידיה הא דחבריה א"ל אביי לרב יוסף ירדו עליה גשמים ונשטשטשו מהו א"ל אם היה רישומן ניכר מותר בעא מיניה רבה בר רב שילא מרב

רש"י

מתני' תרווד · כף קולייר : חף · קס"ד דפותחת של *חף עלמה ושיעורה נפיש מתרווד : כרכר · עץ יש לאורגין וראשו חד : כדי לזרוק בבהמה · דלא טרח איניש למשקל צרור משום עוף להבריחו דבקלא בעלמא דרמי ליה אזיל ליה : **גמ'** והא קיי"ל דשיעורא דרבנן נפיש · גבי לעשות תלאי : חפי פותחת · שינים הקבועים בה ולא היא עלמה ועושים אותם מעלם : חפי פותחת טהורין · דכל זמן שלא חברן בה אינן ראויין לכלום: טמאין · דכלי עלם ככלי מתכות ופשוטיהן טמאין בהכל שוחטין (חולין דף כה:) ולאו משום דמחובר לפותחת וכל המחובר לטהור טהור פותחת יש לה בית קיבול ומקבל מפתח : ושל גל · ואם הפותחת הזאת אינה של כלים כגון של שידה ומגדל אלא של גל כמו *טרוקי גלי כגון דלתות שערי החצר אע"פ שחברן בפותחת הואיל וחבור זה בדלת היא ודלת בנין מחובר לקרקע טהורין : סכוכית · זכוכית ועל שם שסוכין(א)קרי סכוכית ועל שם שהיא זכה קרי זכוכית: והוא שמרגשת · הבהמה בצרור זה בהכאתו : שיעורן בכמה · להתחייב עליהן אי נמי לטלטלן בחצר ולהכניסן לבית הכסא ואידי ואידי חד שיעורא הוא דבמידי דחזי להו מיחייב על הוצאתו : כזית כאגוז כבילה · שלש מכניסין לקינוח ומקנח זו אחר זו אחת כזית ואחת כאגוז ואחת כבילה בתחלה מקנח פי הרעי (ב)בקטנה להסיר רעי הנדבק שם שהגדולה *פוחסת ומלכלך סביבותיו: טורטני · מאזנים יכנים לשם לשקול: מלא היד · בין שלשתן או אפילו הן ד' וה' ובין כולן מלא היד : מקורזלות · (*)ביקוטו' שיהיו ראויות לקינוח: מותר להכניס · בתוך ד' אמות או בחצר דלא ליתסר לטלטוליניהו : כאגוז · כל אחת ואחת: התם מתני' · פלוגתא דאתרוג מתני' היא במסכת סוכה והיא סדורה בפי התלמידים : והכא ברייתא · ויש הרבה תלמידים שלא שנאוה והוא תולה הידועה בשאינה ידועה : כך מחלוקת כאן · ולסימנא בעלמא אמרה דלא תשכח לגירסא דברייתא ואם תשכחנה הזכר ממשנתך דאתרוג : אבל לא הפאיים · כמו שקל פיסת רגב (סנהדרין דף סד·) שקורין גליסט"א דהואיל ומיפרכא לא חזי לקינוח ואסורה לטלטל : כרשיני בבלייתא · הכי מיקרו משום שבבל ארץ לחה היא והמחרישה מעלה רגבים : למשמש · הנצרך ליפנות ואינו יכול ליפנות אמרינן לקמן בפירקין דממשמש בצרור בנקב והוא נפתח וקא סלקא דעתך דקאמר ובשבת אסור למשמש כלל כדרך שממשמשים בחול : ליסתכן · דאמר מר (תמיד פ"א דף כז:) עמוד החוזר מביא אדם לידי הדרוקן : ומשני כלאחר יד · האי כדרך דקאמר רבא כדרך הממשמש בחול בלא שינוי משום השרת נימין אבל כלאחר יד כגון אוחז צרור בב' אלבעותיו שפיר דמי : אם יש מקום קבוע לבה"כ · שאם ישתיירו לו ערבית יקנח בהם שחרית מכניס שם מלא יד : כהכרע · כשיעור המכריע כאגוז נפיש מכזית וזוטר מכבילה : מדוכה קטנה · *מלאכתה לאיסור אסור לטלטל : ואם יש עליה עד · קנוח המעיד שעשויה לכך מותר לטלטלה לקינוח : תחתוניות · פיג"ש : לולבי גפנים · אותן פיצולין הגדלין בגפן וקורין ווידיל"ש : מוריגי בהמה · כל בשר שיש בבהמה העשוי כמורג שהוא פגום וחרוקה כמורג חרוץ חדש כלומר כל מקום שאין הבשר חלק כגון קליפת הלשון וכגון החיך שיש בו כמין קולין וכפגימות וכבית הכוסות : שקינח בו חבירו · אסיד ואחרסית נמי קאי : התולה · שאינו יושב אלמא קינח בו חברו לא חזי לקינוח ורב ששת אמר לעיל אם יש עליה עד מותר : לח · לא חזי יבש חזי : מצד אחד · באותו צד שקינח בו חבירו לא חזי לקינוח אבל בצד שני חזי : דידיה · שהיה קינוח שעליה שלו : ונשטשטשו · אותו עד : מהו · מי בטיל לייחוד דידהו או לא : אי רשומו ניכר מותר · דכיון דמאיס לא חזי לבשמים ולא מיבטל ליה מבית הכסא :

(*) מקורזלות כקור"ש בלע"ז שיהיו חדודות וראויות לקינוח כצ"ל רש"ל

תוספות

חפי פותחת טהורין · פי' בקונטרס שינים של עלם ועושין אותם בפותחת (ג) לפתוח וקודם שלא נקבעו אין ראוין לכלום קבען בפותחת טמאין דכלי עלם כמתכות ופשוטיהם טמאים כדאמר בהכל שוחטין (חולין דף כה:) ולאו משום דמחובר לפותחת והמחובר לטהור טהור פותחת יש לה בית קיבול דמקבלת מפתח ומה שפירש דפשוטי כלי עלם טמאים כדאמר בהכל שוחטין לא דק דהתם לא איירי אלא בגולמי כלי עלם *אבל פשוטי כלי עלם הא תנן ומייתי לה בפ"ק (דף טז:) כלי עץ כלי עור כלי עלם כלי זכוכית פשוטיהן טהורין ומה שפירש דחפין הן של עלם קשה לר"י דגבי כלי מתכות מיתניא בתוספתא דכלים ועוד דאי בשלא נקבעו אין ראויין לכלום אם כן פשיטא דטהורין ומה שפי' שפותחת יש לה בית קיבול לקבל המפתח הא לא חשיב בית קיבול שאין המפתח עשוי לטלטל ע"י אותו בית קיבול כמו הקיטע יוצא בקב שלו (לעיל דף סו·) דטהור כשאין בו בית קיבול כתיתין דפי' בקונט' דמה שמניח ראש שוקו בתוכו לא חשיב בית קיבול שאין השוק מיטלטל על ידו ועוד דפי' דפותחת גורמת טומאה לחף אדרבה תנן במס' כלים בפי"ג (משנה ו) פותחת של עץ וחפין של מתכת טמאה פותחת של מתכת וחפין שלה של עץ טהורה אלמא בתר חפין אזלינן ואע"ג דמשמע דאתיא כרבי נחמיה דלא אזיל בתר מעמיד אלא בתר תשמיש דהיינו חותם בברייתא דשמעתי' נמי נראה לר"י דאתיא כוותיה דקתני סיפא דהכא טבעת של מתכת וחותם של אלמג ר' נחמיה מטהר ונראה לר"י דבחפין של מתכת איירי ואע"פ שלא נקבעו ראוין הם קלת ליתנם בפותחת ואפילו הכי טהורין דגולמי כלי מתכות טהורין קבען בפותחת טמאין שנגמרה מלאכתן וכן משמע בסמוך דטעמא משום נגמר מלאכה דקתני ושל גל אע"פ שחברן לדלת כו' דמשמע מה שקבען לדלת יש לו לגרום טומאה אלא כיון שאין להם פותחת (ד)[וחף] קבוע בגל טהור :

אסור למשמש בצרור · פירש בקונטרס הנצרך לפנות ואינו יכול אסור משום השרת נימין וא"ת והא רבא בדבר שאין מתכוין סבר כר"ש בכפ"ב דבילה (דף כג·) וכה"ג פריך לקמן לרבי יוחנן דאסר משום השרת נימין ויש לומר דהכא במשמוש צרור הוי פסיק רישיה :

ואם לאו כהכרע · ונראה לר"ת כגירסת ר"ח ואם לאו כהכרע מדוכה קטנה של בשמים והכרע פי' רגל כמו כרעי המטה וכן מפרש בירושלמי כמלא רגל מדוכה קטנה של בשמים: (*) **אמר** רב ששת אם יש עליה עד מותר · מילתא באפי נפשה היא פירוש מותר לקנח בה אפילו גדולה יותר מכבילה או אם יש הרבה ממלא היד מותר ליטול כולן דכיון דיש עליהן עד הוכט כולן :

(*) רש"ל וב"ח ומהרש"מ כתבו דזהו דיבור אחד עם דיבור שלמעלה

מהו

עין משפט נר מצוה

כד א מיי' פי"ח מהל' שבת הלכה יב:
כה ב ג שם הלכה יא
כו ד מיי' פכ"ו שם הל' ד סמג לאוין סה טוש"ע א"ח סימן שיב סעיף א:
כז ה מיי' שם טוש"ע שם סעיף ד:
כח ו מיי' שם הל' ט' טור וש"ע שם ס"ה:
כט ז מיי' שם טוש"ע שם סעיף א:
ל ח מיי' שם הל' ד טוש"ע שם סעיף ג:

רבינו חננאל

אם עירב חול בסיד הרא טרכסיד ואסור · וקסבר דהא מתני' חול נמי כדי ליתן על מלא כף סיד. ר' יהודה היא (רב פפא) [רבא] אמר אפי' תימא רבנן. קלקולו זהו תקונו אית ביה ב' פירושים חד לענין שפריה דסיד. האי ברייתא (לאו) לענין שחרירותיה. וקסברי רבנן דסיד שעירב בו חול. אע"פ שהוא מתחזק כן הלך יפיו ומותר בגולה. והכא משו"ה קאמרי חול נמי כדי ליתן על מלא כף סיד. ופירוש שני כיון דלא שרי למיסר ביה בגולה עד שיערב בו חול (הוה ליה) הקלקול דקא מקלקל הוא התקון והלכך משערינן חול נמי כדי ליתן על מלוא כף סיד דחשיב ליה כדי שיהא מותר לסוד בו : צוצלא עוף ממין התורי'. ובלשון חכמים ריציפי. וקורין אותה אל פאכתי': חף *) דתני הכא וחפים דתניא [בברייתא] שיניים [הוא עשוין] מחתיכה של עץ וקורין בלשון פרסי דנר אנגאת מין נודעים בבבל. החפים בנגר שהן תלויין ועומדין כקבורים בתוך העץ שהוא בית הנגר ונקרא אל קפי' ובעץ שהוא הנגר נקבים סבנים להן כשמתקנין נגדן נופלין ונכנסין להן ואלה הן של גל ובהן נסגר והמפתח יש בו חפין בולטין מכוונין כנגדן מכניסין אותו בחלל שבנגר והחפין מעלין את החפין של גל והוא נפתח ואף שחברן בדלת טהורין לעולם [מפני] שהן מחוברים לקרקע. ושבמפתח טהורין עד שיקבעו בפותחת ואז הווין מכלל הכלי : זוז הווין (מצריך) כולן אחד הן. והן כששאל יונין כמה שיעור אבנים מקורזלות [שרשאי להעבירן] בכרמלית יתר מד' אמות ומקנח בהן. ואמרו לו כזית. כאגוז. כביצה. אמר להן (וממטני) [וכי טורטני] יבנים. פירוש היש לן מאזנים שישקל השיעור הזה נמנו וגמרו הכל מותר עד (אלא) [מלא] היד. וכן א"ר ישמעאל ב"ר יוסי משו' אביו וכן הלכה. אבל פלוגתא דר"מ ור' יהודה דפליגין הכא כי היכי דפליגי באתרוג עיקר תרוייהו. (ובדמנו ונגדו) [כדנמנו וגמרו] פיים דקא מפרש ליה (קרי שני גבליאתא) [כרשיני בבלייתא] שהוא אדמה שהיא קרוב להתרך ולהתחתת ואינ' אבנים ולא לבנים שרופי' דקריין אגורי: **אמר רבא** לא ימשמש בצרורות בשבת כדי להחליקן שלא ישרטו את בשרו ונמצא בא לידי כתישה או טחינה. ולא יעשה כדרך שהוא [עושה] ממשמש בחול. מתקיף לה מר זוטרא והיאך יסתכן אלא כלאחר יד. ויש מפרשין כדי לחכך ולנקות את עצמו כדרך שהוא ממשמש בחול. ואף לא יסתכן בעובי שם סינוף אלא מתחכך ומתנקה כלאחר יד · שמוצא שינוי מן החול. ופירוש' דברי ר' ינאי אם יש מקום קבוע לבית הכסא שנפנה בו מטלטל לשם שלש אבנים מקורזלות כל אחד מלא היד לקנח בהן. ואע"פ שיש מקום שנוטלין עד בית הכסא הקבוע אמות הרבה. אבל אין מקום קבוע אלא אם יש בידו אבנים סובב בבקעה לראות אנה ישב אין לו לשטת אלא כהכרע מדוכה קטנה של בשמים. והיינו שמעין פירושא הכרע מדוכה קטנה דאינה של בוכנא שדורכין בו והוא מקנח שמעבירין אותו במדוכה לשחוק בו. וראינו בתלמוד ארץ ישראל מלא רגל מדוכה קטנה של בושם: **אמר** רב ששת אם יש עליה עד מותר. פירש רבינו עד כגון סמרטוט או פקולין כדתנן התם ממשמשת בב' עדים. והן הן תיקוניה ועוותיה. והכי קאמר אע"פ [שקינח] בה כבר הרי הוא מותר ליטלה ולהתקנח בה: **מיתיבי** עשרה דברים מביאין את האדם לידי תחתוניות ואחת מהן המקנח בצרור שקינח בו חבירו. ופירק כמה פירוקין. אם לח הוא לא יקנח בו שמביאו לידי תחתוניות ואם יבש מותר. איבעית אימא אם קינח בו חבירו מצד א' מקנח הוא מצד אחר. ואם קנח חבירו משני צדדין חושש. אבע"א אפי' צרור שהוא קינח בו כבר גם עכשיו חוזר ומקנח ביה. ואם חבירו קינח בו בא הוא לידי תחתוניות: **א"ל** אביי לרב יוסף

*) עיין ערוך ערך חף ה'.

מסורת הש"ס

[ערוך גורס של עץ עלמה ושיעורה וגי' מהרש"א של עלם עלמה]
[גי' הערוך הכרכר]
[לעיל פ.]
[כריתות כח.]

הגהות הב"ח

(א) רש"י ד"ה סכוכית וכו' שסוכין כו קרי: (ב) ד"ה כזית וכו' מקנח פי הכרס בקטנה: (ג) תוס' ד"ה חפי פותחת וכו' של עץ לפתוח וקודם שנקבעו וכו' ותיבת שלא נמחק: (ד) בא"ד אלא כיון שאין להם פותחת וחף קבוע בגל טהור כצ"ל [מדקתני אע"פ שחיברן כדלת וקבען במסמרים] [גמרא] [מיירי] [בפותחת]

גליון הש"ס

גמ' אמר רבא אסור למשמש בצרור. כר"ש מ"ד דשבת כפי' לו להכי כלמש: רש"י ד"ה מדוכה קטנה מלאכתה לאיסור. עיין לקמן דף קכג ברש"י ד"ה הכי נמי עלי ומדוכה וצ"ע :

רב נסים גאון

את ביתו בסיד אלא אם כן עירב בו חול וכו' הדבר שגרם איסור דבר זה הוא מה שאירע לישראל כבית שני מחמת טיטוס הרשע ועיקר דיליה הוא בתוספתא סוטה בפולמוס של טיטוס על עטרות כלות וכו' ושלא יסוד אדם את ביתו בסיד ובביצת הסיד עירב בו חול או תבן הרי זה מותר ר' יהודה אומר עירב בו חול הרי זה טרכסיד ואסור עירב בו תבן הרי זה מותר: **סליק המוציא יין**

עין משפט
נר מצוה

לא א מיי' פכ"ג שם טוש"ע שם סעיף א :
לב ב מיי' פכ"א מהל' שבת הלכה ב סמג לאוין סה טור וש"ע או"ח סימן שיב סעיף ט :
[לב] [ב] מיי' שם פ"ח הלכה א ופרק י הלכה יב :
לג ג שם סעיף ג :
לד ד מיי' פ"ח שם הלכה ג :
[וע"ע תוס' סוכה לו: ד"ה בשבת שלשה]
לה ה שם הלכה ד :
לו ו מיי' שם הל' ה' טוש"ע או"ח סימן שיב סעיף ד :

חסדא ״מהו להעלותם אחריו לגג א"ל *גדול כבוד הבריות שדוחה את לא תעשה שבתורה יתיב מרימר וקאמר לה להא שמעתא איתיביה רבינא למרימר *ר' אליעזר אומר נוטל אדם קיסם משלפניו לחצות בו שיניו וחכמים אומרים לא יטול אלא מן האבוס של בהמה הכי השתא התם אדם קובע מקום לסעודה הכא אדם קובע מקום לבית הכסא אמר רב הונא ״אסור לפנות בשדה ניר בשבת מאי טעמא אילימא משום דוושא אפילו בחול נמי ואלא משום עשבים והאמר ריש לקיש צרור שעלו בו עשבים מותר לקנח בה והתולש ממנה בשבת חייב חטאת אלא דילמא נקיט מעילאי ושדא לתתאי ומיחייב משום דרבה *דאמר רבה [ג] היתה לו גומא וטממה בבית חייב משום בונה בשדה חייב משום חורש גופא ״אמר ר"ל צרור שעלו בו עשבים מותר לקנח בה ״והתולש ממנה בשבת חייב חטאת אמר רב פפי ש"מ מדר"ל האי פרפיסא שרי לטלטולי מתקיף לה רב כהנא אם אמרו לצורך ״יאמרו שלא לצורך אמר אביי פרפיסא הואיל ואתא לידן *לימא ביה מילתא ״היה מונח על גבי קרקע והניחו על גבי יתידות מיחייב משום תוליש היה מונח על גבי יתידות והניחו על גבי קרקע חייב משום נוטע א"ר יוחנן אסור לקנח בחרס בשבת מאי טעמא אילימא משום סכנה אפילו בחול נמי ואלא משום כשפים אפי' בחול נמי לא ואלא משום השרת נימין דבר שאין מתכוין הוא אמר להו רב נתן בר אושעיא גברא רבה אמר מילתא נימא בה טעמא ״לא מיבעיא בחול דאסור אבל בשבת הואיל ואיכא תורת כלי עליו שפיר דמי קמ"ל רבא מתני לה משום השרת נימין וקשיא ליה דר' יוחנן אדר' יוחנן מי א"ר יוחנן אסור לקנח בחרס בשבת אלמא דבר שאין מתכוין אסור והאמר *ר' יוחנן הלכה כסתם משנה °ותנן *נזיר חופף ומפספס אבל לא סורק אלא מחוורתא כדרב נתן בר אושעיא מאי כשפים כי הא *דרב חסדא ורבה בר רב הונא הוו קא אזלי בארבא אמרה להו ההיא מטרוניתא אותבן בהדייכו ולא אותבוה אמרה איהי מילתא אסרתה לארבא אמרו אינהו מילתא שריוהא אמרה להו מאי איעביד לכו
דלא

רש"י

מהו להעלותם אחריו לגג · אם עלה שם לפנות מי חיישינן לטירחא יתירתא או לא: שדוחה את לא תעשה· דכתיב (דברים כב) והתעלמת מהם פרט לזקן ואינו לפי כבודו והכא נמי טלטול דרבנן אלאו דלא תסור אסמכוה רבנן ובמקום כבוד הבריות נדחה : משלפניו · קסמין המוטלין על גבי קרקע ולא אמרינן מוקצין נינהו : לחצות · לטול הבשר שבין השינים ולחצות ביניהן : מן האבוס. שהוא מוכן אלמא העמידו דבריהם במקום כבוד הבריות שפעמים שנראה מבחוץ וגנאי הוא לו : התם אדם קובע לסעודה . והיה לו להכין שם מאתמול : הכא אדם קובע לבה"כ. בתמיה פעמים שמולא אדם שם והולך למקום אחר בית הכסא לא היה מצוי להם בבתיהן שהיו דרין בבתיהן בעלייה מפני דוחק בתים : בשדה ניר . חרישה ראשונה ועומד לזריעה: משום דוושא. ובשדה חבירו מפני שדש את נירו ומתקשה (את) החרישה : משום עשבים . שמחממת לחלוחית הניר עשבים עולין על הצרור וכשהוא מקנח בו נתלשים: מותר לקנח . דאינו מתכוין לתלוש ומותר דהלכה כר"ש : והתולש ממנו . במתכוין חייב דמקום גידולו הוא (א)אע"פ שהוא צרור ואינו עפר: שקיל מעילאי . ממקום גבשושית : ושדי לתתאי . למקום גומא ומשוה החרישה והוי תולדה דחורש : בבית . שייך בנין וזה שמשוה גומות בנין הרצפה הוא ובשדה מתקן החרישה : מדריש לקיש . דאמר מותר לקנח בו ולא אמרינן צרור זה העשבים שעלו מלחלוחית הקרקע הן יונקין וכשמגביהן הרי הוא כעוקרן מגידוליהן : האי פרפיסא . עציץ נקוב שזרעו בו ובתשובת הגאונים מצאתי שעושין חותלות מכפות תמרים וממלאין אותם עפר וזבל בהמה וכ"ב או ט"ו יום לפני ר"ה עושין כל אחד ואחד לשם כל קטן וקטנה שבבית וזורעים לתוכן פול המצרי או קטנית וקורין לו פורפיסא וצומח ובערב ר"ה נוטל כל אחד שלו ומחזירו סביבות ראשו שבעה פעמים ואומר זה תחת זה וזה חליפתי וזה תמורתי ומשליכו לנהר : שרי לטלטולי . ולא אמרינן תולש הוא : לצורך . קינוח כבוד הבריות : חייב משום תולש . דאינו נהנה שוב מריח הקרקע ול"נ דהאי °חייב לאו דווקא אלא אסור משום דדמי לתולש דאי חייב ממש קאמר לצורך היכי שרי רבנן איסור כרת וסקילה משום קינוח . ודומה לו במסכת סנהדרין (דף פב·) הבא על הכותית חייב משום נשג"ז דלאו מדאורייתא היא אלא מדרבנן : משום סכנה . שלא ינתק בו שיני הכרכשא שהיא תלויה בהן : משום כשפים. כדלקמן בשמעתין : השרת נימין. שמשיר את השיער מפני שהוא חדוד : דבר שאין מתכוין הוא. ושמעינן ליה לר' יוחנן דאמר דבר שאינו מתכוין מותר לקמן בשמעתין : לא מיבעיא בחול . שאין איסור טלטול בצרורות דאסור לקנח בחרס משום כשפים שהרי יכול לקנח בצרור : אבל בשבת הואיל ואיכא תורת כלי עליו . לחתות בו אור או לחשוף מים מגבא אימא שפיר דמי דמוטב שיקנח בו מלטלטל צרור : קמ"ל . דלא אי משום סכנה אי משום כשפים : חופף . מחליק שערו : ומפספס . קרפיר : אבל לא סורק . במסרק דודאי משיר שיער ומודה ר' שמעון בפסיק רישיה ולא ימות אבל חופף ומפספס פעמים שאינו משיר וכשמשיר דבר שאין מתכוין מותר : מטרוניתא . נכרית היתה : אמרה מילתא . דכשפים . ואסרתה לארבא ולא זזה ממקומה : אמרי אינהו מילתא . על ידי שם טהרה(ג) :
דלא

תוספות

מהו להעלותם לגג·פי' בקונט' מי חיישינן לטרחא יתירתא וקשה לר"י א"כ הא דפריך (ג) דאסור ליטול קיסם משלפניו תיקשי לכולה שמעתין דשרי לטלטל אבנים מקורזלות ונראה לר"י דהכא מבעיא ליה משום דבית הכסא קרוב על הגג ויכול להכין שם מע"ש ומהדר ליה דאפ"ה שרי ולהכי פריך ליה (ד) דאסור לטלטל קיסם משלפניו לפי שהיה יכול להזמין מאתמול אבל אכולה שמעתא לא מלי פריך שדרכן היה לפנות בשדה ובית הכסא רחוק ולא אטרחוה רבנן להכניס שם מע"ש וגם אם יזמינם שמא יקחם אחר* :

וחכמים אומרים לא יטול אלא מן האבוס כו' · נראה לר"י דלאו דוקא מן האבוס אלא מן הראוי לאבוס דליכא למימר דכשאינו באבוס אסור דבטל אגב קרקע דהא תנן בהמביא כדי יין (ביצה דף לג:) וחכמים אומרים מגבב משלפניו ומדליק אלמא לאו בטל הוא והא דלא שרו בקיסם לחצות שיניו אלא להדליק משום דסברי לא ניתנו עצים אלא להסקה אבל בדבר הראוי לאבוס בהמה שרי אפי' לחצות שיניו ור"א דאמר התם נוטל אדם קיסם משלפניו לחצות שיניו ומגבב מן החצר ומדליק סבר דמה שבבית מוכן לכל מה שירצה אפי' לחצות שיניו אבל שבחצר אינו מוכן אלא להסקה :

והניחו ע"ג יתדות מיחייב משום תולש · האי מיחייב מכת מרדות מדרבנן כדפירש בקונטרס מדשרי ריש לקיש וקשה לר"י דאמרי' בפ"ק דגיטין (דף ז:) א"ר *יוחנן עציץ נקוב המונח ע"ג יתדות באנו למחלוקת ר"ש ורבנן דלר"ש פטור מן המעשר כדמפליג בין ספינה גוששת לשאינה גוששת ולרבנן חייב אמר רבא דילמא לא היא ע"כ לא קאמרי רבנן אלא דספינה דלא מפסיק אויר אבל עציץ דמיפסיק אוירא אפילו רבנן מודו הא. בשמעתין חשבינן ליה כמחובר מדאורייתא אפי' הניחו על גבי יתדות ולא מיחייב משום תולש אלא מדרבנן ונראה לר"י דשמעתין לא סברא דחויא דרבא דהתם* :

והאמר ר' יוחנן הלכה כסתם משנה כו' · וא"ת והא בהגוזל קמא (ב"ק קב·) ובפ"ק דמס' ע"ז (דף ז·) אמר בתרי מסכתות אין סדר למשנה והכא סתם בנזיר ופלוגתא בפרק שני דביצה* (דף כג:) ר' יהודה אומר כל הכלים אין נגררין חוץ מן העגלה שכובשת ואין הלכה כסתם דשמא סתם ואח"כ מחלוקת היא ואין לומר דלר' יוחנן אפי' סתם ואח"כ מחלוקת הלכה כסתם דהא מסקינן בהחולץ (יבמות מב:) אליבא דר' יוחנן דרמי לך לא חש לקימחיה סתם ואח"כ מחלוקת היא ואין הלכה כסתם ותירץ רבינו שמואל מוורדון דבמחלוקת ואח"כ סתם בחדא מסכת לכ"ע הלכה כסתם כדפריש בפ"ק דמס' ע"ז (דף ז·) בהא דפסיק כר"י ·דכל המשנה ידו על התחתונה פשיטא דמחלוקת ואח"כ סתם הוא אבל בתרי מסכתות כל אמוראי סברי דאין הלכה כסתם ור' יוחנן אית ליה דאפי' בתרי מסכתות הלכה כסתם או סתם במתני' ומחלוקת בברייתא דמסתמא סתם לבסוף ואין לנו לומר שסתם רבי קודם ושוב חזר ממה שפסק ואמוראי נינהו אליבא דרבי יוחנן כדאמר באלו טרפות (חולין דף מג·) :

הדרן עלך המוציא יין

רבינו חננאל

ירדו עליהן גשמים ונשטשטו מהן · כך שמעתי פירושו שאם נראו לו אבנים מקורזלות דבוק עם הקרקע מורידה גשמים · וזהו טשטוש · דתניא התם נטשטשו ואין עושין פירות מי חיישינן שמא יהא(כסות) [כבוסה]או בטוחן ואמרו אם היה דישומן ניכר של אבנים מותר לו ליטלן ולקנח בהן:וכי שרא רב חסדא להעלותו אחריו לגג דקאמר גדול כבוד הבריות : **איתיביה** רבינא למרימר וחכ"א אינו נוטל קיסם לחצות בו שיניו · אלא מן האבוס של בהמה· מאי טעמא מפני שהוא מוכן · הכא נמי לא ישול אבנים לקינוח · אלא מרשות שנפנה בו · ולא יעלה לגג · א"ל מרימר הכי השתא · אדם קובע מקום לסעודה · ומאי דליתיה התם לאו מוכן הוא · אבל בית הכסא לא הוה רגילין דקבעין ליה מקום · והלכך מן כל היכא דשקיל מוכן הוא : **אמר** רב הונא אסור לפנות בשדה נירה בשבת · פירוש נירה · חרישה · כדכתיב נירו לכם ניר · ותניא נדשנה קרע שנתים · מ"ט אי משום (רושה) [דוושא] שלא יזיק את בעל השדה · אפי' בחול אסירי · אי משום עשבים הא אמר ר"ל מותר לקנח בו· אלא משום דשקיל מן טוליא ושדי בי ניצא · ומיחייב משום דרבה : **אמר** *) רב פפי שמע מינה מרר"ל האי פרפיסא שרי לטלטלה בשבת · פי' פרפיסא פיים גדול · כהאי דאמרינן (אחורן) [לעיל] מאי פיים א"ר זירא (קרשינן) [כרשיני] בבלייתא דורעין עליו זרעונים בשמים וזולתו וצומחין י.וטה לצרור שעלו בו עשבים · ולשון (פרסי) [פר] דהכא מלשון פרסי בכנפי יונה · אף הזרע הצומח עליו נקרא פר וזהו פרפיסא · וכיון דקא אמר ר"ל מותר לקנח בו קא שמעת מינה רב פפא דשרי לטלטלה : **מתקיף** לה רב כהנא אם אמר לצורך יאמרו שלא לצורך · הא קאמר ר"ל מותר לקנח אבל לטלטולי שלא לצורך לא שרי · והלכך לא צרכינן לדרב פפא : **אמר** אביי האי פרפיסא הואיל ואתא לידן נימא ייה מילתא . היה מונח ע"ג קרקע והניח על גבי יתדות חייב משום תולש כי כשזורעין אותו עושין לו מקום כמו כן או כמו שוליים שיושב עליו שיעור שיניח ע"ג קרקע ואפשר שהוא משרש שם ומתחבר לקרקע

*) עיין ערוך ערך פרסס.

י"ג נימא
[שם איתא ר' זירא]
[עי' תוס' גיטין ז: ד"ה דילמא]
[וע"ע תוס' עירובין לג: ד"ה לא תימא וכו' תמצא על נכון]

מסורת הש"ס

[לקמן קנ: ע"ש וש"נ]
ביצה לג. ע"ש תוספתא דביצה פ"ג
לעיל עג: ע"ש
[לעיל מו. וש"נ]
לעיל נ: נזיר מג.
חולין קה:

הגהות הב"ח

(א) רש"י ד"ה והתולש ממנו וכו' גידולו הוא (ואע"פ וכו' עפר) תא"מ ונ"ב ס"א אינו: (ב) ד"ה אמרי אינהו וכו' שם טהרה . נ"ב ובפ' כל הבשר בחולין דף קה דהס רש"י פי' זה : (ג) תוס' ד"ה מהו וכו' הא דפריך מהא דאסור ליטול : (ד) בא"ד ולהכי פריך ליה מהא דאסור :

גליון הש"ס

גמ' ותנן נזיר חופף. עי' ע"ע מ"ו דכלאים בר"ש שם : רש"י ד"ה חייב משום תולש וכו'.חייב לאו דוקא אלא אסור וכדמשני לעיל דף מ ע"ב מאי חייב מכת מרדות :

Rabbah son of R. Shila asked R. Ḥisda: [81b] Is it permissible to carry them up [the stones] after one to the roof?[6] Human dignity is very important, he replied, and it supersedes a negative injunction of the Torah.[7] Now, Meremar sat and reported this discussion, [whereupon] Rabina raised an objection to Meremar: R. Eliezer said: One may take a chip [lying] before him to pick his teeth therewith;[8] but the Sages maintain: He may take only from an animal's trough?[9] How compare! There, one appoints a place for his meal;[10] but here, does one appoint a place for a privy?[11]

R. Huna said: One may not obey the call of nature in a ploughed field on the Sabbath. What is the reason? Shall we say, because of treading down?[12] Then the same holds good even on weekdays? Again, if it is on account of the grasses,[13]—surely Resh Lakish said: One may cleanse himself with a pebble whereon grass has sprouted, but if one detaches [the grass] thereof on the Sabbath, he incurs a sin-offering? Rather [the reason is] lest he take [a clod] from an
a upper level[1] and throw it below,[2] and he is then liable on account of Rabbah's [dictum], for Rabbah said: If one has a depression and fills it up,—if in the house, he is culpable on account of building; if in the field, he is culpable on account of ploughing.

[To revert to] the main text: Resh Lakish said: One may cleanse himself with a pebble whereon grass has sprouted; but if one detaches [the grass] thereof on the Sabbath, he incurs a sin-offering. R. Pappi said: From Resh Lakish you may infer that one may take up a *parpisa*.[3] R. Kahana demurred: If they said [that it is permitted] in case of need,[4] shall they say [thus] where there is no need![5]

Abaye said: As for *parpisa*, since it has come to hand, we will state something about it. If it is lying on the ground and one places it upon pegs, he is culpable on the score of detaching; if it is lying on pegs and one places it on the ground, he is liable on the score of planting.[6]

R. Joḥanan said: One must not cleanse oneself with a shard on the Sabbath. What is the reason? Shall we say on account of danger?[7] Then on weekdays too [let it be forbidden]? Again if it is on account of witchcraft:[8] it may not [be done] even on weekdays too? Again, if it is on account of the tearing out of hair,—but surely that is unintentional?—Said R. Nathan b. Oshaia to them: [Since] a great man has stated this dictum, let us give a reason for it. [Thus:] it is unnecessary [to state] that it is forbidden on weekdays;[9] but on the Sabbath, since it bears the rank of a utensil, [I
b might think that] it is permitted:[1] therefore he informs us [otherwise].

Raba recited it on account of the tearing out of hair, and found R. Joḥanan to be self-contradictory. [Thus:] did then R. Joḥanan say, One must not cleanse oneself with a shard on the Sabbath, which shows that what is unintentional is forbidden? Surely R. Joḥanan said: The *halachah* is as [every] anonymous Mishnah, and we learnt: A nazirite may cleanse [his hair] and part it, but he must not comb it.[2] But it is clear that it is as R. Nathan b. Oshaia.

What is [the reference to] witchcraft?—R. Ḥisda and Rabbah son of R. Huna were travelling in a boat, when a certain [non-Jewish] matron said to them, 'Seat me near you,' but they did not seat her. Thereupon she uttered something [a charm] and bound the boat;[3] they uttered something, and freed it. Said she

(6) Since he could have carried them up there on the eve of Sabbath, Tosaf. (7) I.e., it is permitted, v. *infra* 94b. (8) Though not designated for this purpose beforehand, it is not regarded as *mukẓeh* (q.v. Glos.). (9) There it is regarded as standing ready for use, but otherwise it is *mukẓeh*, and human dignity, viz., the necessity to clean one's teeth, does not negative this prohibition. (10) Beforehand, and at the same time he could have prepared his toothpicks too. Hence the prohibition retains its force. (11) Surely not! (Cf. p. *supra* 81a, n. b7) (12) The loose ploughed soil, thus spoiling it, the reference being to a neighbour's field. (13) Which sprout on the loose, moist earth, and in picking up a clod for cleansing one may involuntarily detach the grass.

a (1) E.g., a mound or any other protuberance. (2) Into a depression; he thus levels them. (3) Rashi: a perforated pot. Though the earth in it might be regarded as attached to the ground in virtue of the perforation which permits the sap or moisture to mount from the one to the other, yet just as Resh Lakish rules that the pebble is treated as detached in spite of the grass which has grown on it, which is only possible through its lying on the soil, so is this pot too regarded thus. Jast.: a lump of earth in a bag of palm-leaves (v. Rashi in name of תשובת הגאונים). (4) *Sc.* for cleansing, which is necessary. (5) Surely not! (6) Cf. n. a3. 'Culpable' here merely denotes that the action is forbidden, but does not imply liability to a sin-offering, as usual (Rashi and Tosaf.) (7) He may cut himself. (8) As below. (9) Since one can just as easily take a chip or a pebble, to which no suspicion of danger or witchcraft attaches.

b (1) Being preferable to a chip or a pebble, which are not utensils, and in general it is permitted to handle a utensil sooner than that which is not a utensil. (2) V. *supra* 50b for notes. (3) So that it could not proceed further to them, 'What shall I do to you, [82a] seeing that you do not cleanse yourselves with a shard,[4] nor kill vermin on your garments, and you do not pull out and eat a vegetable from a bunch which the gardener has tied together'?[5]

R. Huna said to his son Rabbah, 'Why are you not to be found before R. Ḥisda, whose dicta are [so] keen?' 'What should I go to him for,' answered he, 'seeing that when I go to him he treats me to secular discourses!'[6] [Thus] he tells me, when a man enters a privy, he must not sit down abruptly, nor force himself overmuch, because the rectum rests on three teeth-like glands, [and] these teeth-like glands of the rectum might become dislocated and he [his health] is endangered. 'He treats of health matters,'[7] he exclaimed, 'and you call them secular discourses! All the more reason for going to him!'

If a pebble and a shard lie before one,—R. Huna said: He must cleanse himself with the pebble, but not with the shard;[1] but R. Ḥisda ruled: He must cleanse himself with the shard, and not with the pebble.[2] An objection is raised: If a pebble and a shard lie before one, he must cleanse himself with the shard, not with the pebble—this refutes R. Huna?—Rafram b. Papa interpreted it before R. Ḥisda on R. Huna's view as referring to the rims of utensils.[3]

If a pebble and grass lie before one,—R. Ḥisda and R. Hamnuna [differ therein]: one maintains: He must cleanse himself with the pebble, but not with the grass;[4] whilst the other ruled: He must cleanse himself with the grass, not with the pebble.[5] An objection is raised: If one cleanses himself with inflammable material,[6] his lower teeth[7] will be torn away?—There is no difficulty: the one refers to wet [grass];[8] the other to dry [grass].

If one has a call of nature but does not obey it—R. Ḥisda and Rabina—one said: He has an attack of offensive odour;[9] the other said: He is infected by an offensive smell.[10] It was taught in accordance with the view that he is infected by an offensive smell. For it was taught: One who has a call of nature yet eats, is like an oven which is heated up on top of its ashes, and that is the beginning of perspiration odour.[11]

If one has a call of nature but cannot obey it,—R. Ḥisda said: He should repeatedly stand up and sit down; R. Ḥanan of Nehardea said: Let him move to [different] sides; R. Hamnuna said: Let him work about that place with a pebble; while the Rabbis advise: Let him not think. Said R. Aḥa son of Raba to R. Ashi: If he does not think [of it], he is all the more likely not to be moved? Let him not think of other things, replied he.[12] R. Jeremiah of Difti observed: I myself saw a certain Arab repeatedly arise and sit down until he poured forth like a cruse.

Our Rabbis taught: If one enters [a house] to [partake of] a complete meal,[1] he should [first] walk ten four-cubit lengths—others say, four ten-cubit lengths—be moved, then enter and take his seat.

MISHNAH. [IF ONE CARRIES OUT] A SHARD, [THE STANDARD IS] AS MUCH AS IS NEEDED FOR PLACING BETWEEN ONE BOARD AND ANOTHER:[2] THIS IS R. JUDAH'S VIEW. R. MEIR SAID: LARGE ENOUGH TO SCRAPE OUT THE FIRE THEREWITH; R. JOSE SAID: LARGE ENOUGH TO CONTAIN A REBI'ITH. R. MEIR OBSERVED: THOUGH THERE IS NO PROOF OF THE MATTER, YET THERE IS A HINT: SO THAT THERE SHALL NOT BE FOUND AMONG THE PIECES THEREOF A SHARD TO TAKE FIRE FROM THE HEARTH.[3] SAID R. JOSE TO HIM, THENCE IS PROOF [OF MY VIEW, VIZ.]: OR TO TAKE WATER WITHAL OUT OF THE CISTERN.[4]

GEMARA. (The Scholars asked: Is R. Meir's standard greater or R. Jose's standard greater?)[5] Logically, R. Jose's standard is greater, whereas the verse [quoted indicates that] R. Meir's standard is greater, for should you think that R. Jose's standard is greater, does he [the prophet] [first] curse in respect to a small vessel, and then curse in respect to a large one![6]—Said Abaye:
c Our Mishnah too [means] to scrape out a fire from a large hearth.[1]

SAID R. JOSE TO HIM, THENCE IS PROOF. But R. Jose says well to R. Meir!—R. Meir maintains that he proceeds to a climax: Not only will nothing that is of value to people be found therein, but even that which is of no value to people shall not be found therein.

CHAPTER IX

MISHNAH. R. AKIBA SAID: FROM WHERE DO WE KNOW
d THAT AN IDOL DEFILES BY CARRIAGE LIKE A NIDDAH?[1] BECAUSE IT IS SAID, THOU SHALT CAST THEM [SC. THE IDOLS] AWAY AS A MENSTRUOUS THING; THOU SHALT SAY UNTO IT, GET THEE HENCE:[2] JUST AS A NIDDAH DEFILES BY CARRIAGE, SO DOES AN IDOL DEFILE BY CARRIAGE.[3]

GEMARA. We learnt elsewhere:[4] If one's house adjoins an idol,[5] and it collapses, he must not rebuild it.[6] What shall he do? He must retreat four cubits within his own [ground] and rebuild.

(4) And are thus not exposed to witchcraft—this remark gives the point of the story. (5) But you first untie the bunch. (6) I.e., not on Torah. (7) Lit., 'the life (health) of the creatures'.

(1) Though the first is not a utensil (v. *supra* 81b, n. b1), because the latter is dangerous. (2) Because the former is technically a utensil. (3) Which are rounded and smooth; hence they are not dangerous. (4) Because it injures the flesh (Rashi). Or the reference is to attached (growing) grass, and one must not make use on the Sabbath of that which is attached to the soil. (5) He ignores the prohibition mentioned in the last note, and holds grass to be preferable, because a pebble is not a utensil and may normally not be handled on the Sabbath. (6) Lit., 'over which the fire rules'. (7) I.e., the teeth-like glands supporting the rectum. (8) This is permissible. (9) From his mouth. (10) From the whole body. (11) Which affects the whole body. (12) But concentrate on this.

(1) Lit., 'a fixed meal' as opposed to a mere snack, so that he will have to sit some time there. (2) When they are piled up. Rashi: the boards are not allowed to touch, but are separated by shards to prevent them from warping. *Aruk:* to enable the air to enter and dry them. (3) Isa. XXX, 14. (4) Ibid. The least quantity of water to be counted is a *rebi'ith;* v. first Mishnah of this chapter. (5) Rashal and BaḤ delete this bracketed passage. (6) This is raised as a difficulty. Generally speaking, only a very small shard is required for scraping out a fire from a stove, certainly not one large enough to contain a *rebi'ith*. On the other hand, the prophet would not curse by first observing that not even a small shard will remain, and then add that a large shard will not remain either.

c (1) Which requires a larger shard.

d (1) If one carries a *niddah* (q.v. Glos.), even without actually touching her, he becomes unclean, and R. Akiba teaches that the same applies to an idol. (2) Isa. XXX, 22. (3) Rashi: This Mishnah is quoted here because of its similarity in style to a later Mishnah concerning circumcision on the Sabbath (*infra* 86a). R. Ḥan. and Tosaf.: Since the last Mishnah of the preceding chapter quotes a law which is supported by, though not actually deduced from, a Biblical verse, this chapter commences similarly. Both verses quoted are from Isa. XXX. (4) V. A.Z. 47b. (5) So that its wall is also the wall of the heathen temple, though actually it belongs entirely to him. (6) Since he thereby builds a wall for the temple too.

מסורת הש"ס

[גי' הערוך ליטרח פי' לא יעלים עצמו מלד לנאת]
[לעיל נב: וש"נ]
חולין פז:
לעיל מח. ע"ש
ברכות כג:
ב"ב כג: בילה לט.
[לעיל כט: וש"נ]
[ה"ל מנין ע"י תשבי ערש מנין]
פ"ו מז:

דלא מקנחיתו בחספא. שאוכל לעשות לכם כשפים: ולא קטיל לכו כינא אמנייכו. ואין אתם הורגין כינה בבגדיכם: ולא אכיל לכו ירקא מכישא דאסר גינאה. אין אתם מוליאין שום וכרישא ובצל מאגודה שאוגדין הגננים ואוכלים אלא אתם מתירין האגודה תחילה ש"מ כל הני קשה לכשפים: מותיב לי במילי דעלמא· מושיבני לפניו בדברי חנם שאינו תורה: לא ליתיב בהדיא· במהרה ובחוזק לפי שנפתח הנקב בחוזקה וניתקין שיני הכרכשא ויולאת: ולא ליטרח טפי. פריימבר"א בלע"ז: מקנח בצרור. בשבת אע"פ דלאו בר טלטול הוא בעלמא: ואינו מקנח בחרס. משום סכנה: מקנח בחרס· שיש תורת כלי עליה: באוגני כלים. שהם חלקים ואין מקרעין את הבשר: ואינו מקנח בעשבים. שהעשבים לחים וחותכין את הבשר ורבותינו מפרשים משום תלישה ואיני יודע מהו דאי בעשבים מחוברין מי איכא מאן דשרי וכמדומה אני דמוקמי לה במחוברין ומקנח בהן בחיבורן: ואינו מקנח בצרור. דלאו בר טלטול הוא הלכך מקנח בעשבים כשהן במחובר ולא יזיזם ומשום שימוש במחובר לא מיתסר כדאמרי' בעירובין בפרק ג' (דף לד:) דלא אסרו אלא באילן ובקנים (ג) עוזרדין לפי שהן קשין: שיניו נושרות. שיני הפה מכרכשא: לחין. אין אור שולט בו: רוח רעה. ריח הפה שהזבל מרקב במעיים ויולא ריח דרך פיו: רוח זוהמא. כל גופו מסריח בזיעה מסריחת שהריח נבלע בבשרו ובאבריו והוה בו לזיעה מזוהמת: ואינו יכול לפנות. שאין הנקב נפתח: יסתלק לצדדין. כשבדק עצמו בזוית זו יסתלק לזוית אחרת ויבדוק: טייעא. ישמעאל: הנכנס לסעודת קבע. וגנאי הוא לו אם יצטרך לעמוד מן הסעודה ולפנות: י' פעמים. ימתין בין פעם לפעם ויבדוק עלמו: ואמרי לה ד' פעמים של י' י'. דהכי עדיף· טפי שהילוך מרובה מוריד הזבל לנקביו: **מתני'** בין פצים לחברו. כשמסדרין פלימין ועמודים וקורות ועושין סואר של קורות על הארץ ויש חלל בין זה לזה סומכן מתחתיו שלא יתעקם: זכר לדבר· דחרס חשיב בחתיית אור: לחשוף. לדלות וחבירו חשפי שובל (ישעיה מז) חשפי מים שעל הגתיבה שתלטרכי לעבור הגשמים ושריעת נהרות: מגבא. גומא שמים נקבלין בתוכה: **גמ'** (ג) מסתברא שיעורא דרבי יוסי נפיש ומקרא שיעורא דר' מאיר נפיש. אתקפתא היא כלומר לפי דבריהם נראה שרבי מאיר מחמיר דאמר לחתות בו אור ולא פי' שיעורא וחרס פורתא חזי לחדא גחלת ואילו לקבל רביעית מים נפיש שיעורא וכי מעיינת בקרא לחשוף מים זוטר· דאי ס"ד לחשוף מים נפיש לייט לה שלא יותר בה אפילו כלי קטן והדר אמר כלי גדול וכי דרך המקללים כן: אמר אביי מתני'. דקאמר רבי מאיר לחתות אור מיקידה גדולה קאמר שאפילו גחלת קטנה אינו ראוי לחתות בה אלא בחרס גדול מפני שהוא נכוה: שפיר קאמר ר' יוסי. דמלייט לה בה ש"מ דחזי: אפילו מידי דלא חשיב· כגון לחשוף מים לא לישתכח בה ולעולם לא חשיב שיעורא אלא לחתות אור:

תורה אור

דלא מקנח לכו בחספא ולא קטיל לכו כינא אמנייכו ולא שליף לכו ירקא ואביל לכו מכישא דאסיר גינאה: אמר ליה רב הונא לרבה בריה מאי טעמא לא שכיחת קמיה דרב חסדא דמחדדן שמעתיה אמר ליה מאי איזיל לגביה דכי·אזילנא לגביה מותיב לי במילי דעלמא א"ל מאן דעייל לבית הכסא לא ליתיב בהדיא ולא *ליטרח טפי דהאי כרכשתא אתלת שיני יתיב דילמא משתמטא שיני דכרכשתא ואתי לידי סכנה א"ל הוא עסיק בחיי דברייתא ואת אמרת במילי דעלמא כ"ש זיל לגביה °היו לפניו צרור וחרס רב הונא אמר מקנח בצרור ואין מקנח בחרס ורב חסדא אמר מקנח בחרס ואין מקנח בצרור מיתיבי היו לפניו צרור וחרס מקנח בחרס ואין מקנח בצרור תיובתא דרב הונא *תרגמא רפרם בר פפא קמיה דרב חסדא אליבא דרב הונא באוגני כלים: °היו לפניו צרור ועשבים רב חסדא ורב המנונא חד אמר מקנח בצרור ואין מקנח בעשבים וחד אמר מקנח בעשבים ואין מקנח בצרור מיתיבי *[°] המקנח בדבר שהאור שולטת בו שיניו התחתונות נושרות לא קשיא הא בלחין הא ביבשין הנצרך לפנות *ואינו נפנה רב חסדא ורבינא חד אמר רוח רעה שולטת בו וחד אמר רוח זוהמא שולטת בו תניא כמאן דאמר רוח זוהמא שולטת בו *דתניא °הנצרך לנקביו ואוכל דומה לתנור שהסיקוהו על גב אפרו וזו היא תחלת רוח זוהמא הוצרך ליפנות ואינו יכול ליפנות אמר רב חסדא יעמוד וישב יעמוד וישב רב חנן מנהרדעא אמר יסתלק לצדדין רב המנונא אמר ימשמש בצרור באותו מקום ורבנן אמרי יסיח דעתו אמר ליה רב אחא בריה דרבא לרב אשי כל שכן דכי מסח דעתיה לא מפני אמר ליה יסיח דעתו מדברים אחרים אמר רב ירמיה מדיפתי לדידי חזי לי ההוא טייעא דקם ויתיב וקם ויתיב עד דשפך כקדרה *ת"ר הנכנס לסעודת קבע °הלך י' פעמים של ארבע[ארבע]אמות ואמרי לה ד' פעמים של עשר אמות ונפנה ונכנס וישב במקומו: **מתני'** **חרס כדי ליתן בין פצים לחברו דברי רבי יהודה רבי מאיר אומר כדי לחתות בו את האור רבי יוסי אומר °כדי לקבל בו רביעית אמר רבי מאיר אף על פי שאין ראיה לדבר זכר לדבר °לא ימצא במכיתתו חרש לחתות אש מיקוד אמר ליה רבי יוסי *משם ראיה °ולחשוף מים מגבא(א): **גמ'** (איבעיא להו שיעורא דרבי מאיר נפיש או שיעורא דרבי יוסי נפיש) מסתברא שיעורא דרבי יוסי נפיש ומקרא שיעורא דרבי מאיר נפיש דאי סלקא דעתך שיעורא דרבי יוסי נפיש לייט לה במנא זוטרא והדר לייט לה במנא רבה אמר אביי [מתני' נמי] לחתות אש מיקידה גדולה: רבי יוסי אומר משם ראיה: שפיר קאמר ליה רבי יוסי לרבי מאיר ורבי מאיר לא מיבעיא קאמר לא מיבעיא מידי דחשיב לאינשי דלא לישתכח ליה אלא אפילו מידי דלא חשיב לאינשי לא לישתכח ליה:

הדרן עלך המוציא יין

אמר רבי עקיבא *מניין לעבודה זרה שמטמאה במשא *כנדה שנאמר °תזרם כמו דוה צא תאמר לו מה נדה מטמאה במשא אף עבודה זרה מטמאה במשא: **גמ'** תנן התם *°מי שהיה (ד) ביתו סמוך לעבודה זרה ונפל אסור לבנותו כיצד יעשה כונס לתוך שלו ד' אמות ובונה

היה

הדרן עלך המוציא יין

אמר רבי עקיבא מניין לעבודה זרה כו'. משום דבעי למיתני בהדייהו מניין שמרחיצין את המילה כייל להו להגך דדמיין לה: במשא. אדם הנושאה: תזרם כמו דוה וגו'. בעבודה זרה משתעי: **גמ'** כותלו סמוך לעבודה זרה. שהיה אותו כותל מחילה אף לבית עבודה זרה: אסור לבנותו. דקמהני לעבודה זרה:

אמר רבי עקיבא מניין לע"ז כו'· פי' בקונטרס דנקט לה הכא משום דבעי למיתני מנין שמרחיצין את הקטן ואין נראה דא"כ בההוא הוה ליה להתחיל ועוד דהוה ליה למתנייה בפרק רבי אליעזר דמילה אלא נראה אגב דתנא לעיל בסוף המוציא קראי דאסמכתא גבי חרס נקט נמי הגי קראי דאסמכתא וקרא דתזרם כו' הוא סמוך להאי קראי דאייתי לעיל לא ימלא במכיתתו חרש וגו': **אסור** לבנותו. אפילו למ"ד בפרק קמא דמס' ע"ז (דף יג·) נהנה אסור מהנה מותר ה"מ לגבי מכס שאין נראה כל כך לע"ז כוונתו אלא שנותן כדי שיניחוהו לעבור אבל הכא נראה כאילו בונה לה בית* ר"י: **כונס** לתוך שלו ד"א. במסכת ע"ז פריך עלה והא שביק רווחא לעבודה זרה ומשני לה אבניו

עין משפט נר מצוה

לז א ב מיי' פכ"ו מהל' שבת הלכה ה טוש"ע או"ח סימן שיב סעיף ה:
[לז] [ב] טוש"ע או"ח סימן ג' סעיף יא:
לח ג מיי' פ"ד מהלכות דעות הלכה ג:
לט ד מיי' פי"ח מהל' שבת הלכה י:
א ה מיי' פ"ח מהלכות ע"ז הלכה ה טוש"ע יו"ד סימן קמג סעיף א:

[וע"ע תוספות ע"ז יג. ד"ה אבל מהנה]

[בכה"ג אלפס איתא הנצרך להפנות ואבל רב חסדא ורבינא וכו' ע"ש]

[ומתנין חרס בין הנסרים כדי שיכנס בהן הרוח וייבשו מפני שלחין הן. ערוך ערך פלם]

רש"ל מ"ו

רבינו חננאל

לקרקע. וכיון שמניחו ע"ג יתדות הרי הוא מעבירו ממקו' שמתחבר ומתחייב משום תולש. אבל אם זרעו מעיקרא להניחו ע"ג יתדות בזמן שמניחו על גבי קרקע הרי הכינו במקום שמתחבר לקרקע ונמצא חייב משום נוטע. ולענין חרס מיסברא שיעורא דר' יהודה [זוטר] ור"מ נפיש מיניה ודר' יוסי נפיש מיניה אבל מן קראי שיעורא דר"מ נפיש דאי ס"ד שיעורא דר' יוסי נפיש דההוא כדי לקבל רביעית לייט להו תחלה שלא ימצא דבר קטן שהוא כדי לחתות אש מיקוד והדר לייט שלא ימצא דבר גדול כדי לקבל רביעית ומקשינן היכי אמרת דמקרא דשיעורא דר"מ נפיש מדר' יוסי והלא דבר ידוע שיש לחתות אש בחרס קטנה שאין בה כדי לקבל רביעית. ופרקיה אביי להאי קושיא לא תימא לחתות אש כדי להדליק מטנה במקום אחד אלא לחתות אש מיקידה גדולה כדי להתחמם כנגדה. ומקשי' אי מחשב (קא' השבת) [לענין שבת מאי דהשיב] מקראי ושיעורא דר' מאיר נפיש שפיר קאמר ליה ר' יוסי משם ראיה. דהא חשיב חרס להשוף מים · ומפרקינן לדר"מ דאמר ולחשוף מים לא חשיבותא היא ולא חשיב אלא לחתות אש . ולא מיבעיא קאמר דלא מיבעיא מידי דחשיב דלא שבקינא אלא מאי דלא חשיב נמי לא שבקינא. ולעולם שיעור הוצאה מאי דחשיב הוא: סליק פרק שמיני

פרק ט אמר ר' עקיבא מניין לע"ז שהיא מטמאה במשא כנדה שנאמר תזרם כמו דוה. אגב דתניא אסמכתא מן קראי בסוף המוציא יין לענין שיעור חרס אדכר נמי (הנשאה) [הני משניות]. אסמכתא ראשונה

הגהות הב"ח

(א) במשנה חרס כדי וכו' ולחשוף מים מגבא הוא סוף המשנה ואח"כ מתחיל גמרא מסתברא שיעורא דר' יוסי נפיש: (ב) רש"י ד"ה ואינו מקנח וכו' ובקנים ועוזרדין ופרישין קשין.

ג"ב לשון משנה כרים כלאים וכים מעשרות הפרישין והעוזרדין: (ג) ד"ה מסתברא שיעורא דר' יוסי: (ד) גמ' מי שהיה כותלו סמוך לאשרה:

עין משפט
נר מצוה

א מיי' פ"ח מהלכות משכב ומושב הל"ד:

[ועי' תוס' ע"ז מז: ד"ה אבניו]

ג ב מיי' פ"ו מהלכות שאר אבות הטומאות הלכה ג:

ד ג שם הלכה ב:

היה שלו ושל ע"ז נידון מחצה על מחצה אבניו ועציו ועפריו מטמאים כשרץ שנאמר °שקץ תשקצנו וגו' רבי עקיבא אומר כנדה שנאמר °תזרם כמו דוה מה נדה מטמאה במשא אף ע"ז מטמאה במשא אמר רבה תזרם דאמר קרא נכרינהו מינך כזר צא תאמר לו הכנס אל תאמר לו ואמר רבה במשא דכ"ע לא פליגי דמטמאה דהא אתקש לנדה כי פליגי באבן מסמא רבי עקיבא סבר כנדה מה נדה מטמאה באבן מסמא אף ע"ז מטמאה באבן מטמא ורבנן סברי כשרץ מה שרץ לא מטמא באבן מסמא אף ע"ז לא מטמאה באבן מסמא ולר' עקיבא למאי הלכתא איתקש לשרץ למשמשי' ולרבנן למאי הלכתא איתקש לנדה למשא ולוקשה רחמנא לנבלה אין הכי נמי [א]אלא מה נדה אינה לאברין [ב]אף ע"ז אינה לאברין ואלא הא דבעי רב חמא בר גוריא ע"ז ישנה לאברין או אינה לאברין תיפשוט ליה מהא דלרבנן אינה לאברין רב חמא בר גוריא אליבא דרבי עקיבא בעי לה ור"א אמר באבן מסמא דכ"ע לא פליגי *דלא מטמאה כי פליגי במשא רבי עקיבא סבר כנדה מה נדה מטמאה במשא אף ע"ז מטמא' במשא ורבנן [ג]סברי כשרץ מה שרץ לא מטמאה במשא אף ע"ז לא מטמאה במשא ור"ע למאי הלכתא איתקש לשרץ למשמשי' ורבנן למאי הלכתא איתקש לנדה מה נדה אינה לאברים אף ע"ז אינה לאברים

ורבי

(דברים ז) (ישעיה ל)

היה שלו ושל ע"ז. שהיה חצי מריס הכותל של ע"ז: נדון מחצה על מחצה. המחצה שלו נחשבת בארבע אמות של כניסה לפי שחייבוהו חכמים להרחיקו משלו ארבע אמות וליכנס כולו בתוך שלו: שקץ תשקצנו. לשון שקץ כשרץ שאינו מטמא במשא: נדה מטמאה במשא. דאיתקש [לזב והדוה בנדתה והזב את זובו וגו' (ויקרא טו) וזב מטמא במשא דכתיב (שם) וכל הנוגע בכל אשר יהיה תחתיו יטמא עד הערב והנושא אותם וגו' אף הזב במשמע אותם: באבן מסמא. אבן ששמוה על גבי יתידות וכלים תחתיה כדכתיב (דניאל ו) והיתית אבן חדא ושמת על פום גובא ונדה או זב יושבין עליה אע"פ שלא הכבידו על הכלים טמאים הכלים דכתיב כל אשר יהיה תחתיו: למשמשין. שאין הכלים המשמשין מטמאים לא במשא ולא באבן מסמא: למשא. אבל לא לאבן מסמא דלהכי אהני היקשא דשרץ: ולוקשה לנבלה. דאית בה משא ולית בה אבן מסמא והכי עדיף דתו לא צריך לאקושה לשרץ למעוטי מאבן מסמא: אינה לאברים. אם נחתך אבר ממנה מטמא במשא ובאהל משום תורת אבר מן החי אבל לא משום תורת אבר מן הנדה ונפקא מינה דלא מטמא באבן מסמא: אף ע"ז אינה לאברים. כגון ע"ז של חוליות אבר אבר ממנה אינו מטמא כלל משום ע"ז: דבעי רב חמא. לקמן (דף פג:): אליבא דרבי עקיבא בעי לה. דאקשה לנדה (*למשא) מי אמרינן להא נמי איתקש או דילמא לחומרא מקשינן לקולא לא מקשינן: דלא מטמאה. דהא איתקש לשרץ ובשרץ כתיב מגע ולא כתיב משא: למשמשיה. תירוצא היא:

[רש"א] [גליון] [צ"ל]

אבנין ועליו ועפריו מטמאים כשרץ. ואפי' למ"ד בפ"ג דמסכת ע"ז (דף מה:) ע"ז שנשתברה מאליה מותרת הא מוקי לה בירושלמי כגון שהשתחוה לכל אבן ואבן ולכל עץ ועץ ולכל עפר ועפר דהוי ע"ז שלימה*: **אמר** רבה במשא כ"ע לא פליגי דמטמאה דהא איתקש לנדה. קשה לר"ת מ"ט דרבנן אי אית להו הא דאמר בסוף שמעתין (דף פג:) טומאה דע"ז דרבנן היא ולקולא מקשינן א"כ אמאי מטמאה במשא נימא דהיקישא דנדה דאינה לאיברים והיקישא דשרץ דלא מטמאה במשא ואי סברי רבנן דלחומרא מקשינן אימא אהני היקשא דנדה לטמויי באבן מסמא ודשרץ לטמויי בכעדשה ולר' עקיבא נמי אי לחומרא מקיש אמאי איצטריך למימר דהיקישא דשרץ למשמשיה לימא לטמויי בכעדשה ואי לקולא מקיש לא תטמא אפילו במשא והיקישא דנדה דאינה לאברים והיקישא דשרץ דלא מטמא במשא וכן לר' אלעזר אליבא דר' עקיבא ונראה לר"ת דגרסי' לעיל בספרים אמר רבה תזרם דאמר *קרא נכרינהו מינך כזר לא תאמר לו הכנס אל תאמר לו פירוש כיון דכתיב כבר בריש' וטמאתם את צפוי פסילי כספך וגו' ל"ל תו למימר תזרם כמו דוה אלא לומר שאדם יש להרחיק ואתא למימר אע"ג דשאר קראי נדרשות לקולא משום דטומאת ע"ז דרבנן מנדה ילפינן לחומרא מש"ה קאמר רבה לכ"ע מטמא במשא דאית להו דרשא דתזרם ולרבנן נמי הוית מטמא באבן מסמא כנדה אי לאו דממעטין מדאיתקש לשרץ:

באבן מסמא. פי' בקונטרס אבן מונחת על גבי יתידות ונדה יושבת עליה וכלים תחת האבן וטמא מוכל אשר יהיה תחתיו וקשה דבת"כ מפיק אבן מסמא מוכל המשכב וקרא דכל אשר יהיה תחתיו מוקמינן בפרק בנות כותים (נדה לב:) לעליונו של זב ובת"כ מוקי לה במרכב ועוד דאי מוכל אשר יהיה תחתיו נפקא א"כ אפי' כלים שאין ראוי למשכב ומושב ובת"כ מוכח בהדיא דכלים שאין ראויין למשכב ומושב אין להם אפי' טומאה קלה ועוד אמאי נקט אבן אפי' דף ע"ג יתידות נמי ומפרש ר"ת דאבן מסמא היינו אבן גדולה שהיא כבידה ואין הכלים מרגישים כובד הזב והנדה מחמת כובד האבן ומסמא היינו משא גדולה *שצריכה שימה כדכתיב והיתית אבן חדא ושמת על פום *גובא אך קשה דבת"כ מרבה אבן מסמא מוכל המשכב משמע דמרבה מטעם משכב ומושב ובכל הש"ס משמע דהוי מטעם משא דבמתני' קרי ליה משא ובפ' בתרא דנדה (דף סט:) תנן הזב והזבה מטמאין במשא ומפרש בגמרא מאי משא אבן מסמא ובריש דם הנדה [נדה נה:] ממעט מדוה מאבן מסמא מוהנושא אותם ובתוספתא דכלים תניא אין טומאה לכלי חרס אלא מאוירו ובהיסט הזב ע"ג אבן מסמא והיסט [היינו] משא כדאמר בהעור והרוטב (חולין דף קכד:) אטו נושא לאו היסט הוא משמע ע"ג אבן מסמא שהכלים ע"ג האבן דלא שייך כלל למשכב ומושב ועוד דמדרס כלי חרס טהור וי"ל דהא דמרבה בת"כ אבן מסמא מטעם משכב ומושב היינו כשהזב ע"ג האבן והכלים תחתיה אבל כשיד הטהור או רגלו תחת האבן הוי מטעם משא שהטהור נושא את הטמא או כשאצבעו של זב תחת האבן והכלים עליה טמא מטעם היסט דהיינו משא הזב והיינו היסיט הזב ע"ג אבן מסמא דתוספתא ול"ת בריש דם הנדה (נדה דף נד:) דממעט דם הנדה ממשכב ומושב מהיא יושבת מאי פריך תו אי מה היא מטמאה באבן מסמא אף מדוה נמי מטמאה באבן מסמא כיון דכבר מיעט מאשר היא יושבת מדוה ממשכב ומושב היכי סלקא דעתך תו למימר דמטמא באבן מסמא ואור"י דאבן מסמא נפקא לה משום דרשה דלא מטמא אלא אוכלין ומשקין להכי איצטריך התם למעוטי מדוה אף מאבן מסמא שהיא טומאה קלה: **ורבנן** סברי כשרץ כו'. וא"ת אמאי איצטריך שרץ למעוטי אבן מסמא תיפוק ליה מדאיתקש למת (לקמן דף פג:) וי"ל דכיון דגלי לן קרא דנכרינהו מינך כזר דאית לן לאקשויי לנדה לחומרא לא הוה ממעטי ממת אבן מסמא בע"ז כיון דאיצטריך היקישא דמת לשיעור כזית א"כ לכדאמר בפרק נגמר הדין (סנהדרין דף מז:) מה ע"ז במחובר לא מיתסרא אף קבר במחובר לא מיתסר: **ולרבי** עקיבא למאי הלכתא איתקש לשרץ כו'. תימה לר"י מאי קמיבעיא ליה הא איצטריך לאפוקי שלא יטמא באהל המת דמנדה דילמא לא ילפינן שום קולא דהא בעי רב חמא בר גוריא בסמוך אי ישנה לאברים אע"ג דנדה אינה לאברים ויש לומר דלענין דליכא בע"ז חומרא דמת שפיר ילפינן מנדה ואע"ג דהיקישא דנדה לחומרא קולא נמי אית לן למילף והא דמספקא ליה לענין אברים משום דלא דמי דאברי נדה אין אדם יכול להחזירם, ואברי ע"ז מיהא אומן יכול להחזירם א"כ הא דקאמר למאי הלכתא וכן הא דקא משני למשמשין היינו את"ל דילפינן קולא מנדה: **למשמשיה**. פירש בקונטרס שאין כלים המשמשין לע"ז מטמאין לא במשא ולא באבן מסמא משמע דאי לאו דאיתקש לשרץ הוו מטמו כע"ז באבן מסמא ותימה דלרבנן דהיקישא דשרץ לא אתא למשמשיה מנלן דמשמשין לא מטמו במשא כמו ע"ז עצמה דלקמן קאמר רב אשי אליבא דרבה משמשין בין הן שהסיטו אחרים בין אחרים שהסיטו אותן טהורין ונראה לר"י דאי לאו דאיתקש משמשין לשרץ לא הוה מטמינן להו כלל ורבנן דמטמו למשמשיה מדכתיב שקץ תשקצנו כי חרם הוא משמע כל דבר שהוא חרם פירש שאסור בהנאה הוי כשרץ ומשמשין אסור בהנאה ובזה לא יתיישב פי' הקונטרס דמכי חרם הוא לא משמע למעוטי משמשין דלא מטמו במשא דאין שום יתור לכך אבל הא דמשמשיה טמא משתמע שפיר: **ולוקשה** רחמנא לנבלה. אמאי דהוקשה למת ליכא למיפרך דלוקש לנבלה דהא איצטריך למת לכדדרשינן בנגמר הדין ובקונט' פי' דהכי פריך ולוקשה לנבלה משום דאז לא הוה צריך לאקושה לשרץ: **ורבי** אלעזר אמר כו'. פי' רבינו שמואל דבמילתיה דר' אלעזר ל"ג ור"ע למאי הלכתא איתקש לשרץ למשמשיה דהא איצטריך למעוטה מאבן מסמא כדאמר דכ"ע לא פליגי דלא מטמא באבן מסמא דהא איתקש לשרץ ויש ספרים דל"ג דהא איתקש לשרץ ולפי זה מצינן למימר דטעמא דר' אלעזר דכ"ע לא פליגי דלא מטמא באבן מסמא לאו משום דאיתקש לשרץ אלא בלא שום יתור לא מחמרינן כולי האי לטמאות באבן מסמא ולפי זה גרסי' שפיר ור"ע למאי הלכתא כו' והא דפריך בתר הכי ולוקשה רחמנא לנבלה לא פריך לוקשה לנבלה ותו לא צריך לאקושה לשרץ דהשתא נמי לא צריך לאקושי משום הכי לשרץ אלא הכי פריך דהוה ליה טפי לאקושה לנבלה דדמיא ממש לנבלה לנדה לא דמיא דנדה מטמאה באבן מסמא משא"כ בע"ז:

מיתיבי

דאמר קרא ל"ל נכרינהו כצ"ל רש"ל ומ"כ דלפני תוס' לא היה כתוב האי מימרא דרבה ולכך לא פרשי' תוס' לעיל ואמר רבה

דלא מטמאה דהא איתקש לשרץ כי פליגי כצ"ל רש"ל ועי' רש"י ותוספות ד"ה ור"א

שצריכה שימה והשתא א"ש הא דמייתי בפרק בתרא דנדה והיתית אבן כו'

על פום גובא שצריכה שימה ואתוי אך קשה כצ"ל רש"ל

רבינו חננאל

ראשונה אליבא דר"ע ושארא כולהו לדברי הכל ובהא איפליגו רבה ור' אלעזר אליבא דר"ע ורבנן. רבה סבר דלרבנן לא מסמיא ע"ז באבן מסמא. ופי' אבן מסמא כגון *) אבן (שומא) [שומה] על מושב ועל האבן ע"ז וניטלה ע"ז וניטלה האבן. ובא אדם וישב על אותו מושב והאי היא דכתיב והיושב על הכלי אשר ישב עליו הזב. ותני עלה אפי' ישב על עשרה מצעות זה ע"ג זה אפילו ע"ג אבן מסמא. דאע"ג דהא בזב אמורה נדה נמי ומושב נדה מסמא באבן מסמא. דאמר רבה דסבר ר' עקיבא ע"ז כנדה. אבל לענין משא סבר רבה דאפילו רבנן מודו שהיא מסמאה במשא. ור' אלעזר סבר באבן מסמא כולי עלמא לא פליגי שאין ע"ז מסמא ובמשא הוא

רב נסים גאון

פ"ט כי פליגי באבן מסמא כו'. *)עיקר דילה בתורת כהנים והיושב על הכלי אשר ישב עליו הזב אין לי אלא בזמן שהוא יושב עליו ונוגע בו מנין לעשרה מושבות זה על גבי זה ואפילו על גבי אבן מסמא ת"ל והיושב וכיוצא בו אמרו בנדה ובועלה יכול היא והוא לא יטמאו טומאה חמורה כו' ומנין לי' מושבות זה על גבי זה ואפילו על אבן מסמא ת"ל וכל המשכב ובמסכת נדה בפרק דם הנדה (דף נה) אמרו או מה היא מסמאה באבן מסמא אף דמה נמי מסמא באבן מסמא אמר קרא (ויקרא טו) אתם אתם מיעוטא הוא ובתחלת תוספתא טהרות אמרו זוב הזב ורוקו ושכבת זרעו ומימי רגליו ורביעית מן המת ודם נדה כיוצא במרכב חומר במרכב מבהן וחומר בהן מבמרכב שהן שוה מגען למשאן לטמא אדם ולטמא בגדים מה שאין במרכב חומר במרכב שהמרכב תחת אבן מסמא מה שאין כן בהן ובמשנה נמי בתחילת הסדר יש כזה הענין ובפרק תינוקת (דף סט) שנינו הזב והנדה והזבה והיולדת והמצורע שמתו מסמאין במשא עד שימוק הבשר ובתלמוד אמרו מאי במשא ממש אטו כל מת מי לא מסמא במשא אלא מה במשא באבן מסמא דכתיב (דניאל ו) והיתית אבן חדא ושמת על פום גובא. מה שרץ לא מסמא באבן מסמא אף ע"ז לא מסמא באבן מסמא ודע שהשרץ הזכיר בו הכתוב נגיעה כדכתיב (ויקרא יא) ונוגע בנבלתם ומפרשי ליה רבנן במגע הן מסמאין ואינן מסמאין במשא והואיל ואינו מסמא אלא בנגיעה בלבד כמו כן אינו מסמא על גבי אבן מסמא שהרי לא נגע:

*) עיין ערוך ערך אבן מסמא.

[82*b*] If it belongs to him and to the idol, it is judged as half and half.[7] The stones, timber and earth thereof defile like a [dead] creeping thing [*sherez*], for it is said, *Thou shalt treat it altogether as a creeping thing.*[8] R. Akiba said: [They defile] like a *niddah*, because it is said, '*Thou shalt cast them away* [tizrem] *as a menstruous thing*': just as a *niddah* defiles by carriage, so does an idol defile by carriage. Rabbah observed, *Tizrem*, mentioned in the verse, means 'thou shalt alienate them from thee as a *zar* [stranger].' '*Thou shalt say unto it, Get thee hence*', but thou shalt not say unto
a it, Enter hither.[1]

Rabbah also observed: As for carriage, all agree that it defiles thereby, since it is assimilated to *niddah*. They differ in respect to a stone that closes a cavity:[2] R. Akiba holds, It is like a *niddah*: just as a *niddah* defiles through a cavity-closing stone, so does an idol defile through a cavity-closing stone; while the Rabbis maintain, It is like a creeping thing [*sherez*]: just as a *sherez* does not defile through a cavity-closing stone, so does an idol not defile through a cavity-closing stone.

Now, according to R. Akiba, in respect of which law is it likened to a *sherez*?[3]—In respect of its service utensils.[4] And according to the Rabbis, in respect of which law is it likened to *niddah*?—In respect of carriage. Then let it be likened to *nebelah*?[5]—That indeed is so, but [the analogy with *niddah* teaches:] just as a *niddah* is not [a source of contamination] through her [separate] limbs,[6] so is an idol not [a source of contamination] through its limbs. Then when R. Ḥama b. Guria asked: 'Does the law of an idol operate in respect of its limbs or not?'—solve it for him from this that according to the Rabbis it does not operate in respect of its limbs?—R. Ḥama b. Guria asked it on R. Akiba's view.

But R. Eleazar maintained: In respect of a cavity-closing stone all agree that it does not defile thereby, since it is likened to a *sherez*;[7] they differ only in respect of carriage. R. Akiba holds, It is like a *niddah*: just as a *niddah* defiles through carriage, so does an idol defile through carriage. While the Rabbis argue. It is like a *sherez*: just as a *sherez* does not defile through carriage, so does an idol not defile through carriage. Now, according to R. Akiba, in respect of what law is it likened to a *sherez*?—In respect of its service utensils. And according to the Rabbis, in respect of what law is it likened to a *niddah*?—Just as a *niddah* is not [a source of contamination] through her [separate] limbs, so is an idol not [a source of contamination] through its limbs.

(7) E.g., if the wall is two cubits thick, one cubit only is accounted as his portion, and he must retreat another three cubits. (8) Deut. VIII, 26. *Shakkez teshakkezenu* fr. *shekez*, something loathsome, which is connected with *sherez* (E.V.: *thou shalt utterly detest it*). A *sherez* defiles by its touch, but not when it is merely carried; but v. discussion *infra*.

a (1) I.e., one must absolutely reject it (Tosaf. s.v. אמר). (2) Rashi: a stone resting upon laths, and under it lie utensils. Tosaf.: a stone so heavy that when a *niddah* sits upon it her additional weight makes no difference to the utensils upon which it rests. According to both definitions, the question is whether these utensils are defiled when an idol is placed upon the stone. (3) As it is in the verse, v. *supra* n. d8. (4) The utensils used in an idol's service do not defile through carriage or through a cavity-closing stone. (5) V. Glos. This analogy would give the exact law, whereas the analogy with *niddah* has to be qualified by a further analogy with *sherez*. (6) If a limb e.g., an arm, is cut off from a *niddah*, it defiles as the severed limb of a living human being in general, but not as *niddah*. The practical difference is that it does not defile through a cavity-closing stone. (7) This is the text as emended by Rashal.

[83a] Now according to R. Akiba, in respect of what law is it likened to a *niddah?* [only] in respect of carriage! Then let it be likened to *nebelah?*—That indeed is so, but [the analogy with *niddah*, rather, teaches:] just as *niddah* is not [a source of contamination] through her [separate] limbs, so is an idol not [a source of contamination] through its limbs. Then when R. Ḥama b. Guria asked: 'Does the law of an idol operate in respect of its limbs or not?'—solve it for him from this, according to both the Rabbis and R. Akiba, that it does not operate in respect of its limbs?—R. Ḥama b. Guria learns this as Rabbah, and asked it on R. Akiba's view.

An objection is raised: An idol is like a [creeping thing] *sherez*, and its service utensils are like a *sherez*; R. Akiba maintained: An idol is like a *niddah*, and its service utensils are like a *sherez*. Now, according to R. Eleazar, it is well; but on Rabbah's view, it is a difficulty?—Rabbah answers you: Is it stronger than the Mishnah, which states, 'The stones, timber and earth thereof defile like a *sherez*,' and we explained, What is meant by 'like a *sherez*?' That it does not defile through a cavity-closing stone: here too it means that it does not defile through a cavity-closing stone.

An objection is raised: A heathen man or woman, an idol and its service utensils, they themselves [defile] but not their motion [*hesset*];[1] R. Akiba maintained: They and their *hesset*. Now, as for R. Eleazar, it is well;[1] but on Rabbah's view it is a difficulty?—Rabbah answers you: And [even] on your view, [can you say of] a heathen man and woman too, they but not their motion [*hesset*],—surely it was taught: *Speak unto the children of Israel* [. . . *when any man hath an issue out of his flesh*, etc.]:[2] the children of Israel defile through gonorrhoea, but heathens do not defile through gonorrhoea, but they [the Rabbis] decreed concerning them that they rank as *zabin* in all respects.[3] But Rabbah answers [the difficulty] according to his view, [Thus:] A heathen man or woman: they themselves, their motion [*hesset*], and their cavity-closing stone [all defile]; an idol: it and its motion [*hesset*], but not its cavity-closing stone; R. Akiba maintains: An idol: it, its *hesset* and its cavity-closing stone [defile]. Whilst R. Eleazar interprets it in accordance with his view: A heathen man or woman: they themselves, their motion [*hesset*], and their cavity-closing stone [defile]; an idol: it, but not its motion [*hesset*]. Whilst R. Akiba maintains: An idol: it and its motion [defile].[4]

R. Ashi objected thereto: [If so,] what is [the meaning of] 'they themselves'?[5]—Rather said R. Ashi: This is the meaning: In the case of a heathen man or woman, whether they move others[6] or others move them,[7] [these others] are unclean.[8] If an idol moves others, they are clean;[9] if others move it,[10] they are unclean. [As for] its service utensils, whether they move others or others move them, [these others] are clean. R. Akiba maintained: In the case of a heathen man or woman and an idol, whether they move others or others move them, [these others] are unclean; as for its service utensils, whether they move others or others move them, they are clean.

[In the case of] an idol, as for others moving it, that is well, [for] it is possible; but how is it conceivable for it to move others?—Said Rami son of R. Yeba, Even as we learnt: If a *zab* is on one pan of the scales, and foodstuffs or drinks are in the other pan

(1) *Hesset* is the technical term for uncleanness induced by the motion or shaking caused by a gonorrhoeist (*zab*). E.g., if he moves a bench upon which a clean person is sitting, even without actually touching it, the latter becomes unclean. The Rabbis enacted that heathens defile in the same way as a *zab*. But it is now assumed that *hesset* is used here in the sense that the heathen, etc. are moved by the clean person, which is another expression for their being carried, and it is taught that these do not defile by carriage.

(1) That the first view which is that of the Rabbis, is that they do not defile through carriage. (2) Lev. XV, 2. This introduces the laws of a *zab*. (3) Which includes defilement through carriage. (4) On both interpretations the Baraitha must be emended. (5) If '*hesset*' means 'carriage' (v. *supra* n. a1), what is meant by 'they'? For it cannot mean that they are unclean in themselves, since that is obvious from the fact that we debate whether even their carriage defiles. (6) E.g., by moving or weighing down the bench upon which they are sitting. (7) Which is tantamount to carrying them. (8) Thus he translates: 'they themselves'—i.e., when they are moved by others, and their '*hesset*'—i.e., when they move others. This gives *hesset* its usual connotation. (9) This agrees with Rabbah in accordance with whom R. Ashi explains this Baraitha. It can be explained on similar lines according to R. Eleazar too. (10) I.e., carriage.

ורבי עקיבא למאי הלכתא איתקש לנדה למשא לוקשיה לנבלה אין הכי נמי אלא מה נדה אינה לאברין אף ע"ז אינה לאברין אלא הא דבעי רב חמא בר גוריא ע"ז ישנה לאברים או אינה לאברים תיפשוט ליה מהא בין לרבנן בין לרבי עקיבא דאינה לאברים רב חמא בר גוריא כרבה מתני ובעי לה אליבא דרבי עקיבא מיתיבי ע"ז כשרץ *ומשמשיה כשרץ רבי עקיבא אומר ע"ז כנדה ומשמשיה כשרץ בשלמא לרבי אלעזר ניחא אלא לרבה קשיא °אמר לך רבה מי אלימא ממתני' דקתני עציו ואבניו ועפריו מטמאין כשרץ ואוקימנא מאי כשרץ דלא מטמא באבן מסמא ה"נ דלא מטמא באבן מסמא מיתיבי נכרי ונכרית ע"ז ומשמשיה הן ולא היסטן רבי עקיבא אומר הן והיסטן בשלמא לרבי אלעזר ניחא אלא לרבה קשיא אמר לך רבה וליטעמיך נכרי ונכרית נמי הן ולא היסטן *והתניא °דבר אל בני ישראל וגו' בני ישראל מטמאין בזיבה *ואין נכרים מטמאין בזיבה אבל גזרו עליהן שיהו כזבין לכל דבריהן אלא רבה מתרץ לטעמיה נכרי ונכרית הן והיסטן ואבן מסמא שלהן ע"ז היא והיסטה אבל לא אבן מסמא שלה רבי עקיבא אומר ע"ז היא והיסטה ואבן מסמא שלה ורבי אלעזר מתרץ לטעמיה נכרי ונכרית הן והיסטן ואבן מסמא שלהן ע"ז היא ולא היסטה ורבי עקיבא אומר ע"ז היא והיסטה מתקיף לה רב אשי מאי הן אלא אמר רב אשי הכי קאמר נכרי ונכרית בין הן שהסיטו את אחרים ובין אחרים שהסיטו אותן טמאים ע"ז שהסיטה אחרים טהורין אחרים שהסיטו אותה טמאים משמשיה בין הן שהסיטו את אחרים ובין אחרים שהסיטו אותן טהורים רבי עקיבא אומר נכרי ונכרית וע"ז בין הן שהסיטו את אחרים ובין אחרים שהסיטו אותן טמאים משמשיה בין הן שהסיטו אחרים ובין אחרים שהסיטו אותן טהורין ע"ז בשלמא אחרים שהסיטו אותה משכחת לה אלא היא שהסיטה את אחרים היכי משכחת לה אמר רמי בריה דרב ייבא *כדתנן *הזב בכף מאזנים ואוכלין ומשקין בכף שנייה כרע הזב טמאין כרעו

ויקרא טו

תורה אור

ור' עקיבא למאי הלכתא איתקש לנדה למשא · לחודה לוקשה לנבלה: כרבה מתני לה. דאמר לעיל דר"ע לאבן מסמא נמי אקשה לנדה ולא מצי לאקושה לנבלה: ובעי לה אליבא דר' עקיבא. מי מקיש נמי לענין נדה דאינה לאברים או לא: ניחא. דקתני לרבנן כשרץ אלמא לא מטמיא במשא ממתני'. דמסכת ע"ז אבניו ועציו כו': ה"ג נכרי ונכרית וע"ז ומשמשיה כו'. ול"ג מגע נכרי ונכרית שגזרו חכמים עליהן טומאת זבין: הן ולא היסטן. קס"ד היסטן משמע שהוסטו דהיינו משא ולא כשאר היסיטות שבהש"ס דמשמעו שהטמא הסיט האחרים: בשלמא לר"א ניחא. דקתני ולא היסטן דמשמע דלא מטמא במשא ולקמן פריך מאי הן אי הן טמאין קאמר פשיטא השתא היסטן טמא הס מיבעיא הכי איבעי ליה למתני מגען ולא היסטן: לכל דבריהם(א). אלמא מטמאו במשא דאי לא מטמאו אלא במגע מאי כזבין לימא כטמאי מתים: אלא. הא משבשתא היא ובעי לתרולי ורבה מתרץ לטעמיה ורבי אלעזר לטעמיה: ואבן מסמא שלהן גרסי' גבי נכרי ונכרית בין בתרלתא דרבה בין בדר' אלעזר והכי אמרינן בפרק בתרא דמסכת נדה (דף סט:) נכרי ונכרית מטמאין באבן מסמא: ר' אלעזר מתרץ לטעמיה כו' ע"ז היא ולא היסטה. ולא משאה שאינה מטמאה במשא: מתקיף לה רב אשי מאי הן. אי רבה ורבי אלעזר היסט דברייתא לשון משא משמע להו שהסיטו אחרים דהיינו משא מאי הן והיסטן הן ולא היסטן דקתני בין לר' עקיבא בין לרבנן אי למימרא דהן עלמן טמאים פשיטא דאי טהורים הם היסט מנא להו הכי איבעיא לאיפלוגי ע"ז אין היסטה טמא ר' עקיבא אומר היסטה טמא: אלא אמר רב אשי הכי קאמר נכרי ונכרית בין הן שהסיטו אחרים. והיינו היסטן דקתני בה ככל היסט שבמשנה: בין אחרים שהסיטו אותן. דהיינו משא וזהו הן דקתני בברייתא והכי משמע הן והיסטן דליסנא דברייתא משא שהזכירו חכמים בנכרי ונכרית בין הן שהוסטו על ידי אדם בין היסטן כלומר מה שהסיטו הן טמאין דתורת זבין עליהם דזב שהוסט ע"י אדם או הסיט את האדם ואת כל דבר טמאוהו דתנן (זבין פ"ה משנה ב) כל הנישא על גבי זב טמא והיינו היסט וילפינן לה במסכת נדה (ד' לג·) מוכל הנוגע בכל אשר יהיה תחתיו ומוקמי' לקרא התם ע"כ דה"ק וכל הנוגע בכל אשר יהיה הזב תחתיו דהיינו נישא על גבי הזב: ע"ז שהסיטה את אחרים טהורים. דאיתקש לשרץ להכי שלא תטמא לא בהיסט ולא באבן מסמא ואליבא דרבה קמתרץ לה רב אשי: אחרים שהסיטוה טמאים. דהיינו משא ומודו רבנן דמטמאה במשא דאיתקש לנדה: רבי עקיבא אומר. ע"ז נמי כנכרי ונכרית בין שהסיטה בין שהוסטה וה"ה לאבן מסמא דאיתקש לנדה והכי תני רב אשי לברייתא אליבא דרבה נכרי ונכרית הן המשא שלהן והיסטן ע"ז היא המשא שלה ולא היסטה משמשיה לא הן ולא היסטן ר' עקיבא אומר נכרי ונכרית ע"ז הן והיסטן משמשיה לא הן ולא היסטן וממילא לר' אלעזר מתרץ לה רב אשי הכי נכרי ונכרית הן והיסטן ע"ז ומשמשיה לא הן ולא היסטן ר' עקיבא אומר נכרי ונכרית הן והיסטן ע"ז היא ולא היסטה דבמשא מטמיא ולא באבן מסמא דהוא דומיא דהיסט משמשין לא הן ולא היסטן כך נראה לי סוגיא זו ולא פירשו רבותינו כן והם פירשו מאי הן דאתקפתא דרב אשי אדרבי עקיבא קאי ולא קשיא ליה אלא דתני לה בלשון רבים והכי קשיא ליה כיון דר"ע אע"ז לחודה קאי אמאי תנא הן והיסטה היא והיסטה איבעיא ליה למיתני ולא נהירא לי דקשיא לי טובא בגוה חדא דלא אתקפתא היא דכיון דאמרן דמתני' מחסרתא היא ואוספי מוספינן עלה שפיר מיתני בה [הן] לר"ע בין לרבה דקאמר ר"ע אכולהו קאי וקאמר *הן והיסטן לר' אלעזר נמי קאי אכולהו דהכי קאמר ר' עקיבא ע"ז לענין היסט דהיינו משא כנכרי ונכרית וכולן הן והיסטן והכי קתני רבי עקיבא אומר נכרי ונכרית ע"ז הן והיסטן ועוד מ"ש דלא מיפלגי בין הסיטו להוסטו אלא בתרלתא דרב אשי ומאי דוחקיה לפלוגי בהו אי לאו דהן דברייתא משמע ליה שהוסטו והיסטן משמע ליה שהסיטו ועוד דסוף סוף בתירולא דרב אשי לא מיתרלא אתקפתיה דאי הן משום מגע משמשיה קאמר [לא] הן ולא היסטן הוא ואילו רבי עקיבא הן והיסטן קאמר ואי אנכרי ונכרית הכא נמי ה"מ לתרולי כלישנא קמא ומאי אתקפתיה: היכי משכחת לה. שהאבן יסיט אדם או חפץ אחר: כרע הזב טמאין. שהרי הסיטן זב והיסטו של זב כי האי גוונא כתיב בין בכלים בין באדם בין באוכלין ומשקין בכלים כתיב וכלי חרש אשר יגע בו הזב ותניא בת"כ יכול יטמאנו מאחוריו נאמר כאן בו ונאמר להלן אשר תבושל בו מה להלן מאוירו אף כאן מאוירו א"כ למה נאמר אשר יגע בו פשיטא מי גרע משאר טומאות שמטמאין כלי חרס מאוירן כיון דכתיב גבי שרצים ל"ל למכתבי' הכא אלא להביא מגעו שהוא ככולו ואפי' מאחוריו ואיזהו זה היסטו וגבי אדם נמי וכל אשר יגע בו הזב ואי משום מגע הא כתיב נוגע בבשר הזב אלא להביא מגעו שהוא ככולו ואפי' מאחוריו ואיזה זה היסטו וגבי אוכלין ומשקין תנא וכל כלי עץ ישטף במים אמר ר' שמעון ומה בא זה ללמדנו אם ללמד שיטמא הזב כלי שטף במגע והלא כבר נאמר הנוגע בבשר הזב יכבס בגדיו אם הנוגע בו יכבס בגדיו שהן כלי שטף במגע הוא עצמו לא יטמא כלי שטף במגע אלא למה נאמר וכל כלי עץ וגו' להביא אוכלין ומשקין וכלים הנישאין ע"ג הזב דבסיפיה דקרא דאשר יגע בו הזב כתיב דאוקמינן דמשתעי בהיסט והיינו דתנן כל הנישא על גבי הזב טמא:

כרעו

מיתיבי ע"ז כשרץ ומשמשיה כשרץ. •מברייתא אלים ליה למיפרך ממתני' משום דקתני בה משמשיה משמע דע"ז דומיא דמשמשיה דלא מטמו במשא: **ומשמשיה** בין הן שהסיטו כו'. בשנוייא קמא לא מדכר משמשיה משום דהוי בכלל הן ולא היסטן דברייתא אבל רב אשי הולרך לפרש דמשמשיה לא הן ולא היסטן ולא הוי בכלל הא דקתני בברייתא הן ולא היסטן:

ורבי עקיבא. הרב פור"ת לא גרים משמשיה במילתיה דר"ע דלא פליג במשמשיה ארבנן:

הזב בכף מאזנים כו'. במס' זבים (פ"ד משנה ה) גרסינן הזב בכף מאזנים ומשכב ומושב בכף שנייה כרע הזב טהורין פי' ממדרס ומ"מ טמאין כדין היסט הזב כרעו הן טמאים פי' ממדרס כיון שהזב למעלה הרי נשען עליהן וגירסת הקונט' מיושב יותר אך לא נמצא כן אם לא שברייתא היא בשום מקום:

ע"ז

עין משפט נר מצוה

ה א מיי' פ"ו מהלכות שאר אבות הטומאות הלכה ה:

ו ב מיי' פ"ח מהלכות משכב ומושב הלכה ו סמג עשין רמג:

רבינו חננאל

דפליגי. רבנן סברי לא מטמאה במשא. ור"ע סבר מטמאה במשא. והלכה כרבנן ואליבא דר' אלעזר דרבא משני בשינוייא דחיקי. וטומאת ע"ז דרבנן היא. ולענין הא דמסקינן הין אליבא [דרבא] בין אליבא דר' אלעזר. דלר' עקיבא האי הא איתקש ע"ז לשקץ דכתיב שקץ תשקצנו משום משמשית קשיא למקצת תלמידים כי מכדי משמשי ע"ז אפי' אליבא דר' עקיבא בשקץ היכי קתני לענין בית ע"ז אבניו ועציו ועפריו מטמאין כשרץ. ר"ע אומר כנדה. דאהדרינן דהאי בית היא גופיה ע"ז דתנן בתרה (כתריא) [במשנה] ג' בתים הן. בית שבנה מתחלה לע"ז הרי זה אסור. ואמרינן עלה אמר רב המשתחוה לבית לא אסרו ומותבינן לרבה דאמר במשא כולי עלמא לא פליגי דאה רבנן מודו [דמטמא] קשיא ע"ז כשרץ. ודחי *) (ומותבינן נמי מגע נכרי ונכרית ע"ז ומשמשיה הן [ולא היסטן] · ופרקינן דאמר לרבה וליטעמיך דקאמ' נכרי ונכרי' ולא היסטן ר"ע אומר הן והיסטן. ופי' היסט נדנוד. שאם אמרה הא ברייתא אין נכרי ונכרית נטל אדם קנה או קיסם ונדנד את הבגד אומרין שהסיטן. ומי מטמאין בהיסט הלא גזרה היא שנשא כלום כבר הסיטן. ויש מסים שלא במשא. וכוון עליהן שיהו כזבין מטמאין לכל. שמן המשנה הזו ע"ז מטמא במגע ואין מטמא בהיסט דבריהן והרי הזב מטמא בהיסט הרי נוגע באמת שאינה מטמאה במשא כמו מגע נכרי אלא רבה מפרש טעמיה דרבי אלעזר דנכרי ונכרי' כי הנושאה מסיטה לפי שהוא מתנד' מתרץ לטעמיה. רבה מוקים לה בכתו כדפרשינן לעילא. ור"ע אומר הן והיסטן [ואבן מסמא שלהן ופלינתא] באבן מסמא אבל לענין כל המסיט ע"ז טמא והנושא בכלל מסיט. בשלמא ע"ז ומסלק היסט מן פלוגתא ולר' אלעזר במשא פליגי ניחא הא ברייתא אלא דר' אלעזר מסלק פלוגתא מן נכרי ונכרית לענין בסים. ומוקי לה לפלוגתא לענין ע"ז ומשמשיה בלחוד). מתקיף לה רב אשי מאי הן דפשטא דברייתא הן ולא היסטן ר' עקיבא אומר הן והיסטן בלשון רבים על מגע נכרי ונכרית וע"ז. והאי תירוצא דאמרינן לרבה היא ולא אבן מסמא. ר"ע אומר היא ואבן מסמא. לית בה לענין ע"ז פלוגתא בהסיט כל עיקר. וקאי מפיק לה לברייתא מן פשטא כלל. אבל ר' אלעזר קא מתרץ הן אבל לא הסיטן לרבנן ולר' עקיבא הן והסיטן על ע"ז ומפיק להו נכרי ונכרית בראיה ברורה דהא אימורה כי היכין דאף רבה מפקינן שהרי גזרו עליהן שהן כזבין לכל דבריהן. והא גזירה לענין תרומה ששורפין אותה על מגע גוי והסיטן כדמפרש בתורת כהנים. אבל חולין לא גזרו בהן טומאת נכרי. והכין לישנא דגמרא איצטרכינן למיכתבא משום דמשמש ואית בה חילופי רבה מתרץ לטעמיה נכרי ונכרית הן והיסטן ואבן מסמא שלהן ע"ז היא והיסטה אבל לא אבן מסמא שלה. ר"ע אומר היא ואבן מסמא שלהם ר' אלעזר מתרץ לטעמיה נכרי ונכרית הן והיסטן אבל לא אבן מסמא שלהן. ע"ז היא אבל לא היסטה. ר' עקיבא אומר ע"ז היא והיסטה ומשמשיה הן ולא היסטן. מתקיף לה רב אשי מאי הן והא אתקפתא דרב אשי על מימרא דרבה היא בלחוד. דאילו ר' אלעזר הא קא מתרץ אבל לא היסטן. ור' עקיבא אומר הן והיסטן לענין ע"ז וליכא אתקפתא עליה. ומשום הכין מתרץ רב אשי אליבא דרבה ולא קא מתרץ אליבא דר' אלעזר ולא מכלל דסבר לה כרבה ולא סבר לה כר' אלעזר אלא משום דתרצתא דר' אלעזר תרצא וסומא. ודרבה צריכה עדיין תרצתא. ולא שויא רב אשי תיובתא. אלא תריץ לה תירוצא דחיקא. ולעולם אימא לך דכר' אלעזר סבירא ליה והכין קא מתרץ רב אשי אליבא דרבה האי דקאמרו מאי הן אבל לא היסטן. ר' עקיבא אומר הן והיסטן דאפלגו לענין ע"ז אמר לך רבה הכי קאמר ע"ז ומשמשיה הן אבל לא היסטן שהיסטו הן את אחרים. ר"ע אומר הן והיסטן. אפי' שהיסטו הן את אחרים. ולפום הכין שאילנן. ע"ז שמסיטה היא את אחרים היכי משכחת לה. ופריש רמי בר ייבא כגון שהיתה היא בכף מאזנים ואחרים בכף מאזנים וכרעה ע"ז ותלה נחתא משום יוקרא מכחת שכרעת

*) דברי רבינו אלו מבוללי הכנה ועיין בסוף המסכת.

נדה לד.

[עי' תוס' ב"ב ... ד"ה ונכרי]

הגהות הב"ח

(א) רש"י ד"ה לכל דבריהם. נ"ב ע"ל דף פד ע"ב:

[לפמ"ש תוס' ד"ה הזב כו' אם לא שברייתי' היא כו' צ"ל כדתניא]

הן והיסטן ואבן מסמא שלהן כצ"ל

גליון הש"ס

גמ' אמר לך רבה מי אלימא ממתני'. לעיל ד' יב ע"א עירובין דף סט ע"ב: תוס' ד"ה מיתיבי וכו' מברייתא אלים ליה. עי' לעיל דף יב ע"א תוס' ד"ה מי אלימא:

ז א מיי' פ"ח מהלכות משכב ומושב הלכה א ב:

ח ב מיי' פ"ו מהלכות שאר אבות הטומאות הלכה ד:

ט ג שם הלכה ג ה:

י ד שם הלכה א:

יא ה ו ז מיי' פרק י"ח מהלכות כלים הל"ט:

יב ח מיי' פ"ג מהלכות ת"ת הלכה יב טוש"ע יו"ד סימן רמו סעיף כה:

[לעיל פג:]

כרעו הן טהורין כמאן אזלא הא דתניא "כל הטמאות המסיטות טהורות חוץ מהיסטו של זב *שלא מצינו לו חבר בכל התורה כולה לימא דלא כרבי עקיבא דאי כרבי עקיבא איכא נמי ע"ז אפילו תימא ר' עקיבא תנא זב וכל דדמי ליה *בעי רב חמא בר גוריא ע"ז ישנה לאברים או אינה לאברים היכא דהדיוט יכול להחזירה לא תיבעי לך דכמאן דמחברת דמי כי תיבעי לך היכא דאין הדיוט יכול להחזירה מאי כיון דאין הדיוט יכול להחזירה כמאן דמתברא דמי או דילמא הא לא מחסרה ואיכא דבעי לה להך גיסא היכא דאין הדיוט יכול להחזירה לא תיבעי לך דכמאן דמתברא דמי כי תבעי לך היכא דהדיוט יכול להחזירה מאי כיון דהדיוט יכול להחזירה כמאן דמחברא דמי או דילמא "השתא מיהא קשלפה ושריא תיקו בעי רב אחדבוי בר אמי ע"ז פחותה מכזית מהו מתקיף לה רב יוסף למאי אילימא לענין איסורא לא יהא אלא זבוב בעל עקרון דתניא °וישימו (*להן) בעל ברית לאלהים זה זבוב בעל עקרון *מלמד שכל אחד ואחד עשה דמות יראתו ומניחה בתוך כיסו כיון שזוכרה מוציאה מתוך כיסו ומחבקה ומנשקה אלא לענין טומאה מאי כיון דאיתקיש לשרץ מה שרץ בכעדשה אף ע"ז נמי בכעדשה או דילמא הא איתקיש למת מה מת בכזית אף ע"ז בכזית אמר רב אויא ואיתימא רבה בר עולא ת"ש דתניא "ע"ז פחותה מכזית אין בה טומאה כל עיקר שנאמר °וישלך את עפרה (אל) קבר בני העם מה מת בכזית אף ע"ז בכזית ורבנן למאי הלכתא איתקש לשרץ דלא מטמא במשא לנדה דאינה לאברין למת דלא מטמא בכעדשה אימא לחומרא למאי הלכתא אקשה רחמנא לשרץ לטמויי בכעדשה לנדה לטמויי באבן מסמא אקשה רחמנא למת לטמויי באהל "טומאת עבודה זרה דרבנן היא וקולא וחומרא לקולא מקשינן לחומרא לא מקשינן:

מתני' "מנין לספינה שהיא טהורה שנאמר °דרך אניה בלב ים:

גמ' פשיטא אניה בלב ים היא הא קמ"ל כים מה ים טהור אף ספינה טהורה תניא חנניה אומר נלמדה משק *מה שק מיטלטל מלא וריקן אף כל מיטלטל מלא וריקן לאפוקי ספינה דאינה מיטלטלת מלא וריקן מאי בינייהו איכא בינייהו ספינה של חרס מאן דאמר אניה בלב ים "הא נמי בלב ים היא למ"ד כשק הנך (היא) דכתיבי גבי שק דאי מיטלטלת מלא וריקן אין אי לא לא "אבל ספינה של חרס אע"ג דאינה מיטלטלת מלא וריקן אי נמי ספינת הירדן למ"ד אניה בלב ים היא הא נמי אניה בלב ים היא למ"ד מיטלטלת מלא וריקן הא נמי מיטלטלת מלא וריקן דא"ר חנינא בן עקביא מפני מה אמרו ספינת הירדן טמאה מפני שטוענים אותה ביבשה ומורידין אותה למים א"ר יהודה אמר רב *לעולם אל ימנע אדם את עצמו מבית המדרש ואפי' שעה אחת שהרי כמה שנים נשנית משנה זו בבית המדרש ולא נתגלה טעמה עד שבא רבי חנינא בן עקביא ופירשה אמר רבי יונתן לעולם אל ימנע אדם את עצמו מבית המדרש ומדברי תורה ואפי' בשעת מיתה שנא' °זאת התורה אדם כי ימות באהל אפי' בשעת מיתה תהא עוסק בתורה *אמר ר"ל "אין דברי תורה מתקיימין אלא במי שממית עצמו עליה שנאמר זאת התורה אדם כי ימות באהל אמר רבא

ולחנניה

תורה אור: שופטים ח | מ"ב כג | משלי ל | במדבר יט

רש"י

כרעו הן. ונשאו הן את הזב: טהורין. דתנן כל שהזב נושא עליו טהור חוץ מן הראוי למשכב ומושב האדם אבל כל שאר כלים ואוכלים אין מיטמאין מחמת משכב ומושב כדתניא (לעיל דף נט.) מי שמיוחד לישיבה יצא זה שאומרים עמוד ונעשה מלאכתנו ולמהוי אפילו ראשון לטומאה מחמת משא הזב נמי לא °דכי כתיב משא הזב באדם כתיב והנושא אותם וגו' והא דאמר לעיל נכרי ונכרית וע"ז שהסיטום אחרים טמאים באדם קאמרינן: כל הטמאו' המסיטות. אחרים כגון בכף מאזנים או אדם טמא מת שהסיט את חברו טהורין: שלא מצינו לו. בשאר טומאות שבתורה אלא בזב: וכל דדמי ליה. דאתי מריבויא דזב וע"ז מנדה גמרי דהיינו זב: ישנה לאברים. כגון של חוליות ישנה לטומאתה אבר אבר או לא: דהדיוט יכול להחזירה. שאין צריך אומן לכך: פחותה מכזית. והיא שלמה: לענין איסור. ליאסר בהנאה: ומחבקה ומנשקה. וזהו לשון ברית אהבה וחבה אלמא אדוקים בה וע"ז היא: הא איתקש למת. כדלקמן *אל קבר בני העם: ורבנן למאי הלכתא כו'. אתקפתא היא לרבנן דאמרי אינה מטמאה במשא למאי הלכתא אמרו אליבייהו דאיתקש לנדה דאינה לאברים ולשרץ דלא מטמינן במשא למת דאינה מטמאה בכעדשה כולהו לקולא: אימא. כולהו לחומרא: דרבנן. דכל הנך היקשות דברי קבלה נינהו ואסמכתא בעלמא ושקץ תשקצנו לאו לשון שרץ ממש הוא אלא עיקר קרא לכנות לה שם לגנאי אתא:

מתני' שהיא טהורה. שאינה מקבלת טומאה: בלב ים. הרי היא כים:

גמ' פשיטא אניה בלב ים היא. לאו פירכא היא אלא פירוש למתני': נלמדה משק. שהרי כלי עץ היא והוקשה לשק לענין טומאה: אף כו'. וזו אינה מיטלטל' מלאה דגדולה היא: ספינה של חרס. דלא איתקש לשק: אי נמי ספינת הירדן. איכא בינייהו שהיא קטנה ומיטלטלת מלאה וריקנית לפי שהנהר קטן: הא נמי בלב ים. דים לאו דוקא וכל הנהרות נמי טהורין הן: נשנית משנה זו. של מסכת כלים דתני בה ספינת הירדן טמאה ולא נתגלה הטעם למה:

ולחנניה

תוספות

ע"ז ישנה לאיברים כו'. בשל חוליות מבעיא ליה אבל ע"ז שנשתברה פשיטא ליה דלא מטמאה ולא משום היקישא דנדה פשיטא ליה בנשתברה דדמיא לגמרי לנדה שאין אדם יכול להחזירה דא"כ אמאי קאמר לעיל דמבעיא ליה אליבא דר' עקיבא אליבא דרבנן נמי מלי למיבעי דהא דנפקא להו דע"ז אינה לאיברים מנדה הני מילי כשנשתברה לגמרי אלא ודאי בלא נדה פשיטא ליה דנשתברה טהורה: **כי** תבעי לך היכא דאין הדיוט כו'. לענין טומאה מבעיא ליה כדפי' הקונט' ולעיל נמי מייתי אפלוגתא דרבי עקיבא ורבנן אבל לענין איסורא דאורייתא לא שייך למילף מנדה ואע"ג דאסור בהנאה בטומאה דרבנן מיבעיא ליה אי פרקה אי לאו משמע דבהדיוט יכול להחזירה פשיטא דאסירה אפילו ללישנא בתרא מדבעי לענין טומאה בהדיוט יכול להחזירה דאי איסור הנאה דאורייתא שרי כ"ש דלא מטמא °וקשה לר"י דבפרק ג' דמסכת ע"ז (ד' מט:) פליגי רב ושמואל בע"ז שנשתברה מאליה דרב אמר צריכה לבטל כל קיסם וקיסם ושמואל אמר אין ע"ז צריכה לבטל אלא דרך גדילתה ובעי לאוקמא פלוגתייהו בשברי שברים ומסיק דבע"ז של חוליות עסקינן והדיוט יכול להחזירה קא מיפלגי דרב סבר כיון דהדיוט יכול להחזירה כו' לא בטלה משמע דבאין הדיוט יכול להחזירה אפי' רב מודה דשריא ונראה לר"י דהתם פליגי בחוליות קטנים דכשמתפרקין הוו כעין שברי שברים דקאמר התם מעיקרא אבל הכא מיירי בחוליות גדולות דאפי' שמואל מודה דאסירי בהנאה אפי' אין הדיוט יכול להחזירה: **וישימו** להם בעל ברית וגו'. האי קרא בשופטים כתיב וקשה לר"י למה לא הביא קרא דמלכים (ב א) *זבוב בעל עקרון ולמה ליה לאתויי ברייתא וי"ל דאי מהתם ה"א זבוב גדול היה אלא שהיה לו דמות זבוב לכך מייתי מהכא שהיה קטן כשאר זבובים כדקתני ומניחה בתוך כיסו ודריש לה מדכתיב בעל ברית משמע שכרתו להן ברית להיות כל שעה אצלם ומסברא קאמר זה זבוב בעל עקרון: **מה** מת בכזית אף ע"ז בכזית. תימה [לר"י] לרבי עקיבא אי ישנה לאברים נוקי האי היקישא לקולא דבעי כזית לאברים אבל ע"ז שלימה אפילו אין בה כזית דומיא דמת כשהוא שלם דמטמא אפילו אין בו כזית כדאמר בנזיר בפרק כ"ג (דף נ:) ויש לומר דבמת אפי' אבר שלם שאין בו כזית טמא כדאמרינן נמי התם א"כ כך לי אבר אחד כמו כולה ואם תאמר אכתי מלי לאוקמא היקישא בחוליא אחת שכנגדה במת לא חשיב אבר וי"ל דההיא אפילו כזית לא מטמא דכשברי שברים חשיבא: **נלמדה** משק. דספינה אינה מיוחדת למדרס אף על פי שכל שעה יושבין בה בני אדם מכל מקום עיקרן עשויות לפרגמטיא ואומר בה עמוד ונעשה מלאכתנו דאי ספינה מיוחדת למדרס לא הוה ילפינן משק כדאמרינן בריש אלו מומין (בכורות לה:) דמדרסות לא איתקוש לשק*: **לאפוקי** ספינה שאינה מיטלטלת מליאה. ומה שמיטלטלת בים לא חשיב ליה טלטול כיון דעיקר הילוכה מחמת המים:

נ"ל בעל זבוב אלהי עקרון

רבינו חננאל

שמכרעת סלקין אחרים בכף מאזנים אחרת ונמצאת כנושא אותן וניסוטין מכחה כדתנן בזב. כמאן אזלא הא דתניא כל הטומאות המסיטות אחרי' טהורין חוץ מן הזב. שלא מצינו לו בכל התורה כולה ניחא דלא כר"ע. דאי ר"ע הא אף ע"ז שהסיטה את אחרים טמאין. ודחינן אפילו תימא ר"ע תנא זב וכל דדמי ליה. נמצא דברי רב אשי דפלוגתא דרבה ור' אלעזר בתרצתא דהא מתנית' דר' אלעזר סבר בהיסט שהסיטו אחרים את ע"ז פלוגתא דרבנן ודר' עקיבא. אבל הסיטה היא את אחרים טהורין. ורבה סבר בהיסט שהסיטה ע"ז את אחרים פלוגתייהו. אבל אם הסיטוה אחרים טמאין. ובעיא דרמי בר חמא הא אמרינן כרבה בעי לה ואליבא דר"ע. אבל לרבה לרבנן אינה לאברים. ולר' אלעזר בין אליבא דרבנן ובין אליבא דר' עקיבא אינה לאברים. וכן הלכה: ובעיא דרב אחדבוי בר אמי ע"ז פחותה מכזית לענין איסורא פשטא דאסורא דהא זבוב בעל ע"ז עקרון אסור. אבל לענין טומאה אין בה טומאה של כלום דלהכין איתקש למת ואיתקש לנדה שאינה לאברים. ואיתקש לשרץ שאינה מטמא במשא ולא מצית למימר לחומרא לשרץ כעדשה ולנדה לאבן מסמא. ולמת לאהל משום דטומאת ע"ז דרבנן היא. וכי איכא חומרא וקולא לקולא היא דמקשינן: [מתני'] מנין לספינה שהיא טהורה כו'. פי' שאינה מקבלת טומאה. רבנן דמתני' משום מדמי לה ספינה לים מה הים אין מקבל טומאה אף הספינה אינה מקבלת טומאה. וחנניה מפיק לה למילתא דספינה שאין מקבלת טומאה מן השק דכתיב מכל כלי עץ או בגד או עור או שק מה שק מטלטל מלא וריקן מקבל טומאה לאפוקי ספינה שאינה מטלטלת מלא וריקן. לפיכך אינה מקבלת טומאה. מאי בינייהו איכא בינייהו ספינה של חרס לרבנן [שמדמין] אותה לים אף ספינה של חרס טהורה. ולחנניה שהוא [למד] לטהרת ספינה משק ספינה של חרס [מקבלת] טומאה דא' לן עץ ובגד ועור ושק דכתיבי בענינא גמרינן להו משק נמצא. משק מלמד עליו. אלו הדברים שכתובין בפרשה. וכן מלמד שאין מקבלין טומאה אלא מה שהוא מטלטל מלא וריקן כגון שק אבל כלי חרס אינו כתוב עם השק. לפיכך אין השק מלמד עליו. דאע"פ שאינו מטלטל מלא וריקן מקבל טומאה. אי נמי איכא בין רבנן שלמידין מן הים ובין חנניה שהוא למד מן השק.(ספות) [לענין ספינת] הירדן לרבנן טהורה ולחנניה טמאה מפני שהיא מטלטלת מליאה וריקנית כר' חנניה בן עקביה: אמר (רבה) [רבא]

מסורת הש"ס

[זבחים לז. מנחות נה: בכורות כח. נדה מג. ועי' תוס' בכורות כח. ד"ה שלא]

[צ"ל נ"ל]

(צ"ל להם)

סנהדרין סג: סו:

[לקמן קכג. חגיגה כו: מנחות נו: בכורות לח.]

[כ"ה כד:]

ברכות סג: גיטין נז:

[וע"ע תוס' מנחות לא. ד"ה שידה]

גליון הש"ס

רש"י ד"ה טהורין ולמהוי דכי כתיב משא הזב באדם כתיב. עי' מס' דף נד ע"ב בר"ש ד"ה שאו תוס' ד"ה כי תיבעי וקי' לר"י. ק"ל הא שם מבואר דמדינן ביטול הוא (ולא כן) דהאיבעיא בע"ז של ישראל דלא מהני ביטול אם טהור מטומאה וצ"ע

רב נסים גאון

כמאן אזלא כל הטמאות המסיטות טהורות חוץ מהיסטו של זב שלא מצינו בכל התורה כולה עיקר דילה בתורת כהנים וכלי חרש אשר יגע בו הזב ישבר אין לי אלא כלי חרס מנין לרבות כלי כו' ומאהר שלמדנו שאין מטמאין אותו אלא מאוירו מה ת"ל אשר יגע בו מגע שהוא ככולו הוי אומר זה היסטו ואמרו וכל אשר יגע בו הזב זה הוא היסטו של זב הרי למדנו מיכן שכל מה שיסיטנו הזב טמא וזבה ונדה ויולדת וכל דדמי לזב טומאתן כטומאת הזב ומזה העיקר אמרו במשנה (זבין פ"ד מ"ו) הזב בכף מאזנים ואוכלין ומשקין בכף שנייה וכו' ובאדם לא פרס בין הטהור המסיט את הזב ובין הזב המסיט את הטהור כמו ששנינו (שם פ"ה) המסיט את הזב או שהזב מסיט בו מטמא אוכלין כו' ובתוספתא (זבין פ"ד) אמרו בין שהזב מכריען מטמא אחד כו' ותנן נמי (שם פ"ג מ"א) עלו באילן שכוחו רע ובסוכה שכוחה רע טמא

a and the *zab* outweighs them, they are unclean;[1] [83*b*] if they outweigh [him], they are clean.[2]

With whom does that which was taught agree, [viz.,]: [As for] all unclean things which move [others], they [the things moved] are clean, save [in the case of] moving by a *zab*, for which no analogy[3] is found in the whole Torah. Shall we say that this is not according to R. Akiba, for if according to R. Akiba, there is an idol too?—You may even say that it agrees with R. Akiba: He states *zab* and all that is like thereto.[4]

R. Ḥama b. Guria asked: Does the law of an idol operate in respect to its limbs or not?[5] Now, where an unskilled person can replace it [the limb in the idol], there is no question, for it is as though [already] joined [thereto]. When does the question arise? If an unskilled person cannot replace it, what [then]? Since an unskilled person cannot replace it, it is as broken;[6] or perhaps it is actually not defective?[7] Some there are who put the question in the reverse direction: Where an unskilled person cannot replace it, there is no question, for it is as broken. When does the question arise, if an unskilled person can replace it: what [then]? Since an unskilled person can replace it, it is as though [already] joined [thereto]; or perhaps now it is nevertheless disjoined and loose [separate]?—The question stands over.

R. Aḥedbuy b. Ammi asked: What of an idol less than an olive in size? R. Joseph demurred to this: In respect of what [does b he ask]? Shall we say, in respect of the interdict?[1]—let it be no more than the fly [*zebub*] of Baal Ekron,[2] for it was taught: *And they made Baal-berith their god:*[3] this refers to the fly-god of Baal Ekron. It teaches that everyone made a likeness of his idol[4] and put it in his bag: whenever he thought of it he took it out of his bag and embraced and kissed it![5] But [the question is] in respect of uncleanness: what [is the law]? since it is assimilated to *sherez*,[6] then just as *sherez* [defiles] by the size of a lentil,[7] so an idol too [defiles] by the size of a lentil; or perhaps it is [also] likened to a corpse: just as a corpse [defiles] by the size of an olive,[8] so does an idol [defile] by the size of an olive?—Said R. Awia—others state, Rabbah b. 'Ulla—Come and hear: For it was taught: An idol less than an olive in size has no uncleanness at all, for it is said, *And he cast the powder thereof* [*sc.* of the idol] *upon the graves of the children of the people:*[9] just as a corpse [defiles] by the size of an olive, so does an idol [defile] by the size of an olive.

Now, according to the Rabbis, in respect of what law is it [an idol] likened to *sherez?*—that it does not defile by carriage; to a *niddah?*—that it is not [a source of contamination] through its [separate] limbs; [and] to a corpse?—that it does not defile by the size of a lentil![10] [Why?] Interpret it rather stringently: In respect of what law does the Divine Law liken it to a *sherez?* that it defiles by the size of a lentil; to a *niddah?* that it defiles through a cavity-closing stone; [while] the Divine Law assimilates it to a corpse, [teaching] that it defiles under the law of a covering?[11]—The uncleanness of an idol is [only] by Rabbinical law: [consequently,] where there are lenient and stringent [analogies], we c draw a lenient analogy, but do not draw a stringent analogy.[1]

MISHNAH. HOW DO WE KNOW THAT A SHIP IS CLEAN?[2] BECAUSE IT IS SAID, THE WAY OF A SHIP IN THE MIDST OF THE SEA.[3]

GEMARA. Now, it is obvious that a ship is in the midst of the sea, but we are informed this: just as the sea is clean, so is a ship clean. It was taught: Ḥananiah said: We learn it from a sack:[4] just as a sack can be carried both full and empty, so must everything [which is to be susceptible to defilement] be possible to be carried both full and empty, thus excluding a ship, seeing that it cannot be carried full and empty.[5] Wherein do they differ?—They differ in respect to an earthen ship: he who quotes, '*a ship in the midst of the sea*', [holds that] this too is in the midst of the sea. But as for him who maintains that it must be like a sack: only those [vessels] that are mentioned in conjunction with a sack,[6] if they can be carried full and empty, are [susceptible to uncleanness], if not, they are not [susceptible]; but an earthen ship, even if it cannot be carried full and empty, [is still susceptible to defilement]. Alternatively, [they differ in respect to] a boat of the Jordan:[7] he who quotes, '*a ship in the midst of the sea*', [holds that] this too is a ship in the midst of the sea;[8] but as for him who requires that it be carried full and empty, this too is carried full and empty, for R. Ḥanina b. Akiba said: Why was it ruled that a Jordan boat is unclean? Because it is loaded on dry land and [then] lowered into the water.

Rab Judah said in Rab's name: One should never abstain from [attendance at] the Beth Hamidrash even for a single hour, for lo! how many years was this Mishnah learnt in the Beth Hamidrash without its reason being revealed, until R. Ḥanina b. Akiba came and elucidated it. R. Jonathan said: One should never abstain from the Beth Hamidrash and from Torah, even in the hour of d death, for it is said, *This is the Torah, when a man dieth in a tent:*[1] even in the hour of death one should be engaged in [the study of] the Torah.[2] Resh Laḳish said: The words of the Torah can endure only with him who sacrifices[3] himself for it, as it is said, *This is the Torah, when a man dieth in a tent.*[4]

a (1) Since he thereby moves the foodstuffs or drinks, which is *hesseṭ*. In this way an idol may move others, *sc.* by outweighing them on a pair of scales. (2) For they bear the *zab*, and only articles which are fit for lying or sitting upon, or human beings, are unclean in such a case. (3) Lit., 'companion'. (4) Which includes an idol, since R. Akiba deduces an idol's power to contaminate from a *niddah*, who is akin to a *zab*. (5) V. *supra* 82*b*. (6) And therefore does not defile. (7) All the parts are there, even if not assembled; hence each part should defile.

b (1) One may not benefit in any way from an idol. (2) A Phoenician idol; cf. II Kings I, 2. (3) Judg. VIII, 33. (4) Lit., 'fear'. (5) This shows that it is the same as any other idol, and benefit thereof is certainly forbidden. (6) V. *supra* 82*b*. (7) Less than the size of an olive. (8) That is the least portion of a corpse which defiles. (9) II Kings XXIII, 6. (10) V. *supra* 82*b*. (11) Cf. *supra* 16*b*, n.c7.

c (1) All the verses quoted above as intimating the uncleanness of an idol are only supports (*asmakta*), but not the actual source of the law. Cf. Halevy, *Doroth*, I, 5, ch. 8, pp. 470 *seqq*. (2) I.e., it cannot become unclean. (3) Prov. XXX, 19. (4) A ship is a wooden vessel, and only those wooden vessels which are like a sack can become unclean, since they are assimilated to a sack in Lev. XI, 32. (5) By 'carried' is meant actually as one carries a sack. (6) V. Lev. XI, 32. (7) Owing to the rapid course of the Jordan the boats that plied on it were of canoe-like structure, which could be taken up and carried over the unnavigable stretches. (8) For all rivers are the same, not susceptible to defilement.

d (1) Num. XIX, 14. (2) In the face of the boundless love for the Torah displayed by this dictum, the criticism of Rabbinism as a dry, legalistic system is seen to be shallow and superficial. No system which does not appeal to the warm-hearted emotions could call forth such love. (3) Lit., 'kills'. (4) I.e., this Torah can live only when a man is prepared to die for it—an interpretation that has been historically justified.

Raba said: [84a] Now according to Ḥananiah, carrying by means of oxen is regarded as carrying.[5] For we learnt: There are three waggons: That which is built like a *cathedra*[6] is liable to uncleanness as *midras;*[7] that which is like a bed[8] is liable to uncleanness through the defilement caused by a corpse;[9] that of stones[10] is completely clean. Now R. Joḥanan observed thereon: But if it has a receptacle for pomegranates, it is liable to uncleanness through the defilement of a corpse.[11] There are three chests: a chest with an opening at the side is liable to uncleanness as *midras;*[12] at the
a top, is liable to uncleanness through the defilement of a corpse;[1] but an extremely large one[2] is completely clean.[3]

Our Rabbis taught: The *midras* of an earthen vessel is clean;[4] R. Jose said: A ship too. What does he mean?[5]—Said R. Zebid, He means this: The *midras* of an earthen vessel is clean, but contact therewith renders it unclean,[6] while an earthen ship is unclean, in accordance with Ḥananiah;[7] R. Jose ruled: An [earthen] ship too is clean, in agreement with our Tanna. R. Papa demurred: [If so,] why say, A ship *too?*[8] Rather said R. Papa, This is its meaning: The *midras* of an earthen vessel is clean, whilst contact therewith defiles it; but [in the case of a vessel] of wood, both its *midras* and its touch are unclean; while a boat of the Jordan is clean, in agreement with our Tanna; R. Jose said: A ship too is unclean, in accordance with Ḥananiah.

Now, how do we know that the *midras* of an earthen vessel is clean?—Said Hezekiah, Because Scripture saith, *and whosoever toucheth* his *bed:*[9] this assimilates '*his* bed' to himself [the *zab*]: just as he can be cleansed in a *miḳweh*,[10] so can 'his bed' be cleansed in a *miḳweh*. The School of R. Ishmael taught: *It shall be unto her as the bed of her impurity* [niddah]:[11] this assimilates her bed to herself: just as she can be cleansed in a *miḳweh*, so can 'her bed' be cleansed in a *miḳweh*, thus excluding earthen vessels, which cannot be cleansed in a *miḳweh*.[12]

R. Ela raised an objection: How do we know that a [reed] mat

(5) For the boats of the Jordan are too large to be loaded and carried overland otherwise than by oxen. (6) Short and three sided, like an armchair. (7) Since such are made specifically for sitting; v. *supra* 59a. (8) Long, its purpose being the carriage of goods. (9) I.e., it is susceptible to every form of defilement save *midras*, because it ranks as a utensil, in that it can become unclean, but it is not made for sitting thereon. (10) A cart made for carrying large stones. Its bottom was perforated with large holes, and therefore could not be used to carry articles as small as a pomegranate or less, and for a vessel to be susceptible to defilement it must be able to hold pomegranates. (11) Though the same waggon cannot be moved when full except by oxen. Thus though it is a wooden vessel, and therefore must be capable of being moved full or empty (*supra* 83b), the fact that it can be moved by oxen is sufficient. (12) Because a *zab* can sit on its top without being told 'get up and let us do our work' (v. *supra* 59a), as things can be put in or taken out from the side.

a (1) I.e., it is susceptible to all forms of uncleanness save that of *midras*, because a *zab* if sitting on it would be told to get off it, v. *supra* 66a, n. a9. (2) Lit., 'one that comes in measurement'. (3) It is unfit for lying or sitting upon on account of the opening at the top, and therefore it is not susceptible to *midras*, while since it cannot be moved about owing to its size, it is free from other defilement (v. *supra* 83b). (4) I.e., if a *zab* sits upon it without actually infringing upon the air space within it. (5) A ship is not susceptible to *any* form of defilement. (6) Viz., if a *zab* touches it on the inside. (7) *Supra* 83b. (8) He certainly must mean that it is clean even from defilement through contact; then how explain 'too', which intimates that the first Tanna has stated that a certain article cannot be defiled by contact and R. Jose adds this? (9) Lev. XV, 5. '*His bed*' denotes anything upon which the *zab* has lain, and this passage teaches the law of *midras*. (10) V. Glos. (11) Ibid. 26, q.v. (12) This is deduced from Lev. XI, 33, q.v. Since they cannot be cleansed, they cannot become unclean in the first place through the *midras* of a *zab*.

ולחנניא טילטול על ידי שוורים שמיה טילטול (א)(אין) *דתנן א שלש עגלות הן עשויה כקתידרא טמאה מדרס כמטה טמאה טמא מת של אבנים טהורה מכלום ואמר ר' יוחנן ואם יש בה בית קבול רמונים טמאה טמא מת * ב שלש תיבות הן תיבה *שפתחה מצדה טמאה מדרס מלמעלה טמאה טמא מת ג והבאה במדה טהורה מכלום *ת"ר ד מדרס כלי חרס טהור ר' יוסי אומר. אף הספינה מאי קאמר אמר רב זביד הכי קאמר מדרס כלי חרס טהור ומגעו טמא וספינה של חרס טמאה כחנניא ר' יוסי אומר אף הספינה טהורה כתנא דידן מתקיף לה רב פפא מאי אף (ב) אלא אמר רב פפא הכי קאמר מדרס כלי חרס טהור ומגעו טמא ושל עץ בין מדרסו ובין מגעו טמא וספינת הירדן טהורה כתנא דידן ר' יוסי אומר אף הספינה טמאה כחנניא °ומדרס כלי חרס מנלן דטהור אמר חזקיה דאמר קרא °ואיש אשר יגע במשכבו (ויקרא טו) מקיש משכבו לו מה הוא אית ליה טהרה במקוה אף משכבו נמי אית ליה טהרה במקוה דבי ר' ישמעאל תנא °כמשכב נדתה (שם) יהיה לה מקיש משכבה לה מה היא אית לה טהרה במקוה אף משכבה נמי אית לה טהרה במקוה לאפוקי כלי חרס *דלית ליה טהרה במקוה מתיב ר' אילעא *ה מפץ במת מנין

ודין

[ג"י שפתחה מצדה]

רש"י

ולחנניא. דאמר ספינה המיטלטלת מלאה טמאה אפילו אינה מיטלטלת אלא על ידי שוורים מרוב גודלה הוי טילטול וטמאה: כקתידרא. קצרה ומוקפת משלש לדדין: טמאה מדרס. שלישיבה מיוחדת היא: כמטה. שהיא ארוכה ומתחתיה מקבלת כמטה של עור שאין בה שום נקב: טמאה טומאת מת. כלומר מקבלת שאר טומאות כולן חוץ מטומאת מדרס דכלי הוא לקבל טומאה ולישיבה אינה מיוחדת שטוענין בה פרגמטיא ואומר לו עמוד ונעשה מלאכתנו והא דנקט טמא מת משום דאב הטומאה הוא והכי קאמר אב הטומאה הוא על ידי מת ולא על ידי זב: ושל אבנים. העשויה להוליך בה אבנים: טהורה מכלום. אינה מקבלת שום טומאה לפי שפרוצה מתחתיה נקבים גדולים ולא כלי הוא דכל הכלים שיעורן כרמונים: ואמר רבי יוחנן כו'. אלמא אף על גב דשל עץ איתקש לשק דבעינן מיטלטל מלא וריקן וזו אינה מיטלטלת אלא על ידי שוורים קאמר טמאה טמא מת: תיבה שפתחה מולדה טמאה מדרס. לפי שמשמשת שכיבה עם מלאכתה שמשתמשין בה דרך פתחה ואין צריך לומר לשוכב עליה עמוד ונעשה מלאכתנו: מלמעלה. פתחה כאותן שלנו: טמאה טמא מת. כלומר נעשה אב הטומאה על ידי מת כשאר כל הכלים הראויין לקבל טומאה שאם האהיל אהל המת עליהן נעשין אב הטומאה ולענין שאר טומאות הויין ראשון לטומאה ככל הכלים ולא שמעינן ממתניתין אלא דכלי הוא לטומאה ומדרס לא הויא דאינה מיוחדת לשכיבה דצריך לומר לו עמוד יש מקשין הכל על משנה זו הא דאמר רבי יוחנן בפרק במה אשה (לעיל דף נט:) אף אומר בטומאת מת עמוד ונעשה מלאכתנו והכל הוא בפיהם דכי איתמר ההיא לענין כלי שנשבר ועודנו ראוי למלאכה ולא מעין מלאכה ראשונה וקאמר רבי יוחנן דטהור מטומאתו ראשונה ואומר בו עמוד ונעשה מלאכתנו הראשונה והרי הוא אינו ראוי אבל לומר שתהא מיוחדת למת ולא למלאכה אחרת לא תהא זאת בישראל דהא כתיב (במדבר יט) כל אשר באהל יטמא וכל כלי פתוח וגו' וכל טמא מת שבתלמוד הנזכר אצל מדרס הוא הדין לטמא שרץ או לטומאת נבלה ולא הוזכר מת אלא משום דעל ידי מת נעשה אב הטומאה [כמו] על ידי מדרס שלא בא ללמדנו אלא לומר שהוא כלי מקבל כל טומאה חוץ מטומאת מדרס אם ישב עליו זב אינו נעשה אב הטומאה: הבאה במדה. תיבה גדולה שאינה מיטלטלת ויש לה חלון מלמעלה להשתמש בתוכה: טהורה מכלום. למדרס לא חזיא הואיל וחלולה מלמעלה אינה משמשת שכיבה עם מלאכתה ולשאר טומאות לא חזיא דאינה מטלטלת מליאה ולא איתפרש מה לשון באה במדה ולי נראה על שם אנשי מדות כלומר שצריכה למוד ארכה ורחבה: מדרס כלי חרס טהור. שאם ישב עליו הזב ולא נגע באוירו טהור ואינו מטמא משום מדרס ולקמיה יליף לה מקרא: מאי קאמר. מה ענין ספינה אצל מדרס ספינה טהורה אף מטומאת מגע ולמדרס לא חזיא: ומגעו טמא. אם נגע הזב בתוכו: וספינה של חרס טמאה. במגעה: כחנניא. דיליף טעמא משק וחרס לא איתקש לשק: כתנא דידן. דיליף מבלב ים והא נמי בלב ים היא: מאי אף ספינה. על כרחיך טהורה ממגע קאמר ומאי אף הא לא טיהר תנא קמא כלי ממגע דנימא אף זו כיוצא בו: וספינת הירדן טהורה כתנא דידן. דיליף מבלב ים לא שנא גדולה לא שנא קטנה והוא הדין נמי דמצי לתרוצי וספינה של חרס טהורה בתר דמפכינן דתנא קמא לרבי יוסי אלא משום דשכיחא טפי של עץ משל חרס: משכבו. הוא והמשכב הנזכר כאן: כלי חרס אין לו טהרה במקוה. דכתיב *ישבר אין לו טהרה אלא שבירתו: מפץ. של קנים: במת מניין. שהוא טמא לפי שמצינו שפשוטי כלי עץ טהורין מטומאת מגע שרץ מניין שכלי הראוי למשכב ומושב מקבל טומאת מגע במת:

ודין

תוספות

ולחנניא טילטול על ידי שוורים שמיה טילטול. נראה לר"י אפילו כיש בה מ' סאה תימה לר' יצחק אמאי נקט חנניא הא רבנן נמי לא פליגי בהא דמה שמטהרין ספינת הירדן היינו משום דרך אניה בלב ים (משלי ל) ולאו משום דלא שמיה טילטול ועוד דנראה דספינת הירדן מיטלטלת אפילו על ידי בני אדם דאי אינה מיטלטלת אלא על ידי שוורים אם כן ממתניתין דכלים דתנן ספינת הירדן טמאה הוי מצי לאוכוחי דלחנניה שמיה טילטול:

ואמר רבי יוחנן אם יש בה בית קיבול רימונים כו'. מהא דקתני במטה טמאה טמא מת לא מצי לאתויי ראייה דאיכא למימר שמיטלטלת על ידי בני אדם:

שלש תיבות הן. קשה לר"י דאמאי מייתי לה דאי משום דהיא סיפא דההיא דג' עגלות הן אם כן הוה ליה לאתויי ההיא דג' עריבות שהן בינתים:

הבאה במדה טהורה מכלום. אפתחה למעלה קאי דפתחה מצידה דחזיא למדרס לא בעי מיטלטל מלא וריקן כדאמרי' בבכורות (דף לח.):

אלא אמר רב פפא ה"ק כו' ושל עץ בין מדרסו בין מגעו טמא. תימה לרבינו תם דלמה לו להגיה של עץ וספינת הירדן לא הוה ליה אלא לאפוכי סיפא קמא דלת"ק ספינה של חרס טהורה כתנא דידן ולר' יוסי אף הספינה טמאה כחנניה ואף דרבי יוסי אמגע דקאמר ת"ק דטמא על כן נראה לרבינו תם כגי' ר"ח דגרסינן במילתיה דרב זביד וספינה של חרס טהורה כתנא דידן ורבי יוסי אומר אף הספינה טמאה כחנניא כמו מגע [דכלי חרס] ופריך מאי אף דהשתא לא קאי אעיקר מילתיה דת"ק אלא אדקדוק דבריו דדייקינן הא מגעו טמא אלא א"ר פפא ה"ק כו' וספינה של חרס טמאה כחנניא ר' יוסי אומר אף הספינה טהורה כתנא דידן כמו מדרס כלי חרס דקתני תנא קמא בהדיא דטהור:

מה הוא דאית ליה טהרה במקוה. לאו דוקא נקט מקוה דהא זב בעי מים חיים אלא משום דבעי למינקט מקוה גבי משכב ומושב ולענין מים חיים לא מצרכי' שיהא טעון במשכב ומושב כזב דלא בעינן אלא דדמי ליה פורתא דאית ליה טהרה:

לאפוקי כלי חרס דלית ליה טהרה במקוה. תימה דהא כופת שאור שיחדה לישיבה טמאה מדרס כדאמרינן בהעור והרוטב (חולין דף קכט.) אע"ג דלית ליה טהרה במקוה ואומר רבינו תם דיש במינו בגידולי קרקע טהרה במקוה כגון כלי עץ:

מפץ במת מניין. פירש בקונטרס דמיירי במפץ של עץ ואין נראה לרבינו תם דהא פשוטי כלי עץ יש להם טהרה במקוה כדמוכח בפרק קמא דסוכה (דף טז.) *דאמר מטה מיטהרת איברים ומוקי לה בפשוטי כלי עץ כגון ארוכה ושתי כרעים ואומר ר"ת דהכא במפץ של שיפה ושל גמי דאין לו שום טומאה אלא מדרבנן לבד מטומאת מדרס כדפירש לעיל בפרק במה אשה (דף סו.) והא דפשוטי כלי עץ אית להו טהרה במקוה אומר ר"י דנפקא לן מדכתיב (במדבר לא) וכל כלי עץ תתחטאו דמשמע אפילו פשוטי דומיא דכלי מתכות דכתיבי התם אף על גב דכתיב וכל מעשה עזים ליכא למילף מה מעשה עזים מיטלטל מלא וריקן אף כלי עץ דלא שייך למילף הכי אלא משק כדכתיב (בראשית מב) ויהי הם מריקים שקיהם ולהכי נקט נמי בכל דוכתא מה שק מיטלטל מלא וריקן כו' ולא נקט מה בגד מיטלטל מלא וריקן אף על גב דבגד נמי כתיב גבי שק או בגד או עור או שק:

מה

*) עי' [illegible] סוכה ט"ז [illegible]

עין משפט נר מצוה

יג א מיי' פכ"ז מהלכות כלים הלכה ג:

יד ב שם הלכה א ופכ"ה הלכה טו ופרק כו הלכה ו:

טו ג מיי' פכ"ז שם ופ"ג שם הלכה ג ופ"ו מהלכות טומאת מת הלכה ב:

טז ד מיי' פ"א מהלכות כלים הלכה ח ופי"ח הלכה א:

יז ה מיי' שם פ"א הלכה יג ופכ"ג הלכה א:

רבינו חננאל

ולחנניה טילטול ע"י שוורין שמיה טילטול. פי' הא דקא מטלטל מלא וריקן אפי' על ידי שוורין: שלש עגלות הנה העשויה כקתידרא טמאה מדרס מפני שאדם סומך עליה כדאמרינן בי"ט לענין עגלה של קטן. לפיכך אם דרס טמא עליה. ויש ביניהן דבר חוצץ [או] (ו)נפל עליה מכחו אע"פ שלא נגע בה טמאה. העשויה כמטה טמאה טמא מת. אבל עגלה של אבנים טהורה מכלום ואינה מקבלת טומאה. והיאך היא עגלה של אבנים. עצים מסובכין שתי וערב ועשויין כחלונות חלונות מניחין שם אבנים ומושכין אותן. א"ר יוחנן ואם יש בה בית קיבול רמונים טמאה. פי' כגון שאותן החלונו' רחוקות ואין הרמונים נופלים משם: שלש תיבו' הן שפתחה מצדה טמאה מדרס וזו שנקראת בבבל כוזאנה מפני שיושבין למעל' ממנה. פתחה מלמעלה טמאה טמא מת. והוא הנקרא בבבל צנדוק. הבאה במדה טהורה מכלום. העשויה למוד בהכביל: ת"ר מדרס כלי חרס טהור. ר' יוסי אמר אף הספינה. אתא רב זביד לפרושה מדרס כלי חרס טהור ומגעו טמא. וספינה בין במגע בין במדרס טהורה כרבנן ור' יוסי ספינה של חרס טמאה כחנניה ולא [כתנא] קמא דקא מתקיף לה רב פפא מאי אף דאלמא אטהרה קאי ר' יוסי ולא אטומאה אלא אמר רב פפא ת"ק סבר מדרס כלי חרס טהור. אבל ספינה של טמאה כחנניה ור' יוסי סבר אף הספינה טהורה כרבנן. ומדרס כלי חרס ס"ל דטהור הוא. אמר חזקיה דאמר קרא ואיש אשר יגע במשכבו. מקיש משכבו לו מה הוא דאית ליה טהרה במקוה אף משכבו נמי דבר שיש לו טהרה במקוה הוא טמא מדרס. אבל דבר שאין לו טהרה במקוה אינו מיטמא במדרס. ודבי ר' ישמעאל תנא כמשכב נדתה יהיה לה כענין הזה: מותיב ר'(אלעזר) [אילעא] מפץ במת מניין

רב נסים גאון

אלא אם כן יהיה ההיסט במקום בית הסתרים אז יהיה דינו משונה כמפורש במס' נדה בפרק יוצא דופן (דף מג) אמר ריש לקיש קנה בקומטו של זב והסיט בו את הטהור טהור קנה בקומטו של טהור והסיט בו את הזב טמא מאי טעמא דאמר קרא (ויקרא טו) וכל אשר יגע בו הזב וידיו לא שטף במים זה הסיטו של זב שלא מצינו בכל התורה כולה ואפקיה רחמנא בלשון נגיעה למימרא דהיסט ונגיעה כידו מה התם מבראי אף הבא מבראי ובתורת כהנים אמרו מה ידיו בנראה פרט לבית הסתרים אף כל בשרו בנראה פרט לבית הסתרים דאלמא כי מגיד טהור לזב במקום בית הסתרים טהור הוא ובמס' ע"ז בפרק ר' ישמעאל אומר ג' אבנים זו בצד זו (דף ס) אמרו אמר רב אשי כל שבזב טמא בגוי עושה יין נסך וכל שבזב טהור בגוי אינו עושה יין נסך מיכן אמר ר"ש*) קנה של זב כו' ובבבא קמא בפרק כיצד הרגל (דף יז) אמרו עוד אמר רבא כל שבזב טמא בנזקים משלם נזק שלם כו': אמר רבה ולחנניה טילטול על ידי שוורים שמיה טילטול דתנן ג' עגלות הן העשויה כקתדרא טמאה מדרס כמטה טמאה טמא מת כו' זו המשנה במס' כלים בפרק ג' תריסים וגם בו יש המשנה האחרת ג' תיבות הן וראוי לנו לבאר כי אע"פ שהמת הוא חמור מכל הטמאות וקשה מהן כמו ששנינו במשנה (כלים פ"א מ"ד) חמור מכולם המת שהוא מטמא באהל מה שאין כן כולם מטמאין אינו מטמא משכב ומושב כמו שהוא בתורת כהנים הזב מטמא משכב ומושב לא המת מה אם הזב שאינו מטמא טומאת ז' מטמא משכב ומושב מת שהוא מטמא טומאת ז' אינו דין שיטמא משכב ומושב ת"ל הזב לא המת ר"ש אומר אשר ישכב עליו ואשר ישב עליו את שיש לו שכיבה וישיבה מטמא משכב ומושב ואין זב שמת מטמא משכב ומושב ושאמרו הזב שמת מטמא במשא עד שימוק הבשר מדברי סופרים וטמא מת נידון כמת אינו עושה משכב ומושב (לדבריהם) הזב ולא טמא מת כו' ובתוספתא (כלים פ"א) חומר בבועל נדה מטמא מת שבועל נדה כר תחתון כעליון מה שאין כן בטמא מת ואמרו במשנה ובתוספתא במס' זבין חומר בזב מבמת שהזב עושה משכב ומושב מתחתיו כו' מה שאין המת מטמא טמא מת ששכב על י' מצעות אינו מטמא אלא העליון ששכב עליו והשאר טהורין לפי שלא יעשה משכב ומושב והעליון טמא בנגיעה ולפיכך היו החכמים קורים לכל דבר שאינו מטמא כדין משכב ומושב טמאה טמא מת ולכל דבר שהוא נעשה משכב ומושב היו קורין אותו בשם מדרס בלשון קצרה ולכן כל דבר שהוא מטמא מדרס הוא טמא במגע דהיינו טמא מת לפי הכינוי שכינו לו וכל דבר שאינו ראוי למשכב ומושב הוא טמא טמא מת כדין הנגיעה ואינו מיטמא מדרס וכדבר הזה אמרה המשנה בפרק בא סימן התחתון (נדה מט) כל המיטמא מדרס מטמא טמא מת ויש שהוא מטמא טמא מת וכו' ואמרו בתלמוד (שם) כל המטמא מדרס מטמא טמא מת כל דחזי ליה למדרס מטמא טמא מת ויש שהוא מטמא טמא מת ואינו מטמא מדרס לאיתויי סאה ותרקב דתניא והיושב על הכלי יכול כפה סאה או תרקב וישב עליו יהא טמא ת"ל אשר ישב עליו הזב כל שמיוחד לישיבה יצא זה [שאומרים לו] עמוד ונעשה מלאכתנו ובתוספתא (שם דכלים פ"ג) עריסת בנות טמאה טמא מת היתה משמשת שכיבה הרי זו טמאה מדרס מטה שמוכרין עליה כלים הרי זו טמאה טמא מת היתה משמשת שכיבה וישיבה הרי זו טמאה מדרס ומאלו העיקרים יתברר לך פירוש טומאת מדרס וטמא מת ולפיכך היתה התיבה שפתחה מצידה שהיא ראויה למושב טמאה מדרס ושפתחה מלמעלה שאינה ראויה למושב טמאה טמא מת כמגע ולא טומאת מושב הבין זה ושמור אותו בלבד כי הוא עיקר גדול: יצא כלי חרש דאין כו' דלית ליה טהרה במקוה כמו שכתוב בתורה (ויקרא יא)

ואותו

*) עיין היטיב בתוס' שם ד"ה כל דע"כ הא דבזב טהור לא קאי אקנה בקומטו של זב ודברי רבינו ל"ע.

מסורת הש"ס

כלים פי"ט ופכ"ד מ"ב

ג"ז שם מ"ד

בכורות לח. [תוספתא כלים פ"ב]

[עירובין קד:]

ב"ק כה:

[פי' פירש"י עירובין קד: ד"ה דאין לו טהרה]

הגהות הב"ח

(א) גמ' ד"ה עי' שוורים שמיה טילטול דתנן כצ"ל ותיבת אין נמחק: (ב) שם מאי אף ספינה אלא:

גליון הש"ס

גמ' ומדרס כלי חרס מנלן דטהור. עי' רש"י עירובין דף קד ע"א ד"ה לא ובכורות דף לח ע"א רש"י ד"ה אין מדרס וצ"ע:

עין משפט
נר מצוה

יח א מיי' שם סי"ג ופכ"ג הלכה א:
יט ב מיי' פ"ד מהלכות כלאים הלכה ט סמג לאוין רעט:

ודין הוא ומה פכין קטנים שטהורין בזב טמאים במת *מפץ שטמא בזב אינו דין שיהא טמא במת ואמאי הא לית ליה טהרה במקוה א"ל ר' חנינא שאני התם הואיל ואיכא במינו א"ל *רחמנא ליצלן מהאי דעתא אדרבה רחמנא ליצלן מדעתא דידך וטעמא מאי תרי קראי כתיבי כתיב °ואיש אשר יגע במשכבו וכתיב וכל המשכב אשר ישכב עליו הזב יטמא הא כיצד יש במינו אע"ג דלית ליה טהרה במקוה אין במינו מקיש משכבו לו רבא אמר מדרס כלי חרס טהור מהכא(א) °וכל כלי פתוח אשר אין צמיד פתיל עליו *הא יש צמיד פתיל עליו טהור הוא מי לא עסקינן דיחדינהו לאשתו נדה וקאמר רחמנא טהור: מתני' *ב מנין לערוגה שהיא ששה על ששה טפחים שזורעין בתוכה חמשה זרעונין *ד' על ד' רוחות הערוגה ואחת באמצע שנא' °כי כארץ תוציא צמחה וכגנה זרועיה תצמיח זרעה לא נאמר אלא זרועיה: גמ' מאי משמע אמר רב יהודה כי כארץ תוציא צמחה תוציא חד צמחה חד הרי תרי זרועיה תרי הא ארבע תצמיח חד הא חמשה

וקים

תורה אור
ויקרא טו
במדבר יט
ישעיה סא

רש"י

ודין הוא ומה פכין קטנים. של חרס שטהורין בזב שאינן מטמאין על ידו בשום טומאה דלמדרס לא חזו דאין עשויין לישיבה ועוד שהן של חרס ובמגע לא לטמאו דאין מטמאות אלא מאוירן ואין יכול להכניס אצבעו לתוכן מפני שפיהן צר ובהיסט לא דאפקיה רחמנא בלשון נגיעה דכל שאינו מטמא במגע אינו מטמא בהיסט ובהעור והרוטב (חולין קכד:) אמר נמי הכי לגבי טומאת משא את שבא לכלל מגע בא לכלל משא אע"פ שאפשר ליגע בחוט השערה ותניא בת"כ דשיער הזב מטמא הנ"מ כלי הראוי לנגיעת בשרו ולהכי אפקיה רחמנא בלשון נגיעת בשר כדכתיב (ויקרא טו) והנוגע בבשר הזב: טמאין במת. באהל המת דכתיב (במדבר יט) וכל כלי פתוח: מפץ שטמא בזב. דהא חזי למשכב וכתיב וכל המשכב וגו' ומהכא נפקא לן בעלמא (נדה דף מט:) דכל המטמא במדרס מטמא טומאת מת ואפילו פשוטי כלי עץ: ואמאי. טמא בזב טומאת מדרס: והא לית טהרה במקוה. דכי כתיב טבילה בפרשת שרצים ובפרשת מדין כתיבא והנך כלים דכתיבי התם ילפינן להו טבילה אבל פשוטי כלי עץ שלא נכתבו שם לענין טומאה לא ילפינן להו טבילה ולית להו טהרה במקוה דהא לא כתיבא בהו כי היכי דאוכל ומשקה אין להם טהרה במקוה לפי שלא למדנו להם טבילה בתורה: שאני התם דאיכא במינו. יש בכלי עץ שיש להן טהרה במקוה כגון מקבלים: רחמנא ליצלן מהאי דעתא. דכיון דלדידיה ליכא טהרה במקוה לא שאני מכלי חרס: וטעמא מאי. היכא כתיבא למשום דאיכא במינו אע"ג דבדידיה ליכא [מיטמא נימא] הואיל ואקשיתיה לזב עצמו בעי דתיהוי ליה טהרה לדידיה: כתיב משכבו. מקיש משכבו לו: וכתיב וכל המשכב. אע"ג דלא דמי לזב דהא לא כתיב משכבו: וכל כלי פתוח. כלי חרס קאמר שהטומאה נכנסת לו דרך פתחו: מי לא עסקינן. מי לא משמע במקרא דאפי' ייחדו לאותו כלי לאשתו נדה לישב עליו כל ימיה אמר קרא דמציל על מה שבתוכו באהל המת ואי טמא מדרס היכי מציל והא כל דבר טומאה אין חוצץ בפני הטומאה אלא ש"מ דאין מדרס בכלי חרס הלכך כלי חרס המוקף צמיד פתיל טהור מכלל טומאה ובהיסט נמי לא מטמיא ליה כדפרישית לעיל דכל שלא בא לכלל מגע לא בא לכלל משא לפיכך מציל על מה שבתוכו: מתני' שזורעין בתוכה ה' זרעונין. ולא הוי עירבוב שיש בה כדי להפריש ביניהם הפרש הראוי: ד' מד' רוחות הערוגה. ממלא את כל הרוח עד סמוך לקרן: ואחת באמצע. גרעין אחד ואע"פ שכל אלה הקרנות סמוכין זה לזה ואין ביניהם הרחקה ג' טפחים ויונקים זה מזה אין כאן בית מיחוש דגבי כלאים היכרא הוא דבעינן דלא להוי עירבוב דהא אכלאים קפיד קרא אבל ליניקה לא חיישינן אפילו בכלאי הכרם דאורייתא כדתנן (ב"ב דף כו.) זה סומך לגדר מכאן וזה סומך לגדר מכאן ואע"ג דינקו מתתאי וכ"ש כלאי זרעים דרבנן דלא חיישינן ליניקה כדתנן גבי ראש תור לקמן בשמעתין וגבי ב' שורות והרי יש כאן היכר גדול רוח זו זרועה לפון ודרום וזו זרועה מזרח ומערב אבל בין זרע האמצעי לזרעוני הרוחות צריך הרחקה כדי יניקה דאין שם היכר ואי הוו מקרבי הוי עירבוב והמפרש ד' גרעינין בד' הרוחות טועה דאי ההרחקה משום יניקה ט' זרעונין יש לזרוע בו ד' בד' הקרנות ואחד בכל רוח ורוח באמצעו וא' באמצע הערוגה ויש בין כל אחד ואחד ג' טפחים כשיעור יניקה טפח ומחצה לכל אחד הלכך לכל הרוח הוא ממלא עד סמוך לקרן ואפילו אין בין זרע שברוח זו לזרע שברוח זו ג' טפחים לא איכפת לן דלענין כלאים היכר בעלמא הוא דבעינן כדפרישית: זרועיה. ובגמ' מפרש היכי משמע ה' זרעונים בו' טפחים: גמ' תוציא חד צמחה חד זרועיה תרי תצמיח חד. וששה טפחים דליכא למילף מקרא

(כזה)

קים

תוספות

מה פכין קטנים שטהורין בזב. תימה דמסאה ותרקב ותיבה שפתחה למעלה יכול לעשות ק"ו דלא מטמא מדרס מטמא במת מפץ שמטמא מדרס אינו דין שיטמא במת וי"ל דמה להנך שכן נעשין אב הטומאה מה שאין כן במפץ דכיון שאין לו טהרה במקוה אינו נעשה אב הטומאה כדמוכח בפרק בתרא דעירובין (דף קד:) אבל קשה דמפכים גדולים מצי למיעבד ק"ו דלא מטמו מדרס כדאמר הכא דמדרס כלי חרס טהור ומטמא במת וי"ל דטפי ניחא ליה למיעבד ק"ו מפכים קטנים שטהורין מכל טומאת הזב לגמרי וקשה דבמעיינות הזב מנלן דלא מיטמו פכין קטנים דנהי דבשיער הזב לא מיטמו היינו משום דבעיא ראוי לנגיעת בשר כדפירש בקונטרס דמבשר הזב נפקא טומאת שיער אבל רוקו דכתיב בהדיא וכי ירוק הזב בטהור פשיטא דלא בעיא ראוי לנגיעת בשר וא"ת והיכי עביד ק"ו מפכין קטנים מה לפכין קטנים שכן מטמאין מאוירן תאמר במפץ כו' וליכא למימר דעביד ק"ו הכי מה זב הקל שאין מטמא פכין קטנים מטמא מפץ מת החמור דמטמא פכין קטנים אינו דין שיטמא מפץ דמה [לזב שכן] מטמא במשכב ומושב (ג) וי"ל דאיכא למימר שאר כלים יוכיחו שאין מטמאין מאוירן ומטמאין במת אף אני אביא מפץ מה לשאר כלים שכן נעשין אב הטומאה פכין קטנים יוכיחו*:

שטהורים בזב. שאינו יכול ליגע בתוכם לפי שפיהם צר ובהיסט נמי לא מטמו כדפירש בקונטרס דלא שאינו בא לכלל מגע אינו בא לכלל היסט וא"ת א"כ כלי חרס המוקף צמיד פתיל לא יטמא בהיסט ובפ"ק דנדה (דף ה:) אמר שאינו ניצול במעת לעת שבנדה ובפ' הניזקין (גיטין דף סא:) נמי פריך וליחוש שמא תסיטם אשתו נדה ואור"ת דצמיד פתיל חשיב בא לכלל מגע לפי שעומד ליפתח ולא דמי לקולית נבלה דאמ' בהעור והרוטב (חולין קכו:) מחוסר נקב כמחוסר מעשה דמי ואע"פ שחישב עליה לנוקבה אין טומאה במשא דהתם סתמא אינה עומדת לנקיבה אלא ע"י מחשבה אבל מוקף צמיד פתיל סתמו עומד ליפתח:

מפץ שטמא בזב אינו דין שיטמא במת. מק"ו דהכא קי"ל בכל דוכתא *דכל המטמא מדרס מטמא טמא מת וא"ת כלי חרס המוקף צמיד פתיל יוכיח שטמא בזב דמטמא בהיסט כדפרישית לעיל וטהור במת ואומר ר"ת דלא שייך למימר יוכיח מצמיד פתיל דמה שהוא בהיסט הזב היינו משום דהוי כאילו נגע הזב בתוכו כדאמרי' איזהו מגע שהוא ככולו הוי אומר זה היסטו ובמת אם היה כזית ממנו בתוכו היה טמא: והא לית ליה טהרה במקוה. תימה דבסוף כילד הרגל (ב"ק דף כה:) קאמר עלה דמפץ דהכא וקא מייתי לה בין לטומאת ערב בין לטומאת ז' מה שייך להזכיר טומאת ערב וז' כיון דאין לו טהרה לעולם וי"ל דהאי ק"ו אתי נמי לפשוטי כלי עץ המיוחדים למדרס דטמאים במת ומייתי הא לטומאת ז' אי נמי ברייתא איירי בכל מפצים בין במפץ עץ בין במפץ שיפה וגמי ובמפץ עץ קאמר התם דמייתי ליה לטומאת שבעה דאית ליה טהרה במקוה:

מי לא עסקינן דייחדינהו לאשתו נדה. פי' בקונטרס ואי מיטמא מדרס היכי מציל והלא כל דבר טמא אינו חוצץ בפני הטומאה אלא ש"מ דלא מיטמא מדרס הלכך כלי חרס המוקף צמיד פתיל טהור מכל טומאה ובהיסט נמי לא מטמא דכל שלא בא לכלל מגע אינו בא לכלל משא ואין נראה דודאי מטמא בהיסט כלי חרס מוקף צמיד פתיל כדמוכח בנדה (ה:) ובגיטין (סא:) כדפירשתי לעיל ומפרש ר"ת דמדכתיב וכל כלי דייק דמי לא עסקינן דיחדינהו לאשתו נדה דכל טומאות הבאות דרך גב יש לנו לטהרו מדכתיב וכל הילכך אפילו ייחד להו לישיבה טהורים אבל בהיסט מטמו דטומאה הבאה דרך תוך הוא דחשבינן כאילו נגע בפנים כדאמרינן איזהו מגעו שהוא ככולו הוי אומר זה היסטו ור"י מפרש דלא בעי למימר דמיירי קרא בכל ענין אפי' ישבה עליהם אשתו נדה או היסיטן אלא אם ייחד כלי חרס לאשתו נדה טהור דאין כלי חרס מטמא מדרס דאי (ייחד) טמא לא יליף בצמיד פתיל אע"ג דלא ישבה עליו דאע"פ שבמת אינו מקבל טומאה מגבו כיון דבמדרס יכול לקבל טומאה אין לו לחוץ באהל המת ומסופק ר"י בכך: מניין לערוגה שהיא ו' כו'. י"א דערוגה ו' נפקא לן מדכתיב לחייו כערוגת הבושם (שיר ה) ומשמע לחייו לשון לוחות והם היו ו' על ו' מכלל דערוגה נמי כן היא: ארבע על ארבע רוחות הערוגה. באמצע הרוח כדמוכח בגמרא לפי מה שמפרש בעז"ה ומה שפירש הקונטרס דכלאי זרעים דרבנן אינו נראה לר"י דהא אמרי' בפ' כל הבשר (חולין קטו) כלאי זרעים ליתסרו דהא תיעבתי לך הוא ואין נראה לומר דלהרכבת האילן קרי כלאי זרעים משום דבספ"ק דקידושין (דף לט) מפיק הרכבת האילן משדך לא תזרע כלאים ועוד דהתם בקידושין אמר אההיא מילתא גופא בהמתך לא תרביע כלאים שדך לא תזרע כלאים מה בהמתך בהרבעה אף שדך בהרכבה ומה בהמתך נוהג בין בארץ בין בחו"ל אף שדך נוהג בין בארץ בין בחו"ל ופריך והלא הא כתיב שדך ומשני ההוא למעוטי זרעים שבחו"ל (*ובפ' המביא) משמע דבא"י אסירי מדאורייתא ואפי' לר' יאשיה דאמר אינו חייב עד שיזרע חטה ושעורה וחרצן במפולת יד היינו להתחייב משום כלאי הכרם דלא תזרע כרמך אבל אלאו דלא תזרע שדך מודה דחייב:

וקים

רבינו חננאל

שהוא טמא. עיקר הדבר הזה שלא נאמר במת אלא כל בגד וכל כלי עור וכל מעשה עזים והמפץ שהוא כמין מחצלת שעשויה מן החילף ומן כיוצא בו לא נאמר בה. ואף לא נאמר מפץ בשרץ כי כן כתיב בו מכל כלי עץ או בגד או עור או שק. ומן מתני' כבר גמרינן שהמפץ טמא. דתנן שלשה מפצין הן העשוי לשכיבה טמא מדרס. של צבעים טמא מת ושל גתות טהור מכלום. *) ואפילו דגיתות קאמרינן. דשמואל עביד לה לבנתיה מפצות ביומי תשרי וצריכן למידע מהיכא ילפינן טומאה למפץ במת ובשרץ. ואימרין הני ברייתא בגמ' דבאיזו צד הרגל מועדת לענין דרשת דיו לבא מן הדין להיות כנדון. **) השתא כיון דמפץ לאו כלי עץ הוא ולא בגד ולא עור ולא שק ולא מעשה עזים: ובזב קא דרשינן ליה טומאה דלית ליה טהרה במקוה וקא מטמא מדרס קא מותיב מיניה ר' אלעא למאן דאע"ג דליתיה מהני מידאני עשוי דבר שאין לו טהרה במקוה אין מטמא מדרס. א"ל ר' חנינא הואיל למשכב הוא. ובמחצלת של קנים ויש במינו. פי' כגון שטומאתו מתוך שהוא משכב ויש במין מפצות חשיבה לית ליה טהרה במקוה. דברים שהן ממיני בגד או עור או שק שיש להן טהרה במקוה דהא ליכא טהרה במקוה אלא עליהן הוא אומר כל המשכב אשר ישכב עליו. אבל כלי חרס לדברים הללו. טהרתו במיעוט אין במינו דבר שיש לו טהרה במקוה. ועליהן הוא אומר שיעורו כדתנן מפץ ששה במשכבו. מקיש משכבו לו. ולא היו הדברים ברורים על ששה. תניא בתוספתא לר' אילעא משום הכי קאמר ליה לר' חנינא רחמנא ליצלן מן מפץ שבלה כל זמן שמניחין האי דעתא עד דפריש ליה טעמא דתרין קראי כתיבי אותו על הכסא האשה היושבת רבה אמר מדרס כלי חרס דטהורה מהכא וכל כלי פתוח אשר אין צמיד פתיל עליו טמא הוא הא יש צמיד פתיל טהור. (וכאן דפתים) אע"ג דחזיוה לאשתו נדה למיזגה ולמיסמך עליה טהור הוא: מתני' מניין לערוגה שהיא ששה על ששה טפחים שזורעין בתוכה ה' זרעונים ד' על ד' רוחות ערוגה ואחת

*) טעות גלויה לעין והמתקנים לנכון תבוא עליהם ברכה. ונ"ל ועל דגיתות קאמרינן דשמואל עביד וכו' וכוונתו בזה דלא"ה היה אסור לעמוד ע"ג מפלי בשעת טבילה משום גזירת מרחצאות ועיין בר"ן בפ"ב דשבועות שדהה באמת פירש"י מחמת קושיא זו אמנם לפי דעת רבינו א"ש: **) דברי רבינו הם משוללי הבנה:

מסורת הש"ס

[כתובות מה. ב"ק סה:]

[חולין כה.]

כלאים פ"ג מ"א פסחים לט:

[קידושין לט:]

הגהות הב"ח

(א) גמ' מהכא דכתיב וכל כלי: (ג) תוס' ד"ה מה פכין וכו' דמה לזב שכן מטמא משכב ומושב האמר במת שאין מטמא משכב ומושב וי"ל דאיכא:

וי"ג ובס' מעשר בהמה משמע בהדיא דאסור מדאורי' והוא בבכורות נד.

רב נסים גאון

ואיתו תשברו ואמרו רבותינו ז"ל סלמד שאין לו טהרה אלא שבירה: פכין קטנים שטהורין בזב טמאים במת ממה שאסרה התורה בענין הזב (ויקרא טו) וכלי חרש אשר יגע בו הזב ישבר ולא אסרה וכל כלי חרש למדנו שפכין קטנים טהורין בזב ואמרו במת (במדבר יט) וכל כלי פתוח אפילו כל שהוא וכבר פירשנו בברכות הרי למדנו שפכין קטנים טמאין:

[is susceptible to defilement] through the dead? [84*b*] This follows *a fortiori*: if small [earthen] pitchers which cannot be defiled by
a a *zab*[1] can be defiled through the dead,[2] then a mat, which is defiled by a *zab*,[3] is surely defiled through the dead? But why so [it may be asked], seeing that it cannot be cleansed in a *mikweh*?[4]—Said R. Ḥanina to him: There it is different, since some of its kind [of the same material] are [capable of being cleansed in a *mikweh*].[5] The All Merciful save us from this view! he exclaimed.[6] On the contrary, he retorted, The All Merciful save us from your view! And what is the reason?[7] Two verses are written: [i] *and whosoever touches* his *bed;* and [ii] *every bed whereon he that hath the issue lieth* [*shall be unclean*].[8] How are these [to be reconciled]? If something of its kind [can be cleansed in a *mikweh*], even if that itself cannot be cleansed in a *mikweh* [it is susceptible to *midras*]; but if nothing of its kind [can be cleansed in a *mikweh*], his bed is assimilated to himself.

Raba said: [That] the *midras* of an earthen vessel is clean [is deduced] from the following: *and every open vessel, which hath no covering bound upon it*[, *is unclean*]:[9] hence, if it has a covering bound
b upon it, it is clean.[1] Now, does this not hold good [even] if he had appointed it [as a seat] for his wife, when a *niddah*, yet the Divine Law states that it is clean.[2]

MISHNAH. HOW DO WE KNOW THAT IF A SEED-BED IS SIX HANDBREADTHS SQUARE, WE MAY SOW THEREIN FIVE KINDS OF SEEDS, FOUR ON THE FOUR SIDES, AND ONE IN THE MIDDLE?[3] BECAUSE IT IS SAID, FOR AS THE EARTH BRINGETH FORTH HER BUD, AND AS THE GARDEN CAUSETH ITS SEEDS TO SPRING FORTH:[4] NOT ITS SEED, BUT ITS SEEDS IS STATED.[5]

GEMARA. How is this implied?—Said Rab Judah: *For as the earth bringeth forth her bud: 'bringeth forth'* [denotes] one, [and] *'her bud'* [denotes] one, which gives two; *'her seeds'* [denotes] two,[6] making four; *'causeth to spring forth'* denotes one, making five [in

a (1) They are not susceptible to *midras*, as he cannot sit upon them. Again, an earthen vessel can be defiled only through the contaminating thing coming into contact with its inner air space, which is here impossible, as the neck of a small pitcher is too narrow to permit a *zab* to insert his finger. Furthermore, they cannot become unclean through *hesseṭ*, as *hesseṭ* and contact are interdependent, and only that which is susceptible to the latter is susceptible to the former. (2) They become unclean when under the same roof as a corpse, v. Num. XIX, 15. (3) With the uncleanness of *midras*, since it is fit for lying upon. (4) This is R. Ela's objection: how can the Baraitha state axiomatically that a mat can be defiled by a *zab*? (5) E.g., when they are provided with a receptacle. (6) That a mat should be susceptible to *midras* merely because something else of the same material can be cleansed in a *mikweh*. (7) On what grounds does R. Ḥanina base his thesis? (8) Lev. XV, 4. The first verse implies that the bed must be like himself, on account of the suffix 'his', but not the second, since the suffix is absent there. (9) Num. XIX, 15.

b (1) The contamination must, as it were, penetrate into the inner air space of the vessel, which it is unable to do on account of the covering which interposes as a barrier.—This shows that the reference is to an earthen vessel, where the defilement must enter its atmosphere (cf. *supra* n. a1). (2) Now in such a case it is regarded as a seat, and if it were susceptible to *midras* the cover would not save the vessel from becoming unclean, because whatever is itself liable to defilement cannot constitute a barrier to save something else from same. Hence it follows that an earthen vessel is not subject to *midras* at all. (3) Without infringing the prohibition of sowing diverse seeds (*kil'ayim*) together (Deut. XX, 9). (4) Isa. LXI, 11. (5) Rashi: almost the whole of each side is sown with one species, and one seed is sown in the middle, as in Fig. 1. The shaded part is sown. Though the corners come very near each other, and their roots certainly intermingle, that does not matter, as their very position makes it clear that each side has been sown as a separate strip. But with respect to the middle seed there is nothing to show that it was not sown indiscriminately together with the rest, and therefore a substantial space (three handbreadths) between it and the sides is required. Maim. explains it as in Fig. 2. (6) The minimum number of the plural.

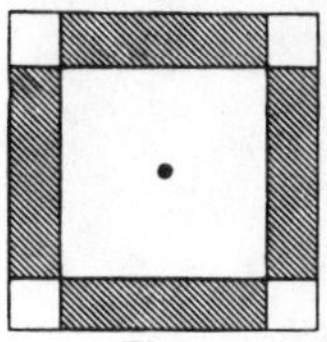

Fig. 1

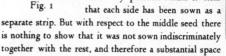

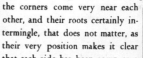

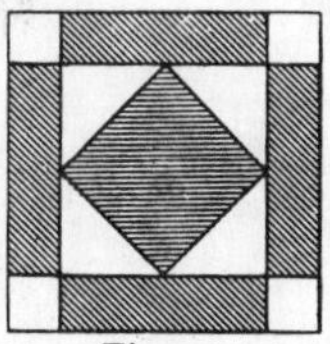

Fig. 2

all], [85*a*] the Rabbis ascertained that five [species sown] in six
a [handbreadths square] do not draw [sustenance] from each other.[1] And how do we know that that which the Rabbis ascertain is of consequence?[2] For R. Ḥiyya b. Abba said in R. Joḥanan's name: What is meant by, *Thou shalt not remove thy neighbour's landmark, which they of old have set?*[3] The landmark which they of old have set thou shalt not encroach upon.[4] What landmarks did they of old set? R. Samuel b. Naḥmani said in R. Joḥanan's name, [Even] as it is written, *These are the sons of Seir the Horite, the inhabitants of the earth:*[5] are then the whole world inhabitants of heaven? But it means that they were thoroughly versed in the cultivation of the earth. For they used to say, This complete [measuring] rod [of land is fit] for olives, this complete [measuring] rod [is fit] for vines, this complete [measuring] rod for figs.[6] *And Horite* [ḥori] implies that they smelled [*merikin*] the earth. *And Hivite* [ḥiwi]? Said R. Papa: [It teaches] that they tasted the earth like a serpent [*ḥiwya*].[7] R. Aḥa b. Jacob said: *Horite* [ḥori] implies that they become free [*ḥorin*] from [the cares of] their property.[8]

R. Assi said: The *internal* area of the seed-bed must be six [handbreadths square], apart from its borders.[9] It was taught likewise: The internal area of the seed-bed must be six [handbreadths square]. How much must its borders be?[10]—As we learnt, R. Judah said: Its breadth must be the full breadth of [the sole of] a foot. R. Zera—others say, R. Ḥanina b. Papa—said: What is R. Judah's reason? Because it is written, *and wateredst it with thy foot:*[11] just as the [sole of] the foot is a handbreadth, so must the border too be a handbreadth.

b Rab said: We learnt of a seed bed in a waste plot.[1] But there is the corner space?[2]—The School of Rab[3] answered in Rab's name: It refers to one who fills up the corners. Yet let one sow

a (1) Hence the implications of the verse are referred to a plot of this size. (2) To base a law thereon. (3) Deut. XIX, 14. (4) By planting so near to your neighbour's border that the roots must draw sustenance from his land, thus impoverishing it. (5) Gen. XXXVI, 20. (6) They knew how to divide up the land for cultivation, and as a corollary they must have known how much earth each species required for its sustenance. It was from them that the Rabbis acquired this knowledge, whose correctness is vouched for by this verse. (7) In both cases for agricultural purposes. (8) Being dispossessed thereof, v. Deut. II, 12. (9) Fallow borders were left around seed-beds for the convenience of treading; the area stated in the Mishnah does not include the borders. (10) That the whole may be technically regarded as a seed-bed, and the laws appertaining thereto (v. *infra*) apply to it. (11) Ibid. XI, 10.

b (1) I.e., the Mishnah refers to such. But if it is surrounded by other beds sown with different seeds, there is only the two handbreadths space occupied by the borders of the two contiguous beds between them, whereas three handbreadths space is required between two rows of different plants. (2) Which can be left unsown. It is then possible to have the bed surrounded by others. (3) The term *Be Rab* may mean either the School founded by Rab or scholars in general; Weiss *Dor*, III, 158.

עין משפט נר מצוה

כ א מיי' שם הלכה י:

וקים להו לרבנן דחמשה בשיתא לא ינקי מהדדי ומנלן דהא דקים להו לרבנן (דחמשא בשיתא) מילתא היא. דא"ר חייא בר אבא א"ר יוחנן מאי דכתיב °לא תסיג גבול רעך [אשר גבלו ראשונים] גבול שגבלו ראשונים לא תסיג מאי גבלו ראשונים אמר רבי שמואל בר נחמני אמר רבי *יונתן (מאי) דכתיב °אלה בני שעיר החורי יושבי הארץ אטו כולי עלמא יושבי רקיע נינהו אלא שהיו בקיאין בישובה של ארץ שהיו אומרים מלא קנה זה לזית מלא קנה זה לגפנים מלא קנה זה לתאנים וחורי שמריחים את הארץ וחוי אמר רב פפא שהיו טועמין את הארץ כחויא רב אחא בר יעקב אמר חורי שנעשו בני חורין מנכסיהן אמר רב אסי ערוגה תוכה ו' חוץ מגבוליה תניא נמי הכי ערוגה תוכה ששה גבוליה בכמה *כדתנן רבי יהודה אומר רוחב כמלא רוחב פרסה א"ר זירא ואיתימא רבי חנינא בר פפא מ"ט דר' יהודה דכתיב °והשקית ברגלך כגן הירק מה רגל טפח אף גבול נמי טפח אמר רב ^א ערוגה בחורבה שנינו והאיכא מקום קרנות אמרי בי רב משמיה דרב בממלא את הקרנות וליזרע מאבראי ולא לימלי מגואי גזירה

ס"א ל"ג | דברים יט | בראשית לו | דברים יא

רש"י

קים להו לרבנן דסתם ערוגה הנזרעת בה ה' זרעונין כך היא מדתה דחמשה זרעונין בשיתא טפחים לא ינקי אמצעי ושברוחות מהדדי דשיעור יניקת כל זרע טפח ומחצה עם מקום הזרע הרי מן הזרע הנזרע (סמוך לגבולה) [בגבול הערוגה] כנגד האמצעי ועד האמצעי ג"ט ומאלו השנים אנו למדים דסבר הגא' דידן שיניקת הזרע טפח ומחצה מדלא קבע מקום לזרע הנזרע אצל הגבול *להושיבו אצל הקרן אלא אפי' אם בא לזורעו כנגד אמצעיתה זורעו אלמא בהרחקת ג' טפחים סגי ואע"ג דלענין כלאים היכרא בעלמא בעינן ולא חיישינן ליניקה כדתנן לקמן במתניתין גבי ראש תור וגבי ב' שורות מיהו הפרש זרעוני ערוגה דלא להוי ערבוב ליכא היכרא בבציר משיעור יניקה דגבי ראש תור ושתי שורות דלקמן איכא היכרא הלכך כי רמיז לן קרא ה' זרעונין בערוגה בת ו' טפחים קאמר: ומנא לן דהא דקים להו לרבנן. בשיעור יניקה מילתא היא למיסמך עלה ולומר בקיאין הן החכמים בעבודת אדמה לידע כמה יונקים שלא תתמה לומר מי הודיע לבריות שיעור יניקה והיך יוכלו לעמוד על כן: גבול רעך. ליטע סמוך למיצר להכחיש קרקעו כשיעור אשר גבלו הראשונים ומי הם ראשונים אמוריים וחויים שהיו בקיאים בכך כדאשכחן בבני שעיר: מלא קנה זה. קנה המדה שבו מודדין הקרקע: לזית. ראוי לגדל זיתים וזה לתאנה והיו יודעין להפריש את הארץ בין קנה לקנה בריחה וטעמה היכן לזיתים והיכן הוא לתאנים וממילא דבקיאים היו בשיעור יניקה: שמריחין. סרס את התיבה ודורשה: וחוי. למה נקרא חוי: שטועמין את הארץ. לאיזה דבר ראויה: כחויא. כנחש שמאכלו עפר: שנעשין בני חורים מנכסיהם. שנטרדו מנחלתם ולא הוצרכו לעבוד אדמתן כדכתיב ובני עשו יירשום (דברים ב): אמר רב אסי ערוגה. שאמרו צריכה להיות ו' חוץ מגבוליה שהיו מניחין בערוגה קרקע חלק סביבות הזריעה למקום דישה כשהוא משקה הזרעים מהלך בגבולין והשמיענו רב אסי דלא תימא ו' עם הגבולין וכשהניח טפח חלק לכאן וטפח חלק לכאן לא תהא ערוגה מקום יניקתה אלא ארבע ואין הפרש בין אמצעי לשכנגדו אלא הגבול אלא טפחיים: בכמה. כמה רחבן להיות ערוגה כהלכתה ותהא עליה תורת הערוגה לכל דבריה כדלקמן להתיר ראש תור ירק הנכנס לה והיוצא ממנה דכי ליתא כשיעורא לא חשיב למיהוי לה קולי שדה: פרסה. פרסת רגל: והשקית ברגלך. להטעין על כתפך מים ולהלך ברגלך סביבותיה להשקותה למ"ל למכתב רגלך לומר שבמקום מהלכו להשקותה כשיעור רגל הוא: אמר רב ערוגה בחורבה שנינו. במשנתנו להתיר בה ה' זרעונין אבל לא שסביבותיה ערוגות שהרי לא פירשו לך אלא הפרש זרעונין שבתוכה ואם תזרע ערוגות סביבותיה לא תוכל להרחיק בין אותן שבתוכה ולזרוע אותן שברוחות הערוגה סמוך לגבול להרחיקה מן האמצעי כשיעורו לפי שאתה מקריבו אצל זרע הנזרע בחברתה אצל גבולה שאין ביניהן אלא שני טפחים של גבולי הערוגה ואנן ג' בעינן: והא איכא מקום קרנות. מאי דוחקיה דלא לאוקומיה בערוגה בין הערוגות מוקפת מכל צד ג' ערוגות שהן ח' כזה*

ולזרוע באמצע וכן בכולן ה' זרעונין והא איכא בכל ערוגה מקום קרנות זוויותיה ואתה יכול להמשיך זרע גרעין שתזרע בצד גבולין של זו לצפון ושל זו לדרום של זו למזרח ושל זו למערב ולזרוע אותן גרעינין אצל הקרנות ואינך צריך להמשיכן מכנגד אותן שבחבירו מפנים אלא הפרש טפח ואמאי אמר רב בערוגה שבחורבה שנינו: בממלא את הקרנות. רב מוקי מתניתין בממלא את כל הרוח של ערוגה לצפון מן המזרח למערב וכן רוח דרומי אבל המזרחי והמערבי זורע מעט ומניח הפרש מכאן ומכאן (כזה)

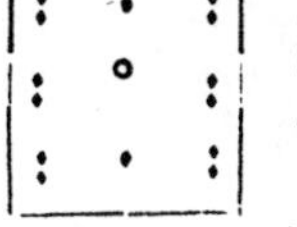

הלכך אי אתה יכול לזרוע עוד בערוגה שאצלה לצפון ושאצלה לדרום מפני עירבוב של ב' הערוגות: וליזרע מאבראי. ויקיפנה ערוגות מכל צד ואת הקרנות שבתוכה לא ימלא (א) ומאי דוחקיה דרב לאוקומיה בערוגה שבחורבה שאין שם אלא היא: גזירה

תוספות

וקים להו לרבנן דחמשה בשיתא לא ינקי. והאמר ר"ת דמכל מקום אילטריך קרא דאי לאו קרא ה"א אע"ג דלא ינקי איכא עירבוב ואסור קמ"ל קרא דבכה"ג ליכא עירבוב ובקרא לחודיה נמי לא סגי דלא הוה ידעינן חמשה בכמה שרי קרא אבל השתא דקים להו לרבנן דחמשה בשיתא לא ינקי אית לן לאוקמי קרא בשיתא וא"ת הכתי ינקי מהדדי דאין כאן ג' טפחים בין זרע לזרע דחסר מקום הזרעים שכל הערוגה אינה רק ששה טפחים ואומר ר"ת דלא קשה מידי דאמות של כלאים שוחקות הן כדמוכח בריש עירובין (דף ג:) ואומר ר"י דה"ג גמירי דחמשה בשיתא לא ינקי עם מקום הזרעים וא"ת יזרעו ט' מינין בערוגה ד' בד' קרנות וד' באמצע כל רוח ואחד באמצע דכל אחד רחוק מחבירו ג' טפחים וי"ל דבכולי האי הוי עירבוב ועוד דאז לא היה יכול לזרוע אלא גרעין אחד מכל מין ומין אבל בחמשה זרעונים יכול לזרוע מארבע מינים הרבה לכל רוח ומיהו קשה לר"י דמנלן לאוקמי קרא בערוגה ו' על ו' אפילו פחות נמי רק שיש באלכסונה ו' ויזרע ד' לד' קרנות ואחת באמצע דהשתא נמי לא ינקי מהדדי וי"ל דסברא דבענין זה אסור פן לא ידקדק לזרוע ממש בסוף הקרן ויש לחוש ליניקה אבל השתא אין צריך לדקדק אלא בגרעין האמצעית ומהאי טעמא נמי אתי שפיר שאין זורעין ט' בערוגה אבל קשה לרשב"א דלוקי בערוגה ה' על ה' דהשתא יש באלכסונה (ו') [ז] דכל אמתא בריבוע אמתא ותרי חומשי באלכסונא ויכול לזרוע בקרנות בלא דקדוק ותירץ לו ר"י דאין להעמיד המקרא בענין זה שאינו שיעור לא ליניקה ולא לשום דבר:

לא תסיג גבול רעך. וא"ת א"כ הזורע כלאים ילקה שתים משום לא תזרע ומשום לא תסיג גבול ובפרק אותו ואת בנו (חולין פב:) אמר הזורע כלאים [כלאים] לוקה שתים משמע דבחד כלאים אינו לוקה אלא אחת °וי"ל דלא לקי אהאי לאו משום דקרא נמי איירי בהסגת גבול ממש דאין לוקין בלאו דניתן להשבון ועוד דהוי לאו שבכללות:

חוי. אור"ת דלאו היינו חוי דשבעה עממין שהרי אינו דורש כלום למה שמם כן אלא בני שעיר גופיה איקרו חוי כדכתיב בת צבעון החוי (בראשית לו):

גבוליה בכמה. פירש בקונטרס דנפקא מינה לענין ראש תור והא דקאמר בסמוך דאין ראש תור בערוגה היינו מערוגה לערוגה ור"י אומר דנפקא מינה למקח וממכר אם מכר לו ערוגה וגבוליה:

דתנן רבי יהודה אומר כו'. אף על גב דרבי יהודה לא מיירי מידי בגבול אלא בהפסק שבין עבודת ירק לירק אחר כדאיתא בפ"ג דכלאים (משנה ג) דתנן היתה שדהו זרועה ירק ומבקש ליטע שם ירק אחר *ר' שמעון אומר עד שיהא התלם מפולש ר' יהודה אומר רוחב כמלא רוחב פרסה נראה להש"ס דכי היכי דחשיב הפסק לענין כלאים חשיב נמי להיות גבול לערוגה:

אמר רב ערוגה בחורבה שנינו. פירש ר"ת דקס"ד שאינו ממלא כל הרוח אלא זורע באמצע כל רוח טפח וג' חומשין ומניח מכל צד לצד קרנות טפחיים וחומש חרב דהשתא זרעוני רוח זה רחוקין מזרעוני רוח האחרת כשיעור אלכסון של טפחיים וחומש על טפחיים וחומש דהוי ג"ט ויותר שני חומשי חומש ופריך והא איכא מקום קרנות שיכול לעשות שם ערוגות אע"פ שלא ירחיק אלא שיעור ב' הגבולים דהשתא איכא טובא בין זרע הפנימית שבאמצע הרוחות ובין זרע החיצונה של צד הקרן דהא איכא ב' גבולין ומקום חרב שהוא ב' טפחים וחומש בכל קרן (ב) ומשני בממלא את הקרנות של מזרח ומערב וברוח צפון ודרום גרעין לכל רוח כאשר תצייר (ג) דבאותה ערוגה איכא הרחקה ג' (כזה)

ואם באת לסבבה בערוגות (אפילו) במקום קרנות לא יהיו ג' טפחים בין זרעוני ערוגה אמצעי לזרעוני ערוגה שבקרנות שאין הפרש ביניהם אלא שיעור שני גבולין אע"פ שיוכל עדיין לזרוע גרעין אחד בכל קרן החיצונית הא מסיק דגזרינן שמא לא ידקדק וימלא קרנות הכי נמי גזרינן בחיצונות שמא ימלא:

וליזרע מאבראי. וליזרע ערוגות לצד קרנות האמצעי כדפרישית ולא ימלא הקרנות דהכי עדיף טפי שיכול להרבות בערוגות:

גזירה

רבינו חננאל

באמצע כו'. עיקרה דמילתא דקים להו לרבנן דה' זרעונים בו' טפחים לא ינקי להדדי וכל דקים להו לרבנן מילתא היא. ואיכא יושבי הארץ שבקיאין בישיבתה של ארץ דברירין להון אלין מילוי ופליקא דהני ששה דערוגה הן מקום זרעונים ואיכא סביביהון גבול טפח ומפרש במתני' היה לו גובל טפח זורע לתוכה י"ג זרעונין. ומפרש' הכא רב אשי דהא ערוגה ו' על ו' חוץ מגבולה. ועיקר דהא מילתא דלא מפסק למהוה בין ירק לירק טפח אחד דהאי הוה מפיק בין ירק לירק טפח אחד. אפילו ערוגה שהיא ה' על ה' הוה אפשר למזרע ח' על ד' רוחותיה וד' באמצע משום דהויא כ"ה טפחים. י"ב מהן הן נזרעין. ודאיצטריכין למימר הכין. דחזינן מרב סעדיה גאון מחסיא דאיסתברא ליה כמן הכין ולאו כי דאיסתברא ליה בהאי אלא קים להו לרבנן דה' זרעונים כל אחד אין פחות מטפח על טפח בו' על ו' לא ינקי מהדדי. והיכי דמי כל זוית טפח ומחצה על טפח ומחצה חרב. ובכל רוח ג"ט אורך רק ברוחב טפח ובאמצע [מין] אחד טפח על טפח דמשכחת בין כל אחד ואחד טפח ומחצה באורך. וכן צורתו*) למראית עין. ודבר זה (סמן) [בזמן] שהזרעונים החמשה נזרעין כולן בתוך הערוגה שהיא ו' על ו' שנמצא הזרעונים נופן של ד' רוחות אוכלין בהן ג' ג' טפחי' באמצע נשארו ג' טפחים. א' ומחצה מיכן וא' ומחצת מיכן ונמצא ד' הקרנות פנויין ולא אפשר למיהוי טפי מן הכי בזמן שארבעה הקרנות פנויין והוא (איכיר) שיעור ו' על ו' והזרעונין בתוכן. אבל אם הזרעונין הרץ לששה אפשר שיהא בה ט' זרעונין שבין כל א' לחבירו טפח ומחצה וד' הקרנות פנויין כי היכי דאיתא בערוגה

*) הציור על זה נמצא בסוף המסכת

נ"ל ר' ישמעאל

מסורת הש"ס

רש"ל להושיבו

[עי' גם כאן יוחנן]

כלאים פ"ג מ"ג

הגהות הב"ח

(א) רש"י ד"ה וליזרע מאבראי וכו' לא ימלא כזה:

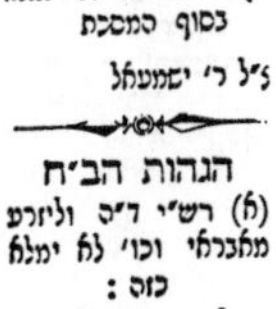

(ב) תוס' ד"ה אמר רב וכו' ב' טפחים וחומש בכל קרן כזה:

(ג) בא"ד גרעין לכל רוח כאשר תצייר כזה:

גליון הש"ס

תוס' ד"ה לא תסיג וכו' וי"ל דלא לקי אהאי לאו. עי' יומא דף לו ע"ב תוס' ד"ה לאו דנבילה:

כא א מיי' שם הל"א :
כב ב ג שם הלכה י :
כג ד ה שם הלכה טו :

*גזירה שמא ימלא את הקרנות ולא יהא אלא ראש תור ירק מי לא תנן *היה ראש תור ירק נכנס לתוך·שדה אחר מותר מפני שנראה סוף שדה אין ראש תור בערוגה ושמואל אמר ערוגה בין הערוגות שנינו והא קא מיתערבי בהדדי [ב]בנוטה שורה לכאן ושורה לכאן אמר עולא בעו במערבא הפקיע תלם אחד על פני כולה מהו אמר רב ששת בא ערבוב וביטל את השורה רב אסי אמר [ג]אין עירובו *מבטל את השורה איתיביה רבינא לרב אשי *הנוטע שתי שורות של קישואין שתי שורות של דילועין שתי שורות של פול המצרי מותר שורה אחת של קישואין ושורה אחת של דילועין ושורה אחת של פול המצרי אסור שאני הכא דאיכא *שראבא אמר רב כהנא א"ר יוחנן [ד]הרוצה למלאות כל גינתו ירק עושה ערוגה ששה על ששה ועוגל בה חמשה וממלא קרנותיה כל מה שירצה והא איכא דביני וביני אמרי דבי רבי ינאי במחריב בין הבינים רב אשי אמר [ה]אם היו זורעין שתי זורען ערב זורען שתי איתיביה רבינא לרב אשי *עבודת ירק בירק אחר ששה טפחים ורואין אותם כטבלא

גזירה שמא ימלא. ואחר כך יזרע בחברתה אצל הגבול מתוכה כאשר זרע האמצעית ולא ישים ללבו עירבוב של שתי הערוגות : ולא יהא אלא ראש תור . כלומר אפילו מילא אותו ואחר כך זרע גרעין אחד בחברתה ואין הפרש כשיעור בינו לבין זרע שבזו מה בכך לא יהא נדון אלא כראש תור ירק הנמשך ובא משדה זו לשדה זו שנראה יפה שאינו מזו שנכנס לה אלא מזו שיוצא ממנה ואיכא היכירא וליניקה לא חיישינן ראש תור קרי ליה לפי שכן דרך לסוף השדה להיות מתקצרת התרישה ולימשך באלכסון כראש תור (כזה) 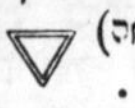 : אין ראש תור בערוגה . אין תורת היתר ראש תור מערוגה לערוגה אלא משדה גדולה לתוך ערוגה או מערוגה לתוך שדה גדולה או משדה גדולה לתוך שדה גדולה אבל שתי ערוגות לא הוי היכר אלא דומה כאילו הן אחת דלא חשיבא כל חדא באפיה נפשה : והא קא (א)מערבי בהדדי. העלין של ערוגה זו בעלין של חבירתה מלמעלה שאין ביניהן אלא שני טפחים של גבולין : בנוטה שורה לכאן ושורה לכאן. ממשיך של רוח זו בצד קרן מזרחית צפונית ושל רוח זו לצד מערבית דרומית וכן כולן להרחיקן שלא יהיו זה כנגד זה כמו שפי' גבי אתקפתא דלעיל דמקום קרנות ולא גזר שמואל שמא ימלא את הקרנות כך נראית שיטה זו בעיני ולא פירשו רבותי כן שהם פירשו קרנות אלו גבולין ויש לי גמגומים בה הרבה גם בכל הש"ס לא שמעתי קרנות אלא זויות ומצאתי לי סמך ביסודו של רבי שמעון הזקן אחי אמי מפי רבינו גרשום אבי הגולה ותשובת רבינו יצחק בן יהודה שהושיבה בג' פנים לא ישרו בעיני : הפקיע. לשון קדיעה שקורע הקרקע כמו מבלאי מכנסי הכהנים היו מפקיעין (סוכה דף נא·) : תלם. מענה שורה : על פני כולה . שהעביר מזרע שבצפון לזרע שבדרום דרך האמצעי וזרעו מאחד המינין או ממין שני מהו מי מבטל תורת שורה הלכות ערוגה בשביל תלם אחד או לא : בא עירבוב וביטל את השורה . ואסור : שתי שורות של קישואים . ואצלן שתי שורות של דלועין ואצלן ב' שורות של פול המצרי ולא בערוגה אלא בשדה גדולה : מותר . דשתי שורות חשיבי למיהוי שדה לנפשייהו והוי היכירא דכל מין ומין מילתא באפי נפשיה : שורה אחת . מכל אחד הוי עירבוב [דלא חשיבא כל חד שדה לנפשה אלמא תלם אחד הוי עירבוב] : דאיכא שראבא . זמורותיהן ארוכות ומתערבות הרבה מלמעלה ונראה עירובן במקומות הרבה : כל גנתו ירק . של הרבה מינין : עושה . כל ערוגותיה מרובעות ו' : ועוגל . בכל ערוגה ה' וזורע בעוגל מין אחד ויש היכר הרבה לדבר ואין צריך להרחיב (ב)בין ערוגה לחברתה וזורע חצי טפח הסובב את כל ערוגה וערוגה משאר מינין לפי שכל אחד ואחד נראה מקומו חלוק לעצמו : והאיכא דביני וביני . הן גבולי הערוגה שאמרנו למעלה ערוגה ו' חוץ מגבולין ואותן גבולין כשיזרעם מחברים את היקף ריבוע הערוגות והוי עירבוב שהרי הם של שני מינין : במחריב בין הביניים . ואינו זורען ולמלאות דקאמר ר' יוחנן לאו דוקא למלאות כל הגנה קאמר אלא שיהיו כל ערוגותיה מליאות ולעולם חוץ מגבוליהן : אם היו . ריבוע הערוגות זרועין שתי זורע בין הביניים ערב : עבודת ירק בירק אחר . כמה שיעור עבודתו להרחיק חבירו ממנו כדי עבודתו : ו' טפחים·לה' זרעונין כמו ששנינו: כטבלא

גזירה שמא ימלא כו' ולא יהא אלא ראש תור . ואפילו ימלא את הקרנות אין כאן עירבוב דהא קרנות אמצעות הולכות כנגד ריבוע הערוגות שסביבותיה והוי כעין ראש תור דשרי אע"ג דאין הרחקה ג' טפחים כיון שיש בהן היכר . אין ראש תור בערוגה לפי שקטנה היא וליכא היכירא :

ושמואל (ג) אמר ערוגה בין ערוגות שנינו . ולצד הקרנות דאפי' מלא הקרנות אין בכך כלום דסבר דיש ראש תור בערוגה :

והא קא מיערבבו אהדדי . שעליהן שלמעלה מעורבבים יחד ואע"ג דאיכא ראש תור מלמטה אסור כיון דמערבי' למעלה העלין דאוירא מבלבל דאפי' לא ינקי מהדדי אסור כדאמרינן (כלאים פ"ז משנה ד) המסכך גפנו ע"ג תבואתו קידש משום דאוירא מבלבל אבל בערוגה אחת ידיעה וליכא עירבוב וכולי האי אין סברא להתיר משום ראש תור :

(ד) בנוטה שורה לכאן ושורה לכאן בנוטה שער ערוגה זו לתוכה וזו לתוכה כדתקנבמס' (כלאים פ"ד מ"ט) ומייתי לה בב"ב (פב:) מעשה בצלמון כו' והיה הופך שער שורה לכאן ועוד תנן בפ"ג דכלאים (משנה ה) נוטע אדם קישות ודלעת בתוך גומא ובלבד שתהא זו נוטה לצד זו וזו לצד זו :

אמר עולא בעו במערבא הפקיע תלם אחד על פני כולה מהו. פי' העמיק תלם א' על פני סביבותיה לד' רוחותיה מהו דבלא העמיק בין לרב בין לשמואל אסור לעשות ערוגות סביבותיה אבל כשחפר והעמיק כשיעור תלם דהיינו טפח בעי אי הוי היכירא כמו בשדה דהוי היכירא כדתנן בכלאים (פ"ג משנה ג) היתה שדהו זרועה ירק כו' *רש"א עד שיהיה התלם מפולש ולעיל הבאתיה א"ר ששת בא עירבוב וביטל את השורה פירוש מבטל הפסק התלם ולא הוי היכירא ותלם היינו שורה ובני ארץ ישראל קרו ליה תלם ובני בבל קרו ליה שורה רב אשי אמר אין עירבוב מבטל השורה :

איתיביה הנוטע שתי שורות כו' מותר. דשתי שורות של דלועין מפסיקין בין קישואין לפול המצרי דקישואין ודלועין לא הוי כלאים דמיככרי כדתנן בסיפא דהך ולעיל הבאתיה נוטע אדם קישות ודלעת בתוך גומא ובלבד כו' וכן דלועין ופול המצרי מינכרי אבל קישואין ופול המצרי הוי כלאים אבל שורה של קישואין כו' אסור דשורה אחת של דלועין לא מפסקה בין קישואין לפול המצרי וכי היכי דקישואין ופול המצרי מבטלין שורה של דלועין שבאמצע ה"נ עירבוב זרעוני הערוגות מבטל תלם שהפקיע ומשני שאני התם דאיכא שראבא שהן גדולים וגסים והכא בזרעונים דקין דלא מבטלי עומק התלם ומפסיק :

אמר ר' יוחנן הרוצה למלאות כל גינתו ירק עושה בה ערוגה ו' על ו' ועוגל כו' . פירוש עושה ערוגה מרובעת ו' על ו' ובתוכה מרובע עוד ה' על ה' ויהיה הפסק בין האמצעי לחיצון חצי טפח מכל צד ועוגל בה בתוך הריבוע הפנימי ה' על ה' וימלא העוגל במין אחד ובקרנות ריבוע הפנימי יזרע מין א' בכל קרן וקרן (כזה)  והשתא הוי בריבוע הפנימי ה' מינין ואע"פ שבין זרע שבתוך העגול לזרע שבקרנות אין הפסק רק משהו אין לחוש דעוגל הוי היכירא בלבד שיהא ג' טפחים בין זרע קרן זה לקרן זה וכן יכול לעשות ערוגות בכל סביבותיה בענין זה דהשתא יש ג"ט בין ערוגה לערוגה דריבוע החיצון חצי טפח חרב וכן לאחרת הרי טפח וב' גבולין שהיו ב' טפחים הרי ג"ט וא"ת מאי איריא ששה אפי' ה' על ה' נמי ועוגל בה ארבע כיון דעוגל חשיב היכירא ויש לומר דעוגל ה' חשיב היכירא אבל ד' לא :

והא איכא ביני וביני . ס"ד דממלא כל הקרנות וזורע בקרנות ריבוע החיצון עד הגבול והרי אין הפסק בין ערוגה זו לאחרת אלא שני טפחים של שני הגבולים ומשני במחריב בין הביניים שמניח חצי טפח הסובב ריבוע הפנימי הכל חרב ואינו ממלא אלא קרנות של ריבוע הפנימי דהשתא יש הרחקה שלש טפחים אי נמי דידע לה שפיר דמניח חצי טפח חרב אלא דפריך אמאי דקאמר למלאות כל גינתו דהשתא אינו ממלא כל גינתו ומשני במחריב כו' ור' יוחנן דקאמר למלאות כל גינתו ירק לבד מן הביניים קאמר איתיביה רבינא לרב אשי עבודת ירק בירק אחר ששה טפחים פי' ערוגה שהתירו בה חמשה זרעונים דהיינו עבודת ירק בירק אחר רואין אותה כטבלא מרובעת הוא דשרי אף על גב דאיכא תערובת ענפים ועלין מלמעלה הא לאו הכי אסור דלא שרי עירבוב אלא בערוגה כהלכתא אבל עוגל ה' אסור דלא חשיב תנא היכרא ומשני דלא בא תנא להחמיר אלא להקל להתיר ראש תור ירק הנכנס לה והיוצא ממנה דבמרובעת שרי אבל בעגולה אין ראש תור ניכר והא דאמר לעיל אין ראש תור ירק לערוגה מערוגה לערוגה קאמר אבל משדה גדולה לערוגה יש ראש תור כן עיקר פי' השמועה ולפי' הקונט' והא איכא מקום קרנות לשון מקום קרנות לא משמע כפירושו וגם מה דמדמה לראש תור וכל הסוגיא מיושבת כפי' ר"ת ומה שפירש"י והא איכא מקום קרנות ויכול להמשיך של זו לצפון ושל זו לדרום ואין צריך להמשיכו מכנגד אותו שבחברתה אלא טפח לא דקדא"כ אינם מרוחקין אלא כמו שעולה האלכסון של טפחיים על טפח ואינו עולה אפי' לשני טפחים ושני חומשים שאלכסון של טפח על טפחיים פחות מאלכסון של טפח על טפח (כזה) : 

מכין

רבינו חננאל

ומן הכין כי אמרו בתלמוד א"ר כהנא בשם ריש לקיש כולהן חוץ לששה אקשו עליה . א"כ ליתני ט' וכן היא . הרי אלו ט' זרעונין סביבי ערוגה ו' על ו' בזמן שהן חוץ לששה ואף זה כהונן הוא אבל אם זרעונים בתוך ששה הן אם אינו מחריב את הארבעת הקרנות אלא מניח טפח ומחצה וזורע טפח אפשר דהוו ח' זרעונים שכולן בתוך ערוגה שהיא ו' על ו' ולא תקינו רבנן הכין אלא לא תקינו ו' בלחוד : אמר רב ערוגה בחורבה שנינו . ואקשינן עליה דהאי דתקינו רבנן ה' זרעונים לתוך ו' ואע"ג דאפשר לעשות ח' לא תקינו אלא ה' בלבד.אלא מפני שתקנו להחריב את ד' הקרנות תקנוהו ה' כדי שיהא יכול לעשו' ערוגות אחרות בכנפי זויות ערוגה זו כגון אלו ואי בחורבה הא איכא קרנות ולמה לו למשבק פנויין ואתינן לפרוקי בממלא את הקרנות לערוגות· ערוגות כהני דפרשינן לעילא . ואע"ג (דהובר)[דבחורבה]הוא. ומקשי' וליזרעולא(ליצלי) [לימלי] ופי' אי חרבה היא ליזרע ח' זרעונין בערוגה שלא יהו קרנות פנויות ולא יזרע כנגדן באלכסון ערוגות ופרקי' האי דגזרו בחרבה שיהו קרנות של ערוגה פנויות שמא ימלא כנגדן ערוגות . ומקשינן ואי הוי בקרנות זרע נמי אפשר דזרע ערוגה בסמוך לה והוא קרן בראש תור אחרת להכניסו לשדה אחרת. מי לא תנן היה ראש תור ירק נכנס לתוך שדה אחרת מותר מפני שנראה כסוף שדה. ופרקי' אין ראש תור בחרבה כי שרי ראש תור מן שדה גדולה שהוא (מופס) [מוכה] דסוף שדה הוא . אבל ערוגה בחורבה לית לה ראש תור מותר כי האי משום דלא מוכח ושמואל אמר ערוגה בין הערוגות שנינו. פירוש בין בחורבה ובין בשדה ואקשינן ליה כי מכדי בין הערוגות הא קא מיערבי זרעים בהדדי . ומפרקינן בנוטה שורה לכאן ושורה לכאן. ואמרינן תרין פירושי חד מנהון שמענוה משום רבינו סעדיה גאון דסמיך בערוגה אחרת לכל מין [אותן] [מינין דהויין שורה לכאן ממין אחד ולא דמי ופירושי' דהוה אמרין ליה רבואתא דילמ' לענין בנוטה שורה לכאן ושורה לכאן אע"פ שהן מינין [אחרים] דקאמר שמואל כיון שהוא עושה בערוג' זו שורה ואינו ערבובי' וכנגדו בערוגה אחרת שורה ואינה ערבוב. וזו נוטה לכאן וזו נוטה לכאן היכרא רבה הוא שהן ב' שורות והוגה דמילי כלאים תלינן בחזיות העין דהא מחיצה אפילו כמחיצת שבת כגון קנים וחבלים מתרת לענין כלאים אף על גב דליכא בינייהו הרחקה משום דאיכא היכרא במחיצה . והכין קאמר שמואל איכא היכרא בב' שורות אחת נוטה לכאן ואחת נוטה לכאן[נ]נודע שב' שדות הן.

ותנן נוטע אדם קישות ודלעת בתוך גומא אחת ובלבד שלא תהא [זה] נוטה אצל זה ולא זו נוטה אצל זו . ובברייתא בתוספתא . מותר אדם לעשות בתוך שדהו תלמיות קטנות של טפח טפח וליתן לתוכן ג' מינין אחד מיכן ואחד מיכן ואחד באמצע . מותר אדם לעשות בתוך שדהו ערוגות קטנות של ו' ו' טפחים וליתן בתוכו ה' ה' מינין ארבעה על ד' רוחות ערוגה ואחת באמצע . ומותר אדם לעשות בתוך שדהו גומא כ... שהיא עמוקה טפח וליתן לתוכה ד' מינין והופכן לארבע רוחותיה.ומותר אדם לעשות בתוך שדהו תלם להיות נוטע קשואין ודלועין אבטיחים ומלפפונות והופכן אלו לצד זה ואלו לצד זה.לפום כן קאמר שמואל נימע ש... לכאן ושורה לכאן : אמר עולא בעין במערבא הפקיע תלם אחד על פני כולה מהו איפרש בה כמה פירושי ולא קא מיסתברין . והכין קא הויינא דעל מימרא דשמואל קאי דקאמר בערוגה בין הערוגות ש...

והתם

כלאים פ"ג מ"ג

סבכל את השורה וביטל השורה את הערוגה רש"ל

[נ"ל שרצא פי' גאון עלין רתכין שאותיין בארץ ורווחין וכנסין אלו באלו ערוך ערך שדן ב]

תוספתא פ"ב דכלאים

הגהות הב"ח

(א) רש"י ד"ה והא קא מיתערבי בהדדי : (ב) ד"ה ועוגל כו' ולא"צ להרחיק בין ערוגה : (ג) תוס' ד"ה וליזרע מלכתחלה וד"ה גזירה וד"ה ושמואל כה דבור א' : (ד) ד"ה בנוטה שורה וד"ה אמר עולא וד"ה איתיביה וד"ה א"ר יוחנן וד"ה הכל כה דיבור אחד :

on the outside,[4] and not fill up the inside? [85b]—It is a preventive measure, lest he fill up the corners. Yet let it not be other than a triangular plot[5] of vegetables? Did we not learn, If a triangular plot of vegetables enters another field,[6] this is permitted, because it is evidently the end of a field?[7]—[The permissibility of] a triangular plot does not apply to a seed-bed.[8]

But Samuel maintained: We learnt of a seed-bed in the midst of [other] seed-beds. But they intermingle?—He inclines one strip in one direction and one strip in another direction.

'Ulla said: They asked in the West [Palestine]: What if a person draws one furrow across the whole?[9] R. Shesheth maintained: The intermingling comes and annuls the strips.[10] R. Assi said: The intermingling does not annul the strips. Rabina raised an objection to R. Ashi: If one plants two rows of cucumbers, two rows of gourds, a and two rows of Egyptian beans, they are permitted;[1] one row of cucumbers, one row of gourds and one of Egyptian beans, they are forbidden?[2]—Here it is different, because there is entanglement.[3]

R. Kahana said in R. Johanan's name: If one desires to fill his whole garden with vegetables,[4] he can divide it into[5] bed[s] six [handbreadths] square, describe in each a circle five [handbreadths in diameter], and fill its corners with whatever he pleases.[6] But there is the [space] between [the beds]?[7]—Said the School of R. Jannai: He leaves the interspaces waste.[8] R. Ashi said: If they [the beds] are sown in the length, he sows them [the interspaces] in the breadth, and *vice versa*.[9] Rabina objected to R. Ashi: The planting[10] of one vegetable with another [requires]

(4) Of the seed-bed, i.e., it need not be in the middle of an unsown plot. (5) Lit., 'an ox-head'. (6) Sown with other crops. Fields were generally ended off in a triangular shape. (7) Though it comes right up to the other crops, one can see that there has been no indiscriminate sowing (cf. note on our Mishnah, *supra* 84b, n. b5); the same should apply here. (8) Because in the proposed case there is nothing to show that the different strips are distinct. (9) Rashi: From north to south, crossing the middle seeds, this furrow being either of one of the five seeds or of a sixth. Tosaf: The furrow is drawn right round the four sides of the plot but deepened (by a handbreadth) and the question is whether this deepening constitutes a distinguishing mark, so that it shall be permitted. (10) I.e., it is not a distinguishing mark, but on the contrary breaks up the separateness of the other strips, and so is forbidden.

a (1) Two rows constitute a field, and therefore each plant is regarded as in a separate field, though they are in proximity to each other. (2) This proves that a single row effects a prohibited intermingling. (3) Their leaves become entangled above as they grow high. On this account they are forbidden.

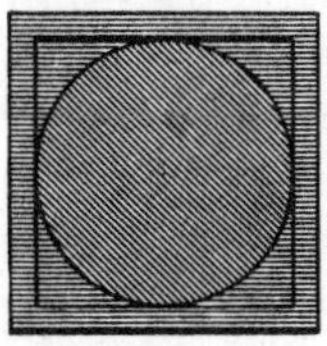

(4) Of different kinds. (5) Lit., 'make'. (6) Thus (see drawing): planting in this way shows that there has been no indiscriminate intermingling. (7) Viz., the borders which are to be left fallow, v. *supra* 85a. (8) R. Johanan's phrase 'his whole garden' is not meant literally, but merely applies to the seed-beds into which it is divided. (9) In this way literally the whole garden can be filled. (10) Lit., 'working'.

six handbreadths [square],[11] and they are regarded [86a] as a square board. Thus it is only permitted as a [square] board, but otherwise it is forbidden?[12]—There [it desires to] teach another leniency in respect thereof, [viz.,] to permit a triangular wedge that issues thence [into another plot or field].[13]

MISHNAH. HOW DO WE KNOW THAT IF ONE [A WOMAN] DISCHARGES SEMEN ON THE THIRD DAY[14] SHE IS UNCLEAN? BECAUSE IT IS SAID, BE READY AGAINST THE THIRD
a DAY.[1] HOW DO WE KNOW THAT A CIRCUMCISED CHILD[2] MAY BE BATHED [EVEN] ON THE THIRD DAY [AFTER CIRCUMCISION] WHICH FALLS ON THE SABBATH? BECAUSE IT IS SAID, AND IT CAME TO PASS ON THE THIRD DAY, WHEN THEY WERE SORE.[3] HOW DO WE KNOW THAT A CRIMSON-COLOURED STRAP IS TIED TO THE HEAD OF THE GOAT THAT IS SENT [TO 'AZAZ'EL]?[4] BECAUSE IT IS SAID, IF YOUR SINS BE AS SCARLET, THEY SHALL BE AS WHITE AS SNOW.[5] HOW DO WE KNOW THAT ANOINTING IS THE SAME AS DRINKING ON THE DAY OF ATONEMENT?[6] THOUGH THERE IS NO PROOF OF THIS, YET THERE IS A SUGGESTION THEREOF, FOR IT IS SAID, AND IT CAME INTO HIS INWARD PARTS LIKE WATER, AND LIKE OIL INTO HIS BONES.[7]

GEMARA. The first clause does not agree with R. Eleazar b. 'Azariah, whilst the second clause does agree with R. Eleazar b. 'Azariah, for if it [the first clause] were according to R. Eleazar b. 'Azariah, we have heard from him that she is clean?[8]—He who does not [wish to] explain [a Mishnah] as [reflecting the views of two] Tannaim learns 'she is clean' in the first clause, and [thus] establishes the whole of it in accordance with R. Eleazar b. 'Azariah. Whilst he who does explain it as [the opinions of two] Tannaim[9] [holds that] the first clause agrees with the Rabbis, while the second is according to R. Eleazar b. 'Azariah.

Our Rabbis taught: If one [a woman] discharges semen on the
b third day, she is clean; this is the view of R. Eleazar b. 'Azariah.[1] R. Ishmael said: This [interval] sometimes comprises four periods,[2] sometimes five, and sometimes six periods.[3] R. Akiba maintained: It [the interval for uncleanness] is always [up to] five periods. And if part of the first period has gone,[4] a part of the sixth period is given her.[5] Now the Rabbis stated this [the following difficulty] before R. Papa—others say, R. Papa said to Raba: As for R. Eleazar b. 'Azariah, it is well: he holds with the Rabbis, who maintain, Abstention [from intimacy] was effected on Thursday.[6] Again, R. Ishmael holds with R. Jose that abstention was effected on Wednesday. But with whom does R. Akiba agree?[7]—After all, R. Akiba holds as R. Jose, [but it is] as R. Adda b. Ahabah said: Moses ascended early in the morning and descended early in the morning. 'He ascended early in the morning,' for it is written, *and Moses rose up early in the morning, and went up unto mount Sinai;*[8] 'he descended early in the morning', for it is written, *Go, get thee down; and thou shalt come up, thou, and Aaron with thee:*[9] this likens descent to the ascent: just as ascent was early in the
c morning, so was descent early in the morning.[1] But why did he [Moses] have to tell them [in the morning]? Surely R. Huna said: The Israelites are holy, and do not cohabit by day![2]—But Raba said: If the house is in darkness, it is permitted. Raba also said—others state, R. Papa: A scholar may cause darkness with his garment, and it is [then] permitted.

(11) I.e., within a bed of this area it is possible to plant a number of different kinds of vegetables, as stated in our Mishnah. (12) This excludes planting in a circle. (13) I.e., when it is planted in this shape the triangular wedge too is permitted. But the plot itself may contain a circle. (14) After cohabitation.

a (1) Ex. XIX, 15. Lit., *'three days'*. The verse continues, *'come not near a woman'*. The Tanna understands this to mean that intercourse was debarred to them for three whole days, including the first day of abstention, before the Giving of the Law, which took place on the fourth day. This proves that a discharge within this period would render her unclean for the day of the discharge, whereas all had to be clean at the Revelation. (2) Lit., 'the circumcised'. (3) Gen. XXXIV, 24. This shows that one is in danger until three days have elapsed, and therefore the Sabbath may be desecrated on its account by bathing the child. (4) V. Lev. XVI, 21-26. (5) Isa. I, 18. By a miracle this crimson coloured strap turned white, thus showing the people that they were forgiven of their sins; v. Büchler, *Sin and Atonement*, p. 327. (6) That the former is interdicted equally with the latter? (7) Ps. CIX, 19. The former is a simile from drinking, the latter from anointing, and the two similes are treated as parallel. (8) V. *infra*. (9) V. B.M. 41a.

b (1) Thus, if she cohabits on Thursday and discharges on the Sabbath, she is clean, no matter at which part of the two days intimacy and discharge took place. (2) *'Onah*, pl. *'onoth*, is the technical term for a day or a night when these are equal. (3) He holds that she is unclean. Now, if cohabitation took place at the very beginning of Thursday evening whilst the discharge occurred at the end of the Sabbath, we have six periods; if at the end of Thursday night, five; and if at the end of Thursday, four. In all cases she is unclean. (4) When intimacy takes place. (5) A discharge up to then defiles her. (6) Whilst the giving of the Law took place on the Sabbath, at the very beginning of which they performed their ritual ablutions to purify themselves, if they had discharged semen on the Friday. Now some may have cohabited at the end of Thursday, and yet they were fit for the Revelation on the Sabbath, which shows that a discharge of semen on the third day does not defile. (7) For the Torah speaks of days, which implies that whether intimacy took place at the beginning or at the end of the day, she would be clean on the third (or, the fourth, according to R. Jose) day, irrespective of the numbers of 'periods' that elapsed. (8) Ex. XXXIV, 4. Though this refers to his second ascent after the breaking of the first tables, it is held to show that he *always* went up early in the morning. (9) Ibid. XIX, 24.

c (1) Hence Moses' order to the Israelites to abstain from intimacy was given early Wednesday morning; this allows five full 'periods' until the beginning of the Sabbath, when they purified themselves. (2) So Moses could have waited for the end of the day.

כטבלא מרובעת כטבלא הוא דשרי הא לאו הכי אסור התם לאקולי בה קולא אחרינא להתיר ראש תור היוצא הימנה:

מתני' מנין לפולטת שכבת זרע ביום השלישי (*שתהא) טמאה שנא' °היו נכונים לשלשת ימים *[א]מנין שמרחיצין את המילה ביום השלישי שחל להיות בשבת שנאמר °ויהי ביום השלישי בהיותם כואבים *[ב]מנין שקושרין לשון של זהורית בראש שעיר המשתלח שנאמר °אם יהיו חטאיכם כשנים כשלג ילבינו [ג]מנין *לסיכה שהיא כשתייה ביוה"כ אע"פ שאין ראיה לדבר זכר לדבר שנא' °ותבא כמים בקרבו וכשמן בעצמותיו:

גמ' רישא דלא כר' אלעזר בן עזריה סיפא כר"א בן עזריה דאי כרבי אלעזר בן עזריה טהורה שמענא ליה מאן דלא מוקי כתנאי תנא רישא טהורה ומוקי לה לכולה כר"א בן עזריה ומאן דמוקים כתנאי רישא רבנן וסיפא כר' אלעזר בן עזריה ת"ר *[ד]פולטת שכבת זרע ביום השלישי טהורה דברי רבי אלעזר בן עזריה רבי ישמעאל אומר פעמים שהן ד' עונות פעמים שהן ה' עונות פעמים שהן ו' עונות ר' עקיבא אומר לעולם ה' *ואם יצאתה מקצת עונה ראשונה נותנין לה מקצת עונה ששית אמרוה רבנן קמיה דרב פפא ואמרי לה רב פפא לרבא בשלמא ר' אלעזר בן עזריה כרבנן דאמרי בה' עביד פרישה ור' ישמעאל כר' יוסי דאמר בד' עביד פרישה אלא רבי עקיבא כמאן לעולם כר' יוסי כדאמר רב אדא בר אהבה *משה בהשכמה עלה ובהשכמה ירד בהשכמה עלה דכתיב °וישכם משה בבקר ויעל אל הר סיני בהשכמה ירד דכתיב °לך רד ועלית אתה ואהרן עמך מקיש ירידה לעליה מה עליה בהשכמה אף ירידה בהשכמה למה ליה למימרא להו והא אמר *רב הונא [ה]ישראל קדושים הן ואין משמשין מטותיהן ביום *הא אמר רבא אם היה בית אפל מותר ואמר רבא ואיתימא רב פפא תלמיד חכם מאפיל בטליתו ומותר והא

שמות יט; בראשית לד; ישעיה א; תהלים קט; שמות לד; שם יט

תורה אור

רש"י

כטבלא מרובעת. אלמא עגולה לאו ערוגה היא: התם. דבעי מרובעת לאחשובה שדה קאמר להתיר ראש תור כו' ולית ליה לר' יוחנן הא דאמר לעיל אין ראש תור בערוגה אי כמי אית ליה מערוגה לערוגה אבל משדה לערוגה יש ראש תור: **מתני'** שהיא טמאה. דיום השלישי אכתי לא מסרחה שכבת זרע וראויה לקלוט ולהיות ולד נוצר הימנה וקרינן שכבת זרע הראוי להזריע: לג' ימים. דהקפיד הכתוב על טומאת קרי במתן תורה *וקס"ד עם יום הפרישה קאמר דבד' בשבת פירשו מנשותיהן וקבלו תורה בשבת שהוא רביעי לאותם ששימשו מטותיה' ברביעי לפני הפרישה וטבלו לילי שבת ולא חש הכתוב אם יפלטו בשבת דמסרח ואינו שכבת זרע הראוי להזריע אבל אם פלטו ע"ש בשלישי טמאות לכך הפרישן שלשה ימים: מנין שמרחיצין. דאף ביום ג' מסוכן הוא: כמים בקרבו וכשמן בעצמותיו. מקיש סיכה לשתיה: **גמ'** רישא. דמתני': דלא כר' אלעזר בן עזריה. דאילו לדידי' שמעינן ליה פולטת ביום השלישי טהורה לקמן בברייתא: וסיפא. דקתני מרחיצין את המילה כו' ר' אלעזר בן עזריה דהוא אמר לה לקמן בפרק ר' אליעזר: מאן דלא מוקי כתנאי. דדחיק ומוקי מתניתין בתרי טעמי או משבש לה ומפרש לה דלא לאוקמי כתנאי משבש לה ואמר משבשתא היא ותני בה טהורה: ומאן דמוקי לה כתנאי. דניחא ליה לאוקומי כתנאי מלמימר משבשתא היא ומלאוקמי בתרי טעמי מוקי כמי להאי כתנאי ופלוגתא היא בהמפקיד (ב"מ מא:) גבי חבית דאמר ר' יוחנן מאן דמתרגם לי חבית אליבא דחד תנא מובילנא ליה מאני לבי מסותא ומוקי רישא ר' ישמעאל וסיפא רבי עקיבא ואי הוה בעי הוה מצי לאוקמי בתרי טעמי ובחד תנא ואיכא דמוקי לה התם בחד תנא ומוקי סיפא בשהניחה במקום שאינו מקומה: ביום השלישי. כגון ששמשה בה' ופלטה שכבת זרע בשבת ל"ש שמשה תחילת ליל חמישי דאישתהי ד' עונות שלמות ליל ה' וה' וליל ו' וו' ל"ש שמשה יום ה' עם חשיכה דלא אישתהי אלא מקצת ה' וליל ו' וו' דליכא אלא ב' עונות שלמות. העונה או יום או לילה: ר' ישמעאל אומר פעמים שהן כו'. בא לחלוק ולומר דפולטת בג' לשימושה טמאה אבל פולטת בד' טהורה ומודיעך לך דמקצת היום ככולו דלא הקפידה תורה אלא במנין של הימים ולא במנין העונות: ופעמים שהם ד' עונות. שלמות שאם שמשה ד' בשבת עם חשיכה פליטתה טמאה עד תחלת שבת: פעמים שהם ה' עונות. כגון ששמשה בתחלת היום של ד': פעמים שהם ו'. כגון ששמשה בתחלת ליל ד' בין השמשות: נותנין לה מקצת עונת ו'. להשלים ה' וכל הפולטת בתוך ה' עונות שלמות טמאה: אמרוה. להא אתקפתא דלקמיה: בשלמא כו'. פלוגתא דרבנן ור' יוסי בברייתא ומייתי לה בהאי פירקא לקמן דלרבנן בה' בשבת פרשו ולר' יוסי בד' ולכ"ע בשבת ניתנו עשרת הדברות וכיון דבשבת נתנו ע"כ בליל שבת טבלו ולא שחרית כדמתרץ לקמן שלא יהו הללו טובלין והללו מהלכין לקבל תורה הלכך בשלמא ר' אלעזר כרבנן דאמרי בחמשה בשבת עבוד פרישה ויש שלא פרשו אלא עם חשיכה ומדטבלו ליל שבת ולא חשו שמא תפלטנה עוד ש"מ דפולטת בג' טהורה ומקצת היום של תשמיש ככולו: ור' ישמעאל. דאומר בג' טמאה בד' טהורה קסבר בד' עבוד פרישה כר' יוסי דהוה ליל שבת רביעי ומיהו יש שלא פירשו עד סמוך לחשיכה וליכא אלא ד' עונות ליל ה' וה' ליל ו' וו' ואפילו הכי משטבלו פליטתן טהורה דלא הקפידה תורה אלא בימים: אלא רבי עקיבא. דאמר כל ה' עונות טמאה אם תפלוט כמאן ומהיכא למד דאעונות קפיד קרא הא ימים כתיב וקיימא לן מקצת היום ככולו: לעולם. ר' עקיבא כר' יוסי ובדרב אדא דאמר משה כל עליותיו בהשכמה עלה וכל ירידותיו בהשכמה הלכך ירידה דכתיב וירד משה מן ההר אל העם ויקדש את העם דהיינו פרישה בהשכמה רביעי היתה ומדהוזקק להפרישן בהשכמה ש"מ עד ה' עונות שלמות קפיד קרא: ופרכינן למה ליה למימרא להו. שחרית בלאו הכי נמי לא הוו משמשי: דקאמר רב הונא. דאין משמשין ביום דכתיב (משלי יט) בוזה דרכיו ימות דבעי לניעותא שלא יסתכלו: תלמיד חכם. שהוא נגוע ולא יסתכל סגי ליה במאפיל בטליתו:

והא

תוספות

מנין לפולטת כו' שנא' היו נכונים לשלשת ימים. אע"פ שבאותה שעה עדיין לא ניתנה תורה מ"מ מסתמא הקפידה תורה על דבר שעתיד להיות טומאה אחר מתן תורה ואע"ג דלא הקפידה על זבין ומצורעין ובועלי נדות היינו משום טעמא דתניא בפרק מי שמתו (ברכות כב.) כתיב והודעתם לבניך ולבני בניך וכתיב יום אשר עמדת לפני ה' אלהיך בחורב מה להלן באימה וביראה וברתת ובזיע כו' מכאן אמרו זבין ומצורעים ובועלי נדות מותרין לקרות בתורה בנביאים ולשנות במשנה ובש"ס בהלכות ובאגדות ובעלי קריין אסורין פירוש דבעל קרי אינו באימה וביראה דמחמת קלות ראש הוא בא:

אע"פ שאין ראייה לדבר זכר לדבר שנאמר ותבא כמים וגו'. ומיהו ראיה גמורה לא הוי משום דקרא לא מישתעי בשתיה אלא ברחילה משום דמשמע מים דומיא דשמן מה שמן מאברא' אף מים מאבראי וקשה לר"י דבפרק בתרא דיומא (דף עו:) קאמר דרחילה איקרי עינוי מנלן א"ר זוטרא מהכא ותבא כמים בקרבו וגו' מים דומיא דשמן מה שמן מאבראי כו' ופריך והא האי תנא איפכא נסיב לה דתנן מנין לסיכה כו' ומאי פריך הא תנא דמתני' קאמר שאין ראיה לדבר אלא זכר לדבר משום דמים דומיא דשמן כדפרישי' ואומר ר"י דפריך הכי דאי חשיבא ראיה גמורה דרחילה כסיכה כדקאמרת לא הוה ליה להאי תנא למעבד מינה אפי' זכר בעלמא קשה לרשב"א דאמאי מייתי האי קרא שאינו אלא זכר בעלמא הוה ליה לאיתויי קרא דלחם חמודות לא אכלתי ובשר ויין לא בא אל פי וסוך לא סכתי (דניאל י) דהוי דרשה גמורה ומיניה נפקא לן בפרק בתרא דיומא (שם) דסיכה איקרי עינוי*:

[וכו' ע' תוס' יומא עו. ד"ה מנין ותוס' נדה לב. ד"ה מנין]

תני רישא טהורה ומוקי לה כו'. אומר ר"י דמשום הכי אינו מגיה למיתני טהורה כדי לאוקמי כולה כרבי אלעזר *אלא בלאו הכי איכא דתני טהורה ואיכא דתני טמאה הלכך מאן דלא מוקי כתנאי נוח לו לשנות כאותן ששונין טהורה ומאן דמוקי כתנאי לא קפיד לשנות טמאה וא"ת אכתי הויא מתני' כתנאי דרישא דמתני' רבי עקיבא קתני לה וסיפא דקתני פולטת טהורה היינו דלא כר"ע דפליג בסמוך אר' אלעזר בן עזריה וי"ל דלא קפיד לאוקמי כתנאי אלא בתרי בבי דסמוכות זו אחר זו אבל אההיא דריש פירקין המרוחקות מההיא דפולטת לא קפיד וא"ת למאן דתני טהורה טפי הוה ליה למנקט במתני' קרא דוקדשתם היום ומחר (שמות יט) דמשמע כרבי אלעזר בן עזריה ואומר ר"י דניחא ליה לאתויי היו נכונים לשלשת ימים דמוכח דמשום פליטת זרע הקפיד דכתיב ביה אל תגשו אל אשה:

פעמים שהן ד' כו'. במלתא דרבי אלעזר בן עזריה ה"מ נמי לשנות בענין זה פעמים שהן שתים פעמים שהן ג' כו' אלא להכי נקט ר' ישמעאל משום דסבר ברביעי עבוד פרישה כרבי עקיבא ובעונות לא בעי למתלי כמו שתולה רבי עקיבא:

בהשכמה עלה. אליבא דרבי עקיבא איירי:

ישראל קדושים הן כו'. ובלאו הכי היו פורשין דאמר *בוזה דרכיו ימות זה המשמש מטתו ביום ועוד דקרא\ן קדושים ואתם תהיו לי ממלכת כהנים וגוי קדוש:

וליטבלו

רבינו חננאל

שורה לכאן ושורה לכאן כדפרישנא לעילא ועלה בען במערבא ואם הפקיע מ צ ד הערוגה תלם אחד על פני כולה ושבקיה ולא זרעיה ומהנותרין זרע בערוגה אחרת ערבוב ולא זרע שורה כדאמר שמואל ב' שורות שורה אחת (שנוטעה) [שנוטה] לכאן ושורה (שנוטעה) [שנוטה] לכאן מהנותרי' בשורה שבזו והפקעת תלם אחד מצדה ופשטה רב ששת לאיסורא ואמר בא עירבוב (ונטל) [וביטל] את השורה אע"פ שהפסיק תלם א'. כיון שורע עירבוב הרי זו שהיא נטועה שורה כאילו אף היא נטועה עירבוב ולא מהניא שורה אלא כנגד שורה שזו נוטה לכאן וזו נוטה לכאן. דהוי היכרא. אבל הכא כיון דהדא עירבוב בטילה לה שורה דאידך ובעירבוב דמיא. וההוא תלם שהפקיעו אם אין בו כדי עבודה לא מהני ואסור. ואתא רב אשי ושריא. ואעפ"כ אין עירבוב מבטל את השורה אלא שורה של זו. והפקעת תלם בזו מתירין אותה: **איתיבי'** רבינא לרב אשי הנוטע שתי שורות של דילועין שתי שורות של קישואין שתי שורות של פול המצרי מותר. שורה אחת של קישואין. שורה אחת של דלועין. שורה אחת של פול המצרי אסור. דאלמא אם ב' שורות הן שהיא נוטה אחת לכאן ואחת לכאן מוכחא מילתא שהן מובדלות זו מזו ומותר. אבל אם יש שורה בשדה זו. ואין בשדה זו שורה שכנגדה אלא עירבוביא היא ואסיר. וצריך להרחיק כדי עבודה. ופריק רב אשי (שאתנן) [שאני] קישואין ודלועין ופול המצרי דאית להו שראבי אבל (דאר) (מינייהו)[שאר המינים] אע"פ שזה נוטע שורה וזה הפקיע תלם אחד מותר. ופי' שראבי עלין רחבין שאוחזין בארץ ורווחן כדאמרינן לענין תני חדא אסור להלך ע"ג עשבים בשבת ותניא אידך מותר אי תימא הא והא ביטות הגשמים ולא קשיא הא דאיכא שראבי והא דליכא שראבי. ואי תימא הא והא דאיכא שראבי ולא קשיא הא [דסיים] מסאני והא דלא[דסיים]מסאני. אבל בזו מן הני אין עירבוב שבזו מבטל שורה שבזו: **אמר רב** כהנא אמר ר' יוחנן הרוצה שימלא את נגתו ירק עושה ערוגה ששה טפחים ועוגל בה חמשה ונמצא ממלא את נגתו ירק כן צורת מרובעת זה ה' על ו' שיש בה ה' עגולין. אקשינן על ר' יוחנן והא איכא בין הבינים. ומפרקינן אמרי דבי ר' ינאי במחריב בין הבינים שמרחיק מה שהוא צריך להרחיק בין כל ירק וירק אלא שנשבר מה שבין העגול למרובע. והרבה הוא נשכר בזאת ולא קא מעיין ר' יוחנן להרחיק את הקרנות כדי שיזרע כנגדן כי איתה הערוגה דהוי ששה על ששה אין בה זריעה אלא י"ג טפחים מכלל ל"ו טפחים ובהעגילו כך ה' עגולים אע"פ שהוא מניח בין ירק לירק כדי צורתו הרי הוא נשכר הרבה: **רב** אשי אמר אם היה זורע שתי זורע את האחר ערב. כגון זה. זורע בזה שתי ובזה ערב כי היכי דליהוי היכרא ואין צריך להרחיק אלא מעט: **איתיביה** רבינא לרב אשי עבודת ירק בירק שנכנס לתוך שרש ירק אחר רואין אותה כטבלא מרובעת. והכי קא מקשי כטבלה מרובעת הוא דשרי הא לאו הכי לא. ופריק רב אשי האי דקאמר כטבלא מרובעת לאו לאחמרי אלא לאקולי בה קלא אחרינא להתיר ראש תור הנכנס לה וראש תור היוצא ממנה: **מתני'** מנין לפולטת שכבת זרע ביום השלישי שהיא טמאה כו'. ותנן התם הפולטת שכבת זרע ביום שלישי טהורה דברי ר' אלעזר בן עזריה. הויא מתניתין דהכא דלא כר' אלעזר בן עזריה. ואקשינן אימא סיפא. מנין שמרחיצין את הקטן ביום השלישי שחל להיות בשבת. ותנן לקמן בהא מסכתא רבי אלעזר בן עזריה אומר מרחיצין את הקטן ביום שלישי שחל להיות בשבת ופריקנן למאן דמוקים כתנאי [תני האני טמאה ורישא רבנן וסיפא ר' אלעזר בן עזריה דלא מוקים

עין משפט נר מצוה

כד א מיי' פ"ג מהלכות מילה הלכה ח טור שו"ע או"ח סימן של סעיף ט:

כה ב מיי' פ"ג מהלכות עבודת יום הכפורים הלכה ד:

כו ג מיי' פ"ג מהלכות שביתת עשור הלכה ט טוש"ע או"ח סימן תריד סעיף א:

כז ד מיי' פ"ה מהלכות שאר אבות הטומאות הל' יא יב סמג עשין רמ:

כח ה מיי' פ"ד מהל' איסורי ביאה הלכה יו"ד טוש"ע או"ח סי' רמ סעיף יא וטור ושו"ע אה"ע סימן כה סעיף ה:

מסורת הש"ס

ס"א וקסבר

[ל"ל שהיא]

לקמן קלד: ע"ש

יומא עז.

שם עו: נדה לב.

מקוואות פ"ח מ"ג [תוספתא מקוואות פ"ו]

[ע' במשנה מכאן ואילך בתוספתא]

[זבחים קא:]

נדה יז. כתובות סה: [שם נו.]

גליון הש"ס

תוס' ד"ה תני רישא וכו' אלא בלאו הכי איכא וכו'. ובענין זה איתא במגילה דף כ ע"ב:

רב נסים גאון סיפא כר' אלעזר בן עזריה הוא זה ששנינו מנין שמרחיצין את הקטן ביום השלישי והדבר זה אמור משום ר' אלעזר בן עזריה בפרק ר' אליעזר אם לא הביא כלי:

עין משפט נר מצוה

כט א מיי' פ"ה מהלכות שאר אבות הטומאות הלכה יג:

ל ב ג מיי' שם הלכ"ז:

והא טבולי יום נינהו אביי בר רבין ורב חנינא בר אבין דאמרי תרווייהו ניתנה תורה לטבול יום יתיב מרימר וקאמר לה להא שמעת' א"ל רבינא למרימר ניתנה קאמרת או ראויה קאמרת אמר ליה ראויה קאמינא וליטבלו ביני שימשי וליקבלו תורה ביני שימשי אמר רבי יצחק °לא מראש בסתר דברתי (א) וליטבלו בצפרא דשבתא וליקבלו תורה בצפרא דשבתא א"ר יצחק שלא יהא הללו הולכין לקבל תורה והללו הולכין לטבילה א"ר חייא ברבי אבא א"ר יוחנן זו דברי ר' ישמעאל ור' עקיבא אבל חכמים אומרים (א) שש עונות שלמות בעינן אמר רב חסדא מחלוקת שפירשה מן האשה *אבל פירשה מן האיש טמאה כל זמן שהיא לחה מתיב רב ששת °וכל בגד וכל עור אשר יהיה עליו שכבת זרע פרט לשכבת זרע שהיא סרוחה מאי לאו שפירשה מן האיש לא שפירשה מן האשה בעי רב פפא *שכבת זרע של ישראל במעי כותית מהו ישראל דדאיגי במצות חביל גופייהו עכו"ם דלא דאיגי במצות לא או דילמא *כיון דאכלין שקצים ורמשים חביל גופייהו ואם תמצי לומר *כיון דאכלי שקצים ורמשים חביל גופייהו בעי בהמה מהו אשה (היא) דאית לה פרוזדור מסרחת אבל בהמה דלית לה פרוזדור לא או דילמא לא שנא תיקו: ת"ר *בששי בחדש ניתנו עשרת הדברות לישראל °רבי יוסי אומר בשבעה בו אמר רבא דכולי עלמא בר"ח אתו למדבר סיני כתיב הכא °ביום הזה באו מדבר סיני וכתיב התם °החדש הזה לכם ראש חדשים *מה להלן ר"ח אף כאן ר"ח ודכולי עלמא בשבת ניתנה תורה לישראל כתיב הכא °זכור את יום השבת לקדשו וכתיב התם °ויאמר משה אל העם זכור את היום הזה מה להלן בעצומו של יום אף כאן בעצומו של יום כי פליגי בקביעא דירחא רבי יוסי סבר בחד בשבא איקבע ירחא ובחד בשבא לא אמר להו ולא מידי משום חולשא דאורחא בתרי בשבא אמר להו °ואתם תהיו לי ממלכת כהנים

בתלתא

(ישעיה מח, ויקרא טו, נדה לד:, שמות יט, שם יב, שם כ, שם יג, שם יט)

תוספות

וליטבלו ביני שימשי וליקבלו תורה ביני שימשי. פירש בקונטרס דלר' עקיבא פריך ור"י אומר דאדר' אלעזר בן עזריה ור' ישמעאל נמי פריך דנילף מהכא דאעונות קפיד קרא דאי אימים לקבלו תורה בי שימשי:

וליטבלו בצפרא דשבתא. הא ודאי לא פריך אלא לר' עקיבא דס"ל דאעונות קפיד קרא דנימא דילמא בעינן שש עונות וכי תימא אם היו פולטות בסוף ליל שבת מתי יטבלו ליטבלו בצפרא דשבתא אבל לר"א ורבי ישמעאל לא פריך דנימא דילמא קפיד רחמנא אעונות דפעמים היא כולא כגון אם שימשה בתחילת הלילה דאי קפדינן אעונות משעברו ה' עונות טהורה והשתא דקפיד אימים איכה טהורה עד יום רביעי ומיהו מצינן למימר דפריך דילמא קפיד אעונות ואימים אתרווייהו לחומרא כששימשה בתחילת הלילה ניזיל בתר יומי וכי שימשה בסוף היום ניזיל בתר עונות: **אמר** ר' יצחק שלא יהא הללו הולכים לקבל תורה. וא"ת א"כ מה צריך רבי יצחק לדרשה דלא מראש בסתר דברתי ויש לומר דאיצטריך דאי לאו הכי ליטבלו בתחילת לילי השבת ומחצות לילה ואילך יקבלו תורה אבל ביום אם היו מאחרים עד שיטבלו כולם היו מתבטלין מת"ת: **אבל** פירשה מן האיש טמאה כל זמן שהיא לחה. הקשה ר"ת דמתני' היא דתנן בפרק דם הנדה (נדה נד:) הזוב והניע והרוק ושכבת זרע מטמאין לחין ואין מטמאין יבישין ומיהו לא קשה כולי האי דאיכא למימר מטמאין לחין תוך ג' ור"ת מפרש דהכא בזכר שנרבע ופלט זרע דומיא דאשה והתם בראה קרי וכן פי' ר"ח: **וכתיב** התם החדש הזה לכם. תימה דבפרק קמא דפסחים (דף ו:) פריך אהאי קרא גופיה ממאי דבריש ירחא קאי וי"ל דודאי בריש ירחא קאי דאמרי' במדרש (מכילתא) שהראהו הקב"ה למשה באצבע ובפסחים לא פריך אלא דבעי למילף מינה הא דאמר רשב"ג שדורשין לפני הפסח בהלכות הפסח שתי שבתות שהרי נביא עומד בר"ח ומזהיר על הפסח וממאי דנביא בריש ירחא קאי וגהי דבראש חדש אמר ליה הקב"ה דילמא משה כשאמר לישראל בארבע' בירחא או בחמשא הוה קאי ומסיק דיליף מדבר ממדבר דבההוא דבאחד לחדש השני אמירת משה לישראל היתה בו ביום כדכתיב באחד לחדש השני ויתילדו על משפחותם וגו' וא"ת דאמאי לא יליף הכא מדבר ממדבר כדיליף התם דהכא נמי כתיב מדבר באו מדבר סיני ויש לומר דעדיפי ניחא ליה למילף הזה הזה ולא מדבר ממדבר:

*__בתלתא__ אמר להו מצות הגבלה. לכ"ע הגבלה קדמה לפרישה דתלתא ויאמר כתיבי וסברא הוא דכל אחד נאמר ביומו בקמא כתיב ואתם תהיו לי וגו' ובבתרא כתיב מצות פרישה ומצות הגבלה ובאמצעי לא כתב ביה מידי שיעשה משה שליחות לישראל ואית לן למישדי מצות הגבלה אההיא אמירה ולא אמצות פרישה שהרי מיד אחר אמירה אחרונה כתיבא מצות פרישה:

היום

רש"י

והא טבולי יום נינהו. כיון דלכולהו שמעינן דבלילי שבת טבלו הוו להו טבולי יום כשקבלו תורה שלא היה להם הערב שמש אחר הטבילה וכיון דהכי הוא איכא למימר דמבע"י טבלו שם ואפ"ה פליטתן טהורה ובצרי להו חדא עונה אליבא דכולהו: ראויה קאמינא. ראויה ליתן לטבולי יום וקסברי הני תנאי לא הקפידה תורה על טבולי יום דלא כתיב הערב שמש אלא לענין קדשים הלכך *כל ג' ימים האמורים לענין פרישה הוזקקו להיות *)קודם טבילה ומיהו לא ניתנה לטבולי יום לפי שטבלו מבעו"י ולא פלטו ואם היו פולטות יחזרו ויטבלו משתחשך אבל לא הוצרכו לכך: וליטבלו בי שמשי וליקבלו תורה בי שמשי. לילי שבת קרי בי שמשא בכל דוכתא מפני שבין השמשות שלו חלוק מכל ימים והוצרך להזכירו בכמה מקומות והכי פריך לר' עקיבא דאמר הקפידה תורה על מנין העונות ולא הקפידה אלא על חמש למה לא קבלוה בלילה מדהמתין עד הבקר איכא למימר שהקפידה על פליטת הלילה ואיכא ו' עונות: *לא בסתר דברתי. במקום ארץ חשך ולילה חשך הוא: ליטבלו בשבתא בצפרא. ולמה הוצרך (ב) לירד בהשכמה דיום א' פרשו עם חשכה בד' ויטבלו בשבת שחרית ואם פלטו לאחר טבילה טהורין דהא עברו ה' עונות שלמות ואם פלטו לילי שבת ונטמאו לא איכפת לן וטובלין שחרית דהא בעל קרי טובל ביומו ואת אמרת ניתנה תורה לטבולי יום ויש ספרים דגרסינן ביה תרי לישני וגרסינן הכי לרבי אלעזר לישמשו ביממא דחמשא לר' ישמעאל לישמשו בליליא דחמשא לרבי עקיבא לישמשו ביממא דארבעה ואומר אני שהוא שיבוש והגורסו טעה ולא ידע לפרש מהו שאמר ר' ישמעאל פעמים שהן ה' עונות כו': אבל חכמים אומרים ו' עונות שלמות. סברי להו כר' יוסי דאמר בארבעה עביד פרישה ובהשכמה כר' עקיבא ולית להו שטבלו בלילי שבת אלא סבירא להו דאותן שטבלו לילי שבת ופלטו לאחר טבילה הוצרכו לטבול בשבת שחרית ולפיכך נתעכבה שכינה מליתן עד הבקר ולא משום לא בסתר דברתי לחודיה: שפירשה מן האשה. כגון פולטת שכבת זרע שקבלה מזכר הוא דאמר ר' אלעזר בן עזריה דבתרי יומי מסרחת מפני שמתחממת בגופה: אבל פירשה מן האיש. על הבגד מטמאה לעולם: כל זמן שהיא לחה. ומיהו משיבשה לא מטמיא דתו לא חזיא להזריע: מאי לאו שפירשה מן האיש. על הבגד ומטהר לה לחה מסרחת דלא קתני פרט לכשיבשה: של ישראל במעי כותית מהו. מי מסרחת בג' ימים כישראלית ואי פלטה ליה בתר ג' טהור הנוגע בטיפה או לא ולהכי נקט שכבת זרע של ישראל דאילו דכותי אמרינן במסכת נדה קריו טהור בפ' בנות כותים (נדה דף לד:): דדייגי במצות. לקיים מצות וחרדים בדבר ומתוך דאגה מתחממין כדכתיב (תהלים לט) חם לבי בקרבי: חביל. חם: דאית לה פרוזדור. בשר כותלי בית הרחם בולט מן השינים ולחוץ ובית הרחם הוי מן השינים ולפנים: אשה אית לה פרוזדור. לפיכך לא שליט בה אויר בגופה ומתחממת: בו' בחדש כו'. דהא דכתיב ויכסהו הענן ששת ימים ויקרא אל משה ביום השביעי סבירא להו כר' יוסי הגלילי דאמר בפ"ק דיומא (דף ד.) זה היה מעשה אחר עשרת הדברות ור' יוסי סבירא ליה דמשה וכל ישראל עומדים לקבל עשרת הדברות ולא בא הכתוב אלא לחלק כבוד למשה: כתיב הכא. הזה הזה לגזירה שוה: מה להלן. זכור את היום הזה בעצמו של יום הזכירה דיציאת מצרים נאמר להו כדכתיב הזה אף כאן בעצמו של יום הזכירה דשבת נאמר להן זכור את יום וגו': בקביעא דירחא. באיזה יום הוקבע החדש: משום חולשא דאורחא גרסינן: בתרי בשבא אמר להו ואתם תהיו לי. ומשה עלה ויקרא אליו כל הענין עד אלה הדברים אשר תדבר וגו' הדברים האלה נאמרו לו למחרת ביאתם כדאמרינן כל עליותיו בהשכמה היו ואפי' למאן דלית ליה בהשכמה ירד דלא אקים אית ליה בהשכמה עלה דהא בהדיא כתיב קרא:

בתלתא

*) נ"ל רק קודם טבילה ולא קודם טהרה [תו"י]

רבינו חננאל

מוקים כתנאי. תני רישא טהורה וכולה ר' אלעזר בן עזריה היא [ועד השתא איכא] תנאי דתני טמאה ואיכא תנאי דתני טהורה. ואיכא רבנן דמפרשי כגירסאה רב מוקים לה כתנאי. ור' יוחנן לא מוקים לה כתנאי. ומן דלא מוקים ליה כתנאי דפרח כמה דיכיל למהוה מתני' אליבא דחד תנא מיפלגא מאני' בתרי לבי מסותא. ואמר רב פפא מוקמינן לה מתניתין כתרי תלתא טעמי. ולא מוקמינן בתרי תלתא תנאי. וכי דפרשינן בפירקין קמאי: **תנן** התם הפולטת ש"ז ביום השלישי טהורה דברי ר' אלעזר בן עזריה. טעמיה דר' אלעזר בן עזריה אפילו ב' עונות שלימות ומשהו והעונה יום או לילה. וקא מיתני בפירוש דר' אלעזר בן עזריה טעמיה יש שם יום וכל שהוא והיא טהורה. כיצד שמשה את ביתה ע"ש קודם לשקיעת החמה ועברו ב' עונות לילי שבת ויום שבת ופלטה במ"ש לאחר שקיעת החמה והרי הוא יום שלישי נמצא יום וכל שהוא והיא טהורה. ויש ב' ימים חסר משהו והיא טמאה. כיצד שמשה את ביתה ע"ש לאחר שקיעת החמה ופלטה באחד בשבת קודם לשקיעת החמה הרי יש כאן ב' ימים חסר משהו והיא טמאה. לפי שאינו יום שלישי עד שתשקע החמה ליכנס יום ב' בשבת. ר' ישמעאל אומר פעמים שהן ד' עונות פעמים שהן ה' פעמים שהן שש. טעמיה דר' ישמעאל שהוא עושה מקצת עונה ככולה וקסבר אין יום שלישי (אחד) [טהורה] פחות מד' עונות שהן ב' ימים שלימים. דקאמר ר' אלעזר בן עזריה ב' עונות שלימו' ומשהו קאמר ר' ישמעאל צריך עונה שלימה לפניהן ועונה שלימה לאחריהן. דקסבר יש פולטת ביום ג' והיא טמאה. כי הא מתני' דאמרינן רישא דלא כר' אלעזר בן עזריה ואלין ד' עונות לר' ישמעאל בעי להו מכלל ג' ימים ולא סגי דהוויין ב' ימים ובעי תחלתן וסופן הנץ החמה ושקיעה. ואי הוה תשמש מן קמי הנץ החמה או שקיעתה אפילו בי"א שעות ומחצה לא מיחשיב. והיכי דמי פעמים שהן ד' וספק כגון ששמשה בסוף לילי אחד בשבת ופלטה בסוף לילי שלישי בשבת הרי כאן ד' שלימות. שמתחלתן וסופן הנץ ושקיעת מכלל ג' ימים. והיכי דמי פעמים שהן חמש כגון ששמשה בתחלת לילי אחד בשבת ופלטה בסוף לילי [שלישי]שבת. אם אתה חושב ד' של יום אחד ויום שני הרי הן משני ימים בלבד לפיכך לא מיחשיב ליה אלא אחד מן יום אחד בשבת ושתים של שני ואחת לילי שלישי. והיכי דמי פעמים שהן ששי כגון ששמשה במקצת יום שבת אחר הנץ החמה ופלטה בסוף לילי שלישי לא מיחשיב יום שבת כל העיקר דלא הוה ליה הנץ החמה ומן יום אחד ויום שני לא מיחשיב אלא (שלשה) [חמש] ולילי שלישי הרי שש.והכין נמי אם שמשה בתחלת לילי אחד בשבת ופלטה בסוף יום שלשה קודם לשקיעת החמה אין כאן ד' עונות שלמות מכלל שלשה ימים כדפרישנא לעילא דלא מיחשיב משלישי אלא אחד. והרי בן שש. יום אחד ויום שני ויום שלישי . ר"ע אומר לעולם חמש . טעמיה דר"ע דשקיל מן הכא להכא וסבר שאם יצאת מקצת עונה ראשונה משלימין לה מקצת עונה ששית ומצריך שפלטה אחר ששים שעות מן התשמיש שהן שיעור ב' ימים ומחצה : **אמרוה** רבנן קמיה דרב פפא ואמרי לה רב פפא לרבא (קמיה דרבא) . בשלמא ר' אלעזר בן עזריה כרבנן דאמרי בחמשה עבד להו משה לישראל פרישה נמצא לישראל פרישה לילי ששי ויום ששי ומשהו מחמישי ומלילי שבת . לפיכך אם שמשה ביום חמישי קודם שקיעת החמה ופלטה בלילי שבת אחר שקיעת החמה טהורה . ר"ע כר' יוסי דאמר בארבעה עבד להו משה פרישה כגון ראפרשינהו בתר חדא שעתא מיום רביעי משכחת ה' עונות בתר חדא שעתא מלילי שבת . כדא"ר עקיבא אם יצאת מקצת עונה ראשונה משלימין לו מקצת עונה ששית . אלא ר' ישמעאל דקמצריך ד' עונות שלימות שמתחלת מתחלת יום או תחלת לילה מתוך ג' ימים כמאן לא כרבנן ולא כר' יוסי . מרבנן מרחק טובא . ומדר' יוסי נמי דהא יומא דארבעה שיצא מקצתו לא מיני למחשביה עונה כי דחשיב ליה ר"ע וארבעי דבידיה חמישי וששי אינון בלחוד ובעאי להו מכלל ג' ימים כמאן קאי ופרקינן לעולם כר' יוסי קאי ר' ישמעאל. ואמר רב אדא בר אבא משה בהשכמה עלה ובהשכמה ירד דאלמא סבר דעבד להו פרישה ביום רביעי בהשכמה קודם הנץ החמה והוה להו חמש עונות מכלל ג' ימים . כדפרשינן לר' ישמעאל בענין פעמים ה' . וסלקא שמעתא ומקשינן בין לר' ישמעאל ובין לר"ע למה ליה למשה רבינו למעבד פרישה לישראל בימא דארבעה והאמר רב הונא ישראל קדושים הן ואין משמשין מטותיהן ביום . ופרקינן איצטריך למשה לאפרושינן והאמר

רבא

מסורת הש"ס

כ"ס ג' רש"ל ויש גורסים כל ג' האמורים ר"ל דעת הלכ"ע לא כר"ע לא ר"י

[ישעיה מ"ח פי"ט לא בסתר דברתי במקום ארץ חשך וכו' קרא מוקדם לקבל דמייתי בסוגיין לא מרלם בסתר דברתי [ע"ש] ומגוס ליכן טעם]

[שם וע"ש לא:]

הגהות הב"ח

(א) גמ' בסתר דברתי וגו' וליטבלו: (ב) רש"י ד"ה ליטבלו בשבתא בצפרא ולמה הוצרך לפרישה דיום רביעי יפרשו עם חשכה וכו' לא איכפת לן דטובלין וכו' לר' ישמעאל לישמשו ביממא לר"ע לישמשו בליליא דארבעה:

הגהות הגר"א

(א) גמ' שש עונות. נ"ב גירסת הגאונים ג' עונות:

גליון הש"ס

גמ' אמר ר"י לא מראש בסתר דברתי זה פסוק בישעיה דף מ"ח ע"ש ולפ"ז צ"ע ליין לא בסתר דברתי זה פסוק ישעיה: גמ' ר' יוסי אומר בשבעה בו. ע' ע"ז דף ג ע"א תוס' ד"ה יום הששי:

[86*b*] But they were *ṭebule yom?*[3]—Abaye b. Rabin and R. Ḥanina b. Abin both say: The Torah was given to *ṭebule yom.* Now Meremar sat and reported this discussion. Said Rabina to him: Do you say that it was given, or that it was fitting [that it should be given]? I mean that it was fitting, he replied.[4]

Yet they should have bathed at twilight and received the Torah at twilight?[5]—R. Isaac quoted [as an answer], *from the beginning I have not spoken in secret.*[6] Yet they could have bathed on the Sabbath morning and received the Torah on the Sabbath morning?[7]—Said R. Isaac. It was unfitting that some should go to receive the Torah whilst others went to *ṭebillah.*[8]

R. Ḥiyya son of R. Abba said in R. Joḥanan's name: These are the views of R. Ishmael and R. Akiba; but the Sages maintain: We require six[9] full periods.[10]

R. Ḥisda said: This controversy is [only] where it [the semen]
a issues from the woman; but if it issues from a man,[1] it is unclean as long as it is moist. R. Shesheth objected: ***And every garment, and every skin, whereon is the seed of copulation, [shall be washed with water and be unclean until the even]***:[2] this excludes semen that is foul.[3] Surely this refers [even] to that which issues from a man?—No: [only] to that which issues from a woman.

R. Papa asked: What of an Israelite's semen within a Cuthean woman?[4] [Do we say,] Because Israelites are anxious about [the observance of] precepts, their bodies are heated,[5] but not so Gentiles, who are not anxious about precepts; or perhaps, as they eat creeping crawling things, their bodies [too] are heated? Now should you say, as they eat creeping crawling things their bodies are heated, what of [semen] within an animal?[6] [Do we say,] A woman, who has a fore-uterus, causes it to become foul, but not so an animal, who has no fore-uterus; or perhaps there is no difference? The questions stand over.

Our Rabbis taught: On the sixth day of the month [Siwan] were the Ten Commandments given to Israel. R. Jose maintained: On the seventh thereof. Said Raba: All agree that they arrived in the Wilderness of Sinai on the first of the month. [For] here it is written, ***on this day they came into the wilderness of Sinai;***[7] whilst elsewhere it is written, ***This month shall be unto you the beginning of months:***[8] just as there the first of the month,[9] so here [too] the first of the month [is meant]. Again, all agree that the Torah was given to Israel on the Sabbath. [For] here it is written, Remember ***the Sabbath day, to keep it holy;***[10] whilst elsewhere it is written, ***And Moses said unto the people,*** Remember ***this day:***[11] just as there,
b [he spoke] on that very day,[1] so here too it was on that very day.[2] [Where] they differ is on the fixing of the New Moon. R. Jose holds that New Moon was fixed on the first day of the week [Sunday], and on that day he [Moses] said nothing to them on account of their exhaustion from the journey. On Monday he said to them,

(3) V. Glos. *ṭebul yom*, pl. *ṭebule yom.* If they had their ritual bath on Friday evening, they would not be thoroughly clean until the following evening, as a *ṭebul yom* does not become clean until the evening after his ablutions. Hence we must assume that they cleansed themselves at the end of Friday, in which case there is one 'period' short on all views. (4) But actually none discharged semen on the Friday, so that they were completely clean. (5) Rashi: According to R. Akiba, if God desired exactly five periods to elapse, why did he postpone Revelation until the morning, which suggests that six periods are necessary? Tosaf. maintains that the difficulty arises on all views. (6) Isa. XLVIII, 16—i.e., the Torah had to be given in broad daylight. (7) If discharge after five 'periods' leaves the woman clean, cohabitation could have been permitted until the very end of Wednesday, and ritual ablution performed on the Sabbath morning, for a subsequent discharge would not matter. (8) V. Glos. (9) Wilna Gaon quotes a reading 'three'. (10) To elapse before discharge shall have no effect.

a (1) E.g., on to a garment. (2) Lev. XV, 17. (3) Being unfit then to engender, it does not defile. (4) For Cuthean v. *supra* 16*b*, n. c4. Here, however, 'Cuthean' is the censor's substitute for 'gentile', which word appears in this passage in Nid. 34*b*, and also in the present discussion. (5) Which makes the semen foul and unfit to engender in three days. (6) This is merely a theoretical question. Bestiality was forbidden on pain of death (Ex. XXII, 18), and Jews were not suspected of this crime (Sanh. 27*b*). (7) Ex. XIX, 1. (8) Ibid. XII, 2. (9) V. Pes. 6*b* and Tosaf. ibid. s.v. מכאי. (10) Ex. XX, 8. (11) Ibid. XIII, 3.

b (1) Of their exodus—implied by '*this*'. (2) I.e., the command to keep the Sabbath, and hence all the Ten Commandments were promulgated on the Sabbath itself.

and ye shall be unto me a kingdom of priests;[3] [87a] on Tuesday he informed them of the order to set boundaries,[4] and on Wednesday they separated themselves [from their wives].[5] But the Rabbis hold: New Moon was fixed on Monday, and on that day he said nothing to them on account of their exhaustion from the journey. On Tuesday he said to them, *and ye shall be unto me a kingdom of priests;* on Wednesday he informed them of the order to set boundaries, and on Thursday they separated themselves. An objection is raised: *And sanctify them to-day and to-morrow:*[6] this is difficult in the view of R. Jose?[7]—R. Jose can answer you: Moses added one day of his own understanding.[8] For it was taught, Three things did Moses do of his own understanding, and the Holy One, blessed be He, gave His approval:[9] he added one day of his own understanding, he separated himself from his wife,[10] and he broke the Tables. 'He added one day of his own understanding': what [verse] did he interpret? *To-day and to-morrow: 'to-day'* [must be] like *'to-morrow'*: just as *'to-morrow'* includes the [previous] night, so *'to-day'* [must] include the [previous] night, but the night of to-day has already passed! Hence it must be two days exclusive of to-day. And how do we know that the Holy One, blessed be He, gave his approval?—Since the *Shechinah* did not rest [upon Mount Sinai] until the morning of the Sabbath.[11] And 'he separated himself from his wife': What did he interpret? He applied an *a minori* argument to himself, reasoning: If the Israelites, with whom the *Shechinah* spoke only on one occasion and He appointed them a time [thereof], yet the Torah said, *Be ready against the third day: come not near a woman:* I, with whom the *Shechinah* speaks at all times and does not appoint me a [definite] time, how much more so! And how do we know that the Holy One, blessed be He, gave his approval? Because it is written, *Go say to them, Return to*
a *your tents,*[1] which is followed by, *But as for thee, stand thou here by me.* Some there are who quote, *with him* [*sc.* Moses] *will I speak mouth to mouth.*[2] 'He broke the Tables': how did he learn [this]? He argued: If the Passover sacrifice, which is but one of the six hundred and thirteen precepts, yet the Torah said, *there shall no alien eat thereof:*[3] here is the whole Torah, and the Israelites are apostates, how much more so![4] And how do we know that the Holy One, blessed be He, gave His approval? Because it is said, *which thou breakest,*[5] and Resh Laḳish interpreted this: All strength to thee[6] that thou breakest it.

Come and hear: *And be ready against the third day:* this is a difficulty according to R. Jose?[7]—Surely we have said that Moses added one day of his own understanding!

Come and hear: The third, the third day of the month and the third day of the week:[8] this is a difficulty according to the Rabbis?[9]—The Rabbis answer you: with whom does this agree? with R. Jose.

In respect of what is [the first] 'the third' [mentioned]?—[In respect] of that which was taught: *And Moses reported the words of the people unto the Lord;*[10] and it is written, *And Moses told the words of the*
b *people unto the Lord.*[1] Now, what did the Holy One, blessed be He, say unto Moses, what did Moses say unto Israel, what did Israel say to Moses, and what did Moses report before the Omnipotent?[2] This is the order of setting boundaries:[3] that is the view of R. Jose son of R. Judah. Rabbi said: At first he explained the penalties [for non-observance], for it is written, *'And Moses reported* [wa-yasheb]', [which implies] things which repel [*meshabbebin*] one's mind.[4] But subsequently he explained its reward, for it is said, *'And Moses told* [wa-yagged]', [which means,] words which draw one's heart like a narrative [*aggadah*]. Some there are who maintain, At first he explained the reward it confers, for it is written, *'And Moses reported* [wa-yasheb]', [which means,] words which appease [*meshibin*] one's mind. Whilst subsequently he explained its penalties, for it is written, *'and Moses told* [wa-yagged'], [meaning], words as hard [unpleasant] to man as worm-wood [*gidin*].

Come and hear: The sixth, the sixth day of the month and the sixth day of the week [Friday]: this is a difficulty according to the Rabbis?[5]—This too agrees with R. Jose. In respect of what

(3) Ex. XIX, 6. (4) V. ibid. 12. (5) Though the reference to this precedes the command to set boundaries, it is nevertheless assumed that events were in this order; v. *infra*. (6) Ibid. 10. (7) For it implies Thursday and Friday, Revelation taking place on the Sabbath. The sanctification consisted in their separation from their wives (v. 14f). (8) The command 'sanctify them' was given him on Wednesday, and he interpreted it as implying three days. (9) Lit., 'agreed with him'. (10) Entirely, after the Revelation. (11) Had Moses' interpretation been incorrect, the *Shechinah* should have alighted Friday morning.
a (1) Deut. V, 30. This was permission to resume marital relations. (2) Num. XII, 8—the same conclusion may be drawn from this. (3) Ex. XII, 43. 'Alien' is interpreted, one whose actions have alienated him from God, v. Targum Onkelos a.l. (4) They are surely unfit to receive the Torah! (5) Ibid. XXXIV, 1. (6) Lit., 'thy strength be well',—an expression of approval. For further notes, v. Yeb., 62a ff. (7) Cf. *supra* n. b7. (8) The meaning of the first 'the third' is discussed *infra*. (9) Since they hold that New Moon was on Monday, the third was on *Wednesday*, not Tuesday. (10) Ibid. 8.
b (1) Ex. XXXIV, 9. (2) Lit., 'the strength'—one of the names of God. The difficulty is this: what conversations took place between v.v. 8 and 9, necessitating a *second* statement by Moses? (3) Though this is mentioned only in v. 12, it is assumed to have been given between Moses' two statements, the second of which signified the people's willingness to set boundaries. (4) Threats of punishment would naturally make the people reluctant to accept the Torah in the first place (Rashi). Jast.: words which chasten, etc. (5) Since they held that New Moon was on Monday, Friday was not the sixth day of the month.

תורה אור

בתלתא אמר להו מצות הגבלה בארבעה עבוד פרישה ורבנן סברי בתרי בשבא איקבע ירחא בתרי בשבא לא אמר להו ולא מידי משום חולשא דאורחא בתלתא אמר להו ואתם תהיו לי בארבעה אמר להו מצות הגבלה בה' עבוד פרישה מיתיבי °וקדשתם היום ומחר קשיא לר' יוסי אמר לך ר' יוסי יום אחד הוסיף משה מדעתו דתניא *ג' דברים עשה משה מדעתו והסכים הקב"ה עמו הוסיף יום אחד מדעתו ופירש מן האשה ושבר את הלוחות הוסיף יום אחד מדעתו מאי דריש היום ומחר היום כמחר מה למחר לילו עמו אף היום לילו עמו ולילה דהאידנא נפקא ליה ש"מ תרי יומי לבר מהאידנא ומנלן דהסכים הקב"ה על ידו דלא שריא שכינה עד צפרא דשבתא ופירש מן האשה מאי דריש נשא קל וחומר בעצמו אמר ומה ישראל שלא דברה שכינה עמהן אלא שעה אחת וקבע להן זמן אמרה תורה °והיו נכונים וגו' אל תגשו אני שבכל שעה ושעה שכינה מדברת עמי ואינו קובע לי זמן על אחת כמה וכמה ומנלן דהסכים הקב"ה על ידו דכתיב °לך אמור להם שובו לכם לאהליכם וכתיב בתריה ואתה פה עמוד עמדי ואית דאמרי °פה אל פה אדבר בו שבר את הלוחות מאי דריש אמר ומה פסח שהוא אחד מתרי"ג מצות אמרה תורה °וכל בן נכר לא יאכל בו התורה כולה [כאן] וישראל מומרים על אחת כמה וכמה ומנלן דהסכים הקב"ה על ידו שנאמר °אשר שברת *ואמר ר"ל °יישר כחך ששיברת ת"ש °והיו נכונים ליום השלישי קשיא לר' יוסי הא אמרינן יום אחד הוסיף משה מדעתו ת"ש שלישי שלישי בחדש ושלישי בשבת קשיא לרבנן אמרי לך רבנן הא מני ר' יוסי היא שלישי למאי לכדתניא °וישב משה את דברי העם אל ה' וכתיב ויגד משה את דברי העם אל ה' מה אמר לו הקב"ה למשה ומה אמר להם משה לישראל ומה אמרו ישראל למשה ומה השיב משה לפני הגבורה זו מצות הגבלה דברי ר' יוסי בר יהודה רבי אומר בתחילה פירש עונשה דכתיב וישב משה דברים שמשבבין דעתו של אדם ולבסוף פירש מתן שכרה דכתיב ויגד משה דברים *שמושכין לבו של אדם כאגדה ואיכא דאמרי בתחילה פירש מתן שכרה דכתיב וישב משה דברים שמשיבין דעתו של אדם ולבסוף פירש עונשה דכתיב ויגד משה דברים שקשין לאדם *כגידין תא שמע ששי ששי בחדש ששי בשבת קשיא לרבנן הא נמי רבי יוסי היא ששי למאי רבא אמר לחנייתן

(שמות יט; שם; דברים ה; במדבר יב; שמות יב; שם לד; שם יט; שם)

בתלתא אמר להו מצות הגבלה. שהדברים שנאמרו לו בשני ירד לערב ואמרן לישראל כדכתיב ויבא משה ויקרא לזקני העם וגו' ולמחרת השכים ועלה וישב משה את דברי העם וגו' כדאמר כל עליותיו בהשכמה היו ובו ביום נאמר לו הנה אנכי בא אליך בעב וגו' ומצות הגבלתם דהשמרו לכם עלות בהר אע"פ שהיא כתובה אחר וקדשתם היום ומחר שהיא מצות פרישה קודם לכן נאמרה דכתיב בההיא עלייה שעלה בשלישי להשיב להקב"ה דברי העם דנעשה (ונשמע) הנה אנכי בא אליך וסיפא דקרא ויגד משה את דברי העם וגו' וכי מה דברי העם יש כאן אלא מצות הגבלה נאמר לו בו ביום ולקמן תניא לה הכי ולערב אמרה לישראל ולמחרת בד' השכים ועלה והגיד שקבלו עליהם מצות הגבלה ונאמרה לו מצות פרישה וקדשתם היום ומחר ואע"פ שיש עוד ג' ימים עד יום שבת האמרינן לקמן לר"י דמשה הוסיף יום אחד מדעתו: היום ומחר. משמע בה' נאמר לו לפרוש ה' וו': אמר לך ר' יוסי. לעולם ברביעי נאמר לו לפרוש ד' וה' והוא הוסיף יום אחד והסכים הקב"ה לדעתו: ופירש מן האשה. לגמרי לאחר מתן תורה מיד משפירש עם חביריו שוב לא חזר לתשמיש: אף היום. צריך להיות לילו עמו והא לא אפשר: וקבע להם זמן. אימתי ידבר עמהם: אמרה תורה והיו נכונים וגו'. (א)פירשו מנשותיהן: ולא קבע לי זמן. לדבורו שאוכל לפרוש קודם לכן: לאהליכם. להתיר נשותיכם לתשמיש שאסרתי לכם: בן נכר. מומר שנתנכרו מעשיו לאביו שבשמים: התורה כולה. תלויה בלוחות הללו וישראל מומרים על אחת כמה וכמה שאינם כדי לה: אשר. אישור שאישרו ושיבחו על שבירתן: ה"ג והיו נכונים ליום השלישי ול"ג והיו נכונים לשלשת ימים: הא אמרן יום אחד הוסיף. והאי קרא דוהיו נכונים ליום השלישי קודשא בריך הוא אמר ליה (ב) ומשה אמר להן היו נכונים לשלשת ימים ולא אמר ליום השלישי אלא פירשו ג' ימים וקרא דכתיב ויהי ביום השלישי בהיות הבקר שלישי לימים שלמים שלילן עמם קאמר: ת"ש. דתניא בברייתא הכי שלישי שלישי בחדש היה שלישי בשבת היה ולקמן בעי שלישי קמא למאי ע"כ במילתא דשלישי קמיירי וקאמר עלה שלישי זה שלישי בחדש: קשיא לרבנן. דשמעינן בחד בשבא איקבע ירחא א"כ על כרחך בתרי בשבת אמר ואתם תהיו בתלתא הגבלה בארבעה פרישה ובשביעי נתנה תורה דהא לכ"ע בשבת נתנה תורה: לכדתניא כו'. והכי קאמר יום שלישי לדברים שהתחיל משה להמשיך לבם של ישראל ולפרש עונשן ומתן שכרן ואותו יום היה שלישי בחדש שלישי בשבת ורבי יוסי קאמר לה: וישב ויגד וכי מה אמר הקב"ה למשה. בין וישב משה דנעשה (ונשמע) לויגד משה שאמר להן לישראל ומה אמרו ישראל למשה על כך שהוצרך משה להגיד למקום והלא לא נאמר בינתים אלא הנה אנכי בא וגו': זו מצות הגבלה. שאע"פ שכתובה אחר מצות פרישה בשלישי נאמרה לו והוצרך להשיב שקבלו עליהן: עונשה. של תורה: משבבין. כמו וילך שובב (ישעיה נז) שמושכין מלקבל שאם יקבלו יענשו הדברים הללו משבבין את לבם מן המקום ואף על פי כן קיבלו עליהן: כגידין. ירק מר: ששי ששי בחדש כו'. לקמיה בעי ששי קמא למאי דהכא ליכא למימר ששי לאותן דברים דבשלמא שלישי דברייתא לעיל איכא למימר דאיירי בהו דהא כל ג' ימים היה משה מדבר באותן הדברים דעל כרחך ויגד משה בד' כתיב דברים שקבלו בג': קשיא לרבנן. דמשמע דבחד בשבא איקבע ירחא:

לחנייתן

היום כמחר. אין זו דרשה גמורה אלא משמע דהיום ממש דאי לאו הכי אין זה מדעתו: ומה ישראל כו'. וא"ת מאי קאמר (*דהוסיף) מדעתו דאורייתא הוא דק"ו ניתן לידרש וי"ל דלא הוי ק"ו גמור דשאני התם משום עשרת הדברות:

וקבע להם זמן. תימה לר"י דהיא הגותנת דמשום שקבע להם זמן וידעו שבאותו יום ודאי תדבר שכינה עמהם הוצרכו לפרוש אבל הוא מספק למה יפרוש וי"ל דלהם נמי איכא ספיקא שמא לא תפלוט והכי עביד ק"ו ומה ישראל שקבע להן זמן וא"כ לא היו צריכים לפרוש משום קרי דביום אחד היה די אפ"ה משום חשש פליטה שהיא קלה הוזקקו לפרוש אני שלא קבע לי זמן ויש חשש קרי שהוא חמור לא כ"ש שיש לי לפרוש:

ואתה פה עמוד עמדי. וא"ת מנלן דפירש משה מדעתו קודם ושוב הסכים הקב"ה על ידו שמא זה הוא צווי גמור שצוה לו לפרוש ותירץ ר"ת דאם איתא דמחמת צווי הקב"ה פירש ולא מדעתו היאך היה מערער אהרן ומרים דכתיב ותדבר מרים ואהרן במשה אלא ודאי מתחלה פירש ממנה לגמרי משה מדעתו ואע"ג דהסכים הקב"ה על ידו מ"מ נתרעמו עליו לפי שאילו לא פירש מדעתו לא היה הקב"ה מסכים דבדרך *שאדם הולך בה מוליכין אותו שהרי לאהרן ומרים לא אמר לפרוש אע"ג שגם עמהם היה מדבר ומיהו קשה דמשמע במדרש שלא ידעו זמן גדול שפירש ממנה גבי אלדד ומידד שהיו מתנבאים שאמרה מרים אשרי נשותיהן של אלו שנתמעט בעליהן פרנסין על הציבור אמרה צפורה אוי להם לנשותיהם של אלו שמיום שנתייחדה שכינה עם אחיך פירש ממני מיד ותדבר מרים ואהרן במשה משמע שלא ידעו קודם לכן וכי לא ידעו הא דכתיב ואתה פה עמוד עמדי ואור"ת דודאי ידעו אבל היו סבורין שפירש ע"פ הדבור עד שאמרה להם צפורה שמדעתו פירש ממנה מתחלה:

ומה פסח כו'. אין זה ק"ו *גמור דהם מומר אסור בפסח שהוא קרבן מ"מ לא היה לו למנוע מליתן להם התורה ולהחזירם בתשובה:

קשיא לרבנן. פי' למה שפירש רבא לעיל דבקביעא דירחא פליגי:

רבינו חננאל

רבא אם היה בית אפל מותר. ואמר רבה (ואיתמר)[ואיתימא]רב פפא ת"ח המאפל בטליתו מותר ומקשינן כי סברי פרישה עבידא אליבא דר' יוסי ור' ישמעאל ור"ע מארבעה ואליבא דר' אלעזר בן עזריה ורבנן מן חמשה. ולכולהו כל אשה ששמשה קודם הפרשה אם פלטה שכבת זרע בלילי שבת טהורה היא תישרי שכינה מליליא דשבתא אמאי איתאחרא עד לצפרא. ופרקינן א"ר יצחק לא מראש בסתר דברתי כן עלתה במחשבה למהוה ביממא והדר אקשינן. אם כן למה לי דעבד פרישה אליבא דר' ישמעאל ור"ע מצפרא ארבעה לר"ע תשמש כולא יומא דארבעה. והרי חמש עונות עד צפרא דשבתא ולר' ישמעאל תשמש עד צפרא דחמשא דהא איכא עד צפרא דשבתא ד' עונות כהלכתן מכלל ג' ימים. ופרקינן א"ר יצחק א"כ יאמרו הללו הולכין לבית הטבילה והללו הולכין לקבל התורה. ואילין שאומרים עליהן הולכין לבית הטבילה אינון נשים שפלטו שכבת זרע בלילי שבת שאילו לא פירשו ביום רביעי הות מיטמא מיניה שפולטת וצריכ' למיטבל לצפרא דשבתא. ואיכא בהא מילתא סוניא ולא שפיר שהללו ילכו לקבל תורה והללו ילכו לבית הטבילה. ואיכא מן דגרסי בהדין קושיא דלעילא נמי. ולר' אלעזר בן עזריה תשמש ביממא דחמשה. ולא צריכה מילתא להכין דר' אלעזר בן עזריה לא איכפת ליה (שמשה) אם [תשמש]בחמש' עד קרוב לשקיעת החמה אם לאו ולא צריך אלא משהו מן חמשה וכולי יומא דמעלי[שבתא]ומשהו מן שבתא דהוא יום שלישי ומקשינן והא טבולי יום נינהו. ומפרקינן ראויה תורה להינתן לטבולי יום. ואיכא דמקדמי וגרסי ליה להאי קושיא ולהאי פירוקא מבתר אוקימתא דמילי דר' ישמעאל ור' עקיבא כר' יוסי ואיכא דגרסי ליה הכא ואית ליה תרין אנפי חד דהויא קושיא על ר"ע דאמר במקצת יומא(דחמש')[דארבעה] עבד להו פרישא וכל אשה שפלטה ש"ז בלילי שבת עד שמשלימין כשיעור הזה מה שיצא מיום חמישי טמאה היא. וכיון שאפשר על דעתא דר"ע שיש אשה שפולט' וטמאה בלילי שבת הרי היא צריכה הערב שמש וכל נשים שהיה להן כן טבולי יום אינון. ועוד אית ליה להאי קושיא אנפא אחרינא כי אמרי' לר' ישמעאל ור"ע למה לי למיעבד להו פרישה דמטיא עד בי שמשא. ליעביד להו פרישה דלא מטיא אלא עד צפרא דשבתא. ופרקינן א"ר יצחק יאמרו הללו הולכין לבית הטבילה והללו הולכין לקבל תורה. ואקשינן למה ליה לר' יצחק לפרוקי כי הדין פירוקא הא טבולי יום נינהו או הות פרישתן עד צפרא דשבתא ואהדרינן אעפ"כ ראוין הוו לקבל התורה והלכך צריכינן לפרוקא דר' יצחק ואע"ג דהאי דקאמרי' והא טבולי יום נינהו משנינן אביי בר אבין ורב חנניא בר אבין תרווייהו דניתנה תורה לטבולי יום מוכחא מלתא דעל נשי קאי ולא בגברי אימיר. הוא כי דסדרנא לשמעתא מפרש בתלמוד א"י שמעתא. א"ר יוחנן טבולי יום קבלו ישראל את התורה. הדא דאת אמר בנשים אבל אנשים כבר טהרו מ"מ וקדשתם היום ומחר א"ר חייא בר אבא א"ר יוחנן זו דברי ר' ישמעאל ור"ע אבל חכ"א ג' עונות שלימות בעינן וכן הלכה. ושכבת זרע שפרשה מלאיש כ"ז שהיא [לחה] טמאה ואפי' פלט אותה [מימים הרבה]. וכי תניא פרט לש"ז שהסריחה דפרשה מן האשה אבל בפרשה מן האיש טמאה כל זמן שהיא ליחה והיכי דמי אפי' הבא על הזכור אם פלט הזכור את שכבת זרעו כ"ז שהיא ליחה טמאה ומנא לן מדקא מיבעיא ליה לרב פפא ש"ז במעי בהמה מהו וקא מסתפקא משום דלית לה פרוזדור. דאלמא פרוזדור דאשה הוא דמסרחא ואם פלטתה אחר ג' עונות שלימות טהורה ובהמה דלית לה פרוזדור מספקא מלתא משום דלא איפשיטא ועבדינן לחומרא אבל זכר דלית ליה פרוזדור לא מסרחא ש"ז במעיו ופשיטא דטמאה. ובמעי נכרית אף אינון הביל גופייהו כישראלי' כד פלטה לה אחר ג' טהורה. ת"ר בששה לחודש נתנו עשר דברות לישראל ר' יוסי אימר בשבעה בו אמר רבה דכ"ע בר"ח סיון באו' מדבר סיני וביום שבת נתנו עשר דברות ובקביעא דסיון פליגי רבנן סברי בתרי בשבא אקבע סיון דההיא שתא ושבת ששה בו ור' יוסי סבר בחד בשבא אקבע ושבת שבעה בו רבנן דסברי בתרין בשבא הוה קבועיה ומפורש בתורה דההוא יומא שחנו במדבר סיני ויחן שם ישראל נגד ההר ומשה עלה אל האלהים ואמר ליה למימר לישראל אתם ראיתם וגו' וקאמרי' רבנן דההוא יומא לא אמר להו משה לישראל מידי משום חולשא דאורחא וטרחיה בשלישי אמר להו האי מימרא ויבא משה וגו' ברביעי עבד להו הגבלה דקאמר והגבלת את העם וגו' ואע"ג דכתיבה בתר הפרשה קבלה היא דהיא הות תחלה. בחמישי

עבד

מסורת הש"ס

יבמות סב. [עי' אדר"נ פ"ב תשיב עוד אחד]

ב"ב יד: יבמות סב. מנחות לט:

[חגיגה יד.]

[תרגום הנני מאכיל את העם הזה לענה מרה כגידין ערוך ערך גד]

הגהות הב"ח

(א) רש"י ד"ה אמרה תורה וכו' יפרשו מנשותיהן: (ב) ד"ה הא אמרן וכו' א"ל למשה ומשה אמר לכן:

גליון הש"ס

גמ' ואמר ר"ל יישר. אשר כמו ישר ובא האל"ף במקום היו"ד וכן אשרו חמוץ (ישעיה א') כמו ישרו חמוץ:

לחנייתן רב אחא בר יעקב אמר למסען וקמיפלגי בשבת דמרה דכתיב °כאשר צוך ה' אלהיך *ואמר רב יהודה אמר רב כאשר צוך במרה מר סבר אשבת איפקוד אתחומין לא איפקוד ומר סבר אתחומין נמי איפקוד ת"ש ניסן שבו יצאו ישראל ממצרים בארבעה עשר שחטו פסחיהם ובחמשה עשר יצאו ולערב לקו בכורות לערב ס"ד אלא (א)מבערב לקו בכורות ואותו היום חמישי בשבת היה מדחמיסר בניסן חמשה בשבת ריש ירחא דאייר שבתא וריש ירחא דסיון חד בשבת קשיא לרבנן אמרי לך רבנן אייר דההיא שתא עבורי עברוה תא שמע דלא עברוה ניסן שבו יצאו ישראל ממצרים בארבעה עשר שחטו פסחיהם בחמשה עשר יצאו ולערב לקו בכורות לערב ס"ד אלא אימא מבערב לקו בכורות ואותו היום חמישי בשבת היה השלים ניסן ואירע אייר להיות בשבת חסר אייר ואירע סיון להיות באחד בשבת קשיא לרבנן הא מני ר' יוסי היא אמר רב פפא ת"ש °ויסעו מאלים ויבאו כל עדת בני ישראל וגו' בחמשה עשר יום לחדש השני ואותו היום שבת היה דכתיב °ובקר וראיתם את כבוד ה' וכתיב °ששת ימים תלקטוהו ומדחמיסר באייר שבתא ריש ירחא דסיון חד בשבת קשיא לרבנן אמרי לך רבנן אייר דההיא שתא עבורי עברוה א"ל רב (ב)חביבי מחוזנאה לרב אשי ת"ש °ויהי בחדש הראשון בשנה השנית באחד לחדש הוקם המשכן תנא אותו יום נטל עשר עטרות ראשון למעשה בראשית ראשון לנשיאים ראשון לכהונה ראשון לעבודה ראשון לירידת האש ראשון לאכילת קדשים ראשון לשכון (ג)שכינה ראשון לברך את ישראל ראשון לאיסור הבמות ראשון לחדשים ומדריש ירחא דניסן דהאי שתא חד בשבא דאשתקד [בד'] בשבת דתניא אחרים אומרים *אין בין עצרת לעצרת ואין בין ר"ה לר"ה (ד) אלא ד' ימים בלבד ואם היתה שנה מעוברת ה' הוה ליה ריש ירחא דאייר מעלי שבתא וריש ירחא דסיון שבתא קשיא בין לרבי יוסי בין לרבנן לר' יוסי שבעה חסרין עבוד לרבנן

תורה אור: דברים ה · שמות טז · שם · שם · שם מ

לחנייתן. שהרי בר"ח חנו והכי קאמר ששי לחנייתן הוא הששי בחדש הוא ששי בשבת: למסען. אף למסען שביום שבאו למדבר סיני נסעו מרפידים: וקא מיפלגי. רב אחא ורבא במצות שבת שנאמר להם במרה אם נצטוו על התחומין בו ביום או לא דכתיב בדברות האחרונות שמור את יום השבת לקדשו כאשר צוך ש"מ קודם הדברות נצטוו בה: ואר"י במרה. דכתיב שם שם לו חק ומשפט (שמות טו): אתחומין לא איפקוד. הלכך כשנסעו מרפידים נסעו בשבת שלא הוזהרו (ה)לילך יותר מאלפים אמה: לערב. לערב משמע לערב הבא: ריש ירחא דאייר שבתא. שהרי ניסן מלא הוא לעולם (ו) א) וריש ירחא דסיון בחד בשבתא: השלים ניסן. נתמלא בשלשים יום לשון שלם *חיסר אייר שהרי אייר חסר כסדרן ומתרמי סיון בחד בשבתא: ואותו היום שבת היה שנא' ובקר וראיתם וגו'. שנתרעמו בו ביום על המן כדכתיב וילונו על משה וגו' להמית את כל הקהל הזה ברעב והבטיחם להוריד להם מן למחר וע"כ בחד בשבת ירד להם מן תחלה שנאמר ששת ימים תלקטוהו וביום השביעי לירידתו שבת לא יהיה בו: ריש ירחא דסיון חד בשבת. כשתשלים לאייר עד ט"ו ויום ט"ו ר"ח סיון: עשר עטרות. ראשון לעשרה דברים: ראשון לבריאת עולם. שאחד בשבת היה: ראשון לנשיאים. להקרבת נשיאים לחנוכת הבית: ראשון לכהונה. אותו היום שמיני למילואים ועבודה באהרן ובניו ועד עכשיו היה בבכורות: ראשון לעבודה. לסדר עבודת ציבור תמידין ושאר קרבנות של תרומת הלשכה: לירידת אש. ותצא אש מלפני ה' ותאכל על המזבח וגו' (ויקרא ט): לאכילת קדשים. במחילה ועד עכשיו היו נאכלים בכל מקום: לשכון. בישראל שכינה שרתה שם כדכתיב ושכנתי בתוכם מכלל דעד השתא לא (ז)שרתה: לברך. ברכת כהנים כדכתיב וישא אהרן את ידיו וגו': לאיסור הבמות. מעכשיו נאסרו שהוא ראוי לפתח אהל מועד כדכתיב ואל פתח אהל מועד לא הביאו: דהאי שתא. שנה השנית ליציאתם הוקם המשכן: ד' ימים. כשאתה קובע כל החדשים כסדרן אחד מלא ואחד חסר הוו ארבעה ימים בין תחלת שנה לתחלת שנה אחרת שמנין חדשי לבנה כסדרן שנ"ד ימים כולן שבועין חוץ מארבעה ימים: ואם היתה שנה מעוברת ה'. דקסבר שני האדרים עבדינן חסרים ופסח דחוי יום אחד לקמן: ז' חסרים עבוד. ולא היו אלא ג' בין פסח לפסח הלכך דאישתקד בה' בשבא ולית ליה דאחרים דאמרי אין מעברין ואין מחסרין שום חדש לצורך אלא לעולם אחד מלא ואחד חסר:

כאשר צוך במרה. ואם תאמר מנא ליה דבמרה איפקוד אשבת דילמא כאשר צוך בפרשת מן דאשכחן דיני שבת כתובין שם את אשר תאפו אפו וגו' וי"ל משום דבכיבוד אב ואם נמי כתיב כאשר צוך ומסתמא כי היכי דהאי כאשר צוך במרה הכי נמי האי וכן מוכח בפרק ד' מיתות (סנהדרין דף נו:) דאיתמר מילתיה דר' יהודה אתרווייהו וא"ת וכיון דבמרה איפקוד אשבת היכי אמרינן בפ' כל כתבי (לקמן קיח:) אלמלי שמרו ישראל שבת ראשונה לא שלטה בהן אומה ולשון שנאמר ויהי ביום השביעי יצאו מן העם ללקוט וגו' וכתיב בתריה ויבא עמלק אמאי קרי להאי שבת ראשונה כיון דבמרה נצטוו והא לא היתה שבת ראשונה דמעיקרא כתיב ויסעו מאילם ויבאו וגו' ואמרינן בסמוך דאותו היום שבת היה ועוד מקשים דמשמע מתוך הפסוקים ששתי שבתות היו קודם ראשונה כשנסעו מאילם ואחר אותו שבת ירד להם המן וכתיב ויהי ביום הששי לקטו לחם משנה וגו' ויניחו אותו עד הבקר וגו' [ויאמר משה אכלוהו היום וגו' ששת ימים תלקטוהו וגו' ויהי ביום השביעי יצאו מן העם ללקוט וגו'] משמע שבשבת שלישית שאחר מרה היא: **ואמר** רב יהודה כאשר צוך במרה. האי קרא במשנה תורה כתיב וליכא למימר (ח)כאשר צוך במתן תורה שהרי משה לא היה מספר אלא על הסדר ובכולהו לא כתיב כאשר צוך: **אתחומין** לא איפקוד. אין נראה לאתויי כר' עקיבא דאמר *תחומין דאורייתא דהא משמע לכ"ע דבסיני לכל הפחות איפקוד אתחומין דלאו דוקא נקט תחומין אלא כלומר הוצאה שהיו מוליכין עמהן כל אשר להן ומר סבר אהוצאה לא איפקוד ומר סבר איפקוד ואע"ג דבפרשת מן כתיב אל יצא איש ממקומו ודרשינן מיניה הוצאה בספ"ק דעירובין (דף יז:) איכא למימר שאחר מתן תורה נאמר אחר שנעשה המשכן [כמו] שאמר הקב"ה להניח צנצנת לפני העדות ומשום דשייכי למילי דמן כתבינהו התם ולמאן דאמר איפקוד אע"פ שבמרה נאמר כתביה התם כדפרישית: **ואותו** יום חמישי בשבת היה ט'. ואם כן ברביעי שחטו פסחיהם ונמצא בשבת שעברה לקחו פסחיהן שאז היה בעשור לחדש ועל כן קורין אותו שבת הגדול לפי שנעשה בו נס גדול כדאמרינן במדרש (שמות רבה פ' כא) כשלקחו פסחיהם באותה שבת נתקבצו בכורות אומות העולם אצל ישראל ושאלום למה היו עושין כך אמרו להן זבח פסח לה' שיהרוג בכורי מצרים הלכו אצל אבותיהם ואצל פרעה לבקש ממנו שישלחו ישראל ולא רצו ועשו בכורות מלחמה והרגו מהן הרבה הה"ד למכה מצרים בבכוריהם: **וכתיב** ששת ימים תלקטוהו. תימה היכי מייתי ראיה מהאי קרא דבשבת היה והלא זה הפסוק נכתב אחר שירד כבר מן שבוע כשהגידו נשיאי העדה למשה שלקטו לחם משנה דכתיב ויאמר משה אכלוהו היום וגו' ששת ימים תלקטוהו והמן כבר ירד מיום ראשון שעבר ואור"י דאע"ג דלא נאמר עד אח"כ מ"מ מוכח שפיר דמשה שכח לומר להם והיה אומר היה לי לומר לכם מה שאמר הקב"ה כשנתן את המן שתלקטוהו ששת ימים ואח"כ אחד בשבת היה: **עשר** עטרות נטל אותו היום. הא דלא חשיב ראשון להקמת המשכן משום דאמרינן במדרש (ויקרא רבה פ' שמיני) שכל ז' ימי המלואים היה משה מעמיד המשכן ומפרקו אי נמי משום דעליה דהקמת המשכן קאי דה"ק אותו היום של הקמת המשכן נטל עשר עטרות אחרות: **ראשון** לאכילת קדשים. ובת"כ במקום אכילת קדשים קתני שחיטתן בצפון: ב)**לרבנן** ח' חסירין עבוד. אומר ר' יצחק דלא הוי צ"ל ח' חסירין עבוד אלא ז' חסירין ואייר דההיא שתא עבורי עברוה כדאמר לעיל אלא משום דלר"י איצטריך למימר דשבעה חסירין עבוד דהא תניא לעיל דאותו יום ה' בשבת היה נקט נמי לרבנן שמנה:

א) יש שכתבו דכך וריש ירחא הוא דבור חדש וכצ"ל וריש ירחא דסיון חד בשבתא שהרי אייר חסר [תו"י]: ב) דבור זה שייך לקמן דף פ"ח

כפה

רבינו חננאל

עבד להו פרישה שלא ינשו אל אשה שלא תפלטו שכבת זרע בשעת [מתן תורה] ותטמא והא פרישנן דר' אלעזר בן עזריא הכין סברי ואף הלכתא דאמרה ר' יוחנן ג' עונות שלימות מעת לעת סלקא לפום הכין ושמעו דברות בצפרא דשבתא דהוא ו' בחודש ר' יוסי דסבר בחד בשבא הוה קבועי אמר לך בחד בשבא לא אמר להו ולא מידי משום חולשא דאורחא. בתרין אמר להו ואתם תהיו לי ממלכת כהנים וגו' בתלתא הגבלה בארבע פרישה וסלקא לר' ישמעאל ור' עקיבא כדפרישנא לעילא ומקשי' אי ר' יוסי דאמר מן צפרא דארבעה עבוד פרישה קרא דכתי' לך אל העם וקדשתם היום ומחר דאלמא היום חמשה ולמחר מעלי דשבתא שמעו דברות. ופריקנ' אמר לך ר' יוסי בארבעה הוא דאמר ליה רחמנא וקדשתם היום ומחר ודרש משה דלאו היום האידנא דהוא יומא דארבעה אלא הכי קאמר ב' ימים דדמי להדדי כי ביום השלישי ירד ה' וצריך למהוי היום כמחר תרויהו לילותיה' עמהם וה"ק יום ומחר שלו ואינון מתחלת חמישי ומנ"ל דהסכימה דעתו לדעת המקום והסכים הקב"ה ע"י דהא לא שראי שכינה עד שבתא ולרבנן היום ומחר חמשה ומעלי ולא צריכי לילו עמו אבל קרא דאמר להו משה לישראל היו נכונים לשלשת ימים לית מוכח ולא קשי לא למר ולא למר. ת"ש שלישי שלישי לחודש שלישי בשבת אלמא ריש ירחא בחד בשבא ופרקי הא מני ר' יוסי היא: ואיבעיא לן האי שלישי דאמר ר' יוסי הוא שלישי לשבת ולחודש ולמאי אצטריך ליה והי יומא ניהו ופירוש כיון דבשני אמר להו ואתם תהיו לי בשלישי וגו' וישב משה והוא יום הגבלה לר' יוסי ב"ר יהודה ולרבי הוא יום שהודיען עונשן ומתן שכרן שמשבבין לבו של אדם דאמר שהודיען עונשה פי' ששוברין לבו של אדם ונפיק מן כי שבבים יהיה עגלי שומרון. ומן ל' ארמי נמי ידוע הוא. שקשין כגידין דקא' דל רגש פרשוהו רבנן בלשון ארמית הרזוקלאלי והוא בטיית הנטלי ואיתא ביום הכפורים לענין מן כזרע גד. ת"ש ששי. ששי בחודש ששי בשבת הא נמי רבי יוסי והאי ששי למאי (דקאמר ביה) [קארי ליה] הכי רבה אמר ששי לחנייתן דאלמא בשבת במסען היו ולא היו מצווין על התחומין באותה שעה. רב אחא בר יעקב אמר אף ביום חנייתן היה מסען והוא חד בשב' ומצווין היו על התחומין. ת"ש ניסן שיצא בו ישראל ממצרים ביום חמישי הוה דמשכחת אייר בז' וסיון בחד בשבא. אמרי לך רבנן אייר דההיא שתא עבורי עברוה וסיון בתרין בשבא. ת"ש דלא עברוה דתניא יום ט"ו בניסן יום חמישי השלים ניסן אירע אייר להיות בשבת חיסר אייר אירע סיון להיות באחד בשבת הא מני ר' יוסי היא. אמר רב פפא ת"ש בחמשה עשר יום לחודש השני אותו היום ע"ש היה ומדט"ו באייר בשבתא ריש ירחא דסיון בחד בשבא ופרקי דעיבורי עברוה לאייר וריש ירח סיון תרין בשבתא א"ל רב חבי מחוזנאה לרב אשי ת"ש ויהי בחודש הראשון בשנה השנית באחד לחודש הוקם המשכן ותניא אותו היום נטל עשר עטרות ראשון למעשה בראשית אלמא חד בשבא היה ומדר"ח ניסן שנה שנית חד בשבת ר"ח ניסן דראשונה ארבע בשבת דתניא אחרים אומרים אין בין עצרת לעצרת ואין בין ראש השנה לראש השנה אלא ד' ימים בלבד ואם היתה שנה מעוברת חמשה וכיון דר"ח ניסן ארבע ר"ח סיון שבת. וקשיא בין לרבנן דאמרי תרין בשבא ובין לר' יוסי דאמר חד בשבא ופרקינן לרבנן ח' חסרין עבוד לר' יוסי ז' חסירין עבוד דכי אמרו אחרים אין בין עצרת לעצרת ד' ימים בזמן שחדשי השנה כס

אחד

מסורת הש"ס

סנהדרין נו:

יש שכתבו שזהו דיבור חדש וגרסי' חיסר אייר עשהו חסר כסדרן רש"ל

[סוטה ל:]

ערכין ט: סוכה נד: ר"ה ו: כ. [תוספתא ערכין פ"א]

הגהות הב"ח

(א) גמ' אלא אימא מבערב: (ב) שם א"ל רב אסי מחוזנאה: (ג) שם ראשון לשכון בישראל ראשון לברכת כהנים ראשון לאיסור הבמות: (ד) שם ואין בין ר"ה לר"ה ואין בין פסח לפסח אלא ד' ימים: (ה) רש"י ד"ה אתחומין וכו' שלא הוזהרו שלא לילך: (ו) ד"ה ריש ירחא וכו' לעולם הס"ד ואח"כ מ"ה וריש ירחא דסיון בחד בשבא שהרי אייר חסר כסדרן ומתרמי סיון בחד בשבתא הס"ד ואח"כ מ"ה השלים וכו' ואח"כ ד"ה חיסר אייר עשהו חסר כסדרן הס"ד והשאר נמחק: (ז) ד"ה לשכון וכו' לא שכן הס"ד: (ח) תוס' ד"ה ואמר ר' יהודה וכו' וליכא למימר. נ"ב וברש"י מס' סנהדרין דף נו מצאתי תירוץ אחר ע"ז ע"ש:

is [the first] 'the sixth' [mentioned]?—Raba said: [87b] [In respect] of their encamping.[6] R. Aha b. Jacob said: [In respect] of their journeying.[7] Now, they disagree about [the precept of] the Sabbath [as communicated to them] at Marah, for it is written, [*Observe the Sabbath day . . .*] *as the Lord thy God commanded thee,*[8] whereon Rab Judah commented in Rab's name: As he commanded
a thee at Marah.[1] One Master holds: They were commanded concerning the Sabbath [in general], but not concerning *tehumin*.[2] Whilst the other Master holds: They were commanded concerning *tehumin* too.[3]

Come and hear: As to the Nisan in which the Israelites departed from Egypt, on the fourteenth day they slaughtered their Passover sacrifices, on the fifteenth they went forth, and in the evening the first-borns were smitten. 'In the evening': can you think so![4] Rather say, The first-borns having been smitten the [previous] evening, and that day was a Thursday. Now, since the fifteenth of Nisan was on a Thursday, the first of Iyar was on the Sabbath,[5] and the first of Siwan was on a Sunday,[6] which is a difficulty according to the Rabbis?—The Rabbis answer you: Iyar in that year was indeed made full.[7]

Come and hear that they did not make it full! As to the Nisan in which the Israelites departed from Egypt, on the fourteenth they killed their Passover sacrifices, on the fifteenth they went forth, and in the evening the first-borns were smitten. 'In the evening': can you think so! Rather, say, The first-borns having been smitten since the [previous] evening, and that day was a Thursday. Nisan was a full month, so that [the first of] Iyar fell on the Sabbath. Iyar was defective, so that [the first of] Siwan fell on a Sunday. This is a difficulty according to the Rabbis?—That agrees with R. Jose.

R. Papa observed, Come and hear: *And they took their journey from Elim, and all the congregation of the children of Israel came unto*
b *the wilderness of Sin . . . on the fifteenth day of the second month.*[1] Now that day was the Sabbath, for it is written, *and in the morning, then ye shall see the glory of the Lord,*[2] and it is written, *Six days ye shall gather it.*[3] Now, since the fifteenth of Iyar was on the Sabbath, the first of Siwan was on a Sunday, which is a difficulty according to the Rabbis?—The Rabbis can answer you: Iyar of that year was made full.

R. Assi[4] of Hozna'ah[5] said to R. Ashi, Come and hear: *And it came to pass in the first month of the second year, on the first day of the month, that the tabernacle was reared up;*[6] [and with reference to this] a Tanna taught: That day took ten crowns.[7] It was the first of the Creation,[8] the first for the princes,[9] the first for the priesthood,[10] the first for [public] sacrifice, the first for the fall of fire [from Heaven],[11] the first for the eating of sacred food,[12] the first for the dwelling of the *Shechinah* in Israel, the first for the [priestly] blessing of Israel,[13] the first for the interdict of the high places,[14] [and] the first of months. Now, since the first of Nisan of that year was on a Sunday, that of the previous year must have been on a Wednesday. For it was taught: Others say, Between one '*Azereth*[15] and another, and between one New Year['s day] and another, there can be a difference of only four days,[16] and in
c a leap year, five [days].[1] Hence the first of Iyar must have fallen on the eve of the Sabbath [Friday], and the first of Siwan on the Sabbath, which is a difficulty according to both R. Jose and the Rabbis?—In R. Jose's view, seven months were declared

(6) The Baraitha states that the sixth day from when they pitched their tents, which was on New Moon, was also the sixth of the month and the sixth day of the week. (7) From Rephidim (v. Ex. XIX, 2). He holds that they left Rephidim and came to the wilderness of Sinai on the same day. (8) Deut. V, 12. This occurs in the second Decalogue, which is a repetition of the first Decalogue. Hence these words, '*as . . . commanded thee*', must have been spoken on the first occasion at Sinai too, and they imply that the Israelites had already been commanded to keep the Sabbath.

a (1) V. Ex. XV, 25. (2) *Tehum* pl. *tehumin*, q.v. Glos. (3) Raba maintains that it was the sixth day from their encamping only, whilst they departed from Rephidim on the previous day, which was the Sabbath, since the law of *tehumin* was as yet non-existent. But R. Aha b. Jacob holds that they must have set out from Rephidim on Sunday too, not on the Sabbath, this law already being in existence. (4) For this implies that the death of the first-borns took place *after* their departure. (5) Nisan containing thirty days. (6) Iyar containing twenty-nine days. (7) Before the calendar was fixed by calculation months might be made full (thirty days) or defective (twenty-nine days) according to the exigencies of the moment.

b (1) Ex. XVI, 1. (2) Ibid. 7. (3) Ibid. 26. Now, the manna first fell on the day after they arrived at Sin, for Moses says '*and in the morning*', i.e., tomorrow, '*ye shall see the glory*', etc., which refers to the manna. Since Moses permitted them to gather it for six days, the first must have been Sunday, and the previous day was the Sabbath. (4) So the text as emended by BaH. (5) (Be-) Hozae, Khuzistan. (6) Ex. XL, 17. (7) I.e., it was pre-eminent in ten things. (8) I.e., it was a Sunday. (9) To make their offerings for the dedication of the Tabernacle, v. Num. VII. (10) When Aaron began to officiate as a priest, v. Lev. IX; before that Divine Service was performed by first-borns. (11) V. ibid. 24. (12) I.e., flesh of sacrifices, which had henceforth to be eaten within a fixed locale, whereas hitherto it might be consumed anywhere. (13) By Aaron, v. ibid. 22. (14) Upon which sacrifices were offered before the erection of the Tabernacle. (15) Lit., 'solemn assembly'—the Feast of Weeks. (16) I.e., one falls four days later in the week than the previous year's, since the Jewish year, which is lunar, consists of three hundred and fifty-four days.

c (1) An extra month of twenty-nine days being intercalated.

defective;[2] [88*a*] in that of the Rabbis', eight months were declared defective.[3]

Come and hear: For it was taught in the Seder 'Olam:[4] As to the Nisan in which the Israelites departed from Egypt, on the fourteenth they slaughtered their Passover sacrifices, on the fifteenth they went out, and that day was the Sabbath eve. Now, since the first of Nisan was the Sabbath eve, the first of Iyar was on a Sunday, and [the first of] Siwan on a Monday. This is a difficulty according to R. Jose?—R. Jose answers you: This agrees with the Rabbis.

Come and hear: R. Jose said: On the second day Moses ascended and descended;[5] on the third he ascended and descended;[6] on the fourth he descended and ascended no more.[7] But since he did not go up,[8] whence did he descend?—Rather [say,] on the fourth he ascended and descended; on the fifth he built an altar and offered a sacrifice thereon; [but] on the sixth he had no time. Surely that was on account of [the giving of] the Torah?[9]—No: it was on account of the preparations for[10] the Sabbath.[11]

A certain Galilean lectured before R. Ḥisda:[12] Blessed be the
a Merciful One who gave a three-fold Torah[1] to a three-fold people[2] through a third[-born][3] on the third day[4] in the third month. With whom does this agree? With the Rabbis.[5]

And they stood under the mount:[6] R. Abdimi b. Ḥama b. Ḥasa said: This teaches that the Holy One, blessed be He, overturned the mountain upon them like an [inverted] cask, and said to them, 'If ye accept the Torah, 'tis well; if not, there shall be your burial.' R. Aḥa b. Jacob observed: This furnishes a strong protest against the Torah.[7] Said Raba, Yet even so, they re-accepted it in the days of Ahasuerus, for it is written, [*the Jews*] *confirmed, and took upon them* [etc.]:[8] [i.e.,] they confirmed what they had accepted long before. Hezekiah said: What is meant by, *Thou didst cause sentence to be heard from Heaven; The earth feared, and was tranquil:*[9] if it feared, why was it tranquil, and if it was tranquil, why did it fear? But at first it feared, yet subsequently it was tranquil.[10] And why did it fear?—Even in accordance with Resh Laḳish. For Resh Laḳish said: Why is it written, *And there was evening and there was morning, the sixth day;*[11] What is the purpose of the additional '*the*'?[12] This teaches that the Holy One, blessed be He, stipulated with the Works of Creation and said thereto, 'If Israel accepts the Torah, ye shall exist; but if not, I will turn you back into emptiness and formlessness.'[13]

R. Simai lectured: When the Israelites gave precedence to '*we*
b *will do*' over '*we will hearken,*'[1] six hundred thousand ministering angels came and set two crowns upon each man of Israel, one as a reward for[2] '*we will do,*' and the other as a reward for '*we will hearken*'. But as soon as Israel sinned,[3] one million two hundred thousand destroying angels descended and removed them, as it is said, *And the children of Israel stripped themselves of their ornaments from mount Horeb.*[4] R. Ḥama son of R. Ḥanina said: At Horeb they put them on and at Horeb they put them off. At Horeb they put them on, as we have stated. At Horeb they put them off, for it is written, *And* [*the children of Israel*] *stripped themselves*, etc. R. Joḥanan observed: And Moses was privileged and received them all, for in proximity thereto it is stated, *And Moses took the tent.*[5] Resh Laḳish said: [Yet] the Holy One, blessed be He, will return them to us in the future, for it is said, *and the ransomed of the Lord shall return, and come with singing unto Zion; and everlasting joy shall be upon their heads;*[6] the joy from of old[7] shall be upon their heads.

R. Eleazar said: When the Israelites gave precedence to '*we will do*' over '*we will hearken,*' a Heavenly Voice went forth and exclaimed to them, Who revealed to My children this secret, which is employed by the Ministering Angels, as it is written, *Bless the Lord, ye angels of His: Ye mighty in strength, that fulfil His word, That hearken unto the voice of His word:*[8] first they fulfil and then they hearken?

R. Ḥama son of R. Ḥanina said: What is meant by, *As the apple tree among the trees of the wood,* [*So is my beloved among the sons*]:[9] why were the Israelites compared to an apple tree? To teach you: just as the fruit of the apple tree precedes its leaves,[10] so did the Israelites give precedence to '*we will do*' over '*we will hearken*'.

c There was a certain Sadducee who saw Raba[1] engrossed in his studies while the finger[s] of his hand were under his feet, and he ground them down, so that his fingers spurted blood. 'Ye rash people,' he exclaimed, 'who gave precedence to your mouth over your ears: ye still persist in your rashness. First ye should have listened, if within your powers, accept; if not, ye should

(2) So there was a difference of *three* days, not four, that year consisting of three hundred and fifty-three days, which makes the first of Siwan fall on a Sunday. (3) Hence the year consisted of three hundred and fifty-two days, and the first of Siwan fell on a Monday. (4) The Seder 'Olam is the earliest extant post-exilic chronicle in Hebrew, and is a chronological record extending from Adam to Bar Kochba's revolt during the reign of Hadrian. Most scholars are agreed in assigning its authorship to R. Ḥalafta, a Tanna of the first century, on the strength of a statement by R. Joḥanan in Yeb. 82*b*. V. J.E., art. Seder 'Olam Rabbah. (5) Hearing, '*and ye shall be . . . a kingdom of priests*' and telling it to the people. (6) Being given the order to set boundaries. (7) Until the Revelation. (8) On the fourth. (9) Which supports the Rabbis that the Torah was given on the sixth of the month. (10) Lit., 'trouble of'. (11) The sixth of the month being Friday, the eve of the Sabbath. (12) In the public lectures or sermons the scholar sat and whispered his statements to a speaker, who conveyed them to the people; this Galilean was probably R. Ḥisda's speaker (generally referred to as '*meturgeman*').
a (1) I.e., the Torah (Pentateuch), Prophets and Hagiographa. (2) Israel consisting of Priests, Levites, and Israelites. (3) *Sc.* Moses, born third after Miriam and Aaron. (4) Of their separation from their wives. (5) For according to R. Jose it was on the fourth day of their separation, Moses having added a day (*supra* 87*a*). (6) Ex. XIX, 17. The translation is literal. E.V. *nether part.* (7) It provides an excuse for non-observance, since it was forcibly imposed in the first place. (8) Esth. IX, 27. (9) Ps. LXXVI, 9. (10) It feared lest Israel would reject the Torah, and became tranquil when Israel accepted it. (11) Gen. I, 31. (12) In the case of the other days it is simply stated, a second day, a third day, etc., 'a' being altogether unexpressed in Hebrew. (13) He thus translates homiletically: and the continuance of morning and evening was depended on *the* sixth day, *sc.* of Siwan, when Israel was offered the Torah. The general idea is: Without law and order as exemplified by the Torah the world must lapse into chaos and anarchy.

b (1) V. Ex. XXIV, 7. Thus they promised to obey God's commands even before hearing them. (2) Lit., 'corresponding to'. (3) Through the Golden Calf. (4) I.e., which they had received at Mount Horeb. Ibid. XXXIII, 6. E.V. '*from mount onwards*'. (5) Ibid. 7. The reference is not clear. V. Rashi. (6) Isa. XXXV, 10. (7) The verse may be translated thus. (8) Ps. CIII, 20. (9) Cant. II, 3. The two lovers in this poem were regarded as God and Israel. (10) Tosaf. observes this is untrue of the apple tree, which grows like all other trees; consequently refer this to the citron tree. As the citron remains on the tree from one year to the next, at which time the tree sheds its leaves of the previous year, the fruit may be said to precede the leaves.

c (1) There were no Sadducees in Raba's time, and the word is probably a censor's substitute for Gentile. In *J.E.* X, 633 bottom it is suggested that he was probably a Manichean. [MS.M: *Min* (v. Glos.)].

רש"י

לרבנן ח' חסרים עבוד. ולא היו בין פסח דאשתקד לפסח דהאידנא אלא כ' ימים ונמלא דאשתקד בע"ש: בשני עלה משה. ושמע ואתם תהיו לי וירד והגיד: בג' עלה. ושמע הגבלה וירד והגיד: בד' ירד. להפריסם: ושוב לא עלה. עד קבלת הדברות שעלו כולם: ומאחר שלא עלה מהיכן ירד. דאמר' בד' ירד ולא אמרת עלה וירד אלא אימא בד' עלה וירד ושוב לא עלה: ובחמישי בנה מזבח. כדכתיב ויבן מזבח תחת ההר: מאי לאו משום תורה. לא היה לו פנאי לעלות שקבלו כולן יחד את הדברות: עליה דרב חסדא. לפני רב חסדא לפי שרב חסדא יושב והדרשן עומד קאמר עליה דדומה כמו שהעומד למעלה מן היושב: אוריאן תליתאי. תורה נביאים וכתובים: לעם תליתאי. כהנים לוים וישראלים: על יד תליתאי. משה תליתאי לבטן מרים אהרן ומשה: ביום תליתאי. לפרישה: תחתית ההר. תחת ההר ממש: גיגית. קובא שמטילין בה שכר: מודעא רבה. שאם יזמינם לדין למה לא קיימתם מה שקבלתם עליכם יש להם תשובה שקבלוה באונס: בימי אחשורוש. מאהבת הנס שנעשה להם: דין. תורה: בתחילה. קודם שאמרו ישראל נעשה ונשמע: יראה. שמא לא יקבלוה ויחזור העולם לתהו ובהו כדר"ל: ולבסוף. כשקבלוה: יום הששי. מאי שנא דכתיב ה' ביום גמר מעשה בראשית: מלמד שהתנה כו'. הששי משמע הששי המיוחד במקום אחר כדאמרי' בעלמא (חולין דף צא:) הירך המיומנת אף כאן ויהי ערב ויהי בקר של גמר בראשית תלוי ביום הששי והוא ו' בסיון שנתנה בו תורה מריבוי דה' דריש ביה כמי הא: שני כתרים. מזיו שכינה: מאה ועשרים. [כל א' וא' נטל כתר]: טענו. הכתרים והכי משמע את עדים [אשר היו להם] מהר חורב: בחורב פרקו. דמשמע כמי ויתנצלו את עדים מהר חורב: ומשה יקח. אותו עדי לשון אחר את האהל לשון בהלו נרו (איוב כט) והוא היה קירון עור פניו: עושי דברו לשמוע. מוכנין לעשות קודם שישמעו ולא כדרך שאר עבדים ששומעים תחילה את הדבר לידע אם יכולין לקבלן עליהם אם לאו: פריו קודם לעליו. כך דרכו וחלוק משאר אילנות חנטת פירותיו קודם לעליו: אצבעתא דידיה. אצבעות ידיו: וקא מייץ בהו. היה ממעכן ברגליו ואינו מבין מתוך טירדא: עמא פזיזא. נמהר: דקדמיתו פומייכו לאודנייכו. קודם ששמעתם אותה היאך היא קשה ואם תוכלו לעמוד בה קבלתם עליכם לקיימה:

דסגינן

גמרא

לרבנן ח' חסרים עבוד ת"ש דתניא בסדר עולם ניסן שבו יצאו ישראל ממצרים בארבעה עשר שחטו פסחיהן בחמשה עשר יצאו ואותו היום ע"ש היה ומדריש ירחא דניסן ערב שבת ריש ירחא דאייר חד בשבא וסיון בתרי בשבא קשיא לר' יוסי אמר לך ר' יוסי הא מני רבנן היא ת"ש רבי יוסי אומר בשני עלה משה וירד בשלישי עלה וירד בד' ירד ושוב לא עלה ומאחר שלא עלה מהיכן ירד אלא ברביעי עלה וירד °בחמישי בנה מזבח והקריב עליו קרבן בששי לא היה לו פנאי מאי לאו משום תורה לא משום טורח שבת דרש ההוא גלילאה עליה דרב חסדא בריך רחמנא דיהב אוריאן תליתאי לעם תליתאי על ידי תליתאי ביום תליתאי בירחא תליתאי כמאן כרבנן: °ויתיצבו בתחתית ההר *א"ר אבדימי בר חמא בר חסא מלמד שכפה הקב"ה עליהם את ההר כגיגית ואמר להם אם אתם מקבלים התורה מוטב ואם לאו שם תהא קבורתכם א"ר אחא בר יעקב מכאן מודעא רבה לאורייתא אמר רבא (א) אעפ"כ הדור קבלוה בימי אחשורוש דכתיב °קימו וקבלו היהודים *קיימו מה שקיבלו כבר *אמר חזקיה מאי דכתיב °משמים השמעת דין ארץ יראה ושקטה אם יראה למה שקטה ואם שקטה למה יראה אלא בתחילה יראה ולבסוף שקטה ולמה יראה כדריש לקיש דאמר *ריש לקיש מאי דכתיב °ויהי ערב ויהי בקר יום הששי ה' יתירה למה לי מלמד שהתנה הקב"ה עם מעשה בראשית ואמר להם אם ישראל מקבלים התורה אתם מתקיימין ואם לאו אני מחזיר אתכם לתוהו ובוהו: דרש ר' סימאי °בשעה שהקדימו ישראל נעשה לנשמע באו ששים ריבוא של מלאכי השרת לכל אחד ואחד מישראל קשרו לו שני כתרים אחד כנגד נעשה ואחד כנגד נשמע וכיון שחטאו ישראל ירדו מאה ועשרים ריבוא מלאכי חבלה ופירקום שנאמר °ויתנצלו בני ישראל את עדים מהר חורב א"ר חמא בר' חנינא בחורב טענו בחורב פרקו בחורב טענו כדאמרן בחורב פרקו דכתיב ויתנצלו בני ישראל וגו' א"ר יוחנן וכולן זכה משה ונטלן דסמיך ליה ומשה יקח את האהל אמר ר"ל עתיד הקב"ה להחזירן לנו שנאמר °ופדויי ה' ישובון ובאו ציון ברנה ושמחת עולם על ראשם שמחה שמעולם על ראשם אמר רבי אלעזר *בשעה שהקדימו ישראל נעשה לנשמע יצתה בת קול ואמרה להן מי גילה לבני רז זה שמלאכי השרת משתמשין בו דכתיב °ברכו ה' מלאכיו גבורי כח עושי דברו לשמוע בקול דברו ברישא עושי והדר לשמוע א"ר חמא *ברבי חנינא מ"ד °כתפוח בעצי היער וגו' למה נמשלו ישראל לתפוח לומר לך מה תפוח זה פריו קודם לעליו אף ישראל הקדימו נעשה לנשמע ההוא צדוקי דחזייה לרבא דקא מעיין בשמעתא ויתבה אצבעתא דידיה תותי כרעא וקא מייץ בהו וקא מבען אצבעתיה דמא *א"ל עמא פזיזא דקדמיתו פומייכו לאודנייכו אכתי בפחזותייכו קיימיתו ברישא איבעי' לכו למשמע אי מציתו קבליתו ואי לא לא קבליתו א"ל אנן

דסגינן

*) יש נוסחאות בר חנינא

תוספות

כפה עליהן הר כגיגית. ואע"פ שכבר הקדימו נעשה לנשמע שמא יהיו חוזרים כשיראו האש הגדולה *שיצאתה נשמתן והא דאמר בפ"ק דמס' ע"ז (דף ג:) כלום כפית עלינו הר כגיגית דמשמע דאם היה כפה עליהן לא היה להן תשובה והכא אמר דמודעא רבה לאורייתא הייט על מה שלא קבלוה אבל מה שלא קיימוה איכא תשובה:

מודעא רבה לאורייתא. והא דאמר בנדרים (דף כה.) שכרת משה ברית עם ישראל על התורה והמצות והשביעם על כך ובפ' אלו נאמרין (סוטה לז:)(ג) שקבלו את כל התורה בהר גרזים ובהר עיבל אור"ת דע"פ הדיבור היה והרי כבעל כרחם אבל בימי אחשורוש קבלו מדעתם מאהבת הנס ומה שכרת עמהן ברית יהושע לעבוד את ה' התם לא קבלו אלא שלא לעבוד ע"ז כדכתיב (יהושע כד) חלילה לנו מעזוב את ה' וכן משמע כוליה ענייגא:

אמר רבא הדר קבלוה בימי אחשורוש. תימה לר"י דבמגילה (דף ז.) גבי אסתר ברוח הקודש נאמרה אמר רב יהודה אמר שמואל אי הואי התם ה"א להו דידי עדיפא מדידהו קיימו וקבלו היהודים קיימו למעלה מה שקבלו למטה ואמר רבא כולהו אית להו פירכא לבר משמואל דלית ליה פירכא והשתא דשמואל נמי אית ליה פירכא דרבא גופיה מוקי האי קרא לדרשה אחריתי ובפ"ק דחגיגה (דף י.) גבי היתר נדרים פורחין באויר קאמר כולהו אית להו פירכא וחשיב פירכא הא דאיצטריך קרא לדרשה אחריתי ואי גרסינן התם רבה אתא שפיר אי נמי ה"ק במגילה כולהו אית להו פירכא שאר תנאים מוקשים בסברתם כדאמר התם אבל שמואל אינו מוקשה כל כך אלא דאיצטריך קרא לדרשה אחריתי*:

[עי' תוס' ע"ז ב: ד"ה כפה ותוס' חגיגה י. ד"ה ואו]

שני כתרים. של הוד היו לפיכך כשנטל משה קרן עור פניו:

ירדו ק"כ ריבוא. מדכתיב ויתנצלו דריש תרי זימני ויש ספרים שכתוב בהן בהדיא ויגלו לא נאמר אלא ויתנצלו °ואע"ג דגדולה מדה טובה ממדת פורענות הכא נמי גדולה היא שמלאך טוב היה קושר שני כתרים ומלאך חבלה לא היה בו כח כי אם להסיר אחד:

פריו קודם לעליו. הקשה ר"ת שהרי אנו רואים שגדל כשאר אילנות ומפרש דתפוח היינו אתרוג וריח אפך כתפוחים מתרגמינן °כריחא דאתרוגא ואתרוג פריו קודם לעליו שדר באילן משנה לשנה ואחר שנה נושרין עליו של אשתקד ובאין עלין אחרים הוי פריו קודם לאותם עלים אך תימה שמביא קרא כתפוח בעצי היער דבהאי קרא לא נמשלו ישראל לתפוח אלא הקב"ה כדכתיב כן דודי בין הבנים וקרא דריח אפך כתפוחים (שיר ז) הוה ליה לאתויי טפי:

ונא

רבינו חננאל

אחד מלא ואחד חסר דהוו ו' שלמין וששה חסרין והוו יומי דשתא שנ"ד דנאכלין ש"נ מנהון בשבועי ומשתיירין ד' אבל כדהוו בה ז' חסרין הוו להו יומי שנ"ג וכד אזלין שביעי משתיירי מינה ג' והלכך כד הוי ראש ניסן דשניית יום אחד בשבת והות בראשונה ז' חסרין הוי ניסן בראשונה בחמשה וסיון בחד בשבא כר' יוסי ואי הוי בשנה ראשונה שמנה חסרין והוו יומא שנ"ב משתיירי מינה תרין וכד הוי ראש ניסן שנייה בחד בשבא הוי ראש ניסן שנה ראשונה במעלי שבתא וראש סיון תרין בשבא כרבנן. ותנן אין פוחתין מארבעה חדשים המעוברין בשנה וכד הווין ד' מעוברין הוו ח' מחוסרין ואפי' למאן דפריש ולא נראה לחכמים לחסר יתר על שמונה: ת"ש רבי יוסי אומר בשני עלה וירד. פי' שני לחנייתן במדבר סיני ובשלישי עלה וירד וברביעי כי תרצהא עלה וירד ובחמישי בנה מזבח והקריב עליו קרבן בששי לא היה לו פנאי ודאי לאו דהוא יום שבת ונתנה בו תורה. וסייעתא לרבנן ודחי ר' יוסי לא אלא הוא דע"ש ומשום טרחא דשבת לא היה לו פנאי: דרש ההוא גלילאה עלי' דרב חסדא בריך רחמנא דיהב אוריין תליתאי ע"י תליתאי לעם תליתאי ביום תליתאי בירח תליתאי ואית רבנן דמרוחין וגרסין כמאן כרבנן וסייעתא דרבנן מן ביום תליתאי יום ג' לפרישה. דאלמא בחמשה עביד להו פרישא כמאן כרבנן ותרין בשבא הוה ר"ח סיון ובששה בו נתנה תורה ומפרשא פלתתא נמי בגמ' דשבעת ימים. צליהתא בלשון ישמעאל א' שקיקה. פתילת הוורד שעושין מצמר נפן צבוע כעין ורד וקורין אותו וורד וכן אמרו (כתובות עד) לענין יצאת וראשה פרועה ופווה בשוק בטווה וורד כנגד פניה. ובלשון פרס נקרא טלנון נודע בבבל:

רב נסים גאון

דרש ההוא גלילאה עלי' דרב חסדא בריך רחמנא דיהב אוריין תליתאי. פי' תורה נביאי' וכתובי'. ביום תליתאי. פי' ביום שלישי לפרישה כרבנן דאמר בחמישי עבד ליה פרישה. ע"י תליתאי ע"י משה שהוא שלישי אהרן ומרים ומשה. לעם תליתאי כהנים לוים וישראל. בירח תליתאי בחודש השלישי ניסן אייר סיון ובסיון ניתנה התורה והוסיפה ההגדה בדבר זה אותותיה משולשים כלומר שהתורה נקרית אמת שנאמר (משלי כג) אמת קנה ואל תמכור ומספר אמת ג' אותיות וישראל בני אבות ג' אברהם יצחק ויעקב משבט שלישי ראובן שמעון לוי ומן לוי נולד משה שעל ידו ניתנה תורה לוי יש בו ג' אותיות משה ג' אותיות ונצפן ג' ירחים כדכתיב (שמות ב) ותצפנהו ג' ירחים ובזה אמרו אמר ר' לוי הא למדתה שכל מעשה אותו היום היה משולש וכנגן זה עוד יש במדרש ילמדנו (תנחומא פרשה יתרו) הלא כתבתי לך שלישים אמר ר' יהושע בן נחמיה הן תורה שאותיותיה משולשות אלף בית גימל והכל היה משולש תורה משולשת תורה נביאים וכתובים משנה משולשת תלמוד הלכות ואגדות תפלה משולשת ערב ובקר וצהרים קרושה משולשת קדוש קדוש קדוש ישראל משולשים כהנים לוים וישראלים ומשה אותיותיו משולשים משבט

מסורת הש"ס

פ"ו ב' ע"ש

שבועות לט.

ע"ז ג.

[ע"ז שם. ע"ש ודף ה. ע"ש]

[כתובות קיב.]

הגהות הב"ח

(א) גמ' אמר רבא אעפ"כ: (ג) תוס' ד"ה מודעא וכו' ובפרק אלו נאמרין אמרו שקבלו:

גליון הש"ס

גמ' בחמישי בנה מזבח. עיין חגיגה דף ו ע"א ברש"י ד"ה ישנה לפני הדיבור: שם בשעה שהקדימו כו'. ע' תשב"ץ ח"ג ענין ס"ד: תוס' ד"ה ירדו וכו' ואף על גב דגדולה מדה טובה יומא דף עו ע"א: שם ד"ה פריו כריחא דאתרוגא. עיין תענית דף כט ע"ב תד"ה של תפוחים:

דסגינן בשלימותא כתיב בן °תומת ישרים תנחם הנך אינשי דסגן בעלילותא כתיב בהו °וסלף בוגדים ישדם: א"ר שמואל בר נחמני א"ר יונתן מאי דכתיב °לבבתני אחותי כלה לבבתני באחת מעיניך בתחילה באחת מעיניך לכשתעשי בשתי עיניך *אמר עולא עלובה כלה מזנה בתוך חופתה אמר רב מרי ברה דבת שמואל מאי קרא °עד שהמלך במסיבו נרדי וגו' אמר *רב ועדיין חביבותא היא גבן דכתי' נתן ולא כתב הסריח *ת"ר (א) *עלובין ואינן עולבין שומעין חרפתן ואינן משיבין עושין מאהבה ושמחין ביסורין עליהן הכתוב אומר °ואוהביו כצאת השמש בגבורתו א"ר יוחנן מאי דכתיב °ה' יתן אומר המבשרות צבא רב כל דיבור ודיבור שיצא מפי הגבורה נחלק לשבעים לשונות תני דבי ר' ישמעאל °וכפטיש יפוצץ סלע *מה פטיש זה נחלק לכמה ניצוצות אף כל דיבור ודיבור שיצא מפי הקב"ה נחלק לשבעים לשונות אמר רב חננאל בר פפא מ"ד °שמעו כי נגידים אדבר למה נמשלו דברי תורה כנגיד לומר לך מה נגיד זה יש בו להמית ולהחיות אף ד"ת יש בם להמית ולהחיות היינו דאמר *רבא למיימינין בה סמא דחיי למשמאילים בה סמא דמותא ד"א נגידים כל דיבור ודיבור שיצא מפי הקב"ה קושרים לו שני כתרים: א"ר יהושע בן לוי מ"ד °צרור המור דודי לי בין שדי ילין אמרה כנסת ישראל לפני הקב"ה רבש"ע אף על פי שמיצר ומימר לי דודי בין שדי ילין °אשכול הכופר דודי לי בכרמי עין גדי מי שהכל שלו מכפר לי על עון גדי שכרמתי לי מאי משמע דהאי כרמי לישנא דמכניש הוא אמר מר זוטרא בריה דרב נחמן כדתנן *כסא של כובס שכורמים עליו את הכלים: וא"ר יהושע בן לוי מאי דכתיב °לחייו כערוגת הבושם כל דיבור ודיבור שיצא מפי הקב"ה נתמלא כל העולם כולו בשמים וכיון שמדיבור ראשון נתמלא דיבור שני להיכן הלך הוציא הקב"ה הרוח מאוצרותיו והיה מעביר ראשון ראשון שנאמר °שפתותיו שושנים נוטפות מור עובר *אל תקרי שושנים אלא ששונים: ואריב"ל כל דיבור ודיבור שיצא מפי הקב"ה יצתה נשמתן של ישראל שנאמר °נפשי יצאה בדברו ומאחר שמדיבור ראשון יצתה נשמתן דיבור שני היאך קיבלו הוריד *טל שעתיד להחיות בו מתים והחיה אותם שנאמר °גשם נדבות תניף אלהים נחלתך ונלאה אתה כוננתה ואמר ר' יהושע בן לוי כל דיבור ודיבור שיצא מפי הקב"ה חזרו ישראל לאחוריהן י"ב מיל והיו מלאכי השרת מדדין אותן שנאמר *°מלאכי צבאות ידודון ידודון אל תיקרי ידודון אלא ידדון: ואריב"ל בשעה שעלה משה למרום אמרו מלאכי השרת לפני הקב"ה רבש"ע מה לילוד אשה בינינו אמר להן לקבל תורה בא אמרו לפניו חמודה גנוזה שגנוזה לך תשע מאות ושבעים וארבעה דורות *קודם שנברא העולם אתה מבקש ליתנה לבשר ודם °מה אנוש כי תזכרנו ובן אדם כי תפקדנו ה' אדונינו מה אדיר שמך בכל הארץ אשר תנה הודך על השמים אמר לו הקב"ה למשה החזיר להן תשובה אמר לפניו רבש"ע מתיירא אני שמא ישרפוני בהבל שבפיהם אמר לו אחוז בכסא כבודי וחזור להן תשובה שנאמר °*מאחז פני כסא פרשז עליו עננו ואמר ר' *נחום מלמד שפירש שדי מזיו שכינתו ועננו עליו אמר לפניו רבונו של עולם תורה שאתה נותן לי מה כתיב בה °אנכי ה' אלהיך אשר הוצאתיך מארץ מצרים אמר להן למצרים ירדתם לפרעה השתעבדתם תורה למה תהא לכם שוב מה כתיב בה לא יהיה לך אלהים אחרים בין עמים אתם שרויין שעובדין ע"ז

תורה אור: משלי יא | שם | שיר ד | שם א | ספטי' ה | תהלים סח | ירמיה כג | משלי ח | שיר א | שם | שם ה | שם | שם | תהלים סח | שם | תהלים ח | איוב כו | שמות כ

רש"י

דסגינן בשלימותא. התהלכנו עמו בתום לב כדרך העושים מאהבה וסמכנו עליו שלא יטעננו בדבר שלא נוכל לעמוד בו: בתחלה. בקבלה שקבלתם אחת הוא אצלכם ולבסוף כשקיימתם שתים יש לבבתני. קרבתני: עלובה. חצופה דעולבנא לישנא דחולפא היא והכי אמר במס' גיטין: מזנה בתוך חופתה. כישראל כשעמדו בסיני ועשו העגל: במסיבו. בחופתו: נתן. עזב ריחו הטוב לאחרים: ועדיין חביבותא היא גבן. אע"פ שהמקרא מספר בגנותו הראה לנו לשון חבה מדלא כתיב הסריח: הנעלבים ואינם עולבים. אחרים באין עליהם בחוצפה ולא הן על אחרים: עושין מאהבת המקום ושמחים ביסורים. על עליבה הבאה עליהם: לבא רב. כל האומות: מה פטיש. מתחלק הסלע על ידו לכמה ניצוצות: למיימינין. (ג) עסוקים בכל כחם וטרודים לדעת סודה כאדם המשתמש ביד ימינו שהיא עיקר: קושרים לו שני כתרים. לדבור שהיה בו ממש ונראה כדכתיב רואים את הקולות (שמות כ): אע"פ שמיצר ומימר לי דודי. בעגל שאמר הורד עדיך: בין שדי ילין. אמר מיד לעשות לו משכן להיות מלומלמת שכינתו בין שני הבדים שנראי' במקדש ראשון כשני שדים דוחקין ובולטין בפרוכת שכנגד הפתח: עין גדי. עון עגל שהוא מין בהמה לשון אחר לשון עכו"ם העורכים לגד שלחן (ישעיה סה): שכרמתי. שאספתי להתאוות אלהות הרבה כדכתיב אלה אלהיך ישראל (שמות לב): שכורמים עליו. שמאספין עליו את הבגדים והוא דף ארוכה ומנוקבת נקבים הרבה ומניח המוגמר תחתיה והכלים מתגמרין מדרך הנקבים לישנא דמיכנש גרסינן: מעביר ראשון. (ג) לגן עדן: מור עובר. על שהעבירן: גשם נדבות. גבי מתן תורה כתיב בספר תהלים: י"ב מיל. זו היא מדת מחניהם והיו הקרובים לדיבור חוזרין מפחד הקול עד קצה המחנה: מדדין אותן. מסייעין אותן להתקרב מעט מעט שהיו חלשים כאשה המדדה את בנה בתחלת הילוכו: ידודון. משמע הם עצמם ידודון: ידדון. מדדין אחרים: תתקע"ד דורות. (ד) באלפים שנה שקדמה תורה לעולם היו עתידין דורות הללו להבראות שנאמר (תהלים קה) דבר צוה לאלף דור °וראה הקב"ה שאין העולם מתקיים בלא תורה כל כך והעבירן ולא בראן ונתנה לכ"ו דורות. הרי שחסרו תתקע"ד מאלף: מה אדיר שמך. אדיר הוא הרבה בארץ ואין ראוי לך ליתן הודך שם כי אם על השמים: פירש שדי מזיו. נוטריקון של פרשז: קנאה

תוספות

ולא כתיב הסריח. לשון מגונה לא היה לו לכתוב אלא כלומר ולא כתב *ערב ריחו דהוה משמע הסריח אלא כתב נתן לשון חביבות: מה פטיש זה מתחלק לכמה ניצוצות. הקשה רבינו שמואל והא קרא משמע דהפטיש מפוצץ את הסלע מדלא כתיב והפטיש יפוצצנו סלע וכן אנו רואין שהפטיש מפוצץ סלעים וליכא למיגרס מה סלע מתחלק לכמה ניצוצות דהא דיבור דהיינו תורה נמשלה לפטיש ולא לסלע ובקונטרס פי' מה פטיש מתחלק הסלע על ידו ואינו מיושב שהדיבור הוא עצמו מתחלק ואינו דמיון גמור ואומר ר"ת דקרא איירי באבן המפוצץ ברזל דאמר *במדרש חזית מעשה באחד שקנה סנפירין ובא לבודקה נתנה על הסדן והכה עליה בקורנס נחלק הפטיש ונשבר הסדן והסנפירין לא זז ממקומו הה"ד וכפטיש יפוצץ סלע ואף על גב דלא כתיב יפוצצנו סלע הרבה פסוקים יש כענין זה אבנים שחקו מים (איוב יד) פי' שחקו אותן מים ואתו שפיר דאמר בפ"ק דקידושין (דף ל:) תנא דבי רבי ישמעאל בני אם פגע בך מנוול זה משכהו לביהמ"ד ואם אבן הוא נמוח שנא' אבנים שחקו מים פירוש שחקו אותם מים ואם ברזל הוא מתפוצץ פירוש אם יצר הרע מתחזק עליו כברזל מתפוצץ שנאמר וכפטיש יפוצץ סלע ואף על פי דהתם מדמה יצה"ר לפטיש וכאן מדמה ד"ת לפטיש אין לחוש °דמקרא אחד יוצא לכמה טעמים: תורה

עין משפט נר מצוה

לא א מיי' פ"ב מהלכות דעות הלכה יג:

[במדרש רבה איכה ד"ה זכו מיניה]

[בקרא כתיב מלכי ועמ"ש הפענח רזא פי' ימדון]

[בסוכה איתא תנחום]

רב נסים גאון

לוי שאותיותיו משולשין מזרע אברהם יצחק ויעקב אבות שלשה בחודש משלש ניסן אייר סיון בסיני שאותיותיו משולשים לשלשה ימים נתקדשו שנאמר (שמות יט) והיו נכונים ליום השלישי: **אמרו** לפניו רבונו של עולם חמדה שגנוזה לפניך תשע מאות ושבעים וארבעה דורות קודם שנברא העולם · הא מילתא נפקא להו לרבנן (ב"ר פכ"ח) מהאי קרא דכתיב (תהלים קה) זכר לעולם בריתו דבר צוה לאלף דור שלפי שמצאו מן יצירת אדם הראשון ועד נתינת התורה כ"ו דור וזה פרטן י' דורות מאדם עד נח וי' מנח עד אברהם ומאברהם עד משה ו' דורות אברהם יצחק יעקב לוי קהת עמרם עד משה ועל ידו ניתנה התורה וכבר שלמו כ"ו דורות ידעו כי התורה היתה גנוזה תתקע"ד דורות וכיון שעברו עליה מימות העולם כ"ו דורות שהן השלמת אלף דור ניתנה התורה כדי שיתקיים דבר צוה לאלף דור:

מסורת הש"ס

גיטין לו: | [שם אי' רבא] | ג"ז שם ויומא כג. | [סנהדרין לד.] | [יומא עב: ע"ש] | כלים פכ"ג מ"ד | [לעיל ל. פסחים קיח.] | [חגיגה יב:] | [חגיגה יד. זבחים קטז.] | [סוכה ה.]

גליון הש"ס

רש"י ד"ה תתקע"ד דורות וכו' וראה הקב"ה שאין העולם מתקיים. במדרש רבה בראשית פ"א איתא ראה הקב"ה שהיו רשעים נתנה לכ"ו דורות ותתקע"ד שתלן בכל דור ודור וכן עזי פנים שבדורות: תוס' ד"ה מה פטיש בסה"ד דמקרא אחד יוצא לכמה טעמים. עי' בברא"ש פ' וארא בפסוק פ':

הגהות הב"ח

(א) גמ' תנו רבנן הנעלבין: (ב) רש"י ד"ה למיימינין כ"ב עי' לעיל דף סג ע"א: (ג) ד"ה מעביר ראשון ראשון לג"ע: (ד) ד"ה תתקע"ד דורות · כ"ב ועיין בחגיגה פרק אין דורשין סוף דף יג וראש דף יד:

not have accepted.' Said he to him, 'We [88*b*] who walked in integrity, of us it is written, *The integrity of the upright shall guide them.*[2] But of others, who walked in perversity, it is written, *but the perverseness of the treacherous shall destroy them.*

R. Samuel b. Naḥmani said in R. Jonathan's name. What is meant by, *Thou hast ravished my heart, my sister, my bride: Thou hast ravished my heart with one of thine eyes?*[3] In the beginning with one of thine eyes; when thou fulfillest, with both thine eyes.[4]

'Ulla said: Shameless is the bride that plays the harlot within her bridal canopy![5] Said R. Mari the son of Samuel's daughter, What verse [refers to this]? *While the king sat at his table, [my spikenard gave up its fragrance].*[6] Said Rab, Yet [His] love was still with us, for *'gave'* is written, not 'made noisome'.

Our Rabbis taught: Those who are insulted but do not insult, hear themselves reviled without answering, act through love and rejoice in suffering, of them the Writ saith, *But they who love Him are as the sun when he goeth forth in his might.*[7]

R. Joḥanan said: What is meant by the verse, *The Lord giveth* a *the word: They that publish the tidings are a great host?*[1]—Every single word that went forth from the Omnipotent was split up into seventy languages.[2] The School of R. Ishmael taught: *And like a hammer that breaketh the rock in pieces:*[3] just as a hammer is divided into many sparks,[4] so every single word that went forth from the Holy One, blessed be He, split up into seventy languages.[5]

R. Ḥananel b. Papa said: What is meant by, *Hear, for I will speak princely things:*[6] why are the words of the Torah compared to a prince? To tell you: just as a prince has power of life and death, so have the words of the Torah [potentialities] of life and death. Thus Raba said; To those who go to the right hand thereof it is a medicine of life; to those who go to the left hand thereof[7] it is a deadly poison. Another interpretation: *'princely'* [denotes] that on every word which went forth from the mouth of the Holy One, blessed be He, two crowns were set.[8]

R. Joshua b. Levi said: What is meant by, *My beloved is unto me as a bundle of myrrh* [ẓeror ha-mor], *That lieth betwixt my breasts?*[9] The congregation of Israel spake before the Holy One, blessed be He, 'Sovereign of the Universe! Though my life be distressed [*meẓar*] and embittered [*memar*], yet my love lieth betwixt my breasts.'[10] *My beloved is unto me as a cluster* [eshkol] *of henna-flowers* [kofer] *in the vineyards of* [karme] *En-gedi:*[11] He to Whom everything belongs [*she-ha-kol shelo*] shall make atonement [*mekapper*] for me for the sin of the kid[12] which I stored up [*karamti*] for myself.[13] Where is it implied that this word *'karme'* connotes gathering?—Said Mar Zuṭra the son of R. Naḥman: Even as we learnt: A fuller's b stool on which linen is heaped up [*kormin*].[1]

R. Joshua b. Levi also said: What is meant by, *His cheeks are as a bed of spices?*[2] With every single word that went forth from the mouth of the Holy One, blessed be He, the whole world was filled with spices [fragrance]. But since it was filled from the first word, whither did the [fragrance of the] second word go?—The Holy One, blessed be He, brought forth the wind from His store-chambers and caused each to pass on in order,[3] as it is said, *His lips are as lilies* [shoshannim], *dropping myrrh that passess on:*[4] read not *shoshannim* but *sheshonim.*[5]

R. Joshua b. Levi also said: At every word which went forth from the mouth of the Holy One, blessed be He, the souls of Israel departed, for it is said, *My soul went forth when He spake.*[6] But since their souls departed at the first word, how could they receive the second word?—He brought down the dew with which He will resurrect the dead and revived them, as it is said, *Thou, O God, didst send a plentiful rain, Thou didst confirm Thine inheritance. when it was weary.*[7]

R. Joshua b. Levi also said: At every single word which went forth from the mouth of the Holy One, blessed be He, the Israelites retreated twelve *mil,* but the ministering angels led them back [*medaddin*],[8] as it is said, *The hosts of angels*[9] *march, they march* [yiddodun yiddodun]:[10] read not *yiddodun* but *yedaddun* [they lead].

R. Joshua b. Levi also said: When Moses ascended on high, the ministering angels spake before the Holy One, blessed be He, 'Sovereign of the Universe! What business has one born of woman amongst us?' 'He has come to receive the Torah,' answered He to them. Said they to Him. 'That secret treasure, which has been hidden by Thee for nine hundred and seventy-four generations c before the world was created,[1] Thou desirest to give to flesh and blood! *What is man, that Thou art mindful of him, And the son of man, that Thou visitest him? O Lord our God, How excellent is Thy name in all the earth! Who hast set Thy glory* [the Torah] *upon the Heavens!'*[2] 'Return them an answer,' bade the Holy One, blessed be He, to Moses. 'Sovereign of the Universe' replied he, 'I fear lest they consume me with the [fiery] breath of their mouths.' 'Hold on to the Throne of Glory,' said He to him, 'and return them an answer,' as it is said, *He maketh him to hold on to the face of His throne, And spreadeth* [PaRSHeZ] *His cloud over him,*[3] whereon R. Naḥman[4] observed: This teaches that the Almighty [*SHaddai*] spread [*PiRash*] the lustre [*Ziw*] of His *Shechinah*[5] and cast it as a protection[6] over him. He [then] spake before Him: Sovereign of the Universe! The Torah which Thou givest me, what is written therein? *I am the Lord thy God, which brought thee out of the Land of Egypt.*[7] Said he to them [the angels], 'Did ye go down to Egypt; were ye enslaved to Pharaoh: why then should the Torah be yours? Again, what is written therein? *Thou shalt have none other gods:*[8] do ye dwell among peoples that engage in

(2) Prov. XI, 3. (3) Cant. IV, 9. (4) Maharsha: A thing may be perceived spiritually and materially. When the Israelites first accepted the Torah they perceived its greatness in spirit only, i.e., in theory (one eye). Having observed it, they saw materially too, i.e., in actual practice (both eyes). (5) Thus did Israel make the Golden Calf at Mount Sinai itself. (6) Ibid. I, 12. I.e., while the King, viz., God, was at Sinai, the Israelites lost their fragrance through sin. (7) Judg. V, 31.

a (1) Ps. LXVIII, 12. (2) The traditional number of the languages of man, i.e., the Torah was given to all humanity. Cf. M. Joseph, *Judaism as Creed and Life,* pp. 157 *seq.* (3) Jer. XXIII, 29. (4) Perhaps referring to the sparks that fly off when it beats the anvil. (5) Commentators differ as to the exact point of the comparison; v. Sanh., 34*a*, n. b9. (6) Prov. VIII, 6. (7) These phrases probably mean, to those who employ it rightly ... wrongly, cf. *supra* 63*a*, n. c5. which seems, however, inapplicable here. (8) The words themselves having substance: cf. the Greek doctrine of the logos. (9) Cant. I, 13. (10) I.e., God is with Israel in all his sorrows. This translation follows Maharsha; Rashi interprets differently—*Ẓeror* and *ha-mor* are connected here with *meẓar* and *memar.* (11) Ibid. 14. (12) *Gedi,* kid standing for small cattle in general, and here referring to the Golden Calf. (13) For future punishment. Thus *eshkol* is connected with *shehakol shelo, kopher* with *mekapper, karme* with *karamti,* and *En-gedi* with *gedi,* a kid.

b (1) V. Kel. XXIII, 4. (2) Cant. V, 13. (3) The fragrance of each word was carried off to the Garden of Eden, leaving room for the next. (4) Ibid. E.V.: *liquid myrrh.* (5) That study, i.e., His words spread fragrance. (6) Ibid. 6. (7) Ps. LXVIII, 10. (8) The word denotes to lead step by step, like one leads a child who can hardly walk. (9) Our texts read: Kings. (10) Ibid. 13.

c (1) Cf. Weber, *Jüdische Theologie,* p. 15 for parallels. (2) Ps. VIII, 5, 2. (3) Job XXVI, 9. (4) In Suk. 5*a* the reading is Tanḥum. (5) Thus *PaRSHeZ* is treated as an abbreviation; in Hebrew the words follow the same order as these letters. (6) Lit., 'cloud'. (7) Ex. XX, 2. (8) Ibid. 3.

[89*a*] idol worship? Again, what is written therein? *Remember the Sabbath day, to keep it holy:*[9] do ye then perform work, that ye need to rest? Again, what is written therein? *Thou shalt not take* [tissa] [*the name ... in vain*]:[10] is there any business [*massa*] dealings among you?[11] Again, what is written therein, *Honour thy father and thy mother;*[12] have ye fathers and mothers? Again, what is written therein? *Thou shalt not murder. Thou shalt not commit adultery. Thou shalt not steal;*[13] is there jealousy among you; is the Evil Tempter among you? Straightway they conceded [right] to the Holy One, blessed be He, for it is said, *O Lord, our Lord, How excellent is Thy name*, etc.[14] whereas '*Who hast set Thy glory upon the heavens*' is not written.[15] Immediately each one was moved to love him [Moses] and transmitted something to him, for it is said, *Thou hast ascended on high, Thou hast taken spoils* [the Torah]; *Thou hast received gifts on account of* a *man:*[1] as a recompense for their calling thee man [*adam*][2] thou didst receive gifts. The Angel of Death too confided his secret to him, for it is said, *and he put on the incense, and made atonement for the people;*[3] and it is said, *and he stood between the dead and the living*, etc.[4] Had he not told it to him, whence had he known it?

R. Joshua b. Levi also said: When Moses descended from before the Holy One, blessed be He, Satan came and asked Him, 'Sovereign of the Universe! Where is the Torah? 'I have given it to the earth,' answered He to him. He went to the earth and said to her, 'Where is the Torah?' '*God understandeth the way thereof*, etc.'[5] she replied. He went to the sea and it told him, '*It is not with me.*' He went to the deep and it said to him, '*It is not in me*,' for it is said. *The deep saith, It is not in me: And the sea saith, It is not with me. Destruction and Death say, We have heard a rumour thereof with our ears.*[6] He went back and declared before Him, 'Sovereign of the Universe! I have searched throughout all the earth but have not found it!' 'Go thee to the son of Amram,' answered He. [So] he went to Moses and asked him, 'Where is the Torah which the Holy One, blessed be He, gave unto thee?' 'Who am I then,' he retorted, 'that the Holy One, blessed be He, should give me the Torah?' Said the Holy One, blessed be He, to Moses, 'Moses, art thou a liar!' 'Sovereign of the Universe!' he replied, 'Thou hast a stored-up treasure in which Thou takest delight every day: shall I keep the benefit for myself?'[7] Said the Holy One, blessed be He, to Moses, 'Moses, since thou hast [humbly] disparaged thyself, it shall be called by thy name, as it is said, *Remember ye the law of Moses My servant.*[8]

R. Joshua b. Levi also said: When Moses ascended on high, he found the Holy One, blessed be He, tying crowns on the b letters [of the Torah].[1] Said He to him, 'Moses, is there no [greeting of] Peace in thy town?'[2] 'Shall a servant extend [a greeting of] Peace to his Master!' replied he: 'Yet thou shouldst have assisted Me,'[3] said He. Immediately[4] he cried out to Him, *And now, I pray thee, let the power of the Lord be great, according as thou hast spoken.*[5]

R. Joshua b. Levi also said: Why is it written; *And when the people saw that Moses delayed* [boshesh] [*to come down from the mount*]?[6] 'Read not *boshesh*' [delayed] but *ba'u shesh* [the sixth hour had come]. When Moses ascended on high, he said to Israel, I will return at the end of forty days, at the beginning of the sixth hour.[7] At the end of forty days Satan came and confounded the world. Said he to them: 'Where is your teacher Moses?' 'He has ascended on high,' they answered him. 'The sixth [hour] has come,' said he to them, but they disregarded him. 'He is dead'—but they disregarded him. [Thereupon] he showed them a vision of his bier, and this is what they said to Aaron, *for* this *Moses, the man*, etc.,[8]

One of the Rabbis asked R. Kahana: Hast thou heard what the mountain of Sinai [connotes]? The mountain whereon miracles [*nissim*] were performed for Israel, he replied. Then it should be called Mount Nisai? But [it means] the mountain whereon a happy augury [*siman*] took place for Israel. Then it should be called, Mount Simanai? Said he to him, Why dost thou not frequent [the academy of] R. Papa and R. Huna the son of R. Joshua, who make a study of *aggadah*. For R. Ḥisda and Rabbah the son of R. Huna both said, What is [the meaning of] Mount Sinai? The mountain whereon there descended hostility [*sin'ah*] toward idolaters.[9] And thus R. Jose son of R. Ḥanina said: It has five names: The Wilderness c of Zin, [meaning] that Israel were given commandments there;[1] the Wilderness of Kadesh, where the Israelites were sanctified [*ḳadosh*], the Wilderness of Kedemoth, because a priority [*ḳedumah*]

(9) Ibid. 8. (10) Ibid. 7. (11) This connects *tissa* with *massa*. [Or, to involve you in a false oath.] (12) Ibid. 12. (13) Ibid. 13-15. (14) Ps. VIII, 10. (15) Showing that they no longer demanded that the Torah be kept in Heaven.

a (1) Ps. LXVIII, 19. (2) I.e., for their disparaging reference to thee as a mere mortal created from the dust (*adamah*); cf. Gen. II, 7, where the Hebrew for 'man' and 'ground' are *adam* and *adamah* respectively. (3) Num. XVI, 47. (4) Ibid. 48. (5) Job. XXVIII, 23. (6) Ibid. 14, 22. (7) Surely it was not given to me alone! (8) Mal. III, 22.

b (1) The 'crowns' or '*Taggin*', as they are generally designated, are three small strokes (*Ẓiyyunim* = daggers) which are written on the top of the letters ש ע ט נ ז ג ץ. For a discussion of their origin and purpose v. *J.E.* art. Taggin. (2) *Shalom* (peace) is the usual greeting in Hebrew. (3) By wishing Me success in My labours. (4) At a later ascent (Rashi). (5) Num. XIV, 17. (6) Ex. XXXII, 1. (7) I.e., at midday. (8) Ibid. (9) They showed their unworthiness by rejecting the Torah.

c (1) *Ẓin* being connected with *ẓiwah*, 'he commanded'.

קנאה יש ביניכם. שאתם באים על ידה לידי רציחה: מסר לו. למדו: באדם בשכר. שחרפוך וקראוך אדם טוער מאדמה לשון שפלות: מסר לו סודו. להקטיר מחתות קטורת בשעת מגפה ולעמוד בין המתים ובין החיים: ואי לאו דאמר ליה. מלאך המות: מנא ידע. הלא בתורה לא נכתב: בדאי אתה. תורה אור בתמיה: קושר כתרים. כגון הנך דאמרי' בפרק הבונה (דף קד.) תגא דקוף לגבי רי"ש וכן שעטנ"ז ג"ץ שצריכין כל אות ג' זיונים כדאמרינן (במנחות דף כט:) ראש הזיי"ן נמתח לימין ולשמאל בגגו מעט וכן ראש השי"ן השמאלי וכן כל ראשי שבע אותיות הללו בכל מקום שהן: אין שלום. אין דרך ליתן שלום: בעירך. במקומך: לעזרני. לומר תצלח מלאכתך: מיד. בעליה אחרת אמר לו יגדל נא כח ה': בא השטן. הוא יצר הרע המחטיא את האדם הוא העולה ומסטין [והאומר] דהוא מדת הדין אין הגון בעיני: כשעלה משה. להר אמר להם לסוף מ' יום אני בא בתוך שש שעות הם סבורים שאותו יום שעלה בו מן המנין הוה והוא אמר להם מ' יום שלימים יום ולילו עמו ויום עלייתו אין לילו עמו שהרי בז' בסיון עלה נמצא יום מ' בי"ז בתמוז היה בי"ז בא שטן ועירבב את העולם והראה דמות חשך ואפילה דמות ענן וערפל וערבוביא לומר ודאי מת משה שהרי באו כבר שש ולא בא ואי אפשר לומר שלא טעו אלא ביום המעונן בין קודם חצות לאחר חצות שהרי לא ירד משה עד יום המחרת שנאמר וישכימו ממחרת וגו': באו שש. שקבע לכם: שנאה לעכו"ם. שלא קבלו בו תורה:

תורה היכן היא. וא"ת וכי שטן לא היה יודע מתן תורה וי"ל דאמרינן במדרש לפניו ילך דבר שטרדו הקב"ה למלאך המות בשעת מתן תורה שלא יקטרג לומר אומה שעתידה לחטוא לסוף מ' יום בעגל אתה נותן להם התורה והוא שטן והוא מלאך המות כדאמרי' בפ"ק דב"ב (דף טז.) ואמרי' נמי בסנהדרין (דף כו:) תושי' שניתנה בתשאי מפני השטן:

לסוף מ' יום אני בא. פירש בקונטרס דאותו יום שעלה בו אינו מן המנין והוא היה אומר להם מ' יום שלימים יום ולילו עמו ויום עלייתו אין לילו עמו שהרי ז' בסיון עלה נמצא יום מ' היה בי"ז בתמוז ואין נראה לר"י בן רבינו מאיר דבהדיא משמע בפ"ק דיומא (דף ד.) דיום עלייה מן המנין דקאמר התם בשלמא לר"ע משכחת להו דבי"ז בתמוז נשתברו הלוחות כ"ד דסיון ושיתסר דתמוז מלו להו מ' יומין ובשיבסר בתמוז נחת אלמא חשיב יום עלייה והיכא מ' יום ומ' לילה כשתחשוב לילה שאחר היום ועוד אם לא תחשוב יום עלייה לא ישלמו מ' ימים אחרונים עד אחר יום הכפורים ושלמו ביוה"כ שאז א"ל הקב"ה למשה סלחתי כדברך גם מה שפרש"י בפרשת כי תשא שבי"ט בתמוז עלה קשה לר"י שאז לא תמצא שלמו מ' ימים אחרונים ביום הכפורים*:

מדבר צין. קשה לר"י דע"כ מדבר צין לאו היינו מדבר פארן דמדבר צין בתחילת דרומה של ארץ ישראל כדכתיב באלה מסעי והיה לכם פאת נגב(א) ממדבר צין על ידי אדום וכתיב ונסב לכם הגבול מנגב וגו' והיו תוצאותיו מנגב לקדש ברנע וקדש ברנע הייני פארן דכתיב בשילוח מרגלים וישלח אותם משה ממדבר פארן ובספר (יהושע יד) כתיב שאמר כלב בשלוח אותי משה מקדש ברנע לרגל את הארץ וכן באלה הדברים כתיב ונבא עד קדש ברנע ומפרש מיד שלוח מרגלים ועוד דכמה מסעות היו ממדבר פארן עד מדבר צין דבסוף בהעלותך כתיב ואחר נסעו העם מחצרות ויחנו במדבר פארן ובאלה מסעי כתיב ויסעו העם מחצרות ויחנו ברתמה א"כ רתמה היינו פארן וחשיב כמה מסעות עד מדבר צין וכן בין פארן לסיני מהלך י"א יום דכתיב אחד עשר יום מחורב דרך הר שעיר עד קדש ברנע א"כ מדבר צין ופארן וסיני לאו הכל אחד ואור"י דהכל מדב' אחד וגדול היה דע"כ סיני הייני פארן דכתי' הופיע מהר פארן ובפרק שור שנגח ד' וה' (ב"ק דף לח.) דרשינן מפארן הופיע ממונן לישראל גבי שור של ישראל שנגח שור של עובד כוכבים פטור ול"ג ברים מסכת ע"ז (דף ב:) מאי בעי בשעיר ומאי בעי בפארן *דהוה משמע דפארן היא אומה אחרת כמו שעיר אלא גרס מאי בעי בשעיר ומאי בעי בתימן וסיני נמי הייני מדבר צין דכתיב מדבר צין היא קדש וסיני איקרי קדש דכתיב בספר (תהלים כט) קול ה' יחיל מדבר יחיל ה' מדבר קדש משמע דהיינו בשעת מתן תורה ומיהו קשה לר"י דהא מדבר קדמות היה מזרחה של ארץ ישראל כדכתיב (דברים ב) ואשלח מלאכים ממדבר קדמות אל סיחון מלך חשבון וגו' שהיתה במזרח של א"י דכתיב (שם ד) בעבר הירדן מזרחה שמש ומדבר צין ופארן הייני בדרומה כמו שמשמע בפסוקים שהבאתי ואיך יהכן דמדבר קדמות הייני מדבר סיני:

עבודת גלולים שוב מה כתיב בה זכור את
יום השבת לקדשו כלום אתם עושים מלאכה
שאתם צריכין שבות שוב מה כתיב בה לא
תשא משא ומתן יש ביניכם שוב מה כתיב
בה כבד את אביך ואת אמך אב ואם יש לכם
שוב מה כתיב בה לא תרצה לא תנאף לא
תגנוב °קנאה יש ביניכם יצר הרע יש ביניכם
תהלים ח מיד הודו לו להקב"ה שנאמר °ה' אדונינו
מה אדיר שמך וגו' ואילו תנה הודך על
השמים לא כתיב מיד כל אחד ואחד נעשה
שם סח לו אוהב ומסר לו דבר שנאמר °עלית
למרום שבית שבי לקחת מתנות באדם
בשכר שקראוך אדם לקחת מתנות אף
במדבר יז מלאך המות מסר לו דבר שנאמר °ויתן את
הקטורת ויכפר על העם ואומר ויעמד בין
המתים ובין החיים וגו' אי לאו דאמר ליה
מי הוה ידע: וא"ר יהושע בן לוי בשעה
שירד משה מלפני הקב"ה בא שטן ואמר
לפניו רבונו של עולם תורה היכן היא אמר
לו נתתיה לארץ הלך אצל ארץ אמר לה
איוב כח תורה היכן היא אמרה לו °אלהים הבין
דרכה וגו' הלך אצל ים ואמר לו אין עמדי
שם הלך אצל תהום א"ל אין בי שנאמר °תהום
אמר לא בי היא וים אמר אין עמדי אבדון
ומות אמרו באזנינו שמענו שמעה חזר
ואמר לפני הקב"ה רבש"ע חיפשתי בכל
הארץ ולא מצאתיה אמר לו לך אצל בן
עמרם הלך אצל משה אמר לו תורה שנתן
לך הקב"ה היכן היא אמר לו וכי מה אני
שנתן לי הקב"ה תורה א"ל הקב"ה למשה בדאי אתה אמר לפניו
רבונו של עולם חמודה גנוזה יש לך שאתה משתעשע בה בכל יום אני
אחזיק טובה לעצמי אמר לו הקב"ה למשה הואיל ומיעטת עצמך תקרא
מלאכי ג על שמך שנאמר °זכרו תורת משה עבדי וגו': וא"ר יהושע בן לוי *בשעה
שעלה משה למרום מצאו להקב"ה שהיה קושר כתרים לאותיות אמר לו
משה אין שלום בעירך אמר לפניו °כלום *יש עבד שנותן שלום לרבו א"ל
במדבר יד היה לך לעזרני מיד אמר לו °ועתה יגדל נא כח ה' כאשר דברת *(אמר) ר' [נ"א ואמר]
שמות לב יהושע בן לוי מ"ד °וירא העם כי בושש משה אל תקרי בושש אלא באו שש
בשעה שעלה משה למרום אמר להן לישראל לסוף ארבעים יום בתחלת שש
אני בא לסוף מ' יום בא שטן ועירבב את העולם אמר להן משה רבכם היכן
הוא אמרו לו עלה למרום אמר להן באו שש ולא השגיחו עליו מת ולא השגיחו
שם עליו הראה להן דמות מטתו והיינו דקאמרי ליה לאהרן °כי זה משה האיש וגו':
א"ל ההוא מרבנן לרב כהנא מי שמיע לך מאי הר סיני א"ל הר שנעשו בו
נסים לישראל הר ניסאי מיבעי ליה אלא הר שנעשה סימן טוב לישראל הר
סימנאי מיבעי ליה א"ל מ"ט לא שכיחת קמיה דרב פפא ורב הונא בריה
דרב יהושע דמעייני באגדתא דרב חסדא ורבה ברי' דרב הונא דאמרי תרווייהו
מאי הר סיני הר שירדה שנאה לעכו"ם עליו והיינו דאמר ר' יוסי בר'
חנינא ה' שמות יש לו מדבר צין שנצטוו ישראל עליו מדבר קדש
שנתקדשו ישראל עליו מדבר קדמות שנתנה קדומה עליו מדבר פארן
שפרו

[וע"ע תוספות בבא קמא סב: ד"ה כדי]

מנחות כט:

[עי' תוספות בבא קמא עג: ד"ה כדי]

[ועי' תוס' ע"ז ב: ד"ה מאי כפין]

גמ' קנאה יש ביניכם. עי' ברש"י בחומש בראשית א כ"ו ובראב"ע שם: שם מיד הודו לו להקב"ה. עי' תורת חיים סנהדרין דף עא ד"ה ולמה נכתבו: שם כלום יש עבד שנותן שלום. עי' מהרש"א בה"א רפ"ד דברכות. וקושייתו ותירוצו בתוס' ב"ק עג ע"ב ד"ה כדי:

הגהות הב"ח
(א) תוס' ד"ה מדבר וכו' פאת נגב מדבר צין:

עין משפט
נר מצוה

לב א מיי' פי"ח מהלכו' שבת הלכה ד:
לג ב שם הלכה ה:
לד ג שם הלכה ח:

מסורת
השי"ס

שפרו ורבו עליה ישראל מדבר סיני שירדה שנאה לעכו"ם עליו ומה שמו חורב שמו ופליגא דר' אבהו דא"ר אבהו הר סיני שמו ולמה נקרא הר חורב שירדה חורבה לעכו"ם עליו: מנין שקושרין לשון של זהורית וכו': כשנים כשני מיבעי ליה א"ר יצחק אמר להם הקב"ה לישראל אם יהיו חטאיכם כשנים הללו שסדורות ובאות מששת ימי בראשית ועד עכשיו כשלג ילבינו: דרש רבא מאי דכתיב °לכו נא ונוכחה יאמר ה' לכו נא בואו נא מיבעי ליה יאמר ה' אמר ה' מיבעי ליה לעתיד לבא יאמר להם הקב"ה לישראל לכו נא אצל אבותיכם ויוכיחו אתכם ויאמרו לפניו רבש"ע אצל מי נלך אצל אברהם שאמרת לו °ידוע תדע ולא בקש רחמים עלינו אצל יצחק שבירך את עשו °והיה כאשר תריד ולא בקש רחמים עלינו אצל יעקב שאמרת לו °אנכי ארד עמך מצרימה ולא בקש רחמים עלינו אצל מי נלך עכשיו יאמר ה' אמר להן הקב"ה הואיל ותליתם עצמכם בי אם יהיו חטאיכם כשנים כשלג ילבינו: א"ר שמואל בר נחמני א"ר יונתן מ"ד °כי אתה אבינו כי אברהם לא ידענו וישראל לא יכירנו אתה ה' אבינו גואלנו מעולם שמך לעתיד לבא יאמר לו הקב"ה לאברהם בניך חטאו לי אמר לפניו רבש"ע ימחו על קדושת שמך אמר אימר ליה ליעקב דהוה ליה צער גידול בנים אפשר דבעי רחמי עלייהו אמר ליה בניך חטאו אמר לפניו רבש"ע ימחו על קדושת שמך אמר לא בסבי טעמא ולא בדרדקי עצה אמר לו ליצחק בניך חטאו לי אמר לפניו רבש"ע בני ולא בניך בשעה שהקדימו לפניך נעשה לנשמע קראת להם °בני בכורי עכשיו בני ולא בניך ועוד כמה חטאו כמה שנותיו של אדם שבעים שנה דל עשרין דלא ענשת עלייהו פשו להו חמשין דל כ"ה דלילותא פשו להו כ"ה דל תרתי סרי ופלגא דצלויי ומיכל ודבית הכסא פשו להו תרתי סרי ופלגא אם אתה סובל את כולם מוטב ואם לאו פלגא עלי ופלגא עליך ואת"ל כולם עלי הא קריבית נפשי קמך פתחו ואמרו (כי) אתה אבינו אמר להם יצחק עד שאתם מקלסין לי קלסו להקב"ה ומחוי להו יצחק הקב"ה בעינייהו מיד נשאו עיניהם למרום ואומרים °אתה ה' אבינו גואלנו מעולם שמך א"ר חייא בר אבא א"ר יוחנן ראוי היה יעקב אבינו לירד למצרים בשלשלאות של ברזל אלא שזכותו גרמה לו דכתיב °בחבלי אדם אמשכם בעבותות אהבה ואהיה להם כמרימי עול על לחיהם ואט אליו אוכיל:

מתני' *[א]המוציא עצים כדי לבשל ביצה קלה [ב]תבלין כדי לתבל ביצה קלה ומצטרפין זה עם זה *[ג]קליפי אגוזין קליפי רמונים איסטים ופואה כדי לצבוע בהן בגד קטן פי סבכה מי רגלים נתר ובורית *קמוליא ואשלג כדי לכבס בגד קטן פי סבכה רבי יהודה אומר כדי להעביר את הכתם:

גמ' תנינא חדא זימנא *קנה כדי לעשות קולמוס אם היה עב או מרוסס כדי לבשל ביצה קלה שבביצים טרופה ונתונה באילפס מהו דתימא התם הוא דלא חזי למידי אבל עצים דחזו לכבא דאקלידא אפילו כל שהוא קמ"ל: תבלין כדי לתבל ביצה קלה: ורמינהו *תבלין שנים וג' שמות ממין אחד או משלשה מינין (ושם אחד) אסורין ומצטרפין זה עם זה ואמר חזקיה במיני

ישעיה א · בראשית טו · בראשית כז · בראשית מו · ישעיה סג · שמות ד · ישעיה סג · הושע יא · ביצה לט. · לעיל עט. · לעיל פ: · ע"ז סו. ערלה פ"ב מ"י

רש"י

ספרו ורבו. דכל אחד נתעברה אשתו זכר במלות שובו נכס לאהליכס °ולא ידענא היכא רמיזא: כשני מיבעי ליה. דומיא דכשלג דלא כתיב כשלגים: ארד עמך אעלך גם עלה. כאן רמז ד' גליות גם ריבויא הוא: יאמר ה'. אתה אמור התוכחה ובך אנו תולין: תורה איר ימחו. הואיל שחטאו ויתקדש שמך בעולם כשתעשה דין בעוברין על דבריך: קראת להן בני בכורי ישראל. שהיה גלוי לפניך שהן עתידין לומר לפניך בסיני נעשה ונשמע לקבל עולך מאהבה כבנים: דל עשרין דלא ענשת להו. שכן מלינו בדור המדבר שלא ענש הקב"ה אלא מכ' שנה ומעלה דכתיב (במדבר יד) במדבר הזה יפלו פגריכם וגו' מבן כ' שנה ומעלה אשר הלינותם עלי: כי אתה אבינו. כנגד יצחק אמרו והוא אמר להם הראו כנגד הקב"ה שהוא אביכם: בשלשלאות של ברזל. כדרך כל הגולים שהרי ע"פ גזרת גלות ירד לשם: בחבלי אדם. בשביל חיבת האדם משכתים למצרים בחבלים ולא בשלשלאות: כמרימי עול על לחייהם. כאדם הסובל ומסייע לבהמתו להרים עולה *מעל צוארה בלוחין ובמקלות: ואט אליו אוכיל. הטיתי לכם כח להכיל את עבודת הפרך:

מתני' ביצה קלה. כבר מפורש* שזה ביצת תרנגולת שהיא קלה לבשל ולא בשיעור כל ביצה שיערו אלא כגרוגרת מביצה קלה: ומצטרפין. כל מיני תבלין זה עם זה: קליפי אגוזים. הגדילה ע"ג הקליפה בעודן לחין: סטים. *קרוג: פואה. *וורנצא: פי סבכה. בראש הסבכה שעשאה בקליעה נותן מעט בגד: נתר. מין אדמה שקורין ניטר"א: קמוליא ואשלג. בגמרא מפרש להו: את הכתם. של דם נדה שאלו הסמנין מעבירין על הכתם של דם נדה בבגד לטהרו: **גמ'** התם. הוא דקולמוס מרוסס לא חזי למידי אלא להסקה: ככא דאקלידא. שן של מפתח: ורמינהו. אמתני' דקתני תבלין מצטרפין שני מינין לכשיעור: ב' וג' שמות. פלפל לבן שחור וארוך או אפילו מן ג' מינין והם (שם אחד) של איסור אסור אם תיבלו בהן את הקדרה: ומצטרפין. לתבלה אם אין בכל אחד כדי לתבל ונצטרפו ותיבלו: ואמר חזקיה. הא דקתני מצטרפין: במיני

תוספות

תבלין שנים ושלשה שמות והן מין אחד. פירש רש"י כמו פלפל ארוך פלפל לבן פלפל שחור ולפי' הא דקתני בסיפא ר"ש אומר ב' שמות ממין אחד או שני מינין משם אחד אין מצטרפין משכחת לה שני מינין משם אחד כעין שמפרש לקמן (דף צ.) תרי גווני אהלא אבל תימה וכי בשביל שיש להם שם אחד יש להן להצטרף יותר מה מועיל השם לגרוס הצירוף כיון שהם שני מינין ואין טעמם בשוה ומפרש ר"ת דג' ענייני איסור כגון של ערלה או של כלאי הכרם ושל אשירה ושל עיר הנדחת קרי ג' שמות °כדאמרינן שלא השם המביאו לידי מכות מביאו לידי תשלומים ובפרק המקבל (ב"מ קיא.) עובר בכל השמות הללו וכן משמע בהדיא בירושלמי בריש פ"ב דמסכת ערלה דקתני התרומה ותרומת מעשר ותרומ' (א) של דמאי והחלה והבכורים עולין באחד ומאה ומצטרפין זה עם זה וקאמר עלה בגמרא לרבי שמעון נצרכה אע"ג דאמר ר"ש אין שני שמות מצטרפין הכא מודה שכולם שם תרומה*:

אסורין ומצטרפין. לכאורה נראה מדתני אסורים ותנא תו מצטרפין דאסורין הייני לאסור את הקדרה ומצטרפין למלקות ואף על גב דלענין חיוב חטאת אמרי' בפ' כלל גדול (לעיל עח.) דחלב (ב)ופיגול ונותר אין מצטרפין למלקות מצטרפין ובפרק בתרא דע"ז (דף סו.) דפליגי אביי ורבא דאביי סבר בתר טעמא אזלינן וקאמר אביי מנא אמינא לה דתנן תבלין ב' וג' שמות כו' א"ב דבתר טעמא אזלינן כולהו חד טעמא נינהו אא"א בתר שמא אזלינן האי שמא לחוד והאי שמא לחוד ורבא אמר הא מני ר"מ היא דאמר כל איסורין שבתורה מצטרפין זה עם זה שנאמר לא תאכל כל תועבה כל שתיעבתי לך הרי הוא בבל תאכל משמע דלאביי אתיא אפי' אליבא דרבנן דר"מ אע"ג דע"כ פליגי עליה לכל הפחות לענין מלקות סבר אביי דלא פליגי אלא בב' מינין אבל בב' איסורין ומין אחד לא והא דאמר ריש לקיש בפרק התערובות (זבחים עח.) הפיגול והנותר והטמא שבללן זה בזה ואכלן פטור אי אפשר שלא ירבה מין על חבירו ויבטלנו ולמלקות איירי דבטמא לא שייך ביה חטאת ועוד מדקאמר התם ש"מ התראת ספק לא שמה התראה ומדמבטלין זה את זה היה משמע דשני איסורין לרבנן דר"מ אין מצטרפין ל"ל דאע"פ שמבטלין זה את זה כשבללן מצטרפין הן למלקות וכן מוכח במעילה בפרק קדשי מזבח (דף יז:) דתנן הפיגול והנותר והטמא (ג) אין מצטרפין וקאמר בגמרא לא שנו אלא לטומאת ידים אבל לאכילה מצטרפין והא דאיצטריך (ד) לאתויי קרא דלאכילה מצטרפין מלא יאכל כי קדש הם כל שבקודש פסול בא הכתוב ליתן לא תעשה על אכילתו פירוש מדנאמרו בלאו אחד מצטרפין לא איצטריך אלא לר"ש דאמר ב' שמות אין מצטרפין ובקודש מודה משום קרא דרבי אליעזר אבל לרבנן אפילו בעלמא מצטרפין והא דתנן בפ' קדשי מזבח (מעילה טו.) הערלה וכלאי הכרם מצטרפין אתיא שפיר כרבנן אליבא דאביי ומיהו לפי זה מצטרפין דרישא לא הוי פירושא כמו אין מצטרפין (ה)דרבי שמעון דלירוף דרבי שמעון הייני לאיסור דאי למלקות הא אית ליה כל שהוא למכות ור"ת מפרש דאסורי' ומצטרפין הכל מיירי להצטרף לאסור את הקדירה ולא למלקות א"נ אסורין בנתינת טעם אם נפלו בקדירה ומצטרפין לאסור בתערובת יבש בלא נתינת טעם והשתא הוי מצטרפין (ו) כמו אין מצטרפין דסיפא דרבי שמעון: [ע' תוס' ע"ז סה: ד"ה כ"ש · ותוס' מעילה יה· ד"ה הני]:

[פי' תוס' ע"ז סו. ד"ה תבלין וכו' והם מין א']

הגהות הב"ח
(א) תוס' ד"ה תבלין וכו' ותרומת מעשר ותרומת מעשר של דמאי והחלה: (ב) ד"ה אסורין וכו' דחלב ודם ופיגול: (ג) בא"ד דתנן הפיגול והנותר אין מצטרפין כצ"ל ותיבת והטמא נמחק: (ד) בא"ד והא דאיצטריך ר' אליעזר לאתויי קרא: (ה) בא"ד ומיהו לפי זה וכו' כמו אין מצטרפין דסיפא דר"ש: (ו) בא"ד והשתא הוי מצטרפין דרישא כמו אין מצטרפין:

פי' עשב שרוחצין בו לכוס הזוהמא [וגי' ס"א קמוניא וע"' סנהדרין מט: ונדה סב.]

[ת"ג על]

[לעיל פ:]

צבע כמו תכלת

עשב שצובעים בו אדום

גליון
השי"ס

רש"י ד"ה שפרו ורבו לא ידענא. עי' ברכות כה ע"ב ברש"י ד"ה מלן שמעת ליה: תוס' ד"ה תבלין וכו' כדאמרי' שלא השם המביאו לידי מכות. מכות דף ד ע"א:

הואיל

was conferred there;[2] the Wilderness of Paran, [89b] because Israel was fruitful [*paru*] and multiplied there; and the Wilderness of Sinai, because hostility toward idolaters descended thereon. Whilst what was its [real] name? Its name was Horeb. Now they disagree with R. Abbahu. For R. Abbahu said: Its name was Mount Sinai, and why was it called Mount Horeb? Because desolation [*ḥurbah*] to idolaters descended thereon.

HOW DO WE KNOW THAT A CRIMSON-COLOURED STRAP IS TIED, etc. [Instead of] *ka-shanim* [like scarlet threads], *kashani* [like a scarlet thread] is required?[3] Said R. Isaac, The Holy One, blessed be He, said to Israel: [Even] if your sins be like these years [*ka-shanim*] which have continued in ordered fashion from the six days of the Creation until now,[4] yet they shall be as white as snow.[5]

Raba lectured: What is meant by, *Go now, and let us reason together, shall say the Lord:*[6] [Instead of] '*Go now*', Come now, is required: [instead of] '*shall say the Lord*', saith the Lord, is required?[7] In the time to come the Holy One, blessed be He, shall say unto Israel, 'Go now to your forefathers, and they will reprove you.'[8] And they shall say before Him, 'Sovereign of the Universe! To whom shall we go? To Abraham, to whom Thou didst say, *Know of a surety* [*that thy seed shall be a stranger . . . and they shall afflict them . . .*],[9] yet he did not entreat mercy for us? To Isaac, who blessed Esau, *And it shall come to pass, when thou shalt have dominion*,[10] and yet he did not entreat mercy for us? To Jacob, to whom Thou didst say, *I will go down with thee into Egypt*,[11] and yet he did not entreat mercy for us? To whom then shall we go
a now? [Rather] let the Lord state [our wrongs]!'[1] The Holy One, shall answer them, Since ye have made yourselves dependent upon Me, '*though your sins be as scarlet, they shall be as white as snow*'.

R. Samuel b. Naḥmani also said in R. Jonathan's name: What is meant by, *For Thou art our father, though Abraham knoweth us not, and Israel doth not acknowledge us: Thou, O Lord, art our father; our Redeemer from everlasting is Thy name?*[2] In the future to come the Holy One, blessed be He, will say to Abraham. 'Thy children have sinned against Me.' He shall answer Him, 'Sovereign of the Universe! Let them be wiped out for the sanctification of Thy Name.' Then shall He say, 'I will say this to Jacob, who experienced the pain of bringing up children: peradventure he will supplicate mercy for them.' So He will say to him, 'Thy children have sinned.' He [too] shall answer Him, 'Sovereign of the Universe! Let them be wiped out for the sanctification of Thy Name.' He shall retort, 'There is no reason in old men, and no counsel in children!' Then shall he say to Isaac, 'Thy children have sinned against me.' But he shall answer Him, 'Sovereign of the Universe! Are they my children and not Thy children. When they gave precedence to "*we will do*" over "*we will hearken*" before Thee, Thou calledst them, *Israel My son, My firstborn*:[3] now they are *my* sons, not *Thy* sons! Moreover, how much have they sinned? How many are the years of man? Seventy. Subtract twenty, for which Thou dost not punish,[4] [and] there remain fifty. Subtract twenty-five which comprise the nights,[5] [and] there remain twenty-five. Subtract twelve and a half of prayer, eating, and Nature's calls, [and] there remain twelve and a half. If Thou wilt bear all, 'tis well; if not, half be upon me and half upon Thee. And shouldst Thou say, they must all be upon me, lo! I offered myself up before Thee [as a sacrifice]!' [Thereupon] they shall commence and say, 'For thou [i.e., Isaac] art our father.' Then shall Isaac say to them, 'Instead of praising me, praise the Holy One, blessed be He,' and Isaac shall show them the Holy One, blessed be He, with their own eyes. Immediately they shall lift up their eyes on high and exclaim, '*Thou, O Lord, art our father; our Redeemer from everlasting is Thy name.*'

R. Ḥiyya b. Abba said in R. Joḥanan's name: It was fitting for our father Jacob to go down into Egypt in iron chains, but
b that his merit saved him,[1] for it is written, *I drew them with the cords of a man, with bands of love; and I was to them as they that take off the yoke on their jaws, and I laid meat before them.*[2]

MISHNAH. IF ONE CARRIES OUT WOOD, [THE STANDARD FOR CULPABILITY IS] AS MUCH AS IS REQUIRED FOR BOILING A LIGHT EGG; [SEASONING] SPICES, AS MUCH AS IS REQUIRED FOR SEASONING A LIGHT EGG; AND THEY COMBINE WITH EACH OTHER.[3] NUTSHELLS, POMEGRANATE SHELLS, WOAD AND MADDER, [THE STANDARD IS] AS MUCH AS IS REQUIRED FOR DYEING THE SMALL PIECE OF CLOTH AT THE OPENING [TOP] OF A NETWORK. URINE, NATRON,[4] LYE,[5] CIMOLIAN EARTH,[6] AND ASHLEG,[7] AS MUCH AS IS REQUIRED FOR WASHING THE SMALL PIECE OF CLOTH AT THE OPENING [TOP] OF A NETWORK; R. JUDAH SAID: AS MUCH AS IS REQUIRED FOR REMOVING THE STAIN.[8]

GEMARA. [But] we have [already] learnt it once: A reed, [the standard is] as much as is required for making a pen. But if it is thick or crushed, as much as is required for boiling the lightest of eggs beaten up and placed in a stew pot?[9]—You might say [That is only] there, because it is unfit for anything [else], but since wood is fit for the tooth of a key, for no matter how little involved [culpability is]; hence we are informed [otherwise].

[SEASONING] SPICES, AS MUCH AS IS REQUIRED FOR SEASONING A LIGHT EGG. But the following contradicts this: Spices
c of two or three designations[1] belonging to the same species or three [different] species are forbidden,[2] and they combine with

(2) I.e., Israel was made pre-eminent by his acceptance of the Torah. [Or, the Torah which preceded Creation, v. Pes. 54a.] (3) Isaiah should employ the singular, parallel to 'snow' in the other half of the sentence. (4) I.e., no matter how deeply sin has eaten into you. (5) Isa. I, 18. (6) Ibid. (7) E.V. is '*come*' and '*saith*', but these translations are inexact. (8) Or, convince you—of your wrong-doing. (9) Gen. XV, 13. (10) Ibid. XXVII, 40. (11) Ibid. XLVI, 4.

a (1) Do Thou rebuke us, not they, for they did not show themselves merciful. (2) Isa. LXIII, 16. (3) Ex. IV, 22. (4) Rashi: As we find God did not punish those up to twenty years of age who accepted the report of the spies; v. Num. XIV, 29. (5) When one sleeps and does not sin.

b (1) Lit., 'caused it for him'—that he went down as Joseph's honoured guest. (2) Hos. XI, 4. (3) To make up the standard. (4) V. Sanh., 49b, n. 5. (5) A sort of soap. (6) A clay used for cleansing. (7) A kind of alkali or mineral used as soap. (8) Caused by a menstruous woman, v. Sanh. 49b. (9) And obviously the same applies to wood.

c (1) Rashi: e.g., black pepper, white pepper, etc. Tosaf.: spices forbidden under various headings, e.g., '*orlah*, *kil'ayim*, etc. (2) If used for seasoning food, the food is interdicted.

each other.[3] And Hezekiah observed; [90a] They learnt this of sweetening condiments,[4] since they are fit for sweetening a dish. Thus it is only because they are fit for sweetening a dish, but otherwise it is not so?—Here too [in our Mishnah] they are fit for sweetening.

NUTSHELLS, POMEGRANATE SHELLS, WOAD AND MADDER, [THE STANDARD IS] AS MUCH AS IS REQUIRED FOR DYEING THE SMALL PIECE OF CLOTH, [etc.]. But this contradicts it: If one carries out dissolved dyes,[5] [the standard is] as much as is required for dyeing a sample colour for wool?[6]—Said R. Naḥman in the name of Rabbah b. Abbuha: That is because no man troubles to steep dyes in order to dye therewith a sample colour for wool.

URINE. A Tanna taught: Urine, until forty days.[7]

NATRON. It was taught: Alexandrian natron, but not natron of Antipatris.[8]

LYE [BORITH]. Rab Judah said: That is sand. But it was taught: *Borith* and sand? Rather what is *Borith?* Sulphur. An objection is raised: To these were added *ḥalbeẓin*[9] and *le'enun*[10] and *borith* and *ahol.*[11] But if you maintain that it is sulphur, is then sulphur subject to *shebi'ith?* Surely it was taught: This is the general rule: Whatever has a root is subject to *shebi'ith,* but that which has no root is not subject to *shebi'ith?* But what is *borith? Ahala.*[1] But it was taught: And *borith* and *ahala?*[2]—There are two kinds of *ahala.*

CIMOLIAN EARTH. Rab Judah said: That is 'pull out stick in.'[3]

ASHLEG. Samuel said: I asked all seafarers and they told me that it is called *shunana;* it is found in the cavity wherein the pearl lies and it is scraped out with an iron nail.

MISHNAH. [IF ONE CARRIES OUT] LONG PEPPER, OF WHATEVER QUANTITY, IṬRAN,[4] OF WHATEVER QUANTITY, VARIOUS KINDS OF PERFUME, OF WHATEVER QUANTITY, VARIOUS KINDS OF METAL, OF WHATEVER QUANTITY, [PIECES] OF THE ALTAR STONES OR THE ALTAR EARTH, MOTH-EATEN SCROLLS OR THEIR MOTH-EATEN MANTLES, OF WHATEVER QUANTITY, [HE IS CULPABLE], BECAUSE THEY ARE STORED AWAY IN ORDER TO BE 'HIDDEN'.[5] R. JUDAH SAID: ALSO HE WHO CARRIES OUT THE SERVICE VESSELS OF IDOLS, OF WHATEVER SIZE, [IS CULPABLE], FOR IT IS SAID, AND THERE SHALL NOT CLEAVE AUGHT OF THE ACCURSED THING TO THINE HAND.[6]

GEMARA. Of what use is any [small] quantity of long pepper? For [dispelling] the [evil] odour of one's mouth.

IṬRAN, OF WHATEVER QUANTITY. What is this good for? For megrim.

VARIOUS KINDS OF PERFUME, OF WHATEVER QUANTITY. Our Rabbis taught: If one carries out a malodorous [perfume], [the standard is] however little: good oil, however little: crimson [dye],[7] however little; and a closed rose,[8] [the standard is] one.

VARIOUS KINDS OF METAL, OF WHATEVER QUANTITY. What is it fit for?—It was taught; R. Simeon b. Eleazar said: Because one can make a small goad out of it.

b Our Rabbis taught: If one says, 'Behold, I vow[1] iron,'[2]—others rule:[3] He must not give less than a square cubit [of sheet iron]. What is it fit for?—Said R. Joseph: To ward off the ravens.[4] Some state, Others rule: He must not give less than a raven barrier. And how much is that?—Said R. Joseph: A square cubit. [If he vows] brass, he must not give less than a silver *ma'ah*['s worth]. It was taught, R. Eliezer said: He must not give less than a small brass hook. What is it fit for?[5]—Said Abaye, The wicks were scraped out and the branches [of the candelabrum] were cleansed therewith.

MOTH-EATEN SCROLLS AND MOTH-EATEN MANTLES. Rab Judah said: The worm [*mekak*] that attacks scrolls, the worm [*tekak*] of silk, the mite [*ela*] of grapes, the worm [*pah*] of figs, and the worm [*heh*] of pomegranates are all dangerous.[6] A certain disciple was sitting before R. Joḥanan eating figs. 'My Master,' he exclaimed, there are thorns in the figs. 'The *pah* [worm] has killed this person,' answered he.[7]

MISHNAH. IF ONE CARRIES OUT A PEDLAR'S BASKET, THOUGH IT CONTAINS MANY COMMODITIES, HE INCURS ONLY ONE SIN-OFFERING. [FOR] GARDEN-SEEDS, [THE STANDARD IS] LESS THAN THE SIZE OF A DRIED FIG; R. JUDAH B. BATHYRA

(3) If there is not sufficient in one to impart a flavour but only in combination with each other. (4) I.e., where the different kinds of spices are all for sweetening. (5) Ready for use. (6) Given to the dyer. (7) After that it loses its efficacy as a cleansing agent, and the standard of the Mishnah does not apply. (8) A city founded by Herod the Great c. 10 B.C.E. in the plain of Kefar Saba. It was the most northerly limit of Judea (Tosaf. Giṭ. VII, 9; Yoma 69a), and about twenty-six miles south of Caesarea. (9) Jast.: bulb of ornithogalum. (10) Jast.: garden-orache. (11) Jast.: an alcalic plant used as soap.—These were added to the list of plants subject to the laws of the seventh year (*shebi'ith*).

(1) Jast.: a mineral substance used for cleansing. Maim. Nid. IX, 6. states that it is a vegetable. (2) This is not the same Baraitha as cited before; v. Maharsha. (3) A popular nickname for Cimolian earth. (4) A kind of resin used for lighting; cf. *supra* 24b. (5) When a sacred thing ceases to be fit for use, it must be 'hidden', i.e., buried or otherwise disposed of in accordance with the regulations stated in Meg. 26b, but not thrown away. (6) Deut. XIII, 17. (7) V. *supra* 48a, n. a11. (8) Lit., 'the virgin of a rose'.

b (1) Lit., 'I (take) upon myself'. (2) To the Temple. (3) 'Others' frequently refers to R. Meir, Hor. 13b. (4) Rashi: spiked sheets of metal were placed on the Temple roof to prevent birds from alighting thereon; v. M.Ḳ. 9a. (5) In the Temple. (6) To him who eats them. (7) They are dangerous worms, not thorns.

במיני מתיקה שנו הואיל וראוין למתק קדירה טעמא דחזו למתק את הקדירה הא לאו הכי לא הכי נמי חזו למתק: קליפי אגוזין וקליפי רמונים סטים ופואה כדי לצבוע בגד קטן: ורמינהי *המוציא סמנים שרויין כדי לצבוע בהן דוגמא לאירא (הא איתמר עלה) אמר רב נחמן אמר רבה בר אבוה לפי שאין אדם טורח לשרות סממנים לצבוע בהן דוגמא לאירא: [א]מי רגלים: תנא מי רגלים עד בן (א) מ' יום: נתר: *תנא נתר אלכסנדרית ולא נתר אנפנטרין: בורית: אמר רב יהודה זה חול והתניא הבורית והחול אלא מאי בורית כבריתא מיתיבי הוסיפו עליהן החלביצין והלעינון והבורית והאהל ואי ס"ד כבריתא כבריתא מי איתא בשביעית (*והתנן) *זה הכלל כל שיש לו עיקר יש לו שביעית ושאין לו עיקר אין לו שביעית אלא מאי בורית אהלא והתניא והבורית ואהלא (אלא) תרי גווני אהלא: קימוליא: אמר רב יהודה שלוף דוץ: אשלג *אמר שמואל שאילתינהו לכל נחותי ימא ואמרו לי שונאנה *שמיה ומשתכח בנוקבא דמרגניתא ומפקי ליה ברמצא דפרזלא: **מתני'** [ב]פלפלת כל שהוא ועטרן כל שהוא מיני בשמים ומיני מתכות כל שהן מאבני המזבח ומעפר המזבח מקק ספרים ומקק מטפחותיהם כל שהוא שמצניעין אותן לגונזן *רבי יהודה אומר אף המוציא משמשי ע"ז כל שהוא שנאמר °ולא ידבק בידך מאומה מן החרם: **גמ'** פלפלת כל שהוא למאי חזיא לריח הפה: עיטרן כל שהוא: למאי חזיא לצילחתא: מיני בשמים כל שהן: ת"ר [ג]המוציא ריח רע כל שהוא שמן טוב כל שהוא ארגמן כל שהוא *ובתולת הוורד אחת: מיני מתכות כל שהן: למאי חזו תניא רבי שמעון בן אלעזר אומר שכן ראוי לעשות ממנה דרבן קטן *ת"ר האומר הרי עלי ברזל אחרים אומרים [ד]לא יפחות מאמה על אמה למאי חזיא אמר רב יוסף לכלייא עורב ואיכא דאמרי אחרים אומרים לא יפחות מכלייא עורב וכמה אמר רב יוסף אמה על אמה *נחשת לא יפחות ממעה כסף *תניא רבי אליעזר אומר לא יפחות מצינורא קטנה של נחשת למאי חזיא אמר אביי *שמהטטין בה את הפתילות ומקנחין הנרות: מקק ספרים ומקק מטפחות: א"ר יהודה מקק דסיפרי תכך דשיראי ואילא דעינבי ופה דתאני והה דרימוני כולהו סכנתא ההוא תלמידא דהוה יתיב קמיה דר' יוחנן הוה קאכיל תאיני אמר ליה רבי קוצין יש בתאנים א"ל קטליה פה לדין: **מתני'** [ה]המוציא קופת הרוכלין אף על פי שיש בה מינין הרבה אינו חייב אלא חטאת אחת *[ו]זרעוני גינה פחות מכגרוגרת ר' יהודה בן בתירה אומר חמשה

זרע

דברים יג

רש"י

במיני מתיקה. עסקינן שטלן מיני מתיקה קדירה אבל מין אחר אין מצטרף ומתניתין לא מפליג: דוגמא לאירא. מעט למר שהוא כמין דוגמא שמראה הצבע לבע"ה כזה תחפוץ או כזה והוא כדי ליתן באירא של קנה של גרדי ושיעורה מועט: לשרות. ומתני' בשאינן שרויין והבא לשרות אינו שורה פחות מכדי בגד קטן: אנפטרין. מקום: הוסיפו עליהם. לענין שביעית: החלבילין. לטרו"ן: והלעונין. לענה: כברית'. גפרית: שיש לו עיקר. שנשרש בארץ ולפי דעתי תורניסא דגרסינן במס' ע"ז* דבר שאין לו שורש (ב) הוא כמו זה ולא כמו שמפרשין אותו פיונ"א: שלוף דוץ. לא איתפרש אבל כך שמו: ברמצא דפרזלא. פורייזורא של ברזל: **מתני'** פלפלת כל שהוא. ואינו פלפל שלנו ובגמרא מפרש כל שהוא למאי חזי: מיני בשמים כל שהן. לריח טוב: מיני מתכות כל שהוא. ראוי לדרבן קטן: שמצניעין אותו לרפואה ל"ג: מקק ספרים. אכילת תולעת אוכלת הספרים ומרקבן ושמו מקק: שמצניעין אותן לגונזן. שכל דבר קדש טעון גניזה: מאומה. אלמא אחשביה קרא לאיסורא והא דתנן (לעיל דף עה:) כל שאינו כשר להצניע כו' ואוקימנא למעוטי עצי אשירה דלא כר' יהודה: **גמ'** לצלחתא. כאב חצי הראש: ריח רע. שמעשנין בהן חולין ותינוקות כגון חלטית להבריח מעליו מזיקין: ארגמן. לבע שצובעין בו ארגמן וטעמא לא איתפרש ול"נ שגם הוא ראוי להריח: בתולת הוורד. עלה של וורד בחור אחת: מיני מתכות כל שהוא. מתני' היא: הרי עלי ברזל. לבדק הבית: לכליא עורב. טבלאות של אמה (ג) היו עושין והן חדין כסכין סביבותיהם ומסמרין חדין בכולן ומחפין בהן גגו של היכל למנוע את העורבים מליישב: ממעה כסף. נחשת שוה מעה כסף: לנורא. מזלג קטן (ד) [כעין] שטוין בו צג זהב ולבדק הבית למאי חזי: שמוחטין בו פתילות · ומנקבין* ראשיהן לעדויי חושכן מוקיי"ר בלע"ז: מקק לסיפרי תכך דשיראי. כל אלו תולעין הן שבכל מין ומין וחלוקין בשמותיהם תכך איילא פה הה: כולהו סכנתא. לאוכלן: קוצים יש בתאנים. היה תולעת יושב ועוקץ בגרונו ודומה שהוא קוץ: קטליה פה לדין · הרגו פה לדין: **מתני'** רוכלין. מוכרי בשמים לקישוטי נשים ויש להן קופות קטנות לצרורות בשמים: אינו חייב אלא חטאת אחת. דכולה חדא הוצאה היא: פחות מכגרוגרת. דאע"ג דכל האוכלין שיעורן כגרוגרת הני כיון דלזריעה קיימי בפחות מכגרוגרת נמי מיחייב:

זרע

תוספות

הואיל וראוין למתק הקדירה. הואיל וממתיקין הוה ליה למימר כדפי' בסוף כלל גדול (דף עו· ושם) וא"ת היכי איירי אי בעתן טעם אפילו שאר מינין נמי ואי אין בהם טועם טעם אפי' מיני מתיקה נמי לא וי"ל דאפילו ביש בהן נותן טעם שרי בשאר מינין דנותן טעם לפגם הוא. ר"י:

מי רגלים בן מ' יום. אין גירסא זו נכונה דמשמע של קטן בן מ' יום ובנדה פרק האשה (דף סג·) גבי ז' סממנין מעבירין קתני כל הני דהכא ומי רגלים וקא בעי התם בגמרא* דילד או מזקן ואית דגרסי של מ' יום ואין נראה דהתם נמי תניא ומי רגלים שהחמיצו וכמה חימוצן שלשה ימים ונראה כספרים דגרסי עד מ' יום דמג' ימים עד מ' מעבירין אותם על הכתם אבל תוך ג' ולאחר מ' אין מעבירין: **בורית** זה החול. ואע"ג דבפ' המוציא (לעיל פ:) יהיב בחול שיעורא אחרינא כדי ליתן על פי כף של סיד אומר רבינו מאיר דהתם מיירי בחול שנותנין בסיד אבל הכא איירי בחול שמלבנין בו את הבגדים ולספרים דגרסי הכא בורית זה אהלא אתי שפיר: **תרי** גווני אהלא. ולעיל דלא שני תרי גווני חול (או לגירסא אחרת תרי גוונא אהלא) משום דקים ליה דליכא בהו תרי גוונין ויש ספרים דגרסי לעיל מאי בורית אהלא ולפי זה אתי שפיר דה"ק לעולם כדאמר מעיקרא דבורית זה אהלא ותרי גווני אהלא:

לא יפחות ממעה כסף. תימה לר"י דלא יפחות מפרוטה הוה ליה למימר כי היכי דתניא בפרק בתרא דמנחות (דף קו:) הרי עלי זהב לא יפחות מדינר זהב כסף לא יפחות מדינר כסף:

מכליא עורב. בערוך כל פי' דבמקדש ראשון מפני רוב קדושה שהיתה בו לא הוה צריך כליא עורב וליתא דבפ"ק דמועד קטן (דף ט·) מוכח בהדיא שהיה במקדש ראשון כליא *עורב:

המוציא קופת הרוכלין אע"פ שיש בה מינין הרבה אינו חייב אלא אחת. תימה דמאי קמ"ל פשיטא דאפילו בהוציא וחזר והוציא אינו חייב אלא אחת כמו בקצר וחזר וקצר כ"ש בבת אחת ואפילו רב יוסף דמחייב אליבא דר' אליעזר בקצר וחזר וקצר בפרק אמרו לו (יומא דף טו·) בהוצאה אחת פשיטא דפטור ותירץ ר"ת דמיירי כגון שנודע לו על מין זה ונתכפר וחזר ונודע לו על מין אחר אפ"ה פטור דהוי הכל כמו דבר אחד ואע"ג דבפרק המצניע (לקמן צג:) תניא ואם היה כלי צריך לו חייב אף על הכלי ומוקי לה רב אשי שטגג בזה ובזה ונודע לו וחזר ונודע לו ובפלוגתא דרבי יוחנן ור"ל דוקא בכלי ואוכלים שבתוכו מחלקין ידיעות אבל באוכלין שבתוך הכלי אפילו כפרות אין מחלקות ור"י מצא בירושלמי אינו הוציא והוציא כלום הוא חייב אלא אחת לא נצרכה אלא לר"א שלא תאמר מינים הרבה יעשו כהעלמות הרבה ויהא חייב על כל אחת ואחת קמ"ל פי' דס"ד דמינים מחלקין כדא"ר יהושע תמחויין מחלקין* ומיהו ה"ל להזכיר ר' יהושע: אם

לה א מיי' פי"ח מהל' שבת הלכה ח:
לו ב ג שם הלכה ה:
לז ד מיי' פ"ב מהלכות ערכין הלכה ט:
לח ה מיי' פי"ח מהל' שבת הלכה כה:
לט ו שם הלכה ו

רב נסים גאון

האומר הרי עלי ברזל לא יפחות מאמה על אמה למאי חזי אמר רב יוסף לכלה עורב · תמצאנו במסכת מדות בפרק ד' ההיכל מאה על מאה על רום מאה האותם ו' אמות וגובהו ארבעים אמה אמה כיור ואמתים [בית] דילפה אמה תיקרה ואמה מעזיבה וג' אמות מעקה ואמה כלה עורב ר' יהודה אומר לא היה כלה עורב עולה מן המדה אלא ד' אמות (עולה) היה מעקה וכבנון זה במנחות (דף קז) בפרק הרי עלי עשרון:

הגהות הב"ח

(א) גמ' מי רגלים עד מ' יום כצ"ל ותיבת בן נמחק: (ב) רש"י ד"ה שיש לו עיקר וכו' שאין לו עיקר הוא כמו: (ג) ד"ה לכליא עורב של אמה על אמה הי': (ד) ד"ה לנורא מזלג קטן הס"ד ואח"כ מ"ה שמוחטין בו פתילות ומקנחין ראשיהן כצ"ל ותיבות שטוינבו זהב לבדק הבית למאי חזי נמחק:

[דף סג.]
לעיל עט.
ע"ז יד. נדה סב.
רש"ל מ"ז ועי' מהרש"א
[וכערכין ו. ד"ה כגון כו' כתבו ישוב נכון ע"ש וכ"כ במנחות קז. ד"ה כלי"]
מנחות קז. ע"ש

מסורת הש"ס

ע"ז יד. וערי' [עוזלא] תורניתא ניהו
נדה סב. ע"ש
[נ"א והתניא]
נדה סב.
[ג"י' הערוך ערך שלג שלגא ובנדה סב. איתא אשלגא]
[פי' תוס' לקמן לד. ד"ה את המת]
[פי' שושן סתום ורבינו האי גאון היה שונה פתילת הוורד שעושין מאמר גפן לבוע כמין וורד וקורין אותו וורד. ערוך ע' ערך בתול]
[מנחות קו:]
[שם קו. ושם איתא ר"א בן יעקב]
[גי' הערוך שמוחטין ועי' ביצה לב:]
לעיל עט.
ומיהו היה לו להזכיר ר' יהושע אלא ר"ל ר"א דמחייב אתולדה במקום אב רש"ל

מ א מיי' פי"ח מהלכות שבת הלכה יח :
מא ב שם הלכה ז :
מב ג שם הלכה יג :
א ד ה מיי' שם הלכה כ כא :

רבינו חננאל

וכי תנן זרע קישואין שנים וזרע דלועין שנים זרע פול המצרי שנים רמינן עלה למה לי שנים במעה אחת ליחייב דהא לענין זבל וחול הדק כדי לזבל כרישה אחת אמר רב פפא כד זריע מזבל אפילו בחטה אחת לפיכך חייב על זבל שיש בו שיעור לזבל אחת אבל לזרוע בתחלה אין אדם טורח להוציא נימה אחת לזריעה: *) אירא ונקרא עירא בלשון ארמי (אוררא) [אודרא] והוא כמין מוך חתיכה קטנה מן הצמר או מן הפשתן או מן צמר של גפנים שאורגין אותן בתוך מטפחות (ספג כמו)[של] טילת נקראת בל'ישמעאל כמל והרבה צובעין אותן. צורי דקל ותורי דקל. (בול שמענן) צורי דקל. הוצין שחולקין אותן לשנים וג' וארבעה וקולעין אות̇ן או שמלפפין אותן ועושין אותן כמין חבל. תורי דקל קליפי חריות והיינו ריתא.**) (דהוה הים רב הונא בו) ויש שפירשוהו נבארא שהוא ליף בלשון ישמעאל ולא דמי כי נבארא סיב נקרא. צפורת כרמים ממיני חגבים רבנן סברי חגב חי [טהור] כל שהוא מפני שמצניעין אותו לקטן לשחק בו כדכתיב התשחק בו כצפור ותקשרנו לנערותיך אבל חגב מת כאוכלין דמי ושיעורו כגרוגרות ודווקא טהור ור' יהודה סבר אף טמא חי כל שהוא ואמרינן ת"ק מ"ט לא אמר חגב חי טמא כל שהוא אמר לך ת"ק לא רגילי אינשי להצניע חגב טמא לקטן לשחק בו דלמא אתי למכליה ואקשי' חגב חי טהור נמי לא ליהבו ליה לקטן דלמא אתי למכליה כשהוא חי ואית ביה משום בל תשקצו דהא רב קאמר ליה לרב כהנא לא תעבר שושיבא אפומך דלא לימרו קא אכיל ליה וקא עבר משום בל תשקצו ושושיבא הוא איל קמצא וכבר העידו על איל קמצא דהוא דכן אמרי לך רבנן לא רגיל סתם קטן למיכל דבר חי והאי דלא יהבי ליה לקטן חגב חי טמא לשחק בו לאו דלמא אכיל ליה כשהוא חי אלא דילמא מאית ואכיל ליה ור' יהודה סבר סתם קטן כשהוא משחק בחגב חי או מאית בין טהור הוא בין טמא הוא קשי ליה ומיספד ספיד ליה אבל מיכל לא אכיל ליה :

הדרן עלך אמר ר"ע

פי' המצניע · כבר מפורש בפירקא קמא כל שאינו כשר להצניע ואין מצניעין כמוהו אם הוציאו בשבת אין חייב עליו אלא המצניעו והשתא אתא ופריש המצניע כלום בחול שאינו כשיעור הוצאה לזרע או לדוגמא או לרפואה והוציאו בשבת חייב עליו בכל שהוא ואלמלא שהצניעו לא היה חייב עליו ואחרים שלא הצניעוהו אין חייבים עליו אלא כשיעורו. למה לי למיתנא המצניע לזרע ליתני המוציא לזרע פי' הכי קאמר אמאי לא תנן המוציא לזרע או לדוגמא או לרפואה מה שהצניעו לכך חייב עליו כל שהוא. ומ"ט אדכרה למחשבה באצנעה ולא אדכרה בהוצאה ואהדרינן. אמר אביי הכא במאי עסקינן כגון שהצניעו ושכחו למה הצניעו וקא מפיק ליה בסתמא פי' אגמרינן דלא אכפת לן מאי קא מכוין בשעת הוצאה בין קא מכוין להוציאו לאותו דבר שהצניעו לו ובין אפקיה בסתמא כיון דמעיקרא הצניעו לאחד מג' דברים הללו או כיוצא בהן אע"פ ששכח למה הצניעו והוציאו בסתם חייב :

תוספות

אם לנטיעה שתים. פי' אותם שהם ראויים לנטיעה אי נמי כלומר במקום שרגילין לנוטען והוי סתמא לנטוע דאי במוציא ממש לנטיעה הא אמר בריש פ' המצניע (לקמן צא·) מחייב היה ר' מאיר במוציא חטה א' לזריעה : **שמצניעין** אותו לחזיר. פירוש שראוי ליתן לעובד כוכבים או למכור לו אבל ישראל אסור לגדל חזיר :

דלא לימרו מיכל קא אכיל ליה ועבר משום בל תשקצו. אומר רשב"א דמשמע מכאן דחגב טהור אין טעון שחיטה מדלא קאמר דלא לימרו דקאכיל ליה בלא שחיטה ועוד דת"ק קאמר בסמוך בחגב חי טמא דילמא מיית ואכיל ליה ובטהור לא חייש והיינו משום דמותר בלא שחיטה ובתוספתא דמסכת תרומות*[פ"ט] תניא אוכל אדם חגבים בין חיין בין שחוטין ואע"ג דאסור לאכול חי משום בל תשקצו מ"מ מותר לחתוך ממנו אבר ולאוכלו על ידי רחילה ואין בו משום אבר מן החי ורש"י הביאו באלו טרפות (חולין דף סו·) מה"ג דמפיק חגבים אין טעונין שחיטה מדכתיב ואת כל נפש החיה הרומשת במים אלו דגים ואת כל נפש השורצת אלו חגבים מדכתיב חגבים אחר דגים משמע דאין. טעונין שחיטה כדגים ואפילו עוף הוה פטרינן ליה בולא כלום אי לאו דהוקש לבהמה כדאמר בהשוחט (שם כז:) א):

ועובר משום בל תשקצו · משמע דשושיבא שרי ואומר ר"ת דבפ"ב דמס' ע"ז (דף לז.) גבי איל קמצא דמפרש רב פפא דהייטו שושיבא ורב חייא בר אשי אמר משמיה דעולא סוסבל וקאמר התם דבראשו ארוך הייטו שושיבא כ"ע לא פליגי דאסור ל"ג דאסור אלא גרס כ"ע לא פליגי דשרי דהכא משמע דשושיבא שרי ולית ביה אלא משום בל תשקצו וסתם מתניתין דפרק אלו טריפות (חולין דף סה:) שרי ראשו ארוך לכך נראה לר"ת דגרס כ"ע לא פליגי דשרי ב) :

הדרן עלך א"ר עקיבא

המצניע וכל אדם אין חייבין עליו אלא כשיעורו. תימה לר"י דאמאי איצטריך למיתני ליה הא תנא ליה חדא זימנא בפרק כלל גדול (לעיל דף עה:) (ו)ושאינו כשר להצניע אינו חייב אלא המצניע* :

רש"י

זרע קישואין. חשוב הוא וחייב בשני גרגרין : המוציא חגב חי (ג) כל שהוא. שמצניעין אותו לקטן לשחק בו כדמפרש רבי יהודה בסיפא דמתני' : מת. הרי הוא כשאר אוכלין וחייב בכגרוגרת : ציפורת כרמים. לקמיה מפרש מאי היא ומאי רפואתו : שמצניעים אותו לקטן כו'. ות"ק מהאי טעמא נמי מחייב ליה בחגב טהור ומיהו אטמא פליג דלא מצנעי ליה לשחק דילמא אכיל ליה כדלקמן : **גמ'** כדי לזבל. אלמא זרע הבא מגרעין אחד חשיב : הא דזריע. מאחר שהן זרועין חשיב כל אחד ואחד ואדם טורח לזבל אחד מהם אבל דלא זריע אין אדם טורח לזרוע גרגיר אחד : המוציא גרעינין. גרעיני תמרה : ביצה קלה. כגרוגרת מבילה שהיא קלה לבשל וזו של תרנגולת : לחשבון. כמו שנותנים לסימן עדות (ג) לכל דיבר פשוט: אחרים אומרים ה'. דעד ד' כללות חשיב אינים ולא מיכשי ואין צריך לתת סימן אבל חמש מיכשי ומותיב סימנא לכולהו: לנישבין. לצוד עופות ובלע"ז ליי"ש : מקשה של חזיר. נימין קשין שבשדרה של חזיר : אחת. דחזיא לאושכפי לתת בראש המשיחה של תפירה : צורי דקלים. נצרים קלופים לעשות סלים : שתים · לשתי בתי נירין : תורי דקל. דקין מצורי והן מן הסיב הגדל סביבותיו °ולא ידעתי למאי *חזי : פיילי ביירי. כך שמו : ומשתכח בדיקלא דחד נבארא. בדקל בחור שלא נכרך עדיין אלא בסיב א' שגדל סביבותיו וכורכו : לחוכמא. לפתוח הלב : גובתא. קנה : שיתין. לאו דוקא אלא מכסהו כסויין הרבה כגון זפת וטעוה על גבה ואדמה:גושפנקי. חותמות : ותלי ליה באיברא דשמאלי. בזרוע השמאלי : וסימן לב כסיל. כגון זה שצריך לפקח לב לשמאלו : ואכיל לאידך פלגא. בתר דאחכים: ואי לא. אכיל ליה אלא שדי ליה : מיעקר תלמודו. וחכמתו שלמד על ידו נעקר ממנו: ות"ק סבר. חגב טמא לא מצנעי' ליה לקטן לשחק: דילמא אכיל. ואפי' למאן דאמר קטן אוכל נבלות אין ב"ד מצווין עליו להפרישו מודה הוא דלא יהבינן ליה בידים דתניא (יבמות דף קד.) לא תאכלום לא תאכילום להזהיר גדולים על הקטנים : אי הכי טהור. אי נמי דילמא אכיל ליה ואי משום דאין בו איסור אבר מן החי דחגב אין טעון שחיטה אית ביה מיהא *משום בל תשקצו במסכת מכות (דף טז:) כדרב כהנא כו' : שושיבא. מין חגב טהור: אלא· לאו משום דחייש דילמא אכיל לי' חי אלא דילמא מיית ואכיל לי' וקאכיל טמא אבל טהור ש"ד : מיספד ספיד ליה. תינוק ולאו אורחיה למיכליה :

הדרן עלך א"ר עקיבא

גמרא

זרע קישואין שנים זרע דילועין שנים זרע פול המצרי שנים (א)°חגב חי טהור כל שהוא מת כגרוגרת צפורת כרמים בין חיה בין מתה כל שהוא שמצניעין אותה לרפואה ר' יהודה אומר אף המוציא חגב חי טמא כל שהוא שמצניעין אותו לקטן לשחוק בו : **גמ'** ורמינהי *זבל וחול הדק כדי לזבל קלח של כרוב דברי ר"ע וחכמים אומרים כדי לזבל כרישא *אמר רב פפא הא דזריע הא דלא זריע לפי שאין אדם טורח להוציא נימא אחת לזריעה : זרע קישואין : ת"ר *המוציא גרעינין אם לנטיעה שתים אם לאכילה כמלא פי חזיר וכמה מלא פי חזיר אחת אם להסיק כדי לבשל ביצה קלה אם לחשבון שתים אחרים אומרים חמש ת"ר °המוציא שני נימין מזנב הסוס ומזנב הפרה חייב שמצניעין אותן לנישבין מקשה של חזיר אחת צורי דקל שתים תורי דקל אחת : ציפורת כרמים בין חיה בין מתה כל שהוא : מאי ציפורת כרמים אמר רב פליא ביארי אמר אביי ומשתכח בדיקלא דחד נבארא ועבדי לה לחוכמא אכיל ליה לפלגא דימיני' ופלגא דשמאליה רמי לה בגובתא דנחשא וחתים לה בשיתין גושפנקי ותלי לה באיברא דשמאלא וסימניך °לב חכם לימינו ולב כסיל לשמאלו וחכים כמה דבעי וגמר כמה דבעי ואכיל ליה לאידך פלגא דאי לא מיעקר תלמודו : ר' יהודה אומר אף המוציא כו' : ותנא קמא סבר לא מאי טעמא דילמא אכיל ליה °אי הכי טהור נמי דהא רב כהנא הוה קאים קמיה דרב והוה קמעבר שושיבא אפומיה אמר ליה שקליה דלא לימרי מיכל קאכיל ליה וקעבר משום °בל תשקצו את נפשותיכם אלא דילמא מיית ואכיל ליה ורבי יהודה אי מיית קטן מיספד ספיד ליה :

תורה אור קהלת י ויקרא יא

הדרן עלך אמר רבי עקיבא

המצניע °לזרע ולדוגמא ולרפואה °והוציאו בשבת חייב בכל שהוא וכל אדם אין חייב עליו אלא כשיעורו חזר והכניסו אינו חייב אלא כשיעורו : **גמ'** למה ליה למיתני המצניע ליתני המוציא לזרע ולדוגמא ולרפואה חייב בכל שהוא אמר אביי הכא במאי עסקינן °כגון שהצניעו ושכח למה הצניעו והשתא קא מפיק ליה סתמא מהו

רש"י

המצניע בכל שהוא. דהא אחשביה : אלא כשיעורו. בכל אחד שיעור המפורש לו בזרעונים חמשה זרע קישואין או דילועין או פול המצרי שנים ובשאר דברים כגון יין או אוכלין או גמי כשיעור המפורש בכלל גדול ובהמוציא: חזר והכניסו . זה שהצניע פחות מכשיעור והוציאו אם חזר ונמלך שלא לזורעו והכניסו : (ד) אינו חייב. בהכנסה זו אלא אם כן יש בו שיעור שלם דכיון דנמלך עליו שלא לזורעו ביטל מחשבתו והרי הוא ככל אדם : **גמ'** ליתני המוציא זרע בכל שהוא חייב. ואף על גב דלא אצנעיה מעיקרא להכי דהא דבעינן שיעורא הייטו טעמא כדאמרן שאין אדם טורח להוציא נימא אחת לזריעה הלכך מוציא סתם פטור עד שיהא בו שיעור אבל זה שהוציא נימא אחת לזריעה בהדיא גלי דעתיה דטרח ואחשביה: אמר אביי. ודאי מוציא לזריעה חייב ואף על גב דלא אצנעיה מעיקרא ומתניתין דבעי מצניע במוציא סתם קאמר כגון לטלטלו מבית לבית דאינו חייב אלא משום דאחשביה בהצנעתו ואם תאמר כבר שנו בכלל גדול (עה:) (ה)כל שאינו כשר להצניע אינו חייב אלא מצניע הא מצניע חייב הכא במאי עסקינן דאיצטריך למתנייה כגון שהצניעו האי מצניע לזרע או לדוגמא ושכח למה מצניעו והשתא מפיק ליה סתמא לטלטלו מבית לבית : מהו

מסורת הש"ס

[לעיל עה:] [לעיל עט.] [תוספתא פ"ט] [ובערוך ערך תר כתב דחזי לתפור פי' דלעת ע"ש]

הגהות הב"ח

(א) גמ' פול המצרי שנים המוציא חגב : (ב) רש"י ד"ה המוציא חגב חי כל שהוא : (ג) ד"ה לחשבון וכו' לסימן לכל כלל ודיבת עדות ... משום בל תשקצו דמאיס הוא וכל דבר מיאוס אית ביה משום בל תשקצו כדאיתא במס' מכות וכו' כצ"ל

א) [וע"ע תוס' ע"ז לח. ד"ה לעולם ותוס' חולין סו. ד"ה כמאי] ב) [בחולין סה: כתבו וכן מצא בספר ישן ובע"ז לז: ד"ה בראשו כתבו וגי' זו נמצאת בפי' ר"ח]

פרק י (ד) רש"י ד"ה חזר והכניסו וד"ה אינו חייב הד"א : (ה) ד"ה אמר אביי וכו' בכלל גדול וכל שאינו כשר להצניע ואין מצניעין כמוהו אינו חייב כצ"ל והד"א עם ד"ה מהו דתימא וד"ה בעלה דכל : (ו) תוס' ד"ה המצניע וכו' בפ' כלל גדול וכל שאין כשר להצניע ואין מצניעין כמוהו אינו חייב :

*) דברי רבינו אלו עד תי' והרבה צובעין אותו שייך לע"א על הא דתניא שם המוציא שרוין כדי לצבוע בהן דוגמא לאירא. **) נראה דצ"ל דסוי תגר רב הונא ביה וכיון רבינו לדעת הש"ס דמגילה (כו ע"ב) ר"פ סוס אסר ריתא כו' ע"ש ועי' בערוך ערך תר התשיעי והבין לתקן ולכוון את דברי רבינו ז"ל.

רב נסים גאון

זרע פול המצרי שנים פול המצרי הוא אל לוביה בלשון ישמעאל והן דמות פולים קטנים ביותר ובאמצעיתן שחור תמצא דבר זה מפורש בתלמוד (ירושלמי כלאים פ"ח) כלאים פול המצרי כד דהוא רטיב אינון צוחין ליה לובי כד דהוא נגיב אינון צוחין ליה פול המצרי : דהא רב כהנא הוה קאי קמיה דרב והוה קא מעבר שושיבא אפומיה שושיבא הוא ממיני ארבה וביאור דבר זה במסכת ע"ז בפרק אין מעמידין (דף לז) מאי איל קמצא רב פפא אמר שושיבא :

סליק פרק אמר רבי עקיבא

גליון הש"ס גמ' אי הכי טהור נמי. עי' משנה למלך פרק י"ז הלכה כו מהל' מ"א: רש"י ד"ה תורי סי' ולא ידעתי למאי חזי כו'. עי' ברכות דף כה ע"ב גרש"י ד"ה מאן שמעת ליה :

RULED: FIVE. [90b] [FOR] CUCUMBER SEED, [THE STANDARD IS] TWO; SEED OF GOURDS, TWO; SEED OF EGYPTIAN BEANS, TWO. IF ONE CARRIES OUT A LIVE CLEAN[8] LOCUST, WHATEVER ITS SIZE; DEAD, [ITS STANDARD IS] THE SIZE OF A DRIED FIG. THE BIRD OF THE VINEYARDS,[9] WHETHER LIVE OR DEAD, WHATEVER ITS SIZE, BECAUSE IT IS STORED AWAY
a FOR A MEDICINE.[1] R. JUDAH SAID: ALSO HE WHO CARRIES OUT A LIVE UNCLEAN LOCUST, WHATEVER ITS SIZE, [IS CULPABLE], BECAUSE IT IS PUT AWAY FOR A CHILD TO PLAY WITH.

GEMARA. But this contradicts it: Manure, or thin sand, [the standard is] as much as is required for fertilizing a cabbage stalk: this is R. Akiba's view. But the Sages maintain: For fertilizing one leek-plant?[2]—Said R. Papa: In the one case it is sown, and in the other it is not, because one does not trouble to carry out a single seed for sowing.

CUCUMBER SEED. Our Rabbis taught: If one carries out kernels [of dates],—if for planting, [the standard for culpability is] two; if for eating, as much as fills the mouth of a swine. And how much fills the mouth of a swine? One. If for fuel, as much as is required for boiling a light egg; if for calculating,[3] two—others say, five.

Our Rabbis taught: If one carries out two hairs of a horse's tail or a cow's tail, he is culpable, because these are laid aside for [bird] snares. Of the stiff bristles of a swine, one [involves liability]; of palm bands,[4] two; of palm fillets,[5] one.

THE BIRD OF THE VINEYARDS, WHETHER LIVE OR DEAD, WHATEVER ITS SIZE. What is the bird of the vineyards?—Said Rab: *Palya be'ari*.[6] Abaye observed: And it is found in a palm tree of [only] one covering, and it is prepared [as food] for [acquiring] wisdom; one eats half of its right [side] and half of its left, places it [the rest] in a brass tube and seals it with sixty [i.e., many] seals and suspends it around his left arm; and the token thereof is, *A wise man's heart is at his right hand; but a fool's heart is at his left*.[7] He acquires as much wisdom as he desires, studies as much as he desires, and [then] eats the other half; for if [he does] not, his learn-
b ing will vanish.[1]

R. JUDAH SAID: ALSO HE WHO CARRIES OUT, etc. But the first Tanna holds, Not so.[2] What is the reason? Lest he [the child] eat it. If so, a clean [locust] is the same, for R. Kahana was standing before Rab and passing a *shoshiba*[3] in front of his mouth. 'Take it away,' said he to him, 'that people should not say that you are eating it and thereby violating [the injunction], *ye shall not make yourselves abominable*.'[4] Rather [the reason is] lest it die and he [the child] eat it. But R. Judah [holds], If it dies the child will indeed weep for it.[5]

CHAPTER X

MISHNAH. IF ONE LAYS [SOMETHING] ASIDE FOR SOWING, FOR A SAMPLE, OR FOR A MEDICINE, AND [THEN] CARRIES IT OUT ON THE SABBATH, HE IS CULPABLE WHATEVER
c ITS SIZE.[1] BUT ALL OTHERS ARE NOT CULPABLE THEREFOR SAVE IN ACCORDANCE WITH ITS STANDARD.[2] IF HE CARRIES IT BACK AGAIN,[3] HE IS LIABLE ONLY IN ACCORDANCE WITH ITS STANDARD.[4]

GEMARA. Why must he teach, IF ONE LAYS ASIDE; let him teach, If one carries out [aught] for sowing, for a sample, or for a medicine, he is culpable, whatever its size?[5]—Said Abaye: We discuss here a case e.g., where one laid it aside and [then] forgot why he laid it aside, and now he carries it out without specifying

(8) I.e., that may be eaten. (9) A species of locust; it is discussed in the Gemara.
a (1) In accordance with the general rule of the Mishnah *supra* 75*b*. (2) Which shows that the seed for a *single* plant entails culpability. (3) E.g., each to denote a certain sum. (4) I.e., made of palm bark. (5) Rashi: made of the bast of palm trees. These are finer than palm bands. (6) Perhaps, 'searcher in forests' (Jast.)—the name of a locust. (7) Eccl. X, 2—i.e., a fool who has to acquire wisdom has to tie this on his left arm.
b (1) Lit., 'be eradicated'. (2) An unclean locust is not laid aside, etc. (3) A species of long-headed locust, which is eatable. (4) Lev. XI, 43. The abomination consists in eating it alive. (5) But not eat it.
c (1) Since by laying it aside he shows that he values it. (2) As stated in the previous chapter. (3) Having carried it out he decides not to sow it, etc., after all, and takes it back into the house. (4) For by changing his mind he removes the artificial value which he first attached to it, and it is the same as any other of its kind. (5) For a definite standard is required only when one carries it out without any specified purpose. But if he states his purpose, he *ipso facto* attaches a value to it.

the purpose: [91a] you might say, His intention has been cancelled;[6] hence we are informed that whenever one does anything, he does it with his original purpose.

Rab Judah said in Samuel's name: R. Meir maintained that one is culpable even if he carries out a single [grain of] wheat for sowing. But that is obvious, [for] we learnt, WHATEVER ITS SIZE?—You might say, WHATEVER ITS SIZE is to exclude [the standard of] the quantity of a dried fig, yet even so [one is not guilty unless there is as much as an olive: hence we are informed [otherwise]. R. Isaac son of Rab Judah demurred: If so,[7] if one declares his intention of carrying out his whole house, is he really not culpable unless he carries out his whole house?—There his intention is null *vis à vis* that of all men.

BUT ALL OTHERS ARE NOT CULPABLE THEREFOR SAVE IN ACCORDANCE WITH ITS STANDARD. Our Mishnah does not agree with R. Simeon b. Eleazar. For it was taught: R. Simeon b. Eleazar stated a general rule: That which is not fit to put away, and such is not [generally] put away, yet it did become fit to a certain person,[1] and he did put it away, and then another came and carried it out, the latter is rendered liable through the former's intention.

Raba said in R. Naḥman's name: If one carries out as much as a dried fig for food, and then decides to [use it] for sowing, or the reverse, he is liable. But that is obvious: consider it from this point of view[2] [and] there is the standard, and consider it from that point of view, [and] there is the standard?—You might say, [Both] removal and depositing[3] must be done with the same intention, which is absent [here]: hence he informs us [otherwise].

Raba asked: What if one carries out half as much as a dried fig for sowing, but it swells[4] and he decides [to use it] for food? Can you argue, Only there[5] is he culpable, because consider it from this point of view [and] there is the standard, and consider it from that point of view and there is the standard: whereas here, since it did not contain the standard of food when he carried it out, he is not culpable. Or perhaps, since he would be culpable for his intention of sowing if he were silent and did not intend it [for another purpose],[6] he is still culpable now? Now, should you rule that since he would be culpable for his intention of sowing if he were silent and did not intend it for another purpose, he is still culpable now: what if one carries out as much as a dried fig for food and it shrivels up and he decides [to keep it] for sowing?[7] Here it is certain that if he remained silent he would not be culpable on account of his
b original intention; or perhaps we regard[1] the present [only]; hence he is culpable? Should you rule that we regard the present, hence he is culpable: what if one carries out as much as a dried fig for food, and it shrivels and then swells up again? Does [the principle of] disqualification operate with respect to the Sabbath or not?[2] The question stands over.

Raba asked R. Naḥman: What if one throws *terumah*[3] of the size of an olive into an unclean house? In respect of what [is the question]? If in respect of the Sabbath,[4] we require the size of a dried fig? If in respect of defilement,[5] we require food as much as an egg?—After all, it is in respect of the Sabbath, [the circumstances being] e.g., that there is food less than an egg in quantity[6] and this makes it up to an egg in quantity.[7] What then: since it combines in respect of defilement, he is also culpable in respect to the Sabbath; or perhaps in all matters relating to the Sabbath we require the size of a dried fig?—Said he to him, We have learnt it: Abba Saul said: As for the two loaves of bread,[8] and the shewbread,[9] their standard is the size of a dried fig.[10] But why so:

(6) Since he forgot it. (7) That according to the Mishnah culpability depends on one's intentions.

(1) He found a use for it. (2) Lit., 'go here'. (3) V. *supra* 2a, n. a5. (4) To the size of a dried fig—i.e., before he deposited it, and he changes his mind likewise before depositing it. (5) In the preceding case. (6) Intention must be verbally expressed, and is not merely mental. (7) V. n. a4.

(1) Lit., 'go after'. (2) The principle of disqualification (lit., 'rejection') is that once a thing or a person has been rendered unfit in respect to a certain matter, it or he remains so, even if circumstances change. Thus here, when it shrivels, it becomes unfit to cause liability, being less than the standard: does it remain so or not? (Of course, if one carries it out thus and deposits it on *another* occasion, he is certainly culpable. But here it became unfit in the course of one act, and the question is whether it can become fit again for the completion of this same act.) (3) V. Glos. (4) Whether his throwing is a culpable act. (5) Whether it becomes unclean. (6) Already in the house. (7) And it alights near the first, touching it, and so both become unclean. (8) V. Lev. XXIII, 17. (9) V. Ex. XXV, 30. (10) I.e., if one carries them out on the Sabbath, this is the minimum quantity involving culpability.

מהו דתימא בטולי בטלה מחשבתו קמ"ל כל העושה על דעת ראשונה הוא עושה אמר רב יהודה אמר שמואל מחייב· היה רבי מאיר אף במוציא חטה אחת לזריעה פשיטא כל שהוא תנן מהו דתימא כל שהוא לאפוקי מגרוגרת ולעולם °עד דאיכא כזית קמ"ל מתקיף לה רב יצחק בריה דרב יהודה אלא מעתה חישב להוציא כל ביתו הכי נמי דלא מיחייב עד דמפיק לכוליה התם בטלה דעתו אצל כל אדם: וכל אדם אין חייבין עליו אלא כשיעורו: מתניתין דלא כרבי שמעון בן אלעזר *דתניא כלל א"ר שמעון בן אלעזר כל שאינו כשר להצניע ואין מצניעין כמוהו והוכשר לזה והצניעו ובא אחר והוציא נתחייב זה במחשבתו של זה אמר רבא אמר רב נחמן הוציא כגרוגרת לאכילה ונמלך עליה לזריעה אי נמי לזריעה ונמלך עליה לאכילה חייב פשיטא זיל הכא איכא שיעורא וזיל הכא איכא שיעורא מהו דתימא בעינן עקירה והנחה בחדא מחשבה והא ליכא קמ"ל בעי רבא הוציא חצי גרוגרת לזריעה °ותפחה ונמלך עליה לאכילה מהו את"ל התם הוא דמיחייב דזיל הכא איכא שיעורא וזיל הכא איכא שיעורא הכא כיון דבעידנא דאפקה לא הוה ביה שיעור אכילה לא מיחייב או דילמא כיון דאילו אישתיק ולא חשיב עליה מיחייב אמחשבה דזריעה השתא נמי מיחייב ואת"ל [א]כיון דאילו אישתיק ולא חשיב עליה מיחייב אמחשבה דזריעה [ב]השתא נמי מיחייב הוציא כגרוגרת לאכילה °וצמקה ונמלך עליה לזריעה מהו הכא ודאי כי אישתיק אמחשבה קמייתא לא מיחייב או דילמא בתר השתא אזלינן ומיחייב ואת"ל [ג]בתר השתא אזלינן ומיחייב הוציא כגרוגרת לאכילה וצמקה וחזרה ותפחה מהו יש דיחוי לענין שבת או אין דיחוי לענין שבת [ד]תיקו: בעא מיניה רבא מרב נחמן [ה]זרק כזית תרומה לבית טמא מהו למאי אי לענין שבת כגרוגרת בעינן אי לענין טומאה כביצה אוכלין בעינן לעולם לענין שבת °וכגון דאיכא פחות מכביצה אוכלין והאי משלימו לביצה מאי מדמצטרף לענין טומאה מיחייב נמי לענין שבת או דילמא כל לענין שבת כגרוגרת בעינן א"ל תניתוה אבא שאול אומר שתי הלחם ולחם הפנים שיעורן כגרוגרת ואמאי לימא מדלענין

יוצא

רש"י

מהו דתימא. כיון דשכח בשעת הוצאה שלא היה זכור בהצנעתו בטלה לו מחשבתו. ואין כאן לא חשיבות מחשבת הצנעה ולא מחשבת הוצאה: קמ"ל. דכל העושה סתם על דעת הראשונה עושה ובחשיבותיה קמא קאי: כל שהוא תנן. וסתם משנה רבי מאיר: לאפוקי מגרוגרת. דשאר אוכלין: אלא מעתה. דמתני' בדעתיה תלינן כדקאמרת משום דעל דעת ראשונה מחשבת ליה שיעורא: חישב להוציא כל ביתו. בהוצאה אחת דלא אחשבה אלא אם כן הוציא כולה כאחד: הכי נמי. דכי אפקא פורתא פורתא לא מיחייב: בטלה דעתיה. ושיעורא דחשיב לאינשי חשיב: וכל אדם אין חייבין אלא כשיעורו. ואע"פ שהוכשר לזה והצניעו: כגרוגרת. איכא שיעורא לאכילה ולהוצאה וכ"ש לזריעה דשיעורא בכל שהוא: ותפחה. ועמדה על גרוגרת קודם הנחה: ונמלך עליה לאוכלה. והניחה מהו: את"ל. בההיא אע"ג דעקירה והנחה לאו בחדא מחשבה הואי מיחייב: התם הוא דזיל הכא כו'. בשעת מחשבה ראשונה היה בו כשיעור למחשבתו ושיעור (א) למחשבה שניה הלכך מילטרפי עקירה והנחה: אבל הכא בעידנא דאפקה לא הוה בה שיעור. למחשבה שניה של הנחה ולא מלטרפי הנחה לעקירה: כיון דאילו אשתיק. בהך שניה אית בה שיעור לזריעה ומיחייב: השתא נמי מיחייב. הואיל ויש שיעור למחשבה אחרונה ובשיעור זה איכא שיעורא למחשבה ראשונה ויותר: לא מיחייב. דהא בשעת הנחה ליכא שיעור למחשבה קמייתא: בתר השתא. בתר מחשבה דהשתא אזלינן לענין הנחה: יש דיחוי. מה שחסרה בינתים אילו הנחה בההיא שעתא לא מיחייב (ב) מי אמרינן תורת דיחוי דנדחה לו מחיוב חטאת ובטלה לה עקירה וכי הדר תפחה והניחה הוי הנחה בלא עקירה: אי לענין טומאה. דמיבעיא לך אם נטמא לטמא טומאת אוכלין או לאו כביצה בעינן: והאי משלימו. שנחה אצלו והשלימו וע"י הנחה זו נטמאו: מאי. מדחשיב הך זריקה לענין טומאה חשיב נמי לענין שבת כאלו הוא כגרוגרת ומיחייב או לא:

שיעורן

תוספות

מתקיף לה רב יצחק. פירש בקונטרס דפריך לאביי וקשה דלמאי נטר ליה עד הכא ואומר הרב פור"ת בשם רבינו שמואל דאדרב יהודה אבזה פריך וה"פ כיון דאמרת דמוליא חטה אחת לזריעה חייב אע"פ שאין רגילות משום דבתר מחשבתו אזלינן ה"נ כשחישב להוציא כל ביתו ניזול בתר מחשבתו ולא נחייבנו בפחות כיון דפחות מיכן אינו חשוב בעיניו ומשני התם בטלה דעתו אצל כל אדם דאין אדם שלא יהא חשוב בעיניו פחות מכן אבל הכא יש בני אדם שחשובה להם חטה אחת לזריעה:

או דילמא בתר השתא אזלינן. משמע דאי בתר השתא אזלינן ליכא למיבעיא מידי מדקאמר את"ל בתר השתא אזלינן הוציא גרוגרת לאכילה וצמקה וחזרה ותפחה מהו ולא מיבעיא ליה אקמייתא ואמאי אכתי תיבעי ליה אי הוה דיחוי אצל שבת או לא כדבעי בסמוך דהא מיד כשצמקה נדחית וי"ל דדוקא ההיא דבסמוך חשיב ליה דיחוי שנדחית בין משיעור ראשון בין משיעור אחרון אבל הכא דמשיעור אחרון מיהא לא נדחית לא חשיב ליה דיחוי:

אי לענין טומאה כביצה אוכלין בעינן. °משמע דלא מקבל אוכל טומאה בפחות מכביצה ומה שהביא *רש"י מת"כ דאוכל מקבל טומאה בכל שהוא דתניא מכל האוכל (ג) שמטמא בכל שהוא יכול יהא מטמא אחרים ת"ל אשר יאכל אוכל הנאכל בבת אחת הוי אומר זה בילת תרנגולת אומר ר"ת דאסמכתא היא דה"כ מעשר ירק מרבינן בת"כ מוכל מעשר הארץ ולא הוי אלא אסמכתא בעלמא והא דפריך בפרק כל שעה (פסחים ד' לג:) למ"ד משקין מיבלע בליעי מהא דתנן טמא מת שסחט זיתים וענבים כביצה מכוונת טהורים ואי מיבלע בליעי אמאי טהורים ומוקי לה בענבים שלא הוכשרו לאימת קא מיתכשרי לכי סחיט להו וכי סחיט להו בציר ליה שיעוריה אתי שפיר גם לפי' הקונטרס דאע"ג דמקבל טומאה בכל שהוא מ"מ בציר ליה שיעורא מלקבל הכשר לפירוש הרב פור"ת דמפרש בשם רש"י בפ' חבית (לקמן קמה:) דאין אוכל מקבל הכשר בפחות מכביצה וטעמא משום דמאשר יאכל נפקא לן לטמא אחרים בכביצה והא כתב אשר יבא עליו מים וכן בפרק אלו עוברין (פסחים מה:) גבי בצק שבסידקי עריבה דמפרש אביי כגון דאיכא פחות מכביצה אוכלין ונגעו בהאי בצק בפסח דאיסורו חושבו מלטרף אע"ג דבלא צירוף פחות מכביצה הוה מצי לאוקמי דנגע שרץ בכזית שבסידקי עריבה בפסח דאיסורו חושבו מקבל טומאה בשאר ימות השנה אי קפיד אין *אי לא לא אלא דלענין קבלת טומאה עצמה לא נפקא לן מינה מידי דבלאו הכי אסורה משום חמץ להכי נקט לענין לטמא אחרים ומייתי רבינו תם ראיה דאין אוכל מקבל טומאה פחות מכביצה דתניא בפרק אלו עוברין (שם מד:) המקפה של תרומה השום והשמן של חולין ונגע טבול יום במקצתן פסל את כולן מקפה של חולין ושום ושמן של תרומה ונגע טבול יום במקצתן לא פסל אלא מקום מגעו והוינן בה מקום מגעו אמאי פסל והא לא הוי כביצה ורש"י ל"ג הכי אלא גרים והא בטל ברובא ומפרש דהכי פריך מקום מגעו אמאי פסול והא בטל שום ושמן אגב מקפה דהא משום הכי קתני ברישא פסל את כולן ואין נראה למחוק הספרים ועוד נהי דבטלי ברישא להחמיר להקל לא אמרינן דבטלי ועוד דלא שייך למימר דבטלי השום והשמן כיון שהן בעין מדקתני לא פסל אלא מקום מגעו ועוד (*דתניא בתוספתא) בד"א בזמן שהיא גוש בקערה משמע שהן בעין ואין להאריך ורש"י חזר בו בכריתות (דף כא:) וגבי פרה מיטמא טומאת אוכלין (חולין דף פב:) והא דאמר בפ"ק דחולין (דף כד:) התורה העידה על כלי חרס אפילו מלא חרדל לאו דוקא חרדל אלא כלומר מלא בילים ומשום דבחרדל איכא טובא ראשון ושני כו' ומקבל טומאה מדרבנן נקט ליה *):

אי לענין שבת כגרוגרת בעינן. הוה מצי למיפרך אמאי נקט זרק ואמאי נקט תרומה ולבית טמא:

כגון דאיכא פחות מכבילה אוכלים כו'. אור"י דלהכי נקט זרק דהשתא בהדי הדדי קא אתיין דלא מחייב לענין שבת עד דנח כדאמר בפרק המוציא (לעיל דף פ:) תוך ג' לרבנן בעיא הנחה על גבי משהו אבל מכנים מכי אתי תוך ג' איכא איסור שבת ואיסור טומאה ליכא עד דמלטרף ולא

*) [וע"ע תוס' פסחים לג. ד"ה לאימת ותוס' [נדה] יז: ד"ה אפילו]

התם

עין משפט נר מצוה

ב א מיי' פי"ח מהל' שבת הלכה כו:
ג ב מיי' שם:
ד ג מיי' שם:
ה ד מיי' שם הל' כז:
ו ה מיי' שם:

רבינו חננאל

ולא תימא בטולי מבטלא למחשבתו אלא כל העושה על דעת מחשבתו ראשונה הוא עושה אמר רב יהודה אמר שמואל מחייב היה רבי מאיר אף במוציא חטה אחת לזריעה פי' הני מילי לענין המצניע אפילו הצניע חטה אחת והוציאה [חייב] וההיא דתנן באידך פרקין זרעוני גינה פחות מגרוגרת ותנן זרע קישואין ודלועין ופול המצרי שנים שיעורין דעלמא דלאו למצניעין שאין אדם מוציא ניטה אחת לזריעה אבל המצניע אפי' אחת חייב עליה וכל אדם שהוציאו סתם בשלא הצניעו אינו חייב עליו אלא כשיעור אע"פ[שהצניע הראשון] ואינו מתחייב במחשבת הראשון ומתניתין דלא כרבי שמעון בן אלעזר אבל אם הוציאו השני מדעת המצניע הראשון חייב ואם הוציא כגרוגרת שהוא כשיעור הוצאה [לאכילה] ומעיקרא היתה מחשבתו לאכילה ונמלך עליה לזריעה או לזריעה ונמלך עליה לאכילהחייב ולא אמרינן צריך שתהא עקירה והנחה בחדא מחשבה ובעיי דרבא לא איפשטו. הוציא חצי גרוגרת לזריעה ותפחה והיא כגרוגרת ונמלך עליה לאכילה בעידנא דעקירה הוה מחייב אמחשבתו ושיעור למחשבתו הואי ובעידנא דהנחה נמי שיעורא היא למחשבתו שבאותה שעה ואילו אשתיק ולא חשיב עליה מחייב אמחשב' דזריעה השתא נמי מחייב הוציא כגרוגרת לאכילה והיתה כשיעור בשעת עקירה וכשצמקה וחסרה נמלך עליה לזריעה דמחייב עליה נמי בשעת הנחה ובתר השתא אזלינן ומחייב אבל אם הוציא כגרוגרת לאכילה וצמקה וחזרה ותפחה ועדיין מחשבתו כדהות אע"פ דבעת עקירה יש בה כשיעור כיון שחסרת בין כך וכך מספקא לן יש דחוי אצל שבת או אין דחוי אצל שבת וקיימא בתיקו.ועקר דהא מלתא דטולה עקירה והנחה במחשבה דאיסורא דקאמרינן (לעיל ד' ה' ב') אמר רב ספרא א"ר אמי א"ר יוחנן המפנה חפצים מזוית לזוית ונמלך עליהן [והוציאן] פטור שלא היתה עקירה משעה ראשונה לכך ומפרשא נמי בגמ' דואלו נערות. בעא מיניה רבא מרב נחמן זרק כזית תרומה לבית טמא מהו (ורמי) כגון שורק מרה"ר לרה"י אי נמי מרשו' היחיד לרה"ר ורשות הרבים באמצע [ושאלינן] למאי קא בעי רבא הא בעיי אי לענין לעולם לענין שבת וכגון [ש]לאו דקא מצטרף לענין [ט]ומאה

שבת כגרוגרת בעינן שאם הוציא אוכלין פחות מכגרוגרת פטור אי לענין טומאה כביצה אוכלין בעינן שאם טימא תרומה פחות מכביצה פטור האי כזית לענין מאי קא מיבעי ליה לרבא ואהדרינן לעולם לענין שבת וכגון שורק לאותו בית טמא תרומה פחות מכביצה ואיתא התם וזרק עכשיו כזית שהוא משלימו לההוא דאיתיה התם לכביצה מאי מדמצטרף לענין טומאה קא מחייב עליה נמי לענין שבת ואי לאו דקא מצטרף לענין טומאה ומחייב עליה לא איחייב עליה לענין שבת ומשום דקא מחשב ליה מחייב כי האי דסוף הזורק יש אוכל אכילה אחת וחייב עליה ארבע חטאות ואשם טמא שאכל חלב והוא נותר מן המוקדשין ביה"כ ר"מ אומר אם היתה שבת והוציא חייב אמרו לו אינו השם ואמרינן עלה אמאי הא אין דרך הוצאה בכך ומהדרינן כיון דאחשביה מחייב הכא נמי הכין או דלמא כל לענין שבת כגרוגרת בעינן א"ל ר"נ תנינא אבא שאול אומר שתי הלחם

מסורת הש"ס

לעיל ע. זבחים מז.

[פסחים לג: נדה יז.]

הגהות הב"ח

(א) רש"י ד"ה התם וכו' ושיעור למחשבתו שניה: (ב) ד"ה יש דיחוי וכו' לא מיחייב חטאת מי: (ג) תוס' ד"ה אי לענין וכו' דתניא מכל האוכל מלמד שמטמא בכל שהוא:

גליון הש"ס

גמ' עד דאיכא כזית. עיין עירובין דף ע"ב ע"ב תד"ה אבל: שם ותפחה ונמלך עליה. עי' מנחות דף נד ע"א תד"ה דמעיקרא: שם וצמקה ונמלך. עיין לעיל עז ע"א תד"ה ועוד: שם וכגון דאיכא פחות מכביצה אוכלין. עיין משנה למלך פ"ד מהל' טו"א: תוס' ד"ה אי לענין. משמע דלא מקבל אוכל טומאה. עי' זבחים דף לא. תד"ה אר"ה:

נ"ל לא קפיד אלא כולם בקיומא כו' רש"ל

[נ"ל דתני בתוספתא שהרי הוא שם פ"ט: ולדרכ' בתוס' פ"ב דטבול יום ליתא וכו' ה"ג בתוס' פסחים שם ד"ה סיג רש"י]

רב נסים גאון

פי' למאי אי לענין שבת כגרוגרת בעינן אי לענין טומאה כביצה אוכלין בעינן. אימא כגרוגרת להוצאת שבת הא אמור בכמה מקומות במשנה (דף עו) המוציא אוכלין כגרוגרת והרבה כזה ואסמכתא דילה מקרא דכתיב (דברים ח) ארץ חטה ושעורה וגפן ותאנה ורמון ואמרו תאנה כגרוגרת להוצאת שבת וכביצה לענין טומאת אוכלין בתורת כהנים [פ' שמיני] אוכל יטמא מלמד שהוא מיטמא בכל שהוא* ת"ל אשר יאכל הא אינו מיטמא אלא בכביצה ובפרק יום הכפורים (יומא פ) תניא ר' אומר כל איסורין שבתורה בכזית חוץ מטומאת אוכלין כו' וטומאת אוכלין מנלן דאמר ר' אבהו אמר ר' אלעזר אמר קרא (ויקרא יא) מכל האוכל אשר יאכל אוכל שאתה יכול לאוכלו בבת אחת ושיערו חכמים שאין בית הבליעה מחזיק יותר מביצת תרנגולת והזכרנו דבר זה בברכות (ופי אל) משנה במסכת מעילה בפרק קודשי מזבח (דף יז) שנינו כל האוכלין מצטרפין לפסול את הגויה בכחצי פרס ומזון ב' סעודות לעירוב וכביצה לטמא טומאת אוכלין וכגרוגרת להוצאת שבת וככותבת ליום הכפורים:

*) יכול יטמא לאחרים בכ"ש

התם

עין משפט
נר מצוה

ז א ב מיי' פי"ד מהל' שבת הלכה יד:
ח ג ד מיי' פי"ב מהל' שבת הלכה יא:
ט ה מיי' פ"ג מהל' גניבה הל' ב טוש"ע ח"מ סי' שנא:
י ו מיי' פי"ג מהל' שבת הלכה יא:

רבינו חננאל

ולחם הפנים שיעורן כגרוגרת וקא דייק מינה רב נחמן דהא מפיק מן המקדש בשבת שתי הלחם ולחם הפנים אע"ג דמפסיל לענין יוצא בכזית לא קא מחייב לענין שבת בשבת עד דהוי כגרוגרת ואם איתא דכיון דאחשביה מיחייב ואע"ג דפחות משיעור הוה מחייב בשבת על כזית בהוצאת שתי הלחם ולחם הפנים ואהדר ליה רבא הכי השתא התם מדאפקיה חוץ לחומת עזרה איפסיל ליה ביוצא ועדיין לא מחייב ליה לענין שבת כל עיקר עד דמפיק ליה לרה"ר אבל הכא לענין האי בעיא דהוא זרק כזית תרומה לבית טמא להשלים אוכל לכביצה שבת וטומאה בהדי הדדי קא אתיין ולא איפשים: חזר והכניסו אינו חייב אלא כשיעור מידעם דאחשביה והצניעו ואפקיה לצורך ואע"ג דלית ביה כשיעור הוצאה מחייב עליה כד מפיק ליה בשבת אי לא איכוין ליה כשיעור צורכיה וחזר והכניסן בחול אם חזר אח"כ לשבת אחרת והוציאו סתם לא מחייב עליה עד דהוי ביה כשיעור הוצאה אא"כ הוא שחזר והכניסו בתורת מצניע אבל אם הכניסו סתם כגון שזרקו לאוצר אע"פ שישנו(בו) [מקומו] ניכר הוא לא אמרינן כיון שהוא מכיר את מקומו במלתיה קאי וחייב על הוצאתו אלא בטוליה בטליה להניא הצנעה קמייתא ודיניה בכל מידעם דלא מחייב עליה אלא בשיעורו: מתני' המוציא אוכלין ונתנן על האסקופה אם האסקופה שנתן עליה רה"ר [חייב] ואם רשות היחיד פטור הא אם חזר והוציאן ממנה לרה"ר חייב [אבל אם האסקופה כרמלית היא דרה"ר עומדת לפניה אם נחו האוכלין בכרמלית וחזר ועקרן מכרמלית והוציאן לרה"ר פטור] אבל אם לא נחו בכרמלית אע"פ שעברו מרה"י לרה"י דרך כרמלית חייב ואשמעינן מתניתין דלא כבן עזאי דתניא המוציא מחנות לפלטיא דרך סטיו חייב ובן עזאי פוטר והוקי האסקופה מפורשין בגמ' דיציאות השבת היכי הויא רה"ר והיכי הויא רה"י והיכי הויא כרמלית. קופה שהיא מליאה פירות ונתונה על האסקופה החיצונה אע"פ שרוב פירות מבחוץ פטור עד שיוציא את כל הקופה סבר חזקיה בקופה של קישואין ושל דלועין מתני' שעדיין מקצת כל קישות וכל דלעת בפנים ולא נתקם מבפנים לחוץ אבל קופה שהיא מלאה פירות אחרים כגון אגוזים ושקדים ותאנים ורמונים וכיוצא בהן וכ"ש חרדל כיון שיש מן הפירות גופן מה שיצא כולן לחוץ יש בו שיעור גרוגרת חייב ואע"פ שהן בתוך הכלי ומקצת הכלי עדיין בפנים ויכול למושכו לפנים ולהכניסו וממילא מה שהוא בחוץ נמשך עם הקופה ונכנס אע"פ שלא נגע בו אלמא קסבר חזקיה אגד כלי לאו שמיה אגד ואית ליה למידק מן מתניתין הדין א"ר זירא דתנן אע"פ שרוב פירות מבחוץ פטור רובה של קישות ורובה של דלעת אבל אם הקישות כולה או הגרוגרת כולה בחוץ חייב ואע"פ שהוא בתוך הכלי ומקצת הכלי בפנים ור' יוחנן סבר אפילו קופה מליאה חרדל ויצא רובה לחוץ כיון שהוא מפורצת ואית ליה נדפאני איגד כלי שמיה איגד ועדיין אגודה היא לפנים ופטור עד שתנתק כולה לחוץ ודייק מן

יוצא בכזית לענין שבת נמי בכזית הכי השתא התם מדאפקיה חוץ לחומת העזרה איפסיל ליה ביוצא אשבת לא מיחייב עד דמפיק ליה לרה"ר הכא שבת וטומאה בהדי הדדי קאתיין: חזר והכניסו אינו חייב אלא כשיעורו: פשיטא אמר אביי הכא במאי עסקינן כגון שזרקו לאוצר ומקומו ניכר מהו דתימא כיון דמקומו ניכר במילתיה קמייתא קאי קמ"ל מדזרקיה לאוצר בטולי בטליה:

מתני' *המוציא אוכלין ונתנן על האסקופה בין שחזר והוציאן בין שהוציאן אחר פטור מפני שלא עשה מלאכתו בבת אחת קופה שהיא מליאה פירות ונתנה על אסקופה החיצונה אע"פ שרוב פירות מבחוץ פטור עד שיוציא את כל הקופה:

גמ' האי אסקופה מאי אילימא אסקופ' רה"ר פטור הא קא מפיק מרה"י לרה"ר אלא אסקופה רה"י בין שחזר והוציאן בין שהוציאן אחר פטור הא קא מפיק מרה"י לרה"ר אלא אסקופה כרמלית והא קמ"ל טעמא דנח בכרמלית הא לא נח בכרמלית מיחייב מתני' דלא כבן עזאי דתניא *המוציא מחנות לפלטיא דרך סטיו חייב ובן עזאי פוטר: קופה שהיא מליאה כו': אמר חזקיה לא שנו אלא בקופה מליאה קישואין ודלועין אבל מליאה חרדל חייב אלמא קסבר אגד כלי לא שמיה אגד ור' יוחנן אמר אפי' מליאה חרדל פטור אלמא קסבר אגד כלי שמיה אגד א"ר זירא מתני' דלא כחזקיה דיקא ודלא כר' יוחנן דיקא דלא כחזקיה דיקא דקתני עד שיוציא את כל הקופה טעמא דכל הקופה הא כל הפירות פטור אלמא קסבר אגד כלי שמיה אגד כרבי יוחנן לא דיקא דקתני אע"פ שרוב פירות בחוץ טעמא דרוב פירות הא כל פירות אע"ג דאגידא קופה מגואי חייב אלמא קסבר אגד כלי לא שמיה אגד ואלא קשיא חזקיה מתרץ לטעמי' ור' יוחנן מתרץ לטעמיה חזקיה מתרץ לטעמיה עד שיוציא את כל הקופה בד"א בקופה מליאה קישואין ודלועין אבל מליאה חרדל נעשה כמי שהוציא את כל הקופה וחייב ר"י מתרץ לטעמיה אע"פ שרוב פירות בחוץ ולא רוב פירות בלבד אלא אפילו כל פירות פטור עד שיוציא את כל הקופה מיתיבי *המוציא קופת הרוכלין ונתנה על אסקופה החיצונה אע"פ שרוב מינין בחוץ פטור עד שיוציא את כל הקופה קס"ד בצררי קשיא לחזקיה אמר לך חזקיה הכא במאי עסקינן באורנסי מתיב רב ביבי בר אביי *הגונב כיס בשבת חייב שכבר נתחייב בגניבה קודם שיבא לידי איסור שבת היה מגרר ויוצא פטור שהרי איסור גניבה ואיסור שבת באין כאחד ואי סלקא דעתך אגד כלי שמיה אגד קדים ליה איסור גניבה לאיסור שבת אי דאפקיה דרך פיו הכי נמי הכא במאי עסקינן דאפקיה דרך שוליו והאיכא מקום חלמה
דאי

*שיעורן כגרוגרת. אם הוליאן לרה"ר בשבת: ואמאי לימא. בכזית מיחייב דהא חשיבה הולאה לענין איפסולי ביולא דאי אכליה הוא עובר בלאו דכל שבקודש פסול בא הכתוב ליתן לא תעשה על אכילתו ואכילה בכזית: חוץ לחומת עזרה. להיקף החיל שלפני עזרת נשים או לעזרת נשים שהיא בחיל: בהדי הדדי אתיין. דעד דאתנח ונלטרף עם השאר *(לא קבל טומאתו מן האויר דהא) לא הוי ביה שיעור: פשיטא. כיון דלא זרעיה בטליה ממחשבה קמייתא והוה ליה ככל אדם: אמר אביי מתניתין בשלא נמלך עליו בפירוש אלא שזרקו לאולר עם פירותיו וזהו ביטול מחשבה מדלא אלנעיה לחודיה ולמיתנייה אילטריך כגון שמקומו ניכר שלא נתערב יפה עם השאר והרי הוא ניכר ביניהם: מ"ד כיון דמקומו ניכר במילתא קמייתא קאי. דהוה ליה כמאן דאלנעיה לחודיה: ה"ג קמ"ל מדזרקיה לאולר בטולי בטליה: **מתני'** על האסקופה. בגמרא מוקי לה באסקופה כרמלית: מלאכתו בבת אחת. עקירה ממקום חיוב והנחה במקום חיוב (א) [והכא] הוה ליה עקירה ממקום חיוב והנחה במקום פטור והדר עקריה ממקום פטור ואנחיה במקום חיוב: עד שיוליא. כלומר אלא אם כן הוליא בראשונה כל הקופה ובגמ' מפרש לה: **גמ'** אי נימא איסקופה רה"ר. כגון גבוהה ט' ורחב ארבעה (ב) ורבים מכתפין עליו דחזיא לרבים לכתופי כדאמר בפ"ק (דף ח.): רשות היחיד. גבוהה י' ורחבה ד' כי חזר והוליאה ליחייב דאיכא עקירה מרה"י והנחה ברה"ר: אלא אסקופה כרמלית. מג' ועד ט' [ולא ט' בכלל] ואיכא מקורה ורחבה ד': הא לא נח מיחייב. ואע"ג דהעבירו דרך כרמלית ולא אמר מהלך כעומד דמי ואיכא הנחת גופו דהוי כהנחת חפץ: מחנות. רה"י: פלטיא. רה"ר: סטיו. מקום מוקף אילטבאות לישב והוא כרמלית דלא בקעיה ביה רבים להדיא: קישואין ודילועין. שהן ארוכין ועדיין יש מהם בפנים וכל מה דאגיד לגואי כל דהו לאו הולאה היא: אבל מליאה חרדל. שהרי יש ממנו כולן בחוץ אע"פ שעל ידי הכלי הוא נאגד לצד פנים חייב דאגד כלי לא שמיה אגד לומר לא יצא כולו ועדיין אגדו בידו בפנים זהו לשון הש"ס לענין שבת כל כמה דלא נפיק ליה כוליה קרי ליה אגוד דאגודו שייך לגבי רשות קמא: בד"א. דעד שיוליא את כל הקופה: במליאה קישואין. שהן ממלאין בארכן את כל רוחב הקופה וכל כמה דלא נפק כולה קופה לא נפיק איכהו (ג): ר' יוחנן מתרץ לטעמיה. תרתי קתני מתני' לא זו אף זו דסיפא [מוכחא] דקתני כל הקופה ולא קתני כל הפירות והכי קאמר אף על פי שרוב הפירות מבחוץ או אפילו כל הפירות מבחוץ נמי פטור עד שיוליא כל הקופה: רוכלין. מוכרי בשמים: קס"ד בצררי. שהיה בה לרור של בשמים שחוקין דכי אפקה למקלת קופה נפיק בההיא פורתא כמה לרורות כולן וקתני פטור אלמא אגד כלי שמיה אגד: באורנסי. אגודות שרשין ארוכין או קנה או קילופה של קנמון שהן ארוכין: הגונב כיס בשבת חייב. בתשלומין ואע"פ שנדון בנפשו שכבר נתחייב בגניבה בשעה שהגביה הכיס בבית הבעלים: היה מגרר ויולא. שלא קנאה בהגבהה אלא בהולאה מבית הבעלים: פטור. מתשלומין: שהרי איסור שבת כו'. ובכתובות פריך אי דאפקיה לרה"ר איסור גניבה ליכא דרשות הרבים לאו מקום קנייה היא ומוקי לה בלדי רה"ר אי נמי שלירוף ידו למטה מג' וקבלה: קדים ליה איסור גניבה לאיסור שבת. דכיון שהוליאו מקלתו קנה כל המעות שמבחוץ שיכול להוליאו דרך פיו ולענין שבת מפטר דאגידי גבי רשות היחיד על ידי הכלי: דרך שוליו. וכיון דלא מצי למשקל לא קני בהגבהתו: הא איכא מקום חלמה. מקום התפירה שיכול לקרוע ולהוליא. חלמה שולדורא כמו בהעור והרוטב (חולין קכג.) שאני עור דחלים:
מפקע

אתון בהדי הדדי ודוקא נקט כזית תרומה דאיכא איסור לאוכלו בטומאה אבל פחות מכזית לא וכן כזית חולין כיון דאין איסור לאוכלו בטומאה לא שייך לומר מיגו דמלטרף לענין טומאה מלטרף לענין שבת וא"ת מ"ש כזית תרומה מחצי זית דהא בתרומה טמאה ליכא אלא עשה כדמוכח בהערל (יבמות דף עג:) דהאוכלה בטומאת עצמה אינו לוקה וחצי זית נמי הא קי"ל כר' יוחנן דחצי שיעור אסור מן התורה (יומא עד.) וי"ל דמ"מ כזית חמיר טפי שהרי זית הוא שיעור ללקות עליו בכל מקום ודוקא לבית טמא אבל לבית טהור לא אע"ג דחשיב ללקות עליו זר האוכלו מ"מ לא חשיב בפחות מגרוגרת כיון דאיסור זרות לא בא ע"י הולאה זו: *פחות מכביצה אוכלין. ה"ה דה"מ למימר דאיכא כבילה אוכלין שאין הם לריכין ללירוף וכזית לבד לריך ללירופן א"נ אור"י דנקט דוקא פחות מכבילה אבל כבילה אפשר דאין מלטרף כיון שקודם לירוף כבר מטמא דילמא שבע לה טומאה דבעיא היא בהקומץ רבה (מנחות כד.) גבי עשרון שחלקו ונטמא אחד מהן והניחו בכלי ונגע טבול יום בטמא מהו מי אמר שבע לה טומאה ולא נטמא הטהור אע"ג דאם היו שניהם טהורים ונגע טבול יום באחד מהן שניהם טמאין דכלי מלרף מה שבתוכו לקדש השתא דשבע לה טומאה לא מלטריף או דילמא לא אמרי' שבע לה טומאה ומשום דהתם מספקא לן נקט פחות מכבילה: קס"ד בלררי קשיא לחזקיה. ואלימא ליה ממתני' משום דהתם קופת הרוכלים אית ביה לררי וכ"ש מדקתני ובה מינין הרבה ומשני באורנסי ובה מינין הרבה אורחא דמילתא נקט וכל המינין ארוכים:
דאי

מסורת הש"ס

שייך מענ"א

רש"ל מ"ז ואינו מוכח די"ל דקאי אקבלת טומאה לטמא אחרים ועי' במהרש"א

לעיל ס:

נ"ל המוציא קופת הרוכלין ובה מינין הרבה ונתנה כו' רש"ל

ב"ק סו. סנהדרין עב. כתובות לא. [תוספ' דב"ק פ"ט]

הגהות הב"ח

(א) רש"י ד"ה מלאכתו וכו' במקום חיוב אבל הכא דהוו ליה: (ב) ד"ה אי נימא וכו' ארבעה. נ"ב ע"ל בפ"ק ד' ח ע"א פי' רש"י דלא בעי' ד' אלא בין רחב בין קצר: (ג) ד"ה במלאהקישואין וכו' איכהו כולהו קס"ד:

גליון הש"ס

גמ' אלמא קסבר אגד כלי שמיה אגד. ע' פסחים דף פה ע"ב תד"ה בנגררין: שם אי דאפקיה דרך פיו ה"נ. עי' בכתו"ש פ"א דכ"מ סימן כג:

רב נסים גאון

התם מדאפקיה חוץ לחומת העזרה איפסיל ליה ביוצא. עיקר זה בתורת כהנים שכל היוצא מן הקדשים חוץ למחיצתו נפסל וישרף באש כמו שנאמר בפירוש פסוק (ויקרא ז) והבשר אשר יגע בכל טמא לא יאכל באש ישרף אין לי טעון שריפה אלא הטמא והנותר ומנין לנשחטה בלילה ושנשפך דמה חוץ לקלעים הלן והיוצא ת"ל לא יאכל כי קודש הוא כל שהוא קודש [פסול] טעון שריפה הבשר לרבות בשר הפנימי שהוא מותר והלא דין הוא הואיל והטמא פסול והיוצא פסול מה הטמא אם נטמא מקצתו כולו פסול אף היוצא אם יצא מקצתו יהא כולו פסול ת"ל והבשר לרבות בשר הפנימי שהוא מותר מיכן אמרו אבר שיצא מקצתו חוץ לחומה בפסחים חותך עד שמגיע לעצם וקולף עד לפרק ומתירו מן הפרק ובמוקדשין גורד כל מקום שהוא יוצא שאין בהם [משום] שבירת העצם ובפרק כיצד צולין את הפסח (פסחים דף פב) שנינו הפסח שיצא או שנטמא ישרף מיד ואמרו בתלמוד בשלמא נטמא דכתיב והבשר אשר יגע בכל טמא אלא יוצא מנלן אלא כל שפסולו בקודש בשריפה הלכתא גמירי לה:
המוציא

let us say, since in respect of [91b] its going out,[11] [the standard is] the size of an olive, in respect of the Sabbath too it is the size of an olive?[12] How compare! There, immediately one takes it without the wall of the Temple Court it becomes unfit as that which has gone out, whereas there is no culpability for the [violation of the] Sabbath until he carries it into public ground. But here the
a Sabbath and defilement come simultaneously.[1]

IF HE CARRIES IT BACK AGAIN, HE IS LIABLE ONLY IN ACCORDANCE WITH ITS STANDARD. But that is obvious?—Said Abaye: What case do we discuss here? E.g., if he throws it on to a store, but its place is [distinctly] recognizable.[2] You might argue, since its place is recognizable, it stands in its original condition;[3] he [the Tanna] therefore teaches us that by throwing it on to a store he indeed nullifies it.[4]

MISHNAH. IF ONE CARRIES OUT FOOD AND PLACES IT ON THE THRESHOLD, WHETHER HE [HIMSELF] SUBSEQUENTLY CARRIES IT OUT [INTO THE STREET] OR ANOTHER DOES SO, HE IS NOT CULPABLE, BECAUSE THE [WHOLE] ACT WAS NOT PERFORMED AT ONCE. [IF ONE CARRIES OUT] A BASKET WHICH IS FULL OF PRODUCE AND PLACES IT ON THE OUTER THRESHOLD, THOUGH MOST OF THE PRODUCE IS WITHOUT,[5] HE IS NOT CULPABLE UNLESS HE CARRIES OUT THE WHOLE BASKET.

GEMARA. What is this threshold? Shall we say, a threshold that is public ground? [How state then] 'HE IS NOT CULPABLE'! Surely he has carried out from private into public ground? Again, if it is a threshold that is private ground, [how state then] 'WHETHER HE [HIMSELF] SUBSEQUENTLY CARRIES IT OUT [INTO THE STREET] OR ANOTHER DOES SO, HE IS NOT CULPABLE'? Surely he carries out from private into public ground? Rather the threshold is a *karmelith*,[6] and he [the Tanna] informs us this: The reason [that he is not culpable] is because it rested in the *karmelith;* but if it did not rest in the *karmelith* he
b would be liable,[1] our Mishnah not agreeing with Ben 'Azzai. For it was taught: If one carries [an article] from a shop to an open place via a colonnade, he is liable; but Ben 'Azzai holds him not liable.[2]

A BASKET WHICH IS FULL OF PRODUCE. Hezekiah said: They learnt this only of a basket full of cucumbers and gourds;[3] but if it is full of mustard, he is culpable.[4] This proves that the tie of the vessel is not regarded as a tie.[5] But R. Joḥanan maintained: Even if it is full of mustard he is not culpable, which proves that he holds that the tie of the vessel is regarded as a tie. R. Zera observed: Our Mishnah implies that it is neither as Hezekiah nor as R. Joḥanan. 'It implies that it is not as Hezekiah', for it states: UNLESS HE CARRIES OUT THE WHOLE BASKET. Thus only the whole *basket;* but if all the produce [is without] he is not culpable, which shows that he holds that the tie of the vessel is regarded as a tie. 'It implies that it is not as R. Joḥanan', for it states: THOUGH MOST OF THE PRODUCE IS WITHOUT: thus only *most* of the produce, but if *all* the produce [is without], though the tie of the basket is within, he is liable, which shows that he holds that the tie of a vessel is not regarded as a tie. But in that case there is a difficulty?[6]—Hezekiah reconciles it in accordance with his view, while R. Joḥanan reconciles it in accordance with his view. Hezekiah reconciles it in accordance with his view: 'UNLESS HE CARRIES OUT THE WHOLE BASKET. When is that? in the case of a basket full of cucumbers and gourds. But if it is full of mustard, it is treated as though HE CARRIED OUT THE WHOLE BASKET, and he is culpable'. While R. Joḥanan reconciles it according to his view. 'THOUGH MOST OF THE PRODUCE IS WITHOUT, and not only most of the produce, but even if all the produce [is without] he is not culpable, UNLESS HE CARRIES OUT THE WHOLE BASKET'.

An objection is raised: If one carries out a spice pedlar's basket and places it on the outer threshold, though most of the kinds [of the spices] are without he is not culpable, unless he carries out the whole basket. Now this was assumed to refer to grains
c [of spices],[1] which is a difficulty according to Hezekiah?—Hezekiah answers you: The reference here is to prickly shrubs.[2]

R. Bibi b. Abaye raised an objection: If one steals a purse on the Sabbath, he is bound to make restitution, since his liability for theft arises before his desecrating of the Sabbath. But if he drags it out of the house he is exempt, since the interdict of theft and the interdict of the Sabbath come simultaneously.[3] But if you think that the tie of a vessel is regarded as a tie,[4] the interdict of theft precedes that of the Sabbath?[5]—If he carries it out by way of its opening,[6] that indeed is so. Here we discuss the case where he carries it out by way of its bottom.[7] But there is the

(11) Beyond the walls of the Temple Court.—These must be consumed within the Temple precincts; if they are taken beyond that they become unfit for food, and the priest who eats them violates a negative injunction. (12) And since we do not reason thus, we see that there is no connection between the standard of culpability for carrying out on the Sabbath and that required for other purposes.

a (1) As it comes to rest the action of throwing is completed, and simultaneously the standard for defilement is reached. (2) He did not actually state that he had changed his mind, but let it be inferred from the fact that he threw it on to a store of other grain. (3) As being destined for separate sowing. (4) I.e., it loses its separate identity, and becomes merely part of the store. (5) In the street. (6) *Supra* 6a.

b (1) Though it was carried out by way of a *karmelith*. (2) V. *supra* 5b. (3) These are long, and are still partly within. (4) Since some of it is entirely in the street. (5) We do not regard all the mustard as one because it is tied together, as it were, by the basket, and treat it the same as cucumbers and gourds. [The 'tie of a vessel' in connection with Sabbath is a technical phrase denoting that side of the vessel in the direction of the domain whence it is carried out (Rashi)]. (6) The Mishnah being self-contradictory.

c (1) E.g., it contained ground spices, which makes it similar to a basket of mustard. (2) 'ῥάμνος, a kind of prickly shrub used for medicinal purposes and carried in long bundles (Jast.). (3) V. Sanh., 72a, n. c1. (4) So that the vessel is still regarded as being within. (5) I.e., he violates the former before the latter. For as soon as part of the purse is outside, all the money within that part is regarded as stolen, since he can take it out through the mouth of the purse as it lies thus. (6) The mouth or opening preceding. (7) Through which he cannot remove the coins; hence he has not stolen them yet.

place of its seams, [92a] which he can rip open[8] if he desires and extract [the coins]?—The reference is to a bar of metal.[9] But since it has straps,[10] he [the thief] can take it out up to its opening, untie [the straps] and take out the bar,[11] whilst the straps [still] unite it to within?[12]—It refers to one that has no straps. Alternatively, it has straps, but they are wound round about it [the purse].[13]

And Raba said likewise: They learnt this only of a basket full of cucumbers and gourds, but if it is full of mustard he is culpable. This proves that he holds that the tie of a vessel is not regarded as a tie. Abaye ruled: Even if it is full of mustard he is not culpable, [which] proves that he holds that the tie of a vessel is regarded as a tie. Abaye [subsequently] adopted Raba's view, while Raba adopted Abaye's view. Now Abaye is self-contradictory, and Raba likewise. For it was taught: If one carries out produce into
a the street,—Abaye said: If in his hand, he is culpable;[1] if in a vessel, he is not culpable.[2] But Raba ruled: If in his hand, he is not culpable;[3] if in a vessel, he is culpable?[4]—Reverse it. 'If in his hand, he is culpable'? But we learnt: If the master stretches his hand without and the poor man takes [an object] from it, or places [an article] therein and he carries it inside, both are exempt?—There it is above three [handbreadths],[5] but here it is below three.[6]

MISHNAH. IF ONE CARRIES OUT [AN ARTICLE], WHETHER WITH HIS RIGHT OR WITH HIS LEFT [HAND], IN HIS LAP OR ON HIS SHOULDER, HE IS CULPABLE, BECAUSE THUS WAS THE CARRYING OF THE CHILDREN OF KOHATH.[7] IN A BACK-HANDED MANNER,[8] [E.G.,] WITH HIS FOOT, IN HIS MOUTH, WITH HIS ELBOW, IN HIS EAR, IN HIS HAIR, IN HIS BELT WITH
b ITS OPENING DOWNWARDS,[1] BETWEEN HIS BELT AND HIS SHIRT, IN THE HEM OF HIS SHIRT, IN HIS SHOES OR SANDALS, HE IS NOT CULPABLE, BECAUSE HE HAS NOT CARRIED [IT] OUT AS PEOPLE [GENERALLY] CARRY OUT.

GEMARA. R. Eleazar said: If one carries out a burden above ten handbreadths [from the street level], he is culpable,[2] for thus was the carrying of the children of Kohath. And how do we know that the carrying of the children of Kohath [was thus]? Because it is written, *by the tabernacle, and by the altar round about:*[3] the altar is likened to the Tabernacle: just as the Tabernacle was ten cubits [high], so was the altar ten cubits high. And how do we know this of the Tabernacle itself?—Because it is written, *Ten cubits shall be the length of a board,*[4] and it is [also] said, *and he spread the tent over the Tabernacle,*[5] whereon Rab commented: Moses our Teacher spread it. Hence you may learn that the Levites were ten cubits tall.[6] Now it is well known that any burden that is carried on staves, a third is above [the porter's height] and two thirds are below: thus it is found that it was very much raised.[7] Alternatively, [it is deduced] from the Ark. For a Master said: The Ark was nine [handbreadths high], and the mercy-seat was one handbreadth; hence we have ten. And it is well known that any burden that is carried on staves, a third is above and two thirds are below: thus it is found that it was very much raised.[8] But deduce it from Moses?—Perhaps Moses was different, because a Master said: The *Shechinah* rests only on a wise man, a strong man, a
c wealthy man and a tall man.[1]

Rab said on R. Ḥiyya's authority: If one carries out a burden on his head[2] on the Sabbath, he is liable to a sin-offering, because the people of Huẓal[3] do thus. Are then the people of Huẓal the world's majority![4] Rather if stated, it was thus stated: Rab said on R. Ḥiyya's authority: If a Huẓalite carries out a burden on his head on the Sabbath, he is liable to a sin-offering, because his fellow-citizens do thus. But let his practice[5] be null by comparison with that of all men?[6] Rather if stated, it was thus stated: If one carries out a burden on his head, he is not culpable.

(8) [The seams of their purses were loosely sewn (Tosaf.)]. (9) And as long as part of it is within he has committed no theft. (10) To close it. (11) Whereby he has already committed the theft. (12) In respect of the Sabbath; hence he has not yet desecrated the Sabbath. (13) So that when he takes it out as far as its opening, the whole bag and straps are outside too.

a (1) Even if his body is in the house, because the tie of his body is not a tie in this respect. (2) If part of the utensil is within, as R. Joḥanan *supra* 91b; this contradicts Abaye's subsequent view. (3) The tie of the body is a tie. (4) [It was known to the redactors of the Talmud that this controversy took place after Abaye and Raba had retracted (Tosaf.)]. (5) And the exemption is because the same person did not effect both the removal and the depositing, not because of the tie of the body. (6) So that it is technically at rest; Cf. *supra* 5a, n. b6 (7) In connection with the Tabernacle in the wilderness, v. Num. VII, 9. The definition of forbidden labour on the Sabbath which involves culpability is learnt from the Tabernacle; v. *supra* 49b. (8) This is the idiom for anything done in an unusual way.

b (1) Of course, if the opening is on top such carrying would be quite usual. (2) Though the space there ranks as a place of non-culpability v. *supra* 6a. (3) Num. III, 26. (4) Ex. XXVI, 16. (5) Ibid. XL, 19. (6) It is now assumed that all Levites were as tall as Moses. (7) The Kohathites carried the altar on staves on their shoulders. Allowing for two thirds of the altar to swing below the top of their heads, the bottom of the altar would still be a third of ten cubits—i.e., three and one third cubits—from the ground, which is considerably more than ten handbreadths. (8) For allowing for Levites of the usual height, viz., three cubits = eighteen handbreadths, and two thirds of the Ark, i.e., six and two thirds handbreadths swinging below the level of their heads, its bottom would still be eleven and one third handbreadths above the ground.—This alternative rejects the deduction from Moses.

c (1) Hence Moses' height may have been exceptional. V. Ned., 38a, n. a4; also Gorfinkle, '*The Eight chapters of Maimonides*', p. 80, for an interesting though fanciful explanation of this passage. (2) Not holding it with his hands at all. (3) V. Sanh., 19a, n. b3. (4) To set the standard for all others. (5) Lit., 'mind'. (6) For since most people do not carry it thus, it is an unusual form of carriage.

מפקע. קורע: בנסכא. שהן חתיכות ארוכות וכל זמן שמקלקלן בפניס לא קנה: ופרכינן וכיון דאיכא שנצין. רצועות שקורין אשטולד"ן: מפיק ליה עד פומיה ושקיל. וכיון דמצי למשקליהו קני ולענין שבת לא מיחייב עד דמפיק להו לשנצין דעל ידו הוא אגוד לרה"י שהרי לא יצאו: ומכרכי עילויה. שאין יכול להוציאו (נ) בלא שנצין: קם אביי בשיטתיה כו'. שניהם חזרו בדבריהם והחליפום: ביד חייב. משילא הפירות ואע"פ שגופו ברשות היחיד ולא אמרינן אגד גופו שמיה אגד: בכלי פטור. כל זמן שיש מקצת הכלי בביתו: ביד פטור. דאגד גופו שמיה אגד דידו בתר גופו גרירא בכלי חייב וקשיא אתרוייהו למה שהחליפו שיטתן: התם למעלה מג'. וטעמא משום דלא נח ולא משום אגד גופה: והכא למטה מג'. דליכא למיפטרי' משום הנחה דכמונח דמי: **מתני'** שכן משא בני קהת. בכתף ישאו (במדבר ז) וימין ושמאל וחיק אורח ארעא ובשם רבינו יצחק בר יהודה מצאתי שאמר בשם רב האי שמפורש בהש"ס ירושלמי ופקודת אלעזר בן אהרן הכהן שמן המאור וקטורת הסמים ומנחת התמיד ושמן המשחה [שמן] אחד בימין [ושמן] אחד בשמאל והקטורת בחיקו והחביתין בכתף: מרפקו. אייסיל"א: פונדתו. אזור חלול: ופיה למטה. אין דרך הולאה בכך אבל פיה למעלה דרך הולאה: שפת חלוקו. שפה התחתונה: **גמ'** המוליא משאוי למעלה מי'. מעבירו באויר בידו ואינו על כתפו וגבוה מן הארץ [עשרה] קאמר דאי במונח על כתפו מתניתין היא והא דתנן (לקמן דף ק:) הזורק ד' אמות בכותל למעלה מעשרה כזורק באויר אלמא אין למעלה מעשרה רשות הרבים דווקא זורק אבל מעביר חייב דיליף מבני קהת במשכן: אשר על המשכן וגו'. בקלעי החצר משתעי: אף מזבח. גובהו י' אמות והוצרך לסובבו בקלעים של י' אמות רחב ומה אני מקיים וג' אמות קומתו (שמות כז) משפת סובב ולמעלה ומה אני מקיים וקומה ה' דקלעים משפת מזבח ולמעלה כך מפורש בזבחים (דף נט:) שהיו הקלעים ט"ו אמות: מכאן אתה למד. דקס"ד שאר הלוים נמי גביהי כמשה: תלתא מלעיל. וכיון דמזבח י' אמות והוא נושא בכתף כדכתיב (במדבר ז) ולבני קהת לא נתן (עגלות) וגו' והלוים י' אמות כי מדלו ליה תילתא למעלה מראשיהן או מכתיפו נמצא גבוה מן הארץ קרוב לשליש של י' אמות דהוו טובא טפי יותר מי' טפחים: ואיבעית אימא. לא גביהי לוים ולאו ממזבח גמרינן דשמא לוים לא גביהי אלא ז' אמות ואין משא דמזבח גבוה מן הארץ אלא ב' או ג' טפחים ומארון גמר לה ר' אלעזר: אשתכח דלמעלה מי' קאי. טובא אפילו אין גובהן של לוים אלא ג' אמות כמוטו הרי י"ח טפחים וארון אינו תלוי למטה מכתפותיהן אלא ו' טפחים וב' שלישי טפח אשתכח דגבוה י' ויותר: וליגמר ממשה. שפרש המשכן ונמצא דגובהן של לוים עשר אמות וכילף מלוים נושאי המזבח: דאמר מר. במסכת נדרים: אנשי הוצל. היו נושאין כדי מים ויין על ראשיהן ואין אוחזין אותם בידים:

תורה אור

דאי בעי מפקע ליה ושקיל בנסכא וכיון דאיכא שנצין מפיק ליה עד פומיה ושרי ושקיל ושנצין אגידי מגואי דליכא שנצין ואיבעית אימא דאית ליה ומכרכי עילויה וכן אמר רבא לא שנו אלא בקופה מלאה קישואין ודלועין אבל מלאה חרדל חייב אלמא קסבר אגד כלי לא שמיה אגד אביי אמר אפילו מלאה חרדל פטור אלמא קסבר אגד כלי שמיה אגד קם אביי בשיטתיה דרבא קם רבא בשיטתיה דאביי ורמי דאביי אדאביי ורמי דרבא אדרבא דאיתמר המוציא פירות לרה"ר אביי אמר ביד חייב בכלי פטור ורבא אמר ביד פטור בכלי חייב איפוך ביד חייב והתנן *פשט בעל הבית את ידו לחוץ ונטל העני מתוכה או שנתן לתוכה והכניס שניהן פטורין התם למעלה מג' הכא למטה מג': **מתני'** המוציא בין בימינו בין בשמאלו בתוך חיקו או על כתיפיו חייב שכן משא בני קהת כלאחר ידו ברגלו בפיו *ובמרפקו באזנו ובשערו ובפונדתו ופיה למטה בין פונדתו לחלוקו *ובשפת חלוקו במנעלו בסנדלו פטור שלא הוציא כדרך המוציאין: **גמ'** אמר ר"א *המוציא משאוי למעלה מעשרה טפחים חייב שכן משא בני קהת ומשא בני קהת מנלן דכתיב °על המשכן ועל המזבח סביב *מקיש מזבח למשכן מה משכן י' אמות אף מזבח י' אמות ומשכן גופיה מנלן דכתיב °עשר אמות אורך הקרש וכתיב °ויפרוש את האהל על המשכן *ואמר רב משה רבינו פרשו מכאן אתה למד גובהן של לויים עשר אמות וגמירי דכל טונא דמידלי במוטות תילתא מלעיל ותרי תילתי מלתחת אישתכח דהוה מידלי טובא ואיבעית אימא מארון *דאמר מר ארון תשעה *וכפורת טפח הרי כאן י' וגמירי דכל טונא דמידלי במוטות תילתא מלעיל ותרי תילתי מלרע אישתכח דלמעלה מי' הוה קאי וליגמר ממשה דילמא משה שאני *דאמר מר אין השכינה שורה אלא על חכם גבור ועשיר ובעל קומה אמר רב משום רבי חייא המוציא משאוי בשבת על ראשו חייב חטאת שכן אנשי הוצל עושין כן ואנשי הוצל *רובא דעלמא אלא אי איתמר הכי איתמר אמר רב משום רבי חייא אחד מבני הוצל שהוציא משוי על ראשו בשבת חייב שכן בני עירו עושין כן ותיבטל דעתו אצל כל אדם אלא אי איתמר הכי איתמר המוציא משוי על ראשו פטור

ואת"ל

במדבר ג | שמות כו | שם מ | [ב"ב כה.] | [נדרים לח.]

דאי בעי מפקע ליה. נראה לר"י שכיסין שלהם לא היו תפורות בחוזק כמו שלנו ולהכי פריך ממקום התפירה ולא ממקום אחר: **ורמי** דאביי אדאביי. °קים ליה להש"ס דהך מילתא דמייתי איתמר בתר דהדור בהו: **התם** למעלה מג'. וההי דלאו שמיה אגד הגא ליכא כדפירש בקונטרס הקשה ה"ר אלחנן לרבה דמוקי מתני' בריש מכילתין (דף ד') כר"ע דאמר קלוטה כמי שהונחה דמיא בהך בבא דמייתי הכא אמאי שניהם פטורין והלא למעלה מג' לר' עקיבא כמו למטה מג' לרבנן וי"ל דרבה סבר אגד גוף שמיה אגד ור"י מפרש התם למעלה מג' ואית לן למימר דשמיה אגד כדאמר בפ"ק (דף ג.) דידו בתר גופו גריר הכא למטה מג' דלאו שמיה אגד: **לאחר** ידו ברגלו. ולספרים דגרס כלאחר ידו י"ל דברגלו הוי פירוש כלאחר ידו ומיהו גירסא קמא ניחא טפי דהכי תניא בברייתא בגמרא: **במרפקו**. (ג)הוא שקורין (א) קוד"א ולא כמו שפירש בקונטרס אייסיל"ש מדתנן באהלות (פ"א מ"ח) רמ"ח אברים באדם שלשים בפיסת היד ו' בכל אצבע שנים בקנה שנים במרפק אחד בזרוע (ד)שנים בכתף כו' משמע דמרפק הוא למטה מן הזרוע וכן בפרק האומר משקלי (ערכין יט:) ידי ורגלי עלי ממלא חבית מים ומכניס ביד עד העציל וברגל עד הארכובה ולעציל קרי ליה במתניתין דהתם במרפקו ותרגום של אצילי ידי מרפקי ידיה (יחזקאל יג) משמע דעציל היינו קוד"א שהוא ביד כנגד ארכובה ברגל ובפ"ב דזבחים (דף יח:) לא יחגרו ביזע שאין חוגרין לא למטה ממתניהם ולא למעלה מאציליהם אלא כנגד אצילי ידיהם ואי אצילי היינו אייסיל"ש היאך יחגרו למעלה מהם ועוד א"כ כנגד אציליהן היאך חוגרים אדרבה שם היא מקום זיעה אלא ודאי היינו קוד"א וכן יש להוכיח מכאן דלא כמפרש דמקום תפילין הוי בקנה למטה ממרפק דבכל מקום אמרינן תפילין בזרוע ובמס' אהלות (פ"א מח) משמע דזרוע הוא למעלה ממרפק ועוד דבפ' האומר משקלי (שם ד' יט:) פריך וביד עד העציל והכתיב והיה לאות על ידך ותנא זה קיבורית ומשני דאורייתא קיבורית כולה פירוש קרויה יד בנדרים הלך אחר לשון בני אדם משמע דמקום תפילין למעלה מן העציל*): **המוציא** בפיו כו'. והא דתנן באמרו לו (כריתות ד' יג:) אם היתה שבת והוליאו בפיו חייב ה"מ אוכלים שדרכן להוליאן בפיו בשעת אכילה: **אישתכח** דלמעלה מי' הוה קאי. דמכתף אדם עד לארץ שלש אמות כדאמר בתרגום מגלת אסתר פרשנדתא אצטליב על תלת אמין וכן כלהו וראשיהם (ה) היו קטועים ומקוה דאמר (יומא לא.) דהוי כל גופו עולה בהן אפילו ראש באמה על אמה ברום ג' אמות דכשיכנס במים יעלו המים למעלה מראשו וכוכין דאמר בסוף המוכר פירות (ב"ב דף ק:*) דאורכן ארבע אמות היינו עם ראש ולואר ועובי הארון עם מה שמשקעין ארון בתוך הכוך טפח או טפחיים וגבי היזק ראיה דהלריך ארבע אמות בריש בבא בתרא (דף ג:) משום לואר וראש ובקל יגביה עלמו שיוכל לראות לכך לריך ארבע אמות והא דאמרינן במי שהוליאוהו (עירובין דף מח:) דמקומו של אדם ארבע אמות היינו כשפושט ידו למעלה מראשו*:

ואת"ל

מתני'

*) [וע"ע תוס' מנחות לז. ד"ה קיבורת ותוס' חולין קו: ד"ה אמר רב ותוס' ערכין יט. ד"ה מרפיקו ותוס' נדה ל: ד"ה שני]

רבינו חננאל

מתניתין כדר' זירא עד שיוציא את כל הקופה הא אם הוציא כל הפירות פטור וחזקיה מתרץ לה למתני' כטעמיה ור' יוחנן מתרץ לה כטעמיה ומותבינן לחזקיה המוציא קופת הרוכלין ונתנה על האסקופה החיצונה אע"פ שרוב מינין מבחוץ פטור עד שיוציא את כל הקופה קס"ד דאית בקופת הרוכלים חפצים קטנים כגון חוליות ומרגליות או כיוצא בהן דציירין בצררי וקאמר אע"פ שרובי הצרורות מבחוץ פטור מפני שאגד כלי [שמיה] אגד עד שיוציא כל הקופה ופריקנא אמר לך חזקיה לית בה בהאי קופה צררי דדמי לאגוזים ותאנים ולחרדל אלא הני מינין דאית בה אורנסי וכיוצא בהן שהן דומין לקישואין ולדלועין שכל אחד מהן נותר ממנו כלום בפנים ובלשון ארמי שנודע עכשיו בינותינו אין אנן יודעין[מהו]אורנסי אלא עצים או קנים שמושך אותן לכרוך עליהן צמר או פשתן והאשה נושאת אותן בידה ומושכה מהן וצריא מיניה חוטי לפילכא ונמצאו אלו הוי בה בקופת הרוכלים ויש להן ארך כקישואין ודלועין מיתיבי ביבי בר אביי הגונב כיס בשבת חייב שכבר נתחייב בגנבה (ואבדה) קודם שבא לידי איסור שבת היה מגרר ויוצא מגרר ויוצא פטור שאיסור שבת ואיסור גניבה באין כאחד. ועיקר הא מלתא שכל המתחייב בנפשו פטור מן התשלומין אבל אם נתחייב בתשלומין קודם שיתחייב בנפשו לא מיפטר. וכי אמר ר' אבין (כתובות לא) הזורק חץ מתחלת ארבע לסוף ארבע וקרע שיראין בהליכתו פטור שעקירה צורך הנחה היא אותיב שם רב ביבי בר אביי כי הא תשובה דקא מותיב מהא מתניתא הגונב כיס בשבת ופריק ליה וה"נ קא מותיב ליה למאן דאמר אגד כלי שמיה אגד מהא מתניתא וקאמר ליה (את) [אם] אמרת מעות המונחים בכיס ופירות המתנחים בקופה אע"פ שהוציא מקצתכים ומקצת הקופה וכבר יצאו מעות הרבה ופירות הרבה לחוץ כיון שאגודים בכיס ומקצת הכיס בפנים פטור והכא קתני היה מגרר ויוצא מגרר ויוצא פטור שהרי איסור שבת ואיסור גנבה באין כאחד ואי הוה אגד כלי שמיה אגד היה זה מתחייב בגניבה קודם שיבוא לידי איסור שבת דמן כד מפיק פורתא מן הכלי לחוץ נתחייב בגניבה דאי בעי שרי ושקיל ולדבריך עדיין לא בא לידי איסור שבת שהרי לא הוציא את כל הכיס וכיון שהוא בא לכלל איסור שבת בהוצאת מקצת הכיס שהרי הגנבה והשבת באין כאחד תיובתא דר' יוחנן ופרקינן אמר לך ר' יוחנן אי אפקי לכיס דרך פיו הכי נמי דמחייב שהרי נתחייב בגנבה קודם שיבוא לידי איסור שבת והא מתניתין לא אתאמרא אלא באפקיה לכיס דרך שוליו דלא מצי למשקל מיניה מידעם עד דמפיק ליה לכוליה ובהכון גנבה ואיסור שבת באין כאחד והדר אקשינן ליה לר' יוחנן והא איכא חלאמא שהוא המקום התפור בשולי הכיס דאי מפקע ליה ודחיק או בפתח דוכתא מן חלאמא דרך שוליו של כיס ושקול מיניה ופריק ר' יוחנן שאם מעות יש בכיס דמצי למעבד הכי ודאי מחייב בגנבה קודם שיבא לידי איסור שבת ולא בהכון עסיק' בהא לאמת (הא ברייתא בכי הא ראית ביה שבא) דלא מצי למשקל מיניה מקצת עד מפיק ליה לכוליה ולא מחייב בגנבה קודם שיבא לידי איסור שבת והדר מקשינן והאיכא שנציא ומפרקינן בדליכא ואי בעית אימא

רב נסים גאון

המוציא בין בימינו בין בשמאלו בתוך חיקו ועל כתיפו חייב שכן משא בני קהת. בגמ' דבני מערבא מפרש כתי' ופקודת אלעזר בן אהרן הכהן שמן המאור ותנ' שמן המאור בימינו וקטורת הסמים בשמאלו ומנחת התמיד של יום תלויה בזרועו שמן המשחה איכן היה נתון ר' אבין בש"ר אלעזר כמין צלוחית קטנה היתה תלויה באפונדתו: **מה** משכן עשר אף מזבח עשר אמות בפרק מבוי (עירובין דף ג) אמרו איבעית אימא מקלעים חמש עשרה אמה לכתף בגובהה הוא דכתי' גבהה והא כתי' וקומה חמש אמות ההוא משפת מזבח ולמעלה כדי שלא יהא כהן עומד ועבודה בידו והעם רואין אותו מבחוץ נתבאר כבר שהמזבח יש בגבהו י' אמות ובמסכת זבחים בפרק קדשי קדשים (דף נט) אמרו ר' יהודה לטעמיה דאמר מזבח דמשה נמי גדול הוה דתניא ה' אמות אורך וה' אמות רוחב רבוע יהיה דברים ככתבן דברי ר' יוסי ר' יהודה אומר נאמר כאן רבוע ונאמר להלן רבוע מה להלן מאמצעיתו הוא מודד אף כאן מאמצעיתו הוא מודד כולה ור' יוסי כי נגמר גזירה שוה בגבהה גמיר דתניא ושלש אמות קומתו דברים ככתבן דברי ר' יהודה ר' יוסי אומר נאמר כאן רבוע ונאמר להלן רבוע מה להלן במזבח הזהב גובהו כשנים ברחבו אף כאן גבהו כשנים ברחבו הא מה אני מקיים וקומה חמש אמות משפת סובב ולמעלה: **דאמר** מר אין השכינה שורה אלא על חכם וגבור ועשיר. עיקר דיליה במסכת נדרים בפרק אין בין מודר הנאה מחברו (דף לח) א"ר יוחנן אין הקב"ה משרה שכינתו אלא על חכם גבור ועשיר ועניו ומנלן ממשה דכתיב (שמות מ) ויפרוש את האהל על המשכן ואמר מר משה פרשו וכתיב (שמות כו) עשר אמות אורך הקרש אימא דאריך וקטין אלא כן הדין קרא דכתיב (דברים ט) ואתפש בשני הלוחות ותניא אורכן ו' ורחבן ו' ועוביין ו' עשיר דכתיב

[זבחים נט:] | [נדרים לח.] | [בכורות מד.] | ערובין ד: | סוכה דף ד: | סנהדרין ז. | נדרים לח. | [פ"ב ביצה ומאה לייבב] | לקמן קמד: | עירובין כח. | כט: | לעיל ג. | לקמן לז.

יא א ב מיי' פי"ג מהל' שבת הלכה ו:
יב ג מיי' פי"ב שם הלכה יג:
יג ד שם הלכה יג:
יד ה שם הלכה יד:

הגהות הב"ח

(א) גמ' דכתיב אשר על המשכן (ב) רש"י ד"ה ומכרכי וכו' שאין יכול להוציאו . נ"ב (ג) תוס' ד"ה במרפקו הוא שקורין קוד"א. נ"ב לקמן בס"פ כנוטל דף ק"ד ע"ב פירש"י גוטים מרפקו אצלי ידיי (ד) בא"ד ואחד בזרוע ושנים בכתף (ה) ד"ה אישתכח וכו' ראשיהם היו:

גליון הש"ס

תוס' ד"ה ורמי דאביי וכו' קים ליה. עיין בתוס' לעיל ע"ב ד"ה הא לן וש"נ:

ואת"ל אנשי הוצל עושין כן בטלה דעתן אצל כל אדם: **מתני'** המתכוין להוציא לפניו ובא לו לאחריו פטור לאחריו ובא לו לפניו חייב באמת אמרו האשה החוגרת בסינר בין מלפניה ובין מלאחריה חייבת שכן ראוי להיות חוזר רבי יהודה אומר אף מקבלי פתקין: **גמ'** מאי שנא לפניו ובא לו לאחריו דפטור דלא אתעביד מחשבתו לאחריו ובא לו לפניו נמי הא לא אתעביד מחשבתו א"ר אלעזר *תברא מי ששנה זו לא שנה זו אמר רבא ומאי קושיא דילמא לפניו ובא לו לאחריו היינו טעמא דפטור דנתכוון לשמירה מעולה ועלתה בידו שמירה פחותה לאחריו ובא לו לפניו היינו טעמא דחייב דנתכוון לשמירה פחותה ועלתה בידו שמירה מעולה אלא מאי קושיא דיוקא דמתני' קשיא המתכוין להוציא לפניו ובא לו לאחריו פטור הא לאחריו ובא לו לאחריו חייב אימא סיפא לאחריו ובא לו לפניו הוא דחייב הא לאחריו ובא לו לאחריו פטור א"ר אלעזר תברא מי ששנה זו לא שנה זו אמר רב אשי מאי קושיא דילמא לא מיבעיא קאמר לא מיבעיא לאחריו ובא לו לאחריו דחייב דאיתעבידא מחשבתו אלא אפילו לאחריו ובא לו לפניו איצטריכא ליה סלקא דעתך אמינא הואיל ולא איתעביד מחשבתו לא ליחייב קמ"ל דנתכוון לשמירה פחותה ועלתה בידו שמירה מעולה דחייב *ולאחריו ובא לו לאחריו תנאי היא דתניא [א]*המוציא מעות בפונדתו ופיה למעלה חייב פיה למטה רבי יהודה מחייב וחכמים פוטרין אמר להן ר' יהודה אי אתם מודים בלאחריו ובא לו לאחריו שהוא חייב ואמרו לו ואי אתה מודה כלאחר ידו ורגלו שהוא פטור אמר ר' יהודה אני אמרתי דבר אחד והן אמרו דבר אחד אני לא מצאתי תשובה לדבריהם והן לא מצאו תשובה לדברי מדקאמר להו אי אתם מודין לאו מכלל דפטרי רבנן וליטעמיך דקאמרי ליה אי אתה מודה מכלל דמחייב רבי יהודה והתניא לאחר ידו ורגלו ד"ה פטור אלא לאחריו ובא לו לאחריו ד"ה חייב לאחר ידו ורגלו דברי הכל פטור כי פליגי בפונדתו ופיה למטה מר מדמי ליה לאחריו ובא לו לאחריו ומר מדמי ליה לאחר ידו ורגלו: באמת אמרו האשה כו': [תנא *כל באמת הלכה היא: רבי יהודה אומר אף מקבלי פתקין]: תנא*) שכן לבלרי מלכות עושין כן: **מתני'** המוציא ככר לרשות הרבים חייב הוציאוהו שנים פטורין לא יכול אחד להוציאו והוציאוהו שנים חייבין ור' שמעון פוטר: **גמ'** אמר רב יהודה אמר רב ואמרי לה אמר אביי ואמרי לה במתניתא תנא זה יכול וזה יכול רבי מאיר מחייב ור' יהודה ור' שמעון פוטרים זה אינו יכול וזה אינו יכול רבי יהודה ור' מאיר מחייבים ורבי שמעון פוטר זה יכול וזה אינו יכול דברי הכל חייב תניא נמי הכי המוציא ככר לרשות הרבים חייב הוציאו שנים רבי מאיר מחייב ורבי יהודה אומר אם לא יכול אחד להוציאו והוציאו שנים חייבין ואם לאו פטורים ורבי שמעון פוטר מנא הני מילי *דתנו רבנן °בעשותה העושה את כולה ולא העושה את מקצתה כיצד שנים שהיו אוחזין *במלגז ולוגזין בכרכר ושובטין בקולמוס וכותבין בקנה והוציאו לרשות הרבים יכול יהו חייבין תלמוד לומר בעשותה העושה את כולה ולא העושה מקצתה

*) [בערוך ערך לבלר פירש לבלר סופרי מלכות חוגרין בסינר ותולין פיתקין במתניהן פעמים שבאין לפנים ופעמים שבאין לאחור]

ויקרא ד

תוספות

ואת"ל אנשי הוצל עושין כן בטלה דעתן אצל כל אדם. משמע דעל אתרא נמי אמר דבטלה דעתן וכן בריש בכל מערבין (עירובין דף כח.) פריך ובבל הוי רובא דעלמא והתניא כו' וכן בתר הכי (ג)פריך ופרסאי הוי רובא דעלמא וקשה דבפ' חבית (לקמן קמד:) גבי של בית מנשיא היו סוחטים ברמונים (ד) ופריך בית מנשיא האי רובא דעלמא ומשני אין דהתקן המקיים קוצים בכרם כו' שכן בערביא מקיימין קוצים לגמליהן ופריך מי דמי ערביא אתרא הוא הכא בטלה דעתו אצל כל אדם וי"ל דהתם חשוב מנהג ערביא דלכל העולם נמי אם היה להם רוב גמלים הוו נמי מקיימי אבל בית מנשיא דחד גברא בטלה דעתו אע"ג דלכל העולם אם היה להם רמונים הרבה היו סוחטין:

רבי יהודה אומר אף מקבלי פיתקין. מפרש רבינו שמואל שיש אדם ממונה למלך שנושא פיתקין של מלך לידע מנין גבוריו וחייליו ובית אוצרותיו ונושאין אותן בכיסיהן התלויין באזוריהן ואותן כיסין חוזרין פעמים לפניהן ופעמים לאחוריהן והוי ממש דומיא דסינר דלעיל שהוא חוזר ות"ק דר' יהודה לא חשיב ליה חוזר והא דמייתי בגמרא תנא שכן לבלרי מלכות עושין כן כלומר שחוזר דבענין זה מיירי רישא (דברייתא) [דמתני']:

תברא מי ששנה זו כו'. ת"ק ה"ל למינקט לאחריו ובא לו לפניו פטור ולתנא בתרא דמחייב הוה לו למינקט לפניו ובא לו לאחריו דהוי רבותא טפי אלא דהשתא לא ידע °שיש בזה שום חילוק:

הא לאחריו ובא לאחריו פטור. לעיל (דף נא:) גבי חזקיה משני נעשה ובפ"ק דקדושין (דף ה:) גבי נתנה היא ואמרה היא ובכמה דוכתי לא משני:

זה אינו יכול וזה אינו יכול ר"מ ורבי יהודה מחייבין. מה שהקשה ריב"א אמאי לא אמרינן חטאת אחד אמר רחמנא ולא שנים ושלשה כדאמר גבי כופר מפורש בפרק ד' וה' (ב"ק דף מ. ד"ה כופר):

רש"י

מתני' המתכוין להוציא לפניו. כגון שצרר מעות בסדינו כדי שיהיו תלוין לפניו ובא לו לאחריו: פטור. דלא נתקיימה מחשבתו וה"ל כמתעסק ולא מתכוין: לאחריו ובא לו לפניו חייב. בגמ' מפרש טעמא: סינר. כעין מכנסיים קטנים וחוגרת אותו לצניעות ואם תלתה בו שום דבר להוציא ובא לו לצד אחר חייבת: שכן ראוי להיות חוזר. דרכו להיות חוזר סביבותיה ומתחלתה ידעה שסופו להתהפך: ר' יהודה אומר אף מקבלי פתקין. של מלך למוסרם לרצים אף הם חייבים בהוצאתן אפילו לא נתקיימה מחשבתן כגון הוציאן על מנת לתתן לרץ זה ונתנו לזה כך לשון רבותי ולבי מגמגם: **גמ'** מי ששנה זו לא שנה זו. ת"ק פטר בתרוייהו ותנא בתרא מחייב בתרוייהו: ועלתה בידו שמירה פחותה. ואכן סהדי דלא ניחא ליה אבל סיפא כל שכן דניחא ליה: דיוקא דמתני' קשיא. דיוקא (א) דמצינן למידק ממתני': לאחריו ובא לו לפניו הוא דחייב. דעלתה בידו שמירה מעולה: וחכמים פוטרין. שאין דרך הוצאה בכך: אני אמרתי דבר אחד. אי אתם מודים כו': והם אמרו דבר א'. אי אתה מודה כו': מכלל דמחייב רבי יהודה. בתמיה הא ודאי דברי הכל פטור דלא מפקי אינשי הכי: לאחריו ובא לו לאחריו דברי הכל חייב. דיש מוציאין כן בשמירה פחותה: לאחר ידו דברי הכל פטור דאין מוציאין כן: מר מדמי לה לאחריו. דשמירה פחותה היא ומר מדמי לה לאחר ידו דלא דמי למוציא לאחריו דהתם משתמרים הן מן הגנבים אבל אלו נופלין מאליהן ואין מוציאין כן: שכן לבלרי מלכות עושין כן. בדעתו למוסרן לזה ואין מוצאו ודבר המלך נחוץ ומלא אחר ומוסרו לו: **מתני'** הוציאו (ב) שנים פטורין. כדילפינן בעשותה יחיד ולא שנים: חייבים. וטעמא מפרש בגמרא: **גמ'** זה יכול. להוציאו לבדו וזה יכול להוציאו לבדו והוציאו שניהם: ר"מ מחייב. דלא דריש בעשותה להכי אלא לפטור יחיד שעשה בהוראת ב"ד כדלקמן: ור' יהודה פוטר. דלאו אורחיה בהכי וסתם מתני' ר' יהודה היא: זה אינו יכול וזה אינו יכול. דאורחייהו להוציא בשנים בהא סבירא ליה לרבי יהודה כרבי מאיר דחייב ורבי שמעון פוטר דיליף מקראי כדלקמן: זה יכול וזה אינו יכול. והוציאו שניהן דברי הכל חייב ולקמן מפרש הי מינייהו חייב: ה"ג הוציאוהו שנים ר' מאיר מחייב ול"ג פטור: ר' יהודה אומר אם לא יכול אחד. כלומר כל אחד ואחד: ואם לאו. אלא זה יכול וזה יכול פטור וממילא דבכי האי גוונא ר' מאיר מחייב: מלגז. פורק"א בת ג' שיניים ומהפכין בה תבואה בגורן והוא מעמר דהוא אב מלאכה: ולוגזין. מאספין השבלין: בכרכר ושובטין. דהוא מיסך כדאמר בפרק כלל גדול (לעיל דף עה) שובט הרי הוא בכלל מיסך: בקנה והוציאוהו כו'. וכל הנך זה יכול וזה יכול ניכהו:

עיגול

רבינו חננאל

לעולם דאיכא ומכרכי עילויה*) והא קושיא איכא דמרוחי ביה ומרבו ביה מילי כגון פירושא ומשוו לה לענין מי שהוציא את הכים דרך שוליו ודרך דחוקה היא ולא סליק טעמייהו וגמ' דיקא הכין הואי והאיכא שנצין בדליכא. והכין פירשוהו רבותינו ובו אתא דילמא לענין מאי דקאי אי דאפקיה דרך פיו הפי נמי דאלמ' מחייב משום דאי בעי שקיל ונמצא בא לידי גנבה קודם שיבא לידי איסור שבת ועלה קא מקשי למה לי אגרויי בכי האי מלתא והיכי [מצי לה]למשקל מדרך פיו קמיה דנפקי' לשוליה והאידנא שניגו דאינן לולאות דידיעין בערי אל בריטה ואל כדאטת די גובי על שוליו בהדי הדדי והכין הוה מנהא דכיסי דההוא וזמן כההיא דתנן כים של שנאצות שניטלו שנאציו טמא נפשם טהור וכי האי(לא) מיצי למשרייה לנישיה אלא מכלפי שולי' דאלמ' צריך להוציא כולוודחינן איכא כיסי דלית להו שנצי [אי נמי] דאית להו שנצי ומכרכי על פומיהו ואינן (עקורין) [כרוכין] כלפי שוליו. ורבא סברה כחזקיה דאגד כלי לאו שמיה אגד ואביי סברה כר"י דאגד כלי שמיה אגד קם אביי בשיטתיה (ורבא)פי' קם בשיטתיה והדר מן מימרא דנפשיה וא' כמימרא דרבא דחייב אלמא אגד כלי לא שמיה אגד כחזקיה קם רבא כשיטתיה דאביי פי' דסבר רבא כאביי דאגד כלי שמיה אגד ואיסקופה מליאה פירות פטור כרבי יוחנן והלכה כרבא דכל היכא דפליגי אביי ורבא הלכתא כרבא לבר יע"ל קג"ם. ורמי דרבא אדרבא ורמי דאביי אדאביי דאיתמר המוציא פירות לרה"ר אמר אביי ביד חייב בכלי פטור ורבא אמר ביד פטור בכלי חייב והשתא דהדר אביי וא' אגד כלי (שמיה) לא שמיה אגד וחייב קשיא הא דקא' הכא בכלי פטור ורבא דקאמר אפילו מליאה חרדל פטור קשיא אהא דקא' הכא בכלי חייב. ואמרינן איפוך אביי אמר בכלי חייב רבא אמר בכלי פטור וקא סלקא דעתך דהא דאביי ורבא כגון שהיה עומד ברה"י והוציא כלי שיש בו פירות לרה"ר וכי אפכינן דהמוציא פירות אבל הא שמעתא דחזקיה ורבי יוחנן קבלה הוא דהדר ביה אביי ממימריה וקם בשיטתיה דרבא דאיפליג עליה רבא ולענין הוציא ביד סליקא ליה דליכא פלוגתא **) דמאן דאמר חייב בזמן ששלשל ידו למטה משלשה ומאן דאמר פטור למעלה משלשה והתם ביציאות השבת כי תני העני חייב אקשינן והא בעינן עקירה מע"ג מקום ארבעה ואמרי' בה כמה טעמי ואיפריכו ולבסוף אמרי' א"ר אבהו כגון ששלשל ידו למטה משלשה וקבלה ואקשינא והא עומד קתני ואוקימנא בשוחה אי נמי דקאי בגומא ואי איתא נפק הך טעמא מהלכתא ואע"ג דלא קמה ביה מתניתין מדאקשינן איכפל תנא לאשמעינן כולהי הני ולא משום דמימרא בטל הוא ובפירקא אחרינא (לקמן בזורק צז.) אמרי' אמר רב חלקיה בר טובי לא תוך שלשה דברי הכל חייב למעלה מעשרה דברי הכל פטור מג' ועד י' באין למחלוקת ר' עקיבא ורבנן ושמעתא דכל פחות מג' כלבוד דמי גמרא גמירי לה ובהא דוכתי מפרשי לה כתיקונה בסייעתא דשמיא והא מלתא דאמרנה לענין קם אביי בשיטתיה דרבא דפרישנא הדר מן מימריה ואמר כמימריה דרבא והני תרווייהו שיטה אית לה דומיא בכמה דוכתי מגמרא. בלולב וערבה אמרי' לוי אמר אתרוג בשמיני נמי אסורה אבוה דשמואל אמר אתרוג בשביעי אסורה בשמיני מותרת קם ר' זירא בשיטתיה דאבוה דשמואל קם אבוה דשמואל בשיטתיה דלוי דא"ר זירא אתרוג שנפסלה אסור לאכילה כל שבעה פירושיה ברור דא"ר זירא כמימרא דאבוה דשמואל קמא שאסורה כל שבעה ובשמיני מותרת והדר אבוה דשמואל כמימרא דלוי. ובהא מסכתא דשבתא בפ' ר"א דתולין אתמר חרדל שלשו מע"ש אמר רב ממחו בכלי ואין ממחו ביד ומפרש אלא אמר שמואל ממחו ביד ואין ממחו בכלי איתמר רבי אלעזר אמר אחד זה ואחד זה אסור למחות ר' יוחנן אמר אחד זה ואחד זה מותר אביי ורבא דאמרי תרווייהו אין הלכה כר' יוחנן קם ר' אלעזר בשיטתא דשמואל פי' הדר מן מאי דאמר זה וזה אסור וא' ממחו ביד ואין ממחו בכלי קם ר' יוחנן בשיטתא דר' אלעזר הדר ביה ר' יוחנן מן מאי דאמר זה וזה מותר ואמר זה וזה אסור כי היכי דהוה א"ר אלעזר מעיקרא אביי ורבא דאמרי תרווייהו הלכה כר' יוחנן מן מאי דהכי קאמר הלכתא לא

*) דברי רבינו אלו מכאן עד תיבת ואינן עקורין כלפי שוליו הם מחוסרי סכנה לפי קוצר דעתו ואולי יש אינה ט"ס בכת"י ומנוה רבה לירד לסוף כוונתו בזה וה' יאיר עינינו במאור תורתו: **) מדברי רבינו נראה שהיה לו גי' אחרת בכאן דאביי ורבא לא פליגי כלל ואביי מיירי למעלה מג' ומשום זה כתב דמאי דמתרץ לעיל דף ה' כגון ששלשל ידו למטה מג' הוא נפיק מהילכתא ועיין תוס' שם ד"ה כגון ובחדושי הרשב"א ז"ל שם ודו"ק:

עין משפט נר מצוה

טו א ב מיי' פי"א מהל' שבת הל' יב סמג לאוין סה:
טז ג מיי' שם הל' יג:
יז ד מיי' שם הל' טו:
יח ה ו שם הל' טז:

מסורת הש"ס

[יבמות יג. כתובות עה: ב"ק מז: ועי' תוס' כתובות עה: פירושו של תברא]

[פי' מזלג ע"ד חילוף האותיות כמו כנש כנס מוסף ערוך]

הגהות הב"ח

(א) רש"י ד"ה דיוקא דמתניתין קשיא דמצינו כצ"ל ותיבת דיוקא נמחק: (ב) ד"ה הוציאוהו שנים: (ג) תוס' ד"ה ואת"ל וכו' בתר הכי פריך כ"ב סוף דף כ"ט: (ד) בא"ד היו סוחטין ברימונים דפריך ובית מנשיא וכו' ומשני אין דהתקן מקיים:

הגהות הגר"א

[א] גמ' דתניא המוציא מעות בפונדתו ופיה למעלה כו'. כ"ב בתוספתא הגי' המתכון להוציא בפונדתו ופיה למעלה והוציא בפונדתו ופיה למטה המתכוין להוציא בפונדתו ופיה למטה ר"י מחייב וחכמים פוטרין וכזה מוכן תשובת ר"י א"א מודים בלאחריו ובא לו לאחריו:

גליון הש"ס

תוס' ד"ה תברא וכו' שיש בזה שום חילוק. עי' תוס' כתובות דף עה ע"ב ד"ה מי ששנה וביבמות דף י ע"ב ד"ה וליתני: לעיל ג.

רב נסים גאון

(שמות לד) פסל לך פסילותן שלך תהא חכם רב ושמואל דאמרי תרווייהו נ' שערי בינה נבראו בעולם וכולם ניתנו למשה חסר א' שנא' (תהלים ח) ותחסרהו מעט מאלהים עניו דכתיב (במדבר יב) והאיש משה עניו מאד:

[92*b*] And should you object, But the people of Huzal do thus,—their practice is null by comparison with that of all men.

MISHNAH. IF ONE INTENDS TO CARRY OUT [AN OBJECT] IN FRONT OF HIM, BUT IT WORKS ROUND[7] BEHIND HIM, HE IS NOT CULPABLE; BEHIND HIM, BUT IT WORKS ROUND BEFORE HIM, HE IS CULPABLE. [YET] IN TRUTH IT WAS SAID: A WOMAN, WHO WRAPS HERSELF ROUND WITH AN APRON, WHETHER [THE ARTICLE IS CARRIED] BEFORE OR BEHIND HER,[8] IS CULPABLE, BECAUSE IT IS NATURAL[9] FOR IT TO REVERSE ITSELF.[10] R. JUDAH SAID: ALSO THOSE WHO RECEIVE NOTES.[11]

GEMARA. What is the difference in [intending to carry it] BEFORE HIM, BUT IT WORKS ROUND BEHIND HIM, that HE IS NOT CULPABLE? [Presumably] because his intention was not fulfilled! But then [if he intended to carry it] BEHIND HIM, BUT IT WORKS ROUND BEFORE HIM, [there] too his intention was not fulfilled!—
a Said R. Eleazar: There is a contradiction:[1] he who learnt the one did not learn the other. Raba said: But what is the difficulty: perhaps [where he intended to carry it] BEFORE HIM, BUT IT WORKS ROUND BEHIND HIM, this is the reason that HE IS NOT CULPABLE, because he intended a strong vigilance whereas he succeeded [in giving it only] a weak vigilance;[2] but [if he intended to carry it] BEHIND HIM, BUT IT WORKED ROUND BEFORE HIM, this is the reason that HE IS CULPABLE, because he intended [only] a weak vigilance whereas he succeeded [in giving it] a strong vigilance.[3] But then what is [R. Eleazar's] difficulty?—The implications of the Mishnah are a difficulty:[4] IF ONE INTENDS TO CARRY OUT [AN OBJECT] IN FRONT OF HIM, BUT IT WORKS ROUND BEHIND HIM, HE IS NOT CULPABLE: hence [if he intends to carry it] behind him and it comes behind him, he is culpable. Then consider the second clause: BEHIND HIM, BUT IT WORKS ROUND BEFORE HIM, only then is he CULPABLE: hence [if he intends to carry it] behind him and it comes behind him, he is not culpable?[5]—Said R. Eleazar: There is a contradiction: he who learnt the one did not learn the other. R. Ashi observed: But what is the difficulty: perhaps he leads to a climax:[6] it is unnecessary [to rule that if he intended to carry it] behind him and it came behind him, he is culpable, since his intention was fulfilled. But even [if he intends to carry it] BEHIND HIM, BUT IT WORKS ROUND BEFORE HIM, it must be [stated]. [For] you might think that I will rule, since his intention was unfulfilled, he is not culpable; therefore he informs us that he intended [only] a weak vigilance whereas he succeeded [in giving it] a strong vigilance, so that he is culpable.

[Shall we say that where he intends to carry it] behind him, and it comes behind him, there is a controversy of Tannaim? For it was taught: If one intends carrying out [an object] in his belt with its opening above, but he carries [it] out in his belt with its opening below, [or] if one intends to carry out in his belt with
b its opening below,[1]—R. Judah rules that he is culpable, but the Sages hold him not culpable. Said R. Judah to them: Do you not admit that [if one intends to carry out an object] behind him and it comes behind him, he is culpable?[2] Whilst they said to him: Do you not admit that [if one carries out an object] as with the back of his hand or with his foot, he is not culpable? Said R. Judah: I stated one argument, and they stated one argument. I found no answer to their argument, and they found no answer to mine. Now, since he says to them, 'Do you not admit,' does it not surely follow that the Rabbis hold that he is not culpable?[3]—Then on your reasoning, when they say to him, 'Do you not admit,' does it follow that R. Judah holds him culpable! But surely it was taught: With the back of his hand or his foot, all agree that he is not culpable! Rather [conclude thus: if one intends to carry out an object] behind him and it comes behind him, all agree that he is culpable; with the back of his hand or foot, all agree that he is not culpable. They differ when [he carries it out] in his belt with its opening below: one Master likens it to [intending to carry it out] behind him and it comes behind him, while the other Master likens it [to carrying] with the back of one's hand or foot.

IN TRUTH IT WAS SAID: A WOMAN, etc. It was taught: Every [statement of] 'In truth [etc.]' is the ***halachah***.[4]

R. JUDAH SAID: ALSO THOSE WHO RECEIVE NOTES. A Tanna taught: Because clerks of the State do thus.[5]

MISHNAH. IF ONE CARRIES OUT A LOAF INTO THE STREET, HE IS CULPABLE; IF TWO CARRY IT OUT, THEY ARE NOT CULPABLE. IF ONE COULD NOT CARRY IT OUT AND TWO CARRY IT OUT, THEY ARE CULPABLE; BUT R. SIMEON EXEMPTS
c [THEM].[1]

GEMARA. Rab Judah said in Rab's name—others state, Abaye said—others again state, it was taught in a Baraitha: If each alone is able,[2]—R. Meir holds [them] culpable, while R. Judah and R. Simeon hold [them] not culpable. If each alone is unable, R. Judah and R. Meir hold [them] culpable, while R. Simeon exempts [them]. If one is able but the other is not, all agree that he is culpable.[3] It was taught likewise: If one carries out a loaf into the street, he is culpable. If two carry it out: R. Meir declares him culpable; R. Judah rules: If one could not carry it out and both carry it out, they are culpable, otherwise they are not culpable; while R. Simeon exempts [them].

Whence do we know this?—For our Rabbis taught: [*And if any one . . . sin . . .*] *in his doing* [etc.]:[4] [only] he who does the whole of it [is culpable], but not he who does part of it. How so? If two hold a pitchfork and sweep [corn together];[5] [or] the shuttle, and press;[6] or a quill, and write; or a cane, and carry it out into the street,[7]—I might think that they are culpable: hence it is stated, '*in his doing*': [only] he who does the whole of it, but

(7) Lit., 'it comes'. (8) I.e., if she hangs anything on it to carry it out, either before or behind her, but it becomes reversed. (9) Lit., 'fit'. (10) Hence she knows of this, and such must be considered her intention. (11) Tosaf.: officials who go out with documents for taking a census, inventories of the State treasury, etc. They carried these in pouches hanging from their belts, which sometimes turned round back to front. R. Judah rules that these too are culpable in such a case.

a (1) Jast. R. Han.: (I take) an oath! (quoted in Tosaf. Keth. 75*b* s.v. תברא). (2) Hence his intention is unfulfilled. (3) Hence his intention was more than fulfilled. (4) [MS.M.: Rather if there is a difficulty the following is the difficulty.] (5) Presumably because such carriage is unnatural, as one cannot exercise a proper vigilance. (6) Lit., 'he states', 'it is unnecessary'.

b (1) This is the reading in the Tosef. Shab. and is thus emended here by Wilna Gaon. Cur. edd.: If one carries out money in his belt with its opening above he is culpable; if its opening is below, R. Judah rules that he is culpable etc. (2) So here too, though carrying an object in a belt with its opening below is unusual. (3) Thus it is dependent on Tannaim. (4) V. B.M. 60*a*. (5) *'Aruk*: they carry their documents in an apron around their loins, and sometimes these are at the front and sometimes at the back.

c (1) From a sin-offering. (2) To carry it out alone. (3) This is discussed *infra*. (4) Lev. IV, 27. (5) Which is forbidden on the ground of binding sheaves, *supra* 73*a*. (6) Which is weaving. (7) All these actions can be done by one man.

not he who does part of it. [93a] [If they hold] a round cake of pressed figs and carry it out into the street, or a beam, and carry it out into the street,—R. Judah said: If one cannot carry it out and both carry it out, they are culpable; if not, they are not culpable. R. Simeon ruled: Even if one cannot carry it out and both carry it out, they are not culpable: for this [reason] it is stated, '*in his doing*', [to teach that] if a single person does it, he is liable; whereas if two do it, they are exempt.

Wherein do they differ? In this verse: *And if one person of the common people shall sin unwittingly, in his doing*, [etc.]. R. Simeon holds: Three limitations are written: '*a person*' shall sin, '*one*' shall sin, '*in*
a *his doing*' he shall sin.[1] One excludes [the case where] one [person] removes an article [from one domain] and another deposits [it in the other domain]; a second is to exclude [the case of] each being able [separately to perform the action]; and the third is to exclude where neither is able [alone]. R. Judah [holds]: one excludes [the case where] one [person] removes and another deposits; the second is to exclude [the case of] each being able; and the third is to exclude [the case of] an individual who acts on the ruling of Beth din.[2] But R. Simeon is consistent with his view, for he maintains: An individual who acts on the ruling of Beth din is liable.[3] While R. Meir [argues]: Is it then written, 'a person shall sin', 'one shall sin', 'in his doing he shall sin'! [Only] two limitations are written:[4] one excludes [the case where] one removes and another deposits; and the other excludes [the case of] an individual who acts on the ruling of Beth din.

The Master said. 'If one is able but the other is not, all agree that he is culpable.' Which one is culpable? Said R. Ḥisda: He who is able. For if the one who is unable,—what does he do then?[5] Said R. Hamnuna to him: Surely he helps him? Helping is no concrete [act], replied he. R. Zebid said on Raba's authority: We learnt likewise: If he [a *zab*] is sitting on a bed and four cloths are under the feet of the bed,[6] they are unclean, because it cannot stand on three;[7] but R. Simeon declares it clean.[8] If he is riding on an animal and four cloths are under its feet, they are clean, because it can stand on three. But why so? surely each helps the other? Hence it must be because we maintain that helping
b is not a concrete [act]. Said Rab Judah of Disḳarta:[1] After all I may tell you that helping is a concrete [act]; but here it is different, because it [the animal] removes it [the foot] entirely [from the ground].[2] But since it alternatively removes one foot and then another, let it be as a *zab* who turns about.[3] Did we not learn, If a *zab* is lying on five benches or five hollow belts:[4] if along their length, they are unclean;[5] but if along their breadth, they are clean. [But] if he is sleeping, [and] there is a doubt that he may have turned [about upon them],[6] they are unclean? Hence[7] it must surely be because we say, Helping is no concrete [act].

a (1) I.e., each of these expressions limits the law to the action of a single individual. (2) And thereby sins; he is not liable to a sin-offering. (3) V. Hor. 2b. (4) Viz., '*one soul*' and '*in his doing*'. (5) He himself can effect nothing. (6) I.e., one cloth under each foot. (7) So that each one is regarded as affording complete support, since the bed cannot stand without it, and therefore the cloth under it is unclean as *midras* (v. *supra* 66a, n. a9)—For a thing to become unclean as *midras* the greater weight of the *zab* must rest on it. (8) Consistently with his view here that where neither can do the work alone, each is regarded merely as a help.

b (1) Deskarah, sixteen *parasangs* N.E. of Bagdad, Obermeyer, p. 146. (2) Hence it is not even regarded as helping. (3) Shifting from one support to another, as in the Mishnah quoted. (4) Probably like long straps, but hollow, and can be used as money pouches. (5) Because he may have shifted from one to another, so that each received the greater part of his weight. (6) And come to be along their length. (7) In the case of the animal.

בעיגול של דבילה והוציאו לרשות הרבים בקורה והוציאו לרה"ר רבי יהודה אומר אם לא יכול אחד להוציאו והוציאוהו שנים חייבין ואם לאו פטורין ר"ש אומר אע"פ שלא יכול אחד להוציאו והוציאוהו שנים פטורים לכך נאמר בעשותה יחיד שעשאה חייב שנים שעשאוה פטורין במאי קמיפלגי בהאי קרא °ואם נפש אחת תחטא בשגגה מעם הארץ בעשותה ר"ש סבר תלתא מיעוטי כתיבי נפש תחטא אחת תחטא בעשותה תחטא חד למעוטי זה עוקר וזה מניח וחד למעוטי זה יכול וזה יכול וחד למעוטי זה אינו יכול וזה אינו יכול ורבי יהודה חד למעוטי זה עוקר וזה מניח וחד למעוטי זה יכול וזה יכול וחד למעוטי יחיד שעשאה בהוראת ב"ד *ור"ש *יחיד שעשאה בהוראת ב"ד חייב ור"מ מי כתיב נפש תחטא אחת תחטא בעשותה תחטא תרי מעוטי כתיבי חד למעוטי זה עוקר וזה מניח וחד למעוטי יחיד שעשאה בהוראת ב"ד: אמר מר זה יכול וזה אינו יכול דברי הכל חייב הי מנייהו מיחייב אמר רב חסדא *זה שיכול דאי זה שאינו יכול מאי קא עביד אמר ליה רב המנונא *דקא מסייע בהדיה אמר ליה *מסייע אין בו ממש אמר רב זביד משמיה דרבא אף אנן נמי תנינא *היה יושב על גבי המטה וארבע טליות תחת רגלי המטה טמאות מפני שאינה יכולה לעמוד על שלש ור' שמעון מטהר *היה רוכב על גבי בהמה וד' טליות תחת רגלי הבהמה טהורות מפני שיכולה לעמוד על ג' ואמאי הא קמסייע בהדי הדדי לאו משום דאמרינן מסייע אין בו ממש אמר רב יהודה מדיסקרתא לעולם אימא לך מסייע יש בו ממש ושאני הבא דעקרה לה לגמרי וכיון דזימנין עקרה הא וזימנין עקרה הא ליהוי כזב המתהפך מי לא תנן *זב שהיה מוטל על ה' ספסלין או על ה' פונדאות לאורכן טמאים לרחבן טהורין ישן ספק מתהפך עליהן טמאין אלא לאו משום דאמרינן מסייע אין בו ממש אמר רב פפי משמיה דרבא אף אנן נמי תנינא
רבי

ויקרא ד | הוריות ג:

תורה אור

רש"י

עיגול וקורה גדולים הן ואין אחד יכול להוציאו : ואם לאו · שיכול אחד להוציאו: נפש תחטא · משמע נפש ולא נפשות : חד למעוטי זה עוקר. מרשות הרבים : וזה מניח · ברשות היחיד דכל כמה דלא כתיב אלא חד מיעוט מסתברא דהאי הוא דממעט דהאי קעביד פלגא והאי פלגא וליכא חד דמסייע בכולהו: וחד · יתורא למעוטי אף על פי דעבדי כי הדדי דהאי עביד כולה והאי עביד כולה ומיהו זה יכול וזה יכול הוא דממעיט דלאו אורחיה למעבדה בתרי : וחד · יתורא למעוטי נו זה אינו יכול וזה אינו יכול דאף על גב דאורחייהו למיעבד בתרי מעטינהו : יחיד שעשה בהוראת ב"ד · הורו ב"ד שחלב מותר והלך היחיד ועשה על פיהם דאנוס הוא ורבי שמעון לטעמיה דאמר בהוריות יחיד שעשה בהוראת ב"ד חייב : תרי מיעוטי כתיבי · נפש אחת חד מיעוטא הוא דאורחיה דקרא לאישתעי הכי : זה שיכול · דאיהו עבדה לכולה : אין בו ממש · מי שאינו אלא מסייע בדבר ואם בא לעשותו לבדו אינו יכול אין בו ממש ולא חשיב מידי ולא מיפטר אידך : אף אנן נמי תנינא · דמסייע אין בו ממש : היה · זב יושב על גבי מטה : וד' טליות · טליתות : שאינה יכולה לעמוד על ג' · וכיון דזה אינו יכול וזה אינו יכול כל אחד ואחד טולי מעשה עביד וגבי מדרס הזב בעינן שינשא רובו עליו בת"כ : ור' שמעון מטהר · ר' שמעון לטעמיה דאמר זה אינו יכול וזה אינו יכול כמי אינו אלא כמסייע ופטור (א)*(נ"א דבעי שיעור זיבה לזה ושיעור זיבה לזה כלומר רובו של זב מכביד על כל אחד ואחד ואפילו מסייע לא הוי) : מפני שיכולה לעמוד על ג' · הלכך כל אחד ואחד ה"ל רביעי ואינו אלא מסייע וסתמא כר' יהודה דזה יכול וזה יכול קרי מסייע : דעקרה ליה לגמרי · עוקרת הרגל מן הארץ ואפי' מסייע לא הוי : ופרכינן ואי טעמא משום דעקרה ליה כיון דזימנין דעקרה האי וזימנין עקרה האי ובכל ג' איכא לספוקי שמא הכבידה עליהן ולא עקרתן לטמינהו מספק כזב (ב) המהפך על ה' פונדאות דמטמינן ליה מספק : פונדאות. כמין חריטין כיסים ארוכים ונותנין בהן מעות ובלעז בריד"ש ורלויין לשמש שכיבה עם מלאכתן שיושב עליהם והם מלאות מעות ופותח פיהם ונוטל ואין צריך לומר לו עמוד ונעשה מלאכתנו : לאורכן · כגון שהיה שוכב על מיעיו או פרקדן ואורכו מוטל על (ג) אורכן : טמאים גרסינן במשנה דטהרות דיש לומר בכל אחת מהן שנישא רובו עליו פעמים על זו ופעמים על זו : לרחבן טהורין · לפי שארכו מוטל על רחבן ואין רובו נישא על אחת מהן : ישן · לו עליהן לרחבן : ספק נתהפך · על ארכו ונמצא כולו נשען על אחת מהן : טמאות · דכל חדא איכא למימר על זו נתהפך אלמא מטמינן מספק והתם נמי אי משום עקירה הוא ניטמינהו מספיקא אלא לאו טעמא משום דכולהו הוו כל חדא וחדא מסייע ואין בו ממש כן נראה בעיני משנה זו ורבותי גורסין לאורכן טהורין ופירשו טעמא דלאורכן טהורין משום דאמרי שמא ביניהן שכב ולא עליהם וקשיא לי א"כ לקולא תלינן ואמאי תני סיפא ספק נתהפך טמאים :
הסוס

תוספות

תלתא מיעוטי כתיבי · והא דנקט בעשותה בברייתא טפי מהנך משום שהוא מיעוט אחרון שבפסוק ובהא פליגי ולא ידע ר"י דאמאי נקט במילתיה דר' שמעון יחיד שעשה חייב כו' ולא נקט לישנא דלעיל העושה את כולה ולא העושה את מקצתה ושמא לישנא דשנים שעשאוה פטורין משמע טפי אפי' זה אינו יכול וזה אינו יכול : חד למעוטי זה עוקר וזה מניח · וזה כתב אות אחת ובא חבירו וכתב אות שניה לא איצטריך קרא אלא אהוצאה דה"א אהכנסה ואהוצא' הוא דקפיד רחמנא וליחייב אפי' בלא הנחה : ה"ג ורבי שמעון יחיד שעשה בהוראת ב"ד לא צריך קרא ול"ג ר"ש לטעמיה דאמר יחיד שעשה בהוראת ב"ד חייב כדפירש בקונטרס דהא תנן בהדיא בפ"ק דהוריות (ד' ג·) הלך ועשה על פיהן בין הביאו כפרתן בין לא כו' ר' שמעון פוטר ומפרש טעמא תולה בב"ד אנוס הוא : אמר מר זה יכול וזה אינו יכול · נראה לר"י דהאי אינו יכול הייט אפי' בעל כח הרבה אלא שהוא נושא הקורה בענין זה בכי האי גוונא שאלמלא אחר לא היה יכול לנשאה לבדו כגון באצבע או תופשה בענין זה שאינו יכול לנשאה לבדו דמה לנו לכחו כיון דהשתא מיהא אינו יכול לנושאה : הי מינייהו מיחייב · לא בעי למימר שיהא פטור אותו שיכול וליחייב שאינו יכול דאין זה סברא אלא קאמר דליתחייב נמי אפילו שאינו יכול כמו לר' יהודה ור"מ דאמרי לעיל זה אינו יכול וזה אינו יכול חייב : אמר רב זביד משמיה דרבא אף אנן נמי תנינא · פירוש דמסייע אין בו ממש קשה לר"י דהכא אית ליה לרב זביד דמסייע אין בו ממש וכן רב אשי בסמוך ובפ"ב דבילה (דף כב.) אמרינן אימר כחל עינא על יד נכרי בשבת א"ל רב אשי מאי דעתיך כו' ואמר רב כהנא חולה שאין בו סכנה אומר לנכרי ועושה הא מסייע בהדיה דקא עמיץ ופתח א"ל איכא רב זביד דקאי כוותך ושני ליה מסייע אין בו ממש משמע דרב זביד ורב אשי סוברים דיש בו ממש ואין לומר דהא דאמר הכא אין בו ממש לא שיפטר לגמרי אלא דאין בו חיוב חטאת דהא מייתי רב אשי לעבודתו כשרה משמע דאפי' פסולא דרבנן ליכא א"כ לענין שבת נמי מנלן שיש בו איסורא דרבנן ומיהו לרב אשי איכא למימר דבתר דשמעה מאמימר סבריה אלא לרב זביד קשה דאיהו גופיה קאמר משמיה דרבא דאין בו ממש ואמימר היה הרבה אחר רבא ואפי' אחר רב פפא שהיה תלמידו של רבא ושמא בתר מעשה דאמימר שמעה רב זביד משמיה דרבא ולא °מרבא עצמו ועוד אור"י דהכי פריך התם והא קא מסייע בהדיה דקא עמיץ ופתח ואע"ג דמסייע אין בו ממש בעלמא הא אית לן למימר דאסרו משום שחיקת סממנין ומשני דאין בו ממש אפילו לענין זה : ור"ש מטהר · פי' בקונטרס דר"ש לטעמיה דפטר זה אינו יכול וזה אינו יכול [ואינו] נראה לרשב"א דשאני התם דגלי רחמנא דאיכא קרא לפטור ונראה דטעמא משום דבעי שיהיה רוב הזב נישא על כל אחד וכן משמע במסכת זבים פ"ד (משנה ה) דתנן הזב בכף מאזנים ומשכב ומושב כנגדו כרע הזב טהורין כרעו הן טמאין ר"ש אומר ביחיד טמאין פי' כשאין אלא משכב אחד או מושב אחד במרובין טהורין שאין כ"א נושא רובו : היה רוכב ע"ג בהמה · בעומדת איירי דאי במהלכת כל שעה עוקרת רגל הא' ועומדת על ג' וטמא מה שתחתיהן שאינה יכולה לעמוד על שתים : מפני שיכולה לעמוד על ג' · וה"ל כל רגל אינו יכול והג' אחרים יכולין : וכיון דזימנין עקרה הא וזימנין הא ליהוי כזב המתהפך · ואפילו ברה"ר טמא : לאורכן טמאין · כן גרים הקונטרס ופי' דטמאין משום דאיכא למימר דכל אחד נושא רובו עליו פעמים על זה ופעמים על זה לרוחבן טהורין שאין רובו נישא על כל אחד מהן ולפי זה אתיא כר"ש דבעי שיהא רוב הזב נישא עליו ור"י אומר דמצי למימר דאתיא אפילו כרבנן וטעמא דטהורות משום דה"ל כל אחד מסייע שאין בו ממש ומהך רישא הוה מצי למיפרך דמטמאין לאורכן מספיקא אלא ניחא ליה למיפרך מסיפא דמפרש בה טעמא אמאי טמאין :
שמשענת

עין משפט נר מצוה

יט א ב מיי' פ"א מהל' שבת הלכה טז :
כ ג מיי' פ"ז מהל' משכב ומושב הלכה ב:
כא ד שם הלכה ו :
כב ה שם הלכה ד :

רבינו חננאל

ישרוף אלא יערב בסוף מי שמת [דף קנח] א"ר עקיבא מודה אני בזה שהנכסים בחזקתן ואמרינן עלה בחזקת מי ר' אילא אמר בחזקת יורשי האם רבי זירא אמר בחזקת יורשי הבן כי סליק ר' זירא קם בשיטתיה דר' (אלעזר) [אילא]קם רבא בשיטתא דר' זירא א"ר זירא שמע מינה אוירא דא"י מחכים פי' משום דהוא הדר למימרא דר' אילא דמן א"י ורבא דמן בבל קם במימרא קמא דר' זירא דהוה אמר בבבל: בין בימינו ובין בשמאלו ובחיקו ועל כתפו הני ארבע דתנן חייב שכן משא בני קהת והוה אמרינן רבוואתא שכן הוה אלעזר בן אהרן נושא ש מ ן המאור וקטורת הסמים ומנחת התמיד ושמן המשחה ואשכחינן בתלמוד א"י שמן המאור בימינו וקטורת הסמים בשמאלו ומנחת התמיד תלויה בזרועו ושמן המשחה ר' אבין בשם ר' אלעזר כמין צלוחה קטנה היתה תלויה באפונדתו: א"ר אלעזר המוציא משאוי למעלה מעשרה טפחים חייב שכן משא בני קהת ומנ"ל דמשא בני קהת למעלה מעשרה טפחים דאשכחינן דמזבח עשר אמות היה גובהו וקא פרסו לוים פריסא עליה וכו' ופרשו עליו כסוי עור תחש ומיכן את למד ללוים שקומתן עשר אמות ואי לאו הכין לא יכלין למפרס פרסא אמזבח ומנ"ל דמזבח גובהו ע ש ר אמות דאיתקש למשכן דכתיב ואת קלעי החצר ואת מסך [פתח] שער (המזבח) [החצר] אשר על המשכן ועל המזבח סביב מקיש מזבח למשכן מה משכן עשר אמות דכתיב עשר אמות אורך הקרש אף מ ז ב ח עשר אמות ואשכחן במשה רבינו שהיתה קומתו עשר אמות דכתיב ויפרוש את האהל על המשכן ואמר רב משה פירשו והא מלתא דגבהה דמזבח עשר אמות אע"ג דכתיב ושלש אמות קומתו מפרשא בגמרא דקדשים בפרק קדשי קדשים והכין אמרי' שם ר' יהודה לטעמיה דאמר מזבח משה גדול היה דתניא ה' אמות אורך וה' אמות רחב רבוע היה המזבח וגו' דברים ככתבן דברי רבי יוסי ר' יהודה[אומר] נאמר כאן רבוע ונאמר להלן רבוע מה להלן מאמצעיתו הוא מודד אף כאן מאמצעיתו הוא מודד ואמרינן ור' יוסי כי גמיר גזירה שוה בגובהא גמירי דתניא ו ש ל ש אמות קומתו דברים ככתבן דברי ר' יהודה ר' יוסי אומר נאמר כאן ר ב ו ע ונאמר להלן במזבח הזהב רבוע מה להלן גובהן כשנים כרחבו אף כאן גובהו כשנים כרחבו א"ל רבי יהודה והלא כבר נאמר ארך החצר מאה באמה ורחב חמשים בחמשים וקומה חמש אמות אפשר כהן עומד ע"ג מזבח ועבודה בידו וכל העם רואין אותו מבחוץ א"ל ר' יוסי ואתה אי אתה אומר כן גבהו והלא כבר נאמר אשר על המשכן ועל המזבח סביב מה משכן עשר אמות אף מזבח עשר אמות ואומר קלעים חמש עשרה אמה לכתף ומה ת"ל וחמש אמות קומתו משפת מזבח ולמעלה ומה ת"ל ושלש אמות קומתו משפת סובב ולמעלה ור' יהודה כי גמיר ג"ש ברוחבה לר' יהודה נמי קא מיתחזי עבודה בידו מי מתחזיא וכיון שקומת הלוים עשר אמות וראה שאפי' המזבח שגבהו עשר אמות הוא נשוי למעלה מי"ט משום דטבעות שהן בתים לבדים קבועות בסוף שליש העליון של מזבח וגמירי דכל טעונא דמידלי במוטות תילתא מלעיל ותרי תילתא מלתחת ומשכחת תילתיה עילאה לעיל מן כתפיהן דהוא ג' אמות (ושליש)[וששה] מכתף לוי ולמטה והויא
בתורת

רב נסים גאון

זב שהיה מוטל על ה' ספסלין או על ה' פונדאות לאורכן טמאין לרחבן טהורין. פירוש דבר זה מצוי בתוספתא (זבים פרק ד) זב שהיה מוטל על ו' כסאות לרחבן טהורות שאין אחד מהן נושא רובו ומשכחת לה

מסורת הש"ס

נ"ל ור' שמעון לטעמי' דאמר יחיד וכו' רש"ל
[נ"ל הא קא]
[ביצה כב.] רש"ל מ"ז
זבין פ"ד מ"ז
ג"ז שם
שם מ"ד

הגהות הב"ח

(א) רש"י ד"ה ור' שמעון וכו' כמסייע ופטור (נ"א דבעי וכו' לא הוי) הא"מ וכ"ב ס"א נמחק הא׳ נ"א כי אינו מפירש"י אלא מפי' התוס' : (ב) ד"ה ופרכינן וכו' כזב המתהפך על : (ג) ד"ה לארכן וכו' מוטל על רחבן וכס"ד :

גליון הש"ס

תוס' ד"ה אמר רב זביד וכו' ולא מרבא עצמו . עיין חולין קיג ע"ב תוס' ד"ה הא דרבינא:

עין משפט נר מצוה

כג א ב מיי' פ"ט מהל' ביאת המקדש הל' יח:
כד ג מיי' פ"א מהל' שבת הלכה טו:
כה ד מיי' פ"ב מהל' גניבה הל' יד סמג עשין עא:
כו ה מיי' פי"ח מהל' שבת הלכה כח:
כז ו מיי' שם הל' יח:

גמרא

רבי יוסי אומר *הסוס מטמא על ידיו החמור על רגליו שמשענת הסוס על ידיו וחמור על רגליו ואמאי הא קא מסייע בהדי הדדי לאו משום דאמרינן מסייע אין בו ממש אמר רב אשי אף אנן נמי תנינא *ר' אליעזר אומר *[א]רגלו אחת על הכלי ורגלו אחת על הרצפה רגלו אחת על האבן ורגלו אחת על הרצפה רואין כל שאילו ינטל הכלי ותינטל האבן יכול לעמוד על רגלו אחת עבודתו כשרה ואם לאו עבודתו פסולה ואמאי הא קא מסייע בהדי הדדי לאו משום דאמרינן מסייע אין בו ממש אמר רבינא אף אנן נמי תנינא *[ב]קיבל בימין ושמאל מסייעתו עבודתו כשרה ואמאי הא קא מסייע בהדי הדדי לאו משום דאמרינן מסייע אין בו ממש ש"מ: אמר מר זה יכול וזה יכול ר"מ מחייב איבעיא להו בעינן שיעור לזה ושיעור לזה או דילמא שיעור אחד לכולם רב חסדא ורב המנונא חד אמר שיעור לזה ושיעור לזה וחד אמר [ג]שיעור אחד לכולן אמר רב פפא משמיה דרבא אף אנן נמי תנינא היה יושב על גבי מטה וארבע טליות תחת ארבע רגלי המטה טמאות מפני שאין יכולה לעמוד על שלש ואמאי ליבעי שיעור זיבה לזה ושיעור זיבה לזה לאו משום דאמרינן שיעור אחד לכולן אמר רב נחמן בר יצחק אף אנן נמי תנינא *צבי שנכנס לבית ונעל אחד בפניו חייב נעלו שנים פטורין לא יכול אחד לנעול ונעלו שנים חייבים ואמאי ליבעי שיעור צידה לזה ושיעור צידה לזה לאו משום דאמרינן שיעור אחד לכולם אמר רבינא אף אנן נמי תנינא *[ד]השותפין שגנבו וטבחו חייבין ואמאי ליבעי שיעור טביחה לזה ושיעור טביחה לזה לאו משום דאמרינן שיעור אחד לכולם ואמר רב אשי אף אנן נמי תנינא שנים שהוציאו קנה של גרדי חייבין ואמאי ליבעי שיעור הוצאה לזה ושיעור הוצאה לזה לאו משום דאמרי' שיעור א' לכולם א"ל רב אחא בריה דרבא לרב אשי דילמא דאית ביה כדי לבשל ביצה קלה לזה וביצה קלה לזה א"כ לישמעינן קנה דעלמא מ"ש דגרדי ודילמא דאית בי' כדי לארוג מפה לזה וכדי לארוג מפה לזה אלא מהא ליכא למשמע מינה תני תנא קמיה דרב נחמן שנים שהוציאו קנה של גרדי פטורין ורבי שמעון מחייב *כלפי לייא אלא אימא חייבין ור"ש פוטר:

מתני' *[ה]המוציא אוכלין פחות מכשיעור בכלי פטור אף על הכלי שהכלי טפלה לו *)את החי במטה פטור אף על המטה שהמטה טפלה לו *את המת במטה חייב וכן [ו]כזית מן המת וכזית מן הנבלה וכעדשה מן השרץ חייב *ורבי שמעון פוטר:

גמ' ת"ר המוציא אוכלין כשיעור אם בכלי חייב על האוכלין ופטור על הכלי ואם היה כלי צריך לו חייב אף על הכלי שמע מינה אוכל שני זיתי חלב בהעלם אחד חייב שתים אמר רב ששת הבא במאי עסקינן כגון ששגג

*) לקמן קמא: עירובין לז:

רש"י

הסוס מטמא בידיו · אם הזב רוכב עליו וטלית תחת אחת מידיו של סוס טמאה אבל תחת רגליו טהורה שאין משענתו על רגליו והא דתנן לעיל ד' טליות תחת רגלי הבהמה טהורות לא כרבי יוסי : כהן העומד·על גבי כלי או אבן או שום דבר החוצץ בינו לבין הרצפה ועבד עבודתו פסולה דכתיב ושרת ככל אחיו הלוים העומדים שתהא עמידתו כשאר אחיו ותנא דבי ר' ישמעאל הואיל ורצפה מקודשת וכלי שרת מקודשין כו' בזבחים : שמאל פסולה לעבודה כדאמר בפ"ק דחולין (דף כב·) כל מקום שנאמר אצבע וכהונה אינו אלא ימין : שיעור לזה · גרוגרת אם אוכל הוא: שיעור זיבה· שיכביד רובו עליו וצריך להיות כאן ד' זבים : נעל אחד בפניו · זו היא צידתו : נעלו שנים פטורין · ור' יהודה הוא דפטר בשניהם יכולין : שיעור · צידת צבי לכל אחד ואחד אלא שמע מינה שיעור אחד לכולן ומדר' יהודה נשמע לר' מאיר בשניהן יכולים דבהא לא פליגי : חייבין לשלם · תשלומי ד' וה' : קנה גרדי · אורחא דמילתא והוא העולה ויורד בשתי : קנה דעלמא · שאינו עומד אלא להסקה דהוי שיעורו כעצים דאילו האי שיעורו כדי אריגה : כלפי לייא · כלפי היכא נהפך דבר זה הא רבי שמעון הוא דפטר שנים שהוציאוהו: **מתני'** את החי במטה · וחי לא מיחייב על הוצאתו דהוא מקיל עצמו ונושא עצמו : וכן כזית מן המת · חייב אם הוציא דהואיל ומטמא הוצאה חשובה היא להציל עצמו מן הטומאה : ור' שמעון פוטר. אפילו במת שלם דהוי מלאכה שאינה צריכה לגופה וכל מלאכה שאינה צריכה (לגופה) אלא לסלקה מעליו הוי מלאכה שאינה צריכה לגופה דברצונו לא באה לו ולא היה צריך לה הלכך לאו מלאכת מחשבת היא לר' שמעון : **גמ'** ופטור על הכלי· שהיא טפילה לאוכל : ואם היה צריך לכלי · להשתמש בו תשמיש אחר מקום שמוליאו שם : חייב · על כל אחד ואחד כי היכי דמיחייב ליה תרתי אתרתי הוצאות בהעלם אחד : ששגג

תוספות

שמשענת הסוס על ידיו·הכי תנן לה במס' זבים פ"ד (מ"ז) היה רוכב על גבי בהמה וארבע טליות תחת רגלי בהמה טהורות מפני שיכולה לעמוד על שלש היתה טלית אחת תחת שתי ידים תחת שתי רגלים תחת יד ורגל טמאה רבי יוסי אומר הסוס מטמא בידיו כו' ונראה לר"י דרבי יוסי לא פליג אלא ארישא אבל אסיפא דקתני תחת שתי רגלים טמאה לא פליג דאף על גב דמשענת הסוס על ידיו דבר פשוט הוא דבלא שתי רגליו לא היה יכול לעמוד קשה לר"י מה ראה רב פפי להביא מסיפא ולא מייתי מרישא ממילתייהו דרבנן כדאייתי לעיל ואומר ר"י דמשום דמרישא איכא לדחויי כדבעי למימר לעיל שאני הכא דעקרה לגמרי אבל אר' יוסי ליכא למידחי דטעמיה משום דעקרה דא"כ לא יטמא הסוס אפילו בידיו דפשיטא נמי דעקרה להו : **ויכול** לעמוד על רגלו אחת עבודתו כשרה ואם לאו פסולה · *מהכא ליכא למיפשט דמין במינו חוצץ דאבן הוא ממין הרצפה ומין בשאינו מינו (א) חוצץ דכלי אינו ממין הרצפה ובעיא הוא בפ' הוציאו לו (יומא דף נח·) בהניח סיב בתוך המזרק וקיבל בו את הדם דודאי סיב מבטל ליה אבל כלי ואבן לא מבטל ליה דאבן נתקלים בה ההולכים שם : **אמר** מר זה יכול וזה יכול רבי מאיר מחייב איבעיא להו כו' : תימה לר"ח דאמאי בעי לה אליבא דרבי מאיר ומאי למיבעי בזה אינו יכול וזה אינו יכול אליבא דר"י דקיימא מתני' כוותיה ונראה דגירסא זו טעות וגרסי' אמר מר זה אינו יכול וזה אינו יכול ואומר ר"י דאין למחוק הספרים משום זה דהא דלא נקט זה אינו יכול כו' משום דאין רגילות באין יכול שלא יהא בו שיעור לכל א' ועל גי' ר"ח קשה לר"י דמאן דבעי שיעור לזה ולזה אטו מי לא שמיע ליה מתני' דמייתי בסמוך לא יכול אחד לנעול ונעלו שנים חייבין אבל לגיר' הספרים דפליגי בזה יכול וזה יכול איכא למימר דבאין יכול מודו כולהו דשיעור אחד לכולן ומאן דמייתי סייעתא מצבי שנכנס לבית אין נראה לו לחלק בין שניהם יכולין לאין יכולין ומיהו °לגי' ר"ח איכא למימר דמאן דבעי שיעור לכל אחד יאמר דצבי שנכנס לאו דוקא אחד אלא כלומר שנים : **ואמאי** ליבעי שיעור טביחה כו'· אבל מגנבו דרישא לא מלי למיפרך דהתם לא בעי שיעור דתשלומי כפל נוהג °בכל דבר ובכל שהוא : **דילמא** דאית ביה כדי לארוג מפה לזה כו' · והא דלא נקט קנה דעלמא לאשמעינן דאע"ג דאין רגילות לארוג שתי מפות בקנה אחד אם יש שיעור לארוג מפה לזה ולזה חייב : **אלא** אימא חייבין ור' שמעון פוטר · ובקנה כבד דה"ל זה אינו יכול וזה אינו יכול : *)**ששגג** על האוכלין והזיד על הכלי· וחייב על הכלי היינו סקילה כפי' רש"י ורבינו שמואל קשה לו לאוקמי ברייתא בחיוב סקילה דבכל דוכתא איירי בחיוב חטאת והגיה הגירסא כגון ששגג על הכלים והזיד על האוכלין ולא התרו בו דליכא באוכלין לא סקילה ולא חטאת ועל הכלי חייב חטאת ואין נראה לר"י לא פי' הקונטרס ולא פי' רשב"ם דכשהזיד באחד אינו חייב חטאת על השני ששגג בו דלא שב מידיעתו הוא כיון שהזיד באחד מהן ונראה דהשתא דמוקי בהזיד בכלי איירי הכל לענין סקילה וה"פ דברייתא המוציא אוכלין כשיעור בכלי חייב סקילה על האוכלין כגון שהתרו בו על האוכלין ופטור על הכלי אם התרו בו משום כלי ואם היה צריך לכלי חייב סקילה אף אם התרו בו משום כלי ופריך והא אף על הכלי קתני משמע דחייב שתים : ובפלוגתא

רבינו חננאל

קומתם עשר אמות צא מהם שש אמות ושני שלישי אמה שארהמזבח נשתייר ג' אמות ושליש שהן כ"ז טפחים והיינו דקא אשתכח דקאמידלי בובא ואי [בעית] אימא מארון דאמר מר ארון' וכפרת טפח ובדים למעל' משליש העליון נשתייר מכתפי לוים ועד סוף ארון פחות מי' טפחים ואפילו אין אנו למדין לטבחן של לוים שהוא עשר אמות אלא אמרינן קומתו מן כתיפו למטה ג' אמות שהן י"ח טפחים צא מהן ו' טפחים ושני שלישים לשני שלישי ארון שלמטה נמצא המשוי למעלה מי"א טפחים ושליש ומקשינן למה לי דקא יליף לקומות הלוים מן קומת מזבח דאתי בהקישא ובגזירה שוה כדמפרש לעילא. נגמר מן משה רבינו דאמ' רב משה רבינו פירש את האהל והוא על ראש עשר אמות ומפרקינן דלמא שאני משה דאמר מר אין השכינה שורה אלא על חכם תבור ועשיר ואיכא למימר שאין שאר הלוים כמוהו לכך אצטריכנן למילף לשאר לוים. והמוציא משוי על ראשו פטור כלישנא בתרא דאפילו אחד מבני הוצל: המתכוין להוציא לפניו ובא לו לאחריו פטור שנתכוין לשמירה מעולה ועלתה בידו שמירה פחותה לאחריו ובא לפניו שנתכוין לשמירה פחותה ועלתה בידו שמירה מעולה כדרכה ולאו כדסליק אדעתא דר' אלעזר דמי ששנה זו לא שנה זו [ודיוקא דקא קשיא] דמדתנן לפניו ובא לאחריו פטור דייקינן שאם נתכוין לאחוריו ובא לאחוריו חייב ומדתנן סיפא לאחוריו ובא לפניו חייב איכא למידק לאחריו ובא לאחריו פטור ואסתברא ליה לר' אלעזר מי ששנה זו לא שנה זו האי נמי לא קם אלא כרב אשי דלא מיבעיא קאמר לא מיבעיא לאחריו ובא לאחריו [דחייב דאיתעבדא מחשבתו אלא אפילו לאחריו ובא לו לפניו דלא איתעבדא מחשבתו גם כן חייב ומסקינן לאחריו ובא לאחריו] דברי הכל היא וכי פליגי רבי יהודה ורבנן בפונדתו ופיה למטה מר מדמי לה לאחריו ובא לאחריו דלאו שמירה מעולה היא חייב ומר מדמי לאחר ידו פטור והלכתא כרבנן. ואשה החוגרות בסינר ומחתה ביה מידעם אפילו נתכוונה לפניה וחזרה לאחריה חייבת שכן ראוי להיות חוזר וקיי"ל כל באמת הל"מ · ולבלרי מלכות חוגרין בסינר ותולין פתקין במתניהם פעמים שבאין לפנים ופעמים שבאין לאחור ואי אכפת להון [חייב]: ולענין שנים שהוציאו כבר דתנן פטורים ואם לא יכול אחד להוציא והוציאו שנים חייבים ור' שמעון פוטר אית בעסק שנים שהוציאו תלתא גווני כל אחד מהן יכול לבדו להוציא אלא שהוציאוהו שנים ר' מאיר מחייב וחכמים פוטרים זה אינו יכול וזה אינו יכול וכשנתחברין שניהם יכולין ר' מאיר ור' יהודה מחייבין ור' שמעון פוטר אחד יכול אחד אינו יכול דברי הכל חייב. ותלמודא דשנים שעשו פטורין בעשותה בעשותה את כולה ולא בעושה מקצתה הא כיצד בזמן שכל אחד מהן יכול כגון לגוז במלגו ושביטה בכרכר וכתיבה בקולמוס במנהגא בעלמא שכל אחד ואחד יכול ואם עשו שנים פטורין אבל כגון הוצאת עיגול של דבילה דטועאי יקירא הוא או קורת דטועאי יקירא היא דכל חד באפי נפשיה לא מצי ביה ושניהם מצי ביה ר' יהודה מחייב ור' שמעון פוטר וקא מיפלגי בהאי קרא ואם נפש אחת תחטא בשגגה בעשותה. ר"ש סבר תלתא מיעוטא כתיבי נפש אחת בעשותה חד למעוטי זה עוקר וזה מניח כגון פשט העני את ידו לפנים ונתן בעה"ב לתוכה והוציא וחד למעוטי זה יכול וזה יכול וחד למעוטי זה אינו יכול וזה אינו יכול ור' יהודה סבר זה אינו יכול וזה אינו יכול לא אימעט ומיעוטא שלישי לאפוקי יחיד שעשה בהוראת ב"ד

רב נסים גאון

בת"כ [סוף פ' מצורע] אשר ישב עליו עד שינשא רובו עליו : **המוציא** אוכלים פחות מכשיעור בכלי פטור אף על הכלי שהכלי טפילה לו . בגמ' דבני מערבא גרסי הא דאת אמר בצריכין לכלים כגון אלין תותיא אבל אם אינן צריכין

גליון הש"ס תוס' ד"ה אמר מר . ומיהו לגי' ר"ח. ק"ל הא ע"כ גם לפרי"י צ"ל כן דאל"כ יקשה נמאן דפשט מד' טליות דתחת רגלי המטה וא"כ ס"ל דאין לחלק בזה בין ז"י וזא"י לזה א"י וזה א"י א"כ מאי פשיט בכדך דמיון שבת לטומאה וממתניתין דזבין אמאי לא פשיט בפשיטותא יותר ממתני' דמסכתין ומדין שבת עצמו מהא דלא יכול אחד לנעול ונעלו שנים אע"כ דמהכא י"ל דנכנסו שנים וא"כ מה הקשה הרי"י על גירסת הר"ח הא גם לשיטתיה צ"ל כן די"ל לאוקמה בנכנסו שנים וצ"ע : תוס' ד"ה ואמאי ליבעי וכו' וכל דבר ובכל שהוא . עיין בב"ק דף סג ע"א תוס' ד"ה דבר שאין מסוים וצע"ק :

מסורת הש"ס

זבים פ"ד מ"ז [ע"ש הגירסא מהופך ועי' תוי"ט]

זבחים כד.

הגהות הגר"א

[א] גמ' הסוס מטמא על ידיו החמור כו'. נ"ל להיפך (וכמ"ש במתני' דזבים ועי' בא"ר שם).

[תוספתא דזבחים פ"א]

הגהות הב"ח

(א) תוס' ד"ה ויכול וכו' ומין בשאינו מינו דחוצץ בכלי שאינו מין הרצפה הוא דבעיא דכפ"ל סי"ל:

לקמן קז.

ב"ק עח: [ע"ש ומנו לייב כ"מ מ. פ"ש]

[לעיל סג:]

[עי' פירש"י בכסמים סו: ועמש"כ רש"י לקמן קכו.]

[עתוס' לקמן לד. ד"ה את]

[עי' תוס' לקמן לד. ד"ה ר"ש]

פיין לדף לד.

R. Papi said in Raba's name, We too learnt thus. [93b] R. Jose said: A horse defiles through its forefeet, an ass through its hindfeet, because a horse rests its weight[8] on its forefeet, while an ass rests its upon its hindfeet.[9] But why so, seeing that they [the feet] help each other [to bear the animal's weight]? Hence it must surely be because we say, Helping is no concrete [act].

R. Ashi said, We too learnt thus: R. Eliezer said: If one foot is on the utensil and the other on the pavement, one foot on the stone and the other on the pavement, we consider: wherever if the utensil or the stone be removed, he can stand on the other foot, his service is valid; if not, his service is invalid.[10] Yet why so, seeing that they [the feet] help each other? Hence it must surely be because we say, Helping is no concrete [act].

Rabina said, We too learnt thus: If he [the priest] catches [the blood] with his right hand, while his left helps him,[11] his service is valid. But why so, seeing that they [the hands] help each other? But it must surely be because we say, Helping is no concrete [act]. This proves it.

The Master said: 'If each alone is able: R. Meir holds [them] culpable.' The scholars asked: Is the standard quantity required for
a each, or perhaps one standard [is sufficient] for all?[1] R. Hisda and R. Hamnuna [differ therein]: one maintains, The standard [is required] for each; while the other rules: One standard [is sufficient] for all. R. Papa observed in Raba's name, We too learnt thus: If he [a *zab*] is sitting on a bed and four cloths are under the feet of the bed, they are unclean, because it cannot stand on three.[2] But why so: let the standard of gonorrhoea be necessary for each?[3] Hence it must surely be because we say, One standard [suffices] for all.

R. Nahman b. Isaac said, We too learnt thus: If a deer enters a house and one person locks [it] before him,[4] he is culpable; if two lock it, they are exempt.[5] If one could not lock it, and both lock it, they are culpable. But why so? let the standard of trapping be necessary for each?[6] Hence it must surely be because we say, One standard [suffices] for all.

Rabina said, We too learnt thus: If partners steal [an ox or a sheep] and slaughter it, they are liable.[7] But why so? let the standard of slaughtering be necessary for each? Hence it must surely be because we say, One standard [suffices] for all.

And R. Ashi [also] said, We too learnt thus: If two carry out a weaver's cane [quill], they are culpable. But why so? let the standard of carrying out be necessary for each? Hence it must surely be because we say, One standard [suffices] for all. Said R. Aha son of Raba to R. Ashi: Perhaps that is where it contains
b sufficient [fuel] to boil a light egg for each?[1]—If so, he [the Tanna] should inform us about a cane in general?[2] why particularly a weaver's?[3] Yet perhaps it is large enough for each to weave a cloth therewith?[4] Hence nothing can be inferred from this.

A tanna[5] recited before R. Nahman: If two carry out a weaver's cane, they are not culpable; but R. Simeon declares them culpable. Whither does this tend![6]—Rather say, They are culpable, while R. Simeon exempts [them].

MISHNAH. IF ONE CARRIES OUT LESS THAN THE STANDARD QUANTITY OF FOOD IN A UTENSIL, HE IS NOT CULPABLE EVEN IN RESPECT OF THE UTENSIL, BECAUSE THE UTENSIL IS SUBSIDIARY THERETO. [IF ONE CARRIES OUT] A LIVING PERSON IN A BED, HE IS NOT CULPABLE EVEN IN RESPECT OF THE BED, BECAUSE THE BED IS SUBSIDIARY TO HIM;[7] A CORPSE IN A BED, HE IS CULPABLE. AND LIKEWISE [IF ONE CARRIES OUT] THE SIZE OF AN OLIVE OF A CORPSE, THE SIZE OF AN OLIVE OF A NEBELAH, OR THE SIZE OF A LENTIL OF A [DEAD] CREEPING THING [SHEREZ], HE IS CULPABLE.[8] BUT R. SIMEON DECLARES HIM EXEMPT.[9]

GEMARA. Our Rabbis taught: If one carries out foodstuffs of the standard quantity, if in a utensil, he is liable in respect of the foodstuffs and exempt in respect of the utensil! but if he needs
c the utensil, he is liable in respect of the utensil too.[1] Then this proves that if one eats two olive-sized pieces of *heleb* in one state of unawareness, he is liable to two [sacrifices]?[2]—Said R. Shesheth:

(8) Lit., 'the leaning of a horse'. (9) The reference is to a cloth placed under the feet of these animals when a *zab* rides upon them. (10) A priest performed the service in the Temple barefooted, and nothing might interpose between his feet and the pavement. (11) Catching the blood of a sacrifice for its subsequent sprinkling on the altar is part of the sacrificial service, and like all other parts thereof must be performed with the right hand.

a (1) When two people carry out an article of food which each could carry out alone, must it be as large as *two* dried figs, so that there is the standard for each, or is one sufficient to render them both culpable? (2) V. *supra a* for notes. (3) 'The standard of gonorrhoea' is that a whole *zab* rests on an article—then it is unclean. Then here too *four zabin* should be lying on the bed for the four cloths to be defiled. (4) So that it cannot escape. This constitutes trapping, which is a culpable labour; v. Mishnah *supra* 73a. (5) Cf. *supra* 92b. (6) Viz., two deers should be required. (7) V. Ex. XXI, 37.

b (1) Mishnah *supra* 89b. (2) The standard of which is to boil a light egg. (3) The standard of which is different; v. next note. (4) This is the standard of a weaver's cane. (5) V. Glos. s.v. (*b*). (6) I.e., surely R. Simeon rules in the opposite direction, that if two perform an action, even if each is unable to do it separately, they are exempt. Jast. translates: towards the tail! i.e., reverse it. (7) Carrying a living person is not a culpable offence, v. *infra* 94a. (8) These are the respective minima which defile. Hence carrying them out of the house ranks as a labour of importance, since a source of contamination is thereby removed. (9) For carrying out a corpse, etc. For its purpose is merely negative, i.e., he does not wish to have the corpse in his house, but does not actually want it in the street; hence it is a labour unessential in itself, and which R. Simeon holds is not a culpable offence, though it is forbidden.

c (1) Thus he is liable to two sacrifices. (2) Surely that is not so, yet the cases are analogous.

What are we discussing here? E.g., [94a] where he sinned unwittingly in respect of the food, but deliberately in respect of the utensil.[3] R. Ashi demurred: But it is stated, 'in respect of the utensil *too*'?[4] Rather said R. Ashi: E.g., where he sinned unwittingly in respect of both, then [one offence] became known to him, and subsequently the other became known to him, this being dependent on the controversy of R. Johanan and Resh Lakish.[5]

[IF ONE CARRIES OUT] A LIVING PERSON IN A BED, HE IS NOT CULPABLE EVEN IN RESPECT OF THE BED. Shall we say that our Mishnah is [according to] R. Nathan, but not the Rabbis? For it was taught: If one carries out an animal, beast,[6] or bird into the street, whether alive or [ritually] killed, he is liable [to a sacrifice]; R. Nathan said: For killed ones he is liable, but for live ones he is exempt, because the living [creature] carries itself!—Said Raba, You may even say [that it agrees with] the Rabbis: the Rabbis differ from R. Nathan only in respect of an animal, beast, and bird, which stiffen themselves;[7] but as for a living person, who carries himself,[8] even the Rabbis agree. R. Adda b. Ahabah observed to Raba, But as to what we learnt: Ben Bathyra permits [it] in the case of a horse.[9] And it was taught: Ben Bathyra permits [it] in the case of a horse, because it is em-
a ployed for work which does not entail liability to a sin-offering [1] And R. Johanan observed, Ben Bathyra and R. Nathan said the same thing.[2] Now if you say that the Rabbis disagree with R. Nathan only in respect of an animal, beast, or bird, because they stiffen themselves, why particularly Ben Bathyra and R. Nathan: surely you have said that even the Rabbis agree?—When R. Johanan said [thus] it was in respect of a horse that is set apart for [carrying] birds. But are there horses set apart for birds? Yes, there are the falconers' [horses].[3] R. Johanan said: Yet R. Nathan agrees in the case of a tied [living being].[4] R. Adda b. Mattenah said to Abaye: But these Persians are like bound [men],[5] yet R. Johanan said, Ben Bathyra and R. Nathan said the same thing?[6] There they suffer from haughtiness,[7] for a certain officer with whom the king was angry ran three *parasangs* on foot.

A CORPSE IN A BED, HE IS CULPABLE.[8] AND LIKEWISE [IF ONE CARRIES OUT] THE SIZE OF AN OLIVE OF A CORPSE, etc. Rabbah b. Bar Hanah said in R. Johanan's name, and R. Joseph said in the name of Resh Lakish: R. Simeon declared exempt [94b]

(3) And 'liable' means to death, for the wilful desecration of the Sabbath. (4) Which implies the *same* liability. (5) V. *supra* 71*b*. Thus according to R. Johanan he is liable to two sin-offerings if he is apprised of each in succession, and then comes to make atonement for both. But in the view of Resh Lakish he is liable to two sacrifices only if he is apprised of one, makes atonement, and is then apprised of the other (Tosaf.). (6) *Behemah* means a domestic animal; *hayyah*, a non-domestic animal. (7) Making themselves a dead weight, and thus they are a real burden. (8) He has natural buoyancy. (9) One may not sell his cattle to a Gentile, because they are used for ploughing, and thereby lose the Sabbath rest to which they are entitled (v. Ex. XX, 10). Horses, however, were not used for ploughing in Mishnaic times, but merely for riding.

a (1) Riding being only Rabbinically prohibited. (2) *Sc.* that it is not a labour to carry a living being, because it carries itself. (3) The falcons which they carry are free and do not stiffen themselves; yet in the view of the Rabbis, who make an exception only in respect of a human being, one would be culpable for carrying out a falcon. Hence R. Johanan specified R. Nathan. (4) Whether human or animal, because these certainly do not carry themselves. (5) Rashi: they ride swathed in their garments and could not walk if they wished to. (6) I.e., Ben Bathyra permits the sale of a horse even to a Persian, showing that even a bound person is not a burden. (7) Their haughty bearing makes them look as if they cannot walk, but actually they are able to quite well. (8) [Tosaf. identifies R. Judah as the authority for this ruling, whose opinion was that there is liability for a labour not essential in itself: cf. *supra* 93*b*, n. b8.]

גמרא

ששגג על האוכלין והזיד על הכלי מתקיף לה רב אשי והא אף על הכלי קתני אלא א"ר אשי כגון ששגג בזה ובזה °ונודע לו וחזר ונודע לו ובפלוגתא *דרבי יוחנן ור"ש בן לקיש: את החי במטה פטור אף על המטה: לימא מתני' רבי נתן היא ולא רבנן דתניא **המוציא בהמה חיה ועוף לרה"ר בין חיין ובין שחוטין חייב רבי נתן אומר על שחוטין חייב ועל חיין פטור *שהחי נושא את עצמו אמר רבא אפילו תימא רבנן ע"כ לא פליגי רבנן עליה דרבי נתן אלא בבהמה חיה ועוף דמשרבטי נפשייהו אבל אדם חי דנושא את עצמו אפילו רבנן מודו א"ל רב אדא בר אהבה לרבא והא דתנן *בן בתירא מתיר בסוס ותניא בן בתירא ב'מתיר בסוס מפני שהוא עושה בו מלאכה שאין חייבין עליו חטאת ואמר רבי יוחנן בן בתירא ורבי נתן אמרו דבר אחד ואי אמרת דלא פליגי רבנן עליה דר' נתן אלא בבהמה חיה ועוף משום דמשרבטי נפשייהו מאי איריא בן בתירא ורבי נתן והאמרת אפילו רבנן מודו כי א"ר יוחנן בסוס המיוחד לעופות ומי איכא סוס המיוחד לעופות אין איכא (*דבי וייארן א"ר יוחנן ג'מודה ר' נתן בכפות א"ל רב אדא בר מתנה לאביי והא הני פרסאי דכמאן דכפיתי דמו וא"ר יוחנן בן בתירא ור' נתן אמרו דבר אחד התם *רמות רוחא הוא דנקיט להו דההוא פרדשכא דרתח מלכא עילויה ורהיט תלתא פרסי בכרעיה: את המת במטה חייב וכן כזית מן המת וכו': *אמר רבה בב"ח א"ר יוחנן וא"ר יוסף אמר רשב"ל פוטר היה ר"ש אף

*)[בערוך' זיידן גרס דביזיידן וע"ש מ"ש בשם רב האי גאון]

רש"י

ששגג על האוכלין והזיד על הכלי. ומאי חייב דקתני מיתה: והא אף קתני. משמע שני חיובין שוין: בפלוגתא דר"י ור"ל. דאיפלוגי בידיעות מחלקות בפ' כלל גדול (לעיל דף עא:) איפלוגי נמי רב ששת ורב אשי הכא רב ששת דלא מוקי לה הכי קסבר דאין ידיעות מחלקות ורב אשי סבר ידיעות מחלקות:

דמשרבטי נפשייהו. משמטים כלפי מטה ומכבידין עצמן להשמיט מיד הנושאן: מתיר בסוס. למוכרו לנכרי מפני שמלאכת הסוס אם היה אדם עושה אותה אין חייב עליה חטאת דלרכיבה עומד והחי נושא את עצמו והא דאסרו למכור בהמה גסה לנכרי משום שאלה ומשום שכירות אסור וסוס אי נמי דמושיל ומוגר לאו איסורא דאורייתא איכא שאין זו מלאכה אלא הסוס וגבי אזהרת שביתת בהמה מלאכה כתיב': ואמר רבי יוחנן גרסינן: דבי וייאדן. של ציידי עופות שנותנין על הסוס עופות כשהן חיין כגון כך ומיהו לצוד שאר עופות *ולא משרבטי נפשייהו דלא קשירי והשתא כמי החי נושא את עצמו ומשום הכי א"ר יוחנן בן בתירא ורבי נתן אמרו דבר אחד: בכפות. בין עוף בין אדם: כמאן דכפיתי דמו. שרוכבים מעוטפין בבגדים רחבים וגם הם עצמן מעונגין מהלך על הארץ: ואמר רבי יוחנן גרסינן: בן בתירא ור' נתן אמרו דבר אחד. והא אמרת מודה ר' נתן בכפות *ואי משום דאוקמינן בסוס המיוחד לעופות משום רבנן אוקמינן דפליגי עליה ולמימר דאילו באדם שניהם שוין לפטור ואי בכפות מודה רבי נתן היכי מתוקמא דבן בתירא כר' נתן משום דחי נושא את עצמו הא בן בתירא מתיר אפילו למכור לפרסיים דכמאן דכפיתי דמו וכל האומות קרי להו נכרים דסבר דכפות נושא את עצמו: רמות רוחא. גסות: הא דלא מסגו בכרעייהו גסות הוא: פרדשכא. סרדיוט:

תוספות

ובפלוגתא דר' יוחנן ור"ל. פי' חייב שתי חטאות לרבי יוחנן כשנודע לו וחזר ונודע לו דידיעות מחלקות ולר"ל אחר (א) שנתכפר נודע לו על אחד ופי' הקונטרס אין נראה לר"י דנהי דלית ליה לרב ששת ידיעות מחלקות מ"מ יעמיד בנודע לו על האחד בשכבר כיפר דכפרה לכ"ע מחלקת:

שהחי נושא את עצמו. תימה לר"י למה פטור דאי משום שהחי מיקל עצמו והלא אפילו במשא קל יותר חייב ואי משום דשנים שעשאו פטורין הא הוי זה יכול וזה אינו יכול שאין הניטל יכול לישא עצמו בלא הנושא והנושא יש בו כח לנושאו אפילו היה מת ואומר ר"י דממשכן גמרינן שלא היו נושאין דבר חי שהתחשים והאילים היו הולכים ברגליהם והחלזון (ב) מיד היו פוצעין אותו טרם ימות דכמה דאית ביה נשמה טפי ניחא ליה כי היכי דליזליל ליבעיה*: אבל אדם חי נושא את עצמו. תימה דבריש נוטל (לקמן דף קמא:) משמע דפליגי נמי באדם דקאמר גבי תינוק רבא כרבי נתן סבירא ליה ואומר רשב"א דקטן כבהמה דמי דמשרביט נפשיה אך קשה לן דבפרק מפנין (שם דף קכח:) תניא מדדין בהמה חיה ועוף בחצר אבל לא ברה"ר והאשה מדדה את בנה ברה"ר ופירש התם בקונטרס דבהמה ברה"ר לא שמא יגביהנה מן הארץ וסתמא כרבנן דר' נתן דמחייבי אבל בנה אי נמי מגבה ליה הא באדם מודו רבנן דחי נושא את עצמו [ושמא ההוא דבפרק נוטל איירי בתינוק בן יומו]: בסוס המיוחד לעופות. ובן בתירא מתיר בסוס בכל הסוסים קאמר ורבנן אוסרין בכל הסוסים משום סוס המיוחד לעופות דלא חילקו חכמים בסוסים: סוסא דבי וייאדן. פר"ח שכן ציידי עופות מניחין עליהן עופות שלהן שצדין בהן עופות אחרים אבל אין לפרש בעופות הנילודין דהני כפותין ניהו והאמר בסמוך דמודה רבי נתן בכפות: והא הני פרסאי. ואיהו לא מפליג למכור לסוס נכרי: *את המת במטה חייב. נראה לר"י דמהכא קים לן בכל דוכתא דאית ליה לר' יהודה מלאכה שאינה צריכה לגופה חייב עליה דמסתמא ת"ק דר"ש היינו רבי יהודה כי ההיא דלעיל זה אינו יכול וזה אינו יכול דת"ק דר"ש היינו ר' יהודה כדמוכח בגמ' ורשב"א אומר דיש להביא מדתנן לעיל (דף ג.) ר' יהודה אומר אף המוציא משמשי ע"ז דהוי מלאכה שאינה צריכה לגופה: *רבי שמעון פוטר. נראה לר"י דמלאכה שאינה צריכה לגופה קרי כשעושה מלאכה ואין צריך לאותו צורך כעין שהיו צריכין לה במשכן אלא לענין אחר כי הצורך שהיתה מלאכה נעשית בשבילו במשכן הוא גוף (איסור) המלאכה ושורשו ולפי זה אתי כולהו שפיר הוצאת המת אין צריך למת ובמשכן היו צריכין לחפצים שהוציאו צד נחש שלא ישכנו אינו צריך לנחש ובמשכן היו צריכין לתחש וחלזון ומפיס מורסא להוציא ליחה המזיקתו ואין עומד להכניס אויר ולהוציא ליחה תמיד אע"פ שנעשה פתח גמור שהרי ראוי (הוא) להכניס ולהוציא אם היה צריך מ"מ לא דמי לפתחים שבמשכן שהיו עומדין להכניס ולהוציא אבל לעשות לה פה דמיא למשכן וחייב והריגת המזיקין אין צריך להם ובמשכן היו צריכין לעורות אילים המאדמים וחופר גומא ואינו צריך אלא לעפרה ובמשכן היו צריכין לגומא לנעוץ בה או לדבר אחר וזב בכיס שלא יטנפו כליו הוי אינה צריכה לגופה שאינו צריך לכיס עצמו ואפילו למנות ראיותיו או נקיים דצריך הכיס מ"מ אין צריך להוצאה זו דה"נ סגי ליה אי יתיב בחד דוכתא ומכבה גחלת שלא יוזקו בה רבים וכחס על הנר ועל השמן או על הפתילה המהובהבת כבר אין צריכין לגופן שבמשכן לא היה כיבוי אלא לעשות פחמין בכיבוי זה ומתקנין על יד כיבוי זה שיהו ראויין למלאכת הצורפין וכיבוי כדי שלא יקדיחו הסממנין בבישולן לא היה במשכן כי זהירים היו שלא להרבות אש יותר מדאי וכן סותר ע"מ לבנות נמי לא מחייב ר' שמעון דבעי שתהא צריכה לגופה אלא כגון שסותר ע"מ לתקן יותר ממה שהיה בתחלה כגון שהבנין האחרון טוב מן הראשון כדמוכח במעתין א) דחס על הנר וכן קורע על (ג) מתו או שובר כלים למירמי אימתא אאינשי דביתיה אין צריכין לגופה דבמשכן היתה קריעה לצורך תיקון דבר ב) הנקרע ואע"ג דבהוצאה לא בעי רבי שמעון שיהא לגמרי כמו שהיה במשכן (ד) דלא בעי מר לעשות לו טס או ס"ת להגיה אע"פ שבמשכן הוצאה הגדבה היתה כדי לתקנה לעשות ממנה משכן וכלים במקלקלים כגון מכבה וסותר וקורע מסתברא דצריך שיהא על מנת לתקן כמו במשכן ולא חשיבי המקלקלים צריכות לגופה עד דהוי לגופו ולגופה והא דלא קרי לה לגופו ולגופה כיון דבעו תרוייהו בכלל לגופה היא אבל לגבי מר וס"ת כיון דלא בעי אלא לגופו דהא לא בעי במר לעשות בו טס ג) וס"ת כדי להגיה בו לא הוי בכלל לגופה ולפי שצריכות לגופה הוי כעין דהוי במשכן כמו שפיר' הוצרך להשמיענו במר דלא בעינן לעשות לו טס כמו שהיה במשכן ורש"י דפירש דברצונו לא היתה באה לו ולא היה צריך לה שאינה אלא לסלקה מעליו כמו צד נחש שלא ישכנו או מכבה גחלת שלא יוזקו בו רבים דברצונו שלא היה בעולם וכן בפרק במה מדליקין (לעיל דף לא:) פירש כחס על הפתילה המהובהבת כבר דאינה צריכה לגופה משום דאין צריך לכיבוי זה ואם לא הובערה מעולם הוה ניחא ליה דהואיל וחס עליה כי אית בה טפי הוה ניחא ליה בה קשה מסותר על מנת לבנות כמו בתחלה וקורע בחמתו למירמי אימתא אאינשי דביתיה דהתם צריך למלאכה ורוצה הוא שיהא בעולם ואין לומר דלא ניחא ליה שיצטרך למירמי אימתא *אם כן מפיס מורסא לעשות לה פה יהא פטור דברצונו היה שלא היה מורסא מעולם וכן קורע יריעה שנפל בה דרנא על מנת לתפור דברצונו לא היה נופל בה וכן תופר בגד קרוע ברצונו שלא היה קרוע אלא צריך לפרש כדפירשתי*: (שייך לע"ב) גדול כבוד הבריות שדוחה את לא תעשה שבתורה. קשה לר"ת דגבי טלטול דהוי איסורא דרבנן לא שרינן משום כבוד הבריות אלא ע"י ככר או תינוק כדאמר בפרק במה מדליקין (לעיל דף ל:) ובפרק כירה (שם דף מג:) °ויש לומר דשאני טלטול דאפשר על ידי ככר או תינוק לכך לא התיר בענין אחר ההכי

א) [לעיל לא:] ב) הנקרע ומיתקן בכך ואע"ג כו' כצ"ל ג) וס"ת אלא כדי לקרות בו כ"ה בס"ה

רבינו חננאל

ופטור מן הקרבן והיכי דמי כגון האי דתנן נשאת ע"פ ב"ד תצא ופטורה מן הקרבן שלא ע"פ ב"ד תצא וחייבת בקרבן ור' שמעון אמר לך יחיד שעשה בהוראת ב"ד לא צריך קרא למעוטיה ור' מאיר דקא מחייב זה יכול וזה יכול אמר לך תרין מיעוטי אינון ואם נפש אחת תחטא בשגגה אחת לאו מיעוטא הוא אלא נפש תחטא בעשותה חד לזה עיקר וזה מניח וחד ליחיד שעשה בהוראת בית דין ובזמן שאחד יכול ואחד אינו יכול והוציאו (שניהם פטורין)[ד"ה חייב].אמר רב חסדא היכול הוא דחייב ואידך שאינו יכול לא קא עביד מידי אלא מסייע הוא ומסייע אין בו ממש ואיסתייע רב חסדא בכמה סייעתא ופש"ן סימן רב זביד משמיה דרבא סייעיה מהא דתני זב היה רוכב ע"ג בהמה וד' טליות תחת ד' רגלי בהמה טהורות מפני שהיא יכולה לעמוד על שלש דחשבת כל חדא מסייעת ומסייע אין בו ממש(וכי)אמר רב יהודה שדסקרתא לעולם אימא לך מסייע יש בו ממש ושאני בהמה דכי עקרא חדא רגל משויא בדעתא למעקר כולהי נופיה אהדרו ליה לאו זמנין עקרא הא וזמנין עקרא הא וכיון דאפילו בעי למעקר כולי גופה ומתחלה עקרא חדא זמנין עקרא הא וזמנין דעקרא הא ולאו חדא בעינא הוא דעקרא או הוה אית ביה ממש במסייע והוה האי זב דרכיב על האי בהמה כזב המתהפך על ה' ספסלין לארכן ויש ספק מתהפך עליהן ממאין דכל רגל מסייעת הוא ספק הא מתעקרא וספק הא מתעקרא לא אמרינן מסייע אין בו ממש.ורב פפי משמיה דרבא סייע מהא ר' יוסי אמר הסוס מטמא [על ידיו] וחמור מטמא ברגליו שמשענת הסוס על [ידיו] וחמור על[רגליו] ואמאי הא קא מסייעת ברגליו בהדי ידים וידים בהדי רגלים לאו משום דאמרי'מסייע אין בו ממש ודרב אשי ורבינא ברירין ומפרשן בתוספתא ובכל הזבחים שקבל דמן: ושמעתתא דבתרא קא גרסין להו אמר מר זה יכול וזה יכול ר' מאיר מחייב איבעיא להו בעינן שיעור לזה ושיעור לזה או דלמא שיעור אחד לכולן ואנחנא הויינא דהא טעותא היא דלא בעו כי האי בעיא אליבא דרבי מאיר דלאו הלכתא כוותי' ולא אמרי אמוראי (פשמ"ש) [פמנ"ש] סימן. אף אנן תנינא אלא אהא קאי האי בעיא זה אינו יכול וזה אינו יכול ר' מאיר ור' יהודה מחייבין ור' שמעון פוטר ובהא הלכה כר' מאיר ור' יהודה והא קאמרינן באין צדין [דף כז] בהדיא רבי יהודה ור"ש הלכה כר' יהודה וכיון דהלכתא זה אינו יכול וזה אינו יכול חייבין עלה בעינן מי צריכינן שיעור לכל חד וחד או חד שיעור לשניהן וסליקא הלכה שיעור אחד לשניהן ופשטה דמתניתין לא יכול אחד להוציאו והוציאו שנים חייבין דאלמא כל אחד מהן בפני עצמן אינו יכול אבל שניהן בהדי הדדי יכולין ואעפ"כ חייבין ולא מצית מימר על זה יכול וזה אינו יכול קאי ולאו אליבא דר' מאיר קאי בעי אלא אליבא דרבנן דפטורין קאמר מי פטרי רבנן אע"פ שהוציאו שניהן שני שיעורין או דלמא אם הוציאו שניהן שיעור אחד פטורי ואם הוציאו שני שיעורין

עין משפט נר מצוה

כח א מיי' פ"ו מהל' שגגות הלכה טו:
כט ב מיי' פי"ב שם הלכה ד:
ל ג מיי' פי"ח שם הלכ' טז:

מסורת הש"ס

[לעיל עה:]
[תוספת' פ"ט]
[לקמן קמא: יומא סו: עירובין קג.]
[פי' רש"ג ורש"א]
ע"ז יד: בכורות ב. [פסחי' נג.]
נ"ל ואי בכפות מודה ר' נתן עד סה"ד ואח"כ שייך ואי משום וכו' עד לפטור וכן הגיה הש"ג מו"ה שכנא ז"ל
[ע"ז ע"א.]
כדפו"י הגי' אמר רבא כו' ור' יוסף אמר ריש לקיש
[שייך לעיל במשנה לג:]
[נ"ז שייך שם]
גיר' הב"י א"כ
[ועי' תוס' חגיגה י: ד"ה מלאכת]

הגהות הב"ח

(א) תוס' ד"ה ובפלוגתא וכו' ולר"ל אחר שנתכפר על אחד חזר ונודע לו על אחר: (ב) ד"ה שהחי וכו' והחלזון. נ"ב ע"ל בדף עה ע"א: (ג) ד"ה ר"ש וכו' וכן קורע בחמתו או שובר כצ"ל ונ"ב עי' בפ' האורג קה ע"ב: (ד) בא"ד דהא לא בעי גבי מר לעשות בו טס:

רב נסים גאון

צריכין לכלים חייב אף על הכלי: ובפלוגתא דר' יוחנן וריש לקיש. עיקר דיליה בפרק כלל גדול (דף עה):

גליון הש"ס

גמ' ונודע לו וחזר ונודע לו. עי' לעיל דף ע ע"א תד"ה המוציא: תוס' ד"ה גדול וי"ל דשאני טלטול דאפשר ע"י ככר. ק"ל הא מבואר לעיל דף מג ע"א דבליכא ככר דשרי טלטול מן הצד רק מטעם דאדם בהול על מתו ואי לא שרית ליה אתי לכבויי ולא שרינן מטעם כבוד הבריות וצ"ע וע' סוכה דף לו ע"ב בתוס' שם:

אף במוציא את המת לקוברו אמר רבא ומודה ר' שמעון במר לחפור בו וספר תורה לקרות בו דחייב פשיטא דאי הא נמי מלאכה שאינה צריכה לגופה היא אלא מלאכה שצריכה לגופה לרבי שמעון היכי משכחת לה מהו דתימא עד דאיכא לגופו ולגופה כגון מר לעשות לו טס ולחפור ספר תורה להגיה ולקרות בו קא משמע לן °ההוא שכבא דהוה בדרוקרא °שרא רב נחמן בר יצחק לאפוקיה לכרמלית א"ל רבי יוחנן אחוה דמר בריה דרבנא לרב נחמן בר יצחק כמאן כר"ש אימר דפטר ר"ש מחיוב חטאת איסורא דרבנן מיהא איכא א"ל האלהים דעיילת ביה את ואפילו לר' יהודה (שרי) דמי קאמינא לרה"ר לכרמלית קאמינא *גדול כבוד הבריות שדוחה את לא תעשה שבתורה *תנן התם [נגעים פ"ז מ"ד] °התולש סימני טומאה והכוה המחיה עובר בלא תעשה איתמר אחת משתים חייב °אחת משלש רב נחמן אמר חייב רב ששת אמר פטור רב נחמן אמר חייב אהני מעשיו דאי משתקלא חדא אחריתי אזלה לה טומאה רב ששת °אמר פטור השתא מיהת הא איתא לטומאה אמר רב ששת מנא אמינא לה דתנן וכן כזית מן המת וכזית מן הנבילה חייב הא חצי זית פטור והתניא חצי זית חייב מאי לאו הא דתניא חייב דאפיק חצי זית מכזית והא דתנן פטור דאפיק חצי זית מכזית ומחצה ורב נחמן אידי ואידי חייב והא דתנן פטור דאפיק חצי זית ממת גדול: **מתני'** °הנוטל צפרניו זו בזו או בשיניו וכן שערו וכן שפמו וכן זקנו וכן הגודלת וכן הכוחלת וכן הפוקסת רבי אליעזר מחייב וחכמים אוסרין משום שבות: **גמ'** אמר ר"א °מחלוקת ביד אבל בכלי (א) חייב פשיטא זו בזו תנן מהו דתימא רבנן בכלי נמי פטרי והא דקתני זו בזו להודיעך כחו דר' אליעזר קא משמע לן ואמר רבי אליעזר °מחלוקת לעצמו אבל לחבירו דברי הכל פטור פשיטא צפרניו תנן מהו דתימא רבי אליעזר לחבירו נמי מחייב והא דקתני צפרניו להודיעך כחן דרבנן קמ"ל: וכן שערו כו': תנא *הנוטל מלא *פי הזוג חייב וכמה מלא פי הזוג אמר רב יהודה שתים והתניא ולקרחה שתים אימא וכן לקרחה שתים תניא נמי הכי *°הנוטל מלא פי הזוג בשבת חייב וכמה מלא פי הזוג שתים רבי אליעזר אומר אחת °ומודים חכמים לר"א במלקט לבנות מתוך שחורות שאפילו אחת חייב °ודבר זה אף בחול אסור משום שנאמר °לא ילבש גבר שמלת אשה [דברים כב] תניא *ר"ש בן אלעזר אומר צפורן וציצין שפירש רובה °מותר ביד מותר בכלי חייב חטאת מי איכא מידי דבכלי חייב חטאת וביד מותר לכתחלה הכי קאמר פירשו רובן ביד מותר בכלי פטור אבל אסור לא פירשו רובן ביד פטור אבל אסור בכלי חייב חטאת אמר רב יהודה הלכה כרבי שמעון בן אלעזר אמר רבה בר בר חנה אמר רבי יוחנן °והוא שפרשו כלפי מעלה ומצערות אותו: וכן הגודלת כו': גודלת כוחלת ופוקסת משום מאי מחייבא אמר רבי אבין א"ר יוסי בר' חנינא גודלת משום אורגת כוחלת משום כותבת פוקסת משום טווה אמרו רבנן קמיה דרבי אבהו וכי דרך אריגה בכך וכי דרך כתיבה בכך וכי דרך טויה בכך אלא א"ר אבהו לדידי מפרשא לי מיניה דר' יוסי בר' חנינא כוחלת

אף במוציא את המת לקוברו. ולא תימא לא פטר אלא במכיחו לחוץ דאין צורך לא לגופו של מוציא ולא לגופה של הוצאה דאפילו הוא צורך המת פטור: מר לחפור בו. שהוא צורך המוציא: מר לעשות לו טס ולחפור. מרה שנרצף פיו וצריך להושיב עליו כמין טס דק שיהא ראוי לחפור: להגיה ולקרות: לאפוקיה לכרמלית. שהיה מוטל בבזיון או בדליקה או בחמה ואי משום טלטול מניח עליו ככר או תינוק: לא תעשה. לאו דלא תסור כי הכא: התולש סימני טומאה. שתי שערות לבנות שהבהרת מטמאה בהן: והכוה את המחיה. מחית בשר חי והוא סימן טומאה בשאת והכוה זה לבטלה משום מחיה ולטהרה: עובר בלא תעשה. דהשמר בנגע הצרעת (דברים כד): אחד מב'. שלא היו בה אלא שתי שערות ותלש האחד: חייב. דשקלא לטומאה שאין מטמאה בפחות מב' דהכי ילפינן לה בת"כ שיער שנים וחייב מלקות: מאי לאו הא דתני חייב דאפיק חצי זית מכזית. דשקליה ובצריה לשיעורא: והא דתני פטור דאפיק חצי זית מכזית ומחצה. דאף על גב דמלמלס לשיעור לאו מילתא היא ולא אמרינן אהני דאי שקיל מיניה פורתא תו ליתא לשיעורא: ממת גדול. דלא אהני מידי: **מתני'** וכן שערו. תולש שער ראשו בידיו: וכן הגודלת. שערה: וכן הכוחלת. עיניה: וכן הפוקסת. יש מרבותי אומרים מתקנת שערה במסרק או בידי' ויש שמפרשין טחה כמין בצק על פניה וכשנוטלו מאדים הבשר*: רבי אליעזר מחייב. בכולם חטאת וחכמים אוסרין משום שבות וטעמא דרבי אליעזר מפרש בגמרא משום מאי מיחייב: **גמ'** מחלוקת ביד. בהא שנוטלן בידו ולא בכלי הוא דפטרי רבנן שאין דרך גזיזה בכך בחול: מהו דתימא בכלי נמי פטרי רבנן. דאין כאן משום גוזז דלא שייך אלא בצמר בהמה: מחלוקת לעצמו. בהא הוא דמחייב ר' אליעזר שיכול לאמן ידו לעצמו לתקנו בלא כלי: אבל לחברו. אין יכול לאמן את ידו ליטול יפה בלי כלי: פשיטא צפרניו תנן. של עצמו: הנוטל מלא פי הזוג. מלא ראש המספרים: חייב. בשבת לרבנן בכלי ולר' אליעזר אף ביד וזהו שיעורו: והא תניא. בההיא ברייתא בסיפא ולקרחה שהזהירה תורה לא תשימו קרחה (דברים יד) שתים הוי קרחה מכלל דפי הזוג לאו ב' שערות נינהו: תניא נמי הכי. כרב יהודה דאמר שתים: רבי אליעזר אומר. באחת הוא חייב ולא בעינן מלא פי הזוג: אחת חייב. שבאחת הוא מקפיד שלא יהא נראה כזקן: שמלת אשה. ודרך הנשים להקפיד על כך ולהתנאות: ציצין. כמין רצועות דקות הפורשות מעור האצבע סביב הצפורן: שפירשו רובן. קרובין לינתק: מי איכא מידי כו'. כיון דבכלי חייב חטאת ביד איכא שבות גזירה אטו כלי: כלפי מעלה. נגד הצפורן התחילו לפרוש דקא מצערו ליה טפי: משום כותבת. שמוליכה מכחול סביב העין כאדם המוליך קולמוס סביב האות: טווה. שמתקנת שערה בין אצבעותיה ופושטתו כשהוא נכרך ולשון השני עושה מלותו בצק כמין חוט: לעצמה

תורה אור

אהני מעשיו דאי משתקלא חדא כו'. באחת מארבע דאי משתקלא חדא אחריתי נמי לא אזלא לה טומאה כ"ע מודו דפטור דהוי כמו חצי זית ממת גדול: **והא** דתנן פטור דאפיק חצי זית ממת גדול. וה"ה דהוה מצי לאוקמיה כגון דליכא אלא חצי זית בלבד אלא דניחא ליה לשנויי בחצי זית ממת גדול דהוי רבותא טפי דאי ליכא אלא חצי זית מן הכל פשיטא דפטור ודווקא חצי זית אבל כזית ממת גדול חייב אע"ג דאי משתקלא זית אחר לא אזלא טומאה מ"מ אהני מעשיו דמשאתכו לא גריר בתר המת וכשיוליאו המת מן הבית וישאר כזית זה יטמא כל הבית וכמלא שעתה בהוצאה זו הוא גורס טהרה: **ממת** גדול. לאו דווקא גדול אלא כלומר מב' זיתים או ג': **אבל** בכלי ד"ה חייב. היינו כרבי יהודה דמחייב במלאכה שאינה צריכה לגופה וא"ת ודילמא רבנן כר"ש סבירא להו ומנא ליה דמחייב בכלי ויש לומר דא"כ ליפלגי בכלי להודיעך כחן דרבנן והא דקאמר מהו דתימא רבנן בכלי נמי פטרי היינו פירושו דס"ל כר"ש וכדפרישית אבל רש"י פירש דפטרי משום דלא שייכא גזיזה אלא בצמר ואין נראה לר"י דבהא ליכא למיטעי דבכל בעלי חיים שייכא גזיזה כדאמר לעיל התולש כנף חייב משום גוזז: **והוא** שפירשו כלפי מעלה. פירש בקונטרס כנגד ראשי אצבעותיו שהן למעלה כשמגביה ידיו ור"ת מפרש שכלפי גוף קרי כלפי מעלה כדאשכחן בפ"ב דנדה (דף יג:) דקאמר מן העטרה ולמעלה והתם היינו לצד הגוף*): **פוקסת**. מה שפירש בקונטרס פוקסת היינו סורקת ביד או במסרק אין נראה דבגמרא משמע דהוי כעין טוויה וסריקה איננה כעין טוויה כלל ועוד דא"כ היה שונה סורקת כדתנן (נזיר דף מב.) נזיר חופף ומפספס אבל לא סורק א): **וכי** דרך אריגה בכך. ואף על גב דקולע נימין חשיבא אריגה כדאמרינן בפרק במה אשה (ג) (לעיל ד' סד.) הכא בשער לא חשיבא אריגה כמו בבגד ועוד דהכא אין סופה להתקיים שעומדת לסתירה: החולב

*) [וע' תוס' מנחות יא: ד"ה מלמטה]

א) [וע"ע תוס' כתובות ד: ד"ה ופוקסת ועי' תוס' מו"ק ט: ד"ה ופוקסת מבואר היטב]

עין משפט נר מצוה

לא א מיי' פט"ו מהל' שבת הלכה כב ופכ"ו הלכה כב סמג לאוין סה טוש"ע א"ח סי' ש"א סעיף ב:

לב ב ג מיי' פ"י מהל' טומאת צרעת הלכה א סמג לאוין שמג:

לג ד ה ו ז ח מיי' פ"ט מהל' שבת הלכה ח ט סמג לאוין סה טוש"ע א"ח סי' שמ סעיף א:

לד ט מיי' פי"ב מהל' ע"ז הלכה י סמג לאוין ס טוש"ע שם וטוש"ע י"ד סי' קפב סעיף ו:

לה י כ מיי' פ"ט מהל' שבת הלכה ט סמג לאוין סה טוש"ע א"ח סי' שכח סעיף לא:

מסורת הש"ס

[עירובין מא: מגילה ג: לעיל פא: ברכות יט: מנחות לז:]

עיין לעיל סד: רש"י ד"ה ולא תיפקס

מכות כ: ע"ש *ג"ל פי הזוג בשבת חייב [תוספתא פ"י ע"ש]

[שם]

הגהות הב"ח

(א) גמ' אבל בכלי ד"ה חייב: (ב) תוס' ד"ה וכי דרך וכו' בפ' במה אשה נ"ב ע"ל נז ע"א גבי תיכי חלילתא ועי' עוד בדף סד ריש ע"א אצל ותולה בצואר כתו:

גליון הש"ס

גמ' שרא ר"נ בר יצחק לאפוקיה לכרמלית. עי' סוכה לו ע"ב הד"ה בשבת: שם אחת משלש. עי' תה"ד סי' מח:

רבינו חננאל

מחייבין חדא דלאו הכי קאמר לא בבעיא ולא בתשובה ועוד דאיפשיטא לן בזה יכול וזה יכול שאע"פ שמוציא כמה שיעורין פטורין הלכך ליכא לאוקמא אלא בענין זה אינו יכול וזה אינו יכול ואמרי' דשיעור אחד לכולן והייבין בו. אמר רב פפא משמיה דרבא אף אנן נמי תנינא היה יושב ע"ג מטה וד' טליות תחת רגלי מטה טמאות מפני שאינה יכולה לעמוד על ג' ואמאי ליבעי שיעור לזה ושיעור לזה פי' שיעור רובו של זב דתנן זב שהיה מוטל על ה' ספסלין לרוחבו טהורין ותני עלה מפני שאין רובו על אחד מהן והכי קאמר הני ד' טליות כל חדא אין רובו עליה ואמאי טמאות אלא לאו משום דשיעור אחד לכולן אמר רב נחמן אף אנן נמי תנינא צבי שנכנס לבית ונעל אחד בפניו חייב נעלו השנים פטורין לא יכול אחד לנעלו ונעלו שנים חייבים ור' שמעון פטור אמאי חייבין ניבעי שיעור צידה לזה ושיעור צידה לזה לאו משום דאמרינן שיעור אחד לכולן ומן הא נמי גמרינן דהא שמעתא לענין זה אינו יכול וזה אינו יכול אמירא חדא מדמפרש לא יכול א' להציאו והציאוהו שנים חייבים ועוד מדר"ש פטור (יפטור) בהא אמר רבינא אף אנן נמי תנינא השותפין שגנבו חייבין עיקר דילה [כב"ק עח] השותפין שגנבו וטבחו פטורין והתניא השותפין שגנבו הייבין אר"נ לא קשיא כאן בשותף שגנב מחבירו כאן בשותף שגנב מעלמא. איתיביה רבא לרב נחמן יכול שותף שגנב מחבירו ושותפין שגנבו יהו הייבין ת"ל וטבחו או מכרו מכרו כלו טבחו כלו אלא אמר רב נחמן לא קשיא כאן בשותף שטבחו לדעת חבירו כאן בשותף שטבחו שלא בדעת חבירו: ואמאי ניבעי טביחה לזה וטביחה לזה והיכי מחייבי שנים בטביחה אחת אלא לאו משום דאמרינן שיעור אחד לכולן אמר רב אשי אף אנן נמי תנינא שנים שהוציאו קנה של גרדי חייבין אע"פ [דסהא לא] שמעינן מינה דשיעור אחד לכולן או צריכי שיעור לכל אחד ואחד מפני שקנה של גרדי יש בו כשני שיעורין וכבר שמענו מן הנך מתניתא דאמרי' שיעור אחד לכולן אלא דגמרינן דלענין זה אינו יכול קיימינן דהיא פלוגתא דר' שמעון ורבנן והא כי תנא תנא קמיה דרב נחמן שנים שהוציאו קנה של גרדי פטורין ור' שמעון מחייב תמה ר"נ ואמר כלפי לייא היכי אמרת הכי הא תנן מתניתין והוציאוהו שנים חייבין ור' שמעון פוטר ותרצה להא ברייתא נמי בהכין הלכך מאי דגרים אמר מר שניהם יכולין ר' מאיר מחייב ואמר עלה איבעיא להו פעותא

רב נסים גאון

גדול כבוד הבריות שדוחה את לא תעשה שבתורה וזה הדבר מיוחד בלאו דלא תסור כמו שפירשו בברכות (דף יט) בפרק מי שמתו ומשכחת לה עוד בסוף פרק הקומץ (דף לז) במסכת מנחות: התולש סימני טומאה והכוה את המחיה עובר בלא תעשה. עיקר זה הוא מה שהזהיר הכתוב (דברים כד) השמר בנגע הצרעת ואמרו רבותינו ז"ל בפירושו שזה הלשון הוא במקום לא תעשה ובכל מקום שכתוב כמותו לא בא לומר אלא שלא תעשה אותו דבר כמו שאמר (עירובין דף צו) אמר ר' אבין אמר ר' אילעאי כל מקום שנאמר השמר פן ואל אינו אלא לא תעשה והזהיר הקב"ה את המצורע שלא יהתוך מה שנראה בבשרו מסימני צרעת ומי שעובר על כך עובר בלא תעשה ומיכן אמר המשנה התולש סימני טומאה והכוה את המחיה עובר בלא תעשה ומשכחת לה בספרי השמר בלא תעשה בנגע זה שיער לבן הצרעת זו המכוה ולפיכך הוצרכנו שיתיר לנו המילה בעת שתתראה בערלה צרעת כמו שאמרו בפרק ר' אליעזר אומר אם לא הביא כלי (דף קלג) תנו רבנן מילה דוחה את הצרעת כו' תנו רבנן ימול ערלתו ואע"פ שיש שם בהרת ומה אני מקיים השמר בנגע הצרעת בשאר מקומות חוץ מן המילה כו' ת"ל בשר ואע"פ שיש שם בהרת וכפ' ואלו הן הלוקין (מכות כב) אמרו מתקיף לה ר' אבהו וליחשוב נמי קוצץ בהרתו ואזהרתיה השמר בנגע

even him who carries out a corpse for burial.[9] Raba observed: Yet R. Simeon admits in the case of [one who carries out] a spade for digging therewith or the Scroll of the Torah to read it, that he is culpable.[10] That is obvious, for if this too should be regarded as a labour unrequired *per se*, how would a labour necessary *per se* be conceivable according to R. Simeon?—You might say, it must be [carried out] both for his requirements and for its own purpose, a e.g., a spade in order to make it into a [metal] plate[1] and for digging, a Scroll of the Law for correcting and reading: [therefore] he informs us [that it is not so].

A dead body was lying in Darukra,[2] which R. Nahman b. Isaac allowed to be carried out into a *karmelith*. Said R. Nahman the brother of Mar son of Rabbana to R. Nahman b. Isaac: On whose authority? R. Simeon's! But perhaps R. Simeon merely exempts [such] from liability to a sin-offering, yet there is a Rabbinical interdict. By God! said he to him, you yourself may bring it in. For [this is permitted] even according to R. Judah:[3] did I then say [that it may be carried out] into the street? I [merely] said, into a *karmelith*: the dignity of human beings is a great thing, for it supersedes [even] a negative injunction of the Torah.[4]

We learnt elsewhere: If one plucks out the symptoms of uncleanness[5] or burns out the raw flesh,[6] he transgresses a negative injunction.[7] It was stated: [If he plucks out] one of two [hairs], he is culpable;[8] one of three: R. Nahman maintained, He is culpable; R. Shesheth said, He is not culpable. R. Nahman maintained, He is culpable: his action is effective in so far that if another is removed the uncleanness departs. R. Shesheth said, He is not culpable: now at all events the uncleanness is present. R. Shesheth observed: Whence do I know it? Because we learnt: AND LIKEWISE [IF ONE CARRIES OUT] THE SIZE OF AN OLIVE OF A CORPSE, THE SIZE OF AN OLIVE OF A NEBELAH, . . . HE IS CULPABLE. This implies, [for] half the size of an olive he is exempt; but it was taught: [For] half the size of an olive he is culpable? Surely [then], where it was taught that he is culpable, [it means] that he carries out half the size of an olive from [a piece as large as] an olive; while where we learnt [by implication] that he is exempt, [it means] that he carries out half the size of an olive from an olive b and a half.[1] But R. Nahman maintains: In both these cases he is culpable;[2] but as to what we learnt that he is exempt, that is where he carries out half the size of an olive of a large corpse.[3]

MISHNAH. IF ONE PARES HIS NAILS WITH EACH OTHER OR WITH HIS TEETH, LIKEWISE [IF ONE PLUCKS] HIS HAIR, LIKEWISE HIS MOUSTACHE, LIKEWISE HIS BEARD; AND LIKEWISE IF [A WOMAN] PLAITS [HER HAIR], LIKEWISE IF SHE PAINTS [HER EYELIDS], LIKEWISE IF SHE ROUGES [HER FACE],[4] —R. ELIEZER DECLARES [THEM] CULPABLE, WHILE THE RABBIS FORBID [THESE ACTIONS] AS A SHEBUTH.[5]

(9) Though that is for the requirements of the dead, he is exempt, since it is not for the requirements of the living. (10) Since it is for his own requirements.

a (1) [*Aliter:* to fix upon it (if blunted) a plate. V. Rashi.] (2) Or, Drukerith, Darkerith, a Babylonian town near Wasit on the lower Tigris; Obermeyer, p. 197. (3) Who holds a labour not required *per se* to be a culpable offence. (4) Hence this is permitted. [Not exactly a Biblical prohibition but an interdict of the Rabbis whose enactments have Biblical force (Rashi). V. Ber. 19*b*.] (5) Viz., the two whitened hairs which are a proof of leprosy; v. Lev. XIII, 3 (the minimum is two hairs). (6) Also a symptom of leprosy, ibid. 10. (7) Deut. XXIV, 8: *Take heed in the plague of leprosy*—this is interpreted as a command not to remove the evidences thereof. (8) Since he thereby effectively removes the symptom of leprosy, the remaining one being insufficient to prove him unclean.

b (1) He is culpable in the first case because his action is effective, but in the second it does not effect anything, and the same applies here. (2) His reasoning is the same as in the case of leprosy. (3) For even if another half is carried out, it makes no difference to the contaminating efficacy of the corpse. (4) One of the explanations of Rashi. V. also Krauss, *T.A.* I, p. 692 n. 293. (5) V. Glos.

◁ *For the continuation of the English translation of this page see overleaf.*

אף במוציא את המת לקוברו אמר רבא ומודה ר' שמעון במר לחפור בו וספר תורה לקרות בו דחייב פשיטא דאי הא נמי מלאכה שאינה צריכה לגופה היא אלא מלאכה שצריכה לגופה לרבי שמעון היכי משכחת לה מהו דתימא עד דאיכא לגופו ולגופה כגון מר לעשות לו טס ולחפור ספר תורה להגיה ולקרות בו קא משמע לן ההוא שכבא דהוה בדרוקרא שרא רב נחמן בר יצחק לאפוקיה לכרמלית א"ל רבי יוחנן אחוה דמר בריה דרבנא לרב נחמן בר יצחק כמאן כר"ש אימר דפטר ר"ש מחיוב חטאת איסורא דרבנן מיהא איכא א"ל האלהים דעיילת ביה את ואפילו לר' יהודה (שרי) דמי קאמינא לרה"ר לכרמלית קאמינא *גדול כבוד הבריות שדוחה את לא תעשה שבתורה *תנן התם התולש סימני טומאה והכוה המחיה עובר בלא תעשה איתמר אחת משתים חייב אחת משלש רב נחמן אמר חייב רב ששת אמר פטור רב נחמן אמר חייב אהני מעשיו דאי משתקלא חדא אחריתי אזלה לה טומאה רב ששת אמר פטור השתא מיהת הא איתא לטומאה אמר רב ששת מנא אמינא לה דתנן וכן כזית מן המת וכזית מן הנבילה חייב הא חצי זית פטור והתניא חצי זית חייב מאי לאו הא דתניא חייב דאפיק חצי זית מכזית והא דתנן פטור דאפיק חצי זית מכזית ומחצה ורב נחמן אידי ואידי חייב והא דתנן פטור דאפיק חצי זית ממת גדול: **מתני'** הנוטל צפרניו זו בזו או בשיניו וכן שערו וכן שפמו וכן זקנו וכן הגודלת וכן הכוחלת וכן הפוקסת רבי אליעזר מחייב וחכמים אוסרין משום שבות: **גמ'** אמר ר"א מחלוקת ביד אבל בכלי (א) חייב פשיטא זו בזו תנן מהו דתימא רבנן בכלי נמי פטרי והא דקתני זו בזו להודיעך כחו דר' אליעזר קא משמע לן ואמר רבי אליעזר מחלוקת לעצמו אבל לחבירו דברי הכל פטור פשיטא צפרניו תנן מהו דתימא רבי אליעזר לחבירו נמי מחייב והא דקתני צפרניו להודיעך כחן דרבנן קמ"ל: וכן שערו כו': תנא *הנוטל מלא *פי הזוג חייב וכמה מלא פי הזוג אמר רב יהודה שתים והתניא ולקרחה שתים אימא וכן לקרחה שתים תניא נמי הכי *הנוטל מלא פי הזוג בשבת חייב וכמה מלא פי הזוג שתים רבי אליעזר אומר אחת ומודים חכמים לר"א במלקט לבנות מתוך שחורות שאפילו אחת חייב ודבר זה אף בחול אסור משום שנאמר לא ילבש גבר שמלת אשה תניא *ר"ש בן אלעזר אומר צפורן שפירש רובה וציצין שפירשו רובן ביד מותר בכלי חייב חטאת מי איכא מידי דבכלי חייב חטאת וביד מותר לכתחלה הכי קאמר פירשו רובן ביד מותר בכלי פטור אבל אסור לא פירשו רובן ביד פטור אבל אסור בכלי חייב חטאת אמר רב יהודה הלכה כרבי שמעון בן אלעזר אמר רבה בר בר חנה אמר רבי יוחנן והוא שפירשו כלפי מעלה ומצערות אותו: וכן הגודלת כו': גודלת כוחלת ופוקסת משום מאי מחייבא אמר רבי אבין א"ר יוסי בר' חנינא גודלת משום אורגת כוחלת משום כותבת פוקסת משום טווה אמרו רבנן קמיה דרבי אבהו וכי דרך אריגה בכך וכי דרך כתיבה בכך וכי דרך טויה בכך אלא א"ר אבהו לדידי מפרשא לי מיניה דר' יוסי בר' חנינא

כוחלת

רש"י

אף במוציא את המת לקוברו. ולא תימא לא פטר אלא במניחו לחוץ דאין צורך לא לגופו של מוציא ולא לגופה של הוצאה דאפילו הוא צורך המת פטור: מר לחפור בו. שהוא צורך המוציא: מר לעשות לו טס ולחפור. מרה שנרצף פיו וצריך להושיב עליו כמין טס דק שיהא ראוי לחפור: להגיה ולקרות: לאפוקיה לכרמלית. שהיה מוטל בבזיון או בדליקה או בחמה ואי משום טלטול מניח עליו ככר או תינוק: לא תעשה. לאו דלא תסור כי הכא: התולש סימני טומאה. שתי שערות לבנות שבבהרת מטמאה בהן: והכוה את המחיה. מחית בשר חי והוא סימן טומאה בשאת והכוה זה לבטלה משום מחיה ולטהרה: עובר בלא תעשה. דהשמר בנגע הצרעת (דברים כד): אחד מב'. שלא היו בה אלא שתי שערות ותלש האחד: חייב. דשקלא לטומאה שאין מטמאה בפחות מב' דהכי ילפינן לה בת"כ שיער שנים וחייב מלקות: מאי לאו הא דתני חייב דאפיק חצי זית מכזית. דשקליה ובצריה לשיעורא: והא דתני פטור דאפיק חצי זית מכזית ומחצה. דאף על גב דמצמצם לשיעור לאו מילתא היא ולא אמרינן אהני דאי שקיל מיניה פורתא תו ליתא לשיעורא: ממת גדול. דלא אהני מידי: **מתני'** וכן שערו. תולש שער ראשו בידיו: וכן הגודלת. שערה: וכן הכוחלת. עיניה: וכן הפוקסת. יש מרבותי אומרים מתקנת שערה במסרק או בידי' ויש שמפרשין טחה כמין בצק על פניה וכשנוטלו מאדים הבשר*: רבי אליעזר מחייב. בכולם חטאת וחכמים אוסרין משום שבות וטעמא דרבי אליעזר מפרש בגמרא משום מאי מיחייב: **גמ'** מחלוקת ביד. בהא שנוטלן בידו ולא בכלי הוא דפטרי רבנן שאין דרך גזיזה בכך בחול: מהו דתימא בכלי נמי פטרי רבנן. דאין כאן משום גוזז דלא שייך אלא בצמר בהמה: מחלוקת לעצמו. בהא הוא דמחייב ר' אליעזר שיכול לאמן ידו לעצמו לתקנו בלא כלי: אבל לחבירו. אין יכול לאמן את ידו ליטול יפה בלי כלי: פשיטא לפרכיו תנן. של עצמו: הנוטל מלא פי הזוג. מלא ראש המספרים: חייב. בשבת לרבנן בכלי לר' אליעזר אף ביד וזהו שיעורו: והא תניא. בההיא ברייתא בסיפא ולקרחה שהזהירה תורה לא תשימו קרחה (דברים יד) שתים הוי קרחה מכלל דפי הזוג לאו ב' שערות נינהו: תניא נמי הכי. כרב יהודה דאמר שתים: רבי אליעזר אומר. באחת הוא חייב ולא בעינן מלא פי הזוג: אחת חייב. שבאחת הוא מקפיד שלא יהא נראה כזקן: שמלת אשה. ודרך הנשים להקפיד על כך ולהתנאות: ציצין. כמין רצועות דקות הפורשות מעור האצבע סביב הצפורן: שפירשו רובן. קרובין לינתק: מי איכא מידי כו'. כיון דבכלי חייב חטאת ביד איכא שבות גזירה אטו כלי: כלפי מעלה. לצד הצפורן התחילו לפרוש דקא מצערו ליה טפי: משום כותבת. שמוליכה מכחול סביב העין כאדם המוליך קולמוס סביב האות: טווה. שמתקנת שערה בין אצבעותיה ופושטתו כשהוא נכרך ולשון השני עושה מאותו בצק כמין חוט:

לעצמה

א) [וע"ע תוס' כתובות ד' ד"ה ופוקסת ועי' תוס' מו"ק ט' ד"ה ופוקסת מבואר היטב]

תוספות

אהני מעשיו דאי משתקלא חדא כו'. באחת מארבע דאי משתקלא חדא אחריתי נמי לא אזלא לה טומאה כ"ע מודו דפטור דהוי כמו חצי זית ממת גדול: **והא** דתנן פטור דאפיק חצי זית ממת גדול. וה"ה דהוה מצי לאוקמיה כגון דליכא אלא חצי זית בלבד אלא דניחא ליה לשנויי בחצי זית ממת גדול דהוי רבותא טפי דאי ליכא אלא חצי זית מן הכל פשיטא דפטור ודווקא חצי זית אבל כזית ממת גדול חייב אע"ג דאי משתקלה זית אחר לא אזלא טומאה מ"מ אהני מעשיו דמשתתא לא גריר בתר המת וכשיוציאו המת מן הבית וישאר כזית זה יטמא כל הבית ונמצא שעתה בהוצאה זו הוא גורם טהרה: **ממת** גדול. לאו דווקא גדול אלא כלומר מב' זיתים או ג': **אבל** בכלי ד"ה חייב. היינו כרבי יהודה דמחייב במלאכה שאינה צריכה לגופה וא"ת ודילמא רבנן כר"ש סבירא להו ומנא ליה דמחייב בכלי ויש לומר דא"כ ליפלגי בכלי להודיעך כחן דרבנן והא דקאמר מהו דתימא רבנן בכלי נמי פטרי היינו פירושו דס"ל כר"ש וכדפרישית אבל רש"י פירש דפטרי משום דלא שייכא גזיזה אלא בצמר ואין נראה לר"י דבהא ליכא למיטעי דבכל בעלי חיים שייכא גזיזה כדאמר לעיל התולש כנף חייב משום גוזז: **והוא** שפירשו כלפי מעלה. פירש בקונטרס כנגד ראשי אצבעותיו שהן למעלה כשמגביה ידיו ור"ת מפרש שכלפי גוף קרי כלפי מעלה כדאשכחן בפ"ב דנדה (דף יג:) דקאמר מן העטרה ולמעלה והתם היינו לצד הגוף*): **פוקסת**. מה שפירש בקונטרס פוקסת היינו סורקת ביד או במסרק אין נראה דבגמרא משמע דהוי כעין טוויה וסריקה אינה כעין טוויה כלל ועוד דא"כ היה שונה סורקת כדתנן (נזיר דף מב.) נזיר חופף ומפספס אבל לא סורק א): **וכי** דרך אריגה בכך. ואף על גב דקולע נימין חשיבא אריגה כדאמרינן בפרק במה אשה (ג) (לעיל ד' סד.) הכא בשער לא חשיבא אריגה כמו בבגד ועוד דהכא אין סופה להתקיים שעומדת לסתירה:

החולב

*) [ועי' תוס' מנחות יא: ד"ה מלמטה]

עין משפט נר מצוה

לא א מיי' פט"ו מהל' שבת הלכה כב ופכ"ו הלכה כג סמג לאוין סה טוש"ע א"ח סי' שי"א סעיף ב:

לב ב ג מיי' פ"י מהל' טומאת צרעת הלכה א סמג לאוין שמג:

לג ד ה ו ז ח מיי' פ"ט מהל' שבת הלכה ח ט סמג לאוין סה טוש"ע א"ח סי' שמ סעיף א:

לד ט מיי' פי"ב מהל' ע"ז הלכה י סמג לאוין ס טוש"ע שם וטוש"ע י"ד סי' קפב סעיף ו:

לה י כ מיי' פ"ט מהל' שבת הלכה ט סמג לאוין סה טוש"ע א"ח סי' שכח סעיף לא:

רבינו חננאל

מחייבין חדא דלאו הכי קאמר לא בבעיא ולא בתשובה ועוד דאיפשיטא לן בזה יכול וזה יכול שאע"פ שמוציא כמה שיעורין פטורין הלכך ליכא לאוקמא אלא בענין זה אינו יכול וזה אינו יכול ואמרי' דשיעור אחד לכולן וחייבין בו. אמר רב פפא משמיה דרבא אף אנן נמי תנינא היה יושב ע"ג מטה וד' טליות תחת רגלי מטה טמאות מפני שאינה יכולה לעמוד על ג' ואמאי ליבעי שיעור לזה ושיעור לזה פי' שיעור רובו של זב דתנן זב שהיה מוטל על ה' ספסלין לרוחבו טהורין ותני עלה מפני שאין רובו על אחד מהן והכי קאמר הני ד' טליות כל חדא אין רובו עליה ואמאי טמאות אלא לאו משום דשיעור אחד לכולן אמר רב נחמן אף אנן נמי תנינא צבי שנכנס לבית ונעל אחד בפניו חייב נעלו השנים פטורין לא יכול אחד לנעלו ונעלו שנים חייבים ור' שמעון פטור אמאי חייבין ניבעי שיעור צידה לזה ושיעור צידה לזה לאו משום דאמרינן שיעור אחד לכולן ומן הא נמי גמרינן דהא שמעתא לענין זה אינו יכול וזה אינו יכול אמירא חדא מדמפרש לא יכול א' להוציאו והוציאוהו שנים חייבים ועוד מדר"ש פטור (יפטור) בהא אמר רבינא אף אנן נמי תנינא השותפין שגנבו חייבין עיקר דילה [בב"ק עח] השותפין שגנבו וטבחו פטורין והתניא השותפין שגנבו חייבין אר"נ לא קשיא כאן בשותף שגנב מחבירו כאן בשותף שגנב מעלמא. איתיביה רבא לרב נחמן יכול שותף שגנב מחבירו ושותפין שגנבו יהו חייבין ת"ל וטבחו או מכרו מכרו כלו טבחו כלו אלא אמר רב נחמן לא קשיא כאן בשותף שטבחו לדעת חבירו כאן בשותף שטבחו שלא בדעת חבירו: ואמאי ניבעי טביחה לזה וטביחה לזה והיכי מחייבי שנים בטביחה אחת אלא לאו משום דאמרינן שיעור אחד לכולן אמר רב אשי אף אנן נמי תנינא שנים שהוציאו קנה של גרדי חייבין אע"פ [דמהא לא] שמעינן מינה דשיעור אחד לכולן או צריכי שיעור לכל אחד ואחד מפני שקנה של גרדי יש בו כשני שיעורין וכבר שמענו מן הנך מתניתא דאמרי' שיעור אחד לכולן אלא דגמרינן דלענין זה אינו יכול קיימינן דהיא פלוגתא דר' שמעון ורבנן והא כי תנא תנא קמיה דרב נחמן שנים שהוציאו קנה של גרדי פטורין ור' שמעון מחייב תמה ר"נ ואמר כלפי לייא היכי אמרת הכי הא תנן מתניתין והוציאוהו שנים חייבין ור' שמעון פוטר ותרצה להא ברייתא נמי בהכין הלכך מאי דגרים אמר מר שניהם יכולין ר' מאיר מחייב ואמר עלה איבעיא להו פעותא

מסורת הש"ס

[עירובין מא: מגילה ג:] לעיל פא. ברכות יט: מנחות לז:

נגעים פ"ז מ"ד

עיין לעיל סד: רש"י ד"ה ולא תיפקום

מכות כ: פ"ש *צ"ל פי הזוג בשבת חייב [תוספתא פ"י ע"ש]

[שם]

תורה אור

דברים כב

הגהות הב"ח

(א) גמ' אבל בכלי ד"ס חייב: (ב) תוס' ד"ה וכי דרך וכו'. בפ' במה אשה כ"ב ע"ל מ ע"א גבי תיכי חלילתא ועי' עוד בדף סד ריש ע"א אבל ותולה בצואר כתו:

גליון הש"ס

גמ' שרא ר"נ בר יצחק לאפוקיה לכרמלית. עי' סוכה לו ע"ב הד"ס בשבת: שם אחת משלש. עי' תס"ד סי' מת:

רב נסים גאון

גדול כבוד הבריות שדוחה את לא תעשה שבתורה וזה הדבר מיוחד בלאו דלא תסור כמו שפירשו בברכות (דף יט) בפרק מי שמתו ומשכחת לה עוד בסוף פרק הקומץ (דף לז) במסכת מנחות: התולש סימני טומאה והכוה את המחיה עובר בלא תעשה. עיקר זה הוא מה שהזהיר הכתוב (דברים כד) השמר בנגע הצרעת ואמרו רבותינו ז"ל בפירושו שזה הלשון הוא במקום לא תעשה ובכל מקום שכתוב כמותו לא בא לומר אלא שלא תעשה אותו דבר כמו שאמר (עירובין דף צו) אמר ר' אבין אמר ר' אילעאי כל מקום שנאמר השמר פן ואל אינו אלא לא תעשה והזהיר הקב"ה את המצורע שלא יחתוך מה שנראה בבשרו מסימני צרעת ומי שעובר על כך עובר בלא תעשה ומיכן אמר המשנה התולש סימני טומאה והכוה את המחיה עובר בלא תעשה ומשכחת לה בספרי השמר בלא תעשה בנגע זה שיער לבן הצרעת זו המכוה ולפיכך הוצרכנו שיתיר לנו המילה בעת שתתראה בערלה צרעת כמו שאמרו בפרק ר' אליעזר אומר אם לא הביא כלי (דף קלב) תנו רבנן מילה דוחה את הצרעת כו' תנו רבנן ימול ערלתו ואע"פ שיש שם בהרת ומה אני מקיים השמר בנגע הצרעת בשאר מקומות חוץ מן המילה כו' ת"ל בשר ואע"פ שיש שם בהרת ובפ' ואלו הן הלוקין (מכות כב) אמרו מתקיף לה ר' אבהו וליחשוב נמי קוצץ בהרתו ואזהרתיה השמר בנגע

בנגע

Continuation of translation from previous page as indicated by ◁

GEMARA. R. Eleazar said: They differ only [where it is done] by hand; but if with an implement, all agree that he is culpable. That is obvious, [for] we learnt, WITH EACH OTHER?—You might say, the Rabbis hold [him] exempt even [if he does it] with an implement, while as to what is stated, WITH EACH OTHER, that is to teach you the extent[6] of R. Eliezer['s ruling]:[7] [hence] he informs us [otherwise].

R. Eleazar also said: They differ only [where one does it] for himself; but [if he does it] for his neighbour, all agree that he is not culpable. That is obvious, [for] we learnt, HIS NAILS?—You might say, R. Eliezer holds [him] culpable even [if he does it] for his neighbour, while as to what is stated, HIS NAILS, that
c is to teach you the extent of the Rabbis[' ruling]:[1] [hence] he informs us [otherwise].

LIKEWISE HIS HAIR, etc. It was taught: If one plucks out a full scissors' edge [of hair], he is culpable. And how much is a full scissors' edge? Said Rab Judah: Two [hairs]. But it was taught: But in respect of baldness [the standard is] two?[2]—Say, and likewise in respect of baldness, [the standard is] two. It was taught likewise: If one plucks out a full scissors' edge [of hair] on the Sabbath, he is culpable. And how much is a full scissors' edge? Two. R. Eliezer said: One. But the Sages agree with R. Eliezer in the case of one who picks out white hairs from black ones, that he is culpable even for one;[3] and this is interdicted even on weekdays, for it is said, *neither shall a man put on a woman's garment.*[4]

It was taught: R. Simeon b. Eleazar said: As for a nail the greater part of which is severed,[5] and shreds [of skin] the largest portions of which are severed [from the body],—by hand it is permitted [wholly to remove them]; [if one severs them] with a utensil, he is liable to a sin-offering. Is there anything which [if done] with a utensil renders one liable to a sin-offering, yet is permitted by hand at the very outset?[6]—This is its meaning: If the greater portions thereof are severed by hand, it is permitted [to remove them wholly]; if done with a utensil one is not culpable, yet it is prohibited. If the greater portions thereof are not severed, [if wholly removed] by hand one is not culpable, yet it is prohibited: with a utensil, one is liable to a sin-offering. Rab Judah said: The *halachah* is as R. Simeon b. Eleazar. Said Rabbah b. Bar Ḥanah in R.
d Johanan's name: Providing they are severed towards the top,[1] so that they pain him.

LIKEWISE IF [A WOMAN] PLAITS, etc. She who plaits, paints or rouges, on what score is she culpable?—R. Abin said in the name of R. Jose son of R. Ḥanina: She who plaits on the score of weaving; she who paints on the score of writing; she who rouges on account of spinning.[2] Said the Rabbis before R. Abbahu: Are then weaving, writing, and spinning done in this way? Rather said R. Abbahu: R. Jose son of R. Ḥanina's [state-

(6) Lit., 'power'. (7) Viz., that even then he is culpable.
c (1) Viz., that he is not culpable even when he pares his own nails. (2) V. Deut. XIV, 1: the prohibition is infringed by the plucking of two hairs. The conjunction *waw* may mean either 'and' or 'but'; it is understood in the latter sense here, and thus implies that there is a different standard for the Sabbath, since both statements are part of the same Baraitha. (3) For its removal makes him look younger; hence it is regarded as a labour. (4) Ibid. XXII, 5. This is interpreted as a general prohibition of effeminacy, which includes the attempt to make oneself look young by such methods. (5) I.e, it is hanging and nearly torn off. (6) Surely not!
d (1) Near the nail. (2) The rouge was drawn out in thread-like lengths, and thus it resembled spinning; v. Tosaf. M.Ḳ. 9b s.v. פוקסת.

ment] was explained to me [thus]: [95a] She who paints [is culpable] on the score of dyeing; she who plaits and rouges, on the score of building. Is this then the manner of building?—Even so, as R. Simeon b. Menassia expounded: ***And the Lord God builded the rib*** [*... into a woman*]:[3] this teaches that the Holy One, blessed be He, plaited Eve['s hair] and brought her to Adam, for in the sea-towns plaiting is called 'building'.

It was taught, R. Simeon b. Eleazar said: If [a woman] plaits [hair], paints [the eyes], or rouges [the face],—if [she does this] to herself, she is not culpable; [if to] her companion, she is culpable. And thus did R. Simeon b. Eleazar say on R. Eliezer's authority: A woman must not apply paint to her face, because she dyes.

Our Rabbis taught: One who milks, sets milk [for curdling],[4] and makes cheese, [the standard is] the size of a dried fig. If one sweeps [the floor], lays the dust [by sprinkling water], and removes loaves of honey, if he does this unwittingly on the Sabbath, he is liable to a sin-offering; if he does it deliberately on a Festival, he is flagellated with forty[5] [lashes]: this is R. Eliezer's view. But the Sages say: In both cases it is [forbidden] only as a *shebuth*.[6]

R. Naḥman b. Guria visited Nehardea. He was asked. If one milks, on what score is he culpable? On the score of milking, he replied. If one sets milk, on what score is he culpable? On the score of setting milk, he replied. If one makes cheese, on what score is he liable? On account of making cheese, he replied. Your teacher must have been a reed-cutter in a marsh, they jeered at him. [So] he went and asked in the Beth Hamidrash. Said they
a to him, He who milks is liable on account of unloading.[1] He who sets milk is liable on account of selecting.[2] He who makes cheese is liable on account of building.[3]

'If one sweeps, lays the dust, and removes loaves of honey,—if he does this unwittingly on the Sabbath, he is liable to a sin-offering; if he does it deliberately on a Festival, he is flagellated with forty [lashes]: this is R. Eliezer's view.' R. Eleazar observed, What is R. Eliezer's reason? Because it is written, ***and he dipped it in the forest of honey***:[4] now, what is the connection between a *forest* and *honey*?[5] But it is to teach you: just as a forest, he who detaches [aught] from it on the Sabbath is liable to a sin-offering, so are loaves of honey, he who removes [honey] therefrom is liable to a sin-offering.

Amemar permitted sprinkling [the floors] in Maḥoza.[6] He argued: What is the reason that the Rabbis said [that it is forbidden]? [It is] lest one come to level up depressions [in the earthen floor]. Here there are no depressions.[7] Rabbah Tosfa'ah[8] found Rabina suffering discomfort on account of the heat—others state, Mar Ḳashisha son of Raba found R. Ashi suffering discomfort on account of the heat. Said he to him. Does not my Master agree with what was taught: If one wishes to sprinkle his house on the Sabbath, he can bring a basin full of water, wash his face in one corner, his hands in another, and his feet in another, and thus
b the house is sprinkled automatically? I did not think of it,[1] he replied. It was taught: A wise woman can sprinkle her house on the Sabbath.[2] But now that we hold as R. Simeon,[3] it is permitted even at the very outset.[4]

MISHNAH. IF ONE DETACHES [AUGHT] FROM A PERFORATED POT, HE IS CULPABLE;[5] IF IT IS UNPERFORATED, HE IS EXEMPT. BUT R. SIMEON DECLARES [HIM] EXEMPT IN BOTH CASES.

GEMARA. Abaye pointed out a contradiction to Raba—others state, R. Ḥiyya b. Rab to Rab: We learnt, R. SIMEON DECLARES [HIM] EXEMPT IN BOTH CASES, which proves that according to R. Simeon a perforated [pot] is treated the same as an unperforated [one]. But the following contradicts it. R. Simeon said: The only difference between a perforated and an unperforated [pot]

(3) Gen. II, 22.
(4) Rashi: Jast.: who beats milk into a pulp. Levy, *Wörterbuch*, s.v. חבין: if one curdles milk in order to press butter out of it; v. also *T.A.* II, 135. (5) Strictly speaking, thirty-nine. (6) V. Glos. This being a Rabbinical interdict, there is neither a sin-offering nor flagellation.
a (1) It is similar thereto, the milk being unloaded from whence it is collected in the cow. As such it is a secondary form of threshing, where the chaff is separated and unloaded, as it were, from the grain. (2) For the whey is thereby selected and separated from the rest of the milk which is to curdle. (3) The solidifying of the liquid is regarded as similar to the act of putting together an edifice. (4) I Sam. XIV, 27, lit. translation. E.V.: *honeycomb*. (5) Surely none at all! (6) V. *supra* 33a, n. c11. (7) All the houses had stone floors. (8) Perhaps of Thospia. Neub. *Géogr.* p. 332: capital of the Armenian district Thospitis.
b (1) Others: I do not agree with it. (2) By the foregoing or a similar device. (3) That what is unintentional is permitted. When one sprinkles it is not his intention that the water should knead together bits of earth and smooth out the depressions. (4) Without resort to any expedient. (5) Cf. *supra* 81b, n. a3.

לעצמה פטורה · שאינה יכולה לבנות יפה ואין דרך בנין אלא אשה לחברתה שרואה ועושה : וכן · מילתא אחריתי דשבת לאיסורא : סרק · לבע אדום הוא הבא בקנים שקורין טיפוניי"ן : המחבץ · המעמיד החלב בקיבה ול"נ מחבץ עושה כמין כלי גמי ונותן הקפוי בתוכו ומי החלב שהן נסיובי נוטפין ולועזין אותן אנקייד"ש : המכבד · את הבית : והמרבץ · במים להרבין את האבק שלא יעלה : חייב חטאת · לקמיה מפרש טעמא דהרודה חלות דבש חייב משום תולש (מחבץ חייב משום בורר) ומכבד ומרבץ משום בונה : אחד זה ואחד זה · אחד שבת ואחד יו"ט : משום שבות · דילמא כי כניס ליה מתמלאין הגומות שבבית מאליהן והוי בנין : קטיל קני באגמא · חותך קנים מן האגם הוה לא ידע לפרש משנה : מפרק · כמו מפרק משאוי שפורק אוכל ממקום שנתכסה בו והוי תולדת דש ואית דאמרי תולדה דקוצר ולא היא דלאו מחובר הוא אלא פקיד ועקיר וקאי בעטיני הדד כתבואה בקשיה ולשון מפרק נמי לא שייך למימר אלא לשון תולש : בורר · אוכל מתוך פסולת : זילחא · לרבץ הבית ורצפת אבנים היתה °בכל העיר: מהבלא · שהיה אבק עולה ומרבה הבל : לאו אדעתאי · לא הייתי זכור ורבותי פירשו לא סבירא לי : אשה חכמה · אשת ת"ח או בת ת"ח ששמעה מאביה: מרבצת ביתה· רוחצת קיתוניות בזוית זו וכוסות בזוית זו : כרבי שמעון · דדבר שאין מתכוין מותר והמרבץ אינו מתכוין להדביק עפר בגומא ולהשוות הבית אלא שלא יעלה אבק : מתני' התולש מעציץ נקוב חייב · דהוי כמחובר דיונק מן הקרקע ע"י הנקב שמריח לחלוחית הקרקע ואפילו הנקב בדופנו : אלא

תורה אור

*כוחלת משום צובעת [ג]גודלת ופוקסת משום בונה וכי דרך בנין בכך אין *כדדרש רבי שמעון בן מנסיא °ויבן ה' אלהים את הצלע מלמד שקילעה הקב"ה לחוה והביאה אצל אדם שכן בכרכי הים קורין לקלעיתא בניתא תניא *ר"ש בן אלעזר אומר גודלת כוחלת ופוקסת לעצמה פטורה לחברתה חייבת וכן היה רבי שמעון בן אלעזר אומר משום רבי אליעזר [ב]אשה לא תעביר *סרק על פניה מפני שצובעת תנו רבנן[ג] *החולב והמחבץ °והמגבן כגרוגרת [ה]המכבד והמרבץ והרודה חלות דבש שגג בשבת חייב חטאת הזיד ביום טוב לוקה ארבעים דברי ר' אליעזר וחכ"א [ו]אחד זה ואחד זה אינו אלא משום שבות רב נחמן בר גוריא איקלע לנהרדעא בעו מיניה חולב משום מאי מיחייב אמר להו משום חולב מחבץ משום מאי מיחייב אמר להו משום מחבץ *מגבן משום מאי חייב אמר להו משום מגבן אמרו ליה רבך *קטיל קני באגמא הוה אתא שאיל בי מדרשא אמרו ליה [ז]חולב חייב משום מפרק [ח]מחבץ חייב משום בורר [ט]מגבן חייב משום בונה המכבד המרבץ והרודה חלות דבש שגג בשבת חייב חטאת הזיד ביו"ט לוקה ארבעים דברי רבי אליעזר *א"ר אלעזר °מ"ט דר' אליעזר דכתיב °ויטבול אותה ביערת הדבש וכי מה ענין יער אצל דבש אלא לומר לך מה יער התולש ממנו בשבת חייב חטאת אף חלות דבש הרודה ממנו בשבת חייב חטאת [י]אמימר שרא זילחא במחוזא אמר טעמא מאי אמור רבנן דילמא אתי לאשויי גומות הבא ליכא גומות רבא (א) תוספאה אשכחיה לרבינא דקא מצטער מהבלא ואמרי לה מר קשישא ברי' דרבא אשכחיה לרב אשי דקא מצטער מהבלא א"ל לא סבר לה מר להא דתניא הרוצה לרבץ את ביתו בשבת מביא עריבה מלאה מים ורוחץ פניו בזוית זו ידיו בזוית זו רגליו בזוית זו ונמצא הבית מתרבץ מאליו א"ל *לאו אדעתאי תנא אשה חכמה מרבצת ביתה בשבת *°והאידנא דסבירא לן כר' שמעון שרי אפי' לכתחלה: **מתני'** *[א]התולש מעציץ נקוב חייב ושאינו נקוב פטור ור"ש פוטר בזה ובזה : **גמ'** רמי ליה אביי לרבא ואמרי לה רבי חייא בר רב לרב תנן רבי שמעון פוטר בזה ובזה, אלמא נקוב לר"ש כשאינו נקוב משוי ליה ורמינהו ר"ש אומר אין בין נקוב לשאינו נקוב אלא

החולב משום דש הוא · כדפי' בקונט' ואתיא ברייתא כר' יהודה דלאמר יש דישה שלא בגידולי קרקע כדפרי' לעיל בפ' כלל גדול (לעיל דף עג:) וכן נראה לר"י דודאי כרבי יהודה אתיא דהא אסרי חכמים ריבון משום שבות ולר"ש שרי לקמן אפילו לכתחלה :

המכבד והמרבץ · תימה דע"כ מיירי דלא הוי פסיק רישיה שישוה הגומות דאי פסיק רישיה היכי שרי לקמן ר"ש לכתחילה הא מודה ר"ש בפסיק רישיה ולא ימות וכיון דלא הוי פסיק רישיה אמאי מחייב ר' אליעזר חטאת האמר בפ' אמר להם הממונה (יומא ד' לד:) גבי צירוף עששיות דדבר דאין מתכוין מותר לר' יהודה מן התורה דלא הוי מלאכת מחשבת וי"ל דבהא פליגי דר' אליעזר סבר דהוי פסיק רישיה ורבנן סברי דלא הוי והא דאמר והאידנא דסבירא לן כר' שמעון שרי לכתחלה אע"ג דאפשר דסבר ר"ש דהוי פסיק רישיה מכל מקום הש"ס סבר כרבנן דלא הוי פסיק רישיה הילכך שרי לכתחלה כיון דקיימא לן כר"ש [עי' תוספות סנהדרין פה. ד"ה ור"ש] :

והרודה חלות דבש · תימה לר"י אמאי לוקה בי"ט ולרבי אליעזר ורבנן נמי לא פליגי אלא משום דלא חשבי לה מלאכה והא תנן בפ"ק דמגילה (דף ז:) אין בין יו"ט לשבת אלא אוכל נפש בלבד ר' יהודה אומר אף מכשירי אוכל נפש וקאמר בגמ' מ"ט דת"ק אמר קרא הוא לבדו יעשה לכם הוא ולא מכשירין ורבי יהודה כתיב הוא וכתיב לכם כאן במכשירין שאפשר לעשותן מעי"ט וכאן במכשירין שא"א כו' מכלל דאוכל נפש שרי רבי יהודה אפי' באפשר ורבנן נמי משמע דלא פליגי אלא במכשירין ולא באוכל נפש ועוד דהך ברייתא כר' יהודה כדפרישית ועוד דבפ' תולין (לקמן דף קלז:) אמרינן דר' אליעזר סבר כרבי יהודה ועדיפא מדרבי יהודה ושרי אפילו אפשר לעשותן מעי"ט וליכא למימר דמיירי ברודה לצורך חול דמכ"מ תקשי למאן דאית ליה הואיל ואי מקלעי ליה אורחין בפרק אלו עוברין (פסחים ד' מו:) ועוד הדבי אליעזר גופיה אית ליה התם* הואיל ולור"י דאיכא לאוקמי ברודה סמוך לחשיכה דלא חזי תו לאורחין אי נמי בדבש שהדבים או אסור בהנאה דלא חזי לאכילה ומיהו תימה לר"י כיון דמותר לגבן בי"ט מן התורה אפילו באפשר (ב) אפילו לא יהא מותר מדרבנן אלא בדלא אפשר אם כן נפל ביתו בי"ט יהא מותר לבנותו בי"ט דמתוך שהותר בנין לצורך דמגבן הוי משום בונה כדאמר בסמוך הותר נמי שלא לצורך ובלבד שיהא צורך היום לאכול בתוכו שלא יכנו שרב ושמש וי"ל דאסור מדרבנן דהוי עובדא דחול כי היכי דאסורין טחינה והרקדה ביו"ט*: **שרא** זילחא במחוזא · תימה דבשילהי תמיד נשחט (שם ד' סה.) תנן כמעשהו בחול כך מעשהו בשבת אלא שהכהנים מדיחים את העזרה שלא ברצון חכמים ומפרש בגמ'* דשלא ברצון חכמים היינו שלא ברצון ר' אליעזר דאי רבנן שבות הוא ואין שבות במקדש דתניא המכבד והמרבץ כו' ומדמוקי מתני' כר"א משמע דמחייב מדאורייתא אפי' בעזרה דאיכא רצפה והכא משמע דברצפה ליכא אשווי גומות; וי"ל דבההיא איכא אשווי גומות טפי שהיו מתמלאות הגומות שבין רובד לרובד א"נ בעזרה נמי לא אסור לר"א אלא משום שבות אטו היכא דליכא רצפה דאיכא חיוב חטאת לר"א וחמיר האי שבות ונוהג אפילו במקדש וכמה שבות אשכחן במקדש (ג) בפ' בתרא דעירובין (דף קב:) אבל לרבנן לא חמיר האי שבות כיון דאפי' בלא רצפה לא הוי לדידהו אלא איסורא דרבנן הלכך אינו נוהג במקדש: **והאידנא** דקי"ל כר"ש שרי אפי' לכתחלה · בה"ג שרי כיבוד מהאי טעמא אפי' בדאולין ואין נראה לר"י דבפרק כל הכלים (לקמן דף קכד:) אמר ר' *אליעזר אף מכבדות של תמרה מותר לטלטלן ופריך אי מחמה לכל בהא לימא ר' *אליעזר אפי' בשל תמרה משמע דפשיטא ליה דליכא מאן דשרי אפי' לרבי שמעון משום דהוי מלאכתו לאיסור ואי שרי לכבד הוי מלאכתו להיתר אלא ודאי כיבוד אסור לכולי עלמא מפני שמזיז עפר ממקומו ולא שרינן הכא לרבי שמעון אלא דווקא ריבוץ : **ורמינהו** רבי שמעון אומר אין בין נקוב כו' · תימה מאי קפריך והא בהך ברייתא נמי קתני כמו במתני' דלכל מילי נקוב כשאינו נקוב בר מלענין הכשר זרעים בלבד ואי קשיא ליה מ"ש שבת מהכשר זרעים אם כן בלא משנה תקשי ליה ברייתא גופה מ"ש להכשר זרעים חשיב נקוב כמחובר ולענין שאר דברים חשוב כתלוש ואומר ר"ת דהכי פריך כיון דלענין שבת חשיב נקוב כשאינו נקוב אף על גב דהוי לקולא ופטור וכן לענין כלאים במסכת כלאים (פ"ז מ"ח) כ"ש לענין הכשר זרעים אית לן לאחשוביה נקוב כשאינו נקוב דהוי לחומרא ובברייתא קתני דנקוב הוי כמחובר לענין הכשר זרעים שאינו מכשיר והכי פירושא דברייתא אין בין נקוב לשאינו

רבינו חננאל

הוא אלא הכין מיבעי למגרס . איבעיא להו בעינן שיעור לזה ושיעור לזה או לאו למגרס קמיה פיסקא מן ברייתא ואעיקר מתניתין קאי דתנן לא יכול להוציאו והוציאו שנים חייבין ור' שמעון פוטר דלא משכחת הא פלוגתא דרבי שמעון ורבנן אלא לענין זה אינו יכול וזה אינו יכול דלענין שניה(אין) יכולין לית מאן דמחייב אלא ר' מאיר ולענין אחד יכול ואחד אינו יכול דברי הכל חייב כמו דאיתא לעיל בשמעתא בהדיא הלכך הא מתני' דרבנן מחייבין ור"ש פוטר אלא בזה אינו יכול וזה אינו יכול ועלה אמרי' הדין בעיא ותשובתו המוציא אוכלין פחות כשיעור בכלי פטור אף על הכלי שהכלי טפילה לו ואם הוציא כשיעור בכלי חייב על האוכלין ופטור על הכלי ואם היה הכלי צריך לו חייב על זה ועל זה כגון שצריך לאוכל וצריך עוד לכלי אי נמי שאין יכול להוציא את האוכל אלא בכלי כגון התותין בא"י וכיוצא בהן ודייקינן מי אתינן למשמע מינה אכל שני זיתי חלב בהעלם אחד דהוא כמי שהוציא אוכל בכלי אחד חייב שתים אמר רב ששת הכא במאי עסקינן כגון ששגג על האוכלין והזיד [על] הכלי פי' והכי קאמר חייב ע"ז חטאת וע"ז (כזית) [כרת].מתקיף לה רב אשי וכו' כגון ששגג בזה ובזה ונודע לו על זה ובפלוגתא דר' יוחנן ור"ל וכבר פרישנא לעיל בכלל גדול והכא קא מסתייע ר"י דאמר חייב שתים [דכתיב] על חטאתו והביא:ואת החי במטה פטור אף על המטה שהמטה טפלה לו אוקימנא באדם את עצמו ודברי הכל בין לר' נתן ובין לרבנן אבל בבהמה חיה ועוף פליגי רבנן ור' נתן רבנן מחייבי עלייהו דסברי אנב ביעותיה משרבטי נפשייהו ומתרשלין ואין נושאין את עצמן ור' נתן פוטר (בחיים) אדא בר אבא לרבא הא דתנן לענין אין מוכרין בהמה גסה לנכרים בן בתירא מתיר בסוס ותניא עלה בן בתירא מתיר בסוס מפני שהוא עושה מלאכה שאין חייבין עליה חטאת וסליק אדעתין ש החי דהוי בן בתירא כר"נ דאמר חי נושא את עצמו ורבנן נמי קאמרי הכי היכי אמר בן בתירא ור' נתן אמרו דבר אחד אלמא רבנן פליגי עלייהו לימא בן בתירא ור' נתן ורבנן אמרו דבר אחד בלבד הוא דמודו אבל כל בהמה חיה ועוף בין חיים בין מתים רבנן מחייבי עלייהו ובן בתירא ור' נתן תרווייהו שאמרו דבר אחד לענין הוצאת בהמה חיה ועוף לאו לענין הוצאת אדם ודתניא שאין חייבין עליה חטאת לאו נשיאת אדם כדאסיקת אדעתין מעיקרא אלא אפי' בסוס המיוחד לעופות קאמר פליגי רבנן עליה ומקשינן ומי איכא סוס מיוחד לעופות ואמרי' איכא (דבי זיירן) [דבי זוירן] הנץ וכיוצא בו שהמלכים

עין משפט נר מצוה

לו א מיי' פכ"א מהל' שבת הלכה כב [כ"ל פכ"ג הל' יב כתב כוחלת משום כותבת וכתב הב"ע בשם ריא"ז ולא ידעתי לו ישוב אם לא שנאמר שנגרסה מיימוני כיס כתוב גם בלישנא בתרא דכוחלת הוי משום כותבת ע"ש ולדעתי צריכים לומר כן גם בסמג לאוין סה שכתב כוחלת משום כותבת וס' הלא ציני בערוך ערך גדל כתב הגרסה במשנה כוחלת משום כותבת גודלת ופוקסת משום בונה מעתק זכינו שגם הרמב"ם והסמג ואחריהם ככל מגרבטורה היה גרסתם כן ושוב אין מקום לתמיהות הפרי' ע"ש] סמג לאוין סה טוש"ע א"ח סי' שג סעיף כה :

לז ב מיי' פכ"ב שם הלכה כו סמג שם טוש"ע שם סעיף כו :

לז [ג] [מיי' פכ"א שם הלכה כג כג טוש"ע שם סעיף כה :]

לז [ג] [מיי' פ"ח שם הלכה ו ופ"ח הל' ז בריש פרק כלל גדול ד' לד. וברא"ש סי' ב]:

לח ג ד מיי' פכ"א מהל' שבת הל' ג ופ"ח הל' י סמג טוש"ע א"ח סי' שלז סעיף א וסי' שלו סעי' ג :

לט ה מיי' פ"ח מהל' שבת הלכה ו סמג שם טוש"ע א"ח סי' שכ סעיף כ :

מ ו מיי' שם הלכה יא ופכ"א הלכה יז סמג שם טוש"ע א"ח סי' שיט סעיף ה :

מא ז מיי' פ"י מהלכות שבת הלכה יג :

מב ח מיי' פכ"א שם הלכה ג סמג שם טוש"ע א"ח סי' שלו סעיף ג :

מג ט מיי' שם וסמג שם טוש"ע שם סעיף ה :

מד י מיי' פ"ח מהל' שבת הל' ג וטוש"ע א"ח סי' שלו סעיף ז :

מסורת הש"ס

ברכות סא. עירובין יח. נדה מה: ע"ש

[תוספ' פ"ו]

[גירסת הערוך שרק פסחים סה. תוספ' פי"ג]

[פי' המקפה גבינה ומקבץ פתיתי החלב לעשותם חריץ של גבינה ערוך]

[סנהדרין נג.]

ב"ע סו. פ:

[ברכות כו. וש"נ]

[עירובין קי:]

[לקמן קח.]

[ע"ש]

[וע' תוס' ביצה ג. ד"ה גזירה שמא]

[סה.]

[צ"ל אלעזר]

[צ"ל אלעזר]

הגהות הב"ח

(א) גמ' רבא תוספאה: (ב) תוס' ד"ה והרודה וכו' אפי' לא יהא מותר. נ"ב עיין פ"ק דמגילה ד' ז: (ג) ד"ה שרא וכו' אשכחן במקדש. נ"ב עיין ע"ל פ' כל הכלים ד' קכג: בד"ה שרי הוא ככל :

גליון הש"ס גמ' והמגבן כגרוגרת. ע' לעיל דף עו ע"ב תד"ה המוציא: גמ' מ"ט דר"א דכתיב ויטבול. ע' פ"י מ"ז דשביעית בפי' הרע"ב : **רש"י** ד"ה זילחא כו' בכל העיר . עי' לעיל כט ע"ב תד"ה גזירה ולקמן דף קנא ע"ב רש"י ד"ה קרקע :

אלא להכשיר זרעים בלבד א"ל לכל מילי רבי שמעון כתלוש משוי ליה ושאני לענין טומאה דהתורה ריבתה טהרה אצל זרעים שנאמר °על כל זרע זרוע אשר יזרע [ויקרא יא] בעא מיניה ההוא סבא מרבי זירא שורש כנגד נקב מה לי א"ר שמעון אישתיק ולא אמר ליה ולא מידי זימנא חדא אשכחיה דיתיב וקאמר ומודה ר"ש שאם ניקב בכדי טהרתו א"ל השתא שורש כנגד נקב בעאי מינך ולא אמרת לי ולא מידי °ניקב בכדי טהרתו מיבעיא אמר אביי ואי איתמר להא דרבי זירא הכי הוא דאיתמר ומודה רבי שמעון שאם ניקב למטה מרביעית *אמר רבא *חמש מדות בכלי חרס ניקב כמוציא משקה טהור מלטמא גיסטרא ועדיין כלי הוא לקדש בו מי חטאת ניקב בכונס משקה טהור מלקדש בו מי חטאת ועדיין כלי הוא להכשיר בו זרעים ניקב כשורש קטן טהור מלהכשיר בו זרעים ועדיין כלי הוא לקבל בו זיתים ניקב כמוציא זיתים טהור מלקבל בו זיתים ועדיין כלי *הוא לקבל בו רימונים *ניקב [פ"ב] כמוציא רימונים טהור מכלום ואם הוקף צמיד פתיל עד שיפחת רובו אמר רב אסי שמעתי כלי חרס שיעורו כמוציא רימון אמר ליה רבא שמא לא שמעת אלא במוקף צמיד פתיל והא רבא הוא דאמר מוקף צמיד פתיל עד שיפחת רובו לא קשיא

הא

רש"י

אלא להכשיר זרעים · הזרועים בתוכו עציץ נקוב אינו מקבל הכשר לטומאה ושאינו נקוב מקבל הכשר דתלוש הוא והא רבי שמעון קאמר ליה וה"נ ר"ש אומר אין בו נקוב כו' דאילו לרבנן איכא טובא דהא מיחייבי אנקוב משום שבת ופטרי אשאינו נקוב: לכל מילי · לשבת ולקנות במשיכה ולא בכסף ולפרוזבול שאינו נכתב אלא על הקרקע: אשר יזרע · כדרך שאדם מוציא לזריעה למעוטי מחובר כל דהו להכי אהני זריעות יתירי דקרא ומיהו שאינו נקוב תלוש גמור הוא: מה לי אמר רבי שמעון · מי מודה דהא במחובר הוא האי שורש ואי תלשו לי' בשבת מיחייב: זימנין · פעם אחרת: שאם ניקב · העציץ בכדי טהרתו ושאם נטמא נטהר בשבירה זו והיינו כמוציא זית דתנן במסכת כלים (פ"ג מ"א) כלי חרס העשוי לאוכלין שיעורו כזיתים ומודה ר' שמעון בהא דחשיב מחובר כל הזרעים שבתוכו דתו לא הוי כלי: ניקב בכדי טהרתו מיבעיא · דהוה לן לספוקי ביה בהנך דלאו כנגד הנקב ולא פשטת להו דכולהו מחובר נינהו: אי אתמר לדרבי זירא · דמודה ר"ש בשום נקב: הכי הוא דאיתמר · שאם ניקב למטה מרביעית שאינו מחזיק רביעית מן הנקב ולמטה דבציר מהכי לאו כלי הוא: חמש מדות גרסי': כמוציא משקה · נקב דק מאד שמשקה יוצא בו: טהור מלטמא גיסטרא · כלומר אם כלי שלם הוא אינו נטהר בכך אבל אם היה שבר כלי והיה ראוי להשתמש בו דמקבל טומאה משנשבר כדתנן הן וקרקרותיהן ודופנותיהן יושבין שלא מסומכין כו' באלו טרפות (חולין דף נד:) וניקב שוב כמוציא משקה אינו טמא עוד משום תורת גיסטרא: גיסטרא · שבר כלי דאין שבר כלי חשוב להצניעו משניקב ולומר הבא גיסטרא (א) אחר ונניח תחתיו לקבל טיף טיף הנוטף מזה אבל אם היה כלי שלם וניקב מעט אין מאבדין אותו אלא אומר הבא גיסטרא אחר ונניח תחתיו: ועדיין כלי הוא לקדש בו מי חטאת · כלומר אם כלי שלם היה וניקב כמוציא משקה עדיין כל תורת כלי עליו ואפי' לקדש בו מי חטאת באפר פרה דבעינן כלי ראוי דכתיב (במדבר יט) מים חיים אל כלי וכ"ש שמקבל טומאה: ניקב כונס משקה · שאם מושיבו על המים נכנס בתוכו דהיינו נקב רחב קצת: טהור מלקדש בו מי חטאת · טהור לאו דוקא אלא כמו טהר יומא (ברכות דף ב.) כלומר בטל לו מתורת כלי לענין מי חטאת: ועדיין כלי הוא לענין הכשר זרעים · הזרועים בתוכו דכתלושין נינהו ואפילו לרבנן שאין נקב זה ראוי להריח לחלוחית הקרקע: ניקב כשורש קטן . הוי טפי מבכונס משקה: טהור מלהכשיר זרעים . לרבנן דהוי עציץ נקוב: ועדיין כלי הוא לקבל בו זיתים · שהוא שיעור לטומאה בכל כלי חרס העשוי לאוכלין סתם כל זמן שלא יחדו לרימונים ומקבל עדיין טומאה: טהור מלקבל בו זיתים · כלומר מלקבל עוד טומאה משום תורת סתם כלי חרס שהרי שיעורן כזיתים ואם היתה עליו טומאה נטהר ממנה: ועדיין כלי הוא לקבל בו רימונים · °שאם יחדו שוב לרימונים מקבל טומאה מכאן ולהבא או אם היה מיוחד לרימונים מתחילה לא נטהר: טהור מכלום · משום כלי אלא א"כ מצניעו לגיסטרא יטמא בתורת גיסטרא: ואם היה מוקף צמיד פתיל · והוא באהל המת אין טומאה נכנסת בו דרך נקב ומציל על כל מה שבתוכו: עד שיפחת רובו . דכל כלי פתוח כתיב (שם) דרך פתח נכנסת לו טומאה ולא דרך נקביו: אלא במוקף צמיד פתיל · שאם ניקב כמוציא רימון אינו מציל:

ברברבי

תוספות

לשאינו נקוב דלכל מילי נקוב ושאינו נקוב שוין ואזלינן לחומרא דבמקום דהוי תלוש חומרא חשבינן תרוייהו כתלוש ואי הוי מחובר חומרא כמו שבת וכלאים חשבינן תרוייהו כמחובר אלא בהכשר זרעים דלא החמירו לאחשובי נקוב כתלוש כשאינו נקוב אלא אוקמוה אדיניה ליחשב כמחובר וי"ל לפי זה דאין תורמין לר"ש מן הנקוב על פירות הגדלים בקרקע כמו באינו נקוב דאזלינן לחומרא ור"י פי' דהכי פריך ר"ש אומר אין בין נקוב לשאינו נקוב אלא הכשר זרעים בלבד וכיון דגבי הכשר זרעים חשוב נקוב כמחובר אע"ג דהוי להקל שאינו מקבל הכשר ש"מ מדאורייתא חשוב כמחובר דאי מדאורייתא חשוב כתלוש היכי הוה מטהרינן להו מדרבנן כשנגעה בהן טומאה כיון דקיבלו הכשר מן התורה ואם כן הא דקתני ברישא דברייתא אין בין נקוב לשאינו נקוב ע"כ לעשות שניהם כמחוברים ולא לעשות שניהם כתלושין כיון דנקוב חשיב מחובר מדאורייתא ובכל מילי נקוב ואינו נקוב כמחוברים חוץ מהכשר זרעים בלבד דאחמיר רבנן לטמויי כשאינו נקוב והשתא משני שפיר שאני לענין טומאה כו' דהתם הוא דכתב רחמנא בהדיא דחשיב נקוב כמחובר אבל לכל מילי חשיב כתלוש ולהכי פטר במתני' אבל קשה לאלו הפירושים דקאמר אלמא נקוב לר"ש כשאינו נקוב משוי ליה משמע דבעי לאיתויי מברייתא דלא משוי נקוב כשאינו נקוב וזה אינו ויש לפרש דה"ק אלמא נקוב לר"ש כשאינו נקוב משוי ליה ורמינהו כו' דאדרבה שאינו נקוב כנקוב משוי ליה ועוד פר"י דה"ק אין בין נקוב לשאינו נקוב לענין מעשר ופאה וכלאים דכיון דכתיב בהו שדך וכרמך וכן במעשר כתיב היוצא השדה שנה שנה חשיבי תלוש בין שאינו נקוב ואין בו חילוק אלא לענין הכשר זרעים וכל דדמי ליה כגון שבת שאינן תלוים בדבר שהוא חשוב שדה אלא בתלוש ומחובר ובהנהו לא הוי נקוב כשאינו נקוב ולפי זה אתי שפיר הא דקאמר אלמא נקוב לר"ש כשאינו נקוב משוי ליה ורמינהו דלא משוי נקוב כשאינו נקוב:

ומודה ר"ש שאם ניקב בכדי טהרתו · פי' כמוציא זית דסתמו של כלי חרס לאוכלין ושיעורן כמוציא זית ונראה לר"י דהיינו טעמא דמודה משום דבטל אגב קרקע כשניקב בכדי טהרתו ודוקא בניקב כמוציא זית אבל בכלי המיוחד למשקין אע"פ שטהרתו בכונס משקה לא אמרי' דבטל דאפי' לרבנן לא חשבי ליה כמחובר בכונס משקה אלא כשורש קטן כדאמר בסמוך:

טהור מלקדש בו מי חטאת · וכ"ש דטהור מלקבל טומאה אם היה מיוחד למשקין: **טהור** מלהכשיר בו זרעים · משמע דכלי חרס בעי נקיבה ודלא כפי' הקונט' בפ"ק דגיטין (דף ז.) שפירש דספינה של חרס דכיון שהיא של עפר חשובה כנקובה ועת לקצר:

ניקב כמוציא רימון טהור מכלום · תימה לר"י היכי קאמר דטהור מכלום והלא אם יחדו לגיסטרא מקבל טומאה כדפי' בקונט' וכפירושו ודאי כן הוא שהרי אפילו אם נשברו בשברים דקים מקבלים השברים טומאה בתורת גיסטרא כשנשאר בשברים שיעור המפורש במסכת כלים (פ"ב משנה ב) ומייתי לה בפ' אלו טריפות (חולין נד:) הדקים שבכלי חרס הן וקרקרותיהן ודופנותיהן יושבין שלא מסומכין שיעורן בכדי סיכת קטן עד לוג ומלוג עד סאה ברביעית כו' ועוד קשה לרשב"א דהוה מצי למימר שש מדות בכלי חרס וי"ל דכשנשבר לגמרי השברים ראויין לגיסטרא אבל כשהכלי שלם אלא שניקב כמוציא רימון אין ראוי לגיסטרא ואפי' יחדו בטלה דעתו אצל כל אדם אבל מתוך פי' הקונט' משמע דכשניקב כמוציא רימון ראוי הוא לגיסטרא דפירש טהור מכלום משום כלי אא"כ מצניעו משום גיסטרא ולפירושו הא דלא נקט ו' מדות דלא מיירי אלא כשיכול להשתמש כדרכן וניקב כמוציא רימון אין ראוי אלא אם כן מטהו על צדו: **שמא** לא שמעת אלא במוקף צמיד פתיל · תימה לר"י דילמא במיוחד לרימונים שמע ואצטריך לאפוקי מדר"א דאמר בסמוך ניקב כמוציא זית אין לו טומאה כו' וי"ל דמשמע דבסתם כלי חרס איירי בלא יחוד וליכא למימר דלענין הכשר זרעים שמע כמ"ד בסמוך שיעורו כמוציא רימון לפירש הקונט' דפירש דלענין הכשר זרעים פליגי דא"כ אמאי נקט כלי חרס אפי' כלי עץ נמי ועוד דרבא סבירא ליה דלענין הכשר זרעים שיעורו כשורש קטן:

הא

עין משפט נר מצוה

מה א מיי' פי"ג מהל' כלים הלכה ב:

רבינו חננאל

שהמלכים צריכין בהן עופות וקורין אותו כאו האחד העוסק [בהן] קורין אותו בלשון פרסי כאויאר ובזמן שהוא יותר מאחד קוראין להן כאוארן ויש להן סוסים מיוחדין לכך לשאת את העופות הדורסין הנקראין כאי ואמרינן א"ר יוחנן הלכה כבן בתירא א"ר יוחנן ואדם כפות מודה רבי נתן שאינו יכול לשאת את עצמו והמוציאו בשבת חייב א"ל רב אדא בר מתנא לאביי והא הני פרסאי דכפיתי דמו שאת רואה אותן שאינן יכולין להלך על רגליהן ואינן יוצאין ובאין אלא רכובין הסוס נושא אותן ובן בתירא מתיר למכרן לנכרים וסבר ליה שהוא עושה מלאכה שאין חייבין עליה חטאת דאלמא אף הכפות בן בתירא פוטר עליו וא"ר יהודה בן בתירא ור' נתן אמרו דבר אחד והא א"ר יוחנן מודה ר' נתן בכפות ופריק ליה אביי דהנך פרסאי יש בהו כח להלך ואף הן נושאין את עצמן ומאי דתקישא להו רמות רוחא מענגין את עצמן מלהלך כענין דכתיב אשר לא נסתה כף רגלה וגו' מהתענג ומרוך וכי בעי למרהט מצי דהא הוא פרדשכא ואיהו פקיד המלך דרתח מלכא עליה והיט תלתא פרסי בכרעיה אבל חולה ודאי ככפות דמי ומחייב ר' נתן על הוצאתו כההיא דגמרא דב' שעירי יוה"כ דתניא עתי אפי' בשבת ואמרי' למאי הלכתא אמר רב ששת שאם חלה מרכיבו [על כתיפו] [illegible] דתני בריש פירקא נוטל אדם את בנו והאבן בידו דאמרינן עלה אמר רבא הוציא תינוק וכיס תלוי לו בצוארו חייב וליחייב משום תינוק רבא כר' נתן סבירא ליה דאמר חי נושא את עצמו וליבטל כיס לגבי תינוק מי לא תנן ואת החי במטה פטור אף על המטה שהמטה טפלה לו מטה לגבי חי מבטל לה כיס לגבי תינוק לא מבטיל ליה. הוציא תינוק מת וכיס תלוי לו בצוארו פטור וליחייב משום תינוק רבה כר' שמעון סבירא ליה [דאמר] כל מלאכה שאינה צריכה לגופה פטור עליה ומדקדקי רבנן בההיא דקא מפטר המוציא את מת דהני מילי דהיכא דלית ליה ריחא דאי אית ליה ריחא נמצאת הוצאתו מלאכה שצריכה לגופה ותניא בפ' א"ר עקיבא [illegible] המוציא ריח רע כל שהוא ואית לה להא מלתא סייעתא בתלמוד א"י ומלתא דמוכחא היא . אמר רבה ומודה ר' שמעון במרא לחפור בו וס"ת לקרות בו דאי מפיק להו חייב ודייקינן בה מאי אצטריך רבה לא שמעינן

רב נסים גאון

בנגע הצרעת: **אמר** רבא ה' מדות בכלי חרש כו' משכחת לה בתורת כהנים כל אשר בתוכו יטמא כמה שיעורו של נקב בכלי חרש בכונס משקה ובכלי שטף במוציא זיתים ובמסכת כלים פרק ג' שיעור כלי חרס לטהר העשוי לאוכלין שיעורו כזיתים העשוי למשקין שיעורו כמשקין כו' הלפס והקדירה שיעורן כזיתים כו' ובפרק ד' שנינו וכן ניסטרא שנתרועעה ואינה מקבלת משקין אע"פ שמקבלת אוכלין טהורה שאין שירין לשירין אי זו היא ניסטרא כל שניטלו אזניה והיו בה חדודין יוצאין ובתוספתא בפ' ג' נסדקה לטפה מאזניה אע"פ שאזניה קיימות הרי זו כניסטרא ואם מתחילה עשאה בלא אזנים נידונת כחבית וכן עוד אמרו אם היתה ניסטרא הרי זו טהורה שלא אמרו שירים לשירים אלא שירים לכלים ובפ' ז' כיצד בודקין כלי חרס לידע אם ניקב בכונס משקה אם לאו מביא עריבה מליאה מים ונותן את הקדירה לתוכה אם כינסה בידוע שבכונס משקה ואם לאו בידוע שבמוציא משקה כו' ומשכחת לה בגמ' במסכת נידה בפרק בא סימן התחתון (דף מח) ושנינו בו כל כלי חרס מכנים ומוציא ויש שהוא מוציא ואינו מכנים ותני עלה מכנים פסול למי חטאת לפי שאמרה תורה במי חטאת (במדבר יט) ונתן עליו מים חיים אל כלי ואם ניקב בכונס משקה יצא מתורת כלי באלו הראיות ובמשנה במסכת פרה בפרק ה' מפני שאין ממלאין ואין מקדשין ואין מזין מי חטאת אלא בכלי ולזה אמרו ניקב בכונס משקה פסול למי חטאת ומשום ניסטרא ו"אמר רב אשי שנין כלי חרס שיעורו בכונס משקה לא אמרו מוציא משקה אלא לענין ניסטרא בלבד מאי טעמא אמר מר זוטרא בריה דרב נחמן לפי שאין אומרין הבא ניסטרא לניסטרא ובפרק כל הבשר (חולין דף קז) אמר רבא כלי שניקב בכונס משקה אין נוטלין ממנו לידים:

ולד:

מסורת הש"ס

תורה אור

ויקרא יא

[עי' תוס' ב"ב קנס. ד"ה ליתמר קמן]

[עי' תוס' עירובין ד: ד"ה כל וכו' ד"ה שיעור]

הגהות הב"ח

(א) רש"י ד"ה גיסטרא וכו' הבא גיסטרא אחר ונניח כצ"ל ותיבת אחר נמחק:

גליון הש"ס

גמ' ניקב בכדי טהרתו מיבעיא. עי' כתובות ע"א ע"א תוס' ד"ה ותיבעי: רש"י ד"ה ועדיין כלי הוא לקבל בו רמונים שאם יחדו. עיין לעיל דף נט ע"א תוס' ד"ה ר' יוחנן וכו' ד' ע"ב תוס' ד"ה כל כלי ונפ"ב מ"ב דכלים בר"ש שם:

[95*b*] is in respect of making [its] plants fit [to become unclean]?[6] —In all respects, answered he, R. Simeon treats it as detached, but in the matter of uncleanness it is different, because the Torah extended [the scope of] cleanness in the case of plants [seeds], for it is said, [*And if aught of their carcase fall*] *upon any sowing seed which is to be sown*, [*it is clean*].[7]

A certain old man asked R. Zera: If the root is over against the hole, what is R. Simeon's ruling then?[8] He was silent and answered him nought. On a [subsequent] occasion he found him sitting and teaching: Yet R. Simeon admits that if it is perforated to the
a extent of making it clean, [there is culpability].[1] Said he to him, Seeing that I asked you about a root that is over against the perforation and you gave me no reply, can there not be a doubt concerning [a pot that is] perforated to the extent of making it clean?[2] Abaye observed: If this [dictum] of R. Zera was stated, it was stated thus: Yet R. Simeon agrees that if it is perforated below [the capacity of] a *rebi'ith*, [there is culpability].[3]

Raba said: There are five principles in the case of an earthen utensil: [i] If it has a perforation sufficient [only] for a liquid to run out, it is clean in that it cannot be defiled when already a mutilated vessel,[4] yet it is still a utensil in respect of sanctifying the water of lustration therein.[5] [ii] If it has a perforation sufficient for a liquid to run in,[6] it is 'clean' in respect of sanctifying the water of lustration therein,[7] yet it is still a utensil to render its plants fit [to become unclean].[8] [iii] If it has a perforation as large as a small root, it is 'clean' in respect of making its plants fit [to become defiled], yet it is still a utensil in that it can hold olives.[9] [iv] If it has a perforation large enough to allow olives to fall out, it is clean in that it cannot hold olives, yet it is still a utensil to
b contain pomegranates.[1] [v] If it has a perforation large enough to allow pomegranates to fall through, it is clean in respect of all things.[2] But if it is closed with an airtight lid, [it ranks as a utensil] unless the greater portion thereof is broken.[3]

R. Assi said: I have heard that the standard of an earthen vessel is [a hole] large enough to allow a pomegranate to fall out.[4] Said Raba to him: Perhaps you heard [this] only of [a vessel] closed with a tight-fitting lid![5] But it was Raba himself who said: If it is closed with a tight-fitting lid, [it ranks as a utensil] unless the greater portion thereof is broken?—There is no difficulty:

(6) Edibles, e.g., grain, vegetables, etc., can be defiled only if moisture has fallen upon them after they were detached from the soil. Now, a perforated pot is regarded as attached to the soil, and therefore its plants cannot become susceptible to uncleanness; whereas an unperforated pot is detached, and so if moisture falls upon its plant, when grown it is henceforth fit to become unclean—This shows that R. Simeon too recognizes this difference. (7) Lev. XI, 37, i.e., if it is in any way attached to the soil it is clean, and this includes a perforated pot. (8) If one tears out that root on the Sabbath (Rashi). Here the root draws sustenance directly from the ground.

a (1) If a utensil becomes unclean and then a hole is made in it large enough for an olive to fall through, it technically ceases to be a utensil and becomes clean. Thus here too, if the perforation is of that size, R. Simeon admits that the pot and its contents, even such as are not over against the perforation, are regarded as attached to the soil. (2) For if the former case is doubtful, surely the latter, where the root may still not be directly over the hole, is even more doubtful. (3) I.e., if the perforation is so low in the sides of the pot that the portion of the pot beneath it cannot hold a *rebi'ith*. Then it is certainly not regarded as a utensil, and its plants are held to grow direct from the ground. Accordingly the perforations spoken of hitherto, and in the Mishnah, are high up in the sides of the pot, and certainly not in the bottom, as is the case with our pots. (4) If the vessel is sound, such a small hole does not deprive it of its character as a utensil and it is still susceptible to uncleanness. But if it was already mutilated, e.g., cracked, this added perforation renders it incapable of becoming unclean. (5) If otherwise sound, v. Num. XIX, 17: putting the water in a utensil is designated sanctification. (6) That is naturally somewhat larger than the preceding. (7) 'Clean' is employed idiomatically to imply that it is not a utensil in respect of what follows; thus one cannot sanctify, etc. (8) V. *supra* n. b6. Even the Rabbis admit that if the perforation is not larger the pot and its contents are treated as detached. (9) And hence susceptible to defilement. If a utensil is not designated for any particular purpose, it must be able to hold olives in order to be susceptible to defilement.

b (1) I.e., if it was explicitly designated for holding pomegranates, it is still a utensil and susceptible to defilement. (2) It is no longer susceptible, or, if it was defiled before it was perforated, it becomes clean. Henceforth it is susceptible to defilement only if its owner puts it aside to use as a mutilated vessel (Rashi). (3) The reference is to Num. XIX, 15, q.v. If the vessel is closed with a tight-fitting lid, its contents too remain clean, unless the greater portion is broken, in which case it does not rank as a vessel and cannot protect its contents from the contamination spread by the corpse. (4) I.e., unless it has such a large hole it ranks as a utensil. (5) I.e., that it affords no protection if it has such a large hole.

[96*a*] the one refers to large ones, the other to small ones.[6]

R. Assi said, They [the Tannaim] learnt. As for an earthen vessel, its standard is [a hole] large enough to admit a liquid, while [one merely] sufficient to allow a liquid to run out was mentioned only in connection with a mutilated vessel.[7] What is the reason?—Said Mar Zuṭra son of R. Naḥman: Because people do not say, 'Let us bring one fragment for another.'[8]

'Ulla said, Two amoraim in Palestine differ on this matter, [viz.,] R. Jose son of R. Abin and R. Jose son of Zabda: One maintains: [the standard is a hole] large enough to allow a pomegranate
a to fall out; while the other rules: As large as a small root.[1] And your sign is, 'whether one increases or whether one diminishes.'[2]

R. Ḥinena b. Kahana said in R. Eliezer's name: As for an earthen vessel, its standard is [a hole] large enough to allow olives to fall out;[3] and Mar Ḳashisha son of Rabbah completes [this statement] in R. Eliezer's name: And then they rank as vessels of dung, stone, or clay,[4] which do not contract uncleanness either by Biblical or by Rabbinical law;[5] but in respect to [the law of] a tight-fitting lid [it ranks as a vessel] unless the greater portion thereof is broken through.[6]

CHAPTER XI

MISHNAH. **IF ONE THROWS [AN ARTICLE] OVER FROM PRIVATE INTO PUBLIC GROUND [OR] FROM PUBLIC INTO PRIVATE GROUND, HE IS CULPABLE. FROM ONE PRIVATE DOMAIN TO ANOTHER, AND PUBLIC GROUND LIES BETWEEN, R. AKIBA HOLDS HIM LIABLE, BUT THE SAGES DECLARE HIM**
b **EXEMPT. HOW SO?[1] IF THERE ARE TWO BALCONIES FACING EACH OTHER IN THE STREET, HE WHO REACHES OVER OR THROWS [AN ARTICLE] FROM ONE TO THE OTHER IS NOT CULPABLE. IF BOTH ARE ON THE SAME STOREY,[2] HE WHO REACHES OVER IS CULPABLE, WHILE HE WHO THROWS IS NOT, FOR THUS WAS THE SERVICE OF THE LEVITES:[3] TWO WAGGONS [STOOD] BEHIND EACH OTHER IN PUBLIC GROUND, [AND] THEY REACHED OVER THE BOARDS FROM ONE TO ANOTHER, BUT DID NOT THROW.**

(6) Rashi: in the case of large ones the greater portion must be broken; but for small ones a hole large enough for a pomegranate to fall out is sufficient. Ri: In the case of large ones a hole large enough etc., is required, but in the case of small ones, where this may be considerably more than half, if the greater portion thereof is broken it is no longer a utensil. (7) V. *supra* 95*b*, n. a4. (8) I.e., when a mutilated vessel springs a leak of this size, people throw it away without troubling to bring another such vessel or a shard to catch its drippings, therefore it is no longer a vessel.

a (1) Rashi: the question is how large the hole of a perforated pot must be in order to render its plants susceptible to defilement (v. *supra* 95*b*, n. b6). R. Tam: they differ in reference to a vessel closed with a tight-fitting lid (cf. *supra* 95*b*, n. b5). (2) I.e., part of a Talmudic dictum, v. Men. 110*a*, the two extremes (v. Raba's enumeration of the five principles, *supra* 95*b*) are taken, and neither of these amoraim takes one of the intermediate standards. (3) A hole of that size renders it clean. (4) I.e., neither glazed nor baked in a kiln. (5) Lit., 'the words of the Scribes'; v. Kid. 17*b*, n. b7. (6) V. *supra* 95*b*, n. b3.

b (1) This explains the view of the Rabbis. (2) I.e., on the same side of the street, which interposes lengthwise. (3) In connection with the Tabernacle in the Wilderness.

עין משפט נר מצוה

מו א מיי' פי"ט מהל' כלים הלכה א:
א ב מיי' פי"ב מהלכות שבת הלכה י סמג לאוין סה טוש"ע א"ח סי' שמו סעיף א:
ב ג מיי' פי"ג שם הלכה יט:
ג ד שם הלכה יח:

גמרא

הא ברברבי והא בזוטרי *אמר רב אסי *שונין כלי חרס שיעורו בכונס משקה ולא אמרו מוציא משקה אלא לענין גיסטרא בלבד מאי טעמא אמר מר זוטרא בריה דרב נחמן לפי שאין אומרים הבא גיסטרא לגיסטרא אמר עולא פליגי בה תרי אמוראי במערבא רבי יוסי בר' אבין ור' יוסי בר זבדא חד אמר כמוציא רמון וחד אמר כשורש קטן וסימניך *אחד המרבה ואחד הממעיט אמר רב חיננא בר כהנא משמיה דרבי אליעזר כלי חרס שיעורו כמוציא זיתים ומר קשישא בריה דרבה מסיים בה משמיה דרבי אליעזר והרי הן ככלי גללים וכלי אבנים וכלי אדמה שאין מקבלין טומאה לא מדברי תורה ולא מדברי סופרים ולענין צמיד פתיל עד שיפחת רובו:

הדרן עלך המצניע

מתני'

הזורק מרשות היחיד לרשות הרבים מרשות הרבים לרשות היחיד חייב *מרשות היחיד לרשות היחיד ורשות הרבים באמצע רבי עקיבא מחייב וחכמים פוטרין כיצד שתי גזוזטראות זו כנגד זו ברשות הרבים המושיט והזורק מזו לזו פטור היו שתיהן בדיוטא אחת המושיט חייב והזורק פטור שכך היתה עבודת הלוים שתי עגלות זו אחר זו ברשות הרבים מושיטין הקרשים מזו לזו אבל לא זורקין:

גמ'

רש"י

ברברבי. ברובו: זוטרי. כמוציא רמון בטל ליה מכלי: שונין. התנאים שונין ברייתא: כלי חרס. דשיעור הראשון האמור בו לבטלו במקלת משום כלי: ככונס משקה. הוא דמבטל ליה מיהא מתורת מי חטאת ולא אמרו נקב מוציא משקה חשוב נקב לכלום אלא לגיסטרא דהתם ודאי אי נקבה הכי כמוציא משקה משדא שדי ליה: שאין אומרים הבא גיסטרא. אחרת לגיסטרא זו להניח תחתיה לקבל הטיפין אבל כלי שלם חסין עליו ומשום נקב פורתא לא שדו ליה ומניחין גיסטרא תחתיו: פליגי בה. בהכשר זרעים: וסימן. דלא תיטעי למימר חד אמר כמוציא זית: אחד המרבה ואחד הממעיט ובלבד שיכוין כו'. *ברייתא היא (מנחות קי.) והיא לך לסימן שאחד מן האמוראים ריבה לשער בגדול שבשלשתן ואחד ממעט לשער בקטן שבשלשתן ולא בבינוני כונס משקה ומוציא משקה ליכא למיטעי בהן לענין זרעים: שיעורו כמוציא זיתים. ליטהר מטומאה: הרי הוא ככלי גללים. שניקב כמוציא זית ואפילו יחדוס לרמונים והא דתנן כלי בעלי בתים שיעורן כרמונים גבי כלי עץ תנינן לה במסכת כלים (פ' יז מ"א):

הדרן עלך המצניע

הזורק רבי עקיבא מחייב. טעמא מפרש בגמרא: כיצד שתי גזוזטראות כו'. רבנן קאמרי להו: גזוזטראות. זיזין היוצאין מן הכותל ומניחין עליהן נסרים להלך: זו כנגד זו. בשני צידי רה"ר והן רה"י שגבוהות י' ורחבות ד': פטור. שלא מצינו זריקה והושטה במלאכת המשכן מרה"י לרשות היחיד ורחב רה"ר מפסיק ביניהן שלא היתה עבודת הלוים כך להושיט קרשים מעגלה לעגלה שבצדה אלא לעגלה שלפניה (ושלאחריה) שארבע עגלות היו לבני מררי שהיו נושאין קרשי המשכן והן הולכין שתים כאחד זו בצד זו כדאמרינן בגמ' וכשהיו פורקין את המשכן לטעון על העגלות היו מעמידין העגלות כדרך הליכתן שתים זו אצל זו סמוך למשכן ושתים זו אצל זו לפניהם דרך הליכתן לאורך רה"ר שהיו רוצים להלך אחר עמוד הענן ההולך לפניהם ופורקי המשכן היו מושיטין הקרשים לאותן שעל שתי העגלות הסמוכות למשכן והן מושיטין לאותן שלפניהם אבל מעגלה לעגלה שבצדה לא היו צריכין להושיט שהרי שתיהן סמוכות לפורקי המשכן: היו שתיהן בדיוטא אחת. כלומר בעלייה אחת באורך רה"ר על פני הבית ויש הפסק רה"ר ביניהם: הזורק פטור. הואיל ולמעלה מי' ולא מצינו זריקה מרה"י לרה"י דרך רה"ר במשכן לא באורך ולא ברוחב: והמושיט חייב. שמצינו הושטה כיוצא בה למעלה מי' במשכן מרה"י לרה"י וקלת אורך רשות הרבים מפסיק ביניהם: שכך היתה עבודת הלוים. ומפרש ואזיל כיצד מצינו כזו בעבודתן שבשתי עגלות זו אחר זו ברשות הרבים פורקי משכן מושיטין לאותן שעל העגלות שאצלן והן מושיטין לאלו שלפניהם אבל לא זורקין שאין אותן קרשים נזרקות מפני כובדן:

גמרא

[נדה מט.]

נ"ל מתניתין [ברכות ה: יז. יומא מב. מנחות קי. שבועות טו.]

לעיל ד.

הגהות הב"ח

(א) תוס' ד"ה הא כו' דקאמר עד שיפחת רובו: (ב) ד"ה ולענין וכו' בנקב כי האי אין נכנסת טומאה:

גליון הש"ס

תוס' ד"ה ולענין צמיד פתיל. ומקשי' דתנן פ"י דמס' כלים ע' תי"ט רפ"ה דאהלות: ד"ה פליגי בה כו' דלענין הכשר זרעים פליגי. עי' זבחים לד ע"ב תד"ה ל"ש בסה"ד לה ע"א:

תוספות

הא ברברבי והא בזוטרי. פי' בקונטרס רברבי ברובו זוטרי כמוציא רמון וקשה לר"י דאין זו שיעור ומה קרי רברבי ומה קרי זוטרי לידע איזה הוא כמוציא רמון ונראה לר"י דברברבי כמוציא רמון ובזוטרי שמוציא רמון הוא יותר מרוב סגי ברוב והא דקאמר עד(א) שתיפחת רובו לא קאי אשיעור דמוציא רמון אלא אשיעור דמוציא זית:

ולענין צמיד פתיל עד שיפחת רובו. פירש רש"י דאין טומאה נכנסת דרך נקב דכל כלי פתוח כתיב דדרך פתחו נכנסת ולא דרך נקב °ומקשינן דתנן בפ"י דמסכת כלים (מ"ב) ואלו מצילין בצמיד פתיל כו' ומצילין בין מפיהם בין מצדיהם משמע דצריך שיהא מוקף צמיד פתיל כשניקב מצדו ועוד דתנן בתר הכי ובמה מקיפין בסיד ובחרסית כו' ובכל דבר שהוא מתמרח ואין מקיפין לא בבעץ ולא בעופרת מפני שהוא פתיל ואינו צמיד משמע דבנקב כל שהוא נכנסת טומאה ועוד דתנן התם ומייתי לה בהגוזל קמא (ב"ק קה.) חבית שניקבה וסתמוה שמרים הצילוה פקקה בזמורה עד שימרח מן הצדדים היו שתים עד שימרח מן הצדדין ובין זמורה לחבירתה ואומר ר"י דאיכא קושיות לפירוש הקונט' דודאי בפתח נכנסת טומאה אפילו דרך נקב קטן ובעינן עד שיסתם לגמרי כל הפתח ולהכי צריך מירוח והא דבין מפיהם בין מצדיהן לא מיירי שניקבו כשבר מן הצד אלא נעשה לצורך פתח והא דהגוזל דחבית שניקבה מיירי כשנפחתה רובה או כמוציא רמון דחשיב כפתח ובעי סתימה מעליא וריב"א הקשה מהא דתנן במסכת כלים (פ"ט משנה ח) נקב העשוי לאוכלין שיעורן כזיתים העשוי למשקין שיעורן כמשקין העשוי לכך ולכך מטילין אותו לחומרא בצמיד פתיל ובכונס משקה פירוש כיון שעשוי למשקים ולאוכלים ויש בו נקב כונס משקה אינו מציל בצמיד פתיל על מה שבתוכו דגזרו אטו ההוא דמיוחד למשקין לחודייהו ולענין קבלת טומאה הוי כלי כיון שמיוחד לאוכלין ובנקב כי האי (ב) נכנסה טומאה ותירץ ר"י דהא דבעי הכא נפחת רובו או כמוציא רמון היינו דוקא בניקב במקום שנשאר עוד שיעור כלי מן הנקב ולמטה כשיעור המפורש בההיא דמייתי באלו טריפות (חולין נה.) אבל ניקב למטה במקום שאין נשאר למטה מן הנקב כשיעור כלי הוי שיעור לאוכלים בכזית ולמשקין בכונס משקה כי ההוא דמסכת כלים (פ"ט משנה ח) ור"ת מפרש במתניתין הכי עד שיפחת רובו מועיל צמיד פתיל אם הנקבים נסתמים אבל בנפחת רובו או במוציא רמון שוב אין מועלת סתימה אלא הוי כאוכלין שגבלן בטיט שאין ניצולין כדאמרינן בריש זבחים (דף ג:) דכיון שנפחת רובו בטלו להו מתורת כלי והא דחבית שנקבה וסתמוה שמרים מיירי בשלא נפחתה כשיעור וסתמו שמרים כל הנקב והא דבעי רבא [התם] (בב"ק שם) (שם) אגף חליה מהו ה"פ אגף חליה וסתמוה שמרים חליה מאי מי הוי סתימה מעליא או לא ומייתי מפקקה בזמורה דלא חשיבא סתימה בלא מירוח בין זמורה לחבירתה הכא נמי לא חשיבא סתימה אגף חליה וסתמוה שמרים חליה ומשני התם לא קאי הכא קאי:

פליגי בה תרי אמוראי. פי' בקונטרס °דלענין הכשר זרעים פליגי ואומר ר"ת דבמסכת עוקצין (פ"ב משנה י) תנן דהכשר זרעים כשורש קטן אלא אמר ר"ת דלענין מוקף צמיד פתיל פליגי: **שיעורן** כמוציא זיתים. ה"ג ברוב ספרים ובפי' ר"ח ורש"י וא"ת מתני' היא במס' כלים (פ"ג מ"א) העשוי לאוכלין שיעורו כזיתים וי"ל דאיצטריך ליה לאשמעינן דלא מהני בה יחוד לרמונים ולאפוקי מדרבא ולהכי מסיים בהו לפרושה הרי הן ככלי אבנים שהם טהורין בכל ענין:

הדרן עלך המצניע

הזורק. כיצד שתי גזוזטראות כו'. תימה לרבה דמוקי פלוגתא דרבי עקיבא ורבנן (לעיל ד' ד.) בקלוטה ופליגי למטה מעשרה לא אתי שפיר כיצד דהא לא קאי אדלעיל דהכא איירי בגזוזטראות למעלה מעשרה דומיא דעגלות ואפילו ר' עקיבא נמי מודה התם ולמאן דמוקי פלוגתייהו למעלה מעשרה אתי שפיר ומיהו יש בירושלמי איכא דתני כיצד ואיכא דלא תני כיצד ומפרש התם דההוא אמורא דמוקי לה למטה מעשרה לא תני כיצד. הוצאה

רבינו חננאל

הא מלתא וכבר פשיטא דאי אמרת מרא לחפור בה וס"ת לקרות בו מלאכה שאינה צריכה לגופה היא היכי משכחת לה לר' שמעון מלאכה שהיא צריכה לגופה ומהדרינן מהו דתימא לית ליה לרבי שמעון משצ"ל עד דאיכא לגופה כגון מר לעשות לו טס וס"ת להגיהו קמ"ל רבא דלא צריך (האי כולה) [כה"ג] אלא אפי' מר לחפור בו וס"ת לקרות בו מודה בו ר"ש [דחייב] והוצאת המת דקא פטר בה ר' שמעון דוקא מקרבן חטאת אבל מ"מ [לכתחלה] (הכי) אסור דקיי"ל כל פטורי שבת פטור אבל אסור לבר מן הנך תלת ולא שרי לכתחלה אלא היכא דכבודו לאפוקי מרה"י לרשות הרבים או לעיליה מרשות הרבים לרה"י (אסור) [מותר] כדקא מפרשינן מעשה דההוא שכבא דשכיב בדרא חדא וקאמר ליה רב נחמן בר יצחק לרב יוחני אחוה דמר בריה דרבנא האלקים דעיילת ביה את ודרית ליה וקא מפרש לא תימא דכר' שמעון קא אמינא ולאו כר' יהודה אלא אפילו לר' יהודה דאמר מלאכה שאינה צריכה לגופה חייב עליה הכא לכרמלי' קאמינ' דלית ביה חיובא אע"ג דאיכא בשאר מילי איסורא [דרבנן] מרה"י או מרה"ר לכרמלית הכא שאני במקום כבוד הבריות שדוחה את לא תעשה והאי ל"ת לאו דלא תסור כדמפורש במנחות סוף פ' הקומץ: פלוגתא דר"ש ור' יהודה בהדיא לא אשכחן היכא פליגו אלא מדוקיהו (במתניין) [שמעינן הכא] דאמרינן (לקמן בהאורג) הקורע בחמתו ועל מתו וכל המקלקלין פטור שניית מתו חמתו אחמתו קשיא. חמתו אחמתו נמי לא קשיא הא רבי יהודה דאמר מלאכה שאינה צריכה לגופה חייב עליה הא ר' שמעון דאמר מלאכה שאינה צריכה לגופה פטור עליה ותוב הא דתנן (לקמן קכא) ועל עקרב שלא תשוך כו' ואמרי' איכא דמתני לה אהא הצד נחש בשבת ומתעסק שלא ישכנו פטור ואם לרפואה חייב מאן תנא אמר רב יהודה א"ר [רבי] שמעון היא דאמר מלאכ' שאינה צריכה לגופה פטור עליה וכן אמר שמואל כל פטורי שבת פטור אבל אסור בר מהני תלת דפטור ומותר וחדא מינייהו הצד נחש בשבת וממאי דפטור מותר הוא דתנן ועל עקרב שלא תשוך ש"מ כי פליגי במתניתין במלאכה שאינה צריכה לגופה פליגי וקשיא לן אי הכי קשיא דשמואל [אדשמואל] דאמר שמואל*) הכא (א') דפטורו [מותר] ומוקי לטעמיה מכופין קערה על גבי הנר אלמא שמואל במלאכה שאינה צריכה לגופה כר"ש ס"ל והא קי"ל דשמואל במלאכה שאינה צריכה לגופה כר' יהודה ס"ל. מיהו [איכא למימר] היכא דאית ביה היזק לרבים כגון גחלת של מתכת וכגון עקרב שלא תישוך כגון הני בלחוד פליגי שמואל על ר' יהודה אבל במלאכה שאינה צריכה לגופה שמואל כרבי יהודה ס"ל: תנן התם בפ"ז דנגעים התולש סימני טמאה והכוה את המחיה עובר בלא תעשה פי' שיער לבן שהפך בשאת והכוה את המחיה להעבירו עובר בלא תעשה עיקרה השמר בנגע הצרעת אלמא אל מעשהו ביד וכדר' אבין א"ר אלעא כל מקום שנאמר השמר פן ואל אינו [אלא] בל"ת: אתמר אם תלש נימא אחת משלש שיער לבן שהפך בבהרת משני נימין דברי הכל חייב אחת משלש רב נחמן אמר חייב אהני מעשיו שקירב דאותו לעבור**) רב ששת אמר פטור השתא מיהא הא איתיה לטמאה ולא עבירה לאיסורה אמר רב ששת מנא אמינא לה דתנן המוציא כזית מן המת חייב ודייקינן מינה אם הוציא כזית חייב הא חצי כזית פטור והתניא המוציא חצי כזית חייב ומשני אמר רב ששת הא דתני חצי כזית חייב דאפיק חצי זית מן כזית שכבר מיעט הטומאה ולפיכך חייב והא דתני פטור דאפיק חצי זית מן כזית ומחצה דלא אהני השתא מידי ואע"פ שקרב מיעוט הטומאה ורב נחמן משני הא דתני חצי זית פטור דאפקוה ממת גדול דהאי שיעורא לא מקרב מיעוטי טומאה אבל חצי זית מכזית ומחצה שקרב הסרת הטומאה חייב וקיי"ל כרב ששת (ומפי עדיף): הנוטל צפורניו זו בזו או בשיניו או בידו שלא בכלי וכן שערו וכן שפמו וכן זקנו שנוטלו בשיניו או בידו שלא בכלי בין לעצמו בין לחבירו אסור משום שבות אבל אם נטלו בכלי כגון אזמל או בנוסטר חייב. וצפורן שפרש רובו וציצין שפירשו רובן כלפי למעלה ומצערות אותו מותר לנוטלן ביד אבל בכלי אסור ואם לא פירש חייב עליהן ביד פטור אבל אסור בכלי חייב חטאת. תנא הנוטל מלא פי הזוג חייב וכמה מלא פי הזוג שתים וכן לקרחה שתים (באבהנום) אבל המלקט שער לבן מתוך שחור אפילו שערה אחת אסור משום לא יהיה כלי גבר על אשה וכן הגודלת וכן הפוקסת ר' אליעזר מחייב חטאת וחכ"א משום שבות ואוקימנא כוחלת משום כותבת גודלת ופוקסת משום בונה: ירושלמי גודלת משום

*) עי' תוס' לעיל דף ג' ע"א ד"ה הלך שהביאו קושיא זו בשם בה"ג וע"ש. **) נראה דצ"ל שקירב למעט הטומאה דאי משתקלא חדא אחריתא אלא לה טומאה.

גמ' מכדי זריקה תולדה דהוצאה היא *הוצאה *גופה היכא כתיבא א"ר יוחנן דאמר קרא °ויצו משה ויעבירו קול במחנה משה היכן הוה יתיב במחנה לויה ומחנה לויה רה"ר הואי וקאמר להו לישראל לא תפיקו ותיתו מרה"י דידכו לרה"ר וממאי דבשבת קאי דילמא בחול קאי ומשום דשלימא לה (א) מלאכה כדכתיב °והמלאכה היתה דים וגו' גמר העברה העברה מיוה"כ כתיב הכא ויעבירו קול במחנה וכתיב התם °והעברת שופר תרועה מה להלן ביום אסור אף כאן ביום אסור אשכחן הוצאה הכנסה מנלן סברא היא מכדי מרשות לרשות הוא מה לי אפוקי ומה לי עיולי מיהו הוצאה אב הכנסה תולדה ומכדי אהא מיחייב ואהא מיחייב אמאי קרי לה האי אב ואמאי קרי לה האי תולדה °נפקא מינה דאי עביד שתי אבות בהדי הדדי אי נמי שתי תולדות בהדי הדדי מיחייב תרתי ואי עביד אב ותולדה דידיה לא מיחייב אלא חדא *ולר"א דמחייב אתולדה במקום אב אמאי קרו לה אב ואמאי קרו לה תולדה הך דהואי במשכן חשיבא קרי לה אב הך דלא הואי במשכן חשיבא לא קרי לה אב אי נמי הך דכתיבא קרי אב והאי דלא כתיבא קרי תולדה והא דתנן *הזורק ד' אמות בכותל למעלה מי' טפחים כזורק באויר למטה מי' טפחים כזורק בארץ והזורק בארץ ד' אמות חייב זרק ד' אמות ברה"ר מנלן דמיחייב אמר ר' יאשיה שכן אורגי יריעות זורקין מחטיהן זה לזה אורגין מחטין למה להו אלא שכן תופרי יריעות זורקין מחטיהן זה לזה ודילמא גבי הדדי הוו יתבי מטו הדדי במחטין דילמא בתוך ארבע הוו יתבי אלא אמר רב חסדא שכן אורג יריעות זורקין בוכיאר ביריעה והלא אוגדו בידו בניסכא בתרא והא במקום פטור קאזלא אלא שכן אורגי יריעות זורקין בוכיאר *לשואליהן ודילמא גבי הדדי הוו יתבי מטו הדדי בחפת ודילמא שלחופי הוו משלחפי ותו מי שאילי מהדדי והתניא *לודא °איש איש ממלאכתו אשר המה עושים ממלאכתו הוא עושה ואינו עושה ממלאכת חבירו ותו מעביר ד' אמות ברה"ר מנלן דמחייב אלא כל ד' אמות ברה"ר גמרא גמירי לה: אמר רב יהודה אמר שמואל מקושש מעביר ארבע אמות ברה"ר הוה במתניתא תנא תולש הוה רב אחא ברבי יעקב אמר מעמר הוה למאי נפקא מינה לכדרב *דאמר רב מצאתי מגלת סתרים בי ר' חייא וכתוב ביה איסי בן יהודה אומר אבות מלאכות ארבעים חסר אחת (ואם עשאן כולם בהעלם אחת) ואינו חייב אלא אחת אחת ותו לא והתנן *אבות מלאכות ארבעים חסר אחת והוינן בה מניינא למה לי וא"ר יוחנן שאם עשאן כולם בהעלם א' חייב על כל אחת ואחת אימא אינו חייב על אחת מהם רב יהודה פשיטא ליה דהמעביר חייב ומתני' פשיטא ליה דתולש חייב ורב אחא בר יעקב פשיטא ליה דמעמר חייב מ"ס הא מיהת לא מספקא ומ"ס הא מיהת לא מספקא: ת"ר מקושש זה צלפחד וכן הוא אומר °ויהיו בני ישראל במדבר וימצאו איש וגו' ולהלן הוא אומר °אבינו מת במדבר מה להלן צלפחד אף כאן צלפחד דברי ר' עקיבא אמר לו ר' יהודה בן בתירא עקיבא בין כך ובין כך אתה עתיד ליתן את הדין אם כדבריך התורה כיסתו ואתה מגלה אותו ואם לאו אתה מוציא לעז על אותו צדיק ואלא

שמות לו
סס
ויקרא כה
שמות לו
במדבר טו
סס כז

תורה אור

גמ' מכדי זריקה תולדה דהוצאה. על כרחיך תולדה היא דלא כמנית באבות מלאכות ותולדה דהוצאה היא שאין לך לתתה תולדת אב אחר דמעין הוצאה היא האמורה באבות מלאכות: מחנה לויה ר"ה היא. שהיו הכל מצויין אצל משה רבינו: מרה"י דידכו. מאהליכם: דשלימא ליה עבידתיה. שהיה הנדבה כדי להשלים: סברא היא. להיות הכנסה תולדת הוצאה שהיא מעין לה כשאר תולדות שהיא מעין מלאכות: מכדי אהאי מיחייב ואהאי מיחייב. כדתנן (לעיל פ"א ב.) פשט העני ידו לפנים: נפקא מינה. דכל אבות מלאכות: שתי אבות. דלא דמיין ושתי תולדות דשתי אבות: ולר"א כו'. במסכת כריתות בפרק אמרו לו: והא דתנן. בפירקין: בכותל. כדמוקי לה בדבילה שמינה ונדבקת: כזורק באויר. ופטור דלא נח ברשות הרבים דאין רה"ר למעלה מעשרה וברה"י נמי לא נח שאינו מקום מסוים שיהא רחבו ד' שהרי לא נח בראש הכותל אלא בפניו: כזורק בארץ. דאויר רה"ר הוא וחייב וכיון דאויר רה"ר הוא ונח בכל דהו מיחייב ורשותא לנפשיה לא הוי לא כרמלית ולא מקום פטור הואיל ובפניו נח ולא נח בראשו שיהא מקום מסוים: תופרי יריעות. מעשה רוקם: גבי הדדי. בתוך אמה אחת ואין צריכין לזרוק אלא להושיט: מטו אהדדי במחטין. כשמותחין את החוט מכין זה את זה במחט: בוכיאר. כלי שקנה של ערב נתון בו שזורקין בין שני דופני היריעה: והלא אגדו בידו. חוט של ערב הוא אוחז והקנה נכרך בחוט ואינו נשמט ממנו: בניסכא בתרא. בחוט האחרון של קנה שהקנה נשמט מהחוט והבוכיאר נופל: ניסכא. זריקה אחרונה של חוט לשון המיסך: והא במקום פטור אזלא. בין דופני היריעה ואין זה רשות הרבים אלא מקום פטור דאין רחב ד': לשואליהן. אורגי יריעה אחרת ויש לו לזה שנים: ה"ג ודילמא שואליהן גביהן הוו יתבין: מטו אהדדי בחפת. אי גבייהו הוו יתבי מגיעין ידו של זה בשל זה בשפת היריעה כשמותחין חוט הערב: בחפת. כמו חפת חלוקו (יומא ד' עז:): שלחופי הוו משלחפי. לעולם גבי הדדי הוו יתבי אלא שאין מכוונים אלא זה נמשך לפנים וזה לאחור: ואין עושה ממלאכת חבירו. שכולם מוכנים בכלי אומנותם ולא הוצרכו לישאול: מעביר ד' אמות הוה. לא תלשן ולא עימרן אלא העבירן ד' אמות לכך נהרג: מעמר. תלושין ומפוזרין היו ועמרן כדאמרן (לעיל ד' עג:) האי מאן דכניף מלחא חייב משום מעמר: מגילת סתרים. שהסתירום לפי שאין כותבין הלכות: ואינו חייב אלא אחת. על כרחיך לענין שוגג קאמר ולחטאת דבמזיד תרי קטלי לא מקטלי ולהכי פריך והא אנן תנן כו': ואינו חייב על אחת מהן. מיתה יש בהן אחת שאינו נהרג עליה ולא פירש איזו היא והשתא לרב יהודה אין זו העבירה שהרי נהרג מקושש עליה ולמתניתא אין תולש באותו ספק: ואלא

הוצאה גופה היכא כתיבא. ואע"ג שהיתה במשכן כדאמר *הם הורידו קרשים מעגלה כו' מכל מקום אי לאו דכתיב לא הוה מחייבי עלה לפי שמלאכה גרועה היא כדפי' לעיל (דף ב.): וממאי דבשבת קאי. ר"ח ל"ג כל זה עד אשכחן הוצאה דהא אפילו בחול קאי נפקא ליה שפיר דהוצאה מלאכה הוא דהא רחמנא קרייה מלאכה כדכתיב ואיש ואשה אל יעשו עוד מלאכה לתרומת הקדש וכתיב ויכלא העם מהביא אלמא קרי להוצאה מלאכה וכן דריש בהדיא בירושלמי:

הכנסה מנלן סברא הוא כו'. וא"ת מה צריך להאי סברא כיון דהוות במשכן כדאמר *הם העלו קרשים לעגלה כו' דהא בסמוך משמע גבי זריקה דאם היתה במשכן הוה אתי ליה שפיר וי"ל דבזריקה נמי איכא סברא מה לי ע"י הולאה מה לי ע"י זריקה דאי לאו סברא לא הוה מחשבינן לה תולדה דהולאה ואי לא הוות נמי במשכן לא הוה מחייבינן עלה מסברא לפי שמלאכה גרועה היא:

ולרבי אליעזר דמחייב אתולדה במקום אב אמאי קרי לה אב כו'. הוה מצי למימר דנפקא מינה לענין התראה כדפי' בפ' כלל גדול (לעיל עג:) ואיכא למימר דהייטו דקמשני הך דהוות במשכן חשיבא כו'. אית דגרסי הך דהוות במשכן חשיבא קרי לה אב והך דלא הוות במשכן חשיבא קרי לה תולדה ולפי זה יש מלאכות דהוו במשכן כגון מנכש ומשקה זרעים דלא חשיבי ולא הוו אבות וכן אי גרסינן דהוות במשכן וחשיבא קרי לה אב אבל אי גרסי' הך דהוות במשכן חשיבא וקרי לה אב הך דלא הוות במשכן לא חשיבא וקרי לה תולדה לפי זה התולדות לא היו במשכן:

אי נמי הך דכתיבא קרי לה אב. הך ליסנא לא איצטריך אלא משום הולאה:

ודילמא שלחופי הוו משלחפי. הכי נמי הוה מצי למיפרך דילמא תוך ארבע אמות הוו יתבי:

[גי' רבינו האי הוצאה מגלן דהוה מלאכה]

הגהות הב"ח
(א) גמ' דשלימא לה עבידתא כדכתיב והמלאכה:

ב"ק ב. לעיל עג. כריתות טז:
לעיל ז: ע.
[כערך שוול גרים הערוך שואליהן פי' מגרמין] [בילקוט ליתא לד']
לעיל ו:
כס"א ל"ג [סס וכ"ב]

ד א מיי' פי"ב מהלכות שבת הלכה ח סמג לאוין סה:
ה ב מיי' פ"ז שם הל' ז:

רבינו חננאל
משום בונה כוחלת משום כותבת פוקסת מכרועא אלנושרי ובלשון ערבית תנער אל אצדג. פוקסת משום צובעת ומדמפרשי רבנן טעמיה דר' אליעזר ש"מ הלכתא כוותיה ויש מי שחולק ואומר הלכה כחכמים דאמרי משום שבות ומ"ד כר' אליעזר מפי עדיף דאיסורא דאורייתא היא ולחומרא עבדינן וכן נמי לענין החולב והמחבץ והמכבד והמרבץ והרודה חלות דבש שוגג בשבת חייב חטאת במזיד ביו"ם לוקה מ' דברי ר' אליעזר וחכמים אומרים א' [זה] ואחד [זה חייב] משום שבות ומדמפרשי אליבא דר' אליעזר ואומר חולב משום מפרק מחבץ משום בורר מגבן משום בונה ש"מ סוגיא דהא שמעתיה כר' אליעזר ויש מי שחולק גם על זה ויש מרבנן דמדקדקי דאמרי כי החולב והמחבץ והמגבן כגרוגרת דברי הכל היא ומסתייעא מהא דגרסינן בפרק אע"פ תניא ר' מרינוס אומר גונח יונק חלב בשבת מ"ט יונק מפרק כלאחר יד הוא ובמקום סכנה לא גזרו רבנן א"ר יוסף הלכה כר' מרינוס ולא שמעינן דאית ליה האי סברא דחולב אסור משום מפרק אלא אליבא דר' אליעזר ורבי מרינוס לא התיר אלא היונק מכלל שהחולב אסור ובסוף פרק חרש שנשא פקחת אסיקנא דיונק מפרק כלאחר יד הוא: שבת דאיסור סקילה גזרו רבנן י"ט דאיסור לאו הוא לא גזרו רבנן וסבירא להו דבהחולב ובמחבץ שמוציא החמאה ובמגבן דברי הכל אסור לא פליגי רבנן עליה דר' אליעזר אלא במכבד ומרבץ וברודה חלות דבש ובהני הלכתא כרבנן וסתיא כוותייהו דהא לא איםנעו מלרבץ אלא משום דחיישינן משום אשווי גומות ואסיקנא והאידנא דסבירא לן כרבי שמעון [דפטר] במלאכה שאינה צריכה לגופה ובדבר שאין מתכוין שרי אפי' לכתחלה לענין כיבוד נמי שרי ואפי' בדהוצי כר' שמעון: הלכתא מחלב בהמה אפי' למאן דסבר דשרי משום שבות אסור וכ"ש למ"ד משום מפרק אסור דמלאכה היא והא דאמר רב חסדא מדברי רבנן נלמד חולב אדם עז לתוך הקדרה אבל [לא] לתוך הקערה כבר פרשה מר' רב יהודאי גאון זצ"ל דבי"ם הוא וכבר פירשנו בפרק חבית:
מתני' התולש מעציץ נקוב חייב משאינו נקוב פטור ר' שמעון פוטר בזה ובזה ורמי ליה אביי לרבא תנן ר' שמעון פוטר הזה ובזה אלמא לר' שמעון לכל מילי נקוב כשאינו נקוב משוי ליה והתנן ר' שמעון [אומר] אין בין נקוב לשאינו נקוב אלא להכשיר זרעים בלבד ופריק רבא לעולם ר' שמעון לכל מילי נקוב כשאינו נקוב משוי לה ואיכא דגרסי כתלוש משוי והדבר אחד הוא פי' כיון דפטור ר' שמעון אפילו בתולש מעציץ נקוב דייקינן מינה דסבר כל מאי דזרע ביה כתלוש דמי ואע"פ שהוא נקוב כשאינו נקוב חשוב והא דשני ביניהון לענין הכשר זרעים דתנן בסוף (פ"ב) דעוקצים עציץ נקוב אינו מכשיר את הזרעים ושאינו נקוב מכשיר את הזרעים וקא מודה בה ר"ש דאלמא זרעים שהן בעציץ שאינו נקוב כתלושין דמי ומים הניתנין עליהן הרי הן בכי יותן ומכשירין אבל עציץ נקוב זרעים שיש בו כמחוברים דמו וכל מים הניתנין בהן אין מכשירין אותן והכא בשבת חשיב הנקוב כשאינו נקוב לפטור והכא בזרעים משני בין נקוב לשאינו נקוב קשיין אהדדי ומשני הכשר זרעים שאני שהתורה רבתה להן טהרה וכי יותן מים על זרע*) זרוע אשר יזרע טהור הוא פי' כל זרע שאינו ראוי עכשיו לזריעה טהור הוא ואין המים מכשירין אותן והא כיון שהוא מחובר כמי שאינו ראוי לזריעה הוא וא"ת שאינו נקוב נמי שאני התם כיון דאינו נקוב לאו זריעה הוא דכל זריעה שאינה בארץ לאו זריעה הוא והאי דאמר לכל מילי כגון ההוא דתנן בכלאים פרק (ז) עציץ נקוב מקדש בכרם ושאינו נקוב אינו מקדש ור"ש אומר זה וזה אסורין ואין מקדשין ולענין כלאים נמי איכא למימר דפליג ר"ש אבל רבנן דבר ברור הוא משנה שלמה בדמאי פרק (ה) שעציץ נקוב הרי הוא כארץ תרם מן הארץ על עציץ נקוב ומן עציץ נקוב על הארץ תרומתו תרומה כו' והלכתא כרבנן שהתולש מעציץ נקוב חייב וגרסינן בסוף פרק חרש שנשא פקחת לא יאמר אדם לתינוק הבא לי קסם אלא מניחו הולש מניחו זורק אמר אביי תולש מעציץ שאינו נקוב בכרמלית מדרבנן וגרסי' נמי במנחות (ד' ע) אמר רב טובי בר קיסנא אמר שמואל הזורע כלאים בעציץ שאינו נקוב אסור אמר אביי מאי קמ"ל בשלמא אי אשמעינן לוקה מכת מרדות מדרבנן שפיר אלא האי דקאמר אסור
*) בקרא דוכי יותן מים לא כתיב כלל אשר יזרע טהור הוא ולכן נראה דצ"ל על כל זרע זרוע אשר יזרע פי' זרע שראוי עכשיו לזריעה אבל כי זרע שאינו ראוי וכו' כצ"ל.

רב נסים גאון

פ"י ולר' אליעזר דמחייב על תולדה במקום אב קול *) ר' אליעזר במסכת (כריתות דף טז) וכבר פירשנו דבריו בפרק כלל גדול ועיקרן בתורת כהנים בפרשת כהן משיח בסדר ויקרא:
*) פירושו כלשון ערבי מאמר ר' אליעזר
ואלא

GEMARA. [96b] Consider: throwing is a derivative of carrying out:[4] where is carrying out itself written?—Said R. Joḥanan, Scripture saith, *And Moses gave commandment, and they caused a proclamation to pass throughout the camp*, [etc.]:[5] now, where was Moses stationed? In the camp of the Levites, which was public ground,[6] and he said to the Israelites, Do not carry out and fetch from your private dwellings into public ground. But how do you know that this was on the Sabbath: perhaps this happened[7] during the week, the reason being that the material was complete[ly adequate], as it is written,
a *For the stuff they had was sufficient*, etc.[1]—The meaning of 'passing through' is learnt from [its employment in connection with] the Day of Atonement, Here it is written, *and they caused a proclamation to pass throughout the camp;* whilst there it is written, *Then shalt thou cause a loud trumpet to pass through* [*sc*. the land]:[2] just as there the reference is to the day of the interdict, so here too the day of the interdict [is meant].[3] We have thus found [an interdict for] carrying out: whence do we know [that] carrying in [is forbidden]?—That is common sense: consider: it is [transference] from one domain to another: what does it matter whether one carries out or carries in? Nevertheless, carrying out is a primary [labour], [whereas] carrying in is a derivative.

Yet let us consider: one is culpable for both: why is one designated a principal and the other a derivative [labour]?—The practical difference is that if one performs two principal or two derivative [labours] together he is liable to two [sacrifices], whereas if he performs a principal [labour] and its derivative he is liable only to one. But according to R. Eliezer, who imposes liability for a derivative [when performed] conjointly with[4] the principal, why is one called a principal and the other a derivative?—That which was of account in the Tabernacle is designated a principal, whereas that which was not of account in the Tabernacle is designated a derivative.[5] Alternatively, that which is written is designated a principal, whereas that which is not written is designated a derivative.

Again, as to what we learnt, 'If one throws [an article] four cubits on to a wall above ten handbreadths, it is as though he throws it into the air;[6] if below ten, it is as though he throws it on to the ground;[7] and he who throws [an article] four cubits along the ground is culpable',[8]—how do we know that he who throws [an article] four cubits in the street is culpable?—Said R. Josiah:
b Because the curtain weavers threw their needles to each other.[1] Of what use are needles to weavers?—Rather [say:] Because the curtain sewers threw their needles to each other. But perhaps they sat close together?—Then they would reach each other with their needles.[2] Yet perhaps they sat within four [cubits] of each other? Rather said R. Ḥisda: Because the curtain weavers threw the clue into the curtain. But the other [worker] still has the distaff in his hand?—He refers to the last manipulation.[3] But it passed through a place of non-liability?[4]—Rather [say:] Because the curtain weavers threw the clue to those who would borrow it from them.[5] Yet perhaps they sat near each other? Then they would touch each other on making the border. Yet perhaps they sat in irregular lines?[6] Moreover, did they borrow from each other? Surely Luda[7] taught: *every man from his work which they wrought:*[8] he wrought of his own work [stuff], but not of his neighbour's.[9] Again, how do we know that if one carries [an article] four cubits in the street, he is culpable? Rather the whole [law of transporting] four cubits in the street is known by tradition.

Rab Judah said in Samuel's name: [The offence of] the gatherer [of sticks][10] was that he carried [them] four cubits over public ground. In a Baraitha it was taught: He cut [them] off.[11] R. Aḥa b. Jacob said: He tied [them] together.[12] In respect of what is the practical difference?—In respect of Rab's [dictum]. For Rab said, I found a secret scroll of the School of R. Ḥiyya, wherein it is written, Issi b. Judah said: There are thirty-nine principal labours, but one is liable only [for] one. One and no more? Surely we learnt, The principal labours are forty less one. And we pondered thereon: why state the number? And R. Joḥanan answered: [To teach] that if one performs all of them in one state of unawareness, he is liable for each separately? Say: for one of these
c he is not culpable.[1] Now, Rab Judah is certain that he who carries [in the street] is culpable; the Baraitha is certain that he who cuts off is culpable; while R. Aḥa b. Jacob is certain that he who binds is culpable. [Thus] one Master holds, This at least is not in doubt, while the other Master holds, That at least is not in doubt.[2]

Our Rabbis taught: The gatherer was Zelophehad. And thus it is said, *And while the children of Israel were in the* wilderness, *they found a man* [*gathering sticks*, etc.];[3] whilst elsewhere it is said, *our father died in the* wilderness;[4] just as there Zelophehad [is meant], so here too Zelophehad [is meant]: this is R. Akiba's view. Said R. Judah b. Bathyra to him, 'Akiba! in either case you will have to give an account [for your statement]: if you are right,[5] the Torah shielded[6] him, while you reveal him; and if not, you cast

(4) On principal and derivative labours v. *supra* 2*b*, n. a2. Throwing is certainly a derivative only, since it is not enumerated in the principal labours *supra* 73*a*; also it must be a derivative of carrying out, for it is not similar to any of the other principal labours. (5) Ex. XXXVI, 6. (6) As everyone had to pass through to gain access to Moses. (7) Lit., 'he stood'.

a (1) Ex. XXXVI, 7. (2) Lev. XXV, 9. (3) *Sc*. the Sabbath. This method of exegesis is called *gezerah shawah*, q.v. Glos. (4) Lit., 'in the place of'. (5) V. *infra* 100*a*. (6) And he is not liable. (7) And since it traverses four cubits, he is culpable. (8) V. *supra* 75*a*.

b (1) Through public ground. (2) When stretching their arms to thread the needles they would strike each other. (3) When the weaver throws the clue through the web for the last time. (4) V. *supra* 6*a*; i.e., it passed between the portions of the curtain, which is certainly not public ground. (5) 'Aruch reads: their apprentices. On both readings the reference is to people working on other curtains, and the clue had to traverse public ground. (6) Crosswise, or in zigzag rows, so that they could work close together without touching each other. (7) An Amora: *Yalkut* reads: Levi. (8) Ex. XXXVI, 4. (9) Having sufficient material of his own. (10) V. Num. XV, 32 *seq*. (11) He cut off twigs or branches from a tree, which is the equivalent of detaching produce from the soil. (12) They were already lying on the ground. Tying them together is the same as binding sheaves.

c (1) V. *supra* 6*b* for notes. (2) As being referred to in Issi's dictum. (3) Num. XV, 32. (4) Ibid. XXVII, 3. (5) Lit., 'if it is as your words'. (6) Lit., 'covered'.

a stigma upon a righteous man.' [97a] But surely he learns a *gezerah shawah?*[7]—He did not learn the *gezerah shawah*.[8] Then of which [sinners] was he?[9]—Of those who *'presumed [to go up to the top of the mountain]*.'[10]

Similarly you read, *And the anger of the Lord was kindled against* them; *and he departed:*[11] this teaches that Aaron too became leprous: this is R. Akiba's view. Said R. Judah b. Bathyra to him, 'Akiba! in either case you will have to give an account: if you are right, the Torah shielded him, while you disclose him; and if not, you cast a stigma upon a righteous man.' But it is written, *'against* them'?[1] That was merely with a rebuke. It was taught in accordance with the view that Aaron too became leprous. For it is written, *And Aaron turned* [wa-yifen] *to Miriam, and behold, she was leprous:*[2] [and] it was taught: [That means] that he became free [*panah*] from his leprosy.[3]

Resh Lakish said: He who entertains a suspicion against innocent[4] men is bodily afflicted, for it is written, [*And Moses ... said,*] *But, behold, they will not believe* me;[5] but it was known[6] to the Holy One, blessed be He, that Israel would believe. Said He to him: They are believers, [and] the descendants of believers, whereas thou wilt ultimately disbelieve. They are believers, as it is written, *and the people believed;*[7] the descendants of believers: *and he* [Abraham] *believed in the Lord*.[8] Thou wilt ultimately disbelieve, as it is said, [*And the Lord said unto Moses and Aaron,*] *Because ye believed not in me*.[9] Whence [is it learnt] that he was smitten?—Because it is written, *And the Lord said furthermore unto him, Put now thine hand into thy bosom,* etc.[10]

Raba—others state, R. Jose b. R. Ḥanina—said: The dispensation of good comes more quickly than that of punishment [evil]. For in reference to the dispensation of punishment it is written, *and he took it out, and behold, his hand was leprous, as white as snow;*[11] whereas in reference to the dispensation of good it is written, *and he took it out of his bosom, and behold, it was turned again as his other flesh:*[12] from his very bosom[13] it had turned again as his other flesh.

But Aaron's rod swallowed up their rods:[14] R. Eleazar observed, It was a double miracle.[15]

FROM ONE PRIVATE DOMAIN TO ANOTHER, etc. Rabbah asked: Do they disagree when it is below ten, and they differ in this: R. Akiba holds, An object caught up is at rest; while the Rabbis hold that it is not as at rest; but above ten all agree that he is not liable, for we do not learn throwing from reaching across. Or perhaps they disagree when it is above ten, and they differ in this: R. Akiba holds, We learn throwing from reaching across; while the Rabbis hold, We do not learn throwing from reaching across; but below ten, all agree that he is culpable. What is the
b reason? An object caught up is as at rest?[1] Said R. Joseph: This question was asked by R. Ḥisda, and R. Hamnuna solved it for him from this: [If one removes an object] from one private domain to another and it passes through the street itself, R. Akiba declares [him] liable, while the Sages exempt [him]. Now, since it states, through the street itself, it is obvious that they differ where it is below ten. Now, in which [case]? Shall we say, in the case of one who carries [it] across: is he culpable only when it is below ten, but not when it is above ten? Surely R. Eleazar said: If one carries out a burden above ten [handbreadths from the street level], he is

(7) V. Glos. That which is so derived is regarded as explicitly stated. (8) Rashi: R. Judah b. Bathyra did not receive this *gezerah shawah* on tradition from his teachers, and no analogy by *gezerah shawah* can be employed unless sanctioned by tradition. 'Aruch: R. Akiba did not learn it from his teachers, but inferred it himself. (9) On the view of R. Judah b. Bathyra. For it is stated, *but he died in his own sin*, ibid. (10) Ibid. XIV, 44. (11) Ibid. XII, 9 q.v.
(1) The plural definitely includes Aaron. (2) Num. XXVII, 10. (3) '*He turned*' is understood to mean, he turned away from, i.e., he was freed. (4) Lit., 'worthy'. (5) Ex. IV, 1. (6) Lit., 'revealed'. (7) Ibid. 31. (8) Gen. XV, 6. (9) Num. XX, 12. (10) Ex. IV, 6; he was smitten with leprosy, ibid. (11) It became leprous only when he took it out. (12) Ibid. 7. (13) I.e., before it was fully withdrawn. (14) Ibid. VII, 12. (15) Lit., 'a *miracle* within a miracle'. It first became a rod again, and as a rod it swallowed up their serpents.
b (1) V. *supra* 4b for notes.

For the continuation of the English translation of this page see overleaf.

ולאו הא גמיר גזירה שוה. וא"כ לא כסתו התורה דהוה ליה כמפורש ומשני רבי יהודה בן בתירא לא גמרה ואין אדם דן ג"ש מעצמו : ואלא. לרבי יהודה : מהיכן הוה. באיזו חטא מת דכתיב כי בחטאו מת : מויעפילו. ויעפילו לעלות וגו' שלא הרשיע כ"כ כחילול שבת : שפנה מצרעתו. קדם ונתרפא : והנה ידו מצורעת. היינו לוקה בגופו : ויוציאה והנה ידו· אחר הוציאה מצורעת כשלג ובמדה טובה כתיב מחיקו והנה שבה : נס בתוך נס. לאחר שחזר ונעשה מטה בלען ולא כשהוא תנין דלא כתיב ויבלע תנין אהרן : ולא ילפינן זורק ממושיט. שהיה בעבודת הלוים למעלה מעשרה מרשות היחיד לרשות היחיד ורשות הרבים באמצע וסיפא דקתני הזורק פטור והמושיט חייב דברי הכל היא : או דילמא למעלה מי' פליגי. ומשום הכי פליגי ופטרי רבנן דאין כאן אויר רה"ר וזורק ממושיט לא ילפינן ורבי עקיבא יליף וסיפא רבנן קאמרי לה : ועובר גרסינן מרה"י לרה"י ועובר ברשות הרבים עצמה. ולא גרסינן בריישא הזורק : והא אמר ר' אלעזר. בהמגיע ויליף ממשא בני קהת דארון : אלא לאו בזורק. מיירי מתניתא כי מתניתין וקתני בברייתא עצמה ובהא הוא דמחייב ר' עקיבא משום דנקלטה באוירו של רה"ר : למעלה מעשרה. דיליף זורק ממושיט : ופליגא דרב חלקיה. הא דר' אלעזר : תוך שלשה דברי הכל חייב. ואע"ג דלא נח מודו דכמונח דמי : פטור. דלא ילפינן זורק ממושיט : באנו למחלוקת. ובקלוטה כמה שהונחה : משום שבות. שזרק מרשותו לרשות חבירו ולאו משום הפסק רה"ר דהוא הדין נמי אם היתה אגא עד שיערבו : ואם היו. שתיהן הרשויות שלו מותר לכתחילה : אסור לזרוק מזה לזה. ואפילו הן שלו דאי משלו לשל חבירו לא הוה שרי שמואל : לאו מי אוקימנא. בעירובין : דמדלי חד ומתתי חד. דמתוך כך צריך להמן ידו מגבוה לנמוך או מנמוך לגבוה טריד בה ודילמא לא זריק על הגג ונופל לרה"ר ואתי לאתויי ולהכי נקט ואתי לאתויי דאילו משום נפילת רה"ר ליכא חיוב חטאת דמתעסק הוא אלא הואיל דלא נתכוון לזרוק לרה"ר : כלבוד דמי. דרשות שאינו גבוה ג' בטל אגל רה"ר : אמר ליה. סברא היא : לפי שאי אפשר. להחליק רה"ר מגבשושית כאילו נלקטו במלקט ורהיטני פלי"נה בלע"ז והן בשני גווני כלים של עץ וברזל חד כעין בתוכו ובהן משוה פני רוחב הקרש ומחליקה הלכך גבשושיות נמי רה"ר : אמר ליה. אי מסברא אפילו ג' נמי : המשלשל. מתחיל לארוג דופני הסוכה בערב כלפי מעלה ומשלשל ובא כלפי מטה : משלשל. מוריד : אם גבוהות מן הארץ ג' טפחים פסולה הא פחות מג' כשרה. דאמרינן לבוד כמי שנכפף עליהן ונשלמו עד למטה הכא לאו טעמא דתילקט הוא נראה לי דהכי גרסינן מאי איכא למימר : התם משום דהויא לה מחיצה שהגדיים בוקעין בה. ובפחות משלשה ליכא בקיעת גדיים : תינח למטה למעלה מאי איכא למימר. למעלה היכא דאמרינן לבוד למעלה בכמה דוכתין כגון מקיפין ג' חבלים דעירובין (דף טז:) וכגון שהרחיק את הסיכוך מן הדפנות ג' טפחים פסולה (סוכה דף יז׳) : כמאן דמלי. מתוך שהוא חוסך ומלא הבלא : אבל שאינו מקורה. כגון חצר : וקא קשיא ליה. בהא דאגמריה רביה :
דברים

תורה אור

ואלא הא גמר גזירה שוה *ג"ש לא גמר אלא מהיכא הוה °מויעפילו הוה כיוצא בדבר אתה אומר °ויחר אף ה' בם וילך מלמד שאף אהרן נצטרע דברי רבי עקיבא אמר לו רבי יהודה בן בתירא עקיבא בין כך ובין כך אתה עתיד ליתן את הדין אם כדבריך התורה כסתו ואתה מגלה אותו ואם לאו אתה מוציא לעז על אותו צדיק ואלא הכתיב בם ההוא בנזיפה בעלמא תניא כמאן דאמר אף אהרן נצטרע דכתיב °ויפן אהרן אל מרים והנה מצורעת תנא שפנה מצרעתו אמר ריש לקיש *החושד בכשרים לוקה בגופו דכתיב °והן לא יאמינו לי וגו' וגליא קמי קוב"ה דמהימני ישראל אמר לו הן מאמינים בני מאמינים ואתה אין סופך להאמין הן מאמינים דכתיב °ויאמן העם בני מאמינים °והאמין בי"י אתה אין סופך להאמין שנאמר °יען לא האמנתם בי וגו' ממאי דלקה דכתיב °ויאמר ה' לו עוד הבא נא ידך בחיקך וגו' : אמר רבא ואיתימא רבי יוסי בר' חנינא מדה טובה ממהרת לבא ממדת פורענות דאילו במדת פורענות כתיב °ויוציאה והנה ידו מצורעת כשלג ואילו במדה טובה כתיב ויוציאה מחיקו והנה שבה כבשרו מחיקו הוא דשבה כבשרו °ויבלע מטה אהרן את מטותם א"ר אלעזר *נס בתוך נס: מרה"י לרה"י כו': *בעי רבה למטה מעשרה פליגי ובהא פליגי דמ"ס אמרינן *קלוטה כמה שהונחה ומר סבר לא אמרינן קלוטה כמה שהונחה אבל למעלה מעשרה דברי הכל פטור ולא ילפינן זורק ממושיט או דילמא למעלה מעשרה פליגי ובהא פליגי דמר סבר ילפינן זורק ממושיט ומר סבר לא ילפינן זורק ממושיט אבל למטה מי' דברי הכל חייב מאי טעמא קלוטה כמה שהונחה דמיא אמר רב יוסף הא מילתא איבעיא ליה לרב חסדא ופשטה ניהליה רב המנונא מהא מרה"י לרה"י ועובר ברשות הרבים עצמה ר' עקיבא מחייב וחכמים פוטרים מדקאמר ברשות הרבים עצמה פשיטא למטה מעשרה פליגי ובמאי אילימא במעביר (א) למטה מעשרה הוא דמחייב למעלה מי' לא מחייב °והאמר ר' *אלעזר המוציא משוי למעלה מעשרה חייב שכן משא בני קהת אלא לאו בזורק ולמטה מעשרה הוא דמחייב למעלה מעשרה לא מחייב ש"מ בקלוטה כמה שהונחה פליגי ש"מ ופליגא דר' אלעזר דאמר ר"א מחייב היה ר' עקיבא אפילו למעלה מי' והאי דקתני רה"ר עצמה להודיעך כחן דרבנן ופליגא דרב חלקיה בר טובי דאמר רב חלקיה בר טובי [א]תוך שלשה דברי הכל חייב למעלה מעשרה דברי הכל פטור מג' ועד י' באנו למחלוקת ר' עקיבא ורבנן תניא נמי הכי בתוך ג' דברי הכל חייב למעלה מי' אינו אלא משום [ב]שבות ואם היו רשויות שלו מותר מג' ועד עשרה ר"ע מחייב [ג]וחכמים פוטרין אמר מר אם היו רשויות שלו מותר לימא תהוי תיובתיה דרב דאיתמר *שני בתים בשני צדי רה"ר רבה בר רב הונא אמר רב [ד]אסור לזרוק מזה לזה ושמואל אמר מותר לזרוק מזה לזה ולאו *מי אוקימנא להההיא [ה]כגון דמידלי חד ומתתי חד דזימנין נפל ואתי לאתויי אמר ליה רב חסדא לרב המנונא ואמרי לה רב המנונא לרב חסדא מנא הא מילתא דאמור רבנן כל פחות מג' *כלבוד דמי אמר ליה לפי שאי אפשר לה לרשות הרבים שתילקט במלקט ובהרהיטני אי הכי ג' נמי ותו הא דתנן *המשלשל דפנות מלמעלה למטה אם הן גבוהין מן הארץ שלשה טפחים פסולה הא פחות מג' כשרה (ב) התם היינו טעמא משום דהויא לה מחיצה שהגדיים בוקעין בה תינח למטה למעלה מאי איכא למימר אלא כל פחות משלשה כלבוד דמי הלכתא גמירי לה *ת"ר מרה"ר לרה"ר ורה"י באמצע רבי מחייב [ו]וחכמים פוטרין רב ושמואל דאמרי תרוייהו לא חייב רבי אלא ברה"י מקורה דאמרינן ביתא כמאן דמליא דמי אבל שאינו מקורה לא אמר רב *חנא אמר רב יהודה אמר שמואל מחייב היה רבי שתים אחת משום הוצאה ואחת משום הכנסה יתיב רב חנא וקא קשיא ליה
למימרא

גזירה שוה לא גמיר· והא תאמר וליגמר מר' עקיבא שהוא קבלה מרבו והו"ת שהיה להם בקבלה מנין ג"ש שבכל התורה וזו היתה יתירה על החשבון לפיכך לא קיבלה :
למימרא

ו א ב ג מיי' פי"ג מהל' שבת הלכה טז סמג לאוין סה :
ז ד ה מיי' פט"ו שם הל' ה סמג שם טוש"ע א"ח סי' שנג סעיף א :
ח ו מיי' פי"ג שם הלכה טז :

רבינו חננאל

מאי קמ"ל דהוי זריעה מדרבנן תנינא משאינו נקוב על הנקוב תרומה ויחזור ויתרום כו' דייקינן לר' שמעון דפטר התולש מעציץ נקוב דבעא מיניה ההוא סבא מר' זירא אם היה שורש הזרע כנגד הנקב מה לי אמר ר' שמעון בזה אשתיק ר' זירא ומנין אשכחיה דיתיב וקאמר ומודה ר' שמעון שאם נקוב בכדי שהרתו פי' במוציא רימון שהתולש ממנו חייב א"ל שורש כנגד הנקב בעינא מינך ולא פשטתה לי לפטורה ניקב בכדי שהרתו מיבעיא. אמר אביי אם איתא לדר' זירא הכי אתמר ומודה ר' שמעון שאם נקב למטה מרביעית פי' הכי קאמר אביי שפיר עבד ר' זירא דלא אהדריליה לההוא סבא דאי אתמר הכי אתמר מודה ר' שמעון שאם ניקב העציץ בארעיתו או קרוב לארעיתו במקום שלא נשאר בו כדי לקבל רביעית דכיון דלית ביה כדי לקבל רביעית בטל מתורת כלי דכי מנקיב עציץ בההוא דוכתא ודאי שרשי הזרעים שיש בו מגיעין לארץ והרי הן כזרועים בארץ והתולש מהן חייב אבל ניקב העציץ מצדו ונשאר בו כדי לקבל רביעית עדיין כלי הוא ואע"פ שהושרש כנגד אותו הנקב איכא למימר שאינו מגיע לארץ ואע"פ שאין דבר חוצץ בינו לבינה עדיין מיבעי אליבא דר' שמעון. אמר רבא ה' מדות בכלי חרס עיקרא כל כלי שנשבר נטהר מיהו לא מחשיב שבור אלא עד שיפסל ממה שהוכן לשמש כגון כלי חרס שהוכן לקיבול משקין מקבל טומאה עד שניקב שיעור הכנסת משקין או הוצאת משקין וכן כלי חרס שהוכן לאוכלין אע"פ שניקב בכונס משקה מקבל טומאה עד שינקב שיעור הוצאת זיתים. כדתנן שיעור כלי חרס לטהר העשוי לאוכלין שיעורו בזיתים עשוי למשקין שיעורו במשקין עשוי לאוכלין ולמשקין מטילין אותו לחומרו בזיתים ולענין רימונים חלוקת אמוראים היא אבל במשנה לא מצינו בכלי חרס שיעור ברימונים ולא הגיעה אלא עד זיתים ולענין כלי עץ או כלי. עור או כיוצא בו הא דתנן כל כלי בעלי בתים שיעורו כרימונים השתא הני חמש מדות דאמר רבא חדא דניקב במוציא משקה טהור מלטמא גסטרא ועדיין כלי הוא לקדש בו מי חטאת משום דגסטרא כלי גדול הוא דמחתין ביה כדים וחצובים והכי דמיא דמקבל מאי דדאיב מינהון ומינטר עיקר גם גסטרא להא מלתא הוכן פעמים שהחבית או הצבא גדולה נשברה לראשה וניטלו אוניה ומכנים אותה ולשומו תחת מטה ותותי מצבי כמו כן ונקראת גיסטרא וכד מינקיב ניסטרא במוציא משקה בטלה מן הדבר שהוכנה לו וליכא כלי חרס דמטהר במוציא משקה בר מגיסטרא בלחוד לפי שאין אומרים הבא גסטרא לגסטרא. פי' אם ניקבה הצבא במוציא משקה או' הבא גיסטרא והנח תחתיה כדי שיקבל מה שיזוב ממנו אבל אם הגיסטרא גופו מוציא משקה אין אומרים הבא גיסטרא לגיסטרא שיקבל מה שיזוב ממנה לקבל ואע"פ שניקב במוציא משקה ותנן גיסטרא שנתרועעה ואינה מקבלת משקין אע"פ שמקבלת אוכלין טהורה שאין שיריים לשיריים פי' שאין שירים לשירים הוא שפירשנו למעלה שהגיסטרא עיקרה : שירי הבית או הצבא שנטלו אוניה וכלי הוא לקדש מי חטאת ועיקרא ההוא דתנן אין ממלאין ואין מקדשין ואין מזין מי חטאת אלא בכלי אשמעינן הבא דגסטרא שנתרועעה ומוציאה משקין תורת כלי עליה וכשרה למי חטאת : שנייה. ניקב בכונס משקה פסול מלקדש בו מי חטאת ועדיין כלי הוא להכשיר בו זרעים כדתנן בנדה פרק ששי כיוצא בו כל כלי חרס שמכנים מוציא ויש מוציא ואינו מכנים ואמרינן עלה מכנים פסול למי חטאת וטהור משום גסטרא דאמר רב אסי שונין כלי החרס שיעורו בכונס משקה לא אמרו במוציא משקה אלא לענין גסטרא בלבד ואמרינן ת"ר כיצד בודקין כלי חרס לידע אם ניקב בכונס משקה אם לאו מביא עריבה מליאה מים ונותן קדירה לתוכה אם כנסה בידוע שבכונס משקה ואם לאו בידוע שבמוציא משקה ר' יהודה אומר כופה אוני קדירה לתוך עריבה ומציף עליה מים אם כנסה בידוע שבכונס משקה ואם לאו בידוע שבמוציא משקה או שופתה ע"ג האור אם האור מעמידה בידוע שבמוציא משקה ואם לא בידוע שבכונס משקה ר' יוסי אומר אף לא שופתה על האור מפני שהאור מעמידה אלא מעמידה ע"ג הרמץ אם רמץ מעמידה בידוע שבמוציא משקה ואם לאו בידוע שבכונס משקה היתה יורדת טפה אחר טפה בידוע שבכונס משקה מאי איכא בין ת"ק לר' יהודה אמר עולא כינוס ע"י הדחק איכא בינייהו אשמעינן אע"פ שרחב הנקב והוסיף על כדי הוצאת משקה והגיע להכנסת משקה עדיין אותו עציץ כשאינו נקוב דמי ומכשיר את הזרעים כדפרשינן לעילא : שלישית. ניקב בשורש קטן טהור מלהכשיר זרעים ועדיין כלי הוא לקבל בו זיתים בהא אשמעינן רבה דלא כר' שמעון דאמר אם ניקב למטה מרביעית וקאמר אפילו ניקב בשורש קטן דאפשר דמתחברין אותו זרעים שיש בו לקרקע ודומה לעציץ נקוב וטהור מלהכשיר זרעים אם לא הגיע הנקב לכדי הוצאת זיתים עדיין כלי הוא ומקבל טומאה. רביעית ניקב במוציא זיתים. אמר רבא אם הוכן מעיקרא זה הכלי לקבל רימונים אע"פ שניקב במוציא זיתים עדיין טמא הוא אבל אם מעיקרא לא הוכן אלא לקבל זיתים כיון שניקב במוציא זיתים טהור והא מלתא פליגי בה רבה סבר דכלי חרס רברבי שיעורו במוציא זיתים לפום דמפרש ליה [לדרב אסי] [ורב אסי] נמי אמר הכין שמעתי והד מהדרי אמוראי דמערבא הד סבר במוציא רימון וחד סבר בשורש קטן וסימניך אחד המרבה ואחד הממעים ורב חנניא בר שלמיא משום ר' אליעזר תני כל כלי חרס בין גדול בין קטן אם ניקב במוציא זיתים טהור וניר קשישא ניסיים בה דר' אליעזר כל כלי חרס שניקב במוציא זיתים הרי הן ככלי גללים וכלי אבנים וכלי אדמה שאין מקבלין טומאה לא מדברי תורה ולא מדברי סופרים והלכתא הכין ובהכין סלקא שמעתתא ולא סליק דצריך כלי חרס במוציא רימון וליתא לדרבא. חמישית ולענין צמיד פתיל עד שיפחת רובה :
פרק יא הזורק מרה"ר לרה"י או מרה"י לרה"ר חייב. אמרינן זריקה תולדה דהוצאה היא והוצאה גופה מייתי לה ר' יוחנן דהיא מלאכה מהא ויצו משה ויעבירו קול במחנה וגו' משה היה יתיב במחנה לויה

[מכות יד: וז"ל הערוך ערך גזר ב' גזרה שוה לא גמיר פי' לא גמיר ר"ע ג"ש אלא הוא דרש מעצמו ע"כ וכזה מיושב קושית התוס' ד"ה ג"ש]
במדבר יד · שם יב · [יומא יט: ע"ש] · שמות ד · ברכות טו · שם · במדבר כ · שמות ד · שם · שם ז
[פסחים קיח: חולין קכז. גיטין עט: ב"ק ע:]
עירובין פה: · [שם] · [פי' סוכה ז:] · שם פו: סוכה טז. · לעיל ד:

הגהות הב"ח

(א) גמ' ובמאי אילימא במעביר. נ"ב פי' ופליגי בכנגת גופו אי כנגת חפץ דמי : (ב) שם הא פחות מג' כשרה מאי איכא למימר התם היינו :

גליון הש"ס

גמ' והאמר ר"א המוציא משוי. עיין עירובין דף לג ע"א תד"ה והא אי בעי :

Continuation of translation from previous page as indicated by ◁

culpable, for thus was the carrying of the children of Kohath. Hence it must surely refer to throwing, and one is culpable only when it is below ten, but not when it is above ten; this proves that they differ in whether an object caught up is as at rest. This proves it.

Now, he [R. Hamnuna] differs from R. Eleazar. For R. Eleazar said: R. Akiba declared [him] culpable even when it is above ten; but as to what is stated, through the street itself,[2] that is to teach you the extent[3] of the Rabbis[' ruling].[4] Now he [R. Eliezer] differs from R. Hilkiah b. Ṭobi, for R. Hilkiah b. Ṭobi said: Within three [handbreadths from the ground], all agree that he is culpable;[5] above ten, all agree that he is not culpable; between three and ten, we come to the controversy of R. Akiba and the Rabbis. It was taught likewise: Within three, all agree that he is liable; above ten, it is [prohibited] only as a *shebuth*,[1] and if they are [both] his own grounds, it is permitted [at the very outset]; between three and ten, R. Akiba ruled [him] culpable, while the Sages exempt him.

The Master said: 'And if they are [both] his own grounds, it is permitted.' Shall we say that this is a refutation of Rab? For it was stated: If there are two houses on the two [opposite] sides of a street, Rabbah son of R. Huna said in Rab's name: One may not throw [an object] from one to another; while Samuel ruled: It is permitted to throw from one to another![2]—But did we not establish that law [as referring] e.g., to [the case] where one [house] is higher and one is lower, so that it [the object] may fall [into the street][3] and he come to fetch it?

R. Ḥisda asked R. Hamnuna—others state, R. Hamnuna asked R. Ḥisda—How do we know this principle which the Rabbis stated, viz.: Whatever is [separated by] less than three [handbreadths] is as joined?[4] Said he to him, Because it is impossible for the street to be trimmed with a plane and shears.[5] If so, the same should apply to three also? Moreover, when we learnt: If one lets down walls from above to below,[6] if they are three handbreadths high above the ground, it [the *sukkah*] is unfit.[7] Hence if [they are] less than three it is fit:[8] what can be said?[9]—There the reason is that it is a partition through which goats can enter.[10] That is well [for] below; what can be said [for] above?[11]—Rather [the fact is] that whatever is [separated by] less than three [handbreadths] is regarded as joined is a law received on tradition.

d Our Rabbis taught: [If one throws[1] an article] from public to public ground, and private ground lies between: Rabbi holds him liable, but the Sages exempt him. Rab and Samuel both assert: Rabbi imposed liability only in the case of covered-in private ground, when we say that the house is as though it were full, but not if it is uncovered.[2] R. Ḥana[3] said in Rab Judah's name in Samuel's name: Rabbi held him liable to two [sacrifices], one on account of carrying out and another on account of carrying in.[4] Now R. Ḥana sat [studying] and this presented a difficulty to

(2) Which implies below ten. (3) Lit., 'power'. (4) Even then they hold that he is not culpable. (5) Because that is regarded as on the ground itself, and therefore at rest.

(1) V. Glos.—The *shebuth* here is that he carries from his domain to his neighbour's, both being private ground. (2) Both houses must belong to the same person, for otherwise Samuel would certainly not permit it. V. 'Er., 85*b* and notes. (3) For the houses not being on the same level, more skill is required to throw from one to the other. (4) *Labud*, v. Glos. (5) The ground cannot be perfectly levelled, and it must contain bumps of that height. Therefore everything within three handbreadths is regarded as joined to the ground. (6) The reference is to the walls of a *sukkah* (booth, v. Lev. XXIII, 42). He takes a wall, e.g., of boards, lowers it, but not right down to the ground, and fastens it to something on top. (7) As the walls are incomplete. (8) For they are then regarded as touching the ground. (9) The *sukkah* not being in a public ground, the reason stated is inapplicable here. (10) Lit., 'cleave'. But they cannot squeeze through a gap less than three. (11) This principle of *labud* operates also where the gap is above; v. e.g., 'Er. 16*b*, Suk. 17*a*; obviously these reasons do not hold good in that case.

d (1) So *supra* 4*b*. (2) V. notes on this passage *supra* 4*b* and 5*a*. (3) Var. lec.: R. Ḥisda. (4) For during its journey it passes out of public into private ground, and enters from private into public ground.

ואלא הא גמר גזירה שוה *ג"ש לא גמר אלא מהיכא הוה °מויעפילו הוה ביוצא בדבר אתה אומר °ויחר אף ה' בם וילך מלמד שאף אהרן נצטרע דברי רבי עקיבא אמר לו רבי יהודה בן בתירא עקיבא בין כך ובין כך אתה עתיד ליתן את הדין אם כדבריך התורה כסתו ואתה מגלה אותו ואם לאו אתה מוציא לעז על אותו צדיק ואלא הכתיב בם ההוא בנזיפה בעלמא תניא כמאן דאמר אף אהרן נצטרע דכתיב °ויפן אהרן אל מרים והנה מצורעת תנא שפנה מצרעתו אמר ריש לקיש *החושד בכשרים לוקה בגופו דכתיב °והן לא יאמינו לי וגו' וגליא קמי קב"ה דמהימני ישראל אמר לו הן מאמינים בני מאמינים ואתה אין סופך להאמין הן מאמינים דכתיב °ויאמן העם בני מאמינים °והאמין בה' אתה אין סופך להאמין שנאמר °יען לא האמנתם בי וגו' ממאי דלקה דכתיב °ויאמר ה' לו עוד הבא נא ידך בחיקך וגו': אמר רבא ואיתימא רבי יוסי בר' חנינא מדה טובה ממהרת לבא ממדת פורענות דאילו במדת פורענות כתיב °ויוציאה והנה ידו מצורעת כשלג ואילו במדה טובה כתיב ויוציאה מחיקו והנה שבה כבשרו מחיקו הוא דשבה כבשרו °ויבלע מטה אהרן את מטותם א"ר אלעזר *נס בתוך נס: מרה"י לרה"י כו': *בעי רבה למטה מעשרה פליגי ובהא פליגי דמ"ס אמרינן *קלוטה כמה שהונחה ומר סבר לא אמרינן קלוטה כמה שהונחה אבל למעלה מעשרה דברי הכל פטור ולא ילפינן זורק ממושיט או דילמא למעלה מעשרה פליגי ובהא פליגי דמר סבר ילפינן זורק ממושיט ומר סבר לא ילפינן זורק ממושיט אבל למטה מי' דברי הכל חייב מאי טעמא קלוטה כמה שהונחה דמיא אמר רב יוסף הא מילתא איבעיא ליה לרב חסדא ופשטה ניהליה רב המנונא מהא מרה"י לרה"י ועובר ברשות הרבים עצמה ר' עקיבא מחייב וחכמים פוטרים מדקאמר ברשות הרבים עצמה פשיטא למטה מעשרה פליגי ובמאי אילימא במעביר (א) למטה מעשרה הוא דמחייב למעלה מי' לא מחייב °והאמר ר' *אלעזר המוציא משוי למעלה מעשרה חייב שכן משא בני קהת אלא לאו בזורק ולמטה מעשרה הוא דמחייב למעלה מעשרה לא מחייב ש"מ בקלוטה כמה שהונחה פליגי ש"מ ופליגא דר' אלעזר דאמר ר"א מחייב היה ר' עקיבא אפילו למעלה מי' והאי דקתני רה"ר עצמה להודיעך כחן דרבנן ופליגא דרב חלקיה בר טובי דאמר רב חלקיה בר טובי *תוך שלשה דברי הכל חייב למעלה מעשרה דברי הכל פטור מג' ועד י' באנו למחלוקת ר' עקיבא ורבנן תניא נמי הכי בתוך ג' דברי הכל חייב למעלה מי' אינו אלא משום שבות ואם היו רשויות שלו מותר מג' ועד עשרה ר"ע מחייב וחכמים פוטרין אמר מר אם היו רשויות שלו מותר לימא תהוי תיובתיה דרב דאיתמר *שני בתים בשני צדי רה"ר רבה בר רב הונא אמר רב אסור לזרוק מזה לזה ושמואל אמר מותר לזרוק מזה לזה ולאו *מי אוקימנא להיא כגון דמידלי חד ומתתי חד דזימנין נפל ואתי לאתויי אמר ליה רב חסדא לרב המנונא ואמרי לה רב המנונא לרב חסדא מנא הא מילתא דאמור רבנן כל פחות מג' *כלבוד דמי אמר ליה לפי שאי אפשר לה לרשות הרבים שתילקט במלקט וברהיטני אי הכי ג' נמי ותו הא דתנן *המשלשל דפנות מלמעלה למטה אם הן גבוהין מן הארץ שלשה טפחים פסולה הא פחות מג' כשרה (ב) התם היינו טעמא משום דהויא לה מחיצה שהגדיים בוקעין בה תינח למטה למעלה מאי איכא למימר אלא כל פחות משלשה כלבוד דמי הלכתא גמירי לה *ת"ר מרה"ר לרה"ר ורה"י באמצע רבי מחייב וחכמים פוטרין רב ושמואל דאמרי תרוייהו לא חייב רבי אלא ברה"י מקורה דאמרינן ביתא כמאן דמליא דמי אבל שאינו מקורה לא אמר רב *חנא אמר רב יהודה אמר שמואל מחייב היה רבי שתים אחת משום הוצאה ואחת משום הכנסה יתיב רב חנא וקא קשיא ליה

למימרא

רש"י

ואלא הא גמיר גזירה שוה. וא"כ לא כסתו התורה דהוה ליה כמפורש ומשני רבי יהודה בן בתירא לא גמרה ואין אדם דן ג"ש מעצמו : ואלא. לרבי יהודה : מהיכן הוה. בחיוו חטא מת דכתיב כי בחטאו מת : מויעפילו. ויעפילו לעלות וגו' שלא הרשיע כ"כ כחילול שבת : שפנה מצרעתו. קדם ונתרפא : והנה ידו מצורעת. היינו לוקה בגופו : ויוציאה והנה ידו. אחר הוציאה מצורעת כשלג ובמדה טובה כתיב מחיקו והנה שבה : נס בתוך נס. לאחר שחזר ונעשה מטה בלען ולא כשהוא תנין דלא כתיב ויבלע תנין אהרן : ולא ילפינן זורק ממושיט. שהיה בעבודת הלוים למעלה מעשרה מרשות היחיד לרשות היחיד ורשות הרבים באמצע וסיפא דקתני הזורק פטור והמושיט חייב דברי הכל היא : או דילמא למעלה מי' פליגי. ומשום הכי פליגי ופטרי רבנן דאין כאן הויה רה"ר וזורק ממושיט לא ילפינן ורבי עקיבא יליף וסיפא רבנן קאמרי לה : ועובר גרסינן מרה"י לרה"י ועובר ברשות הרבים עצמה. ולא גרסינן בריבא הזורק : והא אמר ר' אלעזר. באמצע ויליף ממשא בני קהת דארון : אלא לאו בזורק. מיירי מתניתא כי מתניתין וקתני בברייתא עצמה ובהא הוא דמחייב ר' עקיבא משום דנקלטה באוירו של רה"ר : למעלה מעשרה. דיליף זורק ממושיט: ופליגא דרב חלקיה. הא דר' אלעזר: תוך שלשה דברי הכל חייב. ואע"ג דלא נח נמי דכמונח דמי : פטור. דלא ילפינן זורק ממושיט : באנו למחלוקת. ובקלוטה כמה שהונחה : משום שבות. שזורק מרשותו לרשות חבירו ולאו משום הפסק רה"ר דהוא הדין נמי אם היתה אצלו עד שיערבו: ואם היו. בתיהן הרשויות שלו מותר לכתחילה : אסור לזרוק מזה לזה. ואפילו הן שלו דאי משלו לשל חבירו לא הוה שרי שמואל: לאו מי אוקימנא. בעירובין : דמדלי חד ומתתי חד. דמתוך כך צריך לאמן ידו מגבוה לנמוך או מנמוך לגבוה עביד בה ודילמא לא זריק על הגג ונופל לרה"ר ואתי לאתויי ולהכי נקט ואתי לאתויי דאילו משום נפילת רה"ר ליכא חיוב חטאת דמתעסק הוא אגל הואיל דלא נתכוון לזרוק לרה"ר : כלבוד דמי. דרשות שאינו גבוה ג' בטל אגל רה"ר : אמר ליה. סברא היא : לפי שאי אפשר. להחליק רה"ר מגבשושית כאילו כלקטו במלקט והיטני פלי"נה בלע"ז והן בשני גווני כלים שלען וברזל חד כמין בתוכו ובהן משוה פני רוחב הקרקע ומחליקה הלכך גבשושיות נמי רה"ר: אמר ליה. אי מסברא אפילו ג' נמי: המשלשל. מתחיל לארוג דופני הסוכה בערב כלפי מעלה ומשלשל ובא כלפי מטה : משלשל. מוריד : אם גבוהות מן הארץ ג' טפחים פסולה הא פחות מג' כשרה. דאמרינן לבוד כמי שכפף עליהן ושלמו עד למטה הכא לאו טעמא דתילקט הוא נראה לי דהכי גרסינן מאי איכא למימר: התם משום דהויא לה מחיצה שהגדיים בוקעין בה . ובפחות משלשה ליכא בקיעת גדיים : תינח למטה למעלה מאי איכא למימר. למעלה היכא דאמרינן לבוד למעלה בכמה דוכתין כגון מקיפין ג' חבלים דעירובין (דף טז:) וכגון שהרחיק את הסיכוך מן הדפנות ג' טפחים פסולה (סוכה דף יז:) : כמאן דמלי. מתוך שהוא חוכך ומלא הבלא : אבל שאינו מקורה. כגון חצר : וקא קשיא ליה. בהא דאגמריה רביה :

דברים

תוספות

גזירה שוה לא גמיר. והא תאמר וליגמר מר' עקיבא שהוא קבלה מרבו ואומר ר"ת שהיה להם בקבלה מנין ג"ש שבכל התורה וזו היתה יתירה על החשבון לפיכך לא קיבלה :

למימרא

רבינו חננאל

מאי קמ"ל דהוי זריעה מדרבנן תנינא משאינו נקוב על הנקוב תרומה ויחזור ויתרום כו' דייקינן לר' שמעון דפטר התולש מעציץ נקוב דבעא מיניה ההוא סבא מר' זירא אם היה שורש הזרע כנגד הנקב מה לי' אמר ר' שמעון בזה אשתיק ר' זירא זמנין אשכחיה דיתיב וקאמר ומודה ר' שמעון שאם נקוב בכדי טהרתו פי' במוציא רימון שהתולש ממנו חייב א"ל שורש כנגד הנקב בעינא מינך ולא פשטת לי לפטורה ניקב בכדי טהרתו מיבעיא. אמר אביי אם איתא לדר' זירא הכי אתמר ומודה ר' שמעון שאם נקב למטה מרביעית פי' הכי קאמר אביי שפיר עבד ר' זירא דלא אהדריליה להוא סבא דאי אתמר הכי אתמר מודה ר' שמעון שאם ניקב העציץ בארעיתו או קרוב לארעיתו במקום שלא נשאר בו כדי לקבל רביעית דכיון דלית ביה כדי לקבל רביעית בטל מתורת כלי דכי מנקיב עציץ בההוא דוכתא ודאי שרשי הזרעים שיש בו מגיעין לארץ והרי הן כזרועים בארץ והתולש מהן חייב אבל ניקב העציץ מצדו ונשאר בו כדי לקבל רביעית עדיין כלי הוא ואע"פ שהושרש כנגד אותו הנקב איכא למימר שאינו מגיע לארעא אע"פ שאין דבר חוצץ בינו לבינה עדיין מיבעי אליבא דר' שמעון. אמר רבא ה' מדות בכלי חרס עיקרא כל כלי שנשבר נטהר מיהו לא מחשיב שבור אלא עד שיפסל ממה שהוכן לשמש כגון כלי חרס שהוכן לקיבול משקין מקבל טומאה עד שניקב שיעור הכנסת משקין או הוצאת משקין וכן כלי חרס שהוכן לאוכלין אע"פ שניקב בכונס משקה מקבל טומאה עד שינקב שיעור הוצאת זיתים. כדתנן שיעור כלי חרס לטהר העשוי לאוכלין שיעורו בזיתים עשוי למשקין שיעורו במשקין עשוי לאוכלין ולמשקין מטילין אותו להומרו בזיתים ולענין רימונים חלוקת אמוראים היא אבל במשנה לא מצינו בכלי חרס שיעור ברימונים ולא הגיעה אלא עד זיתים ולענין כלי עץ או כלי עור או כיוצא בו הא דתנן כל כלי בעלי בתים שיעורו כרימונים השתא הני חמש מדות דאמר רבא חדא דניקב במוציא משקה טהור מלטמא גסטרא ועדיין כלי הוא לקדש בו מי חטאת משום דגסטרא כלי גדול הוא דמהתין ביה כדים וחצובים והכי דמיא דמקבל מאי דדאיב מינהון ומינפר עיקר גם גסטרא להא מלתא הוכן פעמים שהחבית או הצבא גדולה נשברה לראשה וניטלו אזניה ומכנים אותה ולשומו תחת מטה ותותי מצבי כמו כן ונקראת גיסטרא וכד מינקיב גיסטרא במוציא משקה בטלה כן הדבר שהוכנה לו וליכא כלי חרס דמטהר במוציא משקה בר מגיסטרא בלהוד לפי שאין אומרים הבא גסטרא לגסטרא. פי' אם ניקבה הצבא במוציא משקה או' הבא גיסטרא והנח תחתיה כדי שיקבל מה שיזוב ממנו אבל אם הגיסטרא גופו מוציא משקה אין אומרים הבא גיסטרא לגיסטרא שיקבל מה שיזוב ממנה לקבל ואע"פ שניקב במוציא משקה ותנן גיסטרא שנתרועעה ואינה מקבלת משקין אע"פ שמקבלת אוכלין טהורה שאין שירים לשיריים פי' שאין שירים הוא שפירשנו למעלה שהגיסטרא עיקרה : שירי הבית או הצבא שנטלו אזניה וכלי היא לקדש מי חטאת ועיקרא ההוא דתנן אין ממלאין ואין מקדשין ואין מזין מי חטאת אלא בכלי אשמעינן הבא דגסטרא שנתרועעה ומוציאה משקין תורת כלי עליה וכשרה למי חטאת : שנייה. ניקב בכונס משקה פסול מלקדש בו מי חטאת ועדיין כלי הוא להכשיר בו זרעים כדתנן בנדה פרק ששי כיוצא בו כל כלי חרס שמכנים מוציא ויש מוציא ואינו מכנים ואמרינן עלה מכנים פסול למי חטאת וטהור משום גסטרא דאמר רב אסי שונין כלי החרס שיעורו בכונס משקה לא אמרו במוציא משקה אלא לענין גסטרא בלבד ואמרינן ת"ר כיצד בודקין כלי חרס לידע אם ניקב בכונס משקה אם לאו מביא עריבה מליאה מים ונותן קדירה לתוכה אם כנסה בידוע שבכונס משקה ואם לאו בידוע שבמוציא משקה ר' יהודה אומר כופה אוגי קדירה לתוך עריבה ומציף עליה מים אם כנסה בידוע שבכונס משקה ואם לאו בידוע שבמוציא משקה או שופתה ע"ג האור אם האור מעמידה בידוע שבמוציא משקה ואם לא בידוע שבכונס משקה ר' יוסי אומר אף לא ישפתה על האור מפני שהאור מעמידה אלא מעמידה ע"ג הרמץ אם רמץ מעמידה בידוע שבמוציא משקה ואם לאו בידוע שבכונס משקה היתה יורדת טפה אחר טפה בידוע שבכונס משקה מאי איכא בין ת"ק לר' יהודה אמר עולא כונס ע"י הדחק איכא בינייהו אשמעינן אע"פ שרחב הנקב והוסיף על כדי הוצאת משקה והגיע להכנסת משקה עדיין אותו עציץ כשאינו נקוב דמי ומכשיר את הזרעים כדפרשינן לעילא : שלישית. ניקב בשורש קטן טהור מלהכשיר זרעים ועדיין כלי הוא לקבל בו זיתים בהא אשמעינן רבה דלא כר' שמעון דאמר אם ניקב למטה מרביעית וקאמר אפילו ניקב בשורש קטן דאפשר דמתחברין אותו זרעים שיש בו לקרקע והומה לעציץ נקוב וטהור מלהכשיר זרעים אם לא הגיע הנקב לכדי הוצאת זיתים עדיין כלי הוא ומקבל טומאה . רביעית ניקב במוציא זיתים . אמר רבא אם הוכן מעיקרא זה הכלי לקבל רימונים אע"פ שניקב במוציא זיתים עדיין טמא הוא אבל אם מעיקרא לא הוכן אלא לקבל זיתים כיון שניקב במוציא זיתים טהור והא מלתא פליגי בה רבה סבר דכלי חרס רברבי שיעורו במוציא זיתים לפום דמיפרש ליה [לדרב אסי] [ורב אסי] נמי אמר הכין שמעתי והד מתרי אמוראי דמערבא חד סבר במוציא רימון וחד סבר בשורש קטן וסימניך אחד המרבה ואחד הממעיט ורב חנניא בר שלמיא משום ר' אליעזר תני כל כלי חרס בין גדול בין קטן אם ניקב במוציא זיתים טהור ומר קשישא מסיים בה דר' אליעזר כל כלי חרס שניקב במוציא זיתים הרי הן ככלי גללים וכלי אבנים וכלי אדמה שאין מקבלין טומאה לא מדברי סופרים והלכתא הכין ובהכין סלקא שמעתתא ולא סליק דצריך כלי חרס במוציא רימון וליתא לדרבא. המישית ולענין צמיד פתיל עד שיפתת רובה :

פרק יא הזורק מרה"ר לרה"י או מרה"י לרה"ר חייב. אמרינן זריקה תולדה דהוצאה היא והוצאה גופה מייתי לה ר' יוחנן דהיא מלאכה מהא ויצו משה ויעבירו קול במחנה וגו' משה היה יתיב במחנה לויה

עין משפט נר מצוה

ו א ב ג מיי' פי"ג מהל' שבת הלכה טז סמג לאוין סה :

ז ד ה מיי' פט"ו שם הל' ח סמג שם טוש"ע א"ח סי' שנג סעיף א :

ח ו מיי' פי"ג שם הלכה טז :

מסורת הש"ס

[מכות יד: וז"ל הערוך ערך גזר ג' גזירה שוה לא גמיר פי' לא גמיר ר"ע ג"ש אלא הוא דרש לעצמו עכ"ל וכזה מיושב קושית התוס' ד"ה ג"ש]

[יומא יט: ע"ש]

[פסחים קיח: חולין קכז.] [גיטין עט. ב"ק פ:]

עירובין פה:

[שם]

[ע' סוכה ו:]

שם טו: סוכה טז.

[לעיל ד:]

תורה אור

במדבר יד | שם יב | שמות ד | שם | שמות ד | שם | שם ז | בראשית טו | במדבר כ

הגהות הב"ח

(א) גמ' ובמאי אילימא במעביר. נ"ב פי' פליגי בהעברת גופו אי בהעברת תכון דמי : (ב) שם הא פחות מג' כשרה הכי איכא למימר התם היינו :

גליון הש"ס

גמ' והאמר ר"א המוציא משוי. עיין עירובין דף לג ע"א תד"ה והא לי בעי :

ט א ב מיי' פי"ט מהל' שבת הלכה ז ויט :
י ג ד מיי' פי"ג שם הלכה כה :
[לעיל עה:]
יא ה מיי' שם הל' טו :

למימרא דמחייב רבי אתולדה במקום אב והתניא רבי אומר *דברים הדברים אלה הדברים אלו ל"ט מלאכות שנאמרו למשה בסיני אמר ליה רב יוסף מר אהא מתני לה וקשיא ליה דרבי אדרבי אנן אדרבי יהודה מתנינן ולא קשיא לן דתניא מרה"י לרשות הרבים ועבר ארבע אמות ברה"ר רבי יהודה מחייב וחכמים פוטרין אמר רב יהודה אמר שמואל מחייב היה רבי יהודה שתים אחת משום הוצאה ואחת משום העברה דאי ס"ד חדא הוא דמחייב מכלל דרבנן פטרי לגמרי הא אפיק לה מרה"י לרה"ר ממאי דילמא לעולם אימא לך ר' יהודה חדא הוא דמחייב ורבנן פטרי לגמרי והיכי משכחת לה כגון דאמר עד דנפקא ליה לרה"ר תנוח ובהא קמיפלגי דר' יהודה סבר אמרינן קלוטה כמה שהונחה ואיתעבידא ליה מחשבתו ורבנן סברי לא אמרינן קלוטה כמה שהונחה ולא איתעבידא ליה מחשבתו אבל אתולדה במקום אב לא מחייב רבי יהודה לא ס"ד דתניא רבי יהודה *מוסיף אף השובט והמדקדק [א]אמרו לו שובט הרי הוא בכלל מיסך מדקדק הרי הוא בכלל אורג מאי לאו דעבדינהו לתרווייהו בהדי הדדי וש"מ מחייב היה רבי יהודה אתולדה במקום אב (א) ממאי דילמא לעולם דעבדה להא לחודה והא לחודה ורבי יהודה אתולדה במקום אב לא מחייב ובהא קמיפלגי דר' יהודה סבר הני אבות נינהו [ב]ורבנן סברי הני תולדות נינהו תדע דקתני רבי יהודה מוסיף אי אמרת בשלמא אבות מאי מוסיף מוסיף אבות אלא אי אמרת תולדות מאי מוסיף איתמר נמי רבה ורב יוסף דאמרי תרווייהו לא חייב רבי יהודה אלא אחת א"ל רבינא לרב אשי ולמאי דסליק אדעתין מעיקרא דמחייב היה ר' יהודה שתים אי להכא קבעי לה להכא לא קבעי לה אי להכא קבעי לה להכא לא קבעי לה אמר ליה *באומר כל מקום שתרצה תנוח: [ג]פשיטא נתכוון לזרוק שמנה וזרק ארבע הרי כתב שם משמעון *נתכוון לזרוק ארבע וזרק שמנה מהו מי אמרינן הא אפיק ליה או דילמא היכא דבעי הא לא נח ולאו היינו דאמר ליה רבינא לרב אשי [ד]וא"ל באומר כל מקום שתרצה תנוח ודקאמרת הרי כתב שם משמעון מי דמי התם כמה דלא כתיב שם לא מכתיב ליה שמעון הכא כמה דלא זריק ארבע לא מיזדרקי ליה תמני: תנו רבנן [ה]הזורק מרשות הרבים לרה"ר ורשות היחיד באמצע ד' אמות חייב
פחות

תוספות

למימרא דמחייב רבי אתולדה במקום אב והתניא כו'. הקשה ה"ר פור"ת מנא ליה דמחייב אתולדה במקום אב דילמא הא דמחייב שתים היינו כשנודע לו וחזר ונודע לו ובפלוגתא דר' יוחנן וריש לקיש *דמחייב אפילו בהוציא והוציא בהעלם אחת ואור"י דאם כן לא היה רב יהודה משמיענו שום חידוש שחייב שתים ועל כרחיך אתא לאשמעינן דרבי מחייב אתולדה במקום אב: לא ס"ד דתניא ר' יהודה מוסיף כו'. לפי מאי דקס"ד דטעמא דרבי יהודה משום דמחייב אתולדה במקום אב אמאי נקט טפי שובט ומדקדק איכא למימר דס"ד דרבנן נמי מחייב אתולדה במקום אב ולא פליגי אלא בשובט ומדקדק ואמרי דלאו היינו תולדה אלא היינו ממש מיסך ואורג אי נמי לא מחייבי רבנן אתולדה במקום אב ולדבריו דרבי יהודה קאמרי: מאי לאו דעבדינהו לתרווייהו בהדי הדדי. אין הלשון מיושב דמשמע דלמסקנא לא קאי הכי וזה אינו דלמסקנא נמי דמפ' דר' יהודה חשיב להן אבות מיירי נמי דעבדינהו לתרווייהו בהדי הדדי דאי בדעבד האי לחודיה והאי לחודיה כדגרסינן בכמה ספרים בהא לא הוה פליגי רבנן עליה דתיפוק ליה דמשום תולדה הוו מחייבי ואומר ר"י דאין למחוק ושפיר גרסינן ליה וה"פ לעולם דעבדה האי לחודיה והאי לחודיה ופליגי במזיד ולענין התראה דלרבי יהודה צריך להתרותו משום שובט ומדקדק ולרבנן משום מיסך ואורג וה"ה דהוה מצי למידחי דעבדינהו לתרווייהו בהדי הדדי ורבי יהודה סבר הני אבות נינהו אלא דניחא ליה לדחויי דעביד האי לחודיה והאי לחודיה דהשתא ע"כ טעמא דר"י לאו משום דמחייב אתולדה במקום אב אלא משום דאבות נינהו: הרי כתב שם משמעון. הך פשיטותא לא קיימא כדמסיק ורבינא נמי דפריך לרב אשי אמילתא דר"י אי להכי קבעי לה להכא לא קבעי לה סבר דלא דמי לכתב שם משמעון דאי דמי לא הוי פריך מידי דהא כי קא בעי דתנוח בסוף ד' כשנחה בתחלת רה"ר ע"י קליטה הרי כתב שם משמעון וכי אזלה תו ד"א ליחייב עלייהו דנעשית מחשבתו ראשונה ולהכי קאמר הש"ס לאו היינו דאמר ליה רבינא לרב אשי דלא הוה ליה לאיתויי מילתיה דרבינא אלא שרוצה לסתור לו אף מה שהיה פשוט לו הרי כתב שם משמעון: הכי גרסינן ודקאמרת הרי כתב שם משמעון מי דמי התם כו'. ואי גרסי' ואמאי והרי כתב שם משמעון אתי נמי שפיר אלא שהוא קושיא ולספרים דגרסינן אמר מר פריך לפי מאי דס"ד מעיקרא:
הניחה

רש"י

דברים הדברים אלה הדברים. גבי שבת דכתיב בויקהל אלה הדברים אשר צוה וגו' דברים משמע תרין ה"א מרבי חד הא תלת אלה בגימטריא תלתין ושם אלו ל"ט כו' ומנייהו למה לי על כרחיך לדעת כמה חטאות אדם מתחייב בהעלם אחד על השבת ואי מחייב אתולדה במקום אב בהעלם אחד הוו להו טובא: אמר ליה רב יוסף. לרב חנא: מר מתני לה · להא דרב יהודה אמר שמואל מחייב היה רבי שתים אהא דרבי: וקשיא ליה דרבי אדרבי · רב יהודה לאו אהא אמרה אלא אדר' יהודה מתני לה ולא קשיא ליה דלא אשכחן בעלמא דפטר ר"י אתולדה במקום אב: מרה"י לרה"ר ועבר ד' אמות ברה"ר · קודם שנוח דאיכא תרתי הוצאה וזריקה ארבע אמות: ה"ג ואחת משום העברה · ורבנן פטרי אהעברה משום דלא סבירא להו קלוטה כמה שהונחה ותהוי כמי שהונחה משילתה בפתח וחזרה ונעקרה ונחה לסוף ד' אבל חייב הוא משום הוצאה: ואיתעביד ליה מחשבתו · שנחה ביציאתה מיד הלכך חייב משום הוצאה אבל משום העברה לא מחייב ואע"ג דחשיב ליה כמה שהונחה ונעקרה והונחה משום דהויא תולדה במקום אב: אף השובט · עם שאר אבות מלאכות להא דאמרן דלכך נמנו שאם עשאן בהעלם א' חייב על כל א' וא': שובט · מכרכר בכרכר: ומדקדק לאחר שמתח החוט של ערב מכה בכרכר בב' וג' מקומות וי"מ מדקדק משוה האריגה כשיש ב' חוטין כרוכין זה עם זה ומובדלים מן השאר משוה אותן בכרכר או במחט: מאי לאו דעבדינהו לכולהו · שובט ומדקדק בהדי שאר מלאכות דהא מוסיף קתני ומיסך ואורג נמנו עם אבות מלאכות ואלה תולדותיה' כדקתני שובט בכלל מיסך: מאי מוסיף · הרי לא נמנו אלא אבות: ולמאי דסלק אדעתא כו' · נהי נמי דמיחייב אתולדה במקום אב הכא לאו תרתי איכא דאי להכא לסוף ד' בעי לה דתנוח הכא לא מיחייב אהעברת ד' דלא עבר מתחלת ד' (מר"ה והעביר) לסוף ד' ברה"ר אלא אהוצאה לחודיה הוא דמיחייב והוצאה אריכא הוא דעבד: ואי להכא · אבל היציאה קבעי לה דתנוח הכא לסוף ד' לא בעי לה דתנוח וליתא לזריקה ד' ולא מיחייב לה דבעינן עקירה מתחילת ד' ברה"ר והנחה לסוף ד' ברה"ר והכא עם יציאת הפתח הא לא נח והעביר לסוף ד' דניחייב אתרווייהו ומיהו אהוצאה הוא דמתחייב דנתקיימה מחשבתו דהא נח ברה"ר: באומר כל מקום שתרצה תנוח · וכיון דלא איכפת ליה הויא ליה קיום מחשבה בתרווייהו: הרי כתב שם משמעון · דתנן לקמן בפ' הבונה (לקמן דף קג) דחייב בב' אותיות ואף על פי שנתכוון למלאכה גדולה: ולאו היינו דבעי מיניה כו' ואמר ליה באומר כו' · הא לא אמר הכי לא מיחייב אלא אם כן נחה במקום מחשבתו הכי נמי בתרווייהו מיפטר לא שנא נתכוון לזרוק שמונה וזרק ארבע לא שנא לזרוק ארבע וזרק שמונה פטור: ה"ג ודקאמרת הרי כתב שם משמעון · ואנתכוון לזרוק שמונה וזרק ד' דפשיטא ליה לחיובא קא מותיב מי דמי התם כל כמה דלא כתב שם לא מכתב שמעון הלכך כי כתב שם בכוונה כתבי' והא עבד ליה מלאכה דיש שם אדם בב' אותיות הללו: הכא כל כמה דלא זריק ד' · שתנוח לסוף ד' לא מזדרק ליה תמניא בתמיה הלכך כי נח לסוף ד' לא נתקיימה מחשבתו ולא דמי לשם משמעון לשון אחר ה"ג אמר מר הרי כתב שם משמעון מי דמי כו' והיא היא: מרה"ר לרה"ר ורה"י באמצע ד"א חייב · אם עבר ברה"ר ד"א ואפי' ע"י צירוף חייב:
פחות

רבינו חננאל

מחנה לויה רה"ר היא וקאמר להו משה לישראל לא תפיקו מבתיכון דהוא רה"י ותיתו לרה"ר והאי דנרסי' בתרה וממאי דבשבת הוה קאי ומשני דגמיר העברה העברה שמיע לן מרבוותא דליתא מעיקרא דשמעתא וגירסני דלאו בקיאין אינון קשיא להון ושפלה הדין גירסא וסוגיא דמשה רבינו בחול הוה קאי במחנה לויה דהוא רה"ר וקאמר לישראל לא תיתי מידי דשלים ליה צורכיה כדכתיב מרבים העם להביא מדי העבודה וגו' ומש"ה ויצו משה ויעבירו קול במחנה וגו' וכתיב והמלאכה היתה דים לכל: ומנלן דהוצאה מרשות לרשות מלאכה היא דדייקינן מדלא אמרה תורה איש ואשה אל יביאו עוד לתרומת הקודש אלא אל יעשו עוד מלאכה קאמרה תורה ולא הוו עבדי מידי אחרינא אלא מפקי ומייתי ש"מ דהבאה קרי לה מלאכה וכיון דאמר להו אל יעשו עוד מלאכה קבילו כדכתיב ויכלא העם מהביא וכיון דהבאה מבתיהון ליתן לגזברים במחנה לויה בחול איקראי מלאכה וקי"ל דכל מלאכה אסור' בשבת איברירה לה מלתא דהוצאה והכנסה נמי מלאכה היא כשם שנמנעו העם מלהוציא ולהביא וליתן לגזברים כך נמנעו הגזברין מלקבל מהן ולהכנים ללשכה ומפורש נמי בירושל' ביציאות השבת שההוצאה קרויה מלאכה: ולר' אליעזר מחייב אתולדה במקום אב והעושה אב ותולדה דידיה מחייב תרתי כאשר הוא מפורש בכריתות וכיון דאהוצאה והכנסה מחייב ואזריקה מחייב אמאי קרי להאי אב ולהאי תולדה ופשוטה היא וכבר פירשנוה למעלה: ואמרי' אשכחן הוצאה וזריקה נמי מרשות לרשות דחייב: הזורק ד' אמות ברה"ר מנלן דחייב א"ר יאשיה שכן אורגי יריעות זורקין מחטיהן זה לזה משום דברה"ר היתה מלאכת המשכן נעשית ואקשינן אורגין מחטין למה להו ותרצינן שכן תופרי יריעות זורקין מחטין ואקשינן תוב ומנלן שהתופרין הללו היו זורקין מחטיהן ארבע אמות ברה"ר שמא זה בצד זה היו יושבין ומשלימין מחט זה לזה ואפילו תימא לא היו זה בצד זה [מ"מ מנ"ל] דד' אמות היו ביניהן דלמא פחות מד' אמות הוו. ונדחת זו דרבי יאשיה ופירק רב חסדא שכן אורגי יריעות זורקין בוכיאן ביריעה ויש שגורסין בוכיאר פי' בוכיאר הקנה שהחוט של ערב תלוי בו שוורקו האורג בתוך היריעה לרחבה להיארג אותו החוט בכלל היריעה ושמעינן מרבותינו הגאונים ש בבבל קורין אותו אל נאוכה ויש מי שאומר אל מכנף ואקשינן עליה והלא אינדו בידו וקיי"ל דכל הזורק דבר ואגדו בידו אינו חייב דהא לא יצא מידו כדמפורש בהמצניע וכדגרסי' סוף הדין-פרקא לענין לכתא ומתנא ובמתניתין דסוף עירובין דף צ"ט הקורא בס"ת על האסקופה הכא נמי עיקר החוט של ערב אצל האורג והוא משימו על הבוכיאן ואורג בו והוא נשמט מאצל האורג ובזה אין חייבין עליו ושנינן בניסכא בתרא פי' החוט של ערב שבסוף שאין אינודו ביד האורג ואקשינן תוב והא אותו מקום שהבוכיאן נזרק בו והוא נפש המסכת מקום פטור הוא ואינו רה"ר ואנן בעינן ד' אמות ברה"ר ונדחה גם הבוכיאן הנזרק ביריעה ושנינן אלא שכן אורגי יריעות זורקין בוכיאר לשוליהן פי' כגון שוליא דנגרי והוא כגון תלמיד המשרת ללמוד מלאכה נקרא שולא ודחינן ודלמא שוליהן גביהן הוו יתבי ולא מרחיקי ד' אמות מהן ושנינן אלא שכן אורגי יריעות זורקין בוכיאר זה לזה דליכא למימר כי האורגין גבי הדדי הוו יתבי דא"כ מטו הדדי בחפא פי' מגיעין זה לזה במסרק שמכסה בו על היריעה ואקשינן תוב וא' ודלמא שלחופי הוו משלחפי כלומר לא היו יושבין זה כנגד זה אלא זה אחורי זה כדגרסי' בפרק המוכר פירות לחבירו בענין כרובין בנס היו עומדין ואתקיף רב אשי ודלמא שלחופי הוו משלחפי או שמא באלכסון או זה יריעתו נתוחה לצפון וזה למערב ובהיות כן יתכן להיות קרובין זה לזה ועוד וכי שואלין היו זה מזה והתני לודא איש איש ממלאכתו אשר המה עושים ממלאכתו היה עושה ולא היה עושה ממלאכת חבירו ועמדו הקושיות הללו בלא פירוק ואקשי תוב ארבעית זורק [בר"ה מנ"ל] מכלל דמעביר פשיטא לן מנא לן דמעביר ד' אמות ברה"ר חייב אלא מעביר גמרא גמירי לה זורק נמי גמרא גמירי לה: מגלת סתרים שהיה כתוב בה אבות מלאכות מ' חסר אחת ואם עשאן כולן בהעלם אחת אינו חייב על אחת מהן כלומר אינו חייב אלא ל"ח חטאות שיש אחת בהן שהוא פטור עליה ונמצא ספק בכולן ואמר שמואל מקשש מעביר ד' אמות ברה"ר הוה פי' כיון שנסקל נתברר כי המעביר ד' אמות ברשות הרבים אינו מן הספיקות אלא ודאי חייב: במתניתא תנא תולש היה והוא הקוצר רב אחא אמר מעמר היה כל אחד מאלו אומרים זו היא הברירה בלא ספק [דחייב] ור' עקיבא שאמר מקשש זה צלפחד נדחו דבריו. ופירשו דלא גמר מפי רבו ג"ש זו אלא הוא לעצמו דן זה וקיי"ל אדם דן ק"ו מעצמו ואין אדם דן ג"ש מעצמו ומוצאת אתה למי- דכל ג"ש דלא גמרא הוא ליכא למיסמך עלה. ור' עקיבא כיון דלא הות גמרא בידיה לפיכך נידחת ולא קבלה ממנו. ואף לא עמד שאהרן נצטרע ואי משום דכתיב ויחר אף ה' בם בנויפה בעלמא: נתברר לנו מספקא קמא דמתניתין כי הזורק מרה"ר לנוח ברה"י או מרה"י לנוח
ברה"ר

לעיל ע. עד מכילתא פ' ויקהל
לעיל עה:
[ב"ק סו:]
[שם]

הגהות הב"ח

(א) גמרא אתולדה במקום אב (ממאי) דילמא וכו' וכהא קא מיפלגי תא"מ ונ"ב ס"ל לעולם אימא לך רבי יהודה אתולדה במקום אב לא מחייב וכהא קא מיפלגי :

him:[5] [97b] Shall we say that Rabbi holds one liable for a derivative [when performed] conjointly with its principal?[6] But surely it was taught, Rabbi said: *Words* [debarim], *the words* [ha-debarim], *these* [eleh] *are the words:* this indicates the thirty-nine labours stated to Moses at Sinai.[7] Said R. Joseph to him: You learn it[8] in reference to this, and so find Rabbi self-contradictory; we learn it in reference to R. Judah['s ruling], and find no difficulty.[9] For it was taught: [If one throws an article] from private to public ground, and it traverses four cubits over the public ground: R. Judah holds [him] liable, whereas the Sages exempt [him]. [Whereon] Rab Judah said in Samuel's name: R. Judah holds [him] liable to two [sacrifices], one on account of transporting [from private ground] and a second on account of carrying over [public ground]. For if you think that he holds him liable to one [only], it follows that the Rabbis exempt [him] completely: but surely he has carried it out from private to public ground? [But] how so? Perhaps I may tell you after all that R. Judah holds him liable to one [only], and the Rabbis exempt [him] completely: yet [as to the question] how is that possible? it is where e.g., he declared, 'Immediately on issuing into the street, let it come to rest'; and they differ in this: R. Judah holds: We say, An object caught up [in the air] is as at rest, and his intention is fulfilled; while the Rabbis hold, We do not say, An object caught up is as at rest, and his intention is
a not fulfilled;[1] but for a derivative [performed] simultaneously with its principal R. Judah does not impose liability?—You cannot think so, for it was taught: R. Judah adds the closing up of the web and the evening of the woof. Said they to him: Closing the web is included in stretching the threads, and evening [the woof] is included in weaving.[2] Does that not mean that one performs both of them together, which proves that R. Judah imposed liability for a derivative [performed] simultaneously with its principal. Why so? perhaps it really means that each was performed separately, R. Judah not imposing liability for a derivative [performed] simultaneously with its principal, and they differ in this: R. Judah holds, These are principal labours; while the Rabbis hold, These are derivatives. The proof [of this assumption] is that it is stated, 'R. Judah *adds* etc.': now, it is well if you agree that they are principal labours [on his view, for then] what does he add? he adds principals; but if you say that they are derivatives, what does he add?[3] It was stated likewise, Rabbah and R. Joseph both maintain: R. Judah imposed liability only for one [sacrifice].

Rabina observed to R. Ashi: But on our original assumption that R. Judah held [him] liable to two,—if he desires it [to alight] here, he does not desire it [to alight] there, and *vice versa?*[4]—Said he to him, It means that he declared, 'Wherever it pleases, let it
b come to rest.'[1]

It is obvious that if one intends throwing [an object] eight [cubits] but throws [it] four, it is as though he wrote SHeM [as part of] SHiMeON.[2] [But] what if one intends throwing [an object] four [cubits] but throws [it] eight: do we say, Surely he has carried it out;[3] or perhaps [we argue] it has not alighted where he desired? But is this not what Rabina observed to R. Ashi, and he answered him, It means that he said, 'Wherever it pleases, let it come to rest'![4] And as to what you say, It is the same as writing SHeM [as part] of SHiMeON: how compare? There, without writing SHeM, SHiMeON cannot be written;[5] but here, without [intentionally] throwing [it] four, cannot one throw it eight?[6]

Our Rabbis taught: If one throws [an object] from public to public ground, and private ground lies between them: [if it traverses] four cubits [over public ground], he is culpable;[7] [98a]

(5) In connection with what he had heard from Rab Judah. (6) V. *supra* 96b. (7) V. *supra* 70a. Now the only purpose of deducing the number is to show that this is the maximum number of sacrifices to which one can be liable; but if one is liable for derivatives in addition to the principal labours there can be far more. (8) What you heard from Rab Judah. (9) For we find nowhere that R. Judah exempts for a derivative performed conjointly with the principal.

a (1) Hence he is not liable on its account. (2) V. *supra* 75a. (3) For only principals are enumerated there. (4) In order to be liable to two it would be necessary that he should carry it out and deposit it in the street, then lift it up and carry it four cubits, and deposit it again. Now it may be argued that an object caught up in the air is as at rest, and therefore immediately it enters the street atmosphere it is as though it alights on the ground, and when it travels further it is as though it is taken up and carried again. But the thrower's intention is that it should come to rest at one place only, either as soon as it emerges into the street or after four cubits; in either case it cannot be regarded as though he deposited it, picked it up, and deposited it again. Hence he can be liable for carrying it out only, but not for its passage in the street (v. Rashi and R. Ḥan.).

b (1) Then it is regarded as though it rested at both places in accordance with this intention. (2) V. *infra* 103a and *supra* 70b, n. b5. Hence here too he is liable. (3) Of its original spot and it has traversed the four cubits he desired, though it has gone further too. (4) But otherwise he is not liable; so here too he should not be liable in either case unless he made such a declaration. (5) Hence when one writes SHeM he does so intentionally, though he also intends to add to it. (6) Surely he can! I.e., one need have no intention to throw it exactly four cubits in order to be able to throw it eight. (The difference is that when one writes SHeM he has performed a labour, whereas when one throws an article, his action is incomplete until it comes to rest.) (7) I.e., over the two public grounds combined.

less than four cubits, he is not culpable. What does this inform us?—This is what he informs us, that [similar] domains combine,[8] and
a we do not say, An object caught up [in the air] is as at rest.[1]

R. Samuel b. Judah said in R. Abba's name in R. Huna's name in the name of Rab: If one carries [an article] four cubits in covered public ground, he is not liable, because it is not like the banners of the wilderness.[2] But that is not so? for the waggons surely were covered,[3] and yet Rab said in R. Ḥiyya's name: As for the waggons, beneath them, between them, and at their sides it was public ground?[4]—Rab referred to the interspaces.[5] Consider: what was the length of the waggons? Five cubits. What was the breadth of the board? A cubit and a half. Then how many [rows] could be placed: three: thus leaving half a cubit, and when you divide it among them [the spaces] they are as joined![6]—Do you think that the boards lay on their width? they were laid on their thickness. Yet even so, what was the thickness of the board? One cubit. How many [rows] were [then] laid? Four, thus leaving a cubit, and when you divide it among them [the spaces] they are as joined![7] Now, on the view that the boards were one cubit thick at the bottom, but tapered to a fingerbreadth, it is well:[8] but on the view that just as they were a cubit thick at the bottom, so at the top too, what can be said?—Said R. Kahana: [They were arranged] in clasped formation.[9] Now, where were they placed: on the top of the waggon. But the waggon itself was

(8) If it travels part of the ground; this does not agree with R. Jose *supra* 80a.
a (1) For if we did, he would be culpable on account of carrying in from public to private ground, even if it does not travel four cubits over the latter. (2) V. *supra* 5a. (3) With the boards of the Tabernacle placed crosswise on top along their length. (4) V. *infra* 99a. The width of the waggons was five cubits, and five cubits' space was allowed between them in the breadth, whilst the boards were ten cubits in length. Hence when placed crosswise on top of the waggons they projected two and a half cubits on both sides; thus the space between them was completely covered over, and yet he states that it was public ground. (5) Between the rows of boards, which were not arranged close to each other. (6) For there was only a quarter cubit = one and a half handbreadths between the rows of boards, whereas a space less than three cubits is disregarded (v. *supra* 97a). (7) For there are three spaces which give two handbreadths for each. (8) As there would be more at the ends than three handbreadths' space between each. (9) I.e., the four rows were not equidistant, but in two rows (as though clasped) at the head and at the tail of the waggon respectively, thus leaving a cubit between them. This was necessary because each row contained three boards, which would give a height of four and a half cubits, and as the thickness was only one cubit they might otherwise topple over.

עין משפט נר מצוה

יב א מיי' פי"ד מהל' שבת הלכה א סמג לאוין סה טוש"ע א"ח סי' שמה סעיף ז ויד:

מסורת הש"ס

פחות מארבע אמות פטור מאי קמ"ל הא קא משמע לן רשויות מצטרפות (א) ודלא אמרינן קלוטה כמה שהונחה: *אמר רב שמואל בר יהודה אמר רב אבא אמר רב הונא אמר רב °המעביר ד' אמות בר"ה מקורה פטור לפי שאינו דומה לדגלי מדבר איני והא עגלות דמקורות הויין *ואמר רב משום רבי חייא °עגלות תחתיהן וביניהן וצדיהן רה"ר כי קאמר רב בדראתא מכדי אורכא דעגלה כמה הואי חמש אמין פותיא דקרש כמה הואי אמתא ופלגא כמה מותיב תלתא פשא ליה פלגא דאמתא כי שדי ליה מר ביני וביני כלבוד דמי מי סברת קרשים אפותייהו הוה מנח להו אחודן מנח להו סוף סומכא דקרש כמה הוי אמתא כמה הוה מותיב ארבעה פשא לה אמתא כי שדי לה מר ביני וביני כלבוד דמי הניחא למ"ד קרשים מלמטן עוביין אמה מלמעלן כלין והולכין עד כאצבע שפיר אלא למ"ד כשם שמלמטן עוביין אמה כך מלמעלה עוביין אמה מאי איכא למימר א"ר כהנא *באטבעי אטבעי היכא מנח להו אגבא דעגלה עגלה גופא מקורה הואי אמר

לעיל ה.

[לקמן לט.]

רש"י

פחות מארבע פטור · דמשום הולכה לא מיחייב דלא אמרינן קלוטה כמה שהונחה: רשויות · השוות: מצטרפות · רשות הרבים זו עם רשות הרבים זו ודלא כר' יוסי דאמר בפרק המוציא יין (עי' פ:) אף בהעלם אחד לרשות אחד חייב לשתי רשויות פטור ועוד קא משמע לן דלא אמרינן קלוטה כמה שהונחה: מקורה · מכוסה: והא עגלות · דמשכן: דמקורות הוו · בקרשים הסדורין עליהן רחבן לאורך העגלה ואורכן לרחבן על ראש דפנותיה וקא סלקא דעתך על פני כל אורך העגלות היו מסודרות: וביניהן · בין עגלה לעגלה שבצדה ואף על פי שראשי הקרשים יוצאים לכאן ולכאן שתי אמות ומחצה לכל רוח וראשי קרשים של עגלה זו מגיעין לראשי קרשים של זו שבצדה שהרי חמש אמות היו בין עגלה לעגלה כדלקמן ורחב עגלה חמש אמות החלל שתי אמות ומחצה ובין הדפנות והאופנים ועובי האופנים שתי אמות ומחצה וי' אמות אורך הקרש וכשאורכה נתון על דופני עגלה לרחבה כמלאו ב' אמות ומחצה בולטין מכל צד ונמצא ריוח שבין ב' העגלות מקורה בראשי קרשים: וצדיהן · ריוח שבין דופן עגלה לאופן ועובי האופן: כי קאמר רב · תחתיהן רה"ר: בדראתא · בריוח שבין שורות הסדר שהיה סודר קרש על קרש סדר אחד ומניחו ריוח וסודר סדר אחר ומניחו ריוח: ה' אמות. כדלקמן: כמה מותיב · כמה סדרים יכול להושיב על אורך דופנותיה תלתא והו לא ומחזיקות ד' אמות וחצי פש ליה ריוח פלגא דאמתא: שדי ליה מר ביני וביני. כשאתה מחלק לריוח שבין הסדרים אין בכל ריוח אלא רביע אמה דהוא טפח ומחצה דה"ל לבוד והייתו מקורה: אחודן מנח להו. דאיכא רווחא טפי: סומכא. עובי: אמתא. כדמשני לקמן עוביין אמה: כמה מותיב. כמה סדרים הוא מסדר: ארבעה. דעל כרחיך כל מה שיכול לסדר על פני אורך העגלה הוא מסדר ואינו מגביה להושיב זו על זו שהרי י"ב קרשים היו לעגלה אחת שמ"ח קרשים היו כ' קרשים לצפון ועשרים לדרום וששה למערב ושנים למקצועות וכיון דרחבן אמה וחצי ומושב אורכן קצר אם אתה מסדר זו על זו הרבה הן נופלות הלכך כמה הוא מותיב ארבע דחמשה בחמשה לא יתבי דאי אפשר לדוחקן ולנמצא להושיב ה' בתוך ה' אמות ועוד מפני בליטת הטבעות: כי שדי מר ביני וביני. לחלקה לאמה זו ג' רווחים שבין ארבע סדרים כלבוד דמי שאין כאן ריוח אלא שני טפחים: הניחא. הא דאמרת שהריוח הזה רשות הרבים הוא למ"ד שעובי הקרשים כלה והולך עד כאצבע איכא למימר דאיכא רווחא טפי בין ד' סדרים: אלא למ"ד כו'. פלוגתא לקמן בשמעתין: אמר רב כהנא באטבעי. בריוח שבין לדי הקרשים שהטבעות קבועות בהם קאמר רב דהוי רשות הרבים כלומר אי אפשר לסדר בה ארבע סדרים כדקאמרת לפי שטבעות קבועין בקרשים כדכתיב (שמות כו) ואת טבעותיהם תעשה זהב שהיה תוחב הבריחים לתוכן לפי שהן גבוהות וכשיושבות על האדנים שאינם אלא אמה מנענעות לפנים או לאחור אלא שהבריחים מחברים את כולם והבריח התיכון מחבר כל ג' הרוחות ומחזיקין זה את זה ואותן טבעות זקופין היו ולא שוכבין והיו רחבין ואי אפשר להן לעמוד זה כנגד זה באותו ריוח לפיכך מושיב שתים זו אצל זו בראש העגלה האחת ופונה לד הטבעות של חיצונה לחוץ ושל פנימית לפנים ואין צריך להניח ריוח ביניהן וכן בראש העגלה השני וכל *אחת הריוח באמצע בין לדי הטבעות כך פירשו רבותי וכך היו גורסין אמר רב כהנא באטבעי אטבעי היכא מנח להו אגבא דעגלה ועגלה גופה מקורה הואי אמר שמואל ביתדות ומפרש אטבעי כמו טבעי ופרכינן הכך רווחא דאטבעי היכא מנח להו אגבא דעגלה כדפרישית והתינח לדיהן וביניהן רשות הרבים אלא תחתיהן היכי הוי רשות הרבים הא עגלה גופה מקורה הואי דקא סלקא דעתך שהיו עשויות כעלייה מלמטה כאותן שלנו שטוענין בהן חול ועפר לבנין:

נ"ל אמה

תוספות

הניחא למ"ד קרשים מלמטה עוביין אמה וכלין והולכין עד כאצבע · הקשה הרב פור"ת ולדידיה מי ניחא והלא כיון שהולכין וכלין עד כאצבע יכולין לסדר ששה סדרים או יותר שיתנו תודו של זה כנגד עביו של זה ויחזיקו ששה סדרים שלש אמות ושלש אצבעות וישארו י"א טפחים לאויר וכי שדית להו ביני וביני כלבוד דמי ותירץ דגנאי הוא להשים לד העב העומד סמוך לקרקע אלא הקצר שהיה למעלה מקום שהיריעות פרוסות עליהן ודמי להא דאמרינן מעלין בקדש ואין מורידין ור"ת תירץ דכמו שהיו פורקין אותן מן המשכן כך היו מניחים על העגלה שהיתה אצל דופן המשכן כי כך היו עושין בלא טורח אבל להופכן היה טורח גדול ורבינו יצחק אומר דשמא מתחלין ולמעלה היו כלין והולכין והשתא אי אפשר לסדר יותר וא"ת מנלן דילפינן ממה שאינו מקורה נילף מן המקורה שבו ויהא המעביר ד' אמות ברשות הרבים מקורה חייב וי"ל דמן האויר יש לנו ללמוד שדומה יותר רשות הרבים ור"י אומר דמהכא לא ילפינן רשות הרבים אלא ממחנה לויה כדאמר לעיל ומהכא לא ילפינן אלא שיעור רשות הרבים דהוי י"ו אמות ומכל מקום אי לאו דתחתיהן וביניהן ולדיהן רשות הרבים לא הוה ילפינן מינייהו שיעור רה"ר:

אטבעי היכא מנח להו אגבא דעגלה עגלה מקורה היא · פירש רש"י דסלקא דעתך שהעגלה היתה מקורה ותימה למה היה סבר לומר כן ועוד דבכל הספרים גרסינן אטבעי היכא מנח להו אגבא דעגלה מה לו להזכיר אטבעי בהך התקפתא לא הוה ליה למימר אלא הא עגלה מקורה היא ועוד דגרסינן לעיל בדראתא ובכל ספרים גרסי' בדרא תתא ולפי גירסתם נמי אין הלשון משמע בין השורות כמו שפיר' ונראה לר"ת כמו שפי' ר"ח בדרא תתא פי' בשורה ראשונה שעדיין לא הניח על העגלה אלא קרשים התחתיים בלבד שאינה מקורה כולה שיש ריוח בין השורות כדמפרש ואזיל אבל כשמסדר שורה שניה ושלישית נסתם האויר שבין השורות שלא היו יכולים להיות מכוונים ולהשימן זה על זה בשוה ממש אלא כל אחד היה בולט לחוץ עד שנסתם כל האויר כמו באריח על גבי לבינה ופריך אורכא דעגלה כמה הוי כו' כלומר אפילו בשורה ראשונה לא היה תחתיהן רשות הרבים כדמפרש ואזיל ומשני אמר רב כהנא באטבעי אע"ג דלא קאמר אלא הדר ביה דודאי כשיש קרשים על העגלה אפילו דרא תתאה לא הוו רשות הרבים תחתיה אלא כי קאמר דהוי רשות הרבים באטבעי שאין על העגלה אלא אטבעי גרידא פי' אטבעי שני עלים נקובים בשני ראשיהן נקובין כעין טבעות לכך קרי להו אטבעי ותוחבין אותן על הקונדיסין העומדין בשני לדי העגלה לרחבה לפניה ולאחריה כדי שלא יפלו הקרשים ולפי שלא נזכר אמורא לעיל אין דרך הש"ס לומר אלא ופריך אטבעי היכא מנחא להו אגבא דעגלה פירוש אחר שנתנו הקרשים על העגלה נותנין עליהן אטבעי טבעות ומסגרות כדפרישית לפניה ולאחריה כדי שיאחזו הקרשים ואז כבר עגלה מקורה היא ולא גרסינן עגלה גופא אלא עגלה מקורה היא ומשני אמר שמואל ביתידות פירוש אטבעי דקאמר רב כהנא לא אותן עלים נקובים המשימין לרוחב העגלה כדפי' אלא ביתידות פירוש שני עלים ארוכים שכמו כן נוקבין אותן בשני ראשיהן ונותנין על הקונדיסין לאורך העגלה ועל אותן עלים נותנין הקרשים כדי שיהו גבוהים למעלה מן האופנים ועשויין כמו אטבעי של רוחב העגלה שלאחר הטעינה ולפי ששמואל אינו כ"א מפרש דברי רב כהנא לא קאמר אלא אבל ר"ח מפרש דהדר ביה משינויא דרב כהנא ואין נראה מדלא קאמר אלא ועוד היאך היה טועה רב כהנא דהא אין רגילות להניח אטבעי עד לאחר טעינה:

ד"ל.

הגהות הב"ח

(א) גמרא מצטרפות ולא אמרינן:

[ז"ל הערוך בע' אטבא פי' אטבי הם המסגרות שמשימין למעלה בעגלות סביב כבית טעונה]

גליון הש"ס

גמ' עגלות תחתיהן וביניהן. עי' עירובין ו ע"א תוד"ה כילד מערבין:

רבינו חננאל

ברשות הרבים ונעשית מחשבתו חייב ופסקא תנינא במתניתין הזורק מרה"י לרה"י אחרת ורה"ר באמצע ר' עקיבא מחייב וחכמים פוטרין ולענין בעיא דרבא למטה מעשרה פליגי פשיטא לן דמודים למעלה מעשרה ברה"ר ונח ברה"ר חייב וכן מושיט מרה"י לרה"ר והיינו מעביר ד' אמות ברה"ר וכמוציא משוי על כתיפו דמי שהרי למעלה מעשרה הוא וכן היה משא בני קהת ומלאכה היא אלא מיהו מושיט מרה"י לרה"ר אע"פ שלא הגיע ברה"ר עד ד' אמות חייב כיון דנח ברה"ר שהרי הוא מוציא מרשות לרשות אבל המגביה חפץ ברה"ר והעבירו ברשות הרבים ולא הכניסו ולא הוציאו מרשות לרשות אם העבירו ד' אמות חייב ואם לאו פטור. אלו כולן פשוטות הן ובעיא דרבה נמי פשוטה היא מדתניא מרה"י לרה"י ועובר ברה"ר עצמה ר' עקיבא מחייב וחכמים פוטרין ודייקינן מדקתני ברה"ר עצמה פשיטא דלמטה מי' פליגי ולא מיתוקמא במעביר כגון מוציא ומושיט דהני אפילו למעלה מי' חייב אלא לאו בזורק ולמטה מי' [הוא] דחייב ר"ע אבל למעלה מעשרה אפילו ר' עקיבא פוטר והכא בהא קא מיפלגי ר' עקיבא סבר אמרי' קלוטה באויר כמה שהונחה דמי ורבנן סברי לא אמרינן קלוטה באויר כמה שהונחה דמי ור' אלעזר פליג וסבירא ליה דרבנן פטרי אפי' למטה מי' ור' עקיבא מחייב אפילו למעלה מעשרה טפחים והאי דקתני ברה"ר עצמה להודיעך כחן דרבנן דהלכתא כוותיהו. והא דאמר רב חלקי' בר טובי תוך שלשה דברי הכל חייב למעלה מי' דברי הכל פטור מחטאת ואינו אסור אלא משום שבות מג' ועד י' ר"ע מחייב וחכמים פוטרין ותניא נמי הכי פליגא אתרוייהו אדר' אלעזר דסבר אפי' (למטה) [למעלה] מי' פליגי ולרב המנונא דסבר למטה מי' פליגי בי' כולהו האי אמרת מג' ועד י' בלבד הוא דפליגי ותניא כוותיה וסוגיין דשמעתין אסור לזורק מרה"י לרה"י ורה"ר באמצע בתוך ג' לדברי הכל ואם זרק חייב חטאת ואע"ג דאמר רבא לקמן (ד' ק') בתוך ג' לרבנן צריך הנחה ע"ג משהו ובהמוציא יין (ד' פ') אוקימנן בזורק מכלל שאם לא נח אפילו ע"ג משהו לא מחייבי רבנן הא *) דרב חלקיה בר טובי

רישא דתניא כוותיה בהדיא מג' ועד י' פטור אבל אסור כרבנן למעלה מעשרה אם אין איתן ב' רשויות שלו אסור לזורק מזו לזו משום שבות ואם הם ב' דיוטאות שלו זו כנגד זו ורה"ר ביניהם (משות) מותר לזורק מזו לזו ואם היתה דיוטא אחת למעלה ואחת למטה שהזורק צריך להעקים ולזרוק אסור משום גזירה גזרינן לזורק דלמא נפלה ברה"ר עצמה ואתי לעיולא מרה"ר לרה"י ותרגומא נמי להא דרב דאמר ב' בתים שלו בשתי צדי רה"ר אסור לזורק מזו לזו דמידלי חד ומיתתי חד כדפרשינא והלכתא כוותיה דרב ובלבד דלמעלה מעשרה נפלו ואסיקנא כל פחות מג' טפחים כלבוד דמי בין למעלה כגון הרחקת סכך מן הדפנות וכיוצא בה ובין למטה הלכתא גמירי לה . ת"ר הזורק מרה"ר לרה"ר ורה"י באמצע ר' מחייב וחכמים פוטרין פי' כגון שזרק מרה"ר ונתכוון לנוח ברה"ר אחר ולא נתכוון כדי שינוח ברה"י וגם לא נח ברה"י אלא עברה בלבד העברה ברה"י ונח ברה"ר שנתכוין כדי שינוח בו ואין ממקום שזרק עד מקום שנח ד' אמות דכיון שאין ביניהם ד' אמות פטרי רבנן ורבי סבר קלוטה באויר כמו שהונחה בקרקע דמו . רב ושמואל דאמרי תרווייהו לא חייב רבי אלא בזמן שעברה ברה"י מקורה דסבר ביתיה כמאן דמליא דמי וכאלו נחה ברה"י ונמצא מכנים ומוציא מרשות לרשות ואע"ג דלית תמן ד' אמות חייב ומפרשא בגיטין בהזורק גט . אבל הזורק דרך רה"י שאינו מקורה לא מחייב ר' ולא אמרינן קלוטה כמו שהונחה: אמר רב יהודה אמר שמואל מחייב היה רבי שתים אחת משום הכנסה ואחת משום הוצאה . ודחי' לה להא הכי והא הכנסה תולדה דהוצאה היא כדתנן בחשבון אבות מלאכות המוציא מרשות לרשות ואע"ג דאוקימנא בתחלת מסכתא זאת תנא כל עקירת חפץ ממקומו הוצאה קרי לה מיהו חדא אב וחדא תולדה . וא"ת מחייב ר' שתים ונמצא מחייב אתולדה במקום אב דידיה והא תניא ר' אומר דברים הדברים אלה הדברים ל"ט מלאכות שנאמרו לו למשה מסיני וכל מאן דאית ליה הילוק מלאכות והללו הן אבות והשאר תולדות ואוקימנא דאינו מחייב אתולדה במקום אב דידיה אלא על האב ועל אתולדה דידיה לא מחייב אלא חדא וא"ל רב יוסף לרב חסדא מר הא שמעתא דרב יהודה אמר שמואל אדר' מתני לה וקשיא ליה . רב יהודה אמר שמואל לא קתני לה אדר' כלל אלא אדר' יהודה מתני לה דתניא הזורק מרה"י לרה"ר ועובר ד' אמות ברה"ר ר' יהודה מחייב וחכמים פוטרין אמר רב יהודה אמר שמואל מחייב היה ר' יהודה שתים אחת משום הוצאה מרשות לרשות ואחת משום מעביר ד' אמות ברה"ר ודחינן מאי דלמא ר' יהודה הדא הוא מחייב כגון דאמ' עד דנפקא לרה"ר תנוח ובהא פליגי ר' יהודה סבר כיון דנפקא לרה"ר קלטתה רה"ר כאילו נחה שם ונעשה מחשבתו ולפיכך חייב.ורבנן סברי לא אמרי' קלוטה כמי שהונחה וכיון שלא נעשית מחשבתו פטור לגמרי דקיי"ל לענין שבת מלאכת מחשבת אסרה תורה אבל אתולדה במקום אב אפילו ר' יהודה לא מחייב ובהכי סלקא שמעתין ואע"ג דטרח למפשט מהא דתניא ר' יהודה מוסיף אף השובט והמדקדק מכלל דהני תולדות נינהו דר' יהודה מחייב אתולדה במקום אב דהויא היא ואסיקנא הני לר' יהודה אבות נינהו ומוסיף להו בהני אבות ואוקמוה רבה ורב יוסף דלא הוה מחייב רבי יהודה אלא אחת וא"ל רבינא לרבא למאי דסליק אדעתין מעיקרא דמחייב ר' יהודה שתים אי האי זורק דעתו שתנוח עם יציאתה לרה"ר ואין דעתו להעבירה ד"א ברה"ר אע"ג דסבר קלוטה כמי שהונחה בהעברה לא מחייב דהא לא נתכוון להעבירה ד"א ברה"ר דהא לא מחייב אלא על מחשבתו כר' יוחנן דאמר המפנה הפצים מזוית לזוית ונמלך עליהן והוציאו לרה"ר פטור שלא היתה עקירה משעה ראשונה לכך. ושני ליה רבא לרבינא באומר הריני זורק ובדעתי כ"מ שתנוח בו הוא רצוני דכל היכא דנח אמרינן הרי נעשית מחשבתו: פשיטא נתכוון לזורק ח"א וזרק ד' הרי כתב שם משמעון וחייב. ואקשינן מי דמי התם כמה דלא כתב שם לא מכתב ליה שמעון וכאלו מתחלה כך היתה מחשבתו כתוב שם ואחריו עון והנה נעשית מחשבתו ולפיכך חייב אבל זורק מי לא יכול לזורק ח"ת בבת אחת כי לא נייה ביניהן כלל ונדחת' נתכוון לזורק ד' אמות וזרק ח' חייב אם אמר

*) עיין תוס' לעיל ד' פ' ד"ה והא ולהלן ד' ק' ד"ה אלמה מ"כ כז:

מסורת הש"ס

אמר שמואל ביתדות
עוביין אמה ומלמעלן כלין והולכין עד
כאצבע שנאמר °יהיו תמים על ראשו ולהלן (שמות כו)
הוא אומר °תמו נכרתו דברי רבי יהודה (יהושע ג)
רבי נחמיה אומר כשם שמלמטן עוביין
אמה כך מלמעלן עוביין אמה שנאמר יחדיו
והכתיב תמים ההוא דליתו שלמין ולא ליתו
דניסרא ואידך נמי הכתיב יחדיו ההוא דלא
לישלחופינהו מהדדי בשלמא למ"ד כשם
שמלמטן עוביין אמה כך מלמעלן עוביין
אמה היינו דכתיב °ולירכתי המשכן ימה (שמות כו)
תעשה ששה קרשים ושני קרשים תעשה
למקצעות דאתי פותיא דהני ממלי ליה
לסומכא דהני אלא למ"ד מלמטן עוביין
אמה מלמעלן כלין והולכין עד כאצבע האי
עייל והאי נפיק דשפי להו כי טורין*:
°והבריח התיכון בתוך הקרשים תנא בנס (שם)
היה עומד °ואת המשכן תעשה עשר יריעות (שם)
אורך היריעה האחת שמנה ועשרים באמה שדי אורכייהו לפותיא דמשכן כמה
הויא עשרין ותמני דל עשר לאיגרא פשא להו ט' להאי גיסא וט' להאי גיסא
לר' יהודה מיגליא אמה דאדנים לר' נחמיה מיגליא אמה דקרשים שדי פותייהו
לאורכא דמשכן כמה הויא ארבעין דל תלתין לאיגרא פשא להו י' לר' יהודה
מכסיא אמה דאדנים לר' נחמיה מיגליא אמה דאדנים °ועשית יריעות עזים (שם)
לאהל וגו' אורך היריעה האחת שלשים באמה וגו' שדי אורכייהו לפותיא דמשכן
כמה הויא תלתין דל עשר לאיגרא פשא להו עשר להאי גיסא ועשר להאי גיסא
לר' יהודה מיכסיא אמה דאדנים לר' נחמיה מיגליא אמה דאדנים תניא נמי
הכי °והאמה מזה והאמה מזה בעודף לכסות אמה של אדנים דברי ר' יהודה ר' (שם)
נחמיה אומר לכסות אמה של קרשים °שדי פותייהו לאורכיה דמשכן כמה
הויא מ' וארבע דל תלתין לאיגרא פשא להו ארבע סרי דל תרתי לכפלא דכתיב
°וכפלת את היריעה הששית אל מול פני האהל פשא להו תרתי סרי בשלמא (שם)
לר' יהודה היינו דכתיב חצי היריעה העודפת תסרח אלא לר' נחמיה מאי
תסרח תסרח מחברותיה תנא דבי ר' ישמעאל למה משכן דומה לאשה שמהלכת
בשוק ושפוליה מהלכין אחריה ת"ר חרוצים היו קרשים וחלולים היו האדנים
ונראין

אמר שמואל ביתדות · לא היו מקורות מלמטה אלא יתדות היו וריוח ביניהן כעין אותן שלט העשויות להביא עצים · ולי נראה פי' דאטבי כמו אטבא דספרי האמור במנחות (ד' לב.) והוא גלוא"ן בלע"ז שמבקע מקל אחד בראשו וטשך בו דפי הקונטרס והכי קאמר רב כהנא באטבי לא היה נותן ריוח בין כל סדרא וסדרא כדקאמרת דמתוך שהסדר גבוה ג' קרשים כל אחד רחבו אמה וחצי ומושבו קצר שהוא אמה של עובי ותו לא הרי הן נופלות זו על זו אלא מושיב שתי שורות של שלש שנים זו אצל זו כמין אטבי שתי צלעות האטבא סמוכות זו לזו כן מושיב לראש העגלה האחת ומחזיקות זו את זו ונמצא מקום מושב הסדר ב' אמות וכן עושה לראש השני ואמת הריוח באמצע ופרכינן היכא מנח להו לקרשים אגבה דעגלה והא עגלה גופה מקורה הואי ותינח לידיהן וביניהן כו' כדפרי' וללשון רבותי אין לשון הגירסא נראה כפירושן ולמה הוזכרו אותן טבעות כאן לשלחופינהו לקרשים שבשני סדרים הפנימית שלא יהו טבעותיהן מכוונין זו כנגד זו: ולהלן הוא אומר תמו נכרתו · מה תמו הנאמר להלן לשון כלייה אף תמים האמור כאן לשון כלייה: שנא' יחדו· כולן שוות: דלא לייתי דנסרא· קרש אחד מב' חתיכות: דלא לישלחופינהו · אחד לפנים ואחד לחוץ אלא מושיב הקרשים מכוונין זה אצל זה שיעמדו הקרשים מכוונים עוביה של זו כנגד עוביה של זו: ואתי פותיא דהני וממלא סומכא דהני · שכשהושיב ששה קרשים למערב נמצא רחבן תשע אמות והמשכן רחבו י' נמצא חסר הכותל חצי אמה לצפון וחצי אמה לדרום ומביא שני קרשים אחד למקצוע זה ואחד למקצוע זה ומושיבן אצל השש ורוחב הקרש אמה וחצי נמצא חצי האמה ממלא וסותם חסרון הקיר מערבי והאמה מכסה עביו של קרש הדרומי החיצון נמצאו הזויות שוין מבחוץ שני חודי הקרשים סמוכין יחד וכן לצפון: האי עייל והאי נפיק · דכיון דקרש אחד שבדרום ושבצפון למעלה כלה בעביו וקרש ההוא נותן במקצוע רחב אמה וחצי נמצא רחב הקרש של מקצוע בולט ויוצא לדרום מלמעלה חוץ מעביו של דרומי וכן לצפון: דשפי להו · לרוחב ב' קרשים שבמקצוע ומקצרן למעלה מרחבן שלא יהיו בולטין: כי טורים · ההרים הללו שהן משופעין [מב' לצדים]: בנס היה עומד · שאחר שהקרשים כולן נתונין באדנים לצפון למערב ולדרום היה נותנו ומבריח לשלשת הרוחות ואין לך אומן יכול לעשות כן ובנס היה נכפף מאליו: דל עשר לאיגרא · לרחב חלל המשכן שהוא י' אמות: לרבי יהודה· דאמר למעלה כלין עוביין של קרשים לכאצבע אינן ממעטין ביריעות וכשפורשן לרחב המשכן טופלות תשע אמות לצפון ומכסין ט' אמות לקרשים מבחוץ ואמה של אדנים מגולה שהאדנים גבהן אמה וחלולין הם והקרשים חרוצין למטה באמצע חצי אמה רחב בגובה אמה ונשאר חצי אמה לכאן וחצי אמה לכאן והן שתי ידות לקרש האחד ומחסר מן הידות מבחוץ ומשני צידיהן לרבוע על עובי דופני האדן כשנועץ שתי הידות בשני אדנים כדי שיהיו הקרשים תכופות ומשולבות אשה אל אחותה ולא יהא עובי האדן מפסיק ביניהן: לרבי נחמיה · דאמר אף מלמעלה עוביין אמה ממעט עובי הקרשים הדרומיות והצפוניות אמה לכאן ואמה לכאן באורך היריעות ואינן טופלות אלא ח' אמות לכל צד: מיגליא אמה מן הקרשים · חוץ לאדנים ואמה דאדנים: שדי פותייהו לאורכא דמשכן · לאחר שחברו ה' יריעות לבד וכל אחת ד' אמות רחב הרי כ' אמות וכנגדן במחברת השנית שהיא של ה' יריעות הרי מ' ל' מהן הויין גג למשכן לאורכו ועשר העודפות: לרבי יהודה דאמר אין עובי קרשים שבמערב ממעט בהו נמצא היו"ד אמות כולן תלויות ומכוסות כל י' אמות של אורך הקרש הרי אף האדנים של צד מערבי מכוסין: ועשית יריעות עזים · אלו יריעות עליונות הפרוסות על יריעות התחתונות העליונות קרויות אהל כלומר לגג ומכסה והתחתונות קרויות משכן עצמו שהן לנוי תכלת וארגמן ותולעת שני: מיכסיא אמה דאדנים · שנשארת מגולה מן התחתונות יכסוה העליונות: לרבי נחמיה מיגליא אמה דאדנים · ועודפה של יריעה זו הולך לכסות אמה דקרשים שלא כסוה התחתונות: בעודף · שיריעות האהל עודפות על יריעות המשכן ב' אמות יהיה סרוח על כיסוי התחתונות לכסות מה שלא כיסוהו: ארבעים וארבע · די"א יריעות היו: תרתי דכפלא · שהיתה נוטה רוחב חצי יריעה על רוח מזרחית שלא היו שם קרשים שהוא פתח למשכן ואין שם אלא מסך פרוש כמו וילון כדכתיב ועשית מסך לפתח האהל וגו': בשלמא לרבי יהודה · דאמר עובי הקרשים לא ממעט ביריעות הייט דכתיב חצי היריעה העודפת בעליונות יותר מן התחתונות תסרח על אחורי המשכן סרוח על כל אורך הקרשים והאדנים של מערב ונגררות בארץ: מאי תסרח · אמה אחת נגררת ותו לא שהרי עובי הקרשים מיעט בה אמה: מחברותיה · חצי היריעה סרוחה מחברותיה אמה ממנה לכסות האדנים ואמה נגררת: ושיפוליה · שולי בגדיה כך היתה יריעה של אחריו נגררת בארץ: חרוצים היו קרשים · כמו שפירשתי חצי אמה באמצע רחבן מלמטה בגובה אמה ונשארין הידות לכאן ולכאן וגם הם חרוצים מבחוץ כשיעור עובי דופן האדן ברחב ובגובה אמה עד הארץ לרבוע על האדן שיהו משולבות קרש *על קרש ולא יפסיק עובי שני האדנים ביניהם: וחלולים היו האדנים · שבאותו חלל היו תוקעין ידות הקרשים: ונראין

דל עשר לאיגרא · בכולה שמעתא אמר דרוחב המשכן י' אמות וקשה לר"י דמנא ליה להש"ס הא דילמא המשכן היה רוחבו י"א אמה והקרשים נאמר שלא היה עוביין אלא חצי אמה ושני קרשים למקצעות המשכן היו סותמות אמת אויר מכאן ואמת אויר מכאן וחצי אמה העודפת ברוחב הקרש כנגד עובי הקרשים שלצד צפון ודרום ומאי חזית למימר איפכא שחצי אמה לכאן וחצי אמה [לכאן] הוא למלאות חסרון הכותל ואמה עובי להיות כנגד עובי הקרש הדרומי והצפוני ואומר ר"י דמבית עולמים ילפינן לה שהיה אורכו ששים אמה ורוחבו עשרים ה"נ במשכן רחבו שליש ארכו: תנא בנס היה עומד · אומר ר"י דהכא דקאמר שבריח התיכון היה מסבב ג' רוחות פליגא אברייתא דמלאכת המשכן דהתם אמר שלא היה נס אלא היו שם חמשה שנים למעלה אחד מתחיל מתחילת אורך המשכן עד חציו והשני מתחיל משם ואילך עד סוף הרוח וכן למטה היו שני בריחים כזה הענין אבל האמצעי היה הולך מרוח מזרח עד רוח מערב והיינו מן הקצה אל הקצה ולא היה מקיף כל שלש רוחות: שתי

רבינו חננאל

אמר כל מקום שתרצה תנוח וכבר פרשנוה בבבא קמא בפרק כיצד הרגל בסופו דקתני התם בפירושא אם אמר כל מקום שתרצה תנוח אין יאי לא לא מחייב. ת"ר הזורק מרה"ר לרה"ר ורה"י באמצע ד' אמות חייב פחות מד' אמות פטור פי' אם יש ממקום שזרק עד שנח בב' הצדדין שהן רה"ר ד' אמות חייב כגון שיש רה"ר בצד זה ב' אמות ובצד אחר ב' אמות אחרות רה"ר שנמצא מעביר ד' אמות ברה"ר וקמ"ל רשויות מצטרפו' אע"ג דרה"י חולק בין ב' רשויות הרבים ולא אמרינן קלוטה כמו שהונחה כלומר קלטתן רה"י טרם תנוח ד' אמות אלא כיון שבזריקה אחת הלך החפץ ד' אמות ברה"ר אע"פ שהן אמות מקוטעות ואינן ארבעתן רצופות ביחד חייב. אמר*) משמיה דרב המעביר ד' אמות ברה"ר מקורה פטור דהא כל מלאכת דשבת מן המשכן גמרינן להו (ולמה)[ולכן] הוא פטור לפי שאינו דומה לדגלי מדבר ואקשינן איני והא עגלות שהיו טעונות קרשי המשכן מקורות היו בזמן שהקרשים עליהן ואמר רב משמיה דרבי חייא עגלות תחתיהן וביניהן וצדיהן רה"ר הן ופרקי' כי אמר רב לפי שאינן דומה לדגלי מדבר בדרא קמא פי' בזמן שלא הניח על העגלות קרשים אלא התחתונים בלבד שאינה מקורה כולה אבל כשיניחו עליה שניים ושלישים ותהא כולה מקורה לא אמר רב ואקשי' מכדי אורך העגלה כמה היא ה' אמות רוחב כל קרש אמה והזי' כמה קרשים טוען בעגלה שלש שאינה מחזקת יותר כי ארכה ה' אמות ורחב ג' קרשים כל קרש אמה וחצי ארבע אמות וחצי נמצאת חצי אמה עודפת העגלה על הקרשים ותן ג' טפחים כי שדית בין קרש לקרש זה העודף כלבוד דמי ואפי' בדרא תתאה עגלה כולה מקורה היא ודחי רב מי סברת קרשים כרחבם היה מטעינם על העגלה אחודן הוה מנח להו ואקשי' תו סוף סוף עובי כל קרש אמה היא כשמסדרן עלה עגלה נותן [ד'] קרשים על העגלה נמצאת עודף בעגלה אמה שהיא ו' טפחים כשתחלקם בין הקרשים יבא ביניהם פחות מג' טפחים שהרי בין ד' קרשים רוצה לחלקם וקיי"ל כל פחות מג' טפחים כלבוד דמי ומכל פנים העגלה אפילו בדרא תתא מקורה היא הניחא למ"ד כדבעינן למימר לקמן קרשים מלמטה עוביין אמה מלמעלה כלין והולכין עד כאצבע פי' הוה הנגר משפע ואוכל בקודש ועולה עד שנמצאת ראש הקרש עוביה אצבע ותחתיה הקרש עביה אמה משכחת לה דמשלבי קרשים מלמטה זו עם זו ומתרפקין ועולין עד שנמצא למעלה ביניהן קרוב לאמה וכיון שיש בין ב' הקרשים אמה ודאי אינן מקורות אלא למ"ד כשם שמלמטה עוביין אמה כך מלמעלה עוביין אמה היכי משכחת לה עגלה שאינה מקורה ופריק רב כהנא תמצא עגלה שאינה מקורה בזמן שאין על העגלה קרשים אלא אטבי בלבד פירוש עגלה זו עשויה ב' קורות ארוכות וב' קצרות בראשיהן כגון מלבנות המטה . והאמצע מגולה ומניחין באמצעה לרחבה קורה יוצאה חוץ לעגלה ב' אמות ומחצה מזה הצד וב' אמות ומחצה מן הצד האחר ומכניסין האופנים בראשי הקורה היוצאות חוץ לעגלה ומטעינין ע"ג העגלה הקרשים תחתיים שניים ושלישים ועוד בארבעת מקצועי העגלה ד' עצים ארוכים קבועים ועומדים כמין כנפי המטה וראשיהן משופעין ואחרי שמטעינין העגלה מביאין ד' קרשים רחבין כשיעור טפחים ונקראין אטבי שנים מהן ארוכים כאורך העגלה וב' מהן ארוכין כשיעור רוחב העגלה נקובים כל אחד נקב בראשו ב' נקבים בכל אחד ואחד ומכנים אלו הקרשים נקביהן בראשי העצים העומדים כמין כנפי הארוכין לאורך העגלה והקצרים לרוחב העגלה ונמצאו אלו העצים הנקראים אטבי כמין מסגרות ונמצאו העצים העומדין בארבעת מקצועי העגלה כמין קירום מחזיקין הקרשים שלא ישמטו לא לארכן ולא לרחבן והן כמין מסגרות שסוגרין בעד הקרשים מכל הצד ואלמלא האטבי היו הקרשים דוחין העצים ונופלין ויש מי שעושין אטבי הללו מן ברזל כענין שפרשנו וכיון שפירק רב כהנא באטבי הקשו עליו וכי תמצא עגלה מגולה ואטבי עליה והלא אטבי לא נעשו אלא להנתן על גבי עגלה טעונה ובעת שהיא טעונה מקורה היא ונדחה רב כהנא ותירגמא שמואל ביתידות פי' יתידות שנים רחבות כמו טפח אגודות בעגלה שנמצא בין יתד ליתד כמו אמה ונמצאת העגלה כולו מגולה היא כולה . והוצרך שמואל להעמידה ביתידות משום דתני ר' חייא תחתיהן ואי אפשר להיות לעגלה תחת ודאי אינה מקורה אלא ביתידות שיש ריוח הרבה ביניהן דליכא למימר בהן כלבוד דמי והוא כדבעינן למימר לקמן כי שיעור ב' עגלות מהלכות זו בצד זו בט"ו אמה ומיכן למדנו דרך רשות הרבים ט"ז אמה אלו ט"ו אמה ואמה יתירה למקום בן לוי כו' . ת"ר קרשים מלמטה עוביין אמה מלמעלן כלין והולכין עד כו' ר' יהודה דרש יהיו תמים על ראשו מלשון כלוי כדכתיב תמו נכרתו והאי דכתיב יחדיו בענין דליהוי משולבין כאחד כשמחברן דומין כאלו אחד הן ולא להוון משתלפי מהדרי ור' נחמיה דייק יחדיו שיהו שוין סופן עד ראשן והא דכתיב תמים דמיתי שלמים ולא מיתי דניסרא בשלמא למ"ד כשם שמלמטן עוביין אמה כך מלמעלן עוביין

*) [רב שמואל בר יהודה אמר ר' אבא אמר רב הונא].

[גירס' הערוך פריו לשון פרסי הוא דבר הרחב ומתקצר והולך למעלה]

גליון הש"ס

גמ' שדי פותייהו. ע"ל דף כח ע"ב תוס' ד"ה ואין קרשים.

צ"ל אל קרש

a covered?[1] [98b]—Said Samuel: [The bottom consisted] of laths.

Our Rabbis taught: The boards were one cubit thick at the bottom, but tapered to a fingerbreadth at the top, for it is said, *they shall be entire* [thammim] *unto the top thereof:*[2] whilst elsewhere it is said, [*the waters . . .*] *ended* [tammu] *and were cut off:*[3] this is R. Judah's view. R. Nehemiah said: Just as their thickness at the bottom was a cubit, so at the top was their thickness a cubit, for it is said, '*and in like manner* [*they shall be entire*]'. But surely '*thammim*' is written?—That [teaches] that they were to come whole,[4] and not divided.[5] And the other too, surely is written '*in like manner*'?—That [teaches] that they were not to erect them irregularly.[6] Now, on the view that just as they were a cubit thick at the bottom, so were they at the top, it is well: thus it is written, *And from the hinder part of the tabernacle westward thou shalt make six boards, And two boards shalt thou make for the corners of the tabernacle:*[7] thus the breadth of these comes and fills in the thickness of those.[8] But on the view that they were a cubit thick at the bottom, while they tapered at the top to a fingerbreadth, one receded and the other protruded?[9]—They were planed mountain-fashion.[10]

And the middle bar in the midst of the boards [*shall pass through from*
b *end to end*].[1] A Tanna taught: It lay[2] there by a miracle.[3]

Moreover thou shalt make the tabernacle with ten curtains. The length of each curtain shall be eight and twenty cubits.[4] Throw their length over the breadth of the Tabernacle; how much was it? twenty-eight cubits. Subtract ten for the roof, and this leaves nine cubits on each side. According to R. Judah, the cubit of the sockets was left uncovered; according to R. Nehemiah, a cubit of the boards was uncovered [too].[5] Cast their breadth over the length of the Tabernacle: how much was it? forty cubits.[6] Subtract thirty for the roof,[7] leaves ten. According to R. Judah the cubit of the sockets was covered; according to R. Nehemiah the cubit of the sockets was uncovered.

And thou shalt make curtains of goats' hair for a tent over the tabernacle: [*eleven curtains shalt thou make them*]. *The length of each curtain shall be thirty cubits,* [*and the breadth of each curtain four cubits*].[8] Cast their length over the breadth of the Tabernacle; how much was it? Thirty. Subtract ten for the roof, which leaves ten [cubits] on each side. According to R. Judah the cubit of the sockets was covered; according to R. Nehemiah the cubit of the sockets was uncovered. It was taught likewise: *And the cubit on one side, and the cubit of the other side, of that which remaineth* [*in the length of the curtains of the tent*]:[9] this was to cover the cubit of the sockets: that is R. Judah's view. R. Nehemiah said: It was to cover the cubit of
c the boards.[1] Cast their breadth over the length of the Tabernacle: how much was it? Forty-four [cubits]. Subtract thirty for the roof leaves fourteen. Subtract two for the doubling over, as it is written, *and thou shalt double over the sixth curtain in the forefront of the tent,*[2] leaves twelve. Now, according to R. Judah, it is well; thus it is written, *the half curtain that remaineth shall hang;*[3] but according to R. Nehemiah, what is meant by [*the half curtain . . .*] *shall hang?*[4]—It shall hang over its companions.[5] The School of R. Ishmael taught: What did the Tabernacle resemble? A woman who goes in the street and her skirts trail after her.[6]

Our Rabbis taught: The boards were cut out and the sockets

a (1) It is assumed that the floor of the waggon was completely closed, like the floor, e.g., of a cement-carrying lorry. How then did Rab state that the space *underneath* the waggon too was public ground? [The translation follows Rashi's reading and interpretation. R. Ḥan and Tosaf. adopt different readings both here and *supra*, 'Rab referred to the interspaces', and explain accordingly.] (2) Ex. XXVI, 24. (3) Josh. III, 17. (4) Translating *thammin* as in E.V. (5) Each board was to be of one piece, not of two joined together (Rashi). Jast. translates: the boards were to be solid, not veneered. (6) Lit., 'they were not to remove them one from another'; but they were all to stand in the same row. (7) Ex. XXVI, 22f. (8) Since the Tabernacle was ten cubits in breadth, and these six boards accounted for nine only, the additional two boards, one at each side, made up the deficiency, whilst the extra cubit left in each fitted exactly over the thickness of the board ranged along the length of the Tabernacle. (9) Obviously these two side boards protruded at the top beyond the attenuated thickness of the boards ranged lengthwise.—'One receded' refers to the latter. (10) These two boards were wider at the bottom and narrower at the top, so that their outward line resembled a mountain slope. 'Aruch reads: like a gusset (*ki tariz*).

b (1) Ex. XXVI, 28. (2) Lit., 'stood'. (3) It was one long straight bar which passed along the three walls; the necessary bending between the angles of the walls was miraculously done by itself. (4) Ibid. 1f. (5) The boards were fitted into sockets (v. 19) one cubit in height. Consequently if the thickness of the top was only one fingerbreadth, practically the whole length of the boards up to the socket was covered by the curtain; (the fingerbreadth and the slightly larger length of the hypotenuse being disregarded). But if the top too was one cubit in thickness, only eight cubits of the boards were covered. (6) I.e., ten curtains each of four cubits in breadth. Ibid. 2. (7) Which was the length of the Tabernacle, twenty boards each one and a half cubits broad. (8) Ibid. 7f. (9) Ibid. 13.

c (1) Left uncovered by the first covering, v. *supra*. (2) Ex. XXVI, 9. (3) Since R. Judah requires only a fingerbreadth for the top thickness of the board, practically two cubits—i.e., half a curtain—hung, i.e., trailed on the floor. (4) Only one cubit was left over, the other being required for the thickness. (5) *Sc.* the lower covering, beyond which the upper fell two cubits. (6) On the ground. So did the Tabernacle's covering trail too.

were grooved;[7] [99a] also, the clasps in the loops[8] looked like stars [set] in the sky.

Our Rabbis taught: The lower curtains [were made] of blue [wool], purple [wool], crimson thread and fine linen,[9] whilst the upper ones were of goats' [hair] manufacture; and greater wisdom [skill] is mentioned in connection with the upper than in connection with the lower. For whereas of the lower ones it is written, ***And all the women that were wise-hearted did spin with their hands;***[10] in reference to the upper ones it is written, ***And all the women whose heart stirred them up in wisdom spun the goats;***[11] and it was taught in R. Nehemiah's name: It was washed [direct] on the goats and spun on the goats.[12]

IF THERE ARE TWO BALCONIES, etc. Rab said in R. Ḥiyya's name: As for the waggons, beneath them, between them, and at their sides it was public ground. Abaye said: Between one waggon and another [as its side] there was [the space of] a full waggon-length. And how much was a waggon-length? five cubits. Why
a was it [this length] necessary: four and a half would have sufficed?[1] —So that the boards should not press [against each other].[2]

Raba said: The sides of the waggon[3] equalled the full [internal] breadth of the waggon, and how much was the [internal] breadth of the waggon? Two cubits and a half.[4] Why was this necessary: a cubit and a half would have sufficed?[5]—In order that the boards should not jump about.[6] Then as to what we have as an established fact that the path [width] of public ground must be sixteen cubits: since we learn it from the Tabernacle,[7]—surely [the public ground] of the Tabernacle was [only] fifteen?[8]—There was an additional cubit where a Levite stood, so that if the boards slipped he would support them.

MISHNAH. AS FOR THE BANK OF A CISTERN,[9] AND A ROCK, WHICH ARE TEN [HANDBREADTHS] HIGH AND FOUR IN BREADTH,[10] IF ONE REMOVES [AUGHT] FROM THEM OR PLACES [AUGHT] UPON THEM, HE IS CULPABLE;[11] IF LESS THAN THIS, HE IS NOT CULPABLE.

GEMARA. Why state, THE BANK OF A CISTERN, AND A
b ROCK: let him [the Tanna] state, 'A cistern and a rock'?[1] [Hence] this supports R. Joḥanan, who said: A cistern together with the bank thereof combine to [give a height of] ten [handbreadths].[2] It was taught likewise: As for a cistern in public ground ten [handbreadths] deep and four broad [square], we may not draw

(7) So that the former fitted into the latter. (8) V. ibid. 10f. (9) V. ibid. 1. (10) Ibid. XXXV, 25. (11) Ibid. 26. (12) V. *supra* 74*b*, n. b4.

a (1) Either for three rows of boards lying on their breadth, which gives exactly four and a half cubits, or for four rows lying on their thickness, thus allowing an additional half cubit to cover the extra space needed for the bars. (2) Rashi: if laid on their breadth. Tosaf: if laid on their thickness, the half cubit being insufficient both for the bars and for freedom of movement of the boards. (3) Which includes the thickness of the sides, the wheels which reached up alongside of them, and the space between the wheels and the sides. (4) So that the sides, as defined in n. a3, were one and a quarter each. (5) To permit the boards to be placed on their thickness *inside* the waggon down its length if necessary. (6) When placed on top, more than one and a quarter cubits would be necessary to support their length firmly. (7) All definitions in connection with work on the Sabbath are learnt thence. (8) Two waggons side by side, each five cubits in width and five cubits' space between them, the whole constituting a public pathway. (9) Formed by the earth dug of it. (10) I.e., four square on top. (11) Because the bank or stone is private ground (v. *supra* 6*a*), whilst the remover stands in public ground.

b (1) This would teach that anything either ten high or ten deep and four square is a private domain. (2) So that the cistern is counted as private ground.

ונראין קרסין בלולאות ככוכבים ברקיע ת"ר יריעות התחתונות של תכלת ושל ארגמן ושל תולעת שני ושל שש ועליונות של מעשה עזים וגדולה חכמה שנאמרה בעליונות יותר ממה שנאמרה בתחתונות דאילו בתחתונות כתיב °וכל אשה חכמת לב בידיה טוו ואילו בעליונות כתיב °וכל הנשים אשר נשא לבן אותנה בחכמה טוו את העזים *ותניא משום ר' נחמיה שטוף בעזים וטווי מן העזים: שתי גזוזטראות כו': *אמר רב משום רבי חייא עגלות תחתיהן וביניהן וצידיהן רה"ר אמר אביי בין עגלה לעגלה כמלא ארך עגלה וכמה ארך עגלה ה' אמות ל"ל בד' ופלגא סגי כי היכי דלא לידחקו קרשים אמר רבא צידי עגלה כמלא רחב עגלה וכמה רחב עגלה שתי אמות ומחצה למה לי באמתא ופלגא סגיא כי היכי דלא לידדו קרשים אלא דקי"ל **דרך רה"ר שש עשרה אמה אנן דגמרינן לה ממשכן דמשכן חמיסרי הואי אמתא יתירא הואי דהוה קאי בן לוי דכי משתלפי קרשים הוה נקיט להו: **מתני'** חולית הבור והסלע שהן גבוהין עשרה ורחבן ארבעה הנוטל מהן והנותן על גבן חייב פחות מכן פטור: **גמ'** למה לי למיתני חולית הבור והסלע ליתני הבור והסלע מסייע ליה לרבי יוחנן דאמר ר' יוחנן *בור וחוליתה מצטרפין לעשרה תניא נמי הכי בור ברה"ר עמוקה י' ורחבה ארבעה אין ממלאין הימנה בשבת

(שמות לה) (שם)

רש"י

ונראין קרסין בלולאות. מילתא אחריתי היא שתי מחברות היו היריעות כל אחת ואחת ה' יריעות תפורות זו עם זו במחט על פני כל ארכן ובאמצע היה מחבר בקרסים מחברת עם מחברת שהיו לולאות בשפת חיצונה של כל מחברת באמצע המשכן אלו כנגד אלו כדכתיב מקבילות הלולאות וגו' (שמות כו): נשא לבן. יתירות חכמה משמע: בין עגלה לעגלה. שבלדה ה' אמות כמלא אורך העגלה: למה לי. אורך העגלה ה' אמות: בארבע ופלגא סגי. שאם מסדרן על רחבן אינו מסדר על ה' אמות יותר מג' והרי בארבע ומחצה יכול לסדרן ואי מסדרן בחודן יותר מד' לא יסדר מפני הפסקת מקום הבריחים שבאמצע הסדרים ובפלגא אמה נמי תסגי ליה: דלא לידחקו. אם בא לסדרן על רחבן: צדי עגלה. חלל שבין דפנות לאופנים ועובי הדופן ועובי האופן: כמלא רחב עגלה. שני הצדדים כמלא רחב חללה דהיינו אמה ורביע לכל צד: למה לי. רחבה תרתי ופלגא אם מפני שאם יצטרך להושיב מן הקרשים לתוכה יכנים: באמתא ופלגא סגי. וישכיבם בה על חודן: כי היכי דלא לידדו קרשים. שלא יהיו הקרשים המוטלים לאורכן על דופנותיה לרחבן מדדין ונוטין לכאן ולכאן שאם מושבות הקרשים קצר מתוך שהן ארוכות ויוצאות לחוץ הרבה יכבד אחד מן הראשין כשהן מדדין בהליכתן ויפלו: חמיסרי הויין. שתי העגלות ההולכות זו בצד זו רחב כל אחת ה' אמות הרי י' וה' אמות ריוח שבין עגלה לעגלה הרי ט"ו ואם תאמר יותר מעשרים הן שהרי הקרשים אורכן י' אמות והן מוטלות על גבי דופני עגלה לרחבה כמלא אורך הקרשים הרי כ' אמה לבד מה שצריך למשוך קרשי כל עגלה ועגלה לצד החיצון של עגלה שלא יגיעו ראשי הקרשים זו בזו ומעכבין את הילוך העגלות אין זה תשובה שהקרשים למעלה מעשרה הן שהעגלה גבוה י' ולגבי רה"ר לית לן למיחשב אלא מקום העגלות וריוח שביניהן שהוא למטה מי' דכל למעלה מי' לאו רה"ר היא הלכך לא חשיב ליה: אמתא יתירתא הואי. עוד צריך להיות ברחב הדרך עודף אמה שתהא חצי אמה לכאן וחצי אמה לכאן לשני לצדדין החיצונות של ב' עגלות: דקאי בן לוי דאי משתלפי. זו מזו ליפול לתוך האויר שביניהם: הוה נקיט להו. נכנס לבין האויר אמה שביניהם ועומד בחצי אמה שיש בין העגלה לצדדין ומתקן את הסדר זו על זו שלא תפול העליונה וכל הדרך הוא מהלך אחורי העגלה וכשרואה אותן משתלפות אל תוך האויר רץ לתוך (א) בליטת הקרשי' שבצדדין עד שמגיע לאמת האויר שביניהם ודוחק עצמו לעמוד בחצי אמה עד שיחזיר הנשלפת למקומה ועל סדרה: **מתני'** חולית הבור. קרקע חפירת הבור נותנין סביבותיו להקיף כמין חומה כמו שאנו נותנין היקף עלים או אבן סביב פי הבור: **גמ'** למה לי למתני חולית הבור והסלע. פשיטא לן דסלע נקט לענין גובהה ובור לענין עומק שנוטל מתוכו ומוציא לרשות הרבים דאי לענין גובהה כגון למוריד מחוליא למטה וכגון דרחבה ארבע למה לי למיתניא כלל הא תנא ליה סלע אלא ודאי למוציא מתוך אוגני בור נקט לה וכיון דהכי הוא חוליא למה לי ליתני הבור לעומק והסלע לגובה: מצטרפין לעשרה. לשויה הבור רה"י ואם הוציא מתוך אוגן חוליא חייב:

תוספות

שתי גזוזטראות כו'. מיירי שסתום למטה בשום דבר ואין גדיים בוקעים תחתיהם או שיש מחיצות למעלה מן הגזוזטרא דתו לא חיישינן לבקיעת גדיים וכן עגלות היו רה"י אע"פ שתחתיהם רה"ר לפי שיש מגוף העגלה עד למעלה מן הקרשים הרבה יותר מעשרה: **בין** עגלה לעגלה כמלא אורך עגלה. לסימנא בעלמא נקטיה ואגב אורחא קמ"ל דאורך עגלה חמש אמות: **כי** היכי דלא לידחקו קרשים. פרש"י אם בא לסדרן על רוחבן וקשה דהא מסיק לעיל דמנח להו אחודן אלא נראה לפרש דלא לידחקו קרשים (ב) אע"ג דדי היה בארבע וחצי לטבעות שהן זו כנגד זו והיו שם אטבעי כדמפרש שהן גלוא"ש מכל מקום מפני כובדן משתרבבים ודוחקין זה לזה אם לא שיש ריוח גדול ביניהם ורחוקין*: **למה** לי באמתא ופלגא סגי. לשיטת רש"י שתי עגלות היו מפורקות זו מזו ויש הפסק ביניהם ה' אמות וכל אחת טעונה לבד משוי של קרשים קשה היאך יכולין קרשים שכל כך כבדין שאורכן עשר אמות ורוחבן אמה וחצי ועוביין אמה לעמוד על ב' אמות ומחצה רוחב ועוד דפריך באמתא ופלגא סגי איך יכול כ"כ כובד גדול לעמוד באמתא ופלגא וכל שכן למ"ד כלין והולכין עד כאצבע שלא היו יכולין לעמוד ועוד היאך היו יכולים שתי עגלות להלך זו בצד זו בט"ו אמות א"כ היו הקרשים נוקשין זה בזה ועוד שצריך לומר לפירושו שהקרשים היו נוטים על האהלים או על החצרות מלמעלה מי' מכל צד ב' אמות ומחצה כמו שפי' בקונטרס בעצמו שהרי אורך שני הקרשים הוא כ' אמה ורה"ר אינו רוחב כי אם ט"ז אמה ועוד מגלן דשתי עגלות היו הולכות זו בצד זו למילף שיהא רה"ר ט"ז אמה שמא היו הולכות כולן זו אחר זו והיה רה"ר קטן או ארבעתן יחד והיה רה"ר גדול הרבה ונראה לר"ת ששתי עגלות היו מחוברות יחד שהיה שם עץ ארוך ט"ו אמה והיו בה ארבע אופנים כמו לשתי עגלות ושתי תיקוני דפנות כמו לשתי עגלות ובין עגלה לעגלה כמו אורך עגלה פירוש בין דופן עגלה זו לדופן עגלה זו ה' אמות ולידי העגלה כמלא רוחב העגלה מכל צד וצד דבין דופן העגלה עם האופן שתי אמות ומחצה ולא כפירוש הקונטרס שפי' אמה ורביע לכל צד ורוחב שתי העגלות עם לידיהן ט"ו אמה ומדופן עגלה זו החיצון לדופן עגלה זו החיצון י' אמות באורך הקרש והיה משכיב הקרש על שתי דופני העגלות ושתי עגלות אחרות לפניהן שאם היו הולכות זו אצל זו היו נוקשות זו בזו וזו אחר זו היו הולכות יפה והשתא פריך שפיר באמתא ופלגא סגי דהואיל ועל שתי העגלות היה משכיבן הוה ס"ד דלא לידדו ומשני דאפילו הכי מידדו:

אמתא יתירא הואי. בצד העגלה דהוי קאי בה בן לוי וצריך לו אמה דגברא באמתא יתיב כדאמר בפ"ק דסוכה (ד' ז:) גבי סוכה העשויה ככבשן ואע"פ שפעמים היה הולך מצד זה ופעמים מצד זה מ"מ היה די לו באמה אחת שמאיזה צד שהיה רוצה ליכנס היה מטה העגלה לצד אחר והיה נכנס בין האהל לעגלה ומתקנס אף על פי שהיה רחוק מן הקרשים שתי אמות ומחצה כשיעור צד העגלה מכל מקום היה יכול להושיט ידו שם ולתקן או על ידי מקל או על ידי שום דבר: **מסייע** ליה לר' יוחנן דאמר בור וחולייתה מצטרפין לעשרה. וא"ת ומה צריך למתני' לאשמעינן הא תניא חדא זימנא בפרק בתרא דעירובין (ד' צט:) בור ברה"ר וחולייתו גבוהה י' טפחים חלון שעל גביו ממלאין ממנו בשבת ומוקי רבי יוחנן בגמרא בסמוכה לה וקא משמע לן דבור וחולייתה מצטרפין לעשרה ויש לומר דדרך תנא להשמיענו בקוצר אע"ג שכבר השמיענו במקום אחר כדאמרינן בריש ברכות (דף ב.) מילתא אגב אורחיה קמ"ל דהעריב שמשו אוכל בתרומה אע"ג דמשנה שלימה היא במס' נגעים (פי"ד מ"ג) העריב שמשו אוכל בתרומה וכהנה רבות בהש"ס אי נמי מיתורא דמתניתין שמעינן דמצטרפין לארבעה ולהשתמש על גבה מיירי משום דמנח עליה מידי ומשתמש כדאמרינן בפרק חלון (עירובין דף עה:) ומיירי כשהחוליא גבוה עשרה דבאינה גבוה י' לא מיחייב נוטל ונותן על גבה והשתא אתי שפיר הא דקתני במתניתין גבוהין עשרה והא דנקט נמי על גבן ואי מתניתין להצטרף לעשרה קאמר ואין החוליא גבוה עשרה לא אתי שפיר הא דקתני גבוה עשרה והנותן על גבן נמי אינו חייב כשמניח על גב החוליא כשאינה גבוה עשרה:

עין משפט נר מצוה

יג א מיי' פי"ד מהל' שבת הלכה א סמג לאוין סה טוש"ע א"ח סי' שמה סעיף ז:

יד ב מיי' פט"ו שם הלכה ט סמג שם טוש"ע א"ח סי' שנד סעיף א:

רבינו חננאל

עוביין אמה היינו דכתיב ולירכתי המשכן ימה תעשה ששה קרשים ושני קרשים תעשה למקוצעות המשכן בירכתים דל פלגא [דאמתא] לחללה בהאי גיסא ופלגא [דאמתא] לחללה בהאי גיסא דאישתייר מעשר אמות חללו של משכן כי חללו של עשר אמות והן ששה קרשים ט' אמות נשארה אמה תשלום עשר אמות למלאות עשר אמות אורך של משכן ואמתא סומכא דקרש מהאי גיסא ואמתא מאידך גיסא היינו דאתיא פותיא דב' קרשים שבמקצועות ממלא לסומכא דהני קרשים ולחללה דאמתא כדאמרן פירוש המשכן עשר אמות הללו כשמעמיד ברוח מערבית ו' קרשים כל קרש רחבו אמה וחצי הרי ט' אמות נשאר מלחלל אמה נמצא פתוח חצי אמה מיכן וחצי אמה מכאן היה מביא ב' קרשים כל קרש רחבו אמה וחצי ומעמידה במקצועות נמצא כל אחד תופס חצי אמה החלל וממלא אמה עובי הקרש האחרון העומד בקצה הצפון שהוא סוף לעשרים קרשים וכן כיוצא בו בקצה הדרום נמצאו מכוונים תמים מלמטן ותמים מלמעלן אין אחד מהם עודף ויוצא על חבירו אלא למ"ד כלין והולכין עד כאצבע האי מעייל. והאי נפיק כי אע"פ שהן מכוונים מלמטן כנגד עביו של קרש הסמוך להן מן הצפון והקרש הסמוך להן מן הדרום. אבל מלמעלן מקום אשר כלו מכלפי עוביו ועומד על כאצבע נמצא כל אחד מב' קרשים הללו של מקצועות המשכן יוצא אמה חסר אצבע מקרשי צפון ודרום ופריק ר"י [כי טורין] דשפי להו כי מידי בלשון ערבי בניקא שעושין בבגדים היא רחבה מלמטה ומשפע ומיצר מלמעלן ובלע"ז גיירי כך באלו ב' קרשי המקצועות היה תחתיתו רחב אמה וחצי והיה הנגד אוכל ועולה כשיפוע עד שיכלה למעלה עד כאצבע כדי שישוו לקרשי צפון ודרום מבחוץ ולא יהיה קרש יוצא וקרש נכנס: **והבריח** התיכון בתוך הקרשים משלש רוחות ואין עץ אחד מבריח ג' רוחות אלא במעשה נס: **כתיב** אורך היריעה האחת שמנה ועשרים באמה רחב חללו של משכן עשר אמות כשתכסה היריעה על המשכן והוא המשכן עומד מכסה החלל עשר אמות נמצאו עודפות ט' אמות מזה הצד חצוני משולשלת על הקרשים וכן בצד הדרומי כיוצא בו לר' יהודה שאמר כי הקרשים למעלה עוביין אצבע בלבד נמצא גג המשכן עשר אמות וט' אמות מצד צפון כיסה הקרש נשארו האדנים מגולין וב' אצבעות מן הקרשים כי כל קרש ארכן (ד') [י'] אמות אמה ממנו ידות מובלעות באדן אבל לר' נחמיה שאמר כי ראשי הקרשים נמי עוביין אמה נמצא חלל המשכן וראשי הקרשים מתכסין מן היריעה י"ב אמה נשארו מכ"ח אמה ט"ז אמה ח' אמות מכסות מקרש שבצפון וח' אמה בקרש שבדרום נמצא מכל קרש בשני הצדדין אמה מגולה והארן הנה זה החשבון לרחב המשכן ועוד כתיב ואת המשכן תעשה עשר יריעות כל יריעה רחבה ד' אמות הרי עשר יריעות מ' אמה והמשכן ארכו ל' כשתכסה המשכן ל' אמה נשארו י' אמות שמשתפעות ויורדות בקרשים אחורי המשכן ונתכסו לר' יהודה הקרשים והאדנים עד קרוב לקרקע אצבע אחת [illegible] קרשים ונשארו האדנים מגולין ועשו יריעות עזים לאהל על המשכן עשתי עשרה יריעות אורך כל היריעה ל' אמה ורחבה ד' אמות נמצאו אלו י"א יריעות בעת שהן מחוברות ל' אמה במ"ד אמות כשמשלו אורך היריעות שהיא ל' אמה לרחבו של משכן מכסה הללו עשר אמות ונשארו אמות משתפעות ויורדות ע"ג הקרשים בצפון וכיוצא בהן בדרום. לר' יהודה מיכסיא דאדנים לא נשארו מגולה מן האדן אלא אצבע לר' נחמיה מיכסיא אמה הקרשים ונשארו האדנים מגולין. תניא נמי הכי [illegible] הכפילה ואמה עובי הקרש [illegible] אמה של אדנים [illegible] וזו שעל הארץ הנה חצי היריעה העודף *) פי' שטף וטוה מן העזים כשהן חיים כדאמרינן (חולין דף קלו) השוטף את רחליו ומעל גבי העזים

*) נראה דחסר וכצ"ל למה המשכן דומה [illegible]

הגהות הב"ח

(א) רש"י ד"ה הוה נקיט וכו' רך לתוך בליטת: (ב) תוס' ד"ה כי היכי דלא לידחקו קרשים לטבעות שהן זו כנגד זו והיו שם לטבעי כדפי' שהן גלוא"ש אע"ג דדי היה בארבע וחצי מ"מ מפני כובדן וכו' ביניהם ודוחק ס"ד:

לעיל צח: [לעיל צח.] [ב"ב נט:] עירובין פח. נט:

רב נסים גאון

הלא דקיימא לן דרך רשות הרבים י"ו אמה ומשתכח עיקר דילה במשנה בפרק המוכר פירות בבבא בתרא (דף צט) דרך היחיד ד' אמות ודרך הרבים י"ו אמה דרך המלך אין לה שיעור הוא

אלא אם כן עשו לה מחיצה גבוה י' טפחים ואין שותין הימנה בשבת אא"כ הכנים לה ראשו ורובו ובור וחוליתה מצטרפין לעשר' בעא מיניה רב מרדכי *מרבא עמוד ברה"ר גבוה י' ורחב ד' °וזרק ונח על גביו מהו מי אמרינן הרי עקירה באיסור הרי הנחה באיסור או דילמא כיון דממקום פטור קאתיא לא א"ל מתניתין היא אתא שייליה לרב יוסף א"ל מתניתין היא אתא שייליה לאביי א"ל מתני' היא אמר להו *כולכו ברוקא דהדדי תפיתו א"ל ואת לא תסברא והתנן הנוטל מהן (א) ונותן על גבן חייב א"ל דילמא מתני' במחט מחט נמי א"א דלא מדליא פורתא דאית ליה מורשא א"נ דרמיא בחריצה אמר רב מישא בעי רבי יוחנן כותל ברה"ר גבוה י' ואינו רחב ארבע ומוקף לכרמלית ועשאו רה"י וזרק ונח על גביו מהו מי אמרינן כיון דאינו רחב ד' מקום פטור הוא או דילמא כיון דעשאו רה"י כמאן דמלי דמיא אמר עולא *קל וחומר לאחרים עושה מחיצה לעצמו לא כ"ש איתמר נמי א"ר חייא בר אשי אמר רב וכן א"ר יצחק א"ר יוחנן כותל ברה"ר גבוה י' ואינו רחב ארבע ומוקף לכרמלית ועשאו רה"י הזורק ונח על גביו חייב לאחרים עושה מחיצה לעצמו לא כ"ש בעי רבי יוחנן בור תשעה ועקר ממנו חוליא והשלימה לעשרה מהו עקירת חפץ ועשיית מחיצה בהדי הדדי קאתו ומיחייב או לא מיחייב °ואם תימצי לומר ²כיון דלא הוי מחיצה עשרה מעיקרא לא מיחייב בור י' ונתן לתוכה חוליא ומיעטה מהו הנחת חפץ וסילוק מחיצה בהדי הדדי קאתו *מיחייב או ²לא מיחייב תיפשוט ליה מדידיה דתנן *הזורק ארבע אמות בכותל למעלה מעשרה טפחים כזורק באויר למטה מעשרה כזורק בארץ והזורק בארץ ארבע אמות חייב *והוינן בה והא לא נח ואמר רבי יוחנן בדבילה שמינה שנינו ואמאי הא קא ממעט מארבע אמות התם לא מבטל ליה הכא מבטל ליה בעי רבא זרק דף ונח על גבי יתידות מהו מאי קמיבעיא ליה הנחת חפץ ועשיית מחיצה בהדי הדדי קאתו היינו דרבי יוחנן כי קמיבעיא ליה לרבא כגון דזרק דף וחפץ על גביו מאי כיון דבהדי הדדי קאתו ²כהנחת חפץ ועשיית מחיצה דמי או דילמא כיון דלא אפשר דלא מידלא פורתא והדר נייח כעשיית מחיצה והנחת חפץ דמי תיקו *אמר רבא ²פשיטא לי מים על גבי מים היינו הנחתן אגוז על גבי מים
לאו

רש"י

מחילה י'. שיהא הממלא עומד לפנים מן המחילה וממלא: ואין שותין הימנה. לעמוד על שפתה ולשאוב בכלי ולהכניס ראשו לחללה ולשתות כדתנן *לא יעמוד אדם ברה"ר וישתה ברה"י שמא ימשוך הכלי אצלו: אלא אם כן הכניס ראשו ורובו. למקום שהוא שותה: הרי עקירה באיסור. מרה"ר: הרי הנחה באיסור. ברה"י: ממקום פטור קאתיא. שאי אפשר שלא הגביה תחילה למעלה מן העמוד שהוא מקום פטור שאינו אויר רה"ר ואויר רה"י נמי לא הוי דכי אמרינן רה"י עולה עד לרקיע ה"מ כנגד רה"י אבל האי מקמי דלימטי לאויר עמוד אגבהיה למעלה מעשרה: מתניתין היא. הנוטל מהן והנותן על גבן חייב: ברוקא דהדדי תפיתו. כולכם רוק אחד אתם רוקקים: ואת לא תסברא. דמתני' היא: במחט. דאינה גבוהה: דאית לה. לסלע מורשא נמוך מי' וכיון דכולה גבוהה י' בר מההיא מורשא ואיהו לא הוי מקום חשוב הוי ליה חורי רשות היחיד: אי נמי דרמיא. מחט בחריץ שבסלע שבראשו ולא נכל מלמעלה מי' אלא לתוך י': מוקף לכרמלית. בכותל זה הקיפו בקעה שהיתה כרמלית ועל ידו נעשית רה"י כגון שהוקף לדירה או לא הקיפו בו °אלא בית סאתים: וזרק. מרה"ר ונח על ראשו מהו: או דילמא כיון. דכותל זה עשאה לכרמלית זו רה"י: כמאן דמלי דמיא. והוי אגל ראשו כארעא סמיכתא כל החלל: לאחרים. כל החלל עשאו רה"י: לעצמו לא כל שכן. ראש הכותל: ועקר ממנה חוליא. והניחו ברה"ר מי מיחייב אע"ג דמקמי עקירה לאו רה"י הוה בשעת עקירה מיהא רה"י הוה: וסילוק מחילה. בהנחה זו נסתלקה מחילת הבור שנתמעטה מעשרה מי מהני האי מיעוטא למיפטריה או לא: בדבילה שמינה. שנדבק בפני הכותל: ואמאי. מיחייב הא מתני' ד' אמות קתני ואפילו מלומלמות וכי נח בפני הכותל נתמעט הזריקה מד' אמות כדי מקום הדבילה וקתני חייב כיון דמעיקרא ד' אמות הוה: התם לא מיבטיל ליה. דבילה הלכך לאו מיעוט הוא: על גבי יתידות. דקות שהיו גבוהות י' ואין רחבות ד' ודף זה רחב ד' עשאו רשות היחיד: מהו. להתחייב בזריקה זו: וחפץ על גביו. ואם תימצי לומר הוא אם תימצי לומר כר' יוחנן דהנחת חפץ ועשיית מחילה בהדי הדדי לא מיחייב הכא ודאי אדף לא מיחייב מיהו אחפץ מהו לחיובי: דלא אפשר דלא מידלי. החפץ מעל הדף בשעת הנחת הדף והדר נייח: כעשיית מחילה. ברישא והדר הנחת החפץ דמי חייב דבשעת הנחתו כבר נעשה דף רה"י: היינו הנחתן. ואם נטל מקלתן והוליא הוה עקירה:
לאו

תוספות

אלא אם כן עשו לה מחילה גבוה י' טפחים. אבל פסין לא מהני אלא בבאר מים חיים או בור הרבים כדתנן בפרק עושין פסין (עירובין דף כב:) אבל בור היחיד עושין לו מחילה כו' ודווקא עמוק י' ורוחב ארבע דהוי רה"י אבל פחות מיכן דהוי כרמלית לא החמירו כל כך ומשתרי שפיר בפסין.

או דילמא כיון דממקום פטור קא אתיא לא. ואם תאמר ומאי קמיבעיא ליה תיפשוט מדתניא בפ"ק (דף ו.) המוציא מחנות לפלטיא דרך סטיו חייב ואחד המושיט ואחד הזורק חייב ואמרינן לעיל (דף צב.) המוציא משוי למעלה מעשרה חייב ומפרש הרב פור"ת דדוקא כשפסק כחו במקום פטור קמיבעיא ליה כגון שזרק למעלה מי' כנגד אויר רה"ר וירד האבן באלכסון ונחה על העמוד דירידה זו אינו מכחו הראשון אלא כח כחו היא וכיון דממקום פטור קא אתיא יש הפסק בין עקירה ראשונה להנחה אבל אם זרק ממש כנגד העמוד שלא הלכה באלכסון כלל אלא הלכה מכחו עד העמוד ודאי חייב ודווקא בזורק מבעיא ליה כדפי' אבל מוציא ומכניס פשיטא ליה דחייב והא דמייתי ראיה מהנוטל והנותן ע"ג חייב הייט משום דמשמע ליה דמיירי בכל ענין בין בזורק בין במושיט כדתניא ברישא הזורק פטור והמושיט חייב והשתא לא דמי למוציא מחנות לפלטיא דרך סטיו דהתם מכחו בא לרה"ר:

ומוקף לכרמלית ועשאו רה"י. אומר ר"י דמשמע דדוקא מוקף לכרמלית דכיון דמוקף לכרמלית אין כ"כ סברא שיעשה רה"י מטעם דלאחרים עושה מחילה אבל מוקפת לרה"ר ועשאו רה"י פשיטא דלעצמו נמי מהני ומשום חורי רה"י ליכא לחיוביה כמו רמיא בחריצא דלעיל דלא ניחא תשמישתיה לגבי רה"י כולי האי על הכותל: לאחרים עושה מחילה כו'. גבי חוליא דבור לא שייך למימר הכי ליחייב המשתמש מרה"ר על גבה כיון שאין החוליא עצמו גבוה י': ואמאי והא קא ממעט מארבע אמות. פירש בקונטרס דמשמע ליה דמיירי אפילו בד' אמות מלומלמות שעובי הדבילה ממעט מד' אמות וקשה לר"י דבענין זה אין נראה שיתחייב כיון שאיגודו בפנים כמו מוציא חצי קופה לרה"ר דאינו חייב עד שיוציאנה כולה לחוץ דאטו אם זרק אדם רומח וכל דבר ארוך כל שהוא יתחייב כיון שראשו אחד יצא חוץ לד' אמות ואם בזורק ד' אמות הכי גמירי לה שיתחייב בכה"ג א"כ היכי פשיט מינה ועוד דאמאי משמע ליה טפי בהאי דזרק ארבע אמות בכותל דהוו מלומלמות משאר ארבע אמות השנויות בכל הש"ס ונראה לר"י דמיירי הכא שזורק חוץ לארבע אמות כמו בכל מקום והכי פריך והא קא ממעט מד' אמות שמקום הדבילה נתבטלה מתורת רשות הרבים שבטל לכותל והרי הוא ככותל עב ולא הוי עוד על גביו רשות הרבים ואם זרק מחט או קוץ ד' אמות ונח על הדבילה או נתקע בתוכו היה פטור דהרי מקום הדבילה נתמעט מדין רשות הרבים ואפ"ה חייב הואיל ובתחילת הזריקה עד קודם הנחה היה שם רה"ר עליו והנחה ומיעוט רה"ר בהדי הדדי קא אתו והכא נמי הוה לן למימר הנחה וסילוק מחילה בהדי הדדי קאתו ומשני התם לא מבטלי ולהכי לא מבטל רה"ר: זרק דף כו' הנחת חפץ ועשיית מחילה כו'. וא"ת אפילו ליכא בקיעת גדיים היכי חשוב לשוייה תחתיו רה"י מ"ש מטרסקל ועמוד ברה"ר גבוה י' ורחב ד' ואין בעיקרו ד' דאמרינן (לקמן דף קא·) זרק ונח על גביו חייב משמע דוקא על גביו אבל תחתיו לא ואומר ר"י כגון שיש שתי מחילות של יתידות ובשלישית אמרינן פי תקרת דף יורד וסותם:

עין משפט נר מצוה

טו א ב מיי' פי"ד מהל' שבת הלכה ג וכו' סמג לאוין סה טוש"ע א"ח סי' שמה סעיף ג.
טז ג מיי' שם הל' כ:
יז ד שם הלכה כא:
יח ה מיי' פי"ג מהל' שבת הלכה ד ופ"ח מהל' טומאת אוכלין הלכה ג:

רבינו חננאל

בלי נויזה היו שוות אותן כדאמרי' (לעיל ד' ע"ד) השוה מע"ג בהמה בשבת ושויה בענין הזה צריכה חכמה יתירה: שתי גזוזטראות שתיהן רה"י הן כל אחת רשות לעצמה ורה"ר ביניהן. המושיט והזורק מזו לזו בתוך י"ם לדברי חכמים פטור אבל אסור וזה על עיקר משנתנו ששנינו מרה"י לרה"י ורה"ר באמצע ר' עקיבא מחייב וחכמים פוטרין אבל המושיט [והזורק] למעל' מעשרה אם היו שתיהן שלו ואין אחת גבוה מן האחרת אלא שתיהן מכוונות זו כנגד זו כבר פירשתי למעלה שמותר להושיט ולזרוק מזו לזו ואם אינן שתיהן שלו אסור להושיט ולזרוק מזו לזו משום [דלא ערבו] ואם חדא מידליא וחדא מיתתא אסור משום גזירה ואם היו הגזוזטראות הללו עומדות למעלה מעשרה ברה"ר מכונות להיותן דיוטא אחת ורשות אחת כיצד שמרכיבין נסר מזו לזו ע"ג רה"ר רחבה ד' טפחים כדי להיותן דיוטא אחת ורשות אחת אם עשה כן מבע"י הרי הן כרשות אחת ומותר לטלטל מזו לזו ע"ג הנסר המתוח מזו לזו ע"ג רה"ר ותנן בעירובין (דף עח) חריץ שהוא עמוק י' ורחב ד' ונתן עליו נסר שרחב ד' טפחים וכן ב' גזוזטראות זו כנגד זו מערבין אחת ואין מערבין שתים פחות מד' מערבין שנים ואין מערבין אחד השתא אם הגזוזטראות הללו הן למעלה מעשרה וניתן עליהן נסר רחב ד"ט מבעוד יום מותר לטלטל מזו לזו שנעשו שתיהן רשות אחת אבל אם קדש [היום] ולא חוברו אסור להושיט מזו לזו בין נסר בין זולתי נסר אסור להושיט אחר שקידש היום והמושיט חייב הוא שכך היו עגלות במדבר היו ב' עגלות זו בצד זו ברה"ר והיו [מושיטין] קרשים ומציבין קרש על ב' עגלות ראשו (זה על זה) [האחד על זו וראשו השני על זו] כנסר שפירשנו ענינו למעלה והו היו שתיהן בדיוטא אחת המושיט מזו לזו חייב שכן היה דרך הלוים שהיו מושיטין הקרשים מזו לזו היא מלאכתן ולפיכך העושה כן בשבת חייב: ירושל' ולא היו זורקין תני בר קפרא כדי שלא לנהוג בזיון בקרשים לפיכך הזורק מזו לזו פטור אבל אסור. וראוי לעמוד בפירוש זה להזהר בו כי עמוק הוא ועלה אמר רב משום ר' חייא עגלות תחתיהן וביניהן וצידיהן רה"ר. אמר אביי בין עגלה לעגלה כמלוא רחב עגלה וכמה אורך עגלה ה' אמות ואקשינן אמאי כיון דג' קרשים מניחין בעגלה בדרא תתאה ועל גבה מניחין אחרים ועולין וכל קרש רחבו אמה וחצי די לעגלה ארכה ד' אמות וחצי כדי שיעור הנחת ג' קרשים ופרקינן הרויח להן חצי אמה כי היכי דלא נידחקו קרשים. אמר רבא וצידי עגלות ב' אמות ומחצה כמלא רחב עגלה ואקשינן למה לי כוליה האי הלא אורך הקרשים מוטלין לרוחב עגלה קצה הקרש בעגלה זו ב' אמות ומחצה וקצתו השני של קרש זה מוטל על העגלה אחרת ב' אמות ומחצה ובין ב' העגלות ה' אמות אמצעיים הקרש תלוי בינהן אפילו אמה אחת ומחצה מן הקצה שלו מכאן בעגלה וכן מן הקצה השני דיו למה ה' אמות בפחות מהכי סגי ושנינן כי היכי דלא לידדו קרשים פי' אם הן שתי אמות ומחצה מיכן ושתי אמות ומחצה מיכן מוטלין בעגלה אפשר שישמט ויורד הקרש ולא יכון נמצא שיעור רוחב העגלה ב' אמות ומחצה וצידה ב' אמות ומחצה כשיעור עגלה וכן בצידה השני נמצא שיעור העגלה וב' צדדיה ז' אמות ומחצה וכשהיו מהלכים במדבר קרשי המשכן היו מוטלין מעגלה זו לעגלה זו והיו הקרשים מוטלין רוחב הקרשים לאורך העגלות נמצאו שיעור העגלות כשמונות קרשי המשכן ומהלכות מתפשטות בדרך ט"ו אמה (דו זו) תחתיהן וביניהן וצידיהן. ואקשינן אלא הא דקי"ל דרך רה"ר ט"ז אמה וכדתנן בפרק המוכר פירות לחבירו ובפרק הכונס צאן לדיר וגמרינן לה ממשכן ממהלך העגלות העגלות הנה אינם אלא ט"ו אמה ומשנינן הוה תמן בעגלות אתא אחריתי פלגא דאמתא מהאי ניסא ופלגא דאמתא דהאי ניסא דהוה קאי בן לוי התם למחזי דאי משלפי קרשים נקיט בהו ומהדר אתבעי למקומן. וכן בגזוזטראות שמכוונות להיות דיוטא אחת ומושיטין נסרים מזו לזו המושיט חייב והזורק פטור שכך היתה עבודת הלוים: מתני' חולית הבור פי' העפר היוצא מן הבור מניחין אותן סביביו כדי שיהא לו כמעקה ואם החוליא גבוה י' ורחבה ד' הרי היא כרה"י. וכן סלע כיוצא בה ואם נטל מרה"ר ונתן על גבו או נטל מעל גבו והניח ברה"י חייב ואם אינה גבוהה י' או גבוהה י' ואינה רחבה ד' אינה כרה"י והעוקר ממנה ומניח ברה"ר פטור וזה מפורש ביציאות השבת בארבע רשויות לשבת נדר ברה"ר גבוהה י' ורחב ד' זו היא רה"י גמורה אבל מקום שיש לו רחב ד' ואינה גבוהה י' אם [אין] גבוהה מן הארץ ג' טפחים הא קיי"ל דכל פחות משלשה דארעא כארעא קאי ואם גבוהה ג' ורחב ד' ולא הגיע לעשרה ככרמלית ובמקום פטור הוא ואינו לא כרה"ר ולא כרה"י ואסור להוציא מרה"י אליו אבל [אינו] רחב ארבעה מותר לכאן ולכאן ובלבד שלא יחליף דהא תניא אדם עומד על האסקופה נוטל מן העני ונותן לו נוטל מבעה"ב ונותן לו ואמרינן האי
אסקופה

מסורת הש"ס

[עירובין נט. לעיל יא.]
[נ"ל מרבה]
[נדה מב. ע"ש פרש"י]
כג"ל
[לקמן ק. וש"נ]
[לעיל ז: וש"נ]
[לעיל סג.]

הגהות הב"ח

(א) גמ' הנוטל מהן והנותן על גבן:

גליון הש"ס

גמ' בעא מיניה רב מרדכי כו' וזורק ונח על גביו. ע' סוכה ד ע"ב תד"ה פחות מג': שם ואם תימצי לומר כיון דלא הוי מחילה. ע' לעיל ח ע"א תד"ה רחבה ששה. רש"י ד"ה מוקף לכרמלית וכו' אלא בית סאתים. עיין לעיל ז ע"א וצ"ע:

[water] from it on the Sabbath,[3] [*99b*] unless a wall ten handbreadths high is made around it;[4] and one may not drink from it on the Sabbath unless he brings his head and the greater part of his body into it,[5] and a cistern and its bank combine to [give a height of] ten.

R. Mordecai asked Rabbah: What of a pillar in the street, ten high and four broad, and one throws [an article] and it alights upon it? Do we say, Surely the removal is [effected] in transgression and the depositing is [effected] in transgression;[6] or perhaps since it comes from a place of non-liability[7] it is not [a culpable action]?—Said he to him, This is [treated in] our Mishnah. He [then] went and asked it of R. Joseph: Said he to him, This is [treated in] our Mishnah. He went and asked it of Abaye. Said he to him, This is [treated in] our Mishnah. 'You all spit with each other's spittle,'[8] cried he to them: Do you not hold thus, they replied. Surely we learnt, IF ONE REMOVES [AUGHT] FROM THEM OR PLACES [AUGHT] UPON THEM, HE IS CULPABLE.[9] But perhaps our Mishnah treats of a needle? he suggested to them!—It is impossible even for a needle not to be slightly raised.—It [the rock] may have a projecting point,[10] or it [the needle] may lie in a cleft.[11]

R. Misha said, R. Joḥanan propounded: What of a wall in a
a street, ten high but not four broad, surrounding a *karmelith*[1] and converting it [thereby] into private ground,[2] and one throws [an article] and it alights on the top of it? Do we say, Since it is not four broad it is a place of non-liability; or perhaps, since it converts it into private ground it is as though it were [all] filled up?[3] Said 'Ulla, [This may be solved] *a fortiori*: if it [the wall] serves as a partition for something else,[4] how much more so for itself![5] This was stated too: R. Ḥiyya b. Ashi said in Rab's name, and thus said R. Isaac in R. Joḥanan's name: In the case of a wall in the street ten high and not four broad, surrounding a *karmelith* and converting it into private ground, he who throws [an article] which alights thereon is culpable: if it serves as a partition for something else, how much more so for itself.

R. Joḥanan propounded: What of a pit nine [handbreadths deep] and one removes one segment from it and makes it up to ten;[6] [do we say] the taking up of the object and the making of the partition come simultaneously, hence he is culpable; or is he not culpable? Now should you say, Since the partition was not ten originally he is not liable: what of a pit ten [deep] and one lays the segment therein and [thus] diminishes it['s depth]? [Here] the depositing of the article and the removal of the partition come simultaneously: is he culpable or not?—You may solve it for him by his own [dictum]. For we learnt: If one throws [an article] four cubits on to a wall,—if above ten handbreadths, it is as though he throws it into the air; if below, it is as though he throws it on to the ground; and he who throws [an article] four cubits along the ground is culpable. Now we discussed this: surely it does not stay there? And R. Joḥanan
b answered: This refers to a juicy cake of figs.[1] Yet why so? Surely it diminishes the four cubits?[2]—There he does not render it as nought;[3] here he does render it as nought.[4]

Raba propounded: What if one throws a board and it alights upon poles?[5] What does he ask? [The law where] the depositing of the article and the constituting of the partition come simultaneously? [but] that is R. Joḥanan's [problem]!—When does Raba ask? e.g., if he throws a board with an article on top of it: what [then]? [Do we say], Since they come simultaneously, it is like the depositing of the article and the making of a partition [at the same time];[6] or perhaps, since it is impossible for it [the article] not to be slightly raised and then alight,[7] it is like the making of a partition and the [subsequent] depositing of an article?[8] The question stands over.

Raba said: I am certain, water [lying] upon water, that is its

(3) Because the well is private ground whilst the drawer stands in the street. (4) For the drawer to stand in private ground. (5) Cf. *supra* 11*a* bottom. (6) I.e., the article is removed from public and deposited in private ground. (7) V. *supra* 6*a*. The object must sail through the air above ten handbreadths in order for it to alight on the top of a column of that height. (8) Your opinions are all traceable to the same source. (9) And in so doing he must lift the object to a height above ten. (10) Part of the top may slope downward and thence project upward, and there the needle lies. In that case it is below ten, and even when picked up does not go above ten. (11) Or groove, likewise below ten.—Thus in R. Mordecai's view the Mishnah does not solve his problem.

a (1) V. Glos. (2) V. *supra* 7*a*. (3) Reaching to the top of the wall, so that the wall and the *karmelith* are one, the whole, including the wall, being private ground. (4) Converting the *karmelith* into private ground. (5) It is certainly private ground, just as the *karmelith* which it converts. (6) [The segment was one handbreadth in thickness and by removing it the pit reaches the depth of ten handbreadths, which constitutes the legal height for the partition of a private domain.]

b (1) V. *supra* 7*b*. (2) For the thickness of the figs must be deducted. Nevertheless he is culpable, and the same reasoning applies to R. Joḥanan's second problem. (3) When he throws the cake of figs on the wall, he does not mean it to become part thereof and cease to exist separately, as it were. (4) For it becomes part of the wall. Hence the two cases are dissimilar. (5) The poles are ten handbreadths high, but not four square, whilst the board is; thus as it rests on these poles it constitutes a private domain. (6) Hence he is not liable, assuming this to be the solution of R. Joḥanan's problem. (7) For it does not stick to the board; hence the board alights first and then this article. (8) Therefore he is culpable.

[natural] rest; a nut upon water, [100a] that is not its [natural] rest. Raba propounded: If a nut [lies] in a vessel, and the vessel floats on water, what [is the law]? Do we regard the nut, and behold it is at rest; or do we regard the vessel, and behold it is not at rest? The question stands over. [In respect to] oil [floating] upon wine, R. Joḥanan b. Nuri and the Rabbis differ. For we learnt: If oil is floating upon wine, and a *ṭebul yom* touches the oil, he disqualifies the oil only. R. Joḥanan b. Nuri said: Both are attached to each other.[9]

a Abaye said: If a pit in the street [is] ten deep and eight broad,[1] and one throws a mat into it, he is culpable; but if he divides it with the mat,[2] he is not culpable.[3] Now according to Abaye, who is certain that the mat annuls the partition,[4] a segment certainly annuls the partition;[5] but according to R. Joḥanan to whom a segment is a problem, a mat certainly does not annul the partition.[6]

Abaye also said: If a pit in the street, ten deep and four broad, [is] full of water and one throws [an object] therein, he is culpable; [but if it is] full of produce and one throws [an object] therein, he is not culpable. What is the reason? Water does not annul the partition,[7] [whereas] produce does annul the partition. It was taught likewise: If one throws [an object] from the sea into a street, or from a street into the sea, he is not liable.[8] R. Simeon said: If there is in the place where he throws [it a separate cavity] ten deep and four broad, he is liable.[9]

MISHNAH. IF ONE THROWS [AN ARTICLE] FOUR CUBITS ON TO A WALL ABOVE TEN HANDBREADTHS, IT IS AS THOUGH HE THROWS IT INTO THE AIR; IF BELOW, IT IS AS THOUGH HE THROWS IT ON TO THE GROUND. AND HE WHO THROWS [AN ARTICLE] FOUR CUBITS ALONG THE GROUND[10] IS CULPABLE.

GEMARA. But it does not stay there?—Said R. Joḥanan: We learnt of a juicy cake of figs.[11]

Rab Judah said in Rab's name in the name of R. Ḥiyya: If one throws [an article] above ten [handbreadths] and it goes and alights in a cavity of any size, we come to a controversy of R. Meir and the Rabbis. According to R. Meir, who holds: We [imaginarily] hollow out to complete it, he is liable; according to the Rabbis who maintain, We do not hollow out to complete it, b he is not liable.[1] It was taught likewise: If one throws [an article] above ten and it goes and alights in a cavity of any size, R. Meir declares [him] culpable, whereas the Rabbis exempt [him].

Rab Judah said in Rab's name: If a [sloping] mound attains [a height of] ten [handbreadths] within [a distance of] four,[2] and one throws [an object] and it alights on top of it, he is culpable. It was taught likewise: If an alley[3] is level within but becomes a slope towards the [main] street,[4] or is level with the [main] street, but becomes a slope within,[5] that alley requires neither a lath nor a beam.[6] R. Ḥanina b. Gamaliel said: If a [sloping] mound attains [a height of] ten [handbreadths] within [a distance of] four, and one throws [an object] and it alights on top of it, he is culpable.

MISHNAH. IF ONE THROWS [AN OBJECT] WITHIN FOUR CUBITS BUT IT ROLLS BEYOND FOUR CUBITS, HE IS NOT CULPABLE; BEYOND FOUR CUBITS BUT IT ROLLS WITHIN FOUR CUBITS, HE IS CULPABLE.[7]

GEMARA. But it did not rest [beyond four cubits]?[8]—Said R. Joḥanan: Providing it rests [beyond four cubits] on something, whatever its size.[9] It was taught likewise: If one throws [an article] beyond four cubits, but the wind drives it within, even if it carries it out again, he is not liable; if the wind holds it for c a moment,[1] even if it carries it in again, he is liable.

Raba said: [An article brought] within three [handbreadths] must, according to the Rabbis, rest upon something, however small.[2] Meremar sat and reported this statement. Said

(9) V. *supra* 5b for notes on the whole passage.

a (1) I.e., eight by four—the pit of course is private ground. (2) E.g., a stiff cane mat, which stands up vertically across the middle of the pit. (3) The thickness of the mat leaves less than four square handbreadths on either side, so that neither is now private ground. (4) As in the previous note. (5) V. the question asked by R. Joḥanan, *supra* 99b. (6) For the mat does not become part of the pit; v. *supra* 99b, n. b3. (7) Hence the pit is private ground in spite of the water. (8) The sea is a *karmelith*, *supra* 6a. (9) Since it stands apart from the rest of the sea. This cavity too is naturally filled with water; hence we see that water does not annul the partition. (10) Or, over the ground, within the height of ten handbreadths. (11) V. *supra* 7b for notes on this and the Mishnah.

b (1) V. *supra* 7b for notes. (2) This renders it too steep to be negotiated in one's ordinary stride, and the top is therefore counted as private ground. (3) This ranks as a *karmelith*, *supra* 6a. (4) Into which it debouches. (5) The ground on the inner side of the entrance is of the same level as the main street for a short distance, but then falls away. (6) To convert it into private ground (v. *supra* 9a), the slope itself being an effective partition. (7) In both cases it did not properly rest before the wind drove it back or forward. (8) Why is he culpable in the latter case? (9) Even not on the ground itself, and stays there momentarily. Rashi: The same holds good if the wind keeps it stationary for a moment within three handbreadths of the ground on the principle of *labud* (v. Glos.). [Wilna Gaon reads: Provided it rests for a little while.]

c (1) Beyond the four cubits. (2) The reference is to the Rabbis' view that an object caught up in the air is not regarded as at rest, in contrast to R. Akiba's ruling that it is as at rest (*supra* 97a). Raba states that the Rabbis hold thus even if the object comes within three handbreadths of the ground: it must actually alight upon something, otherwise it is not regarded as having been deposited.

לאו היינו הנחתן בעי רבא *אגוז בכלי וכלי צף על גבי מים מהו מי אמרינן בתר אגוז אזלינן והא נייח או דילמא בתר כלי אזלינן והא לא נייח תיקו שמן על גבי יין מחלוקת ר' יוחנן בן נורי ורבנן דתנן *שמן שצף על גבי יין ונגע טבול יום בשמן לא פסל אלא שמן ר' יוחנן בן נורי אומר שניהם חיבור זה לזה אמר אביי *בור ברה"ר עמוקה עשרה ורחבה שמנה וזרק לתוכה מחצלת חייב °חילקה במחצלת פטור לאביי דפשיטא ליה דמחצלת מבטלא מחיצה כל שכן חוליא דמבטלא מחיצה לרבי יוחנן דמיבעיא ליה חוליא מחצלת פשיטא דלא מבטלא מחיצת' ואמר אביי [ב]בור ברה"ר עמוקה עשרה ורחבה ארבעה מלאה מים וזרק לתוכה חייב מלאה פירות וזרק לתוכה פטור מ"ט מים לא מבטלי מחיצתא פירות מבטלי מחיצתא תניא נמי הכי הזורק מן הים לאיסרטיא ומן האיסרטיא לים פטור ר"ש אומר אם יש במקום שזורק עמוק עשרה ורחב ארבעה חייב: **מתני'** *[ג]הזורק ארבע אמות בכותל למעלה מעשרה טפחים כזורק באויר למטה מעשרה טפחים כזורק בארץ הזורק בארץ ארבע אמות חייב: **גמ'** *והא לא נח א"ר יוחנן [ד]בדבילה שמינה שנינו א"ר יהודה אמר רב א"ר חייא *זרק למעלה מעשרה והלכה ונחה בחור כל שהוא באנו למחלוקת ר' מאיר ורבנן לר"מ דאמר *חוקקין להשלים מיחייב לרבנן דאמרי [ה]אין חוקקין להשלים לא מיחייב תניא נמי הכי זרק למעלה מעשרה והלכה ונחה בחור כל שהוא ר"מ מחייב וחכמים פוטרין א"ר יהודה אמר רב תל [ו]המתלקט עשרה מתוך ארבע וזרק ונח על גביו חייב תנ"ה [ז]מבוי ששוה לתוכו ונעשה מדרון לרה"ר או שוה לרה"ר ונעשה מדרון לתוכו אותו מבוי אינו צריך לא לחי ולא קורה דבי חנינא בן גמליאל אומר תל המתלקט עשרה מתוך ארבע וזרק ונח על גביו חייב: **מתני'** [ח]זרק לתוך ד' אמות ונתגלגל חוץ לד' אמות פטור חוץ לד' אמות ונתגלגל לתוך ד' אמות חייב: **גמ'** והא לא נח אמר ר' יוחנן [ט]והוא שנח על גבי משהו [עירובין לג:] תניא נמי הכי זרק חוץ לד' אמות ודחפתו הרוח והכניסתו ואע"פ שחזרה והוציאתו פטור אחזתו הרוח משהו אף על פי שחזרה והכניסתו חייב *אמר רבא [י]תוך ג' לרבנן צריך הנחה על גבי משהו יתיב מרימר וקאמר לה להא שמעתא אמר ליה רבינא למרימר לאו

רש"י

לאו היינו הנחתן · ואם נטלו משם לאו עקירה היא: שמן על גבי יין · לענין שבת מחלוקת ר' יוחנן בן נורי ורבנן: דתנן שמן · של תרומה: שצף על גבי יין · של תרומה משום הכי נקט טבול יום משום דפוסל ואינו מטמא הלכך לא פסל אלא שמן בלבד דלאו חיבור הוא למיהוי כחד ואילו הוה טמא הוה מטמא ליה לשמן ושמן פסל ליה ליין: שניהם חיבור · דהוי כחד ופסל אף היין ולענין שבת נמי לרבנן הוה ליה כאגוז על גבי מים ולרבי יוחנן הוה ליה כמים על גבי מים: וזרק לתוכה מחצלת · משום סיפא נקט ליה דבעי למימר חלקה במחצלת פטור לאשמעי' דהנחת חפץ וסילוק מחיצה בהדדי פטור והכא סילוק מחיצה דזיל הכא ליכא ארבעה וזיל הכא ליכא ד' דבצר ליה עובי מקום מחצלת: כל שכן חוליא · דסילוק מחיצה ודאי הוא דמבטיל לה: לרבי יוחנן (א) מחצלת פשיטא ליה דלא מבטלה · דאי נמי אמרינן סילוק מחיצה והנחת חפץ כי הדדי פטור הכא חייב דלא מבטל ליה הלכך לאו סילוק מחיצה היא: וזרק לתוכה · מרה"ר מידי דנייחא כגון אבן או מים: חייב · ולא אמרינן כיון דמלא הוא לא הוי רה"י דמבטל להו מחיצות: מלאה פירות · פטור דבטיל מחיצות כאילו מלאוה עפר: תניא נמי הכי · דמים לא מבטלי מחיצה: מן הים לאיסרטיא · מכרמלית לרה"ר פטור: איסרטיא · הוא סרטיא: ר"ש אומר אם יש · בים במקום שזורק גומא מיוחדת לבדה עמוקה עשרה ורחבה ד' רה"י לעצמה היא ולא הוי כשאר ים אף על גב דים נמי עמוק הוא וממילא שמעינן מדר"ש דמים לא מבטלי מחיצה: **גמ'** רבי מאיר ורבנן · דאיפליגו בחוקקים להשלים בפ"ק דיומא (דף יא:) ובעירובין (ד' יא:) לר"מ דאמר חוקקין להשלים במקו' שיש כדי לחוק הכא חייב דרואין הבור כאלו הוא ארבע: תל המתלקט · שהוא מדרון והולך ומתלקט מעט מעט עד שמגביה י' מתוך ד"א הרי הוא כאלו זקוף כולו והוי רה"י במקום גובהו ואם זרק מרה"ר ונח על גביו חייב ודוקא נקט מתוך ד' אמות דאי מתוך ה' הרי הוא כשאר רשות הרבים דניחא תשמישתיה להילוך: ונעשה מדרון לרה"ר · שהיה קרקע המבוי גבוה מקרקע רה"ר והולך ומשפע אצל פתחו לצד רה"ר או שהיה שוה לרה"ר ונעשה מדרון לתוכה שהיה רה"ר גבוה מקרקע המבוי וכניסת המבוי נמי מן הפתח ולפנים גבוה כקרקע רה"ר ברחב אמה או חצי אמה ואח"כ הוא נעשה מדרון לצד דופן האמצעי: אותו מבוי אינו צריך לחי · דאותו גובה שבצד הפתח הוה ליה מחיצה אף על פי שהוא משפע והולך: **מתני'** זרק חוץ לד"א ונתגלגל כו' חייב · לא שנפל לארץ דא"כ לא איצטריך למימר אלא שהרוח גלגלתהו מן האויר לתוך ד' אמות: **גמ'** והא לא נח · חוץ לד' ואמאי אזלינן בתרה: שנח ע"ג משהו · שעמד קצת ואח"כ נתגלגל והוא הדין אם אחזתו הרוח באויר ועכבתו מעט ואחר כך הכניסתו דחשיב נמי הנחה אם בתוך ג' הוא: ודחפתו הרוח · בעודו באויר: אחזתו משהו · הרוח עכבתו במקומו מעט: לרבנן · דפליגי עליה דר"ע *בזורק מרה"י לרה"י ורה"ר באמצע דלית להו קלוטה כמי שהונחה לא תימא בתוך ג' מודו אלא אפילו תוך ג' נמי צריך שינוח ואם עבר רה"ר כולה פטור ונפקא מינה נמי לזורק ד' אמות וכשבא לנוח והגיע לתוך ג' נזכר שגגתו עד שלא נח פטור כדאמרינן במתני' (דף קב·) עד שתהא תחלתו וסופו שגגה ולא אמרינן עד שלא נזכר הוה ליה מונח:

תוספות

פירות מבטלי מחיצתא · וא"ת ומ"ש מדבילה שמינה דאמרינן לעיל דלא מבטלי ואביי דהכא אית ליה שינויא דבדבילה שמינה שנו כדאמר בפ"ק (דף ז:) זימנין משני ליה בכותל דלית ביה חור ובדבילה שמינה כו' וי"ל דדבילה אינה עומדת כל כך להתבטל שם בכותל כמו שרגילין לבטל פירות בבור כעין תבואה אי נמי דבילה דבר מועט הוא ולא מבטלא אבל בור מלא פירות או חציו מבטל רה"י וה"ה דגרעין אחד או דבר מועט לא מבטל רה"י וא"ת היכי ממעטי הני פירות והא אמר בפרק חלון (עירובין עח:) כל דבר הניטל בשבת אינו ממעט ואפי' אי איירי הכא בטבל שאין ניטל בשבת מ"מ כיון דניטל מן התורה הזורק לתוכו אמאי פטור ואומר ר"י דמן התורה ממעט כל דבר ואפילו הניטל ומדרבנן הוא דגזרו דדבר הניטל אינו ממעט ולהכי לא קאמר מותר לזרוק בתוכו אלא קאמר הזורק לתוכו פטור משמע דאיסורא דרבנן איכא ואפילו בחריץ שבין שתי חצרות אמרו דדבר הניטל אינו ממעט אע"ג דהוי לקולא דלא אסרי אהדדי אבל ק"ק דבפרק חלון (שם) מייתי על בית שמילאוהו תבן דהוי לענין אהל דאורייתא:

והלכה ונחה בחור כל שהוא כו' · בחור מפולש איירי והאי חוקקין להשלים היינו לשוויה מקום ד' כדפי' בפ"ק (דף ז:): **והא** לא נח · וא"ת מאי פריך והתניא לעיל (ד' צז·) תוך ג' ד"ה חייב אע"ג דלא נח ואין נראה לומר דאתוך ד' אמות קאי אמאי פטור הא לא נח וא"כ כשנח אחר כך חוץ לארבע יתחייב דהא (מתניתין) [מכילתין] נמי הכי משמע דאחוץ לד' אמות פריך אמאי חייב וי"ל דפריך לרבא דאמר תוך שלשה לרבנן בעי הנחה ע"ג משהו:

אחזתו הרוח משהו כו' · פי' שעיכבתו ע"ג קרקע או אפי' באויר כדפי' בקונט' דחשיבה אחיזת הרוח כמונח על גבי משהו ונראה דע"ג קרקע (ב) אפי' לר' יהודה דהיינו רבנן דקאמר רבא דצריך הנח' מודה (ג) *)דלא בעינן כדפי' לעיל (דף פ·) ומיהו ק"ק דבסמוך מסקינן איפכא דמתגלגל כיון דאין סופו לנוח לאו כמונח דמי אבל האי כיון דסופו לנוח כמונח דמי וחזר ר"י לפרש דודאי רבי יהודה סבר כר"ע דקלוטה כמו שהונחה (ד) היכא דבעי שתנוח שם כי ההוא דפירקין אבל בההוא דפרק בתרא דעירובין (ד' צז:) היה קורא בספר דלא בעי שתפול שם בעי ר' יהודה הנחה על גבי משהו ורבא קאמר דרבנן דר"ע לית להו קלוטה כמו שהונחה דמיא בשום מקום אפי' רצונו שתנוח שם אפילו תוך ג' ולא ס"ל כברייתא דלעיל דקתני תוך ג' ד"ה חייב אלא סבר כברייתא דהכא דקתני אחזתו הרוח משהו ומתניתין נמי משמע דאיירי בנח משהו כדאוקי ר' יוחנן דומיא דרישא דקתני תוך ד' אמות פטור דאיירי בשנח דאי לאו הכי אמאי מיפטר ורב חלקיה בר טוביה דאמר לעיל תוך שלשה ד"ה חייב מוקי מתניתין בדלא נח ורישא דקתני פטור מיירי כגון שפסק כחו ומחמת הרוח נתגלגל חוץ לארבע:

*) דלא בעינן הנחה כדפי' לעיל דיש חילוק בין מתגלגל ובין אינו מתגלגל כצ"ל

עין משפט נר מצוה

יט א מיי' פי"ד מהל' שבת הלכה כב:
כ ב שם הלכה כג:
כא ג מיי' שם הל' יח סמג לאוין סה טוש"ע א"ח סי' שמה סעיף יב:
כב ד מיי' שם:
כג ה מיי' שם הלכה י וסמג לאוין שם טוש"ע שם סעיף יוד:
כד ו מיי' שם הל' טז:
כה ז מיי' פי"ז שם הל' ד טוש"ע א"ח סי' שסג סעיף לו:
כו ח ט מיי' פי"ג שם הלכה כב:
כז י מיי' שם הל' טז [וע"ש בכ"מ]:

רבינו חננאל

אסקופה מאי היא ואוקימנא [באסקופת] כרמלית ואקשינן עלה סוף סוף איסורא דרבנן איכא ושנינן דלית בה ד' על ד' וכר' יוחנן דאמר מקום שאין בו ד' על ד' מותר לבני רה"ר ולבני רה"י לכתף עליו ובלבד שלא יחליפו השתא דתנינן בחולית הבור והסלע פחות מכאן פטור אם הן פחות בגובה ואין פחות ברוחב הוא פטור אבל אסור ואם פחות ברוחב פטור ומותר בלבד שלא יחליף ודייקינן למה ליה למיתנא חולית הבור והסלע מסייעא ליה לר' יוחנן דאמר בור וחוליתו מצטרפין לעשרה והא דר' יוחנן בהמוצא תפלין (ד' צט) בענין בור ברשות הרבים וחולייתו גבוהה י' טפחים והיכי דמי כגון תל ברה"ר וחקק בו עד ארעית (כנגד) רה"ר מקצתו עשאו ביד ומקצתו עשאו חוליא על הבור וארעית הבור עם רה"ר שוה לו והבור עצמו גבוהה מרה"ר וחולייתו למעלה ממנו אם גבוה הבור וחולייתו שניהם יחדיו עשרה טפחים הרי הן מצטרפין ולמעלה מן החוליא רשות אחרת: וגרסינן בירושל' דקדוק אחד א"ר יוחנן (העומד) [העמוד] והחלול מצטרפין לארבעה והוא שהיה (העומד)[העמוד] רובה עלהחלל והחלל והוא פתיחת הבור (והעומד) [והעמוד] הוא רחב החוליא העומדת שהיא שפת הבור אם נמצא מן השפה אל השפה ד' טפחים אע"פ שיש חלל באמצע הרי הוא רה"י כמו שפירשנו: **בעא** רב מרדכי מרבה עמוד ברה"ר גבוה י' ורחב ד' וזרק ונח על גביו מהו בעיא זו עיקרא כי רה"ר תופשות עד עשרה ומי' ולמעלה מקום פטור הוא לפיכך אם הגביה אדם חפץ מרה"ר ולא הגביהו יותר מי' טפחים אלא לאלתר שהגיע לעשרה הניחו ע"ג העמוד חייב אבל זרקו למעלה מי' מעקם כשהוא ברה"ר ויש במחשבתו שאם יפול ינוח ברה"י אלא שבזריקתו יצא ברה"ר למקום פטור שהוא האויר ואח"כ חזר ונפל ונח ברה"י מי אמרינן הרי עקירה ברה"ר והנחה ברה"י ועביד עקירה והנחה נכנס למקום פטור חייב או דלמא כיון דמקום פטור הוא דקא אתיא פטור ופשטו ליה רבה ורב יוסף ואביי מתניתין היא הלא תראה חוליית הבור והסלע שגבוהין י' ורחבין ד' מכונין הנותן על גבו חייב וכן הנוטל מעל גבו חייב ואי אפשר הנותן והנושא שאין מגביה משהו וימצא יוצא למעלה מעשרה ואח"כ יורד ונח בחוליא או לסלע וכן הנוטל מעל גבו ומניח ברה"ר ואעפ"כ חייב ואקשינן עלייהו ודלמא מתניתין בדבר דק כמו מחט דאפשר למשקליה ולאתוייה בלא הגבהה השיבו לו מחט נמי אי אפשר דלא מידלא פורתא והני מילי דהיות הן ושניא הא שמעתא מדרב חסדא דיציאות השבת כדבעינן לפרושי לקמן **א"ר** מיאשא בעו ר' יוחנן כותל ברה"ר גבוה עשרה ואינו רוחב ד' ומוקף כרמלית ועשאו רה"י וזרק ונח על גביו מהו פי' כגון שהיה הכותל מחיצה בין רה"ר לכרמלית אח"כ בנה כותל בכרמלית שכנגדו ועשה הכרמלית ההיא רה"י מי אמרינן הרי הכותל זה בחזקתו וכיון שאין בו רחב ד' מקום פטור הוא או דלמא כיון שעשאו [רה"י] כמאן דמליא שאר ד"מ דמי ופשטינן כשהיה כותל לכרמלית מקום פטור היה והשתא דהוה ליה כותל רה"י כיון שנח עליו כמאן דנח ברה"י דמי שאם זה הכותל הוא שעושה הכרמלית ההוא רה"י כ"ש שיעשה הכותל ההוא רה"י וכן אמר עולא ק"ו לאחרים נעשה מחיצה לעצמו לא כ"ש וסלקא בהאי טעמא: **בעי** ר' יוחנן בור ברה"ר עמוקה ט' ועקר חוליא ממנו שיש בה טפח ובעקירת החוליא נגמר הבור רה"י כדתניא הריץ עמוק עשרה ורחב ד' זו היא רה"י גמורה והניח החוליא ההוא ברה"ר מאי מי אמרינן עקירת חפץ ממקומו ועשיית מחיצה בהדי הדדי קא אתינן וחייב או לא ופשיטא אם תמצי לומר כיון דבשעת עקירה לא מרה"י עקר ובעקירתו הוא דהוה רה"י לא מחייב אבל זו הבעיא השנית אם הבור עמוק עשרה שהוא רה"י גמורה ועקר חוליא מרה"ר ונתנה לתוכה ובנתינת החוליא לתוכו נתמעט הבור מעשרה מי אמרינן כיון דבשעת התחלת הנחה רה"י גמורה הוא מיחייב או דלמא כיון שבהנחת החוליא נסתלקה המחיצה ונתמעט הבור פטור*) ואקשינן והא לא נח וא"ר יוחנן בדבילה שמינה שנו הלא כיון שעמד ברחוק ד' אמות מצובצבות מן הכותל וזרק בכותל דבילה שמינה ונדבקה בכותל הרי מיעטה הדבילה הד' אמות שבינו ובין הכותל אעפ"כ הוא חייב הכא נמי כיון שהניח החוליא בבור עמוק י' אע"פ שמיעטו החוליא והא חייב ופרקינן שאני התם דדבילה לא מבטל לה ודעתו לנופלה לפיכך לא ממעטא אבל החוליא בטולי מבטל לה לגבי בור ויש לומר

*) נראה דחסר כאן בד' רבינו וצ"ל ותפשוט ליה מדידיה דתנן הזורק וכו' למטה מי' טפחים כזורק בארץ

מסורת הש"ס

לעיל דף כ:
נדה סו: עירובין דף עח: [טבול יום פ"ב מ"ה]
לעיל ז: צז:
[עיל ז: ולהלן:]
ע"ז שם
ע"ז שם וש"נ

הגהות הב"ח

(א) רש"י ד"ה כ"ש וכו' דמבטל לה לרבי יוחנן מחיצות מחצלת פשיטא ליה כצ"ל והד"א: (ב) תוס' ד"ה אחזתו וכו' ונראה דע"ג קרקע. נ"ב כמ"ש אפי' במתגלגל ואפי' לא אחזתו רוח: (ג) בא"ד דלא בעינן כדפי' לעיל. נ"ב בפ' המצניע דף פ ע"ב ד"ה והא אמר: (ד) בא"ד כמו שהונחה דמיא היכא וכו' הסיל דפירקין. נ"ב בדלעיל:

גליון הש"ס

גמ' חולקה במחצלת. עיין בחידושי הרשב"א כאן ע"א ד"ה רחבה שם: [לעיל צז.]

עין משפט
נר מצוה

כח א מיי' פי"ד מהל' שבת הל' ד ויא סמג לאוין סה טוש"ע א"ח סי' שמה סעיף יד:

כט ב ג מיי' שם הל' כד:

ל ד מיי' פ"ג מהלכות עירובין הלכה כה:

לא ה ו מיי' פי"ד מהל' שבת הלכה ה ופט"ו הלכה כ סמג שם טוש"ע א"ח סי' שמה סעיף יח וסי' שנה סעיף א:

[לא] [ז] [מיי' פט"ו שם הלכה יט סמג שם טוש"ע א"ח ריש סי' שנה]

גמרא

לאו היינו מתני' וא"ר יוחנן והוא שנח [א] ע"ג משהו א"ל מתגלגל קאמרת מתגלגל אין סופו לנוח אבל האי כיון דסופו לנוח אע"ג דלא נח כמאן דנח דמי קמ"ל: **מתני'** ״הזורק בים ארבע אמות פטור ״אם *היה רקק מים ורשות הרבים מהלכת בו הזורק לתוכו ד' אמות חייב וכמה הוא רקק מים פחות מעשרה טפחים רקק מים ורשות הרבים מהלכת בו הזורק בתוכו ד' אמות חייב: **גמ'** א"ל ההוא מרבנן לרבא בשלמא הילוך הילוך תרי זימני הא קמ"ל הילוך ע"י הדחק שמיה הילוך תשמיש ע"י הדחק לא שמיה תשמיש אלא רקק רקק תרי זימני למה לי חד בימות החמה וחד בימות הגשמים וצריכי דאי תנא חדא ה"א ה"מ בימות החמה דעבידי אינשי דמסגי לאקורי נפשייהו אבל בימות הגשמים לא ואי אשמעינן בימות הגשמים דכיון דמיטנפי לא איכפת להו אבל בימות החמה לא אביי אמר ״איצטריך סד"א ה"מ היכא דלא הוי ד' אמות אבל היכא דהוי ד' אמות אקופי מקפי ליה רב אשי אמר איצטריך ס"ד אמינא ה"מ היכא דהוה ד' אבל היכא דלא הואי ארבעה מיפסעי פסעי ליה ואזדא רב אשי לטעמיה דאמר רב אשי האי מאן דזריק ונח אגודא דגמלא מיחייב שהרי רבים בוקעין בו: **מתני'** הזורק מן הים ליבשה ומן היבשה לים ומן הים לספינה ומן הספינה לים ומן הספינה לחבירתה פטור ״ספינות קשורות זו בזו מטלטלין מזו לזו אם אינן קשורות אע"פ שמוקפות אין מטלטלין מזו לזו: **גמ'** איתמר ספינה רב הונא אמר מוציאין הימנה זיז כל שהוא וממלא רב חסדא ורבה בר רב הונא אמרי ״עושה מקום ארבעה וממלא רב הונא אמר מוציא הימנה זיז כל שהוא וממלא קסבר כרמלית מארעא משחינן ואוירא מקום פטור הוא ובדין הוא דזיז נמי לא ליבעי אלא כי היכי דליהוי ליה היכרא רב חסדא ורבה בר רב הונא אמרי עושה מקום ארבעה וממלא קסברי ״כרמלית משפת מיא משחינן *מיא ארעא סמיכתא אי לא עביד מקום ארבעה קא מטלטל מכרמלית לרה"י א"ל רב נחמן לרבה בר אבוה ולרב הונא דאמר מוציא הימנה זיז כל שהוא וממלא זימנין דליכא עשרה וקא מטלטל מכרמלית לרה"י אמר ליה גמרינן דאין ספינה מהלכת בפחות מעשרה והא מורשא אית לה אמר רב ספרא גשושי אזלי קמה א"ל רב נחמן בר יצחק לרב חייא בר אבין לרב חסדא ולרבה בר רב הונא דאמרי עושה מקום ארבעה וממלא שופכין דידיה היכי שדי להו וכ"ת דשדי להו באותו מקום מאיסי ליה [ז] דשדי להו אדפנא דספינה והא איכא כחו *כחו בכרמלית לא גזרו ומנא תימרא דתניא ספינה אין מטלטלין לא מתוכה לים ולא מן הים לתוכה רבי

רש"י

לאו היינו מתניתין · דקתני חוץ לארבע אמות ונתגלגל כו' חייב ואמר רבי יוחנן והא שנח הא לא נח לא מדלא אוקמא רבי יוחנן כגון שבא לתוך ג': מתגלגל קאמרת · דבר שהרוח מגלגלו באויר קאמרת: כיון דסופו לנוח · ונזכר עד שלא נח נימא כמונח דמי דהא סופו לנוח וכבר בא לתוך ג':

מתני' וכמה הוא רקק מים · כמה עומקו דנימא אכתי רה"ר הוא ולא נעשה כרמלית · רקק גרבילא"א:

גמ' הילוך הילוך · דנקט תרי זימני רשות הרבים מהלכת בו חד למימרא דאי אין רגילין להלך בו פטור וכי רגילין להלך בו חייב ואע"ג דהילוך ע"י הדחק הוא וחד לאשמעינן דדוקא הילוך ע"י הדחק שמיה הילוך אבל תשמיש לרבים ע"י הדחק כגון גומא תשעה ברה"ר אע"ג דחזיא לאצנועי ביה כומתא וסודרא לא הוי תשמיש למיהוי ההוא גומא רה"ר כעמוד ט' שהרבים מכתפין עליו דאמרינן בפ"ק דהוי רה"ר: אלא רקק תרי זימני למה לי·לאשמעינן הילוך על ידי הדחק אחרינא: דלא הוי ד' אמות · רחב דלא טריחא להו מילתא לעבור בתוכו ונוח לעבור מלהקיף ולילך לראשו שהוא כלה שם: אבל היכא כו'· הדר תניא זימנא אחריתי לאיתויי הא: ה"מ · דהוי ר"ה: היכא דהוי רחבו ד' אמות · דלאו אורחיה למפסעי אלא עברי בגויה: אגודא דגמלא · על דף שבגשר המוטל לרוחב הגשר כשאר הדפים ומובדל מחבירו: חייב · ואע"ג דאיכא דמיפסעו פסעי ולא מנחי כרעייהו עלה איכא טובא דעברי עליה:

מתני' מן הים ליבשה · מכרמלית לר"ה: מן הים לספינה · מכרמלית לרה"י: מטלטלין מזו לזו · ובגמרא פריך פשיטא: שמוקפות · סמוכות זו לזו כמו אין מקיפין שתי חביות (ביצה דף לב:): אין מטלטלין מזו לזו · דמהפסק כרמלית מיפרשי מהדדי ואנן מוקמינן לה בגמרא שהספינות של שני בני אדם וע"י עירוב מטלטל מזו לזו הלכך כי מיפרשי ומפסקה כרמלית בטל עירוב: **גמ'** ספינה · המפרש בספינה בים: מוציא זיז כל שהוא · מדופני הספינה על המים להיכר בעלמא כדמפרש ואזיל: וממלא · מן הים ומכניס לספינה: מקום ארבעה · חלל ד' מוקף מחיצות קטנות ומחיצה תלויה מתרת במים: כרמלית מארעא משחינן · י' של אויר שנתנו חכמים לאיסור כרמלית כדאמרינן בפ"ק (דף ז·) ותופסת עד י' מקרקעית הים משחינן להו ואוירא שהוא למעלה מי' ואפילו הן מים הוי מקום פטור הלכך בהיתירא קא שקיל לכתחלה: דליהוי ליה היכרא · לכרמלית גמורה: ארעא סמיכתא היא · וכל המים כרמלית הן:

סמיכתא · עבה: זימנין דליכא · במים עמוקה עשרה ואי נמי מארעא משחינן כולה כרמלית היא: גמירי אין ספינה מהלכת כו' · דכל היכא דתניא ספינה ולא תני עריבה גדולה היא: והא מורשא אית לה גרסי' · ראש הספינה הולך ומגביה מן המים ואפילו (א) היו המים פחותין מי' אין גוששת שם ואם ממלא כנגד אותו מקום מטלטל מכרמלית לרה"י: גשושי אזלי קמה · בני אדם ממשמשים בכלונסות את עומק המים ואין מניחין לילך הספינה אלא במקום עמוק שמא תמהר לילך ותשכון לארץ במקום מושבה: עושה לה מקום ד' · אלמא כל המים כרמלית הן: שופכין דידיה · מים רעים כגון רחיצת כוסות וקערות: מאיסי ליה · המים שימלא שוב דרך אותו מקום: דשדי להו · בכ"מ שירלה על דופני הספינה והן יורדין לים: והא איכא כחו · כהי דלא זריק להדיא לים מיהו מכחו הן באין לים: עמוקה

תוספות

עושה מקום ארבעה וממלא · פירש בקונטרס עושה מחיצות קטנות ואין נראה לר"ת ולר"י דהא תנן בפרק כילד משתתפים (עירובין דף פז:) גזוזטרא שהיא למעלה מן המים אין ממלאין ממנה מים בשבת אא"כ עשו לה מחיצה גבוה י' ט' אלא עושה מקום (ב) היינו שיהיה הזיז רחב ארבע טפחים כדי שלא יהיו המחילות עשויות לפחות מארבע ולמאן דשרי הכא בזיז כל שהוא לא תקשי דמוקי התם כשאין המים עמוקים י' אי נמי התם גזרינן שמא יעלה הים שירטון כדגזרינן בפרק קמא דעירובין (דף ח·) אבל ספינה לעולם אין מהלכת בפחות מי' ולא שייך למגזר:

גמירי דאין ספינה מהלכת למטה מי' · והא דקאמר בפרק מי שהוליאוהו (עירובין דף מג·) במהלכת ברקק התם מיירי בספינה קטנה אבל הכא בספינות גדולות שטוענין אותן ביותר ונשקעות הרבה במים ואין מהלכות בפחות מי' °ומיהו נ"ל דאף הכלי שדולה בו ונשקע במים הוי למעלה מי' דאי לאו הכי היאך ממלא:

ודילמא מורשא אית לה · פירש ר"ח דילמא יש מורשא לקרקע שסמוך לספינה שהקרקע גבוה שם ואם יוליא דרך שם יהיה למטה מעשרה במקום מילואו כיון שהקרקע גבוה שם אבל רש"י דמפרש מורשא דספינה לא יתכן לשון ודילמא דגרסינן בכל הספרים וגרסינן והא מורשא אית לה:

כחו בכרמלית לא גזרו רבנן · והכי נמי משני בפרק תולין (לקמן דף קמא·) גבי האי מאן דסחי במיא כו' · וק' לר"י דבפרק כילד משתתפין (עירובין דף פה·) אמרי' גבי גזוזטרא שהיא למעלה מן המים לא שנו אלא למלאות אבל לשפוך אסור משום שהמים נדחין מכחו חוץ לארבע אמות אלמא כחו בכרמלית אסור ויש לומר דגזוזטרא פעמים שהיא סמוכה למקום שרה"ר מהלכת וגזרו כחו בכרמלית משום כחו ברשות הרבים אבל בספינה לעולם הוי כחו בכרמלית לא גזרו:

רבינו חננאל

לומר דממעטא בבור ופטור ווו איבעיא לא אפשטא: **בעי** רבא זרק דף ע"ג יתידות כגון פרסקל בראש קנה דנעשה רה"י ואמרינן מאי קא מיבעיא ליה הנחת חפץ ועשיית מחיצה בהדי הדדי היינו בעיא דר' יוחנן ראיבעיא ולא אפשיטא אלא כי קא מיבעיא ליה לרבא כגון שורק דף ויש על גביו חפץ ונח הדף על גבי יתידות והחפץ על גביו מי אמרינן אפי' זה כהנחת חפץ ובהנחתו נעשית מחיצה דמי או דלמא כיון דלא אפשר שלא מידלא החפץ מעט ואח"כ יפול על הדף נמצא שנעשה מחיצה ואח"כ נותן החפץ עליו וחייב ועלתה בתיקו: **אמר** רבא פשיטא לי זרק מים על גבי מים או שעקר מים מרה"י והניחן על גבי מים ברה"ר חייב ווו היא הנחתן זרק או שהניח אגוז על גביהן וצף על גביהן לאו הנחה היא ופטור ואגוז בכלי וכלי ע"ג המים לא אפשיטא שמן על גבי מים פלוגתא דרבי יוחנן בן נורי ורבנן: **אמר** אביי בור ברה"ר עמוק עשרה ורחב ח' זרק לתוכה מחצלת חייב דעדיין חדא רשותא היא אבל נתכוון לחלקה במחצלת הוויין להו ב' בורות ומעוקין עשרה ואין בכל אחד רחב ד' שהרי מיעטן המחצלת מלהיות בכל אחד ד' ויצא מתורת רה"י והרי הן מקום פטור והא דאביי פליגא אדר' יוחנן דהא ר' יוחנן בעי ליה הולא מבטלא מחיצתא או לא וכיון דהולא מיבעיא ליה מחצלת פשיטא ליה דודאי לא מבטלא מחיצתא ועדיין רה"י היא ולאביי דפשיטא ליה דמבטלא מחיצתא כ"ש הולא דודאי מבטלא מ"ט דמיבעיא ליה לר' יוחנן פשיטא ליה לאביי ואם בבור לא ממעטי לה ולא מבטלי מחיצות אבל פירות (שביכר השומן) [שכבירה ושמין] בבור אם נתכלום למעל' פטור דפירי מבטלי מחיצתא וה"מ דבטלינהו גבי בור אבל אי אצנעינהו לפירי בבור למהדר ולמיכל מינייהו לבתר הכי לא ממעטי בבור: **מתני'** הזורק ד' אמות בכותל אם נתכוון לזרוק למעלה מעשרה טפחים בכותל הרי הוא כזורק באויר והזורק באויר פטור ואם נתכוון למטה מי' טפחים בכותל הרי הוא כזורק בארץ והזורק בארץ ד' אמות חייב ואקשינן עלה הזורק למטה מי' טפחים חייב והא לא נח ואוקמא ר' יוחנן בזורק דבילה שמינה שיש בה לחלוחית ונדבקת בכותל חייב שהרי נגמרת מחשבתו כאשר ניסוחה זו היא הנחתה הא דאמר ר' חייא זרק למעלה מי' טפחים בכותל והלכה ונחה בחור שהוא מחלוקת ר' מאיר ורבנן . פירוש כגון שהיה זה החור עצמו כגבוה י' טפחים ומקרקעית החור ולמטה עשרה טפחים מכוונים ואלו היה בחור ד' על ד' דברי הכל כרה"י וחייב הזורק מרה"ר לתוכו ושמעתין בחור דלית ביה ד' על ד' דר' מאיר סבר כל כי האי גוונא חוקקין להשלים וכיון שיש בעובי הכותל לחוק ולהשלימו לחור היה ד' על ד' רואין בכוונת הלב כאלו חקוק הוא ויש בו ד' על ד' וחייב והכ"א אם יש בחור הזה ד' על ד' [חייב] אבל לחוק ולהשלים אין חוקקין כי האי גוונא חקיקה בלבו אלא הרי הוא כגדר גבוה י' טפחים ואינו רחב ד' שהזורק לתוכו פטור והא דר' מאיר וחכמים מפורש בפרק א' דעירובין כיפה ר' מאיר מחייב במזוזה וחכמים פוטרין ושוין שאם יש ברגליה עשרה שחייבת אמר אביי הכל מודין אין ברגליה שלשה ולא כלום יש ברגליה ג' ואינה רחבה ד' ולא כלום הוא כי פליגי היכא דרחבה ד' ויש ברגליה ג' ואינה גבוה י' ויש בה לחוק ולהשלימה לעשרה דר"מ סבר חוקקין להשלים וחכמים סברי אין חוקקין להשלים וזה הוא (ביוה"כ) (בסוכה) פרק א' דחוקקין להשלים ומפורש נמי בפרק המוצא תפלין בעניין מפתח שהוא למעלה מעשרה . אמר אביי ש"מ מהא מתניתא תלת וחדא מינייהו חוקקין להשלים: **ירושלמי** אם יש חור בכותל מחלוקת ר' מאיר וחכמים על דעתיה דר' מאיר יש בו ד' על ד' בין אין בו את רואה את הכותל כנמום על דעתיהו דרבנן אין את רואה את הכותל כנמום אלא כסתום . והך דרב חסדא דיציאות השבת דאמר נעץ קנה ברה"י וזרק ונח על גביו חייב אפי' גבוה מאה אמה שרה"י שלה עולה עד לרקיע לא דמיא להא לא ליבעיא דמרדכי ולא להא דר' חייא דהני בעמוד עומד ברה"ר וחלק רשות לעצמו בגובהו וכותל שהוא ברה"ר ונח בחור שהוא למעלה מי' טפחים אבל דרב חסדא בעמוד ברה"י ועקר אדם חפץ מרה"ר וזורק ברה"י למעלה ונח ע"ג עמוד שהוא ברה"י אפילו ע"ג ק' אמה חייב שכבר זרק מרה"ר לרה"י וקא אמרי' בה אמר אביי ברה"י כ"ע לא פליגי כדרב חסדא והאי חור אם היה בתוך י' לא חשיב לא כרה"ר ולא כרה"י דאתמר הורי רה"ר אביי אמר כרה"ר דמו רבא אמר לא כרה"ר דמו והאי דתנן למטה מי' טפחים כזורק בארץ דקא מוקי לה ר' יוחנן בדבילה שמינה איתיביה רבא לאביי מינה וא"ל אי ס"ד חורי רה"ר כרה"ר למה לי לאוקמה בדבילה שמינה לוקמה בחור . זמנין משני ליה אביי שאני צרור וחפץ דעבידי דהדרי זמנין משני ליה בכותל דלית ביה חור ממאי מדקתני רישא למעלה מי' טפחים כזורק באויר ואי ס"ד בכותל דאית ביה חור אמאי כזורק באויר לוקמא דנח בחור וכי תימא דלית ביה ד' והא רב יהודה אמר רב א"ר חייא זרק למעלה מי' ונח בחור כל שהוא באנו למחלוקת ר"מ ורבנן אלא לאו ש"מ בכותל דלית ביה חור ואע"ג דאביי פריק לנפשיה הלכתא כרבא: **אמר** רב יהודה אמר רב תל המתלקט י"ט מתוך ד' אמות וזרק ונח על גביו חייב · פי' אדם שעומד ברה"ר ועקר מרה"ר והניחו בתל זה כיון דקיי"ל גדר ברה"ר גבוה י' רחבו ד' זו היא רה"י גמורה האי תל נמי רה"י הוא והיכא דמי מתלקט כגון שצידו אחד עומד בנידור י' טפחים מן הארץ כגדר והצד שכנגדו משופע כסדרון וכמין כבש שמתוך ד' אמות בשיפוע המדרגה גובה ועולה י' טפחים כגון זה ד' אמות י' טפחים הציור . אם נח החפץ הזורק על גובהו של תל זה שהוא גובה י' טפחים אע"פ

הגהות הב"ח

(א) רש"י ד"ה והא מורשא וכו' ואפי' המים הן פחותין: (ב) תוס' ד"ה עושה וכו' עושה מקום ארבעה היינו:

הגהות הגר"א

[א] גמרא והוא שנח ע"ג משהו: נ"ב צ"ל והוא שנח משהו:

גליון הש"ס

תוס' ד"ה גמירי ומיהו נ"ל. עיין מג"א סימן רמח סק"ג ביאור להמשך דברי תוספות אלו:

מסורת הש"ס

לעיל ח:
[גיטין ח.]
[לקמן קמא.]

Rabina to Meremar: [100b] Is this not [to be deduced from] our Mishnah, whereon R. Johanan commented, Providing it rests on something, whatever its size?[3]—You speak of [a] rolling [object], replied he; [a] rolling [object] is not destined to rest; but this, since it is destined to rest,[4] [I might argue that] though it did not come to rest, it is as though it had rested:[5] therefore he informs us [that it is not so].

MISHNAH. IF ONE THROWS [AN OBJECT OVER A DISTANCE OF] FOUR CUBITS IN THE SEA, HE IS NOT LIABLE. IF THERE IS A WATER POOL AND A PUBLIC ROAD TRAVERSES IT, AND ONE THROWS [AN OBJECT] FOUR CUBITS THEREIN, HE IS LIABLE. AND WHAT DEPTH CONSTITUTES A POOL? LESS THAN TEN HANDBREADTHS. IF THERE IS A POOL OF WATER AND A PUBLIC ROAD TRAVERSES IT, AND ONE THROWS [AN OBJECT] FOUR CUBITS THEREIN,[6] HE IS LIABLE.

GEMARA. One of the Rabbis said to Raba, As for 'traversing' [mentioned] twice, that is well, [as] it informs us this: [i] traversing
a with difficulty is designated traversing;[1] [ii] use with difficulty is not designated use.[2] But why [state] POOL twice?—One refers to summer, and the other to winter, and both are necessary. For if only one were stated, I would say: That is only in summer, when it is the practice of people to walk therein to cool themselves; but in winter [it is] not [so]. And if we were informed [this] of winter, [I would say that] because they are mudstained they do not object;[3] but in summer [it is] not [so]. Abaye said, They are necessary: I might argue, That is only where it [the pool] is not four cubits [across]; but where it is four cubits [across], one goes round it.[4] R. Ashi said; They are necessary: I might argue, That is only where it [the pool] is four [across];[5] but where it is not four, one steps over it.[6] Now, R. Ashi is consistent with his opinion. For R. Ashi said: If one throws [an object] and it alights on the junction of a landing bridge,[7] he is culpable, since many pass across it.[8]

MISHNAH. IF ONE THROWS [AN OBJECT] FROM THE SEA TO DRY LAND,[9] OR FROM DRY LAND TO THE SEA, FROM THE SEA TO A SHIP[10] OR FROM A SHIP TO THE SEA OR FROM ONE SHIP TO ANOTHER, HE IS NOT CULPABLE. IF SHIPS ARE TIED TOGETHER, ONE MAY CARRY FROM ONE TO ANOTHER. IF THEY ARE NOT TIED TOGETHER, THOUGH LYING CLOSE [TO EACH OTHER], ONE MAY NOT CARRY FROM ONE TO ANOTHER.

GEMARA. It was stated: As for a ship, R. Huna said, A projection, whatever its size, is stuck out [over the side of the ship], and [water] may then be drawn [from the sea]; R. Ḥisda and
b Rabbah son of R. Huna both maintain: One rigs up an enclosure[1] four [handbreadths square] and draws [water].[2] [Now], R. Huna said: A projection, whatever its size, is stuck out, and [water] may then be drawn; he holds that the *karmelith* is measured from the [sea-]bed, so that the air space is a place of non-liability.[3] Hence logically not even a projection is required,[4] but [it is placed there] to serve as a distinguishing mark.[5] R. Ḥisda and Rabbah son of R. Huna both maintain: 'One rigs up an enclosure four square and draws [water]': they hold that the *karmelith* is measured from the surface of the water, the water being [as] solid ground.[6] [Hence] if a place of four [square] is not set up, one transports [the water] from a *karmelith* to private ground.[7]

R. Naḥman said to Rabbah b. Abbuha: But according to R. Huna, who said, 'A projection, whatever its size, is stuck out and [water] may then be drawn',—but sometimes these are not ten,[8] and so one carries from a *karmelith* to private ground?—Said he to him: It is well known that a ship cannot travel in less than ten
c [handbreadths of water].[1] But it has a projecting point?[2]—Said R. Safra: Sounders precede it.[3]

R. Naḥman b. Isaac said to R. Ḥiyya b. Abin: But according to R. Ḥisda and Rabbah son of R. Huna, who maintain, 'One rigs up an enclosure four [square] and draws [water]',—how could he throw out his waste water?[4] And should you answer that he throws it [likewise] through that same enclosure,—it is [surely] repulsive to him![5]—He throws it against the sides of the ship.[6] But there is his force [behind it]?[7]—They [the Sages] did not prohibit one's force in connection with a *karmelith*. And whence do you say this? Because it was taught: As for a ship, one may not carry [e.g., water] from it into the sea or from the sea into it.

(3) Since he does not explain that the object came within three, it follows that even then it must alight on something. (4) It is actually falling when intercepted within three handbreadths from the ground. (5) Hence the thrower is culpable. (6) I.e., it travels four cubits before it rests. That is also the meaning in the previous case.

a (1) Hence the public road that passes through a pool counts as public ground, though one can only traverse it with difficulty. (2) E.g., a pit in the street nine handbreadths deep. Though one can put objects therein, it is inconvenient, and therefore is not the same as a pillar of that height in the street upon which people temporarily place their burdens whilst pausing to rest, and which ranks as public ground (*supra* 8a).—The deduction that such use is not designated use follows from the repetition of traversing, which intimates that *only* traversing with difficulty is regarded as such, but nothing else. (3) To wade through a pool. (4) Instead of wading through it; hence it is not public ground. Therefore it is stated twice, to show that this case too is included. (5) Rashi adds cubits; but the masc. form ארבעה must refer to handbreadths. This reading is also more likely, as otherwise he would not say that if less than four one might step across it.—S. Strashun. (6) And thus avoids it. (7) Perhaps where the bridge joins the quay. (8) Though many, on the other hand, step over it, it does not on that account cease to be ground publicly used, and the same applies above. (9) Which is from a *karmelith* to public ground. (10) I.e., from a *karmelith* to private ground.

b (1) Lit., 'place'. (2) I.e., an enclosure above the water is made, which renders the water immediately below technically private ground, and through this the water is drawn. (3) Only ten handbreadths above the ground rank as a *karmelith*, whilst the space above that is a place of non-liability (*supra* 7a). Hence everything above the surface of the sea, and even the sea itself above ten handbreadths from its bed, fall within the latter category. (4) For one may certainly carry from a place of non-liability. (5) That one may not carry from a real *karmelith*. (6) The sea-bed and the sea count as one, as though the ground of the *karmelith* rose very high. (7) Viz., the ship. (8) Handbreadths from the sea-bed to its surface, so that the whole of the sea is a *karmelith*.

c (1) By *sefina* a large ship is meant, not a small boat. (2) Rashi: the ship has a projecting point (*sc.* a helm), and as that rises out of the water it is possible for it to sail into a draught of even less than ten handbreadths, and should water be drawn at this point one transports from a *karmelith* to private ground. Tosaf. and R. Ḥan. (on the reading preserved in MS.M.): perhaps it (the sea-bed) has a projecting eminence just where the water is drawn, from the top of which there are less than ten handbreadths to the sea surface? (3) Men who sound the depth of the water with long poles, and they take care to avoid such shallows. (4) For it is forbidden to throw from a private ground (the ship) to a *karmelith* (the sea). (5) To draw water subsequently through the same place. (6) Whence it descends into the sea. (7) Even if he does not throw it directly into the sea, he does so indirectly through the exercise of his force.

[101a] R. Judah said: If it is ten [handbreadths] deep [internally] but not ten high,[8] one may transport from it into the sea, but not from the sea into it. Why not from the sea into it: because we [thus] transport from a *karmelith* into private ground? Then from it into the sea, one also transports from private ground to a *karmelith?* Hence it must surely mean on its edge,[9] which proves that they do not forbid one's force in connection with a *karmelith;* this proves it.

R. Huna said: As for the canal boats of Mesene,[10] we may carry in them only within [a distance of] four cubits.[11] But we say this only if they lack [a breadth of] four [handbreadths] at less than three [from the bottom edge]; but if they have [a breadth of] four at less than three, we have no objection; or if they are filled with canes
a and bullrushes,[1] we have no objection.[2] R. Naḥman demurred to this: But let us say, Stretch and bring the partitions down.[3] Was it not taught, R. Jose son of R. Judah said: If one plants a rod in the street, at the top of which is a basket, and throws [an article] and it comes to rest upon it, he is liable: this proves that we say, Stretch and bring the partition down,[4] so here too let us say, Stretch and bring the partition down? R. Joseph demurred to this, Yet did they not hear what was said by Rab Judah in Rab's name, which some trace to R. Ḥiyya: And it was taught thereon, But the Sages exempt [him]?[5] Said Abaye to him: And do you not hold thus? But it was taught: If a pillar in the street [is] ten [handbreadths] high and four broad, but its base is not four, and this narrow portion is three [in height],[6] and one throws [an article] and it alights upon it, he is liable: this proves that we say, Stretch and bring the partitions down;[7] so here too, stretch and bring the partition down. Hence [Abaye continues],[8] this is surely [not] an argument; there[9] it is partition through which goats can pass;[10] but here[11] they are partitions through which goats
b cannot pass.[1] R. Aḥa son of R. Aḥa said to R. Ashi: But in the case of a ship too, there is the passing through of fish? The passing through of fish is not designated passing through, he replied. And whence do you say this? For R. Ṭabla asked Rab: Can a suspended partition make a ruin permissible [for carrying therein]?[2] And he answered him: A suspended partition makes [some-

(8) From the edge of the water. (9) In the latter case the water is not poured directly into the sea but on to the ship's edge, whence it descends into the sea. (10) V. *supra* 37*b*, n. a8. (11) So MS.M. These boats are very narrow and taper to a knife edge in the water. Being thus less than four handbreadths wide at the bottom they do not count as private ground (v. *supra* 6*a*), and therefore one may not carry in them.

a (1) Up to the height where they have a breadth of four. (2) Providing in both cases that they are ten high above the level which gives the breadth of four. (3) I.e., adopt the legal fiction that the sides of the boat drop vertically down to the water, which gives the necessary breadth to make it rank as private ground. (4) For only if we assume imaginary partitions descending from the sides of the basket, which is not ten handbreadths deep itself, have we the necessary conditions for culpability. (5) Which proves that the majority reject this legal fiction. (6) So that the principle of being accounted as joined to the ground from the level which gives a breadth of four does not operate. (7) Otherwise the base would be disregarded, and the sides above would count as partitions suspended in the air, which cannot form a private domain. (8) R. Joseph's question. (9) In the case of the basket set on top of a rod. (10) I.e., even if one adopts that fiction, such imaginary partitions cannot keep goats out! and that is the legal test of a barrier; therefore the Rabbis exempt him. (11) In the case of the boat.

b (1) Being in the water. (2) E.g., the ruins of a hut which has part of a wall hanging from the roof: does this wall make it as though enclosed, so that it ranks as a private domain?

ר' יהודה אומר עמוקה עשרה ואין גבוהה עשרה מטלטלין מתוכה לים אבל לא מן הים לתוכה מ"ש מן הים לתוכה דלא דקא מטלטלין מכרמלית לרה"י מתוכה לים נמי קמטלטל מרשות היחיד לכרמלית אלא לאו אחודה וש"מ *כחו בכרמלית לא גזרו ש"מ אמר רב הונא הני *ביצאתא דמישן אין מטלטלין בהן אלא בארבעה ולא אמרן אלא שאין בפחות משלשה ארבעה אבל יש בפחות מג' ארבעה לית לן בה ואי מלינהו קני ואורבני לית לן בה מתקיף לה רב נחמן ולימא גוד אחית מחיצתא מי לא *תניא ר' יוסי בר' יהודה אומר נעץ קנה ברה"ר ובראשו טרסקל וזרק ונח על גביו חייב אלמא אמרינן גוד אחית מחיצתא ה"נ נימא גוד אחית מחיצתא מתקיף לה רב יוסף ולא שמיעא להו להא דאמר רב יהודה אמר רב ומטו בה משום רבי חייא ותני עלה וחכמים פוטרין אמר ליה אביי ואת לא תסברא והתניא עמוד ברה"ר גבוה עשרה ורחב ד' ואין בעיקרו ד' ויש בקצר שלו ג' וזרק ונח על גביו חייב אלמא אמרינן גוד אחית מחיצתא הכא נמי גוד אחית מחיצתא מידי איריא התם הויא ליה מחיצה שהגדיים בוקעין בה הכא הויא לה מחיצה שאין הגדיים בוקעין בה א"ל רב אחא בריה דרב אחא לרב אשי גבי ספינה נמי הא איכא בקיעת דגים א"ל בקיעת דגים לא שמיה בקיעה ומנא תימרא *דבעא מיניה רבי טבלא *מרבין מחיצה תלויה מהו שתתיר בחורבה וא"ל אין מחיצה תלויה מתרת אלא

רש"י

עמוקה · הספינה : עשרה · לתוכה דהוה רשות היחיד : ואין גבוה · שפתה י' מן המים כגון שמשוקעת במים מכובד משאה : מטלטלים מתוכה לים · דרך דופנותיה כגון שופכין כדמפרש ואזיל דכחו בכרמלית לא גזרו : אבל לא מן הים לתוכה · דאין תשמיש מן הים לתוכה דרך דפנות שאם ימלא וישליך על הדפנות ירדו לקרקעית הספינה ולהכי נקט עמוקה י' דאי אינה עמוקה י' היא גופה כרמלית ומטלטל להדיא אף מן הים לתוכה ואין גבוהה נמי (א) י' דוקא נקט דאי גבוהה י' מותר לטלטל מן הים לתוכה דמכרמלית לרה"י דרך מקום פטור קא מטלטל דצריך להגביה את ידו למעלה מי' ואע"ג דברשות דאורייתא מרה"ר לרה"י מיחייב בכה"ג (לעיל דף ה·) כרמלית מיהא דרבנן היא ולא גזור : אלא לאו אחודה · שופך שופכים על חודה והן יורדין דרך דפנותיה לים : בילאתא · ספינות קטנות וקצרות מלמטה עד כחודו של סכין שקורין קוייט"י : אין מטלטלין בתוכן · דלאו רה"י נינהו שאין ברחבן ארבע מלמטה לפיכך אין מחילותיהן מחילות : ולא אמרן אלא · בשקצה שהן גבוה שלש שאין רחב ד' למטה בעוד שלא הגביה ג' מקרקעיתו ואפי' יש ברחבו י' גובה לא משתרי דכיון דתחתונות לאו מחילה נינהו הוה ליה תלויה : אבל יש בפחות מג' גובה רוחב ד' · שעד שלא הגביהו ג' הרחיבו ד' הרי הן כמי שקרקעיתן עולה עד כאן ומחילותיהן מחילות : אורבני · ערבה דקה : ואי מליכהו · עד מקום רחבן הרי הן כשרות לטלטל אם יש משפת רוחבן ולמעלה י' : ולימא גוד אחית · מכנגד מדת רחבן העליון ולמטה כאילו הן יורדות עד הקרקע מבחוץ : טרסקל · אין עמוק י' ואנו מודדים לו גובה י' שמדת הקנה עולה לו בגובהו והקנה אין רחב ארבעה אלא שאנו אומרים במחילות הטרסקל גוד אחית וכאלו מקיפות את הקנה והוו להו היקף המחילות מן הקרקע ולמעלה לשוייה ראשו רה"י ואם זרק מרה"ר ונח על גביו חייב : ומטו בה · יש שמטין בדבר להכריע ולומר שר' חייא אמר : וחכמים פוטרין · אלמא לא אמרי' גוד אחית להתיר מחילה תלויה : ואת לא תיסברא · דאמרי' כה"ג : ואין בעיקרו · רחב ד' : ויש בקלר שלו ג' · אותו קלר של עיקרו שאינו רחב ד' יש בו גובה ג' והיינו רבותא דליכא למימר לבוד ממקום שכלה רחבו לקרקע אפ"ה הוי רה"י : דאמרי' גוד אחית מחילה · סביב מחילותיה מכנגד רחבה ולמטה כאילו הוא כולו שוה : ה"נ · בבילאתא דמישן נמי נימא גוד אחית : מידי איריא התם כו' · כולה אביי אמר לה לרב יוסף דהא דמייתי ראיה (ג) וחכמים פוטרים כלום ראי' היא לכאן הא דטרסקל דקפטרי רבנן : משום דהויא מחילה שהגדיים בוקעין בה · מלמטה בארץ תחת מחילות הטרסקל שהם פשוטות להלן מן הקנה לכל צד ובקיעת גדיים מעכבת מלמימר גוד אחית שהרי עוברין תחתיה אבל בספינה ליכא בקיעת גדיים שאין לך עובר תחתיהן וכן בעמוד אין דרך להתחכך בו ולעבור תחת שיפועו שאינו אלא מעט : בקיעת דגים לא שמה בקיעה · לפי שאינן נראין : בחורבה · שדרך להיות בה מחילות שנפלו תחתיהן וקיימות מלמעלה ותלויות : מהו שתתיר · לטלטל בחורבה שלא תהא כפרולה לרה"ר : אלא

תוספות

רבי יהודה אומר עמוקה י' ואין גבוהה י' מטלטלין מתוכה לים · וא"ת היכי מייתי סייעתא מדרבי יהודה כיון דרבנן פליגי עליה ואור"י דהא לא פליגי אלא בעמוקה י' וגבוה י' דרבנן סברי דמכרמלית לרה"י דרך מקום פטור אסור אע"ג דרשויות דרבנן ור' יהודה שרי אבל בעמוקה י' ואינה גבוהה י' לטלטל מתוכה לים לא פליגי עליה רבנן והכי איתא בתוספתא[פי"א] דספינה שבים גבוהה י' ועמוקה י' אין מטלטלין מתוכה לים ולא מן הים לתוכה ר' יהודה אומר אם עמוקה י' ואין גבוהה י' כו' וה"ק ר' יהודה בעמוקה י' וגבוהה י' לא מבעי' דמותר לטלטל טלטול גמור הואיל ודרך מקום פטור קא מטלטל אלא גם באינה גבוהה י' יש תקנה לטלטל כגון ע"י כחו כדמפרש הש"ס וקשה לר"י דהשתא לרבי יהודה שרי טלטול דרך מקום פטור ברשויות דרבנן ואפילו רבנן לא פליגי אלא בשאינו עושה הנחה במקום פטור ובפרק כילד משתתפין (עירובין דף פז:) פריך לזעירי דאמר אסור להחליף דרך מקום פטור מכרמלית לרה"י ולזעירי קשיא פלוגתא דרשב"ג ורבנן דפליגי בהא ומשני לה והשתא הא תנאי דהכא דלא כוותיה וי"ל דמ"מ הני תנאי דהתם כיון דמצי לאוקמי כוותי' מוקים להו : מוקף י' ואין גבוהה י' · מהכא אין להקשות למ"ד לעיל מארעא משחינן דהכא מיירי בדליכא זיז כל שהוא להיכרא : הני בילאתא דמישן · לפירש"י דמפרש שהן קצרות מלמטה קשה דכי היכי דבטיל מדין רה"י משום דלית בהו ד' ה"נ ליבטיל מדין כרמלית כדאמר בפ"ק (דף ז·) דאין כרמלית פחותה מד' ואקילו בה רבנן מקולי רה"י דאי הוי מקום ד' (ג) כרמלית ואי לא מקום פטור ועוד מאי פריך לימא גוד אחית מחילה מה מועיל שיהא המחילות מבחוץ כיון שמבפנים אין שם ריוח מקום ד' ולא ניחא תשמישם ודופן הספינה שבקלר מבטל גוד אחית כמו חלוקה במחללת דלעיל ועוד למה לי מליכהו קני ואורבני אע"ג דלא מלאן כיון דיכול למלאות חשיב רה"י כדאמר בפרק חלון (עירובין דף עח·) משום דאי בעי מנח עליה מידי ומשתמש גבי מלאו כולו ביתידות ונראה כפר"ח דבילאתא הם ספינות קטנות העשויות להלך באגמים ועל שם שמהלכות על בלעי המים קרי להו בילאתא ויש להם דפנות וקרקעית העשויות נסרים נסרים ויש חלל בין הנסרים והמים נכנסין שם ויושבין בה כמו במים והיא עשויה כך שאפילו תתהפך אינה נטבעת לעולם וקאמר רב הונא כיון שהיא פרוצה דינה ככרמלית ואין מטלטלין בה אלא בד' ולא אמרו אלא בזמן שאין בין נסר לנסר חלל פחות מג' אבל אם יש בין נסר לנסר חלל פחות מג' כלבוד דמי ואע"ג שהמים נכנסין בה לא חיישינן ונראה דל"ג שאין בפחות מג' ד' ואי מילא כל החלל קני ואורבני מותר לטלטל בכולה : מתקיף לה רב נחמן · למה לך כולי האי לימא גוד אחית מחילתא מי לא תניא רבי יוסי ברבי יהודה אומר וכו' אלמא רואין כאילו דופני הטרסקל יורדין עד עיקרו של קנה ה"נ רואין כאילו דופני הספינה עקומין ומסבבין הנסרים וכמלאו הנסרים מחוברין : וזרק ונח על גביו חייב · למאי דס"ד השתא דאין חילוק בין מחילה דמים לשאר מחילות וס"ד נמי דלא פליגי רבנן עליה דרבי יוסי ברבי יהודה לא מצי לאקשויי אמאי הא תנן בפ' כילד משתתפין (עירובין דף פז:) גזוזטרא שהיא למעלה מן המים אין ממלאין הימנה אא"כ עשו לה מחילה י' מה צריך מחילה י' בלא מחילה י' תסגי כמו בטרסקל דדוקא על גביו חשיב ליה ר' יוסי ברבי יהודה רה"י אבל למטה לא דלהכי לא אהני גוד אחית אי נמי הא דבעינן גבי גזוזטרא מחילה י' היינו לטלטל אבל לזרוק לא בעי מחילה י' כמו בטרסקל והכא הכי פריך לימא גוד אחית דכי היכי דא"ר יוסי בר' יהודה גוד אחית כשאין שם מחילה י' למיהוי רה"י להתחייב ה"נ בספינה שיש שם מחילה י' אית לן למימר גוד אחית אף לטלטל : ויש בקלר שלו ג' · פי' בקונט' גבוה ג' מן הארץ וקשה דאם הוא דק הרבה כמו קנה הוי כמו טרסקל ומבטלי בקיעת גדיים גוד אחית ונראה לר"י דהאי בקלר שלו ג' היינו שיש בעובי הקלר ג' דכיון שיש בעובי הקלר ג' ולמעלה רחב ד' שייך ביה גוד אחית : ומנא תימרא דבעא מיניה ר' טבלא כו' · וא"ת אמאי לא פשיט טפי ממתני' דכילד משתתפין (שם פז:) גזוזטרא שהיא למעלה מן המים וכו' דמשתרי במחילה דלמעלה ואור"י דאי ממתניתין ה"א דה"ה אף בשאר מחילות שאינן של מים מתרת מחילה תלויה ולהכי מייתי מרבי טבלא דמפרש הטעם קל הוא שהקילו חכמים במים : פשיטא

עין משפט נר מצוה

לב א מיי' פט"ו מהל' שבת הלכה כ סמג לאוין סה טוש"ע א"ח סי' שנה סעיף א :

לג ב טוש"ע א"ח סי' שסו סעיף ג בהג"ה:

לד ג מיי' פי"ד מהל' שבת הלכה יח :

לה ד מיי' שם הל' טז:

רבינו חננאל

אע"פ שמצד אחר עולין בו בכבש כשיעור ד' אמות חייב ואפילו מכל סביביו משופע ועולה כיון שגבהו עשרה ושיפועו ד' אמות כרה"י דמיגבהו כגון זה ומפרש בגמ' זבחים (ד' סג). אמר רמי בר אבא כל כבשי כבשים ג"א ומחצה *) לאמה חוץ מכבשו של מזבח ג' אמות ומחצה ואצבע ושליש אצבע אבל אם אין התל עולה לגובה עשרה אלא מתוך שיפועו יתר מד' אמות לא מחשב כרה"י ומפורש במס' עירובין פרק עושין פסין בעא מיניה רחבה מרבה תל המתלקט י' מתוך ד' אמות ורבים בוקעין בו הייבין עליו משום רה"ר אי לא אליבא דרבנן לא תבעי לך השתא ומה התם דניחא תשמישתיה הא אמור רבנן דלא אתו רבים מבטלי מחיצתא הכא דלא ניחא תשמישה לא כל שכן כי תיבעי לך אליבא דר' יהודה ואע"ג דפשיט רבה אליבא דר' יהודה ואפילו במעלות בית [חרון] לאו הלכתא כר' יהודה **) (והא דרבי) דאמר אם היתה דרך הרבים מפסקתה יסלקנה לצדדין וחכ"א אין צריך דעיקר דשמעתא מעלות ומורדות שבא"י אין חייבין עליהן משום רה"ר לפי שאינן כדגלי מדבר ותנן נמי הגיע להר מבליעו והדור למדתו. אמר רבא ל"ש אלא בהר המתלקט י' מתוך ד' אמות אבל הר המתלקט י' מתוך ה' מודדו מדידה יפה רב הונא מתני לה לקולא לא שנו אלא בהר המתלקט י' מתוך ה' אבל הר המתלקט עשרה מתוך ד' אמות אומדו והולך לו· זרק לתוך ד' אמות ונתגלגל חוץ לד' אמות פטור מ"ט שלא היתה מחשבתו חוץ לד' אמות זרק חוץ לד' אמות וחזר לתוך ד' אמות חייב והוא שנח בחוץ לד' אמות ע"ג משהו ואחר שנח התם חזר. זה כבר פירשנוהו למעלה בפלוגתא דרבי עקיבא ורבנן דתנן הזורק מרה"י לרה"י ורה"ר באמצע ר' עקיבא מחייב וחכמים פוטרין דרבנן סברי אע"פ שזרק בתוך ג' ברה"ר שהן כלבוד צריך הנחה ע"ג משהו אבל קלוטה לאו כמי שהונחה דמיא והתם בזורק מרה"י לרה"י ורה"ר באמצע ואע"ג דלא עבר ד' אמות ברה"ר אם נח ברה"ר ע"ג משהו וכן בזורק ברה"ר והעביר בזריקתו מתחלת ד' לסוף ד' אם נח ע"ג משהו חייב ואם לאו פטור אבל המעביר מתחלת ד' לסוף ד' אם כשיעור בבת אחת העביר אם נחה ע"ג משהו חייב ואם לאו פטור דאמרינן לענין המוציא מחנות דרך סטיו משום דר' יוחנן מידי דהוה המעביר חפץ ברה"ר לאו אע"ג דכמה דנקיט ליה ואזיל פטור כי מנח ליה חייב ואע"ג דהמעביר מחנות לפלטיא דרך סטיו לאו כי האי גוונא סלקא מידו לענין מעביר שצריך הנחה הכין הוא והא דאמר רבא הוציא חצי גרוגרת והניחה וחזר והוציא חצי גרוגרת והעבירה דרך עליה חייב כלומר נצטרפת זו עם זו ונעשו כגרוגרת ואקשינן והא לא נח ושנינן כגון דהעבירה למטה מג' דהוא כלבוד' איני והאמר רבא תוך ג' לרבנן צריך הנחה ע"ג משהו ופרקינן כי קאמר רבא בזורק הכא במעביר ולענין דבר שאיגדו בידו ונתגלגל מרה"י מידו ויצא לרה"ר צריך הנחה ברה"ר ע"ג משהו דתנן בענין הקורא בספר על האסקופה ונתגלגל מידו ר' יהודה אומר אפילו אינו מסולק מן הקרקע אלא כמלא חוט גוללו אצלו ואמרינן עלה אלא הא דאמר רבא תוך ג' לרבנן צריך הנחה ע"ג משהו לימא כתנאי א"ל לשמעתיה. אלא כולה ר' יהודה היא והכי קתני הגיע לי' טפחים הופכו על הכתב בד"א בכותל משופע אבל בכותל שאינו משופע אפילו למטה מג' גוללו אצלו דברי ר' יהודה שר'

*) נפלינו שם הגי' ג' אמות לאמה. **) נראה דצ"ל בהא דאמר אם היתה כו' אלא כחכמים דס"ל דא"ל דעיקר דשמעתא וכו'.

מסורת הש"ס

[יקמן קמח.] [כ"ב עג.]

עי' דף ה. עירובין לג:

עירובין יב. ודף טז: ודף מח. ודף פו:

הגהות הב"ח

(א) רש"י ד"ה אבל לא וכו' ואין גבוה י' נמי דוקא : (ב) ד"ה מידי איריא וכו' דמייתי ראיה מדתני וחכמים כצ"ל והד"א עם ד"ה משום: (ג) תוס' ד"ה הני וכו' דאי הוי מקום ד' הוא דהויא כרמלית :

גליון הש"ס

גמ' ויש בקלר שלו ג' · ע' עירובין ד' לג ע"א תוס' ד"ה וכלכלה :

רב נסים גאון

הויא לה מחיצה שהגדיים בוקעין בה · עיקר דילה במסכת כלאים פרק ד' מחיצת הקנים אם אין בין קנה לחברו ג' טפחים כדי שיכנס הגדי הרי זו מחיצה ובתוספתא בפרק ג' כל שהוא פחות מג' צריך שלא יהא בין קנה לחברו ג' טפחים כדי שלא יכנס הגדי דלאלך *) עלי אן כל מחיצה שהגדיים בוקעין בה אינה מחיצה ומשכחת לה בפרק אחד מן עירובין (דף יד) :

*) פירושו בערבי הנה מוכח מזה

לא

לו א מיי' פכ"ו מהל' שבת הלכה יג :

לז ב מיי' פ"ג מהל' עירובין הלכה כה סמג עשין א :

לח ג ד מיי' פט"ו מהל' שבת הל' כב טוש"ע א"ח סי' שמב סעיף ג :

לט ה מיי' פי"ג מהל' טומאת מת הלכה ה :

"אלא במים קל הוא שהקילו חכמים במים ואמאי הא איכא בקיעת דגים אלא ש"מ בקיעת דגים לא שמה בקיעה : ספינות קשורות כו' : פשיטא אמר רבא לא נצרכה אלא להתיר ביצית שביניהן א"ל רב ספרא *משה שפיר קאמרת מטלטלין מזו לזו תנן אלא אמר רב ספרא לא נצרכה אלא לערב ולטלטל מזו לזו וכדתניא ב ספינות קשורות זו בזו מערבין ומטלטלין מזו לזו נפסקו נאסרו חזרו ונקשרו בין שוגגין ובין מזידין בין אנוסין בין מוטעין חזרו להיתרן הראשון ג וכן מחצלות הפרוסות (לר"ה) מערבין ומטלטלין מזו לזו נגללו נאסרו חזרו ונפרשו בין שוגגין בין מזידין בין אנוסין ובין מוטעין חזרו להיתרן הראשון *ד שכל מחיצה שנעשה בשבת בין בשוגג בין במזיד שמה מחיצה איני והאמר רב נחמן לא שנו אלא לזרוק אבל לטלטל אסור כי איתמר דרב נחמן אמזיד איתמר אמר שמואל ואפילו קשורות בחוט הסרבל היכי דמי אי דיכול להעמידן פשיטא אי דאין יכול להעמידן אמאי לעולם דיכול להעמידן ושמואל לאפוקי מדנפשי' קאתי דתנן *ה קשרה בדבר המעמידה מביא לה טומאה בדבר שאין מעמידה אין מביא לה טומאה ואמר שמואל והוא שקשורה בשלשלת של ברזל לענין טומאה הוא דכתיב °בחלל *חרב חרב הרי הוא כחלל אין אבל לענין שבת כיון דיכול להעמידה (היכר בעלמא הוא) אפילו בחוט הסרבל :

במדבר יט

מתני'

פשיטא אמר רבא לא נצרכא כו' · השתא ס"ד דמיירי בשתי הספינות של אדם אחד ולהכי פריך פשיטא וכשאינן קשורות אין מטלטלין דגזירה שמא יפול החפץ אל המים ומטלטל מרה"י לכרמלית ואתי לאתויי אע"ג דלעיל גבי ב' בתים (דף צז·) לא גזרינן דילמא אתי לאתויי הכא בספינות דלא קביעי איכא למיגזר טפי דילמא נפיל ומסיק לא נצרכא אלא לערב ולטלטל וקמ"ל דעירוב מהני בספינות אע"פ שאין קבועות שם דס"ד כיון שאין עתידות להיות שם לא יהנה עירוב קמ"ל דמהני ועוד מפרש ר"י דמעיקרא נמי הוה איירי בספינות של שני בני אדם וע"י עירוב קאמר דמטלטלין מזו לזו ואפ"ה פריך פשיטא דמהני עירוב ולהכי כשאין קשורות אין מטלטלין דלא מהני התם עירוב ומסיק לא נצרכא אלא לערב ולטלטל ואפילו נפסקו כיון דחזרו ונתקשרו וכדתניא כו' : **נפסקו** נאסרו · ולא דמי לעירב דרך הפתח ונסתם דאמר רב הונא ורב יהודה בספ"ק דעירובין (דף יז·) דשבת הואיל והותרה הותרה דהכא כיון דנפסקו הוי כאילו הוי רה"ר ביניהם ואם עירבו ג' בתים (ביניהם) ונפל האמצעי ונעשה רה"ר פשיטא דלא אמרינן הואיל והותרה הותרה : **כי** איתמר דרב נחמן אמזיד איתמר · והא דקתני חזרו להיתרן הראשון אף במזיד לא לגמרי חזרו להיתרן הראשון לטלטל אלא דהוו רה"י דאורייתא ומיהו אספינות לא א"ש דבלא חזרו ונתקשרו הוי רה"י דאורייתא ור"ת מפרש דחזרו להיתרן הראשון אפילו אמזידין ור"ל דאמר דבמזיד לא הוי מחילה אלא לזרוק ולא לטלטל היינו שע"י המחילה נעשה רה"י אבל ספינות דבלאו הכי הוו רה"י כי קשרו אפילו מזיד שרי לטלטל ומחללות הפרוסות ברה"י איירי שיש מחללות מפסיקות בין שתי חלרות נתגלגלו נאסרו שהרי הן כחלר אחת והם עירבו שנים חזרו ונפרשו חזרו להיתירן הראשון ומטלטלי אלו לכאן ואלו לכאן והא דקאמר שכל מחילה הנעשה בשבת שמה מחילה טעמא קא יהיב למילתיה דאפילו היכא דע"י המחילה נעשה רה"י הויא מחילה או לזרוק או לטלטל כ"ש מחילה זו שאינה עשויה אלא להתיר עירוב כבתחלה דהויא מחילה ומסיפא דקתני שכל מחילה הנעשית בשבת כו' פריך לר"נ והויא דכל גגות (עירובין דף לג:) כותל שבין שתי חלרות שנפל ואיכא דשרי התם לטלטל עד עיקר מחילה לא דמי להכא דהתם איירי שלא היה אלא בית אחד בחלר זה ואחד בחלר זה אבל הכא כשיש רבים כאן וכאן אמרינן נתגלגלו נאסרו וצ"ע בשמעתא דדיורין (א) הבאין בשבת (עירובין שם) דאמר שבת הואיל והותרה הותרה :

קשרה בדבר המעמידה מביא לה טומאה · פי' בקונטרס כגון שראשו אחד באהל המת ולא יתכן חדא דמאי קאמר לאפוקי מדשמואל מה שייכא הא לדשמואל דהתם הוא משום חרב הרי הוא כחלל ולא משום קשירה ועוד אמאי קתני קשרה אפילו השלשלת מונחת על הספינה בלא קשירה טמאה ועוד דליפלוגין בהדיא דחרב הרי הוא כחלל ולשון הבאת טומאה כמי לא שייך בכה"ג ונראה לרבינו שמואל דלא גרסינן מביא לה את הטומאה אלא מביאה את הטומאה ומשנה היא בפ"ח דאהלות (משנה ה) ורישא דהך בבא קתני אלו לא מביאין ולא חוללין הזרעים והעוף הפורח וטלית המנפנפת וספינה שהיא שטה על פני המים פירוש שאם יש מתחתיה מת מלד אחד וטהרה מלד אחר אינה מביאה טומאה מלד זה ללד אחר דלא השיבי אהל כיון שמנענעים תמיד וקתני דאם קשרה בדבר המעמידה מביאה את הטומאה ומפרש שמואל והוא שקשרה בשלשלאות של ברזל ולאו דוקא נקט של ברזל אלא כלומר שקשורה בחוזק עד שאינה מתנענעת וזזה ממקומה וכן דרך כשרולה להזכיר דבר חזק מזכיר ברזל כמו אפילו מחילה של ברזל אינה מפסקת (סוטה דף לח:) וכמו נכסי לאן ברזל (ב"ק דף פט·) לפי שהן באחריותו וקשים כברזל ול"ג לענין טומאה הוא דכתיב בחלל חרב הרי הוא כחלל ושיבוש הוא אלא משום דנקט שלשלאות של ברזל טעו לומר דטעמא משום דחרב הרי הוא כחלל אלא גרסינן ה"מ לענין טומאה דבעינן אהל שיהא נח לגמרי אבל גבי שבת שהטעם הוא משום רשות אחת בחוט הסרבל סגי :

סיפא

אלא במים · כגון גזוזטרא שהיא למעלה מן הים דתנן בעירובין (דף פז:) דעושה מחילה תלויה סביב וממלא וכן בור שבין שתי חלרות וחלקו במחילה תלויה מלמעלה ממלא זה מכאן וזה מכאן ואף על פי שלא עירבו (שם דף פו·) : הא איכא בקיעת דגים · גבי גזוזטרא כך תורה אור נראה שיטה זו בעיני ועל מה שפירשו רבותי תמהתי [שהם פירשו] דהאי מידי איריא התם משום דהוה ליה מחילה שהגדיים בוקעים בה רב יוסף קא מהדר ליה לאביי הכי מידי איריא הך דעמוד לדהכא התם משום דהוי מחילה שהגדיים בוקעין בה וצריכה לגוד אחית הלכך אמרינן בה גוד אחית אבל גבי ספינה דליכא בקיעת גדיים לא אמרינן גוד אחית ותמהתי אם אמרו רבותי כן דאי אפשר לאומרו דהא בפ"ק דעירובין בתרי דוכתי (דף יד: וד"ף טז·) אמרינן בקיעת גדיים לעכובי גוד אחית דלא לימריה במחילה תלויה והכא היכי אמרינן דמהני גבי גוד אחית ועוד מאי דוחקיה דרב יוסף לשנויי הכי נימא ליה הא מני רבי יוסי ברבי יהודה היא ואביי גופיה מאי מותיב ליה ואת לא תסברא הא ודאי רבי יוסי ברבי יהודה היא דהא חזינן דחכמים פוטרים גבי טרסקל אלא ע"כ האי מידי איריא מסקנא דמילתיה דאביי היא ולמימר דרבנן קאמרי לה דלא דמיא לטרסקל הלא לספינה : פשיטא · דמטלטלין : לא נצרכא · מטלטלין דמתני' אלא לטלטל מזו לזו דרך בילית קטנה שבין שתי הגדולות ואע"פ שאינה קשורה ניתרת ע"י קשירת שתים החילונות ולא חיישינן דילמא מישתקלא מביניייהו וקא מטלטל דרך אויר כרמלית : בילית · היינו ביליאתא דלעיל: משה · כלומר רבינו בדורו כמשה בדורו : שפיר קאמרת · בתמיה : מזו לזו תנן · משמע שאין אחרת מפסקת ליכנס בה המטלטל הזה : לערב · הא אשמועינן במתניתין דאפילו שתי הספינות לשני בני אדם שצריכין לערב מערבין ומטלטלין : נפסקו · בטל העירוב מפני שנפרדות : שוגגין · שגגת שבת או שגגת מלאכות : מוטעין · מתעסקין בדבר אחר לקושרו ונקשר זה : מחללות הפרוסות · ועשו מחילות הרבה ושבתו יחידים בהן זה בזו וזה בזו : לא שנו · דשמה מחילה : אלא לזרוק · לחייב הזורק מתוכה לרה"ר או להפך : אבל לטלטל · להיות מותר לטלטל בתוכה אסור מדבריהם : אמזיד איתמר · ומשום קנסא ודקתני מתני' חזרו להיתירן הראשון אשוגגין ואנוסין ואמוטעין קאי וכי קתני מזידין אשמה מחילה קאי ולזרוק כרב נחמן : בחוט הסרבל · שקושרין בו את בית הצואר שקורין מונטי"ל : להעמידן · שלא יתפרדו : לאפוקי מדנפשיה · ממילתא דאמר בעלמא דבעינן שלשלאות של ברזל ואשמועינן הכא דלא בעינן כי התם : קשרה · לספינה : בדבר המעמידה מביא לה טומאה · אם היה ראשו אחד קשור באהל המת מביא טומאה לכלים שבספינה ולספינה עצמה כגון ספינת הירדן שמקבלת טומאה כדאמרינן (לעיל דף פג:): ואמר שמואל והוא שקשרה בשלשלת של ברזל · האי קשרה בדבר המעמידה שלשלת של ברזל הוא כדמפרש טעמא ואזיל כלומר קשרה בדבר שרגילין להעמידה בו דהיינו שלשלת מביא טומאה שמטמאה את הספינה *להיות אב הטומאה : בדבר שאינו מעמידה · כלומר שאינו רגיל להעמיד בה כגון מידי דלאו מתכות אין מביא לה טומאה דאילו ספינה לא מיטמאה מחמת אותו כלי להיות אב הטומאה אלא ראשון לטומאה ואינה מטמאה כלים שבתוכה ואשמעינן שמואל הכא דהאי קשורות דמתניתין אף על גב דדבר המעמידה בעינן כל שהוא מעמידה לענין שבת כשר ולא דמי למעמידה דהתם :

מתניתין

[ביצה לח. סוכה נט. חולין גג.]

עירובין כה.

אהלות פ"ח מ"ה [ע"ש]

פסחים יד: יט: עדיות פ"ו חולין ג. רש"ל מ"ז

להיות אב הטומאה והספינה את הכלים שבה דחרב ה"ה כחלל וכו' אבי אבות הטומאה כצ"ל רש"ל

הגהות הב"ח

(א) תוס' ד"ה כי איתמר וכו' וצ"ע בשמעתא דדיורין. נ"ב ספ"ק דעירובין דף יז ע"א

רבינו חננאל

מארעיתא דימא או דנהרא הוא [ומשחינן] מהתם . והוספת עד עשרה טפחים ומן כד מטי לי' טפחים שלימא כרמלית והוות ליה מקום פטור ובדין הוא דזיז נמי לא ליבעי והא דאצריכו ליה זיז כי היכא דלהוי היכירא רב חסדא ורבה בר רב הונא אמרי עושה מקום ד' וממלא קסברי כרמלית משפת מיא משחינן ומיא ארעא סמיכתא היא וצריך לעשות מקום ד' חוץ לספינה כדי שיהא מקום פטור שמעלה המים מן הים או מן הנהר שהן כרמלית לאותו מקום שהוא מקום פטור ומשם מעייל להן לספינה פי' מקום זה כגון תיבה פחותה או סל פחותה ונרס' בירושלמי ואם הוציא מן הים לספינה הרי הוציא מכרמלית לרה"י ואקשינן לרב הונא דאמר מוציא זיז כל שהוא וממלא מן הים לספינה ומנין דליכא י' מארעית נהרא לשפת מיא וקא מטלטל מכרמלית לרה"י ומשני גמירי אין ספינה מהלכת במים שיש בהן פחות מעשרה . ומקשינן ודלמא מורשא איכא . פי' מורשא כמו חפירה שיש בקרקעית הים ליחוש דלמא האי ספינה קיימא בההוא מורשא וסביביו מכרמלית לרה"י ומשני גמירי אין ספינה מהלכת במים שיש בהן פחות מעשרה . ומקשינן ודלמא מורשא איכא . פי' מורשא כמו חפירה שיש בקרקעית הים ליחוש דלמא האי ספינה קיימא בההוא מורשא וסביביו מקום שממלא משם אין בו מקרקעית הים שפת המים י' טפחים וכיון דליתא י' טפחים אותו המים הן כרמלית וקמטלטל מכרמלית לרה"י ופריש רב ספרא נשושי אזלי קמה . כלומר כיון שמגעת הספינה במקום שהמים מעטין מתייראין שמא תשב הספינה בקרקעית הים או שמא תהיה שם סלע ותעבור עליו ותשבר ולפיכך מהלכין בני אדם ספנים מגששין ורואין המים אם הן מי ברכים או פחות או יותר וכיוצא בהם ואם יראו

רב נסים גאון

לא נצרכה אלא להתיר ביצית שביניהם ביצית היא דונית כדגרסי' בפ' המוכר את הספינה (בבא בתרא ד' עג) אמר רבא ביצית ודונית חדא מלתא היא ר' נתן דבבלאה הוה קרי ליה ביצית כדאמרי אינשי ביציאתא דמישאן סומכוס דבר ארעא דישראל הוה קרי ליה דונית כדכתיב (עמוס ד) ואחריתכן בסירות דוגה ומתרגמ' ובנתכן בדוגית צי"ין :

thing] permissible only [101*b*] in water, this being a leniency which the Rabbis permitted in connection with water. But why so: surely there is the passing through of fish? Hence infer from this that the passing through of fish is not designated passing through.

IF SHIPS ARE TIED TOGETHER, etc. This is obvious?—Said Raba, This is necessary only to permit [carrying via] a small boat [lying] between them.[3] Said R. Safra to him, By Moses![4] do you say right? We learnt, ONE MAY CARRY FROM ONE TO ANOTHER![5]—Rather said R. Safra, It is necessary only to [teach that one may] combine them[6] and carry from one to another, and as it was taught: If ships are tied to each other, one may combine them and carry from one to another. If they are separated, they become prohibited. If they are rejoined, whether in ignorance[7] or wilfully, accidentally or erroneously,[8] they revert to their original permitted condition. Likewise, if mats are spread [i.e., hung up],[9] one may combine them and carry from one to another. If they are rolled up, they become prohibited. If they are respread,[10] whether in ignorance or wilfully, accidentally or erroneously, they revert to their original permitted condition. For every partition that is made on the Sabbath, whether ignorantly or wilfully, is designated a partition. But that is not so? For did not R. Naḥman say: They learnt this
a only in respect of throwing,[1] yet it is forbidden to carry [therein]?[2]—R. Naḥman's [dictum] was stated in reference to wilful [erection].[3]

Samuel said: Even if they are tied by a cloak ribbon. How is that: if it can hold them together, it is obvious? If it cannot hold them together, why [does it suffice]?—In truth, it is one that can hold them together, but Samuel comes to discount his own [dictum]. For we learnt: If one ties it [a ship][4] with something that holds it still, it brings defilement to it; with something that does not hold it still, it does not bring defilement to it. Whereon Samuel observed: Providing that it is fastened with iron chains.[5] Now, it is only with respect to defilement where it is written, *one that is slain with a sword,*[6] [teaching,] the sword is like the slain,[7] that that [Samuel's dictum] is so. But with respect to the Sabbath, since it can hold it still, even [if it be] with the ribbon of a cloak, [it is sufficient].

(3) The larger ships being fastened to the opposite sides of the boat. (4) Or, Scholar, great as Moses! (5) Not via a third. (6) By means of an *'erub* (q.v. Glos.), if they belong to different owners. (7) Either of the fact that it is the Sabbath, or that this is interdicted on the Sabbath. (8) While engaged in fastening something else one tied the boats instead. (9) Forming tents, all belonging to separate owners. (10) On the Sabbath.

a (1) The space enclosed by partitions erected on the Sabbath is private ground only in so far that throwing an object therein from public ground is a culpable offence. (2) By Rabbinical law. (3) In which case the Rabbis have imposed the interdict as penalty. (4) If it is a ship that can be defiled (v. *supra* 83*b*). (5) Rashi: If a ship is moored by a chain to a wharf where a corpse is lying and touching the chain. Tosaf. explains the passage quite differently but with emendation of the text. (6) Num. XIX, 16. (7) I.e., metal that touches a corpse has the same degree of uncleanness as the corpse itself (v. Pes. 14*b*), and therefore the chain defiles the ship.

MISHNAH. [102a] IF ONE THROWS [AN ARTICLE] AND RECALLS [THAT IT IS THE SABBATH] AFTER IT LEAVES HIS HAND, AND ANOTHER CATCHES IT,[8] OR A DOG CATCHES IT, OR IT IS BURNT, HE IS NOT LIABLE.[9] IF ONE THROWS [AN ARTICLE] IN ORDER TO INFLICT A WOUND, WHETHER IN MAN OR IN BEAST, AND HE RECALLS [THAT IT IS THE SABBATH] BEFORE THE WOUND IS INFLICTED, HE IS NOT LIABLE. THIS IS THE GENERAL PRINCIPLE: ALL WHO ARE LIABLE TO SIN-OFFERINGS ARE LIABLE ONLY IF THE BEGINNING AND THE END [OF THE FORBIDDEN ACTION] ARE UNWITTING. IF THEIR BEGINNING IS UNWITTING WHILE THEIR END IS WILFUL, IF THEIR BEGINNING IS WILFUL WHILE THEIR END IS UNWITTING, THEY ARE NOT LIABLE, UNLESS THEIR BEGINNING AND END ARE UNWITTING.

a *GEMARA.* Hence if it alighted, he is liable:[1] but surely did he not remind himself, and we learnt, ALL WHO ARE LIABLE TO SIN-OFFERINGS ARE LIABLE ONLY IF THE BEGINNING AND THE END [OF THE FORBIDDEN ACTION] ARE UNWITTING?—Said R. Kahana: The last clause is applicable to a bolt and a cord.[2] [You say,] 'A bolt and a cord'! But is not its tie in his hand?[3]—It means, e.g., that he intended to inflict a wound. But this too we learnt:[4] IF ONE THROWS [AN ARTICLE] IN ORDER TO INFLICT A WOUND, WHETHER IN MAN OR IN BEAST, AND HE RECALLS [THAT IT IS THE SABBATH] BEFORE THE WOUND IS INFLICTED, HE IS NOT LIABLE?—Rather said Raba: It refers to one who carries.[5] But the statement, THIS IS THE GENERAL PRINCIPLE, is stated with reference to throwing? Rather said Raba: Two [contingencies] are taught. [Thus:] 'IF ONE THROWS [AN ARTICLE] and recalls [that it is the Sabbath] after it leaves his hand, or even if he does not recall [it], but ANOTHER CATCHES IT, OR A DOG CATCHES IT, OR IT IS BURNT, HE IS NOT LIABLE'. R. Ashi said: It [the Mishnah] is defective, and teaches this: 'IF ONE THROWS [AN ARTICLE] AND RECALLS [THAT IT IS THE SABBATH] AFTER IT LEAVES HIS HAND, AND ANOTHER CATCHES IT, OR A DOG CATCHES IT, OR IT IS BURNT,
b HE IS NOT LIABLE.[1] But if it alights, he is liable. That, however, is said only if he forgot again;[2] but if he did not forget again, he is not liable, because ALL WHO ARE LIABLE TO SIN-OFFERINGS ARE LIABLE ONLY IF THE BEGINNING AND THE END [OF THE FORBIDDEN ACTION] ARE UNWITTING'.

THIS IS THE GENERAL PRINCIPLE: ALL WHO ARE LIABLE TO SIN-OFFERINGS, etc. It was stated: [If the object travels] two cubits unwittingly, two cubits deliberately, and two cubits unwittingly,[3]—Rabbah ruled, He [the thrower] is not liable; Raba said: He is liable. 'Rabbah ruled, He is not liable': even according to R. Gamaliel, who maintained, Knowledge in respect of half the standard is of no consequence,[4] that is [only] there, because when he completes the standard, he completes it unwittingly, but here that [he completes it] wilfully, it is not so. But to what [does this refer]? If to one who throws, [surely] he is an unwitting offender?[5]—Rather it must refer to one who carries. 'Raba said, He is liable': even according to the Rabbis, who maintained, Knowledge in respect of half the standard is of consequence: that is [only] there, because it is in his power,[6] but here that it is not in his power, it is not so. But to what [does this refer]? If to one who carries, surely it is in his power? Rather it must refer to one who throws.[7]

Raba said: If one throws [an article] and it falls into the mouth of a dog or a furnace, he is culpable. But we learnt, AND ANOTHER CATCHES IT, OR A DOG CATCHES IT, OR IT IS BURNT, HE IS NOT LIABLE?—There that is not his intention; here this is his intention. R. Bibi b. Abaye said, We too have learnt [thus]: A person may eat once, and be liable to four sin-offerings and one guilt-offering on account thereof, [viz.:] An unclean person who
c eats *heleb*, which is *nothar*[1] of sacred food [sacrifices] on the Day of Atonement.[2] R. Meir said: If in addition it is the Sabbath, and he carries it out in his mouth, he is liable.[3] Said they to him, That does not fall under this designation.[4] Yet why so? Surely this is not the normal way of carrying out?[5] But [what you must say is,] since he intends it thus, his design renders it [his mouth] the [right] place;[6] so here too, since he intends [it thus],[7] his design renders it [the mouth of the dog or of the furnace] a place [for depositing].

(8) Before it falls to the ground. (9) The exact meaning is discussed *infra*.

a (1) This assumes that the Mishnah means, AND RECALLS, *and* ANOTHER CATCHES, etc. (2) Tied together. I.e., the second clause can refer only to one who throws a bolt whilst retaining the cord in his hand. If he recollects before it reaches the ground, he can pull it back; hence if he does not pull it back the end (*sc.* its alighting) is deliberate. But if the article has left his hand entirely and he cannot prevent its falling, the end too is regarded as unwitting, whether he recollects or not. (3) That is not throwing at all. (4) Rashi reads: But we learnt this explicitly—why then intimate it in the general principle? (5) *Sc.* the last clause: if he recollects, he can stop before he has traversed four cubits.

b (1) This is all one, not as Raba interprets it. (2) Before it alighted. (3) The thrower or carrier (v. *infra* to which this actually refers) was unaware of the Sabbath (or that throwing is prohibited) during the first two cubits of its passage, recollected for the next two, and forgot again for the last two.—Of course, this is a most unlikely hypothesis—almost impossible in fact. Many similar unlikely contingencies are discussed in the Talmud, and their purpose is to establish the principles by which they are governed and which may then be applied to normal possibilities. (4) Cf. *supra* 71*b*, n. c8. Here too, two cubits is half the standard. (5) Even if he recollects, since it has left his hand and he cannot bring it back. (6) Not to complete the action. (7) Thus there is no controversy, each referring to a different case.

c (1) For *heleb* and *nothar* v. Glos. (2) He is liable to separate sin-offerings because he has violated the interdicts of *heleb*, *nothar*, eating on the Day of Atonement, and the prohibition against an unclean person's consumption of sacred food. Again, since the *heleb* of a sacrifice belongs to the altar, he is liable to a guilt-offering for trespass. (3) On account of carrying. (4) *Sc.* eating, for this liability is on account of carrying, not of eating; v. Ker. 13*b*. (5) One is not liable for performing an action in an abnormal manner. (6) For holding the food in to carry it out. R. Han.: his design renders his mouth the equivalent of a place four handbreadths square, whence and whither removal and depositing can take place. (7) *Sc.* that the dog should catch it, etc.

מתני' הזורק ונזכר מאחר שיצתה מידו קלטה אחר קלטה כלב או שנשרפה פטור זרק לעשות חבורה בין באדם ובין בבהמה ונזכר עד שלא נעשית חבורה פטור *זה הכלל כל חייבי חטאות אינן חייבין עד שתהא תחלתן וסופן שגגה תחלתן שגגה וסופן זדון תחילתן זדון וסופן שגגה פטורין עד שתהא תחילתן וסופן שגגה: גמ' הא נחה חייב והלא נזכר ותנן כל חייבי חטאות אינן חייבין עד שתהא תחלתן וסופן שגגה אמר רב כהנא סיפא אתאן ללכתא ומתנא ומתנא אוגדו בידו הוא כגון שנתכוין לעשות חבורה הא נמי תנינא הזורק לעשות חבורה בין באדם בין בבהמה ונזכר עד שלא נעשית חבורה פטור אלא אמר רבא במעביר והא זה הכלל דקתני אזריקה קתני אלא אמר רבא תרתי קתני הזורק ונזכר מאחר שיצתה מידו אי נמי לא נזכר וקלטה אחר או קלטה כלב או שנשרפה פטור רב אשי אמר חסורי מחסרא והכי קתני הזורק ונזכר מאחר שיצתה מידו קלטה אחר או קלטה כלב או שנשרפה פטור הא נחה חייב בד"א שחזר ושכח אבל לא חזר ושכח פטור שכל חייבי חטאות אינן חייבין עד שתהא תחלתן וסופן שגגה: זה הכלל כל חייבי חטאות כו': איתמר שתי אמות בשוגג שתי אמות במזיד שתי אמות בשוגג רבה אמר פטור רבא אמר חייב רבה אמר פטור אפילו לרבן גמליאל *דאמר אין ידיעה לחצי שיעור התם הוא דכי קא גמר שיעורא בשוגג קא גמר אבל הכא דבמזיד לא ובמאי אי בזורק שוגג הוא אלא במעביר *רבה אמר חייב ואפילו לרבנן דאמרי יש ידיעה לחצי שיעור התם הוא דבידו אבל הכא דאין בידו לא ובמאי אי במעביר הרי בידו ואלא בזורק *אמר *רבה [צ"ל רבא] זרק ונחה בפי הכלב או בפי הכבשן חייב והאנן תנן קלטה אחר או קלטה הכלב או שנשרפה פטור התם דלא מכוין הכא דקא מכוין אמר רב ביבי בר אביי אף אנן נמי תנינא *יש אוכל אכילה אחת וחייב עליה ד' חטאות ואשם אחד הטמא שאכל הלב והוא נותר מן המוקדשין ביוה"כ רבי מאיר אומר אף אם היתה שבת והוציאו [בפיו] חייב אמרו לו אינו מן השם ואמאי הא אין דרך הוצאה בכך אלא כיון דקא מיכוין מחשבתו משויא ליה מקום הכא נמי כיון דקא מיכוין מחשבתו משויא ליה מקום:

הדרן עלך הזורק

רש"י

מתני' הזורק. בשוגג: ונזכר. שהוא שבת: מאחר שיצתה. האבן מידו וקודם שתנוח: קלטה אחר. קס"ד לאחר שנזכר זה קלטה אחר הוו להו שנים שעשאוה וכגון (א) שנעקר ממקומו וקבלאו שקלטה כלב בפיו דלא הויא הנחה דבעינן מקום ד' פטור: גמ' ופרכינן הא נחה. לסוף ד' ברה"ר חייב ואע"ג דנזכר בין עקירה להנחה והא קתני סיפא זה הכלל כו': סיפא. דקתני עד שתהא תחלתן וסופן שגגה: אתאן ללכתא ומיתנא. לכתא עץ קטן שכפול ראשו וצריך לחמורים נושאים דרדורים של יין שתוחבין אותו בשני עקלים שהדרדורים תלויין בהן משני צידי החמור ומחברים בו הדרדורים שיחזיק זה את זה: ומיתנא. חבל כלומר לא מיתוקמא סיפא אלא בזורק לכתא הקשור בחבל קטן כדרכו ואוחז החבל בידו וכשנזכר היה בידו לאחוז החבל ולעכב זריקת הלכתא שלא תנוח הלכך תחילתו שוגג וסופו מזיד ופטור אבל זרק צרור וחפץ שכשנזכר אין בידו לעכבו כוליה שוגג הוא ונזכר דקתני ברישא אשמעינן רבותא דאף על גב דנזכר לא מיפטר מחטאת אא"כ קלטה אחר או כלב: ופרכינן לכתא ומתנא אוגדו בידו. ואפילו כוליה מילתא שוגג לא מיחייב דאין כאן זריקה: כגון שנתכוין לעשות חבורה. בתחלתו בשגגת שבת ונזכר עד שלא נעשית החבורה ולעולם בלכתא ומיתנא וכגון שנתכוין לעשות חבורה כו' דהאי משום זכירה הוא דמיפטר שהיה בידו להחזיר כמלא סופו זדון הא לא נזכר חייב ואע"ג דאגדו בידו דחיוביה לאו משום זריקה הוא אלא משום חבורה: הא בהדיא קתני לה. במתניתין וזה הכלל ע"כ למילתא אחריתי אתא: אלא אמר רבא. זה הכלל למעביר ארבע אמות ברה"ר ונזכר קודם שהעבירו ד' אמות אתא שהיה בידו לעמוד במקום שנזכר אבל זורק לא מיפטר בזכירה: והא כי קתני זה הכלל אזריקה תני לה. דאיירי לעיל מיניה בזורק לעשות חבורה ואי סתם זורק לא מיפטר בזכירה היכי מתני גבי זה הכלל: אלא אמר רבא. רישא מילי מילי קתני לה ותרתי קתני הזורק ונזכר אי נמי לא נזכר וקלטה אחר כו' והדר תני כללא לאתויי מעביר: חסורי מחסרא וכו'. ולעולם חדא קתני: שחזר ושכח. קודם שתנוח דהוה ליה תחילתו וסופו שגגה ואשמעינן נזכר דתנא בה לרבותא דאע"ג דהואי ידיעה בינתיים מיחייב דאין ידיעה לחצי שיעור דהיינו *כאין [צ"ל שאין] בידו להחזיר: ה"ג שכל חייבי חטאות כו': איתמר ב' אמות בשוגג ב' אמות במזיד ב' אמות בשוגג רבה אמר פטור רבא אמר חייב. שתי אמות במזיד שנזכר לאחר שתי אמות ראשונות וחזר ושכח בב' האחרונות: דר"ג. לקמן בפרק הבונה: התם דכי גמר שיעורא בשוגג גמר. הכותב ב' אותיות בב' העלמות דמחייב בה ר"ג באות השניה נגמר השיעור ואף הוא בשוגג אבל הכא בשתי אמצעיות שהן במזיד נגמר השיעור כדמפרש ואזיל לה במעביר ושתי אמצעיות מזיד: שוגג הוא. שהרי אין בידו לעכבה וכיון שחזר ושכח חייב דלא נגמרה מלאכה עד שעת הנחה שהיא לסוף ובשוגג: אלא במעביר. וכיון דבידו לעמוד בסוף ב' אמות האמצעיות אשתכח דגמר שיעורא במזיד: התם הוא דבידו. שלא לחזור ולכתוב השניה הלכך כי חזר ושכח הויא לה שגגה אחריתי ולא גמרה לקמייתא: אבל הכא אין בידו. להחזיר כשנזכר כדמפרש ואזיל בזורק הלכך כולה חדא שגגה היא ומר אמר חדא ומר אמר חדא ולא פליגי: בפי הכבשן. ונשרפה בשלהבת: הכא דקא מיכוין. מחשבתו משויא ליה מקום דהא אחשביה: אכילה אחת. זית אחד: ד' חטאות. משום חלב משום נותר משום אכילת יוה"כ משום טומאת הגוף ואכל קדש: ואשם מעילות. דאפילו הוא כהן גבי אימורים זר הוא: אף אם היתה שבת כו'. ומשום יוה"כ לא מיחייב בהוצאה דקסבר אין עירוב והוצאה ליוה"כ: אינו מן השם. אין חטאת זו משום אכילה אלא משום הוצאה: ואמאי. מיחייב משום הוצאה לדברי הכל הא אין דרך להוציא בפה: מחשבתו. שצריך לאוכלה בהליכתו ואחשבה להוצאה זו בפיו: הדרן עלך הזורק

תוספות

סיפא אתאן ללכתא ומיתנא. אבל רישא מיירי בלא לכתא ומיתנא וה"ה אפילו בלא נזכר פטור כיון שקלטה כלב או נשרפה והא דנקט נזכר לאשמעינן דאפילו בנזכר דוקא קלטה כלב או נשרפה פטור משום דלא נחה הא נחה חייב: אלא אמר רבא במעביר. והוא דחבורה איירי בלכתא ומיתנא ואין ר"י יודע למה הוצרך להשמיטו ההיא דחבורה מה לי חבורה מה לי מעביר וכן לרבא דקאמר תרתי קתני אמאי תנא ההיא דחבורה כיון דתנא הזורק ונזכר פטור ה"נ בחבורה דמ"ש: רב אשי אמר חסורי מחסרא כו'. אין זה ממש חסורי מחסרא דמשנה כמו שהיא שנויה יש לפרש כן אלא כדי לפרשה קאמר בלשון חסורי מחסרא:

ובמאי אי בזורק שוגג הוא. אע"ג דכי גמר שיעוריה במזיד גמר מ"מ כיון דבתחילת זריקה הוי שוגג ואין יכול להחזירה ובהנחה נמי שוגג הוא חשיב כאילו מתחלה ועד סוף הויא חדא שגגה:

אמר רבא זרק בפי כלב. ל"ג ונחה בפי כלב דנחה משמע מעצמה כדא"ר יוחנן בפ"ק (לעיל דף ה.) זרק חפץ ונח לתוך ידו של חבירו חייב ומסיק דקמ"ל אף על גב דלא אחשביה לידיה והכא מסיק דקא מכוין ומחשבתו משויא ליה מקום:

רבי מאיר אומר אם היתה שבת והוציאו בפיו כו'. פי' בקונטרס דלהכי נקט אם היתה שבת דמשום יוה"כ לא מיחייב דאין עירוב והוצאה ליוה"כ ולא הויא מסקנא הכי בפרק אמרו לו (כריתות דף יד.) דנדחו דברי רפרם שהיה מפרש כן ומסיק דנקט שבת כדי להרבות בחטאות ולחייבו אף משום שבת [ויוה"כ]:

והוציאו בפיו חייב. כולהו בהדי הדדי קא אתו °דבליעתו הויא הנחה אע"פ שמהלך כדאמרינן (לעיל דף פ.) כתיבתן זו היא הנחתן ואע"ג דפיו למעלה מי' ואינו רחב ד' בטל הוא אגב רה"ר ולא דמי לבוכיאר ביריעה דאמר בריש פרקין (לעיל דף צו:) דבמקום פטור קא אזיל דהתם מקום קביעות הוה טפי ודמי לטרסקל דאמר בפ"ק (דף ה.) דלמטה מי' הוי רה"ר והכא אפילו למעלה מי' בטל אגב רשות הרבים ועוד דמעביר למעלה מי' כלמטה °וחשיב מונח ברשות הרבים:

הדרן עלך הזורק

עין משפט נר מצוה

מ א מיי' פ"א מהל' שבת הלכה יט ופ"ב מהל' שגגות הלכה א סמג עשין ריג:
מא ב מיי' פי"ג מהל' שבת הלכה יד סמג לאוין סה:
מב ג ד מיי' פ"ו מהל' שגגות הלכה ח:
מג ה ו מיי' פי"ג מהל' שבת הלכה יג:
מד ז מיי' פ"ו מהל' שגגות הלכה ד:

רבינו חננאל

מקום נמוך פחות מי' ומקום גבוה י' טפחים אין מעבירין אותה אלא מחזירין אותה לדרך אחרת · תוב מקשו להני דאמרי עושה מקום ד' כמו שאמרנו כמו תיבה פחותה או סל פחותה וכיוצא בהן וממלא ואע"ג דליכא משפת מיא י' טפחים שופכין דספינה להיכי שדי להו כלומר שופכין שצריך לשופכן כגון מי רגלים וכיוצא בהן היכא שפיך להו וכי תימא באותו מקום (שעשהו ד' הוא ממלא אלא המים) [שעשהו למלא בו המים] הוא שופך שופכין לשם הא קא מימאסו ליה מיא. ומשני שדי להון בדופן של ספינה שהיא מכלל רה"י ואע"ג דשותתין ואולי מדפני ונחתני לים כל כי האי גוונא כחו בכרמלית לא גזרו רבנן וגרסינן בפרק ר' אליעזר דתולין אמר רב יהודה האי מאן דסחי במיא דנהרא בשבתא נינגוב נפשיה וניסק דאי לא קמסיק מיא מכרמלית לרה"י והוא הספינה סוף סוף כי נחית למיסחי קא דחי להו למיא ונמצא מטלטל בכרמלית ושנינן שכוחו בכרמלי' לא גזרו רבנן ומנא תימרא דכחו בכרמלית לא גזרו רבנן דתניא ספינה שבים ר' יהודה אומר עמוקה י' ואינה גבוהה י' מטלטלין מתוכה לים אבל לא מן הים לתוכה ואוקימנא להאי דתני מטלטלין מתוכה לים על חודה של ספינה שהן דפני הספינה וש"מ כחו בכרמלית לא גזרו רבנן פי' עמוקה י' ואינה גבוהה י' כגון שנשתקעו מחיצותיה בים וכשאתה מודד עמוקה של ספינה מבפנים הויא זו טפחים ופעמים יותר אבל משפת הים ולמעלה עד שפת הספינה כיון שנשתקעו מקצת מחיצותיה בים לא הוי גבוהה י' ונמצאת הספינה רה"י והים כרמלית לפיכך הוצאה מן הספינה דרך כחו לא גזרו רבנן אבל להכניס דלא אפשר דרך כחו לא שרו:

ירושלמי א"ר אבין למה מן הים לתוכה אסור מפני הסכנה אמר רב הונא הני ביציאתה דמישן אין מטלטלין בהן אלא בד' אמות · פי' ביצייתא ספינות קטנות העשויות לתשמיש הגדולות כי כשבאות להיכנס בנמל מהלכות לפניה ורואין הקלו המים אם לאו ואם רואין כי קלו המים משליכין העוגין בים שהן ברזילים [גדולים]ומעמידין אותה שם ועוד עשויות לצאת בהם בני הספינה ליבשה וליכנס בהן ולטעון ולפרק האנתיקי שבה ומתוך שהן קלות ומהלכות על ביצת המים לפיכך הם נקראות ביצייתא: מישן · שם מקום וגרסינן בהמוכר את הספינה מכר את ביציית סימכוס אומר מכר את הדוגית ואמר רבא הביצית ודוגית חדא מלתא היא ומפני שמישן הוא מקום אגמי מים עושין ביציית להלך בהן באגמים ויש להן דפנות שהן מחיצותיה וקרקעיתה עשויה נסרים נסרים וביניהם חלל ומי הים והנהר נכנסין בה. והיושבים בה כמו במים יושבין ועושין אותה כך שאפי' אם תתהפך על פניה אינה נטבעת לעולם. ואמר רב הונא כיון שהיא פרוצה ככרמלית דינה ואין מטלטלין בה בשבת אלא בארבע ולא אמרו אלא בזמן שאין בה נסר לנסר חלל פחות מג' טפחים. אבל יש בין נסר לנסר חלל פחות מג' טפחים כיון דכל פחות מג' כלבוד דמי ראין אלו הנסרים כאלו מחוברין איש אל אחיו הן ואע"פ שהמים נכנסין בה לא חיישינן וכרה"י היא ומותר לטלטל בכולה וכן אם היו נסרין פחות מד' ויש בין זה לזה יתר מג' או ג' ומילא את החלל שבין הנסרים קני ואורבני מותר לטלטל בכולה ואתקיף עליה רב

מסורת הש"ס

לעיל ד.

[ועיין תוס' לעיל ד: ד"ה אלא א"ר יוסף ותוס' עירובין צט: ד"ה זרק ונח]

לעיל עח: לקמן קה.

[צ"ל רבא]

עירובין צט.

כריתות יג: שבועות כד: יבמות לד.

[צ"ל שאין]

הגהות הב"ח

(א) רש"י ד"ה קלטה אחר וכו' וכגון. נ"ב ע"ל בדף ה סוף ע"א:

גליון הש"ס

תוס' ד"ה והוציאו וכו' דבליעתו הוי הנחה. ע"ל יא ע"א תד"ה לא יעמוד: בא"ד וחשיב מונח כר"ה ע"ל דף ו ע"א תד"ה התם:

רב נסים גאון

אפי' לרבן גמליאל דאמר אין ידיעה לחצי שיעור. בסוף פ' הבונה (דף קה) חלק רבן גמליאל עם החכמים בכותב ב' אותיות בב' העלמות ובגמ' גרסי במאי קמיפלגי רבן גמליאל סבר אין ידיעה לחצי שיעור וכבר פירשנו איתה בפרק כלל גדול (דף קג): אמר רב ביבי בר אביי אף אנן נמי תנינא יש אוכל אכילה אחת וחייב עליה ד' חטאות ואשם אחד' ומשכחת לה במסכת כריתות בפרק אמרו לו אכלת חלב (דף יג) פי' ד' חטאות בנוי על עיקר המשנה שבתחלת זו המסכת' ל"ו כריתות בתורה ואלו הן טמא שאכל את הקודש והאוכל חלב ודם ונותר ופיגול והאוכל והעושה מלאכה ביום הכפורים כו' ואמרו על אלו חייבין על זדונן כרת ועל שגגתן חטאת ימי שאכל חלב והוא נותר מן המוקדשים ביום הכפורים חייב חטאת משום טמא שאכל את הקודש וחטאת [חלב וחטאת משום אוכל נותר וחטאת] משום אוכל ביום הכפורים הרי ד' חטאות וחייב אשם מעילות כמשה"כ (ויקרא ה) נפש כי תמעול מעל בה' וחטאה בשגגה וכדתנן (מעילה דף יח) הנהנה שוה פרוטה מן ההקדש מעל ואילו היה טהור ואכל את הקודש בשגגה נתחייב אשם מעילות:

סליק פרק הזורק

עין משפט
נר מצוה

א א מיי' פ"י מהל' שבת הלכה יב סמג לאוין סה :
ב ב מיי' שם הל' יח :
ג ג ד מיי' שם הלכה יב :
ד ה מיי' שם הל' יח :
ה ו מיי' שם הלכה יד והלכה טז ופכ"ג הלכה א :
ו ז מיי' שם פ"י הלכה יג:

הבונה כמה יבנה ויהא חייב *הבונה כל שהוא והמסתת והמכה בפטיש ובמעצד (א) *הקודח כל שהוא חייב זה הכלל כל העושה מלאכה ומלאכתו מתקיימת בשבת חייב (וכן) רשב"ג אומר אף המכה בקורנס על הסדן בשעת מלאכה חייב מפני שהוא כמתקן מלאכה: **גמ'** כל שהוא למאי חזיא א"ר ירמיה שכן עני חופר גומא להצניע בה פרוטותיו דכוותה גבי משכן שכן תופרי יריעות חופרין גומא להצניע בה מחטיהן אביי אמר כיון דמשתכי לא עבדי הכי אלא שכן עני עושה פיטפוטי כירה קטנה לשפות עליה קדירה קטנה דכוותה גבי משכן מבשלי סמנין לצבוע יריעות שחסרה מלאכתן עושין פיטפוטי כירה קטנה לשפות עליה יורה קטנה רב אחא בר יעקב אמר *אין עניות במקום עשירות אלא שכן בעה"ב שיש לו נקב בבירתו וסותמו דכוותה גבי משכן שכן קרש שנפלה בו דרנא מטיף לתוכה אבר וסותמו אמר שמואל המצדד את האבן חייב מיתיבי אחד נותן את האבן ואחד נותן את הטיט הנותן את הטיט חייב וליטעמיך אימא סיפא רבי יוסי אומר ואפילו העלה והניח על גבי דימוס של אבנים חייב אלא תלתא בנייני הוו תתא מציעא. ועילא תתא בעי צדודי ועפרא מציעא בעי נמי טינא עילאי בהנחה בעלמא: והמסתת: מסתת משום מאי מיחייב רב אמר משום בונה ושמואל אמר משום מכה בפטיש העושה נקב בלול של תרנגולים רב אמר משום בונה ושמואל אמר משום מכה בפטיש עייל שופתא בקופינא דמרא רב אמר משום בונה ושמואל אמר משום מכה בפטיש וצריכא דאי אשמעינן קמייתא בההיא קאמר רב משום דדרך בנין בכך אבל עושה נקב בלול של תרנגולים דאין דרך בנין בכך אימא מודה ליה לשמואל ואי אשמעינן בהא בהא קאמר רב משום דדמי לבנין *דעבדיה לאוירא אבל שופתא בקופינא דמרא דאין דרך בנין בכך אימא מודה ליה לשמואל ואי אשמעינן בהא בהא קאמר שמואל אבל בהנך תרתי אימא מודה ליה לרב צריכא בעא מיניה רב נתן בר אושעיא מרבי יוחנן מסתת משום מאי מיחייב אחוי ליה בידיה משום מכה בפטיש והאנן תנן המסתת והמכה בפטיש אימא המסתת המכה בפטיש ת"ש

הקודח

רש"י

הבונה. שאמרו באבות מלאכות כמה יבנה כו' : מסתת. מרבע את האבן ומתקנה הכל לפי המקום שיש מקומות שרגילין להחליק ויש מקומות שרגילין לחרוץ בה חריצים בארץ אשכנז: המכה בפטיש. גם הוא באבות מלאכות והוא בלע"ז פי"ק שמפוצץ בו את האבן מן הסלע לאחר שחצב את האבן סביב ומבדיל מן ההר קצת הוא מכה בפטיש מכה גדולה והיא מתפרקת ונופלת וזהו גמר מלאכה של חוצבי אבן וכל הגומר בשבת מלאכה תולדת מכה בפטיש היא : מעצד. אף הוא כמו קורנס גדול של ברזל לבנין של ברזל*: והקודח. נוקב עץ או אבן בכותל : כל שהוא. אכולהו קאי אמסתת ומכה בפטיש ובמעצד והקודח : כל העושה מלאכה ומלאכתו מתקיימת. שיש מתקיימת כיוצא בו [ואין מוסיף עליה] : בשבת. אעושה מלאכה קאי : על הסדן. בלע"ז אינקלומ"א : קורנס. מרטי"ל : מפני שהוא כמתקן מלאכה. ואע"פ שאינו מכה על הפעולה אלא על הסדן ובגמרא מפרש מאי מתקן : **גמ'** דמשתכי · מעלין חלודה המחטין רוא"ל : פטפוטי. רגלי כירה כמין כלי ברזל שקורין טרפיי"ד מעמידין הכירה של חרס : מבשלי סממנים לצבוע שחסרה מלאכתן· שלמלמו למר לצביעתן וחסרה למלאכתן והוצרכו לחזור ולבשל סמנין ולצבוע מעט : יורה קטנה גרסינן הכא : אין עניות במקום עשירות. לא עשו דבר בצמצום אלא הכל מתחלתן דיים והותר : בבירתו. בירה נאה שהוא אוכל ושוכב מקפיד על חור קטן שבה אם מגונה הוא וסותמו בטיט : דרנא. תולעת : המצדד את האבן. מושיבה ומצדדה עד שמתיישבת בקרקעית יסוד הבנין יפה מתוך שהוא מצדדה הוא מכינה תחתיה ומושיבה בארץ חייב ואפילו לא נתן טיט הוי בונה כל שהוא דיש מקיימין כן בלא טיט : הנותן את הטיט חייב . אבל הנותן האבן פטור: דימוס. שורת אבני חומה אלמא בהנחה בעלמא חייב ואפילו לא צידד ועדיפא הא מדשמואל : אלא. לאו קושיא תלתא בנייני הוי : תתא . יסוד החומה תחתית שמושיבין אבנים על הארץ בלא טיט בצדודי ועפר כל עצמו אינו אלא לצדד את האבן שתשב בשוה ולא תטה לכאן ולכאן ויהא עפר סביב לה לסומכה ובההוא אמר שמואל מילתיה וברייתא במיצעא כל הבנין כולו שמן היסוד עד שורה העליונה בעי נמי טינא עם הצידוד : עילאה . דימוס העליון שאין על גביו עוד דימוס אינו חושש אם נטה האבן לצד אחד הלכך בהנחה בעלמא סגי והוא מילתא דרבי יוסי : משום מאי . איזו תולדה מן האבות הוא : מכה בפטיש. גמר מלאכה הוא שהמקום שחרץ חריץ זה לא יחרוץ עוד : לול של תרנגולין . של עץ הוא וסתום ומנקבו שיצא הריח של נוחה ולא יזיק להו : משום מכה בפטיש . שהיא גמר מלאכת הלול וכל מידי דהוא גמר מלאכה חייב משום מכה בפטיש כדאמרי' בפ' כלל גדול (דף עה:): עייל שופתא בקופינא דמרא. *שופתא יתד קטן שתוחבין בתוך בית יד של מרא בהיותו בנקב הברזל להדקו שלא יצא שקורין קאייג"ל : קופינא . הוא חור שבראש המר : מרא . בלע"ז פוסי"ר : מסתת . דרך בנין בכך : ואי אשמעינן בהא. בעושה נקב בלול: דדמי לבנין. שאף בבנין הבתים עושין נקבים לאויר כדקאמר ועבדי לאוירא חורים וחלונות : ואי איתמר בהא . בשופתא : בהא קאמר שמואל · דאי אתרו ביה משום בונה לא מיחייב דלאו בנין הוא : אחוי בידיה . מכה באגרופו על כפו כמכה בפטיש : אימא המסתת המכה בפטיש . וה"ק המסתת שהוא חייב משום מכה בפטיש חייב בכ"ש :

הקודח

תוספות

הבונה· צריך ליתן טעם אמאי תני בונה אחר זריקה והושטה* : **מכה** בפטיש . פי' בקונטרס שמפוצץ בו את הסלע לאחר שחצבה ואין נראה לר"י דבמשכן לא הוה בנין אבנים ולא שייך תנא גמר מלאכה דכלים דהוה במשכן ונקט מכה בפטיש דאבן דלא הוה במשכן אלא נראה לר"י דהאי מכה בפטיש היינו מכוש אחרון שמכה על הכלי בשעת גמר מלאכה : **כל** שהוא למאי חזי . דוקא הכא איצטריך לפרושי דהוה דכוותיה במשכן משום דלא חשיב בנין כל שהוא אבל מוציא עיטרן ופלפלת כל שהוא סברא הוא דמיחייב : **הכי** גרסינן המצדד את האבן חייב . ול"ג משום מכה בפטיש דבמסקנא מוקי לה בתתאה דלא שייך שם מכה בפטיש ועוד דהכי קאי בבונה : **וליטעמיך** אימא סיפא אפילו העלה ע"ג דימוס כו' . ול"ג ר' יוסי אומר אפילו העלה דאי גרסינן ליה מאי קאמר וליטעמיך הא פליגי רבנן עליה ובתוספתא נמי ל"ג ליה : **העושה** נקב בלול . קשה לרב דאמר משום בונה אמאי הפסיק מכה בפטיש בין מסתת לקודח דהוו תרווייהו משום בונה ולשמואל נמי ליתני תרווייהו בהדי הדדי : **האי** מאן דעייל שופתא בקופינא רב אמר חייב משום בונה . ואע"ג דקי"ל *אין בנין בכלים אור"י דהיינו דווקא בהחזרת (ב) בתי תריסין או במנורה של חוליות אבל בנין גמור מיחייב בכלים *כמו בקרקע כדאמרי' בס"פ כירה (לעיל דף מז·) גבי מטה של טרסיים אם תקע חייב חטאת ומחזיר קני מנורה חייב חטאת וקרן עגולה ואין חילוק בין כלים לקרקע אלא במקום שאין חיזוק ואומנות דבכלי לא חשיב בנין ובקרקע חשיב בנין ובפ' בכל מערבין (עירובין דף לה·) גבי נתנו במגדל דמוקי לה רבה ורב יוסף במגדל של עץ דמ"ס כלי הוא ואין בנין בכלים ומ"ס אהל הוא התם מיירי במנעול (ג) וקטיר במיתנא כדמסיק אביי לבסוף ולא הוצרכו לפרש משום דפשיטא דבהכי איירי דבע"א יש סתירה ובנין בכלים וכן משמע מדמוקי אביי במנעול וקטיר במיתנא דהוי כמו חותמות שבכלים הא לאו הכי אסור ובריש סוגיא דפריך ואמאי הוא במקום אחד ועירובו במקום אחר הוא אע"ג דסתם מגדל של עץ הוא דהוי כלי כדמוכח בכמה דוכתי מעיקרא הוה סבר דאיירי שאי אפשר לקחת העירוב אלא על ידי סתירה גמורה : **לול** של תרנגולין . דלא חשיב ליה שמואל בונה אומר ר"י משום דלא חשיב להאי פתח עשוי להכניס ולהוציא : [ועי' לקמן קמו·] : **אבל** בהנך תרתי אימא מודה כו' . ומקמייתא ובתרייתא נמי לא ידעינן מציעתא :

בשלמא

רבינו חננאל

נחמן למה לך כולי האי לימא גוד אחית מחיצתא פי' ראה בלבך כאלו את הותך כמין קלף מן המחיצות שהן דפני הביצית (ומציעו) [ומעמיד] בקרקעיתא ונמצאו הנסרין כולן כאלו מחוברות הוקמי לא תניא ר' יוסי בר יהודה אומר נעץ קנה ברה"ר והניח בראשו טרסקל רחב ד"ט וזרק מרה"ר ונח על גביו חייב. אלמא אמרי' גוד אחית מחיצתא וראין כאלו דפני הטרסקל יורדין עד עיקרו של קנה וכאילו יש בעיקרו ד' טפחים הכא נמי נימא כאלו דפני הספינה עקומין ומסבבין הנסרים ודחי רב יוסף להא דרב נחמן ואמר ליה משם ר' חייא אמרו וחכמים פוטרין אלמא רבנן סברי לא אמרינן גוד אחית מחיצתא וחולקין על ר' יוסי ב"ר יהודה ודחי אביי להא דרב יוסף בשתי דחיות חדא הא איני והתניא עמוד ברה"ר גבוה י' ורחב ד' ואין בעיקרו ד' ויש בקצה שלו ג' וזרק ונח ע"ג חייב אלמא אמרינן גוד אחית מחיצתא כלומר רואין בראיית הלב כאילו הרחב שעל ראשו מגיע עד עיקרו ועוד אפי' רבנן דפליגי עליה דר' יוסי ברבי יהודה התם בקנה שנעץ והניח בטרסקל בראשו דלא אמרינן גוד אחית מחיצתא התם טעמא מאי דכיון שהגדיים בוקעין בעיקר הקנה ועוברין תחת הטרסקל מוכחא מלתא דלית ליה מחיצתא כלל אבל בספינה כיון שאין הגדיים בוקעין באותו חלל שבין הנסרים אפי' רבנן מודו דכי האי גוונא אמרינן גוד אחית מחיצתא . ולא מצא רב יוסף תשובה בשתיהן והשיב רב אחא כלפי אביי ספינה נמי הא איכא בקיעת דגים וכשם שאין אומרין בקנה שיש בראשו טרסקל גוד אחית מחיצתא מפני הגדיים שבוקעין בו כך הספינה אין אומרים גוד אחית מחיצתא מפני הדגים שבוקעין בו כדגרסינן בעירובין פרק ראשון אמר רבא עשה לחי למבוי והגביהו מן הקרקע ג' או שהפליגו מן הכותל ג' לא עשה כלום דהויא לה מחיצ' שהגדיים בוקעין בה ודחה רב אשי להא דרב אחא וא"ל בקיעת דגים לאו שמה בקיעה דהא מחיצה תלויה מתרת במים כרב ואע"פ שהגדיים בוקעין בה אלמא בקיעת דגים לאו שמה בקיעה ואין מחיצה תלויה מתרת בחורבה כרבא בלחי שהגביהו מן הקרקע דהויא מחיצה שהגדיים בוקעין בה וכיון דרב אשי מסייע ליה ואביי ורב נחמן ש"מ שאפילו אין בספינה בפחות מג' ד' מותר לטלטל בכל הביצית : **ספינות** קשורות זו בזו מטלטלין מזו לזו כו' אמרינן פשיטא ואוקמה רב ספרא לא נצרכה אלא לערב ולטלטל מזו לזו ודוקא קשורות אבל מוקפות לא ותניא נמי הכי וסלקא דכל מחיצתא שנעשית בין בשוגג בין במזיד שמה מחיצה היכא דאיתעבידא מחיצה בשבת מותר *) לזרוק אליה ואסור לטלטל משם מפורש בעושין פסין .לענין יבשו מים בשבת ובאו מים בשבת וספינה קשורה בחברתא לא שרי לטלטולי מינייהו עד דמיקטרן בדבר שיכול להעמידה ואפי' בחוט הסרבל ויכול להעמידה הכי הוא מתירה. אבל לענין טומאה פי' שמואל אם הן ספינות קשורות בשלשלת של ברזל ממש שהיא כחרב ונגע בשלשלת זו מת מביאה הטומאה בספינה האחרת שכיון שנגע בה המת נעשת כמת עצמו דקיי"ל חרב הרי הוא כחלל פי' הא דתנן במסכת אהלות פ"ח (מ"ה) קשר את הספינה בדבר שהוא יכול להעמיד כבש את האבן ע"ג הטלית מביאה את הטומאה . פי' שמואל זה השני במשנה זו בדבר שהוא יכול להעמידה . שלשלת של ברזל הוא ממש והוא כגון יש מת בספינה אחת וראש השלשלת נוגעת במת וזו השלשלת קשורה בספינה אחרת נמצאו בו הספינות קשורות זו עם זו בשלשלת. שלשלת זו הנוגעת במת נעשת כמת עצמו דקיי"ל חרב הרי הוא כחלל לפיכך מביא את הטומאה בספינה האחרת : **הזורק** ונזכר לאחר שיצאת מידו שהיא שבת קלטה אחר או קלטה כלב או נשרפה פטור כו' בניינא דמתני' אינו חייב עד שתהיה מתחלת המלאכה עד תשלום המלאכה בשוגג. אבל אם היתה לו ידיעה אחת שגגה**) קודם תשלום המלאכה בידיעה פטור: עד [שיהא] תחלתן וסופן שגגה. ודייקינן מרישא דמתניתין דקתני הזורק ונזכר לאחר שיצאת מידו קלטה אחר פטור וכן אם קלטה כלב וכן אם נשרפה פטור טעמא מאי פטור משום דלא נעשת מחשבתו הא אם נחה במקום שהיתה מחשבתו בעת שזרקה חייב ואע"פ שנזכר לאחר שיצאת מידו הנה היתה לו ידיעה אחר שגגה וחייב ופריק רב כהנא סיפא דקתני עד שתהא תחילתן וסופן שגגה אתאן ללכתא ומתנא. פי' קנה קשור בחוט ארוך שכשיזרקנו לא יאבד אלא מושך בחוט והוא נמשך אחריו כי האי גוונא בעינן תחילה וסוף שגגה שאע"פ שזרקו כיון שנזכר קודם שינוח יכול להחזירו אבל כגון אבן שכיון שיצאה מידו אינו יכול להחזירה אע"פ שנחה אחר זכירתו חייב ודחינן לכתא ומתנא איגודו בידו וכל איגודו בידו אינה זריקה ופריק רב כהנא כגון שזורק זה הקנה לעשות חבורה וקמ"ל עד שתעשה חבורה (במשכת) [בעינן שתמשך] שגגה. ונדחה טעם זה. ופריק רבה כי בעינן תחלה וסוף שגגה במעביר . אבל בזורק לא ורישא דהא מתניתין בזורק ואקשינן עלה והא כי קתני זה הכלל כל חייבי חטאות כו' אזריקה הוא דקתני ונדחה דרבה ופריק רבא מתניתין תרתי קתני חדא הזורק ונזכר לאחר שיצאת מידו אע"פ שנחה במקום מחשבתו פטור וחדא אם לא נזכר וקלטה אחר או כלב או נשרפה פטור דלא אתעבידא מחשבתו. והא (דרבה) [דרבא] והא דרב אשי נמי לא איפריכו מיהו רב אשי דייק הכי ביון דמתניתין כוליה לענין שוגג היא דבבא דרישא קתני ונזכר ומיציעתא נמי הזורק לעשות חבורה ונזכר ובסיפא כולל זה הכלל כל חייבי חטאות כו' הלכך מתניתין כולה בשוגג היא ולא לענין נחה היא אלא

*) עי' בה"ז הלכות ע"ש אות ס' שהביא לשון ר"ה והגיהו .

**) נ"ל ידיעה מתחלה ואח"כ שגגה או שגגה קודם ותשלום המלאכה וכו' .

מסורת הש"ס

[עי' הרי"ס שנתן טעם לזה]

מנחות ט.

ב"ק דף קיט. לועז דולד"ר

גי' רש"ל

[כתובות קו: זבחים פח: מנחות סט. תמיד כט. לח:]

[ביצה דף י.]

[לקמן קמו.]

עיין גיטין לג: רש"י ד"ה שופתא

הגהות הב"ח

(א) במשנה והקודח כל שהוא : (ב) תוס' ד"ה האי מאן וכו' בהחזרת תריסין כצ"ל ותיבת בתי נמחק : (ג) בא"ד במנעול דקטיר:

הגהות הגר"א

[א] גמ' (ולפי') תו"מ וכ"צ וכ"ל שניהם חייבים כצ"ל וכ"ה בירושלמי ואמר שם למי נצרכה סיפא לרבנן ועי' תוס' ד"ה וליטעמיך וכו' :

CHAPTER XII

MISHNAH. [102b] IF ONE BUILDS, HOW MUCH MUST HE BUILD TO BE CULPABLE? HE WHO BUILDS HOWEVER LITTLE, AND HE WHO CHISELS, AND HE WHO STRIKES WITH A HAMMER OR WITH AN ADZE, AND HE WHO BORES [A HOLE],
a HOWEVER LITTLE,[1] IS CULPABLE. THIS IS THE GENERAL PRINCIPLE: WHOEVER DOES WORK ON THE SABBATH AND HIS WORK ENDURES,[2] IS CULPABLE. R. SIMEON B. GAMALIEL SAID: HE TOO IS CULPABLE WHO BEATS WITH THE SLEDGE HAMMER ON THE ANVIL AT THE TIME OF HIS WORK, BECAUSE HE IS AS ONE WHO IMPROVES HIS WORK.[3]

GEMARA. 'HOWEVER LITTLE'—what is that fit for?—Said R. Jeremiah: Because a poor man digs a hole to hide his *peruṭoth* therein.[4] Similarly in connection with the Tabernacle[5] such a labour was performed because those who sewed the curtain dug holes to put away their needles therein. Said Abaye, Since they would rust, they would not do so! Rather [say]: because a poor man makes the feet of a small stove to place a pot upon it. Similarly in connection with the Tabernacle, [such a labour was performed] because those who boiled the dyes for dyeing the curtains, when their materials [the finished dyes] were insufficient, they made the feet of a small stove to place a small kettle upon it. Said R. Aḥa b. Jacob: There is no poverty in the
b place of wealth.[1] Rather [say] because a householder who finds a hole in his dwelling closes it up. Similarly in connection with the Tabernacle, [such a labour was performed] because when a board was attacked by wood-worms, one dropped molten lead into it and closed it.[2]

Samuel said: He who arranges a building stone[3] is culpable.[4] An objection is raised: If one places the stone and another the mortar, he who places the mortar is culpable?[5]—But according to your view, consider the second clause; R. Jose said:[6] Even if one lifts up [the stone] and sets [it] on the row of stones, he is liable? Rather [the fact is that] there are three modes of building, [viz., in connection with] the lower, the middle, and the upper [rows]. The lower requires arranging in place and [filling] earth [around it];[7] the middle[8] requires mortar too; whilst the top merely [requires] placing.[9]

AND HE WHO CHISELS. On what score is a chiseller culpable?—Rab said: On the score of building: while Samuel said: On the score of beating with a hammer.[10] If one makes a hole in a hen-coop,[11]—Rab said: [He is culpable] on account of building; while Samuel said: On account of beating with a hammer. If one inserts a pin through the eyelet of a spade,[12]—Rab said: [He is liable] on account of building; while Samuel said: On account of beating with a hammer. Now, these are [all] necessary. For if we were informed of the first, [I would argue]: in that case Rab rules [so], because such is a mode of building;[13] but if one makes a hole in a hen-coop, seeing that this is not a mode of building, I would maintain that he agrees with Samuel. And if we were informed of this [latter one only],—here does Rab rule [thus], because it is similar to a building, since it is made for ventilation; but [as for inserting] a pin through the eyelet of a spade, which is not a mode of building, I would say that he agrees with Samuel. And if we were told of this [latter one], only here does Samuel rule [thus], but in the former two I would maintain that he
c agrees with Rab:[1] [hence] they are necessary.

R. Nathan b. Oshaia asked R. Joḥanan: On what grounds is a chiseller culpable? He intimated to him with his hand, On account of beating with a hammer. But we learnt, HE WHO CHISELS AND HE WHO BEATS WITH A HAMMER?—Say, 'HE WHO CHISELS,

a (1) 'However little' applies to all the foregoing labours. (2) I.e., it is not necessary to add thereto, which on occasion may be complete in itself. (3) This is explained in the Gemara. (4) *Peruṭah*, pl. *peruṭoth*, a very small coin. Thus we find an instance of very little building, and therefore this sets the standard. Money was hidden in the earth. Cf. B.M. 42a: 'Money can only be guarded by placing it in the earth'; Josephus, *Wars*, V. 7, 2: 'which the owners have treasured up underground against the uncertain fortunes of war'. (5) The labours performed there being the basis for the principal Sabbath labours, v. *supra* 73a.

b (1) This would never be necessary there, for everything was prepared in large quantities. (2) All these are instances of building. (3) Shifting the stone about on the ground until it lies in the right spot. (4) For building, even if no mortar is used. (5) But not the former, which contradicts Samuel. (6) Tosaf. omits 'R. Jose said', and Wilna Gaon makes a somewhat similar emendation. (7) But no mortar, and Samuel refers to this. (8) This means all the rows between the bottom and the top rows. (9) Without the meticulous care needed for the bottom row, since nothing was to go upon it. (10) This being the completion of the work, v. *supra* 75b. (11) For ventilation, etc. (12) Rashi: the pin passed through the handle and made it fast to the blade. (13) Chiselling a stone to smooth it is an essential part of building.

c (1) By reversing the former argument.

WHO BEATS WITH A HAMMER'.[2] Come and hear: [103a] HE WHO BORES A HOLE, HOWEVER LITTLE, IS CULPABLE. As for Rab, it is well: it looks like boring a hole for a building. But according to Samuel,[3] [surely] this is not a completion of work?[4] —The meaning here is that he pierces it with an iron pick and leaves it therein, so that that is the completion of its work.

THIS IS THE GENERAL PRINCIPLE. What does THIS IS THE GENERAL PRINCIPLE add?[5]—It adds the case of hollowing out a *kapiza* in a *kab* measure.[6]

R. SIMEON B. GAMALIEL SAID: HE TOO IS CULPABLE WHO BEATS WITH THE SLEDGE-HAMMER ON THE ANVIL, etc. What does he do?[7]—Rabbah and R. Joseph both say: Because he trains his hand. The sons of Rahabah found this difficult: if so, if one sees a labour [being performed] on the Sabbath and he learns it,[8] is
a he really culpable?[1]—But Abaye and Raba both say: Because those who beat out the [metal] plates of the Tabernacle[2] did thus.[3] It was taught likewise: R. Simeon b. Gamaliel said: Also he who beats with the sledge-hammer on the anvil at the time of his work is culpable, because those who beat out the [metal] plates of the Tabernacle did thus.

MISHNAH. HE WHO PLOUGHS, HOWEVER LITTLE, HE WHO WEEDS AND HE WHO TRIMS [TREES],[4] AND HE WHO CUTS OFF YOUNG SHOOTS, HOWEVER LITTLE, IS CULPABLE. HE WHO GATHERS TIMBER: IF IN ORDER TO EFFECT AN IMPROVEMENT,[5] [THE STANDARD OF CULPABILITY IS] HOWEVER LITTLE; IF FOR FUEL, AS MUCH AS IS REQUIRED FOR BOILING A LIGHT EGG. IF ONE COLLECTS GRASS, IF TO EFFECT AN IMPROVEMENT, [THE STANDARD OF CULPABILITY IS] HOWEVER LITTLE; IF FOR AN ANIMAL['S FODDER], A KID'S MOUTHFUL.

GEMARA. What is it fit for?[6]—It is fit for [planting] the seeds of a pumpkin.[7] Similarly in respect to the Tabernacle, [such a labour was performed] because it is fit for one stalk of [vegetable] dyes.

HE WHO WEEDS AND HE WHO TRIMS [TREES] AND HE WHO CUTS OFF YOUNG SHOOTS. Our Rabbis taught: He who plucks endives and he who cuts greens [shoots],[8] if for [human] consumption, [the standard of culpability is] the size of a dried fig; if for animal [food], a kid's mouthful; if for fuel, as much as is required for boiling a light egg; if in order to improve the soil,[9]
b however little. Are not all in order to improve the soil?[1] Rabbah and R. Joseph both say: They [the Sages] learnt this of an uncleared field.[2] Abaye said: You may even say [that they spoke] of a field that is not uncleared, but in a case where he has no intention.[3] But surely Abaye and Raba both said, R. Simeon admits in a case of, 'cut off his head but let him not die'?[4]—This holds good only when he works in his neighbour's field.[5]

MISHNAH. HE WHO WRITES TWO LETTERS, WHETHER WITH HIS RIGHT OR WITH HIS LEFT HAND, OF THE SAME DESIGNATION OR OF TWO DESIGNATIONS,[6] OR IN TWO PIGMENTS,[7] IN ANY LANGUAGE, IS CULPABLE. SAID R. JOSE: THEY DECLARED ONE CULPABLE [FOR WRITING] TWO LETTERS ONLY BECAUSE [HE MAKES] A MARK, BECAUSE THUS DID THEY WRITE ON EACH BOARD OF THE TABERNACLE, TO KNOW WHICH WAS ITS COMPANION.[8] R. JUDAH SAID: WE FIND A SHORT NAME [FORMING PART] OF A LONG NAME: SHeM AS PART OF SHiMe'ON OR SHeMueL, NOaH AS PART OF NaHOR, DaN AS PART OF DaNieL, GaD AS PART OF GaDDI'eL.[9]

GEMARA. As for his being culpable on account of his right hand, that is well, since that is the [usual] way of writing; but why on account of his left hand, seeing that it is not the [usual] way of writing?—Said R. Jeremiah, They learnt this of a left-handed person. Then let his left hand be as the right hand of all [other] people, and so let him be liable on account of his left, but not his right hand?—Rather said Abaye: [They learned this] of one
c who can use both hands. R. Jacob the son of Jacob's daughter[1] said: The author of this is R. Jose, who said: THEY DECLARED ONE CULPABLE [FOR WRITING] TWO LETTERS ONLY BECAUSE [HE MAKES] A MARK.[2] But since the second clause is R. Jose['s], the first clause is not R. Jose?—The whole is R. Jose.

R. JUDAH SAID: WE FIND, [etc.] Then according to R. Judah, one is culpable only on account of two letters of two designations,[3] but not two letters of the same designation? But surely it was taught: [*If a soul shall sin unwittingly against any of the commandments of the Lord concerning things which ought not to be done,*] *and shall do of one* [*of them*]:[4] I might think that one must write the whole noun or weave a whole garment or make a whole sieve [before he is guilty]; hence '*of one*' is stated. If '*of one*', I might think that even if one writes only one letter or weaves a single thread or makes only

(2) The latter being explanatory of the former. (3) Who holds that boring a hole is not building. (4) For the hole must be filled up subsequently. (5) It is a rule that this phrase always adds something not explicitly mentioned. (6) The *kapiza* was a small measure, less than a *kab*. If one hollows out a *kapiza* in a block of wood that is large enough for a *kab*, one might think that this labour is incomplete for he will probably enlarge it subsequently to a *kab*. Therefore the general principle is stated to teach that this is a complete labour. On the size of a *kapiza* v. *J.E.* XII, 488 I; and 489 Table. (7) How does this constitute a labour? (8) Merely by watching.

a (1) Surely not. (2) For covering the altar. (3) They beat the anvil occasionally, that it might present a smooth surface for the metal plates. (4) By lopping off dead branches, etc. (5) E.g., he cuts off branches or twigs to allow of a more vigorous growth. (6) *Sc.* ploughing very little. (7) 'Ar. and MS.M.: as a cavity for a pumpkin. (8) When very young these are fit for human consumption; a little later they are only fit for animals, and still later, when more hardened, they are used as fuel. (9) To leave room for expansion for the other plants.

b (1) That is their effect, whatever the intention. (2) Where the improvement is unnecessary. (3) Of improving the soil. (4) V. *supra* 75a. This too is inevitable. (5) Since he has no interest in his neighbour's field, the inevitable improvement is disregarded. (6) I.e., the same letter twice or two different letters. (7) E.g., one letter in black and one in red. (8) So that when the Tabernacle was dismantled and subsequently re-erected, the boards should remain in the same order as before. Therefore if one makes any two marks, not particularly letters, he is guilty in R. Jose's view. (9) If one commences writing long names, but writes only part thereof, which forms a complete name in itself, he is liable. The actual transliteration is employed here and in the Gemara below, to show the exact letters referred to.

c (1) Rashi in 'Er. 80a states that the father was an unworthy person, and so he is not mentioned. (2) Even a right-handed person can do that quite easily with his left. (3) I.e., two different letters, since he does not give an example of two identical letters, e.g., SHeSH as part of SHiSHaK. (4) Lev. IV, 2; lit. translation. In a way, '*of*' and '*one*' are contradictory, since '*of*' denotes a portion of an act, whereas '*one*' implies a complete act. This is discussed here, the various views put forward really being attempts to harmonize the two.

הקודח כל שהוא חייב בשלמא לרב מיחזי כמאן דהדר חורתא לבניינא אלא לשמואל לאו גמר מלאכה הוא הכא במאי עסקינן דבזעיה ברמצא דפרזלא ושבקיה בגוויה דהיינו גמר מלאכה: *זה הכלל: זה הכלל לאתויי מאי לאתויי *דחק קפיזא בקבא: רשב"ג אומר המכה בקורנס על הסדן כו': מאי קעביד רבה ורב יוסף דאמרי תרוייהו מפני שמאמן את ידו קשו בה בני רחבה אלא מעתה חזא אומנתא בשבתא וגמר הכי נמי דמיחייב אלא אביי ורבא דאמרי תרוייהו שכן מרדדי טסי משכן עושין כן תניא נמי הכי *רשב"ג אומר אף המכה בקורנס על הסדן בשעת מלאכה חייב שכן מרדדי טסי משכן עושין כן: **מתני'** החורש כל שהוא המנכש והמקרסם והמזרד כל שהוא חייב המלקט עצים אם לתקן כל שהן אם להיסק כדי לבשל ביצה קלה המלקט עשבים אם לתקן כל שהוא אם לבהמה כמלא פי הגדי: **גמ'** למאי חזי *לביזרא דקרא דכוותה גבי משכן שכן ראוי לקלח אחד של סמנין: המנכש והמקרסם והמזרד: ת"ר התולש עולשין והמזרד זרדים אם לאבילה כגרוגרת אם לבהמה כמלא פי הגדי אם להיסק כדי לבשל ביצה קלה אם לייפות את הקרקע כל שהן אטו כולהו לא ליפות את הקרקע נינהו רבה ורב יוסף דאמרי תרוייהו באגם שנו אביי אמר אפילו תימא בשדה דלאו אגם וכגון דלא קמיכוין והא *אביי ורבא דאמרי תרוייהו מודה רבי שמעון בפסיק רישיה ולא ימות לא צריכא דקעביד בארעא דחבריה: **מתני'** הכותב שתי אותיות בין בימינו בין בשמאלו בין משם אחד בין משתי שמות בין משתי (א) סמניות בכל לשון חייב אמר רבי יוסי לא חייבו שתי אותיות אלא משום רושם שכך כותבין על קרשי המשכן לידע איזו בן זוגו א"ר יהודה מצינו שם קטן משם גדול שם משמעון ומשמואל נח מנחור דן מדניאל גד מגדיאל: **גמ'** בשלמא אימין ליחייב משום דדרך כתיבה בכך אלא אשמאל אמאי הא אין דרך כתיבה בכך א"ר ירמיה באטר יד שנו ותהוי שמאל דידיה כימין דכ"ע ואשמאל ליחייב אימין לא ליחייב אלא אמר אביי *בשולט בשתי ידיו רב יעקב *בריה דבת יעקב אמר הא מני ר' יוסי היא דאמר לא חייבו שתי אותיות אלא משום רושם והא מדסיפא ר' יוסי היא רישא לאו ר' יוסי *כולה רבי יוסי היא: א"ר יהודה מצינו: אלא ר' יהודה שתי אותיות והן שני שמות הוא דמחייב שתי אותיות והן שם אחד לא מחייב והתניא ועשה אחת יכול עד שיכתוב כל השם ועד שיארוג כל הבגד ועד שיעשה כל הנפה ת"ל מאחת אי מאחת יכול אפילו לא כתב אלא אות אחת ולא ארג אלא חוט אחד ולא עשה אלא בית אחד בנפה ת"ל

תורה אור: ויקרא ד

רש"י

הקודח. וכל הקודח ע"מ למלאות הוא לתקוע בו יתד ושלא למלאות קרי נוקב: בשלמא לרב. דאמר נקב הוי בנין האי נמי בנין הוא כל שהוא ואע"פ שימלאנו הרי הועיל לבנין שקודח החור: חר חורתא. קדח חור: אלא לשמואל. דאמר נוקב לאו בונה הוא בשלמא נקב דלול איכא למימר מכה בפטיש אבל זה שעומד לסתום לאו גמר מלאכה הוא: דבזעיה ברמצא דפרזלא. במסמר ארוך של ברזל: ושבקיה בגוויה. לאתויי* בה: דחק קפיזא בקבא. בגולם גדול הראוי לחוק בו קב חקק שלש לוגין ואע"פ שעתיד להוסיף יש שמקיימין כן: מאמן ידיו. מרגילם ומכוונם להכאה הראוייה למלאכה מכה גדולה או מכה קטנה: מרדדי טסי משכן. לציפוי קרשים: עושין כן. מכין ג' על הטס ואחת על הסדן להחליק הקורנס שלא יבקע הטס שהוא דק ובעלי מטבע במקומנו ראיתי עושין כן: **מתני'** מקרסם. קוצץ ענפים יבשים מן אילן לתקנו: מזרד. זרדין לחין חדשים של שנה זו ופעמים שהן מרובין ומכחישים האילן ומתייבשין וקוצצין אותם ממנו: אם לתקן. את האילן או את הקרקע וקצצו מן המחובר: ביצה קלה. כגרוגרת מבילת תרנגולת *שקלה היא לבשל מכל הביצים: **גמ'** לביזרא דקרא. לזרוע בתוכה נימא של דלעת ואע"ג דשנינו (לעיל דף נ:) לענין הוצאת זרע דלועין שנים שאין אדם טורח בנימא אחת ה"מ הוצאה דכי מפיק תרתי מפיק כי הדדי שאינו זורע אחת לבדה אבל לענין חרישה כל גומא וגומא באפי נפשה עביד לה: עולשין. עשב שקורין קריספ"ל: זרדין. מין קנים הם ובעודן רכים זורדין אותם למאכל אדם נתקשו מעט ראויין למאכל בהמה יבשו עומדין להסקה: אטו כולהו לא ליפות את הקרקע נינהו. הרי הקרקע מתייפה מאיליו: באגם. שאין צריך ליפות: בארעא דחבריה. °לא איכפת ליה ליפות: **מתני'** בין משם אחד. שתיהן אלפין: משתי שמות. אלף בית: משתי סמניות. אחת בדיו ואחת בסיקרא: בכל לשון. של כל כתבים וגופן של כל אומה ואומה: משום רושם. סימן שהיו עושים בקרשי המשכן מפני שמפרקין אותו וכשיקימוהו לא יחלפו סדר הקרשים ואתא ר' יוסי למימר דאפי' לא כתב אלא רשם שני רשימות בעלמא לסימן חייב: מצינו שם קטן כו'. הא אתא לאשמועינן רבי יהודה דאע"ג שלא נגמר מלאכתו שנתכוין לכתוב תיבה גדולה וכתב מקצת ואותו מקצת הויא תיבה המתקיימת במקום אחר חייב: **גמ'** הא מני רבי יוסי היא. דלא בעי כתיבה אלא רושם בעלמא ובשמאלו רושם מיהא הוה: והן שני שמות. כגון הנך דנקט במתני' שאינן שוות: הא ב' אותיות והן שם אחד. כגון שם משבך או תת מתתנך או חח מחחים לא מיחייב מדלא נקט רבי יהודה חד מהנך: אחת. כולה במשמע: כל השם. התיבה קרוי שם: בית אחד בנפה. לאחר שהסיך נירים של שתי עושה באריגת ערב נירו אחד מלמטה ואחד ממעלה והן קרוין בתים והם עוכבין את השתי כדרך רכיבתו ועומד הארוג ובית אחד אין מתקיים ומשום דלאו חוטין נינהו קרי להו בית כמו בתי נירין שאין לה בתי נירין אחרים:

תוספות

בשלמא לרב מיחזי כמאן דחר חורתא לבניינא. אע"ג דלא דמי לעושה נקב בלול של תרנגולין דהתם עשוי להכניס ולהוציא מ"מ מעט בנין כל דהו מיחייב כמו מעייל שופתא בקופינא דמרא ומכתת אלא לשמואל דמשום בנין כל דהו לא מיחייב אמאי חייב הא אין כאן גמר מלאכה:

אם לבהמה כמלא פי הגדי ואם להיסק. פירוש שאינם ראויין לאכילה דאי לאו הכי מיחייב אשיעורא זוטא כדאמר לעיל (דף עו.) המוציא תבן כמלא פי פרה לגמל חייב:

באגם שנו. ומתני' דלא שייך לאוקמי באגם אומר ר"ת דאיירי באילן יבש שאינו מתקן כלום:

לא צריכא דעביד בארעא דחבריה. פי' בערוך (ערך סכר) דפסיק רישיה דלא ניחא ליה כגון דקעביד בארעא דחבריה וכגון באחר שאינו אוהבו והקוצץ בהרת בשעת מילה שאין לו הנאה מותר לכתחילה ואפילו איסור דרבנן ליכא והתיר ר' חביב שפקקוהו בפשתן להסיר הפקק ולמשוך ממנו יין בשבת אע"פ שא"א שלא יסחוט כשמסיר הפקק והוי פסיק רישיה כיון דאינו נהנה בסחיטה זאת שהיין נופל לארץ מותר ואינו נראה דהא *מפיס מורסא להוציא ממנו ליחה היה אסור אי לאו משום צערא דגופא אע"פ שאינו נהנה כלל בבנין הפתח ואינו מתכוין כלל לבנין הפתח אלא לנקיבה בעלמא וכן הביא רשב"א ממחט של יד ליטול בה את הקוץ דמוקי לה בהנחנקין (סנהדרין דף פד:) כר"ש דאמר מלאכה שאינה צריכה לגופה פטור עליה ומשום צערא שרי ואע"פ שאינו נהנה בחבורה היה אסור אי לאו משום צערא דגופא והא דקאמר לא צריכא דעביד בארעא דחבריה היינו דלא מיחייב חטאת אבל איסורא איכא והא דקאמר בשילהי כל התדיר (זבחים דף צא:) המתנדב יין מביאו ומזלפו על גבי האישים ופריך והא קא מכבה ומוקי לה כר"ש דאמר דבר שאין מתכוין מותר מיירי דלא הוי פסיק רישיה שמזלפו בטיפות דקות א"נ על גבי האיברים אפשר שלא יכבה האש ובפרק לולב הגזול (סוכה דף לג:) גבי אין ממעטין בי"ט משום ר"א בר"ש אמרו ממעטין ופריך והא קא מתקן מנא ומשני כגון שליקטן לאכילה ודבר שאין מתכוין מותר ופריך והא אביי ורבא דאמרי תרוייהו מודה ר"ש בפסיק רישיה ולא ימות ומשני לא צריכא דאית ליה הושענא אחריתי משמע כפי' הערוך דכשאינו נהנה מותר אע"ג דהוי פסיק רישיה וליכא למימר כיון דאית ליה הושענא יתירתא אינו מתקן כלום דא"כ אמאי קאמר התם דסבר לה כאבוה דאמר דבר שאינו מתכוין מותר מיהו י"ל דאותו תיקון מועט כמו מיעוט ענבים דלא אסיר אלא מדרבנן לא גזרו חכמים כשאינו *נהנה:

בארעא דחבריה. פי' דהויא מלאכה שא"צ לגופה: בגלטורי

רבינו חננאל

חסורי מחסרא והכי קתני הזורק ונזכר לאחר שיצאת מידו וקלטה אחר או כלב או נשרפה פטור הא נחה חייב אימתי בזמן שחזר ושכח אבל לא חזר ושכח פטור שכל חייבי חטאות אין חייבין עד שתהא תחילתן וסופן שגגה פלוגתא דרבה ורבא בשתי אמות בשוגג וב' אמות במזיד וב' אמות בזורק ולא איפרשא בהדי' אי בזורק במעביר היא ודברי הכל בפלוגתא דרבן גמליאל וחכמים פליגי דתנן הכותב ב' אותיות בב' העלמות אחת בשחרית ואחת בין הערבים רבן גמליאל מחייב וחכמים פוטרין דאלו התם כתב אות אחת. שהוא חצי שיעור ואמרינן בכלל גדול אמר רבינא כגון שהיתה לו ידיעה בנתיים ורבן גמליאל הוא דאמר אין ידיעה לחצי שיעור אבל הכא אע"פ דהני ד' אמות בשוגג בב' העלמות הן לא דמיא להתם אלא הכא אם מעביר הוא שהעביר שש אמות בבת אחת עלה אמר רבה פטור כגון שהעביר אמתים בשוגג ולאלתר נזכר והעביר אמתים אחרות במזיד ואלתר שכח והעביר אמתים אחרות בשגגה אמר רבה כגון זה אפילו דמאן דמחייב התם כגון שכתב אות אחת בשגגה ולא כתב כלום נזכר ושכח וחזר וכתב אות אחרת בהא מחייב רבן גמליאל דכי גמר שיעורא (דחייבא) [דהיינו] ב' אותיות בשוגג גמר אבל הכא דאינון שתי אמות ג' פעמים ב' אמצעיות שהן נגמר ד' אמות שיעור החיוב במזיד הוה שנמצאת ידיעה מפסקת ורבה דפטר לא פטר אלא במעביר דקאמר אבל הכא כי קא גמר שיעורא במזיד בינייהו קא גמר ואילו זורק כיון שהיתה תחלת הזריקה בשוגג אע"פ שנודע לו לאחר שיצאת מידו כיון שאין בידו להחזיר לא חשיב מזיד ואם זורק הוא עליה אמר רבא חייב כגון שזרק שש אמות בבת אחת בתחלה היה שכח וכשהגיע החפץ לב' אמות נזכר וכשהגיע בסוף ב' אמות האחרונות חזר ושכח אמר לך רבא כגון זה חייב ואפי' לרבנן דפטרי התם דאלו התם לענין הכותב ב' אותיות בב' העלמות היה בידו שלא לכתוב אות [השניה] (וכיון)[והלכך אף]שחזר ושכח את השניה[אינה] מצטרפת עם הראשונה אבל הכא כיון שזרק ויש בכח זריקתו ללכת שש אמות כיון שאין בידו להחזיר את הזורק וארבע מהן בשוגג [היה] אע"פ שיש ביניהן שתים שאינן בשוגג הרי הארבע מצטרפות וחייב עליהן. ורבא לא מחייב אלא בזורק והא קא' התם הוא דבידו אבל הכא לאו בידו ואילו מעביר בידו (ב') הוא. ואיתה לרבה דפטור במעביר ואיתה לדרבא דמחייב בזורק אמר רבא זרק ונחה בפי הכלב או בפי הכבשן חייב ואוקימנא כגון מעיקרא לנוח בפי הכלב או בפי הכבשן ומתני' דקתני קלטה אחר או כלב או שנשרפה פטור בדלא איכון לכך ומשום דלא נעשית מחשבתו הוא דפטור ואע"ג דבעינן עקירה והנחה במקום ד' כיון דאחשביה הוי ליה כאלו אית ביה ד' ומסייע ליה לרב ביבי מהא דתנן בכריתות פרק אמרו לו שנים אכלת חלב [יש] אוכל אכילה אחת וחייב כו' קתני מיהא שאם הוציא ואוכלו חייב ואע"פ שלא הניחו ע"ג מקום ד' אלא כיון שהוא עקרו והניחו בתוך פיו חייב ואקשינן והא אין דרך חיוב הוצאה בכך כלומר אין דרך החיוב אלא בעקירה ממקום ד' והנחה במקום ד' אלא כיון דאחשביה לאנוחיה לפיו כאלו מקום ד' על ד' הוא ה"נ כיון דאחשביה לפי כלב או לפי הכבשן מחשבתו משויא ליה מקום ולא פליגי רבנן עליה דר"מ שהייב אלא כך אמרו לו אינו [מן] השם כלומר מן המנין ד' חטאות אכילה אבל הוצאה לאו משום אכילה חייב אלא משום הוצאה ובהמוציא תפילין (ד' צט) נמי אמרינן דכיון דאחשביה משויא ליה מקום: **הדרן עלך הזורק**

פי"ב הבונה כל שהוא חייב וכו'. הוצרכנו בזאת לב' דברים. אחד להודיע מה צורך לבנין כל שהוא. שני לראות מה בנין כל שהוא היה במשכן. ופירשוהו רבי ירמיה ואביי ורבא אחא כל אחד דרך ידיעה ופשוטה הוא אמר שמואל המצדד את האבן חייב משום מכה בפטיש פי' מצדד מיישב האבן בקרקע כדי לבנות עליה ואסיקנא תלתא בניינא הוו תתאה צדודי ועפרא שכן דרך הבנאין באבני היסוד מצדדין האבנים ומושיבן אותן על העפר. וזהו שאמר שמואל. מציעאה בעי טינא עילאה בהנחה בעלמא והני תלתי המסתת והעושה נקב בלול גדמעייל שופתא בקופינא דמרא רב מחייב להו משום בונה ואם בנה בנין וסותת או בנה בנין או עשה נקב בלול או עייל שופתא בקופינא דמרא בהעלם אחד אינו חייב על הבונה ועשה אחד מאלו אלא חטאת אחת שלא

עין משפט נר מצוה

ז א ב מיי' פ"י מהל' שבת הלכה טו וסמג לאוין סה:
ח ג מיי' פ"ח מהל' שבת הלכה ג:
ט ד ה מיי' שם הלכה ב:
י ו מיי' פ"ח מהל' שבת הלכה ט סמג לאוין סה:
יא ז מיי' שם הלכה י:
יב ח שם הלכה יז:
יג ט י כ שם הלכה יד:
יד ל מיי' פי"א מהל' שבת הלכה יד:

הגהות הגר"א

[א] תוס' ד"ה לא כו' מיירי דלא הוי פ"ר כו' כ"ב כו' רש"י שם ע"ש:

הגהות הב"ח

(א) במשנה משתי סממניות בכל:

תורה אור

ת"ל אחת הא כיצד אינו חייב עד שיכתוב שם קטן משם גדול שם משמעון ומשמואל נח מנחור דן מדניאל גד מגדיאל *רבי יהודה אומר אפילו לא כתב אלא שתי אותיות והן שם אחד חייב כגון שש תת רר גג חח א"ר יוסי וכי משום כותב הוא חייב והלא אינו חייב אלא משום רושם שכן רושמין על קרשי המשכן לידע איזו היא בן זוגו לפיכך שרט שריטה אחת על שני נסרין או שתי שריטות על נסר אחד חייב רבי שמעון אומר °ועשה אחת יכול עד שיכתוב את כל השם עד שיארוג כל הבגד עד שיעשה את כל הנפה ת"ל מאחת אי מאחת יכול אפילו לא כתב אלא אות אחת ואפילו לא ארג אלא חוט אחד ואפילו לא עשה אלא בית אחד בנפה ת"ל אחת הא כיצד אינו חייב עד שיעשה מלאכה שכיוצא בה מתקיימת ר' יוסי אומר *ועשה אחת ועשה הנה פעמים שחייב אחת על כולן ופעמים שחייב על כל אחת ואחת קתני מיהא רבי יהודה אומר אפילו לא כתב אלא שתי אותיות והן שם אחד חייב לא קשיא הא דידיה הא דרביה דתניא רבי יהודה אומר משום רבן גמליאל אפילו לא כתב אלא ב' אותיות והן שם אחד חייב כגון שש תת רר גג חח ור"ש היינו ת"ק וכ"ת אלף אלף °דאאזרך איכא בינייהו דת"ק סבר אלף אלף דאאזרך לא מיחייב ור"ש סבר כיון דאיתיה בגלטורי בעלמא חייב למימרא דר"ש לחומרא והתניא *הקודח כל שהוא חייב המגרר כל שהוא המעבד כל שהוא הצר בכלי צורה כל שהוא רש"א עד שיקדח את כולו עד שיגרור את כולו עד שיעבד את כולו עד שיצור כולו אלא ר"ש הא אתא לאשמעינן עד שיכתוב את השם כולו ומי מצית אמרת הכי והתניא רש"א ועשה אחת יכול עד שיכתוב את השם כולו ת"ל מאחת תריץ ואימא הכי יכול עד שיכתוב את הפסוק כולו ת"ל מאחת ר' יוסי אומר ועשה אחת ועשה הנה פעמים שחייב אחת על כולן ופעמים שחייב על כל אחת ואחת *א"ר יוסי בר' חנינא מ"ט דר' יוסי אחת מאחת הנה מהנה אחת שהיא הנה והנה שהיא אחת אחת שמעון מאחת שם משמעון הנה אבות מהנה תולדות אחת שהיא הנה זדון שבת ושגגת מלאכות הנה שהיא אחת שגגת שבת וזדון מלאכות: א"ר יהודה מצינו שם קטן משם גדול: מי דמי מ"ם דשם סתום מ"ם דשמעון פתוח אמר רב חסדא זאת אומרת סתום ועשאו פתוח כשר מיתיבי °וכתבתם שתהא כתיבה תמה *שלא יכתוב אלפין עיינין עיינין אלפין ביתין כפין כפין ביתין גמין צדין צדין גמין דלתין רישין רישין דלתין היהין חיתין חיתין היהין ווין יודין יודין ווין זיינין נונין נונין זיינין טיתין פיפין פיפין טיתין כפופין פשוטין פשוטין כפופין מימין סמכין סמכין מימין סתומין פתוחין פתוחין סתומין פרשה פתוחה לא יעשנה סתומה סתומה לא יעשנה פתוחה *כתבה כשירה או שכתב את השירה כיוצא בה או שכתב שלא בדיו או שכתב את האזכרות בזהב הרי אלו יגנזו הוא דאמר כי האי תנא דתניא *רבי יהודה בן בתירה אומר נאמר בשני ונסכיהם בששי ונסכיה בשביעי כמשפטם הרי מ"ם יו"ד מ"ם מים מכאן רמז לניסוך מים מן התורה ומדפתוח ועשאו סתום כשר סתום נמי ועשאו פתוח כשר מי דמי פתוח ועשאו סתום

עלויי

ויקרא ד | ישעיה מה | [תוספ' פי"ב] | דברים ו | תענית ב:

ת"ל אחת. שתהא מלאכה שלימה במקום אחד: שם משמעון. ולגבי בגד נמי שני חוטין ובנפה שני בתין שמקיימין (א) כך לפי שאין אדם אורג בגד ביום אחד ועושה נפה בבת אחת ומתחיל ועושה כדי קיום שלא יהא נסתר מאליו: אפילו לא כתב. מתיבה גדולה: אלא ב' אותיות של שם אחד כגון שש תת· והן מתיבות גדולות כגון שש מששבצר משסך שמש תת מתתרלאו תתנו וכ"ש אם נתכוין לקטנה תחילה: שכיוצא בה מתקיימת. ולקמיה פריך היינו ת"ק: ר' יוסי אומר. מפרש למילתיה לקמן: היינו ת"ק. שש תת: וכ"ת אלף אלף דאאזרך. שהם שתי אותיות מתיבה גדולה אבל לא מצינו שהיא תיבה קטנה בכל המקרא: כיון דאיתא בגלטורי. קמיעות וכתבים של מכשפות ושל שמות קורין בלשון לעז"ן של מינין קלוטרוס ורגילין סופרין לכתוב בהן תיבות של שתי אותיות ואינם תיבות במקום אחר: המגרר. כלונסות או קלפים דהויא תולדה דממחק: הקודח כל שהוא. קולט הנקב ואע"פ שלא עבר עובי העץ לראות בעבר השני: כל שהוא. מן האורה: את כולו. כל מה שנתכוין לגרר או לעבד מתחלה בבת אחת: כל השם. כל התיבה: מ"ט דר' יוסי. היכי דריש ליה: אחת מאחת. אחת ה"ל למכתב ולשתוק וכתב מ"ם יתירה [ומהנה יתירא]: הנה מהנה א"נ. הנה הוה ליה למכתב וכתב מהנה מ"ם יתירה ומאחת יתירה הלכך למדרשינהו לכולהו כתבינהו ודרוש אחת הנה בלא מ"ם הכי אחת שהיא הנה הנה שהיא אחת לתרי גווני איכא למידרש משמעותייהו ועשה עבירה אחת והיא לו הנה חייב חטאות הרבה אי נמי ועשה אחת עשייתו חשובה לו כאחת ואע"פ שהנה היו משמע שהרבה עבירות עשה והיינו הנה שהיא אחת הלכך תרוייהו דריש ביה פעמים שהיא כן ופעמים שהיא כן כדמפרש לקמיה: אחת שמעון. כלומר דריש מ"ם יתירה אחת הוי משמע דאינו חייב עד שיכתוב כל התיבה שנתכוין לכתוב: מאחת שם משמעון. כתב מאחת למימר דאפילו לא כתב אלא מקצתה ובלבד שתהא מקויימת (ב) במקום אחר דומיא דאחת דרישיה דקרא: הנה הוי משמע אבות כתב מהנה לרבויי תולדות: אחת שהיא הנה. דאמרן לעיל ה"ד כגון שעשאן בזדון שבת ושגגת מלאכות ואע"ג דכולן אינן אלא חילול שבת אחת מיחייב לכל מלאכה ומלאכה דגופי מלאכות מחלקין הואיל ואיכא שגגה טובא: הנה שהיא אחת שגגת שבת וזדון מלאכות. שאף על פי שהן גופי מלאכות הרבה אינו חייב אלא אחת דחדא שגגה היא: מי דמי כו'. זה שנתכוין לכתוב שם משמעון מ"ם פתוחה כתב והיכי קרי ליה מתקיימת במקום אחר והא לא הויא: וכתבתם. דתפילין ומזוזה: תם. שלם כהלכתה: אלפין עיינין. יש שכותבין כן מפני שדומין בקריאתן: ביתין כפין. דומין בכתיבתן: גמין לדין. דומין בכתיבתן אלא שזה למעלה וזה למטה: זיינין טנין. פשוטין: כפופין. כף פה לדי טן: פשוטין. הכפולות שלהן פשוטות: ממין סמכין. מ"ם סתומה שדומה לסמך: סתומין. מ"ם סתומה: פתוחין. מ"ם פתוחה: כתבה. לספר תורה: כשירה. בדילוגין אריח ולבינה: מכאן רמז כו' כלומר מ"ם דונסכיהם דריש ליה בפתוחה [שמע מינה] בפתוח ועשאו סתום דכשר ומדפתוח ועשאו סתום כשר הוא הדין נמי סתום ועשאו פתוח כגון שם משמעון וכשר להתקיים במקום שם:

עלויי

בגלטורי בעלמא חייב. *פירוש א"א שכותבין בקמיע וכן פירש ר"ח ויש מפרשים א"א היינו אמן אמן (סלה) שכותבין בקמיעין וליתא דהיינו נוטריקון וחייב אפילו באחד ורבנן דפטרי במתני' *פטרי אפילו בב' וג': א"א דלאזרך איכא בינייהו. לאו דוקא דהא ת"ק פטר אפי' שתי אותיות משם אחד עד שיכתוב שם משמעון אלא משום ר"ש נקטיה דאפי' בהא מיחייב: המעבד כל שהוא. לאו דוקא כל שהוא אלא כשיעור המפורש בהמוציא (לעיל דף עט:) ולא נקט כל שהוא אלא לאפוקי מדר"ש דאמר עד שיעבד כל העור: תריץ הכי יכול עד שיכתוב כל הפסוק כו'. וא"ת ומ"מ אריגה מהני דהכא לא מחייב ר"ש עד שיתקן את כולו וי"ל דבאריג שעושה דבר חדש שאינו בעולם מחייב שפיר בשני בתי נירין אבל עיבוד שאינו אלא תיקון העור בעלמא וכן גורר וכל צורה בעי ר"ש עד שיתקן את כולו: טיתין פיפין. מכאן נראה לר"ת שצריך לכוף ראש הטית לתוכה דדמי כעין פ': בשביעי כמשפטם גרסינן. כדמוכח בפרק קמא דתענית (דף ג:) וכן הוא במסורת הגדולה ולא כרש"י *דגרס בשמיני בס"פ לולב וערבה (סוכה דף מז:):

גרוטי

[שני פרושים האלה כתובים בערוך ערך אא]
טו א ב מיי' פי"א מהל' שבת הלכה י: [לקמן קד:]
טז ג מיי' פ"י מהל' שבת הלכה טז:
יז ד מיי' פי"א מהל' שבת הלכה ה:
יח ה מיי' פ"י שם הלכה טז:
יט ו מיי' פ"ז שם הלכה ז:
כ ז מיי' פ"א מהל' תפילין הלכה יט סמג עשין כב טוש"ע א"ח סי' לב סעיף ד וטוש"ע י"ד סי' רעד סעיף ג:
כא ח מיי' וסמג שם טוש"ע א"ח סי' לו סעיף א וטוש"ע י"ד סי' רעד סעיף ה:
כב ט מיי' פ"ז שם הל' יא ופ"ח הלכה א ב סמג עשין כה טוש"ע י"ד סי' רעה סעיף א:
כג י מיי' שם טוש"ע שם סעיף ג:
כד כ ל מיי' פ"א שם הלכה ה סמג שם טוש"ע א"ח סי' לב סעיף ג וטוש"ע י"ד סי' רעא סעיף ו וסי' רעו סעי' ה:

רבינו חננאל

שלא עשה אלא אב ותולדותיה והעושה אב והתולדותיה אינו חייב אלא אחת ושמואל מחייב להני תלת משום מכה בפטיש ואי עביד בנין וחד מהנך חייב תרתי. חד משום בונה וחד משום מכה בפטיש דלאו תולדה דבונה נינהו ובהא פליג רב סבר*) כיון שהמסתת אבני גזיל הוא ואינון אבני דלא משפרין ומשוי להו גזית כדכתיב כל אלה אבני יקרות במדת גזית מגוררות במגירה והויא כמכה אבן בפטיש להשוות עקמו (מיהו) [וכן] נקב בלול נמי כיון דמשום אויר הוא לבנין דמו ותולדת בנין הוא ושמואל סבר נקב לפתוח פה בכלי דמי שהוא סוף מלאכה וכן מכנים ידי הקורדום (בעשהו) אע"פ שכלי הוא רב סבר דיש בנין בכלים ושמואל סבר אין בנין בכלים וגרסינן בכלל גדול משום דרבי יהושע כן כי המסתת חייב משום מכה בפטיש כשמואל ומותבינן לשמואל מהא דתניא הקודח כל שהוא חייב בשלמא לרב דאמר משום בונה היינו דחייב הקודח דמחזי כמי שעושה חור בכותל כדי לבנות שם בנין ותולדת בנין הוא. אלא לשמואל דמחייב הנוקב משום מכה בפטיש שהוא גמר מלאכ' מאי [גמר] מלאכה איכא בקודח והלא הנוקב צריך לקבוע באותו [הנקב] מסמר נמצאת קביעת המסמר הוא הגמר מלאכה ומשני כגון שקדח ברימצא פי' במקדח והניח המקדח במקום שקדח במסמר קבוע באותו העץ שקדח כדי לחזקו שזהו גמר מלאכתו ואשכחן סוגיא דשמעתא בענין המחזיר מטה של פרסים בשבת (לעיל ד' מז) כרב דסבר עיולי שופתא בקופינא והוא יד הקורדום בנקבו שהוא כהחזרת מלבנות המטה ורב ושמואל דאמרי תרווייהו [התם] המחזיר מטה של פרסים בשבת חייב חטאת ומותבינן [מהא] המחזיר קנה מנורה בשבת חייב חטאת קנה של ציידין לא יחזיר ואם החזיר פטור. ר' הימאי אמר המרכיב קרן עגולה חייב קרן פשוטה פטור ופרקינן הוא דאמר כי האי תנא מלבנות המטה וכרעי המטה ולוחים של סקבס לא יחזיר ואם החזיר פטור אבל אסור לא יתקע ואם תקע חייב רשבג"א אם היה רפוי מותר ופשיטא לרבנן בתראי דהני כולהו משום בונה אינון. ומשום הכי מתרינן במן דעביד להו דאמרינן בי רב חמא הואי ההוא מטה גוליתא דהוו מהדרי ליה בשבתא. א"ל ההוא מרבנן לרב חמא מ"ט שריין דמשום בנין מן יהצד הוא ונהי דאיסורא דאורייתא ליכא איסורא מדרבנן [מיהא] איכא א"ל אנא כרבן שמעון ב"ג סברי לי דאמר אם היה רפוי מותר וגרסינן בירושלמי קנה מנורה למה הוא חייב. ר' אבהו בש"ר יוחנן ורב הונא תרווייהו אמרו משום בונה וקי"ל בהני כולהו כרב פי' חק קפיזא בקבא כגון שחקק חריץ בקב מקום שהוא מדת קפיזא ונמצא שעשה כמין השנתות שהיו סימנין בהין: המכה בקורנס על הסדן בשעת גמר מלאכה חייב. אמר רבה ורב יוסף מפני שמאמן את ידיו וסברי בני רחבה דהאי מאמן מלמד את ידיו אומנות הכאה היא ונדחת ומשום אביי ורבא שכן מרדדי טסי משכן עושין כן ותניא נמי הכי ופי' מאמן דאמר רבה ורב יוסף מרגיל את ידיו לאותה מלאכה היא שכן מנהג מרקעי פחים כשמניחין הטס על הסדן מכין תחלה בקורנס על הסדן כשמתחיל במלאכה ולרשב"ג מלאכה גמורה היא ולא דמי לנוטל מגל לקצור ולא קצר ולנוטל קורנס לרדד ולא רידד אלא אותה הכאה מלאכה חשובה (ליתא) [היא] החורש כל שהוא ראויה לעשות גומא לדלעת ובמשכן היו חורשים לקלח אחד של סממנים והמנכש והמלקט עצים קשיא לן מכדי המתקן קרקע בכל שהוא חייב למה לי למיתנא לבהמה כמלוא פי גדי ולהיסק כדי לבשל ביצה קלה אשו בהני לאו מייפה קרקע הוא למה לי שיעורא ומשני רבה ורב יוסף באגם שאין הקרקע מתייפה בליקוט עצים ולא בניכוש לפיכך צריכין שיעור [להתחייב] אביי אמר היכא צריך שיעור בשדה דלא קא מכוין ליפותה ואע"ג דהוא מתייפה אינו חייב אלא בשיעור דקא מכוין ליה אם לבהמה אם להיסק ואקשינן עליה איני והא אביי ורבא דאמרינן תרווייהו מודה ר' שמעון בפסיק רישיה ולא ימות כלומר אפילו ר' שמעון דסבר דבר שאין מתכוין מותר כי האי גוונא דודאי לא אפשר לתלוש מן הקרקע אלא שהקרקע מתייפה מתלישתו ורצונו בכך מחייב ומשני בתולש מן הקרקע שאינו שלו שאין רצונו ליפוי הקרקע כלל לפיכך אינו מתחייב אלא במחשבתו שמתכוין לה: הכותב ב' אותיות בין בימינו בין בשמאלו חייב והא אין דרך כתיבה בכך. ואוקמה ר' ירמיה באיטר שהוא דרכו לכתוב שנמצא שמאלו במקום ימין ואקשינן תוב אי הכי אימינו לא ליחייב דהא כל איטר שמאלו במקום ימינו ונמצא הימין של איטר כי הוא שמאלו ואין דרך כתיבה בכך ונדחה זה. ואוקמה אביי בשולט בב' ידיו דתרווייהו מיומנות הן שנמצא כותב בשתיהן ודרך כתיבה בשתיהן אבל מי שאינו שולט אלא בידו אחת לא מיחייב משום כותב בשבת אלא בזמן שהכותב בידו המיומנת אבל אם כתב בידו אחרת לא מיחייב שאין דרך כתיבה בכך לפיכך איטר שאין שולט אלא בשמאל שמאל דידיה כימין דעלמא היא וחייב עלה ואם כתב בימינו אין דרך כתיבה בכך ולאידך מיחייב עליה. ור' יעקב ברא דבת יעקב אוקמה למיתני' כר"י ומשום רושם הוא ומחייב לפיכך חייב הרושם בין בימינו בין בשמאלו שאינו כותב אלא רושם ואקשינן היכא יכלת

למימר

*) נראה דהסר כאן בד' רבינו ואולי צ"ל רב. סבר דהמסתת צורך בנין הוא וחייב משום בונה ושמואל סבר דכיון שהמסתת וכו'.

[לעיל ע. סנהדרין סב. [כריתות ג. ע"ש]

[לפנינו ברש"י דסוכה מז. ד"ה רב אשי איתא בזה"ל בשביעי כתיב במספרם כמשפטם וכו' ובקרבנות שמיני כתיב במספרם כמשפט וכו']

[לעיל ע. סנהדרין סב. ע"ש]

[מנחות לא: וע"ש בתוס' ד"ה [illegible] כשירה]

הגהות הב"ח

(א) רש"י ד"ה שם משמעון וכו' בתין שמתקיימין כך: (ב) ד"ה מאחת וכו' שתהא מתקיימת במקום:

one mesh of a sieve, [he is culpable]; [103b] therefore *'one'* is stated. How is this [to be reconciled]? One is liable only if he writes a short noun [as part] of a long noun: SHeM as part of SHiMe'oN or SHeMU'eL, NoaḤ as part of NaḤoR, DaN as part of DaNI'eL, GaD as part of GaDDI'eL.[5] R. Judah said: Even if one writes two letters of the same designation, he is liable: e.g., SHeSH, TeTH, RaR, GaG, ḤaḤ.[6] Said R. Jose: Is he then guilty on account of writing? Surely he is guilty only on account of [making] a mark, because marks were made on [each of] the boards of the Tabernacle to know which was its companion. Therefore if one draws one line across two boards, or two lines on one board, he is culpable. R. Simeon said: *'And shall do one'*: I might think that one must write the whole noun or weave a complete garment or make a whole sieve [before he is liable]; therefore it is written, *'of one'*. If *of one*, I might think that even if one writes one letter only, or weaves one thread only, or makes one mesh only in a sieve, [he is guilty]: therefore *'one'* is stated. How is this [to be reconciled]? One is liable only when he performs
a an action the like of which stands [on its own].[1] R. Jose said: *'And shall do one, and shall do them'*: sometimes one sacrifice is incurred for all of them, at others one is liable for each separately.[2] Now it is incidentally taught, R. Judah said: Even if one only writes two letters of the same designation, he is liable?—There is no difficulty: one is his own [view], the other is his teacher's. For it was taught: R. Judah said in R. Gamaliel's name: Even if one only writes two letters of the same designation, he is liable, e.g., SHeSH, TeTH, RaR, GaG, ḤaḤ.

Now R. Simeon, is he not identical with the first Tanna? And should you answer, they differ in respect of the *a'a* of *a'azzereka*:[3] the first Tanna holding, [for writing] the *a'a* of *a'azzereka* one is not liable:[4] while R. Simeon holds, Since it is contained in charms in general,[5] he is culpable,—shall we then say that R. Simeon is more stringent? Surely it was taught: He who bores, however little,[6] he who scrapes,[7] however little, he who tans, however little, he who draws a figure on a vessel, however little, [is culpable]. R. Simeon said: [He is not culpable] unless he bores right through or scrapes the whole of it [the skin] or tans the whole of it or draws the whole of it![8] Rather R. Simeon comes to teach us this: [one is not guilty] unless he writes the whole word. But can you say so? Surely it was taught, R. Simeon said: *'And shall do one'*: you might think that one must write the whole word; therefore *'of one'* is stated?—Answer and say thus: You might think that one must write a complete *sentence*, therefore *'of one'* is stated.

R. Jose said: *'And shall do one, and shall do them'*: sometimes one sacrifice is incurred for all of them, at others one is liable for each separately. Said R. Jose son of R. Ḥanina, What is R. Jose's reason? *'One'*, *'of one'*, *'them'*, *'of them'*: [this implies,] one may be the equivalent of many, and many may equal one. *'One'*, [i.e.,] SHiMe'oN; *'of one'*, [i.e.,] SHeM [as part] of SHiMe'oN; *'them'* [i.e.,] the principal labours; *'of them'*, the derivative labours. 'One is the equivalent of many'—awareness of the Sabbath coupled with unawareness of [the forbidden nature of his] labours. 'Many may equal one'—unawareness of the Sabbath coupled with awareness [of the for-
b bidden nature of his] labours.[1]

R. JUDAH SAID: WE FIND A SHORT NAME [FORMING PART] OF A LONG NAME. Are they then similar: the *mem* of SHeM is closed, whereas that of SHiMe'oN is open?[2]—Said R. Ḥisda: This proves that if a closed [*mem*] is written open,[3] it is valid.[4] An objection is raised: *U-kethabtam*:[5] it must be *kethibah tammah* [perfect writing];[6] thus one must not write the *alef* as an *'ayyin*, the *'ayyin* as an *alef*, the *beth* as a *kaf*, or the *kaf* as a *beth*, the *gimmel* as a *ẓadde* or the *ẓadde* as a *gimmel*,[7] the *daleth* as a *resh* or the *resh* as a *daleth*, the *heh* as a *ḥeth* or the *ḥeth* as a *heh*, the *waw* as a *yod* or the *yod* as a *waw*, the *zayyin* as a *nun* or the *nun* as a *zayyin*, the *ṭeth* as a *pe* or the *pe* as a *ṭeth*, bent letters straight or straight letters bent,[8] the *mem* as a *samek* or the *samek* as a *mem*, closed
c [letters] open or open letters closed.[1] An open section [*parashah*] may not be written closed, nor a closed section open.[2] If one writes it as the 'Song', or if one writes the 'Song' as the general text,[3] or if one writes it without ink, or if one writes the 'Names'[4] in gold, they [the Scrolls thus written] must be 'hidden'.[5]—He [R. Ḥisda] holds with the following Tanna. For it was taught, R. Judah b. Bathyra said: In reference to the second [day] 'We-niskehem [*and their drink-offerings*]' is stated; in reference to the sixth, 'u-nesakehah [*and the drink-offerings thereof*]'; in reference to the seventh, 'ke-mishpaṭam [*after the ordinance*]':[6] this gives *mem*, *yod*, *mem*,[7] [i.e.,] *mayim* [water], whence we have a Biblical intimation of the water libation.[8] Now since if an open letter is written closed, it is valid,[9] a closed [letter] is the same, [viz.,] if a closed letter is written open, it is fit. But how compare! If an open [letter] is

(5) Though examples of proper nouns are given, there is no reason for not assuming that the same does not apply to common nouns too, both here and in the Mishnah. (6) These are complete words in themselves, and also the beginnings of longer words. SHeSH = linen; TeTH = giving; RaR = flowing; GaG = roof; ḤaḤ = hook.

a (1) V. *supra* 102b, n. a2 on Mishnah *supra* 102b. (2) This is explained below. (3) Isa. XLV, 5, E.V.: *I will gird thee*. The word commences with a double *alef* (אאזרך), and a double *alef* does not form an independent word. (4) Since it is not a word. (5) Rashi. Tosaf., and R. Ḥan. Jast.: since it has merely the value of a vowel letter. (6) Even if the wood is not pierced right through. (7) E.g., hair off skin. (8) I.e., the entire figure which he intended to draw.—This proves that he is more lenient.

b (1) V. *supra* 70a and *b* for notes. (2) *Mem* at the end of a word is written ם (closed); in the middle it is written מ (open). (3) In a Scroll of the law, or in a *mezuzah* or phylacteries. (4) Hence when one writes שם with a closed *mem* it is still possible to add thereto as it stands. (5) Deut. VI, 9: E.V.: *and thou shalt write them*. (6) This is a play on *u-kethabtam* by dividing it into two words. (7) The original reads, the *gamma*, this being the ancient name of the letter. In the translation the modern name is used. (8) The medial forms of *kaf*, *pe*, *ẓadde* and *nun* are bent, thus: צ פ נ כ the final forms are straight, thus: ץ ף ן ך.

c (1) This refers to the open and closed *mem*.—Thus this contradicts R. Ḥisda. (2) The *parashiot* (chapters or sections) are either open or closed, the nature of each *parashah* being fixed by tradition. Maimonides and Asheri differ on the definition of 'open' and 'closed', but the present practice is this: Both an open and a closed *parashah* end in the middle of the line, but in an open one the next *parashah* commences on the following line, whereas in a closed *parashah* the next one commences on the same line after a short blank space. V. *J.E.* art. Scroll of the Law, XI, 192 f. (3) The 'Song' refers to the two songs of Moses, Ex. XV, 1-18 and Deut. XXXII, 1-43. The first is written in the form of half bricks set over whole bricks, thus: 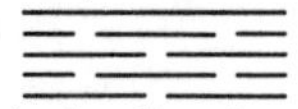 The second is written in seventy double half-columns, thus: 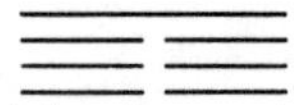 (the unbroken line above represents the ordinary width of the column, and is not part of the Song). (4) Lit., 'the mentions' (of the Divine Name). (5) This is the technical term to indicate that a Scroll is unfit for public use and must be 'hidden', i.e., buried; v. Meg. 26b. (6) V. Num. XXIX, 19, 31, 33. The reference is to the Feast of Tabernacles. (7) Taking one letter out of each of these three words. (8) Which took place on that Feast, v. Ta'an. 2b. For a description of the ceremony v. Suk. 48a and b. The sanctity of this ceremony was disputed by the Sadducees, as stated in the Mishnah a.l.; cf. also Josephus, *Ant*. XIII, 13, 5 and Halevy, *Doroth*, I, 3, 480 *seq*. This may be the reason why R. Judah b. Bathyra sought a hint for it in the Bible. (9) The *mem* of *we-niskehem*, coming as it does at the end, is closed; but it is taken as the first letter of *mayim*, i.e., open; hence it follows that if an open letter is written closed the Scroll is fit.

written closed, [104*a*] it['s sanctity] is enhanced, for R. Ḥisda said: The *mem* and the *samek* which were in the Tables stood a [there] by a miracle.[1] But as for a closed letter which is written open, it['s sanctity] is diminished, for R. Jeremiah—others state, R. Ḥiyya b. Abba—said, [The double form of] *manzapak*[2] was declared by the Watchmen [prophets].[3] (But, is that reasonable: surely it is written, *These are the commandments*,[4] [teaching] that a prophet may henceforth [i.e., after Moses] make no innovations! —Rather they were in existence, but it was not known which were [to be used] medially and which finally, and the Watchmen came and fixed [the mode of their employment]). But still, '*these are the commandments*' [teaches] that a prophet may henceforth make no innovations?[5]—Rather they had forgotten them, and they [the Watchmen] reinstituted them.[6]

It was stated above, R. Ḥisda said: The *mem* and the *samek* which were in the Tables stood [there] by a miracle. R. Ḥisda also said: The writing of the Tables could be read from within and without,[7] e.g., *nebub* [hollow] would be read *buban;—behar* [in the mountain] [as] *rahab; saru* [they departed] [as] *waras*.[8]

The Rabbis told R. Joshua b. Levi: Children have come to the Beth Hamidrash and said things the like of which was not said even in the days of Joshua the son of Nun. [Thus:] *alef Beth* [means] b learn wisdom [*alef Binah*];[1] *Gimmel Daleth*, show kindness to the poor [*Gemol Dallim*]. Why is the foot of the *Gimmel* stretched toward the *Daleth?* Because it is fitting for[2] the benevolent to run after [seek out] the poor. And why is the roof[3] of the *Daleth* stretched out toward the *Gimmel?* Because he [the poor] must make himself available to him.[4] And why is the face of the *Daleth* turned away from the *Gimmel?* Because he must give him [help] in secret,[5] lest he be ashamed of him. *He, Waw*, that is the Name of the Holy One, blessed be He;[6] *Zayyin, Ḥeth, Ṭeth, Yod, Kaf, Lamed:* [this sequence teaches,] and if thou doest thus, the Holy One, blessed be He, will sustain [*Zan*] thee, be gracious [*Ḥen*] unto thee, show goodness [*meṬib*] to thee, give thee a heritage [*Yerushah*], and bind a crown [*Kether*] on thee in the world to come. The open *Mem* and the closed *Mem* [denote] open teaching [*Ma'amar*] and closed [esoteric] teaching.[7] The bent *Nun* and the straight *Nun:* the faithful [*Ne'eman*] if bent [humble], [will ultimately be] the faithful, straightened.[8] *Samek, 'ayyin:* support [*Semok*] the poor [*'aniyyim*]. Another interpretation: devise [*'aseh*] mnemonics [*Simanin*] in the Torah and [thus] acquire [memorize] it.[9] The bent *pe* and the straight *pe* [intimate] an open mouth [*peh*], a closed mouth.[10] A bent *ẓadde* and a straight *ẓadde:* the righteous [*ẓaddik*] is bent [in this world]; the righteous

a (1) The engraving of the Tables went right through from side to side. Consequently the completely closed letters, viz., the *mem* and the *samek*, should have fallen out, and the fact that they did not was a miracle. This assumes that only the closed *mem* was then in use, for it is now assumed that the employment of distinct medial forms was a later innovation. Hence if one writes a closed *mem* instead of an open one, he enhances its sanctity, since that is the older form.—This is historically correct: the present medial forms were probably introduced in order to make it possible to join them to the next letter, and since this was unnecessary in the case of final letters, they were left in their original state. V. *J.E.*, art. Alphabet, Vol. 1, 443[2]. (2) I.e., *mem, nun, ẓadde, pe, and kaf* (מ נ צ פ כ). V. Meg., 2*b*, n. 5. (3) Hence the open letters, dating from a later period, are less sacred. (4) Lev. XXVII, 34. (5) Even such definitive fixing, where none existed before, is held to be an innovation. Weiss, *Dor*, II, p. 8 maintains that this exegesis was directed against Paul's claim to abrogate the Torah. (6) Hence both forms are of equal sanctity. (7) I.e., from both sides. (8) These words do not actually occur in the Ten Commandments written on the Tables, but are given as examples of what words might be legible backwards. For the writing would naturally appear backwards as seen from without and the letters of the words given as examples are fairly easy to read thus. Maharsha assumes that R. Ḥisda found some meaning in these reversed readings.

b (1) Here follows an homiletic interpretation of the names of the Hebrew letters in alphabetical order. (2) Lit., 'the way of'. (3) Lit., 'foot'. (4) And not trouble his benefactor too much, to find him. (5) As though with averted face. (6) These letters form part of the Tetragrammaton. (7) Such which men are forbidden to seek. (8) I.e., upright in the world to come. (Rashi): Jast. (s.v. כפף) faithful when bent, faithful when straightened. (9) Cf. 'Er. 54*b*. (10) The medial (bent) *pe* is almost closed (פ).—'*A time to keep silence, and a time to speak*' (Eccl. III, 7).

◁ *For the continuation of the English translation of this page see overleaf.*

עלויי קא מעלי ליה דאמר רב חסדא *מ"ם וסמ"ך שבלוחות בנס היו עומדין אלא סתום ועשאו פתוח גרועי קא מגרע ליה דאמר ר' ירמיה ואיתימא ר' חייא בר אבא *מנצפך צופים אמרום ותיסברא והכתיב °אלה המצות *שאין הנביא רשאי לחדש דבר מעתה אלא מיהוה הואי מידע לא הוה ידעין הי באמצע תיבה הי בסוף תיבה ואתו צופים תקנינהו *ואכתי אלה המצות שאין הנביא רשאי לחדש דבר מעתה אלא שכחום וחזרו ויסדום גופא א"ר חסדא מ"ם וסמ"ך שבלוחות בנס היו עומדין ואמר רב חסדא כתב שבלוחות נקרא מבפנים ונקרא מבחוץ כגון נבוב בובן (*רהב בהר) סרו ורס: אמרי ליה רבנן לריב"ל אתו דרדקי האידנא לבי מדרשא ואמרו מילי דאפילו בימי יהושע בן נו"ן לא איתמר כוותיהו אל"ף בי"ת אלף בינה גימ"ל דל"ת גמול דלים מ"ט פשוטה כרעיה דגימ"ל לגבי דל"ת שכן דרכו של גומל חסדים לרוץ אחר דלים ומ"ט פשוטה כרעיה דדל"ת לגבי גימ"ל דלימציה ליה נפשיה ומ"ט מהדר אפיה דדל"ת מגימ"ל דליתן ליה בצינעה כי היכי דלא ליכסיף מיניה ה"ו זה שמו של הקב"ה ז"ח ט"י כ"ל ואם אתה עושה כן הקב"ה זן אותך וחן אותך ומטיב לך ונותן לך ירושה וקושר לך כתר לעוה"ב מ"ם פתוחה מ"ם סתומה מאמר פתוח מאמר סתום נו"ן כפופה נו"ן פשוטה נאמן כפוף נאמן פשוט ס"ע סמוך עניים ל"א *סימנין עשה בתורה וקנה אותה פ' כפופה פ' פשוטה פה פתוח פה סתום צד"י כפופה וצד"י פשוטה צדיק כפוף צדיק פשוט היינו נאמן כפוף נאמן פשוט הוסיף לך הכתוב כפיפה על כפיפתו מכאן שנתנה התורה במנוד ראש קו"ף קדוש רי"ש רשע מאי טעמא מהדר אפיה דקו"ף מרי"ש אמר הקב"ה אין אני יכול להסתכל ברשע ומאי טעמא מהדרה תגיה דקו"ף לגבי רי"ש אמר הקב"ה אם חוזר בו אני קושר לו כתר כמותי ומ"ט כרעיה דקו"ף תלויה *דאי הדר ביה ליעייל וליעול בהך מסייע ליה לריש לקיש *) דאמר ר"ל מ"ד °אם ללצים הוא יליץ ולענוים יתן חן בא ליטמא פותחין לו בא ליטהר מסייעים אותו שי"ן שקר תי"ו אמת מאי טעמא שקר מקרבן מיליה אמת מרחקא מיליה שיקרא שכיח קושטא לא שכיח ומ"ט שיקרא אחדא כרעיה קאי ואמת מלבן לבוניה קושטא קאי שיקרא לא קאי א"ת ב"ש אותי תעב אתאוה לו ב"ש בי לא חשק שמי יחול עליו ג"ר גופו טימא ארחם עליו ד"ק דלתותי נעל קרניו לא אגדע עד כאן מדת רשעים אבל מדת צדיקים א"ת ב"ש אם אתה בוש ג"ר ד"ק אם אתה עושה כן גור בדוק ה"ץ ו"פ חציצה הוי בינך לאף ז"ע ח"ס ט"ן ואין אתה מזדעזע מן השטן י"ם כ"ל אמר [שר של] גיהנם לפני הקב"ה רבונו של עולם לים כל אמר הקב"ה אח"ס בט"ע גי"ף אני חס עליהם מפני שבעטו בגי"ף דכ"ץ דכים הם כנים הם צדיקים הם הל"ק אין לך חלק בהן ומרז"ן ש"ת אמר גיהנם לפניו רבונו של עולם מרי זניני מזרעו של שת א"ל א"ל ב"ם ג"ן ד"ס להיכן אוליכן (א) לגן הדס ה"ע ו"ף אמר גיהנם לפני הקב"ה רבונו של עולם עיף אנכי ז"ן ח"ק הללו זרעו של יצחק ט"ר י"ש כ"ת טר יש לי כיתות כיתות של עובדי כוכבים שאני נותן לך:

מתני'

*) יומא לח: ע"ז נה. מנחות כט:

עלויי קא מעלי ליה · שהיתה מם סתומה בלוחות אבל מם פתוחה לא היתה בלוחות כדמפרש מנצפך צופים אמרום וכיון דאמר רב חסדא מם וסמך שבלוחות בנס היו עומדים לא אפשר לאוקומיה אלא בסתומה דהואיל והכתב היה נראה משני עבריהם היה לה ליפול אם לא שבנס היה עומד אבל פתוחה אין בה נס ע"כ מנצפך דרבי ירמיה דאמר צופים אמרום בפתוחים קאמר יש שמקשין סוגיא זו על סוגיא דאמר במגילה דרמינן הא דר' ירמיה אהא דרב חסדא אלמא תרווייהו בסתומין ואין זו קושיא שכן דרך הש"ס המקשן מהפך הסברא כאן כדי שיקשה ובמקום אחר מהפכו לפי הקושיא ואי הוה בעי התם לתרולי כי איתמר דרב חסדא בסתומין ודר' ירמיה בפתוחין הוה מתרץ ליה אלא תירוצא מעליא שני ליה התם וה"נ : מיהוה הוה · תרווייהו ולא (ב) ידעי הי באמצע תיבה כו' : ונקרא מבחוץ · האותיות הפוכות והתיבה הפוכה ולא אשמועינן אלא שהיה החקק נוקב את כל הלוח ולפיכך היו מם וסמך בנס : נבוב בהר סרו · לא היו בלוחות אלא תיבה בעלמא נקט : אלף בינה · למוד תורה : מ"ט פשיט כרעיה דגימ"ל לגבי דלי"ת · ולא לגבי בי"ת : מ"ט פשיט כרעיה דדלי"ת לגבי גימ"ל · ולא לגבי ה"א שמושכה קצת לצד גימ"ל : דלימציה ליה · עני נפשיה ולא יטריחנו לבעל הבית לרוץ אחריו : ה"ו · כמו אני והו (סוכה דף מה.) שמות הם : ומטיב לך · הייטו טי"ת: ירושה · הייטו יו"ד : כתר · הייטו כף: לעולם הבא · הייטו למד : מאמר פתוח ומאמר סתום · יש דברים שנתן רשות לדורשן ויש שאתה מצווה לסותמן כגון מעשה מרכבה : נאמן כפוף · אדם כשר צריך להיות כפוף ועניו וסופו להיות פשוט וזקוף לעולם הבא : סימנים · של סדר שמועות דתנא או אמורא בגירס' דלא תשכח אחת מהן כגון אלו שבש"ס : פה פתוח · בשעת המכניסים פזר* : פה סתום · בשעת המפזרים כנס *אם יש גדול ממך : במנוד ראש · ברתת וענוה יתירה : מ"ט מהדר אפיה דקו"ף מרי"ש · לישנא דמעליא הוא שאחוריו של רי"ש לגבי הקו"ף שאין הקב"ה רוצה להסתכל בפני רשע : תגא דקו"ף · כמין זיי"ן שעושין בסופו של גג קו"ף : כרעיה דקו"ף תליא · שאינה נדבקת עם גגה : ליעול בהך · יקיף תחת רגלי הקו"ף ויכנס בפתח של ימין : מסייעין אותו · ומכינין לו פתח : הוא יליץ · מעצמו יליץ לא יסייעוהו ולא ימנעוהו : ולהם לענוים · ולמדה טובה הוא נמשך : יתן חן · יסייעוהו מן השמים : מקרבן מיליה · אותיותיו קרובות בלשון קרובות כסדרן של אלפא ביתא : אמת מרחקן מיליה · זו בתחילת אל"ף בית וזו באמצע וזו בסוף : אחד כרעא · כל אות ואות שבו עומדת על רגל אחד : אמת מלבן לבוני · מושבין תחתיה אותיותי' כמין לבינה דאל"ף הרי יש לה ב' רגלים ומושבה טוב ורגל השני רחב : אתאוה לו · בתמיה וכן כולן : ע"כ מדת הרשעים · כן הוא כדרש אלו רשעים : אם את בוש · מלחטוא : גר דק גור בדוק · נפסק תגא לצורה תחת כסאי ודוק שמים : לים כל · גיהנם קרוי ים כל לפי שהרוב הולכים שם : אמר שר של גיהנם · לים שלי תן את כל העולם ואפי' ישראל : אמר ליה אח"ס בט"ע גי"ף · אלפא ביתא היא אלא א"ת ב"ש וכולן סדורות בספר יצירה : אני אחוס עליהם על שבעטו בגיף · בניאוף : דכ"ץ · נוטריקון דכים כנים לדיקים : אין לך · גיהנם חלק בהן בישראל : ומרזן שת · ואומר שר של גיהנם זוכני מזרעו של שת · כל העובדי כוכבים וישראל : אל בס · אמר לו הקב"ה לא יהא לך חלק בהם : ג"ן ד"ס . אמר הקב"ה אוליכם לגן הדס לגן עדן : ה"ע ו"ף · הנני עף ברעב : ז"ן ח"ק · הללו זרעו של יצחק הם ולא אתנם לך : ע"ר י"ש כ"ת · שמור לי והמתן יש לי כתות אחרות :

מתני'

גרועי קא מגרע ליה דאמר רבי חייא בר אבא מנצפך צופים אמרום . וא"ת דהכא משמע דבפתוחה קאמר דצופים אמרום ובפ"ק דמגילה (דף ג:) פריך עלה דר' חייא בר אבא מאלה המצות שאין נביא רשאי לחדש דבר ועוד האמר רב חסדא מם וסמך שבלוחות בנס היו עומדים משמע דר' חייא בסתומה איירי ואור"י דהכי קאמר התם ועוד האמר רב חסדא ועוד אי רבי חייא בר אבא בסתומה איירי תקשה נמי דרב חסדא אלא ודאי בפתוחה איירי והא דנקט מנצפך ולא נקט להו כסדר אלפא ביתא משום דמנצפך משמע מן צופים* : נבוב בוכן בהר רהב · תימה דאמאי נקט להו כיון דלא הוה בלוחות : א"ל לר' יהושע בן לוי אתו דרדקי כו' · בירושלמי *ובבראשית רבה (פ' א) קאמר דר' אליעזר ור' יהושע הוו מאותן דרדקי וחולק על הש"ס שלנו והא דאמר בפרקי דר' אליעזר שלא למד ר' *אליעזר תורה אלא עד שהיה גדול הייתו שלא עסק עד שנעשה גדול : אית דגרסי בא ליטמא פותחין לו · כלומר יש לו פתחים ליכנס בא ליטהר מסייעין אותו שפותחין לו פתח ליכנס והיינו דומיא דלעיל דשביק ליה פתח ליכנס ולהגהו דגרסי בא ליטמא פותחין לו צריך לומר דמסייעין אותו הוי טפי מפותחין :

נתכוון

רבינו חננאל

למימר דמתני' ר' יוסי היא והא איכא בתר הכין מימרא דר' יוסי דאלמא רישא לאו ר' יוסי היא. ומוקים לה לכולהו כר' יוסי . א"ר יהודה מצינו שם קטן משם גדול שם משמעון ונח מנחור שהן שתי אותיות מב' שמות . פי' ב' אותיות מב' שמות כגון שם משמעון שי"ן מ"ם והן ב' אותיות וב' שמות כדאמרן שי"ן מ"ם נח מנחור נ"ן חי"ת והן כיוצא בהן אבל ב' אותיות שהן שם אחד כגון גג שזה וזה גימ"ל והן ב' אותיו' בשם אחד. כיוצא בו דד הה חח סס רר שש תת ולישנא דרבנן סס צץ אלו ב' אותיות שהן שם אחד שהן דד הה חח הא הא חית חית וכיוצא בהן . ואקשינן וכי ר' יהודה הכותב ב' אותיות והן ב' שמות כדאמרן הוא דמחייב אבל ב' אותיות והן שם אחד לא מחייב והתניא ועשה אחת יכול שאינו חייב עד שיכתוב את כל השם ת"ל מאחת אפי' מקצת (מאחת)אי מאחת ואפי' מקצתה יכול אפילו לא כתב מן התיבה אלא אות אחת יהא חייב ת"ל אחת הא כיצד אינו חייב עד שיכתוב שם קטן משם גדול שי"ן מ"ם משמעון ושמואל ונח מנחור הן מדניאל ר' יהודה אומר אפילו לא כתב אלא ב' אותיות והן שם אחד כגון שש רר גג חח הה הנה ת"ק שנה סתם שם משמעון ונח מנחור וכולהו ש"מ דכיוצא באלו ב' אותיות שהן. ב' שמות הוא דמחייב ת"ק אבל ב' אותיות שהן שם אחד לא ופליג ר' יהודה עליה בהדיא וקתני כי הכותב ב' אותיות והן שם אחד חייב . קשיא דר' יהודה אדר' יהודה ופרקי' הוא דקתני ר' יהודה במתני' כי הכותב ב' אותיות מב' שמות הוא שהוא חייב כגון שם משמעון וכיוצא בו דידיה הוא . כלומר סברא דידיה שמעה מכאן דליתיה רביה וסברא ולא תנא לה משמיה לפום דפליג על רביה והא דקתני כי חייב אפילו כותב ב' אותיות משם אחד כגון שש תת משם רבן גמליאל רביה שנאה. ואקשינן נמי אליבא דר' שמעון דתני סתם עד שיעשה מלאכה שכיוצא בה מתקיימת.והלא תנא [קמא]לא חייב אות אחת ולא הוט אחד בבגד ולא בית אחד בנפה והלא שם משמעון ונח מנחור כיוצא בהן מתקיימת וכן בבגד וכן בנפה. ונמצא דברי ר' שמעון כת"ק. מה בא ר' שמעון לאשמעינן וכי תימא ב' אותיות שהן שם אחד איכא בינייהו דת"ק לא מחייב ור' שמעון מחייב אי הכי היינו ר' יהודה דהוא נמי ת"ק דר"ש ומחייב כי האי גוונא ולתרווייהו (תני) [קרי] להו ת"ק וכי תימא אין הכי נמי מיהו ר' יהודה אינו מחייב אלא בב' אותיות שהן מלה ידועה כגון שש שהוא מלשון ששה ותת שהוא מלשון נתינה ושש שהוא מלשון ששון . אבל אל"ף אל"ף או בי"ת שאין מהן מלה [בלתי] ידועה כלל אם נתכוין לכתוב אאורך וכתב א"א ר' יהודה לא מחייב בהני כיון דלא משכחת מינייהו שם ולא מלה ידועה ור"ש אמר לך כיון דאיכא בכתיבא כה"ג בגלטורי ומתקיימין כשאר כתיבה (שהיא) מלאכה מתקיימת אני קורא בה וחייב. פי' גלטורי קמיען שכותבין בהן אותיות כגון אא יי וכיוצא בהן*) . ואקשינן תוב וכי ר' יהודה בה מיקל ור' שמעון מחמיר והוא מחייב והא שמעינן ליה לר' שמעון דמקיל בכי האי גוונא דתניא והקודח ר' שמעון אומר עד שיקדח את כולו כו' הנה ר' שמעון מיקל ולא מחייב אלא במאן דעביד כולה מלאכה וכן אינו מחייב אלא עד שיכתוב את כל השם . ואיך אתה אומר כי מחייב ר"ש א"א דאאורך ודחינן לה הכי וכי מצית אמרת דלא מחייב ר"ש אלא עד שיכתוב את כל השם כולו והתניא ר"ש אומר ועשה אחת יכול עד שיכתוב כל השם כולו ת"ל מאחת כו' . והנה אפילו לא כתב אלא מקצת השם חייב ומתרצינן להא מתניתא הכי יכול עד שיכתוב כל הפסוק כולו שנתכוון לכותבו או אפילו נתכוון לכתוב איגרת אינו חייב עד שיכתוב כל מה שנתכוון לו ת"ל מאחת . אפילו מקצת מן האגרת או מקצת מן הפסוק חייב ולעולם מלה שלימה הא דר' יוסי דאמר משום רושם פשוטה היא ומקום שנתכוון לרשום ולא לכתוב חייב ואפילו אינו דבר ידועה ברשימה במה בין בימינו בין בשמאלו חייב : ירושלמי (ה"ג) א"ר אמי והקמות את המשכן כמשפטו וכי יש משפט לעצים אלא [אי זהו] קרש שזכה לינתן בצפון ינתן בצפון לעולם וכן בדרום לפיכך היו רושמין עליהן שלא יחלפו. דבי רב הושעיא ודבי בר פזי הוו עיילין שאלין בשלמא דנשיא בכל יום והוו [אילין] דבי רב הושעיא עיילין ונפקין כו' תרתין זרעין [הוין] בצפורי בולבטיא ופגניא והוון בולבטיא עללין ונפקין ושאלין בשלמא דנשיא בכל יום עללין קודמוהי ונפקין קודמוי והוון פגניא עללין ונפקין בתריהון אזלין פגניא וזכין באורייתא ואתי למיעל קודמוי דבולבטיא אשתאלת לרבנן על ר' יוחנן ודרשה בי מדרשא (תניא) [דבי בנייה] אפילו ממזר ת"ח וכהן גדול

*) עיין בערוך ערך אא .

רב נסים גאון

פי"ב הבונה כמה יבנה . אמרו ליה לר' יהושע בן לוי אתו דרדקי לבי מדרשא ואמרו מילי דאפי' בימי יהושע בן נון לא איתמר כוותייהו בתחלת בראשית דר' אושעיא אמרו מעשה היה ביום סגריר ולא נכנסו חכמים לבית הוועד והיו שם תינוקות אמרו באו ונעשה כצופים כו' ויש אומרים ר"א ור' יהושע ור"ע היו קראו עליהן גם במעלליו יתנכר נער ומשכחת לה בגמ' דבני מערבא בפ' מגילה נקראת (הל' ט) :

האורג

מסורת הש"ס

מגילה ג:

ג"ז שם

[שם ויומא פ. תמורה טז:]

יומא פ.

[נ"ל בהר רהב]

[עי' עירובין נד: אין תורה נקנית יכו']

[מנחות כט: ע"ש]

[ברכות סג.]

[שם]

תורה אור: ויקרא כז; משלי ג

הגהות הב"ח

(א) גמ' להיכן אוליכם לגן : (ב) רש"י ד"ה מיהוה וכו' תרווייהו ולא הוה ידעי :

Continuation of translation from previous page as indicated by ◁

is straightened [in the next world].[11] But that is identical with the faithful bent [and] the faithful straightened?—The Writ added humility[12] to his humility;[13] hence [we learn that] the Torah
c was given under great submissiveness.[1] *Ḳuf* [stands for] *Ḳadosh* [holy]; *Resh* [for] *Rasha'* [wicked]: why is the face of the *Kuf* averted from the *Resh?* The Holy One, blessed be He, said: I cannot look at the wicked. And why is the crown of the *Ḳuf*[2] turned toward the *Resh?* The Holy One, blessed be He, saith: If he repents, I will bind a crown on him like Mine. And why is the foot of the *Ḳuf* suspended?[3] [To show] that if he repents, he can enter and be brought in [to God's favour] through this [opening]. This supports Resh Laḳish, for Resh Laḳish said: What is meant by, *Surely he scorneth the scorners, But he giveth grace unto the lowly?*[4] If one comes to defile himself, he is given an opening;[5] if one comes to cleanse himself, he is helped. *SHin* [stands for] *SHeḳer* [falsehood]; *Taw* [for] *emeTh* [truth]: why are the letters of *SheḲeR* close together, whilst those of *'eMeTH* are far apart?[6] Falsehood is frequent, truth is rare.[7] And why does falsehood [stand] on one foot, whilst truth has a brick-like foundation?[8] Truth can stand, falsehood cannot stand. *AT BaSh:*[9] he that rejects Me [*Othi Ti'ew*], shall I desire [*e Th'aweh*] him? *BaSH:* he that delighteth not in Me [*Bi lo ḥaSHak*], shall My Name [*SHemi*] rest upon him? *GaR:* he has defiled his body [*Gufo*]—shall I have mercy [*aRaḥem*] upon him? *DaḲ:* he has closed My doors [*Dalthothay*]—shall I not cut off his horns [*Ḳarnaw*]?[10] Thus far is the exegesis for the wicked, but the interpretation for the righteous is: *AT BaSH:* If thou art ashamed [to sin] [*aTTah BoSh*], then *GaR DaḲ* [i.e.,] dwell [*GuR*] in heaven [*DoḲ*]. *HaẒ WaF:* there will be a barrier [*ḤaẒiẒah*] between thee and wrath [*aF*]. *Ẓa' ḤaS ṬaN:* nor wilt thou tremble [*miZda'aZe'a*] before Satan [*SaṬaN*]. *YaM KoL:* the Prince of Gehenna said to the Holy One, blessed be He, Sovereign of the Universe! To the sea [*YaM*] let all [*KoL*] be
d consigned.[1] But the Holy One, blessed be He, replieth, *AḤaS, BeṬa, GiF.*[2] I [*ani*] spare [*ḤaS*] them, because they have spurned [*Ba'aṬu*] sensual pleasures [*GiF*]. *DaKaẒ:* they are contrite [*Dakkim*]; they are true [*Kenim*]; they are righteous [*Ẓaddiḳim*]. *HaLaḲ:* thou hast [*LaK*] no portion [*ḤeLeḲ*] in them. *UMaRZaN SHeTH:* the Gehenna cried out before Him, Sovereign of the Universe! My Lord [*MaRi*]! Satiate me [*ZeNini*] with the seed of *SHeTH.*[3] [But] He retorted, *aL BaM* [thou hast nought in them]; *GaN DaS:* Whither shall I lead them? to the Garden [*GaN*] of myrtles [*haDaS*].[4] *Ha! WaF:* the Gehenna cried out before the Holy One, blessed be He, Sovereign of the Universe! I am faint [*'ayeF*] [with hunger]. [To which He replied,] *ZaẒ ḤaḲ:* these are the seed [*Zar'o*] of Isaac [*YiẒḤaḲ*]. *ṬaR YeSH KaT:* Wait [*ṬaR*]! I have [*YeSH*] whole companies [*KiToth*] of heathens whom I will give thee.

(11) Or, righteous when bent, righteous when straight: cf. n. b8. (12) Lit., 'bending'. (13) I.e., particularly emphasized the virtue of humility.
c (1) Lit., 'with bent head'. (2) The upward turn of the 'tittle' or 'dagger' on the upper line of the *Ḳuf*. (3) Not joined to the rest of the letter. (4) Prov. III, 34. (5) I.e., he is permitted, but not actively helped. (6) The three letters of *Sheḳer*, שקר occur together; whereas the three of emeth, אמת are far apart, א being the first, מ the middle, and ת the last letters of the alphabet. (7) I.e., instances of truth are found only at distant intervals. (8) I.e., each of the letters of שקר is insecurely poised on one leg (ש was anciently written ש) whereas those of אמת are firmly set, each resting on two ends, the מ too resting on a horizontal bar. (9) Here follows an interpretation of the letters coupled, the first with the last, the second with the last but one, and so on. (10) Or the passages may be understood affirmatively: though he has rejected Me, yet shall I desire him; etc.
d (1) Rashi: 'all'—i.e., including Israel; the sea, i.e., Gehenna. (2) A combination of letters wherein the first, eighth, and fifteenth are grouped together; similarly the second, ninth and sixteenth, and so on. (3) I.e., with all, both Jews and non-Jews. (4) I.e., of Eden, probably so called here on account of its fragrance: cf. B.B. 75a.

גמרא

עלויי קא מעלי ליה דאמר רב חסדא *מ"ם וסמ"ך שבלוחות בנס היו עומדין אלא סתום ועשאו פתוח גרועי קא מגרע ליה דאמר ר' ירמיה ואיתימא ר' חייא בר אבא *מנצפך צופים אמרום ותיסברא והכתיב °אלה המצות *שאין הנביא רשאי לחדש דבר מעתה אלא מיהוה הואי מידע לא הוה ידעין הי באמצע תיבה הי בסוף תיבה ואתו צופים תקנינהו *ואכתי אלה המצות שאין הנביא רשאי לחדש דבר מעתה אלא שכחום וחזרו ויסדום גופא א"ר חסדא מ"ם וסמ"ך שבלוחות בנס היו עומדין ואמר רב חסדא כתב שבלוחות נקרא מבפנים ונקרא מבחוץ כגון נבוב בובן (*רהב בהר) סרו ורס: אמרי ליה רבנן לריב"ל אתו דרדקי האידנא לבי מדרשא ואמרו מילי דאפילו בימי יהושע בן נו"ן לא איתמר כוותייהו אל"ף בי"ת אלף בינה גימ"ל דל"ת גמול דלים מ"ט פשוטה כרעיה דגימ"ל לגבי דל"ת שכן דרכו של גומל חסדים לרוץ אחר דלים ומ"ט פשוטה כרעיה דדל"ת לגבי גימ"ל דלימציה ליה נפשיה ומ"ט מהדר אפיה דדל"ת מגימ"ל דליתן ליה בצינעה כי היכי דלא ליכסיף מיניה ה"ו זה שמו של הקב"ה ז"ח ט"י כ"ל ואם אתה עושה כן הקב"ה זן אותך וחן אותך ומטיב לך ונותן לך ירושה וקושר לך כתר לעוה"ב מ"ם פתוחה מ"ם סתומה מאמר פתוח מאמר סתום נו"ן כפופה נו"ן פשוטה נאמן כפוף נאמן פשוט ס"ע סמוך עניים ל"א *סימנין עשה בתורה וקנה אותה פ' כפופה פ' פשוטה פה פתוח פה סתום צד"י כפופה וצד"י פשוטה צדיק כפוף צדיק פשוט היינו נאמן כפוף נאמן פשוט הוסיף לך הכתוב כפיפה על כפיפתו מכאן שנתנה התורה במנוד ראש קו"ף קדוש רי"ש רשע מאי טעמא מהדר אפיה דקו"ף מרי"ש אמר הקב"ה אין אני יכול להסתכל ברשע ומאי טעמא מהדרה תגיה דקו"ף לגבי רי"ש אמר הקב"ה אם חוזר בו אני קושר לו כתר כמותי ומ"ט כרעיה דקו"ף תלויה *דאי הדר ביה ליעייל וליעול בהך מסייע ליה לריש לקיש *) דאמר ר"ל מ"ד °אם ללצים הוא יליץ ולענוים יתן חן בא ליטמא פותחין לו בא ליטהר מסייעים אותו שי"ן שקר תי"ו אמת מאי טעמא שקר מקרבן מיליה אמת מרחקא מיליה שיקרא שכיח קושטא לא שכיח ומ"ט שיקרא אחדא כרעיה קאי ואמת מלבן לבוניה קושטא קאי שיקרא לא קאי א"ת ב"ש אותי תעב אתאוה לו ב"ש בי לא חשק שמי יחול עליו ג"ר גופו טימא ארחם עליו ד"ק דלתותי נעל קרניו לא אגדע עד כאן מדת רשעים אבל מדת צדיקים א"ת ב"ש אם אתה בוש ג"ר ד"ק אם אתה עושה כן גור בדוק ה"ץ ו"ף חציצה הוי בינך לאף ז"ע ח"ס ט"ן ואין אתה מזדעזע מן השטן י"ם כ"ל אמר [שר של] גיהנם לפני הקב"ה רבונו של עולם לים כל אמר הקב"ה אח"ס בט"ע גי"ף אני חס עליהם מפני שבעטו בגי"ף דכ"ץ דכים הם כנים הם צדיקים הם הל"ק אין לך חלק בהן ומרז"ן ש"ת אמר גיהנם לפני רבונו של עולם מרי זניני מזרעו של שת א"ל א"ל ב"ם ג"ן ד"ס להיכן אוליכן(א) לגן הדס ה"ע ו"ף אמר גיהנם לפני הקב"ה רבונו של עולם עיף אנכי ז"ץ ח"ק הללו זרעו של יצחק ט"ר י"ש כ"ת טר יש לי כיתות כיתות של עובדי כוכבים שאני נותן לך:

מתני'

*) יומא לח: ע"ז נה. מנחות כט:

ויקרא כז · משלי ג

רש"י

עלויי קא מעלי ליה · שהיתה מם סתומה בלוחות אבל מם פתוחה לא היתה בלוחות כדמפרש מנצפך צופים אמרום וכיון דאמר רב חסדא מם וסמך שבלוחות בנס היו עומדים לא אפשר לאוקומיה אלא בסתומה דהואיל והכתב היה נראה משני עבריהם היה לה ליפול אם לא שבנס היה עומד אבל פתוחה אין בה נס ע"כ מנצפך דרבי ירמיה דאמר צופים אמרום בפתוחים קאמר יש שמקשין סוגיא זו על סוגיא דאמר במגילה דרמינן הא דר' ירמיה אהא דרב חסדא אלמא תרוייהו בסתומין ואין זו קושיא שכן דרך הש"ס המקשן מהפך הסברא כאן כדי שיקשה ובמקום אחר מהפכו לפי הקושיא ולאי הוה בעי התם לתרוצי כי איתמר דרב חסדא בסתומין ודר' ירמיה בפתוחין הוה מתרץ ליה אלא תירוצא מעליא שני ליה התם וה"נ: מיהוה הוה · תרוייהו ולא (ב) ידעי הי באמצע תיבה כו': ונקרא מבחוץ · האותיות הפוכות והתיבה הפוכה ולא אשמועינן אלא שהיה החקק נוקב את כל הלוח ולפיכך היו מם וסמך בנס: נבוב בהר סרו · לא היו בלוחות אלא תיבה בעלמא נקט: אלף בינה · למוד תורה: מ"ט פשיט כרעיה דגימ"ל לגבי דלי"ת · ולא לגבי בי"ת: מ"ט פשיט כרעיה דדלי"ת לגבי גימ"ל · ולא לגבי ה"א שמושכה קלת לצד גימ"ל: דלימליה ליה · עני נפשיה ולא יטריחנו לבעל הבית לרוץ אחריו: ה"ו · כמו אני והו (סוכה דף מה.) שמות הם: ומטיב לך · היינו טי"ת: ירושה · היינו יו"ד: כתר · היינו כף: לעולם הבא · היינו למד: מאמר פתוח ומאמר סתום · יש דברים שנתן רשות לדורשן ויש שאתה מצווה לסותמן כגון מעשה מרכבה: נאמן כפוף · אדם כשר צריך להיות כפוף ועניו וסופו להיות פשוט וזקוף לעולם הבא: סימנים · של סדר שמועות דתנא או אמורא בגירס' דלא תשכח אחת מהן כגון אלו שבש"ס: פה פתוח · בשעת המכנסים פזר*: פה סתום · בשעת המפזרים כנס *אם יש גדול ממך: במנוד ראש · ברתת ועטה יתירה: מ"ט מהדר אפיה דקו"ף מרי"ש · לישנא דמעליא הוא שאחוריו של רי"ש לגבי הקו"ף שאין הקב"ה רוצה להסתכל בפני רשע: תגא דקו"ף · כמין זיי"ן שעושין בסופו של גג קו"ף: כרעיה דקו"ף תליא · שאינה נדבקת עם גגה: ניעול בהך · יקיף תחת רגלי הקו"ף ויכנס בפתח של ימין: מסייעין אותו · ומכינין לו פתח: הוא יליץ · מעצמו יליץ לא יסייעוהו ולא ימנעוהו: ואם לענוים · ולמדה טובה הוא נמשך: יתן חן · יסייעוהו מן השמים: מקרבן מיליה · אותיותיו קרובות בלשון קרובות כסדרן של אלפא ביתא: אמת מרחקן מיליה · זו בתחילת אל"ף בית וזו באמצע וזו בסוף: אחד כרעא · כל אות ואות שבו עומדת על רגל אחד: אמת מלבן לבוני · מושבין תחתיה אותיותי' כמין לבינה דאל"ף הרי יש לה ב' רגלים ומושבה טוב ורגל השני רחב: אתאוה לו · בתמיה וכן כולן: ע"כ מדת הרשעים · כן הוא נדרש אצל רשעים: אם את בוש . מלחטוא: גר דק גור בדוק · נפסק תהא לגורה תחת כסאי ודוק שמים: לים כל · גיהנם קרוי ים כל לפי שהרוב הולכים שם: אמר שר של גיהנם · לים שלי תן את כל העולם ואפי' ישראל: אמר ליה אח"ס בט"ע גי"ף · אלפא ביתא היא אצל א"ת ב"ש וכולן סדורות בספר יצירה: אני אחוס עליהם על שבעטו בגיף · בגיאוף: דכ"ץ · נוטריקון דכים כנים צדיקים: אין לך · גיהנם חלק בהן בישראל: ומרזן שת · והומר שר של גיהנם זונכי מזרעו של שת · כל העובדי כוכבים וישראל: אל בם · אמר לו הקב"ה לא יהא לך חלק בהם: ג"ן ד"ס . אמר הקב"ה אוליכם לגן הדס לגן עדן: ה"ע ו"ף · הנני עף ברעב: ז"ן ח"ק · הללו זרעו של יצחק הם ולא אתנם לך: ט"ר י"ש כ"ת · שמור לי והמתן יש לי כתות אחרות:

מתני'

תורה אור

תוספות

גרועי קא מגרע ליה · דאמר רבי חייא בר אבא מנצפך צופים אמרום . וא"ת דהכא משמע דבפתוחה קאמר דצופים אמרום ובפ"ק דמגילה (דף ג:) פריך עלה דר' חייא בר אבא מאלה המצות שאין נביא רשאי לחדש דבר ועוד האמר רב חסדא מם וסמך שבלוחות בנס היו עומדים משמע דר' חייא בסתומה איירי ואור"י דהכי קאמר התם ועוד האמר רב חסדא ועוד אי רבי חייא בר אבא בסתומה איירי תקשה נמי דרב חסדא אלא ודאי בפתוחה איירי והא דנקט מנצפך ולא נקט להו כסדר אלפא ביתא משום דמנצפך משמע מן צופים*: נבוב בוכן בהר רהב · תימה דאמאי נקט לה כיון דלא הוה בלוחות: א"ל לר' יהושע בן לוי אתו דרדקי כו' · בירושלמי *ובבראשית רבה (פ' א) קאמר דר' אליעזר ור' יהושע הוו מאותן דרדקי וחולק על הש"ס שלנו והא דאמר בפרקי דר' אליעזר שלא למד ר' *אליעזר תורה אלא עד שהיה גדול היינו שלא עסק עד שנעשה גדול: אית דגרסי בא ליטמא פותחין לו · כלומר יש לו פתחים ליכנס בא ליטהר מסייעין אותו שפותחין לו פתח ליכנס והיינו דומיא דלעיל דשביק ליה פתח ליכנס ולהנהו דגרסי בא ליטמא פותחין לו צריך לומר דמסייעין אותו הוי טפי מפותחין:

מסורת הש"ס

מגילה ג:

ג"ז שם

[שם ויומא פ. תמורה טז:]

יומא פ.

[נ"ל בהר רהב]

[עי' עירובין כד: אין הורה נקניה יבי']

[מנחות כט: ע"ש]

[ברכות סג.]

[בס]

הגהות הב"ח

(א) גמ' להיכן אוליכם לגן: (ב) רש"י ד"ה מיהוה וכו' תרוייהו ולא הוה ידעי:

רבינו חננאל

למימר דמתני' ר' יוסי היא והא איכא בתר הכין מימרא דר' יוסי דאלמא רישא לאו ר' יוסי היא. ומוקים לה לכולהו כר' יוסי . א"ר יהודה מצינו שם קטן משם גדול שם משמעון ונח מנחור שהן שתי אותיות מב' שמות . פי' ב' אותיות מב' שמות כגון שם משמעון שי"ן מ"ם והן ב' אותיות וב' שמות כדאמרן שי"ן מ"ם נח מנחור נ"ן ח"ת והן כיוצא בהן אבל ב' אותיות שהן שם אחד כגון גג שזה וזה גימ"ל והן ב' אותיו' בשם אחד. כיוצא בו דד הה חח סס רר שש תת ולישנא דרבנן ממ צץ אלו ב' אותיות שהן שם אחד שהן דד הה חח הא הא חית חית וכיוצא בהן . ואקשינן וכי ר' יהודה הכותב ב' אותיות והן ב' שמות כדאמרן הוא דמחייב אבל ב' אותיות והן שם אחד לא מחייב והתניא ועשה אחת יכול שאינו חייב עד שיכתוב את כל השם ת"ל מאחת אפי' מקצת (מאחת)אי מאחת ואפי' מקצתה יכול אפילו לא כתב מן התיבה אלא אות אחת יהא חייב ת"ל אחת הא כיצד אינו חייב עד שיכתוב שם קטן משם גדול שי"ן מ"ם משמעון ושמואל ונח מנחור והן מדניאל ר' יהודה אומר אפילו לא כתב אלא ב' אותיות והן שם אחד כגון שש רר גג חח הה הנה ת"ק שנה סתם שם משמעון ונח מנחור וכולהו ש"מ דכיוצא באלו ב' אותיות שהן ב' שמות הוא דמהייב ת"ק אבל ב' אותיות שהן שם אחד לא ופליג ר' יהודה עליה בהדיא וקתני כי הכותב ב' אותיות והן שם אחד חייב . קשיא דר' יהודה אדר' יהודה ופרקי' הוא דקתני ר' יהודה במתני' כי הכותב ב' אותיות מב' שמות הוא שהוא חייב כגון שם משמעון וכיוצא בו דידיה הוא . כלומר סברא דידיה שמעה מכאן דליתיה רביה וסברא ולא תנא לה משמיה לפום דפליג על רביה והא דקתני כי חייב אפילו כותב ב' אותיות משם אחד כגון שש תת משם רבן גמליאל רביה שנאה. ואקשינן נמי אליבא דר' שמעון דתני סתם עד שיעשה מלאכה שכיוצא בה מתקיימת. והלא תנא [קמא] לא חייב אות אחת ולא הום אחד בבגד ולא בית אחד בנפה והלא שם משמעון ונח מנחור כיוצא בהן מתקיימת וכן בבגד וכן בנפה. ונמצא דברי ר' שמעון כת"ק. מה בא ר' שמעון לאשמעינן וכי תימא ב' אותיות שהן שם אחד איכא בינייהו דת"ק לא מחייב ור' שמעון מחייב אי הכי היינו ר' יהודה דהוא נמי ת"ק דר"ש ומחייב כי האי גוונא ולתרווייהו (תני) [קרי] להו ת"ק וכי תימא אין הכי נמי מיהו ר' יהודה אינו מחייב אלא בב' אותיות שהן מלה ידועה כגון שש שהוא מלשון ששה ותת שהוא מלשון נתינה ושש שהוא מלשון ששון . אבל אל"ף אל"ף או בי"ת שאין מהן מלה [בל'תי] ידועה כלל אם נתכוין לכתוב אאורך וכתב א"א ר' יהודה לא מחייב בהני כיון דלא משכחת מינייהו שם ולא מלה ידועה ור"ש אמר לך כיון דאיכא בכתיבא כה"ג בגלמורי ומתקיימין כשאר כתיבה (שהיא) מלאכה מתקיימת אני קורא בה וחייב. פי' גלמורי קמיעין שכותבין בהן אותיות כגון אא יי וכיוצא בהן*) . ואקשינן תוב וכי ר' יהודה בה מיקל ור' שמעון מחמיר והוא מחייב והא שמעינן ליה לר' שמעון דמקיל בכי האי גוונא דתניא והקודח ר' שמעון אומר עד שיקדח את כולו כו' הנה ר' שמעון מיקל ולא מחייב אלא בגאן דעביד כולה מלאכה וכן אינו מחייב אלא עד שיכתוב את כל השם . ואיך אתה אומר כי מחייב ר"ש א"א דאאורך ודחינן לה הכי וכי מצית אמרת דלא מחייב ר"ש אלא עד שיכתוב את כל השם כולו והתניא ר"ש אומר ועשה אחת יכול עד שיכתוב כל השם כולו ת"ל מאחת כו' . והנה אפילו לא כתב אלא מקצת השם חייב ומתרצינן להא מתניתא הכי יכול עד שיכתוב כל הפסוק כולו שנתכוון לכותבו או אפילו נתכוון לכתוב איגרת אינו חייב עד שיכתוב כל מה שנתכוון לו ת"ל מאחת . אפילו מקצת מן האגרת או מקצת מן הפסוק חייב ולעולם מלה שלימה הא דר' יוסי דאמר משום רושם פשוטה היא ומקום שנתכוון לרשום ולא לכתוב חייב ואפילו אינו דבר ידועה ברשימה במה בין בימינו בין בשמאלו חייב : ירושלמי (ה"ג) א"ר אמי והקמות את המשכן כמשפטו וכי יש משפט לעצים אלא [אי זהו] קרש שזכה לינתן בצפון ינתן בצפון לעולם וכן בדרום לפיכך היו רושמין עליהן שלא יחלפו. דבי רב הושעיא ודבי בר פזי הוו עיילין שאלין בשלמא דנשיא בכל יום והוו [אילין] דבי רב הושעיא עיילין ונפקין כו' תרתין זרעין [הוין] בצפורי בולבטיא ופגניא והוון בולבטיא עללין ונפקין ושאלין בשלמא דנשיא בכל יום עללין קודמוי ונפקין קודמוי והוון פגניא עללין ונפקין בתריהון אזלין פגניא וזכין באורייתא ואתי למיעל קודמוי דבולבטיא אשתאלת לרבנן על ר' יוחנן ודרשה בי מדרשא (תניא) [דבי בנייה] אפילו ממזר ת"ח וכהן גדול

*) עיין בערוך ערך אא .

רב נסים גאון

פי"ב הבונה כמה יבנה . אמרו ליה לר' יהושע בן לוי אתו דרדקי לבי מדרשא ואמרו מילי דאפי' בימי יהושע בן נון לא איתמר כוותייהו בתהלת בראשית דר' אושעיא אמרו מעשה היה ביום סגריר ולא נכנסו חכמים לבית הוועד והיו שם תינוקות אמרו באו ונעשה כצופים כו' ויש אומרים ר"א ור' יהושע ור"ע היו קראו עליהן גם במעלליו יתנכר נער ומשכחת לה בגמ' דבני מערבא בפ' מגילה נקראת (הל' ט) : האורג

מתני' הכותב שתי אותיות בהעלם אחד חייב *כתב בדיו בסם בסיקרא בקומוס ובקנקנתום ובכל דבר שהוא רושם *על שני כותלי זויות ועל שני לווחי פינקס והן נהגין זה עם זה חייב *הכותב על בשרו חייב המסרט על בשרו ר' אליעזר מחייב חטאת *וחכמים פוטרין *כתב במשקין במי פירות באבק דרכים באבק הסופרים ובכל דבר שאינו מתקיים פטור *לאחר ידו ברגלו בפיו ובמרפיקו *כתב אות אחת סמוך לכתב וכתב על גבי כתב נתכוון לכתוב חי"ת וכתב ב' זיינין אחת בארץ ואחת בקורה כתב על ב' כותלי הבית על שני דפי פנקס ואין נהגין זה עם זה פטור כתב אות אחת נוטריקון ר' יהושע בן בתירא מחייב *וחכמים פוטרין: **גמ'** דיו *דיותא סם סמא סקרא אמר רבה בר בר חנה סקרתא שמה קומוס קומא קנקנתום אמר רבה בר בר חנה אמר שמואל חרתא דאושכפי: ובכל דבר שהוא רושם: לאתויי מאי לאתויי הא דתני *רבי חנניא כתבו במי טריא *ואפצא כשר תני ר' חייא *כתבו באבר בשחור ובשיחור כשר: המסרט על בשרו: תניא *אמר להן רבי אליעזר לחכמים והלא בן סטדא הוציא כשפים ממצרים בסריטה שעל בשרו אמרו לו שוטה היה *ואין מביאין ראיה מן השוטים: כתב אות אחת סמוך לכתב: מאן תנא אמר רבא בר רב הונא דלא כר' אליעזר דאי ר' אליעזר *האמר אחת·על האריג חייב: כתב על גבי כתב: מאן תנא א"ר חסדא דלא כר' יהודה דתניא *הרי שהיה צריך לכתוב את השם ונתכוין לכתוב יהודה וטעה ולא הטיל בו דלת מעביר עליו קולמוס ומקדשו דברי ר' יהודה וחכמים אומרים *אין השם מן המובחר תנא *כתב אות אחת והשלימה לספר *ארג חוט אחד והשלימה לבגד חייב מאן תנא אמר *רבא בר רב הונא ר' אליעזר היא דאמר *אחת על האריג חייב רב אשי אמר אפילו תימא רבנן להשלים שאני *א"ר אמי *כתב אות אחת בטבריא ואחת בציפורי חייב כתיבה היא אלא שמחוסר קריבה והתנן כתב על שני כותלי הבית ועל שני דפי פנקס ואין נהגין זה עם זה פטור התם מחוסר מעשה דקריבה הכא לא מחוסר מעשה דקריבה תנא הגיה אות אחת חייב השתא כתב אות אחת פטור הגיה אות אחת חייב אמר רב ששת הכא במאי עסקינן *כגון שנטלו לגגו של חי"ת ועשאו שני זיינין רבא אמר כגון *שנטלו לתגו של דל"ת ועשאו רי"ש תנא נתכוין לכתוב אות אחת

ועלו

מתני' על שני כותלי זויות · אחת במזרח ואחת בצפון סמוכות זו לזו במקצוע: על שני לוחי פנקס · פנקס של חנוונים כעין אותן של סוחרים שיש להם לוחים הרבה חקוקין וטוחין בשעוה: על שני לוחי פנקס · רבותא אשמועינן דאע"ג דלאו אלוח אחד הם אם נהגין ונקרין זה עם זה שכתובין על שני שפתי הלווחין סמוכים זה לזה חייב: הכותב על בשרו · בדיו: המסרט · במכתב או בסיד: במשקין · כמו מי תותים שמשחירין: או במי פירות · כל פירות: באבק דרכים · בטיט לשון אחר באבק דרכים באצבעו שרט כמו אותיות בעפר נגוב: באבק הסופרי' · עפרורית של קסת הסופר: לאחר ידו · בגב ידו שאחז הקולמוס באצבעותיו והפך ידו וכתב: מרפיקו (א)· אצילי ידיו: כתב אות אחת סמוך לכתב · אלא אות הכתובה זיוג אות להשלימה לשתים: כתב ע"ג הכתב · העביר הקולמוס על אותיות הכתובים כבר וחדשם: נתכוין לכתוב חי"ת · ודילג הקולמוס ולא נראה הגג של חי"ת אלא שני הרגלים ונראה כשני זיינין: על שני כותלי הבית · שאינו במקלוע: על שני דפי פנקס · שעשוי עמודים כמגילה וכתב אות בעמוד זה ואות בזה ואינו יכול לקרבן אלא אם כן יחתוך הפסק שביניהם וה"ה לכותלי הבית רחוקין זה מזה ותנא ברישא שני כותלי הבית דסתמא אין נהגין זה עם זה והדר תנא שני דפי פנקס וה"ה לכותלי הבית ולא זו אף זו קתני: כתב אות אחת על שם נוטריקון · שעשה סימן נקודה עליה לומר שלהבין בה תיבה שלימה כתבה: **גמ'** סמא · אורפימינ"ט: סקרתא· אימני"א לבע אדום שלובעין בה תריסין: קומא · גומא שרף אילן: חרתא דאושכפי · ארמינ"ט: כתבו · לגט: במי טריא · י"א מין פרי וי"א מי גשמים: אפצא · מי עפלים גל"ש: באבר · בעופרת ומשחיר כשהוא משפשף עופרת על הקלף: בשחור · פיחם: שיחור · אדרמינ"ט: הוציא כשפים · שלא היה יכול להוציאן כתובים שהיו החרטומין בודקין כל היוצאים שלא יוציאו כשפים ללמדם לבני מדינה אחרת: שוטה היה · שטות היה בו לעשות מה שאין דרך בני אדם עושים ומסר נפשו על הדבר: א' על האריג · חוט א' ארג על קצת אריג: וטעה ולא הטיל בו דלת · ונמצא שם נכתב במקומו אבל לא בכוונה: מעביר עליו קולמוס · לכוונת שם על כל אותיותיו כאלו הוא כותבו: והשלימה לספר · אות אחרונה של אחת מכ"ד ספרים: מחוסר מעשה דקריבה · אינו מקרבן אלא על ידי קציצה המפסיק ביניהן וכי קאמר רב אמי כגון כתב אחת על שפת לוח זו בטבריה ואחת על שפת לוח זו בצפורי ואתה יכול לקרבן שלא במעשה אלא קריבה בעלמא: ועשאו שני זיינין · והספר לכך צריך: רבא אמר כגון שנטלו לתגא דדלית · דלא הוי אלא הגהת אות אחת ובדבר מועט חייב הואיל וזהו תיקון הספר *דאסור לאדם לשהות ספר שאינו מוגה משום אל תשכן באהליך עולה (איוב יא) והוה ליה ככתב אות אחת והשלימה לספר דאמרן לעיל דחייב ואפי' לרבנן:

ועלו

נתכוין לכתוב ח' וכתב שני זיינין · וא"ת מאי איריא נתכוין לכתוב ח' דלא נעשית מחשבתו אפילו נתכוין לכתוב ז' אחד וכתב שני זיינין פטור כמו נתכוין לזרוק ב' וזרק ד' (לעיל דף עג.) וכן קשה אברייתא דמייתי בגמרא נתכוין לכתוב אות אחת ועלו בידו שתים חייב אמאי חייב מ"ש מנתכוין לזרוק שתים וזרק ד' וי"ל דמיירי כגון שהיה צריך לכתוב שתי אותיות איזה שתי אותיות שיהיו דהשתא נתכוון לדבר איסור וגם נעשית מחשבתו ואפילו הכי פטור כדמפרש בגמ' משום דבעי זיוני וא"ת מאי איריא נתכוין לכתוב חי"ת אפי' נתכוון לכתוב שני זיינין וכתב בלא זיון פטור וי"ל דנקט נתכוין לכתוב ח' לרבותא דדוקא כתב שני זיינין דבעי זיון פטור אבל כתב שתי אותיות אחרות דלא בעו זיון חייב ואע"ג דהשתא מיהא לאחת הוא דמתכוין:

שיחור · פירש רש"י איידרמנ"ט ואין נראה דא"כ מאי הוה קרי ליה רבי חייא בל"א ולא נקט ליה בלשון *מתני': **בן** סטדא · אור"ת דהא בן סטדא דאמרינן הכא דהוה בימי פפוס בן יהודה דהוה בימי רבי עקיבא כדמוכח בפרק בתרא דברכות (דף סא:):

אמר רב חסדא דלא כר' יהודה· וא"ת רב אחא בריבי יעקב דקאמר אההיא דקאמר רב חסדא בפ' שני דגיטין (דף כ.) גט שכתבו שלא לשמה והעביר עליו קולמוס לשמה באנו למחלוקת ר' יהודה ורבנן דתניא נתכוין לכתוב כו' ודחי רב אחא בר יעקב דלמא לא היא ע"כ לא קאמרי (ב) התם גבי תורה אלא משום זה אלי ואנוהו אבל גבי גט מודו א"כ מתני' דהכא כמאן אתיא וי"ל דדוקא בגט שהיה כתוב שלא לשמה הוי כתב עליון כתב לכולי עלמא שהאחרון מתקן יותר מן הראשון שעושהו לשמה אבל כשאין כתב העליון מתקן כלום לכ"ע לא הוי כתב ובהכי מיירי מתני' ואתיא ככ"ע ורב חסדא דקאמר הכא דמתני' אתיא דלא כר"י לטעמיה דקאמר התם גבי גט באנו למחלוקת ר"י ורבנן ומשמע ליה דמתני' דהכא בכל ענין איירי אפי' כשמתקן בכתב האחרון אבל לרב אחא בר יעקב ע"כ מתני' לא איירי בכל ענין דבגט לא מלי איירי: **התם** מחוסר מעשה· בפרק כל המנחות באות מצה (מנחות דף נז:) בהניח בשר על גבי גחלים וגללה בו כגרוגרת בשני מקומות איכא מאן דמחייב ואיכא מאן דפטר מאן דמחייב סבר דלא דמי לכתב על שני כותלי הבית שאין מזיק שם חסרון קריבה כמו כאן:

והתניא

עין משפט נר מצוה

כה א מיי' פי"א מהל' שבת הל' טו סמג לאוין סה:

כו ב מיי' שם הל' יא:

כז ג ד שם הלכה טו:

כח ה שם הלכה טו טוש"ע א"ח סי' שמ סעיף ד ה:

כט ו מיי' שם הל' יד:

ל ז שם הלכה יא:

לא ח שם הלכה יג:

לב ט מיי' פ"ד מהל' גירושין הלכה ג סמג עשין נ טוש"ע אה"ע סימן קכה סעיף ג:

לג י מיי' שם הלכה א טוש"ע שם סעיף ג:

לד כ מיי' פ"א מהל' תפילין הלכה טו טוש"ע י"ד סי' רעו סעיף יב ועיין בב"י:

לה ל מיי' פי"א מהל' שבת הלכה ט:

לו מ מיי' פ"ט מהל' שבת הלכה יח:

לז נ מיי' פי"א שם הלכה יב:

לח ס שם הלכה יג:

רבינו חננאל

ע"ה ממזר ת"ח קודם. ולא תימא הני מילי לפדות ולהחיות ולכסות הא לישיבה לא אלא אפי' לישיבה. ת"ח קודם מ"ם יקרה היא מפנינים מכ"ג שנכנס לפני ולפנים. וקיי"ל כת"ק דמתני' דאפילו ר' יוסי דקי"ל נמוקו עמו. הא (דאינך) [מדאמר]ר' יוסי ב"ר חנינא מ"ם דר' יוסי דדריש ועשה אחת ועשה הנה ומפרש אחת שמעון מאחת שם משמעון שמעינן מיניה דמודי ר' יוסי כי הכותב שם משמעון חייב משום כותב ונרסי' נמי בהזורק מלתא פשיטתא. פשיטא נתכוון לזרוק ח' וזרק ד' הרי כתב שם משמעון וכן נמי בכיצד הרגל וכבר פירשנוה התם. אמר מר א"ר יהודה מצינו שם קטן משם גדול שם משמעון ומשמואל מי דמי מ"ם דשמעון פתוח ומ"ם דשם סתום וכאשר יכתוב שם כזה אינו נקרא שם. ופריק רב חסדא זאת אומרת סתום ועשאו פתוח כשר. ומותבינן עלה וכתבתם על מזוזות ביתך פי' וכתבתם כתב תם. שלא יקרא אלפין עיינין ביתין כפין כלומר שלא תהא צורת בית בלא תגין כמו כ"ף כו' קתני מיהת כו' ולא אותיות פתוחות סתומות ולא סתומות פתוחות כלומר אם יכתוב במזוזה אות שלימה פתוחה סתומה תיגנז מכלל שהיא פסולה. ופרקינן מתני' דמחייב הכותב שם משמעון ופריק רב חסדא זאת אומרת סתום ועשאו פתוח כשר. ר' יהודה בן בתירה היא דדריש סימן לימי החג דרמיזו קראי כלומר ונסכיהם כתוב מ"ם יתירה. ובכולהו כתיב ונסכה והכא כתיב ונסכיה כמשפטם והרי ונסכיהם ונסכיה כמשפטם מי"ם ומצאנו נמי סתום באמצע תיבה כדכתיב לםרבה המשרה ומדפתוח ועשאו סתום כשר כך סתום ועשאו פתוח כשר. ואקשינן בשלמא פתוח ועשאו סתום דעלוי עיילה דלא אות שהיתה כתובה בלוחות חשובה היא ומעולה מן האותיות שנתוספו אח"כ ובלוחות לא היה מ"ם אלא סתומה כרב חסדא דאמר רב חסדא מ"ם וסמ"ך שבלוחות בנס היו עומדין כגון הלובן שלהן אם יש במה להיסמך שאילו נפל הלבן היה נראה לפיכך הם"ם פתוח כיון שהיה חרות בלוחות יש בו עילוי אלא הם"ם הפתוח ואר"ח ירמיה ואיתימא ר' חייא בר אבא מנצפ"ך צופים אמרום. ופריק לעולם מהוה הוו בלוחות הפתוחות והסתומות שאין נביא יכול לחדש דבר וכך היו מתוקנין להיות הפתוחות בראש התיבה ובאמצעה והסתומות בסוף התיבה ורוב העם מן הסופרים ההדיוטים שכחום. והיו כותבין הסתומין בין באמצע תיבה בין בסוף תיבה וכן הפתוחות עד שחזרו ב"ד ותקנום להם כאשר היו מסורין מיוסדין בידיהן וכיון שהיתה ירכתי הכתב מפולשות מצד זה לצד זה קיימא דרב הסדא שהיה נראה מאחוריו הפוך כדרך הנקרא כתב שע"ג זכוכית מאחוריו: כתב אות אחת סמוך לכתב כגון שהיה כתוב נו"ן וכתב תחתיו הי"ת אף על פי כי נמצא נח והנה שם כתוב פטור הוא ודלא כר' אליעזר דאמר האורג חוט אחד על האריג חייב אבל אם היתה מזוזה חסרה אות או ספר היה חסר אות והשלימו אע"פ שלא כתב אלא אות אחת חייב ואפילו לרבנן דקיי"ל להשלים שאני מי טריא בגם ממין שהיה ידוע באותה העת קומא שרף דגרסינן בפרק הראשון כל השרפין יפין לדיו ושרף קטף מן המובחר אבר ועופרת שיחור כלי ברזל שמשרפו. שחור בלשון ישמעאל אל סבאס ואל סודאי. מעשה בבן פטיא שהוציא כשפים ממצרים בשריטה על בשרו אמרו לו שוטה הוא ואין מביאין ראיה מן השוטים. כתב ע"ג כתב פטור אוקמה רב חסדא דלא כר' יהודה דאי ר' יהודה הא כתיבה מעליא היא דאמר מעביר עליו קולמוס ומקדשו: ירושלמי תני עדים שאין יודעין לחתום. אמר ריש לקיש רושם להם בסיקרא והן חותמין בדיו או רושם להם בדיו וחותמין בסיקרא א"ל ר' יוחנן וכי מפני שאנו עוסקין בהלכות שבת נתיר אשת איש אלא מקרעין להן נייר חלק ומרחיב להן הקרע. א"ר חייא בר אבא אילין בני מדינחא עריטין סגין כדבעי כתבין לחבריה כתיב ליה במי מילין ומישדר לחבריה והוא ישפיך עליה דיו שאין בו עפיץ וקליט מקום הכתב עשה כן בשבת מהו ר' יוחנן ור"ל דאמרי תרווייהו דיו ע"ג סיקרא או סיקרא ע"ג דיו חייב ר' יצחק אמר חייב שתים אחת משום כותב ואחת משום מוחק. א"ר אמי כתב אות אחת בטבריא ואות אחת בצפורי חייב כתיבה היא אלא שמחוסרת קריבה זה ששמענו פירוש זה כגון שכתב בקרקע של טבריא שי"ן ובקרקע כנגדו בצפורי [מ"ם] חייב.מ"ט כתיבה שהרי כתב ב' אותיות והן שם אלא שמחוסרת קריבה כלומר אין שם חסר דבר במלאכה אלא אילו האריך המ"ם עד שיקרבנו לשי"ן הרי נתברר הדבר אע"פ שגם עתה המכוון זה האות כנגד זה האות קורא השם הנכתב מחוסר קריבה הוא ואקשינן והתנן על ב' דפי פנקס ואין נהגין זה עם זה פטור. ופרקי' התם לגבי הפנקס מחוסר מעשה קריבה כלומר צריך מעשה לקרב דפי הפנקס שהוא מעשה אחר זולת מעשה הכתיבה. ואם לא קריבה ולא כלום הוא. שאין שם ב' אותיות· ואם תאמר גם זה

צריך

ס"א ר' יהושע פוטר

מגילה יח: גיטין יט.

ג"ז שם בגיטין

[תוספ' פי"ב]

[חולין מט: נדה לג:]

[לקמן קס. וש"נ]

גיטין כ. נד: [מס' סופרים פ"ה הלכה ג

בכ"י רבה וב"ח בחדושי הרי"ן לקמן קס. [כריתות יט:]

[פי' תוס' גיטין יט. ד"ה קנקנתום]

הגהות הב"ח

(א) רש"י ד"ה מרפקו. נ"ב ע"ל בפ' המצניע דף צב ע"א ובמ"ש התוס': (ב) תוס' ד"ה אמר רב חסדא וכו' ע"כ לא קאמרי רבנן התם:

[ע' תוס' מנחות כט: ד"ה ...]

[כתובות יט:]

גליון הש"ס גמ' א"ר אמי כתב אות אחת בטבריא. עיין לעיל דף פ ע"ב תוס' ד"ה בהעלם אחד: תוס' ד"ה בן סטדא · ע' בסה"ד קמג ע"ד. ועיין תוס' חגיגה דף ד' ע"ב ד"ה הוה שכיח.

MISHNAH. [104*b*] IF ONE WRITES TWO LETTERS IN ONE STATE OF UNAWARENESS,[5] HE IS CULPABLE. IF ONE WRITES WITH INK, CHEMICALS, SIKRA,[6] KUMOS,[7] KANKANTUM,[8] OR WITH ANYTHING THAT LEAVES A MARK ON THE ANGLE OF TWO WALLS OR ON THE TWO LEAVES [TABLES] OF A LEDGER, AND THEY [THE TWO LETTERS] ARE READ[9] TOGETHER, HE IS CULPABLE. IF ONE WRITES ON HIS FLESH, HE IS CULPABLE: HE WHO SCRATCHES A MARK ON HIS FLESH, R. ELIEZER DECLARES HIM LIABLE TO A SIN-OFFERING; BUT THE SAGES EXEMPT HIM. IF ONE WRITES
a WITH A FLUID, WITH FRUIT JUICE, WITH ROAD DUST,[1] OR WITH WRITER'S POWDER,[2] OR WITH[3] ANYTHING THAT CANNOT ENDURE, HE IS NOT CULPABLE. [IF ONE WRITES] WITH THE BACK OF HIS HAND, WITH HIS FOOT, WITH HIS MOUTH, OR WITH HIS ELBOW; IF ONE WRITES ONE LETTER NEAR [OTHER] WRITING,[4] OR IF ONE WRITES UPON WRITING;[5] IF ONE INTENDS WRITING A HETH BUT WRITES TWO ZAYYININ; ONE [LETTER] ON THE GROUND AND ANOTHER ON A BEAM; IF ONE WRITES ON TWO WALLS OF THE HOUSE, OR ON TWO LEAVES OF A LEDGER WHICH ARE NOT TO BE READ[6] TOGETHER, HE IS NOT CULPABLE. IF ONE WRITES ONE LETTER AS AN ABBREVIATION,[7] R. JOSHUA B. BATHYRA HOLDS HIM LIABLE, WHILST THE SAGES EXEMPT HIM.

GEMARA. DYo [ink] is *deyutha; SaM* [chemical] is *samma* [orpiment]; *SIKRA:* Rabbah b. Bar Hanah said, Its name is *sekarta. Kumos* is *Kumma. Kankantum:* Rabbah b. Bar Hanah said in Samuel's name, The blacking used by shoemakers.[8]

OR WITH ANYTHING THAT LEAVES A MARK. What does this add?[9]—It adds what was taught by R. Hanina: If he writes it [a divorce] with the fluid of *taria,*[10] or gall-nut [juice], it is valid.[11] R. Hiyya taught: If he writes it with dust,[12] with a black pigment, or with coal, it is valid.

HE WHO SCRATCHES A MARK ON HIS FLESH, [etc.] It was taught, R. Eliezer said to the Sages: But did not Ben Stada bring
b forth witchcraft from Egypt by means of scratches[1] [in the form of charms] upon his flesh?[2] He was a fool, answered they, and proof cannot be adduced from fools.[3]

IF ONE WRITES ONE LETTER NEAR [OTHER] WRITING. Who teaches this?—Said Rabbah son of R. Huna, It does not agree with R. Eliezer. For if [it agreed with] R. Eliezer,—surely he maintained, [for] one [thread] added to woven stuff, he is culpable.[4]

IF ONE WRITES UPON WRITING. Who teaches this? Said R. Hisda, It does not agree with R. Judah. For it was taught: If one had to write the [Divine] Name,[5] but [erroneously] intended to write Judah [*YHWDH*][6] but omitted the *daleth,*[7] he can trace his reed [writing pen] over it and sanctify it: this is R. Judah's view;[8] but the Sages maintain: The [Divine] Name [thus written] is not of the most preferable.

It was taught: If one writes one letter and completes a book[9] therewith, [or] weaves one thread and completes a garment therewith, he is culpable. Who is the authority?—Said Rabbah son of R. Huna, It is R. Eliezer, who maintained: [For] one [thread] added to woven stuff, he is culpable. R. Ashi said, You may even say that it is the Rabbis: completing is different.

R. Ammi said: If one writes one letter in Tiberias and another
c in Sepphoris,[1] he is culpable: it is one [act of] writing but that it lacks being brought together. But we learnt: IF ONE WRITES ON TWO WALLS OF A HOUSE, OR ON TWO LEAVES OF A LEDGER WHICH CANNOT BE READ TOGETHER, HE IS NOT CULPABLE?—There the act of being brought together is lacking;[2] but here the act of bringing together is not lacking.[3]

A Tanna taught: If one corrects one letter, he is culpable. Now, seeing that if one *writes* one letter he is not culpable, if he [merely] corrects one letter he is culpable?[4]—Said R. Shesheth: The circumstances here are e.g., that he removes the roof [i.e., the upper bar] of a *heth* and makes two *zayyinin* thereof. Raba said: E.g., he removes the projection of a *daleth* and makes a *resh* thereof.[5]

(5) V. *supra* 67*b*. (6) A kind of red paint. (7) Ink prepared with gum. (8) Vitriol used as an ingredient of ink. (9) Lit., 'lead'.

a (1) Mixed with water to produce a weak ink.—Others: *in* the dust of the roads, i.e., one traces writing therein with his finger. (2) The refuse of writing material, or the coloured sand strewn over the writing (Rashi and Jast.). Others: *in* writer's powder. (3) Or 'in'. (4) I.e., near a letter already written, so as to complete the word. (5) To make it clearer. (6) Lit., 'lead'. (7) I.e., a letter followed by a short stroke or point to indicate that it is an abbreviation, e.g., ר׳ for רבי. (8) In the above the Hebrew of the Mishnah is translated into the more familiar Aramaic used by the Amoraim. V. Git., 19*a*, n. b2. (9) V. *supra* 103*a*, n. c5. (10) A sort of ink. Rashi: either fruit juice or rain water. V. Low. *Graph. Requisiten*, pp. 158, 161. V. Meg., 17*a*. (11) Hence it must be regarded as durable and therefore involves culpability in connection with the Sabbath. (12) So cur. edd. Rashi reads: with lead.

b (1) Incisions. (2) Which proves that scratches are important, and so one should be liable therefor. In the uncensored text this passage follows: Was he then the son of Stada: surely he was the son of Pandira?—Said R. Hisda: The husband was Stada, the paramour was Pandira. But the husband was Pappos b. Judah?—His mother was Stada. But his mother was Miriam the hairdresser?—It is as we say in Pumbeditha: This one has been unfaithful to (lit., 'turned away from'—*sataht da*) her husband.—On the identity of Ben Stada v. Sanh., 67*a*, n. b5. (3) His action was too unusual to furnish a criterion. (4) V. *infra* 105*a*. The same principle applies here too. (5) The Tetragrammaton; the reference is to a Scroll of the Law, in which the Tetragrammaton must be written with sacred intention. (6) In this word the *waw* (*W*) is a vowel. (7) Thus writing *YHWH*—the Tetragrammaton—after all, but without sacred intention. (8) Thus he counts retracing as writing. (9) Rashi: of one of the Hebrew Scriptures.

c (1) Two towns of Galilee. (2) Before the two letters can be read as one the paper must be cut away, so that they can be put together. (3) E.g., if the letters are written on the edges of two boards. (4) Surely not. (5) In a Scroll of one of the Biblical books. This constitutes a complete labour, because one may not permit a Scroll of Scripture to remain with an error.

A Tanna taught: If one intended writing one letter, [105a] but chanced to write two, he is culpable. But we learnt: HE IS NOT CULPABLE?[6]—There is no difficulty: in the one case it requires crownlets; in the other, it does not require crownlets.[7]

IF ONE WRITES ONE LETTER AS AN ABBREVIATION, R. JOSHUA B. BATHYRA HOLDS HIM LIABLE, WHILST THE SAGES EXEMPT HIM. R. Johanan said in R. Jose b. Zimra's name; How do we know [that] abbreviated forms [are recognized] by the Torah? Because it is written, *for AB [the father of] HaMWN [a multitude of]*[8] *nations have I made thee:*[9] a father [*Ab*] of nations have I made thee; a chosen one [*Bahur*] among nations have I made thee. *HaMWN:* beloved [*Ḥabib*][10] have I made thee among nations; a king [*Melek*] have I appointed thee for the nations; distinguished [*Wathik*] have I made thee among the nations; faithful [*Ne'eman*] a have I made thee to the nations.[1] R. Johanan on his own authority quoted, *aNoKY [I—am the Lord thy God*, etc.].[2] I [*ana*] Myself [*Nafshi*] have written the Script [*Kethibah Yehabith*]. The Rabbis interpreted: Sweet speech [*amirah Ne'imah*], a writing, a gift [*Kethibah Yehibah*]. Others state, *aNoKY* [interpreted] reversed is: Scripture was given [to man] [*Yahibah Kethibah*], faithful are its words [*Ne'emanin amarehah*]. The School of R. Nathan quoted, *Because thy way is perverse [YaRaṬ] before me:*[3] She [the ass] feared [*Yare'ah*], saw [*Ra'athah*], [and] turned aside [*naṬethah*]. The School of R. Ishmael taught: *KaRMeL [fresh ears]*:[4] rounded [*KaR*] and full [*MaLe*]. R. Aha b. Jacob quoted, *and he cursed me with a curse that is grievous [NiMReẒeTh]*.[5] This is an abbreviation: he is an adulterer [*No'ef*], a Moabite, a murderer [*Rozeah*], an adversary [*Ẓorer*], an abomination [*To'ebah*]. R. Nahman b. Isaac quoted, *What shall we speak? or how shall we clear ourselves [NiẒṬaDaḲ]*:[6] We are honest [*Nekonim*], we are righteous [*Ẓaddikim*], we are pure [*Tehorim*], we are submissive [*Dakkim*], we are holy [*Ḳedoshim*].

MISHNAH. IF ONE WRITES TWO LETTERS IN TWO STATES OF UNAWARENESS, ONE IN THE MORNING AND ONE IN THE EVENING, R. GAMALIEL HOLDS HIM LIABLE, WHILST THE SAGES EXEMPT HIM.

GEMARA. Wherein do they differ?—R. Gamaliel holds: Awareness in respect of half the standard is of no account; whilst the Rabbis hold: Awareness in respect of half the standard is of account.[7]

CHAPTER XIII

MISHNAH. R. ELIEZER STATED: HE WHO WEAVES b THREE THREADS AT THE BEGINNING[1] OR ONE [THREAD] ADDED TO[2] WOVEN STUFF, IS CULPABLE; BUT THE SAGES MAINTAIN: WHETHER AT THE BEGINNING OR AT THE END, THE STANDARD [FOR CULPABILITY] IS TWO THREADS. HE WHO MAKES TWO MESHES, ATTACHING THEM EITHER TO THE CROSS-PIECES [NIRIM] OR TO THE SLIPS [ḲEROS], OR IN A WINNOW, SIEVE, OR BASKET, IS CULPABLE. AND HE WHO SEWS TWO STITCHES, AND HE WHO TEARS IN ORDER TO SEW TWO STITCHES [IS LIKEWISE CULPABLE].

GEMARA. When R. Isaac came,[3] he recited: Two. But we learnt THREE?—There is no difficulty: the one refers to thick [threads], the other to thin [ones]. Some explain it in one way, others explain it the reverse. Some explain it in one way: [of] thick threads, three will not break, but two will break;[4] [of] thin threads, even two will not break. Others explain it the reverse: [of] thin [threads], three are noticeable[5] whereas two are not:[6] [of] thick threads, even two are noticeable.

It was taught: He who weaves three threads at the beginning or one thread added to woven stuff, is culpable; but the Sages maintain: Whether at the beginning or at the end, the standard is two threads, and at the selvedge, two threads over the breadth of three meshes. To what is this like? To weaving a small belt c two threads over the breadth of three meshes [in size].[1] [Now,] 'He who weaves three threads at the beginning or one thread added to woven stuff, is culpable': this anonymous [teaching] is in agreement with R. Eliezer. Another [Baraitha] taught: He who weaves two threads added to[2] the border of the web[3] or to the hem,[4] is culpable. R. Eliezer said: Even one. And at the selvedge, two threads over the breadth of three meshes. To what is this like? To weaving a small belt two threads over the breadth of three meshes [in size]. 'He who weaves two threads added to the border of the web or to the hem, is culpable': this anonymous [teaching is] in agreement with the Rabbis.

HE WHO MAKES TWO MESHES, ATTACHING THEM EITHER TO THE CROSS-PIECES [NIRIM]. What does, 'TO THE NIRIM' mean?—Said Abaye: Two in a mesh and one in the cross-piece.

OR TO THE SLIPS [ḲEROS]. What is ḲEROS?—Said Rab: The slips.[5]

AND HE WHO SEWS TWO STITCHES. But we have [already] learnt it in [the list of] principal labours: 'and he who sews two stitches?[6]—Because he wishes to teach the second clause: AND HE WHO TEARS IN ORDER TO SEW TWO STITCHES, he also teaches, AND HE WHO SEWS, [etc.]. But we learnt about tearing too in [the list of] principal labours? Rather because he wishes to teach in a subsequent clause, 'He who tears in his anger or for his dead',[7] he therefore teaches [here], HE WHO SEWS TWO STITCHES.

AND HE WHO TEARS IN ORDER TO SEW TWO STITCHES. How

(6) If he intends writing a *heth* and writes two *zayyinin*. (7) The reference is to a Scroll of the Law, where certain letters, including the ז, are embellished with 'tittles', 'daggers'. If one writes זז instead of a ח (in a Scroll of the law ח is written as a double ז, thus: זז) but without the daggers, he is not culpable; with the daggers, he is culpable. (8) Here too the *waw* is used vocally, but is interpreted consonantally. (9) Gen. XVII, 5. (10) H and Ḥ interchange.

a (1) Thus *AB HaMWN* is interpreted as an abbreviation. (2) Ex. XX, 1. (3) Num. XXII, 32. (4) Lev. XXIII, 14. (5) I Kings II, 8. (6) Gen. XLIV, 16. (7) V. *supra* 71b; 102a.

b (1) Of a garment or a piece of cloth. V. Halevy, *Doroth*, I, 3, pp. 261 *seq.* (2) Lit., 'upon'. (3) From Palestine to Babylon; cf. *supra* 5a, n. b9. (4) Under their own weight. Or, the thickness of the thread prevents them from being closely woven; hence if there are only two they may split. (5) Lit., 'known'. (6) One cannot see that anything substantial has been made; therefore he is not culpable.

c (1) Therefore weaving this amount on the selvedge is a culpable offence. (2) Lit., 'upon'. (3) Or, thickly woven material. (4) Rashi: made at the beginning of the cloth. (5) Jast.: the thrums or slips to which the threads of the warp are attached. (6) *Supra* 73a. (7) *Infra* b.

ועלו בידו שתים חייב והתנן פטור לא קשיא הא דבעי זיוני הא דלא בעי זיוני: כתב אות אחת נוטריקון רבי יהושע בן בתירה מחייב וחכמים פוטרין: א"ר יוחנן משום ר' יוסי בן זימרא מנין ללשון נוטריקון מן התורה שנא' (בראשית יז) °כי א"ב המו"ן גוים נתתיך אב נתתיך לאומות בחור נתתיך באומות המון חביב נתתיך באומות מלך נתתיך לאומות ותיק נתתיך באומות נאמן נתתיך לאומות ר' יוחנן דידיה אמר (שמות כ) °אנכי נוטריקון אנא נפשי כתיבת יהבית רבנן אמרי אמירה נעימה כתיבה יהיבה איכא דאמרי אנכי למפרע יהיבה כתיבה נאמנין אמריה דבי רבי נתן אמרי (במדבר כב) °כי יר"ט הדרך לנגדי *יראה ראתה נטתה דבי רבי ישמעאל תנא (ויקרא כג) *°כרמ"ל כר מלא רב אחא בר יעקב אמר (מלכים א ב) °והוא קללני קללה נמרצ"ת נוטריקון נואף הוא מואבי הוא רוצח הוא צורר הוא תועבה הוא ר"נ בר יצחק אמר (בראשית מד) °מה נדבר ומה נצטד"ק נכונים אנחנו צדיקים אנחנו טהורים אנחנו דכים אנחנו °קדושים אנחנו: **מתני'** *הכותב ב' אותיות בשתי העלמות אחת שחרית ואחת בין הערבים ר"ג מחייב *וחכמים פוטרין: **גמ'** במאי קמיפלגי ר"ג סבר *אין ידיעה לחצי שיעור ורבנן סברי *יש ידיעה לחצי שיעור:

הדרן עלך הבונה

רבי *אליעזר אומר האורג שלשה חוטין בתחילה ואחת על האריג חייב *וחכ"א בין בתחילה בין בסוף שיעורו ב' חוטין *העושה שתי בתי נירין (ב) בנירין בקירוס בנפה בכברה ובסל חייב *והתופר ב' תפירות *והקורע ע"מ לתפור ב' תפירות: **גמ'** כי אתא רבי יצחק תני שתים והאנן תנן ג' לא קשיא הא באלימי הא בקטיני °אמרי לה להאי גיסא ואמרי לה להאי גיסא אמרי לה להאי גיסא אלימי תלתא לא סתרי תרי סתרי קטיני תרי נמי לא סתרי ואמרי לה להאי גיסא קטיני תלתא ידיעי תרי לא ידיעי אלימי תרי נמי ידיעי תניא האורג ג' חוטין בתחילה ואחד על האריג חייב וחכמים אומרים בין בתחילה בין בסוף שיעורן (ג) ב' חוטין ובשפה ב' חוטין ברוחב ג' בתי נירין הא למה זה דומה לאורג צלצול קטן ב' חוטין ברוחב ג' בתי נירין והאורג (ד) ג' חוטין בתחילה ואחד על האריג חייב סתמא כר"א תניא אידך *האורג ב' חוטין על הגס ועל האימרא חייב ר"א אומר אפילו אחד *ובשפה שני חוטין ברוחב שלשה בתי נירין חייב הא למה זה דומה לאורג צלצול קטן שני חוטין על רוחב ג' בתי נירין והאורג ב' חוטין על הגס ועל האימרא חייב סתמא כרבנן: העושה ב' בתי נירין כו': מאי [בנירין] אמר אביי תרתי בבתי (ה) נירא וחדא בנירא: בקירוס: מאי בקירוס אמר רב מצוביתא: והתופר ב' תפירות: הא תנינא באבות מלאכות והתופר ב' תפירות משום דקבעי למיתנא סיפא והקורע ע"מ לתפור ב' תפירות קתני נמי התופר והקורע הא נמי תנינא באבות מלאכות אלא משום דקבעי למיתני סיפא הקורע בחמתו ועל מתו משום הכי קתני [התופר שתי תפירות]: והקורע ע"מ לתפור שתי תפירות: היכי משכחת לה

דעבדה

רש"י

ועלו בידו שתים · הייתו נמי מתכוין לכתוב ח' וכתב שני זיינין : הא · דתנן פטור : דבעי זיוני · שעדיין צריכות ראשי הזיינין לזיינן בתגין שלהן שהזיינין צריכות ג' זוגין ימין ושמאל ולמעלה כדאמרינן במנחות (דף כט:) : מלך נתתיך · נשיא אלהים אתה (בראשית כג) : הכי · מדלא אמר אני : אנא נפשי · אני בעצמי : אמירה · שהיא נעימה : כרמל · גבי מנחת העומר כתיב גרש כרמל שמביאה כשהיא לחה בעוד שהזרע נפוח והכר של קש מלא הימנו : מתני' אחת שחרית ואחת בין הערבים · כיון דהוי"ל שהות בינתים כדי לידע הוה ליה כשתי העלמות : גמ' יש ידיעה לחצי שיעור · לחלק כדי שלא יצטרף עמו חצי האחר :

הדרן עלך הבונה

רבי אליעזר · *אתא לפרושי שיעור אורג שמנו באבות מלאכות (לעיל דף עג·) דתנן התם שני חוטין : בתחילה · אם זו תחלת אריגתו של בגד : ואחת על האריג · אם מוסיף הוא על האריג שיעורו באחת דמצטרף עם האחר : בתי נירין · שנתן ב' חוטין של שתי בנירה שקורין ליצי"ש : בנירין ובקירוס · מפרש בגמרא : בנפה ובכברה · הנך לאו נירין ממש אלא מסרסר ומרכיב חוט א' [של ערב] בשתי מלמטה ואחד מלמעלה ומעמיד השתי בהן כתקנו : גמ' כי אתא ר' יצחק תני · מתני' הכי ר"א אומר האורג ב' חוטין בתחלה ולא פליג ר"א ארבנן אלא באחד על האריג: להאי גיסא · אלימי ג' ולא ב' משום דשנים סתרי דמתוך עוביין אינן נדבקים יפה זה בזה וקטיני בשנים מיחייב : ואמרי ליה להאי גיסא · אלימי שנים חייב : דידיעי · דבר הנראה הוא אבל קטיני בשנים פטור : ובשפה ב' חוטין ברוחב ג' בתי נירין · יש שאורגין סביב [הבגד] השפה באורך הבגד כולו מין אחר של [שתי] ורוחב ברוחב הבגד כשיעור שלשה בתי נירין והאורג בו שני חוטין (ו) חייב: למה זה דומה · כלומר להכי מחייבי באריג קצר כי האי ולא אמרי כמלא רוחב הסיט כדמשערינן במתני' באורג באמצע הבגד : דומה לאורג צלצול קטן · חגורה קצרה שאינה רחבה יותר משלשה בתי נירין : על הגס · אריג הרבה : על האימרא · תחלת הבגד שאורגין בו ערב ממין אחר לאימרא : ובשפה · לאורך השתי כולו עושין אותו : תרתי בבתי נירא וחדא בנירא · ב' פעמי' מרכיב לחוט של שתי בבת נירא דהיינו שקורין ליצ"א : ואחת בנירא · ופעם שלישית מרכיבו על חוט הנירא שקורין ליצ"א המורכב על הקנה : מצוביתא · בירעת גרדין האורגין ברגל הוא וקורין לימיי"ש והיא במקום הקנה העולה ויורד בירעת אריגת נשים שקורין פריש"א : הא תנינא ליה באבות מלאכות · ולמה לי למהדר ולמתנייה הכא הואיל ולא לפרושי בה מידי אתא בשלמא אורג משום פלוגתא ושתי בתי נירין לאשמועינן בנירין ובקירוס ובנפה ובכברה וסל דלא תנא לה (ז) התם :

דעבדה

תוספות

והתניא פטור · אין נראה לר"י לגרוס והתניא דאמאי לא הוה פריך ממתני' ומיהו איכא למימר דממתני' לא קשיא ליה מדקתני וכתב שני זיינין ולא נקט ב' אותיות אחרות דלא בעי זווגי משמע דמשום זיון פטר ליה אבל מברייתא דקתני סתמא פריך שפיר אבל קשה דאי ברייתא היא הא דפריך מינה אמאי נקט נתכוין לכתוב אות אחת ועלו בידו שתים אפי' נתכוין לאותן שתים שכתב וכתבן בלא זיון פטור כיון למוקמי לה בדבעי זיוני דהא בברייתא לא קתני וכתב שני זיינין דטכל לומר דאתי לאשמעינן הא כתב שתי אותיות אחרות דלא בעי זיון חייב כדפירשתי(א) במתניתין לכך נראה דממתני' פריך וגרסינן והתנן :

רבן גמליאל סבר אין ידיעה לחצי שיעור · נראה דטעם *דרשב"ג משום דכתיב או הודע אליו חטאתו ידיעת חטאת הוא דשמה ידיעה אבל ידיעה דלאו חטאת לאו שמה ידיעה :

ורבנן סברי יש ידיעה לחצי כו' · פירש בקונט' הא דנקט אות אחת שחרית ואחת בין הערבים כיון דהוי שהות בינתים כדי לידע חשיב כשתי העלמות ואין נראה חדא דהוה ליה לפרש שיעור שהות ועוד דאמר לעיל כתב אות אחת בציפורי ואות אחת בטבריא חייב אע"ג דמסתמא יש שהות כדי לידע ונראה דמיירי שידע בינתים ואחת שחרית ואחת ערבית נקט לרבותא דאף על גב דיש עם הידיעה הפסק ושהות גדול בינתים מחייב ר"ג :

הדרן עלך הבונה

האורג · אומר ר"י דה"ג וחכ"א בין בתחלה בין בסוף ול"ג בין באמצע בין בסוף דא"כ הוה משמע בסוף הבגד ממש והתם אפי' רבנן מודו דחייב אפילו באחת כדאמרינן סוף פרק הבונה (לעיל דף קד:) אבל אי לא גרסינן באמצע אתי שפיר דבסוף לא בסוף ממש קאמר אלא הכל

עין משפט נר מצוה

לט א ב מיי' פ"ו מהל' שגגות הלכה ח :
א ג מיי' פ"ט מהל' שבת הל' יח סמג לאוין סה:
ב ד מיי' שם הל' טז :
ג ה מיי' פ"י שם הל' כ :
ד ו שם הלכה י :
ה ז מיי' פ"ט שם הל' יח:

רבינו חננאל

צריך להאריך האות האחת ולקרבה לחברתה להיותן נקראות יחדו לא דמי הא להא. דהתם כבר האות כתובה היא. מאי אמרת היא קטנה ורוצה לעשות גדולה. בין קטנה לגדולה לא איכפת לן . לפי' כתיבה [היא] וחייב . תנא הגיה אות אחת חייב . ואקשי' השתא כתב אות אחת פטור המגיה חייב . ופריק רבא כגון שהיה ספר שהיה חסר לרי"ש. ובא להגיהו שנטל [לגגו] של דל"ת ועשאו רי"ש והשלימו לספר דקי"ל כתב אות אחת להשלים דברי הכל חייב. וי"א(כיון)[כגון] שנפלו לתגו של דל"ת מחקו וכתבו רי"ש ודברי אביי פשוטיהן: תנא נתכוון לכתוב אות אחת ועלתה בידו ב' חייב . והתניא פטור ושנינן בדבעי זיונא . פי' כגון צריך לכתוב סי"ת ומדי רהוטו לא הדביק בו (לצלם האחרון ונמצא פאילו פו) איבעי זיונא כדי שיתראו צורת האותיות פטור שעדיין אינה כתובה . ואם לאו חייב.ודוקא שצריך (פו) בענין שכתבו: נוטריקון הוא לשון יון . וסופרי המלכים והשרים שלהם יש להן כתב שקוראין אותו נוטריק' ואומר המלך לסופר כתוב טופס והמלך מסדר לפניו בפיו והסופר כותב מפיו מילי שמשמשת כמה ובשיט· אחת כותב מגלה וזהו נוטריקו: יש מי שאוכל חצי זית חלב בשגגה ונודע לו וחזר ונעלם ממנו ואכל חצי זית אחת רבן גמליאל אומר אין ידיעה לחצי שיעור וכאילו השיעור כולו בשגגה אכלו חייב חטאת וחכמים פוטרין :

הדרן עלך הבונה

פי"ג רבי אליעזר אומר האורג ג' חוטין בתחלה ואחד על האריג חייב . בכלל גדול תנן סתמא. האורג ב' חוטין ולא שנינן בין בתחלה בין בראש הבגד ובין בסופו ע"ג אריג שהוא ארוג כאתמול . וכך הלכה כחכמים ור' אליעזר פליג דסבר פחות מג' חוטין אין מתקיימין אלא נסתרין . הלכך אי בתחלה התחיל באריג צריך ג' חוטין שתהא מלאכה מתקיימת ואם יש חוט אחד ערב ארוג בשתי אם ארג ב' חוטין על גביו חייב · ואם לאו פטור ואם יש ב' חוטין ערב ארוגין בשתי וארג אחד עליהן חייב . וכן אם היו אלף באחד מהן חייב. [הא בקטיני] פי' חוטין דקין אלימי חוטין עבין אמרי לה להאי גיסא ג' בקטיני שהן דקיקי כי השנים כאחד דומה מפני שאין מראין רחב ובאלימי שנים כי רחבן ניכר ואמרי לה להאי גיסא ג' באלימי שהן עבין וקשין ולא חלמי להדדי כי השנים מהן אין נכבשין ואין מתאלצין זה עם זה ובקטיני שנים כי דבק הן ונאחזין זה בזה וחלמי הדדי . והרי פירש במשנה אחרונה כי שיעור רחב ב' חוטין הארוגין מלא הסיט וכאן פירש כי היריעה הנארגת רחבה היא וארג ב' חוטין במקצת רחבה (ואם) [אם] הוא שיעור מה שארג ברחב היריעה מלא סיט חייב ואם היא פחות פטור . ואם זו היריעה הנארגת רחבה כולה פחות מסיט אם היא צרה אפי' ג' בתי נירין בלבד כמו צלצול קטן אם ארג בו ב' חוטין שנמצאת אריגתו מן השפה אל השפה אע"פ שאינן מלא הסיט חייב ולא עוד אלא שאם ארג מאצל שפת הבגד האחת שהוא קרועה אל השאיה שיעור ג' בתי נירין חייב אע"פ שאינן רחב מלא הסיט שדומה לארג צלצול קטן . וצלצול זה כמו אבנט הוא . אבל אם בתוך הבגד שלא מאצל השפה ארג ב' חוטין או יותר אם ישנם ברחב מלא הסיט חייב ואם לאו פטור ; אבל האורג ב' חוטין ברוחב כל שהן אע"פ שאינן בג' בתי נירין על הגס שהוא מקום מעוקם כמין גמא יוונית חוט אחד לכאן וחוט אחד לכאן צבוע שנמצא עמו סימן או על האימרא שהוא רעלם ואל סראו בלשון ישמעאל והוא מלשון חטובות אטון מצרים דמתרגמינן האמרת הטבת שנמצא זה כמו כותב וחייב : העושה ב' בתי נירין . פי' מכנים חוטי השתי בנירין שיעלה זה וירד זה . ויבא הערב ויחזור השתי יעלה התחתון וירד העליון ויבא הערב . קירום . הוא מצובייתא . פי' מסנות אורגין אותה מן הסיב או מן חוטי צמר וכיוצא בהן ומסננין בהן :

מסורת הש"ס

אתי לפלוג אשיעור אורג שמנו חכמים ס"א רב"ל
מנחות כו:ע"ב
[שם]
כריתות יב:
שם ודף יז. [לעיל עא:קב.]
לעיל קד: כריתות יז. יט:
[לעיל עג.]

הגהות הב"ח

(א) תוס' ד"ה והתניא וכו' חייב כדפירש במתניתין : (ב) במשנה שתי בתי נירין בנירים: (ג) גמ' בין בסוף שיעור שתי חוטין : (ד) שם שלשה בתי נירין האורג כצ"ל ואות ו' נמחק: (ה) שם אמר אביי תרתי בבת נירא: (ו) רש"י ד"ה ובשפה וכו' ב' חוטין של ערב חייב : (ז) ד"ה והא תנינן וכו' תנן להו התם :

גליון הש"ס גמ' קדושים אנחנו . ע"ע במדרש במדבר רבה ר"פ מסעי על פסוק נחית כלאן עמך : שם א"ל להאי גיסא . פסחים קח ע"א כ"ב מב ע"ב :

עין משפט נר מצוה

ו א מיי' פ"ח מהל' שבת הל' יז סמג לאוין סה:
ז ב מיי' שם הלכה יח: [ע"ש]
ח ג מיי' פ"ט שם הל' י סמג לאוין סה:
ט ד מיי' שם הל' יד:
י ה שם הלכה יג:
יא ו שם הלכה טו:
יב ז שם הלכה ז:
יג ח שם הלכה יח:
יד ט מיי' פ"י שם הל' י:
טו י טוש"ע י"ד סימן שמ סעיף כח:
טז כ מיי' פ"ט מהל' אבל הלכה יא סמג עשין ב טוש"ע י"ד סי' שמ סעיף ז:
יז ל מ מיי' שם ופי"ב הלכה יב טוש"ע שם סעיף ו:
יח נ מיי' פ"ט שם הל' יא טוש"ע שם סעי' ה:
יט ס מיי' פ"י מהלכות שבת הלכה י ופ"ח הלכה ח ופי"ב הלכה א:
כ ע פ מיי' פ"ב מהל' דעות הלכה ג ופ"ו מהלכות מלכים הלכה י סמג לאוין רכט:
כא צ ק מיי' פי"ב מהל' אבל הל' ב סמג עשין ב [ברי"ף פ"ג דמ"ק דף רלג. וברא"ש שם סי' נט]:

תוספות

הכל חולצין עליו· אומר רשב"א דאפי' אינו רבו חייב כדאמרינן במו"ק (דף כה:) מי תני רבו שמת חכם שמת תני והא דאמר בשילהי פרק אלו מציאות (ב"מ לג.) רבא קרע עליה דההוא גברא דאסבריה זוהמא ליסטרון היינו קרע שאינו מתאחה כדין תלמיד לרב כדתני בפרק אלו מגלחין (מו"ק דף כו.): **דתניא** ר"ש בן אלעזר אומר העומד על המת כו'· משמע ליה להש"ס דמיירי אפי' באינו כשר: **הא** ר' יהודה והא ר"ש. פי' בקונט' דבהאי שיטה כמי משני דלא קשה מתו אמתו והא דלא קאמר אלא משום דלא הוזכר אמורא לעיל וקשה לר"י דע"כ תרוייהו במת דידיה איירי ולא במת דעלמא כדקתני בברייתא דלעיל דיצא ידי קריעה וא"כ הויא מלאכה שצריכה לגופה כיון שהיא לורך מצוה כדמוכח לקמן ונראה לר"י דלא מתרץ אלא חמתו אחמתו אבל בעל מתו לא פליגי דבמת דעלמא פטור דמקלקל הוא ובמת דידיה דאיכא מצוה חשיב מתקן אע"ג דלקמן משמע דלצורך מצוה לא חשיב ר"ש תיקון דהא יליף ממילה והבערת בת כהן דמקלקל בחבורה ובהבערה חייב התם מקלקל הוא לגמרי שאינו צורך אחר אלא מה שהוא צורך מצוה אבל גבי קריעת אבל הוי תיקון הבגד על ידי קריעה שיוכל ללובשו בכל שעה *)ואית (ו) בו חימום ועוד כמו שמחלק לקמן ר"ת דהתם התיקון בא לבסוף שבשעת חבורה והבערה איכה בא הכשר מצוה עד הגמר אבל הכא בשעת קריעה בא התיקון ולא חשיב קלקול: **לא** צריכא דקעבד למירמא אימתא כו'· השתא הוה מצי לאוקמי תרווייהו כר' יהודה ומתני' דלא עבד למירמא אימתא דבלא"ה מוקמינן לקמן כר' יהודה דאמר מקלקל בחבורה פטור אלא דניחא ליה לאוקמי מתני' בדעביד למירמא אימתא דאי בחמתו (ז) פשיטא דפטור:

שרגש עליהן ההר כו'· משום דלא אשכחן דכתיב ביה ויבכו אותו שלשים יום כמו במשה ואהרן. ע"כ תוספות שאנץ. רש"ל:

גמרא

דעבדה כי כיסתא: **מתני'** הקורע בחמתו ועל מתו וכל המקלקלין פטורין והמקלקל ע"מ לתקן שיעורו כמתקן *שיעור המלבן והמנפץ והצובע והטווה כמלא רחב הסיט כפול והאורג שני חוטין שיעורו כמלא הסיט: **גמ'** ורמינהו הקורע בחמתו ובאבלו ועל מתו חייב ואע"פ שמחלל את השבת יצא ידי קריעה לא קשיא הא במת דידיה הא במת דעלמא והא מתו קתני לעולם במת דידיה ובהנך דלאו בני אבילות נינהו ואי חכם הוא חיובי מיחייב *דתניא חכם שמת הכל קרוביו הכל קרוביו ס"ד אלא אימא הכל כקרוביו הכל קורעין עליו הכל חולצין עליו הכל מברין עליו ברחבה לא צריכא דלאו חכם הוא ואי אדם כשר הוא חיובי מיחייב דתניא *מפני מה מתים בניו ובנותיו של אדם כשהן קטנים כדי שיבכה ויתאבל על אדם כשר כדי שיבכה ערבונא שקלי מיניה אלא מפני שלא בכה והתאבל על אדם כשר שכל הבוכה על אדם כשר מוחלין לו על כל עונותיו בשביל כבוד שעשה (א) לא צריכא דלאו אדם כשר הוא ואי דקאי בשעת יציאת נשמה חיובי מיחייב דתניא *ר"ש בן אלעזר אומר העומד על המת בשעת יציאת נשמה חייב לקרוע הא למה זה דומה לס"ת שנשרפה לא צריכא דלא קאי בשעת יציאת נשמה תינח מתו אלא חמתו אחמתו קשיא חמתו אחמתו נמי לא קשיא הא ר' יהודה הא ר"ש הא ר' יהודה דאמר *מלאכה שאין צריכה לגופה חייב עליה הא ר"ש דאמר *מלאכה שאין צריכה לגופה פטור עליה אימר דשמעת ליה לר' יהודה במתקן במקלקל מי שמעת ליה א"ר אבין האי נמי מתקן הוא דקעביד נחת רוח ליצרו וכהאי גוונא מי שרי והתניא *ר"ש בן אלעזר אומר משום חילפא בר אגרא שאמר משום ר' יוחנן בן נורי המקרע בגדיו בחמתו והמשבר כליו בחמתו והמפזר מעותיו בחמתו יהא בעיניך כעובד ע"ז *שכך אומנתו של יצה"ר היום אומר לו עשה כך ולמחר אומר לו עשה כך עד שאומר לו עבוד ע"ז והולך ועובד א"ר אבין מאי קראה לא יהיה בך אל זר ולא תשתחוה לאל נכר איזהו אל זר שיש בגופו של אדם הוי אומר זה יצר הרע לא צריכא דקא עביד למירמא אימתא אאינשי ביתיה כי הא דרב יהודה שליף מצבייתא רב אחא בר יעקב תבר מאני תבירי רב ששת רמי לה לאמתיה מוניני אריש' רבי אבא תבר נכתמא אמר ר"ש בן פזי א"ר יהושע בן לוי משום בר קפרא כל המוריד דמעות על אדם כשר הקב"ה סופרן ומניחן בבית גנזיו שנאמר נודי ספרתה אתה שימה דמעתי בנאדך הלא בספרתך א"ר *יהודה אמר רב כל המתעצל בהספדו של חכם ראוי לקוברו בחייו שנאמר ויקברו אותו בגבול נחלתו בתמנת סרח אשר בהר אפרים מצפון להר געש מלמד שרגש עליהן הר להורגן א"ר חייא בר אבא א"ר יוחנן כל המתעצל בהספדו של חכם אינו מאריך ימים מדה כנגד מדה שנאמר בסאסאה בשלחה תריבנה איתיביה ר' חייא בר אבא לר' יוחנן ויעבדו העם את ה' כל ימי יהושע וכל ימי הזקנים אשר האריכו ימים אחרי יהושע א"ל בבלאי ימים האריכו שנים לא האריכו אלא מעתה למען ירבו ימיכם וימי בניכם ימים ולא שנים *ברכה שאני וא"ר חייא בר אבא א"ר יוחנן אחד מן האחין שמת ידאגו

רש"י

דעבדה· הבגד: כי כיסתא· הולכת ומתקפלת שאין הבגד שוה ובולט בבגד כמין כיס וצריך לקרוע הבגד למטה ומולל לפניו (ב) והתפירה מתיישבת: **מתני'** הסיט כפול· מפרש בגמרא סיט הוא הפסק שבין אצבע לאמה כמו שאדם יכול להרחיבו ואם טוה וליבן וניפץ וצבע שהן כולן אבות מלאכות חוט א' ארוך כשיעור הזה חייב: האורג ב' חוטין שיעורו. ברוחב הבגד כמלא הסיט שאע"פ שלא ארגו על פני כל רוחב הבגד חייב: **גמ'** נראה בעיני דהכי גרסי' ורמינהו הקורע בחמתו ובאבלו ועל מתו חייב ואע"פ כו' ולמאי דגרס הקורע בחמתו ובאבלו ועל מתו אע"פ כו' לא ידענא מאי יצא ידי הקריעה שייך למימר אבחמתו ואמאי נקט בחמתו: יצא ידי הקריעה· שאדם חייב לקרוע על מתו: הא במת דידיה· ברייתא דקתני חייב במת דידיה שחייב לקרוע עליו הלכך קריעה דידיה לאו קלקול הוא אלא תקון: והא מתו· כמי קתני במתני': לעול' במת דידיה· שמוטל עליו לקוברו ומיהו בהנך דלאו בני אבלו' נינהו שאינן מאותן האמורים בפרשת כהנים (ויקרא כא) אביו ואמו בנו ובתו ואחיו ואחותו: ופרכינן ואי חכם הוא זה שמת חיובי מיחייב נמי לקרוע וכיון דמיחייב מתקן הוא ואמאי פטור: חולצין· יוצאים לפניו חלוצי כתף חלוקו קרוע עד שכתיפו חלולה ערומה: מברין עליו ברחבה· שהיו מברין האבלין ברחבה סעודה ראשונה שאבל אוכל אינו אוכל משלו ואסור דקאמר ליה רחמנא ליחזקאל (כד) לחם אנשים לא תאכל: ערבונא שקלי· קודם שיחטא נטלו משכונו: לס"ת שנשרף· הרואה ס"ת שנשרף חייב לקרוע כדאמרינן במו"ק (דף כו.) במגילה ששרף יהויקים דכתיב לא פחדו ולא קרעו בגדים (ג) אף נשמת ישראל הניטלת דומה לו שאין לך ריק בישראל שאין בו תורה ומצות: הא ר' יהודה כו'· ומתו אמתו הכי נמי הוה מצי לתרוצי אלא מעיקרא אהדר לאוקמינהו כחד תנא ולא מתוקמא אלא כר' יהודה דהא מלאכה שאינה צריכה לגופה היא כמוציא את המת (ד) לקוברו: נחת רוח ליצרו· שמשכך את חמתו: מי שרי והא תניא כו'· אלמא לאו מתקן הוא שמלמד ומרגיל את יצרו לבא עליו: בך· משמע בקרבך שאם היה בך תשתחוה לאל נכר לבסוף: שליף מצבייתא· מן הבגד בחמתו להראותם שהוא כועס ויגורו מלפניו: מוניני· ציר של דגים קטנים: נכתמא· כיסוי הכד: נודי ספרתה אתה· לשון לנוד לו (איוב ב): ויקברו אותו· ביהושע כתיב: שרגש (ה) עליהן הר להורגן· שלא הספידו כראוי: מדה כנגד מדה· הוא לא נתאבל על שנתקצרו ימי החכם אף לחייו לא יחושו מן השמים: בבלאי· דמבבל סליק: ימים האריכו· שכלו ימיהם בטוב דחשיב אריכות ימים כדאמרי' בסדר יומא (דף עא.) כי אורך ימים ושנות חיים יוספו וכי יש לך שנים של חיים ושנים שאינם של חיים אמר רבי אלעזר אלו שנותיו של אדם שמתהפכות עליו מרעה לטובה:

רבינו חננאל

הקורע על מתו פטור. ואקשינן וכי מקלקל הוא. והתניא הקורע על מתו ובאבלו אע"פ שחילל שבת יצא ידי קריעה. וכיון שיצא ידי קריעה נמצאת מלאכתו מתקיימת. ובשבת כי האי גוונא חייב. ופריק מתני' בקורע על מת דעלמא דכיון דלא מיחייב בקריעה מקלקל הוא ופטור. וברייתא בקורע על מתו שלו שחייב לקרוע עליו. איני והא בין בזו ובין בזו על מתו קתני ופרקי' מתו דמתני' קרובו שאינו חייב לקרוע עליו מתו דברייתא במי שחייב לקרוע עליו. ואם הוא זה המת שקרע עליו חכם או כשר או היה עומד עליו בשעת יציאת נשמה הקורע בכל אלה אינו חשוב כמקלקל אלא חייב. ואינו פטור אלא הקורע על מי שאין עליו לא חובה ולא מצוה לקרוע וקשה לן דתנן במתני' הקורע בחמתו פטור. ובברייתא תנינן הקורע בחמתו חילל השבת מכלל דחייב ושנינן מתני' ר' שמעון היא דאמר מלאכה שאינה צריכה לגופה פטור עליה. ברייתא ר' יהודה דאמר חייב עליה וראינו לרבותינו שפירשו הכי. היכא שמעינן לר' שמעון דשרי מלאכה שאינה צריכה לגופה מיהא דתנינן את החי במטה פטור אף על המטה שהמטה טפילה לו את המת במטה חייב וכן כזית מן המת וכזית מן הנבילה וכעדשה מן השרץ לר' שמעון פטור ואוקימנא א"ר יוחנן פוטר היה ר"ש אפי' במוציא המת לקוברו ואע"ג דמת לקוברו קאי ואית למימר מלאכה שצריכה לגופה היא. כיון דלאו מידי דמיבעי ליה למיכליה ולא איתהנו מיניה מלאכה שאינה צריכה לגופה [היא] ושרי ר"ש בכה"ג והיכא שמעינן לר' יהודה דאמר [דאמרינן] (לעיל מב) בדבר שאין מתכוין סבר לה כר"ש במלאכה שאינה צריכה לגופה סבר לה כר' יהודה [וגרסינן] (כתובות ה) מהו לבעול בתחלה בשבת דאמרינן במקלקל הלכה כר' יהודה או כר"ש. ותוב כופין קערה ע"ג הנר בשביל שלא תאחוז בקורה כו' א"ר יהודה מעשה בא לפני ריב"ז בערב ואמר חושש אני לו מחטאת. והא דאמרי בכל מקום ר' יהודה היא לא אשכחן לה עיקר אלא מהא. וממאי דקא מפלגי ת"ק ור' יהודה בהא מתני' במלאכה שאינה צריכה לגופה דאמרי' (לקמן ד' קז.) איכא דמתני לה אהא הצד נחש בשבת ומתעסק שלא ישכנו פטור ואם לרפואה חייב מאן תנא א"ר יהודה ר' שמעון היא דאמר מלאכה שאינה צריכה לגופה פטור עליה. אבל דוכתא בהדיא דפליגי עלה בלשון הזה לא אשכחן אלא מהאי דיוקא דאמר הכא שנית מתו אלא אחמתו קשיא אחמתו נמי לא קשיא הא ר' יהודה הא ר' שמעון כדמפרש: ומקשינן אימור דשמעת ליה לר' יהודה מלאכה שאינה צריכה לגופה חייב עליה במתקן דאע"ג דלא קא מכוין כיון דממילא לא הויא מלאכה דניחא ליה חייב במקלקל מי שמעת ליה ופרקי' הקורע בגדיו בחמתו נמי מתקן הוא דכד קניטה דעתיה בכעסיה מתרווח בקריעת בגדיו ונמצא עושה נחת רוח ליצרו. ואקשינן וכי האי גוונא מי מיחייב והתניא הקורע בגדיו בחמתו וכן המשבר כליו וכן המפזר מעותיו בחמתו יהא בעיניך כעובד ע"ז שכך היא אומנות של יצה"ר היום אומר לו עשה כך ולמחר אומר לו עבוד ע"ז כו' ופרקינן לא עבוד בכעסיה הכי אלא מראה עצמו כועס להטיל אימ'

רב נסים גאון

פי"ג ר' אליעזר אומר האורג. חמתו אחמתו לא קשיא הא ר' יהודה הא ר' שמעון הא ר' יהודה דאמר מלאכה שאינה צריכה לגופה חייב עליה הא ר' שמעון דאמר פטור עליה. כבר פירשנו בפרק ראשון אבל דבריהם מתני' ר' יהודה היא דאמר מקלקל בחבורה פטור וברייתא ר' שמעון דאמר מקלקל בחבורה חייב ולא אשכחית עיקר פלוגתא ולא ידעינן לה אבל אדוננו האיי גאון כתב בפירוש זה הפרק כזה הענין והא מילתא דמקלקל בחבורה דקאמרינן פלוגתא דר' יהודה ור' שמעון היא עדיין לא ידעי' פלוגתייהו היכא ניהי ומתניתא דמפרש בה ר' יהודה ור' שמעון במקלקל בחבורה לא שמיע לנא אלא מגמ' ידעינן דפלוגתא

*) עי' תוי"ט ד"ה הקורע על מתו וכו' דמקיים נוסחא ישנה ואין בו חימוס. פי' שע"י הקריעה נסתלק חימומו ע"ש ודלא כרש"ל שהגיה ואית בו חימוס

הגהות הב"ח

גליון הש"ס

is that possible? [105b]—If he made it [the garment] like a pocket.[8]

MISHNAH. HE WHO TEARS IN HIS ANGER OR [IN MOURNING] FOR HIS DEAD,[9] AND ALL WHO EFFECT DAMAGE ARE
a EXEMPT; BUT HE WHO DAMAGES IN ORDER TO REPAIR,[1] HIS STANDARD [FOR CULPABILITY] IS AS FOR REPAIRING. THE STANDARD OF BLEACHING [WOOL], HATCHELLING, DYEING OR SPINNING IT, IS A FULL DOUBLE SIṬ.[2] AND HE WHO WEAVES TWO THREADS TOGETHER, HIS STANDARD IS A FULL SIṬ.

GEMARA. But the following contradicts this: He who rends [his garment] in his anger, in his mourning or for his dead, is guilty, and though he desecrates the Sabbath, he has fulfilled his duty of rending?[3]—There is no difficulty: the one refers to his dead,[4] the other to the dead in general.[5] But he [our Tanna] states, HIS DEAD?—After all, it does refer to his dead,[6] but those for whom there is no duty of mourning?[7] Now, if he [the dead] was a Sage, he is indeed bound [to rend his garments]? For it was taught: If a Sage dies, all are his kinsmen. All are his kinsmen! can you think so? Rather say, all are as his kinsmen, [i.e.,] all must rend [their garments] for him; all must bare [their shoulders] for him,[8] and all partake of the [mourner's] meal for him in a public square![9]—This holds good only if he was not a Sage. But [even] if he was [merely] a worthy man, one is indeed bound [to rend his garments]? For it was taught: Why do a man's sons and daughters die in childhood? So that he may weep and mourn for a worthy man? 'So that he may weep'—is a pledge taken![10] But because he did not weep and mourn for a worthy man, for whoever weeps for a worthy man is forgiven all his iniquities on account of the honour which he showed him!—This holds good only if he was not a worthy man. But if he stood [there] at the
b parting of the soul[1] he is indeed bound? For it was taught, R. Simeon b. Eleazar said: He who stands by the dead at the parting of the soul is bound to rend [his garments]: [for] what does this resemble? A scroll of the Law that is burnt![2]—This holds good only if he was not standing there at the moment of death.

Now, that is well in respect to his dead. But [the two statements concerning tearing] in one's anger are contradictory?—These too cause no difficulty: one agrees with R. Judah, the other with R. Simeon. One agrees with R. Judah, who maintained: One is liable in respect of a labour which is not required *per se;* the other with R. Simeon, who maintained: One is exempt in respect of a labour which is not required *per se.*[3] But you know R. Judah [to rule thus] in the case of one who repairs: Do you know him [to rule thus] in the case of one who causes damage?—Said R. Abin: This man too effects an improvement, because he appeases his wrath. But is it permitted [to effect this] in such a manner? Surely it was taught, R. Simeon b. Eleazar said in the name of Ḥalfa b. Agra in R. Joḥanan b. Nuri's name: He who rends his garments in his anger, he who breaks his vessels in his anger, and he who scatters his money in his anger, regard him as an idolater, because such are the wiles of the Tempter: To-day he says to him, 'Do this'; to-morrow he tells him, 'Do that,' until he bids him, 'Go and serve idols,' and he goes and serves [them].[4] R. Abin observed: What verse [intimates this]? *There shall be no strange god in thee; neither shalt thou worship any strange god:*[5] who is the strange god that resides in man himself? Say, that is the Tempter![6]—This holds good only where he does it in order to instil fear in his household, even as Rab Judah pulled the thrums [of his garment;][7] R. Aḥa b. Jacob broke broken vessels; R. Shesheth threw brine on his maidservant's head; R. Abba broke a lid.

R. Simeon b. Pazzi said in the name of R. Joshua b. Levi in Bar Ḳappara's name: If one sheds tears for a worthy man, the Holy One, blessed be He, counts them and lays them up in His treasure house, for it is said, *Thou countest my grievings: Put thou my tears*
c *into thy bottle; Are they not in thy book?*[1] Rab Judah said in Rab's name: He who is slothful to lament a Sage deserves to be buried alive, because it is said, *And they buried him in the border of his inheritance in Timnath-serah, which is in the hill country of Ephraim; on the north of the mountain of Gaash:*[2] this teaches that the mountain raged against them to slay them.[3] R. Ḥiyya b. Abba said in R. Joḥanan's name: He who is slothful to lament a Sage will not prolong his days, [this being] measure for measure, as it is said, *In measure, when thou sendest her away, thou dost contend with her.*[4] R. Ḥiyya b. Abba objected to R. Joḥanan: *And Israel served the Lord all the days of Joshua and all the days of the elders who prolonged their days after Joshua?*[5]—O Babylonian! answered he, they prolonged 'their *days*',[6] but not years. If so, *that your days may be multiplied, and the days of your children:*[7] [does that mean] days but not years!—A blessing is different.[8]

R. Ḥiyya b. Abba also said in R. Joḥanan's name: When one

(8) Rashi: bulging and creasing, so that part has to be torn open in order for it to be resewn. (9) At the death of one's parents, brothers, sisters, children, wife or husband the garments are rent.
a (1) As in the example mentioned immediately preceding the Mishnah. (2) Rashi: the distance between the tips of the index finger and middle finger when held wide apart, v. Gemara. (3) Sc. for the dead. (4) *Sc.* those enumerated in *supra* n. c9. Since rending is a duty there, it is an act of positive value, and he is liable. (5) Though he rends his garment in grief, it is not actually necessary. (6) I.e., one whom through certain circumstances it is his duty to bury. (7) I.e., other than those enumerated in *supra* n. c9. (8) This was a mourning rite in former times, but is no longer practised. (9) The first meal after the funeral is called the meal of comfort (*se'udath habra'ah*), and is supplied by friends of the mourner. In the case of a Sage all must partake of such a meal. (10) For the future—surely not!
b (1) I.e., at the moment of death. (2) If one sees this he must rend his garments, and even the most ignorant and the most worthless Jew has some knowledge thereof and has fulfilled some of its precepts. (3) V. *supra* 30a. (4) Since then this is forbidden, he cannot be held to effect an improvement. (5) Ps. LXXXI, 10. (6) This shows that no real separate identity was ascribed to the source of evil, of which the Tempter is merely a personification; cf. Joseph, M., *'Judaism as Creed and Life'*, pp. 65-68. (7) To show his anger.
c (1) Ps. LVI, 9. (2) Josh. XXIV, 30. *'Gaash'* is derived from a root meaning to tremble or rage. (3) Because they did not fittingly lament him. (4) Isa. XXVII, 8. (5) Josh. ibid. 31. Thus they lived long in spite of their failure to mourn for Joshua. (6) [Maharsha: Their days seemed prolonged on account of the difficult times they experienced, v. however Rashi.] (7) Deut. XI, 21. (8) [The length of days in the case of a blessing can be only another expression for length of years, cf. n. c6.]

of brothers dies, [106a] all the other brothers should fear. When one of a company dies, the whole company should fear. Some say that this means where the eldest [or chief] dies; others say, where the youngest[9] dies.

AND ALL WHO EFFECT DAMAGE ARE EXEMPT. R. Abbahu recited before R. Johanan: All who cause damage are exempt, except he who wounds and he who sets fire [to a stack of corn]. Said he to him, Go and recite it outside:[1] wounding and setting fire is not a Mishnah;[2] and should you say that it is a Mishnah, wounding refers to one who needs [the blood] for his dog, and setting fire, to one who needs the ashes.[3] But we learnt, ALL WHO EFFECT DAMAGE ARE EXEMPT?[4]—Our Mishnah is [in accordance with] R. Judah, while the Baraitha[5] [agrees with] R. Simeon. What is R. Simeon's reason?—Since a verse is required to permit circumcision [on the Sabbath],[6] it follows that for wounding elsewhere one is liable. And since the Divine Law forbade burning in respect of a priest's [adulterous] daughter,[7] it follows that for kindling a fire in general one is liable. And R. Judah?[8]—There he effects an improvement, even as R. Ashi [said]. For R. Ashi said: What is the difference whether one repairs [the foreskin by] circumcision or one repairs a utensil: what is the difference whether one boils [melts] the lead bar[9] or one boils dyes?

THE STANDARD OF BLEACHING, etc. R. Joseph indicated the double [measure]; R. Ḥiyya b. Ammi showed the single [measure].[10]

MISHNAH. R. JUDAH SAID: HE WHO HUNTS A BIRD [AND DRIVES IT] INTO A TURRET, OR A DEER INTO A HOUSE, IS GUILTY; BUT THE SAGES MAINTAIN: [HE WHO HUNTS] A BIRD

(9) Or, least important.

(1) It is not an authenticated teaching to be admitted to the school. (2) I.e., no Mishnah states that these are exceptions. (3) For medical purposes. Then the wounding and setting fire is beneficial, not a damage-effecting labour. (4) Which refutes R. Abbahu. (5) Cited by R. Abbahu. (6) V. *infra* 132a. (7) Who may not be thus executed on the Sabbath, Sanh. 35b. (8) How does he refute these arguments? (9) Death by fire was carried out by pouring molten lead down the condemned person's throat, Sanh. 52a. (10) [Rashi: The distance between the tips of the index and middle fingers held widely apart, which is the measure of a singel *sit*, is half the distance between the tips of the outstretched thumb and index finger. Thus, whereas R. Joseph using the smaller unit indicated by gesture a double measure to explain the meaning of 'DOUBLE SIT', R. Ḥiyya b. Ammi, using the larger unit, indicated a single measure. For other interpretations v. Jast. s.v. סיט.]

ידאגו כל האחין כולן *אחד מבני חבורה שמת תדאג כל החבורה כולה אמרי לה דמת גדול ואמרי לה דמת קטן: וכל המקלקלין פטורין: *תני ר' אבהו קמיה דר' יוחנן ב כל המקלקלין פטורין חוץ מחובל ומבעיר א"ל *פוק תני לברא חובל ומבעיר אינה משנה ואם ת"ל משנה ג חובל בצריך לכלבו מבעיר בצריך לאפרו והאנן תנן כל המקלקלין פטורין מתניתין *רבי יהודה ברייתא רבי שמעון מ"ט דר' שמעון מדאיצטריך קרא למישרא מילה הא חובל בעלמא חייב ומדאסר רחמנא הבערה גבי בת כהן שמע מינה מבעיר בעלמא חייב ורבי יהודה התם מתקן הוא כדרב אשי דאמר רב אשי מה לי לתקן מילה מה לי לתקן כלי *מה לי לבשל פתילה מה לי לבשל סמנין: שיעור המלבן כו': רב יוסף מחוי *כפול רב חייא בר אמי ד מחוי פשוט:

מתני' *ר' יהודה אומר הצד צפור למגדל וצבי לבית חייב ה וחכ"א צפור למגדל [ביצה כד.] וצבי

רש"י

ידאגו. ייראו מן המיתה: דמת גדול. יש לדאוג הואיל ושלטה מדת הדין בראש הבית: ואמרי לה דמת קטן. שבקלקלה מתחילין מן הקטן*: חוץ מחובל באדם דמקלקל הוא וחייב דתנן (ב"ק פז.) החובל בחברו בשבת פטור (א) מלשלם מפני שנדון בנפשו: ומבעיר. את הגדיש מקלקל הוא וחייב כדתנן (שם דף לד:) והוא שהדליק את הגדיש פטור מן תשלומין מפני שנדון בנפשו: אינה משנה. דאם מקלקל הוא פטור: בצריך. לדם היוצא מן החבלה לכלבו ואם מקלקל הוא אבל מתקן הוא אצל הכלב: והא תנן כל המקלקלין פטורין. ואפי' חובל ומבעיר וקשיין אהדדי ולרבי אבא פריך: מתני' ר' יהודה. דאית ליה מקלקל בחבורה פטור ולא איתפרש היכא ול"נ מתני' ר' יהודה היא דאמר מלאכה שאינה צריכה לגופה חייב עליה הלכך חיובא דחובל בצריך לכלבו ומבעיר בצריך לאפרו משכחת לה דאע"פ דמקלקל הוא אצל מלאכה עצמה מתקן הוא אצל אחרים ולר' יהודה כי האי גוונא מלאכה הוא משום תקון אחרים אבל מקלקל ואינו מתקן פטור ואע"ג דרישא דמתני' אוקימנא כר"ש דקתני קורע על מתו פטור סיפא ר"י: וברייתא ר"ש היא. דאמר מלאכה שאינה צריכה לגופה פטור עליה הלכך אין לך חובל ומבעיר שאין מקלקל ואפי' מבעיר עצים (ב) לקדרתו מקלקל הוא אצל עצים ומה שהוא מתקן אצל אחרים לר"ש לא חשיב דהא מלאכה שאינה צריכה לגופה היא אלא משום דמקלקל בחבלה ובהבערה חייב כדיליף לקמיה: מדאיצטריך קרא. וביום השמיני ביום יתירא ואפי' בשבת ומילה חובל הוא מכלל דשאר מקלקלין בחבורה חייב: ומדאסר רחמנא הבערה דבת כהן. בשבת (*לקמן בפרק ר' אליעזר): מה לי מתקן כלי. הא נמי מתקן גברא הוא ויש מלאכה בתיקון זה: בישול פתילה. שהוא מדליק פתילה של אבר ונותנה לתוך פיה* ודרך בישול הוא זה וחייב על הבישול שאינו מקלקל האבר בבישולו אלא מתקן ולורף: סמנין. של מלאכת המשכן: רב יוסף מחוי. האי הסיט כפול דמתני' כפול ממש ברווח שבין אצבע לאמה מטער שני פעמים: מחוי פשוט. ברווח שבין גודל לאצבע פעם אחד הוא כפול דמתניתא שיש בו כפלים כאותו שבין אמה לאצבע: מתני' הצד צפור. עד שהכניסו למגדל משטיי"ר בלע"ז חייב דזו היא צידתו אבל אם הכניסו לבית אינו ניצוד בכך שיוצא לו דרך חלונות: ולצבי

תוספות

חוץ מחובל ומבעיר א"ל פוק תני לברא כו'. פי' רבינו שמואל דר' אבהו סבר כר"ש דאמר מקלקל בחבורה חייב ור' יוחנן סבר לה כר' יהודה דאמר מקלקל בחבורה ובהבערה פטור וצריך לכלבו ולאפרו לא חשיב מקלקל וחייב אפי' לר' יהודה וכן משמע בסמוך מתוך פי' רש"י וקשה דא"כ אמאי א"ל פוק תני לברא דאטו משום דס"ל כר' יהודה מאן דתנא כר"ש משתקינן ליה דכה"ג פריך בפ"ק דחולין (טו.) ע"כ נראה דר' אבהו ור' יוחנן אליבא דר"ש פליגי דר' אבהו סבר דחובל ומבעיר אע"פ שאינו צריך לכלבו ולאפרו חייב לר' שמעון דגמר ממילה והבערת בת כהן ור' יוחנן סבר דר"ש נמי לא מחייב אא"כ איכא קצת תיקון כגון דצריך לכלבו ולאפרו דמילה והבערה איכא קצת תיקון שהוא צורך מצוה אבל לר' יהודה אפי' צריך לאפרו ולכלבו פטור דאין זה תיקון חשוב דאין דרך לחבול בחבירו כדי ליתן לכלבו או לשרוף גדיש בשביל האפר אע"ג דכל שוחט מקלקל הוא כדאמרי' בפ"ק דחולין (דף ה.) סכין של ע"ז מותר לשחוט בה מודה ר' יהודה לענין שבת דחייב דדוקא לענין ע"ז חשוב מקלקל דכתיב ולא ידבק בידך מאומה מן החרם ולא חשיב ליה נהנה כיון דקלקולו יתר על תקונו ור"ת מפרש דהא דחשיב לר' יהודה מקלקל בצריך לכלבו ואפרו לפי שאין התיקון בא בשעה אלא לאחר מכאן דלאחר שנעשית חבורה בא הדם ולאחר שכלתה ההבערה בא האפר אבל בשוחט בשעת הקלקול בא לו התיקון שמוציאה מידי אבר מן החי וקורע למירמא אימתא אאינשי דביתיה חשוב ליה לר"י נמי תיקון לפי שבשעת הקלקול בא לו התיקון וכן בהריגת המזיקין (לקמן קכא:) חייב לר' יהודה דבא התיקון בשעת הקלקול ולר"ש פטור משום דהויא מלאכה שאינה צריכה לגופה וקורע ע"מ לתפור ומוחק ע"מ לכתוב דמיחייב לכ"ע אע"ג שבשעת הקלקול אינו בא התיקון היינו משום שהקלקול גורם תיקון יותר טוב לבסוף ותיקון גמור הוא שהרי אינו יכול לעשות התיקון אלא ע"י הקלקול:

בחובל וצריך לכלבו כו'. וא"ת ור' אבהו דמחייב אפי' באין צריך לכלבו כיון דאין צריך כלל הויא מלאכה שאינה צריכה לגופה דאע"ג דמחייב ר"ש מקלקל בחבורה מ"מ בעי צריכה לגופה כדאמרי' בריש הנחנקין (סנהדרין פד:) מאן שמעת ליה דאמר מקלקל בחבורה חייב ר"ש האמר מלאכה שאינה צריכה לגופה פטור עליה וכן משמע בפרק כלל גדול (לעיל דף עה.) גבי חלזון ובפרק כל כתבי (לקמן דף קכא:) ובס"פ ספק אכל (כריתות דף כ:) וי"ל דאפי' במקלקל גמור משכחת לה דהויא צריכה לגופה כגון חובל ומבעיר באיסורי הנאה שסבר שיכול ליתן לכלבו ולבשל בו קדרה ור' אבהו אע"ג דלא חשיב צורך מצוה תיקון מ"מ צריכה לגופה חשיב וא"ת צריך לכלבו ולאפרו היכי חשיב צריכה לגופה מ"מ מחופר גומא ואינו צריך אלא לעפרה* וי"ל דלא דמי דהכא הוא צריך לנטילת נשמה כדי לתת לכלבו דהיינו הדם כי הדם הוא הנפש ומבעיר נמי צריך להבערה כדי לעשות אפר כמו מבעיר כדי לבשל קדרה אבל חופר הגומא נעשית מאליה ואינו נהנה ממנה כלום*:

מדאצטריך קרא למישרי מילה כו'. וא"ת למה לי למילף כולה מילתא מהבערת בת כהן דלא דחי שבת דבהבערה איכא נטילת נשמה וחובל נמי לא מחייב אלא משום נטילת נשמה וי"ל דלענין מקלקל בחבורה ליכא למילף מהבערה דהתם התיקון בא בשעת הקלקול אבל לענין מקלקל בהבערה יליף שפיר דלאחר הבערה בא התיקון כדפי' אי נמי אי לאו דילפינן ממילה דמקלקל בחבורה חייב ה"א דרציחה דוחה את השבת דלאו מלאכה היא והבערה לחודה היא דאימעטה משום דמקלקל בהבערה חייב:

דאמר רב אשי מה לי לתקן מילה מה לי לתקן כלי. לאו משום דסבר כר' יהודה אלא מפרש הוא אליבא דר' יהודה: מה לי לבשל פתילה מה לי לבשל סמנין. אין לפרש כמו שבישול סממנין מתקנן להיות יותר חשובים כך פתילה חשובה יותר ע"י בישול דאי היינו טעמא דר' יהודה שאר מיתות ב"ד דלא דחו שבת מנלן כיון דלא שייך בהו תיקון דהבערה לא אסרה תורה אלא משום תיקון פתילה ועוד שריפת בת כהן גופה מנלן דלא דחינן היכא דתיקן הפתילה מאתמול ואומר ר"י דה"פ מה לי בישול פתילה לצורך שריפת בת כהן מה לי בישול סממנין לצורך צביעת בגד דכי היכי דבישול סממנין לצורך צביעה חשוב תיקון ה"נ בישול פתילה לצורך שריפה ומהכא נפקא לן שפיר דכל שאר מיתות ב"ד חשוב תיקון משום מצוה דאי לאו שריפה עצמה חשיבא תיקון משום בישול פתילה לא הוה אסורה אע"פ שמתקנת בכך דכיון שאינה אלא משום שריפה לא הוה חשיב תיקון ולא מיחייב וכן מוציא מרא לחפור לקבור בו מת לר"ש כמו מוציא כיס לקבל בו זיבה בפ"ק (דף יא.) וא"ת בשלמא לר' יהודה שפיר שמעינן דהבערה ללאו יצאת או לחלק מדלא כתב לא תעשה מלאכה בכל מושבותיכם וכתב הבערה ש"מ ללאו יצאת או לחלק כדפרישית בפרק כלל גדול (לעיל דף ע.) [ד"ה הבערה] אלא לר"ש דאיצטריך למיכתב הבערה לחייב מקלקל בהבערה מנא ליה דיצאת ללאו או לחלק וליכא למימר דנפקא ליה לחלק מאחת מהנה כדמפיק ליה ר' יוסי דהא בפרק הבונה (לקמן דף קג:) פליג ר"ש בהדיא אר' יוסי ודריש ליה לדרשה אחריתי וי"ל דנפקא ליה לחלק מהיכא דנפקא ליה לשמואל בפרק כלל גדול (לעיל דף ע.) והשתא אתי שפיר הא דהוה קשה *שמואל דאמר כמאן לא כר' נתן ולא כר' יוסי דהשתא כר"ש ס"ל ובפ"ק דיבמות (דף ו:) קאמר דאיצטריך קרא למיסר הבערה בת כהן משום דהוה סלקא דעתך למישרי מקל וחומר מעבודה דדחיא שבת היינו כר' יהודה דחשיב ליה תיקון אבל לר' שמעון איצטריך קרא בהבערה לחייב כל מקלקל בהבערה הך פלוגתא דמקלקל בחבורה מפרש רש"י דנפקא לן מפלוגתא שאינה צריכה לגופה משמע דלא בעי לר' שמעון צריך לכלבו ולאפרו ולפי זה צריך לומר דר' אבהו כר"ש ור' יוחנן כר' יהודה ואין נראה כדפי' לעיל וצ"ל דהך פלוגתא דמקלקל בחבורה קבלה היתה בידם:

ואין

מסורת הש"ס

[illegible] | ב"ק לד: | [שם ויבמות עז: סנהדרין סב.] | [לעיל יב. עג: וש"נ] | [יבמות ו: וש"נ] | [גיר' הערוך כפופא"שבערך קף ובערך סט ועי' ברמב"ם ובמגיד ועתוס' מנחות לה: ד"ה וכמה וכו'] | [נ"ל יבמות ו: סנהדרין לה:] | סנהדרין נב. | [לעיל עג:] | [וע"ע תוס' סנהדרין פד: ד"ה מאן שמעת] | [עי' תוס' לעיל ע ע"ב ד"ה לא משמע]

הגהות הב"ח

(א) רש"י ד"ה חוץ מחובל וכו' פטור מכולן מפני [וכן גי' רש"ל]: (ב) ד"ה וברייתא וכו' מבעיר עצים באור לקדרתו:

גליון הש"ס

גמ' פוק תני לברא. עירובין ט ע"א ביצה יב ע"ב יומא מג ע"ב יבמות עו ע"ב סנהד' סב ע"א:

עין משפט נר מצוה

כב א מיי' פי"ג מהל' אבל הל' יב סמג שם טוש"ע י"ד סי' שלד סעיף ה:

כג ב ג מיי' פ"א מהל' שבת הל' יז ופ"ח הלכה ז ופ"י הלכה י ופי"ב הלכה א סמג לאוין סה:

כד ד מיי' פ"ט מהל' שבת הלכה ז:

כה ה מיי' פ"י מהל' שבת הלכה יט סמג לאוין סה טוש"ע א"ח סי' שטו סעיף א:

רבינו חננאל

אאינשי ביתיה ואית מן רבנן דטעו ותמהו היכי מקשינן וכי האי גוונא מי מחייב. והא כעובד ע"ז חשיב אטו עובד ע"ז והעושה דברים מכוערים מותר ושניות לקושיא וגרסי מסבריהן וכי האי גוונא מי שרי והתניא ר' שמעון בן אלעזר וכו' *) ואהדרינן להו ואיסורא מי הוי קשיא למ"ד מתקן וחייב הוא ולא מיתוסף בו איסורא אחרינא. אלא לישנא דיקא הכי היא וכה"ג [מי] מיחייב דכיון דאמר [ר' אבין] מתקן הוא משום דעביד נחת ליצרו ומשום הכי מחייב ר' יהודה על מלאכה שאינה צריכה לגופה. אקשינן עליה האי תיקונא הוא אדרבה האי קלקולא רבה הוא משום דמגרת יצרו בעצמו ומקלקל הוא. ולא שמעינן לר' יהודה במקלקל דמחייב נדחה ר' אבין ובטיל פירוקיה לגמרי ואוקימנא לא מחייב ר' יהודה בהא אלא משום דקא עביד למירמא אימתא אאינשי ביתיה וקא מחזי דבחמתיה עביד וקא מכוין לתקוני לאינשי ביתיה וכרב יהודה דהוא שליף מצבייתא כו' דכל כי האי גוונא תיקונא היא ולא קלקולא אלא מיהו מלאכה שאינה צריכה לגופה היא וכל מאן דעביד הכי בשבת לר' יהודה חייב לר' שמעון פטור ומתני' כר' שמעון: פיס' כל המקלקלין פטורין. תני סתמא וברייתא כר' אבהו דמחייב חובל ומבעיר. ואע"ג דאמר ר' יוחנן אינה משנה אלא החובל בצריך לכלבו והמבעיר בצריך לאפרו דלא מקלקלין נינהו מיהו איצטרכינן לברר היכא אמירא החובל והמבעיר שלא לצורך חייב ואהדרינן מתניתין ר' יהודה דאמר מקלקל בחבורה פטור וברייתא ר' שמעון דאמר מקלקל בחבורה חייב ואל תתמה דרישא דמתניתין כרבי שמעון במלאכה שאינה צריכה לגופה וסיפא כר' יהודה במקלקל בחבורה [דבהא] סבר לה כמר ובהא סבר לה כמר ומילתא דמקלקל בחבורה דקאמרי פלוגתא דר' יהודה ור' שמעון היא לא ברירה לן עיקר פלוגתייהו דא היכי ניהו ומתניתא דמפרשא במקלקל בחבורה ר' יהודה פוטר ור' שמעון מחייב. לא שמיע לן אלא מגמרא בלחוד הוא דשמעינן ליה. ובעושה חבורה ומתקן כ"ע לא פליגי דמחייב כי פליגי בעושה חבורה ומקלקל דר' יהודה פוטר וסתם מתניתין כוותיה ור' שמעון אסרי וגרסינן באלו דברים בפסח א"ל רב הונא בר חיננא לבריה כי אזלת לקמיה דר' זריקא בעי מיניה למאן דסבר מקלקל

*) נראה דט"ס יש כאן וצריך תיקון.

רב נסים גאון

דפלוגתא דר' יהודה ור' שמעון היא: מדאצטריך קרא למישרא מילה. עיקר דילה בתורת כהנים וביום השמיני ימול ואפי' בשבת ומה אני מקיים מחלליה מות יומת בשאר מלאכות חוץ ממילה או מקיים אני מחלליה אף במילה ומה אני מקיים ימול חוץ מן השבת ת"ל וביום ואפי' בשבת ובפרק ר' אליעזר (דף קלג) אמרו עוד עד כאן לא פליגי אלא במכשירי מילה אבל מילה עצמה דברי הכל דחיא מנא לן ונאמרו בדבר זה כמה טעמים והעיקר הוא מה שאמר ר' יוחנן כי דבריו שוין עם הברייתא ועליהן אנו סומכין ואיל והוצרך הכתוב לומר וביום להתיר המילה בשבת שהיא מצוה הודיע אותנו שחבורה בעלמא חוץ מן המילה אסור לעשותה וחייב עליה בשבת ומדאסר רחמנא הבערה גבי בת כהן מכלל דמבעיר בעלמא חייב כבר ידעת כי ד' מיתות נמסרו לבית דין סקילה שריפה הרג וחנק וכי בת כהן שזנתה מיתתה בשריפה והיא אחת מן הנשרפין כדכתיב (ויקרא כא) ובת איש כהן כי תחל לזנות וגו' באש תשרף ובמסכת סנהדרין בפרק ד' מיתות (דף נב) זכרו היאך מצות שריפה ואמרו מצות שריפה דנשרפין היו משקעין אותו בזבל עד ארכובותיו ונותנין סודרין קשה לתוך רכה וכורך על צוארו זה מושך אצלו וזה מושך אצלו עד שפותח את פיו ומדליק את הפתילה וזורקה לתוך פיו ופירשו בתלמוד מאי פתילה אמר רב מתנה פתילה של אבר ועל פי זה נאמרה כאן מה לי לבשל פתילה מאי לי לבשל סממנין כלומר פתילה של אבר שתישרף בה בת כהן שזינתה והזהיר הקב"ה את ב"ד שלא ישרפו המתחייב שריפה ביום שבת כמה שנאמר (שמות לה) לא תבערו

וצבי (א) לגינה ולחצר ולביברין [חייב] *רשב"ג אומר לא כל הביברין שוין זה הכלל מחוסר צידה פטור שאינו מחוסר צידה חייב:

גמ' *תנן התם אין צדין דגים מן הביברין בי"ט ואין נותנין לפניהם מזונות אבל צדין *חיה ועוף ונותנין לפניהם מזונות ורמינהו *ביברין של חיות ושל עופות ושל דגים אין צדין מהם ביום טוב ואין נותנין לפניהם מזונות קשיא חיה אחיה קשיא עופות אעופות בשלמא חיה אחיה לא קשיא הא רבי יהודה הא רבנן אלא עופות אעופות קשיא וכי תימא עופות אעופות נמי לא קשיא הא (ב) ביבר מקורה הא ביבר שאינו מקורה והא בית דמקורה הוא ובין לרבי יהודה ובין לרבנן צפור למגדל אין לבית לא אמר רבה בר רב הונא *הכא בצפור דרור עסקינן לפי שאינה מקבלת מרות דתנא דבי ר' ישמעאל למה נקרא שמה צפור דרור מפני שדרה בבית כבשדה השתא דאתית להכי חיה אחיה נמי לא קשיא הא בביבר גדול הא בביבר קטן היכי דמי ביבר גדול היכי דמי ביבר קטן אמר רב אשי כל היכא דרהיט בתריה ומטי לה בחד *)שיחייא ביבר קטן ואידך ביבר גדול אי נמי כל היכא דנפיל טולא דכתלים אהדדי ביבר קטן ואידך ביבר גדול ואי נמי כל היכא דליכא עוקצי עוקצי ביבר קטן ואידך ביבר גדול: רשב"ג אומר וכו': *אמר רב יוסף אמר רב יהודה אמר שמואל הלכה כרבן שמעון בן גמליאל *אמר ליה אביי הלכה מכלל דפליגי א"ל (א)מאי נפקא לך מינה א"ל גמרא גמור זמורתא תהא *ת"ר הצד צבי סומא וישן חייב חיגר וזקן וחולה פטור א"ל אביי לרב יוסף מ"ש הני ומ"ש הני הני עבידי לרבויי הני לא עבידי לרבויי והתניא *חולה חייב אמר רב ששת לא קשיא הא בחולה מחמת אישתא הא בחולה מחמת *אובצנא ת"ר הצד חגבין גזין צרעין ויתושין בשבת חייב דברי רבי מאיר וחכמים אומרים כל שבמינו ניצוד חייב וכל *שאין במינו ניצוד פטור תניא אידך הצד חגבים בשעת הטל פטור בשעת השרב חייב אלעזר בן מהבאי אומר אם היו מקלחות ובאות פטור איבעיא להו אלעזר בן מהבאי ארישא קאי או אסיפא קאי ת"ש *הצד חגבין בשעת הטל פטור בשעת השרב חייב אלעזר בן מהבאי אומר אפילו בשעת השרב אם היו מקלחות ובאות פטור:

מתני' *צבי שנכנס לבית ונעל אחד בפניו חייב נעלו שנים פטורין לא יכול אחד לנעול ונעלו שנים חייבין ור"ש פוטר:

גמ' א"ר ירמיה בר אבא אמר שמואל הצד ארי בשבת אינו חייב עד שיכניסנו לגורזקי שלו: מתני' ישב האחד על הפתח ולא מילאהו ישב השני ומילאהו השני חייב ישב הראשון על הפתח ומילאהו ובא השני וישב בצידו אף על פי שעמד הראשון והלך לו הראשון חייב והשני פטור הא למה זה דומה לנועל את ביתו לשומרו ונמצא צבי שמור בתוכו:

גמ'

*) [גי' הערוך שהיא כגון ריגא אחת ואינו צריך לפוש ביני ביני]

רש"י

*וצבי · ניצוד משהכניסו לביתו ונעל בפניו אבל אם הכניסו לגינה או לחצר אין זו צידה: המחוסר צידה · שקשה לתופסו שם כדמפרש בגמ': גמ' ביברין · קרפיפות מוקפין: אין צדין מהן בי"ט · אלמא לאו ניצוד ועומד קא חשיב ליה ש"מ המכניסו לביבר אין זו צידתו: ואין נותנין לפניהן מזונות · כיון דהן מוקצה לא מצי למטרח עלייהו: הא רבי יהודה · ההיא דאין צדין רבי יהודה היא דבמתניתין לא חשיב לה צידה עד שיכניסו לבית: עופות אעופות קשיא · דהא בין לר' יהודה בין לרבנן צפור למגדל קאמרי: ביבר מקורה · הוי ניצוד: בצפור דרור · מתני' דקתני צפור לבית לא בצפור דרור עסקינן שדרכה לדור בבית כבשדה ושמטת מזוית לזוית: השתא דאתית להכי · לאוקמינהו לתרוייהו כרבנן: חיה אחיה נמי · מוקמי כרבנן: והא ביבר קטן · מתניתין דהכא: והא · מתניתין דביצה בביבר גדול: שיחייא · מרוצה שהוא שוחה לאחוז בה: עוקצי · פיאות להשמט בהן: ואידך · כל מי שאינו כן: מכלל דפליגי · והא אוקימנא דרבנן נמי בביבר קטן אמרי: מאי נפקא לך מינה · כ"ש כיון דלא פליגי עליה הלכתא כוותיה: זמורתא תהא · אומר השמועה בזמירה בעלמא בלא צורך: סומא וישן עבידי לרבויי · לישמט כשמרגישין יד אדם: אובצנא · עייפות שאינו יכול לזוז ממקומו כניצוד ועומד הוא: הגזין · (ג)*מין חגב טהור הוא ונאכלין: במינו ניצוד · כגון חגבים והגזין: שאין במינו ניצוד · צרעין ויתושין שאינן לצורך: חגבים בשעת הטל · עיניהם מתעוורות והרי הן ניצודין ועומדין: מקלחות · הרבה ביחד שהן מזומנות ליקח: ארישא קאי · דאף בשעת הטל אם מקלחות ובאות שרי ואי לא אסור: מתני' צבי שנכנס · מאליו: ונעל אחד בפניו · זו היא צידתו: נעלו שנים פטורים · דהוי להו שנים שעשאוה: לא יכול אחד לנעול · אורחיה הוא לנעול בשנים והרי לכל אחד מלאכה דבלא איהו לא מתעבדא: ורבי שמעון פוטר · לטעמיה דדריש קראי למיפטר זה אינו יכול וזה אינו יכול בפרק המצניע (לעיל צג:): גמ' הצד ארי · אפילו תופסו אין זו צידתו שכשכועס משחית והולך עד שיכניסנו לגורזקי שלו · בית משמר העשוי לו כמין תיבה: מתני' השני חייב · שהוא צדו: הא (ד) למה · שני זה דומה מאחר שנצוד ע"י הראשון: לנועל את ביתו לשומרו · ולא לצוד: ונמצא צבי · שהוא ניצוד כבר שמור בתוכו וכן (ה) אע"פ שעמד הראשון אין זה אלא כשומרו לצבי שהיה לו מאתמול:

תוספות

ואין נותנין לפניהם מזונות · אין לפרש דטעמא משום דדגים מיתזני שפיר במים להכי לא טרחינן דחשיבי כאין מזונותיהם עליך חדא דלאו מילתא דפסיקא היא דלדגים מצויין מזונות ולא לחיה ועוד דבסמוך בעי לאוקמי הא דקתני אין לדין חיה ועוף ואין נותנין לפניהם מזונות בביבר שאינו מקורה וכי בשביל שאינו מקורה מצויין להם מזונות ורש"י דפירש כיון דאין לדין מוקלין נינהו להכי אין נותנין לפניהם מזונות ואין טורחין בשבילם אין נראה כלל דהא תנן לקמן בפ' בתרא (דף קנה:) נותנים מים לפני אווזים ותרנגולים ולפני יוני הרדסיאות אע"ג דמוקלין הן בשבת ונראה לר"י כל היכא דהוי כניצוד ועומד מדאורייתא כגון אווזין ותרנגולין ויוני הרדסיאות ואע"ג דמדרבנן אסור לצודן כדתנן בפרק שמונה שרצים (לקמן דף קז·) חיה ועוף שברשותו הצדן פטור משמע אבל אסור כיון דמדאורייתא כניצוד ועומד נותנין לפניהם מזונות וכן חיה ועוף שבביברין מקורין דחשיב טפי מזונותיהם עליך אבל כאן שמן התורה אין ניצודין לא חשיב מזונותיהן עליך והוי כאותן שהן כל שעה בשדה כמו יוני שובך ויוני עלייה ואתי שפיר לפי זה ההיא דריש אין לדין (ביצה דף כד·) דקתני התם במתניתין רשב"ג אומר זה הכלל המחוסר צידה אסור כו' וקאמר בגמרא היכי דמי מחוסר צידה כגון דאמר הבא מצודה ונצודנו אמר ליה אביי לרב יוסף והרי אווזים ותרנגולים דאמר הבא מצודה ונצודנו ואמר הלך אווזים ותרנגולים ויוני הרדסיאות פטור והשתא קשה מאי פריך והא פטור משמע אבל אסור ובמתניתין קתני נמי רשב"ג אומר מחוסר צידה אסור ולמאי דפי' הכא אתי שפיר דרשב"ג קאי ארישא דקתני אין לדין ואין נותנין לפניהם מזונות וקא אסר רשב"ג במחוסר צידה אף ליתן מזונות וא"כ מחוסר צידה דאורייתא חשיב ליה ולהכי פריך שפיר:

הלכה מכלל דפליגי · אע"ג דר' יהודה פליג מ"מ פריך אביי שפיר דאי לאפוקי מדרבי יהודה אתא לימא אין הלכה כרבי יהודה הכא אתי שפיר דלא קבעי היכי דמי מחוסר צידה דהא כבר פי' דהיכא דאיכא עוקצי ביבר גדול ומסתמא דהייט מחוסר צידה דרשב"ג אבל בריש אין לדין (ביצה דף כד·) קשה אמאי קבעי ה"ד מחוסר צידה הואיל וכבר פי' ביבר גדול וביבר קטן לרבנן ונראה לריב"א משום דהתם קתני במילתייהו חיה ועוף ועלה קאי רשב"ג וקבעי ה"ד מחוסר צידה בעופות אבל אחיה לא קבעי דזה כבר פירש וכן משמע דכל הנהו דמייתי עלה לא מיירי אלא בעופות אבל הכא לא איירו רבנן בעופות אלא בחיה גרידא:

*היכא דנפלי טולא דכתלים · היה להם שיעור הכתלים שוה והיו יודעין שיעורן: (עיין לעיל)

למה זה דומה לנועל ביתו לשומרו ונמצא צבי שמור בתוכו · ואם תאמר מאי אולמא דהך מהך ונראה לריב"א דס"ד דבא וישב בצידו ליתסר משום דמיחזי להוסיף שמירה לצבי הוא בא: וממאי

(א) לקמן קיג· עירובין ס: ביצה כד· ע"ז לב.

עין משפט נר מצוה

כו א ב ג ד מיי' פי' מהל' שבת הלכה כ סמג שם טוש"ע שם סעיף א:

כז ה מיי' שם הל' כא טוש"ע שם סעיף ב:

כח ו מיי' שם הלכה כד טוש"ע שם:

כט ז מיי' וסמג שם טוש"ע שם סעיף ג:

ל ח מיי' שם הלכה כג סמג שם טוש"ע שם סעיף ה:

לא ט מיי' שם הל' יט: [נ"ל אבל צדין חיה ועוף מן הביברין וכ"א במשנה דביצה]

לב י מיי' שם הל' כג סמג שם טוש"ע שם סעיף ו:

רבינו חננאל

בחבורה פטור שחטו שלאלשמו ושלא לאוכליו כו' וכולא שמעתא דקא מפרש ליה בהדא חדא מאי תיקן ולא מפרש מ"ד המקלקל בחבורה פטור מאן הוא אלא מתניתין בהדיא היא כל המקלקלין פטורין בין חובל דמקלקל בחבורה בין דחד מיניה (וקרא) [וקאמר] ר"ש ור' יהודה היא*דשמעינןפלוגתייהו תרסינן בבתולה נשאת אם תמצא לומר דם חבורי מהבר שהבועל בתחלה הוא עושה חבורה הא אמרינן אם תמצא לומר הלכה כר' יהודה דאמר שאין מתכוין אסור מי הואי האי בועל בשבת מקלקל בהאי חבורה אי לא. ואם תימצא לומר מקלקל הוא במקלקל הלכה כר' יהודה או כר' שמעון והכין פירושא הלכה כר' יהודה דאמר מקלקל בחבורה פטור או הלכה כר' שמעון דאמר חייב דאי אמרת הלכה כר' שמעון דאמר מקלקל בחבורה חייב או הלכה כר' יהודה דאמר דבר שאין מתכוין אסור אילו היה כך אסור לבעול בתחלה בשבת וחזינן דמפרש (בספינה) לעולם רב כר' יהודה סבירא ליה דאמר דבר שאין מתכוין אסור. אלא מיהו מקלקל בחבורה הוא ושרי לר' יהודה ואמרי' מ"מ דר' שמעון דאמר חובל ומבעיר אע"פ שמקלקלין חייבין מדאצטריךקרא למישרא מילה בשבת תמרינן דמקלקל בחבורהבעלמא בשבת חייב ואקשינן מילה מתקן הוא כדרב אשי דאמר מה לי לתקן מילה מה לי לתקןכלי מה לי לבשל פתילה מה לי לבשל סמנין ולא נמרי' מינה למקלקלין ומקלקל לא אשכחנן דאיתמר: שיעור המלבן צמר כמלא רחב הסיט כפול וכן המנפץ צמר וכן הצובע וכן הטווה רב יוסף מחוי[כפוף]מעיקר הגודל עד ראש אצבע כשהן דבוקות זו בזו רב חייא בר אמי מחוי פשוט מראש גודל עד ראש אצבע כשהן פשוטות דאעפ"כ אינן הוות זרת:ר' יהודה אומ' הצד צפור למגדל כו' פי' מגדל זה של עץ הוא שחשוב ככלוב גדול אם פתח שער המגדל ועשה תחבולות עד שנכנס הצפור לתוכו וסגר עליו חייב כי כסגרו המגדל תמה הצידה וגם אם הולך אחר צבי והחזירו מיכן ומיכן עד שנכנס לבית חייב כי כיון שנכנס לבית והוא סגר עליו הרי צידו חייב אבל אם

* נלהדפיס יש כאן ואולי צ"ל ומהא הוא דמעיין פלוגתייהו .

מסורת הש"ס

שייך לע"א

[ביצה כג:]

[שם כל השנין ע"ש]

[תוספתא דביצה פ"ג]

[ביצה כד.]

ברכות לג: [לעיל ע: לקמן קיג. קטו. ביצה כד. עירובין ס: ע"ז לב.] [פסחים קי.]

[גיר' הערוך אוכלא פי' עייפות]

[לקמן קז: ביצה לו:]

[תוספתא פ"ג]

לעיל לג:

הגהות הב"ח

(א) גמ' וצבי לבית ולגינה ולחצר: (ב) שם הא בביבר מקורה הא בביבר: (ג) רש"י ד"ה הגזין מין חגב טהור. נ"ב וצ"ע מפ"ק דכתובות דשם משמע דהוא מין שרץ טמא שוב מלאתי קושיא זו בספר פרי חדש סי' פ"א: (ד) ד"ה הא שני זה למה דומה: (ה) ד"ה והמלא וכו' כתוכן כך אפיים:

גליון הש"ס

רש"י ד"ה הגזין מין חגב טהור. עיין ז ע"ב וכתו' פ"א הלכה כא מהל' מאכלות אסורות:

רב נסים גאון

תבערו אש בכל מושבותיכם ביום השבת על פי מה שנתפרש פסוק זה כי בבית דין הוא מדבר כמו שנא' בראש מסכת יבמות (דף ו) מושבות מה תלמוד מכדי שבת חובת הגוף היא וחובת הגוף נוהגת בארץ ובחוצה לארץ מושבות דכתב רחמנא למה לי משום ר' ישמעאל אמר תלמיד אחד לפי שנא' (דברים כא) וכי יהיה באיש חטא משפט מות והומת שומע אני בין בחול בין בשבת ומה אני מקיים (שמות לא) מחלליה מות יומת בשאר מלאכות חוץ ממיתת בית דין ת"ל לא תבערו אש בכל מושבותיכם מה מושבות האמורות להלן בבית דין אף כאן בב"ד ואמר רחמנא לא תבערו אש ועיקר זו הברייתא בסוף מכילתא דר' ישמעאל ואמרו עוד בתלמוד ותיהוי נמי ר' יוסי אימור דאמר ר' יוסי הבערה ללאו יצאת הבערה דעלמא הבערה דבית דין בישול פתילה היא ואמר רב אשי מה לי בישול פתילה מה לי בישול סממנין מיכן למדנו דאסר רחמנא הבערה דבת כהן בשבת ונתחייבו מיכן שהמבעיר בעלמא חייב: רבן גמליאל אומר לא כל הביברין שוין זה הכלל כל מחוסר צידה פטור ושאינו מחוסר צידה חייב. במסכת יום טוב בפרק אין צדין (דף כד) גרסי' היכי דמי מחוסר צידה אמר רב יוסף אמר רב יהודה אמר שמואל כגון דאמרי הבא מצודה ונצודנו ולא יעלה על דעתך שמה שאמרו שם רבן שמעון בן גמליאל אומר לא כל הביברין שוין זה הכלל כל המחוסר צידה אסור ושאינו מחוסר צידה מותר דוחה מה שאמרנו כן אלא השני דברים מעיקר אחד הם והואי כי מה שעומד בביבר והוא עדיין מחוסר צידה פטור מן החטא' כשהוא שגג כי מלאכת הצידה לא נגמרה ואם בעומדו בתוך נשלמה בו הצידה ואינו מחוסר צידה חייב חטאת לפי שעשה מלאכה נגמרה ועל זה העיקר שפירשנו נמצא כל מה שהוא עומד והוא מחוסר צידה אסור ליקח ממנו ביום טוב כי לא נגמרה

INTO A TURRET, [106b] AND A DEER INTO A GARDEN,[11] COURTYARD OR VIVARIUM, IS LIABLE. R. SIMEON B. GAMALIEL SAID: NOT ALL VIVARIA ARE ALIKE. THIS IS THE GENERAL PRINCIPLE: IF IT [STILL] NEEDS TO BE CAUGHT, HE IS EXEMPT;
a IF IT DOES NOT STILL NEED TO BE CAUGHT,[1] HE IS LIABLE.

GEMARA. We learnt elsewhere: Fish may not be caught out of aquaria on a Festival, nor may food be placed before them; but beasts and birds may be caught out of vivaria, and food may be placed before them. But the following contradicts it: As for vivaria of beasts, birds and fish, one may not catch [the animals, etc.] out of them on a Festival, and we may not place food before them: [thus the rulings on] beasts are contradictory, and [the rulings on] birds are contradictory. As for [the rulings on] beasts, it is well: there is no difficulty, one agreeing with R. Judah,[2] the other with the Rabbis.[3] But [the rulings on] birds are contradictory? And should you say, [The rulings on] birds too are not contradictory: one refers to a covered vivarium,[4] whereas the other refers to an uncovered vivarium—[It might be asked]: But a house is covered, yet both R. Judah and the Rabbis hold, Only [if one hunts a bird] into a turret [is he culpable], but not [if he hunts it] into a house?—Said Rabbah b. R. Huna: Here we treat of a free bird,[5] [the reason being] because it does not submit to domestication.[6] For the School of R. Ishmael taught: Why is it called a free bird? Because it dwells in a house [free] just as in the field. Now that you have arrived at this [answer], [the rulings on] beasts too are not contradictory: one refers to a large vivarium, the other to a small vivarium. What is a large vivarium and what is a small vivarium? Said R. Ashi: Where one can run after and catch it with a single lunge, that is a small vivarium; any other is a large vivarium. Alternatively, if the shadows of the walls fall upon each other, it is a small vivarium; otherwise it is a large vivarium.
b Alternatively, if there are not many recesses,[1] it is a small vivarium; otherwise it is a large vivarium.[2]

R. SIMEON B. GAMALIEL SAID, etc. R. Joseph said in Rab Judah's name in Samuel's name: The *halachah* is as R. Simeon b. Gamaliel. Said Abaye to him, [You say,] The *halachah* [etc.]: hence it follows that they [the Rabbis] disagree?[3] And what difference does that make? he replied.[4] Shall one learn a tradition as it were [merely] a song? he retorted.[5]

Our Rabbis taught: If one catches a deer that is blind or asleep, he is culpable; a deer that is lame, aged or sick, he is exempt. Abaye asked R. Joseph: What is the difference between them?—The former try to escape;[6] the latter do not try to escape. But it was taught: [If one catches] a sick [deer] he is culpable?—Said R. Shesheth, There is no difficulty: one refers to [an animal] sick with fever;[7] the other to [an animal] sick through exhaustion.

Our Rabbis taught: He who catches locusts, *gazin*,[8] hornets, or gnats on the Sabbath is culpable: that is the view of R. Meir. But the Sages rule: If that species is hunted, one is liable; if that species is not hunted, one is not liable.[9] Another [Baraitha] taught: He who catches locusts at the time of dew is not liable;[10] at the time of dry heat [midday], is liable. Eleazar b. Mahabai said: If they advance in thick swarms, he is not culpable.[11] The scholars asked: Does Eleazar b. Mahabai refer to the first clause or to the last?—Come and hear: He who catches locusts at the time of dew is not liable; at the time of dry heat, is liable. Eleazar b. Mahabai said: Even at the time of dry heat, if they advance in thick swarms he is not culpable.

MISHNAH. IF A DEER ENTERS A HOUSE AND ONE PERSON SHUTS [THE DOOR] BEFORE IT, HE IS CULPABLE; IF TWO SHUT IT, THEY ARE EXEMPT. IF ONE COULD NOT SHUT IT, AND BOTH SHUT IT, THEY ARE CULPABLE. R. SIMEON DE-
c CLARES [THEM] EXEMPT.[1]

GEMARA. R. Jeremiah b. Abba said in Samuel's name: If one catches a lion on the Sabbath he is not culpable unless he entices it into its cage.

MISHNAH. IF ONE SITS DOWN IN THE DOORWAY BUT DOES NOT FILL IT, AND A SECOND SITS DOWN AND FILLS IT,[2] THE SECOND IS CULPABLE. IF THE FIRST SITS DOWN IN THE DOORWAY AND FILLS IT, AND A SECOND COMES AND SITS DOWN AT HIS SIDE, EVEN IF THE FIRST [THEN] RISES AND DEPARTS, THE FIRST IS CULPABLE WHILE THE SECOND IS EXEMPT. WHAT DOES THIS RESEMBLE? ONE WHO SHUTS HIS HOUSE TO GUARD IT,[3] AND A DEER IS [THEREBY] FOUND TO BE GUARDED THEREIN.[4]

(11) BaḤ reads: into a house, garden, etc. V. Halevy, *Doroth*, I, 3, pp. 233-234 and n. 38 a.l.

a (1) The animal having been driven into a place where it is easy to seize it. (2) In our Mishnah. Since he holds that only when an animal is in a house is it regarded as trapped, it follows that it is not trapped in a vivarium, and therefore if one catches a beast out of a vivarium he is guilty, in accordance with the general principle of the Mishnah. (3) That it is trapped even in a vivarium. (4) In which a bird is regarded as already trapped, and so one may catch a bird out of it on a Festival. (5) Swallow(?). It lives in a house just as in the open and it is difficult to catch it there. But other birds are trapped when driven into a house. (6) Lit., 'authority'.

b (1) Into which the animals may run when chased. (2) On the whole passage v. Beẓ. 23b. (3) But it has just been stated that they too differentiate between large and small vivaria. (4) If the Rabbis do not disagree, the *halachah* is certainly so. (5) I.e., why use words superfluously? (6) Their senses are on the alert and they feel the attempt to take them. Hence they need hunting and catching. (7) That animal tries to escape. (8) Rashi: *hagazin*; a species of wild bees, or locusts, Jast. (9) Nobody hunts gnats or hornets, as they are of no use. (10) Rashi: they are blind then and need no catching. (11) They are easily taken and need no catching.

c (1) In accordance with his view *supra* 92b. (2) Thereby effectively trapping an animal that has entered the house. (3) But not to trap an animal. (4) I.e., a deer which had previously been caught; so here too the first, by filling up the doorway, traps the deer, and the second only guards an animal already caught.

GEMARA. [107a] R. Abba said in R. Ḥiyya b. Ashi's name in Rab's name: If a bird creeps under the skirts [of one's garments], he may sit and guard it[5] until evening. R. Naḥman b. Isaac objected: IF THE FIRST SITS DOWN IN THE DOORWAY AND FILLS IT, AND A SECOND COMES AND SITS DOWN AT HIS SIDE, EVEN IF THE FIRST [THEN] RISES AND DEPARTS, THE FIRST IS CULPABLE WHILE THE SECOND IS EXEMPT. Surely that means, he is EXEMPT, yet it is forbidden?—No: he is exempt, and it is permitted. Reason too supports this: since the second clause teaches, WHAT DOES THIS RESEMBLE? ONE WHO SHUTS HIS HOUSE TO GUARD IT, AND A DEER IS [THEREBY] FOUND TO BE GUARDED THEREIN, it follows that it means, he is EXEMPT, and it is permitted.[1] Others state, R. Naḥman b. Isaac said: We too learnt thus: EVEN IF THE FIRST [THEN] RISES AND DEPARTS, THE FIRST IS CULPABLE, WHILE THE SECOND IS EXEMPT: surely that means, he is EXEMPT, and it is permitted? No: he is EXEMPT, yet it is forbidden. But since the second clause states, WHAT DOES THIS RESEMBLE? ONE WHO SHUTS HIS HOUSE TO GUARD IT, AND A DEER IS [THEREBY] FOUND TO BE GUARDED THEREIN, it follows that he is EXEMPT, and it is permitted. This proves it.

Samuel said: Everything [taught as] involving no liability on the Sabbath involves [indeed] no liability, yet is forbidden, save these three, which involve no liability and are permitted. This [*sc.* the capture of a deer] is one. And how do you know that he is exempt and it is permitted? Because the second clause teaches: WHAT DOES THIS RESEMBLE? ONE WHO SHUTS HIS HOUSE TO GUARD IT, AND A DEER IS THEREBY FOUND TO BE GUARDED THEREIN. A second [is this]: If one manipulates an abscess on the Sabbath, if in order to make an opening for it, he is liable;[2] if in order to draw the matter out of it, he is exempt. And how do you know that he is exempt and it is permitted? Because we learnt: A small needle[3] [may be moved on the Sabbath] for the purpose of extracting a thorn.[4] And the third: If one catches a snake on the Sabbath: if he is engaged therewith [*sc.* in catching it] so that it should not bite him,[5] he
b is exempt; if for a remedy,[1] he is liable. And how do you know that he is exempt and it is permitted?—Because we learnt: A dish may be inverted over a lamp, that the beams should not catch [fire], or over an infant's excrements, or over a scorpion, that it should not bite.[2]

CHAPTER XIV

MISHNAH. REGARDING THE EIGHT REPTILES [SHERA-
c ZIM] WHICH ARE MENTIONED IN THE TORAH,[1] HE WHO CATCHES OR WOUNDS THEM [ON THE SABBATH] IS CULPABLE;[2] BUT [AS FOR] OTHER ABOMINATIONS AND CREEPING THINGS,[3] HE WHO WOUNDS THEM IS EXEMPT; HE WHO CATCHES THEM, BECAUSE HE NEEDS THEM, HE IS LIABLE; IF HE DOES NOT NEED THEM, HE IS EXEMPT; AS FOR A BEAST OR BIRD IN ONE'S PRIVATE DOMAIN, HE WHO CATCHES IT IS EXEMPT; HE WHO WOUNDS IT IS CULPABLE.

GEMARA. Since he [the Tanna] teaches, HE WHO WOUNDS THEM IS CULPABLE, it follows that they have skin.[4] Which Tanna [maintains this]?—Said Samuel, It is R. Joḥanan b. Nuri. For we learnt, R. Joḥanan b. Nuri said: The eight reptiles have skins.[5] Rabbah son of R. Huna said in Rab's name, You may even say [that this agrees with] the Rabbis: the Rabbis disagree with R. Joḥanan b. Nuri only in respect of defilement, because it is written, *And these are they which are unclean unto you*,[6] extending [the law to teach] that their skins are as their flesh; but in respect to the Sabbath even the Rabbis agree. But do they not differ in respect of the Sabbath? Surely it was taught: He who catches one of the eight reptiles mentioned in the Torah, [or] he who wounds them, is culpable: this is R. Joḥanan b. Nuri's view. But the Sages maintain:

(5) To prevent it from flying away.
(1) For obviously one may lock his house in order to guard it. (2) Rashi: either on account of building an opening, or because of mending, for there is no difference between mending a utensil and mending (i.e., healing) a wound. (3) Lit., 'hand-needle'. (4) Because it pains him, and matter which causes pain is similar. (5) '*Mith'assek*' may be understood in the sense of performing indirect labour, i.e., he catches it only incidentally, as he does not need the snake but merely desires to prevent it from doing harm.
(1) The snake's poison can be used medicinally. (2) Though it is thereby caught.
c (1) As unclean, i.e., non-edible; Lev. XI, 29f. (2) These have a skin distinct from the flesh (v. *infra*), and a wound does not completely heal but leaves a scar; this is regarded as a minor degree of killing, i.e., part of the animal's life is taken away. (3) E.g., worms, insects, snakes, etc. (4) V. n. c2. (5) V. Ḥul. 122a. The Rabbis rule that the skins of four of these defile by the same standard as their flesh, viz., the size of a lentil. Thus they hold that their skin is not distinct from their flesh, and R. Joḥanan b. Nuri disputes it. (6) Ibid.

גמ' אמר רבי אבא אמר רב חייא בר אשי אמר רב *נכנסה לו צפור תחת כנפיו יושב ומשמרו עד שתחשך מתיב רב נחמן בר יצחק ישב הראשון על הפתח ומלאהו ובא השני וישב בצדו אף על פי שעמד הראשון והלך לו הראשון חייב והשני פטור מאי לאו פטור אבל אסור [ב]לא פטור ומותר הכי נמי מסתברא מדקתני סיפא למה זה דומה לנועל את ביתו לשומרו ונמצא צבי שמור בתוכו מכלל דפטור ומותר ש"מ איכא דאמרי אמר רב נחמן בר יצחק אף אנן נמי תנינא אע"פ שעמד הראשון והלך לו הראשון חייב והשני פטור מאי לאו פטור ומותר לא פטור אבל אסור הא מדקתני סיפא הא למה זה דומה לנועל את ביתו לשומרו ונמצא צבי שמור בתוכו מכלל דפטור ומותר ש"מ *אמר שמואל [ג]כל פטורי דשבת פטור אבל אסור לבר מהני תלת דפטור ומותר חדא הא וממאי דפטור ומותר דקתני סיפא למה זה דומה לנועל את ביתו לשומרו ונמצא צבי שמור בתוכו ואידך *[ד]המפיס מורסא בשבת אם לעשות לה פה חייב אם להוציא ממנה לחה פטור וממאי דפטור ומותר דתנן *מחט של יד ליטול בה את הקוץ ואידך [ה]הצד נחש בשבת אם מתעסק בו שלא ישכנו פטור אם לרפואה חייב וממאי דפטור ומותר דתנן *כופין קערה על הנר בשביל שלא תאחוז בקורה ועל צואה של קטן ועל עקרב שלא (א) תישך:

הדרן עלך האורג

שמנה [א]שרצים האמורים בתורה הצדן והחובל בהן חייב ושאר שקצים ורמשים החובל בהן פטור הצדן לצורך חייב שלא לצורך פטור [ב]חיה ועוף שברשותו הצדן פטור והחובל בהן חייב: גמ' מדקתני החובל (ב) בהן חייב מכלל דאית להו עור מאן תנא אמר שמואל רבי יוחנן בן נורי היא *דתנן רבי יוחנן בן נורי אומר שמנה שרצים יש להן עורות רבה בר רב הונא אמר רב אפילו תימא רבנן עד כאן לא פליגי רבנן עליה דרבי יוחנן בן נורי אלא לענין טומאה דכתיב °אלה הטמאים לכם *[ח]לרבות שעורותיהן כבשרן אבל לענין שבת אפילו רבנן מודו ולענין שבת לא פליגי והתניא הצד אחד משמנה שרצים האמורים בתורה החובל בהן חייב דברי ר' יוחנן בן נורי וחכמים אומרים אין עור אלא למה

ויקרא יא

רש"י

גמ' תחת כנפיו. תחת כנפי כסותו ואין יכול לצאת שנכנע בפניו מאליו: יושב ומשמרו. כן ואינו צריך לפתוח לו חלון דאינו אלא שומר: לנועל את ביתו. דכל אדם עושין כן: המפיס. מבקע מורסא קויטור"א: אם לעשות לה פה. בתוספתא* תני הכי אם לקולפה ולעשות לה פה כדרך שרופאים של עכשיו עושין דמתקן לה פתח: חייב. משום בונה פתח או משום מתקן כלי מה לי לתקן מכה מה לי לתקן כלי: ואם להוציא לחה. של עכשיו ואינו חושש אם תחזור ותסתום מיד: פטור. ומותר דאין כאן תיקון ורבנן נמי לא גזור בה שבות משום צערא: ומחט של יד. ניטלת בשבת: ליטול בה את הקוץ. והיינו דומיא דלחה דמצער ליה ואינו חושש אם יסתם מיד וקאמר ניטלת לכתחילה מחט של יד היא מחט שתופרין בה בגדים ומשום דקתני בהדה ושל שק לפתוח בה את הדלת קרי לה להאי מחט של יד: קערה. של חרס: כופין. לכתחילה ולא שיכבה את הנר ואשמעינן דכלי ניטל להצלת דבר שאינו ניטל בשבת: על עקרב שלא תשוך. ואע"ג דממילא מתליד:

הדרן עלך האורג

שמנה שרצים. החולד והעכבר וגו' (ויקרא יא): הצדן. חייב שבמינו ניצוד: והחובל בהן חייב. דיש להן עור כדמפרש בגמרא והויא ליה חבורה שאינה חוזרת והויא ליה תולדה דשוחט. לוי"ה. ל"א כיון דיש להן עור נצבע העור בדם הנצרר בו (ג)דחייב משום צובע: ושאר שקצים ורמשים. כגון תולעת ונחשים ועקרבים: החובל בהן פטור. דאין להם עור: שלא לצורך פטור. דאין במינו ניצוד והויא מלאכה שאינה צריכה לגופה ור' שמעון היא כדמוקי לה בגמ': חיה ועוף שברשותו. פטור אם לדן שהרי ניצודין ועומדין: והחובל בהן חייב. דיש להן עור: גמ' שמונה שרצים יש להן עורות. ופליג אדרבנן דאמרי בהעור והרוטב האנקה הכח והלטאה והחומט עורותיהן מטמאין בכעדשה כבשרן אלמא הני ארבעה לית להו עור: אלה הטמאים. בתר האנקה והכח כתיב ודרשינן ה' יתירה דהטמאים לרבות שעורותיהן כבשרן וכתיב אלה למעוטי הנך דקרא קמא החולד והעכבר והצב: אפילו רבנן מודו. דיש להן עור למה

תוספות

וממאי דפטור ומותר דתנן מחט של יד ליטול בה את הקוץ. למאי דמסיק בריש פ' הנחנקין (סנהדרין דף פה:) דאתיא כר"ש אתי שפיר דמיירי אפילו ודאי חביל ומשום שאינה צריכה לגופה שרי אבל לפי מאי דפריך התם והא דתנן מחט של יד ליטול בה את הקוץ ליחוש דילמא חביל לא פשיט הכא מיניה שפיר דבמפיס מורסא דודאי עושה פתח שמא יהא אסור ואומר ר"י דאפילו למאי דס"ד התם פשיט שפיר דמסתבר דככולי עלמא אתיא אפילו כר' יהודה וכיון דרבי יהודה דאסר בעלמא דבר שאין מתכוין אפילו אינו פסיק רישיה שרי הכא משום צערא דגופא לר"ש נמי במפיס מורסא דהוי מלאכה שאינה צריכה לגופה שרי לכתחילה מהאי טעמא:

הדרן עלך האורג

שמנה שרצים החובל בהן חייב. לשון ספי' הקונטר' משום נטילת נשמה עיקר כדפי' בפרק כלל גדול (לעיל דף עה.): הצדן לצורך חייב. וא"ת מ"ש דאיצטריך הכא למיתני טפי הצדן לצורך חייב בכל חיובי דשבת נמי לא מחייב ר"ש אלא לצורך ואומר ר"י דלהכי תנא ליה הכא לאשמעינן דבשאר שקצים ורמשים שאין להן עור צריך שיתכוין לשום צורך דסתמיה לאו לצורך קיימי אבל בשמונה שרצים דרישא דיש להם עור סתמייהו ניצודין לצורך עורן להכי תני לדן בהדי חובל דמחייב נמי משום עור: שלא לצורך פטור. פירש רש"י דאין במינו ניצוד ואינו נראה דהא מאן דפטר אין במינו ניצוד פוטר אפילו לצורך אלא יש לפרש דאפילו במינו ניצוד פטור משום דהויא מלאכה שאינה צריכה לגופה ור"ת מחקו מן הפירושים: אמר שמואל ר' יוחנן בן נורי היא דאמר שמונה שרצים יש להם עור. תימה לר"י דע"כ לא פליגי רבנן עליה דרבי יוחנן אלא לענין טומאה אבל בשבת דילמא מודו ליה דהא עור של עגל הרך הוי כבשר לענין טומאה והחובל בו בשבת חייב וכן עור של עוף מסתמא הוי כבשר שרך הוא ותנן חיה ועוף שברשותו החובל בהן חייב וי"ל דעור של עגל הרך ושל עוף אע"ג דחשיב עור הוי כבשר לענין טומאה משום דרכיכן וראוין לאכילה אבל עור ח' שרצים סבר שמואל דטעמא דרבנן דחשיבי ליה כבשר משום דאזלי בתר גישתא כדמפרש בהעור והרוטב (חולין דף קכב:) ולא משום רכיכות דלא רכיך כולי האי וכיון דלית להו ממשות עור החובל בהן פטור כמו בשאר שקצים ורמשים: ע"כ לא פליגי רבנן אלא לענין טומאה דכתיב אלה הטמאים. וא"ת והא מסקינן בפ' העור והרוטב (שם) דבגישתא קמיפלגי ופי' בקונט' התם דרבנן לא דרשי הטמאים ואיכא למימר דרב דהכא לטעמיה דתני התם תנשמת ולא אזיל בתר גישתא ומיהו בלאו הכי א"א לומר התם כדפי' הקונטרס דלמאי איצטריך למימר התם רב תנא הוא ופליג והא ע"כ ברייתא דדריש הטמאים קיימא כרב ע"כ נראה דרבנן דמתני' דהתם נמי אית להו דרשה דהטמאים אבל לית להו (ד) למינהו הפסיק הענין וכתב הטמאים לרבות ואלה למעט ומוקמינן ריבויא אהנהו ארבע דלית להו גישתא האנקה והכח והלטאה והחומט ורב מרבה כל הנהו דכתיב בתר למינהו וגם תנשמת בכלל וקצת קשה דאמרינן לקמן מאן ת"ק רבי יהודה דאזיל בתר גישתא והא רבנן נמי אזלו בתר גישתא ואפילו הכי דרשי הטמאים וה"כ נימא לרבי יהודה וא"כ נמי נימא עד כאן לא פליג רבי יהודה אלא לענין טומאה דכתיב הטמאים אבל לענין שבת מודה:

עין משפט נר מצוה

לג א מיי' פ"י מהלכות שבת הלכה כג סמג לאוין סה:
לד ב מיי' שם טוש"ע א"ח סי' שט"ז סעי' ז:
לה ג מיי' פ"א מהל' שבת הל' ג סמג שם:
לו ד מיי' שם פ"י הל' יז סמג שם טוש"ע א"ח סי' שכח סעיף כח:
לז ה מיי' שם הל' כה וסמג שם טוש"ע א"ח סי' שטז סעיף ז:
א ו מיי' שם הלכה כא וס"ח שם הלכה ט סמג שם וטוש"ע שם סעיף ח:
ב ז מיי' שם פ"י הל' כד טוש"ע שם סעי' יב:
ג ח מיי' פ"ד מהלכות אבות הטומאות הל' ח סמג עשין רנט:

רבינו חננאל

טרד לצבי עד שנכנס לבינה או לחצר או לביבר בשבת. הרי זו אינה צידה ופטור וחכ"א אפי' טרדו לבינה או לחצר או לביבר וכלאו שם הרי זו צידה וחייב ורמינן מתניתין אהדדי תנא (ביצה דף כג) אבל צדין חיה מן הביברין בי"ט כי חיה שהיא בביבר זו (צידה בביבר) צידתה. וכשנוטלה מן הביבר אינו חשוב כצידה ותניא ביברין של חיה [ושל עופות] אין צדין מהן ביום טוב שמעינן מינה כי חיה שבביבר לאי כצודה דמיא ועכשיו הוא צד אותה ואוקימנא למתני' כחכמים דאמרי הצד חיה לביבר חייב ומשום הכי צדין אותה ביום טוב ובריי'. כר' יהודה אלא עופות אעופות קשיא דמתניתין שריא למיצד עוף מן הביברין ובריי' אוסרת וכי תימא כי שריא מתניתין מביבר מקורה ובריי' אסרה מביבר שאינו מקורה והא בית דמקורה הוא ור' יהודה ורבנן מודו כי הכולא צפור בתוכו בשבת אינו חייב דלא דמו לצד ולאו הוא צד אלא בזמן שצדו למגדל וכל מאן דפטר על זה בשבת אסיר למיצד מיניה בי"ט וכל מאן דמחייב עליה בשבת שרי למיצד מיניה בי"ט וכ"ע על צפור למגדל מחייב בשבת על צפור לבית לא מחייב והכין קשיא היכי שריא מתני' עוף מן הביבר בי"ט ובשבת פטור עליה או היכי אפטר בשבת ובי"ט אוסר אמר רבה בר הונא הכא בצפור דרור עסקינן כו' פי' כי קתני בשבת הצד צפור לבית פטור בצפור דרור ואפי' כד מיבחשה לא חבשה נפשה בצידה לפי שאינה מקבלת מרות אבל צפור אחרת דלא רגילה בבית מאלתר שיסגו' עליה בית מקורה מקבלת מרות וכצודה דמיא וחייב עליה בשבת וכיון שחייב עליה בשבת שרי לצודה בי"ט. השתא דאתית להכי לענין עוף ואוקימתה זו *)ששנויה בשבת בביבר שאינו מקורה והשניה בי"ט בביבר מקורה ונקטינן מהדדי חיה אחיה [נמי כי אקשי] לן ואוקימתיה חדא לר' יהודה וחדא לרבנן לא צריכין להכין אלא מתני' דקתני צדין חיה מן הביברין בביבר קטן ובריי' דתני אין צדין בביבר גדול היכי דמי ביבר גדול[היכי] דמי ביבר קטן ופירשנו בה ג' פירושי וכולן קיימין ואתו הדין פירוקא קרוב לדר' שמעון בן גמליאל דאמר לא כל ביבר המחוסר צידה וצריך למיצדיה בתר הכין פטור עליו בשבת ואסור לצוד ממנו ביו"ט וכל ביבר שאינו מחוסר צידה חייב עליו בשבת וצדין ממנו בי"ט והלכתא כר' שמעון בן גמליאל ומפורש בי"ט היכי דמי מחוסר צידה ואסיקנא שבאות לכלובן ולא בעיין לרבויי פי' רבי' שאורב להן בדרך שהצייד אורב לצודו כדכתיב יארוב במסתר ג' ידכה ישוח ומצפיר להן מיכן ומיכן והכין הצד צבי פתי סומא וישן חייב משום רבויי חיגר או זקן או חולה מחמת אוצנא פטור דלא בעי רבויי חגבין גזין והן מטיני דבורים צירעין ויתושין כל שבמינו ניצוד הצדן בשבת חייב וכל שאין במינו ניצוד הצדן בשבת פטור ודגבים ודאי יש במינו ניצד בשעת הטל אין יכולות לפרוח שאין בהן כח ואין צריכין צידה אלא ניטלת ביד ובשעת השרב אם מלקחות ובאות כמים הנשפכין או כדבר הירוי

*) דברי רבינו צריך ביאור לכאורה דהא מתניתין דא"ל והברייתא הכל ביו"ט מיירי וע"ז קא מהדר הא בביבר מקורה וכו' ול"ע.

הגהות הב"ח

(א) גמ' ועל עקרב שלא ישוך. נ"ב ונ"ע מגמ' דברכות פ' אין עומדין ריש דף לג אבל מלאתי בתוס' לעיל דף ג ד"ה בר מהני תלת דכאן אין הטעם משום סכנה רק מכת מלאכה דלאו צריך לגופיה א"כ בזה אין חילוק בין נחש לעקרב ודו"ק והוא אמת גמור ת"ל: (ב) שם והחובל בהן: (ג) רש"י ד"ה והחובל וכו' ותייב משום: (ד) תוס' ד"ה ע"כ וכו' אבל לית להו דלמינהו הפסיק:

מסורת הש"ס

עדיות פ"ג · לעיל ג. · לקמן פ"ב כתובות ו: עדיות פ"ב מ"ס · לקמן קכב: סנהדרין פד: [עדיות פ"ב מ"ה] · לעיל מג. ודף קכא. · חולין קכב. · [חולין קכב: תוספתא חולין פ"ח]

רב נסים גאון

נגמרה בו הצידה ולכך הוא בשבת פטור לפי שלא עשה מלאכה שהרי מחוסר צידה עדיין ומי שלוקח ממנו ביום טוב עובר על מה שכתוב (במדבר כח) כל מלאכת עבודה לא תעשו מפני שאי אפשר ליקח מה שיש בתוך הביבר אלא בעשיית צידה ולכן אמרו אסור ואם היה אותו ביבר אינו מחוסר צידה מי שרדף אחרי ציד עד שהגיעו לתוכו בשבת חייב כי עשה מלאכה ומה שהוא עומד בתוכו ביום טוב כבר נגמרה בו הצידה ומותר ליטול ולאכול ממנו לפי שמה שהוא לוקח כבר ניצוד ונגמרה בו מלאכה ולא עשה ביום טוב מלאכת עבודה ולפיכך אמרו בי"ט ושאינו מחוסר צידה מותר ואמרו בתוספתא דשבת (פרק יג) הצד יוני עלייה ויוני שובך וציפורים שקיננו בטפיחין או בבירה וכל שמחוסר צידה חייב לפי שעשה מלאכה האווז והתרנגולין ויוני הרדסיות וכל דבר שאין מחוסר צידה פטור מפני שלקח ממה שנגמרה בו הצידה ולא עשה ביום השבת מלאכה ולפיכך הוא פטור כמו שפירשנו נתבאר לך עכשיו כי השני דברים שוין וכי דבר שהייב עליו בשבת מפני שנגמרה מלאכתו מותר לקחת ממנו ביום טוב ובדבר שפטור עליו בשבת מפני שלא נגמרה מלאכתו אסור ליטול ממנו ביום טוב שהרי מחוסר עשייה והרי עשה עבודה ביום טוב וכמו כן עוד התוספתא שוה למשנה ועיקר זה כי צד בשבת לביבר שאינו מחוסר צידה חייב והצד ממנו פטור והצד בשבת לביבר המחוסר צידה פטור והצד ממנו חייב ודברי המשנה הן אמורין בהצד לביבר ודברי התוספתא הן בהצד ממנו ואין ביניהן חלוקה בדין ושמור דבר זה שביארתי לך: סליק פרק האורג

פי"ד שמונה שרצים. וחכמים אומרים לענין טומאה אין עור למה שמנו חכמים. משכחת לה בתורת כהנים הטמאים לרבות עורותיהן יכול עורות כולן ת"ל אלה אלו עורות הטמאים עור

למה שמנו חכמים אדרבה למה שמנו חכמים אין להם עור ואמר אביי הכי קאמר אין עור חלוק מבשר אלא למה שלא מנו חכמים אמר ליה רבא הא למה שמנו חכמים קאמר אלא אמר רבא הכי קאמר אין עור מטמא כבשר אלא למה שמנו חכמים מכלל דרבי יוחנן בן נורי הנך נמי דלא מנו חכמים מטמאין והא קתני ר' יוחנן בן נורי אומר ח' שרצים יש להן עורות ולא מטמאין (א)[אמר רב]אדא בר מתנה תריץ הכי וחכמים אומרים לענין טומאה אין עור למה שמנו חכמים ואכתי לענין שבת לא פליגי והתניא הצד אחד מח' שרצים האמורים בתורה °החובל בהן חייב בשרצים שיש להן עורות ואיזו היא חבורה שאינה חוזרת *נצרר הדם אע"פ שלא יצא רבי יוחנן בן נורי אומר ח' שרצים יש להן עורות אמר רב אשי מאן ת"ק רבי יהודה דאזיל בתר גישתא *דתנן ר' יהודה אומר הלטאה כחולדה אבל רבנן דפליגי עליה דרבי יוחנן לענין טומאה לענין שבת מודו ליה אי הכי האי דברי רבי יוחנן בן נורי דברי רבי יוחנן ומחלוקתו מיבעי ליה תני דברי רבי יוחנן בן נורי ומחלוקתו בעא מיניה לוי מרבי מנין לחבורה שאינה חוזרת דכתיב °היהפוך כושי עורו ונמר חברבורותיו מאי חברבורותיו אילימא דקאי ריקמי ריקמי האי ונמר חברבורותיו נמר גווניו מבעי ליה אלא ככושי מה עורו דכושי אינה חוזרת אף חבורה אינה חוזרת: ושאר שקצים כו': הא הורגן חייב מאן תנא א"ר ירמיה ר"א היא *דתניא ר"א אומר ההורג כינה בשבת כהורג גמל בשבת מתקיף לה רב יוסף עד כאן לא פליגי רבנן עליה דרבי אליעזר אלא בכינה דאינה פרה ורבה °אבל שאר שקצים ורמשים דפרין ורבין לא פליגי ושניהם לא למדוה אלא מאילים רבי אליעזר סבר כאילים מה אילים שיש בהן נטילת נשמה אף כל שיש בו נטילת נשמה ורבנן סברי כאילים מה אילים דפרין ורבין אף כל דפרה ורבה א"ל אביי וכינה אין פרה ורבה *והאמר מר יושב הקב"ה וזן מקרני ראמים ועד ביצי כינים מינא הוא דמיקרי ביצי כינים והתניא טפויי וביצי כינים מינא הוא דמיקרי ביצי כינים °והרי פרעוש דפרה ורבה ותניא הצד פרעוש בשבת רבי אליעזר מחייב °ורבי יהושע פוטר אמר רב אשי צידה אהריגה קרמית עד כאן לא פליגי רבי אליעזר ור' יהושע אלא דמר סבר *דבר שאין במינו ניצוד חייב ומר סבר פטור °אבל לענין הריגה אפילו רבי יהושע מודה: °הצדן לצורך חייב וכו': מאן תנא אמר רב יהודה אמר רב *ר' שמעון היא דאמר מלאכה שאין צריכה לגופה פטור עליה איכא דמתני לה אהא *המפיס מורסא בשבת אם לעשות לה פה חייב אם להוציא ממנה לחה פטור מאן תנא אמר רב יהודה אמר רב ר' שמעון היא דאמר מלאכה שאין צריכה לגופה פטור עליה ואיכא דמתני לה אהא *הצד נחש בשבת אם מתעסק בו שלא ישכנו פטור אם לרפואה חייב מאן תנא אמר רב יהודה אמר רב רבי שמעון היא דאמר מלאכה שאינה צריכה לגופה פטור עליה אמר *שמואל °השולה דג מן *הים כיון שיבש בו כסלע חייב א"ר יוסי בר אבין ובין סנפיריו אמר רב אשי °לא תימא יבש ממש אלא אפילו דעבד רירי אמר מר בר המדורי °אמר שמואל *)°הושיט ידו למעי בהמה ודלדל עובר שבמעיה חייב מאי טעמא אמר רבא בר המדורי אסברא לי לאו אמר רב ששת °האי מאן דתלש כשותא מהיזמי והיגי מיחייב משום עוקר דבר מגידולו הכא נמי מיחייב משום עוקר דבר מגידולו אמר אביי °האי מאן דתלש פיטרא

*) [עי' תוס' ע"ז כו. ד"ה סנר]

רש"י

למה שמנו חכמים. בשחיטת חולין אלו שעורותיהן כבשרן והא ודאי מסכסתא היא אדרבה למה שמנו חכמים אין להם עור דהא עורותיהן כבשרן קאמרי: ואמר אביי הכי קאמר אין עור חלוק מבשר. אלא לאותן ד' שלא מנו חכמים חולד ועכבר וצב ותנשמת אבל האנקה הכח והלטאה והחומט אין עורן חלוק מבשרן ולא הוי חבורה ומ"מ קשיא לרב: א"ל רבא והא למה שמנו קאמר. ולא טעי תנא בין מנו ללא מנו: אין עור מטמא כבשר כו'. והכי קאמרי ליה דקאמרת לענין שבת יש להן עור אבל לענין טומאה עורותיהן כבשרן דאיתרבו מהטמאים אין עור מטמא כבשר אלא לאותן ארבעה שמנו: מכלל דרבי יוחנן כו'. בתמיה והא קתני התם גבי טומאה דכל ח' שרצים לרבי יוחנן בן נורי יש להן עורות: תריץ הכי. סמי מברייתא אלא ותני אין עור למה שמנו חכמים ומיהו לרב לא תקשי דהכי קאמרי ליה לענין שבת מודינא לך דהחובל בהן חייב אבל לענין טומאה פליגא דאין עור לאותן ד' שמנו: בשרצים שיש להן עורות. לאותן ד' שלא מנו: נצרר הדם. נאסף ונקשר במקום אחד שוב אינו חוזר ונבלע: מאן ת"ק. דהך מתניתא דאמר בשרצים שיש להן עורות דמשמע דיש מהן דפטור: רבי יהודה היא. דלענין טומאה לא יליף מאלה הטמאים אלא ההוא דאית ליה גישתא שעורו עב ויש לו עור ממש אינו כבשר ושאינו עב הוי כבשר והלטאה משום דעורה עב משוי ליה כחולדה בהעור והרוטב הלכך לענין שבת נמי לאו עור הוא בשלש מהן אנקה וכח וחומט אבל לרבנן דהעור והרוטב שמנו הלטאה בהך שעורותיהן כבשרן אלמא דטעמייהו לאו משום עור ולאו עור אלא משום דרשה דקרא לענין טומאה הוא דפליגי משום קרא אבל לענין שבת מודו דודאי עור הן: דברי ר' יוחנן בן נורי. דקתני בההיא ברייתא דלעיל לענין שבת כיון דלא איפלגו רבנן עליה אלא לענין טומאה דברי ר' יוחנן בן נורי ומחלוקתו מיבעי ליה: מנין לחבורה שאינה חוזרת. ולמילף דההיא דחוזרת לאו חבורה היא כגון הנך דאין להן עור שנצרר בו הדם חבורתו חוזרת לקדמותה או מכה קטנה שלא נצרר הדם: אילימא דקאי ריקמי ריקמי. ונמר ממש אמר קרא שהוא מנומר בגוונים: אלא ככושי כו'. והאי נמר לשון תמורה היהפוך כושי עורו ונמר חברבורותיו כלומר וימיר חבורת עורו לחזור לקדמותו שלא יתקשה העור במקום המכה: גמל. משום דגדול הוא נקט ליה: מאילים. אילים מאדמים שנשחטו למלאכת המשכן בשביל עורותיהן: והא אמר מר. בשמעתא קמייתא דמס' ע"ז: ביצי כינים. קס"ד כינים קטנים כשיוצאין מביציהן: הטפויין. סירוך הטפויין וביצי כינים מתניתא היא °ולא ידענא היכא תניא: הצד פרעוש. ממקום שאינו ניצוד ועומד כגון מעל גבי קרקע או מבגדיו מבחוץ: להוציא ממנה לחה. מלאכה שאינה צריכה לגופה היא שהפתח היא המלאכה וזה אין צריך (ב) להיות כאן פתח מעכשיו: הצד נחש. כמי הצידה היא המלאכה וזה אינו צריך לצידה אלא שלא תשכנו ואם יודע שתעמוד ולא תזיקנו לא היה צד: השולה דג. שהיה ניצוד ועומד מבעוד יום: כסלע. כרוחב סלע: חייב. משום נטילת נשמה דתו לא חיי: עביד רירי. שנוגעין בו וחוט הרירין *נמשך מן האצבע: דלדל. עקר שהפילתו על ידי דלדול זה: בר המדורי. טעמא דהא מילתא אסברא לי: כשותא. הומלון וגדל מתוך ההיזמי מריח הקרקע שההיזמי יונק ממנו: מיחייב. ואף על פי שאינו מחובר לקרקע כדאמרינן בעלמא (עירובין דף כח: (ג)) מאוירא רבי: פיטרא

תוספות

אמר אביי אין עור חלוק מבשר כו'. מסקנא דפירכא היא מאביי דודאי אליבא דאביי פליגי לענין שבת אבל למאי דמפרש רבא ורב אדא לא פליגי מידי לענין שבת ותימה הוא כיון דלא קיימא שיטיה דאביי היכי פריך מינה: הצד את הפרעוש כו' ר"י פוטר. משמע דפטור אבל אסור ואומר ר"י בשם הרב פורת דאפ"ה אם נושך האדם מותר ליקחנו ולהשליכו מעליו דמשום צער שרי אבל אם הוא באותו ענין על האדם שאינו ירא שישכנו כגון על סרבלו מבחוץ אסור ליטלו אבל יכול להפילו מעליו: יש ספרים דגרסי מ"ט מחייב רבי אליעזר לאו משום דפרה ורבה ושיבוש הוא דהא אפילו בכינה מחייב רבי אליעזר ופרעוש נקט לרבותא דרבי יהושע דאפילו פרעוש פוטר ושינויא נמי דמשני לא משמע דגרים ליה ור"ת נמי מחקו מספרו: כיון שיבש בו כסלע. בניצוד ועומד במים מיירי מדלא מחייב ליה עד שיבש כסלע:

ולא

עין משפט נר מצוה

ד א מיי' פ"ח מהל' שבת הלכה ט סמג לאוין סה טוש"ע א"ח סי' שטז סעיף ח:

ה ב מיי' פי"א שם הל' ב סמג שם טור א"ח סימן שטז:

ו ג ד מיי' פי' שם הלכה כד ופי"א שם הל' ב סמג שם טוש"ע א"ח סי' שטז סעיף ט:

ז ה (מיי' פ"י שם הל' כא) סמג שם טוש"ע שם סעיף ח:

ח ו ז ח מיי' פי"א שם הלכה א:

ט ט י מיי' פ"ח מהל' שבת הלכה ג טוש"ע א"ח סי' שלו סעיף ס:

רבינו חננאל

(הירוי) שהן באות כמו נופלות למקום אחד ואין בהן כח לילך לכאן ולכאן פטור עליהן כאלעזר בן מהבאי ואם מפורחות הן לדעתן חייב: צבי שנכנס לבית. עיקר דבר בעשותה אחת אחד שעשה חייב ב' שעשאו פטורין ומפרש בהמצניע בענין המוציא ככר: אין צידת ארי אלא בהכנסתו (לגדונדקי) [לגורזקי] שלו פי' לכלובו: ישב אחד על הפתח כו' אסיקנא שאם היה צבי רץ כדרכו ונתכוון אדם לנעול בפני עצמו ונעל בפניו ובפני הצבי פטור: נכנסה צפור תחת כנפיו יושב ומשמרה עד שתחשך ומתני' ובא השני וישב בצדו אע"פ שעמד הראשון והלך לו השני מותר לישב ולשמור עד שתחשך: אמר שמואל כל פטורי שבת פטור אבל אסור לבד מהני תלת דפטור ומותר ואלו הן כו' ומפרש (לעיל ג) אע"ג דעביד בהו מעשה איכא אחריני טובא פטור (אף דלא) [אם לא] עביד בהו מעשה:

הדרן עלך האורג

שמונה שרצים האמורין בתורה הצדן והחובל בהן חייב. ודאי זו המפורשות במשנתנו הצדן לצורך חייב שלא לצורך פטור אפי' בח' שרצים היא דאי הוה שנו ח' שרצים לענין צידה והוה מיחייב הצדן בין לצורך ובין שלא לצורך ושאר שרצים ורמשים צדן לצורך [חייב] ושלא לצורך פטור (הוה) מפרש בגמ' טעמא דמילתא ופי' החובל העושה חבורה וכיון דמפרש כי חבורה זו אינה חוזרת שמעינן מינה כי עור הוא שאם נעשית בו חבורה ועשה מקומו צלקת וכיוצא בהו ומדקאמר בשמנה שרצים החובל בהן חייב מכלל שיש להן עור ומוקים לה שמואל כר' יוחנן בן נורי דאמר ח' שרצים יש להן עורות אבל רבנן לא דתנן בהעור והרוטב אלו שעורותיהן כבשרן ומנו האנקה והכח והלטאה והחומט*) ודקתני נמי והתנשמת דאלמא לית להו עורות דכל מאי דאית ליה עור לא מיטמא עורו טומאת נבלות וכד מיעבד טהור והני שרצים עורותיהן כבשרן ור' יוחנן בן נורי פליג בשאר ח' ואוקמה שמואל להא מתניתין כוותיה ורב אמר אפי' תימא רבנן לאו משום דאין להן (לעכבר ולצב ולתולדה) **)עורות טמאו רבנן למשכייהו אלא מדרבינהו קרא אלה הטמאים לכם ודרשי אלה הטמאים לרבות עורותיהן כבשרן אבל לענין חובל בשבת מודו רבנן בה' שרצים שיש להן עורות ואקשי' עלה דרב ולא פליגי והתניא הצד אחד מח' שרצים והחובל בהן חייב דברי ר' יוחנן בן נורי וחכ"א אין עור אלא למה שמנו חכמים ואתמהינן אדרבה למה שמנו חכמים אין להן עור כי עורותיהן כבשרן הוא ופריק ר' אלעא הכי קתני וחכ"א אין עור מטמא כבשר אלא מה שמנו חכמים ואמרו אלו שעורותיהן כבשרן ודייקינן מדקתני חכמים דהני ששנין במשנה ,ואלו שעורותיהן כבשרן הוא דעורן טמא כבשרן והנשארין לא מכלל דר' יוחנן בן נורי דפליג עליהן סבר דאפי' הנשארין מטמאו והא ח' שרצים יש להן עורות קתני דאלמא כולן לא מטמא עורן ונדחת דתריץ רב אדא הכי וחכ"א לענין טומאה אין עור למה שמנו חכמים כלומר אין להן עור אלא כבשר הוא חשוב. ור' יוחנן בן נורי פליג ואמר יש להן עורות ואקשי' וכי לענין טומאה פליגי לענין שבת לא פליגי והתניא הצד אחד משמונה שרצים והחובל בהן חייב בשרצים שיש להן עור ואי זו היא חבורה כל שאינה חוזרת

*) אולי צ"ל ורב תני נמי תנשמת ועי' בחולין דף קכ"ב ע"ב. **) נראה דצ"ל והאנקה והכח והלטאה והחומט.

הגהות הב"ח

(א) גמ' ולא מטמאין אלא אמר רב אדא בר מתנה: (ב) רש"י ד"ה להוציא ממנה וכו' צריך לו להיות: (ג) ד"ה מחייב וכו' כדאמרי' בעלמא עירובין כח ע"ב. נ"ב ע"ש דהמסקנא היא דמארעא קא רבי והערוך גם הוא פי' הכא על פי המסקנא דהתם עיין ערך כשות:

מסורת הש"ס

חולין מה: | שם קכב. | לעיל קו: וש"נ | [לעיל קה: וש"נ] | לעיל ע"א כתובות ו: | [עדיות פ"ב מ"ה] | [עדיות שם] | לעיל ע"א | תענית כד: | [לפרש"י ותוס' בניצוד ועומד וכו' דהיקא מלת הים והרמב"ם ריש פ"י מהל' שבת גרס הספל] | [נמשך עם האצבע כצ"ל] | ירמיה יג | [לעיל ג.]

רב נסים גאון

האנקה והכח והלטאה והחומט ר' יהודה אומר הלטאה כחולדה ר' יוחנן בן נורי אומר ח' שרצים יש להן עורות ומשכחת לה עוד במסכת חולין בפרק העור והרוטב (דף קכב) אלו שעורותיהן כבשרן עור האדם ועור החזיר של ישוב ר' יוסי אומר אף עור חזיר הבר עור חטרת גמל הרכה ועור הראש של עגל הרך ועור בית הפרסות ועור בית הבושת ועור השליל ועור שתחת האליה ועור האנקה והכח והלטאה והחומט ר' יהודה אומר הלטאה כחולדה הרי אלו שמנו אותם חכמים מטמאין עורן כבשרן ואין להן עור שהוא חלוק מבשרן לענין טומאה: מלאכה שאינה צריכה לגופה דפליגי בה ר' יהודה ור' שמעון כבר כתבנוה בפרק יציאות השבת: אמר רב ששת האי מאן דעקר כשותא מהגה והיזמנה חייב משום עוקר דבר מגידולו. משתכח בפרק בכל מערבין (עירובין דף כח) ר' זירא כי הוה חליש מגירסיה הוה אזיל ויתיב אפיתח' דבי ר' יהודה בר אמי אמר כי חלפי רבנן איקום מקמייהו ואקביל אגרא נפק אתא ינוקא אמר ליה מאי אגמרך רבך בכשות אמר ליה כשות בורא פרי האדמה כשות נמי מארעא קא רביא דהא קא חזינן דקטלינן להי להיזמא ומיתא כשותא ובפרק ר"א אומר תולין את המשמרת (דף קלט) אמרו מכריז רב (כמא זמן כשותא) [האי מאן] דבעי למזרע כשותא בברמא נזרע: מאן דתליש פיטוראי הן פטריות שהזכירו

גליון הש"ס

גמ' וסרי פרעוש. עי' כר"ן פ"ק דמסכתין ס ע"ב: שם אמר שמואל הושיט ידו למעי בהמה. עי' בכורות כה ע"א תוס' ד"ה דהוי ליה: רש"י ד"ה הטפויין כו' ולא ידענא. עי' ברכות כה ע"ב ד"ה מאן שמעת ליה וש"נ:

a Only [107b] those which the Sages enumerated[1] have skin. [Whereon it was asked]: On the contrary, Those which the Sages enumerated have no skin?[2] And Abaye said, This is what he [the Tanna] states: Only those not enumerated by the Sages have a skin distinct from the flesh.[3] Said Raba to him: But he states, which the Sages enumerated? Rather said Raba, This is the meaning: the skin of those [reptiles] only which the Sages enumerated defiles like the flesh.[4] Hence it follows that R. Johanan b. Nuri holds that even those which the Sages did not enumerate defile [in this way]? But it is stated, R. Johanan b. Nuri said: The eight reptiles have skins and do not defile?—Rather Said R. Adda b. Mattenah, Reconcile it thus: But the Sages maintain: In respect of defilement those which the Sages enumerated have no skin.

Still, however, do they not differ in respect of the Sabbath? But it was taught: He who catches one of the eight reptiles mentioned in the Torah, [or] he who wounds them, is culpable, [viz.,] in the case of the reptiles which have skins.[5] And what is a wound that does not heal?[6] If the blood becomes clotted, even if it does not issue. R. Johanan b. Nuri said: The eight reptiles have skins![7]—Said R. Ashi, Who is the first Tanna? R. Judah, who maintains that touch is the criterion.[8] For we learnt, R. Judah said: The *halta'ah*[9] is like the weasel. But the Rabbis who disagree with R. Johanan b. Nuri in respect of defilement agree with him in respect of the Sabbath.[10] If so, instead of 'this is the view of R. Johanan b. Nuri,' 'this is the view of R. Johanan b. Nuri and his
b opponents' is required?[1]—Learn: 'this is the view of R. Johanan b. Nuri and his opponents.'[2]

Levi asked Rabbi: How do we know that a wound[3] is such as is permanent?[4]—Because it is written, *Can the Ethiopian change his skin, or the leopard his spots* [habarbarothaw]?[5] What does '*habarbarothaw*' mean: shall we say, that it is covered with spots? Then instead of '*and a leopard* habarbarothaw,' it should read, '*a leopard* gawwanaw [its colours]'? Rather it is parallel to Ethiopian,—just as the skin of an Ethiopian cannot turn, so is a [real] wound one that does not turn [i.e., heal].[6]

BUT OTHER ABOMINATIONS, etc. But if one kills them, he is culpable: which Tanna [holds thus]? Said R. Jeremiah, It is R.

a (1) As those whose skins are the same as their flesh. (2) Since their skin is the same as their flesh. (3) But those enumerated by them have no skin distinct from the flesh, and consequently wounding them involves no liability. On this interpretation the Rabbis differ even in respect of the Sabbath, which contradicts Rab. But on the following explanations there is no difficulty. (4) V. *supra* 107a, n. c5. (5) I.e., the four not enumerated by the Sages. This shows that they differ even in respect of the Sabbath. (6) I.e., which leaves a permanent discolouring—only such entails liability. (7) All involve culpability on the Sabbath. (8) Lit., 'who goes after touch'. (9) A species of lizard. (10) R. Judah holds that the question whether the skin of reptiles is like their flesh or not in the matter of defilement is not settled by deduction from the verse, '*and these are they which are unclean*, etc.' (quoted *supra a*), but is dependent on touch. I.e., if the skin is thick and perceptibly distinct from the flesh, it is not the same as the flesh; otherwise it is. By this criterion the *halta'ah* is like the weasel, since both have thick skins; though if the matter were decided by Scriptural exegesis these two would be dissimilar, as is shown in Hul. 142a. Hence he holds that in respect of the Sabbath too three of these eight have no skin, i.e., if one wounds them he is not guilty, for the skin is thin and not distinct from the flesh. But the Rabbis in Hul. count the *halta'ah* as one of the reptiles whose skin is the same as their flesh, in spite of its thickness. This shows that they settle the matter solely by reference to the verse, and therefore their view, which disagrees with R. Johanan b. Nuri's, applies only to defilement, since the verse is written in that connection, but not to the Sabbath.
b (1) Since the Rabbis agree with him. (2) This is probably not an emendation, but merely implies that it is to be understood thus. (3) For it to involve culpability on the Sabbath. (4) Lit., 'return'. (5) Jer. XIII, 23. (6) On this interpretation *namer* (E.V. *leopard*) is derived from *mur*, to change, and the verse is translated: *Can the Ethiopian change his skin, or turn* (i.e., heal) *his wounds? habarbarothaw* (E.V. *spots*) being derived from *haburah*, a wound.

◁ *For the continuation of the English translation of this page see overleaf.*

ד א מיי' פ"ח מהל' שבת הלכה ט סמג לאוין סה טוש"ע א"ח סי' שטז סעיף ח :
ה ב מיי' פי"א שם הל' ב סמג שם טוש"ע א"ח סימן שטז :
ו ג ד מיי' פ"י שם הלכה כד וטי"א שם הל' ב סמג שם טוש"ע א"ח סי' שטו סעיף ט :
ז ה (מיי' פי' שם הל' כא) סמג שם טוש"ע שם סעיף ח :
ח ו ז ח מיי' פי"א שם הלכה א :
ט ט י מיי' פ"ח מהל' שבת הלכה ג טוש"ע א"ח סי' שלו סעיף ס :

למה שמנו חכמים אדרבה למה שמנו חכמים אין להם עור ואמר אביי הכי קאמר אין עור חלוק מבשר אלא למה שלא מנו חכמים אמר ליה רבא הא למה שמנו חכמים קאמר אלא אמר רבא הכי קאמר אין עור מטמא כבשר אלא למה שמנו חכמים מכלל דרבי יוחנן בן נורי הנך נמי דלא מנו חכמים מטמאין והא קתני ר' יוחנן בן נורי אומר ח' שרצים יש להן עורות ולא מטמאין (א)[אמר רב]אדא בר מתנה תריץ הכי וחכמים אומרים לענין טומאה אין עור למה שמנו חכמים ואכתי לענין שבת לא פליגי והתניא הצד אחד מח' שרצים האמורים בתורה "החובל בהן חייב בשרצים שיש להן עורות ואיזו היא חבורה שאינה חוזרת *נצרר הדם אע"פ שלא יצא רבי יוחנן בן נורי אומר ח' שרצים יש להן עורות אמר רב אשי מאן ת"ק רבי יהודה דאזיל בתר גישתא *דתנן ר' יהודה אומר הלטאה כחולדה אבל רבנן דפליגי עליה דרבי יוחנן לענין טומאה לענין שבת מודו ליה אי הכי האי דברי רבי יוחנן בן נורי דברי רבי יוחנן ומחלוקתו מיבעי ליה תני דברי רבי יוחנן בן נורי ומחלוקתו בעא מיניה לוי מרבי מנין לחבורה שאינה חוזרת דכתיב °היהפוך כושי עורו ונמר חברבורותיו מאי חברבורותיו אילימא דקאי ריקמי ריקמי האי ונמר חברבורותיו נמר גווניו מבעי ליה אלא ככושי מה עורו דכושי אינה חוזרת אף חבורה אינה חוזרת : ושאר שקצים כו' : הא הורגן חייב מאן תנא א"ר ירמיה ר"א היא *דתניא ר"א אומר ההורג כינה בשבת כהורג גמל בשבת מתקיף לה רב יוסף עד כאן לא פליגי רבנן עליה דרבי אליעזר אלא בכינה דאינה פרה ורבה [ב]אבל שאר שקצים ורמשים דפרין ורבין לא פליגי ושניהם לא למדוה אלא מאילים רבי אליעזר סבר כאילים מה אילים שיש בהן נטילת נשמה אף כל שיש בו נטילת נשמה ורבנן סברי כאילים מה אילים דפרין ורבין אף כל דפרה ורבה א"ל אביי וכינה אין פרה ורבה *והאמר מר יושב הקב"ה וזן מקרני ראמים ועד ביצי כינים מינא הוא דמיקרי ביצי כינים והתניא טפויי וביצי כינים מינא הוא דמיקרי ביצי כינים °והרי פרעוש דפרה ורבה ותניא הצד פרעוש בשבת רבי אליעזר מחייב [י]ורבי יהושע פוטר אמר רב אשי צידה אהריגה קרמית עד כאן לא פליגי רבי אליעזר ור' יהושע אלא דמר סבר *דבר שאין במינו ניצוד חייב ומר סבר פטור [ו]אבל לענין הריגה אפילו רבי יהושע מודה : [ה]הצדן לצורך חייב וכו' : מאן תנא אמר רב יהודה אמר רב *ר' שמעון היא דאמר מלאכה שאין צריכה לגופה פטור עליה איכא דמתני לה אהא *המפיס מורסא בשבת אם לעשות לה פה חייב אם להוציא ממנה לחה פטור מאן תנא אמר רב יהודה אמר רב ר' שמעון היא דאמר מלאכה שאין צריכה לגופה פטור עליה ואיכא דמתני לה אהא *הצד נחש בשבת אם מתעסק בו שלא ישכנו פטור אם לרפואה חייב מאן תנא אמר רב יהודה אמר רב רבי שמעון היא דאמר מלאכה שאינה צריכה לגופה פטור עליה אמר *שמואל [י]השולה דג מן *הים כיון שיבש בו כסלע חייב א"ר יוסי בר אבין ובין סנפיריו אמר רב אשי [ז]לא תימא יבש ממש אלא אפילו דעבד רירי אמר מר בר המדורי °אמר שמואל *)[ח]הושיט ידו למעי בהמה ודלדל עובר שבמעיה חייב מאי טעמא אמר רבא בר המדורי אסברא לי לאו אמר רב ששת [ט]האי מאן דתלש כשותא מהיזמי והיגי מיחייב משום עוקר דבר מגידולו הכא נמי מיחייב משום עוקר דבר מגידולו אמר אביי [י]האי מאן דתלש

פיטרא

*) [עי' תוס' ע"ז כו. ד"ה סבר]

רש"י

למה שמנו חכמים. בשחיטת חולין אלו שעורותיהן כבשרן והא ודאי משבשתא היא אדרבה למה שמנו חכמים אין להם עור דהא עורותיהן כבשרן קאמרי : ואמר אביי הכי קאמר אין עור חלוק מבשר. אלא לאותן ד' שלא מנו חכמים חולד ועכבר ולב ותנשמת אבל האנקה הכח והלטאה והחומט אין עורן חלוק מבשרן ולא הוי חבורה ומ"מ קשיא לרב: א"ל רבא והא למה שמנו קאמר. ולא טעי תנא בין מנו ללא מנו : אין עור מטמא כבשר כו'. והכי קאמרי ליה דקאמרת לענין שבת יש להן עור אבל לענין טומאה עורותיהן כבשרן דאיתרבו מהטמאים אין עור מטמא כבשר אלא לאותן ארבעה שמנו : מכלל דרבי יוחנן כו'. בתמיה והא קתני התם גבי טומאה דלכל ח' שרצים לרבי יוחנן בן נורי יש להן עורות : תרין הכי. סמי מברייתא אלא ותני אין עור למה שמנו חכמים ומיהו לרב לא תקשי דהכי קאמרי ליה לענין שבת מודינא לך דהחובל בהן חייב אבל לענין טומאה פליגא דאין עור לאותן ד' שמנו: בשרצים שיש להן עורות. לאותן ד' שלא מנו : נצרר הדם. נאסף ונקשר במקום אחד שוב אינו חוזר ונבלע: מאן ת"ק. דהך מתניתא דאמר בשרצים שיש להן עורות דמשמע דיש מהן דפטור : רבי יהודה היא. דלענין טומאה לא יליף מאלה הטמאים אלא ההוא דאית ליה גישתא שעורו עב ויש לו עור ממש אינו כבשר ושאינו עב הוי כבשר והלטאה משום דעורה עב משוי ליה כחולדה בהעור והרוטב הלכך לענין שבת נמי לאו עור הוא בשלש מהן אנקה וכח וחומט אבל לרבנן דהעור והרוטב שמנו הלטאה בהך שעורותיהן כבשרן אלמא דטעמייהו לאו משום עור ולאו עור אלא משום דרשה דקרא לענין טומאה הוא דפליגי משום קרא אבל לענין שבת מודו דודאי עור הן: דברי ר' יוחנן בן נורי. דקתני בההיא ברייתא דלעיל לענין שבת כיון דלא איפלגו רבנן עליה אלא לענין טומאה דברי ר' יוחנן בן נורי ומחלוקתו מיבעי ליה : מנין לחבורה שאינה חוזרת. ולמילף דההיא דחוזרת לאו חבורה היא כגון הנך דאין להן עור שנצרר בו הדם חבורתו חוזרת לקדמותה או מכה קטנה שלא נצרר הדם : אילימא דקאי ריקמי ריקמי. ונמר ממש אמר קרא שהוא מנומר בגוונים : אלא ככושי כו'. והאי נמר לשון תמורה היהפוך כושי עורו ונמר חברבורותיו כלומר וימיר חבורת עורו לחזור לקדמותו שלא יתקשה העור במקום המכה : גמל. משום דגדול הוא נקט ליה : מאילים. אילים מאדמים שנשחטו למלאכת המשכן בשביל עורותיהן : והא אמר מר. בשמעתא קמייתא דמס' ע"ז : ביצי כינים. קס"ד כינים קטנים כשיוצאין מביציהן : הטפויין. מין הטפויין וביצי כינים מתניתא היא °ולא ידענא היכא תניא:הצד פרעוש. ממקום שאינו ניצוד ועומד כגון מעל גבי קרקע או מבגדיו מבחוץ : להוציא ממנה לחה. מלאכה שאינה צריכה לגופה היא שהפתח היא המלאכה וזה אין צריך (ג)להיות כאן פתח מעכשיו : הצד נחש. נמי הצידה היא המלאכה וזה אינו צריך לצידה אלא שלא ישכנו ואם יודע שתעמוד ולא תזיקנו לא היה צד : השולה דג. שהיה ניצוד ועומד מבעוד יום : כסלע. כרוחב סלע : חייב. משום נטילת נשמה דתו לא חיי : עביד רירי. שטוענין בו וחוט הרירין *נמשך מן האצבע : דלדל. עקר שהפילתו על ידי דלדול זה : בר המדורי אסברא לי. טעמא דהא מילתא : כשותא. הומלון וגדל מתוך ההיזמי מריח הקרקע שההיזמי יונק ממנו : מיחייב. ואף על פי שאינו מחובר לקרקע כדאמרינן בעלמא (עירובין דף כח: (ג)) מאוירא רבי :

פיערא

תוספות

אמר אביי אין עור חלוק מבשר כו'. מסקנא דפירכא היא מאביי דודאי אליבא דאביי פליגי לענין שבת אבל למאי דמפרש רבא ורב אדא לא פליגי מידי לענין שבת ותימה הוא כיון דלא קיימא שינויא דאביי היכי פריך מינה : הצד את הפרעוש כו' ר"י פוטר. משמע דפטור אבל אסור ואומר ר"י בשם הרב פורת דאפ"ה אם נושך האדם מותר ליקחנו ולהשליכו מעליו דמשום צער שרי אבל אם הוא בלותו ענין על האדם שאינו ירא שישכנו כגון על סרבלו מבחוץ אסור ליטלו אבל יכול להפילו מעליו :

יש ספרים דגרסי מ"ט מחייב רבי אליעזר לאו משום דפרה ורבה ושיבוש הוא דהא אפילו בכינה מחייב רבי אליעזר ופרעוש נקט לרבותא דרבי יהושע דאפילו פרעוש פוטר ושיבוש כמו דמשני לא משמע דגרים ליה ור"ת נמי מחקו מספרו :

כיון שיבש בו כסלע. בניצוד ועומד במים מיירי מדלא מחייב ליה עד שיבש כסלע :

ולי

רבינו חננאל

(הירוי) שהן באות כמו נופלות למקום אחד ואין בהן כח לילך לכאן ולכאן פטור עליהן כאלעזר בן מהבאי ואם מפורחות הן לדעתן חייב: צבי שנכנס לבית. עיקר דבר בעשותה אחת אחד שעשה חייב ב' שעשאו פטורין ומפרש בהמצניע בענין המוציא ככר: אין צידת ארי אלא בהכנסתו (לגדונדקי) [לגורזקי] שלו פי' לכלובו : ישב אחד על הפתח כו' אסיקנא שאם היה צבי רץ כדרכו ונתכוון אדם לנעול בפני עצמו ונעל בפניו ובפני הצבי פטור: נכנסה צפור תחת כנפיו יושב ומשמרה עד שתחשך ומתני' ובא השני וישב בצדו אע"פ שעמד הראשון והלך לו השני מותר לישב ולשמור עד שתחשך : אמר שמואל כל פטורי שבת פטור אבל אסור לבד מהני תלת דפטור ומותר ואלו הן כו' ומפרש (לעיל ג) אע"ג דעביד בהו מעשה איכא אחריני טובא פטור (אף דלא) [אם לא] עביד בהו מעשה :

הדרן עלך האורג

שמונה שרצים האמורין בתורה הצדן והחובל בהן חייב. ודאי זו המפורשות במשנתנו הצדן לצורך חייב שלא לצורך פטור אפי' בח' שרצים היא דאי הוה שנו ח' שרצים לענין צידה והוה מיחייב הצדן בין לצורך ובין שלא לצורך ושאר שרצים ורמשים צדן לצורך [חייב] ושלא לצורך פטור (הוה) מפרש בגמ' טעמא דמילתא ופי' החובל העושה חבורה וכיון דמפרש כי חבורה זו אינה חוזרת שמעינן מינה כי עור הוא שאם נעשית בו חבורה ועשה מקומו צלקת וכיוצא בהו ומדקאמר בשמנה שרצים החובל בהן חייב מכלל שיש להן עור ומוקים לה שמואל כר' יוחנן בן נורי דאמר ח' שרצים יש להן עורות אבל רבנן לא דתנן בהעור והרוטב אלו שעורותיהן כבשרן ומנו האנקה והכח והלטאה והחומט*) ודקתני נמי והתנשמת דאלמא לית להו עורות דכל מאי דאית ליה עור לא מיטמא עורו טומאת נבלות וכד מיעבד טהור והני שרצים עורותיהן כבשרן ור' יוחנן בן נורי פליג בשאר ח' ואוקמה שמואל להא מתניתין כוותיה ורב אמר אפי' תימא רבנן לאו משום דאין להן (לעבבר ולצב ולהולדה) **)עורות טמאו רבנן למשכייהו אלא מדרבינהו קרא אלה הטמאים לכם ודרשי אלה הטמאים לרבות עורותיהן כבשרן אבל לענין הובל בשבת מודו רבנן בח' שרצים שיש להן עורות ואקשי' עלה דרב ולא פליגי והתניא הצד אחד מח' שרצים והחובל בהן חייב דברי ר' יוחנן בן נורי וחכ"א אין עור אלא למה שמנו חכמים ואתמהינן אדרבה למה שמנו חכמים אין להן עור כי עורותיהן כבשרן הוא ופריק ר' אלעא הכי קתני וחכ"א אין עור מטמא כבשר אלא מה שמנו חכמים ואמרו אלו שעורותיהן כבשרן ודייקינן מדקתני חכמים דהני ששנינן במשנה ואלו שעורותיהן כבשרן הוא דעורן טמא כבשרן והנשארין לא מכלל דר' יוחנן בן נורי דפליג עליהן סבר דאפי' הנשארין מטמאו והא ח' שרצים יש להן עורות קתני דאלמא כולן לא מטמא עורן ונדחת דתריץ רב אדא הכי וחכ"א לענין טומאה אין עור למה שמנו חכמים כלומר אין להן עור אלא כבשר הוא חשוב. ור' יוחנן בן נורי פליג ואמר יש להן עורות ואקשי' וכי לענין טומאה פליגי לענין שבת לא פליגי והתניא הצד אחד משמונה שרצים והחובל בהן חייב בשרצים שיש להן עור ואי זו היא חבורה כל שאינה חוזרת

*) אולי צ"ל ורב תני נמי תנשמת ועי' בחולין דף קכ"ב ע"ב. **) נראה דצ"ל והאנקה והכח והלטאה והחומט.

רב נסים גאון

האנקה והכח והלטאה והחומט ר' יהודה אומר הלטאה כחולדה ר' יוחנן בן נורי אומר ח' שרצים יש להן עורות ומשכחת לה עוד במסכת חולין בפרק העור והרוטב (דף קכב) אלו שעורותיהן כבשרן עור האדם ועור החזיר של ישוב ר' יוסי אומר אף עור חזיר הבר עור חטרת גמל הרכה ועור הראש של עגל הרך ועור בית הפרסות ועור בית הבושת ועור השליל ועור שתחת האליה ועור האנקה והכח והלטאה והחומט ר' יהודה אומר הלטאה כחולדה הרי אלו שמנו אותם חכמים מטמאין עורן כבשרן ואין להן עור שהוא חלוק מבשרן לענין טומאה : מלאכה שאינה צריכה לגופה דפליגי בה ר' יהודה ור' שמעון כבר כתבנוה בפרק יציאות השבת : אמר רב ששת האי מאן דעקר כשותא מהגה והיזמנה חייב משום עוקר דבר מגידוליו. משתכחה בפרק בכל מערבין (עירובין דף כח) ר' זירא כי הוה חליש מגירסיה הוה אזיל ויתיב אפיתחא דבי ר' יהודה בר אמי אמר כי חלפי רבנן איקום מיקמייהו ואקביל אגרא נפק אתא ינוקא אמר ליה מאי אגמרך רבך בכשות אמר ליה כשות בורא פרי האדמה כשות נמי מארעא קא רביא דהא קא חזינן דקטלינן להי להיזמא ומיתא כשותא ובפרק ר"א אומר תולין את המשמרת (דף קלט) אמרו מכריז רב (מנא זבן כשותא) [האי מאן] דבעי למיזרע כשותא בברמא ניזרע: מאן דתליש פיטוראי הן פטריות שהזכירו

גליון הש"ס גמ' וה"ר פרעוש. עי' בר"ן פ"ק דמסכתין ה ע"ב : שם אמר שמואל הושיט ידו למעי בהמה. עי' בכורות כה ע"א תוס' ד"ה דהוי ליה : רש"י ד"ה הטפויין כו' ולא ידענא. עי' ברכות כה ע"ב ד"ה מאן שמעת ליה וש"נ :

הגהות הב"ח

(א) גמ' ולא מטמאין אלא אמר רב אדא בר מתנה : (ב) רש"י ד"ה להוציא ממנה וכו' לריך לו להיות : (ג) ד"ה מחייב וכו' כדאמרי' בעלמא עירובין כח ע"ב. נ"ב ע"ש דהמסקנא היא דמלתא קא רבי והגירוך גם הוא סי' הכא על פי המסקנא דהתם עיין ערך כשות :

חולין פה

שם קכב.

יבמות יג

לעיל קו: וש"נ

[לעיל קה: וש"נ]

לעיל ע"א כתובות ה: [עדיות פ"ב מ"ה]

[עדיות שם] לעיל ע"א

תענית כד:

[לפרש"י ותוס' בנילוד ועומד וכו' דהיקא מלת הים והרמב"ם ריש פי"א מהל' שבת גרס הספל]

[נמשך עם האצבע כצ"ל]

Continuation of translation from previous page as indicated by ◁

Eliezer. For it was taught, R. Eliezer said: He who kills vermin on the Sabbath is as though he killed a camel on the Sabbath. R. Joseph demurred to this: The Rabbis disagree with R. Eliezer only in respect to vermin, which does not multiply and increase, but as for other abominations and creeping things, which multiply and increase, they do not differ [therein]. And both learn it from none but the rams.[7] R. Eliezer holds, It is as the rams: just as there was the taking of life in the case of the rams, so whatever constitutes the taking of life [is a culpable offence]. While the Rabbis argue, It is as the rams: just as rams multiply and increase, so

c are all which multiply and increase [of account].[1] Said Abaye to him, Do not vermin multiply and increase? But a Master said: 'The Holy One, blessed be He, sits and sustains [all creatures], from the horns of wild oxen to the eggs of vermin'?[2]—It is a species called 'eggs of vermin'. But it was taught: *Tippuyyi*[3] and the eggs of vermin?—The species is called 'eggs of vermin'. But there is the flea, which multiplies and increases, yet it was taught, If one catches a flea on the Sabbath: R. Eliezer declares him liable, while R. Joshua exempts [him]?—Said R. Ashi: You oppose catching to killing! R. Eliezer and R. Joshua disagree only in that one Master holds: If the species is not hunted, one is liable; whilst the other Master holds: He is exempt. But in respect to killing even R. Joshua agrees.

HE WHO CATCHES THEM BECAUSE HE NEEDS THEM, HE IS LIABLE, etc. Which Tanna [rules thus]?—Said Rab Judah in Rab's name: It is R. Simeon, who maintains, One is not culpable on account of a labour unrequired *per se*.[4] Others learn it in reference to this: If one manipulates an abscess on the Sabbath,—if in order to make an opening for it, he is liable; if in order to draw the matter out of it, he is exempt. Which Tanna [rules thus]? Said Rab Judah in Rab's name: It is R. Simeon, who maintains: One is not culpable on account of a labour unrequired *per se*. Others again learn it in reference to this: If one catches a snake on the Sabbath: if he is engaged therewith [in catching it] so that it should not bite him, he is exempt; if for a remedy, he is liable.[5] Which Tanna [rules thus]? Said Rab Judah in Rab's name, It is R. Simeon, who maintains: One is not culpable on account of a labour unrequired *per se*.

d Samuel said: If one removes a fish from the sea,[1] as soon as the size of a *sela'* thereof becomes dry, he is liable.[2] R. Jose b. Abin observed: Provided it is between the fins.[3] R. Ashi said: Do not think literally dry, but even if it forms slimy threads.[4]

Mar Bar Hamduri said in Samuel's name: If one inserts his hand in an animal's bowels and detaches an embryo that is inside her, he is culpable. What is the reason? Said Raba: Bar Hamduri explained it to me: Did not R. Shesheth say: If one plucks cuscuta from shrubs and thorns, he is culpable on account of uprooting something from the place of its growth;[5] so here too he is culpable on account of uprooting something [*sc*. the embryo] from the

(7) Which were killed for the sake of their skins, which were dyed red and used in the Tabernacle. Thus killing was a labour of importance in the Tabernacle, and hence ranks as a principal labour; v. *supra* 49*b*.

c (1) In that killing them renders one liable. (2) 'Eggs of vermin' is assumed to mean its progeny. (3) Name of certain small insects. (4) V. *supra* 105*b*. (5) V. end of last chapter for notes.

d (1) Rashi and Tosaf. both explain that this refers to a fish that was already caught before the Sabbath. In that case 'from the sea' is unintelligible. Maim. in *Hilchoth Shabbath* beginning of ch. XI reads 'from a bowl', which is preferable. V. Marginal Gloss. [Rashi, however, did not seem to read 'from the sea']. (2) For taking life, as it cannot live after that.—There is no culpability for catching, since it was caught before the Sabbath. (3) But a dryness in any other part does not mean that the fish can no longer live. (4) I.e., it becomes partially dry only, so that the moisture adheres to one's finger in slimy threads. (5) But not for detaching from the soil, as cuscuta was not held to be attached to the soil; v. 'Er. 28*b*.

place of its growth. Abaye said: He who plucks [108a] fungus from the handle of a pitcher is liable on account of uprooting something from the place of its growth. R. Oshaia objected: If one detaches [aught] from a perforated pot, he is culpable; if it is unperforated, he is exempt?—There, that is not its [normal place for] growing; but here this is its [normal place for] growing.[6]

AN ANIMAL OR A BIRD, etc. R. Huna said: *Tefillin* may be written upon the skin of a clean bird. R. Joseph demurred: What does he inform us? That it has a skin![7] [But] we have [already] learnt it: HE WHO WOUNDS IT IS CULPABLE?[8]—Said Abaye to him, He informs us much. For if we [deduced] from our Mishnah, I might object, Since it is perforated all over,[9] it may not [be thus used]; hence he informs us as they say in the West [Palestine]: Any hole over which the ink can pass is not a hole.

a R. Zera objected: [*And he shall rend it*] *by the wings thereof:*[1] this is to teach that the skin is fit.[2] Now if you think that it is [a separate] skin, how can Scripture include it?[3]—Said Abaye to him, It is [indeed a separate] skin, but the Divine Law includes it.[4] Others state, R. Zera said: We too learnt thus: '*By the wings thereof*'; this is to include the skin. Now, if you say that it is [a separate] skin, it is well: hence a verse is required for including it. But if you say that it is not skin, why is a verse required for including it? Said Abaye to him, In truth I may tell you that it is not [a separate] skin, yet it is necessary. I might argue, Since it is covered with splits [holes], it is repulsive. [Hence] we are informed [otherwise].

Mar son of Rabina asked R. Naḥman b. Isaac: May *tefillin* be written upon the skin of a clean fish? If Elijah will come and declare, he replied. What does 'if Elijah will come and declare' mean? Shall we say, whether it has a [separate] skin or not,—but we see that it has a skin? Moreover we learnt: The bones of a fish and its skin afford protection in the tent wherein is a corpse![5] Rather [he meant]: If Elijah comes and tells [us] whether its foul smell[6] evaporates or not.

Samuel and Ḳarna were sitting by the bank of the Nehar Malka,[7] and saw the water rising and becoming discoloured. Said Samuel to Ḳarna, A great man is arriving from the West who suffers from stomach trouble, and the water is rising to give him a welcome. Go and smell his bottle![8] So he went and met Rab. He asked him, How do we know that *tefillin* may be written only on the skin of a clean [edible] animal? Because it is written, *that*
b *the Law of the Lord may be in thy mouth,*[1] [meaning] of that which is permitted in thy mouth, he replied. How do we know that blood is red? he asked.[2]—Because it is said, *and the Moabites saw the water over against them as red as blood.*[3] How do we know that circumcision [must be performed] in that [particular] place?

(6) The reference being to a moss or fungus which sprouts up in such places. (7) Distinct from its flesh. (8) Which shows that it has a distinct skin, v. *supra* 107a, n. c2. (9) Lit., 'it has holes (and) holes'—where the feathers are set.

a (1) Lev. I, 17. The reference is to a fowl burnt-offering, whose wings were burnt upon the altar. (2) To be burnt on the altar, it being unnecessary to skin the bird first. (3) It should be the same as the skin of an animal, which must be first removed, v. 6. (4) This verse shows that the skin of a bird is not the same as that of an animal. (5) If food is in a vessel which is covered by the bones or the skin of a fish, or if the whole vessel, which is closed, is made from these materials, the food is protected from contamination; v. Num. XIX, 15.—Thus the skin is mentioned as a separate entity. (6) Lit., 'filth'. (7) The Royal Canal. The Canal connecting the Euphrates and the Tigris at Nehardea and Maḥoza respectively; Obermeyer, 244f. (8) Examine his knowledge—a humorous allusion to Ḳarna's ability to judge whether wine was good or not merely by smelling the bottle, Keth. 105a. V. Obermeyer, op. cit., p. 247 and notes.

b (1) Ex. XIII, 9. (2) Only blood that is red or of colours akin to redness defiles a woman as a menstruant (Nid. 19a), and this was the point of his question. (3) II Kings III, 22.

◁ *For the continuation of the English translation of this page see overleaf.*

מסורת הש"ס

פיטרא מאונא דחצבא מיחייב משום עוקר דבר מגידולו מתיב רב אושעיא *התולש מעציץ נקוב חייב ושאינו נקוב פטור התם לאו היינו רביתיה הכא היינו רביתיה: חיה ועוף כו': אמר רב הונא *כותבין תפילין על גבי עור של עוף טהור אמר רב יוסף מאי קמ"ל דאית ליה עור תנינא החובל בהן חייב א"ל אביי טובא קמ"ל דאי ממתניתין הוה אמינא כיון דאית ביה ניקבי ניקבי לא קמ"ל *כדאמרי במערבא כל נקב שהדיו עוברת עליו אינו נקב מיתיבי רבי זירא °בכנפיו להכשיר את העור ואי ס"ד עור הוא היכי מרבי ליה קרא א"ל אביי עור הוא ורחמנא רבייה איכא דאמרי א"ר זירא אף אנן נמי תנינא בכנפיו לרבות את העור אי אמרת בשלמא עור הוא היינו דאיצטריך קרא לרבוייה אלא אי אמרת לאו עור הוא אמאי איצטריך קרא לרבוייה אמר ליה אביי לעולם אימא לך לאו עור הוא ואיצטריך סד"א כיון דאית ביה פירצי פירצי מאיס קמ"ל בעא מיניה מר בריה דרבינא מרב נחמן בר יצחק מהו לכתוב תפילין על גבי עור של דג טהור א"ל אם יבא אליהו ויאמר מאי אם יבא אליהו ויאמר אילימא אי דאית ליה עור אי דלית ליה עור הא חזינן דאית ליה עור ועוד התנן *עצמות הדג ועורו מצילין באהל המת אלא אם יבא אליהו ויאמר אי פסקא זוהמא מיניה אי לא פסקא זוהמא מיניה: שמואל וקרנא הוו יתבי אגודא דנהר מלכא חזינהו למיא דקא דלו ועכירי א"ל שמואל לקרנא גברא רבה קאתי ממערבא וחייש במעיה וקא דלו מיא לאקבולי אפיה קמיה זיל תהי ליה אקנקניה אזל אשכחיה לרב א"ל מניין שאין כותבין תפילין אלא על גבי עור בהמה טהורה א"ל דכתיב *°למען תהיה תורת ה' בפיך מן המותר בפיך *מניין לדם שהוא אדום שנאמר °ויראו מואב מנגד את המים אדומים כדם *מניין למילה שבאותו מקום נאמר כאן ערלתו ונאמר להלן ערלתו מה להלן דבר שעושה פרי אף כאן דבר שעושה פרי אימא לבו דכתיב °ומלתם את ערלת לבבכם אימא אזנו דכתיב °הנה ערלה אזנם דנין ערלתו תמה מערלתו תמה ואין דנין ערלתו תמה מערלת שאינה תמה א"ל *מאי שמך קרנא א"ל יהא רעוא דתיפוק ליה קרנא בעיניה לסוף עייליה שמואל לביתיה אוכליה נהמא דשערי וכסא דהרסנא ואשקייה שיכרא ולא אחוי ליה בית הכסא כי היכי דלישתלשל לייט רב ואמר מאן דמצערן לא לוקמוה ליה בני וכן הוה: כתנאי מניין למילה שבאותו מקום נאמר כאן ערלתו ונאמר להלן ערלתו מה להלן דבר שעושה פרי אף כאן דבר שעושה פרי דברי ר' יאשיה ר' נתן אומר אינו צריך הרי הוא אומר °וערל זכר אשר לא ימול את בשר ערלתו מקום שניכר בין זכרות לנקבות: *ת"ר כותבין תפילין על גבי עור בהמה טהורה ועל גבי עור חיה טהורה ועל גבי עור נבלות וטרפות שלהן ונכרכות בשערן ונתפרות בגידן והלכה למשה מסיני א) שהתפילין נכרכות בשערן ונתפרות בגידן אבל אין כותבין לא על גבי עור בהמה טמאה ולא על גבי עור חיה טמאה ואינו צריך לומר על גבי עור נבלה וטרפה שלהן ואין נכרכין בשערן ואין נתפרות בגידן וזו שאילה שאל *ביתוסי אחד את ר' יהושע הגרסי מניין שאין כותבין תפילין על עור בהמה טמאה דכתיב °למען תהיה תורת ה' בפיך מדבר המותר בפיך אלא מעתה על גבי עור נבלות וטרפות אל יכתבו א"ל אמשול לך משל למה"ד לשני בני אדם שנתחייבו הריגה למלכות אחד הרגו מלך ואחד הרגו איספקליטור ב) איזה מהן משובח הוי אומר זה שהרגו מלך אלא מעתה יאכלו אמר ליה התורה אמרה °לא תאכלו כל נבלה ואת אמרת יאכלו א"ל קאלוס: **מתני'** אין עושין הילמי בשבת אבל

ויקרא א | שמות יג | מ"ב ג | דברי' י | ירמי' ו | בראשית יז | דברים יד

א) לעיל כח: ב) [שר הטבחים ת"י רב ספקלטוריא. ערוך]

רש"י

פיטרא. פטריות בולי"ן: מאונא דחצבא. פעמים שהוא גדל בשפת הדלי ממים: ושאינו נקוב פטור. משום דלא מחובר בקרקע עולם הוא: לאו היינו רביתיה. דאין דרך זריעה שם אבל אלו שאמרנו הוא עיקר גידולן: נקבי נקבי. מקום מושב נוצה: לא ניכתוב. דרחמנא אמר *וכתבתם כתיבה תמה שלימה ולא מופסקת: בכנפיו. בעולת העוף משתעי שיסיסענו בעוד כנפיו בו *ומקטיר כנפיו כל כנפי הגוף בלו"ש בלע"ז נוצה הוא הדקה שהיא בבשר כמין למר שאין לה שרשים קשים: להכשיר את העור. לימדך הכתוב שאינו צריך הפשט כעולת בהמה שפסל בה את העור: פירצי. הייט נקבי: מאי אם יבא אליהו ויאמר. היתר ואיסור אין תלוי בו דלא בשמים היא: והתנן עצמות הדג ועורו מצילין באהל המת. לפי שאין מקבלין טומאה כדתניא בת"כ עור יכול עורות שבים כו' ועצמות הדג נמי דכלי עצם דמקבלים טומאה מכל מעשה עזים ילפינן לה להביא דבר הבא מן העזים מן הקרנים ומן הטלפים* אבל דגים לא וכל שאינו מקבל טומאה חוצץ בפני הטומאה ומשנה זו במס' כלים: דהוו דלו. גליון מגביהן: לאקבולי אפיה. לעשות מחילה סביביו כשהוא נפנה על דופני הספינה שלא יראה גילויו. ע"א לקנח: ועכירי. ענין נער משום נערו שאף הוא עכור ומפני שלא היה רוח מנשבת וראה המים נעשין גלין הבין שלכבוד אדם גדול הוא והנהר היה משוך מא"י לבבל: תהי. הריח בו בקנקנו אם יין הוא או החמיץ כמו בת תיהא דאמר גבי יין נסך (ע"ז ד' סו:) כלומר בדקהו אם חכם הוא אם לאו: מנין לדם שהוא אדום. דגבי נדה דם כתיב ותנן (נדה דף יט.) ה' דמים טמאים באשה וכולן משום דמראיתן אדומה אף על גב דשחור תנא בהו אמרינן שחור אדום הוא אלא שלקה: ונאמר להלן ערלתו. גבי נטיעה (ויקרא יט): תמה. באותיותיה ערלתו: ואין דנין ערלתו מערלת. דאין זו אמירה תמה שאינו מפורש בתוך התיבה ערלת מה: תיפוק קרנא בעיניה. הבין בו שלנסותו בא: אוכליה נהמא דשערי. כדי לשלשל דרופא היה שמואל: ולא אחוי ליה בית הכסא. שמתוך כך מתהפך ומתבלבל הזבל במעיו ומתמוגג כולו: ונכרכות. האיגרות: בשערן. של אלו ואחר כך מכניסן בדפוסי הקציצה שלהן: אספקלטור. שר הטבחים בלשון יוני: זה שהרגו מלך. ואלו לקו ע"י בורלן: קאלוס. משובח טעם זה: **מתני'** הילמי. שלמויי"א:

[מנחות לד.] | לעיל קה. [נ"ל ומקטיר] | חולין קיט: | [חולין כה:] | [בליסס"י מ"א] | [לעיל כח: מכות יא.] נדה יט. [תוספ' פט"ו] | [ב"ב פט.] | [מסכת סופרים פ"א הל' א וב' בשינוי לשון קצת] | מסכת סופרים פ"א הלכה ב

תוספות

ואי ס"ד עור הוא היכי מרבי ליה קרא. תימה לר"י הא אפילו נוצה שבכנפים מרבה קרא וי"ל דבהמה נמי אשכחן שהיה קרב שיער שבזקן תיישים ולמר שבראש רחלים כדאמרינן בזבחים (דף פה:) ובחולין (דף נ.) דלא קפיד קרא אלא אהפשט עור וה"נ אע"פ שהנוצה קריבה אי עור הוא צריך הפשט:

ר"ח ל"ג וקדלו מיא לאקבולי אפיה אלא הכי גרס חזנהו שמואל למיא דקדלו ועכירי אמר שמואל גברא רבה קאתי וחש במעיה פי' שמע שמואל שמועה שאדם גדול היה בא בספינה וידע שמואל שישתה מן הנהר אותו אדם גדול ומתוך כך יחוש במעיו לפי שהמים היו עכורים מחמת הרוח שהיה מבלבלם ולפי ששמואל היה רופא מומחה א"ל לקרנא זיל תהי ליה בקנקניה פי' תראה אם הוא חכם וראוי לכבדו אביאנו לביתי ואעשה לו רפואה ואכבדו לפי מה שראוי לו: **מניין** לדם שהוא אדום. וכל אותן ד' מינין דמרבינן* מדמיה דמיה יש בהן צד אדמומית:

[נדה יט.]

איזה מהן חשוב אותו שהרגו מלך. וא"ת תינח מתו מחליהן נחורות ועקורות מאי איכא למימר וי"ל כיון דמתו שרי א"כ מן המותר בפיך לאו דוקא אלא ממין המותר בפיך קאמר: **אין** עושין הילמי בשבת. הלכה כרבנן דבפרק קמא דעירובין (דף יד:) אמר אין הלכה כר' יוסי לא בהילמי ולא בלחיין ואמר נמי התם פוק חזי מאי עמא דבר ופי' בקונטרס וכבר נהגו העם בלחי משהו וכיון דאין הלכה כר' יוסי בלחיים כ"ש בהילמי דאפילו רב הונא בר חיננא דפליג התם בלחיים מודה בהילמי ושרי לעשות מי מלח בשבת ליתן על עופות ללויין ואם נותן מלח על העופות ואח"כ נותן משקין עליהם שרי אפילו לרבי יוסי שהשמנונית ממתיק המלח כמו שמן ועלין:

עין משפט נר מצוה

י א מיי' פ"א מהלכות תפילין הלכה י ופ"א מהל' כלים הל' ד סמג עשין כב כה טוש"ע א"ח סי' לב סעיף יב וטוש"ע י"ד סי' רעא סעיף א [וברא"ש בהל' ס"ת הלכה ב]:

יא ב מיי' פ"א מהל' תפילין הל' כ טוש"ע א"ח סי' לב סעי' יג:

יב ג מיי' פ"ו מהל' מעשה קרבנות הל' כא סמג עשין קפ:

יג ד מיי' פ"ו מהל' טומאת מת הלכה א:

יד ה מיי' פ"א מהל' תפילין הל' י סמג עשין כב וכה טוש"ע א"ח סי' לב סעיף יב וטוש"ע י"ד סי' רעא סעיף א [וברא"ש בהלכות ס"ת הלכה ב]:

טו ו מיי' פ"ה מהל' איסורי ביאה הל' ו [טוש"ע י"ד סי' קפא סעי' א]:

טז ז מיי' פ"א מהל' תפילין הלכה י סמג עשין כב וכה טוש"ע א"ח סי' לב סעיף יב וטוש"ע י"ד סי' רעא סעיף א [ובאלפסי בהל' תפילין דף עא: וברא"ש שם הלכה ד]:

יז ח מיי' פ"ג שם הלכה א ח סמג שם טוש"ע א"ח סי' לב סעיף מד

יח ט מיי' שם הלכה א וט' טוש"ע שם סעיף מט.

רבינו חננאל

נצרר הדם אע"פ שלא יצא. ר' יוחנן בן נורי אומר ח' שרצים יש להן עורות מדקתני בהא מתניתא בשרצים שיש להן עורות. אלמא דרבנן הוא דאית להו חלוקה במקצת שמונה שרצים ומקצתן אבל ר' יוחנן בן נורי אכולה מחייב ומחייב דהכא בשבת כוותיה וקשיא לרב ופריק רב אשי אליבא דרב ואמר ת"ק דמפליג בין מקצת שרצים למקצתן לאו חכמים אינון אלא ר' יהודה דאזיל בתר גישתא דתנן רבי יהודה אומר הלטאה כחולדה אבל רבנן דפליגי התם על ר' יוחנן בן נורי לענין טומאה פליגי. אבל לענין שבת מודו ליה. ואקשינן אי הכי הא ברייתא דתניא הצד א' מח' שרצים האמורין בתורה והחובל בהן חייב דברי ר' יוחנן בן נורי דברי ר' יוחנן בן נורי ומחלקותו הוה ליה למיתנא דמשמע אפי' רבנן דפליגי עליה לענין טומאה הכא מודו ליה ופרקי' תני דברי רבי יוחנן בן נורי ומחלקותו פירוש חבורה מלשון חברבורות. כגון יחת מתחתתים יגל מגלגל מכלת מכלכול וכיוצא בהן ודייקינן מדקתני החובל בהן פטור. מכלל שההורגן חייב. ומוקים לה ר' ירמיה כר' אלעזר דאמר ההורג כינה בשבת כהורג גמל בשבת ודחי רב יוסף ואמר אפי' תימא רבנן מחייבי ליה דלא פטרי רבנן אלא כגון כינה דאינה פרה ורבה אבל שקצים ורמשים דפרו ורבו מחייבי ההורגן ושניהן דרשו מאילים האמורים במעשה המשכן ועורות אילים שהורגים אותן ליטול עורותיהן כדפרישנן דכל מלאכה ממעשה המשכן גמרי להו. והריגת מזיקין מפרשינן לה בכל כתבי הקדש. ואקשי ליה אביי לרב יוסף שהקב"ה זן ביצי כינים והתניא הספויין וביצי כינים אלמא יש ביצים לכינים והן בלשון ארמית נכי ובלשון ישמעאל ציבאן ופרעושים ודאי יש להן ביצים ולא פטר ר' יהושע*) את ההורגן ולא פטר את הצדן ואמר מר רב יהודה גאון זצ"ל דהוא מרבנן קשישי ראשונים דהוו מימנעי מלצוד פרעוש בשבת ואפי' על בשרם ולא מנעון למשקל כינים כדמפרש בריש מס' דא: **פיסקא** הצדן לצורך חייב ושלא לצורך פטור כו' המפים מורסא בשבת והצד נחש בשבת אע"ג דאוקמינהו רב לר"ש דאמר מלאכה שאינה צריכה לגופה פטור עליה קיי"ל כשמואל דאמר בהו דאינן פטור ומותר: **אמר** שמואל [השולה] דג מן הים. אם הוציאו מן הים ולא שהה כדי יציאת נפש עד שהחזירו לים פטור שהרי לא עקר דבר מגידולו וגם לא הרגו ולא העתיקו נמי ממקום חיותו לגמרי אבל אם הניחו ביבשה עד שיבש בו כסלע לחלוחית המים חייב א"ר יוסי בר אבין ולא אמרו שיבש אלא בין סנפירין של דג ששם חייו. וכיון שיבש שם כאילו מת וזו השמועה של ר' יוסי בר' אבין מפורש בתענית פ' סדר תעניות האלו רב אשי אמר לא תימא יבש ממש אלא אפי' (דברירה) [דעבד רירי] פי' דרירי של דג יוצא מתוך פיו הנה נטה למות ואינו חוזר בחיותו וכמת הוא חשוב והשולה אותו חייב. הא דאמר שמואל הכניס ידו למעי בהמה ודלדל עובר שבמעיה חייב ואסיקנא חיוביה משום עוקר דבר מגידולו כדרב ששת דמאן דתלש [כשותא] מהיזמי והיגי [חייב] ומפרש בפ' בכל מערבין דקטלין לה להיזמתא ויבשה כשותא: **אמר** אביי האי מאן דתלש פיטורא מאונא דחצבא חייב משום עוקר דבר מגידולו. פי' פיטורא זה ממיני כמהין ופטריות ומפורש בגמ' ברכות פ' כיצד מברכין אמר אביי מירבא קא רבו מן ארעא ומינק מן אוירא ינקי עיקר שלהן מן הקרקע ולא מיתמר בהן גידולי הארץ והכין נמי להעוקר פטריות מן אונא דחצבא אע"פ שהוא כלי חרס יוצא ונגדל ומאוירא ינקי. וכמה דאית לפיטורא במקום גידולו אית ביה כח דיניק מן אוירא. וכד מיעקר לא יניק מאוירא: **מותיב** רבה אושעיא תולש מעציץ נקוב חייב ומשאינו נקוב פטור דאלמא פיטורא באונא דחצבא כעשב בעציץ [שאינו] נקוב דמי ופרקינן התם לאו היינו רביתיה. הכא היינו רביתיה.

*) ע"ס יש כאן ונראה דל"ל ולא פטר ר"י אלא את הצדן אבל לא את ההורגן.

רב נסים גאון

שהזכירו במסכת ברכות (דף מ) על כמהין ופטריות אומר שהכל נהיה בדברו והקשינו וכמהין ופטריות לאו מגידולי קרקע נינהו ורמינהי כו' ופריק אביי מרבי מארעא קא רבי מינק מאוירא קא יניק:

מעלה

Continuation of translation from previous page as indicated by ◁

—'*His 'orlah*'[4] is stated here, and '*its 'orlah*'[5] is stated elsewhere: just as there something that produces fruit [is meant], so here too something [the limb] that produces fruit [is meant]. Perhaps it means the heart, for it is written, *Circumcise therefore the foreskin of your heart?*[6] Perhaps it means the ear, for it is written, *behold, their ear is uncircumcised?*[7]—We learn the complete [word] '*orlatho* from the complete [word] '*orlatho*, but we do not learn the complete '*orlatho* from '*orlath*, which is incomplete.[8] 'What is your name?' he asked. Ḳarna. 'May it be [His] will that a horn [ḳarna] shall sprout out from between his eyes!' he retorted.[9] Subsequently Samuel took him into his house, gave him barley bread and a fish pie to eat, and strong liquor to drink,[10] but did not show him the privy, that he might be eased.[11] Rab cursed, saying, He who causes me pain, may no sons arise from him. And thus it was.

This is a controversy of Tannaim. How do we know that circumcision [must be performed] in that place? '*Orlatho* is stated here, and '*orlatho* is stated elsewhere: just as there something that produces fruit [is meant], so here too something that produces fruit [is meant]: that is R. Josiah's view. R. Nathan said: It is unnecessary: surely it is said, *And the uncircumcised male who is not circumcised in the flesh of his foreskin:* [that indicates] the place where the male sex is differentiated from the female sex.

Our Rabbis taught: *Tefillin* can be written upon the skin c of clean animals and upon the skin of clean beasts,[1] and upon the skin of their *nebeloth* or *ṭerefoth*,[2] and they are tied round with their hair,[3] and sewn with their tendons. And it is a *halachah* from Moses at Sinai[4] that *tefillin* are tied round with their hair and sewn with their tendons. But we may not write [them] upon the skin of unclean animals or upon the skin of unclean beasts, and the skin of their *nebeloth* and *ṭerefoth* need not be stated;[5] nor may they be tied round with their hair or sewn with their tendons. And this question a certain Boethusian[6] asked R. Joshua the grits dealer: How do we know that *tefillin* may not be written upon the skin of an unclean animal? Because it is written, '*that the law of thy Lord may be in thy mouth*', [implying] of that which is permitted in thy mouth. If so, they should not be written on the skin of *nebeloth* and *ṭerefoth?* Said he to him, I will give you a comparison. What does this resemble? Two men who were condemned to death by the State, one being executed by the king and the other by the executioner. Who stands higher? Surely he who was slain by the king![7] If so, let them be eaten? The Torah saith, *Ye shall not eat any nebelah*,[8] he retorted, yet you say, let them be eaten! Well spoken![9] admitted he.

MISHNAH. ONE MAY NOT PREPARE [PICKLING] BRINE ON

(4) Gen. XVII, 14, in connection with circumcision (E.V. *foreskin*). (5) Lev. XIX, 23, in reference to the fruit of a tree within the first three years of its planting, which may not be eaten (E.V. *uncircumcision*). (6) Deut. X, 16. This question of course was not meant seriously, but was put merely to point out that 'circumcision' is mentioned in connection with other organs too. (7) Jer. VI, 10. (8) '*Orlatho*' is written in both verses quoted by Rab, whereas '*orlah* and '*orlath* are written in the verses proposed by Ḳarna. (9) He was probably annoyed at Ḳarna's temerity in thus examining him. (10) All this he gave him to act as a laxative. (11) This, too, was part of the treatment. Samuel was a doctor.

c (1) *Behemah* denotes a domestic animal; *ḥayyah*, a wild animal. (2) V. Glos. (3) The slips of parchment are rolled up and tied round with hair of these animals. (4) V. *supra* 28b, n. c7. (5) As unfit. (6) The Boethusians were a sect similar to the Sadducees, and disagreed with the Pharisees on certain religious beliefs, such as immortality and its concomitant, reward and punishment in the Hereafter, and resurrection, which they rejected; and in certain practices, viz., the date of Pentecost and the method of preparing incense on the Day of Atonement (Men. X, 3; Tosaf. Yoma I, 8—the parallel passage in Yoma 39a has 'Sadducees'). The opinion most generally held is that the Boethusians were a variety of the Sadducees. (7) Similarly, *nebeloth* and *ṭerefoth* may be regarded as slain by God. (8) Deut. XIV, 21. (E.V.: '*of anything that dieth of itself*'). (9) No argument can override an explicit statement to the contrary.

פיטרא מאונא דחצבא מיחייב משום עוקר דבר מגידולו מתיב רב אושעיא *התולש מעציץ נקוב חייב ושאינו נקוב פטור התם לאו היינו רביתיה הכא היינו רביתיה: חיה ועוף כו': אמר רב הונא *כותבין תפילין על גבי עור של עוף טהור אמר רב יוסף מאי קמ"ל דאית ליה עור תנינא החובל בהן חייב א"ל אביי טובא קמ"ל דאי ממתניתין הוה אמינא כיון דאית ביה ניקבי ניקבי לא קמ"ל *כדאמרי במערבא ^בכל נקב שהדיו עוברת עליו אינו נקב מיתיבי רבי זירא °בכנפיו להכשיר את העור ואי ס"ד עור הוא היכי מרבי ליה קרא א"ל אביי עור הוא ורחמנא רבייה איכא דאמרי א"ר זירא אף אנן נמי תנינא בכנפיו ^לרבות את העור אי אמרת בשלמא עור הוא היינו דאיצטריך קרא לרבוייה אלא אי אמרת לאו עור הוא אמאי איצטריך קרא לרבוייה אמר ליה אביי לעולם אימא לך לאו עור הוא ואיצטריך סד"א כיון דאית ביה פירצי פירצי מאים קמ"ל בעא מיניה מר בריה דרבינא מרב נחמן בר יצחק מהו לכתוב תפילין על גבי עור של דג טהור א"ל אם יבא אליהו ויאמר מאי אם יבא אליהו ויאמר אילימא אי דאית ליה עור אי דלית ליה עור הא חזינן דאית ליה עור ועוד התנן *עצמות הדג ועורו מצילין באהל המת אלא ^אם יבא אליהו ויאמר אי פסקא זוהמא מיניה אי לא פסקא זוהמא מיניה: שמואל וקרנא הוו יתבי אגודא דנהר מלכא חזינהו למיא דקא דלו ועכירי א"ל שמואל לקרנא גברא רבה קאתי ממערבא וחייש במעיה וקא דלו מיא לאקבולי אפיה קמיה זיל תהי ליה אקנקניה אזל אשכחיה לרב א"ל מניין שאין כותבין תפילין אלא על גבי עור בהמה טהורה א"ל דכתיב *°למען תהיה תורת ה' בפיך מן המותר בפיך *מניין לדם שהוא אדום שנאמר °ויראו מואב מנגד את המים אדומים כדם *מניין למילה שבאותו מקום נאמר כאן ערלתו ונאמר להלן ערלתו מה להלן דבר שעושה פרי אף כאן דבר שעושה פרי אימא לבו דכתיב °ומלתם את ערלת לבבכם איבא אזנו דכתיב °הנה ערלה אזנם דנין ערלתו תמה מערלתו תמה ואין דנין ערלתו תמה מערלת שאינה תמה א"ל *מאי שמך קרנא א"ל יהא רעוא דתיפוק ליה קרנא בעיניה לסוף עייליה שמואל לביתיה אוכליה נהמא דשערי וכסא דהרסנא ואשקייה שיכרא ולא אחוי ליה בית הכסא כי היכי דלישתלשל לייט רב ואמר מאן דמצערן לא לוקמוה ליה בני ולכן הוה: כתנאי מניין למילה שבאותו מקום נאמר כאן ערלתו ונאמר להלן ערלתו מה להלן דבר שעושה פרי אף כאן דבר שעושה פרי דברי ר' יאשיה ר' נתן אומר אינו צריך הרי הוא אומר °וערל זכר אשר לא ימול את בשר ערלתו מקום שניכר בין זכרות לנקבות *ת"ר כותבין תפילין על גבי עור בהמה טהורה ועל גבי עור חיה טהורה ועל גבי עור נבלות וטרפות שלהן ^ונכרכות בשערן ^ונתפרות בגידן והלכה למשה מסיני *שהתפילין נכרכות בשערן ונתפרות בגידן אבל אין כותבין לא על גבי עור בהמה טמאה ולא על גבי עור חיה טמאה ואינו צריך לומר על גבי עור נבלה וטרפה שלהן ואין נכרכין בשערן ואין נתפרות בגידן וזו שאילה שאל *ביתוסי אחד את ר' יהושע הגרסי מניין שאין כותבין תפילין על עור בהמה טמאה דכתיב °למען תהיה תורת ה' בפיך מדבר המותר בפיך אלא מעתה על גבי עור נבלות וטרפות אל יכתבו א"ל אמשול לך משל למה"ד לשני בני אדם שנתחייבו הריגה למלכות אחד הרגו מלך ואחד הרגו איספקליטור ^איזה מהן משובח הוי אומר זה שהרגו מלך אלא יאכלו אמר ליה התורה אמרה °לא תאכלו כל נבלה ואת אמרת יאכלו א"ל קאלוס: **מתני'** אין עושין הילמי בשבת אבל

א) [לעיל כח:] ב) [בר' טעבחים ת"י רב ספקלטוריא. ערוך]

רש"י

פיטרא. פטריות בולי"ן: מאונא דחצבא. פעמים שהוא גדל בשפת הדלי ממים: ושאינו נקוב פטור. משום דלא מחובר בקרקע עולם הוא: לאו היינו רביתיה. דאין דרך זריעה שם אבל אלו שאמרנו הוא עיקר גידולן: נקבי נקבי. מקום מושב נוצה: לא ניכתוב. דרחמנא אמר *וכתבתם כתיבה תמה שלימה ולא מופסקת: בכנפיו. בעולת העוף משתעי שיפסענו בעוד כנפיו בו *ומקטיר כנפיו כל כנפי הגוף בלו"ש בלע"ז נוצה הוא הדקה שהיא בבשר כמין צמר שאין לה שרשים קשים: להכשיר את העור. לימדך הכתוב שאינו צריך הפשט כעולת בהמה שפסל בה את העור: פירצי. היינו נקבי: מאי אם יבא אליהו ויאמר. היתר ואיסור אין תלוי בו דלא בשמים היא: והתנן עצמות הדג ועורו מצילין באהל המת. לפי שאין מקבלין טומאה כדתניא בת"כ עור יכול עורות שבים כו' ועצמות הדג נמי דכלי עצם דמקבלים טומאה מכל מעשה עזים ילפינן לה להביא דבר הבא מן העזים מן הקרנים ומן הטלפים* אבל דגים לא וכל שאינו מקבל טומאה חוצץ בפני הטומאה ומשנה זו במס' כלים: דהוו דלו. גליין מגביהן: לאקבולי אפיה. לעבות מחילה סביביו כשהוא נכנס על דופני הספינה שלא יראה גילויו. ע"א לקנח: ועכירי. ענין עכר משום עכרו שאף הוא עכור ומפני שלא היה רוח מנשבת ורואה המים נעשין גלין הבין שלכבוד אדם גדול הוא והנהר היה מבוך מא"י לבבל: תהי. הריח בו בקנקנו אם יין הוא או החמיץ כמו בת תיהא דאמר גבי יין נסך (ע"ז ד' סו:) כלומר בדקהו אם חכם הוא אם לאו: מנין לדם שהוא אדום. דגבי נדה דם כתיב ותנן (נדה דף יט.) ה' דמים טמאים באשה וכולן משום דמראיתן אדומה אף על גב דשחור תנא בהו אמרינן שחור אדום הוא אלא שלקה: ונאמר להלן ערלתו. גבי נטיעה (ויקרא יט): תמה. באותיותיה ערלתו: ואין דנין ערלתו מערלת. דאין זו אמורה תמה שאינו מפורש בתוך התיבה ערלת מה: תיפוק קרנא בעיניה. הבין בו שלגלגו בו: אוכליה נהמא דשערי. כדי לשלשל דרופא היה שמואל: ולא אחוי ליה בית הכסא. שמתוך כך מתהפך ומתבלבל הזבל במעיו ומתמוגג כולו: ונכרכות. האיגרות: בשערן. של אלו ואחר כך מכניסן בדפוסי הקציצה שלהן: אספקליטור. שר הטבחים בלשון יוני: זה שהרגו מלך. ואלו נקו ע"י בוראן: קאלוס. משובח טעם זה: **מתני'** הילמי. שלמוייר"א בלע"ז: אבל

תוספות

ואי ס"ד עור הוא היכי מרבי ליה קרא. תימה לר"י הא אפילו נוצה שבכנפים מרבה קרא וי"ל דבהמה נמי אשכחן שהיה קרב שיער שבזקן תישים ולמר שבראש רחלים כדאמרינן בזבחים (דף פה:) ובחולין (דף כ.) דלא קפיד קרא אלא אהפשט עור וה"ג אע"פ שהעולה קריבה אי עור הוא צריך הפשט:

ר"ח ל"ג וקדלו מיא לאקבולי אפיה אלא הכי גרס חזנהו שמואל למיא דקדלו ועכירי אמר שמואל גברא רבה קאתי וחש במעיה פי' שמע שמואל שמועה שאדם גדול היה בא בספינה וידע שמואל שישתה מן הנהר אותו אדם גדול ומתוך כך יחוש במעיו לפי שהמים היו עכורים מחמת הרוח שהיה מבלבלם ולפי ששמואל היה רופא מומחה א"ל לקרנא זיל תהי ליה בקנקניה פי' תראה אם הוא חכם וראוי לכבדו אביאנו לביתי ואעשה לו רפואה ואכבדנו לפי מה שראוי לו:

מניין לדם שהוא אדום. וכל אותן ד' מינין דמרבינן* מדמיה דמיה יש בהן צד אדמונית:

איזה מהן חשוב אותו שהרגו מלך. וא"ת תינח מתו מאליהן נחורות ועקורות מאי איכא למימר וי"ל כיון דמתו שרי א"כ מן המותר בפיך לאו דוקא אלא ממין המותר בפיך קאמר:

אין עושין הילמי בשבת. הלכה כרבנן דבפרק קמא דעירובין (דף יד:) אמר אין הלכה כר' יוסי לא בהילמי ולא בלחיין ואמר נמי התם פוק חזי מאי עמא דבר ופי' בקונטרס וכבר נהגו העם בלחי משהו וכיון דאין הלכה כר' יוסי בלחיים כ"ש בהילמי דאפילו רב הונא בר חיננא דפליג התם בלחיים מודה בהילמי ושרי לעשות מי מלח בשבת ליתן על עופות צלויין ואם נותן מלח על העופות ואח"כ נותן משקין עליהם שרי אפילו לרבי יוסי שהשמנונית ממתיק המלח כמו שמן: עלין

מסורת הש"ס

[מנחות לד.] — לעיל נה. [ג"ל ומקטיר] — חולין קיז: — [חולין כה:] — [לעיל כח. מכות יח. נדה יט. [תוספ' פ"ט]] — [ב"ב פט:] — [מסכת סופרים פ"א הל' א וכו' כביוי לשון קלת] — מסכת סופרים פ"ה הלכה ב — ויקרא א — שמות יג — דברי' י — ירמי' ו — בראשית יז — שמות יג — דברים יד

עין משפט נר מצוה

י א מיי' פ"א מהלכות תפילין הלכה י ופ"א מהל' כלים הל' ד סמג עשין כב כה טוש"ע א"ח סי' לב סעיף יב וטוש"ע י"ד סי' רעא סעיף א [וברא"ש בהל' ס"ת הלכה ב]:

יא ב מיי' פ"א מהל' תפילין הל' כ טוש"ע א"ח סי' לב סעי' יג:

יב ג מיי' פ"ו מהל' מעשה קרבנות הל' כא סמג עשין קפ:

יג ד מיי' פ"ו מהל' טומאת מת הלכה א:

יד ה מיי' פ"א מהל' תפילין הל' י סמג עשין כב וכה טוש"ע א"ח סי' לב סעיף יב וטוש"ע י"ד סי' רעא סעיף א [וברא"ש בהלכות ס"ת הלכה ב]:

טו ו מיי' פ"ה מהל' איסורי ביאה הל' ו [טוש"ע י"ד סי' קפח סעי' א]:

[נדה יט.]

טז ז מיי' פ"א מהל' תפילין הלכה י סמג עשין כב וכה טוש"ע א"ח סי' לב סעיף יב וטוש"ע י"ד סי' רעא סעיף א [ובאלפסי בהל' תפילין דף עה: וברא"ש שם הלכה ד]:

יז ח מיי' פ"ג שם הלכה א ח סמג שם טוש"ע א"ח סי' לב סעיף מד:

יח ט מיי' שם הלכה א וט' טוש"ע שם סעיף מט.

רבינו חננאל

נצרר הדם אע"פ שלא יצא. ר' יוחנן בן נורי אומר ח' שרצים יש להן עורות מדקתני בהא מתניתא בשרצים שיש להן עורות. אלמא דרבנן הוא דאית להו חלוקה במקצת שמונה שרצים ומקצתן אבל ר' יוחנן בן נורי אכולה מחייב ומחייב דהכא בשבת כוותיה וקשיא לרב ופריק רב אשי אליבא דרב ואמר ת"ק דמפליג בין מקצת שרצים למקצתן לאו חכמים אינון א"א ר' יהודה דאזיל בתר גישתא דתנן רבי יהודה אומר הלטאה כחולדה אבל רבנן דפליגי התם על ר' יוחנן בן נורי לענין טומאה פליגי. אבל לענין שבת מודו ליה. ואקשינן אי הכי הא ברייתא דתניא הצד א' מח' שרצים האמורין בתורה והחובל בהן חייב דברי ר' יוחנן בן נורי דברי ר' יוחנן בן נורי ומחלקותו הוה ליה למיתנא דמשמע אפי' רבנן דפליגי עליה לענין טומאה הכא מודו ליה ופרקי' תני דברי רבי יוחנן בן נורי ומחלקותו פירוש חבורה שלשון הברבורות. כגון יחת שתתחתים יגל מגלגל מכלת מכלכול וכיוצא בהן ודייקינן מדקתני החובל בהן פטור. מכלל שההורגן חייב. ומוקים לה ר' ירמיה כר' אלעזר דאמר ההורג כינה בשבת כהורג גמל בשבת ודחי רב יוסף ואמר אפי' תימא רבנן מחייבי ליה דלא פטרי רבנן אלא כגון כינה דאינה פרה ורבה אבל שקצים ורמשים דפרו ורבו מחייבי ההורגן ושניהן דרשו מאילים האמורים במעשה המשכן ועורות אילים שהורגים אותן ליטול עורותיהן כדפרישנן דכל מלאכה ממעשה המשכן גמרי להו. והריגת מזיקין מפרשינן לה בכל כתבי הקדש. ואקשי ליה אביי לרב יוסף שהקב"ה זן ביצי כינים והתניא הספוין וביצי כינים אלמא יש ביצים לכינים והן בלשון ארמית נכי ובלשון ישמעאל ציבאן ופרעושים ודאי יש להן ביצים ולא פטר ר' יהושע*) את ההורגן ולא פטר את הצדן ואמר מר רב יהודה גאון זצ"ל דהוא מרבנן קשישי ראשונים דהוו מימנעי מלצוד פרעוש בשבת ואפי' על בשרם ולא מנעון למשקל כינים כדמפרש בריש מס' דא: **פיסקא** הצדן לצורך חייב ושלא לצורך פטור כו' המפיס מורסא בשבת והצד נחש בשבת אע"ג דאוקמינהו רב לר"ש דאמר מלאכה שאינה צריכה לגופה פטור עליה קיי"ל כשמואל דאמר בהו דאינון פטור ומותר: **אמר** שמואל [השולה] דג מן הים. אם הוציאו מן הים ולא שהה כדי יציאת נפש עד שהחזירו לים פטור שהרי לא עקר דבר מגידולו וגם לא הרגו ולא העתיקו נמי ממקום היותו לגמרי אבל אם הניחו ביבשה עד שיבש בו כסלע להלוהית המים חייב א"ר יוסי בר אבין ולא אמרו שיבש אלא בין סנפירין של דג ששם חייו. וכיון שיבש שם כאילו מת וזו השמועה של ר' יוסי בר' אבין מפורש בתענית פ' סדר תעניות האלו רב אשי אמר לא תימא יבש ממש אלא אפי' (דבריירה) [דעביד רירי] פי' דרירי של דג יוצא מתוך פיו הנה נטה למות ואינו חוזר בחיותו וכמת הוא חשוב והשולה אותו חייב. הא דאמר שמואל הכניס ידו למעי בהמה ודלדל עובר שבמעיה חייב ואסיקנא חיוביה משום עוקר דבר מגידולו כדרב ששת דמאן דתלש [כשותא] מהיזמי והיגי [חייב] ומפרש בפ' בכל מערבין דקטלין לה להיזמתא ויבשה כשותא: **אמר** אביי האי מאן דתלש פיטורא מאונא דחצבא חייב משום עוקר דבר מגידולו. פי' פיטירא זה ממיני כמהין ופטריות ומפורש בגמ' ברכות פ' כיצד מברכין אמר אביי מירבא קא רבו מן ארעא ומינק מן אירא ינקי עיקר שלהן מן הקרקע ולא מיתמר בהן גידולי הארץ והכין נמי להעוקר פטריות מן אונא דהצבא אע"פ שהוא כלי חרס יוצא ונגדל ובאוירא ינקי. וכמה דאית לפיטורא במקום גידולו אית ביה כח דיניק מן אוירא. וכד מיעקר לא יניק מאוירא: **מותיב** רבה אושעיא תולש מעציץ נקוב חייב ומשאינו נקוב פטור דאלמא פיטוראבאונא דחצבא כעשב בעציץ [שאינו] נקוב דמי ופרקינן התם לאו היינו רביתיה. הכא היינו רביתית.

*) ע"ס יש כאן ונראה דצ"ל ולא פטר ר"י אלא את הצדן אבל לא את ההורגן.

רב נסים גאון

שהזכירו במסכת ברכות (דף מ) על כמהין ופטריות אומר שהכל נהיה בדברו והקשינו וכמהין ופטריות לאו מגידולי קרקע נינהו ורמינהי כו' ופריק אביי מרבי מארעא קא רבי מינק מאוירא קא יניק:

מעלה

אבל עושה הוא את מי המלח וטובל בהן פתו ונותן לתוך התבשיל *א"ר יוסי והלא הוא הילמי בין מרובה ובין מועט ואלו הן מי מלח המותרין נותן שמן לכתחלה לתוך המים או לתוך המלח: **גמ'** מאי קאמר א"ר יהודה אמר שמואל ה"ק אין עושין מי מלח מרובין אבל עושה הוא מי מלח מועטין: א"ר יוסי והלא הוא הילמי בין מרובין בין מועטין: איבעיא להו רבי יוסי לאסור או להתיר אמר רב יהודה להתיר מדלא קתני רבי יוסי אוסר א"ל רבה הא מדקתני סיפא ואלו הן מי מלח המותרין מכלל דר' יוסי לאסור אלא אמר רבה לאסור וכן אמר רבי יוחנן לאסור תניא נמי הכי אין עושין מי מלח מרובין לתת לתוך הכבשין שבתוך גיסטרא אבל עושה הוא מי מלח מועטין ואוכל בהן פתו ונותן לתוך התבשיל א"ר יוסי וכי מפני שהללו מרובין והללו מועטין הללו אסורין והללו מותרין יאמרו מלאכה מרובה אסורה מלאכה מועטת מותרת אלא אלו ואלו אסורין הן ואלו הן מי מלח המותרין נותן שמן ומלח או שמן ומים ובלבד שלא יתן מים ומלח לכתחלה: (עזין צנון ואתרוג סימן): תני רבי יהודה בר חביבא אין עושין מי מלח עזין מאי מי מלח עזין רבה ורב יוסף בר אבא דאמרי תרווייהו כל שהביצה צפה בהן וכמה אמר אביי תרי תילתי מילחא ותילתא מיא למאי עבדי לה א"ר אבהו למורייסא תני רבי יהודה בר חביבא אין מולחין צנון וביצה בשבת רב חזקיה משמיה דאביי אמר צנון אסור וביצה מותרת אמר רב נחמן מריש הוה מלחנא פוגלא אמינא אפסודי קא מפסידנא ליה דאמר שמואל פוגלא חורפי מעלי כיון דשמענא להא דכי אתא עולא ואמר במערבא מלחי *כישרי כישרי ממלח לא מלחנא טבולי ודאי מטבילנא תני ר' יהודה בר חביבא אתרוג צנון וביצה אילמלא קליפתן החיצונה אינן יוצאין מבני מעיים לעולם כי אתא רב דימי אמר מעולם לא טבע גברא בימא דסדום אמר רב יוסף הפוכה סדום והפוכה מילה גברא הוא דלא טבע כשורא טבע אמר ליה אביי לא מיבעיא קאמר לא מבעיא כשורא דאפילו בכל מימות שבעולם לא טבע אלא אפילו גברא דטבע בכל מימות שבעולם בימא דסדום לא טבע למאי נפקא מינה כי הא דרבין הוה שקיל ואזיל אחוריה דרבי ירמיה אגודא דימא דסדום אמר ליה מהו למימשי מהני מיא בשבת א"ל שפיר דמי מהו למימץ ולמיפתח אמר ליה זו לא שמעתי כיוצא בה שמעתי דאמר ר' זירא זימנין א"ל משמיה דרב מתנה וזימנין אמר לה משמיה דמר עוקבא ותרווייהו משמיה דאבוה דשמואל ולוי אמרין חד אמר יין בתוך העין אסור על גב העין מותר וחד אמר רוק תפל [אפילו] על גב העין אסור תסתיים דאבוה דשמואל הוא דאמר יין בתוך העין אסור על גב העין מותר מדאמר שמואל שורה אדם פיתו ביין ונותנו על גב העין בשבת דשמיעא ליה ממאן לאו דשמיעא ליה מאבוה וליטעמיך הא דאמר שמואל רוק תפל אפי' ע"ג העין אסור דשמיעא ליה ממאן אילימא דשמיעא ליה מאבוה אלא לוי ולא חדא אמר אלא חדא שמיעא ליה מאבוה וחדא שמיעא ליה מלוי ולא ידעינן הי מאבוה הי מלוי אמר מר עוקבא אמר שמואל שורה אדם קילורין מע"ש ונותן על גב עיניו בשבת ואינו חושש בר ליואי הוי קאי קמיה דמר עוקבא חזייה דהוה מייץ ופתח אמר ליה כולי האי ודאי לא שרא מר שמואל שלח ליה רבי ינאי למר עוקבא לישדר לן מר מהנך קילורין דמר שמואל שלח ליה שדורי משדרנא לך דלא תימא צר עין אנא אלא הכי אמר שמואל טובה טיפת צונן שחרית ורחיצת ידים ורגלים בחמין ערבית מכל קילורין שבעולם תניא נמי הכי אמר רבי מונא משום רבי יהודה טובה טיפת צונן שחרית ורחיצת *ידים ורגלים ערבית מכל קילורין שבעולם הוא היה אומר א) יד לעין תיקצץ ב) יד לחוטם תיקצץ יד לפה תיקצץ יד לאוזן תיקצץ יד לחסודה תיקצץ יד לאמה תיקצץ יד לפי טבעת תיקצץ יד לגיגית

א) מסכת כלה ב) [עי' תוס' נדה יג: ד"ה דינא]

רש"י

אבל עושה כו'. מפרש בגמ': והלא הוא הילמי בין רב בין מעט. ואם המרובים אסורים אף המועטים אסורים ואם אלו מותרים אף אלו מותרין ובגמרא מפרש דלחומרא א"ר יוסי דכולן לאיסור מפני שהוא כמעבד מתקן את האוכל הנתון לתוכו כדי שיתקיים: ואלו הן המותרין נותן שמן לתוך מים בתחלה. קודם שיתן המלח נותן שמן לתוך המלח בתחלה קודם שיתן המים דהשמן מעכב שאין המלח מתערב יפה עם המים ומתיש את כחו מהיות מי מלח עזין אבל לא יתן מים ומלח תחילה אפילו נותן שמן לבסוף דבשעה שנותן מים ומלח יחד הוא נראה כמעבד: גמ' מאי קאמר. מאי הילמי ומאי מי מלח: לאסור או להתיר. האי דקאמר שניהן שוין לאיסור או להיתר: כבשין. ירק שכובש להתקיים: גיסטרא. כלי שבור של חרס ואינו ראוי לכל תשמיש כשלם ומקצין אותו לכך: שהביצה צפה בהם. כח המלח מעכבת מלשקוע: למורייסא. של דגים: אין מולחין צנון וביצה. ג' וד' חתיכות יחד שהמלח מעבדן ונעשין קשין והוי תיקון: מריש הוה מלחנא פוגלא. בשבתא: פוגלא. צנון: כשרי. תלין גבוהים עיגול על עיגול: מימלח לא מלחנא. שתים יחד: טבולי. בשעת אכילה מטבילנא ואכילנא: קליפה חיצונה. דביצה היא החלבון אלא איידי דתני בהדי אתרוג וצנון קליפה נקט בה נמי לשון קליפה: אין יוצאין מבני מעים. שמתקשרין ומתקשין ונעצרין: לא טבע גברא בימא דסדום. מפני שהמים מלוחין וכח מליחתן מעכבו מלטבוע: והפוכה מילה. דברים האמורים בה הפוכין: כשורא טבע. בתמיה: מהו למימשי מהני מיא גרסינן. מי אסור משום רפואה דגזור רבנן בכל רפואות בשבת משום שחיקת סממנין ואלו מרפאות את העין: שפיר דמי. דלאו מוכחא מילתא דלרפואה עביד אף על פי שמרפאין שרי דטעמא דרפואה דאסירא ליתא אלא גזירה שמא ישחוק סממנין דדמי לטחינה שהוא אב מלאכה: מהו למימץ ולמפתח. לשון אין מעמצין את המת (לקמן דף קנא:) עוצם עיניו כשהוא רוחץ מהן בשבת מהו שיסגיר ויפתח עיניו כדי שיכנס מהן לעין: כיוצא בו שמעתי. דהיכא דמוכחא מילתא דלרפואה עביד אסור ומימץ ומפתח נמי מוכחא מילתא והא אסהדותא דרב דימי דאמר לא טבע גברא בימא דסדום נפקא לן מינה הא כיון דמליחי טובא מסו ואסר למימץ ולמפתח: זימנין א"ל וכו'. שקבל משניהם: ותרווייהו. רב מתנה ומר עוקבא: משמיה דאבוה דשמואל ולוי אמרי. תרתי מילי אמור חדא משמיה דאבוה דשמואל וחדא משמיה דלוי: חד אמר. או אבוה דשמואל או לוי: יין בתוך העין. דעמיץ ופתח אסור דמוכחא מילתא: על גב העין מותר. דאמרי לרחיצה בעלמא עבדי: רוק תפל. שלא טעם כלום משניעור משנתו: אפילו על גב עין אסור. דמוכחא מילתא דלרפואה דאילו לרחיצה מאיס להכי נקט רוק תפל לפי שהוא חזק ומרפא: וליטעמיך כו'. א"כ לוי ולא חדא אמר בתמיה והא חדא משמיה אתמר כדאמרן: שורה. במים: קילורין. לוזי"א בלע"ז: ונותן ע"ג עיניו. דלדידיה כיון דאצרכוה לשרותה מע"ש איכא היכרא וליכא למיגזר ומאן דחזיכהו סבר דרחילה בעלמא היא דכסבר שהוא יין: כולי האי ודאי לא שרא. דמוכחא מילתא: מר עוקבא הוה שכיח גבי מר שמואל ואב ב"ד היה בימיו כדאמרינן לעיל (דף נה: ובמועד קטן דף טז:): טיפת צונן. לתת בעיניו: ורחיצת ידים ורגלים בחמין ערבית. נמי מאירה העינים: הוא היה אומר. ר' מונא: יד לעין. שחרית קודם שיטול ידיו: תיקצץ. נוח לו שתקצץ שרוח רעה שורה על היד ומסמתו וכן כולן: לחסודה. ריבדא דכוסילתא פלימא"ה בלע"ז: לפי טבעת. נקב הרעי שעגול כטבעת: תיקצץ. ולא תגע שוב בעין או באוזן קודם נטילה:

לגיגית

עין משפט גר מצוה

יט א ב מיי' פכ"ב מהל' שבת הלכה י סמג לאוין סה טוש"ע א"ח סי' שכא סעיף ב:

כ ג ד מיי' שם טוש"ע שם סעיף ג:

כא ה ו מיי' פכ"א מהל' שבת הלכה כה סמג שם טוש"ע א"ח סי' שכח סעיף כ:

כב ז ח מיי' שם טוש"ע שם סעיף כא:

כג ט טוש"ע א"ח סי' ד סעיף ג:

כד י שם סעיף ד:

כה כ מיי' פכ"א מהל' איסורי ביאה הל' כג טוש"ע אה"ע סי' כג סעיף ד:

כו ל טוש"ע א"ח סי' ד סעיף ד:

מסורת הש"ס

עירובין יד:

[ס"א כישי כישי פירוש תתיכות תתיכות' ערוך ערך כשר]

[נ"א רחיצת ידים ורגלים בחמין ערוך ערך קלר]

גליון הש"ס

גמ' ונותן על גב עיניו. עי' לעיל דף יח ע"א תד"ה ומתרפאת:

רבינו חננאל

מפרשי רבנן עשב בעציץ שאינו נקוב כתלוש דמי כדמפרש בסוף המצניע והאי פטורא באונא דהצבא לאו כתלוש דמי הלכך התם לאו עוקר דבר מגידולו (דהוא רביתיה) והכא עוקר דבר מגידולו: והלכתא כדרב הונא שכותבין תפלין על עוף טהור ואע"ג דאית ביה ניקבי כיון שהדיו עובר עליו כשר ואע"ג דדחו אביי לסייעדיה מן ושסע אותו בכנפיו לרבות את העור וקאמר לעולם אימא לך לאו עור הוא ואיצטריך כו' דיחוי בעלמא הוא דדחי ומתניתין החובל בהן חייב: **בעא** מר בריה דרב מרב נחמן מהו לכתוב תפלין על עור של דג טהור. אסיקנא אם יבא אליהו ויאמר פסקה זוהמא מיניה בשעובדין אותו ואי לא לא. (פי') דשמואל וקרנא דהוו יתבי וחזו למיא דדלו ועכירי כו' הוה שמיע ליה לשמואל דגברא רבה אתי ממערבא בההוא יומא וכיון דחזא למיא דעכירי. אמר בדעתיה אי אפשר דלא שתי מינייהו והוה בריר להו דכל מאן דשתי מהנהו מיא בעידן דעכירי חייש במעיה. ועל זה אמר גברא רבה דקא אתי חייש במעיה. תהי בקנקניה. פי' כגון טעום יין שבזה הקנקן מלשון קרנא הוה תהי בחמרא (כתובות ד' קה) כלומר חזי גמריה וכיון דחזא דהוא רב גדול צוה שמואל את קרנא ועייליה לביתיה ואכלי' אוכל דמשלשל ולא אודעיה מקום בית הכסא דאיכון לאיסויי מן חשש דבמעיה וכיון דאיצער רב ולא ידע דלאסוייה הוא דעבד הכי לטייה לא לקיים ליה ברא למאן דמצערן לצעריה ולא איקיים ליה לשמואל ברא אלא בנתא וכיון דאיתידע ליה לרב דלאסויה הוא דעביד ליה הכי ולטותיה איתקיימא בשמואל חש דלא תחלש דעתיה ואדבריה על נפשיה כדמפרש בב"ק פרק מרובה (דף פ') והייט מעשה (דיסוריה) [דסוגיין] ולטייה נמי לקרנא ונפקא ליה[קרן] של בשר בעינו. פי' קאלוס בלשון יון טוב כלומר הודה לדבריו. וא"ל טב מה שאמרת. והלכה כת"ק דמתני': **מתני'** אין עושין הילמי בשבת אבל עושה הוא מי מלח. וכי תימא *)היכי בברייתא אין עושין מי מלח מרובין לתת לתוך הכבשין שבתוך הגסטרא. אבל עושה הוא מי מלח מועטים (וטובל) [ואוכל] בהן פתו ונותן לתוך התבשיל וכן הלכה ואע"ג דר' יוסי אוסר מי מלח אין הלכה כמותו דגרסי' בתחלת עירובין אמר רב יהודה אמר שמואל אין הלכה כרבי יוסי לא בהלמי ולא בלחיים: **ירושלמי** כל מי שנותנין לתוכה ביצה ושוקעת זו היא מי מלח אינה שוקעת זו היא הילמי תני ר' יהודה בר חביבא אין עושין מי מלח עזין והן שהביצה צפה בהן והלכתא כוותיה. ואם הביצה שוקעת בהן מותרין וכיון דאמר הביצה צפה בהן הזכיר לא טבע בימא דסדום כלומר כל מים מלוחים עזין צפין בהן: למימלח פוגלא א[...] במילחא שרי: יין לתוך העין אסור ע"ג העין מותר. כשמואל דאמר שורה אדם פתו ביין ונותן ע"ג העין ואינו חושש. רוק תפל אפילו ע"ג העין אסור. וכן קילורין שהוא שרן מ[...] מי סדום ע"ג העין שרי אבל מיפתח ומימץ עיינא בין בסממנא וקילורי בין במיא דסדום כדאמר ליה מר עוקבא לבר לואי כוליה לא שרא מר שמואל. פי' חסודה בלשון ערבי אל[...] חויא

*) נראה דצ"ל היכי פירושא דמילתא הכי מפרשא בברייתא וכו'.

a THE SABBATH,[1] [108*b*] BUT ONE MAY PREPARE SALT WATER AND DIP HIS BREAD INTO IT OR PUT IT INTO A STEW. SAID R. JOSE, BUT THAT IS BRINE, WHETHER [ONE PREPARES] MUCH OR LITTLE?[2] RATHER THIS IS THE SALT WATER THAT IS PERMITTED: OIL IS FIRST PUT INTO THE WATER[3] OR INTO THE SALT.[4]

GEMARA. What does he [the first Tanna] mean?[5] Said Rab Judah in Samuel's name, He means this: One may not prepare a large quantity of salt water, but one may prepare a small quantity of salt water.

SAID R. JOSE, BUT THAT IS BRINE, WHETHER [ONE PREPARES] MUCH OR LITTLE? The scholars asked: Does R. Jose [mean] to forbid [both] or to permit [both]?—Said Rab Judah: He [means] to permit [both], since it is not stated, R. Jose forbids. Said Rabbah to him: But since the final clause states, RATHER THIS IS THE SALT WATER THAT IS PERMITTED, it follows that R. Jose [means] to forbid [in the first clause]! Rather said Rabbah: He [means] to forbid; and thus did R. Joḥanan say: He [means] to forbid. It was taught likewise: One may not prepare a large quantity of salt water for putting into preserved vegetables in a mutilated vessel;[6] but one may prepare a little salt water and eat his bread therewith or put it into a stew. Said R. Jose: Is it just because this is in large quantity and this is in small, that the one is forbidden and the other is permitted? then it will be said, Much work is forbidden but a little work is permitted! Rather both are forbidden, and this is the salt water that is permitted: one puts oil and salt [mixed into water] or oil and water [over salt], but provided that water and salt are not mixed at the outset.

b [Mnemonic: Strong, radish and citron.][1] R. Judah b. Ḥabiba recited: We may not prepare strong salt water. What is strong salt water?—Rabbah and R. Joseph b. Abba both say: Such that an egg floats in it. And how much is that?—Said Abaye: Two parts of salt and one part of water. For what is it made? Said R. Abbahu: For *muries.*[2]

R. Judah b. Ḥabiba recited: One may not salt a radish or an egg on the Sabbath.[3] R. Hezekiah said in Abaye's name: Radish is forbidden, but an egg is permitted. R. Naḥman said: Originally I used to salt radish, arguing, I do indeed spoil it, for Samuel said, Sharp radish is [more] beneficial. But when I heard what 'Ulla said when he came,[4] viz., In the West [Palestine] they salt them slice by slice,[5] I no longer salt them,[6] but I certainly do drop them [in salt].[7]

R. Judah b. Ḥabiba recited: A citron, radish, and egg, but for their outer shell,[8] would never leave the stomach.[9]

When R. Dimi came,[10] he said: No man ever sank in the Lake of Sodom.[11] R. Joseph observed: Sodom was overturned and the statement about it is topsy-turvy:[12] No man sank [in it], but a plank did?[13] Said Abaye to him, He states the more surprising thing.[14] It is unnecessary [to mention] a plank, seeing that it does not sink in any water; but not even a man, who sinks in all [other] waters of the world, [ever] sank in the Lake of Sodom. What difference does that make?—Even as it once happened that Rabin was walking behind R. Jeremiah by the bank of the Lake of Sodom, [and] he asked him, May one wash with this water on the Sabbath?[15]—It is well, he replied.[16]

c Is it permissible to shut and open [one's eyes]?[1] I have not heard this, he answered, [but] I have heard something similar; for R. Zera said, at times in R. Mattenah's name, at others in Mar 'Uḳba's name, and both [R. Mattenah and Mar 'Uḳba] said it in the names of Samuel's father and Levi: one said: [To put] wine *into* one's eye[2] is forbidden; [to put it] *on* the eye, is permitted.[3] Whilst the other said: [To put] tasteless saliva,[4] even on the eye, is forbidden. It may be proved that it was Samuel's father who ruled, '[To put] wine *into* one's eye is forbidden; *on* the eye, is permitted': for Samuel said: One may soak bread in wine and place it on his eye on the Sabbath. Now, from whom did he hear this, surely he heard it from his father?—But then on your reasoning, when Samuel said: [To apply] tasteless saliva even *on* the eye is forbidden; from whom did he hear it? Shall we say that he heard it from his father,—then Levi did not state any one [of these laws]![5] Hence he [must have] heard one from his father and one from Levi, but we do not know which from his father and which from Levi.

Mar 'Uḳba said in Samuel's name: One may steep collyrium [an eye salve] on the eve of the Sabbath and place it upon his eyes on the Sabbath without fear.[6] Bar Lewai was standing before Mar 'Uḳba, and saw him opening and shutting [his eyes].[7] To this extent Mar Samuel certainly did not give permission, he observed to him. R. Jannai sent [word] to Mar 'Uḳba, Send us some of Mar Samuel's eye-salves.[8] He sent back [word], I do indeed send [them] to you, lest you accuse me of meanness; but thus did Samuel say: A drop of cold water in the morning, and bathing the hands and feet in hot water in the evening, is better than all the eye-salves in the world. It was taught likewise: R. Muna said in R. Judah's name: A drop of cold water in the morning

d and bathing the hands and feet [in hot water][1] in the evening is better than all the eye-salves in the world. He [R. Muna] used to say: If the hand [be put] to the eye, let it be cut off;[2] the hand to the nose, let it be cut off: the hand to the mouth, let it be cut off; the hand to the ear, let it be cut off; the hand to the vein [opened for blood letting], let it be cut off; the hand to the membrum, let it be cut off; the hand to the anus, let it be

a (1) This is forbidden under 'salting', v. *supra* 73*a*. (2) Salt water prepared for dipping bread into it, is in fact brine, even though it is usually prepared in a smaller quantity than one generally prepares brine. (3) In such a case the salt cannot mix thoroughly with the water and loses some of its effectiveness. (4) Before the salt is put into the water. The oil weakens the salt in both cases. (5) Surely brine and salt water are identical. (6) Which is specially set aside for pickling.

b (1) A mnemonic is a string of words to aid the memory. (2) A pickle containing fish hash and sometimes wine (Jast.). (3) A number of slices at the same time (Rashi). (4) Cf. *supra* 5*a*, n. b9. (5) Eating the one before the next is salted. (6) More than one slice. Two slices at once (Rashi). (7) Each radish as I eat it. (8) This refers to the white of the egg, not what is generally called the shell. (9) They are very constipating. (10) V. *supra* 5*a*, n. b9. (11) Owing to its high specific gravity due to its large proportion of salt. (12) Lit., 'overturned'. (13) Surely a plank is even lighter. (14) Lit., 'he says, it is unnecessary (to state)'. (15) Its saltiness conferred healing properties upon it; hence the question, since one may not heal on the Sabbath. (16) For it is not evident that one washes himself for that reason. [Healing is forbidden only for fear lest one crushes the necessary ingredients, but it is not labour in itself: consequently the Rabbis did not impose this interdict unless one is obviously performing a cure.]

c (1) Several times in succession, for the salt to enter and heal them. The purpose is more obvious here. (2) By opening and shutting it. This is similar to Rabin's question. Thus the saltiness of the Lake of Sodom has a practical bearing in law. (3) For it looks as though he is merely washing himself. (4) I.e., saliva of a person who has tasted nothing after sleeping. (5) Surely one was reported in his name! (6) Of transgression. (7) For the salve to enter right in. (8) Samuel was a doctor.

d (1) So the text as emended in 'Aruch. (2) It causes it injury, and so the rest. In nearly all cases it means before washing in the morning.

cut off; the hand [109a] to the vat,[3] let it be cut off: [because] the [unwashed] hand leads to blindness, the hand leads to deafness, the hand causes a polypus.[4]

It was taught, R. Nathan said: It[5] is a free agent, and insists [on remaining on the hands] until one washes his hands three times.

R. Joḥanan said: Stibium removes [cures] the Princess,[6] stops the tears, and promotes the growth of the eye-lashes. It was taught likewise, R. Jose said: Stibium removes the Princess, stops the tears, and promotes the growth of the eye-lashes.

Mar 'Uḳba also said in Samuel's name: Leaves[7] have no healing properties.[8] R. Joseph said: Coriander has no healing properties. R. Shesheth said: Cuscuta has no healing properties. R. Joseph observed: Coriander is injurious even to me.[9] R. Shesheth observed: Eruca is beneficial even to me.[10]

Mar 'Uḳba further said in Samuel's name: All kinds of cuscuta are permitted, except *teruza*.[11]

a R. Ḥisda said: To glair roast meat[1] is permitted; to make hashed eggs[2] is forbidden. Ze'iri's wife made [it] for Ḥiyya b. Ashi,[3] but he did not eat it. Said she, 'I have made this for your teacher [Ze'iri] and he ate, yet do you not eat'!—Ze'iri follows his view. For Ze'iri said: One may pour clear wine and clear water through a strainer on the Sabbath, and he need have no fear.[4] This proves that since it can be drunk as it is,[5] he does nothing;[6] so here too, since it can be eaten as it is,[7] he does nothing.

Mar 'Uḳba also said: If one knocks his hand or foot, he may reduce the swelling with wine, and need have no fear. The scholars asked: What about vinegar? Said R. Hillel to R. Ashi, When I attended R. Kahana's academy they said, Not vinegar.[8] Raba observed: But the people of Maḥoza,[9] since they are delicate, even wine heals them.[10]

Rabina visited R. Ashi: He saw that an ass had trodden on his foot, and he was sitting and reducing the swelling in vinegar.[11] Said he to him, Do you not accept R. Hillel's statement, Not vinegar? [A swelling on] the back of the hand or on the foot is different, he replied.[12] Others state, He saw him reducing the swelling in wine. Said he to him, Do you not agree with what Raba said, The people of Maḥoza, since they are delicate, even wine heals them, and you too are delicate? [A swelling on] the hand or on the foot is different, he replied, for R. Adda b. Mattenah said in Rab's name, [A blow on] the hand or on the foot is like an internal wound, and the Sabbath may be desecrated on its account.

Our Rabbis taught: One may bathe in the water of Gerar,[13]
b in the water of Ḥammethan,[1] in the water of Essa,[2] and in the water of Tiberias,[3] but not in the Great Sea [the Mediterranean], or in the water of steeping,[4] or in the Lake of Sodom. But this contradicts it: One may bathe in the water of Tiberias and in the Great Sea, but not in the water of steeping or in the Lake of Sodom. Thus [the rulings on] the Great Sea are contradictory.—Said R. Joḥanan, There is no difficulty: one agrees with R. Meir, the other with R. Judah. For we learnt: All seas are like a *miḳweh*,[5] for it is said, *and the gathering of* [miḳweh] *the waters called He seas:*[6] this is R. Meir's view. R. Judah said: The Great Sea [alone] is like a *miḳweh*, *'seas'* being stated only because it contains many kinds of waters.[7] R. Jose maintained: All seas [including the Great Sea] purify when running,[8] but they are unfit for *zabim*, lepers, and to be sanctified as the water of lus-

(3) Which is to be filled with wine. (4) A morbid growth in the nose. (5) The evil spirit that rests on the hands during the night. The belief in same is held to have been borrowed from the Persians, and many regulations were based thereon; v. Weiss, *Dor*, II, p. 13. (6) The name of a demon afflicting the eye, also a certain disorder of the eye. Var. lec.: בת חורין, the Nobleman's daughter, likewise with the same meaning. (7) *'Alin*. Rashi: the name of a certain herb. (8) Therefore they may be applied to the eye on the Sabbath (Ri). (9) Who am blind. (10) Though I possess good eyesight already. (11) A kind of cucumber or melon possessing medicinal properties. These are used for no other purpose; hence they are forbidden (cf. *supra* 108*b*, n. b16).

a (1) Rashi; R. Ḥan.: to strain off the juice of melon, which is taken as a laxative. V. Tosaf. a.l. (2) I.e., a hash of roasted eggs beaten up. (3) Rashi: roast meat glaired. (4) Of transgression. (5) Without straining. (6) Though one may not filter muddy wine on the Sabbath. (7) Without the covering of eggs. (8) Its purpose is too obviously medicinal. (9) V. *supra* 33*a*, n. c11. (10) Their skin is so delicate that even wine acts like vinegar upon it. Hence they would only use it medicinally, and therefore it is forbidden. (11) It was the Sabbath. (12) A bruise there is dangerous. (13) Gerar was the seat of a Philistine prince (Gen. X, 19; XX, 1 *et seq*; I Chron. IV, 39) whose site has not been identified with certainty. Some think it was southwest of Kadesh; others, that it was south of Gaza.

b (1) The word means 'hot springs'. It was a town a mile away from Tiberias. (2) Supposed to be east of the lake of Tiberias, v. Neub. *Géogr*. p. 38; Jast. s.v. (3) Though all these are salty, it is permitted, as it does not seem that one is bathing particularly for medicinal purposes (v. *supra* 108*b*, n. b16). (4) In which flax was steeped. (5) V. Glos. They are like a *miḳweh* in all respects, and not like a spring. The difference between these two are: (i) a *zab* can have his ritual bath in a spring, but not in a *miḳweh*; (ii) the water of a spring, but not of a *miḳweh*, is fit for sprinkling upon a leper (Lev. XIV, 5) and for mixing with the ashes of the red heifer (Num. XIX, 17); (iii) the water of a spring purifies when running, whereas a *miḳweh* purifies only when its water is still (v. *supra* 65*a* bottom and *b* top and notes a.l.).—Since R. Meir maintains that all seas are alike, he draws no distinction in respect to bathing either, and permits it in the Great Sea too. (6) Gen. I, 10. (7) Many different rivers flow into the sea, hence the plural; but actually the verse refers to the Great Sea only. Thus he draws a distinction between the Great Sea and other seas, and so he also forbids bathing therein on the Sabbath. (8) Since that is the nature of seas.

*לגינית תקצץ יד מסמא יד מחרשת יד מעלה פוליפוס תניא רבי נתן אומר בת חורין היא זו ומקפדת עד שירחוץ ידיו ג' פעמים א"ר יוחנן *פוך מעביר בת (א) מלך ופוסק את הדמעה ומרבה שיער בעפעפים תניא נמי הכי רבי יוסי אומר פוך מעביר בת מלך ופוסק את הדמעה ומרבה שיער בעפעפים ואמר מר עוקבא אמר שמואל עלין אין בהם משום רפואה אמר רב יוסף כוסברתא אין בה משום רפואה אמר רב ששת כשור אין בהן משום רפואה אמר רב יוסף כוסברתא אפילו לדידי קשה לי אמר רב ששת גרגירא *אפילו לדידי מעלי ואמר מר עוקבא אמר שמואל כל מיני כשות שרו לבר מטרוזא אמר רב חסדא שריקא טויא שרי פיעפועי ביעי אסור דביתהו דזעירי עבדא ליה לחייא בר אשי ולא אכל אמרה ליה לרבך עבדי ליה ואכל ואת לא אכלת זעירי לטעמיה דאמר זעירי *נותן אדם יין צלול ומים צלולין לתוך המשמרת בשבת ואינו חושש אלמא כיון דמשתתי הכי לאו מידי קעביד הכא נמי כיון דמיתכיל הכי לאו מידי קעביד ואמר מר עוקבא מי שנגפה ידו או רגלו צומתה ביין ואינו חושש איבעיא להו חלא מאי אמר רב הלל לרב אשי כי הוינא בי רב כהנא אמרי חלא לא אמר רבא והני בני מחוזא כיון דמפנקי אפילו חמרא נמי מסי להו רבינא איקלע לבי רב אשי חזייה דדריכא ליה חמרא אגבא דכרעיה ויתיב קא צמית ליה בחלא אמר ליה לא סבר לה מר להא דאמר רב הילל חלא לא א"ל גב היד וגב הרגל שאני איכא דאמרי חזייה דקא צמית ליה בחמרא אמר ליה לא סבר לה מר להא דאמר רבא הני בני מחוזא כיון דמפנקי אפי' חמרא נמי מסי להו ומר נמי הא מפנק אמר ליה גב היד וגב הרגל שאני *דאמר רב אדא בר מתנה אמר רב גב היד וגב הרגל הרי הן כמכה של חלל ומחללין עליהן את השבת ת"ר רוחצים במי גרר במי חמתן במי עסיא ובמי טבריא אבל לא בים הגדול ולא במי משרה ולא בימה של סדום ורמינהו רוחצים במי טבריא ובים הגדול אבל לא במי משרה ולא בימה של סדום קשיא ים הגדול אים הגדול א"ר יוחנן לא קשיא הא ר"מ הא ר' יהודה *דתנן כל הימים כמקוה שנאמר °ולמקוה המים קרא ימים דברי ר"מ ר' יהודה אומר ים הגדול כמקוה ולא נאמר ימים אלא שיש בו מיני ימים הרבה רבי יוסי אומר כל הימים מטהרין בזוחלין ופסולים לזבים ולמצורעים ולקדש בהן מי חטאת מתקיף לה רב נחמן בר יצחק אימור

א) [וע"ע תוס' לקמן קמז. ד"ה דיעבד ותוס' חולין עו: ד"ה אלא נור]

רש"י

לגינית. שמטילין בה שכר: תיקצץ. דלא תיגע קודם נטילת שחרית: יד. לעין מסמא קודם נטילה: יד. לאוזן מחרשת: יד. לפה או לחוטם: מעלה פוליפוס. ריח החוטם והפה ול"נ דיד לאמה לאו לענין שחרית נקט לה אלא משום דמביא לידי קרי ובמסכת נדה (דף יג:) אמרינן בה תקצץ *משום האי טעמא ומשום דתניא בה נמי לטותא דתיקצץ תנייה נמי גבי הנך וכן יד לפי טבעת למשמש בה תדיר מביאתו לידי תחתוניות: בת חורין היא. הרוח השורה על הידים לפני נטילה: ומקפדת. בנטילתו לנוטלה יפה עד שישפוך מים יפה ג' פעמים על ידיו: פוך. אם נותנו בעיניו: מעביר בת מלך. אם הזיקה לעיניו: עלין. כך שם העשב: אין בהם משום רפואה. באכילתו להאיר העינים דלא מסו: כוסברתא. אלייאנדר"א: אפילו לדידי. דמאור עינים אנא קשה לי לכאב העין אם אוכלנו: גרגירא. אורוג"א: אפילו לדידי. °דמאור עינים אנא מעליא לי: כל מיני כשות שרי. למיכל בשבת כדתנן במתני' כל האוכלים אוכל אדם לרפואה דלא מוכחא מילתא: לבר מטרוזא. שאין אדם אוכל אלא לרפואה ומוכחא מלתא: שריקא טויא. לשרוק ולטוח שמן וביצים מגולגלין על הצלי כשהוא חם משחשכה שרי ובלבד שלא יהא רותח כדי לבשל ולא אמרינן דמי למתקן: פיעפועי ביעי. לטרוף ביצים מגולגלין בקערה: אסור. דמתחזי כמאן דבעי למשדינהו בקדרה: עבדא ליה. שריקא טויא: לרבך. זעירי: משמרת. שמסננין בה שמרים: כיון דמשתתי הכי. שראוי לשתותו כמו שהוא בלא סינון: דמיתכיל הכי. בלא שירקא: שנגפה. שנכשלה ולקתה לשון פן תגוף (תהלים צא) דם מגפתה (מכשירין פ"ו מ"ח): צומתה ביין. לשכך הדם: דמפנקי. מעונגין הן וכל דבר שהוא חזק קצת קשה לבשרן וצומתה: דדריכא ליה תמרא. חמור דרך לו על רגלו: שאני. שמכתו קשה ומסוכן ומחללין עליו את השבת: רוחצין במי גרר. ואע"פ שהן מלוחין קצת דרך לרחוץ בהן בחול ולא מוכחא מילתא דלרפואה היא: אבל לא בים הגדול. לקמן מפרש טעמא: ולא במי משרה. ששורין בו פשתן ואין דרך רחיצה בהן אלא לרפואה דמסו וכן בימה של סדום דמליח טובא ואין רוחצין בה אלא לרפואה ומוכחא מילתא: הא. דקתני רוחצים בים הגדול ר"מ היא דמשוי כל הימים כי הדדי ולא מפליג בין ים הגדול לשאר הימים: והא. דתני אין רוחצין רבי יהודה היא דמפליג בין ים הגדול לשאר ימים: כל הימים כמקוה. לכל תורת מקוה ואין להם תורת מעיין ומה בין מקוה למעיין המעיין כשר לטבילת זב והזאת לפור מצורע דמים חיים הן ולקדש מי חטאת דבכולהו מים חיים כתיב בזב כתיב (ויקרא טו) ורחץ בשרו במים חיים במצורע כתיב (שם יד) אל כלי חרש על מים חיים במי חטאת כתיב (במדבר יט) מים חיים אל כלי ומטהר טמאים הטובלים במימיו כשהן זוחלין ומקלחים שהרי זה דרכו של מעיין כל עצמן זוחלין הן ומקוה שהן מים מכונסין אם הטביל במימיו דרך זחילתן במקום קטפרס אינה טבילה עד שיהא במקום אשבורן שלו קווין ועומדין והכי תניא בת"כ אי מה מעיין מטהר בזוחלין אף מקוה מטהר בזוחלין ת"ל אך (ב) מעיין מטהר בזוחלין והמקוה באשבורן זהו פירוש מטהר בזוחלין בכל מקום ואני לא שמעתיו כן ואין המקוה כשר לטבילת זב ולהזיית מצורע ולקדש מי חטאת וכל הימים כמקוה שהכתוב קראן מקוה: רבי יהודה אומר. לא קרא הכתוב מקוה אלא לים הגדול דביה משתעי קרא במעשה בראשית ששם נקוו כל מי בראשית: ולא נאמר ימים. בלשון רבים אלא מפני שמעורבין בו מיני ימים הרבה שכל הנחלים הולכים אל הים: רבי יוסי אומר כל הימים. וים הגדול תורת מעיין מים זוחלין עליהן לענין שהם מטהרין בזוחלין מפני שדרך להיות נחלים זוחלין עליהן וזה דרכן אבל פסולין הן לתורת מים חיים דהכתוב קראן מקוה:

תוספות

עלין אין בהם משום רפואה. פי' בקונטרס דבאכילה מיירי ואין נראה לר"י אלא איירי להשים על העין דבהכי איירי כולה סוגיא ועוד אי באכילה מיירי היכי אסר רב ששת גרגירא כיון דמאכל בריאין הוא והתנן כל האוכלים אוכל אדם לרפואה: (ג) לדידי אפילו כוסברתא קשי לי. קשה לר"י א"כ אמאי איצטריך למימר רב יוסף כוסברתא אין בו משום רפואה כיון דמזקת לעינים כ"ש דלא מרפאה ואומר ר"י דה"ק אין בה משום רפואה כלומר יש שטועין וסבורין שיש בה רפואה ואין בה רפואה אלא מזקת לעינים ויכול להיות שמהגה אותו בשום ענין: שריקא טויא. פירש ר"ח מים שמסננים ממעי אבטיח ושותים כדי לשלשל ור"ל דמותר לסנן מים שבמעיין כדמסיק כיון דמיתכיל הכי לאו מידי קעביד אבל פעפועי ביעי אסור דלא מיתכיל בלא סיטון שפיר והשתא אתי שפיר לפי' ר"ח דשייכא הא מלתא להכא דמיירי ברפואה: רוחצין במי גרר במי חמתן במי טבריא. והא דתנן בפ' חבית (לקמן דף קמז:) הרוחץ במי מערה במי טבריא ודייק בגמרא דיעבד אין לכתחילה לא התם מיירי ברוחץ בגומא דדמיא למרחץ אבל בנהר מותר לכתחילה כדפרישית לעיל בפרק כירה (לעיל לט: ד"ה והא) ורבינו נסים כתב במגילת סתרים דהא דקתני הרוחץ דיעבד אין לכתחילה לא משום מי מערה אבל במי טבריא אפילו לכתחילה שרי ולא קתני במי טבריא אלא ללמד על מי מערה שהן חמין דומיא דמי טבריא וטעמא משום דמי טבריא מגולין אבל מערה מכוסה היא כדאמר בשור שנגח את הפרה (ב"ק דף נ:) דמערה עבידא דמטללא וכפיש הבלא ותיישינן שמא יזיע ומש"ה לכתחילה לא א): רבי יוסי אומר כל הימים מטהרין בזוחלין. נראה לריב"א דטעמא משום דכל שעה הולכים ושבים מכאן לכאן והוי כזוחלין הלכך יש להם לטהר בזוחלין כמו שאר נהרות אבל מים חיים אינם שהרי אינם נובעים הלכך מיסתבר טפי מה שהכתוב קראן מקוה היינו לפוסלן ממים חיים: הא ר"מ והא רבי יהודה. תימה היכי מדמי הא פלוגתא לפלוגתא דלעיל דמיירי ברפואה:

חיויא

מסורת הש"ס

[וכן איתא במסכת כלה]

פי' כחול עינים

[עי' יומא יח: ...]

לקמן קלט:

ע"ז כח.

פרה פ"ח מ"ח מקוואות פ"ה משנה ד

עין משפט נר מצוה

כז א טוש"ע א"ח סי' ד סעיף ה:

כח ב שם סעיף ג:

כט ג סמג לאוין סה טוש"ע א"ח סימן שכח סעיף כד:

ל ד ה ו מיי' פכ"א מהל' שבת הלכה כג סמג שם טוש"ע שם סעיף כט:

לא ז מיי' פ"כ שם הל' ה סמג שם טוש"ע שם סעיף ו:

לב ח שם סעיף מד:

לג ט מיי' פ"ט מהלכות מקוואות הלכה יב סמג עשין רמח:

רבינו חננאל

תניא ר' (יוסי) [נתן] אומר בת חורין היא. פי' רוח רעה ששורה על [גב] העין יש לה כבוד ברוחות כבן חורין בבני אדם ואינה עוברת עד ג' פעמים ופוך מעבירה*). אמר שמואל עלין אין בהן משום רפואה. פי' עלי ירק לצנן העין אין בהן משום רפואה ושרי וכן כסברתא וכן כשות אין בהן משום רפואה. ורב יוסף דהוי סני נהורא הוה אמר אפי' אנא כוסברתא קשיא לי דאלמא מכאיב העין ורב ששת נמי סני נהורא הוה ואמ' אפי' לדידי גרגירא מעלי דמשפה גלגל העין. כל מיני קשות מותר להניח ע"ג העין בשבת בר מטרוזה ולא בריר לן יפה מאי היא שריקא טויא גם היא **) ואמרו כי הן מי של מיעי אבטיחים שמסננין אותן במשמרת ושותין אותן לבדן ויפין הן לשילשל. וכן פעפועי ביעי ועיקר דהוה שתי להן לטעמיה דאמר נותן אדם מים צלולין ויין צלול לתוך המשמרת בשבת ואינו חושש אלמא כיון דמישתתי הכי לאו מידי קא עבוד הכא נמי בשירקא טויא כיון שנאכל עם האבטיח ועם מעיו אף בזמן דשפי להו במשמרת לאו מידי עבוד. ומפורש בגמרא דיוה"כ כי זעירי רביה דרב חייא בר אשי תלמידו דזעירי הוא ***) דהוא נמי תלמידו דרב הוה ניחא לי משום הכא דרב אשי הוה. אמר מר עוקבא מי שנגפה ידו או רגלו צומתה ביין ואינו חושש אבל חומץ לא ואי מפנק אפי' חמרא אסור אא"כ ישנה מכה של חלל שמחללין עליה השבת: מי גרר ומי חמתן המים שלהן חמין הן כמו חמי טבריא.

*) עי' ערוך ערך בת חורין.

**) נראה דחסר איזה תיבות וצ"ל גם היא אינו בריר לן ואמרו וכו'.

***) דברי רבינו אלו מסוללי הבנה ואולי דנפל איזה ט"ס בדבריו וצ"ע.

הגהות הב"ח

(א) גמ' פוך מעביר בת חורין ופוסק וכו' ר' יוסי וכו' בת חורין ופוסק:

(ב) רש"י ד"ה כל הימים וכו' ת"ל אך מעיין מעיין מטהר:

(ג) תוס' ד"ה עלין וכו' לרפואה הס"ד ואח"כ מ"ה כוסברתא אפי' לדידי קשה:

גליון הש"ס

רש"י ד"ה אפי' לדידי דמאור עינים. ע' בכתובות מו' ובגליון כעל פג"א פ' נת:

רב נסים גאון

מעלה פוליפוס. במס' כתובות בפרק המדיר (דף עז) אמרו מאי בעל פוליפוס אמר רב יהודה אמר שמואל ריח החוטם בממניתא תאנא ריח הפה: אמר רב יוסף כוסברתא אפי' לדילי קשה לי אמר רב ששת גרגירא אפי' לדילי מעלי לי. רב יוסף ורב ששת היו מאורי עינים ואמר רב יוסף בדרך הבא' כי הכוסבר מזיק לעין אפי' לו שהוא סומא וכמו כן אמר רב ששת כי הגרגיר הוא מועיל אפי' לסומים ותמצא רב יוסף אמר בפרק החובל (בבא קמא דף פז) מריש הוה אמינא מאן דאמר לי הלכה כר' יהודה דאמר סומא פטור מהמצות עבידנא יומא טבא לרבנן דאמינא לא מיפקדנא ועבידנא מצות השתא דשמעתא להא דאמר ר' חנינא גדול המצווה ועושה אדרבה מאן דאמר לי לית הלכתא כר' יהודה עבידנא יומא טבא לרבנן ואיתא נמי בגמ' בפרק האשה (קידושין דף לא) ורב ששת הרי אמרו בכמה מקומות דברים שמוכיחים שהוא סומא בברכות בפרק תפלת השחר (דף ל) כי הא דרב חסדא ורב ששת הוו קא אזלי באורחא קם רב חסדא וקא מצלי תפלת הדרך אמר ליה רב ששת לשמעיה מאי קעביד רב חסדא וכו' ובפרק הרואה מקום (שם נח) רב ששת נפק למיחזי מלכא אמר ליה ההוא מינא בר בי רב חצבי לנהרא כגני לא אמר ליה השתא חזית דאנא ידענא טפי מינך כי אתא מלכא פתח רב ששת קא מבריך ליה למלכא אמר ליה ההוא מינא כי לא חזית מאי מברכת ובפרק ערבי פסחים (דף קטז) דבר שמוכיח על שניהן והוא כשאמר רב אחא בר יעקב סומא פטור מלומר הגדה הקשו עליו איני והאמר רבינא לדילי *) אמר לי רב ששת שאלתינהו לרבנן דבי רב יוסף מאן אמר הגדתא ואמרו לי רב יוסף ואיך תאמר שהסומא פסול לומר הגדה והרי אלו סומין ואמרי הגדתא ובפרק מי שאחזו (גיטין דף סח) אמרו על רב ששת שאמר לשמעיה מאי חזית אמר ליה ציפתא דדשא אמר ליה הדר מינה ובגמ' דבני מערבא בפרק יציאות השבת (הלכה ג) ואיש אמונים מי ימצא זה ר' זעירא דר' זעירא לית אנן צריכין חששין לשמועתא דרב ששת דהוא נברא מפתחה: דביתהו דזעירי אנסיבא ליה לר' חייא בר אשי עבדא ליה ולא אכל אמרה ליה לרבך עבדי ואכל ואת לא אכלת. בפ' יום הכפורים (יומא עז) אמרי דר' חייא בר אשי תלמיד זעירי (לדבריהם) [הוי. דאמר התם] איבעיא להו רבה לגבי תלמידא מהו אמר רב יצחק בר דנא לדידי חזי לי לזעירי דאזל לבי רב חייא בר אשי תלמידיה רב אשי אמר ההוא רב חייא בר אשי הוא דאזל לגבי זעירי רביה: גב היד וגב הרגל הרי הן כמכה של חלל. עיקר זה במסכת ע"ז בפרק אין מעמידין (דף כח) אמר רבה בר בר חנה א"ר יוחנן כל מכה שמחללין עליה את השבת אין מתרפאין מהן מאי בינייהו גב היד וגב הרגל דאמר רב אדא בר אהבה אמר רב גב היד וגב הרגל הרי הן כמכה של חלל ומחללין עליה את השבת ואמרו ומהיכן מכה של חלל פירש ר' אמי מן שפה ולפנים ובגמרא דבני מערבא כל שהוא מן החלל ולפנים מרפאין אותן בשבת תמן אמרין בשם ר' יוחנן נבות ידים ורגלים סכנה: ר' יוסי אומר כל הימים מטהרין בזוחלין ופסולין לזבים ולמצורעים ולקדש מהן מי חטאת. אלו השלשה (תנאים) [דברים] שמר

*) הלשון משובש קצת ולפנינו שם הגי' שאלתינהו לרבנן דבי רב יוסף מאן דאמר אגדתא בי רב יוסף אמרו רב ששת וכצ"ל כאן.

עין משפט
נר מצוה

לד א ב מיי' פכ"א מהל' שבת הלכה כא סמג לאוין סה טוש"ע א"ח סי' שכח סעיף מד :

לה ג מיי' שם הלכה כב טוש"ע שם סעיף לז :

מסורת השש"ס

אימור דפליגי לענין טומאה וטהרה לענין שבת מי שמעת להו אלא אמר רב נחמן בר יצחק לא קשיא הא דאישתהי הא דלא אישתהי במאי אוקימתא לבתרייתא דלא אישתהי אי דלא אישתהי אפילו במי משרה נמי דהתניא רוחצין במי טבריא ובמי משרה ובימה של סדום ואף על פי שיש לו חטטים בראשו במה דברים אמורים שלא נשתהא אבל נשתהא אסור אלא ים הגדול אים הגדול לא קשיא [א]הא ביפין שבו הא ברעים שבו מי משרה אמי משרה נמי לא קשיא [ב]הא דאישתהי הא דלא אישתהי : **מתני'** [ג]אין אוכלין *איזביון בשבת לפי שאינו מאכל בריאים אבל אוכל הוא את יועזר ושותה אבוברואה *כל האוכלין אוכל אדם לרפואה וכל המשקין שותה חוץ ממי דקלים וכוס עיקרין מפני שהן לירוקה אבל שותה הוא מי דקלים לצמאו וסך שמן עיקרין שלא לרפואה : **גמ'** אמר רב יוסף אזוב אברתה בר המג איזביון אברתה בר הינג עולא אמר מרוא חיורא עולא איקלע לבי רב שמואל בר יהודה אייתו לקמיה מרוא חיורא אמר היינו אזוב דכתיב באורייתא רב פפי אמר שומשוק א"ר ירמיה מדיפתי כוותיה דרב פפי מסתברא *דתנן מצות אזוב שלשה קלחין ובהן שלשה גבעולין ושומשוק הוא דמשתכחא הכי למאי אבלי ליה לקוקאיני במאי אבלי ליה בשבע תמרי אוכמתא ממאי הויא מקימחא דשערי (במנא) דחליף עליה ארבעין יומין : אבל אוכל הוא את יועזר : מאי יועזר פותנק למאי אבלי לה לארקתא במאי אבלי לה בשבע תמרי חיוורתא ממאי הויא מאומצא ומיא אליבא ריקנא ומבישרא שמנא אליבא ריקנא ומבישרא דתורא אליבא ריקנא מאמגוזא אליבא ריקנא ומגירי דרוביא אליבא ריקנא ומשתי מיא אבתריה ואי לא ליבלע תחלי היוורתא ואי לא ליתיב בתעניתא וליתי בישרא שמנא ולישדי אגומרי ולימיץ גרמא וליגמע חלא ואיכא דאמרי חלא לא משום דקשי לכבדא ואי לא לייתי גורדא דאסינתא דגרידא מעילאי לתתאי ולא מתתאי לעילאי דילמא נפקא איידי פומיה ולישלקה בשיכרא בי שיבבי ולמחר נסכרינון לנקבין דידיה ולישתי וכי מפני אפשיחה דדקלא : ושותין אבוברואה : מאי אבוברואה חומטריא מאי חומטריא חוטרא יחידאה למאי עבדי לה לגילויא ואי לא ליתי חמשא כלילי וחמשא כוסתא דשיכרא ונישלוקינהו בהדי הדדי עד דקיימא אאנפקא ונישתי אימיה דרב אחדבוי בר אמי עבדה ליה להההוא גברא חד כלילא וחד כוסתא דשיכרא שלקה ואישקיתיה ושגרא תנורא וגרפתיה ואותביתיה לבינתא בגוויה ונפק כהוצא ירקא רב אויא אמר רביעתא דחלבא מעיזא חיורתא רב הונא בר יהודה אמר לייתי אתרוגא חליתא ולחייקיה ולימלייה דובשא ולותבה בי מיללי דנורא וליכליה רבי חנינא אמר מי רגלים בני ארבעים יום *ברזינא לזיבורא רביעאה לעקרבא פלגא ריבעא לגילויא ריבעא אפילו לכשפים מעלו אמר רבי יוחנן אניגרון ואבנגר ותירייקה מעלו בין לגילויא בין לכשפים האי מאן דבלע חוויא לוכליה כשותא במילחא ולירהטיה תלתא מילי רב שימי בר אשי חזייה לההוא גברא דבלע חוויא אידמי ליה כפרשא אוכליה כשותא במילחא וארהטיה קמיה תלתא מילי ונפק מיניה גובי גובי איכא דאמרי רב שימי בר אשי בלע חוויא אתא אליהו אידמי ליה כפרשא אוכליה כשותא במילחא וארהטיה קמיה תלתא מילי ונפק מיניה גובי גובי האי מאן דטרקיה חוויא ליתי עוברא דחמרא חיורתא וליקרעיה ולותביה עילויה והני מילי דלא אישתכח טרפה ההוא בר

אימור דפליגי לענין טומאה וטהרה . ומשום קרא : לענין שבת . דטעמא משום רפואה הוא מי שמעת להו : הא דאישתהי . בגווייהו אסור דמוכחא מלתא דלרפואה קא מכוין : הא דלא אישתהי . אלא רחץ ויצא מותר : בתרייתא . דקתני רוחצין בדלא אישתהי : חטטין . מאלנ"ץ : שלא נשתהי . בתוך המים דנראה כמיקר בעלמא : ביפין . שכן רוחצין בהן בחול לרחיצה שאינה לרפואה : ברעים . אין רוחצין דמוכחא מלתא דלרפואה ותרוייהו בדאישתהי : מי המשרה אמי המשרה לא קשיא. הך דקתני רוחצין במי המשרה אהנך תרתי דלעיל דקתני אבל לא במי המשרה הא דאישתהי הא דלא אשתהי **מתני'** איזביון . מפרש בגמרא שאינו מאכל בריאים ומוכחא מלתא דלרפואה אכיל ליה : אבל אוכל הוא את יועזר . שהרבה אוכלין אותו כשהן בריאין : ממי דקלים . מפרש בגמרא : וכוס עיקרין . משקה שנותנין לתוכו עיקרי ירקות ובשמים ובגמרא מפרש ליה : מפני שהן לירוקה . לחולי של ירקון ואינו מאכל בריאים : לצמאו . אם אינו חולה : **גמ'** אמר רב יוסף אזוב . דאורייתא שהוכשר להזאה הוא שקורין אברתא בר המג : איזביון . דמתניתין הוא שקורין אברתא בר הינג ויש מרבותי מפרשים בר המג שגדל במקום גמי בר הינג שגדל בין ההגים רוגל"ן : עולא אמר . אזוב דאורייתא הוא מרוא חיורא בלע"ז שלוי"א: שומשוק . הוא אזוב דאורייתא : ג' קלחים . דאגודה כתיב ואין אגודה פחות מג': ובהן ג' גבעולין . בכל קלח ג' גבעולין קנים דקים כעין של קנבוס: לקוקייני . תולעים שבבני מעים : דחליף עליה מ' יומי . משנטחן : פותנק . בלע"ז פולא"ל : לארקתא . תולעים שבכבד: ממאי הוי . החולי : מאומצא . בשר בגחלים : אליבא ריקנא . קודם אכילה : ומגירי דרובייא. לולבי תילתן כעין לולבי גפנים : רוביא . תילתן פיגרי : ומשתי מיא בתרייהו. האוכל אחד מאלו קודם אכילה ושותה אחריו מים : ואי לא . אי לית ליה פותנק א"כ אכליה ולא איתסי : תחלי . שחלי כרישון : לימוץ גרמא. יהא מולץ אבר יפה מאותו בשר וימץ שמנו בפיו : גורדא דאסינתא . קליפה גרודה מן הסנה : מעילאי לתתאי . שתהא גרודה מלמעלה למטה : דלמ"א נפקא. התולעים : איידי פומיה . דרך פיו : בי שבבי . בין השמשות בחשכותא דשמשי . ל"א בי שבבי בבית אחד משכניו שלא יריח הוא הריח שהוא קשה לו : נסכרינן לנקבים דיליה . יסתום נחיריו שלא יריח ל"א יסתום נחיריו ונקבי אזניו שלא יצא כח המשקה מגופו : מפני אפשיחה . מקום שנפשח הדקל אישברנקי"ר : חוטרא יחידאה . עץ הגדל יחידי בלא ענף : לגילויא . מי שבתה מים מגולין : חמשה כלילי . וורדין : כוסתא דשיכרא . כוסות : עד דקיימי אאנפקא . שיעמדו על מדה מחזקת אנפק והיא רביעית הלוג כדאמרינן בחזקת הבתים (ב"ב נה:) : ושגרא תנורא . הסיקה תנור : וגרפתיה . מגחלים שילטנן קלת ואותבה לבינתא בגויה . שישב עליה ולא יכוה : ונפק מיניה . הקיא החרס שבלע : הוצא . עלה של לולב : אתרוג חליתא . מתוק : ולחייקיה . לגויה יחקוק בתוכו חקק : וליתבה בי מיללי דנורא . מניחו ע"ג גחלים לוחשות שיתבשל האתרוג בדבש : בני מ' יום . שעברו עליהם מ' יום . ל"א של תינוק בן מ' יום : ברזינא לזיבורא . כוס קטן מאד ושמו ברזינא מאותן מי רגלים שותין למי שנשכתו צרעה ומתרפא : רביעתא לעקרב . רביעית לוג למי שעקצו עקרב : פלגא ריבעא לגילויא . חצי לוג : רבעא לוג : אניגרון ואבנגר ותירייקי מים שנשלק בהם בנגרי מין עשב ששמו בנגרי וסתם אניגרון מי שלק תרדין כדאמרינן (ברכות דף לה:) אניגרון מיא דסילקא ותירייקי צרי : אידמי ליה כפרשא . תופסו ומייסרו שהפחד והמרוצה והכשות מתישין כחו (א) ומחמם ומת הנחש בתוכו: גובי . חתיכות חתיכות יצא הנחש ממנו גובי טרונצו"ן בלע"ז : דטרקיה . נשכו : עוברא דחמרא חיורתי . עובר הנקבה במעי חמורה לבנה : דלא אשתכח טרפה . האם :

רבינו חננאל

ושלשתן מותר לרחוץ בהן אע"פ [שהן] חמין. ואין רוחצין בימא של סדום אבל בים הגדול סבר לה ר' יוחנן פלוגתא . ר' מאיר אסר ור' יהודה שרי ואתקיף רב נחמן בר יצחק עליה עד כאן לא פליגי אלא לענין טומאה וטהרה אי עלתה לטבילה אי לא אבל לענין שבת לא פליגי ומשני אם נשתהה בים הגדול בשבת כדי להתרפאות אסור ואם לא נשתהה מותר ואקשינן במאי אוקימתא להא ברייתא דקתני רוחצין בים הגדול בדלא אישתהי אימא סיפא ולא במי משרה [ואי]לא אישתהי אפי' במי משרה נמי שרי.דתניא רוחצין במי טבריאובמי משרה וימא של סדום ואע"פ שיש לו חטטין בראשו בד"א בשלא נשתהה (אסור) אבל נשתהה אסור ופרקי' כי אמרי שהיה במי משרה אבל בים הגדול יפים ורעים אמרינן . הא דתניא רוחצין בים הגדול במים יפין שבו דלא מסו. הא דתניא אבל לא בים הגדול ברעים שבו דמסו. מי דקלים.המעין היוצא במערבא מבין איתן ג' שתילים ובירושלמי שונין מי דקרין שדוקרין את המרה . אבוב רועה פי' בלשון ישמעאל אנבוב אל רעאי או עצאה אל רעאי :

רב נסים גאון

אמר בהן הכתוב מים חיים נאמר בזב (ויקרא טו) ורחץ בשרו במים חיים וזה מיוחד בזב בלבד ולא בזבה כמו שיש בתוספתא (זבים פרק ג) חומר בזב מה שאין בזבה שהזב טעון ביאת מים חיים וזבה אינה טעונה ביאת מים חיים והמצורע נאמר בו (ויקרא יד) ושחט את הצפור האחת אל כלי חרש על מים חיים ונאמר בפירוש דבר זה מים חיים ולא מים מלוחין ולא מים פושרין ולא מים מכובין ולא מים מנטפין וזה מיוחד בהזאתו של מצורע לבד אבל טבילתו אין צריך מים חיים ובזה נאמר (שם) ורחץ במים אפי' במי מקוה ולא דין הוא ומה אם הזב שאינו טעון הויית מים חיים טעון ביאת מים חיים מצורע שהוא טעון הויית מים חיים אינו דין שיטען ביאת מים חיים תלמוד לומר ורחץ במים ואפי' במי מקוה וקידוש מי חטאת נאמר בו (במדבר יט) ולקחו לטמא ונאמר בו ונתן עליו מים חיים אל כלי ונאמר בפירוש במי מעין הכתוב מדבר ובפסחים בגמ' דכל שעה (דף לד) נאמר ונתן עליו מים חיים אל כלי שתהא חיותן בכלי מדקאמר ונתן אלמא תלושין נינהו ומדקאמר מים חיים אלמא מחוברים נינהו אלא מעלה ובמס' סוטה בפרק היה מביא את מנחתה (דף טז) אמרו ונתן עליו אלמא אפר ברישא וכתיב מים חיים אל כלי כיצד רצה זה נותן רצה זה נותן ורבנן [אל] כלי דוקא עליו לערבן ואימא עליו דוקא כלי שתהא חיותן בכלי וכו' ובמשנת מקואות בפרק א' שנינו למעלה מהן מים חיים (שהן טעונין טבילה) [שבהן טבילה לזבים] והזיה למצורעין וכשרין לקדש מהן מי חטאת : לקוקני הם תולעים נקראים בלשון ישמעאל חב אל קרע ותמצא בפ' אלו טריפות (חולין ד' סז) : והלכתא

[במסכת שבמשניות אי' איזוב יון]

ברכות לח. יומא מט.

סוכה יג. פרה פי"א מ"ט

הגהות הב"ח
(א) רש"י ד"ה אידמי וכו' כחו ומתחמם ומת :

[פי' הערוך אחד מד' ברביעית]

tration.[9] R. Naḥman b. Isaac demurred: [109*b*] Say that they differ in respect to uncleanness and purity; but do you know them [to differ] in respect of the Sabbath?[10] Rather said R. Naḥman b. Isaac: There is no difficulty: in the one case he tarries [there];[11] in the other he does not tarry [there]. To what have you referred the second [Baraitha]? Where he does not tarry! If he does not tarry, [it is permitted] even in the water of steeping too. For it was taught: One may bathe in the waters of Tiberias and in the water of steeping and in the Lake of Sodom, even if he has scabs on his head. When is that? If he does not tarry [there]; but if he tarries [there], it is forbidden!—Rather [reply thus]: [The rulings on] the Great Sea are not contradictory: one refers
a to its wholesome [water]; the other to its malodorous [water].[1] [The rulings on] the water of steeping too are not contradictory: in the one case he tarries; in the other he does not tarry.

MISHNAH. WE MAY NOT EAT GREEK HYSSOP ON THE SABBATH, BECAUSE IT IS NOT THE FOOD OF HEALTHY PEOPLE;[2] BUT WE MAY EAT YO'EZER[3] AND DRINK ABUB RO'EH.[4] A MAN MAY EAT ANY KIND OF FOOD AS A REMEDY, AND DRINK ANY LIQUID,[5] EXCEPT WATER OF PALM TREES[6] AND A POTION[7] OF ROOTS, BECAUSE THEY ARE [A REMEDY] FOR JAUNDICE; BUT ONE MAY DRINK WATER OF PALM TREES FOR HIS THIRST AND RUB HIMSELF WITH OIL OF ROOTS WITHOUT MEDICAL PURPOSE.

GEMARA. R. Joseph said: Hyssop[8] is *abratha bar hemag;*[9] Greek hyssop is *abratha bar henag.*[10] 'Ulla said: [Hyssop is] white *marwa* [sage]. 'Ulla visited R. Samuel b. Judah [and] they set white *marwa* before him. Said he to them, That is the hyssop prescribed in Scripture. R. Pappi said, It is *shumshuk* [marjoram]. R. Jeremiah
b of Difti[1] said: Reason supports R. Pappi. For we learnt: 'The law of hyssop [requires] three stalks [each] containing three calyxes'; and *shumshuk* is found to have that shape. For what is it eaten?—[As a remedy] for worms. With what is it eaten?—With seven black dates. By what is it [the disease of worms] caused?—Through [eating] barley-flour forty days old.

BUT ONE MAY EAT YO'EZER. What is YO'EZER?—Pennyroyal.[2] For what is it eaten? [As a remedy] for worms in the bowels[3] With what is it eaten? With seven white dates. Through what is it caused? Through [eating] raw meat[4] and [drinking] water on an empty stomach; through [eating] fat meat on an empty stomach or ox meat on an empty stomach; through nuts on an empty stomach; shoots of fenugreek on an empty stomach and drinking water after it.[5] But if not,[6] let him swallow white cress. If not, let him fast, then bring fat meat and cast it on the coals, suck out a thick piece and drink vinegar. But others say, not vinegar, because it affects the liver. If not, let him procure the scrapings of a thorn bush which was scraped from top to bottom but not from below and upward, lest [the worms] issue through his mouth, and boil them in strong liquor[7] at twilight.[8] On the morrow let him stop up his orifices[9] and drink it: And when he eases himself, he must do so on the stripped parts of a palm tree.

AND DRINK ABUB RO'EH. What is ABUB RO'EH? *Ḥumtarya* [eupatorium]. What is *ḥumtarya?* The lonely staff.[10] What is it prepared for? [As a remedy for] one who drank uncovered water.[11] If not,[12] let him bring five roses and five glasses of strong liquor, boil
c them together until they amount to an *anpak*,[1] and drink it. The mother of R. Aḥadbuy b. Ammi prepared [a potion of] one rose and one glass of strong liquor for a certain man. She boiled them up, made him drink it, lit the stove and swept it out, placed bricks in it,[2] and it [the poison of the snake] issued like a green palm-leaf. R. Awia said: A quarter [*log*] of milk from a white goat.[3] R. Huna b. Judah said: Let him obtain a sweet citron, scoop it out, fill it with honey, set it on burning embers [to boil], and then eat it. R. Ḥanina said: [One drinks] urine forty days old[4] [as a remedy]; a *barzina*[5] for [the sting of] a wasp; a quarter [*log*] for a scorpion [bite]; an eighth [of a *log*] for uncovered water; a quarter is efficacious even against witchcraft. R. Joḥanan said: *Elaiogaron*,[6] *kangad*,[7] and *theriac* are efficacious against both uncovered water and witchcraft. If one swallows a snake, he should be made to eat cuscuta with salt and run three *mils*. R. Shimi b. Ashi saw a man swallow a snake; thereupon he appeared to him in the guise of a horseman,[8] made him eat cuscuta with salt and run three *mils* before him, [and] it issued from him in strips.[9] Others say: R. Shimi b. Ashi swallowed a snake, thereupon Elijah came,[10] appeared to him in the guise of a horseman, made him eat cuscuta with salt and run three *mils* before him, [and] it issued from him in strips.

If one is bitten by a snake, he should procure an embryo of a white ass, tear it open, and be made to sit upon it; providing, however, that it was not found to be *ṭerefah*. A certain [110*a*]

(9) I.e., to be mixed with the ashes of the red heifer. (10) Which is totally different. (11) Then it is obvious that his purpose is to effect a cure.

a (1) The latter is forbidden, since no one would bathe therein for cleanliness. (2) But obviously a medicine. (3) A certain plant. (4) Lit., 'shepherd's flute'—name of a plant (Eupatorium) used for medicinal purposes (Jast.). (5) Provided that they are eaten and drunk without healing intentions too. (6) Explained *infra* 110*a*. (7) Lit., 'cup'. (8) Prescribed in the Torah for purification, e.g., Lev. XIV, 4. (9) So they called it. (10) *Abratha* is probably *Artemisia abrotanum*, and with the designations *bar hemag* (of the bush) and *bar henag* (of the shrub) the names of two sub-species of hyssop were meant.

d (1) V. *supra* 10*a*, n. b5. (2) *Mentha pulegium*; Jast. (3) Fluke worms(?). (4) *Umẓa* is meat roasted directly on coals or pickled in a strong acid. (5) That probably applies to all the foregoing. (6) If pennyroyal is unobtainable or has failed to cure. (7) Mead, or beer. (8) Or the text may mean, 'in a neighbour's house', so that the sufferer himself should not smell it, lest the smell affect him. (9) Either his nostrils, so as not to smell it when drinking, or his nostrils and ears, that the strength of the potion should not pass out of his body. (10) Name of a drink made of liver-wort (Jast.). (11) Water left uncovered over night might not be drunk, lest a snake had drunk of it—a necessary precaution in Eastern countries. (12) V. n. b6.

c (1) A quarter of a *log*, B.B. 58*b*. (2) For the sufferer to sit on. (3) Is a good remedy for this. (4) Or, of a babe forty days old. (5) A small measure, one thirty-second of a *log*. (6) A sauce of oil and garum, to which wine is sometimes added (Jast.). (7) A kind of chevril. (8) Rashi: in order to frighten him, which would help to kill the snake. (9) The snake was broken up within him. (10) Elijah was thought to appear quite frequently to favoured persons: cf. B.M. 59*b*; Sanh. 113*a*; Keth. 61*a*, *passim*.

officer of Pumbeditha was bitten by a snake. Now there were thirteen white asses in Pumbeditha; they were all torn open and found to be *ṭerefah*. There was another on the other side of Pumbeditha, [but] before they could go and bring it a lion devoured it. [Thereupon] Abaye observed to them, 'Perhaps he was bitten
a by a snake of the Rabbis,[1] for which there is no cure, as it is written, *and whoso breaketh through a fence,*[2] *a serpent shall bite him?*'[3] 'Indeed so, Rabbi,' answered they. For when Rab died, R. Isaac b. Bisna decreed that none should bring myrtles and palm-branches to a wedding feast to the sound of a *ṭabla,*[4] yet he went and brought myrtle and palm-branches at a wedding to the sound of the *ṭabla;* [so] a snake bit him and he died.

If a snake winds itself around a person, let him go down into water, put a basket over its head and force it [the snake] away from himself, and when it goes on to it [the basket], he should throw it into the water, ascend and make off.

If a man is scented by a snake,[5] if his companion is with him, he should make him ride four cubits.[6] If not, let him jump a ditch.[7] If not, let him cross a river; and at night place his bed on four barrels and sleep under the stars,[8] and bring four cats and tie them to the four legs of the bed. Then he should fetch rubbish[9] and throw it there, so that when they hear a sound they [the cats] will devour it.

If a man is chased by one [a snake], he should flee into sandy places.[10]

If a woman sees a snake and does not know whether it has turned its attention to her or not, let her remove her garments and throw them in front of it; if it winds itself around them, its mind is upon her; if not, its mind is not upon her. What can she do? She should cohabit [with her husband] in front of it. Others say, That will even strengthen its instincts. Rather she should take some of her hair and nails and throw them at it and say, 'I am menstruous'.

If a snake enters a woman, let her spread her legs and place them on two barrels; fat meat must be brought and cast on the burning coals; a basket of cress must be brought together with
b fragrant wine and placed there, and be well beaten together.[1] They should take a pair of tongs in their hand, for when it smells the fragrance it will come out, so that it can be seized and burnt in the fire, as otherwise it will re-enter.

ANY KIND OF FOOD etc. What does 'ANY KIND OF FOOD' include?—It includes milt [taken as a remedy] for the teeth, and vetches for the bowels. What does 'ANY LIQUID' include?—It includes caperjuice in vinegar.

EXCEPT WATER OF PALM TREES. It was taught: Except water that pierces. He who teaches, water that pierces, [calls it thus] because it pierces the gall.[2] And he who says, WATER OF PALM TREES, that is because it comes forth from [between] two palm trees. What is water of palm trees?[3]—Rabbah b. Beruna said: There are two *tali*[4] in the west [Palestine] and a spring of water issues from between them. The first cup [thereof] loosens, the second causes motion, and the third passes out just as it enters. 'Ulla said: I myself drank Babylonian beer and it is more efficacious than these [waters];[5] provided, however, that one had discontinued [drinking] it for forty days.[6]

R. Joseph said: Egyptian beer consists of one part barley, one part safflower, and one part salt. R. Papa said: One part wheat, one part safflower, and one part salt. And the token is *sisane.*[7] And it is drunk between Passover[8] and Pentecost; upon him who is constipated it acts as a laxative, while him who suffers with diarrhoea it binds.

AND A POTION OF ROOTS. What is a POTION OF ROOTS? Said R. Joḥanan: The weight of a *zuz*[9] of Alexandrian gum is brought, a *zuz* weight of liquid alum and a *zuz* weight of garden crocus, and they are powdered together. For a *zabah*, a third thereof [mixed] with wine [is efficacious] that she shall not become barren. For jaundice two thirds thereof [mixed] with beer [is
c drunk], and he [the sufferer] then becomes impotent.[1] 'For a *zabah*, a third thereof [mixed] with wine [is efficacious] that she shall not become barren': but if not,[2] let them procure three

a (1) I.e., as a punishment for disobeying the Rabbis. (2) Rabbinical laws were often so called; cf. Aboth, I, 13. (3) Eccl. X, 8. (4) A bell or a collection of bells forming an instrument specially used at public processions, weddings, etc. (5) Which pursues him. (6) To break the track of the scent. (7) The water breaks the scent. (8) So that the snake cannot attack him either from below or above. (9) Rashi: branches, twigs, etc., which rustle and make a noise when anything passes over them. 'Ar: refuse of reeds. (10) Where the snake cannot follow.

b (1) To cause their fragrance to ascend. (2) I.e., makes it function. (3) BaḤ deletes this question. (4) A species of palms. (5) *Sc.* of the well just mentioned. (6) Otherwise the system does not react to it. (7) A basket made of twigs. *Sisane* contains two *sameks;* thus R. Joseph (יוסף) mentioned barley (שעורים) —the *samek* and *sin* being interchangeable. (8) Lit., 'the sacrifice'. (9) Three and five hundred eighty-five thousandth grammes; v. *J.E. Weights and Measures,* XII, p. 486: Other Weights and Table on p. 489.

c (1) Though cured of his illness. (2) If it is unavailable or fails to cure.

לו א טוש"ע א"ח סי' שכח סעיף לז:

בר קשא דפומבדיתא דטרקיה חויא הוה *תליסר חמרי חיורתא בפומבדיתא קרעינהו לכולהו ואישתכחו טריפה הואי חדא בההוא גיסא דפומבדיתא עד דאזלי מייתי לה אכלה אריה אמר להו אביי דילמא *חויא דרבנן טרקיה דלית ליה אסותא דכתיב °ופורץ גדר ישכנו נחש אמרו ליה אין רבי דכי נח נפשיה דרב גזר רב יצחק בר ביסנא דליכא דלימטייה אסא וגידמי לבי הילולא [בטבלא] ואזל איהו אמטי אסא וגידמי לבי הילולא בטבלא טרקיה חויא ומית האי מאן דכרכיה חויא לינחות למיא ולישחוף דיקולא ארישא ולהדקיה מיניה וכי סליק עילויה לישדיה למיא וליסלוק וליתי האי מאן דמיקני ביה חויא אי איכא חבריה בהדיה לירכביה ארבע גרמידי ואי לא *לישואר נגרא ואי לא ליעבר נהרא ובליליא לותביה לפוריא אארבעה חביתא וניגני בי כוכבי ולייתי ד' שונרי וליסרינהו בארבעה כרעי דפורייה וליתי *שחפי ולישדי התם דכי שמע קלי אבלי ליה האי מאן דרהיט אבתריה לירהיט בי חלתא האי איתתא דחזיא חויא ולא ידעה אי יהיב דעתיה עילוה אי לא יהיב דעתיה עילוה תשלח מאנה ונשדייה קמיה אי מכרך בהו דעתיה עילוה ואי לא לא יהיב דעתיה עילוה מאי תקנתה תשמש קמיה איכא דאמרי כ"ש דתקיף ליה יצריה אלא תשקול ממזיה ומטופרה ותשדי ביה ותימא *דישתנא אנא האי איתתא דעייל בה חויא ליפסעה ולתבוה אתרתי חביתא וליתי בישרא שמנה ולישדי אגומרי וליתי אגנא דתחלי וחמרא ריתתנא ולותבו התם ולימרוקינהו בהדי הדדי ולינקוט צבתא בידה דכי מירח ריחא נפיק ואתי ולישקליה וליקלייה בנורא דאי לא הדר עילוה: כל האוכלין כו': כל האוכלין לאיתויי מאי **לאיתויי טחול לשינים וכרשינין לבני מעיים כל המשקין לאיתויי מאי לאיתויי מי צלפין בחומץ א"ל רבינא לרבא מהו לשתות מי רגלים בשבת א"ל תנינא כל המשקין שותה ומי רגלים לא שתו אינשי: חוץ ממי דקלים: תנא חוץ ממי דקרים מאן דתנא מי דקרים שהם דוקרים את המרה ומאן דאמר מי דקלים שיוצאין מן שני דקלי (א) מאי מי דקלים אמר רבה בר ברונא תרתי תלאי איכא במערבא ונפקא עינא דמיא מבינייהו כסא קמא מרפי אידך משלשל ואידך כי היכי דעיילי הכי נפקי אמר עולא לדידי שתי שיכרא דבבלאי ומעלי מינייהו והוא דלא רגיל ביה ארבעין יומין רב יוסף אמר זיתום *המצרי תילתא שערי ותילתא קורטמי ותילתא מילחא רב פפא אמר תילתא חיטי ותילתא קורטמי ותילתא מילחא (וכמונא) *וסימניך סיסאני ושתי להו בין דבחא לעצרתא דקמיט מרפי ליה ודרפי קמיט ליה: וכוס עקרין: מאי כוס עקרין אמר ר' יוחנן לייתי מתקל זוזא קומא אלכסנדריא ומתקל זוזא גביא גילא ומתקל זוזא כורכמא רישקא ולישחקינהו בהדי הדדי לזבה תלתא בחמרא ולא מיעקרא לירקונא תרין בשיכרא ומיעקר לזבה תלתא בחמרא ולא מיעקרא ואי לא לייתי תלתא

קפיזי

רש"י

בר קשא. ממונה למלך וישראל היה: דילמא חויא דרבנן. שעבר על נידוי חכמים ונחש הנושכו על כך אין לו רפואה לפיכך לא כמלא לו רפואה: אין רבי. אין רבינו כך היה: דכי נח נפשיה דרב גזר רב יצחק. שיהיו ממעטים משמחה אותה שנה ולא יהא אדם מביא אסא וגידמי להילולא בטבלא שהיו רגילים להביא הדס וענפי דקלים לשמוח לפני החתן והכלה וכשמביאים אותן לפניהם מקשקשים לפניהם בשוק בבואם בתופים וזוגין טבלא אשקליט"א וגזר שלא יקשקשו לפניהם עוד: דכרכיה. נכרך סביבותיו: ולישחוף דיקולא. סל: ארישיה. דחויא למעלה מראשו: ולהדקיה מיניה. יוריד הסל מעט מעט לצד הנחש ויבדיל בו הנחש מבשרו שיעלה על הסל שאם אוחזו בידו או מנתקו בחזקה יכעוס וישכנו: וכי סליק. הנחש על הסל ימהר וישליכנו במים ויברח לו: דמיקני ביה חויא. כועס ורודף אחריו ומריח ריח פעמיו ורודפו: לירכביה ארבע גרמידי. שיפסקו עקבי פעמיו ולא יוכל להריחם: לישואר נגרא. חריץ של מים ידלוג: ארבע חביתא. שלא יעלה אליו מהר ולא יריח ריחו: בי כוכבי. במקום גלוי שלא יעלה דרך הגג ויפיל עצמו עליו: שחפי. ענפים וקסמים וכל דבר המקשקש זה בזה ומשמיע קול כשיעבור עליהן וירגישו החתולים ויאכלוהו: בי חלתא. בין החולות שאין נחש יכול לרוץ שם ויחזור לאחוריו: אי יהיב דעתיה עלה. לתאות תשמיש: תשלח מאנה. תפשוט בגדיה ותשליכם לפניה: מאי תקנתא. אי יהיב דעתיה עלה: תשמש קמיה. עם בעלה ותתגנה בפניו: ותשדי ביה. ותזרק ביה: דשתנא אנא. דרך נ"ש לי ולאחר בעלמא הוא: דעייל בה חויא. כשהוא תאב לה נכנס כולו באותו מקום: ליפסעה. יפסקו את רגליה זה מזה: אתרתי חביתי. מקצתה על זו ומקצתה על זו כדי שיפתח רחמה: ונישדי אגומרי. כי היכי דניסליק ריחא: אגנא תחלי. סל מלא שחליים: ריתתנא. שיש לו ריח טוב: וליתבו התם. על גבי קרקע תחת מושבה: וליטרוקינהו בהדדי. היין והשחליים כדי שיעלה הריח: צבתא. איטנליי"ש: דאי לא. קלי ליה הדר עילוה: לאיתויי טחול לשינים. ואע"פ שקשה לבני מעיים: כרשינין לבני מעיים. ואע"פ שקשה לשינים כדאמרינן בברכות (דף מד:) סד"א כיון שקשים לאדם לאו אורחיה למיכלינהו אי לאו לרפואה שיש בהם ומוכחא מילתא וניתסר קמ"ל: צלפים. פרי של צלף קפריי"ר: תלאי. דקלים נטיעות מין תמרים שנקרא בלשון ארמי תלאי: כסא קמא. דשתו מהגהו מיא: מרפי. זבל שבמעים במקלת: אידך. כוס שני: משלשל. מאד: היכי דעיילי. צלולים: הכי נפקי. שמנקין המעיים מן הרעי מראשונים: והוא דלא רגיל. למשתי שיכרא כבר עברו מ' יום: רב יוסף אמר זיתום המצרי. הוא מי דקרים ועל שם שדוקרים את החולי: תלתא קורטמי. כרכום: סיסני. כלי שנותנין בו תמרים כדאמרינן בעלמא (ב"מ דף סז:) ואי אגבהינהו בסיסני קננהו וסימניך דלא תחליף שמעתתא שם כלי זה יהא לך סימן שיש בו שני סמכין רב יוסף אמר שערי: בין דבחא לעצרתא. בין פסח לעצרת: דקמיט. עצור: קומא אלכסנדרית. שרף אילנות של אלכסנדריא: גביא גילא. אלו"ם בלע"ז: כורכמא רישקא. כרכום של גן קרו"ג אורייכטל הגדל בגנים: לזבה. הנך תלתא מיני לישקייה בחמרא: ולא מיעקרא. אינה נעקרת מלילד לפי שהיין מפיג חוזקן של סמנים ומתרפאה מן החולי: לירקונא תרי. מינייהו לישתי בשיכרא וזהו רפואתו: ומיעקר. מלהוליד: לזבה תלתא בחמרא. הדר נקט ליה משום הנך רפואות דנקט ואזיל: ואי לא כו'. כולהו לא מעלי אלא לזבה:

קפיזא

תוספות

חויא דרבנן טרקיה דלית ליה אסותא. אע"ג דגבי בן דמא בן אחותו של ר' ישמעאל בפרק ב' דמס' ע"ז (דף כז:) קאמר שלא עבר על דברי חבירים שנאמר ופורץ גדר ישכנו נחש אע"ג דלא הוה ליה אסותא שהרי מת התם לא היה לו רפואה מזומנת אבל הכא שהרפואה היתה מזומנת ונאבדה ממנו במזל רע קאמר דלית ליה אסותא: וליתי אגנא דתחלי. משמע הכא דהנחש אוהב שחליים וכן בשלהי דנדרים (דף נא:) דקאמר ליה נואף לבעל לא תיכול מהני תחלי דטעמינהו חויא וא"כ יש בהן משום גילוי (ב) ובפרק ב' דמס' ע"ז (ל: ושם) אמר דשחליים אין בהם משום גילוי וי"ל דהתם לא ממש שחליים קאמר אלא בהנך דאמר התם (מס' ע"ז דף סז.) וכן היו עושין בערבי שבתות בצפורי [נותנין חומץ לתוך גריסין] והיו קורין אותו שחליים אי נמי בשלהי נדרים (דף נא:) מיירי דהוה ביה חלא כדמסקינן התם במס' ע"ז (דף ל:) אבל אית בהו חלא מיגרי בהו והכא נמי חמרא מיגרי בהו: רב יוסף אמר זיתום המצרי. ר"ת כל הך מילתא מחק מספרו ואומר דל"ג (ג) אלא ברישא אלו עוברין (פסחים מב:) ונראה לר"י שמחקה משום דזיתום המצרי מותר לשתות כדתניא בפרק בתרא (דף קנו.) ושוין שבוחשין את השתית ושותין זיתום המצרי ואומר ריב"א דאין צריך למחוק דרב יוסף לא קאי לפרש מי דקרים דמתני' אלא אמילתיה דעולא קאי דאמר שיכרא בבלאי מעלי מינייהו ואומר רב יוסף דזיתום המצרי מעלי מינייהו מיהו משמע כפירוש הקונט' דאמתני' קאי מדלא קאמר בהדיא זיתום המצרי מעלי מינייהו: סיסאני. ולא קאמר וסימניך סמך סמך כדאמר בשלהי במה אשה (לעיל סו.) משום דשערי לא כתיב בסמך:

והתניא

רב נסים גאון

והלכתא קוקאני אסירי מנמנם כורא ועיילין ליה באוסיא: אניגרון מפרש בברכות פ' כיצד מברכין על הפירות (דף לה) אמר רבא בר שמואל מיא דסילקי: ותימא ליה דישתנא אנא. במס' ע"ז בפ' אין מעמידין (ד' כד) אמרו אמר רב אשי כמן קרו פרסאי לנדה דשתנא מהכא כי דרך נשים לי: כל האוכלין לאיתויי טחול לשינים וכרישין לבני מעים. בפרק כיצד מברכין על הפירות (דף מד) תנו רבנן טחול יפה לשינים וקשה לבני מעים כרישין יפים לבני מעים וקשים לשינים: חוץ ממי דקלים. בגמ'

הגהות הב"ח

(א) גמ' שיוצאין משני דקלים (מאי מי דקלים) תא"מ ונ"ב ס"א איתו: (ב) תוס' ד"ה וליתי וכו' משום גילוי ואע"ג דבפ"ב דע"ז אמר: (ג) ד"ה רב יוסף וכו' ואומר דל"ג לה אלא ברישא:

[פ"רש"י לקמן קיט. ד"ה פריסר עיליתי] [ע"ז כז:] [בערוך ערך שור גי' הערוך לשוור] [גירסת הערוך שחפי דקניא פי' קליפות קנים] [ע"ז יח. כד:] [ברכות מד:] [פסחים מג: ע"ש] [שם פ"ג ברש"י]

תורה אור: קהלת י

תורה אור

קפיזי שמכי פרסאי ונישלוק בחמרא ונשקייה ונימא לה קום מזוביך ואי לא לותבה אפרשת דרכים ולינקטה כסא דחמרא בידה וליתי איניש מאחורה וליבעתה ולימא לה קום מזוביך ואי לא ליתי בונא דכמונא ובונא דמוריקא ובונא דשבלילתא ונישלוק בחמרא ונשקייה ונימא לה קום מזוביך ואי לא ליתי שיתין שיעי דדנא ולשפיה ולימא לה קום מזוביך ואי לא ליתי *פשטינא ולישלוק בחמרא ולשפיה ונימא לה קום מזוביך ואי לא ליתי חרנוגא דהיגתא רומיתא וליקלי וליסבה בשחקי דכיתנא בקייטא ובשחקי דעמר גופנא בסיתוא ואי לא ליכרי שבע בירי וליקלי בהו שבישתא ילדה דערלה ולינקטה כסא דחמרא בידה ולוקמה מהא ולותבה אהא ולוקמה מהא ולותבה אהא ואבל חדא וחדא לימא לה קום מזוביך ואי לא לייתי סמידא וליסבה מפלגא לתתאי ולימא לה קום מזוביך ואי לא ליתי ביעתא דנעמיתא וליקלי וליסבה בשחקי דכיתנא בקייטא ובשחקי דעמר גופנא בסיתוא ואי לא ליפתח לה חביתא דחמרא לשמה ואי לא לנקיט שערתא דמשתכחת בכפותא דכודנא חיורא אי נקטה חד יומא פסקה תרי יומי ואי נקטה תרי יומי פסקה תלתא יומי ואי נקטה תלתא יומי פסקה לעולם: לירקונא תרין בשיכרא (א) ומעיקר ואי לא לייתי רישא דשיבוטא דמילחא ולישלוק בשיכרא ולישתי ואי לא לייתי *מוניני דקמצי ואי ליכא מוניני דקמצי לייתי *מוניני דנקירי ולעייליה לבי בני ולישפייה ואי ליכא בי בני לוקמיה בין תנורא לגודא אמר רבי יוחנן הרוצה שיחממנו יקנחנו בסדינו רב אחא בר יוסף חש ביה עבד ליה רב כהנא ואיתסי ואי לא ליתי תלתא קפיזי תמרי פרסייתא ותלתא קפיזי דקירא דנישתרופי ותלתא קפיזי אהלא תולענא ולישלוקינהו בשיכרא ולישתי ואי לא ליתי עילא בר חמרא וליגלח מציעתא דרישא ולישביק ליה דמא מאפותיה ולותביה ארישיה וליזדהר מעיניה דלא ליסמי להו ואי לא ליתי רישא דברחא דמנח בכיבשא ולישלוק בשיכרא ולישתי ואי לא ליתי דבר אחר חוטרנא וליקרעיה ולותביה אליביה ואי לא ליתי כרתי מכבתותא דמישרי ההוא טייעא דחש ביה אמר ליה לגינאי שקול גלימאי והב לי מישרא דכרתי יהיב ליה ואכלה א"ל אושלן גלימיך ואיגני ביה קלי איכרך גנא ביה כד איחמם וקם נפל פורתא פורתא מיניה: לירקונא תרין בשיכרא ומיעקר *ומי שרי והתניא [ג]מניין לסירוס באדם שהוא אסור ת"ל °ובארצכם לא תעשו בכם ויקרא כב לא תעשו דברי ר' חנינא הני מילי היכא דקא מיכוין הכא מעצמו הוא דאמר ר' יוחנן [ד]הרוצה שיסרס תרנגול יטול כרבלתו ומסתרס מאליו והאמר רב אשי רמות רוחא הוא דנקיטא ליה אלא בסרים והאמר ר' חייא בר אבא אמר ר' יוחנן

הכל

והתניא מניין לסירוס (ג)שהוא אסור. וא"ת אפילו לא אסור סירוס תיקשי ליה דליתסר משום פריה ורביה וכ"ת משום דהוי מלי לשנויי ביש לו בנים הא משמע בסוף הבא על יבמתו (יבמות דף סה:) גבי דביתהו דר' חייא דאי הוה מיפקדה אפריה ורביה לא הוה שתיא סמא דעקרתא אע"ג דהוי לה שתי נקבות ושני זכרים משום בבקר זרע [את] זרעך ולערב אל תנח ידך (קהלת יא) ובאשה לא שייך סירוס אוקי במסקנא לרבי יוחנן בן ברוקה דמחייב בפריה ורביה בעקרה וזקנה ולא מוקי ביש לה בנים ויש לומר דמסירוס ניחא ליה למפרך משום דאיכא למ"ד בפרק הבא על יבמתו (שם דף סא:)כיון דקיימא פריה ורביה תו לא צריך: **תלמוד** לומר ובארצכם לא תעשו. מכאן קא דריש והא דאמר בחגיגה (דף יד:) שאלו את בן זומא מהו לסרוסי כלבא אמר להו בארצכם לא תעשו כל שבארצכם לא תעשו התם נפקא לן מארץ כדמפרש בשאלתות דרב אחאי* דהא חובת הגוף הוא מה לי בארץ מה לי בחו"ל אלא האי בארץ לכל אשר בארץ אתא והכא מכם דריש כדפי' ומה שמפרש בשאלתות* דהא דאסר לשתות סמא דעקרתא היינו כרבי יהודה דאמר דבר שאין מתכוין אסור ואע"ג דקי"ל כר"ש דשרי היינו דוקא בשבת משום דבעינן מלאכת מחשבת אבל בכל התורה כולה סבירא לן כרבי יהודה ואין נראה לר"י דבכל התורה כולה קי"ל כר"ש דשרי כדמשמע לעיל בפ' המוציא (פא:) דאמרי' דרבי יוחנן כבר כסתם משנה דנזיר חופף ומפספס וכו' והיינו כרבי שמעון דשרי דבר שאינו מתכוין וכן משמע בפרק כל פסולי המוקדשין (בכורות דף לד·) דשמואל סבר כר"ש בכל התורה כולה דדבר שאין מתכוין שרי גבי המקיז דם בבכור דפסק שמואל התם כר"ש דשרי להקיז ופריך עד השתא לא אשמועינן שמואל דדבר שאין מתכוין מותר דאמר רב חייא בר אשי כו' ואי יש חילוק בין שבת לדעלמא איצטריך התם שפיר לפסוק כר"ש אע"ג דכבר אשמעינן דבשבת הלכה כר"ש והכא אתיא אפילו לר' שמעון דפסיק רישיה הוא דודאי יסתרס בשתיי' כוס עיקרין:

להביא

קפיזי. כלי מחזיק ג' לוגין: שמכי. בצלים: פרסאי. גדולים הם: קום מזוביך. חדלי מזוביך כמו ויעמוד השמן (מלכים ב ד): וליבעתה. יבעתנה בלי ידיעתה פתאום: בונא. מלא אגרוף: מוריקא. כרכום: שבלילתא. תלתן פנגרי"ג: שיעי דדנא. מגופת חבית ולשייפיה. לכשישורו במים: פשטינא. עשב שאינו גדל בקומה אלא הולך ופשט על גבי קרקע: חרנוגא. מין עשב הוא שגדל אצל ההיגים: היגתא רומיתא. מין הגא הוא שנקראת רומי"ת: וליסבה בשחקי דכיתנא. יקחו אותו האפר בבלאי בגדי פשתן בקיץ: דעמר גופנא. קוטו"ן: ליכרי שב בירי. שבעה גומות: שבישתא דערלה. זמורות של כרם ילדה: ולינקטה כסא דחמרא. יאחוז כוס של יין בידה ותשב על הגומא: ולוקמה מהא. מעל גומא זו יושיבוה על זו ועל כל עמידה נימא לה קום מזוביך: קמחא דסמידא. קמח סולת: וליסבה. יסוכו אותה ממנו: דנעמיתא. בת היענה: ליפתח לה חביתא דחמרא לשמה. כלומר יין הרבה תשתה תמיד: שערתא דמשתכח בכפותא דכודנא חיורתי. שעורה הנמצאת בגללי פרדה לבנה: אי נקטא. לה בידה חד יומא פסקה מזובה תרי יומי אית דגרס נקטה חדא נימא גרעין אחד: לירקונא. דאמרן לעיל קומא וגביא גילא וכורכמא תרי בשיכרא ומיעקר: ואי לא. דלית ליה אי נמי עביד ולא אהני: רישא דשיבוטא. ראש דג ששמו שיבוטא: דמילחא. שהוא מלוח: מוניני דקמצי. ציר חגבים: דנקירי. מין עופות קטנים: ולישייפיה. ישפשפוהו בו: בין תנור לגודא. בין תנור לכותל במקום חם שיזיע וילא החולי: הרוצה שיחממנו. לזה: יקנחנו בסדינו. יעטפנו בסדינו יפה או בסדין של חולה אחר של חולי זה: עבד ליה רב כהנא. רפואה זו של סדין: קירא דנישתרופי. שעוה הלפה וטופת מכוורת שנתמלאה ועודפת: אהלא. אלויין: תולענא. אדום: עילא בר חמרא. עייר בן אתונות: וליגלח. החולה: מציעתא דרישיה. אמצעית ראשו: ולישבוק ליה דמא מאפותיה. יקיז לעייר ממצחו: ולותביה ארישיה. ישפך הדם על התגלחת: ולזדהר מעיניה. שלא יכנס מדם זה בעיניו: רישא דברחא. של איל: דמנח בכבשא. כבוש בחומץ או בציר: דבר אחר חוטרנא. חזיר טלוא (ב) בחברבורות מנומר: מכבתותא דמישרי. מאמצע הערוגה שהם חריפים: אושלן גלימיך. השאילני הטלית: ואיגני בה. ואישן בה: קלי. מעט: איכריך גנא. נכרך בה וישן בה: נפל פורתא פורתא. קדחה הטלית מחום חריפת החולי שילא עם הזיעה ונפלה חתיכות דקות: ומי שרי. לשתות כוס עיקרין: לא תעשו. קרי ביה לא תעשו: ומסתרס מאליו. ואע"ג דסירוס אסור בידים: והא אמר רב אשי. דההוא לאו סירוס הוא אלא רמות רוחא נקיטא ליה לתרנגול ומשניטל אודו הוא מתאבל ואינו משמש אבל בסירוס אפילו ממילא אסור: אלא בסרים. הך דשרי למישתי כוס של עיקרין במי שהוא סרים כבר עסקינן:

הכל

עין משפט נר מצוה

לז א מיי' פט"ז מהלכות איסורי ביאה הל' יא סמג לאוין קכ טוש"ע אה"ע סי' ה סעיף יב:

לח ב מיי' שם הלכה י' טוש"ע שם סעי' יא:

לט ג מיי' שם טוש"ע שם סעיף יג בהג"ה:

[פרשת אמור סימן קה]

[שם]

רב נסים גאון

דבני מערבא (הלכה ג) גרסי ר' בא שאל לרב ירמיה מה ניתני דיקלין או דקרין אמר ליה דקרין שהן דוקרין את המרה אמר ר' יונה לא מסתברא אלא דקלין שהן יוצאין מבין ב' דקלין ובסוף פ' כיצד מברכין על הפירות (שם) נמי גרסי אית תנאי תאנו מי דקרים ואית תנאי תאנו מי דקלים מאן דאמר מי דקרים שהן דוקרין את המרה ומאן דאמר מי דקלים שהן יוצאין מבין שני דקלים:

הגהות הב"ח

(א) גמ' בשיכרא ומיעקר ואי לא: (ב) רש"י ד"ה דבר אחר וכו' טלוא. נ"ב טלוא תרגם אונקלוס רקועתא וכן הוא בב"ק דף קיח ע"ב: (ג) תוס' ד"ה והתניא מנין לסירוס באדם שהוא אסור:

מסורת הש"ס

[גיר' הערוך פשישנא פי' עשב שאינו גם אלא רחב]

פי' ציר של ארבה ערוך [שאין בציר שום ארבה כלומר מנקורי ערוך ערך מטני]

[110b] *kapiza*[3] of Persian onions, boil them in wine, make her drink it, and say to her, 'Cease your discharge.' But if not, she should be made to sit at cross-roads, hold a cup of wine in her hand, and a man comes up from behind, frightens her and exclaims, 'Cease your discharge!' But if not, a handful of cummin, a handful of saffron, and a handful of fenugreek are brought and boiled in wine, she is made to drink it, and they say to her, 'Cease your discharge'. But if not, let sixty pieces of sealing clay of a [wine] vessel be brought, and let them smear her[4] [therewith] and say to her, 'Cease your discharge'. But if not, let one take a fern,[5] boil it in wine, smear her with it and say to her, 'Cease your discharge'. But if not, let one take a thistle growing among Roman thorns,[6] burn it, and gather it up in linen rags in summer and in cotton rags in winter. If not, let one dig seven holes and burn therein a young shoot of *'orlah*,[7] put a cup of wine into her hand, then make her rise from one [hole] and seat her on the next, make her rise from that and seat her on the following [and so on], and at each one he should say to her, 'Cease your discharge'. But if not, let one take fine flour, rub her from the lower half downwards and say to her, 'Cease your discharge'. If not, let him take an ostrich egg, burn it, and wrap it in linen rags in summer and in cotton rags in winter. If not, let him broach a barrel of wine specially for her sake. If not, let him fetch barley grain which is found in the dung of a white mule: if she holds it one day, it [her discharge] will cease for two days; if she holds it two days, it will cease for three days; but if she holds it three days, it will cease for ever.

'For jaundice two thirds thereof with beer [is drunk], and he [the sufferer] then becomes impotent.' But if not, let him take the head of a salted *shibuṭa*,[8] boil it in beer and drink it. If not, let him take brine of locusts. If brine of locusts is not available,
a let him take brine of small birds,[1] carry it into the baths and rub himself [therewith]. If there are no baths, he should be placed between the stove and the wall.[2]

R. Joḥanan said: If one wishes to make him [the sufferer from jaundice] warm, he should wrap him well[3] in his sheet. R. Aḥa b. Jacob suffered therewith, so R. Kahana treated him thus and he recovered. But if not, let him take three *ḳapiza* of Persian dates, three *ḳapiza* of dripping wax,[4] and three *ḳapiza* of purple aloes, boil them in beer and drink it. If not, let him take a young ass; then he [the invalid] shaves half his head, draws blood from its forehead and applies it to his [own] head, but he must take care of his eyes, lest it [the blood] blind him. If not, let him take a buck's head which has lain in preserves [vinegar], boil it in beer and drink it. If not, let him take a speckled swine, tear it open and apply it to his heart: If not, let him take porret [leeks] from the wastes of the valley.[5] A certain Arab suffered with it. Said he to a gardener, Take my robe and give me some leeks from the wastes of the valley.[6] He gave them to him [and] he ate them. Then he requested, Lend me your robe and I will sleep in it. He singed it, wrapped himself therein and slept. As he became heated through and got up, it fell away from him bit by bit.[7]

'For jaundice two [thirds thereof] with beer, and he becomes impotent.' But is this permitted? Surely it was taught: How do we know that the castration of a man is forbidden? From the verse, *neither shall ye do thus in your land:*[8] [this means], ye shall not do [thus] to yourselves: the words of R. Ḥanina!—That is only if he intends [it so], but here it is automatic. For R. Joḥanan said: If one wishes to castrate a cock, let him cut off its crest, and it is automatically castrated.[9] But R. Ashi said: There it suffers from
b conceit?[1] Rather [the reference here is to] one who is [already] a castrate.[2] But R. Ḥiyya b. Abba said in R. Joḥanan's name: [111a]

(3) V. *supra* 103a, n. c6. (4) Rashi: after soaking it in water. (5) *Pastina*. The word means a low, spreading plant. (6) Jast.: probably *corduelis spinosa*. (7) V. Glos. (8) Name of a fish, probably mullet (Jast.).
a (1) 'Aruch: clear fish brine. (2) To make him perspire. (3) Or, rub him. (4) That drips down from an overful honeycomb. (5) Jast., who also suggests an alternative: of the after-crops of valleys. Rashi: from the middle of the furrow, where the leeks are sharp. (6) Or, as Rashi. V. preceding note. (7) From the feverish heat of the sleeper. (8) Lev. XXII, 24: v. preceding part of the verse. (9) Thus direct castration only is prohibited, but not indirect, and the same applies here.
b (1) It grieves that its crest is removed and refuses to copulate, but actually it is not castrated. (2) Who suffers from jaundice.

All agree that if one prepares it [a meal-offering] as leaven after another has prepared it as leaven,[3] he is culpable; because it is said, *It shall not be baked leaven,*[4] *it shall not be made leaven.*[5] If one castrates after another has castrated, he is culpable, for it is said, *That which hath its stones bruised, or crushed, or broken, or cut away,*[6] [*ye shall not offer unto the Lord; neither shall ye do thus in your land*]:[7] now, if one is guilty for cutting [them] away, how much more so for breaking them![8] But it is to teach[9] that if one castrates after another, he is culpable![10]—Rather it refers to an old man.[11] But R. Joḥanan said: It was those very [remedies][12] which restored me to my youth?[13]—Rather the reference [here] is to a woman.[14] But according to R. Joḥanan b. Beroḳa, who said: Concerning both [man and woman] it is said, *And God blessed them: and God said unto them, Be fruitful and multiply,*[15] what can be said?—The reference [here] is to an old woman[16] or to a barren woman.

MISHNAH. IF ONE'S TEETH PAIN HIM, HE MUST NOT SIP VINEGAR THROUGH THEM,[17] BUT MAY DIP [HIS BREAD IN VINEGAR] IN THE USUAL MANNER,[18] AND IF HE IS CURED, HE IS CURED. IF ONE'S LOINS PAIN HIM, HE MUST NOT RUB THEM WITH WINE OR VINEGAR, BUT HE MAY ANOINT THEM WITH OIL,[1] YET NOT ROSE OIL.[2] ROYAL CHILDREN MAY ANOINT THEIR WOUNDS WITH ROSE OIL, SINCE IT IS THEIR PRACTICE TO ANOINT THEMSELVES THUS ON WEEKDAYS. R. SIMEON SAID: ALL ISRAEL ARE ROYAL CHILDREN.

GEMARA. R. Aḥa the Long, i.e., R. Aḥa b. Papa, pointed out a contradiction to R. Abbahu. We learnt: IF ONE HAS TOOTHACHE, HE MUST NOT SIP VINEGAR THROUGH THEM. Shall we say vinegar is beneficial to the teeth,—but it is written, *As vinegar to the teeth, and as smoke to the eyes?*[3]—There is no difficulty: the one refers to vinegar of fruit;[4] the other to acid. Alternatively, both refer to acid: one means where there is a wound; the other, where there is no wound.[5] If there is a wound it heals; if there is no wound it loosens [the teeth in the gums].

HE MUST NOT SIP VINEGAR THROUGH THEM. But it was taught, He must not sip and eject, yet he may sip and swallow?—Said Abaye, When we learnt our Mishnah we too learnt of sipping and ejecting. Raba said, You may even say [that it refers to] sipping and swallowing: the one holds good before the dipping, the other after the dipping.[6] But let us say, Since it is permitted before the dipping, it is permitted after the dipping too,[7] for we know that Raba accepts this argument.[8] For Raba said: There is nothing which is permitted on the Sabbath and forbidden on the Day of Atonement:[9] since it is permitted on the Sabbath, it is permitted on the Day of Atonement too?—He retracted from the present statement.[10] How do you know that he retracted from this statement: perhaps he retracted from the other?—You cannot think so, for it was taught: All who are obliged to perform *ṭebillah* may do so in the normal way, both
b on the ninth of Ab and on the Day of Atonement.[1]

IF ONE'S LOINS PAIN HIM, etc. R. Abba b. Zabda said in Rab's name: The *halachah* is as R. Simeon. Shall we say that Rab holds with R. Simeon?[2] Surely R. Simeon son of R. Ḥiyya said in

(3) I.e., the first kneads the dough after it was leaven, a second shapes it, and a third bakes it. (4) Lev. VI, 10. (5) Ibid. II, 11. The repeated prohibition shows that every separate act of preparation entails guilt. (6) E.V. *cut;* from the present discussion it appears, however, that the Talmud translates the word '*cut away*'. (7) Ibid. XXII, 24. (8) Then why mention it? (9) Lit., 'bring'. (10) Hence even a castrate may not drink this potion. (11) Who is in any case unable to beget children. (12) The reference is to the remedies mentioned in Giṭ. 70a. (13) And made me potent again. (14) Who is not commanded to procreate: hence she may sterilize herself. (15) Gen. I, 28. This is understood as a positive command. (16) Who certainly cannot regain her youth in this respect. (17) This is healing, which is forbidden on the Sabbath. (18) And eat the vinegar-soaked bread.

a (1) Since this is done even without intention of healing. (2) Which ordinary people use only as a remedy. (3) Prov. X, 26. (4) Rashi: Wine not fully matured in the grapes—that is injurious. (5) Or, swelling. (6) Bread dipped in vinegar was eaten before meals. Before one has done this he may sip vinegar for his tooth, as it merely looks like a substitute for soaked bread. But if he has already eaten, he is obviously sipping it now as a remedy only. (7) For a thing cannot be permitted during one portion of the Sabbath and forbidden during the other. (8) Lit., 'he accepts "Since"'. (9) In the matter of labour. (10) *Sc.* that which differentiates between before and after dipping.

b (1) It was in reference to this that Raba stated that what is permitted on the Sabbath is permitted on the Day of Atonement, and he is supported by a Baraitha. (2) I.e., with his lenient rulings relating to the Sabbath.

*הכל מודים *במחמץ אחר מחמץ שהוא חייב שנאמר °לא תאפה חמץ °לא תעשה חמץ *במסרס אחר מסרס שהוא חייב שנאמר °ומעוך וכתות ונתוק וכרות אם על כרות חייב על נתוק לא כל שכן אלא להביא נותק אחר כורת שהוא חייב ואלא בזקן *והאמר ר' יוחנן הן הן החזירוני לנערותי אלא באשה *ולר' יוחנן בן ברוקא דאמר על שניהם הוא אומר °ויברך אותם אלהים ויאמר להם פרו ורבו מאי איכא למימר בזקינה אי נמי בעקרה: **מתני'** *החושש בשיניו לא *יגמע בהן את החומץ אבל מטבל הוא כדרכו ואם נתרפא נתרפא החושש במתניו לא יסוך (א) יין וחומץ אבל *סך הוא את השמן ולא שמן וורד *בני מלכים סבין שמן וורד על מכותיהן שכן דרכן לסוך בחול *ר"ש אומר כל ישראל בני מלכים הם: **גמ'** רמי ליה רב אחא אריכא דהוא רב אחא בר פפא לר' אבהו תנן החושש בשיניו לא יגמע בהן את החומץ למימרא דחומץ מעלי לשינים והכתיב °כחומץ לשינים וכעשן לעינים לא קשיא הא בקיוהא דפרי הא בחלא ואיבעית אימא הא והא בחלא הא דאיכא מכה הא דליכא מכה איכא מכה מסי ליכא מכה מרפי: לא יגמע בהן את החומץ: *והתניא לא יגמע ופולט אבל מגמע ובולע אמר אביי כי תנן נמי מתני' מגמע ופולט תנן רבא אמר אפי' תימא מגמע ובולע כאן לפני טיבול כאן לאחר טיבול ונימא מדלפני טיבול שרי לאחר טיבול נמי שרי דשמעינן ליה לרבא דאית ליה הואיל דאמר רבא ליכא מידי דבשבת שרי וביום הכפורים אסור הואיל דבשבת שרי ביוה"כ נמי שרי הדר ביה רבא מהך ממאי דמהך הדר ביה דילמא מההיא הדר ביה לא ס"ד *דתניא כל חייבי טבילות טובלין כדרכן בין בט' באב בין ביוה"כ: החושש במתניו כו': אמר ר' אבא בר זבדא אמר רב הלכה כר' שמעון למימרא דרב כר' שמעון סבירא ליה *והאמר רב שימי בר חייא משמיה דרב האי *מסוכרייא דנזייתא אסור

תורה אור: ויקרא ו · שם כב · בראשית א · משלי י

רש"י

הכל מודים · אע"פ שנחלקו בבכור שאחזו דם אי מקיזין או אין מקיזין דהוי מטיל מום בבעל מום ואיכא למאן דשרי להקיזו ולעשות בו מום מודין הם במחמץ מנחה אחר מחמץ שכל עשיותיה של מנחה נאסרו בחימוץ: דכתיב לא תאפה חמץ לא תעשה חמץ. אפייה בכלל היתה ולמה יצאת להקיש אליה מה אפייה מיוחדת שהיא מעשה וחייבין עליה בפני עצמה כו'* והכל מודים שאם לשה הראשון בחימוץ ובא השני וערכה בחימוץ והשלישי אפאה כולם חייבין: כורת · שאינו נותקן לגמרי אלא חותכן ותלויין בכיס: אלא בזקן · שפסק מלידה: והא אמר ר' יוחנן · בפרק מי שאחזו במסכת גיטין: הן הן החזירוני לנערותי. הרפואות האמורות שם למי שאיטו בריא בתשמיש ואמר ר' יוחנן לאחר שזקנתי החזירוני אותן רפואות לנערותי לתשמיש אלמא זקן מוליד: אלא באשה · שאינה מצווה בפריה ורביה כדאמרי' ביבמות פרו ורבו ומלאו את הארץ וכבשוה איש דרכו לכבש ואין דרכה של אשה לכבש: **מתני'** מטבל כדרכו · מאכלו ופתו בחומץ: לא יסוך בהן יין וחומץ · דאין אדם סך אותו אלא לרפואה: אבל לא שמן וורד · לפי שדמיו יקרין ואינו מצוי ומוכחא מילתא דלרפואה עביד: שכן דרכן לסוך בחול · בלא מכה: **גמ'** קיוהא · יין שלא נתבשל כל צרכו בענביו קשה לשינים: ליכא מכה מרפי · לומת הבשר והשינים נרפים רחוקין זה מזה דשייללי"ר מתחלנות: לא יגמע ופולט · דמוכח דלרפואה היא: לפני טיבול · לפני אכילה מותר שדרכן היה לטבול בחומץ בכל יום והרואה אומר זהו טיבולו ולאחר טיבול אסור הכל יודעין שכבר סעד וטבל כל צרכו: ונימא מדלפני טיבול שרי כו' · דאין לך שאסור למקלת השבת ומותר למקלתו דהא שמעינן לרבא בפרק י"ט במסכת ביצה דאמר גבי טבילה הואיל בכי האי גוונא דקתני התם דאין מטבילין כלים בשבת ואדם טובל ואמרינן כלים מ"ט לא אמר רבא מפני שנראה כמתקן כלי אבל אדם נראה כמיקר ואמרי' תינח בשבת דשריא רחילה ביוה"כ דאסור רחילה והכל יודעין דטובל הוא ומתקן עצמו מאי איכא למימר הא איכא למיגזר אטו מתקן עור לבי ואמר רבא ליכא מידי דאיסור שבת דבשבת לישתרי וביוה"כ ליתסר והואיל ובשבת לא הוה למיסריה ביוה"כ נמי לא גזור עליה: הכא גרסי' הדר ביה רבא מהא · דקודם טיבול ומוקי מתניתין במגמע ופולט כאביי וזו נאמרה תחלה והדר ביה: דילמא מההיא הדר ביה · וסבר דביום הכפורים אסור לטבול ולא אמרינן הואיל וההיא איתמר ברישא: למימרא דרב · בקולי (נ"א בכולי) שבת סבירא ליה כר' שמעון והא אמר כו': האי מסוכרייא · בגד כורכין בברזא חבית של חרס מפני שאין הנקב שוה: אסור

תוספות

להביא נותק אחר כורת כו'. פירש"י דכורת הייט שכורת ביצים ממקום חיבורן ועדיין הם בכיס ונותק הוי שנותקן מן הכיס ומשליכן לארץ קשה לר"י דבפרק על אלו מומין (בכורות דף לט:) קאמר דנתוק וכרות לא הוי מום בגלוי דהא איתנהו פי' איתנהו בכיסם ונראה לר"י דכרות הוי שלא נכרתו לגמרי ממקום חיבורן אלא עדיין מעורים קצת ונתוק הייט שניתקו לגמרי אלא שהם בכיס: **אלא** בזקן · הכא לא שייך למיסר משום מסרס אחר מסרס דזקנה לאו סירוס היא: **בזקנה** ובעקרה. באשה נמי לא שייך בה מסרס אחר מסרס דאין שייך בה סירוס: **כי** תנן נמי מתניתין במגמע ופולט תנן · וסיפא דקתני אבל מטבל הוא כדרכו ה"ה דה"מ למיתני במגמע ובולע אלא אורחא דמילתא נקט: **לא** ס"ד דתניא כל חייבי טבילות טובלין כדרכן · תימה מנא לן דמהא הדר ביה דילמא מטעם דמפרש התס* דאין מטבילין בשבת משום דמיחזי כמתקן כלי ויפרש דאסור לטבול משום גזירה שמא יעבירנו ד' אמות ברה"ר או כשאר טעמי דמפרש התם והני טעמי לא שייכי באדם הלכך מותר ביוה"כ בלא טעמא דהואיל דלכולהו אמוראי לא פריך התם ביוה"כ ליתסר אלא לרבא ואומר ר"י דלא מסתבר להפוכי תרי מילי משום חדא דתרי מילי נינהו חדא מטעם דנראה כמתקן וחדא הא מילתא דאית ליה הואיל ולהכי ניחא ליה טפי למימר דהדר מהך דהכא ויהיו שני דבריו קיימים וא"ת ונוקי הך ברייתא דטובלין כדרכן כמ"ד טבילה בזמנה מצוה ורבא כמ"ד לאו מצוה וי"ל משום דטבילה בזמנה מצוה לא הוה שרינן איסור תיקוני מנא ובפרק כל כתבי הקדש (לקמן דף קכא:) משמע דאפי' למ"ד טבילה בזמנה לאו מצוה טובלין כדרכן כל חייבי טבילות דתניא התם ר' יוסי אומר מן המנחה ולמעלה אינו צריך לטבול משמע דאי בעי טביל אע"ג דסבירא (ג) טבילה בזמנה לאו מצוה וא"ת דתניא בפרק בתרא דיומא (פח:) הזב והזבה ובועל נדה וטמא מת טובלין ביוה"כ טמא מת היכי טביל ומה תועלת לו אותה טבילה הא אין טבילה בלא הזאה והזאה לא דחי יוה"כ כי היכי דלא דחיא שבת כדאמרינן בפסחים פרק אלו דברים (דף סט:) וליכא למימר שתועיל לו טבילה לענין שיוכל להזות למחר דהא תנן בסוף מסכת פרה דהוא עצמו טובל בלילה ומזה ביום משמע שצריך להזות ביום שטבל וי"ל דלעולם אין צריך לטבול ביום הזאה והתם קמ"ל דיכול לטבול בלילה אע"ג דטבילה היא כתחלת הזאה דאין הזאה בלא טבילה והזאה ביום היא א"נ התם איירי בטבילה דלאחר הזאה כדאמר בספרא הקדים טבילה להזאה לא עשה ולא כלום משמע דאיכא נמי טבילה לאחר הזאה: **טובלין** כדרכן בין בט' באב בין כו' · בפ"ק דתענית (דף יג:) פליג עליה ר' חנינא סגן הכהנים ואמר כדי הוא בית אלהינו לאבד עליו טבילה אחת בשנה והלכתא כוותיה כדאמר בירושלמי: **למימרא** דרב כר"ש ס"ל · פי' בקונט' למימרא דרב בכולי שבת כר' שמעון סבירא ליה ולי נראה דאם כן הוה ליה לאקשויי מכרכי דזוזי דרב אסר בפרק קמא (דף יט:) וכמה אמוראין דמחלקין באיסורי שבת כדאמר בפרק מפנין (לקמן קכח.) במוקצה לאכילה סבר לה כר' יהודה במוקצה לטלטול כו' ונראה לר"ת דמשמע ליה דטעמא דר' שמעון במתני' משום דשרי דבר שאין מתכוין ות"ק אסר ליה אפי' לתענוג משום דזימנין לרפואה קעביד ואסר בעלמא דבר שאין מתכוין ור"ש דמקיל בעלמא קשרי נמי הכא בשאין מתכוין לרפואה והשתא אתי שפיר: **האי** מסוכרייתא דנזייתא אסור להדוקה ביומא טבא · פי' סתימת גיגית של שכר אסור להדוקה משום סחיטה כדפירש בקונטרס וכן פירש ר"ח אף על גב דלא אשכחן דהוה חיים לסחיטה אלא גבי מים כדאמר בפרק ואלו קשרים (לקמן דף קיג:) גבי היה מהלך בשבת ופגע באמת המים דאמר לנחות במיא אתי לידי סחיטה ובפרק חבית (לקמן דף קמז:) אמר הרוחץ במי מערה ונסתפג באלונטית לא יביאנה בידו ומפרש בגמרא משום דאתי לידי סחיטה ובפרק שואל (לקמן דף קמח.) ובריש המביא כדי יין (ביצה דף ל.) גבי הני נשי דלא משניין ניפרוס סודרא פירוש על הכד דלמא (ג) מישמיט במיא ואתי לידי סחיטה אבל גבי יין לא גזרינן משום סחיטה כדאמר בפרק תולין (לקמן דף קלט:) מסננין את היין בסודרין וטעמא

מסורת הש"ס

[מנחות:ע"ש בכורות לג:] · [מנחות נה:] · גיטין ע. · יבמות סה: · גיטין מג. קדושין לה. · ביצה יח: ע"ז כח. · [גי' הערוך ינמא] · [עי' תוס' לקמן קלד: ד"ה ואין] · [לעיל סו. וש"נ] · ביצה יח: · שם ותענית יג: · בכורות כה. ע"ש כתובות ו. · [גי' הערוך מסוברייא]

עין משפט נר מצוה

מ א מיי' פי"ב מהלכות מעשה קרבנות הל' יד סמג לאוין של:
מא ב מיי' פט"ו מהל' א"ב הלכה ט י סמג לאוין קכ טוש"ע אה"ע סי' ה סעיף יא:
מב ג מיי' שם הלכה ו טוש"ע שם סעיף יב:
מג ד מיי' פכ"א מהל' שבת הלכה כג סמג לאוין סה טוש"ע א"ח סי' שכח סעיף א:
מד ה מיי' שם הלכה כד סמג שם טוש"ע שם סי' שכה סעיף לב:
מה ו טוש"ע שם סי' שכ סעיף יח:

רבינו חננאל

החושש בשיניו לא יגמע בהן את החומץ איני והא תניא לא יגמע ויפלוט אבל מגמעובולע ומשני אביי כי תנן נמי מתני' לא יגמע ויפלוט תנן. רבא אמר אפי' תימא מגמע ובולע והא דתניא שרי לפני טבול כלומ' קודם אכילה שרי. מתניתין דאסר לגמע ולבלוע לאחר והוא לאחר אכילה וממאי דטיבול לשון אכילה הוא דתנן הביאו לפניו מטביל בחזרת עד שמגיע לפרפרת הפת ותוב אבל מטבל במיני תרגימא. ר' יצחק מטבל בירקי. תניא נמי הכי השמש מטבל בבני מעים וטעמא מאי שהחומץ קודם אכילה אינו מרפא אבל לאחר אכילה מרפא. ומפורש בתלמוד א"י מודים חכמים לר' במגמע חומץ של תרומה אחר טיבולו שמשלם קרן וחומש. שהחומץ מיישב את הנפש. ודברי ר' מפורשי ביוה"כ ואקשינן לרבא' והא מדלפני טיבול שרי לאחר טיבול נמי שרי. דשמעינן ליה לרבא דאית ליה הואיל דגרסי' בי"ט פרק [ב'] דתנן [התם] מטבילין כלים מלפני השבת. כ"ע מיהת כלים בשבת לא מ"ט וכל חד אמר טעמא. רבא אמר מפני שנראה כמתקן כלי. ואקשי' אי הכי אדם נמי. ושנינן אדם נראה כמקר ומהוינן בימות הגשמים ובמים הרעים נ"כ אית ליה אנפא שלא נראה כמתקן כלום ואקשי' התינח בשבת ויוה"כ מי שרי ברחיצה דאמרת נראה כמיקר. אמר רבא הואילואישתרי טבילה בשבת אשתרי נמי ביוה"כ הכא נמי לימא רבא הואיל ולפני טיבול שרי לאחר טיבול נמי שרי וקמה קשיא זו על רבא ושנינן הדר ביה רבא ואמר בין לפני טיבול בין לאחר טיבול שרי. ומוקים לה למתני' כדאביי דאמר לא יגמע ויפלוט תנן אבל לגמע ולבלוע שרי. ואקשי' ממאי דהאי דטיבול הדר ביה דלמא מטבילה דיוה"כ הדר ביה ואמר אין טובלין. ושנינן לא דהא תניא בהדיא כל חייבי טבילות טובלין כדרכן בין בט' באב בין ביוה"כ. אלמא אמרי' הואיל והתירה טבילה בשבת התירה נמי ביוה"כ. וכך פירשנו שמועה זו ביום טוב **החושש בשיניו** לא יסוך יין וחומץ אבל סך הוא שמן ולא שמן וורדים כו'. שמעינן מינה בני מלכים דרגילי בסיכת שמן וורד בחול לא מסי להו בשבת *) והוא חשוב להן. לפיכך בשבת אסור הלכך בני מלכים ושכיח להו ורגילי ביה לא מסי להו ושרי אבל שאר בני אדם דלא שכיח להו ולא רגילי ביה מסי לפיכך אסור. ר"ש אומר כל ישראל בני מלכים. כלומר כל ישראל מותרין בשמן וורד אמר רב הלכה כר"ש. ודייקינן (לרבי) [דרבי] שמעון **)לטעמיה לפיכך שנה כל אדם סך כדרכו ואינו מתכוין לרפואה ואם נתרפא נתרפא ואקשי' למימרא דרב כר' שמעון סבירא ליה דאמר דבר שאין מתכוון מותר. לפיכך פסק הלכה כר' שמעון והאמרי משמיה דרב האי מסובריא דנזייתא אסור להדוקא ביומא טבא. פי' כגון

*) נראה דל"ל אבל שאר בני אדם דלא רגילי בהו וסוא חשוב להן לפיכך בשבת אסור וכו'. **) נראה דל"ל לטעמי' דס"ל דדבר שאינו מתכוין מותר לפיכך וכו'.

הגהות הב"ח

(א) במשנה לא יסוך בהן יין: (ב) תוס' ד"ה לא ס"ד וכו' אע"ג דסבירא ליה טבילה: (ג) ד"ה האי וכו' על הכד דילמא מישמיט במיא:

רב נסים גאון

והאמר ר' יוחנן הן הן החזירוני לנערותי. עיקר דילה במסכת גיטין בפרק מי שאחזו קורדיקוס (דף ע) אמר אביי מי שאינו בקי בדרך ארץ ליתי תלתא בביזי קרטמי דחדיי ופרוקינהו וניסלוק כל יומא חדא מינייהו ונימזוג בחמרא ונישתי אמר ר' יוחנן הן הן החזירוני לנערותי: **ולר'** יוחנן בן ברוקא דאמר על שניהם הוא אומר ויברך אותם אלהים. במשנת יבמות (דף סה) בסוף פרק הבא על יבמתו:

אסור להדוקיה ביומא טבא בהדיא אפילו ר"ש מודה *דאביי ורבא דאמרי תרוויהו מודה ר"ש בפסיק רישיה ולא ימות והאמר *רב חייא בר אשי אמר רב הלכה כר' יהודה ורב חנן בר אמי אמר שמואל הלכה כר"ש ורב חייא בר אבין מתני לה בלא גברי רב אמר הלכה כר' יהודה ושמואל אמר הלכה כר"ש אלא אמר רבא *אני וארי שבחבורה תרגימנא ומנו רבי חייא בר אבין הלכה כר"ש ולאו מטעמיה מאי הלכה כר' שמעון ולאו מטעמיה אילימא הלכה כר"ש דשרי ולאו מטעמיה דאילו ר"ש סבר מסי ורב סבר לא מסי וסבר רב לא מסי והא מדקתני בני מלכים סכין על גבי מכותיהן שמן וורד מכלל דמסי אלא הלכה כר"ש דשרי ולאו מטעמיה דאילו ר"ש סבר אף ע"ג דלא שכיח שרי ורב סבר אי שכיח אין ואי לא שכיח לא ובאתרא דרב שכיח משחא דוורדא:

הדרן עלך שמנה שרצים

*ואלו קשרים שחייבין עליהן קשר הגמלין וקשר הספנין וכשם שהוא חייב על קישורן כך הוא חייב על היתרן ר"מ אומר כל קשר שהוא יכול להתירו באחת מידיו אין חייבין עליו: **גמ'** מאי קשר הגמלין וקשר הספנין אילימא קטרא דקטרי בזממא וקטרא דקטרי באיסטרידא האי קשר שאינו של קיימא הוא אלא קיטרא דזממא גופיה ודאיסטרידא גופה: ר"מ אומר כל קשר כו': בעי רב אחדבוי *אחוי דמר אחא עניבה לר"מ מהו טעמיה דר"מ משום דיכול להתירו באחת מידיו הוא והא נמי יכול להתירו או דילמא טעמא דר"מ משום דלא מיהדק והא מיהדק תיקו: **מתני'** יש לך קשרין שאין חייבין עליהן כקשר הגמלין וכקשר הספנין קושרת אשה מפתח חלוקה וחוטי סבכה ושל פסקיא ורצועות מנעל וסנדל ונודות יין ושמן וקדירה של בשר ראב"י אומר קושרין לפני הבהמה בשביל שלא תצא: **גמ'** הא גופא קשיא אמרת יש קשרין שאין חייבין עליהן כקשר הגמלין וכקשר הספנין חיובא הוא דליכא הא איסורא איכא והדר תני קושרת אשה מפתח חלוקה אפילו לכתחילה הכי קאמר יש קשרין שאין חייבין עליהן כקשר הגמלין וכקשר הספנין ומאי ניהו קיטרא

רש"י

אסור להדוקיה · בנקב משום סחיטה ואע"ג דלא קא מכוין לסחוט אלמא לא ס"ל כר"ש בדבר שאין מתכוין: הלכה כר' יהודה · בדבר שאין מתכוין דאסור: בלי גברי · מתני לה לפלוגתא דרב ושמואל בלא אמוראים האומרים משמם אלא הם עצמם נחלקו בה: תרגימנא · דלא תיקשי דרב אדרב: הלכה כר"ש · דשרי בשמן וורד: אבל לא מטעמיה · דאין הטעם כדבריו: דאילו ר"ש סבר מסי · ואפ"ה שרי דאין לך דמותר לזה ואסור לזה: מכלל דמסי · אפי' לת"ק דאי לאו דמסי למאי איצטריך ליה: אע"ג דלא שכיח · שמן וורד במקומו של זה הסך ממנו ודמיו יקרים והכל יודעין שאינו סכו אלא לרפואה שרי דכל ישראל בני מלכים הם ור' יהודה אוסר דמוכחא מילתא ורב נמי כר"י ס"ל אלא במקומו הוא דשרי דשכיח דסכין שמן וורד ולא מוכחא מילתא:

הדרן עלך שמנה שרצים

ואלו קשרים · המנוין באבות מלאכות דקתני* הקושר והמתיר קשר של קיימא שאינו מתירו לעולם דומיא דקושרי חוטי יריעות הנפסקות: קשר הגמלין וקשר הספנין · בגמרא מפרש להו: כך הוא חייב על היתרן · כדילפי' בכלל גדול (לעיל דף עד:) מציידי חלזון שצריכין לפרקים להתיר קשרי רשתות הקיימות כדי לקצרן או להרחיבן: שיכול להתירו · דלא הדקיה: אין חייבין עליו · ואפי' עשאו לקיימא: **גמ'** זממא · מנקבין לנאקה בחוטמ' ונותנין בה טבעת של רצועה וקושרין אותה ועומדת שם לעולם וכשרוצה לקושרה לבהמה קושר רצועה ארוכה באותה טבעת וקושרין בה ופעמים שמתירה: קטרא דקטרי בזממא · זהו קשר הרצועות שקושרין בטבעת: איסטרידא · גם הוא כמין טבעת שעושין מן עקל או מן רצועה בנקב שבראש הספינה ואותו קשר מתקיים וכשרוצה להעמידו קושר רצועה באותה טבעת ומעמידה בה וכשרוצה להתיר מתיר הרצועה ונוטלה: קטרא דקטרי באסטרידא · קשר רצועה הארוכה: עניבה · ומהדקה שפיר לר"מ מהו: **מתני'** יש לך קשרין שאין חייבין עליהן · חטאת כמו שחייבין על קשר הגמלין אלא פטור אבל אסור ובגמרא מפרש הי ניהו: מפתח חלוקה · כמו שיש לגלחים כעין לשונות לכאן ולכאן וקושרים של ימין בכתף שמאל ושל שמאל בכתף ימין דכיון דכל יומא שרו ליה לא דמי מידי לקשר של קיימא ומותר לכתחילה: סבכה · קוייפ"א: ושל פסקיא· אזור רחב וחוטין תלויין בראשו לקושרו בהן וקורין פינדור"ס: ונודות יין· של עור שכופפין פיהם וקושרין: וקדרה של בשר· פעמים שקושרין בגד לפיה: קושרין בפני הבהמה · אבל ברוחב הפתח: **גמ'** קיטרא

תוספות

וטעמא משום דאין אדם חושש לסוחטו כיון דע"י סחיטה אינו יכול לנקותו מריחו וחזותו גם אין דרך לסחוט בגד לצורך משקה שבו אבל מ"מ אסור לסחוט דכי סחיט ליה מתלבן הבגד קצת והוי מכבס או משום מפרק כמו סוחט זיתים וענבים כדאמרי' בפרק מפנין (לקמן קכח:) אם היתה צריכה שמן חבירתה מביאה לה בשערה ופריך והא אתי לידי סחיטה אלמא יש סחיטה בשמן ובפרק תולין (לקמן דף קמא·) קאמר רבא לא ליהדוק איניש אודרא אפומא דשישא דילמא אתי לידי סחיטה ופי' בקונט' כד של שמן ובפרק נוטל (לקמן דף קמג·) ספוג אם יש לו בית אחיזה מקנחין בו ואם לאו אין מקנחין בו משום סחיטה ולהכי אסור להדוקה וא"ת דאמר בפרק בתרא דיומא (דף עז:) ההולך להקביל פני רבו או פני אביו או פני מי שגדול הימנו עובר עד צוארו במים ואינו חושש ואמר נמי בפ"ב דביצה (דף יח·) גבי טבילת כלים בשבת דנדה שאין לה בגדים מערמת וטובלת בבגדיה ולא גזרינן דילמא אתי לידי סחיטה וי"ל דמלוה שאני ואם תאמר היכי שרי התם ליכנס בבגדיה ונדה נמי איך טובלת בבגדיה נימא שרייתו זהו כיבוסו כדאמרי' בזבחים בפרק דם חטאת (דף צד:) וי"ל דדוקא היכא דאיכא טיפת דם או טינוף אמר שרייתו זהו כיבוסו דבהכי איירי בפ' דם חטאת ומצא ר"י מוגה בספר הישר דלא אמר שרייתו זהו כיבוסו בדבר שאינו כ"א לכלוך כמו סיפוג באלונטית וקינוח ידים במפה והני שהולכין במים עם הבגדים הוי נמי דרך לכלוך ולא דרך נקיון ועל תינוק שלכלך בגדי אמו במי רגלים אין לזרוק עליו מים דשרייתו זהו כיבוסו ושמע ר"י מפי הנשים שהתיר ר"ת [ליטול ידיה] ולקנח ידיה בבגד כיון שהוא דרך לכלוך כדי שתוכל להתפלל ולברך ואין נראה לר"י שהרי היא מתכוונת לטהר הלכלוך ודרך רחיצה וליבון הויא זה הקינוח:

מודה ר"ש בפסיק רישיה · והא דאמר גבי לא ליהדוק איניש אודרא אפומא דשישא דילמא אתי לידי סחיטה ולא הוי פסיק רישיה יש לחלק דהתם מיירי בכיסוי שאינו בולע כ"כ וגם אינו סותמו כל כך בחוזק שאינו חושש רק שיהא מכוסה אבל הכא שהוא בלד הגיגית בולע הרבה וגם מהדקו בחוזק כדי שלא יצא היין והוי פסיק רישיה:

ושלש מחלוקות בדבר · אית ספרים דל"ג ליה:

הדרן עלך שמנה שרצים

ואלו קשרים · עניבה לר"מ מהו · וא"ת אמאי לא פשיט מדתנן לקמן אבל דלי שנפסק לא יהא קושרו אלא עונבו ומוכח' בפ"ק דפסחים (ד' יא·) דהנהו רבנן הייגו ר"מ דפריך התם מינה לרבנן שהם ר"מ וי"ל דהתם נמי פריך מספק אם הנהו רבנן הם ר"מ כמו שמסתפק כאן: אימור

עין משפט נר מצוה

מו א מיי' פכ"א מהל' שבת הלכה כב סמג לאוין סה טוש"ע א"ח סי' שכ סעיף א:

א ב מיי' פי"ו מהל' שבת הלכה א סמג לאוין סה טוש"ע א"ח סי' שיז סעיף א:

ב ג מיי' שם הלכה ז:

ג ד מיי' שם הלכה ג:

ד ה מיי' שם הל' א ב סמג שם טוש"ע שם:

מסורת הש"ס

[לעיל פט. קג. לקמן קיז. קכב: קלג. קמג. סוכה לג: כתובות ו. בכורות כה:] [ביצה לו:]

[קידושין מח: סנהדרין מ: כ"ב פח.]

[לעיל עג.]

[במשנה שבמשניות וכו' בפי' הרב והרמב"ם איתא אלו]

ג"א דמן אחא פי' שם מקו

רבינו חננאל

מוך*) או כיוצאבו דבר שסותמין בו פי החבית אמר רב אסור לאמץ סתימתו דאתי לידי סחיטה והנה אע"פ שאינו מתכוין לסחיטה אלא לסתימת פי החבית בלבד כיון שסוחט אסור דלא כר' שמעון. ושנינן במסובריא דנזייתא אפי' ר' שמעון מודה כיון דאי אפשר ליה דלא להדוקי' ודאי מתחילה סוחט הוא וכי האיגונא ר' שמעון מחייב דמודה ר' שמעון בפסיק רישיה ולא ימות וכבר פירשנוהו למעלה.ואכתי רב כר' שמעון סבירא ליה והא בהדיא אמרי' רב הלכה כר' יהודה אמר ושמואל אמר הלכה כר' שמעון. ומשני (רב אמר)הכי אמר רב הלכה כר' שמעון ולאו מטעמיה דאילו ר' שמעון אע"ג דלא שכיח שרי וכו' ואע"ג דהוא דר"ש סלקא בפרק המקבל בשיטה. דגרסי' התם אמר אביי רשב"ג ור' שמעון ור' ישמעאל ור"ע כולהו סבירא להו כל ישראל בני מלכים ולית הלכתא כחד מנייהו ה"מ בהא סברא בלחוד דקם ליה בהדייהו. אבל דבר שאין מתכוין בהדיא קיי"ל דהלכתא כוותיה הלכך אע"ג דשמן [וורד] ע"כ מסי אם סך הוא כדרכו ואינו מתכוין לרפואה אע"ג שמתרפא בין בדוכתא דשכיח שמן וורד בין בדוכתא דלא שכיח שרי. פי' מודה ר' שמעון בפסיק' רישיה ולא ימות כל היכא דעביד מידעם בשבת דאפשר שיבא לידי איסור ולא מיכוון להוא איסורא שרי למיעבד ההוא עבידתא ולא אסרינן ליה גזירה שלא יבא לידי אותו איסור והוא כגון הגורר מטה כסא וספסל דאפשר לעשות בגרירתו (להן) חריץ ואפשר לגוררן ברפיון בלא עשיית חריץ אע"פ שנעשה מותר אבל כגון האומר כוונתי לחתוך ראש זה העוף לאכילה לכלב ואין כוונתו להמיתו. כגון זה מודה ר"ש שחייב שאע"פ [שאינו מכוין כיון] שאי אפשר לו לחתוך ראש העוף אלא עד שימיתהו וכן המתקנח בספוג שאין לו עור בית אחיזה עתה אם יאמר להתקנח ואין כוונתו לסחוט נתירהו לו והלא אי אפשר לאדם להתקנח בספוג שאין לו עור בית אחיזה ולא יסחוט כגון זה אומר מי איכא דפסיק רישיה ולא ימות וכן*) מסובריא דנזייתא פי' נזייתא כדות של יין או של שכר.מסובריא הוא הנקב העשוי להוציא בו יין בזמן שהיין שותת ויוצ אם בא אדם לסתמו ולהדקו ואומר למנוע שפיכות היין אני מתכוון (נתכוונתי) ולא לסתום הפתח בהא קאמר רב מודה ר' שמעון. וכן לענין נר שהוא אחר הדלת ותניא פותח ונועל ואם כבתה כבתה. ואמר (לקמן קכ) דלייט רב עלה דכיון דהמקום רחוק הוא אי אשר לפתוח ולנעול אלא אם יכבה. ובענין הזה מודה ר"ש בפסיק רישיה ולא ימות וכבר פרשני כל דבר שאינו מתכוון מותר: **הדרן עלך שמונה שרצי**

ואלו קשרים שחייבין עליהן קשר הגמלים כו'. קשר גמלים קטרא. אסיקנא קיטרא דזממא גופיה. פי' [עושין] נקבים לחוטמיה דגמל ומחתין ביה יתר וקטרין ביה אפסר קטן והיינו זממא וקשר של קיימא הוא ובה כן קטרי בההוא אפסר חבל ארוך שמושכין בו הגמל והוא קיטרא דקטרין בזממא איסתדירא הוא אסקריא דספינתא והוא התורן וקטרין ביה חבל והוא קשר של קיימא. והדר קטרי בההוא איסתדירא חב אחד דעייליה ביה נינדי מושכי הקלע כשבאין להרימו על הספינה כדי שתסע והוא קטרא דקטרי באיסתדירא. בעי רב אחדבוי מדאח"ה פי' (חדחאה) [אחה] שם מקום ידוע מתא דאהא. פי' עניב בדבעינן למיבר לקמן. ואסיקנא האי קטרא דקטרי בזממא ודקטרי באיסתדירא חיובא ליכא איסורא מיהא איכא אבל מפתחי חלוק אע"פ דאית ליה תרתי דשי כי (היכי דאית **) אשתא) למני שרי למיקטרינהו לתרוייה ילא אמרי' דחדא מנייהו בטולי בטלה אלא תרווייהו שרי למיקטרינהו.פי' פסיקיא חגורה כדמתרגמינן (ישעיה ג') ותחת חגורה נקפה [ואתר דהוה אסרן פסקיא]. והוא המיין של נשים:פי' סבכה וקאיה בל' ערבי שרי למק בהנהו

*) עיין ערוך ערך סבר ס'.

**) נראה דצ"ל דאיתא הטתא למני וכו'.

Rab's name: The stopper of the brewing vat[3] [111b] may not be forced into [the bung-hole] on a Festival![4]—There even R. Simeon agrees, for Abaye and Raba both maintain: R. Simeon agrees in the case of 'cut off his head but let him not die'.[5] But R. Ḥiyya b. Ashi said in Rab's name: The *halachah* is as R. Judah,[6] while R. Ḥanan b. Ammi said in Samuel's name: The *halachah* is as R. Simeon. Further, R. Ḥiyya b. Abin recited it without [intermediary] scholars:[7] Rab said: The *halachah* is as R. Judah; while Samuel ruled: The *halachah* is as R. Simeon?—Rather said Raba, I and a lion of the company,[8] viz., R. Ḥiyya b. Abin, explained it: [Rab said:] The *halachah* is as R. Simeon, but not on account of his view. What is meant by 'The *halachah* is as R. Simeon, but not on account of his view?' Shall we say, 'The *halachah* is as R. Simeon', that it is permitted; 'but not through his reason', for R. Simeon holds [that] it heals,[9] whereas Rab holds that it does not heal? Does then Rab hold that it does not heal? But surely, since he [the Tanna] states, ROYAL CHILDREN MAY ANOINT THEIR WOUNDS WITH ROSE OIL, it follows that [all agree] that it does heal? But 'the *halachah* is as R. Simeon', that it is permitted; 'but not through his reason': for whereas R. Simeon holds that in spite of its being rare it is permitted, Rab holds: Only if it is common [is it permitted], but not if it is
a rare,[1] and in Rab's place rose oil was common.

CHAPTER XV

MISHNAH. NOW, THESE ARE THE KNOTS WHICH
b ENTAIL CULPABILITY:[1] CAMEL-DRIVERS' KNOTS AND SAILORS' KNOTS. AND JUST AS ONE IS GUILTY FOR TYING THEM, SO IS HE GUILTY FOR UNTYING THEM. R. MEIR SAID: ANY KNOT WHICH ONE CAN UNTIE WITH ONE HAND ENTAILS NO GUILT.

GEMARA. What are CAMEL-DRIVERS' KNOTS AND SAILORS' KNOTS? Shall we say, the knot which is tied through the nose ring[2] and the knot which is tied through the ship's ring,[3] but these are non-permanent knots?[4]—Rather it means the knot of the nose ring itself and of the ship's ring itself.[5]

R. MEIR SAID: ANY KNOT, etc. R. Aḥadbuy the brother of Mar Aḥa asked: What of a slip-knot[6] on R. Meir's view: is R. Meir's reason because it can be untied with one hand, and this too can be untied;[7] or perhaps R. Meir's reason is that it is not well-fastened,[8] whereas this is well-fastened? The question stands over.

MISHNAH. YOU HAVE SOME KNOTS WHICH DO NOT ENTAIL GUILT LIKE FOR CAMEL-DRIVERS' KNOTS AND
c SAILORS' KNOTS.[1] A WOMAN MAY TIE UP THE OPENING OF HER CHEMISE, THE RIBBONS OF HER HAIR-NET AND OF HER GIRDLE,[2] THE LACES OF HER SHOES OR SANDALS, PITCHERS OF WINE AND OIL, AND THE MEAT POT.[3] R. ELEAZAR B. JACOB SAID: ONE MAY TIE [A ROPE] IN FRONT OF AN ANIMAL,[4] THAT IT SHOULD NOT GO OUT.

GEMARA. This is self-contradictory: you say, YOU HAVE SOME KNOTS WHICH DO NOT ENTAIL GUILT LIKE FOR CAMEL-DRIVERS' KNOTS AND SAILORS' KNOTS; thus there is indeed no guilt, but there is a prohibition. Then he [the Tanna] teaches: A WOMAN MAY TIE UP THE OPENING OF HER CHEMISE, [which means] even at the very outset?—This is what he says: YOU HAVE SOME KNOTS WHICH DO NOT ENTAIL GUILT LIKE FOR CAMEL-DRIVERS' KNOTS AND SAILORS' KNOTS, and

(3) In which beer is kept during the process of brewing. The stopper was made of soft materials, such as rags, wound round the bung. (4) For thereby the moisture which it previously absorbed is wrung out, and this is forbidden. But it is unintentional, whereas R. Simeon holds that such is permitted, v. *supra* 75a. (5) V. *supra* 75a, n. a8. (6) Viz., that whatever is unintentional is forbidden. (7) Lit., 'men'. (8) I.e., one of our great scholars. (9) Yet it is permitted to all because a thing cannot be permitted to one and forbidden to another.

a (1) Where it is evident that it is applied as a remedy.

b (1) Tying knots is a principal labour, *supra* 73a. (2) Rashi: a ring was inserted through the camel's nose (this ring was of cord, and had to be knotted after passing through the nose—R. Ḥan., and the same appears from the Gemara) and when it was to be tethered a long rope was tied thereto. The reference is to the knot that is made in tying this long rope. (3) Rashi: a ring at the head of the ship, through which a rope was passed and tied when the ship was moored. Jast. translates: the loop which they made when attaching the sail to the rigging. (4) Only a permanent knot entails guilt, and these are naturally untied when the camel or the ship moves on. (5) Which are permanent. (6) Or, loop, which, however, is strongly fastened. (7) Hence it does not involve guilt. (8) An ordinary knot must be quite loose if it can be untied with one hand.

c (1) Nevertheless they are forbidden. The Gemara explains which are meant. (2) Rashi. Jast.: the cords of the breast bandage. (3) All these are tied and untied daily, and therefore are not permanent. (4) I.e., across the stable entrance.

which are they? [112*a*] The knot which is tied through the nose ring and the knot which is tied through the ship's ring: [for these] there is indeed no guilt, nevertheless there is a prohibition.[5] But some are permitted at the outset. And which are they? [A WOMAN] MAY TIE UP THE OPENING OF HER CHEMISE.

THE OPENING OF HER CHEMISE. But that is obvious?—This is necessary only where it has two pairs of bands:[6] you might say, One of these is disregarded:[7] hence he informs us [that we do not fear this].

AND THE RIBBONS OF HER HAIR-NET. But that is obvious?—This is necessary [to teach] only where it is roomy:[8] you might
a say, She will remove it [thus]:[1] hence he informs us that a woman is careful over[2] her hair and will [first] untie it.

AND THE LACES OF HER SHOES OR SANDALS. It was stated: If one unties the laces of his shoes or sandals,—one [Baraitha] taught: He is liable to a sin-offering; another taught: He is not liable, yet it is forbidden; while a third taught: It is permitted in the first place. Thus [the rulings on] shoes are contradictory, and [those on] sandals are contradictory?—[The rulings on] shoes are not contradictory: when it teaches, 'he is liable to a sin-offering', it refers to cobblers' [knots];[3] 'he is not liable, but it is forbidden'—that refers to [a knot] of the Rabbis;[4] 'it is permitted in the first place', refers to [the knots] of the townspeople of Mahoza.[5] [The rulings on] sandals too are not contradictory: when it states that 'one is liable to a sin-offering', it refers to [sandals] of travellers[6] tied by cobblers; 'one is not liable yet it is forbidden', refers to amateur knots[7] tied by [the wearers] themselves; 'it is permitted at the outset', refers to sandals in which two go out,[8] as was the case with Rab Judah. For Rab Judah, brother of R. Salla the Pious, had a pair of sandals, at times he went out in them, at others his child. He went to Abaye and asked him, How is it in such a case?—One is liable to a sin-offering [for tying them], he replied. I do not even understand[9] why [though] one is not liable for this yet it is forbidden, and you tell me that one is liable to a sin-offering. What is the
b reason?[1]—Because on weekdays too, he replied, at times I go out in them, at others the child. In that case, said he, it is permitted at the outset.

R. Jeremiah was walking behind R. Abbahu in a *karmelith*, when the lace of his sandal snapped.[2] What shall I do with it? enquired he.—Take a moist reed that is fit for an animal's food and wind it about it, he replied. Abaye was standing in front of[3] R. Joseph,[4] when the lace of his sandal snapped. What shall I do with it? asked he.—Let it be, he replied.[5] Wherein does it differ from R. Jeremiah's [case]?—There it was not guarded;[6] here it is guarded. But it is still a utensil,[7] seeing that I could change it from the right [foot] to the left?[8]—Said he to him: Since R. Johanan explained [the law] on R. Judah's view, it follows that the *halachah* is as R. Judah.[9] To what does this refer?—For it was taught: If the two ears of the sandal[10] or its two strappings are broken, or if the entire sole is removed, it is clean.[11] If one of its ears or strappings [is broken], or if the greater part of the sole is removed, it is unclean. R. Judah said: If the inner one is broken, it is unclean;[12] if the outer, it is clean. Whereon 'Ulla—others state, Rabbah b. Bar Hanah—said in R. Johanan's name: Just as the controversy in respect to uncleanness, so is there a controversy in respect to
c the Sabbath,[1] but not in respect to *halizah*.[2] Now we discussed this: To whose [view] does R. Johanan refer? Shall we say, To that of the Rabbis, [and he states], since it is a utensil in respect to uncleanness, it is also so in respect to the Sabbath, but not in respect to *halizah*, where it is not a utensil? Surely we learnt: If she removes the left[-foot shoe] from the right foot,[3] the *halizah* is valid?[4] [Shall we] on the other hand [say that he refers] to R. Judah's [ruling]: [and means], since it is not a 'utensil' in respect to defilement, it is not a 'utensil' in respect to the Sabbath either, but that is not so in respect to *halizah*, where it is a 'utensil': [it may be asked against this]: Perhaps we rule, If she removes the left[-foot shoe] from the right foot the *halizah* is valid, only where it is a 'utensil' for its own function;[5] but here it is not a 'utensil' for its *own* function, seeing that R. Judah said: If the outer is broken, it is clean, which proves that it is not a 'utensil?'[6]—In truth, [R. Johanan referred] to R. Judah's view: say, And it is *likewise* so in respect to *halizah*, and he informs us this: When do we say, If she removes the left [-foot shoe] from the right foot the *halizah* is valid, [only] where

(5) For though temporary only, as stated *supra* 111*b*, they are frequently left there a long time, and so are forbidden. (6) Lit., 'entrances'. The chemise ties up by two pairs of bands or strings. It can be put on and removed even when one set is actually tied, though of course with difficulty. (7) I.e., when she removes it she may leave one pair tied, which makes it a permanent knot; since we do not know which may be left, both should be forbidden. (8) Not closely fitting, so that it can be removed from the head even when tied.
a (1) Without untying the ribbons. (2) Lit., 'spares'. (3) Rashi: when the cobbler inserts the lace in the shoe, he ties it there permanently.—Perhaps the shoes and its laces were so arranged that part of the lace was permanently fastened. (4) Sometimes they tied it very loosely, so that the shoe could be removed and put on without untying. Thus whilst not actually permanent to involve a sin-offering, it is semi-permanent, hence forbidden. (5) Who were particular that all their garments should fit exactly. Hence their shoes too were tightly fastened and had to be untied every time they were put on or off.—Perhaps they are mentioned in particular because being well-to-do they thought more of dress; cf. Obermeyer, p. 173. (6) *Taya'a*, specially Arabian caravan merchants. (7) Lit., 'balls'. (8) They are worn by two different people on occasion. Hence they must be tied exactly each time, and therefore the knot is temporary.—In the other two the differences are the same as in the case of shoes. (9) Lit., 'it presents a difficulty to me'.
b (1) Abaye asked this: why do you think that it ought to be permitted? (2) With the result that the sandal fell off his foot. (3) Tosaf. in Hag. 23*a* s.v. ונפסקה reads: was walking behind. (4) Rashi: in a courtyard. (5) Do not pick it (the sandal) up to put away. (6) In a *karmelith* others might take it. (7) Why should it not be allowed to handle the sandal? (8) A sandal had two strappings, perhaps like loops, through which the laces were inserted, one on the outside and the other on the inside of the foot. Now, if the inner one is broken, it can be mended, and though it is not very seemly to walk in sandals with the strappings or laces merely knotted together, nevertheless it does not matter, as it is not very noticeable on the inner part of the foot. But if the outer one is broken, one would not walk out in it until a new one is inserted; consequently it ceases to be a 'utensil', and may not be handled on the Sabbath (cf. *supra* 28*b*, n. b3). In Abaye's case the outer strap was broken, hence R. Joseph's ruling. But Abaye argued that by changing the sandal to the other foot this would become the *inner* strapping, hence it should be permitted. Presumably their sandals were not shaped exactly to the foot, and were interchangeable. (9) That it ceases to be a 'utensil' if the outer is broken. (10) At the back, by means of which the sandal is held when it is tied up. (11) For here too it ceases to be a 'utensil'. (12) For it is still a 'utensil'.
c (1) If it is a utensil in respect of the former, it is likewise so in respect of the latter, and may be handled on the Sabbath. (2) V. Glos. (3) In the ceremony of *halizah* the shoe must be removed from the right foot. (4) Because they are interchangeable. But then it should also be regarded as a shoe in respect to *halizah* even if the *outer* strapping is broken. (5) I.e., it is at least fully fit for the *left* foot. (6) Even in respect of its own foot.

קיטרא דקטרי בזממא וקיטרא דקטרי באיסטרידא חיובא הוא דליכא הא איסורא איכא ויש שמותרין לכתחילה ומאי נינהו קושרת מפתחי חלוקה : מפתח חלוקה : פשיטא לא צריכא דאית ליה תרי דשי מהו דתימא חדא מינייהו בטולי מבטיל קא משמע לן : וחוטי סבכה : פשיטא לא צריכא דרויחא לה מהו דתימא מישלף שלפא לה קא משמע לן דאשה חסה על שערה ומישרא שריא לה : ורצועות מנעל וסנדל : איתמר התיר רצועות מנעל וסנדל תני חדא חייב חטאת ותניא אידך פטור אבל אסור ותניא אידך מותר לכתחילה קשיא מנעל אמנעל קשיא סנדל אסנדל מנעל אמנעל לא קשיא הא דקתני חייב חטאת בדאושכפי פטור אבל אסור בדרבנן מותר לכתחלה בדבני מחוזא סנדל אסנדל לא קשיא הא דקתני חייב חטאת בדטייעי דקטרי אושכפי פטור אבל אסור בדחומרתא דקטרי אינהו מותר לכתחילה בסנדל דנפקי ביה בי תרי כדרב יהודה דרב יהודה אחוה דרב סלא חסידא הוה ליה ההוא זוגא דסנדלי זמנין דנפיק ביה איהו זימנין נפיק ביה ינוקיה אתא לקמיה דאביי א"ל כה"ג מאי א"ל חייב חטאת א"ל השתא פטור אבל אסור קא קשיא לי חייב חטאת קאמרת לי מאי טעמא א"ל משום דבחול נמי זימנין נפיקנא ביה אנא זימנין נפיק ביה ינוקא א"ל אי הכי מותר לכתחילה *רבי ירמיה הוה קאזיל בתריה דר' אבהו בכרמלית איפסיק (א) רצועה דסנדליה אמר ליה מאי ניעבד לה א"ל שקול גמי לח דחזי למאכל בהמה וכרוך עילויה אביי *הוה קאי קמיה דרב יוסף איפסיק ליה רצועה אמר ליה מאי איעביד ליה א"ל שבקיה מאי שנא מדרבי ירמיה [ג]התם לא מינטר הכא מינטר והא מנא הוא דאי בעינא הפיכנא ליה מימין לשמאל א"ל מדקמתרץ רבי יוחנן אליבא דרבי יהודה [ג]ש"מ הלכה כרבי יהודה מאי היא *דתניא [ד]סנדל שנפסקו שתי אזניו או שתי תרסיותיו או שניטל כל הכף שלו טהור אחת מאזניו או אחת מתרסיותיו [ה]או שניטל רוב הכף שלו טמא ר' יהודה אומר נפסקה פנימית טמא החיצונה טהור ואמר עולא ואיתימא רבה בר בר חנה אמר ר' יוחנן כמחלוקת לענין טומאה כך מחלוקת לענין שבת אבל לא לענין הליצה והוינן בה [ר' יוחנן] אליבא דמאן אילימא אליבא דרבנן מדלענין טומאה מנא הוי לענין שבת נמי מנא הוי אבל לא לחליצה דלאו מנא הוא *והתנן [ו]חלצה של שמאל בימין חליצתה כשרה ואלא אליבא דרבי יהודה *מדלענין טומאה לאו מנא הוא לענין שבת נמי לאו מנא הוא אבל לא לחליצה דמנא הוא אימר דאמרי' חלצה של שמאל בימין חליצת' כשרה היכא דלמילתי' מנא הוא הכא למילתיה לאו מנא הוא דהא אמר ר' יהודה נפסקה החיצונה טהור אלמא לאו מנא הוא לעולם אליבא דר' יהודה אימא וכן להליצה והא קמשמע לן דכי אמרינן חלצה של שמאל בשל ימין חליצתה כשרה היכא דלמילתיה

תוספות

אימור דאמרי' חליצתה כשרה היכא דלמילתיה מנא הוא · והא דלא מוקים לה אליבא דרבנן אבל לא לחליצה משום דלמילתיה דהיינו בשמאל לאו מנא הוא היינו טעמא משום דכיון דמנא הוא לדידהו לשבת ולטומאה אף על גב דלמילתיה לאו מנא הוא כשר הוא לחליצה כיון דשל שמאל בימין חליצתה כשרה אבל לר' יהודה דלמילתיה לאו מנא הוא ולמידי אחרינא נמי לאו מנא הוא מסתבר דלאו מנא הוא לחליצה : סנדל

רש"י

קיטרא דקיטרי בזממא · רצועה ארוכה שמכניסין בטבעת אסור לכתחילה לקושרה שם מפני שפעמים שמניח שם שבוע או שבועיים וקושר ומתיר ראש האחד שנתון ביתד או בעמוד שאסור בו האנקה והגמל : תרתי דשי · שתי פתחים היינו אותן לשוטות והווין זו למעלה וזו למטה זו לימין וזו לשמאל ואם אינה מתרת אלא האחד יכולה לפושטה וללובשה בדוחק : מהו דתימא חדא מינייהו בטולי מבטיל לה · ותיהוי קשר של קיימא וכיון דלא ידעי הי מינייהו תרווייהו ליתסרו קא משמע לן : פשיטא · דהא כל יומי שריא לה : דרויחא · לא דחקתו בראשה אלא קושרתו בריוח שיכולה להוציא מראשה כשהיא קשורה : מהו דתימא מישלף שלפא לה · מראשה הכי והוה לה קשר של קיימא : חייסה על שערה · שמא תוציא בדוחק ותינתק שערה ודפסקיא נמי איכא לשנויי כה"ג מהו דתימא מחתא ליה דרך רגלה ויוצאה קמ"ל דלא עבדה הכי משום לניעותא : בדאושכפי · בקשר שהאושכף עושה כשתוחב הרצועה במנעל קושר קשר מתוכו שלא תוכל לצאת והוא קיים לעולם : בדרבנן · כשקושרים סביב רגלים אין קושרין בדוחק שפעמים שחולצו כשהוא קשור ונועלו כשהוא קשור ומיהו קשר של קיימא לא הוי שבשעת הטיט מתירין אותו וקושרין אותו בדוחק שלא ידבק בטיט וישמט מרגליו : בדבני מחוזא · שהם רחבי לבב ומקפידים על לבושיהן ונעליהן להיות מכוונין וקושרין אותו בדוחק וצריך להתירו ערבית : בדטייעי דקטרי אושכפי · בסנדלים של ישמעאלים סוחרים שהאושכפים קושרים בהן הרצועות בקשר קבוע : בדחומרתא דקטרי אינהו · אלו סנדלים של שאר אנשים שאין רצועות קבועות בהן ע"י אומן אלא הם עצמן קושרין אותם בחומרתא בעלמא וקושרין ומתירין ופעמים שמתקיים שבת או חדש : דנפקי בי תרי · וצריך כל אחד ואחד לקשור לפי רגלו הלכך בכל יום קושרו ומתירו : כה"ג · שאני מתירו עכשיו ונועל בני ושבת היתה : השתא פטור אבל אסור הוה קשיא לי · אמאי אסור : מ"ט · קשיא לך : א"ל משום דבחול נמי · אני מתירו בכל יום וקושרו התינוק לפי רגלו : אי הכי מותר לכתחילה · ומעיקרא סבר דלא רגיל למעבד הכי וקטרא דאושכפי הוה שרגיל להיות קבוע : איפסיק רצועה דסנדליה · ונפל הסנדל מרגלו שע"י הרצועה הוא עומד שהסנדל פתוח מעל גביו וצדדיו של עץ או של עור שלוק וקשה והרצועות נקשרות על גב הרגל ומעמידות אותו: שקול גמי לח דחזי למאכל בהמה. דראוי לטלטול : וכרוך · במקום הרצועה ונועלו עד שתכנס: אביי הוה קאי קמיה דרב יוסף · בחצר: שבקיה · במקום שנפל מרגלך ולא תטלנו בידך להכניסו : ומ"ש מדר' ירמיה· דשרא ליה ר' אבהו לנועלו ע"י גמי : התם · בכרמלית כגון בקעה לא הוה מינטר : והא מנא הוא · ואמאי אסור לטלטלו והא עדיין תורת מנעל עליו : דאי בעינא הפיכנא מימין לשמאל . שהסנדל יש לו שתי תרסיות והן של עור מקום קביעות הרצועות אחת מבחוץ ואחת מבפנים לבין שני רגלים כעין שיש למנעלים שלנו וכשנפסק הפנימי ראוי הוא לתקנו ואע"ג שתיקונו ניכר וגנאי הוא מיהו לצד פנים לא מיתחזי וכשנפסקה חיצונה אינו הגון שוב לתקנו והך דאביי חיצונה איפסיק משום הכי אסריה רב יוסף אפילו לטלטלו וא"ל אביי והא אכתי מנא הוא דהפיכנא ליה לרגל האחרת ונמצאת החיצונה פנימית : א"ל מדקא מתרץ רבי יוחנן · למילתיה דר"י לקמן ומפרש לה : ש"מ הלכה כר"י דאמר משנפסקה החיצונה לאו מנא הוא : אזניו · שבצדי גב הרגל שאוחזו בהן כשנועלו : תרסיותיו · מקום קביעות הרצועות : הכף שול"א בלע"ז שתחת פרסות הרגל : טהור · דתו לא מתקני ליה וא"נ מתקני ליה חדוש הוא והשתא מיהא בטיל ליה : (ב) טמא · לא פרחה טומאה מעליו דאכתי מנא הוא ואפילו נפסקה החיצונה דאי בעי מפיך ליה מימין לשמאל ונמצאת חיצונה נעשית פנימית : ואמר עולא גרסי' אליבא דמאן · מהכי תנאי א"ר יוחנן דמאי דסבירא ליה לענין טומאה ס"ל לענין טלטול שבת אבל לענין חליצה מודה לבר פלוגתיה : אילימא לרבנן · אשמעינן רבי יוחנן דכי היכי דלענין טומאה משוי ליה מנא לענין שבת נמי מנא הוא אבל לחליצה לאו מנא הוא ואינו כשר לחליצה והא אנן תנן חלצה בסנדל של שמאל בימין שהחליצה ברגל ימיני ואם נעל בו סנדל שמאל וחלצה כשר ואי נפסקה חיצונה דסנדל של שמאל אמאי לא הוה כשר לחלוץ הואיל ובעלמא סנדל הוא משום דחזי להפוכי ה"נ חזי להפוכי : אלא אליבא דר"י · אמרה ר' יוחנן למילתיה ולאשמעינן דבחליצה מודה ר"י דמנא הוא כגון שנפסקה חיצונה של שמאל הופכו לימין וחולץ וכדתנן של שמאל בימין חליצתה כשירה : אימר דאמרינן חליצה כשירה · היכא דלא נפסקו תרסיותיו : דלמילתיה · ברגל העשוי לו מנא הוא : הכא למילתיה לאו מנא הוא · דהא ר"י לענין טומאה ושבת לאו מנא משוי ליה : אימא וכן לחליצה · כדמפרש ואזיל ואשמעינן דכי אמרינן חלצה כו' ואליבא דרבנן לא מצינן לאוקמיה

מסורת הש"ס

גיר' התוס' בחגיגה כג. ד"ה ונפסקה אביי קא אזיל בתר רב יוסף

תוספתא דכלים ב"ב פ"ד

יבמות קא

[לקמן קכג.]

הגהות הב"ח

(א) גמ' רבי ירמיה כו' איפסיק ליה רצועה : (ב) רש"י ד"ה טמא לא ז"ל קודם ד"ה טהור דתו לא:

עין משפט נר מצוה

ה א ב ג מיי' פ"י מהל' שבת הלכה ד סמג לאוין סה טוש"ע א"ח סי' שח סעיף טו :

ו ד ה מיי' פ"ז מהלכות כלים הלכה יב יג ופכ"ד הלכה ד :

ז ו מיי' פ"ד מהל' יבום הלכה יט סמג עשין נה טוש"ע אה"ע סי' קסט סעיף כב בהג"ה :

רבינו חננאל

בהנהו חוטי שערה דמשרא הוא דשריא ליה ולא שיפה להו מעוף . רצועות מנעל וסנדל אית בהוא ג' בבי קיטרי דקטרי אושכפי להויא רצועה במנעל עצמו המתירה חייב חטאת . והני רצועות הנמשכות מגופו של מנעל שקושרין אותו על הרגל ועל השוק (אחר שני עלין המנעל) אחר שנועלין הנך מותר לכתחלה לקשרן ולהתירן וזהו דבני מחוזא והן נמי קשר חיצון של רצועות שהוא למעלה מן השוק ומן הרגל. אם מעיקרא קשרן לשום כך הרצען קשר של קיימא שכשנועל ההוא מנעל מכנים רגליו באותן הרצועות ואינו מתירן כל עיקר ההוא נמי המתירן חייב עליו חטאת אבל זה הקשר החיצון שלא קשרו האומן אלא כל אדם קושרו מהיכי דניהא ליה מרווח או צר או כגון מסני רבנן שכל אחד מעמידו על חפצו כד רויח למיסם ולמישלף בניחותא כגון זה המתירו פטור. שהרי מעשה הדיוט הוא אבל אסור להתירו לכתחלה דהוא קא מוקים ליה על חפצו וקשרו כמין קשר של קיימא לפי שאין דעתו להתירו ולשנותו. ומשני דבני מחוזא דעבידן להתירן ולקשרן בכל זמן דכד בעי למרהט שרי ליה וקמים ליה וכד בעי לסנויי בניחותא כי הלוכן דרבנן מרפי ליה כי הא גוונא מותר להתירו לכתחלה. וסנדל כי הלין אנפין אית ביה . סנדל דטייעי כגון קצת האי דקרו ליה השתא תאסומא דעביד ליה לפי מידת אסתורא דכרעיה וקטר ליה קיטרא מעליא . אם התירו חייב חטאת . ודחומרתא פי' מכנפין כולהי רצועות ומעיילין בחומרתא דכד בעי מעייק והדר קטיר מאבראי דחומרתא וכד בעי מרווח כגון האי פטור אבל אסור . וסנדל המוכן לשנים דחומרא דכד בעי האי למסיימיה מרווח ליה וכד בעי אחרינא למסיימיה קמיט ליה ודאי הני לא קטרי קשר של קיימא מעיקרא דניח ליה להתירו ונייח ליה נמי לאידך להתירו הלכך לכתחלה [שרי]. הא דר' ירמיה דאיפסיק ליה רצועה דסנדליה וא"ל ר' אבהו שקול גמי לח דחזי למאכל בהמה וכרוך עליה ואתייה. קיי"ל דהאי גמי לח דא"ל כי היכי דאיתכשר להנטל בשבת דהאי כיון דאחזי למאכל בהמה הוה ליה דבר הניטל בשבת. כמו ככר או תינוק ושרי לאיתויי פחות מד' אמות כר' יצחק דאמר מוליכו פחות פחות מד' אמות . ולא תימא כיס בלבד שרו ליה דאדם בהול על ממונו . ואי לא שרית ליה אתי לאתויה ד' אמות בר"ה אלא כל דבר שצריך לו מדתנן המוציא תפלין מכניסן זוג זוג . ובשעת הסכנה מכסן והולך לו בד"א בסכנת גוים אבל בסכנת לסטין מוליכן פחות פחות מד' אמות וה"מ בדוכתא דלא מינטר . אבל בדוכתא דמינטר לישבקיה בדוכתא כרב יוסף ואע"ג דא"ל אביי אי בעינא אפיכנא ליה . לא היישינן ליה. יש רבנן דהוו מפרשי אפיכנא ליה מימין לשמאל וכיון דאפיכנא ליה הויא לה רצועה דאיפסיקא (וסדורא דפיש לבראי ומיהדק קליל) ומשתני ליה ואנן לא קא מתחזי לנא היכי הוי הכין אלא הפוך מקום עקיבו לראשו ואוחזו באצבעותיו ואמר ליה כיון דמסגינא ביה אע"פ בהיפוך כלי הוא ואמאי אסור לטלטוליה ואמר ליה רב יוסף מדמתרץ ר' יוחנן אליבא דר' יהודה דכד מפסיק סנדל אע"ג דאפשר להפוכיה לאו מנא היא ש"מ דהלכתא כר' יהודה . מאי דר' יהודה דתניא סנדל שנפסקה אחת מאונה או אחת מתרסיותיו או שניטל כל הכף טמא ב' אזניו או ב' תרסיותיו אי שניטל רוב הכף טהור ר' יהודה אומר נפסקה הפנימית טמא החיצונה טהור פי' קסבר ר' יהודה אע"פ שלא נפסקה אלא האוזן החיצונה של סנדל בלבד נפיק ליה מתורת כלי וטהור ות"ק סבר אם נפסק אחת מאזניו או אחת מתרסיותיו עדיין כלי הוא אינו יוצא מתורת כלי עד שיפסקו שתיהן ולר' יהודה כיון שנפסק האוזן החיצונה כבר יצא מתורת כלי וטהור הוא ואע"פ שיכול להפכו לזה הסנדל ברגלו האחרת ולשום האוזן החיצונה פנימית . וקמתרץ ר' יוחנן אליבא דר' יהודה דאמר עולא ואיתימא רבה בר בר חנה אמר ר' יוחנן כמחלוקת לטומאה כך מחלוקת לענין שבת . אבל לא לחליצה פי' כל דהוא כלי לקבל טומאה גם הוא כלי לינטל בשבת וכל שיצא מתורת כלי לענין טומאה אף יצא מתורת כלי לענין שבת ואינו ניטל ומשום הכי אצרכיה רב יוסף למישבקיה ודלא לטלטוליה בשבת . והיכי מתרץ דר' יוחנן אליבא דר' יהודה דקתני ר' יוחנן אבל לא לחליצה והוי בה רבא אליבא דמאן קאמר ר' יוחנן אבל לא להליצה אילימא אליבא [דרבנן] דסברי בפסיקת אוזן אחת לא נפיק מתורת כלי ואמר ר' יוחנן כי לא נפיק מתורת כלי אליבא דרבנן לא לענין טומאה ולא לענין שבת. אבל לענין חליצה

עין משפט
נר מצוה

ח א מיי' פי"ז מהל' כלים הלכה יב :
ט ב ג מיי' פי"ז מהל' כלים הלכה ג :
י ד ה מיי' פ"י מהלכות שבת הל' ג סמג לאוין סה טוש"ע א"ח סי' שיז סעיף ו :

[לעיל מז. וש"נ]

מסורת הש"ס

כלים פכ"ו מ"ד
עירובין כד. כפ"ל מ"ז

ברכות מא. עירובין ד. כד. סוכה ו. כלים פי"ז מ"א

[ע"ז: עירובין כד.] שקלים ח: ע"ש

גיר' ר' יוסי דמן יוקרת

דלמילתיה מנא הוא אבל הכא למילתיה לאו מנא הוא ומי א"ר יוחנן הכי והאמר *רבי יוחנן הלכה כסתם משנה *ותנן *סנדל שנפסקה אחת מאזניו ותיקנה טמא מדרס *(נפסקה שניה ותיקנה טהור מלטמא מדרס אבל טמא מגע מדרס) מאי לאו לא שנא פנימית ולא שנא חיצונה לא פנימית דוקא אבל חיצונה מאי טהור אי הכי אדתני נפסקה שניה ותיקנה טהור מן המדרס אבל טמא מגע מדרס ניפלוג (א) בדידה בד"א שנפסקה פנימית אבל חיצונה טהור אמר רב יצחק בן יוסף תהא משנתנו בסנדל שיש לו ארבע אזנים וארבע תרסיותים *שלא לשבור דבריו של ר' יוחנן כי אתא רבין אמר רב חנן בר אבא אמר רב הלכה כרבי יהודה ורבי יוחנן אמר אין הלכה כר' יהודה ומי א"ר יוחנן הכי והא מדמתרץ ר' יוחנן אליבא דר' יהודה ש"מ כר' יהודה סבירא ליה א) אמוראי נינהו ואליבא דרבי יוחנן *תנן התם *כל כלי בעלי בתים שיעורן כרמונים בעי (ב) (רבי) חזקיה ניקב כמוציא זית וסתמו וחזר וניקב כמוציא זית וסתמו עד שהשלימו למוציא רימון מהו אמר ליה ר' יוחנן רבי *שנית לנו סנדל שנפסקה אחת מאזניו ותיקנה טמא מדרס נפסקה שניה ותיקנה טהור מן המדרס אבל טמא מגע מדרס ואמרינן לך מאי שנא ראשונה דהא קיימא שניה שניה נמי (ג) מתקנה ראשונה ואמרת לן עליה פנים חדשות באו לכאן *הכא נמי פנים חדשות באו לכאן *קרי עליה לית דין בר אינש איכא דאמרי כגון דין בר אינש *אמר ר' זירא אמר רבא בר זימונא אם ראשונים בני מלאכים אנו בני אנשים ואם ראשונים בני אנשים אנו כחמורים ולא כחמורו של *ר' חנינא בן דוסא ושל רבי פנחס בן יאיר אלא כשאר חמורים : ונודות יין ושמן : פשיטא לא צריכא דאית ליה תרתי אוני מהו דתימא חדא מינייהו בטולי מבטל לה קמ"ל : קדירה של בשר : פשיטא לא צריכא דאית לה ב) שלאבא מהו דתימא בטולי מבטל לה קמ"ל : *רבי אליעזר בן יעקב אומר קושרה כו' : פשיטא *לא צריכא דאית לה תרתי איסרי מהו דתימא חדא

לאוקמיה לדרבי יוחנן ולמימר וכן לחליצה ולאשמעינן דמנא הוא דא"כ מאי אתא לאשמעי' ר' יוחנן כיון דלמילתיה מנא הוא בהדיא תנן לה מתניתין ומשום דאפכי לא מיפסל דתנן חלצה בשל שמאל בימין חליצתה כשרה והיינו דאמר לעיל דמתרץ רבי יוחנן אליביה דר' יהודה : ומי אמר ר' יוחנן הכי · דהלכה כר' יהודה : טמא מדרס · אם היה של זב והיה טמא מדרס לא טהר מטומאתו כשנפסקה ועודנו אב הטומאה : מאי לאו · אפילו חיצונה ומשום דחזי לאפוכי ולתקנה וה"ה אע"ג דלא תיקנה דע"כ אי כשנפסקה פרחה לה טומאתה תו לא הדרה אלא להכי נקט תקנה משום סיפא לאשמעינן רבותא דאע"ג דתיקנה לראשונה כי הדר נפסקה שניה טהור מן המדרס : אדתני נפסקה שניה · אע"פ שתקנה טהור מן המדרס דכיון שנפסקו שתיהן בטיל ליה : אבל טמא מגע מדרס · והוי ראשון לטומאה דעדיין כלי הוא *דחזי למילתיה(ד) דהא מיתקנה ראשונה ואף למדרס הוא ראוי אי הוה נעיל ליה זב מכאן ולהבא מיהו מטומאת מדרס קמייתא דהויא עליה טהו' כדאמרינן לקמן פנים חדשות באו לכאן וכל תורת מנעל שהיתה עליה בשעת קבלת טומאה ראשונה הלכה לה וכיון דכלי הוא הוי ראשון שהרי נגע בעצמו כשהיה אב הטומא' וכל זמן שהוא כלי וראוי לקבל טומאה לא טהר מטומאת המגע :

הגה"ה מתחילה היה הגיר' כך ברש"י · והוה ראשון לטומאה דעדיין כלי הוא לאשתמושי ביה תשמיש אחרינא ומאב הטומאה טהור דלא הוי מיוחד עוד למנעל והוי ראשון שהרי נגע בעצמו כשהיה אב הטומאה · ואח"כ הגיה רש"י בדבריו :

ניפלוג כו' · למה לי למינקט נפסקה שניה דנפסקו שתיהן הא ע"כ הא שניה החיצונה היא ומשום היא לחודה הוה ליה למיתני טהור מן המדרס : תהא משנתנו · הך דמדרס : ד' אזנים וד' תרסיותים · והך דנפסק' שניה דקתני תרווייהו בחיצונות קאמר וסתמא כרבי יהודה דכיון דנפסקו חיצונות טהור : שלא לשבר דבריו של רבי יוחנן · דאמר הלכה כרבי יהודה : אמוראי נינהו · רבה בר בר חנה אמרה להאי דלעיל והא רבין אמרה : כל כלי בעלי בתים · לגבי כלי עץ תנא לה במסכת כלים : שיעורן כרימונים · לטהר מטומאתן אבל פחות מכאן חיים עליה ולא מבטיל ליה : וחזר וניקב כמוציא זית · אלא נקב הראשון : עד שהשלים · הסתימה למוציא רימון : הא מתקנה ראשונה · ולא בטל מתורת מנעל : פנים חדשות · משירדה לו טומאת מדרס נתחדשו פנים הללו ואין זו הראשון שכבר נתקלקל בו כדי ביטולו : לית דין בר איניש · אלא מלאך : כגון דין בר איניש · גברא בעלא : חמורו דר' פנחס · מפורש בהכל שוחטין (חולין דף ז·) ודרבי חנינא במסכת תענית (ד' כד·) ג) : תרתי אוני · אזנים שכופלים לתוכו ובאחת מהן יכול להוציא היין : שלאבא · ברלו"ן : מהו דתימא מבטל ליה · לקשר שעל פיה ומוציא מה שבתוכו דרך שלאבא : תרי איסורי · שני חבלים קושר ברחב הפתח זה למעלה מזה לישנא אחרינא תרי איסורי שקושרין היום בשני לידי הפתח ולא היתה תלויה בה מאתמול :
חדא

סנדל שנפסקה אחת מאזניו ותיקנה כו' . פירש בקונטרס דהוא הדין לא תיקנה טמא מדרס דאי כשנפסקה פרחה לה טומאה תו לא הדרה לה והדין עמו דלא מצינו טומאה ישנה (ה) אלא בכלי מתכות ולעיל נמי אמרי' ניטלה אחת מאזניו ואחת מתרסיותיו טמא והא דנקט ותיקנה פירש בקונטרס דנקט משום סיפא לאשמעינן דאע"ג דתיקנה כי נפסקה שניה טהור מן המדרס אבל משום דקתני סיפא אבל טמא מגע מדרס לא נקט ותיקנה דאפילו לא תיקנה ונפסקה שניה טמא מגע מדרס כדפי' בקונט' משום דעדיין כלי הוא לאישתמושי ביה תשמיש אחרינא וקשה דתנן בהדיא בסיפא דהך משנה במסכת כלים בפ' כ"ו (משנה ד) לא הספיק לתקן את הראשונה עד שנפסקה שניה טהור ורש"י בעצמו חזר בו והגיה אבל טמא במגע מדרס (ו) דעדיין כלי הוא וחזי למילתיה דהא איתקנה לראשונה והשתא נקט ברישא דוקא ותיקנה דאי לא תיקנה כי נפסקה שניה אינו טמא אפילו מגע מדרס כדקתני סיפא בהדיא ואגב דנקט ברישא ותיקנה נקט נמי בסיפא :
אבל טמא מגע מדרס · הקשה ה"ר שמעון אמאי טמא מגע מדרס הא שבע לה טומאה ובהקומץ רבה (מנחות כד·) בעי רבא גבי עשרון שחלקו מי אמרינן שבע לה טומאה או לאו וליכא למימר כיון שדרס עליו הזב ברגלו יחף דבא לו מדרס ומגע (ז) מדרס יחד דבבת אחת לא אמרינן שבע לה טומאה כדמוכח בהקומץ רבה (ג"ז שם) א"כ איכא פנים חדשות למגע מדרס כמו למדרס אלא על כרחך אחר שנטלה הראשונה וניתקנה בא לו מגע מדרס כמו שפירש בקונט' שנוגע בעצמו ואם כן נימא דשבע לה טומאה ולפי' הקונט' קמא ניחא דאפילו נפסקו שתי אזניו טמא מגע מדרס ומפרש ה"ר שמעון דלא אמרינן שבע לה טומאה כשהטומאה באה לו מגופו כמו הכא שטומאת מגע באה לו שנוגע בעצמו כדפי' בקונטרס ולפירושו אתיא כרבי מאיר דאמר טומאת בית הסתרים מטמא דמה שנוגע בעצמו טומאת בית הסתרים היא וזהו דוחק דבפ' בהמה המקשה (חולין דף עב:) ובפ' העור והרוטב (שם דף קכט:) פריך בפשיטות טומאת בית הסתרים היא משמע דלא קי"ל כר"מ ובפרק שני דעירובין (דף כד·) פירש בקונטרס דבשעת פרישתו דאוזן קיבל טומאה מאביו ואין נראה דבפרק בהמה המקשה (חולין דף עב:) אמרינן דבעינן דבאות מבגד גדול ונראה לר"י כשתיקן אוזן ראשונה באה לו לאוזן טומאת מדרס ומגע מדרס יחד והסנדל בטל לאוזן דאי אפשר להיות טומאה לזה בלא זה :
נפלוג וניתני בדידה בד"א · קשה לר"י אדפריך ניפלוג וניתני [נ"ל דמתני'] בדידה תיקשי ליה גופה (*דברייתא) אמאי טמא מגע מדרס הלא כיון שנפסקה החיצונה בטל לה מתורת כלי ואומר ר"י דהוה בכלל קושיית הש"ס דניפלוג וניתני בדידה וממילא ידעינן דטמא מגע מדרס איתו אמת : עד שהשלימו למוציא רמון מהו · והא דתנן במסכת כלים (פי"ז מ"ד) רימונים שאמרו שלשה אחוזים זה בזה לא שהשיעור בשלשה רימונים אלא מפרש מה שאמר למעלה הרימון לא גדול ולא קטן אלא בינוני וקאמר דהיינו בינוני כשלשה האחוזים זה בזה וגדילים יחד אבל הרימונים הגדילים אחד אחד או שנים הם גדולים ואותן שגדילים ארבעה יחד הם קטנים ד) :
רבי שנית לנו סנדל · תמוה לה"ר אלחנן אמאי לא מייתי ההיא סייעתא למטה דמתניה מקמי הך (כלים פי"ח משנה ו) מטה שהיתה טמאה מדרס נשברה ארוכה ותיקנה טמאה מדרס נשברה שניה ותקנה טהורה מן המדרס אבל טמאה מגע מדרס אם לא הספיק לתקן את הראשונה כו' :
לא צריכא דאית לה שלאכא · לא גרסינן דאית לה תרי שלאכי דלמה צריך לתרי שלאכי כיון שיש לו פתח :
כלל

א) יש גורסין אחר זה ואיבעית אימא ר"י קאמר לה אליבא דר"י וליה לא ס"ל: ב) [גיר' הערוך שלבא פי' כגון דדי הכיור שמקלחין · המים אע"ג דיכול לארוקי המרק מן השליבה מותר להתירו] ג) [במסכת תענית לא נמצא מחמורו של ר"ח בן דוסא כלום רק מחמורו של רבי יוסי דמן יוקרת נזכר שם בתענית כד. ואולם רש"י דכאן שכתב להדיא ודר"ח אפשר דקא מכוין אהא דאי' באבות דר' נתן ספ"ח עובדא דחמורו של רבי חנינא בן דוסא ע"ש מבואר] ד) [וע"ע תוס' עירובין ד: ובסוכה ו. ד"ה שיעורן]

רבינו חננאל

חליצה טומאה אינו כשר ולאו ככלי הוא . והא לדברי הכל אם נפסקה האוזן הפנימית כלי גמור הוא . ואי מפסק החיצונה מהפיך ליה לסנדל ומשוי ליה פנימית . ותניתן בהדיא לענין חליצה דאי אפיך לסנדל של שמאל בימין וחלץ כשר . דתנן חלצה בשל שמאל בימין חליצתה כשרה . אלא כי קאמר ר' יוחנן אבל לא לחליצה אליבא דר' יהודה דסבר בפסיקת אוזן החיצונה יצא מתורת כלי לגמרי ולענין שבת ולענין טומאה מודה ליה ר' יוחנן לר' יהודה וסבר לה כותיה . אבל לא לחליצה . דסבר ר' יוחנן לחליצה כלי כשר הוא. ומדתנן חלצה בשל שמאל בימין חליצתה כשרה . ודחי' אימור דאמר רבנן חלצה בשל שמאל בימין כשר דבמקומו כלי מעליא הוא כלומר ברגלו השמאל סנדל מעולה הוא. אבל הכא שנפסקה אונו החיצונה דילמא (אליבא דרבנן) קא' בלבד הוי באותה הרגל לאו סנדל מעליא הוא שהרי נפסקה אזנו החיצונה ומן שנפסל באתריה דלא הוי באתריה מנא . איך הוי מנא באתריה דלאו דידיה הוא ונדחו אלו הדברים . ולא עמדה כדרך שאמרנו כי לענין טומאה ושבת וחליצה יש ביניהן הפרש לא אליבא דרבנן ולא אליבא דרבי יהודה והדרנן לתירוצא וכן לחליצה . כלומר תורת כלי בחליצה כתורת כלי בענין שבת ובטומאה ואליבא דרבי יהודה דאמר בפסיקת אוזן החיצונה בלבד הוא יוצא מתורת כלי . ואקשינן וממאי דכי אמר ר' יוחנן וכן לחליצה למיפסל סנדל שנפסקה אוזן החיצונה' דילמא אליבא דרבנן קאמר דלא מיפסל עד דמפסקו ב' אוניו. ושנינן הא לא איצטריך ר' יוחנן לאשמעינן דהא תנינא החולץ משמאל בימין חליצתה כשרה הכא נמי כי משתני חיצונה למיהוי פנימית כשר. דהא לרבנן במקומה נמי כלי הוא . ולא הוה צריך ר' יוחנן למימרה ולא איצטריך אלא אליבא דרבי יהודה ומדקא מתרץ ר' יוחנן אליבא דר' יהודה ש"מ הלכה כר' יהודה לענין שבת דאע"ג דיכול להפוכה לחיצונה ולהשוייה פנימה לא הויא מנא והני ב' אונים דאמר ת"ק דמיפסקן לאו הני אונים שמשני צידי סנדל אלא ב' אונים מצד אחד . וסנדל זה יש לו ד' אונים ב' מצד זה וב' מצד זה. רבנן סברי [כיון] דלא מפסקן הני תרתי דמצד אחר לא נפיק מתורת כלי . ר' יהודה סבר מכד מפסקה חיצונה בטל מהיות כלי דסמכיה על אוזן החיצונה והיא שאוחזת את כף הרגל אבל פנימית לאו סמכא עלה והאי דקתני שאם נפסק כל הכף כולו עדיין טמא הוא ואם נפסק רוב הכף שלו טהור דייקינן מדקתני בנפסק רוב הכף שלו ולא קתני שלו בכלל

הגהות הב"ח

(א) גמ' ניפלוג וניתני בדידה: (ב) שם בעי חזקיה כצ"ל ותיבת רבי נמחק: (ג) שם שניה נמי הא מתקנה: (ד) רש"י ד"ה אבל טמא וכו' דחזי למילתיה קמייתא דהא כצ"ל ודיבור זה צ"ל קודם דבור המתחיל מאי לאו: (ה) תוס' ד"ה סנדל וכו' טומאה ישנה. נ"ב בפ"ק דף טז: (ו) בא"ד אבל טמא מגע מדרס והוי ראשון לטומא' דעדיין כלי הוא דחזי למילתא קמיי' דהא איתקנה: (ז) ד"ה אבל וכו' דבא לו מדרס ומגע זב יחד :

גליון הש"ס

גמ' שלא לשבור דבריו של ר"י. כזה לעיל מו ע"א : שם שנית לנו סנדל. יש לעיין אמאי לא מייתי ממתני' הקודמ' פי"ח מ"ז דכלים וצ"ע :

רב נסים גאון

פרק טו אלו קשרים אם ראשונים מלאכים אנן בני אנשים [ואם ראשונים כבני אנשים אנו כחמורים ולא] כחמורו של ר' חנינא בן דוסא. משכחת עיקר דילה באבות דר' נתן (פרק ח) והוא המעשה מעשה בחמורו של ר' חנינא בן דוסא שנגנבה ליסטים וחבשוה בחצר והניחו לה שעורים תבן ומים ולא היתה אוכלת ולא היתה שותה אמרו מה אנו מניחין זו עד שתמות ותבאש החצר עלינו פתחו לה דלת והוציאוה לחוץ הלכה עד שהגיעה אצל פתחו של ר' חנינא בן דוסא שמע בנו קולה והכירה אמר דומה קולה לקול בהמתנו אמר לו בני עמוד לפניה ופתח לה דלת

[112b] it is a 'utensil' for its own function, but here it is not a 'utensil' for its own function.[7]

Now, did R. Joḥanan say thus?[8] Surely R. Joḥanan said, The *halachah* is as an anonymous Mishnah,[9] and we learnt: If one of the ears of a sandal is broken and he repairs it, it [the sandal] is unclean as *midras*.[10] (If the second is broken [too] and he repairs
a it, it is clean in that it is not defiled as *midras*,[1] but it is unclean as that touched by *midras*.)[2] Does not [this mean that] there is no difference whether it is the inner or the outer?[3]—No, [it refers] only [to] the inner. Then what if the outer [is broken]? [Would it be] clean! If so, instead of teaching, If the second is broken [too] and he repairs it, it is clean in that it is not defiled as *midras*, but it is unclean as that touched by *midras*, let him [the Tanna] draw a distinction in that very matter and teach: When is that? if the inner is broken; but [if] the outer [is broken] it is clean?—Said R. Isaac b. Joseph: Let our Mishnah[4] treat of a sandal which has four ears and four strappings, so as not to overthrow[5] the words of R. Joḥanan.

When Rabin came,[6] he said: R. Ḥanan b. Abba said in Rab's name: The *halachah* is as R. Judah; while R. Joḥanan said: The *halachah* is not as R. Judah. But did R. Joḥanan say thus: surely since R. Joḥanan explained [the law] on the basis of R. Judah's view, it follows that he agrees with R. Judah?—There is [a controversy of] amoraim as to R. Joḥanan's opinion.

We learnt elsewhere: As for all utensils belonging to private people, their standards are [holes as large] as pomegranates.[7] Hezekiah asked: What if it [a utensil] receives a hole [large enough] for an olive to fall through, and he [the owner] closes it, then it receives another hole[8] [large enough] for an olive to fall through, and he closes it, [and so on] until it is made large enough for a pomegranate to fall through? Said R. Joḥanan to him, You have taught us: If one of the ears of a sandal is broken and he repairs it, it [the sandal] is unclean as *midras*; if the second is broken and he repairs it, it is clean in that it is not defiled as *midras*, but it is unclean as that touched by *midras*. Now we asked you: Why is it different [when] the first [is broken],—because the second is sound? But [when] the second [too] is broken, the first is [already] repaired? And
b you answered us: A new entity[1] has arrived hither;[2] here too, a new entity has arrived hither! [Thereupon] he [Hezekiah] exclaimed concerning him, This one is not the son of man![3] Others say, Such a one is indeed the son of man![4] R. Zera said in Raba b. Zimuna's name: If the earlier [scholars] were sons of angels, we are sons of men; and if the earlier [scholars] were sons of men, we are like asses, and not [even] like asses of R. Ḥanina b. Dosa and R. Phinehas b. Jair,[5] but like other asses.

PITCHERS OF WINE OR OIL. But that is obvious?—This is necessary only where they have two spouts;[6] you might say, He [the owner] may completely disregard one:[7] therefore he [the Tanna] informs us [that we do not fear this].

THE MEAT POT. But that is obvious?—This is necessary only where it has a [screwed-in] stopper: you might say, He [the owner] may completely abandon [it]:[8] hence he informs us [that we do not fear this].

R. ELIEZER B. JACOB SAID: ONE MAY TIE, etc. But that is obvious? This is necessary only where there are two cords: you

(7) And this is the statement referred to above that R. Joḥanan explained the law on the view of R. Judah. (8) That the *halachah* is according to R. Judah. (9) I.e., one not taught in the name of any Rabbi. (10) If it belonged to a *zab*. V. *supra* 66a, n. a9.

a (1) I.e., it loses the *midras* defilement which it contracted previously. (2) I.e., it is unclean in the first degree, which is one degree below *midras* itself. It retains this lesser degree of defilement, because we regard it as having touched itself, as it were, when it was unclean as *midras*.—Rashal deletes the bracketed passage here. (3) Which is against R. Judah. (4) The cited anonymous Mishnah (Kel. XXVI, 4). (5) Lit., 'break'. (6) V. *supra* 5a, n. b9. (7) If they are unclean, and then broken, the holes being large enough to allow a pomegranate to fall through, they cease to be utensils and become clean; cf. *supra* 95b. (8) At the side of the first.

b (1) Lit., 'face'. (2) I.e., subsequent to the shoe being defiled as *midras*, the breaking of both loops and their mending so change the shoe as to make it virtually a different utensil, not the one which was defiled. (3) He is superhuman. (4) He is a man in the full sense of the word. (5) The allusions are explained in Ḥul. 7a and Ta'an. 24a. (6) And the Mishnah refers to tying them up. (7) Lit., 'make it as nought', and use the other only; cf. *supra* 112a, n. 7. (8) *Sc.* the cloth which he ties on top, as he can unscrew the stopper and take the food out that way.

might say, [113a] He [the owner] may completely disregard one;[9] hence he [the Tanna] informs us [that we do not fear this].

R. Joseph said in Rab Judah's name in Samuel's name: The *halachah* is as R. Eliezer b. Jacob. Said Abaye to him, [You say,] The *halachah* [etc.]: hence it follows that they [the Rabbis] disagree?[10] And what difference does that make? he replied. Shall the accepted tradition be [merely] like a song? he retorted.[11]

MISHNAH. A BUCKET [OVER A WELL] MAY BE TIED WITH
a A FASCIA[1] BUT NOT WITH A CORD;[2] BUT R. JUDAH PERMITS IT. R. JUDAH STATED A GENERAL RULE: ANY KNOT THAT IS NOT PERMANENT ENTAILS NO CULPABILITY.

GEMARA. What CORD is meant. Shall we say an ordinary [bucket] cord? [How then state] R. JUDAH PERMITS IT?—[Surely] it is a permanent knot? Rather it refers to a weaver's rope.[3] Shall we say that the Rabbis hold, We preventively forbid a weaver's cord on account of an ordinary one,[4] while R. Judah holds, We do not preventively forbid? But the following contradicts it: If the cord of a bucket is broken, one must not tie it [together] but merely make a loop [slip-knot]; whereas R. Judah maintains: One may wind a hollow belt or a fascia around it, providing that he does not tie it with a slip-knot. [Thus] R. Judah's [views] are self-contradictory and [similarly] the Rabbis'?—The Rabbis' [views] are not self-contradictory: one rope may be mistaken for[5] another,[6] [whereas] looping cannot be mistaken for knotting.[7] R. Judah's [views] are not self-contradictory: there it is not because looping may be mistaken for knotting, but [because] looping itself is [a form of] knotting.[8]

R. Abba said in the name of R. Ḥiyya b. Ashi in Rab's name: A man may bring a cord from his house and tie it to a cow and [its] trough.[9] R. Aḥa the Long, that is R. Aḥa b. Papa, refuted R. Abba: If a cord [is attached] to a trough, one may tie it to [his] cow; and if [attached] to a cow, one may tie it to a trough, provided however, that he does not bring a cord from his house and tie it to the cow and the trough?—There [the reference is to] an ordinary cord; here [we treat of] a weaver's cord.

Rab Judah said in Samuel's name: A weaver's implements may
b be handled on the Sabbath.[1] Rab Judah was asked: What of the upper beam and the lower beam?[2]—Yes and No, and he was uncertain about it.[3] It was stated: R. Naḥman said in Samuel's name: A weaver's implements may be handled on the Sabbath, even the upper beam and the lower beam, but not the [vertical] rollers.[4] Raba asked R. Naḥman: Why are rollers different, that it is not [permitted]? Shall we say, because one makes holes?[5] But the holes are made automatically![6] For we learnt: If one stores turnips or radishes under a vine, provided some of their leaves are

(9) He will untie only the lower one, and the animal can leave the stable by stooping. (10) Surely not, seeing that this is exactly similar to the other cases. (11) V. *supra* 57b, 106b.

a (1) A band or fillet. (2) The first is certainly not permanent, but the second may be left there, and thus a permanent knot will have been tied on the Sabbath. (3) He needs this and will not abandon it there. (4) The former ought to be permitted, since the knot is only temporary (v. preceding note), and the only reason for prohibiting it is that we fear that otherwise one may fasten an ordinary rope too. (5) Lit., 'interchanged with'. (6) As in n. a4. (7) No one will think that if the former is permitted the latter is too. (8) In his view.

(9) Without fear of subsequently leaving one end tied, in which case it becomes a permanent knot.

b (1) For a permissible use, though of course their normal use is forbidden on the Sabbath. (2) Jast.: the upper beam on which the warp depends; the lower beam, the roller on which the web is wound as it advances.—Do we say that since these are costly the weaver is careful not to use them for any purpose but their own, and hence they may not be handled even for a legitimate use? (3) Lit., 'it was weak in his hand'. (4) Perforated rollers used by women in weaving. (5) The roller is set in the ground, and in pulling it out one naturally dislodges the earth around it and thus makes a hole. (6) I.e., they cannot be regarded as made by him.

For the continuation of the English translation of this page see overleaf.

חדא מינייהו · אחד מן הראשים [ונל"א] חד מינייהו מבטל ליה כשיוליא הבהמה לא יתיר אלא תחתון ויוליאנה בדוחק : מכלל דפליגי · בתמיה ואמאי איפלגו הא דמי להנך דלעיל: **מתני'** קושרין דלי בפסקיא · ע"פ הבור דפסקיא לא מבטל [ליה] התם : אבל לא בחבל · דמבטל ליה התם והוי קשר של קיימא תורה אור

חדא מינייהו בטולי מבטיל קמ"ל אמר רב יוסף אמר רב יהודה אמר שמואל הלכה כרבי אליעזר בן יעקב *א"ל אביי הלכה מכלל דפליגי אמר ליה מאי נפקא לך מינה אמר ליה *גמרא גמור זמורתא תהא : **מתני'** *קושרין דלי בפסקיא אבל לא בחבל רבי יהודה מתיר כלל אמר רבי יהודה כל קשר שאינו של קיימא אין חייבין עליו : **גמ'** חבל דמאי אי לימא חבל דעלמא רבי יהודה מתיר קשר של קיימא הוא אלא (א) חבל דגרדי למימרא דרבנן סברי גזרינן חבל דגרדי אטו חבל דעלמא ורבי יהודה סבר לא גזרינן ורמינהו *חבל דלי שנפסק לא יהא קושרו אלא עונבו *ורבי יהודה אומר כורך עליו פונדא או פסקיא ובלבד שלא יענבנו קשיא דר' יהודה אדרבי יהודה קשיא דרבנן אדרבנן דרבנן אדרבנן לא קשיא חבל בחבל מיהלף עניבה בקשירה לא מיחלפא דר' יהודה אדרבי יהודה לא קשיא התם לא משום דמיחלפא עניבה בקשירה אלא עניבה גופה קשירה היא א"ר אבא *אמר רב חייא בר אשי אמר רב מביא אדם חבל מתוך ביתו וקושרו בפרה ובאיבוס איתיביה רבי אחא אריכא דהוא רבי אחא בר פפא לרבי אבא חבל שבאיבוס קושרו בפרה ושבפרה קושרו באיבוס ובלבד שלא יביא חבל מתוך ביתו ויקשור בפרה ובאיבוס התם חבל דעלמא הכא חבל דגרדי אמר רב יהודה אמר שמואל *כלי קואי מותר לטלטלן בשבת בעו מיניה מרב יהודה כובד העליון וכובד התחתון מהו *אין ולאו ורפיא בידיה איתמר אמר רב נחמן אמר שמואל כלי קואי מותר לטלטלן בשבת אפילו כובד העליון וכובד התחתון אבל לא את העמודים א"ל רבא לרב נחמן מאי שנא עמודים דלא אילימא דקעביד גומות גומות ממילא קא הויין דתנן *הטומן לפת וצנונות תחת הגפן אם מקצת עליו מגולין אינו חושש לא משום כלאים ולא משום שביעית ולא משום מעשר וניטלין בשבת בשדה לא אתי לאשויי גומות הכא בבית אתי לאשויי גומות בעא מיניה ר' יוחנן מרבי יהודה בר ליואי כלי קואי כגון כובד העליון וכובד התחתון מהו לטלטלן בשבת אמר ליה אין מטלטלין מה טעם לפי שאין ניטלין : **מתני'** מקפלין את הכלים אפילו ארבעה וחמשה פעמים ומציעין את המטות מלילי שבת לשבת אבל לא משבת למוצאי שבת רבי ישמעאל אומר מקפלין את הכלים ומציעין את המטות מיום הכיפורים לשבת *וחלבי שבת קריבין ביום הכיפורים אבל לא של יוה"כ בשבת ר"ע אומר לא של שבת קריבין ביום הכיפורים ולא של יום הכיפורים קריבין בשבת: **גמ'** אמרי דבי רבי ינאי לא שנו אלא באדם אחד אבל בשני בני אדם לא ובאדם אחד נמי לא אמרן אלא בחדשים אבל בישנים לא וחדשים נמי לא אמרן אלא בלבנים אבל בצבועים לא ולא אמרן אלא שאין לו להחליף אבל יש לו להחליף לא *תנא של בית רבן גמליאל לא היו מקפלים כלי לבן שלהן מפני שהיה להן להחליף אמר רב הונא אם יש לו להחליף יחליף ואם אין לו להחליף ישלשל בבגדיו מתקיף לה רב ספרא והא מיתחזי כרמות רוחא כיון דכל יומא לא קעביד והאידנא הוא דקא עביד לא מיתחזי כרמות רוחא °וכבדתו מעשות דרכיך וכבדתו שלא יהא מלבושך של שבת כמלבושך של חול וכי הא *דרבי יוחנן קרי למאניה מכבדותי מעשות דרכיך שלא יהא הילוכך של שבת כהילוכך של חול ממצוא חפצך *חפציך אסורין חפצי שמים מותרין ודבר דבר שלא

רש"י

שהרי קשור ותלוי שם תמיד : ורבי יהודה מתיר · בגמרא מפרש : **גמ'** בחבל דגרדי · פליגי דלריך לה ולא מבטל לה : חבל דלי שנפסק · באמלעיתו : לא יהא קושר · דקשר של קיימא הוא לעולם : כורך עליו · מחבר שני ראשי הפיסוק זה על זה וכורך עליהם פונדא אזור חלול או פסקיא פיישול"א : ובלבד שלא יענבנו · לחבל דר"י סבר גזרינן עניבה אטו קשירה ורבנן לא גזרו : מיחלף · אינו ניכר בין זה לזה ואי שרינן בדגרדי אתי למישרי בדעלמא : וקושרו בפרה · ראשו אחד והשני באבוס ולא חיישינן שמא כשיתיר הפרה לא יתיר אלא הקשר שבראשה ויבטל החבל באבוס שיהא מוכן לכך או יתיר שבאבוס ויבטל אותו שבפרה ונמלא האחד של קיימא : כלי קואי · כלי אורגים ואיידי דאיירי בחבל דגרדי נקט לה הכא : מותר לטלטלן · לשני הקנים לתשמיש אחר והשמיענו דאין גרדי מקפיד עליהם ולא הוי מלאכתן לאיסור : כובד העליון והתחתון · אנשובל"ש : מהו · מי אמרינן איידי דיקירי לא חזו כתמייהו לתשמיש אחרינא והוה ליה דבר שמלאכתו לאיסור : ורפיא בידיה · רפויה היתה התשובה בפיו אם לאסור אם להתיר : העמודים · טריור"ש בלע"ז אותם המנוקבות שאורגין בהן הגסים : דקא עביד גומא · כשאולגן מן הארץ שהן תקועות בגומא מזיז העפר ועביד גומא מקום העמוד : מקצת עליו מגולין · משום ניטלין בשבת נקט לה דאי לא הוי מגולין אין לו במה לאוחזה : אינו חושש · לפי שאינה מושרשת : ולא משום מעשר . להיות בטילה בנטיעה זו וכשנוטלה יצטרך לחזור ולעשר : לפי שאין ניטלין · אף בחול מפני כובדן הלכך כל מלאכתן לכך : **מתני'** מקפלין את הכלים · בגדים כשפושטן מקפלין מפני שמתרככין מכיבוסם ומתקמטי' כשאינן מקופלים : אפי' ד' וה' פעמים · כדי לחזור וללובשן בו ביום : מיוה"כ לשבת · כגון אם חל יוה"כ להיות בע"ש : קריבין ביוה"כ · שחל להיות במוצאי שבת : **גמ'** בשני בני אדם · כשמקפלין אותן מפשטין קמטיהן ונראין כמתקנין : ישנים · קיפולן מתקן יותר מן החדשים שהחדשים קשין מאליהן ואין ממהרין לקמוט : לבועין · קיפולן מתקן : יש לו · אחרים להחליף היום לה : כלי לבן שלהן : רבותא נקט וכל שכן לבועים : יש לו להחליף יחליף · מי שיש לו בגדים לבד מאותן שלבש בחול יחליפם בשבת : ישלשל בבגדיו · כלפי מטה שיראו ארוכים והוא מדת עשירים יושבים בביתם ואינם צריכים לגלק בגדיהם מן הארץ בשביל מלאכה וכבוד שבת הוא : מכבדותי · שמכבדין בעליהן : שלא יהא הילוכך כו' · לקמן מפרש להו : ממצוא חפצך · כי ההוא דאמרינן בעירובין (דף לח:) לא יטייל אדם לסוף שדהו בשבת לידע מה היא צריכה [אחר השבת] : חפצי שמים מותרים · כגון פוסקים לדקה ומשדכין על התינוקות ליארס (לקמן קנ.) : שלא

תוספות

כלל אמר ר"י · תימה היכא קאי אי אמילתיה קמייתא התם מתיר לגמרי והכא קתני אין חייבין עליו משמע הא איסורא איכא כדדייק הש"ס לעיל וי"ל דה"ק כל קשר שאינו של קיימא אין חייבין עליו הא של קיימא חייבין עליו ואפי' עניבה לאפוקי מדרבנן דאמרו עניבה לאו היינו קשירה א"נ אמאי דקתני ברישא אין חייבין עליהם קאי רבי יהודה :

התם חבל דעלמא הכא חבל דגרדי · וקמ"ל רב דלא גזרינן חבל דגרדי אטו חבל דעלמא וכר' יהודה א"נ אפי' רבנן מודו דאפי' בחבל דעלמא לא שכיח שיהיה קשר של קיימא כשקושרו בפרה ובאבוס ולהכי לא גזור בחבל דגרדי :

מקפלים כלים כו' · מכאן למדנו דאסור לקפל טליתות של ב"ה לפי שהם צורך מחר : **אבל** יש לו להחליף לא · ולנו שיש לנו להחליף אסור ומספק ר"י אי קרי יש לו להחליף כשאין לו יפה כזה : שלא

עין משפט נר מצוה

יא א מיי' וסמג שם טוש"ע שם סעיף ד :
יב ב מיי' שם הלכה ב טוש"ע שם סעיף א:
יג ג מיי' שם הלכה ס טוש"ע שם סעיף ה :
יד ד ה מיי' שם הל' ג טוש"ע שם סעיף ז :
טו ו ז מיי' פכ"ו מהל' שבת הלכה א :
טז ח מיי' פכ"ג מהל' שבת הלכה ז :
יז ט מיי' פכ"ג מהל' שבת [הלכה כב] סמג לאוין סה טוש"ע א"ח סי' שב סעיף ג :
יח י מיי' פ"ל שם הל' ג ופ"ה מהל' דעות הל' ט סמג עשין ג טוש"ע א"ח סי' רסב סעיף ב :
יט כ מיי' פכ"ד שם הלכה א סמג שם ולאוין סה טוש"ע א"ח סי' שו סעיף א :
כ ל מיי' שם הל"ה טוש"ע שם סעיף ו :

מסורת הש"ס

לעיל מו: קיו: [וש"נ] ביצה כד. ע"ז לב: פסחים יח.

פסחים שם [עירובין נו. יב: סוכה לג:]

כ"ה א"ר חייא א"ר יוחנן

[לקמן קמ:]

[לקמן קטז: ב"מ יד: קידושין סה.]

כלאים פ"ה מ"ט לעיל כ: עירובין עז.

[יומא מו. סוכה כד:]

[תוס' פי"ג]

ב"ק נח: סנהדרין נד:

[לקמן קנ.]

הגהות הב"ח

(א) גמ' אלא בחבל דגרדי :

רבינו חננאל

כולן אלא קתני כל הכף כולו סתמא והאי כף סתמא שאם נפסק עדיין טמא הוא ככף של תרסיות קתני והוא שבמקום העקב ומאזן לאזן הוא סביב העקב והאי דקתני הכף שלו שאם נפסק רובו טהור הכף של סנדל שהוא מן הסנדל גופו אם ניטל רובו טהור . ואקשי' ומי סבר לה ר' יוחנן כר' יהודה והאמר ר' יוחנן הלכה כסתם משנה. ותנן סנדל שנפסקה אחת מאזניו ותיקנה טמא מדרס . מאי לאו לא שנא פנימית ול"ש חיצונה כיון דמשתריא חדא מינייהו טמא . ודחי' לא נפסקה פנימית שנינן אבל נפסקה חיצונה טהור ואמרי' אי אישתביקא בכללא אפשר לשנויי כדקאמרת . אלא מדקתני סיפא נפסק שניה ותיקנה טהור מן המדרס אבל טמא מגע מדרס דהא פריש בה ומפרש סוף מאי דאית בה ואי דוקא פנימית קתני אדמפרש אם נפסקה אח"כ שניה ותיקנה נפלוג בקמייתא וניתני בד"א שנפסקה פנימית אבל נפסקה חיצונה טהור ופרקי' אמר רב יצחק ב"ר יוסף תהא משנתנו בסנדל שיש לו ד' אונים וד' תרסיותים ובהאי סנדל תנינן נפסקה אחת מאזניו סתם משמע אפי' חיצונית והוא כגון סנדל שיש לו ב' אונים פנימיות זו מצד זו וב' חיצונות זו מצד זו שאם תפסק אחת מן החיצונות הא קיימא חברתא בדוכתא דהיא נמי חיצונית ובחדא פנימית וכנגדה חדא חיצונה סגיא ומשום הכי טומאתו של סנדל בדוכתא קיימא אבל היכא דליכא חיצונה אלא חדא ונפסקה בטל ההוא סנדל מתורת כלי דפנימית לחיזוק בעלמא עבידא . ודרך הסנדל אזן אחת חיצונה ואזן אחת פנימית ויש שעוש' שתים שתים אם תפסק האחת תשאר האחרת במקומה ועל זה שנינו נפסקה טמא . כי

אתא רבין אמר משמיה דרב הלכה כר' יהודה ור' יוחנן אמר אין הלכה כר' יהודה ואסיקנא אמוראי נינהו ואליבא דר' יוחנן כלומר יש אמורא שאומר מדמתרץ ר' יוחנן אליבא דר' יהודה ש"מ הלכתא כר' יהודה ויש [illegible]

רב נסים גאון

[illegible]

גליון הש"ס רש"י ד"ה מותר לטלטלן וכו' ולא הוה מלאכתו לאיסור. ע"ל קכג ע"ב תד"ה רתת: שם ד"ה מהו וכו' והו"ל דבר שמלאכתו לאיסור. ע"ל קכג ע"א תד"ה כסוי :

Continuation of translation from previous page as indicated by ◁

uncovered, he need have no fear on account of *kil'ayim*, the seventh year, or tithes, and they may be removed on the Sabbath?[7]—In a field one will not come to level [fill up] the holes; [whereas] here in the house one will come to level the holes.[8]

R. Joḥanan asked R. Judah b. Lewai: As for a weaver's implements, e.g., the upper beam and the lower beam, may they be handled on the Sabbath?—They may not be handled, answered he. What is the reason? Because they cannot be taken up [moved].[9]

MISHNAH. ONE MAY FOLD UP GARMENTS EVEN FOUR OR
c FIVE TIMES,[1] AND SPREAD THE SHEETS ON THE BEDS ON THE NIGHT OF THE SABBATH[2] FOR [USE ON] THE SABBATH, BUT NOT ON THE SABBATH FOR [USE ON] THE CONCLUSION OF THE SABBATH. R. ISHMAEL SAID: ONE MAY FOLD UP GARMENTS AND SPREAD THE SHEETS ON THE BEDS ON THE DAY OF ATONEMENT FOR [USE ON] THE SABBATH;[3] AND THE FATS OF THE SABBATH[4] MAY BE OFFERED [BURNT ON THE ALTAR] ON THE DAY OF ATONEMENT,[5] BUT NOT THOSE OF THE DAY OF ATONEMENT ON THE SABBATH. R. AKIBA SAID: NEITHER MAY THOSE OF THE SABBATH BE OFFERED ON THE DAY OF ATONEMENT, NOR MAY THOSE OF THE DAY OF ATONEMENT BE OFFERED ON THE SABBATH.

GEMARA. The School of R. Jannai said: They learnt this only of one man, but [it may] not [be done] by two men.[6] And even of one man, we said [this] only of new [garments],[7] but not of old [ones]. And even of new [garments], we said this only of white, but not of coloured [ones].[8] And we said this only if he has no others to change, but if he has others to change it is not permitted. It was taught: [The members] of the household of R. Gamaliel did not fold up their white garments, because they had [others] for changing.

R. Huna said: If one has a change [of garments],[9] he should change [them], but if he has nothing to change into, he should lower his garments.[10] R. Safra demurred: But this looks like ostentation?—Since he does not do this every day, but [only] now [on the Sabbath], it does not look like ostentation.

d *And thou shalt honour it, not doing thine own ways:*[1] '*and thou shalt honour it*', that thy Sabbath garments should not be like thy week-day garments, and even as R. Joḥanan called his garments 'My honourers'.[2] '*Not doing thine own ways*', that thy walking on the Sabbath shall not be like thy walking on weekdays.[3] '*Nor finding thine own affairs*':[4] thine affairs are forbidden, the affairs of Heaven [religious matters] are permitted. '*Nor speaking thine own words:*'

(7) V. *supra* 50*b* bottom *et seq*. for notes. Thus we do not say that in removing them from the ground he makes holes. (8) And for fear of this it is forbidden. (9) Even on weekdays, owing to their heaviness. Hence they are utensils whose exclusive purpose is a labour forbidden on the Sabbath (cf. *supra* 36*a*, n. b8).

c (1) Every time one takes them off, if they are to be worn again on the Sabbath. (2) I.e., Friday night. (3) Rashi: e.g., if the former falls on Friday.—Nowadays this can never happen, but it was possible in the age of the Mishnah, when the beginning of each month was fixed by direct observation. (4) I.e., the fats of sacrifices offered on the Sabbath. (5) If it follows the Sabbath. The fats were burnt during the night following the day in which the sacrifice was offered up. (6) When two men fold up garments they naturally smooth out the creases, and thus repair them, as it were. (7) They have less creases, and also the cloth is harder, and so the folding does not smooth them out. (8) Their creases are more easily smoothed out.—Perhaps their method of dyeing had that effect on the cloth. (9) For the Sabbath. (10) Wear them lower down, to make them look longer.—Wealthy men who did not work in the field generally wore longer garments than workers.

d (1) Isa. LVIII, 13. The reference is to the Sabbath. (2) The garments dignify the person. (3) This is explained *infra*. (4) Ibid. E.V.: *pleasure*.

חדא מינייהו בטולי מבטיל קמ"ל אמר רב יוסף אמר רב יהודה אמר שמואל הלכה כרבי אליעזר בן יעקב *א"ל אביי הלכה מכלל דפליגי אמר ליה מאי נפקא לך מינה אמר ליה *גמרא גמור זמורתא תהא: **מתני'** *קושרין דלי בפסקיא אבל לא בחבל רבי יהודה מתיר כלל אמר רבי יהודה כל קשר שאינו של קיימא אין חייבין עליו: **גמ'** חבל דמאי אי לימא חבל דעלמא רבי יהודה מתיר קשר של קיימא הוא אלא (א) חבל דגרדי למימרא דרבנן סברי גזרינן חבל דגרדי אטו חבל דעלמא ורבי יהודה סבר לא גזרינן ורמינהו *חבל דלי שנפסק לא יהא קושרו אלא עונבו *ורבי יהודה אומר כורך עליו פונדא או פסקיא ובלבד שלא יענבנו קשיא דר' יהודה אדרבי יהודה קשיא דרבנן אדרבנן דרבנן אדרבנן לא קשיא חבל בחבל מיחלף עניבה בקשירה לא מיחלפא דר' יהודה אדרבי יהודה לא קשיא התם לא משום דמיחלפא עניבה בקשירה אלא עניבה גופה קשירה היא א"ר אבא *אמר רב חייא בר אשי אמר רב מביא אדם חבל מתוך ביתו וקושרו בפרה ובאיבוס איתיביה רבי אחא אריכא דהוא רבי אחא בר פפא לרבי אבא חבל שבאיבוס קושרו בפרה ושבפרה קושרו באיבוס ובלבד שלא יביא חבל מתוך ביתו ויקשור בפרה ובאיבוס התם חבל דעלמא הכא חבל דגרדי אמר רב יהודה אמר שמואל *כלי קוואי מותר לטלטלן בשבת בעו מיניה מרב יהודה כובד העליון וכובד התחתון מהו *אין ולאו ורפיא בידיה איתמר אמר רב נחמן אמר שמואל כלי קוואי מותר לטלטלן בשבת אפילו כובד העליון וכובד התחתון אבל לא את העמודים א"ל רבא לרב נחמן מאי שנא עמודים דלא אילימא דקעביד גומות גומות ממילא קא הויין דתנן *הטומן לפת וצנונות תחת הגפן אם מקצת עליו מגולין אינו חושש לא משום כלאים ולא משום שביעית ולא משום מעשר וניטלין בשבת בשדה לא אתי לאשוויי גומות הכא בבית אתי לאשוויי גומות בעא מיניה ר' יוחנן מרבי יהודה בר ליואי כלי קוואי כגון כובד העליון וכובד התחתון מהו לטלטלן בשבת אמר ליה אין מטלטלין מה טעם לפי שאין ניטלין: **מתני'** מקפלין את הכלים אפילו ארבעה וחמשה פעמים ומציעין את המטות מלילי שבת לשבת אבל לא משבת למוצאי שבת רבי ישמעאל אומר מקפלין את הכלים ומציעין את המטות מיום הכיפורים לשבת *וחלבי שבת קריבין ביום הכיפורים אבל לא של יוה"כ בשבת ר"ע אומר לא של שבת קריבין ביום הכיפורים ולא של יום הכיפורים קריבין בשבת: **גמ'** אמרי דבי רבי ינאי לא שנו אלא באדם אחד אבל בשני בני אדם לא ובאדם אחד נמי לא אמרן אלא בחדשים אבל בישנים לא וחדשים נמי לא אמרן אלא בלבנים אבל בצבועים לא ולא אמרן אלא שאין לו להחליף אבל יש לו להחליף לא *תנא של בית רבן גמליאל לא היו מקפלים כלי לבן שלהן מפני שהיה להן להחליף אמר רב הונא אם יש לו להחליף יחליף ואם אין לו להחליף ישלשל בבגדיו מתקיף לה רב ספרא והא מיתחזי כרמות רוחא כיון דכל יומא לא קעביד והאידנא הוא דקא עביד לא מיתחזי כרמות רוחא °וכבדתו מעשות דרכיך (ישעיה נח) וכבדתו שלא יהא מלבושך של שבת כמלבושך של חול וכי הא *דרבי יוחנן קרי למאניה מכבדותי מעשות דרכיך שלא יהא הילוכך של שבת כהילוכך של חול ממצוא חפצך *חפציך אסורין חפצי שמים מותרין ודבר דבר

שלא

רש"י

חדא מינייהו · אחד מן הראשים [ונל"א] חד מינייהו מבטל ליה כשיוליא הבהמה לא יתיר אלא תחתון ויוליאנה בדוחק: מכלל דפליגי · בתמיה ואמאי איפלגו הא דמי להנך דלעיל: **מתני'** קושרין דלי בפסקיא · ע"פ הבור דפסקיא לא מבטל [ליה] התם: אבל לא בחבל · דמבטל ליה התם והוי קשר של קיימא שהרי קשור ותלוי שם תמיד: ורבי יהודה מתיר · בגמרא מפרש: **גמ'** בחבל דגרדי · פליגי דצריך לה ולא מבטל לה: חבל דלי שנפסק · באמצעיתו: לא יהא קושר · דקשר של קיימא הוא לעולם: כורך עליו · מחבר שני ראשי הפיסוק זה על זה וכורך עליהם פונדא אזור חלול או פסיקיא פיישול"א: ובלבד שלא יענבנו · לחבל דר"י סבר גזרינן עניבה אטו קשירה ורבנן לא גזרו: מיחלף · אינו ניכר בין זה לזה ואי שרינן בדגרדי אתי למישרי בדעלמא: וקושרו בפרה · ראשו אחד והשני באבוס ולא חיישינן שמא כשיתיר הפרה לא יתיר אלא הקשר שבראשה ויבטל החבל באבוס שיהא מוכן לכך או יתיר שבאבוס ויבטל אותו שבפרה ונמצא האחד של קיימא: כלי קוואי · כלי אורגים ואיידי דאיירי בחבל דגרדי נקט לה הכא: מותר לטלטלן · לשני הקנים לתשמיש אחר ואשמעינן דאין גרדי מקפיד עליהם °ולא הוי מלאכתן לאיסור: כובד העליון והתחתון · אנשובל"ש: מהו · מי אמרינן איידי דיקירי לא חזו לתשמייהו לתשמיש אחרינא °והוה ליה דבר שמלאכתו לאיסור: ורפיא בידיה · רפויה היתה התשובה בפיו אם לאסור אם להתיר: העמודים · טריזו"ש בלע"ז אותם המנוקבות שאורגין בהן הגשים: דקא עביד גומא · כשחולצן מן הארץ שהן תחובות בגומא מזיז העפר ועביד גומא מקום העמוד: מקצת עליו מגולין · משום ניטלין בשבת נקט לה דאי לא הוי מגולין אין לו במה לאוחזה: אינו חושש · לפי שאינה מושרשת: ולא משום מעשר. להיות בטילה בנטיעה זו וכשנוטלה יצטרך לחזור ולעשר: לפי שאין ניטלין · אף בחול מפני כובדן הלכך כל מלאכתן לכך: **מתני'** מקפלין את הכלים · בגדים כשפושטן מקפלין מפני שמתרככין מכיבוסם ומתקמטי' כשאינן מקופלים: אפי' ד' וה' פעמים · כדי לחזור וללובשן בו ביום: מיוה"כ לשבת · כגון אם חל יוה"כ להיות בע"ש: קריבין ביוה"כ · שחל להיות במוצאי שבת: **גמ'** בשני בני אדם · כשמקפלין אותן מפשטין קמטיהן ונראין כמתקנין: ישנים · קיפולן מתקנן יותר מן החדשים שהחדשים קשין מאליהן ואין ממהרין לקמוט: צבועין · קיפולן מתקנן: יש לו · אחרים להחליף היום לא: כלי לבן שלהן · רבותא נקט וכל שכן צבועים: יש לו להחליף יחליף · מי שיש לו בגדים לבד מאותן שלבש בחול יחליפם בשבת: ישלשל בבגדיו · כלפי מטה שיראו ארוכים והוא מדת עשירים היושבים בביתם ואינם צריכים לסלק בגדיהם מן הארץ בשביל מלאכה וכבוד שבת הוא: מכבדותי · שמכבדין בעליהן: שלא יהא הילוכך כו' · לקמן מפרש להו: ממצוא חפצך · כי ההוא דאמרינן בעירובין (דף לח:) לא יטייל אדם לסוף שדהו בשבת לידע מה היא צריכה [אחר השבת]: חפצי שמים מותרים · כגון פוסקים לדקה ומשדכין על התינוקות ליארס (לקמן קנ.): שלא

תוספות

כלל אמר ר"י · תימה היכא קאי אי אמילתיה קמייתא התם מתיר לגמרי והכא קתני אין חייבין עליו משמע הא איסורא איכא כדדייק הש"ס לעיל וי"ל דה"ק כל קשר שאינו של קיימא אין חייבין עליו הא של קיימא חייבין עליו ואפי' עניבה לאפוקי מדרבנן דאמרו עניבה לאו היינו קשירה א"נ אמאי דקתני ברישא אין חייבין עליהם קאי רבי יהודה: התם חבל דעלמא הכא חבל דגרדי · וקמ"ל רב דלא גזרינן חבל דגרדי אטו חבל דעלמא וכר' יהודה א"נ אפי' רבנן מודו דאפי' בחבל דעלמא לא שכיח שיהיה קשר של קיימא כשקושרו בפרה ובאבוס ולהכי לא גזור בחבל דגרדי: מקפלים כלים כו' · מכאן למדנו דאסור לקפל טליתות של ב"ה לפי שהם צורך מחר: אבל יש לו להחליף לא · ולנו שיש לנו להחליף אסור ומספקא ר"י אי קרי יש לו להחליף כשאין לו יפה כזה: שלא

מסורת הש"ס

לעיל מז: קו: [וש"נ] ב"ק כד: ע"ז לג: פסחים יח. · פסחים שם · [עירובין נו. ע"ז: סוכה לג:] · כ"א א"ר חייא א"ר יוחנן · [לקמן קמ:] · [לקמן קנז: ב"מ יד: קידושין סה.] · כלאים פ"א מ"ט לעיל נ: עירובין עז. · [יומא מו. סוכה נד:] · [תוס' פי"ג] · ישעיה נח · ב"ק לה: סנהדרין לד: · [לקמן קנ.]

הגהות הב"ח

(א) גמ' אלא בחבל דגרדי:

עין משפט נר מצוה

יא א מיי' וסמג שם טוש"ע שם סעיף ד:
יב ב מיי' שם הלכה ב טוש"ע שם סעיף א:
יג ג מיי' שם הלכה ה טוש"ע שם סעיף ה:
יד ד ה מיי' שם הל' ג טוש"ע שם סעיף ז:
טו ו ז מיי' פכ"ו מהל' שבת הלכה א:
טז ח מיי' פכ"ג מהל' שבת הלכה ז:
יז ט מיי' פכ"ב מהל' שבת [הלכה כב] סמג לאוין סה טוש"ע א"ח סי' שב סעיף ג:
יח י מיי' פ"ל שם הל' ג ופ"ה מהל' דעות הל' ט סמג עשין ל טוש"ע א"ח סי' רסב סעיף ג:
יט כ מיי' פכ"ד שם הלכה א סמג שם ולאוין סה טוש"ע א"ח סי' שו סעיף א:
כ ל מיי' שם הל"ה טוש"ע שם סעיף ו:

רבינו חננאל

כולן אלא קתני כל הכף כולו סתמא והאי כף סתמא שאם נפסק עדיין טמא הוא ככף של תרסיות קתני והוא שבמקום העקב ומאזן לאוזן הוא סביב העקב והאי דקתני הכף שלו שאם נפסק רובו טהור הכף של סנדל שהוא מן הסנדל גופו אם ניטל רובו טהור. ואקשי' ומי סבר לה ר' יוחנן כר' יהודה והאמר ר' יוחנן הלכה כסתם משנה. ותנן סנדל שנפסקה אחת מאזניו ותיקנה טמא מדרס. מאי לאו לא שנא פנימית ול"ש חיצונה כיון דמשתריא חדא מינייהו טמא. ודחי' לא נפסקה פנימית שנינן אבל נפסקה חיצונה טהור ואמרי' אי אישתביקא בכללא אפשר לשנויי כדקאמרת. אלא מדקתני סיפא נפסק שניה ותיקנה טהור מן המדרס אבל טמא מגע מדרס דהא פריט בה ומפרש סוף מאי דאית בה ואי דוקא פנימית קתני אדמפרש אם נפסקה אח"כ שניה ותיקנה נפלוג בקמייתא וניתני בד"א שנפסקה פנימית אבל נפסקה חיצונה טהור ופרקי' אמר רב יצחק ב"ר יוסף תהא משנתנו בסנדל שיש לו ד' אזנים וד' תרסיותים ובהאי סנדל תנינן נפסקה אחת מאזניו סתם משמע אפי' חיצונית והוא כגון סנדל שיש לו ב' אזנים פנימיות זו מצד זו וב' חיצונות זו מצד זו שאם תפסק אחת מן החיצונות הא קיימא חברתא בדוכתא דהיא נמי חיצונית ובחדא פנימית וכנגדה חדא חיצונה סגיא ומשום הכי טומאתו של סנדל בדוכתא קיימא אבל היכא דליכא חיצונה אלא חדא ונפסקה בטל ההוא סנדל מתורת כלי דפנימית לחיזוק בעלמא עבידא. ודרך הסנדל אזן אחת חיצונה ואזן אחת פנימית ויש שעוש' שתים שתים אם תפסק האחת תשאר האחרת במקומה ועל זה שנינו נפסקה טמא. כי אתא רבין אמר משמיה דרב הלכה כר' יהודה ור' יוחנן אמר אין הלכה כר' יהודה ואשכחנא אמוראי נינהו ואליבא דר' יוחנן כלומר יש אמורא שאומר מדמתרץ ר' יוחנן אליבא דר' יהודה ש"מ הלכתא כר' יהודה ויש מי שאומר כי בפירוש א"ר יוחנן אין הלכה כר' יהודה ואע"ג דמספקא לן הי מנייהו דוקא כיון דאשכחנא רב יוסף דעבד עובדא כר' יהודה ורב נמי אמר הלכה כר' יהודה ורב יצחק בר יוסף נמי מתרץ וא' תהא משנתנו בסנדל שיש לו ד' אזנים וד' תרסיותים כדי שלא לשבור דבריו של ר' יוחנן עבדינן כר' יהודה: תנן כל כלי בעלי בתים שיעורן כרימונים בעי חזקיה ניקב כמוציא זית וסתמו וחזר וניקב נקב אחר דהוו נקבים זה בצד זה וכל אחד סותמו קודם שניקב הנקב האחר והוו להו כולהו במוציא רימון מי אמרינן כיון דאית בהו ככולהו שיעור רימון טהור אותו כלי מטומאתו או דלמא כיון דבעידנא דכד ניקב האי ניקבא הנקב הראשון סתום היה וכיון שנסתם כאילו לא ניקב הוא וכיוצא בה בעי בעושין פסין [כ"ד ע"א] פרץ אמה וגדרה פרץ אמה וגדרה עד שהגיע [ליותר מי'] מהו וא"ל ר' יוחנן לא שנית לנו סנדל שנפסקה אחת מאזניו ותיקנה טמא מדרס נפסקה שניה ותיקנה טהור מן המדרס אבל טמא מגע מדרס. פי' כשתפסק אחת מאזניו והוא טמא מדרס עדיין טומאתו עליו שבפסיקת אוזן אחת לא יצאה מתורת כלי ועמד ותיקנה כשתפסק השניה אע"פ שהראשונה מתוקנת היתה בשעה שנפסקה השניה בפסיקה שניה טהר מן המדרס שהיה טמא ופרחה אותה הטומאה אבל דומה כאלו נגע באותו ראשון שהיה טמא מדרס ונמצא זה השני טמא מגע מדרס ואליבא דרבנן איזו אוזן שנפסקה תחלה בין הפנימית בין החיצונית ונפסקה שניה אחריה כך דינה אבל אליבא דר' יהודה אם נפסקה החיצונית לאלתר טהור אבל אם נפסקה פנימית תחלה הרי היא כטומאתו וכשתפסק החיצונית טהור מן המדרס ולא יכלת לאוקומה הא מתני' אליבא דר' יהודה ולפום הדין פירושה דחזקיה ור' יוחנן בסנדל שיש לו ב' אזנים דקאמר מ"ש ראשונה אי מיפסקה אינו טהור דהא קיימא שניה אי אמרת חיצונה נפסקה תחלה הרי טהור מאלתר ואי אמרת פנימית נפסקה תחלה הכי [היכי] מקשי ליה שניה נמי אי מיפסקא לא לטהר דהא קיימא ראשונה ומ"ש(פנימית) [מפנימית]בדקיימא לר' יהודה אלא הכין אליבא

רב נסים גאון

דלת והנח לה שעורים תבן ומים עמד והניח לפניה שעורים תבן ומים והיתה אוכלת ושותה לפיכך אמרו כשם שהצדיקים הראשונים חסידים כך בהמתן חסידין ומעשה חמורו של ר' פנחס בן יאיר מפרש בפרק א' מן שחיטת חולין (דף ז) ר' פינחס בן יאיר הוה אזיל לפדיון שבויים כו' איקלע לההוא אושפיזא רמו שעריה להמריה ולא אכלה נקרונהו ולא אכל המושינהו לא אכל אמר להו דילמא לא מעשרן עשרונהו ואכל אמר להו עני זה הולך לעשות רצון קונו ואתם מאכילין אותו טבלין ואיתא נמי במסכת דמאי (פרק א) ובמסכת שקלים דבני מערבא (פרק ה): יש לו להחליף יחליף אין לו להחליף ישלשל בבגדיו. בבראשית דר' הושעיא (פרשה יא) משכחת לה ומפרש בתוספתא ויברך אלהים את יום השביעי ברכו בעטיפה ר' הונא אמר צריך להחליף אבין בר חסדאי אמר צריך לשלשל ר' ירמיה ור' זעירא אמרו צריך לשלשל:

ורחצת

גליון הש"ס רש"י ד"ה מותר לטלטלן ולא הוה מלאכתן לאיסור. ע"ל קכב ע"ב תד"ה רתת: שם ד"ה מהו וכו' והו"ל דבר שמלאכתו לאיסור. ע"ל קכג ע"א תד"ה כסיכי:

מסורת הש"ס

עין משפט נר מצוה

כא א מיי' פכ"ד שם הלכה ד סמג שם טוש"ע א"ח סי' שז סעיף א :
כב ב מיי' שם הלכה א סמג שם טוש"ע א"ח סי' שא סעיף ח :
כג ג (מיי') סמג שם טוש"ע א"ח סי' שא סעיף ג :
כג [ג] [מיי' שם הלכה ד טוש"ע שם סעי' א]:
כד ד טוש"ע שם סעי' א בהג"ה :

שלא יהא דבורך של שבת כדבורך של חול (א) *דבור אסור הרהור מותר בשלמא כולהו לחיי אלא שלא יהא הילוכך של שבת כהילוכך של חול מאי היא כי הא דאמר רב הונא אמר רב ואמרי ליה אמר ר' אבא אמר רב הונא היה מהלך בשבת ופגע באמת המים אם יכול להניח את רגלו ראשונה קודם שתעקר שניה מותר ואם לאו אסור מתקיף לה רבא היכי ליעביד ליקף קמפיש בהילוכא ליעבר זימנין דמיתווסן מאני מיא ואתי לידי סחיטה אלא בהא כיון דלא אפשר שפיר דמי אלא כדבעא מיניה ר' מר' ישמעאל בר' יוסי [ג] מהו לפסוע פסיעה גסה בשבת א"ל וכי בחול מי הותרה שאני אומר *פסיעה גסה נוטלת *אחד מחמש מאות ממאור עיניו של אדם ומהדר ליה בקידושא דבי שמשי בעא מיניה ר' מר' ישמעאל בר' יוסי מהו לאכול אדמה בשבת א"ל וכי בחול מי הותרה שאני אומר אף בחול אסור מפני שהוא מלקה *אמר ר' אמי כל האוכל מעפרה של בבל כאילו אוכל מבשר אבותיו וי"א כאילו אוכל שקצים ורמשים דכתיב וימח את כל היקום וגו' אמר ריש לקיש *למה נקרא שמה שנער שכל מתי מבול ננערו לשם א"ר יוחנן למה נקרא שמה מצולה שכל *מתי מבול נצטללו לשם [וי"א כאילו אוכל] שקצים ורמשים והא ודאי איתמחויי איתמחו אמרי (ב) כיון דמלקי גזרו ביה רבנן דהא ההוא גברא דאכל *גרגישתא ואכל תהלי וקדחו ליה תחליה בלביה ומית ורחצת וסכת ושמת שמלותיך א"ר אלעזר אלו בגדים של שבת תן לחכם ויחכם עוד אמר רבי אלעזר זו רות המואביה ושמואל הרמתי רות דאילו נעמי קאמרה לה ורחצת וסכת ושמת שמלותיך עליך וירדת הגורן ואילו בדידה כתיב ותרד הגורן והדר ותעש ככל אשר צותה חמותה שמואל דאילו עלי קאמר ליה שכב והיה אם יקרא אליך ואמרת דבר ה' כי שומע עבדך ואילו בדידי' כתיב ביה ויבא ה' ויתיצב ויקרא כפעם בפעם שמואל שמואל ויאמר שמואל דבר כי שומע עבדך ולא אמר דבר ה' ותלך ותבא ותלקט בשדה אמר רבי אלעזר שהלכה ובאת הלכה ובאת עד שמצאה בני אדם המהוגנין לילך עמהם ויאמר בועז לנערו הנצב על הקוצרים למי הנערה הזאת וכי דרכו של בועז לשאול בנערה אמר ר' אלעזר דבר חכמה (ג) ראה בה שני שבלין לקטה שלשה שבלין אינה לקטה במתניתא תנא דבר צניעות ראה בה עומדות מעומד נופלות מיושב וכה תדבקין עם נערותי וכי דרכו של בועז לדבק (ד) עם הנשים א"ר אלעזר כיון דחזא ותשק ערפה לחמותה ורות דבקה בה אמר שרי לאידבוקי בה ויאמר לה בועז לעת האוכל גשי הלום א"ר אלעזר רמז רמז לה עתידה מלכות בית דוד לצאת ממך דכתיב ביה הלום שנאמר ויבא המלך דוד וישב לפני ה' ויאמר מי אנכי אדני ה' ומי ביתי כי הביאתני עד הלום וטבלת פתך בחומץ א"ר אלעזר מכאן שהחומץ יפה לשרב ר' שמואל בר נחמני אמר רמז רמז לה עתיד בן לצאת ממך שמעשיו קשין כחומץ ומנו מנשה ותשב מצד הקוצרים א"ר אלעזר מצד הקוצרים ולא בתוך הקוצרים רמז רמז לה שעתידה מלכות בית דוד שתתחלק ויצבט לה קלי ותאכל אמר רבי אלעזר ותאכל בימי דוד ותשבע בימי שלמה ותותר בימי חזקיה ואיכא דאמרי ותאכל בימי דוד ובימי שלמה ותשבע בימי חזקיה ותותר בימי רבי *דאמר מר אהורידיה דרבי הוה עתיר משבור מלכא במתניתא תנא ותאכל בעולם הזה ותשבע לימות המשיח ותותר לעתיד לבא: ותחת כבודו יקד יקד כיקוד אש *א"ר יוחנן ותחת כבודו ולא כבודו ממש *ר' יוחנן לטעמיה דר' יוחנן קרי למאניה מכבדותי ר"א אומר *ותחת כבודו תחת כבודו ממש ר' שמואל בר נחמני אמר תחת כבודו כשריפת בני אהרן *מה להלן שריפת נשמה וגוף קיים אף כאן שריפת נשמה וגוף קיים א"ר אחא בר אבא אמר רבי יוחנן

מנין

[פסחים מג.]

תורה אור

רש"י

שלא יהא דבורך של שבת כדבורך של חול · כגון מקח וממכר וחשבונות : הרהור מותר · להרהר בלבו כך וכך יציאות אני צריך להוציא על שדה זו : אם יכול להניח רגלו ראשונה · שעקר מצד זה להניח לצד זה: קודם שתעקר שניה · שאין רחבה יותר מכדי פסיעה ורגלו אחת לצד זה ושניה לצד זה : מותר · אף לדלג ולעקור את זו קודם שנחה ראשונה: אסור · לקפוץ : ליקף . למקום שהאמה כלה שם : ליעבר · שישים רגלו במים : זימנין דמיתווסן מאניה · ישורו במים : שפיר דמי · לדלג : מהו לפסוע פסיעה גסה · מי עבר משום מעשות דרכיך פסיעה גסה יותר מאמה פסיעה בינונית אמה : קידושא דבי שמשי · השותה מיין של קידוש בלילי שבתות : מהו לאכול אדמה· ארזיל"א בלע"ז מי גזרו בה משום שחיקת סמנים כשאר רפואה או לא : שהיא מלקה · מביא לידי חולי : מבשר אבותיו · שמתו שם בגולה : שקצים ורמשים הא ודאי אתמחויי אתמחו ולא נעשו עפר : אלא כיון דמלקי . גזור בה משום אוכל שקצים ורמשים : קדחו ליה תחלא· נקלטו השחלים באדמה וגדלו במעיו ונגע בלבו ומת : שמלותיך · וכי ערומה היתה אלא שמלות מיוחדות והייטו דשבת : ותרד הגורן והדר ותעש · שם סכה ולבשה שמלות נאות שלא יפגשו בה כשהיא מקושטת ויאמרו זונה היא : שמואל · שהיתה שכינה קוראה לו מתוך ההיכל ולא היה יודע מי קורא לו וכתיב התם ויבן עלי כי ה' קורא לנער ויאמר לו לך שכב והיה אם יקרא אליך ואמרת דבר ה' כי שומע עבדך והוא לא רצה להזכיר השם שמא אין זו שכינה: בני אדם המהוגנין · שבקוצרים לילך עמהם : לישאל בנערה · כל נערות גברותא היה דרכו לישאל מי הן א"כ מסתכל בהן היה : שני שבלין לקטה · כשהיא רואה שני שבלין שנפלו מן הקוצרים לוקטתן אבל שלש שוכבות יחד אין לוקטתן דהכי היא מתניתין (פאה פ"ו משנה ה) שני שבלים לקט ג' אינו לקט : עומדות · שבלים עומדות שכח בועז לוקטת מעומד דשכחת קמה נמי הוי שכחה : נופלות · אותן שנשרו מן הקוצרים לוקטת מיושב ואינה שחה ליטלן משום צניעות : רמז רמז לה · רוח הקדש נזרקה בו : מצד הקוצרים · כל הקוצרים הפסיקו בינו לבינה ולא הושיבה בתוכם או אצלו רוח הקדש נזרקה בו ולרמז שמלכות בית דוד היוצאת משניהם עתידה ליחלק דאילו ישבה בתוכם לא היה זה רמז הפסקה בין שניהם : ותאכל ותשבע · לשון עושר הוא דוד שלמה וחזקיה כתיב בהן עושר שהיו מביאים להן כל מלכי ארץ מנחה : אהורידיה · ממונה על הסוסים ופרדות שלו : ותחת כבודו . איידי דאיירי בקרא בפלוגתא דרבי יוחנן ור"א ורבי שמואל בר נחמני נקטיה להאי הכא : ה"ג רבי יוחנן אומר תחת כבודו ולא כבודו ממש רבי יוחנן לטעמיה דר"י קרי למאניה מכבדותי רא"א תחת כבודו ממש ר' שמואל בר נחמני אומר תחת כבודו כשריפת בני אהרן כו' והכי פירושא בין לרבי יוחנן בין לר"א גופן נשרף אלא רבי יוחנן משמע ליה תחת כבודו כמו תחת רגליו לשון תחתית וכבודו הייטו בגדיו וה"ק תחת בגדיהם של חיילותיו של סנחריב יקד יקוד ולא בגדיהם נשרפו ור"א משמע ליה תחת לשון חליפין כמו ישלם תחת השור (שמות כא) משום דר"א לא קרי למאני' מכבדותיה לכך ע"כ כבודו הייטו גופו וה"ק כבודו ממש ישרף ותחתיו יהא אפר ושריפה כיקוד אש ורבי שמואל משמע ליה תחת כר' יוחנן וכבודו כר"א הלכך קרא כר' יוחנן מידרש ותחת כבודו נשרף ולא כבודו ממש והאי כבודו גופו הוא והלכך כשריפת בני אהרן שריפת נשמה וגוף קיים כדאמרינן בסנהדרין בד' מיתות (ד' נב:) :

מנין

תוספות

שלא יהא דבורך של שבת כדבורך של חול · פי' בקונטרס כגון מקח וממכר ואין נראה לר"ת דהא כבר נפקא ממצוא חפצך אלא אומר ר"ת כדאמר בויקרא רבה (פ' לד) ר"ש בן יוחי הוה ליה אימא סבתא דהות מישתעיא סגיא אמר לה אימא שבתא הוא שתקה משמע שאין כל כך לדבר בשבת כמו בחול ובירושלמי אמרי' בטורח התירו בשאלת שלום בשבת :

ואפילו

רבינו חננאל

דר' יוחנן איכא לאוקומה להאי בעיא כי ראשונה לר' יוחנן בסנדל שיש לו ד' אזנים וכו' סימרא באזניו החיצונות בלבד דאי מפסקא חדא סמיך על חבירתה והכי קאמר מאי שנא ראשונה דהא קיימא שניה ומקשינן שניה נמי הא מתקנא ראשונה[ודוקא]אי פסקי תרוייהו טהור . וא"ל ר' יוחנן לחזקיה דאמרת לן פנים חדשות באו לכאן כיון דתרווייהו איפסיקו בתר דאיפסקי ליה אע"ג דהדא חדא איתקנא ההוא [תקנתא] חדש הוא וכמאן דליתיה דמי והכא נמי לענין כל כלי בעלי בתים כיון שנקבן נקבין הרבה עד שהגיע לשיעור הוצאת רמון אע"ג דמיתקני כיון דפנים חדשות אתקינו טהור והכין נמי לענין פרץ אמה וגדרה כו' ואמר חזקיה על ר' יוחנן לית לן בר אינש אלא מלאך הוא אימא דאמר כגון דין בר אינש ומאן דליתיה הכי כבהמה הוא כנגד זה : קיטרי נודות יין ושמן אע"ג דאית ליה ב' אוני שרי ליה להתירן לתרווייהו ולא אמרינן דחד מינייהו בטלה וכן קדירה של תבשיל מותר להתירה ואע"ג דאית ליה שלבא . פי' כגון דדי הכיור שמקלחין מים אע"ג דיכול לאודוקי המרק מן השלבא מותר להתירה : קושרין דלי בפיסקיא . שהוא אבנט מפני שאינו קשר קיימא אבל לא בחבל. אוקימנא בחבל הגרדי ומשום גזירה. ור' יהודה מתיר סבר חבל דגרדי אי קטיר ליה בדלי קשר של עראי הוא ולאורתא שרי ליה מן הדלי משום דבעי ליה למלאכתו . לפי' כיון שאינו קשר של קיימא שרי ולא גזרי חבל דגרדי אטו חבל דעלמא ורמינן עלה [מי גזרי רבנן אטו חבל דגרדי] (אי ניגרדי רבנן) הא תנן חבל דלי שנפסק לא היה קשרו אלא עונבו . ר' יהודה אומר כורך עליו פונדא וכו' ולא קא גזרו רבנן עניבה אטו קשירה · ושנינן קשירת חבל הגרדי בחבל דעלמא מיחלף לפיכך גזרינן אבל עניבה בקשירה הכירא רבה היא לפיכך לא גזרינן. לר' יהודה נמי דאסר בעניבה לאו משום דגזר עניבה אטו קשירה אלא משום דסבר עניבה קשירה מעולה היא . והאי דאמרי' בלולב הגזול כו' ובפרק המוצא תפילין דר' יהודה סבר עניבה קשירה מעולה היא הכא עיקרה ודרבא נמי תימא בחבל דגרדי דמתח ביה . דלא קטר ליה קשר של קיימא : כלי קיואי הן כלי אומנות . הארוג כגון האבנט והככר שהיריעה תלויה בו מלמעלה והככר שפשוטה עליו מלמטה מותר לטלטלו בשבת אבל העמודים התקועין בארץ אע"פ שכשעוקרן אינו מתכוין לעשות גומא והגומא ממילא קא מתגליא אעפ"כ אסור לטלו בשבת גזירה דילמא אתי לאשווי גומות ואע"ג כי הלפת וצנון הטמונים תחת הגפן אם היו מקצת עלין מגולין ניטלין בשבת ולא גזרינן דילמא אתי לאשווי גומות התם שדה ולא איכפת ליה בגומות לפיכך לא גזרינן אבל בית דקפיד בגומא גזרינן דילמא אתי לאשווי גומות. אדם אחד מקפל כלים מלילי שבת לשבת ובשבת מצפרא לפניא ולשבת אחרת אבל שנים אין מקפלין כלי אחד דהוה ליה כמעשה אומן ואחד נמי אינו מקפל אלא כלים חדשים אבל ישנים לא דקיפולן מחזירן כחדשים ונמצאת כי היא מלאכה וצבועים נמי פאכה (צבועים) [ציביעיה] בדלא מקפלן משום הכי כמלאכה היא חשוב וכי אמרינן שמקפל אדם מתחלת יום שבת לסופו בשאין לו בגדים אחרים להחליף אבל יש לו להחליף אינו מקפל: דיבור שאסור בשבת מפורש בפרק שואל אדם מחבירו ודר' זירא אמר רב ואמרינן לה א"ר אבא אמר רב הונא אירחיא לה מדרבא והיכא דלא ניחא ליה לאקיפי דלא לאפושי הילוכא ולא ניחא ליה למיעבר במיא דלא ליתוסי מאניה ואתי לידי סחיטה קפיץ ליה לאמת המים ושרי אלא אוקימנא שלא יהא הילוכך של שבת כהילוכך של חול אלא כדי [שניה] ראשונה קודם שתיעקר שניה ולא יהא מנהגו שיהיו פסיעותיו גסות בשבת. פי' רבב כגון קירא והילקוסתא הנודע בבבל הלב ונפטא וזפת וכיוצא בהם :

הגהות הב"ח

(א) גמרא כדיבורך של חול דבר דבור אסור: (ב) שם איתמחויי איתמחו אלא כיון: (ג) שם אמר ר' אליעזר דבר חכמה. נ"ב פירוש דבר הלכה וכן איתא בפרק בתרא דנדה דף סט ע"ב שלשה דברי חכמה ומפרש הלכה: (ד) שם דרכו של בועז (לדבק) תא"מ ונ"ב ס"א לדבר :

[לקמן קנ.]
ברכות מג: תענית ז:
[זבחים קיג:]
פי' טיט נקי [ע' פרש"י יבמות קו: ובב"מ מ. ד"ה גרגישתא ובפרש"י כתובות ס: ד"ה גרגישתא]
ב"מ פה.
סנהדרין לד.
סנהדרין שם
[ב"ק לא:]
[סנהדרין לד: וע"ש ומגלה ליבנ]
[סנהדרין נב:]

רב נסים גאון

ורחצת וסכת ושמת שמלותיך אמר ר' אלעזר אלו כלים של שבת. בגמ' דפיאה גרסי בני מערבא (פרק ח) אמר ר' חנינא צריך אדם שיהא לו שני עיטופין אחד לחול ואחד לשבת מה טעם שנאמר (רות ג) ושמת שמלותיך עליך וכי ערומה היית אלא אלו בגדי שבת כדדרש ר' שמלאי בציבורא בכון חבריא לקיבולה אמרו ליה ווי לנא כעטיפתנו בחול כך עטיפתנו בשבת אמר להם אעפ"כ אתם צריכין לשנות: מה שריפת בני אהרן שריפת נשמה וגוף קיים . משכחת לה בסנהדרין בפרק ד' מיתות (דף נב) תניא אבא יוסי בן (ראסי) [דוסתאי] אומר ב' חוטין של אש יצאו מבית קודש הקדשים ונחלקו לד' ונכנסו ב' בחוטמו של זה וב' בחוטמו של זה ושרפום והכתיב (ויקרא י) ותאכל אותם אותם ולא בגדיהם :

[113b] that thy speech [conversation] on the Sabbath should not be like thy speech on weekdays.[5] *'Speaking'*: speech is forbidden, but thought [about mundane matters] is permitted. Now, as for all [the rest], they are intelligible; but what is meant by, 'that thy walking on the Sabbath shall not be like thy walking on weekdays'?—As R. Huna said in Rab's name—others state, R. Abba said in R. Huna's name: If one is walking on the Sabbath and comes to a stream of water, if he can put down his first foot[6] before lifting the second,[7] it is permitted;[8] otherwise it is forbidden.[9] Raba demurred: What shall he do? Shall he go round it? Then he increases the walking [distance]![10] Shall he cross it [walking through]? His garments may be soaked in water and he is led to wringing [them] out![11] Rather [in such a case], since it is impossible [otherwise], it is permitted [to jump across]. But [what is meant][12] is as Rabbi asked R. Ishmael son of R. Jose: Is it permitted to take great strides on the Sabbath?[13]—Who then permitted it on weekdays? he replied; for I maintain that a long stride takes away a five hundredth part of a man's eyesight,[14] and it is restored to him by the evening *Kiddush*.[15]

Rabbi asked R. Ishmael son of R. Jose: May one eat earth on the
a Sabbath?[1]—Who then permitted it on weekdays? he replied. For I maintain, It is forbidden even on weekdays, because it causes illness.

R. Ammi said: He who eats earth of Babylon is as though he ate the flesh of his ancestors;[2] some say, It is as though he ate of abominations and creeping things, because it is written, *And he dissolved every living thing*, etc.[3] Resh Lakish said, Why is it [Babylon] called Shinar? Because all the dead of the Deluge were shaken out [deposited] thither [*nin'aru lesham*]. R. Johanan said: Why was it called *Mezulah* [depth]? Because all the dead[4] of the Deluge were dumped[5] there.

'Some say, It is as though he ate of abominations and creeping things.' But these were certainly completely dissolved?[6] Rather because they cause illness the Rabbis forbade them. For a certain man ate *gargishta*[7] and [then] ate cress, and the cress sprouted up into his heart[8] and he died.

Wash thyself therefore, and anoint thee, and put thy raiment upon thee.[9] R. Eleazar said: This refers to the Sabbath garments. *Give instructions to a wise man, and he will be yet wiser.*[10] R. Eleazar said: This alludes to Ruth the Moabitess and Samuel of Ramah.[11] 'Ruth'—for whereas Naomi said to her, *Wash thyself therefore, and anoint thee, and put thy raiment upon thee, and get thee down to the threshing-floor;* yet of her it is written, *And she went down unto the threshing-floor,* and [only] subsequently, *and did according to all that her mother-in-law bade her.*[12] 'Samuel': for whereas Eli said to him, *Lie down: and it shall be, if He call thee, that thou shalt say, Speak, Lord, for Thy servant heareth;*[13] yet of him it is written, *And the Lord came, and stood, and called as at other times, Samuel, Samuel. Then Samuel said,*
b *Speak; for Thy servant heareth,*[1] but he did not say, Speak, Lord.[2]

And she went and came and gleaned in the field.[3] R. Eleazar said:

(5) E.g., business talk is forbidden. (6) On the other side of the stream. (7) From this side of the stream—i.e., he can negotiate the stream in a single stride. (8) Even to jump across. (9) To jump across. (10) Which is more tiring and certainly not preferable on the Sabbath. (11) Which is forbidden. (12) By 'that thy walking on the Sabbath, etc.' (13) Or does it not seem in keeping with the restfulness that should characterize the Sabbath. (14) Lit., 'the light of a man's eyes'. (15) By drinking the wine of *Kiddush*, q.v. Glos.

a (1) Is the chewing of earth, perhaps as a cure, so similar to the crushing of medicinal ingredients, that it is forbidden just as is the latter? (2) Who died there. (3) Gen. VII, 23. It is now assumed that they became earth. (4) Var. lec.: waters. (5) Or, sunk—*niztallelu*. (6) They did not become earth. (7) A certain reddish clay. (8) It took root and grew in the *gargishta*. (9) Ruth III, 3. (10) Prov. IX, 9. (11) I.e., the prophet. (12) Ruth III, 6.—She reversed the order, lest she be met on the way thus adorned, and suspected of being a harlot. (13) I Sam. III, 9.

b (1) I Sam. III, 10. (2) Being uncertain if it was God's voice. (3) Ruth II, 3.

◁ *For the continuation of the English translation of this page see overleaf.*

בא אמיי' פכ"ד שם הלכה ד סמג שם טוש"ע א"ח סי' שו סעיף א:
בב ב מיי' שם הלכה א סמג שם טוש"ע א"ח סי' שו סעיף ח:
בג ג (מיי') סמג שם טוש"ע א"ח סי' שא סעיף ג:
בג [ג] [מיי' שם הלכה ד טוש"ע שם סעי' א]:
בד ד טוש"ע שם סעי' א בהג"ה:

שלא יהא דבורך של שבת כדבורך של
חול (א) *דבור אסור הרהור מותר בשלמא
כולהו לחיי אלא שלא יהא הילוכך של
שבת כהילוכך של חול מאי היא כי הא
דאמר רב הונא אמר רב ואמרי ליה אמר ר'
אבא אמר רב הונא היה מהלך בשבת
ופגע באמת המים אם יכול להניח את רגלו
ראשונה קודם שתעקר שניה מותר ואם
לאו אסור מתקיף לה רבא היכי ליעביד
ליקף קמפיש בהילוכא ליעבר זימנין
דמיתווסן מאני מיא ואתי לידי סחיטה
אלא גהא כיון דלא אפשר שפיר דמי אלא כדבעא מיניה ר' מר'
ישמעאל בר' יוסי [ג] מהו לפסוע פסיעה גסה בשבת דא"ל וכי בחול מי
הותרה שאני אומר *פסיעה גסה נוטלת *אחד מחמש מאות ממאור עיניו
של אדם ומהדר ליה בקידושא דבי שמשי בעא מיניה ר' מר' ישמעאל
בר' יוסי מהו לאכול אדמה בשבת א"ל וכי בחול מי הותרה שאני אומר
אף בחול אסור מפני שהוא מלקה *אמר ר' אמי כל האוכל מעפרה של
בבל כאילו אוכל מבשר אבותיו וי"א כאילו אוכל שקצים ורמשים דכתיב
°וימח את כל היקום וגו' אמר ריש לקיש *למה נקרא שמה שנער שכל מתי
מבול ננערו לשם א"ר יוחנן למה נקרא שמה מצולה שכל *מתי מבול
נצטללו לשם [וי"א כאילו אוכל] שקצים ורמשים והא ודאי איתמחויי איתמחו
אמרי (ב) כיון דמלקי גזרו ביה רבנן דהא ההוא גברא דאכל *גרגישתא ואכל
תחלי וקדחו ליה תחליה בלביה ומית °ורחצת וסכת ושמת שמלותיך א"ר
אלעזר אלו בגדים של שבת °תן לחכם ויחכם עוד אמר רבי אלעזר זו
רות המואביה ושמואל הרמתי רות דאילו נעמי קאמרה לה ורחצת וסכת
ושמת שמלותיך עליך וירדת הגורן ואילו בדידה כתיב ותרד הגורן והדר
ותעש ככל אשר צותה חמותה שמואל דאילו עלי קאמר ליה °שכב
והיה אם יקרא אליך ואמרת דבר ה' כי שומע עבדך ואילו בדידי' כתיב
ביה ויבא ה' ויתיצב ויקרא כפעם בפעם שמואל שמואל ויאמר שמואל דבר
כי שומע עבדך ולא אמר דבר ה' °ותלך ותבא ותלקט בשדה אמר רבי
אלעזר שהלכה ובאת הלכה ובאת עד שמצאה בני אדם המהוגנין לילך
עמהם °ויאמר בועז לנערו הנצב על הקוצרים למי הנערה הזאת וכי דרכו
של בועז לשאול בנערה אמר ר' אלעזר דבר חכמה (ג) ראה בה שני שבלין
לקטה שלשה שבלין אינה לקטה במתניתא תנא דבר צניעות ראה בה
עומדות מעומד נופלות מיושב °וכה תדבקין עם נערותי וכי דרכו של
בועז לדבק (ד) עם הנשים א"ר אלעזר כיון דחזא °ותשק ערפה לחמותה ורות
דבקה בה אמר שרי לאידבוקי בה °ויאמר לה בועז לעת האוכל גשי
הלום א"ר אלעזר רמז רמז לה עתידה מלכות בית דוד לצאת ממך דכתיב
ביה הלום שנאמר °ויבא המלך דוד וישב לפני ה' ויאמר מי אנכי אדני
ה' ומי ביתי כי הביאתני עד הלום °וטבלת פתך בחומץ א"ר אלעזר
מכאן שהחומץ יפה לשרב ר' שמואל בר נחמני אמר רמז רמז לה עתיד
בן לצאת ממך שמעשיו קשין כחומץ ומנו מנשה °ותשב מצד הקוצרים
א"ר אלעזר מצד הקוצרים ולא בתוך הקוצרים רמז רמז לה שעתידה
מלכות בית דוד שתתחלק °ויצבט לה קלי ותאכל אמר רבי אלעזר ותאכל
בימי דוד ותשבע בימי שלמה ותותר בימי חזקיה ואיכא דאמרי ותאכל
בימי דוד ובימי שלמה ותשבע בימי חזקיה ותותר בימי רבי *דאמר מר
אהוריריה דרבי הוה עתיר משבור מלכא במתניתא תנא ותאכל בעולם הזה
ותשבע לימות המשיח ותותר לעתיד לבא: °ותחת כבודו יקד יקוד כיקוד
אש *א"ר יוחנן ותחת כבודו ולא כבודו ממש *ר' יוחנן לטעמיה דר' יוחנן
קרי למאניה מכבדותי ר"א אומר *ותחת כבודו תחת כבודו ממש ר' שמואל
בר נחמני אמר תחת כבודו כשריפת בני אהרן *מה להלן שריפת נשמה וגוף
קיים אף כאן שריפת נשמה וגוף קיים א"ר אחא בר אבא אמר רבי יוחנן
מנין

שלא יהא דבורך של שבת כדבורך של חול · פי' בקונטרס כגון מקח וממכר ואין נראה לר"ת דהא כבר נפקא ממצוא חפצך אלא אומר ר"ת כדאמר בויקרא רבה (פ' לד) ר"ש בן יוחי הוה ליה אימא סבתא דהות מישתעיא סגיא אמר לה אימא שבתא הוא שתקה משמע שאין כל כך לדבר בשבת כמו בחול ובירושל' אמרי' בטורח התירו בשאלת שלום בשבת: ואפילו

שלא יהא דבורך של שבת כדבורך של חול · כגון מקח וממכר וחשבונות : הרהור מותר · להרהר בלבו כך וכך יליאות אני לריך להוליא על שדה זו : אם יכול להניח רגלו ראשונה · שעקר מצד זה להניח לצד זה: קודם שתעקר שניה · שאין רחבה יותר מכדי פסיעה ורגלו אחת לצד זה ושניה לצד זה : מותר · אף לדלג ולעקור את זו קודם שנחה ראשונה: אסור · לקפוץ : ליקף . למקום שהאמה כלה שם : ליעבר · שישים רגלו במים : זימנין דמיתווסן מאניה · ישורו במים : שפיר דמי · לדלג : מהו לפסוע פסיעה גסה · מי עבר משום מעשות דרכיך פסיעה גסה יותר מאמה פסיעה ביטונית אמה : קידושא דבי שמשי · השותה מיין של קידוש בלילי שבתות : מהו לאכול אדמה · ארזיל"א בלע"ז מי גזרו בה משום שחיקת סמנים כשאר רפואה או לא : שהיא מלקה · מביא לידי חולי : מבשר אבותיו · שמתו שם בגולה : שקצים ורמשים הא ודאי אתמחויי אתמחו ולא נעשו עפר : אלא כיון דמלקי . גזור בה משום אוכל שקצים ורמשים : קדחו ליה תחלה · נקלטו השחלים באדמה וגדלו במעיו ונגע בלבו ומת : שמלותיך · וכי ערומה היתה אלא שמלות מיוחדות והיינו דשבת : ותרד הגורן והדר ותעש · שם סכה ולבשה שמלות נאות שלא יפגעו בה כשהיא מקושטת ויאמרו זונה היא : שמואל · שהיתה שכינה קוראה לו מתוך ההיכל ולא היה יודע מי קורא לו וכתיב התם ויבן עלי כי ה' קורא לנער ויאמר לו לך שכב והיה אם יקרא אליך ואמרת דבר ה' כי שומע עבדך והוא לא רצה להזכיר השם שמא אין זו שכינה: בני אדם המהוגנין · שבקוצרים לילך עמהם : לישאל בנערה · כל נערות שרואה היה דרכו לישאל מי הן א"כ מסתכל בהן היה : שני שבלין לקטה · כשהיא רואה שני שבלין שנפלו מן הקוצרים לוקטתן אבל שלש שוכבות יחד אין לוקטתן דהכי היא מתניתין (פאה פ"ו משנה ה) שני שבלים לקט ג' אינו לקט : עומדות · שבלים עומדות ששכח בועז לוקטת מעומד דשכחת קמה נמי הוי שכחה : נופלות · אותן שנשרו מן הקוצרים לוקטת מיושב ואינה שחה ליטלן משום צניעות : רמז רמז לה · רוח הקדש נזרקה בו : מצד הקוצרים · כל הקוצרים הפסיקו בינו לבינה ולא הושיבה בתוכם או אלנו רוח הקדש נזרקה בו ולרמז שמלכות בית דוד היוצאת משניהם עתידה ליחלק דאילו ישבה בתוכם לא היה זה רמז הפסקה בין שניהם : ותאכל ותשבע · לשון עושר הוא דוד שלמה וחזקיה כתיב בהן עושר שהיו מביאים להן כל מלכי ארץ מנחה : אהוריריה · ממונה על הסוסים ופרדות שלו : ותחת כבודו . איידי דאיירי בקרא בפלוגתא דרבי יוחנן ור"א ורבי שמואל בר נחמני נקטיה להאי הכא : ה"ג רבי יוחנן אומר תחת כבודו ולא כבודו ממש רבי יוחנן לטעמיה דר"י קרי למאניה מכבדותי ר"א תחת כבודו ממש ר' שמואל בר נחמני אומר תחת כבודו כשריפת בני אהרן כו' והכי פירושא בין לרבי יוחנן בין לר"א גופן נשרף אלא רבי יוחנן משמע ליה תחת כבודו כמו תחת רגליו לשון תחתית וכבודו הייטו בגדיו וה"ק תחת בגדיהם של חיילותיו של סנחריב יקוד יקוד ולא בגדיהם נשרפו ור"א משמע ליה תחת לשון חליפין כמו ישלם תחת השור (שמות כא) משום דר"א לא קרי למאני' מכבדותיה לכך ע"כ כבודו הייטו גופו וה"ק כבודו ממש ישרף ותחתיו יהא אפר ושריפה כיקוד אש ורבי שמואל משמע ליה תחת כר' יוחנן וכבודו כר"א הלכך קרא כר' יוחנן מידרש ותחת כבודו נשרף ולא כבודו ממש והאי כבודו גופו הוא והלכך כשריפת בני אהרן שריפת נשמה וגוף קיים כדאמרינן בסנהדרין בד' מיתות (ד' נב:) :

רבינו חננאל

דר' יוחנן איכא לאוקומה להאי בעיא כי ראשונה לר' יוחנן בסנדל שיש לו ד' אזנים וכו' סימרא באזניו החיצונות בלבד דאי מפסקא חדא סמיך על חבירתה והכי קאמר מאי שנא ראשונה דהא קיימא שניה ומקשינן שניה נמי הא מתקנא ראשונה [ודוקא] אי פסקי תרוייהו טהור . וא"ל ר' יוחנן לחזקיה דאמרת לן פנים חדשות באו' לכאן כיון דתרווייהו איפסיקו בתר דאיטמי ליה אע"ג דהדרא חדא איתקנא ההוא [תקנתא] חדש הוא וכמאן דליתיה דמי והכא נמי לענין כל כלי בעלי בתים כיון שנקבן נקבין הרבה עד שהגיע לשיעור הוצאת רמון אע"ג דמיתקני כיון דפנים חדשות אתקינו טהור והכין נמי לענין פרק אשה ונדרה כו' ואמר חזקיה על ר' יוחנן לית לן בר אינש אלא מלאך הוא אימא דאמר כגון דין בר אינש ומאן דליתיה הכי כבהמה הוא כנגד זה : קיטרי נודות יין ושמן אע"ג דאית ליה ב' אוני שרי ליה להתירן לתרווייהו ולא אמרינן דחד מינייהו בטלה וכן קדירה של תבשיל מותר להתירה ואע"ג דאית ליה שלבא . פי' כגון דדי הכיור שמקלחין מים אע"ג דיכול לאודוקי המרק מן השלבא מותר להתירה : קושרין דלי בפיסקיא . שהוא אבנט מפני שאינו קשר קיימא אבל לא בחבל. אוקימנא בחבל הגרדי ומשום גזירה. ור' יהודה מתיר סבר חבל דגרדי אי קפיר ליה בדלי קשר של עראי הוא ולאורתא שרי ליה מן הדלי משום דבעי ליה למלאכתו . לפי' כיון שאינו קשר של קיימא שרי ולא גזרי חבל דגרדי אטו חבל דעלמא ורמינן עלה [מי גזרי רבנן אטו חבל דגרדי] (אינידגרדי רבנן) הא תנן חבל דלי שנפסק לא היה קשרו אלא עונבו . ר' יהודה אומר כורך עליו פונדא וכו' ולא קא גזרו רבנן עניבה אטו קשירה · ושנינן קשירת חבל הגרדי בחבל דעלמא מיחלף לפיכך גזרינן אבל עניבה בקשירה הכירא רבה היא לפיכך לא גזרינן.לר' יהודה נמי דאסר בעניבה לאו משום דגזר עניבה אטו קשירה אלא משום דסבר עניבה קשירה: מעולה היא . והאי דאמרי' בלולב הגזול כו' ובפרק המוצא תפילין דר' יהודה סבר עניבה קשירה מעולה היא הכא עיקרה ודרבא נמי תימא בחבל דגרדי דסתח ביה . דלא קטר ליה קשר של קיימא : **כלי** קיואי הן כלי אומנות . האורג כגון האכסן והככר שהיריעה תלויה בו מלמעלה והככר שפשוטה עליו מלמטה מותר לטלטלו בשבת אבל העמודים התקועין בארץ אע"פ שכשעוקרן אינו מתכוין לעשות גומא והגומא ממילא קא מתגליא אעפ"כ אסור לטלו בשבת גזירה דילמא אתי לאשווי גומות ואע"ג כי הלפת וצנון הטמונים תחת הגפן אם היו מקצת עלין מגולין ניטלין בשבת ולא גזרינן דילמא אתי לאשוויי גומות התם שדה ולא איכפת ליה בגומות לפיכך לא גזרינן אבל בית דקפיד בגומא גזרינן דילמא אתי לאשוויי גומות. אדם אחד מקפל כלים מלילי שבת לשבת ובשבת מצפרא לפניא ולשבת אחרת אבל שנים אין מקפלין כלי אחד דהוה ליה כמעשה אומן ואחד נמי אינו מקפל אלא כלים חדשים אבל ישנים לא דקיפולן מחזירן כחדשים ונמצאת כי היא מלאכה וצבועים נמי פאכה (צבועים)[ציבעיה] בדלא מקפלן משום הכי כמלאכה היא חשוב וכי אמרינן שמקפל אדם מתחלת יום שבת לסופו בשאין לו בגדים אחרים להחליף אבל יש לו להחליף אינו מקפל: **דיבור** שאסור בשבת מפורש בפרק שואל אדם מחבירו ודר' זירא אמר רב ואמרינן לה א"ר אבא אמר רב הונא אידחיא לה מדרבא והיכא דלא ניחא ליה לאקיפי דלא לאפושי הילוכא ולא ניחא ליה למיעבר במיא דלא ליתוסי מאניה ואתי לידי סחיטה קפיץ ליה לאמת המים ושרי אלא אוקימנא שלא יהא הילוכך של שבת כהילוכך של חול אלא כדי [שיניח] ראשונה קודם שתיעקר שניה ולא יהא מנהגו שיהיו פסיעותיו גסות בשבת . פי' רבב נכון קירא והילקוסתא הנודע בבבל הלב ונפטא וזפת וכיוצא בהם :

רב נסים גאון

ורחצת וסכת ושמת שמלותיך אמר ר' אלעזר אלו כלים של שבת.בגמ' דפיאה גרסי בני מערבא(פרק ח) אמר ר' חנינא צריך אדם שיהא לו שני עיטופין אחד לחול ואחר לשבת מה טעם שנאמר (רות ג) ושמת שמלותיך עליך וכי ערומה היית אלא אלו בגדי שבת כדדרש ר' שמלאי בציבורא בכון חבריא לקיבלוה אמרו ליה ויי לנא כעטיפתנו בחול כך עטיפתנו בשבת אמר להם אעפ"כ אתם צריכין לשנות: **מה** שריפת בני אהרן שריפת נשמה וגוף קיים . משכחת לה בסנהדרין בפרק ד' מיתות (דף נב) תניא אבא יוסי בן (ראסי) [דוסתאי] אומר ב' חוטין של אש יצאו מבית קודש הקדשים ונחלקו לד' ונכנסו ב' בחוטמו של זה וב' בחוטמו של זה ושרפוה והכתיב (ויקרא י) ותאכל אותם אותם ולא בגדיהם :

[לקמן קנ.]
ברכות מג: תענית י:
[זבחים קיג:]
[שם ע"ש פלוגתא דר"י ור"ל מהופך]
פי' ערך נקי [ע' פרש"י יבמות קו: ובב"מ מ. ד"ה גרגישתא ובפרש"י כתובות ס: ד"ה גרגישתא]
ב"מ פה.
סנהדרין לד.
סנהדרין נב.
[ב"ק לא:]
[סנהדרין נב:]

הגהות הב"ח

(א) גמרא כדיבורך של חול דבר דבור אסור: (ב) שם איתמחויי איתמחו אלא כיון: (ג) שם אמר ר' אליעזר דבר חכמה. נ"ב פירוש דבר הלכה וכן איתא בפרק בתרא דנדה דף סט ע"ב שלשה דברי חכמה ומפרש הלכה: (ד) שם דרכו של בועז (לדבק) תא"מ ונ"ב ס"א לדבר :

Continuation of translation from previous page as indicated by ◁

She repeatedly went and came until she found decent men whom to accompany. *Then said Boaz unto his servant that was set over the reapers, whose damsel is this?*[4] Was it then Boaz's practice to enquire about damsels?[5]—Said R. Eleazar: He perceived a wise dealing[6] in her behaviour, two ears of corn[7] she gleaned; three ears of corn she did not glean.[8] A Baraitha taught: He perceived modest behaviour in her, the standing ears[9] [she gleaned] standing; the fallen [she gleaned] sitting. *And cleave here by my maidens:*[10] was it then Boaz's practice to cleave[11] to the women?[12]—Said R. Eleazar, As soon as he saw that, *'and Orpah kissed her mother-in-law; but Ruth cleaved unto her,'*[13] he said, It is permitted to cleave unto her. *And at meal-time Boaz said unto her, Come hither:*[14] Said R. Eleazar, He intimated to her,[15] The royal house of David is destined to come forth from thee, [the house] whereof *'hither'* is written, as it is said, *Then David the king went in, and sat before the Lord; and he said, Who am I, O Lord God, and what is my house, that Thou hast brought me hither?*[16]

And dip thy morsel in vinegar.[17] R. Eleazar said: Hence [it may be deduced] that vinegar is beneficial in hot weather. R. Samuel b. Naḥmani said: He intimated to her, A son is destined to come forth from thee whose actions shall be as sharp[18] as vinegar; and who was it, Manasseh. *And she sat beside the reapers:*[19] R. Eleazar observed: At the side of the reapers, but not in the midst of the reapers: he [Boaz] intimated to her[20] that the Kingdom of the
c House of David was destined to be divided.[1] *And he reached her parched corn, and she did eat [and was sufficed, and left thereof]:*[2] Said R. Eleazar: *'She ate'* in the days of David, *'she was sufficed'* in the days of Solomon, *'and she left over'* in the days of Hezekiah.[3] Some there are who interpret, *'She ate'* in the days of David and Solomon, and *'she was sufficed'* in the days of Hezekiah, *'and she left over'* in the days of Rabbi.[4] For a Master said, Rabbi's house steward was wealthier than King Shapur.[5] In a Baraitha it was taught: *'And she ate'*, in this world; *'and she was sufficed'*, in the days of the Messiah: *'and she left over'*, in the future that is to come.[6]

And beneath his glory shall he kindle a burning like the burning of a fire.[7] R. Joḥanan said: That which is *'beneath'* his glory [shall be burnt], but 'glory' is not literal.[8] R. Joḥanan is consistent with his opinion, for R. Joḥanan called his garments 'my honourers'. R. Eleazar said, *'and beneath his glory'* means literally instead of his glory.[9] R. Samuel b. Naḥmani interpreted: *'And beneath his glory'* [must be understood] like the burning of the sons of Aaron; just as there the burning of the soul [is meant], while the body remained intact,[10] so here too, the burning of the soul, while the body remains intact.[11]

(4) Ibid. 5. (5) Surely he did not ask about every maiden gleaning in the field! (6) Lit., 'a matter of wisdom'. BaḤ, quoting Nid. 69*b*, translates: a knowledge (lit., 'matter of *halachah*'). (7) That fell from the reapers. (8) In accordance with the law stated in Pe'ah VI, 5.—This fact attracted his attention. (9) Which the reapers forgot to cut down; these belong to the poor. (10) Ruth II, 8. (11) Var. lec.: speak. (12) The question as based on the verse is not clear, v. Maharsha. (13) Ibid. I, 14. (14) Ibid. II, 14. (15) Under the action of the Holy Spirit. (16) II Sam. VII, 18. E.V.: *'thus far'*; Heb. in both verses, *halom*. (17) Ruth II, 14. (18) Lit., 'hard', 'grievous'. (19) Ibid. (20) By seating her thus.

c (1) Just as the reapers made a division between her and him. (2) Ruth II, 14. (3) This metaphorically indicates the progressive stages of prosperity during the reigns of these three monarchs. (4) R. Judah the Prince, who was a descendant of the House of David. (5) Shapur I, King of Persia and a contemporary of Samuel (third century). (6) Cf. Sanh., 90*a*, n. d3. (7) Isa. X, 16. (8) For the literal meaning of *'glory'* in reference to a man is his body, the flesh which gives him his beauty; hence beneath his *'glory'* would have to mean his soul, which R. Joḥanan regards as unsuited to the context. Therefore *'glory'* must refer to his garments, which dignify him, whilst *'beneath his glory'* denotes the body. (9) *Taḥath* means both 'beneath' and 'instead'. He too maintains that the body shall be burnt and translates, instead of his glory—*sc.* his body—there shall be the ashes to which it is reduced. (10) V. Sanh. 52*a*. (11) He translates *taḥath* 'beneath', like R. Joḥanan, and *'glory'* his body, like R. Eleazar, and hence arrives at this conclusion.—In Sanh. 94*a* R. Eleazar's view and R. Samuel b. Naḥmani's are combined.

R. Aḥa b. Abba said in R. Joḥanan's name: [114a] Whence do
a we learn change of garments[1] in the Torah? Because it is said, *And he shall put off his garments, and put on other garments,*[2] and the School of R. Ishmael taught: The Torah teaches you manners: In the garments in which one cooked a dish for his master, one should not mix a cup [of wine] for his master.[3]

R. Ḥiyya b. Abba said in R. Joḥanan's name: It is a disgrace for a scholar to go out with patched shoes into the market place. But R. Aḥa b. Ḥanina did go out [thus]?—Said R. Aḥa son of R. Naḥman: The reference is to patches upon patches. R. Ḥiyya b. Abba also said in R. Joḥanan's name: Any scholar upon whose garment a [grease] stain is found is worthy of death,[4] for it is said, *All they that hate me* [mesanne'ai] *love* [merit] *death:*[5] read not *mesanne'ai* but *masni'ai* [that make me hated, i.e., despised].[6] Rabina said: This was stated about a thick patch.[7] Yet they do not differ: one refers to the upper garment [coat], the other to a shirt.

R. Ḥiyya b. Abba also said in R. Joḥanan's name: What is meant by the verse, *Like as my servant Isaiah hath walked naked and barefoot?*[8] '*Naked*' means in worn-out garments; '*barefoot*' in patched shoes.

We learnt elsewhere: A grease stain upon a saddle constitutes an interposition.[9] R. Simeon b. Gamaliel said: [The inferior limit is] as much as an Italian *issar.*[10] On garments: [if the stain is] on one side, it does not interpose; [if] on both sides,[11] it interposes. R. Judah said in R. Ishmael's name: Even on one side it interposes.[12] R. Simeon b. Lakish asked R. Ḥanina: In the case of a saddle,
b [can the stain be] on one side, or [must it be] on both sides?[1] I have not heard this, he replied, but have heard something similar. For we learnt, R. Jose said: [The garments] of *banna'im:* [a stain even] on one side [interposes]; of uncultured persons, [only a stain] on both sides [interposes].[2] And surely a saddle does not stand higher than the garment of an ignoramus![3] What are *banna'im?*—Said R. Joḥanan: These are scholars, who are engaged all their days in the upbuilding of the world.[4]

R. Joḥanan also said: Who is the scholar to whom a lost article is returned on his recognition thereof?[5] That [scholar] who is particular to turn his shirt.[6] R. Joḥanan also said: Who is the scholar that is appointed a leader of the community? He who when asked a matter of *halachah* in any place can answer it, even

a (1) As an act of honour. (2) Lev. VI, 4. (3) In Talmudic times liquor was diluted with water. (4) This expression merely denotes strong indignation—a scholar should set a high standard of cleanliness. (5) Prov. VIII, 36. The speaker is learning personified. (6) For a scholar who has no pride in his personal appearance brings contempt upon his learning. (7) Jast.; v. however, Rashi. (8) Isa. XX, 3. (9) When an article is unclean and requires *ṭebillah* (v. Glos.), nothing may interpose between it and the water; otherwise the *ṭebillah* is invalid. With respect to stains, etc., if one generally objects to them, they are an interposition; if not, they are not an interposition. A grease stain belongs to the former category. (10) A certain coin. The stain must be at least that size for it to interpose. (11) The greasiness having soaked through. (12) V. Kel. IX, 5, 6.

b (1) In R. Ishmael's view. (2) The former are more fastidious than the latter. R. Jose disagrees with R. Judah and maintains that according to R. Ishmael a stain on the garments of *banna'im* (explained below as meaning scholars) interposes even if it is on one side only.—This passage is cited to show that scholars must be particular. (3) I.e., an uncultured person. On '*am ha-areẓ* v. *supra* 13*a*, n. a1. (4) *Banna'im*, lit. means builders. Frankel, *Zeitschrift für die Religiösen Interessen des Judentums'*, 1846 p. 455 maintains that the term *banna'im* was originally applied to the Essenes.—Ignorance is the greatest enemy of stability, but it should be noted that the phrase (disciple of the wise) (*talmid ḥakam*) always denoted scholarship plus piety. (5) Lit., 'on impression of the eye'. The ordinary person in claiming a lost article must state identification marks, but a scholar is believed if he simply states that he recognizes it; B.M. 23*b*. (6) For the seams and rough edges to be on the inside. It appears that not all were particular about this.

◁ *For the continuation of the English translation of this page see overleaf.*

מנין לשנוי בגדים מן התורה שנא' ופשט את בגדיו ולבש בגדים אחרים *ותנא דבי רבי ישמעאל לימדך תורה דרך ארץ בגדים שבישל בהן קדירה לרבו אל ימזוג בהן כוס לרבו *אמר רבי חייא בר אבא אמר רבי יוחנן גנאי הוא לת"ח שיצא במנעלים המטולאים לשוק והא רבי אחא בר חנינא נפיק אמר רבי אחא בריה דרב נחמן בטלאי על גב טלאי (א) ואמר רבי חייא בר אבא אמר ר' יוחנן כל תלמיד חכם שנמצא רבב על בגדו חייב מיתה שנאמר כל משנאי אהבו מות *אל תקרי משנאי אלא משניאי רבינא אמר רבד איתמר ולא פליגי הא בגלימא הא בלבושא ואמר רבי חייא בר אבא אמר ר' יוחנן מאי דכתיב כאשר הלך עבדי ישעיהו *ערום ויחף ערום בבגדים בלואים ויחף במנעלים המטולאים *תנן התם רבב על המרדע חוצץ רשב"ג אומר עד כאיסר האיטלקי ועל הבגדים מצד אחד אינו חוצץ משני צדדין חוצץ רבי יהודה אומר משום רבי ישמעאל אף מצד אחד חוצץ בעא מיניה רבי שמעון בן לקיש מר' חנינא מרדעת מצד אחד או משני צדדין אמר ליה זו לא שמעתי כיוצא בה שמעתי דתנן* רבי יוסי אומר של בנאין מצד אחד ושל בור משני צדדין ולא תהא מרדעת חשובה מבגדו של עם הארץ מאי בנאין אמר רבי יוחנן אלו תלמידי חכמים שעוסקין בבנינו של עולם כל ימיהן ואמר רבי יוחנן איזהו תלמיד חכם שמחזירין לו אבידה בטביעות העין זה המקפיד על חלוקו להופכו ואמר רבי יוחנן *איזהו ת"ח שממנין אותו פרנס על הציבור *זה ששואלין אותו דבר הלכה בכל מקום ואומר ואפי' במסכת כלה *ואמר רבי יוחנן איזהו ת"ח שבני עירו מצווין לעשות לו מלאכתו זה שמניח חפצו ועוסק בחפצי שמים והנ"מ למיטרח בריפתיה ואמר רבי יוחנן איזהו תלמיד חכם כל ששואלין אותו הלכה בכל מקום ואומרה למאי נפקא מינה למנוייה פרנס על הציבור אי בחדא מסכתא באתריה אי בכוליה תנויה בריש מתיבתא ר' שמעון ב"ל אמר *אלו כלים האוליירין הבאין ממדינת הים למימרא דחיורי נינהו והאמר להו רבי ינאי לבניו בני אל תקברוני לא בכלים לבנים ולא בכלים שחורים לבנים שמא לא אזכה ואהיה כחתן בין אבלים שחורים שמא אזכה ואהיה כאבל בין חתנים אלא בכלים האוליירין הבאין ממדינת הים אלמא סומקי נינהו לא קשיא הא בגלימי הא בלבושי: ר' ישמעאל אומר מקפלין כו': ת"ר עולת שבת בשבתו*) לימד על חלבי שבת שקריבין ביום הכיפורים יכול אף של יוה"כ בשבת ת"ל בשבתו דברי רבי ישמעאל ר' עקיבא אומר עולת שבת בשבתו לימד על *חלבי שבת שקרבים ביו"ט יכול אף ביוה"כ ת"ל בשבתו כשתמצא לומר לדברי רבי ישמעאל נדרים ונדבות קריבין ביו"ט וכי איצטריך קרא ליוה"כ לדברי ר"ע *נדרים ונדבות אין קרבין ביו"ט וכי איצטריך קרא למישרא בי"ט אמר ר' זירא כי

*) [נ"ל בשבת וכ"א בסמוך לקמן במילתיה דרבי עקיבא והוי"ט העתיק ת"ר עולת שבת לימד וכו']

רש"י

מנין לשינוי בגדים. שהוא דרך כבוד לפני המקום: ולבש בגדים אחרים. והוציא את הדשן הזקיקו הכתוב ללבוש בגדים פחותים בשעת הוצאת הדשן שאינה עבודה חשובה כדי שלא ימאסו בגדיו החשובים שעובד בהן עבודת אכילה ושתיה כגון קיטור וניסוך: ותנא דבי ר' ישמעאל. בדרשא דהאי קרא: בגדים שבישל בהם קדירה לרבו. דומיא דהוצאת הדשן: אל ימזוג בהם כוס לרבו. לפיכך הוזקק ללבוש בגדים פחותים: רבב. שומן וחלב: חייב מיתה. שצריך להיות חשוב והגון לכבוד תורתו: משניאי. שממאסין עצמן בעיני הבריות והבריות אומרים אוי להם ללומדי התורה שהם מאוסים ומגונים נמצא זה משניא את התורה: רבד איתמר. שכבת זרע *לשון מרבדים רבדתי ערשי (משלי ז) ריפדתיו וקישטתיו בבשמים מינים המכניסים תאוה ותזקק לי: בגלימא. שהוא עליון אפי' רבב: בלבוש. שהוא תחתון רבד אין רבב לא: על המרדעת. של חמור: חוצץ. כל דבר חוצץ לענין טבילה(ב) דקפיד עליה וכל חציצה שמקפיד עליו חוצצת: תנן התם. במסכת מקוואות ונקט לה (ג) משום דבעי למימר של בנאים כו' לומר שדרך תלמיד חכם מקפיד על לבושיו: משני לצדדין. שהיה בו הרבה עד שנבלע בבגד ונראה לצד שני: מרדעת מצד אחד או מב' לצדדין. לר' ישמעאל דאמר בבגד מצד אחד מרדעת מאי אמר בה: ר' יוסי אומר של בנאים. פליג אדר' יהודה ואמר לר' ישמעאל בגד של בנאים דהיינו תלמידי חכמים שמקפידין על לבושיהן מצד אחד ושל בור מב' לצדדין: שמחזירים לו אבדה בטביעות עין. כיון שאמר אני מכירה אע"פ שאינו נותן בה סימן כדאמר באלו מציאות (ב"מ כג:): המקפיד על חלוקו להופכו. לובשו כשהוא הפוך מקפיד עליו והופכו שמקפיד עליו שלא יראו התפירות המגונות ואימרי החלוק: בכל מקום. בכל הש"ס ואפי' במסכת כלה דלא רגילי בה אינשי וזה נתן לבו וגרסה מסכת כלה ברייתא היא כלה בלא ברכה אסורה לבעלה כנדה: ת"ח שבני עירו מצווין לעשות מלאכתו. כדאמר בפרק ז' דיומא (דף עב:) כתוב א' אומר ועשית לך ארון עץ וכתוב אחד אומר ועשו ארון עצי שטים וגו': למיטרח בריפתיה. דבר שאינו יכול לטרוח בו וחייו תלויין בו: אם יודע להשיב במסכת שהוא עוסק בה ממנים אותו פרנס באתריה: ואם בכולי תנויה. דקאי בהא מסכת ומהדר במסכת אחריתי: אלו כלים האוליירין. הא דתנן בנאין מצד אחד היינו כלים של אוליירין בלנים שיש להם אלונטיאות חשובות להתעטף בהם בני אדם חשובים בצאתם מן המרחץ ומקפידים על טינוף מעט ובנאים לשון בי בני (לעיל דף לג:): למימרא דחיורי נינהו. מדמקפידין על רבב שעליהם דאילו סומקי לא מיגנו בטינוף פורתא: שמא לא אזכה. ואשב בין אותן שנדונין בגיהנם שרומין *לשולי קדירה: גלימי. סומקי: חלבי שבת. כגון אברי תמיד של בין הערבים קריבים במוצאי שבת והוא יום הכפורים: עולת שבת בשבתו. משמע למידרש בלא וי"ו ומשמע דעולת שבת קריבה בשבת אחרת לימד על חלבי שבת כו': יכול אף של יוה"כ בשבת ת"ל בשבתו. וי"ו מיעוטו הוא בשבתו ולא בשבת אחרת: שקריבים בי"ט. שחל להיות במוצאי שבת: נדרים ונדבות· פלוגתא היא במסכת ביצה (דף יט.) ור' ישמעאל סבירא ליה כמאן דאמר קריבין הלכך כיון דנדרים ונדבות שיכול להמתין ולשחטן בחול ולהקריבן נשחטים ונקרבין ביום טוב קל וחומר בחלבי שבת שנשחטו כדרכן בזמנן וניתותרו הלכך לא איצטריך קרא עולת שבת בשבתו אלא ליום הכפורים:

תוספות

ואפילו במסכת כלה. פי' בקונט' דלא רגילי בה אינשי והוא נתן לבו לגורסה ובקדושין פי' לגריעותא בפרק האיש מקדש (דף מט:) גבי ע"ת שאני תלמיד (ד) אין אומרים כשמעון בן עזאי וכשמעון בן זומא אלא כל ששואלין אותו דבר הלכה ואפי' במסכת כלה ופי' בקונטרס אפי' במס' כלה שהיא קלה ונראה דהכא משמע (ואומר) דנקט ליה משום חשיבות שיודע אפי' במסכת כלה דלא רגילי בה אינשי ראוי למנותו פרנס אבל התם קתני דבר אחד מתלמודו משמע אפי' לא למד אלא מסכת כלה ואמר הימנה דבר אחד הרי זה חכם ומיהו בפירוש רש"י דקידושין וכן בפי' רבינו חננאל אין כתוב בהן דבר אחד מתלמודו ורבינו יצחק מפרש דהאי מסכת כלה הייינו דרשות הסדורות מהלכות החג כדאמרינן בלא יחפור (ב"ב כב.) רב נחמן בר יצחק ריש כלה הוה וקאמר איזהו ת"ח שראוי למנותו על הציבור באתריה כדאמר בסמוך במסכתי' באתריה כגון שיודע להשיב בכל מקום שישאלוהו באותה מסכת אפי' במס' כלה שרגילין בה ראוי למנותו בעירו אבל בכיר מהכי אין ראוי למנותו והא דהוצרך לתנור ולהשמיענו בסמוך אי במסכתיה באתריה אע"ג דכבר השמיענו כאן לפי שרוצה לחלק בין מסכת לכוליה הש"ס *והשתא הוי דהכא כי ההוא דקידושין (דף מט:):

הא בלבושא הא בגלימא. הא דר' ינאי בגלימא כדמשמע בפ' כל היד (נדה דף כ.) גבי שחור כחרת ור' יוחנן אמר אלו כלים האוליירין הבאין ממדינת הים למימרא דאוכמי נינהו והאמר ר' ינאי כו' לא קשיא הא בגלימא הא בפתורי דר' ינאי בגלימא דהיא סומקי דשחורים לא הוו כדמסיק הכא אבל פתורי הוו אוכמי ולבושא חיורי:

חלבי שבת קריבין ביוה"כ. אומר ר"י דכל היכא דקתני תרי שבי דהוו בהדי הדדי אתיא כאחרים דאמרי אין בין עצרת לעצרת אלא ד' ימים בלבד והכי מפרש הש"ס בפ' בתרא דסוכה (דף נד:):

ליתקע

עין משפט נר מצוה

כה א ב מיי' פ"ה מהל' דעות הלכה ט ופ"ה מהלכות יסודי התורה הלכה יא:

כו ג מיי' פ"ג מהלכות מקוואות הלכה ד סמג עשין רמח:

כז ד מיי' שם הלכה ג:

כח ה טוש"ע חו"מ סי' רסב סעיף כא:

כט ו טוש"ע או"ח סימן קלו בהג"ה:

ל ז טוש"ע יו"ד סימן רמג סעיף א ב:

לא ח מיי' פ"א מהל' תמידין ומוספין הלכה ז סמג עשין קפ:

לב ט מיי' פ"א מהלכות חגיגה הלכה ח י:

רבינו חננאל

ת"ח שנמצא רבב על בשרו חשוב כמשניאי התורה שאין ב"א דבקי' בו שלא יתלכלך מלבושם ממנו. רבד מל' מרבדים רבדתי ערשי. פי' דם יבש כדגרסי' בנדה פ' תינוקת ריבדא דכוסילתא. אמר רמי בר אבא האי ריבדא דכוסילתא עד ג' יומין לא חייץ מכאן ואילך חייץ. כל תלמיד שנמצא דם על בגדו מכוער הוא שמא יראה ככתם. וזה הדבר אם הוא בטלית שמתכסה בה העליונה הרי זה מכוער אבל אם הוא שמציע תחתיו (או) [אולי] דם מאכולת הוא אפשר דלא הוה לי' טלית אחרת וגנא בה. כדתניא התם הרגה מאכולת תולה לא הרגה אינה תולה דברי ר' שמעון בן גמליאל. וחכ"א בין הרגה בין לא הרגה תולה. ארשב"ג לדבריי אין (סוף)[קץ] לדבריהם אין סוף לדברי אין קץ שאין אשה טהור' לבעלה שאין מטה אלא שיש עליה כמה טיפי דמים לדבריהם אין סוף וכו'. תנן התם במקוואות פ' ט' אלו חוצצין בכלים הזפת והמור כו' עד על המרדעת חוצץ כו' רבב זהו ממיני זפת הא דתניא בסיפא דהא מתניתין ר' יוסי אומר של בנאין מצד א' חוצץ כו' פי' ר' יוחנן בנאין אלו ת"ח שעוסקין בבניינו של עולם וקפדי על רבב שעל בגדיהן לכבסו ולהוציאו כדי שלא יהו מן המשניאין לפיכך אפילו בצד אחד נראה חוצץ ולא עלתה לו טבילה אבל בגדי הבורים אם עבר מצד לצד חוצץ ואם לאו אינו חוצץ וכן הלכה: וא"ר יוחנן איזהו ת"ח כל שמחזירין לו אבידה בטביעות עין זה המקפיד על חלוקו להופכו וכן אמרו איזהו ת"ח שממנין אותו פרנס על הצבור זה ששואלין אותו דבר הלכה בכל מקום ואומרה ואיזהו שבני עירו מצווין לעשות מלאכתו מי שמניח חפציו ועוסק בחפצי שמים ר"ל אמר בנאין אלו אוליירין הבאים ממדינת הים. ואקשי' למימר דכלי אוליירין חיורי נינהו שהזפת מצד אחד נודע בהן. והאמר ר' ינאי לבניה אל תקברוני בלבנים ולא בשחורים אלא באוליירין אלמא סומקי נינהו. ושנינן המלבושים לבנים הן כגון מני כסותא. והגלימא כגון מאני דמתעטפי בהן סומקי הוו: ר' (שמעון) [ישמעאל] סבר חלבין שנתותרו ביוה"כ קריבין בשבת אבל שנתותרו מן השבת אין קריבין ביוה"כ. ור' עקיבא סבר לא של שבת קריבין ביוה"כ ולא של יוה"כ בשבת. ונרסינן ביומא בפרק א"ר אלעזר משום בר קפרא. אומר היה ר"מ איברי עולת חול שניתותרו עושה להן מערכה וסודרן אפילו בשבת. ואמרינן למאי איצטריך אפילו בשבת הא הנינא והיום חמש. א"ר אחא בר יעקב איצטריך אטינא הני מילי היכא דחל יוה"כ למיהוי אחר השבת דחלבי שבת קריבין ביוה"כ אבל באמצע שבת אימא לא קמ"ל: אמר רבא [האי] מאן [דלא] חש לקמחיה בכל יום תנו

מסורת הש"ס

ויקרא ו · משלי ח · ישעיה כ · במדבר כח

לקמן קיט. [יומא כג:] · כתובות מג: ע"ש · [ברי"ף פי' דם יבש וכתב הר"ן שהוא מלשון ריבדא דכוסילתא מ"ק כח. ועי' בערוך ערך רבב] · [עי' יומא פו.] · מקוואות פ"ט משנה ה' ו' · [שם במשנה] · תענית י: · קידושין מט: · יומא עב: · דף כ. · [פסחים נח. ביצה יט. כ: סנהדרין נו.] · [עי' תוס' לעיל כד: ד"ה ולא]

הגהות הב"ח

(א) גמ' בטלאי על גבי טלאי וה"מ בפנתא אבל בגילדא לית לן בה ואמר ר' חייא: (ב) רש"י ד"ה חוצץ וכו' לענין טבילה היכא דקפיד: (ג) ד"ה תנן התם וכו' ונקט לה הכא משום: (ד) תוס' ד"ה ואפילו וכו' שאני תלמיד חכם אין:

רב נסים גאון

גנאי הוא לתלמידי חכמים שיצאו במנעלים המטולאים · במס' ברכות בפרק כיצד מברכין על הפירות (דף מג) תנו רבנן ששה דברים גנאי לתלמיד חכם אל יצא כשהוא מבושם לשוק ואל יצא יחידי בלילה ואל יצא במנעלים המטולאים בשוק[וכו']: תנן התם על המרדעת חוצץ. עיקר זאת המשנה בפרק ט' ממס' מקואות אלו חוצצין בכלים הזפת והמור כו' על המרדעת חוצץ רבן שמעון בן גמליאל אומר עד

גליון הש"ס תוס' ד"ה ואפילו כו' והשתא הוי דהכא כי ההוא דקידושין · ועי' תשב"ץ ח"א סימן לג:

Continuation of translation from previous page as indicated by ◁

in the Tractate Kallah.[7] R. Joḥanan also said: Who is the scholar whose work it is the duty of his townspeople to perform?[8] He who abandons his own interest and engages in religious affairs; yet that is only to provide[9] his bread.[10]

R. Joḥanan also said: Who is a scholar? He who is asked a *halachah* in any place and can state it. In respect of what practical matter?—To appoint him a leader of the community: if [he is well-versed only] in one Tractate, [he can be appointed] in his own
c town; if in the whole [field of] learning,[1] [he can be appointed] as the head of an academy.[2]

R. Simeon b. Laḳish said: This means[3] the court robes [*olaryin*][4] that come from overseas. Shall we say that they are white? But R. Jannai said to his sons, 'My sons, bury me neither in white shrouds nor in black shrouds. White, lest I do not merit,[5] and am like a bridegroom among mourners: black, in case I have merit, and am like a mourner among bridegrooms. But [bury me] in court garments [*olaryin*] that come from overseas. This proves that they are coloured.—There is no difficulty: one refers to robes,[6] the other to shirts.[7]

R. ISHMAEL SAID: ONE MAY FOLD UP, etc. Our Rabbis taught: *The burnt-offering of the Sabbath, on the Sabbath thereof:*[8] this teaches concerning the fats of the Sabbath, that they may be offered [burnt] on the Day of Atonement. One might think, Those of the Day of Atonement [can] also [be burnt] on the Sabbath, therefore it is stated, '*on the Sabbath thereof*': this is R. Ishmael's opinion. R. Akiba said: '*The burnt-offering of the Sabbath on the Sabbath thereof*': this teaches concerning the fats of the Sabbath, that they can be offered on a Festival.[9] One might think, On the Day of Atonement too, therefore it is stated, '*on the Sabbath thereof.*'
d When you examine the matter,[1] according to R. Ishmael's opinion, vows[2] and freewill-offerings[3] may be sacrificed on a Festival, hence the verse is required in respect of the Day of Atonement.[4] [But] on the view of R. Akiba, vows and freewill-offerings cannot be sacrificed on a Festival; hence the verse is required to permit [the burning of the fats on] Festivals.

(7) A short tractate of that name. Rashi: Though this is not generally studied. Others: the laws of Festivals (*Kallah* was the name given to the general assemblies in Elul and Adar, when the laws of the Festivals were popularly expounded). V. Kid., 49*b*, nn. a3-4. (8) V. Yoma 72*b*; cf. Aboth III, 5 and note a.l. in Sonc. ed. The present passage supports the thirteenth century interpretation quoted there, and suggests that it was similarly interpreted in Talmudic ages too. (9) Lit., 'take trouble over'. (10) I.e., he can only demand the necessities of existence.

c (1) Jast. the Mishnah, [Kaplan, J. op. cit. p. 250 understands this as a technical term denoting the summary embodying conclusions arrived at in schools as a result of the discussions based on the Mishnah]. (2) It may be observed that it is automatically assumed that the leader of a community must be a scholar, for Jewry sought to promote an aristocracy of learning, not of birth. Cf. Halevi, *Doroth*, I, 3, pp. 640 *seq*. (3) Resh Laḳish gives his definition of the garments of '*banna'im*'. (4) Jast. Rashi reads: *olyarim* (from Gk. ὀλεάριος): costly wraps used by wealthy persons at the baths. (5) To be amongst the righteous. (6) Upper garments, which were coloured. (7) Or, chemises. These were white. (8) Num. XXVIII, 10. This is interpreted with and without the 'thereof' (the suffix ו). Thus: (i) The burnt-offering of one Sabbath may be completed (i.e., its fat burnt on the altar) on another Sabbath; (ii) The burnt-offering of one Sabbath must be completed on that self-same Sabbath. In this connection it must be observed that the Day of Atonement too is designated Sabbath in Lev. XXIII, 32. (9) Following the Sabbath.

d (1) Lit., 'when you find to say'. (2) I.e., vowed sacrifices. (3) For the difference v. R.H. 6*a*. Both, of course, are voluntary sacrifices. (4) For if even voluntary offerings, which can be brought on weekdays, may be sacrificed on a Festival, it goes without saying that fats left over from the obligatory public sacrifices of the Sabbath can be burnt in the evening, even if it is a Festival, and no verse is necessary to teach this. Consequently the verse must be referred to the Day of Atonement.

°מניין לשנוי בגדים מן התורה שנא' °ופשט את בגדיו ולבש בגדים אחרים *ותנא דבי רבי ישמעאל לימדך תורה דרך ארץ בגדים שבישל בהן קדירה לרבו אל ימזוג בהן כוס לרבו *אמר רבי חייא בר אבא אמר רבי יוחנן *גנאי הוא לת"ח שיצא במנעלים המטולאים לשוק והא רבי אחא בר חנינא נפיק אמר רבי אחא בריה דרב נחמן בטלאי על גב טלאי (א) ואמר רבי חייא בר אבא אמר ר' יוחנן כל תלמיד חכם שנמצא °רבב על בגדו חייב מיתה שנאמר °כל משנאי אהבו מות *אל תקרי משנאי אלא משניאי רבינא אמר רבד איתמר ולא פליגי הא בגלימא הא בלבושא ואמר רבי חייא בר אבא אמר ר' יוחנן מאי דכתיב °כאשר הלך עבדי ישעיהו *ערום ויחף ערום בבגדים בלואים ויחף במנעלים המטולאים *תנן התם רבב על המרדע חוצץ רשב"ג אומר עד כאיסר האיטלקי ועל הבגדים מצד אחד אינו חוצץ משני צדדין חוצץ רבי יהודה אומר משום רבי ישמעאל אף מצד אחד חוצץ בעא מיניה רבי שמעון בן לקיש מר' חנינא מרדעת מצד אחד או משני צדדין אמר ליה זו לא שמעתי כיוצא בה שמעתי דתנן* רבי יוסי אומר של בנאין מצד אחד ושל בור משני צדדין ולא תהא מרדעת חשובה מבגדו של עם הארץ מאי בנאין אמר רבי יוחנן אלו תלמידי חכמים שעוסקין בבנינו של עולם כל ימיהן ואמר רבי יוחנן איזהו תלמיד חכם שמחזירין לו אבידה בטביעות העין זה המקפיד על חלוקו להופכו ואמר רבי יוחנן *איזהו ת"ח שממנין אותו פרנס על הציבור *זה ששואלין אותו דבר הלכה בכל מקום ואומר ואפי' במסכת כלה *ואמר רבי יוחנן איזהו ת"ח שבני עירו מצווין לעשות לו מלאכתו זה שמניח חפצו ועוסק בחפצי שמים והנ"מ למיטרח בריפתיה ואמר רבי יוחנן איזהו תלמיד חכם כל ששואלין אותו הלכה בכל מקום ואומרה למאי נפקא מינה למנוייה פרנס על הציבור אי בחדא מסכתא באתריה אי בכוליה תנויה בריש מתיבתא ר' שמעון ב"ל אמר *אלו כלים האוליירין הבאין ממדינת הים למימרא דחיורי נינהו והאמר להו רבי ינאי לבניו בני אל תקברוני לא בכלים לבנים ולא בכלים שחורים לבנים שמא לא אזכה ואהיה כחתן בין אבלים שחורים שמא אזכה ואהיה כאבל בין חתנים אלא בכלים האוליירין הבאין ממדינת הים אלמא סומקי נינהו לא קשיא הא בגלימי הא בלבושי:

ר' ישמעאל אומר מקפלין כו': ת"ר °עולת שבת בשבתו*) לימד על חלבי שבת שקריבין ביום הכיפורים יכול אף של יוה"כ בשבת ת"ל בשבתו דברי רבי ישמעאל ר' עקיבא אומר עולת שבת בשבתו לימד על *חלבי שבת שקרבים ביו"ט יכול אף ביוה"כ ת"ל בשבתו כשתמצא לומר לדברי רבי ישמעאל נדרים ונדבות קריבין ביו"ט וכי איצטריך קרא ליוה"כ לדברי ר"ע *נדרים ונדבות אין קרבין ביו"ט וכי איצטריך קרא למישרא בי"ט אמר ר' זירא

כי

*) [נ"ל בשבת וכ"א בסמוך לקמן במילתיה דרבי עקיבא והוי"ט העתיק ת"ר עולת שבת לימד וכו']

רש"י

מניין לשינוי בגדים. שהוא דרך כבוד לפני המקום: ולבש בגדים אחרים. והוציא את הדשן הזקיקו הכתוב ללבוש בגדים פחותים בשעת הוצאת הדשן שאינה עבודה חשובה כדי שלא ימאסו בגדיו החשובים שעובד בהן עבודת אכילה ושתיה כגון קיטור וניסוך: ותנא דבי ר' ישמעאל. בדרשא דהאי קרא: בגדים שבישל בהם קדירה לרבו. דומיא דהוצאת הדשן: אל ימזוג בהם כוס לרבו. לפיכך הוזקק ללבוש בגדים פחותים: רבב. שומן וחלב: חייב מיתה. שצריך להיות חשוב והגון לכבוד תורתו: משניאי. שממאסין עצמן בעיני הבריות והבריות אומרים אוי להם ללומדי התורה שהם מאוסים ומגונים נמצא זה משניא את התורה: רבד איתמר. שכבת זרע *לשון מרבדים רבדתי ערשי (משלי ז) ריפדתיו וקישטתיו בבשמים מינים המכניסים תאוה ותזקק לי: בגלימא. שהוא עליון אפי' רבב: בלבוש. שהוא תחתון רבד אין רבב לא: על המרדעת. של חמור: חוצץ. כל דבר חוצץ לענין טבילה(ב) דקפיד עליה וכל חציצה שמקפיד עליו חוצצת: תנן התם. במסכת מקוואות ונקט לה (ג) משום דבעי למימר של בנאים כו' לומר שדרך תלמיד חכם מקפיד על לבושיו: משני צדדין. שהיה בו הרבה עד שנבלע בבגד ונראה לצד שני: מרדעת מצד אחד או מב' צדדין. לר' ישמעאל דאמר בבגד מצד אחד מרדעת מאי אמר בה: ר' יוסי אומר של בנאים. פליג אדר' יהודה ואמר לר' ישמעאל בגד של בנאים דהיינו תלמידי חכמים שמקפידין על לבושיהן מצד אחד ושל בור מב' צדדין: שמחזירים לו אבדה בטביעות עין. כיון שאמר אני מכירה אע"פ שאינו נותן בה סימן כדאמר באלו מציאות (ב"מ כג:): המקפיד על חלוקו להופכו. לובשו כשהוא הפוך מקפיד עליו והופכו שמקפיד עליו שלא יראו התפירות המגונות ואימרי החלוק: בכל מקום. בכל הש"ס ואפי' במסכת כלה דלא רגילי בה אינשי וזה נתן לבו וגרסה מסכת כלה ברייתא היא כלה בלא ברכה אסורה לבעלה כנדה: ת"ח שבני עירו מצווין לעשות מלאכתו. כדאמר בפרק ז' דיומא (דף עב:) כתוב א' אומר ועשית לך ארון עץ וכתוב אחד אומר ועשו ארון עצי שטים וגו': למיטרח בריפתיה. דבר שאינו יכול לטרוח בו וחייו תלויין בו: אם יודע להשיב במסכת שהוא עוסק בה ממנים אותו פרנס באתריה: ואם בכולי הגויה. דקאי בהא מסכת ומהדר במסכת אחריתי: אלו כלים האוליירין. הא דתנן בנאין מצד אחד היינו כלים של אוליירין בלנים שיש להם אלונטיאות חשובות להתעטף בהם בני אדם חשובים בצאתם מן המרחץ ומקפידים על טינוף מעט ובנאים לשון בי בני (לעיל דף לג:): למימרא דחורי ניהו. מדמקפידין על רבב שעליהם דאילו סומקי לא מינכר בהו טינוף פורתא: שמא לא אזכה. ואשב בין אותן שנדונין בגיהנם שרומין *לשולי קדירה: גלימי. סומקי: חלבי שבת. כגון אברי תמיד של בין הערבים קריבים במוצאי שבת והוא יום הכפורים: עולת שבת בשבתו. משמע למידרש בלא וי"ו ומשמע דעולת שבת קריבה בשבת אחרת לימד על חלבי שבת כו': יכול אף של יוה"כ בשבת ת"ל בשבתו. וי"ו מיעוטו הוא בשבתו ולא בשבת אחרת: שקריבים בי"ט. שחל להיות במוצאי שבת: נדרים ונדבות. פלוגתא היא במסכת ביצה (דף יט.) ור' ישמעאל סבירא ליה כמאן דאמר קריבין הלכך כיון דנדרים ונדבות שיכול להמתין ולשחטן בחול ולהקריבן נשחטים ונקרבין ביום טוב קל וחומר בחלבי שבת שנשחטו כדרכן בזמנן וניתותרו הלכך לא איצטריך קרא עולת שבת בשבתו אלא ליום הכפורים:

כי

תוספות

ואפילו במסכת כלה. פי' בקונט' דלא רגילי בה אינשי והוא נתן בלבו לגורסה ובקדושין פי' לגריעותא בפרק האיש מקדש (דף מט:) גבי ע"מ שאני תלמיד (ד) אין אומרים כשמעון בן עזאי וכשמעון בן זומא אלא כל ששואלין אותו דבר הלכה ואפי' במסכת כלה ופי' בקונטרס אפי' במס' כלה שהיא קלה ונראה דהכא משמע (ואומר) דנקט ליה משום חשיבות שיודע אפי' במסכת כלה דלא רגילי בה אינשי ראוי למנותו פרנס אבל התם קתני דבר אחד מתלמודו משמע אפי' לא למד אלא מסכת כלה ואמר הימנה דבר אחד הרי זה חכם ומיהו בפירוש רש"י דקידושין וכן בפי' רבינו חננאל אין כתוב בהן דבר אחד מתלמודו ורבינו יצחק מפרש דהאי מסכת כלה היינו דרשות הסדורות מהלכות החג כדאמרינן בלא יחפור (ב"ב כב.) רב נחמן בר יצחק ריש כלה הוה וקאמר איזהו ת"ח שראוי למנותו על הציבור באתריה כדאמר בסמוך במסכתי' באתריה כגון שיודע להשיב בכל מקום שישאלוהו באותה מסכת אפי' במס' כלה שרגילין בה ראוי למנותו בעירו אבל בציר מהכי אין ראוי למנותו והא דהוצרך לחזור ולהשמיענו בסמוך אי במסכתיה באתריה אע"ג דכבר השמיענו כאן לפי שרוצה לחלק בין מסכת לכוליה הש"ס °והשתא הוי דהכא כי ההוא דקידושין (דף מט:):

הא בלבושא הא בגלימא. הא דר' ינאי בגלימא כדמשמע בפ' כל היד (נדה דף כ.) גבי שחור כהרת ור' יוחנן אמר אלו כלים האוליירין הבאין ממדינת הים למימרא דאוכמי ניכהו והאמר ר' ינאי כו' לא קשיא הא בגלימא הא בפתורי דר' ינאי בגלימא דהיא סומקי דשחורים לא הוו כדמסיק הכא אבל פתורי הוו אוכמי ולבושא חיורי:

*חלבי שבת קריבין ביוה"כ. אומר ר"י דכל היכא דקתני תרי שבי דהוו בהדי הדדי אתיא כאחרים דאמרי אין בין עצרת לעצרת אלא ד' ימים בלבד והכי מפרש הש"ס בפ' בתרא דסוכה (דף נד:):

ליתקע

עין משפט נר מצוה

כה א ב מיי' פ"ה מהל' דעות הלכה ט ופ"ה מהלכות יסודי התורה הלכה יא:
כו ג מיי' פ"ג מהלכות מקוואות הלכה ד סמג עשין רמח:
כז ד מיי' שם הלכה ג:
כח ה טוש"ע חו"מ סי' רסב סעיף כא:
כט ו טוש"ע או"ח סימן קלו בהג"ה:
ל ז טוש"ע יו"ד סימן רמג סעיף א ב:
לא ח מיי' פ"א מהל' תמידין ומוספין הלכה ז סמג עשין קפ:
לב ט מיי' פ"א מהלכות חגיגה הלכה ח י:

רבינו חננאל

ת"ח שנמצא רבב על בשרו חשוב כמשניאי התורה שאין ב"א דבק' בו שלא יתלכלך מלבושם ממנו. רבד מל' מרבדים רבדתי ערשי. פי' דם יבש כדגרסי' בנדה פ' תינוקת ריבדא דכוסילתא. אמר רמי בר אבא האי ריבדא דכוסילתא עד ג' יומין לא חייץ מכאן ואילך חייץ. כל תלמיד שנמצא דם על בגדו מכוער הוא שמא יראה ככתם. וזה הדבר אם הוא בטלית שמתכסה בה העליונה הרי זה מכוער אבל אם הוא שמציע תחתיו (או) [אולי] דם מאכולת הוא אפשר דלא הוה לי' טלית אחרת וגנא בה. כדתניא התם הרגה מאכולת תולה לא הרגה אינה תולה דברי ר' שמעון בן גמליאל. וחכ"א בין הרגה בין לא הרגה תולה. ארשב"ג לדברי אין(סוף)[קץ] לדבריהם אין סוף לדברי אין קץ שאין אשה טהור' לבעלה שאין מטה אלא שיש עליה כמה טיפי דמים לדבריהם אין סוף וכו'. תנן התם במקוואות פ' ט' אלו חוצצין בכלים הזפת והמור כו' עד על המרדעת חוצץ כו' רבב זהו מטיני ופת הא דתניא בסיפא דהא מתניתין ר' יוסי אומר של בנאין מצד א' חוצץ כו' פי' ר' יוחנן בנאין אלו ת"ח שעוסקין בבניינו של עולם וקפדי על רבב שעל בגדיהן לכבסו ולהוציאו כדי שלא יהו מן המשניאין לפיכך אפילו בצד אחד נראה חוצץ ולא עלתה לו טבילה אבל בגדי הבורים אם עבר מצד לצד חוצץ ואם לאו אינו חוצץ וכן הלכה: וא"ר יוחנן איזהו ת"ח כל שמחזירין לו אבידה בטביעות עין זה המקפיד על חלוקו להופכו וכן אמר איזהו ת"ח שממנין אותו פרנס על הצבור זה ששואלין אותו דבר הלכה בכל מקום ואומרה ואיזהו שבני עירו מצווין לעשות מלאכתו מי שמניח חפציו ועוסק בחפצי שמים ר"ל אמר בנאין אלו אוליירין הבאים ממדינת הים. ואקשי' למימר דכלי אוליירין חיורי נינהו שהוזפת מצד אחד נודע בהן. והאמר ר' ינאי לבניה אל תקברוני בלבנים ולא בשחורים אלא באוליירין אלמא סומקי נינהו. ושנינן המלבושים לבנים הן כגון מני כסותא. והגלימא כגון מאני דמתעטפי בהן סומקי הוו: ר' (שמעון) [ישמעאל] סבר חלבין שנתותרו ביוה"כ קריבין בשבת אבל שנתותרו מן השבת אין קריבין ביוה"כ. ור' עקיבא סבר לא של שבת קריבין ביוה"כ ולא של יוה"כ בשבת. וגרסינן ביומא בפרק א"ר אלעזר משום בר קפרא. אומר היה ר"מ איברי עולת חול שניתותרו עושה להן מערכה וסודרן אפילו בשבת. ואמרינן למאי איצטריך אפילו בשבת הא תנינא והיום חמש. א"ר אחא בר יעקב איצטריך אמינא הני מילי היכא דחל יוה"כ למיהוי אחר השבת דחלבי שבת קריבין ביוה"כ אבל באמצע שבת אימא לא קמ"ל: אמר רבא [האי] מאן [דלא] חש לקמחיה בכל יום תנו עד

מסורת הש"ס

ויקרא ו | לקמן קיט. [יומא כג:] | ברכות מג: ע"ש | משלי ח | [נרי"ף פי' דם יבש וכתב הר"ן שהוא מלשון ריבדא דכוסילתא מ"ק כח. ועי' בערוך ערך רבד] | ישעיה כ | [עירובין נג. מגילה כח.] | [עי' יומא מז.] | מקוואות פ"ט משנה ס' ו' | [שם במשנה] | תענית י: | קידושין מט: | יומא עב: | נדה כ. | במדבר כח | [פסחים נח. ביצה יט. כ: סנהדרין לו.] | [עי' תוס' לעיל כד: ופסחים נט: ד"ה ולא] | [ר"ה יז.]

הגהות הב"ח

(א) גמ' בטלאי על גבי טלאי וה"מ בפנתא אבל בגילדה לית לן בה ואמר ר' חייא: (ב) רש"י ד"ה חוצץ וכו' לענין טבילה היכא דקפיד: (ג) ד"ה תנן התם וכו' ונקט לה הכא משום: (ד) תוס' ד"ה ואפילו וכו' שאני תלמיד חכם אין:

רב נסים גאון

גנאי הוא לתלמידי חכמים שיצאו במנעלים המטולאים · במס' ברכות בפרק כיצד מברכין על הפירות (דף מג) תנו רבנן ששה דברים גנאי לתלמיד חכם אל יצא כשהוא מבושם לשוק ואל יצא יחידי בלילה ואל יצא במנעלים המטולאים בשוק[וכו']: תנן התם על המרדעת חוצץ. עיקר זאת המשנה בפרק ט' ממס' מקואות אלו חוצצין בכלים הזפת והמור כו' ועל המרדעת חוצץ רבן שמעון בן גמליאל אומר עד

גליון הש"ס תוס' ד"ה ואפילו כו' והשתא הוי דהכא כי ההוא דקידושין · ועי' תשב"ץ ח"א סימן לג:

עין משפט
נר מצוה

לג א מיי' פ"ה מהלכות שבת הלכה כא :
לד ב שם הל' יח יט כ:
לה ג שם הלכה כא :
לו ד מיי' פ"א מהלכות שביתת עשור הל"ג טוש"ע או"ח סימן תריא סעיף ב :

*כי הוינא בבבל הוה אמרי הא דתניא [א]יוה"כ שחל להיות ע"ש לא היו תוקעין ובמוצאי שבת לא היו מבדילין דברי הכל היא כי סליקנא להתם אשכחיתיה ליהודה בריה דרבי שמעון בן פזי דיתיב וקאמר ר' עקיבא היא דאי רבי ישמעאל כיון דאמר חלבי שבת קריבין ביום הכיפורים ליתקע כי היכי דלידעי דחלבי שבת קריבין ביום הכיפורים ואמינא ליה אנא *כהנים זריזין הן אמר ליה מר קשישא בריה דרב חסדא לרב אשי מי אמרינן כהנים זריזין הן והתנן *[ב]שלש להבטיל את העם ממלאכה שלש להבדיל בין קודש לחול *כדאמר אביי לשאר עמא דבירושלים הכא נמי לשאר עמא דבירושלים וליתקע כי היכי דלידעי דשרי בקניבת ירק מן המנחה ולמעלה אמר רב יוסף לפי שאין דוחין שבות להתיר ורב שישא בריה דרב אידי אמר שבות קרובה התירו *שבות רחוקה לא התירו ושבות קרובה התירו *והתנן [ג]יום טוב שחל להיות ערב שבת תוקעין ולא מבדילין מוצאי שבת מבדילין ולא תוקעין ואמאי ליתקע כי היכי דלידעי דשרי בשחיטה לאלתר אלא מחוורתא כדרב יוסף אמר רבי זירא אמר רב הונא ואמרי לה אמר רבי אבא אמר רב הונא [ד]יוה"כ שחל להיות בשבת אסור בקניבת ירק אמר רב מנא תנא (א) מנין ליוה"כ שחל להיות בשבת שאסור בקניבת ירק ת"ל °שבתון (שמות טז) שבות למאי אילימא למלאכה והכתיב °לא (שם כ) תעשה כל מלאכה אלא לאו אקניבת ירק ש"מ אמר רבי חייא בר אבא אמר רבי יוחנן יוה"כ שחל להיות בשבת מותר בקניבת ירק מיתיבי מנין ליוה"כ שחל להיות בשבת שאסור בקניבת ירק ת"ל שבתון שבות למאי אילימא למלאכה והכתיב לא תעשה כל מלאכה אלא לאו בקניבת ירק לא לעולם למלאכה ולעבור עליה בעשה· ול"ת תניא כוותיה דרבי יוחנן יוה"כ שחל להיות בשבת מותר

כי הוינא בבבל. כשלמדתי תורה בבבל קודם שעליתי לא"י : לא היו תוקעין. שש תקיעות שתוקעין בע"ש להבטיל ולהבדיל משום דיוה"כ קודש כשבת ואסור בכל מלאכה: ובמוצ"ש · אם חל בו יוה"כ: לא היו מבדילין. בתפלה המבדיל בין קדש לקדש כמו שמבדילין בי"ט שחל להיות במוצ"ש : דברי הכל היא. לא הוה מסיקנא אדעתאי דתיהוי בפלוגתא דרבי ישמעאל ורבי עקיבא דמתני' : רבי עקיבא היא. דחשיב ליה יוה"כ כשבת הלכך לא בעי למתקע להבדיל בין זה לזה להיכרא דלא תקעינן אלא בין יום קל ליום חמור וכי היכי דבשבת לא תקעי להבדיל כהנים מלהקריב חלבי שבת ביוה"כ ביוה"כ נמי לא תקעינן להבדילן מלהקריב חלבי יוה"כ בשבת : דאי ר' ישמעאל. כיון דקיל ליה יוה"כ משבת ליתקע להבטיל מהקריב חלבי יוה"כ בשבת ובתקיעה זו יביטו שהוא יום הקל ולכשיחול יוה"כ במוצאי שבת ולא יתקעו ידעו שמותר להקריב בו חלבי שבת : זריזים הם. בקיאים הן בכל ואין צריכין סימן דכתיב בהן יורו משפטיך ליעקב (דברים לג) : והתנן. במסכת סוכה : ג' להבטיל כו'. ומני להו בתקיעות שבמקדש אין פוחתין מכ"א תקיעות במקדש וקס"ד מדתקעי' להו במקדש להיכרא דכהני' תקעי להו : כדאמר אביי. בסדר יומא בפרק ג' גבי נברשת שעשתה הילני המלכה על פתחו של היכל בשעה שהחמה זורחת ניצוצות יוצאות הימנה והכל יודעים שזמן ק"ש הגיע ומותבינן ורמינהו הקורא ק"ש עם אנשי משמר לא יצא אלמא לאו בזימנא קריין ואמר אביי הא סימן דנברשת לשאר עמא שיקראו ק"ש בעונתה : וליתקע. בין לר"ע בין לרבי ישמעאל לאודועי דקל הוא משבת דיוה"כ שרי בקניבת ירק תלוש לנתק העלין מן הקלחין כדי להשוותם שיהו מוכנים לחתכן ולפרמן דאמרינן לקמן דשרי משום דהוי עינוי שרואה ומזמן ואינו אוכל : קניבה. כי ההיא דכלל גדול (לעיל עג:) האי מאן דקניב סילקא אלא דהתם במחובר והכא בתלוש : לפי שאין דוחין שבות להתיר. תקיעת שופר שבות הוא וקאמרת דלידחיה להודיע היתר בקניבת ירק אין דוחין שבות להתיר אלא לאסור כגון יו"ט שחל להיות בע"ש תוקעין להבטיל ולהבדיל : ורב ששת בריה דרב אידי אמר לעולם דוחין שבות להתיר. אי הוה מיבעי' לן היתרא אידנא אבל השתא דלא מיבעי לן קניבת ירק ביוה"כ שחל להיות בע"ש שהרי בשבת לא יבשלום ולא תהא תקיעה זו אלא להודיענו היתר בשנה אחרת שיחול יה"כ באמצע שבת לא התירו : שבות קרובה. כלומר דחיוב שבות התירו לצורך דבר קרוב ולא לצורך דבר רחוק : תוקעין. להבטיל את העם ממלאכה המותרת ביו"ט כגון אוכל נפש ולהבדיל בין הקודש ובין החול : ולא מבדילין. בתפלה ועל הכוס דלא תקט לומר הבדלה אלא ביציאת קודש ובכניסת חול ולא בכניסת קדש וביציאת חול דהתם שייך לקדושי יומא וקדוש יום שמקדשין על היין הוי היכירא דיליה : מוצאי שבת. ואם חל יו"ט במוצאי שבת מבדילין בתפלה ועל הכוס המבדיל בין קודש לקודש מפני שהקודש חמור יוצא ונכנס קל : ולא תוקעין. מבעוד יום להבטיל ולהבדיל דהא היוצא חמור והיום לא עשו שום מלאכה : ואמאי. אי ס"ד דוחין שבות להתיר לצורך דבר קרוב יתקע משחשיכה לידע דשרי בשחיטה לאלתר : אסור בקניבת ירק. ולא מבעי בשבת דעלמא דאסור משום שבות דקטרח משבת לחול אלא אפילו אידנא דיש כאן עינוי דהא בשאר יוה"כ שאסר שבות אסור זה מותר השתא דחל בשבת לא שרו רבנן : אמר רב מנא תנא כו' : ת"ל. בשבת בראשית שבתון שבת קדש ושבתון משמע שבות : ולמאי. באיזה קניבה אסר לן קרא : אילימא במלאכה. כגון מחובר : הא כתיב לא תעשה כל מלאכה. והא תו למה לי : אלא לאו לקניבת ירק. בעלמא בתלוש דמידי דלאו מלאכה קאי עליה בעשה דשבתון שבות וכיון דמדאורייתא אסור בכל שבתות השנה הכא לא שרינן ליה משום עגמת נפש למידחי איסור דאורייתא ובשאר יוה"כ שרי לעגמת נפש ואע"ג דכתיב ביה נמי שבתון שבות לאו ממלאכה הוא אלא מכל דבר המעכב מלהתענות מדסמכינן לועניתם הכי דרשינן לה בפרק בתרא דיומא (דף עד.) לרחילה וסיכה ודומין להם :

ליתקע כי היכי דלידעו דחלבי שבת קריבין ביום הכפורים. הך תקיעה בע"ש קאמר כדפירש בקונטרס אבל יוה"כ שחל באחד בשבת לא תקעי במוצאי שבת להודיע שיוה"כ הוא קל דאדרבה מתוך התקיעה יהא נראה שהוא חמור דכל תקיעות שתוקעין בע"ש או עי"ט תוקעין בכניסת חמור והכי אמר בסמוך י"ט שחל במוצ"ש מבדילין ולא תוקעין ולא תקעי להודיע דחלבי שבת קריבין בי"ט ומיהו התם דבר ידוע הוא שי"ט קיל הוא משבת והא דפריך עלה בסמוך ואמאי ליתקע כי היכי דלידעי דשרי שחיטה לאלתר אותה תקיעה אינה אלא להודיע שהוא לילה ולא להודיע שי"ט קל הוא משבת והא דלא קאמר הכא ליתקע כי היכי דלידעו דחלבי יוה"כ אין קריבין בשבת דהא כי לא תקעי נמי מחמת שבת ויוה"כ שוין אין קריבין של זה בזה אם כן התקיעה אינה מוכחת שלא יהיו קריבין של יוה"כ בשבת והא נמי לא בעי למיפרך ולידביל במוצאי שבת דלידעי דחלבי שבת קריבין ביוה"כ דהא אפי' מבדיל בבית הכנס' ברבים אין פרסום בהבדלה כמו בתקיעה :

וליתקע כי היכי דלידעו דשרי בקניבת ירק. ה"ה דהוה מצי למיפרך אליבא דר' ישמעאל ליתקע כי היכי דלידעו שמליעין את המטות מיוה"כ לשבת אלא ניחא ליה למיפרך לכ"ע :

אמר רב יוסף לפי שאין דוחין שבות להתיר. לעיל כי פריך ליתקע כי היכי דלידעו דחלבי שבת קריבין כו' לא הוה מצי לשנויי הכי דאין זו התרה מה שמתירין להקריבם אלא חומרא הוא שיקטירו האימורים ולא יבאו לידי נותר ויש חומרא בדבר שחייבין להקטירם :

אלא לקניבת ירק. נראה לר"י דאסמכתא בעלמא הוא דאי מדאורייתא ביוה"כ נמי ליתסר והא דאמר בפרק כלל גדול (לעיל עג:) האי מאן דקניב סילקא חייב שתים התם מיירי במחובר והכא איירי בתלוש כדפירש בקונטרס ולא דמי להא דאמר בפרק כלל גדול א) האי מאן דפריס סילקא חייב משום טוחן דהתם מיירי כשעושה חתיכות דקות מאד והכא מיירי כשעושה חתיכות גדולות : לעולם למלאכה. וקניבת ירק דברייתא היינו שעושים דק דק דהוי איסור דאורייתא דדמי לטוחן א"כ במחובר : ואמאי ליתקע כי היכי דלידעו דשרי בשחיטה. לעיל לא להודיע די"ט קיל אלא להודיע שהוא לילה וכן אומר ר"י מה שתוקעים במוצאי יוה"כ אינו אלא להודיע שהוא לילה ויאכלו את בניהם שהתענו וגם להכין סעודת מוצאי יוה"כ שהיא כעין י"ט ב) כמו שיסד הפייטן ג) אחר גמר מילוי אכול בדלוי ורצוי ולא כמחזורים שכתוב בהן שהתקיעה זכר ליובל כי למה תוקעין בכל שנה ושנה וכי היה יובל בכל שנה ושנה :

הדרן עלך ואלו קשרים

א) [דף עד: וע"ש תוס' ד"ה האי מאן] ב) [ועי' תוס' לקמן קיז: ד"ה אבל לא כו'] ג) [בפזמון של מנחה ליוה"כ]

סוכה נד
[לעיל כ. וש"נ]
סוכה נג:
יומא לז:
[פסחים מ.]
חולין כו:

הגהות הב"ח
(א) גמ' אמר רב מנא תניא נמי הכי מנין ליוה"כ :

הגהות הגר"א
[א] גמ' דר' יוחנן. נ"ל דרב הונא (ר"ל לגי' הרמב"ם ומ"מ) :

רבינו חננאל

*) השתא הוא בפלוגתא דרבי ישמעאל ור"ע: אמר ר' זירא כי הוינן בבבל הוה אמרי' הא דתניא יוה"כ שחל להיות ערב שבת לא היו תוקעין ובמוצ"ש לא היו מבדילין דברי הכל היא . כלומר מפני מה תוקעין בע"ש כדי להבדיל מן המלאכה כיון שע"ש יוה"כ הוא אין שם מלאכה שצריכין תקיעה להבטילן . וכן הבדלה כדי להתיר העם למלאכה וכיון שמוצ"ש יוה"כ אין בו התר מלאכה לפיכך אין צריך להבדלה . וא"ר זירא כי סליקי להתם ואשכחתיה ליהודה בריה דר"ש בן פזי דאומר הא מתני' ר"ע היא דלא שני ליה בין שבת ליוה"כ דהא לא חלבי שבת קריבין ביוה"כ ולא של יוה"כ בשבת לפיכך לא צריך הכירא בין האי להאי . אלא לר' ישמעאל דשני ליה ליתקע במ"ש ליוה"כ דליהוי הכירא לכהנים להקריב מה שנותר מחלבי שבת וא"ל ר' זירא אפי' לר' ישמעאל ושני ליה בין שבת ליום הכיפורים כהנים זריזין הן ויודעין שחלבי שבת קריבין ביוה"כ לפיכך לא בעי תקיע' ואבדלת' איני דכהנים זריזין הן והתנן ג' להבדיל בין [קודש] לחול ושנינן הא דתנן להבדיל בין קדש לחול אינה שנויה לגבי כהנים אלא לישראל בלבד . כדאמר אביי התם ביומא לענין נברשת של זהב שעשת הילני על פתח ההיכל להודיע עת ק"ש דלאו לכהנים איתעביד אלא לשאר עמא דבירושלים . ואקשי' תוב וליתקע בהדי הבדלה לשאר עמא דנידעו דשרי להו קניבת ירק מן המנחה ולמעלה · דהא קי"ל דבשבת אסור לקנב ירק ולהניח לערב משום בורר . ואמרינן (לעיל ע"ד) אמר אביי בורר ואוכל לאלתר בורר ומניח לאלתר אבל שלא לאלתר לא יברור . ובסוף אמרוה קמיה דרבה ואמר דשפיר אמר נחמני . אבל ביוה"כ מותר לברור ולקנב מן המנחה ולמעלה ולהניח במוצאי יוה"כ . ומפרק רב יוסף לפי שאין דוחין שבות להתיר . פי' תקיעה אסורה משום שבות . דדרשי כל מלאכת עבודה יצאו תקיעת שופר ורדיית הפת שהן חכמה ואינה מלאכה ולא דחו שבות לא בשבת ולא ביוה"כ בתקיעה להתיר קניבת ירק אי הוה איכא מילתא למיסרא משום מלאכ' [הוא] דדחי שבות ותוקעין אבל למישרא קניבת ירק לא דחו שבות ותקעי. רב שישא בריה דרב אידי אמר שבות קרובה התירו שבות רחוקה לא התירו . פי' אפילו תימא דוחין שבות להתיר מידי דאית ליה רשות למיעבדיה בקרובה דוחין שבות (משום) להתירו . אבל מידי דרחיק ולית ליה למיעבדיה בקרובה אין דוחין שבות להתירו . וקניבת ירק ביוה"כ לאלתר אלא מן המנחה ולמעלה . איני והתנן יו"ט שחל להיות ע"ש תוקעין ולא מבדילין . ולאחר שבת מבדילין ולא תוקעין . ואי אמרת רשות קרובה התירו ליתקע במיעל יו"ט שחל להיות לאחר שבת כי היכי דנידעו דשרי לשחיטה לאלתר . ועמדה הקושיא . ונדחה הא דרב שישא . ואסיק' אלא מחוורתא כדר' יוסף . וקשי לן בהא שמעתא הא דאמר רב יהודה בריה דר"ש בן פזי הא מתניתא ר' עקיבא היא דאי ר' ישמעאל הא אמר חלבי שבת קריבין ביוה"כ ליתקע במ"ש ליוה"כ כי היכי דנידעו וחלבי שבת ביוה"כ קריבין . וקשיא לן וכי יש תקיעה במ"ש דאמר ליתקע במ"ש . והיו מן החכמים מפרשין ואמרי' האי גירסא מאן דגרים ליתקע שעותא הוא . אלא הכי קאמר דאי ר' ישמעאל היא ניבדיל כי היכי דלידעו דחלבי שבת קריבין ביוה"כ . וקמפרש בתלמוד א"י דגרסינן ר' זעירא בשם רב חסדא יוה"כ שחל להיות ע"ש אין תוקעין לאחר שבת אין מבדילין . אימא כר"ע ברם כר' ישמעאל מבדיל שכן חלבי שבת קריבין ביוה"כ . א"ר זעירא קומי ר' מנא אפילו כר' ישמעאל לא יבדיל כלום הוא אלא להתיר דבר שהוא אסור אילו הקטיר חלבי שבת בשבת שמא אינו מותר ופירוקא דר' זירא בתלמודא דילן היינו טעמא דלא מבדילינן משום דכהנים זריזין טפי עדיף . וטעמא דרב שישא בריה דרב אידי נמי אינגליא לן

*) לכאורה תמוה דהא ר"י ור"ע לא פליגי רק בחלבי שבת אי קרבין ביוה"כ אבל בחלבי חול ליכא מאן דפליג ועי' תוס' שם ד"ה אבל ובמל"מ בפ"ד מהל' מעשה הקרבנות הלכה ג' והו"ק.

רב נסים גאון

עד כאיסר האיטלקי : כדאמר אביי לשאר עמא דבירושלים. ומשכחת דברי אביי במס' יומא בפרק אמר להן הממונה (דף לז) דתנן הילני אמו עשתה נברשת של זהב על פתח ההיכל. תאנא בשעה שחמה זורחת ניצוצות יוצאות ממנה ויודעין שהגיע זמן קרית שמע. מיתיבי הקורא קרית שמע כו' אמר אביי לשאר עמא דבירושלים : סליק פרק אלו קשרים

R. Zera said: [114b] When I was in Babylon[5] I thought,[6] That which was taught, If the Day of Atonement fell on the eve of the Sabbath [Friday], it [the Shofar] was not sounded,[7] while [if it fell] at the termination of the Sabbath, *habdalah* was not recited,[8] is a unanimous opinion. But when I emigrated thither [to Palestine], I found Judah the son of R. Simeon b. Pazzi sitting and saying, This is according to Akiba [only];[9] for if [it agrees with] R. Ishmael,—since he maintains, The fats of the Sabbath may be offered on the Day of Atonement, let it [the *Shofar*] be sounded, so that it may be known that the fats of the Sabbath can be offered on the Day of Atonement.[10] Whereupon I said to him, The priests[11] are zealous.[12]

Mar Ḳashisha son of R. Ḥisda said to R. Ashi: Do we then say, Priests are zealous? Surely we learnt: Three [blasts were blown] to cause the people to cease work; three, to distinguish between
a the holy [day] and weekdays?[1]—As Abaye answered,[2] it was for the rest of the people in Jerusalem; so here too it was for the rest of the people in Jerusalem.

Yet let it [the *Shofar*] be blown, so that they might know that the trimming of vegetables is permitted [on the Day of Atonement] from the [time of] *minḥah*[3] and onwards?[4]—Said R. Joseph: Because a *shebuth*[5] is not superseded in order to give permission.[6] While R. Shisha son of R. Idi answered: A *shebuth* [of] immediate[7] [importance] was permitted; a *shebuth* [of] distant [importance] was not permitted.[8] But did they permit a *shebuth* [of] immediate [importance]? Surely we learnt: If a Festival falls on Friday, we sound [the *shofar*] but do not recite *habdalah*;[9] [if it falls] at the termination of the Sabbath, we recite *habdalah*[10] but do not sound [the *shofar*].[11] But why so: let it be sounded so that it may be known that killing [animals for food] is permitted immediately [the Sabbath ends]?[12] Rather it is clear that it is as R. Joseph [answered].

R. Zera said in R. Huna's name—others state, R. Abba said in R. Huna's name: If the Day of Atonement falls on the Sabbath, the trimming of vegetables is forbidden. R. Mana said, It was taught likewise: How do we know that if the Day of Atonement falls on the Sabbath, the trimming of vegetables[13] is forbidden?
b Because it is said, *Shabbathon;* it is a *shebuth.*[1] Now, in respect of what [is it stated]: shall we say, In respect of labour,[2]—surely it is written, *thou shalt not do any work?*[3] Hence it must surely refer to the trimming of vegetables;[4] this proves it.

R. Ḥiyya b. Abba said in R. Joḥanan's name: If the Day of Atonement falls on the Sabbath, the trimming of vegetables is permitted. An objection is raised: How do we know that if the Day of Atonement falls on the Sabbath, the trimming of vegetables is forbidden? Because *shabbathon* is stated: it is a *shebuth*. In respect of what: shall we say in respect of labour, —surely it is written, *'thou shalt not do any work'?* Hence it must surely refer to the trimming of vegetables!—No: in truth it refers to actual work, but [it is stated] to [show that] one violates an affirmative and a negative injunction on account thereof.[5] It was taught in accordance with R. Joḥanan: If the Day of Atonement

(5) R. Zera was a Babylonian who studied at home first and then emigrated to Palestine. (6) Lit., 'said'. (7) As on ordinary Fridays, *supra* 35*b*. (8) In the evening prayer, V. Glos. When a Festival falls on Sunday, *habdalah* is recited in the evening to signify that there is a distinction between the holiness of the Sabbath and that of Festivals. (9) Since he maintains that the fats of the Sabbath may not be burnt on the Day of Atonement and *vice versa*, he evidently holds that they each enjoy equal sanctity. Therefore neither *habdalah* nor the sounding of the *shofar* is required, for these are necessary only to mark a difference in the degree of sanctity. (10) For the sounding of the *shofar* would teach that the Day of Atonement possessed a lower degree of holiness. (11) Who burn the fats. (12) They take care to know the law and need no reminder.

a (1) This was done in the Temple, and he assumed that it was in order to remind the priests. (2) In reference to another matter; v. Yoma 37*b*. (3) V. Glos. (4) In this it differs from the Sabbath, when it is forbidden. V. *infra*. (5) V. Glos.; the blowing of the *shofar* is a *shebuth*. (6) But only where it is necessary to emphasize prohibitions, e.g., if Friday is a Festival, so that many things permitted thereon are forbidden on the Sabbath. (7) Lit., 'near'. (8) If it were of immediate importance, the *shebuth* would have been permitted. But in any case when the Day of Atonement falls on Friday, the vegetables, even if trimmed, cannot be cooked on the Sabbath. So that the sounding of the *shofar* would only be of importance for subsequent Days of Atonement, and in such a case the *shebuth* is not superseded. (9) On Friday evening, because *habdalah* is recited only when a more stringent holiness is left behind. (10) On Saturday evening. (11) Saturday afternoon. (12) For the preparation of food is permitted on Festivals, Ex. XII, 16. (13) I.e., cutting away those parts of vegetables which are not edible. The reference is of course to unattached vegetables.

b (1) Ex. XVI, 23: E.V. (*solemn*) *rest*. Here it is translated as *shebuth*, and thus intimates such labour as trimming vegetables. (2) I.e., the word forbids actual labour, e.g., the trimming of vegetables that are still attached to the soil, *supra* 73*b*.—The discussion here treats of vegetables already cut off from the ground. (3) Ex. XX, 9, hence *shabbathon* is superfluous. (4) The verse is merely a support (*asmakta*), the prohibition being a Rabbinical one only (Ri). (5) *Shabbathon* is an affirmative command, bidding one to rest.

falls on the Sabbath, [115a] the trimming of vegetables is permitted. Nuts may be cracked and pomegranates scraped from the [time of] *minḥah* and onwards, on account of one's vexation.[6] The household of Rab Judah trimmed cabbage. Rabbah's household scraped pumpkins. Seeing that they were doing this [too] early,[7] he said to them, A letter has come from the west in R. Joḥanan's name [to the effect] that this is forbidden.[8]

CHAPTER XVI

a *MISHNAH*. ALL SACRED WRITINGS[1] MAY[2] BE SAVED FROM A CONFLAGRATION,[3] WHETHER WE READ THEM OR NOT;[4] AND EVEN IF THEY ARE WRITTEN IN ANY LANGUAGE, THEY MUST BE HIDDEN.[5] AND WHY DO WE NOT READ [CERTAIN OF THE SACRED WRITINGS]? BECAUSE OF THE NEGLECT OF THE BETH HAMIDRASH.[6]

GEMARA. It was stated: If they are written in Targum[7] or in any [other] language,—R. Huna said: They must not be saved from a fire; while R. Ḥisda ruled: They may be saved from a fire. On the view that it is permissible to read them,[8] all agree that they must be saved. They differ only according to the view that they may not be read. R. Huna says: We may not save [them], since they may not be read. R. Ḥisda says: We must save [them], because of the disgrace to Holy Writings.[9] We learnt: ALL SACRED WRITINGS MAY BE SAVED FROM A FIRE, WHETHER WE READ THEM OR NOT, AND EVEN IF THEY ARE WRITTEN IN ANY LANGUAGE. Surely WHETHER WE READ THEM refers to the Prophets, whilst OR NOT refers to the Writings, AND EVEN IF THEY ARE WRITTEN IN ANY LANGUAGE, though they may not be read [publicly], yet he [the Tanna] teaches that they MAY BE SAVED, which refutes R. Huna?—R. Huna can answer you: Is that logical? Consider the second clause: THEY MUST BE HIDDEN: seeing b that they must be saved,[1] need hiding be mentioned?[2] But R. Huna explains it in accordance with his view, while R. Ḥisda explains it according to his. R. Huna explains it in accordance with his view. WHETHER WE READ THEM, [i.e.,] the Prophets; OR NOT, [i.e.,] the Writings. That is only if they are written in the Holy Tongue [Hebrew], but if they are written in any [other] language, we may not save them, yet even so they must be hidden. R. Ḥisda explains it according to his view: WHETHER WE READ THEM, [i.e.,] the Prophets, OR NOT, [i.e.,] the Writings; EVEN IF THEY ARE WRITTEN IN ANY LANGUAGE, we must still save them. And this is what he states: And [even] their worm-eaten [material] MUST BE HIDDEN.

An objection is raised: If they are written in Targum or in any [other] language, they may be saved from the fire: this refutes R. Huna?—R. Huna answers you: This Tanna holds, They may be read. Come and hear: If they are written in Egyptian,[3] Median, a trans[-Euphratean][4] Aramaic, Elamitic,[5] or Greek, though they may not be read, they may be saved from a fire: this refutes R. Huna?—R. Huna can answer you: It is [a controversy of] Tannaim. For it was taught: If they are written in Targum or in any language, they may be saved from a fire. R. Jose said: They may not be saved from a fire. Said R. Jose: It once happened that my father Ḥalafta visited R. Gamaliel Berabbi[6] at Tiberias and found him sitting at the table of Joḥanan b. Nizuf with the Targum of the Book of Job in his c hand[1] which he was reading. Said he to him, 'I remember that R. Gamaliel, your grandfather, was standing on a high eminence on the Temple Mount, when the Book of Job in a Targumic version was brought before him, whereupon he said to the builder, "Bury it under the bricks."[2] He [R. Gamaliel II] too gave orders, and they hid it.'[3] R. Jose son of R. Judah said: They overturned a tub of mortar upon it. Said Rabbi: There are two objections to this: Firstly, how came mortar on the Temple Mount?[4] Moreover, is it then permitted to destroy them with one's own hands? For they must be put in a neglected place to decay of their own

(6) Lit., 'grief of the soul'. It would be very vexing if the breaking of the Fast had to be delayed whilst these are prepared (*Baal Ha-Ma'or* V. Marginal Gloss.; Rashi explains it differently). (7) Before the time of *minḥah*. (8) Such letters afford examples of early Rabbinic Responsa.

a (1) E.g., the Torah, Prophets, and Writings. (2) In this connection 'may' is the equivalent of 'must', and similarly in the Gemara. (3) By being moved from one domain to another on the Sabbath. V. next Mishnah. (4) The reference is to public readings. There was (and is) public reading from the Prophets but not from the Writings (Hagiographa). Rashi quotes another explanation: even private individuals did not read the Writings (on the Sabbath), because public lectures were given on that day, which left no time for private reading. (5) If they become unfit for use. V. *supra* 90a, n. a5. (6) The public lectures would be neglected. For a general discussion on the manner, etc. of these lectures v. Zunz, *G.V.* Ch. 20. (7) The Aramaic translation of the Pentateuch and other portions of the Bible are called Targum—the translation *par excellence*. But v. Kaplan, op. cit. pp. 283 *seq*. (8) Publicly; v. Meg. 8*b*. (9) It disgraces them if they are allowed to be burnt like something worthless.

b (1) On your hypothesis. (2) Obviously if they have sufficient sanctity to be saved on the Sabbath they must not be simply thrown away when no longer fit for use. (3) Or, Coptic. (4) עברית so Jast.: perhaps the reference is to Hebrew in transliteration. (5) Of Elam, south of Assyria. (6) A title of scholars most frequently applied to disciples of R. Judah ha-Nasi and his contemporaries, but also to some of his predecessors (as here), and sometimes to the first Amoraim (Jast.). V. Naz., 19*a*, n. 1.

c (1) This shows that a Targum of Job existed already in the middle of the first century C.E. This is not identical with the extant Targum, which on internal evidence must have been composed later; v. *J.E.* art. *Targum*, Vol. XII, p. 62; Zunz, *G.V.* 64 *seq*. (2) Lit., 'the course (of stones)'. (3) The spread of works inimical to Judaism, both through the rise of Christianity and false claimants to the Messiahship, caused the Rabbis to frown upon books other than those admitted to the Holy Scriptures, even such as were not actually inimical thereto.—Weiss, *Dor*, I, 212, 236. (4) A mixture of lime and sand was used, but not mortar, which is made of earth and water.

מותר בקניבת ירק *(ואמר רבי חייא בר אבא אמר רבי יוחנן יום כיפורים שחל להיות בחול) מפצעין באגוזים ומפרכסין ברימונים מן המנחה ולמעלה מפני *עגמת נפש דרב יהודה מקנבי כרבא דבי רבה גרדי קארי כיון דחזא דהוו קא מחרפי אמר להו אתא איגרתא ממערבא משמיה דר' יוחנן דאסיר:

הדרן עלך ואלו קשרים

כל כתבי הקדש מצילין אותן מפני הדליקה בין שקורין בהן ובין שאין קורין בהן. (א)אע"פ שכתובים בכל לשון *טעונים גניזה ומפני מה אין קורין בהם מפני ביטול בית המדרש: **גמ'** איתמר [ב]היו כתובים תרגום או בכל לשון רב הונא אמר אין מצילין אותן מפני הדליקה ורב חסדא אמר מצילין אותן מפני הדליקה אליבא דמאן דאמר ניתנו לקרות בהן דכולי עלמא לא פליגי דמצילין כי פליגי אליבא דמאן דאמר לא ניתנו לקרות בהן רב הונא אמר אין מצילין דהא לא ניתנו לקרות בהן רב חסדא אמר מצילין משום בזיון כתבי הקדש תנן כל כתבי הקדש מצילין אותן מפני הדליקה בין שקורין בהן בין שאין קורין בהן (ב)אע"פ שכתובין בכל לשון מאי לאו שקורין בהן נביאים ושאין קורין בהן כתובים אע"פ שכתובין בכל לשון דלא ניתנו לקרות בהן וקתני מצילין ותיובתא דרב הונא אמר לך רב הונא ותסברא אימא סיפא טעונין גניזה השתא אצולי מצילינן גניזה מיבעי אלא רב הונא מתרץ לטעמיה ורב חסדא מתרץ לטעמיה רב הונא מתרץ לטעמיה בין שקורין בהם נביאים ובין שאין קורין בהם כתובים במה דברים אמורים שכתובין בלשון הקדש אבל בכל לשון אין מצילין ואפילו הכי גניזה בעו רב חסדא מתרץ לטעמיה בין שקורין בהן נביאים ובין שאין קורין בהן כתובים אע"פ שכתובין בכל לשון נמי מצילין והכי קאמר ומקק שלהן טעונין גניזה מיתיבי היו כתובים תרגום (ג)וכל לשון מצילין אותן מפני הדליקה תיובתא דרב הונא אמר לך רב הונא האי תנא סבר ניתנו לקרות בהן ת"ש היו כתובין גיפטית מדית עיברית עילמית יוונית אע"פ שלא ניתנו לקרות בהן מצילין אותן מפני הדליקה תיובתא דרב הונא אמר לך רב הונא תנאי היא דתניא *היו כתובין תרגום ובכל לשון מצילין אותן מפני הדליקה ר' יוסי אומר אין מצילין אותן מפני הדליקה אמר ר' יוסי *מעשה באבא חלפתא שהלך אצל רבן גמליאל בריבי לטבריא ומצאו שהי' יושב על שלחנו של (*יוחנן הנזוף) ובידו ספר איוב תרגום והוא קורא בו אמר לו זכור אני ברבן גמליאל אבי אביך שהיה עומד ע"ג מעלה בהר הבית והביאו לפניו ספר איוב תרגום ואמר לבנאי שקעהו תחת הנדבך אף הוא צוה עליו וגנזו ר' יוסי ברבי יהודה אומר עריבה של טיט כפו עליו אמר רבי שתי תשובות בדבר חדא וכי טיט בהר הבית מנין ועוד וכי מותר לאבדן ביד אלא מניחן במקום התורפה והן *מרקיבין מאליהן מאן תנאי אילימא

רש"י

מותר בקניבת ירק. דשבות לאו איסורא דאורייתא הוא אלא דרבנן והכא משום עגמת נפש שמתקן ואינו אוכל והרי קרוב לעינוי שרי ודווקא מן המנחה ולמעלה שהוא שואף ומצפה לעת אכילה ואיכא עגמת נפש טפי: כיון דחזי דהוי קא מחרפי. מקדימין לפני המנחה דהשתא לאו עגמת נפש הוא: אמר להו. לאינשי ביתיה: אתא איגרתא ממערבא כו'. כי היכי דלקבלו מיניה:

הדרן עלך ואלו קשרים

כל כתבי הקדש. כגון תורה נביאים וכתובים ולא תימא תורה לחוד הוא דשרי למיטרח ולאצולי ולא שאר ספרים: מצילין אותן. כדקתני לקמן למבוי שאינו מפולש וטירחא בעלמא הוא דשרי (ד) בה וחסרון עירוב כדמפרש בגמרא: בין שקורין בהן. כגון נביאים שמפטירין בהן בשבת בבית הכנסת: בין שאין קורין בהן. כגון כתובים ורבינו הלוי אמר דאפי' יחידים אין קורין בהן כדקתני טעמא משום ביטול בית המדרש דמשכי לבא ובשבת היו דורשין דרשה לבעלי בתים שעסוקין במלאכה כל ימות החול ובתוך הדרשה היו מורין להן הלכות איסור והיתר וטוב להן לשמוע מלקרות בכתובים: ואע"פ שכתובין בכל לשון. ואיכא למאן דאמר לקמן לא ניתנו לקרות בהן מצילין אותן: טעונין גניזה. אסור להניחן במקום הפקר ובגמרא מתרץ לה ורבותי פירשו דהאי בכל לשון דקאמר אכתובים קאי ולא אנביאים ומדומה אני מפני שמצינו ביונתן בן עוזיאל שאמרו תרגום הן נופרשין כך ואני אומר אף בנביאים אם אמר יונתן לא כתבו ולא ניתנו ליכתב והכי מפרש במסכת מגילה (דף ט.) ומאן דאסר בכולהו אסר בר מס"ת יוונית משום מעשה דתלמי המלך ולא מפליג התם בין נביאים לכתובים: מפני בטול בית המדרש. שהיה קבוע בשבת כדפרישית לעיל: **גמ'** איתמר היו כתובין תרגום. אכתובים קאמר ול"נ אכל כתבי הקדש קאי: אליבא דמאן דאמר ניתנו לקרות בהן. מותר לקרות בכתבי הקדש הכתובין בכל לשון במסכת מגילה (דף ח:) ואין בין ספרי' ותפילין ומזוזות אלא שהספרים נכתבין בכל לשון: לא ניתנו. (*רבן גמליאל) פליג עלה ואמר אף ספרים לא התירו שיכתבו אלא יוונית: ואע"פ שכתובין בכל לשון. ולא ניתנו לקרות דמדקאמר אף על פי מכלל דלא ניתנו לקרות בהן דאי ניתנו מאי גריעותייהו: אימא סיפא. לדידך דאמרת אע"פ שכתובין בכל לשון אמצילין קאי אימא סיפא על כרחיך מילתא באנפיה נפשיה הוא וטעונין גניזה בחול פשיטא השתא בשבת מצילינן להו גניזה בחול מיבעיא: ואפילו הכי בעו גניזה. ודקתני ואע"פ שכתובין בכל לשון לאו אהצלה קאי אלא אטעונין גניזה והכי קאמר אף על פי שכתובים בכל לשון ובשבת אין מצילין אותן בחול מיהא טעונין גניזה: ומקק שלהם. אם בלו ונעשו רקבון אף המקק רקבובית (ה) של אכילת התולעים טעונין גניזה: עברית. כתב של עבר הנהר: אבא חלפתא. אבא של רבי יוסי חלפתא שמו: רבן גמליאל בריבי. לא שהיה בנו של רבי אלא אדם גדול קרי בריבי: רבן גמליאל אבי אביך. הוא רבן גמליאל הזקן ורבן גמליאל שהיה בדורו של חלפתא הוא אבי אביו של רבינו הקדוש: גב מעלה בהר הבית. שבהר הבית היו מעלות כשהוא הולך וגבוה כדתנן במסכת מדות (פ"ב מ"ג): נדבך. שורת אבני הבנין: טיט בהר הבית מנין. וכי בטיט היו בונין והלא בטרכסיד היו בונים חול וסיד מעורבין וטיט לא הוי אלא עפר ומים: התורפה. גלוי והפקר: מאן תנאי. דקאמר רב הונא לעיל תנאי היא מאן מהני תנאי קאי כרב חסדא ומאן כרב הונא: אילימא

תוספות

כל כתבי הקדש מצילין אותן מפני הדליקה כו'. אומר ר"ת דכולא האי פירקא איירי כשנפלה דליקה באותו בית או באותו חצר דכיון שהאש שם ודאי בהול הוא ואי שרית ליה אתי לכבויי כדמפרש בגמרא אבל נפלה דליקה בבית אחר מותר להציל הכל:

אליבא דמ"ד ניתנו לקרות בהן כ"ע לא פליגי דמצילין. והשתא ספרים שלנו מצילין דנתנו לקרות בהן משום עת לעשות לה' הפרו תורתך כדאמרינן בהניזקין (גיטין ס.): **לא** ניתנו לקרות בהן. פירש רש"י דהיינו רבן שמעון בן גמליאל דפליג במתניתין בפ"ק דמגילה (דף ח:) דאף ספרים לא התירו שיכתבו אלא יוונית ופירש הרב פור"ת דהיינו טעמא כיון דלא ניתנו ליכתב אסור לקרות בהן משום דדברים שבכתב אסור לאומרן בעל פה וקשה דאין זה אי אתה רשאי לאומרו בע"פ כיון שאינו אומרו בלשון הקדש אלא באותו לשון כשהן כתובין דהא שרי למימר בעל פה תרגום [*]במתרגם רב יוסף:

עילמית יוונית. אומר ר"י דאתיא כרבי יהודה דאסר שאר ספרים לכתוב יוונית ולא התיר אלא בס"ת בלבד אבל רבנן שרו אף בשאר ספרים כדאמר בפ"ק דמגילה (דף ט.):

ובידו ספר איוב תרגום. משמע שבימי התנאים כבר נעשה תרגום כתובים וכן תניא במגילה (דף כא:) (ו)במגילה ובהלל אפילו עשרה קורין ועשרה מתרגמין מה שאין כן בתורה אע"פ שיונתן לא עשאו מ"מ שוב נעשה בימי התנאים ודלא (ז)כאומרים דתרגום של כתובים רב יוסף עשאו*:

רבינו חננאל

מהתם. דגרסי' התם א"ר ישמעאל אחוי דר' ברכיה ויבדיל שכן הוא מותר להדיח כבשים ושלקות. כלומר דברים שאסורי' בשבת ומותרי' ביוה"כ ומשני לא מן המנחה ולמעלה מותר להדיח דאלמא שבת דחוקה היא ויבדיל מן המנחה ולמעלה. ושנינן מה נפשך כוס אין כאן נר אין כאן במה מבדילין א"ר אבין בתפלה: וראינו שפירש בה רבינו האיי הגאון נר ישראל יחיה ויפרה לעד. האי קושטא קושטיא היא מיהו מחויא מילתא דבערב יוה"כ נמי הות תקיעה להבטיל העם מן המלאכה ולהבדיל בין קודש לחול ולערבי יו"ט נמי איכא טובא אלא מיהו כד הוי ערב יוה"כ ועיו"ט חול. אלא כד הוי קודש לא תקעינן. ואע"ג דלא מיפרשא בתקיעות שהיו במקדש. דייקינן מהא דתנן בפ' קמא דשחיטת חולין (דף כו:) כל מקום שיש הבדלה אין תוקעין וכל מקום שיש תקיעה אין הבדלה כיצד יו"ט שחל להיות ערב שבת תוקעין אבל לא מבדילין מכלל דביו"ט שאינו ע"ש היו מבדילין אבל לא תוקעין*) מכלל דאי הוה יו"ט בתר חול היו תוקעין וראוי לדעת דהני כולהו שמעתתא אליבא דאחרים. אבל לדילן לא מיתרמי לן יוה"כ סמוך לשבת לא מלפניה ולא מאחריה. ומפרש בגמרא דהליל. דכד מיקלע כפורים בחד בשבא מדחינן ליה. ומקשינן ומי דחינן והתנן חלבי שבת קריבין ביוה"כ. וא"ר זירא כי הוינא בבבל אמרי' הא דתניא יוה"כ שחל להיות ע"ש לא היו תוקעין ובמוצ"ש לא היו מבדילין דברי הכל היא. ופרקי' ההיא מתניתא אחרים היא דתניא אחרים אומרים אין בין עצרת לעצרת אין בין ר"ה לר"ה אלא ד' ימים. ואם היתה שנה מעוברת חמשה. וגרסינן בירושל' בתחלת מגילה. א"ר יוסי לית כאן חל להיות בשני חל להיות בשבת דאם חל להיות י"ד בשני צומא רבא בחד בשבא. ואם חל בשבת צומא רבא בעירובתא שמעינן מינה דאע"ג דסתם משנה היא דהויה היא ומשנת יחיד היא ולאו דסמכא היא. וכן כל משנה והלכה שהיא כיוצא בה. וכולן בדן ואודן בה תלוין שהלכה למשה מסיני שלא לקבוע יוה"כ סמוך לשבת בין מלפניה בין מאהריה ולענין קניבת ירק הלכתא יוה"כ שחל להיות בשבת אסור בקניבת ירק ואפילו מן המנחה ולמעלה. ואם חל להיות בחול מפצעין באגוזים ומפרכין ברמונים ומותר בקניבת ירק מן המנחה ולמעלה אבל [משום] מינדר [מילתא אסרוהו]: הדרן עלך ואלו קשרים

פרק טז כל כתבי הקדש מצילין אותן מפני הדליקה בין שקורין בהן בין שאין קורין בהן. פירוש קורין בהן בצבור. תורה הפרשה בתורה ואפטרתא בנביאים ושאין קורין בהן בצבור כתובים. איתמר היו כתובין תרגום ובכל לשון רב הונא אמר אין מצילין אותן מפני הדליקה. רב חסדא אמר מצילין ובכתבי הקדש שמתורגמין בלשון אחר בין בכתב עברי בין בכתב אחר. ר' יוסי אמר לא ניתנו לקרות בהן דא"ר יוסי מעשה באבא חלפתא שהלך אצל רבן גמליאל לטבריא ומצאו יושב על שולחנו של יוחנן בן הנזוף ובידו ספר איוב תרגום א"ל רבי זכור אני את רבן גמליאל אבי אביך שהיה עומד ע"ג מעלה בהר הבית והביאו לפניו ספר איוב תרגום ואמר לבנאי שקעהו תחת הנדבך. אף הוא צוה עליו ונגנז ור' נמי הכי קאמר מניחו במקום התורפה והן כלין מאליהן. ולפום הכי תנא ר' יוסי אין מצילין אותן.

*) הכר וצ"ל ומדתנן יו"ט שחל כמו"ש מבדילין ולא תוקעין.

עין משפט נר מצוה

א א מיי' פ"י מהלכות ס"ת הלכה ג טוש"ע יו"ד סימן רפב סעיף ה:
ב ב מיי' פכ"ג מהלכות שבת הלכה כו סמג לאוין סה טוש"ע או"ח סימן שלד סעיף יב:

מסורת הש"ס

[פי' שלא יהא טורח במוצאי היום בקניבה ותהא נפשו עגומה עליו וכן מפצעין באגוזי' ומפרכין ברמונים ודוקא מן המנחה ולמעלה שמאחר שהוא קרוב לעת האוכל דומה למי שיש לו פת בסלו ולא אתי למיכל מינייהו אבל קודם המנחה אסור גזרינן דילמא אתי למיכל מינה ורב"י פי' בזה שאמרו משום עגמת נפש בענין אחר ולא ישר בעיני עכ"ל בעל המאור]

[תוספ' פי"ד]

[מס' סופרים פ"ה הט"ו]

[בתוספתא אי' ר' יוחנן בן ניזוף]

ס"א מתאבדין

הגהות הגר"א

[א] גמ' מותר. נ"ל אסור: [ב] שם (ואמר רחב"א א"ר"י) תא"מ: [ג] שם בחול. נ"ב מותר כן הוא גירסת הרמב"ם ומ"מ (ועמ"ש רבינו בא"ח סימן תרי"א סק"ד):

הגהות הב"ח

(א) במשנה ואע"פ שכתובין: (ב) גמ' ואע"פ כו' ואע"פ כו' ולא ניתנו: (ג) שם תרגום ובכל לשון: (ד) רש"י ד"ה מצילין וכו' דשרי בהו וחסרון: (ה) ד"ה ומקק שלהן וכו' רקבובית. נ"ב עי' לעיל דף ל ע"א: (ו) תוס' ד"ה ובידו וכו' ובהלל ובמגילה אפילו עשרה: (ז) בא"ד ודלא כאומרים. נ"ב כלומר אבל קודם זה לא נעשה בימי התנאים ולא גרסי ועשרה מתרגמין וכמו שפירש"י במגילה אלא כבר נעשה בימי התנאים כמו שמוכח הכא:

גליון הש"ס

תוס' ד"ה לא ניתנו. כדמתרגם ר"י. עיין בב"ק דף ג ע"ב בתוס' ד"ה כדמתרגם:

עין משפט
נר מצוה

ג א מיי' שם הלכה כו סמג שם טוש"ע שם:
ד ב מיי' וסמג שם טור שו"ע שם סעיף יד:
ה ג מיי' שם טוש"ע שם סעיף יב:
ו ד מיי' פ"ב מהלכות מגילה הלכה ט סמג עשין ד טוש"ע או"ח סימן תרלא סעיף א:
ז ה ו ז ח מיי' פרק כג מהלכות שבת הלכה כח סמג לאוין סה טור שו"ע או"ח סימן שלד סעיף יב:

תורה אור

אילימא תנא קמא *דרבי יוסי ודילמא בהא קמיפלגי מר סבר ניתנו לקרות בהן ומר סבר לא ניתנו לקרות בהן אלא רבי יוסי ותנא דגיפטית *ת"ר אהברכות בוהקמיעין אע"פ שיש בהן אותיות של שם ומעניינות הרבה שבתורה אין מצילין אותן מפני הדליקה אלא נשרפים במקומן [הן ואזכרותיהן] מכאן אמרו כותבי ברכות כשורפי תורה מעשה באחד שהיה כותב בצידן באו והודיעו את רבי ישמעאל והלך רבי ישמעאל לבודקו כשהיה עולה בסולם הרגיש בו נטל טומוס של ברכות ושקען בספל של מים ובלשון הזה אמר לו רבי ישמעאל גדול עונש האחרון מן הראשון בעא מיניה ריש גלותא מרבה בר רב הונא גהיו כתובין בסם ובסיקרא בקומוס ובקנקנתום בלשון הקדש מצילין אותן מפני הדליקה או אין מצילין תיבעי למ"ד מצילין תיבעי למ"ד אין מצילין תיבעי למ"ד אין מצילין הני מילי היכא דכתיבי תרגום ובכל לשון אבל הכא דכתיבי בלשון הקדש מצילין או דילמא אפי' למ"ד מצילין ה"מ היכא דכתיבי בדיו דמיקיים אבל הכא כיון דלא מיקיים לא א"ל אין מצילין והא רב המנונא תנא מצילין א"ל *אי תניא תניא מאי תניא אמר רב אשי כדתניא *אין בין [מגילה ח:] ספרים למגילה אלא שהספרים נכתבים בכל לשון דומגילה עד שתהא כתובה אשורית על הספר ובדיו בעא מיניה רב הונא בר חלוב מרב נחמן ס"ת שאין בו ללקט שמונים וחמש אותיות כגון פרשת ויהי בנסוע הארון מצילין אותה מפני הדליקה או אין מצילין א"ל ותיבעי לך פרשת ויהי בנסוע הארון גופה ההיכא דחסר פרשת ויהי בנסוע לא קמיבעיא לי דכיון דאית ביה הזכרות אע"ג דלית ביה שמונים וחמש אותיות מצילין כי קא מיבעיא לי ס"ת שאין בו ללקט מאי א"ל ואין מצילין איתיביה זתרגום שכתבו מקרא ומקרא שכתבו תרגום וכתב עברית מצילין מפני הדליקה ואצ"ל תרגום שבעזרא ושבדניאל ושבתורה תרגום שבתורה מאי ניהו °יגר שהדותא [בראשית לא] ואף על גב דלית בה שמונים וחמש אותיות כי תניא ההיא איבעיא להו הני שמונים וחמש אותיות מכונסות או מפוזרות רב הונא אמר מכונסות רב חסדא אמר אפילו מפוזרות מיתיבי ס"ת שבלה אם יש בו ללקט שמונים וחמש אותיות כגון פרשת ויהי בנסוע הארון מצילין ואם לאו אין מצילין תיובתא דרב הונא *תרגמה רב חסדא אליבא דרב הונא חבתיבות ת"ר °ויהי בנסוע [במדבר י] הארון ויאמר משה פרשה זו עשה לה הקב"ה סימניות מלמעלה ולמטה לומר שאין

רש"י

אילימא ת"ק. כרב חסדא ור' יוסי כרב הונא: דילמא. טעמא דת"ק משום דקסבר ניתנו לקרות בהן והאי דר' יוסי קאי כרב הונא מיהו כרב חסדא לא קאי ולא חד דהא רב חסדא אפי' למ"ד לא ניתנו קאמר מצילין: הברכות. מטבע ברכות שטבעו חכמים כגון י"ח ושאר ברכות: ומעניינות הרבה. מפרשיות שהיו כותבין בקמיעין פסוקים ללחש כגון כל המחלה וכגון לא תירא מפחד לילה: נשרפין במקומן. אם נפלה דליקה בשבת: כשורפי תורה. שהרי לא יצילם בשבת: לבודקו. אם אמת היה הדבר: טומוס. קבוצת קונטריסים: היו כתובין. תורה נביאים וכתובים: תיבעי למ"ד. בנכתבים בכל לשון מצילין תיבעי למ"ד אין מצילין: דלא מיקיים. אין מתקיים כדיו: הא רב המנונא תנא מצילין: מאי תניא. היכא תניא: מדקאמר מגילה בדיו. וקתני דהוא מן הדברים שבין ספרים למגילה ש"מ שאר ספרים נכתבים בסם ובסיקרא: בר חלוב. שם אדם: פ"ה אותיות. זהו שיעור לספר תורה שנמחק או בלה להיות עומד בקדושתו: כגון פרשת ויהי בנסוע הארון. שהוא ספר לעצמו כדלקמן ויש בה פ"ה אותיות: ללקט. שנשארת כאן תיבה ובמקום אחר תיבה: מהו. להצילן: ותיבעי לך לפרשת ויהי בנסוע הארון גופה. שנכתבה לבדה וחסרה אות מהו להצילה: שאין בו כדי ללקוט. ובאותו ליקוט עצמו ליכא אזכרות: תרגום שבתורה. יגר שהדותא ושבנביאים כגון כדנא תימרון להום (ירמיה י) שכתבו מקרא [א"נ] התרגום שבעזרא כתבו מקרא: כתב עברית. אותיות גדולות הן ואין דומות לכתב אשורית אף ע"פ שכתובין בלשון הקדש אלא שכתב האותיות משונות: ואין צ"ך לומר תרגום שבעזרא ושבדניאל ושבתורה. שכתבו תרגום כהלכתו: להשלים. אם היה בו כדי ללקט ותרגום זו משלימו מצטרף ומצילין בשבילו: תיובתא דרב הונא. דמדקתני ללקט מכלל דמפוזרות נינהו: בתיבות. הא דקתני ללקט דמשמע מפוזרות לא ללקט אות ואות לבד אלא ללקט תיבה שלימה תיבה כאן ותיבה כאן עד פ"ה אותיות וכי פליגינן באותיות המפוזרות: עשה לה סימניות מלמעלה ומלמטה. להבדיל' מן הסמוכות לה: למעלה ולמטה. בתחלה ובסוף ויהי בנסוע הארון:

שאין

תוספות

היו כתובים בסם ובסיקרא כו'. משמע דפשיטא ליה שאין קורין בהן דאי קורין בהן פשיטא דמצילין כדאמר לעיל וקשה לרשב"א דבסמוך משמע דפשיטא ליה לריש גלותא גופיה דקורין בהן דקאמר והתניא מצילין והיינו ההוא ברייתא דמייתי שהספרים נכתבים בכל לשון ומגילה עד שתהא כתובה אשורית על הספר ובדיו אבל שאר ספרים נכתבין שלא בדיו ולפי מה שאפרש בסמוך דהך ברייתא איירי לענין הגלה אתי שפיר ולעולם אין קורין בהן:

אבל הכא כיון דלא מקיים לא. אע"ג דבפ"ב דגיטין (דף יט.) קרי להו דבר שמתקיים דתנן בכל כותבין בסם ובדיו ובסקרא ובקומוס ובקנקנתוס ובכל דבר שמתקיים אומר ר"י דהתם קרי ליה מתקיים טפי ממשקין ומי פירות דקתני התם בסיפא דאין כותבין בהן אבל אין מתקיימין כמו דיו אבל קשה לר"י דתנן בפ"ב דסוטה (דף יז:) גבי מגילת סוטה אין כותבין לא בקומוס ולא בקנקנתוס שנאמר ומחה כתב שיכול למחוק אלמא קומוס וקנקנתוס מתקיימין יותר מדיו ואומר ר"י דלעולם אין מתקיימין כמו דיו ואין יכול למחות כמו דיו לפי שנבלעין בקלף:

מגילה עד שתהא כתובה אשורית על הספר ובדיו. משמע דשאר ספרים לא בעי ספר ודיו וקשה דבפ' המוציא יין (לעיל דף עט:) משמע דספר תורה בעי ספר דתני' על הגייר ועל המטלית פסולה ומוקי לה בס"ת וה"ה על הדיפתרא אע"ג דלא חשיב ליה לענין פסול ה"נ לא חשיב ליה לענין כשרות דקתני על הקלף ועל הדוכסוסטוס כשירה ולא קתני דיפתרא ועוד תנן במסכת סופרים (פ"א) אין כותבין לא ע"ג דיפתרא ולא ע"ג נייר מחוק ועוד דמגילה פסולה אדיפתרא כדתנן פ"ב דמגילה (דף יז.) וכן מגילת סוטה פסולה אדיפתרא כדאמר בפ"ב דסוטה (דף יז:) משום דבעיא ספר וכ"ש ס"ת דנקראת כמה פעמים ספר ודיו נמי צריך כדאמר בפרק הבונה (לעיל קג:) כתבה שלא בדיו או שכתב האזכרות בזהב הרי אלו יגנזו ותירץ הרב יוסף דס"ת ודאי בעי ספר ודיו והכא איירי דווקא בשאר ספרים והא דלא קתני אין בין ספרים לס"ת ומגילה משום דס"ת נכתבים בכל לשון להכי לא עריב לה ואכתי קשה לר"י דתנן בפ"ק דמגילה (דף ח:) אין בין ספרים לתפילין ומזוזות אלא שהספרים נכתבין בכל לשון כו' ופריך בגמרא וספרים נכתבין בכל לשון ורמינהו מקרא שכתבו תרגום ותרגום שכתבו מקרא וכתב עברי אינו מטמא את הידים עד שיכתבנו בכתב אשורית על הספר ובדיו ומשני כאן בספרים כאן במגילה ורב אשי משני כי תניא ההיא בשאר ספרים ורבי יהודה היא אלמא בשאר ספרים נמי בעי רבי יהודה ספר ודיו והוא הדין לרבנן דלא אשכחן דפליגי רבנן עליה אלא בכתב אשורית אבל בספר ודיו לא אשכחן דפליגי ועוד קשה דשביק רב אשי התם שינויא קמא דמוקי לה במגילה ומסייע ליה ברייתא דהכא דקתני בהדיא דמגילה בעי שתהא כתובה אשורית וספר ודיו ורב אשי גופיה מייתי לה הכא ונראה לר"י דדוקא לענין הגלה מיתניא הך ברייתא דאין בין ספרים למגילה אלא שהספרים נכתבין בכל לשון ואפי' בלא ספר ודיו חשיבו לענין דמצילין אותו מפני הדליקה אע"ג דלא חזו לקריאה משום דיש בהו אזכרות אבל במגילה אין מצילין אלא א"כ ראויה לקריאה שתהא כתובה אשורית על הספר ובדיו לפי שאין בה הזכרה ולמ"ד א"כ תקשה מברייתא דהכא דאמר לעיל כל היכא דלא ניתנו לקרות בהן אין מצילין וי"ל דהא מסיק לעיל תנאי היא:

מיתיבי ס"ת שבלה אם יש בה כדי ללקט כו'. השתא משמע דמלשון ללקט קא פריך דמשמע אפי' מפוזרות ותימה א"כ אמאי קא בעי מעיקרא מכונסות או אפי' מפוזרות פשיטא דאפי' מפוזרות מדבעא רב הונא ס"ת שאין בו ללקט משמע הא יש בו ללקט מצילין אע"פ שהן מפוזרות:

רבינו חננאל

ושאר תנאי*) (דתנן) [דאמרי] מצילין לא מסיים מן מינהון סבר ניתנו לקרות בהן. ומאן מנהון סבר לא ניתנו לקרות בהן אלא האי תנא דגפטית. דתני אע"פ שלא ניתנו לקרות בהן מצילין אותן. ות"ק דר' יוסי בניתנו לקרות בהן פליג. וקי"ל כרב הונא דרב חסדא לגביה תלמיד הוא. והא דתנינן כל כתבי הקדש מוקים לה רב הונא בתרי בבי. כל כתבי הקדש מצילין אותן מפני הדליקה בין נביאי' שקורין בהן בין כתובים שאין קורין בהן. בד"א בכתבי הקדש הכתובים בלשה"ק [אבל אי הוי] אינון כתבי הקדש כתובי' בכל לשון אין מצילין אותן מפני הדליקה ואפי' הכי טעונין גניזה והא ברייתא דתניא הברכות והקמיעות אע"פ שיש בהן של שם ומעניינות של תורה הרבה אין מצילין אותן מפני הדליקה ונגנזין במקומן הלכה היא. והלכה כדתנא רב המנונא שאם היו כתובים בסם ובסיקרא מצילין אותן אע"פ שאינו דבר של קיימא. ולענין בעיא דרב הונא בר חלוב מרב נחמן סוגיא דשמעתא. כל ס"ת דאית ביה פיסקא דאית ביה שם אע"ג דאין בו ללקט פ"ה אותיות מצילין אותו. והאי דתניא יגר שהדותא מצילין אותו להשלים דאי איכא פ"ה אותיות אע"ג שמהן יגר שהדותא מצילין אותו. והלכתא כרב הונא דהני פ"ה אותיות מכונסות ולא מפוזרות. ופי' מכונסות כדתרגמא רב חסדא אליבא דרב הונא בתיבו' אי יכול ללקט פ"ה אותיות מס"ת מתוך תיבות שלימות מצילין אותו כגון דמשכחת בראשית והיא מניה לשש. ויצא מניה לארבע. ואלה מניה לארבע. ויקרא מניה לחמש כולן תיבות שלימות עשרים (וא"ו) [או] פחות או יתר שמנין אותיותיהן פ"ה. אבל אותיות שמתוך תיבות שאינן שלימות אין מצילין כגון ויאמר מכלל ויאמר. אבר מכלל אברם או אברהם וכיוצא בהן. כל שנמצאת תיבה שלימה מונין אותיותיה להעלות לפ"ה אותיות וכל תיבה מקצתה מטושטשת אין אותיותיה המוגהות עולות למנין פ"ה. ומשו"ה אמרן ללקט ואע"פ שהתיבות מפוזרו' במקומו' רחוקין זה מזה: גליונים של ס"ת. איבעיא אם מצילין אותן ולא איפשיטא. ס"ת שנמחק מקום המחק אין מצילין אותו ואם לאו אין מצילין אותו. וליפוק ליה משום גליון. בלה שאני כלומר אם מצילין מפני הגליונים לא הוה צריך לדקדוקי בתר פ"ה אותיות. ושנינן בלה שאני מכלל כי אם לא בלה מצילין אותו מפני הגליונין אע"פ שאין בו ללקט פ"ה אותיות. ת"ש ס"ת שנמחק אם יש בו כדי ללקט פ"ה אותיות מצילין אותו ואם לאו אין מצילין אותו. ושנינן נמחק לא קא מיבעיא לן דכי קדוש כי איכא כתב. כי ליכא כתב לא קדוש. כי קא מיבעיא לי גליונות של מעלה ושל מטה ושבין דף לדף ושבין פרשה לפרשה שבתחילת הספר ושבסופו (מ"ש) [כאי]. ת"ש גליונין של מעלה ושל מטה שבין דף לדף שבין פרשה לפרשה שבתחלת הספר ושבסופו מטמאין את הידים. ושנינן דילמא כי חשיבי אגב ס"ת. אבל גליונים דלא ממטו את הידים לאו כוותיה אינון. וכיון דבעיא זו לא איפשיטא מחמרינן בבזיון כתבי קדש. ומצילין אותן הגליונין מפני הדליקה בשבת ותוב מהא דתניא הגליונין וספרי המינין אין מצילין אותן מפני הדליקה. סיגו דדחינן ומוקמינן לה גליונין של ספרי מינין. ואקשינן מכלל דספרי מינין גופיהן מצילין. ושנינן הכי ספרי מינין הרי הן כגליונין. כלומר כשם שהגליונין שאין כתיבה עליהן אין להן כבוד ואין מצילין אותן. כך ספרי מינין מכלל שהגליונין של ס"ת מצילין אותן. והני ספרי מינין. ספרי תורה שכתבן מין איתן דקי"ל כר"נ דאמר גקימיט ס"ת שכתבו מין ישרף. כתבו נכרי יגנז. נמצא ביד מין יגנז. ביד נכרי אמרי לה יגנז ואמרי לה קורין בו. אבל הספרים שחיברו אותן המינין דברי הבל ישרפו. דהא כתבי קדש שכתובין תרגום אפילנו בהו אם

*) נראה מזה דרבינו לא היה גורס אילימא ת"ק דר"י ודילמא בהא קמיפלגי רק היה לו גי' אחרת דזה וצ"ע.

מסורת הש"ס

ז"ל ור' יוסי

[לעיל סא: ע"ש] [תוספתא פי"ד] מ"ס פ' טו הלכה ד]

[חגיגה יג: מו"ק ד. יומא לא: יבמות קיב: נדרים יט: זבחים טו: לא: לז: מנחות קז: בכורות ז. חולין צג. תמורה לא: נדה כג: ועי' פרש"י]

[לעיל נג: ע"ש]

accord.[5] Which Tannaim [differ on this question]?[6] [115b] Shall we say the first Tanna and R. Jose,—but perhaps they differ in this: one Master holds, It is permitted to read them; while the other holds, It is not permitted to read them?[7] Rather [they are] R. Jose and the Tanna [who taught the law] about the Egyptian [script].

Our Rabbis taught: Benedictions and amulets, though they contain letters of the [Divine] Name and many passages of the Torah, must not be rescued from a fire but must be burnt where they lie,[8] they together with their Names. Hence it was said,' They who write down Benedictions are as though they burnt a Torah.[9] It happened that one was once writing in Sidon. R. Ishmael was informed thereof, and he went to question him [about it]. As he was ascending the ladder, he [the writer] became aware of him, [so] he took a sheaf of benedictions and plunged them
a into a bowl of water. In these words[1] did R. Ishmael speak to him: The punishment for the latter [deed] is greater than for the former.

The Resh Galutha[2] asked Rabbah son of R. Huna: If they are written with paint [dye], *siḳra*,[3] gum ink, or calcanthum,[4] in Hebrew, may they be rescued from a fire or not? This is asked whether on the view that we may save[5] or that we may not save. It is asked on the view that we may not save: that may be only if they are written in Targum or any [other] language; but here that they are written in Hebrew, we may rescue [them]. Or perhaps even on the view that we may save [them], that is only when they are written in ink, which is lasting; but here, since it [the writing] is not permanent, [we may] not [rescue them]?—We may not save [them], answered he. But R. Hamnuna recited, We may save [them]?—If it was taught, it was taught, replied he.[6] Where was it taught?—Said R. Ashi, Even as it was taught: The only difference between the [other] Books[7] and the Megillah[8] is that the Books can be written in any language, whereas a *Megillah* must be written in Assyrian,[9] on a Scroll, and in ink.[10]

R. Huna b. Ḥalub asked R. Naḥman: A Scroll of the Law in which eighty-five letters cannot be gathered,[11] such as the section, *And it came to pass when the Ark set forward* [etc.],[12] may it be saved from a fire or not?—Said he, Then ask about the section, *'and it*
b *came to pass*, etc.,' itself![1]—If the section, '*And it came to pass*, etc.,' is defective [through effacing], I have no problem, for since it contains the Divine Name, even if it does not contain eighty-five letters we must rescue it. My only problem is about a Scroll of the Law wherein [this number] cannot be gathered: what then? We may not save it, he answered.

He refuted him: If Targum is written as *Miḳra*,[2] or *Miḳra* is written in Targum or in Hebrew characters,[3] they must be saved from a fire, and the Targum in Ezra, Daniel and the Torah [the Pentateuch] go without saying. Now, what is the Targum in the Torah? [The words], *Yegar sahadutha;*[4] and though it does not contain eighty-five letters [it must be saved]?—That was taught in respect of completing [the number].[5]

The scholars asked: These eighty-five letters, [must they be] together or [even] scattered? R. Huna said: [They must be] together; R. Ḥisda said: Even scattered. An objection is raised: If a Scroll of the Law is decayed, if eighty-five letters can be gathered therein, such as the section, '*and it came to pass when the ark set forward* etc.,' we must save it; if not, we may not save it. This refutes R. Huna?[6]—R. Ḥisda expounded it on the basis of R. Huna's [ruling as referring] to words.[7]

Our Rabbis taught: '*And it came to pass when the ark set forward that Moses said*, [etc.]': for this section the Holy One, blessed be He, provided signs above and below,[8] to teach [116a] that

(5) The objection to writing down the Targum was probably due to the fear that it might in time be regarded as sacred. V. also Kaplan, op. cit., p. 285. (6) *Sc.* whether they may be rescued from a fire. (7) And the question whether they may be saved depends on whether they may be read. (8) Lit., 'in their place'. (9) Since should fire break out they may not be saved (Rashi).

a (1) Lit., 'this language.' (2) V. *supra* 48a, n. b7. (3) A red paint. (4) Vitriol used as an ingredient of shoe-black and of ink (Jast.). (5) Holy writings written in other languages. (6) Then I am wrong. (7) Comprising the Bible—i.e., the Torah, Prophets and Hagiographa. (8) The Book of Esther. (9) The modern square Hebrew characters, which superseded the older Hebrew, viz., Syriac or Samaritan form. V. Meg., 8b, n. c4 and Sanh., 22a, n. a4. (10) Ri: this is only in respect of saving them from a fire. Other books even if not written on a scroll and in ink must be saved, whereas for a *Megillah* these conditions are necessary. (11) I.e., the whole Scroll is effaced and eighty-five clear letters cannot be found in it. This is the minimum for a Scroll to retain its sanctity. (12) Num. X, 35-36. That contains eighty-five letters, and as stated *infra* it is designated a separate 'Book'.

b (1) If it is written separately upon a piece of parchment, and one or more of its letters are effaced. (2) I.e., if the Biblical passages which are in Aramaic in the original are written in Hebrew, as practically the whole of the Pentateuch (*miḳra*—lit., 'reading') is. (3) Samaritan script. V. *supra*, n. a9. (4) Gen. XXXI, 47, q.v. (5) I.e., if the Scroll contains eighty-five uneffaced letters including *yegar sahadutha*, it must be saved. (6) Because 'can be gathered' implies that they are scattered. (7) It contains complete words scattered about which total to eighty-five letters. They differ where all the eighty-five letters are scattered, the Scroll containing no complete words at all. (8) I.e., at the beginning and at the end.—In the Scrolls the section is preceded and followed by a reversed *nun*, which distinguishes and divorces it from the adjoining passages.

a this is not its place. Rabbi said: It is not on that account,[1] but because it ranks as a separate Book. With whom does the following dictum of R. Samuel b. Naḥmani in R. Jonathan's name agree: *She* [Wisdom] *hath hewn out her seven pillars:*[2] this refers to the *seven* Books of the Law? With whom? With Rabbi.[3] Who is the Tanna that disagrees with Rabbi? It is R. Simeon b. Gamaliel. For it was taught, R. Simeon b. Gamaliel said: This section is destined to be removed from here and written in its [right place].[4] And why is it written here? In order to provide a break between the first [account of] punishment and the second [account of] punishment.[5] What is the second [account of] punishment?—*And the people were as murmurers,* [etc.].[6] The first [account of] punishment?—*And they moved away from the mount of the Lord,*[7] which R. Ḥama b. R. Ḥanina expounded [as meaning] that they turned away from following the Lord. And where is its [rightful] place?—In [the chapter on] the banners.[8]

The scholars asked: The blank spaces of a Scroll of the Law, may we rescue them from fire or not?—Come and hear: If a Scroll of the Law is decayed, if eighty-five letters can be gathered therein, such as the section *'and it came to pass when the ark set forward,'* we must save it; if not, we may not save it. But why so? conclude [that it may be saved] on account of its blank space?[9]—That which is decayed is different.[10] Come and hear: If a Scroll of the Law is effaced, if eighty-five letters can be gathered therein, such as the section, *'and it came to pass when the ark set forward,'* we must save it; if not, we may not save it. But why so: conclude [that we must
b save it] on account of its blank space?[1]—As for the place of the writing, I have no doubt, for when it was sanctified it was on account of the writing, [and] when its writing goes its sanctity goes [too]. My problem is only in respect of [the blank spaces] above and below, between the sections, between the columns, [and] at the beginning and the end of the Scroll. Yet conclude [that it must be saved] on that account?[2]—It may mean [there] that one had cut off [the blank spaces] and thrown them away.

Come and hear: The blank spaces above and below, between the sections, between the columns, at the beginning and at the end of the Scroll, defile one's hands.[3]—It may be that [when they are] together with the Scroll of the Law they are different.[4] Come and hear: The blank spaces[5] and the Books of the Minim[6] may not be saved from a fire, but they must be burnt in their place, they and the Divine Names occurring in them. Now surely it means the blank portions of a Scroll of the Law? No: the blank spaces in the Books of Minim. Seeing that we may not save the Books of Minim themselves, need their blank spaces be stated?—This is its meaning: And the Books of Minim are like blank spaces.

It was stated in the text: The blank spaces and the Books of the Minim, we may not save them from a fire. R. Jose said: On weekdays one must cut out the Divine Names which they contain, hide them,[7] and burn the rest. R. Tarfon said: May I bury my son if I would not burn them together with their Divine Names if they came to my hand. For even if one pursued me[8] to slay me, or a snake pursued me to bite me, I would enter a heathen Temple [for refuge], but not the houses of these [people], for the latter know [of God] yet deny [Him], whereas the former are ignorant and deny [Him], and of them the Writ saith, *and behind the doors*
c *and the posts hast thou set up thy memorial.*[1] R. Ishmael said: [One can reason] *a minori:* If in order to make peace between man and wife the Torah decreed, Let my Name, written in sanctity, be blotted out in water,[2] these, who stir up jealousy, enmity, and wrath between Israel and their Father in Heaven, how much more so;[3] and of them David said, *Do not I hate them, O Lord, that hate Thee? And am I not grieved with those that rise up against Thee? I hate them with perfect hatred: I count them mine enemies.*[4] And just as we may not rescue them from a fire, so may we not rescue them from a collapse [of debris] or from water or from anything that may destroy them.

R. Joseph b. Ḥanin asked R. Abbahu: As for the Books of *Be Abedan,*[5] may we save them from a fire or not?—Yes and No, and he was uncertain about the matter.[6] Rab would not enter a *Be Abedan,* and certainly not a *Be Niẓrefe;*[7] Samuel would not enter a *Be Niẓrefe*, yet he would enter a *Be Abedan*. Raba was asked: Why did you not attend at the *Be Abedan?* A certain palm-tree stands in the way, replied he, and it is difficult for me [to pass it].[8] Then we will remove it?—Its spot will present diffi-
d culties to me.[1] Mar b. Joseph said: I am one of them[2] and do not fear them. On one occasion he went there, [and] they wanted to harm him.[3]

Imma Shalom, R. Eliezer's wife, was R. Gamaliel's sister. Now,

a (1) Lit., 'designation'. (2) Prov. IX, 1. (3) Since that section is a separate Book, the portions of Numbers preceding and following it are also separate Books; hence there are seven in all. (4) Viz., in the section dealing with the disposition of the Israelites according to their banners and their travelling arrangements, Num. II. (5) So as to relieve the gloomy effect that would otherwise be produced. (6) Num. XI, 1 *seq*. (7) Ibid. X, 33. (8) But in the future, when all evil and its consequent retribution has ceased, this section will be inserted in its right place. (9) And since we do not reason thus, it follows that the margin may not be saved. (10) For the parchment of the margins too is perished. The question is where the parchment is quite sound, but the writing is effaced.

b (1) Which is now the entire Scroll. (2) Even if the place of the writing is no longer sacred, if the margins must be saved, the entire Scroll must be saved *ipso facto*. (3) Cf. *supra* 14*a*. This proves that they have the same sacred character as the rest of the Scroll. (4) The writing there being sound. (5) Jast. s.v. גליון translates, the gospels, though observing that here it is understood as blanks. V. Herford, R.T., *'Christianity in the Talmud'*, p. 155 n. (6) Sectarians. The term denotes various kinds of Jewish sectarians, such as the Sadducees, Samaritans, Judeo-Christians, etc., according to the date of the passage in which the term is used. The reference here is probably to the last-named. V. *J.E.*, art. Min; Bacher in *REJ*. XXXVIII, 38. Rashi translates: Hebrew Bibles written by men in the service of idolatry. (7) V. *supra* 90*a*, n. a5. (8) Lit., 'him'—he meant himself but used the third person owing to a reluctance to speak even hypothetically of evil befalling himself.

c (1) Isa. LVII, 8; they know of the true God, but have rejected Him, thrusting Him out of sight, as it were. (2) The reference is to the trial of a wife accused of adultery; v. Num. V, 23f. (3) Not only do they themselves go astray from God, but lead many others astray from Him. (4) Ps. CXXXIX, 21f. (5) The meeting place of early Christians where religious controversies were held (Jast.). Rashi: the books written for the purpose of these controversies; v. also Weiss, *Dor*, III, p. 166 and n. 13. [The meaning of *Be Abedan* is still obscure in spite of the many and varied explanations suggested; e.g., (*a*) House of the Ebionites; (*b*) *Abadan* (Pers.) 'forum'; (*c*) *Beth Mebedhan* (Pers.) 'House of the chief Magi'; v. Krauss's *Synagogale Altertümer*, p. 31]. (6) V. *supra* 113*a*. (7) בי נצרפי; a meeting place of the Nazarenes, Jewish Christians, where local matters were discussed and religious debates were held. (Levy). [Ginzberg, *MGWJ* LXXVIII, p. 23 regards it as the name of a Persian house of worship meaning the Asylum of Helplessness]. (8) This of course was merely an evasion.

d (1) It will leave a hole and render the road impassable. (2) I am well acquainted with them. (3) Uncensored text adds: R. Meir called it (the Gospel) *'Awen Gilyon*, the falsehood of blank paper; R. Joḥanan called it *'Awon Gilyon*, the sin of etc. On the whole passage v. Herford, op. cit., pp. 161-171.

שאין זה מקומה ר' אומר לא מן השם הוא זה אלא מפני שספר חשוב הוא בפני עצמו כמאן אזלא הא דא"ר שמואל בר *נחמן א"ר יונתן (משלי ט) °חצבה עמודיה שבעה אלו שבעה ספרי תורה כמאן כר' מאן תנא דפליג עליה דר' רשב"ג הוא דתניא רשב"ג אומר עתידה פרשה זו שתיעקר מכאן ותכתב במקומה ולמה כתבה כאן כדי להפסיק בין פורענות ראשונה לפורענות שנייה פורענות שנייה מאי היא (במדבר יא) °ויהי העם כמתאוננים פורענות ראשונה (שם) °ויסעו מהר ה' וא"ר *חמא בר' חנינא שסרו מאחרי ה' והיכן מקומה אמר רב אשי בדגלים °איבעיא להו הגליונין של ס"ת מצילין אותן מפני הדליקה או *אין מצילין אותן מפני הדליקה ת"ש ס"ת שבלה אם יש בו ללקט שמונים וחמש אותיות כגון פרשת ויהי בנסוע הארון מצילין ואם לאו אין מצילין ואמאי תיפוק ליה משום גיליון דידיה בלה שאני ת"ש ס"ת שנמחק אם יש בו ללקט שמונים וחמש אותיות כגון פרשת ויהי בנסוע הארון מצילין ואם לאו אין מצילין ואמאי תיפוק ליה משום גיליון דידיה מקום הכתב לא קמיבעיא לי דכי קדוש אגב כתב הוא דקדוש אזל כתב אזלא לה קדושתיה כי קמיבעיא לי של מעלה ושל מטה שבין פרשה לפרשה שבין דף לדף שבתחלת הספר שבסוף הספר ותיפוק ליה משום ההוא °דגייז ושדי ת"ש *בהגליונין של מעלה ושל מטה שבין פרשה לפרשה שבין דף לדף שבתחלת הספר שבסוף הספר מטמאין את הידים דילמא אגב ס"ת שאני ת"ש גהגיליונין וספרי מינין אין מצילין אותן מפני הדליקה אלא נשרפין במקומן הן ואזכרותיהן מאי לאו גליונין דספר תורה לא גליונין דספרי מינין (א) השתא ספרי מינין גופייהו אין מצילין גליונין מבעיא הכי קאמר וספרי מינין הרי הן כגליונים גופא *הגליונים וספרי מינין אין מצילין אותם מפני הדליקה רבי יוסי אומר בחול קודר את האזכרות שבהן וגונזן והשאר שורפן א"ר טרפון *°אקפח את בני דשאם יבאו לידי שאני אשרוף אותם ואת האזכרות שבהן השאפי' אדם רודף אחריו להורגו ונחש רץ להכישו נכנס לבית ע"ז ואין נכנס לבתיהן של אלו שהללו מכירין וכופרין והללו אין מכירין וכופרין ועליהן הכתוב אומר (ישעיה נז) °[ו]אחר הדלת והמזוזה שמת זכרונך א"ר ישמעאל ק"ו *ומה לעשות שלום בין איש לאשתו אמרה תורה שמי שנכתב בקדושה ימחה על המים הללו שמטילין קנאה ואיבה ותחרות בין ישראל לאביהן שבשמים על אחת כמה וכמה ועליהם אמר דוד (תהלים קלט) °הלא משנאיך ה' אשנא ובתקוממיך אתקוטט תכלית שנאה שנאתים לאויבים היו לי וכשם שאין מצילין אותן מפני הדליקה כך אין מצילין אותן לא מן המפולת ולא מן המים ולא מדבר המאבדן בעי מיניה (ב)יוסף בר חנין מר' אבהו הני ספרי דבי אבידן מצילין אותן מפני הדליקה או אין מצילין *אין ולאו ורפיא בידיה רב °לא אזיל לבי אבידן וכ"ש לבי נצרפי שמואל לבי נצרפי לא אזיל לבי אבידן אזיל אמרו ליה לרבא מ"ט לא אתית לבי אבידן אמר להו דיקלא פלניא איכא באורחא וקשי לי ניעקריה דוכתיה קשי לי מר בר יוסף אמר אנא מינייהו אנא ולא מסתפינא מינייהו זימנא חדא אזיל בעו לסכוניה אימא שלום דביתהו דרבי אליעזר אחתיה דרבן גמליאל הואי הוה ההוא *פילוסופא בשבבותיה

דהוה

רש"י

שאין זה מקומה. שאינה ראויה לכאן דלאו בהליכות מסעות משתעי לעיל מינה אלא בדגלים היתה ראויה ליכתב בפרשת במדבר סיני: לא מן השם הוא זה. לא זה השם של טעמי הסימניות דמקומה הוא דפרשה זו בתחלת מסע שנסעו מהר סיני *איירי כדכתיב לעיל מיניה (ג) ויהי בחדש השני בשנה השנית בעשרים לחדש נעלה הענן וגו': ז' ספרי תורה. דפרשה זו ספר לעצמו נמצא שלמעלה ספר לעצמו [ושלמטה ספר לעצמו] הואיל וזה מקומה נמצא ספר וידבר נחלק לג' ספרים: עתידה פרשה זו. לעתיד שיהו כל הפורעניות בטלין ולא ידאגו לפורענות ויצר הרע בטל: מאחרי ה'. בתוך ג' ימים למסעם התאוו האספסוף תאוה להתרעם על הבשר כדי למרוד בהקב"ה: הגליונין. קלפים חלקים וקס"ד השתא דבכל לדדין שיהו חלקים קמיבעיא ליה כגון חלק שלמעלה ושלמטה ושנמחק כתבו ונעשה חלק: בלה שאני. דכיון שבלה אף הגליון בטל וכי מיבעיא ליה שהגליונין קיימים אלא שהכתב הלך: ותיפוק ליה משום גליון דידיה. דהיינו כל הספר תורה: מקום הכתב. שנמחק: לא מבעיא לי. דודאי מיגרע גרע דכי קדיש מעיקרא לאו לשם גליון חלק קדיש אלא אדעתא דכתב וכיון דאזל ליה כתב פקע מקדושתיה: של מעלה ומטה. דמתחלה לשם חלק קדיש והשתא כשנמחק כתב הספר נמי חלק הוא: ה"ג ותיפוק ליה משום ההוא דגייז ושדי. והכי פירושא ותיפוק לי' דאע"ג דאין בו כדי ללקט פ"ה אותיות הוה ליה למיתני בברייתא מצילין משום ההוא ריוח של מעלה ומטה אלא לאו פשוט מיניה דאין מצילין ומשני דגייז ושדי שנחתכו הגליונים ולא נשתייר בו אלא מקום הכתב: שבתחלת הספר ושבסוף הספר. שכולן היו כתובין כמגילה כס"ת ואמרי' בב"ב בפ"ק (דף יג:) ראשו כדי לגול עמוד סופו כדי לגול היקף להקיף כל הכרך: מטמא את הידים. אם נגע בו ונגע בתרומה פוסלה דמגזירת י"ח דבר היא (לעיל דף יד.): דילמא אגב ס"ת. שלא נמחק כתב הספר אלא כולו קיים וזה נגע בגליונים וכי מבעיא לן בנמחק הספר ואין כאן קדושה אלא משום גליון ששמשו בעודו קיים: ספרי מינין. משרתים לע"ז וכתבו להן תורה נביאים כתובים כתב אשורית ולשון הקודש: וספרי המינין גופייהו מצילין. בתמיה: ספרי המינין הרי הן כגליונים. כקלפים חלקים שלא נכתב בהם מעולם: קודר. חותך חתיכות הקלף מקום השם: שאפי' רודף אדם להורגו. על עצמו קאמר: שהללו. נכרים העובדים ע"ז אינן מכירין שהרי בכך גדלו וכך למדום אבותם: ואחר הדלת והמזוזה שמת זכרונך. זכרון הוא בידך ואינה שכחה לך אלא שהשלכת אותי אחרי הדלת: כך אין מצילין אותן. אפי' בחול: דבי אבידן. ספרים שכתבו להם המינין להתווכח עם ישראל ומקום שמתווכחים שם קרי ליה בי אבידן: אין ולא. זימנין אמר ליה אין זימנין א"ל לא: לבי נצרפי. ע"ז וכך שמה: וקשה לי. שסורשן נעשו גבשושית ולדחותם בקש בא: אמרי ליה ניעקריה קשה לי דוכתיה. שתהא שם גומא אי נמי נסיתיו וקשה לי ריחו וכל זה שהיו מתיראין רב ורבא מלכת לבי אבידן שמא מתוך שיתווכחו יעמדו עליהם. ויהרגום: מינייהו אנא. מכירי הם: פילוסופא. *מין°:

תוספות

פורענות ראשונה ויסעו וא"ר חנינא שסרו מאחרי השם. °פי' בקונטרס שמאז התחילו לשאול בשר ואומר ר"י דאין נ"ל כן אלא פורענות ראשונה כדאמר במדרש (ילמדנו) ויסעו שנסעו מהר סיני דרך שלשת ימים כתינוק היוצא מבית הספר שבורח לו והולך לו כך היו בורחים מהר סיני דרך שלשת ימים לפי שלמדו הרבה תורה בסיני אמר הקב"ה (ד)נסמוך פורענות לפורענות לאו אלא נפסוק פרשת ויהי בנסוע הארון*: ספרי מינין כו' א"ר טרפון כו'. אומר ר"י דמיירי בנמלאו ביד מינין דאי כתבן מין הא אמר בפרק השולח (גיטין דף מה:) נמצא ביד מין יגנז כתבו מין ישרף ודוחק לומר דאתי כר"ט ודלא כרבנן ורבי יוסי: כך אין מצילין אותן לא מן המים כו'. דלא תימא דוקא מן הדליקה אין מצילין משום דאי שרית ליה אתי לכבויי אלא אפילו היכא דליכא למיגזר מידי אסור לטלטלן ולהוציאן והך סיפא כרבנן דלרבי טרפון לא איצטריך: פילוסופא. מין כדפי' בקונטרס ורבינו שמע [מיהודי אחד שבא מארץ יון ואמר] דבלשון יון פלוספוס הוא דוד החכמה ואית דגרסי פילא סבא והוא לשון לצון שחוק כדאמר באיכה רבתי דפלי ביהודאי פירוש שחק ונתלוצץ:

ושמואל

עין משפט נר מצוה

ח א מיי' פכ"ג מהלכות שבת הלכה כז טוש"ע או"ח סימן שלד סעיף כ:

ט ב מיי' פ"ט מהלכות שאר אבות הטומאות הלכה ו:

י ג ד מיי' פ"ו מהלכות יסודי התורה הלכה ח ופ"א מהלכות תפילין הלכה יג טור שו"ע או"ח סימן שלד סעיף כא וטור שו"ע יו"ד סימן רפא סעיף א: [עי' תוי"ט פ"ה דאבות משנה ד]

יא ה טוש"ע יו"ד סימן קנז סעיף ג:

רבינו חננאל

אם מצילין אותן מפני הדליקה אי לא. ספרי מינין מיבעיא. ואלו פ"ה אותיו' כנגד פרשת ויהי בנסוע הארון. ופרשת ויהי בנסוע הארון ספר בפני עצמו הוא. ומקומו בדגלים ולמה נכתב כאן. להפסיק בין פורענו' ראשונה שהיא ויסעו מהר ה' וגו' לפורענות שנייה. שהיא ויהי העם כמתאוננים וגו': ספרי דבי אבידן. חצר ידועה ויש בה ספרי הכמות מכל אומה ויש בה ספרי תור' קדש ונביאים וכתובי' כתובי' בלשה"ק. ומפני שאינו ידוע מי כתבו או ישראל או זולתן. אמרו על ר' אבהו שהיה הדבר רפיא בידיה להורות עליהן להצילן או לא. וזה [בי] אבידן היו מתקבצין שם חכמי' ונבונים מכל אומה ונושאין ונותנין בדברי חכמה. וכן בי נצרפי. מהו בבי נצרפי היתה שם ע"ז. דגרסי' בע"ז איזו היא אשירה סתם. אמר שמואל כגון דאמרי הני תמרי נהווינן לשכרא דבי נצרפי ושתו ליה ביום אידם. אמר אמימר אמרו לי סבי (דשם בריתא) [דפומבדיתא] הלכתא כשמואל והני מילי אלה שהיו באותו זמן (הן) שעד אותה שעה לא טוכסין להן הטוכסוסין שהן עכשיו בידיהן אלא כתועין היו יש מהן שומרין התורה ויש מהן שאינן שומרין וכולן קוראין אותה ויש מי שהיה קוראה בלשה"ק כיון דאסיקנא קוראין בהן בתורה ובנביאים. אבל בכתובים אין קוראין בהן.

רב נסים גאון

פט"ז כמאן אזל הא דא"ר שמואל בר נחמני חצבה עמודיה שבעה אלו ז' חומשי תורה כמאן כר'. דר' סבר ויהי בנסוע הארון ספר בפני עצמו א"כ על דעת ר' מתחילת ספר וידבר עד ויהי בנסוע הארון ספר בפני עצמו ופרש' ויהי בנסוע הארון ספר בפני עצמו ומן שם עד סוף ספר וידבר ספר בפני עצמו נחלק ספר וידבר לג' ספרים הרי ג' ספרי וידבר עם ד' ספרים הנשארים יהיו הכל ז' ובבראשי' דר' אושעיא בפרשת אלה תולדות יצחק (פרשה סד) תניא כוותיה ויקרא אותה שבעה כנגד ספר וידבר שהוא משלים ז' ספרי תורה והלא ה' הם אלא בר קפרא עבד מן ספר וידבר עד ויהי בנסוע הארן ספר בפני עצמו ויהי בנסע הארן ספר בפני עצמו מן תמן ועד סיפיה דספרא ספר בפני עצמו: בי נצרפי מן בתי ע"ז ומשכחת במסכת עירובין בפרק חלון (דף פ) ובמסכת ע"ז בפרק כל הצלמין (דף מח) אי זו היא אשירה סתם אמר רב כל שכומרין משמרין אותה ואין טועמין מפירותיה ושמואל אמר כגון דאמרי הני תמרי נינהו לשיכרא דבי ניצרופי ושתו ליה ביום אידם:

מסורת הש"ס

נמי' דאיירי לעיל מיניה

[ג"ל נחמני]

[תענית כט.]

ידים פ"ג מ"ד ע"ש

[תוספתא' פי"ד]

[לעיל יז.] [זבחים יג.]

[סוכה נג: נדרים סו: מכות יא. חולין קמא.]

[לעיל קיג. וש"נ]

[פירוש חוזה בכוכבי' ערוך]

[ועי' ע"ז דף נד: פירש רש"י פילוסופין חכמי האומות]

הגהות הב"ח

(א) גמ' דספרי מינין (השתא ספרי וכו' מבעיא הא"מ) ונ"ב ג"י רש"י וספרי מינין גופייהו מצילין: (ב) שם בעי מיניה רב יוסף: (ג) רש"י ד"ה לא מן השם וכו' כדכתיב לעיל מיניה ויהי בשנה השנית בחדש השני בעשרים בחדש: (ד) תוס' ד"ה פורעניות וכו' אמר הקב"ה לא נסמוך פורענות לפורענות אלא:

גליון הש"ס

גמ' איבעיא להו הגליונין. עי' מגילה דף לב ע"א תוס' ד"ה הלוחות: שם דגייז ושדי. עי' תשובות זכרון יוסף סימן יא ויב: שם אקפח את בני. לעיל דף יז ע"א זבחים דף יג ע"ב: שם לא אזיל לבי אבידן עי' ע"ז דף יז ע"א תוס' ד"ה הרחק: רש"י בד"ה פילוסופא מין. עי' מס' ד"א רבה פ"ה: תוס' ד"ה פורענות פי' בקונטרס. עי' תוי"ט פ"ה מ"ד דאבות:

עין משפט
נר מצוה

יב א מיי' פכ"ג מהל' שבת הלכה יט סמג לאוין סה :
יג ב מיי' שם הלכה כח סמג שם טוש"ע או"ח סימן של"ד סעיף טו טז :
יד ג מיי' שם הלכה כו טור שו"ע שם סעיף יז יח :
טו ד מיי' פ"א מהלכות ק"פ הלכה טז :

רבינו חננאל

חזר ופירש מפני מה אין קוראין בכתובים מפני ביטול בהמ"ד ומסייעא לה הא דתני העוסק במקרא מדה שאינה מדה כו'. ובית תלמוד ספי עדיף [מהעוסק] במקרא. אמר רב לא שנו שאין קורין בהן אלא בזמן בית המדרש. פי' בשעה שהחכמים יושבי' במדר' ומתעסקין בתלמוד. אבל שלא בזמן בהמ"ד כגון שכבר עמדו בעלי מדרש ונכנסו לבתיהן קורין. ושמואל [אמר] במקום שיש מדרש קבוע כו'. ואסקה רב אשי הכי לעולם כדקאמרינן מעיקרא. אמר רב אין קורין בזמן בהמ"ד כדאמרן אבל בזמן שלא בהמ"ד קורין. ושמואל אמר בין בזמן בהמ"ד בין שלא בזמן בהמ"ד אין קורין. דסבירא ליה כר' נחמיה וגזירה היא משום שטרי הדיוטות והלכתא כלישנא קמא בזמן בית המדרש אין קורין שלא בזמן בית המדרש קורין: ירושלמי (ה"א) אמר ר' יהושע בן לוי הדא אגדתא הכותבה אין לו חלק. הדורשה מתחרך. השומעה אינו מקבל שכר. מיומוי לא איסתכלית בה אלא חד זמן. ואשכחית כתוב בה קע"ה פרשיו' דיבור אמירה צווי שכתוב בתורה כנגד שנות[של] אהע"ה. שנא' לקחת מתנות באדם. וכתיב האדם הגדול בענקים. קמ"ז מזמורו' שכתוב בתילים כנגד שנות יעקב אבינו ללמד שכל קילוסין שישראל (עושין הללויה) מקלסין להקב"ה כנגד שנותיו של יעקב שנא' ואתה קדוש יושב תהלות ישראל קכ"ג פעמים שישראל עונין הללויה כנגד שני אהרן שנאמר הללויה הללו אל בקדשו לקדושו לאהרן קדוש ה' אפילו כן הוינא מיבעיא בליליא: מצילין תיק הספר עם הספר. אמרי רבנן דהאי תיק קאי לחודיה. ונוטלין ממקו' שהוא עם הספר וכן תיק [של] תפילין: י"ד שחל להיות בשבת ר' ישמעאל בנו של ר' יוחנן בן ברוקא אומר מפשיטין את הפסח עד החזה. סבר כיון דאיתעביד ליה צורך גבוה שיכול להוציא החלבים לא יפשוט יותר מזה. ורבנן סבר מפשים כולו. וטעמא כל פעל ה' למענהו. מאי למענהו לעשות כבוד לקדשים: פי' יומא דאסתנא יום שמנשבת רוח צפון שאין הבשר מסריח בו. רבא אמר שלא יהו קדשים מוטלין בעורותיהן כנבילה. אבל אם הוא מוטל בשלחן של זהב שהוא דרך כבוד לא יפשיט יותר למטה מן החזה וכו'. וגרסי' בפסחים בפרק תמיד [נשחט] שהיו מפשיטין. דתנן י"ד שחל להיות בשבת מניח ידו על כתף חבירו כו'. ואמרינן עלה. תנא כל אחד נוטל פסחו בעורו ומפשילו לאחוריו. אמר רב עיליש טייע. פי' שהערביים מפשילין כליהן לאחוריהן. ור' ישמעאל בנו של ר' יוחנן בן ברוקא מוקים למענהו שלא יוצא האמורין קודם הפשטת העור כדי שלא ידבק שיער העור בחלבים: אמרו ליה רבנן (אין) [אי] מצילין תיק הספר עם הספר לא נפשוט (עור עם החזה) [את הפסח מעורו]. אמר להן מי דמי. הצלת תיק טלטול בעלמא הפשטת עור מלאכה דקא בעי ליה לעור. אמר רב אשי בתרי פליגי עליה במלאכה ובטלטול. והכי קאמרי ליה תינח הפשטה שהיא מלאכה טלטול מאי דאיכא

תוספות

ושמואל דאמר כר' נחמיה. ולא פליג אדרב דשפיר מודה דלמתני' דמפרש טעמא מפני ביטול בית המדרש קורין שלא בזמן בית המדרש אלא בא לומר דר' נחמיה פליג עלה דמתני': **וכ"ש** בשטרי הדיוטות. פירש בקונטרס אגרות ותימה דנהגו העולם לקרות בכתב ואגרות השלוחים ממקום למקום ולטלטלן ודאי שרי דהא ראויין לצור ע"פ צלוחית ונראה לר"י דלא קרי שטרי הדיוטות אלא שטרי חובות וכיוצא בהן אבל אגרות שרי דפעמים שיש בהן פקוח נפש ואפי' יודע שאין בו פקוח נפש מתיר ר"ת דלא הוי שטרי הדיוטות כיון שאין צריך למה שכתוב בה לפי שיודע מה שבאיגרות ואם אינו יודע שמא יש בו צורך גדול או פקוח נפש ושרי וכ"מ בירושלמי דקאמר מפני מה אין קורין בכתבי הקדש מפני שטרי הדיוטות שאם אתה אומר לו שהוא מותר אף הוא אומר מה בכך אם אתעסק בשטרותי משמע דווקא כעין חובות ושטרות קאמר וכן פי' רש"י לקמן *גבי גזירה [לקמן קמט.] שלא יקרא בשטרי הדיוטות דבשטרי מקח וממכר קאמר וכן הגיה בפי' כתב ידו ומיהו אותן מלחמות הכתובין בלע"ז נראה לרבינו יהודה דאסור לעיין בהן דלא גרע מהא דתניא בפ' שואל (לקמן קמט.) כתב שתחת הצורה והדיוקנאות אסור לקרות בהן בשבת ואפי' בחול לא ידע ר"י מי התיר דהוי"ל כמושב לצים:

פליגי בטלטול כו'. פי' אחר שנפשט כל העור פליגי דרבנן שרו לטלטל שעדיין צריך לבשר שלא יתלכלך ור' ישמעאל אסר אבל כשאינו מופשט אלא עד החזה שרי לכ"ע לטלטל כדמוכח בסמוך ואע"ג דר' ישמעאל לא שרי להפשיט אלא עד החזה מ"מ פליגי במופשט כולו כגון שעבר בהפשיט אי נמי בתמידים ומוספים דמותר להפשיטן: הכא

דהוה שקיל שמא דלא מקבל שוחדא בעו לאחוכי ביה אעיילא ליה שרגא דדהבא ואזול לקמיה אמרה ליה בעינא דניפלגי לי בנכסי דבי נשי אמר להו פלוגו א"ל כתיב לן במקום ברא ברתא לא תירות א"ל מן יומא דגליתון מארעכון איתנטלית אורייתא דמשה ואיתיהיבת ספרא אחריתי וכתיב ביה ברא וברתא כחדא ירתון למחר הדר עייל ליה איהו חמרא לובא אמר להו שפילית לסיפיה דספרא וכתב ביה אנא לא למיפחת מן אורייתא דמשה אתיתי [*ולא לאוספי על אורייתא דמשה אתיתי] וכתיב ביה במקום ברא ברתא לא תירות אמרה ליה נהור נהוריך כשרגא א"ל רבן גמליאל אתא חמרא ובטש לשרגא: ומפני מה אין קורין כו': אמר רב לא שנו *אלא בזמן בית המדרש אבל שלא בזמן בהמ"ד קורין ושמואל אמר אפילו שלא בזמן בית המדרש אין קורין איני והא נהרדעא אתריה דשמואל הוה ובנהרדעא *פסקי סידרא בכתובים במנחתא דשבתא אלא אי איתמר הכי איתמר אמר רב לא שנו אלא במקום בהמ"ד אבל שלא במקום בהמ"ד קורין ושמואל אמר בין במקום בהמ"ד בין שלא במקום בהמ"ד בזמן בהמ"ד אין קורין שלא בזמן בית המדרש קורין ואזדא שמואל לטעמיה °דבנהרדעא פסקי סידרא דכתובים במנחתא דשבתא רב אשי אמר לעולם כדאמרן מעיקרא ושמואל כרבי נחמיה דתניא *אע"פ שאמרו כתבי הקדש אין קורין בהן אבל שונין בהן ודורשין בהן נצרך לפסוק מביא ורואה בו א"ר נחמיה מפני מה אמרו כתבי הקדש אין קורין בהן כדי שיאמרו בכתבי הקדש אין קורין וכ"ש בשטרי הדיוטות: **מתני'** ב מצילין תיק הספר עם הספר ותיק התפילין עם התפילין ואע"פ שיש בתוכן מעות ג ולהיכן מצילין אותן למבוי שאינו מפולש בן בתירא אומר אף למפולש: **גמ'** *ת"ר ארבעה עשר שחל להיות בשבת מפשיטין את הפסח עד החזה דברי רבי ישמעאל בנו של רבי יוחנן בן ברוקה וחכ"א ד מפשיטין את כולו בשלמא לרבי ישמעאל בנו של ר' יוחנן בן ברוקה דהא איתעביד ליה צורך גבוה אלא לרבנן מ"ט אמר רבה בר בר חנה א"ר יוחנן דאמר קרא °כל פעל ה' למענהו [משלי טז] והכא מאי למענהו איכא רב יוסף אמר שלא יסריח רבא אמר *שלא יהו קדשי שמים מוטלין כנבלה מאי בינייהו איכא בינייהו דמנח אפתורא דדהבא אי נמי יומא דאסתנא ורבי ישמעאל בנו של רבי יוחנן בן ברוקה האי *פעל ה' למענהו מאי עביד ליה שלא יוציא את האימורין קודם הפשטת העור מ"ט אמר רב הונא בריה דרב נתן משום נימין אמר רב חסדא אמר מר עוקבא מאי אהדרו ליה חברייא לרבי ישמעאל בנו של רבי יוחנן בן ברוקה הכי קאמרי ליה אם מצילין תיק הספר עם הספר לא נפשיט את הפסח מעורו מי דמי התם טלטול הכא מלאכה אמר רב אשי בתרתי פליגי פליגי בטלטול ופליגי במלאכה והכי קאמרי ליה אם מצילין תיק הספר עם הספר לא נטלטל עור אגב בשר מי

רש"י

דהוה שקיל שמא דלא מקבל שוחדא. היה מוליא עליו שם שאינו מקבל שוחד מבעלי דינין הבאין לפניו והיה מקבלו בסתר: א"ל. פילוספא לר"ג מיומא דגליתון כו': שפילית. כל סוף הדבר הוא תחתית שלו ושייך למימר שפילית לסיפיה: נהור נהורך כשרגא. תורה אור הגהר אורך כשרגא רמזה שנתנה לו מנורה בשוחד: אמר לו ר"ג אתא חמרא ובטשא. דחפתו לארץ כלומר אני נתתי בשוחד*[והכל כדי שישמעו המתאספים שם נבלותו ומי הוא]: בזמן בית המדרש. קודם אכילה היו דורשים: שלא בזמן בית המדרש. לאחר אכילה לא דרשו משום שכרות: פסקי סדרא בכתובים. *[היו רגילים לקרא בבהמ"ד פרשה בכתובים]: במקום בהמ"ד. שהחכם דורש דהיינו בבהמ"ד אבל בעלמא קורין: בין במקום בהמ"ד כו' בזמן בהמ"ד אין קורין. לפי שמבטלו מלילך אצל הדורש אבל שלא בזמן בהמ"ד כגון לאחר אכילה קורין: ושמואל. דאמר לעיל אפילו לאחר אכילה אין קורין: כר' נחמיה. אמרה למילתיה דלית ליה טעמא דאין קורין משום בטול אלא כדי שיאמרו קל וחומר לשטרי הדיוטות ומיהו שמואל הנהיג במקומו כדברי חכמים דמתניתי' דאמרי טעמא (דמתני') משום ביטול תורה הלכך לאחר אכילה דליכא דרשה קורין: שונין בהן. כגון מדרש שה"ש וקהלת: שטרי הדיוטות. כגון של חשבונות או איגרות השלוחות למלא חפץ: **גמ'** עד החזה. מתחיל מרגליו האחרונים עד החזה שיוכל להוציא אימורים שהקטר חלביו דוחין שבת ותו לא מפשיט מידי עד אורתא דלורך הדיוט הוא: למענהו. לכבודו: שלא יסריח. שהעור מחממו ומסריחו ואין זה כבודו להיות פרס אוכלי שולחנו מגואל: אפתורי דדהבא. שאינו מוטל בבזיון אבל לשמא יסריח חייש רב יוסף ורבא לא חייש עד אורתא: יומא דאסתנא. רוח צפונית שהיא ביגונית לא חמה ולא צנה כדאמרינן ביבמות בפרק הערל (דף עב.) ואיזו רוח המסרחת רוח מזרחית בשעת החום כדאמרינן בגיטין (דף לא:) אפילו שכבת זרע שבמעי אשה מסרחת בו דכתיב (הושע יג) יבא קדים רוח ה' ממדבר עולה וגו' יש מפרשין יומא דאסתנא רוח דרומית שהיא צוננת אמת שרוח דרומית צוננת אבל אסתנא על כרחיך צפונית היא ונוחה כדאמר בעלמא (עירובין ד' סה.) צריכא שמעתא צילותא כיומא דאסתנא ורוח דרומית היא בלשון ארמי יומא דשותא: קודם הפשטת העור. עד החזה: מ"ט. עור לאימורין מאי קא עביד: משום נימין. של צמר הנדבקין באימורין: חברייא. בני מחלוקתו: אם מצילין. בשבת: תיק עם הספר. ואע"פ שיש בתוכו מעות ומשום כבוד הספר שהוא צורך גבוה עבדינן בהדיה הלכת מעות שהן צורך הדיוט: לא נפשיט את הפסח. בתמיה משום צורך גבוה לא שרי צורך הדיוט בהדיה: התם. תיק ומעות דקמייתי ראיה מיניה טלטול בעלמא הוא: הכא. גבי פלוגתייהו דפסח דאיירי בה הפשטה מלאכה גמורה דהפשטה מאבות מלאכות היא: בתרתי פליגי. גבי פסח פליגי בטלטולו דאסר רבי ישמעאל לטלטל [הפסח] אחר שהוציא אימוריו אפי' מחמה לצל משום עור דלאו בר טלטול הוא (א)ולא דמי לשלחין דאמרן בבמה טומנין (לעיל מט.) שמטלטלין אותן דהתם עור בהמה גסה דחזי למישטחיה ולמיזגא עליה: והכי קאמרי ליה. תשובה לענין טלטול: לא נטלטל עור אגב בשר. דהוי כמי כבוד שמים דבשר דומיא דספר ומותר לטלטלו מחמה לצל ואגב בשר יטלטלו עור המחובר בו: מי

מסורת הש"ס

גי' רש"ל
גי' רש"ל
בספרים ישנים ליתא אלא
[היינו הפטרה עי' תוס' לעיל כד. ד"ה שאלמלא וכו' וכ"כ תוספות לגדול במגילה כא. ד"ה ואין מפטירין]
[תוספ' פי"ד מ"ש פט"ו הלכה ג ע"ש]
לקמן קנב: מנחות סג: [תוספ' דפסחי' פ"ו]
[זבחים פה:]
[נ"י כל פעל]

הגהות הב"ח

(א) רש"י ד"ה בתרתי פליגי וכו' דלאו בר טלטול הוא הס"ד ואחר כך מ"ה והכי קאמרי ואח"כ ד"ה לא נטלטל וכו' המחובר בו ולא דמי לשלחין וכו'. נ"ב הך קושיא היא אף לחברייא וע"ל בתוס' פ' במה טומנין דף מט בד"ה טומנין בשלחין:

גליון הש"ס גמ' דבנהרדעא פסקי סדרי. ע"ל דף כד ע"א תוס' ד"ה שאלמלא:

a certain philosopher[4] lived in his vicinity, [116*b*] and he bore a reputation that he did not accept bribes.[5] They wished to expose him,[6] so she brought him a golden lamp, went before him, [and] said to him, 'I desire that a share be given me in my [deceased] father's estate.' 'Divide,' ordered he. Said he [R. Gamaliel] to him, 'It is decreed for us, Where there is a son, a daughter does not inherit.' [He replied], 'Since the day that you were exiled from your land the Law of Moses has been superseded[7] and another book[8] given, wherein it is written, 'A son and a daughter inherit equally.'[9] The next day, he [R. Gamaliel] brought him a Lybian ass. Said he to them, 'Look[10] at the end of the book, wherein it is written, I came not to destroy the Law of Moses nor[11] to add to the Law of Moses,[12] and it is written therein, A daughter does not inherit where there is a son.' Said she to him, 'Let thy light shine forth like a lamp.'[13] Said R. Gamaliel to him, 'An ass came and knocked the lamp over!'[14]

AND WHY DO WE NOT READ [THEM], etc. Rab said: They learnt this only for the time of the Beth Hamidrash, but we may read [them] when it is not the time of the Beth Hamidrash. But Samuel said: We may not read them [on the Sabbath] even when it is not the time of the Beth Hamidrash. But that is not so, for Nehardea was Samuel's town, and in Nehardea they closed the prescribed lesson [of the Pentateuch] with [a reading from]
a the Hagiographa at *minḥah* on the Sabbath?[1] Rather if stated it was thus stated: Rab said, They learnt this only in the place of the Beth Hamidrash; but we may read [them] elsewhere than in the Beth Hamidrash. While Samuel said: Whether in the place of the Beth Hamidrash or elsewhere, at the time of the Beth Hamidrash[2] we may not read [them]; when it is not the time of the Beth Hamidrash we may read them. And Samuel is consistent with his view, for in Nehardea they closed the prescribed lesson [of the Pentateuch] with[3] [a reading from] the Hagiographa. R. Ashi said, In truth, it is as we first stated, Samuel [ruling] according to R. Nehemiah.[4] For it was taught: Though they [the Sages] said, Holy writings may not be read, yet they may be studied, and lectures thereon may be given. If one needs a verse, he may bring [a Scroll] and see [it] therein. R. Nehemiah said: Why did they rule, Holy Writings may not be read? So that people may say, If Holy Writings may not be read, how much more so secular documents![5]

MISHNAH. ONE MAY SAVE THE SHEATH OF A SCROLL TOGETHER WITH THE SCROLL, AND THE CONTAINER OF TEFILLIN[6] TOGETHER WITH THE TEFILLIN, EVEN IF IT [ALSO] CONTAINS MONEY. AND WHITHER MAY WE RESCUE THEM? INTO A CLOSED ALLEY; BEN BATHYRA RULED: EVEN INTO AN OPEN ONE.[7]

GEMARA. Our Rabbis taught: If the fourteenth [of Nisan] falls on the Sabbath, the Passover sacrifice is flayed as far as the
b breast:[1] this is the view of R. Ishmael son of R. Joḥanan b. Beroḳah. But the Sages maintain: We flay the whole of it. As for R. Ishmael son of R. Joḥanan b. Beroḳah, it is well, [the reason being] that the requirements for the Sanctuary[2] have been fulfilled;[3] but what is the reason of the Rabbis?—Said Rabbah b. Bar Ḥanah in R. Joḥanan's name: Because Scripture saith, *The Lord hath made every thing for his own purpose*.[4] But what is there here *'for his own purpose?'* R. Joseph said: So that it should not putrefy.[5] Raba said: So that Divine sacrifices should not lie like a *nebelah*. Wherein do they differ?—They differ where it is lying on a gold table,[6] or if it is a day of the north wind.[7] Now R. Ishmael son of R. Joḥanan b. Beroḳah, how does he dispose of this [verse], *'The Lord hath made every thing for his own purpose'?*—[That teaches] that one must not draw out the *emurim*[8] before the stripping of the skin.[9] What is the reason?—Said R. Huna son of R. Nathan: On account of the threads.[10]

R. Ḥisda observed in Mar 'Uḳba's name: What did his companions answer to R. Ishmael son of R. Joḥanan b. Beroḳah?—They argued thus with him: If the sheath of a Scroll may be rescued together with the Scroll, shall we then not flay the Passover sacrifice of its skin?[11] How compare! There it is [mere] handling, whereas here it is work.[12]—Said R. Ashi, They differ in two things, viz., in respect of both handling and labour, and they argue thus with him: If the sheath of a Scroll may be saved together with the
c Scroll, shall we not handle the skin on account of the flesh.[1] [117*a*]

(4) Rashi: *min* (i.e., sectarian). (5) He was a judge. (6) Lit., 'make sport of him'. (7) Lit., 'taken away'. (8) The reading in Cod. Oxford is: and the law of the Evangelium has been given. (9) There is no passage in any known Gospel that a son and daughter inherit alike. (10) Lit., 'descend to'. (11) Var. lec.: but; v. Weiss, *Dor*, I, p. 233, n. 1. (12) Cf. Matt. V, 17 *seq.* (13) Alluding to the lamp which she presented him on the preceding day. (14) This story is discussed in Bacher, *Ag. d. Pal. Am.* II, p. 424 n. V. also R.T. Herford, op. cit., pp. 146-154, though his conjecture that the story ends with a covert gibe at Christianity is hardly substantiated.

a (1) As a *hafṭarah* (q.v. Glos.) after the Reading of the Law: so Jast. V. Rashi; cf. *supra* 24*a*. [*Aliter:* They expounded a part of Scripture from the Hagiographa etc. V. Bacher, *Terminologie* s.v. סדרא]. (2) I.e., when the public lectures are given. (3) The text should read בכתובים as above, not דכתובים. (4) But he does not state his own view there. (5) E.g., bills, documents relating to business transactions, etc. (6) I.e., the bag or box in which they are kept. (7) This is discussed *infra*.

b (1) Starting from the hind legs. One can then remove the fats which are to be burnt on the altar (these are called *emurim*, lit., 'devoted objects'), the burning being permitted on the Sabbath. Since the rest of the skin must be flayed only in order to reach the portion which he himself will eat in the evening, this is regarded as having a secular purpose, and therefore must be left for the evening. (2) Lit., 'the Most High'. (3) When it is flayed thus far, as explained *supra* note 1. (4) I.e., His honour. Prov. XVI, 4. (5) It is not in keeping with the honour due to God that the meat of the sacrifices offered to Him should turn putrid. (6) One may still fear putrefaction, but it is certainly not lying like a *nebelah*. Hence according to R. Joseph it must be completely stripped even so, but not according to Raba. (7) Which keeps the meat fresh. (8) V. n. b1. (9) As far as the breast. (10) Of wool, which would otherwise adhere to the fats, etc. (11) Surely the two are identical, for the sheath too is not sacred, just as the flaying of the skin after the breast has been reached serves a secular purpose only. (12) Flaying being a principal labour, v. *supra* 73*a*.

c (1) Rashi: R. Ishmael holding that once the *emurim* have been drawn out the animal may not be handled because of the skin, while the Rabbis argue that on the contrary since the flesh itself might be handled the skin may be likewise in virtue thereof. According to this they differ where the animal has only been partially flayed. Tosaf. interprets the passage differently.

How compare! There it [the sheath] had become as a stand to that which is permitted,[2] whereas here it [the skin] had become a stand to a thing that is forbidden![3] Rather they say thus to him, If we may save the sheath of a Scroll together with the Scroll, though it also contains money,[4] shall we not handle the skin on account of the flesh? How compare! There it [the sheath] became a stand for something that is forbidden [the money] and something that is permitted [the Scroll]; whereas here the whole has become a stand for that which is forbidden?—Rather they say thus to him: If a sheath containing money may be brought from elsewhere to save a Scroll of the Law with it, shall we not handle the skin in virtue of the flesh? And how do we know that itself? Shall we say, since one need not throw them [the coins] out when it contains them,[5] he may bring it [the sheath] too? How compare! There, in the meanwhile the fire may alight [upon the Scroll];[6] but here, let them be thrown out in the meantime?[7] Rather said Mar son of R. Ashi: In truth it is as we originally explained it; and as to your objection, There it is [mere] handling, whereas here it is work,—[that is answered] e.g., that he does not require the skin.[8] But Abaye and Raba both say: R. Simeon agrees in

a a case of 'cut off its head but let it not die?'[1]—He removes it [the skin] in strips.[2]

AND WHITHER MAY WE RESCUE THEM, etc. What is an open [alley] and what is a closed [one]?—R. Ḥisda said: [If it contains] three walls and two stakes,[3] it is a closed alley; three walls and one stake, it is an open alley. And both of them[4] are based on R. Eliezer['s opinion]. For we learnt: To make an alley eligible,[5] Beth Shammai maintain: [It requires] a stake and a beam;[6] Beth Hillel say: Either a stake or a beam; R. Eliezer said: Two stakes.[7] Said Rabbah to him, If there are three walls and one stake, do you call it open![8] Moreover, according to the Rabbis, let us save thither even foodstuffs and liquids?[9] Rather said Rabbah, [it is to be explained thus]: [If it contains] two walls and two stakes,[10] it is a closed alley; two walls and one stake, it is an open alley, and both[11] are based on [the view of] R. Judah. For it was taught: Even more than this did R. Judah say: If one owns two houses on the opposite sides of the street, he can place a stake or a beam at each side and carry between them. Said they to him: A street cannot be made fit for carrying by an *'erub* in this way.[12] Said Abaye to him, But according to you too, on [the view of] the Rabbis let us save thither even foodstuffs and liquids?[13]

(2) *Sc.* the Scroll, which may be handled, even if there is no fire. (3) *Sc.* the flesh, which may not be handled until the evening before which it is not required (Rashi). Tosaf.: the flesh may be handled *now*, but before the sacrifice was killed the whole animal was *mukzeh*. (4) Which by itself may not be handled. (5) V. Mishnah. (6) If one should first have to empty the sheath of its money. (7) Whilst carrying the sheath to the Scroll it can be emptied of its money without loss of time. (8) Hence the flaying is unintentional, as far as the skin is concerned.—On this explanation they differ only in respect of skinning the animal, as was first suggested.

a (1) V. *supra* 75a, n. a8. (2) Not as one piece. It is not even real flaying then, and only counts as a *shebuth* (Rashi). (3) I.e., it is a cul-de-sac leading off a street, and stakes are planted in the ground at either side of the opening. These stakes legally count as a fourth wall, and thus the alley is regarded as entirely enclosed. (4) The Rabbis and Ben Bathyra. (5) To rank technically as an 'alley' wherein carrying on the Sabbath is permitted under certain conditions. (6) A stake at the side of the entrance and a beam across it. (7) Ben Bathyra however holds that in order to save holy writings R. Eliezer too is more lenient. (8) Surely not, even if it be conceded that two stakes are required to make it fit. (9) I.e., where it is closed with two stakes carrying should be entirely permitted therein, and not restricted to holy writings. [The Rabbis state *infra* 120a that foodstuffs may be saved by carrying them into a courtyard furnished with an *'erub*, but not into an alley.] (10) I.e., it is open at each end, and a stake is placed at both entrances. (11) V. n. a4. (12) V. *supra* 6a bottom for notes. Ben Bathyra holds that where the saving of holy writings is in question R. Judah is more lenient. (13) Seeing that in your opinion the Rabbis hold with R. Judah that two partitions and two stakes render the space fit for carrying.

מי דמי התם נעשה בסיס לדבר המותר הכא נעשה בסיס לדבר האסור אלא הכי קאמרי ליה אם מצילין תיק של ספר עם הספר ואע"פ שיש בתוכו מעות לא נטלטל עור אגב בשר מי דמי התם נעשה בסיס לדבר האסור ולדבר המותר הכא כולו נעשה בסיס לדבר האסור אלא הכי קאמרי ליה אם מביאין תיק שיש בתוכו מעות מעלמא להציל בו ספר תורה לא נטלטל עור אגב בשר והיא גופה מנלן אילימא דמדהיכא דאית ביה לא שדי להו איתויי נמי מייתינן מי דמי התם אדהכי והכי נפלה דליקה הכא אדהכא והכי לישדינן אלא אמר מר בר רב אשי לעולם כדאמרינן מעיקרא ודקא קשיא לך *הכא טלטול והכא מלאכה כגון דלא קבעי ליה לעור והא *אביי ורבא דאמרי תרווייהו מודה ר"ש בפסיק רישיה ולא ימות דשקיל ליה *בברזי: ולהיכן מצילין אותן וכו': היכי דמי מפו' היכי דמי שאינו מפולש אמר רב חסדא שלש מחיצות ושני לחיין זהו מבוי שאינו מפולש ג' מחיצות ולחי אחד זהו מבוי המפולש ותרווייהו אליבא דרבי אליעזר דתנן *הכשר מבוי ב"ש אומרים לחי וקורה וב"ה *אומרים או לחי או קורה ר' אליעזר אומר שני לחיים א"ל רבה ג' מחיצות ולחי אחד מפולש קרית ליה ועוד לרבנן נציל לתוכו אוכלין ומשקין אלא אמר רבה שתי מחיצות ושני לחיין זהו מבוי שאינו מפולש שתי מחיצות ולחי אחד זהו מבוי המפולש ותרווייהו אליבא דרבי יהודה *דתניא יתר על כן אמר ר' יהודה מי שיש לו שני בתים בשני צדי ר"ה עושה לחי מיכן ולחי מיכן או קורה מיכן וקורה מיכן ונושא ונותן באמצע אמרו לו אין מערבין רה"ר בכך א"ל אביי לדידך נמי לרבנן נציל לתוכו אוכלין ומשקין אלא

רש"י

(א)מי דמי. תיק הספר נעשה בסיס לדבר המותר לטלטלו בלא שום דליקה דספר בר טלטול הוא ולדבר האסור כגון מעות: הכא. האי עור נעשה בסיס לדבר שכולו אסור בטילטול שהבשר אסור לטלטלו דלא חזי לאכילה עד אורתא דפסח אינו נאכל אלא בלילה וגלי ורבי ישמעאל לית ליה כבוד שמים בנאכל להדיוט ואפילו הוי עור תורת כלי עליו מיתסר משום דהוי בסיס לאיסור וכ"ש דהוא גופיה לאו בר טלטול הוא: אם מביאין תיק שבתוכו מעות. דהוי בסיס לדבר שכולו אסור ומניח בו ספר להצילו ואינו צריך להשליך המעות כדמפרש ואזיל לא נטלטל עור אגב הבשר: אי נימא דמדהיכא דאית ביה. מעות עם הספר לא שדי להו לא מצריך ליה תנא דידן למשדינהו כדקתני ואע"פ שיש בתוכו מעות: איתויי נמי מייתינן. מעלמא מאחת זוית הבית תיק ובתוכו מעות להניח בתוכו ספר ולהציל: מי דמי. היכא דהספר מונח עם המעות להיכא דהוא בא עכשיו להביאו עם המעות ולתת בו ספר: התם. דספר ומעות בתוכו להכי לא מצרכינן ליה למשדינהו: דילמא אדהכי והכי נפלה דליקה. על הספר: הכא. אדמייתי ליה נישדינהו דרך ביאתו: כדאמרינן מעיקרא. דלא פליגי אלא בהפשטה ומייתי רבנן ראיה מתיק הספר דמתני' דמצילין מעות אגב ספר נרכי הדיוט אגב נרכי גבוה הואיל וליכא שהות למשדינהו וה"נ אגב נרכי גבוה דכל פעל ה' למענהו יפשיט: ודקשיא לך כו' דלא בעי ליה לעור. אינו צריך לו לעור ואינו מתכוין להפשיט משום עור ולא דמי להפשט אילים ותחשים דמשכן: והא ר"ש מודה בפסיק רישיה ולא ימות. והכא אע"ג דלא מיכוין מיפשיט הוא: דשקיל ליה בברזי. בחתיכות דקות מפשיט וחותך דאין דרך הפשטה בכך ולאו מלאכה הוא אלא שבות: שני לחיים. לפתח שאין לו מחיצה: זהו מבוי שאינו מפולש. כלומר מבוי הניתר בכל הלכותיו בין בעירוב בין בשאר דברים וכל היתר שאר מבואות יש לו כגון שיתופי מבואות: ותרווייהו. רבנן ובן בתירא סבירא להו כר"א דאמר אין מבוי ואפילו סתום ניתר בלחי א' ואשמעינן בן בתירא דבהצלת כתבי הקדש לא בעינן לחיים כרבי אליעזר: מפולש קרית ליה. נהי נמי דבעי ר' אליעזר לחיים מיהו מפולש לא מיקרי: ועוד לרבנן. דאמרי לשאינו מפולש וקאמרת דהיינו מבוי הניתר בכל הלכותיו: נציל לתוכו אף אוכלין ומשקין. כמו לחצר המעורבת ואמאי פלגינהו מהדדי דגבי ספר קתני למבוי שאינו מפולש וגבי אוכלין קתני להיכן מצילין אותן לחצר המעורבת דמשמע אבל למבוי לא: שתי מחיצות. מכאן ומכאן: שני לחיין. לחי לכל פתח ופתח: אליבא דרבי יהודה. דאמר בשתי מחיצות סגי ושני לחיים ואתא בן בתירא למימר דלגבי ספר מודה ר' יהודה דסגי בחד דג' מחיצות הוו: לדידך נמי. איכא למיפרך כאתקפתא דלעיל: לרבנן. כיון דאמרת דתרוייהו כר' יהודה לרבנן דאמרי לשאינו מפולש ומפרשי ליה לשאינו חסר כלום כר' יהודה דלא בעי אלא שתי מחיצות ושני לחיים אי הכי לרבנן יציל לתוכו אוכלין ומשקין כמו לחצר המעורבת:

תוספות

הכא נעשה בסיס לדבר האסור. פי' בקונטרס שהבשר אסור לטלטל שהרי אינו ראוי לאכילה עד הלילה ואינו נראה דא"כ היכי קאמר לא נטלטל עור אגב בשר כיון דבשר אסור לטלטל ונראה דלכ"ע בשר מותר לטלטל אע"ג דמאן דשרי *בשר תפל בעלמא לטלטל היינו משום דחזי לכלבים והכא נמי לא חזי לכלבים מ"מ משום בזיון קדשי שמים שרי לכ"ע ובטלטול עור אגב בשר הוא דפליגי והא דקאמר הכא דהוי בסיס לדבר האסור היינו קודם שנשחטה היה בסיס לדבר האסור שכל הבהמה מוקצה היא מטלטול:

מי דמי התם אדהכי והכי נפלה דליקה. וא"ת אמאי לא קאמר התם נעשה בסיס לדבר המותר ולדבר האסור הכא נעשה בסיס לדבר האסור גרידא וי"ל דאין נראה לו לחלק כיון דהשתא סבור שיכול לנער מעות מן הכיס ואפילו הכי א"צ לנער ושרי כל שהוא עושה להצלת ס"ת ה"ה דשרי להביא תיק שיש בו מעות גרידא:

אדהכי והכי לשדינהו. משמע דאי לא מצי למשדי המעות הוה מצי להביא התיק עם המעות להביא בו ס"ת וא"כ כשאינו מופשט אלא עד החזה מותר לכ"ע לטלטל הואיל ולא מצי שדי ליה ולא פליגי אלא כשהופשט לגמרי כדפי' לעיל:

דשקיל ליה בברזי. פירש בקונט' דאיכא שבות בכה"ג וקשה דהוה ליה למיתני בפסחים בפרק אלו דברים (דף סה:) הפשט דדחי שבת בהדי הנהו שבות דקתני התם דדחו שבת ונראה לר"י דליכא אפילו שבות דאינו מפשיט כשיעור חשיבות עור יחד ולא דמי למפיס מורסא דהתם פתח קעביד אך שא"צ לו וכן לד מזיקין מ"מ לד הוא אבל הכא דלא קא עביד הפשט אפי' שבות ליכא:

(*דשקיל ליה בברזי). וא"ת דתני' בסוף תמיד נשחט (פסחים סה:) תנא *חשכה כל אחד ואחד נוטל פסחו בעורו אם כן לאו בברזי מיה מופשט ומשמע דבשבת איירי דאמתני' דהתם קאי דקתני ארבעה עשר שחל בשבת ואיכא למימר דלא קאי אשבת א"כ נוטלו בעורו שנפשט עד החזה ועוד אומר ר"י דאיכא למימר דרבנן לדברי רבי ישמעאל קאמרי לדידן מותר להפשיט לגמרי לדידך אודי לן מיהא דמותר להפשיט בברזי וא"ת לפי זה ה"ל למיחשב התם דחיית הפשט וי"ל דפלוגתא לא קא מיירי דלר' ישמעאל לא דחי ליה הפשט כלל ואע"ג דחשיב הרכבתו והבאתו מחוץ לתחום דפליגי בה ר"ע ור' אליעזר לא חשיב לה פלוגתא דר"א דשמותי הוא ועוד דמההיא פלוגתא ילפינן דהזאה אינה דוחה להכי קתני לה:

שלש מחיצות ושני לחיים כו'. השתא האי דמפרש לה הכי ומוקי תרווייהו אליבא דר"א ולא בעי למימר שלש מחיצות ולחי א' אינו מפולש ובלא לחי זהו מפולש והוה מפרש אליבא דהלכתא היינו משום דסבר דבלא לחי כלל לא הוה שרי בן בתירא דהוי כרמלית ולא דמי לחצר שאינה מעורבת דסיפא:

ועוד לרבנן נציל לתוכו אוכלין ומשקין. (ואמאי נקט חצר מעורבת) ולא דמפלגי בין חצר מעורבת למבוי הוה לן לפלוגי בין מבוי משותף למבוי שאינו משותף דבמשותף יהא מותר להציל לתוכו אוכלין ומשקין ואמאי נקט חצר מעורבת:

אלא אמר רבה כו'. תימה מה תירץ רבה מקושיא דנציל לתוכו אוכלין ומשקין ואומר ר"י דרבה רוצה לומר דרבנן סברי כרבי יהודה דוקא לנורך הצלת כתבי הקדש ולא לנורך אחר ואביי פריך משום דאינו נראה לו סברא שיסברו כר' יהודה לחצאין ומשני אביי ג' מחיצות כו' ואביי לא סברי רבנן כר"א לחצאין דר"א להצלת כתבי הקדש סגי בלחי אחד כדמכיים ואזיל ואפילו נרבי אליעזר כו':

הא

רבינו חננאל

דאינון סברי מטלטלין העור ע"ג בשר מקום שחיטה כל חד לדוכתיה והוא אסר. ואהדרו ליה אם מטלטלין להציל תיק של ספר אנו לא נטלטל עור אגב בשר ואהדר להו מי דמי תיק נעשה בסיס לס"ת שמותר לטלטלו. עור נעשה בסיס לבשר אסור לטלטלו. אלא הכי קאמרו ליה כו' ודחה ר' ישמעאל מי דמי. התם תיק נעשה בסיס לס"ת שהוא מותר. ולמעות שהן אסורין הכא בבשר כולן אסור. והדר רב אשי ואמר הכי אהדרו ליה אם מביאין בעלמא תיק שיש בו מעות להציל לו ס"ת אנו לא נטלטל עור אגב בשר. והא מנ"ל אי נימא דדייקית מינה מה התיק שיש בו מעות וס"ת אינך מסיר המעות מתוך התיק ומציל הס"ת לא אתה מציל אפי' המעות כך אם יש מעות בתיק והצרכת להביאו להציל ס"ת אינך מסיר המעות מתוכו דילמא שני התם במקום שכבר הגיעה הדליקה עד הספר ואם יתעסק בהשלכת המעות תאכלם. אבל במקום דהדליקה לא הגיעה [עדיין] והולכין להביא תיק להציל הספר. אם יש בתיק מעות אסור לטלטלן עד שישליכם. ושני רב אשי לעולם כדאמרינן מעיקרא. ודקא אמרת התם בתיק טלטול הכא בעור כגון דמתכוין לגלות הבשר ואין כוונתו לעור. ואקשינן והא אביי ורבא דאמרי תרווייהו מודה ר"ש דסבר דבר שאינו מתכוין שרי בפסיק רישיה ולא ימות כגון זה אמרינן באומר המפשיט דאינו מתכוין לעור ולא דמי לפסיק רישיה ולא ימות. [...]מה לאומר הנני מתתך ראש זה העוף ואין כוונתי לשוחטו כגון זה אפי' לר' שמעון שוחט הוא. ואסקי' דשקיל ליה בברזי. פי' ברזי נקבים והכי קאמר מאן דמבזע ליה כשהוא מפשיטו מוכחא מילתא דלא [...] לעור ולא דמי לפסיק רישיה ולא ימות. ולהיכן מצילין אותו למבוי שאינו מפולש וכן הלכה. ולית הלכתא כבן בתירא דאמר אפילו למבוי המפולש והיכי דמי מבוי שאינו מפולש. שמצילין בו כתבי הקדש:

אסקה

עין משפט נר מצוה

טז א מיי' פי"ז מהלכות שבת הל' ג סמג עשין ה טוש"ע או"ח סימן שסג סעיף ג וסעיף יד:

לקמן קכת.

[ערוך פי' ברזא נקבים והכי קאמר מאן דבזע לי' לעור כשהוא מפשיטו מוכחא מילתא דלא בעי לעור ואין לו הנאה ממנו ולא דמי לפסיק רישא עכ"ל ולפי פי' זה יתיישב קושית התוס' ד"ה דשקיל הא דתניא בתמיד נשחט תנא חשכה וכו']

רפ"ל מ"ז

[מלת חשכה ליתא שם ע"ש]

מסורת הש"ס

[צ"ל התם]

לעיל פה: קנ. קיח: לקמן קכ: קלג. קמג. סוכה לג: [ביצה לו.] כתובות ו. בכורות כה.

עירובין יא:

לעיל ו. עירובין יב: כב. נט: לה.

הגהות הב"ח

(א) רש"י ד"ה (מי דמי. וכו' כגון מעות הכא האי וכו' אסור בטלטול) תא"מ וכ"ב וע"א ועיקר מי דמי תיק הספר נעשה בסיס לדבר המותר לטלטלו בלא שום דליקה דספר בר טלטול הוא הכא האי עור נעשה בסיס לדבר האסור בטלטול כו':

עין משפט
נר מצוה

יז א מיי' פי"ז מהל' שבת הלכה ב ופכ"ג הלכ"ו סמג לאוין סה ועשין א טור שו"ע או"ח סימן שלד סעיף יז וסימן שסג סעיף א ג יד:

יח ב מיי' פכ"ג שם הלכ"א וסמג שם טור ושו"ע או"ח סימן שלד סעיף א:

יט ג מיי' פרק כ"ב שם הלכה טז סמג שם טוש"ע או"ח סימן שלה סעיף ב:

כ ד מיי' שם טור שו"ע שם סעיף ג:

כא ה מיי' פ"ב מהלכות יו"ט הלכה ד טור שו"ע או"ח סימן תצח סעיף י:

כב ו מיי' פכ"ג מהלכות שבת הלכה כה טור שו"ע או"ח סימן שלד סעיף ג:

כג ז מיי' שם טור שו"ע שם סעיף ד:

כד ח מיי' פכ"ב שם הל"א סמג שם טור ושו"ע או"ח סימן רנד סעיף ה:

כה ט טוש"ע או"ח סי' רנ סעיף א:

כו י כ מיי' פ"ל שם הלכה ט סמג עשין ל טור שו"ע או"ח סימן רעד סעיף א ב וסימן רפט סעיף א:

כז ל טוש"ע או"ח סימן שלד סעיף ב בהג"ה:

כח מ מיי' וסמג שם טוש"ע או"ח סימן רצא סעיף א:

הא דתניא נשברה לו חבית בראש גגו. הקשה הרב פורת אמאי לא פריך ממתניתין דריש חבית (לקמן קמג:) דתנן חבית שנשברה מצילין ממנה מזון שלש סעודות ואומר לאחרים בואו והצילו לכם ובלבד שלא יספוג ותירץ דההיא איכא למימר כגון שהחבית בכרמלית דחיישינן שמא יעביר כלי ד' אמות בכרמלית אבל בהך ברייתא קתני בהדיא בראש גגו ור"י תירץ דהתם מיירי כשנשפך היין לארץ דחיישינן שמא יספוג אומר ה"ר שמואל בשם ר"ת דדוקא נשברה לו חבית אבל נסדקה ועושה טיף טיף מותר להביא כלים לקלוט ולצרף דאינו בהול כל כך להביא כלים דרך רה"ר כמו כשנשברה:

כלי אחר ויקלוט כלי אחר ויצרף. אומר ר"י דזו אף זו קתני לא מבעי' לקלוט דמינכר שמציל דאסור אלא אפילו לצרף דלא מינכר כולי האי שהוא מציל אסור: **הציל** פת נקיה לא יציל פת הדראה. אומר ר"י כשאפו בי"ט של פסח מצות מסולת נקיה שיש לו די לצורך י"ט אין אופין אחריהן פת של הדראה אלא מתחילה יעשה של הדראה ואחרי כן יעשה הנקיה:

אבל לא משבת ליום הכפורים. פירש בקונטרס למוצאי יוה"כ וא"ת פשיטא דחול גמור הוא ומ"ש משבת למוצאי שבת וי"ל דמטה לאכול במוצאי יוה"כ כדפי' לעיל(ב) (דף קיד:) ועוד לפי שהתענו מותר יותר אי נמי ליום הכפורים עצמו קאמר ולהאכיל התינוקות:

והתנא דבי רבי ישמעאל כל מלאכת עבודה לא תעשו. וא"ת ואמאי מייתי קרא *דכל מלאכת עבודה דכתיב גבי י"ט הא אפי' בשבת דכתיב לא תעשה מלאכה סתם ולא כתיב עבודה שרי לתקוע ולרדות מן התורה כדמשמע הכא דלאשבת מייתי לה ופירש רבינו שמואל דגרס *כל מלאכה לא תעשו ורשב"א מפרש דלעולם מכל מלאכת עבודה אימעיט תקיעה ורדייה ושבת ילפינן מי"ט דאין בין י"ט לשבת אלא אוכל נפש בלבד כדכתיב אך אשר יאכל לכל נפש (שמות יב):

שהיא חכמה ואינה מלאכה. וכיון דמדאורייתא שריא אע"ג דמדרבנן אסירא כדאמר בר"ה השנה (דף לג.) אין מעכבין את התינוקות מלתקוע הא נשים מעכבין הכא הוה לן למישרי משום ג' סעודות:

במנחה

(ויקרא כג)

[צ"ל לא תעשה כל מלאכה שמות כ]

אלא אמר רב אשי [א]שלש מחיצות ולחי אחד זה מבוי שאינו מפולש ג' מחיצות בלא לחי זהו מבוי המפולש ואפילו לרבי אליעזר דאמר בעינן לחיים הני מילי לאוכלין ומשקין אבל לספר תורה בחד לחי סגי:

מתני' [ב]מצילין *מזון ג' סעודות הראוי לאדם הראוי לבהמה כיצד נפלה דליקה בלילי שבת מצילין מזון ג' סעודות בשחרית מצילין מזון ב' סעודות במנחה מזון סעודה אחת ר' יוסי אומר לעולם מצילין מזון שלש סעודות:

גמ' מכדי בהיתרא קטרח נציל טפי אמר רבא *מתוך שאדם בהול על ממונו אי שרית ליה אתי לכבויי א"ל אביי אלא הא דתניא *נשברה לו חבית בראש גגו מביא כלי ומניח תחתיה *ובלבד שלא יביא כלי אחר ויקלוט כלי אחר ויצרף התם מאי גזירה איכא ה"נ גזירה שמא יביא כלי דרך רה"ר גופא [ג]נשברה לו חבית בראש גגו מביא כלי ומניח תחתיה ובלבד שלא יביא כלי אחר ויקלוט כלי אחר ויצרף [ד]נזדמן לו אורחין מביא כלי אחר וקולט כלי אחר ומצרף ולא יקלוט ואחר כך יזמין אלא יזמין ואח"כ יקלוט °ואין מערימין בכך משום רבי יוסי בר יהודה אמרו מערימין לימא בפלוגתא דרבי אליעזר ור' יהושע קמיפלגי דתניא *אותו ואת בנו שנפלו לבור רבי אליעזר אומר מעלה את הראשון על מנת לשוחטו והשני עושה לו פרנסה במקומו בשביל שלא ימות רבי יהושע אומר [ה]מעלין את הראשון על מנת לשוחטו ואינו שוחטו ומערים ומעלה את השני רצה זה שוחט רצה זה שוחט ממאי דילמא עד כאן לא קאמר רבי אליעזר התם דאפשר בפרנסה אבל הכא דלא אפשר לא ועד כאן לא קאמר רבי יהושע התם משום דאיכא צער בעלי חיים אבל הכא דליכא צער בעלי חיים לא ת"ר *[ו]הציל פת נקיה אין מציל פת *הדראה פת הדראה מציל פת נקיה [ז]ומצילין מיום הכפורים לשבת אבל לא משבת ליום הכפורים ואין צריך לומר משבת ליום טוב ולא משבת לשבת הבאה ת"ר* [ח]שכח פת בתנור וקידש עליו היום מצילין מזון שלש סעודות ואומר לאחרים בואו והצילו לכם וכשהוא רודה לא ירדה במרדה אלא בסכין איני והא *תנא דבי רבי ישמעאל(א) °לא תעשה כל מלאכה יצא תקיעת שופר ורדיית הפת שהיא חכמה ואינה מלאכה *כמה דאפשר לשנויי משנינן א"ר חסדא [ט]לעולם ישכים אדם להוצאת שבת שנאמר °והיה ביום הששי והכינו את אשר יביאו לאתר *'אמר ר' אבא בשבת חייב אדם לבצוע על שתי ככרות דכתיב לחם משנה *אמר רב אשי חזינא ליה לרב כהנא דנקט תרתי ובצע חדא אמר לקטו כתיב רבי זירא [כ]הוה בצע אכולה שירותיה אמר ליה רבינא לרב אשי והא מיחזי כרעבתנותא אמר ליה כיון דכל יומא לא עביד והאידנא הוא דקעביד לא מיחזי כרעבתנותא רבי אמי ורבי אסי [ל]כי מיקלע להו ריפתא דעירובא שרו עילויה אמרי הואיל ואיתעביד בה חדא מצוה ליתעביד בה מצוה אחרינא: **כיצד** נפלה דליקה כו': *ת"ר כמה סעודות חייב אדם לאכול בשבת [מ]שלש רבי חידקא אומר ארבע א"ר יוחנן ושניהם מקרא אחד דרשו °ויאמר משה אכלוהו היום כי שבת היום לה' היום לא תמצאהו בשדה רבי חידקא סבר הני תלתא היום לבר מאורתא ורבנן סברי בהדי דאורתא תנן נפלה דליקה בלילי שבת

מצילין

תורה אור

אלא אמר רב אשי כו'. בין רבנן ובין בן בתירא כר' אליעזר סבירא להו דבעי ג' מחיצות וב' לחיים בעלמא והכא לגבי ספר אמרי רבנן מודה ר' אליעזר בלחי אחד ובן בתירא אמר דמודה ר' אליעזר אף בלא לחי: בחד לחי סגי ליה. מילתא דרבנן קא מפרשי:

מתני' נפלה דליקה בלילי שבת. קודם אכילה: שחרית. קודם סעודה: לעולם הוא מציל. הואיל ויומא בר הכי הוא ובהיתרא טרח דהא בני טלטול נינהו ולחצר המעורבת ואפי' טובא הוה שרי ליה אי לאו משום גזירה וכדמפרש בגמרא: **גמ'** מכדי בהיתרא קטרח. חזו לטלטול ולחצר המעורבת: ואי שרית ליה. לאתחולי בהצלה כולי האי מתוך שהוא בהול מיכסי ליה שבת ואתי נמי לכבויי: ויקלוט. קילוח הנופל מן האויר: ויצרף. סמוך לגג כעין שאיבה אלא שאינו ראוי לשאוב שהגג חלק והיין אינו בגומא מצרף כלי לגג שיזוב מן הגג לכלי והוא אוחז הכלי בידו: התם מאי גזירה איכא. כיון דמידי דהתירא הוא אמאי לא יקלוט ויצרף: שמא יביא כלי כו'. מתוך שהוא מחזר על כלים הרבה ישכח ויביא: ולא יקלוט ואח"כ יזמין. אורחים דבשעת קליטה לא מיבעיא ליה: אין מערימין בכך. לזמן אורחים שאינן צריכין לאכול ויותירו: שנפלו לבור. בי"ט ואין שניהם ראוים לשחיטה ביום אחד: ואינו שוחטו. שמוצא לו עלילה שמא חברו שמן ממנו: עד כאן לא קאמר ר' אליעזר. דאין מערימין: הציל פת נקיה. לשלש סעודות: לא יציל פת הדראה. פת קיבר שניטל הדרה לפי שאין ערמה כשרה לומר פת הדראה נוחה לי: אבל לא משבת ליום הכפורים. כגון אם חל יוה"כ באחד בשבת דהא לא אכיל עד לאורתא ולאורתא ליטרח ולייתי: ואין צריך לומר משבת לי"ט. דיכול להכין בו ביום: מרדה. כלי שרודין בו הפת ומפרידין אותו מכותל התנור שנדבק בה לא ירדה אותו במרדה שהוא דרך חול: ישכים אדם. בע"ש לטרוח ולזמן הוצאת שבת: והכינו את אשר יביאו לאתר. בשעת הבאה הכנה והבאה בהשכמה היא דכתיב וילקטו אותו בבקר בבקר (שמות טז): לבצוע. ברכת המוציא: נקיט תרתי. אוחזן בידו: לקטו כתיב. דמשמע אחיזה אבל בליעה לא כתיב משנה: בצע לכוליה שירותיה. פרוסה גדולה ודי לו בה לאותה סעודה ולכבוד שבת ונראה כמחבב סעודת שבת להתחזק ולאכול הרבה: כי מקלע להו. פעמים שהעירוב בביתם ופעמים בבית אחד משאר בני אדם: שרו ביה. היינו ברכת המוציא שהיא התחלת אכילה. שרו מתחילין: תלתא היום. למנין שלש סעודות בא:

לעולם

מסורת הש"ס

[לקמן קכ.]

לקמן קכ:

[לעיל מג: ע"ש]

[לקמן קמג:]

ביצה לז. [תוספתא דביצה פ"ג] [לקמן קכ:]

[תוס' פי"ד]

[גי' הערוך בערך רד הדראה פי' לחם עב ובלע"ז אדר"ו]

[שם]

שמו' טז

שם טז

לקמן קלח: ע"ש ר"ה כט: ע"ש

[לקמן קכח: וש"נ]

[ברכות לט:]

ברכות לט:

כתובות סד:

שמות טז

הגהות הב"ח

(א) גמ' והא תנא דבי ר' ישמעאל לא תעשו. נ"ב עי' בפי' ר"א דמילה דף קלא ע"ב דגורס קרא דכל מלאכת עבודה לא תעשו:

(ב) תוס' ד"ה אבל וכו' כדפי' לעיל. נ"ב בס"פ אלו קשרים ממש וכ"כ התוס' סוף יומא דף פא בד"ה והאמר רב:

גליון הש"ס

גמ' ואין מערימין בכך. מו"ק דף יב ע"ב:

רבינו חננאל

אסקה רב אשי ג' מחיצות ולחי א' והוא מבוי שאינו מפולש שאין בו שיתוף ולא עירוב וזה להציל כתבי הקדש אבל אוכלין ומשקין אין מצילין אלא לחצר המעורבת דהלכת' כת"ק. והא דאמר רבה ב'מחיצות ולחי אחד זהו מפולש. ב' מחיצות וב' לחיים זהו שאינו מפולש. ואליבא דר' יהודה דאמר מי שיש לו ב' בתים בב' צדי רה"ר עושה לחי מכאן ולחי מכאן או קורה מיכן וקורה מיכן ונושא ונותן באמצע והכי פי' דכר פסיק לה לרה"ר לרחבה מב' צדיה ב' בתים עושה לחי מיכן ולחי מיכן ומערב ונושא ונותן באמצע. והתם איכא פלוגתא דת"ק (וחנינא) [וחנניה] ורב אמר הלכה כת"ק. ושמואל אמר הלכה (כחנינא)[כחנניה].וקאי במבוי שיש בו ב'מחיצו' בלבד כנגד זו וב' פתחים יש לו זה כנגד זה והאי איכא עליה לחי או קורה מיכן ולחי או קורה מיכן. לר' יהודה דלא מצריך דלת יכול לערב אותו. א"ל אביי א"כ למר נמי כיון שמתערב יצילו לתוכן אוכלין ומשקין. ובא רב אשי ופירק. וסלקא כותיה: מצילין מזון ג' סעודות. ואקשינן מכדי בהיתרא קא טרח דקתני להיכן מצילין לחצר המעורבת נציל טפי. ופרקי אמר רבה מתוך שאדם בהול על ממונו דאי שרית ליה להציל כל מאי דבעי אתי לכבויי. א"ל אביי ואלא הא דתניא נשברה לו חבית בראש גגו מביא כלי ומניח תחתיה ובלבד שלא יביא כלי אחר ויקלוט כלי אחר ויצרף. התם מ"ט לא יביא כלי אחר ויקלוט כלי אחד ויצרף והא בהיתרא קא טרח. אהדר ליה רבה התם נמי גזרו עליה דאי שרית לאתויי כלי [אחר יביא כלי] דרך רה"ר וכיון שנאסר מלהביא כלי אחר הרי זה מייאש ולא פשיט באיסורא. והא דמי שנשברה לו חבית בראש גגו. סלקא דלאו בפלוגתא דר' אליעזר ור' יהושע היא. ולענין פת בתנור הלכתא כי הא דתניא שכח פת בתנור וקדש עליה היום מציל מזון ג' סעודות. ואומר לאחרים בואו והצילו לכם. ולא ירדה במרדה אלא בסכין. ואע"ג דתנא דבי שמואל כל מלאכת עבודה לא תעשו. יצא תקיעת שופר ורדיית הפת שהיא חכמה ואינה מלאכה. כמה שאפשר לשנויי משנינן: **אמר** רב חסדא לעולם ישכים אדם להוצאת שבת שנאמר והיה ביום הששי והכינו את אשר יביאו לאתר. והלכתא כר' אבא דאמר חייב אדם לבצוע על ב' ככרות בשבת.

ואיתא

[117b] Rather said R. Ashi: Three walls and one stake, that is a closed alley; three walls without a stake, that is an open alley. And even according to R. Eliezer who maintains [that] we require two stakes, that is only in respect of foodstuffs and liquids, but for a Scroll of the Law one stake is sufficient.

MISHNAH. FOOD FOR THREE MEALS MAY BE SAVED, THAT WHICH IS FIT FOR MAN, FOR MAN, THAT WHICH IS FIT
a FOR ANIMALS, FOR ANIMALS.[1] HOW SO? IF A FIRE BREAKS OUT SABBATH NIGHT,[2] FOOD FOR THREE MEALS MAY BE SAVED; [IF] IN THE MORNING, FOOD FOR TWO MEALS MAY BE SAVED; AT [THE TIME OF] MINḤAH, FOOD FOR ONE MEAL.[3] R. JOSE SAID: AT ALL TIMES WE MAY SAVE FOOD FOR THREE MEALS.[4]

GEMARA. Consider: He labours[5] in that which is permissible;[6] then let us save more?—Said Raba: Since a man is excited over his property, if you permit him [to save more], he may come to extinguish [the fire]. Said Abaye to him, Then as to what was taught: If one's barrel [of wine] is broken on the top of his roof he may bring a vessel and place [it] underneath, provided that he does not bring another vessel and catch [the dripping liquid][7] or another vessel and join it [to the roof][8]—what preventive measure is required there?—Here too it is a preventive measure lest he bring a utensil through the street.

[To turn to] the main text: If one's barrel is broken on the top of his roof, he may bring a vessel and place it underneath, provided that he does not bring another vessel and catch [the dripping liquid] or another vessel and join it [to the roof]. If guests happen to visit him, he may bring another vessel and catch [the dripping liquid], or another vessel and join it [to the roof]. He must not catch [the liquid] and then invite [the guests], but must first invite [them] and then catch [the liquid]; and one must not evade the
b law in this matter.[1] In R. Jose son of R. Judah's name it was said: We may evade [the law]. Shall we say that they disagree in the [same] controversy [as that] of R. Eliezer and R. Joshua? For it was taught: If an animal[2] and its young[3] fall into a pit,[4]—R. Eliezer said: One may haul up one of them [lit., the first] and [must slaughter it], for the second, one makes provision where it lies, so that it should not die. R. Joshua said: One may haul up the first in order to kill it, but if one does not kill it, then one practices an evasion, and hauls up the second and kills whichever one desires![5]—How so? perhaps R. Eliezer rules thus only there, because provisio can be made, but not here, seeing that that is impossible. An perhaps R. Joshua rules thus only there because suffering of dum animals is involved; but not here that there is no suffering c dumb animals?[6]

Our Rabbis taught: If he saved bread [made] of fine flour, h must not save coarse bread; [if he saved] coarse bread, he ma [still] save a fine [flour] bread.[7] And one may save on the Da of Atonement for the Sabbath,[8] but not on the Sabbath for th Day of Atonement,[9] and it goes without saying [that one must no rescue food] on the Sabbath for a Festival, or on a Sabbath fo the following Sabbath.

Our Rabbis taught: If one forgets a loaf in an oven, and th
c day becomes holy upon him,[1] food for three meals may be saved, and he may say to others, 'Come and save for yourselves.' An when he removes [the bread], he must not remove it with a *mardeh* but with a knife.[4] But that is not so, for the School of R. Ishma taught: *Thou shalt not do any work*:[5] the blowing of the *shofar* and th removal of bread [from the oven] are excluded as being an art not work?—As much as is possible to vary [it][6] we do so.

R. Ḥisda said: One should always make early [preparations] against the termination of the Sabbath, for it is said, *And it sha come to pass on the sixth day, that they shall prepare that which they brin in*[8]—[i.e.,] immediately.

R. Abba said: On the Sabbath it is one's duty to break bread over two loaves, for it is written, *twice as much bread*.[10] R. Ash said: I saw that R. Kahana held two [loaves] but broke bread ove one, observing, *'they gathered'* is written.[11] R. Zera broke enoug bread for the whole meal.[12] Said Rabina to R. Ashi: But that look like greed?—Since he does not do this every day, he replied, bu only now [the Sabbath], it does not look like greed, he replied.[1] R. Ammi and R. Assi, when they came across the bread of a *'erub*, would commence [their meal] therewith,[14] observing, 'Sinc one precept has been performed with it,[15] let another precept b performed with it.'

HOW SO? IF A FIRE BREAKS OUT, etc. Our Rabbis taught How many meals must one eat on the Sabbath? Three. R. Ḥidk said: Four. R. Joḥanan observed, Both expound the same verse *And Moses said, Eat that to-day; for to-day is a Sabbath unto the Lord to-day ye shall not find it in the field*.[16] R. Ḥidka holds: These thre
d 'to-days' are [reckoned] apart from the evening;[1] whereas th Rabbis hold, They include [that of] the evening. We learnt

a (1) I.e., three meals per person and per animal, taking into account what is fit for man and what is fit for beast. (2) Before the first meal has been eaten. (3) In each case food may be saved for as many meals as will yet be required for that Sabbath. (4) Whenever the fire breaks out. (5) Lit., 'troubles'. (6) Food may be handled on the Sabbath, and he carries it out into a courtyard provided with an *'erub* (*infra* 120a), whither carrying is permitted in any case. (7) As it falls through the air. (8) I.e., set it near the roof, so that the liquid may flow along the roof and into the vessel. These are forbidden because it is manifest that the vessels are brought in order to save the wine or oil.

b (1) I.e., he may not invite guests merely as a pretence, and when the wine is saved they will not drink it after all, but only guests who have not yet dined will drink it. (2) Lit., 'it'. (3) The reference is to animals that may be eaten. These may not be slaughtered together with their young on the same day. V. Lev. XXII, 28. (4) On a Festival. (5) V. Beẓ. 37a. (6) It is noteworthy that to save animals from suffering is regarded as a stronger reason for desecrating the Festival than to save one from personal loss. (7) There is n evasion in saying that he prefers the latter, hence it is still a Sabbath need (8) This is permitted, as the food is required immediately the Sabbath com mences. (9) Which falls on Sunday. This is forbidden, as he can procure foo on the termination of the Fast.

c (1) I.e., the Sabbath commenced. (2) Before the bread is burnt. (3) A baker' shovel; the oven tool generally used for removing bread. (4) To emphasiz that it is the Sabbath. (5) Ex. XX, 10. (6) Viz., the usual procedure, so tha the Sabbath may not be treated like a weekday. (7) On Friday. (8) Ibid XVI, 5. (9) I.e., to recite the benediction. (10) Ibid. 22. (11) Ibid. On merely requires two loaves before him, thus 'gathering' double the usual por tion, but recites the benediction over one loaf. (12) I.e., he cut off so muc bread, reciting the blessing over it. (13) But is manifestly in honour of the Sab bath. (14) I.e., they said the blessing over it. (15) *Sc.* that of *'erub*. (16) Ibid. 25

d (1) Each *'to-day'* denotes one meal, and a fourth is the meal on Friday night

IF A FIRE BREAKS OUT SABBATH NIGHT, [118a] FOOD FOR THREE MEALS MAY BE SAVED: surely that is where one has not [yet] eaten?[2]—No: it is where he has [already eaten]. [IF] IN THE MORNING, FOOD FOR TWO MEALS MAY BE SAVED: surely that is where one has not yet eaten? No: [where] he has eaten. AT [THE TIME OF] MINḤAH, FOOD FOR ONE MEAL: surely that is where one has not eaten?—No: [where] he has eaten. But since the final section states, R. JOSE SAID: AT ALL TIMES WE MAY SAVE FOOD FOR THREE MEALS, it follows that the first Tanna holds [that] three [are required]. Hence it is clear that our Mishnah does not agree with R. Ḥidḳa.

Now, as to what we learnt: He who has food for two meals must not accept [relief] from the *tamḥuy:* food for fourteen meals, must not accept from the *ḳuppah*,[3]—who [is the authority for this], [for] it is neither the Rabbis nor R. Ḥidḳa? If the Rabbis, there are fifteen meals; if R. Ḥidḳa, there are sixteen?[4]—In truth, it is the Rabbis, for we say to him [the recipient], 'What you require to eat at the conclusion of the Sabbath, eat it on the Sabbath.'[5] Shall we say then that it agrees [only] with the Rabbis and not with R. Ḥidḳa?—You may even say [that it agrees with] R. Ḥidḳa: we say to him, 'What you require to eat on the eve of the Sabbath [before nightfall], eat it on the Sabbath.'[6] And the whole day of Sabbath eve [Friday] we make him spend in fasting?[7] Rather the author of this is R. Akiba, who said: Treat thy Sabbath like a weekday rather than be dependent on men.[8]

Now, as to what we learnt: 'A poor man travelling from place to place must be given not less than a loaf [valued] at a *pundion* when four *se'ahs* cost one *sela*';[1] if he stays overnight, he must be given the requirements for spending the night; while if he spends the Sabbath there, he must be given food for three meals'[2]—shall we say that this is [according to] the Rabbis [only], not R. Ḥidḳa?—In truth, it may [agree with] R. Ḥidḳa, [the circumstances being] e.g., where he [already] has one meal with him, so we say to him, 'Eat that which you have with you.' And when he departs, shall he depart empty-handed![3]—We provide him with a meal to accompany him. What is meant by 'the requirements of spending the night?'—Said R. Papa: A bed and a bolster.

Our Rabbis taught: The plates in which one eats in the evening [Friday night] may be washed for eating in them in the morning; [those which are used] in the morning may be washed to eat in them at midday; [those used] at midday are washed to eat in them at *minḥah;* but from *minḥah* and onwards they may no longer be washed;[4] but goblets, [drink-]ladles and flasks, one may go on washing [them] all day, because there is no fixed time for drinking.

R. Simeon b. Pazzi said in the name of R. Joshua b. Levi in Bar Ḳappara's name: He who observes [the practice of] three meals on the Sabbath is saved from three evils: the travails of the Messiah,[5] the retribution of Gehinnom,[6] and the wars of Gog and Magog.[7] 'The travails of the Messiah': *'day'* is written here;[8] whilst there it is written, *Behold, I will send you Elijah the prophet before the great and terrible* day *of the Lord comes.*[9] 'The retribution of Gehinnom': *'day'* is written here; whilst there it is written, *That* day
b *is a day of wrath.*[1] 'The wars of Gog and Magog': *'day'* is written here; whilst there it is written, *in that* day *when Gog shall come.*[2]

R. Joḥanan said in R. Jose's name: He who delights in the Sabbath is given an unbounded heritage, for it is written, *Then shalt thou delight thyself in the Lord, and I will make thee to ride*

(2) Thus proving that our Mishnah disagrees with R. Ḥidḳa. (3) *Tamḥuy* is the charity plate, the food collected from contributors and distributed daily; *ḳuppah* lit., 'heap', 'pile'), the communal charity, from which weekly grants were made every Friday for food. With two meals one has enough for the day; with fourteen he has enough for the week, hence he must not accept relief from either respectively; v. Pe'ah VIII, 7. (4) In the week. (5) Just before its termination. (6) I.e., after nightfall. (7) It is virtually a fast if he must postpone his second meal to the night. (8) Hence if he has fourteen meals he can eat two on the Sabbath rather than receive charity.—This saying of R. Akiba is sometimes quoted nowadays to show that one may even desecrate the Sabbath rather than descend to charity. It is quite obvious that R. Akiba had no such thing in mind but merely meant that one should not seek to obtain the extra luxuries of the Sabbath through charity.

a (1) A *pundion* = one twelfth of a *denar* = one forty-eighth of a *sela*'. A loaf of that size is sufficient for the average two meals. (2) V. Pe'ah ibid. (3) Surely not. (4) Since they are not required for the Sabbath any more. (5) The advent of the Messiah was pictured as being preceded by years of great distress. (6) Purgatory. (7) Also a time of intense suffering. (8) V. *supra* 117*b* bottom. (9) Mal. III, 2. (E.V. IV, 5). This is understood to refer to the advent of the Messiah.

b (1) Zeph. I, 15. (2) Ezek. XXXVIII, 18. Since *'day'* is mentioned three times in connection with the Sabbath meals (*supra* 117*b*), their observance will save one from the bitter experiences of these three 'days'.

מצילין מזון ג' סעודות מאי לאו דלא אכל לא דאכל שחרית מצילין מזון שתי סעודות מאי לאו דלא אכל לא דאכל במנחה מצילין מזון סעודה אחת מאי לאו דלא אכל לא דאכל והא מדקתני סיפא רבי יוסי אומר לעולם מצילין מזון ג' סעודות מכלל דתנא קמא ג' סבירא ליה אלא מחוורתא מתני' דלא כרבי חידקא והא *דתנן מי [א]שיש לו מזון שתי סעודות לא יטול מן התמחוי מזון ארבע עשרה לא יטול מן הקופה מני לא רבנן ולא רבי חידקא אי רבנן חמסרי הויין אי רבי חידקא שית סרי הויין לעולם רבנן דאמרינן ליה מאי דבעית למיכל באפוקי שבתא אכליה בשבתא לימא רבנן היא ולא ר' חידקא אפי' תימא ר' חידקא דאמרינן ליה מאי דבעית למיכל במעלי שבתא אכליה לאורתא וכולי יומא דמעלי שבתא בתעניתא מותבינן ליה אלא הא מני רבי עקיבא היא דאמר *[ב]עשה שבתך חול ואל תצטרך לבריות *והא דתנן [ג]אין פוחתין לעני העובר ממקום למקום מככר בפונדיון מד' סאין בסלע לן נותנין לו פרנסת לינה ואם שבת נותנין לו מזון ג' סעודות לימא רבנן היא ולא ר' חידקא לעולם ר' חידקא כגון דאיכא סעודה בהדיה דאמרינן ליה הא דאיכא בהדך אכליה וכי אזיל בריקן אזיל דמלווינן ליה סעודה בהדיה מאי פרנסת לינה אמר רב פפא פוריא ובי סדיא: ת"ר [ד]קערות שאכל בהן ערבית מדיחן לאכול בהן שחרית שחרית מדיחן לאכול בהן בצהרים בצהרים מדיחן לאכול בהן במנחה מן המנחה ואילך שוב אינו מדיח אבל כוסות וקיתוניות וצלוחיות מדיח והולך כל היום כולו לפי שאין קבע לשתיה א"ר שמעון בן פזי א"ר יהושע בן לוי משום בר קפרא [ה]כל המקיים שלש סעודות בשבת ניצול משלש פורעניות מחבלו של משיח ומדינה של גיהנם וממלחמת גוג ומגוג מחבלו של משיח כתיב הכא יום וכתיב התם °הנה אנכי שולח לכם את אליה הנביא לפני בוא יום וגו' מדינה של גיהנם כתיב הכא יום וכתיב התם °יום עברה היום ההוא ממלחמת גוג ומגוג כתיב הכא יום וכתיב התם °ביום בא גוג א"ר יוחנן משום רבי יוסי כל המענג את השבת נותנין לו נחלה בלי מצרים שנאמר °אז תתענג על ה' והרכבתיך על במתי ארץ והאכלתיך

נחלת

תורה אור

מלאכי ג | צפניה א | יחזקאל לח | ישעיה נח

לעולם מצילין מזון ג' סעודות. מדלא אמר ארבע לית ליה דרבי חידקא: מכלל דתנא קמא שלש סעודות סבירא ליה. דבהאי לא איפליגו אלא דת"ק סבר מה שעבר כבר לא יציל ולרבי יוסי יציל: תמחוי. קערה גדולה היא וגובין בה גבאים מאכל מבעלי בתים ומחלקין לעניים ב' סעודות ליום מיום ליום: לא יטול. כיון דיש לו כמלא גזל לעניים: קופה. מעות הן לפרנס עניים בני טובים דזיל להו מילתא דתמחוי ומתחלקין מע"ש לע"ש: י"ד סעודות לא יטול מן הקופה. שהרי יכול להמתין לע"ש הבאה אבל כשיש לו מזון י"ב יטול שהרי לא תחלק עוד עד שיגיע ע"ש והרי לשבעה ימי שבת צריכין י"ד סעודות: אכליה בשבתא. שהרי תאכלנה סמוך לערב ולא תצטרך לאכול בלילה ואף על גב דאמרינן לקמן לעולם יסדר אדם שלחנו במוצאי שבת ה"מ למאן דאפשר ליה: בתעניתא מותבינן ליה. בתמיה: אלא הא מני ר' עקיבא היא. ולענין סעודת שבת במאן דאפשר ליה איכא למימר כרבנן ואיכא למימר כרבי חידקא ומיהו האי דצריך לבריות יעשה שבתו חול ולא יטיל על אחרים כבוד שבתותיו: אין פוחתין לעני העובר ממקום למקום. שאינו לן בלילה אצלם: מככר. הלקוח בפונדיון כשהשער ד' סאין בסלע והפונדיון אחד מי"ב בדינר דהוא אחד ממ"ח בסלע ושיערו לו חכמים ככר זו לשתי סעודות היום והלילה: לן נותנין לו פרנסת לינה. לקמן מפרש מאי היא שהרי סעודה של לילה בכלל ככר היא וככר זו משערינן בעירובין (דף פב:) למזון שתי סעודות לעירובי תחומין: ואם שבת. אצלם בשבת: מאי פרנסת לינה. הא קבל ליה סעודת הלילה: בי סדיא. לבדין פולטר"א להניח תחת מראשותיו: שוב אינו מדיחן. דאין הדחה זו אלא לחול: חבלו של משיח. כדאמרי' בכתובות (דף קיג:) דור שבן דוד בא בו קטיגוריא בתלמידי חכמים שנאמר ועוד בה עשיריה וגו' חבלי לשון חבלי יולדה (הושע יג): בלי מצרים. כלומר אין לה קץ: אז תתענג. בתר וקראת לשבת עונג כתיב:

נחלת

פאה פ"ח מ"ז | פסחי' קיב. קיג. | פאה פ"ח מ"ז ב"ב ט.

במנחה מצילין מזון סעודה אחת. מכאן משמע דזמן אכילה שלישית בשבת היא מן המנחה ולמעלה דלא כאותם שמחלקין סעודת שחרית ומברכין בינתים ומיהו מהא דאמרינן בפסחים בפ"ק (דף יג.) י"ד שחל להיות בשבת משייר מזון שתי סעודות אין ראיה מדאין משיירין מזון ג' סעודות שאין לעשות ב' סעודות שחרית דהא כיון שאוכל הכל שחרית חשיב כסעודה אחת ועוד אומר ר"י שיש כאן איסור ברכה שאינה צריכה כדאי' בפ' בא לו (יומא דף ע.) גבי ובעשור שבחומש הפקודים דקאמר וניתי ס"ת אחרינא ונקרי א"ר שמעון בן לקיש מפני ברכה שאינה צריכה: **מככר** בפונדיון כו'. הייט כר' יוחנן בן ברוקא דחשיב ככר בפונדיון מד' סאין בסלע שתי סעודות דעירוב ופליג התם (עירובין דף פב:) ארבי מאיר ורבי יהודה שאומרים התם שיעור אחר:

והא דתנן אין פוחתין כו' נימא רבנן היא ולא רבי חידקא. אומר ר"י דאין לפרש שבת נותנין לו מזון ג' סעודות דהייט כשבא שם בע"ש לעת האוכל דמסתמא ישבות שם שאין רגילות כל כך ללכת ערב שבת ובשביל שבת נותנים לו סעודה אחת יותר ממה שנותנין לו בשאר ימים דא"כ היכי ניחא לרבנן והלא מן הכל אין לו כי אם ד' סעודות אחת שהביא עמו דמלוינן בהדיה ושלשה שנתנו לו וכשיאכל אחת בערב שבת לא ישארו בידו רק ג' סעודות ואותן יאכל בשבת וא"כ תיקשי נמי לרבנן וכי אזיל ריקן אזיל כדפריך בסמוך ומיהו איכא למימר דבסמוך לרבנן נמי פריך אבל קשה דכי משני דמלוינן ליה סעודה בהדיה לא תירץ כלום לר' חידקא דאין לו לשבת כ"א שלש סעודות ולר' חידקא צריך ד' ונראה לר"י דכשבא בע"ש לעת האוכל נותנין לו מזון ב' סעודות כמו בשאר ימים ואם בא לשבות שם מוסיפין לו עוד ג' סעודות וקאמר לימא רבנן היא ולא רבי חידקא דלרבנן ניחא שיש בידו ה' סעודות בתחילת שבת ואותה שהביא עמו יאכל בע"ש ומאותן ה' סעודות יאכל ג' בשבת ואחת במוצאי שבת ואחת יוליך עמו אלא לרבי חידקא כשיאכל ד' בשבת ואחת להוליך עמו למחר א"כ מה יאכל במוצאי שבת וליכא למימר דאמרינן ליה מה דהוה לך למיכל באפוקי שבתא אכול בשבתא כדאמרי' לעיל דהתם אמרינן ליה כדי שלא יהא ניזון מן הצדקה אבל הכא כבר הוא ניזון ולהכי נוטל כל צרכו ומשני דאיכא סעודה בהדיה המתרץ היה סבור שהיה פשוט למקשה שהסעודה שיוליך עמו נותנין לו באחד בשבת אע"פ שבשאר ימים נותנין לו סעודה שיוליך עמו עם אחרות בע"ש אין נותנין לו אותה עד שילך לפי שאינו הולך מיד עד אחר השבת ולכך היה סבור שהמקשה לא היה יודע שהביא סעודה עמו ואין לו בתחלת השבת אלא ד' להכי משני ליה דאיכא סעודה בהדיה והמקשה משיב דפשיטא ליה דאיכא סעודה בהדיה אך קשה ליה כיון דמתרגמת דאכיל לכולהו וכי אזיל בריקן אזיל שכמו שהביא עמו לכאן כן ישאנה עמו בלאתו מכאן ומשני דמלוינן ליה כו':

דמלוינן סעודה בהדיה. וא"ת א"כ אמאי נותנים לו ב' סעודות כיון שמביא אחת עמו יתנו לו אחת ויאכל אחת והאחת יוליך עמו וי"ל דאין מחלקין תמחוי בלילה אלא ביום בזמן הסעודה ולכך נותנין לו שנים שיאכל אחת מיד ואחת בלילה במקום שיהיה ואחת להוליך עמו למחר: **לפי** שאין קבע לשתיה. מכאן יש ללמוד בלילה כשרוצה להתענות למחר לאחר אכילה אע"פ שאינו יכול לאכול אם לא התנה לפי שמסתמא כשבירך סילק דעתו מלאכול מלשתות ודאי לא סילק דעתו כדאמר הכא דאין קבע לשתיה והיכא דלא שכיח יין אע"ג דסילק דעתו מן היין מ"מ ממים לא סילק דעתו ומיהו אומר ר"י דשמא דוקא בימיהם שהיו קובעין עצמן לשתיה אחר אכילה אמרו דאין קבע לשתיה אבל לדידן לא וריב"א פירש במסכת תענית (דף יב.) שאף לאחר שישן מותר לשתות על פי הירושלמי ואין ר"י רוצה להקל. כל כך כיון שלא נזכר בהדיא, בש"ס שלנו [עיין תוספות תענית יב: ד"ה נים]:

רוכס

ל א מיי' פ"ט מהלכות מתנות עניים הלכה יג סמג עשין קסב טור שו"ע יו"ד סימן רנג סעיף א ב:

לא ב מיי' פ"ל מהלכות שבת הלכה ז סמג עשין ל טוש"ע או"ח סי' רמב:

לב ג מיי' פ"ז מהלכות מ"ע הלכה ח סמג עשין קסב טוש"ע יו"ד סימן רנ סעיף ד:

לג ד מיי' פכ"ג מהלכות שבת הלכה ז סמג לאוין סה טוש"ע או"ח סימן שכג סעיף ו:

לד ה מיי' פ"ל שם הלכה ט סמג עשין ל טוש"ע או"ח סימן רצא סעיף א:

רבינו חננאל

ואיתא בפ' כיצד מברכין: ת"ר כמה סעודות חייב אדם לוכל בשבת ג'. פי' א' בלילה וב' ביום. וכן הלכה. ולפיכך שנינו שמציל מזון ג' סעודו' ומתני' מחוורתא דלא כר' חידקא: **כלי** מאכל אינו מדיח אלא מה שצריך לוכל בו בשבת. לפי זמן סעודותיו אבל כלי שתיה כל היום. שאין קבע לשתיה:

נחלת יעקב אביך וגו' לא כאברהם שכתוב בו °קום התהלך בארץ לארכה וגו' ולא כיצחק שכתוב בו °כי לך ולזרעך אתן את כל הארצות האל אלא כיעקב שכתוב בו °ופרצת ימה וקדמה וצפונה ונגבה ר"נ בר יצחק אמר ניצול משעבוד גליות כתיב הכא והרכבתיך על במתי ארץ וכתיב התם °ואתה על במותימו תדרוך אמר רב יהודה אמר רב כל המענג את השבת נותנין לו משאלות לבו שנאמר °והתענג על ה' ויתן לך משאלות לבך עונג זה איני יודע מהו כשהוא אומר וקראת לשבת עונג הוי אומר זה עונג שבת במה מענגו רב יהודה בריה דרב שמואל בר שילת משמי' דרב אמר בתבשיל של תרדין(א) ודגים גדולים וראשי שומין רב חייא בר אשי אמר רב אפי' דבר מועט ולכבוד שבת עשאו הרי זה עונג מאי היא א"ר פפא כסא דהרסנא אמר ר' חייא בר אבא א"ר יוחנן כל המשמר שבת כהלכתו אפי' עובד ע"ז [כדור] אנוש מוחלין לו שנאמר °אשרי אנוש יעשה זאת וגו' מחללו אל תקרי מחללו אלא מחול לו אמר רב יהודה אמר רב אלמלי שמרו ישראל שבת *ראשונה לא שלטה בהן אומה ולשון שנאמר °ויהי ביום השביעי יצאו מן העם ללקוט וכתיב בתריה ויבא עמלק אמר רבי יוחנן משום רבי שמעון בן יוחי *אלמלי משמרין ישראל שתי שבתות כהלכתן מיד נגאלים שנא' °כה אמר ה' לסריסים אשר ישמרו את שבתותי וכתיב בתריה והביאותים אל הר קדשי וגו' אמר ר' יוסי *יהא חלקי מאוכלי שלש סעודות בשבת א"ר יוסי יהא חלקי מגומרי הלל בכל יום איני והאמר מר הקורא הלל בכל יום הרי זה מחרף ומגדף כי קאמרינן בפסוקי דזמרא א"ר יוסי יהא חלקי ממתפללים עם דמדומי חמה *א"ר חייא בר אבא א"ר יוחנן מצוה להתפלל עם דמדומי חמה א"ר זירא מאי קרא °ייראוך עם שמש ולפני ירח דור דורים וא"ר יוסי יהא חלקי ממתי בחולי מעיים דאמר מר *רובן של צדיקים מתים בחולי מעיים וא"ר יוסי יהא חלקי ממתי בדרך מצוה וא"ר יוסי יהא חלקי ממכניסי שבת בטבריא וממוציאי שבת בצפורי וא"ר יוסי יהא חלקי ממושיבי בהמ"ד ולא ממעמידי בהמ"ד וא"ר יוסי יהא חלקי מגבאי צדקה ולא ממחלקי צדקה *וא"ר יוסי יהא חלקי ממי שחושדין אותו ואין בו אמר רב פפא לדידי חשדן ולא הוה בי א"ר יוסי חמש בעילות בעלתי ונטעתי חמשה ארזים בישראל ומאן אינון ר' ישמעאל ברבי יוסי ור' *אלעזר בר"י ור' חלפתא בר"י ור' אבטילס בר"י ורבי מנחם בר' יוסי והאיכא ורדימס היינו מנחם ואמאי קרי ליה ורדימס *שפניו דומין לוורד למימרא דרבי יוסי מצות עונה לא קיים אלא אימא חמש בעילות בעלתי ושניתי *אמר רבי יוסי מימי לא קריתי לאשתי אשתי ולשורי שורי אלא לאשתי ביתי ולשורי שדי אמר ר' יוסי מימי לא נסתכלתי במילה שלי איני והאמרו ליה לרבי מאי טעמא קראו לך רבינו הקדוש אמר להו מימי לא נסתכלתי במילה שלי ברבי מילתא אחריתי הוה ביה שלא הכנים ידו תחת אבנטו וא"ר יוסי מימי לא ראו קורות ביתי אימרי חלוקי וא"ר יוסי מימי לא עברתי על דברי חברי יודע אני בעצמי שאיני כהן אם אומרים לי חבירי עלה לדוכן אני עולה *וא"ר יוסי מימי לא אמרתי דבר וחזרתי לאחורי אמר רב נחמן *) תיתי לי דקיימית ג' סעודות בשבת אמר רב יהודה תיתי לי דקיימית עיון תפלה אמר רב הונא בריה דרב יהושע תיתי לי דלא סגינא ד' אמות בגילוי הראש אמר רב ששת תיתי לי דקיימית מצות תפילין ואמר ר"נ תיתי לי דקיימית מצות ציצית אמר ליה רב יוסף לרב יוסף בריה דרבה אבוך במאי זהיר טפי אמר ליה בציצית יומא חד הוה קא סליק בדרגא איפסיק ליה חוטא ולא נחית ואתא כמה דלא רמיה ואמר אביי תיתי לי דכי חזינא צורבא מרבנן דשלים מסכתיה עבידנא

*) [לקמן ריש קיט. ז"ל רש"י תיתי לי ישולם שכרי ובבכורות ל. ז"ל רש"י תיתי לי שכר טוב ועי' תוס' בבכורות ל: ד"ה שמא]

תורה אור: בראשית יג | שם כו | שם כח | דברים לג | תהלים לז | ישעיה נח | ישעיה נו | שמות טז | ישעיה נו | תהלים עב

רש"י

נחלת יעקב. ולא נחלת אברהם ויצחק: לארכה ולרחבה. ארץ זו ולא יותר: הארצות האל. ותו לא: תבשיל של תרדין. חשוב הוא: ראשי שומין. חשובים היו להן: כסא דהרסנא. דגים קטנים מטוגנים בשמן קרביהן ובקמח: דור אנוש. התחילו לעבוד ע"ז דכתיב (בראשית ד) אז הוחל לקרוא וגו': בתריה. בתר ההיא פרשתא: הרי זה מחרף ומגדף. שנביאים הראשונים תיקנו לומר בפרקים לשבח והודיה כדאמרינן בערבי פסחים (דף קיז.) וזה הקוראה תמיד בלא עתה אינו אלא כמזמר שיר ומתלוצץ: פסוקי דזמרא. שני מזמורים של הילולים הללו את ה' מן השמים הללו אל בקדשו: דמדומי חמה. כשהיא אדומה שחרית אחרי הנץ מיד היא אדומה וערבית סמוך לשקיעתה: עם שמש. עם זריחתה: ולפני ירח. קודם אור הירח בעוד השמש לא שקעה: ממתי מחולי בני מעיים. שמתייסרין ביסורין ומתמרקין עונותיהן: ממכניסי שבת בטבריא. מפני שהיא עמוקה ומחשכת מבעוד יום וסבורין שחשכה וממוציאי שבת בצפורי שיושבת בראש ההר ובעוד כשהחמה שוקעת נראית שם אור גדול ומאחרין לצאת: ממושיבי בית המדרש. חזנים מאספי תלמידים בכל יום לבא: ממעמידי. ממונים לעת האוכל לומר הגיע עת לעמוד ולאכול: ממחלקי. לעניים לדקה דאמרינן בבבא בתרא פ"ק (דף ח:) לדקה נגבית בשנים ומתחלקת בשלשה והמחלקים אותה עליהם לבדוק לפי הצריך לכל אחד ואחד ופעמים שקרובין דעתם לרחם על זה ולחלוק יותר מן הצורך שאומדין אותו בהרווחה ואומדין את חברו בצמצום: בעלתי ושניתי. כדי שיהיו זכרים דאמר מר הרוצה שיהיו בניו זכרים יבעול וישנה (עירובין דף ק:): לא קריתי לאשתי אשתי. שאף שיחת חולין שלי יש ללמוד הימנה חכמה: אשתי ביתי. שהיא עיקר של בית: ולשורי שדי. שהוא עיקר של שדה דכתיב ורב תבואות בכח שור (משלי יד): לא נסתכלתי כו'. מרוב צניעות: והא אמרו לו כו'. וא"כ לרבי יוסי נמי הוה ליה למיקרייה רבינו הקדוש: תחת אבנטו. מן האבנט ולמטה: לא ראו קורות כו'. (ב)כשפושט חלוקו [פושטו] כמו שהוא לובשו דרך ראשו ומכסה את עצמו תחלה משום צניעות בסדינו מתחת ויושב במטתו: לא אמרתי דבר וחזרתי לאחורי. שאם בא מי שאמרתי עליו דבר ושאל אם אמרתי כן עליו לא חזרתי בי לאמר איני כדבריו לפי שמתחלה אמת אמרתי וקסבר כל מילתא דמתאמרא באפי מרה לית בה משום לישנא בישא וכן מפרש במסכת ערכין (דף טו:): דקיימתי מצות תפילין. שלא הלך ארבע אמות בלא תפילין וכן לענין ציצית: עד דרמיה. שתקנה וזה לשון תליית ציצית כדאמרינן בעלמא (תענית ד' כב.) לא רמי חוטי: דשלים מסכתיה. שגרסה:

עבידנא

תוספות

רובם של צדיקים מתים בחולי מעיים. פי' בקונטרס למרק עונותיהם ור"י אומר כי יש במדרש *למרק אכילה מן המעיים להיות נקיים וטהורים כמלאכי השרת: אימא ה' בעילות בעלתי ושניתי. ובירושלמי משני דיבמות היו ולא רצה לקיים בהן מצות עונה אלא רק כדי לקיים מצות יבום דהיינו ביאה ראשונה: אילו היו אומרים לי חברי עלה לדוכן. לא ידע ר"י מה איסור יש בזר העולה לדוכן אם לא משום ברכה לבטלה של כהנים אמרה תורה לברך את ישראל: עיון תפלה. פי' בכוונת הלב וכן ההיא דאלו דברים שאוכל מפירותיהן בעולם הזה (לקמן דף קכז.) דחשיב עיון תפלה אבל הא דאמר בברכות (דף לב: ונה.) המעיין בתפלתו סוף בא לידי כאב לב ההוא עיון דמצפה מתי יעשה הקב"ה בקשתו שסבור שתפלתו מקובלת כדמייתי עלה תוחלת ממושכה מחלה לב וכן ההיא *דאמר ר"י שלשה דברים מזכירין עוונותיו של אדם קיר נטוי ועיון תפלה [ומוסר דין לשמים על חבירו] והא דאמר בפרק גט פשוט (ב"ב קסד:) שלשה דברים אין אדם ניצול מהם בכל יום לשון הרע והרהור עבירה ועיון תפלה אין לפרש שמצפה מתי תיעשה בקשתו שהרבה בני אדם ניצולים מזה אלא הוה כי ההוא דשמעתין כלומר שאינו מתכוין בתפלה שאי אפשר ליזהר כדאמרינן בירושלמי* מחזיקנא טיבו לרישא דכי מטא למודים מנפשיה כרע*:

בתליסר

עין משפט נר מצוה

[בראשית רבה פרשה פב]

לה א מיי' פ"ל מהל' שבת הלכה ז סמג עשין ל טור שו"ע או"ח סימן רמב:

לו ב מיי' פ"ז מהלכות תפלה הלכה יב טור ש"ע או"ח סימן נא סעיף ח:

לז ג מיי' פ"ג מהלכות תפילה הלכה א' סמג עשין יט טוש"ע או"ח סימן פט סעיף א וסימן רלג סעיף א [ברי"ף כאן ובפ"ה דברכות דף ט. וכן ברא"ש כאן ושם סי' ה']:

לח ד טור שו"ע או"ח סימן רסא סעיף ב וסימן רצג סעיף א:

לט ה מיי' פכ"א מהל' איסורי ביאה הלכה ט טוש"ע אה"ע סימן כג סעיף ז בהגה:

מ ו ז טוש"ע או"ח סימן ב סעיף א ו:

[ברכות נה.]

מא ח טוש"ע יו"ד סי' רמו סעיף כו בהג"ה:

[פרק היה קורא הלכה י]

[ועי' תוס' ברכות לג: ד"ה כל]

רב נסים גאון

אמר ר' יוסי יהא חלקי עם מכניסי שבת בטבריא ועם מוציאי שבתות בציפורי. לפי שטבריא היתה נמוכה והחמה שוקעת שם בעוד יומם והיו יושביה מקבלין עליהן השבת משקיעת החמה אצלם ושקיעתה לשם קודם שקיעתה במקומות הגבוהין ומי שמקבל עליו הכנסת השבת מאותה השעה הרי עשה סייג לעצמו והוא משובח ומעולה מן היושבים במקומות הגבוהין ובהרים וכנגדן מוציאי שבת בציפורי שהיא גבוהה מפי ומאחרין לשם פני המזרח להכסיף ושוהין ומאדימין והיו מקבלין עליהן שימור השבת עד שמכסיפין פני המזרח התחתון והעליון ולפיכך הן משובחים בזה הענין יותר מאנשי טבריא ובמסכת ראש השנה בפרק יו"ט של ראש השנה (דף לא) משכחת וטבריא עמוקה מכולן שנאמר (ישעיה כט) ושפלת מארץ תדברי ובמסכת מגילה בפרק מגילה נקראת (דף ו) ולמה נקראת שמה ציפורי אמר רב פפא שיושבת בראש ההר כצפור והרי נתברר לך מיכן כי טבריא נמוכה וציפורי גבוהה:

גליון הש"ס

גמ' יהא חלקי ממכניסי שבת בטבריא. ברבינו יונה פ"ח דברכות דף מג ע"א כתב די"מ שבטבריא היו מגמרים הכלים בע"ש מפני כבוד שבת שיריחו ריח טוב ובציפורי היו מגמרים במ"ש והיו עושין כן לכבוד שבת שהיו מרלין הצער שיש להם מהנפש יתירה שהיה להם בשבת ועתה בפרידת השבת צריכין למוגמר להריח ריח טוב עיין שם. וכעין זה כ' באגודה. והר"י מיגאש בתשובה סימן מ"ה כ' יהא חלקי וכו' היינו עם אותם שבהתחלת שבת המה בטבריא ובהפוקי יומא הם בציפורי כי טבריא וציפורי תוך תחום אחד ומקדמי ומאחרי שבת: תוס' ד"ה אילו וכו' לא ידע ר"י וכו' וכזה לקמן קלא ע"ב תוס' ד"ה קמ"ל. וקלא ע"א תוס' ד"ה מי סברת ובכתובות דף לג ע"א תוס' ד"ה תימה:

מסורת הש"ס

[ע"ל פ"ו ע"ב תוס' ד"ה כאשר]

[עי' תוס' נדה יג: ד"ה עד שיכלו]

[עי' תוס' בכורות ל: ד"ה שמא וכו']

ברכות כט:

[כתובות קג:]

מו"ק יח:

בדפו"י אליעזר

[סוטה לו:]

גיטין נב:

ערכין טו:

[פ"ש ברש"י]

הגהות הב"ח

(א) גמ' בתבשיל של תרדין. נ"ב בעירובין ראש ד' ס"ט אמר רב חסדא תבשיל של תרדין יפה ללב וטוב לעינים וכל שכן לבני מעים ואמר אביי והוא דיתיב אבי תפי וכו' ובס"פ מרובה דף פ"ב ע"א חמשה דברים נאמרו בשום משביע ומשחין ומצהיל פנים ומרבה הזרע והורג כנים שבבני מעים ומכניס אהבה ומוציא קנאה ובפ' כיצד מעברין ריש דף נ"ו פירש"י לשבח ולא לגנאי וע"ש: (ב) רש"י ד"ה לא ראו קורות כו' כשפושט חלוקו. נ"ב ס"א לא היה הופכו מרוב צניעות כשפושטו כו':

upon the high places of the earth; and I will feed thee [118b] *with the heritage of Jacob thy father*, etc.[3] Not like Abraham, of whom it is written, *Arise, walk through the land in the length of it*, etc.;[4] nor like Isaac of whom it is written, *for unto thee, and unto thy seed, I will give all these lands, etc.;*[5] but like Jacob, of whom it is written, *and thou shalt spread abroad to the west, and to the east, and to the north, and to the south.*[6] R. Naḥman b. Isaac said, He is saved from the servitude of the Diaspora: here it is written, *and I will make thee to ride upon the high places of the earth;* whilst there it is written, *and thou shalt tread upon their high places.*[7]

Rab Judah said in Rab's name: He who delights in the Sabbath is granted his heart's desires, for it is said, *Delight thyself also in the Lord; and He shall give thee the desires of thine heart.*[8] Now, I do not know what this '*delight*' refers to; but when it is said, *and thou shalt call the Sabbath a delight,*[9] you must say that it refers to the delight of the Sabbath.[10]

Wherewith does one show his delight therein?—Rab Judah son of R. Samuel b. Shilath said in Rab's name: With a dish of beets, large fish, and heads of garlic. R. Ḥiyya b. Ashi said in Rab's name: Even a trifle, if it is prepared in honour of the Sabbath, is delight. What is it [the trifle]?—Said R. Papa: A pie of fish-hash.

R. Ḥiyya b. Abba said in R. Joḥanan's name: He who observes the Sabbath according to its laws, even if he practises idolatry
a like the generation of Enosh,[1] is forgiven, for it is said, *Blessed is Enosh*[2] *that doeth this . . .* [*that keepeth the Sabbath* meḥallelo *from profaning it*]:[3] read not *meḥallelo* but *maḥul lo* [he is forgiven].

Rab Judah said in Rab's name: Had Israel kept the first Sabbath, no nation or tongue would have enjoyed dominion over them, for it is said, *And it came to pass on the seventh day, that there went out some of the people to gather;*[4] which is followed by, *Then came Amalek.*[5] R. Joḥanan said in the name of R. Simeon b. Yoḥai: If Israel were to keep two Sabbaths according to the laws thereof, they would be redeemed immediately, for it is said, *Thus saith the Lord concerning the eunuchs that keep My Sabbaths,*[6] which is followed by, *even them will I bring to My holy mountain*, etc.[7]

R. Jose said: May my portion be of those who eat three meals on the Sabbath. R. Jose [also] said: May my portion be of those who recite the entire *Hallel*[8] every day. But that is not so, for a Master said: He who reads *Hallel* every day blasphemes and reproaches [the Divine Name]?[9]—We refer to the 'Verses of Song'.[10]

R. Jose said: May my portion be of those who pray with the red glow of the sun.[11] R. Ḥiyya b. Abba said in R. Joḥanan's name: It is virtuous to pray with the red glow of the sun. R. Zera observed: What verse [intimates this]? *They shall revere Thee with* [i.e., at the time of] *the sun* [*rise*], *and before the moon* [shines],[12] *throughout all generations.*[13]

(3) Isa. LVIII, 14. (4) Gen. XIII, 17. (5) Ibid. XXVI, 3. (6) Ibid. XXVIII, 14. (7) Deut. XXXIII, 29. The underlying idea is probably the same as that of Heine's 'Princess Sabbath'. (8) Ps. XXXVII, 4. (9) Isa. LVIII, 13. (10) The emphasis on the importance of observing the Sabbath with those meals and as a day of delight was meant according to Weiss (*Dor* I, 121) to counteract the ascetic tendencies of the Essenes.

a (1) Gen. IV, 26. According to tradition idolatry commenced in his days. (2) E.V. '*the man*'. (3) Isa. LVI, 2. (4) Ex. XVI, 27. This refers to the manna, in connection with which the Sabbath is mentioned for the first time explicitly. (5) Ibid. XVII, 8. (6) Isa. LVI, 4. (7) Ibid. 7. (8) Lit., 'praise' Ps. CXIII-CXVIII, which was inserted in the service on Festivals, *Ḥanukkah*, and New Moon—on the latter occasion, as well as from the third day of Passover, chs. CXV, 1-11 and CXVI, 1-11 are omitted. (9) Because its recital was instituted for special occasions only, and by reading it every day he treats it as a mere song. (10) The name given to Ps. CXLV-CL which are designated here as *Hallel* on account of the term 'praise' recurring in them; v. Elbogen, *Der Jüdische Gottesdienst*, p. 83, § 2. (11) Rashi. Jast.: The time in the morning and the evening when the sun appears to stand still or be silent, viz., dawn and sunset. (12) I.e., at sunset. (13) Ps. LXXII, 5. Cf. R. Joḥanan's statement in Ber. 9*b* on the *wathikin* (R. Zera quotes this verse there too, which makes it probable that the same time is referred to there and here); Elbogen, op. cit. p. 246.

◁ *For the continuation of the English translation of this page see overleaf.*

נחלת יעקב אביך וגו' לא כאברהם שכתוב בו °קום התהלך בארץ לארכה וגו' ולא כיצחק שכתוב בו °כי לך ולזרעך אתן את כל הארצות האל אלא כיעקב שכתוב בו °ופרצת ימה וקדמה וצפונה ונגבה ר"נ בר יצחק אמר ניצול משעבוד גליות כתיב הכא והרכבתיך על במתי ארץ וכתיב התם °ואתה על במותימו תדרוך אמר רב יהודה אמר רב כל המענג את השבת נותנין לו משאלות לבו שנאמר °והתענג על ה' ויתן לך משאלות לבך עונג זה איני יודע מהו כשהוא אומר וקראת לשבת עונג *הוי אומר זה עונג שבת במה מענגו רב יהודה בריה דרב שמואל בר שילת משמי' דרב אמר בתבשיל של תרדין(א) ודגים גדולים וראשי שומין רב חייא בר אשי אמר רב אפי' דבר מועט ולכבוד שבת עשאו הרי זה עונג מאי היא א"ר פפא כסא דהרסנא אמר ר' חייא בר אבא א"ר יוחנן כל המשמר שבת כהלכתו אפי' עובד ע"ז [כדור] אנוש מוחלין לו שנאמר °אשרי אנוש יעשה זאת וגו' מחללו אל תקרי מחללו אלא מחול לו אמר רב יהודה אמר רב אלמלי שמרו ישראל שבת *ראשונה לא שלטה בהן אומה ולשון שנאמר °ויהי ביום השביעי יצאו מן העם ללקוט וכתיב בתריה ויבא עמלק אמר רבי יוחנן משום רבי שמעון בן יוחי *אלמלי משמרין ישראל שתי שבתות כהלכתן מיד נגאלים שנא' °כה אמר ה' לסריסים אשר ישמרו את שבתותי וכתיב בתריה והביאותים אל הר קדשי וגו' אמר ר' יוסי *יהא חלקי מאוכלי שלש סעודות בשבת א"ר יוסי [ב]יהא חלקי מגומרי הלל בכל יום איני והאמר מר הקורא הלל בכל יום הרי זה מחרף ומגדף כי קאמרינן בפסוקי דזמרא א"ר יוסי יהא חלקי ממתפללים עם דמדומי חמה *א"ר חייא בר אבא א"ר יוחנן [ג]מצוה להתפלל עם דמדומי חמה א"ר זירא מאי קרא °ייראוך עם שמש ולפני ירח דור דורים וא"ר יוסי יהא חלקי ממתי בחולי מעיים דאמר מר *רובן של צדיקים מתים בחולי מעיים וא"ר יוסי יהא חלקי ממתי בדרך מצוה וא"ר יוסי °[ד]יהא חלקי ממכניסי שבת בטבריא וממוציאי שבת בצפורי וא"ר יוסי יהא חלקי ממושיבי בהמ"ד ולא ממעמידי בהמ"ד וא"ר יוסי יהא חלקי מגבאי צדקה ולא ממחלקי צדקה *וא"ר יוסי יהא חלקי ממי שחושדין אותו ואין בו אמר רב פפא לדידי חשדן ולא הוה בי א"ר יוסי חמש בעילות בעלתי ונטעתי חמשה ארזים בישראל ומאן אינון ר' ישמעאל ברבי יוסי ור' *אלעזר בר"י ור' חלפתא בר"י ור' אבטילס בר"י ורבי מנחם בר' יוסי והאיכא ורדימס היינו מנחם ואמאי קרי ליה ורדימס *שפניו דומין לורד למימרא דרבי יוסי מצות עונה לא קיים אלא אימא חמש בעילות בעלתי ושניתי *אמר רבי יוסי מימי לא קריתי לאשתי אשתי ולשורי שורי אלא לאשתי ביתי ולשורי שדי אמר ר' יוסי [ה]מימי לא נסתכלתי במילה שלי איני והאמרו ליה לרבי מאי טעמא קראו לך רבינו הקדוש אמר להו מימי לא נסתכלתי במילה שלי ברבי מילתא אחריתי הוה ביה שלא הכנים ידו תחת אבנטו וא"ר יוסי [ו]מימי לא ראו קורות ביתי אימרי חלוקי וא"ר יוסי מימי לא עברתי על דברי חברי יודע אני בעצמי שאיני כהן אם אומרים לי חבירי עלה לדוכן אני עולה *וא"ר יוסי מימי לא אמרתי דבר וחזרתי לאחורי אמר רב נחמן *) תיתי לי דקיימית ג' סעודות בשבת אמר רב יהודה תיתי לי דקיימית עיון תפלה אמר רב הונא בריה דרב יהושע [ז]תיתי לי דלא סגינא ד' אמות בגילוי הראש אמר רב ששת תיתי לי דקיימית מצות תפילין ואמר ר"נ תיתי לי דקיימית מצות ציצית אמר ליה רב יוסף לרב יוסף בריה דרבה אבוך במאי זהיר טפי אמר ליה בציצית יומא חד הוה קא סליק בדרגא איפסיק ליה חוטא ולא נחית ואתא כמה דלא רמיה ואמר אביי תיתי לי דכי [ח]חזינא צורבא מרבנן דשלים מסכתיה עבידנא

*) [לקמן ריש קיט. ז"ל רש"י תיתי לי ישולם שכרי ובבכורות ל. ז"ל רש"י תיתי לי שכר טוב ועי' תוס' בבכורות ב: ד"ה שמא]

תוספות

רובם של צדיקים מתים בחולי מעיים . פי' בקונטרס למרק עונותיהם ור"י אומר כי יש במדרש *למרק אכילה מן המעיים להיות נקיים וטהורים כמלאכי השרת : **אימא** ה' בעילות בעלתי ושניתי . ובירושלמי משני דיבמות היו ולא רצה לקיים בהן מצות עונה אלא רק כדי לקיים מצות יבום דהיינו ביאה ראשונה : **אילו** היו אומרים לי חברי עלה לדוכן. °לא ידע ר"י מה איסור יש בזר העולה לדוכן אם לא משום ברכה לבטלה של כהנים אמרה תורה לברך את ישראל: **עיון** תפלה . פי' בכוונת הלב וכן ההיא דאלו דברים שאוכל מפירותיהן בעולם הזה (לקמן דף קכז.) דחשיב עיון תפלה אבל הא דאמר בברכות (דף לב: ונה.) המעיין בתפלתו סוף בא לידי כאב לב ההוא עיון דמצפה מתי יעשה הקב"ה בקשתו שסבור שתפלתו מקובלת כדמייתי עלה תוחלת ממושכה מחלה לב וכן ההיא *דאמר ר"י שלשה דברים מזכירין עוונותיו של אדם קיר נטוי ועיון תפלה [ומוסר דין לשמים על חבירו] והא דאמר בפרק גט פשוט (ב"ב קסד:) שלשה דברים אין אדם ניצול מהם בכל יום לשון הרע והרהור עבירה ועיון תפלה אין לפרש שמצפה מתי תיעשה בקשתו שהרבה בני אדם ניצולים מזה אלא הוה כי ההוא דשמעתין כלומר שאינו מתכוין בתפלה שאי אפשר ליזהר כדאמרינן בירושלמי* מחזיקנא טיבו לרישא דכי מטא למודים מנכסיה כרע* : בתליסר

רש"י

נחלת יעקב · ולא נחלת אברהם ויצחק : לארכה ולרחבה . ארץ זו ולא יותר : הארצות האל . ותו לא : תבשיל של תרדין . חשוב הוא : ראשי שומין . חשובים היו לכן : כסא דהרסנא . דגים קטנים מטוגנים בשמן קרביהן ובקמח : דור אנוש . התחילו לעבוד ע"ז דכתיב (בראשית ד) אז הוחל לקרוא וגו' : בתריה . בתר ההיא פרשתא : הרי זה מחרף ומגדף . שנביאים הראשונים תיקנו לומר בפרקים לשבח ולהודיה כדאמרינן בערבי פסחים (דף קיז.) וזה הקוראה תמיד בלא עתה אינו אלא כמזמר שיר ומתלוצץ : פסוקי דזמרא . שני מזמורים של הילולים הללו את ה' מן השמים הללו אל בקדשו : דמדומי חמה . כשהיא אדומה שחרית אחרי הנץ מיד היא אדומה וערבית סמוך לשקיעתה : עם שמש . עם זריחתה : ולפני ירח . קודם אור הירח בעוד השמש לא שקעה : ממתי מחולי בני מעיים. שמתייסרין ביסורין ומתמרקין עונותיהן : ממכניסי שבת בטבריא . מפני שהיא עמוקה ומחשכת מבעוד יום וסבורין שחשכה וממוציאי שבת בצפורי שיושבת בראש ההר ובעוד כשהחמה שוקעת נראית שם אור גדול ומאחרין לצאת : ממושיבי בית המדרש . חזנים מאספי תלמידים בכל יום לבא : ממעמידי . ממונים לעת האוכל לומר הגיע עת לעמוד ולאכול : ממחלקי . לעניים לדקה דאמרינן בבבא בתרא פ"ק (דף ח:) לדקה נגבית בשנים ומתחלקת בשלשה והמחלקים אותה עליהם לבדוק לפי הצריך לכל אחד ואחד ופעמים שקרובין דעתם לרחם על זה ולחלוק יותר מן הצורך שאומדין אותו בהרווחה ואומדין את חברו בצמצום : בעלתי ושניתי · כדי שיהיו זכרים דאמר מר הרוצה שיהיו בניו זכרים יבעול וישנה (עירובין דף ק:) : לא קריתי לאשתי אשתי . שאף שיחת חולין שלי יש ללמוד הימנה חכמה : אשתי ביתי . שהיא עיקר של בית : ולשורי שדי . שהוא עיקר של שדה דכתיב ורב תבואות בכח שור (משלי יד): לא נסתכלתי כו'. מרוב צניעות : והא אמרו לו כו' . וא"כ לרבי יוסי נמי הוה ליה למיקרייה רבינו הקדוש : תחת אבנטו . מן האבנט ולמטה : לא ראו קורות כו'. (ג)כשפושט חלוקו [פושטו] כמו שהוא לובשו דרך ראשו ומכסה את עצמו תחלה משום צניעות בסדינו מתחת ויושב במטתו : לא אמרתי דבר וחזרתי לאחורי . שאם בא מי שאמרתי עליו דבר ושאל אם אמרתי כן עליו לא חזרתי בי לאמר איני כדבריו לפי שמתחלה אמת אמרתי וקסבר כל מילתא דמתאמרא באפי מרה לית בה משום לישנא בישא וכן מפרש במסכת ערכין (דף טו:) : דקיימתי מצות תפילין. שלא הלך ארבע אמות בלא תפילין וכן לענין ציצית : עד דרמיה . שתקנה וזה לשון תליית ציצית כדאמרינן בעלמא (תענית ד' כב.) לא רמי חוטי : דשלים מסכתיה. שגרסה: עבידנא

עין משפט נר מצוה

[בראשית רבה פרשה פב]

לה א מיי' פ"ל מהל' שבת הלכה ז סמג עשין ל טור שו"ע או"ח סימן רמב :
לו ב מיי' פ"ז מהלכות תפלה הלכה יב טור שו"ע או"ח סימן נא סעיף ח :
לז ג מיי' פ"ג מהלכות תפילה הלכה א' סמג עשין יט טוש"ע או"ח סימן פט סעיף א וסימן רלג סעיף א [ברי"ף כאן ובפ"ה דברכות דף כו. וכן ברא"ש כאן ושם סי' כ'] :
לח ד טור שו"ע או"ח סימן רסא סעיף ב וסימן רצג סעיף א :
לט ה מיי' פכ"א מהל' איסורי ביאה הלכה כג טוש"ע אה"ע סימן כג סעיף ז בהגה :
מ ו ז טוש"ע או"ח סימן ב סעיף א ו :
[ברכות נה.]
מא ח טוש"ע יו"ד סי' רמו סעיף כו בהג"ה :

[פרק היה קורא הלכה י]
[ועי' תוס' ברכות לב: ד"ה כל]

רב נסים גאון

אמר ר' יוסי יהא חלקי עם מכניסי שבת בטבריא ועם מוציאי שבתות בציפורי. לפי שטבריא היתה נמוכה והחמה שוקעת שם בעוד יומם והיו יושביה מקבלין עליהן השבת משקיעת החמה אצלם ושקיעתה לשם קודם שקיעתה במקומות הגבוהין ומי שמקבל עליו הכנסת השבת מאותה השעה הרי עשה סייג לעצמו והוא משובח ומעולה מן היושבים במקומות הגבוהין ובהרים וכנגדן מוציאי שבת בציפורי שהיא גבוהה טפי ומאחרין לשם פני המזרח להכסיף ושוהין ומאדימין והיו מקבלין עליהן שימור השבת עד שמכסיפין פני המזרח התחתון והעליון ולפיכך הן משובחים בזה הענין יותר מאנשי טבריא ובמסכת ראש השנה בפרק יו"ט של ראש השנה (דף לא) משכחת וטבריא עמוקה מכולן שנאמר (ישעיה כט) ושפלת מארץ תדברי ובמסכת מגילה בפרק מגילה נקראת (דף ו) ולמה נקראת שמה ציפורי אמר רב פפא שיושבת בראש ההר כצפור והרי נתברר לך מיכן כי טבריא נמוכה וציפורי גבוהה :

גליון הש"ס

גמ' יהא חלקי ממכניסי שבת בטבריא ברבינו יונה פ"ח דברכות דף מג ע"א כתב די"מ שבטבריא היו מגמרים הכלים בע"ש מפני כבוד שבת שריחו ריח טוב ובציפורי היו מגמרים במ"ש והיו עושין כן לכבוד שבת שהיו מראין הצער שיש להם מהנפש יתירה שהיה להם בשבת ועתה בפרידת השבת צריכין למוגמר להריח ריח טוב עיין שם . וכעין זה כ' באגודה . והר"י מיגאש בתשובה סימן מ"ה כ' יהא חלקי וכו' היינו עם אותם שבתחלת שבת המה בטבריא ובאפוקי יומא הם בציפורי כי טבריא וציפורי תוך תחום אחד ומקדמי ומאחרי שבת : תוס' ד"ה אילו וכו' לא ידע ר"י וכזה לקמן קלא ע"ב תוס' ד"ה קמ"ל . וקלח ע"א תוס' ד"ה מי שברת ובכתובות דף כד ע"א תוס' ד"ה תימא :

הגהות הב"ח

(א) גמ' בתבשיל של תרדין. נ"ב בעירובין ריש ד' ס"ט אמר רב חסדא תבשיל של תרדין יפה ללב וטוב לעינים וכל שכן לבני מעים ואמר אביי והוא דיתיב אבי תפי וכו' ובס"פ מרובה דף פ"ב ע"א חמשה דברים נאמרו בשום משביע ומשחין ומצהיל פנים ומרבה הזרע והורג כנים שבבני מעים ומכנים אהבה ומוציא קנאה ובפ' כיצד מעברין ריש דף נ"ו פירש"י לשבת ולא לגנאי וע"ש : (ג) רש"י ד"ה לא ראו קורות כו' כשפושט חלוקו . נ"ב ס"א לא היה הופכו מרוב צניעות שכשפושטו כו' :

[עי' תוס' נדה יג: ד"ה עד שיכלו]
[עי' תוס' בכורות ב: ד"ה שמא וכו']
ברכות כג:
[כתובות קג:]
מו"ק יח:
בדפוסי אליעזר
[סוטה לו:]
גיטין נב:
ערכין טו: [פ"ש כתב"י]

Continuation of translation from previous page as indicated by ◁

R. Jose also said: May my lot be of those who die with bowel b trouble,[1] for a Master said, The majority of the righteous die of trouble in the bowels. R. Jose also said: May my portion be of those who die on the way to the performance of a religious duty.[2] R. Jose also said: May my lot be of those who welcome the Sabbath in Tiberias and who let it depart in Sepphoris.[3] R. Jose also said: May my lot be of those who seat [pupils] in the Beth Hamidrash,[4] and not of those who order [them] to rise [depart] from the Beth Hamidrash.[5] R. Jose also said: May my lot be of those who collect charity, but not of those who distribute charity.[6] R. Jose also said: May my lot be of those who are suspected whilst innocent.[7] R. Papa said: I was suspected [of something] of which I was free.[8]

R. Jose said: I cohabited five times and planted five cedars in Israel. Who are they? R. Ishmael son of R. Jose, R. Eleazar[9] son of R. Jose, R. Ḥalafta son of R. Jose, R. Abṭilos son of R. Jose, and R. Menaḥem son of R. Jose. But there was Wardimos?—Wardimos and Menaḥem are identical, and why was he called Wardimos? Because his face was like a rose [*werad*]. Shall we say that R. Jose did not fulfil his marital duties?[10]—Rather say, I cohabited five times and repeated.[11]

R. Jose said: I have never called my wife 'my wife' or my ox 'my ox', but my wife [I called] 'my home,' and my ox 'my field'.

R. Jose said: I have never looked at my circumcised membrum. But that is not so, for Rabbi was asked, Why were you called 'Our holy Teacher?' Said he to them, I have never looked at my c membrum?[1]—In Rabbi's case there was another thing to his credit, viz., he did not insert his hand beneath his girdle. R. Jose also said: The beams of my house have never seen the seams of my shirt.[2]

R. Jose also said: I have never disregarded the words of my neighbours. I know of myself that I am not a priest, [yet] if my neighbours were to tell me to ascend the dais,[3] I would ascend [it].[4] R. Jose also said: I have never in my life said anything from which I retracted.[5]

R. Naḥman said: May I be rewarded[6] for observing three meals on the Sabbath. Rab Judah said: May I be rewarded for observing devotion in prayers.[7] R. Huna son of R. Joshua said: May I be rewarded for never walking four cubits bareheaded.[8] R. Shesheth said: May I be rewarded for fulfilling the precept of *tefillin*.[9] R. Naḥman also said: May I be rewarded for fulfilling the precept of fringes.

R. Joseph asked R. Joseph son of Rabbah: Of what is thy father most observant? Of fringes, he replied. One day he was ascending a ladder[10] when a thread [of his fringes] broke, and he would not descend until [another] was inserted.

Abaye said: May I be rewarded for that when I saw that a

b (1) The suffering involved effects atonement (Rashi). (2) I.e., while engaged in the performance of a good deed (Maharsha). (3) In Tiberias, which was situated in a valley, the Sabbath commenced rather earlier, whilst in Sepphoris, which was on a mountain, it terminated rather later than elsewhere. (4) Rashi: the ushers who collect the pupils. (5) To adjourn for meals. (6) It is very difficult to perform the latter with absolute impartiality, as personal predilections are apt to intervene. (7) Lit., 'and it is not in him'. (8) V. *infra* 140*b*, n. a10 and Ber. 8*b*. (9) Var. lec.: Eliezer. (10) Except on five occasions. (11) Cf. 'Er. 100*b*.

c (1) Which shows that this modesty was peculiar to him. (2) I.e., he did not turn his shirt inside out when he undressed but pulled it over his head whilst sitting up in bed, so that he remained covered as much as possible out of modesty. (3) When the priests recite the priestly blessing; v. Num. VI, 22-27. (4) Though he certainly would not recite the blessing with the other priests, which is forbidden, but merely stand there (Maharsha). (5) Rashi refers this to his opinions on other people: even if unfavourable he did not retract even in the owner's presence, because he did not state them in the first place without being perfectly sure of their truth. (6) Lit., 'may it (*sc.* reward) come to me'. (7) I did not pray mechanically.—The same phrase is used in a derogatory and possibly opposite sense elsewhere, v. Ber. 55*a*, B.B. 164*b*. (8) Cf. *infra* 156*b*. (9) V. Glos. Rashi: he never walked four cubits without wearing his *tefillin;* similarly with respect to fringes. (10) Or, stairs.

disciple had completed his tractate, [119a] I made it a festive day for the scholars. Raba said: May I be rewarded for that when a disciple came before me in a lawsuit, I did not lay my head upon my pillow before I had sought [points in] his favour.[1] Mar son of R. Ashi said: I am unfit to judge in a scholar's lawsuit. What is the reason? He is as dear to me as myself, and a man cannot see [anything] to his own disadvantage.

R. Ḥanina robed himself and stood at sunset of Sabbath eve [and] exclaimed, 'Come and let us go forth to welcome the queen Sabbath.'[2] R. Jannai donned his robes on Sabbath eve and exclaimed, 'Come, O bride, Come, O bride!'

Rabbah son of R. Huna visited the home of Rabbah son of R. Naḥman, [and] was offered three *se'ahs* of oiled cakes. 'Did you know that I was coming?' asked he. 'Are you then more important[3] to us than it [the Sabbath]?' replied he.[4]

R. Abba bought meat for thirteen *istira peshiṭa*[5] from thirteen butchers[6] and handed it over to them [his servants][7] as soon as the door was turned[8] and urged them, 'Make haste, Quick, Make haste, Quick!'[9]

R. Abbahu used to sit on an ivory stool and fan the fire. R. 'Anan used to wear an overall;[10] for the School of R. Ishmael taught: The clothes in which one cooks a dish for his master, let him not pour out[11] a cup [of wine] for his master in them. R. Safra would singe the head [of an animal]. Raba salted *shibuṭa*.[12] R. Huna lit the lamp. R. Papa plaited the wicks. R. Ḥisda cut up the beetroots. Rabbah and R. Joseph chopped wood. R. Zera kindled the fire. R. Naḥman b. Isaac carried[13] in and out,[14] saying, 'If R. Ammi and R. Assi visited me, would I not carry for them?'[15] Others state: R. Ammi and R. Assi carried in and out, saying, 'If R. Joḥanan visited us, would we not carry before him?'[16]

Joseph-who-honours-the-Sabbaths had in his vicinity a certain gentile who owned much property. Soothsayers[1] told him, 'Joseph-who-honours-the-Sabbaths will consume all your property.'[2] [So] he went, sold all his property, and bought a precious stone with the proceeds, which he set in his turban. As he was crossing a bridge the wind blew it off and cast it into the water, [and] a fish swallowed it. [Subsequently] it [the fish] was hauled up and brought [to market] on the Sabbath eve towards sunset. 'Who will buy now?' cried they. 'Go and take them to Joseph-who-honours-the-Sabbaths,' they were told, 'as he is accustomed to buy.' So they took it to him. He bought it, opened it, found the jewel therein, and sold it for thirteen roomfuls[3] of gold *denarii*.[4] A certain old man met him [and] said, 'He who lends to the Sabbath,[5] the Sabbath repays him.'

Rabbi asked R. Ishmael son of R. Jose, The wealthy in Palestine, whereby do they merit [wealth]?[6]—Because they give tithes, he replied, as it is written, '*Asser te'asser*[7] [which means], give tithes ['*asser*] so that thou mayest become wealthy [*tith'asser*].[8] Those in Babylon, wherewith do they merit [it]?—Because they honour the Torah, replied he. And those in other countries, whereby do they merit it?—Because they honour the Sabbath, answered he. For R. Ḥiyya b. Abba related: I was once a guest of a man in Laodicea,[9] and a golden table was brought before him, which had to be carried by sixteen men; sixteen silver chains were fixed in it, and plates, goblets, pitchers and flasks were set thereon,[10] and upon it were all kinds of food, dainties and spices. When they set it down they recited, *The earth is the Lord's, and the fulness thereof;*[11] and when they removed it [after the meal] they recited, *The heavens are the heavens of the Lord; But the earth*
c *hath He given to the children of men.*[1] Said I to him, 'My son! whereby hast thou merited this?' 'I was a butcher,' replied he, 'and of every fine beast I used to say, "This shall be for the Sabbath"'. Said I to him, 'Happy art thou that thou hast [so] merited, and praised be the Omnipresent who has permitted thee to enjoy [all] this.'

The emperor said to R. Joshua b. Ḥanania,[2] 'Why has the Sabbath dish such a fragrant odour?' 'We have a certain seasoning,' replied he, 'called the Sabbath, which we put into it, and that gives it a fragrant odour.' 'Give us some of it,' asked he. 'To him who keeps the Sabbath,' retorted he, 'it is efficacious; but to him who does not keep the Sabbath it is of no use.'

The Resh Galutha[3] asked R. Hamnuna: What is meant by the verse, [*and thou shalt call* ...] *the holy of the Lord honourable?*[4]—This[5] refers to the Day of Atonement, replied he, in which there is neither eating nor drinking, [hence] the Torah instructed, Honour it with clean [festive] garments. *And thou shalt honour it:*[6] Rab said: By fixing [it] earlier;[7] Samuel maintained: By postponing [it].[8] The sons of R. Papa b. Abba asked R. Papa: We, for instance, who have meat and wine every day, how shall we mark a change?—If you are accustomed to [dine] early,[9] postpone it, if you are accustomed to [dine] late, have it earlier, answered he.

R. Shesheth used to place his scholars in a place exposed to the sun in summer, and in a shady place in winter, so that they

(1) Certainly not in a spirit of partiality, but because he had such a high opinion of scholars that he felt that they would not engage in a lawsuit unless they know right to be on their side (Maharsha). (2) Cf. Elbogen, op. cit., p. 108. (3) Lit., 'better'. (4) We prepared them in honour of the Sabbath. (5) An *istira peshiṭa* = a half *zuz*. (6) To make sure that some of it at least would be the best obtainable. 'Thirteen' is not meant literally, but merely denotes many; cf. *infra* n. b4. (7) Or, paid them. (8) Lit., 'by the pivot of the door'. (9) All in honour of the Sabbath. (10) Whilst attending to the cooking etc. (11) Lit., 'mix'. (12) A kind of fish, probably mullet. (13) Lit., 'carried'. (14) Whatever was necessary for the Sabbath. (15) E.g., place a seat for them. (16) The point of all these statements is that the Rabbis did not think it beneath their dignity to engage in menial labour in honour of the Sabbath.

(1) Lit., 'Chaldeans'. (2) It will eventually pass into his possession. (3) R. Tam translates: vessels. (4) This, of course is an exaggeration, and merely implies much money, 'thirteen' often being used figuratively in that sense, cf. *supra* n. a6 and Ḥul 95*b* (Rashi). (5) I.e., expends money in its honour. (6) The verb denotes to obtain through merit. (7) E.V. '*Thou shalt surely tithe*', Deut. XIV, 22. (8) A play on words. (9) Several towns bore this name. (10) *Ḳebu'oth* denotes that they were fastened thereto—probably by the chains. (11) Ps. XXIV, 1.
c (1) Ps. CXV, 16. (2) The emperor referred to is Hadrian, his contemporary, with whom he had much intercourse; cf. Gen. Rab. X, 3; Ḥul. 59*b*, 60*a*; Ber. 56*a*. (3) V. *supra* 48*a*, n. b7. (4) Isa. LVIII, 13. (5) '*The holy of the Lord*'. (6) Ibid. With reference to the Sabbath. (7) One honours the Sabbath by dining at an earlier hour than usual. (8) To a later hour, as one eats then with a better appetite—this view would naturally commend itself to Samuel on medical grounds. (9) Rashi: with reference to the midday meal.

מסורת הש"ס

עין משפט נר מצוה

מב א טוש"ע חו"מ סי' טו סעיף א:

מג ב מיי' פ"ל מהלכות שבת הלכה ג סמג עשין ל טוש"ע או"ח סי' רסב סעיף ג:

מד ג מיי' שם הלכה ו סמג שם טור שו"ע או"ח סימן ר"נ סעיף א:

מה ד טוש"ע או"ח סי' תרי סעיף ד:

[וע"ע תוס' ב"ב קנג: ד"ה עיליתא]

מו ה מיי' פ"ל שם הל"ח וסמג שם טוש"ע או"ח סימן רפח סעיף ו:

עבידנא יומא טבא לרבנן · לתלמידים ראש ישיבה היה: תיתי לי · ישולם שכרי: דכי אתי צורבא מרבנן כו'. שחיבת תלמידי חכמים עלי: דלא מזיגנא רישא אבי סדיא. איני מניח ראשי על הכר: כמה דלא מהפיכנא ליה בזכותיה. עד שאראה אם יש בדבריו לזכותו: מתעטף · בבגדים נאים: בואי כלה. הכי קרי ליה לשביתת שבת מתוך חביבות: טחיי. רקיקין טחין פניהן בשומן אליה או בשמן: מי עדיפת לן מינה. כלום אתה חשוב לנו מן השבת לכבוד שבת הכנוס ולא היינו יודעים שתבא: מתליסר טבחי. לטעום בשבת מן המובחר: אסתירי. סלעים אסתירי פשיטי סלעים מדינ' והן א' מח' בסלע צורי והיינו חצי דינר: ומשלים להו אצינורא דדשא. לפני בואם להביא לו הבשר היה מזמן להן מעותיהן על פתחן ואומר להן אשור הייא התאשרו והתחזקו מהר באומנותיכם למהר ולחזור ולמכור ולהתעסק בצרכי שבת ולי נראה ומשלים להו אציטרא דדשא כשהיה מביא ראשונה היה נותנה לשמשין המכינים סעודתו על פתח ביתו ולא היה נכנס אלא ממהר לחזור ולהביא אחרת ואמר להן לשמשין אשור הייא התאשרו מהר להכין את זו בעוד שאלך להביא את זו: אתכתקא דשינא. פסטו"ל של שן שחשוב היה ועשיר: ומושיף נורא. נופח מאש נורא לכבוד השבת ורבינו לוי גרס אתכתקא דשאגא תדהר: לביש גונדא · כלי שחור להודיע שהיום אינו כדי להתנהג בחשיבות מלהתעסק בתבשילי שבת ולא יטנף בגדיו בבישול קדירות: דתנא דבי רבי ישמעאל כו'. דבישול קדירה מטנף בגדים: מחריך רישא. אם היה שם ראש בהמה לחרוך מחרכו הוא בעצמו: פריס. לשון פרומים מחתך: מלחת לצותי. מליח האור בעצים דקים: מכתף ועייל מכתף ונפיק. בע"ש יוצא ונכנס להביא תמיד משואות כלי תשמיש ובגדי חופש ומגדים כאדם שמקבל את רבו בביתו ומראה לו[דברים יד] שהוא חשוב עליו וחרד לכבודו לטרוח ולהרבות בשבילו: מוקר שבי. מכבד שבתות: אמרי ליה כלדאי. לההוא נכרי: כלדאי. חוזים בכוכבים: אכיל להו · סופך ליפול בידו: אותבה בסייניה. עשה לו כובע של לבד ושבלו במשבצות של[תהלים כד] זהב וקבע בו מרגליות וקבע את זו[שם] עמהם: סייניה. כובע ורבינו הלוי[קטו] גרס בסדיניה בסודרו ולשון הגון לי והוא לשון ר' יצחק ב"ר יהודה: תריסר עיליתי דדינרי. עליות מלאות דינרי זהב °וגוזמא בעלמא הוא כלומר הון עתק מאד כך פירש[ישעיה נח] רבינו הלוי וכן בכל מקום כגון תליסר גמלי ספיקי טריפתא (חולין דף נה:) וכן תליסר טבחי דלעיל: במה הן זוכין. לעושר גדול כזה: לה' הארץ. דאין אנו רשאין ליהנות עד שנברך שמו בברכת הלחם: והארץ נתן לבני אדם. ע"י מתנתו נהנינו הטובה הזאת: מאי דכתיב ולקדוש ה' מכובד. מדכתיב וקראת לשבת עונג מכלל דלקדוש ה' לאו אשבת קאי: וכבדתו. אשבת מהדר דאי ביוה"כ הא כתיב ביה מכובד: להקדים. זמן סעודת שבת לזמן סעודת חול וזהו כבודו: לאחר. וזהו כבודו שהוא מתאוה לאכול: במאי נשנייה. במאי נשניוהו משאר ימים: אי רגיליתו לאקדומי. סעודתכם בבקר אחרוה: רב ששת סגי נהור היה ואינו רואה עת האכילה וכשהיה דורש בשבת מושיב התלמידים במקום שתגיע שם החמה לעת האוכל כדי שילטערו וימהרו לקום: דמטי טולא. שילטנהו: הייא. מהר:

[כתובות קה:]

ב"ק לג. ע"ש

ב"א מעילי ולמכסי

[נ"ל דכתיב וקראת לשבת עונג רבי אבא וכו' וכ"א בחולין קיח.]

לעיל קיד. [יומא כג:]

תורה אור

עבידנא יומא טבא לרבנן אמר רבא °תיתי לי דכי אתא צורבא מרבנן לקמאי לדינא לא מזיגנא (א)רישי אבי סדיא כמה דלא מהפיכנא בזכותי' אמר מר בר רב אשי פסילנא ליה לצורבא מרבנן לדינא מ"ט *דחביב עלי כגופאי ואין אדם רואה חובה לעצמו *ר' חנינא מיעטף וקאי אפניא דמעלי שבתא אמר בואו ונצא לקראת שבת המלכה רבי ינאי לביש מאניה *(ב)מעלי שבת ואמר בואי כלה בואי כלה רבה *בר רב הונא איקלע לבי רבה בר רב נחמן קריבו ליה תלת סאוי טחיי א"ל מי הוה ידעיתון דאתינא אמרו ליה מי עדיפת לן מינה *רבי אבא זבן בתליסר אסתירי פשיטי בישרא מתליסר טבחי ומשלים להו אצינורא דדשא ואמר להו °אשור *הייא אשור הייא °ר' אבהו הוה יתיב אתכתקא דשינא ומושיף נורא רב ענן לביש גונדא *דתנא דבי רבי ישמעאל בגדים שבישל בהן קדירה לרבו אל ימזוג בהן כוס לרבו *רב ספרא מחריך רישא רבא מלח שיבוטא רב הונא מדליק שרגי רב פפא גדיל פתילתא רב חסדא פרים סילקא רבה ורב יוסף מצלחי ציבי ר' זירא מצתת צתותי רב נחמן בר יצחק מכתף ועייל מכתף ונפיק אמר אילו מקלעין לי ר' אמי ור' אסי מי לא מכתיפנא קמייהו ואיכא דאמרי ר' אמי ורבי אסי מכתפי ועיילי מכתפי ונפקי אמרי אילו איקלע לן רבי יוחנן מי לא מכתפינן קמיה יוסף מוקיר שבי הוה ההוא נכרי בשבבותיה דהוה נפישי נכסיה טובא אמרי ליה כלדאי כולהו נכסי יוסף מוקר שבי אכיל להו אזל זבנינהו לכולהו ניכסי זבן בהו מרגניתא אותבה בסייניה בהדי דקא עבר מברא אפרחיה זיקא שדייה במיא בלעיה כוורא אסקוה אייתוה אפניא דמעלי שבתא אמרי מאן זבין כי השתא אמרי להו זילו אמטיוהו לגבי יוסף מוקר שבי דרגיל דזבין אמטיוה ניהליה זבניה קרעיה אשכח ביה מרגניתא זבניה בתליסר עיליתא דדינרי דדהבא פגע ביה ההוא סבא אמר מאן דיזיף שבתא פרעיה שבתא בעא מיניה רבי מר' ישמעאל ברבי יוסי עשירים שבא"י במה הן זוכין א"ל בשביל שמעשרין שנאמר °עשר תעשר *עשר בשביל שתתעשר[דברים יד] שבבבל במה הן זוכין א"ל בשביל שמכבדין את התורה ושבשאר ארצות במה הן זוכין א"ל בשביל שמכבדין את השבת דאמר רבי חייא בר אבא פעם אחת נתארחתי אצל בעל הבית בלודקיא והביאו לפניו שלחן של זהב משוי ששה עשר בני אדם וששה עשרה שלשלאות של כסף קבועות בו וקערות וכוסות וקיתוניות וצלוחיות קבועות בו ועליו כל מיני מאכל וכל מיני מגדים ובשמים *וכשמניחים אותו אומרים °לה' הארץ ומלואה וגו' *וכשמסלקין[תהלים כד] אותו. אומרים °השמים שמים לה' והארץ נתן לבני אדם אמרתי לו בני[שם קטו] במה זכית לכך אמר לי קצב הייתי ומכל בהמה שהיתה נאה אמרתי זו תהא לשבת אמרתי לו [אשריך שזכית] וברוך המקום שזיכך לכך א"ל קיסר לרבי יהושע בן חנניא מפני מה תבשיל של שבת ריחו נודף אמר לו תבלין אחד יש לנו ושבת שמו שאנו מטילין לתוכו וריחו נודף אמר לו תן לנו הימנו אמר לו כל המשמר את השבת מועיל לו ושאינו משמר את השבת אינו מועיל לו א"ל ריש גלותא לרב המנונא מאי דכתיב °ולקדוש ה'[ישעיה נח] מכובד א"ל °זה יוה"כ שאין בו לא אכילה ולא שתיה אמרה תורה כבדהו בכסות נקיה °וכבדתו רב אמר להקדים ושמואל אמר לאחר אמרו ליה בני רב פפא בר אבא לרב פפא כגון אנן דשכיח לן בישרא וחמרא כל יומא במאי נישנייה אמר להו אי רגיליתו לאקדומי אחרוה אי רגיליתו לאחרוה אקדמוה רב ששת בקיטא מותיב להו לרבנן היכא דמטיא שימשא בסיתוא מותיב להו לרבנן היכא דמטיא טולא כי היכי דליקומו הייא ר' זירא מהדר

בתליסר עיליתא דדינרי. אומר ר"ת דעיליתא שם כלי הוא כדאמרינן בריש כילד מעברין (עירובין דף נג:) עלת נקפת בכדה*: רב אמר להקדים ושמואל אמר לאחר. ולא פליגי אלא רב איירי בדרכו לאחר ושמואל איירי בדרכו להקדים כדאמרינן בסמוך: ומלא

[חולין קיח.]

סי' מהר וכ"כ בסוף עמוד זה

קדושין מא.

ע"י תוס' שם

תענית ט.

[עי' תוספות ברכות לה: ד"ה כאן]

רבינו חננאל

ורבנן הני דעבדי צרכי שבת בנפשייהו. כגון ר' אבהו דהוה [יתיב] (הציבי) אתכתקא דשינא ומשיף נורא. ורב חנן דשגר תנורא ורב הונא גדיל פתילתא. ורב חסדא מדליק שרגי ורב פפא פרים סילקי. רבה ורב יוסף צלחי ציבי כולהו כדמפרש בגמרא בריש האיש מקדש. שקיום המצוה באדם עצמו טפי עדיף יתר מבשלוחו: וכבדתו שמשנה זמן סעודתו בהקדמה או באיחור. ויחיד המתפלל בעצמו אומר ויכולו:

הגהות הב"ח

(א) גמ' לא מזיגנא רישא אבי: (ב) שם לביש מאניה במעלי:

גליון הש"ס

גמ' אשור הייא. גיטין דף לד ע"א: רש"י ד"ה תליסר עיליתא דדינרי וכו' וגוזמא בעלמא. עי' ברכות דף כ ע"א בתוס' ד"ה תליסר מתיבתא:

מהדר

מהדר אזוזי זוזי דרבנן א"ל במטותא מינייכו לא תחללוניה אמר *רבא ואיתימא ר' יהושע בן לוי *אפי' יחיד המתפלל בע"ש צריך לומר ויכולו דאמר רב המנונא כל המתפלל בע"ש ואומר ויכולו מעלה עליו הכתוב כאילו נעשה שותף להקב"ה במעשה בראשית שנאמר ויכולו אל תקרי ויכולו(א) אלא ויכלו אמר רבי אלעזר מניין שהדיבור כמעשה שנאמר °בדבר ה' שמים נעשו אמר רב חסדא אמר מר עוקבא כל המתפלל בע"ש ואומר ויכולו שני מלאכי השרת המלוין לו לאדם מניחין ידיהן על ראשו ואומרים לו °וסר עונך וחטאתך תכופר תניא ר' יוסי בר יהודה אומר שני מלאכי השרת מלוין לו לאדם בע"ש מבית הכנסת לביתו אחד טוב ואחד רע ׳וכשבא לביתו ומצא נר דלוק ושלחן ערוך ומטתו מוצעת מלאך טוב אומר יהי רצון שתהא לשבת אחרת כך ומלאך רע עונה אמן בעל כרחו ואם לאו מלאך רע אומר יהי רצון שתהא לשבת אחרת כך ומלאך טוב עונה אמן בעל כרחו אמר ר' אלעזר ׳לעולם יסדר אדם שלחנו בע"ש אע"פ שאינו צריך אלא לכזית ואמר ר' חנינא ׳לעולם יסדר אדם שלחנו במוצאי שבת אע"פ שאינו צריך אלא לכזית חמין במוצאי שבת מלוגמא פת חמה במוצאי שבת מלוגמא ר' אבהו הוה עבדין ליה באפוקי שבתא עיגלא תילתא הוה אכיל מיניה כולייתא כי גדל אבימי בריה א"ל למה לך לאפסודי כולי האי נשבוק כולייתא ממעלי שבתא שבקוהו ואתא אריא אכליה אריב"ל ׳כל העונה אמן יהא שמיה רבא מברך בכל כחו קורעין לו גזר דינו שנאמר °בפרוע פרעות בישראל בהתנדב עם ברכו ה' מ"ט בפרוע פרעות משום דברכו ה' רבי חייא בר אבא א"ר יוחנן אפילו יש בו שמץ של עבודה זרה מוחלין לו כתיב הכא בפרוע פרעות וכתיב התם °כי פרוע הוא(ב) אמר ריש לקיש כל העונה אמן בכל כחו פותחין לו שערי ג"ע שנאמר °פתחו שערים ויבא גוי צדיק שומר אמונים *אל תיקרי שומר אמונים אלא שאומרים אמן *מאי אמן א"ר חנינא אל מלך נאמן א"ר יהודה בריה דרב שמואל משמיה דרב אין הדליקה מצויה אלא במקום שיש חילול שבת שנאמר °ואם לא תשמעו אלי לקדש את יום השבת ולבלתי שאת משא וגו' והצתי אש בשעריה ואכלה ארמנות ירושלים ולא תכבה מאי ולא תכבה אמר רב נחמן בר יצחק בשעה שאין בני אדם מצויין לכבותה אמר אביי לא חרבה ירושלים אלא בשביל שחללו בה את השבת שנאמר °ומשבתותי העלימו עיניהם ואחל בתוכם אמר ר' אבהו לא חרבה ירושלים אלא בשביל שביטלו ק"ש שחרית וערבית שנאמר °הוי משכימי בבקר שכר ירדפו וגו' וכתיב °והיה כנור ונבל תוף וחליל ויין משתיהם ואת פועל ה' לא יביטו וכתיב °לכן גלה עמי מבלי דעת אמר רב המנונא לא חרבה ירושלים אלא בשביל שביטלו בה תינוקות של בית רבן שנאמר °שפוך על עולל בחוץ וגו' מה טעם שפוך משום דעולל בחוץ אמר עולא לא חרבה ירושלים אלא מפני שלא היה להם בושת פנים זה מזה שנאמר °הובישו כי תועבה עשו גם בוש לא יבושו וגו' אמר ר' יצחק לא חרבה ירושלים אלא בשביל שהושוו קטן וגדול שנאמר °והיה כעם ככהן וכתיב בתריה *הבוק תבוק הארץ אמר רב עמרם בריה דר"ש בר אבא א"ר שמעון בר אבא א"ר חנינא לא חרבה ירושלים אלא בשביל שלא הוכיחו זה את זה שנאמר °היו שריה כאילים לא מצאו מרעה מה איל זה ראשו של זה בצד זנבו של זה אף ישראל שבאותו הדור כבשו פניהם בקרקע ולא הוכיחו זה את זה א"ר יהודה לא חרבה ירושלים אלא בשביל שביזו בה ת"ח °שנאמר °ויהיו מלעיבים במלאכי האלהים ובוזים דבריו ומתעתעים בנביאיו עד עלות חמת ה' בעמו עד [ל] אין מרפא מאי עד לאין מרפא אמר רב יהודה אמר רב ׳כל המבזה ת"ח אין לו רפואה למכתו אמר רב יהודה אמר רב מאי דכתיב °אל תגעו במשיחי ובנביאי אל תרעו אל תגעו במשיחי אלו תינוקות של בית רבן ובנביאי אל תרעו אלו ת"ח אמר ריש לקיש משום רבי יהודה נשיאה אין העולם מתקיים אלא בשביל הבל תינוקות של בית רבן א"ל רב פפא לאביי דידי ודידך מאי א"ל אינו דומה הבל שיש בו חטא להבל שאין בו חטא ואמר ריש לקיש משום ר"י נשיאה ׳אין מבטלין תינוקות של בית רבן אפי' לבנין בית המקדש ואמר ר"ל לר"י נשיאה כך מקובלני °מאבותי ואמרי לה מאבותיך ׳כל עיר שאין בה תינוקות של בית רבן מחריבין אותה רבינא אמר מחרימין אותה *ואמר רבא לא חרבה ירושלים אלא בשביל שפסקו ממנה אנשי אמנה שנאמר °שוטטו בחוצות ירושלים וראו נא [ודעו ובקשו ברחובותיה אם תמצאו איש] (אם יש איש) עושה משפט מבקש אמונה ואסלח לה איני והאמר רב קטינא *אפי' בשעת כשלונה של ירושלים לא פסקו ממנה אנשי אמנה שנאמר °כי יתפש איש באחיו בית אביו (לאמר) שמלה לכה קצין תהיה לנו דברים שבני אדם מתכסין בהן כשמלה ישנן בידיך *והמכשלה הזאת תחת ידך

דברים

רש"י

מהדר אזוזי זוזי דרבנן. כשהיה רואה אותן זוגות זוגות ומדברין בתורה מחזר אחריהם ואומר להם במטותא מנכון לכו והתעסקו בעונג שבת ולא תחללוניה לבטל תענוגים: ויכלו. הקב"ה וזה שמספר בשבחו של מקום ובשבח של שבת: יסדר אדם שלחנו בע"ש. ללילי שבת: במוצ"ש. נמי כבוד שבת ללוות ביציאתו דרך כבוד כאדם המלוה את המלך בצאתו מן העיר: חמין. לשתות ולרחוץ: מלוגמא. רפואה: אכליה אריא. לעגל הראוי לשחוט: בכל כחו. בכל כוונתו: בפרוע פרעות. ביטול פורעניות כגון פרוע דמתרגמין בטל: בהתנדב עם ברכו. כשמתנדבין ישראל לברך את בוראן: כי פרוע. כי פרעו אהרן ע"ז והכי קאמר בהבטל פריעות ע"ז שתפתקע ותשתכח שלא יזכר עונש משום התנדב עם הוא: אל מלך נאמן. כך מעיד על בוראו שהוא אל מלך נאמן: שאין בני אדם מצויין לכבותה. בשבת: בבקר. בזמן ק"ש וכן מאחרי בנשף: והיה כנור ונבל. בסיפיה דקרא ואת פועל ה' לא יביטו לא שמו לב ליחד שמו על בריותיו: שפוך על עולל. רישא דקרא ואת חמת ה' נלאיתי הכיל שפוך וגו' שפוך החמה בנקמה בשביל שעולל לחוץ ובטלין מבית רבן: הובישו כי תועבה עשו וגו'. סיפיה דקרא גם בוש לא יבושו וגם הכלם לא כו': במשיחי אלו תינוקות של בית רבן. שדרך תינוקות למושחן בשמן*: ובנביאי אלו תלמידי חכמים. שנאמר ונביא לבב חכמה (תהלים צ): מחריבין. איכא שיור: מחרימין. ליכא שיור: מתכסין בהן כשמלה. כששואלין אותן טעמי תורה הללו עושין עצמן כמעלימין את דבריהם מפני שאינן יודעים להשיב: ישנן בידך. אתה בקי לפיכך קצין תהיה לנו ותלמדנו חכמה:

דברים

תורה אור

תוספות

ומצא נר דלוק ושולחן ערוך. וא"ת דאמר בריש ערבי פסחים (דף ק:) ושוין שאין מביאין את השולחן אא"כ קידש וי"ל דערוך הוא במקום אחר אלא שאין מביאין אותו עד אחר הקידוש כי היכי דתיתי סעודתא ביקרא דשבת כדאיתא בשאלתות דרב אחאי *ודוקא בימיהם שהיו להם שלחנות קטנים לפני כל אחד ואחד אבל שלנו גדולים הם וקשה לטלטלם*(ג): כל העונה אמן יהא שמיה רבא בכל כחו. פי' בכל כוונתו וכן פירש רש"י ור"י אומר דיש בפסיקתא במעשה דר' ישמעאל בן אלישע דקאמר התם כשישראל נכנסים לבתי כנסיות ואומרים יהא שמיה רבא מברך בקול רם מבטלים גזירות קשות:

א"ר חנינא אל מלך נאמן. צריך להזהר בו בשעה שאומר אמן:

אידי

עין משפט נר מצוה

מז א מיי' פכ"ט מהל' שבת הלכה ז סמג עשין ל טוש"ע או"ח סי' רסח סעיף א:

מח ב מיי' פ"ל שם הל' ה סמג שם טור שו"ע או"ח סימן רסב סעיף א:

מט ג מיי' שם הלכה ה וסמג שם:

נ ד מיי' וסמג שם טור שו"ע או"ח סימן ש:

נא ה מיי' פ"ט מהלכות תפלה הלכה א טוש"ע או"ח סימן נו סעיף א [וברב אלפס ברכות פא דף ע"ו: וברא"ש שם סימן יט]:

[פרשת יתרו סימן נד]

[וע"ע תוס' פסחים ק: ד"ה שאין]

נב ו מיי' פ"ו מהלכות ת"ת הלכה יא טור שו"ע יו"ד סימן רמג סעיף ז:

נג ז מיי' פ"ב שם הל"ב טוש"ע יו"ד סי' רמה סעיף יג [וברב אלפס פ"ב דב"ב דף קסג: וברא"ש פ"ג דמו"ק סי' ס"א]:

נד ח מיי' שם הלכה א טוש"ע שם סעיף ז [וברב אלפס שם]:

הגהות הב"ח

(א) גמ' אל תיקרי ויכלו אלא ויכלו: (ב) שם כי פרוע הוא כי פרעו אהרן אמר ריש לקיש: (ג) תוס' ד"ה ומצא וכו' וקשה לטלטלם. נ"ב פי' אחר קידוש שלא להפסיק כל כך בין קידוש לסעודה אנו רגילין לפרוס מפה ולקדש:

שמות לב

סנהדרין קי:

ישעיה ה

חגיגה יד.

[חגיגה שם. גיטין מג.]

גליון הש"ס

גמ' שנא' ויהיו מלעיבים במלאכי האלהים. עיין שאלתות נדרים דף כ ע"ב מאן מוש"ש רבנן: שם כך מקובלני מאבותי. עיין ב"מ דף פד ע"א ד"ה אי סדרת:

מסורת הש"ס

[בהרא"ש ובטור סי' רסח איתא אמר רב וכו' ואמר רב המנונא כל המתפלל וכו' וכ"ה בשאלתות סי' א]

[כדאי' לעיל ?]

שופטים ה

ישעיה כו

[סנהדרין קיט:]

ירמיה יז

יחזקאל כב

ישעיה ה

שם

שם

ירמיה ו

שם

[פי' תתרוקן]

ישעיה כד

איכה א

דה"ב לו

דה"א טז

ירמיה ה

ישעיה ג

[חגיגה יד.]

should arise quickly.[10] R. Zera [119*b*] used to seek out pairs of scholars[11] and say to them, 'I beg of you, do not profane it.'[12]

Raba—others state, R. Joshua b. Levi—said: Even if an individual prays on the eve of the Sabbath, he must recite, *And* [*the heaven and the earth*] *were finished* [*etc.*];[1] for R. Hamnuna said: He who prays on the eve of the Sabbath and recites '*and* [*the heaven and the earth*] *were finished,*' the Writ treats of him as though he had become a partner with the Holy One, blessed be He, in the Creation, for it is said, *Wa-yekullu* [*and they were finished*]; read not *wa-yekullu* but *wa-yekallu* [and they finished].[2] R. Eleazar said: How do we know that speech is like action? Because it is said, *By the word of the Lord were the heavens made.*[3] R. Ḥisda said in Mar 'Uḳba's name: He who prays on the eve of the Sabbath and recites '*and* [*the heaven and the earth*] *were finished,* the two ministering angels who accompany man place their hands on his head and say to him, *and thine iniquity is taken away, and thy sin purged.*[4]

It was taught, R. Jose son of R. Judah said: Two ministering angels accompany man on the eve of the Sabbath from the synagogue to his home, one a good [angel] and one an evil [one]. And when he arrives home and finds the lamp burning, the table laid and the couch [bed] covered with a spread, the good angel exclaims, 'May it be even thus on another Sabbath [too],' and the evil angel unwillingly responds 'amen'. But if not,[5] the evil angel exclaims, 'May it be even thus on another Sabbath [too],' and the good angel unwillingly responds, 'amen'.

R. Eleazar said: One should always set his table on the eve of the Sabbath, even if he needs only the size of an olive. While R. Ḥanina said: One should always set his table on the termination of the Sabbath, even if he merely requires as much as an olive.[6] Hot water after the termination of the Sabbath is soothing; fresh [warm] bread after the termination of the Sabbath is soothing.[7]

A three-year old[8] calf used to be prepared for R. Abbahu on the termination of the Sabbath, of which he ate a kidney. When his son Abimi grew up he said to him, Why should you waste so much? let us leave over a kidney from Sabbath eve. So he left it over, and a lion came and devoured it.[1]

R. Joshua b. Levi said: He who responds, 'Amen, May His great Name be blessed,' with all his might, his decreed sentence[2] is torn up, as it is said, *When retribution was annulled*[3] *in Israel, For that the people offered themselves willingly, Bless ye the Lord:*[4] why '*when retribution was annulled*'? Because they blessed the Lord. R. Ḥiyya b. Abba said in R. Joḥanan's name: Even if he has a taint of idolatry, he is forgiven: it is written here, '*when retribution was annulled* [bifroa' pera'oth]'; whilst elsewhere it is written, *And Moses saw that the people were broken loose* [parua']; *for Aaron had let them loose.*[5]

Resh Laḳish said: He who responds 'Amen' with all his might, has the gates of Paradise opened for him, as it is written, *Open ye the gates, that the righteous nation which keepeth truth* [shomer emunim] *may enter in:*[6] read not '*shomer emunim*' but '*she'omrim amen*' [that say, amen]. What does 'amen' mean?—Said R. Ḥanina: God, faithful King.[7]

Rab Judah son of R. Samuel said in Rab's name: An [outbreak of] fire occurs only in a place where there is desecration of the Sabbath, for it is said, *But if ye will not hearken unto me to hallow the Sabbath day and not to bear a burden ... then will I kindle a fire in the gates thereof, and it shall devour the palaces of Jerusalem, and it shall not be quenched.*[8] What does '*and it shall not be quenched*' mean?—Said R. Naḥman b. Isaac: At the time when no people are available to quench it.

(10) This was on the Sabbath. He himself was blind, and he did not wish them to stay too long in the Beth Hamidrash. (11) Engaged in *halachic* discussions. (12) The Sabbath, by neglecting its delights and good cheer.

a (1) Gen. II, 1. (2) 'They' referring to God and to him who praises God for the Creation. (3) Ps. XXXIII, 6. (4) Isa. VI, 7. (5) If everything is in disorder and gloomy. (6) That too honours the Sabbath, just as a royal visitor is not allowed to depart without a retinue accompanying him. (7) That would not be difficult to obtain, as bread is baked very quickly in the East. (8) Or, a third grown; or, third born.

b (1) The calf that would have been killed. (2) If Heaven has decreed evil for him. (3) *Sic.* E.V.: '*For that the leaders took the lead*'. (4) Judg. V, 2. (5) Ex. XXXII, 25; the reference is to the idolatrous worship of the Golden Calf. (6) Isa. XXVI, 2. (7) Interpreting it as an abbreviation: *el melek ne'eman.* (8) Jer. XVII, 27.

◁ *For the continuation of the English translation of this page see overleaf.*

מהדר אזוזי זוזי דרבנן א"ל במטותא מינייכו לא תחללוניה אמר *רבא ואיתימא ר' יהושע בן לוי "אפי' יחיד המתפלל בע"ש צריך לומר ויכולו דאמר רב המנונא כל המתפלל בע"ש ואומר ויכולו מעלה עליו הכתוב כאילו נעשה שותף להקב"ה במעשה בראשית שנאמר ויכולו אל תקרי ויכולו(א) אלא ויכלו אמר רבי אלעזר מניין שהדיבור כמעשה שנאמר °בדבר ה' שמים נעשו אמר רב חסדא אמר מר עוקבא כל המתפלל בע"ש ואומר ויכולו שני מלאכי השרת המלוין לו לאדם מניחין ידיהן על ראשו ואומרים לו °וסר עונך וחטאתך תכופר תניא ר' יוסי בר יהודה אומר שני מלאכי השרת מלוין לו לאדם בע"ש מבית הכנסת לביתו אחד טוב ואחד רע "וכשבא לביתו ומצא נר דלוק ושלחן ערוך ומטתו מוצעת מלאך טוב אומר יהי רצון שתהא לשבת אחרת כך ומלאך רע עונה אמן בעל כרחו ואם לאו מלאך רע אומר יהי רצון שתהא לשבת אחרת כך ומלאך טוב עונה אמן בעל כרחו אמר ר' אלעזר "לעולם יסדר אדם שלחנו בע"ש אע"פ שאינו צריך אלא לכזית ואמר ר' חנינא "לעולם יסדר אדם שלחנו במוצאי שבת אע"פ שאינו צריך אלא לכזית חמין במוצאי שבת מלוגמא פת חמה במוצאי שבת מלוגמא ר' אבהו הוה עבדין ליה באפוקי שבתא עיגלא תילתא הוה אכיל מיניה כולייתא כי גדל אבימי בריה א"ל למה לך לאפסודי כולי האי נשבוק כולייתא ממעלי שבתא שבקוהו ואתא אריא אכליה אריב"ל "כל העונה אמן יהא שמיה רבא מברך בכל כחו קורעין לו גזר דינו שנאמר °בפרוע פרעות בישראל בהתנדב עם ברכו ה' מ"ט בפרוע פרעות משום דברכו ה' רבי חייא בר אבא א"ר יוחנן אפילו יש בו שמץ של עבודה זרה מוחלין לו כתיב הכא בפרוע פרעות וכתיב התם °כי פרוע הוא(ב) אמר ריש לקיש כל העונה אמן בכל כחו פותחין לו שערי ג"ע שנאמר °פתחו שערים ויבא גוי צדיק שומר אמונים *אל תיקרי שומר אמונים אלא שאומרים אמן *מאי אמן א"ר חנינא אל מלך נאמן א"ר יהודה בריה דרב שמואל משמיה דרב אין הדליקה מצויה אלא במקום שיש חילול שבת שנאמר °ואם לא תשמעו אלי לקדש את יום השבת ולבלתי שאת משא וגו' והצתי אש בשעריה ואכלה ארמנות ירושלים ולא תכבה מאי ולא תכבה אמר רב נחמן בר יצחק בשעה שאין בני אדם מצויין לכבותה אמר אביי לא חרבה ירושלים אלא בשביל שחללו בה את השבת שנאמר °ומשבתותי העלימו עיניהם ואחל בתוכם אמר ר' אבהו לא חרבה ירושלים אלא בשביל שביטלו ק"ש שחרית וערבית שנאמר °הוי משכימי בבקר שכר ירדפו וגו' וכתיב °והיה כנור ונבל תוף וחליל ויין משתיהם ואת פועל ה' לא יביטו וכתיב °לכן גלה עמי מבלי דעת אמר רב המנונא לא חרבה ירושלים אלא בשביל שביטלו בה תינוקות של בית רבן שנאמר °שפוך על עולל בחוץ וגו' מה טעם שפוך משום דעולל בחוץ אמר עולא לא חרבה ירושלים אלא מפני שלא היה להם בושת פנים זה מזה שנאמר °הובישו כי תועבה עשו גם בוש לא יבושו וגו' אמר ר' יצחק לא חרבה ירושלים אלא בשביל שהושוו קטן וגדול שנאמר °והיה כעם ככהן וכתיב בתריה *הבוק תבוק הארץ אמר רב עמרם בריה דר"ש בר אבא א"ר שמעון בר אבא א"ר חנינא לא חרבה ירושלים אלא בשביל שלא הוכיחו זה את זה שנאמר °היו שריה כאילים לא מצאו מרעה מה איל זה ראשו של זה בצד זנבו של זה אף ישראל שבאותו הדור כבשו פניהם בקרקע ולא הוכיחו זה את זה א"ר יהודה לא חרבה ירושלים אלא בשביל שביזו בה ת"ח °שנאמר °ויהיו מלעיבים במלאכי האלהים ובוזים דבריו ומתעתעים בנביאיו עד עלות חמת ה' בעמו עד [ל] אין מרפא מאי עד לאין מרפא אמר רב יהודה אמר רב "כל המבזה ת"ח אין לו רפואה למכתו אמר רב יהודה אמר רב מאי דכתיב °אל תגעו במשיחי ובנביאי אל תרעו אל תגעו במשיחי אלו תינוקות של בית רבן ובנביאי אל תרעו אלו ת"ח אמר ריש לקיש משום רבי יהודה נשיאה אין העולם מתקיים אלא בשביל הבל תינוקות של בית רבן א"ל רב פפא לאביי דידי ודידך מאי א"ל אינו דומה הבל שיש בו חטא להבל שאין בו חטא ואמר ריש לקיש משום ר"י נשיאה "אין מבטלין תינוקות של בית רבן אפי' לבנין בית המקדש ואמר ר"ל לר"י נשיאה כך מקובלני °מאבותי ואמרי לה מאבותיך "כל עיר שאין בה תינוקות של בית רבן מחריבין אותה רבינא אמר מחרימין אותה *ואמר רבא לא חרבה ירושלים אלא בשביל שפסקו ממנה אנשי אמנה שנאמר °שוטטו בחוצות ירושלים וראו נא [ודעו ובקשו ברחובותיה אם תמצאו איש] (אם יש איש) עושה משפט מבקש אמונה ואסלח לה איני והאמר רב קטינא *אפי' בשעת כשלונה של ירושלים לא פסקו ממנה אנשי אמנה שנאמר °כי יתפש איש באחיו בית אביו (לאמר) שמלה לכה קצין תהיה לנו דברים שבני אדם מתכסין בהן כשמלה ישנן בידיך *והמכשלה הזאת תחת ידך

דברים

רש"י

מהדר אזוזי זוזי דרבנן. כשהיה רואה אותן זוגות זוגות ומדברין בתורה מחזר אחריהם ואומר להם במטותא מכון לכו והתעסקו בעונג שבת ולא תחללוניה לבטל תענוגים: ויכלו. הקב"ה וזה שמספר בשבחו של מקום ובשבח של שבת: יסדר אדם שלחנו בע"ש. בלילי שבת: במוצ"ש. נמי כבוד שבת ללוות ביציאתו דרך כבוד כאדם המלוה את המלך בצאתו מן העיר: חמין. לשתות ולרחוץ: מלוגמא. רפואה: אכליה אריא. לעגל הראוי לשחוט: בכל כחו. בכל כוונתו: בפרוע פרעות. ביטול פורעניות כגון פרוע דמתרגמין בטל: בהתנדב עם ברכו. כשמתנדבין ישראל לברך את בוראן: כי פרוע. כי פרעו אהרן ע"ז והכי קאמר בהבטל פריעות ע"ז שתפקע ותשתכח שלא יזכר עונש משום התנדב עם הוא: אל מלך נאמן. כך מעיד על בוראו שהוא אל מלך נאמן: שאין בני אדם מצויין לכבותה. בשבת: בבקר. בזמן ק"ש וכן מאחרי בנשף: והיה כנור ונבל. בסיפיה דקרא ואת פועל ה' לא יביטו לא שמו לב ליחד שמו על בריותיו: שפוך על עולל. רישא דקרא ואת חמת ה' נלאיתי הכיל שפוך וגו' שפוך החמה בנקמה בשביל שעולל לחוץ ובטלין מבית רבן: הובישו כי תועבה עשו וגו'. סיפיה דקרא גם בוש לא יבושו וגם הכלם לא כו': במשיחי אלו תינוקות של בית רבן. שדרך תינוקות למושחן בשמן*: ובנביאי אלו תלמידי חכמים. שנאמר ונביא לבב חכמה (תהלים צ): מחריבין. היכא שיור: מחרימין. ליכא שיור: מתכסין בהן כשמלה. כששואלין אותן טעמי תורה הללו עושין עצמן כמעלימין את דבריהם מפני שאין יודעים להשיב: ישנן בידך. אתה בקי לפיכך קצין תהיה לנו ותלמדנו חכמה:

תוספות

ומצא נר דלוק ושולחן ערוך. וא"ת דאמר בריש ערבי פסחים (דף ק:) ושוין שאין מביאין את השולחן אא"כ קידש וי"ל דערוך הוא במקום אחר אלא שאין מביאין אותו עד אחר הקידוש כי היכי דתיתי סעודתא ביקרא דשבת כדאיתא בשאלתות דרב אחאי *ודוקא בימיהם שהיו להם שלחנות קטנים לפני כל אחד ואחד אבל שלנו גדולים הם וקשה לטלטלם*(ג): כל העונה אמן יהא שמיה רבא בכל כחו. פי' בכל כוונתו וכן פירש רש"י ור"י אומר דיש בפסיקתא במעשה דר' ישמעאל בן אלישע דקאמר התם כשישראל נכנסים לבתי כנסיות ואומרים יהא שמיה רבא מברך בקול רם מבטלים גזירות קשות:

א"ר חנינא אל מלך נאמן. צריך להרהר בו בשעה שאומר אמן: אידי

עין משפט נר מצוה

מז א מיי' פכ"ט מהל' שבת הלכה ז סמג עשין ל טוש"ע או"ח סי' רסח סעיף א:

מח ב מיי' פ"ל שם הל' ה סמג שם טור שו"ע או"ח סימן רסב סעיף א:

מט ג מיי' שם הלכה ה וסמג שם:

נ ד מיי' וסמג שם טור שו"ע או"ח סימן ש:

נא ה מיי' פ"ט מהלכות תפלה הלכה א טוש"ע או"ח סימן נו סעיף א [וכרב אלפס ברכות פג דף ע"ו: וברא"ש שם סימן יט]:

[פרשת יתרו סימן נד]

[וע"ע תוס' פסחים ק: ד"ה שאין]

נב ו מיי' פ"ו מהלכות ת"ת הלכה יא טור שו"ע יו"ד סימן רמג סעיף ז:

נג ז מיי' פ"ב שם הל"ב טוש"ע יו"ד סי' רמה סעיף יג [וכרב אלפס פ"ב דב"ב דף קסג: וברא"ש פ"ג דמו"ק סי' ס"א]:

נד ח מיי' שם הלכה א טוש"ע שם סעיף ז [וכרב אלפס שם]:

הגהות הב"ח

(א) גמ' אל תיקרי ויכולו אלא ויכלו: (ב) שם כי פרוע הוא כי פרעו אהרן אמר ריש לקיש: (ג) תוס' ד"ה ומצא וכו' וקשה לטלטלם. נ"ב פי' אחר קידוש שלא להפסיק כל כך בין קידוש לסעודה אנו רגילין לפרוס מפה ולקדש:

שמות לב

סנהדרין קי:

ישעיה ה

ישעיה כד

גליון הש"ס

גמ' שנא' ויהיו מלעיבים במלאכי האלהים. ע"ד שאחז"ל נדרים דף כ ע"ב מאן מה"ש רבנן: שם כך מקובלני מאבותי. עיין ב"מ דף פד ע"א ד"ה אי סדרת:

חגיגה יד.

[חגיגה שם. גיטין מג.]

מסורת הש"ס

[בהרא"ש וטור סי' רסח איתא אמר רב וכו' ואמר רב המנונא כל המתפלל וכו' וכ"א בשאלתות ברא"שית סי' א]

[כדאי' לעיל ..]

תהלים לג

ישעיה ו

תוספתא

ישעיה כו

[סנהדרין קי.]

ירמיה יז

יחזקאל כב

שם

שם

ירמיה ו

שם

[פי' תתרוקן]

איכה א

דה"ב לו

דה"א טז

ירמיה ה

ישעיה ג

[חגיגה יד.]

Continuation of translation from previous page as indicated by ◁

Abaye said: Jerusalem was destroyed only because the Sabbath was desecrated therein, as it is said, *and they have hid their eyes from My sabbaths, therefore I am profaned among them.*[9]

R. Abbahu said: Jerusalem was destroyed only because the c reading of the *shema'*[1] morning and evening was neglected [therein], for it is said, *Woe unto them that rise up early in the morning, that they may follow strong drink* [etc.]; and it is written, *And the harp and the lute, the tabret and the pipe, and wine, are in their feasts: but they regard not the work of the Lord;* and it is written, *Therefore my people are gone into captivity, for lack of knowledge.*[2]

R. Hamnuna said: Jerusalem was destroyed only because they neglected [the education of] school children; for it is said, *pour it out* [*sc.* God's wrath] *because of the children in the street:*[3] why pour it out? Because the child is in the street.[4]

'Ulla said: Jerusalem was destroyed only because they [its inhabitants] were not ashamed of each other, for it is written, *Were they ashamed when they committed abomination? nay, they were not at all ashamed* [. . . *therefore they shall fall*].[5]

R. Isaac said: Jerusalem was destroyed only because the small and the great were made equal, for it is said, *And it shall be, like people like priest;* which is followed by, *The earth shall be utterly emptied.*[6]

R. Amram son of R. Simeon b. Abba said in R. Simeon b. Abba's name in R. Ḥanina's name: Jerusalem was destroyed only because they did not rebuke each other: for it is said, *Her princes are become like harts that find no pasture:*[7] just as the hart, the head of one is at the side of the others's tail, so Israel of that generation hid their faces in the earth,[8] and did not rebuke each other.

Rab Judah said: Jerusalem was destroyed only because scholars were despised therein: for it is said, *but they mocked the messengers of God, and despised His words, and scoffed at His prophets, until the wrath of the Lord arose against His people, till there was no remedy.*[9] What does '*till there was no remedy*' intimate? Said Rab Judah in Rab's name: He who despises a scholar, has no remedy for his wounds.

Rab Judah said in Rab's name: What is meant by, *Touch not Mine anointed, and do My prophets no harm?*[10] '*Touch not Mine anointed*' d refers to school children;[1] '*and do My prophets no harm*', to disciples of the Sages. Resh Laḳish said in the name of R. Judah the Prince:[2] The world endures only for the sake of the breath of school children. Said R. Papa to Abaye, What about mine and yours?—Breath in which there is sin is not like breath in which there is no sin, replied he. Resh Laḳish also said in the name of R. Judah the Prince: School children may not be made to neglect [their studies] even for the building of the Temple. Resh Laḳish also said to R. Judah the Prince: I have this tradition from my fathers—others state, from your fathers: Every town in which there are no school children shall be destroyed. Rabina said: It shall be laid desolate.[3]

Raba said: Jerusalem was destroyed only because men of faith[4] ceased therein: for it is said, *Run ye to and fro in the streets of Jerusalem, and see now, and know, and seek in the broad places thereof, if ye can find a man, if there be any that doeth justly, that seeketh faithfulness; and I will pardon her.*[5] But that is not so? For R. Ḳaṭṭina said: Even at the time of Jerusalem's downfall men of faith did not cease therein, for it is said, *When a man shall take hold of his brother in the house of his father, saying, Thou hast clothing, be thou our ruler:*[6] [this means,] things wherewith men cover themselves as [with] a garment[7] are in thy hand. *And let this stumbling*[8] *be under thy*

(9) Ezek. XXII, 26. God's name is profaned when the holy city lies in ruins.
c (1) V. Glos. (2) Isa. V. 11-13. (3) Jer. VI, 11. (4) Instead of having schools provided for him. (5) Ibid. 15. (6) Isa. XXIV, 2f. 'People' is understood as a synonym for the humble masses; 'priest' symbolizes the great. (7) Lam. I, 6. (8) A metaphor for deliberately shutting their eyes to evil. (9) II Chron. XXXVI, 16. (10) I Chron. XVI, 22.

d (1) Whom it was customary to anoint with oil, cf. *supra* 10*b*. (2) *Nesi'ah*, Judah II. (3) This is more thorough-going than the former. (4) I.e., men completely truthful and trustworthy. (5) Jer. V, 1. (6) Or, judge, Isa. III, 6. (7) Rashi: when questioned on learning they hide themselves, pretending not to hear, because they cannot answer. (8) E.V. '*ruin*'.

hand:[9] [120*a*] things of which people are not sure[10] unless they [first] stumble over them[11] are in thy hands; [therefore] *be thou our judge. In that day* [yissa] *shall he lift up* [his voice] *saying, I will not be an healer:*[12] '*yissa*' denotes nought but swearing, and thus it is said, *Thou shalt not take* [tissa] *the name of the Lord* [*thy God in vain*].[13] *I will not be a binder up* [ḥobesh]: I will not be of those who shut themselves up [*ḥobeshe*] in the Beth Hamidrash. *And*
a *in my house is neither bread nor clothing:* I possess no *mikra*,[1] *mishnah*, or *gemara*.[2]—How does that follow: perhaps it is different there, for had he said to them, 'I have studied them' [the reasons of the Law], they would have retorted, 'Then tell [them] to us'? Then let him say that he had learnt and forgotten: why [state] '*I will not be a binder up*' at all?[3]—There is no difficulty: here it is in connection with learning;[4] there in connection with worldly affairs.

MISHNAH. ONE MAY SAVE A BASKET FULL OF LOAVES, EVEN IF IT CONTAINS [SUFFICIENT FOR] A HUNDRED MEALS, AND A ROUND CAKE OF PRESSED FIGS,[5] AND A BARREL OF WINE, AND HE [THE OWNER] MAY SAY TO OTHERS, 'COME AND SAVE FOR YOURSELVES'; AND IF THEY ARE WISE, THEY MAKE A RECKONING WITH HIM AFTER THE SABBATH.[6] WHITHER MAY THEY BE SAVED? INTO A COURTYARD PROVIDED WITH AN 'ERUB. BEN BATHYRA SAID: EVEN INTO A COURTYARD UNPROVIDED WITH AN 'ERUB. AND THITHER HE MAY CARRY OUT ALL THE UTENSILS [HE REQUIRES] FOR HIS USE;[7] AND HE PUTS ON ALL THAT HE CAN PUT ON AND WRAPS HIMSELF IN ALL WHEREWITH HE CAN WRAP HIMSELF;[8] R. JOSE SAID: [ONLY] EIGHTEEN GARMENTS.[9] THEN HE MAY PUT ON [GARMENTS] AFRESH[10] AND CARRY THEM OUT, AND SAY TO OTHERS, 'COME AND RESCUE WITH ME.'[11]

b *GEMARA*. But he [the Tanna] teaches in the first clause,[1] three meals, but no more?—Said R. Huna, There is no difficulty: here it means that he comes to save [the whole basket simultaneously]; there he comes to collect [food]: if he comes to save, he may save all;[2] if he comes to collect, he may collect only for three meals. R. Abba b. Zabda said in Rab's name: Both are where one comes to collect, yet there is no difficulty: here it is into the same courtyard;[3] there it is into another courtyard.

R. Huna the son of R. Joshua asked: What if one spreads out his garments, collects and places [therein], collects and places [therein]?[4] Is it like one who comes to save,[5] or like one who comes to collect?—[Come and hear]:[6] Since Raba said, R. Shizbi misled R. Ḥisda by teaching, 'Provided that he does not procure a vessel which holds more than three meals', it follows that it is like one who comes to save,[7] and it is permitted. R. Naḥman b. Isaac

(9) Ibid. (10) Lit., 'do not stand by them'. (11) They must first make mistakes before they arrive at certainty. (12) Or, a binder up. (13) Ex. XX, 7. This is an injunction against false swearing.

a (1) Scriptural knowledge. (2) Gemara, which was often substituted by the censors for Talmud, is generally understood to mean the discussion on the Mishnah; v. however Kaplan, *Redaction of the Talmud* pp. 195-7, where he maintains that *gemara* does not mean discussions but the final decisions arising out of the discussions.—Returning to our text, we see that there were 'faithful', i.e., truthful men in Jerusalem who confessed their ignorance and refused office on that account. (3) This proves that he was animated by a desire for truth, and thus contradicts Raba. (4) In this respect they were truthful. (5) Although it is very large. (6) They may demand payment for their labour. (7) On that day e.g., plates, glasses, etc. (8) And thus saves them from the fire. (9) Which are normally worn; v. *Gemara infra*. (10) Having taken off the first; this is the first Tanna's view, not R. Jose's. (11) In the same manner.

b (1) *Sc.* the Mishnah *supra* 117*b*. (2) In the basket, no matter how much it contains. (3) *Sc.* that of the house which is on fire. (4) More than three meals. (5) The whole simultaneously, since it is all to be carried out together. (6) V. BaḤ. (7) For Raba evidently holds that one may bring a vessel and collect more than for three meals—the reference is to the Baraitha *supra* 117*b*: 'If one's barrel burst on the top of his roof' etc.

◁ *For the continuation of the English translation of this page see overleaf.*

מסורת הש"ס

דברים שאין אדם עומד בהן · על בוריין לאומרן כהלכתן : אלא אם כן נכשל בהן . עד שאומרן ב' וג' פעמים בשיבוש דהיינו טעמי תורה המסותרין : לא אהיה חובש . איני רגיל להיות חובש חבוש בבהמ"ד. אהיה הורגלתי כמו שחוק לרעהו אהיה (איוב יב) אני הוה : וממאי . דמשום דיש בהן אמנה הוא דילמא על כרחיך לריכים שישיבו האמת : דאי אמר להו גמירנא. אותן טעמי תורה : אמרי ליה . שואלים אימא לן : ומשני הוה ליה למימר גמר ושכח מאי לא אהיה חובש . מודה הוא על האמת שלא יגע בתורה : בדברי תורה . היו נאמנין ואין מתהללים על שקר :

תורה אור

דברים שאין בני אדם עומדין עליהם אלא אם כן נכשלים בהן ישנן תחת ידיך קצין תהיה לנו (ישעיה ג) °ישא ביום ההוא לאמר לא אהיה חובש וגו' אין ישא אלא לשון שבועה וכן הוא אומר לא תשא את שם ה' לא אהיה חובש לא אהיה מחובשי עצמן בבית המדרש ובביתי אין לחם ואין שמלה שאין בידי לא *מקרא ולא משנה ולא גמרא וממאי דילמא שאני התם דאי אמר להו גמירנא אמרו ליה אימא לן הוה ליה למימר גמר ושכח מאי לא אהיה חובש כלל לא קשיא כאן בדברי תורה כאן במשא ומתן : **מתני'** *מצילין סל מלא ככרות אע"פ שיש בו מאה סעודות ועיגול של דבילה וחבית של יין ואומר לאחרים בואו והצילו לכם ואם היו פיקחין עושין עמו חשבון אחר השבת להיכן מצילין אותן ב לחצר המעורבת בן בתירה אומר אף לשאינה מעורבת *ג ולשם מוציא כל כלי תשמישו °ד ולובש כל מה שיכול ללבוש ועוטף כל מה שיכול לעטוף ר' יוסי אומר י"ח כלים ה וחוזר ולובש ומוציא ואומר לאחרים בואו והצילו עמי : **גמ'** והא תנא ליה *רישא ג' סעודות ותו לא אמר רב הונא לא קשיא כאן בבא להציל כאן בבא לקפל ו בא להציל מציל את כולן בא לקפל אינו מקפל אלא מזון ג' סעודות *ר' אבא בר זבדא אמר רב אידי ואידי בבא לקפל ולא קשיא כאן לאותה חצר כאן לחצר אחרת בעי רב הונא בריה דרב יהושע פירש טליתו וקיפל והניח מאי כבא להציל דמי או כבא לקפל דמי (א) מדאמר רבא אטעיה רב שיזבי לרב חסדא ודרש ובלבד שלא יביא כלי שהוא מחזיק יותר מג' סעודות ש"מ ז כבא להציל דמי ושפיר דמי א"ל רב נחמן בר יצחק לרבא מאי טעותא אמר ליה דקתני *ובלבד שלא יביא כלי אחר ויקלוט כלי אחר ויצרף כלי אחר הוא דלא אבל בההוא מנא כמה דבעי מציל : ועיגול של דבילה כו' : ח חשבון מאי עבידתיה מהפקירא קזכו אמר רב חסדא מדת חסידות שנו כאן אמר רבא חסידי אגרא דשבתא שקלי אלא אמר רבא הכא בירא שמים עסקינן (ב) °ולא ניחא ליה דליתהני מאחרים ובתגם נמי לא ניחא ליה דליטרח והכי קאמר ואם היו פיקחין דידעי דכה"ג לאו שכר שבת הוא עושין עמו חשבון לאחר השבת : ולהיכן מצילין כו' : מ"ש הכא דקתני לכם ומ"ש הכא דקתני עמי אמרי גבי מזונות קתני לכם משום דלא קא חזו (ג) אלא מזון ג' סעודות אבל גבי לבושים קתני עמי משום דקחזי ליה לכולי יומא: ת"ר לובש (ד) מוציא ופושט וחוזר ולובש ומוציא ופושט ואפילו כל היום כולו דברי רבי מאיר רבי יוסי אומר שמנה עשר כלים ואלו הם שמנה עשר כלים °מקטורן *אונקלי ופונדא קלבוס של פשתן וחלוק *ואפיליות ומעפורת °ושני ספרקין ושני מנעלים ושני אנפילאות וב' פרגד וחגור שבמתניו וכובע שבראשו וסודר שבצוארו : **מתני'** ר' שמעון בן ננס אומר פורסין °עור של גדי על גבי שידה תיבה ומגדל שאחז בהן את האור מפני שהוא מחרך י ועושין מחיצה בכל הכלים בין מלאין בין ריקנים בשביל שלא תעבור הדליקה רבי יוסי אוסר בכלי חרס חדשים מלאין מים לפי שאין יכולין לקבל את האור והן מתבקעין ומכבין את הדליקה : **גמ'** אמר רב יהודה אמר רב טלית שאחז בה האור מצד אחד נותנין עליה מים מצד אחר ואם כבתה כבתה מיתיבי *ל טלית שאחז בה האור מצד אחד פושטה ומתכסה בה ואם כבתה כבתה וכן ספר תורה שאחז בו האור פושטו וקורא בו ואם כבה כבה הוא

מתני' ועיגול של דבילה . שהוא גדול ויש בו סעודות הרבה : ואם היו פקחין . לישאל שכרן כפועלים : כל כלי תשמישו . שצריכין לו לאותו היום כגון כוסות וקיתוניות : י"ח כלים . מפרש להו בגמרא שכן דרך ללובשן בחול יחד אבל טפי מהכי לא ואיט פושטן לחזור וללבוש ולהציל אחרים : **גמ'** בבא להציל . [שהציל] בסל [אחד] כדקתני סל מלא ככרות ואיט טורח אלא להצילן מתוך הדליקה בבת אחת מציל כל מה שבסל דהא חדא זימנא הוא מה לי פורתא מה לי טובא : בבא לקפל . סלים הרבה זה עם זה לטרוח [ולאוספם] ולחזור ולהוציא מזון ג' סעודות הוא דיכול להציל בסלים הרבה ותו לא שכל א' טורח בעלמו הוא : פירש טליתו וקיפל והניח . הביא אוכלין והניח וחזר והביא והניח מהו : כבא להציל דמי . הואיל ואין כאן אלא כלי אחד ובפעם אחת הוא מוליאם : או כבא לקפל דמי . הואיל וטורח לאסוף ולכנוס : אטעייה רב שיזבי לרב חסדא . *[עד] שדרש לפניו והודה לו רב חסדא והאי מתני' דאמרן לעיל (דף קיז:) נשברה לו חבית בראש גגו מביא כלי ומניח תחתיה ודרש רב שיזבי לרב חסדא ובלבד שלא (ה) יתן כלי המחזיק יותר משלש סעודות והודה לו רב חסדא ומדאמר רבא אטעייה שמע מינה טעותא הוא דאפילו מחזיק סעודות הרבה מותר כיון דחד מנא הוא והאי כמקפל וטתן בכלי אחד דמי דהא מעט מעט הוא טופל *ומטפטף בו ש"מ בחד מנא כבא להציל דמי : מאי טעותא . מנא לך דטעותא הוא בידיה : אמר ליה . מדקתני בה בברייתא : ובלבד שלא יביא כלי אחר כו' . ש"מ כלים טובא הוא דאסירי אבל בחד שפיר דמי : מהפקירא וכו' . דהא הצילו לכם קאמר להו לצרכיהם ואם פקחים הם יעכבו הכל הוה ליה למיתני : מדת חסידות . שמחזירין לו : חסידי אגרא דשבתא שקלי . בתמיה אם חסידים הם יש להם לוותר משלהם בכל דבר שיש בו כדנוד עבירה ואע"ג דלאו שכר שבת גמור הוא שהרי לא התנה ומהפקירא קא זכו מיהו חסיד לא מיקרי אא"כ מוותר משלו : הכא בירא שמים עסקינן . המציל הזה ירא שמים הוא ולא חסיד לוותר משלו : דלא ניחא ליה דליתהני מאחריני . בזכייה דהפקירא דידע דלא-מרלונו הפקירו : ובתגם נמי לא ניחא ליה דליטרח . דלאו חסיד הוא (ו) ולמחול על שלו : והכי קאמר כו' . כלומר דהאי אם היו פקחין דמתני' לאו פקחין בדין קאמר ליטול את הראוי להם דאם כן יעכבו הכל הוה ליה למתני אלא לאו הכי קאמר הגי יראי שמים אם פקחין הן בהלכות שבת דידעי דכה"ג לאו שכר שבת הוא דמעיקרא לאו אדעתא דשכר פעולה נחית עושין עמו חשבון והכי קאמר אדרב חסדא כמי קאי אלא לא שבקיה לרב חסדא לסיימיה למילתיה : *לחצר המעורבת . ואפי' הכי טובא לא ליטל כדאמר לעיל (דף קיז:) מתוך שבהול אי שרי לאיעסוקי בהצלה טולי האי אתי לכבויי : מקטורן . מנטי"ל : אונקלי . לבוש רחב כעין שריגיש"א ובלשון ערבי מתשיא"ה : פונדא . אזור חלול מעל למדיו : קלבוס . נביי"ש : חלוק . קמיש"א על בשרו : ואפליון . סדין להתעטף בו טלו : מעפורת . לעטף ראשו : ושני ספרקין . פייסול"ש : אנפילייאות . קלנט"ש של למר : פרגוד . גנליי"ש ובלשון אשכנזי קי הוז"ן : חגור . על חלוקו מבפנים : וסודר שבצוארו . ותלויין ראשיו לפניו לקנח בו פיו ועיניו : **מתני'** עור של גדי . לח : מפני שהוא מחרך-מן האור ובלע"ז רטריי"ט ואיט נשרף ומתוך כך הוא מגין על התיבה : בין מלאים . מים : שאינן יכולין לקבל כח האור . מפני שחדשים הם : הוא

[Margin notes on the right, top to bottom:] ס"א מעם · עירובין לה: · לעיל קיז: · [לעיל יט:] · ס"י · לעיל קיז: עירובין לט: · [ל"ל ומטלטל עי' רש"א] · [פי' בגד רקיק שלובש אדם על בשרו ערוך] · [תוספתא פי"ד] · [שייך לעיל במשנה]

אידי ואידי בבא לקפל . פירש הרב פורת דלקפל היינו אפי' בא לקפל דלר' אבא אין חילוק בין לקפל בין להציל דאפילו להציל בחצר אחרת לא שרי אלא מזון ג' סעודות אבל אין נראה לומר דלהציל שרי אפילו מאה סעודות בחצר אחרת גם לרבי אבא דאם כן הוה ליה לאוקומי מתני' אידי ואידי בחצר אחרת וכאן בבא לקפל וכאן בבא להציל : **נותן** מים מצד זה . פירש רשב"ם לאו דוקא על הטלית דהא קי"ל בפ' דם חטאת (זבחים לד:) דבבגד שרייתו זהו כיבוסו ולעיל בסוף פרק שמנה שרצים (דף קיא·) פירשתי:

גרס

עין משפט נר מצוה

נה א מיי' פכ"ג מהל' שבת הל' כב כג סמג לאוין סה טור שו"ע או"ח סימן שלד סעיף ו [וסימן אא סעיף מד] :

נו ב מיי' שם הלכה כ טוש"ע שם סעיף יז :

נז ג מיי' שם טור שו"ע שם סעיף ז :

נח ד ה מיי' שם הלכה כה טור שו"ע שם סעיף ח :

נט ו ז מיי' שם הלכה כב כג טור שו"ע שם סעיף ו :

ס ח ט מיי' שם הלכה כד טור שו"ע שם סעיף ט :

סא י כ מיי' פרק יב שם הלכה ד ה סמג שם טוש"ע שם סעיף כב:

סב ל מיי' שם הלכה ו טור שו"ע שם סעיף כג כד :

רבינו חננאל

מצילין סל מלא ככרות ואע"ג שיש בו ק' סעודות . אקשינן איני והא תני רישא מצילין מזון ג' סעודות ותו לא ושני רב הונא לא קשיא רישא בבא לקפל . פי' כגון שמקבץ מתוך הבית ממקומות [הרבה] ונותן בכמה כלים שאין לו להציל אלא מזון של ג' סעודות בלבד . סיפא במציל כולו בכלי אחד כמות שהוא . ואע"פ שאין זה הטעם כאשר פירשנו.כי רישא במקפל ונותן בכלים שנים ושלשה . וסיפא במציל סל אחד כמות שהוא מפורש (היבננותו סו') . בעי רב הונא בריה דר' יהושע פירש טליתו וקיפל והניח וקיפל והניח מהו . כבא לקפל דמי או כבא להציל דמי . דמצלי לן שאם קיפל בכלי אחד ונטלו . וחזר וקיפל בכלי אחר ונטלו זהו לקפל פשיטא שאינו מציל אלא מזון ג' סעודות . וכי קא מבעיא שקיפל והניח בתוך טליתו וחזר וקיפל והניח בתוך טליתו מי אמרינן כיון שמקפל ומביא כמקפל דמי ואסור . או דילמא כיון שהוא מניחן בתוך טלית אחד אחד ונוטלן כאחד כבא להציל דמי ושרי . ומיפרשא נמי הא בגמ' בסוף יציאות השבת . הנהו תרי תלמידי . מר מציל בחד מנא ומר מציל בתרי מני קספלני בפלוגתא דר' אבא בר זבדא ורב הונא . הכין גמרא ומינמר מינה דלקפל בתרי תלתא מני כדפרישנא לעילא ואסיר לרב הונא ושרי לר' אבא בר זבדי ומסתייע נמי בתלמוד ׳. דאמרי על מצילין סל מלא ככרות מכיון שכולו גוף אחד כמין שכולה סעודה אחת היא והאי במימרא דרב הונא ובא ר' אבא בר זבדא ופירק פירוק אחר . ואמר רישא דמתני' במציל לחצר אחרת שאין לו להציל אלא מזון ג' סעודות בלבד בין בכלי א' בין בב' ג' כלים . וסיפא במציל באותו חצר שיש לו להציל אפילו ק' סעודות בין בכלי אחד בין בכמה כלים. ולענין בעיא דרב הונא בריה דר' יהושע פשט

מדאמר רבא הא מילתא אטעייה רב שיזבי ודרש ובלבד שלא יבא כלי אחד מחזיק יותר מג' סעודות . ש"מ כבא להציל דמי ש"מ . והכי קא גמרין מדקאמר רבא דבטעותא דרש רב חסדא שלא יביא כלי מחזיק יותר מג' סעודות. שמעינן מינה כי אפילו אם יביא כלי שמחזיק כל מה שהוא חפץ ויקפל ויניח בו ויטלנו כולו בבת אחת שפיר דמי. א"ל רב נחמן בר יצחק מאי טעותא. פירוש מנ"ל דטעותא היא דילמא דוקא אמר רב שיזבי . אהדר ליה רבא לא ס"ד מדקתני לענין מי שנשברה לו חבית בראש גגו מביא כלי ומניח תחתיה ובלבד שלא יביא כלי אחר ויקלוט כלי אחר ויצרף . כלי אחר לא יביא . הא בכלי אחד כמה דבעי נהוי וכן הלכה . וכיון שדרך בני אדם להזמין אורחים בשבת אומרים לאחרים בואו והצילו לכם . אבל להציל הוא ואח"כ להזמין אסור: ואם היו פקחין עושין עמו חשבון לאחר השבת . אוקימנא בירא שמים ולא ניחא ליה לאיתהניי מאחריני ובתגם [נמי לא ניחא ליה למטרח] . והכי פירושא דמתני' אם היו פקחין שיודעין דכי האי גוונא לאו שכר שבת הוא הואיל ומהפקירא קא זכו ואינון האי דמהדרו ליה לבעה"ב מתנה מדידהו הוא עושין חשבון כשיעור שכרן ושקלי ליה . ושארא שבקי ליה לבעה"ב . סוגיא דשמעתא שהחסיד גדול הוא מירא שמים . ולשם מוציא כל כלי תשמישו. לרבנן בחצר המעורבת . לבן בתירא אף לשאינה מעורבת . ולובש כל מה שהוא יכול ללבוש ועוטף כל מה שהוא יכול להתעטף. ואפי' יתר מי"ח כלים. וכן הלכתא. וקי"ל שמותר להערים : ירושלמי תני אין מערימין. ר' יוסי בר אבין אמר מערימין . ועל זו

הגהות הב"ח

(א) גמ' לקפל דמי תא שמע מדאמר רבא : (ב) שם בירא שמים עסקינן דלא · (ג) שם דלא קא חזי ליה אלא : (ד) שם תנו רבנן לובש ומוציא : (ה) רש"י ד"ה אטעייה וכו' ובלבד שלא יביא כלי : (ו) ד"ה ובתגם וכו' דלמחול :

גליון הש"ס

מתני' ולובש כל מה שיכול ללבוש. ע"ל דף סה ע"ב: גמ' מקטורן אונקלי ופונדא. עי' לעיל דף נט ע"ב תוס' ד"ה תרי סמייני : שם ושני ספרקין. נזכר במתני' פרק כ"ט משנה ג דכלים: מתני' עור של גדי. עיין לעיל דף מט ע"א תוס' ד"ה טומנין :

Continuation of translation from previous page as indicated by ◁

observed to Raba: Why is it an error?—He replied: Because it is stated, 'provided that he does not bring another vessel and catch [the dripping liquid] or another vessel and join it [to the roof]': [thus] only another vessel may not [be brought], but he may save as much as he desires in the same vessel.

AND A ROUND CAKE OF PRESSED FIGS, etc. What have we to do with a reckoning? Surely they acquire it from *hefker*?[8]—Said R. Ḥisda: They spoke here of pious conduct.[9] Will pious men take payment for the Sabbath? objected Raba.[10] Rather said Raba, We refer here to a God-fearing person, who does not wish to benefit from others, yet is unwilling to trouble for nothing,[11] and this is its meaning: AND IF THEY ARE WISE, that they know that
c in such a case it is not payment for the Sabbath,[1] THEY MAKE A RECKONING WITH HIM AFTER THE SABBATH.

WHITHER MAY THEY BE SAVED, etc. Why does he state here [SAVE] FOR YOURSELVES, whilst there he states, RESCUE WITH ME?—I will tell you: in connection with food he states, FOR YOURSELVES, because food for three meals only is fit for himself; but in connection with garments he states, RESCUE WITH ME, because they are fit for him all day.[2]

Our Rabbis taught: He may put on, carry out, and take off, then again put on, carry out, and take off, even all day: this is R. Meir's view. R. Jose said: [Only] eighteen garments. And who comes to save,[7] and it is permitted. R. Naḥman b. Isaac these are the eighteen garments: a cloak, undertunic,[3] hollow belt,[4] linen [sleeveless] tunic, shirt, felt cap, apron, a pair[5] of trousers, a pair of shoes, a pair of socks, a pair of breeches, the girdle round his loins, the hat on his head and the scarf round his neck.[6]

MISHNAH. R. SIMEON B. NANNOS SAID: ONE MAY SPREAD A GOAT SKIN[7] OVER A BOX, CHEST, OR TRUNK[8] WHICH HAS CAUGHT FIRE, BECAUSE HE SINGES;[9] AND ONE MAY MAKE A BARRIER WITH ALL VESSELS, WHETHER FULL [OF WATER] OR EMPTY, THAT THE FIRE SHOULD NOT TRAVEL ONWARD. R. JOSE FORBIDS IN THE CASE OF NEW EARTHEN VESSELS FILLED WITH WATER, BECAUSE SINCE THEY CANNOT STAND THE HEAT, THEY WILL BURST AND EXTINGUISH THE FIRE.[10]

GEMARA. Rab Judah said in Rab's name: If a garment catches fire on one side, water may be poured on to it on the other, and if it is [thereby] extinguished, it is extinguished. An objection is raised: If a garment catches fire on one side, one may take it off and cover himself with it, and if it is extinguished, it is extinguished; and likewise if a Scroll of the Law catches fire, one may spread
d it out and read it, and if it is extinguished, it is extinguished?[1]

(8) V. Glos. Seeing that he tells them to save it for *themselves*, it is theirs altogether. (9) A pious man will not take advantage of the fire to keep the food for himself. (10) Surely not. (11) *Ḥasiduth* (piety) however is a higher stage than God-fearingness.
c (1) Since it is actually *hefker* and they do not stipulate for payment beforehand. (2) He may wish to change many times during the day, so that he needs all for himself. (3) Jast.: an easy dress worn in the house and, under the cloak, in the street, but in which it was unbecoming to appear in public. (4) A money bag. (5) Lit., 'two'. (6) Some of these translations are only approximate: Felt-cap and hat, as well as 'trousers' and 'breeches' were obviously garments both worn at the time. (7) Rashi: which is damp. (8) Lit., 'turret'.—Three kinds of boxes or chests are meant. (9) But does not burn it and at the same time it protects the boxes. (10) Which is forbidden as a principal labour, v. *supra* 73a.
d (1) In each case probably the motion extinguishes it if the flame is very small. But the Tanna does not permit water.

דברים שאין אדם עומד בהן · על בוריין לאומרן כהלכתן : אלא אם כן נכשל בהן . עד שאומרן ב' וג' פעמים בשיבוש דהיינו טעמי תורה המסותרין : לא אהיה חובש . איני רגיל להיות חובש חבוש בבהמ"ד. אהיה הורגלתי כמו שחוק לרעהו אהיה (איוב יב) אני הוה : וממאי . דמשום דיש בהן אמנה הוא דילמא על כרחך נריכים שישיבו האמת : דאי אמר להו גמירנא. אותן טעמי תורה : אמרי ליה. שואלים אימא לן : ומשני הוה ליה למימר גמר ושכח מאי לא אהיה חובש. מודה הוא על האמת שלא יגע בתורה : בדברי תורה. היו נאמנין ואין מתהללים על שקר :

תורה אור

דברים שאין בני אדם עומדין עליהם אלא אם כן נכשלים בהן ישנן תחת ידיך קצין תהיה לנו °ישא ביום ההוא לאמר לא אהיה חובש וגו' אין ישא אלא לשון שבועה וכן הוא אומר לא תשא את שם ה' לא אהיה חובש לא אהיה מחובשי עצמן בבית המדרש ובביתי אין לחם ואין שמלה שאין בידי לא *מקרא ולא משנה ולא גמרא וממאי דילמא שאני התם דאי אמר להו גמירנא אמרו ליה אימא לן הוה ליה למימר גמר ושכח מאי לא אהיה חובש כלל לא קשיא כאן בדברי תורה כאן במשא ומתן: **מתני'** *מצילין סל מלא ככרות אע"פ שיש בו מאה סעודות ועיגול של דבילה וחבית של יין ואומר לאחרים בואו והצילו לכם ואם היו פיקחין עושין עמו חשבון אחר השבת להיכן מצילין אותן לחצר המעורבת בן בתירה אומר אף לשאינה מעורבת *ולשם מוציא כל כלי תשמישו °ולובש כל מה שיכול ללבוש ועוטף כל מה שיכול לעטוף ר' יוסי אומר י"ח כלים וחוזר ולובש ומוציא ואומר לאחרים בואו והצילו עמי: **גמ'** והא תנא ליה *רישא ג' סעודות ותו לא אמר רב הונא לא קשיא כאן בבא להציל כאן בבא לקפל בא להציל מציל את כולן בא לקפל אינו מקפל אלא מזון ג' סעודות *ר' אבא בר זבדא אמר רב אידי ואידי בבא לקפל ולא קשיא כאן לאותה חצר כאן לחצר אחרת בעי רב הונא בריה דרב יהושע פירש טליתו וקיפל והניח וקיפל והניח מאי כבא להציל דמי או כבא לקפל דמי (א)מדאמר רבא אטעיה רב שיזבי לרב חסדא ודרש ובלבד שלא יביא כלי שהוא מחזיק יותר מג' סעודות ש"מ כבא להציל דמי ושפיר דמי א"ל רב נחמן בר יצחק לרבא מאי טעותא אמר ליה דקתני *ובלבד שלא יביא כלי אחר ויקלוט כלי אחר ויצרף כלי אחר הוא דלא אבל בההוא מנא כמה דבעי מציל: ועיגול של דבילה כו': חשבון מאי עבידתיה מהפקירא קזכו אמר רב חסדא מדת חסידות שנו כאן אמר רבא חסידי אגרא דשבתא שקלי אלא אמר רבא הכא בירא שמים עסקינן (ב)ולא ניחא ליה דליתהני מאחרים ובתנם נמי לא ניחא ליה דליטרח והכי קאמר ואם היו פיקחין דידעי דכה"ג לאו שכר שבת הוא עושין עמו השבון לאחר השבת: ולהיכן מצילין כו': מ"ש הכא דקתני לכם ומ"ש הכא דקתני עמי אמרי גבי מזונות קתני לכם משום דלא קא חזו (ג)אלא מזון ג' סעודות אבל גבי לבושים קתני עמי משום דקחזי ליה לכולי יומא: ת"ר לובש (ד) מוציא ופושט וחוזר ולובש ומוציא ופושט ואפילו כל היום כולו דברי רבי מאיר רבי יוסי אומר שמנה עשר כלים ואלו הם שמנה עשר כלים °מקטורן *אונקלי ופונדא קלבוס של פשתן וחלוק *ואפיליות ומעפורת °ושני ספרקין ושני מנעלים ושני אנפילאות וב' פרגד וחגור שבמתניו וכובע שבראשו וסודר שבצוארו: **מתני'** ר' שמעון בן ננס אומר פורסין °עור של גדי על גבי שידה תיבה ומגדל שאחז בהן את האור מפני שהוא מחרך °ועושין מחיצה בכל הכלים בין מלאין בין ריקנים בשביל שלא תעבור הדליקה רבי יוסי אוסר בכלי חרס חדשים מלאין מים לפי שאין יכולין לקבל את האור והן מתבקעין ומכבין את הדליקה: **גמ'** אמר רב יהודה אמר רב טלית שאחז בה האור מצד אחד נותנין עליה מים מצד אחר ואם כבתה כבתה מיתיבי *טלית שאחז בה האור מצד אחד פושטה ומתכסה בה ואם כבתה כבתה וכן ספר תורה שאחז בו האור פושטו וקורא בו ואם כבה כבה הוא

מתני' ועיגול של דבילה. שהוא גדול ויש בו סעודות הרבה : ואם היו פקחין. לישאל שכרן כפועלים : כל כלי תשמישו. שצריכין לו לאותו היום כגון כוסות וקיתוניות : י"ח כלים. מפרש להו בגמרא שכן דרך ללובשן בחול יחד אבל טפי מהכי לא ואינו פושטן לחזור וללבוש ולהציל אחרים : **גמ'** בבא להציל. [שהציל] בסל [אחד] כדקתני סל מלא ככרות ואינו טורח אלא להצילן מתוך הדליקה בבת אחת מציל כל מה שבסל דהא חדא זימנא הוא מה לי פורתא מה לי טובא : בבא לקפל. סלים הרבה זה עם זה לטרוח [ולאוספם] ולחזור ולהוציא מזון ג' סעודות הוא דיכול להציל בסלים הרבה ותו לא שכל א' טורח בעצמו הוא : פירש טליתו וקיפל והניח. הביא אוכלין והניח וחזר והביא והניח מהו : כבא להציל דמי. הואיל ואין כאן אלא כלי אחד ובפעם אחת הוא מוציאם : או כבא לקפל דמי. הואיל וטורח לאסוף ולכנוס : אטעייה רב שיזבי לרב חסדא. *[עד]שדרש לפניו והודה לו רב חסדא והא מתני' דאמרן לעיל (דף קיז:) נשברה לו חבית בראש גגו מביא כלי ומניח תחתיה ודרש רב שיזבי לרב חסדא ובלבד שלא (ה)יתן כלי המחזיק יותר משלש סעודות והודה לו רב חסדא ומדאמר רבא אטעייה שמע מינה טעותא הוא דאפילו מחזיק סעודות הרבה מותר כיון דחד מנא הוא והאי כמקפל וטתן בכלי אחד דמי דהא מעט מעט הוא טופל *ומטפטף בו ש"מ בחד מנא כבא להציל דמי : מאי טעותא. מנא לך דטעותא הוא בידיה : אמר ליה. מדקתני בה בברייתא : ובלבד שלא יביא כלי אחר כו'. ש"מ כלים טובא הוא דאסירי אבל בחד שפיר דמי : מהפקירא וכו'. דהא הצילו לכם קאמר להו לצרכיהם ואם פקחים הם יעכבו הכל הוה ליה למיתני : מדת חסידות. שמחזירין לו : חסידי אגרא דשבתא שקלי. בתמיה אם חסידים הם יש להם לוותר משלהם בכל דבר שיש בו נדנוד עבירה ואע"ג דלאו שכר שבת גמור הוא שהרי לא התנה ומהפקירא קא זכו מיהו חסיד לא מיקרי אא"כ מוותר משלו : הכא בירא שמים עסקינן. המציל הזה ירא שמים הוא ולא חסיד לוותר משלו : דלא ניחא ליה דליתהני מאחריני. בזכייה דהפקירא דידע דלא-מרצונו הפקירו : ובתנם נמי לא ניחא ליה דליטרח. דלאו חסיד הוא (ו)ולמחול על שלו: והכי קאמר כו'. כלומר דהאי אם היו פקחין דמתני' לאו פקחין בדין קאמר ליטול את הראוי להם דאם כן יעכבו הכל הוה ליה למתני אלא לאו הכי קאמר הני יראי שמים אם פקחין הן בהלכות שבת דידעי דכה"ג לאו שכר שבת הוא דמעיקרא לאו אדעתא דשכר פעולה נחית עושין עמו חשבון והכי קאמר אדרב חסדא נמי קאי אלא לא שבקיה לרב חסדא לסיימיה למילתיה : *לחצר המעורבת. ואפי' הכי טובא לא ליצול כדאמר לעיל (דף קיז:) מתוך שבהול אי שרי לאיעסוקי בהצלה כולי האי אתי לכבויי : מקטורן. מנטי"ל : אונקלי. לבוש רחב כעין שריגש"א ובלשון ערבי מחשיא"ה : פונדא. אזור חלול מעל למדיו : קלבוס. גבי"ש : חלוק. קמיש"א על בשרו : אפליון. סדין להתעטף בו כולו : מעפורת. לעטף ראשו : ושני ספרקין. פיישול"ש : אנפילאות. קלנצו"ש של למר : פרגוד. גנליי"ש ובלשון אשכנז קני הוז"ן : חגור. על חלוקו מבפנים : וסודר שבצוארו. ותלויין ראשיו לפניו לקנח בו פיו ועיניו : **מתני'** עור של גדי. לח : מפני שהוא מחרך. מן האור ובלע"ז רטריי"ט ואינו נשרף ומתוך כך הוא מגין על התיבה : בין מלאים. מים : שאינן יכולין לקבל כח האור. מפני שחדשים הם: הוא

אידי ואידי בבא לקפל. פירש הרב פורת דלקפל היינו אפי' בא לקפל דלר' אבא אין חילוק בין לקפל בין להציל דאפילו להציל בחצר אחרת לא שרי אלא מזון ג' סעודות אבל אין נראה לומר דלהציל שרי אפילו מאה סעודות בחצר אחרת גם לרבי אבא דאם כן הוה ליה לאוקומי מתני' אידי ואידי בחצר אחרת וכאן בבא לקפל וכאן בבא להציל: **נותן** מים מצד זה. פירש רשב"ס לאו דוקא על הטלית דהא קי"ל בפ' דם חטאת (זבחים לד:) דכבגד שרייתו זהו כיבוסו ולעיל בסוף פרק שמנה שרצים (דף קיא.) פירשתי:

גרס

עין משפט נר מצוה

נה א מיי' פכ"ג מהל' שבת הל' כב כג סמג לאוין סה טור שו"ע או"ח סימן של"ד סעיף ו [וסימן שא סעיף מד] :
נו ב מיי' שם הלכה כ טוש"ע שם סעיף יז:
נז ג מיי' שם טור שו"ע שם סעיף ז :
נח ד ה מיי' שם הלכה כה טור שו"ע שם סעיף ח :
נט ו ז מיי' שם הלכה כב כג טור שו"ע שם סעיף ו :
ס ח ט מיי' שם הלכה כד טור שו"ע שם סעיף ט :
סא י כ מיי' פרק יב שם הלכה ד ה סמג שם טוש"ע שם סעיף כב:
סב ל מיי' שם הלכה ו טור שו"ע שם סעיף כג כד :

רבינו חננאל

מצילין סל מלא ככרות ואע"ג שיש בו ק' סעודות . אקשינן איני והא תני רישא מצילין מזון ג' סעודות ותו לא ושני רב הונא לא קשיא רישא בבא לקפל . פי' כגון שמקבץ מתוך הבית ממקומות [הרבה] ונותן בכמה כלים שאין לו להציל אלא מזון של ג' סעודות בלבד . סיפא במציל כולו בכלי אחד כמות שהוא . ואע"פ שאין זה הטעם כאשר פירשנו. כי רישא במקפל ונותן בכלים שנים ושלשה . וסיפא במציל סל אחד כמות שהוא מפורש (היבננוהו מו') . **בעי** רב הונא בריה דר' יהושע פירש טליתו וקיפל והניח וקיפל והניח מהו . כבא לקפל דמי או כבא להציל דמי . דמצלי לן שאם קיפל בכלי אחד ונטלו . וחזר וקיפל בכלי אחר ונטלו זהו לקפל פשיטא שאינו מציל אלא מזון ג' סעודות . וכי קא מבעיא שקיפל והניח בתוך טליתו וחזר וקיפל והניח בתוך טליתו מי אמרינן כיון שמקפל ומביא כמקפל דמי ואסור . או דילמא כיון שהוא מניחן בתוך טלית אחד אחד ונטלן כאחד כבא להציל דמי ושרי . ומיפרשא נמי הא בגמ' בסוף יציאות השבת . הנהו תרי תלמידי . מר מציל בחד מנא ומר מציל בתרי מני קמפלגי בפלוגתא דר' אבא בר זבדא ורב הונא . הכין גמרא ומינגר מינה דלקפל בתרי תלתא מני כדפרישנא לעילא ראסיר לרב הונא ושרי לר' אבא בר זבדי ומסתייע נמי בתלמוד . דאמרי על מצילין סל מלא ככרות מכיון שכולו גוף אחד כמין שכולה סעודה אחת היא והאי במימרא דרב הונא ובא ר' אבא בר זבדא ופירק פירוק אחר . ואמר רישא דמתני' במציל לחצר אחרת שאין לו להציל אלא מזון ג' סעודות בלבד בין בכלי א' בין בב' ג' כלים . וסיפא במציל באותו חצר שיש לו להציל אפילו ק' סעודות בין בכלי אחד בין בכמה כלים. ולענין בעיא דרב הונא בריה דר' יהושע פשטם מדאמר רבא הא מילתא אטעייה רב שיזבי ודרש ובלבד שלא יבא כלי אחד מחזיק יותר מג' סעודות . ש"מ כבא להציל דמי ש"מ . והכי קא גמרין מדקאמר רבא דבטעותא דרש רב חסדא שלא יביא כלי מחזיק יותר מג' סעודות. שמעינן מינה כי אפילו אם יביא כלי שמחזיק כל מה שהוא חפץ ויקפל ויניח בו ויטלנו כולו בבת אחת שפיר דמי. א"ל רב נחמן בר יצחק מאי טעותא. פירוש מנ"ל דמעותא היא דילמא דוקא אמר רב שיזבי . אהדר ליה רבא לא ס"ד מדקתני לענין מי שנשברה לו חבית בראש גגו מביא כלי ומניח תחתיה ובלבד שלא יביא כלי אחר ויקלוט כלי אחר ויצרף . כלי אחר לא יביא . הא בכלי אחד כמה דבעי נהוי וכן הלכה . וכיון שדרך בני אדם להזמין אורחים בשבת אומרים לאחרים בואו והצילו לכם . אבל להציל הוא ואח"כ להזמין אסור: **ואם** היו פקחין עושין עמו חשבון לאחר השבת . אוקימנא בירא שמים ולא ניחא ליה לאיתהניי מאחריני ובחנם [נמי לא ניחא ליה למטרח] . והכי פירושא דמתני' אם היו פקחין שיודעין דכי האי גוונא לאו שכר שבת הוא הואיל ומהפקירא קא זכו ואינון האי דמהדרו ליה לבעה"ב כגון מתנה מדידהו הוא עושין חשבון כשיעור שכרן ושקלי ליה . ושארא שבקי ליה לבעה"ב . סוגיא דשמעתא שהחסיד גדול הוא מירא שמים . ולשם מוציא כל כלי תשמישו. לרבנן בחצר המעורבת . לבן בתירא אף לשאינה מעורבת . ולובש כל מה שהוא יכול ללבוש ועוטף כל מה שהוא יכול להתעטף. וכן הלכתא. וקי"ל שמותר להערים : **ירושלמי** תני אין מערימין. ר' יוסי בר אבין אמר מערימין . ועל זו

הגהות הב"ח

(א) גמ' לקפל דמי תא שמע מדאמר רבא : (ב) שם בירא שמים עסקינן דלא · (ג) שם דלא קא חזי ליה אלא : (ד) שם תנו רבנן לובש ומוציא : (ה) רש"י ד"ה אטעייה וכו' ובלבד שלא יביא כלי : (ו) ד"ה ובחנם וכו' דלמחול :

גליון הש"ס

מתני' ולובש כל מה שיכול ללבוש. ע"ל דף סה ע"ב: גמ' מקטורן אונקלי ופונדא. עי' לעיל דף נט ע"ב תוס' ד"ה תרי המייני : שם ושני ספרקין. נזכר במתני' פרק כ"ט משנה ג דכלים : מתני' עור של גדי. עיין לעיל דף מט ע"א תוס' ד"ה טומנין :

הוא דאמר כר' שמעון בן ננס אימר דאמר רבי שמעון בן ננס מפני שהוא מחרך גרם כיבוי מי אמר אין מדקתני סיפא רבי יוסי אוסר בכלי חרס חדשים מלאים מים שאינן יכולים לקבל את האור והן מתבקעין ומכבין את הדליקה מכלל דתנא קמא שרי ת"ר נר שעל גבי טבלא מנער את הטבלא והיא נופלת ואם כבתה כבתה אמרי דבי רבי ינאי לא שנו אלא בשוכח אבל במניח נעשה בסיס לדבר האסור תנא נר שאחורי הדלת פותח ונועל כדרכו ואם כבתה כבתה לייט עלה רב אמר ליה רבינא לרב אחא בריה דרבא ואמרי לה רב אחא בריה דרבא לרב אשי מאי טעמא לייט עלה רב אילימא משום דרב סבר לה כרבי יהודה ותנא קתני לה כר' שמעון משום דרב סבר לה כר' יהודה כל דתני כר' שמעון מילט לייט ליה אמר ליה בהא אפילו ר' שמעון מודה דהא אביי ורבא דאמרי תרוייהו מודה רבי שמעון בפסיק רישיה ולא ימות אמר רב יהודה פותח אדם דלת כנגד (א)מדורה בשבת לייט עלה אביי במאי עסקינן אילימא ברוח מצויה מאי טעמיה דמאן דאסר אי ברוח שאינה מצויה מאי טעמא דמאן דשרי לעולם ברוח מצויה מר סבר גזרינן ומר סבר לא גזרינן: עושין מחיצה כו': למימרא דרבנן סברי גרם כבוי מותר ור' יוסי סבר גרם כבוי אסור והא איפכא שמעינן להו דתניא עושין מחיצה בכלים ריקנין ובמלאין שאין דרכן להשתבר ואלו מלאין שאין דרכן להשתבר כלי מתכות רבי יוסי אומר אף כלי כפר שיחין וכלי כפר תנניה אין דרכן להשתבר וכי תימא איפוך מתני' ורבי יוסי דברייתא לדבריהם קאמר ומי מצית אפכת לה והאמר רבה בר תחליפא משמיה דרב מאן תנא גרם כבוי אסור ר' יוסי אלא לעולם לא תיפוך ובריתא כולה ר' יוסי היא וחסורי מחסרא והכי קתני עושין מחיצה בכלים ריקנין ובמלאים שאין דרכן להשתבר ואלו הן כלים שאין דרכן להשתבר כלי מתכות וכלי כפר שיחין וכלי כפר חנניה נמי אין דרכן להשתבר שר' יוסי אומר אף כלי כפר שיחין וכלי כפר תנניה אין דרכן להשתבר ורמי דרבנן אדרבנן ורמי דרבי יוסי אדרבי יוסי דתניא הרי שהיה שם כתוב לו על בשרו הרי זה לא ירחוץ ולא יסוך ולא יעמוד במקום הטינופת נזדמנה לו טבילה של מצוה כורך עליה גמי ויורד וטובל רבי יוסי אומר לעולם יורד וטובל כדרכו ובלבד שלא ישפשף שאני התם דאמר קרא ואבדתם את שמם מן המקום ההוא לא תעשון כן לה' אלהיכם עשייה הוא דאסור גרמא שרי אי הכי הכא נמי כתיב לא תעשה [כל] מלאכה עשייה הוא דאסור גרמא שרי מתוך שאדם בהול על ממונו אי שרית ליה אתי לכבויי אי הכי קשיא דרבנן אדרבנן ומה התם דאדם בהול על ממונו שרי הכא לא כל שכן ותסברא האי גמי היכי דמי אי דמיהדק קא הוי חציצה אי לא מיהדק עיילי ביה מיא חציצה תיפוק ליה משום דיו בלחה דתניא הדם והדיו הדבש והחלב יבשין חוצצין לחים אין חוצצין מכל מקום קשיא אלא אמר רבא בר רב שילא היינו טעמייהו דרבנן דקסברי אסור לעמוד בפני השם ערום מכלל דר"י סבר מותר לעמוד בפני השם ערום דמנח ידיה עילויה לרבנן נמי דמנח ידיה עילויה זימנין דמשתלי ושקיל ליה לר' יוסי נמי זימנין דמשתלי ושקיל ליה אלא אי דאיכא גמי ה"נ הב"ע לאהדורי אגמי רבנן סברי טבילה

רש"י

גמ' הוא דאמר כר"ש. דשרי לעטובי דליקה בעור גדי: גרס כיבוי. כי האי גוונא כשמגיע למים הוא כבה: מי אמר. דילמא הא דקתני במתני' ועושין מחיצה בכל הכלים לאו בחדשים המתבקעים קאמר: נר. דולק קרוסיי"ל: אלא בשכח. דשכחו מבעוד יום על הטבלא שלא מדעת: אבל מניח נעשית. טבלא בסיס לדבר האסור ואסור לטלטלה כדי לנערה: לייט עליה. על כל המורין כן: כר' יהודה. דאמר דבר שאין מתכוין אסור: בפסיק רישיה. והכא נמי הרוח מכבהו: כנגד המדורה. ואע"פ שרוח מנשבת ומבעיר האור: מאי טעמא דמאן דאסר. אין דרך להבעיר ברוח מצויה ולא פסיק רישיה ולא ימות הוא: אף כלי כפר שיחין. חרס העשוי מאותו עפר חזק הוא ואין משתבר אלמא לר' יוסי בגרם כבוי טפי מיקל מדרבנן: וכי תימא איפוך מתני'. ותני ברישא דברי ר' יוסי וחכמים אוסרין בכלי חרס חדשים כו': ור' יוסי דברייתא. דמשמע דבהגהו דפקעי מודה דהא כפר שיחין וכפר חנניה הוא דקשרי: לדבריהם קאמר להו. לדידי כל הכלים שרו דגרם כבוי מותר אלא לדידכו נהי דאסריתו גרם כבוי אודו לי מיהת דבהני אפילו גרם ליכא: כורך עליו גמי. קס"ד השתא כדי שלא ימחק את השם במים אלמא לרבנן גרם מחק אסור ולר' יוסי שרי: ובלבד שלא ישפשף. דהוי מוחק בידים: ותסברא. דהכא נמי דאצרכוה רבנן משום שלא ימחק הוא: האי גמי היכי דמי. להגין עליו: אי דמיהדק. שלא יכנסו בו מים וימחק הוי חצילה: ואי בלא מיהדק. לבשרו: עיילי ביה מיא. ואינו מגין מלמחוק: תיפוק ליה דמשום דיו. בלא גמי נמי חיין דיו ומשני בלחה: מכל מקום קשיא. גמי לרבנן למה להו: מכלל דלר' יוסי כו'. בתמיה והא כתיב לא יראה בך ערות דבר (דברים כג): אלא אי איכא גמי הכי נמי. דמודה ר' יוסי דלריך לכרוך עליו גמי ולא סגי ליה לאנוחי ידיו עליו דילמא מישתלי ושקיל ליה לידיה:

תוספות

גרם כיבוי מי אמר. וא"ת הא קתני מתני' בין מלאים בין ריקנים ומאי רבותא איכא טפי במלאים אי לאו דמיירי בדרכן להשתבר וי"ל דס"ד דמיירי בכלים שאין דרכן להשתבר וקמ"ל דלא גזרינן אטו כלים שדרכן להשתבר:

מנער את הטבלא והיא נופלת ואם כבתה כבתה. אומר ר"י דמיירי דליכא שמן בנר דאי איכא שמן בנר חייב שהרי שופך ממנו והוי כמסתפק ממנו דחייב משום מכבה כדאמר בפ"ב דביצה (דף כב:) ובירושלמי מוקי לה בנר שכבה ולא קתני בהך ברייתא ואם כבתה כבתה ואתא לאשמעינן היתר טלטול ע"י ניעור לר' יהודה דאסר טלטול בנר שכבה אי נמי אפילו לר"ש ובנר גדול כגון קערה ועששית דמודה ר"ש כדאמר בפרק [כירה] (דף מד·) או כשיש אפר וגחלת אלא שכבה השלהבת: פותח ונועל כדרכו. אע"פ שע"י כן מתנדנד הנר ומתרחק השמן מן השלהבת או מתקרב והוי מכבה או מבעיר אבל אין לפרש משום כיבוי דרוח דאחורי הדלת ליכא רוח ועוד דא"כ הוה ליה למימר פותח אדם דלת כנגד הנר כדקאמר בסמוך כנגד המדורה ועוד דתיכא פותח נועל מאי איסורא איכא אלא·כדפרישית ואי לאו משום כיבוי והבערה משום טלטול אין לאסור דבנעילת דלת לא חשיב טלטול וגם לא הוי בסיס לדבר האסור דבית חשוב הוא ובטל אגב בית אי נמי בשכח דלא הוי בסיס: מר סבר גזרינן. הלכך צריך ליזהר שלא לפתוח הדלת לפני המדורה אפילו ברוח מצויה דהא לייט עלה אביי דהוי בתראה והנ"מ כשהמדורה קלת קרובה אצל הדלת: והא איפכא שמעינן להו. לאו דווקא איפכא דר' יוסי דברייתא הוי כמו מתני' דאסר דרכו להשתבר אלא היינו איפכא דבמתניתין מחמיר ר' יוסי טפי מדרבנן ובברייתא מיקל טפי: וכי תימא איפוך מתני' כו'. וא"ת מ"מ תקשה דבמתני' לא אסרי רבנן אלא חרס חדש ובברייתא אסרי אפי' ישן מדנקט כלי מתכות וי"ל דנקט בברייתא כלי מתכות משום דאין חילוק בהם בין חדשים לישנים וה"ה כלי חרס ישן: והאמר רבה כו'. ואם תאמר ואמאי לא מפיך ברייתא דטפי אית לן לאפוכה ממתני' והוי אתי נמי שפיר הא דרבה בר תחליפא וכימא דרבנן לדברי ר' יוסי קאמרי ואינהו שרי אף בכלי חרס חדש וי"ל דהתלמוד לא קאמר אלא דאפילו מפיך מתני' לא אתי שפיר אלא על כרחיך ברייתא אית לן לתרולי וכיון דאתיא להכי לא צריך להפוכה אלא למימר חסורי מיחסרא: אי הכי קשה דרבנן אדרבנן. בלאו הכי הוה קשיא דרבנן אדרבנן אלא משום דהשתא פריך מכ"ש קאמר אי הכי *):

*) [ועי' תוס' עירובין לג: ובכילה ח: וכתובות ג: וב"מ לג. שבועות מה: ד"ה אי הכי]

רבינו חננאל

אמרינן בגמרא דפורפת על האבן ועל האגוז כו' תיבעי למאן דאמר מערימין תיבעי למ"ד אין מערימין. ואמר לאחרים בואו והצילו עמי שכן דרך בני אדם להשאיל כליו בשבת·פי' י"ח כלים דקא"ר יוסי [מקטורין] כמו מעיל · ובלשון ישמעאל כרכום שיש לו בית ראש ועושה לו הלובשו ויש לו לולאות וקרסים (שהוא הווה) [שמחברן והוא] כמו מלבוש : אונקלי . בגד דקיקי שנקרא מערקה שלובש אדם על בשרו וחולם כל גופו וכן שנינו (מגילה כ"ד) בענין תפלין של יד ציפהו זהב ונתנו על בית יד של אונקלי שלו הרי זה דרך החיצונים : פונדא · גם היא מגעת עד למטה מטבורו של אדם וקורין לו בלשון פרסי פֶּשֶׁת · תקשר כחשב אפודה והיא אפוד האמורה בתורה ויש בה כסים כסים כנגד הלב ותחת הידים : קנבוס של פשתן · חלוק התחתון שלובשין אותו ונקרא גלאלה · חלוק הוא המלובש העליון וקורין לו ורבנין: שני. ספרקים *) ויש שגורס סובריקין והם בלשון יון המכנסים ושמעו שאמר הגאון נס' דח' דם תפנקי שמלבישין בהן הידים עד האציל ויש בהן בתי אצבעות שני מנעלים כמשמען : שני פרגוד . בלשון ישמעאל טראבי : אנפליאות . גם הם מנעלים לשוקים עליון האנין שעל השוקים מן העור · מעפורת והגור שבמתנים וכובע הרי י"ח כלים : ר' שמעון בן ננס אומר פורשין עור של גדי כו'. אמר רב יהודה טלית שאחז בה האור מצד אחד נותן עליה מים מצד אחר ואם כבתה כבתה · והא ודאי גרם כיבוי הוא · ואקשינן עליה ממתנית' דקתני פושטה ומתכסה בה אבל מים שהן גרם כיבוי לא קתני ואתגינן לאוקמיה לרב יהודה כר' שמעון בן ננס ולא קם · דר' שמעון בן ננס לא קאמר אלא מפני שהוא מחרך הא גרמא בידים לא קאמר אלא קם רב יהודה כרבנן · דתנן עושין מחיצה בכל הכלים בין מלאים בין ריקנין דשרו גרם כיבוי ור' יוסי אוסר גרם כיבוי והלכה כרבנן וכרב יהודה : נר שעל גבי טבלא איתא דאוקמה דבי ר' ינאי בשכח נר שעל גבי טבלא · אבל המניח נר על טבלא נעשה טבלא בסים לנר שהיא מוקצה מחמת איסור ואסור לטלטוליה' ודתנא תנא קמיה דרב ולייט עלה רב · היכא דידע שבודאי כשפותח ונועל יכבה הנר מפני שהדלת נוגעת בו ומכבתו שאסור דבהא אפי' ר"ש מודה דהוי פסוק רישיה ולא ימות · אבל אי גרם בעלמא שרי : אמר רב יהודה אמר שמואל פותח אדם דלת כנגד המדורה בשבת ואינו חושש · ואע"פ שהרוח מלבה את האש לייט עלה אביי דחשיב ליה כמבעיר את האש ואי רוח שאינה מצויה היא והוא שמניף ומושבה לא פליגי דאסיר. כי פליגי ברוח מצויה · (רב) [אביי] סבר גזרינן ברוח מצויה אטו רוח שאינה מצויה · ומר סבר לא גזרינן והלכתא כאביי וקאמרינן בגמרא דהכונס צאן לדיר בנזיקין חמלבה ואין בליבויו כדי ללבותה פטור · ואקשינן אמאי פטור · ליהוי כי זורה ורוח מסייעתו · ואמרינן בה כמה טעמי · סימן ברו"ש · אמר אביי כגון שליבה מצד זה וליבתה הרוח מצד אחר רבא אמר כגון שליבה ברוח מצויה וליבתו הרוח שאינה מצויה · רב זירא אמר דצמדא צמידי · רב אשי אמר היכא אמרינן זורה ורוח מסייעתו לענין שבת דמלאכת מחשבת אסרה תורה · אבל הכא גרמא בעלמא היא ותרמא בנזקין פטור· ש"מ דכיון דמשוי אורחא אפי' לרוח מצויה ללבות ומחשב לכן אסור בשבת דהיינו מלאכת מחשבת: פתיא דשמעתא דר' יוסי מתיר בכלים מליאין מים כגון כלי מתכות וכלי כפר חנניה וכפר שיחין שהרש שלהן חזק ואינן מתבקעין באור · ואע"פ שאין גרם כיבוי אסור כגון הני שקי · ור' יוסי דשרי

ההיא

*) עיין ערוך ערך ספרק

עין משפט נר מצוה

סג א ב מיי' פי"ב מהל' שבת הלכה ו סמג לאוין סה טוש"ע או"ח סימן רעז סעיף ג :
סד ג מיי' שם פ"ה הל' יז טוש"ע שם ס"א :
סה ד מיי' שם טוש"ע שם סעיף ב :
סו ה ו מיי' פ"ו מהל' יסודי התורה הל' ו סמג עשין ג :
סז ז מיי' פ"ב מהלכות מקואות הלכה ב סמג לאוין קיא טוש"ע יו"ד סימן קצח סעיף טו :
סח ח מיי' פ"ו מהל' יסודי התורה הל"ו:

מסורת הש"ס

לקמן קכט. ודף קמג: · לעיל סט: קג. קיא. קלג: קלג. [קמג:] ביצה לו. סוכה לג: כתובות ו. בכורות כה. · יומא ח. כח. [מס' סופרים פ"ה הל"ו] · דברים יב · שמות כ · לעיל קכ: · פסחים סה: מנחות כא. זבחים לה.

הגהות הב"ח

(א) גמ' כנגד המדורה :

גליון הש"ס

גמ' הרי זה לא ירחוץ. עי' נדה דף סו ע"ב תוס' ד"ה אם סמוך : שם דמנח ידיה עלויה. עי' בתרומת הדשן סימן י' :

רב נסים גאון

מאי טעמא לייט עלה רב אי נימא דרב סבר לה כר' יהודה תמצא בירורו בפ' במה מדליקין (לעיל דף כב) רב אמר אין הלכה כר' שמעון בגרירה מכלל דכר' יהודה סבירא ליה דפליג על ר' שמעון ואסר דבר שאינו מתכוין ובסוף פ' שמונה שרצים (לעיל דף קיא) ובפרק בתולה נשאת (כתובות דף ו) הלכה אמרו אמר רב הלכה כר' יהודה ורב חייא בר אבין מתני לה בלא גברי רב אמר הלכה כר' יהודה ושמואל אמר הלכה כר' שמעון ותניא כוותיה בבכורות בפרק כל פסולי המוקדשין (דף לד) הרי מיכן למדנו שרב סבר דבר שאין מתכוין אסור כר' יהודה :

[120*b*]—He rules as R. Simeon b. Nannos.[2] Yet perhaps R. Simeon b. Nannos said [merely], BECAUSE HE SINGES: but did he rule [thus] of indirect extinguishing?[3]—Yet, since the final clause teaches, R. JOSE FORBIDS IN THE CASE OF NEW EARTHEN VESSELS FILLED WITH WATER, BECAUSE SINCE THEY CANNOT STAND THE HEAT THEY WILL BURST AND EXTINGUISH THE FIRE, it follows that the first Tanna permits it.

Our Rabbis taught: If a lamp is on a board, one may shake [tip up] the board and it [the lamp] falls off, and if it is extinguished, it is extinguished. The School of R. Jannai said: They learnt this only if one forgot [it there]; but if he placed [it there], it [the board] became a stand for a forbidden article.[4] A Tanna taught: If a lamp is behind a door, one may open and close [it] naturally, and if it is extinguished[5] it is extinguished. Rab cursed this [ruling]. Said Rabina to R. Aḥa the son of Raba—others state, R. Aḥa the son of Raba to R. Rashi—why did Rab curse this? Shall we say because Rab holds with R. Judah,[6] whereas the Tanna teaches as R. Simeon? Because Rab holds with R. Judah, if one teaches as R. Simeon, shall he curse him!—Here, he replied, even R. Simeon agrees, for Abaye and Raba both said: R. Simeon agrees in a case of 'cut off his head and let him not die.'[7]

Rab Judah said: One may open a door opposite a fire on the Sabbath.[8] Abaye cursed this. What are the circumstances? If there is a normal wind [blowing], what is the reason of the one a who forbids?[1] If there is an abnormal wind, what is the reason of the one who permits?[2]—In truth, it refers to a normal wind: one Master holds, we prohibit preventively;[3] whilst the other Master holds, We do not prohibit preventively.

ONE MAY MAKE A BARRIER, etc. Shall we say that the Rabbis hold, Indirect extinguishing[4] is permitted, while R. Jose holds that it is forbidden? But we know them [to maintain] the reverse. For it was taught: One may make a barrier of empty vessels and of full vessels which are not liable to burst; and these are the full vessels which are not likely to burst: metal vessels. R. Jose said: The vessels of Kefar Shiḥin and Kefar Ḥananiah[5] too are not likely to burst![6] And should you answer, Reverse our Mishnah, while R. Jose of the Baraitha argues on the view of the Rabbis;[7] [it may be asked], But can you reverse them? Surely Rabbah b. Taḥlifa said in Rab's name: 'Which Tanna holds that indirect extinguishing is forbidden? R. Jose'! Hence in truth you must not reverse it, the whole of the Baraitha being [the view of] R. Jose, but there is a lacuna, and it was thus taught: One may make a barrier with empty vessels and with full vessels that are not likely to burst, and these are the vessels which are not likely to burst: metal vessels, and the vessels of Kefar Shiḥin and Kefar Ḥananiah too are not likely to burst. For R. Jose maintains: The vessels of Kefar Shiḥin and Kefar Ḥananiah too are not likely to burst.

Now, the Rabbis are self-contradictory and R. Jose is self-contradictory. For it was taught: If one has the [Divine] Name written on his skin, he must not bathe nor anoint [himself] nor stand in an unclean place. If he must perform an obligatory *ṭebillah*, he b must wind a reed[1] about it and descend and perform *ṭebillah*. R. Jose said: He may at all times descend and perform *ṭebillah* in the ordinary way, provided that he does not rub [it]?[2]—There it is different, because Scripture saith, *And ye shall destroy their name out of that place. Ye shall not do so unto the Lord your God:*[3] only [direct] action is forbidden, but indirect action is permitted. If so, here too it is written, *thou shalt not do any work:*[4] only [direct] action is forbidden, but indirect action is permitted?—Since a man is excited over his property, if you permit him [indirect action], he may come to extinguish it. If so, the Rabbis are self-contradictory: if there, though a man is excited over his property, it is permitted, how much more so here?—Now, is that logical:[5] this reed, how is it meant? If it is wound tightly, it is an interposition;[6] [while] if it is not wound tightly the water enters. ([You speak of] 'an interposition' that follows from the ink?[7]—The reference is to wet [ink], for it was taught: Blood, ink, honey, and milk, if dry [on the skin] constitute an interposition; if moist, they do not constitute an interposition.) Yet still there is the difficulty?[8]—Rather said Raba b. Shila, This is the reason of the Rabbis: because they hold one must not stand nude in the presence of the Divine Name. Hence it follows that R. Jose holds that one may stand nude in the presence of the Divine Name?[9]—He places his hand upon it. Then according to the Rabbis too, let him place his hand upon it?—He may chance to forget and remove it. Then according to R. Jose too, he may forget and remove it?—Rather [reply thus]. If a c reed is available, that is indeed so.[1] The discussion is about going

(2) Just as the fire may be arrested by a goatskin, so may it be arrested by water, seeing that it is not poured directly on the flame. (3) Such as water. (4) *Sc.* the lamp, which may not be handled on the Sabbath, and then the same applies to the board too; cf. *supra* 117*a* and note a.l. (5) By the draught. (6) That even an unintentional action is forbidden. (7) V. *supra* 75*a*, n. a8. (8) *Medurah* is a fire for heating, e.g., in the fire place, and the door is opened for the draught to fan it.

a (1) It is generally insufficient to fan it into a blaze, hence it is not a case of 'cut off his head' etc. (2) It will certainly make it burn up. (3) Because if that is permitted, one will think that the door may be opened even if an abnormal wind is blowing. (4) Lit., 'a cause of extinguishing'. (5) Kefar means a village or country town. The former was probably near Shiḥin in the vicinity of Sepphoris; the latter was a town in Galilee. The earthen vessels made there were fire proof. (6) This shows that he too permits only such. The Baraitha is thus not actually the reverse of the Mishnah, but generally speaking we see that R. Jose is more lenient in the former, whereas in the Mishnah he is more stringent (Tosaf.). (7) Thus R. Jose himself holds that even if they are likely to burst they are permitted, but he argues that even on the more stringent view of the Rabbis the vessels of Kefar Shiḥin etc. should be permitted too.

b (1) As assumed at present in order to prevent effacement of the Name. (2) Intentionally with his hands.—Thus the Rabbis forbid even an indirect action, whereas R. Jose forbids only a direct action. (3) Deut. XII, 3f. (4) Ex. XX, 9. (5) That the need of a reed according to the Rabbis is to prevent effacement. (6) Between the water and the flesh, which invalidates *ṭebillah*. (7) With which the Name is written. This interrupts the thread of argument: if you object to the reed because it is an interposition, what of the ink itself? (8) About the reed. Why do the Rabbis insist on a reed?—This difficulty is raised to show that the Rabbis' view has nothing to do with the question whether indirect action is permitted or not. (9) Surely not.

c (1) All agree that it must be used—even R. Jose, the reason being that one may not stand nude in the presence of the Name.

to seek a reed:[2] the Rabbis hold, [121a] *Ṭebillah* in its [due] time is not obligatory,[3] hence we seek [it]; whereas R. Jose holds, *Ṭebillah* in its [due] time is obligatory, hence we do not seek [it].

Now, does then R. Jose hold, *Ṭebillah* in its [due] time is obligatory? Surely it was taught: A *zab* and a *zabah*, a male leper and a female leper, he who cohabits with a *niddah*,[4] and he who is defiled through a corpse, [perform] their *ṭebillah* by day.[5] A *niddah* and woman in confinement [perform] their *ṭebillah* at night.[6] A *ba'al ḳeri*[7] must proceed with *ṭebillah* at any time of the day.[8] R. Jose said: [If the mishap happened] from *minḥah* and beyond he need not[9] perform *ṭebillah*.[10]—[The author of] that is R. Jose son of R. Judah who maintained: [One] *ṭebillah* at the end suffices for her.[11]

MISHNAH. IF A GENTILE COMES TO EXTINGUISH, WE DO NOT SAY TO HIM, 'EXTINGUISH IT' OR 'DO NOT EXTIN-
a GUISH,' BECAUSE HIS RESTING IS NOT OUR OBLIGATION.[1] BUT IF A MINOR COMES TO EXTINGUISH, WE MUST NOT PERMIT HIM,[2] BECAUSE HIS RESTING IS OUR OBLIGATION.

GEMARA. R. Ammi said: In the case of a conflagration they [the Rabbis] permitted one to announce, 'Whoever extinguishes [it] will not lose [thereby].' Shall we say that this supports him: IF A GENTILE COMES TO EXTINGUISH, WE DO NOT SAY TO HIM, 'EXTINGUISH' OR 'DO NOT EXTINGUISH,' BECAUSE HIS RESTING IS NOT OUR OBLIGATION: thus we [merely] may not say to him, 'Extinguish [it],' but we may say, 'Whoever extinguishes [it] will not lose [thereby].' Then consider the second clause: WE DO NOT SAY TO HIM, . . . 'DO NOT EXTINGUISH': but neither may we say to him, 'Whoever extinguishes [it] will not lose [thereby]?'[3] Rather no deduction can be made from this.[4]

Our Rabbis taught: It once happened that a fire broke out in the courtyard of Joseph b. Simai in Shiḥin, and the men of the garrison at Sepphoris[5] came to extinguish it, because he was a steward of the king.[6] But he did not permit them, in honour of the Sabbath, and a miracle happened on his behalf, rain descended and extinguished [it]. In the evening he sent two *sela'* to each of them, and fifty to their captain. But when the Sages heard of it they said, He did not need this, for we learnt: IF A GENTILE COMES TO EXTINGUISH, WE DO NOT SAY TO HIM, 'EXTINGUISH' OR 'DO NOT EXTINGUISH'.

BUT IF A MINOR COMES TO EXTINGUISH, WE MUST NOT PERMIT HIM, BECAUSE HIS RESTING IS OUR OBLIGATION. You may
b infer from this [that] if a minor eats *nebeloth*,[1] it is the duty of Beth din to restrain him?[2]—Said R. Joḥanan: This refers to a minor acting at his father's desire.[3] Then by analogy, in respect to the Gentile, he [too] acts at the Jew's desire: is this permitted? —A Gentile acts at his own desire.[4]

MISHNAH. A DISH MAY BE INVERTED OVER A LAMP, THAT THE BEAMS SHOULD NOT CATCH [FIRE], AND OVER AN INFANT'S EXCREMENT, AND OVER A SCORPION, THAT IT SHOULD NOT BITE. R. JUDAH SAID: AN INCIDENT CAME BEFORE R. JOḤANAN B. ZAKKAI IN ARAB,[5] AND HE SAID, I FEAR ON HIS ACCOUNT [THAT HE MAY BE LIABLE TO] A SIN-OFFERING.[6]

GEMARA. Rab Judah and R. Jeremiah b. Abba and R. Ḥanan b. Raba visited the home of Abin of Neshiḳya.[7] For Rab Judah

(2) I.e., whether one must postpone the *ṭebillah* until he obtains it. (3) Even an obligatory *ṭebillah* need not be performed just when it is due. (4) Which defiles him—such coition is strictly forbidden. (5) The seventh day from their defilement. They can perform *ṭebillah* any time after dawn, even if it is not yet seven full days of twenty-four hours each from the time of defilement, and even if this falls on the Day of Atonement. (6) The evening following the day which completes their period of uncleanness, the full period being required in their case. This holds good even if the evening belongs to the Day of Atonement. (7) Lit., 'one whom a mishap has befallen'—a euphemism for one who discharged semen. By Rabbinical law he requires *ṭebillah* before he can engage in the study of Torah. (8) Lit., 'the whole day'. Even if he discharged semen in the late afternoon of the Day of Atonement, he may perform *ṭebillah* on the same day and need not wait for the evening, because *ṭebillah* in its right time is obligatory. [A non-obligatory bath is prohibited on the Day of Atonement.] (9) [Var. lec. he may not, v. Tosaf. a.l.] (10) Because *ṭebillah* at its right time is not obligatory, which is the point of the objection. The circumstances here are that he has already recited all the prayers of the day (Tosaf.), or at least *minḥah*, while the *ne'ilah* (concluding) service may be recited at night. (11) The reference is to a woman who gave birth without knowing exactly when, what, and whether it was with or without a gonorrhoeic discharge. The first view is that all possibilities must be taken into account and she must perform *ṭebillah* at the due times posited by these. R. Jose b. R. Judah, however, rules that a single *ṭebillah*, performed at the end of the whole period that is in doubt, is sufficient, though actually the right time may have been earlier, for in any case *ṭebillah* at the time when it becomes due is not obligatory.

a (1) Lit., 'their obligation'. It is not the duty of Israelites to see that he rests on the Sabbath, hence we need not forbid him. On the other hand by Rabbinical law one must not instruct a Gentile to work—hence we may not tell him to extinguish the fire. (2) Lit., 'we do not hearken to him'. (3) For the second clause merely states that it is unnecessary to stop him, which implies, however, that one must not give him a hint to extinguish. (4) For one clause of the Mishnah must be exact, even in respect of its implication, whereas the other clause is not to be stressed so far, and it is not known which is exact. (5) [The Acropolis mentioned in Josephus, *Vita* 67]. (6) [Agrippa II, v. Klein, S., *Beiträge* p. 66, n. 1 and Graetz, *MGWJ*, 1881, p. 484].

b (1) V. Glos.; i.e., any forbidden food. (2) Lit., 'to keep him away'.—In Yeb. 114a this is in doubt. (3) But where he acts entirely of his own accord it may not be so. (4) Though he knows that the Jew too desires it, he may nevertheless act on his own accord. But a minor is more likely to be directly influenced by what he understands to be his father's wish. (5) [Near Sepphoris, v. Klein *Beiträge* p. 75]. (6) Since the snake was not pursuing him, his action may constitute trapping, which involves a sin-offering. (7) A town in Babylonia.

טבילה בזמנה לאו מצוה ומהדרינן ור' יוסי סבר טבילה בזמנה מצוה ולא מהדרינן וסבר ר' יוסי טבילה בזמנה מצוה *והתניא *הזב והזבה המצורע והמצורעת בועל נדה וטמא מת טבילתן ביום נדה ויולדת טבילתן בלילה בעל קרי טובל והולך כל היום כולו ר' יוסי אומר מן המנחה ולמעלה אינו *צריך לטבול ההיא ר' יוסי בר' יהודה היא *דאמר דייה טבילה באחרונה: **מתני'** *[ב]נכרי שבא לכבות אין אומרים לו כבה ואל תכבה מפני שאין שביתתו עליהן אבל קטן שבא לכבות אין שומעין לו מפני ששביתתו עליהן: **גמ'** *א"ר אמי [ג]בדליקה התירו לומר כל המכבה אינו מפסיד נימא מסייע ליה נכרי שבא לכבות אין אומרים לו כבה ואל תכבה מפני שאין שביתתו עליהן כבה הוא דלא אמרינן ליה הא כל המכבה אינו מפסיד אמרינן ליה אימא סיפא אל תכבה לא אמרינן ליה וכל המכבה אינו מפסיד נמי לא אמרינן ליה אלא *מהא ליכא למשמע מינה ת"ר *מעשה ונפלה דליקה בחצירו של יוסף בן סימאי בשיחין ובאו אנשי גיסטרא של ציפורי לכבות מפני שאפטרופוס של מלך היה ולא הניחן מפני כבוד השבת ונעשה לו נס וירדו גשמים וכיבו לערב שיגר לכל אחד מהן שתי סלעין ולאפרכוס שבהן חמשים וכששמעו חכמים בדבר אמרו לא היה צריך לכך שהרי שנינו נכרי שבא לכבות אין אומרים לו כבה ואל תכבה: אבל [ד]קטן שבא לכבות אין שומעין לו מפני ששביתתו עליהן: שמעת מינה *קטן אוכל נבלות ב"ד מצווין עליו להפרישו אמר רבי יוחנן [ה]בקטן העושה לדעת אביו דכוותה גבי נכרי דקא עביד לדעתיה דישראל מי שרי נכרי לדעתיה דנפשיה עביד: **מתני'** *[ו]כופין קערה על גבי הנר בשביל שלא תאחוז בקורה ועל צואה של קטן ועל עקרב שלא תישך *א"ר יהודה מעשה בא לפני רבן יוחנן בן זכאי בערב ואמר חוששני לו מחטאת: **גמ'** רב יהודה ורב ירמיה בר אבא ורב חנן בר רבא איקלעו לבי אבין דמן נשיקא לרב יהודה ורב ירמיה בר אבא אייתו

רש"י

טבילה בזמנה מצוה. דכתיב והיה לפנות ערב ירחץ במים (דברים כג): לאו מצוה. ואי לא משכח גמי אהדרנא לישתהי עד למחר ולמ"ד לאו מצוה קרא עצה טובה קמ"ל כדי שיעריב שמשו ביום לאחר טבילה שאם ימתין לטבול עד הלילה לא יהא לו הערב שמש עד ליל המחרת: הזב והזבה כו'. ברייתא זו אגב יוה"כ שנויה בתוספתא דיומא (פ"ד): הזב והזבה והמצורע ובועל נדה וטמא מת טובלין ביום. משהאיר המזרח ביום השביעי שלהם וטעמא(א) בפ"ב דמגילה (דף כ.) מקרא דביום השביעי מקצת שביעי ספירה ואם חל שביעי שלהם ביוה"כ טובלין כדרכן לאכול תרומה לערב: נדה ויולדת. טובלות כדרכן בלילי יוה"כ אם חל שביעי שלהם בערב יוה"כ שאינה יכולה לטבול ביום ז' דכתיב בה תהיה בנדתה בהוייתה תהא כל ז' (פסחים דף צ:): בעל קרי. שצריך טבילה לדברי תורה מדברי סופרים ואפי' אין (ב) אוכל טהרות לבו ביום: טובל כל היום כולו. ואע"פ שראה קרי מן המנחה ולמעלה לאחר שהתפלל תפלת המנחה שהרי הוא יכול להמתין עד שתחשך ויטבול לתפלת ערבית אפ"ה טובל ביו"כ מבעוד יום אע"פ שאסור ברחיצת הרשות דטבילה בזמנה מצוה: ר' יוסי אומר מן המנחה ולמעלה. אם ראה קרי לאחר שהתפלל תפלת מנחה שהרי הוא יכול להמתין עד שתחשך ויטבול ויתפלל תפלת ערבית ותפלת נעילה נמי ס"ל שיכול להתפלל בלילה כרב דאמר (יומא דף פז:) תפלת נעילה פוטרת של ערבית: אין צריך לטבול. ביום משום זמן טבילה דלאו מצוה לטבילה בזמנה: דייה לטבילה שתהא באחרונה. במסכת נדה בפרק המפלת גבי אשה שיצאה מלאה ובאה ריקנית ואינה יודעת מתי ילדה דמצרכינן לה נ"ה טבילות לספק ד' טבילות שעליה טבילת זכר לז' או טבילת נקבה לשבועיים ובלילה או שמא יולדת זכר בזוב וצריכה אף טבילת זבה ביום שבעה לספורים שלה או יולדת נקבה בזוב היתה ומשום דלא ידעינן מתי ילדה ואימתי מטי זמן טבילה דידה מצרכינן לה טבילה כל לילה וכל יום שיש לספוקי בזמן טבילתה ופליג ר' יוסי ברבי יהודה עלה ואמר דייה לטבילה שתהא באחרונה לסוף ספורים של נקבה דהיינו לסוף שלש שבועים שאם ילדה נקבה בזוב טמאה שבועיים ללידתה וז' נקיים בשביל הזיבה ולא אמרינן טבילה בזמנה מצוה: **מתני'** אין אומרים לו כבה. °אמירה לנכרי משום שבות: ולא תכבה. אין צריך למחות בידו אלא יניחנו ויכבה: שאין שביתתו. של נכרי עליהן דישראל אינו מוזהר על שביתתו של נכרי שאינו עבדו: **גמ'** כבה הוא דלא אמרינן ליה. שעושהו שלוחו ממש: הא כל המכבה אינו מפסיד כו'. ונכרי מדעתיה דידיה עביד שריא: אל תכבה הוא דלא אמרינן ליה. שאינו צריך למחות בידו ומיהו גילוי דעתא דלא יפסיד בדבר נמי לא משתרי דאי גילוי דעתא שרי למה ליה למיתני סיפא אין צריך למחות: אלא מהכא ליכא למישמע מיניה. דודאי מתניתין לאו כולה דוקא אלא חדא מינייהו דוקא או רישא או סיפא ותנא אידך אטו ההיא ולא ידעינן הי מינייהו דוקא דנגמר מיניה: גיסטרא. שלטון: אפטרופוס. ממונה על ממונו: שמעת מינה קטן אוכל נבילות בית דין מצווין להפרישו. ותקשי לר' יוחנן *דאמר ביבמות (דף קיד.) לרבה בר בר חנה דאירכסו ליה מפתחות של בית המדרש ברשות הרבים בשבת דבר טלי' וטליא ליטיילי התם דאי משכחי להו מייתי להו: על דעת אביו. בקטן שידע להבחין שהכבוי זה נוח לאביו ועושה בשבילו: נכרי אדעתיה דנפשיה עביד. ואפילו יודע שנוח לו לישראל הוא להנאת עצמו מתכוין שיודע שלא יפסיד: **מתני'** כופין קערה. של חרס: על גבי הנר. ובלבד שלא יכבה ואע"פ שנוטל כלי להצלת קורה שאינה ניטלת בשבת הא אותבינן מינה (דף מג.) לרבי יצחק דאמר אין כלי ניטל אלא לדבר הניטל ושנייה בצריך למקומו: מעשה בא. כפיית כלי על עקרב: בערב. מקום: חוששני לו מחטאת. כיון דלא היה עקרב רץ אחריו איני יודע אם חייב משום צידה אם לאו וחוששני לומר חייב חטאת הוא: אייתו

תוספות

הכי גרסי' ר' יוסי אומר מן המנחה ולמעלה אינו צריך לטבול· וכן גירסת רש"י ור"ת אבל לא גרסי' אינו יכול לטבול דאפי' מאן דסבר טבילה בזמנה לאו מצוה °שרי לטבול כדמשמע בסוף מסכת יומא (דף פז:) דפריך לרב דאמר תפלת נעילה פוטרת של ערבית משום דקסבר דתפלת נעילה בלילה והתניא אור יוה"כ כו' נעילה מתפלל שבע ומתודה בערבית כו' ומשני תנאי היא דתניא כל חייבי טבילות טבילתן ביום נדה ויולדת טובלין בלילה בעל קרי טובל והולך עד המנחה דסבר תפלת נעילה בלילה וטבילה בזמנה לאו מצוה ר' יוסי אומר כל היום כולו טובל דתפלת נעילה ביום אלמא אע"ג דת"ק סבר דטבילה בזמנה לאו מצוה אפ"ה קתני כל חייבי טבילות טבילתן ביום אפילו טמא מת וטמא שרץ שאין צריכין טבילה לתפלה יכולין לטבול והא דפירש בקונטרס דר' יוסי כרב דאמר תפלת נעילה בלילה לא דק דבשלהי יומא (דף פח.) פריך מהך ברייתא דר' יוסי אדר"י דהכא קאמר מן המנחה ולמעלה א"צ לטבול ובההיא קאמר כל היום ומשני דהכא איירי בדצלי כבר תפלת נעילה והתם בדלא צלי ובכולהו רבי יוסי דלא כרב: **רבי** יוסי בר' יהודה היא. וא"ת א"כ בשילהי יומא (דף פח.) מנא ליה לרב דהוא ת"ק דברייתא קמייתא דקאמר דבעל קרי טובל עד המנחה אתי כוותיה דתפלת נעילה בלילה דילמא איירי בדצלי וטבילה בזמנה לאו מצוה ור' יוסי סבר מצוה ותנא קמא דהכא הוא ר' יוסי דהתם ויש לומר דסבר דר' יוסי דהכא ודהתם מסתמא חד תנא הוא ותרווייהו רבי יוסי ברבי יהודה דאיירי בטבילת בעל קרי ביוה"כ וא"כ קשיא ר' יוסי בר' יהודה אדר' יוסי בר' יהודה וע"כ אית לן לשנויי הא דצלי והא דלא צלי: **אין** אומרים לו כבה. אפי' באיסור דרבנן אמירה לנכרי שבות כדאמרינן לקמן בפרק שואל (דף קנ.) לא יאמר אדם לחבירו שכור לי פועלים כו' דמוקי לה בחברו נכרי וכן מוכח בפרק הדר (דף סז:) גבי נייתי חמימי מגו ביתא: **אלא** מהא ליכא למישמע מינה. מ"מ קי"ל כר' אמי ובירושלמי אמר שעשה ר' אמי מעשה כזה: **שמע** מינה קטן אוכל נבלות בית דין מצווין עליו להפרישו. נ"ל דמוקי מתניתין כרבי יהודה דאמר מלאכה שאינה צריכה לגופה חייב עליה או כר"ש וכשצריך לאותו כיבוי כגון לעשות פחמין דבאיסורא דרבנן מוכח בפרק חרש (יבמות קיד.) דאין ב"ד מצווין להפרישו ונראה דמיירי בקטן שלא הגיע לחינוך דבהגיע לחינוך כיון שחייב לחנכו כ"ש דצריך להפרישו שלא יעשה עבירה וכל הנהו דפריך ביבמות הוה מצי לשנויי כשהגיע לחינוך אלא דניחא ליה לאוקמי בכל ענין והא דבעי לאיתויי התם דאין ב"ד מצווין להפרישו מדקתני תינוק יונק והולך וקתני ובגדול אסור משמע דוקא גדול אבל קטן אפי' בהגיע לחינוך שרי התם ע"כ גדול לאו דוקא בר עונשין דהא במסקנא מפרש טעמא משום דסתם תינוק מסוכן הוא אצל חלב והאי טעמא לא שייך אלא בבן שתים או שלש שנים: כל

מסורת הש"ס

פסחים ו: יומא ו. פח. ע"ש [תוספתא יומא פ"ד ע"ש]

[צ"ל יכול וכ"א ביומא פח.]

יבמות קיד.

כתובות ע:

[ברכות כב. וש"נ]

יבמות קיד. נדה מו: [גיטין נה.]

לעיל מג. קז.

[לקמן קמו.]

הגהות הב"ח

(א) רש"י ד"ה הזב והזבה והמצורע וכו' וטעמא מפרש בפ"ב דמגילה: (ב) ד"ה בעל קרי וכו' אוכל טהרות הס"ד ומיהו לבו ביום נמחק:

וכן פירש הר"ן ותקשי לר' יוחנן וכו' וכבר העיר הב"י בטור או"ח סי' שמג דבתוספתות דידן איתא בהוא עובדא דמפתחות ר' פדת ור' יוחנן ספוקי מספקא ליה ועי' בכ"מ סוף הלכות מאכלות אסורות הלכה כז

עין משפט נר מצוה

סט א מיי' פ"א מהלכות מקואות הלכה ו ופ"ג מהלכות שביתת עשור הלכה ב ג ופ"ד מהלכות איסורי ביאה הלכה ו סמג עשין רמג טוש"ע או"ח סימן תקנד סעיף ח וסי' תרגג סעיף יא יב וטוש"ע יו"ד סימן קנז סעיף ג וסימן שפא סעיף ה [מרי"ף פ"ב דשבועות דף רלב וברא"ש בהלכות מקואות סי' לו]:

ע ב מיי' פ"ו מהלכות שבת הלכה ד ופי"ב הלכה ז סמג לאוין סה טוש"ע או"ח סימן שלד. סעיף כה:

עא ג מיי' פי"ב שם וסמג שם טוש"ע שם סעיף כו:

עב ד ה מיי' פי"ב שם ופכ"ד הלי"א ופי"ז מהל' מאכלות אסורו' הל' כז כח ופ"ג מהלכות אבל הלכה יב סמג שם ולאוין קמח טוש"ע שם סעיף כה וסימן שמג וטוש"ע יו"ד סימן שעג סעיף א בהגה"ה:

עג ו מיי' פי"ב הלכות שבת הלכה ד סמג לאוין סה טוש"ע או"ח סימן רעז סעיף ה וסימן שלד סעיף כג בהגה"ה:

רבינו חננאל

גרם מחיקת שם משום דאמר לך התם עשייה אסור גרמא שרי רבנן בשבת גרמא כמו מלאכת מחשבת היא ואסור. ואע"ג דכתיב לא תעשה כל מלאכה. (כל מלאכה)מדאורייתא עשייה אסורה מיהו גזרו רבנן אפי' גרמא משום דקי"ל אדם בהול על ממונו אי שרית ליה אתי לכבויי. תוב אקשינן דרבנן אדרבנן התם בגרם מחיקת השם מצרכי ליה נמי לח. והכא שרו בגרם כיבוי. ואקשינן עלה האי נמי לח היכי דמי אי דקטור ומיהדק הוא גופיה חייץ בטבילה. ואי לא מיהדק עיילי ביה מיא ומסקי לשם ולא מהני נמי לח לשם שכתוב על בשרו מידי ולא איפרקא הא קושיא. תוב אקשינן עליה ותיפוק ליה דדיו גופיה שהשם כתוב בו שחוצץ. ופרקינן הב"ע בדיו לחה שאינ' חוצצת. דתניא הדם והדיו והדבש והחלב יבישין חוצצין לחים אין חוצצין. ופרקי' על קושיא הראשונה רבנן דאסרי לטבול עד דכריך על השם נמי לח לאו משום דסבירא להו גרם מחיקת השם אסור דכל גרמא שרי. והכא משום דאסור לעמוד בפני השם ערום מצריכי נמי לח. וכיון דלא צריך אלא לכסויי השם ומסילא ידעינן שאין מהדק הנמי לח ולא איכפת ליה אי עיילי מיא דלא חייש לגרם מחיקה. ואקשינן וכי ר' יוסי מתיר לעמוד בפני השם. ושנינן לר' יוסי מכסהו לשם בידו ויטבול. אי הכי לרבנן נמי ניכסייה בידית ונדחות זה הפירוק. ופרקינן לדברי הכל אסור לעמוד בפני השם ערום. ואי איכא נמי וכיוצא בו לכרוך על השם ולטבול בזמניה דכ"ע דכריך. כי פליגי היכא דליכא מידי מצוי וצריך להדורי ולאתויי. ר' יוסי אומר טבילה בזמנו מצוה ואתיא מצוה זו ודחה לעמידת ערום בפני השם וטביל בדלא מיכסי*). ורבנן סברי טבילה בזמנה לאו מצוה הלכך לא הדרי. ואקשינן איני דהי' יוסי סבר טבילה בזמנה מצוה והתנן בעל קרי טובל כל היום כולו. ר' יוסי אומר מן המנחה ולמעלה אינו צריך לטבול ואוקימנא **) בדצלי. ואמרינן אי צלי ליה מנחה מקמי דליחזי קרי מ"ט דרבנן דמחייבי ליה למיטבל

*) נראה דצ"ל כאן ולא בעי לאהדורי אגמי ורבנן סברי טבילה בזמנה לאו מצוה הלכך בעי אהדורי. **) לפנינו בגמ' ליתא להך אוקימתא אולי כוונתו להסוגיא דיומא דף פ"ח ע"ב.

רב נסים גאון ההיא ר' יוסי בר' יהודה היא דתניא ר' יוסי בר' יהודה אומר דייה לטבילה באחרונה משכחת לה במס' נדה (דף כט) בפרק המפלת: שמעת מינה קטן אוכל נבילות בית דין מצווין עליו

גליון הש"ס רש"י ד"ה אין אומרים לו וכו' אמירה לנכרי משום שבות. עי' ע"ז דף טו ע"א ברש"י ד"ה נכי דלרביעה: תוס' ד"ה ה"ג וכו' שרי לטבול כדמשמע. ע"ל דף קיח ע"א תוס' ד"ה לא ס"ד:

עד א מיי' פ"ט מהלכות י"ט הלכה יד טוש"ע או"ח סימן שח סעיף טו:
עה ב ג מיי' פכ"ו מהל' שבת הלכה יג סמג לאוין סה טוש"ע או"ח סימן שח סעיף לד:
עו ד ה מיי' פי"א שם הלכה ד סמג שם טור ש"ע או"ח סימן שטז סעיף י:
עז ו מיי' פכ"א שם הלכה ב ופכ"ו הלכה יג סמג שם טור או"ח שם סעיף יא:
עח ז ח מיי' פ"א מהלכות שבת הל"ד סמג שם טור ש"ע שם סעיף ז:
עט ט מיי' פכ"ה מהל' שבת הלכה יא טור ש"ע או"ח סימן רעט סעיף ז:

כל המזיקין נהרגין בשבת. אף על גב דתנן במתניתין ועל עקרב שלא ישוך איצטריך לאשמעינן דהריגה נמי שרינן דסלקא דעתך דאסירא משום דמיפרסמא מילתא טפי מצידה ומהאי טעמא נמי פליג רב הונא בסמוך ואסר הריגה:

ברצין אחריו וד"ה. פי' בקונט' דרבי יהושע בן לוי ברצין אחריו ואי פקוח נפש וברייתא באין רצין וכר"ש וקשה דא"כ תקשה מהך ברייתא לרבא בר רב הונא דשרי להרוג נחשים ועקרבים בשבת דע"כ באין רצין אחריו מיירי דאי ברצין אחריו אמאי אין רוח חסידים נוחה הימנו לפירוש הקונטרס דברצין אחריו איכא פקוח נפש ועוד בגיותי שהרג נחש ומיבעיא לן אי שפיר עבד תיפשוט מהכא דלא שרינן לר"ש באין רצין אלא ה' בלבד ועוד קשה לר"י דלישנא דהכא מתרצנא לה משמע לברייתא עצמה ונראה לר"י לפרש דברייתא ברצין אחריו וד"ה פירוש אפילו ר' יהודה מודה דחמשה שרי להרוג ברצין אחריו אבל שאר אסור להורגן אפילו רצין אחריו לר' יהודה ור' יהושע בן לוי כר"ש דשרי שאר(א) אפילו באין רצין אחריו ורב הונא דאסר בסמוך לא סבר כרבי יהושע בן לוי ונראה לר"י וכן פירש ר"ח שאין להקל כרבי יהושע בן לוי אלא כהנהו אמוראי דלקמן דלא שרו אלא בדריסה לפי תומו:

גמ' איתו להו פורייתא לרב חנן בר רבא לא אייתו ליה אשכחיה מתני ליה לבריה ועל צואה של קטן מפני קטן א"ל אבין שטיא מתני שטותא לבניה והלא היא עצמה מוכנת לכלבים וכ"ת דלא חזיא ליה מאתמול והתניא נהרות המושכין ומעיינות הנובעין הרי הן כרגלי כל אדם ואלא היכי אתנייה אימא על צואה של תרנגולים מפני קטן ותיפוק ליה דהוי גרף של רעי וכ"ת גרף של רעי אגב מנא אין איהו גופיה לא והא ההוא עכבר דאישתכח באיספרמקי דרב אשי ואמר להו נקוטו בצוציתיה ואפקוה באשפה וקטן באשפה מאי בעי ליה בחצר חצר נמי גרף של רעי הוא [א] באשפה שבחצר: ועל עקרב שלא תישך: א"ר יהושע בן לוי כל המזיקין נהרגין בשבת מתיב רב יוסף חמשה נהרגין בשבת ואלו הן זבוב שבארץ מצרים וצירעה שבנינוה ועקרב שבחדייב ונחש שבא"י וכלב שוטה בכל מקום מני אילימא ר' יהודה הא אמר מלאכה שאינה צריכה לגופה חייב עליה אלא לאו ר"ש והני הוא דשרי אחריני לא אמר ר' ירמיה ומאן נימא לן דהא מתרצתא היא דילמא משבשתא היא אמר רב יוסף אנא מתנינא לה ואותיבנא לה ואנא מתריצנא לה ברצו אחריו ודברי הכל תני תנא קמיה דרבא בר רב הונא ההורג נחשים ועקרבים בשבת אין רוח חסידים נוחה הימנו א"ל ואותן חסידים אין רוח חכמים נוחה מהם ופליגא דרב הונא דרב הונא חזייה להההוא גברא דקא קטיל זיבורא א"ל שלימתינהו לכולהו ת"ר נזדמנו לו נחשים ועקרבים הרגן בידוע שנזדמנו לו להורגן לא הרגן בידוע שנזדמנו להורגו ונעשה לו נס מן השמים אמר עולא ואיתימא רבה בר בר חנה א"ר יוחנן בנישופין בו א"ר אבא בר כהנא פעם אחת נפל אחד בבהמ"ד ועמד ניותי אחד והרגו אמר רבי פגע בו כיוצא בו איבעיא להו פגע בו כיוצא בו דשפיר עביד או לא ת"ש דר' אבא בריה דר' חייא בר אבא ור' זירא הוו יתבי אקילעא דבי ר' ינאי נפק מילתא מבינייהו בעו מיניה מר' ינאי מהו להרוג נחשים ועקרבים בשבת אמר להו צירעה אני הורג נחש ועקרב לא כ"ש דילמא לפי תומו דאמר רב יהודה רוק דורסו לפי תומו ואמר רב ששת נחש דורסו לפי תומו ואמר רב קטינא עקרב דורסו לפי תומו אבא בר מרתא דהוא אבא בר מניומי הוה מסקי ביה דבי ריש גלותא זוזי אייתוהו קא מצערא ליה הוה שדי רוקא אמר להו ריש גלותא אייתו מאנא סחיפו עלויה אמר להו לא צריכתו הכי א"ר יהודה רוק דורסו לפי תומו אמר להו צורבא מרבנן הוא שבקוהו אמר ר' אבא בר כהנא א"ר חנינא פמוטות של בית רבי מותר לטלטלן בשבת א"ל ר' זירא בניטלין בידו אחת או בשתי ידים א"ל

גמ' איתו להו פורייתא. מטות לישב עליהן: לא אייתו ליה. והושיבוהו לארץ: מפני קטן. שלא יטפח בו ויתלכלך: א"ל. רב חנן שהיה כעוס ומתכוין להקניטו לר' אבין: והלא מוכנת לכלבים. ולמה לי לכפות כלי יפנוה משם שהרי ראויה לטלטל: דלא חזיא מאתמול. שהיום נולדה: נהרות המושכים כרגלי כל אדם. משום דמידי דנייד הוא ולא קני שביתה ואע"פ שבא מתוך לתחום כל אדם מוליכן למקום שעירב לו לילך מיהו שמעינן מינה דמותרין בטלטול ואע"ג דמאתמול לא הוי הכי קמן כיון דאורחייהו בהכי דעתיה עלייהו ה"נ כיון דאורחיה דקטן בהכי דעתיה עליה דלכי תיתי יאכילנה לכלבים: א"ל ר' אבין. ואלא היכי אתנייה: צואה של תרנגולים. דלא חזיא לכלבים ושל קטן דקתני מתניתין שמטפח בה קטן קאמר ובשביל הקטן אמר כופין: תיפוק ליה דגרף של רעי הוא. דמאיס ולפנייה דהא קי"ל במסכת ביצה גרף של רעי מותר להוציאו לאשפה: וכי תימא גרף של רעי דמותר אגב מנא אין. הא דקי"ל מותר להוציאו משום דרמי במנא דגרף הייט כלי חרס העשוי לכך ואגב מנא הוא דשרי לטלטולי אבל בפני עצמו לא והכא לאו במנא רמי: באספרמקי. בשמים: בצוציתיה. בזנבו אלמא בלאו מנא נמי מטלטלי ליה: ומשני באשפה. דלא רמי קמייהו ולא גרף של רעי הוא: קטן באשפה מאי בעי. סתם אשפה ברה"ר הוא ומאי בעי קטן התם דקא מיכסי ליה בשביל קטן: ומשני בחצר. דשכיח קטן התם קס"ד בחצר דלאו אשפה וקפריך סוף סוף גרף של רעי הוא ומשני באשפה שבחצר: כל המזיקין. ההורגין: נהרגין בשבת. וקס"ד אפי' אין רצין אחריו ומשום דס"ל כר"ש דמלאכה שאינה צריכה לגופה מדרבנן היא דאסירא והכא לא גזור: (נהרגין בשבת. אפי' אין רצין אחריו) משום דס"ל דסתמן הורגין הן: הא אמר חייב עליה. והיכי שרי במלאכה גמורה כשאין רצין אחריו דליכא פקוח נפש: ומאן לימא לן ט'. דרב יוסף הוא מתני ליה כדלקמן ולא בדבי ר' חייא ור' אושעיא מיתנייא וכל מתניתא דלא מתנייא בתוספתא דר' חייא ור' אושעיא איכא לספוקי במשבשתא ולא מותבינן מינה: אנא תנינא לה. במתניתא דידי ואנא אותבינא בבי מדרשא אדר' יהושע בן לוי: ואנא מתרצנא לה. דלא תיקשי כי אמר ר' יהושע בן לוי כל המזיקין נהרגין ברצין אחריו קאמר דפקוח נפש הוא: ודברי הכל. ואפי' לר' יהודה והא דחמשה נהרגין כשאין רצין אחריו ור' שמעון: אין רוח חסידים נוחה הימנו. דעתן של חסידים אינה מעורבת עמו שאין הגון בעיניהם על מה שעשה: נוחה. עריבה אין מתרצין במעשיו: אמר ליה. רבא לתנא: ואותן חסידים. הנוהגין אותו על כך אין רוח חכמים עריבה עמהם להיות נוחה ומיושבת במה שרואין במדת חסידים הללו דשפיר עביד דאי לא מזיקין השתא סופן להזיק בשעת כעסן: שלימתינהו לכולהו. הרגת את כולן כלומר מה אהני בהא אכתי טובא איכא אלמא לאו שפיר עבד והא דרבא פליג אדאבוה: שנזדמנו לו להורגן. לכך באו לידו שזימן לו המקום לאבדן לפי שהיו עתידות להזיק וגלגלו זכות על ידי זכאי: לא הרגן בידוע שנזדמנו לו להרוג אותו. והראה לו הקב"ה שחטא אלא שנעשה לו נס: בנישופין בו. בכה"ג קתני בידוע שנזדמנו להורגו נישופין כן דרך הנחש עושה כעין שריקה כשהוא רואה שונאו וכועס: ניותי. על שם מקומו וישראל היה: דשפיר עביד. וכיוצא בו דקאמר לאו לנגחי הוא אלא הנחש רודף ונעשה זה כיוצא בו: או לא. וכיוצא בו דקאמר לנגחי הוא: לרעה אני הורג. בשבת לכלות מזיקין ואף על פי שאינה מועדת כאלו: לא כל שכן. אלמא שפיר עביד: דילמא לפי תומו. לא שיעמוד עליו ויהרגנו להדיא אלא כשהוא הולך לתומו ונחש או עקרב בפניו אין צריך לישמט ממנו אלא דורסו והולך ואם מת בדריכתו ימות הואיל ולא נתכוין דדבר שאין מתכוין לר' יהודה מדרבנן הוא ולענין מזיקין לא גזור: רוק דורסו לפי תומו. שאין מתכוין למרח ולאשוויי גומות דאף על גב דממילא ממרח הוא כי לא מיכוין שרי משום מאיסותא: הוה שדי רוקא. היה רוק מוטל לפניהם ושבת היתה: פמוטות. מנורות ולא של חוליות היו: של

ביצה לב. עירובין מ.מת. [תוספתא ביצה פ"ד]

ביצה לו:

[לעיל עג וש"נ]

[פסחים נט:]

[יומא פד. יבמות קכ.]

[פ"ל ואמר]

הגהות הב"ח

(א) תוס' ד"ה ברצין וכו' כר' שמעון דשרי שאר מזיקין אפילו:

הגהות הגר"א

[א] גמ' באשפה שבחצר כו' נ"ב גירסת הרי"ף בחצר אחרת:

גליון הש"ס

גמ' והלא היא עצמה מוכנת לכלבים. ע"ל דף יע ע"ב תוס' ד"ה שמן: רש"י ד"ה דלמא לפי תומו וכו' דדבר שאין מתכוין לר"י מדרבנן. ע"ל דף מא ע"ב תוס' ד"ה מיחם:

רבינו חננאל

ביומא ליתעכב עד לאורתא ולטבול. ומסקינן משום דסברי רבנן אע"ג דצלי ליה טבילה בזמנה מצוה ור' יוסי סבר טבילה בזמנה לאו מצוה היא האי ר' יוסי בר' יהודה דגרסינן בנדה פרק המפלת בענין טועה. ר' יוסי בר"י אומר דייה לטבול באחרונה דקסבר טבילה בזמנה לאו מצוה היא. וזה רבי יוסי דהיה (אומר) שם כתוב על בשרו. אסיקנא בגמרא דשבעת ימים (ביומא דף ז') דטבילה בזמנה מצוה פליגי ונתבררה בסוף יום הכפורים דהא לר' יוסי בר"י יהודה היא ואיכא אהריתי התם לר' יוסי דאמר כל היום כולו כשר לטבילה. דאלמא סבר טבילה בזמנה מצוה] היא: א"ר אמי בדליקה התירו לומר כל המכבה אינו מפסיד. וכן הלכה: נכרי שבא לכבות אין אומרים לו כבה ואל תכבה אלא מניחין אותו. ואין אומרים לו כבה וגם אין מונעין אותו מלכבות. אבל קטן העושה לדעת אין מניחין אותו לכבות: אריב"ל כל המזיקין נהרגין. אסיקנא כשהן רצין אחריו. אבל אין רצין אחריו אין נהרגין אלא אלו בלבד. זבוב שבארץ מצרים. וצירעה שבנינוה ועקרב שבחדייב ונחש שבא"י וכלב שוטה בכ"מ. פי' נישופין כדכתיב הוא ישופך ראש ואתה תשופנו עקב: רוק וכן נחש וכן עקרב אם דורסן לפי תומן שפיר דמי ושרי: א"ר חנינא פמוטות של בית רבי מותר לטלטלן בשבת. א"ל ר' זירא בניטלין בידו אחת

רב נסים גאון

להפריש מאי דשקלינן וטרינן בהא מילתא איתא במס' יבמות (דף קיד) בפרק החרש שנשא פיקחת: סוף סוף גרף של רעי הוא ונפקיה כבר פירשנו בפרק כירה כי עיקר השמועה שיש בה התרת זה הדבר בפרק משילין פירות (ביצה דף לו): ר' יהודה אומר כל מלאכה שאינה צריכה לגופה חייב עליה כבר פירשנוה בפרק יציאות השבת ואמרנו כי עיקרה הן דברי ר' יהודה שאמרם כאן בזו המשנה מעשה בא לפני

and R. Jeremiah b. Abba [121*b*] couches were brought; for R. Ḥanan b. Raba none was brought.[8] Now, he found him reciting to his son, AND OVER AN INFANT'S EXCREMENT, on account of the infant.[9] Said he to him, 'Abin! a fool recites nonsense to his son:[10] surely that itself is fit for dogs!'[11] And should you say a that it was not fit for him from yesterday,[1] surely it was taught: Flowing rivers and gushing springs are as the feet of all men?[2] Then how shall I recite it?—Say: Over the excrement of fowls, on account of an infant.[3] But deduce it[4] because it is [as] a vessel for excrements.[5] And should you answer, The vessel of excrements is only [permitted] in virtue of the utensil,[6] yet that itself may not [be carried out],—but a mouse was found in R. Ashi's spices, and he said to them [his servants], 'Take it by the tail and throw it out?'[7]—This refers to a dung heap.[8] But what business has an infant with a dung heap?[9]—It is in the courtyard.[10] But in a courtyard too it is a vessel of excrements?—It refers to a dung heap in the courtyard.

AND OVER A SCORPION, THAT IT SHOULD NOT BITE. R. Joshua b. Levi said: All [animals, etc.] that cause injury[11] may be killed on the Sabbath. R. Joseph objected: Five may be killed on the Sabbath, and these are they: the Egyptian fly, the hornet of Nineweh, the scorpion of Adiabene,[12] the snake in Palestine, and a mad dog anywhere. Now, who [is the authority?] Shall we say, R. Judah? Surely he maintains, One is guilty on account of a labour b not required for itself?[1] Hence it must be R. Simeon, and only these are permitted, but not others?—Said R. Jeremiah, And who tells us that this is correct: perhaps it is corrupt? Said R. Joseph: I recited it and I raised the objection, and I can answer it: This is where they are pursuing him, and is unanimous.[2]

A Tanna recited before Raba son of R. Huna: If one kills snakes or scorpions on the Sabbath, the spirit of the pious[3] is displeased with him. He retorted, And as to those pious men, the spirit of the Sages is displeased with *them*. Now, he disagrees with R. Huna, for R. Huna saw a man kill a wasp. Said he to him, 'Have you wiped them all out?'[4]

Our Rabbis taught: If one chances upon snakes and scorpions, and he kills them, it is manifest that he had chanced upon them in order to kill them; if he does not kill them, it is manifest that he had chanced upon them that they should kill him, but that a miracle was performed by Heaven on his behalf. 'Ulla said:—others state, Rabbah b. Bar Ḥanah said in R. Joḥanan's name—That is when they hiss at him.[5]

R. Abba b. Kahana said: One [of them] once fell in the Beth Hamidrash, and a Nabatean[6] arose and killed it.[7] Said Rabbi: A similar one must have attacked him. The scholars asked: 'A similar one must have attacked him' [means] that he had done well, or not?[8]—Come and hear: For R. Abba, son of R. Ḥiyya b. Abba, and R. Zera were sitting in the anteroom of R. Jannai's academy, [when] something issued from between them.[9] [So] they asked R. Jannai: May one kill snakes and scorpions on the Sabbath?—Said he to them: I kill a hornet, how much more so snakes and c scorpions! But perhaps that is [only] incidentally,[1] for Rab Judah said: One can tread down saliva incidentally:[2] and R. Shesheth said, One can tread down a snake incidentally, and R. Kaṭṭina said, One may tread down a scorpion incidentally.[3]

Abba b. Martha, who is Abba b. Minyomi, owed money to the house of the Resh Galutha. [So] they brought him [before the Resh Galutha]; he distressed him [and] he[4] spat out saliva,[5] [whereupon] the Resh Galutha ordered, 'Bring a vessel and cover it'. Said he to them, 'You do not need this, [for] thus did Rab Judah say: One can tread down saliva incidentally.' 'He is a scholar,' remarked he [the Resh Galutha]; 'let him go'.

R. Abba b. Kahana said in R. Ḥanina's name: The candlesticks[6] of Rabbi's household may be handled on the Sabbath. R. Zera asked him: [Does that mean] where they can be taken

(8) He had to sit on the ground. (9) To prevent him from dabbling with it. (10) This rude remark was made in spleen at his host's discourtesy. (11) *Mukeneth*, Lit., 'stands prepared'. Hence it may be handled and therefore one can carry it out altogether; why then overturn a dish upon it?

a (1) *Sc.* Friday; thus it is newly-created, as it were, on the Sabbath (technically called *nolad* v. Glos.), and as such may not be handled. (2) On the Sabbath or Festival an article may be carried, where carrying is permitted through an *'erub*, only where its owner may go, i.e., it is 'as the feet of its owner'. But this does not apply to the water of a flowing river, and every man may carry it whither he himself may go, though not all may go to the same place (v. Beẓ. 39*a*). Now, that which comes on the Sabbath from without the *teḥum* (v. Glos.) may not be taken anywhere within the *teḥum*. But although the water of a flowing river does come from without, it may be carried within. This shows that though that particular water was not there on the Friday, it is regarded as fit on the Sabbath, because it was naturally expected. Hence the same applies to the excrement: though it did not exist before the Sabbath, it was expected, and therefore may be handled, seeing that it can be put to a legitimate use. (3) V. *supra* n. b9. But this may not be handled itself, because it is not fit for dogs.—He interprets the Mishnah thus. (4) That one may carry it out. (5) Which may be cleared away on account of its repulsiveness. (6) Which contains the excrements. (7) And a mouse is the same as excrement. (8) Which stands apart. (9) Which was usually in the street. (10) It is now assumed that this refers to the excrement, not the dung heap. (11) Rashi: that kill. (12) A district of Assyria between the rivers Lycus and Caprus.

b (1) *Supra* 12*a*, 31*b*; the present killing falls within the same category. (2) I.e., R. Joshua's statement refers to this case. But in the Baraitha they are not pursuing him, and it is taught on R. Simeon's view. (3) Heb. *ḥasidim*. Here probably no particular sect is meant. Weiss, *Dor*, I, 109, maintains that the early *Ḥasidim* are probably referred to. (4) Sarcastically. I.e., you have achieved nothing, and should not have done it on the Sabbath. (5) Otherwise it is not to be assumed that they were meant to kill him. (6) Rashi, a Jew from Nabatea. (7) This was on a Sabbath. (8) Did Rabbi speak seriously or sarcastically? (9) Or, the question came up (for discussion) between them.

c (1) Lit., 'in one's simplicity'—i.e., not intentionally, but in the course of his walking. (2) I.e., on Sabbath, despite the possibility of levelling thereby some grooves in the soil. (3) Thus the question remains unanswered. (4) Abba. (5) There happened to be saliva spat out. V. Rashi. (6) Rashi: a one-piece lamp; v. *supra* 44*a*, n. a6.

up with one hand, or [even] with two hands? [122*a*] Such as those of your father's house, he replied.[7]

R. Abba b. Kahana also said in R. Ḥanina's name: The litters[8] of Rabbi's household may be handled on the Sabbath. R. Zera asked him: [Does that mean] those that can be moved by one man, or [even] by two men? Like those of your father's house, he replied.

R. Abba b. Kahana also said: R. Ḥanina permitted Rabbi's household to drink wine [carried][9] in gentile coaches[10] [sealed] with one seal.[11] I do not know whether it is because of his agreement with R. Eliezer[12] or because of the [Gentile's] fear of the Nasi's household.[13]

MISHNAH. IF A GENTILE LIGHTS A LAMP, AN ISRAELITE MAY MAKE USE OF ITS LIGHT; BUT IF [HE DOES IT] FOR THE SAKE OF THE ISRAELITE, IT IS FORBIDDEN. IF HE DRAWS
a WATER[1] TO GIVE HIS OWN ANIMAL TO DRINK, AN ISRAELITE MAY WATER [HIS] AFTER HIM; BUT IF [HE DRAWS IT] FOR THE ISRAELITE'S SAKE, IT IS FORBIDDEN. IF A GENTILE MAKES A STAIRWAY TO DESCEND BY IT,[2] AN ISRAELITE MAY DESCEND AFTER HIM; BUT IF ON THE ISRAELITE'S ACCOUNT, IT IS FORBIDDEN. IT ONCE HAPPENED THAT R. GAMALIEL AND THE ELDERS WERE TRAVELLING IN A SHIP, WHEN A GENTILE MADE A STAIRWAY FOR GOING DOWN, AND R. GAMALIEL AND THE ELDERS DESCENDED BY IT.

GEMARA. Now these are [all] necessary. For if we were informed [about] a lamp, that is because a lamp for one is a lamp for a hundred; but as for water, [I might say] let us forbid it,[3] lest he come to increase [the quantity drawn] on the Israelite's account.[4] What is the need of [the ruling about] a stairway?[5]—He tells us the story of R. Gamaliel and the elders.

Our Rabbis taught: If a Gentile gathers herbs,[6] an Israelite may feed [his cattle therewith] after him, but if [he gathers] on the Israelite's account, it is forbidden. If he draws water to give his cattle to drink, an Israelite may water [his] after him, but if on the Israelite's account, it is forbidden. When is that? If he does not know him; but if he knows him it is forbidden. But that is not so? For R. Huna said in R. Ḥanina's name: A man may stand his cattle on grass on the Sabbath,[7] but not on *mukẓeh*[8] on the Sabbath![9]—It means that he stands in front of it [the animal],[10] and so it goes [there] and eats.

The Master said: 'When is that? If he does not know him; but if he knows him, it is forbidden.' But R. Gamaliel [is a case
b where] he knew him?[1]—Said Abaye: It was not [made] in his presence.[2] Raba said: You may even say that it was in his presence: 'a lamp for one is a lamp for a hundred.'[3] An objection is raised: R. Gamaliel said to them, 'Since he did not make it in our presence, let us go down by it?'—Say: 'Since he made it, let us go down by it.'

Come and hear: If a city inhabited by Israelites and Gentiles contains baths where there is bathing on the Sabbath, if the majority are Gentiles, one [an Israelite] may bathe therein immediately;[4] if the majority are Israelites, one must wait until hot water could be heated.[5]—There, when they heat, they do so with a view to the majority.[6]

Come and hear: If a lamp is burning at a banqueting party:[7] if the majority are Gentiles, one may make use of its light; if the majority are Israelites, it is forbidden; if half and half, it is for-

(7) Small ones. But heavy ones generally have an appointed place and may not be moved. (8) For carrying people. (9) V. MS.M. (10) Left in the charge of Gentiles. (11) To prevent the Gentiles from tampering with it. Normally two seals are required. (12) In A.Z. 31*a*, that for wine only one seal is required. (13) Which would prevent the Gentile from tampering with the wine.

a (1) From a pit in the street. (2) Rashi: a gangway from a large ship to dry land. (3) Even when the Gentile draws it for his own use. (4) Whilst ostensibly drawing it for himself. (5) That is analogous to a lamp—the same stairway suffices for many as for one. (6) As animal fodder. (7) I.e., on grass attached to the soil, and we do not fear that he may thereby come to cut grass for his animal. (8) Fodder stored away for later use; this may not be handled on the Sabbath as *mukẓeh* (v. Glos.); hence its designation. (9) Lest he take it and feed the animal. But grass cut on the Sabbath is also *mukẓeh* and may not be handled, since it was not fit for handling as detached before the Sabbath. (10) Barring its way to elsewhere and so making it go on to the detached grass; but he does not actually lead the animal himself; then it is permitted.

b (1) Since he travelled with R. Gamaliel in the boat. (2) Then the Gentile certainly did not make it for him. (3) He needed the gangway for himself, and there is no extra work even if he had R. Gamaliel in mind. But one may not cut more grass on the Jew's account. (4) After the Sabbath, because it was heated primarily for Gentiles. (5) After the Sabbath, so as not to benefit from the heating of the water on the Sabbath. Now, the water had to be heated for the Gentiles in any case, and there is no real difference between heating for one or for many; further, it was not heated in the Jews' presence, yet one must not benefit from it. This contradicts both Abaye and Raba. (6) Hence it is regarded as specifically for Jews. (7) Having been lit on the Sabbath.

א"ל כאותן של בית אביך ואמר ר' אבא בר כהנא אמר ר' חנינא קרונות של בית רבי מותר לטלטלן בשבת א"ל ר' זירא בניטלין באדם אחד או בשני בני אדם א"ל כאותן של בית אביך ואמר ר' אבא בר כהנא התיר להם ר' חנינא לבית רבי לשתות יין בקרונות של נכרי *בחותם אחד ולא ידענא אי משום דסבר לה *כר' אליעזר אי משום אימתא דבי נשיאה: **מתני'** ב נכרי שהדליק את הנר משתמש לאורו ישראל ואם בשביל ישראל אסור מילא מים להשקות בהמתו משקה אחריו ישראל ואם בשביל ישראל אסור עשה נכרי כבש לירד בו יורד אחריו ישראל ואם בשביל ישראל אסור מעשה ברבן גמליאל וזקנים שהיו באין בספינה ועשה נכרי כבש לירד בו וירדו בו ר"ג וזקנים: **גמ'** וצריכא דאי אשמעינן נר משום דנר לאחד נר למאה אבל מים ליגזר דילמא אתי לאפושי בשביל ישראל וכבש ל"ל מעשה דרבן גמליאל וזקנים קמ"ל ת"ר ג נכרי שליקט עשבים מאכיל אחריו ישראל ואם בשביל ישראל אסור מילא מים להשקות בהמתו משקה אחריו ישראל ואם בשביל ישראל אסור ד בד"א שאין מכירו אבל מכירו אסור איני *והאמר רב הונא אמר רבי חנינא ה מעמיד אדם בהמתו על גבי עשבים בשבת אבל לא על גבי מוקצה בשבת ו דקאים לה באפה ואזלא היא ואכלה אמר מר בד"א שאין מכירו אבל מכירו אסור הא רבן גמליאל מכירו הוה אמר אביי שלא בפניו הוה רבא אמר ז אפי' תימא בפניו נר לאחד נר למאה מיתיבי *אמר להן רבן גמליאל הואיל ושלא בפנינו עשאו נרד בו אימא הואיל ועשאו נרד בו תא שמע *ח עיר שישראל ונכרים דרין בתוכה והיתה בה מרחץ המרחצת בשבת אם רוב נכרים מותר לרחוץ בה מיד אם רוב ישראל ימתין בכדי שיחמו חמין התם כי מחממי אדעתא דרובא מחממי תא שמע ט נר הדלוק במסיבה אם רוב נכרים מותר להשתמש לאורה אם רוב ישראל אסור מחצה על מחצה אסור התם נמי כי מדלקי אדעתא

רש"י

של בית אביך. דקטנות היו אבל גדולות אדם קובע להם מקום: קרונות. עשויות לבני אדם: אי משום דסבר כרבי אליעזר. דאמר במסכת ע"ז (דף לא.) יין מותר בחותם אחד: אי משום אימתא דבי נשיאה. שהיה הנכרי המביאו ירא מן הנשיא שהיה שליט על פי המלכות ומשום דאיירי ר' אבא בר כהנא לעיל גבי נחש נקט כל הני בשמיה: **מתני'** אם בשביל ישראל אסור. מדרבנן: מילא מים. מבור ברה"ר: כבש. עושין בספינה גדולה לירד בו מספינה ליבשה: **גמ'** נר לאחד נר למאה. כיון דנכרי לצרכו הדליקו ליכא למימר דבשביל ישראל אפיש: כבש למה לי. הא דומיא דנר הוא כבש לאחד כבש למאה: מאכיל אחריו ישראל. את בהמתו ואחריו דוקא נקט בכולהו דנכרי לצורך עצמו עביד: אבל מכירו אסור. קס"ד דעביד נמי אדעתא דידיה: מעמיד אדם בהמתו על גבי עשבים. מחוברים: בשבת. לרעות וליכא למיגזר שמא יתלוש ויאכיל: ואיטו מעמידה ע"ג מוקצה. שמא יטול בידו ויאכיל והא נמי מוקצין נינהו לגבי טלטול דאתמול הוו מחוברין: דקאים ליה באפה. שלא תפנה למקום אחר: ואזלא ואכלה. אבל הוא איטו עומד על העשבים קרוב להם דניחוש לשמא יטול ויאכיל: מכירו הוה. שהרי בספינה היה בא עמו: שלא בפניו הוה. כשעשאו לא היה רבן גמליאל שם דניכוין ליה: נר לאחד נר למאה. כבש לאחד כבש למאה אבל גבי עשבים כשהוא מכירו מרבה בשבילו: הואיל ושלא בפנינו כו'. קשיא לרבא דשמעינן מינה דבפניו אסור ואע"פ שאין כאן מרבה בשבילו: אימא הואיל ועשאו נרד בו. וטעמא לאו משום שלא בפניו הוא אלא הכי הוה מעשה: מותר לרחוץ בה מיד. למוצאי שבת: בכדי שיחמו חמין. שלא יהנה במה שהקדימו להחם בשבת וכן בכל מעשה שבת נתנו חכמים שיעור להמתין לערב בכדי שיעשו והא הכא דחימום לאחד חימום למאה דבבת אחת מחממין וקתני אם רוב ישראל דהוי דומיא דמכירו דמסיק אדעתיה לעשות אף בשבילו אסור ואע"ג דשלא בפניו וקשיא בין לאביי בין לרבא: אדעתא דרובא מחממי. ועיקר חילול השבת בשבילם אבל נכרי וישראל דנכרי אדעתא דנפשיה הוא דעביד שרי לאביי שלא בפניו ולרבא אפי' בפניו: נר הדלוק במסיבה. של בני אדם: אם רוב ישראל אסור. והא הכא דהוי דומיא דמכירו הואיל ורובא נינהו אסיק דעתיה להדליק אף בשבילם וקתני אסור: אדעתא

תוספות

של בית אביך. פי' שהם גדולים או קטנים דאית להו חידקי כמו שפירשתי לעיל (דף לה.*): **משתמש** ישראל לאורה. ולא גזרינן שמא ידליק כדגזרינן בפ"ק דביצה (דף ג.) פירות הנושרין שמא יעלה ויתלוש ובמשקין שזבו שמא יסחוט משום דסחיטה ותלישה הם קלים לעשות ואדם להוט אחריהם לפי שהן דבר אכילה אבל בכל הני דהכא אינן קלין לעשות כל כך ואין אדם להוט אחריהן: **ואם** בשביל ישראל אסור. נראה דאסור לכל ישראל דדוקא בחוץ לתחום דרבנן אמר בפרק בכל מערבין (עירובין דף מ.) ובאין לדין (ביצה דף כה.) הבא בשביל ישראל זה מותר לישראל אחר אבל באיסורא דאורייתא כי הכא לא ואע"ג דישראל המבשל בשבת בשוגג יאכל התם לא חיישינן אי שרית ליה לאכול דילמא אתי לבשולי במזיד דהא איכא איסור סקילה וחמיר עליה אבל בנכרי העושה לצורך ישראל אי שרית ליה אתי למימר לנכרי לעשות בשבילו ולא דמי להא דאמר לעיל* נכרי שבא לכבות אין אומרים לו כבה ואל תכבה והכא אסור כשעושה בשביל ישראל דכי אמרינן דנכרי אדעתא דנפשיה קא עביד הנ"מ בכיבוי וכיוצא בו שאין ישראל נהנה במעשה הנכרי אבל הכא שגוף ישראל נהנה במעשה של נכרי לא אמרינן אדעתא דנפשיה קעביד הואיל והנכרי מתכוין להנאתו כך פירש רבינו שמשון הזקן: **משקה** אחריו ישראל ואם בשביל ישראל אסור. אומר ר"ת מדנקט בהמתו ולא נקט מילא מים לעצמו דווקא להשקות בהמתו אסור משום שלא היה יכול להביאה לתוך הבור אבל הוא עצמו שרי דמטפס ועולה מטפס ויורד וכיון שיכול ליכנס לתוך הבור ולשתות לא אסרו לו בשביל שמילא אותם נכרי והא דאסרינן בגמרא נכרי שליקט עשבים לצורך ישראל אע"ג דישראל יכול להעמיד בהמתו על גבי העשבים במחובר אומר ר"ת דהתם נמי איירי בתרי עברי דנהרא שלא היה יכול *להביא הבהמה לשם ואע"ג דהך בבא דמילא מים משום חידוש דהיתרא קתני לה כדמוכח בגמרא מיהא בהמתו משום איסורא נקט לה וה"ר אליהו הביא ראיה להתיר מפירות שיצאו חוץ לתחום וחזרו שלא הפסידו היתירן הראשון כדאמר בפרק מי שהוציאוהו (עירובין דף מא:) ה"ה המים שמתחלה היה יכול(א) לבא שם והביאו דרך רה"ר דשרו ולא דמי דהתם לא אתעבידא בהו איסורא דאורייתא מיהו לענין אותו ישראל עצמו לא מצינו חילוק ור"י אומר דה"ה לישראל עצמו אסור והאי דנקט בהמתו לאשמעינן רבותא דלא גזרינן דילמא אתי לאפושי בשביל ישראל שבהמה רגילה לשתות הרבה אבל ישראל עצמו פשיטא דשותה אחריו דליכא למיחש כולי האי דילמא אתי לאפושי דבדלייה אחת מושך הרבה לצורכו ולצורך ישראל ולפי זה אם נמשכו המים לצורך ישראל זה אסור לכל ישראל אי איכא איסורא דאורייתא כגון שמביאם דרך רה"ר או מרה"י לרה"ר אבל בכרמלית שרי לישראל אחר ויש שרצו לומר דדוקא שתיה אסורה אבל לרחוץ ידיו ורגליו ושאר תשמישין שרי כדאמר בפרק חרש (יבמות דף קיד.) רבי יצחק אירכסו ליה מפתחות דבי מדרשא כו' אמר ליה דבר טליא וטליתא ליטיילו התם דאי משכח להו מייתי להו אלמא יכולין ליהנות ממפתחות להשתמש בהם בשבת ואין נראה לר"י כלל דהתם אין עושין לדעת ישראל ועוד דהרי כבש ונר וכמה דברים דאסור להשתמש בהם בשבת כשנעשין לצורך ישראל ה"נ לא שנא שתיה לא שנא שאר תשמישין אסירי: **איני** והאמר רב הונא אמר רב חנינא מעמיד אדם כו' אבל לא על גבי מוקצה. והני עשבים נמי מוקצין נינהו שנלקטו היום מן המחובר וא"ת ולימא דהך ברייתא רבי שמעון היא דלית ליה מוקצה וי"ל דמשני לה אפילו כר' יהודה א"נ מודה ר"ש במוקצה דמחובר כדפי' בקונטרס בפרק אין צדין (ביצה דף כד:) מדלא ליקטן מאתמול אקצינהו והוי כגרוגרות וצימוקים ובריש ביצה (דף ג.) דאסר פירות הנושרים משום גזירה שמא יעלה ויתלוש ולא אסר להו משום מוקצה משום דמוכנים לעורבים כי ההיא דמקום שנהגו (פסחים דף נו:) והכא איירי כשאין הבהמה יכולה לבא ולאכול מן המחובר ולהכי הוי מוקצה א"נ עשבים מוקצין הם אפילו לר"ש לפי שאינו יושב ומצפה שילקטום אבל בנר יושב ומצפה מתי יכבה כדאמרינן לעיל (דף מו:) וכן פירות הנושרין יושב ומצפה מתי יפלו ולהכי אי לאו טעמא דשמא יעלה ויתלוש הוו שרו: **מעמיד** אדם בהמתו ע"ג עשבים בשבת. כדדרשי' במכילתין למען ינוח שורך וחמורך וגו' יכול לא יניחנו תולש לא יניחנו עוקר ת"ל למען ינוח ואין זה נוח אלא לצער. ר"ת: **אמר** אביי שלא בפניו הוה. נראה לר"י דמודה אביי דנר לאחד נר למאה אלא דסבר דהכא אם היה בפניו עיקר היה נעשה לצורך ר"ג שהיה נשיא ושר וראש בספינה אהדרינהו:

מסורת הש"ס

[ע"ז לא.]

[עירובין עט.]

[תוספתא פי"ד]

לקמן קנא. מכשירין פ"ב מ"ט

הגהות הב"ח

(א) תוס' ד"ה משקה וכו' שמתחלה היה יכול לילך ולשתות שם והביאו נכרי דרך רה"ר:

עין משפט נר מצוה

[ד"ה ואפילו]

פ א מיי' פי"ג מהלכות מאכלות אסורות הל"י סמג לאוין קלח טור שו"ע יו"ד סימן קיח סעיף א וסימן קל סעיף ב:

פא ב מיי' פ"ו מהלכות שבת הלכה ב ג סמג לאוין סה טוש"ע או"ח סימן רעו סעיף א וסימן שכה סעיף יא ויב:

פב ג ד מיי' וסמג שם טוש"ע או"ח סימן שכה סעיף י יא:

פג ה ו מיי' פכ"א מהל' שבת הלכה לו סמג שם טוש"ע או"ח סימן שכד סעיף יג וסימן שכה סעיף יא:

פד ז מיי' פ"ו שם הל"ד וסמג שם טור שו"ע שם:

פה ח מיי' שם הלכה ז סמג שם טוש"ע או"ח סימן שכו סעיף יג:

[דף קכא.]

פו ט מיי' שם הלכה ד סמג שם טוש"ע שם סימן רעו סעיף ב:

רבינו חננאל

או בב' ידים. אמר ליה כאותן של בית אביך ש"מ דניטלת בידו אחת שרי. ניטלת בב' ידים לא איתברירא לן בהדיא. וכן קרונות של בית רבי הניטלין בב' בני אדם לא איפשיטא. והתיר ר' חנינא לשתות יין הבא בקרונות של נכרים בחותם אחת ולא ידענא אי משום דסבר לה כר' אליעזר אי משום אימתא דבי נשיאה: נכרי שהדליק את הנר. ת"ר נכרי שליקט עשבים מאכיל אחריו ישראל ואם בשביל ישראל אסור. וכן מילא מים להשקות בהמתו וכו'. בד"א

להביא הבהמה לשם ואין זה דוחק דדומיא דמתני' איירי האי בתרי עברי דנהרא שאין הבהמה יכולה לירד לבור ואע"ג דהך בבא וכו' כצ"ל רש"ל

רב נסים גאון

לפני רבן יוחנן בן זכאי בערב ואמר חושש אני לו מחטאת: אי משום דסבר לה כר' אליעזר דלא חייש לזיופא ומימרא דר' אליעזר במס' ע"ז אין מעמידין בהמה (דף לא) דתניא אחד הלוקח וא' השוכר בית כו' ר' אליעזר מתיר בשתיית ואמרו מר סבר כי פליגי רבנן עליה דר' אליעזר בחותם אחד כו' ובפ' השוכר את הפועלין (שם דף סט) אמרו וכי מאחר דקיימא לן כוותיה דרשב"ג וכוותיה דר' אליעזר דלא חייש לזיופא:

סליק פרק כל כתבי הקודש

אדעתא דרובא מדלקי שמואל איקלע לבי אבין תורן אתא ההוא נכרי אדליק שרגא אהדרינהו שמואל לאפיה כיון דחזא דאייתי שטר וקא קרי אמר *[א]אדעתא דנפשיה הוא דאדליק אהדרינהו איהו לאפיה גבי שרגא:

הדרן עלך כל כתבי

כל [ב]הכלים ניטלין בשבת ודלתותיהן עמהן אע"פ שנתפרקו (בשבת) שאינן דומין לדלתות הבית לפי שאינן מן המוכן [ג]נוטל אדם קורנס לפצע בו את האגוזין קרדום לחתוך בו את הדבילה מגירה לגור בה את הגבינה מגריפה לגרוף בה את הגרוגרות את הרחת ואת *המלגז לתת עליו לקטן את הכוש ואת הכרכר לתחוב בו *[ד]מחט של יד ליטול בו את הקוץ ושל סקאים לפתוח בו את הדלת: **גמ'** כל הכלים ניטלין ואע"פ שנתפרקו בשבת ולא מיבעיא בחול אדרבה בשבת מוכנין על גבי אביהן בחול אין מוכנין על גבי אביהן אמר אביי הכי קאמר כל הכלים ניטלין בשבת ודלתותיהן עמהן אע"פ שנתפרקו בחול ניטלין בשבת ת"ר *[ה]דלת של שידה ושל תיבה ושל מגדל נוטלין אבל לא מחזירין ושל לול של תרנגולים לא נוטלין ולא מחזירין בשלמא של לול של תרנגולים קסבר כיון דמחברי בארעא יש בנין בקרקע יש סתירה בקרקע אלא של שידה ושל תיבה ושל מגדל מאי קסבר אי קסבר יש בנין בכלים יש סתירה בכלים ואי אין סתירה בכלים אין בנין בכלים אמר אביי לעולם קסבר יש בנין בכלים ויש סתירה בכלים ושניטלו קאמר א"ל רבא [שתי תשובות בדבר] חדא דנוטלין קתני ועוד מאי אבל לא מחזירין אלא אמר רבא קסבר *[ו]אין בנין בכלים ואין סתירה בכלים וגזירה שמא יתקע: נוטל אדם קורנס כו': אמר רב יהודה קורנס של אגוזין לפצע בו את האגוזין אבל של נפחין לא קסבר דבר שמלאכתו לאיסור אפילו לצורך גופו אסור א"ל רבה אלא מעתה סיפא דקתני ואת הרחת ואת המלגז לתת עליו לקטן רחת ומלגז מי מייחדי ליה לקטן אלא אמר רבה קורנס של נפחין לפצע בו האגוזין קסבר

דבר

אדעתא דרובא · הלכך ישראל עיקר ומחצה על מחצה נמי ליכא למיקם עלה דמלתא דאיכא למימר עיקר דעתיה דמדליק בשביל ישראל ואיכא למימר עיקר דעתיה דמדליק בשביל נכרי אבל נכרי וישראל והמדליק עצמו משתמש לאורה ודאי עיקר אדעתא דידיה עביד וכיון דנר לאחד נר למאה שרי: תורן · מקום: דאייתי שטר · ההוא דאדלקה:

הדרן עלך כל כתבי

כל הכלים ניטלין בשבת ודלתותיהן עמהם · כל הכלים שיש להם דלתות כגון שידה תיבה ומגדל ניטלין בשבת ודלתות שיש להם בלן עמהן ניטלין עמהן: ואע"פ שנתפרקו · הדלתות מן הכלים ניטלין ואין דומין לדלתות הבית שאין ניטלין לפי שדלתות הבית אינן מן המוכן לטלטל שאינן כלי אבל אלו הן כלי אגב אביהן: קורנס · מרטי"ל: דבילה · אחר שעשאה עיגול עבה היא מאד וקשה כגבינה וצריך קורדום לחותכה: ומגירה · כעין סכין ויש בו פגימות הרבה: לגור בה את הגבינה · לחתכו ולחלקו לפי שממהרת לחתוך דבר עב: מגריפה · ווד"יל: לגרוף בה את הגרוגרות · מן החביות: רחת · פאל"א: מלגז · כמין עתר שקורין פורק"א של ברזל ולו ג' שיניים ומהפכין בו קש בגורן: לתת עליו לקטן · מזונות: כוש · פלך פוסי"ל: כרכר · רא"יל: לתחוב בו · לאכול בו תותים וכל פרי רך: מחט של יד · מחט קטן שתופר בו בגדים: ושל סקאים · מחט גדולה שתופרים בה שקים: לפתוח בו את הדלת · מי שאבד מפתחו: **גמ'** ולא מיבעיא בחול · קא סלקא דעתך ואע"פ שנתפרקו אבשבת דקתני רישא קאי ומשמע אע"פ שנתפרקו היום מותרים ולא מיבעיא אם נתפרקו מאמש: אדרבה · מאי אע"פ שייך למתני הא ודאי נתפרקו בשבת איכא למישרי משום דכי קדיש יומא הוו מוכנין לטלטל אגב אביהן: הכי קאמר כו' · ואע"פ לא ארבותא דנתפרקו בשבת קאי אלא ארבותא דנתפרקו או בחול או בשבת קאי ולא מיבעיא כשהן מחוברין: נוטלין · משמע מסלקין אותן בשבת [*מהיתר] ציר שלהן: לול · בנין העשוי לתרנגולין: לא נוטלין ולא מחזירין · כדמפרש ואזיל חזרתו בנין ממש הוא וסילוקו סתירה גמורה היא: מאי קסבר · שמתיר סילוקו ואוסר חזרתו: אי קסבר יש בנין בכלים · וחזרתו בנין על כרחיך אם יש בנין יש סתירה ואמאי נוטלין: ושניטלו קאמר · וה"ק דלת של תיבה שידה ומגדל שניטלו אין מחזירין: מאי אבל · כיון דלא תנא נוטלין לא שייך למיתני אבל: לעולם קסבר אין סתירה ואין בנין · הלכך נוטלין ומיהו אין מחזירין מדרבנן: גזירה שמא יתקע · בחוזקה בסכין ויתדות והוה ליה גמר מלאכה וחייב משום מכה בפטיש: קורנס של אגוזים · המיוחד לפציעת אגוזים הוא דקתני מתניתין דנוטלין אותו למלאכתו משום דעיקרו למלאכת היתר: אבל של נפחים · דעיקרו למלאכת איסור לא: לצורך גופו · שגופו צריך עוד למלאכה אחרת של היתר אין מטלטלין אותו לאותה מלאכה וכ"ש אם אין צריך לגופו אלא לפחת מקומו דאין מטלטלין: מי מייחדי לקטן · בשלמא כולהו הני דמתני' איכא לאוקמא בעשויין ומיוחדין לכך בר מהני דליכא דעביד להו להכי:

דבר

אהדרינהו שמואל לאפיה · מיירי שהיה לכל הפחות מחצה על מחצה דמשום נר לאחד נר למאה לא משתריא אלא היכא שהוא ניכר שהוא עושה לצרכו דהו לא גזרינן אפילו במכירו שמא ירבה בשבילו: הדרן עלך כל כתבי

כל הכלים הניטלין בשבת דלתותיהן עמהם גרסינן ול"ג כל הכלים ניטלין דטובא איכא דאין ניטלין כגון מסר הגדול ויתד של מחרישה דאפילו ר"ש מודה כדאיתא בשילהי מכילתין (דף קנז.) וכגון חצוצרות* בת תרי כורי דאסר רבה בשילהי במה מדליקין (דף לה:) וכן חצוצרות לרבי יהודה* ונר ישן* מ"ר: **אדרבה** בשבת מוכנין אגב אביהן · אע"ג דלקמן בפירקין (דף קכד:) אמר איפכא גבי שברי כלי חרס דשרי לטלטל יותר כשנשברו בע"ש משנשברו בשבת לא דמיא דהכא אכתי כלי הוא שעדיין עומד למלאכה ראשונה וראוי להתחבר הכיסוי עם הכלי אבל לקמן לא חשיב כלי אלא מחמת שעומד למלאכה אחרת הלכך כשנשבר בשבת אסור טפי דהוי נולד: **לעולם** קסבר יש בנין בכלים כו' · וכשניטלו מטלטלין קאמר וה"פ הברייתא דלת של שידה תיבה ומגדל ניטלין פירוש מטלטלין כשניטלין ולא כפירוש הקונטרס דמפרש שניטלין דקתני היינו שניטלו קאמר כלומר כשניטל אין מחזירין אותן דלא יתכן לפרש כן ניטלין דסיפא אלא לשון טלטול הוא כדפרשתי ופריך והא(א) נמי נוטלין קתני ועוד מאי אבל לא מחזירין דלא שייך למיתני אמילתיה דלא (דמיא) [שייך] כלל למאי דאיירי בה דמעיקרא קאמר ניטלין שמותר לטלטל ואין בו איסור מוקצה והדר קאמר אבל לא מחזירין שהוא משום איסור בנין מאי ענין זה אצל זה לא שייך כה"ג למיתני אבל כלל: **רחת** ומלגז מי מייחדי ליה לקטן · ורב יהודה ידע ליה לסיפא אלא דילמא הוה מוקי לה בשיחדה לכך ככל הנך דמתניתין ואם תאמר והאמר רב יהודה אמר שמואל בפרק אלו קשרים (לעיל דף קיג.) כלי קיואי מותר לטלטל בשבת דהיינו לצורך גופו אע"פ שמלאכתו לאיסור ואין לומר (דמשמע) דשמואל קאמר ליה וליה לא סבירא ליה מדבעי מיניה מרב יהודה כובד עליון וכובד התחתון מהו אין ולאו ורפיא בידיה משמע דס"ל הכי ועוד דרב יהודה גופיה בסוף כירה (לעיל ד' מו·) קאמר שרגא דמישחא שרי לטלטולי ואין לומר דמיירי כשייחדו להיתר כדמוקי רב יהודה הנך דמתני' דהא כלי קיואי לא משמע שייחדו דאם כן אפילו כובד העליון וכובד תחתון נמי ויש לומר דלא אסר רב יהודה אלא דומיא דפיצוע אגוזים שהיא מלאכה גרועה לגבי קורנס שמיוחד למלאכה חשובה וכן כל הנך דמתניתין הוה אסור בלא ייחוד דמלאכת היתר שלהן מלאכה גרועה היא לגבי הנך כלים שמיוחדין למלאכה חשובה אבל כלי קיואי ושרגא דמשחא מותר לטלטל לצורך גופן דמלאכה שלהן חשובה יותר מפיצוע אגוזים:

בסיכי

עין משפט
נר מצוה

נז א טור שו"ע שם:

א ב מיי' פכ"ב מהלכות שבת הלכה כה ופכ"ה הלכה יב סמג לאוין סה טוש"ע או"ח סימן שח סעיף ח:

ב ג מיי' שם הלכה ז טוש"ע שם סעיף ג:

ג ד מיי' שם הלכה ח טוש"ע שם סעיף יא:

[עי' לעיל לה. תוס' ד"ה ואפילו]

[לעיל נו.]

[לעיל מד.]

ד ה מיי' פכ"ב שם הלכה כה טור שו"ע שם סעיף ט:

ה ו מיי' שם הלכה כו סמג שם טוש"ע או"ח סימן שיד סעיף א:

פירוש מולג [ובמשנה שבמשניות איתא המולג]

רבינו חננאל

בנכרי שאינו מכירו אבל אם מכירו אסור. ת"ש עיר של ישראל ונכרים דרין בה':

הדרן עלך כל כתבי הקודש

פר"ז כל הכלים ניטלין בשבת כו'. באנו לפרש מתי נפרקו בשבת או אפי' בחול. ואוקמה אביי להא מתני' אע"פ שנתפרקו בחול ניטלין בשבת לפי שאינן דומין דלתות הכלים לדלתות הבית. כי דלתות הבית קבועין בקרקע ולא הוכנו להיטלטל. אבל הכלים הוכנו לטלטול וכ"ש דלתותיהן. ופשוטה היא. ומפרקינן* גזירה שמא יתקע. פי' שמא יתקע בה מסמר או יתד וכדומה להן: נוטל אדם קורנס לפצוע בו אגוזים וכו'. בא רב יהודה להעמיד משנתנו ע בקורנס המוכן לפצוע אגוזים. ולא כל קורנס מותר. אלא זה בלבד. אבל קורנס של נפחים וכדומה להן אפילו לצורך גופו אסור. ואקשי' עלה רבה אלא מעתה סיפא דקתני ואת הרחת ואת המלגז לתת עליו לקטן. פי' לתת עליו מאכל לקטן כגון תבשיל. רחת ומלגז [מי] מכינין בנ"א לתבשיל

*) נראה דחסר בדברי רבינו וצ"ל דלת של שידה ושל תיבה ושל מגדל נוטלין אבל לא מחזירין

מסורת הש"ס

לעיל קז. סנהדרין פד:

[תוספתא פ"ט]

[עירובין לה. ביצה י. יא: כב.]

ירש"ל ובספי' איתא מהיכר וכן איתא ברא"ש בד"ה לעולם

הגהות הב"ח

(א) תוס' ד"ה לעולם וכו' ופריך והא ניטלין קתני ולא תני נמי נתפרקו כו' ועוד מאי אבל:

bidden?[8]—There too, when they light it, [122*b*] they do so with a view to the majority.

Samuel visited the house of Abin of Toran.[9] A Gentile came and lit a lamp, [whereupon] Samuel turned his face away.[10] On seeing that he [the Gentile] had brought a document and was reading it, he observed, 'He has lit it for himself'; [so] he [too] [Samuel] turned his face to the lamp.

CHAPTER XVII

a *MISHNAH*. IMPLEMENTS MAY[1] BE HANDLED ON THE SABBATH AND THEIR LIDS[2] WITH THEM, EVEN IF THEY ARE DETACHED [ON THE SABBATH], FOR THEY ARE NOT LIKE THE DOORS OF A HOUSE, WHICH ARE NOT OF MUKAN.[3] A MAN MAY TAKE A HAMMER TO SPLIT NUTS, A CHOPPER TO CUT [A ROUND OF] PRESSED FIGS, A SAW FOR SAWING CHEESE, A SPADE TO SCOOP DRIED FIGS,[4] A WINNOWING SHOVEL AND A PITCH-FORK TO PLACE [FOOD] UPON IT FOR A CHILD, A REED OR A WHORL TO STICK [FOOD], A SMALL NEEDLE[5] TO REMOVE A THORN, AND A SACK [NEEDLE] TO OPEN A DOOR THEREWITH.[6]

GEMARA. ALL UTENSILS MAY BE HANDLED, ... EVEN IF THEY ARE DETACHED on the Sabbath,[7] while it goes without saying [if detached] on a weekday;[7] on the contrary, on the Sabbath they stand 'prepared' in virtue of their origin;[8] [whereas if detached] on a weekday, they do not stand 'prepared' in virtue of their origin?[9]—Said Abaye, This is its meaning: ALL UTENSILS MAY BE HANDLED ON THE SABBATH, THEIR DOORS WITH THEM, EVEN IF THEY ARE DETACHED on a weekday, they may be handled on the Sabbath.

b Our Rabbis taught: The door of a box, chest, or coffer[1] may be removed, but not replaced; that of a hen-roost may neither be removed nor replaced. As for that of a hen-roost, it is well! he holds that since they [the hen-roosts] are attached to the ground, [the interdict of] building applies to the ground and that of demolishing applies to the ground;[2] but as for that of a box, chest, or coffer, what is his opinion? If he holds, [The interdict of] building applies to utensils, then that of demolishing [too] applies to utensils; whilst if there is no [prohibition of] demolishing in respect to utensils, there is no [prohibition of] building in respect to utensils [either]?[3]—Said Abaye: In truth he holds: There is [the prohibition of] building in the case of utensils, and there is [that of] demolishing in respect of utensils, but he means, Those that were removed [may not be replaced].[4] Said Raba to him, There are two objections to this: one, since he teaches that they may be removed; and two, how [explain] '*but* not replaced?'—Rather said Raba: He holds, [The interdict of] building does not apply to utensils, and the interdict of demolishing does not apply to utensils, yet it is a preventive measure, lest he fix it firmly.[5]

A MAN MAY TAKE A HAMMER, etc. Rab Judah said: [This means,] a nut hammer to split nuts therewith, but not a smith's [hammer]: he holds, An article whose function is a forbidden labour is forbidden [even] when required for itself.[6] Said Rabbah to him: If so, when the second clause teaches, A WINNOWING SHOVEL AND A PITCH-FORK, TO PLACE [FOOD] UPON IT FOR A CHILD, are a winnowing shovel and a pitch-fork set aside specially for a child?[7] Rather said Rabbah: [It means] a smith's hammer to split nuts therewith; he holds, [123*a*] An article whose function

(8) This contradicts Raba. (9) MS.M. To Abitoran. (10) So as not to benefit from it.

a (1) Tosaf. reads: ALL UTENSILS WHICH MAY, etc., for in fact there are many that may not be handled. (2) Those that have doors or lids, e.g., a chest or coffer. (3) V. Glos. The doors of a house, if detached, may not be handled on the Sabbath, because they are not parts of utensils which stand 'prepared' for handling. But the doors of utensils are like the utensils themselves. (4) Out of the barrel. (5) Lit., 'hand-needle'. (6) If the key is lost. (7) This is now the assumed meaning and implication of the Mishnah. (8) Lit., 'father'. If they became detached on the Sabbath since they were fit to handle at the beginning of the Sabbath, when they were part of the whole, they remain so for the whole Sabbath. (9) For when the Sabbath commenced they were not part of the utensil.

b (1) Lit., 'tower' or 'turret'—a large box or chest. (2) I.e., it is like fitting or removing a house door, which constitutes building and demolishing; v. *supra* 73*a*. (3) Thus removing and refitting should be the same. (4) Thus only one law is stated; the doors of a chest, box, and coffer, if detached (before the Sabbath), may not be refitted. (5) Nailing or screwing it on, which is certainly labour; hence he must not put it back at all. (6) For a permitted labour. I.e., since the normal function of a smith's hammer is to perform labour forbidden on the Sabbath, it may not be handled even for a permitted purpose. (7) Surely not!

is a forbidden labour is permitted when required for itself.

a Abaye raised an objection to Rabbah: A mortar,[1] if containing garlic, may be moved;[2] if not, it may not be moved?[3]—The author of this is R. Nehemiah, he replied, who maintains, A utensil may be handled only for the purpose of its [normal] use.[4] He objected to him: Yet both hold alike that if he has [already] cut meat upon it, it may not be handled?[5]—He thought of answering him that this agrees with R. Nehemiah, but when he heard R. Ḥinena b. Shalmia's dictum in Rab's name: All agree in respect of the dyer's pins, tubs, and beams:[6] since one is particular about them he appoints a [special] place for them; so here too one appoints a special place for it [the pestle].[7]

It was stated, R. Ḥiyya b. Abba said in R. Joḥanan's name: We learnt [in our Mishnah] of a goldsmith's hammer; R. Shaman b. Abba said: We learnt of a spice hammer. He who says a spice [hammer], all the more so a goldsmith's [hammer].[8] He who says a goldsmith's,—but one is particular about a spice [hammer].[9]

A REED OR A WHORL, etc. Our Rabbis taught: If an unripe fig was hidden in straw,[10] or a cake which was hidden in live coals,[11] and part thereof is uncovered, it may be handled;[12] but if not, it may not be handled. R. Eleazar b. Taddai said: One impales them on a reed or a whorl, and they [the straw or coals] are shaken off of their own accord. R. Naḥman said: The *halachah* is as R.

b Eleazar b. Taddai. Shall we say that R. Naḥman holds, Indirect[1] handling is not designated handling?[2] Surely R. Naḥman said: 'A radish, if it is the right way up, is permitted; if it is reversed,[3] it is forbidden.[4]—R. Naḥman retracted from that [ruling].

A SMALL NEEDLE TO REMOVE A THORN, etc. Raba son of Rabbah sent to R. Joseph: Let our Master teach us, What of a needle from which the eye or the point has been removed?[5]—We have learnt it, he replied: A SMALL NEEDLE TO REMOVE A THORN: now, what does it matter to the thorn whether it has an eye or not? He [thereupon] put an objection to him: If the eye or the point of a needle is removed, it is clean?[6]—Said Abaye: You oppose defilement to the Sabbath! [For] defilement we require a working *utensil*,[7] [whereas] in respect to the Sabbath we require anything that is fit, and this too is fit for removing a splinter. Raba observed, He who raises the objection does so rightly: since it is not a utensil in respect to defilement, it is not a utensil in respect to the Sabbath.

An objection is raised: A needle, whether with or without an eye, may be handled on the Sabbath, while one with an eye was specified only in respect to defilement?[8]—Abaye interpreted it on the view of Raba as referring to unfinished utensils, for sometimes he may decide to use it thus and make it rank as a utensil; but if the eye or point is removed one throws it away among the rubbish.[9]

Causing a new-born babe to vomit,[10] R. Naḥman forbids, while R. Shesheth permits. R. Naḥman said: Whence do I rule thus?

a (1) For pounding garlic. (2) On account of the garlic, to which the mortar is merely subsidiary. (3) Since its essential function is forbidden, it may not be moved even for a permitted purpose, which refutes Rabbah. (4) V. *supra* 36a. Whereas our Mishnah disagrees with R. Nehemiah. (5) The reference is to a pestle: Beth Shammai rule that it must not be handled on a Festival for cutting meat thereon, because its normal use, *sc.* pounding, is forbidden on a Festival; Beth Hillel permit it, so as not to hinder the joy of the Festival. But if the meat has already been cut upon it, so that the permissive reason no longer holds good, Beth Hillel admits that it may not be handled. (6) Rashi and Jast. (7) Whence it is not to be moved for any other purpose but its own. This lays a stronger prohibition upon it; hence it may not be handled. (8) That it may be used, and the more so as an ordinary smith's hammer—in agreement with Rabbah. (9) Not to use it for anything else, lest it become too soiled for subsequent use on spices. (10) For it to ripen. Straw is *mukzeh* for making bricks. (11) Before the Sabbath. (12) Since the straw or the coals themselves need not be handled.

b (1) Lit., 'from the side'. (2) V. *supra* 43b. (3) Lit., 'from top to bottom . . . from bottom to top'. (4) The reference is to a detached radish stored in loose earth in the ground: if it is the right side up, one may pull it out, because since the top of the radish is broader than the bottom he does not dislodge any earth; but if reversed, the loose soil will naturally cave in, hence it is tantamount to handling the soil and is forbidden, though it is only indirect handling. (5) Does it still rank as a utensil and permitted to be handled on the Sabbath? (6) Which shows that it is not a utensil. (7) But if the eye or point is removed the needle is no longer a utensil. (8) V. *supra* 52b. This refutes Raba. (9) Not regarding it as a utensil at all. (10) By inserting the finger in its mouth in order to relieve it of its phlegm (Jast.). Rashi: To manipulate and ease a child's limbs.

דבר שמלאכתו לאיסור לצורך גופו מותר איתיביה אביי לרבה *מדוכה אם יש בה שום מטלטלין אותה ואם לאו אין מטלטלין אותה א"ל הא מני ר' נחמיה היא דאמר *אין כלי ניטל אלא לצורך תשמישו איתיביה (*ב"ש אומרים אין נוטלין את העלי לקצב עליו בשר [א]וב"ה מתירין) *ושוין שאם קצב עליו בשר שאסור לטלטלו סבר לשנויי ליה כר' נחמיה כיון דשמעה להא דאמר רב חיננא בר שלמיא משמיה דרב הכל מודים בסיכי זיירי ומזורי דכיון דקפיד עלייהו מייחד להו מקום ה"נ מייחד להו מקום איתמר ר' חייא בר אבא אמר ר' יוחנן [ב]קורנס של זהבים שנינו רב שמן בר אבא אמר קורנס של בשמים שנינו מאן דאמר דבשמים כ"ש דזהבים מאן דאמר של זהבים אבל דבשמים קפיד עלייהו: ואת הכוש ואת הכרכר כו': *ת"ר פגה שטמנה בתבן וחררה שטמנה(א) בגחלים אם מגולה מקצתה מותר לטלטלה ואם לאו אסור לטלטלה ר"א בן תדאי אומר [ג]תוחבין בכוש או בכרכר והן מנערות מאיליהם אמר רב נחמן הלכה כר"א בן תדאי למימרא דסבר רב נחמן *טלטול מן הצד לא שמיה טלטול *והאמר רב נחמן האי פוגלא מלמעל' למטה שרי ממטה למעלה אסיר הדר ביה רב נחמן מההיא: מחט של יד ליטול בה כו': שלח ליה רבא בריה דרבה לרב יוסף ילמדנו רבינו מחט שניטל חררה או עוקצה מהו א"ל תניתוה מחט של יד ליטול בה את הקוץ וכי מה איכפת ליה לקוץ בין נקובה לבין שאינה נקובה איתיביה *מחט שניטל חררה או עוקצה טהורה אמר אביי טומאה אשבת קרמית *טומאה כלי מעשה בעינן לענין שבת מידי דחזי בעינן והא נמי חזיא למשקלא בה קוץ אמר רבא מאן דקמותיב שפיר קמותיב *מדלענין טומאה לאו מנא הוא לענין שבת נמי לאו מנא הוא מיתיבי *[ד]מחט בין נקובה בין שאינה נקובה מותר לטלטלה בשבת ולא אמרו נקובה אלא לענין טומאה בלבד *תרגמא אביי אליבא דרבא בגולמי עסקינן זימנין דמימלך עלייהו ומשוי להו מנא [ה]אבל היכא דניטל חררה או עוקצה אדם זורקה לבין גרוטאות *אסובי ינוקא רב נחמן *אסיר ורב ששת [ו]שרי אמר רב נחמן מנא אמינא לה דתנן *אין עושין אפיקטויזין

[גמ' שוליים: רש"ל מ"ז · [לקמן קכד. ביצה יא.] · עירובין מג. · לקמן קכד: · נ"ל אוסר]

רש"י

דבר שמלאכתו לאיסור · אם צריך בשבת לגופו(ב) של מלאכה אחרת של היתר מותר: מדוכה · שדוכין בה שום: אם יש בה שום מטלטלין אותה · אגב השום: ואם לאו אין מטלטלין · כגון לישב עליה כיון דעיקר מלאכתו לשחיקה דהיא מלאכת איסור משום טוחן: תשמישו · תשמיש המיוחד לו: ושוין · ב"ש וב"ה שנחלקו בנוטלין את העלי לקצב עליו בשר ביו"ט: שאם קצב עליו בשר · שעשה לצורך שמחת יו"ט: שאסור לטלטלו · דהאי דקשרו ב"ה משום שמחת יו"ט קשרו אלמא משום דעלי מלאכתו לאיסור לכתישת טרגים וטיסני וקליפת עלים לעבד בהן עורות אסור: הכל מודים · רבנן דאיפלגו אדר' נחמיה: בסיכי זיירי ומזורי · כלי צבעין הן ורבינו הלוי פירש כלי אורגין סיכי הן עמודין זיארי הן קנים שבשתי ומזורי כובד עליון ותחתון ונראין נראה לי דזייארי לשון עוצרים הן כמו מעצרתא זיירא (ע"ז דף ס·): דקפיד עלייהו · האומן שלא יתלכלכו ושלא יתעקמו: מייחד להם מקום · מקצה להן בידים: הני נמי · [ג]עלי ומדוכה: קורנס של זהבים · אע"פ דקפיד עליה קצת שצריך שיהא חלק לרדד טסין אפ"ה כיון שמתקן על ידי הכאה שמכה על הסדן לא מקפי ליה וכ"ש של שאר נפחים כרבה: בשמים · לשחוק בו: קפיד עליה · שלא ימאס: פגה · תאנה שלא בשלה כל צרכה וטומנין בתבן להתבשל ותבן מוקצה הוי לטיט: אם מגולה מקצתה · שיכול לאוחזה במקום המגולה דאפי' טלטול מן הצד ליכא שאין צריך להגביה התבן אלא מגביה מקום המגולה והתבן נשמט ונופל: פוגלא · צנון תלוש שהטמינו בארץ ונתגלה ראשו: מלמעלה למטה שרי · אם היה העליון שלה למעלה והקצר למטה וכשהוא שולפה אוחזה מעליון שלה לתחתון שלה ורוחב הצנון למעלה מותר דליכא טלטול לעפר כלל שהרי נתגלה ראשו: ממטה למעלה אסור · שמזיז עפר לפי שהגומא קצרה מלמעלה ורוחב הצנון מלמטה ואע"ג דטלטול עפר מן הצד הוא שאינו אוחזו ממש בידו: חררה · חור שלה: עוקצה · פויינט"א: מהו · לטלטלה מי בטל תורת כלי מינה או לא: כלי מעשה · שמעשה שלו קיים: ולא אמרו נקובה · להיות תורת כלי עליה יותר משאין נקובה אלא לענין טומאה וקס"ד דבנטל חור שלה קאמר דלענין טומאה בטל שם כלי מינה ולטלטול שרי: בגולמי · גולמי מחטין העומדות לינקב דנקובה נגמרה מלאכתה ושאינה נקובה אינה נגמרה מלאכתה הלכך לענין טומאה הוא דלא הוי כלי אבל בטלטול שריא דחזי לקוץ: דמימליך · ולא נקיב לה: ומשוי לה מנא · כמות שהיא ולנטילת קוץ: גרוטאות · שברי מתכות אדם זורק' לבין גרוטאו' ובטל שם כלי מינה: אסובי ינוקא · להחליק סדר אבריו כשהוא נולד אבריו מתפרקין וצריך ליישבן: אסיר · דדמי למתקן: אפיקטויזין

תוספות

בסיכי זיירי ומזורי · פי' בערוך* פי' סיכי הם יתדות המוכנין לנפץ בהן משי וכיוצא בה תרגום יתדות סיכי זיירי כלי עץ כמו קרשים שכובשין בהן בגדים דתנן (לקמן דף קמא·) מכבש של בעלי בתים מזורי כלי עץ שהכובס מכה בו הבגדים על האבן שמלבנו ואלו כלים מקפיד עליהם שלא יתעקמו ולא יתפגמו שלא יתקלקלו הבגדים והמשי ומסיח דעתו מלטלטלן וכן מפרש בירושלמי זיירי דין עצר ביה מזורא דין חביט ביה ולפי' הקונט' דמפרש מזורי כובד עליון וכובד תחתון נ"ל דסבירא ליה כמאן דאסר בפרק אלו קשרים (לעיל דף קיג·): **הא** נמי מייחד לה מקום · מ"מ משום שמחת יו"ט מותר לטלטלו לקצב עליו בשר: *)**הדר** ביה רב נחמן מההיא · מסתברא דמההיא הדר ביה מדאמר בפרק תולין (לקמן דף קמא·) אמרי בי רב תניא דלא כרב נחמן: **פגה** שהטמינה כו' · [ה]מיירי שהניחה שם ע"מ ליטלה אבל אם הניחה שם לכל השבת הוי בסיס לדבר האסור כדאמר לקמן בפרק נוטל (ד' קמב:) גבי אבן שעל פי החבית לא שנו אלא בשוכח אבל במניח נעשה בסיס לדבר האסור: **האי** פוגלא · וא"ת האי פוגלא היכי דמי אי במניח מ"ט דמאן דשרי מלמטה למעלה הא אפילו ניעור לא שרי כ"ש טלטול מן הצד ואי בשכח מ"ט דמאן דאסר אפי' טלטול גמור שרי לצורך לטלטל אגב היתר לקמן בפרק נוטל (קמא. וד' קמב:) במעות שעל גבי הכר בצריך למקומו דמטלטלו בעודן עליו ואבן שעל פי החבית כשהוא בין החביות מגביה ומטה כ"ש טלטול מן הצד וי"ל דמניח על מנת ליטלה איירי אע"ג דכשכח דמי כמו טמן וכיסה בדבר שאינו ניטל בסוף במה טומנין (לעיל דף נא·) דשרי לנער משום דאין מניח לכל השבת ובעצמות וקליפין דריש ביצה (ד' ב·) דשרי ב"ה לסלק את הטבלא ולנער מ"מ לא היה לו להניח באותו ענין שיצטרך טלטול מן הצד ועצמות וקליפין לא מסתייה דלא ליכח בהן על גבי השלחן וטמן וכיסה דפרק במה טומנין (לעיל ד' נא·) אין לחוש כיון דאפשר בניעור, דאפילו טלטול מן הצד איכא א): **מדלענין** טומאה לאו מנא לענין שבת נמי לאו מנא · תימא הא תנן לקמן *כל הכלים הניטלין שבריהן ניטלין אע"ג דלענין טומאה לא הוי מנא כשנשבר אלא על ידי ייחוד לפי' הקונטרס דסוף המצניע (לעיל דף צה:) י"ל דה"פ מדלענין טומאה [ו]לאו מנא אפי' על ידי ייחוד דכיון דניטל חררה או עוקצה לא מהני ביה ייחוד לענין שבת נמי לאו מנא היא אבל היכא דהוה מנא לענין טומאה ע"י ייחוד איכא למימר דהוי מנא לענין שבת אפי' בלא ייחוד כיון דיכול להיות כלי לענין טומאה וכן משמע בסמוך דתרגמא אביי אליבא דרבא בגולמי דזימנין דמימלך עלייהו ומשוי להו מנא משמע דלהכי מותר לטלטל אע"ג דטהורה היא דהכתי לא מימלך עלה כיון שראוי ליחדה להיות כלי ב): **אסובי** יטקא · לאו היינו לפופי יטקא דשרי בפרק במה אשה (לעיל דף סו:) ולקמן בסוף חבית (דף קמז:) דהיינו שכורכין אותו בבגדים וקושרים בחגורה רחבה וכן פירש בקונטרס בסוף מפנין ג) כי היכי דלא תקשי דרב נחמן אדרב נחמן דשרי התם לפופי והכא אסר אסובי והא דתנן בפ' חבית (שם) אין מעצבין את הקטן פריך לה התם מההיא דלפופי ומוקי לה בחומרי שדרה דמיחזי כבונה וקשה דמייתי לה מאין עושין אפיקטויזין שהוא תיקוני גברא כדפירש בקונטרס הוה ליה לאתויי מסיפא דאין מעצבין את הקטן דהוי נמי תקוני יטוקא ודמי טפי שהכל דרשו מעגין בקטן מעגין אסובי ופירש רבינו תם דהכי נמי מייתי מסיפא דלא שמעין לתיקוני מן ... אין מעצבין :

רבינו חננאל

לתבשיל וכדומה לו. ולא מצא רב יהודה פירוקי והעמיד רבה משנתנו בקורנס של נפחים וה"ה לכל קורנס. ושמעינן מינה דכל דבר שמלאכתו אפי' לאיסור כגון מלאכת הקורנס של נפחים שהן עושי מלאכת כלי נחשת וברזל. ומלאכתם [זו] שהוכנו לכך אסורה בשבת. אם הוצרכו [לומר] [לדבר] שהוא מותר בשבת. כגון פיצוע אגוזים שהנהנת מאכל ואינה מלאכה מותר. ואקשינן עליה והא מדוכה אם יש בה שום מטלטלין [אותה] ואם לאו אין מטלטלין אותה. דכיון שמלאכתה לאיסור היא אפי' לצורך גופה אין מטלטלין אותה. ופריק ליה מני מתניתא ר' נחמיה היא דאמר אין כלי ניטל אלא לצורך תשמישו. פי' מצאנו ר' נחמיה שאמר בפי' אפי' טלית ואפי' [תרווד] אין ניטלין אלא לצורך והיא טלית ללבישה. ותרווד לאכל בו ומתני' דקתני נוטל אדם קורנס לפצוע בו [וקרדום] (ומדוכה) דלא כר' נחמיה. ותוב אקשי' עליה ושוין שאם קצב עליו בשר ופשוטה היא. ומוקמינן להני מתניתא לדברי הכל ואפילו לרבנן ומודו רבנן במדוכה ובעלי דכיון דקפיד עליה מכין עליה מקום ונמר בדעתו שלא לטלטלן מאותו מקום. לפיכך אסור לטלטלן מן המקום המוכן להם. ודין אלו כדין סיכי זיירי ומזורי. פי' סיכי הן יתדות המכונין לנער בהן משי וכדומה לו. והן תרגום של יתדות סיכי. זיירי. כלי עץ כגון קרשים שכובשין בהן הבגדים. כדתנן מכבש של בעלי בתים. מזורי כלי עץ שהכובס מכה בו הבגדים על אבן בעת שמלבנן. ואלו כולן קפיד עליהן שלא יתעותו או יפגמו. שאם יפגמו יקרעו הבגדים והמשי. לפיכך מסיח דעתו מטלטלן ונעשו מוקצים ועל כן אסור לטלטלן. וכך זה מפורשין בתלמוד א"י. בזייר די [בסכונה] עצר ביה · במזורה. די חבוט ביה (בביבאנא) די כתיש ביה. ונתברתו דברי משנתנו כי כל הקורנס מותר לפצוע בו אגוזין ואפי' קורנס של זהבים. ובקורנס של בשמים חלק בר' חייא בר

ושומשן ואם אין בהם מקום מגולה בחררה בלא גחלים . ובפגה בלא תבן אסור לטלטלן . ואלעזר בן תדאי סבר ...

עין משפט נר מצוה

ו א טוש"ע או"ח סימן תלט סעיף ה :

ז ב מיי' פכ"ה מהלכות שבת הלכה ז סמג לאוין סה טוש"ע או"ח סימן שח סעיף ג [ועי' בכ"י]:

ח ג מיי' שם הלכה טו סמג שם טוש"ע או"ח סימן שח סעיף ט :

ט ד ה מיי' שם הלכה ח סמג שם טוש"ע או"ח סימן שח סעיף יא :

י ו מיי' פ"ב מהלכות שבת הלכה יד וכ"ה הלכה לא טור וש"ע או"ח סימן שח סעיף ט :

מסורת הש"ס

[ערך זיירי] · [לקמן קכד. תוספתא פי"ד] · [לעיל נו. וש"נ] · ביצה יח. · [לעיל מג: לקמן קמא.] · שם · לעיל נב: כלים פי"ג מ"ה · [לעיל ס.] · [לעיל קיב.] · לעיל נב: [תוספ' דכלים ב"מ פ"ב] · [לעיל נב: וש"נ]

הגהות הב"ח

(א) גמ' וחררה שטמנה · נ"ב לשון רש"י בעירובין דף עז וחררה שטמינה בגחלים ...

(ב) רש"י ד"ה דבר שמלאכתו וכו' לגופו למלאכה כצ"ל ותיבת של נמחק :

גליון הש"ס

רש"י ד"ה הני נמי עלי ומדוכה. ע"ל ...

א) [ועי' תוס' לעיל דף מג. ד"ה או שמטן] ב) [ועי' תוס' חולין נב. ד"ה שיעורן] ג) [דף קכט:] *) שייך לקמן קודם ד"ה מדלענין

רב נסים גאון

הכל מודין בסיכי זיארי ומזורי . בגמרא דבני מערבא גרסי זירה דו עצר בה מזורי דו חבט בה וסיכי הן יתדות וגלוי הוא הדבר וידוע לכל :

עין משפט נר מצוה

יא א מיי' פכ"ו מהל' שבת הלכה ז:
יב ב מיי' פ"א מהלכות כלים הלכה י:
יג ג מיי' שם פ"ב הל"ב:
יד ד ה מיי' פכ"ה מהל' שבת הלכה ט סמג לאוין סה טור ושו"ע או"ח סימן שח סעיף א:
טו ו מיי' שם הלכה ג טוש"ע שם סעיף ג ד:
טז ז מיי' פ"ה מהלכות תמידין ומוספין הלכה יא:
יז ח מיי' פ"א מהלכות ק"פ הלכה יד:

[במשנה שבמשניות ליתא ר' יוסי אומר וכן מוכח מסוגיא דלקמן קנז. ע"ש אבל בעירובין לה. איתא סבר לה כר' יוסי דאמר כל הכלים ניטלין וכו' וצ"ע וכן ברי"ף ורא"ש איתא ר' יוסי אומר כל הכלים וכו']

[וע"ע תוס' מנחות נז. ד"ה לא סדור ותוספות עירובין דף קב: ד"ה והעליון]

אפיקטויזין בשבת ורב ששת התם לאו אורחיה הכא אורחיה אמר רב ששת מנא אמינא לה דתנן מחט של יד ליטול בה את הקוץ ורב נחמן התם פקיד הכא לא פקיד: **מתני'** קנה של זיתים אם יש קשר בראשו מקבל טומאה ואם לאו אין מקבל טומאה *בין כך ובין כך ניטל בשבת: **גמ'** אמאי פשוטי כלי עץ הוא *ופשוטי כלי עץ אינן מקבלין טומאה מ"ט *דומיא דשק בעינן תנא משמיה דר' נחמיה בשעה שמהפך בזיתים הופכו ורואה בו: **מתני'** *ר' יוסי אומר *כל הכלים ניטלין חוץ מן המסר הגדול ויתד של מחרישה: **גמ'** אמר ר"נ *האי °אוכלא דקצרי כיתד של מחרישה דמיא אמר אביי חרבא דאושכפי וסכינא דאשכבתא וחצינא דנגרי כיתד של מחרישה דמי ת"ר *בראשונה היו אומרים שלשה כלים ניטלין בשבת מקצוע של דבילה ווזהמא ליסטרן של קדרה וסכין קטנה שעל גבי שלחן התירו וחזרו והתירו וחזרו והתירו עד שאמרו כל הכלים ניטלין בשבת חוץ מן מסר הגדול ויתד של מחרישה מאי התירו וחזרו והתירו וחזרו והתירו אמר אביי התירו דבר שמלאכתו להיתר לצורך גופו וחזרו והתירו דבר שמלאכתו להיתר לצורך מקומו וחזרו והתירו דבר שמלאכתו לאיסור לצורך גופו אין לצורך מקומו לא ועדיין בידו אחת אין בשתי ידיו לא עד שאמרו כל הכלים ניטלין בשבת ואפי' בשתי ידים א"ל רבא מכדי התירו קתני מה לי לצורך גופו מה לי לצורך מקומו אלא אמר רבא התירו דבר שמלאכתו להיתר בין לצורך גופו ובין לצורך מקומו וחזרו והתירו מחמה לצל וחזרו והתירו דבר שמלאכתו לאיסור לצורך גופו ולצורך מקומו אין מחמה לצל לא ועדיין באדם אחד אין בשני בני אדם לא עד שאמרו כל הכלים ניטלין בשבת אפילו בשני בני אדם *איתיביה אביי מדוכה אם יש בה שום מטלטלין אותה ואם לאו אין מטלטלין אותה הכא במאי עסקינן מחמה לצל איתיביה *ושוין שאם קצב עליו בשר שאסור לטלטלו הכא נמי מחמה לצל אמר ר' חנינא *) בימי נחמיה בן חכליה נשנית משנה זו דכתיב °בימים ההמה ראיתי ביהודה דורכים גתות בשבת ומביאים הערימות אמר ר' אלעזר קנין ומקלות גלוסטרא ומדוכה כולן קודם התרת כלים נשנו קנין דתנן *לא סידור הקנין ולא נטילתן דוחה את השבת מקלות דתנן *מקלות דקין חלקין היו שם ומניחו על כתפו ועל כתף חבירו ותולה ומפשיט (*אמר) רבי אלעזר ארבעה עשר שחל להיות בשבת מניח ידו

*) [עי' תוס' ב"ק לד. ד"ה בימי]

תורה אור: נחמיה יג

רש"י

אפיקטויזין · להקיא שותה משקים ומקיא ולא לרפואה אלא להריק את מעיו שיוכל לאכול ולשתות [היום] הרבה כדאמרי' בפרק חבית ואע"ג דלא גזור בה משום שחיקת סממנין דהא לאו לרפואה היא אסור משום דמתקן גברא: הכא אורחיה · והרי הוא כמי שמאכילו ומשקהו: ליטול בה את הקוץ · אלמא תקוני גברא במידי דלאו לרפואה דליכא משום שחיקת סממנין שרי: פקיד · הקוץ הזה אינו מחובר בו אלא מופקד ונתון שם והוצאה זו אינו תיקון: הכא לא פקיד · ודמי למלאכה שמסדרן ומכניסן למקום חבור: **מתני'** קנה של זיתים · לאחר מסיקתן נוכר במעטן ושמנן מתאסף בתוכן ונוח לצאת ויש לו קנה להפכן בו ולבדוק אם כמרו כל צרכן ומגיען לבית הבד: אם יש קשר בראשו · כעין פקק של קנה קולמוס: מקבל טומאה · דכלי הוא לפי שעב בראשו קצת: ואם לאו · לא דמי לכלי ובגמ' מפרש לה: **גמ'** ואמאי · כי יש בו קשר בראשו נהי נמי דקשר משוי ליה מנא מיהו פשוטי כלי עץ הוא שאפילו חלול הוא אין חללו עשוי לקבל כלום: הופכו ורואה · בחלל ראשו שמשתייר שם ע"י שהוא פקוק בקשר מן השמן הזב מן הזיתים ובודק בו אם הגיעו לעצור וזו היא לו קבלה בחלל שלו ואם לאו שאין קשר בראשו אין השמן נראית שם מפני שאינו פקוק וכולו חלל הלכך לאו לקבל הוא עשוי והוי פשוטי כלי עץ ובין כך ובין כך ניטל בשבת דהא כלי הוא להפוך בו זיתים: **מתני'** מסר הגדול · מגירה גדולה שעשויה לקצוץ קורות: ויתד של מחרישה · הוא כלי גדול העשוי כסכין שבו עושין חריץ של תלם המענה קולטר"א בלע"ז דהנך קפיד עלייהו ומייחד להם מקום דלא חזו למלאכה אחרת: **גמ'** אוכלא דקצרי · כלי נחושת העשוי כנפה נקבים נקבים והוא של כובסים ונותנו על הבגדים ומזלף בו המים עליהן וי"מ שמגמרין מוגמר מתחתיו והבגדים מונחין עליו ומתגמרין דרך הנקבים: חרבא דאושכפי · סכין של רצענין: וסכינא דאשכבתא · סכין של בית המקולין שהקצבין מקצבין בו בשר: חצינא · דולויר"א כל הני קפדי עלייהו משום דמפגמי ומקצי להו בידים: ג' כלים · ותו לא ולקמן אמרינן דבימי נחמיה בן חכליה בבית שני גזרו על טלטול כל הכלים כדי לגדור גדר להחמיר באיסורי שבת מפני שהיו מקילין בה: מקצוע · איזמל שמחתכין בו דבלה יעשהו במקצועות מתרגמינן באיזמליהון (ישעיה מד): זוהמא לסטרון · כף גדולה שמסלקין בו זוהמא של קדרה: וסכין קטן · שחותכין בו לחם ובשר ואוכלין דהני תדירין בתשמיש: התירו · עוד כשראו שחזרו להזהר קצת באיסור שבת וחזרו והתירו כשנזהרו יותר וחזרו והתירו ולקמיה מפרש מאי כולהו הנך התירו: עד שאמרו · עוד חזרו והתירו את הכל עד שאמרו הכל ניטלין חוץ מן המסר הגדול כו': התירו · לטלטל דבר שעיקר מלאכתו בחול להיתר לדבר המותר בשבת התירו לטלטל לצורך גופו אם הוצרך להשתמש בגוף הכלי אבל לא משום שהוצרך למקומו: וחזרו והתירו · את אלו לצורך מקומו: וחזרו והתירו אף מי שמלאכתו לאיסור · והוצרך לו בשבת לגופו למלאכת היתר ומיהו לא הותרו אלו לצורך מקומו: כל הכלים · הללו שאמרנו חוץ מן המסר הגדול דלא שרי לא לצורך גופו ולא לצורך מקומו ואביי דמתרץ הכי הדר ביה לגבי רבה דאמר לעיל קורנס של נפחים שניטו לדבר שמלאכתו לאיסור שרי לצורך גופו: א"ל רבא מכדי · לצורך התירו בפעם ראשונה: מה לי גופו מה לי מקומו · תרווייהו צורך נינהו: מחמה לצל · שאינו צריך לו עכשיו לא לגופו ולא למקומו אלא חס עליו שמא יתבקע בחמה: עד שאמרו · היינו עוד היתר אחרינא כל הכלים אפי' גדולים ומיהו לכדאוקימנא של היתר אפי' מחמה לצל ושל איסור לצורך גופו או מקומו: אין מטלטלין אותה · בשלמא לדידי אין מטלטלין אותה לצורך מקומה קאמר אלא לדידך אמאי: משנה זו · דלעיל בראשונה היו אומרין ג' כלים ותו לא משום דהוו מזלזלים בשבתות דכתיב בימים ההמה וגו': קנים ומקלות כו' · משניות הן כדמפרש ואזיל: קודם התרת כלים · מנין האחרון שהותרו כולן לצורך גופן לאביי ולרבא אף לצורך מקומו: לא סידור הקנים · שהיו נותנין במערכת לחם הפנים בין חלה לחלה להפרידן ליכנס הרוח ביניהן שלא יתעפשו: ולא נטילתן · מן המערכה ישנה: דוחה את השבת · אלא נכנס בע"ש ונוטל הקנים ולמחר מסלק המערכה הישנה ומסדר החדשה בלא קנים ולמוצאי שבת נכנס ונותן הקנים ביניהן זו נשנית קודם היתר מנין הראשון דהא מלאכתן להיתר וקאסר להו לצורך גופן: מקלין דקין וחלקין היו · בעזרה בפסח שחל להיות י"ד בחול:

ידו

תוספות

וסכינא דאשכבתא · פירש בקונטרס סכין שהקצבים מקצבין בה בשר וי"מ סכין שמוחטין בה שמקפיד שלא תיפגם ויש ליזהר שלא לטלטלו אפי' לצורך גופו דהוי כיתד של מחרישה דאפי' ר"ש מודה כדאמרינן בסוף מכילתין (דף קנז:):

מקצוע של דבילה · לא חשיב אלא כלים דלאו בני קיבול דהא פשיטא דכוסות וקערות ולגוזיות היו מטלטלין:

איתיביה אביי מדוכה · בשלמא לדידי מוקמינן לצורך מקומו וה"מ לשנויי כר' נחמיה כדשני לעיל ואביי נמי הוה ידע דהא משני ליה רבה הכי לעיל אלא פריך לרבא אולי יאמר תירוץ אחר ורבא לא בעי לשנויי כר' נחמיה דלית הלכתא כוותיה ורבה דמשני ליה כר' נחמיה משום דמשמע ליה אין מטלטלין אותם בשום ענין: **הכא** נמי מחמה לצל · והא דנקט נקצב עליו בשר אע"ג דלצורך גופו ומקומו נמי שרי לאשמעינן דאפילו בהא פליגי ב"ש דלא שרו מחמת שמחת יו"ט:

לא סידור קנים · אע"ג דאין שבות(א) במקדש כמה שבותים *אשכחן במקדש *שגזרו פעמים לצורך כי הכא בקנים ומקלות לפי שהיו מחללים את השבת: *הרי היא ככל הכלים · אע"ג דקודם התרת כלים נשנית איכא למימ' ככל הכלים כעין כוסות וקערות:

הא

עיין לקמן דף קנז.

מסורת הש"ס

[חולין כה.]

לעיל פג: חגיגה כו: מנחות נז: [בכורות לח.]

לקמן קנז. עירובין לה.

[גי' הערוך בערך אבל אובלא וע"ש פירושו בשני אופנים]

[תוספ' פט"ז]

[לקמן קכד.]

ביצה יא. [תוספ' ביצה פ"א]

מנחות צו.

פסחים סה.

[צ"ל ר' אלעזר אומר]

הגהות הב"ח

(א) תוס' ד"ה לא סידור וכו' דאין שבות כ"כ ע"ל פרק המצניע דף צג בתוס' ד"ה שלא זילותא:

גליון הש"ס

תוס' ד"ה לא וכו' אשכחן במקדש. ע"ל דף קכו ע"א תוס' ד"ה המונח:

רבינו חננאל

ממטן למעלן אסיר. פי' אם יש לאדם פוגלא טמונה בתבן או אפילו בעפר תיחוח עומדת כעין נטועה ראשה טמונה ועליה מגולין עכשיו כשבא לנוטלה אם אוחז בעלים ומושך הראש ומסלקה זהו ממעלה למטה. אע"פ כשמגביה התבן והעפר משתרבב במקומן ויורד שרי אבל לאחוז קצה הראש הטמונה ולהגביהה ממטה למעלה לא. אלמא שטלטול מן הצד שמיה טלטול. ומפרקינן הדר ביה מההיא. מחט שניטל חררה או עוקצה. פי' חרירה הנקב שלה. עוקצה ראשה הוא. חידודה תרגמה אביי אליבא דרבא בגלמי והן פשוטין כדתנן גלמי כלי מתכות טהורין פשוטיהן טמאין ואלו הן וכו'. והן חוטי ברזל משוכין וחותך אותן חתיכות חתיכות ולוקח מהן האומן כשיעור אורך מחט ומחדד ראשה האחת ונוקב הקצה השני ונעשה מחט. וקודם שיחדדנה וינקבנה נקראת אותה החתיכה גולם. כגון זו וכיוצא בה שהן עומדות להעשות כלי ניטלין בשבת. אבל מחט שניטל חררה או עוקצה אסור. גרוטאות הוא לשון יון. ופתרונו כלי מוכן להטיל בו התגר כלי נחושת או כלי ברזל שבורין שיזדמנו לו לקנותם קונה ומשליכם לאותו כלי כדי להתיכם. ונקראין גרוטאות ומיכן נהגו לקרות לתגר גרוטאות:

אסובי ינוקא. פי' כשנופל ערלת הגרון של תינוק משימה החיה את אצבעותיה בפיו ומסלקת אותה הערלה. ופעמים שמקיא התינוק ועל זה אקשינן עלה והא אין עושין אפיקטויזין בשבת כו'. ורבותינו הגאונים אמרו פי' אחר. ואנן כתבנו מה שקבלנו מרבותינו: **מתני'** קנה של זיתים כו'. ואמרינן אמאי פשוטי כלי עץ הוא ואין מקבלין טומאה. ומפרקינן תנא משמיה דר' נחמיה בשעה שמהפך בו את הזיתים הופכו ורואה בו. ולא פי' מה הוא רואה בו. אבל פירשו בתלמוד א"י. קנה שהתקינו להיות בודק בו הזיתים. כיצד הוא יודע אם מלוכלך במשקה בידוע שנגמרה מלאכת המעטן. ואם לאו בידוע שלא נגמרה מלאכת המעטן. א"ל ר' מנא לא תני שמואל אלא להיות שולה בו הזיתים. כלומר יש בו בית קבול: **אמר** רב נחמן האי אובלא דקצרי כיתד של מחרישה דמי. ואסור לטלטלה. אובלא. אבן גדולה שנותן הכובס עליה היריעה שרוצה ללבנה והיא שרויה במים ומכה עליו במזורי. מכה ומהפך ומכה. ועוד שורה ומכה. ואחרי שישלים שוטחה ומייבשה. ועוד חוזר ושורה אותה פעם אחר פעם עד שתתלבן היטב. וי"א כלי חרס מנוקב שטופין אותו ע"ג גחלים ומקטרן בגפרית הכלים ללבנן. אמר אביי חרבא דאשכפתא. וסכינא דאשכבתא וחצינא דנגרי כיתד של מחרישה דמו ואסור לטלטלם. חרבא דאשכפי. איזמל של שכף כדמתרגמינן עשה לך חרבות צורים. איזמלין חריפין. סכינא דאשכבתא. סכין המיוחדת לשחיטה בלבד. חצינא דנגרי הוא גרזן. והוא המעצד של חרש כיון דקפדי אפגמיהו קבע ליה מקום ומסיח דעתו מלעשות בהן מלאכה אחרת הללו וכיוצא בהן שהן מוקצה מחמת חסרון כיס אסור לטלטלן בשבת. והרי מפורש בסוף פרק מי שהחשיך דכולהו הני היינו טעמא דאסירי משום דמוקצה מחמת חסרון כיס נינהו. ואפילו ר' שמעון מודה דתנן סתמא לדברי הכל כל הכלים ניטלין בשבת חוץ מן המסר הגדול ויתד של מחרישה. מקצוע של דבילה כלי ברזל שחותכין בו דבילה. וזומליסטרון תרווד שמהפך בו הקדירה. כדתנן זומליסטרא שנטל כפה טמאה מפני המזלג וכו'. א"ר חנינא בימי נחמיה בן חכליה נשנית משנה זו דכתיב בימים ההמה ראיתי ביהודה דורכים גיתות בשבת. כיון שראום כך שהקילו בשבת אסרו להן כל הכלים ושרי להן הא דתנן רבנן. בראשונה היו אומרים שלשה כלים ניטלין בשבת מקצוע של דבילה וזומליסטרון של קדירה. וסכין קטנה. כיון שנגדרו וחזרו לדקדק בשמירת שבת היו מתירין להן והולכין עד שהתירו הכל חוץ ממסר הגדול ויתד של מחרישה. וכך הוא מפורש בתלמוד א"י: **א"ר** אלעזר קנים ומקלות וקלוסטרא ומדוכה כולם קודם התרת כלים נשנו. ולפיכך נשנו באיסור. קנים הם קנים של לחם הפנים. והן שנוין במס' מנחות

רב נסים גאון

בשעה שמהפך בו זיתים הופכו ורואה בו. בגמ' דבני מערבא גרס' דבי ר' ינאי אמרי קנה שהתקינו להפך בו זיתים כיצד הוא יודע אם היה מלוכלך במשקה בידוע שנגמר מלאכת המעטן ואם לאו בידוע שלא נגמרה מלאכת המעטן אמר לון ר' לא תני שמואל אלא להיות שולה בו את הזיתים ומשום הכי אמרי דמקבל טומאה והואיל וככלי קיבול דמי. אמר רב נחמן האי אוכלא דקצרי כיתד של מחרישה דמי אוכלא דקצרי הוא כלי שרוצה לדלעת ומנוקב הוא כולו נקבין ובו מזלפין מים הכובסין על הבגדים ומשכחת לה בפ' כל ישראל יש להם חלק (סנהדרין דף לג) אמרו מנקבין אותו ככברה אמר אביי כאוכלא דקצרי:

a Because we learnt: One must not use an emetic[1] [123b] on the Sabbath.[2] And R. Shesheth?[3]—There it is unnatural, whereas here it is natural.[4] R. Shesheth said, Whence do I rule thus? Because we learnt: A SMALL NEEDLE TO REMOVE A THORN.[5] And R. Naḥman?—There it is [externally] deposited,[6] whereas here it is not [externally] deposited.[7]

MISHNAH. A CANE FOR OLIVES,[8] IF IT HAS A BULB ON TOP,[9] IS SUSCEPTIBLE TO DEFILEMENT; IF NOT, IT IS NOT SUSCEPTIBLE TO DEFILEMENT. IN BOTH CASES IT MAY BE HANDLED ON THE SABBATH.

GEMARA. Why so? It is a flat wooden utensil, and these are not susceptible to uncleanness; what is the reason? We require [something] similar to a '*sack*'?[10]—It was taught in R. Nehemiah's name: When he turns the olives he reverses it and looks at it.[11]

MISHNAH. R. JOSE SAID: ALL UTENSILS MAY BE HANDLED, EXCEPT A LARGE SAW AND THE PIN OF A PLOUGH.[12]

GEMARA. R. Naḥman said: A fuller's trough[13] is like the pin of a plough. Abaye said: A cobbler's knife and a butcher's b chopper and a carpenter's adze are like the pin of a plough.[1]

Our Rabbis taught: At first they [the Sages] ruled, Three utensils may be handled on the Sabbath: A fig-cake knife,[2] a pot soup-ladle,[3] and a small table-knife. Then[4] they permitted [other articles], and they permitted again [still more], and they permitted still further, until they ruled: All utensils may be handled on the Sabbath except a large saw and the pin of a plough. What is meant by 'then they permitted [other articles], and they permitted again [still more], and they permitted still further'?—Said Abaye: [First] they permitted an article whose function is for a permitted purpose, provided it was required for itself;[5] then they further permitted an article whose function is for a permitted purpose, even when its place is required; then they further permitted an article whose function is for a forbidden purpose, provided it was required for itself,[6] but not when its place is required. Yet still [these might be handled] with one hand only, but not with two hands,[7] until they [finally] ruled, All utensils may be handled on the Sabbath even with both hands. Raba observed to him, Consider: he [the Tanna] teaches, they permitted [other things], what difference is it whether they are required for themselves or their place is needed?[8] Rather said Raba: [First] they permitted an article whose function is for a permitted purpose, both when required for itself or when its place is required; then they further permitted [it to be moved] from the sun to the shade;[9] then they further permitted an article whose function is for a forbidden purpose [to be moved] only when it is required for itself or when its place is required, but not from the sun to the shade. Yet [it c might] still [be moved] by one person only, but not by two,[1] until thy ruled: All utensils may be handled on the Sabbath, even by two persons.

Abaye put an objection to him: A mortar containing garlic may be handled; if not, it may not be handled?[2]—We treat here of [moving it] from the sun to the shade. He refuted him: And both hold alike that if he had cut meat upon it it may not be handled?[3]—Here too it means from the sun to the shade.

R. Ḥanina said: This Mishnah[4] was taught in the days of Nehemiah the son of Hacaliah, for it is written, *In those days I saw in Judah some treading winepresses on the Sabbath, and bringing in sheaves.*[5]

R. Eleazar said: [The laws about] canes, staves, fastenings, and mortar[6] were all learnt before the permission re [the handling of] utensils. 'Canes', for we learnt: Neither the placing of the canes nor their removal supersedes the Sabbath.[7] 'Staves', as we learnt: There were thin smooth staves there, which one placed on his shoulder and his fellow's shoulder, then he suspended [the sacrifice d upon them] and skinned it.[1] R. Eleazar said: If the fourteenth [of

a (1) In order to leave room for more food. (2) V. *infra* 147a. (3) How does he explain that? (4) Hence it is the same as feeding an infant. (5) And this is similar. (6) The thorn is laid in the flesh, as it were, but has not entered the system. (7) But is within the system, and to bring it out by causing vomiting is like mending a person, which is similar to repairing a utensil (cf. *supra* 106a). (8) Used for stirring a mass of maturing olives to see whether they are fit for pressing. (9) Closing one end of the reed. (10) Which has a receptacle. The reference is to Lev. XI, 32. (11) Viz., at the oil which penetrates the hollow reed; for this a bulbous (closed) top is required, which turns the cane into a utensil technically containing a receptacle. (12) One is very particular not to use these for any purpose but their own, and this makes them *mukẓeh*. (13) Rashi: (i) A sieve-like perforated tub placed above the linen; water is poured over it, whereby the linen is sprinkled through the holes. Or (ii) the same, the linen being placed inside and incense is burnt underneath, so that the fragrance ascends and perfumes the garments.

b (1) They may not be handled. (2) I.e., for cutting a cake of pressed figs. (3) זוהמא ליסטרן (v. *infra*, n. c5). Rashi: for removing the scum of the soup. (4) When they saw that the people became more strict in Sabbath observance. (5) I.e., when it was required for use, but not when its place was required. (6) To use it in a permitted labour. (7) I.e., if too heavy for one hand they might not be handled. (8) When they permitted the one they would certainly simultaneously permit the other. (9) To avoid scorching; though here neither the article itself is required for use, nor the place where it lies.

c (1) Cf. *supra*, n. b7. (2) Abaye can explain that it may not be handled when its place only is required, since its normal function is forbidden; but how can Raba explain it? (3) V. *supra a* for notes. (4) *Sc.* the first ruling which permitted only three utensils to be handled but forbade all others. (5) Neh. XIII, 15. To counteract this laxity the Rabbis had to be particularly severe.—v. Halevy: *Doroth*, I, 3, pp. 310–345 for the dates of the Rabbinical enactments, and particularly pp. 344 *seqq.* for the present passage. Weiss, *Dor*, I, p. 57, n. 2 argues that the Greek form of the word זומליסטרון (this is the form given in Kel. XIII, 2, though it is variously corrupted elsewhere—Gk. ζωμάρυστρον = ζωμήρυσις) proves that this ruling must be much later, certainly not before the Greeks spread in Palestine and the Jews became acquainted with them. This is not conclusive: the original enactment may have employed a Hebrew word which was changed later in the academies, when the Greek form became more familiar. (6) The Gemara proceeds to state these laws. (7) Canes were placed between the loaves of showbread, to permit the air to circulate about them, so that they should not become mouldy. The loaves were set from one Sabbath to the next. Since the canes might not be handled then, they would have to be removed on Friday and rearranged at the conclusion of the Sabbath. Thus for a short while the loaves would be without them.

d (1) These staves were placed in the Temple court and used for the Passover sacrifice in the manner stated.

Nisan] fell on a Sabbath, one placed [124a] his hand upon his fellow's shoulder, and his fellow's hand [rested] upon his shoulder, and so [the animal] was suspended and skinned.[2] 'A fastening', as we learnt: If a door-bolt has on its top a fastening contrivance,[3] R. Joshua said: One may shift it from one door and hang it on another on the Sabbath;[4] R. Tarfon said: It is like all utensils, and may be moved about in a courtyard. 'A mortar': that which we have stated.[5] Said Rabbah, Whence [does that follow]: perhaps in truth I may argue that they were learnt after the permission re utensils. [Thus:] what was the reason of [placing] canes? On account of mouldiness; but in that short while[6] they would not become mouldy. As for the staves, it was possible [to act] as R. Eleazar [stated]. The fastening may be as R. Jannai, who said: We treat here of a courtyard not provided with an *'erub*:[7] [now,] R. Joshua holds, The inside of the door[8] is as within, so one carries a utensil of the house through the courtyard;[9] whereas R. Tarfon holds that the inside of the door is as without, so one carries a utensil of the courtyard in the courtyard. As for a mortar, that agrees with R. Nehemiah.[10]

MISHNAH. ALL UTENSILS MAY BE HANDLED WHETHER REQUIRED OR NOT REQUIRED. R. NEHEMIAH SAID: THEY MAY BE HANDLED ONLY WHEN REQUIRED.

GEMARA. What does REQUIRED AND NOT REQUIRED
a mean?—Rabbah[1] said: REQUIRED: an article whose function is for a permitted purpose [may be moved] when required itself; NOT REQUIRED: an article whose function is for a permitted purpose [may be moved] when its place is required;[2] but an article whose function is for a forbidden purpose may [be handled] only when required itself,[3] but not when its place is required. Whereupon R. Nehemiah comes to say that even an article whose function is for a permitted purpose [may be handled] only when required itself, but not when its place [alone] is required. Said Raba to him: If its place is required, do you call it: NOT REQUIRED! Rather said Raba: REQUIRED: an article whose function is for a permitted purpose [may be handled] whether required itself or its place is required: NOT REQUIRED [means] even from the sun to the shade; whilst an article whose function is for a forbidden purpose [may be moved] only when required itself or its place is required, but not from the sun to the shade. Whereupon R. Nehemiah comes to say that even an article whose function is for a permitted purpose [may be moved] only when required

(2) But the staves might not be used then. (3) This had a thick head and could be used as a pestle. (4) *Shometah* implies that it may be pushed from one to the other, but not picked up in the usual way. (5) *Supra* 123*b*. Now R. Eleazar maintains that all these prohibitions held good only before the extended permission in respect to utensils, by which they were abolished. (6) V. *supra* 123*b*, n. c7. (7) Many houses open into the courtyard. Utensils may not be carried from the houses into the yard, but those already in the yard from before the Sabbath may be moved about therein. (8) Where the fastening contrivance is to be found. (9) Which if done in the normal way is forbidden; therefore it may only be 'shifted' (v. n. 4). (10) Who maintains that no utensil may be moved for any but its normal use. Hence all four may have been taught after the extended permission was given: the first two remain forbidden because there was no need for handling them at all, the third is connected with the interdict of carrying from one domain to another, whilst the fourth represents an individual view.

a (1) Alfasi and Asheri read: Abaye. (2) Though the article itself is not. (3) For a permitted labour.

For the continuation of the English translation of this page see overleaf.

מסורת הש"ס

ידו על כתף חבירו ויד חבירו על כתיפו ותולה ומפשיט גלוסטרא דתנן* א נגר שיש בראשו גלוסטרא ר' יהושע אומר שומטה מן פתח זה ותולה בחבירו בשבת ר' טרפון אומר הרי הוא ככל הכלים ומיטלטל בחצר מדוכה הא דאמרן אמר רבה ממאי דילמא לעולם אימא לך לאחר התרת כלים נשנו קנים טעמא מאי משום איעפושי בהאי פורתא לא מיעפש מקלות אפשר כר' אלעזר גלוסטרא כדרבי ינאי דאמר רבי ינאי בחצר שאינה מעורבת עסקינן רבי יהושע סבר תוך הפתח כלפנים דמי וקמטלטל מנא דבתים בחצר ור' טרפון סבר תוך הפתח כלחוץ דמי ומנא דחצר בחצר קא מטלטל מדוכה ר' נחמיה היא: **מתני'** ב כל הכלים ניטלין לצורך ושלא לצורך *ר' נחמיה אומר אין ניטלין אלא לצורך: **גמ'** מאי לצורך ומאי שלא לצורך אמר *רבה לצורך דבר שמלאכתו להיתר לצורך גופו שלא לצורך דבר שמלאכתו להיתר לצורך מקומו ודבר שמלאכתו לאיסור לצורך גופו אין לצורך מקומו לא ואתא רבי נחמיה למימר ואפילו דבר שמלאכתו להיתר לצורך גופו אין לצורך מקומו לא אמר ליה רבא לצורך מקומו שלא לצורך קרית ליה אלא אמר רבא ג לצורך דבר שמלאכתו להיתר בין לצורך גופו בין לצורך מקומו שלא לצורך ואפי' מחמה לצל ד ודבר שמלאכתו לאיסור לצורך גופו ולצורך מקומו אין מחמה לצל לא ואתא רבי נחמיה למימר ואפילו דבר שמלאכתו להיתר לצורך גופו ולצורך מקומו אין מחמה לצל לא יתיב רב ספרא ורב אחא בר הונא ורב הונא בר חנינא ויתבי וקאמרי לרבה אליבא דרבי נחמיה הני קערות היכי מטלטלינן אמר להו רב ספרא מידי דהוה אגרף של רעי אמר ליה אביי לרבה למר אליבא דרבי נחמיה הני קערות היכי מטלטלינן להו אמר ליה רב ספרא חברין תרגמה מידי דהוה אגרף של רעי איתיביה אביי לרבא* מדוכה אם יש בה שום מטלטלין אותה ואם לאו אין מטלטלין אותה הכא במאי עסקינן מחמה לצל איתיביה *ושוין שאם קיצב עליו בשר שאסור לטלטלו הכא נמי מחמה לצל והא דתנן *ה אין סומכין את הקדירה בבקעת וכן בדלת והא בקעת דביום טוב דבר שמלאכתו להיתר הוא אלמא דבר שמלאכתו להיתר בין לצורך גופו בין לצורך מקומו אסור התם(א) מאי טעמא כיון דבשבת דבר שמלאכתו לאיסור הוא גזירה יו"ט אטו שבת וכי תימא שבת גופיה תישתרי דהא דבר שמלאכתו לאיסור לצורך גופו ולצורך מקומו שרי ו הני מילי היכא דאיכא תורת כלי עליו היכא דליכא תורת כלי עליו לא °ומי גזרינן והתנן* ז משילין פירות דרך ארובה ביום טוב ח אבל לא בשבת ומי לא גזרינן והתנן* ט אין בין יו"ט לשבת אלא אוכל נפש בלבד אמר רב יוסף לא קשיא הא ר' אליעזר הא רבי יהושע *דתניא אותו ואת בנו שנפלו לבור ר' אליעזר אומר מעלה את הראשון על מנת לשוחטו ושוחטו והשני עושה לו פרנסה במקומו בשביל שלא ימות ר' יהושע אומר מעלה את הראשון על מנת לשוחטו ואינו שוחטו ומערים ומעלה את השני רצה זה שוחט רצה זה שוחט *ממאי דילמא עד כאן לא קאמר ר' אליעזר התם אלא דאפשר לפרנסה אבל היכא דלא אפשר לפרנסה לא אי נמי עד כאן לא קאמר רבי יהושע התם דאפשר בהערמה אבל היכא דלא אפשר בהערמה לא אלא אמר רב פפא לא קשיא הא בית שמאי הא בית הלל דתנן בית שמאי אומרים

אין

ידו על כתף חברו · דלא מטלטלי מקלות: גלוסטרא · דתנן רבי יהושע אמר נגר שיש בראשו גלוסטרא שראשה עב וראוי לדוך בו שום וטעלין בו דלת: שומטה מפתח זה ותולה בחברו · ואע"ג דלריך לגופו לתלותו בחברו ולנועלה בו שומטו ע"י גרירה אבל טלטול גמור לא ואע"פ שמלאכתו להיתר לא שרי ליה לצורך גופו: מדוכה הא דאמרן · לעיל אע"ג דשנייה רבא לעיל מחמה לצל ואביי שנייה לצורך מקומו שינויי דחיקי נינהו אלא קודם התרת כלים נשנו: קנים טעמא מאי · מסדרין אותם במערכה: משום איעפושי · דלא סמכינן אניסא ומשום ההוא פורתא שהישנה מתעכבת בלא קנים מלילי שבת לשבת והחדשה משבת למוצ"ש לא מיעפשי: כדר"א · מניח ידו על כתף חבירו: שאינה מעורבת · שהרבה בתים פתוחים לה ולא עירבו דכלים ששבתו בבתים אסור להוציאן לחצר וששבתו בחצר מותר לטלטלן בחצר שהחצר כולו רשות לעצמו הוא והבתים מיוחדים לכל איש ביתו: תוך הפתח · שנטל הנגר משם: וקא מטלטל מנא דבית בחצר · הלכך שומטה אין דטלטול מן הצד היא אבל טלטול גמור לא: מדוכה רבי נחמיה היא · דאמר* ובעירובין (דף לה:) אפילו טלית ואפי' תרווד אין ניטלין אלא לצורך תשמיש המיוחד: **מתני'** ה"ג במתניתין כל הכלים ניטלין לצורך כו': **גמ'** מאי לצורך ומאי שלא לצורך אמר רבה כו'· לצורך דשרי תנא קמא הייט דבר שמלאכתו להיתר ומטלטלו לצורך גופו: שלא לצורך דבר שמלאכתו להיתר · ומטלטלו שלא לצורך גופו אבל צריך למקומו: ודבר שמלאכתו לאיסור לצורך גופו. הוא דאישתרי אם צריך לו למלאכת היתר אבל שלא לצורך גופו ואע"ג דצריך למקומו לא ורבה לטעמיה דאמר לעיל (דף קכג:) גבי קורנס של נפחים נמי מותר לצורך גופו: א"ל רבא כו' אלא אמר כו' · ולרבא דמוקי אליבא דרבי נחמיה דלצורך גופו ולצורך מקומו מותר ע"כ האי לצורך גופו כגון שזה התשמיש מיוחד לו דתניא לקמן בפרק חבית (דף קמו.) רבי נחמיה אומר אפילו תרווד ואפילו טלית אין ניטלין אלא לצורך תשמישן וצורך מקומו נמי לרבא כלצורך גופו ותשמישו דמי ולרבה צורך גופו הוא דשרי רבי נחמיה ודוקא לתשמיש המיוחד לו ובין לרבה ובין לרבא דוקא דבר שמלאכתו להיתר אבל דבר שמלאכתו לאיסור אפילו לצורך גופו לא שרי רבי נחמיה דהאי צורך גופו לאו תשמיש המיוחד לו הוא דהא מיוחד למלאכת איסור: לרבה אליבא דרבי נחמיה · דאמר דבר שמלאכתו להיתר לצורך מקומו לא: הני קערות· לאחר אכילה היכי מטלטל להו לסלקן מלפניו: ואם לאו אין מטלטלין אותה. בשלמא לרבה כגון דאין צריך לגופה [אלא למקומה] אלא לדידך אמאי: וכן בדלת · אוקימנא במסכת ביצה וכן הדלת אין סומכין בבקעת וביו"ט קיימי: והא בקעת ביו"ט מלאכתה להיתר היא· דלהסקה חזי וקיימא וקאסר לטלטלה לצורך גופו למלאכה אחרת וכל שכן לצורך מקומה: ומשני התם(ג) טעמא כיון דבשבת אסור דהא בקעת בשבת מלאכתה לאיסור היא ביום טוב נמי אסור גזירה י"ט אטו שבת: משילין פירות דרך ארובה ביום טוב · בהדיא תנן אבל לא בשבת פירות השטוחים על הגג לייבשן וראה גשמים ממשמשים ובאין משילן לארץ דרך ארובת הגג דלא טריחא מילתא דנופלין מאליהן אלמא דלא גזרינן ופרכינן ומי לא גזרינן והתנן אין בין כו': לא קשיא הא. דתנן משילין דשרי טירחא ביו"ט משום איבוד ממון רבי יהושע היא שהתיר להעלות בהמה בהערמה מן הבור: והא · דתנן אין בין כו' ר"א היא: דאפשר בהערמה · דמיחזי כמאן דעביד לצורך יו"ט אבל גבי משילין דליכא הערמה לדמויי להתירא לא:

אין

הא ר"א · ההיא דאין בין אע"ג דבפ"ק דמגילה (דף ז:) דייקינן עלה הא לענין מכשירי אוכל נפש זה וזה שוין וקאמר מתני' דלא כרבי יהודה ור"א סבירא ליה כר"י ועדיפא מדרבי יהודה כדאמר בריש תולין (לקמן דף קלז:) איכא למימר דההוא תנא סבר לה כוותיה בחדא דגזרינן י"ט אטו שבת ופליג עליה במכשירין ועוד יש לומר דאין בין דפ"ק דמגילה מיירי במילי דאורייתא ואין בין דהכא הייט דתנן במשילין (ביצה ד' לז:) דמיירי במילי דשבות ואיט מענין אחד תדע דהכי פריך עלה בפ' משילין כדפריך הכא בשמעתא ולא פריך בפ"ק דמגילה והא דדייק התם הא לענין מכשירין זה וזה שוין לא דייק בפרק משילין:

הא

עין משפט נר מצוה

יח א מיי' פכ"ו מהלכות שבת הלכה ט סמג לאוין סה טוש"ע או"ח סימן שיג סעיף א:

יט ב ג מיי' פכ"ה שם הלכה ג סמג שם טוש"ע או"ח סימן שח סעיף ד:

כ ד מיי' שם טוש"ע שם סעיף ג:

כא ה מיי' פ"ד מהלכות יו"ט הלכה יא טור שו"ע או"ח סימן תקג סעיף ג:

כב ו מיי' פכ"ה מהל' שבת הלכה ו טוש"ע או"ח סימן שח סעיף ז:

כג ז מיי' פ"ה מהלכות יו"ט הלכה ה טור שו"ע או"ח סימן תקכא סעיף א:

כד ח טוש"ע או"ח סימן שלא סעיף ז:

כה ט מיי' פ"א מהלכות יו"ט הלכה א סמג לאוין עה טוש"ע או"ח סימן תצה סעיף א:

[גי' הרי"ף והרא"ש אביי]

לקמן קלז: ביצה כח. לז: מגילה ז: [תוספתא דמגילה פ"א]

ס פי"א מ"ד [ושם ליתא להך תיבה נגר שיש בראשו]

לקמן קמו.]

[לעיל לז. וש"נ

לעיל קכג.]

:וביצה יח.]

ביצה לב:

...ה לה: לז.

ביצה לז. [תוספתא ביצה פ"ג]

...ה לז. ע"ש]

הגהות הב"ח

(א) גמ' התם ...יטו טעמא ...ון דבשבת: ...רש"י ד"ה ומשני התם ...נו טעמא:

גליון הש"ס

...'ומי גזרינן ...תנן משילין. ע"ל דף כג ע"ב תוספות ...ד"ה גזירה:

רבינו חננאל

שאסור בשבת סידורן ונטילתן מתוך לחם הפנים. מקלות מפורש במס' פסחים. בזמן שחל י"ד להיות בשבת אסר ר' אלעזר לטלטל מקל ולהניחו על כתיפו ועל כתף חבירו לתלות הפסח בו ולהפשיטו. וכן גלוסטרא. היא משנה בכלים פ' י"א שאסר ר' יהושע לטלטלה בשבת. תוספתא דכלים בתחלת בב"מ קלוסטרא ר' טרפון מטמא וחכמים מטהרין. ברוריה אומר שומטה מפתח זה ותולה בחבירו בשבת. כשנאמרו דברים לפני ר' יהושע אמר יפה אמר ברוריה. והוא ...נין הזה בעירובין בסופו. מדוכה זו שאמרנו למעלה אלו כולן כלים הן וקודם התרת כלים נשנו שאסור לטלטלן בשבת. (* אבל אחר התרת כלים מותרין הן וחלק רבא על רבי אלעזר ואמר דלמא אחר ...רת כלים נשנו ואסורין הן לעולם. ודבריו פשוטין הן: מתני' כל הכלים הניטלין לצורך ניטלין לצורך ושלא לצורך כו'. פירש רבא משנה זו לצורך דבר שמלאכתו להיתר כגון קערות וכוסות וכדומה להן. ...מותר לכתחלה לטלטלן לאכול ולשתות בהן הללו מותרין לטלטלן בין לצורך גופו לאכול בהן בין לצורך מקומו לפנותן כדי לישב במקומן. דבר שמלאכתו לאיסור כגון קורנס של נפחים וכדומה לו לצורך גופו ...כול בהן(מותר) [כגון] לפצוע בו אגוזין מותר. אבל לצורך מקומן אסור. ורבי נחמיה אמר אפילו דבר שמלאכתו להיתר כגון קערות וכדומה להן לצורך גופו לאכול בהן מותר. אבל אחר שיאכל בהן אסור לטלטלן ...צורך]מקומן. ועל זה הקשה ליה אביי לרבה למר אליבא דר' נחמי' הני קערות כלומר שאינו מטלטלן אלא לצורך אכילה בהן אחר שיאכל אדם היאך מטלטלן ומסלקן מן השולחן. והשיבו לו כבר נתקשה זה לרב ...רא חברין. ופירק מידי דהוה אגרף של רעי ושל מימי רגלים נוטלן ושופכן וכו'. דתניא בתוספתא גרף של רעי שמותר לטלטל לדברי הכל. ובזמן שאמר רבה דברים הללו השיבו רבא לצורך מקומו שלא לצורך ...רית ליה. אלא אמר לצורך דבר שמלאכתו להיתר בין לצורך גופו בין לצורך מקומו. שלא לצורך אפילו מחמה לצל. ודבר שמלאכתו לאיסור לצורך גופו ולצורך מקומו אין. מחמה לצל לא. ואתא ר' נחמיה ...ימר דאפילו דבר שמלאכתו להיתר לצורך גופו ולצורך מקומו אין. מחמה לצל לא. מותיב אביי (לרבה) [לרבא] לדידך דאמרת דבר שמלאכתו לאיסור אפילו לצורך מקומו מטלטל והרי מדוכה שאינה מטלטלת אלא ...ורך גופה אם יש בה שום. אבל אין בה שום לצורך מקומה אסור לטלטלו ופירק ליה הכא במאי עסקינן בשצריך לטלטלה להסירה מן החמה שלא תיבקע ולהניחה בצל. וכן שאר השמועה כולה פשוטה

היא

*) דברי רבינו כמות שהם אין להם הבנה ונראה דצ"ל אבל רבה אמר דלאחר התרת כלים וכו'

Continuation of translation from previous page as indicated by ◁

:self or its place is required, but not from the sun to the shade. Now, R. Safra, R. Aḥa b. Huna, and R. Huna b. Ḥanina sat nd reasoned: According to Rabbah on R. Nehemiah's view, how nay we move plates?[4]—Said R. Safra to them, By analogy with pot of excrement.[5] Abaye asked Rabbah: According to you on R. Nehemiah's view, how may we move plates?—R. Safra our olleague has answered it, By analogy with a pot of excrement, e replied.

Abaye objected to Raba: A mortar, if containing garlic, may be andled; if not, it may not be handled?—We treat here of [moving :] from the sun to the shade. He [further] objected to him: And oth hold alike that if he had already cut meat upon it, it may not e moved?[1]—Here too it means from the sun to the shade. Now, s to what we learnt: 'One may not support a pot with a leg, nd the same applies to a door',[2]—but surely a log on a Festival an article whose function is for a permitted purpose,[3] which hows that an article whose function is for a permitted purpose nay not [be handled] whether required itself or its place is eeded?[4]—There this is the reason: since on the Sabbath it is an rticle whose function is for a forbidden purpose, it is preventively orbidden on Festivals on account of the Sabbath.[5] And should ou say, Let the Sabbath itself be permitted, since an article whose unction is for a forbidden purpose may be [handled] when required itself or its place is required,—that is only where it comes within the category of a utensil, but not where it does not come within the category of a utensil.[6]

Yet do we enact a preventive measure? Surely we learnt: Produce[7] may be dropped down through a skylight[8] on Festivals, but not on the Sabbath?[9]—Do we then not preventively prohibit? Surely we learnt: The only difference between Festivals and the Sabbath is in respect of food for consumption?[10]—Said R. Joseph, There is no difficulty: the one is [according to] R. Eliezer; the other, R. Joshua. For it was taught: If an animal[11] and its young fall into a pit,[12]—R. Eliezer said: One may haul up one of them [lit., the first] in order to slaughter it, and must slaughter it; and as for the other, provisions are made where it lies in order that it should not die. R. Joshua said: One hauls up the first in order to kill it, but he does not kill it, then he practises an evasion and hauls up the second, and kills whichever he de-
c sires.[1] How so? Perhaps R. Eliezer rules [thus] only there, because provisions can be made, but not where provisions can not be made. Or perhaps R. Joshua rules thus only there, since an evasion is possible; but not where an evasion is impossible? Rather said R. Papa: There is no difficulty: one is [according to] Beth Shammai; the other, Beth Hillel. For we learnt, Beth Sham-

(4) After eating the last Sabbath meal, seeing that they re not required for further use on the Sabbath. (5) Which may be removed ecause it is repulsive, and the same applies to dirty plates.
ɪ) V. *supra* 123*a* notes. (2) On Festivals. V. Beẓ. 32*b*. (3) *Sc.* it is used or fuel. (4) For even the first is forbidden here, and the second all the nore so. (5) If the former is permitted, it may be thought that the latter oo is permitted. (6) A log does not rank as a utensil. (7) Spread out on he roof to dry. (8) When it is about to rain. (9) V. Beẓ. 35*b*. Thus we do not argue as in n. b5. (10) Which may be prepared on Festivals, e.g., by baking, cooking, etc., but not on the Sabbaths. Thus on all other matters they are alike. (11) Lit., 'it'. (12) On a festival, when one may haul up the animal for slaughtering only. On the other hand, it is forbidden to slaughter an animal together with its young on the same day (Lev. XXII, 28).
c (1) V. *supra* 117*b* for notes. Just as R. Joshua permits both animals to be brought up, so he permits one to lower the produce on a Festival to avoid financial loss.

ידו על כתף חבירו ויד חבירו על כתיפו ותולה ומפשיט גלוסטרא דתנן* [א]נגר שיש בראשו גלוסטרא ר' יהושע אומר שומטה מן פתח זה ותולה בחבירו בשבת ר' טרפון אומר הרי הוא ככל הכלים ומיטלטל בחצר מדוכה הא דאמרן אמר רבה ממאי דילמא לעולם אימא לך לאחר התרת כלים נשנו קנים טעמא מאי משום איעפושי בהאי פורתא לא מיעפש מקלות אפשר כר' אלעזר גלוסטרא כדרבי ינאי דאמר רבי ינאי בחצר שאינה מעורבת עסקינן רבי יהושע סבר תוך הפתח כלפנים דמי וקמטלטל מנא דבתים בחצר ור' טרפון סבר תוך הפתח כלחוץ דמי ומנא דחצר בחצר קא מטלטל מדוכה ר' נחמיה היא: **מתני'** [ב]כל הכלים ניטלין לצורך ושלא לצורך *ר' נחמיה אומר אין ניטלין אלא לצורך: **גמ'** מאי לצורך ומאי שלא לצורך אמר *רבה לצורך דבר שמלאכתו להיתר לצורך גופו שלא לצורך דבר שמלאכתו להיתר לצורך מקומו ודבר שמלאכתו לאיסור לצורך גופו אין לצורך מקומו לא ואתא רבי נחמיה למימר ואפילו דבר שמלאכתו להיתר לצורך גופו אין לצורך מקומו לא אמר ליה רבא לצורך מקומו שלא לצורך קרית ליה אלא אמר רבא [ג]לצורך דבר שמלאכתו להיתר בין לצורך גופו בין לצורך מקומו שלא לצורך ואפי' מחמה לצל [ד]ודבר שמלאכתו לאיסור לצורך גופו ולצורך מקומו אין מחמה לצל לא ואתא רבי נחמיה למימר ואפילו דבר שמלאכתו להיתר לצורך גופו ולצורך מקומו אין מחמה לצל לא יתיב רב ספרא ורב אחא בר הונא ורב הונא בר חנינא ויתבי וקאמרי לרבה אליבא דרבי נחמיה הני קערות היכי מטלטלינן אמר להו רב ספרא מידי דהוה אגרף של רעי אמר ליה אביי לרבה למר אליבא דרבי נחמיה הני קערות היכי מטלטלינן להו אמר ליה רב ספרא חברין תרגמה מידי דהוה אגרף של רעי איתיביה אביי לרבא* מדוכה אם יש בה שום מטלטלין אותה ואם לאו אין מטלטלין אותה הכא במאי עסקינן מחמה לצל איתיביה *ושוין שאם קיצב עליו בשר שאסור לטלטלו הכא נמי מחמה לצל והא דתנן *[ה]אין סומכין את הקדירה בבקעת וכן בדלת והא בקעת דביום טוב דבר שמלאכתו להיתר הוא אלמא דבר שמלאכתו להיתר בין לצורך גופו בין לצורך מקומו אסור התם(א) מאי טעמא כיון דבשבת דבר שמלאכתו לאיסור הוא גזירה יו"ט אטו שבת וכי תימא שבת גופיה תישתרי דהא דבר שמלאכתו לאיסור לצורך גופו ולצורך מקומו שרי [ו]הני מילי היכא דאיכא תורת כלי עליו היכא דליכא תורת כלי עליו לא [ז]ומי גזרינן והתנן* [ח]משילין פירות דרך ארובה ביום טוב [ח]אבל לא בשבת ומי לא גזרינן והתנן* [ט]אין בין יו"ט לשבת אלא אוכל נפש בלבד אמר רב יוסף לא קשיא הא ר' אליעזר הא רבי יהושע *דתניא אותו ואת בנו שנפלו לבור ר' אליעזר אומר מעלה את הראשון על מנת לשוחטו ושוחטו והשני עושה לו פרנסה במקומו בשביל שלא ימות ר' יהושע אומר מעלה את הראשון על מנת לשוחטו ואינו שוחטו ומערים ומעלה את השני רצה זה שוחט רצה זה שוחט *ממאי דילמא עד כאן לא קאמר ר' אליעזר התם אלא דאפשר לפרנסה אבל היכא דלא אפשר לפרנסה לא אי נמי עד כאן לא קאמר רבי יהושע התם דאפשר בהערמה אבל היכא דלא אפשר בהערמה לא אלא אמר רב פפא לא קשיא הא בית שמאי הא בית הלל דתנן בית שמאי אומרים

אין

רש"י

ידו על כתף חברו · דלא מטלטלי מקלות : גלוסטרא · דתנן רבי יהושע אמר נגר שיש בראשו גלוסטרא שראשה עב וראוי לדוך בו שום וטעלין בו דלת : שומטה מפתח זה ותולה בחברו · ואע"ג דצריך לגופו לתלותו בחברו ולנעולה בו שומטו ע"י גרירה אבל טלטול גמור לא ואע"פ שמלאכתו להיתר לא שרי ליה לצורך גופו : מדוכה הא דאמרן · לעיל אע"ג דשנייה רבא לעיל מחמה לצל ואביי שנייה לצורך מקומו שינויי דחיקי נינהו אלא קודם התרת כלים נשנו : קנים טעמא מאי · מסדרין אותם במערכה : משום איעפושי · דלא סמכינן אכיסא ומשום ההוא פורתא שהישנה מתעכבת בלא קנים מלילי שבת לשבת והחדשה משבת למוצ"ש לא מיעפשי : כדר"א · מניח ידו על כתף חבירו: שאינה מעורבת · שהרבה בתים פתוחים לה ולא עירבו דכלים ששבתו בבתים אסור להוציאן לחצר וששבתו בחצר מותר לטלטלן בחצר שהחצר כולו רשות לעצמו הוא והבתים מיוחדים לכל איש ביתו : תוך הפתח · שנטל הנגר משם:וקא מטלטל מנא דבית בחצר · הלכך שומטה אין דטלטול מן הצד היא אבל טלטול גמור לא : מדוכה רבי נחמיה היא· דאמר* בעירובין (דף לה·) אפילו טלית ואפי' תרווד אין ניטלין אלא לצורך תשמיש המיוחד: **מתני'** ה"ג במתניתין כל הכלים ניטלין לצורך כו' : **גמ'** מאי לצורך ומאי שלא לצורך אמר רבה כו'· לצורך דשרי תנא קמא היינו דבר שמלאכתו להיתר ומטלטלו לצורך גופו: שלא לצורך דבר שמלאכתו להיתר · ומטלטלו שלא לצורך גופו אבל צריך למקומו : ודבר שמלאכתו לאיסור לצורך גופו. הוא דאישתראי אם צריך לו למלאכת היתר אבל שלא לצורך גופו ואע"ג דצריך למקומו לא ורבה לטעמיה דאמר לעיל (דף קכב:) גבי קורנס של נפחים נמי מותר לצורך גופו : ה"ל רבה כו' אלא אמר כו' · ולרבא דמוקי אליבא דרבי נחמיה דלצורך גופו ולצורך מקומו מותר ע"כ האי לצורך גופו כגון שזה התשמיש מיוחד לו דתניא לקמן בפרק חבית (דף קמו.) רבי נחמיה אומר אפילו תרווד ואפילו טלית אין ניטלין אלא לצורך תשמישן ולצורך מקומו נמי לרבא כלצורך גופו ותשמישו דמי ולרבה לצורך גופו הוא דשרי רבי נחמיה ודוקא לתשמיש המיוחד לו ובין לרבה ובין לרבא דוקא דבר שמלאכתו להיתר אבל דבר שמלאכתו לאיסור אפילו לצורך גופו לא שרי רבי נחמיה דהאי לצורך גופו לאו תשמיש המיוחד לו הוא דהא מיוחד למלאכת איסור : לרבה אליבא דרבי נחמיה · דאמר דבר שמלאכתו להיתר לצורך מקומו לא : הני קערות· לאחר אכילה היכי מטלטל להו לסלקן מלפניו : ואם לאו אין מטלטלין אותה . בשלמא לרבה כגון דאין צריך לגופה [אלא למקומה] אלא לדידך אמאי : וכן בדלת · אוקימנא במסכת ביצה וכן הדלת אין סומכין בבקעת וביו"ט קיימי : והא בקעת ביו"ט מלאכתה להיתר היא· דלהסקה חזי וקיימא וקאסר לטלטלה לצורך גופו למלאכה אחרת וכל שכן לצורך מקומה: ומשני התם(ב) טעמא כיון דבשבת אסור דהא בקעת בשבת מלאכתה לאיסור היא ביום טוב נמי אסור גזירה י"ט אטו שבת : משילין פירות דרך ארובה ביום טוב · בהדיא תנן אבל לא בשבת פירות השטוחים על הגג לייבשן וראה גשמים ממשמשים ובאין משילן לארץ דרך ארובת הגג דלא טריחא מילתא דטופלין מאליהן אלמא דלא גזרינן ופרכינן ומי לא גזרינן והתנן אין בין כו': לא קשיא הא. דתנן משילין דשרי טירחא ביו"ט משום איבוד ממון רבי יהושע היא שהתיר להעלות בהמה בהערמה מן הבור : והא · דתנן אין בין כו' ר"א היא : דאפשר בהערמה · דמיחזי כמאן דעביד לצורך יו"ט אבל גבי משילין דליכא הערמה לדמויי להתירא לא :

אין

תוספות

הא ר"א · והיא דאין בין אע"ג דבפ"ק דמגילה (דף ז:) דייקינן עלה הא לענין מכשירי אוכל נפש זה וזה שוין וקאמר מתני' דלא כרבי יהודה ור"א סבירא ליה כר"י ועדיפא מדרבי יהודה כדאמר בריש תולין (לקמן דף קלז:) איכא למימר דההוא תנא סבר לה כוותיה בחדא דגזרינן י"ט אטו שבת ופליג עליה במכשירין ועוד יש לומר דאין בין דפ"ק דמגילה מיירי במילי דאורייתא ואין בין דהכא הייט דתנן במשילין (ביצה ד' לז:) דמיירי במילי דשבות ואינו מענין אחד תדע דהכי פריך עלה בפ' משילין כדפריך הכא בשמעתא ולא פריך בפ"ק דמגילה והא דדייק התם הא לענין מכשירין זה וזה שוין לא דייק בפרק משילין :

הא

מסורת הש"ס

[א] כלים פי"א מ"ד [ושם ליתא להך תיבות נגר שיש בראשו]
[לקמן קמו.]
[לעיל לג. וש"נ]
[לעיל קכג.]
[ס: וביצה יא.]
ביצה לב:
ביצה לה: לו.
ביצה לז. [ותוספתא ביצה פ"ג]
[ביצה לז. ע"ש]
[גי' הרי"ף והרא"ש אביי]
לקמן קלז: ביצה כח. לז: מגילה ז: [תוספתא דמגילה פ"א]

עין משפט נר מצוה

יח א מיי' פכ"ו מהלכות שבת הלכה ט סמג לאוין סה טוש"ע או"ח סימן שיג סעיף א :
יט ב ג מיי' פכ"ה שם הלכה ג סמג שם טוש"ע או"ח סימן שח סעיף ד :
כ ד מיי' שם טוש"ע שם סעיף ג :
כא ה מיי' פ"ד מהלכות יו"ט הלכה יא טור שו"ע או"ח סימן תקב סעיף ג :
כב ו מיי' פכ"ה מהל' שבת הלכה ז טוש"ע או"ח סימן שח סעיף ז :
כג ז מיי' פ"ה מהלכות יו"ט הלכה ה טור שו"ע או"ח סימן תקכא סעיף א :
כד ח טוש"ע או"ח סימן שלח סעיף ז :
כה ט מיי' פ"א מהלכות יו"ט הלכה א סמג לאוין עה טוש"ע או"ח סימן תצה סעיף א :

הגהות הב"ח

(א) גמ' התם היינו טעמא כיון דבשבת : (ב) רש"י ד"ה ומשני התם היינו טעמא :

גליון הש"ס

ז' ומי גזרינן והתנן משילין. ע"ל דף כג ע"ב תוספות ד"ה גזירה :

רבינו חננאל

שאסור בשבת סידורן ונטילתן מתוך לחם הפנים . מקלות מפורש במס' פסחים . בזמן שחל י"ד להיות בשבת אסר ר' אלעזר לטלטל מקל ולהניחו על כתיפו ועל כתף חבירו לתלות הפסח בו ולהפשיטו. וכן גלוסטרא . היא משנה בכלים פ' י"א שאסר ר' יהושע לטלטלה בשבת . תוספתא דכלים בתחלת בב"מ קלוסטרא ר' טרפון מטמא וחכמים מטהרין. ברוריה אומר שומטה מפתח זה ותולה בחבירו בשבת.כשנאמרו דברים לפני ר' יהושע אמר יפה אמר ברוריה . והוא בין הזה בעירובין בסופו. מדוכה זו שאמרנו למעלה אלו כולן כלים הן וקודם התרת כלים נשנו שאסור לטלטלן בשבת . (* אבל אחר התרת כלים מותרין הן וחלק רבא על רבי אלעזר ואמר דלמא אחר התרת כלים נשנו ואסורין הן לעולם. ודבריו פשוטין הן : מתני' כל הכלים הניטלין לצורך ניטלין לצורך ושלא לצורך כו'. פירש רבא משנה זו לצורך דבר שמלאכתו להיתר כגון קערות וכוסות וכדומה להן . מותר לכתחלה לטלטלן לאכול ולשתות בהן הללו מותרין לטלטלן בין לצורך גופו לאכול בהן בין לצורך מקומו לפנותן כדי לישב במקומן . דבר שמלאכתו לאיסור כגון קורנס של נפחים וכדומה לו לצורך גופו יכול בהן(מותר) [כגון] לפצוע בו אגוזין מותר. אבל לצורך מקומן אסור. ורבי נחמיה אמר אפילו דבר שמלאכתו להיתר כגון קערות וכדומה להן לצורך גופו לאכול בהן מותר. אבל אחר שיאכל בהן אסור לטלטלן לצורך] מקומן . ועל זה הקשה ליה אביי לרבה למר אליבא דר' נחמי' הני קערות כלומר שאינו מטלטלן אלא לצורך אכילה בהן אחר שיאכל אדם היאך מטלטלן ומסלקן מן השולחן. והשיבו לו כבר נתקשה זה לרב ספרא חברין . ופירק מידי דהוה אגרף של רעי שמותר לטלטל לדברי הכל . דתניא בתוספתא גרף של רעי ושל מימי רגלים נוטלן ושופכן וכו' . ובזמן שאמר רבה דברים הללו השיבו רבא לצורך מקומו שלא לצורך קרית ליה. אלא אמר לצורך דבר שמלאכתו להיתר בין לצורך גופו בין לצורך מקומו . שלא לצורך אפילו מחמה לצל . ודבר שמלאכתו לאיסור לצורך גפו ולצורך מקומו אין . מחמה לצל לא . ואתא ר' נחמיה למימר דאפילו דבר שמלאכתו להיתר לצורך גופו ולצורך מקומו אין. מחמה לצל לא. מותיב אביי (לרבה) [לרבא] לדידך דאמרת דבר שמלאכתו לאיסור אפילו לצורך מקומו מטלטל והרי מדוכה שאינה מטלטלת אלא לצורך גופה אם יש בה שום. אבל אין בה שום לצורך מקומה אסור לטלטלו ופירק ליה הכא במאי עסקינן בשצריך לטלטלה להסירה מן החמה שלא תיבקע ולהניחה בצל . וכן שאר השמועה כולה פשוטה היא

*) דברי רבינו כמות שהם אין להם הבנה ונראה דצ"ל אבל רבה אמר דלאחר התרת כלים וכו'

עין משפט נר מצוה

בו א מיי' פ"א מהלכות יו"ט הלכה ד סמג לאוין עה טוש"ע או"ח סימן תקיח סעיף א :

כז ב מיי' פכ"ה מהלכו' שבת הלכה ג סמג לאוין שם טוש"ע או"ח סימן שח סעיף ג :

כח ג מיי' פכ"ו שם הלכה ב סמג שם טוש"ע שם סעיף מט :

[ביצה לז. ע"ש ובפרש"י שם]

כט ד מיי' פכ"ה מהל' שבת הלכה יב סמג שם טוש"ע או"ח סימן שח סעיף ו :

ל ה מיי' פכ"ו שם הלכה ב טוש"ע או"ח סימן שח סעיף יז :

לא ו ז ח מיי' שם הל' ג טוש"ע שם סעיף ז:

[גי' הרי"ף והרא"ש דאביי]

מסורת הש"ס

*אין מוציאין את הקטן ואת הלולב ואת ספר תורה לרה"ר ובית הלל מתירין אימר דשמעת להו לבית שמאי הוצאה טלטול מי שמעת להו *וטלטול *גופיה לאו משום הוצאה היא ואף רב סבר לה להא דרבא דאמר רב מר שלא יגנב זהו טלטול שלא לצורך ואסור טעמא שלא יגנב אבל לצורך גופו ולצורך מקומו מותר איני והא רב כהנא איקלע לבי רב ואמר אייתו ליה שותא לכהנא ליתיב עליה לאו למימרא דדבר שמלאכתו לאיסור לצורך גופו אין לצורך מקומו לא הכי אמר להו שקולו שותא מקמי כהנא ואי בעית אימא התם מחמה לצל הוה רב מרי בר רחל הוה ליה ההיא בי סדיותא בשמשא אתא לקמיה דרבא אמר ליה מהו לטלטולינהו אמר ליה שרי אית לי אחרינא חזו לאורחין אית לי נמי לאורחים אמר ליה גלית אדעתיך *דכרבה סבירא לך *לכולי עלמא שרי לדידך אסיר אמר רבי אבא אמר רבי חייא בר אשי אמר רב מכבדות של מילתא מותר לטלטלן בשבת אבל של תמרה לא רבי אלעזר אומר אף של תמרה במאי עסקינן אילימא לצורך גופו ולצורך מקומו בהא לימא רב של תמרה לא והא רב כרבא סבירא ליה אלא מחמה לצל בהא לימא ר' אלעזר אף של תמרה [א]לעולם מחמה לצל אימא וכן אמר רבי אלעזר: **מתני'** *כל הכלים הניטלין בשבת שבריהן ניטלין עמהן ובלבד שיהו עושין מעין מלאכה שברי עריבה לכסות בהן את פי החבית שברי זכוכית לכסות בהן את פי הפך רבי יהודה אומר ובלבד שיהו עושין מעין מלאכתן שברי עריבה לצוק לתוכן מקפה ושל זכוכית לצוק לתוכן שמן: **גמ'** אמר רב יהודה אמר שמואל מחלוקת שנשברו מערב שבת דמר סבר מעין מלאכתן אין מעין מלאכה אחרת לא ומר סבר אפילו מעין מלאכה אחרת אבל נשברו בשבת דברי הכל מותרין הואיל ומוכנין על גבי אביהן מותר מותיב רב זוטראי *מסיקין בכלים ואין מסיקין בשברי כלים דנשברו אימת אילימא דנשברו מערב יום טוב עצים בעלמא נינהו אלא לאו ביום טוב וקתני מסיקין בכלים ואין מסיקים בשברי כלים אלא אי איתמר הכי איתמר אמר רב יהודה אמר שמואל מחלוקת שנשברו בשבת דמר סבר מוכן הוא ומר סבר נולד הוא אבל מערב שבת דברי הכל מותרין הואיל והוכנו למלאכה מבעוד יום תני חדא מסיקין בכלים ואין מסיקין בשברי כלים ותניא אידך *כשם שמסיקין בכלים כך מסיקין בשברי כלים ותניא אידך אין מסיקין לא בכלים ולא בשברי כלים הא רבי יהודה הא רבי שמעון הא רבי נחמיה *אמר רב נחמן הני ליבני דאישתיור מבניינא שרי לטלטולינהו דחזו למיזגא עלייהו שרגינהו ודאי אקצינהו אמר רב נחמן אמר שמואל חרס קטנה מותר לטלטל בחצר אבל בכרמלית לא ורב נחמן דידיה אמר אפילו בכרמלית אבל ברה"ר לא ורבא אמר אפילו ברה"ר ואזדא רבא לטעמיה דרבא הוה קאזיל בריתקא דמחוזא אתווסאי מסאניה טינא אתא שמעיה שקל חספא וקא מכפר ליה רמו ביה רבנן קלא אמר לא מיסתייא דלא גמירי מיגמר נמי מגמרי אילו בחצר הואי מי לא הוה חזיא לכסויי ביה מנא הכא נמי חזיא לדידי אמר רב יהודה אמר שמואל מגופת חבית שנכתתה(א) מותר לטלטל בשבת תניא נמי הכי *מגופה שנכתתה היא ושבריה מותר לטלטלה בשבת ולא *יספות ממנה שבר לכסות בה את הכלי ולסמוך בה כרעי המטה ואם זרקה באשפה אסור מתקיף לה רב פפא אלא מעתה זריק ליה לגלימיה ה"נ דאסור אלא אמר רב פפא

אם

רש"י

אין מוציאין · הוצאה שלא לצורך דלא אישתרי לכתחלה ביו"ט טפי מבשבת אלא אוכל נפש והך דמשלין ב"ה : טלטול מי שמעת להו . דמשוי יו"ט לשבת : טלטול לאו צורך הוצאה · בתמיה הלכך אי מזלזלת בטלטול מזלזלת בהוצאה : להא דרבא · דאמר צורך מקומו כצורך גופו : מר · פוסו"ר : שלא יגנב · דומיא דמחמה לצל ואסור בדבר שמלאכתו לאיסור: שותא · (ב)מצודה : לאו למימרא כו' · למה לי לפרושי בהדיא דליתיב עלה לאו משום למימרא דהאי דשרי לטלטולי משום דצורך גופו הוא : שקילו שותא מקמיה כהנא · דניתוב על מקומה קאמר וצורך מקומה הוא דהוה : מחמה לצל הוה · במקום הרע לה היתה ואי לאו דפריש בהדיא ליתיב עלה מאן דחזי סבר דמחמה לצל שרי ולמקומה לא היה צריך דלימא שישב במקומה : בי סדיותא · כרים של צבד שקורין פילטר"א : בי שמשי · בחמה : אמר ליה שרי · רבא לטעמיה דאמר דבר שמלאכתו להיתר אף מחמה לצל מותר : אית לי אחריני · איני צריך לגופו : דכרבה סבירא לך · דאמר מחמה לצל אסור והלכה כרבא דאמר דבר שמלאכתו להיתר שרי לגמרי ודבר שמלאכתו לאיסור לצורך גופו ומקומו מותר מחמה לצל ושלא יגנב אסור: מכבדות · אישקוב"א שמכבדים בהן את השולחן: של מילתא · (ג)בגדים לכבד שולחן שמלאכתו להיתר : של תמרה · כעין שלנו לכבד את הבית דאסור משום אשויי גומות דמודה רבי שמעון בפסיק רישיה ולא ימות : לצורך גופו · למלאכת היתר: אלא מחמה לצל בהא לימא רבי אלעזר אף של תמרה · דבר שמלאכתו לאיסור ליכא מאן דשרי מחמה לצל : וכן אמר רבי אלעזר · של מילתא מותר של תמרה אסור מחמה לצל : **מתני'** מעין מלאכה · שום מלאכה ואפי' אינה מעין הראשונה : לצוק לתוכה מקפה · עבה דומיא דעיסה מעורבת במים : **גמ'** הואיל ומוכנין על גבי אביהן · כשקדש היום : מסיקין בכלים · ביו"ט שהרי ראוין לטלטל ויטלטל ויתנם לתוך האור : ואין מסיקין בשברי כלים · דהוו להו מוקצין ולא חזו לטלטול : עצים בעלמא נינהו. דהא מאתמול להסקה קיימי : וקתני אין מסיקין · ולא אמרינן מוכנין היו אגב אביהן אלא אמרינן נולד נינהו ואסירי : מר סבר מוכן הוא · כיון דראוי לשום מלאכה ומר סבר נולד הוה דמאתמול לאו להאי מלאכה הוה קאי הלכך מעין מלאכתו בעינן : הא רבי יהודה · מסיקין בכלים ואין מסיקין בשברי כלים דאית ליה מוקצה ונולד כלים לאו מוקצה נינהו שברים נולד נינהו : והא · דתני מסיקין בשניהם : רבי שמעון · דלית ליה מוקצה ולית ליה נולד : והא · דתניא אף בכלים אין מסיקין : רבי נחמיה היא · דאמר אין כלי ניטל אלא לצורך תשמישו המיוחד לו והאי לאו מיוחד הוא לו דלאו להסקה קאי : דאישתיור · שהשלים בניינו וניתותר ומהשתא לא קיימי לבנין אלא לישב עליהם ותורת כלי עליהם: שרגינהו · אי סדרן זו על זו ודאי אקצינהו לצורך בנין אחר: בחצר · דשכיחי בה כלים שהחרס הזה ראוי להם לכיסוי ותורת כלי עליו : אבל לא בכרמלית. אפי' בתוך ד' אמות דלא שכיחי ביה מאני ולא חזי לכסויי: אפילו בכרמלית . הואיל ולאו רה"ר הוא שכיחי דאזלי ויתבי התם וחזי לכסות בו רוק : ורבא אמר אף ברה"ר · כיון דבחצר כלי הוא בעלמא נמי לא פקע שם כלי מיניה : בריתקא · שם רה"ר : אתווסאי מסאניה טינא · נתלכלך מנעלו בטיט: כפר ליה · מקנחו: אמר רבא לא מסתייה דלא גמירי · מה אסור מה מותר: אלא מיגמר נמי מגמרי . מלמדין שיבוש שבידם לאחרים: לדידי . לקינוח ולעו"ג דלא שכיח הרי שם כלי עליו בחצר: שנכתתה · החבית: (ד)מגופה · של חבית שנכתתה החבית : היא · המגופה : ושבריה · של חבית ניטלין בשבת דחזו לכיסוי מנא : לא יספות. (ה)יתקן להתיר בליטותיו ועוקציו בשבת דעביד כלי והוי מכה בפטיש : ואם זרק · מגופה זו לאשפה בטלה מתורת כלי : זרקיה לגלימיה · בשבת לאשפה ה"נ דאסור לטלטולי :

מבעוד

תוספות

הא רבי נחמיה · דסבירא ליה דאין כלי ניטל אלא לצורך תשמישו הרגיל בחול כדמפרש בפרק במה מדליקין (לעיל דף לו·) והאי נמי אין רגיל בחול לשרוף אותו: **ורבא** אמר אפילו ברה"ר · ובהני דנשברו בע"ש קאמר דאי בנשברו בשבת האמר בפרק נוטל (לקמן דף קמב:) דרבא אית ליה מוקצה וכל שכן נולד :

אם

מסורת הש"ס: ביצה יב. לג. · ס"א אמו טלטול לאו צורך הוצאה היא · [ע"ז כח:] · חולין יד: · לעיל כט: כט. לקמן קמג. ביצה לג. · ביצה שם · ביצה לג: · [תוספ' פט"ו] · [ערוך בערך ספת פי' לא יחתוך. פי' אחר לא יחכך]

רבינו חננאל

היא והלכתא כרבנן וכדמוקים לה רבה . דהכין סוגיא דשמעתא כולה . וזה שאמר רב שקולו שיתא מקמי כהנא. פי' שיתא שריתא והיא קורה כדמתרגמינן בצל קורתי בטלל שירותי . וי"א חבילה . וי"א רשת כדכתיב ויפרשו עליו גוים בשחתם נתפש . ושיתא היא שהתא . פי' מכבדת ממאטא שמכבדין הבית בהן . הנהו בי סדוותא . פי' כסתות והוא כגון כרים וכסתות : מתני' כל הכלים הניטלין בשבת שבריהן ניטלין [עמהן] ובלבד שיהו עושין מעין מלאכה וכו'. ר' יהודה אומר ובלבד שיהו עושין מעין מלאכתן כו' . פי' מקפה . מרק . בא רב יהודה משמיה דשמואל להעמיד מחלוקת ר' יהודה ות"ק כשנשברו מע"ש . ולא עמד אלא כשנשברו בשבת . דת"ק סבר מוכן הוא . ור' יהודה סבר מעין מלאכה אחרת כנולד הוא כדמפרש בגמרא דהכל שוהטין . אבל מע"ש דברי הכל מותרין . ואפילו לר' יהודה הואיל והוכנו למלאכה אחרת מבעו"י ואינו כנולד בשבת וקיי"ל כרבנן . וכלישנא בתרא דשמואל בין נשברו בשבת בין נשברו מע"ש . מעין מלאכה סגיא . תני חדא מסיקין בכלים ואין מסיקין בשברי כלים . פירוש בקעת שברי עצים שמסיקין בהן כדכתיב ויבקע עצי עולה. ותניא אידך כשם שמסיקין בכלים כך מסיקין בשברי כלים . ותניא אידך אין מסיקין לא בכלים ולא בשברי כלים לא קשיא הא ר' יהודה הא ר"ש הא ר' נחמיה. הא דתני אין מסיקין בשברי כלים ר' יהודה דמתניתין היא דחשיב בשברי כלים בנולד . והא דתני מסיקין בזה ובזה ר"ש היא דלית ליה מוקצה . ומיפרשא בגמ' דבמה מדליקין . והא דתני אין מסיקין לא בזה ולא בזה ר' נחמיה היא דאמר אין כלי ניטל אלא לצורך תשמישו . ומפורש במס' יו"ט פרק המביא כדי יין . והא דאמר רב נחמן אמר שמואל לענין ליבני דאישתייר מבניינא שרגינהו אקצינהו אפילו לר' שמעון דהני כגרוגרות וכצמוקים דמו . דאית ליה מוקצה . וזה שאמר חרס קטנה מותר לטלטלה בחצר . הואיל וראוי לכסות בו כלי שבחצר . אבל בכרמלית שאין בו כלי לא ורב נחמן סבר כיון שהמוציא מרשות הרבים לכרמלית או המכנים אינו חייב זימנין דעייל ליה לחצר וחזי ליה . ורבא סבר אפילו ברה"ר חזי לכפורי ביה טינא ושרי לטלטולי בטעמיה . וזה שאמר רב יהודה אמר שמואל מגופת חבית שנכתתה מותר לטלטלה. פי' מגופת כסוי שסותם פי החבית מלשון יגיפו הדלתות [ולא יספות]. פי' לא יחתוך הוא . כדתנן סופת באבטיח.ותניא נמי הכי כולן פשוטות הן.

הגהות הב"ח

(א) גמ' אמר שמואל מגופת חבית שנכתתה היא ושבריה מותר וכו' מגופת חבית שנכתתה : (ב) רש"י ד"ה שותא מצודה . נ"ב וכן פי' בעל המאור על סכה שותא דסוו מגנו עלה בי הרי דפ' הגוזל ומאכיל דף קיז אבל הכא פי' כמו שריתא דהיינו קורה כמו סכה שריתא דבי ר' ספת דפ' המוצא תפילין דף קב ע"א : (ג) ד"ה של מילתא של בגדים הס"ד ואח"כ מ"ה מותר לכבד בהן השלחן : (ד) ד"ה שנתכתתה החבית (מגופה וכו' החבית) תא"מ ונ"ב ס"א אין זה : (ה) ד"ה לא יספות לא יתקן להסיר :

רב נסים גאון

הא ר' יהודה והא ר' שמעון והא ר' נחמיה. דברי ר' יהודה ור"ש בפרק במה מדליקין (דף כט) אמר רב יהודה אמר רב מסיקין בכלים ואין מסיקין בשברי כלים דברי ר' יהודה ור' שמעון מתיר ודברי ר' נחמיה הן שנאמרו כן במשנה ר' נחמיה אומר אין ניטלין אלא לצורך וכמו שתירץ רבא ואמר ואתא ר' נחמיה למימר אפילו דבר שמלאכתו להיתר לצורך גופו ולצורך מקומו אין אבל מחמה לצל לא ובתוספתא (פט"ו) ר' נחמיה אומר אפילו טליתו ואפילו תרווד אין ניטלין אלא לצורך בברייתא שנאמר בה אין מסיקין לא בכלים ולא בשברי כלים הן דברי ר' נחמיה ובמס' יו"ט בפרק המביא כדי יין (דף לג) הזכירו עוד זה הדבר ואמרו תרי תנאי ואליבא דר' נחמיה כלומר קצת התנאים סוברין כי ר' (יהודה) [נחמיה] שאני ליה בין שבות שבת לשבות יום טוב :

הגהות הגר"א [א] גמ' לעולם מחמה לצל . נ"ב גי' הגאונים ור"א כר"ש סבירא ליה דדבר שאין מתכוין מותר :

mai say: [124b] One may not carry out an infant, a *lulab*,[2] or a Scroll of the Law into the street;[3] but Beth Hillel permit it.[4] But perhaps you know[5] Beth Shammai [to rule thus only in respect of] carrying out; do you know them [to rule likewise in respect of] handling?—Is then handling itself not [forbidden on account of] carrying out?[6]

Now, Rab too holds this [view] of Raba. For Rab said: [Moving] a hoe lest it be stolen is unnecessary handling, and is forbidden.[7] Thus only when it is in order that it should not be stolen, but if it is required for itself or its place is required, it is permitted. But that is not so? For R. Kahana visited Rab's house, whereupon he ordered, Bring a log of wood[8] for Kahana to sit. [Now] surely that was to imply that a thing whose function is for a forbidden purpose[9] [may be handled] only when required itself,[10] but not [merely] when its place is required?—This is what he a said to them: Remove the log from Kahana's presence.[1] Alternatively, there it was [moved] from the sun to the shade.[2]

R. Mari b. Rachel[3] had some pillows[4] lying in the sun. He went to Raba and asked him, May these be moved?—It is permitted, replied he.[5] [But] I have others?[6]—They are of use for guests. I have [some] for guests too?—You have revealed your opinion that you agree with Rabbah,[7] observed he: to all others

it is permitted, but to you it is forbidden.

R. Abba said in the name of R. Ḥiyya b. Ashi in Rab's name: Table brushes[8] [made] of cloth may be handled on the Sabbath, but not [those made] of palm[-twigs];[9] R. Eleazar maintained: Even [those made] of palm[-twigs]. What are we discussing: Shall we say [where they are handled] when required in themselves or their place is required, shall Rab rule here 'but not [those made] of palm[-twigs]'? Surely Rab agrees with Raba?[10] Again, if it means from the sun to the shade, shall R. Eleazar rule here 'even [those made] of palms'?[11]—In truth [it means] from the sun to the shade: say, And thus did R. Eleazar rule.[12]

MISHNAH. ALL UTENSILS WHICH MAY BE HANDLED ON THE SABBATH, THEIR FRAGMENTS MAY BE HANDLED TOO,[13] PROVIDED, HOWEVER, THAT THEY CAN PERFORM SOMETHING IN THE NATURE OF WORK. [THUS]: THE FRAGMENTS OF A KNEADING TROUGH [THAT CAN BE USED] TO COVER THE MOUTH OF A BARREL THEREWITH, [AND] THE FRAGMENTS OF A GLASS, TO COVER THEREWITH THE MOUTH OF A CRUSE. R. JUDAH MAINTAINED: PROVIDED THAT THEY CAN PERFORM SOMETHING IN THE NATURE OF THEIR OWN

---

(2) The palm branch; v. Lev. XXIII, 40. (3) On Festivals, for only the preparation of food is permitted. Hence the Mishnah stating that this is the only difference, etc., agrees with Beth Shammai. (4) Therefore the law that produce may be dropped, etc., agrees with Beth Hillel. (5) Lit., 'hear'. (6) Carrying out naturally involves handling, and the latter was forbidden on account of the former.—So Rashi in Beẓ. 37*a*, which seems the correct interpretation on the present reading. But the reading there, as well as a variant here, is: 'is not handling a (pre)requisite of carrying out'? (v. Rashi and Marginal Gloss.). Hence handling is forbidden because it partakes of the nature of carrying out. Thus when Beth Shammai prohibit carrying out they also prohibit handling. (7) Just as moving it from the sun to the shade. (8) BaH. Rashi and Jast. translate: a trap. (9) A log is used as fuel, which, of course, is

forbidden on the Sabbath. Trapping too (according to Rashi's translation) is forbidden. (10) And therefore he emphasized that it was wanted for a seat.
a (1) That he may sit in its place. (2) Therefore he emphasized the true purpose, so that they might not think that it was moved for that reason alone. (3) His father at the time of his conception was not a Jew; hence he is called by his mother's name. (4) Or, bolsters. (5) In accordance with his view *supra* 124*a*, q.v. (6) So I do not need these for themselves. (7) Or, Abaye, *supra* 124*a*. (8) For clearing the crumbs off the table, which is permitted. (9) I.e., brooms used for sweeping the floor, which is forbidden. (10) Permitting this. (11) None permit this. (12) Like Rab, the former version of R. Eleazar's view being incorrect. (13) Lit., 'with them'. (The words are, however, rightly omitted in MS.M.]

◁ *For the continuation of the English translation of this page see overleaf.*

בו א מיי' פ"א מהלכות יו"ט הלכה ד סמג לאוין עה טוש"ע או"ח סימן תקיח סעיף א:

בז ב מיי' פכ"ה מהלכו' שבת הלכה ג סמג לאוין שם טוש"ע או"ח סימן שח סעיף ג:

כח ג מיי' פכ"ו שם הלכה ב סמג שם טוש"ע שם סעיף מט:

[ביצה לז. ע"ש ובפרש"י שם]

כט ד מיי' פכ"ה מהל' שבת הלכה יב סמג שם טוש"ע או"ח סימן שח סעיף ו:

ל ה מיי' פכ"ו שם הלכה ב טוש"ע או"ח סימן שח סעיף יז:

לא ו ז ח מיי' שם הל' ג טוש"ע שם סעיף ז:

[גי' הרי"ף והרא"ש דכאביי]

*אין מוציאין את הקטן ואת הלולב ואת ספר תורה לרה"ר ובית הלל *מתירין אימר דשמעת להו לבית שמאי הוצאה טלטול מי שמעת להו *וטלטול *גופיה לאו משום הוצאה היא ואף רב סבר לה להא דרבא דאמר רב [ג]מר שלא יגנב זהו טלטול שלא לצורך ואסור טעמא שלא יגנב אבל לצורך גופו ולצורך מקומו מותר איני והא רב כהנא איקלע לבי רב ואמר אייתו ליה שותא לכהנא ליתיב עליה לאו למימרא דדבר שמלאכתו לאיסור לצורך גופו אין לצורך מקומו לא הכי ?אמר להו שקולו שותא מקמי כהנא ואי בעית אימא התם מחמה לצל הוה רב מרי בר רחל הוה ליה ההיא בי סדיותא בשמשא אתא לקמיה דרבא אמר ליה מהו לטלטולינהו אמר ליה שרי אית לי אחרינא הזו לאורחין אית לי נמי לאורחים אמר ליה גלית אדעתיך *דכרבה סבירא לך *לכולי עלמא שרי לדידך אסיר אמר רבי אבא אמר רבי חייא בר אשי [ג]אמר רב מכבדות של מילתא מותר לטלטלן בשבת אבל של תמרה לא רבי אלעזר אומר אף של תמרה במאי עסקינן אילימא לצורך גופו ולצורך מקומו בהא לימא רב של תמרה לא והא רב כרבא סבירא ליה אלא מחמה לצל בהא לימא ר' אלעזר אף של תמרה [א]לעולם מחמה לצל אימא וכן אמר רבי אלעזר: **מתני'** *[ג]כל הכלים הניטלין בשבת שבריהן ניטלין עמהן ובלבד שיהו עושין מעין מלאכה שברי עריבה לכסות בהן את פי החבית שברי זכוכית לכסות בהן את פי הפך רבי יהודה אומר בלבד שיהו עושין מעין מלאכתן שברי עריבה לצוק לתוכן מקפה ושל זכוכית לצוק לתוכן שמן: **גמ'** אמר רב יהודה אמר שמואל מחלוקת שנשברו מערב שבת דמר סבר מעין מלאכתן אין מעין מלאכה אחרת לא ומר סבר אפילו מעין מלאכה אחרת אבל נשברו בשבת דברי הכל מותרין הואיל ומוכנין על גבי אביהן מותר מותיב רב זוטראי *מסיקין בכלים ואין מסיקין בשברי כלים דנשברו אימת אילימא דנשברו מערב יום טוב עצים בעלמא נינהו אלא לאו ביום טוב וקתני מסיקין בכלים ואין מסיקים בשברי כלים אלא אי איתמר הכי איתמר אמר רב יהודה אמר שמואל מחלוקת שנשברו בשבת דמר סבר מוכן הוא ומר סבר נולד הוא אבל מערב שבת דברי הכל מותרין הואיל והוכנו למלאכה מבעוד יום תני חדא מסיקין בכלים ואין מסיקין בשברי כלים ותניא אידך *כשם שמסיקין בכלים כך מסיקין בשברי כלים ותניא אידך אין מסיקין לא בכלים ולא בשברי כלים הא רבי יהודה הא רבי שמעון הא רבי נחמיה *אמר רב נחמן [ה]הני ליבני דאישתיור מבניינא שרי לטלטולינהו דחזו למיזגא עלייהו שרגינהו ודאי אקצינהו אמר רב נחמן אמר שמואל [ו]חרס קטנה מותר לטלטל בחצר אבל בכרמלית לא ורב נחמן דידיה אמר אפילו בכרמלית אבל ברה"ר לא ורבא אמר [ז]אפילו ברה"ר ואזדא רבא לטעמיה דרבא הוה קאזיל בריתקא דמחוזא אתווסאי מסאניה טינא אתא שמעיה שקל חספא וקא מכפר ליה רמו ביה רבנן קלא אמר לא מיסתייא דלא גמירי מיגמר נמי מגמרי אילו בחצר הואי מי לא הוה חזיא לכסויי ביה מנא הכא נמי חזיא לדידי אמר רב יהודה אמר שמואל מגופת חבית שנכתתה(א) מותר לטלטל בשבת תניא נמי הכי *מגופה שנכתתה היא ושבריה מותר לטלטלה בשבת ולא *[ח]יספות ממנה שבר לכסות בה את הכלי ולסמוך בה כרעי המטה ואם זרקה באשפה אסור מתקיף לה רב פפא אלא מעתה זריק ליה לגלימיה ה"נ דאסור [ח]אלא אמר רב פפא

אם

אין מוליאין · הואיל ושלא לצורך דלא איסתרי לכתחילה ביו"ט טפי מדשבת אלא אוכל נפש והך דמשילין ב"ה: טלטול מי שמעת להו. דמשוי יו"ט לשבת: טלטול לאו צורך הוצאה · בתמיה הלכך אי מזלזלת בטלטול מזלזלת בהוצאה: להא דרבא · דאמר צורך מקומו כצורך גופו: מר · פוסו"ר: שלא יגנב · דומיא דמחמה לצל ואסור בדבר שמלאכתו לאיסור: שותא · (ג)מגודה: לאו למימרא כו' · למה לי לפרושי בהדיא דליתיב עלה לאו משום למימרא דהאי דשרי לטלטולי משום דצורך גופו הוא: שקילו שותא מקמיה כהנא · דניתוב על מקומה קאמר וצורך מקומה הוא דהוה: מחמה לצל הוה · במקום הרע לה היתה ואי לאו דפריש בהדיא ליתיב עלה מאן דחזי סבר דמחמה לצל שרי ולמקומה לא היה צריך דלימא שישב במקומה: בי סדיותא · כרים של לבד שקורין פילטר"א: בי שמשי · בחמה: אמר ליה שרי · רבא לטעמיה דאמר דבר שמלאכתו להיתר אף מחמה לצל מותר: אית לי אחריני · איני צריך לגופו: דכרבה סבירא לך · דאמר מחמה לצל אסור והלכה כרבא דאמר דבר שמלאכתו להיתר שרי לגמרי ודבר שמלאכתו לאיסור לצורך גופו ומקומו מותר מחמה לצל ושלא יגנב אסור: מכבדות · איסקוב"א שמכבדים בהן את השולחן: של מילתא · (ג)בגדים לכבד שולחן שמלאכתו להיתר: של תמרה · כעין שלנו לכבד את הבית דאסור משום אשויי גומות דמודה רבי שמעון בפסיק רישיה ולא ימות: לצורך גופו · למלאכת היתר: אלא מחמה לצל בהא לימא רבי אלעזר אף של תמרה · דבר שמלאכתו לאיסור ליכא מאן דשרי מחמה לצל: וכן אמר רבי אלעזר · של מילתא מותר של תמרה אסור מחמה לצל: **מתני'** מעין מלאכה · שום מלאכה ואפי' אינה מעין הראשונה: לצוק לתוכה מקפה · עבה דומיא דעיסה מעורבת במים: **גמ'** הואיל ומוכנין על גבי אביהן · כשקדש היום: מסיקין בכלים · ביו"ט שהרי ראוין לטלטל ויטלטל ויתנם לתוך האור: ואין מסיקין בשברי כלים · דהוו להו מוקצין ולא חזו לטלטול: עצים בעלמא נינהו. דהא מאתמול להסקה קיימי: וקתני אין מסיקין · ולא אמרינן מוכנין היו אגב אביהן אלא אמרינן נולד נינהו ואסירי: מר סבר מוכן הוא · כיון דראוי לשום מלאכה ומר סבר נולד הוה דמאתמול לאו להאי מלאכה הוה קאי הלכך מעין מלאכתו בעינן: הא רבי יהודה · מסיקין בכלים ואין מסיקין בשברי כלים דאית ליה מוקצה ונולד כלים לאו מוקצה נינהו שברים נולד נינהו: והא · דתני מסיקין בשניהם: רבי שמעון · דלית ליה מוקצה ולית ליה נולד: והא · דתניא אף בכלים אין מסיקין: רבי נחמיה היא · דאמר אין כלי ניטל אלא לצורך תשמישו המיוחד לו והאי לאו מיוחד הוא לו דלאו להסקה קאי: דאייתור · שהשלים בנייתו וניתותר ומהשתא לא קיימי לבנין אלא לישב עליהם ותורת כלי עליהם: שרגינהו · אי סדרן זו על זו ודאי אקצינהו לצורך בנין אחר: בחצר · דשכיחי בה כלים שהחרס הזה ראוי להם לכיסוי ותורת כלי עליו: אבל לא בכרמלית. אפי' בתוך ד' אמות דלא שכיחי ביה מאני ולא חזי לכסויי: אפילו בכרמלית. הואיל ולאו רה"ר הוא שכיחי דאזלי ויתבי התם וחזי לכסות בו רוק: ורבא אמר אף ברה"ר · כיון דבחצר כלי הוא בעלמא נמי לא פקע שם כלי מיניה: בריתקא · שם רה"ר: איתווסאי מסאניה טינא · נתלכלך מנעלו בטיט: כפר ליה · מקנחו: אמר רבא לא מסתייה דלא גמירי · מה אסור מה מותר: אלא מיגמר נמי מגמרי. מלמדין שיבוש שבידם לאחרים: לדידי. לקינוח ואע"ג דלא שכיח הרי שם כלי עליו בחצר: שנכתתה · החבית: (ד)מגופה · של חבית שנתכתתה החבית: היא · המגופה: ושבריה · של חבית ניטלין בשבת דחזו לכיסוי מנא: לא יספות. (ה)יתקן להסיר בליטותיו ועוקציו בשבת דעביד כלי והוי מכה בפטיש: ואם זרק · מגופה זו לאשפה בטלה מתורת כלי: זרקיה לגלימיה · בשבת לאשפה ה"נ דאסור לטלטולי:

מבעוד

היא והלכתא כרבנן וכרמוקים לה רבה. דהכין סוגיא דשמעתא כולה. וזה שאמר רב שקולו שיתא מקמי כהנא. פי' שיתא שריתא והיא קורה כדמתרגמינן בצל קורתי בצל שירותי. וי"א חבילה. וי"א רשת כדכתיב ויפרשו עליו גוים בשחתם נתפש. ושיתא היא שהתא. פי' מכבדת מטאטא שמכבדין הבית בהן. הנהו בי סדוותא. פי' כסתות והוא כגון כרים וכסתות: **מתני'** כל הכלים הניטלין בשבת שבריהן ניטלין [עמהן] ובלבד שיהו עושין מעין מלאכה וכו'. ר' יהודה אומר ובלבד שיהו עושין מעין מלאכתן כו'. פי' מקפה. מרק. בא רב יהודה משמיה דשמואל להעמיד מחלוקת ר' יהודה ות"ק כשנשברו מע"ש. ולא עמד אלא כשנשברו בשבת. דת"ק סבר מוכן הוא. ור' יהודה סבר מעין מלאכה אחרת כנולד הוא כדמפרש בגמרא דהכל שוהמין. אבל מע"ש דברי הכל מותרין. ואפילו לר' יהודה הואיל והוכנו למלאכה אחרת מבעו"י ואינו כנולד בשבת וקיי"ל כרבנן. וכלישנא בתרא דשמואל בין נשברו בשבת בין נשברו מע"ש. מעין מלאכה סגיא. תני חדא מסיקין בכלים ואין מסיקין בשברי כלים. פירוש בקעת שברי עצים שמסיקין בהן כדכתיב ויבקע עצי עולה. ותניא אידך כשם שמסיקין בכלים כך מסיקין בשברי כלים. ותניא אידך אין מסיקין לא בכלים ולא בשברי כלים לא קשיא הא ר' יהודה הא ר"ש הא ר' נחמיה. הא דתני אין מסיקין בשברי כלים ר' יהודה דמתניתין היא דחשיב בשברי כלים בנולד. והא דתני מסיקין בזה ובזה ר"ש היא דלית ליה מוקצה. ומיפרשא בגמ' דבמה מדליקין. והא דתני אין מסיקין לא בזה ולא בזה ר' נחמיה היא דאמר אין כלי ניטל אלא לצורך תשמישו. ומפורש במס' יו"ט פרק המביא כדי יין. והא דאמר רב נחמן אמר שמואל לענין ליבני דאישתייר מבניינא שרגינהו אקצינהו אפילו לר' שמעון דהני כגרוגרות וכצמוקים דמו. דאית ליה מוקצה. וזה שאמר חרס קטנה מותר לטלטלה בחצר. הואיל וראוי לכסות בו כלי שבהצר. אבל בכרמלית שאין בו כלי לא ורב נחמן סבר כיון שהמוציא מרשות הרבים לכרמלית או המכנים אינו חייב זימנין דעייל ליה לחצר והוי ליה. ורבא סבר אפילו ברה"ר חזי לכפורי ביה טינא ושרי לטלטולי בטעמיה. וזה שאמר רב יהודה אמר שמואל מגופת חבית שנכתתה מותר לטלטלה. פי' מגופת כסוי שסותם פי ההבית מלשון יגיפו הדלתות [ולא יספות]. פי' לא יתתוך הוא. כדתנן סופת באבטיה.ותניא נמי הכי כולן פשוטות הן.

ביצה יב. | ס"א אמו טלטול לאו צורך הוצאה היא | [ע"ז כח:] | חולין יח. | לעיל כט: לקמן קנו. ביצה לב. | ביצה שם | ביצה לג. | [תוספ' ספ"ז] | [ערוך בערך ספת פי' לא יתחך. פי' אחר לא יחכך]

הגהות הב"ח

(א) גמ' אמר שמואל מגופת שנכתתה היא ושבריה מותר וכו':

מגופת חבית שנכתתה: (ב) רש"י ד"ה שותא מגודה. נ"ב וכן פי' בעל המאור על ההוא שותא דהוה בי הרי דפ' הגוזל ומאכיל דף קיז אבל הכא פי' כמו שריתא דהיינו קורה כמו ההוא שריתא דבי ר' המונח תפילין דף קב ע"א: (ג) ד"ה של מילתא של בגדים הס"ד ואח"כ מ"ה מותר לכבד בהן השלחן שנתכתתה החבית (מגופה וכו' החבית) תא"מ ונ"ב ס"א אין זה: (ה) ד"ה לא יספות לא יתקן

רב נסים גאון

הא ר' יהודה והא ר' שמעון והא ר' נחמיה. דברי ר' יהודה ור"ש בפרק במה מדליקין (דף כט) אמר רב יהודה אמר רב מסיקין בכלים ואין מסיקין בשברי כלים דברי ר' יהודה ור' שמעון מתיר ודברי ר' נחמיה הן שנאמרו כן במשנה ר' נחמיה אומר אין ניטלין אלא לצורך וכמו שתירץ רבא ואמר ואתא ר' נחמיה למימר אפילו דבר שמלאכתו להיתר לצורך גופו ולצורך מקומו אין אבל מחמה לצל לא ובתוספתא (פט"ו) ר' נחמיה אומר אפילו טליתו ואפילו תרווד אין ניטלין אלא לצורך בברייתא שנאמר בה אין מסיקין לא בכלים ולא בשברי כלים הן דברי ר' נחמיה ובמס' יו"ט בפרק המביא כדי יין (דף לג) הזכירו עוד זה הדבר ואמרו תרי תנאי ואליבא דר' נחמיה כלומר קצת התנאים סוברין כי ר' (יהודה) [נחמיה] שאני ליה בין שבות שבת לשבות יום טוב:

הגהות הגר"א [א] גמ' לעולם מחמה לצל. נ"ב ג' הגאונים ור"א כר"ש סבירא ליה דדבר שאין מתכוין מותר:

Continuation of translation from previous page as indicated by ◁

b [FORMER] WORK;[1] [THUS:] THE FRAGMENTS OF A KNEADING TROUGH, TO POUR A THICK MASS THEREIN;[2] OR OF A GLASS, TO POUR OIL THEREIN.

GEMARA. Rab Judah said in Samuel's name: The controversy is only if they were broken from the eve of the Sabbath, one Master holding: Only [provided they are fit for] something in the nature of their *own* [former] work, but not for something in the nature of a different work; whereas the other Master holds: Even [if fit] for something in the nature of a different work. But if they are broken on the Sabbath, all agree that they are permitted,[3] since they are ***mukan***[4] in virtue of their origin.[5]

R. Zuṭrai objected: 'We may heat [an oven] with utensils, but not with fragments of utensils'.[6] Now when were these broken? Shall we say that they were broken from the eve of the Festival,—then they are simply pieces of wood.[7] Hence it must surely be on the Festival, yet he teaches, 'We may heat with utensils, but not with fragments of utensils'?[8]—Rather if stated, it was thus stated: Rab Judah said in Samuel's name: The controversy is only if they are broken on the Sabbath, one Master holding that they are ***mukan***, whilst the other Master holds that they are *nolad*.[9] But [if broken] on Sabbath eve, all hold that they are permitted, since they were ***mukan*** for work from the day time.[10]

One [Baraitha] taught: We may heat with utensils, but not with fragments of utensils; another was taught: Just as we may heat with utensils, so may we heat with fragments of utensils: whilst a third taught: We may heat neither with utensils nor with fragments of utensils. One agrees with R. Judah, one with
c R. Simeon, and the last with R. Nehemiah.[1]

R. Naḥman said: The bricks that are left over from a building may be handled, since they are fit to sit on.[2] [But] if he places them in rows, then he has certainly set them apart.[3]

R. Naḥman said in Samuel's name: A small shard may be moved about in a courtyard, but not in a ***karmelith***.[4] But R. Naḥman [giving] his own [view] maintained: Even in a ***karmelith***,[5] but not in the street; whereas Raba said. Even in the street.[6] Now, Raba is consistent with his view. For Raba was walking in the manor of Maḥoza,[7] when his shoes became soiled with clay; [so] his attendant came, took a shard, and wiped it off. The Rabbis [his disciples] rebuked him.[8] Said he, It is not enough that they have not learnt—they would even teach! If it were in a courtyard, would it not be fit for covering a utensil? Here too I have a use for it.

Rab Judah said in Samuel's name: The bung of a barrel which is broken in pieces may be handled on the Sabbath. It was taught likewise: If a bung is broken in pieces [both] it and the fragments thereof may be handled on the Sabbath. But one must not trim a fragment thereof to cover a vessel or support the legs of a bed[9] therewith; but if one throws it away on the dung heap, it is forbidden.[10] R. Papa demurred: If so, if one throws away his robe,

b (1) I.e., similar to that performed by the whole utensil. (2) Like the dough kneaded in the trough. (3) Whatever their present use. (4) V. Glos. (5) V. ***supra* 122*b***, n. a8. (6) On Festivals. (7) Which may certainly be used. (8) Which refutes Samuel's view reported by Rab Judah. (9) Newly created (v. Glos.). As a fragment it has only just come into existence, and therefore must not be used on the Sabbath. (10) I.e., from before the commencement of the Sabbath they stood to be used as fuel, and so they are regarded as ready for their new function.

c (1) (i) R. Judah: both *mukẓeh* and *nolad* are forbidden, hence the prohibition of fragments. (ii) R. Simeon: *mukẓeh* and *nolad* are permitted, hence both fragments and vessel are permissible; (iii) R. Nehemiah: a utensil may be handled on the Sabbath or Festival only for its normal function, hence the prohibition of both. (2) And the last few may possibly be kept for that purpose. (3) For another building; hence they are ***mukẓeh*** and must not be handled. (4) In the former vessels may generally be found for which the shard can be used as a cover, but not in the latter. (5) Where people sometimes sit down; one can cover saliva with this. (6) Since it is a utensil in a courtyard, it remains so elsewhere. (7) V. ***supra* 59*b***, n. b8 and B.B. 12*b*, n. a4. (8) Lit., 'lifted their voice against him'. (9) V. *supra* 43*a*, n. b2. Here, however, it is probably meant literally. (10) Because the owner has shown that it has ceased to be a utensil in his eyes.

a is that too prohibited?[1] Rather said R. Papa: [125a] If he threw it away whilst yet day,[2] it is forbidden.

Bar Hamduri said in Samuel's name: Shreds of reeds detached from a mat may be handled on the Sabbath. What is the reason? —Said Raba, Bar Hamduri explained it to me: What is the [reed-] mat itself fit for? For covering the earth. These too are fit for covering dirt.

R. Zera said in Rab's name: Pieces of silk of aprons may not be handled on the Sabbath. Said Abaye: This refers to rags less than three [fingerbreadths] square, which are of no use to rich or poor.[3]

Our Rabbis taught: The fragments of an old oven[4] are like all utensils which may be handled in a courtyard: this is R. Meir's view. R. Judah said: They may not be handled. R. Jose testified in the name of R. Eleazar b. Jacob concerning the fragments of an old oven that they may be handled on the Sabbath, and concerning its lid [of the oven] that it does not require a handle.[5] Wherein do they differ?—Said Abaye: where they perform something in the nature of work, but not in the nature of their own [former] work,[6] R. Judah being consistent with his view, and R. Meir with his.[7] Raba demurred: If so, instead of disputing about the fragments of an oven, let them dispute about the fragments of utensils in general? Rather said Raba: They dispute about the fragments of the following oven. For we learnt: If he sets it [the oven] over the mouth of a pit or a cellar and places a stone there,—R. Judah said: If one can heat it from underneath and it is [thereby] heated above, it is unclean; if not, it is clean. But the Sages maintain: Since it can in any wise be heated, it is unclean.[8] And wherein do they differ? In this verse; *Whether oven, or range of pots, it shall be torn*
b *down: they are unclean, and shall be unclean unto you.*[1] R. Judah holds: Where tearing down is wanting it is unclean, whilst where tearing down is not wanting it is not unclean.[2] Whereas the Rabbis hold: '*They shall be unclean unto you*' [implies] in all cases.[3] But the Rabbis too, surely it is written, '*it shall be torn down*'?—That is [intended] in the opposite direction:[4] for one might argue, Since it is attached to the ground, it is like the very ground itself;[5] therefore it informs us [otherwise].[6] And the other [R. Judah] too, surely '*they shall be unclean unto you*' is written?—That [is explained] as Rab Judah's dictum in Samuel's name. For Rab Judah said in Samuel's name: They differ only in respect of the first firing,[7] but at the second firing,[8] even if it is suspended to a camel's neck.[9] 'Ulla observed: And as for the first firing, according to the Rabbis, even if it is
c suspended from a camel's neck![1] R. Ashi demurred: If so, instead of disputing about the fragments of the oven, let them dispute about the oven itself;[2] [for] seeing that the oven itself, according to R. Judah, is not a utensil, need the fragments [be mentioned]? Rather said R. Ashi: In truth it is as we originally stated, and [the controversy is] where it [the fragment] can serve as a [baking] tile,[3] whilst R. Meir argues on R. Judah's opinion. [Thus:] according to my view, even if they [the fragments] can perform something in the nature of [any] work;[4] but even on your view, you must at least agree with me [here] that in such a case, it is its *own* work. But R. Judah [argues]: It is dissimilar. There it is heated from within, here it is heated from without; there it stands, here it does not stand.

'R. Jose testified in the name of R. Eleazar b. Jacob concerning the fragments of an old oven, that they may be handled on the Sabbath, and concerning its lid, that it does not require a handle.' Rabina said: In accordance with whom do we handle nowadays the oven lids of the town Meḥasia[5] which have no handle? In accordance with whom? R. Eleazar b. Jacob.

MISHNAH. IF A STONE [IS PLACED] IN A PUMPKIN SHELL,[6] AND ONE CAN DRAW [WATER] IN IT AND IT [THE STONE] DOES NOT FALL OUT,[7] ONE MAY DRAW [WATER] IN IT; IF NOT, ONE MAY NOT DRAW [WATER] IN IT.[8] [125b] IF A [VINE-]BRANCH[9]

---

a (1) Surely not! (2) I.e., on Friday before the commencement of the Sabbath. (3) Cf. *supra* 26b. (4) I.e., one that has already been fired, so that the clay whereof it is made is hardened and fit for its work. (5) In order that it shall be permissible to handle it on the Sabbath. There is also an opposing view, v. *infra* 126b. (6) E.g., they are fit for covering a barrel, but one cannot bake in them. (7) As expressed in the Mishnah *supra* 124b. (8) The reference is to an oven. In ancient days this consisted merely of walls, without a separate bottom, and was set upon the ground and plastered thereto. Now, here the oven is set over the walls of a pit, not actually on the ground, and a stone is placed between the oven and the pit as a wedge. R. Judah maintains that if the oven is so placed, e.g., its walls almost correspond to those of the pit, that if a fire is made *beneath* the oven, in the pit's atmosphere, the oven itself is heated (sufficiently for its work), it is an 'oven' in the technical sence (as stated below) and is susceptible to defilement. But if the fire must be placed in the atmosphere of the oven, it is not an 'oven' and cannot be defiled. (Rashi).

b (1) Lev. XI, 35. (2) *Yuttaẓ*, fr. *nathaẓ*, is generally applicable to the tearing down or demolishing of anything attached to the soil, e.g., a house. Now, since the Bible orders that if an oven is defiled it shall be torn down, it follows that it must be so closely joined to the soil that one can speak of tearing it down. Otherwise the Scriptural law does not apply to it, because technically it is 'torn down' from the very time that it is fixed. Hence in the present case if it is not so closely joined to the ground that one can make a fire in the pit on which it stands and thereby heat the oven, it is likewise 'torn down' *ab initio*, and therefore is not an 'oven' which can be defiled. By 'unclean' and 'not unclean' susceptibility and non-susceptibility to uncleanness is meant. (3) For the repetition is emphatic. (4) *Sc.* it teaches not leniency but greater stringency, as explained. (5) Which of course, cannot be defiled. (6) Viz., that even where it shall be 'torn down', as defined in n. b2, is applicable, it is still liable to defilement, and all the more so where it is inapplicable. (7) I.e., it had never yet been fired when it was set over the pit. The first firing hardens the clay and technically completes the manufacture of the oven, and R. Judah holds that in this case it cannot be completed at all, for the reasons stated, and so it never becomes an oven. (8) I.e., it was originally set upon the ground in the usual manner, fired, and then removed to the pit. (9) It is unclean, since it is already an 'oven' from the first firing. This extended possibility of defilement is taught by the emphatic repetition, '*and it shall be unclean unto you*'.

c (1) Wherever it is, it is unclean.—It is in reference to the fragments of this oven that R. Meir and R. Judah dispute, seeing that in the first place it was not absolutely completed. (2) Whether it may be handled on the Sabbath. (3) Tiles which were heated to bake something placed upon them. Thus it can still be used in a manner akin to its original function, but not altogether so, for originally one baked *inside* the oven, whereas now the food to be baked must be placed on top. (4) They may be handled. (5) V. *supra* 11a, n. 7. (6) Used for drawing water. As the pumpkin was too light to sink, a stone was used to weight it. (7) Being securely fastened. (8) The stone is then like any other stone, which may not be handled, and the pumpkin too may not be handled, because it serves as a stand for a forbidden article (cf. *supra* 117a top). (9) Or, rod.

מסורת הש"ס

תורה אור

אם זרקה מבעוד יום לאשפה אסורה אמר בר המדורי אמר שמואל *קרומיות של מחצלת מותר לטלטלם בשבת מ"ט אמר רבא בר המדורי אסברא לי מחצלת גופא למאי חזיא לכסויי ביה עפרא הני נמי חזיין לכסויי בהו טינופת א"ר זירא אמר רב *שירי פרוזמיות אסור לטלטלן בשבת *אמר אביי במטלניות שאין בהן ג' על ג' דלא חזיין לא לעניים ולא לעשירים: ת"ר *שברי תנור ישן הרי הן ככל הכלים הניטלין בחצר דברי ר"מ ר' יהודה אומר אין ניטלין העיד ר' יוסי משום ר"א בן יעקב על שברי תנור ישן שניטלין בשבת ועל כיסויו שאינו צריך בית יד במאי קמיפלגי אמר אביי בעושין מעין מלאכה ואין עושין מעין מלאכתן קמיפלגי ואזדא ר' יהודה לטעמיה ור"מ לטעמיה מתקיף לה רבא אי הכי אדמיפלגי בשברי תנור ליפלגו בשברי כלים בעלמא אלא אמר רבא בשברי דהאי תנור קמיפלגי דתנן *נתנו על פי הבור או על פי הדות ונתן שם אבן רבי יהודה אומר אם מסיק מלמטה והוא נסוק מלמעלה טמא ואם לאו טהור וחכמים אומרים הואיל והוסק מ"מ טמא ובמאי (ויקרא יא) קמיפלגי בהאי קרא °תנור וכירים יותץ טמאים הם וטמאים יהיו לכם רבי יהודה סבר מחוסר נתיצה טמא שאין מחוסר נתיצה טהור ורבנן סברי טמאים יהיו לכם מ"מ ורבנן נמי הכתיב יותץ ההוא לאידך גיסא דסלקא דעתך אמינא כיון דחבריה בארעא כגופא דארעא דמי קמ"ל ואידך נמי הכתיב טמאים יהיו לכם ההיא כדרב יהודה אמר שמואל דאמר רב יהודה אמר שמואל מחלוקת בהיסק ראשון אבל בהיסק שני אפילו תלוי בצואר גמל אמר עולא והיסק ראשון לרבנן אפילו תלוי בצואר גמל מתקיף לה רב אשי אי הכי אדמיפלגי בשברי תנור ליפלגו בתנור גופה השתא תנור גופה לרבי יהודה לא הוי מנא שבריו מיבעיא אלא אמר רב אשי לעולם כדאמרן מעיקרא ובעושה מעשה טפקא ורבי מאיר לדבריו דרבי יהודה קאמר לדידי אפילו בעושין מעין מלאכה אלא לדידך אודי לי מיהא דכהאי גוונא מלאכתו הוא ורבי יהודה לא דמי התם הסקו מבפנים הכא הסקו מבחוץ התם מעומד הכא לאו מעומד: העיד ר' יוסי משום רבי אליעזר בן יעקב על שברי תנור ישן שניטלין בשבת ועל כיסויו שאינו צריך בית יד: אמר רבינא כמאן מטלטלינן האידנא כיסוי דתנורי דמתא מחסיא דאין להם בית אחיזה כמאן כר"א בן יעקב: **מתני'** *האבן שבקירויה אם ממלאין בה ואינה נופלת ממלאין בה ואם לאו אין ממלאין בה

זמורה

מבעוד יום· גלי דעתיה מאתמול דלאו מנא הוא: קרומיות של מחצלת· שנפרדו מן מחצלת ישנה: בר המדורי אסברא לי· בר המדורי פירש לי טעמו של דבר: לכסות בה עפרא· עומד לכסות בו צואה א"נ שלא יעלה האבק: שירי פרוזמיות· טליתות כדאמר בסוכה (דף יא.) רמא תכלתא בפירזמא דאיכשי ביתיה: תנור ישן· שכבר הוסק וחרסיו קשים וחזו למלאכה: הרי הן ככל הכלים· לקמיה מפרש פלוגתייהו וטעמייהו: ועל כיסויו· של תנור שאינו צריך בית יד דבלאו בית אחיזה מטלטלין ליה ופלוגתא היא במתניתין דאיכא למ"ד בעינן בית אחיזה: מעין מלאכה· כגון לכסות בהן פי חבית: ואין עושין מעין מלאכתן· לאפות: ואזדא ר"מ לטעמיה· דאמר במתני' לא בעינן מעין מלאכתן: דהאי תנור· העשוי כעין זה ששנוי במשנה זו שאני מביא לך שלא נתקן כל צרכו מתחילתו ובשבר קמיפלגי: נתנו על פי הבור. תנורים שלהם עשוין כקדירות גדולות ואין להן שולים ומושיבו לארץ ומדביק טיט סביבותיו לעשותו עב שיחזיק חומו והיא קרויה טפילה והיא מגעת לארץ ומתוך כך הבל שלו קיים ואם נתנו על פי הבור או על פי הדות שהיא כעין בור אלא שהבור בחפירה והדות בבנין ונתן שם אבן בינו לבין דופן הבור לדוחקו שלא יפול ויהא עומד באויר: רבי יהודה אומר· אם דופנותיו למעלה קרובים לדופני הבור שלא הוצרך לתת ביניהם אלא אבן דקה ואין אויר ניכר בין דופני התנור לדופני הבור שיעכב את היסק התנור אלא יועילו לו דופני הבור להחזיק את חומו ושוליו קרובים לשולי הבור שאם מסיקין אותו מלמטה שעושין האור בבור והתנור ניסוק (א)מלמעלה בתוכו מאור דרך שוליו או שהתנור בתוך חלל הבור באויר והיסק עולה סביב דופנותיו וניסוק כגון שקצר מלמטה ורחב מלמעלה או הבור רחב מלמטה ופיו קצר טמא: ואם לאו· אלא נסוק כשאר תנורים מתוכן טהור כדמפרש טעמא דבעינן מחוסר נתילה שיהא קרוב להיות מחובר וכי אינו קרוב לארץ אין לך תנור נתוץ מזה ואין לך לקיים בו תנור וכירים יותץ דנתילה לא שייכא אלא בבנין מחובר וכשאין מחובר שבירה שייכא ביה: טמאים הם וטמאים יהיו לכם· דכפל ביה קרא רבויא הוא שאע"פ שאינו מתוקן כל צרכו: ההוא לאידך גיסא· האי יותץ לאו לאגמורי קולא אתא ולמימר דהאי ליכא לקיומי ביה נתילה כגון זה שאינו בנוי ומחובר וממילא הוא נתוץ דליהוי טהור דהדר תנא ביה קרא וטמאים יהיו לכם לרבויי אלא לאגמורי חומרא אתא דלא תימא כל התנורים העשוים כהלכתן ומחוברים לארץ הרי הן כשאר בתים וקרקע דמי הואיל וחברן ולא לקבל טומאה קמ"ל יותץ דאע"ג דשייכא ביה לשון נתילה כלומר דמחובר הוא טמא וכ"ש (א) דמחוסר נתילה: בהיסק ראשון· שלא הוסק מעולם והיסק ראשון שנחלקו בו דההוא משוי ליה כלי כדתנן במס' כלים (פ"ה) איזהו גמר מלאכתו משיסיקנו לאפות בו סופגנין בההיא פליג ר' יהודה ואמר דאינו ראוי ליעשות כלי: אבל בהיסק שני· שמתחלה נעשה כשאר תנורים מחובר לארץ או לאבן עב והוסק שם ונעשה כלי וסוף נטלו משם ונתנו על פי הבור וכאן נטמא מודה ר' יהודה דאיתרבאי מוטמאים יהיו לכם: ואפילו תלוי בצואר גמל· אא"כ חלקו כדין טהרת תנור שצריך לשבור אף את חרסו ואינו נטהר בנטילתו שלם ממקומו: אמר עולא היסק ראשון לרבנן· דאמרי מריבוי דקרא ואע"ג דאין הבל שלו מתקיים יפה מקבל טומאה לא תימא נתנו ע"פ הבור דוקא אלא אפילו תלאו בצואר גמל והוסק שם היסק ראשון טמא: מתקיף לה רב אשי· אדרבא דאוקי פלוגתא דטלטול שברי תנור ישן דלעיל בשברים דכי האי תנור(ב) דהוא גופיה לר' יהודה לאו מנא הוא: כדאמרן מעיקרא· בעושין מעין מלאכה ולא מעין מלאכתן ושברי תנור מעליא קאמר ודקשיא לך אמאי נקט תנור ליפלוג בשברי כלי בהאי איצטריכא ליה ובעושין קצת מעין מלאכת אפייה כגון מעשה טפקא רעפים שקורין טובל"ש שמסיקין אותם ואופין בהן כך שברים אלו רחבים ומיהו אין להן תוך להסיקם מבפנים אלא מבחוץ כרעפים ולאו משום דבעי רבי מאיר מעין מלאכתן אלא משום דרבי יהודה נקט לה: ור"מ לדבריו דר' יהודה· נקט תנור וקאמר לדידי אפילו עושין מעין מלאכה כדאמר במתניתין: מעומד· בתנור אופין מעומד שהפת דבוקה בדופני התנור ועומדת ואינה מוטלת בשכיבה ע"ג שוליו כרעפים שהן שוכבות על רחבן: כיסוי דתנורי דמתא מחסיא· כיסוי תנור של אותו מקום לא היה להן בית אחיזה· תנור מפני שפיו למעלה יש לו כסוי שלא יצא הבל שלו לאחר שהדביק בו הפת מכסהו: **מתני'** האבן שבקירויה· דלעת יבישה חלולה וממלאין בה מים ומתוך שהיא קלה אינה שואבת אלא לפה ונותנין בה אבן להכבידה: אם ממלאין בה ואינה נופלת· שקשורה יפה לפי הקירויה שויא כלי: ואם לאו· הרי היא כשאר אבנים ואין מטלטל את הקירויה דשויא בסיס לאבן שעשאה:

א) בתוס' יו"ט פכ"ה דכלים משנה ו העתיק לשון רש"י וכ"ש שהיינו מחוסר נתילה וכצ"ל

אם זרקה מבעוד יום· השתא לא פריך אלא מעתה זרק לגלימא מבעוד יום דכיון דלא היה מוכן מבעו"י ליכא לדמויי לגלימי: **מחצלת** גופה למאי חזיא· לרווחא דמילתא מפרש הכי אע"ג דלא בעי מעין מלאכה ראשונה כדאמר רב נחמן לעיל חרס קטנה מותר לטלטלה בחצר משום דחזיא לכסויי בה מנא: **הרי** הן ככל הכלים הניטלין בחצר. לאו דוקא בחצר לרב נחמן ולרבא דשרו בכרמלית ורה"ר: **בשעושין** מעין מלאכה ואין עושין מעין מלאכתן· והא דנקט תנור ישן דשברי תנור חדש אין ראוין לכלום: **בשברי** דהאי תנור קמיפלגי· לפי תירוץ זה תימה הא דנקט תנור ישן דבהיסק ראשון פליגי: **כמאן** כר' אליעזר בן יעקב· ה"ה דה"מ למימר כרבי יוסי דשרי לקמן* לטלטל כיסוי כלים שאין להם בית אחיזה בכלי דחבריהו בארעא אלא משום דמשנת ר' אליעזר בן יעקב קב ונקי:

ואזדו

עין משפט נר מצוה

לב א מיי' פכ"ו מהל' שבת הלכה ח טור שו"ע או"ח סימן שח סעיף יב:

לג ב מיי' שם טוש"ע שם סעיף יג:

לד ג מיי' שם הל' יד:

לה ד מיי' פכ"ה מהל' שבת הלכה יג טור שו"ע או"ח סימן שח סעיף י:

לו ה מיי' פט"ו מהלכות כלים הלכה ח:

לז ו מיי' פכ"ה מהלכות שבת הלכה יח טוש"ע או"ח סימן שט סעיף ג:

[סוכה נג.]

[דף קכו:]

[פי' תוספות לקמן קכו: ד"ה כיון וכו']

[תוספ' פט"ו]

כלים פ"ה מ"ז

הגהות הב"ח

(א) רש"י ד"ה ר' יהודה וכו' והתנור ניסוק בתוכו מלמעלה לאור: (ב) ד"ה מתקיף וכו' האי תנור הסיד ואח"כ מ"ס בתנור גופיה:

רבינו חננאל

אתוטאי מסאני סינא. נטנפו מנעלין בטיט. פי' קרומיות. שירי מחצלאות שבלו. וזה שאמר ר' זירא אמר רב שירי פרוזמיות אסור לטלטלן בשבת. פרוזמיות. פירוש טליתות. כדאמרינן התם. רב יהודה רמי תכלתא בפריזמא דאינשי ביתיה. פי' תלא ציצית בטלית של אשתו. ופשוטה היא: ת"ר שברי תנור ישן. ס"א שירי תנור ישן הרי הן ככל הכלים וניטלין בחצר דברי ר' מאיר ר' יהודה אומר אין ניטלין. העיד ר' יוסי וכו'. ואמרינן במאי קא מיפלגי בעושין מלאכה ואין עושין מעין מלאכתן. ור"מ לטעמיה דהוא ת"ק דמתני'. וקיי"ל סתם משנה ר"מ דשרי. אע"פ שאין עושין מעין מלאכתן. ור' יהודה לטעמיה דאסר ולא קא שרי אלא בעושין מעין מלאכתן. ואתקף עליה רבא ולא מצא פירוק. ואוקים רבא פלוגתיהן בשברין דהאי תנור. דכיון דתנינן בפ' המביא כדי יין ת"ר תנור וכירים חדשים הרי הן ככל הכלים הניטלין בחצר. אבל אין סכין אותן שמן וכו' הוצרכו להודיע כי תנור חדש הראוי לאפות בו ניטל בחצר ושבריו כיוצא בו. ומצאנו חלוקה בתנור חדש לענין טומאה והאומר מקבל טומאה סבר הואיל ויתכן לאפות בו כלי גמור הוא. ושבריו כיוצא בו. והואיל וככלים חשובין ניטלין. ופירשו חלוקתן לענין טומאה וה"ה לטלטול. דתנן נתנו ע"פ הבור או ע"פ הדות ונתן שם אבן. ר' יהודה אומר אם מסיק מלמטה והוא ניסוק מלמעלה טמא ואם לאו טהור. וחכ"א הואיל והוסק מ"מ טמא. וכך פירושו תנור שנתנו ע"פ הבור או ע"פ הדות ונתן שם אבן בפי הבור או בפי הדות. סבר ר' יהודה אם מסיק מלמטה בבור או בדות וניסק מלמעלה התנור הרי הוא כבנוי בקרקע ונגמרה מלאכתו ונעשה כלי לאפות בו ומקבל טומאה ואם לאו לא נגמרה מלאכתו וחשוב הוא כקדירה שלא *)בפת' לה פת או לתת לתוכה תבשיל. שאין דרך התנור לאפות בו והוא תלוי. וחכ"א כיון שנתן בפי הבור אבן ויכול להסיקו על האבן הרי הוא כלי לאפות בו. והיא כלי לקבל טומאה. וחלוקתן בזה הפסוק תנור וכירים יותץ. ר' יהודה סבר מדאמר קרא יותץ מכלל שצריך להיות בנוי ואם [לאו] אינו כלי. ורבנן סברי טמאים מ"מ ואפילו אינו בנוי: **תוספתא** ומודה ר' יהודה בתנור שנתנו ע"פ הבור או ע"פ הדות ונתן שם אבן ומירחו בטיט מן הצדדים שהוא טמא. וחכ"א בין כך ובין כך טמא. ועל זו הדרך סוגיא דהא שמעתא. ואתקיף לה רב אשי לרבא על זה שאמר ולא מצא פירוקי והעמיד רב אשי דברי אביי ולא בטעמו. אלא העמיד חלוקתם בשברי תנור שאופין עליהם מעשה טפקא. ופירושו שנותנין זה השבר ע"ג אבנים ומסיקין אש מלמטה ומרתיחין אותן השברין ומדבקין הפת מלמעלה וקיי"ל כר' אליעזר והא רבינא פירש דמטלטלינן כיסוי דתנורי כר' אליעזר: **מתני'** האבן שבקירויה וכו'. פי' מביאין קרא יבשה ומוציאין בני מעיה ועושה אותה חללה. ועושין אותה כגון זרנוקא לדלות בה מים מן הבור ואינה שוקעת במים אלא היא צפה ע"פ המים ואין יכולין למלאות בה מים וכשרוצין להכבידה נותנין בתוכה אבן מהודקת שלא תהיה מתנדנדת וממלאין בה מים מן הבורות. וזה פי' האבן שבקירוי'

*) נ"ל שלא נגמרה שאינה ראויה לאפות

רב נסים גאון

דתנן נתנו על פי הבור או על פי הדות וכו'. זו המשנה במס' כלים בפרק ה' (משנה ו) תנור שנתן בו עפר עד חציו מעפר ולמטה מטמא במגע מעפר ולמעלה מטמא באויר נתנו על פי הבור או על פי הדות וכו' ועיקר זה הוא מה שנאמר בתורת כהנים (פ' שמיני פ"ט) [אי] מה כלי חרש בשמו אף תנור שלא הוסק [תנור] שמו ת"ל אך מאימתי מקבל טומאה משיסיקנו כדי לאפות בו סופגנין יותץ טמאים הם את

זמורה שהיא קשורה בטפיח ממלאין בה בשבת *פקק החלון ר"א אומר בזמן שהוא קשור ותלוי פוקקין בו ואם לאו אין פוקקין בו וחכ"א בין כך ובין כך פוקקין בו :

גמ' *תנן התם אבן שעל פי החבית מטה על צידה והיא נופלת אמר רבה א"ר אמי א"ר יוחנן **לא שנו אלא בשוכח אבל במניח נעשה בסיס לדבר האסור ורב יוסף א"ר אסי א"ר יוחנן לא שנו אלא בשוכח אבל במניח נעשה כיסוי להחבית אמר רבה *מותבינן אשמעתין האבן שבקירויה אם ממלאין בה ואינה נופלת ממלאין בה ולא היא התם כיון דהדקה שויא דופן אמר רב יוסף ומותבינן אשמעתין אם לאו אין ממלאין בה ולא היא התם כיון דלא הדקה בטולי בטלה במאי קמיפלגי מר סבר בעינן מעשה ומר סבר לא בעינן מעשה ואזדו לטעמייהו דכי אתא רב דימי א"ר חנינא ואמרי לה א"ר זירא א"ר חנינא פעם אחת הלך רבי למקום אחד ומצא נדבך של אבנים ואמר לתלמידיו צאו וחשבו כדי שנשב עליהן למחר ולא הצריכן רבי למעשה ור' יוחנן אמר הצריכן רבי למעשה מאי אמר להו רבי אמי אמר צאו ולמדום אמר להו רבי אסי אמר צאו ושפשפום אמר להו איתמר ר' יוסי בן שאול אמר סואר של קורות הוה ור' יוחנן בן שאול אמר גשוש של ספינה הוה מ"ד גשוש כ"ש סואר ומ"ד סואר אבל גשוש קפיד עליה : זמורה שהיא קשורה כו' : קשורה אין לא קשורה לא לימא מתניתין דלא כרשב"ג דתניא *חריות של דקל שגדרן לעצים ונמלך עליהן לישיבה צריך לקשור רבן שמעון בן גמליאל אומר אין צריך לקשור אמר רב ששת אפי' תימא רשב"ג הכא במאי עסקינן במחוברת באביה אי הכי קא משתמש במחובר לקרקע למטה מג' רב אשי אמר אפי' תימא בתלושה גזירה שמא יקטום : פקק החלון כו' : *אמר רבה בר בר חנה א"ר יוחנן *הכל מודים שאין עושין אהל עראי בתחלה ביו"ט וא"צ לומר בשבת לא נחלקו אלא להוסיף שר"א אומר אין מוסיפין ביו"ט וא"צ לומר בשבת וחכ"א מוסיפין בשבת וא"צ לומר ביו"ט : וחכ"א בין כך ובין כך פוקקין בו : מאי בין כך ובין כך אמר ר' אבא אמר רב כהנא בין

רש"י

זמורה · של גפן : שהיא קשורה בטפיח · פך ששואבין בו מן הבור או מן המעין : ממלאין בה · דהויא כלי להך זמורה : ותלוי · שאינו נגרר בארץ שהחבל שהוא קשור בו אינו מגיע לארץ : אין פוקקין בו · דמיחזי כמוסיף על הבנין : בין כך ובין כך · בגמרא מפרש לה : גמ' תנן התם . לקמן בהאי מסכתא : האבן שעל פי החבית · והוצרך ליטול מן היין שבתוכה : מטה · החבית על צדה והיא נופלת : לא שנו · דמותר לטלטל החבית והאבן עליה דקתני ואם היתה בין חביות שירא להטותה שם שלא תפול האבן על החביות שבצדה מגביה ומטה על צדה והיא נופלת : בשוכח · האבן עליה שלא במתכוין : אבל במניח נעשית · החבית בסיס לאבן שהיא דבר האיסור ואין מטלטל את החבית: ורב יוסף א"ר אסי · לקולא אמר ר' יוחנן לא שנו דהוצרך להטות את החבית ולא ניתן לטלטל האבן להדיא: אלא בשוכח · דלא נתכוין לעשותה כלי : אבל במניח נעשה · האבן כיסוי לחבית ומגלה אותה כדרכה: אשמעתין · על שמועה שלי שאמרתי במניח אין האבן נעשה כלי : ממלאין בה · אלמא אבן נעשה כלי : דהדקה · שקשרה יפה : ואם לאו אין ממלאין · ולא אמרינן נעשה כלי בהנחה בעלמא וקשיא לדידי דאמרי לעיל במניח נעשה כיסוי לחבית : ולא היא · לא קשיא לי דהתם הואיל ובלא קשירה לא חזיא למלאות דהא נפלה והאי לאו הדקה בטולי בטלה מתורת כלי גלי דעתיה דלא חשיב ליה אבל כיסוי חבית הנחה משויא ליה כלי : ואזדו לטעמייהו · ר' אמי ור' אסי : נדבך של אבנים · אבנים סדורות ומוקצות לבנין : מאי אמר להו · מאי מעשה הצריכן לרבי יוחנן : צאו ולמדום · סדרו אותם והשיבום כדי שלא נצטרך ליגע בהם למחר לפי שאין הזמנה במעשה [*כל דהו] מועלת לאבן לעשותה כלי ור' אמי לטעמיה דאמר לעיל אין אבן נעשית כלי בהנחה : לנודום · כדאמרי' במו"ק (דף יב.) עושה להם למודים לסדר נסרים על פי הבור : ושפשפום · מן הטיט שיהו נאות לישב ולמחר תלמדום דבמעשה כל דהו נעשה כלי : סואר של קורות · הוה ולא אבנים : סואר · סדר של קורות חדשות שמסדרין אותן לבנין כדי שלא יתעקמו : גשוש · עץ ארוך שמגששים בו המים לפני הספינה לידע שהוא בעומקו שתוכל ספינה להלך בהן : קפיד עליה · שלא יתעקם ומייחד ליה מקום ומקלה ליה בידים ואפי' לר"ש אסור לטלטלו דמוקצה מחמת חסרון כיס אפי' ר"ש מודה : שאינה קשורה לא · ואפי' יש עקמומית בראשה כעין מזלג שראוי לתלות בה טפיח ולמלאות ויושב עליה : שגדרן לעצים · שחתכן להיסק : צריך לקשור · מע"ש : באביה · בגפן : והא קא משתמש במחובר · ואפילו קשורה מבעוד יום ליתסר : למטה מג'. סמוך לקרקע וכגון לשאוב מן המעין שאינו עמוק ומותר להשתמש באילן למטה מג' כדאמרי' בפרק בתרא דעירובין (דף צט:) היו שרשיו גבוהין מן הארץ ג' לא ישב עליהם : גזירה שמא יקטום · שמא למחר תהיה לו ארוכה ויקטמנה מתוך שהיא רכה ונוחה לקטום ונמצא עושה כלי וחייב משום מכה בפטיש אבל בחריות לישיבה ליכא למיגזר הכי הלכך במחשבה סגי : שאין עושין אהל עראי · לפרוס מחצלת על ד' מחיצות או על ד' קונדסים להיות צל לאהל מן החמה ודוקא גג אבל מחילה לאו אהל הוא ושרי לפורסה לצניעות כדאמרי' עירובין (ד' צד.) בעובדא דשמואל ופקק החלון דמתני'*) משום דבנין קבוע הוא ומיחזי כמוסיף על הבנין : להוסיף · כגון שהיה מחצלת פרוסה עליהן וכרוכה ונשאר בה אויר ולמחר פושטה דומיא דפקק דמוסיף בעלמא הוא : בין

*) גי' רש"ל הוי למעלה בגג ולא מן הצד אבל הר"ן מקיים פי' רש"י דהכא

תוספות

ואזדו לטעמייהו · תימה היכי הוה רבי אסי לטעמיה אדרבה פליגי דהכא קאמר ר' אסי נעשה כיסוי לחבית בהנחה גרידא בלא שום מעשה וגבי נדבך אמר ר' אסי צאו ושפשפום אמר להן דהיינו מעשה שהצריכן רבי ועוד קשה גבי נדבך קאמר דסגי בשפשוף ולקמן גבי כיסוי כלים א"ר אסי א"ר יוחנן והוא שיש בהם תורת כלי ויש לומר דכיסוי חבית סגי לה בהנחה שדרכו לעשותו כל דהו דלא בעי תיקון ומעשה גמור כשאר כיסוי כלים ונדבך של אבן מסותת ומרובע לבנין סגי להו בשפשוף שאין צריך עוד תיקון ומ"מ הוי ר' אסי לטעמיה דכי היכי דמיקל רבי אסי גבי נדבך ה"נ הכא והא דקאמר ר' אסי בפרק במה טומנין (עיל דף נ.) חריות של דקל ישב אע"פ שלא קשר התם רב (אסי) ה) גרסינן אי נמי ראויין הם לישיבה טפי מאבנים:

הכל מודים שאין עושין אהל עראי בתחלה · פי' בקונ' דלא אסיר אהל אלא למעלה בגג אבל בדפנות לא כדמוכח בעובדא דשמואל בכל גגות (עירובין דף צד.) דאיתמר חצר כותל שנפלה רב אמר אין מטלטלין אלא בד' אמות ושמואל אמר זה מטלטל עד עיקר המחילה וזה מטלטל עד עיקר המחילה והא דרב לאו בפירוש איתמר אלא מכללא דשמואל הוה יתיב בההוא חצר נפל גודא דביני אמר להו שמואל שקולו גלימא נגודי ליה אהדרינהו רב לאפיה כו' ושמואל למה ליה למיעבד הכי האמר זה מטלטל עד עיקר המחילה כו' שמואל לצניעותא בעלמא הוא דעבד אלמא משמע דאהל דדפנות שרי למיעבד הכי ורב שהיה מקפיד לאו משום עשיית אהל דשרי כדפרישית אלא הוה קפיד אמאי דהוו מטלטלין גלימא ד' אמות בחצר וקשה דע"כ שייך איסור אהל אפילו בדפנות כדאיתא בעירובין בפרק מי שהוציאוהו (דף מד. ושם) גבי עשיית דופן סוכה דפריך התם והאמר רבה בר בר חנה אמר רבי יוחנן הכל מודים שאין עושין אהל עראי בתחילה ומשני הא בדופן שלישית והא בדופן רביעית אלא נראה לר"ת דשפיר שייך בדפנות אהל היכא דמחילה מועלת להיתר ולהכי בדופן שלישית דהויא מחילה ומכשר ליה לסוכה חשיב עשיית אהל בתחלה אבל דופן רביעית אינה אלא תוספת בעלמא הואיל וכבר הסוכה היתה כשרה ועיקר פלוגתין דר"א ורבנן איתא באהל כבעשיית דופן דפקק החלון משמע בחלון שבכותל דאי בגג מיירי הוה ליה למימר ארובה כמו ששנינו משילין פירות דרך ארובה (ביצה דף לה:) ומיהו באהל שבגג נמי פליגי כדמוכח לקמן בפרק תולין (דף קלז:) דמייתי הך גבי תליית משמרת שהיא כעין גג וכן משמע בפרק בתרא דעירובין (דף קב.) דאמר הנהו דיכרי דהוו בי רב הונא ביממא בעו טולא ובליליא בעו אוירא אתא לקמיה דרב אמר ליה כרוך בודיא ושייר בה טפח דלמחר הוא מוסיף על אהל עראי ומותר ומשמע דהיינו נמי תוספת אהל עראי דפליגי רבי אליעזר ורבנן ועובדא דשמואל דכל

ה) נ"ל אסי. רש"א.

עין משפט נר מצוה

לח א מיי' פכ"ה מהל' שבת הלכה יז סמג לאוין סה טוש"ע או"ח סימן שח סעיף כב וסימן שט סעיף ד :

לט ב מיי' שם פכ"ו הל' כא סמג שם טור ושו"ע או"ח סימן שח סעיף כה:

מ ג מיי' פכ"ג מהלכות שבת הלכה ז :

מא ד ה מיי' פכ"ב מהל' שבת הלכה כז סמג לאוין סה טוש"ע או"ח סימן שטו סעיף א :

מב ו מיי' שם טוש"ע שם סעיף ב :

מסורת הש"ס: לקמן קלז: עירובין מד סוכה כז: · [לקמן קמב: ע"ש] · [לעיל קכ: לקמן קמב: ע"ש] · [קידושין כ וש"נ] · לעיל נ: ולקמן קכו: גי' רש"א · לקמן קלז: עירו' מד. סו: [תוספ' סוכה פ"א]

רבינו חננאל

וזה שאמר רבי צאו ולמדום עשו להם לימודים. יש מי שאומר עיניני בהן. כלומר לימוד בעינן בלא מעשה ור"א לימודים כגון זה ששנינו במסכת משקין. ר' יהודה אומר עושה לו לימודים בשביל שלא יתחיק. והן כיסויי עצים ועליהם פים (שרוצים מעשים) [שהצריכן למעשה] וראיתן הא דגרסינן בבמה טומנין תני רבה בר רב הונא קמי דרב חריות של דקל שגדרום לעצים ונמלך עליהם לישיבה צריך לקשר רשב"ג אומר אין צריך לקשר. ואהדרינן מאן תנא דפליג עליה דרשב"ג. ר' חנינה בן עקביא היא שהלך למקום א' ומצא חריות של דקל שגדרום לעצים כו': פיסקא זמורה שהיא קשורה בטפיח כו'. זמורה היא כגון אמיר והיא זמורה של כרם ארוכה כמו חבל וטפיח הוא כלי בדלי. ואמרה המשנה אם זמורה זו היתה קשורה בזה הכלי ממלאין בה בשבת שעשאה מאתמול במקום חבל ועשה בה מעשה ואם לאו אסור לחשב עליו בשבת להיותו חבל. ואמרינן לימא מתניתין דלא כרשב"ג. דהא רשב"א בחריות שגדרן לעצים ונמלך עליהן לישיבה אין צריך לקשר. ופריק רב ששת זמורה זו מחוברת באביה. כלומר מחוברת בקרקע. ואם לא קשרה מאתמול ביבשה. ואינה דומה לחריות של דקל שהן גזורין. ואקשינן אי הכי משתמש במחובר ופריקו למטה משלשה. כדתנן היו שרשין גבוהין מן הארץ שלשה טפחים לא ישב עליהן. אם גבוהין ג' טפחים הוא דאסירו. הא בפחות מהן מותר לישב עליהן. מיהא שמעינן דפחות מג' במחובר לקרקע בקרקע דמי ומותר להשתמש בו. ויש שאומרים כי המים הם קרובים בפחות משלש' ולא אתי למחתך. רב אשי אמר אפילו תימא בתלושה גזירה שמא יקטום: מתני' פקק החלון. כגון מסך העשוי לסתום החלון בין אם הוא מבגד בין מזולתו בזמן שקשור ותלוי פוקקין בו. ואם לאו אין פוקקין בו.

אמר (רבא) [רבה] בר בר חנה א"ר יוחנן הכל מודין שאין עושין אהל עראי בתחלה ביו"ט . ואין צ"ל בשבת . לא נחלקו אלא להוסיף . פי' שאם היה בו פקק פוקק במקצת החלון . ר' אליעזר אוסר למושכן כנגד כל החלון . וחכמים מתירים (וזהו) להוסיף כיוצא בו בסוף המוצא תפילין הנהו דכרי דהוו לרב הונא דביממא בעו טולא ובליליא בעו אוירא . ואמר ליה רב כרוך בודיא עלייהו ושייר בה טפח ולמחר פרסיה

רב נסים גאון

את שיש לו נתיצה ואת שאין לו נתיצה אין לו טומאה : **אי הכי קא משתמש במחובר למטה מג'** מכלל כי מה שיהיה מדבר המחובר לקרקע קרוב מהארץ פחות מג' טפחים מותר להשתמש בו ואין איסור משום שבות [רק] מה שהוא גבוה מן הארץ ג' טפחים ותמצא עיקר זה במשנה במס' עירובין בפרק המוצא תפילין (דף צט) אילן שהוא מיסך על הארץ אם אין נופו גבוה מן הארץ ג' טפחים **לא ישב** עליהן ודבר זה אין בו חלוקה אבל חלקו רבא ורב ששת בשרשי אילן הבאים מלמעלה מג' לתוך ג' ובפ' בכל מערבין (שם דף לג) תניא נתנו באילן בתוך ג' מותר לטלטל : **סליק פרק כל הכלים**

a IS TIED TO A PITCHER,[1] ONE MAY DRAW [WATER] WITH IT ON THE SABBATH. AS FOR THE STOPPER OF A SKYLIGHT, R. ELIEZER SAID: WHEN IT IS FASTENED[2] AND SUSPENDED,[3] ONE MAY CLOSE [THE SKYLIGHT] WITH IT; IF NOT, ONE MAY NOT CLOSE [THE SKYLIGHT] WITH IT.[4] BUT THE SAGES MAINTAIN: IN BOTH CASES WE MAY CLOSE [THE SKYLIGHT] WITH IT.

GEMARA. We learnt elsewhere: If a stone is on the mouth of a cask [e.g., of wine], one tilts it on a side and it falls off.[5] Rabbah said in R. Ammi's name in R. Johanan's name: They learnt this only if one forgets [it there]; but if he places [it there],[6] it [the barrel] becomes a stand for a forbidden article.[7] Whereas R. Joseph said in R. Assi's name in R. Johanan's name: They learnt this only if one forgets [it there]; but if he places [it there], it [the stone] becomes a covering of the barrel.[8] Rabbah said: An objection is raised against my teaching: IF A STONE [IS PLACED] IN A PUMPKIN SHELL, AND ONE CAN DRAW [WATER] IN IT AND IT DOES NOT FALL OUT, ONE MAY DRAW [WATER] IN IT?[9] But it is not [analogous]: there, since it is firmly fastened, it is made as a wall [of the vessel]. R. Joseph said: An objection is also raised against my teaching: IF NOT, ONE MAY NOT DRAW [WATER] IN IT?[10] But it is not [analogous]: there, since he did not fasten it firmly, he really made it as nought.[11]

Wherein do they differ? One Master [R. Ammi] holds: An
b act of labour is required;[1] while the other Master [R. Assi] holds: An act of labour is not required. Now, they are consistent with their views. For when R. Dimi came,[2] he said in R. Ḥanina's name—others state, R. Zera said in R. Ḥanina's name: Rabbi once went to a certain place and found a course of stones,[3] whereupon he said to his disciples, Go out and intend [them,][4] so that we can sit upon them to-morrow; but Rabbi did not require them [to perform] an act of labour. But R. Joḥanan said, Rabbi did require them [to perform] an act of labour. What did he say to them?[5]—R. Ammi said: He said to them, Go out and arrange them in order.[6] R. Assi said: He said to them, 'Go out and scrape them' [free of mortar, etc.].[7] It was stated: R. Jose b. Saul said: It was a pile of beams;[8] R. Joḥanan b. Saul said: It was a ship's sounding pole.[9] Now he who says [that it was] a sounding pole, all the more so a pile [of beams];[10] but he who says that [it was] a pile, but one is particular about a sounding pole.[11]

IF A VINE-BRANCH IS TIED, etc. Only if it is tied, but not otherwise? Must we say that our Mishnah does not agree with R. Simeon b. Gamaliel? For it was taught: As for the dried branches of a palm tree which one cut down for fuel, and then he changed his mind, [intending them] for sitting [thereon], he must tie them together.[12] R. Simeon b. Gamaliel said: He need not tie them together.—Said R. Shesheth, You may even say [that it agrees with] R. Simeon b. Gamaliel: we treat here of one [a branch] that is attached to its parent stock.[13] If so, he makes use of what
c is attached to the soil?[1]—It is below three.[2] R. Ashi said: You may even say that it refers to a detached [branch]: it is a preventive measure, lest he cut [i.e., shorten] it.[3]

AS FOR THE STOPPER OF A SKYLIGHT, etc. Rabbah b. Bar Ḥanah said in R. Joḥanan's name: All agree that we may not make for the first time a temporary building on a Festival, whilst on the Sabbath it goes without saying. They differ only in respect of adding [to a building]: R. Eleazar maintaining, We may not add on a Festival, whilst on the Sabbath it goes without saying; whereas the Sages rule: We may add on the Sabbath, whilst it is superfluous to speak of a Festival.

BUT THE SAGES MAINTAIN: IN BOTH CASES WE MAY CLOSE [THE SKYLIGHT] WITH IT. What does 'IN BOTH CASES' mean?

a (1) To let it down into the well. (2) By a cord to the wall. (3) In the air, the cord being too short to allow it to reach the ground. (4) For it looks like adding to the building. (5) If he wishes to draw wine, v. *infra* 142*b*. (6) Before the Sabbath. (7) *Sc.* the stone, which may not be handled. (8) Hence the stone itself may be handled and removed, and it is unnecessary to tilt the barrel. (9) Which shows that the stone is now part of the vessel. (10) Which shows that it is not part of the vessel. (11) Since the pumpkin is not fit for drawing water, as the stone will fall out. But here it is enough for his purpose to place the stone upon the barrel, therefore the stone becomes part of the barrel in virtue of that act.

b (1) For the stone to count as part of the barrel, and mere placing is not an act of labour. (2) V. *supra* 5*a*, n. b9. (3) Arranged in order, and waiting to be used in building. This renders them *mukẓeh*. (4) Express your intention of sitting on them to-morrow (the Sabbath), so that they may not be *mukẓeh*. (5) In R. Joḥanan's view. (6) That they may be ready for sitting upon without further handling, R. Ammi holding, as above, that mere disposition does not make them a utensil. (7) But they can be arranged for sitting on the Sabbath itself. Thus these views are consistent with those expressed above. (8) Not stones. (9) With which the depth of the water is sounded. (10) They certainly could have sat upon the latter. (11) Not to use it for anything else, lest it be bent or warped. Therefore it is *mukẓeh* and must not be handled. (12) V. *supra* 50*a*. (13) *Sc.* the vine. Hence if it is not tied to the pitcher before the Sabbath, it remains part of the vine and must not be handled.

c (1) Even if tied before the Sabbath it is still that and is forbidden. (2) Handbreadths from the ground. Such may be used, v. 'Erub. 99*b*. (3) On the Sabbath, if it is not fastened to the pitcher before. Hence even R. Simeon b. Gamaliel agrees.

—R. Abba said in R. Kahana's name: [126a] Whether it is fastened or not, providing that it was prepared.[4] Said R. Jeremiah to him, But let the Master say, Whether it is suspended or not, providing that it is fastened;[5] for Rabbah b. Bar Ḥanah said in R. Joḥanan's name: Just as there is a controversy here, so is there a controversy in respect of a dragging bolt.[6] For we learnt: With a dragging bolt, one may lock [the door] in the Temple, but not in the country;[7] but one that is laid apart [on the ground][8] is forbidden in both places. R. Judah said: That which is laid apart [is permitted] in the Temple; and that which is dragged, in the country. Now it was taught: Which is a dragging bolt wherewith we may close [a door] in the Temple but not in the country? That which is fastened [to the door] and suspended, one end reaching the ground. R. Judah said: Such is permitted even in the country. But which is forbidden in the country? That which is neither fastened nor suspended, but which one removes and places in a corner. Further, R. Joshua b. Abba said in 'Ulla's name: Who a is the Tanna of 'a dragging bolt?'[1] It is R. Eleazar![2]—Said he to him, I hold with the following Tanna. For it was taught: If a private individual prepares[3] a cane for opening and shutting [a door] therewith: if it is tied and suspended to the door, he may open and shut [it] therewith; if it is not tied and suspended, he may not open and shut [it] therewith. R. Simeon b. Gamaliel ruled: If it is prepared,[4] even if it is not fastened.[5]

R. Judah b. Shilath said in R. Assi's name in R. Joḥanan's name: The *halachah* is as R. Simeon b. Gamaliel. Now, did R. Joḥanan

(4) For this purpose before the Sabbath. (5) Before the Sabbath, i.e., explain the Mishnah stringently, instead of leniently. (6) Lit., 'a bolt that is dragged'. I.e., a door-bolt, fastened to the door, but one end thereof drags on the floor. (7) 'Country' is employed technically to denote all places except the Temple.—Since it is fastened to the door, it is as though built thereto, and therefore the prohibition of handling it is only a Rabbinical one, which was imposed in the country but not in the Temple. (8) It is not fastened at all, but when removed from the sockets it is simply placed on the ground.

a (1) Requiring both that it be fastened and suspended. (2) Whereas R. Judah will agree with the Rabbis. From this passage we see that all agree that it must be tied. (3) I.e., sets aside. (4) I.e., since it has been devoted to this purpose. (5) It may be used for opening and shutting. R. Abba rules in accordance with this.

"בין קשור בין שאינו קשור והוא שמתוקן א"ל ר' ירמיה ולימא מר בין תלוי ובין שאינו תלוי והוא שקשור דאמר רבה בר בר חנה א"ר יוחנן כמחלוקת כאן כך מחלוקת בנגר הנגרר *דתנן נגר הנגרר נועלין בו במקדש אבל לא במדינה והמונח כאן וכאן אסור ר' יהודה אומר המונח *במקדש והנגרר במדינה ותניא איזהו נגר הנגרר °שנועלין בו במקדש אבל לא במדינה כל שקשור ותלוי וראשו מגיע לארץ ר' יהודה אומר [ב]זה אף במדינה מותר אלא איזהו שבמדינה אסור כל שאינו לא קשור ולא תלוי ושומטו ומניחו בקרן זוית ואמר רבי יהושע בר אבא משמיה דעולא מאן תנא נגר הנגרר ר"א היא א"ל אנא דאמרי כי האי תנא דתניא *קנה שהתקינו בעה"ב להיות פותח ונועל בו בזמן שקשור ותלוי בפתח פותח ונועל בו אין קשור ותלוי אין פותח ונועל בו רשב"ג אומר מתוקן אע"פ שאינו קשור אמר רב יהודה בר שילת אמר רב אסי א"ר יוחנן [ג]הלכה כרשב"ג ומי אמר רבי יוחנן הכי והתנן כל כסויי הכלים

שיש

בין קשור כו' · כלומר אפילו קשירה לא צריך : והוא שמתוקן · מוכן מאתמול לכך : א"ל רבי ירמיה · אמאי פסיק ליה מר לקולא : לימא מר · דלא פליגי רבנן אלא אתנו"ס דרבי אליעזר בעי קשור ותלוי ואפילו קשור אם ראשו נגרר לארץ חשיב ליה רבי אליעזר כשומטו מן הקרקע ובונה בו לכתחלה ורבנן אמרי ליה בין תלוי בין נגרר פוקקין בו ובלבד שיהא קשור : דאמר רבה בר בר חנה · בתלייה הוא דפליגי ולא בקשירה דמדמי לה לפלוגתא דנגר הנגרר והתם לדברי הכל קשור בעינן : נגר · יתד שתוקעין בחור שבמפתן ונועלין בו את הדלת:הנגרר. כדמפרש שקשור בדלת אלא שראשו נגרר לארץ: נועלין בו במקדש · דכיון דקשור בו מיוחד ועומד הוא לכך וכבר נבנה בנין זה מבעוד יום ואין בו אלא גזירת שבות מדבריהם ואין שבות במקדש : והמונח · שאינו קשור כלל אלא כשהוא שומטו מן החור מניחו ע"ג קרקע הלכך כשתוקעו בשבת בונה הוא ואיסורא דאורייתא הוא אף במקדש : המונח מותר במקדש · דכיון דמתוקן מאתמול להכי לאו בונה הוא : שקשור ותלוי · ראשו העליון אבל ראשו התחתון מגיע לארץ: מאן תנא נגר הנגרר · אסור דבעי תרתי : ר"א היא · דאמר גבי פקק החלון תרתי בעינן מכלל דר' יהודה כרבנן אלמא רבנן קשירה בעו : כי האי תנא· דאפי' קשירה לא בעי כרבן שמעון בן גמליאל דאמר מתוקן בהזמנה בעלמא ואע"פ שאינו קשור : שהתקינו · שהזמינו : אמר רב יהודה גרסינן ולא גרסינן ואמר :

דכל גגות (עירובין צד·) דפריך ושמואל למה ליה למיעבד הכי וקאמר זה מטלטל כו' לאו משום דלאו הוה אמר אין מטלטלין בו אלא בד' אמות דאז הוה ניחא ליה אלא אז כמי היה קשה היכי עביד הכי כיון דמחילה מתרת לטלטל בחצר הוה כעשיית אהל עראי בתחלה ואסור כדפרישית לעיל ומהאי טעמא היה מקפיד רב דס"ל שאין מטלטלין אלא בד' אלא משום דהש"ס ידע דסבר שמואל דזה מטלטל עד עיקר המחילה ניחא למיפרך למה הוצרך לעשות מחילה :

בין קשור בין שאינו קשור והוא שמתוקן · נראה לר"ת דלאו בתיקון של מעשה אלא במחשבה בעלמא כדמוכח לקמן דאמר כרשב"ג ס"ל דאמר מתוקן אע"פ שאינו קשור דהיינו במחשבה ומשמע דלגמרי ס"ל כוותיה דגבי ר' יוחנן דוקא הוא דאמר בסמוך סבר לה כוותיה בחדא ופליג עליה בחדא ופריך ולימא מר בין תלוי בין שאינו תלוי והוא שקשור כרבי יהודה דבעי קשירה וטעמא משום טלטול ולא משום בנין דאי משום בנין מאי ראיה מנגר שצריך קשירה לפקק והא בפקק לא שייך בנין אלא תוספת אהל עראי ותוספת אהל עראי שרו רבנן בלא שום קשירה כדמוכח במי שהוליאוהו (דף מד·) :

והמונח כאן וכאן אסור · פי' רש"י שכשתוקעו בשבת בונה הוא ואיסורא דאורייתא איכא ואינו משמע שיהא בו איסורא דאורייתא כיון שאינו מבטלו שם אלא נראה לר"ת דכולה מילתא בנגר הנגרר ליכא איסורא אלא משום טלטול וכי ההיא דקנה שהתקינו בעה"ב להיות פותח ונועל בו דמיירי משום טלטול ואפ"ה בעי ר"א קשור ותלוי יותר משאר כלי תשמיש שדי להם בתיקונם לפי שהם תשמיש בית מידי דהוי אכיסוי קרקעות שהחמירו בהם להצריכם בית אחיזה אע"ג דהכי משום שבות נאסר טלטולם במקדש כקנים וכמקלות דלעיל אבל בשום בנין ליכא איסורא כלל אפילו מדרבנן וקשה לר"ת מנלן דאפליגו רבי אליעזר ורבנן בתוספת אהל עראי כיון דאפליגו בטלטול דילמא בחד הוא דאיפליגו ותירץ ר"ת בספר הישר דא"כ הוה ליה למנקט פלוגתייהו במילתא דלא שייכא ביה תוספת אהל כי ההיא דנגר הנגרר ומדנקט פלוגתא בפקק החלון דשייך ביה תוספת אהל ש"מ דפליגי בהאי וליכא למימר דדווקא בהאל פליגי ולא בטלטול דהא בההיא דנגר לא שייך אלא איסור טלטול אפ"ה איפלוג בה ר"א ורבנן דע"כ איבעי לן למימר דת"ק דנגר היינו ר"א דרבנן שרו אפילו בפקק החלון כ"ש בנגר דלא שייך איסור אהל אלא איסור טלטול אלא ודאי בתרתי פליגי דר"א אסר בפקק החלון ומשום טלטול בשאין תורת כלי גמור עליו ואפי' יש עליו תורת כלי גמור כגון שיש לו בית יד אסור מ"מ משום תוספת אהל עראי כיון דבטלי' בפקק ורבנן דשרו אפי' אין עליו תורת כלי דלית להו לא משום טלטול ולא משום אהל :

רבי יהודה אומר כו' · ובעירובין מסקינן אמר רב יהודה אמר שמואל הלכה כרבי יהודה וקשה לר"י דהא שמואל גופיה סבר לעיל בפרק במה טומנין (דף נ·) גבי חריות של דקל שגדרן לעצים דבמחשבה בעלמא סגי דאיתמר רב (יהודה) אומר קושר ושמואל אמר חושב וקאמר התם דשמואל ס"ל כרשב"ג דאמר חריות של דקל שגדרן לעצים ונמלך עליהן לישיבה א"ל לקשר וא"כ היכי קאמר הלכה כרבי יהודה דבעי קשירה משום איסור טלטול דהא לא שייך איסור בנין בההיא דנגר הנגרר אלא איסור טלטול ומשום איסור טלטול בעי רבי יהודה קשירה כדפירשתי וליכא לפרושי דבנגר הנגרר דהכא לאפוקי מאיסור בנין הוא דבעי קישור אבל משום איסור טלטול לא הוה בעי קישור אלא במחשבה בעלמא כרשב"ג א"כ מאי קא מהדר ליה ר' אבא בר כהנא לר' ירמיה אנא דאמרי כי האי תנא כו' דילמא מאי דלא בעי התם רשב"ג אלא מתוקן אע"פ שאינו קשור היינו משום דהתם ליכא אלא איסור טלטול דהתם ודאי לא מיירי מידי בבנין דקאמר קנה שהתקינו בעה"ב להיות פותח ונועל (א) ומדקתני פותח ונועל משמע שאינו נועל באותו קנה עצמו דהוה ליה למיתני שהתקינו לנעול בו אלא משמע שהוא כעין מפתחות שלנו שיש מהם שמושכין המנעול שבדלת לכאן ולכאן כך הקנה מושך המנעול אבל הקנה עצמו אינו במקום המנעול א"כ פשיטא דכה"ג לא שייך בנין בהאי קנה אלא משום איסור טלטול הוא ומיהו אין ראיה מזה דבהאי קנה מיירי כדפרישית מדקתני פותח ונועל דהא כה"ג קתני בתוספתא חבילי עצים וסוכה של קוצים שעשאן דלת לפירצה ולחצר אם היו קשורות ותלויות פותחין ונועלין בהן אם לאו כו' מיהו אומר ר"י דאפילו הוה מפרש ההיא דקנה שהתקינו כו' דשייך ביה בנין ובמקום מנעול הוה ולהכי פשיט מיניה רבי אבא בר כהנא דס"ל כרשב"ג דאמר דכי הוי מתוקן אע"פ שאינו קשור כפיק מתורת איסור בנין לא הוי אתי שפיר (דה"א) מדקאמר הש"ס בסמוך וכ"ת הכא נמי דאיכא תורת כלי עליהן והתניא חריות של דקל כו' והיכי מוכח מההיא דחריות של דקל דהא דאמר מתוקן אע"פ שאינו קשור היינו בלא תורת כלי אלא במחשבה בעלמא דלמא באיסור טלטול הוא דלא מצריך רשב"ג אלא מחשבה אבל באיסור בנין הוה בעי שיתקעהו ויכינהו ויעשו בו מעשה שיהא תורת כלי עליו על כן נראה לר"י דבהכי פליגי רבי אבא בר כהנא ורבי יוחנן ורב יהודה דעירובין (דף קב·) דאינהו סבירא להו דבההיא דנגר לא שייך אלא איסור טלטול ואיהו ס"ל דשייך בנין בנגר הנגרר ולהכי בעי קישור לאפוקי מאיסור בנין והשתא אתיא שמעתין שפיר דלא מיירי מידי באיסור בנין לא בההוא דנגר ולא בההיא דקנה והשתא נמי ההיא דקנה משום טלטול · מ"ר :

שקשור ותלוי וראשו מגיע לארץ · פירוש ראשו העליון תלוי וראשו התחתון מגיע לארץ כדפירש בקונטרס ונראה לרשב"א דאפילו שני הראשים מונחים לארץ אלא שקשור דשרי במקדש והאי דנקט כהאי גוונא לאשמעינן דאפ"ה אסור במדינה והשתא אתי שפיר הא דתנן במשנה והמונח כאן וכאן אסור היינו שאינו קשור ולא תלוי כלל דאי אמרת דוקא נקט ראשו מגיע לארץ אבל שני הראשים מונחין בארץ אסור במקדש אע"פ שקשור אם כן השתא לא הוי מונח דרבי יהודה כמונח דתנא קמא דמונח דרבי יהודה על כרחיך היינו שאינו לא קשור ולא תלוי ושומטו ומניחו בקרן זוית דלאי אמרת כמו מונח דת"ק שני ראשים מונחים בארץ אלא שקשורין היכי קאמר המונח במקדש ההוא אפילו במדינה שרי דלא אסר רבי יהודה אלא דוקא שאינו קשור כלל :

וכ"ת

עין משפט נר מצוה

מג א ב מיי' פכ"ב מהלכות שבת הלכה ל ופכ"ו הלכה י סמג לאוין סה טוש"ע או"ח סימן שיג סעיף א :

מד ג מיי' פכ"ו שם הלכה י :

רבינו חננאל

עליהן מוסיף על אהלי עראי הוא ושפיר דמי . וחכ"א בין כך ובין כך פוקקין בו . ומיבעיא לן מאי בין כך ובין כך אמר רבה בר כהנא בין קשור בין שאינו קשור אותו פקק פוקקין בו . והוא שמתוקן . כלומר שהתקינו לפקק בו . היכי דמי תיקון זה כדאמרינן בסוף המוצא תפילין : ת"ר סיכי קמצים וחבילי עצים שהתקינן לפירצה שבחצר. בזמן שקשורין ותלוין נועלין בשבת ואין צ"ל ביו"ט . א"ל ר' ירמיה ולימא מר בין תלוי בין שאינו תלוי והוא שקשור כלומר כבר נעשה בו מעשה לשום כלי . דאמר רבה ב"ב חנה א"ר יוחנן כמחלוקת כאן בפקק החלון כך חלוקתן בנגר הנגרר בקשור ותלוי בלבד . אבל לא לענין מקדש ומדינה . ותניא בסוף עירובין . איזהו נגר הנגרר שנועלין בו במקדש אבל לא במדינה: שומטו ומניחו בקרן זוית . דייקינן מינה סדקתני ושומטו ומניחו מכלל שאם הוא קשור שאם אינו יכול לשומטו ולהניחו בקרן זוית שפיר דמי . ואמרינן מאן תנא נגר הנגרר צריך להיות קשור ותלוי ר אליעזר והא ר' יוחנן סבר כי חכמים חלוקי, על ר' אליעזר סבירא להו כר' יהודה דאסר בשאינו קשור ולא תלוי ולא בתלוי אבל אם הוא קשור אע"פ שאינו תלוי שרי . וא"ל ר' אבא לר' ירמיה אנא דאמרי והוא שמתוקן אע"פ שאינו לא קשור ולא תלוי כי הא מתניתא דתני בקנה שהתקינו בעה"ב להיות פותח ונועל בו . ואמר רשב"ג מתוקן אע"פ שאינו קשור ואמר משמיה דר' יוחנן הלכה כרשב"ג דקאי רשב"ג כחכמים. ואקשינן היכי אמר ר' יוחנן הלכת

מסורת הש"ס

עירובין קב.

[צ"ל מותר במקדש]

[תוספ' פט"ז]

הגהות הב"ח

(א) תוס' ד"ה ר' יהודה וכו' פותח ונועל בו מדקתני פותח ונועל בו משמע :

גליון הש"ס

גמ' שנועלין בו במקדש אבל לא במדינה . עיין פי"א מ"ד דכלים :

כה א ב ג מיי' פכ"ה מהלכות שבת הל' יג סמג לאוין סה טוש"ע או"ח סימן שח סעיף י:

א ד ה מיי' פכ"א מהל' שבת הלכה ב ופכ"ו הלכה טו סמג לאוין סה טוש"ע או"ח סימן שלג סעיף א:

שיש להם בית אחיזה ניטלין בשבת ואמר רב יהודה בר שילא אמר רב אסי אמר רבי יוחנן והוא שיש תורת כלי עליהן וכי תימא הכא נמי דאיכא תורת כלי עליו ומי בעי רשב"ג תורת כלי עליו והתניא *חריות של דקל שגדרן לשם עצים ונמלך עליהן לישיבה צריך לקשר רשב"ג אומר אין צריך לקשר רבי יוחנן סבירא ליה כוותיה בחדא ופליג עליה בחדא דרש רבי יצחק נפחא אפתחא דריש גלותא הלכה כרבי אליעזר מתיב רב עמרם *ומדבריהם למדנו שפוקקין ומודדין וקושרין בשבת א"ל [אביי] מאי דעתיך משום דקתני סתמא נגר הנגרר נמי סתמא היא ואפי' הכי *מעשה רב: **מתני'** (*כל) כיסוי הכלים שיש להם בית אחיזה ניטלין בשבת א"ר יוסי בד"א *בכיסוי קרקעות אבל בכיסוי הכלים בין כך ובין כך ניטלין בשבת: **גמ'** אמר רב יהודה בר שילא א"ר אסי א"ר יוחנן והוא שיש תורת כלי עליהן דכ"ע כסוי קרקעות אם יש להן בית אחיזה אין אי לא לא כסוי הכלים אע"ג דאין להם בית אחיזה כי פליגי בכלים דחברינהו בארעא מ"ס גזרינן ומ"ס לא גזרינן לישנא אחרינא כי פליגי בכיסוי תנור מר מדמי ליה לכיסוי קרקע ומר מדמי ליה לכיסוי כלים:

הדרן עלך כל הכלים

מפנין *אפילו ארבע וחמש קופות של תבן ושל תבואה מפני האורחים ומפני בטול בהמ"ד *אבל לא את האוצר מפנין תרומה טהורה ודמאי ומעשר ראשון שניטלה תרומתו ומעשר שני והקדש שנפדו והתורמוס היבש מפני שהוא מאכל *לעזים *אבל לא את הטבל ולא את מעשר [ראשון] שלא נטלה תרומתו ולא את מעשר שני והקדש שלא נפדו ולא *את הלוף ולא את החרדל ר' שמעון בן גמליאל *מתיר בלוף מפני שהוא מאכל עורבין חבילי קש וחבילי עצים וחבילי זרדים אם התקינן למאכל בהמה מטלטלין אותן ואם לאו אין מטלטלין אותן: **גמ'** השתא חמש מפנין ארבע מיבעיא *אמר רב חסדא ארבע מחמש (*איכא דאמרי ארבע מאוצר קטן) וחמש מאוצר גדול ומאי אבל לא את האוצר שלא יתחיל באוצר תחלה ומני רבי יהודה היא דאית ליה מוקצה ושמואל אמר ארבע וחמש כדאמרי

וכי תימא הכא נמי דאיכא תורת כלי עליו. פי' בקונטרס שיהא ראוי לעשות שום תשמיש אחר ואין נראה לר"ת כי למה יש לנו להצריך שלדבר אחר יהא ראוי כיון שראוי לדבר זה אלא נראה לר"ת דה"פ דאיכא תורת כלי עליו שתיקנו ועשה בו מעשה והכינו לכך שמאחר שלכך תיקנו והכינו לכך יש תורת כלי עליו אפילו אינו ראוי לדבר אחר כמו חריות של דקל שאינן ראוין לשום תשמישאלא לישיבה אף על פי כן(ד) יכול להכינם ולטלטלם בשבת והבנים כמו אמרינן לעיל לאו ושיפשפו ועוד אי תורת כלי עליהם ממש לריכא למימר דכלי ניטל לצורך גופו והא דאמרי' בעירובין (ד' קב.) נגר הנגרר עשה לו בית יד מהו א"ל בוכנא קאמרת פירוש ושרי לאו משום דאי לא הוה כבוכנא ע"י הבית יד הזה הוה אסור דאפילו לא חזי למילתא אחריתי כיון שתקנוהו בידים לכך היה מותר אפי' בלא בית יד אלא נראה לר"י דההיא מיירי בנקמז דאסור לעיל מיני' בסמוך משום דמיחזי כבונה פי' שנועץ הנגר בתוך הנקב שבמפתן עד(ה) בתוך הארץ כדפירש בקונטרס התם ועלה קאי הא עשה לו בית יד באותו נגר שנקמז אי נמי שמואל לטעמיה דסבר דטעמא דרבי יהודה משום בנין אפילו בלא נעילת נגר בארץ וכן נראה יותר כי נקמז אין פתרונו נעילה בארץ אלא דומה שהוא מעין נשמט רק שאינו נשמט ממש כדמוכח בברייתא שהביא למעלה דקתני נגר אם נשמט כולו אסור נקמז מותר רבי יהודה אומר נקמז אע"פ שאינו נשמט ולא נודע פירוש נקמז היטב ובירושלמי גרסינן נגר דר' אליעזר הוה קטיר בגמי נשמט אסור נקמז רבי יעקב בר אחא מורה ברא"ש אלבעותיו(ו):

ומדבריהן למדנו שפוקקין ומודדין. ואע"ג דטפיח לא מבטל ליה כמו פקק כדאמרי' בפרק הישן (סוכה דף כה.) גבי סדין איכא למימר דמבטל ליה טפי מסדין ולא מצי למימר נמי פקק דמטה שאני כדאמרי' בשילהי מכילתין (ד' קנז:) גבי מדידה דהתם לא הוי איסור כל כך אלא משום דהוי כעובדא דחול אבל פקק דמשום תוספת אהל דדמי לבנין ליכא למישרי משום מצוה:

הדרן עלך כל הכלים

מפנין ארבע וחמש קופות. בירושלמי מפרש כמה שיעור קופות כההוא דתנן* שלשה קופות של שלשה סאין של

שיש להן בית אחיזה. בית יד: ה"ג ואמר רב יהודה והוא שיש תורת כלי עליהן. שהכיסוי ראוי להשמיש (א)עצמו הוא דניטלין בשבת ואם אין תורת כלי עליו לא אמרינן כיסוי כלי הוא כלי ודלתות שידה תיבה ומגדל דתנא מתני' טטלין יש תורת כלי עליהן דראויין ליסב עליהן ולתת עליהן מזונות לקטן ולקמן מפרש אמאי בעינן בית אחיזה הואיל ותורת כלי עליהן אלמא לרבי יוחנן מידי דליכא תורת כלי עליו לא מטלטלין והאי קנה מאי תורת כלי עליו איכא אי משום דפותח ונועל בו אין זו תורת כלי עליו אלא תורת בנין: וכ"ת הכא נמי דאיכא תורת כלי עליו. שראוי להפך בו זיתים או לפצע בו אגוזים(ב):*) (תורת כלי עליו. אפי' אינו ראוי לדבר אחר): סבירא ליה כוותיה בחדא. דמתוקן ואע"פ שאינו קשור: ופליג עליה בחדא. דבעי תורת כלי: הלכה כרבי אליעזר. דבעינן קשור ותלוי: מדבריהם למדנו. בפ' בתרא בימי אביו של ר' לדוק ובימי אבא שאול בן בטנית שפקקו את המאור בטפיח וקשרו את המקידה בגמי לידע אם יש בגיגית פותח טפח והתם מפרש לה וקתני מדבריהם למדנו: שפוקקין. את המאור בדבר שאינו קשור ותלוי: וקושרין. קשר שאינו של קיימא לכתחלה: ומודדין. מקוה ומטלטלות: מאי דעתיך. דמותבת לרבי יצחק נפחא מהא מצי לשנויי לך הא מני רבנן היא ואי משום דקתני לה סתמא מותבת ליה דמדסתם לן כרבנן הלכתא כוותייהו: נגר הנגרר. נמי סתמא. קתני לה וסתם לן בהא כרבי אליעזר דאסור: מעשה רב. למילף מיניה דכיון דסמיך למיעבד עובדא לקולא ש"מ הלכתא היא:

מתני' בכיסוי קרקע. כגון כיסוי בור ודות דהוי כבונה אי לאו דמוכחא בית אחיזה דילה דלמשקיל ולהדורי עביד: **גמ'** א"ר יוחנן והוא שיש תורת כלי עליהם. דכיסויין הללו חזו לתשמיש דעלמא אבל כיסוי כלי לא אמרינן כלי הוא: ודכ"ע. משום דאוקמא ר' יוחנן בשיש תורת כלי עליהן איצטריכא ליה למימר דכי פליגי רבנן בכלים דחבריניהו בארעא פליגי דאילו כלים דעלמא אע"ג דלית להו לכיסוייהן בית אחיזה מיטלטלי דכיון דאיכא תורת כלי עליהן קיימי מה לי איכא בית אחיזה מה לי ליכא בית אחיזה אלא בכיסוי כלים המחוברי' לקרקע כגון תנור וכירים הוא דפליגי משום דדמו במקצת לכיסוי בור ודות וגזרינן הכי אטו הכי:

הדרן עלך כל הכלים

מפנין. אם צריך למקומן להושיב שם אורחים להסב בסעוד' או תלמידים לדרשה ולא חיישינן לטרחא דשבת: אבל לא את האוצר. מפרש בגמרא: מפנין תרומה טהורה. כלומר ומהו מפנין דבר הראוי כגון אלו תרומה טהורה דחזי לבהמת כהן אבל תרומה טמאה לא דאפילו לבהמת כהן לא חזיא בשבת דאע"ג דבחול חזיא כדתניא בכל שעה בפסחים (דף לב.) שאם רצה כהן מרילה לפני הכלב בשבת וביום טוב לא חזיא דזו היא ביעורה מן העולם או להיסק או לבהמה ואין מבערין תרומה טמאה וקדשים טמאין ביום טוב כדתנן (לעיל דף כג:) ואין מדליקין בשמן שריפה ביום טוב ואוקימנא *טעמא משום דאין שורפין קדשים ביום טוב: (ג)לוף. מין קטניות שאינו ראוי חי אפילו לבהמה: לעורבין. כגון עשירים שמגדלין עורבין לגדולה: זרדים. מין קנים הם שמזרדים כשהן רכים ואוכלים אותם: **גמ'** ארבע מחמש. אם לא היה שם אלא כשיעור ה' קופות לא יפנה אלא ד' מהם שאסור לגמור את האוצר דילמא חזי גומות בקרקעיתו ומשוי להו: מאוצר גדול. ואם יש הרבה אין מפנין אלא חמש דחיישינן לטירחא: מאי אבל לא את האוצר. שלא יגמור את האוצר לא מצית אמרת דהא מרישא שמעינן ארבע וחמש: תחלה. אם לא התחיל בו להסתפק ממנו כבר למאכלו או למאכל בהמתו דאם כן הוה ליה מוקצה ומתניתין רבי יהודה היא: כדאמרי

*) ס"א ל"ג ומ"כ שלפני רש"י היה הגירסא בגמרא אחר ברייתא דחריות אלמא לא בעי רשב"ג תורת כלי עליו ומציין רש"י בזה

רבינו חננאל

כרשב"ג ורשב"ג שרי אע"פ דליכא תורת כלי עליו. ור' יוחנן שמעי' ליה דבעי תורת כלי. ואוקימנא בקנה שהתקינו להיות נועל ופותח בו בדאיכא תורת כלי עליו ובהא א"ר יוחנן הלכתא כרשב"ג. אבל בחריות של דקל שגדרן לעצים דשרי רשב"ג בלא קישור לא סבר לזה ר' יוחנן כוותיה. ועליהן [אמר דר'] יוחנן סבר לה כוותיה בחדא ופליג עליה בחדא: **דרש** ר' יצחק נפחא אפתחא דבי ריש גלותא הלכתא כר' אלעזר שאין פוקקין (עליו) [בו] אם [לא שהוא] קשור ותלוי. ואותבה ר' (עולא) [רב עמרם] מהא דתנן בסוף שבת מדבריהן למדנו שפוקקין ומודדין וקושרין בשבת. א"ל אביי לרב (עזרא) [עמרם] למה אותיבתיה מהא מפני שהיא שנויה סתם. וקיי"ל הלכה כסתם משנה. נגר הנגרר נמי סתמא היא. והיא שנויה סתם אליבא דר' אלעזר. ושני ליה אע"פ דהא סתמא והא סתמא. הא סתמא דפוקקין ומודדין וקושרין בשבת עבדו בה עובדא ומעשה רב וזו הלכה למעשה והלכתא כחכמים ונדחה דרישא דר' יצחק נפחא. ואמרינן בתלמוד א"י. א"ר יוחנן אתיא יחידאה דהכא סתמא דהתם. ויחידאה דהתם כסתמא דהכא. פי' יחידאה דהכא דהוא ר' אלעזר דפקק החלון בסתמא דנגר נגרר [ויחידאי דנגר הנגרר] (דהוא ר' יהודה כסתמא) [דפקק החלון דהכ"א] בין כך ובין כך פוקקין בו: **כל** כסויי הכלים שיש להן בית אחיזה ניטלין בשבת. א"ר יוסי בד"א בכסויי קרקעות וכו'. א"ר יהודה בר שילא א"ר אסי א"ר יוחנן והוא שיש תורת כלי עליהן. ואמרינן כולי עלמא בכסוי קרקעות אם יש להן בית אחיזה שרי ואי לא אסיר לטלטלן. כגון כסויי הבארות וכסויי הדות וכיוצא בהן. כסויי כלים כגון כדות ופיטסים וכיוצא בהן אע"פ שהן להן בית אחיזה מותר לטלטלן לנלותם ולכסותם. כי פליגי בכסויי כלים וחיברו בקרקע. ר' יוסי לא גזר ות"ק סבר גזרינן והלכתא כוותיה: הדרן עלך פרק כל הכלים

פי"ח **מפנין** אפילו ד' וה' קופות של תבן. פי' מפנין מעתיקין התבואה ממקום למקום מלשון ופניתי הבית. ופנו את הבית. אקשינן על משנתנו. השתא ה' מפנין ד' מיבעיא ופריק רב חסדא ארבע מחמש וה' מאוצר גדול. ומאי אבל לא את האוצר שלא יתחיל באוצר תחלה ומני ר"י היא דאית ליה מוקצה ובא שמואל ופריק פירוק אחר ודברים פשוטין הן. אבל סוגיא דשמעתא כרב חסדא דמתניתא סתמא תנן כוותיה. שאין מתחילין

רב נסים גאון

פי"ז ר' יהודה היא דאמר מוקצה ור' שמעון לית ליה מוקצה אצל כל פתמא (פי' עיקר הדברים) בפרק במה מדליקין וכבר פירשנו זה בפרק יציאות השבת:

לקמן קנז.

[לעיל כא: וש"נ]

[עי' תוס' לקמן קנח. ד"ה אבל]

[בשקלים פ"ג מ"ב]

לעיל ב. [ודף קכה:]

הגהות הב"ח

(א) רש"י ד"ה ה"ג וכו' להשמיש לעצמו הוא: (ב) ד"ה וכ"ת הכא וכו' אגוזים הס"ד ואחר כך מ"ה אין צריך לקשר אלמא דאיכא תורת כלי עליו: (ג) רש"י ד"ה לוף תז"מ. וכ"ב ס"א תורמוס: (ד) תוס' ד"ה וכי תימא וכו' אלא לישיבה אעפ"כ. נ"ב ועי' בא"ר"י: (ה) בא"ד עד לתוך הארץ: (ו) בא"ד מורה ברא"ש אלבעותיו כזה V:

ביצה לה:

[שם לו.]

ס"א לעזים

[ב"מ קיג.]

[עי' תוס' לקמן קכח. ד"ה רשב"ג]

[עי' תוס' לעיל ס: ד"ה בשמת ע"ש דהשתיק אמר רב חסדא ד'מאוצר קטן וה' מאוצר גדול]

[שם כג:]

say thus? Surely we learnt: All lids of vessels [126b] which have a handle, may be handled on the Sabbath. Whereon R. Judah b. Shila said in R. Assi's name in R. Joḥanan's name: Providing that they have the character of utensils.[6] And should you answer, Here too [it means] where it ranks as a utensil,[7]—does then R. Simeon b. Gamaliel require it to have the character of a utensil? Surely it was taught: As for the dried branches of a palm tree which one cut down for fuel and then changed his mind, [intending them for sitting thereon], he must tie them together.[8] R. Simeon b. Gamaliel said: He need not tie them together![9]—R. Joḥanan agrees with him in one[10] and disagrees with him in the other.[11]

a R. Isaac the smith[1] lectured at the entrance of the Resh Galutha:[2] The *halachah* is as R. Eliezer. R. Amram objected: And from their words we learn that we may close [a skylight], measure [a *mikweh*], and tie [a temporary knot] on the Sabbath![3]—Said Abaye to him, What is your view: because it is taught anonymously?[4] [But the Mishnah concerning] a dragging bolt is also anonymous![5]—Yet even so an actual incident is weightier.[6]

MISHNAH. ALL LIDS OF UTENSILS WHICH HAVE A HANDLE MAY BE HANDLED ON THE SABBATH. SAID R. JOSE, WHEN IS THAT SAID? IN THE CASE OF LIDS OF GROUND [BUILDINGS],[7] BUT THE LIDS OF UTENSILS MAY IN ANY CASE BE HANDLED ON THE SABBATH.

GEMARA. R. Judah b. Shila said in R. Assi's name in R. Joḥanan's name: Provided that they have the character of a utensil. All agree: Covers of ground [buildings may be handled] only if they have a handle but not otherwise; covers of utensils, even if they have no handle. Where do they differ? In respect of utensils joined to the ground: one Master holds: We forbid [them] preventively,[8] while the other Master holds, We do not forbid preventively. Another version: Where do they differ? In
b respect of an oven cover:[1] one Master likens it to the cover of a ground [building], while the other Master likens it to the cover of utensils.

CHAPTER XVIII

MISHNAH. IT IS PERMITTED TO REMOVE EVEN FOUR OR FIVE BASKETS OF STRAW OR PRODUCE [GRAIN] TO MAKE ROOM FOR GUESTS OR ON ACCOUNT OF THE NEGLECT OF THE
c BETH HAMIDRASH,[1] BUT NOT THE STORE.[2] ONE MAY CLEAR AWAY CLEAN TERUMAH, DEM'AI,[3] THE FIRST TITHE WHOSE TERUMAH HAS BEEN SEPARATED,[4] REDEEMED SECOND TITHE AND HEKDESH,[5] AND DRY LUPINES, BECAUSE IT IS FOOD FOR GOATS.[6] BUT [ONE MAY] NOT [CLEAR AWAY] ṬEBEL,[3] THE FIRST TITHE WHEREOF TERUMAH HAS NOT BEEN TAKEN, UNREDEEMED SECOND TITHE OR HEKDESH, LOF[7] OR MUSTARD. R. SIMEON B. GAMALIEL PERMITS [IT] IN THE CASE OF LOF, BECAUSE IT IS FOOD FOR RAVENS.[8] AS FOR BUNDLES OF STRAW,[9] TWIGS, OR YOUNG SHOOTS, IF THEY WERE PREPARED AS ANIMAL FODDER, THEY MAY BE MOVED; IF NOT, THEY MAY NOT BE MOVED.[10]

GEMARA. Seeing that five may be cleared away, need four be stated?—Said R. Ḥisda: [It means] four out of five.[11] Some
d there are who state, Four of a small store,[1] and five of a large store. And what does BUT NOT THE STORE mean?[2] That one must not commence [dealing] with a store for the first time;[3] and which [Tanna] rules [thus]? It is R. Judah, who accepts [the interdict of] *mukẓeh*. But Samuel said: [It means] four or five

(6) I.e., the lids themselves must be fit for use as vessels. But how can a cane rank as a utensil? (7) E.g., if the cane may be used for stirring olives in the vat. (8) V. *supra* 50a, n. a1. (9) They may be handled without tying, though they are certainly not utensils. (10) That if it is prepared it need not be tied. (11) Holding that they must have the character of a utensil.

a (1) Many of the Rabbis were tradesmen or workers; e.g., R. Joḥanan the cobbler; R. Papa, who was a brewer; Hillel at one time a wood-cutter. (2) V. *supra* 48a, n. b7. (3) V. Mishnah *infra* 157a. The reference there is to a cloth that is not fastened and suspended, and yet we may close a skylight with it. (4) You assume that that proves the *halachah* is so, for otherwise you could simply answer that it represents the Rabbis' view only and is not a final ruling. (5) And there R. Eliezer's view is stated. (6) In the Mishnah *infra* 157a it is not merely a theoretical ruling but bears on actual practice. Therefore one may assume that it states the final ruling, and this refutes R. Isaac. (7) E.g., the lid or cover of a pit built in the ground. When they have a handle they are obviously not part of the pit and are meant to be put on and taken off. But otherwise they seem to be there permanently: hence placing them there is like building, and removing them is like demolishing. (8) Lest they be confused with the lid of ground-buildings.

b (1) V. *supra* 125a, n. a8 for its construction.

c (1) Caused by lack of room for the disciples. (2) Explained *infra*. (3) V. Glos. (4) The first tithe belonged to the Levite; a tenth thereof, called *terumah* ('separation'), was given to the priest. (5) The second tithe was to be eaten by its Israelite owner in Jerusalem. Both it and *hekdesh*, q.v. Glos., could be redeemed, whereby they became like ordinary produce, save in a few respects, and then consumed. (*Hekdesh*, i.e. an animal dedicated as a sacrifice, might be redeemed only if it received a blemish.) (6) Var lec.: for the poor. (7) Jast.: a plant similar to colocasia, with edible leaves and root, and bearing beans. It is classified with onions and garlic. (8) Which some wealthy people bred. (9) Or, stubble. (10) This is the reason of the others too which may not be moved, viz., because they cannot be used even as animal fodder. (11) If the entire store consists of five, only four may be removed, but not all, lest depressions in the ground are revealed which may be levelled on the Sabbath.

d (1) Var. lec. omit: 'Some there are . . . small store'. (2) It cannot mean that the whole store must not be cleared away, since on the present interpretation that is already implied in the first clause. (3) If he had not already started using it for food, either for himself or for his animals, before the Sabbath, it is *mukẓeh* and must not be touched.

[127a] just as people speak; yet if one desires even more may be cleared away. And what does BUT NOT THE STORE mean? That one must not complete[ly remove] the whole of it, lest he come to level up depressions;[4] but one may indeed commence therewith.[5] And who [rules thus]? It is R. Simeon, who rejects [the interdict of] *mukzeh*.

Our Rabbis taught: One must not commence with a store for the first time, but he may make a path through it to enter and go out. 'He may make a path'! but surely you say, 'One must not commence'?—This is its meaning: one may make a path through it with his feet as he enters and goes out.[6]

Our Rabbis taught: If produce is heaped together [for storage] and one commenced [using] it on the eve of the Sabbath, he may take supplies from it on the Sabbath; if not, he may not take supplies from it on the Sabbath: this is R. Simeon's view; but R. Aha permits it. Whither does this tend![7]—Rather say: this is R. Aha's view; but R. Simeon permits it.

A Tanna taught: What is the standard quantity for produce that is heaped together?—A *lethek*.[8] R. Nehumi b. Zechariah asked Abaye: What is the standard quantity for produce that is heaped together? Said he to him, Surely it was said: The standard quantity for produce that is heaped together is a *lethek*.

The scholars asked: These four or five baskets that are stated,
a [does it mean] only in four or five baskets, but not more,[1] which shows that it is better to minimize one's walking; or perhaps it is better to minimize the burden?[2] Come and hear: For one [Baraitha] taught: One may clear away even four or five tubs of pitchers of wine and oil; whereas another was taught: In ten or fifteen. Surely they differ in this, viz., one Master holds: It is better to minimize the walking; while the other Master holds: It is better to reduce the burden?—No: All hold that it is better to reduce the walking: do you think that ten or fifteen refers to 'tubs'? [No]; it refers to the pitchers, yet there is no contradiction: here [in the first, the reference is] where they can be carried [only] singly in a tub;[3] whereas there, where they can be carried in twos, and there, where they can be carried in threes,[4] of the size of the jugs of Harpania.[5]

The scholars asked: These four or five that are stated, [does it mean] even if he has more guests; or perhaps it all depends on the [number of] guests? And should you say that it all depends on the number of guests, can one person clear [them] away for all of them, or perhaps each man must do so for himself?—Come and hear: For Rabbah said in R. Ḥiyya's name: Rabbi once went to a certain place; seeing that the place was too cramped for the disciples, he went out to a field and found it full of sheaves, whereupon Rabbi cleared the whole field of the sheaves.[6] While R. Joseph related in R. Oshaia's name: R. Ḥiyya once went to a certain place; seeing that the place was too cramped for the disciples, he went out to a field and found it full of sheaves, whereupon R. Ḥiyya cleared the whole field of the sheaves. This proves that it all depends on the [number of] guests. But still the question remains, Can one person clear [them] away for all, or perhaps each man must do so for himself?—Come and hear: 'And Rabbi cleared the sheaves.' Then on your view, did Rabbi personally
b clear [them]?[1] But he gave orders that it [the field] be cleared, yet after all each [acted] for himself.[2]

TO MAKE ROOM FOR THE GUESTS, etc. R. Johanan said: Hospitality to wayfarers[3] is as 'great' as early attendance at the Beth Hamidrash, since he [the Tanna] states, TO MAKE ROOM FOR GUESTS OR ON ACCOUNT OF THE NEGLECT OF THE BETH HAMIDRASH. R. Dimi of Nehardea said: It is 'greater' than early attendance at the Beth Hamidrash, because he states, TO MAKE ROOM FOR GUESTS, and then, AND ON ACCOUNT OF THE NEGLECT OF THE BETH HAMIDRASH. Rab Judah said in Rab's name: Hospitality to wayfarers is greater than welcoming the presence of the *Shechinah*, for it is written, *And he said, My Lord, if now I have found favour in Thy sight, pass not away*, etc.[4] R. Eleazar said: Come and observe how the conduct of the Holy One, blessed be He, is not like that of mortals. The conduct of mortals [is such that] an inferior person cannot say to a great[er] man, Wait for me until I come to you; whereas in the case of the Holy One, blessed be He, it is written, *and he said, My Lord, if now I have found*, etc.

R. Judah b. Shila said in R. Assi's name in R. Johanan's name: There are six things, the fruit of which man eats in this world, while the principal remains for him for the world to come, viz.: Hospitality to wayfarers, visiting the sick, meditation in prayer, early attendance at the Beth Hamidrash, rearing one's sons to the study of the Torah, and judging one's neighbour in the scale of merit.[5] But that is not so? For we learnt: These are the things which man performs and enjoys their fruits in this world, while the principal remains for him for the world to come, viz.: honouring one's parents, the practice of loving deeds,[6] and making peace between man and his fellow, while the study of the Torah sur-
c passes them all:[1] [this implies], these only, but none others?

(4) V. *supra* 126b, n. c11. (5) I.e., the reverse of n. d3. (6) This is not handling. (7) Surely it should be reversed, since R. Simeon always rejects *mukzeh*. (8) Half a *kor* = fifteen *se'ahs*. But less does not constitute a store, and the prohibition of *mukzeh* does not apply to it in any case.

a (1) I.e., must they actually be carried away thus, but not broken up into smaller quantities and then removed? (2) Hence they may certainly be broken up into smaller quantities. (3) Being too large to be carried more than one at a time. (4) Which gives ten or fifteen pitchers in five piles. (5) דקורא, jugs enclosed in wicker-work. Harpania was a rich agricultural town of Mesene, south of Babylon, famous for its wicker-work manufactured from the fibre of palm leaves; v. Obermeyer, p. 200. (6) To make room for the disciples.

b (1) Surely not. (2) Thus the question remains unanswered. (3) The word means both guests and wayfarers. (4) Gen. XVIII, 3; he thus left God, as it were, to attend to the wants of the three wayfarers. [On this interpretation he was speaking to God, and begged Him to remain whilst he saw to his guests v. Shebu. 35b.] (5) I.e., seeking a favourable interpretation of his actions, even when they look suspicious. (6) Not merely alms-giving.

c (1) Not because knowledge in itself is a great virtue, but because it is the foundation and condition of real piety; cf. Ab. II, 6; also, 'Learning is great, because it leads to (good) deeds'.

כדאמרי אינשי ואי בעי אפילו טובא נמי מפנין ומאי *אבל לא את האוצר שלא יגמור כולו(א) דילמא אתי אשוויי גומות אבל אתחולי מתחיל ומני ר"ש היא דלית ליה מוקצה ת"ר אין מתחילין באוצר תחילה אבל עושה בו שביל כדי שיכנס ויצא עושה בו שביל והא אמרת אין מתחילין הכי קאמר עושה בו שביל ברגליו בכניסתו וביציאתו תנו רבנן תבואה *צבורה בזמן שהתחיל בה מע"ש מותר להסתפק ממנה בשבת ואם לאו אסור להסתפק ממנה בשבת דברי ר"ש ר' אחא מתיר כלפי לייא אלא אימא דברי ר' אחא ורבי שמעון מתיר תנא כמה שיעור תבואה *צבורה לתך בעא מיניה רב נחומי בר זכריה מאביי שיעור תבואה *צבורה בכמה אמר ליה הרי אמרו שיעור תבואה צבורה לתך איבעיא להו הני ארבע וחמש קופות דקאמר בארבע וחמש קופות אין טפי לא אלמא למעוטי בהילוכא עדיף או דילמא למעוטי משוי עדיף ת"ש דתני חדא מפנין אפילו ארבע וחמש קופות של כדי שמן ושל כדי יין ותניא אידך בעשר ובחמש עשרה מאי לאו בהא קמיפלגי דמר סבר מעוטי בהילוכא עדיף ומר סבר מעוטי במשוי עדיף לא דכ"ע מעוטי בהילוכא עדיף ומי סברת בעשר ובחמש עשרה אקופות קאי אכדין קאי ולא קשיא הא דמשתקלי חד חד בקופה והא דמישתקלי תרי תרי והא דמשתקלי תלתא תלתא ובדקורי דהרפניא איבעיא להו הני ארבע והמש דקאמר אע"ג דאית ליה אורחין טובא או דילמא הכל לפי האורחין ואת"ל הכל לפי האורחין חד גברא מפני לכולהו או דילמא גברא(ב) גברא מפני לנפשיה ת"ש דאמר רבה אמר רבי חייא פעם אחת הלך רבי למקום אחד וראה מקום דחוק לתלמידים ויצא לשדה ומצא שדה מלאה עומרים ועימר רבי כל השדה כולה (שמע מינה הכל לפי האורחין) ורב יוסף א"ר הושעיא פעם אחת הלך ר' חייא למקום אחד וראה מקום דחוק לתלמידים ויצא לשדה ומצא שדה מלאה עומרים ועימר ר' חייא כל השדה כולה שמע מינה הכל לפי האורחין ועדיין תבעי לך חד גברא מפני ליה לכולא או דילמא כל גברא וגברא מפני לנפשיה ת"ש ועימר רבי ולטעמיך רבי בדנפשיה עימר אלא צוה ועימר ולעולם כל חד וחד מפני לנפשיה: מפני האורחין וכו': א"ר יוחנן גדולה הכנסת אורחין כהשכמת בית המדרש דקתני מפני האורחין ומפני בטול בית המדרש ורב דימי מנהרדעא אמר יותר מהשכמת בית המדרש דקתני מפני האורחין והדר ומפני בטול בית המדרש *אמר רב יהודה אמר רב גדולה הכנסת אורחין מהקבלת פני שכינה דכתיב ויאמר *(ה') אם נא מצאתי חן בעיניך אל נא תעבור וגו' א"ר אלעזר בא וראה שלא כמדת הקב"ה מדת בשר ודם מדת ב"ו אין קטן יכול לומר לגדול המתן עד שאבא אצלך ואילו בהקדוש ברוך הוא כתיב ויאמר *(ה') אם נא מצאתי וגו' אמר רב יהודה בר שילא א"ר אסי א"ר יוחנן ששה דברים אדם אוכל פירותיהן בעולם הזה והקרן קיימת לו לעולם הבא ואלו הן הכנסת אורחין וביקור חולים *ועיון תפלה והשכמת בית המדרש והמגדל בניו לתלמוד תורה והדן את חברו לכף זכות איני והא אנן *)תנן אלו דברים שאדם עושה אותם ואוכל פירותיהן בעולם הזה והקרן קיימת לו לעולם הבא ואלו הן כיבוד אב ואם וגמילות חסדים והבאת שלום שבין אדם לחברו ות"ת כנגד כולם **) [הני אין מידי אחרינא לא] הני

*) פאה פ"ק מ"א קדושין לט: ע"ש   **) ס"א

רש"י

כדאמרי אינשי · תשבון קטן תחילה ואם יצטרך ליותר יפנה יותר משום הכי נקט ד' ברישא והדר חמשה וה"ה אפילו טובא : שלא יגמור · משום אשויי גומות : ברגלו · מפנה ברגלו לכאן ולכאן דרך הליכתו דלא הוי טלטול : תבואה צבורה · מוכחא מילתא דהוקצה לאוצר : להסתפק · להאכיל לבהמתו : אסור דברי ר"ש ורבי אחא כו' : כלפי לייא · כנגד היכן פונה הדבר הזה האמור להיפך ר"ש מתיר מוקצה בכל מקום וכאן הוא מחמיר : לייא · היכן כגון אלבי לנהרא כגני לייא דברכות (דף נח.) : לתך · אבל בציר מהכי לאו אוצר הוא : לתך · חצי כור הוא ט"ו סאין : בד' וה' קופות אין טפי לא · בקופות עצמן הוא יפנה וימלאם אם ירצה או שק בכתפו שיעור קופה בפעם אחת אבל טפי להלך יותר מה' פעמים כגון לפנות בכלים קטנים וירבה בהילוך לא : למעוטי בהילוכא עדיף · ואע"ג דאפושי משוי הוא : או דילמא מעוטי משוי עדיף · ואם בא לפנות בכלים קטנים כשיעור ה' קופות מותר ולרב חסדא קבעי לה דאמר ה' דוקא : בי' ובט"ו · קס"ד אקופות קאי לומר שמפנה בקופות קטנות וירבה בהילוך : אכדין קאי · ולא פליגי והכי קאמר בי' בט"ו יפנה באותן ה' קופות : הא דמשתקלי חדא חדא בקופה · הך דתניא ד' וה' ולא נחת למניינא דכדין איירי בכדין גדולים דמשתקלי חדא בקופה והך דתנא בי' וט"ו איירי בכדים בינונים ובכדין קטנים עשר כדמשתקלי תרי תרי בקופה ט"ו כדמשתקלי תלתא תלתא בקופה דקטנים : בי דקורי דהרפניא · *בכדין של הרפניא : איבעיא להו · אליבא דרב חסדא : דחוק לתלמידים · שאין מקום לתלמידים להושיב : ועימר · פנה את העומרים וכרמלית הואי ובפחות פחות מד' אמות : ת"ש ועימר רבי · אלמא חד גברא פניכהו : רבי בנפשיה עימר · בתמיה וכי אורחיה דנשיא בהכי : כהשכמת ביהמ"ד · מדשוי להו במתני' כי הדדי : מהשכמת בית המדרש · דתנא דידן אקדמה ברישא : אל נא תעבור · והניחו והלך לקבל האורחים: ועיון תפלה · לכוין בתפלתו : הכי

תוספות

של כדי שמן ושל כדי יין · והא דתנן בפ' המביא (ביצה דף כט:) כדי יין לא יביאם בסל ובקופה היינו ממקום רחוק דמיחזי כעובדין דחול אבל הכא בביתו : דבולי עלמא למעוטי בהלוכא עדיף · לא מצי למימר למעוטי במשוי עדיף דההיא דקתני ד' וה' קופות לא מצי סבר הכי דא"כ הוה ליה למיתני בעשר וט"ו כשיעור ה' קופות וא"ת והא תנן בפרק אין צדין (שם דף כה.) שחטה בשדה לא יביאנה במוט ובמוטה אלא מביאה לאיברים אף על גב דמפיש בהילוכא התם שאני דאיכא טירחא יותר מדאי להביאה שלימה א"נ משום דמיחזי כמוליכה למכור בשוק והא דאמרינן בריש שואל (לקמן דף קמח.) היכי ליעבד דמליא בחצבא רבא תימלי בחצבא זוטא קא מפשא בהילוכא דמליא בחצבא זוטא תמלא בחצבא רבא קא מפשא במשוי התם כיון שנהגו למלאות המים בחצבא רבא או בחצבא זוטא קשה להם לשנות מכמות שנהגו: אע"ג דאית ליה אורחין טובא או דילמא הכל לפי האורחין · מכאן יש להוכיח דהא דתנן במתניתין ד' וה' קופות הוי אפי' בשביל אדם אחד דאי הוי נמי לפי האורחין אמאי נקט ד' וה' ועוד מדלא מספקא ליה אי חד מפני כולהו או כל חד לנפשיה אלא באת"ל הכל לפי האורחין משמע הא אם אמר אף על גב דאיתרמו ליה אורחין טובא ליכא לאיסתפוקי ואי אמרינן דד' וה' קופות הוי לפי האורחין אכתי איכא לספוקי אי חד גברא מפני לכולהו או כל חד מפני לנפשיה אלא משמע דפשיטא דד' וה' אינן לפי האורחין אלא אפילו לצורך אדם אחד : ולטעמיך רבי בנפשיה עימר · פי' כל השדה כולה : דכתיב ויאמר ה' אם נא מצאתי חן וגו' · קסבר כמאן דאמר בשבועות (דף לה:) דהאי השם קדש דאיכא מאן דאמר התם שהוא חול שלמלאכים היה מדבר שהיה מזמינם : אוכל מפירותיהן בעולם הזה · בפ"ק דקדושין (דף לט:) מפ' דהיינו אם היתה *שקולה מכרעת דשכר מצות בהאי עלמא ליכא : כיון

עין משפט נר מצוה

ב א מיי' פכ"ו מהל' שבת הלכה טו טוש"ע שם :

ג ב ג מיי' שם הלכה יד וטו :

ד ד טוש"ע שם סעיף כ:

ה ה ו מיי' וסמג שם טוש"ע שם ס"ג :

ו ז מיי' פי"ד מהלכות אבל הלכה ב :

ז ח סמג עשין יב :

ח ט מיי' פ"ה מהלכות דעות הלכה ז ופכ"ג מהלכות סנהדרין הלכה י טוש"ע ח"מ סימן יז סעיף י :

ט י מיי' פ"ג מהלכות ת"ת הלכה ג סמג שם טוש"ע י"ד סימן רמו סעיף יח :

וכן משנה דהכא פליגא אר' יעקב דס"ל בסוף פרק קמא דקדושין דשכר מצוה כו' רש"ל · ואפשר לפרש כוונת התוספות בלא הגה"ה שרוצים ליישב שם למאי דלא תירצו התם הקושיא באופן אחר דהני מצות הקרן כולה קיימת לעוה"ב לאפוקי שאר מצות ומתרצי תוס' דא"א לפרש כן דשכר מצוה בהאי עלמא ליכא אליבא דכ"ע ולא פליגי התם אר"י אלא בפירות ודוק כ"מ ומהרש"א גרס דשכר מצוה בהאי עלמא איכא :

מסורת הש"ס

[ביצה לו.]

[חלת צבורה ליתא בהלכות פרש ויל"א סי' יא]

[ג"ז ליתא שם]

[ג"ז ליתא שם]

[עי' בפרש"י ב"מ פד. ותוס' חולין ד. ד"ה דקורא]

[שבועות לה:]

ברא"ם בית יח

[נ"ל אדני]

[נ"ל אדני]

[עי' תוספות לעיל קיח: ד"ה עיון ותוספות ברכות לב: ד"ה כל ותוס' ב"ב קסד: ד"ה עיון]

הגהות הב"ח

(א) גמ' שלא יגמור כולו (דילמא וכו' גומות) תא"מ ונ"ב ס"א: (ב) שם או דילמא גברא וגברא:

גליון הש"ס

גברא גדולה הכנסת אורחים · עי' ב"מ דף פו ע"א ובתוספות שם ד"ה מזייה:

רבינו חננאל

מתחילין באוצר תחלה ולא בתבואה צבורה . ומדבעא רב נחומי כמה שיעורי תבואה צבורה · ותנא כמה שיעור תבואה צבורה לתך ש"מ דהלכתא כתני מתניתא מדקפחינן לפרושי טעמייהו ויש מי שאומר הלכתא כשמואל דמוקים למתניתין כרבי שמעון דלית ליה מוקצה והלכתא כוותיה . ולתך זה האמור כאן הוא שיעור הקופות ששנינו במשנתנו · ואע"ג דלא איתאמרא בהדיא בגמרא דילן הא איתפרש בתלמוד א"י · ר' זעירא שאל לר' יאשיה כמה שעור הקופות · א"ל נלמד סתום מן המפורש דתנינן תמן בג' קופות של ג' ג' סאין תורמין את הלשכה · ושיעור לתך הצי כור והוא ט"ו סאין · נמצא שעור המשנה והברייתא שיעור אחד · וכדאוקמה רב חסדא למתני' ד' מה' · והכין שמעתא דא סלקא ועלה קמבעיא לן מעוטי בהלוכא עדיף או מעוטי במשוי עדיף · ואמרי' ת"ש דתני חדא מפנין אפילו ד' וה' קופות של כדי יין וכדי שמן · ותניא אידך בעשר ובחמש עשרה · ואוקימנא להו דכ"ע מעוטי בהילוכא עדיף · ושיעורם אחד הם · ואכדין קאי ולא אקופות והא מתניתא דקתני חמש הכין פירושא · חמש כדות גדולות שאין מכילה הקופה יותר מכדה אחת · והא מתניתא דקתני בעשר כדות בחמש קופות והן בינוניות שנמצאו ב' כדות בכל קופה והא דתני ט"ו ג' כדות בכל קופה והא דמשתקלי תלת כדי בכל קופה כגון דקורי הרפניא פי' כדות שעושין בהרפניא והן קטנות ונוטלות ג' ג' בקופה שנמצא שיעור משקל כל כדה קטנה סאה והבינונית סאה וחצי · והגדולה ג' סאין . ותוב איבעיא לן הני דקא מפנינן ד' או ה' קופות מפני האורחין אע"פ דאית ליה אורחין הרבה אין לו רשות לפנות יותר מזה השיעור או דילמא הכל לפי האורחין ועוד בעיא אחרת כשמפנין אחד מפנה לכולן או כל אחד מפנה לעצמו ואיפשיטא שמעתא הכל לפי האורחין אם יש לו אורחין הרבה מפנין להן כל צרכן. ובאנו לדקדק מדקתני ועימר רבי את כל השדה שאחד מפנה לכולן (ולא עמר) [ודחינן וליטעמיך] וכי ר' בעצמו עימר אלא צוה ועימרו · ולעולם כל חד וחד לנפשיה וכיון דלא איפשיט בהדיא חד מפנהו לכולהו מחמרינן לפנויי כל דחד וחד לנפשיה דאיסורא הוא. וסתמא לחומרא · זה נכון לפנות כל אחד לעצמו ומסתייעא הא מילתא מהא (לעיל דף קכ"ה ע"ב) דא"ר חנניה פעם אחד הלך למקום אחד ומצא נדבך של אבנים ואמר לתלמידיו צאו וחשבו כדי שנשב עליהן למחר ולא סמך במחשבתו שלו אלא הצריך כל אחד לעצמו וכדר' אסי ור' אמי אליבא דר' יוחנן כל אחד כטעמיה. פי' נדבך של אבנים אבנים סדורות זו ע"ג זו · ושפשפום לפשפשם ברגליהם. סואר של קורות נתונות זו ע"ג זו · גשוש בלשון ישמעאל עירים ספינות · נגדר בלשון ישמעאל מתרו ופינוי לבית המדרש ולאורחים והכנת מקום לישיבתם שניהם שוין בדבר מצוה ושאר השמועה פשוטה היא · והא דתנן מפנין ד' ה' קופות · ה"מ לדבר מצוה מדקתני מפני האורחין ומפני

רב נסים גאון

במה שיעור תבואה לתך · הלתך הוא חצי כור והוא ט"ו כי הכור הוא ל' סאה והכור והחומר מדה אחת כי תרגום חומר כורא כמו שאתה מוצא ביחזקאל (מה) האיפה והבת תוכן אחד להם ואמר התרגום מכילת וביתא סוקס חד יהי לכון סכום תלת סאין למיסב מעשר כורא הרי נתברר לו מיכן כי החומר הוא כור וכי הבת היא ג' סאין ואמר אחר כך כי עשרת הבתים חומר נמצא שיעור הכור ל' סאין ושם אמר (הושע ג) וחומר שעורים ולתך שעורים ואמרו חכמינו בפרק גיד הנשה (חולין דף צג) אלו ארבעים וחמשה צדיקים החומר ל' ולתך ט"ו הכל מ"ה נתקיים לך כי הכור הוא שני לתכים :

י א מיי' פכ"ה מהלכות שבת הלכה כ:
יא ב שם הלכה יט:
יב ג מיי' פ"י מהלכות מעשר הלכה יא:
יג ד מיי' פ"ג מהלכות תרומות הלכה יג סמג עשין קלג טוש"ע יו"ד סימן שלא:
יד ה מיי' פכ"ה מהל' שבת הלכה יז:

[בר"ף וברא"ש איתא שרב הרגל]

[ועי' תוספות עירובין לא. ד"ה דמאי ותוס' סוכה לה: ד"ה דאי בעי]

כיון דחזיא לכהן שפיר דמי · אע"ג דאמר בשילהי כירה (לעיל דף מז:) דבגדי עניים לעשירים לא הכא לכ"ע חזיא אלא איסורא הוא דרביע עליה אבל התם לא חזו מחמת גריעותא ומהאי טעמא נמי לא אמרינן התם טעמא דבסמוך דאי בעי מפקר לנכסיה והא דאמר בפרק כל הכלים (לעיל ד' קכה:) שירי פרוזמיות שאין בהן ג' על ג' אין מטלטלין אותן משמע הא יש בהן שלש על שלש מטלטלים היינו לעניים א"כ אפילו לעשירים בבית עניים: **דאי** בעי מפקר לנכסיה · הוה מצי למימר כדלעיל כיון דחזי אלא כיון דמשכח טעמא דאפי' לדידיה מצי חזי אמר ובפרק כל שעה (פסחים דף לה:) ובפרק שלשה שאכלו (ברכות ד' מז:) איצטריך להאי טעמא*: **האי** אידגן · מדנקט אידגן משמע אפי' לא ראה פני הבית תימה אכתי אפילו הקדימו בכרי נמי לא לחייב אלא באידגן וראה פני הבית וי"ל דאי לא כתב והרמותם ה"א דכולם חייבין אפילו לא אידגן השתא דכתי' קרא מוקמי ליה במסתבר דהיינו לא אידגן שאפילו ראה פני הבית לא היה חייב א"כ י"ל הא דנקט אידגן היינו ככל דינו שראה פני הבית אלא דמילתא דפסיקא נקט דאיכא למאן דאמר בבא מציעא (ד' פח:) דלא בעינן ראיית פני הבית אלא בזיתים וענבים דלאו בני גורן נינהו: **הא** קמ"ל דאין חומש מעכב · ואף על גב דמבעיא לן בפרק הזהב (שם דף נד:) אי מעכב אי לא ולא פשיט מהכא משום דהוה מצי למידחי דאגב אחרינא תנייה: אבל

הני נמי *(בגמילות חסדים שייכי ל"א הני) בהני שייכי ת"ר הדן חבירו לכף זכות דנין אותו לזכות ומעשה באדם אחד שירד מגליל העליון ונשכר אצל בעה"ב אחד בדרום שלש שנים ערב *יוה"כ אמר לו תן לי שכרי ואלך ואזון את אשתי ובני אמר לו אין לי מעות אמר לו תן לי פירות אמר לו אין לי תן לי קרקע אין לי תן לי בהמה אין לי תן לי כרים וכסתות אין לי הפשיל כליו לאחוריו והלך לביתו בפחי נפש לאחר הרגל נטל בעה"ב שכרו בידו ועמו משוי ג' חמורים אחד של מאכל ואחד של משתה ואחד של מיני מגדים והלך לו לביתו אחר שאכלו ושתו נתן לו שכרו אמר לו בשעה שאמרת לי תן לי שכרי ואמרתי אין לי מעות במה חשדתני אמרתי שמא פרקמטיא בזול נזדמנה לך ולקחת בהן ובשעה שאמרת לי תן לי בהמה ואמרתי אין לי בהמה במה חשדתני אמרתי שמא מושכרת ביד אחרים בשעה שאמרת לי תן לי קרקע ואמרתי לך אין לי קרקע במה חשדתני אמרתי שמא מוחכרת ביד אחרים(א) היא ובשעה שאמרתי לך אין לי פירות במה חשדתני אמרתי שמא אינן מעושרות ובשעה שאמרתי לך אין לי כרים וכסתות במה חשדתני אמרתי שמא הקדיש כל נכסיו לשמים א"ל העבודה כך היה הדרתי כל נכסי בשביל הורקנוס בני שלא עסק בתורה וכשבאתי אצל חבירי בדרום התירו לי כל נדרי ואתה כשם שדנתני לזכות המקום ידין אותך לזכות ת"ר *מעשה בחסיד אחד שפדה ריבה אחת בת ישראל ולמלון השכיבה תחת מרגלותיו למחר ירד וטבל ושנה לתלמידיו ואמר (*להן) בשעה שהשכבתיה תחת מרגלותי במה חשדתוני אמרנו שמא יש בנו תלמיד שאינו בדוק לרבי בשעה שירדתי וטבלתי במה חשדתוני אמרנו שמא מפני טורח הדרך אירע קרי לרבי אמר להם העבודה כך היה ואתם כשם שדנתוני לכף זכות המקום ידין אתכם לכף זכות תנו רבנן פעם אחת הוצרך דבר אחד לתלמידי חכמים אצל מטרוניתא אחת שכל גדולי רומי מצויין אצלה אמרו מי ילך אמר להם ר' יהושע אני אלך הלך רבי יהושע ותלמידיו כיון שהגיע לפתח ביתה חלץ תפיליו ברחוק ארבע אמות ונכנס ונעל הדלת בפניהן אחר שיצא ירד וטבל ושנה לתלמידיו ואמר *(להן) בשעה שחלצתי תפילין במה חשדתוני אמרנו כסבור רבי לא יכנסו דברי קדושה במקום טומאה בשעה שנעלתי במה חשדתוני אמרנו שמא דבר מלכות יש בינו לבינה בשעה שירדתי וטבלתי במה חשדתוני אמרנו שמא ניתזה צינורא מפיה על בגדיו של רבי אמר להם העבודה כך היה ואתם כשם שדנתוני לזכות המקום ידין אתכם לזכות: מפנין תרומה טהורה וכו': פשיטא לא צריכא דמנחה ביד ישראל מהו דתימא כיון דלא חזיא ליה אסור קמ"ל כיון דחזיא לכהן שפיר דמי: ודמאי (וכו'): דמאי הא לא חזי ליה *כיון דאי בעי מפקר ליה לנכסיה והוה עני וחזיא ליה השתא נמי חזי ליה *דתנן מאכילין את העניים דמאי ואת האכסניא דמאי ואמר רב הונא תנא ב"ש אומרים אין מאכילין את העניים דמאי ואת האכסניא דמאי וב"ה אומרים מאכילין את העניים דמאי ואת האכסניא דמאי: ומעשר ראשון שניטלה תרומתו וכו': פשיטא לא צריכא שהקדימו בשבולים ונטלה הימנו תרומת מעשר ולא נטלה הימנו תרומה גדולה וכי הא *)דא"ר אבהו אר"ל מעשר ראשון שהקדימו בשבולין פטור מתרומה גדולה שנא' °והרמותם ממנו תרומת ה' מעשר מן המעשר מעשר מן המעשר אמרתי לך ולא תרומה גדולה ותרומת מעשר מן המעשר *א"ל רב פפא לאביי א"ה אפי' הקדימו בכרי נמי ליפטר א"ל עליך אמר קרא °מכל מתנותיכם תרימו וגו' ומה ראית האי אידגן והאי לא אידגן: ומעשר שני וכו': פשיטא לא צריכא שנתן את הקרן ולא נתן את החומש הא קמ"ל דאין חומש מעכב: והתורמס היבש כו': דווקא יבש אבל לח לא מ"ט כיון דמריר לא אכלה: אבל

*) ברכות שם עירובין לא: פסחים לה: ביצה יג:

ה"ג הני נמי בהני שייכי · הכנסת אורחים וביקור חולים היינו גמילות חסדים ועיון תפלה היינו בכלל גמילות חסדים דכתיב (משלי יא) גומל נפשו איש חסד *השכמת בית המדרש וגידול בנים לתלמוד תורה היינו תלמוד תורה דן את חבירו לכף זכות בכלל הבאת שלום דמתוך שהוא מכריעו לזכות ואמר לא חטא לי בזאת אנוס היה או לטובה נתכוון יש שלום ביניהן ורבי יוחנן לפרש לך אתא דבכלל ג' דמתניתין איתנהו להנך ו' ואיכא נמי לכבוד אב ואם ורבי יוחנן לא פליג עליה: בפחי נפש · בדאבון נפש: מוחכרת · שנותנה לחברו בכך וכך כורין לשנה: °כל היכא דאמרינן* מעשה בחסיד אחד או רבי יהודה בן בבא או רבי יהודה ברבי אלעאי: ריבה · נערה: שאינו בדוק לרבי · שאינו מכיר במדותיו לסמוך עליו ולהניחה אצלו: מטרוניתא · נכרית: דבר מלכות · וצריך להעלימו: צינורא · רוק וגזרו על הנכרים שיהיו כזבים לכל דבריהם: מאכילין לעניים דמאי · לא אסרוהו עליהם מפני שצריכים לחזר על פתח ע"ה וסמכו על שרוב עמי הארץ מעשרין: אכסניא · (א)חיל של מלך ישראל ומטילו על בני העיר לפרנסן*: שניטלה תרומתו · קס"ד תרומת מעשר שהלוי נותן לכהן וכ"ש תרומה גדולה שיש על ישראל להפריש והפרישו קודם שנתן המעשר ללוי: שהקדימו בשבולין · לתרומה ישראל היה לו להפריש תרומה גדולה תחילה דכתיב (שמות כב) מלאתך ודמעך לא תאחר מלאתך אלו בכורים מכאן שהמקדים תרומה לבכורים לוקה ודמעך זו תרומה שאם הקדים מעשר לתרומה לוקה והנ"מ משנתמרח בכרי לוקה אם הקדים מעשר לתרומה אבל הקדים למעשר קודם לתרומה בשבלים אינו לוקה: והרמותם ממנו · בלוים כתיב גבי תרומת מעשר: מכל מתנותיכם וגו' · נמי בלוים כתיב גבי תרומת מעשר וקאמר את כל תרומת ה' כל משמע כל לד תרומה שבו: האי · דנתמרח: אידגן · וחלה עליו חובת תרומה כדכתיב (דברים יח) ראשית דגנך הלכך כי שקלה לוי בעי אהדורי לכהן תרי ממאה שבו בראשה והדר אחד מעשרה: דמריר · שהוא מר: שלא

תורה אור

כאן חסר ונפש היינו תפלה דכתי' גבי חנה ואשפוך את נפשי לפני ה' ש"א ע"ר"ש ברכות כ: ד"ה טורף נפשו וכן הוכח כר"ש סלה פ"א מ"ט

[כ"ק קג:]

הגהות הב"ח

(א) גמ' אמרתי שמא מוחכרת ביד אחרים וכשמא כצ"ל ותיבת היא נמחק: (ב) רש"י ד"ה אכסניא חיל של מלך ישראל נ"ב כ"כ פירש"י בפרק כל מערבין דף לא וכן בפרק כל שעה דף לה אבל התוספות בפ' שלנו פי' עוד פי' אחר חיל של נכרים כו' ע"ש דף מו:

גליון הש"ס

רש"י ד"ה כל היכא דאמרינן מעשה וכו' עיין דבר נחמד בזה בברכת הזאת תמורה דף טו ע"ב: [*צ"ל להם]

[צ"ל להם]

ברכות מז. ודמאי

ברכות מז. דמאי פ"ג מ"א עירובין יז: לא: פסחים לה: סוכה לה:

במדבר יח

תמורה ה:

°במדבר יח

רבינו חננאל

ומפני ביטול בהמ"ד שהן מצות כדרב יהודה אמר שמואל דאמר גדול הכנסת אורחין · וכדר' יוחנן דאמר אחד משמשה דברים שאדם אוכל מפירותיהן בעוה"ז והקרן קיימת לו לעולם הבא: **מפנין** תרומה טהורה אע"פ שהיא בביתו של ישראל הואיל וראויה לכהן היום מטלטלין אותה ושפיר דמי וכן דמאי והדמאי כיון דאילו הפקיר כל נכסיו ויהיה עני מותר לאוכלו אע"פ שעכשיו לא הפקיר נכסיו מותר לטלטלו · והוא הלוקח תבואה מעם הארץ שאינו יודע אם הוציא מעשר ממנה אם לאו כי התרומה לא נחשדו עמי הארץ עליה (ודאי) והיו מפרישין אחד מחמשים והוא בבינונית ונתנו לכהן אבל המעשר היו הרבה ע"ה שלא היו מפרישין אותו ונותנין ללוי · וחייבו חכמים הקונה מעם הארץ שאינו יודע אם הוציא מעשר ממנה אם לאו להפריש מ ז ו התבואה חלק אחד ממאה שהיא תרומת מעשר שהוא א' וכל תרומה כאוכל תרומה והוא עון מיתה · וזה פירושו ישראל שיש לו מאה סאין תבואה חייב לתת לכהן ב' סאין מהן והיא נקראת תרומה גדולה וחייב לתת עשרה מהן פחות מעט והוא נקרא מעשר ראשון וחייב הלוי לתת מן העשרה סאין שנתן לו ישראל סאה אחת לכהן והוא שאמר הכתוב והרמותם ממנו תרומת ה' מעשר מן המעשר · נמצא הסאה שביד כהן שהיא תרומת מעשר שנתן לו הלוי אחד ממאה מן התבואה שביד ישראל וכיון שראו שע"ה לא היו מפרישין מעשר לכהן שחייב בו מיתה [לכן חייבהו להפריש] אבל המעשר שהוא בלאו לא חייבהו מספק · וזה מפורש בגמרא יומא *)

פ"ק דיוחנן העביר הודיית המעשר בסוף מס' סוטה ודמאי זה כיון שהוא ספק מעושר ספק אינו מעושר התירוהו מפני חיי נפש לאכסניא ולעניים (בפירושו). וזה שאמר ר"ל מעשר ראשון שהקדימו בשבולין פטור מתרומה גדולה פי' חייבה התורה להפריש תרומה ומעשר מן הדגן שכבר נעשה גורן כדכתיב ראשית דגנך תירושך ויצהרך כו' ואינו נקרא דגן אלא אחרי דישתו בגורן והעמדתו כרי והתורה אמרה להפריש מן הדגן ראשון תרומה גדולה ואחריו מעשר ראשון. ואחריו שנה ראשונה ושניה מעשר שני · ושנה שלישית אינו מפריש מעשר [שני] אלא מעשר עני. ואינו חייב להפריש כל אלו אלא אחרי שיקצור וינדו ויעמיד כרי בגורן לפיכך אמר ר"ל אם בא ישראל מי שהיו לו עשרה עומרין שבלין וקודם שיכניסן לגורן לדוש נתן מהן עומר אחד מעשר ללוי הלוי אינו חייב לתת ממנו אלא תרומת מעשר לכהן שהשבלין לא נתחייבו אלא בתרומה ולא במעשר והביא טעם לדבריו מן המקרא הזה והקשה עליו רב פפא למה הוצרכת לדחוק הדבר בשבולין אפילו בכרי הקדים והפריש המעשר קודם שיפרוש התרומה ליפטר ולא יהא חייב הלוי להפריש ממנו אלא תרומת מעשר · ופירק לו כיון שהעמידו כרי אידגן וקרינא ביה מכל מתנותיכם תרימו שכולל הכל · ומעשר שני והקדש שנפדו הוצרך להזכירו התנא להודיע שאם לא נתן החומש מעכב

*) כפ"ק דף ע' ע"א ובסוף סוטה במשנת דיוחנן כ"ג העביר הודיית המעשר ובגמ' שם כ"ג.

רב נסים גאון

שמא צינורא ניתזה מפיה על רבי · פי' צינורא שינתז מפי האדם כשהוא מדבר למטרונית והיא נכרית ונגע בו מרוקה הוצרך לטבול כי רוקן של נכרים גזרו עליו חכמים טומאה ועיקר זה הוא מה שאמר הקב"ה בענין הזב (ויקרא טו) וכי ירוק הזב בטהור יכול אפילו רקק ולא נגע יהא טמא ת"ל בטהור ובתוספתא זבין בפרק חמישי אמרו ורירו וכיחו ומימי האף שלו הרי הן כרוקו דמעת עינו ודם מגפתו וחלב האשה מטמאין טומאת משקה זובו ורוקו ומימי רגליו מטמאים טומאה חמורה וזאת התורה מיוחדת בישראל בלבד אבל לא בנכרים והחכמים הם שגזרו עליהם שיהו כזבין לכל דבריהם ותמצא כיוצא בזה במס' נדה בפרק בנות כותים (דף לד) כשאמר בית שמי דם הנכרית טהור הקשה להם מזו הברייתא ולא חלקו בית שמי אלא בדמה בלבד אבל רוקה אין מי שחולק בו כי הוא טמא ושורפין עליו את התרומה וכבר פירשו טעמם של בית שמי שטיהרו דמה (וטיהרו) [וטמאו] רוקה ומימי רגליה דשכיחי גזרו בהו רבנן דמה דלא שכיחא לא גזרו בה רבנן ובית הלל הכל אצלם טמא ושם במסכת שקלים (פ"ח מ"א) שנינו כל הרוקין הנמצאים בירושלים טהורין חוץ משל שוק העליון וגרסי בתלמוד בני מערבא ר' אבון בשם ר' יהושע של גוים היה שם ובמשנת טהרות בפרק ה' (משנה ח) שנינו שוטה אחד בעיר או נכרית או כותית כל הרוקין שבעיר טמאין וקודם לכן בפרק ד' אמרו על ו' ספיקות שורפין את התרומה אחד מהן ספק הרוקין שבעיר טמאין כבר נתבאר לך עכשיו ונתקיים מכל מה שהקדמנו כי רוק הנכרים טמא וכי גזירה דרבנן היא ובפרק השבת (דף טו) אמרו ספיקות באושא גזור עליהן ולפיכך הוצרך ר' יהושע בן חנניא טבילה ותמצא יומא בפרק הוציאו לו את הכף (דף מז) אמרו עליו על רבי ישמעאל בן קימחית שיצא ודבר עם ערבי אחד בשוק וניתזה צינורא מפיו על בגדו ונכנס ישבאב אחיו ושימש תחתיו ובחומר בקודש (חגיגה דף כג) תמצא גזירת צינורא דעם הארץ וזה בענין הקודש: **מפנין** תרומה טהורה ודמאי · כבר פירשו

[127*b*]—These too are included in the practice of loving deeds. Another version: these are included in those.[2]

Our Rabbis taught: He who judges his neighbour in the scale of merit is himself judged favourably. Thus a story is told of a certain man who descended from Upper Galilee and was engaged by an individual in the South for three years. On the eve of the Day of Atonement[3] he requested him, 'Give me my wages that I may go and support my wife and children.' 'I have no money,' answered he. 'Give me produce,' he demanded; 'I have none,' he replied. 'Give me land.'—'I have none.' 'Give me cattle.'—'I have none.' 'Give me pillows and bedding.'—'I have none.' [So] he slung his things behind him and went home with a sorrowful heart.[4] After the Festival his employer took his wages in his hand together with three laden asses, one bearing food, another drink, and the third various sweetmeats, and went to his house. After they had eaten and drunk, he gave him his wages. Said he to him, 'When you asked me, "Give me my wages," and I answered you, "I have no money," of what did you suspect me?' 'I thought, Perhaps you came across cheap merchandise and had purchased it therewith.' 'And when you requested me, "Give me cattle," and I answered, "I have no cattle," of what did you suspect me?' 'I thought, they may be hired to others.' 'When you asked me, "Give me land,' and I told you, "I have no land," of what did you suspect me?' 'I thought, perhaps it is leased to others.' 'And when I told you, "I have no produce," of what did you suspect me?' 'I thought, Perhaps they are not tithed.' 'And when I told you, "I have no pillows or bedding," of what did you suspect me?' 'I thought, Perhaps he has sanctified all his property to Heaven.' 'By the [Temple] service!' exclaimed he, 'it was even so; I vowed away all my property because of my son Hyrcanus, who would not occupy himself with the Torah, but when I went to my companions in the South they absolved me of all my vows. And as for you, just as you judged me favourably, so may the Omnipresent judge you favourably.'

a Our Rabbis taught: It happened that a certain pious man[1] ransomed an Israelite maiden [from captivity]; at the inn he made her lie at his feet. On the morrow he went down, had a ritual bath, and learnt with his disciples. Said he to them, 'When I made her lie at my feet, of what did you suspect me?' 'We thought, perhaps there is a disciple amongst us who[se character] is not clearly known[2] to our Master.'[3] 'When I descended and had a ritual bath, of what did you suspect me?' 'We thought, perhaps through the fatigue of the journey the Master was visited by nocturnal pollution.' 'By the [Temple] Service!' exclaimed he to them, 'it was even so. And just as you judged me favourably, so may the Omnipresent judge you favourably.'

Our Rabbis taught: The scholars were once in need of something from a noblewoman where all the great men of Rome were to be found. Said they, 'Who will go?' 'I will go,' replied R. Joshua. So R. Joshua and his disciples went. When he reached the door of her house, he removed his *tefillin*[4] at a distance of four cubits, entered, and shut the door in front of them. After he came out he descended, had a ritual bath, and learnt with his disciples. Said he to them, 'When I removed my *tefillin*, of what did you suspect me?' 'We thought, our Master reasons, "Let not sacred words enter a place of uncleanness".' 'When I shut [the door], of what did you suspect me?' 'We thought, perhaps he has [to discuss] an affair of State with her.' 'When I descended and had a ritual bath, of what did you suspect me?' 'We thought, perhaps some spittle spurted from her mouth upon the Rabbi's
b garments.'[1] 'By the [Temple] Service!' exclaimed he to them, 'it was even so; and just as you judged me favourably, so may the Omnipresent judge you favourably.'

WE MAY CLEAR AWAY CLEAN TERUMAH, etc. But that is obvious?—It is necessary [to teach it] only where it is lying in the hand of an Israelite; you might say, Since it is of no use[2] for him, it is forbidden [to handle it]; he [the Tanna] informs us therefore [that] since it is fit for a priest it is permitted.

DEM'AI, etc. But *dem'ai* is not fit for him?—Since if he desired he could renounce [ownership of] his property and become a poor man, whereby it would be fit for him, it is fit for him now too. For we learnt: The poor may be fed with *dem'ai* and billeted soldiers may be given *dem'ai*. And R. Huna said, It was taught: Beth Shammai maintain: The poor may not be given *dem'ai* as food, nor billeted soldiers; but Beth Hillel rule: The poor may be given *dem'ai* as food, and [likewise] billeted soldiers[3].

AND THE FIRST TITHE WHOSE TERUMAH HAS BEEN SEPARATED. But that is obvious?—It is necessary [to teach it] only where he anticipated [the separation of] the first tithe in the ears, and separated *terumah* of tithe but not the great *terumah*.[4] And this is as the following dictum of R. Abbahu in the name of Resh Lakish: First tithe which one anticipated in the ears is exempt from the great *terumah*, for it is said, *then ye shall offer up an heave-offering of it for the Lord, a tithe of the tithe:*[5] I ordered thee [to offer] a tithe of the tithe, but not the great *terumah* plus the *terumah* of the tithe of the tithe. R. Papa said to Abaye: If so, even if he anticipates
c it in the stack,[1] he should be exempt?—For your sake Scripture writes, *out of all your gifts ye shall offer every heave-offering of the Lord.*[2] And what [reason] do you see [to interpret thus]?[3]—The one has become corn [*dagan*], while the other has not become corn.[4]

AND THE SECOND TITHE, etc. But that is obvious?—It is necessary [to teach it] only where the principal has been given but not the fifth:[5] thus he informs us that the fifth is not indispensable.[6]

AND DRY LUPINES, etc. Only dry, but not moist. What is the reason? Since it is bitter, she [the goat] will not eat it.

(2) Hospitality and visiting the sick belong to the practice of loving deeds; early attendance at the Beth Hamidrash and rearing one's children to the study of the Torah are included in the study of the Torah; while judging one's neighbour favourably enables peace to be made between a man and his fellow and between a husband and wife, as each can be persuaded to take a charitable view of the other's actions. As for meditation in prayer, Rashi includes it in the practice of loving deeds—to one's own soul—as it is written, *the man of love doeth good to his own soul* (Prov. XI, 17). Maharsha includes it in peace-making—between God and man. (3) Alfasi and Asheri read: Festival. (4) Lit., 'with blasting of spirit'.

a (1) חסיד אחד, the phrase generally designates either R. Judah b. Baba or R. Judah b. Ila'i (Rashi). (2) Lit., 'tested', 'examined'. (3) So you could not trust him. (4) Which were then worn during the day.

b (1) Which by Rabbinical law affects levitical purity; cf. *supra* 15*b*, 17*b*. (2) Lit., 'not fit'. (3) V. Dem. III, 1. (4) The great *terumah* is a portion of the produce, unspecified by Scriptural law, which the Israelite must give to the priests; for *terumah* of the tithe, v. n. on Mishnah. The great *terumah* was to be separated first and then first tithe. But here the order was reversed, and the Israelite separated the tithe whilst the grain was yet in the ears. (5) Num. XVIII, 26.

c (1) I.e., when it is no longer in the ears but has been piled up in stacks. (2) Num. XVIII, 29; i.e., *all* is an extension, and shows that the offering is due even in such a case. 'For your sake' or, 'concerning you'—to refute this possibility. (3) To apply the limitation of the first verse to the one case and the extension of the second to the other—perhaps it should be reversed. (4) The priestly due, i.e., the great *terumah*, is '*the firstfruits of thy corn*' (Deut. XVIII, 4). Hence once it is piled up as corn it is due, and one cannot evade his obligations by reversing the order of the gifts. (5) When one redeemed the second tithe he had to add a fifth of its value. (6) To the validity of the redemption, and the redeemed produce may be consumed anywhere, even though the fifth has not been added.

[128*a*] BUT NOT ṬEBEL, etc. That is obvious?—It is necessary [to teach it] only of *ṭebel* made so by Rabbinical law, e.g., if it was sown in an unperforated pot.[7]

NOR THE FIRST TITHE, etc. That is obvious?—It is necessary [to teach it] only where it had been anticipated in the pile, the tithe having been separated but not the great *terumah*. You might argue as R. Papa proposed to Abaye:[8] hence he [the Tanna] informs us [that it is] as Abaye answered him.

NOR THE SECOND TITHE, etc. That is obvious?—It is necessary [to teach it] only where they have been redeemed, but not in accordance with their laws; [i.e.,] the [second] tithe was redeemed by uncoined metal,[9] for the Divine Law states, *And thou shalt bind up* [we-ẓarta] *the money in thine hand*,[10] [implying], that which
a bears a figure [*ẓurah*];[1] [and] *hekdesh* which was secularized by means of land,[2] for the Divine Law states, Then he shall give the money and it shall be assured to him.[3]

NOR LOF. Our Rabbis taught: We may handle *ḥaẓab*,[4] because it is food for gazelles, and mustard, because it is food for doves. R. Simeon b. Gamaliel said: We may also handle fragments of glass, because it is food for ostriches. Said R. Nathan to him: If so, let bundles of twigs be handled, because they are food for elephants. And R. Simeon b. Gamaliel?[5] Ostriches are common, [whereas] elephants are rare. Amemar observed: Provided he has ostriches. R. Ashi said to Amemar: Then when R. Nathan said to R. Simeon b. Gamaliel, 'let bundles of dried branches be handled, because they are food for elephants',—if one has elephants, why not? But [he means,] they are fit for [elephants]; so here too they are fit for [ostriches].[6]

Abaye said: R. Simeon b. Gamaliel, R. Simeon, R. Ishmael, and R. Akiba, all hold that all Israel are royal children. 'R. Simeon b. Gamaliel', as stated.[7] 'R. Simeon': for we learnt: Royal children may anoint their wounds with oil, since it is their practice to anoint themselves thus on weekdays. R. Simeon said: All Israel are royal children. 'R. Ishmael and R. Akiba': for it was taught: If one is a debtor for a thousand *zuz*, and wears a robe a hundred *manehs* in value, he is stripped thereof and robed with a garment that is fitting for him. It was taught in the name of R. Ishmael, and it was taught in the name of R. Akiba: All Israel are worthy of that robe.

BUNDLES OF STRAW, TWIGS, etc. Our Rabbis taught: Bundles of straw, bundles of branches, and bundles of young shoots,[8] if one prepared them as animal fodder, may be handled; if not, they may not be handled. R. Simeon b. Gamaliel said: Bundles which can be taken up with one hand may be handled; with two
b hands, may not be handled. As for bundles of *si'ah*,[1] hyssop and *koranith*:[2] if they were brought in for fuel, one must not draw on them [for food] on the Sabbath; [if brought in] as animal fodder, he may draw on them on the Sabbath; and he may break [it] with his hand and eat [thereof], provided that he does not break it with a utensil. And he may crush it and eat, provided that he does not crush a large quantity with a utensil: the words of R. Judah. But the Sages maintain: He may crush [it] with the tips of his fingers and eat, provided, however, that he does not crush a large quantity with his hands in the [same] way as he does on weekdays; the same applies to *ammitha*, the same applies to *higgam* [rue], and the same applies to other kinds of spices. What is *ammitha?*—*Ninya*.[3] [What is] *si'ah?*—Said Rab Judah: *Si'ah* is *ẓithre*;[4] *ezob* is *abratha* [hyssop];[5] *koranith* is what is called *koranitha*. But there was a certain man who asked, 'Who wants *koranitha*,' and it transpired [that he meant] thyme?—Rather *si'ah* is *ẓithre*, *ezob* is *abratha*, and *koranitha* is *ḥashe* [thyme].

It was stated: Salted meat may be handled on the Sabbath; unsalted[6] meat,—R. Huna says: It may be handled; R. Ḥisda rules: It may not be handled. 'R. Huna says: It may be handled'? But R. Huna was Rab's disciple, and Rab agrees with R. Judah who accepts [the prohibition of] *mukẓeh?*[7]—In [the interdict of] *mukẓeh* in respect of eating he agrees with R. Judah;[8] in [the interdict] of *mukẓeh* as regards handling he agrees with R. Simeon.[9]

'R. Ḥisda rules: It may not be handled.' But R. Isaac b. Ammi visited R. Ḥisda's house and he saw a [slaughtered] duck being moved from the sun into the shade, and R. Ḥisda observed, I
c see here a financial loss.'[1]—A duck is different, because it is fit as raw meat.

Our Rabbis taught: Salted fish may be handled; unsalted fish may not be handled;[2] meat, whether unsalted or salted, may be handled; [and this is taught anonymously as R. Simeon].[3]

Our Rabbis taught: Bones may be handled because they are

(7) Cf. *supra* 95*a* Mishnah. By Scriptural law it is not *ṭebel* at all, and one would think that the produce might therefore be handled. (8) That it is exempt; *supra* 127*b* bottom. (9) *Asimon*. V. B.M. 47*b* for the meaning of the term. (10) Deut. XIV, 25.

a (1) The image stamped on a coin. This connects *ẓarta* with *ẓurah*. (2) I.e., land was given in order to redeem it. (3) I.e., it can be redeemed by money, but not by land. Actually there is no such verse, but v. B.M., 54*a*, n. c1. (4) Jast.: a shrubby plant, probably cistus. (5) How does he answer this? (6) And they may be handled even if one has no ostriches. (7) He permits *lof* to be handled because it is food for ravens, which only wealthy people—who are the same as princes—kept. (8) BaḤ on the basis of Ṭur O.Ḥ. 308, 28 omits the last-mentioned here, though retaining it in the Mishnah.

b (1) Jast.: a plant classified with hyssop. *Satureia Thymbra* (savory). (2) Jast.: thyme or origanum. (3) Jast.: Bishop's weed. Rashi: mint (4) *Satureia*; v. n. b1. (5) Used as a remedy for indigestion, v. *supra* 109*b*. (6) Lit., 'unsavoury'. (7) Which applies to unsalted meat, since it is not fit for food. (8) That which is normally unfit for food may not be eaten, even if its owner wishes. (9) That it is permitted.

c (1) If you leave it in the sun. Thus they moved it at his orders. (2) Because it cannot be eaten, nor will it be given to dogs, as one does not give to dogs what can be made fit for man. (3) Hence raw meat is permitted. Rashal, however, deletes the bracketed passage; v. Tosaf.

*אבל לא את הטבל וכו' : פשיטא לא צריכא בטבל טבול מדרבנן(א) שזרעו בעציץ שאינו נקוב : [ב]ולא מעשר ראשון וכו' : פשיטא לא צריכא שהקדימו· בכרי שנטל ממנו מעשר ולא נטלה ממנו תרומה גדולה מהו דתימא כדאמר ליה רב פפא לאביי קמ"ל כדשני ליה אביי : [ג]ולא את מעשר שני וכו' : פשיטא לא צריכא דנפדו ולא נפדו כהלכתן מעשר שפדאו על גבי אסימון דרחמנא אמר [ב"מ מז:] °וצרת הכסף בידך *דבר שיש בו צורה (דברים יד) הקדש שחיללו על גבי קרקע דרחמנא אמר ונתן הכסף וקם לו : [ד]ולא את הלוף : ת"ר *מטלטלין את החצב מפני שהוא מאכל לצביים ואת החרדל מפני שהוא מאכל ליונים רשב"ג אומר אף מטלטלין שברי [תוספ' פט"ו] זכוכית מפני שהוא מאכל לנעמיות אמר ליה רבי נתן אלא מעתה חבילי זמורות יטלטלו מפני שהוא מאכל לפילין ורשב"ג נעמיות שכיחי פילין לא שכיחי אמר אמימר [ה]והוא דאית ליה נעמיות אמר רב אשי לאמימר אלא דקאמר ליה ר' נתן לרשב"ג חבילי זמורות יטלטל מפני שהוא מאכל לפילין אי אית ליה פילין אמאי לא אלא ראוי ה"נ ראוי *אמר אביי רשב"ג ורבי שמעון ורבי ישמעאל ורבי עקיבא כולהו סבירא להו כל ישראל בני מלכים הם רשב"ג הא דאמרן ר' שמעון *דתנן בני מלכים סכין על גבי מכותיהן שמן וורד שכן דרכן של בני מלכים לסוך בחול *ר"ש אומר כל ישראל בני מלכים הם ר' ישמעאל ור' עקיבא דתניא [ו]הרי שהיו נושין בו אלף מנה ולבוש *איצטלא בת ק' מנה מפשיטין אותו ומלבישין אותו איצטלא הראויה לו תנא משום רבי ישמעאל ותנא משום רבי עקיבא כל ישראל ראוין לאותה איצטלא :

חבילי קש וחבילי כו' : תנו רבנן *[ז]חבילי קש וחבילי עצים(ג) וחבילי זרדים אם התקינן למאכל בהמה מטלטלין אותן ואם לאו אין מטלטלין אותן רשב"ג אומר הבילין הניטלין ביד אחד מותר לטלטלן בשתי ידים אסיר לטלטלן *[ח]חבילי *סיאה אזוב וקורנית הכניסן לעצים אין [א] מסתפק מהן בשבת למאכל בהמה מסתפק מהן בשבת וקוטם ביד ואוכל ובלבד שלא יקטום בכלי ומולל ואוכל ובלבד שלא ימלול בכלי הרבה דברי רבי יהודה וחכמים אומרים °מולל בראשי אצבעותיו ואוכל ובלבד שלא ימלול בידו הרבה כדרך שהוא עושה בחול וכן באמיתא וכן בפיגם וכן בשאר מיני תבלין *מאי אמיתא ניניא סיאה אמר רב יהודה (סיאה) צתרי אזוב אברתא קורנית קורניתא שמה והא ההוא דאמר להו מאן בעי קורניתא ואישתכח חשי אלא סיאה צתרי אזוב אברתא קורניתא חשי : איתמר בשר מליח מותר לטלטלו בשבת בשר [ב] תפל רב הונא אמר מותר לטלטלו רב חסדא אמר אסור לטלטלו רב הונא אמר מותר לטלטלו °והא *רב הונא תלמיד דרב הוה ורב כר' יהודה סבירא ליה דאית ליה מוקצה במוקצה לאכילה סבר לה כרבי יהודה °במוקצה לטלטל סבר לה כרבי שמעון רב חסדא אמר אסור לטלטלו והא רב יצחק בר אמי איקלע לבי רב חסדא וחזא ההוא בר אווזא דהוו קא מטלטלו ליה משמשא לטולא ואמר רב חסדא חסרון כיס קא חזינן הכא שאני בר אווזא דחזי לאומצא ת"ר [ט]דג מליח מותר לטלטלו דג תפל אסור לטלטלו [י]בשר בין תפל ובין מליח מותר לטלטלו (*וסתמא כרבי שמעון) תנו רבנן [ל]מטלטלין את העצמות מפני שהוא מאכל לכלבים בשר

שלא ניטלה תרומתו · קא סלקא דעתך שלא ניטלה תרומת מעשר שלו : אסימון · שאין עליו צורה : חצב · עשב שמשריש בעומק כנגדו ואין שרשיו מתפשטין ובו *תיחם יהושע את הארץ לישראל : נעמיות · בנות היענה : יטלטלו · ראוי הוא להיות לו פילין ולהאכילן : על מכותיהן · בשבת ולא גזר משום שחיקת סממנין : שכן דרכן לסוך · בלא מכה הלכך לאו מוכחא מילתא דלרפואה : התקינן · הזמינן : אסור לטלטלן · ואפילו הזמינם למאכל בהמה דטירחא היא : סיאה אזוב וקורנית · לקמיה מפרש לה : הכניסן לעצים · לייבשן : שלא יקטום בכלי · כדרך חול כדאמרן (לעיל דף עד:) האי מאן דפרים סילקא דמי לטוחן · במילתיה דרבי יהודה גרסינן מולל ואוכל ובלבד שלא ימלול בכלי הרבה וחכמי' אומרים מולל בראשי אצבעותיו ובלבד שלא ימלול בידו הרבה כדרך חול כך מצאתי בתוספתא דרבנן מחמרי דבכולי ידא אסור אלא בראשי אצבעותיו ומהו מולל כגון אם בא לאכול הזרע מולל השרביטין שהזרע בתוכם : וכן באמיתא · לקמיה מפרש מאי אמיתא : ניניא · מינט"א : פיגם · רוד"א : צתרי · שדריא"ה לוי"ה ל"א פוליאול : אברתא · איסכי"א : חשי · שדריא"ה וללשון הראשון לא פורש : בשר תפל · שאינו מלוח ומאן דגרים תפוח היא היא : מותר לטלטלו · דלית ליה מוקצה בטלטול : במוקצה לאכילה סבר לה כר' יהודה · כלומר באיסור מוקצה לענין אכילה סבר לה כרבי יהודה דאסר לאוכלו(ג) ובאיסור מוקצה לטלטול סבר לה כרבי שמעון : בר אווזא · שחוט : משמשא לטולא · שלא יסריח : ואמר להו רב חסדא חסרון כיס חזינא הכא· שאתם מניחים אותה בשמש ומתחמם וסלקוהו על פיו מחמה לצל : באומצא · כשהוא חי אוכלין אותו בלא מלח : דג תפל אסור לטלטלו · דאינו ראוי לכלוס ולכלבים לאו דעתיה למישדייה אבל מליח נאכל חי על ידי מלחו : בשר

*אבל לא את הטבל · והא דאמר(ד) רבה בפרק כירה (לעיל דף מג·) טבל מוכן הוא אצל שבת שאם עבר ותיקנו מתוקן ה"מ לענין ביטול כלי מהיכנו שלא החמירו כמו לענין טלטול בידים : שפדאו אגב האסימון · הא דנקט אסימון הייט דלא כרבי דוסא דפרק הזהב (ב"מ דף מז:) והוה מצי למימר מעות הניתנות סימן לבית המרחץ לד"ה אלא משום דאם כן מאי קמ"ל אבל השתא קמ"ל כרבנן : ונתן הכסף וקם לו · אין הפסוק כן אלא ויסף חמישית כסף ערכך עליו וקם לו (ויקרא כז) ודרך הש"ס לקצר ולומר בלשון אחר קצר כי ההיא דפרק הדר (עירובין דף סה·) רבי חנינא ביומא דרתח לא מצלי שנאמר בצר אל יורה ובפרק הרואה (ברכות דף נה:) שנאמר כל החלומות הולכים אחר הפה וקשה לר"י נימא כסף דוקא וכ"ת דשוה כסף ככסף חדא דגבי נזקין מצרכינן קרא ישיב לרבות שוה כסף ועוד דאם כן אפילו קרקע נמי ומנלן למעוטי קרקע ואומר ר"י דמכלל ופרט נפקא כדתנן בבכורות בפרק יש בכור לנחלה (דף נא·) אין פודין לא בעבדים ולא בקרקעות ולא בהקדשות ומפרש בגמרא דבעי למימר ולא הקדשות בכל אלו לענין פדיון בכור דרשינן התם כלל ופרט ופדויו מבן חדש כלל בכסף פרט תפדה חזר וכלל מה הפרט מפורש דבר המיטלטל כו' ה"נ איכא למימר בפדיון הקדשות וגתן כלל כסף פרט וקם לו חזר וכלל כו' מיהו בת"כ דריש ליה מקרא אחרינא וכל ערכך יהיה בשקל הקדש מה ת"ל לפי שנאמר(ה) תפדה יכול בעבדים ושטרות וקרקעו' ת"ל בשקל הקדש אין לי אלא סלעים מניין לרבות כל דבר המיטלטל ת"ל ופדה בערכך א"כ למה נאמר בשקל פרט לעבדים ושטרות וקרקעות אלא כן דרך הש"ס שאינו מביא עיקר הדרשה כמו שרגיל להביא *](כתובות דף מו:) בנעוריה בית אביה כל שבח נעורים לאביה אע"ג דההוא בהפרת נדרים הוא דכתיב וכן הרבה : רשב"ג אומר אף מטלטלין שברי זכוכית · משמע דמודה לת"ק דמתיר חרדל והא דתנן רשב"ג מתיר בלוף וכל שכן דמתיר בחרדל : הכניסן לעצים אין מסתפק · איכא למימר דה"ק הא סתמא נעשה כמי שהכניסן למאכל בהמה כי היכי דלא תקשה רישא לסיפא : דחזי לאומצא · מכאן ראיה דדם האברים שלא פירש מותר דקאמר דחזי לאומצא אע"ג דלא מליח * : דג תפל אסור לטלטלו · תימה מדשרי בשר תפל אלמא כר"ש אתיא אם כן דג תפל נמי לישרי כמו בשר תפל וי"ל דדג תפל אינו ראוי לכלבים אי נמי כר' יהודה אתיא ודג תפל אע"פ שראוי לכלבים אסור לטלטלו דכל מידי דחזי לאינש לא מקצה לכלבים בשר תפל מותר לטלטלו לרבי יהודה מפני שהוא מאכל לאיה : מטלטלין את העצמות · לר' יהודה דאית לי' מוקצה מיירי כגון שלא הי' עליה' בשר מאתמול: בשר

עין משפט נר מצוה

[שייך לעיל קכו: על המשנה]

טו א ב ג מיי' פכ"ס מהל' שבת הל' יט :

טז ד ה מיי' פכ"ו מהל' שבת הל' [טו] יז סמג לאוין סה טוש"ע א"ח סימן שח סעיף כט :

יז ו מיי' פ"א מהלכות מלוה ולוה הלכה ז ופ"ג מהלכות ערכין הל' טו סמג עשין לג טוש"ע ח"מ סימן לז סעיף כח :

יח ז מיי' פכ"ו מהלכות שבת הלכה יח סמג לאוין סה ועשין קלה טוש"ע א"ח סימן שח סעיף כח :

יט ח ט מיי' שם ופכ"א שם הלכה יט סמג שם טוש"ע א"ח סימן שכא סעיף א ובסימן שיט סעיף ו :

כ י מיי' פכ"ו שם הלכה טו סמג שם טוש"ע א"ח סי' שח סעיף לב :

כא כ מיי' שם טוש"ע שם סעיף לא :

כב ל מיי' שם טוש"ע שם סעיף כט בהג"ה:

[המורה מקום זה לא דק דאדרבה שם בכתובות מו: וכן שם מ: ובקדושין ג: פריך הש"ס עלה ומסיק ג"כ דההיא בהפרת נדרים הוא דכתיב אבן כוונתם אגמרא דב"ק פז. וע"ש בתוספות ד"ה כיון וע"ע בתוס' עירובין טו: ד"ה בכתיבה וכו' מבואר היטב וע"ע תוספות מו"ק ח. ד"ה נ"ל ומגילה ג. ד"ה וילן ודף כ. ד"ה דכתיב וביבמות סח. ד"ה אי נת וסנהדרין לד: ד"ה דכתיב וזבחים קיז. ד"ה והתורה ובכריתות טו. ד"ה עדות וסוכה ל. ד"ה כי יקריב בכורות יד. ד"ה סוב]

מסורת הש"ס

[ב"ב נו.]

[ב"מ מז:]

[תוספ' פט"ו]

[שם]

ר"ל פיאה

[לקמן קמ. ע"ש]

[ביצה מ.]

תס"ל מ"ז

ב"מ קיג:

לעיל קיא.

[לעיל סז. וש"נ]

פי' מעיל ותגורה

[ב"ב כב:]

הגהות הב"ח

(א) גמ' בטבל טבול מדרבנן וכגון שזרע בעציץ: (ב) שם וחבילי עצים (וחבילי זרדין) תא"מ וכ"כ עי' במה שכתב הטור א"ח סי' ש"ח משמע לסדיא דלא גרסי' בברייתא וחבילי זרדין אבל במתניתין גרסינן וחבילי זרדין ע"ש : (ג) רש"י ד"ה במוקצה וכו' דאסור לאוכלו ובמוקצה לאיסור טלטול סבר: (ד) תוס' ד"ה אבל וכו' דאמר רב יוסף בפרק כירה : (ה) ד"ה ונתן וכו' לפי שנאמ' ופדה בערכך יכול בעבדים:

רבינו חננאל

מעכב: אסימון מטבע שאין עליו צורה · ולא את הלוף ולא את החרדל · רשב"ג מתיר בלוף וכו' והא דרשב"ג פשיטה חבילי קש וחבילי עצים וכו'. חצבי עשב הוא והוא העשב (שכן) [שבו] תיחם יהושע לישראל את הארץ · הא מתני' סתמא היא וכוותה עבדינן דהא מתנית' נמי דברי הכל הוא · ורשב"ג דאמר אין מותר לטלטל אלא חבילה הניטלת בידו אחת מוקמינן ליה בחבילות שהכניסן למאכל בהמה דכל פתח של תורה לחומרא עבדינן . ותוב מתניתין סתמא תני וכוותה עבדינן וליכא לאוקמא רשב"ג מפרש דהא לא קתני איפתי ולא במה: חבילי סיאה · ציתרי · אזוב אברתא. וקורנית (האשי) [חשי] כולן מיני אזוב הן. הכניסן לעצים להדליק מהן אין מסתפק מהן בשבת למאכל בהמה מסתפק מהן בשבת *)דקי"ל אבל דחזי ליה וקוטם ואוכל ובלבד שלא יקטום בכלי ובמלילה חלקו ר' יהודה וחכמים והלכה כחכמים שאמרו מילל בראשי אצבעותיו ואוכל ובלבד שלא ימלול בידו הרבה כדרך שהוא עושה בחול · וכן באמיתא וכן בפינם וכן בשאר מיני תבלין וקי"ל כחכמים · אמיתא · נענע : בשר תפוח חלק בו רב הונא ורב חסדא · רב הונא אמר מותר לטלטלו ורב חסדא אמר אסור לטלטלו · והלכתא כרב הונא דרב חסדא לגבי רב הונא תלמיד הוא · ותוב רב הונא קאי כר' שמעון דקי"ל כוותיה ואפילו רב דסבר כר' יהודה במוקצה לאכילה במוקצה לטלטול כר' שמעון סבירא ליה ואי חזי לאומצא פי' ואם ראוי להיאכל נא אפי' רב חסדא מודה שמותר לטלטלו

*) אולי צ"ל וה"ה אם הכניסן סתמא דקי"ל דלעתי' אבל דחזי ליה ועי' תוס' כאן ד"ה הכניסן .

רב נסים גאון

בפרק שלשה שאכלו כאחת כי הוא הדבר הנדמה דמי מתוקן ומי אינו מתוקן ובארנו שם עיקר גזירתו : אסימון הוא מטבע בפ' הזהב (ב"מ דף מז) מאי אסימון פולסא ומה שהוא בענין זה אסור לפדות בו את המעשר שני כי הכתוב פי' שצריך מטבע שיש עליו צורה דכתיב (דברים יד) וצרת הכסף בידך דבר שיש עליו צורה : ת"ר מטלטלין את החצב זה חצב הוא צמח משלח שרשיו למטה בקרקע בצדק בלא הטייה והוא מה שאמרו בפרק חזקת הבתים (ב"ב דף נה) אמר ר' אסי אמר ר' יוחנן המצר והחצב מפסיקין בנכסי הגר וכו' ואמרו מאי חצובא אמר רב יהודה אמר רב שבו תיחם יהושע את הארץ לישראל

הגהות הגר"א [א] גמ' אין מסתפק מהן בשבת למאכל בהמה · נ"ב למאכל מסתפק מהן בשבת : [ב] שם מותר לטלטל בשבת בשר תפל · נ"ב ג"י הגאונים ורי"ף תפוח ועי' רשב"א

גליון הש"ס גמ' והא ר"ה תלמיד דרב · ביצה דף מ ע"א · ב"ק קטו ע"א · ועיין ב"ב דף קנג ע"א תוספות ד"ה שלחו ליה (קנ"ב ע"ב) : שם במוקצה לטלטל ס"ל כר' שמעון · עיין לעיל דף יט ע"ב תוספות ד"ה °הני כרכי דזוזי · ולקמן דף קלט ע"ב השייך לדף קמ ע"ב תוספות ד"ה תלא דכבלא · ועיין במהרש"א ביצה דף לג ע"א בתוספות ד"ה אין סומכין :

בשר תפוח מפני שהוא מאכל לחיה מים מגולין מפני שהן ראויין לחתול רשב"ג אומר כל עצמן אסור לשהותן מפני הסכנה: **מתני'** *[א]כופין את הסל לפני האפרוחים כדי שיעלו וירדו תרנגולת שברחה דוחין אותה עד שתכנס מדדין עגלין וסייחין* [(א)]אשה מדדה את בנה אמר רבי יהודה [ב]אימתי בזמן שהוא נוטל אחת ומניח אחת אבל אם היה גורר אסור: **גמ'** אמר רב יהודה אמר רב בהמה שנפלה לאמת המים מביא כרים וכסתות ומניח תחתיה ואם עלתה עלתה מיתיבי *בהמה שנפלה לאמת המים עושה לה פרנסה במקומה בשביל שלא תמות פרנסה אין כרים וכסתות לא לא קשיא [ג]הא דאפשר בפרנסה הא דאי אפשר בפרנסה אפשר בפרנסה אין ואי לא מביא כרים וכסתות ומניח תחתיה והא *קא מבטל כלי מהיכנו סבר מבטל כלי מהיכנו דרבנן *[ד]צער בעלי חיים דאורייתא ואתי דאורייתא ודחי דרבנן: [ה]תרנגולת שברחה וכו': דוחין אין מדדין לא תנינא להא דת"ר [ו]מדדין בהמה חיה ועוף בחצר אבל לא את התרנגולת תרנגולת מאי טעמא לא אמר אביי משום דמקפיא נפשה תני חדא מדדין בהמה וחיה ועוף בחצר אבל לא ברה"ר והאשה מדדה את בנה [ז]ברה"ר ואצ"ל בחצר ותניא אידך אין עוקרין בהמה וחיה ועוף בחצר אבל דוחין בהן שיכנסו הא גופא קשיא אמרת אין עוקרין אבל דדויי מדדינן [(ג)]הדר אמרת דוחין אין מדדין לא אמר אביי סיפא אתאן לתרנגולת אמר אביי [ח]האי מאן דשחיט תרנגולת לכבשינהו לכרעיה בארעא אי נמי נידל להו מידל דדילמא מנח להו לטופריה בארעא ועקר להו לסימנים: **מתני'** [ט]אין מילדין את הבהמה ביום טוב אבל מסעדין ומילדין את האשה בשבת וקורין לה חכמה ממקום למקום ומחללין עליה את השבת וקושרין את הטיבור רבי יוסי אומר *אף חותכין *וכל צרכי מילה עושין בשבת: **גמ'** כיצד מסעדין רב יהודה אמר אוחז את הולד שלא יפול לארץ רב נחמן אמר דוחק בבשר כדי שיצא הולד תניא כוותיה דרב יהודה *כיצד מסעדין [י]אוחזין את הולד שלא יפול לארץ ונופח לו בחוטמו ונותן לו דד לתוך פיו כדי שינק אמר רשב"ג [כ]מרחמין היינו על בהמה טהורה ביו"ט היכי עביד אמר אביי מביא בול של מלח ומניח לה בתוך הרחם כדי שתזכור צערה ותרחם עליו ומזלפין מי שליא על גבי ולד כדי שתריח ריחו ותרחם עליו ודוקא טהורה אבל טמאה לא מ"ט טמאה לא מרחקא ולדא ואי מרחקא ולדא לא מקרבא: [ל]מילדין את האשה וכו': מכדי תנא ליה מילדין את האשה וקורין לה חכמה ממקום למקום ומחללין עליה את השבת לאתויי מאי לאתויי הא דתנו רבנן [מ]אם היתה צריכה לנר חבירתה מדלקת לה את הנר ואם היתה צריכה לשמן חבירתה מביאה לה שמן ביד ואם אינו ספק ביד מביאה בשערה ואם אינו ספק בשערה מביאה לה בכלי אמר מר אם היתה צריכה לנר חבירתה מדלקת לה את הנר פשיטא [נ]לא צריכא בסומא מהו דתימא כיון דלא חזיא אסור קא משמע לן איתובי מיתבא דעתה סברא אי איכא מידי חזיא חבירתא ועבדה לי: אם היתה צריכה לשמן וכו': [ס]תיפוק ליה משום סחיטה רבה ורב יוסף דאמרי תרווייהו אין סחיטה בשיער רב אשי אמר אפי' תימא יש סחיטה בשיער מביאה לה בכלי דרך שערה *דכמה דאפשר לשנויי משנינן אמר רב יהודה אמר שמואל חיה כל זמן שהקבר פתוח בין אמרה צריכה אני *)בין לא אמרה צריכה אני מחללין עליה את השבת נסתם הקבר בין אמרה צריכה

*) ס"א בין אמרה איני צריכה

[Tosafot]

בשר תפוח מפני שהוא מאכל לחיה · תימה לימא מפני שהוא מאכל לכלבים וי"ל דכרבי יהודה אתיא ואינו מסריח כפירוש הקונטרס אלא חזי ליה וכל מידי דחזי ליה לאינש לא מקלה לכלבים אבל מפני שהוא מאכל לחיה מותר לטלטלו דכל ישראל בני מלכים הם ורב חסדא דלא שרי בשר תפל מהאי טעמא לית ליה כל ישראל בני מלכים:

אין עוקרין בהמה חיה ועוף · לספרים דגרסי רה"ר קך ברייתא פליגא אקמייתא בתרתי דדייקין הא דדויי מדדינן אפילו ברה"ר ולעיל קתני דווקא בחצר ותו סיפא דמוקמת לתרנגולת דאין מדדין ברה"ר ולעיל קתני דאפי' בחצר לא ולספרים דגרסי אין עוקרין בהמה חיה ועוף בחצר אתי שפיר: **קמ"ל** איתובי מיתבא דעתה · אע"ג דבפרק בתרא דיומא (דף פג·) אמר חולה אין מאכילין אותו ביוה"כ אלא ע"פ מומחה והכא[(ה)] שריא משום יתובי דעתא היינו שיותר יכולה היולדת להסתכן על ידי פחד שתתפחד שמא אין עושין יפה מה שהיא צריכה ממה שיסתכן החולה ברעב:

רבה

[Rashi]

בשר תפוח · מסריח: לחתול · לא מזיק ליה ארס דנחש שאף הנחשים היא אוכלת: מפני הסכנה · שמא ישתה אדם מהם: **מתני'** כופין סל בפני האפרוחים · אשמעינן דכלי ניטל לדבר שאינו ניטל בשבת ורבי יצחק משני לה *בפ"ג בצריך למקומו: שברחה · מן הבית: דוחין · בידים: מדדין עגלים · אוחז בצוארו ובצדדין וגוררו ומסייעו[(ג)] ומנענע לו ברגליו: אשה מדדה את בנה · אוחזתו בזרועותיו מאחוריו ומסייעתו והוא מניע רגליו והולך: שנוטל אחת ומניח אחת · שהתינוק מניע את רגליו כשמניח אחת מגביה אחת: אבל גורר אסור · מפני שנושאתו: **גמ'** ואי לא · כגון שהמים עמוקין: והא קמבטל כלי מהיכנו · דמשהניחם תחתיה אין יכול לטלטלן דדומה לסותר בנין[(ד)] מדרבנן: צער בעלי חיים דאורייתא · שנאמר עזוב תעזוב עמו ואיכא מאן דדריש טעמא דקרא משום צער בעלי חיים באלו מציאות (ב"מ דף לב:): מדדין לא · שלא יהא אוחזה בגפיה ורגליה נוגעין לארץ ומוליכה: דמקפיא נפשה · מגבהת עצמה מן הארץ ונמצא זה מטלטל אבל אווזים כשאוחזין בגפיהן הן מהלכין ברגליהן ומיהו ברה"ר לא משום שמא יגביה מן הארץ ונמצא נושא דסתמא כרבנן דפליגי עליה דרבי נתן בהמצניע (לעיל דף צד·) גבי המוציא חיה ועוף בין חיין בין שחוטין חייב והאשה מדדה את בנה אפילו ברה"ר דאי נמי מגביה ליה חי נושא את עצמו דהכי מוקמינן התם דבאדם מודו רבנן לרבי נתן: מקפיא · כגון אקפו ידייכו דחגיגה (דף טז:): אין עוקרין · רגליה לגמרי מן הארץ דמוקצה היא לטלטלה: דדויי מדדינן · אוחזה בשני לדדיה בידו ומדדה והוה טלטול טפי מדחייה שדחפה מאחריה: סיפא · דקתני דוחין אבל לא מדדין: אתאן לתרנגולת · ורישא בשאר עופות: לכבשינהו לכרעיה בארעא · כדי שיתכפלו ולא יוכל להתחזק עליהן: אי נמי לידליהו · יגביהנו שלא יהו רגליו נוגעות לארץ: **מתני'** מסעדין · מפרש בגמרא: חכמה · מילדת: אין מילדין את הבהמה ביום טוב · דאיכא טרחא יתירה: אבל מסעדין · אותה בי"ט: ומיילדין אשה בשבת · ואין צריך לומר שמסעדין וכל שכן ביום טוב: וקושרין הטיבור · של ולד שהוא ארוך שאם לא יתקשר ויכרך בשום דבר יצאו מעיו אם יגביהו התינוק: **גמ'** דוחק · בבשר של בהמה לפנים שיהא הולד בולט לחוץ: ונופח לו בחוטמו · שנחיריו סתומין מ בריריו: ונותן דד · של אמו בתוך פיו: מרחמין · מאהבין את ולדה עליה: בול של מלח · מלא אגרוף דכייב לה וזוכרת צער לידה ומרחמה את הולד אם רחקתו: מי שליא · שורין את השליא במים: לא מרחקה · אין דרכה לרחק: מביאה לה שמן · דרך רה"ר: ביד · בכפה ולא בכלי דכמה דאפשר משנינן: בשערה · ככה שערה שמן וכשבאה אצלה מקנחתו ואין כאן חילול שבת כיון שאין דרך הולאה בכך: פשיטא · דהא פקוח נפש דוחה שבת: תיפוק ליה משום סחיטה · למה לא הביאה לה בכלי שלא תחלל שבת בהולאה הכא נמי הא קמחללה בסחיטה: אין סחיטה בשיער · שהוא קשה ואין בולע: דרך שערה · כורכת הכלי בראשה בשערה: חיה · יולדת: קבר · בית הרחם: צריכה

צריכה

[עין משפט נר מצוה]

כג א מיי' פכ"ה מהל' שבת הלכה כה סמג לאוין סה טוש"ע א"ח סימן שח סעיף לט:

כד ב מיי' פי"ח שם הלכה טו סמג שם טוש"ע שם סעיף מא:

כה ג מיי' פכ"ה שם הלכה כו וסמג שם טוש"ע א"ח סימן שה סעיף יט:

כו ד מיי' פי"ג מהלכות רוצח וש"כ הלכה יג סמג עשין פ פא ולאוין קסט טוש"ע ח"מ סימן ערב סעיף ט בהג"ה:

כז ה ו מיי' פכ"ה מהל' שבת הלכה כו סמג לאוין סה טוש"ע א"ח סי' שח סעיף מ:

כח ז שם סעיף מא:

כט ח [מיי' פ"ג מהל' שחיטה הל' יד] סמג עשין טוש"ע י"ד סי' כד סעיף כ [וברב אלפס חולין פ"ב דף רסא]:

ל ט י מיי' פ"ד מהל' יו"ט הלכה טז סמג לאוין עה טוש"ע א"ח סימן תקכב סעיף א וסימן תקכג סעיף ג:

[ב"מ לב:]

לא כ מיי' שם טוש"ע שם ס"ד:

לב ל מ נ מיי' פ"ב מהלכות שבת הלכה יא סמג לאוין סה טוש"ע א"ח סי' של סעיף א:

[בש"ע א"ח סימן ש"ל סעיף ז פסק הלכתא כרבי יוסי וכן דעת הרמב"ם]

[מסורת הש"ס]

[צ"ל לעיל בפ"ג מג:]

[לעיל מג.]

[ב"מ לב.]

[לעיל קיז:]

[לקמן קמא. ביצה לג.]

[לקמן קלג.]

[תוספ' פט"ז]

הגהות הב"ח

(א) במשנה ואשה מדדה: (ב) גמ' וסדר אמרת: (ג) רש"י ד"ה מדדין וכו' ומסייעו ליגך ומנענע: (ד) ד"ה והא קא מבטל וכו' לסתור בנין מבטל כלי מהיכנו מדרבנן לער בעלי חיים:(ה) תוס' ד"ה קמ"ל וכו והכא שריא משום וכו' היינו לפי שיותר:

[לעיל מג· וש"נ ועי"ש תוספות ד"ה דמבטל]

גליון הש"ס

גמרא תיפוק ליה משום סחיטה · עיין לקמן דף קמה ע"א תוספות ד"ה כבשים:

רבינו חננאל

לטלטלו: דג תפל אסור לטלטלו בשר בין חי ובין מליח מותר לטלטלו · ת"ר מטלטלין את העצמות מפני שהן מאכל לכלבים בשר תפוח מפני שהוא מאכל לחיה וזו היא דתניא כוותיה דרב הונא מים מגולין מפני שהן ראוין לחתול · ומתניתא אלין הלכתא אינון דליכא דפליג · ואליבא דב"ה נשנו דתנן ב"ה אומרים מגביהין מעל השלחן עצמות וקליפין: כופין את הסל לפני האפרוחים שיעלו ושירדו · בהמה שנפלה לאמת המים אם אפשר לה בפרנסה עושין לה פרנסה במקומה · ואם אי אפשר לה בפרנסה מביא כרים וכסתות ומניח תחתיה ואם עלתה עלתה ואף על גב דמבטל כלי מהיכנו · מדרבנן היא · וצער ב"ח דאורייתא ואתא דאורייתא ודחה דרבנן · תרנגולת שברחה דוחין אותה עד שתכנס אבל אין מדדין אותה אפי' בחצר משום דמקפיא נפשה ואע"פ ששאר בהמה חיה ועוף מדדין בחצר אבל לא ברה"ר תרנגולת אפילו בחצר לא אלא אסור לדדותם אפילו בחצר · האשה מדדה את בנה ברה"ר וכ"ש בחצר והא דאמר ר' יהודה אימתי בזמן שנוטל אחת ומניח אחת אבל אם היה גורר אסור [היינו] ברה"ר בלבד שאם נוטל התינוק רגלו אחת ונשען על רגלו האחרת נמצא כמהלך אבל אם אינו נשען על רגליו אלא כשמדדתו גורר רגליו נמצאת נושאתו ברה"ר ואסור אבל בחצר מותר לטלטלו ולשאת אותו והא דאמר אביי מאן דשחיט תרנגולת ליכבשינה לכרעתא בארעא · אי נמי תידלינהו דילמא מנח להן לטופראה בארעא ועקרה להו לסימנים הלכתא היא: **מתני'** אין מילדין את הבהמה ביו"ט אבל מסעדין כיצד מסעדין · רב יהודה אומר אוחז בולד שלא יפול לארץ והלכתא כמותו · דתניא כוותיה · כיצד מסעדין אוחז בולד שלא יפול לארץ ונופחו לו בחוטמו ונותן דד לתוך פיו כדי שיינק כו' · וקיי"ל דמסעדין ומרחמין דתנינן ביו"ט אבל לא בשבת ומילדין את האשה בשבת וקורין לה חכמה ממקום למקום ומחללין עליה את השבת · ואסיקנא שמדלקת לה חברתה את הנר ואפילו אם היא סומא מותר להדליק לה נר בשבת דקיי"ל ייתובי מייתבא דעתה סברא אי איכא מידי חזייא חברתאי ועבדא לי · ואם היתה צריכה לשמן מביאה לה שמן כרב אשי דאמר מביאה לה בכלי דרך שערה נועצת כלי של שמן בשערה כדי שלא [יהא] הוצאה ביד כדרך המוציאין ומסקנא כמה דאית לשנויי משנינן ואם צריכה למאכל מביאין לה · מר זוטרא מתני אמר רב יהודה אמר שמואל חיה כל זמן שהקבר פתוח · פירוש הקבר בית הרחם · בין אמרה צריכה אני ובין אמרה איני צריכה מחללין עליה את השבת · נסתם (הכלי) [הקבר] אמרה צריכה

רב נסים גאון

כדי שיתפרש תחומין אחד מחבירו ויאמינו בכך לענין עירובן של תחומים ושיתופם כי השרשים שהוא משלח בקרקע מוכיחים על הגבולים ועל פי זה אמרו שם במסכת יום טוב (פרק אין צדין דף כה) חצובא סקטע רגליהון דרשיעיא שהוא דבר שאין בו רוח חיים ובצמיחתו משלח שרשיו בארץ במשפט והרשעים מעקמין דרכיהם ואין הולכין בדרכיו של הקב"ה כמו שראוי להם לכן דרכם באפילה: **צער** בעלי חיים דאורייתא מה שאמר הקב"ה (שמות כג) כי תראה חמור שונאך רובץ תחת משאו ואמרו בבא מציעא בפרק אלו מציאות (דף לב) מצוה מן התורה לפרוק דקסבר תנא דידן צער בעלי חיים דאורייתא ורבי יוסי הגלילי סבר צער בעלי חיים דרבנן וסבר (אביי) [רב יהודה] בכאן כתנא קמא דצער בעלי חיים דאורייתא וביטול כלי מהיכנו דרבנן משכחת לה בפרק כירה (לעיל דף מג) דתנן אין נותנין כלי תחת הנר לקבל בו את השמן ואמר רב חסדא אין נותנין כלי תחת התרנגולת לקבל ביצתה כו' ופירש רב יוסף טעמא בכך ואמר היינו טעמא דרב חסדא דקא מבטל כלי מהיכנו והא מרבנן הוא:

סליק פרק מפנין

food for dogs; [128b] putrid meat, because it is food for beasts; uncovered water,[4] because it is fit for a cat. R. Simeon b. Gamaliel said: It may not be kept at all, because of the danger.[5]

MISHNAH. A BASKET MAY BE OVERTURNED BEFORE FLEDGLINGS, FOR THEM TO ASCEND OR DESCEND.[6] IF A FOWL RUNS AWAY [FROM THE HOUSE], SHE IS PUSHED [WITH THE HANDS] UNTIL SHE RE-ENTERS. CALVES AND FOALS MAY BE MADE TO WALK, AND A WOMAN MAY MAKE HER SON WALK.[7] R. JUDAH SAID: WHEN IS THAT? IF HE LIFTS ONE [FOOT] AND PLACES [ANOTHER] DOWN; BUT IF HE DRAGS THEM IT IS FORBIDDEN.[8]

GEMARA. Rab Judah said in Rab's name: If an animal falls into a dyke, one brings pillows and bedding and places [them] under it, and if it ascends it ascends. An objection is raised: If an animal falls into a dyke, provisions are made for it where it lies so that it should not perish. Thus, only provisions, but not pillows and bedding?—There is no difficulty: here it means where provisions are possible; there, where provisions are impossible. If provisions are possible, well and good;[9] but if not, one brings pillows and bedding and places them under it. But he robs a utensil
a of its readiness [for use]?[1]—[The avoidance of] suffering of dumb animals is a Biblical [law], so the Biblical law comes and supersedes the [interdict] of the Rabbis.[2]

IF A FOWL RUNS AWAY. We may only push [it], but not make it walk. We have here learnt what our Rabbis taught: An animal, beast, or bird may be made to walk in a courtyard, but not a fowl. Why not a fowl?—Said Abaye, Because she raises herself.[3]

One [Baraitha] taught: An animal, beast, and bird may be made to walk in a courtyard, but not in the street; a woman may lead her son in the street, and in the courtyard it goes without saying. Another taught: An animal, beast, and bird may not be carried[4] in a courtyard, but we may push them that they should enter. Now this is self-contradictory. You say, We may not carry, which implies that we may certainly make them walk; then you say, we may only push but not lead?—Said Abaye: The second clause refers to a fowl.

Abaye said: When one kills a fowl he should [either] press its legs on the ground or else lift them up,[5] lest it places its claws on the ground and tears its organs loose.[6]

MISHNAH. ONE MAY NOT DELIVER AN ANIMAL [IN GIVING BIRTH] ON A FESTIVAL, BUT ONE MAY ASSIST IT. WE MAY DELIVER A WOMAN ON THE SABBATH, SUMMON A MIDWIFE FOR HER FROM PLACE TO PLACE, DESECRATE THE SABBATH ON HER ACCOUNT, AND TIE UP THE NAVEL-STRING. R. JOSE SAID: ONE MAY CUT [IT] TOO. AND ALL THE REQUIREMENTS OF CIRCUMCISION MAY BE DONE ON THE SABBATH.

GEMARA. How may we assist? Rab Judah said: The new-born [calf, lamb, etc.] is held so that it should not fall on the earth. R. Naḥman said: The flesh is compressed in order that the young should come out. It was taught in accordance with Rab Judah. How do we assist? We may hold the young so that it should
b not fall on the ground, blow into its nostrils,[1] and put the teat into its mouth that it should suck. R. Simeon b. Gamaliel said: We stimulate pity[2] to a clean animal[3] on a Festival. What was done?—Said Abaye: A lump of salt was brought and placed in its womb so that it [the mother] might remember its travails[4] and have pity upon it; and we sprinkle the water of the after-birth[5] upon the newly-born [animal] so that its mother might smell it and have pity upon it. Yet only [in the case of] a clean [animal], but not an unclean one. What is the reason? An unclean animal does not spurn its young, and if it does spurn it, it does not take it back.[6]

ONE MAY DELIVER A WOMAN, etc. Consider: He [the Tanna] teaches, ONE MAY DELIVER A WOMAN AND SUMMON A MIDWIFE FOR HER FROM PLACE TO PLACE, then what does AND DESECRATE THE SABBATH ON HER ACCOUNT add?—It adds the following taught by the Rabbis: If she needs a lamp, her neighbour may kindle a lamp for her. And if she needs oil, her neighbour brings her oil[7] in her hand;[8] but if that in her hand is insufficient, she brings it in her hair; and if that in her hair is insufficient, she brings it to her in a vessel.

The Master said: 'If she needs a lamp, her neighbour may kindle a lamp for her.' That is obvious?—This is necessary [to be taught] only in the case of a blind [woman]: you might argue, Since she cannot see it, it is forbidden; hence he informs us that we tranquillize her mind, [as] she reasons, if there is anything [required] my friend will see it and do it for me.

'If she needs oil, etc.' [But] deduce it on the grounds of wringing
c out?[1]—Rabbah and R. Joseph both answer: [The interdict of] wringing out does not apply to hair. R. Ashi said: You may even say that wringing out does apply to hair: she brings it to her in a vessel by means of her hair,[2] [because] as much as we can vary it we do so.[3]

Rab Judah said in Samuel's name: If a woman is in confinement, as long as the uterus is open, whether she states, 'I need it,' or 'I do not need it,' we must desecrate the Sabbath on her account. If

(4) V. *supra* 109b, n. b11. (5) To a human being who may drink it. (6) Into or from the hen-coop. (7) The verb refers to the short hop-like steps made by a child when he is just learning to walk. (8) As the mother in effect carries him. The reference is to a public domain. (9) Lit., 'yes'.

a (1) Because once he places the bedding under the animal, he may no longer remove it on Sabbath, v. *supra* 43a. (2) The prohibition of depriving a utensil on a Sabbath of its readiness for use, with the result that one carries it. This is forbidden as *mukzeh*. The broad humaneness of this is striking, particularly when it is remembered that it antedates by many centuries any similar view elsewhere. Cf. *supra* 117b, n. b6. (3) But ducks when held by their wings actually walk. (4) Lit., 'you may not remove' (their feet from the ground simultaneously). (5) So that they cannot touch the ground at all. (6) Viz., the windpipe and the gullet. If these are torn loose before being cut the animal or bird is unfit for food.

b (1) To clear them of their mucus, etc. (2) [I.e., arouses the maternal instinct of the animal for its young. Tosef. reads: 'pity *in*']. (3) I.e., one permitted as food. (4) In giving birth. (5) Water in which the placenta was soaked. (6) Lit., 'bring it near'—in spite of these expedients. (7) Through the street. (8) But not in a vessel, if it can be avoided.

c (1) I.e., if she brings it in her hair she must then wring it out, which is just as much forbidden as carrying it in a vessel. Since this is so, why not carry it ordinarily? (2) The vessel is attached to her hair. (3) When the Sabbath must be desecrated, we do it in as unusual a manner as possible.

the uterus is closed, whether she says, [129a] 'I need it' or 'I do not need it,' we may not desecrate the Sabbath for her:[4] that is how R. Ashi recited it. Mar Zuṭra recited it thus: Rab Judah said in Samuel's name: If a woman is in confinement, as long as the uterus is open, whether she says, 'I need it' or 'I do not need it,' we desecrate the Sabbath for her. If the uterus is closed, if she says, 'I need it,' we desecrate the Sabbath for her; if she does not say, 'I need it,' we do not desecrate the Sabbath for her.[5] Rabina asked Meremar: Mar Zuṭra recited it in the direction of leniency, [while] R. Ashi recited it in the direction of stringency; which is the law?—The law is as Mar Zuṭra, replied he: where [a matter of] life is in doubt we are lenient.

From when is the opening of the uterus?—Abaye said: From when she sits on the seat of travail. R. Huna son of R. Joshua said: From when the blood slowly flows down; others state, From when her friends carry her by her arms.[6] For how long is the opening of the uterus?—Abaye said: Three days: Raba said in Rab Judah's name: Seven; others maintain: Thirty.

The scholars of Nehardea said: A lying-in woman [has three periods: from] three [days after confinement], seven [days], and thirty [days]. From three [days], whether she says, 'I need it'
a or she says, 'I do not need it,'[1] we desecrate the Sabbath for her. [From] seven [days], if she says 'I need it,' we desecrate the Sabbath for her; if she says, 'I do not need it,' we do not desecrate the Sabbath for her. [From] thirty days, even if she says, 'I need it,' we may not desecrate the Sabbath for her,[2] yet we may do so by means of a Gentile,[3] as R. 'Ulla the son of R. Ilai, who said: All the requirements of an invalid may be done by means of a Gentile on the Sabbath, and as R. Hamnuna, who said: In a matter entailing no danger [to life], one bids a Gentile and he does it.

Rab Judah said in Samuel's name: For a woman in confinement [the period is] thirty days. In respect of what law? The scholars of Nehardea said: In respect of a ritual bath.[4] Raba observed: We said this only if her husband is not with her;[5] but if her husband is with her, he makes her warm. Even as R. Ḥisda's daughter performed *ṭebillah* within thirty days in her husband's absence,[6] caught a chill, and was carried in a bed to [her husband] Raba at Pumbeditha.

Rab Judah said in Samuel's name: We may make a fire for a lying-in woman on the Sabbath [in the winter].[7] Now it was understood from him, only for a lying-in woman, but not for an invalid; only in winter, but not in summer. But that is not so: there is no difference between a lying-in woman and any [other] invalid, and summer and winter are alike. [This follows] since it was stated, R. Ḥiyya b. Abin said in Samuel's name: If one lets blood and catches a chill, a fire is made for him even on the Tammuz [summer] solstice.[8] A teak chair was broken up for Samuel;[9] a table [made] of juniper-wood was broken up for Rab Judah. A footstool was broken up for Rabbah, whereupon Abaye said to Rabbah, But
b you are infringing, *thou shalt not destroy?*[1] '*Thou shalt not destroy*' in respect of my own body is more important to me, he retorted.

Rab Judah said in Rab's name: One should always sell [even] the beams of his house and buy shoes for his feet. If one has let blood and has nothing to eat, let him sell the shoes from off his feet and provide the requirements of a meal therewith. What are the requirements of a meal?—Rab said: Meat; while Samuel said: Wine. Rab said meat: life for life. While Samuel said, Wine: red [wine] to replace red [blood].

(Mnemonic: SHeNiMSaR.)[2] For Samuel on the day he was bled[3] a dish of pieces of milt was prepared; R. Joḥanan drank until the smell [of the wine] issued from his ears; R. Naḥman drank until his milt swam [in wine]; R. Joseph drank until it [the smell] issued from the puncture of bleeding.[4] Raba sought wine of a [vine] that had had three [changes of] foliage.[5]

R. Naḥman b. Isaac said to his disciples: I beg of you, tell your wives on the day of blood-letting, Naḥman is visiting us.[6] Now, all artifices are forbidden, save the following artifice, which is permitted. Viz., if one is bled and cannot [buy wine],[7] let him take a bad *zuz*[8] and go to seven shops until he has tasted as much as a *rebi'ith*.[9] But if not,[10] let him eat seven black dates, rub his temples with oil, and sleep in the sun. Ablaṭ[11] found Samuel sleeping in the sun. Said he to him, O Jewish Sage! can that which is injurious be beneficial? It is a day of bleeding, replied he.[12] Yet it is not so, but there is a day when the sun is beneficial for the
c whole year, [viz.,] the day of the Tammuz [summer][1] solstice, and he said to himself, I will not reveal it to him.[2]

(Mnemonic: Sparingly, wind, taste, tarry.) Rab and Samuel both say: If one makes light of the meal after bleeding his food will be made light of by Heaven, for they say; He has no compassion for his own life, shall I have compassion upon him! Rab and Samuel both say: He who is bled, let him not sit where a wind can enfold [him], lest the cupper drained him [of blood] and reduced it[3] to [just] a *rebi'ith*,[4] and the wind come and drain him [still further], and thus he is in danger. Samuel was accustomed to be bled in a house [whose wall consisted] of seven whole bricks[5] and a half-brick [in thickness]. One day he bled and felt himself [weak]; he examined [the wall] and found a half-brick missing.

Rab and Samuel both say: He who is bled must [first] partake of something and then go out; for if he does not eat anything, if he meets a corpse his face will turn green; if he meets a homicide

(4) As there is no danger of life. Asheri, however, reads: If she says, 'I need it', we desecrate (the Sabbath); if she does not say, 'I need it', we do not desecrate. (5) Asheri reads: If she says, 'I do not need it', we do not desecrate (the Sabbath); if she does not say, 'I do not need it', we do desecrate. (6) I.e, when she cannot walk.
a (1) Var. lec.: or she does not say, 'I need it'; similarly *infra*. (2) For she certainly does not need it and is in no danger. (3) Lit., 'Syrian'. (4) Which she must not take until thirty days for fear of a cold. (5) After the ritual bath, which she takes in order to eat *terumah*, etc. (6) Lit., 'not in her husband's presence'. (7) Lit., 'in the rainy season'. This is bracketed in the text. (8) Tammuz is the fourth month of the year, corresponding to about July. (9) For a fire, other wood being unavailable.
b (1) Deut. XX, 19, q.v.; this is understood as a general prohibition of wasteful destruction of any sort. (2) V. *supra* 25a, n. b1. *SH*=*SH*emuel (Samuel); *N*=R. JoḥaNan; *M*=R. NaḥMan; *S*=R. JoSeph; *R*=Raba. (3) Lit., 'when he did the thing'. (4) I.e., the hole made in his flesh when he was bled. Jast. s.v. כוילתא translates: until the puncture was healed up. (5) I.e., wine in its third year. (6) That they may prepare substantial meals! (7) Having no money. (8) I.e., a worn-out one which is not accepted as current coin. (9) A quarter of a *log*. Wine was tasted before buying; at each shop he would taste the wine and then proffer the coin, which, of course, would be refused. (10) He does not even possess such a coin. (11) A Persian sage and friend of Samuel, v. A.Z. 30a. (12) And I require heat.
c (1) Var. lec. Tebeth (winter). (2) Samuel possessed medical knowledge and did not wish to reveal trade secrets. (3) Lit., 'set it'. (4) Which was held to be the minimum quantity of blood which can sustain life. (5) A whole brick is three handbreadths.

צריכה אני · לחילול: בין שאמרה אין צריכה אני · וחברותיה אומרות שהיא צריכה מחללין: באגפיה · בזרועותיה שאינה יכולה להלך: חיה ג' ימים וז' ימים ול' יום · הוזכרו בה לחילוק הלכות חילול שבת ל' מז' עד השלמת ל' וכן ז' מג' עד השלמת ז': כל צרכי חולה · והא חיה עד ל' יום סתמא חולה היא: דבר שאין בו סכנה · חולה שאם לא יעשו לו רפואה זו אין מסוכן למות ומ"מ צריך הוא לה: אומר לארמאי ועושה · אבל דבר שיש בו סכנה ישראל עצמו עושה לו: לטבילה · עד ל' יום לא תטבול מפני הצינה: שאין בעלה עמה · והיא טובלת לטהרות: בעלה מחממה · לאחר טבילה בתשמיש והגוף מתחמם מן הגוף: מדורה · היסק גדול: הקיז דם · וכ"ש חולה: צלחו ליה תכתקא דשאגא · לא מצאו עצים מוכנים להיסק ביום הקזה וגזה ובקעו כסא של תדהר שהוא מעולה בדמים: פתורא דיונה · מין ארז הוא ורבינו הלוי אמר(א) בוי"ש: *רבה צלחו ליה שרשיפא · ספסל: ויקח מנעלים · שאין לך ביזוי מן המהלך יחף בשוק: (מאי) צרכי סעודה · (צרכי) סעודת הקזה: ביומא דמלתא · דהקזה: דטחלי · טחול סומקא חלף סומקא: עד דנפיק תיהי · הריח: מאוניה · מאזכיו מריחין היין: מריבדא דכוסילתא · נקבי כלי האומן שבבשרו פלימ"א: עד דקפי טחליה · טחול שלו צף ביין: בר תלתא טרפי · בן ג' שנים שטענה אמו משנקלט ג' עלין חדשין: לרבנן · לתלמידיו: אמרו נחמן איקלע לגבן · הרבו בסעודה כאילו אני סועד אצלכם: בר מהאי ערמה · דמפרש ואזיל: ולא אפשר ליה · לקנות יין: לשקול זוזא מכא · זוז רע ופחות שאינו יוצא בהוצאה: וליזיל לשב חנותא · ודרך הלוקחים לטועמו תחלה שיהא טוב ויטעום וכשיתן לו הזוז והחנווני ימצאהו רע ולא יקבלנו והוא ילך לחנות אחרת ויעשה כן: ואי לא · דאין לו זוז רע: ולישוף משחא בצידעיה · ברקתו והתמרים והשומן מחממין אותו: בישא מי הוה טבא · חום השמש שהוא קשה לאדם כלום מטיב לו: היכא דכריך זיקא · *אינדרו"ן שיש בו חלונות והרוח נכנסת בהם נכרכת · ומתגלגלת באינדרו"ן: דילמא שפי ליה אומנא · מריקו מדמו כמו השופה יין לחבירו (ב"מ דף ס·): ומוקי ליה ארביעתא · לא הניח בו דם אלא כדי חייו דהיינו רביעית והדר אתי ליה זיקא ושייף ליה מדם הנותר בגופו ומחסרו משיעורו ומסתכן: שב לביני ואריחא · עובי החומה ז' לבינים מוטלין לרחבן זה אצל זה דכל לבינה ג"ט ואריחא אריח חצי לבינה טפח ומחצה: ארגיש בנפשיה · הרגיש בעצמו שהוא נחלש: חסר חד אריחא · החומה היתה חסירה מעוביה אריח:

תורה אור

*צריכה אני בין לא אמרה צריכה אני אין מחללין עליה את השבת רב אשי מתני הכי מר זוטרא מתני הכי אמר רב יהודה אמר שמואל חיה כל זמן שהקבר פתוח בין אמרה צריכה אני ובין אמרה אין צריכה אני מחללין עליה את השבת נסתם הקבר אמרה *צריכה אני מחללין עליה את השבת לא אמרה צריכה אני אין מחללין עליה את השבת א"ל רבינא למרימר מר זוטרא מתני לקולא ורב אשי מתני לחומרא הלכתא כמאן א"ל הלכה כמר זוטרא *ספק נפשות להקל מאימתי פתיחת הקבר אמר אביי *משעה שתשב על המשבר רב הונא בריה דרב יהושע אמר [ב]משעה שהדם שותת ויורד ואמרי לה [ג]משעה שחברותיה נושאות אותה באגפיה עד מתי פתיחת הקבר אמר אביי שלשה ימים רבא אמר משמיה דרב יהודה שבעה ואמרי לה שלשים אמרי נהרדעי [ד]חיה ג' ז' ול' ג' בין אמרה צריכה אני ובין *אמרה לא צריכה אני מחללין עליה את השבת ז' אמרה צריכה אני מחללין עליה את השבת אמרה לא צריכה אני אין מחללין עליה את השבת ל' אפי' אמרה צריכה אני אין מחללין עליה את השבת אבל עושין ע"י ארמאי *כדרב עולא בריה דרב עילאי דאמר כל צרכי חולה נעשין ע"י ארמאי בשבת *וכדרב המנונא דאמר רב המנונא *[ה]דבר שאין בו סכנה *אומר לנכרי ועושה אמר רב יהודה אמר שמואל לחיה ל' יום למאי הלכתא אמרי נהרדעי לטבילה אמר רבא לא אמרן אלא שאין בעלה עמה אבל בעלה עמה בעלה מחממה כי הא דברתיה דרב חסדא טבלה בגו תלתין יומין שלא בפני בעלה ואצטניאת ואמטוי לערסה בתריה דרבא לפומבדיתא *אמר רב יהודה אמר שמואל [ו]עושין מדורה לחיה בשבת (בימות הגשמים) סבור מינה לחיה אין לחולה לא בימות הגשמים אין בימות החמה לא (*ולא היא ל"ש חיה ול"ש חולה ל"ש בימות הגשמים ול"ש בימות החמה מדאתמר) אמר רב חייא בר אבין אמר שמואל [ז]הקיז דם ונצטנן עושין לו מדורה אפי' בתקופת תמוז שמואל צלחו ליה תכתקא דשאגא רב יהודה צלחו ליה פתורא דיונה לרבה צלחו ליה שרשיפא וא"ל אביי לרבה והא קעבר מר משום °בל תשחית *א"ל בל תשחית דגופאי עדיף לי אמר רב יהודה אמר רב לעולם ימכור אדם קורות ביתו ויקח *מנעלים לרגליו הקיז דם ואין לו מה יאכל ימכור מנעלים שברגליו ויספיק מהן צרכי סעודה מאי צרכי סעודה רב אמר בשר ושמואל אמר יין רב אמר בשר נפשא חלף נפשא ושמואל אמר יין סומקא חלף סומקא: (סימן שנמסר) *שמואל ביומא דעבד מילתא עבדי ליה תבשילא דטחלי ר' יוחנן שתי עד דנפיק תיהיא מאוניה ורב נחמן שתי עד דקפי טחליה רב יוסף שתי עד דנפיק מריבדא דכוסילתא רבא מהדר אחמרא בר תלתא טרפי אמר להו רב נחמן בר יצחק לרבנן במטותא מינייכו ביומא דהקזה אמרו לביתייכו נחמן אקלע לגבן וכולהו אערומי אסירי בר מהאי ערמה דשרי מאן דעביד מילתא ולא אפשר ליה לישקול זוזא מכא וליזיל לשב חנותא עד דטעים שיעור רביעתא ואי לא ליכול שב תמרי אוכמתא ולישוף מישחא בצידעיה וניגני בשמשא אבלט אשכחיה לשמואל דגני בשמשא א"ל חכימא דיהודאי בישא מי הוי טבא א"ל יומא דהקזה הוא ולא היא אלא איכא יומא דמעלי בה שמשא בכוליה שתא יומא דנפלה ביה תקופת *תמוז וסבר לא איגלי ליה: (היקיל ברוח טעמא שהה סימן) רב ושמואל דאמרי תרוייהו כל המקיל בסעודת הקזת דם מקילין לו מזונותיו מן השמים ואומרים הוא על חייו לא חס אני אחוס עליו רב ושמואל דאמרי תרוייהו האי מאן דעביד מילתא לא ליתיב היכא דכריך זיקא דילמא שפי ליה אומנא ומוקים ליה ארביעתא ואתי זיקא ושאיף מיניה ואתי לידי סכנה שמואל הוה רגיל ועבד מילתא בביתא דשב לביניא ואריחא יומא חדא עבד וארגיש בנפשיה בדק וחסר חד אריחא רב ושמואל דאמרי תרוייהו האי מאן דעביד מילתא ליטעום מידי והדר ליפוק דאי לא טעים מידי אי פגע בשכבא ירקא אפיה אי פגע במאן דקטל נפשא מית אי פגע בדבר

רבא משמיה דרב יהודה אמר שבעה · לכאורה משמע דרבא לטעמיה דבפרק הדר (עירובין דף סח·) גבי ההוא ינוקא דאישתפוך חמימיה אמר להו רבא נישיילה לאימיה אם צריכה ניחיימו אגב אימיה דמסתמא ביום שמיני היה קודם מילה שהיה צריך חמין למולו דלאחר מילה מסוכן הוא ובלא אימיה ביום שמיני מחללין עליו שבת והיינו לאחר שבעה דבנכנסה הקבר בעינן צריכה מיהו ללישנא דאמרי לה צרבא שלשים תיקשי למה צריכה ועוד דבקונטרס פי' התם ניחיימו אגב אימיה ע"י נכרי וכן פירש ר"ח לכך יש לפרש דאביי ורבא ואמרי לה מר אמר חדא ומר אמר חדא ולא פליגי וכולהו קיימו כנהרדעי*:

רבינו חננאל

צריכה אני מחללין עליה את השבת אמרה איני צריכה אין מחללין עליה את השבת ומסקינן לה לשמעתא דא"ל מרימר לרבינא הלכתא פי' הא דמר זוטרא ספק נפשות להקל והוצרכנו לדקדק מאימתי פתיחת הקבר כדי לחלל באותו העת את השבת לעשות צרכי החיה · ואמר אביי משתשב על המשבר · ואמר רב הונא בריה דרב יהושע משעה שהדם שותת ויורד כו' ודייקי מדלא אמר רב הונא עד שיתחיל הדם להיות שותת ש"מ קודם שתשב על המשבר קאמר וכאביי עבדינן *ולא מחללי שבתא אלא עד שיהא שותת · קדם שותת ויורד ותשב על המשבר אבל דהא דאמר אביי משום רב יהודה עד מתי פתיחת הקבר ג' ימים בלבד אין הלכה כמותו · ולא כרבא דאמר משמיה דרב יהודה שבעה · אלא קיי"ל כנהרדעא דאמרי חיה ג' ז' ושלשים · ג' בין אמרה צריכה אני בין אמרה איני צריכה מחללין עליה את השבת · ז' אמרה צריכה אני מחללין עליה את השבת אמרה איני צריכה אין מחללין עליה את השבת · סתמא עבדינן כמר זוטרא לקולא · שלשים אפילו אמרה צריכה אני אין מחללין עליה את השבת · אלא עושין לה ע"י ארמאי כדרב עולא בריה דרב עילאי דאמר כל צרכי הולד נעשין ע"י ארמאי בשבת וכדרב המנונא דאמר דבר שאין בו סכנה אומר לנכרי ועושה · חיה לא תטבול בתוך שלשים יום שמא תצטנן אמר רבא לא אמרן אלא שאין בעלה עמה · אבל בעלה [עמה בעלה] מחממה · אמר רב יהודה אמר שמואל עושין מדורות לחיה בשבת סבור מינה לחיה אין לחולה לא [בימות הגשמים אין] בימות החמה לא וכו' ומסקינן משמא דשמואל הקיז דם ונצטנן עושין לו מדורה ואפילו בתקופת תמוז · שמעינן מינה אפילו לחולה ואפילו בימות החמה · שמואל צלחו ליה תכתקא דשאגא · פי' שמואל הקיז דם ולא היה לו עצים מוכנים להדליק ולהתחמם בהן ובקעו לו שידה שהיו עציה עצי שאגא והן יקרים להודיע שאם יתמהמה עד שיביאו לו עצים יסתכן וכדתרגם ויבקע עצי העולה וצלח אעי דעלתא · רב יהודה צלחו ליה פתורא פי' שולחן העשוי מעצי ‏יָ‏נֵ‏ם והן יקרים פי' יאבנוס · ורבה צלחו ליה שרשיפא והוא הדום לכסא וכולן מעם אחד· שאם לא ימהרו להתחמם יסתכנו

*) נ"ל ולא מחללי שבתא עד שתהא הדם שותת ויורד ותשב על המשבר וכו' וכ"כ הרי"ף כאן משמיה דרבותא ופשט דכוונתו על דברי רבינו כאן:

לג א ב ג מיי' פ"ב מהל' שבת הלכה יג סמג לאוין סה טוש"ע א"ח סימן של סעיף ג:
לד ד מיי' שם טוש"ע שם ס"ד:
לה ה מיי' שם הלכה י סמג שם טוש"ע א"ח סי' שכח סעיף יז:
לו ו מיי' שם הלכה יד סמג שם טוש"ע א"ח סימן של סעיף ו:
גי' רא"ש אמרה איני צריכה אין מחללין לא אמרה איני צריכה מחללין
לז ז מיי' וסמג שם טוש"ע א"ח סימן שכח סעיף יח:
[וע"ע תוס' בגיטין ע: ד"ה אע"ג]
[שם ע"ש]
*[עיין רש"י גיטין ע: ד"ה כדאמר רבא]
ס"א ז"א וס"ג לא איתמר אמר ר"ח כו'
[לקמן קמ:]
[עי' פסחים קיב.]

גי' רא"ש אמרה צריכה אני מחללין לא אמרה צריכה אין כו'
בן גי' הערוך בערך שרפרף אולם הגאון מהרי"ף הגיה כאן שצ"ל רבה
[יומא פג. סד: כתובות ו. ב"ק מד: ל. ב"ב נ: סנהדרין עט.]
ס"י הגירסא לא אמרה צריכה וכן לקמן
[ביצה כב.]
ביצה שם וכו' שאלתות פרש' שמות סי' לח ריא ואמר רב המנונא דבר שאין בו וכו'
עירובין עט:
אין זה בלעז כ"א לשון תלמ' אכסדרא דבי רב כאינדרונא צעלית' מנחות לג:
חולין קיח.]
ס"א סבת

הגהות הב"ח
(א) רש"י ד"ה פתורא דיונה כו' מויי"ש · נ"ב עצי ברותים:

גליון הש"ס
גמרא משעה שתשב על המשבר · עיין ס"ן מ"ד אהלות כר"ש:

עין משפט נר מצוה

[וע"ע תוספות כתובות ג. ד"ה שבתי דינין]

לח א מיי' פ"ד מהלכות דעות הלכה יח:

לט ב מיי' שם הל' ג:

מ ג מיי' שם הלכה יט טוש"ע א"ח סי' רמ סעיף טו:

מא ד מיי' פ"ד מהלכות דעות הלכה יח:

מב ה ש"ע א"ח סימן תסח סעי' י בהג"ה:

מג ו מיי' פ"ב מהלכות שבת הלכה יא יג סמג לאוין סה טוש"ע א"ח סימן של סעיף ז:

גמרא

בדבר אחר קשה לדבר אחר רב ושמואל דאמרי תרווייהו האי מאן דעביד מילתא לישהי פורתא והדר ליקום דאמר מר *ה' דברים קרובין למיתה יותר מן החיים ואלו הן אכל ועמד שתה ועמד ישן ועמד הקיז דם ועמד שימש מטתו ועמד אמר שמואל פורסא דדמא כל תלתין יומין ובין הפרקים ימעט ובין הפרקים יחזור וימעט ואמר שמואל פורסא דדמא חד בשבתא ארבעה ומעלי שבתא אבל שני וחמישי לא דאמר מר מי שיש לו זכות אבות יקיז דם בשני ובחמישי שב"ד של מעלה ושל מטה שוין כאחד בתלתא בשבתא מאי טעמא לא משום דקיימא ליה מאדים *בזווי מעלי שבתא נמי קיימא בזווי כיון דדשו ביה רבים שומר פתאים ה' (תהלים קטז) אמר שמואל ד' דהוא ד' ד' דהוא ארביסר ד' דהוא עשרים וארבעה ד' דליכא ארבע בתריה סכנתא ר"ח ושני לו חולשא שלישי לו סכנה מעלי יומא טבא חולשא מעלי יומא דעצרתא סכנתא וגזרו רבנן אכולהו מעלי יומא טבא משום יומא טבא דעצרת דנפיק ביה זיקא ושמיה טבוח דאי לא קבלו ישראל תורה הוה טבח להו לבשרייהו ולדמייהו אמר שמואל אכל חטה והקיז דם לא הקיז אלא לאותה חטה והנ"מ לרפואה אבל לאוקולי מיקל המקיז דם שתייה לאלתר אבילה עד חצי מיל איבעיא להו שתייה לאלתר מעלי אבל בתר הכי קשי או דילמא לא קשי ולא מעלי תיקו איבעיא להו אכילה עד חצי מיל הוא דקמעלי הא בתר הכי ומקמי הכי קשי או דילמא לא קשי ולא מעלי תיקו *מכריז רב מאה קרי בזוזא מאה רישי בזוזא מאה שפמי ולא כלום אמר רב יוסף כי הוינן בי רב הונא יומא דמפגרי ביה רבנן אמרי האידנא יומא דשפמי הוא ולא ידענא מאי קאמרי: וקושרין הטבור: ת"ר *קושרין הטבור ר' יוסי אומר אף חותכין וטומנין השליא כדי שיחם הולד אמר רשב"ג בנות מלכים טומנות בספלים של שמן בנות עשירים בספוגים של צמר בנות עניים במוכין *אמר רב נחמן אמר רבה בר אבוה אמר רב הלכה כר' יוסי ואמר רב נחמן אמר רבה בר אבוה אמר רב מודים חכמים לר' יוסי בטבור של שני תינוקות שחותכין מ"ט דמנתחי אהדדי ואמר רב נחמן אמר רבה בר אבוה אמר רב כל האמור בפרשת תוכחה עושין לחיה בשבת שנאמר ומולדותיך ביום הולדת אותך לא כרת שרך ובמים לא רחצת למשעי והמלח לא המלחת והחתל לא חתלת (יחזקאל טז) ומולדותיך ביום הולדת מכאן שמיילדים את הולד בשבת לא כרת שרך מכאן שחותכין הטבור בשבת ובמים לא רחצת למשעי מכאן שרוחצין הולד בשבת והמלח לא המלחת מכאן שמולחין הולד בשבת והחתל לא חתלת מכאן שמלפפין הולד בשבת:

הדרן עלך מפנין

רש"י

בדבר אחר · חזיר: קשה לדבר אחר · לרעת שהחזירים מנוגעים הם כדאמרינן בקדושין (ד' מט:) י' קבים נגעים ירדו לעולם תשעה נטלו חזירים: אכל ועמד · מהר לעמוד פתאום אחר שאכל שובעו: פורסא דדמא · זמן הקזה כמו בפרוס הפסח (שקלים פ"ג מ"א): בין הפרקים · פירקי שטתיו כגון לאחר מ' שנה: ימעט · בהקזה לא יקיז בכל חדש אלא לב' חדשים: ובין הפרקים יחזור וימעט · לאחר ששים יקיז לג' חדשים לפי שאין כחו עליו ואין דמו חם וגופו מלטנן כשמחסר דמו: שב"ד של מעלה ושל מטה שוין · אדם נדון בכל יום וב"ד יושבין בעיירות בב' ובה' מתקנת עזרא ואילך (ב"ק ד' פב.) וכיון דיום הדין ופקידה היא שטתיו נזכרים: דקיימא ליה מאדים בזווי · שמזל מאדים משמש בו בשעות זוגות ומזל מאדים ממונה על החרב ועל הדבר ועל הפורעניות והזוגות קשין שהן רשות לשדים כדאמר בפסחים (ד' קי:) והפורעניות מוכנין של"מ חנכ"ל סדר השעות כשנתלו המאורות והמזלות שעה ראשונה של ד' בשבת שימש שבתאי ובשניה לדק ואחריו מאדים ואחריו חמה ואחריו נוגה ואחריו כוכב ואחריו לבנה נמלאו ז' המזלות לז' השעות וחוזרים חלילה לעולם נמצא בסדר זה לעולם סימני מזלות המשמשין בתחלת לילי השבוע כלכ"ש חל"ם מולאי שבת שעה ראשונה שלו כוכב תחלת ליל שני לדק וכן בסדר הזה וסדר תחלת סימני הימים חל"ם כלכ"ש שעה ראשונה של אחד בשבת חמה ושל שני בשבת לבנה ושל שלישי בשבת מאדים נמלא מאדים חוזר בו חלילה בשעה שמינית ביום והיא זוגות אבל שאר ימים אין מאדים בזוגות שלהם אם לא בלילה ובלילה אין דרך להקיז: מעלי שבתא נמי קיימא מאדים בזווי · שהרי שעה ראשונה של יום נוגה לפי הסדר של חל"ם כלכ"ש תחלת הימים וכיון שתחלתו נוגה וסדר הליכתן של"ם חנכ"ל נמלאו מתחילין לחזור חלילה בשעה רביעית נמלא מאדים בשעה ששית: כיון דדשו ביה רבים · הורגלו בו מפני דוחקן שיהיו קרובים לסעודת שבת ואמרינן בפירקין דלעיל (ד' קיח:) כבוד שבת בדגים גדולים ובמסכת ע"ז (ד' כט:) אמרינן שני לדם דג: ארבע דהוא ד' · ד' בשבת שהוא ד' לחדש או ארביסר לחדש או כ"ד לחדש כולהן קשה להקזה: ד' דליכא ד' בתריה · שאין ד' ימים עד סוף החדש ואיכא דאמרי דליכא ד' בשבת בתריה באותו חדש ולאו כן: ה"ג ר"ח ושני לו חולשא שלישי לו סכנתא: אכל חטה והקיז דם לא הקיז אלא לחטה · שהאוכל מכביד את האדם והקזה שאחר אכילה אינו מועיל אלא לאותו כובד: וה"מ · במקיז לרפואה: אבל אקולי · מי שיש לו דם המכביד עליו אפי' לאחר אכילה מקיז ומיקל: מאה רישי בזוזא · כלומר אם יהיו בזול מאד קנה ראשי בהמה ואם לאו אל תקח שאינך בריאין לאכול: מאה קרי · דלועין: מאה שפמי · כמו על שפם (ויקרא יג) גרווינ"ן בלעז שפתים של בהמה: יומא דמפגרי ביה רבנן · שהיו התלמידים מתעצלין מלבא בבית המדרש קרי ליה יומא דשפמי כלומר היום הזה אבד לו ואין בו תועלת: וטומנין את השליא · כדמפרש רשב"ג שהיא רפואה להתחמם הולד: ספוגין של צמר · צמר מנופץ: של שני תינוקות · תאומים וקשורין טבורן זה בזה: משום דמנתחי מהדדי · זה אילך וזה אילך ונמצאו מסוכנין: בפרשת תוכחה · שהוכיח יחזקאל לישראל את חסדי הקב"ה שעמהן: תוכחה · לשון לכו ונוכחה (ישעיה א) להתווכח ולהודיע מי הוא שסרח על שכנגדו: למשעי · לטוח ולהחליק בשרו: שמולחין · ובשרו מתקשה: מלפפין · אנמליו"ן בלע"ז ולאו הייט אסובי יטקא דאמרן לעיל בפרק כל הכלים (דף קכג:) דהא שמעינן ליה לרב נחמן דאסר אלא *לפופי בעלמא כמו שעושין בחגורות ופסיקיאות: הדרן עלך מפנין

[וכן איתא לעיל סו: לפופי יטקא בשבת שפיר דמי וע"ש בפרש"י וכן עוד לקמן קמז: ובפרש"י שם]

תוספות

מי שיש לו זכות אבות · וקודם תקנת עזרא אע"פ שהיו דנין בכל יום שהיו צריכים לא היו קובעים ליסב בכל יום*:

דקאי מאדים בזווי · ברביעי נמי קאי מאדים בזווי בסוף היום אלא לא חשו חכמים לכך דאין דרך להקיז כל כך בסמוך ללילה:

דליכא ארבע בתריה · שאין ד' ימים עד סוף החדש כדפירש בקונטרס דליכא למימר רביעי בשבת דהא ד' דהוא עשרין וארבע הייני דליכא רביעי בתריה:

מאה רישי בזוזא מאה קרי בזוזא · לפירוש הקונטרס תימה מה שייך הכא ור"ח גרים מאה קרני בזוזא ומפרש מאה רישי מאה ראשי בני אדם (ונראה) שהיה מנהג קצוב לספר לגלח בזוזא וכן מנהג ק' קרני להקיז בזוזא כמו קרנא דאומנא (לקמן דף קנד:) אבל מאה שפמי לתקן השפה בולא כלום דבשכר גילוח והקזה היה מתקן השפה וביום שהיה מתקן שפמו לא היה נוטל כלום ועל כן היה למשל כל מי שהיה יגע ולא עלה בידו שכרו היו קורין אותו יומא דשפמי:

מפגרי רבנן · תשש כחם והיו מתחלשין ולא יכלו למיגרס כדכתיב (ש"א ל) וירדוף דוד הוא וארבע מאות איש (עמו) ויעמדו מאתים איש אשר פגרו מעבור את נחל הבשור:

כל האמור בפרשת תוכחה · לאו מקרא מפיק אלא מסתמא כיון שבא בפרשת תוכחה אם כן לער הוא אם אין עושין והקילו חכמים לעשות ובכולן אין בהן איסורא דאורייתא:

הדרן עלך מפנין

מסורת הש"ס

גיטין ע.

[עיין תוספות עירובין נו. ד"ה ואין]

[תוספ' פט"ו]

[לעיל קכח: והטבור לא היה כתוב בה כדאמר רב נחמן הלכה כר' יוסי ועיין בי"א סימן של]

[מכאן עד יומא דשפמי תמצא פירוש יפה בערוך ערך פגר בשינוי הנוסח']

גליון הש"ס

גמרא כיון דדשו ביה רבים שומר פתאים. עיין חסיד סי' רי"א: רש"י ד"ה מלפפים וכו' בחגורות ופסיקיאות. עיין לקמן דף קמז ע"ב ברש"י ד"ה בחומרי סדרא וכו' ועי' בתשובת אדמת קודש חלק א"ח סי' ח:

רבינו חננאל

יסתכנו · פי' זוזא מכא · זוז מעוך שנמעך מטבע הצורה ונראה כאסימון · דעביד מלתא · באותו היום שמקיז דם · פורסא דדמא כל תלתין יומין · פי' גבול הדם לבחורים כל שלשים יום · בין הפרקים הגיע לחמשים שנה ימעט · יוציא משנים חדשים [או] ג' חדשים · פעם אחת עוד בין הפרקים בא בימים יחזור ימעט מששה חדשים לששה חדשים או משנה לשנה וזה הפי' קיבלנוהו מרבותינו קבלה: **בתלתא** קאי מאדים בזווי. פי' בשתי שעות שהן זוגות יום שלישי שעה שמינית מאדים ושעה שתים ועשרים מאדים ושכך סידור הכוכבים חל"ם כצנ"ש בימים נמצא יום אחד שעה ראשונה כוכב חמה יום שני שעה ראשונה כוכב לבנה · יום ג' שעה ראשונה כוכב מאדים יום ד' שעה ראשונה כוכב [כוכב] · יום ה' שעה ראשונה כוכב צדק יום ו' שעה ראשונה כוכב נוגה · יום ז' שעה ראשונה כוכב שבתי וסידורן חל"ם כצנ"ש בימים כצנ"ש חל"ם בלילות וסידוריהן חנכ"ל שצ"ם · וכיון שביום ג' עומד מאדים בשעה שמינית והן זוגות ובשעה כ"ב והן זוגות חיישינן לסכנה · וכיוצא בזה בשני ובחמישי משום הכי חיישינן לסכנה · כי מאדים הוא ממונה על הדם ואקשינן עלה והא יום ו' הוא דמעלי שבתא דקאי מאדים בשעה ששית ובשעה עשרים והן זוגות · ואמרת פורסא דדמא חד בשבא וארבעה ומעלי שבתא . ולא מצאו לו פירוק · והשיב אע"פ שהוא כן כיון דדשו בה רבים להקיז ביום ששי שומר פתאים ה' · מאה רישי בזוזי מאה קרני בזוזא שפמי ולא כלום פי' היה מנהג קצוב כי הספר מגלח מאה ראשי כלומר מאה ראשי בני אדם נוטל שכרו זוז אחד וכן (א' מדוגמא) [המשים] מאה קרן כלומר מאה קרן של זכוכית והוא ריבדא דכוסילתא נוטל בשכרו בק' קרן זוז אחד. אבל לתקן הזקן וליטול השפה ולתקנו לא היה מנהג ליקח האומן כלום אלא אותן בני אדם שמגלח ראשם או עושה להן ריבדא דכוסילתא נוטל שכרו כאשר אמרנו מתקן זקנם ונוטל שפמם בחנם. וכן היה הדין ויום שהיה האומן עושה השפמות לא היה נוטל שכר והיה הולך לביתו ריקם. ועל כן היה למשל כל מי שהיה יגע ולא [היה] עולה בידו (סבר) [שכר] היה קורא אותו יומא דשפמי. מיפגרי תשש כחם והוו מתחלשי ינעים ויעפים ולא יכלי למיגרס כדכתיב וירדף דוד הוא וארבע מאות איש ויעמדו מאתים איש אשר פגרו מעבור וגו' הוו אמרי יומא דשפמי*): וקושרין את הטיבור. ר' יוסי אומר אף חותכין את הטיבור כל צרכי מילה עושין בשבת אמר רב נחמן אמר רבה בר אבוה הלכה כרבי יוסי שחותכין בשבת טיבור תינוק אחד וכ"ש טיבור ב' תינוקות שבזה אפילו חכמים מודים שמחתך מ"ט משום (דמתחזי) [דמנתחו] אהדדי · ואמר רב נחמן אמר רבה בר אבוה אמר רבכל האמור בפרשת תוכחה עושין לחיה בשבת שנא' ומולדותיך ביום הולדת אותך מיכן שמיילדין לחיה בשבת לא כרת שרך מיכן שחותכין את הטיבור בשבת ובמים לא רוחצת למשעי מיכן שמרחיצין את הולד בשבת והחתל לא חתלת מיכן שמלפפין הולד בשבת ואמרינן בתלמוד א"י ומחללין עליה את השבת שמואל אמר עושין לה מדורה אפילו בתקופת תמוז וקושרין את הטיבור כהדא אמתיה דבר קפרא נפקא מיילדה בשבת אתת ושאלת לר' וא' לה אזלון ושאלון לחייתא · אמרה לה ליכא חייא אמר לה זילי עבידי כמנהגך אמרה ליה ליכא מנהג אמר לה איזיל חתיך כר' יוסי כבמתניתא וכל צרכי חיה עושין בשבת תני השליא הזאת בשבת עשירין טומנין אותה בשמן והעניים בתבן ובחול אלו ואלו טומנין אותה בארץ כדי ליתן ערבון בארץ [לארץ]: הדרן עלך מפנין

*) עיין בערוך ערך פגר .

he will die; and if he meets [129b] a swine,[6] it [the meeting] is harmful in respect of something else.[7]

Rab and Samuel both say: One who is bled should tarry awhile and then rise, for a Master said: In five cases one is nearer to death than to life. And these are they: When one eats and [immediately] rises, drinks and rises, sleeps and rises, lets blood and rises, and cohabits and rises.

Samuel said: The correct interval for blood-letting is every thirty days; in middle age[8] one should decrease [the frequency];[9] at a [more] advanced age[10] he should again decrease [the frequency]. Samuel also said: The correct time for blood-letting is on a Sunday, Wednesday and Friday, but not on Monday or Thursday, because a Master said: He who possesses ancestral merit may let blood on Monday and Thursday, because the Heavenly Court
a and the human court are alike then.[1] Why not on Tuesday?—Because the planet Mars rules at even-numbered hours of the day.[2] But on Friday too it rules at even-numbered hours?—Since the multitude are accustomed to it,[3] *'the Lord preserveth the simple.'*[4]

Samuel said: A Wednesday[5] which is the fourth [of the month], a Wednesday which is the fourteenth, a Wednesday which is the twenty-fourth, a Wednesday which is not followed by four [days][6]—[all] are dangerous.[7] The first day of the month and the second [cause] weakness; the third is dangerous. The eve of a Festival [causes] weakness; the eve of Pentecost is dangerous, and the Rabbis laid an interdict upon the eve of every Festival on account of the Festival of Pentecost, when there issues a wind called Ṭaboaḥ,[8] and had not the Israelites accepted the Torah it would absolutely have killed them.[9]

Samuel said: If one eats a grain of wheat and [then] lets blood, he has bled in respect of that grain only.[10] Yet that is only as a remedy,[11] but if it is to ease one,[12] it does ease.[13] When one is bled, drinking [is permissible] immediately; eating until half a *mil*.[14] The scholars asked: [Does this mean], immediate drinking is beneficial, but after that it is injurious; or perhaps [after that] it is neither harmful nor beneficial?—The question stands over. The scholars asked: Is eating beneficial only until half a *mil*, but before or after it is harmful; or perhaps it is [then] neither harmful nor beneficial? The question stands over.

Rab announced: A hundred gourds for one *zuz*, a hundred
b heads for one *zuz*, a hundred lips for nothing.[1] R. Joseph said: When we were at R. Huna's academy, on a day that the scholars took a holiday they would say, 'This is a day of lips,' but I did not know what they meant.

WE TIE UP THE NAVEL-STRING. Our Rabbis taught: We tie up the navel-string. R. Jose said: We cut [it] too; and we hide the after-birth, so that the infant may be kept warm. R. Simeon b. Gamaliel said: Princesses hide [it] in bowls of oil, wealthy women in wool fleeces, and poor women in soft rags.

R. Naḥman said in Rabbah b. Abbuha's name in Rab's name: The *halachah* is as R. Jose. R. Naḥman also said in Rabbah b. Abbuha's name in Rab's name: The Sages agree with R. Jose in the case of the navel-string of twins, that we cut them. What is the reason? Because they pull upon each other.[2]

R. Naḥman also said in Rabbah b. Abbuha's name in Rab's name: All that is mentioned in the chapter of rebuke[3] is done for a lying-in woman on the Sabbath. As it is said, *And as for thy nativity, in the day thou wast born thy navel was not cut, neither wast thou washed in water to cleanse thee; thou wast not salted at all, nor swaddled at all.*[4] *'And as for thy nativity, in the day thou wast born'*: hence an infant may be delivered on the Sabbath; *'thy navel was not cut'*: hence the navel-string is cut on the Sabbath: *'neither wast thou washed in water to cleanse thee'*: hence the infant is washed on the Sabbath; *'thou wast not salted at all'*: hence the infant is salted on the Sabbath; *'nor swaddled at all'*: hence the infant is swaddled on the Sabbath.

(6) Lit., 'something else'. (7) Viz., leprosy, which this may cause. (8) Lit., 'at the middle stages', viz., from forty onwards (Rashi). (9) The body then begins to lose heat, and frequent bleeding may be injurious. (10) Rashi: from the age of sixty.
a (1) The court used to meet on Mondays and Thursdays, v. B.Ḳ. 82a. One's transgressions are punished in a time of natural risk. Cf. *supra* 32a. (2) Jast. *Ma'adim* lit., means the reddener. The hours as well as the months were thought to stand under the influence of planets which moulded their nature. The planet Mars represented war and pestilence and retribution, whilst the even-numbered hours of the day were regarded as particularly susceptible to disaster. This double combination was therefore very dangerous, and blood-letting might have serious results. (3) *Sc.* bleeding on Friday. (4) Ps. CXVI, 6. (5) Lit., 'fourth' day of the week. (6) In the same month (Rashi). (7) For bleeding. (8) Lit., 'slaughter'. (9) Lit., 'their flesh and blood.'

(10) I.e., bleeding immediately after a meal serves only to lighten one of that meal, but has no wider effects. (11) If it is done as a remedy it is ineffective. (12) E.g., if one suffers from high blood-pressure. (13) Even if performed immediately after a meal. (14) I.e., as long as it takes to walk that distance—about nine minutes; v. *supra* 34b, 35a.
b (1) Rashi: gourds and animal-heads are but slightly beneficial, and they are worth having only when a hundred can be bought for one *zuz*; but the lips of animals are quite worthless. Tosaf., reading with R. Han. קרני instead of קרי translates: a hundred (surgeons') horns (i.e., bleedings) for one *zuz*, a hundred heads (i.e., hair cuttings) for one *zuz*, a hundred lips (trimmings of moustaches) for nothing, as this was free if done at the same time as the bleeding or hair cutting. Thus 'a day of lips' became a proverbial description of a day without profit. (2) Which endangers their lives. (3) Wherein Ezekiel rebukes the Jews; ch. XVI. (4) Ezek. XVI, 4.

CHAPTER XIX

MISHNAH. [130a] R. ELIEZER SAID: IF ONE DID NOT
a BRING AN INSTRUMENT ON THE EVE OF THE SABBATH,[1] HE MUST BRING IT ON THE SABBATH UNCOVERED;[2] BUT IN [TIMES OF] DANGER[3] HE HIDES IT ON THE TESTIMONY OF WITNESSES. R. ELIEZER SAID FURTHER: ONE MAY CUT TIMBER TO MAKE CHARCOAL FOR MANUFACTURING IRON.[4] R. AKIBA STATED A GENERAL PRINCIPLE: ANY [MANNER OF] WORK WHICH COULD BE PERFORMED ON SABBATH EVE DOES NOT SUPERSEDE THE SABBATH; BUT THAT WHICH COULD NOT BE PERFORMED ON SABBATH EVE DOES SUPERSEDE THE SABBATH.

GEMARA. The scholars asked: Is R. Eliezer's reason[5] out of love for the precept,[6] or perhaps it is because of suspicions?[7] What is the practical difference? Whether it may be brought covered on the testimony of witnesses. If you say it is out of love for the precept, it must be uncovered and not hidden. But if you say it is because of suspicions, it is well even if hidden: what then? It was stated, R. Levi said: R. Eliezer ruled thus only out of love for the precept. It was taught likewise: He must bring it uncovered, and he must not bring it covered: this is R. Eliezer's opinion.[8] R. Ashi said: Our Mishnah too proves this, because it states, BUT IN TIMES OF DANGER HE HIDES IT ON THE TESTIMONY OF WITNESSES; thus in times of danger only, but not when there is no danger. This proves that it is out of love for the precept: this proves it.

Another [Baraitha] taught: He brings it uncovered, but he must not bring it covered: this is R. Eliezer's view. R. Judah said in R. Eliezer's name: In times of danger it was the practice to
b bring it hidden on the testimony of witnesses.[1] The scholars asked: The witnesses which he mentions, [does it mean] he and another one, or perhaps he and another two?—Come and hear: BUT IN [TIMES OF] DANGER HE HIDES IT ON THE TESTIMONY OF WITNESSES: if you agree to say he and two [others], it is well; but if you say he and another, what witnesses [are there]?[2]—Such as are eligible to testify elsewhere.[3]

R. ELIEZER SAID FURTHER [etc.]. Our Rabbis taught: In R. Eliezer's locality they used to cut timber to make charcoal for making iron on the Sabbath. In the locality of R. Jose the Galilean they used to eat flesh of fowl with milk. Levi visited the home of Joseph the fowler [and] was offered the head of a peacock in milk, [which] he did not eat. When he came before Rabbi he asked him, Why did you not place them under the ban?[4] It was the locality of R. Judah b. Bathyra, replied he, and I thought, Perhaps he has lectured to them in accordance with R. Jose the Galilean. For we learnt: R. Jose the Galilean said: It is said, *Ye shall not eat any* nebelah,[5] and it is said, *Thou shalt not seethe a kid in its mother's milk:*[6] [this teaches,] that which is forbidden on the score of *nebelah* may not be seethed in milk. Now since a fowl is prohibited when *nebelah*, you might think that one must not seethe it in milk; therefore it is stated, '*in its* mother's *milk*', hence a fowl is excluded, since it has no mother's milk.

R. Isaac said: There was one town in Palestine where they
c followed R. Eliezer,[1] and they died there at the [proper] time.[2] Moreover, the wicked State[3] once promulgated a decree against Israel concerning circumcision,[4] yet did not decree [it] against that town.

It was taught, R. Simeon b. Gamaliel said: Every precept which they accepted with joy, e.g., circumcision, as it is written, *I rejoice at thy word, as one that findeth great spoil,*[5] they still observe with joy. While every precept which they accepted with displeasure,[6] e.g., the forbidden degrees of consanguinity, as it is written, *And Moses heard the people weeping throughout their families,*[7] [i.e.,] on account of the affairs of their families,[8] they still perform them with strife, for there is no marriage settlement which does not contain a quarrel.[9]

It was taught, R. Simeon b. Eleazar said: Every precept for which Israel submitted to death at the time of the royal decree, e.g., idolatry and circumcision,[10] is still held firmly in their minds. Whereas every precept for which Israel did not submit to death at the time of the royal decree, e.g., *tefillin*, is still weak in their hands.[11] For R. Jannai said: *Tefillin* demand a pure body, like Elisha-the-man-of-the-wings. What does this mean?—Abaye said: That one must not pass wind while wearing them; Raba said: That one must not sleep in them. And why is he called 'the man of-the-wings'? Because the wicked State once proclaimed a decree against Israel that whoever donned *tefillin* should have his brains pierced through; yet Elisha put them on and went out into the streets. A quaestor saw him: he fled before him, and the latter gave pursuit. As he overtook him, he [Elisha] removed them from his head and held them in his hand, 'What is that in your hand?' he demanded, 'The wings of a dove,' was his reply. He stretched out his hand and the wings of a dove were found therein. Hence he is called 'Elisha-the-man-of-the-wings.' And why did he tell him the wings of a dove rather than that of other birds? Because the Congregation of Israel is likened to a dove, as it is said, *as the wings of a dove covered with silver, and her pinions with*
d *yellow gold:*[1] just as a dove is protected by its wings, so with the Israelites, their precepts protect them.[2]

R. Abba b. R. Adda said in R. Isaac's name: They once forgot to bring a knife on Sabbath eve, so they brought it on the Sabbath

a (1) A knife for circumcision. (2) That all may see it. (3) When circumcision is forbidden by the State, as during the reign of Antiochus Epiphanes before the Maccabean revolt; v. I Macc. I, 48, 60, 11, 46. It was again forbidden during the Hadrianic persecution; cf. Mek. *Yithro, Ba-Ḥodesh*, VI; Graetz, *Geschichte* IV, 154. (4) For a circumcision knife. Thus R. Eliezer permits not only circumcision but even its preparatory adjuncts, though these could have been prepared before the Sabbath. (5) For requiring the knife to be brought uncovered. (6) One must show how precious is circumcision that he even desecrates the Sabbath on its account. (7) That would otherwise attach to the bringer, that he was unlawfully desecrating the Sabbath. (8) The emphatic repetition shows that it must not be hidden on any account.

b (1) 'It was the practice' implies that this is not a mere theoretical ruling but an actual account of what happened in the past. As R. Eliezer died before the Hadrianic wars, this must refer to the days of the persecution by Antiochus.—Weiss, *Dor*, II, p. 131, n. 1. (2) There is only one, as obviously he cannot be counted. (3) In truth it may be he and another, nevertheless there are two who know the purpose of his carrying, and they are referred to as witnesses, since two in general can testify. Yet two *independent* witnesses may not be required, since there is no actual lawsuit. (4) For infringing the dietary laws. (5) Deut. XIV, 21. (6) Ibid. 22—these laws are stated successively.

c (1) In respect of circumcision. (2) Never prematurely. (3) Rome. (4) Forbidding it; v. *supra* n. a3. (5) Ps. CXIX, 162. This is understood to refer to circumcision, which is a single 'word', i.e., command, which preceded the bulk of Mosaic legislation (this dating back to Abraham, Gen. XVII, 10), and which the Jew, in virtue of being circumcised, ceaselessly performs. (6) Lit., 'quarrelling'. (7) Num. XI, 10. (8) Viz., because they were now interdicted in marriage. (9) Lit., 'in which they (the parties concerned) throw no discord'. (10) Cf. *supra* n. a3. Antiochus demanded idol worship too; later, Caligula made a similar demand; v. Graetz, *History* (Eng. trans.) Vol. II, pp. 188 *seqq.*; cf. also Weiss, *Dor*, II, p. 5. (11) V. Weiss, op. cit., p. 134.

d (1) Ps. LXVIII, 14. (2) Cf. also *supra* 49a and notes a.l.

תורה אור

רבי אליעזר אומר אם לא הביא כלי מע"ש מביאו בשבת מגולה ובסכנה מכסהו ע"פ עדים ועוד אמר *ר"א כורתים עצים לעשות פחמין לעשות (כלי) ברזל *כלל אמר ר"ע °כל מלאכה שאפשר לעשותה מע"ש אינה דוחה את השבת (ומילה) שאי אפשר לעשותה מע"ש דוחה את השבת:

גמ' איבעיא להו טעמא דר"א משום חבובי מצוה או דילמא משום חשדא למאי נפקא מינה לאתויי מכוסה ע"פ עדים אי אמרת משום חבובי מצוה מגולה אין מכוסה לא אלא אי אמרת משום חשדא אפי' מכוסה שפיר דמי מאי איתמר א"ר לוי לא אמרה ר"א אלא לחבובי מצוה תניא נמי הכי מביאו מגולה ואין מביאו מכוסה דברי ר"א אמר רב אשי מתני' נמי דיקא דקתני ובשעת הסכנה מכסהו ע"פ עדים בסכנה אין שלא בסכנה לא שמע מינה משום חבובי מצוה שמע מינה תניא אידך מביאו מגולה ואין מביאו מכוסה דברי ר"א ר' יהודה אומר משום ר"א נוהגין היו בשעת הסכנה שהיו מביאין מכוסה ע"פ עדים איבעיא להו עדים דקאמר איהו וחד או דילמא הוא ותרי ת"ש ובסכנה מכסהו ע"פ עדים אי אמרת °בשלמא הוא ותרי שפיר אלא אי אמרת הוא וחד מאי עדים שראוים להעיד במקום אחר: ועוד אמר ר"א: *ת"ר במקומו של ר"א היו כורתין עצים לעשות פחמין לעשות ברזל בשבת במקומו של ר' יוסי הגלילי היו אוכלין בשר עוף בחלב לוי איקלע לבי יוסף רישבא קריבו ליה רישא *דטוותא בחלבא לא אכל כי אתא לקמיה דרבי א"ל אמאי לא תשמתינהו א"ל אתריה דר' יהודה בן בתירה הוה ואמינא דילמא דרש להו כר' יוסי הגלילי *דתנן ר' יוסי הגלילי אומר נאמר °לא תאכלו כל נבלה ונאמר °לא תבשל גדי בחלב אמו את שאסור משום נבלה אסור לבשל בחלב עוף שאסור משום נבלה יכול יהא אסור לבשל בחלב ת"ל בחלב אמו יצא עוף שאין לו חלב אם א"ר יצחק עיר אחת היתה בא"י שהיו עושין כר"א והיו מתים בזמנן ולא עוד אלא שפעם אחת גזרה מלכות הרשעה גזרה על ישראל על המילה ועל אותה העיר לא גזרה: תניא רשב"ג אומר כל מצוה שקיבלו עליהם בשמחה כגון מילה דכתיב °שש אנכי על אמרתך כמוצא שלל רב °עדיין עושין אותה בשמחה וכל מצוה שקבלו עליהם בקטטה °כגון עריות דכתיב °וישמע משה את העם בוכה למשפחותיו *על עסקי משפחותיו עדיין עושין אותה בקטטה דליכא כתובה דלא רמו בה תיגרא תניא ר"ש בן אלעזר אומר כל מצוה שמסרו ישראל עצמן עליהם למיתה בשעת גזרת המלכות כגון עבודת כוכבים ומילה עדיין היא מוחזקת בידם וכל מצוה שלא מסרו ישראל עצמן עליה למיתה בשעת גזרת המלכות כגון תפילין עדיין היא מרופה בידם *דא"ר ינאי תפילין צריכין גוף נקי כאלישע בעל כנפים מאי היא אמר אביי שלא יפיח בהם רבא אמר שלא יישן בהם ואמאי קרו ליה אלישע בעל כנפים שפעם אחת גזרה מלכות הרשעה גזרה על ישראל שכל המניח תפילין על ראשו יקרו את מוחו והיה אלישע מניח תפילין ויצא לשוק וראהו קסדור אחד רץ מלפניו ורץ אחריו כיון שהגיע אצלו נטלן מראשו ואחזן בידו א"ל מה בידך אמר לו כנפי יונה פשט את ידו ונמצאו בה כנפי יונה לפיכך היו קוראין אותו בעל כנפים *מאי שנא כנפי יונה דא"ל ולא א"ל שאר עופות משום דדמיא כנסת ישראל ליונה שנאמר °כנפי יונה נחפה בכסף ואברותיה בירקרק חרוץ מה יונה זו כנפיה מגינות עליה אף ישראל מצות מגינות עליהן: א"ר אבא בר רב אדא א"ר יצחק פעם אחת שכחו ולא הביאו איזמל מערב שבת והביאוהו בשבת [דרך גגות ודרך חצירות] שלא

דברים יד / שם
תהלים קיט
במדבר יא
תהלים סח

רש"י

רבי אליעזר אומר אם לא הביא כלי · איזמל למול את התינוק וקאי אמתניתין דפרקין דלעיל* דסליק מיניה וכל צרכי מילה עושין בשבת: מגולה · בפני הכל ובגמרא מפרש אמאי מצריך ליה לגלוייה: ובסכנה · שגזרו ארמאים על המילה: מכסהו ע"פ עדים · שיעידו שאיזמל של מצוה הוא מביא ולא יחשדוהו: כלל אמר ר"ע · נחלק על ר"א במכשירי מצוה שאין דוחין הואיל ואפשר לעשותן מע"ש: [ושאי אפשר לעשות מע"ש · כגון] מילה עצמה שא"א לה ליעשות דזמנה ביום השמיני דוחה שבת: **גמ'** טעמא דר"א · דאמר מגולה אין מכוסה לא: משום חיבוב מצוה · להודיע שחביבה מצוה עליו שמחלל שבת עליה: משום חשדא · שלא יחשדוהו שהוא נושא שאר חפציו וסיפא דמתני' דקתני ובסכנה מכסהו ע"פ עדים ודאי משום חשדא הוא אלא רישא מיבעיא לן דוקא מגולה קאמר אבל מכוסה ע"פ עדים שלא בשעת הסכנה לא ומשום חיבוב מצוה או לאו דוקא מגולה דטעמיה משום חשדא וה"ה למכוסה על פי עדים: אי אמרת בשלמא הוא ותרי שפיר · היינו דמיקרו עדים אלא הוא וחד מי מיקרי עדים איהו לגביה נפשיה מי מיקרי עד: ומשני שראוים להעיד במקום אחר · לעולם הכא עדות לא שייכא דלאפוקי מחשדא בעלמא הוא ואין כאן לא דיני ממונות ולא דיני נפשות שיהו שנים(א) ומאי קרו להו עדים דאיכא גילוי מילתא ע"י השני ושנים קרו עדים בעדות אחריתי שאינו נוגע בה: לעשות ברזל · לאיזמל של מילה: היו אוכלין בשר עוף בחלב · כדלקמן: רישבא · לייד עופות: נאמר לא תאכלו כל נבלה ונאמר · באותו פסוק עצמו לא תבשל גדי משמע כל האסור משום נבלה נוהג בו איסור בשר בחלב: שש אנכי על אמרתך · אמירה יחידה שקדמה לשאר אמירות והיא מילה שישראל עושין ושש עליה דכל שאר מצות אינן מוכיחות כל שעה כגון תפילין ומזוזה וציצית דאינן כשהוא בשדה וערום בבית המרחץ אבל זו מעיד עליהם לעולם כדאמרינן במנחות (דף מג:) בדוד שראה עצמו בבית המרחץ ונצטער אמר אוי לי שאני ערום מכל מצות כיון *שנסתכל במילה נתיישבה דעתו: בשמחה · שעושין משתה: על עסקי משפחותיו · שנאסר להם קרובות: מרופה · רפויה: דא"ר ינאי תפילין צריכות גוף נקי · שלא יפיח אלמא לא זהירי בהו ושמעינן מינה דלא מסרו עליה אלא אלישע לבדו: יקרו · פוריי"ר בלעז לשון יקרוה עורבי נחל (משלי ל) ולשון תנקר לא נעלה (במדבר טז): את מוחו · שכנגד תפילין: קסדור · ממונה: מגינות *עליהן · אינה נלחמת בחרטומיה אלא בכנפיה: דרך

תוספות

רבי אליעזר אומר אם לא הביא כלי כו' מביאו בשבת מגולה · °וא"ת ויביאו התינוק אצל כלי דהשתא ליכא איסור שבת כלל דהאי טעה את עצמו וי"ל דקטן צריך לאמו הוא ואחר המילה היה צריך להחזירו לאמו ואז הוי כפות(ג) לפי שהוא חולה כדאמרינן ביומא (דף סו:) אפי' תימא ר' נתן חולה שאני וגם אמו שהיא מסוכנת לא תוכל לבא אצל התינוק ועוד י"ל כיון דיותר בקל יביא הכלי משיביא התינוק שרי ר"א כדי למהר המצוה כדמוכח בגמרא דאמר פעם אחת שכחו ולא הביאו איזמל מע"ש והביאו בשבת שלא ברצונו שהביאו דרך אגרות וגגות וקרפיפות והיו יכולין להביא דרך רה"ר אלמא דשרי ר"א דרך רה"ר דהוי דאורייתא (ג) °כדי למהר המצוה אע"פ שיכול לעשות [בענין] דליכא אלא איסורא דרבנן: **שש** אנכי · במדרש (שוחר טוב) למנצח על השמינית כתיב הנדרש על המילה שהיא בשמיני וכן אמרי'(ד) (פר"א פ' כ"ט) ויעש אברהם משתה גדול ביום הגמל את יצחק ביום ה"ג מל את יצחק דהיינו ביום השמיני דמילה כמנין ה"ג · ר"ת: **אמר** ליה כנפי יונה · הרי שלא מסר עצמו לומר תפילין הן · רבינו שמואל: שלא

מסורת הש"ס

[קכח:]
[מכר לקמן קלו. ובעירובין קב: קג.]
יבמות יד. חולין קטז. ע"ש
[נ"ל דטווסא עיין בערוך פירושו] חולין קיג.
יומא עה.
[נ"ל שנזכר]
לעיל מט.
[מנחות מג: לעיל מט. [illegible]] [נ"ל [illegible]]

הגהות הב"ח

(א) רש"י ד"ה ומשני וכו' ואמאי קרי להו: (ב) תוס' ד"ה ר' אליעזר וכו' ואז הוי כפות: נ"ב עיין בפרק סמאלים דף לד ע"א: (ג) בא"ד כדי למהר המצוה · נ"ב עיין בסוף עירובין דף קג ע"ב בתוספות ד"ה מה לי: (ד) ד"ה שש וכו' וכן אמרי' במדרש ויעש אברהם:

עין משפט נר מצוה

א א מיי' פ"ב מהלכות מילה הלכה ו סמג עשין כח טוש"ע א"ח סי' שלא סעיף ו וטוש"ע י"ד סימן רסו סעיף ב:

ב ב טוש"ע י"ד סימן רסה סעיף יב:

ג ג מיי' פ"ט מהלכות איסורי ביאה הל' יח סמג לאוין קכד:

פסחים סו. שם: יבמות יד. מנחות עב. נו.

רבינו חננאל

פרק יט

רבי אליעזר אומר אם לא הביא כלי מערב שבת מביאו בשבת מגולה וכו' ואיבעיא לן האי דקתני ר' אליעזר אומר מביאו מגולה משום חבובי מצוה הוא או משום שלא יחשדוהו שהוציא חפציו טמונים לפיכך מגליהו שיראו שסכין של מצוה הוא · ופשטנא דמשום חבובי מצוה הוא היכא דליכא סכנה ותוב איבעיא לן האי דתנא במתניתא רבי יהודה משום רבי אליעזר [אומר] נוהגים היינו בסכנה מביאין אותו (בסכנה) מכוסה ע"פ עדים הני עדים שנים אחרים זולתו המביאו או דלמא הוא ואחרים ולא איפשטא בהדיא: לוי איקלע לבי יוסף רישבא קריבו ליה רישא דטווסא בחלבא לא אכל כי אתא לקמיה דר' א"ל מ"ט לא שמתינהו א"ל אתרא דר' יהודה בן בתירא ואמרי דלמא דריש להו כרבי יוסי הגלילי דסבר יצא עוף שאין לו חלב אם: א"ר יצחק עיר אחת היתה בא"י שהיו עושין כר' אליעזר והיו מתיה מתין בזמנן ולא עוד אלא שפעם אחת גזרה מלכות הרשעה גזרה על ישראל על המילה ועל אותה העיר לא גזרה *) כל השבח ואין הלכה כר"א ולא כר' יוסי הגלילי שמתיר בשר עוף בחלב ולא כרבי ינאי שאמר תפילין צריכין גוף נקי כאלישע בעל כנפים ומפרשי רבנן כי לא אמר רבי ינאי אלא בשעת הגזרה וסמיך דהוא עריק ועבדי ליה נס אמר ראבין בר רב אדא א"ר יצחק פעם אחת שכחו ולא הביאו איזמל מע"ש והביאוהו

*) נראה דנ"ל לאחר כל השבח הזה מ"מ אין הלכה כר"א וכו'

גליון הש"ס

גמ' בשלמא הוא ותרי · עיין תשובת הרא"ש ח"א סי' פ"ט: תוס' ד"ה רבי אליעזר וכו' וא"ת ויביאו התינוק · עיין לעיל דף לד ע"א תוספות ד"ה אבל אדם: בא"ד כדי למהר המצוה · עיין עירובין דף קג ע"ב תוס' ד"ה מה לי:

ד א מיי׳ פ״ב מהלכות מילה הלכה ו סמג עשין כח טוש״ע א״ח סימן שלא סעיף ו וטוש״ע י״ד סימן רסו סעיף ב :

ה ב מיי׳ פ״ג מהלכות עירובין הלכה יח סמג עשין דרבנן א טוש״ע א״ח סימן שעב סעיף א :

ו ג מיי׳ פ״ה מהלכות עירובין הלכה טו סמג שם טוש״ע א״ח סימן שפה :

ז ד מיי׳ פ״ה מהלכות שבת הלכה יז סמג שם טוש״ע א״ח סימן שסג סעיף כו :

שלא ברצון ר״א מתקיף לה רב יוסף שלא ברצון ר״א אדרבה ר״א הוא דשרי וכי תימא שלא ברצון ר״א דשרי אפילו ברה״ר אלא ברצון רבנן דאסרו דרך רה״ר ושרו דרך גגות דרך חצירות וקרפיפות ומי שרי *והתניא *כשם שאין מביאין אותו דרך רה״ר כך אין מביאין אותו לא דרך גגות ולא דרך קרפיפות ולא דרך חצירות אלא אמר רב אשי שלא ברצון ר״א ומחלוקתו אלא ברצון ר״ש *דתנן ר״ש אומר אחד בגגות(א) ואחד קרפיפות ואחד חצירות כולן רשות אחד הן לכלים ששבתו בתוכן ולא לכלים ששבתו בתוך הבית בעא מיניה רבי זירא מר׳ אסי מבוי שלא נשתתפו בו מהו לטלטל בכולו מי אמרינן כחצר דמי מה חצר אע״ג דלא ערבו מותר לטלטל בכולו האי נמי אע״ג דלא נשתתפו בו מותר לטלטל בכולו או דילמא לא דמי לחצר דחצר אית ליה ד׳ מחיצות האי לית ליה ד׳ מחיצות א״נ חצר אית ליה דיורין האי לית ביה דיורין שתיק ולא א״ל ולא מידי זימנין אשכחיה דיתיב וקא אמר אמר ר״ש בן לקיש משום ר׳ יהודה הנשיא פעם אחת שכחו ולא הביאו איזמל מע״ש והביאוהו בשבת והיה הדבר קשה לחכמים היאך מניחין דברי חכמים ועושין כר״א חדא דר״א שמותי *הוא ועוד יחיד ורבים *הלכה כרבים וא״ר אושעיא שאילית את רבי יהודה הגוזר ואמר לי מבוי שלא נשתתפו בו הוה ואייתוהו מהאי רישא להאי רישא א״ל ס״ל למר מבוי שלא נשתתפו(ב) מותר לטלטל בכולו וא״ל אין א״ל והא זימנין בעאי מינך ולא אמרת לי(ג) הכי *דילמא אגב שיטפך רהיט לך גמרך א״ל אין אגב שיטפא רהיטא לי גמרי *איתמר אמר רבי זירא אמר רב מבוי שלא נשתתפו בו אין מטלטלין בו אלא בד׳ אמות אמר אביי הא מילתא אמרה רבי זירא ולא פירשה עד דאתא רבה בר אבוה ופירשה דאמר רב נחמן אמר רבה בר אבוה אמר רב גמבוי שלא נשתתפו בו עירבו חצירות עם בתים אין מטלטלין בו אלא בד׳ אמות לא עירבו חצירות עם בתים מותר לטלטל בכולו אמר ליה רב חנינא חוזאה לרבה מאי שנא כי עירבו חצירות עם בתים דניתקו חצירות ונעשו בתים ורב לטעמיה *דאמר רב דאין המבוי ניתר בלחי וקורה עד שיהו בתים

רש״י

דרך גגות ודרך חצירות · שלא עירבו זו עם זו ואיכא איסורא דרבנן : שלא ברצון ר״א ומחלוקתו · קאמר דר״א אפילו ברה״ר שרי ואינהו דאייתו דרך חצרות גלי אדעתייהו דאין מכשירי מילה דוחין שבת ושלא ברצון החלוקין עליו דאסרי דרך חצרות דהעמידו חכמים דבריהם דאיסור (*) שבת אף במקום כרת : אלא ברצון ר״ש · שמתיר אף לדבר הרשות : דתנן ר״ש אומר אחד גגות כו׳ כולן · ואפילו הן של בעלים הרבה מטלטלין מזה לזה דלא אסרו מרשות לרשות אלא בתים : קרפיפות · אם של בית סאתים הוא מטלטל בכולו ואם יותר ולא הוקף לדירה קרי ליה רשות אחת לגבי חבירו או לגבי חצר לטלטל ב׳ אמות בזה וב׳ אמות בזה להוציא ולהכניס מזה לזה : ששבתו בתוכן · שכשקדש היום היו בתוכו ולא בתוך הבית דאילו שבתו כלים בבית לא מיבעיא היכא דלא עירבו בני בתי החצר דאפילו מבית לחצר לא יוציאו כלי הבית אלא אפילו עירבו ומטלטל מבית לחצר לא יוציאו כלי הבית מחצר זו לחברתה שלא עירבו עמה : שלא נשתתפו בו · עירוב דחצירות במבוי קרי שיתוף : מהו לטלטל · בתוכו בכולו כלים ששבתו בתוכו ולהוציא מן החצר לתוכו פשיטא לן דאסור וכן ממנו לחצר : מה חצר אע״ג דלא עירבו · הרבה בתים שבחצר ביחד ואסור להכניס ולהוציא מבתים לחצר ומחצר לבתים : מותר לטלטל בכולו · מה שנמצא בתוכו או בגדיו שהוציאן מן הבית לתוכו דרך מלבוש *פוסטן ומטלטלן בכולו לדברי הכל דג׳ מחלוקות הן בעירובין בפרק כל גגות לדברי ר׳ מאיר גגין רשות לעצמן ומטלטלין מזה לזה ואפילו של בעלים הרבה וחצרות רשות לעצמן לטלטל מזו לזו בלא עירוב כלים ששבתו בתוכם אבל לא מגגין לחצרות וקרפיפות רשות לעצמן ולדברי חכמים גגין וחצרות רשות אחת וקרפיפות רשות אחת ולדברי ר״ש כולן רשות אחת חוץ מן הבתים : א״נ חצר אית ביה דיורין · כלומר עשויה להשתמש בה תדיר : האי אין בו דיורין · שהדיורין בבתים הן והבתים פתוחין לחצירות וחצירות למבוי : זמנין · פעם אחרת : אשכחיה · רבי זירא לר׳ אסי : שמותי הוא · ברכוהו כדאמרינן בהזהב (ב״מ דף נט:) ובתלמוד ירושלמי *מפ׳ שמותי הוא מתלמידי שמאי היה : וא״ר אושעיא · לאותן שהיה קשה עליהן מה ששמעו : שאילית את רבי יהודה הגוזר · המל את התינוקות : ואייתוהו מהאי רישא · שהיה התינוק בבית שבראש המבוי והאיזמל בבית שבראש האחר שכנגדו עד כאן דברי ר׳ אסי : א״ל · רבי זירא אלמא ס״ל למר מדאמר ליה להא ולא קשיא לך ביה מידי סבירא לך מותר לטלטל בכולו : הכי גרסינן והא זמנין בעאי מינך ולא אמרת דילמא אגב שיטפא אתיא לך · כשהיית שטוף בגרסתך לחזור על שמועה זו דר״ל עם מרוצת גרסתך אתיא לך כך דר׳ אושעיא בהדא דאיתמר עלה : ולא פירשה · אימתי מותר ואימתי אסור : עירבו חצרות · שבמבוי עם בתיהם שבני הבתים מוציאין לחצרותיהן שעירבו בתים הפתוחים לחצר יחד וכן בני חצר האחרת אבל בני החצרות לא נשתתפו במבוי : אין מטלטלין · במבוי אפי׳ כלים ששבתו בתוכו אלא בד׳ : לא עירבו חצרות עם בתיהן · שאסורים בני הבתים להוציא מבתיהן לחצריהם : מותר לטלטל בכולו · כלים ששבתו בתוכו ולקמיה מפרש טעמא : ונעשו בתים · בטלו לגבי הבתים ואין שם חצרות עליהם : בתים

תוספות

שלא ברצון ר״א דשרי אפי׳ ברה״ר · קשה לרשב״א הא אמרינן לקמן בפירקין (דף קלג·) כל מקום שאתה מוצא עשה ולא תעשה אם אתה יכול לקיים את שניהם מוטב כו׳ והכא כיון דאפשר לקיים את שניהם להביאו דרך גגות וחצירות וקרפיפות אמאי יביאו אותו דרך רה״ר וליכא למימר דלגבי מילה דגלי רחמנא בה דדחי שבת כדדרשינן לקמן לא אמרינן הכי דהא לקמן(ד) גבי בשר אפי׳ במקום בהרת יקוץ כו׳ אמרינן כדר״ל דאמר ר״ל כל מקום שאתה מוצא כו׳ : ומי שרי והתניא · וא״ת ולוקמי שהביאו דרך חצר מעורבת דהוי כרצון חכמים ושלא כרצון ר״א דשרי אפי׳ דרך רה״ר וי״ל דבכה״ג לא הוה(ה) שרי ר״א מן רה״ר כיון שיכול להביאו דרך חצר מעורבת בהיתר גמור א״נ לישנא דשכחו לא משמע כן דאי היתה מעורבת לא ה״ל למימר שכחו אלא לא חשו להביאו מע״ש כיון דבשבת אפשר להביאו בהיתר גמור אבל כי מסיק ברצון ר״ש אתי שפיר דקאמר שכחו שאם היו נזכרין מע״ש היו מביאין משום דפליגי רבנן עליה : ברצון ר״ש · ה״ה דהוה מצי למימר ברצון ר״מ שהביאו דרך גגות מגג לגג או דרך חצרות מחצר לחצר כדמוכח בפרק כל גגות (עירובין דף פט·) דאית ליה כל גגות העיר רשות אחת הן וכן חצרות וקרפיפות אלא נקט ר׳ שמעון דקי״ל כוותיה : לכלים ששבתו לתוכו · וכן היה אותו איזמל : דרבי אליעזר שמותי הוא · מב״ש וכן מוכח בירושלמי במסכת תרומות בפרק סאה תרומה דתנן התם סאה תרומה טמאה שנפלה למאה סאין טהורין בית שמאי אוסרים וב״ה מתירין כו׳ עד לאחר שהודו ר״א אומר תירום ותישרף ואמר בגמרא(ו) בן פזי ורבי אייבו בר נגרי הוו יתבין ואמרי תנינן אחר שהודו ר״א אומר תירום ותישרף מי הודה למי א״ר אסי מתניתין אמרה כן לאחר שהודו ר״א אומר תירום ותישרף ר״א לאו שמותי הוא הרי משמע דשמותי הוא מתלמידי ב״ש דמיכה קא פשיט דב״ש הודו לב״ה · ר״ת* : ניתקו חצרות ונעשו בתים · פירוש וחשיב כאילו אין כאן חצר כלל שהחצר נעשה בית וכשלא עירבו חשיבי בתים כליתנהו ומיהו חצר לא חשיב כליתא אע״פ שאסור לטלטל *) מתוכו למבוי כיון שאין(ז) דרך מפסיק בינו למבוי לא חשוב [כסתום] אבל בתים כסתומות חשיבי כיון שהחצר מפסיק בינם למבוי ודוקא היכא דלא נשתתפו בעינן בתים וחצרות פתוחין לתוכו אבל נשתתפו לא בעינן ומשני אפשר דמבטלי רשות גבי חד דהשתא איכא בית דלא חשיב כסתום ולא אמר נמי ניתקו חצרות כולם כיון דשאר הבתים אסורין בחצר ופריך בית איכא בתים ליכא ולא מצי למימר דבטלי רשות גבי תרי שהם היו אוסרין זה על זה ולא מצי למימר שהשנים עירבו דהא מדקאמר רב לא עירבו משמע לא עירבו כלל :

רבינו חננאל

בשבת שלא כרצון רבי אליעזר ושקלינן וטרינן בה ואוקמא רב אשי שלא כרצון ר׳ אליעזר דשרי אפילו דרך רה״ר ושלא ברצון מחלוקתו והם החכמים שחולקים על ר׳ אליעזר ואומרים אפילו דרך גגות ודרך חצירות וכו׳ דרבי עקיבא סבירא ליה כוותיהון אלא כרצון ר׳ שמעון דשרי דרך גגות דתנן ר׳ שמעון אומר אחד גגות ואחד חצירות ואחת קרפיפות כו׳ · בעא ר׳ זירא מר׳ אמי מבוי שלא נשתתפו בו מהו לטלטל בכולו כו׳ ושתק ר׳ אמי ולא השיב לו זמנין אשכחיה דאמר אמר ר״ל משום רבי יהודה נשיאה פעם אחת שכחו ולא הביאו אזמל מע״ש והביאוהו בשבת והיה הדבר קשה לחכמים היאך מניחין דברי חכמים ועושין כר׳ אליעזר שהן דברי יחיד ועוד רבי אליעזר שמותי הוא כלומר מתלמידי שמאי הוא · א״ר אושעיא שאילית את ר׳ יהודה הגוזר פי׳ המל ואמר לי מבוי שלא נשתתפו בו הוה ואתיוה מהאי רישא להאי רישא אמינא ליה סבירא ליה למר מבוי שלא נשתתפו בו מותר לטלטלו בכולן א״ל אין כו׳ · אתמר ר׳ זירא אמר רב מבוי שלא נשתתפו בו אין מטלטלין בו אלא בארבע · ר׳ זירא לא פירש שמועה זו היטב עד דאתא רב נחמן אמר רבה בר אבוה ופרשה משמיה דרב הכי מבוי שלא נשתתפו בו אם עירבו חצרות עם בתיהם אין מטלטלין בו אלא בארבע לא עירבו חצרות עם בתיהם מותר לטלטל בכולו א״ל רב חנינא חוזאה לרבא מפני מה כי עירבו עם בתיהם אין מטלטלין באותו מבוי אלא בארבע דניתקו חצרות ונעשו בתים כלומר כיון שעירבו נעשו בתי החצר והחצר רשות אחת ורב לטעמיה דאמר אין מבוי ניתר בלחי וקורה עד שיהו בתים

*) פי׳ ר״ל לדבריו דס״ל דבתים אין לה וא״כ אינו ניתר בלחי וקורה ולו לא ס״ל ר״ש דרשות א׳ הן וא״כ גם חצר אין לה וא״כ היאך אמר וחצירות איכא ועי׳ בטוא״ח סימן שעב וברמב״ם פ״ג מה״ע ומשכחת ליה לר״ש מבוי דניתר בלחי וקורה כמ״ש התוספות לקמן דבטלי רשות לגבי תרי ואותן תרי עירבו יחד וכוונת התוספות להקשות בין על עירבו ובין על לא עירבו וכדי שלא תאמר דזהו שמקשה המקשה באומרו בתים איכא חצרות ליכא בעירבו ע״כ פירשו התוספות דמ״ש ניתקו חצירות פירוש וחשיב כאלו כו׳

הגהות הב״ח

(א) גמ׳ אחד גגות ואחד חצרות ואחד קרפיפות רשות אחת : (ב) שם שלא נשתתפו בו מותר : (ג) שם ולא אמרת לי דילמא כצ״ל ותיבת הכי נמחק : (ד) תוס׳ ד״ה שלא וכו׳ דהא לקמן · נ״ב דף קלג ע״א : (ה) ד״ה ומי שרי וכו׳ שרי ר״א דרך רה״ר כיון : (ו) ד״ה דרבי אליעזר וכו׳ ואמר בגמרא רבי יהודה בן פזי : (ז) ד״ה ניתקו וכו׳ כיון שאין דבר מפסיק :

גליון הש״ס

רש״י ד״ה מותר לטלטל בכולו וכו׳ פוסטן ומטלטלן · תמי׳ לי הא מ״מ כיון דשבתו בבית אסור לטלטלן וכדאיתא להדיא עירובין דף לא בכומתא וסודרא ועע״ג : תוספות ד״ה דר״א שמותי וכו׳ וכן מוכח בירושלמי . עיין נדה דף לד ע״ב תוספות ד״ה ואומר :

נ״ע שבת

פסחים נא.

עירובין כג. נט. עד. פט. צא.

[לעיל מ: ברכות ס. וש״נ]

[נדה נג:]

עירובין עג:

סוף פרק ט דשביעית

עירובין ס. [ע״ש נ״ש] ושם עג:

[נדה ז:]

[ועי׳ תוספות נדה ז: ד״ה שמותי הוא]

through roofs and courtyards,[3] [130b] [this being] against the will of R. Eliezer. R. Joseph demurred: [You say] 'against the will of R. Eliezer'! on the contrary, it is R. Eliezer who permits it? And if you say, 'against the will of R. Eliezer' who permits it even through the street;[4] but only with the consent of the Rabbis, who forbid [it to be carried] through the street yet permit it through roofs, courtyards, and enclosures,[5]—yet is this permitted? Surely it was taught: Just as one may not bring it through the street, so may one not bring it through roofs, through enclosures, or through courtyards?—Said R. Ashi: It was not with the consent of R. Eliezer and his opponent[s], but with the consent of R. Simeon. For we learnt, R. Simeon said: Roofs, enclosures
a and courtyards are all one domain[1] in respect of utensils which spent the Sabbath therein,[2] but not in respect of utensils which rested in the house.[3]

R. Zera asked R. Assi: In the case of an alley in which they [its residents] have not become partners,[4] what about carrying in the whole of it?[5] do we say it is like a courtyard: just as a courtyard, even if an *'erub* has not been made, it is permitted to carry in the whole of it,[6] so this too, though they have not become partners in it,[7] it is permitted to carry in the whole of it; or perhaps it is unlike a courtyard; for a courtyard has four walls [partitions], whereas this has not four walls; alternatively, a courtyard has tenants,[8] whereas this has no tenants? He was silent and said nothing to him. On a subsequent occasion he [R. Zera] found him [R. Assi] sitting and stating: 'R. Simeon b. Lakish said in the name of R. Judah the Prince: They once forgot to bring a knife on Sabbath eve, so they brought it on the Sabbath. Now this matter was difficult for the Sages [to understand]: how could they abandon the opinion of the Sages and act as R. Eliezer: firstly, since R. Eliezer was [a follower] of Beth Shammai;[9] and further, [where] an individual and many [are in dispute], the *halachah* is as the many? Whereupon R. Oshaia said: I asked R. Judah the circumciser, and he told me, It was an alley wherein they [its residents] had not become partners, and they brought it [the knife] from one end to the other. Said he to him: Do you then hold that in the case of an alley in which they had not become partners, it is permitted to carry in the whole of it? Yes, he replied.' Said he [R. Zera] to him [R. Assi], But I once asked [it of] you and you did not answer me: perhaps in the rapid course [of your review] your
b tradition sped [back] to you?[1] Yes, he replied; in the course of my review my tradition sped [back] to me.

It was stated, R. Zera said in Rab's name: In the case of an alley in which no partnership had been made, one may not carry therein save within four cubits. Abaye observed, R. Zera stated this law but did not explain it, until Rabbah b. Abbuha came and explained it. For R. Naḥman said in Rabbah b. Abbuha's name in Rab's name: In the case of an alley in which no partnership has been made, if the courtyards[2] are combined with the houses,[3] one may not carry therein [the alley] save within four cubits; [but] if the courtyards are not combined with the houses, one may carry over the whole of it.[4] R. Ḥanina Ḥoza'ah[5] said to Rabbah: Why does it differ when the courtyards are combined with the houses? [Presumably] because the courtyards have been transformed[6] and are become houses,[7] Rab being consistent with his view; for Rab said: An alley does not become permitted

(3) For which no *'erub* (q.v. Glos.) had been provided. It is normally forbidden to carry through such by Rabbinical law. (4) It is a general principle (*infra* 133a) that where a positive command and a negative command are in question, both should be fulfilled wherever possible; hence it might be argued that R. Eliezer too agrees that it should not be carried through the street, since there is an alternative (Tosaf.). Yet it may be that since R. Eliezer's ruling is largely in order to emphasize the great esteem in which the precept is held (*supra* 130a), the Talmud felt that he would require it to be carried through the streets. (5) *Karpifoth;* v. *supra* 7a.

a (1) Carrying from one to another is permitted. (2) I.e., which were there from the beginning of the Sabbath, v. 'Er. 91a. (3) I.e., which were in the house at the beginning of the Sabbath.—Here the knife belonged to the former category (Tosaf.). (4) By means of an *'erub*; v. *supra* 23a. (5) *Sc.* utensils which were there at the commencement of the Sabbath. (6) Not from a house into the courtyard or from one courtyard into another, but in that courtyard itself. (7) This is the technical term in respect of an alley, whereby it all ranks as a single and private domain for its residents. (8) I.e., the residents of the houses which open into it put it to private use. (9) So Rashi and Tosaf. on the strength of a statement in J. Sheb. IX, end; this does not mean that he actually belonged to the School of Shammai, but generally adopted their views (v. Weiss, *Dor*, II, p. 83, n. 2), which were always disregarded in favour of Beth Hillel's. Rashi suggests another meaning: he was under a ban (v. B.M. 59b).

b (1) I.e., you recalled it. [*Aliter:* 'In the rapid course (of your study) your tradition escaped you', i.e., R. Oshaia's statement. V. Strashun]. (2) That open into the alley. (3) Which give on the courtyards. I.e., all the houses served by the same courtyard are combined by means of an *'erub*, so that they may carry to and fro between the houses and the courtyard belonging to same; but the courtyards themselves have not been made common partners in the alley. (4) *Sc.* utensils which were in the *alley* at the beginning of the Sabbath. (5) Of Be Ḥozae. V. *supra* 51b, n. b4. (6) Lit., 'torn away'—from their original designation. (7) I.e., they are now part of the houses and not courtyards at all.

[for carrying] through a stake and a beam unless [131a] houses and courtyards[8] open into it, whereas here we have houses but not courtyards?[9] Then even if they are not combined, let us regard these houses as though closed [up],[10] so we have courtyards
a but not houses?—They can all renounce[1] their rights in favour of one.[2] But even so, we have a house, but not houses?[3]—It is possible that from morning until midday [they renounce their rights] in favour of one, and from midday until evening in favour of another.[4] But even so, when there is one there is not the other?—Rather said R. Ashi: What makes the courtyards interdicted [in respect of the alley]? [Of course] the houses; and these are non-existent.[5]

R. Ḥiyya b. Abba said in R. Joḥanan's name: Not in respect of everything did R. Eliezer rule that the preliminary preparations of a precept[6] supersede the Sabbath, for lo! the two loaves[7] are an obligation of the day,[8] yet R. Eliezer did not learn them[9] from aught but a *gezerah shawah*.[10] For it was taught, R. Eliezer said: Whence do we know that the preliminaries of the two loaves supersede the Sabbath? 'Bringing' is stated in connection with the '*omer*,[11] and 'bringing' is stated in connection with the two loaves:[12] just as with the 'bringing' stated in connection with the '*omer*, its
b preliminaries[1] supersede the Sabbath, so with the 'bringing' stated in connection with the two loaves, their preliminaries supersede the Sabbath. These must be free,[2] for if they are not free one can refute [this analogy]: as for the '*omer*, [its preliminaries supersede the Sabbath] because if one finds it [already] cut,[3] he must cut [other sheaves]; will you [then] say [the same] in the case of the two loaves, seeing that if one finds [the wheat therefor] cut he does not cut [any more]? In truth they are indeed free. [For] consider: it is written, *then ye shall bring the sheaf of the firstfruits of your harvest unto the priest:*[4] what is the purpose of '*from the day that ye brought*'? Infer from it that it is in order to be free. Yet it is still free on one side only, while we know R. Eliezer to hold that where it is free on one side [only], we deduce, but refute?—'*Ye shall bring*' is an extension.[5]

What is it to exclude?[6] Shall we say that it is to exclude the *lulab*,[7] surely it was taught: The *lulab* and all its preliminaries supersede the Sabbath: this is R. Eliezer's view! Again, if it is to exclude *sukkah*,[8]—surely it was taught: The *sukkah* and all its preliminaries supersede the Sabbath: this is R. Eliezer's view! Again, if it is to exclude unleavened bread,—surely it was taught: Unleavened bread and all its preliminaries supersede the Sabbath: this is R. Eliezer's view! If, on the other hand, it is to exclude the *shofar*,[9]—surely it was taught: The *shofar* and all its preliminaries supersede the Sabbath: this is R. Eliezer's view!—Said R. Adda b. Ahabah: It is to exclude fringes for one's garment and *mezuzah* for one's
c door.[1] It was taught likewise: And they agree that if one inserts fringes in his garment or affixes a *mezuzah* to his door,[2] he is culpable. What is the reason? R. Joseph said: Because no [definite] time is appointed for them. Said Abaye to him, On the contrary,

(8) I.e., two courtyards with two houses opening into each. V. 'Er. 5a and 73b. (9) And for this reason when the courtyards are combined with the houses it is not permissible to carry save within four cubits. (10) Since one cannot carry from the houses into the alley on account of the intervening courtyards. [The courtyards were in *front* of the houses.]

a (1) Lit., 'annul'. (2) The tenants of all the houses save one can renounce their rights in the courtyard in his favour; the courtyard is then his, and he may carry from his house into it. (3) Whereas Rab needs at least two houses, v. *supra* n. 8. (4) Thus we have houses. (5) Rab holds ('Er. 74a) that a roof, courtyards, enclosures, and the alley are all one domain, and carrying is permitted from one to another, provided, however, that the houses are not combined with the courtyards, so that no utensils belonging to the houses are to be found in the courtyards which might then be carried into the alley. Hence the same applies to carrying in the alley itself: for if there are no houses at all a formal partnership is unnecessary, and carrying in the alley is permitted, just as from the alley into the courtyard. Since the houses are not combined with the courtyards and no utensils may be moved from the former into the latter, for all practical purposes the houses are non-existent: therefore one may carry over the whole of the alley itself. (6) As distinct from the precept itself. (7) Which are offered on the Feast of Weeks, v. Lev. XXIII, 17. (8) *Sc.* the Feast of Weeks, and must not be postponed for the next day. (9) That their baking supersedes the Sabbath; not the baking, but the offering '*unto the Lord*' is the actual precept, the former being merely a necessary preparation. (10) V. Glos. But if he held that *all* preparations supersede the Sabbath, he would not require the *gezerah shawah* in this particular case. (11) V. Glos. (12) Ibid. vv. 15, 17.

b (1) Viz., the reaping, grinding, and sifting; Men. 72a. (2) I.e., *from the day that ye brought* (v. 15) and '*ye shall bring*' (v. 17) must have no other purpose than this *gezerah shawah*. There are three views on this matter: (i) Both parts of the *gezerah shawah* must be free, otherwise it can be refuted if they are dissimilar in other respects; (ii) Only one part must be free; and (iii) Even if both parts are required for another teaching too, the *gezerah shawah* cannot be refuted. (3) But not for the express purpose of fulfilling the precept. (4) Lev. XXIII, 10. (5) Since Scripture could write, *and ye shall offer a new meal-offering unto the Lord out of your habitations*, etc. The extension embraces the preliminaries of bringing, and intimates that these supersede the Sabbath. (6) R. Joḥanan's statement that R. Eliezer did not rule that the preliminaries of *all* precepts etc. (7) V. Glos. and Lev. XXIII, 40. (8) V. Glos. and ibid. v. 42. (9) V. Glos. and ibid. v. 24.

c (1) These must not be inserted or affixed on the Sabbath. (2) On the Sabbath.

*בתים וחצרות פתוחין לתוכו והכא בתים איכא חצרות ליכא כי לא עירבו נמי ליחזינהו להני בתים כמאן דסתימי דמו וחצרות איכא ובתים ליכא אפשר דמבטלי ליה רשותא דכולהו לגבי חד סוף סוף בית איכא בתים ליכא אפשר דמצפרא ועד פלגא דיומא לגבי חד מפלגיה דיומא ולפניא לגבי חד סוף סוף בעידנא דאיתיה להאי ליתיה להאי אלא אמר רב אשי מי גרם לחצרות שיאסרו בתים וליכא אמר ר' חייא בר אבא א"ר יוחנן °לא לכל אמר ר' אליעזר מכשירי מצוה דוחין את השבת שהרי שתי הלחם חובת היום הן ולא למדן ר"א אלא מגזירה שוה דתניא ר' אליעזר אומר מניין למכשירי שתי הלחם שדוחין את השבת נאמרה הבאה בעומר ונאמרה הבאה בשתי הלחם מה הבאה האמורה בעומר מכשירין דוחין את השבת אף הבאה האמורה בשתי הלחם מכשירין דוחין את השבת מופני דאי לא מופני איכא למיפרך מה לעומר שכן אם מצא קצור קוצר תאמר בשתי הלחם שאם מצא קצור אינו קוצר לאי אפנויי מופני מכדי כתיב °והבאתם את עומר ראשית קצירכם אל הכהן *ביום הביאכם למה לי ש"מ לאפנויי ואכתי מופנה מצד אחד הוא ושמעינן ליה לר' אליעזר *דאמר מופנה מצד אחד למידין ומשיבין °תביאו רבויא הוא למעוטי מאי אילימא למעוטי לולב *והתניא לולב וכל מכשיריו דוחין את השבת דברי ר"א ואלא למעוטי סוכה והתניא סוכה וכל מכשיריה דוחין את השבת דברי ר"א ואלא למעוטי מצה והתניא מצה וכל מכשיריה דוחין את השבת דברי רבי אליעזר ואלא למעוטי שופר והתניא שופר וכל מכשיריו דוחין את השבת דברי ר"א אמר רב אדא בר אהבה למעוטי ציצית לטליתו ומזוזה לפתחו תניא נמי הכי ושוין שאם צייץ טליתו ועשה מזוזה לפתחו שהוא חייב מאי טעמא אמר רב יוסף לפי שאין קבוע להם זמן אמר ליה אביי אדרבה מדאין קבוע להם זמן כל

רש"י

בתים וחצרות. שני בתים פתוחים לשתי חצרות שתים לכל חצר ושתי חצרות פתוחות למבוי: כמאן דסתימי דמי. דהא לגבי מבוי כמאן דסתימי הוו דהא חצרות מפסיקות בינתים שאין הבתים מוציאין להם: אפשר דמבטלי. בני הבתים שבחצר רשות שיש להם בחצר לגבי חד מינייהו והוי כל החצר שלו ומותר להוציא מביתו לחצר: סוף סוף בית איכא. בכל חצר בתים ליכא ורב בעי שני בתים לכל חצר: אלא אמר רב אשי. טעמא לאו משום בתים וחצרות פתוחות לתוכו הוא דרב בין עירבו בין לא עירבו מכיון דפתיחי שתי חצרות למבוי ושני בתים לכל חצר תורת מבוי עליו וניתר בלחי וקורה והיינו טעמא דכי עירבו בחצרות ולא נשתתפו במבוי אסור לטלטל בו וכי לא עירבו שרי: מי גרם לחצירות שיאסרו. על המבוי להצריכו שיתוף להוציא מן החצירות לתוכו: בתים. הוא דגרמי לו דאי לאו משום בתים הוו להו חצרות ומבוי רשות אחת דרב דאמרה להא מלתא כר"ש סבירא ליה דאמר בעירובין (דף עד.) גג וחצר וקרפף ומבוי כולן רשות אחת הן ומטלטלין מזה לזה ואמר רב הלכה כר' שמעון והוא שלא עירבו בתים עם החצרות דלא שכיחי מאני דבתים בחצר הלכך לענין טלטול בתוכו נמי כי לא עירבו חצרות עם הבתים שרי דהוה להו כמו שנשתתפו בו דמי גרם לו למבוי ליאסר והצריך לשיתוף בתים גרמו לו ואינם שהרי נסתלקו ממנו ומותר להוציא מן החצרות למבוי כאילו נשתתפו ובנשתתפו לא מספקא לן דמותר לטלטל בכולן: לא לכל אמר רבי אליעזר. לא בכל מכשירי מצוה אמר כן ולקמן מפרש הי מכשירי מצוה אתא למעוטי: שתי הלחם. דעצרת חובת יום הן ואין לאחרן עד למחר: ולא למדן רבי אליעזר· דאפילו תדחה שבת אלא בגזירה שוה ואי בכל מכשירי מצוה שעיקר המצוה נוהגת בשבת אמר מכשיריה כמותה למה לי גזירה שוה: מה הבאה האמורה בעומר מכשיריה. דהיינו קצירה טחינה והרקדה שלה דוחין את השבת כדאמרינן במנחות (דף עב:) בחריש ובקציר תשבות מה חריש רשות אף קציר רשות יצא קצירת העומר שהיא מצוה: שכן (א) מצא קצור. שלא לשם עומר מצוה לקצור לשמה דכתיב וקצרתם והבאתם הלכך קצירה גופיה מצוה היא תאמר בשתי הלחם שלא נאמר בהן קצירה: לאי. באמת: מצד אחד. הבאה דעומר מופנה הבאה דשתי הלחם אינה מופנה דצריכה לגופה: ושמעינן ליה לרבי אליעזר דאמר. גזירה שוה שאינה מופנה משני לדדיה אלא מצד אחד למדין ממנה אם אין להשיב אבל אם יש להשיב משיבין ובמסכת יבמות בפרק מצות חליצה* [דף ע:] שמעינן ליה דאמר הכי דקתני חליצה בשמאל פסולה ורבי אליעזר מכשיר דלא יליף רגל רגל ממצורע ופרכינן ורבי אליעזר לא יליף ממצורע והא תניא ר"א אומר מניין לרציעה שהיא באוזן ימנית נאמר כאן אוזן ונאמר להלן אוזן וכו' ומשנינן אזן אזן מופנה רגל רגל לא מופנה והאי לאו מופנה דקאמרינן משני לדדין קאמר דרגל דכתיב בחליצה איצטריכא לגופה אבל מצד אחד מופנה הוא דפרשת מצורע מופנה הוא ההיא דעני דכולהו כתיבין במצורע עשיר: תביאו ריבויא הוא. דהא והקרבתם מנחה חדשה סמיך ומצי למיכתב ממושבותיכם לחם תנופה ותביאו יתירה הוא: למעוטי מאי. הא דאמר רבי יוחנן לעיל לא לכל אמר רבי אליעזר למעוטי הי מכשירים אתי דלא דחי שבת: וכל מכשיריו. כגון לקוצצו מן המחובר: למעוטי ציצית. שלא יתלנה בטליתו בשבת כדמפרש טעמא ואזיל:

תוספות

אפשר דמבטלי רשות כו'. וא"ת כי עירבו חצרות נמי עם בתים מצינן למימר שיש חצר למבוי כגון שביטלו אותו של חצר זה לרשות דכולהו שיש להם במבוי לגבי חצר אחרת ויכולין לטלטל מן החצר למבוי הא לא בעי לאקשויי °דאיכא למ"ד בעירובין (דף סו:) אין ביטול רשות מחצר לחצר ועוד דבלאו הכי פריך שפיר: מפלגא דיומא לפניא. רב לטעמיה דאמר במסכת עירובין (דף סח:) מבטלין וחוזרין ומבטלין: מי גרם לחצרות. אנן קי"ל דאפילו עירבו חצרות עם בתים מותר לטלטל (ב) דהא רב דאסר בעירבו לטעמיה דפסיק כרבי שמעון דוקא בלא עירבו אבל רבי יוחנן פסיק כר"ש בין עירבו בין לא עירבו וכר' יוחנן קי"ל: לא לכל אמר רבי אליעזר מכשירי מצוה דוחין את השבת. לקמן מפרש דאתא למעוטי ציצית ומזוזה וה"פ לא (ג) כל מצות הנוהגות בשבת אמר ר' אליעזר שמכשירין ידחו שבת שהרי שתי הלחם כו' ומשמע לכאורה דאי לא דאשכחן דמצריך ר' אליעזר ג"ש הוה גמרינן לציצית ומזוזה ממילה וכיון דמכשיריה דחו שבת ותימה הוא היכי שייך למילף ציצית ומזוזה ממילה דמילה דין הוא דמכשיריה דוחין שבת דהיא עצמה דוחה שבת אבל ציצית ומזוזה אין במצותן דחיית שבת: תאמר בשתי הלחם שאם מצא קצור אינו קוצר. תימה מאי קא פריך דהיא גופה נילף מינה מה העומר שאף על פי שמצא קצור קוצר אף שתי הלחם אם מצא קצור קוצר ונילף מינה תרתי מכשירין וקצירה ותירץ ר"ת דהא לא דמי דנילף מינה קצירה שהרי בעצרת יהיו כל החיטין והשעורין קצורים ולא משמע דאתיא ג"ש אלא (ד) מכשירין דדחו שבת א"כ י"ל דהא לא מצי למימר נילף קצירה דמהיכא נפקא לן קצירת העומר דדחיא שבת מדכתיב בחריש ובקציר תשבות כדדרשינן במנחות בשילהי ר' ישמעאל (דף עב:) מה חריש רשות אף קציר רשות יצא קצירת העומר שהיא מצוה וגלי רחמנא דליכא למילף אלא לגבי העומר דכתיב ביה נמי קציר ולא לגבי שתי הלחם דלא כתיב בהו קציר ועל כרחך ודאי היינו טעמא דיליף גבי עומר קצירה משום דכתיב ביה קציר דאי לאו הכי מ"ש דיליף טפי גבי עומר מגבי שתי הלחם דהא נמי נימא יצא קצירת שתי הלחם שהיא מצוה: ושוין שאם צייץ טליתו כו' מ"ט כו'. תימה מה צריך טעם לזה אלא משום דלא אשכחן דרבינהו קרא דכל אימך מצרכינן קרא לקמן דלא גמרי מהדדי ומיהו יש לומר דאיכא למילף ציצית ומזוזה מסוכה דמאי פרכת שכן נוהגת בלילות כבימים מזוזה נמי נוהג בלילות כבימים וכן ציצית לרבנן דפליגי עליה דרבי שמעון בפרק התכלת (מנחות דף מג.) דלא דרשי וראיתם אותו פרט לכסות לילה אלא °פרט לכסות סומא ולהאי טעמא דפרישית דמסוכה יליף צריך לומר דציצית (ה) אם עבר זמנה בטלה דאי לאו הכי איכא למפרך מה לסוכה שכן אם עבר זמנה בטלה דמסתבר דמילה אם עבר זמנה לא בטלה שאותה מילה עצמה שהוא מיחייב בשמיני הוא עושה בתשיעי שאם מל בשמיני לא היה חוזר ומל בתשיעי אבל (ו) סוכה ציצית ומזוזה בכל יומא מיחייב בהן אפילו קיימם היום חייב לקיימם למחר הלכך כשעבר היום ולא עשאם מצות היום לא יקיים עוד לעולם ואם תאמר ומסוכה היכי מצי למילף וכן כל הנך דלקמן דפריך ניכתוב רחמנא בהאי וניתי הנך וניגמרו מיניה אדרבה נגמר מכיבוד אב ואם ומבנין בית המקדש דלא דחו שבת כדאיתא

רבינו חננאל

בתים וחצרות פתוחין לתוכו והכא כיון שערבו כאלו אין שם חצר וכולן (בתים) [חצרות] נינהו ואפי' נשתתפו כיון שאין שמבטלין שתופן באותו מבוי. כך יש לומר כי לא עירבו נמי כיון שהן אסורין להוציא מן הבית לחצר חשב אותן הבתים כאלו סתומין הן שאין להם רשות להשתמש מן הבתים לחצר וחצר איכא בית ליכא. לטעמיה דרב [illegible]

רב נסים גאון

ואכתי מופנה מצד א' הוא ושמעינן ליה לר' אליעזר דאמר מופנה מצד אחד למדין ומשיבין [illegible]

מסורת הש"ס: [עירובין ס: יב: סג: עד.] · ויקרא כג · שם · [צ"ל מיום] · יבמות ע: · סוכה מג.

הגהות הב"ח

(א) רש"י ד"ה שכן אם מצא: (ב) תוס' ד"ה מי גרס וכו' מותר לטלטל בכולי דהא רב: (ג) ד"ה לא לכל וכו' וה"פ לא לכל מצות: (ד) ד"ה תאמר וכו' אלא למכשירין: (ה) ד"ה ושוין וכו' דציצית ומזוזה אם עבר: (ו) בא"ד אבל ציצית ומזוזה כצ"ל ותיבת סוכה נמחק:

גליון הש"ס

גמ' לא לכל ר"א מכשירי מצוה. עי' בס' [illegible] בלקוטי': רש"י ד"ה ושמעי' ליה לר"א וכו' מופנה הוא אלא דעני' עי' ברש"י יבמות דף ע ע"ב ד"ה ושמעי' ליה לר"א וצ"ע: תוס' ד"ה אפשר וכו' דאיכא למ"ד בעירובין. עי' עירובין דף עג ע"ב תוס' ד"ה אלא פשיטא: תוס' ד"ה ושוין אלא פרט לכסות סומא. וכ"כ רש"י סוכה יא ע"א ד"ה לפרזומא ועיין בשער המלך פ"ג מהל' ציצית:

[illegible]

**) [illegible]

כל שעתא ושעתא זמניה הוא אלא אמר רב נחמן א"ר יצחק ואיתימא רב הונא בריה דרב יהושע *הואיל ובידו להפקירן: אמר מר לולב וכל מכשיריו דוחין את השבת דברי ר"א מנא ליה לר"א הא אי מעומר ושתי הלחם שכן צורך גבוה אלא אמר קרא °ביום *ביום אפילו בשבת ולמאי הלכתא אילימא לטלטול איצטריך קרא למישרי טלטול אלא למכשיריו ורבנן ההוא מיבעי ליה ביום ולא בלילה ור"א ביום ולא בלילה מנא ליה נפקא ליה °מושמחתם לפני ה' אלהיכם שבעת ימים ימים ולא לילות ורבנן איצטריך ס"ד אמינא נילף שבעת ימים (א) מסוכה מה להלן ימים ואפילו לילות אף כאן ימים ואפילו לילות קמ"ל וליכתוב רחמנא בלולב וניתו הנך ונילפו מיניה משום דאיכא למיפרך מה ללולב שכן טעון ארבעה מינים: סוכה וכל מכשיריה דוחין את השבת דברי רבי אליעזר מנא ליה לר"א הא אי מעומר ושתי הלחם שכן צורך גבוה הוא אי מלולב שכן טעון ארבעה מינים אלא גמר שבעת ימים (ג) מלולב מה להלן מכשיריו דוחין את השבת אף כאן נמי מכשיריו דוחין את השבת וליכתוב רחמנא בסוכה וניתי הנך וניגמור מיניה משום דאיכא למיפרך מה לסוכה שכן נוהגת בלילות כבימים: מצה וכל מכשיריה דוחין את השבת דברי ר"א מנא ליה לר"א הא אי מעומר ושתי הלחם שכן צורך גבוה אי מלולב שכן טעון ארבעה מינים אי מסוכה שכן נוהגת בלילות כבימים אלא גמר חמשה עשר חמשה עשר מחג הסוכות מה להלן מכשיריה דוחין את השבת אף כאן מכשיריה דוחין את השבת וליכתוב רחמנא במצה וניתו הנך וליגמור מיניה משום דאיכא למיפרך מה למצה שכן נוהגת בנשים כבאנשים: שופר וכל מכשיריו דוחין את השבת דברי ר"א מנא ליה לר"א הא אי מעומר ושתי הלחם שכן צורך גבוה אי מלולב שכן טעון ארבעה מינים אי מסוכה שכן נוהגת בלילות כבימים אי ממצה שכן נוהגת בנשים כבאנשים אלא אמר קרא °יום תרועה יהיה לכם ביום אפילו בשבת ולמאי אילימא לתקיעה הא *תנא דבי שמואל כל מלאכת עבודה לא תעשו יצתה תקיעת שופר ורדיית הפת שהיא חכמה ואינה מלאכה אלא למכשירין ורבנן ההוא מיבעי ליה ביום ולא בלילה ור"א ביום ולא בלילה מנא ליה נפקא ליה °מביום הכפורים תעבירו שופר בכל ארצכם וגמרי מהדדי וליכתוב רחמנא בשופר וליתו הנך וליגמרו מיניה מתקיעת שופר דראש השנה ליכא למיגמר שכן מכנסת זכרונות של ישראל לאביהן שבשמים מתקיעות [שופר] דיוה"כ ליכא למיגמרי *דאמר מר תקעו ב"ד שופר נפטרו עבדים לבתיהם ושדות חוזרות לבעליהן: (אמר מר) מילה וכל מכשיריה דוחין את השבת דברי רבי אליעזר מנא ליה לר"א הא אי מכולהו גמר כדאמרינן ועוד מה להנך שכן

ויקרא כג | שם | במדבר כט | ויקרא כה | ר"ס

רש"י

כל שעתא זמניה הוא. וכיון שיש לו טלית בכל יום שמשהה בלא ציצית עובר בעשה °ואפילו מונחת בקופסא הלכך כל יומא רמיא מצותיה עליה: הואיל ובידו להפקירן. ונפקי מרשותיה ולאו עליה רמיא חובתיה: אי מעומר ושתי הלחם. וגמר במה מצינו: ביום ואפילו בשבת. מדלא כתיב בראשון לדרשא אתא בכל יום שהוא ראשון לחג: ולמאי איצטריך לרבויי. להאי ואפילו בשבת אי נימא לטלטל כדמשמע קרא לקיחה טלטול בעלמא הוא ועדיין במתן תורה לא נאסר טלטול דאיצטריך קרא למישרי להאי: אלא למכשיריו. דאיסורא דאורייתא הוא: מה להלן ימים ואפילו לילות· כדילפינן במסכת סוכה (דף מג·): וליכתוב רחמנא בלולב. דמכשירין דחו: וניתו. עומר ושתי הלחם מיניה ולמה ליה דכתביה בכולהו: אי מלולב. במה מצינו מלולב שהוא מצוה ומכשיריו דוחין אף סוכה שהיא מצוה מכשיריה דוחין: גמר ז' ימים כו'. ובג"ש אתי ליה ואע"ג דאיכא מופנה משני לדדים דהא גבי לולב חד שבעת ימים הוא דכתיב ודרשינן לר' אליעזר למעוטי לילות כיון דגלי רחמנא בעומר ושתי הלחם ולולב גילוי מילתא בעלמא הוא ולא פרכינן עלה גימגום (ג): וניתו הנך. עומר ושתי הלחם מינה: אי מסוכה שכן נוהגת בלילות כבימים. ואילו מצה לילה הראשון חובה ותו לא כדאמרינן בפסחים (דף קכ·): ונכתוב רחמנא. בהדיא במצה ונגמרו הנך כולהו מיניה: בנשים כבאנשים. כדילפינן בפסחים (ד' מג:) לא תאכל עליו חמץ שבעת ימים וגו' כל שישנו בבל תאכל חמץ ישנו בקום אכול מצה ונשים איתנהו בבל תאכל חמץ דכל מצות לא תעשה בין שהזמן גרמא בין שאין הזמן גרמא חייבות לאפוקי סוכה ולולב דליתנהו בנשים דמצות עשה שהזמן גרמא היא: ולמאי. האי קרא הי מילתא דתרועה אתא למישרי בשבת אי לתקיעה לא איצטריך דאפילו תקיעת הרשות לית בה איסורא דאורייתא: מלאכת עבודה. של טורח: וגמרי מהדדי. במסכת ראש השנה (דף לג:) שאין תלמוד לומר בחדש השביעי דהא בכמה קראי כתב לן דיוה"כ בחודש השביעי מה ת"ל בחודש השביעי שיהו כל תרועות משל חדש השביעי שוות: נפטרו עבדים לבתיהם. קריאת דרור דיובל תלויה בה הלכך חשיבא: אי מכולהו. מאחת מכולן: כדאמרינן. איכא למיפרך בכל הנך חדא לד חמור האמור בה לעיל: שאם

תוספות

כדאיתא בפ"ק דיבמות (דף ו·) וי"ל דהכא הכי גמרי מה מצינו בהנך שמצות נוהגות בשבת ומכשיריה דחו שבת אף כל שמצות נוהגות בשבת מכשיריה דחו שבת הלכך לא שייך למילף מכיבוד דהיינו המצוה עצמה ולא מכשיריה דשחוט לי בשל לי היינו כיבוד עצמו כשמתקן לו מאכלו והבנין נמי הוי מצוה אחת שצוה הקדוש ברוך הוא לבנות בית המקדש: **סד"א** נילף שבעת ימים משבעת ימים מסוכה. וא"ת היכי תיסק אדעתיה לדון ג"ש הא אין אדם דן ג"ש מעצמו אא"כ למדה מרבו וי"ל דשמא בעלמא ניתנה למדרש*: **קמ"ל**. °ולא ידענא השתא האי שבעת ימים למאי אתיא דאע"ג דדרשינן בפ"ק דפסחים (דף ה·) מה שביעי שביעי לחג אף ראשון ראשון לחג הא איכא למידרש משבעה בלא ימים:

שכן טעון ארבעה מינים. אף על גב דעומר ושתי הלחם נמי מביאין עמהן כבשים ויין לניסוך ושמן למנחות שאני ד' מינין שבלולב דמעכבין זה את זה כדאמר בפרק הקומץ (מנחות דף כז·) ובפרק התכלת (שם דף מה:) [אמרינן] הכבשים אין מעכבין לא את העומר ולא את שתי הלחם *והיינו טעון ד' מינין שאין מצות לולב כלל בלא ד' מינין אבל באלו יכולה להיות מצותן בלא ד' מינין. הר"ב פור"ת: **אי** מעומר כו'. הכא לא דייקא תלמודא למילף מביניהו דהכי אורחיה דתלמודא זימנין דייק וזימנין לא דייק ואי הוה דייק הוה משכח פירכ' הרב פור"ת א"כ מילתא דאתיא במה הצד טרח וכתב לה קרא כמו מילתא דאתיא בקל וחומר והאי דקאמר תלמודא ניכתוב רחמנא בהאי ותיתי אידך מיניה פירוש ומאי צריך קרא היינו משום דאי בלא מה הצד הוה מצי למילף הך מצוה מאידך לא הוה כתב רחמנא קרא כיון דהוה פשוט כל כך דלא דמי למילתא דאתיא בק"ו דהוא פשוט יותר: **שבעת** ימים (ד) מלולב. מופנה הוה משני לדדים גבי לולב לא איצטריך דאע"ג דדרשינן ימים ולא לילות מיהו לא הוה צריך למיכתב שבעת כלל דהוה מצי למיכתב ושמחת לפני וגו' בימים והוי לשון שבעת מיותר לג"ש וא"ת ור' אליעזר היכי דריש ימים ולא לילות כיון דאית ליה ג"ש היא גופה נילף מסוכה מה להלן ימים אפילו לילות אף לולב ימים ואפי' לילות ויש לומר דלית לן למילף בג"ש מילתא דלשון ג"ש גופא מוכחא דאינו כן דימים משמע ולא לילות:

ואי מסוכה שכן נוהגת בלילות כבימים. משמע דבעי למימר תאמר במצה שאינה נוהגת בלילות כבימים ואדרבה עיקר מצותה בלילה הראשון שנאמר בערב תאכלו מצות (שמות יב) והכי הוה מצי למימר שכן נוהגת בימים ובלילות:

נפקא ליה מביום הכפורים. וגמרינן מהדדי כדדרשינן בראש השנה* שיהו כל התקיעות של חודש השביעי שוות כדפירש בקונטרס ורבנן סברי דלא שייך לאקשויי אלא לומר שסדר תקיעות יהיו שוין לענין סדר תקיעות מייתי·לה התם אבל לזמן דיום ודאי לא איתקש דע"כ זמנם אינו שוה שזה בראש חודש וזה בעשור לחודש: והשניה

רבינו חננאל

אומל לא שרינן בכי האי גוונא דבהדיא קיי"ל הלכתא כרבנן*) וכללי' דרבי עקיבא דאמר כל מלאכה שאפשר לה לעשות מע"ש אינ' דוחה את השבת והבאת אומל כיון שאפשר לו להביאו מע"ש ולא הביאו אין הבאתו דוחה את השבת אפילו לענין עשיית פסח דכרת הוא לא מייתינן אומל למול בנו או עבדו כדי שיותר לו לעשות פסח ולא שנא להו לרבנן לא דרך רה"ר ולא דרך גגות וקרפיפות וחצרות הכל אחד הוא ובכל אסור ואשכחנן בתלמוד א"י עובדא ולא הביאוהו בשבת. ואמרינן בכל מקום (רב עביד) מעשה רב דגמרינן מינה. וזה הוא המעשה. ר' שמואל בר אבודומי הוה ליה עובדא למגזר לרב ששעא בריה אנשיון למיתי אומל שאל לר' [מנא]· אמר להון ידחה למחר. שאל לר' יצחק בן אלעזר אמר להון משחוק [קנדיטון] לא אנשיתון ומיתי אומל אנשיתון ידחה למחר: א"ר חייא בר אבא. א"ר יוחנן לא לכל א"ר אליעזר מכשירי מצוה דוחין את השבת שהרי שתי הלחם חובת היום הן ולא למדם ר' אליעזר אלא מג"ש נאמרה הבאה בעומר שנאמר והבאתם את עומר וגו' ונאמרה הבאה בשתי הלחם שנאמר ממושבותיכם תביאו לחם תנופה שתים וגו'. מנין שהעומר דוחה שבת'. גרסינן באחרית פרק ר' ישמעאל אומר העומר היה בא בשבת מג' סאין וכו'. ת"ר תקריב את מנחת בכוריך מה ת"ל לפי שמצות העומר להביא מן הקמה מניין שאם לא מצא קמה יביא מן העומרין ת"ל תקריב כו' עד תקריב לפי שמצותו לקצור בלילה. מניין שאם קצר ביום כשר ודוחה שבת ת"ל תקריב כל שהוא תקריב מ"מ תקריבו אפי' בשבת אפילו ביום בטומאה. ותוב תניא (בתו"כ) בסוף פרשת אמור אל הכהנים (ובפסחים עז ובמנחות ע"ב) רבי אומר וידבר משה את מועדי ה' מה ת"ל לפי שלא למדנו שדוחין את השבת אלא הפסח והתמיד שכתוב בהן במועדו מניין לרבות העומר והקרב עמו. שתי הלחם והקרב עמהן שידחו שבת ת"ל וידבר משה את מועדי ה' קבעו מועד אחד לכולן ופשוטה היא זו ההלכה כולה. ואפי' ר' אליעזר שמתיר במכשירי מצוה מודה. שאם ציץ טליתו ועשה מזוזה בפתחו בשבת שהוא חייב ואמרינן מ"ש הני ואוקימנא הואיל ובידו להפקירן. פי' כי הציצית הוא חובת הבגד וכיון שהפקיר אינו בגדו וכן הבית [דף לג:]

מסורת הש"ס

[עי' תוספות מנחות מד· ד"ה טלית]

סוכה מג·

לעיל קיז: ע"ש

ר"ס כט:

הגהות הב"ח

(א) גמ' נילף שבעת ימים משבעת ימים מסוכה: (ב) שם אלא גמר שבעה ימים משבעת ימים מלולב: (ג) רש"י ד"ה גמר ז' ימים וכו' גימגום סס"ד ואחר כך מ"ס ונכתוב רחמנא בהדיא בסוכה וניתי הנך עומר ושתי הלחם ולולב מינה: (ד) תוס' ד"ה שבעת ימים משבעת ימים מלולב מופנה הוה משני לדדין דגבי לולב נמי לא איצטריך:

גליון הש"ס

רש"י ד"ה כל שעתא וכו' ואפי' מונחת בקופסא. עי' מנחות דף מ[א] ע"א תוס' ד"ה טלית: תוס' ד"ה קמ"ל ולא ידענא. כעי' זה לעיל ד[ף] קי"ח ע"ב תד"ה אלו הן וש"כ:

---

*) עיין היטב בריי"ף כאן דדחה כל הראיות שהביא רבינו ע"ש

since no time is appointed for them, [131b] every moment[3] is the [proper] time for them?—Rather said R. Naḥman b. Isaac—others state, R. Huna son of R. Joshua: Because it is in one's power to renounce their ownership.[4]

The Master said: 'The *lulab* and all its preliminaries supersede the Sabbath: this is R. Eliezer's view.' Whence does R. Eliezer know this? If from the *'omer* and the two loaves, [that may be] because they are requirements of the Most High?[5]—Rather Scripture saith, [*And ye shall take ye*] *on the* [*first*] *day* [... *branches of palm trees*, etc.]:[6] '*on the day*' [intimating,] even on the Sabbath.[7] Now in respect of which law?[8] Shall we say, in respect of handling?[9] Is a verse necessary to authorize handling![10] Hence it must be in respect of its preliminaries.[11] And the Rabbis?[12]—That is required [to teach], by day,[13] but not by night. Then R. Eliezer: whence does he [learn] 'by day but not by night'?—He deduces it from, *and ye shall rejoice before the Lord your God seven* days:[14] days only, not nights. And the Rabbis?[15]—It is necessary: you might argue, Let us learn [the meaning of] seven days from the seven days of *sukkah:* just as there 'days' [means] and even nights,[16] so here too 'days', and even nights: hence it teaches us [otherwise]. Then let the Divine Law state it[17] in the case
a of *lulab*, and these [others][1] could be adduced and learnt therefrom?[2]—Because one could refute [the analogy]: as for *lulab*, [its preliminaries supersede the Sabbath] because it requires four species.[3]

'The *sukkah* and all its preliminaries supersede the Sabbath: this is R. Eliezer's view.' Whence does R. Eliezer learn this? If from the *'omer* and the two loaves,—[there it may be] because they are requirements of the Most High; if from *lulab*,—[that may be] because it requires four species! Rather [the scope of] '*seven days*' is deduced from the '*seven days*' of *lulab:* just as there its preliminaries supersede the Sabbath, so here too its preliminaries supersede the Sabbath.[4] Then let the Divine Law write it in connection with *sukkah*, and these [others] could be adduced and learnt therefrom?—Because one could refute [the analogy]: as for *sukkah*, that is because it [the precept] is binding by night just as by day.

'Unleavened bread and all its preliminaries supersede the Sabbath: this is R. Eliezer's view.' Whence does R. Eliezer know this? If from the *'omer* and the two loaves,—[there it may be] because they are requirements of the Most High? If from *lulab*,—because it requires four species? If from *sukkah*,—because it is binding by night just as by day? Rather the meaning of '*the fifteenth* [*day*]' is learnt from the Festival of Tabernacles:[5] just as there its preliminaries supersede the Sabbath, so here too its preliminaries supersede the Sabbath. Then let the Divine Law state it in connection with unleavened bread, and these [others] could be adduced and learnt therefrom?—Because one could refute [the analogy]: as for unleavened bread, that is because it is obligatory upon women just as upon men.[6]

'The *shofar* and all its preliminaries supersede the Sabbath: this is R. Eliezer's view.' Whence does R. Eliezer know this? If from the *'omer* and the two loaves,—because they are requirements of the Most-High? If from *lulab*,—because it requires four species? If from *sukkah*,—because it is binding by night just as by day? if from unleavened bread,—because it is obligatory upon women just as upon men?—Rather Scripture saith, *It is a day of*
b *blowing of trumpets unto you:*[1] [it must be blown] by day, even on the Sabbath. And in respect of what?[2] Shall we say in respect of blowing [the *shofar*],—but the School of Samuel[3] taught: *Ye shall do no servile work:*[4] the blowing of the *shofar* and the removal of bread [from an oven] are excluded as being an art, not work.[5] Hence [it must be] in respect of [its] preliminaries. And the Rabbis?—That is required [to teach], by day but not by night. Then R. Eliezer, whence does he learn, by day but not by night?—He deduces it from, *in the Day of Atonement shall ye send abroad the trumpet throughout all your land*,[6] and these[7] are learnt from each other.[8] Now, let the Divine Law state it in connection with *shofar*, and these [others] can come and be learnt therefrom?—One cannot learn from the blowing of the *shofar* on New Year, because it brings the remembrance of Israel to their Father in Heaven.[9] One cannot learn from the blowing of the *shofar* on the Day of Atonement [either], because a Master said: When the Beth din blew the *shofar*, slaves departed to their homes and
c estates reverted to their [original] owners.[1]

Circumcision and all its preliminaries supersede the Sabbath: this is R. Eliezer's view. Whence does R. Eliezer learn this? If he learns [it] from all [the others, the objection is] as we stated.[2]

(3) Lit., 'hour'. (4) Thus, when he comes to do it on the Sabbath, he could renounce ownership of the garment or the house, in which case these precepts are no longer incumbent on him. (5) I.e., they are a direct offering. (6) Lev. XXIII, 40. (7) For '*on the first*' suffices: hence '*day*' teaches that the ceremony must be performed whatever the day. (8) Is this intimation necessary? (9) Permitting the handling of the *lulab* on the Sabbath. (10) Surely not, for the interdict of handling is only Rabbinical. (11) E.g., carrying the *lulab* through the streets, which would otherwise be Biblically forbidden. (12) How do they interpret the superfluous 'day'? (13) The *lulab* precept has to be performed by day. (14) Ibid. (15) Do they not admit that it can be deduced from this latter verse? (16) This is deduced in Suk. 43*a*. (17) This law that the preliminaries supersede the Sabbath.

a (1) *Sc.* the *'omer* and the two loaves. (2) That there too it is thus: why are separate verses required? (3) Viz., those enumerated in Lev. XXIII, 40. Hence it is important that even its preliminaries supersede the Sabbath. (4) Since this analogy is based on a *gezerah shawah*, it cannot be refuted as before, when the suggested analogy was based purely on logical grounds. (Rashi). (5) Lev. XXIII, vv. 6 and 39. (6) They too must partake thereof; v. Pes. 43*b*. But the precepts of *lulab* and *sukkah* are not incumbent upon women.

b (1) Num. XXIX, 1. (2) Does 'day' extend the law even to the Sabbath? (3) This is rather unusual. Generally we have 'the School of R. Ishmael', and the present passage is so quoted *supra* 117*b* in cur. edd. R. Han. however, reads 'the School of Samuel' there too, and it is likewise so in R.H. 29*b* in cur. edd. Weiss, *Dor*, III, p. 169 maintains that the reference is to a collection of Baraithas compiled by Samuel. It may also be observed that the verse quoted here is not the same as that quoted *supra* in cur. edd., though Tosaf.'s reading is identical in both places. It is barely possible that two different Baraithas are referred to, both making the same deduction but from different verses. (4) Lev. XXIII, 25. (5) Hence no verse is required to teach that it is permitted. (6) Ibid. XXV, 9. (7) *Sc.* the blowing of the *shofar* on New Year and on the Day of Atonement. (8) As shown in R.H. 33*b*. (9) Hence it is so important that even its preliminaries supersede the Sabbath. But the same may not apply to other precepts.

c (1) In accordance with Lev. XXV, 10. Hence this too was of particularly great importance. (2) Each differs in some respect.

Moreover, as for those, [132a] [they may supersede the Sabbath] because if their time passes they are annulled![3] Rather this is R. Eliezer's reason: Because Scripture saith, *and in the eighth day the flesh of his foreskin shall be circumcised*,[4] [implying] even on the Sabbath.[5] Then let the Divine Law write it in connection with circumcision, and these [others] can come to be deduced thence?—Because one can refute [the analogy]: as for circumcision, that is because thirteen covenants were made in connection therewith.[6]

Now, the Rabbis disagree with R. Eliezer only in respect of the preliminaries of circumcision; but as for circumcision itself, all hold that it supersedes the Sabbath: whence do we know it?—Said 'Ulla, It is a traditional law;[7] and thus did R. Isaac say, It is a traditional law.

An objection is raised: How do we know that the saving of life supersedes the Sabbath? R. Eleazar b. 'Azariah said: If circumcision, which is [performed on but] one of the limbs of man, supersedes the Sabbath, the saving of life, *a minori*, must supersede the Sabbath. Now if you think that it is a traditional law, can one argue *a minori* from a traditional law? Surely it was taught, R. Eleazar said to him: Akiba! [That] a bone [of a corpse] the size of a barley grain defiles[8] is a traditional law, whereas [that] a quarter
a [*log*] of blood [of a corpse] defiles is [deduced by you] *a minori*,[1] and we do not argue *a minori* from a traditional law!—Rather said R. Eleazar: We learn *'a sign'* [written in connection with circumcision from] *'a sign'* [written in connection with the Sabbath].[2] If so, let *Tefillin*, in connection with which *'sign'*[3] is written, supersede the Sabbath?[4]—Rather *'covenant'* is learnt from *'covenant'*.[5] Then let [the circumcision of] an adult, in connection with whom *'covenant'* is written,[6] supersede the Sabbath?[7]—Rather *'generations'* is learnt from *'generations'*.[8] Then let fringes, in connection with which *'generations'* is written,[9] supersede the Sabbath?[10]—Rather said R. Naḥman b. Isaac: We learn *'sign,' 'covenant,'* and *'generations'* from *'sign,' 'covenant'* and *'generations,'* thus excluding the others in connection with each of which only one is written.

R. Joḥanan said: Scripture saith, *in the* [*eighth*] *day, 'in the day'* [implying] even on the Sabbath.[11] Resh Laḳish objected to R. Joḥanan: If so, those who lack atonement,[12] in connection with
b whom *'in the day'* is written,[1] do they too supersede the Sabbath?[2]—That is required [for teaching], by day but not by night.[3] But this too[4] is required [for teaching], by day but not by night?—That is deduced from, *and he that is eight* days *old*.[5] But this too can be derived from, *in the day that he commanded* [*the children of Israel to offer their oblations*, etc.]?[6]—Though it may be derived from, *'in the day that he commanded*, [etc.]', yet it [the other verse] is necessary: you might argue, Since the Merciful One had compassion upon him, [permitting him] to bring [a lesser sacrifice] in poverty, he may bring [it] at night too: hence we are informed [otherwise]. Rabina demurred: If so,[7] let a *zar* and an *onen*[8] be eligible for them?[9]—Surely Scripture brought him back.[10]

R. Aḥa b. Jacob said, Scripture saith, *'the eighth'*, [intimating] the eighth, even if it is the Sabbath. But this *'eighth'* is required to exclude the seventh?—That follows from, *'and he that is* eight *days old'*. Yet they are still required, one to exclude the seventh and the other to exclude the ninth, for if [we deduced] from one [verse only] I might say, only the seventh is excluded, since its time [for circumcision] has not [yet] arrived, but from the eighth onward that is the [right] time? Hence it is clear [that it must be explained] as R. Joḥanan.

It was taught in accordance with R. Joḥanan and not as R. Aḥa b. Jacob: '[*And in*] *the eighth* [*day the flesh of his foreskin*] *shall be circumcised*': even on the Sabbath. Then to what do I apply, *every one that profaneth it shall surely be put to death?*[11] To labours other than circumcision. Yet perhaps it is not so, but [it includes] even circumcision, whilst to what do I apply *'in the eighth ... shall be circumcised'*: [To all days] except the Sabbath? Therefore *'in the day'* is stated, [teaching], even on the Sabbath.

Raba observed: Why was this Tanna content at first, and what
c was his difficulty eventually?[1]—He argues thus: '[*in*] *the eighth ... shall be circumcised*': even on the Sabbath. Then to what do I apply, *'every one that profaneth it shall be put to death'?* To labours other than circumcision, but circumcision supersedes it. What is the reason? It [follows] *a minori*. If leprosy, which suspends the sacrificial

(3) They must be performed at a certain time or not at all. But circumcision, though obligatory for the eighth day from birth, can and must be performed afterwards if not done then. (4) Lev. XII, 3. (5) It cannot be to teach that circumcision itself is performed on the Sabbath, because as stated *infra* that is already known by tradition, hence it must refer to its preliminaries. (6) In the passage enjoining circumcision upon Abraham and his descendants (Gen. XVII) *'covenant'* is mentioned thirteen times, which shows its great importance. (7) Rashi: Received from Moses on Sinai. (8) A nazirite by its touch, and he must commence again (cf. Num. VI, 9-12).

a (1) R. Akiba deduced *a minori* from the former that if a nazirite is under the same covering as a quarter *log* of blood taken from a corpse he is defiled, just as in the first case; v. Naz. 57*a*. (2) Circumcision: *and it shall be a* sign *of a covenant betwixt me and you* (Gen. XVII, 11); Sabbath: *for it is a sign between me and you* (Ex. XXXI, 13). Since both are so designated, it follows that the former must be performed even on the latter. (3) Deut. VI, 8: *And thou shalt bind them for a* sign *upon thine hand*. (4) [Probably, one should be permitted to carry them on him in the street on the Sabbath]. (5) V. n. 2 for circumcision; Sabbath: *Wherefore the children of Israel shall keep the Sabbath ... for a perpetual* covenant (Ex. XXXI, 16). (6) Gen. XVII, 14: *And the uncircumcised male who is not circumcised in the flesh of his foreskin ... hath broken my* covenant. In Ḳid. 29*a* this is referred to an adult whom his father had omitted to circumcise, and it throws the obligation upon himself. (7) Whereas it is stated *infra* that it supersedes the Sabbath only when performed on the eighth day. (8) Sabbath: *to observe the Sabbath throughout their* generations (Ex. XXXI, 16); circumcision: *every male throughout your* generations (Gen. XVII, 12). (9) Num. XV, 38: *bid them ... make them fringes ... throughout their* generations. (10) I.e., let it be permitted to insert them in garments on the Sabbath. (11) This is according to the Rabbis. R. Eliezer, as stated *supra*, utilizes this in respect of the preliminaries. Hence he holds that circumcision itself is a traditional law, whilst he learns that life saving is permitted from a Scriptural verse (Yoma 85*b*). (12) This is the technical designation of all unclean persons who must offer a sacrifice as part of their purification rites, viz., a *zab* and a *zabah*, a leper, and a woman after childbirth.

b (1) E.g., *this shall be the law of the leper in the* day *of his cleansing* (Lev. XIV, 2); similarly the rest. (2) They are surely not permitted to bring their offerings on the Sabbath, for only public sacrifices were permitted on them. (3) Sacrifices may not be offered up at night. (4) *'Day'* written in connection with circumcision. (5) Gen. XVII, 12. (6) Lev. VII, 38. (7) That the leniency shown in poverty might be regarded as permitting other things which normally invalidate the sacrifice. (8) V. Glos. for both. (9) *Sc.* to offer these sacrifices. A *zar* may kill the sacrifice, but cannot perform any of the other services in connection therewith. (10) In fact we see that this leniency was not extended to permission to offer at night: thus in all other respects the poor are governed by the same rules as the rich. (11) Ex. XXXI, 14.

c (1) Why does he assume at first that the eighth naturally supersedes the Sabbath, whereas subsequently he finds a difficulty in this assumption and proposes to reverse it?

שכן אם עבר זמנה בטלה אלא היינו טעמא דרבי אליעזר דאמר קרא °וביום השמיני ימול בשר ערלתו ואפילו בשבת וליכתוב רחמנא במילה וליתו הנך וליגמור מיניה משום דאיכא למיפרך מה למילה שכן נכרתו עליה שלש עשרה בריתות: ע"כ לא פליגי רבנן עליה אלא במכשירי מילה אבל מילה גופה דברי הכל דוחה שבת מנלן אמר עולא הלכה וכן אמר רבי יצחק הלכה מיתיבי *מניין לפיקוח נפש שדוחה את השבת רבי אלעזר בן עזריה אומר מה מילה שהיא אחת מאיבריו של אדם דוחה את השבת קל וחומר לפיקוח נפש שדוחה את השבת ואי סלקא דעתך הלכה קל וחומר מהלכה מי אתי והתניא *אמר לו רבי אלעזר (*בן עזריה) עקיבא עצם כשעורה מטמא הלכה ורביעית דם קל וחומר ואין דנין קל וחומר מהלכה אלא אמר רבי אלעזר אתיא אות אות אלא מעתה תפילין דכתיב בהן אות לידחי שבת אלא אתיא ברית ברית גדול דכתיב ביה ברית לידחי שבת אלא אתיא דורות דורות ציצית דכתיב ביה דורות לידחי שבת אלא אמר רב נחמן בר יצחק דנין אות ברית ודורות מאות ברית ודורות לאפוקי הנך דחד חד הוא דכתיב בהן ור' יוחנן אמר אמר קרא ביום *ביום אפילו בשבת אמר ליה ריש לקיש לרבי יוחנן אלא מעתה מחוסרי כפרה דכתיב בהו ביום הכי נמי דדחו שבת ההוא מיבעי ליה ביום ולא בלילה האי נמי מיבעי ליה ביום ולא בלילה ההוא מבן שמנת ימים נפקא האי נמי מביום צוותו נפקא אע"ג דנפקא מביום צוותו אצטריכא סד"א הואיל וחס רחמנא עליה לאתויי בדלות בלילה נמי ליתי קמ"ל מתקיף לה רבינא אלא מעתה יהא זר כשר בהן ויהא אונן כשר בהן הא אהדריה קרא רב אחא בר יעקב אמר אמר קרא שמיני שמיני אפילו בשבת האי שמיני מיבעי ליה למעוטי שביעי שביעי מבן שמנת ימים נפקא ואכתי מיבעי ליה חד למעוטי שביעי וחד למעוטי תשיעי דאי מחד הוה אמינא שביעי הוא דלא מטא זמניה אבל משמיני ואילך זמניה הוא אלא מחוורתא כדרבי יוחנן תניא כוותיה דרבי יוחנן ודלא כרב אחא בר יעקב שמיני ימול אפילו בשבת ומה אני מקיים °מחלליה מות יומת בשאר מלאכות חוץ ממילה או אינו אלא אפי' מילה ומה אני מקיים שמיני ימול חוץ משבת ת"ל ביום אפילו בשבת אמר רבא האי תנא מעיקרא מאי קא ניחא ליה ולבסוף מאי קא קשיא ליה הכי קאמר שמיני ימול אפילו בשבת ומה אני מקיים מחלליה מות יומת בשאר מלאכו' חוץ ממילה אבל מילה דחיא מ"ט ק"ו הוא ומה צרע' שדוחה את העבודה ועבודה

תורה אור: ויקרא יב · שמות לא

רש"י

שאם עבר זמנן בטלין · הילכך דחו: וביום השמיני ימול ואפילו בשבת · ומילה גופה דדחיא שבת אמרינן לקמן הלכה למשה מסיני אייתר ליה ביום למכשיריה: י"ג בריתות · נאמרו לאברהם בפרשת מילה (בראשית יז): והא תניא · במסכת נזיר: עקיבא עצם כשעורה הלכה · שהיה ר"ע דן ק"ו מניין לרביעית דם המת שהנזיר מגלח על אהלה ק"ו מה עצם כשעורה שאינו מטמא באהל נזיר מגלח על מגעו ומשאו רביעית דם שמטמאה באהל דכתיב ועל כל נפש מת לא יבא אינו דין שהנזיר מגלח עליה ואמר ליה רבי אלעזר עקיבא עצם כשעורה הלכה למשה מסיני שיהא נזיר מגלח עליה ורביעית דם אתה בא ללמוד ממנה בק"ו ואין דנין קל וחומר מהלכה דלא ניתנה תורה שבעל פה לידרש בי"ג מדות: אתיא אות אות · בשבת כתיב (שמות לא) כי אות היא ובמילה כתיב (בראשית יז) והיה לאות ברית מה להלן שבת אף כאן שבת: אלא מעתה · אי הך ג"ש דאות האמורה בשבת נאמרה בסיני לידרש שתיבה זו לדרשה נאמרה ליגמר מינה נמי לתפילין: אלא אתיא ברית ברית · ההוא דאות אות לא נאמרה בסיני ואין אדם דן גזרה שוה מעצמו אלא הך דברית ברית נאמרה בסיני ובשבת כתיב ברית (שמות לא) לדורותם ברית עולם: גדול · בן שלש עשרה דהוי מילה שלא בזמנה: דכתיב ביה ברית · וערל זכר אשר לא ימול וגו' את בריתי הפר (בראשית יז) והאי קרא בגדול כתיב מדמחייב ליה כרת שאם לא מלו אביו חייב למול את עצמו ולידחי שבת ואנן אמרינן לקמן דאפילו יום טוב אינה דוחה אלא בזמנה: דורות דורות · בשבת כתיב לדורותם ברית עולם ובמילת קטן כתיב (שם) ובן שמנת ימים ימול לכם כל זכר לדורותיכם: ביום ואפילו בשבת · מדלא כתיב בשמיני ימול ולר' אליעזר דאפקיה למכשירין מילה עצמה הלכה היא ופיקוח נפש לא אתיא ליה בק"ו ממילה אלא מקראי נפקא ליה כדאמרינן בפרק בתרא דיומא*: מחוסרי כפרה · כל טמאין שהוצרכו לקרבן זב וזבה יולדת ומצורע נאמר בהן וביום השמיני: ביום לוותו · את בני ישראל להקריב את קרבניהם (ויקרא ז) ביום ולא בלילה: אלא מעתה · משום דהוכשר להביא בדלות מכשירין בה שאר פסולין: יהא זר ואונן כשר בהן · אונן עד שלא נקבר מתו פסול לעבודה דכתיב (שם כא) בכהן גדול לאביו ולאמו לא יטמא ומן המקדש לא יצא ולא יחלל והכי משמע אף ביום שמתו אביו ואמו אינו צריך לצאת מן המקדש אלא מקריב אונן ולא יחלל ועבודתו לא תהא מחוללת בכך הא אחר שלא יצא חילל: הא אהדריה קרא · לפסול בהן לילה דכתיב בהו וביום כדאמרינן וכיון דלענין לילה תורת כל הקרבנות עליהן לענין זר ואונן נמי תורת קרבן עליהן: שמיני · כל שהוא שמיני ואפילו בשבת וביום למעוטי לילה: תניא כוותיה דר' יוחנן · דיליף מוביום: מעיקרא מאי ניחא ליה · לאוקמי שמיני דווקא ואפילו בשבת ודחי מחלליה מות יומת אלא שאר מלאכות מאיזה טעם נראה לו כן: ולבסוף · כשהיפך דבריו ואמר או אינו אלא אפי' מילה בכלל מחלליה מות יומת דהוא דווקא ודחי שמיני ימול אלא שאר ימים: מאי קשיא ליה · בטעמא הראשון: אבל מילה דחיא · שבת בק"ו ותיגמר מיניה למידחי מחלליה מות יומת אלא שאר מלאכות ולמימר שמיני דווקא קאמר ואפי' ביום שבת: ומה צרעת שדוחה את העבודה · אזהרה שהזהירה תורה על הצרעת שלא לקוץ בהרתו כדתניא (מכות דף כב:) השמר בנגע הצרעת אזהרה בקוצץ בהרתו הכתוב מדבר והחמירה תורה באזהרה זו לדחות העבודה כדקיימא לן בפסחים (דף סז:) דטומאת מת נדחית בקרבן צבור ולא זבין ומצורעי' ובטלים לעשות פסח ולא אמרינן יקוצו בהרתן ויאכלו פסחים או הכהן יקוץ בהרתו ויעבוד אם הכהנים טמאין בצרעת והקהל טהורין:

תוספות

והתניא אמר ליה רבי אלעזר כו' · ול"ג והתנן דכל זה אינו במשנה: ההיא מבן שמונת ימים נפקא · תימה דתניא בת"כ ומייתי לה בפרק הערל (יבמות עב:) השמיני ימול דתניא יכול בין ביום ובין בלילה ת"ל ביום אין לי אלא שנימול לח' נימול לט' לי' ולי"א מניין שאינו נימול אלא ביום ת"ל וביום ובפ"ב דמגילה (דף כ:) נמי אמר אין מוהלין אלא ביום דכתיב וביום השמיני ויש לומר דסמיך אבן שמנת ימים ודרשא פשוטה נקט: אלא מעתה יהא זר ואונן כשר בהן · לאו דווקא נקט זר דהא בכולהו בזב וזבה ויולדת ומצורע כתב בהו כהן:

הא אהדריה קרא · והוה ליה דבר שיצא מן הכלל לידון בדבר החדש לאתויי בדלות שאי אתה יכול להחזירו לכללו לפסול לילה ואונן עד שיחזירנו הכתוב לכללו בפירוש הרי החזירה בפירוש ופסל לילה וה"ה אונן וקשה ואמאי לא קאמר דאהדריה קרא מדכתיב כהן ולא זר ושמא לשום דרשא אחריתי אתא:

תניא כוותיה דרבי יוחנן ודלא כרב אחא בר יעקב · ודלא כרב נחמן בר יצחק דאמר אתיא אות ברית דורות לא הוי דאיהו מודה דדרשינן ביום כדדרשינן בברייתא ואות ברית דורות אתא למכשירין וביום למילה גופה ולית ליה למילה הלכה אע"ג דר' יוחנן אית ליה *הלכה לר' אליעזר [כדפי' רש"י והאי ברייתא דדרשי ביום אתיא כרבנן דביום] אילטריך למילה גופה ולהכי לא קאמר אלא דלא כרב אחא דברייתא מוכחא בהדיא דלא בעיא למדרש שמיני ימול · מ"ר: מה צרעת שדוחה את העבודה · תימה ולימא קל וחומר איפכא ותדחה עבודה את הצרעת שיקוץ בהרתו כדי לעשות עבודה ומה שבת שדוחה את המילה ומילה דוחה את הצרעת עבודה דוחה אותה צרעת שנדחה מפני מילה אינו דין שתהא עבודה דוחה אותה והא דאמרינן בפסחים בפרק אלו דברים (דף סז:) וישלחו מן המחנה כל צרוע וכל זב וכל טמא לנפש אם טמאי מתים משתלחין זבים ומצורעים לא כ"ש אלא יש לך שעה שזבין ומצורעים משתלחים ואין טמאי מתים משתלחים ואיזה זה פסח הבא בטומאה

רבינו חננאל

כיוצא בו . עד כאן לא פליגי ר' אליעזר ורבנן אלא במכשירי מילה אבל במילה עצמה דברי הכל דחיא שבת . מנלן עולא ור' אסי ור' יצחק נפחא כולהי אימרי הלכה ומותבינן עליהן . מניין לפקוח נפש שדוח' שבת נענה ר' אלעזר בן עזריה ואמר ומה מילה שהיא אחד מאבריו של אדם דוחה שבת ק"ו לפקוח נפש שדוחה את השבת ואי ס"ד הלכה ק"ו מהלכה(מייתי)[מי אתי]. והתניא א"ל ר' עקיבא עצם כשעורה הלכה ורביעית דם ק"ו ואין דנין ק"ו מהלכה וכו' לבטלו וזה מפורש בנזיר פר' כ"ג ונזיר אןמטמאין לקרוביהן וכו' . ובטלו דברי מי שאמר הלכה היא ובא ר' אלעזר ללמדו בג"ש באות אות משבת . ונדחו דבריו ובא רב נחמן בר יצחק ולמדו באות ברית ודורו' בשבת כתיב לעשות את השבת לדורותם ברית עולםביני ובין בני ישראל אות היא לעולם במילה כתיב ואתה את בריתי תשמור אתה וזרעך אחריך לדורותם וכתיב ונמלתם את בשר ערלתכם והיתה לאות ברית ביני וביניכם . ר' יוחנן אמר אמר קרא וביום השמיני ימול בשר ערלתו ביוםאפילו בשבת אקשינן עליה ר"ל אי הכי אפילו מחוסרי כפרה כגון מצורע והזבה דכתי' בהןוביום השמיני יקח שני כבשים וגו' ובזבה כתיב וביום השמיני תקח לה שתי תורים הכי נמי כיון דכתיב בהו וביום יקריבו קרבנותיהםאפילו בשבת והא קיי"ל אין קרבן יחיד דוחה את השבת ופירק לו זה שכתוב במחוסרי כפרה וביום למעוטי לילה · עוד הקשה לו ר"לוכל קשיא שהקשה לו פירק ר' יוחנן וחזר רבינא להתקיף על פירוק ר' יוחנן ופריק סד"א הואיל וחס רחמנא עליה לאתויי בדלות בלילה נמי ליתי קמ"ל וביום . התקיף רבינא אי הכי אמ' דחס עליהן או אינו כשר בהן ולא יטריחם להמתין עד שימצאו כהן טהור כשר לטהרם ופריק הא אהדריה קרא כלומר אע"פ שחס עליו והקל בקרבנו החזיר לטהרת הכהן שנאמר והביא אותםביום השמיני לטהרתו אל הכהן וגו' ואתא רב אחא בר יעקב עוד להוציאו שהמילה מותרת בשבת מדכתיב וביוםהשמיני ימול כלומר איזה יפול שמיני אין לך לא להקדים ולא לאחר ונתקשה ולא עמדו דבריו ואמרינן אלא מחוורתא כר' יוחנן דאפקיה מן וביום . וסוגיא דשמעתיה כר' יוחנןודתניא כותי'. ולא כר' אחא בר יעקב:

רב נסים גאון

איצטריך סלקא דעתך אמינא הואיל וחס רחמנא עליה לאיתויי בדלות בלילה נמי ליתי קמ"ל מתקיף לה רבינא [אלא]מעתה יהא זר ואונן כשר בהן חייבנו הקב"ה בתורת הקרבנות שנקריבם ביום ולא בלילה שנאמר (ויקרא ז) אשר צוה ה' את משה ביום צותו את בני ישראל ופירש ביום צותו למדנו לכל הקרבנות כולם שאינן כשירין אלא ביום ובפרק הקורא את המגילה (דף כ) שנינו כל היום כשר לסמיכה לשחיטה כו' ובתלמוד אמרו לסמיכה ולשחיטה דכתיב (ויקרא ג) וסמך ושחט ואיתקש סמיכה לשחיטה ובשחיטה כתיב (שם יט) ביום זבחכם לקמיצה והגשה והזייה בכולהי כתיב ביום צותו והזהיר האונן והזר עם כל המנויין במשנה שלא יקרבו להקריב קרבן כמו שאמרה המשנה (זבחים דף טו) כל הזובחים שקיבל דמן זר ואונן כולם פסולין ובגמ' גרסי זר מנלן דתני לוי (ויקרא כב) דבר אל אהרן ואל בניו וינזרו למעוטי מאי כו' אלא הכי קאמר וינזרו מקדשי בני ישראל ולא יחללו כלומר בני ישראל ראוי להם שיתרחקו מן הקדשים ולא יקריבו אותן שלא יחללום שאם יקרבו אליהם ויקריבו אותם מחללים אותם ואמר עוד (במדבר יח) וזר לא יקרב ונאמר בעונש (שם) והזר הקרב יומת ובאונן עוד אמרו מנלן דכתיב (ויקרא כא) ומן המקדש לא יצא ולא יחלל הא אחר שלא יצא חילל וכשאמרנו כי המחוסר כפרה והוא המצורע ששלמו ימי טהרתו ועדיין לא הקריב קרבן לא נאמר בו וביום השמיני אלא לחייב הקרבת קרבנו ביום ולא בלילה הקשינו לאמר כי דבר זה ידוע הוא לפי שכתב כן במקום אחר ביום צותו וממנו ידענו חיוב הקרבת כל הקרבנות ביום ולא בלילה והואיל וכן אין אנו צריכין לשנותו לנו עוד ופירק האומר דבר זה ואמר שמה שאמר כאן וביום השמיני אינו לשנות אלא שאנו צריכין לאותו דבר מפני שמצאנו שהקל כאן על המצורע ואמר בו (ויקרא יד) ואם דל הוא ואין ידו משגת מה שלא הקל על זולתו מכלל הטמאים והם זב וזבה ואילמלי שאמר בו וביום השמיני לחייב הקרבת קרבנו ביום היה עולה על דעתנו הואיל והיקל עליו הכתוב שדי לו בשתי תורים או ב' בני יונה להטאתו ולעולתו ושינה בינו ובין שאר הטמאות בדבר זה והם הנזכרים אחריו הזב והזבה כמו כן נמי ראוי שיקריב קרבנותיו בלילה ולא היינו לומדין משפטו משאר הקרבנות שנאמר בהן ביום צותו הילכך הוצרכנו להשמיענו וביום השמיני כדי שירחיק מדעתנו סברא זו התקיף (רבא) [רבינא] ואמר הואיל ואתה אומר כי לפי שהקל עליו הכתוב שיביא שתי תורים או שני בני יונה מה שאין כן בזולתו לא נלמוד משאר הקרבנות כלום ממשפטיו מפני שיצא מכללם מחמת שייחדו הכתוב בדבר זה ואילמלא שאמר הכתוב וביום השמיני היינו מתירים הקרבת קרבנותיו בלילה לפי דבר זה ראוי להיות הזר והאונן וכל המנויין

[תוספ' פס"ז] יומא פה: מכילתא פרשת כי תשא · פסחים פה: נזיר נז. [בפסחים ובנזיר ליתא] · [סנהדרין נט:] · [דף פה:]

תוספות

בטומאה אלמא דצרעת דוחה את העבודה נימא דהיינו כל זמן שהיא עליו ובק"ו נילף שיקוץ בהרתו כדי לעשות עבודה ועוד קשה לימא רציחה תוכיח שדוחה את העבודה ואינו דוחה שבת אף אני אביא מילה וכי תימא מילה עדיפא שדוחה צרעת הדוחה את העבודה אכתי נימא קבורת מת מצוה תוכיח דעדיפא ממילה שדוחה את המילה מולאחותו הדוחה את הצרעת הדוחה את העבודה הדוחה את השבת אפילו הכי לא דחיא שבת ויש לומר דהכי נמי הוה מצי למימר איפכא ורציחה תוכיח או קבורת מת מצוה תוכיח אלא דניחא ליה לומר שיהא דוחה דנפקא ליה מביום דמילה דחיא שבת ועושה מתחילה ק"ו להעמיד דבריו וסותרו אחר כך שאינו ק"ו כלל א) ופריך ליה מיניה וביה: **הדר** אמר ממאי דשבת חמירא דילמא צרעת חמירא · תימה דבברייתא דלעיל מסיק איפכא דלאו משום דצרעת חמירא אלא משום (ג) גברא דלא חזי ורבא גופיה סבירא ליה הכי לקמן ועוד למאי דקאמר השתא מנלן דצרעת דוחה את העבודה אימא דעבודה דוחה הצרעת מק"ו ומה שבת חמורה [צרעת לא כ"ש והאומר ר"י דלהאי לישנא] צריך לומר דגרסינן רבה הכא ולית ליה דרבא דלקמן דטעמא משום דגברא לא חזי וסבירא ליה כרב ספרא דפליג עליה דרבא לקמן והא דפשיט להו לרבה ורב ספרא דצרעת דוחה עבודה מצי למימר דמקרא נפקא להו אבל רבא דס"ל גברא לא חזי לדידיה לא בעי קרא ועוד נראה לרשב"א ב) דאפי' ליכא קרא דצרעת דוחה עבודה אתי שפיר אפילו לרב ספרא דלא קאמר רב ספרא שיהא הטעם ודאי דצרעת דוחה עבודה משום חומרא דצרעת אלא איכא למימר הכי ואיכא למימר הכי הילכך בברייתא דלעיל סתר ק"ו דקאמר וממאי דצרעת חמירא דילמא משום גברא דלא חזי והכא ולקמן על מילתא דרבא דחיקן בע"א ממאי דשבת חמירא דילמא צרעת חמירא שכן דוחה את העבודה וזיל הכא קא מדחי ליה וזיל הכא קא מדחי ליה ומהאי טעמא נמי ליכא למילף ביה ק"ו דעבודה תדחי צרעת דשבת דחמורה דוחה צרעת לא כ"ש דדילמא אין לתלות משום חומרא אלא משום (ג) גברא לא חזי: **האי** עשה ולא תעשה הוא · השמר היינו לאו ולעשות היינו עשה כדפי' בקונטרס ואע"ג דאמר בסוף פרק הקומץ (מנחות דף לו:) השמר דלאו לאו השמר דעשה עשה מכל מקום לאו מצות עשה הוא אלא לא תעשה ג) דאמר רחמנא הזהר פן תקוץ בהרת תימה היכי מצינן למימר דלעשות אתא לעשה הא אמר לקמן דאיצטריך לעשות אי אתה עושה אבל אתה עושה בסיב שעל גבי רגלו ויש לפרש דעשה שמעינן מדכתיב ד) לשמור ואם תאמר והא אמר בסמוך היכא אמרינן דאתי עשה ודחי את לא תעשה כגון מילה בצרעת אלמא דליכא בצרעת אלא לאו ואר"ת דלא נקטינן אלא לסימנא בעלמא ואם תאמר והא דקי"ל דלאו עשה דוחה את לא תעשה ועשה נגמר ממילה בצרעת דדחי וי"ל מה למילה *שכן נכרתו עליה י"ג בריתות*:

גמרא

ועבודה דוחה את השבת מילה דוחה אותה שבת שנדחית מפני העבודה אינו דין שתהא מילה דוחה אותה ומאי או אינו דקאמר הדר אמר וממאי דצרעת חמורה דילמא שבת חמורה שכן יש בה עונשין ואזהרות הרבה (*אי נמי) וממאי משום דחמירא צרעת היא דילמא משום גברא הוא דלא חזי ומה אני מקיים שמיני ימול חוץ משבת °תלמוד לומר ביום אפילו בשבת: תנו רבנן °מילה דוחה את הצרעת בין בזמנה בין שלא בזמנה °יום טוב אינה דוחה אלא בזמנה בלבד מנהני מילי דתנו רבנן °ימול בשר ערלתו °ואע"פ שיש שם בהרת יקוץ ומה אני מקיים °השמר בנגע הצרעת בשאר מקומות חוץ ממילה או אינו אלא אפילו מילה ומה אני מקיים ימול בשר ערלתו בזמן שאין בה בהרת ת"ל בשר ואע"פ שיש שם בהרת אמר רבא האי תנא מעיקרא מאי ניחא ליה ולבסוף מאי קשיא ליה הכי קאמר ימול בשר ערלתו ואע"פ שיש בהרת ומה אני מקיים השמר בנגע הצרעת בשאר מקומות חוץ ממילה אבל מילה דוחה את הצרעת מ"ט דאתיא מק"ו ומה שבת חמורה מילה דוחה אותה צרעת לא כ"ש ומאי או אינו דקאמר הדר קאמר ממאי דשבת חמירא דילמא צרעת חמירא שכן דוחה את העבודה ועבודה דוחה את השבת ת"ל בשר ואע"פ שיש שם בהרת לישנא אחרינא מילה דוחה את הצרעת מ"ט דאתי עשה ודחי לא תעשה ומאי או אינו דקאמר הדר קאמר אימר דאמרינן דאתי עשה ודחי את לא תעשה גרידא האי עשה ולא תעשה הוא ומה אני מקיים ימול בשר ערלתו בזמן שאין בה בהרת ת"ל בשר ואע"פ שיש שם בהרת תינח גדול דכתיב בהו בשר קטן נמי כתיב ביה בשר בינוני מנלן אמר אביי אתיא מבינייא מגדול לא אתיא שכן ענוש כרת מקטן לא אתיא שכן מילה בזמנה הצד השוה שבהן שכן נימולין ודוחין את הצרעת אף כל שנימולין דוחין את הצרעת רבא אמר מילה בזמנה דוחה לא צריכא קרא מק"ו אתיא ומה שבת דחמירא דוחה צרעת לא כל שכן אמר ליה רב ספרא לרבא ממאי דשבת חמירא דילמא צרעת חמירא שכן דוחה את העבודה ועבודה דוחה את השבת התם לאו משום דחמירא צרעת אלא משום דגברא הוא דלא חזי אמאי ויקוץ בהרתו ויעבוד מחוסר טבילה הוא תינח נגעים טמאים נגעים *טהורים מאי איכא למימר אלא א"ר אשי *היכא אמרינן דאתי עשה ודחי ל"ת כגון מילה בצרעת א"נ ציצית וכלאים דבעידנא דמתעקר לאו קא מוקי' עשה הכא בעידנא דמתעקר ללאו לא קא מוקים עשה והא דרבא ורב ספרא תנאי

רש"י

ועבודה · חמורה היא שדוחה שבת בתמידין ומוספין וקרבנות צבור שזמנם קבוע : מילה דוחה אותה · את הצרעת כדתניא לקמן ימול בשר ערלתו אפילו במקום בהרת יקוץ : ומה או אינו דקאמר · דמשמע או אינו כן כמו שאמרנו אלא אפי' מילה נמי בכלל מחלליה מאי קשיא ליה דקא הדר ביה : הדר אמר תנא · לנפשיה ממאי דצרעת חמורה משבת דתימא ק"ו : דילמא שבת חמורה כו' · דהאי דצרעת דוחה עבודה ממאי דמשום חומרא דצרעת היא דילמא הא דלא אמרינן ליה יקוץ משום דגברא דלא חזי הוא כדלקמן דאי נמי קייץ מחוסר טבילה והערב שמש והיום לא יעבוד (א) וטבול יום דמצורע כמצורע הילכך מחלליה מות יומת אפילו במילה ועל כרחך שמיני ימול תדחה אלא שאר ימים : בין שלא בזמנה · כגון קטן חולה והמתינו לו עד שיבריא : בשר · ריבויא הוא ולדרשה : ה"ג ל"א מאי טעמא אתי עשה ודחי לא תעשה · מ"ט מילה דוחה צרעת דאתי עשה דימול ודחי לא תעשה דהשמר (ג) לך דהכי קי"ל בפ"ק דיבמות (דף ג:) דאתי עשה ודחי לא תעשה: האי עשה ולא תעשה הוא · השמר לא תעשה הוא ולעשות ככל אשר יורו (דברים כד) היינו עשה : תינח גדול · בר עונשין דכתיב ביה בשר וערל זכר אשר לא ימול את בשר ערלתו (בראשית יז) והאי בבר עונשין משתעי מדמחייב ליה כרת וקטן נמי בזמנה ביום השמיני כתיב ביה בשר וביום השמיני ימול בשר ערלתו : בינוני · כגון שלא בזמנה ולאו בר עונשין ואביו מצווה עליו נפקא לן מהמול לכם כל זכר (קדושין דף כט·) : אתיא מבינייא · הצד השוה שבהן שנימולו ודוחין את הצרעת אף אני אביא בינוני שנימול וידחה הצרעת : לא צריכא קרא כו' · וכי אתיא קרא לשלא בזמנה של בינוני : דגברא לא חזי · קס"ד מפני שהוא טמא והיינו דפריך ויקוץ ויטהר ויעבוד : מחוסר טבילה · ולא חזי לעבודה בהאי יומא ומשום למחר דליתא לעבודה קמן לא מדחי : נגעים טהורין · כגון בהק ופרחה בכוליה ובכולהו איתרבו לאיסור קציצה בסיפרי אין לי אלא משנזקק לטומאה עד שלא נזקק לטומאה מניין ת"ל ככל אשר יורו : אלא אמר רב אשי · הא דאמרינן שבת חמירא מצרעת אע"ג דדחייה צרעת לעבודה לאו חומרא דידה הוא אלא היינו טעמא כי אמרינן אתי עשה ודחי לא תעשה כגון מילה בצרעת דבשעת קציצה דמיעקר לאו מקיים עשה וכן ציצית דכלאים בשעת לבישה מיעקר לאו ומקיים עשה אבל צרעת הנקצצת משום עבודה בעידנא דמיעקר לאו דקציצה אכתי לא מקיים עשה דעבודה הילכך מידחיא עבודה ולאו חומרא דצרעת הוא : תנאי · רבא אמר מילה בזמנה לא צריכא קרא · והילכך האי בשר דכתיב בה אם אינו ענין לזמנה תנהו ענין לשלא בזמנה ולאו אינו דקתני הוא מפרש רבא כלישנא אחרינא :

רבינו חננאל

הגהות הב"ח

רב נסים גאון

service,[2] [132b] whilst the sacrificial service supersedes the Sabbath,[3] yet circumcision supersedes it:[4] then the Sabbath, which is superseded by the sacrificial service, surely circumcision supersedes it. And what is the 'or perhaps it is not so' which he states? —He then argues [thus]: yet whence [does it follow] that leprosy is more stringent? Perhaps the Sabbath is more stringent, since there are many penalties and injunctions in connection therewith. Further, whence [does it follow] that it[5] is because leprosy is more stringent, perhaps it is because the man is not fit;[6] whilst to what do I apply, '*in the eighth ... shall be circumcised*', [to all days] except the Sabbath? Therefore '*in the day*' is stated, teaching, even on the Sabbath.

Our Rabbis taught: Circumcision supersedes leprosy, whether [performed] at its [proper] time[7] or not at its [proper] time; it supersedes Festivals only [when performed] at its [proper] time. How do we know this?—Because our Rabbis taught: '*The flesh of*
a *his foreskin shall be circumcised*'; even if a *bahereth*[1] is there it must be cut off. Then to what do I apply, '*Take heed in the plague of leprosy*'?[2] To other places, but excluding the foreskin. Or perhaps it is not so, but [it includes] even the foreskin, while how do I apply, '*the flesh of his foreskin shall be circumcised*', when it does not contain a *bahereth!* Therefore '*flesh*' is stated, intimating even when a *bahereth* is there. Raba observed: This Tanna, why was he content at first, and what was his difficulty eventually?—He argues thus: '*The flesh of his foreskin shall be circumcised*': even if a *bahereth*' is there. Then to what do I apply: '*Take heed in the plague of leprosy*'? To other places, excluding the foreskin, yet circumcision supersedes leprosy. What is the reason? Because it is inferred *a minori:* if circumcision supersedes the Sabbath, which is stringent, how much more so leprosy. And what is the 'or perhaps it is not so' which he states? He then argues: how do we know that the Sabbath is more stringent: perhaps leprosy is more stringent, since it supersedes the sacrificial service, while the sacrificial service supersedes the Sabbath? Therefore *flesh* is stated, intimating, even when a *bahereth* is there. Another version: circumcision supersedes leprosy: what is the reason? Because a positive command[3] comes and supersedes a negative command.[4] Then what is the 'or is it not so' which he states? He then argues: Perhaps we rule that a positive command comes and supersedes a negative command [only in the case of] a negative command by itself, but this is a positive command plus a negative command.[5] Then how do I apply, *the flesh of his foreskin shall be circumcised?* When it does not contain a *bahereth*. Therefore *flesh* is stated, intimating, even when a *bahereth* is there.

Now, this is well of an adult, in connection with whom '*flesh*' is written; of an infant too '*flesh*' is written; but whence do we
b know one of intermediate age?[1]—Said Abaye, It is inferred from the other two combined:[2] it cannot be inferred from an adult [alone], since there is the penalty of *kareth*[3] [in his case]; it cannot be inferred from an infant [eight days old], since [there] it is circumcision at the proper time. The feature common to both is that they must be circumcised and they supersede leprosy: so all who must be circumcised supersede leprosy.

Raba said: [That] circumcision at the proper time supersedes [leprosy] requires no verse, [for] it is inferred *a minori:* If it supersedes the Sabbath, which is [more] stringent, how much more so leprosy! Said R. Safra to Raba: How do you know that the Sabbath is [more] stringent, perhaps leprosy is [more] stringent, seeing that it supersedes the sacrificial service, whilst the sacrificial service supersedes the Sabbath?—There it is not because leprosy is more stringent but because the person is unfit. Why so? Let him cut off the *bahereth* and perform the service?—He [still] lacks *ṭebillah*. This is well of unclean eruptions! what can be said of clean eruptions?[4]—Rather R. Ashi said: Where do we rule that a positive command comes and supersedes a negative one? E.g., circumcision in [the place of] leprosy, or fringes and *kil'ayim*,[5] where at the very moment that the negative injunction is disregarded[6] the
c positive command is fulfilled;[1] but here at the moment that the negative injunction is disregarded the positive command is not fulfilled.[2]

(2) It is stated *infra* that one may not cut away a leprous bright spot in order to be clean, and this holds good even on Passover: individuals may not do so in order to bring the Passover sacrifice, nor may priests to enable them to perform the sacrificial service. (3) Public sacrifices being brought thereon. (4) The injunction not to cut away a leprous bright spot is disregarded when it is on the foreskin which is to be circumcised. (5) *Sc.* the reason that the sacrificial service does not supersede leprosy. (6) For, as stated *infra*, even if the bright spot is cut away he is still unfit to offer the Passover sacrifice until he performs *ṭebillah* and the sun sets. (7) The eighth day from birth.

a (1) A bright, snow-white spot (v. Neg. I, 1) on the skin, which is a symptom of leprosy (Lev. XII, 2 *seq.*). (2) Deut. XXIV, 8; this is interpreted as an injunction against cutting away a leprous bright spot, etc. (3) To circumcise. (4) Not to cut the *bahereth* away. (5) Negative: *Take heed in the plague of leprosy*, '*Take heed*' always being so regarded; positive: *that thou observe diligently*, etc.

b (1) The following three passages are applied to three different cases of circumcision: (i) *And the uncircumcised male who is not circumcised in the flesh of his foreskin, that soul shall be cut off from his people* (Gen. XVII, 14)—this applies to an adult whom his father did not circumcise as an infant. (ii) *And in the eighth day the flesh of his foreskin shall be circumcised* (Lev. XII, 3)—this is a command to the father of the child. (iii) *Every male among you shall be circumcised* (Gen. XVII, 10)—this is a general command, e.g., to the Beth din, for a child to be circumcised after his eighth day if not circumcised at the proper time. Now, '*flesh*' is written in (i) and (ii), but not in (iii), which refers to a child of intermediate age, i.e., between eight days and thirteen years and a day, when he becomes an adult. (2) Lit. 'from between them'. (3) V. Glos. (4) E.g., where the leprosy covers the whole skin (v. Lev. XII, 12f). Even then it must not be cut away and supersedes the sacrificial service. (5) V. Glos. and Deut. XXII, 11f: *Thou shalt not wear a mingled stuff, wool and linen together. Thou shalt make thee fringes upon the four borders of thy vesture.* The juxtaposition of these two laws is interpreted as showing that the former is suspended in the case of fringes, and the garment may be of linen while the fringes are of wool. (6) Lit., 'uprooted'.

c (1) I.e., the latter is fulfilled through the disregard of the former. (2) The cutting away of the *bahereth* itself is not a fulfilment of the command to offer a Passover sacrifice, but merely preliminary thereto, so that the fact that leprosy supersedes the sacrificial service is no mark of the stringency of leprosy.

Now, this [discussion] of Raba and R. Safra [133a] is [a controversy between] Tannaim. For it was taught: '*Flesh*', and even if a *bahereth* is there, '*it shall be circumcised*': the words of R. Josiah. R. Jonathan said: This is unnecessary: if it supersedes the Sabbath [which is more] stringent, how much more so leprosy.[3]

The Master said: '"*Flesh*", and even if a *bahereth* is there, "*it shall be circumcised*": the words of R. Josiah.' Why is a verse required for this: it is an unintentional act,[4] and an unintentional act is permitted?—Said Abaye, This is only necessary according to R. Judah, who maintains: An unintentional act is forbidden. Raba said, You may even say [according to] R. Simeon: R. Simeon admits in the case of 'cut off his head but let him not die.'[5] Now, does not Abaye accept this reasoning? Surely Abaye and Raba both said, R. Simeon admits in the case of, 'cut off his head but let him not die'?—After hearing it from Raba he accepted its logic.

Others recite this [dictum] of Abaye and Raba in reference to the following: *Take heed in the plague of leprosy, that thou observe diligently, to do* [etc.]:[6] '*to do*' thou art forbidden,[7] but thou mayest effect it by means of bast on the foot or a pole on the shoulder, and if it goes it goes.[8] But what need of a verse for this: it is an unintentional act, and an unintentional act is permitted?—Said Abaye: It is only necessary according to R. Judah, who maintains: An unintentional act is forbidden. But Raba said: You may even say [that it agrees with] R. Simeon, yet R. Simeon admits in the case of 'cut off his head but let him not die.' Now, does not Abaye accept this reasoning? Surely Abaye and Raba both said, R. Simeon admits in the case of 'cut off his head but let him not die'? After hearing it from Raba, he accepted its logic.

Now Abaye on R. Simeon's view,[1] how does he utilize this [word] '*flesh*'?—Said R. Amram: As referring to one who asserts that it is his intention to cut off his *bahereth*.[2] That is well of an adult: what can be said of an infant?[3] Said R. Mesharsheya: It refers to the infant's father who asserts that it is his [specific] intention to cut off his son's *bahereth*. Then if there is another,[4] let another perform it; for R. Simeon b. Laḳish said: Wherever you find a positive command and a negative command [in opposition], if you can fulfil both of them, it is preferable;[5] but if not, let the positive command come and supersede the negative command?[6]—This is where there is no stranger.

The Master said, 'It supersedes Festivals only [when performed] at its [proper] time. How do we know this? Hezekiah said, and the School of Hezekiah taught likewise: Scripture saith: *And ye shall let nothing of it remain until the morning; [but that which remaineth of it] until the morning [ye shall burn with fire]*:[7] now [the second] *until the morning* need not be stated: What then is the teaching of, *until the morning?* Scripture comes to appoint the second morning for its burning. Abaye said: Scripture saith, the *burnt-offering of the Sabbath* [shall be burnt] *on its Sabbath*,[8] but not the burnt-offering of weekdays on the Sabbath, nor the burnt-offering of weekdays on Festivals. Raba said: Scripture saith, [*no manner of work shall be done in them save that*
b *which every man must eat*], *that only may be done of you*:[1] '*that*', but not its preliminaries; '*only*', but not circumcision out of its proper time, which might [otherwise] be inferred *a minori*. R. Ashi said: [*On the seventh day is a Sabbath of*] *holy rest* [shabbathon][2] is an affirmative precept, thus there is an affirmative and a negative precept in respect of Festivals, and an affirmative precept cannot supersede a negative plus an affirmative precept.[3]

R. AKIBA STATED A GENERAL PRINCIPLE, etc. Rab Judah said in Rab's name: The *halachah* is as R. Akiba. And we learnt similarly in respect to the Passover sacrifice: R. 'Akiba stated a general principle: Any labour which can be performed on the eve of the Sabbath does not supersede the Sabbath; slaughtering [the Passover sacrifice], which can not be done on the eve of the Sabbath,[4] supersedes the Sabbath; and Rab Judah said in Rab's name: The *halachah* is as R. Akiba. And these are necessary. For if he informed us [of the *halachah*] in connection with circumcision, —it is only there that the preparatory requirements which could be done the previous day do not supersede the Sabbath, since there is no *kareth*;[5] but as for the Passover sacrifice, where there is *kareth*,[6] you might argue, Let them [the preliminaries] supersede the Sabbath. And if he told us [the *halachah*] about the Passover sacrifice, —that is because thirteen covenants were not made in connection therewith; but as for circumcision, seeing that thirteen covenants were made in connection therewith[7] I would say, Let them [the preliminaries] supersede the Sabbath. Thus they are necessary.[8]

MISHNAH. WE PERFORM ALL THE REQUIREMENTS OF
c CIRCUMCISION ON THE SABBATH. WE CIRCUMCISE,[1] UNCOVER [THE CORONA],[2] SUCK [THE WOUND],[3] AND PLACE A COMPRESS AND CUMMIN UPON IT.[4] IF ONE DID NOT CRUSH [THE CUMMIN] ON THE EVE OF THE SABBATH, HE MUST CHEW [IT] WITH HIS TEETH AND APPLY [IT TO THE WOUND]; IF HE DID NOT BEAT UP WINE AND OIL ON THE EVE OF THE SABBATH,[5] EACH MUST BE APPLIED SEPARATELY. WE MAY NOT MAKE A ḤALUḲ[6] FOR IT IN THE FIRST PLACE, BUT MUST WRAP A RAG ABOUT IT. IF THIS WAS NOT PREPARED FROM THE EVE OF THE SABBATH, ONE WINDS IT ABOUT HIS FINGER[7] AND BRINGS IT, AND EVEN THROUGH ANOTHER COURTYARD.

(3) Thus R. Josiah learns circumcision at the proper time supersedes leprosy from '*flesh*', whilst the same for circumcision after the eighth day must be inferred from the common feature (v. *supra* 132*b*), this agreeing with R. Safra's rejection of Raba's argument. Whereas R. Jonathan infers the former *a minori*, so that 'flesh' may be applied to the other case, as Raba. (4) *Sc.* the cutting way of the *bahereth*. (5) V. *supra* 75*a*, n. a8. (6) Deut. XXIV, 8. (7) Lit., 'thou mayest not do'. I.e., one may not intentionally cut off a *bahereth*. (8) I.e., one need not refrain from wearing a tight shoe of bast or carrying a heavy burden on his shoulder, though these may remove the *bahereth*.

(1) Before he accepted Raba's dictum. (2) In order to be rendered clean. Yet even so it is permitted for the sake of circumcision. (3) Eight days old. He has no intention, yet '*flesh*' is written in his case too (v. *supra* 132*b* n. b1). (4) Available to perform the circumcision—the prohibition concerning the *bahereth* will not apply to him, since he has no interest in the child's ritual cleanness. (5) Thus, if a stranger performs it, the positive command of circumcision is fulfilled without violating the injunction of leprosy, since the stranger has no such intention. (6) And thus the question remains: what need is there for the word '*flesh*' in the case of the infant? (7) Ex. XII, 10. (8) Num. XXVIII, 10.

b (1) Ex. XII, 16. (2) Lev. XXIII, 3. (3) V. *supra* 24*b* and 25*a* for notes. From all the foregoing we see that labour which can be done on weekdays or which belongs primarily to weekdays does not supersede Festivals even in the fulfilment of a precept, and the same applies here. (4) If the fourteenth of Nisan falls on the Sabbath. (5) When circumcision is postponed. (6) For not offering it. (7) V. *supra* 132*a* top. (8) V. Pes. 66*a*.

c (1) Cut off the foreskin. (2) *Peri'ah*. By splitting the membrane and pulling it down. (3) *Meẓiẓah*. Nowadays the suction is accomplished by means of a glass cylinder. (4) To make the wound heal. (5) This too was applied to the wound. (6) A kind of shirt-shaped bandage placed over the membrum and tied at the corona, to prevent the flesh from growing back and recovering the membrum. (7) As though it were a garment, so that it shall not be carried just like on weekdays.

תנאי היא דתניא *בשר ואף על פי שיש שם בהרת ימול דברי רבי יאשיה רבי יונתן אומר אינו צריך שבת המורה דוחה צרעת לא כ"ש: אמר מר בשר אע"פ שיש שם בהרת ימול דברי רבי יאשיה *הא למה לי קרא דבר שאין מתכוין הוא ודבר שאין מתכוין מותר אמר אביי לא נצרכא אלא לרבי יהודה דאמר דבר שאין מתכוין אסור רבא אמר אפילו תימא ר"ש מודה ר"ש בפסיק רישיה ולא ימות והא *אביי ורבא דאמרי תרוייהו מודה רבי שמעון בפסיק רישיה ולא ימות בתר דשמעה מרבא סברה איכא דמתני להא דאביי ורבא אהא °השמר בנגע הצרעת לשמור מאד ולעשות *לעשות אי אתה עושה *אבל (א) עושה אתה בסיב שעל גבי רגלו ובמוט שעל גבי כתפו ואם עברה עברה והא למה לי קרא דבר שאין מתכוין הוא ודבר שאין מתכוין מותר אמר אביי לא נצרכא אלא לרבי יהודה דאמר דבר שאין מתכוין אסור ורבא אמר אפילו תימא רבי שמעון ומודה רבי שמעון בפסיק רישיה ולא ימות והא אביי ורבא דאמרי תרווייהו מודה ר' שמעון בפסיק רישיה ולא ימות לבתר דשמעיה מרבא סברה ואביי אליבא דרבי שמעון האי בשר מאי עביד ליה אמר רב עמרם באומר לקוץ בהרתו הוא מתכוין תינח גדול קטן מאי איכא למימר אמר רב משרשיא באומר אבי הבן לקוץ בהרת דבנו הוא קא מתכוין ואי איכא אחר ליעביד אחר *דאמר ר"ש בן לקיש *כל מקום שאתה מוצא עשה ולא תעשה אם אתה יכול לקיים שניהם מוטב ואם לאו יבא עשה וידחה לא תעשה דליכא אחר: °אמר מר יום טוב אינה דוחה אלא בזמנה בלבד מנא הני מילי *אמר חזקיה וכן תנא דבי חזקיה אמר קרא °לא תותירו ממנו (ה)עד בקר שאין ת"ל עד בקר מה ת"ל עד בקר בא הכתוב ליתן לו בקר שני לשריפתו אביי אמר אמר קרא °עולת שבת בשבתו ולא עולת חול בשבת ולא עולת חול בי"ט רבא אמר אמר קרא °הוא לבדו יעשה לכם הוא ולא מכשירין לבדו ולא מילה שלא בזמנה דאתיא מק"ו רב אשי אמר °שבתון עשה הוא והוה ליה י"ט עשה ול"ת ואין עשה דוחה את לא תעשה ועשה: כלל אמר ר"ע וכו': *אמר רב יהודה אמר רב הלכה כר"ע ותנן נמי גבי פסח כי האי גוונא *כלל אמר ר"ע כל מלאכה שאפשר לה לעשותה מע"ש אינה דוחה את השבת שחיטה שאי אפשר לעשותה מע"ש דוחה את השבת ואמר רב יהודה אמר רב הלכה כר"ע וצריכא דאי אשמעינן גבי מילה התם הוא דמכשירין (ג) אפשר לעשות מאתמול לא דחו שבת דליכא כרת אבל פסח דאיכא כרת אימא לידחו שבת ואי אשמעינן גבי פסח משום דלא נכרתו עליה י"ג בריתות אבל מילה דנכרתו עליה י"ג בריתות אימא לידחו שבת צריכא:

מתני' *עושין כל צרכי מילה [בשבת] מוהלין ופורעין ומוצצין ונותנין עליה איספלנית וכמון *אם לא שחק מע"ש °לועס בשיניו ונותן אם לא טרף יין ושמן מע"ש ינתן זה בעצמו וזה בעצמו ואין עושין לה חלוק לכתחילה אבל כורך עליה סמרטוט אם לא התקין מע"ש כורך על אצבעו ומביא ואפי' מחצר אחרת: גמ'

תוספתא נגעים פ"ג · דברים כד · במדבר כח · שמות יב · במדבר כח · שמות יב · ויקרא כג

רש"י

תנאי היא · דאיכא דנפקא ליה מילה בזמנה מק"ו כרבא וכי אתא קרא לשלא בזמנה ואיכא דלא נפקא ליה בק"ו ואיצטריך למילה בזמנה כרב ספרא ושלא בזמנה אתיא מבינייא: לרבי יהודה · רבי יאשיה דמצריך קרא להכי כרבי יהודה סבירא ליה: מודה ר' שמעון בפסיק כו' · הילכך אי לא רבי קרא לא עבדי: סברה · נתן בה דעתיה וקבל ממנו: ה"ג לעשות עושה אתה בסיב שעל רגלו ובמוט שעל גבי כתיפו · ואינו צריך להזהר (*) מלדחות ציב שקושר מנעלו ברגלו ומשאוי על כתיפו: ואם עברה · הבהרת בכך עברה ואינו חושש לה להכי כתיב לעשות שמותר לעשות מלאכתו: ואביי אליבא דר' שמעון · מעיקרא מקמי דסברה האי בשר מאי עביד ליה: באומר לקוץ · גדול שהוא בר עונשין ואומר למוהל לקוץ בהרתו בכוונה ליטהר: קטן · דלא ידע לכווני מאי איכא למימר ועל כרחיך בתרווייהו כתיב בשר כדאמרי' לעיל ובשר דכתיב גבי קטן ביום השמיני ל"ל: באומר אבי הבן לקוץ · דמתכוין לטהרו והוא מוזהר דלא ליעבד בידים ובמתכוין: ואי איכא אחר · שאינו חושש לטהרו ליעבד אחר ולא ליקו אב להתם ואע"ג דרבייה קרא שהרי אתה יכול לקיים עשה בלא עקירת לאו לר' שמעון דהא אחר לא מיכוין ולא עבר ואמר ריש לקיש כו' ורבויא למאי אתא: שאין תלמוד לומר עד בקר · תניינא והנותר ממנו עד בקר דמאי למכתב והנותר באש תשרפו (ג) אלא אשריפה קאי והכי קאמר והנותר ממנו בזמן שאסרתי לך דהייתו בקר ראשון כשיבא בקר שני שהוא חולו של מועד תשרפו אבל בי"ט לא אלמא מידי דחול לא עבדינן בי"ט ופסח קרבן י"ד בניסן הוא שהוא חול ומילה שלא בזמנה כמי מידי דחול הוא דבשבת זו לא היה זמנה: ולא עולת חול בי"ט · אברי תמיד של ע"ש אין קרבין בי"ט ומילה שלא בזמנה כמי כעולת חול בי"ט דמי: דאתיא בק"ו · שנדחה ומה צרעת שדוחה עבודה מילה שלא בזמנה דוחה אותה כדאמרינן לעיל(ד) שבת שנדחית מפני עבודה אינו דין שמילה שלא בזמנה דוחה אותה להכי איצטריך לבדו: ואין עשה · דמילה דוחה לא תעשה ועשה אבל בזמנה איתרבי מביום אפילו בשבת: גבי פסח · כל מלאכה שאפשר לה לעשות מע"ש כגון הבאתו מחוץ לתחום ותיכת יבלתו: וצריכא · למימר בתרווייהו הלכה כר"ע דמכשירין לא דחו: מילה בזמנה ליכא כרת · דקטן לאו בר עונשין הוא ואבוה לא מיחייב עליה כרת: **מתני'** מוהלין · חותך את הערלה: ופורעין · את העור המכסה ראש הגיד: ומוללין · את הדם ואף על גב דהיא עשיית חבורה שאין הדם ניתק מחיבורו אלא על ידי (ה) המלילה: איספלנית · תחבושת: לועס בשיניו · כמה דאפשר לשנויי משנינן: לא טרף יין ושמן · כך היו רגילין והיא רפואה שמערבין וטורפין בקערה יין ושמן יחד כדרך שטורפין ביצים בקערה: חלוק · כעין כיס דחוק היו עושין ומלבישים את ראש הגיד עד העטרה וקושרים שם כדי שלא יחזור העור לכסות את הגיד: לא התקין · לא הזמין: כורך על ידו · דרך מלבוש לשנותו מדרך הולכה בחול:

א) [נ"ל עד בקר והנותר ממנו עד בקר באש תשרופו וכ"א בפסחים : ב) [וע"ע תוס' יומא יג. ד"ה הלכה ותוס' זבחים מ"ה ד"ה הלכתא] ג) [ואמילתא דר"ע לא בעי צריכותא דאשמעי' בכל דוכתא מאי דדחי שבת כ"כ תוס' במנחות]

תוספות

ואביי אליבא דר' שמעון · ולרבי יונתן לא מיבעיא ליה דמוקי ליה בינוני ולאביי נמי דאמר לעיל דבינוני אתי מבינייא מצי למימר דסבר ר' יונתן מילתא דאתי בק"ו טרח וכתב לה קרא:

באומר לקוץ בהרתו הוא מתכוין · וא"ת אם כן אמאי קאמר אביי לא נצרכא אלא לרבי יהודה הא לר"ש נמי איצטריך כדאמר הכא ויש לומר דלשון ברייתא משמע דמיירי בלא מתכוין מדלא קתני בשר אע"ג דמתכוין לקוץ בהרת ימול:

ותנן נמי גבי פסח כה"ג אמר רב יהודה אמר רב הלכה כר"ע · והכא לא פריך הילכתא למשיחא משום דנפקא מינה גבי מילה אע"ג דגבי מילה נמי פסיק הכי מ"מ לאלומי פיסקא דמילה פסיק נמי גבי פסח אגב דפסיק גבי מילה דתילף מינה שפסק ברור הוא לכל דבר (ג):

וצריכא דאי אשמעינן · אדרב יהוד' קאי דפסיק כר"ע הכא והתם דאי אדרבי עקיבא א"כ בפ' שתי הלחם (מנחות דף צו·) דקתני נמי כלל אמר ר"ע הוה ליה למימר וצריכא וכן פירש בקונטרס ג):

עושין כל צרכי מילה בשבת · אע"ג דלעיל נמי קתני (ו)בשילהי מפנין (ד' קכח:) התם תני לה אגב גררא דמילי דתיקון אבל הכא עיקר :

מסורת הש"ס

[יומא נד:] · צ"ל מלדחוק · [שם] · לעיל פס. קי. קיז: ולק' קמג. [ביצה לו.] סוכה לג: כתובות ו. בכורות כס. · במות כ: נזיר מא. נח. מנחות מ. · לעיל כד: פסחים פג: תמורה ד: ע"ש · [פסחים סט:] · פסחים סו. סט: יבמות יד. מנחות עב. ודף צו. · [לעיל קכח:] · [ע' תוס' עמוד ב ד"ה לועס]

עין משפט נר מצוה

י א מיי' פ"י מהלכות טומאת צרעת הלכה א סמג לאוין שמב :

יא ב מיי' פ"ג מהלכות ציצית הלכה ו :

יב ג מיי' פ"א מהלכות קרבן פסח הלכה יח סמג עשין רנג :

יג ד מיי' פ"ב מהלכות מילה הל' ו סמג עשין כח טוש"ע א"ח סי' שלא סעיף א טוש"ע י"ד סי' רסו סעיף ב :

יד ה מיי' שם הל' ז סמג שם וטוש"ע א"ח שם סעיף ז וטוש"ע י"ד שם סעיף ג :

רבינו חננאל

והנגם והחרש והשוטה והשכור ובעלי נגעים טהורין פסולין באדם וכשרין בבהמה כו' פי' כל זמן שיש בכהן נגעים טהורים פסול לעבודה חתכו טהר מיד ואין צריך טבילה: מודה ר' שמעון בפסיק רישי' ולא ימות פי' כי ר' שמעון מודה בדבר שהוא ברור כגון אדם שחותך ראש אדם ואומר שאין כוונתו להמיתו אלא להוציא את סמנו שאין שומעין לו אלא דנין אותו דין כל הורג נפש כך כל דבר שמתברר (מעשין) [שיעשה] לאותה מלאכה אין אומרין שלא היתה כוונתו לכך. וכה"ג אפילו ר' שמעון מודה. ואביי אליבא דר' שמעון קודם שישמע מרבא. מודה ר' שמעון בפסיק רישית ולא ימות דהוה מוקים ליה כר' יהודה ולא כר' שמעון הוה אמר דר"ש פליג נמי בהא דסבר ר' שמעון חתיכות הערלה והצרעת עליה דבר שאין מתכוין הוא שאין כוונתו לחתוך הצרעת אלא למול בנו וכי האי לר' שמעון שרי ולא צריך קרא למשריית אם כן אביי אליבא דר' שמעון האי בשר ערלתו מאי עביד ליה אמר רב משרשיה באומר לקוץ בהרתו הוא מתכוין כלומר בדבר מוכיח שמתכוין לקוץ בהרתו בא הכתוב להתירו ואקשינן תינח גדול פי' שיש בו דעת יש לומר כן מתכוין לקוץ בהרתו קטן שאין בו דעת למה כתוב בו בשר להתיר חתיכת צרעת במילה ואמרי' קטן נמי מתכוין אביו בזה במולו לבנו לחתוך בהרת בנו ואמרי' בעת שיש בהרת בערלת הקטן ימול אחר זולתו אבי הבן. שהאחר אין מתכוין לחתוך הבהרת ודבר שאין מתכוין לר' שמעון שרי ולא הוה צריך קרא למישריה דאמר רבי שמעון בן לקיש כל מקום שאתה מוצא עשה ולא תעשה פי' כגון זה עשה שנאמר וביום השמיני ימול בשר ערלתו. לא תעשה השמר בנגע הצרעת שהוא לאו כאשר פירשנו למעלה. ואם יש בהרת בערלה וימול אחר זולתו אבי הבן נתקיימה המילה שהיא עשה ונתקיימה חתיכת הצרעת שלא בכוונה שלא הזהירה התורה אלא במתכוין והאחר לא נתכוון ואין אומר יבא עשה וידחה לא תעשה אלא אם אין כח כלל לקיים שניהם ופרקינן דליכא אחר ואם נאמר להמתין עד שיבא אחר וימול ביטלנו וביום השמיני ימול שהוא עשה: ובאנו לפרש עוד תשלום הברייתא: **אמר** מר י"ט אינו דוחה אלא בזמנו. פי' אין מילה דוחה י"ט אלא הנימול ביום ח' שהוא זמנו בלבד ואמרינן מנא הני מילי ופירשו חזקיה*) מן הקדשים שמעונין שריפה והוא עשה כדכתיב

*) חסר קצת וכצ"ל ופי' חזקיה דילפינן זה מנותר מן קדשים וכו'.

הגהות הב"ח

(א) גמ' אבל אתה עושה אותו בסיב: (ב) שם דאפשר לעשות: (ג) רש"י ד"ה שאין ת"ל וכו' באש תשרפו אלמא דאשריפה קאי וכו' דחול הוא דבי"ט זו לא: (ד) ד"ה דאתיא וכו' כדאמרינן לעיל י"ט שנדחית: (ה) ד"ה ומוללין וכו' אלא ע"י (המלילה) תז"מ ונ"ב ס"א הכורה: (ו) תוס' ד"ה עושין וכו' קתני לה בשילהי:

רב נסים גאון

והיינו מפרישין אותו לענין דיניו מכלל הקרבנות אבל הואיל ונאמר בו וביום השמיני באר לנו בזה חזרתו לכלל הקרבנות בכל עניניו והשבתו אליהן בכל תנאותיהן חוץ מקרבן עולה ויורד המפורש בו בלבד וזה שהוצרכתי לפרש דבר זה לפי שראיתיו מסובך אצל כל התלמידים וביארתיו כדי שיתגלה ויתברר: **אימור** דאמרי' אתי עשה ודחי לא תעשה לא תעשה גרידא לא תעשה ועשה מי דחי לא תעשה גרידא הוא לא תעשה הכי יחיד*) שאין עמו כרת כמו (דברים כה) לא תחסום שור בדישו (שם כב) לא תחרוש בשור ובחמור (ויקרא י"ט) לא תקיפו פאת ראשכם ודומה להם ויתוסף עם זה מה שנאמר במבטא השמר פן ואל כגון (דברים כד) השמר בנגע הצרעת (שמות לד) פן תכרת ברית ליושב הארץ (שם טז) אל יצא איש ממקומו גם הן אזהרות לאו ומי שיעבר עליהם עובר על לא תעשה כמו שאמרו בתלמוד (עירובין דף צו וב"ג) השמר פן ואל אינן אלא לשון לא תעשה ומה שנמצא בתורה ממצות לא תעשה מה שאין בו כרת ולא מיתת בית דין ולא ניתוסף עליו עשה אותו דבר הוא הנקרא לאו גרידא ודינו שכשאירע עם מצות עשה במקום אחד נקיים מצות עשה ולא נחוש לאזהרת לאו ועיקר זה מצוי במסכת יבמות בפ' א' (דף ג) וכן אמרו שם אימור דאמרי' דאתי עשה ודחי לא תעשה לא תעשה גרידא לא תעשה שיש בה כרת מי דחי ותו לא תעשה גרידא מנלן דדחי דכתיב (דברים כב) לא תלבש שעטנז וכתיב גדילים תעשה לך ידענו כי זה לא תעשה אינו שוה בכל דבר אלא מיוחד הוא וכי הציווי שנאמר אחריו הוא תנאי עליו וכי לא בא להזהיר אלא על לבישת כלאים חוץ ממצות ציצית אבל מה שהוא מעורב מחוטי פשתן עם הטלית של צמר שהיא מצוה אינו נכנס בזו האזהרה אלא מותר הוא ואמרו חכמים שדבר זה עיקר הוא שנסמך עליו וכי כל אזהרה שאין עמה כרת שבתורה כך היא דרכה שבעת שאירע חיוב מצות עשה נדחה האזהרה שהיא לא תעשה ונקיים הציווי שהוא עשה ותבוא מצות עשה ותדחה לא תעשה כי האזהרה של לאו על זה התנאי נאמרה ובזה הפירוש שפירשנו יסיר מלבך ספק גדול שמסתפקין בו בני אדם ושואלין עליו והוא שאומרין מאחר שאנו יודעין שאזהרת לאו קשה מציווי עשה היאך יבא עשה וידחה האזהרה של לאו שהוא חמורה

*) נ"ל לא תעשה יחידי שאין עמו כרת.

גליון הש"ס רש"י ד"ה שאין ת"ל וכו' י"ד בניסן הוא שהוא חול. עיין בטורי אבן במגילה בחגי מלואים דף מז ע"ב ד"ה אף כאן:

טו א מיי' פ"ב מהלכות מילה הל' ד ו טוש"ע א"ח סי' של"א סעיף ג וטוש"ע י"ד סי' רסו סעיף ב':
טז ב מיי' פ"ז מהל' ס"ת הלכה ד ופ"ז מהל' לולב הל' ו סמג עשין כה ולאוין שסד טוש"ע א"ח סימן תרנו:
יז ג מיי' פ"א מהלכות דעות הלכה ו:
[שייך לעמוד א במשנה]
יח ד מיי' פ"ג מהלכות קידוש החדש הל' ד:
יט ה מיי' פ"ה מהל' תמידין ומוספין הל' ד סמג עשין קל:
כ ו מיי' פ"ב מהלכות שגגות הלכה ט:
כא ז מיי' פ"ב מהל' מילה הל' ב סמג עשין כח טוש"ע י"ד סי' רסד סעיף ג:
כב ח טוש"ע א"ח סי' ד סעיף כ:

תורה אור

גמ' מכדי קתני כולהו כל צורכי מילה לאתויי מאי לאתויי הא דת"ר "המל כל זמן שהוא עוסק במילה חוזר בין על הציצין המעכבין את המילה בין על הציצין שאין מעכבין את המילה פירש על ציצין המעכבין את המילה חוזר על ציצין שאין מעכבין את המילה אינו חוזר מאן תנא פירש אינו חוזר אמר רבה בר בר חנה אמר רבי יוחנן רבי ישמעאל בנו של ר' יוחנן בן ברוקה היא דתניא *ארבעה עשר שחל להיות בשבת מפשיט (*אדם) הפסח עד החזה דברי רבי ישמעאל בנו של ר' יוחנן בן ברוקה וחכ"א מפשיטין את כולו ממאי עד כאן לא קאמר ר' ישמעאל בנו של ר' יוחנן בן ברוקה התם (א) משום דלא בעינן °זה אלי ואנוהו אבל הכא דבעינן זה אלי ואנוהו הכי נמי *דתניא זה אלי ואנוהו 'התנאה לפניו במצות עשה לפניו סוכה נאה ולולב נאה ושופר נאה ציצית נאה ספר תורה נאה וכתוב בו לשמו בדיו נאה בקולמוס נאה בלבלר אומן וכורכו בשיראין נאין אבא שאול אומר ואנוהו הוי דומה לו 'מה הוא חנון ורחום אף אתה היה חנון ורחום אלא אמר רב אשי הא מני רבי יוסי היא דתנן *'בין שנראה בעליל ובין שלא נראה בעליל מחללין עליו את השבת רבי יוסי אומר נראה בעליל אין מחללין עליו את השבת ממאי דילמא עד כאן לא קאמר ר' יוסי התם (ב) דלא ניתנה שבת לידחות אבל הכא דניתנה שבת לידחות הכי נמי אלא אמרי נהרדעי רבנן דפליגי עליה דרבי יוסי היא דתנן *"ארבעה כהנים נכנסין שנים בידם שני סדרים ושנים בידם שני בזיכין וארבעה מקדימין לפניהם שנים ליטול שני סדרים ושנים ליטול שני בזיכין המכניסין עומדים בצפון ופניהם לדרום והמוציאין עומדים בדרום ופניהם לצפון אלו מושכים ואלו מניחין טפחו של זה בצד טפחו של זה משום שנאמר °לפני (ה') תמיד ר' יוסי אומר אפילו אלו נוטלין ואלו מניחין אף זה היה תמיד ת"ר מהלקטין את המילה ואם לא הילקט ענוש כרת מני א"ר כהנא אומן מתקיף לה רב פפא אומן לימא להו אנא עבדי פלגא דמצוה אתון עבידיתו פלגא דמצוה אלא אמר רב פפא גדול מתקיף לה רב אשי גדול בהדיא כתיב ביה °וערל זכר אשר לא ימול אלא אמר רב אשי לעולם אומן 'וכגון דאתא בין השמשות דשבת ואמרו ליה לא מספקת ואמר להו מספקינא ועבד ולא איסתפק ואישתכח דחבורה הוא דעבד וענוש כרת: מוצצין וכו': אמר רב פפא 'האי אומנא דלא מייץ סכנה הוא ועברינן ליה פשיטא מדקא מחללי עליה שבתא סכנה הוא מהו דתימא האי דם מיפקד פקיד קמ"ל חבורי מיחבר ודומיא דאיספלנית וכמון מה איספלנית וכמון כי לא עביד סכנה הוא אף ה"נ כי לא עביד סכנה הוא: ונותנין עליה איספלנית: אמר אביי *אמרה לי אם איספלניתא דכולהון כיבי שב מינאי תרבא וחדא קירא רבא אמר קירא וקלבא רישינא דרשה רבא במחוזא קרעינהו בני מיומי אסיא למנייהו אמר להו שבקי לכו חדא דאמר שמואל "האי מאן דמשי אפיה ולא נגיב טובא נקטרו ליה חספניתא

(שם כה) (בראשית יז) (שמות טו) [קידושין לא: וש"נ]

גדול בהדיא כתיב ביה · אע"ג דבכמה דוכתין תניא מה שבהדיא בפסוק איבעי (ז) למתני גדול שלא מל ענוש כרת:
***לועס** בשיניו · אף על גב דלאחר מילה חולה שיש בו סכנה הוא מ"מ כמה דאפשר לשנויי משנינן: הכא

גמ' מכדי קתני · במתניתין: כולהו · כל דברים העשוים למילה מוהלין ופורעין ומוללין כו' למה לי דתנן כללא ברישא עושין כל צרכי מילה: ציצין · שיורי ערלה ובמתני'(ג) מפרש אלו הן ציצין המעכבין ויש שאינן מעכבין כגון בשר שאינה חופה רוב העטרה אלא מיעוטה ומה היא עטרה שורה גבוה המקפת בגיד סביב שממנה הגיד משפע ויורד לצד הקרקע ומשפע ויורד לצד הגוף: המל · בשבת: כל זמן שהוא עוסק בה · שלא סילק ידו אם ראה שנשתיירו בה ציצין בין מעכבין את המילה שאינה כשרה עד שיחתכם בין שאין מעכבין חוזר וחותך דכולא חדא מילתא היא והרי ניתנה שבת לדחות אצלה: פירש · שסילק ידיו: על המעכבין חוזר · שהרי הן כמילה עצמה: ועל שאין מעכבין אינו חוזר · דהוי כהתחלה בפני עצמה ועל אלו לא ניתן לחלל את השבת והיינו דקתני כל צרכי מילה ואפילו ציצין שאין מעכבין חוזר עליהם כל זמן שלא פירש: מאן תנא פירש אינו חוזר · ומשום דפירש חשיב ליה חזרה מילתא לנפשה והואיל ולא עיכוב מצוה נינהו לא הדר: מפשיט הפסח עד החזה. (ד)והיינו פירש דתנן במסכת תמיד (פ"ד מ"ב) גבי הפשיטו שהיה מתחיל מן הרגלים והיה מפשיט ויורד עד שמגיע לחזה הגיע לחזה חתך את הראש ונתנו למי שזכה בו ואח"כ הכרעיים ומירק והפשיט כו' שמעי' מיניה משהגיע לחזה סילק ידיו מן ההפשט והתחיל להתעסק בניתוח קלא וגבי עולה דכולה כליל מירק והפשיט ומנתח הידים תחילה אחר הראש וגבי פסח נמי משהפשיט עד החזה דיכול להוציא אימוריו(ה) בלא נימין קורעו ומוציאן מיד והוה ליה פירש מן ההפשט וקאמר רבי ישמעאל שוב אינו גומר ומפשיט משום דכיון דפירש הויא חזרה מילתא דאתחלתא לנפשה ושלא לצורך גבוה דומיא דציצין דלא מעכבין: דלא בעינן זה אלי ואנוהו · דלאחר נטילת האימורין אין הידור מצוה ביפוי בשר אבל יפוי מילה מצוה היא: הוי דומה לו · ולשון אנוהו אני והוא אעשה עצמו כמותו לדבק בדרכיו: בין שנראה · החדש: בעליל · בגילוי לכל ויש לדעת שראוהו בית דין והקרובים להם ואין צריך לרואין חוץ לתחום לחלל שבת ולבא ולהעיד לפני ב"ד מחללין: ר' יוסי אומר כו' · אלמא אע"ג דאיכא מצוה כיון דלאו לצורך גבוה הוא לא מחללינן והכא נמי פירש דהוי אתחלתא דחילול כי הכא בלא צורך גבוה לא מחללינן: לא ניתנה שבת לדחות · אפילו בהתחלתה דהא נראה בעליל אבל הכא כיון שנתנה שבת לדחות להתחיל בה המילה הכי נמי דכי פירש והדר לאו אתחלתא לנפשה היא והוי כמו שלא פירש וגומר כל מלותו: רבנן דפליגי עליה דרבי יוסי · גבי לחם הפנים: ארבעה כהנים נכנסין · להיכל בשבת לסדור לחם הפנים: שני סדרים · שתים מערכות של לחם: שני בזיכין · שתי כפות מלאות לבונה כדכתיב (ויקרא כד) ונתת על המערכת לבונה זכה: מקדימין לפניהם שנים ליטול · מן השלחן שני סדרים הישנים: ושנים ליטול שני בזיכין · והשלחן היה נתון ארכו ממזרח למערב ואלו עומדין מזה לרוחב השלחן בצפון ואלו עומדין לנגדו לדרום ודווקא מכניסין לצפון דכל צפון ענין חשיבות היא כדאמרינן במסכת סוכה (דף נו.) גבי חילוק לחם הפנים למשמרה הנכנסת והיוצאת הנכנסין חולקין בצפון כדי שיראו (ו) נכנסין: רבי יוסי אומר אפילו אלו נוטלין · תחילה ומסלקין כולה מן השלחן ולאחר שעה מניחין אלו: אף זה תמיד · ומה אני מקיים תמיד שלא ילין שלחן בלא לחם ולרבנן אי שקלי ושבקי ליה והדר מסדרי לא מיקרי להו תמיד אלא התחלה אחריתי ונמצא שמתעכב שלחן בלא לחם וגבי פירש נמי כי הדר אתי מילתא אחריתי היא ולרבי יוסי דאמר כי שבקי והדר מתחלי נמי תמיד הוא דחדא מילתא הוא הכא נמי פירש חוזר אע"פ שאין מעכבין דכולה גמר מילתא היא: מהלקטין · בציצין המעכבין: מני · כרת זו של מי הוא: אמר רב כהנא אומן. ענוש כרת ובשבת קאי שחילל שבת ולא עשה מצוה: ונימא אנא עבדי פלגא · כלומר הואיל וכשהתחיל ברשות התחיל וחבורה שעשה ברשות עשה אמאי חייב נימא להו לכו אתם וסיימו המלאכה: אלא אמר רב פפא · בגדול שמל קמיירי ובחול וענוש כרת דקאמר משום מילה קאמר דעדיין ערל הוא: וכגון דאתא בין השמשות · דכל היום כשר למילה *ואמרו ליה לא מספקת לגמור ביום כהילכתה ותעשה חבורה בשבת בלא מצוה וענוש כרת ומיהו מיתה ליכא דלא אתרו ביה למיתה ולא קבל עליו התראה וכרת איכא דלהתחלה ברשות לא התחיל ולא ניתנה שבת לדחות אלנו בשעה זו: מהו דתימא · מתניתין לא אשמעינן דמחלל שבתא עלה דדם מיפקד פקיד מופקד ועומד שם כנתון בכלי ובמציצה אין חבורה ואין כאן איסור תורה ומשום הכי שרי ולאו משום סכנה ואומנא דלא מייץ בחול לאו סכנתא היא ולא ניעבריה: קא משמע לן דדם חיבורי מיחבר · כשיוצא ע"י מציצה ואפילו הכי שרי משום סכנה מדקתני במתני' גבי איספלנית וכמון: שב מינאי תרבא · ז' מנות של חלב: וחדא דקירא · שעוה: קירא וקלבא רישינא · הוא זפת של עץ שמוציאים ממנו שלא ע"י האור והיא לבנה: קרעינהו למנייהו · שהפסיד להם לגלות רפואה זו: שבקי לכו חדא · שלא גיליתי: חספניתא

לעיל קטז: מנחות סג: [תוספתא פסחים פ"ד] [נזיר ב: ע"ש] סוכה יא: מכילתא פרשת בשלח [מס' סופרים פ"ג הל' יג] ר"ס כח: מנחות סד. מנחות ז. לט: פסחים ד. יומא כח: (מגילה כ.)

הגהות הב"ח

(א) גמ' התם אלא משום דלא: (ב) שם ר' יוסי התם אלא משום דלא ניתנה בשבת: (ג) רש"י ד"ה ציצין וכו' ובמתני'. נ"ב לקמן דף קלז סוף ע"א: (ד) ד"ה מפשיטין את הפסח עד וכו': (ה) להוציא אימוריו נ"ב ע"ל בפרק כ"כ דף קטז בסוף הדף: (ו) ד"ה ושנים ליטול וכו' כדי שיראו שהן נכנסין: (ז) תוס' ד"ה גדול וכו' איבעי ליה למיתני:

רבינו חננאל

והנותר ממנו עד בוקר באש תשרופו ואין שריפת קדשים דוחה י"ט דתנינן בגמרא בפ' כיצד צולין את הפסח. דתנן העצמות והגידים והנותר ישרפו בששה עשר חל ששה עשר להיות בשבת ישרפו בי"ז שאינו דוחה את השבת ולא את יו"ט וקיימא לן דמילה שלא בזמנה אפילו יו"ט אינו דוחה דתנן שני יו"ט של ר"ה נימול לי"ב ללמדך שאין עשה דוחה י"ט כן המילה שלא בזמנה אינה דוחה י"ט ואין לומר אי הכי אפי' מילה בזמנה כי מילה בזמנה בפירוש אמרה תורה וביום ואפי' בשבת וכ"ש י"ט אביי פירשו מעולת שבת בשבתו כו' רבא אמר הוא ולא מכשיריו פי' עשיית אוכל נפש דוחה י"ט ולא מכשירי אוכל נפש. כגון חטיבת עצים מן היער לבשל ביו"ט וכדומה(לו) [הוא] לבדו ולא מילה שלא בזמנה הבאה בק"ו וזהו ק"ו שאמר רבא ומה אוכל נפש שאע"פ שהיא באזהרת שמחה אינה (מנוח שדוחה) [דוחה] יו"ט לשחוט ולבשל ולאפות וכיוצא בהן מילה שלא בזמנה שאע"פ שהיא בלא זמנה מצוה היא ומעכבתו מלאכול בתרומה. אינו דין שדוחה י"ט בא לבדו למעט המילה שלא בזמנה. רב אשי אמר שבת שבתון עשה הוא וי"ט עשה ול"ת עשה שבתון ולא תעשה כל מלאכה לא תעשה נמצא כתיב ביו"ט עשה ול"ת והמילה עשה בלבד. ולא אתי עשה דמילה ודחי את לא תעשה ועשה דיו"ט: מתני' כלל א"ר עקיבא כל מלאכה שאפשר [לעשות] מע"ש דוחה את השבת וכו'. אמר רב יהודה אמר רב הלכה כר' עקיבא: מתני' עושין כל צרכי מילה בשבת מוהלין ופורעין כו' אמרינן כי מכדי קתני מוהלין ופורעין ומוצצין כו' עושין כל צרכי מילה למה לי לאתויי הא דתנו רבנן המל כל זמן שעוסק במילה חוזר בין על ציצין המעכבין את המילה בין על הציצין שאינן מעכבין את המילה חוזר על שאין מעכבין אינו חוזר. ואמרינן מאן תנא פירש ואתא רבה בר בר חנה לאוקומה כר' (שמעון) [ישמעאל] בר' יוחנן בן

רב נסים גאון

חמורה ממנו ומדרך הידוע שהחמור דוחה הקל ולא עוד אלא שפעמים שעולה על דעתן שיש בענין הזה ענין חזרה בדבר הראשון והתשובה הוא מה שהקדמנו שהאזהרה של לאו כך נאמרה מיוחדת וכי הציווי של עשה תנאי הוא בה וכן אמרו רז"ל (ספרי פ' תצא) מחלליה מות יומת וביום השבת שני כבשים בני שנה שניהן בדיבור אחד נאמרו ערות אשת אחיך ויבמה יבוא עליה שניהן בריבור אחד נאמרו מה שאי אפשר לבשר ודם לומר שנא' אחת דיבר אלהים שתים זו שמענו הבן דבר זה ושמור אותו כי הוא ספק גדול והרי גלינו אותו ומזה העיקר אמרו רז"ל בתלמוד כל מקום שאתה מוצא עשה לא תעשה אם אתה יכול לקיים את שניהם מוטב ואם לאו יבא עשה וידחה לא תעשה וסבר (רבינא) [רבא] כי לא תעשה שבקודש מוצא מזה העיקר וכי לא ידחה מפני עשה ולא שוה עמו רב אשי בדבר זה כמו שנאמר בשחיטת קדשים בפרק דם חטאת (דף צז) אמאי וניתי עשה ונידחי לא תעשה אמר רבינא אין עשה דוחה את לא תעשה שבמקדש דתניא כו' רב אשי אמר יקדש עשה הוא ואין עשה דוחה את לא תעשה ועשה ובמס' נזירות בפ"ב נזירין(דף נח)אמרו עוד (ומאי דקא מודי ליה) [ומאן דמוקים]לקרא למידחא לא תעשה ועשה לאו גרידא מנא ליה יליף מגדילים דאמר קרא לא תלבש שעטנז הא גדילים תעשה לך מהן וכל מה שתמצא בתלמוד דאתי עשה ודחי לא תעשה מזה העיקר שהקדימו הוא וזה הדין בלאו גרידא בלבד אבל לא לא תעשה ועשה וכל שכן לא תעשה שיש בו כרת אין עשה דוחה אותם ואנו מבארין לך זה ונאמר

GEMARA. [133*b*] Consider: He [the Tanna] states them all [separately]: what is ALL THE REQUIREMENTS OF CIRCUMCISION to include?—It is to include that which our Rabbis taught: He who circumcises,[8] as long as he is engaged in the circumcision, he returns both for the shreds [of the corona] which invalidate the circumcision and for those which do not invalidate the circumcision.[9] Once he has withdrawn,[10] he returns on account of the shreds which invalidate the circumcision, but not for the shreds which do not invalidate the circumcision.

Who teaches: Once he has withdrawn, he must not return?—Said Rabbah b. Bar Ḥanah in R. Johanan's name: It is R. Ishmael the son of R. Joḥanan b. Berokah. For it was taught: If the fourteenth [of Nisan] falls on the Sabbath, the Passover sacrifice is flayed as far as the breast: this is the view of R. Ishmael the son of R. Joḥanan b. Berokah. But the Sages maintain: We flay the whole
a of it.[1] But how so? R. Joḥanan may rule [thus] only there, because we do not require [the application of the verse,] *This is my God, and I will adorn him;*[2] but here that we require, '*This is my God, and I will adorn him*',[3] that indeed is so![4] (For it was taught: *This is my God, and I will adorn him:* [i.e.,] adorn thyself before Him in [the fulfilment of] precepts. [Thus:] make a beautiful *sukkah* in His honour,[5] a beautiful *lulab,* a beautiful *shofar,* beautiful fringes, and a beautiful Scroll of the Law, and write it with fine ink, a fine reed[-pen], and a skilled penman, and wrap it about with beautiful silks. Abba Saul interpreted, and I will be like him:[6] be thou like Him: just as He is gracious and compassionate, so be thou gracious and compassionate.)—Rather said R. Ashi, Which [Tanna] is this? It is R. Jose. For we learnt: Whether it is clearly visible or it is not clearly visible,[7] the Sabbath is desecrated on its account.[8] R. Jose ruled: If it is clearly visible, they must not desecrate the Sabbath for it.[9] But how so? Perhaps R. Jose rules [thus] only there, because the Sabbath was not given to be superseded;[10] but here that the Sabbath was given to be superseded,[11] it indeed is so?[12]—Rather said the scholars of Nehardea: It is the Rabbis who disagree with R. Jose. For we learnt: Four priests
b entered:[1] two held two courses [of loaves] in their hands, and two held two censers;[2] and four preceded them, two in order to remove the two courses,[3] and two to remove the two censers. Those who brought in [the new loaves and frankincense] stood in the north facing the south,[4] while those who carried [them] out stood in the south facing the north:[5] these withdrew [the old] and these laid down [the new], the handbreadth of one at the side of the handbreadth of the other,[6] because it is said, [*And thou shalt set upon the table shewbread*] *before Me* alway.[7] R. Jose said: Even if these remove and the other replace [it later], that too constitutes '*alway*'.[8]

Our Rabbis taught: The membrum must be trimmed,[9] and if one does not trim it, he is punished with *kareth.* Who? R. Kahana said: The surgeon.[10] R. Papa demurred 'The surgeon'! he can say to them, 'I have performed half of the precept: do you perform half of the precept.'[11] Rather said R. Papa: An adult.[12] R. Ashi demurred: Of an adult it is explicitly stated, *and the uncircumcised male who is not circumcised in the flesh of his foreskin, [that soul shall*
c *be cut off from his people*]?[1] Rather said R. Ashi: In truth it means the surgeon: e.g., if he came at twilight on the Sabbath, and they warned him, 'you have no time,'[2] but he insisted, 'I have time': so he performed it but had not time [to complete it]. Thus the net result is[3] that he [merely] made a wound,[4] hence he is punished with *kareth.*[5]

WE SUCK OUT, etc. R. Papa said: If a surgeon does not suck [the WOUND], it is dangerous and he is dismissed. Is it not obvious? since we desecrate the Sabbath for it, it is dangerous?[6]—You might say that this blood is stored up, therefore he informs us that it is the result of a wound, and it is like a bandage and cummin: just as when one does not apply a bandage and cummin there is danger, so here too if one does not do it there is danger.[7]

WE PLACE A COMPRESS UPON IT. Abaye said: Mother told me,[8] A salve [compress] for all pains [is made of] seven parts of fat and one of wax. Raba said: Wax and resin.[9] Raba taught this publicly at Maḥoza, [whereupon] the family of Minyomi the doctor tore up their [bandage] cloths.[10] Said he to them. Yet I have left you one [cure unrevealed]. For Samuel said: He who washes his face and does not dry it well, scabs will break out on

(8) On the Sabbath. (9) This is what the Mishnah includes. (10) From circumcising, thinking it finished.

a (1) V. *supra* 116*b*. When one reaches the breast he temporarily ceases flaying in order to remove the fats; this cessation is analogous to withdrawing in the case of circumcision, and R. Ishmael rules that he must not return to complete the flaying. (2) Ex. XV, 2. Or perhaps, and I will adorn myself for His sake. Once the fats are removed for sacrificial purposes there is no adornment of the precept in trimming the flesh and making it look presentable. (3) The cutting away even of the shreds which does not invalidate circumcision is nevertheless an adornment thereof. (4) And may be permitted even by R. Ishmael. (5) Lit., 'before Him'. (6) Reading אנוהו as a combination אני והוא I and He (have to act alike). (7) Viz., the crescent of the New Moon, which had to be seen and attested by two witnesses before the Beth din could sanctify the beginning of the month, v. R.H. 21*b*. (8) By the two witnesses appointed to look out for it. They must come to the Beth din to testify, even if it is the Sabbath and they are without the *teḥum* (q.v. Glos.), though since it is clearly visible the Beth din is in any case aware of its presence. (9) Because it is unnecessary. The same applies to the shreds which do not invalidate the circumcision. (10) From the very outset there was no need to desecrate the Sabbath, since the new moon is clearly visible to all. (11) On account of the circumcision. (12) That one must cut away all shreds.

b (1) The Temple on the Sabbath to set the shewbread. (2) Of frankincense for the loaves, v. Lev. XXIV, 7. (3) Of the previous week's loaves. (4) Because the Table was placed east to west, and the priests stood at its side facing its breadths. (5) I.e., opposite the other priests across the Table. (6) I.e., the withdrawing and the replacing were almost simultaneous. (7) Ex. XXV, 30. (8) I.e., '*alway*' merely indicates that a night must not pass without shewbread lying upon the table. But the Rabbis hold that an interval would mark a new placing, not a *continuation* of the old, and so '*alway*' would be unfulfilled. Similarly, when one withdraws from circumcision, to return for the shreds is a new act, hence not permitted unless these invalidate circumcision. (9) I.e., the shreds which invalidate the circumcision must be removed; this appears to be the interpretation of Rashi and R. Ḥan. Jast.: (One may) trim the preputium by splitting and drawing it upwards so as to form a pouch around the denuded cone. V. R. Ḥan. second interpretation. (10) Because he violated the Sabbath without completely fulfilling the precept. On this interpretation the reference is to the Sabbath. (11) I.e., his labour was certainly permitted as far as it went. (12) It refers to an adult who circumcises himself on weekdays, and he is punished by *kareth* because he remains uncircumcised on account of these shreds.

c (1) Gen. XVII, 14; *supra* 132*b*, n. b1. Why then state it here? (2) To perform the whole of the circumcision before the day ends. (3) Lit., 'it is found'. (4) It is not regarded as circumcision. (5) Because he had no right even to start. (6) Otherwise it would not be permitted, as it is not actually part of circumcision. (7) If the blood were held to be stored up in a separate receptacle, as it were, there would be no desecration of the Sabbath in sucking it out, and therefore the fact that it is done on the Sabbath would not prove that its omission is dangerous. But since it comes out as a result of a wound, i.e., the pressing causes a wound and thus forces out the blood, it is permitted only because its omission is dangerous. (8) She was really his foster-mother, v. Ḳid. 31*b*. (9) רישינא is a commentator's Gloss; v. Jast. (10) They had not more need for them, the secret now being known to all. The phrase may also mean: they tore their garments (in despair and vexation).

him. [134a] What is his remedy? Let him wash it well in beet juice.[11]

IF ONE DID NOT CRUSH [IT] ON THE EVE OF THE SABBATH. Our Rabbis taught: The things which may not be done for circumcision on the Sabbath may be done on Festivals: cummin may be crushed, and wine and oil may be beaten up together on its account. Abaye asked R. Joseph: Wherein does [the powdering of] cummin on Festivals differ? [Presumably] because it can be used in a dish?[1] then wine and oil too are fit for an invalid on the Sabbath? For it was taught: One may not beat up wine and oil for an invalid on the Sabbath. R. Simeon b. Eleazar said in R. Meir's name: One may indeed beat up wine and oil. R. Simeon b. Eleazar related, R. Meir was once suffering internally,[2] and we wished to beat up wine and oil for him, but he would not permit us. Said we to him, Your words shall be made void in your own lifetime! Though I rule thus, he replied, yet my colleagues rule otherwise, [and] I have never[3] presumed to disregard the words of my colleagues. Now he was stringent in respect to himself, but for all others it is permitted?—There it need not be well beaten, whereas here it needs to be well beaten. Then let us do likewise here too and not mix it well?—That is what he teaches, EACH MUST BE APPLIED SEPARATELY.[4]

Our Rabbis taught: One may not strain mustard grain through its own strainer,[5] nor sweeten it with a glowing coal.[6] Abaye asked R. Joseph: Wherein does it differ from what we learnt: An egg may be passed through a mustard strainer?[7] There it does not look like selecting,[8] whereas here it looks like selecting,[9] he replied. 'Nor sweeten it with a glowing coal'. But surely it was taught, One may sweeten it with a glowing coal?—There is no difficulty: one refers to a metal coal, the other to a wood coal.[10] Abaye asked R. Joseph: Wherein does it differ from [roasting] meat on coals?[11]—There it is impossible,[12] whereas here it is possible.[13]

Abaye asked R. Joseph: What about cheese-making?[1]—It is forbidden, answered he. Wherein does it differ from kneading [dough]?—There it is impossible, here it is possible, replied he.[2] But the people of Nehardea say: Freshly-made[3] cheese is palatable?—They mean this: even freshly-made cheese is palatable.[4]

ONE MAY NOT MAKE A ḤALUḲ FOR IT, etc. Abaye said, Mother told me: The side-selvedge of an infant's *haluk* should be uppermost,[5] lest a thread thereof stick and he [the infant] may become privily mutilated.[6] Abaye's mother used to make a lining[7] for half [the *haluk*].[8]

Abaye said: If there is no *haluk* for an infant, a hemmed rag should be brought, and the hem tied round at the bottom[9] and doubled over at the top.[10]

Abaye also said: Mother told me, An infant whose anus is not visible should be rubbed with oil and stood in the sun, and where it shows transparent it should be torn crosswise with a barley grain, but not with a metal instrument, because that causes inflammation.

Abaye also said: Mother told me, If an infant cannot suck, his lips are cold. What is the remedy? A vessel of burning coals should be brought and held near his nostrils, so as to heat it; then he will suck.

Abaye also said: Mother told me, If an infant does not breathe,[11] he should be fanned with a fan, and he will breathe.

Abaye also said: Mother told me, If an infant cannot breathe easily,[12] his mother's after-birth should be brought and rubbed over him, [and] he will breathe easily.

Abaye also said: Mother told me, If an infant is too thin, his mother's after-birth should be brought and rubbed over him
c from its narrow end to its wide end;[1] if he is too fat, [it should be rubbed] from the wide to the narrow end.

Abaye also said: Mother told me, If an infant is too red, so that the blood is not yet absorbed in him,[2] we must wait until his blood is absorbed and then circumcise him. If he is green, so that he is deficient in blood,[3] we must wait until he is full-blooded and then circumcise him. For it was taught, R. Nathan said: I once visited the sea-towns,[4] and a woman came before me who had circumcised her first son and he had died and her second son and he had died; the third she brought before me. Seeing that he was [too] red I said to her, Wait until his blood is absorbed. So she waited until his blood was absorbed and [then] circumcised him and he lived; and they called him Nathan the Babylonian after my name. On another occasion I visited the province of Cappadocia,[5] and a woman came before me who had circumcised her first son and he had died and her second son and he had died; the third she brought before me. Seeing that he was green, I examined him and saw no covenant blood[6] in him. I said to her, Wait until he is full-blooded; she waited and [then] circumcised him and he lived, and they called him Nathan the Babylonian, after my name.

(11) Or, water in which vegetables were thoroughly boiled.

(1) Hence since it is permitted for this purpose, it is permitted for circumcision too. (2) Lit., 'in his bowels'. (3) Lit., 'throughout my days'. (4) Which means that they may be poured together but not mixed well. (5) On Festivals. (6) The heat made the mustard more palatable. (7) To render the egg clear. (8) Because all of it passes through. (9) Because some of the inferior grains remain on top.—Nevertheless it is not actual selecting, because even they are fit for use (Toasf.). (10) The latter is forbidden, as it is extinguished in the process, which is prohibited on Festivals. (11) Though this puts them out. (12) That the meat should be roasted before the Festival and be just as tasty. (13) The mustard grains could have been sweetened the previous day.

(1) On Festivals. (2) V. *supra* nn. a12–13. (3) Lit., 'of the (same) day'. (4) But it is still more so when it is made the previous day. (5) I.e., not facing the flesh. (6) When the *haluk* is pulled away. (7) Lit., 'covering'. (8) I.e., she left the seam or selvedge on the inner side, but lined it half way down, so that it should not touch the membrum. (9) Of the membrum, so as not to touch the wound. (10) Thus the edge is on the outside. (11) I.e., gives no signs of life (Rashi and Jast.). 'Ar.: does not urinate. (12) Rashi. Jast.: cry.

c (1) Starting with the former and continuing until the latter.—This is symbolical: even so should the infant progress (Rashi). (2) Into his limbs, but it is still on the under-surface of the skin. This makes circumcision dangerous. (3) Lit., 'the blood has not yet fallen into him'. (4) Tyre, etc. (5) A district of Asia Minor. (6) The blood which circumcision causes to flow is so designated. Thus circumcision would be physically dangerous, and furthermore even if performed it would be inadequate, as covenant blood is required.

*חספניתא מאי תקנתיה לימשי טובא במיא דסילקא: לא שחק מערב שבת: תנו רבנן דברים שאין עושין למילה בשבת עושין לה ביו"ט *שוחקין לה כמון וטורפין לה יין ושמן א"ל אביי לרב יוסף מאי שנא כמון בי"ט דחזי לקדרה יין ושמן חזי נמי בשבת לחולה דתניא *אין טורפין יין ושמן לחולה בשבת אמר ר"ש בן אלעזר משום ר"מ אף טורפין יין ושמן א"ר שמעון בן אלעזר פעם אחת חש רבי מאיר במעיו ובקשנו לטרוף לו יין ושמן ולא הנחנו אמרנו לו דבריך יבטלו בחייך אמר לנו אע"פ שאני אומר כך וחבירי אומרים כך °מימי לא מלאני לבי לעבור על דברי חבירי הוא ניהו דמחמיר אנפשיה אבל לכולי עלמא שרי התם לא בעי ליבא הכא בעי ליבא הכא נמי ניעביד ולא לילך היינו דקתני נותן זה בפני עצמו וזה בפני עצמו: ת"ר אין מסננין את החרדל במסננת שלו ואין ממתקין אותו בגחלת א"ל אביי לרב יוסף מאי שנא מהא *דתנן נותנים ביצה במסננת של חרדל א"ל התם לא מיחזי כבורר הכא מיחזי כבורר ואין ממתקין אותו בגחלת והתניא ממתקין אותו בגחלת לא קשיא כאן בגחלת של מתכת כאן בגחלת של עץ א"ל אביי לרב יוסף מ"ש *מבישרא אגומרי א"ל התם לא אפשר הכא אפשר א"ל אביי לרב יוסף מהו לגבן א"ל אסור מ"ש מלישה א"ל התם לא אפשר הכא אפשר והא אמרי נהרדעי גבינה בת יומא מעליא הכי קאמרי דאפילו גבינה בת יומא מעליא: אין עושין לה חלוק כו': אמר אביי *אמרה לי אם האי חלוק דינוקא לפניה לסיטרא *לעילאי דילמא מידביק (א)גרדא מיניה ואתי לידי כרות שפכה אימיה דאביי עבדא כיסתתא לפלגא אמר אביי האי ינוקא דלית ליה חלוק לייתי בליתא דאית ליה שיפתא וליכרכיה לשיפתא לתתאי ועייף ליה לעילאי ואמר אביי אמרה לי אם האי ינוקא דלא ידיע מפקתיה לשייפיה מישחא ולוקמיה להדי יומא והיכא דזיג ליקרעיה בשערתא שתי וערב אבל בכלי מתכות לא משום דזריף ואמר אביי אמרה לי אם האי ינוקא דלא מייץ מיקר (ב)דקר פומיה מאי תקנתיה ליתו כסא גומרי ולינקטיה ליה להדי פומיה דחיים פומיה ומייץ ואמר אביי אמרה לי אם האי ינוקא דלא *מנשתיה לינפפיה בנפוותא ומנשתיה ואמר אביי אמרה לי אם האי ינוקא דלא *מעוי ליתו סליתא דאימיה ולישרקיה עילויה ומעוי ואמר אביי אמרה לי אם האי ינוקא דקטין לייתו לסילתא דאימיה ולישרקיה עילויה מקוטנא לאולמא ואי אלים מאולמא לקוטנא ואמר אביי אמרה לי אם האי ינוקא דסומק דאכתי לא איבלע ביה דמא א]ליתרחו ליה עד דאיבלע ביה דמא ולימהלוה דירוק ואכתי לא נפל ביה דמיה ליתרחו עד דנפל ביה דמיה ולימהלוה *דתניא א"ר נתן פעם אחת הלכתי לכרכי הים ובאת אשה לפני שמלה בנה ראשון ומת שני ומת שלישי הביאתו לפני ראיתיו שהוא אדום אמרתי לה המתיני לו עד שיבלע בו דמו המתינה לו עד שנבלע בו דמו ומלה אותו וחיה והיו קורין אותו נתן הבבלי על שמי שוב פעם אחת הלכתי למדינת קפוטקיא ובאת אשה אחת לפני שמלה בנה ראשון ומת שני ומת שלישי הביאתו לפני ראיתיו שהוא ירוק הצצתי בו ולא ראיתי בו דם ברית אמרתי לה המתיני לו עד שיפול בו דמו והמתינה לו ומלה אותו וחיה והיו קורין שמו נתן הבבלי על שמי:

מתני'

א) [גי' הערוך ליתרהו ועי' במוסף הערוך ערך תרה וברש"י גיטין סח: ד"ה תרתי גבי]

רש"י

חספניתא. פניו מתבקעות ואני אומר שהוא מין שחין שקורין אינייר"א והוא (בגרב) ובחרס שכתוב בתורה (דברים כח) *וחספניתא תרגום של חרס: במיא דסילקא. מרק תרדין: חזי לחולה. שאין בו סכנה: יבטלו. דהאי נמי חולה הוא: אבל לכולי עלמא שרי. ר"מ וסתם מתני' ר"מ ואמאי תנן נותן זה בעצמו וזה בעצמו: התם. גבי שאר חולים: לא בעו ליבא. לטרפו ולערבו יפה יפה: ולא לילך. לא יערבנו כל כך: ומתרץ היינו דקתני נותן זה בעצמו וזה בעצמו. שמערב ואינו לוכך: אין מסננין את החרדל. בי"ט: במסננת שלו. טעמא מפרש לקמיה דמיחזי כבורר שמשליך הסובין שלו:

ואין ממתקין אותו בגחלת. כדרך שרגילין לכבות לתוכו את הגחלת או אבן ניסוקת: נותנין ביצה במסננת של חרדל. ומסננה בתוכו לייפות מראיתו: לא מיחזי כבורר. שכולה יוצאה דרך המסננת ואין משייר שם פסולת: בגחלת של עץ. אסור דשייך בה כיבוי לפי שעושה פחם גחלת של מתכת לא שייך בה כיבוי דאינו נעשה פחם: ומ"ש מבישרא אגומרי. שצולין בי"ט ואע"ג דמכבה: לא אפשר. לצלות מאתמול דבעינא שביחא טפי אבל חרדל אפשר מאתמול: לגבן. גבינה: מאי שנא מלישה. שלשין פת ביום טוב והאי נמי כלישה דמיא: לא אפשר. דפת חמה מעליא טפי הכא אפשר מאתמול: אימא אף גבינתא בת יומא מעליא. וכ"ש דאתמול: לפניה לסטריה לעילאי. לאימרא שבשפת פיה יהפוך ויקפל למעלה שלא תהא סמוכה לבשרו מפני שראש מקום חתך הבגד שם הוא ויוצאין ממנו גרדין שקורין פיינד"ץ ודלמא מדביקא גרדתא מיניה במכה וכשבא להפשיט החלוק מעל המילה ישמוט ויקרע את ראש הגיד ומשוי ליה כרות שפכה: אימיה דאביי. אומנתו: עבדא. לתינוקות הבאים לידה לתקן מילתן: כיסתתא לפלגא. דמילה כיס היתה עושה של בגד לפניס בתוך החלוק ותופרתו מתוכו בתוך החלוק ומגיע למטה עד חצי החלוק כדי לחוץ בין האימרא ובין המילה: לייתי בליתא. מעט שחק של בגד שיהא בו אימרא לפי שהאימרא מהדקה יפה בבשר שלא ישמט החלוק מן הגיד: וליפכיה לשפתיה לתתאי. לתחתית ראש הגיד יתן השפה וראש השני החלק יהא למעלה: ולעפפיה לעילאי. אותו ראש העליון החלוק יקפל ויקפול כלפי חוץ מפני הגרדין שלא ידבקו במכה: דלא ידיע ביה מפקתיה. שאין ניכר בו נקב בית הרעי ששם הולאת זבלו: לישייפיה מישחא. שהשמן מאהיל הבשר: ולוקמיה להדי יומא. נגד השמש: והיכא דזיג. שנלול כזכוכית בידוע שהחלל כנגדו: בשערתא. בראש השעורה שהוא חדוד: דזריף. מנפחו אינפליי"ר בלע"ז: דלא מייץ. שלא יכול לינק: מיקר הוא דקר פומיה. נלטננו שפתיו ואין בו כח למוץ בהן: לייתו כסא דגומרי. תשטח גחלים על דף או על כלי: ולוקמה להדי פומיה. ויעמיד אצל פיו: דחיים פומיה. שיתחמם פיו: ומייץ. ויינק: דלא מינשתא. שאין נשימה ניכרת בו שאין דופק כנגד לבו כדרך כל אדם: לינפפיה בניפוותא. יניפו עליו בנפה שקורין וא"ן: דלא מעוי. אין רוחו נכנס ויוצא יפה אלייכ"א בלע"ז: סליתא דאימיה. שליא שנולדה עמו: ולישרקיה עליה. יחליקנה על בשרו כמו אישתרוקי אישתריקו (ע"ג ד' מ:) אשאולדי"ר: דקטין. שהוא דק: מקוטנא לאולמא. השליא ראשה א' קצר וראשה אחד רחב יחליקוה עליו מראש הקצר יתחילו וימשכו לצד הרחב כלומר כן ירחיב זה ויתעבה: ואי אלים. ולא מחמת בריאות אלא נפוח לישרקיה עליה מאולמא לקוטנא: דסומק. כל בשרו אדום: לא איבלע ביה דמיה. בבשרו דעכשיו כל דמו מלוי בין עור לבשר וכשמוהלין אותו יוצא כל דמו: ליתרחו ליה. ימתינו מלמולו: לא נפל ביה דמא. לא בא בו דם ומתוך כך חלש הוא ואין בו כח וממהר לחלוש ולמות: לכרכי הים. ה"ג ראיתיו שהיה ירוק הצצתי בו ולא היה בו דם ברית תרתי לגריעותא חדא דאי מהיל ליה לא נפק מיניה דמא והטפת דם ברית מצוה כדכתיב (זכריה ט) גם את בדם בריתך ועוד דמסוכן הוא ומשום חולשא שלא נולד בו עדיין דם:

מתני'

תוספות

הכא מיחזי כבורר. מיהו בורר לא הוי שגם הפסולת ראוי לאכילה ולא דמי למשמרת דריש תולין (לקמן ד' קלז:) דאיכא למ"ד חייב משום בורר:

מי

עין משפט נר מצוה

[בתרגום שלפנינו ליתא ובע"ז כח: פירש רש"י חספניתא סדקין שבפני אדם]

כג א מיי' פ"ב מהלכות מילה הל' יוד סמג עשין כח טוש"ע י"ד סי' רסו סעיף ו:

כד ב ג מיי' פ"ג מהל' י"ט הלכה יז סמג לאוין עה טוש"ע א"ח סי' תקי סעיף ג

[וברב אלפס ביצה פ"ב קלג: ע"ש וברא"ש שם סי' כג]:

כה ד שם סעיף ה:

כו ה טוש"ע י"ד סי' רסד סעיף ג בהג"ה:

כז ו ז מיי' פ"א מהל' מילה הלכה יז טוש"ע י"ד סי' רסג סעיף א:

רבינו חננאל

ברוקה. ולא קשה ופשוטה היא ובא רב אשי להעמידה כר' יוסי דנראה בעליל ואיפשיטא במנחות בתחלת פ' ר' ישמעאל הכי לאו א"ר יוסי התם כיון דאפשר לא טרחינן הכא נמי כיון דאפשר לא טרחינן ונדחת גם זו ואתו נהרדעי ואוקמוה כרבנן דפליגי עליה דר' יוסי במנחות פרק שתי הלחם נילושות דתנן ד' כהנים נכנסים ב' בידם ב' סדרים וב' בידם ב' בזיכין וד' מקדמין לפניהם ב' ליטול ב' סדרים וב' ליטול ב' בזיכין המכניסין עומדין בצפון ופניהם לדרום והמוציאין עומדים בדרום ופניהם לצפון. אלו מושכין ואלו מניחין טפחיים של זה בצד טפחו של זה שנא' לפני תמיד. ר' יוסי אומר אפילו אלו נוטלין ואלו מניחין אף זו היתה תמיד. שמעינן מדבריהם שאי' אלו מושכין ואלו מניחין. פי' מושכין את לחם הפנים לא שמערין אותו מעל השלחן כולו אלא מושכין אותו מעט מעט ומתגלה מקצת השלחן ובאותו מקצת המגולה מניחין הלחם המכניסין החדש. וכן עושין טפחו של זה בצד טפחו של זה וסבירא להו שאם נטלו הישן מעל השלחן אין מחזירין אותו אלא כיון שסילק הלחם הישן ונשאר השלחן שעה אחת בלא לחם עברו על הכתוב לפני תמיד ואע"פ שיש לו רשות להדר הא חדש [הוא] מהא שמעינן שהפורש מן המצוה אין לו עוד לחזור עליה להדרה. ומצאנו בתלמוד א"י המל ימול מיכן לשתי מילות אחת למילה ואחת לפריעה. אחת למילה ואחת לציצין כדברי ר' עקיבא ולר' ישמעאל דסבירא ליה דברה תורה כלשון בני אדם נפקא ליה מהא דא"ר יהודה בן פזי אז אמרה חתן דמים למולות מיכן ב' מילות למילה ולפריעה למילה ולציצין:

ת"ר מהלקטין את המילה ואם לא הלקטו ענוש כרת. פי' מהלקטין יש מי שאומר מלקטן הציצין המעכבין את המילה כולן וכן סבירא לן ויש מי שאומר מהלקטין מלשון ילקוט שהערלה היא כמו ילקוט ובתוכו העטרה וצריך לחתוך הילקוט כולו לגלות העטרה ואם לא חתכו כולו כאלו לא מל והמל אם לא הילקט בשבת כל הציצין המעכבין את המילה כאלו לא מל וחילל השבת וענוש כרת. והאי דאמרו לא מספקת אינה התראה ואינו מתכוון לחלל את השבת אלא לעשות מצוה מכוון וכיון שלא עשה חייב (כדרבי)[כרת] מפני שלא הניח כיון שנכנסה השבת מוציצין. אע"ג דהאי דם מחבר הוא כיון דאי' סכנה דמיא לאספלנית וכמון ועבדינן לה בשבת פי' אספלנית: רטיה קירא שעוה והיא פסולת הדבש: חספניתא כעין קרום הצומח בעור הפנים ומתקלף ובלשון ישמעאל אל כופה סילקא בלשון ישמעאל סילק: טורפין. מערבין. פי' פילתא שילא

מסורת הש"ס

[פי' כעין קרום הצומח בעור הפנים ומתקלף. ערוך]

[תוספ' פי"ג]

לקמן קלט:

[ביצה כג.]

[קידושין לא: וש"נ]

[גי' הערוך בערך סטר אבראי]

חולין מז: [תוספ' פט"ז ע"ש]

הגהות הב"ח

(א) גמ' דילמא מידביק גרדתא מיניה: (ב) שם מיקר הוא דקר:

גליון הש"ס

גמ' מימי לא מלאני לבי. לעיל דף קיח ע"ב:

פי' שאין יכול להצתין ערוך ע' צתם

[פי' שאין מוציא הבל מהוטמו ערוך]

רב נסים גאון

ונאמר כי כל מצות לא תעשה שבתורה שענש בה כרת לא דחיא לה מצות עשה כי התנאי שנא' בערות אשת אחיך שהוא היתר היבום בה שנאמר (דברים כה) יבמה יבא עליה לא בא אלא באשת אח גרידתא שאינה אסורה אלא משום אשת אח בלבד אבל באחות אשתו שהיא אשת אחיו ודומה לה מן ט"ו נשים המנויין במשנה לא נאמר בהן תנאי להתיר הייבום ואילו נשאו ראובן ושמעון שתי אחיות ומת ראובן ובן אין לו אין לאשתו על שמעון לא חליצה ולא ייבום ולא אתי עשה דאמר רחמנא יבמה יבא עליה ודחי (ויקרא יח) ואשה אל אחותה לא תקח שענש בה הכתוב כרת ובזה אמרה המשנה ט"ו נשים פוטרות צרותיהן וכו' ואמרו בתלמוד (יבמות דף ח) בסוף הדבר רבא אמר ערוה לא צריכא קרא דאין עשה דוחה את לא תעשה שיש בו כרת וכמו כן אם יהיה לא תעשה שאין בו כרת אבל נוסף עליו עשה שנמצא באותה מצוה עשה ולא תעשה אין לנו נמי לדחותה במצות עשה לפי שיצאת מן כלל לאו גרידא כמפני הציווי שנתוסף עליה ואפילו שתי מצות עשה שהן זו כנגד זו ואין אחת מכרעת מחברתה אין לנו לדחות אחת מהן מפני האחרת כמו שנאמר בתלמוד בפרק תמיד נשחט (פסחים דף נט) בשלמא לתנא קמא יבא עשה דפסח שיש בה כרת וידחה עשה דהשלמה שאין בו כרת אלא לר' ישמעאל בנו של ר' יוחנן בן ברוקא מכדי האי עשה והאי עשה מאי אולמית דהאי עשה מהאי עשה וכל שכן אם יהיה עשה ולא תעשה שמן הדין לסיים אותם יותר מלקיים העשה בלבד שכנגדם אלא אם יהיה דבר מיוחד שייחדו הכתוב או החכמים שנעשה כמו שהוא מפורש ואנו מזכירים עיקר שתקיש לו כל מה שתמצא מזה הענין ונאמר אמר הקב"ה ביום אחד לחודש השביעי שהוא יום ראש השנה (ויקרא כג) יהיה לכם שבתון זה מקרא מלא בציווי השביתה ואמר עוד מלאכת עבודה לא תעשו הזהיר בו מלעשות מלאכות מיוחדות נמצא עלינו בקידוש היום עצמו עשה ולא תעשה עוד ציונו בו לתקוע בשופר שנאמר (במדבר כט) יום תרועה יהיה לכם ובעת שלא תיקננו השופר מערב יום טוב והוצרכנו ביום טוב עצמו לתקוע בשופר לקיים המצוה ואי אפשר להיות דבר זה אלא עד שנחתוך השופר ונתקן אותו ונחלל קדושת היום ראוי לנו שנניח מצות שופר שהיא עשה ולא נחלל היום שיש בחיוב קידושו עשה ולא תעשה שאי אפשר שיבא עשה בלבד וידחה עשה ולא תעשה יחדו וכגון זה מילה שלא בזמנה והוא מי שנתאחר לאחר יום ח' מחמת חולי שאירע לתינוק או מפני הספק כמו ששנינו (לקמן דף קלז) בין השמשות ערב שבת נימול לי' יום טוב אחר שבת נמול לי"א וכשתהיה מילה שלא בזמנה אינה מותרת ביום טוב כי יום טוב יש בו עשה ולא תעשה ולא יבא עשה של מילה ודחי עשה ולא תעשה של יום טוב אלא בזמנה שהוא יום ח' ודאי שבו נאמר (ויקרא יב) וביום השמיני ימול ואמרו בפירוש וביום ואפי' בשבת אבל שלא בזמנה אפי' יום טוב אינה דוחה שאין עשה דוחה את לא תעשה ועשה אלא נזיר מצורע כי פירש בראיות ברורות שעשה ידחה את לא תעשה ועשה שבו וביאור זה כי הקב"ה צוה הנזיר שיגדל שער ראשו מאחר שהקדים האזהרה

עין משפט נר מצוה

כח א מיי' פ"ב מהל' מילה הלכה ח וס"ג מהל' שבת הלכה יד סמג עשין כח טוש"ע א"ח סי' של"א סעיף ט:

כט ב ג מיי' פכ"א מהל' שבת הלכה כו טוש"ע א"ח סי' שכח סעיף כב:

ל ד ה מיי' שם טוש"ע שם סעיף כג:

מסורת הש"ס

לעיל פו. ע"ש

תורה אור

מתני' מרחיצין את הקטן בין לפני המילה ובין לאחר המילה ומזלפין עליו ביד אבל לא בכלי ר"א בן עזריה *אומר מרחיצין את הקטן ביום השלישי שחל להיות בשבת שנאמר °ויהי ביום השלישי בהיותם כואבים (בראשית לד) ספק ואנדרוגינוס אין מחללין עליו את השבת ורבי יהודה מתיר באנדרוגינוס: **גמ'** והא אמרת רישא מרחיצין רב יהודה ורבה בר אבוה דאמרי תרוייהו כיצד תני מרחיצין את הקטן בין לפני מילה בין לאחר מילה כיצד מזלפין עליו ביד אבל לא בכלי אמר רבא והא מרחיצין קתני אלא אמר רבא הכי קתני מרחיצין את הקטן בין מלפני מילה בין לאחר המילה ביום הראשון כדרכו וביום השלישי שחל להיות בשבת מזלפין עליו ביד אבל לא בכלי ר"א בן עזריה אומר מרחיצין את הקטן ביום השלישי שחל להיות בשבת שנאמר ויהי ביום השלישי בהיותם כואבים תניא כוותיה דרבא מרחיצין הקטן בין לפני מילה בין לאחר מילה ביום ראשון כדרכו וביום השלישי שחל להיות בשבת מזלפין עליו ביד ר"א בן עזריה אומר מרחיצין את הקטן ביום השלישי שחל להיות בשבת ואע"פ שאין ראיה לדבר זכר לדבר שנאמר ויהי ביום השלישי בהיותם כואבים וכשהן מזלפין אין מזלפין לא בכוס ולא בקערה ולא בכלי אלא ביד אתאן לתנא קמא מאי אע"פ שאין ראיה לדבר זכר לדבר משום דגדול לא סליק בישרא הייא קטן סליק ביה בישרא הייא ההוא דאתא לקמיה דרבא אורי ליה כשמעתיה איחלש רבא אמר אנא בהדי תרגימנא דסבי למה לי אמרו ליה רבנן לרבא והתניא כוותיה דמר אמר להו מתניתין כוותייהו דיקא ממאי מדקאמר רבי אלעזר בן עזריה אומר מרחיצין את הקטן ביום השלישי שחל להיות בשבת אי אמרת בשלמא תנא קמא מזלפין קאמר היינו דקאמר ליה ר"א בן עזריה מרחיצין אלא אי אמרת תנא קמא מרחיצין ביום הראשון קאמר ומזלפין ביום השלישי האי רבי אלעזר בן עזריה אומר מרחיצין אף מרחיצין מיבעי ליה כי אתא רב דימי אמר רבי אלעזר הלכה כר"א בן עזריה הוו בה במערבא הרחצת כל גופו או הרחצת מילה אמר להו ההוא מרבנן ורבי יעקב שמיה מסתברא הרחצת כל גופו דאי ס"ד הרחצת מילה מי גרע מחמין על גבי מכה דאמר רב אין מונעין חמין ושמן מעל גבי מכה בשבת מתקיף לה רב יוסף ולא שני לך בין חמין שהוחמו בשבת לחמין שהוחמו מע"ש מתקיף לה רב דימי וממאי דהכא בחמין שהוחמו בשבת פליגי דילמא בחמין שהוחמו בע"ש פליגי אמר אביי אנא בעאי דאישני ליה וקדם ושני ליה רב יוסף מפני שסכנה הוא לו איתמר נמי כי אתא רבין א"ר אבהו א"ר אלעזר ואמרי לה א"ר אבהו א"ר יוחנן *הלכה כר"א בן עזריה בין בחמין שהוחמו בשבת בין בחמין שהוחמו מע"ש בין הרחצת כל גופו בין הרחצת מילה מפני שסכנה היא לו: גופא אמר רב אין מונעין חמין ושמן מעל גבי מכה בשבת ושמואל אמר נותן חוץ למכה ושותת ויורד למכה מיתיבי *אין נותנין שמן וחמין על גבי מוך ליתן על גבי מכה בשבת התם משום סחיטה תא שמע אין נותנין חמין ושמן על גבי מוך שעל גבי מכה בשבת התם נמי משום סחיטה תניא כוותיה דשמואל *אין נותנין חמין ושמן על גבי מכה בשבת אבל נותנין חוץ למכה ושותת ויורד למכה תנו רבנן *נותנין על גבי המכה מוך יבש וספוג יבש אבל לא גמי יבש ולא כתיתין יבשין קשיא כתיתין אכתיתין לא קשיא *הא בחדתי הא בעתיקי אמר אביי שמע מינה הני כתיתין מסו: ספק ואנדרוגינוס כו': תנו רבנן °ערלתו (ויקרא יב) ערלתו ודאי דוחה את השבת ולא

רש"י

מתני' ומזלפין עליו. את החמין: ביד. אבל לא בכלי ובגמ' פריך הא אמרת רישא מרחיצין דמשמע כדרכו והדר תני אפילו לזלף עליו בכלי אסור: ספק. כגון ספק בן ח' חדשים [וספק בן ט'] דהוא כאבן בעלמא ואין מילתו דוחה שבת (וספק בן ט'): ר' יהודה מתיר באנדרוגינוס. דאיתרבי מקרא כדמפרש בגמ' לקמן: **גמ'** והא אמרת רישא מרחיצין. ואפילו כדרכו: כיצד קתני. מרחיצין דרישא לאו כדרכו הוא דתנא סיפא לפרושי כיצד מרחיצין כגון לזלף ביד ואפילו ביום ראשון: תניא כוותיה דרבא כו' ה"ג ביום השלישי מזלפין עליו ביד ולא גרסינן אבל לא בכלי: אתאן לת"ק. הך סיפא תנא קמא אמרה דאילו ר"א אפילו הרחצה כדרכו שרי: משום דגדול לא סליק בישרא הייא. היינו טעמא דמעשה שכם לאו ראיה גמורה היא משום דגדול אין מכה שבבשרו מעלה ארוכה מהר אבל קטן נתרפא מידי סכנתו מהר: אורי ליה כשמעתיה. התיר לו הרחצה כדרכו ביום ראשון שחל להיות בשבת: איחלש. נעשה חולה והיה דואג שמא על כך נענש: אמר בהדי תרגימנא דסבי למה לי. מה היה לי לחלוק כנגד זקנים הללו רב יהודה ורבה בר אבוה שפירשו שאסור להרחיץ: אי אמרת בשלמא ת"ק מזלפין. ביום ראשון קאמר ולא איירי בהרחצה כלל אלא בזילוף היינו דאתא ר"א בן עזריה ופליג ואמר מרחיצין: אלא אי אמרת תנא קמא נמי מרחיצין אמר בשני הימים ולא פליג ר"א אלא איום שלישי דקאמר ת"ק מזלפין אף מרחיצין ביום השלישי מיבעי ליה: הוו בה. דייקי בה: דאי ס"ד הרחצת מילה מי גרע מחמין על גבי מכה. דשרי והכא אסרי רבנן בשלישי (*לגמרי): ולא שני כו'. והכא גבי מילה בהוחמו בשבת עסקינן הלכך בשלישי דליכא סכנתא לא: אמר אביי אנא בעאי דאישני ליה. אני הייתי רוצה לתרץ אתקפתא זו כדשני ליה רב יוסף מפני שסכנה היא לו: וקדם רב יוסף ושנייא ליה. דודאי מתניתין חמין שהוחמו בשבת נמי שרי בימים הראשונים ולר"א אף בשלישי מפני שמניעת חמין סכנה היא לו: אין נותנין כו'. קס"ד גזרה משום שחיקת סמנין כשמואל דטעמיה משום הכי הוא והיינו דקאמר אבל נותן חוץ למכה דלא מוכחא מילתא דלרפואה: מוך יבש וספוג יבש. דלאו לרפואה היא אלא שלא ישרטו בגדיו הקשים מכתו: אבל לא כתיתין יבישים (א) וגמי יבש. חתיכות בגדים דקות משום דמסו וגזרו משום שחיקת סמנין: קשיא כתיתין אכתיתין. רישא שרי מוך יבש דהיינו כתיתין וסיפא אסר כתיתין: חדתי. חדשים שלא היו על גבי מכה מעולם מסו עתיקי לא מסו: ה"ג שמע מינה הני כתיתין מסו: ערלתו ודאי דוחה השבת. דבהאי קרא וביום השמיני דילפינן מיניה אפילו בשבת כתיב בסיפיה ערלתו דמשמע מיעוטא ערלתו של זה ולא של אחר ולמעוטי ספק אתא: אנדרוגינוס

תוספות

מי גרע מחמין על גבי מכה. והיכי אסרי רבנן בשלישי אע"ג דאיכא למימר דרב אמרה למילתיה כר"א בן עזריה דפסקינן לעיל הלכתא כוותיה משמע ליה דלכ"ע קאמר ועוד דאפילו לר"א בן עזריה פריך דמשמע דשרי בשלישי משום סכנה מדמייתי קרא ויהי ביום השלישי ורב איירי במכה שאין בה סכנה: **ואין** מונעין חמין ושמן. פירש ה"ר יוסף פורת בשם רבינו שמואל דבמעורבת יחד איירי דאי כל חד באפי נפשיה מאי קמ"ל בשמן מתני' היא בפ' שמנה שרצים (לעיל דף קי"א) אבל סך הוא את השמן והיינו אפילו על גבי מכה מדקתני בני מלכים סכין ע"ג מכותיהן שמן וורד מכלל דבשאר שמן מותר לאחר אפילו ע"ג מכה ושמואל נמי היכי הוה פליג: ולא

רבינו חננאל

מקטמא לאולמא ממקום הדק לעבה: ת"ר דברים שאין עושין למילה בשבת עושין לה ביו"ט שוחקין כמון וטורפין לה יין ושמן יין בפ"ע ושמן בפ"ע אבל ע"י ליכא [אסור]. פי' ליכא עירוב יין ושמן להוליך השמן בתוך היין על [ידי] עירוב. (אבל) א"ל אביי לרבה מהו לגבן. פי' לגבן ביו"ט לקפות גבינה לקבץ פיתותי החלב הקפוי ולעשותם חריץ של גבינה. א"ל אסור לגבן. א"ל והלא גיבון כמו לישת העיסה שנותן מים בקמח ומולל בידיו ועושה פתיתין ומוסיף מים ומקבץ הפתיתין ועושה אותם עיסה. כך מקפה החלב בטוכמסו ואחר שיקפה בכלי ויעמוד מכניס ידו ופיתתו. ואח"כ מכניס ידו ומגבן מתוך הכיס. הנה גיבון ולישה מלאכתן שוה מפני מה זה מותר וזה אסור ופירק לו קמח אי אפשר לאוכלו אלא ע"י לישה ביומו. והחלב אפשר לאכלו חלב או לעשותו גבינה בערב. אקשינן עלה והא אמרו נהרדעי גבינה בת יומא מעליא והנה היא כמו הלישה וכששהפת חמה מעליא כך הגבינה בת יומא מעליא ופריק ליה הכי קאמר אפילו בת יומא מעליא מכלל שבת שנים ושלשה ימים מעליא טפי ואפילו בת יומא מעליא: אין עושין למילה חלוק לכתחילה אבל כורך עליה סמרטוט: מתניתין מרחיצין את הקטן בין לפני המילה ובין לאחר המילה ומזלפין עליו אבל לא בכלי. ואקשי היאך קתני מזלפין מכלל שרחיצה אסורה והא רישא דמתניתין קתני מרחיצין ופרקי' רב יהודה ורבה בר אבוה אמר כך סידור המשנה מרחיצין את הקטן בין לפני המילה ובין לאחר המילה. והרחצה זו כיצד היא ע"י זילוף היא ביד אבל לא בכלי. ואקשי עליהו רבה והא מרחיצין קתני וזילוף אינה רחיצה ופריק רבא משנתנו הא דקתני מרחיצין ביום ראשון של מילה אם היא שבת רחיצה כדרכו בין לפני המילה בין לאחר המילה וביום השלישי שחל להיות בשבת מזלפין ביד אבל לא בכלי ותניא כוותיה דרבא ואע"ג דתניא כוותיה לפום דקדוקא דמתניתין לא מיתוקמה כתירוציה דהא רבה כנפשיה אורי כשמעתיה ואיחלש ועיין במתניתין שפיר וחזא דלכאורה כתירוציה דרבא. וכי עיין בה

הגהות הב"ח

(א) רש"י ד"ה אבל לא כתיתין יבישים חתיכות כצ"ל ותיבות וגמי יבש נמחק:

רש"ל מ"ו וא"ל למחוק וקאי למאי דהסכים רבא לפי סבר דדיקאטוטייהו ולא התיר ת"ק אפי' לזלף ביום ג'

רב נסים גאון

האזהרה עליו שלא יגלחנו שנאמר (במדבר ו) גדל פרע שער ראשו אחר שאמר תער לא יעלה על ראשו הרי הוא בדבר זה מוזהר בלאו ומצווה בעשה וחייב המצורע בעת טהרתו לגלח כל שער שבגופו שנאמר (ויקרא יד) והיה ביום השביעי יגלח את כל שערו וכשיתנגע הנזיר בצרעת ויגיע יום ז' שהוא חייב לגלח בו אמרו חכמים שמצות גילוח של צרעת דוחה עשה ולא תעשה שיש עליו לענין נזירותו וכי מה שאמר הכתוב לענין מצורע את ראשו אחר שאמר יגלח את כל שערו לא בא אלא לענין נזיר שנאמר בו תער לא יעבור על ראשו לומר כי זו המצוה אינו חייב בה אלא בעת שלא תהיה בו צרעת אבל בעת שיהיה בגופו צרעת יגלח את ראשו אפי' שער ראשו שהזהרתיו שלא יגלחנו בימי נזירותו חייב לגלח אם היה צרוע נתקיים לנו מזה שבנזיר מצורע לבדו יבא עשה ודחי לא תעשה ועשה ובראש מס' יבמות (דף ה) אמרו אלא דקיימא לן דאין עשה דחי לא תעשה ועשה ליגמר מנזיר דאתי עשה ודחי לא תעשה ועשה אלא מנזיר לא גמרינן שכן ישנן בשאלה ובארו כי דבר זה הוא מיוחד בו לבדו ולא בזולתו וכי בכל התורה כולה לא אתי עשה ודחי לא תעשה ועשה והזהר לשמור אלו העיקרים שפירשנו שהן מתבארים לך כל דבר כשתמצא בתלמוד מעין אלו הענינים: **תינח** גדול דכתיב ביה בשר קטן נמי כתיב ביה בשר בינוני מנלן פי' כבר ידענו כי הקטנים פטורים ממצות והשכר והעונש הם תלויין בחיוב המצות ומאחר שנדע כי לא חייב הכתוב במצות אלא לפי שיש בו עניני החיוב כגון שהביא ב' שערות ושהגיע למספר שני האנשים ושיצא מגבול הנערות אז הוא בן עונשין וכיון שראינו שענש הכתוב מי שלא נימול שנאמר (בראשית יז) וערל זכר אשר לא ימול את בשר ערלתו ונכרתה וגו' ידענו כי דבר זה מיוחד הוא באנשים גדולים ולא בנערים ומצאנו כתב בו בשר ערלתו להודיענו שהמילה דוחה את הצרעת על דרך העיקר שהקדמנו דאתי עשה ודחי לא תעשה וכי בעת שתהיה בערלה בהרת ימול ויחתוך אותה וידחה מה שכתוב (דברים כד) השמר בנגע הצרעת והצרכנו שיבאר לנו דבר זה להסיר מדעתנו מה שהיה עולה עליו שמה היינו סוברים כי זה שכתב (שם) לשמור מאד ולעשות הוא דבר מוסף על הלאו והוה ליה לא תעשה ועשה ואין המילה דוחה אותן שאין עשה דוחה את לא תעשה ועשה והסיר ממנו סברא זו והודיענו שהוא לא תעשה בלבד והמילה דוחה אותה והו שאמרו תינח גדול דכתב ביה בשר והקטן גמי שהוא בן ח' ימים נאמר בו וביום השמיני ימול בשר ערלתו ידענו כי המילה ביום ח' תדחה (עוד) את הצרעת נשאר לנו לשאול על הבינוני והוא שעברו עליו ח' ימים ולא נימול מפני מאורע שאירע לו כגון שהיה חולה או שהיה בו ספק התחיה המילה ראויה בו בעת שיש בהרת בערלתו או לא ולפיכך אמרו בינוני מנלן ובאה התשובה משם אביי דאתיא מבינייא ומשם רבא מילה בזמנה [לא] צריכא קרא כו' ופירוש על דעת אביי שהמילה מותרת בבינוני במקום שיש בהרת נלמוד מגדול וקטן כמו ששנינו (ריש ספרא) בבנין אב משני כתובים הצד השוה שבהן כו' וכן הוא הילוך הדבר בכאן כי הבינוני לא יתכן שנלמוד מן הגדול לפי שהגדול ענוש כרת לכך התירו בו הכתוב חתיכת הבהרת אבל הבינוני שאין בו חיוב כרת אין דבר זה מותר בו וכמו כן לא נלמוד דבר זה מן הקטן כי הקטן מילתו בזמנה ביום ח' והיא דוחה את השבת ולפיכך התיר הכתוב חתיכת הבהרת אבל הבינוני שאין מילתו בזמנה לא ומאחר שלא יכולנו ללמוד דבר זה מאחד מהן חיברנו אותם ביחד וקיימנו דבר עיקר מהם שהבינוני מותר לחתוך בהרת מערלתו וכן הילוכו של דבר בענין זה בינוני מנלן אמר אביי אתיא מבניינא מה לגדול שכן ענוש כרת קטן יוכיח שאינו ענוש כרת מה לקטן שכן מילה בזמנה גדול יוכיח שאין מילה בזמנה וחזר הדין הצד השוה שבהן שמילתו דוחה את הצרעת אף אני אביא בינוני שתהא מילתו דוחה את הצרעת ורבא לא הוצרך לדבר זה כי הוא סובר כי בשר ערלתו שנאמר בבן שמנת ימים לא בא להתיר מילת בן שמונת ימים במקום שיש בהרת כי זה נלמדנו מקל וחומר השתא שבת חמורה דוחה צרעת קלה לא כל שכן והואיל ואינו צריך לבן ח' ימים הועיל להתיר המילה בבינוני במקום שיש בהרת: לא צריכא אפי' ר' יהודה דאמר דבר שאינו מתכוין אסור כבר פירשנו זה בפ' כירה. לבדו ולא מילה שלא בזמנה

MISHNAH. [134b] WE MAY BATHE THE INFANT BOTH BEFORE AND AFTER THE CIRCUMCISION, AND SPRINKLE [WARM WATER] OVER HIM BY HAND BUT NOT WITH A VESSEL. R. ELEAZAR B. 'AZARIAH SAID: WE MAY BATHE AN INFANT ON THE THIRD DAY [OF CIRCUMCISION] WHICH FALLS ON THE SABBATH, BECAUSE IT IS SAID, AND IT CAME TO PASS ON
a THE THIRD DAY, WHEN THEY WERE SORE.[1] AS FOR ONE WHO IS DOUBTFUL,[2] AND AN HERMAPHRODITE, WE MAY NOT DESECRATE THE SABBATH ON THEIR ACCOUNT; BUT R. JUDAH PERMITS [IT] IN THE CASE OF AN HERMAPHRODITE.

GEMARA. But you say in the first clause, WE MAY BATHE?[3] —Rab Judah and Rabbah b. Abbuha both said: He [the Tanna] teaches how [it is to be done]. [Thus:] WE MAY BATHE THE INFANT BOTH BEFORE AND AFTER THE CIRCUMCISION. How? WE SPRINKLE [WARM WATER] OVER HIM BY HAND, BUT NOT WITH A VESSEL. Raba objected: But he states, WE MAY BATHE?[4] Rather said Raba, He teaches thus: WE MAY BATHE THE INFANT BOTH BEFORE AND AFTER CIRCUMCISION on the first day in the normal manner; but on the third day which falls on the Sabbath, WE SPRINKLE [WARM WATER] OVER HIM BY HAND BUT NOT WITH A VESSEL. R. ELEAZAR B. 'AZARIAH SAID: WE MAY BATHE AN INFANT ON THE THIRD DAY WHICH FALLS ON THE SABBATH, BECAUSE IT IS SAID, AND IT CAME TO PASS ON THE THIRD DAY, WHEN THEY WERE SORE. It was taught in accordance with Raba: We may bathe the infant before and after the circumcision on the first day in the normal manner, but on the third day which falls on the Sabbath we besprinkle him by hand. R. Eleazar b. 'Azariah said: We may bathe an infant on the third day which falls on the Sabbath, and though there is no proof, there is an allusion thereto, for it is said, '*And it came to pass on the third day, when they were sore*'. And when they sprinkle, they sprinkle neither with a glass nor with a dish nor with a vessel, but only by hand—this agrees with the first Tanna. Why [does he say,] though there is no proof, there is an allusion thereto?[5]— Because an adult's flesh does not heal quickly, whereas an infant's
b does.[1]

A certain [person] came before Raba, [and] he gave him a ruling in accordance with his view.[2] [Then] Raba fell ill. Said he: What business did I have with the interpretation of the older scholars?[3] [Thereupon] the Rabbis said to Raba: But it was taught in accordance with the Master? Our Mishnah supports them, he replied. How so? Since it states, R. ELEAZAR B. 'AZARIAH SAID: WE MAY BATHE THE INFANT ON THE THIRD DAY WHICH FALLS ON THE SABBATH. It is well if you assume that the first Tanna means [that] we may [merely] sprinkle: hence R. Eleazar b. 'Azariah says to him, We may bathe. But if you explain that the first Tanna means, We may bathe on the first day and sprinkle on the third day, then [instead of] this [statement], R. ELEAZAR B. AZARIAH SAID: WE MAY BATHE, it should have said, 'WE MAY ALSO BATHE [ON THE THIRD DAY].'

When R. Dimi came,[4] he said in R. Eleazar's name: The *halachah* is as R. Eleazar b. 'Azariah. In the West [Palestine] they pondered thereon: is the bathing of the whole body [permitted], or [only] the bathing of the membrum? Said one of the Rabbis, named R. Jacob, It is logical [that it means] the bathing of the whole body. For should you think, the bathing of the membrum,— is this worse [less important] than hot water on a wound? For Rab said, One does not withhold hot water and oil from a wound on the Sabbath.[5] R. Joseph demurred: And do you not admit a distinction between hot water heated on the Sabbath and hot water heated on the eve of the Sabbath?[6] To this R. Dimi demurred: And whence [does it follow] that they differ here in respect of hot water heated on the Sabbath? Perhaps they differ in respect of hot water heated on the eve of the Sabbath?—Said Abaye, I wanted to answer him, but R. Joseph anticipated [me]
c and answered him: Because it is a danger for him.[1] It was stated likewise: When Rabin came,[2] he said in R. Abbahu's name in R. Eleazar's name—others state, R. Abbahu said in R. Joḥanan's name: The *halachah* is as R. Eleazar b. 'Azariah in respect of both hot water heated on the Sabbath and hot water heated on the eve of the Sabbath, whether for the bathing of the whole body or for the bathing of the membrum, because it is dangerous for him.

[To turn to] the main text: 'Rab said: One does not withhold hot water and oil from a wound on the Sabbath. But Samuel said: One must place it outside the wound, and it flows down on to the wound'. An objection is raised: One may not put oil and hot water on a rag to apply it to a wound on the Sabbath?—There it is on account of wringing out.[3] Come and hear: One may not pour hot water and oil on a rag which is on a wound on the Sabbath?—There too it is because of wringing out. It was taught in accordance with Samuel: One may not apply hot water and oil to a wound on the Sabbath, but one may put it outside the wound, and it flows down on to the wound.

Our Rabbis taught: One may apply dry wadding or a dry sponge to a wound[4] but not a dry reed or dry rags [of cloth]. [The rulings on] rags are contradictory?[5] There is no difficulty: the one treats of new [rags];[6] the other of old.[7] Abaye observed: This proves that rags heal.

ONE WHO IS DOUBTFUL, AND AN HERMAPHRODITE, etc. Our Rabbis taught, [*And in the eighth day the flesh of*] his *foreskin* [*shall be circumcised*]:[8] '*his foreskin*', [the foreskin of] one who is certain[9] supersedes the Sabbath, [135a] but [of] one in doubt

a (1) Gen. XXXIV, 25. This shows that the third day is a dangerous period, and therefore the infant may be bathed even on the Sabbath. (2) One who is born prematurely, and he may be an eight months' child. The Rabbis held that such could not possibly live, and therefore the Sabbath might not be violated for his circumcision. (3) Which implies in the normal manner, *sc.* in a bath. (4) Sprinkling is not bathing. (5) Surely this is a *proof* that the third day is dangerous.

b (1) The verse quoted, q.v., treats of the former. (2) Permitting the infant to be bathed on the first day, which was a Sabbath, in the usual way. (3) *Sc.* Rab Judah and Rabbah b. Abbuha. I.e., 'why did I interfere and disregard it?' He regarded his illness as a punishment. (4) V. *supra* 5a, n. b9. (5) Whereas according to the present interpretation the first Tanna permits even sprinkling on the first day only, but not on the third. (6) Rab refers to the latter, while R. Joseph assumed that the Mishnah refers to the former.

c (1) Hence the Mishnah must certainly refer to water heated on the Sabbath. (2) V. *supra* 5a, n. b9. (3) One may pour too much on the rag and then wring it out, which is forbidden. (4) These are not intended for healing but merely as a protection. (5) A dry rag too is a fragment, and it is permitted. (6) These heal and are forbidden. (7) Which do not heal (Rashi). R. Ḥan. reverses it. (8) Lev. XII, 3; '*day*' includes the Sabbath, *supra* 132a. (9) I.e., who is certainly subject to the obligation.

does not supersede the Sabbath; '*his foreskin*' [of] one who is certain supersedes the Sabbath, but an hermaphrodite does not supersede the Sabbath. R. Judah maintained: An hermaphrodite supersedes the Sabbath and there is the penalty of *kareth*. '*His foreskin*': [of] one who is certain supersedes the Sabbath, but [of]
a one born at twilight[1] does not supersede the Sabbath; *his foreskin:* one who is certain supersedes the Sabbath, but one who is born circumcised does not supersede the Sabbath, for Beth Shammai maintain: One must cause a few drops of the covenant blood to flow from him, while Beth Hillel rule: It is unnecessary. R. Simeon b. Eleazar said: Beth Shammai and Beth Hillel did not differ concerning him who is born circumcised that you must cause a few drops of the covenant blood to flow from him, because it is a suppressed foreskin:[2] about what do they differ? about a proselyte who was converted when [already] circumcised: there Beth Shammai maintain: One must cause a few drops of the covenant blood to flow from him; whereas Beth Hillel rule: One need not cause a few drops of the covenant blood to flow from him.

The Master said: 'But [of] one that is doubtful does not supersede the Sabbath.' What does this include?[3]—It includes the following which was taught by our Rabbis: For a seven-months' infant[4] one may desecrate the Sabbath, but for an eight-months' infant one may not desecrate the Sabbath.[5] For one in doubt whether he is a seven-months' or an eight-months' infant, one may not desecrate the Sabbath. An eight-months' infant is like a stone and may not be handled, but his mother bends [over] and suckles him because of the danger.[6]

It was stated: Rab said: The *halachah* is as the first Tanna;[7] while Samuel said: The *halachah* is as R. Simeon b. Eleazar. A circumcised child was born to R. Adda b. Ahabah. He took him to
b thirteen circumcisers,[1] until he mutilated him privily.[2] I deserve it for transgressing Rab's [ruling], said he. Said R. Naḥman to him, And did you not violate Samuel's [ruling]? Samuel ruled thus only of weekdays, but did he rule thus of the Sabbath?—He [R. Adda b. Ahabah] held that it is definitely a suppressed foreskin.[3] For it was stated: Rabbah said: We *suspect* that it may be a suppressed foreskin;[4] R. Joseph said: It is *certainly* a suppressed foreskin.

R. Joseph said: Whence do I know it? Because it was taught, R. Eliezer ha-Ḳappar said: Beth Shammai and Beth Hillel do not disagree concerning him who is born circumcised, that one must cause a few drops of the covenant blood to flow from him. Concerning what do they differ? As to whether the Sabbath is desecrated on his account: Beth Shammai maintain, We desecrate the Sabbath on his account; while Beth Hillel rule: We must not desecrate the Sabbath on his account. Does it then not follow that the first Tanna holds, We desecrate the Sabbath for him?[5] But perhaps the first Tanna maintains that all agree that we may not desecrate the Sabbath for him?—If so, R. Eliezer ha-Ḳappar comes to teach us Beth Shammai's view![6] But perhaps he means this: Beth Shammai and Beth Hillel did not disagree in this matter![7]

R. Assi said: He whose mother is defiled through confinement must be circumcised at eight [days], but he whose mother is not
c defiled through confinement[1] is not circumcised on the eighth day,[2] because it is said, *If a woman conceive seed, and bear a man child, then she shall be unclean,* etc. . . *And in the eighth day the flesh of his foreskin shall be circumcised.*[3] Said Abaye to him, Let the early generations[4] prove [the reverse], where the mother was not defiled through confinement,[5] yet circumcision was on the eighth

a (1) On Friday, and it is not known whether it was then Friday or the Sabbath. (2) I.e., the foreskin which seems absent is pressed to the membrum. (3) For the various cases of doubt are enumerated in detail. (4) I.e., one born after seven months of pregnancy. (5) The Rabbis held that such could not possibly live; hence there is no point in desecrating the Sabbath by circumcising him. (6) To herself, if she is not eased of her milk. (7) Who taught that Beth Shammai and Beth Hillel disagree about a child who is born circumcised; the *halachah* then naturally being as Beth Hillel.

b (1) That they might cause a few drops of the covenant blood to flow. It was the Sabbath, and they all refused. (2) Eventually he performed the operation himself unskilfully, with that result. (3) There is no element of doubt at all, and therefore it must be done even on the Sabbath. (4) It is only because of this doubt that some drops of blood must be made to flow. (5) Even in Beth Hillel's opinion. Hence Beth Hillel must hold that it is certainly a suppressed foreskin. (6) Surely that is of no interest, since the *halachah* is as Beth Hillel. (7) Thus: the first Tanna maintains that Beth Shammai and Beth Hillel agree that we may not desecrate the Sabbath; hence their controversy must refer to weekdays, Beth Hillel holding that no blood-flow at all is required, whereupon R. Eleazar ha-Ḳappar stated that this is incorrect, there being no dispute in respect to weekdays, for even Beth Hillel necessitate a blood-flow, and they differ only in respect of the Sabbath. On this interpretation he informs us of Beth Hillel's view in respect to weekdays.

c (1) E.g., if the child is not born in the usual manner but extracted through the cesarean section; or if a Gentile woman gives birth and becomes a proselyte the following day. (2) But immediately. (3) Lev. XII, 2f. Thus the two are interdependent. (4) Viz., those preceding the giving of the Torah. (5) The law of defilement being as yet non-existent.

ולא ספק דוחה את השבת ערלתו ודאי דוחה את השבת [א]ולא אנדרוגינוס דוחה את השבת רבי יהודה אומר אנדרוגינוס דוחה את השבת וענוש כרת ערלתו ודאי דוחה את השבת [ב]ולא נולד בין השמשות דוחה את השבת ערלתו ודאי דוחה את השבת [ג]ולא נולד כשהוא מהול דוחה את השבת שב"ש אומרים צריך להטיף ממנו דם ברית וב"ה אומרים אינו צריך *א"ר שמעון בן אלעזר לא נחלקו ב"ש וב"ה *[ד]על נולד כשהוא מהול שצריך להטיף ממנו דם ברית מפני שערלה כבושה היא על מה נחלקו על גר שנתגייר כשהוא מהול שבית שמאי אומרים [ה]צריך להטיף ממנו דם ברית ובה"א א"צ להטיף ממנו דם ברית: אמר מר ולא ספק דוחה את השבת לאתויי מאי לאתויי הא דתנו רבנן *[ו]בן שבעה מחללין עליו את השבת ובן ח' אין מחללין עליו את השבת ספק בן ז' ספק בן ח' אין מחללין עליו את השבת *בן שמונה הרי הוא כאבן ואסור לטלטלו אבל אמו שוחה ומניקתו מפני הסכנה איתמר רב אמר הלכה כת"ק ושמואל אמר הלכה כר"ש בן אלעזר רב אדא בר אהבה אתיליד ליה ההוא ינוקא כשהוא מהול אהדריה אתליסר מהולאי עד דשוייה כרות שפכה אמר תיתי לי דעברי אדרב אמר ליה רב נחמן ואדשמואל לא עבר איניש דאמר שמואל בחול בשבת מי אמר (א) הוא סבר ודאי ערלה כבושה היא דאיתמר רבה אמר חיישינן שמא ערלה כבושה היא רב יוסף אמר ודאי ערלה כבושה היא אמר רב יוסף מנא אמינא לה דתניא רבי אליעזר הקפר אומר לא נחלקו ב"ש וב"ה על נולד כשהוא מהול שצריך להטיף ממנו דם ברית על מה נחלקו לחלל עליו את השבת ב"ש אומרים מחללין עליו את השבת וב"ה אומרים אין מחללין עליו את השבת לאו מכלל דת"ק סבר מחללין עליו את השבת ודילמא ת"ק דברי הכל אין מחללין קאמר אם כן רבי אליעזר הקפר טעמא דב"ש אתא לאשמעינן דילמא ה"ק *לא נחלקו ב"ש וב"ה בדבר זה: *) אמר ר' אסי כל שאמו טמאה לידה נימול לשמונה וכל שאין אמו טמאה לידה אין נימול לשמנה שנאמר °אשה כי תזריע וילדה זכר וטמאה וגו' וביום השמיני ימול בשר ערלתו א"ל אביי דורות הראשונים יוכיחו שאין אמו טמאה לידה ונימול לשמנה א"ל *נתנה תורה ונתחדשה

*) [נ"ל אמר רבה אמר ר' אסי כל שאמו וכו' וכן איתא בשאלתות פ' לך לך סי' ט וכ"א כרי"ף והרא"ש]

ויקרא יב

[ב"ב קי:]

רש"י

אנדרוגינוס. ספק הוא ונולד בין השמשות נמי ספק זמנו הוא ספק אינו זמנו וכן נולד מהול ספק שמא ערלה כבושה היא העור דבוק בבשר ולקמיה פריך ספק קמא לאתויי מאי הואיל ותני כל הני ספיקי: רבי יהודה אומר כו'. לקמיה יליף מילתיה: שב"ש אומרים צריך להטיף כו'. ואפילו הכי מודו דשבת לא דחי: שצריך להטיף. חיישינן שמא ערלה כבושה היא: על גר. דליכא שום ספק ערלה כגון ערבי מהול: בן ח' אין מחללין עליו. שהרי כמת הוא ואין מילתו מצוה ואי קשיא א"כ לאו חילול הוא שהרי הוא כמחתך בבשר מת לקמן נמי מוקי האי חילול במכשירי מילה ואליבא דר' אליעזר: מפני הסכנה. מפני שחלב הרבה (ה) בדדיה ומביאה לידי חולי: כת"ק. אליבא דב"ה דאמר א"צ להטיף ממנו דם ברית: אהדריה אתליסר מהולאי. שיטיפו ממנו דם ברית ולא רצו משום דשבת הואי ואפילו לב"ש ספק הוא ואין מחללין: עד דשוייה כרות שפכה. והוא עצמו מלו ועשאו כרות שפכה שחתך מן הגיד: אדרב. דאמר א"צ להטיף: בשבת מי אמר. הא ספיקא הוא: והוא סבר. רב אדא סבר דודאי ערלה כבושה היא ומחללינן: חיישינן. הא דאמר ר"ש בן אלעזר לדברי הכל צריך להטיף אספיקא קאמר ובחול שמא ערלה כבושה היא ולענין שבת נמי ודאי לא מחללינן: ודאי ערלה כבושה היא. ומחללינן: לאו מכלל דת"ק. דר' אליעזר הקפר סבר דברי הכל מחללין והנא דאמרי כוותיה: ה"ג וממאי דילמא מכלל דת"ק סבר דברי הכל אין מחללין א"כ רבי אליעזר טעמא דב"ש אתא לאשמעינן כו'. א"כ דתנא לעיל מיניה אמר דברי הכל אין מחללין ר' אליעזר הקפר דאתא לאיפלוגי ולמימר דלאו דברי הכל הוא דהא לב"ש מחללין מאי רבותא אשמעינן דב"ש פליגי בה הא ב"ש במקום ב"ה אינה משנה *ומשנינן דילמא הכי קאמר ר' אליעזר לת"ק דאמר בשבת לדברי הכל אין מחללין ופלוגתייהו בחול דלב"ה א"צ להטיף ממנו דם ברית הא ליתא דלא נחלקו בדבר זה אלא ודאי צריך ובשבת הוא דפליגי וטעמא דב"ה אתא לאשמעינן דבחול צריך ולאפוקי מת"ק דאמר לב"ה לא צריך: כל שאין אמו טמאה לידה. כגון יוצא דופן ונכרית שילדה ולאחר נתגיירה אין בנה ממתין עד שמנה אלא נימול מיד: דורות הראשונים. מאברהם עד מתן תורה שנתנה מילה ולא נהגו טומאה: ונתחדשה

[תוספ' פט"ז] יבמות עה. [תוספ' פט"ז] יבמות פ. ב"ב כ: [לעיל מג. יבמות כח. ב"ק לד. סוכה טו.]

תוספות

ולא ספק דוחה את השבת. נראה לר"י דאסמכתא בעלמא הוא ולא איצטריך קרא להכי דהיכי תיסוק אדעתיה לחלל את השבת ולא ידענא אם הוא בר חיוב מילה או לא כדמפרש לקמן דספק נולד לז' או לח' ומשום נולד בין השמשות לא איצטריך נמי קרא דמוטב דתיבטל מצות מילה בשמיני מספיקא בשב ואל תעשה ואל יחלל שבת בידים מספק אלא נראה לר"י דעיקר האי קרא אתא לאנדרוגינוס שאינו דוחה שבת ונולד כשהוא מהול ומיהו לא מחד ערלתו נפקי דאין סברא לומר שקולים ויבואו שניהם אלא תרי קראי כתיבי חד במילה בזמנה וביום השמיני ימול בשר ערלתו וחד במילה שלא בזמנה *)דגדול וערל זכר אשר לא ימול בשר ערלתו (בראשית יז) א"נ קרא אתא לאנדרוגינוס ונולד כשהוא מהול מסברא ידעינן דאין צריך להטיף דם ברית ר"י. א"נ עיקר קרא לנולד כשהוא מהול ולאנדרוגינוס לא צריך קרא דהא נפקא ליה לר' יהודה לקמן לאנדרוגינוס טעון מילה מדכתיב כל זכר ורבנן הוו דרשי לדרשה אחריתי: לא נחלקו על נולד כשהוא מהול שצריך להטיף ממנו דם ברית כו' על מה נחלקו על גר שנתגייר. השתא משמע דיותר יש להצריך הטפה לנולד כשהוא מהול מלנתגייר כשהוא מהול דהא לנולד כ"ע מודו ובגר איכא פלוגתא וא"כ לקמן דפסיק רב הלכה כת"ק ומשמע דכוותיה קי"ל מדקאמר רב אדא בר אהבה תיתי לי דעברי אדרב וכיון דקי"ל כת"ק בנולד כשהוא מהול שאין צריך להטיף ממנו דם ברית כ"ש גר שנתגייר כשהוא מהול וה"ג לא פסקו כן אלא פסקו דקטן א"צ וגר צריך ובקטן ודאי כדין פסקו כשמועתו ובגר נמי נראה לר"י שסמכו אההיא דיבמות דפרק החולץ (דף מו:) דתניא הרי שבא ואמר מלתי ולא טבלתי מטבילין אותו ומה בכך דברי רבי יהודה ור' יוסי אומר אין מטבילין וא"ת דא"צ להטיף ממנו דם ברית בנתגייר כשהוא מהול לרבי יוסי אמאי אין מטבילין הרי הוא מהול לפניט מאי נפקא מינה אם לא מלו אותו ב"ד לא יהא אלא ערבי מהול וגבעוני מהול אלא ודאי צריך להטיף ממנו דם ברית ולכך אין מטבילין דאינו גר עד שימול ויטבול ונראה לרשב"א לתת טעם בדבר שהרי הסברא הפוכה מסברא דשמעתין והיינו טעמא דבין קטן שנולד כשהוא מהול ובין גר שנתגייר כשהוא מהול דין הוא דשניהם היו טעונים הטפת דם ברית אי לאו דדרשינן הכא דקטן אין צריך להטיף ממנו משום דכתיב ערלתו ודוקא בקטן דגלי גלי בגר דלא גלי לא גלי ור"ח פסק איפכא מה"ג: בן שמנה הרי הוא כאבן ואסור לטלטלו. נראה לר"י דעכשיו מותר לטלטל כל תינוקות שאין אנו בקיאין ועולם כמו ספק בן ח' ספק בן ט' ופעמים שהאשה מתעברת סמוך לטבילתה ופעמים שאינה מתעברת ומותר למולו בשבת ממ"נ כדאמרינן לקמן (דף קלו.) אפילו הוא בן שמנה ודאי כגון שלא בא על אשתו אלא פעם אחת ופירש וילדה לסוף ח' אפילו הכי נראה לר"י דמותר לטלטלו ולמולו בשבת אם אין ריעותא בשערו ובציפרניו כדאמר בפרק הערל (יבמות דף פ:) דאמרינן האי בר שבעה הוא ואישתהוי אישתהי: מפני הסכנה. סכנת חלב כשיש הרבה בדדין ולא חיישינן שמא תטלטל אותו ולא(ג) ידע רשב"א מאי איריא מפני הסכנה דאפילו לא יהא אלא לצער בעלמא מותר* אפילו (ד) היא לחלוב עצמה ולהוציא חלב שבדדין אע"פ שהיא מלאכה שאינה צריכה לגופה דחמיר איסורא טפי מאיסור טלטול נראה דשרי מידי דהוה אמפיס מורסא דשרינן משום צערא: מכלל דת"ק סבר ד"ה מחללין. ר' אליעזר הקפר ור"ש בן אלעזר תרווייהו קיימי את"ק וה"ק ליה ר"א הקפר לר"ש בן אלעזר לא כך יש להשיב על דברי ת"ק אלא הכי אית לן למימר לא נחלקו כו' והשתא דייק שפיר מכלל דת"ק סבר וכו'. פירוש רשב"א:

*) נ"ל דגדול וכדרך אם אינו ענין לשלא בזמנו שאף לודאי אינו דוחה

כתנאי

אפי' לחלוב בעצמה כצ"ל ותיבת היא נמחק

הגהות הב"ח

(א) גמ' מי אמרינהו סבר: (ב) רש"י ד"ה מפני הסכנה וכו' שחלב הרבה. נ"ב ובמס' יבמות דף פ פירש"י משום סכנת שניהם: (ג) תוס' ד"ה מפני הסכנה וכו' שמא תטלטל אותו ולא ידענא מאי איריא כצ"ל ותיבת רשב"א נמחק: (ד) בא"ד אפי' לחלוב בעצמה כצ"ל ותיבת היא נמחק:

עין משפט נר מצוה

לא א ב ג מיי' פ"א מהל' מילה הלכה יא סמג עשין כח טוש"ע א"ח סי' שלא סעי' ה וטוש"ע י"ד סי' רסו סעיף ח וסעיף י:
לב ד מיי' שם הלכה א סמג שם טוש"ע יד סי' רסג סעי' ד:
לג ה מיי' וסמג שם ומיי' פי"ד מהל' איסורי ביאה הלכה ה טוש"ע י"ד סי' רסח סעי' א:
לד ו מיי' פ"א מהל' מילה הלכה יד ופכ"ה מהל' שבת הלכה ו טוש"ע א"ח סי' של סעי' ז ח וי"ד סי' רס"ו סעי' יא בהג"ה:

רבינו חננאל

יאות איתברר ליה כתירוציה דרב יהודה ורבה בר אבוה. דאי כתירוצי' דידיה דאוקמא למתניתין שאמרו חכמים מרחיצין ביום ראשון בשבת כדרכו ומולפין ביום שלישי שחל להיות בשבת ר' אלעזר בן עזריה אומר אף מרחיצין ביום שלישי שחל להיות בשבת היה צריך לומר מפני שאמרו חכמים יום ג' שחל להיות בשבת מולפין בא הוא ואמר מולפין ואף מרחיצין אלא מכיון (כולא)[דלא]אמר כך שמעינן מינה שלא הזכירו חכמים ביום ג' שחל להיות בשבת לא רחיצה ולא זילוף. ומפילא שמעינן דלית להו לרבנן ביום השלישי לא רחיצה ולא זילוף. ר' אלעזר בן עזריה אומר מרחיצין את המילה ביום השלישי שחל להיות בשבת שנאמר ויהי ביום השלישי בהיותם כואבים וכ"ש ביום ראשון וקיי"ל כר' אלעזר בן עזריה דאמרי' א"ר אבהו א"ר יוחנן הלכה כר' אלעזר בן עזריה בין בחמין שהוחמו בשבת ובין חמין שהוחמו בע"ש. בין הרחצת כל גופו בין הרחצת מילה. מפני שסכנה היא לו: גופא אמר רב אין מונעין חמין ושמן מע"ג מכה בשבת ושמואל אמר נותנין חוץ למכה ושותת ויורד למכה. ואע"ג דקיי"ל רב ושמואל הלכה כרב באיסורי הכא הלכה כשמואל דתניא כוותיה, אין נותנין חמין ושמן ע"ג מכה בשבת אבל נותן חוץ למכה ושותת ויורד למכה. תני רב נותנין ע"ג מכה מוך יבש וספוג יבש אבל לא נמי יבש ולא כתיתין יבשין. קשיא כתיתין אכתיתין. רישא קתני נותנין ע"ג המכה מוך יבש והוא כתיתין והדר תני ולא כתיתין יבשין ופרקינן לא קשיא הא בחדתי והוא מוך יבש מותר שאין חשובין כרטיה. אבל כתיתין ישנין אסורין. ועלה אמר אביי ש"מ האי נקרא מטו. פי' נקרא היא כתיתין והן סמרטוטין יבשים שיש עליהם סינוף צואה ריעי. כדגרסינן בע"ז ליתו נקרא מקיקלתא כו': ת"ר ערלתו ערלתו ודאי דוחה את השבת ולא ספק דוחה את השבת ערלתו ודאי דוחה את השבת ולא אנדרוגינוס דוחה את השבת וכו' אמר מר ולא ספק דוחה את השבת לאתויי הא דתנו רבנן בן ז' מחללין עליו את השבת בן ח' אין מחללין עליו את השבת ספק בן ח' אין מחללין עליו את השבת בן ח' הרי הוא כאבן ואסור לטלטלו בשבת. אבל אמו שוחה עליו ומניקתהו מפני הסכנה. (צריך לכתוב תשלום הברייתא כמות שהיא בתוספתא). אתמר רב אמר הלכתא כת"ק דברייתא דאמר הא דתני ולא נולד כשהוא מהול דוחה את השבת שבית שמאי אומרים צריך להטיף ממנו דם ברית ובה"א אין צריך להטיף ממנו דם ברית ושמואל אמר הלכה כר' שמעון בן אלעזר שאמר לא נחלקו בית שמאי ובית הלל על הנולד מהול שצריך להטיף ממנו דם ברית דכיון שר' שמעון בן אלעזר סתמא א' יש לומר לא אמר אלא בחול אבל בשבת לא אמר דומיא דסיפא דקתני סיפא על מה נחלקו על גר שנתגייר כשהוא מהול שב"ש אומרים צריך להטיף ממנו דם ברית ובה"א אין צריך וברור הוא שאין מילה לגר בשבת ועל זה אמר שמואל הלכה כר' שמעון בן אלעזר והוא בחול ולא בשבת. וחלקו עוד בנולד כשהוא מהול רבה ורב יוסף רבה אמר חיישינן שמא ערלה כבושה היא ורב יוסף אמר ודאי ערלה כבושה היא וראינו דברי רבה שהן שוין בשבת דרב אמר הלכה כת"ק ודקדקנו דברי ת"ק שאמר ולא נולד כשהוא מהול דוחה את השבת ועל זה הלוקת ב"ש וב"ה ועליו אמרו ב"ה אין צריך להטיף ממנו דם ברית בשבת. ויש לומר אפילו בחול דהא סתם קאמר אין צריך להטיף ממנו דם ברית ומסתברא כרבה דאמר שמא ערלה כבושה היא. ומשמא אין מחללין את השבת ובירור דבר זה דברי רבה שאמר מנא אמינא לה. דתניא ר' אליעזר הקפר אומר לא נחלקו ב"ש [וב"ה על הנולד כשהוא מהול שצריך להטיף ממנו דם ברית ועל מה נחלקו לחלל עליו את השבת שבית

רב נסים גאון

בזמנה דאתיא מקל וחומר וגם זה פירשנו בפ' במה מדליקין: מילה דנכרתו עליה י"ג בריתות. מפורשין הן בתורה (בראשית יז) ואלו הן ואתה את בריתי תשמר ואתנה בריתי אני הנה בריתי והקימותי את בריתי לברית עולם ואתה את בריתי תשמור והיתה בריתי בבשרכם לברית עולם את בריתי הפר והקימותי את בריתי לברית עולם את בריתי אקים את יצחק*: ולא שאני לך בין חמין שהוחמו בשבת לחמין שהוחמו מערב שבת. תמצא נשיאות ונתינות שבדבר זה ומה שנאמר עליו בפ' כירה (ד' לח) דתנן מעשה שעשו אנשי טבריא שהביאו סילון של צונן לתוך אמה של חמין אמרו להם חכמים אם בשבת כחמין שהוחמו בשבת אסורין ברחיצה[וכו'] ומותרין בשתיה ואוקימנה כר' שמעון דאסורין להשתטף בהן כל גופו ולענין חמין שהוחמו מערב שבת אמר שמואל לא הותרו לרחוץ בהן אלא פניו ידיו ורגליו ותניא כוותיה דשמואל חמין שהוחמו מערב שבת למחר רוחץ בהן פניו ידיו ורגליו אבל לא ירחוץ בהן כל גופו ולר' שמעון מותר להשתטף בהן כל גופו ובפרק חבית (דף קמז) תמצא שיחזק דבר זה של ר' שמעון שמתיר להשתטף בהן כל גופו אסור להרחיץ בהן כל גופו: בן ח' הרי הוא כאבן. לפי מה שנולד לח' חדשים אי אפשר לו לחיות כל עיקר ותמצא פירושו בבראשית דר' אושעיא (פרשה יד) וייצר בב' יצירות יצירה לאדם ויצירה לחוה

יצירה

* פה חסרון וכפול וכלי סדרים והמעיין בפרשה ימצאם במלואם וכסדרם.

ונתחדשה הלכה איני והא איתמר יוצא דופן *ומי שיש לו שתי ערלות רב הונא ורב חייא בר רב חד אמר מחללין עליו את השבת וחד אמר [א]אין מחללין עד כאן לא פליגי אלא לחלל עליו את השבת [ב]אבל לשמנה ודאי מהלינן ליה *הא בהא תליא כתנאי יש יליד בית שנימול לאחד ויש יליד בית שנימול לשמנה יש מקנת כסף שנימול לאחד ויש מקנת כסף שנימול לשמנה יש מקנת כסף שנימול לא' ויש מקנת כסף שנימול לשמונה כיצד [ג]לקח שפחה מעוברת ואח"כ ילדה זהו מקנת כסף הנימול לשמונה לקח שפחה וולדה עמה זו היא מקנת כסף שנימול לאחד ויש יליד בית שנימול לשמנה [ד]כיצד לקח שפחה ונתעברה אצלו וילדה זהו יליד בית הנימול לשמנה רב חמא אומר ילדה ואח"כ הטבילה זהו יליד בית שנימול לאחד הטבילה ואחר כך ילדה זהו יליד בית הנימול לשמנה ותנא קמא לא שני ליה בין הטבילה ואח"כ ילדה בין ילדה ואח"כ הטבילה דאע"ג דאין אמו טמאה לידה נימול לשמנה (אמר רבא) בשלמא לר' חמא משכחת לה יליד בית נימול לא' יליד בית נימול לח' מקנת כסף נימול לא' ומקנת כסף נימול לח' ילדה ואח"כ הטבילה זהו יליד בית שנימול לאחד הטבילה ואח"כ ילדה זהו יליד בית שנימול לח' מקנת כסף נימול לשמנה כגון שלקח שפחה מעוברת והטבילה ואח"כ ילדה מקנת כסף נימול לאחד כגון שלקח זה שפחה וזה עוברה אלא לת"ק בשלמא כולהו משכחת להו אלא יליד בית נימול לאחד היכי משכחת לה א"ר ירמיה בלוקח שפחה לעוברה הניחא *למ"ד קנין פירות לאו כקנין הגוף דמי אלא למ"ד קנין פירות כקנין הגוף דמי מאי איכא למימר אמר רב משרשיא בלוקח שפחה ע"מ שלא להטבילה *תניא ר"ש בן גמליאל אומר [ה]כל ששהה ל' יום באדם אינו נפל שנאמר ופדויו (במדבר יח) מבן חדש תפדה [ו]שמנת ימים בבהמה אינו נפל שנאמר ומיום השמיני והלאה ירצה (ויקרא כב) לקרבן וגו' הא לא שהה ספיקא הוי

רש"י

ונתחדשה הלכה. דמי שאמו טמאה לידה נימול בח' ולא אחר: יוצא דופן. שנקרעת אמו: שתי ערלות. שני עורות זה על זה* ואמרי לה שני גידין: אבל לשמנה ודאי מהלינן. ואע"ג דיוצא דופן אין אמו טמאה לידה: הא בהא תליא. וחילול שבת תלי במילה לח' דמי שנימול לח' דוחה שבת ומי שאינו נימול לח' אינו דוחה השבת דכי כתיב וביום השמיני דילפינן מיניה ואפילו בשבת בנימול לח' כתיב: כתנאי. הא דרב אסי: ה"ג הא מילתא בשאלתות דרב אחאי* כיצד לקח שפחה (א) ואחר כך ילדה זהו מקנת כסף שנימול לשמונה לקח שפחה וולדה עמה זהו מקנת כסף שנימול לאחד לקח שפחה ונתעברה אצלו וילדה זהו יליד בית שנימול לח' רבי חמא אומר הטבילה ואחר כך ילדה זהו יליד בית שנימול לח' ילדה ואח"כ הטבילה זהו יליד בית שנימול לא' בשלמא לר' חמא משכחת לה יליד בית כדקתני מקנת כסף שנימול לשמנה כגון שלקח שפחה ואחר כך ילדה נימול לח' נמי כגון שלקח שפחה וולדה עמה אלא לת"ק כו' ובספרים שלנו כתיב נימול לאחד נמי כגון שלקח זה שפחה וזה עוברה ונראה בעיני דהא דלא גרים בשאלתות כגון שלקח זה שפחה וזה עוברה משום דקשיא ליה מאי דוחקיה לאוקמיה בשני לקוחות ולשנויי גירסא דסיפא מרישא דקתני לקח שפחה וולדה זהו מקנת כסף שנימול לח': יש יליד בית שנימול לח'. דתרי קראי כתיבי ביליד בית ומקנת כסף חד כתיב ביה ח' וחד לא כתיב ביה ח' (בראשית יז) המול ימול יליד ביתך ומקנת כספך ולא מפרש ביה לח' ימים וכתיב (שם) ובן שמונת ימים ימול לכם כל זכר לדורותיכם יליד בית ומקנת כסף ומסתברא דהאי דמפרש ביה לשמנה היינו היכא דדמי לישראל מעליא שנולד בביתו של ישראל משקנאו דדומיא דלכם בעינן דכתיב בההוא קרא ימול לכם כל זכר והדר יליד בית ומקנת כסף הלכך לקח שפחה מעוברת וילדה הרי זה מקנת כסף דגוף שלם הוא במעי אמו וקנאו שנימול לח' דדומיא דלכם הוא שנולד ברשותו של ישראל לקח שפחה וולדה עמה שכבר ילדתו ואע"פ שלא עברו עליו ח' ללידתו מלו מיד כדכתיב המול ימול וגו' דלאו דומיא דלכם הוא לקח שפחה ונתעברה אצלו לא הוי עובר מקנת כסף אלא יליד בית שנימול לח' דדומיא דלכם הוא ולקמיה מפרש יליד בית הנימול לאחד אליבא דת"ק: רבי חמא אומר. הטבילה לשם עבדות וחלה עליה שם תורת שפחת ישראל דנתחייבה בכל מלות שהאשה חייבת בהן והויא טמאה לידה זהו יליד בית שנימול לח': ילדה והטבילה זהו יליד בית שנימול לאחד. דכל שאין אמו טמאה לידה אין ממתינין לו לח' כרב אסי: בשלמא לרבי חמא. דשני בין הטבילה ואחר כך ילדה לילדה ואח"כ הטבילה: משכחת לה. כולהו יליד בית נימול לאחד ילדה ואח"כ הטבילה יליד בית נימול לח' הטבילה ואח"כ ילדה ושניהם בשנתעברה אצלו דלא הוי מקנת כסף. מקנת כסף נימול לח' כגון שלקח שפחה מעוברת וילדה לאחר שהטבילה. מקנת כסף הנימול לח' כגון שלקח זה שפחה וזה עוברה דכיון דאין לבעל העובר חלק באמו לאו דומיא דלכם הוא ה"ה נמי דמצי לפלוגי במקנת כסף בין ילדה ואחר כך הטבילה בין הטבילה ואחר כך ילדה ולמימר מקנת כסף נימול לח' כגון שלקח שפחה מעוברת ועוברה וילדה ואחר כך הטבילה אלא רבותא אשמעינן דאפילו בהטבילה ואח"כ ילדה משכחת לה והא דשני מקנת כסף נימול לא' לרבי חמא מלת"ק ולא אמר כגון שלקח שפחה וולדה עמה משום דאם כן ילדה קודם טבילה היא ומאי איריא טולד קודם שלקחה אפילו טולד משלקחה נמי לרבי חמא נימול לא': אלא יליד בית נימול לא' היכי משכחת לה. הא ודאי דומיא דלכם הוא הואיל ולאו בטומאת לידה תליא לדידיה: בלוקח שפחה לעוברה. ואפילו מישראל דהוי' טמאה לידה שכבר טבלה לאו דומיא דלכם הוא הואיל ואין לו חלק באמו: הניחא כו'. פלוגתא דר"ל ורבי יוחנן בבבא בתרא (דף קלו:): שלקחה על מנת שלא להטבילה. דלא שייכא בה תורת חיובא דמלות כלל דלאו דומיא דלכם הוא אבל לטומאת לידה לא חיישינן בילדה ואח"כ הטבילה: ופדויו. בבכור אדם כתיב: מבן חדש. מדתלי בהכי שמע מינה עכשיו נתברר שהוא בן קיימא ולא קודם לכן: הא לא שהה. שלשים יום באדם ובבהמה ח' ימים ספיקא הוי הש"ס פריך עלה:

מימהל

תוספות

כתנאי יש יליד בית כו'. תימה היכי משמע ליה מתוך הך ברייתא דרבי חמא תלי טעמא בטומאת לידה לעולם אימא לך דסבר יוצא דופן נימול לח' והאי דמצריך טבילה בשפחה משום דבענין אחר אינה חשובה גיורת עד שתטבול כדנפקא לן ביבמות בפרק החולץ (דף מו:):

כגון שלקח זה שפחה וזה עוברה. פירש בקונטרס דהוי מצי למימר כגון שלקח שפחה מעוברת וילדה קודם טבילה אלא רבותא נקט דאפילו בטבלה ואח"כ ילדה משכחת לה מקנת כסף נימול לא' וקשה לר"י דא"כ ת"ק דלעיל ה"ל למינקט נמי הך רבותא ולמאי קאמר (ב) מקנת כסף נימול כו' אפילו לקח מעוברת נמי אלא שלקח זה שפחה וזה עוברה אלא ודאי לקח זה שפחה וזה עוברה הוי שפיר דומיא דלכם וכגירסת שאילתות דרב אחאי. נראה לר"י דגרס כגון שלקח שפחה וולדה עמה מיהו תימה לר"י דהוה מצי למינקט רבותא אפילו בלא ולדה עמה כגון שלקח שפחה מעוברת וילדה קודם טבילה וי"ל דניחא ליה למינקט כדקתני בברייתא במילתיה דת"ק ועוד אומר ר"י דמשום דהנך קראי נימול לאחד ונימול לשמונה דיליד בית ומקנת כסף כתיבי בפרשת לך לך הלכך ניחא לאשכוחינהו בכה"ג דשייך קודם מתן תורה דלא הוה טבילה ואע"ג דיליד בית נימול לא' לר' חמא לא משכחת לה אלא אחר מתן תורה בילדה ואח"כ טבלה מיהו כל מה שיכול לקיים לפני מתן תורה מקיים:

כגון שלקחה ע"מ שלא להטבילה. וכדמפר' ביבמות בפרק החולץ (דף מה:) דלקח על מנת שלא לגיירו יכול להשהותו הרבה:

כל ששהה שלשים יום באדם וח' ימים בבהמה. אינן שוין דיום שמנה כלאחר שמנה כדמוכח לקמן דעבד להו עיגלא תילתא ביומא דשבעה וקאמר אי איתרחיתו עד לאורתא הוה אכלינן מיניה ויום שלשים כלפני שלשים כדתנן בבכורות בפ' יש בכור לנחלה (דף מט.) ואפילו רבי עקיבא דפליג לא קאמר אלא דמספקא אם הוא כלפני שלשים או כלאחר שלשים ולענין אבילות אפילו ר"ע מודה דהוה כלפני שלשים משום דהלכה כדברי המיקל באבל:

מימהל

עין משפט נר מצוה

לה א מיי' שם הלכה יא טוש"ע א"ח סי' של סעיף ה וי"ד סי' רסו סעיף י:

לו ב מיי' שם הלכה ז סמג עשין כח טוש"ע י"ד סי' רסב סעיף ג וסימן רסו סעיף י:

לז ג ד מיי' שם הלכה ד ה סמג שם טוש"ע י"ד סי' רסז סעיף א:

לח ה מיי' שם הלכה יג וע"א מהל' יבום וחליצה הלכה כב ופ"ב מהל' רוצח ושמירת נפש הלכה ו ופ"א מהל' אבל הלכה ו סמג עשין נא ועשין דרבנן ב טוש"ע י"ד סי' שמ סעיף ל וסי' שעג סעיף ד וסי' שעח סעיף ו וטוש"ע א"ח סי' תקנו סעיף ד:

לט ו מיי' פ"ד מהל' מאכלות אסורות הלכה ד (ופ"ג מהל' איסורי מזבח הלכה ח) סמג לאוין עה וקלג עשין קעח:

רבינו חננאל

שמאי] אומרים מחללין ובה"א אין מחללין ודייק רבה מדברי ר' אליעזר הקפר מכלל דת"ק סבר דברי הכל אין מחללין ואמר רבה אנא דאמרי כת"ק לדברי הכל ואקשינן על הדין דוקיא דרבה א"כ ר' אליעזר הקפר טעמא דב"ש אתא לאשמעינן כלומר אם ת"ק אמר דברי הכל מחללין ור' אליעזר הקפר אמר כי ב"ה סבירא להו אין מחללין למה חלק על ת"ק. ת"ק אמר דברי הכל אין מחללין והוא עוד אמר כי בה"א אין מחללין והלכה כמותם. לא בא אלא לפרש טעמא דב"ש מה הוצרך לזה. והא בהדיא קיי"ל ב"ש במקום ב"ה אינה משנה פריק רבה דלמא ת"ק אמר לא נחלקו אלא בלהטיף ממנו דם ברית ור' אליעזר הקפר אמר לא נחלקו בזה אלא לחלל עליו את השבת נחלקו. וביקש רבה להעמיד דבריו כב"ה אליבא דתנא [קמא] ולא נתברר אבל עמדו דבריו כב"ה אליבא דר' אליעזר הקפר ונמצאו דבריו ודברי רב שאמר הלכה כת"ק דבר אחד. וקיי"ל הלכתא כרב באיסורי. ועוד רבה ורב יוסף הלכתא כרבה בר משדה קנין ומחצה הלכך כוותייהו עבדינן וקיי"ל דעלד כשהוא מהול צריך להטיף ממנו דם ברית בחול שמא ערלה כבושה היא. ואם חל ח' שלו בשבת אין מחללין עליו את השבת וכן הלכה. ומעשה דרב אדא בר אהבה ברור הוא והזכירוהו בתלמוד א"י כלשון הזה. רב אדא בר אהבה איתליד ליה חד בר (בן) [בי] מסמסם ביה פית רבי אבין אמר פצוע דכא נעשה ונתענה עליו ומת. גר שנתגייר כשהוא מהול אין לו תקנה אבל הוא בעצמו לא: אמר רבה אמר רב אסי כל שאמו טמאה לידה נימול לשמונה כו' מסתברא שלא בא רבה אלא למעט בן הנכרית שאין אמו טמאה לידה. אם יקנהו אין נימול לח' שבן בת ישראל ובן הגיורת ובן השפחה אמה טמאה לידה שכך שנינו בענין אשה כי תזריע בני ישראל בענין הזה. ואין הנכרים בענין הזה או בני ישראל אין לי אלא בני ישראל מניין לרבות את הגיורת ואת השפחה בין משוחררת ובין שאינה משוחררת ת"ל אשה כי תזריע וילדה זכר וטמאה גו' הא אפילו שפחה טמאה ומקשינן עלה וכל שאמו טמאה לידה נימול לשמונה ומי שאין אמו טמאה לידה אינו נימול לשמנה. והרי יוצא דופן שאין אמו טמאה לידה דתניא וילדה עד שתלד ממקום הולד פרט ליוצא דופן ר' שמעון אומר יוצא דופן הרי הוא כילוד וחייבין עליו קרבן ובלבד שהוא פטור מחמש סלעים ואתמר יוצא דופן ומי שיש לו ב' ערלות רב הונא ורב חייא בר רב חד אמר מחללין עליו את השבת וחד אמר אין מחללין עליו את השבת · עד כאן לא פליגי לחלל עליו את השבת אבל ודאי לשמונה מהלינן ליה. ופרקי' הא בהא תליא האומר מחללין עליו את השבת סבר נימול לח' והאומר אין מחללין סבר אינו נימול לשמונה ואמרי דדברי רבה כתנאי זה התנא שאמר לקח שפחה ועוברה עמה נימול לח'. פי' קנה שפחה גויה ועוברה נמצא זה העובר מקנת כסף וקודם שיטבלנה עודה בגיותה ילדתו כיון שיגיע ליום שמיני חייב למולו ואע"פ שילדתו בגיותה שאינה טמאה לידה ואמר התנא זהו מקנת כסף הנימול [לשמונה]. דלא כרבה ורב אחא אמר ילדה כו'. קיי"ל דכולהו תנאי מא"י אינון לפיכך קרי להו רבי בר מתלת דוכתי. ואע"ג דתנאי אינון קרי להו רב. רב אבא בהאשה שנפלו לה נכסים. ורב אבא נמי בג' שאכלו כאחד. ורב חמא בהדא דוכתא. ורב אחא אמר ילדה ואח"כ הטבילה מאחר שאין אמו טמאה לידה אינו נימול לשמונה אלא ליום אחד כרבה. וזהו שאמר רבה לרב חמא הבעי טבילה משכחת לה יליד בית נימול לשמונה כגון שהטבילה ואח"כ ילדה. מקנת כסף נימול לשמונה כגון שלקח שפחה ועוברה עמה. וגם זו הטבילה ואח"כ ילדה ומפני מה לא פירש בה טבילה כיון שהפרש מקודם לזה בין הטבילה ואח"כ ילדה ובין ילדה ואח"כ הטבילה. (מימי) [מי] לא שמעת לה לקח שפחה ועוברה עמה. זהו מקנת כסף שנימול לשמונה. לקח

רב נסים גאון

יצירה לט' ויצירה לז' רב הונא אמר נוצר לט' ונוצר לז' הי לח' אינו חי: הניחא למאן דאמר קנין פירות [לאו] כקנין הגוף דמי אלא למאן דאמר קנין פירות (לאו) כקנין הגוף דמי. ומחלוקת היה על זה בין ר' יוחנן ובין ריש לקיש ותמצא מחלוקתם בהרבה מקומות מן התלמוד במס' גיטין בפרק השולח גט לאשתו (דף מז) איתמר המוכר שדהו לפירות ר' יוחנן אמר מביא וקורא ריש לקיש אמר מביא ואינו קורא ר' יוחנן אמר מביא וקורא קנין פירות כקנין הגוף דמי ריש לקיש אמר מביא ואינו קורא קנין פירות לאו כקנין הגוף דמי ובבבא בתרא בפרק יש נוחלין (קלו) מכר הבן בחיי האב וכו' ובמס' יבמות בפרק החולץ (לו) כמו כן וזאת

מסורת הש"ס

[עי' רש"י יבמות עב. ד"ה מי שיש לו] [יבמות עב.] [פרשת לך לך סימן ט] [מגילה ו: נזיר יח: תמורה יח.] ב"ק פח: ב"מ ג. ב"ב כב. קלו. יבמות לו: [גיטין מז. מח. ערכין כו.] [יבמות שם ודף פ: נדה מד: תוספ' פט"ו]

הגהות הב"ח

(א) רש"י ד"ה הא מילתא וכו' כיצד לקח שפחה מעוברת ואח"כ וכו' שנימול לשמונה כגון שלקח שפחה מעוברת והטבילה ולאחר ואח"כ ילדה: (ב) תוס' ד"ה כגון שלקח זה וכו' לך כרבותא ולמאי קאמר לקח שפחה וולדה עמה זו היא מקנת כסף שנימול לאחד אפילו לקח מעוברת נמי:

גליון הש"ס

גמ' שלקח זה שפחה וזה עוברה. עיין בשער המלך פי"ב מהל' נדה הלכה י ובקצות החושן סי' רע סעיף א ובספר כתובה בדף יא: בתד"ה לא"כ: שם שמנת ימים בבהמה. עי' מנחות דף לז ע"א תד"ה סומא אני:

day![6]—The Torah was given, replied he, [135b] and then a new law was decreed.[7] But that is not so? for it was stated: If one is extracted through the cesarean section, or has two foreskins,[8]—R. Huna and R. Ḥiyya b. Rab [differ thereon]: one maintains, We desecrate the Sabbath for them; whilst the other holds, We do not desecrate the Sabbath for them. Thus, they differ only concerning the desecration of the Sabbath for them, but we certainly circumcise them on the eighth day?—One is dependent on the other.[9]

This is a controversy of Tannaim: [For it was taught], There is [a slave] born in his [master's] house who is circumcised on the first [day], and there is one born in his [master's] house who is circumcised on the eighth [day]; there is [a slave] bought with money who is circumcised on the first [day], and there is [a slave] bought with money who is circumcised on the eighth day. 'There is [a slave] bought with money who is circumcised on the first [day], and there is [a slave] bought with money who is circumcised on the eighth day.' How so? If one purchases a pregnant female slave and then she gives birth, that [the infant] is an acquired slave who is circumcised at eight days. If one purchases a female slave together with her infant child, that is a slave bought
a with money who is circumcised on the first day.[1] 'And there is [a slave] born in [his] master's house who is circumcised on the eighth day'. How so? If one purchases a female slave and she conceives in his house and gives birth, that is [a slave] born in his [master's] house who is circumcised at eight days. R. Ḥama said:[2] If she gives birth and then has a ritual bath,[3] that is [a slave] born in his [master's] house who is circumcised on the first day; if she has a ritual bath and then gives birth, that is [a slave] born in his [master's] house who is circumcised at eight days. But the first Tanna allows no distinction between one who [first] has a ritual bath and then gives birth and one who gives birth and then has a ritual bath, so that though his mother is not defiled through her confinement he is circumcised on the eighth day.[4] Raba said:[5] As for R. Ḥama, it is well: we find [a slave] born in his [master's] house who is circumcised on the first day, and one who is circumcised on the eighth day; one bought with money who is circumcised on the first day, and one bought with money who is circumcised on the eighth day. [Thus:] if she gives birth and then has a ritual bath, that is [a slave] born in his [master's] house who is circumcised on the first day; if she has a ritual bath and then gives birth, that is [a slave] born in the house
b who is circumcised on the eighth [day].[1] 'One bought with money who is circumcised on the eighth [day]': e.g., if one purchases a pregnant female slave and she has a ritual bath and then gives birth; 'one bought with money who is circumcised on the first day': e.g., where one buys a [pregnant] female slave and another buys her unborn child.[2] But according to the first Tanna, as for all [others] it is well: they are conceivable.[3] But how can [a slave] born in the house be found who is circumcised on the first day?[4] —Said R. Jeremiah: In the case of one who buys a female slave for her unborn child.[5] This is satisfactory on the view that a title to the usufruct is not as a title to the principal; but on the view that a title to the usufruct is as a title to the principal, what can be said?[6]—Said R. Mesharsheya: [It is possible] where one buys a female slave on condition that he will not subject her to a ritual bath.[7]

It was taught, R. Simeon b. Gamaliel said: Any human being who lives[8] thirty days is not a *nefel*,[9] because it is said, *And those that are to be redeemed of them from a month old shalt thou redeem.*[10] An animal [which lives] eight days is not a *nefel*, for it is said, *and from the eighth day and henceforth it shall be accepted for an*
c *oblation*, etc.[1] This implies that if it [an infant] does not last

(6) In accordance with God's command to Abraham; v. Gen. XVII, 12. (7) Viz., that the two are interdependent. (8) Two skins on top of each other. Or, two separate membra. (9) The infant who must be circumcised on the eighth day must be circumcised even on the Sabbath, since that is deduced from (*eighth*) day (*supra* 132a); but where the eighth day is unnecessary the Sabbath may not be desecrated.

a (1) Of purchase, even if he is not eight days old yet. (2) [Probably R. Ḥama the father of R. Oshaia, v. Hyman, *Toledoth* II p. 456]. (3) By this rite she enters the Jewish household as slave, becoming liable to all duties enjoined upon a Jewish woman. V. next note. (4) These laws centre on Gen. XVII, 12, 13: *And he that is eight days old shall be circumcised among you, every male throughout your generations, he that is born in the house, or bought with money of any stranger, which is not of thy seed* (v. 12). *He that is born in thy house, and he that is bought with thy money, must needs be circumcised* (v. 13). Whereas v. 12 specifies circumcision for the eighth day, v. 13 does not, which implies at the earliest possible moment. Now it is logical that v. 12 refers to a slave who is as like as possible to a full Jew, that being the implication of '*among you*', intimating those that are similar to you, viz., one born in his master's house after he was purchased, i.e., his mother was bearing him when she was bought; whilst v. 13 applies to a slave who is unlike a full Jew, viz., he was already born before he was bought. R. Ḥama draws this distinction: If his mother has a ritual bath, whereby she formally becomes a Jewish-owned slave in that she is bound to observe all the laws incumbent upon Jewesses in general, so that her confinement renders her unclean just like a Jewess, and then she gives birth, the infant is circumcised on the eighth day. But otherwise the infant is not like a Jewish-born child, and is circumcised on the first day. But the first Tanna ignores this distinction: thus R. Assi's ruling is a matter of controversy between the first Tanna and R. Ḥama. (5) Maharam deletes this.

b (1) Both of these refer to a slave who conceived in her master's house, so that the infant is not '*bought with money*'. (2) Since the latter does not own the mother, the child is not like a Jewish-born infant, and therefore he is circumcised on the first day. (3) As already stated *supra*. (4) Since he rejects the distinction based on when the mother had her ritual bath, one born in the house is certainly similar to a Jew. (5) Even if he buys her from a Jew, and she has already had her ritual bath and is subject to the uncleanness of confinement, the child is nevertheless unlike a Jewish child, since his owner has no share in the mother. (6) V. B.B. 136a; the mother is the principal, while the child is the usufruct. On the latter view he is like a Jewish-born child. (7) There her child is certainly unlike a Jewish-born one. (8) Lit., 'tarries'. (9) A non-viable, premature birth. (10) Num. XVIII, 16. Since he must then be redeemed, it follows that he is viable.

c (1) Lev. XXII, 27.

[so long], it is doubtful; [136a] how then can we circumcise him?[2] —Said R. Adda b. Ahabah: We circumcise him in either case: if he is viable, he is rightly circumcised; whilst if not, one [merely] cuts flesh.[3] Then as to what was taught, If there is doubt whether he is a seven-months' [infant] or an eight-months', we must not desecrate the Sabbath on his account:[4] why so? let us circumcise him in either case: if he is viable, he is rightly circumcised; if not, you [merely] cut flesh?—Mar the son of Rabina said: R. Neḥumi b. Zechariah and I explained it: We do indeed circumcise him; this [teaching] is required only in respect of the preliminaries of circumcision, this being in accordance with R. Eliezer.[5]

Abaye said, This is dependent on Tannaim:[6] *And if any beast, of which ye may eat, die:* [*he that toucheth the carcase thereof shall be unclean until the even*];[7] this is to include an eight-months' [animal],[8] [teaching] that *shechitah*[9] does not render it clean.[10] R. Jose son of R. Judah and R. Eleazar son of R. Simeon maintain: Its *shechitah* does render it clean. Surely they differ in this: one Master holds, It is a living creature;[11] whilst the other Master holds, It is [technically] dead?—Said Raba: If so, instead of disputing on the matter of uncleanness and cleanness, let them dispute on the question of consumption.[12] Rather [say then] all hold that it is [technically] dead, but R. Jose son of R. Judah and R. Eleazar son of R.
a Simeon argue, It is as a *ṭerefah:*[1] a *ṭerefah*, though indeed it is dead, does not *shechitah* render it clean?[2] So here too it is not different. But the Rabbis [reason]: it is unlike a *ṭerefah*, for a *ṭerefah* had a period of fitness,[3] whereas this one enjoyed no period of fitness. And should you object, what can be said about a *ṭerefah* from birth?[4] There *shechitah* is efficacious for its kind, whereas here *shechitah* is not efficacious for its kind.[5]

The scholars asked: Do the Rabbis disagree with R. Simeon b. Gamaliel[6] or not?[7] Should you answer [that] they differ, is the *halachah* as he or not?—Come and hear: If a calf is born on a festival, one may slaughter it on a festival![8]—What case do we treat of here? Where we know for certain that its months [of bearing] were complete.[9] Come and hear: And they agree that if it is born together with its blemish, it is *mukan*![10] Here too [it is said] where its months [of bearing] were complete. Come and hear: For Rab Judah said in Samuel's name: The *halachah* is as R. Simeon b. Gamaliel. 'The *halachah* [is thus]' implies that they [the Rabbis] disagree.[11] This proves it.

Abaye said: If it falls from a roof or is devoured by a lion, all hold that it was viable.[12] When do they differ? if it yawns and dies.[13] One Master holds: It was viable; whilst the other Master holds: It was [technically] dead. What is the practical difference? Whether
b it frees the mother from Levirate marriage.[1]

'If it falls from a roof or is devoured by a lion, all hold that it was viable.' But surely R. Papa and R. Huna the son of R. Joshua visited the house of R. Iddi b. Abin's son, who prepared a third-born calf[2] for them on its seventh day [from birth], whereupon they said to him, 'Had you waited with it until evening[3] we would have eaten thereof: now we will not eat thereof'![4]—Rather [say thus:] If it yawns and dies, all agree that it was dead [non-viable]; they differ where it falls from a roof or is devoured by a lion, one Master holding that it was viable; the other Master, that it was dead.[5]

A child was born to the son of R. Dimi b. Joseph, [and] it died within thirty days. [Thereupon] he sat and mourned for it.[6] Said his father to him, 'Do you wish to eat dainties?'[7] 'I know for certain that its months [of pregnancy] were complete, he replied. R. Ashi visited R. Kahana: a mishap befell him within the thirty days.[8] Seeing him sitting and mourning for it, he said to him, 'Does the Master not agree with what Rab Judah said in Samuel's name: The *halachah* is as R. Simeon b. Gamaliel?'—'I know for certain that its months were complete,' replied he.

It was stated: If it died within thirty days,[9] and she [the mother] arose and was betrothed,[10]—Rabina said in Raba's name: [136b]

(2) On the eighth day which falls on the Sabbath, seeing that he may be non-viable, in which case there is really no obligation to circumcise him at all. (3) Which cannot be regarded as the inflicting of a wound (this is the form of labour to which circumcision belongs), since the infant is already as dead. (4) V. *supra* 135a. (5) *Supra* 130a; but here the Sabbath may not be violated for the preliminaries. (6) *Sc.* whether a non-viable infant is so completely regarded as dead that the infliction of a wound on it is merely flesh cutting. (7) Lev. XI, 39. (8) I.e., a calf born in the eighth month of bearing instead of in the usual ninth. (9) V. Glos. (10) For even if ritually slaughtered, it may not be eaten, since it was non-viable (v. *supra* 135a, n. a5; the same applies to animals), and therefore it is the same as though it had died of itself. (11) Therefore *shechitah* renders it clean, just as in the case of any other animal that is permitted as food. (12) According to the first Tanna *shechitah* should make it fit for food, but not according to the others.

a (1) An animal suffering with some disease or illness on account of which it may not be eaten after *shechitah*. It too is regarded as technically dead. (2) This is deduced by the Rabbis from the present verse. (3) Before it contracted that disease. (4) Lit., 'the womb'. (5) An animal born at nine months belongs to the *species* where *shechitah* counts, though this particular one is an exception. But no eight-months' animal is rendered fit for food by *shechitah*. (6) *Supra* 135b bottom. (7) The question is whether they permit a young animal to be eaten before it is eight days old. (8) Though it is only one day old. (9) Then it is definitely viable. (10) V. Glos. The reference is to a firstling born blemished on a festival. A firstling might not be eaten before it received a blemish and we are taught here that this animal is *mukan* and may be eaten on the day of its birth. V. Beẓ. 26b. (11) Cf. *supra* 106b. (12) I.e., if the infant dies through an *external* cause before thirty days, we assume that it was viable. Hence if he was an only child and survived his father, no matter by how short a time, his mother is free from Levirate marriage (v. Deut. XXV, 5), since his father did have a son. Similarly in the case of an animal, if slaughtered before it is eight days old it may be eaten, because we assume that it was viable. (13) I.e., it dies naturally within thirty days, having shown very little vitality.

b (1) V. *supra* n. a12. (2) I.e., the third which its mother had calved. *Aliter:* (*a*) a third-grown calf; (*b*) a calf in its third year. (3) When it would have been eight days old. (4) Though it was slaughtered. (5) Hence the attitude of R. Papa and R. Huna b. R. Joshua. (6) I.e., he performed the ritual mourning rites which are obligatory upon a bereaved father. (7) Lit., 'throat-ticklers'; Jast.: Which friends send to mourners—i.e., you should not mourn for him, seeing that he was non-viable. (8) I.e., his child died within thirty days from birth. (9) V. *supra* n. a13; the same case is referred to here. (10) At a later date, thinking that the child had freed her from the levirate obligation.

מימהל היכי מהלינן ליה אמר רב אדא בר אהבה *מלין אותו ממה נפשך אם חי הוא שפיר קא מהיל ואם לאו מחתך בבשר הוא ואלא הא דתניא ספק בן ז' ספק בן ח' אין מחללין עליו את השבת אמאי נימהליה ממה נפשך אם חי הוא שפיר קא מהיל °ואם לאו מחתך בבשר הוא אמר מר בריה דרבינא אנא ורב נחומי בר זכריה תרגימנא מימהיל הכי נמי מהלינן ליה לא נצרכה אלא למכשירי מילה *ואליבא דרבי אליעזר אמר אביי כתנאי °וכי ימות מן הבהמה אשר היא לכם לאכלה להביא [ב]בן שמנה שאין שחיטתו מטהרתו רבי יוסי ברבי יהודה ור' אלעזר בר"ש אומרים שחיטתו מטהרתו מאי לאו בהא קא מיפלגי דמר סבר חי הוא ומ"ס מת הוא אמר רבא אי הכי אדמיפלגי לענין טומאה וטהרה ליפלגי לענין אכילה אלא דכולי עלמא מת הוא ורבי יוסי ברבי יהודה ורבי אלעזר ברבי שמעון סברי כטרפה טרפה לאו [ג]אף על גב דמתה היא שחיטתה מטהרתה הכא נמי לא שנא ורבנן לא דמי לטרפה טרפה היתה לה שעת הכושר האי לא היתה לה שעת הכושר וכ"ת טרפה מבטן מאי איכא למימר התם יש במינה שחיטה °[ד]הכא אין במינה שחיטה איבעיא להו מי פליגי רבנן עליה דרבן שמעון בן גמליאל או לא אם תמצי לומר פליגי הלכה כמותו או אין הלכה כמותו ת"ש *[ה]עגל שנולד ביום טוב שוחטין אותו בי"ט הכא במאי עסקינן [ו]דקים ליה בגוויה שכלו לו חדשיו ת"ש *ושוין [ז]שאם נולד הוא ומומו עמו שזה מן המוכן ה"נ שכלו לו חדשיו ת"ש דאמר רב יהודה אמר שמואל הלכה כרבן שמעון בן גמליאל *הלכה מכלל דפליגי ש"מ אמר אביי [ח]נפל מן הגג או אכלו ארי דברי הכל חי הוא כי פליגי שפיהק ומת מר סבר חי הוא ומר סבר מת הוא למאי נפקא מיניה [ט]לפטור מן הייבום נפל מן הגג או אכלו ארי דברי הכל חי הוא והא רב פפא ורב הונא בריה דרב יהושע איקלעו לבי בריה דרב אידי בר אבין ועביד להו עיגלא תילתא בימא דשבעה ואמרי ליה [י]אי איתרחיתו ליה עד לאורתא הוה אכלינן מיניה השתא לא אכלינן מיניה אלא כשפיהק ומת דברי הכל מת הוא כי פליגי בנפל מן הגג ואכלו ארי מר סבר מת הוא ומר סבר חי הוא בריה דרב דימי בר יוסף אתיליד ליה ההוא ינוקא בגו תלתין יומין שכיב יתיב קמתאביל עילויה אמר ליה אבוה צוּרוניתא קבעית למיכל אמר ליה [כ]קים לי ביה שכלו לו חדשיו רב אשי איקלע בי רב כהנא איתרע ביה מילתא בגו תלתין יומין חזייה דיתיב וקא מתאבל עילויה אמר ליה לא סבר ליה מר להא דאמר רב יהודה אמר שמואל הלכה כרבן שמעון בן גמליאל אמר ליה קים לי בגויה שכלו לו חדשיו *איתמר מת *)בתוך שלשים ועמדה ונתקדשה אמר רבינא משמיה דרבא אם

*) [עי' תוס' בכורות מט. ד"ה מה ותוס' יבמות לו: ד"ה מת וכו' שכתבו דרש"י דהכא גורס בסוף בלשים]

רש"י

מימהל היכי מהלינן. שום קטן ביום השמיני בשבת דילמא נפל הוא ולא חזי למול ועושה חבורה שלא לשם מצוה: אם חי הוא. כלומר אם כלו לו חדשיו שפיר קא מהיל: מחתך בבשר. שחוטה הוא ולא חבורה היא: לא נצרכה. הא דקתני אין מחללין אלא לענין מכשירי מילה לרבי אליעזר דאמר דחו שבת ה"מ דקים ליה בגויה שכלו לו חדשיו שעברו °ט' חדשים משמשה עד שילדתו ולא שמשה כל ימי עיבורה אבל ספק אין מכשיריו דוחין דילמא לאו בר מימהל הוא ומחלל שבת בעשותו פחמים וברזל: כתנאי. נפל גמור אם חשוב כמת כדקאמר רב אדא בר אהבה דליתא אלא מחתך בבשר או לא והויא חבורה: לאכלה להביא בן ח'. דכוליה קרא דריש ליה בתורת כהנים מן הבהמה מקצת בהמה מטמאה ומקצת אינה מטמאה פרט לטרפה ששחטה ומדממעיט טרפה ששחטה מכלל דבטהורה קאי אשר היא לכם להביא בהמה טמאה לפי שפרשה ראשונה דכתיב בה לכל הבהמה אשר היא מפרסת פרסה ואיננה מעלת גרה וגו' מוקי לה התם באבר מן החי הכתוב מדבר ופרשה זו במתה ודאי לאכלה להביא בן ח' חדשים שאף שחיטתו מיתה ומטמאה: מר סבר חי הוא. לפיכך שחיטתו מטהרתו: לענין אכילה. אי מותר באכילה בשחיטתו אם לאו: טרפה. שחיטתה מטהרתה מלטמא כדפרישית: היתה לה שעת הכושר. לישחט וליטהר קודם שנטרפה: מי פליגי. למישרי ולד של בהמה בתוך ח' ימים: שוחטים אותו ביו"ט. ולאו מוקצה שהרי בין השמשות נמי היה מוכן אגב אמו מיהו שמעינן מינה דמותר לבו ביום: ושוין. רבי יהודה ורבי שמעון שנחלקו ברואין מומין ביו"ט במסכת ביצה שאם נולד היום הוא ומומו עמו שהוא מן המוכן ומותר לבקר מומו ביו"ט דלא דמי כמתקן ביו"ט דלא איתחזק באיסורא ומוקמינן לה התם כגון דיתבי דייני התם וראוהו בשעת לידה מיד: נפל מן הגג או אכלו ארי. שמת מחמת מיתה הבאה לו בתוך ל' ממקום אחר דברי הכל בחזקת כלו לו חדשיו קאי דאי לאו הך מיתה לא הוה מת הילכך חי הוא ובאדם הוי ולד ופוטר את אמו מן החליצה וגבי בהמה נמי סתם ולד בהמה ששחט בתוך ח' מותר באכילה דלא חזינא ביה ריעותא ורוב היולדות אינן מפילות: שפיהק. °בייליי"ר בלע"ז כלומר לאחר לידתו לא ראו בו אלא חיות מעט שפיהק ומת וגבי אדם קאי: ה"ג ועבדו (א)עגלא תילתא בימא דשבעה: איתרחיתו. מלשוחטו עד אורתא שהוא ליל שמיני: הוה אכלינן מיניה· דמקצת היום ככולו כדכתיב (ויקרא כב) והיה שבעת ימים תחת אמו הא לילה חזי ומיהו מיום השמיני הוא דירצה דאורתא לאו בת הקרבה היא כדכתיב (שם ז) ביום צוותו להקריב אבל מכלל נפל נפקי ליה וחזי לאקדושי כדאמרינן בזבחים (דף יב·) °לילה לקדושה יום להרצאה והלכך לענין חולין חזי מאורתא למישחטיה ומיכל אלמא מאן דס"ל כרשב"ג פליג במיתה הבאה לו ממקום אחר ואמר ספיקא הוא: שכיב בגו תלתין. ללידתו: א) צוורוניתא. מטעמים שמאכילין את האבל: קא בעית למיכל. לכך אתה מתאבל חנם: איתרע מילתא· אבילות: בגו תלתין יומין. ללידת הולד: מת הולד ב) בתוך ל'. ללידתו ולא היה לאביו בן אלא הוא ג) וטלד לאחר מיתת אביו ועל ידו היו פוטרין אמו מן החליצה אם היה בר קיימא: ועמדה ונתקדשה. לאחר זמן לפי שסבורה שאינה זקוקה ליבם: אם

א) [במו"ק כ: גרס רש"י לידונייה' ופי' סעודת אבל כמו גיר' הערוך שהביאו תוס' הכא ד"ה צודניתא] ב) [צ"ל בסוף ע"פ עדות' של תוס' יבמות ובכורות] ג) [צ"ל ואתי לאחר מיתת אביו] ד) [ור"ל דאי לאו הכי מה בא רשב"ג להוסיף על מילתא דרבי]

תוספות

מימהל היכי מהלינן ליה. מכאן משמע דלא איירי רשב"ג בבן שמנה (ב) דוקא אלא בספק ולדות וכן משמע לקמן דקאמר ת"ש עגל שנולד בי"ט שוחטין אותו בי"ט ודאי דכלו לו חדשיו ואת"ל דלא איירי רשב"ג אלא בודאי בן שמנה הוה ליה לדחויי הב"ע בספק ולדות ועוד קאמר לקמן נפל מן הגג ואכלו ארי דברי הכל חי הוא ואי בודאי בן ח' איירי היכי תיסק אדעתיה לומר ד"ה חי הוא ובכולהו דלקמן נמי דמוקמינן בדקים ליה בגוויה שכלו לו חדשיו וקשה לר"י מהא דאמרינן בפ' הערל (יבמות דף פ:) איזהו בן ח' כל שלא כלו לו חדשיו רבי אומר שערו וצפרניו מוכיחין עליו כו' דאמר ההיא בר שבעה הוא ואישתהויי אישתהי ופריך (ג) הא דעבד רבה תוספאה עובדא באשה שהלך בעלה למדינת הים ואישתהי עד תריסר ירחי שתא כמאן כרבי כיון דאיכא רשב"ג דאמר אישתהי *דתני כל ששהה כו' כרבי עבד אלמא משמע בהדיא דבודאי בן ח' איירי מדמוכח מיניה דמשתהי כרבי ומנא ליה דילמא לעולם ס"ל דלא משתהי ובספק ולדות איירי רשב"ג כדפרישית ואור"י דע"כ בודאי בן ח' נמי איירי דהא בתוספתא דמכילתין מיתני מילתיה דרשב"ג בתר מילתיה דרבנן ורבי דיבמות ואפלוגתייהו קאי דאיירי בבן ח' וא"ת ובשמעתין מנלן דבספק ולדות ס"ל לרשב"ג הא לא שהה ספיקא הוי דילמא קסבר ולד מעליא הוי ולא איירי כלל בספק ולדות אלא בודאי בן ח' ויש לומר דדייקינן מדקתני כל ששהה דכל משמע לרבות ספק דווקא שהה הא לא שהה ספיקא הווי והא דמבעיא לן לקמן אי פליגי רבנן עליה דרשב"ג היינו בספק ולדות דבן ח' ודאי בהדיא קתני לה בתוספתא וא"ת והיכי פשיט לקמן מדאמר רב יהודה אמר שמואל הלכה כרשב"ג מכלל דפליגי בספק ולדות תאמר דלעולם לא פליגי בספק ולדות וכי פסיק רב יהודה כוותיה הנ"מ בודאי בן ח' וי"ל דא"כ ה"ל למיתני הלכה כר' (ד) דליכא למימר דלא קאמר הלכה כרבי משום דבעי הוכחת סימנין שערו וצפרניו אבל רשב"ג לא בעי דהא פשיטא דבן ח' שלא גמרו שערו וצפרניו לכ"ע לא חי ומדנקט רשב"ג ש"מ דבספק ולדות איירי ופסק בכולא מילתא כוותיה והשתא נמי אין צריך לדקדק (ה) מכל דבלאו הכי יש להוכיח דבספק ולדות איירי כמו שהוכחתי ד) ר"י: צודניתא. גרס בערוך*) לשון לידה ומזונות: ואם

*) [ערך צד ג]

עין משפט נר מצוה

מ א מיי' פ"א מהל' מילה הלכה יד סמג עשין כח טוש"ע י"ד סי' רסו סעיף יא בהג"ה:

מא ב ג ד מיי' פ"ב מהל' שאר אבות הטומאות הלכה ו:

מב ה ו מיי' פ"ב מהל' יום טוב הלכה א סמג לאוין עה טוש"ע א"ח סי' תצח סעיף ה:

מג ז מיי' שם הלכה ז טוש"ע שם סעיף ט:

מד ח ט מיי' פ"א מהל' יבום הלכה ה סמג עשין נ טוש"ע אה"ע סי' קנו סעיף ד:

מה י מיי' פ"ד מהל' מאכלות אסורות הלכה ד סמג לאוין עה וקלג טוש"ע י"ד סי' טו סעיף ב:

[ר"ל מדקתני כל ששהה ולא תני אם שהה כרבי עבדי]

מו כ מיי' פ"א מהל' אבלות הלכה ז סמג עשין מד"ס ב טוש"ע י"ד סי' שעד סעיף ח [ברי"ף כאן ובפ"ג דמו"ק דף רל: וכן ברא"ש כאן ובתם סי' לג]:

רבינו חננאל

זה שפחה והוא עובר זהו יליד בית שנימול לאחד דברי הכל הוא. כי פליגי בילדה ואח"כ הטבילה ת"ק סבר גם זה יליד בית נימול לשמונה. ורב אחא סבר זה יליד בית נימול לאחד. ושאר השמועה פשוטה היא: תניא רשב"ג אומר כל ששהה באדם שלשים יום אינו נפל שנאמר ופדויו מבן חדש תפדה. שמונת ימים בבהמה אינו נפל שנאמר ומיום השמיני והלאה ירצה וגו'. הא לא שהה ספק הוי ווה שאנו מלין כל קטן בן ח' ימים הלא אמר רשב"ג קודם ל' יום ספק נפל הוא ואין מחללין עליו את השבת ומלין אתו בן ח' ימים שמא נפל הוא. ופרקי' מלין אותו ממה נפשך אי חי הוא שפיר קא מהיל. ואי נפל הוא מחתך בבשר הוא ולא מלאכה היא ומקשינן אלא הא דתניא ספק בן ז' או בן ח' אין מחללין עליו את השבת אמאי (נימא) [נימהליה] ליה ממ"נ ופרקינן מימהל ה"נ ומהלינן ליה לא נצרכה אלא למכשירי מילה ואליבא דר' אליעזר ולית הלכתא הכי דשנויא היא ואשנויא לא סמכינן ואם יש להקשות עוד אי הכי אם המילה היתוך בשר היא ואינה מלאכה אפילו מילה שאינה בזמנה יהא נימול בשבת מחתך בבשר הוא. ופירקו כי מילה דחי מלאכה היא כי מתקן הוא כי כיון שחותך הערלה מתקנו לאכול תרומה ולשחוט עליו אביו את הפסח: לאכלה להביא בן ח' שאין שחיטתו מטהרתו פי' זו בהמה נשה טהורת שילדת למ' חדשים היא. ומיבעיא לן רשב"ג פליגי רבנן עליה אי לא ופשטינן דפליגי רבנן עליה והלכתא כוותיה דאמר רב יהודה אמר שמואל הלכה כרשב"ג ואי לא דפליגי הלכה למה. אמר אביי נפל מן הגג ואכלו אריה. דברי הכל כמו חי הוא. [כי] פליגי שפיהק ומת ומקשינן עליה מדרב פפא ורב הונא בריה דר' יהושע דאיקלעו לבי בריה דרב אידי בר אבין ועבד להו עיגלא תלתא ביומא דשבעא ואמר ליה אי אהרתו עד לאורתא הוה אכלינן מיניה. והרי זה נשחט ולא אכלו ממנו שאמרו כיון שלא שהה ח' ימים כנפל חשוב ואין שחיטתו מתירתו באכילה. והדר ביה ואמר אלא שפיהק ומת דברי הכל מת הוא כי פליגי בנפל מן הגג או [אכ]לוהו אריה ושמעינן מהאי מעשה דרב פפא ורב הונא בריה דרב יהושע שאם נשחט קודם ח' ימים אסור באכילה ואינו מותר אלא מלילי ח' והלאה (לקרבן) הלכך לילי שמיני מותר באכילה ולקרבן פסול. ואין כשר לקרבן אלא מיום השמיני והלאה וזה שאמר אביי. וכי ימות מן הבהמה אשר היא לכם לאכלה להביא בן שמונה ימים שאין שחיטתו מטהרתו. ר' יוסי בר יהודה ור' אלעזר בר' שמעון אומרים שחיטתו מטהרתו: ברייתא זו שנויה בתורת כהנים. לח' חדשים חלוקתם. דתני בהדיא במתניתא דבי ר' חייא

רב נסים גאון

זאת אחת מג' הלכות כריש לקיש כמו שאמר רבא הלכתא כריש לקיש בהני תלת הדא הא אבל בכל מקום שיש מחלוקת בין ר' יוחנן וריש לקיש הלכה כר' יוחנן לבר מהני תלת: אמר אביי כתנאי לאכלה להביא בן ח' שאין שחיטתו מטהרתו עיקר דבר זה שנוי בתורת כהנים (ויקרא יא) וכי ימות מן הבהמה אשר היא לכם לאכלה וכי ימות הרי זו מיתה ודאי מן הבהמה יש מן הבהמה מטמאה ויש מן הבהמה שאין מטמאה פרט לטריפה ששחטה ונתבאר לנו בזה הכתוב בהמה [טרפה] ששחטה אינה מטמאה ונשאו ונתנו בדבר זה הרבה ואמרו באמצע הדברים בן ח' יוכיח שיש למיני שחיטה ואין שחיטתו מטהרתו ולאחר

מסורת הש"ס

ויקרא יא

[לעיל קל.]

חולין נח: ביצה ו:

חולין שם ביצה כו:

[לעיל קו: וכ"נ]

יבמות לו:

הגהות הב"ח

(א) רש"י ד"ה ה"ג ועביד להו עגלא תלתא: (ב) תוס' ד"ה מימהל וכו' בבן שמונה ודאי דוקא אלא: (ג) בא"ד ופריך אלא הא דעבד: (ד) בא"ד הוה ליה למיתני הלכה כרבי וכרשב"ג דליכא: (ה) בא"ד אין צריך לדקדק מכל כמו שהוכיח ר"י דבלאו הכי יש להוכיח דבספק ולדות איירי הס"ד:

גליון הש"ס

גמ' ואם לאו מחתך בבשר הוא. עי' מ"א סי' תקכו ס"ק יא. ועי' בירושלמי פ"ז דיבמות הלכה ז: שם הכא אקמיניה שחיטה. עי' חולין עד ע"א תד"ה בנפקעת: רש"י ד"ה לא נצרכה. ט' חדשים משמשה. עי' תב"ש סי' טו ס"ק טו: ד"ה שפיהק ביילי"ר בלע"ז. עי' נדה סג ע"א תד"ה מפסקת: ד"ה הוה אכלינן מיניה וכו' לילה לקדושה. ועי' בתוס' שם זבחים יב ע"א ד"ה יום וצ"ע:

*אם אשת ישראל היא חולצת אם אשת כהן היא אינה חולצת ורב *שרביא משמיה דרבא אמר אחת זו ואחת זו חולצת אמר ליה רבינא לרב שרביא באורתא אמר רבא הכי לצפרא הדר ביה אמר ליה שריתוה יהא רעוא דתשרו תרבא: ר' יהודה מתיר וכו': אמר רב שיזבי אמר רב חסדא לא לכל אמר רבי יהודה אנדרוגינוס זכר הוא שאם אתה אומר כן בערכין יערך ומנלן דלא מיערך *דתניא °הזכר ולא טומטום ואנדרוגינוס יכול לא יהא בערך איש אבל יהא בערך אשה תלמוד לומר הזכר ואם נקבה היא זכר ודאי נקבה ודאית ולא טומטום ואנדרוגינוס וסתם

ויקרא כז

רש"י

אם אשת ישראל היא. אם אינו כהן זה שנתקדשה לו ומותר בחלוצה: חולצת. מן הספק ואח"כ תנשא ואם כהן הוא שאם תחלוץ תהא אסורה לו סמכינן אדרבנן ואמרינן להו נפל הוא ואינה חולצת: לאורתא אמר רבא הכי. כדקאמרת דאחת זו ואחת זו חולצת: ולצפרא הדר ביה. ואמר אשת כהן אינה חולצת: אמר ליה. רב שרביא לרבינא: שריתוה. בלא חליצה ועבריתו אדרבנן שמעון. יהא רעוא דתשרון חלב באכילה: לא לכל אמר ר"י. לא לכל דבר אמר ר"י דאנדרוגינוס זכר הוא אלא לענין מילה בלבד דיליף ליה מריבויא דקרא כדלקמן: שאם אתה אומר. זכר הוא לכל דבר: בערכין יערך. האומר ערכו עלי יעריכוהו: הזכר. ה' יתירא קדריש וגבי נקבה דריש ואם יתירא ולא טומטום ואנדרוגינוס: והא

תוספות

ואם אשת כהן היא אינה חולצת· הקשה ה"ר משה מבהייס ותחלוץ ומה בכך הא אמרי' בס"פ שני דיבמות (דף כג·) דספק חלוצה היכא דנכנסה שריא דתנן התם אם קדמו וכנסו אין מוציאין מידם ואמרינן בגמ' *תני שילא אפילו שניהם כהנים מ"ט חלוצה דרבנן ועל ספק חלוצה לא גזרו ואומר רבי דהאי דאינה חולצת בשמעתין לא משום שאם חלצה (לא) יהא מחויב להוציאה אלא כיון דאפשר בלא חליצה מוטב שלא תחלוץ שלא להוציא לעז על בניה כעין שמצינו בפרק בתרא דיבמות (דף קיט·) דתנן האשה שהלך בעלה וצרתה למדינת הים ובאו ואמרו לה מת בעליך לא תנשא ולא תתייבם עד שתדע שמא מעוברת צרתה ואמר בגמ' *ולעולם אמר זעירי ג' לעלמה ט' לחבירתה וחולצת ממ"נ פי' שאם נתעברה צרתה וילדה מותרת לשוק בלא חליצה ואם לא נתעברה הרי חליצה פוטרת ר' יוחנן אמר לעלמה ג' לחבירתה לעולם ופריך ותחלוץ ממ"נ ומשני גזירה שמא יהא ולד של קיימא ונמצא מצריכה כרוז לכהונה ולירכה דילמא איכא דהוי בחליצה ולא הוה בהכרזה ואמרו קא שרו חלוצה לכהונה אלמא אנו מעגנין אשה זו לעולם משום טעמא דנמצא מצריכה כרוז לכהונה ולכך אין אנו מניחים לחלוץ וכל שכן הכא שיש לימנע יותר מחליצה ואיכא למיחש טפי שלא יאמרו קא שרו חלוצה לכהן. מ"ר: ואם אשת כהן היא אינה חולצת· דחי הוא אפילו כי לא שהה כדבכן כדאי' בהחולץ (יבמות דף לו: ושם) והא דאמרינן לעיל דהלכה כרשב"ג היינו דוקא באשת ישראל אבל באשת כהן לא קי"ל כוותיה להצריכה חליצה הואיל ואשת כהן היא. מ"ר: **דתניא** הזכר ולא טומטום ואנדרוגינוס. השתא משמע דדריש מלשון זכר ונקבה ולא מיותרא דה' דהזכר ואם נקבה דאם לא כן מאי קפריך בסמוך ומ"ש גבי מילה מאי קרא צריך במילה לרבות אנדרוגינוס והא אדרבה צריך מיעוט גבי ערכין למעוטי אנדרוגינוס אלא ע"כ לאו מיותרא דקרא ממעט ליה מערך איש ואשה אלא ממשמעות דזכר ונקבה הלכך צריך קרא במילה לרבות אנדרוגינוס וכ"מ כמי דגבי קידוש ממעט אנדרוגינוס בלא שום ייתור כדמוכח בפרק טרף בקלפי ביומא (דף מג· ושם) דאמר תנן התם הכל כשרים לקדש כו' ומפרש אשה מנלן אמר קרא ונתן ולא ונתנה כו' ומההיא טעמא דממעט אשה ממעט אנדרוגינוס וקשה לרבי דבנדה פרק המפלת (דף כח: ושם) מייתינן הך מילתא דערכין וקאמר טעמא דכתב רחמנא הזכר ואם נקבה הא מזכר ונקבה לחוד לא הוה ממעט להו אלמא מיותרא דואם וה' דהזכר קדריש ואומר רבי דודאי מיותרא קדריש כדמשמע התם והא דאיצטריך כל זכר גבי מילה לרבות אנדרוגינוס כי היכי דלא נילף מערכין ומשום הכי גבי קידוש לא צריך קרא למעט אנדרוגינוס דילפינן מערכין וממילה לא ילפינן דאית לן למילף מערכין לחומרא ופסול לקדש והא דאמר רב בהמפלת (גם זה שם) טומטום ואנדרוגינוס שראו לובן ואודם כאחת אין חייבין על ביאת מקדש ושורפין עליו את התרומה ונפקא ליה התם ביאת מקדש מדכתיב מזכר ועד נקבה תשלחו זכר ודאי נקבה ודאית ולא טומטום ואנדרוגינוס ופריך התם וכל היכא דכתיב זכר ונקבה למעוטי טומטום ואנדרוגינוס והתניא כו' דטעמא דכתב רחמנא הזכר ואם נקבה כו' והשתא מאי קפריך דבלא יתור נמי שפיר ממעט טומטום ואנדרוגינוס משום דילפינן מערכין וי"ל דכי גמרי מערכין לחומרא כמו גבי קידוש אבל לקולא לפוטרו מביאת מקדש כשראה לובן ואודם כאחת. לא ילפינן מערכין אלא אדרבה ילפינן ממילה לחומרא לחייבו על ביאת מקדש מיהו קשה לרבי מהא דתני בבכורות בפרק אלו מומין (דף מב· ושם) הזכר ולא הנקבה כשהוא אומר למטה זכר שאין תלמוד לומר להוציא טומטום ואנדרוגינוס והשתא אמאי איצטריך קרא למעט טומטום ואנדרוגינוס שאינם קדושים לעולה תיפוק ליה משום דילפינן מערכין לחומרא דהיינו חומרא שאין קדושה חלה עליהם וצריך להביא קרבן אחר ובדוחק אומר ר"י דאדרבה היא קולא שאם לא מצא אלא אנדרוגינוס יהא יושב ובטל כעין שמצינו גבי סוכה בפרק לולב הגזול (דף לו:) דתניא ר' יהודה אומר אין סוכה נוהגת אלא בד' מינים שבלולב והדין נותן ומה לולב שאינו בלילות כבימים כו' אמרו לו כל דין שתחלתו להחמיר וסופו להקל אינו דין לא מצא ד' מינין יהא יושב ובטל ומיהו לא דמיא שפיר דההיא דהתם ודאי סופו להקל שאם לא ימצא ד' מינים כל ימי סוכה נמצא המצוה עוברת וא"א לעשותה עוד אפילו ימצא אחרי כן אבל גבי קרבן אם אינו מוצא עכשיו אלא אנדרוגינוס אחר זמן ימצא וא"כ תחילתו *וסופו להחמיר הוא ועוד אומר רבי דההוא קרא דהזכר גבי עולת נדבה הוא דכתיב ולא גבי חובה הלכך לא שייך התם יהא יושב ובטל כיון שאינו מחויב שום קרבן. מ"ר: **הזכר** ולא טומטום ואנדרוגינוס. בבכורות בפרק (א) אלו מומין (מב· ושם) אמר סמי מכאן טומטום דתנן התם טומטום ואנדרוגינוס אין שוחטין עליו לא במקדש ולא במדינה רבי ישמעאל אומר אין מום גדול מזה וחכ"א אינו בכור אלא נגזז ונעבד ואמר בגמ' אר"ח מחלוקת באנדרוגינוס אבל טומטום דברי הכל ספיקא הוא וקדוש מספיקא אמר ליה (ב) אלא מעתה בערכין יערך אלמה תניא הזכר ולא טומטום ואנדרוגינוס ומשני סמי מכאן טומטום ומשמע דהכי פריך אלמה תניא הזכר ולא טומטום (ג) וכיון דאמרת דספיקא היא איצטריך קרא למעוטי ספיקא ומאי קשיא דבשלמא בההיא סוגיא דלעיל דהתם פריך גבי אנדרוגינוס איצטריך קרא למעוטי ספיקא שפיר פריך שהרי אין סברא לומר שיהא ספק לפסוק דודאי ברור למקרא אם הוא זכר או נקבה ואם הוא אמת שהפסוק חושבו זכר למה ימעטו שלא יהא קדוש לעולה ואם קרא חשיב ליה נקבה א"ל לכתוב למעטו (ד) *אלא טומטום ודאי צריך קרא שיש מהן זכרים ויש מהן נקבות וכי האי גוונא שייך שפיר למקרא למעטו כיון שהוא ספק לנו אם הוא זכר או נקבה כעין שמצינו גבי מעשר בהמה דתנן בפ' בתרא דבכורות (דף נח:) ומייתי לה בפ"ק דב"מ (דף ו:) קפץ אחד מן המנויין לתוכן כולן פטורין ומפרש התם טעמא דעשירי וודאי אמר רחמנא ולא עשירי ספק וכן בנגעים ספק בהרת קדמה לשער לבן או שער לבן קדם לבהרת ונפקא לן בשלהי מסכת נזיר (דף סה·) דטהור מדכתיב לטהרו או לטמאו שפתח הכתוב תחילה בטהרה ונראה לר' דה"פ מילתא דרב חסדא אבל טומטום קדוש מספיקא משום דלכל כמה דמצינן לאוקמי קרא למעט אנדרוגינוס דממעטי להו רבנן מדכתיב הזכר כדדריש התם לעיל לית לן לאוקמי לקרא למעוטי טומטום משום דאם הוא זכר ודאי אין סברא למעוטי ואם הוא נקבה אין צריך קרא דהשתא פריך שפיר מערכין דלא הוה לן למעוטי טומטום כיון דאיכא לאוקמי קרא לאנדרוגינוס לית לן למעוטי טומטום מיניה דליכא למימר ואם נקבה לאנדרוגינוס לא איצטריך דכבר מיעטוה מהזכר (ה) מ"מ הוה אמינא כהי דמעטיה קרא מערך איש מיהו לא גרע מאשה ויהא לו לכל הפחות ערך אשה הלכך לאנדרוגינוס נמי איצטריך ואם נקבה לפיכך הוצרכו לתרץ סמי מכאן טומטום והא דתני בפ"ק דחגיגה (דף ד· ושם) זכורך להוציא טומטום ואנדרוגינוס ולא פריך מינה בבכורות לרב חסדא וליסני סמי מכאן טומטום ונראה לר' משום דקרא יתירא (ו) למעט טומטום דתרי זכורך כתיבי והא דפריך בפ"ק דחגיגה בשלמא אנדרוגינוס איצטריך סד"א הואיל ואית ליה זכרות ליחייב קמ"ל דבריה הוא בפני עצמו אלא טומטום ספיקא הוא איצטריך קרא למעוטי ספיקא ומשני כשביליו מבחוץ ונראה לרבי דשפיר פריך דהתם ודאי לא הוה צריך קרא למעוטי טומטום דפשיטא בלא קרא דלא מייתי עולת ראייה דהיכי נעביד מספיקא לא מייתי על תנאי דאם נקבה הוא תהא עולת נדבה דהא עולת ראייה לא בעי סמיכה ואסור לסמוך משום עבודה בקדשים [ועולת נדבה בעי סמיכה] ואם לא יסמוך טוב שלא יביא כמו שמצינו גבי פסח בפסחים פרק האשה (דף פח:) דתניא חבורה שנתערבו עורות פסחיהן ונמצאה יבלת באחת מהן כולן יצאו לבית השריפה ופטורין מלעשות פסח שני כו' עד דפריך וניתי מותר הפסח ומשני משום סמיכה דאילו מותר הפסח בעי סמיכה ואילו פסח לא בעי סמיכה אלמא משום סמיכה נמנעים מלעשות פסח כ"ש מלהביא עולת ראייה ובבכורות על מילתא דרב חסדא לא הוה מצי לשנויי כשביליו מבחוץ דכ"ש דלא הוה ליה לקרא למעוטיה · מ"ר. וקשה לי לרב חסדא אמאי ממעט רב בנדה טומטום

עין משפט נר מצוה

מז א מיי' פ"ב מהל' יבום הלכה כא סמג עשין נ טוש"ע אה"ע סי' קסד סעיף ז:

[שם כד·]

מח ב מיי' פ"א מהל' ערכין הלכה ה:

[דף קיט:]

רבינו חננאל

ודבי ר' אושעיא איזה בן ח' כל שלא יצאו לו חדשיו. ר' אומר סימנים ניכרין בו שערו וצפרניו שלא גמרו וכדורקשבן שמנה חדשים באדם נפל כך בן ח' בבהמה גסה וכן ד' בדקה נפל. רשב"ג אומר כל ששהה באדם ל' יום אינו נפל וכו'. והלכתא כת"ק דאמר בן שמנה אין שחיטתו מטהרתו אלא אמרינן מת היה ונבילה היא ומטמאה שאין שחיטה מועלת בנבילה דתנינן מתניתין סתמא כוותיה בפרק בהמה המקשה לילד ופירשנוהו שם. מי יש במינו שחיטה מי אין במינו שחיטה בן ח' חי אין שחיטתו מטהרתו. לפי שאין למינו שחיטה. וסוגיא דשמעתא שאין שחיטתו מטהרתו בפחות משמנה ימים אלא בדמוחזק לן שכלו חדשיו כגון שהיתה הבהמה קשורה לו בביתו ט' חדשים לגסה וה' לדקה וילדה וברי לן שלא עלה [עליה] זכר בביתו וזה ששנינו במשנתנו סתם תינוק בן יום א' מטמא בזיבה. ומטמא בנגעים ומטמא בטמא מת. וזוקק ליבום ופוסל מן היבום ומאכיל בתרומה ופוסל בתרומה ונוחל ומנחיל והורגו חייב והרי הוא לאביו ולאמו ולכל קרוביו כחתן שלם ואמרינן בגמרא למאי הלכתא אמר רב פפא לענין אבלות לימא מתניתין דלא כרשב"ג דתניא רשב"ג אומר כל ששהה באדם ל' יום אינו נפל הא לא שהה (ספק) ספיקא הוי. ומפרקינן דקים ליה ביה שכלו לו חדשיו. ודין כל השנוים במשנה זאת דינם אחד במוחזק לן ביה שכלו לו חדשיו ומיהא הוו (מיתא) [מתאבלין] באלי בריה דרב דימי בריה דרב יוסף ורב כהנא בינוקא דשכיב בגו תלתין יומין דהוו מוחזקין שכלו לו חדשיו: איתמר מת בתוך ל' ועמדה ונתקדשה אמר רבינא משמיה דרבא אם אשת ישראל היא חולצת אם אשת כהן היא אינה חולצת ורב שרביא משמיה דרבא אמר אחת זו ואחת זו חולצת. א"ל רבינא לרב שרביא באורתא אמר רבא הכי כי דאמרת לצפרא הדר ביה. א"ל יהא רעוא דתשרי תרבא כלומר עתה תאסר ואחר שעה תתירה. יהי רצון שתתיר אף החלב. והלכתא כרבינא משמא דרבא. והאמר רבינא והדר ביה רבא מההיא: ר' יהודה מתיר באנדרוגינוס פי' למולו בשבת אמר רב שיזבי אמר רב חסדא לא לכל

מסורת הש"ס

[יבמות איתא משרשיא]

בכורות מב· ערכין ד: נדה כח:

[גירי' רש"א וסופו להחמיר הוא הלכך לא שייך התם יושב ובטל ועוד סבר רבי כו' ולא גבי חובה והוי קולא כיון שאינו מחויב שום קרבן]

ס"א אלא טומטום די"ל שהמקרא חושבו לא זכר ולא נקבה די"ש מהם זכרים כו'

הגהות הב"ח

(א) תוס' ד"ה הזכר וכו' בבכורות בפרק על אלו מומין וכו' אין לך מום גדול:
(ב) בא"ד אמר ליה רבה אלא מעתה וכו':
(ג) בא"ד דכיון דאמרת:
(ד) בא"ד אלא טומטום די"ש לומר שאין המקרא חושבו לא זכר ולא נקבה די"ש מהן זכרים:
(ה) בא"ד מהזכר דמ"מ ה"א נהי:
(ו) בא"ד דקרא יתירא איכא למעט:

רב נסים גאון

ולאחר כן אסרו לאכלה להביא בן ח' שאין שחיטתו מטהרתו כלומר בן ח' חדשים בבהמה גסה מהורה על דעת כמו שאמרו בפרק א' מסכת בכורות (דף ח) בבהמה גסה יולדת לט' חדשי ומה שתלד בהמה גסה מהורה בחודש ח' הרי הוא כמת ולא תועיל בו השחיטה להוציאו מידי נבילה לענין הטומאה כמו שמועלת בטריפה מכאן הראיה שהקדמנו ממה שאסרו ויש מן הבהמה שאינה מטמאה פרט לטריפה ששחטה

If she is an Israelite's wife,[11] she must perform *ḥaliẓah;*[12] but if she
a is a priest's wife,[1] she does not perform *ḥaliẓah.*[2] But R. Sherabia[3] ruled in Raba's name: Both the one and the other must perform *ḥaliẓah*. Rabina said to R. Sherabia: In the evening Raba did rule thus, but the [following] morning he retracted.[4] You would permit her,[5] he retorted: would that you permitted forbidden fat!

R. JUDAH PERMITS, etc. R. Shizbi said in R. Ḥisda's name: Not in respect of everything did R. Judah rule [that] an hermaphrodite is a male; for if you do say thus, in the case of vows of valuation[6] let him be subject to valuation. And how do we know that he is not subject to 'valuation'? Because it was taught: '[*And thy estimation shall be of*] *the male* [*from twenty years old,* etc.]:[7] but not a *ṭumṭum*[8] or an hermaphrodite. You might think that he does not come within the valuation of a man, yet he does come within the valuation of a woman; therefore it is stated, . . . *the male . . . and if it be a female:*[9] a certain male, a certain female,

(11) I.e., if her second husband is an Israelite, i.e., not a priest, and may marry a *ḥaluẓah* (q.v. Glos.).—Betrothal was the first stage of marriage, and binding like marriage; v. Kid., 2*a*, n. 9. (12) V. Glos.: for the child may have been non-viable.

a (1) Who may not marry a *ḥaluẓah*. (2) But may assume that her child was viable, relying on the majority of births, and therefore she has no levirate obligation. (3) In Yeb. 36*b* the reading is: R. Mesharsheya. (4) Ruling that she need not perform *ḥaliẓah* if she is a priest's wife. (5) Without *ḥaliẓah*, thus disregarding the view of R. Simeon b. Gamaliel. (6) *'Arakin*,—vows whereby one offers his own or another person's *'valuation'* to the Temple. The valuations were fixed and dependent on the age and sex of the person concerned, v. Lev. XXVII, 1ff. (7) Lev. XXVII, 3. (8) One whose genitals are hidden or undeveloped, so that his sex is doubtful. In Bek. 42*a* the Talmud deletes *'ṭumṭum'* from this passage. (9) Ibid. 4.

but not a *ṭumṭum* or an hermaphrodite'. [137a] And an anonymous [statement in the] Sifra[10] is according to R. Judah.[11] R. Naḥman b. Isaac said: We too learnt likewise: All are eligible to sanctify,[12] save a deaf-mute, an imbecile, and a minor. R. Judah admits a minor, but invalidates a woman and an hermaphrodite. This proves it. And why is circumcision different?[13] Because it is written, every *male among you shall be circumcised.*[14]

MISHNAH. IF A MAN HAS TWO INFANTS, ONE FOR CIRCUMCISION AFTER THE SABBATH AND THE OTHER FOR CIR-
a CUMCISION ON THE SABBATH, AND HE ERRS[1] AND CIRCUMCISES THE ONE BELONGING TO AFTER THE SABBATH ON THE SABBATH, HE IS CULPABLE.[2] [IF HE HAS] ONE FOR CIRCUMCISION ON THE EVE OF THE SABBATH AND ANOTHER FOR CIRCUMCISION ON THE SABBATH, AND HE ERRS AND CIRCUMCISES THE ONE BELONGING TO THE EVE OF THE SABBATH ON THE SABBATH,—R. ELIEZER HOLDS [HIM] LIABLE TO A SIN-OFFERING;[3] BUT R. JOSHUA EXEMPTS [HIM].[4]

GEMARA. R. Huna recited: He is culpable;[5] Rab Judah recited: He is not culpable. 'R. Huna recited: He is culpable'; because it was taught, R. Simeon b. Eleazar said: R. Eliezer and R. Joshua did not differ concerning a man who has two infants, one for circumcision on the Sabbath and another for circumcision after the Sabbath, and he errs and circumcises the one belonging to after the Sabbath on the Sabbath, that he is culpable. About what do they disagree? About him who has two infants, one for circumcision on the eve of the Sabbath and another for circumcision on the Sabbath, and he errs and circumcises the one belonging to the eve of the Sabbath on the Sabbath, R. Eliezer declaring [him] liable to a sin-offering, while R. Joshua exempts [him]. Now, both learn it from nought but idolatry:[6] R. Eliezer holds, it is like idolatry: just as idolatry, the Divine Law decreed, Do not engage [therein], and if one engages [therein] he is culpable, so here too it is not different. But R. Joshua [argues]: there there is no precept [fulfilled], whereas here there is a precept.

'Rab Judah recited; He is not culpable.' For it was taught, R. Meir said: R. Eliezer and R. Joshua did not differ concerning a man who has two infants, one for circumcision on the eve of the Sabbath and another for circumcision on the Sabbath, and he errs and circumcises the one belonging to the eve of the Sabbath on the Sabbath, that he is not culpable. About what do they disagree? About him who has two infants, one for circumcision after the Sabbath and another for circumcision on the Sabbath, and he errs and circumcises the one belonging to after the Sabbath on the Sabbath, R. Eliezer declaring [him] liable to a sin-offering, while R. Joshua exempts him. Now, both learn it from nought save idolatry: R. Eliezer holds, It is like idolatry: just as idolatry, the Divine Law decreed, Do not engage [therein], and if one engages [therein] he is culpable, so here too it is not different. But R.

(10) The *halachic* midrash on Leviticus, in which this passage occurs. (11) This principle was laid down by R. Joḥanan; v. Sanh., 86*a*, n. a1.—Thus R. Judah does not regard him as a male in this respect. (12) The waters of lustration by placing the ashes therein; v. Num. XIX, 17. (13) That an hermaphrodite is considered a male. (14) Gen. XVII, 10: '*every*' is an extension, and teaches the inclusion of an hermaphrodite.

a (1) Lit., 'forgets'. (2) For unwittingly desecrating the Sabbath. For since circumcision is obligatory from the eighth day only, this is not circumcision, but the mere inflicting of a wound, which entails culpability. (3) For though he has actually fulfilled a precept, nevertheless circumcision after the proper time does not supersede the Sabbath. (4) He erred through the fulfilment of a precept, viz., because he was occupied with the circumcision of the second, which actually was to be done that day; he also did fulfil a precept by circumcising the first, and R. Joshua holds that in such a case one is not culpable. (5) In the first clause of the Mishnah, as our text. (6) The obligations to all sin-offerings are learnt from the unwitting offence of idolatry, which serves as a model; v. Num. XV, 29-30 (v. 30 is understood to refer to deliberate idolatry, and shows that the preceding verses refer to all unwitting offences which are similar thereto).

◁ *For the continuation of the English translation of this page see overleaf.*

תורה אור

(א) *וסתם ספרא רבי יהודה אמר רב נחמן בר יצחק אף אנן נמי תנינא *"הכל כשרים לקדש חוץ מחש"ו רבי יהודה מכשיר בקטן ופוסל באשה ואנדרוגינוס ש"מ ומאי שנא מילה משום דכתיב °המול לכם כל זכר: מתני' *מי שהיו לו שני תינוקות אחד למול אחר השבת ואחד למול בשבת ושכח ומל את של אחר השבת בשבת חייב אחד למול בע"ש ואחד למול בשבת ושכח ומל את של ע"ש בשבת רבי אליעזר מחייב חטאת °ורבי יהושע פוטר: גמ' רב הונא מתני חייב רב יהודה מתני פטור רב הונא מתני חייב דתניא אמר ר"ש בן אלעזר לא נחלקו רבי *אלעזר ור' יהושע על מי שהיו לו ב' תינוקות אחד למול בשבת ואחד למול אחר השבת ושכח ומל את של אחר השבת בשבת שהוא חייב על מה נחלקו על מי שהיו לו ב' תינוקות א' למול בע"ש וא' למול בשבת ושכח ומל את של ע"ש בשבת שר' אליעזר מחייב חטאת ורבי יהושע פוטר ושניהם לא למדוה אלא מעבודת כוכבים ר' אליעזר סבר כעבודת כוכבים מה עבודת כוכבים אמר רחמנא לא תעביד וכי עביד מיחייב ה"נ לא שנא ורבי יהושע התם דלאו מצוה הכא מצוה רב יהודה מתני פטור דתניא א"ר מאיר [ב]לא נחלקו ר"א ורבי יהושע על מי שהיו לו ב' תינוקות אחד למול בע"ש ואחד למול בשבת ושכח ומל את של ע"ש בשבת שהוא פטור על מה נחלקו על מי שהיו לו ב' תינוקות אחד למול אחר השבת וא' למול בשבת ושכח ומל את של אחר השבת בשבת שר"א מחייב חטאת ורבי יהושע [ג]פוטר ושניהם לא למדוה אלא מעבודת כוכבים ר"א סבר כעבודת כוכבים מה עבודת כוכבים אמר רחמנא לא תעביד וכי עביד מיחייב ה"נ לא שנא ור' יהושע התם לא טריד מצוה הכא טריד מצוה *תני ר' חייא אומר היה ר"מ לא נחלקו רבי *אלעזר ורבי יהושע על מי שהיו לו ב' תינוקות א' למול בע"ש וא' למול בשבת ושכח ומל את של ע"ש בשבת שהוא חייב על מה נחלקו על מי שהיו לו ב' תינוקות א' למול אחר השבת וא' למול בשבת ושכח ומל של אחר השבת בשבת *שר"א מחייב חטאת ור' יהושע פוטר השתא רבי יהושע סיפא דלא קא עביד מצוה פוטר רישא דקא עביד מצוה מחייב אמרי דבי ר' ינאי רישא כגון שקדם ומל של שבת בע"ש דלא ניתנה שבת לידחות סיפא ניתנה שבת לידחות א"ל רב אשי לרב כהנא רישא נמי ניתנה שבת לידחות לגבי תינוקות דעלמא להאי גברא מיהא לא איתיהיב: מתני' *[ד]קטן נימול לשמנה לתשעה ולעשרה ולאחד עשר ולי"ב לא פחות ולא יותר הא כיצד כדרכו לשמנה נולד לבין השמשות נימול לט' ביה"ש של ע"ש נימול לעשרה יו"ט לאחר השבת נימול לאחד עשר ב' ימים של ר"ה נימול לשנים עשר קטן החולה אין מוהלין אותו עד שיבריא: גמ' *אמר שמואל [ה]חלצתו חמה נותנין לו כל ז' להברותו איבעיא להו מי בעינן מעת לעת ת"ש דתני *לודא יום הבראתו כיום הולדו מאי לאו מה יום הולדו לא בעינן מעת לעת אף יום הבראתו לא בעינן מעת לעת לא עדיף יום הבראתו מיום הולדו דאילו יום הולדו לא בעינן מעת לעת ואילו יום הבראתו בעינן מעת לעת: מתני' *[ו]אלו הן ציצין המעכבין את המילה בשר החופה את רוב העטרה ואינו אוכל בתרומה [ז]ואם היה בעל בשר מתקנו מפני מראית העין

מל

רש"י

והא סתם ספרא הוא דבתורת כהנים תניא לה וסתם ספרא רבי יהודה*: לקדש. מי חטאת לתת אפר על המים: מכשיר בקטן ופוסל באשה. טעמיה מפרש בסדר יומא בפ"ג: ובאנדרוגינוס. שמע מינה דרבי יהודה כאשה משוי ליה: כל זכר. ריבויא הוא:

מתני' ושכח ומל את של אחר השבת בשבת חייב. דטעה בדבר מצוה ולא עשה מצוה הוא ועבד ליה חבורה שלא לצורך ובהא אפילו רבי יהושע מודה: אחד למול בשבת ואחד למול בע"ש ושכח ומל את של ע"ש בשבת ר"א מחייב חטאת. דמילה שלא בזמנה אינה דוחה שבת ואע"ג דטעה בדבר מצוה שהיה טרוד באותו של שבת ומתוך כך טעה בזה ואף בזה עשה מצוה שהרי ראוי הוא למול אלא שאינו דוחה שבת [ס"ל] לר"א טעה בדבר מצוה ועשה מצוה שיש בה חיוב חטאת חייב ורבי יהושע פוטר דס"ל טעה בדבר מצוה ועשה מצוה פטור:

גמ' רב הונא מתני. במתניתין ברישא חייב לדברי הכל כדתנינן לה אנן: ורב יהודה מתני ברישא פטור. דמוקי לה בשכח ומל את של ע"ש בשבת ופלוגתא היא בשל אחר השבת בשבת: שהוא חייב. דאע"ג דטריד במצוה וטעה בה כיון דלאו מצוה שעדיין לא הגיע זמנו למול חייב: אלא מע"ז. שהוקשו כל חטאות שבתורה לחטאת ע"ז דכתיב תורה אחת יהיה לכם וגו' בפרשת שלח לך אנשים גבי קרבן ע"ז: ור' יהושע התם. עובד עבודת כוכבים לא עשה מצוה: ה"ג רב יהודה מתני פטור דתניא אמר ר"מ לא נחלקו ר"א ורבי יהושע על שהיו לו שני תינוקות אחד למול ע"ש כו': ה"ג ורבי יהושע התם לא טריד במצוה הכא טריד במצוה. טרוד להתעסק במצוה גמורה שהרי אחד מהם זמנו היום וטרוד לבו למהר ולעשות ומתוך טרדו טעה ומל את זה שאין בו מצוה כלל: ושכח ומל של ע"ש בשבת שהוא חייב. לקמיה מתרץ לה: דלא ניתנה שבת לידחות. שאין לו תינוק שיהא זמנו היום הלכך לא היה טרוד היום במצוה שלא היה מוטל עליו כלום לעשות ולא היה לו לטעות: מתני' נולד בין השמשות נימול לט'. שהרי ליום שמיני של מחר הוא נימול ושמא בין השמשות יום הוא ונימול לט': היה היום ע"ש. א"א למולו בשבת הבאה דשמא ט' הוא והויא ליה מילה שלא בזמנה ואינה דוחה שבת וצריך להמתין עד לאחר השבת שהוא עשירי: חל יו"ט להיות אחר השבת. אין מילה שלא בזמנה דוחה אותו ונימול לי"א: גמ' חלצתו חמה. נסלק ממנו החולי ויצא מגופו: דתני לודא. שם חכם: יום הבראתו כיום הולדו. ממתינין לו כיום הולדו: מאי לאו. יום הולדו דווקא קאמר דלא בעינן מעת לעת: לא. כיום הולדו דקתני למיתב ליה ז' מיהו עדיף יום הבראתו מהא דבעינן מעת לעת ומהא ליכא למשמע מידי: מתני' ציצין. רצועות של בשר שנשארו מן הערלה: עטרה. היא שפה גבוה המקפת את הגיד סביב וממנה משפע ויורד לראשו: ואינו אוכל בתרומה. אם כהן הוא דילפינן ביבמות (ד' ע:) שערל אסור בתרומה: ואם היה בעל בשר. שהיה שמן ונראה בשר שלמעלה מערלתו לאחר שניטלה ערלה כולה כאילו אותו בשר חוזר וחופה את הגיד: מתקנו. ומשפע באיזמל מאותו עובי: מפני מראית העין. שלא יהא נראה כערל:

פרע

תוספות

טומטום שראה לובן ואודם מביאת מקדש וכ"ת משום דאיכא קרא יתירא (ג) דדריש לה לטומטום דכתיב מזכר ועד נקבה תשלחו ואי למעוטי אנדרוגינוס גרידא לא ה"ל למיכתב אלא זכר לא היא דאי לא כתב אלא זכר א"כ ה"א אשה לא מחייב' בביאת מקדש מדכתיב זכר ולא כתיב אדם ושמא י"ל דלית ליה לרב דר"ח דאיכא אמורא נמי דפליג עליה בבכורות וא"ת ומאי איצטריך רב למעוטי אנדרוגינוס והא איהו ס"ל בפרק הערל ביבמות (דף פג.) דאנדרוגינוס ספיקא הוא (ג) ואיצטריך קרא למעוטי ספק מיהו הא לא קשיא דה"א כשראה לובן ואודם כאחת יתחייב ממ"כ אבל הא תימה כיון דסבר רב אנדרוגינוס ספיקא הוא אמאי קאמר רב מזכר ועד נקבה זכר ודאי נקבה ודאית ואם הוא זכר ימעט אותו מזכר ואם הוא נקבה ימעט אותו מנקבה ומיהו י"ל דמשום טומטום נקטיה דפעמים הוי זכר ופעמים הוי נקבה:

הזכר ולא טומטום ואנדרוגינוס. תימה לרבי דבפרק אלו מומין (בכורות דף מב.) גבי בכור מצריך הזכרים למעוטי טומטום ואנדרוגינוס משמע התם דמהזכר לחודיה לא הוה ממעט לה והכא ממעטין ליה מהזכר לחודיה:

מל

עין משפט נר מצוה

מט א מיי' פ"ו מהל' פרה הלכה ב סמג עשין רלב:

נ ב ג מיי' פ"ב מהל' שגגות הלכה ח:

נא ד מיי' פ"א מהל' מילה הלכה יב סמג עשין כח טוש"ע י"ד סי' רסו סעיף ח:

נב ה מיי' שם הלכה טז סמג שם טוש"ע י"ד סי' רסב סעיף ב:

נג ו ז מיי' פ"ב מהל' מילה הלכה ג ה סמג שם טוש"ע י"ד סי' רסד סעיף ה ו:

רבינו חננאל

א"ר יהודה אנדרוגינוס זכר הוא. שאם אי אתה אומר כך יערך ומנ"ל דלא מערך דתניא הזכר ולא טומטום ואנדרוגינוס כו' ופשוטה היא ומסקינן בה ומאי שנא גבי מילה דכתיב המול לכם כל זכר כל לרבות. ויש מי שאומר הלכתא כרבנן דאמרי ספק ואנדרוגינוס אין מחללין עליו את השבת ואין הלכה כר' יהודה ומרחזינן רב חסדא דריש לטעמיה דר' יהודה ש"מ הלכתא כוותיה: מתניתין מי שהיו לו ב' תינוקות אחד למול אחר השבת ואחד למול בשבת ושכח ומל את של אחר השבת בשבת חייב וכו' [ואמרינן בגמ'] רב התנא מתני חייב ורב יהודא מתני פטור פי' רב הונא מתני חייב דמוקים ליה למתניתין לר"ש דאמר ר"ש לא נחלקו ר' אליעזר (ור"ש) [ור' יהושע] על מי שהיו לו *) דקיי"ל סתם משנה ר' מאיר ובהא תנא דבי ר' חייא פליגי עליה ורב הונא דמוקים לה כר' שמעון כוותיה עבדינן וחלוקת ר' אליעזר ור' יהושע דברים ברורין הן. (שנים) ושניהם מע"ז למדוה דהא איתקשא כל התורה כולה לע"ז ר' אליעזר סבירא כע"ז מה ע"ז אמרה תורה לא תעבוד ואם תעבוד ע"ז בשגגה מכל מקום חייב חטאת. כן אמרה תורה בשבת. המחלל השבת בשגגה מ"מ חייב חטאת. ור' יהושע סבר התם לגבי ע"ז לא נתכוין לקיים המצוה הכא בשבת נתכוין לקיים מצות מילה. לפיכך פטור הוא והלכתא כר' יהושע וכדמתניתין ר' שמעון: אחד למול ערב שבת ואחד למול בשבת ושכח ומל את של שבת בע"ש ואת של ע"ש בשבת פטור כי מ"מ מצוה עשה. ואע"פ שטל בס'. אבל בזמן ששכח ומל את של אחר השבת בשבת כיון שלא עשה מצוה כי בו' מלו אפילו ר' יהושע מודה שחייב חטאת. וכן הלכה וכל היכא דפליג ר' אליעזר ור' יהושע הלכה כר' יהושע חוץ ממקומות ידועים. וזה אינו מהם. וכן רב הונא הלכתא כוותיה דשכיח גבי ריש גלותא ונרסינן הלכתא כוותין או הלכתא מתנייתו כו': מתניתין קטן נימול לשמונה לתשעה כו' קטן חולה אין מלין אותו עד שיבריא. אמר שמואל חלצתו חמה נותנין לו כל ז' להברותו והלכתא כשמואל דיהבינן ליה מאחר שחלצתו חמה שבעת ימים

מסורת הש"ס

[סנהדרין פו:]

[עירובין לו: וש"נ] יומא מג. יבמות עב: ערכין ג.

פרה פ"ה מ"ד

פסחים עב. כריתות יט:

[צ"ל אליעזר]

פסחים עב. ע"ש [צ"ל אליעזר]

[יבמות לד:]

ערכין ח:

יבמות עא.

ג"ז שם:

הגהות הב"ח

(א) גמ' וסתם ספרא ר' יהודה. נ"ב וע"ע מן מס' נדה דף מו: (ג) תוס' ד"ה הזכר יתירא למעוטי לה לטומטום: (ד) בא"ד ספיקא הוא וכי איצטריך:

גליון הש"ס

מתני' ור' יהושע פוטר. עי' מנחות דף סד ע"א תד"ה ואפי' נתכפר:

*) [נראה לעין דחסר פה כמה תיבות וכצ"ל על מי שהיו לו שני תינוקות אחד למול בשבת ואחד למול אחר השבת ומל של אחר השבת בשבת שהוא חייב וכו' ורב יהודה מתני פטור דתניא אמר ר"מ וכו' ומהדר ואוקמי מתני' כר"מ משום דקיי"ל דסתם משנה ר"מ וכו']

רב נסים גאון

אף אנן נמי תנינא הכל כשרין לקדש חוץ מחרש שוטה וקטן כו'. זו המשנה במס' פרה בפרק ה' ולענין קידוש מי חטאת נתכוונה.*) לומר שבעת שישארו ציצין המעכבין את המילה הרי הוא ערל עדיין ואם הוא כהן אסור לוכל בתרומה כמו ששנינו בבהמה המקשה לילד: ששחטה ותמצא כמותה בשחיטת חולין (עב) בפרק בהמה המקשה לילד: בתלמוד המחלוקת שהיתה בין ר' אליעזר ובין ר' עקיבא בתורת כהנים במה שכתוב (ויקרא כב) איש איש מזרע אהרן ומה שכתוב (שם) תושב כהן ר' אליעזר גמר לערל בגזירה שוה לערל מפסח ור' עקיבא אמר איש איש לרבות את הערל: במס' יבמות (דף ע) הערל וכל הטמאין לא יאכלו בתרומה והזכירו

*) זה לפרש את המשנה אלו הן ציצין כו'

אבל

Continuation of translation from previous page as indicated by ◁

Joshua [argues:] There he is not preoccupied with a precept,
b whereas here he is preoccupied with a precept.[1]

R. Hiyya taught, R. Meir used to say: R. Eliezer and R. Joshua did not differ concerning him who has two infants, one for circumcision on the eve of the Sabbath and one for circumcision on the Sabbath, and he errs and circumcises the one belonging to the eve of the Sabbath on the Sabbath, that he is culpable. About what do they disagree? About a man who has two infants, one for circumcision after the Sabbath and another for circumcision on the Sabbath, and he errs and circumcises the one belonging to after the Sabbath on the Sabbath, R. Eliezer declaring [him] liable to a sin-offering, while R. Joshua exempts him. Now if R. Joshua exempts him in the second clause, though he does not fulfil a precept, shall he declare him culpable in the first clause, where
c he does fulfil a precept![1]—The School of R. Jannai said: The first clause is, e.g., where the [infant] belonging to the Sabbath was previously circumcised on the eve of the Sabbath, so that the Sabbath does not stand to be superseded;[2] but in the second clause the Sabbath stands to be superseded. Said R. Ashi to R. Kahana: [But] in the first clause too the Sabbath stands to be superseded in connection with infants in general?—Nevertheless as far as this man [is concerned] it does not stand to be superseded.

MISHNAH. AN INFANT IS TO BE CIRCUMCISED ON THE EIGHTH, NINTH, TENTH, ELEVENTH, AND TWELFTH [DAYS], NEITHER EARLIER NOR LATER. HOW SO? IN THE NORMAL COURSE, IT IS ON THE EIGHTH; IF HE IS BORN AT TWILIGHT, ON THE NINTH;[3] AT TWILIGHT ON SABBATH EVE, ON THE TENTH;[4] IF A FESTIVAL FOLLOWS THE SABBATH, ON THE ELEVENTH;[5] IF THE TWO DAYS OF NEW YEAR [FOLLOW THE SABBATH], ON THE TWELFTH.[6] AN INFANT WHO IS ILL IS NOT CIRCUMCISED UNTIL HE RECOVERS.

GEMARA. Samuel said: When his temperature subsides [to normal], we allow him full seven days for his [complete] recovery. The scholars asked: Do we require twenty-four hours' days?[7]—Come and hear: For Luda taught: The day of his recovery is like the day of his birth. Surely that means, just as with the day
d of his birth, we do not require a twenty-four hours' day,[1] so with the day of his recovery, we do not require a twenty-four hours' day?—No: the day of his recovery is stronger than the day of his birth, for whereas with the day of his birth we do not require a twenty-four hours' day, with the day of his recovery we do require a twenty-four hours' day.

MISHNAH. THESE ARE THE SHREDS WHICH INVALIDATE CIRCUMCISION: FLESH THAT COVERS THE GREATER PART OF THE CORONA; AND HE MUST NOT PARTAKE OF TERUMAH.[2] AND IF HE IS FLESHY,[3] HE MUST REPAIR IT FOR APPEARANCES'

b (1) He is anxious to carry out the obligation which rests on him and this preoccupation excuses his error. Rab Judah accordingly reads the Mishnah quite differently, and in accordance with the present view.

c (1) Surely not, v. *supra* n. a4. (2) There is no infant left for whom the Sabbath must be violated. There was therefore no preoccupation with a precept and the error consequently was inexcusable, hence he is culpable. (3) As it may have been night already, and circumcision must not take place *before* the eighth. (4) *Sc.* the following Sunday week. (5) The following Monday week. (6) In Palestine all Festivals are of one day's duration, in accordance with Scripture, save New Year, which is of two days.—In the last three cases the infant cannot be circumcised on the following Friday, in case it is the seventh day, nor on the Sabbath or Festival, in case Friday was the eighth day, and circumcision after its proper time does not supersede them. (7) Lit., 'from time to time'. Must we wait seven whole days to the hour, or can we circumcise any time on the seventh day?

d (1) E.g., we do not wait eight full days to the hour for a normal circumcision, but perform it any time on the eighth day. (2) If he is a priest and was thus inadequately circumcised, v. Yeb. 70a. (3) So that though the circumcision was correctly performed the foreskin nevertheless looks as though it was uncircumcised.

(א) *וסתם ספרא רבי יהודה אמר רב נחמן בר יצחק אף אנן נמי תנינא **הכל כשרים לקדש חוץ מחש"ו רבי יהודה מכשיר בקטן ופוסל באשה ואנדרוגינוס ש"מ ומאי שנא מילה משום דכתיב °המול לכם כל זכר: מתני' *מי שהיו לו שני תינוקות אחד למול אחר השבת ואחד למול בשבת ושכח ומל את של אחר השבת בשבת חייב אחד למול בע"ש ואחד למול בשבת ושכח ומל את של ע"ש בשבת רבי אליעזר מחייב חטאת °ורבי יהושע פוטר: גמ' רב הונא מתני חייב רב יהודה מתני פטור רב הונא מתני חייב דתניא אמר ר"ש בן אלעזר לא נחלקו רבי *אלעזר ור' יהושע על מי שהיו לו ב' תינוקות אחד למול בשבת ואחד למול אחר השבת ושכח ומל את של אחר השבת בשבת שהוא חייב על מה נחלקו על מי שהיו לו ב' תינוקות א' למול בע"ש וא' למול בשבת ושכח ומל את של ע"ש בשבת שר' אליעזר מחייב חטאת ורבי יהושע פוטר ושניהם לא למדוה אלא מעבודת כוכבים ר' אליעזר סבר כעבודת כוכבים מה עבודת כוכבים אמר רחמנא לא תעביד וכי עביד מיחייב ה"נ לא שנא ורבי יהושע התם דלאו מצוה הכא מצוה רב יהודה מתני פטור דתניא א"ר מאיר [ג]לא נחלקו ר"א ורבי יהושע על מי שהיו לו ב' תינוקות אחד למול בע"ש ואחד למול בשבת ושכח ומל את של ע"ש בשבת שהוא פטור על מה נחלקו על מי שהיו לו ב' תינוקות אחד למול אחר השבת וא' למול בשבת ושכח ומל את של אחר השבת בשבת שר"א מחייב חטאת ורבי יהושע [ו]פוטר ושניהם לא למדוה אלא מעבודת כוכבים ר"א סבר כעבודת כוכבים מה עבודת כוכבים אמר רחמנא לא תעביד וכי עביד מיחייב ה"נ לא שנא ור' יהושע התם לא טריד מצוה הכא טריד מצוה *תני ר' חייא אומר היה ר"מ לא נחלקו רבי *אלעזר ורבי יהושע על מי שהיו לו ב' תינוקות א' למול בע"ש וא' למול בשבת ושכח ומל את של ע"ש בשבת שהוא חייב על מה נחלקו על מי שהיו לו ב' תינוקות א' למול אחר השבת וא' למול בשבת ושכח ומל של אחר השבת בשבת *שר"א מחייב חטאת ור' יהושע פוטר השתא רבי יהושע סיפא דלא קא עביד מצוה פוטר רישא דקא עביד מצוה מחייב אמרי דבי ר' ינאי רישא כגון שקדם ומל של שבת בע"ש דלא ניתגד שבת לידחות סיפא ניתנה שבת לידחות א"ל רב אשי לרב כהנא רישא נמי ניתנה שבת לידחות לגבי תינוקות דעלמא להאי גברא מיהא לא איתיהיב: מתני' *[ד]קטן נימול לשמנה לתשעה ולעשרה ולאחד עשר ולי"ב לא פחות ולא יותר הא כיצד כדרכו לשמנה נולד לבין השמשות נימול לט' ביה"ש של ע"ש נימול לעשרה יו"ט לאחר השבת נימול לאחד עשר ב' ימים של ר"ה נימול לשנים עשר קטן החולה אין מוהלין אותו עד שיבריא: גמ' *אמר שמואל [ה]חלצתו חמה נותנין לו כל ז' להברותו איבעיא להו מי בעינן מעת לעת ת"ש דתני *לודא יום הבראתו כיום הולדו מאי לאו מה יום הולדו לא בעינן מעת לעת אף יום הבראתו לא בעינן מעת לעת לא עדיף יום הבראתו מיום הולדו דאילו יום הולדו לא בעינן מעת לעת ואילו יום הבראתו בעינן מעת לעת: מתני' *[ו]אלו הן ציצין המעכבין את המילה בשר החופה את רוב העטרה ואינו אוכל בתרומה [ז]ואם היה בעל בשר מתקנו מפני מראית העין

מל

תורה אור: בראשית יז

והא סתם ספרא הוא דבתורת כהנים תניא לה וסתם ספרא רבי יהודה*: לקדש. מי חטאת לתת אפר על המים: מכשיר בקטן ופוסל באשה. טעמיה מפרש בסדר יומא בפ"ג: ובאנדרוגינוס. שמע מינה דרבי יהודה כאשה משוי ליה: כל זכר. ריבויא הוא: מתני' ושכח ומל את של אחר השבת בשבת חייב. דטעה בדבר מצוה ולא עשה מצוה הוא ועבד ליה חבורה שלא לצורך ובהא אפילו רבי יהושע מודה: אחד למול בשבת ואחד למול בע"ש ושכח ומל את של ע"ש בשבת ר"א מחייב חטאת.. דמילה שלא בזמנה אינה דוחה שבת ואע"ג דטעה בדבר מצוה שהיה טרוד באותו של שבת ומתוך כך טעה בזה ואף בזה עשה מצוה שהרי ראוי הוא למול אלא שאינו דוחה שבת ס"ל לר"א טעה בדבר מצוה ועשה מצוה שיש בה חיוב חטאת חייב ורבי יהושע פוטר דס"ל טעה בדבר מצוה ועשה מצוה פטור: גמ' רב הונא מתני. במתניתין ברישא חייב לדברי הכל כדתנינן לה אנן: ורב יהודה מתני ברישא פטור. דמוקי לה בשכח ומל את של ע"ש בשבת ופלוגתא היא בשל אחר השבת בשבת: שהוא חייב. דאע"ג דטריד במצוה וטעה בה כיון דלאו מצוה שעדיין לא הגיע זמנו למול חייב: אלא מע"ז. שהוקשו כל חטאות שבתורה לחטאת ע"ז דכתיב תורה אחת יהיה לכם וגו' בפרשת שלח לך אנשים גבי קרבן ע"ז: ור' יהושע התם. עובד עבודת כוכבים לא עשה מצוה: ה"ג רב יהודה מתני פטור דתניא אמר ר"מ לא נחלקו ר"א ורבי יהושע על שהיו לו שני תינוקות אחד למול ע"ש כו': ה"ג ורבי יהושע התם לא טריד במצוה הכא טריד במצוה. טרוד להתעסק במצוה גמורה שהרי אחד מהם זמנו היום וטרוד לבו למהר ולעשות ומתוך טרדו טעה ומל את זה שאין בו מצוה כלל: ושכח ומל של ע"ש בשבת שהוא חייב. לקמיה מתרץ לה: דלא ניתנה שבת לידחות. שאין לו תינוק שיהא זמנו היום הלכך לא היה טרוד היום במצוה שלא היה מוטל עליו כלום לעשות ולא היה לו לטעות: מתני' נולד בין השמשות נימול לט'. שהרי ליום שמיני של מחר הוא נימול ושמא בין השמשות יום הוא ונימול לט': היה היום ע"ש. א"א למולו בשבת הבאה דשמא ט' הוא והויא ליה מילה שלא בזמנה ואינה דוחה שבת וצריך להמתין עד לאחר השבת שהוא עשירי: חל יו"ט להיות אחר השבת. אין מילה שלא בזמנה דוחה אותו ונימול לי"א: גמ' חלצתו חמה. נשלף ממנו החולי ויצא מגופו: דתני לודא. שם חכם: יום הבראתו כיום הולדו. ממתינין לו כיום הולדו: מאי לאו. יום הולדו דווקא קאמר דלא בעינן מעת לעת: לא. כיום הולדו דקתני למיתב ליה ז' מיהו עדיף יום הבראתו מהא דבעינן מעת לעת ומהא ליכא למשמע מידי: מתני' ציצין. רצועות של בשר שנשארו מן הערלה: עטרה. היא שפה גבוה המקפת את הגיד סביב וממנה משפע ויורד לראשו: ואינו אוכל בתרומה. אם כהן הוא דילפינן ביבמות (ד' ע·) שערל אסור בתרומה: ואם היה בעל בשר. שהיה שמן ונראה בשר שלמעלה מערלתו לאחר שניטלה ערלה כולה כאילו אותו בשר חוזר וחופה את הגיד: מתקנו. ומשפע באיזמל מאותו עובי: מפני מראית העין. שלא יהא נראה כערל:

פרע

טומטום שראה לובן ואודם מביאת מקדש וכ"ת משום דאיכא קרא יתירא (ג) דדריש לה לטומטום דכתיב מזכר ועד נקבה תשלחו ואי למעוטי אנדרוגיטס גרידא לא ה"ל למיכתב אלא זכר לא היא דאי לא כתב אלא זכר א"כ ה"א אשה לא מחייב' בביאת מקדש מדכתיב זכר ולא כתיב אדם ושמא י"ל דלית ליה לרב דר"ח דאיכא אמורא נמי דפליג עליה בבכורות וא"ת ומאי איצטריך רב למעוטי אנדרוגיטס והא איהו ס"ל בפרק הערל ביבמות (דף פג·) דאנדרוגיטס ספיקא הוא (ג) ואיצטריך קרא למעוטי ספק מיהו הא לא קשיא דה"א כשראה לובן ואודם כאחת יתחייב ממ"נ אבל הא תימה כיון דסבר רב אנדרוגיטס ספיקא הוא אמאי קאמר רב מזכר ועד נקבה זכר ודאי נקבה ודאית ואם הוא זכר ימעט אותו מזכר ואם הוא נקבה ימעט אותו מנקבה ומיהו י"ל דמשום טומטום נקטיה דפעמים הוי זכר ופעמים הוי נקבה:

הזכר ולא טומטום ואנדרוגינוס. תימה לרבי דבפרק אלו מומין (בכורות דף מב·) גבי בכור מצריך הזכר הזכרים למעוטי טומטום ואנדרוגיטס משמע התם דמהזכר לחודיה לא הוה ממעט לה והכא ממעטין ליה מהזכר לחודיה:

מל

עין משפט נר מצוה

מט א מיי' פ"ו מהל' פרה הלכה ג סמג עשין רלב:

נ ב ג מיי' פ"ב מהל' שגגות הלכה ח:

נא ד מיי' פ"א מהל' מילה הלכה יב סמג עשין כח טוש"ע י"ד סי' רסו סעיף ח:

נב ה מיי' שם הלכה עז סמג שם טוש"ע י"ד סי' רסב סעיף ב:

נג ו ז מיי' פ"ב מהל' מילה הלכה ג ה סמג שם טוש"ע י"ד סי' רסד סעיף ה ו:

רבינו חננאל

א"ר יהודה אנדרוגינוס זכר הוא. שאם אי אתה אומר כך יערך ומנ"ל דלא מערך דתניא הזכר ולא טומטום ואנדרוגינוס כו' ופשוטה היא ומסקינן בה ומאי שנא גבי מילה דכתיב המול לכם כל זכר כל לרבות. ויש מי שאומר הלכתא כרבנן דאמרי ספק ואנדרוגינוס אין מחללין עליו את השבת ואין הלכה כר' יהודה ומדחזינן רב חסדא דריש לטעמיה דר' יהודה ש"מ הלכתא כוותיה: מתניתין מי שהיו לו ב' תינוקות אחד למול אחר השבת ואחד למול בשבת ושכח ומל את של אחר השבת בשבת חייב וכו' [ואמרינן בגמ'] רב הונא מתני חייב ורב יהודא מתני פטור פי' רב הונא מתני חייב דמוקים ליה למתניתין לר"ש דאמר ר"ש לא נחלקו ר' אליעזר (ור"ש) [ור' יהושע] על מי שהיו לו *) דקיי"ל סתם משנה ר' מאיר ובהא תנא דבי ר' חייא פליגי עליה ורב הונא דמוקים לה כר' שמעון כוותיה עבדינן וחלוקת ר' אליעזר ור' יהושע דברים ברורין הן. (שנים) ושניהם מע"ז למדוה דהא איתקשא כל התורה כולה לע"ז ר' אליעזר סבירא כע"ז מה ע"ז אמרה תורה לא תעבוד ואם תעבוד ע"ז בשגגה מכל מקום חייב חטאת. כן אמרה תורה בשבת. המחלל השבת בשגגה מ"מ חייב חטאת. ור' יהושע סבר התם לגבי ע"ז לא נתכוין לקיים המצוה הכא בשבת נתכוין לקיים מצות מילה. לפיכך פטור הוא והלכתא כר' יהושע וכדמתניתין ר' שמעון: אחד למול ערב שבת ואחד למול בשבת ושכח ומל את של שבת בע"ש ואת של ע"ש בשבת פטור כי מ"מ מצוה עשה. ואע"פ שמל בס'. אבל בזמן ששכח ומל את של אחר השבת בשבת כיון שלא עשה מצוה כי בו' מלו אפילו ר' יהושע מודה שחייב חטאת. וכן הלכה וכל היכא דפליג ר' אליעזר ור' יהושע הלכה כר' יהושע חוץ ממקומות ידועים. וזה אינו מהם. וכן רב הונא הלכתא כוותיה דשביח גבי ריש גלותא וגרסינן הלכתא כוותין או הלכתא

מסורת הש"ס

[סנהדרין פו·]

[עירובין לו: וש"נ] יומא מג. יבמות עב: ערכין ג. פרה פ"ה מ"ד

פסחים עב. כריתות יט:

[צ"ל אליעזר]

פסחים עב. ע"ש [צ"ל אליעזר]

[יבמות לד·]

ערכין ח:

יבמות עא.

ג"ז שם:

הגהות הב"ח

(א) גמ' וסתם ספרא ר' יהודה. נ"ב וע"ע מן מס' נדה דף מו: (ג) תוס' ד"ה הכא יתירא למעוטי לה לטומטום: (ד) בא"ד ספיקא הוא וכי איצטריך:

גליון הש"ס

מתני' ור' יהושע פוטר. עי' מנחות דף סד ע"א תד"ה ואפי' נתכפר:

כוותייכו כו': מתניתין קטן נימול לשמונה לתשעה כו' קטן חולה אין מלין אותו עד שיבריא. אמר שמואל חלצתו חמה נותנין לו כל ז' להברותו והלכתא כשמואל דיהבינן ליה מאחר שחלצתו חמה שבעת ימים

*) [נראה לעין דחסר פה כמה תיבות וכצ"ל על מי שהיו לו שני תינוקות אחד למול בשבת ושכח ואחד למול אחר השבת ושכח ומל של אחר השבת בשבת שהוא חייב וכו' ורב יהודה מתני פטור דתניא אמר ר"מ וכו' ומהדר אוקמי מתני' כר"מ משום דקיי"ל דסתם משנה ר"מ וכו']

רב נסים גאון

שישרפה ותמצא כמותה בשחיטת חולין (עב) בפרק בהמה המקשה לילד: אף אנן נמי תנינא הכל כשרין לקדש חוץ מחרש שוטה וקטן כו'. זו המשנה במס' פרה בפרק ה'. ולענין קידוש מי חטאת נתכוונה.*) לומר שבעת שישארו ציצין המעכבין את המילה הרי הוא ערל עדיין ואם הוא כהן אסור לוכל בתרומה כמו ששנינו בגמ' יבמות (דף ע) הערל וכל הטמאין לא יאכלו בתרומה והזכירו בתלמוד המחלוקת שהיתה בין ר' אליעזר ובין ר' עקיבא בתורת כהנים במה שכתוב (ויקרא כב) איש איש מזרע אהרן ומה שכתוב (שם) תושב כהן ר' אליעזר גמר לערל בגזירה שוה לערל מפסח ור' עקיבא אמר איש איש לרבות את הערל;

אבל

*) זה לפרש את המשנה אלו הן ציצין כו'

עין משפט נר מצוה

נד א מיי' פ"ב מהל' מילה הלכה ד סמג עשין כח טוש"ע י"ד סי' רסד סעיף ד :
נה ב מיי' שם הלכה ג טוש"ע שם סעי' ה:
נו ג מיי' שם הלכה ה טור וש"ע שם סעיף ו:
נז ד מיי' פ"ג מהל' מילה הלכה א סמג שם טוש"ע י"ד סי' רסה סעיף א:
נח ה מיי' שם הלכה ד סמג שם טוש"ע י"ד סי' רסה סעיף ה:
נט ו מיי' שם הלכה ה סמג שם טוש"ע י"ד סי' רסז סעיף יב:
א ז מיי' פכ"א מהל' שבת הלכה יז ופ"ג מהל' י"ט הלכה יז סמג לאוין סה עם טוש"ע א"ח סי' שטו סעי' ט וסי' שיט סעיף ט וסי' תקי סעיף ד:

מסורת הש"ס

תורה אור

אמל ולא פרע את המילה כאילו לא מל:
גמ' *אמר רבי אבינא א"ר ירמיה בר אבא אמר רב בבשר החופה את רוב גובהה של עטרה: ואם היה בעל בשר וכו': [שם] אמר שמואל קטן המסורבל בבשר רואין אותו כ"ז שמתקשה ונראה מהול אינו צריך למול ואם לאו צריך למול במתניתא תנא *רשב"ג אומר גקטן המסורבל בבשר רואין אותו כל זמן שמתקשה ואינו נראה מהול צריך למולו ואם לאו אינו צריך למולו מאי בינייהו איכא בינייהו נראה ואינו נראה: מל ולא פרע: ת"ר *דהמל אומר אקב"ו על המילה אבי הבן אומר אקב"ו להכניסו בבריתו של אברהם אבינו העומדים (א) אומרים כשם שנכנס לברית כך יכנס לתורה לחופה ולמע"ט והמברך אומר אשר קידש ידיד מבטן חוק בשארו שם וצאצאיו חתם באות ברית קדש על כן בשכר זאת אל חי חלקנו (ב) צוה* להציל ידידות שארינו משחת למען בריתו אשר שם בבשרנו בא"י כורת הברית. ההמל את הגרים אומר ברוך אתה ה' אלהינו מלך העולם אקב"ו על המילה והמברך אומר אקב"ו למול את הגרים ולהטיף מהם דם ברית שאילמלא דם ברית לא נתקיימו שמים וארץ שנאמר (ירמיה לג) °אם לא בריתי יומם ולילה חוקות שמים וארץ לא שמתי בא"י כורת הברית והמל את העבדים אומר אקב"ו על המילה והמברך אומר אקב"ו למול את העבדים ולהטיף מהם דם ברית [נדרים לא:] *שאילמלא דם ברית חוקות שמים וארץ לא נתקיימו שנאמ' אם לא בריתי יומם ולילה חוקות שמים וארץ לא שמתי בא"י כורת הברית:

הדרן עלך רבי אליעזר דמילה

רבי אליעזר אומר תולין את המשמרת בי"ט ונותנין לתלויה בשבת וחכ"א אאין תולין את המשמרת בי"ט ואין נותנין לתלויה בשבת אבל נותנין לתלויה ביו"ט:
גמ' השתא ר"א אוסופי אהל עראי לא מוספינן למיעבד לכתחלה שרי מאי היא דתנן *פקק החלון ר"א אומר בזמן שקשור ותלוי פוקקין בו ואם לאו אין פוקקין בו וחכ"א בין כך ובין כך פוקקין בו ואמר רבה בר בר חנה א"ר יוחנן *הכל מודים שאין עושין אהל עראי בתחלה בי"ט ואין צ"ל בשבת לא נחלקו אלא להוסיף שר"א אומר אין מוסיפין בי"ט ואין צ"ל בשבת וחכ"א מוסיפין בשבת ואין צ"ל ביום טוב ר"א סבר לה כרבי יהודה דתניא *אין בין יום טוב לשבת אלא אוכל נפש בלבד רבי יהודה מתיר אף מכשירי אוכל נפש אימר דשמעינן ליה לר' יהודה במכשירין שאי אפשר לעשותם מערב יום טוב במכשירין שאפשר לעשותם מעיו"ט מי שמעת ליה דר"א עדיפא מדרבי יהודה: וחכ"א: איבעיא להו תלה מאי אמר רב יוסף תלה חייב חטאת א"ל אביי אלא מעתה תלא כוזא בסיכתא הכי נמי דמיחייב אלא

פרע. גילה: גמ' רוב גובהה. לא תימא רוב העטרה דקתני מתני' רוב היקפה אלא אפילו רוב גובהה במקום אחד: קטן המסורבל בבשר. פלטר"י בלע"ז שמן ועב ולאחר שנימול נראה כמכסהו: כל זמן שמתקשה. ומתוך הקישוי מתפשט בשרו בדשמואל גרסינן ונראה מהול במתניתא גרסינן ואינו נראה מהול: איכא בינייהו נראה ואינו נראה. לשמואל נראה מהול הוא דאין צריך למולו הא נראה ואינו נראה צריך למתניתא אינו נראה הוא דצריך הא נראה ואינו נראה אינו צריך: אשר קידש ידיד מבטן. יצחק קרי ידיד על שם אשר אהבת (בראשית כב): מבטן. דקודם שנולד נתקדש למצוה זו דכתיב (שם יז) אבל שרה אשתך וגו' והקימותי את בריתי אתו היינו מילה: בשארו. בבשרו: שם. חק של מילה: ולצאצאיו. אחריו: חתם באות. זו של ברית קדש: צוה להציל ידידות שארינו משחת. מגיהנם דכתיב גם את בדם בריתך שלחתי אסיריך מבור אין מים בו (זכריה ט):

הדרן עלך ר' אליעזר דמילה

תולין את המשמרת. שמסננין בה שמרי יין ומותח פיה לכל צד בעגול ונעשה כאהל על חלל הכלי שקורין אשטנד"א ואע"ג דעביד אהל שרי בי"ט כדמפרש בגמרא אבל בשבת מיתלא לכתחילה לא אבל אם תלויה היא נותנין לתוכה שמרים ומסנן דאין דרך בורר בכך: גמ' פקק החלון. כגון ארובת הגג: אלא להוסיף. כגון פקק זה שאינו אלא תוספת עראי על האהל: סבר ליה כרבי יהודה. הלכך הכא שרי דמכשירי אוכל נפש הוא: שאי אפשר לעשותן מעי"ט. כגון שפוד שנרצם בי"ט: עדיפא. חזקה דהוא שרי אפילו מכשירין שאפשר מעיו"ט: תלה כוזא בסיכתא. תלה כלי קטן במגוד: ה"נ דמיחייב. והכא מאי חיובא איכא באהל עראי בנין גמור לא הוי ומדרבנן הוא דמיתסר: אלא

מל ולא פרע את המילה כאילו לא מל. תימה אמאי איצטריך למיתני האי כיון דכבר תנא דבשר החופה את רוב העטרה מעכב המילה וכי לא פרע עדיין רוב עטרה מכוסה: אבי הבן אומר כו'. רבינו שמואל גרים אבי הבן ברישא והדר המל אומר וכבר הנהיג לעשות כן לברך אבי הבן קודם המילה משום דלהכניסו להבא משמע כדאמרינן בפ"ק דפסחים (ד' ז: ושם) בלבער כ"ע לא פליגי דלהבא משמע ועוד *דכל המצות מברך [שם] עליהן עובר לעשייתן ור"ת החזיר המנהג לקדמותו וגרס המל ברישא והדר אבי הבן כמו שכתוב בכל הספרים וכן מוכח כולה סוגיא מדקאמר העומדים שם אומרים כשם שהכניסו לברית מכלל שכבר הכניסו ועוד דגבי גר דבסמוך גרס ברישא המל כו' והדר המברך אומר אקב"ו למול את הגרים ונראה הוא שזהו כנגד ברכת אבי הבן והתם א"א לשנות הגירסא שיש באותה ברכה להטיף מהן דם ברית כו' ברוך כורת הברית משמע דכל זה הוא אחר המילה ועוד דהמברך מברך לעולם אחר המילה כמו במילת קטן והיא דפסחים ה"פ בלבער כ"ע לא פליגי דלהבא משמע טפי מלשעבר ומיהו לשעבר נמי משמע כי פליגי בעל ביעור מר סבר דמשמע מעיקרא טפי מלהבא ומר סבר להבא נמי משמע כמו מעיקרא והא דאמרינן דכל המצות מברך עובר לעשייתן ה"מ כשהמברך עצמו עושה המצוה: ידיד מבטן. אומר ר"ת שהוא אברהם אבינו שנקרא ידיד שנאמר (ירמיה יא) מה לידידי בביתי כדדרשינן במנחות בפרק כל המנחות (ד' נג: ושם) ושלשת האבות נזכרים חוק בשארו שם הוא יצחק ולאצאיו חתם באות ברית קדש הוא יעקב ולאצאיו הוא ובניו כמו שתרגם יונתן הצאצאים והצפיעות בניא ובני בניא (ישעיה כב) כלומר יוצאי חלציו*: במצותיו וצונו למול את העבדים. שנאמר יליד בית ומקנת כסף (בראשית יז):

הדרן עלך ר' אליעזר דמילה

תולין. אבל נותנין לתלויה ביום טוב. וצריך לפרש ולומר שאם היה עושהו מאתמול לא היה טוב כל כך וחזק והא דתניא בפרקין דלעיל (ד' קלד. ושם) דאין מסננין את החרדל במסננת שלו בי"ט אם היה עושהו מאתמול לא היה מתקלקל: דרבי אליעזר עדיפא מדר"י. תימה ולר"א תיקשה ליה הנהו קראי דדריש בפ"ק דמגילה (ד' ז:) דקאמר ורבי יהודה כתיב הוא וכתיב לכם ולא קשיא כאן במכשירין שאפשר וכו' וכ"ת ר"א הוה דריש הוא לדרשה אחריתא א"כ מנ"ל התם דרבי יהודה הוה מפליג לימא דרבי יהודה הוה דריש ליה לדרשה אחריתי כר' אליעזר ונראה דבדאורייתא מודה ר' אליעזר דמכשירין דאפשר אסורים *וכי שרי להו הכא ה"מ באהל עראי דאינו אלא מדרבנן גזירה אטו אהל קבע כדאמרינן בביצה בפרק המביא (ד' לב:) מיהו קשה מנ"ל דעדיפא דילמא בהא מודה אפילו רבי יהודה:

*) [ועי' תוס' מנחות נג. ד"ה בן]

רבינו חננאל

מעת לעת להבראותו. וזה מפורש ביבמות בפר' הערל וכל הטמאים: מתני' ואלו הן ציצין המעכבין את המילה. א"ר אבינא א"ר ירמיה בר אבא אמר רב בשר החופה את רוב גובהה של עטרה וכו' וכן הלכתא. ואם הוא בעל בשר מתקנו מפני מראית העין כלומר אע"פ שהציצין הללו אינן חופין רוב גובהה של עטרה מתקנו מפני שלא יהא נראה כערלה: אמר שמואל קטן המסורבל בבשר רואין אותו כל זמן שמתקשה [ונראה מהול אין צריך למול במתניתא תנא רשבג"א קטן המסורבל בבשר רואין אותו כ"ז שמתקשה] שאינו נראה מהול צריך למול ואמרי' מאי בינייהו איכא בינייהו [נראה] ואינו נראה צריך למול לרשב"ג דאמר ואינו נראה מהול כלל צריך למול אבל אם נראה ואינו נראה אינו צריך למול. פי' מסורבל מסובב בבשר כדכתי' כפיתו בסרבליהון וכו'. מל ולא פרע את המילה וכו'. פי' מי שמל ולא פרע את המילה כלומר לא קרע את העור וגילה את העטרה כאלו לא מל:

הדרן עלך ר' אלעזר אם לא הביא. עז ותהלה לאל אבי. שית עזר גלילין. חלץ באזר והחלין. בפ' ר' אליעזר תולין:

ר' אליעזר אומר תולין את המשמרת ביו"ט וכו' ואקשי' עלה השתא ר' אליעזר להוסיף באהל עראי מחמיר ואמר אין מוסיפין לכתחלה (שאי) [מאי היא]. דתנן פקק החלון ר' אליעזר אומר בזמן שקשור ותלוי פוקקין בו כו' ופקק זה כגון מסך לסתום בו חללו של חלון ואמר רבה בר בר חנה א"ר יוחנן הכל מודים שאין עושין אהלי עראי בתחלה ביו"ט ואין צריך לומר בשבת לא נחלקו אלא להוסיף שר' אליעזר אומר אין מוסיפין ביו"ט ואין צ"ל בשבת וחכ"א מוסיפין בשבת ואין צ"ל ביו"ט ומפרקינן ר' אליעזר סבר לה כר' יהודה דתניא אין בין יו"ט לשבת אלא אוכל נפש בלבד. ר' יהודה אומר אף מכשירי אוכל נפש וזה שמתיר ר' אליעזר לעשות אהל לכתחלה ביו"ט לתלות המשמר מפני שהוא מכשירי אוכל נפש כדי לשמר היין לשתות בשמחת יו"ט ונמצא ר' אליעזר מיקל מר' יהודה שר' יהודה אינו מתיר אלא במכשירין שאי אפשר לעשותן מעיו"ט אבל במכשירין שאפשר לעשותן מעיו"ט כגון שימור היין וכדומה לו אוסר ור' אליעזר מתיר אפילו בזה. ואין הלכה

יבמות עב. ע"ש
[תוספ' פס"ז]
[מנחות מב: תוספ' ברכות פ"ו כל הענין עד סופו]
הג"מ יעב"ץ ז"ל ניקד זוס בחיריק

הגהות הב"ח

(א) גמ' העומדין שם אומרים כשם שהכניסתו לברית כך תכניסהו לתורה כצ"ל ותיבת ולמע"ט נמחק: (ב) שם תלתא לורט זוס:

לעיל קכב. עירובין מד: סוכה כז:
[תוספ' סוכה פ"א לעיל קכה: וש"נ]
[תוספ' מגילה פ"א] ביצה כח. לו: מגילה ז: לעיל ס: קכד:
[עי' תוס' דפסחים סח: ד"ה מה ראים רשות]

SAKE. [137b] IF ONE CIRCUMCISES BUT DOES NOT UNCOVER THE CIRCUMCISION,[4] IT IS AS IF HE HAS NOT CIRCUMCISED.

GEMARA. R. Abina said in the name of R. Jeremiah b. Abba in Rab's name: [This means,] the flesh that covers the greater part of the height of the corona.

AND IF HE IS FLESHY, etc. Samuel said: If an infant['s membrum] is overgrown with flesh, we examine him: as long as he appears circumcised when he forces himself,[5] it is unnecessary to recircumcise him; but if not he must be recircumcised. In a Baraitha it was taught: R. Simeon b. Gamaliel said: If an infant['s membrum] is overgrown with flesh, we examine him: if he does not appear circumcised when he forces himself, he must be recircumcised: otherwise he need not be recircumcised. Wherein a do they differ?—They differ where it is only partially visible.[1]

IF ONE CIRCUMCISES BUT DOES NOT UNCOVER THE CIRCUMCISION. Our Rabbis taught: He who circumcises must recite: '... Who hast sanctified us with Thy commandments, and hast commanded us concerning circumcision.' The father of the infant recites, '... Who hast sanctified us with Thy commandments and hast commanded us to lead him into the covenant of our father Abraham.' The bystanders exclaim, 'Even as he has entered the covenant, so may he enter into the Torah, the marriage canopy, and good deeds.' And he who pronounces the benediction recites: '... Who hast sanctified the beloved one[2] from the womb; He set a statute in his flesh, and his offsprings he sealed with the sign of the holy covenant. Therefore as a reward for this, O living God Who art our portion, give command to save the beloved of our flesh from the pit, for the sake of Thy covenant which Thou hast set in our flesh. Blessed art Thou, O Lord, Who makest the covenant.' He who circumcises proselytes says, 'Blessed art Thou, O Lord our God, King of the universe, Who hast sanctified us with Thy commandments and hast commanded us concerning circumcision.' He who pronounces the benediction recites, '... Who hast sanctified us with Thy commandments and hast commanded us to circumcise proselytes and to cause the drops of the blood of the covenant to flow from them, since but for the blood of the covenant Heaven and earth would not endure, as it is said, *If not My covenant by day and by night, I had not appointed the ordinances of heaven and earth.*[3] Blessed art Thou, O Lord, Who makest the covenant.' He who circumcises slaves recites: '... Who hast sanctified us with Thy commandments and hast commanded us concerning circumcision.' While he who pronounces the benediction recites: '... Who hast sanctified us with Thy commandments and hast commanded us to circumcise slaves and to cause the drops of the blood of the covenant to flow from them, since but for the blood of the covenant the ordinances of heaven and earth would not endure, as it is said, *If not My covenant by day and night, I had not appointed the ordinances of heaven and earth*. Blessed art Thou, O Lord, b Who makest the covenant.'[1]

CHAPTER XX

MISHNAH. R. ELIEZER STATED: ONE MAY SUSPEND A STRAINER ON FESTIVALS, AND POUR [WINE] THROUGH c A SUSPENDED [STRAINER] ON THE SABBATH.[1] BUT THE SAGES RULE: ONE MAY NOT SUSPEND A STRAINER ON FESTIVALS, NOR POUR [WINE] THROUGH A SUSPENDED [STRAINER] ON THE SABBATH, BUT WE MAY POUR [IT] THROUGH A SUSPENDED [STRAINER] ON FESTIVALS.

GEMARA. Seeing that R. Eliezer [holds] that we may not [even] add to a temporary tent, can it be permitted to make [one] in the first place?[2] What is this allusion? For we learnt: As for the stopper of a skylight,—R. Eliezer said: When it is fastened and suspended, one may close [the skylight] with it; if not, one may not close [the skylight] with it. But the Sages maintain: In both cases you may close [the skylight] with it. Whereon Rabbah b. Bar Ḥanah said in R. Joḥanan's name: All agree that a temporary tent may not be made on Festivals, whilst on the Sabbath it goes without saying. They differ only in respect of adding [to a tent]; R. Eliezer maintaining, One may not add on a Festival, whilst on the Sabbath it goes without saying; whereas the Sages rule: One may add on the Sabbath, whilst it is superfluous to speak of Festivals![3]—R. Eliezer agrees with R. Judah. For it was taught: The only difference between Festivals and the d Sabbath is in respect of food for consumption.[1] R. Judah permits the preliminary preparations of food for consumption too.[2] But say that we know R. Judah [to rule thus] of preparations which could not be done on the eve of the Festival; do you know him [to rule thus] of preparations which could be done on the eve of the Festival?—R. Eliezer's [ruling] goes further than R. Judah's.[3]

BUT THE SAGES RULE, [etc.]. The scholars asked: What if one does suspend [it]?—R. Joseph said: If one suspends [it] he is liable to a sin-offering. Said Abaye to him: If so, if one hangs a

(4) I.e., the corona, by splitting the membrane and pulling it down.—He did not perform the *peri'ah*. V. *supra* 133a. (5) To cause his bowels to function.

a (1) Lit., 'he appears and does not appear'. Samuel maintains that unless it is fully visible he must be circumcised, whereas the Baraitha teaches that only where it is quite invisible is recircumcision required. (2) Rashi refers this to Isaac; Tosaf. to Abraham. (3) Jer. XXXIII, 25.

b (1) The emphasis on the extreme importance of circumcision was probably meant to counteract the early Christian teaching, which abrogated circumcision entirely in order to attract converts; v. Weiss, *Dor*, II, 9. It is perhaps noteworthy that in the present passage it is precisely in connection with proselytes and slaves that this is so much emphasized.

c (1) When a strainer is 'suspended', i.e., set over the vessel which receives the liquid, a 'tent' is technically made, in that the strainer covers the vessel like the top of a tent cover and protects that which is beneath it. R. Eliezer permits this on Festivals but not on the Sabbath. Again, when the liquid, e.g., wine, is poured through the strainer, the lees are separated from the wine; nevertheless he does not regard this as 'selecting' (v. *supra* 73a) and permits it on the Sabbath. A cloth strainer is probably meant; v. *T.A.* II, p. 243. (2) As he does permit it in the Mishnah. (3) This means that R. Eliezer forbids even adding to a temporary tent.

d (1) V. *supra* 60b, n. 8. (2) The suspending of a strainer falls within this category. (3) For he permits it even in the latter case.

pitcher on a peg, is he too liable?[4] [138a] Rather said Abaye: It is [forbidden] by Rabbinical law, in order that one should not act in the very way he acts on weekdays.

Abaye collected some general principles of Baraithas, and he recited: One must not stretch out a leather bag,[5] a strainer, a canopy,[6] or a camp chair;[7] and if he does he is not culpable, but it is forbidden. One must not make a permanent tent, and if he does he is liable to a sin-offering. But a bed, chair, three-legged stool, and a footstool may be set up at the very outset.[8]

NOR POUR [WINE] THROUGH A SUSPENDED [STRAINER] ON THE SABBATH. The scholars asked: What if one does strain [wine]? —R. Kahana said: If one strains he incurs a sin-offering. R. Shesheth demurred: Is there aught for which the Rabbis impose a sin-offering whereas R. Eliezer permits it at the very outset? To this R. Joseph demurred: Why not? Surely there is a 'golden city',[9] where R. Meir imposes a sin-offering, while R. Eliezer gives permission at the very outset. What is this? For it was taught: A woman must not go out with a 'golden city', and if she does go out, she is liable to a sin-offering: this is R. Meir's view: but the Sages rule: She may not go out [with it], yet if she goes out she is not culpable. R. Eliezer maintained: A woman may go out with a 'golden city' at the very outset!—Said Abaye to him, Do you think that R. Eliezer refers to R. Meir, who rules that she is liable to a sin-offering? He refers to the Rabbis, who maintain that there is no culpability, though it is forbidden; whereupon

a he said to them, It is permitted at the very outset.[1]

On what grounds is he warned?[2]—Rabbah said: On the grounds of selecting;[3] R. Zera said: On the score of sifting.[4] Rabbah said, Reason supports my view: What is usual in selecting? One takes the edible matter and leaves the refuse, so here too he takes the edible [the wine] and leaves the refuse. R. Zera said, Reason supports my view: what is usual in sifting? The refuse [remains] on top whilst the edible matter [falls] below, so here too,—the refuse [remains] on top whilst the edible matter [drops] below.

Rami b. Ezekiel recited: One must not spread a doubled-over sheet;[5] yet if he does he is not culpable,[6] but it is forbidden. If a thread or a cord was wound about it,[7] it may be spread at the very outset. R. Kahana asked Rab: What about a canopy?[8] A bed too is forbidden. What about a bed? A canopy too is permitted, he replied. What about a canopy and a bed? A canopy is forbidden, replied he, while a bed is permitted. Yet there are no contradictions: when he said, A bed too is forbidden, [he meant

b one] like that used by the Carmanians.[1] When he said to him, A canopy too is permitted, [he referred to] one like Rami b. Ezekiel['s].[2] A canopy is forbidden while a bed is permitted refers to one like ours.[3] R. Joseph said: I saw the canopy beds of R. Huna's house stretched out at night and thrown down in the morning.[4]

Rab said in R. Ḥiyya's name: A [door] curtain may be hung up and taken down.[5] And Samuel said in R. Ḥiyya's name: [138b]

(4) Surely not. Here too it is not a real building and is forbidden by Rabbinical law only. (5) *Gud* is a broad leather bag into which wine or milk was poured. It was stretched out at night tent-wise for the liquid to cool in the night air. (6) Rashi: whose top is a handbreadth in width. Alfasi and Maim.: whose top is less than a handbreadth in width. (7) Jast. Tosaf.: a framework over which the leather seat was stretched; this is like the making of a tent. (8) If they have fallen. The covers or tops of these are *permanently* spread, so no 'tent' is made. (9) This was a kind of ornamental headdress containing a picture of Jerusalem; v. *supra* 59*b*.

(1) Abaye's reasoning is difficult to follow unless he means that R. Eliezer was altogether ignorant of R. Meir's view (Tosaf. and marginal Gloss.). (2) A deliberate offence is not punishable unless the transgressor is previously warned that his proposed action is forbidden on such and such a score; in the case of the violation of the Sabbath he must be advised under what category of labour his action is prohibited. The selection here is in regard to the straining of wine. (3) He is warned that straining is tantamount to selecting. (4) V. *supra* 73*a* for these two labours. (5) Tent-wise over a pole, the ends being fastened to the ground, so that the whole forms a tent under which he can lie (R. Ḥan.). (6) Because the top or roof of this improvised tent is less than a handbreadth in width. (7) The sheet was already on the pole from before the Sabbath, and a thread or cord was attached thereto by means of which it might be pulled down. When it is pulled down one merely adds to a temporary or improvised tent, and this Baraitha permits it. (8) V. *supra* n. 6.

b (1) Inhabitants of Carmania, a province of the ancient Persian empire, with the capital Carmana. Others: a frame used by vendors of linen garments. On both translations the frameworks were such that they were taken apart and then set up; this constitutes a forbidden labour. (2) I.e., one about which a cord was wound, and which he permits in this passage. (3) V. *supra* n. 8. (4) Which shows that they may be taken apart—he was speaking of the Sabbath—and in the same way they may be set up. (5) It is not a 'tent', since it has no roof.

אלא אמר אביי **מדרבנן היא שלא יעשה כדרך שהוא עושה בחול מנקיט אביי חומרי מתניתא ותני [ב]הגוד והמשמרת כילה וכסא גלין לא יעשה ואם עשה פטור אבל אסור [ג]אהלי קבע לא יעשה ואם עשה חייב חטאת [ד]אבל מטה וכסא טרסקל ואסלא מותר לנטותן לכתחילה: ואין נותנין לתלויה בשבת: איבעיא להו שימר מאי אמר רב כהנא [ה]שימר חייב חטאת מתקיף לה רב ששת מי איכא מידי דרבנן מחייבי חטאת ורבי אליעזר שרי לכתחילה מתקיף לה רב יוסף אלמה לא הרי עיר של זהב דר"מ מחייב חטאת ורבי אליעזר שרי לכתחילה מאי היא °דתניא *לא תצא אשה בעיר של זהב ואם יצאה חייבת חטאת דברי ר"מ וחכמים אומרים לא תצא ואם יצאה פטורה *ר"א אומר יוצאה אשה בעיר של זהב לכתחילה א"ל אביי מי סברת ר"א אדר"מ קאי דאמר חייבת חטאת אדרבנן קאי דאמרי פטור אבל אסור ואמר להו איהו מותר לכתחילה *[ו]משום מאי מתרינן ביה רבה אמר משום בורר רבי זירא אמר משום מרקד אמר רבה כוותי דידי מסתברא מה דרכו של בורר נוטל אוכל ומניח הפסולת אף הכא נמי נוטל את האוכל ומניח את הפסולת אמר ר' זירא כוותי דידי מסתברא מה דרכו של מרקד פסולת מלמעלה ואוכל מלמטה אף הכא נמי פסולת מלמעלה ואוכל מלמטה תני רמי בר יחזקאל [ז]טלית כפולה לא יעשה ואם עשה פטור אבל אסור היה כרוך עליה חוט או משיחה מותר לנטותה לכתחילה בעא מיניה רב כהנא מרב כילה מהו א"ל אף מטה אסורה מטה מהו א"ל אף כילה מותרת כילה ומטה מהו א"ל כילה אסורה ומטה מותרת ולא קשיא הא דקאמר אף מטה אסורה בדקרמנאי הא דקאמר ליה אף כילה מותרת כדרמי בר יחזקאל כילה אסורה ומטה מותרת כדדידן אמר רב יוסף חזינא להו לכילי דבי רב הונא דמאורתא נגידו ומצפרא חביטא רמיא *אמר רב משום רבי חייא [ח]וילון מותר לנטותו ומותר לפורקו ואמר שמואל משום רבי חייא (עירובין קב:)

בילת

רש"י

אלא אמר אביי מדרבנן. קאסרי לה חכמים דמתניתין דלא שבקינן ליה למיתליה למיעבד עובדא דחול: מנקיט. מלקיט: חומרי מתנייתא. כללות של ברייתות: חומר קשר כלומר כללות שמלא בברייתות בגוד לבדה ובמשמרת לבדה ובכילה לבדה ובכסא גלין לבדה ושכאן כולן הפטורין אבל אסורין בחומר אחד והמותרים לכתחילה בחומר אחד: הגוד. הוא עור של בהמה תפור ופיו רחב מאד ויש לו שנלים ועוברי דרכים ממלאין אותו יין או חלב במקום שתוקעין שם אהליהם ללון ושוטחין אותו ופיו מתוח ע"ג יתידות והרוח עוברת מתחתיו ומלטכן שלא יתקלקל היין והוי דומה לאהל לאחר שנמתח: כילה. שיש [א] בגגה טפח: וכסא גלין. כמו מטה גללניתא דכירה (לעיל דף מז:) והוא שם מקום ומפרקין מטותיהן וכסאותן וטוענין אותן עמהן וחוזרין ומחזירין אותן: לא יעשה. דאהל ערלי ניכהו וכסא גלין נמי גזרה שמא יתקע בחוזק: אבל מטה. שלנו המחוברת ועומדת אם היתה זקופה או מוטה על לדיה מותר לנטותה לישבה על רגליה ואע"ג דהשתא עביד אהל שרי דלא מידי עביד אלא ליתובא בעלמא: כסא טרסקל. כך שמו ובלעז פלודסטויי"ל ועליונו של עור ומקפלין אותו וכשמסלקין אותו סומכין אותו לכותל וכשרוצה לישב עליו נוטהו ויושב על ד' רגלים: ואסלא. עשוי כעין כסא טרסקל אבל עור הפרוש עליו נקוב לבית הכסא מותר לנטותו לכתחילה דהא עביד וקאי: שימר. נתן שמרים לתלויה וסינן: חייבת חטאת. דלאו תכשיט הוא אלא משוי: פטור. דתכשיט הוא ולכתחילה אסור דילמא שלפא ומחויא: יוצאה אשה. דמאן דרכה למיפק בעיר של זהב אשה חשובה ואשה חשובה לא שלפא ומחויא: משום מאי מתרינן ביה. למשמר: משום בורר. דהאי נמי בורר הוא: כוותי דידי מסתברא. דאי אתרו ביה משום בורר התראה היא: דנוטל אוכל ומניח פסולת. *ולרבא ה"ה נמי דאי אתרו ביה משום מרקד הויא התראה אבל לרבי זירא אי אתרו ביה משום בורר לאו התראה היא דלא דמי לבורר שהאוכל למטה ופסולת למעלה מה שאין כן בבורר קטנית שהפסולת למטה: טלית כפולה לא יעשה. לשטוח טליתו על גבי ארבע יתידות ליסן תחתיה וראשיו מתכפלין לכאן ולכאן לגד הארץ והויא ליה לכתלים להגן מן החמה דהוי אהלא: כרוך עליה. מבעוד יום: חוט או משיחה. ונתנה על הגס שעל הקנוף כשהיא מכופלת וכרך עליה חוט למשכה בו לפורסה לכאן ולכאן מותר למושכה בו בשבת דמוסיף על אהל עראי הוא ואינו כעושה לכתחילה: כדקרמנאי. היינו גללניתא* שפורקה ומחזירה והוא שם מקום לשון אחר קרמנאי מוכרי בגדי פשתן מוכרין עליהן: כדרמי. כרך עליה חוט: כדדידן. מטה שהיתה זקופה והוא מושיבה על רגליה: דמאורתא נגידו ומלפרא חביטא. בלילי שבת ראיתים פרוסות ולבקר ראיתים מושלכים לארץ אלמא מותר לפורקה וה"נ מותר לנטותה: וילון. מסך שכנגד הפתח: מותר לנטותו. שאין אהל אלא מי שעשוי כעין גג:

כילת

תוספות

אלא אמר אביי מדרבנן. ואף על גב דתלא כוזא בסיכתא אפילו איסור דרבנן ליכא במילי דרבנן שייך שפיר לחלק אבל אי במשמרת מדאורייתא אסור אין שייך לחלק. מ"ר: כסא גלין. לא כפי' הקונטרס מטה גללניתא דשלהי כירה ואסור משום שמא יתקע דכולה שמעתא איירי באיסור אהל אלא היינו [כעין] מטה שפורסין עליה עור ואסור משום אהל כשמושיב תחילה המטה ואחר כך פורס העור דהוי ממטה למעלה ואסור כדאיתא בכילה בפ' המביא כדי יין (ד' לג:) דפוריא אסור מלמטה למעלה. מ"ר: כסא טרסקל. יש בהן עור וכשרוצה לישב עליו נוטה העור ויושב על ד' רגלים כדפירש בקונטר' וכגון שהוא קבוע בכסא דאם לא כן היה אסור לנטותו כדאמר בפ' המביא (שם דף לג:) אמר רב יהודה האי מדורתא מלמעלה למטה שרי פירוש כשטוכין עצים מכאן ומכאן ונותנין עליהם עצים ארוכים ארכן לרחב של אלו ובמביא תחילה עצים שטותן למעלה ואחרי כן עצים שמכאן ומכאן אינו כן דרך עשיית אהל לעשות הגג תחילה ואחריו הדפנות ושרי וכה"ג קרי מלמעלה למטה מלמטה למעלה אסור וכן ביעתא פירוש כשטותנין ביצים ע"ג האסכלא שקורין גרדיי"ל וכשנותנין הביצים תחילה ואוחז בהן בידו עד שמביא הכלי תחתיהן שרי דהיינו מלמעלה למטה וכן קידרא שמושיבה על שתי חביות שלריך לאוחזה בידו ואחר כך לסדר תחתיה החביות וכן חביתא חביות שמסדרין באולר ומושיבין אחת על גבי שתים וכן פוריא לפרוס העור תחילה באויר ואח"כ להביא המטה תחתיו ומיהו יש לפרש הך דשמעתא באינו קשור ומיירי כגון שעושה מלמעלה למטה אבל משמע דבכל ענין מיירי. מ"ר. וכל הנהו דאסרינן בבילה אומר ר"ת דדווקא דברים שיש להם מחילה עד לארץ אבל להושיב הקדרה על טרפיד בי"ט שרי אפילו מלמטה למעלה להביא הטרפיד תחילה ואחר כך להושיב הקדרה וכן להושיב השולחן על גבי ספסלין וביעתא וקידרא וחביתא ופוריא י"ל שיש להם מחילה. מ"ר: מי סברת דר' אליעזר קאי אדר"מ כו'. °לא ידע רבי מאי קמשני*): מה דרכו של בורר. לא תקשה אההיא דשילהי כלל גדול (לעיל דף עד.) כמו שפי' שם (בד"ה בורר ואוכל): כרך עליה חוט או משיחה מותר לנטותה. כגון ששייר בה טפח דבענין אחר לא הוה שרי כדאשכחן בפרק בתרא דעירובין (דף קב.) כרוך בודיא ושייר בה טפח למחר פושטה דמוסיף על אהל עראי הוא אי נמי כריכת חוט או משיחה מועלת בלא שייר בה טפח: בעא מיניה רב כהנא מרב כו'. ונראה לר"י ששאל לו סתם בכל כילות אם הם מותרות אמר ליה אפילו מטה יש מהן שאסורות הדר בעא אם כל מטות אסורות אמר ליה אף כילות מותרות אמר ליה כיון שאין אתה מחלק בשניהם מהו להשוותן כילה ומטה ובמקום שאסור בזה כנגדו אסור בזה א"ל כילה אסורה ומטה מותרת וכן יש לפרש ההיא דפרק אלו טרפות (חולין דף נג.) יש דרוסה לחתול א"ל אף לחולדה יש דרוסה לחולדה א"ל אף לחתול אין דרוסה לחתול ולחולדה יש דרוסה או אין להם דרוסה א"ל לחתול יש דרוסה ולחולדה אין דרוסה ומפרש התם דבגדיים וטלאים יש דרוסה לחתול ולא לחולדה ובאימרי רברבי אין דרוסה אפילו לחתול ובעופות יש דרוסה אפילו לחולדה ויש ליישב כעין שפירש הר"ר ילחק בן ר"מ (פי') התם שכששיה עוסק באימרי שאלו אם יש דרוסה לחולדה וכן כולם. מ"ר: אף כילה מותרת כדרמי בר יחזקאל. הוה מצי למימר כי ההיא דשניטו בסמוך לכילי דבי רב הונא וי"ל כדרמי בר יחזקאל הוו:

*) [נ"ל פירושו דאף אם לא קאי אר"מ מ"מ הדבר תמוה איך יחלקו בסברות רחוקות כ"כ אם לא שלא ידע ר"א מסברת ר"מ כלום וזהו כוונת התוס']

שאין

עין משפט נר מצוה

ב א ב מיי' פכ"א מהל' שבת הלכה יז ופכ"ב שם הלכה כח סמג לאוין סה טוש"ע א"ח סימן שטו סעיף ג ד ו : ג נ מיי' פכ"ב שם הלכה כו :
ד ד מיי' שם הלכה כח סמג שם טוש"ע שם סעיף ה :
ה ה מיי' פ"ח מהל' שבת הלכה יד סמג שם.
ו ו מיי' שם הלכה יא ופכ"א הלכה יז סמג שם:
ז ז ח מיי' פכ"ב מהל' שבת הלכה כט סמג שם טוש"ע א"ח סי' שטו סעיף י :

רבינו חננאל

הלכה כר' אליעזר: מתני' וחכ"א אין תולין את המשמרת ביו"ט. איבעיא לן תלא מאי וסליקא חיובא מדרבנן (ובלבד)שלא יעש' כדרך שהוא עושה בחול. מנקיט אביי חומרי מתנייתא ותני הגוד והמשמרת כילה וכסא [גלין] לא יעשה ואם עשה פטור אבל אסור כלומר איסורא דרבנן. אהל קבוע לא יעשה ואם עשה חייב חטאת אבל המטה והכסא והטרסקל והאסלא מותר לנטותו בתחלה. פי' משמרת הא דאמרן והיא מסננת של יין. גוד הוא חמת מים. בלולב [וערבה] (הגזול)(דף מח) משכיה דההוא גברא דעבדיע ליה נודא. ומלינן ביה מיא והולכי דרכים נועצים יתידות בארץ וקושרין (אחת) [אותו] זה בחוטין עבין ותולין אותו באלו היתידות להצטנן מימיו. כילה שיש בגגה טפח כסא גלין הוא של חוליות. טוענין עליו קרשים ויושבין עליו וכשעומדין פורקין אותו מטה כגון הא דידן ולא ברירא לן מלאכתה אלא דברים מוכיחין שהיא מטה (גיליתא) [גללניתא]. והכרעים שמחזיר רפויין הן ולפיכך היא מותרת כדאמרינן (לעיל מז ע"ב) אם היה רפוי מותר. ולגבה היא עשויה במסמרים והיא זקופה ומרביצה לישן עליה הואיל ולגבה עשויה אינה חשובה כאהל וכן כסא לשבת בו וזה שאמר גורר אדם מטה וכסא וספסל שלשתן טעם אחד הן. טרסקל הוא קערה פשוטה כגון שלחן קטן וכדתניא ר' יוסי בר' יהודה נעץ קנה ברה"ר והניח בראשו טרסקל וזרק ונח על גביו גם זה לגביו עשוי לאכול בו. או לתת בו חפצים. אסלא הוא ספסל של ברזל. דתנן האסלא טמא המדרס וטמא מת (פרשה) [ופירושו] היא טמאה מדרס. והברזל טמא טמא מת. וספסל זה של ברזל. ועליו עור נטוי לישב עליו. ותנן עור האסלא וחלל שלו מצטרפין לטפח ואמרינן בתחלת עירובין מאי עור אסלא אמר רבה בר בר חנה א"ר יוחנן עור אסלא עור כסא של בית הכסא והוא שאמרנו ספסל של ברזל נטוי עליו עור נקוב באמצע כשיעור סיס הן חסר הן יתר ויושב עליו אדם ותחתיו נרף כדי לקבל בו הרעי לפיכך נקרא עור כסא של בית הכסא אלו כולן מותר לנטותן בתחלה. ואין נותנין לתלויה בשבת ר' אליעזר דתני ונותנין לתלויה בשבת סבר מותר לשמר בתחלה בשבת וחכמים אוסרין ואיבעיא לן אליבא דרבנן שימר מאי ואמר רב כהנא חייב חטאת ופי' שימור בשוגג חייב חטאת דלא אשכחן במזיד בשבת חייב חטאת. אלא כל שהוא בשבת בשוגג חייב חטאת במזיד חייב מיתה ועל זה הטעם אמרו משום מאי מתרינן ביה רבה אמר משום בורר' ר' זירא אמר משום מרקד. סבר בורר ומרקד שניהן אבות מלאכות הן ובורר ומרקד כעין דבר אחד הן ולא נחלקו בשמותן אלא מפני שהיה במקדש ולמה (רבא) [רבה] ור' זירא אלא להודיעך שאם התרו בו משום מרקד אליבא דרבה אינו חייב וכן אליבא דר' זירא אם התרו בו משום בורר. והלכתא כר' זירא: תאני רמי בר יחזקאל טלית כפול לא יעשה ואם עשה פטור אבל אסור. פי' אדם שקפל טלית וקשרה בין ב' כתלים והדביק קצוות הטלית בארץ ונכנס לישן תחתיה בגגה כאמצע ושיפוע ויורדת למטה בארץ כמלוא קומת אדם ברוחב אהל עראי הוא. ומפני שאין בגגה טפח ולא בפחות משלשה לפיכך פטור אבל אסור. ואם היו עליה חוטין מאתמול ונטה אותה מותר. והא דבעי רב כהנא מרב כילה מהו א"ל אף מטה אסורה מכלל שגם כילה אסורה פי' מטה דקרמינא. היא מטה של פרסיים. ורב לטעמיה דאשכחינן בסוף כירה רב ושמואל דאמרי תרווייהו המחזיר מטה של פרסיים בשבת חייב חטאת ומסתברא דהאי מטה של פרסיים לא יתכן לו להחזירה אלא אם יתקע לפי שמלבנותיה וכרעיה דחוקין ואינן נשלבין אלא אם יתקע בהן וכיון שתקע בהן חייב כולה היא כילה שיש בגגה טפח או בפחות משלשה סמוך לגגה טפח. שמצינו באהלי טומאה טפח והנה נטה אהל

גליון הש"ס

גמ' דתניא לא תצא אשה. עיין סב ע"א: תוס' ד"ה מי סברת וכו' לא ידע. עיין לעיל קיח ע"ב תוד"ה אלו כיה ושם:

הגהות הגר"א

[א] רש"י ד"ה כילה שיש בגגה טפח. נ"ב אבל הרי"ף והרמב"ם כתבו דוקא שאין בגגה וכו' סמוך בגגה טפח :

[לקמן קמ.] — לעיל נט: תוספ' פ"ה — עדיות פ"ב מ"ז — [פי' תוס' לעיל נט: ד"ה משום ותוס' ב"ק ב. ד"ה ורבי אליעזר] — [צ"ל ולרבה] — [פי' לעיל מז:]

רב נסים גאון

פרק ר' אליעזר אומר תולין: אבל מטה כסא טרסקל ואסלא מותר לנטותן לכתחילה. משכחת לה בעירובין בפרק מבוי (דף י) מאי עור אסלא אמר רבה בר בר חנה אמר ר' יוחנן עור כסא של בית הכסא:

יש:הכנסו

ח א מיי' פכ"ב מהל' שבת הלכה לא טוש"ע א"ח סי' שטו סעיף יח:

ט ב ג מיי' פכ"ב מהל' שבת הלכה לא סמג שם טוש"ע א"ח סי' שטו סעיף מ:

י ד מיי' שם טוש"ע שם סעיף מא:

יא ה מיי' שם הלכה לב סמג שם טוש"ע א"ח סי' שטו סעיף יב:

יב ו מיי' פכ"ו שם הלכה ו סמג שם טוש"ע שם סי' שח סעיף טז:

יג ח מיי' פי"א מהל' שאר אבות הטומאות הלכה ב:

יד ט מיי' פ"ט מהל' טומאת מת הלכה ו ופי"ג מהל' כלים הלכה א ג:

*כילת חתנים מותר לנטותה ומותר לפורקה אמר רב ששת בריה דרב אידי *לא אמרן אלא שאין בגגה טפח אבל יש בגגה טפח אסורה וכי אין בגגה טפח נמי לא אמרן אלא שאין בפחות משלשה סמוך לגגה טפח אבל יש בפחות משלשה סמוך לגגה טפח אסור[א] ולא אמרן אלא שאין בשיפועה טפח אבל יש בשיפועה טפח *שפועי אהלים כאהלים דמו ולא אמרן אלא דלא נחית מפוריא טפח אבל נחית מפוריא טפח אסור: *ואמר רב ששת בריה דרב אידי האי סיאנא שרי והאיתמר סיאנא אסור לא קשיא הא דאית ביה טפח הא דלית ביה טפח אלא מעתה שרביב בגלימא טפח ה"נ *דמיחייב *אלא לא קשיא הא דמיהדק הא דלא מיהדק שלח ליה רמי בר יחזקאל לרב הונא אימא לן איזי הנך מילי מעלייתא דאמרת לן משמיה דרב תרתי בשבת וחדא בתורה שלח ליה הא דתניא גוד בכיסנא מותר לנטותה בשבת אמר רב לא שנו אלא בב' בני אדם אבל באדם אחד אסור אמר אביי וכילה אפילו בי' בני אדם אסור אי אפשר דלא מימתחא פורתא אידך מאי היא דתניא *)כירה שנשמטה אחת מירכותיה מותר לטלטלה שתים אסור רב אמר אפילו אחד נמי אסור גזירה שמא יתקע תורה דאמר רב עתידה תורה שתשתכח מישראל שנאמר °והפלא ה' את מכותך *הפלאה זו איני יודע מהו כשהוא אומר °לכן הנני יוסף להפליא את העם הזה הפלא ופלא הוי אומר הפלאה זו תורה ת"ר *כשנכנסו רבותינו לכרם ביבנה אמרו עתידה תורה שתשתכח מישראל שנאמר °הנה ימים באים נאם ה' אלהים והשלחתי רעב בארץ לא רעב ללחם ולא צמא למים כי אם לשמוע את דברי ה' וכתיב °ונעו מים עד ים ומצפון ועד מזרח ישוטטו לבקש את דבר ה' ולא ימצאו דבר ה' זו הלכה דבר ה' זה הקץ דבר ה' זו נבואה ומאי ישוטטו לבקש את דבר ה' אמרו עתידה אשה שתטול ככר של תרומה ותחזור בבתי כנסיות ובבתי מדרשות לידע אם טמאה היא ואם טהורה היא ואין מבין אם טהורה היא ואם טמאה היא בהדיא כתיב ביה °מכל האוכל אשר יאכל אלא לידע אם ראשונה היא ואם שניה היא ואין מבין °הא נמי מתניתין היא כדתנן *השרץ שנמצא בתנור הפת שבתוכו שניה שהתנור תחילה מספקא להו הא דאמר ליה רב אדא בר אהבה לרבא ליחזייה האי תנורא כמאן דמלי טומאה ותיהוי פת ראשונה א"ל לא אמרינן ליחזייה האי תנורא כמאן דמלי טומאה *דתניא יכול יהו כל הכלים מיטמאין באויר כלי חרס ת"ל כל אשר בתוכו יטמא מכל האוכל אשר יאכל °אוכלין (א) מטמאין באויר כלי חרס ואין כלים מטמאין באויר כלי חרס תניא רבי שמעון בן יוחי אומר חס ושלום שתשתכח תורה מישראל שנאמר °כי לא תשכח מפי זרעו אלא מה אני מקיים ישוטטו לבקש את דבר ה' ולא ימצאו שלא ימצאו

הלכה

*) [ערוך פי' כירה זו כלי מתכת הוא וכל זמן שתורת כלי עליה מותר לטלטלה לצורך מקומה לפיכך אם אחת מירכותיה נשמטה עדיין היא כלי שיכולה לעמוד בשלש אבל אם נטלו שתים בטלה מתורת כלי שאינה יכולה לעמוד בשתים]

תורה אור: דברים כח; ישעיה כט; עמוס ח; שם; ויקרא יא; דברים לא. פסחים כ: כלים פ"ח מ"ה

רש"י

כילת חתנים. לא דמיא לשאר כילות שאר כילות פרוסות על גבי קינוף שהיא לד' רגלים ויש לה גג דהוי אהל ושל חתנים על גבי נקליטין שאינם אלא שנים באמצעית המטה וקנה נתון עליהם והבגד נתון עליו ונופל לכאן ולכאן ואין לה גג טפח הלכך לאו אהל הוא: בפחות מג'. שהיא הולכת ומתפשטת למטה: ולא אמרן אלא שאין בשיפועה טפח. שאין כל לד ולד (ב) נפשט למטה להתרחק טפח מכנגד אמצעיתו דהיינו שאין ברחבו למטה טפחיים וכילת חתנים אינה עשויה ליסן תחתיה: אבל נחתא מפוריה טפח. ההוא טפח הוה קיר לאהל והמטה נעשית לו גג: כייאנא. כובע של לבד פלטר"ן: אסור. לצאת בו בשבת ולקמיה מפרש ואזיל: הא דאית ביה טפח. שהוא מתפשט להלן מראשו טפח אסור משום אהלא: אלא מעתה שרביב בגלימיה טפח. הניח טליתו על ראשו כדרך שהוא מתעטף (ג) והרחיקה להלן מראשו טפח: אלא. טעמא לאו משום אהל הוא אלא משום שלא יגביהנו הרוח מראשו ואתי לאתויי ארבע אמות הלכך מיהדק בראשו שפיר שרי לא מיהדק אסור: תרתי בשבת וחדא בתורה. שהיית רגיל לומר שני דברים משמו בהלכות שבת ואחת בתורה כדלקמן: גוד בכיסנא. גוד ברלועותיו ומונח על מקום קבוע שלו: מותר לנטותו בשבת. והא דאמרן לעיל פטור אבל אסור היכא דלא הוי מתוקן בכיסנין: בב' בני אדם. לא מימתח ליה שפיר: באדם אחד: ממתח ליה שפיר שמותחו על יתד זו וקושרו בה וחוזר ומותחו על זו וקושרו בה כך פירשו רבותי וכן מצאתי בתשובת הגאונים ואיני יודע מהו: אידך. דשבת מאי היא: מירכותיה. פטפוטים שלה כעין רגלים: שמא יתקע. כשמחבר לה הרגל יתקענה בחוזק והוי בונה אבל *(ת"ק) היכא דלא נשמטה אלא אחת לא חיים למתקע כולי האי: הפלא ופלא. סיפא דקרא ואבדה חכמת חכמיו: בכרם. על שם שהיו יושבין שורות שורות ככרם: זו הלכה. כדכתיב (דברים ה) [להגיד לכם] את דבר ה' דהייתו תורה: זו נבואה. לדכתיב (הושע א) דבר ה' אשר היה אל הושע וגו': זה הקץ. °לא ידענא מהיכא: בהדיא כתיב. ותורה שבכתב הרי כתובה ומונחת יקראו ויראו: שהתנור תחלה. שנטמא מן האויר כדכתיב (ויקרא יא) אל תוכו והוא חוזר ומטמא אוכלין שבתוכו מן האויר: כמאן דמלי טומאה. כשנפל השרץ באוירו דהא בלא נגיעה מטמא והלכך כמאן דמלי טומאה הוא ותהוי פת ראשונה: לא ס"ד. למיהוי כמאן דמלי טומאה: דתניא יכול יהו כל הכלים טמאים מאויר כלי חרס. שאם היה כלי אחר בתוכו שיטמא מחמת השרץ שבאויר החיצון או מחמת שיטמאנו אויר כלי החיצון שהוא טמא: תלמוד לומר כל אשר בתוכו יטמא. וסמיך ליה מכל האוכל אשר יאכל: אוכלין ומשקין שבתוכו טמאים ולא כלים שמע מינה תרתי חדא דלא אמרינן חזייה כמאן דמלי טומאה דאם כן אם כלי שטף הוא הפנימי שמטמא מגבו יהא טמא דהא נגע בטומאה אלא לא אמרינן חזייה כמאן דמלי טומאה ואוכלין ומשקין שבחילון הוא דמטמאי מחמת הכלי שהכלי ראשון והם שניים אבל כלים לא דהוא"ל דאין טומאה זו באה אלא מחמת הכלי אשמעינן האי קרא שאין כלי שאינו אב הטומאה מטמא כלי:

תוספות

שאין בשיפועה טפח. הרבה יש תימה (ד) איך יתכן זה דא"כ למה הוא ראוי אם לכל השיפוע אין טפח ויש לפרש כגון שהסדין שפרוס על הכילה מונח על גבי קנים מרובים ולא פשטו הסדין היטב ומונח ונופל בין קנה לקנה כעין שורות דיש עכשיו בין כל קנה שיפוע ואין באותו שיפוע טפח ודוחק וי"מ שאין בשיפוע טפח בגובה י' דכשילא השיפוע טפח אין משם עד למטה גובה י' דלא חשיב אהל כדאשכחן בפ"ק דסוכה (דף י:) דבכילה כי הך מותר ליסן בסוכה דאמר רב יהודה אמר שמואל מותר ליסן בכילת חתנים אע"פ שיש לה גג והוא שאינה י' טפחים ואין נראה לר"י דודאי כהי דגבי סוכה לא חשיב אהל וכן לגבי ק"ש כדאיתא התם (דף י:) מיהו לגבי שבת חשיב ואסירי שהרי משמרת וביעתא וקידרא וחביתא אסירי משום אהל ולא משמע שיש בגובהן י' טפחים. מ"ר. ועוד קשה מדלקמן גבי כפיפה מצרית ובשם רבינו שמואל פי' דל"ג להאי לישנא כלל שיפועי אהלים כאהלים דמו דבסוף פ"ק דסוכה (דף יט:) מסקינן דשיפוע אהלים לאו כאהלים דמו ואי משום הא לא איריא דיש לפרש דהתם באין בשיפועו טפח והכא כשיש בשיפועו טפח:

הא דמהדק. פירש ר"ח שאינו נכפף דאז נראה כעין אהל דלא מהדק שהוא נכפף ואז אין נראה כעין אהל:

דבר ה' זה הקץ. דכתיב גבי גלות שבעים לכלות דבר ה' מפי ירמיה (עזרא א). מ"ר:

ולישלח

רבינו חננאל

קבוע וחייב חטאת במטה של פרסיים כדאמרן תוב בעא מיניה כילה מהו וא"ל אף מטה מותרת מכלל ששתיהן מותרות כילה שאין בגגה טפח ויש עליה חוטין קשורין מאתמול והוא כגון הטלית שאמר רמי בר יחזקאל ומטה היא גליתא מטה שהמחזירה אין צריך לתקע שלבנותיה וכרעיה אינן דוחקות וברפיון נכנסין ויוצאין. תוב בעא מיניה כילה ומטה מהו. א"ל כילה אסורה ומטה מותרת. פי' כילה אסורה שיש בגגה טפח. ומטה מותרת כדידן. והיא מטה גליתא שהיו מחזירין אותה בשבת בבית רב חמא ומפורש בסוף פרק כירה. והני כילי דבי רב הונא ודבי רב פפא ורב הונא בריה דרב יהושע דהוו מאורתא נגידין ובצפרא חביטא רמיין. יש מי שאומרים משלבות היו בארץ שאסור לטלטלן בשבת ואנו קבלנו מרבותינו כי נטויות היו מע"ש ומשוכות למעלה כמין כפולות ובבקר הי' משפיעין ומשרבבין אותן למטה ונמצאו מוסיפין כחכמים שחולקין על ר' אליעזר ואומרים מוסיפין באהלי עראי בשבת ואין צ"ל ביו"ט וכדאמרינן בהמוצא תפילין הנהו דיכרי דהוו בי רב הונא דביממא בעי טולא ובליליא בעו אוירא אתו לקמיה דרב א"ל זיל כרוך (פוריא) [בודיא] ושייר בה טפח ולמחר פושטה דמוסיף על אהל עראי הוא ושפיר דמי. ובתרה א' הא שמעתא דשמואל כילת חתנים וכו' שמעינן מינה דכולהו חד טעמא אינון אמר רב משום ר' חייא וילון פי' פרוכת מותר לנטותו ומותר לפרקו וזה בזמן שכרוכין עליו ב' חוטין או משיחות דלא גרע מטלית כפולה כילת חתנים כדאמרן שאין בגגה טפח ולא בפחות מג' סמוך לגגה טפח וגם אינה יורדת למטה מן המטה טפח. צ"ע שכעין שמועה זו בפרק מי שהוציאוהו נוים: גמ' פעם אחת לא נכנסו לנמל עד שהשכחת ונתקשה בעינינו הדבר מכמה פנים וכולן נכוחים למבין. ועוד מפני מה כשנתפרקו אפי' על הארץ למה מניחין אותן ובין לצורך גופן ובין לצורך מקומן שרי. ואנו פירשנו מה שקבלנו. ולפי שהוא מלאכת שמים הזכרנו דברים ודברי זולתנו שאמרו מוטלות ומושלכות לארץ היו לא כתבנו הפירכא שעל הדברים הללו. וראינו סיוע על הטעם שהזכרנו כי קבלנוהו ומניין של דברים הללו בפרק המוצא תפילין שנורות רבותינו בענין תוספת אהלים. כלומר טעם אחד הן. ולולי כן הקושיא היה מקשה מהן: סיינא. כובע שמשמשין בני אדם בראשיהן יוצא כמין פסל מן הראש כשיעור טפח הן יתר. ואנן ראינוהו פעמים רבות ועושין אותו להאהל על הפנים שלא יכם השמש. וכשהוא מהודק ביותר ואינו נכפף כבגד חשוב כאהל ואסור: הא דתנן גוד בכיסנא מותר פי' חמת שיש עליה חוטין או משיחות קשורין מצדדיה מותר לנטותה בשבת באותן היתידות המוכנין לה. אמר רב בשני בני אדם מותר אבל באדם אחד אסור. כי צריך לתת חוטי הצד האחד ולפיכך אסור שנמצא נוטה אהל. וזה שאמר אביי בכילה שיש בגגה טפח שאסור לנטותה בשבת אפילו בעשרה בני אדם אי אפשר דלא מימתחא ביה פורתא פשוטה היא. והא דתניא כירה שנשמטה אחת מירכותיה מותר לטלטלה ב' אסור לטלטלה. כירה זו כלי מתכות היא וכל זמן שתורת כלי עליה מותר לטלטלה לצורך מקומה. לפיכך אם נשלה אחת מירכותיה עדיין כלי היא שיכולה לעמוד בג' אבל אם ניטלו ב' בטלה מתורת כלי שאינה יכולה לעמוד בשתים. רב אמר אפילו אחת אם ניטלה אסור לטלטלה שמא יתקע והלכתא כרב: אמר רב עתידה תורה שתשתכח מישראל שנאמר והפלא ה' את מכותך וגו' ושאר השמועה פשוטה היא. והא דרב אדא בר אהבא דאמר ליה לרבא ליחזייה לתנור כמאן דמלי טומאה

רב נסים גאון

כשנכנסו רבותינו לכרם ביבנה. כבר פירשו בברכות בגמ' דבני מערבא וכי כרם שם אלא אלו תלמידי חכמים שהם עשוים שורות שורות ככרם:

עירובין קב: ע"ש לעיל מט: ע"ש
[סוכה יט:]
עירובין קב: וסם
[תמורה ג: מכות יג: ע"ש]
[תוספ' עדיות פ"א]
עיין רש"ל

הגהות הב"ח

(א) גמ' אוכלין ומשקין מט': (ב) רש"י ד"ה ולא אמרן כו' לד ולד נתפשט למטה: (ג) ד"ה אלא מעתה וכו' מתעטף כה על ראשו והרחיקה: (ד) תוס' ד"ה שאין וכו' תימה. נ"ב ובעירובין דף קב תירץ רש"י על כל קושיא כאן תירוץ שכתבו התוס' כאן:

הגהות הגר"א

[א] גמ' (ולא אמרן אלא שאין בשיפועה טפח אבל יש בשיפועה טפח שפועי אהלים כאהלים דמו) הא"מ ונ"ב הרמב"ם ז"ל לה (ועמ"ש רבינו בא"ח סי' שטו סעיף כא):

גליון הש"ס

גמ' הא נמי מתני' היא. עי' חולין קי ע"א תוד"ה דתנן הכבד: רש"י ד"ה זה הקן. עי' ברכות כה ע"ב רש"י ד"ה מאן שמעת ליה וש"נ:

A bridal bed may be set up and it may be dismantled.[6] R. Shesheth son of R. Idi said: That was said only where its roof is not a handbreadth [in width],[7] but if its roof is a handbreadth, it is forbidden. And even if the roof is not a handbreadth, this was said only where there is not [the width of] a handbreadth within three [handbreadths] from the top; but if there is a handbreadth within three from the top, it is forbidden. And this is said only if its slope is less than a handbreadth, but if its slope is a handbreadth, the slopes of tents are as tents.[8] And it was said only if it does not descend a handbreadth below the bed; but if it descends a handbreadth below the bed, it is forbidden.

R. Shesheth son of R. Idi also said: A peaked cap[9] is permitted. But it was stated: A peaked cap is forbidden?—There is no diffi-
a culty: in the one case it is a handbreadth [in size];[1] in the other it is not a handbreadth. If so, if one lets his cloak protrude a handbreadth,[2] is he too culpable?[3]—Rather [say] there is no difficulty: here it is tightly fitted [on his head]; there it is not tightly fitted.[4]

Rami b. Ezekiel sent to R. Huna: Tell us, pray, those well-favoured dicta which you told us [formerly] in Rab's name, two about the Sabbath and one about Torah. He sent [back] to him: As to what was taught, It is permitted to stretch the leather bag[5] by its thongs,[6] Rab said: They learnt this only of two men: but [if done] by one man, it is forbidden.[7] Abaye said: But a canopy, even [if stretched] by ten men, is forbidden, [for] it is impossible that it shall not be somewhat stretched.

What is the other [dictum]? For it was taught: If one of the shafts of a stove falls off, it [the stove] may be handled; if both [fall off], it may not be handled.[8] Rab said: Even if one [falls out] it is forbidden, lest he [re]fix it.[9]

'[And one about] Torah': for Rab said: The Torah is destined to be forgotten in Israel, because it is said, *Then the Lord will make thy plagues wonderful:*[10] now, I do not know what this wonder is, but when it is said, *Therefore, behold, I will proceed to do a wonderful work among this people, even a wonderful work and a wonder [and the wisdom of their wise men shall perish]*,[11] it follows that this wonder refers to Torah.

Our Rabbis taught: When our Masters entered the vineyard
b at Yabneh,[1] they said, The Torah is destined to be forgotten in Israel, as it is said, *Behold, the days come, saith the Lord God, that I will send a famine in the land, not a famine of bread, nor a thirst for water, but of hearing the words of the Lord.* And it is said, *And they shall wander from sea to sea, and from the north even to the east; they shall run to and fro to seek the word of the Lord, and shall not find it.*[2] '*The word of the Lord*' means *halachah*; '*the word of the Lord*' means 'The End';[3] '*the word of the Lord*' means prophecy. And what does '*they shall run to and fro to seek the word of the Lord*' mean? Said they, A woman is destined to take a loaf of *terumah* and go about in the synagogues and academies to know whether it is unclean or clean, and none will know[4] whether it is clean or unclean. But that is explicitly stated, *All food which may be eaten* [. . . *shall be unclean*]?[5] Rather to know whether it is a first degree or a second degree [of uncleanness],[6] and none will know. But that too is a Mishnah. For we learnt: If a [dead] creeping thing[7] is found in an oven, the bread within it is a second, because the oven is a first?[8]—They will be in doubt over what R. Adda b. Ahabah asked Raba: Let us regard this oven as though it were filled with uncleanness,[9] and let the bread be a first? He replied, We do not say, Let us regard this oven as though it were filled with uncleanness. For it was taught: You might think that all utensils become unclean in the air space of an earthen vessel: therefore it is stated, *whatsoever is in it shall be unclean . . . all food therein which may be eaten:* food and liquids become unclean in the air space of
c an earthen vessel.[1] It was taught, R. Simeon b. Yoḥai said: Heaven forfend that the Torah be forgotten in Israel, for it is said, *for it shall not be forgotten out of the mouths of their seed.*[2] Then how do I interpret, *they shall run to and fro to seek the word of the Lord, and shall*

(6) V. *supra* 138a, n. a6, also *T.A.* II, p. 457, n. 311, where it is understood as a sedan chair or litter. (7) It being spread over a very narrow pole. (8) Hence it is forbidden. By 'its slope' is meant the distance at the base from the vertical. Obviously such is unfit for use, and Rashi observes that a bridal bed was not for sleeping. This is unsatisfactory, and Tosaf. suggests other interpretations but rejects them too as equally unsatisfactory. V. 'Er. 102b, n. 15. (9) Jast.: A felt cap with a shade in front.

a (1) It may not be worn on the Sabbath, as it technically forms a tent. (2) He winds it about his head so as to protrude this distance. (3) Read with Asheri, 'is it too forbidden'? (4) Rashi: In the latter case a peaked cap is forbidden, not as a 'tent' but lest the wind blow it off and he come to carry it. (5) V. *supra* 138a, n. 5. (6) The interdict *supra a* is only where it is unprovided with thongs or straps. (7) Rashi: two men do not stretch it well; but one person is forced to tie one end to a stake, stretch it, and then tie the other end to another stake, whereby it becomes a tent. Rashi however is dissatisfied with this explanation and states that he does not understand it, nor are other commentators more satisfactory. (8) The shafts are the four feet upon which it stands. (9) Which is labour. But the first view is that it can stand well enough with one shaft missing to make this fear unlikely. (10) Deut. XXVIII, 59. (11) Isa. XXIX, 14.

b (1) Whither R. Joḥanan b. Zakkai transported or founded an academy after the destruction of the second Temple. 'Vineyard' is a metaphor for the academy, because the scholars sat in rows like vines, J. Ber. IV, 1. The time referred to here is probably that of the Hadrianic persecutions. (2) Amos VIII, 11f. (3) The designated time of redemption, when the Messiah will appear. Tosaf. finds the analogy for this interpretation in Ezra I. (4) Lit., 'understand'. (5) Lev. XI, 34. Surely the Written Law will be available. (6) V. *supra* 13b, n. b6. (7) *Sherez*, which defiles utensils and food. (8) The *sherez* touches the oven, which in turn touches the bread. The Rabbis could not imagine complete forgetfulness even of the Mishnah. (9) For immediately the *sherez* enters the air space of the oven, even before it actually touches it, it defiles, hence one should regard the *sherez* as though completely filling it.

c (1) But if the *sherez* were regarded as completely filling the oven, utensils therein too should be unclean, as though they touched the *sherez*, for direct contact therewith does defile them. Thus in the future it will be doubtful whose view, R. Adda b. Ahabah's or Raba's, is correct. (2) Deut. XXXI, 21.

not find it? They will not find [139*a*] a clear *halachah* or a clear Mishnah[3] in any place.[4]

It was taught, R. Jose b. Elisha said: If you see a generation overwhelmed by many troubles, go forth and examine the judges of Israel, for all retribution that comes to the world comes only on account of the judges of Israel, as it is said, *Hear this, I pray you, ye heads of the house of Jacob, and rulers of the house of Israel, that abhor judgment, and pervert all equity. They build up Zion with blood, and Jerusalem with iniquity. The heads thereof judge for reward, and the priests thereof teach for hire, and the prophets thereof divine for money; yet will they lean upon the Lord*, etc.[5] They are wicked, but they place their confidence in Him Who decreed, and the world came into existence.[6] Therefore the Holy One, blessed be He, will bring three punishments upon them answering to the three sins which they cultivate,[7] as it is said, *Therefore shall Zion for your sake be ploughed as a field, and Jerusalem shall become heaps, and the mountain of the house as the high places of a forest.*[8] And the Holy One, blessed be He, will not cause His Divine Presence to rest upon Israel until the wicked judges and officers cease out of Israel, for it is said, *And I will turn My hand upon thee, and thoroughly purge away thy dross, and will take away all thy tin. And I will restore thy judges as at the first, and thy counsellors as at the beginning*, etc.[9]

'Ulla said: Jerusalem shall be redeemed only by righteousness,[10] as it is written, *Zion shall be redeemed with judgment, and her converts with righteousness.*[1]

R. Papa said: When the haughty cease to exist [in Israel], the magi[2] shall cease [among the Persians]. When the judges cease to exist [in Israel], the *chiliarchi*[3] shall cease. 'When the haughty cease to exist [in Israel], the magi shall cease [among the Persians]'; as it is written, *And I will purely purge away thy haughty ones.*[4] When the judges cease to exist [in Israel], the *chiliarchi* shall cease; as it is written, *The Lord hath taken away thy judgments, He hath cast out thine enemy.*[5]

R. Melai[6] said in the name of R. Eleazar son of R. Simeon: What is meant by the verse, *The Lord hath broken the staff of the wicked, the sceptre of the rulers?*[7] '*The Lord hath broken the staff of the wicked*' refers to the judges who become a staff for their sheriffs;[8] '*the sceptre of the rulers*' refers to the scholars in the families of the judges.[9] Mar Zuṭra said: This refers to the scholars who teach the laws of the public[10] to ignorant judges.[11]

R. Eleazar b. Melai said in the name of Resh Laḳish: What is meant by the verse, *For your hands are defiled with blood, and your fingers with iniquity; your lips have spoken lies, your tongue muttereth wickedness?*[12] '*For your hands are defiled with blood*': this refers to the judges: '*and your fingers with iniquity*', to the judges' scribes;[13] '*your lips have spoken lies*'—to the advocates of the judges;[14] '*your tongue muttereth wickedness*'—to the litigants.

R. Melai also said in the name of R. Isaac of Magdala: From the day that Joseph departed from his brothers he did not taste wine, for it is written, [*The blessings of thy father ... shall be on the head of Joseph*], *And on the crown of the head of him who was a nazirite* [*since his*
b *departure*] *from his brethren.*[1] R. Jose b. R. Ḥanina said: They too did not taste wine, for it is written, *And they drank, and drank largely with him:*[2] which implies [that they did] not [drink] until then. And the other?[3]—There was no extensive drinking,[4] yet there was [moderate] drinking.[5]

R. Melai also said: As a reward for, *and when he seeth thee, he shall be glad in his heart,*[6] he was privileged to wear the breastplate of judgment upon his heart.

The citizens of Bashkar[7] sent [a question] to Levi: What about [setting up] a canopy [on the Sabbath]; what about cuscuta in a vineyard?[8] what about a dead man on a Festival?[9] By the time he [the messenger] arrived [at Levi's home] Levi had died. Said Samuel to R. Menashia, If you are wise, send them [an answer]. [So] he sent [word] to them: 'As for a canopy, we have examined it from all aspects and do not find any aspect by which it can be permitted'. But let him send them [a permissive ruling] in accordance with Rami b. Ezekiel?[10]—[He did not do this] because they were not learned in the law.[11] 'Cuscuta in a vineyard is a [forbidden] mixture'. But let him send them [a reply] in accordance with R. Tarfon. For it was taught: As for cuscuta, R. Tarfon maintains: It is not *kil'ayim*[12] in a vineyard; while the Sages rule: It is *kil'ayim* in a vineyard. And it is an established principle: The view of
c him who is lenient in respect to Palestine,[1] is *halachah* without Palestine?—[Likewise] because they were not learnt in the law. Rab announced: He who wishes to sow cuscuta in a vineyard, let him sow.[2] R. Amram the pious would ban [a person] for this. R. Mesharsheya would give a *peruṭah*[3] to a Gentile child to sow it for him.[4] Then let him give it to an Israelite child?—He would come to adhere [to this practice when he grew up]. Then let him give it to an adult Gentile?—He might come to substitute an Israelite for him.

As for a corpse, he sent [word to them]: Neither Jews nor Syrians [non-Jews] may occupy themselves with a corpse, neither on the first day of a Festival nor on the second.[5] But that is not so? For R. Judah b. Shilath said in R. Assi's name: Such a case happened in the synagogue of Ma'on[6] on a Festival near the

(3) I.e., an absolute and definite ruling, completely intelligible and not subject to controversy. (4) Lit., 'in one place'. I.e., in any of the places whither they shall wander (Maharsha). (5) Mic. III, 9-11. (6) This phrase is now liturgical. (7) Lit., 'which is in their hand'. (8) Ibid. 12. (9) Isa. I, 25f. (10) I.e., through the exercise of righteousness.
(1) Isa. I, 27. (2) The Guebres, who caused the Jews much suffering under the Sassanians, cf. Sanh., 74*b*, n. a6. (3) [גזירפטי (Pers. *Wezirpat*, a ruler, Funk, Schwarz, *Festschrift*, p. 432) the name of a class of oppressive Persian officers.] (4) Deriving סיגיך from סגי, great, haughty. (5) Zeph. III, 15. (6) MS. O.: Simlai. (7) Isa. XIV, 5. (8) They support their underlings in evil; or, support them in their refusal to summon the defendant to court or to enforce the court verdict unless they are well-paid for it (Rashi). (9) I.e., unfit judges appointed by the scholars of their family. (10) הלכות צבור. Probably laws concerning communal matters, the imposts of levies for communal and charitable purposes; v. Herzog, *The Main Institutions of Jewish Law*, Vol. 1, XXIII. (11) Rashi: the judges being appointed in reliance that these scholars would guide them in law, whereas they subsequently act of their own accord in many cases. (12) Isa. LIX, 3. (13) Who record verdicts falsely. (14) Rashi: who instruct the litigants how to plead. V. Aboth, I, 8, n. 1.

b (1) Gen. XLIX, 26. E.V.: '*of him that was separate from his brethren*'. A nazirite is forbidden wine, Num. VI, 2-3. (2) Gen. XLIII, 34. (3) R. Melai: why does he omit the brothers? (4) Lit., 'no drunkenness'. During the period of separation. (5) On the part of the brothers. (6) Ex. IV, 14—the reference is to Aaron. (7) Cas'kar, the chief town in the Mesene region, on the right bank of the old Tigris; directly opposite, on the left bank, lay Wasit, and the two are to some extent identified; v. Obermeyer, pp. 91-3. (8) Does it infringe the prohibition against divers plants being sown together? v. Deut. XXII, 9. (9) What arrangements are permissible for handling him, the funeral, etc. (10) Who permits its spreading when it is furnished with cords, v. *supra* 138*a*. (11) They would go still further. (12) V. Glos.

c (1) Lit., 'the land' *par excellence*. (2) V. Halevy, *Doroth*, I, 3, p. 137 (סט). (3) A small coin. (4) He agreed with Rab, nevertheless he did it in an unusual manner, so as not to encourage laxity. (5) Though the second is only a Rabbinical institution. (6) A town near Tiberias.

הלכה ברורה ומשנה ברורה במקום אחד: תניא רבי יוסי בן אלישע אומר אם ראית דור שצרות רבות באות עליו צא ובדוק בדייני ישראל *שכל פורענות שבאה לעולם לא באה אלא בשביל דייני ישראל שנאמר °שמעו נא זאת ראשי בית יעקב וקציני בית ישראל המתעבים משפט ואת כל הישרה יעקשו בונה ציון בדמים וירושלים בעולה ראשיה בשוחד ישפוטו וכהניה במחיר יורו ונביאיה בכסף יקסומו ועל ה' ישענו וגו' *רשעים הן אלא שתלו בטחונם במי שאמר והיה העולם לפיכך מביא הקב"ה עליהן ג' פורעניות כנגד ג' עבירות שבידם שנאמר °לכן בגללכם ציון שדה תחרש וירושלים עיין תהיה והר הבית לבמות יער *ואין הקב"ה משרה שכינתו על ישראל עד שיכלו שופטים ושוטרים רעים מישראל שנאמר °ואשיבה ידי עליך ואצרוף כבור סגיך ואסירה כל בדיליך ואשיבה שופטיך כבראשונה ויועציך כבתחלה וגו' *אמר עולא אין *ירושלים נפדה אלא בצדקה שנאמר °ציון במשפט תפדה ושביה בצדקה אמר רב פפא אי בטלי יהירי בטלי אמגושי אי בטלי דייני בטלי *גזירפטי אי בטלי יהירי בטלי אמגושי דכתיב ואצרוף כבור סגיך אי בטלי דייני בטלי גזירפטי דכתיב °הסיר ה' משפטיך פנה אויבך אמר רבי מלאי משום ר"א בר' שמעון מ"ד °שבר ה' מטה רשעים שבט מושלים שבר ה' מטה רשעים אלו הדיינין שנעשו מקל לחזניהם שבט מושלים אלו ת"ח שבמשפחות הדיינין מר זוטרא אמר אלו תלמידי חכמים שמלמדים הלכות ציבור לדייני בור אמר ר"א בן מלאי משום ר"ל מאי דכתיב °כי כפיכם נגואלו בדם ואצבעותיכם בעון שפתותיכם דברו שקר לשונכם עולה תהגה כי כפיכם נגואלו בדם אלו הדיינין ואצבעותיכם בעון אלו סופרי הדיינין שפתותיכם דברו שקר אלו עורכי הדיינין לשונכם עולה תהגה אלו בעלי דינין ואמר רבי מלאי משום ר' יצחק מגדלאה מיום שפירש יוסף מאחיו לא טעם טעם יין דכתיב °ולקדקד נזיר אחיו ר' יוסי בר' חנינא אמר אף הן לא טעמו טעם יין דכתיב °וישתו וישכרו עמו מכלל דעד האידנא לא (הוה שיכרות) ואידך שיכרות הוא דלא הוה שתיה מידהא הוה ואמר רבי מלאי בשכר °וראך ושמח בלבו זכה לחשן המשפט על לבו: שלחו ליה בני בשכר ללוי כילה מהו כשותא בכרמא מהו מת בי"ט מהו אדאזיל נח נפשיה דלוי אמר שמואל לרב מנשיא אי חכימת שלח להו כילה חזרנו על כל צידי כילה ולא מצינו לה צד היתר ולישלח להו כדרמי בר יחזקאל לפי שאינן בני תורה כשותא בכרמא עירבובא ולישלח להו כדר"ט דתניא *כישות ר' טרפון אומר אין כלאים בכרם וחכמים אומרים כלאים בכרם וקי"ל *כל המיקל בארץ הלכה כמותו בחו"ל לפי שאינן בני תורה מבריז רב האי מאן דבעי למיזרע כשותא בכרמא ליזרע רב עמרם חסידא מנגיד עילויה רב משרשיא יהיב ליה פרוטה לתינוק נכרי וזרע ליה וליתן ליה לתינוק ישראל אתי למיסרך וליתן ליה לגדול נכרי אתי לאיחלופי בישראל מת שלח להו מת לא יתעסקו ביה לא יהודאין ולא ארמאין לא ביום טוב ראשון ולא ביום טוב שני איני והאמר רבי יהודה בר שילת אמר רבי אסי עובדא הוה בבי כנישתא דמעון ביום טוב הסמוך לשבת ולא

רש"י

הלכה ברורה. בטעמים שלא יהא בה מחלוקת: ג' עבירות. בשחד ישפוטו במחיר יורו ונביאיה בכסף יקסמו: ג' פורעניות. שדה תחרש עיין תהיה ולבמות יער: ויועציך כבתחלה. ואחר כך יקרא לך עיר הצדק לשרות בה שכינה: אי בטלי יהירי. ישראל מתייהרים בבלורית ובמלבושי יהירות כפרסים הללו: בטלי אמגושי. יבטלו מסיתים ומדיחים המשניאים אותנו: סגיך. הם גסי הרוח שמגדלין עצמן לשון ישגה מאד (איוב ח) ואח"כ ואסירה כל בדיליך אלו אותם המבדילים שונאי ישראל מן הקב"ה בשקריהם ובפחזותם: בטלי דייני. רשעים מישראל שמטין דין: בטלי. מעל ישראל: גזירפטי. נוגשי שוטרי עובדי כוכבים: שנעשו מקל לחזניהם. לשמשיהן נותנין יד והויין להן לחזק לומר לא אהיה שליח ולהזמין את פלוני לב"ד אם לא תרבה שכר ואחר פסק דין לא ארדנו ליכנס למשכנו: שבט מושלים. מקל אגרופין של מושלים היינו דיינים רשעים שת"ח שבמשפחותם להם למקל ולאגרוף שעל ידיהם היו מעמידין אותן ומחפין עליהם ועושין סניגרון לדבריהם: לדייני בור. שבהבטחת אותן ת"ח מעמידין דייני בור לדון את כל הבא והרבה דינין שאין נמלכים בהן ומטין אותן: כפיכם נגואלו בדם אלו הדיינין. שכפיהן פשוטין לקבל שוחד ומטין את הדין ונוטלין ממון מן הבעלים שלא כדין ונותנו לשכנגדו והרי הוא כנוטל נשמתו: סופרי הדיינין. שכותבין שטרות של רמיה: עורכי הדיינין. מלמדין את בעלי דינין לטעון: עמו. מכלל דעד השתא לא: זכה לחשן המשפט. שכנגד הלב שהיה גדול ממנו וקודם למשה נגלית שכינה על אהרן כדכתיב (שמואל א ב) הנגלה נגליתי אל בית אביך ונאמרה לו נבואה של מצרים הכתובה (ביחזקאל כ) עד וימרו בי ואעפ"כ לא נתקנא בו בזאת: בני בשכר. שם מקום: כילה מהו. לנטותה בשבת: כשותא. הימלון שגדל על ההגא מהו בכרמא ירק הוא וכלאים בכרם או אילן הוא ואינו כלאים בכרם: ולישלח להו. צד היתר בה: כדרמי בר יחזקאל. כרך עליה חוט או משיחה: ומשני לפי שאינן בני תורה. ומקילי טפי: עירבובא. כלאים: וקי"ל. בברכות בפרק כילד גבי ערלה וה"ה לכלאים שאף היא מצוה התלויה בארץ ואינה נוהגת מן התורה אלא בארץ: יהיב פרוטה לתינוק נכרי. קסבר בחוץ לארץ שרי ומיהו כל כמה דאפשר משני שלא ילמדו להקל:

תוספות

ולישלח להו כר"ט. הא לא פריך לישלח להו כר' יאשיה דאמר אינו חייב עד שיזרע חטה ושעורה וחרצן במפולת יד דשמא הם לא שאלו כשותא בכרמא מהו אלא היכא שעשה לדין איסור כלאים ג' מינים כאחד ועוד שמא לא ס"ל כר' יאשיה ואע"ג דקי"ל כר' יאשיה בספ"ק דקדושין (דף לט.) א"נ לא להריתו [לא] קי"ל כר' יאשיה ואמר נמי בברכות פרק מי שמתו (דף כב.) נהוג עלמא כתלת סבי כר' אילעי בראשית הגז כרבי יאשיה בכלאים כר' יהודה בן בתירא בדברי תורה מיהו י"ל שלא היו סבורין כן דהא קאמר נמי נהוג כרבי יהודה בדברי תורה ואפ"ה פליגי עליה אמוראי טובא בשמעתא דהתם וקאמר נמי כרבי אילעי בראשית הגז דאמר אינו נוהג אלא בארץ ואפ"ה אמרינן בחולין בשילהי פ' הזרוע (דף קלו.) אמר רב חסדא האי טבחא דלא מפריש מתנתא ליהוי בשמתא דה' אלהי ישראל ואמר נמי דרבא קנים אטמא ואפילו רב נחמן גופיה דאמר נהוג עלמא כתלת סבי אמר התם דקנים גלימא וא"ת נהי דלא ס"ל כר' יאשיה מ"מ לישלח להו כרבי יאשיה דכל המיקל בארץ הלכה כמותו בחו"ל וי"ל דלא שייך למימר הכי אלא במין של איסור דהמתירו חושבו מין היתר בארץ הלכה כמותו בחו"ל אבל בדבר שאינו תלוי אלא בזריעה חטה ושעורה וחרצן במפולת יד בהא לא אמר הלכה כמותו בחו"ל. מ"ר:

רב עמרם חסידא מנגיד עלה רב משרשיא יהיב ליה פרוטה לנכרי כו'. קשיא לי אמאי הא אמרינן לעיל דהלכה כר"ט דמיקל בחו"ל וצריך לומר דבמקומם לא היו בני תורה:

וליתן ליה לתינוק ישראל. אומר רבי שקבלה הוא בידינו שזה המקשה רב אחא בר יעקב והיינו הא דאמר בעירובין בשילהי בכל מערבין (דף מ: ושם) גבי ברכת זמן על הכוס ביוה"כ דמפרש התם דלא אפשר דהיכי ליעביד כו' ליתביה לתינוק לית הלכתא כרב אחא בר יעקב דילמא אתי למיסרך ולא מלינו במקום אחר דאית ליה לרב אחא האי סברא וי"מ דהוא ההוא דפ' בתרא דנדה (דף סז:) דאתקין בימאה דתמניא משום גנבי ולא חיישינן לסרך בתה במקום לורך ולא נהירא דמאי שנא דנקיט טפי רב אחא בר יעקב מכל שאר אמוראי דהתם ועל ההיא דהתם אומר ר"ת שמותר ליתן לתינוק לשתות כוס של ברכה כי מיקלע מילה ביוה"כ ולא חיישינן דילמא אתי למיסרך כיון שאין זה מנהג [בקבוע] ולא דמי לכוס דיוה"כ דאי הוו יהבי ליה אתי למיסרך אף כשיהיה גדול כיון שעושין מנהג לשתות בכל שנה ושנה ביוה"כ:

עין משפט נר מצוה

טו א מיי' פכ"ג מהל' סנהדרין הלכה ט סמג לאוין רו טוש"ע ח"מ סי' ח סעיף ג:

כ"ג הרש"ל והריעב"ז מחקו

טז ב מיי' פ"י מהל' מתנות עניים הלכה א סמג עשין קסב טוש"ע י"ד סי' רמז:

[גיר' הערוך ערך גז ז' גאזי דפאטי פי' סריסי ושוטרי השרים ובערך יסיר גרס גזירפטי פי' רשעים]

רבינו חננאל

ותהוי פת ראשונה הכא הוא מפורש בפסחים בסוף פ"א: וזה שהשיב רב מנשיא לבני בי בשכר על הכילה ועל הכשות בכרם ועל המת ביו"ט כולן לאיסור לפי שאינן בני תורה. מהא שמעינן שאפילו דברים המותרים כגון אלו וכדומה להן המסורין לעם הארץ אין אדם רשאי להורות להן להיתר אלא יחמיר עליהן

מסורת הש"ס

[יבמות סג. ע"ש ב"ב ה. ע"ש]

[יומא עא:]

סנהדרין לח: [צ"ל ישראל וכ"ה ברמב"ם וכטור וע"ע מ"ש על הגליון סנהדרין לח.]

[תוספ' סוף פרק ג דכלאים]

ברכות לו:

עין משפט נר מצוה

יז א מיי' פ"א מהל' י"ט הלכה כג סמג לאוין עה טוש"ע א"ח סי' תקכו סעיף א :
יח ב מיי' שם טוש"ע שם סעיף ד :
יט ג מיי' פי"ט מהל' שבת הלכה כ סמג לאוין סה טוש"ע א"ח סי' שא סעיף לט :
כ ד מיי' שם טוש"ע שם סעיף לח וסי' יג סעיף א :
כא ה מיי' פ"ג מהל' י"ט הלכה יז סמג לאוין עה טוש"ע א"ח סי' תקי סעיף ד :
[ועי' תוס' ביצה ו. ד"ה והאידנא]
כב ו מיי' פ"ז שם הלכה ח סמג שם טוש"ע שם סי' תקלג סעיף א :
כג ז מיי' פכ"ג מהל' שבת הלכה ב סמג שם טוש"ע שם סי' שיד סעיף יא :
כד ח טור א"ח סימן שלט :
כה ט מיי' פ"ח מהל' שבת הלכה יד ופכ"א הלכה יז סמג שם טוש"ע א"ח סי' שיט סעיף ט :
כו י מיי' פ"ח שם ופ"ג מהלכות י"ט הלכה יז סמג שם טוש"ע שם סעיף טו :
כז כ ל מ נ מיי' פ"ח מהל' שבת הלכה יד ופכ"א הלכה יז סמג שם טוש"ע שם סעיף י ויא :
כח ס ע מיי' פכ"ב שם הלכה לג טוש"ע שם סעיף יב :
כט פ מיי' שם סמג שם טוש"ע א"ח סי' שטו סעיף יג :
ל צ טוש"ע שם סימן שיט סעיף יג :
לא ק שם סעיף יד :

גמרא

ולא ידענא אי מלפניה אי מלאחריה ואתו לקמיה דרבי יוחנן ואמר להו יתעסקו ביה עממין *ואמר רבא [א]מת בי"ט ראשון יתעסקו בו עממין [ב]ביום טוב שני יתעסקו בו ישראל ואפילו ביו"ט שני של ראש השנה מה שאין כן בביצה לפי שאינן בני תורה : א"ר אבין בר רב הונא אמר רב חמא בר גוריא [ג]מתעטף אדם בכילה ובכסכסיה ויוצא לרה"ר בשבת ואינו חושש מ"ש מדרב הונא *דאמר רב הונא אמר רב [ד]היוצא בטלית שאינה מצוייצת כהילכתה בשבת חייב חטאת ציצית לגבי טלית חשיבי ולא בטלי הני לא חשיבי ובטלי אמר (א) רבה בר רב הונא [ה]מערים אדם על המשמרת ביו"ט לתלות בה רמונים ותולה בה שמרים אמר רב אשי והוא דתלה בה רמונים מאי שנא מהא דתניא *[ו]מטילין שכר במועד לצורך המועד שלא לצורך המועד אסור אחד שכר תמרים ואחד שכר שעורים אע"פ שיש להן ישן מערים ושותה מן החדש התם לא מוכחא מילתא הכא מוכחא מילתא אמרו ליה רבנן לרב אשי חזי מר האי צורבא מרבנן ורב הונא ב"ר חיון שמיה ואמרי לה רב הונא בר' חלוון שמיה [ז]דשקל ברא דתומא ומנח בברזא דדנא ואמר לאצנועיה קמיכוינא ואזיל [ח]ונאים במברא ועבר להך גיסא וסייר פירי ואמר אנא למינם קמיכוינא אמר להו הערמה קאמרת הערמה בדרבנן היא וצורבא מרבנן לא אתי למיעבד לכתחילה : **מתני'** [ט]נותנין מים ע"ג השמרים בשביל שיצולו [י]ומסננין את היין [א] בסודרין *ובכפיפה מצרית *[כ]ונותנין ביצה במסננת של חרדל ועושין אנומלין בשבת ר' יהודה אומר בשבת בכוס ביו"ט בלגין ובמועד בחבית רבי צדוק אומר הכל לפי האורחין : **גמ'** *אמר זעירי [ל]נותן אדם יין צלול ומים צלולין לתוך המשמרת בשבת ואינו חושש אבל עכורין לא מיתיבי רבן שמעון בן גמליאל אומר טורד אדם חבית של יין יינה ושמריה ונותן לתוך המשמרת בשבת ואינו חושש תרגמה זעירי [ל]בין הגיתות שנו : [מ]מסננין את היין בסודרין : אמר רב שימי בר חייא [נ]ובלבד שלא יעשה גומא : [ס]ובכפיפה מצרית : אמר רב חייא בר אשי אמר רב [ע]ובלבד שלא יגביה מקרקעיתו של כלי טפח אמר *רב [פ]האי *)פרונקא אפלגיה דכובא שרי אבוליה כובא אסור אמר רב פפא [צ]לא ניהדק איניש (ג) **)צינייתא בפומיה דכוזני דחביתא משום דמיחזי כמשמרת דבי רב פפא [ק]שאפו שיכרא ממנא למנא (ג) אמר ליה רב אחא מדיפתי לרבינא האיכא ניצוצות לבי רב פפא לא חשיבי : ונותנין ביצה במסננת : תני יעקב קרחה לפי

*) [עי' תוס' ביצה לב: ד"ה מלמטה למעלה] **) ג"י הערוך בערך לבת א' לא נהדק איניש לבתא אפומא דכוזינתא

רש"י

ולא ידענא אי מלפניה. אם חל י"ט בע"ש ומת בו ביום ומפני שלא יוכלו להתעסק בו למחר התירו לקוברו ע"י עממים : אי מלאחריה. והוא מת בשבת ומפני שנשתהא כבר והיה מסריח התירו : מת ביו"ט ראשון כו'. מת שנשתהא כגון שמת בשבת ולמחר היה יו"ט : מה שאין כן בבילה. דאין ר"ה שוה לימים טובים של גליות דאילו ר"ה חמיר יו"ט שני דיליה ונולדה בזה אסורה בזה : מתעטף אדם בכילה. שהוא כסדין ומתעטף בה דרך מלבוש : וכסכסיה. רצועות התלויות בה ולא אמרינן הך רצועות לאו לצורך עיטוף נינהו והוה משאוי ההוא שעתא שאין כיסכסין עשויין אלא לנטותה באהל : חייב חטאת. ואילו לא היתה מצויילת כלל לא מיחייב דהא לבושיה הוא אלמא הציציות הויין לו משאוי הואיל ואינן כמלותו אינן צריכין לה ומן הבגד ממש אינן דליחשבינן כוותיה : חשיבי. משום דשל תכלת הן ולא בטלי והוו בה משוי : מערים אדם על המשמרת ביו"ט. לרבנן דאמרי אין תולין את המשמרת ביום טוב ואוקימנא דטעמא לאו משום אהל אלא משום עובדא דחול מערים ותולה אותה לצורך רמונים דלאו עובדין דחול נינהו ומסנן בה שמרים הואיל ונתלית דהא אמרינן נותנין לתלויה ביו"ט : והוא דתלי בה רמונים. ברישא דמוכח מילתא דמעיקרא לאו לשמרים תלייה : מטילין. ברשי"ר בלע"ז : במועד. בחולו של מועד : מערים ושותה מן החדש. אלמא בלא שום הוכחה מותר להערים : התם לאו מוכחא מילתא. דמילתא דאיסורא הוא דהרואה אומר לצורך המועד הוא שאין הכל יודעין שיש לו מן הישן הכא מוכחא מילתא לאיסור דסתם תולה משמרת לשמרים הוא תולה ואי לא יהיב בה רימונים ברישא להכיר בעלמא כי יהיב בה שמרים מוכח דלהכי תלייה : ברא דתומא. ללע של שום : ומנח בברזא דדנא. מקום שיש בו נקב בחבית והיין יוצא [ב] נותנו שם בשבת לסתום והוי כמתקן ומערים לכתחילה : ואומר לאצנועיה. להאי ברא דתומא מיכוינא ועוד עביד אחריתי אזל נאים במברא בספינה רחבה העשויה לעבור המים והיא של נכרי ויודע הוא שיעבירנה הנכרי לצד האחר : וסייר פירי. ומשמר שם פירות כרמו ונמלא שהנכרי מעבירו במים בשבת : הערמה בדרבנן היא. ה"נ הך הערמה לאו באיסורא דאורייתא הוא אלא באיסורא דרבנן דא"כ עביד ממש בלא הערמה אדרבנן הוא דעבר הלכך כיון דצורבא מרבנן הוא לא אחמירו עליה דהוא לא אתי למעבד לכתחילה להדיא בלא הערמה לעבור שם לפני הכל : **מתני'** נותנין מים. בשבת ע"ג שמרים הנתונים במשמרת מבעוד יום : כדי שיצולו. שיהו צלולין לזוב*) את היין מפני הקמחים שקורים ייג"ש : בסודרין ובכפיפה מצרית. העשויה מצורי דקל : כפיפה. סל : ונותנין ביצה במסננת. שהחרדל נתון בה להסתנן וקולטת את הפסולת ואף הביצה החלמון שלה נוטף ומסתנן עמו והוה ליה לחרדל למראה והחלבון שהוא קשור נשאר למעלה ורבינו הלוי פירש סיטונה של ביצה לתוך תבשיל היא ולא לתוך חרדל ובמסננת של חרדל הוא דשרי משום שינוי ויורד לתוך הקערה שהוא כלי שני ומתלבן התבשיל : אינומלין. פוטו"ן : לגין. גדול מכוס וקטן מחבית : **גמ'** טורד. מערבב : בין הגתות שנו. שכל היינות עכורין ושותין אותן בשמריהם הלכך אין כאן תיקון דבלאו הכי משתתי : שלא יעשה גומא. מן הסודר בפי הכלי כי עובדא דחול אי נמי אתי לידי סחיטה : שלא יגביה. הכפיפה מקרקעית (ד) כלי התחתון טפח כמדת אהל : פרונקא. בגד שטוחין על גיגית יין לכסותה : אפלגא דכובא שרי. דלאו אוהלא הוי : לא ניהדק איניש ליניית בפומא דכוזי דחביתא. כלי חרס קטן שמערין בו יין מחבית לא יתן בפיו קסין וקסמים בחוזקה לפי שאין לך מסננת גדולה מזו : שפו שיכרא. כל היכא דתני לשון שפוי בנחת הוא והפסולת נשאר בשולי הכלי : והאיכא ניצוצות. קטנות הגישופות באחרונה מתוך הפסולת שקורין ברי"ש והנהו מוכחן דבורר הוא : ניצוצות בי רב פפא לא חשיבי. (ה) שחנוני מטיל שכר היה כדאמרינן בבבא מליעא (דף סה:) ובפסחים (דף קיג:) הלכך אינו מקפיד לניצוצות כל כך וכשמגיע לניצוצות משליך הן ופסולתן לחוץ ותחילת שפייתן (ו) מן הפסולת ניכר דלאו בורר הוא : לפי

*) כאן יש ערבוב דברים ע"י חסרון נקודות המבדילות וצ"ל כדי שיצולו. שיהיו צלולין לזוב : את היין. מפני הקמחים וכו'. ועי' פירש"י להרי"ף

תוספות

יום טוב שני יתעסקו בו ישראל. ובבילה (ד' ו') מסקינן בתר הך מילתא אמר רבינא האידנא דאיכא חברי חיישינן פירוש ולא יתעסקו בו ישראל פן ילוו עליהם חברי לעשות מלאכה ביו"ט כיון שרואין שעושין בשביל מת ומעשה היה והוליכו מת חוץ לתחום ביו"ט והלכו אחריו בסוסים להתעסק במת וכעס ר"ת אף על ההולכים ברגל בלא סוסים ושמע רבי דטעמו משום דמסיק רבינא האידנא דאיכא חברי ולדידן אע"ג דליכא למיחש יש לאסור כיון דמסיק הכי גם יש לירא פן ילוו השרים להתעסק במלאכתן ולכתוב מה שהם רוצים ושלח להם ר"ת בני בשכר אינם בני תורה בני מלאון (ז) (אותה העיר) בני תורה* :

ציצית חשיבי ולא בטלי. שאינם מבוטלין לפי שחשובים הם בעיניו שדעתו ליתן בטלית ציצית רביעית כך פי' ר"ח : הא לא חשיבי ובטלי על זה סמך רבי להניח באבנטו רצועות התלויות בו ויש שקושרים בהם בתי שוקים דבטלי דלא חשיבי כולי האי : מאי שנא מהא דתניא כו'. פי' [וס"ל כרבי יוסי בר' יהודה דאמר מערימין] לעיל בכ' כל כתבי (דף קיז:) :

*תלא דבישרא כו'. לא כפירוש הקונטרס דפי' בשר מליח שתלו ליבשו דהל"ל הא בפרק מפנין דמה שייך הכא ועוד למה מזכיר תלא ועוד מוכח לעיל בפרק מפנין (דף קכח.) דדג מליח נמי חזי לאומצא ועוד דהכא בטלטול איירי ואמרינן לעיל דרב במוקצה לטלטל סבר לה כר"ש ונראה כפי' הערוך דמשום תלא נקטיה ובלא בשר אלא תלא דבשרא לא ממאיס ושרי לטלטולי ושל דגים מאיס והוי מוקצה מחמת מיאוס והשתא אתי שפיר באיסור דתלא כעין כיסא דירקא ור' פי' לנו דלתלא דבשרא רגיל להיות בו תורת כלי אבל של דגים לא ולא משום מוקצה מחמת מיאוס דלא איירי שמעתין במוקצה מחמת מיאוס. מ"ר : אבל

רבינו חננאל

לאיסור. וזה שאמר מתעטף אדם בכילה וכוסכיא ויוצא בה לרה"ר פי' כוסכיא חופין ומשיחות שעליה. הלכה היא דקא מקשינן עלה מדרב הונא דאמר היוצא בטלית שאינה מצוייצת כהלכתה כגון שתלה ציצית בג' כנפי הטלית והניח הרביעית אותן חוטי הציצית כיון שאינה מצוייצת בד' כנפות שלה אינה חשובה ציצית דמצוה. וכחוטין דעלמא הן חשובין והיוצא בה חייב חטאת ופרקינן ציצית לגבי טלית חשיבי ולא בטלי שלב האדם רוצה בקיומן כי בדעתו שיתלה הרביעית וילבשנה. אבל כוסכיא לגבי כילה אינו צריך להן ובטלי : והא דאמר רבה בר בר חנה מערים אדם על המשמרת ביו"ט לתלות בה רמונים ותולה בה שמרים אליבא דרבנן שאסורים לתלות ולשמר לכתחלה ואע"פ שהיא אסורה והוא דתלה לה רמונים כרב אשי ואע"ג דאמרינן מ"ש מהא דתניא מטילין שכר במועד וכו' התם בשכר במועד לא מוכחא מלתא הכא במשמרת מוכחא מילתא ולשמר הוא תולה ואם תלה בה רמונים אין ואי לא לא. והא דאמרו ליה לרב אשי על רב הונא בר חיון. ואמרי לה בר חילון דהוה שקיל ברא דתומיא ומנח בבירזא דדנא פי' שהיה נוטל ראש שום ונותנו בנקב של חבית שיוצא ממנו היין ולא היה מסתפק מאותה חבית אלא חבית שבאוצר והיה מערים וסותם הנקב בראש השום והיה אומר להצניע ראש השום אני צריך ועוד היה הולך וישן במעברא וכו' אמר להו רב אשי הערמה מדרבנן היא והערמה לכתחלה ת"ח לא עבדי : ונותנין המים על השמרים בשביל שיצלו אמר זעירי נותן אדם יין צלול ומים צלולין לתוך המשמרת בשבת ואינו חושש אבל עכורין לא . ואם בין הגתות הוא שעדיין היין תוסס ואינו צלול טורד אדם חבית יינה ושמריה בשבת ואינו חושש ואפילו אליבא דרבנן וליכא דפליג בהא ומסנן | את היין בסודרין אמר רב שימי בר חייא ובלבד שלא יעשה גומא. פי' שלא ימשוך קצות הסודר למעלה וישאר כמו גומא באמצעיתו . ובכפיפה מצרית . ואמרינן משמיה דרב שלא יגביה מקרקעיתו של כלי טפח. שכן מצינו באהלי טומאה טפח: וכל מקום שיש בו חלל טפח כאהל חשוב ואין עושין אהלי עראי לכתחלה בשבת: פראנקא. פי' כאוי בפי הקנקן ויש בו נקבים קטנים. לסנן בו היין כאשר יציקוהו בקנקן. אם יהיה זה הכיסוי בחצי פי הכלי אינו מסנן . ואם הוא בכל הפה של כלי הרי הוא כמסננת ונראה כמשמר היין במשמרת : וי"א פרונקא טלית של בגד שעשאו לכסוי כובא כדאמרי' בתחלת במה טומנין ומ"ש מפרונקא דמר ואומר עוד בע"ז פרק אין מעמידין בהמה בפונדקאות פש ליה חמרא בכובה צייריה בפרונקיא פי' נשאר לו יין בכלי קשר פי הכלי בסמרטוטין: לא ניהדוק צבתא בפומא דכווא משום דמחזי כמשמרת . פי' צבתא בפומא דכווא מוך חדש וכדומה לו והוא מלשון מצאי צבתים או כרוכות וי"א לוף של דקל וכדומה לו : ונותנין ביצה במסננת של חרדל .תני יעקב קרחה לפי

הגהות הב"ח

(א) גמ' לא חשיבי ובטלי אמר [illegible]

(ז) תוס' ד"ה יו"ט שני כו' בני מלאון (אותה העיר) [illegible]

הגהות הגר"א

[א] במשנה ומסננין את היין. [illegible] סודר כן פסק הר מב"ם אבל הטור כתב דכ"ש במשמרת דמותר וקאמר סודר דמים בו אסור משא"כ במשמרת כמ"ש בגמרא ומים כו' והרשב"א פירש דקאמר סודרין דאפילו עכור מותר (ועמ"ש רבינו בא"ח סי' שיט) :
[ב] רש"י בד"ה ומנח בברזא דדנא כו' והיין יוצא כו'. נ"ב והיין דווקא יוצא (ועמ"ש רבינו בא"ח ס"ס שיד) :

גליון הש"ס מתני' ומסננין את היין בסודרין . עי' לקמן קמא ע"א תוד"ה האי מסוכרייתא : תוס' ד"ה תלא כו' ושל דגים מאיס . עי' יש ע"ב תוד"ה הני כרכי .

Sabbath, [139b] though I do not know whether it preceded or followed it,[7] and when they went before R. Joḥanan, he said to them: Let Gentiles occupy themselves with him [the dead]. Raba too said: As for a corpse,[8] on the first day of Festivals Gentiles should occupy themselves with him; on the second day of Festivals Israelites may occupy themselves with him, and even on the second day of New Year, which is not so in the case of an egg?[9]—[Here too] because they were not learned in the law.

R. Abin b. R. Huna said in R. Ḥama b. Guria's name: A man may wrap himself in a canopy sheet and [tie it] with its cords to go out into the street on the Sabbath without fear.[10] How does this differ from R. Huna's [dictum], for R. Huna said in Rab's name: If one goes out on the Sabbath wearing a garment not provided with [proper] fringes as required by law, he is liable to a
a sin-offering?[1]—Fringes are important in relation to the cloak, hence they are not merged [therein]; these are not of [separate] importance, and [so] are accounted as nought.

Rabbah[2] son of R. Huna said: A man may employ an artifice in connection with a strainer on a festival, suspending it for pomegranates yet straining lees therein.[3] Said R. Ashi: Provided he does place pomegranates in it.[4] How does it differ from what was taught: One may brew beer on the [intermediate days of a] Festival[5] when it is required for the Festival, but if not required for the Festival it is forbidden: [this applies to] both barley beer and date beer. Though one has old [beer], he may practise an evasion[6] and drink of the new?—There the matter is not evident;[7] here the matter is evident.[8]

The scholars said to R. Ashi: See, sir, a Rabbinical disciple, whose name is R. Huna b. Ḥiwan—others state, R. Huna b. Ḥilwon—who took peel of garlic,[9] placed it in the bung hole of a barrel, and asserted, 'My intention is to put it away [here].'[10] He also went and dozed in a ferry and thus crossed to the other side and looked after his fruit, asserting, 'My intention was to sleep.' Said he to them, You speak of an artifice: it is an artifice [in connection with] a Rabbinical [interdict],[11] and a disciple of the Rabbis will not come to do this at the very outset.[12]

MISHNAH. WATER MAY BE POURED OVER LEES IN ORDER TO CLARIFY THEM, AND WINE MAY BE STRAINED THROUGH CLOTHS AND THROUGH A BASKET MADE OF PALM TWIGS; AND AN EGG MAY BE PASSED THROUGH A MUSTARD STRAIN-
b ER;[1] AND ENOMLIN[2] MAY BE PREPARED ON THE SABBATH. R. JUDAH SAID: ON THE SABBATH [IT MAY ONLY BE MADE] IN A GOBLET; ON FESTIVALS, IN A LAGIN;[3] AND ON THE INTERMEDIATE DAYS OF FESTIVALS IN A BARREL. R. ZADOK SAID: IT ALL DEPENDS ON THE [NUMBER OF] GUESTS.

GEMARA. Ze'iri said: One may pour clear wine and clear water into a strainer on the Sabbath without fear,[4] but not turbid [liquids]. An objection is raised: R. Simeon b. Gamaliel said: One may stir up a barrel of wine, [i.e.,] the wine and the lees, and pour it into a strainer on the Sabbath without fear![5]—Ze'iri explained it: They learnt this of the season of the wine pressing.[6]

WINE MAY BE STRAINED THROUGH CLOTHS. R. Shimi b. Ḥiyya said: Provided that one does not make a hollow.[7]

AND THROUGH A BASKET MADE OF PALM TWIGS. R. Ḥiyya b. Ashi said in Rab's name: Provided he does not lift it [the basket] a handbreadth from the bottom of the vessel.[8]

Rab said: [Spreading] a rag over half a cask [to cover it] is permitted; over the whole cask, is forbidden.[9]

R. Papa said: A man must not stuff chips into the mouth of a
c cask jug,[1] because it looks like a strainer. R. Papa's household poured wine slowly from one vessel to another.[2] R. Aḥa of Difti[3] objected: But there is the residue?[4]—The residue had no value in R. Papa's household.[5]

AN EGG MAY BE PASSED THROUGH A MUSTARD STRAINER. R.

(7) I.e., whether the Festival fell on Friday on which day the death occurred, so that it had to be buried on the same day, or whether it fell on Sunday and the death occurred on the Sabbath, so that the burial could not be delayed any longer. (8) Of a person who died on a Sabbath which was followed by a Festival. (9) An egg laid on the first day of any Festival except New Year may be eaten on the second day too. But in respect to a corpse New Year is the same as other Festivals. (10) Of transgression.

a (1) The garment has fringes, but since they are not in accordance with the law they are regarded not as part thereof but as a burden which entails a sin-offering. Thus here too, since the normal function of the cords is to spread the sheet, not to tie it round a person, they constitute a burden. (2) Var. lec.: R. Abin. (3) Lit., to suspend pomegranates therein, but he suspends lees therein. (4) For some time. (5) I.e., the intermediate days of Passover and Tabernacles, which enjoy semi-sanctity, being treated as profane in some respects and as holy in others. (6) Of the law. (7) The evasion is not obvious, for a person who sees him brew beer does not know that he has sufficient already for the festival. (8) That he is evading the law, unless he actually puts pomegranates in it, since its usual function is to strain them. (9) Jast. R. Han.: a head of garlic. (10) But actually it was to prevent the wine from running out, and thus he repaired the barrel, as it were. (11) For even if he did these without an artifice he would only violate a Rabbinical, not a Scriptural interdict. (12) Without an artifice—hence he does nothing wrong.

b (1) Rashi: the strainer contains mustard, and when the egg is poured upon it the yolk passes through and the white remains on top. R. Halevi (quoted by Rashi): the egg is strained into a dish, not into mustard, but a mustard strainer is specified in order that the action on the Sabbath, though permitted, shall be done differently from what it is on weekdays. (2) V. Gemara *infra*. (3) Larger than a goblet (כוס) but smaller than a barrel (חבית). (4) Of transgression. (5) Though the liquid is turbid through the stirring. (6) All wine is turbid then and drunk thus; hence it is not made fit for drinking (which would be forbidden on the Sabbath) by being put through the strainer. (7) The cloth must be taut and not form a hollow. (8) Which receives the wine. Otherwise it forms a 'tent', v. *supra* 137b, n. c1. (9) In the latter case a 'tent' is made.

c (1) I.e., a jug used for taking wine out of a cask; the chips act as a strainer. (2) So as to leave the sediment behind. (3) V. *supra* 10a, n. b5. (4) The last drops percolating through the dregs left behind in the first vessel, which shows that their purpose was to strain the wine. (5) He was a beer brewer (B.M. 65b) and could afford to throw away the little wine left at the bottom together with the chips, thus leaving nothing at all there to show their real motive.

Jacob Ḳarḥah recited: [140*a*] Because it is only done for colouring.[6]

It was stated: If mustard grain is kneaded on Sabbath eve,—on the morrow, Rab said: One must crush [dissolve] it[7] with a utensil, but not by hand.[8] Said Samuel to him: 'By hand'! Does one then crush it every day by hand—is it asses' food? Rather said Samuel: He must crush it by hand, but not with a utensil. It was stated, R. Eleazar said: Both the one and the other are forbidden; while R. Joḥanan ruled: Both the one and the other are permitted. Abaye and Raba both say: The *halachah* is not as R. Joḥanan. R. Joḥanan [subsequently] adopted R. Eleazar's thesis, while R. Eleazar adopted Samuel's thesis. Abaye and Raba both said [then]: The *halachah* is as R. Joḥanan.

Abaye's mother[9] prepared [it] for him, but he would not eat [it]. Ze'iri's wife prepared [some] for R. Ḥiyya b. Ashi, but he would not eat [it]. Said she to him, 'I prepared it for your teacher [Ze'iri] and he ate, whilst you do not eat!'

Raba b. Shaba said: I was standing before Rabina and I stirred [the mustard] for him with the smooth [inner] part of the garlic, and he ate it.

Mar Zuṭra said: The law is not as all these opinions, but as the following which was stated: If mustard is kneaded on the eve of the Sabbath, on the morrow one may crush [dissolve] it both by hand or with a utensil; he may pour honey in it, yet he must not beat it up but may mix them. If cress was chopped up on the eve of the Sabbath, on the morrow one may put oil and
a vinegar into it and add *ammitha*[1] thereto; and he must not beat them up but may mix them. If garlic was crushed on the eve of the Sabbath, on the morrow one may put beans and grits therein, yet he must not pound them, but may mix them, and one may add *ammitha* to it. What is *ammitha?*—*Ninya.*[2] Abaye observed: This proves that *ninya* is good for [seasoning] cress.

AND ENOMLIN MAY BE PREPARED ON THE SABBATH. Our Rabbis taught: *Enomlin* may be prepared on the Sabbath but *aluntith* may not be prepared on the Sabbath. What is *enomlin* and what is *aluntith?*—*Enomlin* is [a mixture of] wine, honey, and pepper. *Aluntith* is [a mixture of] old wine, clear water and balsam, which is prepared as a cooling [draught] in the baths.[3] R. Joseph said: I once entered the baths after Mar 'Uḳba; on leaving I was offered a cup of [such] wine, and I experienced [a cooling sensation] from the hair of my head [right] down to my toe nails; and had I drunk another glass I would have been afraid lest it be deducted from my merits in the future world.[4] But Mar 'Uḳba drank it every day?—Mar 'Uḳba was different, because he was accustomed to it.

MISHNAH. HILTITH[5] MUST NOT BE DISSOLVED IN WARM WATER,[6] BUT IT MAY BE PUT INTO VINEGAR; AND ONE MUST NOT CAUSE LEEKS TO FLOAT,[7] NOR RUB THEM;[8] BUT THEY MAY BE PUT INTO A SIEVE[9] OR A BASKET.[10] STUBBLE MAY NOT BE SIFTED THROUGH A SIEVE, NOR PLACED ON AN EMINENCE, FOR THE CHAFF TO DROP DOWN; BUT ONE MAY
b TAKE IT UP IN A SIEVE AND PUT IT INTO THE MANGER.[1]

GEMARA. The scholars asked: What if one does dissolve [it]? R. Adda of Naresh[2] maintained before R. Joseph: If one dissolves [it] he is liable to a sin-offering. Said Abaye to him: If so, if one soaks[3] raw meat in water, is he too liable?[4] Rather said Abaye: It is a Rabbinical [prohibition], that one should not act as he does during the week. R. Joḥanan asked R. Jannai: May *ḥiltith* be dissolved in cold water? It is forbidden, replied he. But we learnt: ḤILTITH MUST NOT BE DISSOLVED IN WARM WATER, implying that it is permitted in cold water? If so,[5] what is the difference between you and me? Our Mishnah is [the opinion of] an individual. For it was taught: *Ḥiltith* may be dissolved neither in warm nor in cold water; R. Jose said: In warm water it is forbidden; in cold it is permitted.

What is it made for? [As a remedy] for asthma.[6] R. Aḥa b. Joseph suffered with asthma. He went to Mar 'Uḳba, [who] advised him, 'Go and drink three [gold *denar*] weights of *ḥiltith* on three days.' He went and drank it on Thursday and Friday. The following morning he went and asked [about it] in the Beth Hamidrash.[7] Said they to him, The school of R. Adda—others state, the school of Mar son of R. Adda recited: One may drink a *ḳab* or two *ḳabs* without fear.[8] About drinking, said he, I do not ask.[9] My question is, What about dissolving it? R. Ḥiyya b. Abin observed to them: This case happened to me,[10] and I went and consulted R. Adda b. Ahabah, but he could not inform me. [So] I went and asked R. Huna, and he answered me, Thus did Rab say: He may dissolve [it] in cold water and place it in the sun. Is this [only] according to him who permits [dissolving]?—[No.] It is even according to him who forbids [it]: that is only if one had not drunk at all; but here, since he had drunk [it] on Thursday and Friday, if he would not drink it on the Sabbath he would be endangered.

c R. Aḥa b. Joseph was walking along, leaning[1] on the shoulder of R. Naḥman b. Isaac, his sister's son. When we reach R. Safra's house, lead me in, he requested.[2] When they arrived [there] he led him in. How about rubbing [the stiffness out of] linen[3] on the Sabbath? asked he; is his intention to soften the linen, and it is permitted, or perhaps his intention is to make it whiter,[4] which is forbidden?—His intention is to soften it, replied he, and it is permitted. When he went out he [R. Naḥman] enquired, What did you ask him? I asked him, What about rubbing linen on the Sabbath, replied he, and he answered me, It is permitted. But let the Master inquire about a scarf?[5] I do not ask about a scarf, because I asked it of R. Huna and he decided it for me. Then let the Master solve this from a scarf?—There it looks like making it whiter,[6] but here it does not look like making it whiter.

(6) *Sc.* when the yolk is poured into a stew; but actually both yolk and white are fit for food, and therefore this is not an act of 'selecting' (v. Mishnah 73*a*). (7) In water. (8) He regards the latter as the usual way, and therefore it is forbidden on the Sabbath. (9) V. *supra* 66*b*, n. a3.
a (1) A kind of cress or pepperwort (*Lepidum sativum*) Jast. (2) Jast.: ammi, Bishop's weed. Rashi: mint. (3) Hence it partakes somewhat of the nature of a medicine, and therefore it is forbidden. (4) A second glass would inevitably have killed me but for a miracle, which would be ultimately debited to my account. (5) Jast.: *assa foetida*, an umbelliferous plant used as a resin in leaves, for a spice and for medicinal purposes. (6) To be drunk medicinally. (7) I.e., pour water over them to make the refuse float up so that it can be removed. (8) By hand, likewise to remove the refuse. (9) And the refuse *may* fall through. (10) Probably an open-work basket is meant which may act somewhat as a sieve. Though sifting is forbidden, these are permitted, because even if the refuse does fall through it is only incidental.
b (1) Though some chaff may fall through, this is unintentional, the Mishnah agreeing with R. Simeon that whatever is unintentional is permitted. (2) V. *supra* 60*a*, n. a11. (3) The Hebrew is the same for dissolves and soaks. (4) Surely not. (5) That you do not accept me as a greater authority on the Mishnah than yourself. (6) Lit., 'heaviness of heart'. (7) To ask whether he might take it on Sabbath. (8) Of transgression. (9) If the *ḥiltith* is dissolved before the Sabbath. (10) Lit., 'it was not in his hand'.
c (1) Lit., 'supporting himself. (2) He was an old man. (3) When it is starched. The rubbing softens it and makes it whiter. (4) Lit., 'to beget whiteness'. (5) Or, turban. (6) One is more particular about a scarf.

לפי שאין עושין אותה אלא לגוון איתמר חרדל שלשו מע"ש למחר אמר רב ממחו בכלי אבל לא ביד א"ל שמואל ביד אטו כל יומא ממחו ליה ביד מאכל חמורים הוא אלא אמר שמואל ממחו ביד ואינו ממחו בכלי אתמר ר"א אמר אחד זה ואחד זה אסור ורבי יוחנן אמר אחד זה ואחד זה מותר אביי ורבא דאמרי תרוייהו אין הלכה כרבי יוחנן קם רבי יוחנן בשיטתיה דר"א קם רבי אלעזר בשיטתיה דשמואל אביי ורבא דאמרי תרוייהו הלכה כרבי יוחנן *אימיה דאביי עבדא ליה ולא אכל דביתהו דזעירא עבדא ליה לרב חייא בר אשי ולא אכיל א"ל לרבך עבידי ליה ואכל ואת לא אכלת אמר רבא בר שבא הוה קאימנא קמיה דרבינא ובחשי ליה בשופתא דתומא ואכל °אמר מר זוטרא *לית הלכתא ככל הני שמעתתא אלא כי הא דאתמר חרדל שלשו מע"ש למחר ממחו בין ביד בין בכלי ונותן לתוכו דבש ולא יטרוף אלא מערב שחליים ששחקן מע"ש למחר נותן לתוכן שמן וחומץ וממשיך לתוכן אמיתא ולא יטרוף אלא מערב שום שריסקו מע"ש למחר נותן לתוכו פול וגריסין ולא ישחוק אלא מערב וממשיך את אמיתא לתוכן *מאי אמיתא נינייא אמר אביי ש"מ האי נינייא מעליא לתחלי: ועושין אנומלין בשבת: *ת"ר עושין אנומלין בשבת ואין עושין *אלונטית ואיזו היא אנומלין ואיזו היא אלונטית אנומלין יין ודבש ופלפלין אלונטית יין ישן ומים צלולין ואפרסמון דעבדי לבי מסותא למיקר אמר רב יוסף זימנא חדא עלית בתר מר עוקבא לבי באני כי נפקי אתאי אשקיין חמרא חד כסא וחשי מבינתא דראשי ועד טופרא דכרעי ואי אשקיין כסא אחרינא הואי מסתפינא דלמא מנכו לי מזכותא דעלמא דאתי והא מר עוקבא דשתי כל יומא שאני מר עוקבא דדש ביה: **מתני'** אין שורין את החילתית בפושרין אבל נותן לתוך החומץ ואין שולין את הכרשינין ולא שפין אותן אבל נותן לתוך הכברה או לתוך הכלכלה אין כוברין את התבן בכברה ולא יתננו על גבי מקום גבוה בשביל שירד המוץ אבל נוטל הוא בכברה ונותן לתוך האיבוס: **גמ'** איבעיא להו שרה מאי תרגמא רב אדא נרשאה קמיה דרב יוסף שרה חייב חטאת א"ל אביי אלא מעתה שרה אומצא במיא הכי נמי דמיחייב אלא אמר אביי *מדרבנן שלא יעשה כדרך שהוא עושה בחול בעא מיניה רבי יוחנן מר' ינאי מהו לשרות את החלתית בצונן א"ל אסור והא אנן תנן אין שורין את החלתית בפושרין הא בצונן מותר א"ל *א"כ מה בין לי ולך מתניתין יחידאה היא דתניא *אין שורין את החלתית לא בחמין ולא בצונן רבי יוסי אומר בחמין אסור בצונן מותר למאי עבדי ליה ליוקרא דליבא רב אחא בר יוסף חש ביוקרא דליבא אתא לקמיה דמר עוקבא א"ל זיל שתי תלתא תיקלי חילתתא בתלתא יומי אזל אישתי חמשא בשבת ומעלי שבת לצפרא אזל שאל בי מדרשא אמרו ליה תנא דבי רב אדא ואמרי לה תנא דבי מר בר רב אדא שותה אדם קב או קביים ואינו חושש אמר להו לשתות לא קמיבעיא לי כי קא מיבעיא לי לשרות מאי אמר להו רב חייא בר אבין בדידי הוה עובדא ואתאי שאילתיה לרב אדא בר אהבה ולא הוה בידיה אתאי שאילתיה לרב הונא ואמר הכי קאמר רב שורה בצונן ומניח בחמה כמאן דשרי אפילו למאן דאסר ה"מ היכא דלא אישתי כלל אבל הכא כיון דאישתי חמשא ומעלי שבתא אי לא שתי בשבת מיסתכן מיסתמיך ואזיל רב אחא בר יוסף אכתפיה דרב נחמן בר יצחק בר אחתיה א"ל כי מטינן לבי רב ספרא עיילינא כי מטו עייליה בעא מיניה מהו לכסכוסי כיתניתא בשבתא לרכוכי כיתניתא קא מיכוין ושפיר דמי או דילמא לאולודי חיורא קמיכוין ואסיר א"ל לרכוכי קא מיכוין ושפיר דמי כי נפק אתא א"ל מאי בעא מר מיניה א"ל בעי מיניה מהו לכסכוסי כיתניתא בשבתא ואמר לי שפיר דמי ותבעי ליה למר סודרא סודרא לא קא מיבעיא לי דבעי מרב הונא ופשיט לי *ותיפשיט ליה למר מסודרא א"ל התם מיחזי כי אולודי חיורא הכא לא מיחזי כאולודי חיורא אמר רב חסדא האי כיתניתא

משלפו

רש"י

לפי שאין עושין(א) אלא לגוון · למראה שהחלמון יפה לגוון ולא החלבון הלכך אידי ואידי אוכל הוא ואין כאן ברירת פסולת מאוכל : ממחו · דישטיפדי"ר בלע"ז במים או ביין : ממחו בכלי · משמע זהו שינוי שלו : ואינו ממחו ביד · דממחו ליה שפיר טפי : אלא אמר שמואל ממחו ביד · שאין זה דרכו בחול : קם ר' יוחנן בשיטתיה דר"א · חזר בו ואסר : אביי ורבא דאמרי תרוייהו הלכה כר' יוחנן · דאסר : לרבך · לזעירי : בשופתא דתומא · אמלעי של שום : ולא יטרוף · כדרך שטורפין ביצים בקערה בכף דרך טריפה שמכה בכח : שחליים · כרישין והיו שוחקין אותם במים : ממשיך · נותן : אמיתא · מינט"א בלע"ז : מעליא לתחלי · לערב עם שחליים : ואין עושין אלונטית · שאינה למשקה למה אלא לצנן לאחר המרחץ ודוגמת רפואה : וחשי מבינתא דרישא · הרגשתי בלבתו משערת ראשי עד לפרסי רגלי : מנכו לי מזכיותי · אם הייתי ניצול ממנו שלא אמות : שתי כל יומא · ולא היה מזיקו : דדש ביה · רגיל בו : **מתני'** חילתית · חלטי"ש בלשון ישמעאל ובלע"ז לזרי"א ושורין אותו בפושרין ושותין אותן המים לרפואה : אבל נותן · החלתית : בתוך החומץ · ומטבל בו מאכלו ולקמיה מפרש אמאי אין שורין : ואין שולין את הכרשינין · מציף עליהם מים בכלי לברור פסולתן כדתנן במסכת ביצה (דף יד:) אף מדיח ושולה : ולא שפין אותן · ביד להסיר פסולת דהוה ליה בורר : אבל נותן לתוך הכברה · ואע"פ דפעמים שהפסולת נופל דרך נקבי הכברה ונמצא נתברר מאליו : תבן · הוא שעושין מן הקש מחתכין אותו במוריגין ועושה כל זנב(ב) השבולת תבן: מוץ. הוא מוזקן השבולת העליון ואינו ראוי למאכל וכוברין אותו(ג) בכברין שיפול המוץ : אבל נוטל(ד) בכברה · ליתן בתוך האבוס ואע"פ שהמוץ נופל °מאליו כר"ש דאמר דבר שאין מתכוין מותר : **גמ'** שרה · חילתית בפושרין מאי : אומצא · בשר חי : שלא יעשה כו' · לא שבקוה רבנן למעבד עובדי דחול : אם כן · דלא ידענא לפרושי מתני' טפי מינך מה בין לי ולך : מתניתין יחידאה היא · ור' יוסי אמרה אבל לרבנן אף בצונן אסור : ליוקרא דליבא · שלבו כבד עליו : תלתא תקלי חילתתא · משקל ג' זהובים : שאיל בי מדרשא · מה יעשה בשבת : לשתות לא קמיבעיא לי · דבלאו רפואה משקה הוא ותנן כל המשקין שותה (לעיל דף קט:) : לשרות · דתנן מתניתין אין שורין : כמאן דשרי · בעיא הוא הך דרב לימא כרבי יוסי דשרי בצונן אבל לרבנן אסור : עיילנא · הכניסני ואיש זקן היה : לכסכוסי כיתניתא · חלוק כתונת של פשתן שנתכבסה והרי היא קשה ומשפשפה בין שתי ידיו והיא מתרככה ואף הליבון שלה מלהיל על ידי השפשוף : אולודי חיורא · הליבון מלהיל : התם מיחזי כאולודי חיורא · שמקפיד על ליבונו וזוהרו של סודר יותר מכיתניתא .

משלפא

עין משפט נר מצוה

לב א מיי' פ"ח מהל' שבת הל' יד ופכ"ב הלכה יב סמג לאוין סה טוש"ע א"ח סי' שכא סעיף טו :

לג ב ג מיי' פכ"ב שם טוש"ע שם סעיף טז:

לד ד מיי' שם טוש"ע שם סעיף יז :

לה ה מיי' פ"ד מהל' דעות הלכה יז :

לו ו מיי' פכ"א מהל' שבת הלכה ז סמג לאוין סה טוש"ע א"ח סי' שכא סעיף יח :

לז ז (מיי' פ"ח מהל' שבת) סמג לאוין סה טוש"ע א"ח סי' שיט סעיף ח :

לח ח מיי' פכ"א שם הלכה לג סמג שם טוש"ע א"ח סי' שכד סעיף א :

לט ט י כ מיי' פכ"א שם הלכה כב ופכ"ב שם הל' ז סמג שם טוש"ע א"ח סי' שכא סעיף יח :

[ע' תוס' כתובות כד. ד"ה לית]

מ ל מ מיי' פכ"ב שם הלכה יז סמג שם טוש"ע א"ח סי' שב סעיף ה :

רבינו חננאל

לפי שאין עושין אותה אלא לגוון . פי' לצבעו להתראות בו גוונא של ביצה מאכל המרס . פי' זה המאכל מטורס הוא כדתנן (נתן) [נטל] את הדם ונתנו למטרס בו על הרובד הרביעי וי"א מאכל חמורים הוא כלומר אינו מאכל ב"א אלא מאכל חמורים הוא: חרדל שלשו מע"ש חלקו עליו רב ושמואל ור' יוחנן ור' אלעזר ודבריהן פשוטין הן ומר זוטרא דהוא בתרא אמר לית הלכתא ככל הני שמעתתא אלא כי הא דתניא חרדל שלשו מע"ש למחר מניחו בין ביד בין בכלי ונותן לתוכו דבש ולא יטרוף אלא מערב. שום שריסקו מע"ש למחר נותן לתוכו פול או גריסין ולא ישחוק אלא מערב . וממשיך את האמיתה לתוכה מאי אמיתה ננחה. אנומלין יין ושמן ודבש ופלפלין. אלונתית יין ישן ומים צלולין ואפרסמון : אין שורין את החלתית בפושרין אבל נותן לתוך החומץ ומיבעיא לן שרה מאי . ומסקנא שרה אמר אביי איסורא מדרבנן וא"ר יוחנן מתניתין יחידאה היא והוא ר' יוסי אבל חכ"א בין בחמין בין בצונן אסור וסוגיא דשמעתא אם שרה מאתמול לשתות חלתית בשבת מותר . אבל לשרותו אסור אפילו בצונן . ואם שרה קודם השבת ועכשיו בשבת חושש אם לא ישתה מסתכן מותר לו לשרות בתוכו ולהניחה בחמה : לכסכוסי כיתונתא . פי' לרכוכי קא מיכוון ושרי או דלמא לאולודי וכו' . פי' לקבץ מקצת הבגד של פשתים לתוך ידו לשופו מפני שרוחצין הבגד ומתייבש בשמש או ברוח עומד אנסו פי' קשה ורוצה לרככו נותן הבגד לתוך ידיו ומוליך ומביא ידיו עד שיעשה הבגד ההוא כמו קפולין קטנים כמין קמטין כי הא דא"ר זירא בפ' חבית (דף קמז) מאי מרזב כנון*) כסכוסי מאני דמתחזי כמרזב וכי הא דתנן בפ' האשה שהיא עושה צריכה:צריכה לכסכס ג' פעמים על כל דבר ודבר ואמרי' בגמ' בעי ר' ירמיה אמטויי חד ואיתויי [חד] או דלמא אמטויי [חד] ואיתויי [תרתי] תיקו: וכן עוד מפורש בתלמוד א"י בענין מוליך ומביא שבלולב . מהא שמעינן דכיסכוס כעין שפשוף הוא ומתקבץ הבגד פי' יתכמש ונראה קמטין קמטין וכשלובשו מתפשט וכדאמרינן אמר רב כהנא ואיתמא רב יהודה טיט שעל בגדו מכסכסו מבפנים . ומרקדי להאי כיתונתא . שמעינן מנה דסודרא ליתיה כתינתא ולא יתכן לומר שהוא צמר שאם הוא צמר איך אומר לו היה לך ללמוד פשתים מצמר . והדבר רחוק ביניהם ואינה אלא צמר גפן שזה קרוב לזה ופשט

*) לפנינו בגמ' איתא גם כיסו בגלייתא

מסורת הש"ס

[ע' קדושין לא:]

[לעיל קכח.]

ע"ז ל.

[שם איתא אלונתית אבל בערוך גרס כגי' שלפנינו]

[לעיל קלח.]

[חולי' קלד:] [תוספ' פי"ז]

הגהות הב"ח

(א) רש"י ד"ה לפי שאין עושין אותה אלא: (ב) ד"ה תבן וכו' כל זנב השבלים תבן : (ג) ד"ה מוץ וכו' בכברה כדי שיפול: (ד) ד"ה אבל נוטל הוא בכברה ונותן לתוך האבוס :

גליון הש"ס

גמ' אמר מר זוטרא לית הלכתא ככל הכי שמעתתא. עיין כתובות דף כ"ד ע"א תוס' ד"ה לית הלכתא : רש"י ד"ה אבל נוטל וכו' נופל מאליו כר"ש. עיין לעיל דף כ"ד ע"א ברש"י ד"ה כלאים דתבלים: ס"א לאיסורא

רב נסים גאון

אין שורין את הכרשינין . גרסי' בגמ' דבני מערבא תני אין שורין את הכרשינים משום בורר ולא שפין אותן משום דש אין כוברין את התבן משום מרקד . גורפין מלפני הפטם וסלקין לצדדין מפני הרעי בגמ' דבני מערבא גרסי מה שהפטם אוכל ומותיר הרעי אוכל :

הרעי

עין משפט
נר מצוה

מא א ב מיי' פכ"ס מהל' שבת הל' יח סמג לאוין סה טוש"ע א"ח סי' שח סעיף מז :
מב ג מיי' פכ"ו מהל' שבת הל' טז סמג שם טוש"ע שם סעיף כז וכח :
מג ד מיי' פ"ז מהל' ברכות הלכה ג :
מד הו מיי' פכ"ו מהל' שבת הלכה יט סמג לאוין סה טוש"ע א"ח סי' שכד סעיף טו :
מה ז מיי' שם טוש"ע שם סעיף יד :

רבינו חננאל

רב חסדא דלרכובי מיכוון ושרי. אמר רב חסדא הא כיתניתא משלפה לדילא מקניא. פי' למשוך הבגד ששוטחו בקנה להנגב ונעשה נגוב וישאר הקנה במקומו. ולא מטלטלין מותר אבל למשוך הקנה מן הבגד ולטלטלו בשבת אסור שהקנה אינו כלי להטלטל בחצר. אמר רבא ואם כלי קוואי מותר. פי' אם הוא הבגד שטוח בכלי האורג וכלי האורג נקראין כלי קוואי כדאמרינן בפרק ואלו קשרים שחייבין עליהן. אתמר אמר רב נחמן אמר שמואל כלי קוואי מותר לטלטלו בשבת ואפי' כובד העליון וכובד התחתון אבל לא את העמודים ותוב בעא מיניה ר' יוחנן מרבי יהודה בר לוי כלי קוואי כגון כובד העליון וכובד התחתון כו'. האי תלא דבשרא פי' יתד של עץ עשוי לתלות בו בשר ופעמים שתולין בו זולתו [שרי לטלטולי] אבל העץ שתולין בו דגים. כיון שהדגים ריחם רע וקשה אין תולין בו דבר אחר ומסיחין דעתן ממנו ומוקצה מחמת מיאוס הוא ואסור : מדנהר אבא. שם מקום הוא : ציפיתא חדתא. פי' מחצלת חדשה בורא בחדא ידא. כגון אבן שאין לה דמים ולא צורך. ומפני שהסתירה מהן נתייקרה בעיניהם ופייסוהו להראותה להן : מתני' אין שולין את הכרשינין ולא שפין כו' גורפין מלפני הפטם ומסלקין לצדדים כו'. פי' גורפין המאכל של בהמה מלפני הפטם ומאכל שאר בהמות מסלקין לצדדין דברי ר' דוסא חכמים אוסרין ואיבעיא לן רבנן ארישא פליגי והיא גורפין [או] אסיפא פליגי והוא שמסלקין לצדדין ואמרינן ת"ש וחכ"א אחד זה ואחד זה לא יסלקנו לצדדין. ש"מ רבנן אתרווייהו פליגי. אמר רב חסדא מחלוקת באבוס של כלי ואפי' בזה חכמים אוסרין אבל באבוס של קרקע דברי הכל אסור לגרוף

*משלפו לדידה מקניא שרי קניא ממנה אסור אמר רבא *ואם כלי קוואי הוא מותר אמר רב חסדא האי *כישתא דירקא אי חזיא למאכל בהמה שרי לטלטולי ואי לא אסיר אמר רב חייא בר אשי אמר רב האי *תליא דבשרא שרי לטלטולי דכוורי אסיר אמר רב קטינא העומד באמצע המטה כאילו עומד בבריסה של אשה ולאו מילתא היא ואמר רב חסדא בר בי רב הבין ירקא ליזבין אריכא כישא כי כישא ואורכא ממילא ואמר רב חסדא בר בי רב דזבין קניא ליזבין אריכא טונא כי טונא ואורכא ממילא ואמר רב חסדא בר בי רב [*דלא נפישא ליה ריפתא] לא ליכול ירקא משום דגריר ואמר רב חסדא אנא לא בעניותי אכלי ירקא ולא בעתירותי אכלי ירקא בעניותי משום דגריר בעתירותי דאמינא היכא דעייל ירקא ליעול בשרא וכוורי (א) ואמר רב חסדא בר בי רב דלא נפישא ליה ריפתא לא ליבצע בצועי ואמר רב חסדא בר בי רב דלא נפישא ליה ריפתא *לא ליבצע מ"ט דלא עביד בעין יפה ואמר רב חסדא אנא מעיקרא לא הואי בצענא עד דשדאי ידי בכולי מנא ואשכחי [ביה כל צרכי] ואמר רב חסדא האי מאן דאפשר ליה למיכל נהמא דשערי ואכל דחיטי קעבר משום בל תשחית ואמר רב פפא האי מאן דאפשר למישתי שיכרא ושתי חמרא עובר משום בל תשחית ולאו מילתא היא *בל תשחית דגופא עדיף ואמר רב חסדא בר בי רב דלית ליה משחא נימשי במיא דחריצי ואמר רב חסדא בר בי רב דזבין אומצא ליזבין אונקא דאית ביה תלתא מיני בישרא וא"ר חסדא בר בי רב דזבין כיתוניתא ליזבן מדנהר אבא ונִיחוורה כל תלתין יומין דמפטיא ליה תריסר ירחי שתא ואנא ערבא מאי כיתוניתא כיתא נאה וא"ר חסדא בר בי רב לא ליתיב אציפתא חדתא דמכליא מאניה וא"ר חסדא בר בי רב לא לישדר מאניה לאושפיזיה לחווריה ליה דלאו אורח ארעא דילמא חזי ביה מידי ואתי למגניא אמר להו רב חסדא לבנתיה תיהוי צניעתן באפי גברייכו לא תיכלון נהמא באפי גברייכו לא תיכלון ירקא בליליא לא תיכלין תמרי בליליא ולא תשתון שיכרא בליליא ולא תיפנון היכא דמפני גברייכו וכי קא קארי אבבא איניש לא תימרון מנו אלא מני נקיט *מרגניתא בחדא ידיה וכורא בחדא ידיה מרגניתא אחוי להו וכורא לא אחוי להו עד דמיצטערן והדר אחוי להו : אין שולין את הכרשינין* : מתני' דלא כי האי תנא דתניא ר"א בן יעקב אומר אין משגיחין בכברה כל עיקר :

מתני' גורפין מלפני הפטם ומסלקין לצדדין מפני הרעי דברי רבי דוסא וחכמים אוסרין נוטלין מלפני בהמה זו ונותנין לפני בהמה זו בשבת :

גמ' איבעיא להו רבנן ארישא פליגי או אסיפא פליגי או אתרוייהו פליגי ת"ש דתניא וחכמים אומרים אחד זה ואחד זה לא יסלקנו לצדדין אמר רב חסדא מחלוקת באיבוס של קרקע אבל באיבוס של כלי דברי הכל מותר ואיבוס של קרקע מי איכא למאן דשרי הא קא משוי גומות אלא אי איתמר הכי איתמר א"ר חסדא מחלוקת באיבוס של כלי אבל באיבוס של קרקע דברי הכל אסור : ונוטלין מלפני בהמה : תנא חדא נוטלין מלפני בהמה שפיה יפה ונותנין לפני בהמה שפיה רע ותניא אידך נוטלין מלפני בהמה שפיה רע ונותנין לפני בהמה שפיה יפה אמר אביי אידי ואידי מקמי חמרא לקמי תורא שקלינן מקמי תורא לקמי חמרא לא שקלינן והא דקתני נוטל מלפני בהמה שפיה יפה בחמור דלית ליה רירי ונותנין לפני בהמה שפיה רע בפרה

דאית

אבל באיבוס של קרקע דברי הכל אסור · אע"ג דמתכן שריקן לרבי שמעון (לעיל דף כט·) הכא רגילות הוא להתכוין לאשווי גומות והייפיק ספי שמא יתכוין :
הקש

משלפא לדידה מקניא · כשמותחין אותה לגנבה תוחבים קנה מבית יד לבית יד וכשנוטלה בשבת ישלפנה מן הקנה ולא הקנה ממנה דלא חזי לטלטולי דלהסקה קאי : ואם כלי קוואי היא · קנה של אורגים דתורת כלי עליו שרי : תליא דבשרא · בשר מליח התלוי לייבשו ומלא האבל קרי תליא : שרי · דנאכל הוי בהומא : דכוורי · אין נאכלין חיין : באמצע מטה · שאיש ואשתו רגילין בה לישן : כאילו עומד כו'. דמהדר : לזבין אריכא · אגודה ארוכה של כרוב אגוד ושל כרישין ארוכים : כישא כי כישא · שכל אגודות הגנין שוות בעובין שלכולן מדה אחת לחבל שהוא אגוד בו : ואורכא ממילא · כלומר ארכו של זה שהוא ארוך מחבירו הוא משתכר בו : קניא · חבילי קנים לעצים : לא ליכול ירקא · ירק חי (ג)כרישין לירפו"ל ושחליים: משום דגריר ליבא · ומאכילו להם הרבה ואין לו : לא ליבלע בלועי · מורשיליונ"ש בלע"ז לא יאכל עכשיו מעט פת שימלא לו ולאחר שעה מעט מפני שאין לו דרך שביעה אלא יצרף ויאכל יחד : מעיקרא · קודם שנתעשרתי : עד דשדאי ידי בכולא מנא · כשהייתי ממשמש בסל ומוצא בו פת הרבה הייתי מברך המוציא : דלית ליה משחא · שהיו סכין ידיהן שמן קודם מים אחרונים להעביר את הזוהמא : במיא דחריצי · הנקוים יחד וגדל עליהם ירקרוקית עבה ונוחה כשמן : אונקא · צואר : תלתא מיני בשרא · יטעום בו ג' מיני מטעמים שמן וכחוש וגיד הצואר : מדנהר אבא · מאותו מקום שפשתנו יפה : דמפטיא ליה תריסר ירחי שתא ואנא ערבא · אני ערב בדבר שתתקיים לו שנה שלימה ותפטיהו שלא יצטרך לקנות חלוק : כיתא נאה · כת נאה ראויה להושיב בעליה בכת נאה : אציפתא חדתא · מחצלת חדשה של גמי לח ולחלוחית הגמי מבלה הבגדים : לאושפיזא · לפונדקית שלו לא ישלח חלוקו ללבן : דילמא חזיא בהו · קרי ומגניא עליה : לא תיכלון נהמא באפי גברייכו · פעמים תאכל הרבה ותתגנה עליו : לא תיכלון ירקא בלילה · מפני ריח הפה : שיכרא ותמרי · משלשלין ומביאין לידי הפחה : היכא דמפני גברייכו · בגילוי בפניהם בשדות ואפילו שלא בפניהם שמכיר מקומו ומקומכם ונמאסת' לו בזכרו : לא תימרון מנו · מי הוא לשון זכר לא תרגילו לשונכם לדבר עם זכרים : אלא מני · מי היא : נקיט מרגניתא בחדא ידיה וכורא בחדא ידיה · כשבעליך ממשמש בך להתאוות ליך לתשמיש ואוחז הדדים בידו אחת והאחרת עד אותו מקום : מרגניתא אחוין ליה. הדדין המביאי' לו שתתרבה תאותו ומקום תשמיש אל תמציאי לו מהר כדי שיתרבה תאותו וחיבתו ויצטער הדר אחוי ליה : כורא · לשון כור נורפין (לעיל דף עה·) לשון אחר בור לשון בור שוחה : מתניתין · דקתני אבל נותנין לתוך הכברה :

מתני' גורפין מלפני הפטם · שור שמפטמין אותו גורפין אבוס שלפניו בשבת לתת לתוכו התבן והשעורין ולא יתערב בהן עפרורית ויקוץ במאכלו : ומסלקין תבן (ג) שלפניו לצדדין כשהוא רב כדי שלא ידרסנו ברעי: וחכמים אוסרים · מפ' בגמ' אהיא : ונוטלין מלפני בהמה זו · שעורין ותבן ונותנין לפני זו ולא אמרינן טלטול דלא חזי הוא אלא ודאי חזי הוא דאין בהמה קצה במאכל הניטל מלפני חבירתה : **גמ'** ארישא פליגי · אגורפין ואסרי לגרוף משום דפעמים שהאבוס של קרקע וקא מכוין לאשווי גומות שלא יפלו השעורים לתוכו : או אסיפא פליגי · ומשום דלא חזי שיש בו(ד) שנמאס במדרס רגליו : תא שמע · דאתרוייהו פליגי : אחד זה ואחד זה · אחד גריפת האבוס ואחד תבן שלפניו לא יסלקנו לצדדין : של קרקע · כעין שעושין גדר קטן לפני בהמה ונותנין מאכל לפנים ממנו דאיכא למיחש לאשויי גומות : מחלוקת באבוס של כלי · וגזרו רבנן גזרה אטו של קרקע : שפיה יפה · לקמיה מפרש : אידי ואידי · שתיהן המשניות סבירא להו : מקמי חמרא לקמי תורא שקלינן · שאינו מטיל רירין ואין מה שלפניו נמאס וראוי לתתו לפני שור : מקמי תורא לקמי חמרא לא שקלינן ·

דאית

מסורת הש"ס

[לעיל קיג.]
[בערוך איתא הוצא]
[עי' תוס' לעיל קלט: ד"ה תלא]
[עי' תוס' עירובין נה: ד"ה כל עיר וכו' נראה דלא גרסי להנך ד' תיבות]
ברכות מו:
[לעיל קכט.]
[גירס' אחרינא ופירושו עי' בערוך ערך בזר א'] נ"ל וכו'

הגהות הב"ח

(א) דלא נפישא ליה ריפתא (לא ליבלע וכו' יפה) תא"מ ונ"ב ס"א לא ליבלע בלועי והשאר נמחק וככי משמע מפירש"י :
(ב) רש"י ד"ה לא ליכול ירקא ירק חי · נ"ב עיין פרק כיצד מעברין בדף נה במ"ש התוס' בד"ה כל עיר :
(ג) ד"ה ויסלק תבן מלפניו לצדדין :
(ד) ד"ה או אסיפא וכו' שיש בו מה שנמאס :

R. Ḥisda said: As for linen, [140*b*] to draw it away from the cane is permitted; to draw out the cane from it is forbidden.[7] Raba said: But if it is a weaver's implement, it is permitted.[8]

R. Ḥisda said: A bunch of vegetables, if fit as food for animals, may be handled; if not, it is forbidden.

R. Ḥiyya b. Ashi said in Rab's name: A meat hook[9] is permitted [to be handled]; a fish [hook] is forbidden.[10]

R. Ḳaṭṭina said: He who stands in the middle of a [marital]
a bed is as though he stood on a woman's stomach.[1] But this is incorrect.

R. Ḥisda also said: When a scholar buys vegetables, let him buy long ones, for one bunch is like another [in thickness], and so the length [comes] of itself.[2]

R. Ḥisda also said: When a scholar buys canes,[3] let him buy long ones; one load is like another, so the length [comes] of itself.

R. Ḥisda also said: When a scholar has but little bread, let him not eat vegetables, because it whets [the appetite]. R. Ḥisda also said: I ate vegetables neither when poor nor when rich.[4] When poor, because it whets [the appetite]; when rich, because I say, Where the vegetables are to enter, let fish and meat enter![5]

R. Ḥisda also said: If a scholar has but little bread he should not divide [his meal].[6] R. Ḥisda also said: If a scholar has but little bread he should not break [bread].[7] What is the reason?—Because he does not do it generously.[8] R. Ḥisda also said: Formerly I would not break [bread] until I had passed my hand through the whole of my wallet and found there as much as I needed.

R. Ḥisda also said: When one can eat barley bread but eats wheaten bread he violates, *thou shalt not destroy*.[9] R. Papa said: When one can drink beer but drinks wine, he violates, *thou shalt not destroy*.[10] But this is incorrect: *Thou shalt not destroy*, as applied to one's own person, stands higher.[11]

R. Ḥisda also said: When a scholar has no oil, let him wash with pit water.[12]

R. Ḥisda also said: If a scholar buys raw meat he should buy the neck, because it contains three kinds of meat.

R. Ḥisda also said: When a scholar buys linen [underwear],
b he should buy it from the Nehar Abba[1] and wash[2] it every thirty days, and I guarantee that it will relieve him [from buying another] for a full year. What does *kitonitha* [underwear] mean? *Kitta na'ah* [fine flax].[3]

R. Ḥisda also said: A scholar should not sit upon a new mat, because it destroys the garments.[4]

R. Ḥisda also said: A scholar should not send his garments to his host[5] for washing, for this is not in good taste, lest he see something[6] and he come to despise him.

R. Ḥisda advised his daughters: Act modestly before your husbands: do not eat bread before your husbands,[7] do not eat greens at night,[8] do not eat dates at night nor drink beer at night,[9] and do not ease yourselves where your husbands do,[10] and when someone calls at the door, do not say 'who is he' but 'who is she?'[11] He [R. Ḥisda] held a jewel in one hand and a [valueless] seed grain in the other; the pearl he showed them but the seed grain he did not show them until they were suffering,[12] and then he showed it to them.[13]

ONE MUST NOT CAUSE LEEKS TO FLOAT. Our Mishnah[14] does not agree with the following Tanna. For it was taught, R. Eliezer b. Jacob said: One must not look at the sieve at all.[15]

MISHNAH. ONE MAY SWEEP OUT [THE MANGER] FOR A STALL OX,[16] AND MOVE [THE REMNANTS] ASIDE FOR THE SAKE
c OF A GRAZING ANIMAL:[1] THIS IS R. DOSA'S VIEW, BUT THE SAGES FORBID IT. ONE MAY TAKE [FODDER] FROM ONE ANIMAL AND PLACE IT BEFORE ANOTHER ANIMAL ON THE SABBATH.[2]

GEMARA. The scholars asked: Do the Rabbis disagree with the first clause, or with the second, or with both?—Come and hear: For it was taught, But the Sages maintain: Both the one and the other[3] must not be moved on a side.[4]

R. Ḥisda said: They differ in respect of a ground manger,[5] but all agree that a manger which is a vessel[6] is permitted. But is there any opinion that a ground manger is permitted: surely one levels the holes?—Rather if stated, it was thus stated: R. Ḥisda said: They differ in respect of a vessel manger, but all hold that a ground manger is forbidden.

ONE MAY TAKE [FODDER] FROM ONE ANIMAL [etc.]. One [Baraitha] taught: One may take [fodder] from before an animal that is fastidious and place [it] before an animal that is not fastidious; while another taught: One may take [fodder] from before an animal that is not fastidious and place [it] before an animal that is fastidious. Abaye observed: Both [Baraithas hold] that one may take from an ass [to put] before an ox, but not from an ox [and place it] before an ass. Now, when it is taught, 'One may take from before an animal that is fastidious', it refers to an ass, which does not drop saliva [into its food]; 'and place [it] before

(7) Linen was hung up on a cane passing through the sleeves to dry. A cane must not be handled on the Sabbath, being regarded as *mukẓeh*, as it stands to be used as fuel. (8) For it is then a utensil, which may be handled. (9) Lit., 'a suspender of meat'—i.e., a hook. Tosaf. and Jast. (10) The first was more like a utensil than the second.

a (1) Because he is incited to impure thoughts. (2) I.e., the additional length is extra value—presumably the price was not increased. (3) For fuel. (4) Or, I would eat vegetables neither when rich nor when poor. (5) Which are more nutritious. (6) Eat a little now and a little later, as at no time will he have enough. (7) To distribute it among the guests at a meal. (8) MS.M. deletes the two intervening passages. (9) Deut. XX, 19. I.e., it is wasteful extravagance. (10) Was his attitude influenced by the fact that he was a beer brewer? (11) To consume better food and drink is beneficial, not wasteful. (12) The scum thickens it into a semblance of oil.

b (1) A canal in the Bagdad region; Obermeyer, p. 239. (2) Lit., 'whiten'. (3) Jast. Rashi: the upper class—its wearer is fit to be a member of the upper classes—a play on words, of course. (4) Being hard, it injures the texture. (5) The keeper of the boarding house where he stays. (6) A euphemism for semen. (7) You may eat too much. (8) Because of their odour. (9) Because of their laxative properties. (10) Even in their absence. (11) I.e., 'who is it' but in the feminine, not the masculine form. (12) With curiosity, to know what he was holding. (13) To prove the folly of curiosity (Jast. s.v. בזרא, which 'Aruch reads instead of כורא). (14) Which continues, BUT THEY MAY BE PUT INTO A SIEVE. (15) I.e., one must not handle it for any purpose on the Sabbath. (16) If it contains chips, etc., they may render the straw repulsive and cause the animal to go off its feed.

c (1) Which is ordinarily fed on pasture.—R. Ḥan. and Jast. Rashi translates: one may move aside the straw, if there is much, lest the animal tread it into the dung. (2) Because the second will eat it, and therefore it is not unnecessary handling. (3) *Sc.* fodder in a manger and straw lying in front of an animal. (4) Thus they disagree with both clauses. (5) I.e., a small low fenced enclosure on the ground. The Rabbis forbid it lest one comes to level up holes in the ground. (6) I.e., a real manger.

an animal that is not fastidious', to a cow, [141a] which drops saliva.[7] And when it is taught, 'One may take [fodder] from before an animal that is not fastidious', it refers to an ass, which is not particular about what it eats;[8] 'and put [it] before an animal that is fastidious,' to a cow, which is particular about what it eats.[9]

MISHNAH. ONE MUST NOT MOVE STRAW [LYING] UPON A BED WITH HIS HAND, YET HE MAY MOVE IT WITH HIS BODY. BUT IF IT IS FODDER FOR ANIMALS, OR A PILLOW OR A SHEET WAS UPON IT BEFORE NIGHTFALL, HE MAY MOVE IT WITH
a HIS HAND.[1] ONE MAY UNDO A HOUSEHOLDER'S CLOTHES PRESS,[2] BUT NOT FORCE IT DOWN.[3] BUT A LAUNDERER'S [PRESS] MAY NOT BE TOUCHED.[4] R. JUDAH SAID: IF IT WAS UNDONE BEFORE THE SABBATH, ONE MAY UNFASTEN THE WHOLE AND REMOVE IT.

GEMARA. R. Naḥman said: A radish, if it is the right way up, it is permitted; if it is reversed, it is forbidden.[5] R. Adda b. Abba said, The scholars[6] said, We learnt [a Mishnah] in disagreement with R. Naḥman: ONE MUST NOT MOVE STRAW [LYING] UPON A BED WITH HIS HAND, YET HE MAY MOVE IT WITH HIS BODY. BUT IF IT IS FODDER FOR ANIMALS, OR A PILLOW OR A SHEET WAS UPON IT BEFORE NIGHTFALL, HE MAY MOVE IT WITH HIS HAND: this proves, indirect[7] handling is not designated handling;[8] this proves it.

Rab Judah[9] said: To crush peppergrains one by one with a knife-handle is permitted; in twos, it is forbidden.[10] Raba said: Since he does it in a different way,[11] crushing even many [is permitted] too.

Rab Judah also said: If one bathes in water, he should first dry himself[12] and then ascend, lest he come to carry[13] four cubits in a
b *karmelith*.[1] If so, when he enters[2] too, his force propels the water four cubits,[3] which is forbidden?—They did not prohibit one's force in a *karmelith*.

Abaye—others state, Rab Judah—said: One may scrape off the clay from his foot on to the ground, but not on to a wall. Said Raba, Why not on to a wall? because it looks like building?[4] but it is ignorant building?[5] Rather said Raba: He may scrape it off on to a wall but not on to the ground, lest he come to level holes. It was stated, Mar son of Rabina said: Both are forbidden; R. Papa said: Both are permitted. According to Mar son of Rabina, whereon shall he scrape it? He scrapes it on a plank.[6]

Raba said: A man should not sit on the top of a stake,[7] lest an article roll away from him[8] and he come to fetch it.

Raba also said: One must not bend sideways a cask [which is standing] on the ground,[9] lest he come to level hollows.

Raba also said: One must not squeeze a cloth stopper into the mouth of a jug, lest he come to wring [it] out.

R. Kahana said: As for the clay [mire] on one's garment, he may rub off from the inside but not from the outside.[10] An objection is raised: One may scrape off the clay from his shoes with the back of a knife, and that which is on one's garment he may scrape off with [even][11] his finger nail, providing that he does not rub it. Surely that means that he must not rub it at all?—No: he must not rub it from the outside but only from the inside.

R. Abbahu said in R. Eleazar's name in R. Jannai's name: A

(7) Hence the cow will eat after the ass. (8) It eats fodder even when it contains thorns and thistles. (9) Spurning thorns and thistles.

a (1) V. *supra* 50a for notes. (2) The two boards of the press fitted on to four perforated rods: the upper board was pressed down and pegs were inserted in the holes to keep it there. The press may be undone by withdrawing these pegs, because the clothes are required for the Sabbath. (3) As the clothes will be wanted during the week, but not on the Sabbath. (4) This was screwed down very tightly, and undoing it would resemble taking a utensil to pieces. (5) V. *supra* 123a for notes. (6) *Be rab* may mean either the academy founded by Rab, or scholars in general, v. Weiss, *Dor*, III, 158. (7) Lit., 'from the side.' (8) Cf. *supra* 43b, n. b1. (9) Asheri in Bez. I, 21 reads: R. Huna. (10) Because then it looks like grinding. (11) From usual, which is in a mill or a mortar. (12) I.e., the part of his body that is not in the water. (13) The water upon him.

b (1) V. Glos. (2) Lit., 'goes down'. (3) His weight makes the water spurt that distance. (4) *Sc.* the addition of clay to the wall. (5) Lit., 'a field labourer'. I.e., surely none but the ignorant would think of building in such a manner. (6) Lying on the ground. (7) At the entrance to an alley, whereby carrying therein is permitted; v. *supra* 9a, n. a2. (8) Without the entrance, where it is public ground. (9) Text as emended by BaḤ. (10) In the latter case he looks as though he desires to wash the garment, though it is not actual washing. (11) So Wilna Gaon.

דאית לה רירי והא דקתני נוטלין מלפני בהמה שפיה רע בחמור דלא דייק ואכיל ונותנין לפני בהמה שפיה יפה בפרה דדייקא ואכלה: **מתני'** *[א]הקש שעל גבי המטה לא ינענעו בידו אלא מנענעו בגופו ואם היה מאכל בהמה או שהיה עליו כר או סדין מנענעו בידו [ב]מכבש של בעלי בתים מתירין אבל לא כובשין ושל כובסין לא יגע בו ר' יהודה אומר אם היה מותר מע"ש מתיר את כולו ושומטו: **גמ'** *אמר רב נחמן האי פוגלא מלמעלה למטה שרי מלמטה למעלה אסיר אמר רב אדא בר אבא אמרי בי רב תנינא דלא כרב נחמן הקש שע"ג המטה לא ינענעו בידו אבל מנענעו בגופו ואם היה מאכל בהמה או שהיה עליו כר או סדין מנענעו בידו ש"מ *[ג]טלטול מן הצד לא שמיה טלטול ש"מ אמר רב *[ד]יהודה הני פלפלי מידק חדא חדא בקתא דסכינא שרי תרתי אסיר רבא אמר [ה]כיון דמשני אפילו טובא נמי *אמר רב יהודה [ו]מאן דסחי במיא לינגיב נפשיה ברישא והדר ליסליק דילמא אתי לאתויי ד' אמות בכרמלית אי הכי כי קא נחית נמי קא דחי כחו ד' אמות ואסיר *כחו בכרמלית לא גזרו אמר אביי ואיתימא רב יהודה טיט שע"ג רגלו מקנחו בקרקע ואין מקנחו בכותל אמר רבא מ"ט בכותל לא משום דמיחזי כבונה הא בנין חקלאה הוא אלא אמר רבא [ז]מקנחו בכותל ואין מקנחו בקרקע דילמא אתי לאשויי גומות איתמר מר בריה דרבינא אמר אחד זה ואחד זה אסור רב פפא אמר אחד זה ואחד זה מותר למר בריה דרבינא במאי מקנחי ליה בקורה *אמר רבא (א)[ח]לא ליתיב איניש אפומיה דליחייא דילמא מיגנדרא ליה חפץ ואתי לאתויי ואמר רבא [ט]לא ליצדד איניש כובא(ג) דילמא אתי לאשויי גומות ואמר רבא [י]לא ליהדוק איניש אודרא בפומא דשישא [כ]דילמא אתי לידי סחיטה אמר רב כהנא [ל]טיט שע"ג בגדו מכסכסו מבפנים ואין מכסכסו מבחוץ מיתיבי טיט שע"ג מנעלו מגררו בגבסכין [א] ושעל בגדו מגררו בצפורן ובלבד שלא יכסכס מאי לאו שלא יכסכס כלל לא שלא יכסכס מבחוץ אלא מבפנים א"ר אבהו א"ר אלעזר אמר ר' ינאי מגררין מנעל חדש אבל לא ישן

במה

דאית לה רירי · ואימאים והא דקרי לה הכא פיה יפה והכא פיה רע כדמפרש ואזיל פיה יפה דלית ליה רירי פיה רע דלא דייק ואכיל שאוכל קוצים ודרקנים : **מתני'** הקש שעל המטה · וסתמא להסקה ומוקצה הוא ובא לשכב עליו ומנענעו כדי שיהא נח ורך לשכב : לא ינענעו בידו · דמוקצה הוא : אבל מנענעו בגופו . בכתפיו וטלטול מן הצד הוא דלא שמיה טלטול : או שהיה עליו כר או סדין · דגלי דעתיה דאקלייה לשכיבה מעתה תורת כלי עליו : מכבש · פריס"א שני לווחים ארוכים וכבדים וסודרין בגדים על התחתון ומורידין העליון עליו וכובשים את הבגדים על ידי יתדות שיש עמודים קבועין מנוקבין בארבע הפיאות של התחתונות והעליונה מנוקבת בארבע זויותיה ועולה ויורדת בעמודים וכפי מה שהוא רוצה לכבוש מורידה ותוחב יתד בנקב העמוד ואינה יכולה לעלות: מתירין · את המכבש שנוטל את היתד והוא ניתר דהיינו צורך שבת שנוטל את הכלים : אבל לא כובשין · דהיינו צורך חול : ושל כובסין לא יגע בו · מפני שהוא עשוי לתקן הבגדים ותוחבו בחוזקה ומיהדק והתרה שלו דומה לסתירה : **גמ'** האי פוגלא · כגון שטומנין בקרקע להתקיים כשבא לחלצו מלמעלה למטה שרי אם היה ראשה מלמעלה ועוקצה מלמטה וחוללה מראשה העבה תחילה ועוקצה נמשך אחריה מותר לפי שהגומא רחבה מלמעלה ואין מזיזין הקרקע כשהוא שומטה אבל אם חוללה מלמטה למעלה שתחתונה נתון למעלה וראש עליונה שהוא עב נתון למטה והוא שומטה מסופה לראשה אסור לפי שהגומא קצרה מלמעלה וכשהוא חוללה מזיז העפר ומטלטלו ואע"ג דטלטול מן הצד הוא שמיה טלטול ואסור : תניא דלא כר"נ · דאילו ממתניתין שמעינן דלא שמיה טלטול דקתני מנענעו בגופו : מידק. דייק: חדא חדא · לאו טוחן הוא אלא כלאחר יד : דקמשני · שלא ברחים ושלא במדוכה : לאתויי ד' אמות · מים שעליו : קא דחי כחו · את המים ד' אמות : אחד זה ואחד זה אסור · זה משום בונה וזה משום אשויי גומות : אחד זה ואחד זה מותר · אין דרך מתכוין בכך וקי"ל כר"ש : בקורה · בעץ המוטל על הקרקע(ג): אפומא דלחייא · של מבוי דליכא הכירא : אודרא · מוכין שסותמין בהן פי הפך : שישא · פך : מכסכסו · משפשפו : מבפנים · דלא מוכחא מילתא לאיתחזויי כמלבן ומלבן ממש לא הוי דאין נותן שם מים : כסכוס דמי למכבס : אבל לא ישן · שקולפו והוי ממחק :

במה

הקש שע"ג המטה · בריש פרק כירה (דף לו:) פי' מה הוא קש : **הני** פלפלי מידק חדא ט'· פירש ר"ת *בשאלתות דרב אחאי בפרשת אמור אל הכהנים מפרש דבי"ט איירי וקשה לר' דהוה ליה לפרש בהדיא כיון דבמכילתין לא איירי אלא בשבת ועוד היכי אסר רב יהודה טולי האי בפלפלין הא אפילו מלח צריכא בפ"ק דביצה (ד' יד·) במדוך של עץ אלא נראה לרבי דהכא בשבת איירי ואגב דאיירי בטלטול ע"י שינוי מייתי ליה הכא ובכולה שמעתא נמי מייתי מילי דשבת טובא אע"ג דלא שייכן הכא טולי האי אבל בי"ט נראה לר"י דשרי בלא שינוי אפי' במדוך של אבן כשאר תבלין דתנן בפ"ק דביצה (שם) ב"ה אומר תבלין נדוכין במדוך של אבן והמלח במדוך של עץ ואמרי' בגמרא דכ"ע מלח בעי שינוי מ"ט רב הונא ורב חסדא חד אמר כל הקדרות צריכות מלח ואין כל הקדרות צריכות תבלין וחד אמר כולן מפיגין טעמן ומלח אין מפיגה טעמא מאי בינייהו איכא בינייהו דידע מאי בעי בשולי(ד) אי נמי מוריקא פירוש כרכום אינה מפיגה טעמא למ"ד משום הפגת טעם אסור ולמ"ד משום כל הקדרות כו' שרי א"כ פלפלין דהכא נמי שרי דאין כל הקדרות צריכות פלפלין וא"כ (ס"א ואי נמי) למ"ד נמי משום הפגת טעם פלפלין שרו דצריך לומר נמי שמפיגים טעמם מדלא קאמר איכא בינייהו פלפלין ומיהו אומר רבי דאין זה דקדוק שצריך לפרש שם בע"א דקשיא למ"ד דשרי מוריקא משום דאין כל הקדרות צריכות מוריקא א"כ יהא מותר לקוצרו ולחותכו מן המחובר אע"כ צריך לפרש יש בו הפגת טעם ולא כשאר תבלין להכי שרי למ"ד אין כל הקדרות כו' כיון דאיכא נמי קצת הפגת טעמא והשתא אתי שפיר דלקצור אסור ומהשתא אין ראיה להתיר פלפלין דשמא אין בהם הפגת טעם כלל ומיהו אומר ר"י דע"כ הם מפיגין טעמם דתנן בפ"ב דביצה (ד' כג·) ג' דברים רבי אלעזר בן עזריה מתיר וחכמים אוסרין שוחקין את הפלפלין ברחים שלהן והיכי הוה שרי רבי אלעזר בן עזריה אי לא מפיגין טעמא ואין סברא לומר דבהא פליגי רבי אלעזר בן עזריה ורבנן דמר סבר דמפיגין טעמא ומר סבר אין מפיגין טעמא אלא מדשרי ר' אלעזר בן עזריה ש"מ דמפיגין טעמא ורבנן דאסרי משום דברחים שלהם מיחזי טפי כי עובדא דחול ועוד תניא בהדיא בתוספתא דביצה בתר פלוגתא דבית שמאי ובית הלל הפלפלין כתבלין על כן נראה לר"י דמותר לכתוש פלפלין ביום טוב אפילו במדוך של אבן ומיהו היכא דידע מאי קדרה בעי בשולי אסור במדוך של אבן דלא ידענא כמאן הלכתא ואזלינן לחומרא ולא שייך למימר בשל סופרים הלך אחר המיקל היכא דהם הוא קולא בדבר אחד חומרא הוא בדבר אחר מיהו במדוך של עץ ממ"נ שרי אפי' במדוכה של אבן כעין שלנו שקורין מורטייר כיון שהמדוך של עץ דלא אסרינן התם היכא דידע מאי קדרה בעי בשולי אלא בלא שינוי ושומין הנדוכים בי"ט נראה לר"י דשרי אפי' ידע מאי קדרה בעי בשולי לפי שמפיגין טעמן יותר מדאי ושרי מידי דהוי אשוחט ומבשל דשרי לכ"ע אפילו יודע מאי קדרה בעי בשולי דנראה הוא דהפגת טעם היינו שתש כח התבלין ואינם חדין כל כך ויכול לתקן הדבר כשמרבה התבלין אבל הפגת טעם שומין אין יכול לתקן מידי דהוה אשוחט ואופה ומבשל וגם רוח רעה שורה עליהן [נדה יז.] אם דכן מערב י"ט(ה) אפילו במדוך של אבן או של ברזל שרי ועוד דאין נראה שיהו בכלל תבלין דלא מיקרי תבלין אלא ירקות כעין כמון אבל שומין ובצלים אינם בכלל תבלין*): **דילמא** אתי לאשויי גומות·אע"ג דרבא ס"ל בסוף פ"ב דביצה (ד' כג·) בדבר שאין מתכוין כר"ש גזרינן הכא כשיהא עסוק לקנח רגלו ישכח שבת ויתכוין לאשויי גומות כעין שמליט בפ' בתרא דעירובין (ד' קד.) דנשים המשחקות באגוזים ובתפוחים אסור דילמא אתי לאשויי גומות כלומר במתכוין שמשכחת שבת מחמת שחוק שלהן: **אודרא** אפומא דשישא·פי' בפ"ח שרלים (לעיל ד' קיא:) [בד"ה האי מסוכרייתא שם ע"א] :

*) [וע"ע תוס' ביצה יד· ד"ה בית הלל]

[צ"ל וכן בשאלתות]

מו א מיי' פכ"ב מהל' שבת הלכה כב סמג לאוין סה טוש"ע או"ח סי' שיא סעיף ח :

מז ב מיי' פכ"ו שם הל' יב סמג שם טוש"ע או"ח סי' שב סעיף ד :

מח ג מיי' פכ"ב שם הל' יד טו סמג שם טוש"ע או"ח סי' שיא סעיף ח :

מט ד מיי' פכ"א שם הלכה כ סמג שם טוש"ע או"ח סי' שכא סעיף ז :

נ ה מיי' פט"ו שם הל' כב סמג שם טוש"ע או"ח סימן שכו סעיף ז :

נא ו מיי' פכ"א שם הל' כ סמג שם טוש"ע או"ח סימן שב סעיף ו :

נב ז מיי' פי"ז שם הל' יז טוש"ע או"ח סי' שסה סעיף ה :

נג ח טוש"ע או"ח סי' שלז סעיף ד :

[ברא"ש ביצה פ"א סי' כא איתא רב הונא]

נד ט מיי' פכ"ב שם הלכה טו סמג שם טוש"ע שם סי' שב סעיף טו :

נה י מיי' פכ"ב שם הלכה יז סמג שם טוש"ע או"ח סי' שב סעיף ז :

לעיל ל.

לעיל קכג.

[לעיל מג: קכג.]

[צ"ל ואמר]

[ילק' קא.]

לקמן קמח: ביצה ל.

הגהות הב"ח

... גמ' אמר ... ליתיב ... תא"מ ... אלפסי ... ישתמש ... אינים וע"ל ... בדף קמח : ... שם כובא ... רעה דילמ': ... רש"י ד"ה ... בקורה וכו' ... קרקע הכ"ד ... א"כ מ"ה לא ... לידדד לא ... ידדנה ... להושיבה ... ד"ד:(ד)תוס' ... ה הני וכו' ... מאי בעי ... שוליה למ"ד ... משום כל ... הקדרות כו' ... אסור ולמ"ד ... משום הפגת ... ם שרי אי ... מי מוריקא ... וכו' א"כ ... פלפלין נמי ... י דהכא נמי ... כל הקדרות ... (ה) בא"ד ... מערב י"ט ... הלכך אפי' ... במדוך :

הגהות הגר"א

... גמ' ושעל ... גדו מגררו ... פורן . נ"ב ... וכ"ה בגב ... סכין :

רבינו חננאל

הקש שע"ג המטה לא ינענעו בידו אבל מנענעו בגופו: אמר רב נחמן האי פוגלא מלמעלה למטה שרי ממטה למעלה אסור . יש מי שאומרים לא ינררה ויש מי שאומרים מותר לגררה ממעלה וכבר פירשנו דברי רב נחמן בפרק כל הכלים . אמר רב יהודה [הני] פלפלי [מידק] חדא חדא בקתא דסכינא שרי למידק . פי' ביו"ט אבל בלדכן אסור דהא אין מפיגין טעמן והוה ליה למידק מעיו"ט . רבא אמר כיון דמשני אפי' טובא והלכתא כרבא ביו"ט ויש מי שמתיר כי האי גוונא אפי' בשבת : טיט שע"ג רגליו הלכתא כמר בריה דרבנא דאמר בין בקרקע ובין בכותל ולא שרי אלא בקורה בלבד . ואמר רבא לא לצדד איניש כובא בארעא דלא אתו לאשויי גומות ואמר רבא לא ליהדוק איניש אודרא בפומיה דשישא דלמא אתו לידי סחיטה . פי' לא ידחוק אדם מוכין שרויין בפי

שישא שמא יבא לידי סחיטה טיט שעל בגדו מכסכסו מבפנים ואין מכסכסו מבחוץ או מגררו בצפורן כסכסו כבר פירשנוהו למעלה . וכל אלו שאמר רבא אסור אחד בשבת ואחד ביו"ט לא שנא

במנעל

רב נסים גאון

טיט שעל גבי מנעל איכא חספא דרבא משכחת לה בפרק כל הכלים ניטלין בשבת (דף קכד) רבא הוה קאזיל בריסתקא דמחוזא איתווס מסאניה בטינא אתא שמעיה שקל חספא יקא מכפר ליה : תני

במה מגררו א"ר אבהו בגב סכין א"ל ההוא סבא סמי דידך מקמי הא דתני רבי חייא *[א]אין מגררין לא מנעל חדש ולא מנעל ישן [ב]ולא יסוך את רגלו שמן והוא בתוך המנעל או בתוך הסנדל אבל סך את רגלו שמן ומניה בתוך המנעל או בתוך הסנדל וסך כל גופו שמן ומתעגל ע"ג קטבליא ואינו חושש אמר רב חסדא לא שנו אלא לצחצחו אבל לעבדו אסור פשיטא [ג]ותו לצחצחו מי איכא מאן דשרי אלא אי איתמר הכי איתמר אמר רב חסדא [ד]לא שנו אלא שיעור לצחצחו אבל שיעור לעבדו אסור ת"ר [ה]לא יצא קטן במנעל גדול אבל יוצא הוא בחלוק גדול [ו]ולא תצא אשה במנעל מרופט ולא תחלוץ בו [ז]ואם חלצה חליצתה כשרה ואין יוצאין במנעל חדש באיזה מנעל אמרו במנעל של אשה תני בר קפרא ל"ש אלא [ח]שלא יצאה בו שעה אחת מבעוד יום אבל יצאה בו מע"ש מותר תני חדא [ט]שומטין מנעל מעל גבי אימוס ותניא אידך אין שומטין לא קשיא הא ר' אליעזר הא רבנן *דתנן מנעל שעל גבי *אימוס רבי אליעזר מטהר [י]וחכמים מטמאים הניחא לרבא *דאמר דבר שמלאכתו לאיסור בין לצורך גופו בין לצורך מקומו מותר שפיר אלא לאביי דאמר *לצורך גופו מותר לצורך מקומו אסור מאי איכא למימר הכא במאי עסקינן ברפוי דתניא רבי יהודה אומר אם היה רפוי מותר טעמא דרפוי הא לא רפוי לא הניחא לאביי דאמר דבר שמלאכתו לאיסור לצורך גופו מותר לצורך מקומו אסור שפיר אלא לרבא דאמר בין לצורך גופו בין לצורך מקומו מותר מאי איריא רפוי אפי' לא רפוי נמי ההיא דרבי יהודה משום דרבי אליעזר הוא דתניא ר' יהודה אומר משום רבי אליעזר אם היה רפוי מותר:

הדרן עלך תולין

נוטל *[א]אדם את בנו והאבן בידו וכלכלה והאבן בתוכה [ב]ומטלטלין תרומה טמאה עם הטהורה ועם החולין רבי יהודה אומר אף מעלין את המדומע באחד ומאה: **גמ'** אמר רבא [ג]הוציא תינוק חי וכיס תלוי בצוארו חייב משום כיס תינוק מת וכיס תלוי לו בצוארו פטור תינוק חי וכיס תלוי לו בצוארו חייב משום כיס וליחייב נמי משום תינוק רבא כרבי נתן סבירא ליה *דאמר חי נושא את עצמו וליבטל כיס לגבי תינוק מי לא תנן *את החי במטה פטור אף על המטה שהמטה טפילה לו מטה לגבי חי מבטלי ליה כיס לגבי תינוק לא מבטלי ליה תינוק מת וכיס תלוי לו בצוארו פטור וליחייב משום תינוק רבא כר"ש ס"ל דאמר *כל מלאכה שא"צ לגופה פטור עליה תנן נוטל אדם את בנו והאבן בידו אמרי דבי רבי ינאי [ד]בתינוק שיש לו געגועין על אביו אי הכי מאי

[עירובין צד: לעיל צד:]

תוספות

במנעל מרופט כו' ואם חלצה חליצתה כשרה · ול"ת אמאי גזרינן בפרק מצות חליצה (יבמות דף קב·) מנעל אטו מנעל מרופט כיון דדיעבד חליצתה כשרה ואומר ר"י דגזרינן אטו מרופט יותר מדאי שאינו חופה רוב רגלו דאם חלצה בו אין חליצתה כשרה ·

ההיא דרבי יהודה משום דרבי אליעזר היא · מכאן ראיה דרבי יהודה שרי דבר שמלאכתו לאיסור לצורך גופו ולצורך מקומו כמו שפירשתי בסוף פרק במה מדליקין (דף מד:) ד"ה הא ר"י:

הדרן עלך תולין

נוטל. רבא כרבי נתן ס"ל. פירש' בפ' המצניע(א) (לעיל ד' צד·):

תינוק מת וכיס תלוי בצוארו פטור· דאגב מרדיה מבטיל ליה לכיס א"כ תינוק חי הוא צריך לכיס לטייל בו התינוק אבל תינוק מת מה צריך לכיס והוי מלאכה שאינה צריכה לגופה(ב) ופטור שלא הוציא כדרך המוציאין: **אי** הכי מאי איריא אבן אפי' דינר נמי · אי אמרת בשלמא דתרווייהו מבטל להו בין אבן ובין דינר ואין כאן טלטול מוקצה כלל הייני דנקט אבן משום דאי נפיל לא אתי אבוה לאתויי אבל דינר אי נפיל אתי אבוה לאתויי לא אלא אי אמרינן דתרווייהו לא בטלי ואפ"ה שרינן איסור מוקצה כשמטלטל התינוק עם האבן משום געגועין בדינר נמי ליסרי דלא שייך למימר דילמא אתי אבוה לאתויי דמאי נפקא לן מינה דהשתא נמי דאיכא איסור מוקצה שרינן ליה משום געגועין ומשני דאע"פ שיש איסור מוקצה כשמטלטל התינוק עם האבן ושרינן ליה משום געגועין מיהו יש לנו להחמיר במוקצה יותר כשמטלטלו בידים משמטלטלו אגב תינוק אף על גב דבההיא שעתא נמי איכא מוקצה הלכך גזרינן דילמא נפיל בדינר ואתי אבוה לאתויי. כך פירש רבינו שמואל:
ונשדיניהו

רש"י

במה מגררו · לחדש : והוא בתוך המנעל · מפני שהמנעל נהנה ממנו וכמאן מעבדו : מתעגל · מתגלגל : קטבליא · עור שלוק שטוחין ממנו משטחות לשלחן ולמטה : אלא לצחצחו · לא שנו דאסור לסוך שמן לרגלו ונותנו בתוך המנעל אלא שמתכוין לצחצחו למנעל : ולצחצחו מי שרי · במתכוין הא איכא למיגזר אטו לעבדו : שיעור לצחצחו. שלא היה כ"כ שמן הניסוך לעור מגופו כדי לעבד לעור אלא לצחצחו ומיהו איכו אפי' לצחצח לא מתכוין : לא יצא · אדם קטן במנעל שהוא גדול לו משום דנפל מרגלו ואתי לאתויי : אבל יוצא בחלוק גדול · דלא נפיל מיניה ולמישלף ואתויי לא חיישינן דלא קאי ערום בשוק : מרופט · קרוע מלמעלה דגנאי הוא לה וכי חייכי עלה שלפה ומייתי לה : ולא תחלוץ בו · לכתחילה דלאו נעל מעליא הוא : במנעל חדש · כדמפרש ואזיל שלא יצאה בו מבעוד יום ובאשה קיימינן דאשה מקפדת אם אינו מכוון למדת רגלה אבל יצאה בו כבר הכירה בו דמכוון הוא לה או אינה מקפדת : אימוס · פורמ"ה : ר' אליעזר מטהר · אלמא לאו כלי הוא ובשבת נמי אסור לטלטלו : הניחא לרבא דאמר · בפ' כל הכלים דבר שמלאכתו לאיסור בין שהוא צריך להשתמש בגופו של כלי בין שאינו צריך אלא למקומו מותר לטלטלו מאחר שתורת כלי עליו שפיר איכא לאוקומי להא דתני שומטין כרבנן דכיון דכלי הוא והאימוס נמי כלי הוא ואף על גב דמלאכתו דאימוס לאיסור לתקן מנעלין מטלטלין לאותו אימוס משום לצורך מקומו דהיינו מנעל שהאימוס נתון לתוכו : אלא לאביי · כהי נמי דמנעל שעל האימוס לרבנן כלי הוא אימוס מיהא מלאכתו לאיסור הוא וזה ששומט ממנו את המנעל אינו צריך לגופו של אימוס והיכי מטלטל ליה : ברפוי · שהמנעל נשמט מאליו וא"צ לטלטל האימוס : הא לאו רפוי לא · וע"כ טעמא משום דאימוס אסור לטלטל לצורך מקומו : ה"ג ההיא רבי יהודה משום רבי אליעזר הוא · כי אמרה ליה ר' יהודה להאי דמפליג בין רפוי לשאינו רפוי אליבא דרבי אליעזר אמר דאמר מנעל שעל האימוס לאו גמר כלי הוא כל זמן שמחוסר הוצאה ולענין שבת נמי אסור לטלטלו משום דלאו כלי הוא והשמעינן דרפוי לאו מחוסר הוצאה הוא ומותר לטלטלו דאילו לרבנן אף על גב דאין רפוי מותר דטעמא דשאין רפוי אסור לרבי יהודה לאו משום אימוס הוא אלא משום מנעל גופיה :

הדרן עלך תולין

נוטל. והאבן בידו · בחצר ולא אמרי' דמטלטל לאבן : עם הטהורה · אגב הטהורה ואגב חולין אבל טמאה באפי נפשה לאו בת טלטול היא : אף מעלין את המדומע · סאה תרומה שנפלה לק' של חולין דקי"ל דעולה מותר להעלותו לסאה תרומה מהן בשבת ויהיו החולין מותרין ולא אמרינן מתקן הוא ובגמרא מפרש טעמא : **גמ'** חייב משום כיס · ולא משום תינוק כדמפרש ואזיל משום כיס מיהו חייב ולא אמרינן איהו לא מפיק ליה אלא תינוק קא מפיק ליה ולקמיה פריך לה ממתניתין : פטור · לגמרי כדמפרש ואזיל : מטה לגבי חי מבטל לה · להיות טפילה לו שהרי צריך לה : מלאכה שאינה צריכה לגופה · ומוציא מת לקוברו מלאכה שא"צ לגופה היא כדאמר בהמצניע* וכיס שהיה תלוי בצוארו לשחק בו אגב מרדיה מבטל ליה לגבי תינוק שמת ולא חשיב ליה ההיא שעתא : והאבן בידו · מדשרי ליה בטלטול בחצר ש"מ לאו כמאן דנקיט לה איהו לאבן דמי ולגבי כיס היכי מחייבת ליה : בתינוק שיש לו געגועין על אביו · שאם לא יטלנו יחלה ולא העמידו טלטול שלא בידים במקום סכנה ואע"ג דלאו סכנת נפש גמורה אלא סכנת חולי :
התי

עין משפט נר מצוה

נו א מיי' פכ"ב מהלכות שבת הלכה יח סמג שם טוש"ע או"ח סי' שכ סעיף ה :

נז ב ג ד מיי' (שם הל' יח) ופכ"ג הלכה י סמג שם טוש"ע או"ח סי' שכז סעיף ד :

נח ה מיי' פי"ט שם הל' טו סמג שם טוש"ע או"ח סי' שא סעיף ז :

נט ו מיי' וסמג שם טוש"ע או"ח סי' שג סעיף יג :

ס ז מיי' פ"ד מהל' יבום הלכה יט סמג עשין נב טוש"ע אה"ע סימן קסט סעיף כא כב :

סא ח מיי' פי"ט מהל' שבת הלכה טו סמג לאוין סה טוש"ע או"ח סי' שג סעיף יג :

סב ט מיי' פכ"ו מהל' שבת הלכה יג סמג שם טוש"ע א"ח סי' שח סעיף יד :

סג י מיי' פכ"ד מהלכות כלים הלכה ה :

א ב מיי' פכ"ב מהלכות שבת הלכה טז סמג לאוין סה טוש"ע או"ח סי' שט סעיף א :

ב ג מיי' פי"ח מהלכות שבת הלכה יז :

ג ד מיי' פכ"ה שם הל' טו סמג שם טוש"ע א"ח סי' שט סעיף א :

כלים פכ"ו מ"ד [סנהדרין סח.]

לעיל קכד.

רבינו חננאל

וגירור מנעל הלכה כדתני ר' חייא אין מגררין לא מנעל חדש ולא מנעל ישן. ולא יסוך רגלו שמן והוא בתוך המנעל או בתוך הסנדל. אבל סך את רגלו בשמן ומניחה בתוך המנעל או בתוך הסנדל וסך כל גופו שמן ומתעגל ע"ג קטבליא. פי' ספרה. ואינו חושש ואמר רב חסדא לא שני אלא אם נתן שמן מעט שיעור לצחצחו אבל שיעור לעבדו אסור. [אבל] לצחצחו אסור וכ"ש לעבדו. וכן הלכה: ת"ר לא יצא קטן במנעל גדול אבל יוצא הוא בחלוק גדול. פי' של אדם גדול ולא תצא אשה במנעל מרופט רפוי שמתרבב מן הרגל כמו שאמור אם יטעום עבדך את אשר אכל ואת אשר אשתה מיכן [ואמר לקמן] (קלג) ששפתותיהן של זקנים מתרפסות ואין יכול לקפוץ שפתותיו לטעום החך המאכל וכן עוד לא תצא אשה במנעל חדש בשבת אא"כ יצאה בו שעה אחת מבע"י: תני חדא שומטין מנעל מע"ג האימוס בשבת. אימוס זה דפוס של מנעל ואליבא דרבנן שאומרין מנעל שע"ג אימוס כלי היא ומקבל טומאה. ותניא אידך אין שומטין הא לרבי אליעזר דאמר מנעל ע"ג אימוס אינו כלי ואינו מקבל טומאה דתנן בסדר טהרות בבא בתרא פ' סנדל עמק' וכיס של שנצות מנעל על האימוס ר' אליעזר מטהר וחכמים מטמאין. פי' ר' אליעזר מטהר סבר מנעל על האמים אינו כלי לפיכך אינו מטמא ובשבת אסור לשומטו וחכמים שמטמאין סברי מנעל על האמום כבר נגמרה מלאכתו וכלי הוא לקבל טומאה. וכיון שהוא כלי מותר לשומטו בשבת והלכה כחכמים ואקשינן עלה הניחא לרבא דאמר דבר שמלאכתו לאיסור כבנין האימים וכיוצא בו מכלי אומנות מלאכה בין לצורך מקומו מותר לטלטלו שפיר לטעמייהו דרבנן דסברי שומטין מנעל מעל אמים בשבת אלא (לאבין) [לאביי] דאמר לצורך גופו בלבד שרי אמום מאי לצורך גופו איכא דשומטין ומפרקינן הכא במאי עסקינן ברפוי כלומר מנעל זה רפוי הוא על האמום ואינו צריך להגביהו אלא מושך המנעל מעליו ונשאר האמום דתניא ר' יהודה אומר אם היה רפוי מותר והורנו להקשות על זה הפירוק לרבא ופשוטה היא ופריק רבא הא ר' יהודה משום ר' אליעזר היא כלומר אפילו ר' אליעזר שאמר אין שומטין סבר הני מילי בשאינו רפוי מהודק לטלטליה ולאשתומיה אבל אם היה רפוי שמושך המנעל והאמום נשאר במקומו מותר לשומטו אבל חכמים סבירא להו אע"פ שאינו רפוי אלא מהודק אם אינו לצורך גופו מותר לטלטלו לצורך מקומו :

הדרן עלך רבי אליעזר אומר תולין

פרק כא נוטל אדם את בנו והאבן בידו כו'. אמר רבא הוציא תינוק חי וכיס תלוי לו בצוארו חייב משום כיס תינוק מת וכיס תלוי לו בצוארו פטור. פי' תינוק מת לקברו והכיס עמו כדאמר ר"ש לקיש

רב נסים גאון

תני בר קפרא לא שנו אלא שלא יצאת בו שעה אחת מבעוד יום. בגמ' דבני מערבא בפרק במה אשה יוצאה (הלכה ג) ובפרק כל ישראל יש להם חלק (הלכה א) גרסי' כמה שיעורו והכין גרסי' לא ילבש אדם מנעלים וסנדלים

הגהות הב"ח

(א) תוס' ד"ה נוטל וכו' בפ' המצניע. נ"ב ד' צד בד"ה אבל אדם: (ב) ד"ה תינוק וכו' שאינה צריכה לגופה אי נמי אפי' צריך לו פטור שלא הוציאה :

גליון הש"ס

גמ' ולא יסוך את רגלו שמן. וכן איתא בירושלמי ספ"ח דשביעית לענין שמן שביעית:

[תוספ' פ"ד] [נ"ל אימום וכן הוא בערוך ובמשנה דכלים ובמפרשים בעלוין] [לעיל קכב:] לעיל מו. לעיל צד. [עירובין קג. יומא סו:] [לעיל קג: וש"נ] [דף צד:]

new shoe may be scraped, but not an old one. [141*b*] With what does one scrape it?—Said R. Abbahu: With the back of a knife. A certain old man said to him, Delete your [teaching] on account of what R. Ḥiyya taught: One must not scrape either a new shoe or an old one, nor must he rub his foot with oil while it is in the
a shoe or sandal;[1] but one may rub his foot with oil and place it in his shoe or sandal; he may also oil his whole body and roll himself on a leather spread without fear.[2] R. Ḥisda said: They learnt this only [if his intention is] to polish it;[3] but [if it is] to dress it,[4] it is forbidden. 'To dress it'? surely that is obvious? Moreover, does any one permit it [if he desires] to polish it?—Rather if stated, it was thus stated: R. Ḥisda said: They learnt this only of a quantity [sufficient merely] to polish it; but [if] the quantity[5] [is sufficient] to dress it, it is forbidden.

Our Rabbis taught: A small[-footed] man must not go out with the shoe of a large[-footed] man,[6] but he may go out with [too] large a shirt. A woman must not go out with a gaping shoe,[7] nor may she perform *ḥaliẓah* therewith; yet if she does perform *ḥaliẓah* therewith, the *ḥaliẓah* is valid. And one must not go out with a new shoe: of what shoe did they rule this? Of a woman's shoe.[8] Bar Ḳappara taught: They learnt [this] only where she had not gone out therein one hour before nightfall;[9] but if she went out therein on the eve of the Sabbath, it is permitted.

One [Baraitha] taught: A shoe may be removed from its last; while another taught: It may not be removed. There is no difficulty: one is [according to] R. Eliezer, the other [according to] the Rabbis. For we learnt: If a shoe is on the last,—R. Eliezer declares it clean, while the Sages declare it is unclean.[10] This is well according to Raba, who maintained: It is permitted [to handle] an article whose function is for a forbidden purpose, whether it is required itself or for its place: then it is correct. But on Abaye's view that it may be [handled] for itself, but it is forbidden [to
b handle it] when its place is required,[1] what can be said?[2]—We treat here of one [a shoe] that is loose [on the last].[3] For it was taught, R. Judah said: If it is loose, it is permitted [to remove it]. The reason [then why it is permitted] is because it is loose. But if it is not loose it is not [permitted]? This is well on Abaye's view that an article whose function is for a forbidden purpose may be [handled] when required for itself, but not when its place [only] is required: then it is correct. But according to Raba, who maintains, It is permitted [to handle it] both when required for itself or when its place is required, what can be said: [for] why particularly a loose [shoe],—even if not loose too it is thus?—That[4] represents R. Judah's view in R. Eliezer's name. For it was taught: R. Judah said in R. Eliezer's name: If it is loose, it is permitted.[5]

CHAPTER XXI

MISHNAH. A PERSON MAY TAKE UP HIS SON WHILE HE HAS A STONE IN HIS HAND OR A BASKET WITH A STONE IN IT; AND UNCLEAN TERUMAH MAY BE HANDLED TOGETHER
c WITH CLEAN [TERUMAH] OR WITH ḤULLIN.[1] R. JUDAH SAID: ONE MAY ALSO REMOVE[2] THE ADMIXTURE [OF TERUMAH IN ḤULLIN] WHEN ONE [PART IS NEUTRALIZED] IN A HUNDRED [PARTS].[3]

GEMARA. Raba said: If one carries out[4] a live child with a purse hanging around its neck, he is culpable on account of the purse; a dead child with a purse hanging around its neck, he is not culpable. 'A live child with a purse hanging around its neck, he is culpable on account of the purse.' But let him be culpable on account of the child?—Raba agrees with R. Nathan, who maintained, A living [person] carries himself.[5] But let the purse be counted as nought in relation to the child? Did we not learn, [If one carries out] a living person in a bed, he is not culpable even in respect of the bed, because the bed is subsidiary to him?—A bed is accounted as nought in relation to a living person,[6] but a purse is not accounted as nought in relation to the child.

'A dead child with a purse hanging around its neck, he is not culpable.' But let him be culpable on account of the child?—Raba agrees with R. Simeon, who maintained: One is not culpable
d on account of a labour unrequired *per se*.[1]

We learnt: A PERSON MAY TAKE UP HIS SON WHILE HE HAS A STONE IN HIS HAND?'[2]—The School of R. Jannai said: This

a (1) Because the oil incidentally softens the leather, which is forbidden. (2) Of transgression. (3) When he puts his oiled foot in the shoe or sandal his purpose is to polish the leather. (4) To soften the leather or make it more pliable. (5) Of oil rubbed on to the foot. (6) Lest it fall off, and he come to carry it. (7) Rashi. Jast.: 'a flappy (outworn) shoe'—either because she may be laughed at and so she will take it off (Rashi), or it fall off, and she come to carry it. (8) She is particular about the fit, and if it is not exact, she may remove and carry it. 'New' means never worn at all. (9) Lit., 'while it was yet day—Friday.' (10) 'Clean' and 'unclean' mean not susceptible and susceptible to uncleanness respectively. R. Eliezer holds that as long as it is on the last it is not a completely finished article, whereas only such can become unclean. Since it is not a finished article, it may not be handled on the Sabbath. The view of the Rabbis is the reverse.

b (1) V. notes *supra* 123*b*. (2) For the function of the last is a forbidden one, and in removing the shoe one must necessarily handle the last, though he does not require the use of the last itself, and according to Abaye that is forbidden. (3) So that the last is not handled at all. (4) The Baraitha which makes a distinction between where it is loose or not. (5) Though R. Eliezer holds that as long as it is on the last it is not completely finished (v. *supra*) and therefore may not be handled, that is only if it is tightly fitted on it, so that there is some difficulty in removing it. But if it is loose and comes off easily he admits that it is finished; hence it ranks as an article, is susceptible to defilement, and may be handled on the Sabbath.

c (1) Although the stone or the unclean *terumah* by itself may not be handled as *mukẓeh*. (2) Lit., 'take up'. (3) If one part of *terumah* is accidentally mixed with a hundred parts of *ḥullin* it is neutralized and the mixture is permitted to non-priests. Nevertheless, since it does contain some *terumah*, though it cannot be distinguished from the rest, one part must be removed, and R. Judah permits this on the Sabbath. (4) From a private into a public domain. (5) V. *supra* 94*a*. (6) Since the bed is required for him.

d (1) V. *supra* 30*a*; carrying out a dead child comes under this category, *supra* 94*b*. (2) This proves that the man is not regarded as himself holding the stone, which would be forbidden. Hence by analogy he does not carry out the purse suspended around the child's neck; why then is he culpable on its account?

refers to a child who pines for his father.[3] If so, [142*a*] why particularly a stone? the same applies to a *denar!* Why did Raba say: They learnt only a stone, but a *denar* is forbidden?—In the case of a stone, if it falls down the father will not come to fetch it, [but] with a *denar*, if it falls down the father will come to fetch it. It was taught in accordance with Raba: If one carries out his garments folded up and lying on his shoulder, or his sandals or his rings in his hands, he is liable; but if he was wearing them, he is not culpable. If one carries out a person with his garments upon him, with his sandals on his feet and his rings on his hands,[4] he is not culpable. Hence if he carried them as they are[5] he would be culpable.[6]

A BASKET WITH A STONE IN IT: yet why? let the basket be [regarded as] a stand for a forbidden article?[7]—Said Rabbah b. Bar Ḥanah in R. Joḥanan's name: We treat here of a basket full of produce.[8] Then let the produce be thrown out, and let the stone be thrown out, and then we can collect [the produce] by hand?[9]—As R. Elai said [elsewhere] in Rab's name: The reference is to fruit which becomes soiled, so here too [we treat] of fruit which becomes soiled.[10] Then let one shake it [the basket] about?[11] —Said R. Ḥiyya b. Ashi in Raba's name: We treat here of a broken
a basket, so that the stone itself becomes a wall for the basket.[1]

[UNCLEAN] TERUMAH MAY BE HANDLED, etc. R. Ḥisda said: They learnt [this] only where the clean [*terumah*] is underneath and the unclean is on top; but if the clean [*terumah*] is on top and the unclean underneath, one must take the clean and leave the unclean.[2] But if the clean is underneath too, let him throw off [the unclean] and take it?—Said R. Elai in Rab's name: We treat of fruit which becomes soiled. An objection is raised: One may handle unclean *terumah* together with clean *terumah* or with *ḥullin*, whether the clean is on top and the unclean is below, or the unclean is on top and the clean is underneath; this refutes R. Ḥisda?—R. Ḥisda answers you: Our Mishnah [means that] it is required for itself;[3] the Baraitha is where its place is required.[4] What compels R. Ḥisda to interpret our Mishnah as meaning that it is required for itself?[5]—Said Raba, Our Mishnah, by deduction, supports him. For the second clause[6] states: If money is lying on a cushion, one shakes the cushion, and it falls off. Whereon Rabbah b. Bar Ḥanah said in R. Joḥanan's name: They learnt this only if it [the cushion] is required for itself; but if its place is required, one removes it while it [the money] is upon it. And since the second clause means that it is required for itself, the first clause too means that it is required for itself.

R. JUDAH SAID: ONE MAY ALSO REMOVE, etc. Yet why? surely he makes it fit?[7]—R. Judah agrees with R. Eliezer, who maintains: The *terumah* lies as a [separate] entity.[8] For we learnt: If a *se'ah* of *terumah* falls into less than a hundred,[9] and thus they become a [forbidden] mixture, and then some of the mixture falls else-
b where,[1] R. Eliezer said: It creates a [forbidden] mixture as though it were certain *terumah*,[2] but the Sages maintain: The mixture creates a [forbidden] mixture only in proportion.[3] [But] say that you know him [to rule thus] with stringency; do you know him [to rule thus] with lenience?[4]—Rather [reply thus]: He [R. Judah] rules as R. Simeon, as we learnt: If a *se'ah* of *terumah* falls into a hundred,[5] and one has no time to remove [it] until another falls in, it is [all] forbidden;[6] but R. Simeon permits it.[7] Yet how [does this follow]? Perhaps there they differ in this: viz., the first Tanna holds: Though they fell in consecutively it is as though they fell in simultaneously, so that each falls into fifty; whereas R. Simeon holds: The first is neutralized in the hundred, and this one is neutralized in a hundred and one?[8]—Rather [reply thus]: He [R. Judah] rules as R. Simeon b. Eleazar. For it was taught, R. Simeon b. Eleazar said: One may cast his eyes at one side and eat from the other.[9] Yet does he agree with him? [142*b*]

(3) If he does not take him up he may sicken with pining, though it will not actually endanger him: hence since the father does not actually handle the stone himself he is permitted to take him up. (4) I.e., the man is wearing them. (5) If the person carried were holding, not wearing them. (6) This is analogous to Raba's dictum, for a purse suspended from a child's neck is not in the position of being worn. (7) V. *supra* 47*a*, n. b4. (8) So that the basket serves as a stand for a permitted thing. (9) And replace it in the basket. Why did they permit to carry the stone? (10) If thrown on the ground, e.g., figs and grapes. (11) Until the stone lies at a side, when it can be thrown out without affecting the produce.

a (1) By filling up the gap. (2) And there is no reason for handling the unclean. (3) I.e., he wishes to eat the *terumah*. Therefore if the clean *terumah* is on top he can simply take it and leave the rest. (4) He needs the place where the utensil containing it is standing: therefore he must remove them—*sc.* the clean and the unclean—together, whatever their position. (5) So that he has to explain the Mishnah as referring to when the unclean *terumah* is on top. (6) *Sc.* the Mishnah *infra* 142*b*. (7) For use. This should be preventively forbidden out of consideration for that which is made fit by means of labour. (8) Since one part is to be removed, it is as though the *terumah* therein lay separate and distinct, and therefore the whole mixture is fit for use in any case. (9) *Se'ahs* of *ḥullin*.

b (1) I.e., into another pile of produce. (2) *Sc.* as though it were *all terumah* and therefore it can only be neutralized by a hundred times its quantity. Thus he regards the *terumah* as distinct. (3) E.g., if a *se'ah* of *terumah* falls into nine *se'ahs* of *ḥullin* in the first place, and then a *se'ah* of the mixture falls into another heap of produce, this second *se'ah* is regarded as containing one tenth of a *se'ah* of *terumah* only, and if the second pile contains ten *se'ahs* it neutralizes it. (4) As in our Mishnah, where this view would result in greater lenience. (5) Hence it is neutralized, but that one *se'ah* of the whole must be removed. (6) Since there are now two *se'ahs* of *terumah* in one hundred of *ḥullin*. (7) It is now assumed that his reason is because he regards the first *se'ah* as lying distinct and apart, and therefore the second *se'ah* alone is counted, and that too is neutralized. (8) Hence on the contrary, instead of regarding the *terumah* as a thing apart, he maintains that it becomes entirely one with the *ḥullin*. (9) I.e., he may decide to remove a *se'ah* from one side of the pile and then, without actually removing it, eat from the other. Thus the removing is not essential.

מאי איריא אבן אפילו דינר נמי אלמה אמר רבא "לא שנו אלא אבן אבל דינר אסור אבן אי נפלה לה לא אתי אבוה לאיתויי דינר אי נפיל אתי אבוה לאתויי תניא כוותיה דרבא "המוציא כליו מקופלים ומונחים על כתפו וסנדליו וטבעותיו בידו חייב ואם היה מלובש בהן פטור "המוציא אדם וכליו עליו וסנדליו ברגליו וטבעותיו בידיו פטור ואילו הוציאן כמות שהן חייב: כלכלה והאבן בתוכה: ואמאי תיהוי כלכלה בסיס לדבר האסור אמר רבה בר בר חנה אמר ר' יוחנן הבא בבכלכלה מלאה פירות עסקינן ולישדינהו לפירי ונישדי לאבן "ונינקטינהו בידים כדרבי אלעי אמר רב בפירות המיטנפין "ה"נ בפירות המיטנפין ולינערינהו נעורי *אמר רב חייא בר אשי אמר רבא "הבא בבכלכלה פחותה עסקינן דאבן גופה נעשית דופן לכלכלה: "מטלטלין תרומה וכו': אמר רב חסדא לא שנו "אלא שטהורה למטה וטמאה למעלה אבל טהורה למעלה וטמאה למטה שקיל ליה לטהורה ושביק ליה לטמאה וכי טהורה למטה נמי לישדינהו ולינקטינהו אמר רבי אלעי אמר רב "בפירות המיטנפין עסקינן מיתיבי מטלטלין תרומה טמאה עם הטהורה ועם החולין בין שטהורה למעלה וטמאה למטה בין שטמאה למעלה וטהורה למטה תיובתא דרב חסדא אמר לך רב חסדא "מתניתין לצורך גופו ברייתא לצורך מקומו מאי דוחקיה דרב חסדא לאוקמי מתניתין לצורך גופו אמר רבא מתני' כוותיה דייקא דקתני סיפא מעות שעל הכר מנער את הכר והן נופלות ואמר רבה בר בר חנה אמר רבי יוחנן לא שנו אלא לצורך גופו אבל לצורך מקומו מטלטלו ועודן עליו ומדסיפא לצורך גופו רישא נמי לצורך גופו: רבי יהודה אומר אף מעלין וכו': ואמאי "הא קא מתקן רבי יהודה כר' אליעזר סבירא ליה דאמר תרומה בעינא מחתא *דתנן סאה תרומה "שנפלה לפחות ממאה ונדמעו ונפל מן המדומע למקום אחר רבי אליעזר אומר מדמעת כתרומת ודאי וחכמים אומרים "אין המדומע מדמע אלא לפי חשבון אימר דשמעת ליה לחומרא לקולא מי שמעת ליה אלא הוא דאמר כר"ש כדתנן *"סאה תרומה שנפלה למאה ולא הספיק להגביה עד שנפלה אחרת הרי זו אסורה ור"ש מתיר וממאי דילמא התם בהא קמיפלגי דתנא קמא סבר אע"ג דנפלו בזה אחר זה כמאן דנפל בבת אחת דמי והא להמשין נפלה והא להמשין נפלה ור"ש סבר קמייתא בטיל במאה והא תיבטיל במאה והד אלא הוא דאמר כרבי שמעון בן אלעזר דתניא ר' שמעון בן אלעזר אומר *נותן עיניו בצד זה ואוכל מצד אחר ומי סבר ליה כוותיה

והא

רש"י

אתי לאתויי · וטעמא לאו משום טלטול הוא דאפילו לאוחזו בידו והתינוק מהלך ברגליו אסר ליה רבא דילמא נפיל ואתי לאתויי וכיון דלאו סכנת נפש היא לא שרו ביה טלטול: תניא כוותיה דרבא · דכי נקט לה עליון כמאן דאפקא תחתון גופיה דמי ומיחייב: וסנדליו וטבעותיו בידו · בקומצו שלא כדרך מלבוש: המוציא אדם וכליו עליו · מלובש בהן: וטבעותיו בידיו · באצבעותיו מדלא תנא בידו כדנקט רישא: פטור · דבגדיו בטלי לגביה ועליו הוא פטור כרבי נתן: ואילו הוציאן כמות שהן · שהיה אותו עליון אחוז בהן ולא מלובש חייב הנושא והיינו כרבא: תיהוי כלכלה בסיס · והיא עצמה תיאסר: מלאה פירות · דעיקר נעשית בסיס לפירות הלכך אבן מיטלטלת אגב כלי ופירות שהוא מותר: ונינקטינהו בידים · ילקטם מעל הארץ בידיו ויחזירם לכלכלה ויטלטלם ולמה התירו אבן לטלטל אגב כלי ופירות: בפירות המיטנפין · בפירות מבושלין ורכין מאד כגון תאנים ותותים וענבים שאם ישליכם לארץ יטנפו: ולנעריניהו נעורי · עד שיסתלקו הפירות מן האבן לתוך הכלכלה נגררין וישליך האבן לבדה בנעורתה: פחותה · שנפחית דופנה או שוליה: וטמאה למעלה · והוא צריך לטהורה ואינו יכול ליטול הטמאה בידים לפי שהיא מוקצה לפיכך יטלטל הכל עד השלחן וישליך הכל עליו ויטול הטהורה: לישדינהו · לארץ כולן: ולינקטינהו · לטהורה ביד ויחזירנה לכלכלה: מתני' לצורך גופו · שצריך לטהורה לגופה לאוכלה הלכך אי לאו דטהורה למטה לא שרו ליה לטלטולי לטמאה אלא שקיל לטהורה וממטי לה לשלחן: ברייתא לצורך מקומו · שצריך למקום הכלי וע"כ כיון הוא צריך לסלקו משם ושרו ליה רבנן לטלטל האי אטו האי: ומאי דוחקיה כו' · דאיצטריך למימר לא שנו אלא שהטמאה למעלה לשבקי כדקס"ד בין שטמאה למעלה בין שטמאה למטה ולוקמי בצריך למקומו: אלא לצורך גופו · שצריך לכר לשכב עליו שם ולא לסלקו לפיכך לא התירו לו ליטלו עם המעות אלא מנערו במקומו אבל צריך למקום הכר מטלטל הכל ביחד: ומדסיפא כו' רישא נמי לצורך גופו · הלכך אי הוה טהורה למעלה לא הוי שרי ליה לטלטולי טמאה כדקתני גבי מעות מנערו ונופלות ומטלטל היתרא לחודיה: הא קמתקן · שמביאה לידי היתר ונגזר ביה אטו תיקון שע"י מלאכה: כר"א דאמר תרומה · הואיל וניתנה להעלות אחת שירדה בעינא מחתא כאילו מונחת לבדה ואינה מעורבת הלכך לא קמתקן מידי: מדמעת · זה שנפרד משם ואוסר צ"ט של חולין כאילו היא תרומה ודאי: וחכ"א אין המדומע מדמע · חולין אחרים אלא לפי חשבון התרומה שבמדומע כגון אם תחילתו נדמע ס' של חולין ע"י סאה תרומה וחזרה סאה ממנו ונפלה לתוך אחרים לא חשבינן תרומה אלא ס' שבסאה זו ומדמע עד צ"ט שכנגדו ואם יש חולין יותר מק' כנגדו עולה: אימר דשמעת ליה · לר"א דאמר תרומה כמאן דמחתא בעינא: לחומרא · לדמעה כתרומה ודאי: לקולא · דלא ליהוי המעלה אותה בשבת כמתקן: מי אמר · הא ודאי מתקן הוא ע"כ: הוא דאמר · רבי יהודה דמתני' כרבי שמעון דאמר לקולא נמי כמאן דמחתא בעינא דמיא: למאה · וראויה להעלותה ויתכשרו החולין: עד שנפלה אחרת · ועכשיו אין בה חולין כדי להעלותה באחד וק': ר"ש מתיר · קס"ד משום דס"ל קמייתא כמאן דמחתא בעינא דמיא ונמצאת אחרונה זו נופלת בתוך ק' של חולין: בטל בק' · והוו להו כולהו חולין ומיהו כיון דצריך להעלותה ע"כ המעלה מתקנו: נותן עיניו · במדומע בצד זה להעלותו לתרומה ואוכל בצד אחר הלכך הואיל ובלא העלאה מתחיל ואוכל אין תיקון בהעלאתו:

אלא

[ות פ"ב ורס יב. ע"ש]

[ות פ"ב מ"ח]

[ורות נט. צ"ע תוס' במחשבה ס' מנחות נה. ד"ה במחשבה]

תוספות

ונשדינהו לפירי ונשדייה לאבן · ואם תאמר גבי קטן נמי נשדייה לאבן מידו ואמאי שרי לטלטולי עם האבן וי"ל אם ישליכו מידו יצעק התינוק ויבכה וא"ת מ"מ דלא שרינן לטלטל תינוק אלא כשיש לו געגועין תיבטל אבן אגב תינוק כמו שהיא בטלה אגב כלכלה מלאה פירות וי"ל דאינו צריך כל כך טלטול התינוק וא"ת אפילו אין הכלכלה מלאה פירות תיבטל האבן אגבה כי היכי דבטלי בפ"ב דביצה (דף כא:) שיורי הכוס אגב הכוס אי לאו דאיסורי הנאה נינהו וי"ל שאני שיורי דגריעי יותר מדאי ובטלו טפי וכן צ"ל מתוך שמעתא גופה דביצה כמו שפירשתי לעיל בסוף כירה (דף מז: בד"ה הוה):

ונשדינהו לפירי ונשדייה לאבן כו' · וא"ת מכל מקום נינקטינהו לפירי בידים ויניח האבן בכלכלה והא אמרינן לקמן לא שנו אלא שטהורה למטה וטמאה למעלה אבל טהורה למעלה וטמאה למטה שקיל לה לטהורה ושביק לה לטמאה והיינו על כרחך בידיו דאי זריק לה בכלי א"כ גם בטמאה למעלה יכול לזורקה בכלי אלא שמע מינה דשקיל לה בידיו וא"כ הכי נמי ניסקלינהו לפירי בידיו וי"ל דמיירי שפי הכלכלה צר הוא ואינו יכול להכניס שם ידיו אי נמי י"ל דהסיא דלקמן מיירי בתרומה שהיא בכלים קטנים בתוך הקופה שאין דרך להניח טמאה וטהורה ביחד אלא בכלים זה בפני עצמו וזה בפ"ע ולהכי מצי שקיל לטהורה שהיא למעלה בידיו אבל כלכלה דהכא אין כאן כלים ולא מצי נקיט להו בידיו פן יפול לארץ והשתא לא צריכא לשינויא קמא דפירות המיטנפין דהא כיון דאבן עצמה הוי דופן לכלכלה אפי' הוי שדי לפירות ולאבן והדר שקיל לפירי ושבק לאבן לא הוי ליה במאי לאנחינהו כיון שהכלכלה פחותה*) שהאבן נעשה לה דופן · והא דלא קאמר אלא לפי שלא הוזכר המורא לעיל · א"כ השתא יש להעמיד נמי בפירות המיטנפין דאל"כ נוכל להשליך הסל בקרקע ולהוליך בכלכלה מעט מעט כמה שתוכל להחזיק עד מקום הפחת · מ"ר:

הבא נמי בפירות המיטנפין · וא"ת אכתי יטלם בידו ויניחם בתוך כלי אחר או על גבי טבלא או ע"ג סודר כדמוכח בסמוך גבי תרומה דאמר רב חסדא לא שנו אלא שטהורה למטה וטמאה למעלה אבל טהורה למעלה וטמאה למטה שקיל לטהורה ושביק הטמאה ואע"ג דמוקמינן נמי בפירות המיטנפין וי"ל דהתם מיירי כגון שטהורה מונחת בכלים קטנים בפני עצמה וכן הטמאה ואותם כלים מונחים בתוך כלי אחד גדול והיו כלים של טהורה למעלה מכלים של טמאה דיכול ליקח סלי טהורה ולהניחם ע"ג קרקע אבל אם מונחת זו על גב זו בלא שום כלי כי הכא שהפירות מונחים ביחד בהא ודאי לא אמר שביק לה לטמאה ושקיל לה לטהורה · מ"ר:

שנפלה לפחות מק' חולין · מכאן משמע דתרומה עולה באחד ומאה עם האיסור ורש"י לא פירש כן בפרק גיד הנשה (חולין דף צט:) גבי כל איסורין שבתורה במאה דלפירו' שיטתו לא אתי' מסקנא הכי*):

*) [ועי' תוס' חולין לט: ד"ה לא]

והא

עין משפט נר מצוה

ד א מיי' וסמג שם ושו"ע שם:

ה ב ג מיי' פ"ח מהל' שבת הלכה יז ופ"ט הלכה יט:

ו ד טוש"ע א"ח סי' שלה סעיף ה:

ז ה מיי' פכ"ה שם הל' טז טוש"ע א"ח סי' שם סעיף ג:

ח ו מיי' שם טוש"ע שם סעיף ג:

ט ז ח ט י מיי' שם הלכה כ:

יכ (מיי' פכ"ג שם הלכה ט והלכה טו):

יא ל מיי' פי"ג מהל' תרומות הל' ג:

יב מ שם הלכה י:

רבינו חננאל

פטור היה ר' שמעון במוציא את המת לקברו והלכתא כרבא דקאי כר' שמעון דסבר כל מלאכה שאינה צריכה לגופה פטור עליה. ובפרק יציאות השבת אוקימנא להא דתני זב שיצא בכיס שלו בשבת פטור כר' שמעון דסבר מלאכה שאינה צריכה לגופה פטור ולא תימא מלאכה צריכה לגופה כגון מר לעשות פה וס"ת להגיהו אלא אפי' מר לחפור בו וס"ת לקרות בו מלאכה צריכה לגופה היא וכי לא פטר ר' שמעון אלא מלאכה שאינה צריכה לגופה אבל מלאכה שצריכה לגופה אפי' ר' שמעון מחייב ותניא כרבא המוצ"א כלים מקופלין ומונחין לו על כתפו וסנדליו וטבעתו בידו חייב. ואם היה מלובש בהן פטור. המוציא אדם וכליו וסנדליו ברגליו וטבעתו בידו פטור. שאלו הוציא כמות שהן חייב והלכתא כוותיה: מתני' מטלטלין תרומה טמאה עם הטהור' אוקמה רב חסדא למתניתין הא בשטהורה למטה וטמאה למעלה ואותבוה הא מטלטלין תרומה טמאה עם הטהורה ועם החולין בין טהורה למטה וטמאה למעלה ובין טהורה למעלה וטמאה למטה. ופרקה רב חסדא מתני' לצורך גופו כדי לאכלו. שאינו מותר לו לטלטלו אלא הראוי לו לאכילה. ובריתא לצורך מקומו שצריך לפנות המקום לבית המדרש או לאורחים שמותר לו לטלטל לצורך מקומו. אפילו מה שאינו ראוי לאכילה. ואמרינן מאי דוחקיה דרב חסדא לאוקימנא למתני' לצורך גופו אמר רבא מתניתא קשיתיה דקתני סיפא מעות שעל הכר נוער את הכר והן ניפלות ואוקימנא ר' יוחנן לצורך גופו דאי לצורך מקומו אפי' עודן עליו מטלטלן ואמר רב חסדא לא מוקמינן מתניתין בתרי טעמי ומדסיפא לצורך גופו רישא נמי לצורך גופו: פיסקא דמתני' ר' יהודה אומר אף מעלין את המדומע באחד ומאה. פי' מדומע תרומה שנפלה בחולין ודימעה מעלין אותה אם יש שם מאה ואחד

רב נסים גאון

וסנדלים חדשים אלא אם כן הילך בהן מבעוד יום כמה יהא הילוך; בני ביתיה דבר קפרא אמרין (מדבית רבא דבר קפרא אמרין) מן דבית

דבר קפרא עד בית רבה דר' הושעיא צפראי אמרין מכניסתא דבבלאי עד דרתיה דר' חמא בר חנינא סבראי אמרין מן סדרא רבה עד חנותיה דר' הושעיא: הניחא לרבא דאמר דבר שמלאכתו לאיסור בין לצורך

בין לצורך מקומו מותר שפיר אלא לאביי דאמר דבר שמלאכתו לאיסור לצורך גופו מותר לצורך מקומו אסור מאי איכא למימר · ומשכחת עיקר דיליה בפרק כל הכלים ניטלין בשבת (דף קכג):

כא נוטל אדם את בנו ר' יהושע אומר אף מעלין את המדומע באחד ומאה: פירושו שבעת שיפול חלק אחד תרומה בצ"ט חלקים חולין כולן אסורין לישראל וימכרו לכהן ואם יפול חלק במאה חלקים מוציאן

והא מיפליג פליג עילויה דתניא *רבי יהודה אומר מעלין את המדומע באחד ומאה רבי שמעון בן אלעזר אומר נותן עיניו בצד זה ואוכל מצד אחר דרבי יהודה עדיפא מדר"ש בן אלעזר: **מתני'** *האבן שע"פ החבית מטה על צדה והיא נופלת היתה בין החביות מגביה ומטה על צדה והיא נופלת מעות שעל הכר מנער את הכר והן נופלות *היתה עליו *לשלשת מקנחה בסמרטוט היתה של עור נותנין עליה מים עד שתכלה: **גמ'** אמר רב הונא אמר רב *לא שנו אלא בשוכח אבל במניח נעשה בסיס לדבר האסור: [היתה בין החביות כו']: מאן תנא דכל היכא דאיכא איסורא והיתרא בהיתרא טרחינן באיסורא לא טרחינן אמר רבה בר בר חנה אמר רבי יוחנן רשב"ג היא דתנן *הבורר קטנית ביו"ט ב"ש אומרים בורר אוכל ואוכל וב"ה אומרים בורר כדרכו בחיקו ובתמחוי *ותניא אמר רשב"ג במה דברים אמורים שהאוכל מרובה על הפסולת אבל פסולת מרובה על האוכל דברי הכל בורר אוכל והא הכא דכי אוכל מרובה על הפסולת דמי הכא נמי כיון דאי בעי למישקל לא משתקיל ליה יין עד דשקיל לה (א) לאבן כפסולת מרובה על האוכל דמי: היתה בין החביות מגביה: תניא רבי יוסי אומר היתה החבית מונחת באוצר או שהיו כלי זכוכית מונחין תחתיה מגביה למקום אחר ומטה על צדה והיא נופלת ונוטל הימנה מה שצריך לו ומחזירה למקומה: מעות שעל הכר: אמר רב חייא בר אשי אמר רב לא שנו אלא בשוכח אבל במניח נעשה בסיס לדבר האסור אמר רבה בר בר חנה אמר ר' יוחנן לא שנו אלא לצורך גופו אבל לצורך מקומו מטלטלו ועודן עליו וכן תני חייא בר רב מדיפתי לא שנו אלא לצורך גופו אבל לצורך מקומו מטלטלו ועודן עליו: מעות שעל הכר מנער וכו': א"ר אושעיא שכח ארנקי בחצר מניח עליה ככר או תינוק ומטלטלה אמר רב יצחק שכח לבינה בחצר מניח עליה ככר או תינוק ומטלטלה אמר רבי יהודה בר שילא אמר ר' אסי פעם אחת שכחו דסקיא מלאה מעות בסרטיא ובאו ושאלו את ר' יוחנן ואמר להן הניחו עליה ככר או תינוק וטלטלוה אמר מר זוטרא הלכתא ככל הני שמעתתא בשוכח רב אשי אמר אפילו שכח נמי [לא] *ולא אמרו *ככר או תינוק אלא למת בלבד אביי מנח כפא אכיפי רבא מנח סכינא אבר יונה ומטלטלה אמר רב יוסף כמה חריפא שמעתתא דדרדקי אימר דאמור רבנן בשוכח לכתחילה מי אמור אמר אביי אי לאו *דאדם חשוב אנא כפא אכיפי למה לי הא חזו למיזגא עלייהו אמר רבא אנא אי לאו דאדם חשוב אנא סכינא אבר יונה למה לי הא חזי לי לאומצא טעמא דחזי לאומצא הא לא חזי לאומצא לא *למימרא דרבא כרבי יהודה סבירא ליה והאמר רבא לשמעיה טווי לי בר אווזא ושדי מיעיה לשונרא

התם

תוספות

שאוכל מרובה על הפסולת · פי' בקונטרס משום דהשתא הוי טרחא יתירא למישקליה לאוכל ואינו נראה לר"י דאי משום טרחא הוי מאי קאמרי בסמוך הכא נמי כיון דאי בעי למישקל לא מישתקיל ליה עד דשקיל ליה לאבן כפסולת מרובה על האוכל דמי היכי הוי משום האי טעמא כפסולת מרובה על האוכל ולכך הוצרך רש"י לפרש דל"ג עד דשקיל ליה לאבן על כן נראה לר"ת דטעמא משום דכי אוכל מרובה על הפסולת הוה פסולת כבטל לגבי רובו ומותר ליטלו מן האוכל ולזורקו אבל פסולת מרובה על האוכל לא בטיל ליה פסולת *לגבי אוכל והשתא אתי שפיר גירסת הספרים דגבי חבית נמי כיון דאי בעי למישקל לא מתקיל ליה (ה) עד דשקיל ליה לאבן כפסולת מרובה על האוכל דמי דכיון שאין יכול כלל ליטול מן היין בלא נטילת האבן לא חשיב כבטיל לגבי האוכל כיון שהאוכל אינו ניכר כלל ואינו יכול ליטול הימנו כשהאבן על פי החבית · מ"ר · והא דמוקי לה בספ"ק דביצה (ד' יד: ושם) כגון דנפיש בטרחא וזוטר בשיעורא *אאוכל קאי ולא אפסולת ולפירש"י קאי אפסולת ולא אאוכל [וע"כ לא יברור הפסולת דנפיש בטירחא]:

לא שנו אלא בשכח · וא"ת תרתי דרב למה לי וי"ל חדא מכלל חבירתה איתמר והא לא תקשה תרתי מתני' למה לי דהוה אמינא אבן ודאי שרי בשכח שנראה טפי ככיסוי החבית אבל מעות שעל גבי הכר אפילו בשכח ה"א דאסיר:

רש"י

ואמר כיון דאפשר ליה למיעבד עונג שבת בכה"ג ליתן עיניו בצד זה ולאכול בצד אחר אין מעלין: דרבי יהודה עדיפא · מיקל טפי פורתא ואמר כיון דיכול ליתן (עליו) עיניו בצד זה ולאכול בצד זה לא הוי מתקן בהעלאתו ומעלין: **מתני'** מטה על צדה · מטה חבית על צדה אם צריך ליטול מן היין והאבן נופלת ולא יטלנה בידים: היתה בין החביות · ויירא שלא תפול האבן על החביות וישברם: מגביה · לחבית כולה ומסלקה מבין החביות ושם מטה על צדה: לשלשת · שום דבר מיאוס כגון רוק או צואה: מקנחה בסמרטוט · ולא יתן עליה מים דסתם כר של בגד הוא ובגד שרייתו במים הוא כבוסו: היתה · לשלשת זו על כר של עור דלאו בר כיבוס הוא: נותן עליה מים עד שתכלה · ומיהו כיבוס ממש לא (ב) והואיל וכתם כרים וכסתות רכים נינהו שייך למימר בהו כיבוס בעורות רכין ומיהו שרייתן לא זהו כבוסן וכן מפורש בזבחים בפרק דם חטאת: **גמ'** לא שנו · מטה על צדה דחבית: אלא בשכח · ששכח האבן עליה בין השמשות ולא מדעת: נעשה חבית בסיס לדבר האסור · ואסור להטותה שאף החבית מוקצה: מאן תנא · דמתניתין דקתני מגביה ומטה על צדה דאית ליה דכי טרח מטרח בחבית דהוי היתרא ולא יטול האבן ממש דהוי איסורא ואע"ג דהשתא נמי אבן מטלטל בהדי חבית: רבן שמעון · אליבא דבית הלל: בורר אוכל ואוכל · המאכל יטול והפסולת ישאר בכלי: בורר כדרכו · נוטל פסולת ומניח אוכל אם ירצה: כשהאוכל מרובה על הפסולת · דאי שקיל אוכל מפיש בטרחא: דברי הכל בורר אוכל · דבהיתירא טרח ולא באיסורא ופרכינן והא הכא דמתניתין דאוכל מרובה על הפסולת וכי מגביה האבן עם החבית טרח טפי והוה (ג) למשקל פסולת כר"ש: כיון דאי בעי למשקל · לכולי יין מן החבית לא משתקיל ליה יין שבשוליה עד דשקיל ומגבה לה לחבית כפסולת מרובה דמי דאי בתחלתו לא מגבה לה לחבית סוף סוף מיבעי ליה לאגבוהה או להבית הלכך הוה ליה מפיש בטרחא: ה"ג לא משתקל ליה (ד) עד דשקיל לה ול"ג עד דשקיל לה לאבן: היתה החבית מונחת באוצר · כלומר במקום מכונס שאוצרין שם חביות הרבה ודואג שמא יטלה ותפול האבן על החבית שאצלה: לא שנו · דמנער: נעשה · הכר בסיס למעות ואף הכר אסור בטלטול: לא שנו · דמנערה ואינו מטלטלה בעודן עליה: אלא שצריך לגופו · של כר לשכב עליו הלכך בניעור סגיא ושדי ליה באתרייהו: אבל צריך למקומו · של כר מטלטלו עם המעות למקום אחר: דסקיא מלאה מעות גרסינן: בסרטיא · רה"ר: הניחו עליה ככר או תינוק · דליהדרי לטלטלה אגבייהו תוך ד' אמות וטלטלוה פחות פחות מד' אמות או במחילה של בני אדם כדאמרי' בעירובין (דף מג:): בשוכח · אבל במניח מדעת מערב (יום) שבת לא התירו לו לטלטלה ע"י ככר או תינוק: אלא למת · משום כבוד הבריות כשמוטל בחמה: אביי מנח כפא אכיפי · מניח תרווד על העומרים לטלטלן אגב תרווד: אבר יונה · חי [בלא] מליח: חריפא שמעתא דרדקי · סבורים הם שהם חריפים: אימר דאמור רבנן · בארנקי ודסקיא מניח עליה ככר או תינוק בשכחה ובמקום התורפה ומשום הפסד ממון: אמר אביי · אנא שפיר מטלטלנא כיפי ואפילו בלא תרווד: אי לאו דאדם חשוב אנא · ואנא מחמיר על עצמי שלא ילמדו ממני להקל בהכורין: כפא אכיפי למה לי · בלאו כפא נמי שרי לטלטליכהו דהא חזו למיזגא עלייהו: לאומצא · לאוכלו חי בשבת שיש בני אדם שדעתן יפה ואוכלים בשר חי וקרו לה אומצא: הא לא חזי לאומצא לא · ואע"ג דחזו לשונרא דאמרינן מוכן לאדם לא הוי מוכן לכלבים: כר' יהודה · במסכת ביצה (ד' ו:): טווי לי בר אווזא · ביום טוב: ושדי מיעיה לשונרא · אלמא מטלטל להו משום שונרא ואע"ג דאהידנא לא חזי לאדם דלאו אורח ארעא למיכלא ביום טוב ומיהו מאתמול לאדם הוו קיימי:

התם

עין משפט נר מצוה

יג א מיי' פכ"ה מהל' שבת הל' יז טוש"ע א"ח סי' שט סעיף ד:

יד ב מיי' פכ"ה שם הל' יח טוש"ע א"ח סי' שב סעיף ט:

טו ג מיי' פכ"ה שם הלכה יז טוש"ע א"ח סי' שט סעיף ד:

טז ד מיי' פ"ג מהל' יו"ט הל' טו סמג לאוין עה טוש"ע א"ח סי' תקי סעיף ב:

צ"ל לגבי אוכל והאוכל לגבי פסולת משום דכתיב וע"כ נראה לאו אהאוכל והשתא כו'

יז ה מיי' פכ"ה מהל' שבת הלכה יז טוש"ע א"ח סי' שט סעיף ה:

יח ו מיי' פכ"ה שם הלכה כא סמג שם טוש"ע א"ח סי' שיא סעיף ט:

צ"ל האוכל קאי שהאוכל נפיש בטרחא ולפי"ה בורר אוכל הואיל וזוטר בשיעורא ולא בטל ליה פסולת

רבינו חננאל

ואקשינן אמאי והא קא מתקן שיבלא תמצא עושה מעשה בשבת ופרקי' ר' יהודה דאמר כי מעלין את המדומע כר' אליעזר סבירא ליה דאמר תרומה בעינא מחתא. פי' תרומה שנפלה בחולין אין מחשבין אותה שנתערבה בכל החולין אלא כאילו נתונה במקום אחד היא וכשנוטל ממאה ואחד סאין סאה אנן אומרין כי היא היא התרומה. אבל שאר החולין מתוקנין היו מקודם. ולא היה אסור אלא זו הסאה שנוטלה במקום התרומה שנפלה בלבד. דתנן סאה של תרומה שנפלה לפחות ממאה ונדמעו ונפל מן המדומע למקום אחד. ר' אליעזר אומר מדומע כתרומה ודאי. פי' סאה תרומה שנפלה לתוך חמשים סאין חולין ועוד נפלה מאלו החמשים ואחד סאין סאה אחת לששים סאה חולין ר' אליעזר סבר הכל אסור חמשים הראשונים וששים האחרונים שאני אומר הסאה של תרומה עצמה היא שנפלה בששים האחרונים לפי שאין המדומע עולה אלא בא' ומאה ואין באחד מהן מאה בעת נפילתה בהן וחכ"א אין המדומע מדמע אלא לפי חשבון פי' סאה שנפלה לחמשים סאין ונפלה מאלו החמשים סאין לפחות מחמשים מדמעת אבל אם נפלה סאה לששים סאין עולה לפי שאילו היתה סאה במאה סאין ואחת היתה עולה וחזרנו עוד להקשות אימור דשמעת ליה לר' אליעזר שמחשב מכלל נ"א סאין הללו הסאה האחת שנפלה לס' סאין אחרות תרומה כולה. ומדמעת עד מאה ואחת להומרא לקולא לתקן בשבת מי שמעת ליה ולא

עמדה ופירקנן פירוק אחר והוא ר' יהודה סבר לה כר' שמעון דתנן סאה של תרומה שנפלה למאה חולין ונדמעו ולא הספיק להגביהה עד שנפלה האחרת הרי זו אסורה ור' שמעון מתיר ת"ק סבר כיון שלא הגביהה נמצא שנפלו ב' סאין למאה סאין ואין עולין כי פחות ממאה הן. ור' שמעון סבר מאותה העת שנפלה סאה תרומה לסאה חולין הותרו הסאה. ונשארו חולין בהכשרן. וסאה אחת בתוכן תרומה התרומה היא אסורה בלבד וכשנפלה אחר כן עוד סאה אחרת תרומה עליהן על מאה חולין נפלה ועולה כו' ופרקי' לה ודברים פשוטין הן. והדרנן ומוקמינן ר' יהודה דמתני' כר' שמעון בן אלעזר דאמר נותן עיניו בצד זה כלומר מחשב להוציא התרומה מצד זה ואוכל מצד אחר ש"מ כי התרומה מחתא במקום אחד. ואקשינן וכי ר' יהודה כר' שמעון בן אלעזר סבירא ליה והא מפלג פליג עליה דתניא ר' יהודה אומר מעלין את המדומע באחד ומאה ר' שמעון אומר נותן עיניו בצד זה ואוכל מצד זה וכפרקי' דר' יהודה עדיפא שר' יהודה מתיר אפי' להעלותה ור' שמעון אינו מתיר להעלותה אלא לתת עיניו בצד זה ולאכול מצד זה. ותרווייהו סבירא להו סאה תרומה שנפלה למאה חולין בעת שנפלה למאה מותרין הן ובתקונן הן ואין צריכין תיקון אלא סילוק סאה אחת שהן בלבד במקום התרומה: פיסקא האבן שעל

מסורת הש"ס

[תוספ' פט"ז]

[לעיל קכה:]

זבחים לד.

[פי' צואת תרנגולים · ערוך]

[לעיל קכא: ע"ש]

ביצה יד:

ג"ז שם ע"ש

[לעיל ל: מג:]

[לעיל נא. וש"נ]

ביצה לג.

הגהות הב"ח

(א) גמ' דשקיל לה כפסולת כצ"ל ותיבת לאבן נמחק: (ב) רש"י ד"ה נותן וכו' כיבוס ממש לא דהואיל: (ג) ד"ה דברי הכל וכו' והוה ליה למשקל: (ד) ד"ה ה"ג לא משתקיל ליה יין עד: (ה) תוס' ד"ה שהאוכל וכו' לא משתקיל ליה יין עד:

גליון הש"ס

גמ' מאן תנא דכל היכא דאיכא איסורא והיתרא. עיין לעיל דף נא ע"ב תוס' ד"ה אינו נוטל:

רב נסים גאון

מוציאין חלק אחד והשאר מותר לישראל ותמצא עיקר דבר זה בספרי מכל חלבו את מקדשו ממנו שאם נפל לתוכו הרי זה מקדשו מיכן אמרו תרומה עולה באחד ומאה אין לי אלא תרומה טהורה ותמצא **בשבעת תרומות ותוספות תרומות** מזה הענין הרבה ועיקרו מה שהזכרנו' ובגמ' דערלה בפרק ב' (ירושלמי פ"ב הלכה א) מניין שהן עולין אמר ר' יונה כ"ה (במדבר יח) מכל חלבו את מקדשו ממנו דבר שאתה מרים ממנו שאם יפול לתוכו הרי זה מקדשו וכמה הוא אחד מכאה ואיתא נמי בפרק ד' דתרומות התרומות צריך להרים כמה שהוא במשנה במסכת ערלה בראש פרק ב' התרומה ותרומת מעשר של דמאי מצטרפין זה עם זה ואינו צריך להרים וכו' וטעמו של דבר לפי שהתרומות והחלה והביכורים הם נכסי כהן וצריך להרים תרומה ויתנה ואם לא ירים ויתן לו הרי זה גוזל ממנו ואין להם בעלים שראויין להם לפיכך אינו צריך להרים

surely he disagrees? For it was taught, R. Judah said: One removes the admixture [of *terumah* in *hullin*] when one part [is neutralized] in a hundred and one parts;[10] R. Simeon b. Eleazar said: One casts his eyes at one side and eats from the other?[11]—R. Judah's [ruling] goes beyond R. Simeon b. Eleazar's.[12]

MISHNAH. IF A STONE IS ON THE MOUTH OF A CASK
a [OF WINE], ONE TILTS IT ON A SIDE AND IT FALLS OFF.[1] IF IT [THE CASK] IS [STANDING] AMONG [OTHER] CASKS,[2] HE LIFTS IT OUT, TILTS IT ON A SIDE, AND IT FALLS OFF. IF MONEY IS LYING ON A CUSHION, ONE SHAKES THE CUSHION, AND IT FALLS OFF. IF DIRT[3] IS UPON IT, ONE WIPES IT OFF WITH A RAG;[4] IF IT IS OF LEATHER,[5] WATER IS POURED OVER IT UNTIL IT DISAPPEARS.

GEMARA. R. Huna said in Rab's name: They learnt this only where one forgot [it there], but if he placed [it there], it [the cask] becomes a stand for a forbidden article.

IF IT IS [STANDING] AMONG [OTHER] CASKS, etc. Which Tanna holds that wherever there is something permitted and something forbidden, one must occupy oneself with what is permitted, not with what is forbidden?[6]—Said Rabbah b. Bar Hanah in R. Johanan's name, It is R. Simeon b. Gamaliel. For we learnt: If one selects beans on a festival, Beth Shammai maintain: He must select the edible [beans] and eat them;[7] whereas Beth Hillel rule: He may select in the usual way[8] into his lap or into a plate. Now it was taught, R. Simeon b. Gamaliel said: When was this said? When the edible exceeds the non-edible;[9] but if the non-edible exceeds the edible, all agree that he must select the edible. But here it is analogous to where the edible exceeds the non-edible?[10]—Since he cannot take [the whole of] the wine, should he desire it, unless he lifts it up, it is analogous to where the non-edible exceeds the edible.[11]

IF IT IS [STANDING] AMONG [OTHER] CASKS, HE LIFTS IT OUT. It was taught, R. Jose said: If the cask is lying among a store [of casks], or if glassware is lying under it, he lifts it out elsewhere, tilts it on a side, so that it falls off, takes thereof what he requires, and replaces it.

IF MONEY IS LYING ON A CUSHION: R. Hiyya b. Ashi said in Rab's name: They learnt this only where one forgot [it there]; but if
b he placed [it there],[1] it [the cushion] became a stand for a forbidden article. Rabbah b. Bar Hanah said in the name of R. Johanan: They learnt this only when it is required for itself; but if its place is required, one may remove it [the cushion] while they [the coins] are yet upon it. And thus did Hiyya b. Rab of Difti[2] recite: They learnt this only when it is required for itself; but if its place is required, one may move it while they are yet upon it.

IF MONEY IS LYING ON A CUSHION, ONE SHAKES, etc. R. Oshaia said: If one forgets a purse in a courtyard, he places a loaf or a child thereon and moves it. R. Isaac said: If one forgets a brick in a courtyard, he places a loaf or a child thereon and moves it. R. Judah b. Shila said in R. Assi's name: They once forgot a saddle-bag full of money in the street, and went and consulted R. Johanan and he told them, Place a loaf or a child thereon and move it.[3] Mar Zutra said: The law is as all these rulings, where one forgets. R. Ashi said: Even if one forgets, this is still not [permitted], and they permitted [the expedient of] a loaf or a child only in connection with a corpse.[4]

Abaye placed a ladle on a pile of sheaves;[5] Raba placed a knife on a young dove[6] and handled it. Said R. Joseph: How keen are the rulings of children![7] assume that the Rabbis ruled thus when one forgets: but was it said [that it is permitted] at the very outset?
c Abaye retorted: But that I am a person of importance,[1] would I need a ladle on sheaves: surely they are fit for reclining thereon.[2] Raba retorted: But that I am a person of importance, would I need a knife on a young dove? surely it is fit for me as raw meat.[3] Thus the reason is because it is fit as raw meat; but if it were not fit as raw meat it might not [be handled]:[4] shall we say that Raba agrees with R. Judah?[5] But surely Raba said to his servant, Roast me a duck[6] and throw its entrails to a cat?[7] [143a]—

(10) One hundred and one is stated inclusively. (11) Thus R. Judah insists on actual removal. (12) He agrees with R. Simeon b. Eleazar but adds that since mere intention suffices to make the mixture fit, one can also remove the *se'ah* on the Sabbath.

a (1) When he wishes to draw the contents. (2) And the falling stone might cause damage. (3) E.g., secretion, spittle, etc. (4) But not with water, which is forbidden as washing. (5) Which is not such as is washed with water. (6) As here: one must not handle the stone, a forbidden article, but the whole cask, which is a permitted object, even though the stone lies upon it. (7) Leaving the non-edible beans in the bowl. (8) I.e., he can remove the non-edible beans, if he wishes. (9) Then Beth Hillel permit the latter to be picked out, because it is less trouble. (10) For there is more trouble in lifting out the whole cask than in simply removing the stone. (11) Eventually he must lift out the cask and tilt it in order to obtain the wine at the very bottom; hence there is no more trouble in lifting it out now.

b (1) Before the Sabbath. (2) V. *supra* 10a, n. b5. (3) Less than four cubits at a time, since carrying in a street is forbidden; or, within a barrier formed by a chain of persons, v. 'Er. 43*b*. (4) V. *supra* 30*b*. (5) To handle the latter in virtue of the former. (6) Killed, raw and unsalted. (7) Said sarcastically.

c (1) Who sets an example. (2) Hence I may handle them in any case, and I place the ladle there merely because I do not wish to encourage laxity of observance. (3) Which used to be eaten in his days. (4) Though it would still be fit for dogs; thus fitness for dogs does not permit handling by humans. (5) Who holds the view expressed in the preceding note; v. Bez. 6*b*. (6) It was a festival. (7) Thus he permitted him to handle it, though unfit for human beings just then, entrails not being eaten on Festivals: nevertheless on the previous day, before the festival commenced, they would have been fit for human beings too.

There, since they would putrefy,[8] his mind was [set] upon them from the previous day.[9]

Logic too indicates that Raba agrees with R. Judah. For Raba lectured: A woman must not enter a wood-shed to take thence a wood poker;[10] and if a wood poker is broken [on a Festival], it may not be used as fuel on the Festival, because we may heat with utensils but not with fragments of utensils. This proves it.[11]

MISHNAH. BETH SHAMMAI SAY: ONE MAY REMOVE BONES AND [NUT]SHELLS FROM THE TABLE;[12] BUT BETH HILLEL RULE: ONE MUST TAKE AWAY THE WHOLE BOARD AND SHAKE IT.[13] ONE MAY REMOVE FROM THE TABLE CRUMBS LESS THAN THE SIZE OF AN OLIVE AND THE PANICLES OF BEANS AND LENTILS, BECAUSE THEY ARE FOOD FOR ANIMALS. AS FOR A SPONGE, IF IT HAS A LEATHERN HANDLE, ONE MAY WIPE [THE BOARD] WITH IT; IF NOT, ONE MAY NOT WIPE [THE
a BOARD] WITH IT.[1] [THE SAGES MAINTAIN]:[2] IN EITHER CASE IT MAY BE HANDLED ON THE SABBATH[3] AND IS NOT SUSCEPTIBLE TO DEFILEMENT.[4]

GEMARA. R. Naḥman said: As for us, we have no other [view] but that Beth Shammai agree with R. Judah, and Beth Hillel with R. Simeon.[5]

ONE MAY REMOVE CRUMBS FROM THE TABLE. This supports R. Joḥanan. For R. Joḥanan said: Crumbs less than an olive in size may not be wantonly[6] destroyed.[7]

PANICLES OF BEANS. Who is the authority? [Apparently] R. Simeon, who rejects [the interdict of] *mukẓeh*?[8] Then consider the final clause: AS FOR A SPONGE, IF IT HAS A LEATHERN HANDLE, ONE MAY WIPE [THE BOARD] WITH IT; IF NOT, ONE MAY NOT WIPE WITH IT: this agrees with R. Judah, who maintains, That which is unintentional is forbidden?[9]—Here even R. Simeon agrees, for Abaye and Raba both maintained: R. Simeon admits in a case of 'cut off his head but let him not die.'[10]

The kernels of Syrian dates[11] may be handled, since they are fit [for cattle] on account of their parent source,[12] but those of
b Persian [dates] are forbidden.[1] Samuel handled them in virtue of [a piece of] bread.[2] (Mnemonic: *SHaRNaS SHaPaZ*.)[3] Samuel is consistent with his view, for Samuel said: One may carry out all his requirements with bread.[4] Rabbah handled them in virtue of a bowl [flask] of water. R. Huna the son of R. Joshua made them as a pot of excrements.[5] Said R. Ashi to Amemar: But may we make a pot of excrements at the outset?[6] R. Shesheth threw them away [spat them out] with his tongue. R. Papa threw them behind the couch.[7] It was said of R. Zechariah b. Eucolos that he would turn his face to the back of the couch and throw them away.

(8) If left until the evening after the Festival. (9) Intending them for cats, and therefore they are *mukan* (q.v. Glos.). (10) For wood in a shed is generally meant for fuel, not to be used as a utensil. (11) That Raba accepts the interdict of *mukẓeh*, in accordance with R. Judah. (12) By hand, though they are not even fit for a dog—dry and hard bones are referred to—for Beth Shammai do not accept the interdict of *mukẓeh*. (13) But the bones and nutshells may not be handled, Beth Hillel accepting the interdict of *mukzeh*.

a (1) For fear of wringing out the absorbed moisture. (2) This is omitted in some versions. (3) When dry. (4) Being neither a wooden utensil, a garment, a sack, nor metal, and only these can become unclean. (5) R. Judah accepts the interdict of *mukẓeh*; R. Simeon does not. Hence the views ascribed to Beth Shammai and Beth Hillel respectively in our Mishnah must be reversed. (6) Lit., 'by hand'. (7) Rashi: since the Mishnah states, ONE MAY REMOVE, implying that they are removed by hand, and must not be thrown away. Tosaf. rejects this deduction: moreover, it appears from Ber. 52*b* that 'may be destroyed' is the correct reading. Accordingly, Tosaf. reads there: . . .*may be* wantonly destroyed, the deduction being from the statement, BECAUSE THEY ARE FOOD FOR ANIMALS, which may be destroyed. (8) For on Judah's view it is *mukẓeh*, since it was together with the edible portion before the Sabbath when it was not *mukan* for animals. (9) The unintentional act is that in holding it water is wrung out. (10) V. *supra* 75*a*, n. a8. (11) These were of an inferior quality and only fit for cattle. (12) Lit., 'their mother'. *Sc.* the date itself, v. n. 8, the case here being the reverse.

b (1) Because the dates themselves were fit for human beings. (2) Similar to the cases given *supra* 142*b*. (3) V. *supra* 32*b*, n. b6. *SH*=*SH*emuel (Samuel), *R*=Rabbah; *N* = R. Hu*N*a; *S* = R. A*S*hi, *SH* = *SH*esheth, *P* = R. *P*apa; Z = R. *Z*echariah. (4) *Supra* 50*b*. (5) He collected all the kernels in front of him; the quantity made them repulsive and he could treat them as a pot of excrements, which may be removed. (6) Surely not. Thus he disagrees with R. Huna. (7) Upon which he reclined while eating.

התם כיון דמסרח דעתיה עילויה מאתמול הכי נמי מסתברא דרבא כר' יהודה סבירא ליה *דדרש רבא "אשה לא תכנס לבית העצים ליטול מהן אוד ואוד שנשבר אסור להסיקו ביום טוב לפי *שמסיקין בכלים ואין מסיקין בשברי כלים שמע מינה: **מתני'** *ב"ש אומרים *"מעבירין מעל השלחן עצמות וקליפין וב"ה אומרים *מסלק את הטבלא כולה ומנערה מעבירין (א) מלפני השלחן פירורין פחות מכזית ושער של אפונין ושער עדשים מפני שהוא מאכל בהמה "ספוג אם יש לו עור בית אחיזה מקנחין בו ואם לאו אין מקנחין בו (ב) *(וחכמים אומרים) בין כך ובין כך *ניטל בשבת ואינו מקבל טומאה: **גמ'** *אמר רב נחמן אנו אין לנו אלא ב"ש כרבי יהודה וב"ה כרבי שמעון: מעבירין (ג) מלפני השלחן פירורין: מסייע ליה לר' יוחנן *דאמר רבי יוחנן "פירורין שאין בהן כזית אסור לאבדן ביד: שער של אפונין: מני ר"ש היא דלית ליה מוקצה אימא סיפא ספוג אם יש לו בית אחיזה מקנחין בו ואם לאו אין מקנחין בו אתאן לר' יהודה דאמר דבר שאין מתכוין אסור בהא אפילו ר"ש מודה *דאביי ורבא דאמרי תרוייהו מודה ר"ש בפסיק רישיה ולא ימות "הני גרעינין דתמרי ארמייתא שרו לטלטולינהו הואיל וחזיין אגב אמן ודפרסייתא אסור שמואל מטלטל להו אגב ריפתא: (שרנ"ם שפ"ז סימן): שמואל לטעמיה *דאמר שמואל "עושה אדם כל צרכו בפת *רבה מטלטל להו אגב לקנא דמיא רב הונא בריה דרב יהושע עביד להו כגרף של ריעי א"ל רב אשי לאמימר *"וכי עושין גרף של ריעי לכתחילה רב ששת זריק להו בלישניה רב פפא זריק להו אחורי המטה *אמרו עליו על רבי זכריה בן אבקולס "שהיה מחזיר פניו אחורי המטה וזורקן:

הדרן עלך נוטל אדם את בנו

רש"י

התם כיון דמסרח · מעייא אי מלנע ליה עד אורתא: מאתמול דעתיה עליה · לשונרא ובין השמשות נמי מוכן לבהמה הוה: אוד· פורגו"ן דהשתא עלים להסקה ניתנו ולא לטלטול כלי: ואוד שנשבר · ביו"ט: בשברי כלים · שנשברו היום דהוו להו נולד: ש"מ · דכרבי יהודה סבירא ליה דאית ליה מוקצה:

מתני' מעבירין · בידים מעל השלחן: עצמות · קשין שאינן ראויין לכלב: וקליפין · של אגוזים דלית להו לב"ש מוקצה: וב"ה אומרים מסלק את הטבלא · שיש תורת כלי עליה אבל לא יטלטל הקליפין בידים כרבי יהודה: מעבירין מעל השלחן · סתמא היא: פירורין פחות מכזית · וכ"ש כזית כדמפרש טעמא שהם מאכל בהמה: ושער של אפונין · שרביטין של קטנית שהקטנית גדל בהם: אפונין · ייס"ש: עור בית אחיזה · [בית אחיזה] של עור שיאחזנו בו: מקנחין בו · טבלא: אין מקנחין בו · שכשאוחזו נסחט בין אצבעותיו: ניטל בשבת · כשהוא נגוב: ואינו מקבל טומאה · דאינו לא כלי עץ ולא בגד ולא שק ולא מתכת: **גמ'** אנו אין לנו · אין אנו סומכין על משנתינו כמות שהיא שנויה אלא מוחלפת שיטתה וב"ש כרבי יהודה כו': אסור לאבדן ביד · מדקתני מעבירין בידים ולא זריק להו: דלית ליה מוקצה · דאי ר' יהודה מאתמול לאו לבהמה קיימי שהרי האוכל היה עמהן והיום לוקח מהם: שאין מתכוין · שאין מתכוין לסחוט: גרעינין · של תמרים והם לבהמה: ארמייתא · תמרים רעים הם ומאכילין התמרים עצמן לבהמה הלכך אגב אימייהו לבהמה נמי קיימי: פרסייתא · תמרים טובים הם ואין מאכילין אותן לבהמה: כל צרכו · משתמש בו ואין כאן משום בזיון וממחהו בתבשיל: לקנא דמיא · ספל של מים: גרף של ריעי · נוטלן לפניו כשאוכל התמרים עד שנמאסות בעיניו ונוטלן אותן מפניו כגרף של ריעי ונותנן לבהמה: זריק להו בלישני' · אל עבר השלחן: אחורי המטה · שהוא מיסב עליה:

הדרן עלך נוטל

תוספות

התם כיון דמסרח · ומתקלקל ואין ראוי למאכל אדם מאתמול דעתיה עילויה ליתנו לבהמה אע"ג דבשער של אפונין ושל עדשים אסרינן לרבי יהודה אע"ג דחזו למאכל בהמה וכן גרעינין דלעיל בפרק במה מדליקין (דף כט:) דאמרינן לרבי יהודה אבל אין מסיקין בגרעינין מ"מ הכא שרי כדפי' התם: **ליטול** מהן אוד · נראה לר"ת כפירוש ה"ג דאסירי משום תיקוני מנא דלפירו' זה (ד) דאע"ג דלא מתקלא ליה גזרינן שלא יבא לידי תיקון כלי: **עצמות** וקליפין · לא כפירוש הקונטרס דפירש אפילו קשין ואין ראויין לאכילת כלבים *דהאי תנא אמרינן בגמרא דכרבי שמעון סבירא ליה ור"ש בעי לכל הפחות ראויות למאכל בהמה דקתני מעבירין מעל השלחן פירורין כו' מפני שהוא מאכל בהמה ומוקמינן בגמרא כוותיה:

אנו אין לנו אלא ב"ש כר"י כו' · במסכת עדיות לא מיתניא בהדי קולי ב"ש וחומרי ב"ה והיינו כרב נחמן והא דלא מייתי סייעתא מהתם משום דמאי אולמא דהא מהא:

פירורין שאין בהן כזית אסור לאבדן ביד · פי' בקונט' מדקתני מעבירין ולא קתני זורקין וקשה לרבי דברישא נמי קתני מגביהין מעל השלחן עצמות וקליפין ולא קתני זורקין אע"פ שמותר לאבדן ביד ועוד דאמרינן בברכות בריש אלו דברים (דף נב:) וב"ה אומרים אם שמש ת"ח הוא נוטל פירורין שיש בהן כזית ומניח פירורין שאין בהן כזית ומסייע ליה לר' יוחנן דאמר פירורין שאין בהן כזית מותר לאבדן ביד ואי אפשר ליגרס התם אסור *ונראה לר' דהכא גרסי' מותר ודייק מדאצטריך למיתני מפני שהוא מאכל בהמה דהיינו משמע דלא חזי לאדם והוו כשאר מאכל בהמה ומותר לאבדן · מ"ר:

ואם לאו אין מקנחין בו · אית ספרים דגרסי וחכ"א בין כך ובין כך מקנחין בו ולא יתכן דאמר בגמרא דבאין לו עור בית אחיזה אפילו ר"ש מודה דאסור משום דפסיק רישיה הוא וה"ר יצחק מדנפירא גרס בין כך ובין כך אין מקנחין בו כרבי יהודה דאמר דבר שאין מתכוין אסור ואין נראה לר"י דהא בגמרא משמע דברישא מודה ר' יהודה (ה) דאמר אימא סיפא ספוג אם יש לו עור בית אחיזה· מקנחין בו ואם לאו אין מקנחין בו אתאן לרבי יהודה אם כן בין כך ובין כך אין מקנחין בו לא רבי יהודה ולא ר' שמעון אלא ודאי לא גרסינן ליה כלל · מ"ר:

שמואל מטלטל להו אגב ריפתא · אף על גב דכר"ש סבירא ליה דשרי לקמן בפרק בתרא (דף קנו:) נבלה שנתנבלה בשבת מיהו מחמיר היה משום דהוה אדם חשוב כאביי ורבא דלעיל · ר"ת: **רבא** מטלטל להו אגב לקנא דמיא · ואם תאמר והא רבא סבר לעיל כר"י דאית ליה מוקצה ואטו לקנא דמיא היכי שרי לכתחילה ויש לומר דשני לן בין היכא דאפשר למיעבד האי טלטול מאתמול להיכא דלא אפשר דכיפין ובר יונה היו מאתמול בידו והיה יכול לטלטלם אבל הני גרעיני תמרה לא אפשר ושרי אפילו לרבי יהודה ואף לאדם חשוב דאמר בבילה פרק יו"ט (דף כח:) דאמר ליה אביי לרב יוסף הני סופלי לחויתא היכי שדינן ביומא טבא לרבי יוסי דאמר לכם ולא לכלבים חזיין להסקה כו' בשבת מאי איכא למימר מטלטלין להו אגב ריפתא כדשמואל אלמא דאפילו רב יוסף דלא בעי למישרי לעיל אגב כפא וסכינא אפילו דבר הראוי לאדם שרי התם גרעיני תמרה אגב ריפתא:

הדרן עלך נוטל אדם את בנו

יט א מיי' פ"ד מהל' י"ט הלכה יא סמג לאוין עה טוש"ע א"ח סי' תקז סעיף ג:
כ ב מיי' פכ"ו מהלכות שבת הלכה טו סמג לאוין סה טוש"ע א"ח סי' שח סעיף כז:
כא ג מיי' פכ"ה שם הלכה טו סמג שם טוש"ע א"ח סי' שח סעיף ז:
כב ד מיי' פ"ז מהל' ברכות הלכה ט טוש"ע א"ח סי' קפ סעיף ד
[עי' תוס' ביצה ב: ד"ה מגביהין]
[עי' תוס' ביצה ב. ד"ה וכ"ס]
כג ה מיי' פכ"ו מהל' שבת הלכה טו סמג לאוין סה טוש"ע א"ח סי' שח סעיף ג:
כד ו מיי' פ"ז מהלכות ברכות הל' ט טוש"ע א"ח סי' קפ סעיף א:
כה ז מיי' פכ"ה מהל' שבת הלכה כד ופכ"ו הלכה יג סמג לאוין סה טוש"ע א"ח סי' שח סעיף לו:
כו ח מיי' פכ"ו שם הל' טו טוש"ע שם סעיף ג:
[עי' תוס' מנחות נח: ד"ה ואיכא דאמרי דזהו מסוגיות הפוכות]

מסורת הש"ס

ביצה לג. וכם
[שם לב.] לעיל כח. כט. וקכד:
לקמן קנו. [ביצה ב. תוספ' פי"ז מתני' איפכא ע"ש]
נ"א מקנחין בו וניטל
[לקמן קנו: פ"ש ביצה ב:]
ברכות נב: ע"ש
לעיל קג. קיא: קכ: וקלג. סוכה לג: כתובות ו. בכורות כה. [ביצה לו.]
ברכות לט: לעיל קיז: ביצה לט.
[ד"ל רבא ע' תוס' ד"ה רבא]
[ביצה ל'-לו:]
[תוספ' פי"ז]

רבינו חננאל

פי החבית מטה על צדה והיא נופלת. אמר רב הונא אמר רב לא שנו אלא בשוכח אבל במניח נעשה בסים לדבר האסור. פי' נעשת החבית כגון לאבן ואסור להטות החבית כלל. והלכתא כוותיה דרבא דר' אמי אמר ר' יוחנן קאי כוותיה. בפרק כל הכלים: **היתה** בין החביות מגביהה מטה על צדה כו'. תניא (א') ר' יוסי אומר היתה החבית מונחת באוצר או שהיו כלי זכוכית מונחין תחתיה מגביהה למקום אחד ומטה על צדה ונוטל מה שצריך לו ומחזירה למקומה. מעות שעל הכר נמי אוקמוה משמ' דרב בשוכח אבל במניח נעשת הכר בסים למעות ואסור אפילו לנערן ואמר רבה משמיה דר' יוחנן לא שנו אלא לצורך גופו כגון שצריך (סבר) לישב עליו אבל אם הוא צריך למקומו· מטלטלין ועודן עליו. וכן תני חייא בר רב מדפתי והא דא"ר הושעיא שכח ארנקי בחצר ור' יצחק דאמר שכח לבינה בחצר ויהודה בר שילא דאמר שכחו דסקיא מלאה מעות בסטין ואמרו שמניח עליה ככר או תינוק ומטלטלו ואמר מר זוטרא הלכתא ככל הני שמעתתא בשכח ולית הלכתא כוותייהו אלא הלכתא כרב אשי דהוא בתראה דאמר לא אמרו ככר או תינוק אלא למת בלבדי אביי מנח כפא פי' תרווד אכיפי הן כגון כיפה של צמר ורבא מנח סכינא אבר יונה והוא מליח אבל היה מבושל והיה מטלטל בן יונה אגב סכינא אמר שאלו מותרין לטלטלן בשבת דתניא בראשונה היו אומרים ג' כלים מותרין בשבת מקצוע של דבילה וזומלוסטרין וסכין קטנה שע"ג השלחן וכפה היא זומליסטרון כדתנן ניטלה כיפה מטאה משום מולג · ואקשינן על רבה טעמא דחזי לאומצא הא לא חזי לאומצא לא דהא מוקצה הוא כלומר כר' יהודה סבירא ליה ולא כר' שמעון דאי ר' שמעון לית ליה מוקצה אלא אפילו בשר תפוח שרי לטלטוליה וכל בשר אחר בין חי בין מליח. ותוב אקשינן עליה ומי סבר לה רבא כר' יהודה והא א"ל רבא לשמעיה טוי לי בר אווזא ביו"ט ושדי מיעיא לשונרא דאי כר' שמעון דאי כר' יהודה הא אמר כל דבר שאינו מוכן לאכילה אסיר לטלטלו ואפילו בהמה לא היה מתיר לבודקה אלא באשפה שאם תמצא טריפה יניחנה באשפה. ומסקנא דשמעתא דרבה כר' יהודה ס"ל ופשוטה היא: **מתני'** בה"א מגביהין מעל השולחן עצמות וקליפין וכו'. אמר רב נחמן אנו אין לנו אלא ב"ש כר' יהודה וב"ה כר' שמעון מעבירין מעל גבי השלחן פירורין פחות מכזית מסייע ליה לר' יוחנן דאמר פירורין שאין בהן כזית מותר לאבדן ביד. ספוג אם יש לו עור בית אחיזה מקנחין בו ואם לאו אין מקנחין בו אפילו לר' שמעון דהא אי אפשר שלא לסחוט באחוז בספוג אלא אם יש לו עור בית אחיזה: גרעינין דתמרי. ארמי ארמייתא שרי לטלטולי הואיל וחזיין על גב איטן. פי' רכים הן ונאכלין עם התמרים עצמן. דפרסייתא שמואל מטלטלינהו ואגב ריפתא וכו' שמעתא: **הדרן עלך נוטל אדם**

הגהות הב"ח

(א) במשנה מעבירין מעל השלחן פירורין: (ב) שם ומקנחין בו (וחכ"א) תא"מ ונ"ב רש"י והתוספות ולאפסי לא גרסי וחכ"א אבל מפי' המשניות להרמב"ם

מחמת דגרס לה: (ג) גמ' מעבירין מעל השלחן פירורין: (ד) תוס' ד"ה ליטול וכו' דלפירוש זה אע"ג: (ה) ד"ה ואם לאו וכו' מודה ר' יהודה דאמרינן אימא:

רב נסים גאון

רבא כר' נתן סבירא ליה דאמר חי נושא את עצמו· עיקר דבריו של ר' נתן בפרק המצניע (דף צד) ר' נתן אומר על השחוטין חייב על החיים פטור מפני שהחי נושא את עצמו. רבא כר' שמעון סבירא ליה דאמר מלאכה שאינה צריכה לגופה פטור עליה ועיקר דבריו של ר' שמעון גם בפרק המצניע (דף נג) דתנן וכן כזית מן המת וכעדשה מן השרץ חייב ור' שמעון פוטר ונרסי' בגמ' אמר רבה אמר ר' רב יוסף אמר ריש לקיש פוטר היה ר' שמעון אף במוציא את המת לקוברו וכבר פירשנו זה בפרק יציאות השבת: **הכי** נמי מסתברא דרבא כר' יהודה סבירא ליה דדרש רבא אשה לא תכנס לבין העצים ליטול מהן אוד אוד שנשבר ביום טוב אסור להסיקו לפי שמסיקים בכלים ואין מסיקין בשברי כלים וזה שיטה לדברי ר' יהודה שאמר במשנה בפ' במה מדליקין (ד' כט) ואין מסיקין בשברי כליםדברי ר' יהודה הואיל וסברא ליה כוותיה בנולד במוקצה נמי דתנן בסוף מסכתא (לקמן דף קנו) ר' יהודה אומר אם לא היתה נבילה מערב שבת אסורה לפי שאינה מן המוכן כר' יהודה סבירא ליה ולכך אמר סכינא אבר יונה למה לי הא הזי לאומצא דדייקת מינה הא לא חזי לאומצא לא וכמו שאמר בתחילת מסכת יום טוב (דף ג) דאית ליה מוקצה אית ליה נולד ודלית ליה מוקצה לית ליה נולד כי הכלל עיקר אחד חוזר והיא ההכנה: **אמר** רב נחמן אנו אין לנו אלא בית שמאי כרבי יהודה ובית הלל כרבי שמעון וכן אמרו עוד מני ר' שמעון היא דלית ליה מוקצה ועיקר דברי רבי יהודה ור' שמעון בפרק כירה (דף מד) וכבר פירשנוה למעלה. אתאן לרבי יהודה דאמר דבר שאין מתכוין אסור עיקר דבריו של ר' יהודה במשנה במסכת בכורות (דף לג) ובמס' יום טוב (דף כג) וכבר פירשנו דבריו גם במס' זו בפ' כירה: **סליק פרק נוטל**

רבא

עין משפט
נר מצוה

א א ב מיי' פכ"ב מהל' שבת הלכה טו סמג לאוין סה טוש"ע א"ח סי' שלה סעיף א:

ב ג מיי' שם פכ"א הל' יא טוש"ע שם סעיף ה:

[בפסקי תוספות איתא כסותו]

ג ד ה ו מיי' פכ"א מהל' שבת הלכה יב סמג שם טוש"ע א"ח סי' שכ סעיף א:

ד ז מיי' פ"י מהלכות טומאת אוכלין הל' ד:

ה ח שם הל' ס ופ"א מהל' משכב ומושב הלכה טו:

[עיין תוס' ביצה ג. ד"ה ר"י אמר]

חבית *שנשברה מצילין הימנה מזון שלש סעודות ואומר לאחרים באו והצילו לכם ובלבד שלא יספוג *אין סוחטין את הפירות להוציא מהן משקין ואם יצאו מעצמן אסורין ר' יהודה אומר אם לאוכלין היוצא מהן מותר ואם למשקין היוצא מהן אסור *חלות דבש שריסקן מע"ש ויצאו מעצמן אסורין (א) ורבי אליעזר מתיר: **גמ'** תנא לא יספוג ביין ולא יטפח בשמן שלא יעשה כדרך שהוא עושה בחול ת"ר נתפזרו לו פירות בחצר מלקט על יד על יד ואוכל אבל לא לתוך הסל ולא לתוך הקופה שלא יעשה כדרך שהוא עושה בחול: אין סוחטין את הפירות: *אמר רב יהודה אמר שמואל מודה היה רבי יהודה לחכמים בזיתים וענבים מ"ט כיון דלסחיטה נינהו יהיב דעתיה ועולא אמר רב חלוק היה ר' יהודה אף בזיתים וענבים ורבי יוחנן אמר הלכה כרבי יהודה בשאר פירות ואין הלכה כרבי יהודה בזיתים וענבים אמר רבה אמר רב יהודה אמר שמואל מודה היה רבי יהודה לחכמים בזיתים וענבים ומודים חכמים לרבי יהודה בשאר פירות א"ל רבי ירמיה לרבי אבא אלא במאי פליגי א"ל לכי תשכח אמר רב נחמן בר יצחק מסתברא בתותים ורמונים פליגי דתניא זיתים שמשך מהן שמן וענבים שמשך מהן יין והכניסן בין לאוכל בין למשקין היוצא מהן אסור תותים שמשך מהן מים ורמונים שמשך מהן יין והכניסן לאוכלין היוצא מהן מותר למשקין ולסתם היוצא מהן אסור דברי רבי יהודה וחכמים אומרים בין לאוכלין בין למשקין היוצא מהן אסור וסבר רבי יהודה סתם אסור *והתנן חלב האשה מטמא לרצון ושלא לרצון חלב בהמה אינו מטמא אלא לרצון אמר ר' עקיבא קל וחומר הוא ומה חלב האשה שאינו מיוחד אלא לקטנים מטמא לרצון ושלא לרצון חלב הבהמה שמיוחד בין לקטנים בין לגדולים אינו דין שיטמא בין לרצון ובין שלא לרצון אמרו לו אם טמא חלב האשה שלא לרצון שדם מגפתה טמא יטמא חלב הבהמה שלא

רש"י

חבית. מצילין הימנה מזון ג' סעודות · ואפילו בכלים הרבה דאילו בחד מנא אמרי' בכל כתבי הקדש (לעיל דף קכ·) דכמה דבעי מציל: לכם · כל אחד מזון ג' סעודות: ובלבד שלא יספוג · שלא ישים ספוג במקום היין לחזור ולהטיפו בכלי גזירה שמא יסחוט: אין סוחטין את הפירות · דהוה ליה מפרק (ב) תולדה דדישה: אסורין · גזירה שמא יסחוט לכתחילה: רבי יהודה אומר אם לאוכלין · הם מכונסין אותם פירות היוצא מהן מותר דלא ניחא ליה במה שזבו וליכא למגזר בהן שמא יסחוט: ואם למשקין · מכונסין אסורין דניחא ליה במאי דנפקא מינייהו ונתקיימה מחשבתו ואיכא למיגזר שמא יסחוט והכי אמרי' בביצה דטעמא דמשקין שזבו משום שמא יסחוט הוא: חלות דבש · מאחר שמרוסקין הדבש זב מאליו מתוך השעוה ואין דרך לסוחטו הלכך רבי אליעזר מתיר וחכמים אוסרין גזירה אטו שאינן מרוסקין דילמא מרסק להו (ג): **גמ'** ויטפח · מכניס בו כפו והשמן נדבק בה ומקנחו בשפת הכלי ואסרוה משום עובדין דחול: מודה ר' יהודה בזיתים · דאע"ג דהכניסן לאוכלין היוצא מהן אסור דכיון דרובן לסחיטה קיימי כי אתו לידי משקה יהיב דעתיה למיהוי ניחא ליה בהכי: אפי' בזיתים וענבים · הואיל והני לאוכלין כנסו: מסתברא בתותים ורמונים פליגי · דאיכא דבעו להו למשקין הלכך משוו להו רבנן כזיתים וענבים ור' יהודה פליג עלייהו אבל שאר פירות ליכא דבעי להו למשקין הלכך מודו רבנן בהם: שמשך · זב מאליהן כמו נהרות המושכין (לעיל דף קכא·): והכניסן · מתחילתן בין לאוכלין בין למשקין כו' דרמונים קרי יין משום דאית להו קיוהא: וחכ"א כו' · והא דנקט רב נחמן לישנא דמסתברא ולא אמר בהדיא דבתותים ורמונים פליגי משום דאיכא למימר פליגי בתותים ורמונים וה"ה לשאר פירות ולהודיעך כחו דרבי יהודה נקט להו ואי משום ברייתא דלקמן דשמעינן מינה דמודים חכמים לרבי יהודה בשאר פירות לאו בהדיא שמעינן לה דאיכא למימר רבי יהודה היא כדפרכינן עלה: וסבר רבי יהודה סתם · שלא פירש לאוכל ולא למשקה הוי המשקה הזב מהן אסור: והתנן חלב האשה מטמא · מכשיר: לרצון ושלא לרצון · בין שיצא ממנה לרצון בין שיצא שלא לרצון שהחלב קרוי משקה שנאמר ותפתח את נאד החלב ותשקהו (שופטים ד): חלב הבהמה אינו מטמא אלא אם כן יצא לרצון · ואי לא לא חשיב משקה ואם נגע בו שרץ אינו מקבל טומאה וטעמא מפרש לקמיה: שדם

תוספות

חבית · ובלבד שלא יספוג · אפילו יש לו עור בית אחיזה דליכא חשש סחיטה אסור כדמפרש בגמרא שלא יעשה כדרך שעושה בחול: **מלקט** על יד על יד ואוכל · נראה דל"ג ואוכל מדקתני סיפא אבל לא לתוך הסל ולא לתוך הקופה משמע הנך דווקא אסירי משום עובדא דחול אבל לתוך *כפו שרי: **ורבי** יוחנן אמר הלכה כרבי יהודה בשאר פירות · בריש מסכת ביצה (דף ג· ושם) רבי יוחנן רמי דר' יהודה אדרבי יהודה תנן ר"י אומר אם לאוכלין היוצא מהן מותר אם למשקין כו' אלמא כל לאוכלין אוכלא דאיפרת הוא ורמינהו ועוד אמר ר"י מתנה אדם על הכלכלה של פירות ביו"ט ראשון ואוכלה בשני וכן ביצה שנולדה בראשון אוכלה בשני בשני אין בראשון לא ואמר רבי יוחנן מוחלפת השיטה וצריך לומר דההיא דמתנה אדם מחליף דאי מתני' מחליף אם כן במאי דנקט הכא ר' יהודה הוה ליה למינקט רבנן וה"ל למימר הלכה כרבנן בשאר פירות · מ"ר · *ולי נראה דאפילו אפיך מתני' אתי שפיר כעין שמצינו בב"ק בפרק הגוזל קמא (דף נו:) דתנן גזל בהמה והוכחשה עבדים והזקינו משלם כשעת הגזלה ר"מ אומר בעבדים אומר לו הרי שלך לפניך ואמר בגמרא אמר רבי חנינא בר אבדימי אמר רב הלכה כר"מ ופריך ורב שביק רבנן ועביד כר"מ כו' עד דמסיק דרב מתניתין איפכא אתנא' אלמא אע"פ שהיה שונה במתניתין וחכ"א בעבדים אומר לו הרי שלך לפניך וה"ל למימר השתא הלכה כחכמים אפ"ה נקט ר"מ לפי מה שהאחרים שונין המשנה ה"נ נקט רבי יוחנן רבי יהודה בשמעתין וכן נמי מצינו בשילהי פ"ק דסוכה (דף יט:) דתנן העושה סוכתו כמין צריף ר"א פוסל וחכמים מכשירין ואמרינן בגמרא אביי אשכחיה לרב יוסף דגני בכילת חתנים בסוכה א"ל כמאן כר"א ה"ל שבקת רבנן ועבדת כר"א אמר ליה ברייתא איפכא תניא השתא היה לו להשיב רב יוסף כרבנן ולא כר"א כיון דאיהו איפכא תני אלא כן דרך הש"ס בכל מקום· נראה לי: **הלכה** כר' יהודה בשאר פירות· אע"ג דבריש ביצה (ד' ג·) גזר ר' יוחנן ביצה שנולדה ביו"ט משום משקין שזבו והכא לא גזר בשאר פירות י"ל דשייך טפי לגזור בביצה לפי שהיא עומדת ליסחט מן התרנגולת *ודרך לגומעה חיה אבל שאר פירות אין עומדים ליסחט כלל · מ"ר: **שמשך** מהן שמן כו' · פי' בקונט' שמשך זב מאליהן כמו נהרות המושכין ולפירושו צריך לומר הכניסן בין לאוכלין כו' היינו הכניסן מתחילתן ואין הלשון משמע כן ועוד קשה לר"י דאי משך מאליו קאמר גבי תותים שמשך מהם מים ה"ל למימר שמשכו או שנמשכו דמים בכל מקום לשון רבים ועוד קשה לר"י אם כן הך ברייתא הוה תיובתא דרב ורבי יוחנן דאמרי לעיל חלוק היה רבי יהודה בזיתים וענבים דהכא משמע דבזיתים וענבים מודה אלא נראה לר"י דמשך האדם קאי וסחטן תחילה ושוב הכניסן דהשתא לרב ורבי יוחנן דסברי חלוק היה רבי יהודה בזיתים וענבים נקט דוקא משך דאיכא למיחש טפי דילמא יהיב דעתיה לסחוט משקה אחר שהכניסו נמי לאכילה מאחר שסחטן תחילה להוציא מהן משקה הא לא משך לא ולשמואל דאמר מודה רבי יהודה בזיתים וענבים נקט משך משום רבותא דתותים ורמונים דאפילו משך הכניסן לאוכלין היוצא מהן מותר · מ"ר: **חלב** האשה מטמא לרצון ושלא לרצון · והא דתנן במסכת מכשירין (פ"ה) כל משקה שתחילתו לרצון אף על פי שאין סופו לרצון או שסופו לרצון אף על פי שאין תחלתו לרצון מכשיר לא דמי רצון דהתם לרצון דהכא דהתם מיירי בשעת נפילתן על הזרעים שיהא לרצון דבעינן יותן דומיא דכי יתן מה יתן דניחא ליה אף יותן דניחא ליה אבל הכא מיירי בשעת פרישה מן האשה או מן הבהמה: **לרצון** ושלא לרצון · כדמפרש בסמוך טעמא משום דדם מגפתה טמא וחלב ודם חד הוא דדם נעכר ונעשה חלב ולא צריכין למה שפי' בקונט' משום דאיקרי משקה שנאמר ותפתח את נאד החלב ותשקהו ונראה לר"י דהא דאיצטריך לפרש האי טעמא בפ' דם נדה (נדה דף נה:) גבי חלב האשה הנ"מ לרבי עקיבא דשמעתין דלית ליה טעמא (*) דפרישה או למאן דלית ליה דם נעכר ונעשה חלב אבל לרבנן דשמעתין לא צריך (ד) כדפרישית דחלב האשה אלא דוקא לטמא חלב בהמה לרצון · *מ"ר: מחמיר

(*) נ"א ועוד ור"י לא איירי רק משאר פירות גם מזיתים וענבים אבל מתותים ורמונים אינו מזכיר כלום דעתו מבא"כ ר' יהודה דאמר כפי' תותים ורמונים אם הכניסן לאוכלין היוצא מהן מותר וכן דומין לביצה ואפ"ה ס"ל דבראשון אסור בביצה וע"כ רמי ליה אהדדי במסכת עירובין לט. ובמס' ביצה ויותר פשוט שלא ן להגיה כלום וצ"ל ודרך לגומעה וצ"ל לייבב דאף אם עומדת לסחיטה ומ"מ צריך עוד תיקון ואינו ראוי לדמות למשקין שזבו שא"צ שום תיקון ע"ז אמר ודרך כו':

רבינו חננאל

חבית שנשברה מצילין הימנה מזון ג' סעודות וכו' תנא לא יספוג ביין בכפיו ולא יטפח בשמן ביד כדרך שהוא עושה בחול. לא יטפח כדאמרינן בכל מקום טופח ע"מ להטפיח וכדתנן בפרק החובל בחבירו וכו'. מעשה באחד שפרע ראשה של אשה כו' עד שמרה עומדת על פתח הצירה ושיבר הפך בפניה. ובה כאיסר שמן. גילתה ראשה והיתה מטפחת ומנחת על ראשה וכו': ת"ר נתפזרו לו פירות בחצירו מלקט על יד על יד ואוכל. אבל לא לתוך הסל ולא לתוך הקופה שלא יעשה כדרך שהוא עושה בחול וכו' וחלקו רב יהודה אמר שמואל ורב ועולא כל חד וחד מעמיד חלוקת ר' יהודה וחכמים ור' יוחנן אמר הלכה כר' יהודה בשאר פירות ואין הלכה כמותו בזיתים וענבים. א"ר אבא אמר רב יהודה אמר שמואל מודה היה רבי יהודה לחכמים בזיתים וענבים ומודים חכמים לרבי יהודה בשאר פירות · ובמאי פליגי בתותים ורמונים דתניא זיתים שמשך מהן שמן וענבים שמשך מהן יין והכניסן בין לאוכלין בין למשקין היוצא מהן אסור. תותים שמשך מהן מים ורמונים שמשך מהן יין והכניסן לאוכלין היוצא מהן מותר למשקין ולסתם היוצא מהן אסור דברי ר' יהודה והכ"א בין לאוכלין בין למשקין היוצא מהן אסור נמצאת חלוקת ר' יהודה וחכמים בתותים ורמונים ובה א"ר יוחנן הלכה כר' יהודה בשאר פירות וכיון שפסק ר' יוחנן הלכה כר' יהודה הוצרכנו לברר דבריו ולפיכך אמרינן וסבר ר' יהודה סתם אסור והתנן

מסורת הש"ס

ביצה ג. חולין יד:

לעיל יט:

חולין יד:

מכשירין פ"ו מ"ח כריתות יג.

י"ג דפריסית

[ועי' תוס' נדה יט: ד"ה כתיב ככא]

הגהות הב"ח

(א) במשנה ור"א מתיר. נ"ב ר' אלעזר גרסי' עי' בפירש"י בפ' דשבת דף יט ריש ע"ב: (ב) רש"י ד"ה אין סוחטין וכו' מפרק דהוא תולדה. (ג) ד"ה חלות וכו' להו הס"ד ואח"כ מ"ה ולא *טפה: (ד) תוס' ד"ה לרצון וכו' לא צריך לחלב האשה כדפי' אלא:

CHAPTER XXII

a *MISHNAH*. [143b] IF A CASK [OF WINE] IS BROKEN,[1] ONE MAY SAVE THEREOF THE REQUIREMENTS[2] FOR THREE MEALS, AND HE [THE OWNER] CAN SAY TO OTHERS, 'COME AND SAVE FOR YOURSELVES', PROVIDED THAT HE DOES NOT SPONGE IT UP.[3] FRUIT MAY NOT BE SQUEEZED IN ORDER TO EXPRESS THEIR JUICES:[4] IF THEY EXUDE OF THEIR OWN ACCORD THEY ARE PROHIBITED. R. JUDAH SAID: IF [THEY STAND] AS EATABLES,[5] THAT WHICH EXUDES FROM THEM IS PERMITTED; BUT IF FOR LIQUIDS,[6] THAT WHICH EXUDES FROM THEM IS PROHIBITED. IF HONEYCOMBS ARE CRUSHED ON THE EVE OF THE SABBATH AND IT [THE HONEY] EXUDES SPONTANEOUSLY, IT IS FORBIDDEN; BUT R. ELEAZAR[7] PERMITS IT.

GEMARA. A Tanna taught: One must not sponge up wine nor dab up oil,[8] so that he should not act as he does during the week.

Our Rabbis taught: If one's produce is scattered in his courtyard, he may collect a little at a time and eat it,[9] but not into a basket or a tub, so that he should not act as he does during the week.

FRUIT MAY NOT BE SQUEEZED, [etc.]. Rab Judah said in Samuel's name: R. Judah agreed with the Sages in respect to olives and grapes. What is the reason? Since they are [normally]
b for expressing, he puts his mind to them.[1] But 'Ulla said in Rab's name: R. Judah disagreed in respect of olives and grapes too. While R. Joḥanan said: The *halachah* is as R. Judah in the case of other produce, but the *halachah* is not as R. Judah in the case of olives and grapes. Rabbah said in Rab Judah's name in Samuel's name: R. Judah agreed with the Sages in respect of olives and grapes, while the Sages agreed with R. Judah in respect of other produce. Said R. Jeremiah to R. Abba: Then wherein do they differ? When you find it [I will tell you,] he replied.[2] R. Naḥman b. Isaac said: It is reasonable that they differ in the case of mulberries and pomegranates.[3] For it was taught: If one draws off oil from olives, or wine from grapes,[4] and [then] carries them in,[5] whether as eatables or for their liquids, that which exudes from them is forbidden. If one draws fluid out of mulberries or juice[6] out of pomegranates, and [then] carries them in, as eatables, that which exudes from them is permitted; [if he carries them in] for their liquid or without specifying [their purpose], that which exudes from them is forbidden: the words of R. Judah. But the Sages maintain: Whether for eating or for drinking, that which exudes from them is forbidden.

Now, does R. Judah hold that if it [the purpose] is unspecified, it [the exuding liquid] is forbidden? But surely we learnt: A woman's milk defiles,[7] [whether it flows] with or without [the woman's] desire; a cow's milk defiles only [when it flows] with [its owner's] desire.[8] Said R. Akiba, It [the reverse] follows *a minori*: if woman's milk, which is set apart for infants only, defiles [whether it flows] with or without [her] desire, then cow's milk, which is set apart for both infants and adults, surely defiles
c [whether it flows] with or without [the owner's] desire.[1] [Said they to him]: If a woman's milk is unclean[2] without [her] desire, that may be because the blood of her wound is unclean;[3] shall

a (1) On the Sabbath. (2) Lit., 'food'. (3) I.e., he must not absorb the spilt wine in a sponge, lest he wring it out (into a vessel), which is forbidden. (4) This is forbidden under threshing, v. *supra* 73*a*. (5) E.g., dates which are intented for eating. (6) E.g., dates intended for honey. (7) This is the reading *supra* 19*b*, R. Eleazar b. Shammua' being the Tanna that is meant—Rashi ibid; v. BaḤ. Cur. edd. R. Eliezer. (8) With his hands, which he then wipes on the edge of a vessel so that the oil runs unto it. (9) This implies that he may collect only what he intends eating there and then. Tosaf. however, favours the deletion of 'and eat it'.

b (1) If they exude their liquid he does not mind, or is even pleased. (2) Probably: if you think carefully about it you will find the answer yourself. (3) Which were not usually pressed for juice. (4) Ri. (v. Tosaf. a.l.) Rashi translates; if oil oozes out of olives, etc.—of its own accord. (5) To the house for storing. 'Then' is added on the Ri's explanation. Rashi: he had (previously) carried in. (6) Lit., 'wine'. (7) I.e., if it falls on a food-stuff it makes it liable to defilement, cf. *supra* 12*a*, n. a1, likewise, it is defiled itself if it comes into contact with a dead *shereẓ* (q.v. Glos.)—Rashi, Maim. and Asheri in Maksh. VI, 8. (8) Cf. *supra* 12*a*, n. a1.

c (1) For the power of rendering food susceptible to uncleanness depends upon whether the fluid is regarded as a liquid or not. Hence since cow's milk is more widely used as a liquid than woman's milk, its power in this respect cannot be less than that of the latter. (2) In the same sense as in *supra*, n. b7. (3) Likewise in the same sense; Nid. 55*b*.

cow's milk be unclean [144a] without [the owner's] desire, though the blood of its wound is clean? I am more stringent in the case of milk than in the case of blood, replied he, because if one milks[4] as a remedy[5] it [the milk] is unclean, whereas if one lets blood as a remedy it is clean. Said they to him: Let baskets of olives and grapes prove it, for the liquid that exudes from them with [their owner's] desire is unclean; without [their owner's] desire, is clean. Now does not 'with desire' mean that he [the owner] is pleased therewith;[6] whilst 'without [his] desire' means that it [the purpose] is unspecified?[7] Now if olives and grapes, which stand to be pressed, yet where [the juice exudes] without desire it is nothing: how much more so mulberries and pomegranates, which do not stand to be pressed?[8]—No: 'with desire' means that it is unexpressed, whilst 'without desire' means that he [the owner] revealed his mind, saying, 'It does not please me'. An alternative answer is: baskets of olives and grapes are different, [for] since it stands to be wasted,[9] he [the owner] indeed renounces it beforehand.[10]

We have [thus] found that R. Judah agrees with the Rabbis in the case of olives and grapes. How do we know that the Rabbis
a agree with R. Judah in the case of other fruits?[1] Because it was

(4) A cow, or if one draws off a woman's milk. (5) Not because the milk is required, but because its presence in the animal or woman may be injurious to them. (6) I.e., from his explicit statements we understand that he is pleased therewith.—It may be observed that where fruit is kept for its juice, its exuding is regarded as in conformity with the owner's desire, whether he actually wanted it just then or not. (7) In which case it is clean, because it is not regarded as a liquid. This must at least represent the view of R. Judah, whose range of liquids is more restricted than that of the Rabbis. (8) And since according to R. Judah it is not a liquid in respect of defilement, when it exudes on the Sabbath it should be permitted.—This is the point of the difficulty. (9) *Sc.* the liquid that exudes. Thus 'baskets' is intentionally stated here, for the juice runs out through the holes. (10) Hence it certainly does not exude with his desire. But if the fruit is in other utensils which conserve the liquid, it is regarded as exuding with his desire even where he said nothing.

a (1) Excluding mulberries and pomegranates.

שלא לרצון [א]שדם מגפתה טהור אמר להן מחמיר אני בחלב מבדם שהחולב לרפואה טמא [ב]והמקיז לרפואה טהור אמרו לו סלי זיתים וענבים יוכיחו [ג]שהמשקין היוצאין מהן לרצון טמאין שלא לרצון טהורים מאי לאו לרצון דניחא ליה שלא לרצון בסתמא ומה זיתים וענבים דבני סחיטה נינהו שלא לרצון ולא כלום תותים ורמונים דלאו בני סחיטה נינהו לא כ"ש לא לרצון בסתמא שלא לרצון דגלי אדעתיה דאמר לא ניחא לי ואיבעית אימא שאני סלי זיתים וענבים כיון דלאיבוד קיימי מעיקרא אפקורי מפקרי להו אשכחן ר' יהודה דמודי לרבנן בזיתים ובענבים רבנן דמודו ליה לרבי יהודה בשאר פירות מנלן דתניא סוחטין בפגעין

רש"י

שדם מגפתה. של אשה אם נגף רגלה או ידה וכל חבורה שילא ממנה דם כדאמר בפרק דם הנדה (נדה דף נה:) דם חללים דהיינו דם הרוג קרוי משקה שנאמר ודם חללים ישתה ודם מגפתו מפרש התם דדם חללים הוי דמה לי קטליה כוליה מה לי קטליה פלגא: וחלב. כדם מגפתו דדם נעכר ונעשה חלב ודם מגפתה כתמיה שלא לרצון הוא וטמא: יטמא חלב הבהמה שלא לרצון. בתמיה שהרי דם מגפתה טהור דבהמה לאו בכלל חלל הוא ומיהו דם שחיטה מכשר משום דאיתקש למים דכתיב (דברים יב) על הארץ תשפכנו כמים: מחמיר ע"כ אני בחלב. לטמאו אף שלא לרצון מבדם: שהחולב. לרפואת הבהמה שלא יזיקנה חלבה טמא דהא לרצון הוא והמקיז דם לבהמתו לרפואה טהור דדם מגפתה היא והואיל והחולב לרפואה טמא אף הנוטף שלא לרצון טמא: אמרו לו. אינו דומה שלא לרצון ליוצא לרצון שהרי סלי זיתים וענבים יוכיחו שהמשקה כו': שלא לרצון בסתמא. וקתני טהורין דלא חשיב משקה אי רבי יהודה קאמר לה קשיא ואי רבנן קאמרי כל שכן טהורין לרבי יהודה דהא מידי דלרבנן משקה הוא לרבי יהודה לאו משקה הוא וכ"ש מידי דלרבנן לאו משקה והשתא ומה זיתים וענבים כו' והוא הדין מצי למירמי נמי זיתים וענבים אזיתים וענבים דקתני לעיל דמודה בהו רבי יהודה דאף לאוכלין היוצא מהן אסור אלא הא אלימא ליה לאקשויי דתותים ורמונים דלאו בני סחיטה נינהו קתני לעיל דכהם אסור והכא קתני דאפי' זיתים וענבים סתמא לאו למשקה: דגלי דעתיה. בהדיא ואמר לא ניחא לי והוי גילוי דעתא טפי מהכניסו לאוכלין: ואיבעית אימא שאני סלי זיתים וענבים וכו'. ודווקא נקט סלין שהמשקה הנוטף מהן נופל לארץ והולך לאיבוד הלכך סתמא לא ניחא ליה: אפקורי מפקיר. לההוא משקה אבל שאר כלים אפילו תותים ורמונים אימא לך סתמא למשקה:

תוספות

מחמיר אני בחלב מבדם שהחולב לרפואה טמא והמקיז לרפואה טהור. א"כ מאי דמטמינן חלב האשה לאו מחמת דם הוא דדם נעכר ונעשה חלב דא"כ חולב לרפואה טהור כמו דם אלא ודאי משום דכתיב ותפתח את נאד החלב ואומר רבי דבחנם נקט חולב לרפואה דהכי נמי הו"מ להשיב לרבנן מחלב בהמה גופה שדמה טהור (א) וחלבה טמא א"כ החלב אינו טמא מחמת דם אלא משום דכתיב ותפתח את נאד החלב וא"כ שלא לרצון נמי מהאי טעמא יהא טמא. מ"ר: סלי זיתים וענבים יוכיחו שמשקה היוצא מהן לרצון טמא שלא לרצון טהור. בשילהי מסכת מכשירין מסיים לא אם אמרת בסלי זיתים וענבים שהרי תחילתו אוכל וסופו משקה תאמרו בחלב שתחילתו וסופו משקה: מאי לאו לרצון דניחא ליה ושלא לרצון בסתמא. ולרצון ושלא לרצון דגבי חלב אשה ליכא למימר דמיירי בשלא לרצון בסתמא ודווקא בסתמא אבל אמר לא ניחא לי אינו מטמא דהא לפי מה שפירשתי הטעם משום דם מגפתה אפי' אמר לא ניחא לי נמי מטמא אלא משמע דשלא לרצון דקתני בכולהו באשה ובהמה וזיתים וענבים מיירי בכל ענין בין מסתמא בין אמר לא ניחא לי: תותים ורימונים דלאו בני סחיטה נינהו. תימה לי מאי קשה דילמא הא דתניא לעיל גבי תותים ורמונים למשקין ולכתם היוצא מהן אסור הנ"מ במשך דוקא והכא בלא משך איירי הלכך שלא לרצון דהיינו בסתמא לא חשיב משקה: לא לרצון בבהמה ושלא לרצון דגלי דעתיה דאמר לא ניחא לי. (ב)דתניא התם בכריתות פרק אמרו לו (דף יג.) התירו (ג) לו למגע טמא מת להניק את בנה ובנה טהור ופריך בנה אמאי טהור כיון דינק חלב איטמי ליה מהלב וכי תימא לא איתכשר איתכשר בטיפה המלוכלכת ע"פ הדד ואע"ג דחלב אשה משקה הוא ואין צריך הכשר [משמע ליה] דמה שהוא בפי התינוק שהתינוק יונק חשיב כאוכל וצריך הכשר לפי שזהו מאכלו של תינוק וקאמר דאיתכשר בטיפה המלוכלכת בפי הדד דהוי משקה ככהם הלב דלאו לאוכל בעי ליה ומשני רב נחמן אמר רבה בר אבוה (ד) בתקיפה אחת שלא הניח טיפה המלוכלכת ע"פ הדד אמר רבא שתי תשובות בדבר חדא דקא הזינן ליה לפומיה דינוקא דמלא חלבא ועוד מקום חלב מעין הוא דהא תנן חלב האשה מטמא לרצון ושלא לרצון מאי היא דלא ניחא ליה וקתני מטמא פי' אלמא חשיבא כמעין מדמטמאה שלא לרצון וכיון דחשוב כמעין גם בפי התינוק נמי יהא חשוב כמשקה כמו שהם היה מעין ואין צריך הכשר כך צריך לפרש דאת"ל דאינו מזכיר מעין אלא כלומר דכמשקה חשיב א"כ מאי צריך למימר שלא לרצון מאי היא כו' דמדקתני לרצון מטמא הו"מ למיפרך אלמא לרצון חשיב כי משקה ואשה דמניקה את בנה לרצון הוא אלא אמר רבא כו' עד ולרבא מקום חלב מעין הוא ולא צריך הכשר והתנן האשה שנטף חלב מדדיה ונפל לאויר התנור התנור טמא וקשיא לן במאי איתכשר ואמר ר' יוחנן בטיפה המלוכלכת ע"פ הדד והשתא קשה לר"י מאי קאמר במאי איתכשר דמדבעי הכשר אלמא אוכל חשיב ליה וא"כ איך יטמא אוכל את התנור והא אין אוכל מטמא כלי ואומר ר"י דה"פ וקשיא לן במאי איתכשר כלומר לא מבעיא שאין התנור טמא אלא חלב הנוטף מדדיה גופה אמאי יהא טמא הא לא איתכשר ומשני בטיפה המלוכלכת ע"פ הדד ואותה טיפה עצמה המלוכלכת ע"פ הדד תטמא התנור שהיא חשובה משקה ומשקה מטמא כלי כדאמרינן בפ' קמא דמכילתין (דף יג:) והשתא פריך שפיר לרבא דאמר דאפילו אמר לא ניחא לי מטמא חלב האשה דחשיב משקה והכא חשיב ליה אוכל אבל לר"נ אמר רבה בר אבוה אתי שפיר דהכא דאמר לא ניחא לי ודאי חשיב ליה אוכל ונטף חלב מדדיה חשיב לא ניחא ליה כיון שהוא נופל לאויר תנור ואזיל לאיבוד דודאי לא ניחא ליה ועוד פריך התם לרבא מדתניא ט' משקין בזב הזיעה וליחה סרוחה והריעי טהורים מכלום דמעת עינו ודם מגפתו וחלב האשה מטמא טומאת משקין ברביעית רוקו וזובו ומימי רגליו מטמא טומאה חמורה בכל שהוא ואי אמרת מקום חלב מעין הוא חלב באשה נמי יטמא טומאה חמורה בכל שהוא כזובו ורוקו וקשה לרבי מאי קפריך לעולם מעין הוא ואפ"ה לא יטמא טומאה חמורה משום דבעינן דומיא דרוק כדאיתא בנדה (ד' נו.) מה רוק שמתגלגל ויוצא וחוזר ונבלע אף כל שמתגלגל ויוצא וחוזר ונבלע יצא חלב שבאשה שמתגלגל ויוצא ואינו חוזר ונבלע ותימה הוא לומר דמה שהוא חוזר ונבלע גרם לו ליחשב כמעין ומכל מקום ודאי כן הוא וצריך לומר דמה שהיה חושבו רבא כמעין להיות חשיב משקה בפי התינוק היינו משום דסלקא דעתיה שחוזר ונבלע ומייתי ראיה מן המשנה דחוזר ונבלע הוא מדקתני מטמא שלא לרצון דהיינו אמר לא ניחא לי א"כ חוזר ונבלע הוא דאי לאו הכי אם אמר לא ניחא ליה לא יהיה מטמא והשתא פריך ליה מהכא דאינו חוזר ונבלע אלמא מקום חלב האשה לאו מעין הוא ופריך אי הכי קשה הא דקתני מטמא שלא לרצון ומשני מי סברת שלא לרצון דלא ניחא ליה לא שלא לרצון בסתמא דדעתיה דתינוק קרובה גבי חלב אבל אמר לא ניחא ליה טהור והאי דנטף חלב מדדיה ונפל לתוך התנור כאומר לא ניחא ליה חשיב דודאי לא ניחא ליה כיון שהלך לאיבוד והא דקאמר שלא לרצון בסתמא היינו כשנופל בקערה שאינו הולך לאיבוד דמהני טעמא דדעתיה דתינוק קרובה גבי חלב לאחשוביה אז כמשקה ובפי התינוק לעולם כאוכל חשיב והשתא קשה לר"י חדא דבמסקנא מסקינן איפכא לרצון בסתמא ושלא לרצון דאמר לא ניחא ליה ודומיא דהך דזיתים וענבים הוי ההוא דחלב האשה דאי לאו הכי לא שייך למימר יוכיחו וכ"ת ס"ל כאיבעית אימא דאמר שאני סלי זיתים וענבים כיון דלאיבוד קיימא אפקורי מפקר להו אכתי קשה דדומיא דהכי אית לן למימר בחלב האשה דאזיל לאיבוד וא"כ היינו כאומר לא ניחא ליה והתם מטמא דוקא סתמא אבל לא ניחא ליה טהור ועוד קשה לרבי מאי קאמר התם אלא קשה הא מתני' וקאמר נמי מי סברת שלא לרצון לא ניחא ליה וקאמר דלא ניחא (ה) טהור ואמאי והא טעמא שלא לרצון טמא היינו משום דחשיב דם מגפתו דדם נעכר ונעשה חלב כדפי' לעיל וא"כ גם אמר לא ניחא ליה נמי יהא טמא. מ"ר:

מי

עין משפט נר מצוה

ו א ב מיי' פ"י מהלכות טומאת אוכלין הל"ג:

ז ג מיי' פ"א שם הלכה ג ופ"י הלכה יב:

רבינו חננאל

והתנן במס' מכשירין אמרו לו זיתים וענבים יוכיחו שהמשקין היוצא מהן לרצון טמאין פי' מקבלין טומאה. מפני שהן משקין והמשקין אין צריכין הכשר ושלא לרצון טהורין כלומר אוכלין הן. וכיון שלא הוכשרו אינן מטמאין. ובאנו להעמיד משנה זו לרצון דניחא ליה. שלא לרצון בסתמא להודיע כי אפילו זיתים וענבים דבני סחיט' נינהו סתמא אוכל הן. וכ"ש תותים ורמונים. ואמרינן לא. פי' לרצון דמתניתין בסתמא. וכל סתם משקה הוא חשוב. ופי' שלא לרצון דגלי אדעתא בפי' שאין רצונו להוציא מהן משקין. (איכא) [איבעיא] תימא שאני סלי זיתים וענבים כיון שהסלין לאו בני קיבול משקה הן דבר ידוע הוא שכל משקה השותת מהן לעפר והולך וזהו לאיבוד כאילו מעיקרא הפקירן וכשאינן חשובין ולפיכך הן טהורין. תוב אתינן לפרושי דרבנן מודו לי' לר' יהודה בשאר פירות מהא דתניא סוחטין בפגעים. יש מי שאומר ספיגיל ובפרישין ובעוזרדין אבל לא ברמונים. ואוקימנא אפילו תימא רבנן כיון דלא בני סחיטה נינהו אפילו לכתחלה. ושל בית מנשיא היו סוחטין בהול ברמונים ועושין מסטו יין של רמונים כלומר שהרמונים בני סחיטה נינהו כזיתים וענבים ואסור לסוחטן בשבת. אמר רב נחמן הלכה כשל בית מנשיא בן מנחם. ואמרינן וכי מנשיא תנא הוא. ואוקימנא האי תנא

הגהות הב"ח

שייך לעמוד קודם

(א) תוס' ד"ה מחמיר וכו' שדמה טהור. נ"ב ובתוספות י"ט סוף מס' מכשירין מתרץ קושיא זו דבאמת דם בהמה לשתיה מכשיר כמו חלב שהוא לשתיה ע"כ מוכרח לומר מדם הקזה והחולב לרפוא' ע"ש: (ב) ד"ה לא לרצון וכו' לא ניחא לי תניא כצ"ל ואות ד' נמחק: (ג) בא"ד התירו לה למגע טמא מת: (ד) בא"ד אמר רבה בר אבוה שינק בתקיפה: (ה) בא"ד וקאמר דלא ניחא ליה טהור:

בפגעין ובפרישין ובעוזרדין אבל לא ברמונים ושל בית מנשיא בר מנחם היו סוחטין ברמונים וממאי דרבנן היא דילמא ר' יהודה היא ותהוי נמי ר' יהודה אימר דשמעת ליה לר' יהודה יצאו מעצמן סוחטין לכתחילה מי שמעת ליה אלא מאי אית לך למימר כיון דלאו בני סחיטה נינהו אפילו לכתחילה אפילו תימא רבנן כיון דלאו בני סחיטה נינהו אפילו לכתחילה ש"מ רבנן היא ש"מ של בית מנשיא בר מנחם היו סוחטין ברמונים אמר רב נחמן הלכה כשל בית מנשיא בר מנחם א"ל רבא לרב נחמן מנשיא בן מנחם תנא הוא וכי תימא הלכה כי האי תנא דסבר לה כשל מנשיא בן מנחם ומשום דסבר כמנשיא בן מנחם הלכה כמותו מנשיא בן מנחם הוי *רובא דעלמא אין דתנן *המקיים קוצים בכרם ר"א אומר קדש וחכ"א [א]אינו מקדש אלא דבר שכמוהו מקיימין וא"ר חנינא מ"ט דרבי *אליעזר שכן בערביא מקיימין קוצי שדות לגמליהם מידי איריא דערביא אתרא הכא בטלה דעתו אצל כל אדם אלא היינו טעמא כדרב חסדא דאמר רב חסדא תרדין שסחטן ונתנן במקוה פוסלין את המקוה בשינוי מראה והא לאו בני סחיטה נינהו אלא מאי אית לך למימר כיון דאחשבינהו הוה להו משקה ה"נ כיון דאחשבינהו הוה להו משקה רב פפא אמר משום דהוי דבר שאין עושין ממנו מקוה לכתחילה [ב]וכל דבר שאין עושין ממנו מקוה לכתחילה פוסל את המקוה בשינוי מראה *תנן התם [ג]נפל לתוכו יין או חומץ ומוחל ושינה מראיו פסול מאן תנא דמוחל משקה הוא אמר אביי רבי יעקב היא *דתניא ר' יעקב אומר [ד]מוחל הרי הוא כמשקה ומה טעם אמרו מוחל היוצא בתחלה טהור לפי שאינו רוצה בקיומו ר"ש אומר מוחל אינו כמשקה ומה טעם אמרו מוחל היוצא מעיקול בית הבד טמא לפי שאי אפשר לו בלא ציחצוחי שמן מאי בינייהו איכא בינייהו דאתי בתר איצצתא רבא אמר משום דהוי דבר שאין עושין הימנו מקוה ופוסל את המקוה בשינוי מראה אמר רב יהודה אמר שמואל [ה]סוחט אדם אשכול של ענבים לתוך הקדרה אבל לא לתוך הקערה אמר רב חסדא מדברי רבינו נלמד *[ו]חולב אדם עז לתוך הקדרה אבל לא לתוך הקערה [ז]אלמא קסבר משקה הבא לאוכל אוכל הוא מתיב רמי בר חמא *[ח]זב שחולב את העז החלב טמא ואי אמרת משקה הבא לאוכלין אוכל הוא במאי איתכשר *כדאמר ר' יוחנן בטיפה המלוכלכת ע"פ הדד הכא נמי בטיפה המלוכלכת ע"פ הדד מתיב רבינא *[ט]טמא מת שסחט זיתים וענבים כביצה

רש"י

בפגעין. פרונ"ש בלע"ז ולהוציא מימיהן לשתות: ובפרישין. קויידונ"ץ: ובעוזרדין. קורמ"ש דלאו אורחייהו בהכי ואין כאן משום דש: אבל לא ברמונים. דאורחייהו בהכי: ושל בית מנשיא. היו רגילין לסחוט רמונים בחול אלמא איכא דסחיט להו הלכך בשבת אסור: אלא מאי אית לך למימר. לר' יהודה כיון דלאו בני סחיטה כו' וכי היכי דלרבי יהודה שרי לכתחילה מהאי טעמא מהשתא אפי' תימא רבנן ושרו ליה מהאי טעמא: מנשיא תנא הוא. בתמיה וכי איצא פליג למימר דבשבת אסור דתימא הלכתא כוותיה והא לא הוזכר אלא לדברי התנא לראיה דהאי תנא הוא סבר כוותיה: וכ"ת. הא דאמר הלכה כשל בית מנשיא ה"ק הלכה כהאי תנא דאסר ברימונים הואיל וקאי מנשיא כוותיה דסוחטין רימונים בחול אלמא בני סחיטה נינהו: הוי רובא דעלמא. דמשום איהו לחודיה נשווי דרך רמונים לסחיטה: קוצים. קרדונ"ש: מקדש. את התבואה משום כלאים דזריעה הוא: ואמר רבי חנינא כו'. אלמא משום חד מקום דאחשבינהו משוינן להו דבר חשוב: אתרא. הוא וחשיבות דרבים הוי חשיבותא: הכא. חד גברא לחודיה הוא נימא בטלה דעתו: אלא היינו טעמא. דרב נחמן דאמר הלכה אין סוחטין: כרב חסדא. אע"ג דלעלמא לא חשיב כיון דאחשיב איהו הוי לדידיה משקה והכי מפרש רב נחמן לברייתא דלעיל סוחטין בפגעין ובפרישין למתק הפרי ולא לצורך המשקה אבל לא ברימונים ואפילו למתקן (א) דשל בית מנשיא היו סוחטין בחול לצורך משקה הלכך בשבת אסור אפי' למתק הואיל ואיכא חד דעביד לשם משקה ולא משום דמנשיא רובא דעלמא אלא חיישינן אי שרית ליה למתק אתי למעבד לשום משקה וכיון דאיהו מחשב ליה הוי משקה ומיחייב אבל בפגעין ליכא (ב) למיחש דאין אדם עושה אותו למשקה: בשינוי מראה. לא בשלשת לוגין דלא הוזכרו שלש לוגין אלא במים שאובין אבל שאר משקין לא פסלי אא"כ נשתנה מראה המקוה על ידיהן: רב פפא אמר. טעמא דתרדין לאו משום חשיבותא דאחשבינהו הוא ולעולם לאו משקה נינהו והא דמפסיל משום דכל דבר שאין עושין ממנו מקוה שאינו מים או שלג או ברד פוסל את המקוה בשינוי מראה: נפל לתוכו. של מקוה יין או חומץ או מוחל והוא כמין מים וזב מן הזיתים וג' מינים יש בו כשטוענן מתחילה במעטן להתחמם ולהתבשל מאליהן מוחל זב מהן והוא צלול כמים ולאחר שעמדו ימים ודחקו זה את זה חוזר מוחל לזוב מהן והוא קרוב להיות כשמן ולאחר שעלרן להוציא שמנן בבית הבד ומשתהה התפוח של גפת בעקלים שהוא אגוד בהן בבית הבד חוזר מוחל וזב מהן: מאן תנא דמוחל משקה הוא. קס"ד דאין מקוה נפסל אלא על ידי משקה ואפילו בשינוי מראה: בתחילה. בתחלת טעינתן של זיתים: מעקול בית הבד. לאחר שנסחט שמנו או לפני סחיטתו: מאי בינייהו. במאי פליגי הואיל ותרווייהו מודו דמוחל היוצא בתחילה טהור והיוצא מעקל בית הבד טמא באיזה מוחל נחלקו דלמר הוי משקה וטמא ולמר לא הוי משקה וטהור: דאתי בתר איצצתא. לאחר שהתחילו להתחמם ודחקו זה את זה ונשתהה הכומר ימים: רבא אמר. קמייתא דקתני מוחל פוסל מקוה דברי הכל הוא ומשום דהוי כו': לתוך הקדרה. של תבשיל לתקנו דמוכחא מילתא דלאו למשקה בעי ליה אלא לאוכל [ג]ואין זה דרך פריקתו והוי כמפריד אוכל מאוכל: אבל לא לתוך הקערה. דזמנין דלמשקה קאי ואף על גב דבקערה לא שתי איניש לא מוכחא מילתא ואיכא איסור: אלמא. מדקאמר סוחט לתוך הקדרה קסבר כו': החלב טמא. שהזב מטמא כל דבר במשא והרי הוסט הקילוח ולא קמפליג בין לתוך הקדרה בין לתוך הכוס: ואי אמרת אוכל הוא. הא אין אוכל מקבל טומאה שלא בהכשר והאי במאי איתכשר: כדאמר רבי יוחנן. במסכת כריתות גבי האשה שנטף חלב מדדיה: בטיפה המלוכלכת על פי הדד. טיפה ראשונה מלכלכת בה פי הדד בדעת וטחה ליחלב וההיא הוי משקה כשהם חלב דלאו לאוכל בעי ליה: טמא מת שסחט זיתים וענבים כבילה

תוספות

מי דמי ערביא אתרא הוא. וא"מ למיפרך הניחא לרבי אליעזר לרבנן מאי איכא למימר אלא פריך דאפילו לרבי אליעזר לא ניחא ומה שקשה מאכשי הולל דפרק המצניע (לעיל דף צב:) פירשתי שם (ד"ה ואת"ל): ה"נ כיון דאחשביה הוו להו משקה. תחילה ס"ד דסוחטין בפגעין כו' היינו סחיטה ממש אבל השתא אי אפשר לומר דהא פשיטא דאסור דכיון דאחשביה הוה להו משקה אלא סוחטין דקתני היינו בליי"ר בלע"ז למתק הפרי כדפי' בקונטרס: אמר אביי ר' יעקב היא. קשה לי לימא דהאי מוחל דקתני היינו במוחל היוצא מעקול בית הבד ודברי הכל וכי תימא מדקתני מוחל סתמא משמע דבכל מוחל איירי לא היא דע"כ אפי' לרבי יעקב לא איירי בכל מוחל דהא מודה דמוחל היוצא בתחילה טהור וי"ל דמוחל היוצא מעקול בית הבד לא הוה קרינן ליה מוחל סתם כיון דאי אפשר לו בלא צחוחי שמן: חולב אדם עז כו'. נראה לר"ת דהיינו דווקא בי"ט דחזיא בהמה לאכילה הוי כמו אוכלא דאיפרת אבל בשבת לא חזיא לשחיטה כמו דם חשיבא שהבהמה היא כפסולת וכשחולב הוי כנוטל אוכל מתוך פסולת וכן משמע בבה"ג דבי"ט איירי ומיהו סחיטת זיתים וענבים דשרי לעיל לתוך הקדירה היינו אפי' בשבת כיון דאשכול חזיא לאכילה: כבילה

[לעיל נב. ושם נסמן]

ח א מיי' פ"ה מהלכות כלאים הל"ח טוש"ע יו"ד סימן רצו סעיף יד:
ט ב מיי' פ"ז מהלכות מקוואות הלכה א סמג עשין רמח:
י ג מיי' שם והלכה ט סמג שם טוש"ע יו"ד סימן רא סעיף כה:
יא ד מיי' פ"י מהלכות טומאת אוכלין הלכה יג ופי"א הלכה ו:
יב ה מיי' פ"ח מהלכות שבת הל"י סמג לאוין סה טור שו"ע או"ח סימן שכ סעיף ד:
יג ו ז מיי' שם וסמג שם טור שו"ע או"ח סימן תקה:
יד ח ט מיי' פ"ט מהל' טומאת אוכלין הל"ב:

כלאים פ"ה מ"ח ב"ב קנו:

[צ"ל אלעזר]

הגהות הב"ח

(א) רש"י ד"ה כרב חסדא וכו' ואפילו למתקן הואיל דשל בית וכו': (ב) בא"ד למיחש נמחק דאין אדם:

מקוואות פ"ז מ"ד

תוספ' דטהרות פרק י'

[עי' תוס' מג: ד"ה מפרק וכו']

טהרות פ"ב מ"ג

כריתות יג. פסחים לג: טהרות פ"ג מ"ג

גליון הש"ס

רש"י ד"ה לתוך הקדירה ואין זה דרך פריקתו. עיין לעיל דף קט ע"ב תוספות ד"ה מפרק

רבינו חננאל

דאמר סוחטין בפגעין ובפרישין ובעוזרדין אבל לא ברמונים וסבר לה כמנשיא בן מנחם שסוחט בחול ברמונים להוציא מהן מים וכן כמו זיתים וענבי' וקיי"ל כוותיה ואקשינן וכי מנשיא הוה רובא לעלמא. ומהדרינן אין. כי הא דתנן המקיים קוצים בכרם וכו' ואוקימנא אע"פ שאין דרך בני אדם לקיים קוצים בכרם כיון שבערביא מקיימין קידש הכא נמי אע"פ שאין דרך בני אדם לסחוט רמונים בחול כיון שסוחטין של בית מנשיא בחול בשבת אסור לסחוט ודחינן ערביא מקום בני אדם רבים ומנשיא אדם אחד הוא ובטלה דעתו אצל [כל] בני אדם ואתינן לטעמא אחריתי אלא האי תנא כטעמיה דרב חסדא דאמר תרדין שסחטן ונתנן למקוה פסלו תמקוה. בשנוי מראה וכיון שהזכרנו פסולות המקוה אצרינן. תנן התם [נפל] לתוכו יין ומוהל כו' פי' מוהל המים היוצאים מעוקל בית הבד עת שטוען קורות בית הבד על הזיתים הטחונין והוא מי הזיתים ויש בהן צחצוחי שמן: איצצאי דוחק. כדגרסינן בפרק המפקיד (דף מ ע"א)

אמר ר' יהודה אמר שמואל סוחט אדם אשכול של ענבים בתוך הקדירה אבל לא לתוך הקערה. אמר רב חסדא מדברי רבינו נלמד חולב אדם עז לתוך הקדירה אבל לא לתוך הקערה אלמא קא סבר משקה הבא לאוכל אוכל הוא. ואותביה רמי [בר חמא] זב שחלב עז החלב טמא. כלומר (טמא) [שטימא אותה] הזב בנגיעתו. וא"ת אוכל הוא במאי אתכשר ופרקינן כר' יוחנן דאמר איתכשר בטפה המלוכלכת על

רב נסים גאון

פכ"ב רבא אמר משום דהוה דבר שאין עושין ממנו מקוה לכתחילה וכל דבר שאין עושין ממנו מקוה לכתחילה פוסל את המקוה בשינוי מראה. עיקר דיליה בתורת כהנים מקוה מים לא מקוה כל המשקין כולן פרט לשנפל בתוכו מי כבשין ומי צבעין ושינו את מראיו ובתוספתא טבול יום (פרק א) חומר במשקין שאין להן טהרת הגוף ואין להן טהרה מטומאתן ואינן מטהרין בגוף ופוסלין את המקוה בשינוי מראה מה שאין כן במים: כדאמר ר' יוחנן בטיפה על פי הדד. משכחת לה במס' כריתות בפרק אמרו לו אכלת חלב (דף יג) ולרבא מקום חלב מעין הוא ולא צריך הכשר והתנן האשה שחלב מדדיה ונפל לאויר תנור תנור טמא וקשיא לן במאי איתכשר ואמר ר' יוחנן בטיפה מלוכלכת ע"פ הדד ואין

taught: One may express [144b] plums, quinces and sorb-apples,[2] but not pomegranates, and [indeed] the household of Menasia b. Menahem used to express pomegranates.[3] And how do you know that this is the [ruling of] the Rabbis: perhaps it is R. Judah['s view]?—Even granted that it is R. Judah['s]: when have you heard R. Judah [to permit the juice], when it exudes of itself: have you heard him [to rule that] we may express it at the very outset?[4] But what you must answer is since they are not intended for pressing, [it is permitted] even at the outset; consequently even if it is assumed to be the ruling of the Rabbis, since they are not intended for pressing [it is permitted] at the very outset. Hence it follows that this [agrees with] the Rabbis [too].[5] This proves it.

'The household of Menasia b. Menahem used to express pomegranates.' R. Naḥman said: The *halachah* is in accordance with the household of Menasia b. Menahem. Said Raba to R. Naḥman: Was then Menasia b. Menahem a Tanna?[6] And should you say [that you mean], The *halachah* is as this Tanna[7] because he agrees with the [practice of] Menasia b. Menahem: just because he agrees with Menasia b. Menahem, the *halachah* is as he! Does Menasia b. Menahem represent the majority of people?[8]—Yes. For we learnt: If one maintains thorns in a vineyard,—R. Eleazar said: They are forbidden;[9] but the Sages maintained: Only that the like of which is [normally] kept[10] creates an interdict. Now R. Ḥanina said: What is R. Eleazar's reason? Because in Arabia the
a thorns of fields are kept for the camels.[1] How compare! Arabia is a [whole] region, but here his practice[2] counts as nought in relation to that of all [other] people!—Rather this is the reason,[3] as R. Ḥisda. For R. Ḥisda said: If beets are expressed and [the juice] poured into a *mikweh*,[4] it renders the *mikweh* unfit on account of changed appearance.[5] But these are not normally expressed?[6] What you must then answer is that since he assigned value thereto,[7] it ranks as liquid;[8] so here too, since one assigns a value thereto, it ranks as a liquid.[9] R. Papa said: The reason is that it is something wherewith a *mikweh* may not be made in the first place, and everything wherewith a *mikweh* may not be made in the first place renders a *mikweh* unfit through changed appearance.[10]

We learnt elsewhere: If wine, vinegar, or secretion [of olives][11] falls therein [a *mikweh*] and changes its appearance, it is unfit.[12] Which Tanna holds that secretion [of olives] is a liquid?[13]—Said Abaye, It is R. Jacob. For it was taught, R. Jacob said: The secretion is as a liquid, and why did they [the Sages] rule, The secretion which exudes at the beginning[14] is clean?[15] Because one does not desire to keep it. R. Simeon said: Secretion is not as a liquid, and why did they rule, The secretion that exudes from
b the bale made up for the press[1] is unclean? Because it cannot but contain particles of diluted oil. Wherein do they differ?[2] They differ in respect to what oozes after [the olives have been subject to their own] pressure. Raba said: The reason is because it is something whereof a *mikweh* may not be made, and such renders a *mikweh* unfit through change of colour.[3]

Rab Judah said in Samuel's name: One may squeeze out a cluster of grapes into a pot,[4] but not into a plate.[5] R. Ḥisda observed: From our master's words we may learn [that] one may milk a goat into a pot [of food], but not into a plate. This proves that he holds: a liquid that unites with[6] a [solid] foodstuff is [accounted] a foodstuff. Rami b. Ḥama objected: If a *zab* milks a goat, the milk is unclean.[7] But if you say, A liquid that unites with a [solid] foodstuff is a foodstuff, whereby did it become susceptible?[8]—As R. Joḥanan said [elsewhere], By the drop [of milk] smeared on the nipple: so here too by the drop smeared on the nipple.[9] Rabina objected: If a person unclean through a corpse

(2) Because their juice is not normally expressed, and therefore that is not akin to threshing, which is the reason of the prohibition in the case of other fruits. (3) On weekdays, which shows that pomegranates are intended for this. (4) Surely not. (5) For the same logic holds good on their view too. (6) Of course not. The practice of this household is merely quoted, but he himself could give no ruling. (7) Who forbids with pomegranates. (8) That the *halachah* should be decided by his practice. (9) Lit., 'sanctified'. Viz., the grapes, on account of the mixture of plants; Deut. XXII, 9. (10) I.e., a plant which is wanted and valuable, which excludes thorns.

a (1) Thus Arabian practice decides the law, and the same is true here. (2) Lit., 'mind'. (3) For R. Naḥman's ruling that one may not press pomegranates. (4) V. Glos. (5) The water is stained red and no longer looks like water. (6) Hence their juice should be of no account. (7) *Sc.* the juices. (8) Which can invalidate a *mikweh*. (9) Viz., the juice of pomegranates. Rashi: R. Naḥman accordingly explains the Baraitha thus:—One may squeeze plums, etc., not for their juice, since this would automatically give the juice a value of its own as a liquid, which in turn prohibits squeezing, but in order to improve the taste of the fruit. But not pomegranates, even to improve the fruit, for since *some*, as the house of Menasia b. Menahem, squeeze it for the sake of the juice, should you permit the former the latter too may be done. This does not apply to plums etc. which no-one squeezes for the sake of their juice. (10) Yet no value is assigned thereto and the juice is not a liquid. (11) A fluid given off by olives before the actual oil is expressed. It is in fact a kind of diluted oil. (12) V. Mik. VII, 4. (13) To invalidate a *mikweh*. (14) When the olives are first loaded in the press, but before they are actually pressed. (15) It does not render food susceptible to defilement; v. *supra* 12a, n. a1.

b (1) Jast.: a bale of loose texture containing the olive pulp to be pressed. This fluid denotes a further stage than the previous. (2) Since both admit that the first fluid is clean, while that which oozes from the olive pulp is unclean, in respect of what do they disagree? (3) That is why the serial fluid makes the *mikweh* unfit; accordingly that ruling agrees with all. (4) Of food, for obviously the juice will not be drunk separately but is meant to season the food; as such it remains a food, i.e., a solid, itself. (5) As it may then be drunk separately, notwithstanding that one does not generally drink from a plate. (6) Lit., 'comes into'. (7) A *zab* defiles everything through *hesseṭ* (v. *supra* 83a, n. a1); here too he exercises *hesseṭ* on the milk. (8) To defilement, for no foodstuff can be unclean unless a liquid has previously fallen upon it (v. *supra* 12a, n. a1).—The law is stated generally, which implies that it is so even if he milks it into a pot of food. (9) The milker smears the first drop around the nipple, to facilitate the flow. This drop of course counts as a liquid, and all the subsequent milk is touched thereby.

squeezes out olives or grapes [145a] exactly as much as an egg [in quantity], it is clean.[10] Hence if more than an egg [in quantity], it [the juice] is unclean; but if you say, A liquid that unites with a [solid] foodstuff is a foodstuff, whereby did it become susceptible?—He raised the objection and he himself answered it: It refers to squeezing out into a plate.

R. Jeremiah said, This is dependent on Tannaim: If one smooths [the surface of dough] with grapes [grape juice], it does not become susceptible [to defilement];[1] R. Judah maintained: It is made susceptible. Do they not differ in this: one Master holds, A liquid that unites with a [solid] foodstuff is a foodstuff, while the other Master holds that it is not a foodstuff?—Said R. Papa. All hold, A liquid that unites with a foodstuff is not a foodstuff,[2] but here they differ in respect of a liquid that will eventually be destroyed:[3] one Master holds, It is [accounted] a liquid; while the other Master holds, It is not a liquid. And [they differ] in the [same] controversy as that of these Tannaim. For it was taught: If one splits olives[4] with unclean hands, they are rendered susceptible;[5] if in order to salt them,[6] they are not rendered susceptible; if in order to know whether the olives are ripe[7] for gathering[8] or not, they do not become susceptible; R. Judah said: They do become susceptible. Now, surely they differ in this, viz., one Master holds: A liquid that stands to be destroyed[9] is [accounted] a liquid, while the other Master holds that it is not a liquid![10]—Said R. Huna the son of R. Joshua: These [latter] Tannaim [indeed] differ in respect of a liquid that stands to be destroyed, while the former Tannaim[11] differ in respect of liquid whose purpose is to polish [the dough].[12]

R. Zera said in R. Ḥiyya b. Ashi's name in Rab's name: A man may squeeze a bunch of grapes into a pot [of food], but not into a plate; but [one may squeeze] a fish for its brine even into a plate.[1] Now, R. Dimi sat and stated this ruling. Said Abaye to R. Dimi, You recite it in Rab's name, hence it presents no difficulty to you; [but] we recite it in Samuel's name, so it presents a difficulty to us. Did Samuel say, '[One may squeeze] a fish for its brine even into a plate'? Surely it was stated: If one presses out [pickled] preserves,[2]—Rab said: If for their own sake,[3] it is permitted; if for their fluid,[4] he is not culpable, nevertheless it is forbidden. But with boiled preserves, whether for their own sake or for their fluid, it is permitted. While Samuel ruled: Both with [pickled] preserves and boiled preserves, if for their own sake, it is permitted; if for their fluid, he is not culpable, yet it is forbidden![5]—By God! replied he, '*Mine eyes have beheld, and not a stranger*':[6] I heard it from R. Jeremiah's mouth, and R. Jeremiah from R. Zera, and R. Zera from R. Ḥiyya b. Ashi, and R. Ḥiyya b. Ashi from Rab.

To turn to [the main] text: 'If one presses out [pickled] preserves,—Rab said: If for their own sake, it is permitted; if for their fluid, he is not culpable, nevertheless it is forbidden. But with boiled preserves, whether for their own sake or for their fluid, it is permitted. While Samuel ruled: Both with [pickled] preserves and boiled preserves, if for their own sake, it is permitted; if for their fluid, he is not culpable, yet it is forbidden. R. Joḥanan said: Both with [pickled] and boiled preserves, if for their own sake, it is permitted; if for their fluid, he is liable to a sin-offering'. An objection is raised: One may squeeze [pickled] preserves on the Sabbath for the requirements of the Sabbath, but not against the termination of the Sabbath; but one must not express olives and grapes, and if he does, he is liable to a sin-offering: this is a difficulty according to Rab, Samuel, and R. Joḥanan?—Rab reconciles it with his view, Samuel with his, and R. Joḥanan with his. 'Rab reconciles it with his view': One may squeeze [pickled] preserves on the Sabbath for the requirements of the Sabbath, but not against the termination of the Sabbath. When is this said? when it is [done] for their own sake; but if for their fluid, he is not culpable, yet it is forbidden; while [as for] boiled preserves, whether [done] for their own sake or for their fluid, it is permitted. But one must not express olives and grapes, and if he does he is liable to a sin-offering. 'Samuel explains it according to his view': One may squeeze [pickled] preserves on the Sabbath for the requirements of the Sabbath, [and] the same applies to boiled preserves. When is this said? When it is for their own sake; but if for their fluid, he is not culpable, yet it is forbidden. And one must not express olives and grapes, and if he does, he is liable to a sin-offering. 'R. Joḥanan explains it according to his view': One may squeeze [pickled] preserves for the requirements of the Sabbath, but not against the termination of the Sabbath. This applies to both [pickled] and boiled preserves. When is that said? When it is for their own sake; but he must not squeeze them for their fluid, and if he does, it is as though he squeezed olives and grapes, and he is liable to a sin-offering.

R. Ḥiyya b. Ashi said in Rab's name: By the words of the c Torah[1] one is culpable for the treading out of olives and grapes alone. And the School of Menasseh taught likewise: By the words of the Torah one is culpable for the treading out of olives and grapes alone. And a witness [attesting] what he heard from[2]

(10) This person defiles food, and in turn the food, if not less than the size of an egg in quantity, defiles liquids. Here the man does not touch the expressed juice. Now from the very first drop that issues the residue is less than the necessary minimum, and therefore it cannot defile the liquid that follows. V. Toh. III, 3; v. Pes., 33b, n. a2.

(1) Presumably the flour was kneaded with eggs, which do not render it susceptible, and the first Tanna teaches that the grape juice does not do so either. (2) So cur. edd., which Rashi and Tosaf. support. Wilna Gaon states that the reading of the Geonim, as well as that of Alfasi, is: is a foodstuff. (3) For the heat of the oven will dry it up. (4) Rashi: to soften them. (5) To defilement through the liquid that oozes out because he is pleased with it, since the olives are softened thereby, v. *supra* 12a, nn. a1–4. (6) When very hard they cannot take salt, and therefore he desires to soften them slightly, but not so much that the juice oozes out; hence he is not pleased therewith. (7) Lit., 'have arrived'. (8) Whether they are soft enough for the oil to be easily expressed. (9) The liquid which oozes out of course is lost. (10) And similarly do the Tannaim of the former Baraitha differ on the same question. (11) Who discuss the smoothing of dough. (12) But the question of waste does not enter here, because this liquid serves a definite purpose, giving the dough a brighter colour.

b (1) Because it is a foodstuff, not a drink, and the squeezing merely separates its composite parts, viz., the brine from the flesh. (2) I.e., raw vegetables, preserved or pickled in wine or vinegar. (3) I.e., he wishes to eat them, and they bear too much moisture at present. (4) He actually wishes to drink its fluid. (5) Now the squeezing of boiled preserves is like that of a fish for its brine. Thus Samuel is self-contradictory. (6) Job XIX, 27. That Rab is the authority for the reported ruling.

c (1) Pentateuchal law. (2) Lit., 'from the mouth'.

תורה אור

כביצה מכוונת טהור הא יותר מכביצה טמא ואי אמרת משקה הבא לאוכל אוכל הוא במאי איתכשר הוא מותיב לה והוא מפרק לה בסוחט לתוך הקערה א"ר ירמיה כתנאי *המחליק בענבים לא הוכשר רבי יהודה אומר הוכשר מאי לאו בהא קמיפלגי מ"ס משקה הבא לאוכל אוכל הוא ומ"ס לאו אוכל הוא אמר רב פפא דכולי עלמא [א] משקה הבא לאוכל לאו אוכל הוא והכא במשקה הבא לאיבוד קמיפלגי מר סבר משקה הוא ומ"ס לאו משקה הוא ובפלוגתא דהני תנאי דתניא *המפצע בזיתים בידים מסואבות הוכשר לסופתן במלח לא הוכשר לידע אם הגיעו זיתיו למסוק אם לאו לא הוכשר רבי יהודה אומר הוכשר מאי לאו בהא קמיפלגי דמ"ס משקה העומד לאיבוד משקה הוא ומ"ס לאו משקה הוא אמר רב הונא בריה דרב יהושע הני תנאי במשקה העומד לאיבוד פליגי והנך תנאי במשקה העומד לצחצחו קמיפלגי א"ר זירא אמר רב חייא בר אשי אמר רב סוחט אדם אשכול של ענבים לתוך הקדרה אבל לא לתוך הקערה ודג לצירו אפילו לתוך הקערה יתיב רב דימי וקאמר לה להא שמעתא א"ל אביי לרב דימי אתון משמיה דרב מתניתון ולא קשיא לכו אנן משמיה דשמואל מתנינן לה וקשיא לן מי אמר שמואל דג לצירו אפי' לתוך הקערה והאיתמר כבשים שסחטן אמר רב לגופן מותר למימיהן פטור אבל אסור ושלקות בין לגופן בין למימיהן מותר ושמואל אמר אחד כבשים ואחד °שלקות לגופן מותר למימיהן פטור אבל אסור א"ל האלהים °עיני ראו ולא זר (כלו כליותי בחקי וגו') מפומיה דר' ירמיה שמיע לי ור' ירמיה מר' זירא ור' זירא מרב חייא בר אשי ורב חייא בר אשי מרב: גופא כבשים שסחטן אמר רב לגופן מותר למימיהן פטור אבל אסור ושלקות בין לגופן בין למימיהן מותר ושמואל אמר אחד זה ואחד זה לגופן מותר למימיהן פטור אבל אסור רבי יוחנן אמר אחד כבשים ואחד שלקות לגופן מותר למימיהן חייב חטאת מיתיבי סוחטין כבשים בשבת לצורך השבת אבל לא למוצ"ש וזיתים וענבים לא יסחוט ואם סחט חייב. חטאת קשיא לרב קשיא לשמואל קשיא לר' יוחנן רב מתרץ לטעמיה שמואל מתרץ לטעמיה ר' יוחנן מתרץ לטעמיה רב מתרץ לטעמיה סוחטין כבשים בשבת לצורך השבת אבל לא למוצ"ש בד"א לגופן אבל למימיהן פטור אבל אסור ושלקות בין לגופן בין למימיהן מותר וזיתים וענבים לא יסחוט ואם סחטן חייב חטאת שמואל מתרץ לטעמיה סוחטין כבשים בשבת לצורך השבת הוא הדין לשלקות בד"א לגופן אבל למימיהן פטור אבל אסור וזיתים וענבים לא יסחוט ואם סחט חייב חטאת ר' יוחנן מתרץ לטעמיה סוחטין כבשים לצורך השבת אבל לא למוצ"ש אחד כבשים ואחד שלקות בד"א לגופן אבל למימיהן לא יסחוט ואם סחט נעשה כמי שסחט זיתים וענבים וחייב חטאת אמר רב חייא בר אשי אמר רב °דבר תורה אינו חייב אלא על דריסת זיתים וענבים בלבד וכן תני דבי מנשה דבר תורה אינו חייב אלא על דריסת זיתים וענבים בלבד *ואין עד מפי עד כשר אלא

כבילה מכוונת טהור · משנה היא במסכת טהרות ומפרש בה בהדיא ובלבד שלא יגע במשקה שאינו נוגע אלא באוכל וכיון דכבילה מכוונת הוא לכי סחיט טיפה קמייתא חסר ליה מכבילה ואין האוכל אע"פ שהוא טמא מטמא המשקה שאין אוכל מטמא אחרים בפחות מכבילה אבל אם היה נוגע במשקה איטמי ליה משקה מטיפה ראשונה שהמשקה מקבל טומאה בכל שהוא וה"נ תני בה בהדיא יותר מכבילה טמא שכיון שילאה טיפה ראשונה נטמאה בכבילה וטמא מת דווקא נקט שאינו מטמא בהיסט וה"ה לטמא שרץ וכל טמאי מגע וטמא מת לרבותא נקט דהוי אב הטומאה משום דקתני סיפא אבל זב שסוחט זיתים וענבים אפי' גרגיר יחידי טמא שכיון שילאה טיפה ראשונה נטמא המשקה במשא הזב: ואי אמרת כו' · דקס"ד אפי' סוחט לתוך הקדירה: כתנאי · משקה הבא לאוכל אוכל הוא או משקה הוא: המחליק בענבים · נתוס המחליק פני ככרותיו בענבים שסוחט המשקה על הככר: הוכשר · האוכל *הענבים הוכשרו: הבא · לצורך אוכל כגון שסחטן לשם הפת: ה"ג דכ"ע משקה הבא לאוכל לאו אוכל הוא · אלא משקה הוא והיינו טעמא דמ"ד לא הוכשר שמתחילה נכתנו אדעתא דאזיל לאיבוד שהאוכל שואבו ושורפו: המפצע בזיתים · בלעי"ז כדי שיהיו רכין: הוכשר · דניחא ליה במשקה דטייף עלייהו שמתוך כך הם מרבים טעם: לסופתן במלח · שמתוך שהן קשין אין המלח נדבק בהן ומפצעם לרככן מבחוץ מעט: לא הוכשר · דלא מכוין למשקה דידהו דליעקר: לידע אם הגיעו זיתיו למסוק · צריך הוא לראות אם שומנו נוח לצאת מיהו המשקה אזיל לאיבוד: הני תנאי · דמפצע ודאי במשקה העומד לאיבוד פליגי כדאמרי' אבל תהי דמחליק לאו בעומד לאיבוד פליגי דלאו לאיבוד אזל שהרי לנאות האוכל נתנו והרי מנאתו אלא במשקה העומד לנאתו לאוכל קא מיפלגי דא"כ משקה הבא לאוכל משקה הוא ה"מ היכא דקא שריף ליה א"נ שטר ביה ריפתא דתורת משקה עביד אבל לנאתו פליגי: ודג לצירו · שהיפה דג להוציא צירו לאו משקה הוא אלא אוכלין: כבשין · ירק חי כבוש ביין וחומץ: לגופו · אם לאכול הכבשים סוחטן ממשקה הנקף עליהן והנבלע בהן מותר לכתחילה דלא מפרק הוא הואיל ולאו למשקה הוא צריך: פטור · שאין זה נפרק שאין המשקה הזה יוצא מן הכבשים שלא גדל בתוכן אבל אסור אטו זיתים וענבים: שלקות · אפילו למימיהן לאו משקה ניכהו אלא אוכל: למימיהן פטור אבל אסור · והא שלקות דומיא דדג לצירן הוא ולא שרי ליה שמואל לכתחילה: עיני ראו ולא זר · הא דבעינא למימר לך דמשמיה דרב איתמר: סוחטין כבשין · ולא מפליג בין לגופן בין למימיהן ושרי לכתחילה וקשיא לכולהו דליכא בהו דשרי כבשין למימיהן לכתחילה: דבר תורה · כלומר אסרה תורה מלאכה ודריכת זיתים וענבים הוא דהויא מלאכה אבל שאר דריכות לאו אורחייהו בהכי ולאו מלאכה ניכהו:

לעדות

כביצה מכוונת טהור · פי' בקונטרס שאע"פ שהאוכל טמא אינו מטמא את המשקה שאין אוכל מטמא בפחות מכבילה והאי טעמא לא ניחא אלא למ"ד בפרק כל שעה (פסחים דף לג: ושם) משקים מיפקד פקידי אבל למ"ד התם מיבלע בליעי טמאים המשקין מאליהן כיון שנגע באוכל [ומשני התם דבמתני' מיירי בענבים שלא הוכשרו לאימת מתכשרי לכי סחיט להו וכי סחיט להו בליר שעוריה והשתא לפי' רש"י מה בכך] מיד כשילאה הטיפה ראשונה (א) נטמאה הואיל ואוכל מקבל טומאה בכל שהוא ומה שהקשה ר"ת לפירו' פי' לעיל בריש המצניע (דף צא.):

דכ"ע משקה הבא לאוכל לאו אוכל הוא · לא מצינן למימר דכ"ע אוכל הוא (ב) א"כ מ"ט דמ"ד הוכשר:

אם הגיעו זיתיו למסוק כו' · מה שקשה ליה לרב נחמן דמפרש בפ"ק (דף יז:) דגזרו לבצור בטהרה משום דפעמים שאדם הולך כו' · שם פירשתי בד"ה גוזרני:

כבשים שסחטן לגופן מותר למימיהן פטור אבל אסור · רב לטעמיה דאמר לקמן דבר תורה אינו חייב אלא על דריכת זיתים וענבים ולפירוש הקונטרס דפי' משום דאתי המשקה מעלמא קשה לרבי אמאי גזרו להדוקי אודרא אפומא דשישא בשלהי תולין (לעיל דף קמא.) שמא יסחוט הא אפילו סחיט ליכא איסור דאורייתא מיהו י"ל דהתם רבא דקאמר לה וס"ל כר' יוחנן דמחייב חטאת:

ורבי יוחנן אמר אחד כבשין ואחד שלקות לגופן מותר למימיהן חייב חטאת · ובדג לצירו נמי הוה מחייב ר' יוחנן חטאת לתוך הקערה דדג לצירו מדמינן לשלקות בכולה שמעתיה דפריך מדשמואל דשלקות אההיא דדג לצירו ופי' ר"ח דהלכה כר' יוחנן דקיי"ל כוותיה לגבי רב ושמואל ושמעינן ממילתא דר"י שאסור לסחוט כבשים ושלקות למימיהן ואם סחט חייב חטאת ולא הפריש בסחיטה בין קדירה לקער' אלא הכל אסור מתוך אלו דברים מתברר שאין הלכה לא כשמואל ולא כרב שאמרו סוחט אדם אשכול של ענבים לתוך הקדירה ויש שמעמידין דברי רב ושמואל ביו"ט מדדייק רב חסדא מדברי שמואל כן ואין לנו להדורי אפירכי ולאפוקי שמעתא מדוכתיה אלא ודאי בשבת קאמרי רב ושמואל ואין הלכה כמותן לא בשבת ולא ביו"ט ע"כ פי' ר"ח ומה שדקדק מדלא מפליג ר' יוחנן משמע דמיירי אפילו לתוך הקדירה אין זה דיוק דהא רב ושמואל נמי אסרי סתמא בכבשים (ג) למימיהן ואע"ג דשרו לסחוט בהדיא אשכול של ענבים לתוך הקדירה ומה שדחה דברי המעמידין דברי רב ושמואל ביו"ט אומר ר"ת שהדין עמו אבל דברי רב חסדא ביום טוב כדפירשתי לעיל:

בהמה

טו א מיי' פ"א מהלכות טומאת אוכלין הל"ד:

טז ב טוש"ע או"ח סימן שכ סעיף ח:

רש"ל ועי' מהרש"א

יז ג מיי' פ"ח מהלכות שבת הל"י ופכ"א הל' יג סמג לאוין סה טוש"ע או"ח שם סעיף ז:

יח ד מיי' פ"ח שם הל"י ופכ"א הלכה יב:

יט ה מיי' פי"ב מהלכות גרושין הלט"ו סמג עשין נ טור שו"ע אה"ע סימן יז סעיף ג:

רבינו חננאל

פי הדף שנפסלה מאוכל והיא מכשרת במשקה ואותיב רבינא טמא מת שסחט זיתים וענבי' וכו' ופרקינן בסוחט לתוך הקערה שהוא ודאי משקה . ומפני מה לא פירק פירוק זה לגבי חולב עז חדא מתרי תלתא טעמא קאמר . א"ר ירמיה כתנאי . המחלק בענבים לא הוכשר . פי' מחלק משפשף פעמים שמתמצה בהן משקין . ומחליקין בו . ולפיכך אמר ר' יהודה הוכשר שכך משקה גמור הוא . ות"ק אמר משקה הבא לאוכל הוא וכאוכל הוא חשוב ואינו מכשיר ובא רב הונא ופירש כי התנאין החולקין במחלק במחליק בענבים פליגי במשקה העומד לצחצחו ואלו החולקין במפצע זיתים בידים מסואבות פליגי . במשקה העומד לאיבוד . א"ר זירא א"ר חייא בר אשי אמר רב סוחט אדם אשכול של ענבים לתוך הקדרה אבל לא לתוך הקערה וכן פירושו כל דבר הנסחט בקדירה הוא אוכל ומותר ולתוך הקערה משקה הוא ואסור . זולתי הדג שאפילו סחיטתו בקערה שרי . והא דאתמר כבשים שסחטן אמר רב לגופן מותר וכו' . דברים פשוטין יהן . ואין צריכין לפנים ולא לפני פנים. אמנם צריכין אנו לברר כמי ההלכה . לפיכך אנו מזכירין דברי כולן : גופא כבשים שסחטן כגון ירקות וראשי לפתות וכרוב וכל הדומה להן . אמר רב לגופן מותר כלומר סחטן להסיר מימיהן ולאכלן מותר . אבל אם כוונתו למימיהן והוא צירן פטור אבל אסור. ושלקות כגון ירקות וכדומה להן שלקן מקודם השבת ונשארו מימיהן בהן וכן דגים מלוחין בין לגופו בין למימיהן מותר. ושמואל אמר אחד כבשים ואחד שלקות לגופן מותר למימיהן פטור אבל אסור ור' יוחנן אמר אחד כבשים וא' שלקות לגופן מותר למימיהן חייב חטאת ומותבינן עלייהו סוחטין כבשים בשבת לצורך השבת אבל לא למוצ"ש.זיתים וענבים לא יסחוט ואם סחט חייב חטאת קשיא לרב וקשיא לשמואל וקשיא לר' יוחנן וכל אחד מהן מתרץ מתניתא דא לטעמיה ודבריהן

פשוטין הן אבל אנחנו כותבין תירוץ . טעמא דר' יוחנן דהלכתא כוותיה דקיי"ל כל היכא דפליגי רב ושמואל ור' יוחנן הלכה כר' יוחנן. ולפיכך מדקדקינן בדבריו להעמיד הלכה על בוריו. ר' יוחנן מתרץ לטעמיה סוחטין כבשים בשבת לצורך השבת. אבל לא למוצ"ש ואחד כבשים ואחד שלקות לגופן אבל למימיהן לא יסחוט ואם סחט נעשה כמי שסחט זיתים וענבים וחייב חטאת . ולא הפריש בסחיטתן למימיהן בין קדירה לקערה אלא הכל אסור . דהא סחיטת זיתים וענבים בין לקדירה ובין לקערה למימיהן הוא צריך . וא"ר יוחנן שהסוחט כבשים ושלקות למימיהן כסוחט זיתים וענבים וחייב חטאת . ומתוך אלו הדברים מתברר שאין הלכה לא כשמואל ולא כרב שאומ' סוחט אדם אשכול של ענבים לתוך הקדירה אבל לא לתוך הקערה . ויש שמעמיד דברי (רבינו) רב ושמואל ביו"ט. מדדייק רב חסדא מדברי שמואל . ואמר מדברי רבינו נלמד חולב אדם עז לתוך הקדירה אבל לא לתוך הקערה כדי לקיים דבריהם להיות הלכה ואינן דבריהם נכונים שאפילו ביו"ט כל אילו אסורין ולינק בפיו מן הבהמה ביו"ט אסור וכ"ש לחלוב כדגרסינן בסוף פרק חרש [שנשא] פקחת . אבא שאול אומר נוהגין היינו שיונקין מן בהמה טהורה ביו"ט ואקשינן עליה היכי דמי אי דאיכא סכנה אפילו בשבת שרי אי דליכא סכנה אפילו ביו"ט אסור . ומפרקי' לא צריכא דאית בה צערא (וסברא) [וקסבר] מפרק כלאחר יד הוא.שבת דאיסור סקילה הוא גזור רבנן. י"ט דאיסור לאו לא גזור רבנן. הנה אפי' לינק ביו"ט לא התירו אלא במקום שיש צער כ"ש לחלוב במקום שאין צער שודאי אסור . ואין לנו להדורי אפירכי ולאפוקי שמעתא מדוכתא אלא ודאי זה שאומר סוחט אדם לתוך הקדירה אבל לא לתוך הקערה בשבת אמרו . ושאמר רב חסדא ביו"ט הוא ואין הלכה כמותם לא בשבת ולא ביו"ט וכך קיבלנו מרבותינו והא דתנא דבי מנשה דבר תורה אינו חייב אלא על דריכת זיתים וענבים בלבד. לא קשיא הא דר' יוחנן *) ושאר פירות זולתי זיתים וענבים סלקא שמעתא כר' יהודה דאמר לאוכלין היוצא מהן מותר

למשקין

*) [נראה דר"ל דהתנא דבי מנשה לא כו' למעט רק שאר פירות אבל לא כבשים ושלקות אך לגבוה לריכה תיקון קצת. ועי' בר"ץ כאן]

מעשרות פ"א מ"ח

ז"ל והענבים ואיירי בפת שנילוש במי פירות ועכשיו הוכשר

איוב יט

יבמות סז: ודף קכב. בכורות לו. מו:

הגהות הב"ח

(א) תוס' ד"ה כבילה וכו' הטיפה ראשונה הוכשר הואיל ואוכל וכו' בריש המצניע. נ"ב דף צא בד"ה אי לענין וע"ש: (ב) ד"ה דכ"ע וכו' דא"כ מ"ט: (ג) ד"ה ור' יוחנן וכו' אסרי סתמא בכבשים ובשלקות למימיהן:

הגהות הגר"א

[א] גמ' משקה הבא לאוכל לאו אוכל הוא . נ"ב גירסת הגאונים אוכל הוא . עי' רשב"א וכ"כ הרי"ף ע"ש:

גליון הש"ס

גמ' שלקות לגופן מותר למימיהן . עי' לעיל דף עג ע"ב תוס' ד"ה וצריך לעצים:

לעדות אשה · לומר לאשה מת בעליך דאקילו בה רבנן משום עיגונא וכל דמקדש אדעתא דרבנן *מקדש *ואפקועי רבנן לקדושין מיניה: לעדות בכור · בכור ביד כהן כשנתנו ישראל לו שלם ואירע לו בו מום קי"ל בבכורות (דף לה.) נחשדו כהנים להטיל מום בבכור ואין נאמן לומר מום זה נפל בו מאליו וצריך להביא עדים ואמרינן התם דאשה כשרה לעדות זו: אימא לעדות שהאשה כשרה לה · והאי נמי כשרה לה: גברא יתירא · ר"ש דמתני' ר"א תנן בה: אתא לאשמעינן · בתמיה כלומר מה בא ללמדנו אם לא זאת: מתני' כל שבא בחמין · כלומר שנתבשל: שורין אותו בחמין · כדי שיהא נמוח: וכל שלא בא בחמין · כגון בשר יבש שאוכלין אותו חי ע"י הדחק: מדיחין אותו. ולא אמרי' זהו בישוליה אבל לא שורין: חוץ מן המליח ישן · דג מליח של שנה שעברה: וקוליים האיספנין · שם דג שאוכלין אותו מחמת מלחו ע"י הדחה בחמין והנך אפילו הדחה נמי לא שזהו גמר מלאכתן והוי בשול: גמ' כגון מאי. הוי בא בחמין שחוזרין ושורין אותו בחמין: תרנגולתיה דר' אבא · מבשלה ושורה אותה ימים רבים בחמין למחות מאליה ואוכלה לרפואה: בר תלתא טרפי · בן ג' שנים: אתנוסי · הייתי נאנס להקיא מחמת מיאוס: רייק · רוקק מכותחא דבבלאי כשזוכרו שהיה מאוס בעיניו: אמר רב יוסף כו'. קשה היה בעיניו שנמאסין בני בבל על בני ארץ ישראל אמר אנו נמי יש לנו לרוק מתרנגולתיה דר' אבא שהם אוכלים: ועוד כותח · אינו מאוס כל כך בעיני שאר בני מערבא: דהא אמר רב גזא כו'· ושאילו מיניה אותו כותח: בריחי. חולים: הדיח · קוליים מאי: חייב חטאת · דהוי בישול: מפני מה עופות שבבבל שמנים · משל א"י: כלך · לכה לך אלא שקיצר הלשון: למדבר עזה · והיא מא"י: מועדים שבבבל שמחים · רגילים לשמוח במועדים יותר מא"י: מפני שהם עניים · וכל השנה אין להם שמחה במאכל ומשתה ואין להם מרגוע ממלאכה לפיכך במועדים כל שמחתם: מצויינין · מלויינין עצמן בלבושים נאים: מלויינין · מקושטין: שאינן בני תורה · כל כך לכבדם כבני ארץ ישראל מחמת תורתם מכבדים אותם מחמת לבושיהן שנראין חשובים: דרדקי · בחורים שלא הגיעו לסברא: מפני שלא גלו · העופות כמו אותן של א"י כדאמרינן לקמן: שאנן מואב מנעוריו וגו' · סיפיה דקרא על כן עמד טעמו בו אלמא הגולין מפיגין טעמן ושמנן: נ"ב שנה · משגלו בימי צדקיה בחרבות ירושלים עד שנפקדו בימי כורש ואז עלו מהם לייסד את הבית י"ח שנים קודם גמר הבנין שהיא לסוף ע' שנה בשנת שתים לדריוש כדאמרי' במגילה (דף יא:): וכולן חזרו. הבהמות ועופות ואף הדגים חוץ מן קוליים האספנין וכולן חזרו דהא עד בהמה כתיב ומכלל דמכאן ואילך הדור חוץ מקוליים כדמפרש: הני מדרי דבבל מהדרי מיא לעין עיטם · מדרונות שבבבל מחזירין מים הנשפכים בהן לעין עיטם שהוא מקום גבוה שבא"י שאותו מעיין מביא מים לבית טבילת כה"ג ביוה"כ דמתוקן בחומת עזרה על גבי שער המים כדאמרינן בסדר יומא (דף לא.) עין עיטם גבוה מקרקע העזרה כ"ג אמות והילך מחזירין שיש בפרת סילוטות וסולמות למטה מן הקרקע (הים) ודרך אותן סולמות חוזרין המים לא"י וחוזרין וטבלין במעייטות והדגים חזרו דרך אותן סולמות שטוחים להעלותן יותר מדרך פרת עצמו: והאי · קוליים האספנין: כיון דלא שריר שדריה · אין קשה שדרה שלו: לטבריה · לבוז ולהטיל עליהם עול ולא שמתכוונין לבטלן משמחת הרגל אבל הקללה גרמה לכך: קומטין · *לשון לעז הוא שלטון: בולשת · חיל המלך: ליפורי וטבריה מא"י: שאינן במקומם · שמא"י גלו לשם והגולה למקום נכרי מליין עצמו במלבושים שיהא חשוב: במתא שמאי · בעירי איני צריך להתכבד אלא בשמי שאני ניכר בו: בלא מתא · במקום שאינה עירי: תותבאי · כבודי תלוי בשמלתי שמלתו מתרגמינן תותביה (שמות כב): ציצין · לילין למחין: הבאים · אותן של יעקב שיבאו לבבל ישרשו ויעשו ציצין ופרחים לתורה וסייעתא אתיא לר' יוחנן דטעמא דמלויינין לאו לפי שאינן בני תורה כדרבי אסי אלא לפי שאינן במקומן:

כשבא

תורה אור

בהמה בגימטריא . אסמכתא בעלמא היא דנ"ב נפקא לן בלאו גימטריא כדפי' בקונטרס :

סובר

אלא לעדות אשה בלבד *איבעיא להו עד מפי עד לעדות בכור מהו רב אמי אסיר ורב אסי שרי א"ל רב אמי לרב אסי והא תנא דבי מנשיא אין עד מפי עד כשר אלא לעדות אשה בלבד אימא לעדות שהאשה כשרה לה בלבד רב יימר אכשר עד מפי עד לבכור קרי עליה מרימר יימר שרי בוכרא *והלכתא עד מפי עד כשר לבכור: חלות דבש: כי אתא רב הושעיא מנהרדעא *אתא ואייתי מתניתא בידיה זיתים וענבים שריסקן מע"ש ויצאו מעצמן אסורין ור"א ור"ש מתירין אמר רב יוסף גברא יתירא אתא לאשמעינן א"ל אביי טובא קמ"ל דאי ממתניתין הוה אמינא התם הוא דמעיקרא אוכלא ולבסוף אוכלא אבל הכא דמעיקרא אוכלא ולבסוף משקה אימא לא קמ"ל: **מתני'** *כל שבא בחמין מערב שבת שורין אותו בחמין בשבת וכל שלא בא בחמין מערב שבת מדיחין אותו בחמין בשבת חוץ מן המליח הישן (ודגים מלוחין קטנים) *וקוליים האיספנין שהדחתן זו היא גמר מלאכתן: **גמ'** כגון מאי אמר רב ספרא כגון תרנגולתא דר' אבא ואמר רב ספרא זימנא חדא איקלעית להתם ואוכלן מיניה ואי לא רבי אבא דאשקיין חמרא בר תלתא טרפי איתנסי רבי יוחנן רייק מכותח דבבלאי אמר רב יוסף ולירוק אנן מתרנגולתא דרבי אבא ועוד אמר רב גזא זימנא חדא איקלעית להתם ועבדית כותח דבבלאי שאילו מיניה *כל בריחי מערבא: כל שלא בא בחמין וכו': הדיח מאי אמר רב יוסף הדיח חייב חטאת אמר מר בריה דרבינא אף אנן נמי תנינא חוץ ממליח ישן וקוליים האיספנין שהדחתן זו היא גמר מלאכתן שמע מינה יתיב רבי חייא בר אבא ורבי אסי קמיה דרבי יוחנן ויתיב רבי יוחנן וקא מנמנם אמר ליה רבי חייא בר אבא לרבי אסי מפני מה עופות שבבבל שמנים א"ל כלך למדבר עזה ואראך שמנים מהן מפני מה מועדים שבבבל שמחים מפני שהן עניים מפני מה ת"ח שבבבל מצויינין לפי שאינן בני תורה מפני מה עובדי כוכבים מזוהמי' מפני שאוכלין שקצי' ורמשי'* איתער בהו רבי יוחנן אמר להו דרדקי לא כך אמרתי לכם °אמור לחכמה אחותי את *אם ברור לך הדבר כאחותך שהיא אסורה לך אומרהו ואם לאו לא תאמרהו אמרו ליה ולימא לן מר איזה מהן מפני מה עופות שבבבל שמנים מפני שלא גלו שנאמר °שאנן מואב מנעוריו ושקט הוא אל שמריו ובגולה לא הלך והכא מנלן דגלו דתניא *רבי יהודה אומר נ"ב שנה לא עבר איש ביהודה שנאמר °על ההרים אשא בכי ונהי וגו' מעוף השמים ועד בהמה נדדו הלכו בהמ"ה בגימטריא חמשין ותרתין הוו א"ר יעקב א"ר יוחנן כולן חזרו חוץ מקוליים האיספנין *דאמר רב הני מדרי דבבל מהדרי מיא לעין עיטם והאי כיון דלא שריר שדריה לא מצי סליק מפני מה מועדים שבבבל שמחים מפני שלא היו באותה קללה דכתיב °והשבתי כל משושה חגה חדשה ושבתה וכל מועדה וכתיב °חדשיכם ומועדיכם שנאה נפשי היו עלי לטורח *מאי היו עלי לטורח א"ר אלעזר אמר הקב"ה לא דיין לישראל שחוטאין לפני אלא שמטריחין אותי לידע איזו גזירה קשה אביא עליהן א"ר יצחק אין לך כל רגל ורגל שלא באתה בולשת לציפורי ואמר רבי חנינא אין לך כל רגל ורגל שלא בא לטבריה אגמון וקמטון ובעל זמורה מפני מה ת"ח שבבבל מצויינין לפי שאינן (א) בני מקומן דאמרי אינשי במתא שמאי בלא מתא תותבאי °הבאים ישרש יעקב יציץ ופרח ישראל תני רב יוסף אלו תלמידי חכמים שבבבל שעושין ציצין ופרחים לתורה מפני מה עובדי כוכבים מזוהמין שלא עמדו על הר סיני שבשעה

שבא

עין משפט נר מצוה

[ועי' שבות יעקב חלק ב' סימן קטו]

כ א מיי' פ"ב מהלכות בכורות הלכה טו סמג עשין ריא טוש"ע יו"ד סימן שיד סעיף ה :

כא ב מיי' פכ"א מהל' שבת הלכה טו טור שו"ע או"ח סימן רנב סעיף ה וסי' שכ סעיף ב:

כב ג מיי' פכ"ב שם הלכה ח סמג לאוין סה טוש"ע או"ח סימן שיח סעיף ד :

כג ד מיי' פ"כ מהלכות סנהדרין הלכה ז סמג עשין כו טור שו"ע חו"מ סימן י סעיף א :

רבינו חננאל

למשקין היוצא מהן אסור . והא דתניא סוחטין בפגעים ובפרישין ובעוזרדין אבל לא ברמונים דשל בית מנשיא בן מנחם היו סוחטין ברמונים אמר רב נחמן הלכה כשל בית מנשיא בן מנחם וסלקא שמעתא דאסור לסחוט ברמונים בשבת. והא דתני אין עד מפי עד כשר אלא לעדות אשה בלבד . אוקימנא לעדות שהאשה כשרה לה והלכתא עד מפי עד כשר לבכור . פי' עד מפי עד נאמן להעיד על בכור בהמה טהורה שזה המום שיש בו אפי' שראוי לבוא בידי אדם הוא לא נפל בו מידי אדם ובזו העדות החכם מתירו להאכל במומו וכ"ש בעדות גדולה מזו. ומפורש כך בבכורות פ' כל פסולי המוקדשי'. וסלקא שמעתא התם דהלכתא כרשב"ג דאמר אפילו בנו ובתו נאמנים ויש מי שאומר כי עד מפי עד נאמן בבכור אדם ומעות הוא בידו : חלות דבש שריסקן מע"ש ויצאו מעצמן אסורין ור' אלעזר ור"ש מתירין . כי אתא רב הושעיא מנהרדעא אתא ואייתי מתניתא בידיה זיתים וענבים שריסקן מע"ש ויצאו מעצמן אסורים . ור' אלעזר ור"ש מתירין . והא מתניתא מסייעא נמי לר' יוחנן : מתני' כל שבא בחמין מלפני השבת וכו' . ומיבעיא לן כגון מאי . ואמר רב ספרא כגון תרנגולתא דר' אבא שהיתה מלוחה ביותר וכשמבקשין לאוכלה שורין אותה במים חמין . אמר רב ספרא כגון זו התרנגולת אם הובאה בחמין מלפני השבת מותר לשרותה בחמין בשבת ולאוכלה . ואם לאו אסור לשרותה ומותר להדיחה והמליח הישן וקוליים האיספנין

רב נסים גאון

ואין עד מפי עד כשר אלא לעדות אשה בלבד כשאמר כי מת בעלה התירוה בית דין לינשא ואע"פ שהמועט העתיק דבר זה מזולתו וכמו שביארו דבר זה בפרק אשה שהלך בעלה וצרתה (דף קכב) והוחזקו להיות משיאין עד מפי עד וכו': עד מפי עד בבכור מהו. עיקר דיליה במסכת בכורות בפרק כל פסולי המוקדשין (דף לה) דתניא ר' יהושע בן קפוסאי אומר בכור בי כהן צריך ב' מן השוק להעיד עליו רבן שמעון בן גמליאל אומר אפילו בנו ובתו ואמרו הלכתא כרבן שמעון ודוקא בנו ובתו אבל אשתו לא מאי טעמא אשתו כגופו דמיא ועוד אמרו איבעיא להו עד מפי עד מהו לעדות בכור אמר ליה תני אלא לעדות אשה כשירה לו וכבר נתברר לנו שבתו כשירה והואיל ואשה כשירה לעדות בכור עד מפי עד נמי כשר לעדות בכור וכן פסקה ההלכה וזה שאמרו בבכור בהמה אבל בבכור אדם לא. גרסינן בפרק י' יוחסין (דף עד) ג' נאמנין על הבכור חיה ואמו ואביו חיה לאלתר אמו כל ז' אביו לעולם: כגון תרנגלתיה דר' אבא . כך פירשה אדונינו האיי גאון ז"ל תרנגולת שמבשלין אותה ומוציאין אותה מהמרק וממלאין אותה בתבלין וכשרוצה לאכול ממנה שורין אותה במים חמים ואוכלים אותה כאילו היא חמה : סליק פרק חבית

[יבמות נ:]

בכורות לו. ע"ש

לעיל יט:

לעיל לט.

[דג שבמקומות האספניא ושמו בלשון סקודש שיבוטא ערוך אספנין]

[עי' לעיל כח.]

הגהות הב"ח

(א) גמ' לפי שאינן במקומן כצ"ל ותיבות בני נמחק:

ב"ב טז:

סנהדרין ז:

[יומא כד.]

בכורות מד:

[מגילה יא:]

לשון קומטוס כמו קומוס ולשון רומי הוא עי' רש"י סוטה יד ד"ה בסתרה

another witness is valid [145b] in evidence concerning a woman alone.[3] The scholars asked: What about a witness [attesting] what he heard from another witness in evidence relating to a
a firstling?[1]—R. Ammi forbids [the admission of his testimony]; while R. Assi permits it. Said R. Ammi to R. Assi, But the School of Menasseh taught: A witness testifying what he heard from another witness is valid in testimony concerning a woman alone? —Say: Only in testimony for which a woman is valid.[2] R. Yemar recognized as fit a witness [testifying] from the mouth of another witness in respect to a firstling, [whereupon] Meremar called him 'Yemar who permits firstlings.'[3] Yet the law is, A witness [testifying] from the mouth of another witness is valid in respect to firstlings.

HONEYCOMBS. When R. Oshaia came from Nehardea, he came and brought a Baraitha with him:[4] If one crushes olives and grapes on the eve of the Sabbath, and they [their juices] ooze out of themselves, they are forbidden; but R. Eleazar and R. Simeon permit them. R. Joseph observed. Does he come to inform us of another person?[5]—Said Abaye to him, He comes to tell us much. For if [we learnt] from our Mishnah [alone], I would argue, Only there [is it thus], since it [the honey] was a [solid] foodstuff originally and is now a foodstuff; but here that they [the grapes, etc.] were originally a foodstuff but now[6] a fluid, I would say, It is not so. Hence he informs us [otherwise].

MISHNAH. WHATEVER WAS PUT INTO HOT WATER BEFORE THE SABBATH MAY BE STEEPED [AGAIN] IN HOT WATER ON THE SABBATH; BUT WHATEVER WAS NOT PUT INTO HOT WATER BEFORE THE SABBATH MAY [ONLY] BE RINSED WITH HOT WATER ON THE SABBATH, EXCEPT OLD SALTED [PICKLED]
b FISH, [SMALL SALTED FISH],[1] AND THE COLIAS OF THE SPANIARDS,[2] BECAUSE RINSING COMPLETES THEIR PREPARATION.[3]

GEMARA. What, for example?[4] R. Safra said: E.g., R. Abba's fowl[s].[5] R. Safra also said: I once paid a visit there [Palestine] and ate thereof, and but for R. Abba who made me drink wine of three foliages[6] I would have been in danger.[7] R. Joḥanan expectorated at [the mention of] Babylonian *kutaḥ*.[8] Said R. Joseph: Then we [Babylonians] should expectorate at R. Abba's fowl![9] Moreover, R. Gaza has related, I once paid a visit there [in Palestine] and prepared some Babylonian *kutaḥ*, and all the invalids of the West [Palestine] asked me for it.

WHATEVER WAS NOT PUT INTO HOT WATER, etc. What if one does rinse [them]?[10]—R. Joseph said: If one rinses them, he incurs a sin-offering. Mar the son of Rabina said, We too learnt thus: EXCEPT OLD SALTED [PICKLED] FISH, AND THE COLIAS OF THE SPANIARDS, BECAUSE THEIR RINSING COMPLETES THEIR PREPARATION: this proves it.[11]

R. Ḥiyya b. Abba and R. Assi were sitting before R. Joḥanan, while R. Joḥanan was sitting and dozing. Now, R. Ḥiyya b. Abba asked R. Assi, Why are the fowls in Babylonia fat?[12] Go to the wilderness of Gaza, replied he, and I will show you fatter ones.

(3) He is valid to attest a man's death, so that his wife may remarry v. Yeb. 90b.
a (1) A firstling of animals may not be eaten until it receives a blemish accidentally, which must be proved by witnesses. (2) A woman is a valid witness only in certain matters, which includes a firstling's blemish, and in these hearsay too is admissible. (3) Said in a critical spirit. (4) Lit., 'in his hand'. (5) What purpose does this Baraitha serve? The same principle is expressed in our Mishnah by R. Eleazar, and he merely tells us that it is also R. Simeon's view. (6) Lit., 'at the end'.

b (1) Var. lec. omits this. (2) A kind of tunny-fish. (3) V. *supra* 39a top for notes. (4) Is put into hot water and then steeped again. (5) Which he boiled and kept many days in hot water until they dissolved; then he ate them as a remedy. (6) I.e., in the third year. (7) I was moved to expectorate, so sickly was it. (8) He disliked it so much. (9) The disparagement of the Babylonian delicacy gave him offence. (10) The old salted fish etc. (11) Since it completes their preparation it is the equivalent of boiling. (12) Fatter than the Palestinian ones.

◁ *For the continuation of the English translation of this page see overleaf.*

תורה אור

בהמה בגימטריא. אסמכתא בעלמא היא דנ"ב נפקא לן בלאו גימטריא כדפי' בקונטרס: סוכר

אלא לעדות אשה בלבד *איבעיא להו עד מפי עד לעדות בכור מהו רב אמי אסיר ורב אסי שרי א"ל רב אמי לרב אסי והא תנא דבי מנשיא אין עד מפי עד כשר אלא לעדות אשה בלבד אימא לעדות שהאשה כשרה לה בלבד רב יימר אכשר עד מפי עד לבכור קרי עליה מרימר יימר שרי בוכרא "והלכתא עד מפי עד כשר לבכור: חלות דבש: כי אתא רב הושעיא מנהרדעא *אתא ואייתי מתניתא בידיה זיתים וענבים שריסקן מע"ש ויצאו מעצמן אסורין "ור"א ור"ש מתירין אמר רב יוסף גברא יתירא אתא לאשמעינן א"ל אביי טובא קמ"ל דאי ממתניתין הוה אמינא התם הוא דמעיקרא אוכלא ולבסוף אוכלא אבל הכא דמעיקרא אוכלא ולבסוף משקה אימא לא קמ"ל: **מתני'** *"כל שבא בחמין מערב שבת שורין אותו בחמין בשבת וכל שלא בא בחמין מערב שבת מדיחין אותו בחמין בשבת חוץ מן המליח הישן (ודגים מלוחין קטנים) *וקולייס האיספנין שהדחתן זו היא גמר מלאכתן: **גמ'** כגון מאי אמר רב ספרא כגון תרנגולתא דר' אבא ואמר רב ספרא זימנא חדא איקלעית להתם ואוכלן מיניה ואי לא רבי אבא דאשקיין חמרא בר תלתא טרפי איתנסי רבי יוחנן רייק מכותח דבבלאי אמר רב יוסף ולירוק אנן מתרנגולתא דרבי אבא ועוד אמר רב גזא זימנא חדא איקלעית להתם ועבדית כותח דבבלאי שאילו מיניה *כל בריחי מערבא: כל שלא בא בחמין וכו': הדיח מאי אמר רב יוסף הדיח חייב חטאת אמר מר בריה דרבינא אף אנן נמי תנינא חוץ ממליח ישן וקולייס האיספנין שהדחתן זו היא גמר מלאכתן שמע מינה יתיב רבי חייא בר אבא ורבי אסי קמיה דרבי יוחנן ויתיב רבי יוחנן וקא מנמנם אמר ליה רבי חייא בר אבא לרבי אסי מפני מה עופות שבבבל שמנים א"ל כלך למדבר עזה ואראך שמנים מהן מפני מה מועדים שבבבל שמחים מפני שהן עניים מפני מה ת"ח שבבבל מצויינין לפי שאינן בני תורה מפני מה עובדי כוכבים מזוהמי' מפני שאוכלין שקצי' ורמשי'* איתער בהו רבי יוחנן אמר להו דרדקי לא כך אמרתי לכם °אמור לחכמה אחותי את *"אם ברור לך הדבר כאחותך שהיא אסורה לך אומרהו ואם לאו לא תאמרהו אמרו ליה ולימא לן מר איזה מהן מפני מה עופות שבבבל שמנים מפני שלא גלו שנאמר °שאנן מואב מנעוריו ושקט הוא אל שמריו ובגולה לא הלך והכא מנלן דגלו דתניא *רבי יהודה אומר נ"ב שנה לא עבר איש ביהודה שנאמר °על ההרים אשא בכי ונהי וגו' מעוף השמים ועד בהמה נדדו הלכו בהמ"ה בגימטריא חמשין ותרתין הוו א"ר יעקב א"ר יוחנן כולן חזרו חוץ מקולייס האיספנין *דאמר רב הני מדרי דבבל מהדרי מיא לעין עיטם והאי כיון דלא שריר שדריה לא מצי סליק מפני מה מועדים שבבבל שמחים מפני שלא היו באותה קללה דכתיב °והשבתי כל משושה חגה חדשה ושבתה וכל מועדה וכתיב °חדשיכם ומועדיכם שנאה נפשי היו עלי לטורח *מאי היו עלי לטורח א"ר אלעזר אמר הקב"ה לא דיין לישראל שחוטאין לפני אלא שמטריחין אותי לידע איזו גזירה קשה אביא עליהן א"ר יצחק אין לך כל רגל ורגל שלא באתה בולשת לציפורי ואמר רבי חנינא אין לך כל רגל ורגל שלא בא לטבריה אגמון וקמטון ובעל זמורה מפני מה ת"ח שבבבל מצויינין לפי שאינן (א) בני מקומן דאמרי אינשי במתא שמאי בלא מתא תותבאי °הבאים ישרש יעקב יציץ ופרח ישראל תני רב יוסף אלו תלמידי חכמים שבבבל שעושין ציצין ופרחים לתורה מפני מה עובדי כוכבים מזוהמין שלא עמדו על הר סיני שבשעה שבא

רש"י

לעדות אשה · לומר לאשה מת בעליך דאקילו בה רבנן משום עיגונא וכל דמקדש אדעתא דרבנן *מקדש *ואפקועי רבנן לקדושין מיניה: לעדות בכור · בכור ביד כהן כשנתנו ישראל לו שלם ואירע לו בו מום קי"ל בבכורות (דף לה.) נחשדו כהנים להטיל מום בבכור ואין נאמן לומר מום זה נפל בו מאליו וצריך להביא עדים ואמרינן התם דאשה כשרה לעדות זו: אימא לעדות שהאשה כשרה לה · והאי נמי כשרה לה: גברא יתירא · ר"ש דמתני' ר"א תנן בה: אתא לאשמעינן · בתמיה כלומר מה בא ללמדנו אם לא זאת: **מתני'** כל שבא בחמין · כלומר שנתבשל: שורין אותו בחמין · כדי שיהא נמוח: וכל שלא בא בחמין · כגון בשר יבש שאוכלין אותו חי ע"י הדחק: מדיחין אותו. ולא אמרי' זהו בישוליה אבל לא שורין: חוץ מן המליח ישן · דג מליח של שנה שעברה: וקולייס האיספנין · שם דג שאוכלין אותו מחמת מלחו ע"י הדחה בחמין והנך אפילו הדחה נמי לא שזהו גמר מלאכתן והוי בשול: **גמ'** כגון מאי. הוי בא בחמין שחוזרין ושורין אותו בחמין: תרנגולתיה דר' אבא · מבשלה ושורה אותה ימים רבים בחמין למחות מאליה ואוכלה לרפואה: בר תלתא טרפי · בן ג' שנים: אתנוסי · הייתי נאנס להקיא מחמת מיאוס: רייק · רוקק מכותחא דבבלאי כשזוכרו שהיה מאוס בעיניו: אמר רב יוסף כו'. קשה היה בעיניו שנמאסין בני בבל על בני ארץ ישראל אמר אנו נמי יש לנו לרוק מתרנגולתיה דר' אבא שהם אוכלים: ועוד כותח · אינו מאוס כל כך בעיני שאר בני מערבא: דהא אמר רב גזא כו'· ושאילו מיניה אותו כותח: בריחי · חולים: הדיח · קולייס מאי: חייב חטאת · דהוי בישול: מפני מה עופות שבבבל שמנים · משל א"י: כלך · לכה לך אלא שקיצר הלשון: למדבר עזה · והיא מא"י: מועדים שבבבל שמחים · רגילים לשמוח במועדים יותר מא"י: מפני שהם עניים · וכל השנה אין להם שמחה במאכל ומשתה ואין להם מרגוע ממלאכה לפיכך במועדים כל שמחתם: מצויינין · מציינין עצמן בלבושם נאים: מקושטין: שאינן בני תורה · כל כך לכבדם כבני ארץ ישראל מחמת תורתם מכבדים אותם מחמת לבושיהן שנראין חשובים: דרדקי · בחורים שלא הגיעו לסברא: מפני שלא גלו · העופות כמו אותן של א"י כדאמרינן לקמן: שאנן מואב מנעוריו וגו' · סיפיה דקרא על כן עמד טעמו בו אלמא הגולין מפיגין טעמן ושמנן: נ"ב שנה · משגלו בימי צדקיה בחרבות ירושלים עד שנפקדו בימי כורש ואז עלו מהם לייסד את הבית י"ח שנים קודם גמר הבנין שהיא לסוף ע' שנה בשנת שתים לדריוש כדאמרי' במגילה (דף יא:): וכולן חזרו. הבהמות ועופות ואף הדגים חוץ מן קולייס האספנין וכולן חזרו דהא עד בהמה כתיב ומכלל דמכאן ואילך הדור חוץ מקולייס כדמפרש: הני מדרי דבבל מהדרי מיא לעין עיטם · מדרונות שבבבל מחזירין מים הנשפכים בהן לעין עיטם שהוא מקום גבוה שבא"י שאותו מעיין מביא מים לבית טבילת כה"ג ביוה"כ דמתוקן בחומת עזרה על גבי שער המים כדאמרינן בסדר יומא (דף לא.) עין עיטם גבוה מקרקע העזרה כ"ג אמות והילך מחזירין שיש בפרת סילונות וסולמות למטה מן הקרקע (הים) ודרך אותן סולמות חוזרין המים לא"י וחוזרין וטובעין במעיינות והדגים חזרו דרך אותן סולמות שטוחים להעלותן יותר מדרך פרת עצמו: והאי · קולייס האספנין: כיון דלא שריר שדריה · אין קשה שדרה שלו: לטבריה · לבוז ולהטיל עליהם עול ולא שמתכוונין לבטלן משמחת הרגל אבל הקללה גרמה לכך: קומטין · *לשון לעז הוא שלטון: בולשת · חיל המלך: ליפורי וטבריא מא"י: שאינן במקומם · שמא"י גלו לשם והגולה למקום נכרי מציין עצמו במלבושים שיהא חשוב: במתא שמאי · בעירי אני צריך להתכבד אלא בשמי שאני ניכר בו: בלא מתא · במקום שאינה עירי: תותבאי · כבודי תלוי בשמלתי שמלתו מתרגמינן תותביה (שמות כב): ציצין · למחין: הבאים · אותן של יעקב שיבאו לבבל ישרשו ויעשו ציצין ופרחים לתורה וסייעתא אתיא לר' יוחנן דטעמא דמצויינין לאו לפי שאינן בני תורה כדרבי אסי אלא לפי שאינן במקומן:

כשבא

רבינו חננאל

למשקין היוצא מהן אסור . והא דתניא סוחטין בפגעים ובפרישין ובעוזרדין אבל לא ברמונים דשל בית מנשיא בן מנחם היו סוחטין ברמונים אמר רב נחמן הלכה כשל בית מנשיא בן מנחם וסלקא שמעתא דאסור לסחוט ברמונים בשבת והא דתני אין עד מפי עד כשר אלא לעדות אשה בלבד . אוקימנא לעדות שהאשה כשרה לה והלכתא עד מפי עד כשר לבכור . פי' עד מפי עד נאמן להעיד על בכור בהמה טהורה שזה המום שיש בו אפי' שראוי לבוא בידי אדם הוא לא נפל בו מידי אדם ובזו העדות החכם מתירו להאכל במומו וכ"ש בעדות גדולה מזו. ומפורש כך בבכורות פ' כל פסילי המוקדשי'. וסלקא שמעתא התם דהלכתא כרשב"ג דאמר אפילו בנו ובתו נאמנים ויש מי שאומר כי עד מפי עד נאמן בבכור אדם וטעות הוא בידו : חלות דבש שריסקן מע"ש ויצאו מעצמן אסורין ור' אלעזר מתיר . כי אתא רב הושעיא מנהרדעא אתא יאייתי מתניתא בידיה זיתים וענבים שריסקן מע"ש ויצאו מעצמן אסורים . ור' אלעזר ור"ש מתירין . והא מתניתא מסייעא נמי לר' יוחנן : מתני' כל שבא בחמין מלפני השבת וכו' . ומיבעיא לן כגון מאי . ואמר רב ספרא כגון תרנגולתא דר' אבא שהיתה מלוחה ביותר וכשמבקשין לאוכלה שורין אותה במים חמין . אמר רב ספרא כגון זו התרנגולת אם הובאה בחמין מלפני השבת מותר לשרותה בחמין בשבת ולאוכלה . ואם לאו אסור לשרותה ומותר להדיחה והמליח הישן וקוליים האיספנין

רב נסים גאון

ואין עד מפי עד כשר אלא לעדות אשה בלבד כשאמר כי מת בעלה התירוה בית דין לינשא ואע"פ שהמועט העתיק דבר זה מזולתו וכמו שביארו דבר זה בפרק אשה שהלך בעלה וצרתה (דף קכב) והוחזקו להיות משיאין עד מפי עד וכו': **עד מפי עד בבכור מהו.** עיקר דיליה במסכת בכורות בפרק כל פסולי המוקדשין (דף לה) דתניא ר' יהושע בן קפוסאי אומר בכור בי כהן צריך ב' מן השוק להעיד עליו רבן שמעון בן גמליאל אומר אפילו בנו ובתו ואמרו הלכתא כרבן שמעון ודוקא בנו ובתו אבל אשתו לא מאי טעמא אשתו כגופו דמיא ועוד אמרו איבעיא להו עד מפי עד מהו לעדות בכור אמר ליה תני אלא לעדות אשה כשירה לו וכבר נתברר לנו שבתו כשירה והואיל ואשה כשירה לעדות בכור עד מפי עד נמי כשר לעדות בכור וכן פסקה ההלכה וזה שאמרו בבכור בהמה אבל בבכור אדם לא. גרסינן בפרק י' יוחסין (דף עד) ג' נאמנין על הבכור חיה ואמו ואביו חיה לאלתר אמו כל ז' אביו לעולם: כגון תרנגלתיה דר' אבא . כך פירשה אדונו האיי גאון ז"ל תרנגולת שמבשלין אותה ומוציאין אותה מהמרק וממלאין אותה בתבלין וכשרוצה לאכול מטמנה שורין אותה במים חמים ואוכלים אותה כאילו היא חמה : סליק פרק חבית

עין משפט נר מצוה

[ועי' שבות יעקב חלק ב' סימן קטו]

כ א מיי' פ"ב מהלכות בכורות הלכה טו סמג עשין ריא טוש"ע יו"ד סימן שיד סעיף ס :

כא ב מיי' פכ"א מהל' שבת הלכה טז טור שו"ע או"ח סימן רנג סעיף ה וסי' שכ סעיף ב:

כב ג מיי' פכ"ב שם הלכה ח סמג לאוין סה טוש"ע או"ח סימן שיח סעיף ד :

כג ד מיי' פ"כ מהלכות סנהדרין הלכה ז סמג עשין כז טור שו"ע חו"מ סימן י סעיף א :

מסורת הש"ס

[יבמות לא:] · בכורות לו. ע"ש · לעיל יט: · לעיל לט. · [דג שבמקומות האספניא ושמו בלשון הקודש שיבוטא ערוך ערך אספן] · [עי' לעיל כח.]

הגהות הב"ח

(א) גמ' לפי שאינן במקומן כצ"ל ותיבת בני נמחק :

ב"ב טז: · סנהדרין ז: · [יומא נד.] · בכורות מד: · [מגילה לא:]

לשון קומטוס כמו קומוס ולשון רומי הוא עי' רש"י סוטה יד ד"ה גסטרא

Continuation of translation from previous page as indicated by ◁

Why are the festivals in Babylon [so] joyous? Because they [its inhabitants] are poor.[13] Why are the scholars in Babylonia distinguished [in dress]? Because they are not well learned.[14] Why are idolaters lustful? Because they eat abominable and creeping things. R. Johanan awoke thereat [and] said to them, Children!
c did I not thus teach you: *Say unto wisdom, Thou art my sister:*[1] if the matter is as clear to thee as that thy sister is interdicted to thee, say it; but if not do not say it? Said they to him, Then let the Master tell us some of these? Why are the fowls of Babylonia fat? Because they were not sent into exile, as it is said, *Moab hath been at ease from his youth, and he hath settled on his lees . . . neither hath he gone into captivity. [Therefore his taste remaineth in him, and his scent is not changed]*.[2] And how do we know that they suffered exile here [in Palestine]? Because it was taught, R. Judah said: For fifty-two years no man passed through Judea, as it is said, *For the mountains will I take up a weeping and wailing, and for the pastures of the wilderness a lamentation, because they are burned up, so that none passeth through . . . both the fowl of the heavens and the beast* [behemah] *are fled, they are gone:*[3] the numerical value of *behemah* is fifty-two.[4] R. Jacob said in R. Johanan's name: They all returned save the colias of the Spaniards. For Rab said: The water courses of Babylonia carry back the water to the fountain of Etam;[5] but these [colias], since their spine is not firm, could not go up.[6] Why are the festivals in Babylonia joyous? Because they were not subject to that curse, whereof it is written, *I will also cause all her mirth to cease, her feasts, her new moons, her Sabbaths, and all her solemn assemblies;*[7] and it is written, *Your new moons and your appointed feasts My soul hateth: they are a trouble unto Me.*[8] What does '*they are a trouble unto Me*' mean?—Said R. Eleazar: The Holy One, blessed be He, saith, Not enough is it for Israel that they sin before Me, but that they trouble Me to know which evil decree I am to bring upon them. R. Isaac said: There is no single festival when troops
d did not come to Sepphoris.[1] R. Hanina said: There is no single festival when there did not come to Tiberias a general with his suite and centurions.[2]

Why are the scholars of Babylonia distinguished [in dress]? Because they are not in their [original] homes,[3] as people say, In my own town my name [is sufficient]; away from home, my dress.[4] *In days to come shall Jacob take root, Israel shall blossom* [yaziz] *and bud* [ufarah].[5] R. Joseph recited, This refers to scholars in Babylonia who wreathe blossoms [*zizin*] and flowers [*perahim*] around the Torah.[6]

Why are idolaters lustful? Because they did not stand at

(13) And live drably during the rest of the year, therefore they appreciate the festivals all the more. (14) Lit., 'they are not sons of (i.e., they do not possess) the Torah'.—Hence they have nothing else but dress to distinguish them.

c (1) Prov. VII, 4. (2) Jer. XLVIII, 11. The verse is quoted to show the adverse physical effects of exile. (3) Ibid. IX, 9 (E.V. 10). (4) I.e., ב = 2; ה = 5; מ = 40; ה = 5. Thus he translates: the fowl of the heavens is fled for fifty-two (years). Of course, the fifty-two years of desolation are based on historical figures (Meg. 11*b*), and this verse is merely quoted as a support or hint. (Tosaf.). (5) The highest eminence in Palestine (Zeb. 54*b*). According to Josephus (Ant. VIII, 7 § 3) it was sixty stadia south of Jerusalem, and it supplied the city with water. The *mikweh* used by the High Priest on the Day of Atonement, which was situated above the Water Gate, was also drawn thence (Yoma 31*a*).—Thus as the water flowed from Babylonia it carried along the fish which had migrated from Palestine. (6) The whole discussion was probably a mere *jeu d'esprit* as a relaxation after serious study. (7) Hos. II, 13. (8) Isa. I, 14.

d (1) In upper Galilee. They were quartered on the Jews and naturally hindered the joy of the festival. (2) אנגמון lit., 'cane bearer', but MS.O. reads: הגמון, a general. For קומטון Jast. suggests that קומים (= *comites*, members of the imperial cabinet) should be read. בעלי זמורה = rod bearers, i.e., centurions. (3) I.e., they hail from Palestine. (4) There I must make myself known and distinguished through dress.—This is certainly a more charitable explanation than the previous. (5) Isa. XXVII, 6. (6) This is in support of R. Johanan's estimate of the Babylonian scholars.

Mount Sinai. For when [146a] the serpent came upon Eve he injected a lust into her:[7] [as for] the Israelites who stood at Mount Sinai, their lustfulness departed; the idolaters, who did not stand at Mount Sinai, their lustfulness did not depart.[8] R. Aḥa son of Raba asked R. Ashi. What about proselytes?—Though they were not present, their guiding stars[9] were present, as it is written, [*Neither with you only do I make this covenant and this oath*], *but with him that standeth here with us this day before the Lord our God, and also with him that is not here with us this day*.[1] Now he differs from R. Abba b. Kahana, for R. Abba b. Kahana said: Until three generations the lustful [strain] did not disappear from our Patriarchs: Abraham begat Ishmael, Isaac begat Esau, [but] Jacob begat the twelve tribes in whom there was no taint whatsoever.[2]

MISHNAH. ONE MAY BREAK OPEN A CASK IN ORDER TO EAT RAISINS THEREOF, PROVIDED THAT HE DOES NOT DESIGN MAKING A UTENSIL;[3] AND ONE MAY NOT PERFORATE THE BUNG OF A CASK:[4] THIS IS R. JUDAH'S RULING; BUT THE SAGES PERMIT IT. AND ONE MUST NOT PIERCE IT AT THE SIDE THEREOF,[5] WHILE IF IT IS PERFORATED[6] ONE MUST NOT PLACE WAX UPON IT, BECAUSE HE CRUSHES IT.[7] R. JUDAH SAID: [SUCH] AN INCIDENT CAME BEFORE R. JOḤANAN B. ZAKKAI IN ARAB[8] AND HE SAID, I FEAR ON HIS ACCOUNT [THAT HE MAY BE LIABLE] TO A SIN-OFFERING.

GEMARA. R. Oshaia said: They learnt this only of pressed [raisins]; but not when they are loose [apart].[9] 'But not if they are loose [apart]'? An objection is raised: R. Simeon b. Gamaliel said: One may bring a cask of wine, strike off its head with a sword, and place it before guests on the Sabbath, and he need have no fear![10]—That is [according to] the Rabbis: our Mishnah is [according to] R. Nehemiah.[11] Now, what compels R. Oshaia to establish our Mishnah as agreeing with R. Nehemiah, so that it refers to pressed [raisins]; let him explain it as referring to loose [raisins] and [in agreement with] the Rabbis?—Said Raba, Our Mishnah presents a difficulty to him: why particularly teach 'RAISINS': let him [the Tanna] teach 'fruit?' Hence it follows thence that the reference is to pressed [raisins].

One [Baraitha] taught: One may untie, unravel, or cut
b through the wicker wrappers of raisins and dates.[1] Another was taught: One may untie, but not unravel or cut. There is no difficulty: one agrees with the Rabbis; the other with R. Nehemiah. For it was taught, R. Nehemiah said: Even a spoon, even a robe, and even a knife may be handled only when required for their [usual] function.

R. Shesheth was asked: What about piercing a cask with a spit[2] on the Sabbath? does he intend [making] an opening, so it is forbidden, or perhaps his intention is to be generous[3] and it is permitted?—He intends [making] an opening, replied he, and it is forbidden. An objection is raised: R. Simeon b. Gamaliel said: One may bring a cask of wine and strike off its head with a sword?—There his intention is certainly to be generous: but here, if he really means to be generous, let him open it.[4]

ONE MAY NOT PERFORATE THE BUNG, etc. R. Huna said: The controversy is [in respect of a hole] at the top;[5] but all agree that it is forbidden at the side,[6] and thus he teaches, ONE MUST NOT PIERCE IT AT THE SIDE THEREOF. But R. Ḥisda maintained: The controversy is in [respect of a hole] at the side, but all agree that it is permitted on the top, and as to what he teaches, ONE MUST NOT PIERCE IT AT THE SIDE THEREOF, there it refers
c to the cask itself.[1]

Our Rabbis taught: One may not pierce a new hole[2] on the Sabbath, but if one comes to add,[3] he may add; but some say, One may not add. But they all agree that one may pierce an old hole[4] at the very outset. Now as to the first Tanna, wherein does it differ from [boring] a new hole, which may not [be done]? [Presumably] because an opening is [thereby] effected! Then in adding too an opening is improved [effected]?[5]—Said Rabbah: By the words of the Torah[6] every opening which is not made for putting in and taking out is not an opening, and it was the Rabbis who forbade it[7] on account of [the ventilation of] a hen-coop, which is made to permit the fresh air to enter and the fumes to pass out.[8] Hence 'if one comes to add, he may add': [for] in a hen-coop one will certainly not come to add,

(7) Cf. II Esdras IV, 30. (8) The idea is that the serpent infected Eve (i.e., the human race) with lust, from which, however, those who accept the moral teachings of the Torah are freed. Cf. B.B. 16a: The Holy One, blessed be He, created the evil passions, but He also created the Torah as their antidote. Thus this passage does not teach the doctrine of 'Original Sin', which Judaism rejects; v. Hertz, *Genesis*, pp. 59-60, 'Jewish view on the "Fall of Man"'. V. also Weiss, *Dor*, II, p. 9. (9) On *mazzal* v. Sanh., 94a, n. 10.

(1) Deut. XXIX, 14f. The teachings of Judaism and its spiritual ennoblement were freely meant for all mankind. (2) Even before the Revelation at Sinai. (3) I.e., a proper opening for the cask; this constitutes a labour. (4) If it is tightly fitted in the cask, so that wine etc., may be poured out through the perforation. R. Ḥan. regards the bung as the whole cover fitted into the top of the cask. (5) This is explained in the Gemara. (6) And one wishes to close the holes. (7) I.e., he spreads it, which is forbidden. (8) V. *supra* 121a, n. b5. (9) If the raisins are pressed together, a knife must be handled for cutting them out, and at the same time the barrel may be broken open with it. But if they are loose, so that a knife or axe is not required, it may not be handled merely for breaking the cask open. (10) Of violating the Sabbath. (11) That a utensil may be handled only for its normal use.

b (1) Unripe dates and raisins were packed in wrappers made of plaited palm branches, to ripen. If the wrapper is tied with a cord one may untie it, unravel its strands, or cut it. (2) I.e., by forcing it between the splices. (3) Lit., 'a good eye'—i.e., to widen the opening so that the wine may flow freely, not niggardly, but he does not mean to make a permanent opening. (4) By withdrawing the bung, when the wine would flow no less freely. (5) There the Rabbis permit it, because it is unusual to make an opening there, but rather the whole bung is removed. (6) As an opening is sometimes made there in preference to withdrawing the stopper from the top, lest dust etc., fall in. 'Side' and 'top' both refer to the bung or lid, viz., the side of the bung and the top of the bung, but not to the sides of the cask itself.

c (1) Not the bung. (2) In a vessel. (3) I.e., enlarge an existing hole. (4) Which became stopped up. (5) מתקן may mean both effected and improved.—By enlarging the hole he completes its work. (6) By Pentateuchal law. (7) *Sc.* the hole under discussion, as the wine is not poured into the barrel through it. (8) V. *supra* 102b.

כשבא נחש על חוה · כשנתן לה עלה לאכול מן העץ בא אליה דכתיב (בראשית ג) הנחש השיאני לשון נשואין : גרים מאי · שלא היו על הר סיני מהיכן פסקה זוהמא : מזלייהו הוו · בסיני וכל שעמדו על הר סיני נתקדשו ונטהרו ונתרפאו מכל מום ואף עורים ופסחים שהיו בישראל כדתניא בספרי: תורה אור

ופליגא · הא דאמרן דלא פסקה זוהמא עד סיני : מתני' שובר אדם חבית · מליאה גרוגרות בסכין או בסייף לאכול ממנה גרוגרות דאין במקלקל שום איסור בשבת : ובלבד שלא יתכוין לעשות כלי · לנוקבה יפה בפתח נאה : אין נוקבין מגופה · הדבוקה (ג) בפה החבית לעשות נקב אלא נוטל את כולה אבל כי נקיב לה מתקן פתחא : וחכמים מתירין · דאין דרך פתח לחבית בכך : ולא יקבנה מלידה · בגמרא מפרש לה : שהוא ממרח · ויש כאן משום ממחק: בערב · מדינה* : מחטאת · שמא מירח השעוה לדובקה בדופני הכלי סביב הנקב : גמ' לא שנו · דשובר החבית ומטלטל הסייף לכך : אלא בדרוסות· שהגרוגרות דרוסות בעיגול וחותכין ממנו בקורדום או בסייף ואיידי דמטלטל סייף לחתוך גרוגרות תבר ביה נמי לחבית: אבל מפורדות · שא"ל לחתכן לא יטלטל סייף לשבור החבית(ד)דמתני' ר' נחמיה דאמר אין כלי ניטל אלא לתשמיש המיוחד לו כדמוקי לקמן : ואינו חושש · ואע"ג דיין לאו למהתכיה קאי : רבנן היא · דפליגי אדר' נחמיה ואמרי כל הכלים ניטלים לצורך ושלא לצורך : חותלות · כלי של כפות תמרים ועושין כמין סלים ונותנים לתוכן תמרים רעים להתבשל: מתיר · אם הכסוי קשור בחבל : אבל לא מפקיע · סותר שרשרות החבל בכלי : ולא חותך · דאין כלי ניטל אלא לצורך תשמישו וסכין אינו עשוי לכך : למיברז · לתחוב פויינדור"א בלע"ז : בבורטיא · ברומח לתוחבו בדופניה לנקוב : לעין יפה · להרחיב מולא היין בנקב גדול מדלא נקיב ליה כדרך הנוקבין נקב עגול ויפה : התם ודאי לעין יפה קמיכוין·שמרחיב פיה למטה ממגופתה כדקתני מתיז את ראשה שפת פיה: לפתוחי מיפתח· יטול מגופתה : למעלה·בראש המגופה התם הוא דשרו רבנן דלאו אורחא למיעבד פתחא התם אלא נוטל כל המגופה : אבל מלדה · זמנין דעבדי לה משום פתחא ואינו רוצה לפותחה למעלה שלא יפול עפר או פסולת ביין : היינו דקתני ולא יקבנה מלדה· ואמגופה קאי ודברי הכל: מחלוקת מן הצד · התם הוא דקאסר רבי יהודה משום דאיכא דעבדי ליה פתחא : אין נוקבין נקב חדש· בכלי : נקב ישן · שנסתם דכי חוזר ופותח לאו כעושה פתח הוא שהרי עשוי ועומד וסתימתו לאו כלום : אוסופי נמי קמתקן פתחא · שמרחיבו ויש כאן משום גמר מלאכה : הבלא · סרחון שלא ימותו התרנגולין : ואם בא להוסיף מוסיף · ולא גזרינן דילמא אתי לאוסופי בלול של תרגולין דלא מוסיף איניש עליה:

משום

*שבא נחש על חוה הטיל בה זוהמא ישראל שעמדו על הר סיני פסקה זוהמתן עובדי כוכבי' שלא עמדו על הר סיני לא פסקה זוהמתן א"ל רב אחא בריה דרבא לרב אשי גרים מאי א"ל אע"ג דאינהו לא הוו מזליידהו הוו דכתיב °את אשר ישנו פה עמנו עומד היום לפני ה' אלהינו ואת אשר איננו פה וגו' ופליגא דר' אבא בר כהנא דא"ר אבא בר כהנא עד שלשה דורות לא פסקה זוהמא מאבותינו אברהם הוליד את ישמעאל יצחק הוליד את עשו יעקב הוליד י"ב שבטים שלא היה בהן שום דופי : מתני' *[א]שובר אדם את החבית לאכול הימנה גרוגרות ובלבד שלא יתכוין לעשות כלי ואין נוקבין מגופה של חבית דברי ר' יהודה *וחכמים [ב]מתירין ולא יקבנה מצדה ואם [ג]היתה נקובה לא יתן עליה שעוה מפני שהוא ממרח אמר ר' יהודה *מעשה בא לפני רבן יוחנן בן זכאי בערב ואמר חוששני לו מחטאת : גמ' א"ר אושעיא ל"ש אלא דרוסות אבל מפורדות לא ומפורדות לא מיתיבי ר' שמעון בן גמליאל אומר מביא אדם את החבית של יין ומתיז ראשה בסייף ומניחה לפני האורחים בשבת ואינו חושש ההיא רבנן (א) מתני' רבי נחמיה היא ומאי דוחקיה דרבי אושעיא לאוקמי מתניתין כרבי נחמיה ובדרוסות לוקמה במפורדות ורבנן אמר רבא מתני' קשיתיה מאי איריא דתני גרוגרות ליתני פירות אלא ש"מ בדרוסות תניא חדא [ד]חותלות של גרוגרות ושל תמרים מתיר ומפקיע וחותך ותניא אידך מתיר אבל לא מפקיע ולא חותך לא קשיא הא רבנן הא ר' נחמיה *דתניא ר' נחמיה אומר אפי' תרווד ואפילו טלית ואפילו סכין אין ניטלין אלא לצורך תשמישן [א] בעו מיניה מרב ששת °מהו למיברז חביתא בבורטיא בשבתא לפיתחא קמיכוין ואסיר או דילמא לעין יפה קמיכוין ושרי א"ל [ה]לפיתחא קא מכוין ואסיר מיתיבי רשב"ג אומר [ו]מביא אדם חבית של יין ומתיז ראשה בסייף התם ודאי לעין יפה קמיכוין הכא אם איתא דלעין יפה קמיכוין לפתוחי מיפתח : אין נוקבין מגופה וכו' : אמר רב הונא מחלוקת למעלה [ז]אבל מן הצד דברי הכל אסור והיינו דקתני לא יקבנה מצדה ורב חסדא אמר מחלוקת מן הצד אבל על גבה דברי הכל מותר והא דקתני לא יקבנה מצדה התם בגופה דחבית תנו רבנן [ח]אין נוקבין נקב חדש בשבת ואם בא להוסיף מוסיף ויש אומרים [ט]אין מוסיפין ושוין שנוקבין (ג) נקב ישן לכתחילה. ותנא קמא מאי שנא מנקב חדש דלא דקא מתקן פיתחא אוסופי נמי קא מתקן פיתחא אמר רבה [י]דבר תורה כל פתח שאינו עשוי להכנים ולהוציא אינו פתח ורבנן הוא דגזור משום לול של תרנגולין *דעביד לעיולי אוירא ולאפוקי הבלא ואם בא להוסיף מוסיף אוסופי ודאי בלול של תרנגולים לא אתי לאוסופי

משום

שובר אדם את החבית לאכול הימנה גרוגרות · בגמרא מוקי לה בדרוסות לרבי נחמיה אבל לרבנן דרבי נחמיה שרי אפילו מפורדות ותימה לרבי מהא דתנן בפרק בכל מערבין (עירובין דף לד: ושם) גבי עירוב נתנו במגדל ונועל בפניו ואבד המפתח הרי זה עירוב ופריך בגמרא אמאי הוא במקום אחד ועירובו במקום אחר הוא ומשני רב ושמואל דאמרי תרווייהו הכא במגדל של (ה) בנין עסקינן ור"מ היא כו' ואמאי מבעי ליה לאוקמא הכי ומעיקרא נמי מאי קאמר והלא יכול לשבר ולפתוח את המגדל וליטול את העירוב כי היכי דהכא שרי לשבר החבית וליטול הגרוגרות ואם בא לחלק בין נטילת העירוב לנטילת הגרוגרות א"כ קשה היכי מוקי לה התם כר' מאיר ונראה דהתם אסור לשבר את המגדל והכא דשרי לשבר את החבית משום דמיירי במוסתקי כדמוקי לה בביצה פרק המביא כדי יין (דף לג: ושם) ומפ' רש"י התם דהיינו חבית שבורה ומדבקין שבריה בשרף של עץ שעושה ממנו זפת וקורין רייש"א ומש"ה דוקא חבית שרי דמחמת גריעותו לא חיים עליה וליכא למיחש שמא יתכוין לעשות כלי וכן כולה שמעתא דהכא במוסתקי ואע"ג דהתם בביצה לא מוקמינן הכי אלא לר"א דפריך ולית ליה לר"א הא דתנן שובר אדם את החבית כו' ועלה משני מתני' במוסתקי מ"מ אפילו לרבנן מיבעי לאוקמי הכי דרבנן לא פליגי אדר"א דקאמר לא יקטמנו פי' לא יקטום את ההדס להריח בו אלא משום דאיהו סבירא ליה דבקטימת קיסם חייב חטאת כשקוטמו להצות בו שיניו וא"כ אי לא מוקמינן לה במוסתקי עלייהו איכא למיפרך ולית להו הא דתנן כו' הלכך מיבעי לן למימר דאליבא דכולהו מיירי מתניתין במוסתקי והשתא אתיא שמעתא שפיר · מ"ר · ובגמ' ירושלמי בפרק בכל מערבין מגלאתי הדא דתימא במגדל של אבן אבל במגדל של עץ נעשה כשובר החבית לאכול ממנה גרוגרות :

מתיר ומפקיע וחותך. אומר רבי מההיא דעירובין (דף לד:) יש ללמוד דהא דאמרינן (ביצה דף לא:) חותמות שבכלים מתיר ומפקיע וחותך היינו כגון דקטיר במיתנא אבל פותחת של עץ ושל מתכת אסור לשבר ולהפקיע מדקשיא ליה התם אמאי הוא במקום אחד ועירובו במקום אחר דפשיטא ליה שאינו יכול להפקיע הפותחת וליטול העירוב אע"פ שסתם מגדל שבכל הש"ס הוא כלי כמו הלד לבי לבית ולפור למגדל וכי ההיא דבריש כל הכלים (לעיל קכב:) ובמסקנא נמי לא בעי לאוקומי אלא בקטיר במיתנא דהיינו דוקא חותמות שבכלים אבל דבר שהוא חזק כעין פותחת לא הוה שרי ת"ק · מ"ר* :

הא רבנן והא ר' נחמיה · תימה לי אמאי לא מוקי תרווייהו כר' נחמיה והא דקתני מתיר מפקיע וחותך ביו"ט והא דקתני מתיר אבל לא מפקיע וחותך בשבת דאיכא תנא דס"ל הכי אליבא דר' נחמיה בביצה בפ' המביא כדי יין (לב:) וי"ל דניחא ליה למימר חדא כרבנן מדנימא תרווייהו כר' נחמיה :

משום

[דברים כט] [שם סוף כב:] [יבמות קג:] [לעיל קכה. פ"כ"י שם מקום] [פ"א ר' יוסי מתיר] [לעיל קכה.] [ביצה לג:] [עירובין לה. ביצה לב: [תוספתא פט"ו]] [ועי' תוס' עירובין לה: ד"ה נעי סכינא] [לעיל קב:]

עין משפט נר מצוה

כד א מיי' פכ"ג מהל' שבת הלכה ב סמג לאוין סה טוש"ע או"ח סימן שיד סעיף א :

כה ב מיי' שם טוש"ע שם סעיף ו :

כו ג מיי' שם הלכה יא טוש"ע שם סעיף יא:

כז ד שם סעיף ח :

כח ה ו ז מיי' שם הל' ב טור שו"ע שם סעיף ו :

כט ח ט מיי' שם הל"א טוש"ע שם סעיף א:

ל י מיי' שם הל"א ופ"י הלכה טז סמג שם :

הגהות הב"ח

(א) גמ' ההיא רבנן היא מתניתין : (ב) שם בנקב ישן : (ג) רש"י ד"ה אין נוקבין וכו' הדבוקה בפי החבית : (ד) ד"ה אבל מפורדות וכו' החבית הס"ד ואח"כ מ"ה ואינו חושש וכו' קאי הס"ד ואח"כ מ"ה ההיא רבנן הוא וכו' ושלא לצורך הס"ד ואח"כ מ"ה מתני' ר' נחמיה היא דאמר אין כלי וכו' לקמן הס"ד ואח"כ מ"ה חותלות וכו' תמרים ועשוין כמין סלים:(ה) תוס' ד"ה שובר וכו' במגדל של לבנים עסקי' :

הגהות הגר"א

[א] גמ' בעו מיני' מרב ששת מהו למיברז . נ"ב ר"ל במקום שנקב אסור אם ברומח מותר טוב :

גליון הש"ס

גמרא מהו למיברז חביתא. ע"ל דף מח ע"ב תוס' ד"ה וכי מה בין :

רבינו חננאל

אם לא הביאם בחמין מלפני השבת אפילו להדיחן בשבת אסור ואם עבר והדיחן חייב חטאת שנגמר מלאכה . פי' מכותא מכותתא היא . ויש מי שאומר כותא כותחא היא בדיחי במערבא חולים שבמערב : מתני' שובר אדם את החבית לאכול ממנה גרוגרות כו' . א"ר הושעיא לא ששובר את החבית לאכול ממנה גרוגרות אלא דרוסות אבל מפורדות אינו שובר החבית אלא מוציא גרוגרות ואוכל ואינו שובר . ואוקימנא למתניתין כר' נחמיה . מדקתני גרוגרות ולא קתני פירות . והא דתניא רשב"ג אומר מביא אדם חבית של יין ומתיז ראשה בסייף ומניחה לפני האורחים בשבת ואינו חושש לרבנן . וכן הא דתני חותלות של תמרים ושל גרוגרות ומתיר ומפקיע וחותך לרבנן והא דתני מתיר אבל לא מפקיע ולא חותך ר' נחמיה דאמר אפילו תרווד ואפילו טלית אין נוטלין אלא לצורך תשמישן : בעו מיניה דרב ששת מהו למיברז חביתא בבורטיא . פי' לנקוב חבית ברומח . ויש שאומר במקדח ומסקנא לפיתחא קא מיכוין ואסיר : פיס' אין נוקבין מגופה של החבית . פי' מגופה כסוי החבית דברי ר' יהודה וחכמים מתירין והלכה כחכמים . והני מילי שיהא הנקב בגג הכסוי אבל לנקב נקב בצד הכסוי אסור כדתנן לא יקבנה מצדה שהוא דברי הכל . וכרב הונא דהלכתא כוותיה . דהוא לגביה דרב חסדא רבו וליתא לדרב חסדא: ת"ר אין נוקבין נקב חדש בשבת . ואם בא להוסיף מוסיף ואקשינן עלה למה אסור לנקוב נקב חדש שנמצא מתקן פתח גם בהוסיפו בנקב ומרחיבו נמצא מתקן פתח . ולמה מותר ופריך רבא מן התורה כל פתח שאינו עשוי להכנים ולהוציא אינו חשוב פתח . ואלו הנקבים כולן אין מכניסין בהן אלא להוציא הן עשויין לבלבד ומתירין . ורבנן גזרו על כל נקב בבית התרנגולין דהא הנקרא לול של תרנגולים כדכתיב ובלולים יעלו . וזה לול של תרנגולים שעשוי להכניס בו רוח ולהוציא הבחמות ולא כמין פתח נעשה . ומפני שדרך בני אדם להרחיב בלול של תרנגולים כי מתיירא שלא יכנס מכנו הנחש ויזיק אותן . וכיון שאין דרך בני אדם להרחיבה לא גזרו ברחבתו כל נקב . והוא טעם ת"ק . וי"א

מישום ריחשא וי"א אין מוסיפים זימנין דלא תקניה מעיקרא ואתי לארוחי ביה דרש רב נחמן משום רבי יוחנן הלכה כיש אומרים: *ושוין שנוקבין נקב ישן לכתחלה: אמר רב יהודה אמר שמואל לא שנו אלא במקום העשוי לשמר אבל לחזק אסור היכי דמי *לישמר היכי דמי לחזק °א"ר חסדא למעלה מן היין זהו לשמר למטה מן היין זהו לחזק (א) רבא אמר ג)למטה מן היין נמי זהו לשמר והיכי דמי לחזק כגון שניקבה למטה מן השמרים א"ל אביי לרבא תניא דמסייע לך *ד)בית סתום יש לו ארבע אמות פרץ את פצימיו אין לו ד' אמות ה)בית סתום אינו מטמא כל סביביו פרץ את פצימיו מטמא כל סביביו גוזבתא רב אסר ושמואל שרי ו)מהתך לכתהלה דכ"ע לא פליגי דאסור אהדורי דכ"ע לא פליגי דשרי כי פליגי דהתיכה ולא מתקנא מאן דאסר גזרינן דילמא אתי למיחתך לכתהלה ומאן דשרי ז)לא גזרינן כתנאי אין הותכין שפופרת ביו"ט וא"צ לומר בשבת נפלה (אין) מהזירין אותה בשבת ואין צריך לומר ביו"ט ור' יאשיה מיקל ר' יאשיה אהייא אילימא ארישא הא קמתקן מנא אלא אסיפא ת"ק נמי מישרא קשרי אלא דחתיכה ולא מתקנא איכא בינייהו מ"ס גזרינן ומ"ס לא גזרינן דרש רב שישא בריה דרב אידי משמיה דר' יוחנן הלכה כר' יאשיה: ואם היתה נקובה וכו': מישהא רב אסר ושמואל שרי מאן דאסר ח)גזרינן משום שעוה ומאן דשרי לא גזרינן אמר ליה רב שמואל בר בר חנה לרב יוסף בפירוש אמרת לן משמיה דרב מישחא שרי אמר טבות ריש בא אמר שמואל האי טרפא דאסא אסור מ"ט רב ייסר מדפתי אמר גזירה משום מרזב רב אשי אמר ט)גזירה שמא יקטום מאי בינייהו [א] איכא בינייהו דקטים ומנחי בי סדיא רב אסר ושמואל כ)שרי ברכין דבולי עלמא לא פליגי דשרי ל)בקשין דכ"ע לא פליגי דאסור כי פליגי במיצעי מאן דאסר מיהוי כמשוי ומאן דשרי לא מיהוי כמשוי והא דרב לאו *בפירוש איתמר אלא מכללא איתמר [נדפו"ם ס.] דרב איקלע להוא אתרא דלא הוה ליה רווחא נפק יתיב בכרמלית אייתו ליה בי סדיא לא יתיב מאן דחזא סבר משום דבי סדיא אסור ולא היא דרב אברוזי מבריז בי סדיא שרי °ומשום כבוד רבותינו לא יישב עליו ומאן נינהו רב כהנא ורב אסי: **מתני'** *מ)נותנין [ביצה לג.] תבשיל לתוך הבור בשביל שיהא שמור ואת המים היפים ברעים בשביל שיצננו ואת הצונן בחמה בשביל שיחמו *מי שנשרו כליו בדרך במים מהלך בהן ואינו [ביצה לג:] חושש הגיע לחצר החיצונה שוטחן בחמה [ג] אבל לא כנגד העם: **גמ'** פשיטא מהו דתימא ניגזור משום אשויי גומות קא משמע לן: ואת המים היפים ברעים: פשיטא סיפא איצטריכא ליה ואת הצונן בחמה הא נמי פשיטא מהו דתימא ניגזור דילמא אתי לאטמוני ברמץ קמ"ל: ל)מי שנשרו וכו': *אמר רב יהודה אמר רב כ)כל מקום שאסרו חכמים מפני מראית העין אפילו בחדרי חדרים אסור תנן שוטחן בחמה אבל לא כנגד העם תנאי היא דתניא שוטחן בחמה אבל לא כנגד העם ר"א ור"ש נ)אוסרין אמר רב הונא המנער

רש"י

משום ריחשא· שלא יכנס בו שרץ כגון *נמייה וחולדה שממיתים את התרנגולים: זימנין דלא תקיה מעיקרא · שיהא כדי להוציא הבל ולהכניס את האויר: לא שנו · דנוקבין: אלא במקום · דסתימה זו לא נעשית אלא לשמור ריח היין שלא יצא ויתקלקל וכיון דלאו סתימה מעליותא עבדי לה לאו כלום הוא: לחזק · שיחזק הכלי שלא יצא יינו הואיל וסתימה מעלייתא היא כי הדר נקיב לה הוי כפותח לכתחלה: למטה מן היין נמי לשמר הוא · כיון דלאו כובד היין נשען עליו סגי ליה בסתימה כל דהו: למטה מן השמרים · אגל שוליו שכל כובד היין נשען שם: תניא דמסייע לך · דלא פקע שם פתח מיניה אלא בסתימה מעלייתא: בית סתום יש לו ד"א · קיי"ל בבבא בתרא חצר מתחלקת לפי פתחיה לפי פתח הבתים הפתוחין לה אם באו לחלק את החצר בין שנים שהיה לזה בית שפתוחין לו לחצר שני פתחים ולזה בית שפתוחין לו לחצר ד' פתחים נוטל נכל פתח ארבע אמות בחצר נגד פתחו למדת רוחב פתחו והשאר חולקין בשוה ואם נסתם אחד מהם קודם חלוקת החצר ולא פירץ את פצימיו אלא סתם בין שני הפצימין אינו מפסיד [דין] פתחו בכך פירץ את פצימיו והח"כ סתמו פקע שם פתח מיניה: בית סתום · והמת בתוכו אינו מטמא סביביו: פרץ פצימיו · וסתמו נעשה קבר ומטמא סביביו ד"א כדאמרי' בסוטה (ד' מד·) מת תופס ד"א לטומאה וגזרה דרבנן שמא יאהיל ולא יבין: גובתא · לתקוע קנה חלול בנקב החבית שילא היין דרך הקנה: מחתך · רוגיי"ר לתקנה למדת הנקב: אהדורי · אם נפלה: ולא מתקנא · לא ניתנה בנקב לידע אם למדתו היא: אי לימא ארישא · לחותכה ולשפותה: משחא · שמן עב אסור · למרחו: טרפא דאסא · ליתן עלה של הדס בנקב החבית שתעלה עשוי כמרזב והיין זב דרך שם: גזירה משום מרזב · שמא יכין מרזב: שמא יקטום · העלה מן הענף וכיון דקטמיה הוה ליה כמתקן כלי כדתניא במסכת ביצה (דף לג:) לחוות בו שיניו לא יקטמנו ואם קטמו חייב חטאת: בי סדיא · לבדין שקורין פלטר"ש ועשויין לקפלן תחתיו במקום הכר או הכסת: רב אסר · להביאו דרך מלבוש דרך רשות הרבים כשהוא מעוטף בו: ברכין · שדרכן להתחמם בהן: דשרו · דמלבוש הן: ולא הוה ליה רווחא · בבית למקום מושבם של תלמידים: ומשום כבוד רבותינו · שלא היה להן דבר לישב עליו ויושבין על גבי קרקע: רב כהנא ורב אסי · תלמידי חברים היו לו*: **מתני'** לתוך הבור · שאין בו מים: שיהא שמור · שלא יסריח מחמת החום: ואת המים היפים ברעים · כלי מלא מים יפים לתוך מקוה מים רעים להשתמר (ג) שיצונו ולא יחמו: מי שנשרו · שנפלו למים בשבת: לחצר החיצונה · הסמוכה למבוא העיר בתוך העיר שהוא מקום משתמר: שוטחן בחמה · ליבשן: אבל לא כנגד העם · שיחשדוהו שכבסן: **גמ'** פשיטא · דטתנין תבשיל לתוך הבור: גומות · שבקרקע הבור שיהו שוין להושיב הקדרה:

המנער

תוספות

משום ריחשא · ולאו פתחא אחרינא דליכא למיחש לריחשא לא גזרינן דדוקא אבו טול של תרנגולין גזרינן דלא מסקי אינשי אדעתייהו שיהא עשוי להכניס ולהוציא:

פריץ פצימיו מטמא כל סביביו · פי' בקונטרס כל סביביו ד' אמות כקבר ואין נראה לזקיני הרב ר' שמשון זצ"ל דכיון דמסיימי מחילתא ולית לן למיחש שמא יעלה על הבית ויאהיל עליו ולא ידע לית לן למימר דמטמא ד' אמות כל סביביו כדמוכח בסוטה פרק משוח מלחמה (ד' מד·) גבי חצר הקבר העומד בתוכה טהור הני מילי חצר הקבר דמסיימא מחילתא אבל מת בעלמא תפיס ומשמע דבמת נמי היכא דמסיימא לא נטמא כל סביביו ד' אמות אלא נראה לו דהכי פי' זיזין בולטין מחוץ לבית מכל צד ויש בהם פותח טפח בכל אחד אם הבית סתום ועדיין נראית בו צורת הפתח הוא מטמא בסתמו של מת עומד לצאת דרך הפתח פרץ פצימיו וחזר ובנאו כשאר כותל ולא נותר בו כלל פתח מטמא כל סביביו דכל חד וחד איכא לספוקי דילמא דרך אותו מקום יצא מן הבית מיהו לאו פירכא היא כולי האי מה שהקשה לפירוש הקונטרס די"ל שלא חלקו חכמים במת ועוד נראה דלא קשה כלל לפי' הקונטרס דבית נמי לא מסיימי מחילתא בהוא מטמא הנוגע בכתלים אפילו לא יעלה על גביו כקבר שמטמא במגע אפילו מן הצד כדתניא בספרי בפרשת פרה אדומה או בקבר זה קבר סתום או אינו אלא קבר פתוח אמרת ק"ו ומה אהל שמקבל טומאה אינו מטמא מכל צדדין כשהוא פתוח קבר שאינו מקבל טומאה אינו דין שלא יטמא מכל צדדין כשהוא פתוח הא למה כשהוא סתום מטמא אף הנוגע מן הצד:

הלכה כרבי יאשיה · הלכך מותר לתת לכתחילה גובתא שקורין קנזיי"ל בחבית:

משום מרזב. פי' הרב פור"ת שלא יבוא ליתן על גגו מרזב וקשה דבגובתא נמי נגזר אלא נראה לרבי כפי' הקונט' שלא יתקן מרזב לייטו שיפול היין בתוכו וילך למרחוק דכשלוקח עלה של הדס ומקפלו כעין מרזב נראה כעושה מרזב אבל בגובתא שאינו עושה בו שום מעשה לא גזרינן · מ"ר:

אייתי ליה בי סדיא · בי מילעי הוה דלי לאו הכי היכי איתמר מכללא:

מי שנשרו כליו במים · בדרך גרסינן) לשון נפילה לא כפי' הקונטרס לעיל בפרק במה אשה (דף כה·) שנשרו במי גשמים דהא אמרינן בביצה בפרק משילין (דף לה:) מאן דתני מנשירין לא משתבש כדתנן מי שנשרו כליו במים בדרך אלמא לשון נפילה הוא · ג) מ"ר:

א) ר"ל דגרסי' הנו"ן דנשרו בקמץ לשון נפילה דאלו הנו"ן בחירק הוי לשון שרייה. רש"ל ג) [ועי' תוס' ביצה לה: ד"ה מי שנשרו]

רבינו חננאל

וי"א אין מוסיפין דזמנין דלא תקניה מעיקרא ואתי לארוחי ביה הלכתא כוותיה דדרש רב נחמן בר רב חסדא משמיה דר' יוחנן הלכה כי"א . ושוין שנוקבין נקב ישן לכתחלה ואמר רב יהודה משמיה דשמואל אינו מותר לפתוח נקב ישן אלא במקום העשוי לשמר פי' להוציא היין מן השמרים אבל לחזק אסור פי' היה נקב בחבית וסתמו שלא יהא שותת . וחלקו רב חסדא ורבה והלכתא כרבה דתניא מסייעתו ואלו דברי רבה רבה אמר למטה מן היין נמי זהו לשמר ומותר לפותחו והיכי דמי לחזק כגון שנקבה למטה מן השמרים דמוכחא מלתא שאין אדם עושה נקב בקרקעיתא של חבית להוציא יין ולא לשמר . עשאי מפני כשמפנה החבית הופכה על פיה. וזה הנקב כיון שסתמו נעשה סתום . זה בגופה של הבית ובטל מלהיות נקב בו וחשוב כפתח בית הנסתם בפירוץ פצימין שנסתלק ממנו דין פתח לגמרי . גובתא שהיא שפופרת של קנה או של עצים שנותנין בנקב החבית או ביד הנוד של יין להיות מושכין ממנו יין מן החבית או מן הנוד . רב אסר ושמואל שרי ואוקימנא חלוקתן בשפופרת חתוכה. ואינה מתוקנת להכניסה לנקב אבל לחתוך דברי הכל אסור . ואם היא חתוכה ומתוקנת דברי הכל מותר להחזירה בנקב החבית או בנוד למשוך ממנה יין . והעמדנו עוד חלוקת רב ושמואל כתנאי . דתניא אין חותכין שפופרת ביו"ט ואין צ"ל בשבת . נפלה מחזירין בשבת . ואין צ"ל ביו"ם . ור' יאשיה מיקל ודייקי' עלה ר' יאשיה אהייא מיקל אילימא ארישא שאמר ת"ק אין חותכין כלומר אין חותכין מקנה גדול חתיכה לעשות' שפופרת הא ר' יאשיה מיקל בהא קא מתקן כלי בשבת אלא שאמר ת"ק נפלה מחזירין אותה . בהא ליטא ר' יאשיה מיקל מי החמיר שיאמר בזה מיקל הלא בזה גם ת"ק מותר קאמר . ותריצנא אלא לאו דחתיכה ולא מתקנה איכא בינייהו וכך הציעה . אין עושין שפופרת ביו"ט ואין צ"ל בשבת . ואפי' חתכה ולא מתקנה אסור אבל אם היתה כבר בחבית ונפלה מחזירין אותה בשבת ואין צ"ל ביו"ט ור' יאשיה מיקל בחתיכה ולא מתקנה נמצאו דברי רב כת"ק ודברי שמואל כר' יאשיה והלכה כר' יאשיה ודרש רב שישא בריה דרב אידי משמא דר' יוחנן הלכתא כר' יאשיה וזה שאמר חתכה ולא מתקנה לאו שצריכה תיקון כלי כגון סכין וכדומה לו אלא תיקון ביד בלבד . ואם צריכה תיקון בסכין או זולתו סכין כלי אחר אסורה . ואם היתה החבית נקובה לא יתן עליה שעוה מפני שממרח. כלומר סותם כדאמרינן התם לענין חבית שניקבה וסתמה שמרים כו' מורח מן הצדדין. וכיון דר' יהודה דמתניתין וריב"ז ורב ושמואל אמרי ש"מ שאסור לתת שעוה בחבית . וכן משחא. רב אסר גזירה במשחא אטו שעוה. והלכתא כוותיה: טרפא דאסא. פי' עלה הדס שנותנין על הנקב של חבית להיות מקלח בו היין ולא יהיה שותת בדופני החבית . לדברי הכל אסור ליטול עלה של הדס בשבת ולשומו בנקב של חבית כמרזב . ואפילו רב אשי לא התיר אלא שאם היה הנקב מושך ממנו *) אבל לתתו לכתחלה אוסר : בי סדיא רב אסר ושמואל שרי אין זה מקומו אלא בשביל שהזכיר השמועות שחלקו בהן רב אסר ושמואל שרי נסבה בגררא . ופשוטה היא . כסת זו שחלקו בה כסת בינונית לא דקה ולא קשה . ומסקינן בה אפילו זו מותר לטלטלה: נותנין תבשיל בתוך הבור בשביל שיהא שמור. פי' בור זה אין בו מים ונותן התבשיל בקרקעיתו מהו דתימא לגזור דלמא אתי לאשויי גומות קמ"ל דלא גזרינן . ואת המים היפים ברעים פשיטא ואת הצונן בחמה פשיטא מהו דתימא לגזור דלמא אתי לאשויי גומות **) ברמץ קמ"ל דלא גזרינן : מתני' מי שנשרו כליו בדרך כו'. אמר רב יהודה אמר רב כל מקום שאסרו חכמים מפני מראית העין אפילו בחדרי חדרים אסור . איני והא תנן שוטחן בחמה אבל לא כנגד העם ואוקימנא

*) נראה דצ"ל מונח בנקב מותר למשוך ממנו . **) אינו מובן ואולי צ"ל דלמא אתי לאטמוני ברמץ וכדאיתא בגמ'.

עין משפט נר מצוה

לא א ב מיי' פכ"ג מהלכות שבת הל"א סמג לאוין כה טוש"ע א"ח סימן שיד סעיף ב:

לב ג מיי' פ"ב מהלכות שכנים הלכ' ו טוש"ע חו"מ סימן קנב סעיף ז:

לג ד מיי' פ"ו מהלכות טומאת מת הל"ה:

לד ה ו מיי' פכ"ב מהל' שבת הלכה ו סמג לאוין סה טוש"ע א"ח סימן שיד סעיף ט:

לה ז מיי' שם הלכה יא סמג שם טור ש"ע שם סעיף יא:

לו ח שם סעיף ט:

לז ט מיי' פי"ט מהל' שבת הלכה יז סמג שם טוש"ע א"ח סימן שא סעיף לט:

לח כ מיי' פכ"ב מהל' שבת הלכה ... סמג שם טור א"ח סימן שיט:

לט ל מ נ מיי' שם הל"כ סמג לאוין סה טור ש"ע א"ח סימן שא סעיף מה:

מסורת הש"ס

עי' לעיל נא: רש"י ד"ה קטנה ושם מבמא שממיים וחולדה חיים כן

[פי' להוציא היין מן השמרים. ערוך ערך חזק פ"ב]

ב"ב יב.

[כדאיתא סנהדרין לו:]

לעיל סד: ביצה ס. ע"ז יב.

הגהות הב"ח

(א) גמ' רבא אמר למטה וכו' א"ל אביי לרבא: (ב) רש"י ד"ה ולא כיון וכו' להסתמר שיצננו ולא יחמו:

הגהות הגר"א

[א] גמ' איכא בינייהו דקטים ומנח. נ"ב פי' שהוא קטום ויש עוד טרפא קטומים סוד. וז"ש ומנחי אבל גירסא כרי"ף והרא"ש וב"פ ומנח: [ב] שם שוטחן בחמה. כ"כ דווקא (ועמ"ש רבינו בא"ח סימן ש"ל ס"ק קי"ט)

גליון הש"ס

גמ' אמר ר"ח למעלה מן היין זהו לשמר. ג"י כרי"ף למעלה מן היין זהו לחזק למטה מן היין זהו לשמר רבה אמר למעלה וכו': שם ומשום כבוד רבותינו לא ישב. עי' שבועות דף מז ע"א תוס' ד"ה שוס יתיב:

[146b] on account of insects.[9] Yet 'some say, One may not add': Sometimes one may not make it [the hole] [properly] in the first place, and so come to enlarge it. R. Naḥman lectured on the authority of R. Joḥanan: The *halachah* is as 'some maintain'.

But they all agree that you may pierce an old hole at the very outset! Rab Judah said in Samuel's name: They learnt this only where it was done in order to conserve [the fragrance];[10] but if in order to strengthen it [the cask], it is forbidden.[11] How is it [when it is] to conserve, and how is it [when meant] to strengthen?[12] —Said R. Ḥisda: If it is above the [level of the] wine, its purpose is to conserve; if below the [top of the] wine, its purpose is to
a strengthen.[1] Rabbah said: [If] below the [top of the] wine, that too is to conserve. Then how is it to strengthen?—E.g., if it was pierced below the lees.[2]

Abaye said to Rabbah, Something which supports you was taught: A closed house has four cubits; if one had broken open its door-frame, it does not receive four cubits.[3] A closed house [room] does not defile all around it; if he had broken through the door-frame, it defiles all around it.[4]

[The insertion of] a tube,[5] Rab forbids, while Samuel permits. As for cutting it in the first place,[6] all agree that it is forbidden; [again], all agree that replacing it[7] is permitted. They differ only where it is cut but not made to measure:[8] he who forbids [its insertion] [holds that] we preventively prohibit [it], lest he come to cut it out in the first place; while he who permits it, [holds that] we do not preventively prohibit.

This is dependent on Tannaim: One may not cut a tube on a Festival, and it is superfluous to speak of the Sabbath. If it falls out,[9] it may be replaced on the Sabbath, and it goes without saying on Festival[s]. While R. Josiah is lenient. To what does R. Josiah refer. Shall we say, to the first clause? Surely he prepares a
b utensil![1] Again, if to the second clause, the first Tanna too certainly permits it! Hence they must differ where it is cut but not made to measure: one Master holds, we preventively prohibit, while the other Master holds, We do not preventively prohibit. R. Shisha son of R. Idi lectured in R. Joḥanan's name: The *halachah* is as R. Josiah.

WHILE IF IT IS PERFORATED, etc. Oil [to stop up the hole], Rab forbids, while Samuel permits.[2] He who forbids [holds]: We preventively prohibit on account of wax;[3] while he who permits [holds]: We do not preventively prohibit. R. Samuel

(9) One does not make the ventilation hole too large for fear of insects, worms, etc., entering. (10) I.e., the hole was closed up for that purpose. The closing is done quite feebly, and there is no real work in re-opening it. (11) To re-open it, because it was firmly closed and its re-opening is tantamount to making a new hole. (12) What is the general rule which determines its purpose?

a (1) That the wine should not drip out. (2) There it has to bear the weight of all the wine and so must be strengthened. (3) If a number of houses open into a common courtyard and their owners wish to divide it, each to have his own privately, each receives four cubits along the breadth of the courtyard for every door to his house that gives upon it, and the rest is shared equally. Now, if one of the doors had been walled up, but without its frame being broken through, its owner can still claim the four cubits for it; but if the frame was first broken through and then it was closed up, it ceases to count as a door, and the four cubits are lost. V. B.B. 12*a*. (4) If a room containing a corpse is closed, i.e., the door is walled up, the defilement of the corpse does not extend beyond it. But if the door-frame was first broken and then walled up, so that no aperture at all is visible, the house is regarded as a grave and defiles everything around it to a distance of four cubits.—Thus an opening must be absolutely closed before it ceases to count as such, and the same applies to the cask. (5) I.e., into a barrel, as a pipe. (6) To the required size of the hole. (7) *Sc.* a fitted tube which had fallen out. (8) It had not been tested in the hole to see whether it fits exactly. (9) From the bottle, where it serves as a pipe.

b (1) Surely he does not permit the making of a tube! (2) Rab forbids thick semi-solid oil to be spread over the hole, while Samuel permits it. (3) The spreading of wax too may be regarded as permissible if one is allowed to spread oil.

◁ *For the continuation of the English translation of this page see overleaf.*

עין משפט נר מצוה

לא א ב מיי' פכ"ב מהלכות שבת הל' לא סמג לאוין סה טוש"ע או"ח סימן שיד סעיף ב:
לב ג מיי' פ"ב מהלכות שכנים הל' ז טוש"ע חו"מ סימן קעג סעיף ז:
לג ד מיי' פ"ו מהלכות טומאת מת הל' א:
לד ה ו מיי' פכ"ב מהל' שבת הלכה ו סמג לאוין סה טוש"ע או"ח סימן שיד סעיף ט:
לה ז מיי' שם הלכה יא סמג שם טוש"ע שם סעיף יא:
לו ח שם סעיף ט:
לז ט מיי' פי"ט מהל' שבת הלכה יז סמג שם טוש"ע או"ח סימן שא סעיף לט:
לח כ מיי' פכ"ב מהל' שבת הלכה ט טור או"ח סימן שיח:
לט ל מ נ מיי' שם הל"כ סמג לאוין סה טור ש"ע או"ח סימן שא סעיף מה:

רבינו חננאל

וי"א אין מוסיפין דזמנין דלא תקניה מעיקרא ואתי לארוחי ביה הלכתא כותיה דדרש רב נחמן בר רב חסדא משמיה דר' יוחנן הלכה כי"א. ושוין שנוקבין נקב ישן לכתחלה ואמר רב יהודה משמיה דשמואל אינו מותר לפתוח נקב ישן אלא במקום העשוי לשמר פי' להוציא היין מן השמרים אבל לחזק אסור פי' היה נקב בחבית ופתמו שלא יהא שותת. וחלוק רב חסדא ורבה ורבא כרבה דתניא דמסייעתו ואלו דברי רבה רבה אמר למטה מן היין נמי זהו לשמר ומותר לפתחו והיכי דמי לחזק כגון שנקבה למטה מן השמרים דסתימה מעלייתא היא שאין אדם עושה נקב בקרקעיתה של חבית להוציא יין ולא לשמר. עשאו מפני כשנפתחה החבית הוסיפה על פיה. ואם הנקב בין השמרים נעשה סתום. זה בנוסף של הבית ובטל מלהיות נקב בו וחשוב כפתח בית הנסתם בפירוק פציפין שנסתלק מפני דין פתח לגמרי. גובתא שהיא שפופרת של קנה או של עצים שנותנין בנקב של חבית או ביד הנוד של יין להיות מושכין ממנו יין מן החבית או מן הנוד. רב אסר ושמואל שרי ואוקימנא דלוקחן בשופרות התחתיה ואינה מתוקנת להכניסה לנקב אבל להתקין דברי הכל אסור. ואם היתה התחוב ומתוקנת דברי הכל מותר להחזירה בנקב התחבית או בנוד לאשוך מבנה יין. והעמדנו עד הלוקת רב ושמואל כתנאי. דתניא אין הותכין שפופרת ביו"ט ואין צ"ל בשבת. נפלה מחזירין בשבת. ואין צ"ל ביו"ט. ור' יאשיה מיקל ודייק' עלה ר' יאשיה אהייא אילימא ארישא שאבר ת"ק אין דותכין כלומר אין חותכין סכנה גדול תתיכהלעשות' שפופרת הא ר' יאשיה מיקל בהא קא מתקן כלי בשבת אלא שאסר ת"ק נפלה מחזירין אותה.

מסורת הש"ס

עי' לעיל נא. רש"י ד"ה קטנה ופס מבמע שנמייה וחולדה מיום כן

[פי' להוציא היין מן השמרים. ערוך ערך חזק פ"ט]

כ"ב יב.

הגהות הב"ח

(א) גמ' רבה אמר למטה וכו' א"ל אביי לרבה: (ב) רש"י ד"ה ואת המים וכו' להשתמר שלצנו ולא יחמו:

הגהות הגר"א

[א] גמ' איכא בינייהו דקטים ומנחי כו' פי' שהוא קטום ויש עוד הרבה קטומים סור. וז"ש ומנחי אבל גירסת הרי"ף והרא"ש וב"י ומנחי. [ב] שם שוטחן בחמה. ר"ל דווקא (ועמ"ש רבינו בא"ח סימן ש"א ס"ק קס).

גליון הש"ס

גמ' אמר ר"ח למעלה מן היין זהו לשמר. ג' רש"י למעלה מן היין זהו להזק למטה מן היין זהו לשמר רבה אמר למעלה וכו': שם ומשום כבוד רבותינו לא ישב. עי' שבועות דף מז ע"ב תוס' ד"ה סוה יתיב:

[כדאיתא סנהדרין לו:]

לעיל סד. ביצה ס. ע"ז יב.

משום ריחשא · ואטו פתחא אחרינא דליכא למיחש לריחשא לא גזרינן דדוקא אטו נקב של תרנגולין גזרינן דלא מסקי אינשי אדעתייהו שיהא עשוי להכניס ולהוציא :

פרץ פצימיו מטמא כל סביביו · פי' בקונטרס כל סביביו ד' אמות כקבר ואין נראה לזקני הרב ר' שמשון זצ"ל דכיון דמסיימי מחיצתא ולית לן למיחש שמא יעלה על הבית ויאהיל עליו ולא ידע לית לן למימר דמטמא ד' אמות כל סביביו כדמוכח בסוטה פרק משוח מלחמה (ד' מד·) גבי חצר הקבר העומד בתוכה טהור הני מילי חצר הקבר דמסיימא מחיצתא אבל מת בעלמא תפיס ומשמע דבמת נמי היכא דמסיימא לא נטמא כל סביביו ד' אמות אלא נראה לו דהכי פי' זיזין באותו בית שבולטין מחוץ לבית מכל צד ויש בהם פותח טפח בכל אחד אם הבית סתום ועדיין נראית בו צורת הפתח אינו מטמא שסתמו של מת עומד לצאת דרך הפתח פרץ פצימיו וחזר ובנאו כשאר כותל ולא נותר בו כלל פתח מטמא כל סביביו דכל חד וחד איכא לספוקי דילמא דרך אותו מקום יצא מן הבית מיהו לאו פירכא היא כולי האי מה שהקשה לפירוש הקונטרס די"ל שלא חלקו חכמים במת ועוד נראה דלא קשה כלל לפי' הקונטרס דבית נמי לא מסיימי מחיצתא בהוא מטמא הנוגע בכתלים אפילו לא יעלה על גביו כקבר שמטמא במגע אפילו מן הצד כדתניא בספרי בפרשת פרה אדומה או בקבר זה קבר סתום או אינו אלא קבר פתוח אמרת ק"ו ומה אהל שמקבל טומאה אינו מטמא מכל לצדדין כשהוא פתוח קבר שאינו מקבל טומאה אינו דין שלא יטמא מכל לצדדין כשהוא פתוח הא למה כשהוא סתום מטמא אף הנוגע מן הצד :

הלכה כרבי יאשיה · הלכך מותר לתת לכתחילה גובתא שקורין רזי"ל בחבית : **משום** מרזב · פי' הרב פור"ת שלא יבוא ליתן על גגו מרזב וקשה דבגובתא נמי נגזר אלא נראה לרבי כפי' הקונט' שלא יתקן מרזב לייננו שיפול היין בתוכו וילך למרחוק דכשלוקח עלה של הדס ומקפלו כעין מרזב נראה כעושה מרזב אבל בגובתא שאינו עושה בו שום מעשה לא גזרינן · מ"ר :

אייתי ליה בי סדיא · בי מילעי הוה דהוי לאו הכי היכי איתמר מכללא : **מי** שנשרו כליו במים · בדרך גרסינן (א) לשון נפילה לא כפי' הקונטרס לעיל בפרק במה אשה (דף סה·) שנשרו במי גשמים דהא אמרינן בביצה בפרק משילין (דף לה:) מאן דתני מנשירין לא משתבש כדתנן מי שנשרו כליו במים בדרך אלמא לשון נפילה הוא · ב) מ"ר :

א) ר"ל דגרסי' הנו"ן דנשרו בקמץ לשון נפילה דאלו הנו"ן בחירק הוי לשון שריה. רש"א
ב) [ועי' תוס' ביצה לה: ד"ה מי שנשרו]

משום ריחשא וי"א אין מוסיפים זימנין דלא תקניה מעיקרא ואתי לארוחי ביה דרש רב נחמן משום רבי יוחנן הלכה כיש אומרים: ושוין שנוקבין נקב ישן לכתחלה: אמר רב יהודה אמר שמואל לא שנו אלא במקום העשוי לשמר אבל לחזק אסור היכי דמי *לישמר היכי דמי לחזק א"ר חסדא למעלה מן היין זהו לשמר למטה מן היין זהו לחזק (א) רבא אמר למטה מן היין נמי זהו לשמר והיכי דמי לחזק כגון שניקבה למטה מן השמרים א"ל אביי לרבא תניא דמסייע לך *בית סתום יש לו ארבע אמות פרץ את פצימיו אין לו ד' אמות בית סתום אינו מטמא כל סביביו פרץ את פצימיו מטמא כל סביביו גובתא רב אסר ושמואל שרי מהתך לכתהלה דכ"ע לא פליגי דאסור אהדורי דכ"ע לא פליגי דשרי כי פליגי דחתיכה ולא מתקנא מאן דאסר גזרינן דילמא אתי למיחתך לכתחלה ומאן דשרי לא גזרינן כתנאי אין חותכין שפופרת ביו"ט וא"צ לומר בשבת נפלה (אין) מחזירין אותה בשבת ואין צריך לומר ביו"ט ור' יאשיה מיקל ר' יאשיה אהייא אילימא ארישא הא קמתקן מנא אלא אסיפא ת"ק נמי מישרא קשרי אלא דחתיכה ולא מתקנא איכא בינייהו מ"ס גזרינן ומ"ס לא גזרינן דרש רב שישא בריה דרב אידי משמיה דר' יוחנן הלכה כר' יאשיה: ואם היתה נקובה וכו': מישחא רב אסר ושמואל שרי מאן דאסר גזרינן משום שעוה ומאן דשרי לא גזרינן אמר ליה רב שמואל בר בר חנה לרב יוסף בפירוש אמרת לן משמיה דרב מישחא שרי אמר טבות ריישבא אמר שמואל האי טרפא דאסא אסור מ"ט רב ייִמר מדפתי אמר גזירה משום מרזב רב אשי אמר גזירה שמא יקטום מאי בינייהו (א) איכא בינייהו דקטים ומנחי בי סדיא רב אסר ושמואל שרי ברכין דכולי עלמא לא פליגי דשרי בקשין דכ"ע לא פליגי דאסור כי פליגי במיצעי מאן דאסר מיהוי כמשוי. ומאן דשרי לא מיהוי כמשוי והא דרב לאו *בפירוש איתמר אלא מכללא איתמר דרב איקלע להוא אתרא דלא הוה ליה רווחא נפק יתיב בכרמלית אייתו ליה בי סדיא לא יתיב מאן דחזא סבר משום דבי סדיא אסיר ולא היא דרב אברוזי מבריז בי סדיא שרי ומשום כבוד רבותינו לא יישב עליו ומאן נינהו רב כהנא ורב אסי: **מתני'** *נותנין תבשיל לתוך הבור בשביל שיהא שמור ואת המים היפים ברעים בשביל שיצננו ואת הצונן בחמה בשביל שיחמו *מי שנשרו כליו בדרך במים מהלך בהן ואינו חושש הגיע לחצר החיצונה שוטחן בחמה (ב) אבל לא כנגד העם: **גמ'** פשיטא מהו דתימא ניגזר משום אשויי גומות קא משמע לן: ואת המים היפים ברעים: פשיטא סיפא איצטריכא ליה ואת הצונן בחמה הא נמי פשיטא מהו דתימא ניגזור דילמא אתי לאטמוני ברמץ קמ"ל: מי שנשרו וכו': *אמר רב יהודה אמר רב כל מקום שאסרו חכמים מפני מראית העין אפילו בחדרי חדרים אסור תנן שוטחן בחמה אבל לא כנגד העם תנאי היא דתניא שוטחן בחמה אבל לא כנגד העם ר"א ור"ש אוסרין אמר רב הונא

המנער

משום ריחשא · שלא יכנס בו שרץ כגון *נמייה וחולדה שממיתים את התרנגולים : זימנין דלא תקניה מעיקרא · שיהא כדי להוציא הבל ולהכניס את האויר : לא שנו · דנוקבין : אלא במקום · דסתימה זו לא נעשית אלא לשמור ריח היין שלא יצא ויתקלקל וכיון דלאו סתימה מעליותא עבדי לה לאו כלום הוא : לחזק · שיחזק הכלי שלא יצא ייננו הואיל וסתימה מעלייתא היא כי הדר נקיב לה הוי כפותח לכתחלה : למטה מן היין נמי לשמר הוא · כיון דלאו כובד היין נשען עליו סגי ליה בסתימה כל דהו : למטה מן השמרים · אצל שוליו שכל כובד היין נשען שם : תניא דמסייע לך · דלא פקע שם פתח מיניה אלא בסתימה מעלייתא : בית סתום יש לו ד"א · קיי"ל בבבא בתרא חצר מתחלקת לפי פתחיה לפי פתח הבתים הפתוחין לה אם באו לחלק את החצר בין שנים שהיה לזה בית שפתוחין לו לחצר שני פתחים ולזה בית שפתוחין לו לחצר ד' פתחים נוטל לכל פתח הרבע אמות בחצר נגד פתחו למדת רוחב פתחו והשאר חולקין בשוה ואם נסתם אחד מהם קודם חלוקת החצר ולא פירק את פצימיו אלא סתם בין שני הפצימין אינו מפסיד [דין] פתחו בכך פירק את פצימיו ואח"כ סתמו פקע שם פתח מיניה : בית סתום · והמת בתוכו אינו מטמא סביביו : פרץ פצימיו · וסתמו נעשה קבר ומטמא סביביו ד"א כדאמר בסוטה (ד' מד·) מת תופס ד"א לטומאה וגזרה דרבנן שמא יאהיל ולא יבין : גובתא · לתקוע קנה חלול בנקב חבית שילך היין דרך הקנה: מחתך · רונגיי"ר לתקנה למדת הנקב: אהדורי · אם נפלה : ולא מתקנא · לא ניתנה בנקב לידע אם למדתו היא : אי לימא ארישא · לחתיכה ולשפופרת : משחא · שמן עב אסור · למרחו : טרפא דאסא · ליתן עלה של הדס בנקב החבית שהעלה עשוי כמרזב והיין זב דרך שם : גזירה משום מרזב · שמא יכין מרזב : שמא יקטום · העלה מן הענף וכיון דקטמיה הוה ליה כמתקן כלי כדתניא במסכת ביצה (דף לג:) לחטוט בו שיניו לא יקטמנו ואם קטמו חייב חטאת : בי סדיא · לבדין שקורין פלטור"ש ועשויין לקפלן תחתיו במקום הכר או הכסת : רב אסר · להביאו דרך מלבוש דרך רשות הרבים כשהוא מעוטף בו : ברכין · שדרכן להתחמם בהן : דשרו · דמלבוש הן : ולא הוה ליה רווחא · בבית למקום מושבם של תלמידים : ומשום כבוד רבותינו · שלא היה להן דבר לישב עליו ויושבין על גבי קרקע : רב כהנא ורב אסי · תלמידי חברים היו לו*: **מתני'** לתוך הבור · שאין בו מים : שיהא שמור · שלא יסריח מחמת החום : ואת המים היפים ברעים · כלי מלא מים יפים לתוך מקוה מים רעים להשתמר (ב) שיצונו ולא יחמו: מי שנשרו · שנפלו למים בשבת: לחצר החיצונה · הסמוכה למבוא העיר בתוך העיר שהוא מקום משתמר: שוטחן בחמה· ליבשן : אבל לא כנגד העם · שיחשדוהו שכבסן : **גמ'** פשיטא. דטתנין תבשיל לתוך הבור: גומות · שבקרקע הבור שיהו שוין להושיב הקדרה :

המנער

בהא לימא ר' יאשיה מיקל מי החמיר שיאמר בזה מיקל הלא בזה גם ת"ק מותר קאמר . ותריצנא אלא לאו דחתיכה ולא מתקנה איכא בינייהו וכך הציעה . אין עושין שפופרת ביו"ט ואין צ"ל בשבת . ואפי' חתכה ולא מתקנה אסור אבל אם היתה כבר בחבית ונפלה מחזירין אותה בשבת ואין צ"ל ביו"ט ור' יאשיה מיקל בחתיכה ולא מתקנה נמצאו דברי רב כת"ק ודברי שמואל כר' יאשיה והלכה כר' יאשיה ודרש רב שישא בריה דרב אידי משמא דר' יוחנן הלכתא כר' יאשיה ווה שאמר חתכה ולא מתקנה לאו שצריכה תיקון כלי כגון סכין וכדומה לו אלא תיקון ביד בלבד . ואם צריכה תיקון בסכין או זולתו סכין כלי אחר אסורה. ואם היתה החבית נקובה לא יתן עליה שעוה מפני שממרח. כלומר סותם כדאמרינן התם לענין חבית שניקבה וסתמה שמרים כו' מורח מן הצדדין. וכיון דר' יהודה דמתניתין וריב"ז ורב ושמואל אסרי ש"מ שאסור ליתן שעוה בחבית . וכן משחא. רב אסר גזירה במשחא אטו שעוה. והלכתא כוותיה: טרפא דאסא. פי' עלה הדס שנותנין על הנקב של חבית להיות מקלח בו היין ולא יהיה שותת בדופני החבית . לדברי הכל אסור ליתן עלה של הדס בשבת ולשומו בנקב של חבית כמרזב . ואפילו רב אשי לא התיר אלא שאם היה הנקב מושך ממנו *) אבל לתתו לכתחלה אוסר : בי סדיא רב אסר ושמואל שרי אין זה מקומו אלא בשביל השמועות שחלקו בהן רב אסר ושמואל שרי נסבה בגררא . ופשוטה היא . כסת זו שחלקו בה כסת בינונית לא דקה ולא קשה . ומסקינן בה אפילו זו מותר לטלטלה: נותנין תבשיל בתוך הבור בשביל שיהא שמור. פי' בור זה אין בו מים ונותן התבשיל בקרקעיתו מהו דתימא לגזור דלמא אתי לאשויי גומות קמ"ל דלא גזרינן . ואת המים היפים ברעים פשיטא ואת הצונן בחמה פשיטא מהו דתימא לגזור דלמא אתי לאטמוני ברמץ קמ"ל דלא גזרינן : מתני' מי שנשרו כליו בדרך כו'. אמר רב יהודה אמר רב כל מקום שאסרו חכמים מפני מראית העין אפילו בחדרי חדרים אסור . איני והא תנן שוטחן בחמה אבל לא כנגד העם ואוקימנא

*) נראה דצ"ל מונח בנקב מותר למשוך ממנו . **) אינו מובן ואולי צ"ל דלמא אתי לאטמוני ברמץ וכדאיתא בגמ'.

Continuation of translation from previous page as indicated by ◁

b. Bar Ḥanah observed to R. Joseph: You distinctly told us in Rab's name [that with] oil [it] is permitted

Ṭabuth the fowler[4] said in Samuel's name: [To shape] a myrtle leaf[5] is forbidden. What is the reason?—R. Yemar of Difti[6] said: It is a preventive measure on account of [the making of] a pipe. R. Ashi said: It is a preventive measure lest one pluck it [from the tree]. Wherein do they differ? They differ where it is [already] plucked and [others too] are lying about.[7]

[To wear] linen sheets,[8] Rab forbids, while Samuel permits.[9] Of soft ones all agree that it is permitted;[10] in the case of hard ones all agree that it is forbidden.[11] They differ in respect of medium ones: he who forbids [holds that] they look like a burden; while he who permits [holds that] they do not look like a burden. Now, this [view] of Rab was stated not explicitly but by inference.
c For Rab visited a certain place where he had no room.[1] So he went out and sat in a *karmelith*. Linen sheets were brought him,[2] [but] he did not sit [upon them]. He who saw this thought that it was because linen sheets are forbidden. Yet that is not so, for Rab had indeed announced [that] linen sheets are permitted, but he did not sit on them out of respect for our masters: and who are they? R. Kahana and R. Assi.[3]

MISHNAH. A DISH MAY BE PLACED IN A PIT FOR IT TO BE GUARDED, AND WHOLESOME WATER INTO NOISOME WATER FOR IT TO BE COOLED, OR COLD WATER IN THE SUN FOR IT TO BE HEATED. IF ONE'S GARMENTS FALL INTO WATER ON THE ROAD, HE MAY WALK IN THEM WITHOUT FEAR. WHEN HE REACHES THE OUTERMOST COURTYARD[4] HE MAY SPREAD THEM OUT IN THE SUN, BUT NOT IN SIGHT OF THE PEOPLE.[5]

GEMARA. [But] it is obvious?[6]—You might say, Let us preventively forbid it on account of the levelling of depressions;[7] hence he [the Tanna] informs us [otherwise].

AND WHOLESOME WATER, [etc.] It is obvious?—The second clause is required: OR COLD WATER IN THE SUN, [etc.]. That too is obvious?—You might say, Let us preventively forbid it, lest he come to put it away in [hot] ashes;[8] therefore he teaches us [otherwise].

IF ONE'S GARMENTS FALL, [etc.] Rab Judah said in Rab's name: Wherever the Sages forbade [aught] for appearance's sake,
d it is forbidden even in the innermost chambers.[1] We learnt: HE MAY SPREAD THEM OUT IN THE SUN, BUT NOT IN SIGHT OF THE PEOPLE?—It is [a controversy of] Tannaim. For it was taught: He may spread them out in the sun, but not in sight of the people; R. Eleazar and R. Simeon forbid it.

(4) Rashi. Others: = ריש בי אבא, the head of the family (in Ta'an. 10a). (5) One may not shape a myrtle leaf into a funnel or pipe and insert it into the mouth of a bottle or cask. (6) V. *supra* 10a, n. b5. (7) There are plenty of leaves, so that there is no fear that one may pluck it, hence it is permitted (Wilna Gaon); but the first reason still holds good. R. Ḥan. explains it thus: All agree that one may not make a funnel and insert it in the hole of a cask, but they differ where the leaf was already lying in the hole as a funnel from before the Sabbath. According to R. Yemar it is still forbidden to pour wine through it, lest he make a funnel, but according to R. Ashi it is permitted, since there is no fear of plucking a leaf from the tree. (8) Which are folded together and used as a pillow or bolster. (9) Rab forbids a person to wrap them about himself and walk through the streets, thus wearing them as a garment, while Samuel permits it. (10) They give warmth and therefore may certainly be regarded as a garment. (11) They give no warmth and are merely a burden.

c (1) Rashi: for his disciples. (2) Tosaf: of medium quality, neither hard nor soft. (3) They were his disciple-colleagues (v. Sanh. 36b), and it was not fitting that he should enjoy a comfort which had not been provided for them. (4) Within the town. (5) Lest they suspect him of having washed them on the Sabbath. (6) That a dish may be placed in a pit. (7) He may find depressions in the floor of the pit and level them. (8) Which is forbidden.

d (1) V. Beẓ. 9a.

R. Huna said: [147*a*] If one shakes out his cloak[2] on the Sabbath, he is liable to a sin-offering.[3] Now, we said this only of new ones, but in the case of old ones we have nought against it; and this is said only of black ones, but in the case of white or red ones we have nought against it; [but in any case there is no culpability] unless he is particular about them.[4]

'Ulla visited Pumbeditha. Seeing the scholars shaking their garments he observed, 'The scholars are desecrating the Sabbath.' Said Rab Judah to them, 'Shake them in his presence, [for] we are not particular at all [about the clothes].' Abaye was standing before R. Joseph. Said he to him, 'Give me my hat.' Seeing some dew upon it he hesitated to give it to him. 'Shake it and throw it off,' he directed, '[for] we are not particular at all.'

R. Isaac b. Joseph said in R. Johanan's name: If one goes out on the Sabbath with a cloak folded up [and] lying on his shoulders, he is liable to a sin-offering.[5] It was taught likewise: Clothes vendors who go out on the Sabbath with cloaks folded up [and] lying on their shoulders are liable to a sin-offering. And they [the Sages] said this not of clothes vendors alone but of all men, but that it is the nature of merchants to go out thus. Again, if a shopkeeper goes out with coins bound up in his wrapper, he is liable to a sin-offering. And they said this not of a shopkeeper alone but of all men, but that it is a shopkeeper's nature to go out thus. And runners may go out with the scarfs on their shoulders;[6] and they said this not of runners alone but of all men, but that it is the
a nature of runners to go out thus.[1]

R. Judah said: It once happened that Hyrcanus, son of R. Eliezer b. Hyrcanus, went out on the Sabbath with the scarf on his shoulder, but that a thread [thereof] was wound round his finger.[2] But when the matter came before the Sages they said, [It is permitted] even if a thread is not wound about one's finger. R. Naḥman b. R. Ḥisda lectured in R. Ḥisda's name: The *halachah* is [that it is permissible] even if a thread is not wound about his finger.

'Ulla visited the academy of Assi b. Hini [and] was asked: Is it permitted to make a *marzeb* on the Sabbath? Said he to them, Thus did R. Ilai say: It is forbidden to make a *marzeb* on the Sabbath. What is a *marzeb?*—Said R. Zera: The capes[3] worn by Babylonian women.[4] R. Jeremiah was sitting before R. Zera [and] asked him, How is it thus? It is forbidden, replied he. And how is it thus? It is forbidden, replied he.[5] R. Papa said: Adopt this general rule: Whatever [is done] with the intention of gathering it [the skirts] up[6] is forbidden; whatever is for adornment is permitted. Just as R. Shisha son of R. Idi used to adorn himself with his cloak.[7]

When R. Dimi came,[8] he said: On one occasion Rabbi went out into the field with the two ends of his cloak lying on his shoulder. [Thereupon] Joshua b. Ziruz, the son of R. Meir's father-in-law, said to him: Did not R. Meir declare one liable to a sin-offering in such a case?[9] Was R. Meir so very particular?[10]
b he exclaimed. [So] Rabbi let his cloak fall. When Rabin came,[1] he said: It was not Joshua b. Ziruz but Joshua b. Ḳapusai, R. Akiba's son-in-law. Said he: Did not R. Akiba declare one liable to a sin-offering in such a case? Was R. Akiba so very particular? he exclaimed. [So] Rabbi let his cloak fall. When R. Samuel b. R. Judah came, he said: It was stated that this [question] was asked.[2]

MISHNAH. IF ONE BATHES IN THE WATER OF A PIT[3] OR IN THE WATER OF TIBERIAS[4] AND DRIES HIMSELF EVEN WITH TEN TOWELS, HE MUST NOT FETCH THEM IN HIS HAND.[5] BUT TEN MEN MAY DRY THEIR FACES, HANDS, AND FEET ON ONE TOWEL AND FETCH IT IN THEIR HANDS. ONE MAY OIL AND [LIGHTLY] MASSAGE [THE BODY], BUT NOT KNEAD[6] OR SCRAPE.[7] YOU MUST NOT GO DOWN TO A WRESTLING GROUND,[8] OR INDUCE VOMITING,[9] OR STRAIGHTEN AN INFANT['S LIMBS],[10] OR SET A BROKEN BONE. IF ONE'S HAND OR FOOT IS DISLOCATED, HE MUST NOT AGITATE IT VIOLENTLY IN COLD WATER BUT MAY BATHE IT IN THE USUAL WAY, AND IF IT HEALS, IT HEALS.

GEMARA. THE WATER OF A PIT is taught analogous to THE WATER OF TIBERIAS: just as the water of Tiberias is hot, so [by] the water of a pit hot [water is meant]; [and furthermore, it states] IF ONE BATHES: only if it is done, but not at the outset.[11]

(2) Rashi: to free it from the dust. Tosaf.: he shakes off the dew. (3) As it is tantamount to washing it. (4) He would never put them on thus; then the dusting is tantamount to washing. But if he is not particular about the dust there is no culpability in any case. (5) The part which is thrown over the shoulder is considered a burden. (6) These were swift runners, e.g., for carrying express messages. In *T.A.* I, p. 603, n. 530*b*, it is conjectured that the סודר (scarf) was their only garment, apart from a loincloth.

a (1) Even if they are folded up and not hanging down (Wilna Gaon and 'Aruk) —though presumably they are wound round their necks in the first place. (2) To prevent it from falling off. (3) Lit., 'pouches'. (4) Formed by drawing up the skirts of their garments backwards and attaching it with ribbons, thus shaping it like a tube or gutter, which is the meaning of *marzeb*. (5) He gathered up his skirts in various ways and asked him whether such were permissible on the Sabbath. (6) Rashi: to remain so permanently. Wilna Gaon, citing Maim.: to prevent it from being torn or soiled. Jast. translates: with the intention of creasing. (7) After putting it on he would smooth and straighten it out to make it more becoming. This is permitted even on the Sabbath. (8) V. *supra* 5*a*, n. b9. (9) For it is not wearing but carrying a burden. (10) As to call this a burden.

b (1) V. *supra* 5*a*, n. b9. (2) The incident did not actually happen, but the question was asked in the academy: Rabbi thought of permitting it, but was dissuaded when told of R. Meir's (or, R. Akiba's) view. (3) Which had been heated. (4) Which was naturally hot—Tiberias possessed thermal springs. (5) Even if carrying is permitted, e.g., in his house or where an *'erub* has been provided. (6) I.e., massage strongly. (7) With a scraper, perhaps a strigil, to invigorate the circulation. (8) So Jast. Heb. *Kordima*. MS.M. and Jer. read: לפילוטא i.e., the clay ground (of the brickyard). Rashi translates: the name of a river. (9) By means of an emetic. (10) By manipulation. (11) For otherwise the Mishnah should read: one may bathe.

המנער טליתו בשבת חייב חטאת ולא אמרן אלא בחדתי אבל בעתיקי לית לן בה ולא אמרן אלא באוכמי אבל בחיורי וסומקי לית לן בה והוא דקפיד עלייהו עולא איקלע לפומבדיתא חזא רבנן דקא מנפצי גלימייהו אמר קמחללין רבנן שבתא אמר להו רב יהודה נפוצי ליה באפיה אנן לא קפדינן מידי אביי הוה קאי קמיה דרב יוסף א"ל הב לי כומתאי [חזא דאיכא] טלא עליה הוה קמחסם למיתבה ליה א"ל נפוץ שדי אנן לא קפדינן מידי *אמר רב יצחק בר יוסף א"ר יוחנן היוצא בטלית מקופלת מונחת לו על כתיפו בשבת חייב חטאת תנ"ה סוחרי כסות היוצאים בטליתות מקופלות ומונחות על כתיפן בשבת חייבין חטאת ולא סוחרי כסות בלבד אמרו אלא כל אדם אלא שדרכן של מוכרין לצאת כך ותנוני היוצא במעות הצרורין לו בסדינו חייב חטאת ולא חנוני בלבד אמרו אלא כל אדם אלא שדרכו של חנוני לצאת כך *והרטנין *יוצאין בסודרין [א] שעל כתיפן ולא רטנין בלבד אמרו אלא כל אדם אלא שדרכן של רטנין לצאת בכך א"ר יהודה מעשה בהורקנוס בנו של רבי אליעזר בן הורקנוס שיצא בסודר שעל כתיפו בשבת אלא שנימא כרוכה לו באצבעו וכשבא הדבר לפני חכמים אמרו אפילו אין נימא כרוכה לו באצבעו דרש רב נחמן בר רב חסדא משמיה דרב חסדא הלכה אע"פ שאין נימא כרוכה לו באצבעותיו עולא איקלע לבי אסי בר היני בעו מיניה מהו לעשות מרזב בשבת אמר להו הכי אמר רבי אלעי אסור לעשות מרזב בשבת מאי מרזב אמר ר' זירא כיסי בבלייתא ר' ירמיה הוה יתיב קמיה דר' זירא א"ל חכי מאי א"ל אסור והכי מאי א"ל אסור אמר רב פפא *נקוט האי כללא בידך כל אדעתא דלכנופי [ב] אסור כל דלהתנאות שרי כי הא דרב שישא בריה דרב אידי מתנאה בסדינו הוה כי אתא רב דימי אמר פעם אחת יצא רבי לשדה והיו שני צידי טליתו מונחין על כתיפו אמר לפניו יהושע בן זירוז בן חמיו של רבי מאיר בזו לא חייב ר' מאיר חטאת אמר ליה דקדק רבי מאיר עד כאן שלשל רבי טליתו כי אתא רבין אמר לא יהושע בן זירוז הוה אלא יהושע בן כפוסאי היה חתנו של ר' עקיבא אמר בזו לא חייב ר' עקיבא חטאת אמר לו דקדק ר"ע עד כאן שלשל רבי טליתו כי אתא רב שמואל בר רב יהודה אמר נשאל איתמר: **מתני'** הרוחץ במי מערה ובמי טבריא ונסתפג אפילו בעשר אלונטיאות לא יביאם בידו אבל עשרה בני אדם מסתפגין באלונטית אחת פניהם ידיהם ורגליהם ומביאין אותן בידן סבין וממשמשין* אבל לא מתעמלין ולא מתגררין אין יורדין *לקורדימא *) ואין עושין אפיקטויזין ואין מעצבין את הקטן ואין מחזירין את השבר מי שנפרקה ידו ורגלו לא יטרפם בצונן אבל *רוחץ הוא כדרכו ואם נתרפא נתרפא: **גמ'** קתני מי מערה דומיא דמי טבריא מה מי טבריא חמין אף מי מערה חמין *הרוחץ דיעבד אין לכתחילה לא מכלל דלהשתטף

*) לעיל קכג.

רש"י

המנער טליתו · מן העפר: חייב חטאת · דזהו ליבונה: אלא באוכמי · שהאבק מקלקל מראיתה וקפיד עליה: והוא דקפיד עלייהו · ללובשן עד שינערם: קמחללי (א) שבתא · וגלימי אוכמי הוו: לא קפדינן · לא איכפת לן אם יש עליה אבק הלכך כלו ליבון הוא: כומתאי · כובעי: הוה קא מחסם. לשון לא תחסום (דברים כה): למיתבא ליה · שצריך לנער הטל מעליה: בטלית מקופלת · לאחר שנתנה על ראשו הגביה שיפוליה על כתפיו: חייב חטאת · שאין זה דרך מלבוש: והרטנין · על שם מקום: נימא כרוכה על אצבעו · שלא יפול מכתפיו: בר היני: מרזב · מפרש לקמיה: כיסי בבלייתא · שמסלקין בגדיהם מן הארץ כשהן ארוכין וכופלין אותן כלפי מעלה פרונצי"ש ומחזיקין אותן [ג] ע"י חוטין והיינו כמין כיס וכמו מרזב: אסור. משום תקוני מנא: הכי מאי · קולטו חלוקו (בפניו) בענין אחד ושואלו כגון זה מרזב או לא וחוזר וקולטו בענין אחר ושואלו: לכנופי · שיהא מתוקן תמיד להעמיד קיפולו לעולם: להתנאות · לפי שעה: מתנאה בסדינו · אחר שנתעטף היה מתקנו על גופו ומייפו ובחול קאמר כלומר אלמא דאורחיה בהכי וה"ה לשבת: שני צידי טליתו · שבימינו ובשמאלו לצד הקרקע: בן זירוז בזו לא חייב ר"מ חטאת · בתמיה דאין זה דרך מלבוש אלא דרך משוי: דקדק ר"מ ע"כ · בתמיה לחייב חטאת בדבר הדומה להיות מותר כזה שאינה מקופלת ואחוריה טפלין למטה מכתפיו אלא שצידיה היו מונחין על כתפו: שלשל · הורידה למטה שקבל דבריו: נשאל איתמר. לא אירע מעשה זה לרבי אלא שאלו לפניו מהו לנאת בו ובקש להתיר עד שאמרו לפניו משום רבי מאיר חייב חטאת דאיהו סבר הואיל ואינה מקופלת שהרי אחוריה היו טפלין למטה מן כתפיו אלא שצידיה היו מונחים על כתפיו הוה סבר דרך מלבוש הוא: **מתני'** מי מערה · מי מקוה מקורה (ב) שהוא חם ואין חומו יולא ודוקא חמין נקט ומש"ה קתני הרוחץ דיעבד: ונסתפג · וקינח: אפי' בעשר אלונטיות · סדינין שמקנחין בהן וסיפג בהן זה אחר זה ורבותא היא דלא נפישי מיא בכל חד אפ"ה לא יביאם בידו בתוך ביתו אפי' ע"י עירוב שמא ישכח ויסחט בבואו: אבל עשרה בני אדם · הואיל ומרובין הן מדכרי אהדדי: מסתפגין באלונטית אחת · והיינו נמי רבותא דחדא אלונטית לעשרה (ג) נפישא ביה מיא אפילו הכי מביאין אותה בידים: פניהם ידיהם ורגליהם · אורחא דמילתא נקט וה"ה לכל גופם: סכין · שמן בשבת: וממשמשין · ביד על כל הגוף להנאה: אבל לא מתעמלין · לשפשף בכח: ולא מתגררין · גרסינן במגררת שקורין אשטריי"א דהוי עובדא דחול: לקורדימא · שם הנהר ובגמ' מפרש טעמא: אפיקטויזין · להקיא: ואין מעצבין את הקטן · לשון ידיך עצבוני (איוב י) שמתקנים ומייבשין עצמותיו וחוליות שדרתו כמדת ללמו ובגמרא אמר טעמא: ואין מחזירין את השבר · עצם שנשבר. כל רפואה אסורה משום שחיקת סמנין: נפרקה · אלוייש"ר בלעז שיצא העצם מפרק שלו: לא יטרפס · לשון ביצים טרופות בקערה (חולין דף סד.):

תוספות

המנער טליתו · פי' ר"ח מן הטל שעליו דהיינו כיבוס וליבון חייב חטאת וכן משמע דהוי דומיא דכומתא דרב יוסף אבל בניעור מן העפר כדפירש בקונטרס אין נראה שיהא שייך ליבון:

היוצא בטלית מקופלת · איידי דאיירינן במי שנשרו כליו בדרך שאין דרך הוא לקפל טליתו נקטיה הכא:

הרטנין · רטנין כמו הרהטנין *(הערודפי' הרלים): **מהו** לעשות מרזב. נראה לרבי דלענין איסור הוצאה איירי כמו טלית של ד' כנפות ולוקח שני לידי כותב טליתו של לד ימינו ונותן על כתף השמאלית ואינו פושטו על כתף אלא מקופל ומונח על כתפו והיינו דקאמר מאי מרזב כיסי בבלייתא שקורין פרונגלדר"ה דכשהוא מונח כמו שפירשתי יש בו כיסים מרובים וכל כיסא וכיסא נראה כמין מרזב ומיבעיא ליה אי איכא איסור הוצאה בכך כיון שאינה דרך מלבוש והיינו דקאמר כל אדעתא לכנופי אסור דהיינו כמו שפירשתי ששני לידי הימין מקובלים ומונחים על כתף השמאלית שיכול לילך במהרה ולא יכביד עליו טליתו אדעתא דלהתנאות שפיר דמי והיינו כשאין לידי טליתו מקובלין אלא לד אחד מונחת על כתפו הגל נוארו ולד האחר טפל על שכמו עד הזרוע ואין בו שום כיסוי והיינו שלשל רבי טליתו דבסמוך שלשל אותו כמו שפירשתי כעין להתנאות והיינו דרך מלבוש וכן פירש בערוך ערך מרזב אסור לעשות מרזב בשבת פירוש כשיעטוף אדם טליתו ויקפיל שני קצותיו כעין דרך קיפול ויניחנה על שכמו השמאלית ויחזור ויקפל שאר הטלית שבלד הימין ויניחנה בכתפו רק מה שפירש שקורין מרזב מה שטליתו מוספלת מהנה ומהנה וחלל כנגד השדרה דנראה כמין מרזב אינו נראה לרבי דא"כ מאי קאמר בתר הכי מאי מרזב כיסי בבלייתא הלא אינו עשוי כעין כיסא · מ"ר:

אף מי מערה חמין · (ד) שהוחמו בחור דאי בחמי טבריא שרי לכתחילה כדאמר בפרק כירה (ד' מ. ושם) והניחו להן חמי טבריא ובפרק שמונה שרצים (ד' קט: ושם) א):

דיעבד אין · אמי מערה קאי ולא תנא במתני' חמי טבריא אלא למידק אף מי מערה חמין ב):

דתניא

א) עי' רש"א ורש"ל . ב) [ועי' תוספות לעיל קט. ד"ה רוחצין ותוס' חולין טו: ד"ה אלא נור]

כשיתעטף אדם טליתו ויקפל ב' קצותיה כמין כרך קיפול ויניחה על כתפו השמאלית ויחזור ויקפל שאר הטלית המשולשל בצידו הימין מניחה בכתפו הימין ונמצאת טליתו מקופלת מהנה ומהנה ומופשלת על כתפיו וחלל כנגד השדרה ונראה כמין מרזב . וכענין זה היה קשר (כישי) [כישא] בבלייתא שהיו קושרין ב' כריתות וקורין אותה כישא וכיסכוסי מאני*) . וי"א זולתי פירוש זה. אבל חובה עלינו לומר בלשון רבותינו ומה שקיבלנוהו . וכרב פפא שהוא בתראה עבדינן ואמר כללא כל אדעתא לכנופי אסור . כל להתנאות שפיר דמי וכדרב שישא בריה דרב אידי שהיה מתנאה בסדינין כי אתא רב דימי אמר פעם אחת יצא רבי לשדה והיו ב' צידי טליתו מונחין לו על כתפו ושאר הטלית כרוכה ומופשלת לו לאחוריו . אמר לפניו יהושע בן זירוז בן חמיו של ר"מ בזו לא חייב ר"מ חטאת . כלומר זה המעשה דומה לרטנין שיוצאין בסודרין בסדינין מקובצין ולא משולשין על כתפיהן ור' מאיר לא היה בזה מחייב חטאת**) אי לא אסורה מדרבנן . א"ל ר' דקדק ר"מ עד כאן שלשל רבי טליתו: **מתני'** הרוחץ במי מערה כו'. אוקימנא

*) עיין בערוך ערך מרזב א'. **) [אולי צ"ל אלמא דאסורה מדרבנן ואפשר דרבינו מפרש בזו לא חייב ר"מ חטאת בניחותא דחטאת לא היה מחייב רק הוי אוסר מדרבנן וצ"ע בזה] .

רבינו חננאל

ואוקימנא ליה דרב כתנאי: אמר רב הונא המנער טליתו בשבת חייב חטאת . פי' המנער כדכתיב התנערי מעפר וכדגרסינן התם ומנערה אחת לשלשים. אם יש אבק בבגד חדש שחור ומקפיד עליו . או אם יש עליו דבר מינוף אוסר רב הונא לנפצו . אבל אם הוא בגד ישנו לבן או אדום ולא קפיד עלייהו שרי וכן הלכה . וזה שראה עולא לרבנן דהוו נפצי גלימייהו ואמר הני מחללי שבתא . רבנן דפומבדיתא במלבושין דלא קפדי עלייהו הוו נפצי . (אמתא) [כומתא] הוא כמין כובע של ראש במקום סודר כדאמרינן בפרק השולח גט לאשתו האי אמתא דהזה שכיב מרה אתת בכת קמיה.ואמרה ליה עד אימת תיתעבד ותזיל התיא אמתא שקל כומתיה ושדא בה אמר ליה קני הא וקני נפשיך . כלומר קני נפשיך בחליפין . וי"א כומתא הוא כגון כאן דומה לגביע והוה באותו הטמנ' מינוף . והוה אביי מהסס . כלומר מתיירא כדאמרינן התם חזייה דהוה קא מהסס . א"ל רב יוסף לאביי נפוץ שדי אנן לא קפדינן מידי: היוצא בטלית מקופלת ומונחת לו על כתפו כגון אלו מוכרי כסות שמקפלין ומפשילין אותן על כתפיהו . אתמר משמיה דר' יוחנן חייב חטאת ותניא כוותיה והכי הלכתא וכן נמי היוצא וצרורין לו בסדינו מעות חייב חטאת אבל הרטנין שהם הרצים יוצאין בסודר שעל כתפיהן . ולא אלו בלבד אלא כל אדם . והנכון להיות כרוך בצוארו . או נימא כרוכה לו באצבעו . כהורקנוס בר' אליעזר. ואע"ג דאמר משמא דר' יוחנן הלכה אע"פ שאין נימא כרוכה לו על אצבעו: **עולא** איקלע לבי אסי בר (חני) [היני] בעא מיניה מהו לעשות מרזב בשבת א"ל הכי אמר ר' אלעזר אסור . כך קבלנו מרבותינו שיש בידם קבלה כי מרזב זה

עין משפט נר מצוה

מ א מיי' פי' מהלכות שבת הלכה יח סמג לאוין סה טוש"ע או"ח סימן שב סעיף א:

מא ב מיי' פי"ט שם הלי"ט סמג שם טור ש"ע או"ח סימן שא סעיף כט:

[בערך רטן וסיים שם הרלים יוצאין בסודר שעל כתפיהן מקובץ ולא מסולשל בשביל שלא יעכבו לרוץ]

מב ג שם סעיף לב לג:

מג ד מיי' שם טור ש"ע שם סעיף לד:

מד ה שם סעיף לא:

מה ו מיי' פכ"ב שם הלכה כ טור ש"ע או"ח סימן שכו סעיף א:

מסורת הש"ס

לעיל נח.

[תוספתא פ"ו]

ס"א היוצאין וכן גי' ר"מ

[יומא כ. מגילה כב:]

ס"א בבני מעיים ר"א לפלומא ס"א טובל

[עי' תוס' חולין ב. ד"ה המניח ועי' תוס' סוטה ב. ד"ה המקנא דיעבד]

הגהות הב"ח

(א) רש"י ד"ה קמחללי רבנן שבתא: (ב) ד"ה מי מערה וכו' מקורה שהוחם ואין חומו: (ג) ד"ה מסתפגין וכו' אלונטית לעשרה בני אדם נפישו: (ד) תוס' ד"ה אף מי מערה חמין בחמין שהוחמו וכו' ובפ' שרצים וכו' ולא דקאמר דיעבד אין אמי מערה וכו' וכו' וכו' וכו' וכו' וכו' וכו' וכו' וכו' וכו'

הגהות הגר"א

[א] גמ' יוצאין בסודרין שעל כתפן . נ"ב פי' אפילו מקופל . וז"ש רטנין ר"ל הרלים . ערוך ורמב"ם: [ב] שם כל אדעתא דלכנופי . נ"ב פי' הרמב"ם שלא יקרעו או שלא יתלכלכו: [ג] רש"י ד"ה כסוי בבלייתא ומחזיקין אותן . נ"ב אבל הרמב"ם כתב אפילו בידו או על כתפו:

גליון הש"ס

רש"י ד"ה חייב חטאת · דזהו ליבונה . עיין לעיל דף קמא ע"א רש"י ד"ה מכבנים וצ"ע:

עין משפט נר מצוה

מו א ב מיי׳ פכ״ב מהל׳ שבת הלכה יט טור שו״ע או״ח סימן שא סעיף מח :
מז ג ד מיי׳ פי״ט שם הלכה יט סמג לאוין סה טוש״ע שם סעיף לד :
מח ה ו מיי׳ פכ״א מהל׳ שבת הלכה כח סמג שם טוש״ע או״ח סימן שכו סעיף ג :
מט ז מיי׳ וסמג שם טוש״ע שם וסימן שכה סעיף מג :
נ ח מיי׳ שם :
נא ט מיי׳ שם הלכה ל טוש״ע או״ח סימן שכז סעיף ג :
נב י מיי׳ שם הלכה כט טוש״ע או״ח סי׳ שא סעיף מו בהג״ה :
נג כ ל מיי׳ שם הלכה לא סמג שם טוש״ע או״ח סי׳ שכח סעיף לט:
[בגיטין אי׳ סוכני וחומס]
נד מ מיי׳ וסמג שם טור שו״ע או״ח סימן של סעיף י :
נה נ מיי׳ פכ״ב שם הלכה כו :
[שייך לעיל במשנה]

תוספות

דתניא א״ר כשהיינו למדין תורה כו׳ · מסתמא יחידי היה שלא היה אלא אחד מתלמידיו עמו כשהיה רוחץ כדתניא במקום שנהגו (פסחים דף נא·) שלא ירחוץ תלמיד עם רבו ואם היה רבו צריך לו מותר ומסתמא ר״ש לא היה צריך אלא לאחד כשהיה רוחץ וכשהיו שבים לביתם היה התלמיד נושא האלונטית בפני עצמה שר״ש לא היה נושא עמו דהא ס״ל שיחיד מותר להביאה ולא חיישינן לסחיטה והא דקאמר היינו ר״ל כל אחד ואחד בפני עצמו כשהיה מגיע יומו לשמש רבו ולעיל בפ׳ כירה (דף מ:) גרסינן מעשה בתלמיד של ר׳ מאיר שנכנס אחריו לבית המרחץ ויש ספרים דגרסי תלמידיו ואינו ובכל הספרים גרסי לקמן בפרק שואל (דף קנא:) תלמידו · מ״ר :

צריך לקשר שני ראשיה למטה · בגיטין בפ׳ הנזקין (דף נט.) מפרש דסכניתא הוא בגד דק דאמרינן *סוכני וחומר כי אמגוזא ופלגא דאמגוזא ומשום הכי צריך לקשר שני ראשיה למטה שלא יפריחנו מעליו הרוח ואתי לאתויי או משום דנראה כעין משוי לפי שהוא דק מאד ואינו נראה מלבוש אא״כ נראה קשור :

*__אין__ מעצבין את הקטן · פירשתי [ברים כל הכלים] (דקכ״ג.) ד״ה אסוכי:

גמרא

דלהשתטף כל גופו אפי׳ לכתחילה שפיר דמי מני ר״ש היא *דתניא לא ישתטף אדם בין בחמין בין בצונן דברי ר״מ ר״ש מתיר ר׳ יהודה אומר בחמין אסור בצונן מותר : ונסתפג אפילו בעשר אלונטיות : רישא רבותא קמ״ל וסיפא רבותא קמ״ל רישא רבותא קמ״ל דאפילו הני דלא נפישי בהו מיא כיון דחד הוא אתי לידי סחיטה וסיפא רבותא קמ״ל אפילו הני דנפישי בהו מיא כיון דרבים נינהו מדכרי אהדדי : *תנו רבנן מסתפג אדם באלונטית ומניחה בחלון ולא ימסרנה לאוליירין מפני שחשודים *על אותו דבר רבי שמעון אומר מסתפג באלונטית אחת ומביאה בידו לתוך ביתו אמר ליה אביי לרב יוסף הלכתא מאי אמר ליה הא ר׳ שמעון הא רבי הא שמואל הא ר׳ יוחנן ר׳ שמעון הא דאמרן רבי *דתניא אמר רבי כשהיינו למדין תורה אצל ר׳ שמעון בתקוע היינו מעלין שמן ואלונטית מחצר לגג ומגג לקרפף עד שהיינו מגיעין אצל מעין שהיינו רוחצין בו שמואל דאמר רב יהודה אמר שמואל מסתפג אדם באלונטית ומביאה בידו לתוך ביתו ר׳ יוחנן דאמר ר׳ חייא בר אבא א״ר יוחנן הלכה מסתפג אדם באלונטית ומביאה בידו לתוך ביתו ומי א״ר יוחנן הכי והא״ר יוחנן *הלכה כסתם משנה ותנן ונסתפג אפילו בעשר אלונטיות לא יביאם בידו ההוא כבן חכינאי מתני לה א״ר חייא בר אבא אר״י האוליירין מביאין בלרי נשים לבי בני ובלבד שיתכסה בהן ראשן ורובן סכניתא (א) צריך לקשר ב׳ ראשיה למטה א״ר חייא בר אבא א״ר יוחנן למטה מכתפיים אמר להו רבא לבני *מחוזא כי מעבריתו מאני לבני חילא שרביבו בהו למטה מכתפיים : סכין וממשמשין : *ת״ר סכין וממשמשין בבני מעיים בשבת ובלבד שלא יעשה כדרך שהוא עושה בחול היכי עביד ר׳ חמא בר חנינא אמר סך ואח״כ ממשמש ר׳ יוחנן אמר סך וממשמש בבת אחת : אבל לא מתעמלין : א״ר חייא בר אבא א״ר יוחנן אסור לעמוד בקרקעיתה של דיומסת מפני שמעמלת ומרפא אמר ר׳ יהודה אמר רב כל ימיה של דיומסת עשרים ואחד יום ועצרת מן המנין איבעיא להו עצרת (בתחלה) להאי גיסא או להאי גיסא ת״ש דאמר שמואל כולהו שקייני *מדיבחא ועד עצרתא מעלו דילמא התם הוא דכמה דקריר עלמא מעלי אבל הכא משום הבלא הוא כיון דחמים עלמא טפי מעלי אמר רבי חלבו חמרא דפרוגייתא ומיא דדיומסת קיפחו עשרת השבטים מישראל רבי אלעזר בן ערך איקלע להתם *אימשיך בתרייהו איעקר תלמודיה כי הדר אתא קם למיקרי בספרא בעא למיקרא °החדש הזה לכם *אמר החרש היה לבם בעו רבנן רחמי עליה והדר תלמודיה והיינו דתנן *ר׳ נהוראי אומר הוי גולה למקום תורה ואל תאמר שהיא תבא אחריך שחבריך יקיימוה בידך ואל בינתך אל תשען *תנא לא ר׳ נהוראי שמו אלא ר׳ נחמיה שמו ואמרי לה ר׳ אלעזר בן ערך שמו ולמה נקרא שמו ר׳ נהוראי שמנהיר עיני חכמים בהלכה : אבל לא מתגררין : ת״ר *אין גוררין במגררת בשבת רשב״ג אומר אם היו רגליו מלוכלכות בטיט ובצואה גורר כדרכו ואינו חושש רב שמואל בר יהודה עבדא ליה אימיה מגררתא דכספא : אין יורדין לקורדימא וכו׳ : מאי טעמא משום פיקא : ואין עושין אפיקטויזין בשבת : אמר רבה בר בר חנה אמר רבי יוחנן לא שנו אלא בסם אבל ביד מותר תניא רבי נחמיה אומר אף בחול אסור מפני הפסד אוכלין : ואין מעצבין את הקטן : אמר רבה בר בר חנה אמר ר׳ יוחנן *לפופי ינוקא בשבת שפיר דמי והאנן תנן אין מעצבין התם בחומרי שדרה דמיחזי כבונה : ואין מחזירין את השבר : אמר רבי חנא *) בגדתאה אמר שמואל הלכה

הדרן עלך חבית

*) [עמ״ש רש״י ברכות נד: וע״ע פרש״י ביבמות סז. ד״ה בגדתאה]

[חשודין לשרופה ונותנין אותה לאחרים. ערוך ערך ע״ב] — ברכות ה. — סנהדרין קא. — פסחים מב: — שמות יב — [תוספ׳ פי״ז] — [לעיל סו: ע״ש]

רש״י

גמ׳ דלהשתטף · שוטפן על גופו דלאו דרך רחיצה היא שרי לכתחילה אפי׳ בחמין : סיפא · אבל עשרה בני אדם כו׳ : ומניחה בחלון · הסמוכה לכותל המרחץ : לאוליירין · בלנים : על אותו דבר · סחיטה : הא רבי והא ר״ש כו׳ : הרי כל אלו שמתירין : מחצר לגג כו׳ · ר״ש לטעמיה דאמר בעירובין (דף פט·) אחד גגות אחד חצירות ואחד קרפיפות כולן רשות אחת הן לטלטל מזה לזה ואפילו של בעלים הרבה : עד שהיינו מגיעין כו׳ · ומסתמא לא היו מניחין אותה על המעין במקום הפקר : כבן חכינאי מתני לה. דברי בן חכינאי מסיים בה ולאו סתמא : האוליירין · בלנין : מביאין בלרי נשים · סדינים שהנשים מסתפגין בהם מותר להביאן דרך מלבוש לבית המרחץ : סכניתא · סודר גדול [א] שתלוי לו בין כתפיו וראשו עטוף בו : צריך לקשור שני ראשיה · זה בזה שלא תפול מראשו: כי מעבריתו מאני לבני חילא · כשתביאו בגדי העובדי כוכבי׳ בני החיל המוטלי׳ עליכם לשמשן ואתם מביאים להם בשבת דרך רשות הרבים : שרביבו בהו למטה מכתפיים · שלא יהיו שוליהם מונחים בכתפיכם אלא משוכי׳ למטה שיהא נראה לבוש : סך ואח״כ ממשמש · [דקסבר] בחול ממשמש ואחר כך סך : דיומסית* · שם נהר שמימיו מלוחים : שמעמלת · מחממת : ומרפא · שהטיט מלוח : כל ימיה · ימי רפואתה : להאי גיסא כו׳ · מתחלת הימים או בסוף : שקייני · משקין לרפואה : מדבחא לעצרת · אלמא עצרת בסוף : חמרא דפרוגיתא · שם מדינה שיינה משובח : קפחו עשרת השבטים · שהיו בעלי הנאה ועסוקים בכך ולא היו עוסקים בתורה ויצאו לתרבות רעה : להתם · לפורגיתא ודיומסית : אימשיך בתרייהו · אחר היין והרחיצה : איעקר תלמודיה · נעקר תלמודו ושכחו : החרש היה לבם : הוי גולה למקום תורה. אם ת״ח אתה אל תשב אלא במקום ת״ח חברך ואל תאמר תלמידים הם יבואו אלי ודי לי בכך למה אהיה גולה : שחביריך יקיימוה בידך · שתהא רגיל אצלם וכשתשנה מסכת אחת והם אחרת תשמענה ותהא סדורה בפיך ואל תשתכח הימנה : ואל בינתך אל תשען. לומר חכם גדול אני וזכרן וכשאחזור פרק זה או מסכת זו לא תשתכח חברתה ממני : מגררת · אשטריי״ל ואדם מגרר בה : מגרדתא דכספא · לשבת : משום פיקא · טיט של אותו נהר מחליק ובגדי האדם נישורין במים כשהוא נופל ואתי לידי סחיטה : אלא בסם · דדמי לרפואה וגזירה ° משום שחיקת סמנין : אבל ביד · להכניס יד לתוך גרונו עד שיקיא מותר : מפני הפסד אוכלין · שבמעיו ומתוך כך הוא רעב וחוזר ואוכל : לפופי · אונמלוטי״ר כמו שעושי׳ לקטן שיתיישבו אבריו ולא יתעקם : בחומרי שדרה · חוליות של שדרה שנתפרקה אחת מהן ולאחר זמן קמיירי דלאו ביום לידה (ג) אמרי׳ (לעיל דף קכט:) כל האמור בפ׳ תוכחה דיחזקאל עושין לחיה בשבת :

רבינו חננאל

אוקימנא למתני׳ הרוחץ בחמין דיעבד אבל לכתהלה לרחוץ בחמין אסור . ולהשתטף בחמין נמי אפי׳ כל גופו מותר כר״ש דתניא לא ישתטף אדם בין בחמין בין בצונן דברי ר״מ . ור״ש מתיר . ר׳ יהודה אומר בחמין אסור ובצונן מותר . אע״פ דתנינן סתמא כר״ש לית הלכתא כוותיה דהא בפירוש נמי תנינן סתמא כוותיה (לעיל דף לח) . מעשה שעשו אנשי טבריא כו׳ *) (ואע״ג דאמר עולא הלכה כאנשי טבריא הא אמר ליה רב נחמן תברינהו לסילונייהו אנשי טבריא) ואוקימנא כר״ש . ופסקי׳ בגמרי׳ אמר רבה בר בר חנה א״ר יוחנן הלכה כרבי יהודה ודקדק רב יוסף על רבה בר בר חנה וא״ל בפירוש שמיעא לך דהלכתא כר׳ יהודה או מכללא אמרתיה . א״ל בפירוש שמיעא ליה .
וכיון דפסק ר׳ יוחנן בפירוש הלכה כר׳ יהודה כוותיה עבדינן: ומסתפג אפי׳ בעשר אלונטיות ולא יביאם בידו ואע״פ שאין בהם מים מרובין . דכיון דחד הוא . דלמא מינשי ועביד סחיטה . אבל אם היו ב״א הרבה אפילו אם מסתפגין כולן באלונטית אחת והיא שרוי במים כיון דרבים נינהו מדכרי אהדדי ולא אתו לידי סחיטה . ומותר להביאה בידים בחצר או מן הגג וכרומה לו מקום שמותר לו לטלטל: אוליירין הם השמשים בני אדם הנכנסין במרחץ והן חשודין בזמה שמא יטמאו לונטיות זו בשכבת זרעם. א״ל אביי לרב יוסף והלכתא מאי כו׳ והלכתא כי הא דא״ר חייא בר רבה א״ר יוחנן הלכה מסתפג אדם באלונטית ומביאה בידו לתוך ביתו . ומקשינן עלה הא״ר יוחנן הלכה כסתם משנה ותנן מסתפג אדם אפילו בעשר אלונטיות ולא יביאם בידו . ומפרקי׳ מתני׳ ר׳ יוחנן לא תאני לה סתמא . אלא כבן חכינאי מתני לה. בתלמוד א״י בפ׳ כירה ר׳ חנניה בן עקיבא התיר הבאת לונטיות: סכינתאי א״ר אבין בר רב חסדא א״ר יוחנן צריך לקשר ב׳ ראשיה למטה . א״ר חייא בר אבא א״ר יוחנן למטה מכתפים. וכן זה שאמר רבא לבני מחוזא כי מעבריתו מני דבני חילא שרביבו להו למטה מכתפים . שלא להראות משא בכתף: בלרין נשים לבי בני. פי׳ דהא קן של נשים כשמביאין להן האוליירין במרחץ לא התירו אלא עד שיתכסה בהן ראשו ורובו: סכין וממשמשין והלכתא כר׳ יוחנן דאמר סך וממשמש בבת אחת והוא משמוש ביד בקלות . אבל לא מתעמלין . פי׳ פושטין ומקפלין זרועותיהם לפניהן ולאחריהן וכן רגליהן ע״ג ירכותיהן ומתחממין ומזיעין והוא כמין מעשה רפואה ואסור . וכן אסור לעמוד בשבת בקרקעיתה של דיומסת מפני שמעמלת ומרפאה: חמרא דפרוגתא יין של פרוגיתא והוא שם מקום ומיא דדימסת גם הוא שם מקום . כלומר יין של פרגיתא ומיא של דיומסת טובים הם וערבין ונמשך לב שותה אותן בהן ואינו רוצה להניחם ומתאחר שם ואותן מקומות אין בהן בני תורה והמתאחר שם זמן הרבה מתקפח ושכח תלמודו . אבל לא מתגרדין . גירוד זה הוא חיכוך בכלי כי הא דתנן רבנן אין גורדין במגרת בשבת רשבג״א אם היו רגליו מלוכלכות בטיט ובצואה גורד כדרכו ואינו חושש. רב ושמואל בר יהודה עבדא ליה אמיה מגריתא דכספא להתחכך בה: אין יורדין לקירומא . ס״א לפילומא פי׳ בקעה ויש שם מים ותחתיו טיט כמו טפל. ואם יבקע ויטבע בו אינו יכול לעלות עד שמתקבצין הרבה ב״א ומעלין אותו משם. יש מי שאומרים הרוחץ באותה בקעה מצטנן ואותן המים משלשלין בני מעיו **) . וזה פי׳ ביקא . פי׳ אפיקטויזין קיא. אמר רבה בר בר חנה א״ר יוחנן לא שנו אלא בסם שהוא אסור אבל ביד מותר . ואין מעצבין את הקטן כו׳ . פי׳ מושכין אבריו של קטן ומיישב בידו הוליות של שזירה אחת על חברתה וזהו עיצוב מלשון עצבון: לפופי ינוקא לחבר אברים של תינוק. וכדתרגם ויחבר ולפיף : ואין מחזירין את השבר אמר רב הונא בגדתאה אמר שמואל מחזירין

*) לכאורה נראה דמהיכא ואע״ג עד תברינהו לסילונייהו אנשי טבריא שייך להלן אחר תיבות כוותיה עבדינן ודו״ק
**) עי׳ ערוך ערך פלס א׳

[עי׳ פירש״י עירובין סג. ד״ה מחוזא וברש״י פסחי׳ ה. ד״ה מחוזא וברש״י ב״מ נט. סוד שם עז. ד״ס אוכלסא דמחוזא]

מסורת הש״ס

לעיל לט:
עירובין לא. [מנחות עב.]
[וכישעיה כח א גרס ומיא דדיומסית וכן גרס רד״ק שם]
[לעיל מו. וש״נ]
אדר״נ ספי״ד
אבות פ״ד משנה י״ד
עירובין יג: ע״ש

הגהות הב״ח

(א) גמרא סכניתא אמר ר׳ אבין בר רב חסדא א״ר יוחנן צריך לקשר שני וכו׳ ואמר ר׳ חייא:
(ג) רש״י ד״ה בחומרי וכו׳ ביום לידה לא אמרינן. נ״ב סוף פ׳ מפנין ע״ש ברש״י בפי׳ דלפופי הוא על ידי תגורות ופסיקיות :

הגהות הגר״א

[א] רש״י ד״ה סוכניתא סודר גדול. נ״ב אבל הרמב״ם פי׳ קטן שאין מכסה ראשו ורובו :

גליון הש״ס

גמ׳ אמר החרש היה לבם. עי׳ דבר נחמד בקרבים בליקוטים שבסוף הספר : רש״י ד״ה אלא בסם וכו׳ משום שחיקת סמנין . ע״ל דף קמ ע״ב ברש״י ד״ה אפיקטויזין :

Hence [147*b*] sousing the whole body[12] is well [permitted] even
a at the very outset.[1] Who [is the authority for this]? It is R. Simeon. For it was taught: A man must not souse the whole of his body, either with hot or with cold water: this is R. Meir's view; but R. Simeon permits it. R. Judah said: It is forbidden with hot water, but permitted with cold.

AND DRIES HIMSELF EVEN WITH TEN TOWELS. The first clause informs us of the most surprising ruling, and the second clause informs us of the most surprising ruling. 'The first clause informs us of the most surprising ruling': even these, which do not contain much water, [are forbidden]; for since there is only one person, he will come to wring it out. 'And the second clause informs us of the most surprising ruling': even these, though they contain very much water [are permitted]; for since there are many, they will remind each other.[2]

Our Rabbis taught: A man may dry himself with a towel and place it on the window-sill, but he must not give it to the bath attendants, because they are suspected of that thing.[3] R. Simeon said: One may dry himself with one towel and bring it home.[4] Abaye asked R. Joseph: What is the law? Said he to him, Lo! there is R. Simeon; lo! there is Rabbi; lo! there is Samuel; lo! there is R. Johanan.[5] 'R. Simeon', as we have stated. 'Rabbi': for it was taught, Rabbi said: When we learnt Torah at R. Simeon['s academy] in Tekoa,[6] we used to carry up oil and towels from the courtyard to the roof and from the roof to an enclosure,[7] until we came to the fountain where we bathed. 'Samuel': for Rab Judah said in Samuel's name: A person may dry himself with a towel and carry it home [wrapped round] his hand.[8] 'R. Johanan': for R. Hiyya b. Abba said in R. Johanan's name: The *halachah* is: A person may dry himself with a towel and carry it home [wrapped round] his hand. Yet did R. Johanan say thus: surely R. Johanan said, The *halachah* is as an anonymous Mishnah, whereas we learnt: AND DRIES HIMSELF EVEN WITH TEN TOWELS, HE MUST NOT FETCH THEM IN HIS HAND?—He recited this as Ben
b Hakinai['s view].[1]

R. Hiyya b. Abba said in R. Johanan's name: The bath attendants may bring women's bathing clothes to the baths, providing that they cover their heads and the greater part of their bodies in them.[2] As for a *sabnitha*,[3] R. Hiyya b. Abba said in R. Johanan's name: One must tie its two bottom ends.[4] R. Hiyya b. Abba also said in R. Johanan's name: [That means] below the shoulders.[5] Raba said to the citizens of Mahoza: When you carry the apparel of the troops,[6] let them drop below your shoulders.[7]

ONE MAY OIL AND LIGHTLY MASSAGE [THE BODY]. Our Rabbis taught: One may oil and massage the bowels [of an invalid] on the Sabbath, provided this is not done as on weekdays. How then shall it be done?—R. Hama son of R. Hanina said: They must first be oiled and then massaged.[8] R. Johanan said: The oiling and massaging must be done simultaneously.

BUT [ONE MAY] NOT KNEAD. R. Hiyya b. Abba said in R. Johanan's name: One may not stand on the mud of Diomsith,[9] because it stimulates [the body] and loosens [the bowels]. Rab Judah said in Rab's name: The complete period of Diomsith is twenty-one days, and Pentecost is included.[10] The scholars asked: Does Pentecost belong to this end or to that end?[11]—Come and hear: For Samuel said: All potions [medicines] [taken] between
c Passover and Pentecost are beneficial.[1] Perhaps that is [only] there, where it is beneficial [only] as long as the weather is cold: but here it is on account of the heat,[2] [so] when the weather is warm it is [even] more beneficial.

R. Helbo said: The wine of Perugitha[3] and the water of Diomsith cut off the Ten Tribes from Israel.[4] R. Eleazar b. 'Arak visited that place. He was attracted to them,[5] and [in consequence] his learning vanished. When he returned, he arose to read in the Scroll [of the Torah].[6] He wished to read, *Hahodesh hazeh lakem* [*This month shall be unto you*, etc.],[7] [instead of which] he read *haharesh hayah libbam*.[8] But the scholars prayed for him, and his learning returned. And it is thus that we learnt, R. Nehorai said: Be exiled to a place of Torah, and say not that it will follow thee, for thy companions will establish it in thy possession;[9] and do not rely on thine own understanding.[10] A Tanna taught: His name was not R. Nehorai but R. Nehemiah; whilst others state, his name was R. Eleazar b. 'Arak, and why was he called R. Nehorai? Because he enlightened [*manhir*] the eyes of the Sages in *halachah*.[11]

BUT [ONE MAY] NOT SCRAPE. Our Rabbis taught: One may not scrape with a strigil on the Sabbath. R. Simeon b. Gamaliel said: If one's feet are soiled with clay and dirt he may scrape them off in the usual way, without fear. R. Samuel b. Judah's mother made him a silver strigil.

YOU MAY NOT GO DOWN TO A WRESTLING GROUND. What
d is the reason? Because of sinking [in the clay soil].[1]

ONE MAY NOT INDUCE VOMITING ON THE SABBATH. Rabbah b. Bar Hanah said in R. Johanan's name: They learnt this only [when it is effected] by a drug, but it may be done by hand.[2] It was taught, R. Nehemiah said: It is forbidden even during the week, because of the waste of food.

OR STRAIGHTEN AN INFANT['S LIMBS]. Rabbah b. Bar Hanah said in R. Johanan's name: To swaddle an infant on the Sabbath is permitted. But we learnt: YOU MAY NOT STRAIGHTEN?[3]—There it refers to the spinal vertebrae, which appears as building.[4]

ONE MAY NOT SET A BROKEN BONE. R. Hana of Bagdad

(12) As opposed to an actual bath.
a (1) Even in hot water. (2) Should one forget himself and wish to wring it out. (3) *Sc.* of wringing it out and giving it to others. V. 'Er., 88*a* notes. (4) Presumably wrapped about him as a garment, or where an *'erub* is provided. (5) All these have stated their view, and surely they furnish a reliable guide. (6) Near Bethlehem in Judea. (7) V. *supra* 7*a*. (8) V. n. a4.
b (1) Not anonymously. (2) So that they are brought as garments. (3) 'Aruch; Cur. edd. *saknitha*. Rashi: a large cloth covering, falling over the shoulders. Maim: a small cloth, not large enough to cover the head and the greater part of the body. (4) So that it should not fall off. (5) So that it looks like wearing apparel. (6) To the baths. The troops (non-Jewish) were billeted in Jewish houses (Cf. Ta'an. 21*a*), and the Jews had to perform such offices as bringing their bathing outfits to the baths, carrying them through the streets. (7) V. *supra* 147*a*, n. 5. (8) On weekdays it was reversed. (9) Jast.: identical with Emmaus, a town in the plain of Judea renowned in Talmudic days for its warm springs and luxurious life. (10) Only twenty-one days in the year does one derive medical benefit from Diomsith, and Pentecost is included in those twenty-one days. (11) I.e., does the period commence with Pentecost or end with it?
c (1) Hence Pentecost ends the period. (2) I.e., the healing properties of Diomsith reside in the heat of its springs. (3) A place in northern Israel famous for its wine. A similar statement is made in Lev. Rab. about the wine of Pelugto, near Tiberias, and probably the two are identical. (4) They were so much pre-occupied with these pleasures that they neglected learning and lost faith, which ultimately led to their exile and disappearance. (5) *Sc.* its inhabitants and their luxurious life. (6) In Talmudic days the weekly lesson of the Pentateuch was read by a number of the congregation, each of whom read a part. (7) Ex. XII, 2. (8) Their hearts were silent; or perhaps it is an unintelligible phrase. Each word differs only by one letter from the original to which in turn it bears some resemblance, and the story is quoted as an illustration of the seductive powers of Diomsith! (9) Intellectual intercourse is essential if one is to retain his learning. (10) V. Ab. IV, 14. (11) If R. Nehorai was identical with R. Eleazar b. 'Arak, his statement was thus a result of personal experience.
d (1) This makes walking a labour (Jast.). Rashi: the clay of that river (v. n. on Mishnah) is slippery, and so one may fall into the water, saturate ones garments, and then wring them out. R. Han.: a man may easily sink into the soft mud, thus giving many people the labour of hauling him out. (2) By thrusting the finger down the throat. (3) And that is the purpose of swaddling. (4) If one is dislocated it may not be reset.

said in Samuel's name: [148a] The *halachah* is that one may reset a fracture.[5] Rabbah b. Bar Ḥanah visited Pumbeditha. He did not attend Rab Judah's session, [so] he sent Adda the waiter to him and said, 'Go and seize him.'[6] So he went and seized him. When he [Rabbah] appeared, he found him [Rab Judah] lecturing, One may not reset a fracture. Said he to him, Thus did R. Ḥana of Bagdad say in Samuel's name: The *halachah* is that one may reset a fracture. Said he to him, Surely Ḥana is one of ours and Samuel is one of ours,[7] yet I have not heard this; did I then not summon you justly?[8]

IF ONE'S HAND IS DISLOCATED, etc. R. Awia was sitting before R. Joseph, when his hand became dislocated.[9] How is it thus? asked he. It is forbidden. And how is it thus?[10] It is forbidden. In the meantime his hand reset itself.[11] Said he to him, what is your question? Surely we learnt, IF ONE'S HAND OR FOOT IS DISLOCATED HE MUST NOT AGITATE IT VIOLENTLY IN COLD WATER, BUT MAY BATHE IT IN THE USUAL WAY, AND IF IT HEALS, IT HEALS. But did we not learn: ONE MAY NOT SET A FRACTURE, he retorted, yet R. Ḥana of Bagdad said in Samuel's name, The *halachah* is that one may set a fracture.[1]—Will you weave all in one web?[2] he replied; where it was stated it was stated, but where it was not stated it was not stated.[3]

CHAPTER XXIII

MISHNAH. A MAN MAY BORROW PITCHERS OF WINE AND PITCHERS OF OIL FROM HIS NEIGHBOUR, PROVIDED HE DOES NOT SAY TO HIM, 'LEND [THEM] [HALWENI] TO ME';[1] AND SIMILARLY A WOMAN [MAY BORROW] LOAVES FROM HER NEIGHBOUR. IF HE DOES NOT TRUST HIM HE LEAVES HIS CLOAK WITH HIM [AS A PLEDGE] AND MAKES A RECKONING WITH HIM AFTER THE SABBATH. IN THE SAME WAY, IF THE EVE OF PASSOVER IN JERUSALEM FALLS ON A SABBATH, ONE LEAVES HIS CLOAK WITH HIM [THE VENDOR] AND RECEIVES HIS PASCHAL LAMB[2] AND MAKES A RECKONING WITH HIM AFTER THE FESTIVAL.

GEMARA. Raba son of R. Ḥanan asked Abaye: Wherein does *halweni* differ from *hash'ileni?*[3] In the case of *hash'ileni*, he replied, he [the lender] will not come to write it down;[4] whereas [if he says] *halweni* he will come to write it down. But since on weekdays it sometimes happens that one wishes to say *halweni* but says *hash'ileni*, yet he is not particular[5] and comes to write it down, so on the Sabbath too he may come to write it down?[6]—On the Sabbath, he replied, since the Rabbis permitted *hash'ileni* only, but not *halweni*, the matter is distinguishable and he will not come to write.

Raba son of R. Ḥanan said to Abaye: Consider! The Rabbis said, Regarding all actions on Festivals, as far as it is possible to vary, we vary them;[1] then the women who fill their pitchers on Festivals, why do they not vary [their way of doing it]?—Because it is impossible. How should they do it: shall those who [usually] draw [water] with a large pitcher [now] draw [it] with a small pitcher? Then they increase the amount of walking! Shall those who [usually] draw [water] with a small pitcher [now] draw

(5) He held that this is the correct reading of the Mishnah. (6) Rashi: take his coat until he comes. (7) They are both of our district. (8) Otherwise we would have remained in error. (9) Lit., 'his hand changed'—from its place. (10) He manipulated his hand in various ways and asked of each whether it was permitted on the Sabbath. (11) Lit., 'was healed'.

a (1) Which shows that the text may be corrupt, and so the same may apply to the present quotation. (2) Will you apply the same argument to all? (3) You cannot assume that the text is corrupt here too.

b (1) This is explained in the Gemara. (2) If one forgot to buy an animal before the Sabbath, he leaves his cloak as a pledge with a vendor on the Sabbath, and takes an animal, but must not actually buy it then, fixing its price. (3) Both mean 'lend me', the first implying for a considerable time, the second for a short period (Rashi).—The Mishnah forbids the use of the first term. [Tosaf.: in the first case the object itself passes into the possession of the borrower; in the second, the borrower enjoys only right of use in the object while the object itself remains the possession of the lender. V. Tosaf. a.l., Ḳid. 47*b* and Rappaport J. *Das Darlehen* pp. 29ff.] (4) He expects to remember it in any case. (5) He allows him to keep it for a long time, though the request was only *hash'ileni*. (6) Thinking that the borrower may keep it a long time.

c (1) So as not to do them in the same way as during the week, even where they are permitted.

ה"הלכה מחזירין את השבר רבה בר בר חנה איקלע לפומבדיתא לא על לפירקיה דרב יהודה שדריה לאדא דיילא א"ל זיל גרביה אזיל גרביה אתא אשכחיה דקא דריש אין מחזירין את השבר א"ל הכי אמר רב חנא בגדתאה אמר שמואל הלכה מחזירין את השבר א"ל הא חנא דידן והא שמואל דידן ולא שמיע לי ולאו בדינא גרבתיך : מי שנפרקה ידו כו' : רב אויא הוה יתיב קמיה דרב יוסף שניא ליה ידיה א"ל הכי מאי אסור והכי מאי א"ל אסור אדהכי איתפח ידיה א"ל מאי תיבעי לך הא תנן מי שנפרקה ידו או רגלו לא יטרפם בצונן אבל (א) רוחץ כדרכו ואם נתרפא נתרפא א"ל ולא תנן אין מחזירין את השבר ואמר רב חנא בגדתאה אמר שמואל הלכה מחזירין את השבר אמר ליה *כולהו בחדא מחיתא מחיתנהו היכא דאיתמר איתמר היכא דלא איתמר לא איתמר :

הדרן עלך חבית

שואל אאדם מחבירו כדי יין וכדי שמן ובלבד שלא יאמר לו בהלויני וכן האשה מחבירתה ככרות ואם אינו מאמינו מניח טליתו אצלו ועושה עמו חשבון לאחר שבת וכן ערב פסח בירושלים שחל להיות בשבת מניח טליתו אצלו ונוטל את פסחו ועושה עמו חשבון לאחר יום טוב : **גמ'** א"ל רבא בר רב חנן לאביי מאי שנא השאילני ומאי שנא הלויני אמר ליה השאילני לא אתי למיכתב הלויני אתי למיכתב והא כיון דבחול זימנין דבעי למימר ליה הלויני וא"ל השאילני ולא קפיד עילויה ואתי למיכתב בשבת נמי אתי למיכתב א"ל (בחול דלא שנא כי א"ל הלויני ל"ש כי א"ל השאילני לא קפדינן עילויה אתי למיכתב) בשבת כיון דהשאילני הוא דשרו ליה רבנן הלויני לא שרו ליה מינכרא מילתא ולא אתי למיכתב *א"ל רבא בר רב חנן לאביי מכדי אמרו רבנן גכל מילי דיום טוב כמה דאפשר לשנויי משנינן הני נשי דמליין חצבייהו מיא מ"ט לא משנין דמשום דלא אפשר היכי לעבדי דמליין בחצבא רבא לימלו בחצבא זוטא הא קא מפשו בהילוכא דמליין בחצבא זוטא לימלו בחצבא רבא קא מפשו במשוי

רש"י

הלכה מחזירין את השבר · סבירא ליה לשמואל מחזירין תנן : אדא דיילא · מכשטר"ל ממונה : גרביה · קח בגדו עד שיבא : אתא · רבה אשכחיה לרב יהודה כו' : הא חנא דידן · ממקומו הוא ולא שמעתי זאת מפיו עד הנה : ולאו בדינא גרבתיך · בתמיה שאילו לא באת לא למדתי : שניא ליה ידיה · נשתנית ידו ממקומה אשולשיי"ר בלע"ז : הכי מאי · היה עושה בענינים הרבה ושואל : בחדא מחיתא מחיתנהו · באריגה אחת ארגתו*: היכא דאיתמר · דמתניתין לאו דוקא תנן איתמר :

הדרן עלך חבית

שואל. שלא יאמר הלויני. מפרש בגמרא: שחל להיות בשבת. ולא נזכר מע"ש לקנות: לאחר יו"ט · ליום שלישי : **גמ'** הלויני משמע לזמן מרובה וקיי"ל במסכת מכות (דף ג:) סתם הלואה ל' יום ואתי מלוה זה לכתוב על פנקסו כך וכך הלויתי כדי שלא ישכח: א"ל וכיון דבחול נמי זימנין דבעי למימר הלויני ואמר השאילני : ולא קפיד עליה · והויא הלואה: בשבת נמי · כי אמר השאילני סבר דהלואה היא ואתי למכתב ומאי היכר איכא : ה"ג א"ל בשבת כיון דהשאילני שרו ליה רבנן הלויני לא שרו ליה מינכרא מילתא ולא אתי למכתב: אמרו רבנן · במסכת ביצה : כל כמה דאפשר לשנויי משנינן · דאמרינן המביא כדי יין לא יביאם בסל ובקופה כו' : בנכתמא

תוספות

שואל אדם מחבירו כדי יין וכדי שמן ובלבד שלא יאמר לו הלויני. פירש רש"י טעמא משום דסתם הלואה ל' יום ולפי שהוא לזמן מרובה יותר משאלה אתי למיכתב וקשה לר"ת דסתם שאלה (ג) ל' יום כדאמר במנחות בהתכלת (דף מד.*) טלית שאולה כל ל' יום פטורה מן הציצית ואמרינן נמי התם הדר בפונדקי' בא"י והשוכר בית בחו"ל כל ל' יום פטור מן המזוזה מכאן ואילך חייב במזוזה אלמא דסתם שאלה ל' יום איתא והכי פטורה כל ל' יום דאמר שאולה היא אבל מכאן ואילך נראה כמו שלו ומיהו יכול לומר לרש"י לאו משום דאי מתבע ליה לדינא בתוך ל' יום שאין צריך להחזיר דודאי היה חייב להחזיר (ג) דעבידי אינשי דמשאלי פחות משלשים יום אבל טפי לא משאלי הלכך עד ל' יום אמרי אינשי שאולה היא ור"י פירש לנו דהייתו טעמא בשאלה לפי שהיא חוזרת בעין לא אתי למיכתב אבל לשון הלואה אינו חוזר בעין ואתי למיכתב ואע"ג דכי שאיל מיניה כדי יין וכדי שמן לא הדרי בעין מ"מ מתוך שמזכיר לו לשון שאלה זכור הוא ולא אתי למיכתב. מ"ר וכן פירש ה"ר פורת :

אתקין רבא במחוזא דדרו בדוחקא כו' · ברוב ספרים אינו כתוב כאן ולא בפירוש רש"י ובריש המביא כדי יין (ביצה דף ל. ושם) נראה שהוא מקומו וזה לשון פירוש הקונטרס בביצה דדרו בדוחקא משוי שאדם יחיד נושא בחול על כתיפו בטורח אם בא לשאתו לצורך יום טוב ביו"ט כגון חבית או שק מלא פירות ישאנו ביו"ט בדיגלא עתר שקורין פורק"א כדרך טעאי מלח למכור מפני שצריך לשנות וכשמשנה ישנה להקל משאו ולא להרבות טורח ביו"ט ועתר זה טח לשאת בו משא כבד וכשנושא בו חבית הנישאת בכתף ישנה להקל דדרו בדיגלא משוי חבית גדולה שרגילה לשאת בדיגלא לידרו באגרא ישאוהו ביו"ט בב' בני אדם במוט על כתפים דהייתו נמי שינוי להקל דדרו באגרא במוט על כתפים לידרו ביו"ט אותו משוי באכפא במוט בידים משום שינוי ואפילו אינו להקל מ"מ שינוי הוא ואינו מרבה טורח בשינוי דדרו באכפא ניפרוס סודרא קל הוא ואינו מכביד ושינוי בעלמא הוא ולהגנע עד כאן לשונו ומשמע מתוך פירושו דכל אלה משוי אחד להם בשוה ואין זה נושא יותר אלא שנושא משאו בענין אחר ממה שהיה רגיל וזה דחקו שאם כפרש שכל אלו ממעטים משאם מאשר היו רגילים לשאת קשיא הא דאמר בסמוך (ד) מפשי בהילוכא משמע מפירושא דאגרא נושאים שני בני אדם שפיר במוט בשנים ויש בו משוי שני בני אדם שנושאים כל מה שרגילין לשאת בדיגלא ודיגלא היא משוי שני בני אדם כדמשמע בבבא מציעא בס"פ השוכר את האומנים (דף פג.) וקשיא לר' דהתם משמע נמי דאגרא אין בו משוי לשני בני אדם דאמר התם דדרו באגרא ואיתבר משלם פלגא מ"ט נפיש לחד וזוטר לתרי ודמי לפשיעה ודמי לאונס בדיגלא משלם כולה משמע דלא הוי זוטר לתרי נראה דאגרא לשום אדם אינו נראה עובדא דחול כמו דיגלא ומשום הכי דדרו בדיגלא לידרו באגרא ואע"פ שמפיש בהילוכא יכול לשנות כיון שאינו נראה כל כך עובדא דחול והשתא אתי שפיר דדרו באגרא לידרו באכפא אע"פ שבודאי מרבה במשאוי הוא בנושא בידים המוט מכשנושאו על כתיפו מ"מ כיון שאינו נראה עובדא דחול כמו אגרא יכול לעשות כעין שמלינו גבי בהמה מסוכנת דתנן בביצה (דף כה·) שחטה בשדה לא יביאנה במוט אלא מביאה בידו אברים אברים ותנן נמי (דף כט: ושם) בהמביא כדי יין לא יביאם בסל ובקופה אלא מביא הוא על כתפיו או לפניו אלמא הני אע"ג דמפשי בהילוכא כיון שאינו עושה כל כך כדרך שעושה בחול יש לו לשנות וההיא דבסמוך דמליין בחצבא זוטא ודמליין בחצבא רבה תרווייהו עובדא דחול ובענין שנושאים זה נושאים זה הלכך אין לו לשנות לא להקל ולא להכביד כדפי' טעמא וההיא דלעיל בריש מפנין (דף קכז·) לא שייכא עובדא דחול שאינו מטלטל אלא בבית מזוית לזוית. מ"ר · וההיא דשחטה בשדה פירש בריש מפנין (ג"ז שם) בע"א וכמו שפירש כאן עיקר ועוד קשה לי לפי' הקונטרס דדרו באכפא אמאי ניפרוס סודרא עליה הוה ליה למימר לידרו באגרא כיון שאינו משנה להכביד יותר מאכפא כמו שמשמע נמי מתוך פירושו ולפירוש רבי אתי שפיר :

ניפרוס

עין משפט נר מצוה

נו א טוש"ע או"ח סימן שכג סעיף מז :

נז ב שם סעיף ל :

[ועי' תוספות שם ד"ה טלית]

א ג ד מיי' פכ"ג מהל' שבת הלכה יב סמג לאוין סה טור ש"ע או"ח סימן שז סעיף יא :

ב ה מיי' פ"ה מהלכות י"ט הלכה א ב סמג לאוין עה טוש"ע או"ח סימן תקי סעיף ח :

ג ו מיי' שם טוש"ע שם סעיף י וסימן שכג סעיף ה :

רבינו חננאל

מחזירין את השבר. רבה בר בר חנה לא על (פי')לפירקי' דרב יהודה שדריה לאדא דייאלא א"ל זיל גרד ביה אזל גרביה.פירוש*) משכיהו והביאהו מלשון פרץ נחל מעם גר כלומר הבריחהו . כדגרסינן בפרק בנות כותים נדות מעריסתן . שילא בר אבינא עבד עובדא כרב. כי קא ניחא נפשיה דרב . א"ל לרב אסי זיל צניעיה ואי לא צאית גרדיה הוא סבר גרדית א"ל ופי' הכהו וכו' : מי שנפרקה ידו או רגלו פי' שף מבוכניה לא יטרפן בצונן אבל רוחץ כדרכו ואם נתרפא נתרפא ורב אויא דשניא ליה ידיה והיה אומר לרב יוסף ומראה בידו אם יעשה בידו כך או כך מותר או אסור עד שהיה מראה לו כדי שיראנו מה שהתירו חכמים חזרת ידו למקומה ונתרפא :

הדרן עלך חבית

פרק כ"ג שואל אדם מחבירו כדי יין וכדי שמן ובלבד שלא יאמר לו הלויני כו'. ואוקימנא דחיישינן שמא יכתוב **) וכןשאם יאמר לו הלויני גוערין בו ואומרים לו אסור לומר כן ביום שבת לשון הלואה מינכרא מלתא ולא אתי למכתב וכיון שהזכיר א"ל רבא בר רב חנן לאביי נסיב

*) עיין בערוך בשלם ערך גרד א'

**) אינו מובן לכאורה ואולי דסים לו גירי' הספרים בגמרא כמוסגר בתאי לבנם וסובא כתיי' הרשב"א כאן ומפרש רבינו דכחלוק סוא דבשבת כיון שאם אומר הלוני קפדינן עלוהי יש לו היכירא ולא אתי למכתב מלשון שאלה וכו' ודו"ק :

מסורת הש"ס

[עי' פרש"י חולין נח:]

רש"ל מ"ז

[לעיל קכח: וש"נ] ביצה ל. ע"ש

הגהות הב"ח

(א) גמ' לא יטרפם בצונן (אבל רוחץ) תא"מ ונ"ב ס"א אבל טובל: (ב) תוס' ד"ה שואל וכו' דסתם שאלה נמי ל' יום: (ג) בא"ד היה חייב להחזיר אלא דעבידי: (ד) ד"ה אתקין וכו' דאמר בסמוך הא קא מפשי בהילוכא :

גליון הש"ס

מתני' שואל אדם מחבירו . עי' בירושלמי פ"ח דשביעית על מ"ד סוכה כר"ש שם :

תורה אור

ניפרום סודרא אתי לידי סחיטה נבסייה בנבתמא זימנין דמיפסק ואתי למקטריה הלכך לא אפשר וא"ל רבא בר רב חנן לאביי תנן *לא "מספקין ולא מטפחין ולא מרקדין ביו"ט וקא חזינן דעבדין ולא אמרינן להו ולא מידי ולטעמיך הא דאמר *רבא *לא ליתיב איניש אפומא דלחייא דילמא מיגנדר ליה חפץ ואתי לאיתויי והא קא חזינן (א) נמי דמותבי חצבי ויתבן אפומא דמבואה ולא אמרינן להו ולא מידי אלא הנח לישראל *מוטב שיהו שוגגין ואל יהו מזידין *סבור מינה הנ"מ בדרבנן אבל בדאורייתא לא "ולא היא ל"ש בדרבנן ול"ש בדאורייתא דהא תוספת דיוה"כ דאורייתא היא וקא חזינן להו דקאכלי ושתו עד שתחשך ולא אמרי' להו ולא מידי: וכן אשה מחבירתה ככרות: בשבת הוא דאסיר אבל בחול שפיר דמי לימא מתני' דלא כהלל דתנן *וכן היה הלל אומר "לא תלוה אשה ככר לחבירתה עד שתעשינה דמים שמא יוקרו חטין ונמצאו באות לידי רבית אפילו תימא הלל "הא באתרא דקייץ דמיה הא באתרא דלא קייץ דמיה: ואם אינו מאמינו: איתמר הלוואת יו"ט רב יוסף אמר לא ניתנה ליתבע *ורבה אמר "ניתנה ליתבע רב יוסף אמר לא ניתנה ליתבע דאי אמרת ניתנה ליתבע אתי למיכתב רבה אמר ניתנה ליתבע דאי אמרת לא ניתנה לא יהיב ליה ואתי לאימנועי משמחת יו"ט תנן אם אינו מאמינו מניח טליתו אצלו אי אמרת בשלמא לא ניתנה ליתבע משום הכי מניח טליתו אצלו ועושה עמו חשבון לאחר שבת אלא אי אמרת ניתנה ליתבע אמאי מניח טליתו אצלו ליתן ליה ולתבעיה אמר לא בעינא דליקום בדינא ודיינא מתיב רב אידי בר אבין *"השוחט את הפרה וחילקה בראש השנה אם היה חדש מעובר משמט ואם לאו אינו משמט ואי לא ניתנה ליתבע מאי משמט שאני התם דאיגלאי מילתא דחול הוא ת"ש מסיפא אם לאו אינו משמט אי אמרת בשלמא ניתנה ליתבע היינו דקתני אינו משמט אלא אי אמרת לא ניתנה ליתבע (ב) אמאי אינו משמט דאי יהיב ליה שקיל מכלל דרישא אי יהיב ליה לא שקיל רישא צריך למימר ליה משמט אני סיפא לא צריך למימר ליה משמט אני כדתנן *"המחזיר חוב בשביעית יאמר לו משמט אני ואם אמר לו אעפ"כ יקבל ממנו משום שנאמר °וזה דבר השמטה רב אויא שקיל משכונא *רבה בר עולא מערים איערומי: וכן ערב פסח: א"ר יוחנן *"מקדיש אדם פסחו בשבת וחגיגתו ביו"ט נימא מסייע ליה וכן ערב פסח בירושלים שחל להיות בשבת מניח טליתו אצלו ונוטל את פסחו ועושה עמו חשבון לאחר יו"ט הכא במאי עסקינן בממנה אחרים עמו על פסחו דמעיקרא מיקדש וקאי והא אנן תנן *"אין נמנין על הבהמה בתחילה ביו"ט שאני הכא כיון דרגיל אצלו כמאן דאימני ביה מעיקרא דמי והא תני רבי הושעיא הולך אדם אצל רועה הרגיל אצלו ונותן לו טלה לפסחו ומקדישו ויוצא בו התם נמי כיון דרגיל אצלו אקדושי (ג) ליה מעיקרא והא מקדיש קתני הקדש עילוי מדרבנן ומי אמר ר' יוחנן הכי *והא אמר ר' יוחנן הלכה כסתם משנה ותנן *"לא מקדישין ולא מעריכין ולא מחרימין ולא מגביהין תרומות ומעשרות כל אלו ביו"ט אמרו ק"ו בשבת לא קשיא כאן בחובות שקבוע להן זמן כאן בחובות שאין קבוע להן זמן: **מתני'** מונה אדם את אורחיו ואת פרפרותיו מפיו אבל לא מן הכתב מפיס אדם עם בניו ועם בני ביתו על השולחן ובלבד שלא יתכוין לעשות מנה גדולה כנגד מנה קטנה *ומטילין חלשין על הקדשים ביו"ט אבל לא על המנות:

גמ'

רש"י

בנבתמא · כיסוי: זימנין דמיפסק כו' · כיון דמגרכת ליה כיסוי קטר ליה בכד וזימנין דמיפסק ואתי למקטריה והיא קשר של קיימא דאסור מדאורייתא: ואתי לידי סחיטה · ודקאמר במסכת ביצה ניפרום סודרא עלויה כו' (ד) [התם] בדבר יבש קא מיירי: אין מספקין · כף אל כף משום אבל: מטפחין · על הלב: מרקדין · לשמחה וטעמא מפרש במסכת ביצה שמא יתקן כלי שיר: אפומא דלחייא · לפי שאין ניכר כל כך בין מבוי לרה"ר: ואתי לאתויי · חפץ המתגלגל תוך ד' אמות: ומגנדר אגביהן ומייתין ליה ל"ג: בשבת הוא דאסור · לומר הלויני משום מכתב: הא בחול שרי . ולא חיישינן לרבית ואף על גב דבלשון הלואה קאמר ליה: באתרא דקייץ דמייהו · דככרות לא אתי לידי רבית שאם יוקירו יתן דמיהן: לא ניתנה ליתבע · בב"ד שאין ב"ד נזקקין לה לעולם: בדינא ודיינא · לא לבא לדין ולא לברור דיין ולהטריח את עצמו: השוחט את הפרה וחילקה בראש השנה· של מוצאי שביעית ללוקחים ובהקפה וקיי"ל שביעית משמטת בסופה דכתיב מקץ: אם היה חדש · אלול מעובר ועשו ראש השנה שני ימים משמט דיום טוב ראשון של סוף שביעית היה ונמצאת זו הלואת שביעית ואם לאו הויא לה הלואת מוצאי שביעית ואינו משמט: ל"ג אי אמרת בשלמא כו' ה"ג ואם לא ניתנה ליתבע מאי משמט הואיל ואין ב"ד נזקקין לכופו שמוטה היא ועומדת: דחול הוא · שהרי חדש מעובר ולא הוי יו"ט עד למחר הלכך אי לאו דשביעית הוא סוה גבי: ואם לאו אינו משמט · אלמא ניתנה ליתבע ומשני מאי אינו משמט דאי יהיב ליה שקיל: מכלל דרישא אי יהיב ליה לא שקיל· בתמיה: רישא · דהלואת שביעית היא אי נמי יהיב ליה לוה צריך למימר ליה מלוה משמט אני: (ה) ואם אמר. לוה אעפ"כ איני חפץ שישמטו יקבל ממנו: דבר השמטה · אפילו מקבל חובו יזכיר לו שמיטה בדבורו: שקיל משכונא · בשעת הלואה מהלואת יו"ט: מערים איערומי · לאחר י"ט לוקח ממנו שום חפץ ומעכבו: פסחו בשבת · אם חל י"ד בשבת: וחגיגתו ביו"ט · ביום הקרבתה מותר להקדיש ואע"ג דתנן אלו הן משום שבות אין מקדישין הני כיון דהקרבתן דוחה קדושתן דוחה: בממנה אחרים עמו · כדכתיב (שמות יב) במכסת נפשות: על פסחו · שהיה קדוש ועומד מאתמול: אקדושי · מקדיש ליה רועה מע"ש שהרי יודע שזה סומך עליו: עילוי · מעלה בעלמא שיקדישו בעלים: הא · דקתני אין מקדישין בחובות שאין קבוע להן זמן קאי שאין הקרבתן דוחה שבת: **מתני'** פרפרותיו · מיני מעדנים: אבל לא מן הכתב · אם כתב מע"ש כך וכך אורחים פלוני ופלוני זמנתי כדי שלא ישכחם לא יקרא באותו כתב בשבת ובגמ' מפרש טעמא: מפיס · לשון פיים מטיל פיים לחלק מי מגיע כל מנה ומנה: ובלבד שלא יתכוין לעשות כו' · שיהו המנות שוות ולא תהא אחת גדולה ואחת קטנה לזכות בגדולה הזוכה ע"פ הגורל והמתחייב ע"פ הגורל לקטנה יטלנה ובגמ' מפרש טעמא: חלשים · גורלות: על הקדשים · בין הכהנים: אבל לא על המנות · בגמרא מפרש:

גמ'

תוספות

ניפרום סודרא עליה אתי למסחטיה · מכאן מייתי ר"ת ראיה דביין ושמן לא שייכא סחיטה לעיל בשלהי שמונה שרצים (דף קיא: בד"ה האי מסוכרייהא) פירשתי: **לא** מספקין ולא מטפחין · לא כפי' הקונטרס משום דא"כ מאי איריא ביו"ט אפי' בחול המועד נמי אסור כדתנן במועד קטן פרק בתרא (דף כח:) נשים במועד מענות אבל לא מטפחות אלא נראה לרבי משום שמחה רגילין לספק ולטפח בהשמעת קול ואסור שמא יתקן כלי שיר כדמפרש בהמולא תפילין (עירובין דף קד.): **וכן** היה הלל אומר · כרבנן דפליגי עליה באיזהו נשך (ב"מ ד' עה.) וקי"ל:

רבה אמר ניתנה ליתבע · הלכה כרבה לגבי רב יוסף: ורב אויא ורבה בר עולא מחמרי אנפשייהו כ"ה בס"א:

דאי אמרת ניתנה ליתבע אתי למיכתב · אע"פ שמזכיר לו לשון שאלה:

דאיגלאי מילתא דבחול הויא · ורב יוסף לא מיירי אלא בשבת ויו"ט ודאי:

והא אנן תנן אין נימנין כו' · פירש ה"ר פורת בשם רבינו שמואל דל"ג ליה חדא דמה שייך להקשות מנמנין של רשות לנמנין של מצוה ועוד דמפרש התם בביצה פרק אין צדין (דף כז:) מאי אין נמנין אין פוסקין דמים בתחילה לבהמה ביו"ט הרי אני עמך בסלע הריני עמך בשתים אבל אומר לו הריני עמך לשליש ולרביע:

ולמ"ד

עין משפט נר מצוה

ד א מיי' פכ"ג מהלכות שבת הלכה ה סמג לאוין סה טוש"ע או"ח סימן שלט סעיף ג וסימן תקכד סעיף א:

ה ב מיי' פ"א מהלכות שביתת עשור הלכה ז סמג לאוין סה וסט טור ושו"ע או"ח סימן תרח סעיף ג:

ו ג מיי' פ"י מהלכות מלוה ולוה הלכה ב סמג לאוין קצג טוש"ע יו"ד סימן קסב סעיף א:

[נ"ל רבה]

ז ד שם סעיף ג:

[כ"ב ס: ועי' תוס' לעיל נה. ד"ה ואע"ג ותוס' ב"ב ס: ד"ה מוטב ותוס' ע"ז ד. ד"ה שהי']

ח ה מיי' פ"ד מהלכות י"ט הלכה כה טוש"ע או"ח סימן תקכה סעיף א:

ט ו מיי' פ"ט מהלכות שמיטה ויובל הלכה ה סמג עשין קמט:

י ז מיי' שם הלכה כח סמג לאוין רעא טור ושו"ע חו"מ סימן סז סעיף לו:

יא ח מיי' פכ"ג מהלכו' שבת הלכה יד ופ"א מהלכות קרבן פסח הל"ט סמג עשין רכג:

יב ט מיי' פ"ד מהלכות י"ט הלכה יט סמג לאוין סה טוש"ע או"ח סימן תק סעיף א:

יג י מיי' פכ"ג מהלכות שבת הלכה יד סמג לאוין סה ועה טור ש"ע או"ח סימן שלט סעיף ד וסימן תקכד סעיף א:

רבינו חננאל

להא . דא"ל תנן לא מספקין ולא מרקדין ולא מטפחין . בגדרא . ופשוטה היא. ומיפרשא נמי בגמ' דהמביא כדי יין בפס' יו"ט וכן שואלת אשה מחברתה ככרות . ודייקינן מינה בשבת הוא דאסור מכלל דבחול שרי מתניתין דלא כהלל כו' ומסקינן בה אפילו תימא כהלל באתרא דקייצי דמי . ואם אינו מאמינו מניח טליתו אצלו ועושה עמו חשבון לאחר שבת. אתמר הלואת יו"ט רב יוסף אמר לא נתנה ליתבע רבא אמר ניתנה ליתבע ואתינן למיגמר מן מתניתין תנן ואם אינו מאמינו מניח טליתו אצלו כו' ולא גמרינן מינה דלא מיפרשא בהדיא כחד מינייהו ומותבינן לרב יוסף מהא דתנן השוחט את הפרה וחילקה בראש השנה אם היה חדש מעובר משמט . פי' אם היה אלול מעובר נמצא יום לקיחתו חלק מן הפרה יום חול שר"ה מחר הוא וכיון שנושה בו דמי בשר הפרה שלקח מאתמול דכיון שנכנסה שנה שביעית משמטת לדברי רבא ניחא כי נתנה ליתבע ומלוה נושה בו וכשנכנסת שביעית משמטת אלא לרב יוסף דאמר לא נתנה ליתבע אמאי צריך למיתנא משמטת בלאו הכי פטור הוא מלשלם . ואפילו בשאר שני שבוע דהא לא ניתנה ליתבע . ופריק רב יוסף שאני התם דכיון דאיגלאי מלתא דחול היא (ניתנה ליתבע דהא מלוה דחול היא) ואנן לא קאימנא אלא הלואת יו"ט ואסיקנא למשמע מסיפא ואם לאו אינו משמט לרבא דאמר ניתנה ליתבע דתובעו ונפרע ממנו [ניחא] אלא לרב יוסף דאמר לא ניתנה ליתבע קשיא כיון דתני אינו משמט הלא משמע דתובע ונפרע ממנו ואינו יכול לומר לו כי השביעית השמיטתו ופריק רב יוסף לעולם לא נתנה ליתבע והמלוה אינו יכול ליתבע אלא אם יביא הלה ויפרע יקבל ואינו צריך לומר משמט אני. ואקשינן עליה מכלל דרישא אי יהיב ליה מעצמו לא שקיל . ופריק רב יוסף ואמר רישא אם מחזיר לו צריך שיאמר לו משמט אני . דהא נושה בו מלוה אבל ספק שאינו נושה בו מלוה אם יבא לחשבון אינו צריך לומר לו משמט אני אלא יקבל כדתנן המחזיר חוב בשביעית צריך שיאמר משמט אני . ואם אמר לו אעפ"כ יקבל ממנו משום שנאמר וזה דבר השמטה ומפורש ענין זה בפ' השולח גט לאשתו. וראינו רבותינו שהיו מעמידין השמועה זו כרב יוסף. חדא (דרבה) [דרבא] לגבי רב יוסף תלמיד הוא ועוד סוגיא דשמעתא רובה כרב יוסף ריהטא ועוד מדחינן רב אויא מקבל משכונא מכלל שאם אין בידו משכון אינו יכול ליתבע . ותוב רבא בר עולא מיערם איערומי כלומר לא היה תובעו בהדיא אלא היה אומר לו הלויני וכאשר יתן לו ויבאו המעות לידו אומר לו יש לי אצלך הלואת יו"ט נשתלמתי אתם מכלל כי הלואת יו"ט כי האי גוונא יתכן אבל בהדיא לא ניתנה ליתבע וראינו תשובה לגאון ופסיק כרבא . ואמר רבא בתרא הוא . וקיי"ל דהלכתא כבתראי וכן הדעת נוטה : וכן ערב פסח בירושלים כו'. א"ר יוחנן מקדיש אדם פסחו בשבת וחגיגתו ביו"ט נימא מסייעא ליה וכן ערב פסח כו' ופשוטה היא. הא דתני ר' הושעיא ומקדישו אוקמינא. הקדיש עלוי מדרבנן ואקשינן עלה והא תנא דאמר הלכה כסתם משנה ותנן אין מקדשין ואין מעריכין ואין מחרימין ומפרקינן הא דא"ר יוחנן מקדיש בשבת בחובות הקבוע להן זמן . כגון פסח שאם לא יעשנו היום אינו יכול לעשותו למחר והיא מצוה עוברת והא

דיתנן

מסורת הש"ס

ביצה ל. וד' לו:

לעיל קמח. ביצה ל.

[ביצה ל. ע"ש]

הגהות הב"ח

(א) גמ' קא חזינן נמי דמותבי תצבייהו וכו' הנח להן לישראל: (ב) שם מאי אינו משמט דאי יהיב ליה: (ג) שם אקדושי מקדיש ליה מעיקרא: (ד) רש"י ד"ה ואתי לידי סחיטה וכו' סודרא עלויה כו' כיון ושמן קמיירי: (ה) ד"ה רישא וכו' משמט אני ואם אמר לו הלוה אעפ"כ נ"ל וכו"ל:

שביעית פ"י משנה ב

ג"ז שם גיטין לז:

כ"ל רבא פסחים סו: [ועי' תוספות חגיגה ח. ד"ה משום ותוס' בכורות נג. ד"ה ולאי]

[לעיל טו. וש"נ]

פסחים סו: ביצה לו:

[עי' תוס' לקמן קמט:]

דברים טו

ביצה כז:

[גי' רי"ף אלפס והרא"ש ורבא]

it with a large one? Then they increase the burden! [148b] Shall one spread a cloth? Then he may come to wring it out! Shall one cover it with a lid? It [the string wherewith it is tied] may break and he will come to knot it.[2] Therefore it is impossible.

Raba son of R. Ḥanan also said to Abaye: We learnt, One must not clap [the hands], beat [the breast], or dance[3] on Festivals. Yet we see that they do it, and do not rebuke them in any way? —Then on your reasoning, when Rabbah said: A man should not sit on the top of a stake, lest an article roll away from him and he come to fetch it,[4]—yet we see [women][5] who carry pitchers and sit at the entrance of alleys, and we do not rebuke them? But leave Israel: better that they should [sin] in ignorance than deliberately. Now, he understood from this that that [principle] holds good only in respect of Rabbinical [enactments] but not Scriptural laws.[6] Yet that is not so: there is no difference between a Rabbinical and a Scriptural law. For lo! the addition to the Day of Atonement is Scriptural,[7] yet we see them [women] eat and drink until it is dark and do not rebuke them.

AND SIMILARLY A WOMAN [MAY BORROW] LOAVES FROM HER NEIGHBOUR, [etc.]. Only on the Sabbath is it forbidden, but on weekdays it is well. Shall we say that our Mishnah does not agree with Hillel, for we learnt: And thus Hillel used to say: A woman must not lend a loaf to her neighbour without first valuing it, lest wheat advances and they [the lender and the
a borrower] come to [transgress the prohibition of] usury?[1]—You may even say [that it agrees with] Hillel: the one is in a place where its value is fixed; the other, where its value is not fixed.[2]

IF HE DOES NOT TRUST HIM. It was stated: As for a loan made on a Festival,—R. Joseph said: It cannot be claimed;[3] whilst Rabbah[4] said: It can be claimed. 'R. Joseph said: It cannot be claimed', for if you say that it can be claimed, he [the lender] will come to record it. 'Rabbah said: It can be claimed', for if you say that it cannot, he will not lend him, and so he will come to abstain from the joy of the Festival.

We learnt: IF HE DOES NOT TRUST HIM, HE LEAVES HIS CLOAK WITH HIM: now, it is well if you say that it cannot be claimed, therefore he must leave his cloak with him and make a reckoning with him after the Sabbath. But if you say that it can be claimed, why must he leave his cloak with him: let him lend it and then [re-]claim it?—He says, I do not wish to stand at court and before judges.

R. Idi b. Abin objected: If one kills a cow and apportions it on New Year, [then] if the month was prolonged it cancels [the debt]; but if not, it does not cancel the debt.[5] But if it cannot be claimed,[6] what does it cancel!—There it is different, because it is
b [retrospectively] revealed that it was a weekday.[1] Come and hear [a refutation] from the second clause: 'but if not, it does not cancel the debt'. Now, it is well if you say that it can be claimed, hence he teaches [that] it does not cancel [the debt]; but if you say that it cannot be claimed, then what is meant by 'it does not cancel [the debt]'?—That if he [the debtor] pays him, he accepts it: whence it follows that the first clause means that [even] if he pays him he must not accept![2]—In the first clause he must tell him, 'I release it,' while in the second he need not say, 'I release it'. As we learnt: If one repays a debt in the seventh year he [the creditor] must tell him, 'I release it;' but if he [the debtor] replies, '[I repay] even so,' he may accept it from him, for it is said, *And this is the word*[3] *of the release.*[4]

R. Awia used to take a pledge.[5] Rabbah[6] b. 'Ulla had recourse to an artifice.[7]

IN THE SAME WAY, IF THE EVE OF PASSOVER, etc. R. Joḥanan said: One may sanctify his Passover sacrifice on the Sabbath[8] and his Festival sacrifice on the Festival.[9] Shall we say that we can support him: IN THE SAME WAY, IF THE EVE OF PASSOVER IN JERUSALEM FALLS ON A SABBATH, ONE LEAVES HIS CLOAK WITH HIM AND RECEIVES HIS PASCHAL LAMB, AND MAKES A RECKONING WITH HIM AFTER THE FESTIVAL?[10]—[No.] We treat here of one who assigns shares to others together with himself in his Passover sacrifice,[11] so that it stands sanctified from before. But we learnt: One may not enrol [to share] in an animal on the
c Festival in the first place?[1]—Here it is different: since he is a *habitué* of his, it is as though he had enrolled for it beforehand. But R. Oshaia taught: 'A man can go to a shepherd to whom he is accustomed to go and he gives him a sheep for his Passover sacrifice, and he sanctifies it and fulfils his obligation therewith?—There too, since he is accustomed to go to him, he [the shepherd] does indeed sanctify it beforehand.[2] But he states, 'he sanctifies it'?[3] —This sanctification is a Rabbinical preferment.[4] But did R. Joḥanan say thus? Surely R. Joḥanan said: The *halachah* is [always] as an anonymous Mishnah, whereas we learnt: One may not sanctify, vow a 'valuation',[5] devote,[6] or separate *terumoth* and tithes: all these were said of Festivals, and how much more so of the Sabbath!—There is no difficulty: One refers to obligatory offerings for which there is a fixed time;[7] the other refers to obligations for which there is no fixed time.

MISHNAH. A MAN MAY COUNT HIS GUESTS AND HIS DAINTY PORTIONS BY WORD OF MOUTH, BUT NOT FROM WRITING. A MAN MAY CAST LOTS WITH HIS SONS AND THE MEMBERS OF HIS HOUSEHOLD FOR THE TABLE,[8] PROVIDED THAT HE DOES NOT INTEND TO OFFSET A LARGE PORTION AGAINST A SMALL ONE.[9] AND [PRIESTS] MAY CAST LOTS FOR SACRIFICES ON FESTIVALS, BUT NOT FOR THE PORTIONS.[10]

(2) With a permanent knot, which is forbidden. (3) The former two in grief, the third in joy. (4) V. *supra* 141*a*. (5) V. BaḤ. (6) Both cases mentioned here are Rabbinical. (7) The fast must begin before the Day of Atonement actually commences, and this is deduced from Scripture; v. Yoma 81*b*.

a (1) V. B.M. 75*a*. (2) If the price of the loaf is fixed (and our Mishnah refers to such) even Hillel agrees, because if it advances the lender will make an allowance when it is returned. (3) In a court of Law. (4) Alfasi and Asheri read: Raba. (5) This refers to New Year following the seventh year, debts contracted during which are void (v. Deut. XV, 1, 2). The months consist of either thirty or twenty-nine days; in the former case the following month is celebrated with two days as New Moon, the first of which is the last day of the previous month. Now if a butcher kills a cow and divides it among his customers on credit on the first New Year's day following the seventh year: if the previous month, Elul, consisted of thirty days, this New Year's Day was really the last day of Elul, i.e., of the seventh year, and therefore the debt cannot be claimed. But if Elul consisted of twenty-nine days, this New Year's Day is the first of the eighth year, hence the debt can be claimed.—New Year, of course, is a Festival. (6) *Sc.* a debt contracted on *any* Festival.

b (1) *Sc.* the last day of Elul, in spite of the fact that it was celebrated as New Year. (2) Surely not! The year of release does not actually cancel debts but merely deprives the creditor of his right to exact them. (3) E.V. '*manner*'. (4) Deut. XV, 2. I.e., the creditor must *inform* the debtor of the release. (5) From anyone who borrowed from him on a Festival. (6) Var. lec.: Raba. (7) Rashi: after the Festival he would take an article from the debtor and then detain it. (8) I.e., when the eve of Passover falls on the Sabbath. (9) An animal must be formally sanctified before it may be offered as a sacrifice. This may not be done on Sabbaths or Festivals, but since two animals are actually offered on those days respectively they may be sanctified too, if that was not done previously. (10) And of course he would have to sanctify it on the same day. (11) Those who participate in the sacrifice must formally enrol themselves as members to share in that particular animal (v. Ex. XII, 4). Thus the payment is merely for a share in an animal which is already consecrated.

c (1) Because it is regarded as transacting business, v. Beẓ. 27*b*. (2) I.e., the shepherd sanctifies it on the festival even on his behalf. (3) I.e., when he receives it. (4) I.e., the Rabbis held it more fitting that the owner too should sanctify the animal, but actually that has already been done. (5) Heb. מעריכין. This is the technical term for a vow to give one's own or another person's 'valuation' to the Temple. V. Lev. XXVII, 1ff. (6) Heb. מחרימין, i.e., renounce an object by dedicating it absolutely for priestly use; v. Lev. XXVII, 28f. (7) E.g., the Passover sacrifice and Festive offerings. Such may be sanctified on the Sabbath and Festivals, as otherwise the obligation must remain unfulfilled. (8) Which portion of the food shall belong to each. (9) The portions must be alike in size, not one larger and one smaller, so that the first drawn by lot shall receive the largest, etc. (10) This is explained in the Gemara.

GEMARA. [149a] What is the reason?—R. Bibi said: It is a preventive measure, lest he erase.[1] Abaye said: It is a preventive measure, lest he read.[2] Wherein do they differ?—They differ where it is written high up on the wall: according to him who says, Lest he erase, we do not fear; but according to him who says, Lest he read [secular documents], we do fear. Now, as to him who says, 'Lest he erase', let us fear lest he read [secular documents]? Moreover, have we no fear that he may erase?[3] Surely we learnt: One may not read by the light of a lamp; whereon Rabbah said: Even if it is as high as twice a man's stature, even if it is as high as [the measurement of] two ox-goads, or even as ten houses on top of each other, he must not read?[4]—Rather they differ where it is written on the wall and is low down: according to him who says, 'Lest he erase', we fear; [but] according to him who says, 'Lest he read [secular documents]', we do not fear, [for] one will not confuse a wall with a document.[5]

Now, according to him who says, 'Lest he read [etc.]', let us fear lest he erase?—Rather they differ where it is engraved on a tablet or a board: on the view that it is 'lest he erase', we have no fear; but on the view that it is 'lest he read', we do fear. But according to him who says, lest he erase, let us fear lest he read [etc.]? And should you answer, a tablet or a board cannot be confused with a document,—surely it was taught: A man may count how many shall be within and how many without[6] and how many portions he is to set before them, from writing on a wall, but not from writing on a tablet or a board. How is it meant? Shall we say that it is indeed written, wherein does one differ from the other? Hence it must surely mean that it is engraved, yet he states, 'from writing on the wall, but not from writing on a tablet or a board'?—Rather [say thus]: In truth [they differ] where it is written high up on the wall, and as for your difficulty about Rabbah's [ruling], [the ruling] of Rabbah is dependent on Tannaim. For it was taught: A man may count his guests and his dainty portions by word of mouth, but not from writing. R. Aḥa permits [it] from writing on the wall. How is it meant: Shall we say that it is written low down,—then let us fear lest he erase it? Hence it must surely mean that it is written high up, which proves that Rabbah's [ruling] is dependent on Tannaim.

Now these Tannaim are as the following: For it was taught:
b One must not look in a mirror on the Sabbath;[1] R. Meir permits [one to look] in a mirror that is fixed to the wall. Why is one fixed to the wall different?—[Presumably] because in the meanwhile[2] he will recollect![3] then even if it is not fixed, he will recollect?—We treat here of a metal mirror, and [the reason is] in accordance with R. Naḥman's [dictum] in Rabbah b. Abbuha's name. For R. Naḥman said in Rabbah b. Abbuha's name: Why was it ruled that a metal mirror is forbidden? Because a man usually removes straggling hairs with it.[4]

Our Rabbis taught: The writing under a painting or an image[5] may not be read on the Sabbath. And as for the image itself, one must not look at it even on weekdays, because it is said, *Turn ye not unto idols.*[6] How is that taught?—Said R. Ḥanin: [Its interpretation is,] Turn not unto that conceived in your own minds.[7]

A MAN MAY CAST LOTS WITH HIS SONS, etc. Only with his sons and household, but not with strangers:[8] what is the reason?—As Rab Judah said in Samuel's name. For Rab Judah said in Samuel's name: The members of a company who are particular
c with each other[1] transgress [the prohibitions of] measure, weight,

(1) He may find too many names on the list and erase some before instructing his servant to invite the guests. (2) Secular documents. (3) If the list is high up. (4) V. *supra* 11a. Though he could not reach the lamp to tilt it; hence the same reasoning applies here. (5) No one is likely to think that since he may read something written on a wall he may also read business documents. (6) I.e., how many guests shall be placed at the top of the table—'within' the privileged circle—and how many at the bottom—'without'.

b (1) Lest he see uneven locks of hair and trim them. (2) While he goes for a pair of scissors. (3) That it is the Sabbath. (4) Its edge being sharpened. Now the first Tanna forbids all mirrors, drawing no distinctions; whilst R. Meir does draw a distinction. That is similar to the matter just debated. (5) I.e., the written legend beneath a picture. (6) Lev. XIX, 4. (7) Tosaf.: the interdict is only against images (or perhaps statues—Jast.) made for idolatrous purposes, but others are permitted. (8) For otherwise the Tanna would simply teach, A MAN MAY CAST LOTS.

c (1) I.e., members of a company at one table, each of whom has his own provisions, and when one borrows from another, are particular to weigh, measure, or count, that the exact quantity may be returned.

מסורת הש"ס

עין משפט נר מצוה

יד א ב ג מיי' פכ"ג מהלכות שבת הל"ט סמג לאוין סה טור שו"ע או"ח סימן שז סעיף יב:

טו ד ה מיי' פכ"ב מהל' שבת הלכה יד סמג שם טור שו"ע או"ח סימן שב סעיף יג:

טז ו מיי' פכ"ג שם הלכה יט סמג שם טור שו"ע או"ח סימן שז סעיף טו:

יז ז מיי' פ"ב מהלכות ע"ז הלכה ב סמג לאוין יד טוש"ע יו"ד סי' קמב סעיף טו:

יח ח מיי' פ"ז מהלכות גניבה הלכה י סמג לאוין עה [אבל הפוסקים השמיטו מטעם שכ' הב"י בחו"מ סוף סי' תקי"ז]:

גמ' מ"ט רב ביבי אמר גזירה שמא ימחוק אביי אמר גזירה שמא יקרא בשטרי הדיוטות מאי בינייהו א"ב דכתב אכותל ומידלי למ"ד שמא ימחוק לא חיישינן ולמ"ד שמא יקרא חיישינן ולמ"ד שמא ימחוק ניחוש שמא יקרא ותו לשמא ימחוק לא חיישינן *והתניא *לא יקרא לאור הנר *ואמר רבה אפי' גבוה שתי קומות אפי' גבוה שתי מרדעות אפי' עשרה בתים זה ע"ג זה לא יקרא אלא איכא בינייהו דכתב אכותל ומיתתי למאן דאמר שמא ימחוק חיישינן למ"ד שמא יקרא לא חיישינן גודא בשטרא לא מיחלף ולמ"ד שמא יקרא ליחוש שמא ימחוק אלא איכא בינייהו דחייק אטבלא ואפינקס למ"ד שמא ימחוק לא חיישינן למ"ד שמא יקרא חיישינן ולמ"ד שמא ימחוק ליחוש שמא יקרא וכ"ת טבלא ופינקס בשטרא לא מיחלף והתניא *מונה אדם כמה מבפנים וכמה מבחוץ וכמה מנות עתיד להניח לפניהם [ג]מכתב שעל גבי הכותל אבל לא מכתב שעל גבי טבלא ופינקס היכי דמי אילימא דכתיב מיכתב מ"ש הכא ומ"ש הכא אלא לאו דחייק וקתני מכתב שעל גבי הכותל אבל לא מכתב שע"ג טבלא ופינקס אלא לעולם דכתב אכותל ומידלי ודקא קשיא לך דרבה דרבה תנאי היא דתניא [ו]מונה אדם את אורחיו ואת פרפרותיו מפיו אבל לא מן הכתב ר' אחא מתיר מכתב שעל גבי הכותל היכי דמי אילימא דכתיב מתתא ליחוש שמא ימחוק אלא לאו דכתב ומידלי וש"מ דרבה תנאי היא ש"מ והני תנאי כהני תנאי דתניא *[ד]אין רואין במראה בשבת *רבי מאיר מתיר במראה הקבוע בכותל מ"ש הקבוע בכותל דאדהכי והכי מדכר שאינו קבוע נמי אדהכי והכי מדכר הכא במראה של מתכת עסקינן וכדרב נחמן אמר רבה בר אבוה דא"ר נחמן אמר רבה בר אבוה [ה]מפני מה אמרו מראה של מתכת אסורה מפני *שאדם עשוי להשיר בה נימין המדולדלין תנו רבנן *[ו]כתב המהלך תחת הצורה ותחת הדיוקנאות אסור לקרותו בשבת [ז]ודיוקנא עצמה אף בחול אסור להסתכל בה משום שנאמר °אל תפנו אל האלילים מאי תלמודא (ויקרא יט) אמר רבי חנין אל תפנו אל מדעתכם: **מפיס** אדם עם בניו וכו': עם בניו ועם בני ביתו אין ועם אחר לא מאי טעמא כדרב יהודה אמר שמואל *דאמר רב יהודה אמר שמואל [ח]בני חבורה המקפידין זה על זה עוברין משום מדה ומשום משקל ומשום מנין ומשום לווין ופורעין ביו"ט וכדברי

[תוספ' פי"ח]

[תוספ' פי"ח]

[ב"ב כב.]

רש"י

גמ' מ"ט · אבל לא מן הכתב: שמא ימחוק · מן האורחין שיראה שלא הכין להם כל צרכם ויתחרט שזימן יותר מן הראוי וימחוק מן הכתב כדי שלא יקראם השמש: כל הני שמא יקרא בשטרי הדיוטות של מקח וממכר קאמר (א): דכתב · מגייהא אכותל בדיו: ומידלי · שאינו מגיע לשם למחוק: (אפילו גבוה שאינו מגיע לשם למחוק): אפילו גבוה · שאינו מגיע שם להטות הנר אסור דהואיל ונמוך אסור גבוה נמי אסור שלא תחלוק: ומיתתי · שנמוך ויכול להגיע שם ולמחוק: ולמ"ד שמא יקרא · היכא דליכא למיחש לשמא יקרא ליחוש לשמא ימחוק: דחייק · בסכין בתוך העץ בטבלא שאין טוחה למחוק והדהכי מדכר וליכא למיחש למחוק: גודא · כותל: פינקס · כעין לוחות של סוחרים: כמה בפנים וכמה בחוץ · את מי ומי אושיב בפנים במקום המכובד ואת מי ומי אושיב בחוץ שאינה כל כך ספונין: אבל לא מכתב שעל גבי טבלא ופינקס · דגודא בשטרא לא מיחלף אבל טבלא ופינקס מיחלף: [דכתיב מיכתב · כתב של דיו]: אלא לעולם דכתב אכותל ומידלי · שאינו יכול למחוק ולשמא יקרא לא חיישינן דגודא בשטרא לא מיחלף ודקשיא לך דאע"ג דמידלי ליתסרי כדרבה דאמר גבי נר אפילו י' בתים: דרבה תנאי היא · דאיכא דחייש לשלא תחלוק באיסור שבת דרבנן ואיכא דמפליג: ליחוש לשמא ימחוק · דהא ר' אחא כותל דוקא נקט ואי מתתי מה לי כותל מה לי אגרת: אין רואין במראה · מירואי"ר לפי שהרואה במראה אינו צריך אלא לתקן שערות ראשו וזקנו הלכך חיישי' שמא יראה נימין המדולדלות שאינן שוות עם שאר השער *ויגלחן: דאדהכי והכי · שילך להביא תער או מספרים: מדכר · שהוא שבת: של מתכת · שאינו צריך להביא מספרים שהיא עצמה מגלחת השער: כתב המהלך תחת הצורה ותחת הדיוקנאות · כגון בני אדם המציירים בכותל חיות משונות או דיוקנות של בני אדם של מעשים כגון מלחמת דוד וגלית וכותבין תחתיה זו צורת חיה פלונית וזו דיוקנית פלוני ופלונית: אסור לקרותו בשבת · שמא יקרא בשטרי הדיוטות: אל מדעתכם · אל אשר אתם עושים מדעת לבבכם ואלא שלכם. אלילים לשון חללים: עם בניו ובני ביתו אין עם אחר לא · מדלא תנא ומפיס על המנות: משום לווין ופורעין · דגזור בהו רבנן שמא יכתוב: המקפידין · שאין מוחלים ומוותרין זה לזה: וכדברי

תוספות

ולמ"ד שמא ימחוק ליחוש שמא יקרא · ולא מסיק אדעתיה גודא בשטרא לא מיחלף: **בשטרי** הדיוטות · פי' בקונט' של מקח וממכר ולעיל בפרק כל כתבי (דף קטז: ושם) פירש איגרות השלוחות למנות חפן: **אלא** איכא בינייהו דכתיב אכותל ומתתאי · ולא ידענא אמאי נקט מתתאי כיון דס"ד דכ"ע אית להו דרבה: **אילימא** דכתיב מיכתב מ"ש הכא מ"ש הכא. פירוש תרווייהו יהא אסור שמא ימחוק: **לעולם** דכתב אכותל ומידלי ודקשיא לך דרבה דרבה תנאי היא · לפירוש הקונטרס צ"ל דהשתא דמוקי לה דכתיב אכותל ומידלי למ"ד שמא ימחוק איכא דאית ליה דרבה ולמ"ד שמא יקרא לית ליה דרבה והשתא מיבעיא לן למימר דבדרבה פליגי תנאי כי היכי דפליגי אמוראי דהכא ובריתא קמייתא מיתוקמא שפיר דכתיב מכתב אכותל ומידלי דכולהו אמוראי גודא בשטרא לא מיחלף וקשה לפירוש זה דהשתא לא הוה פלוגתייהו כדהוה מוקמת לה מעיקרא למאן דאמר שמא ימחוק לא חיישינן למאן דאמר שמא יקרא חיישי' וה"ר פורת פירש דאביי ורב ביבי תרוייהו לית להו דרבה דפליגי בכתב אכותל ומידלי למאן דאמר שמא ימחוק לא חיישינן כיון דמידלי ולית לן דרבה ולשמא יקרא נמי לא חייש קסבר גודא בשטרא לא מיחלף ולמ"ד שמא יקרא חייש דקסבר גודא בשטרא מיחלף ואביי לא הוה מוקי פלוגתייהו דרבי אחא ורבנן (ב) כרבה דא"כ ר' אחא ע"כ לית ליה דאביי דשרי בכותל אלמא קסבר גודא בשטרא לא מיחלף וא"כ כמאן סבירא ליה דאפילו רבנן לא פליגי עליה דר' אחא אלא משום דאית להו דרבה וגזרינן שמא ימחוק אלא הוה מפרש אביי דכ"ע לית להו דרבה ולא חיישינן לשמא ימחוק במידלי ובגודא בשטרא מיחלף פליגי והא דקאמר ש"מ דרבה תנאי היא הו"מ למימר ודאי לכ"ע לית להו דרבה כדמפרש לאביי אלא דלא מצי למוכח הא בהדיא ולהכי קאמר דתנאי היא וליכא לאקשויי לרבה והא לא מצי למימר דפליגי (ג) בחייק מיחק רבי אחא ורבנן ובגודא בשטרא מיחלף פליגי אבל כ"ע אית להו דרבה משום דסברא הוא כיון דחייק ואיתא כמי בכותל פשיטא דבהא לא הוי אמרי רבנן דגודא בשטרא מיחלף וצריך לאוקמא השתא ברייתא דלעיל דחייק מיחק למאן דסבר גודא בשטרא מיחלף וקשה קצת לפירוש זה דה"ל למימר דכ"ע (ד) לית להו דרבה ואביי ורב ביבי בגודא אי מיחלף בשטרא פליגי: **ודיוקני** עצמה אף בחול אסור · נראה דבשויה לשם עבודת גלולים אמר אבל (ה) לנוי מותר כדמשמע מבנן של קודשים דלא הוו מסתכלי בצורתא דזוזא (ע"ז דף נ:) מכלל דאחריני הוו מסתכלי *: **בני** חבורה המקפידין זה על זה עוברין משום משקל ומשום מדה ומשום מנין · פירוש לפי שמקפידין זה על זה עוברין אפילו על מה שאין שאר בני אדם עוברין משום מדה כדאמרינן בביצה (דף כט.) יכול אדם לומר לחבירו מלא לי כלי זה אבל לא במדה פירוש כלי שמודדין בו אסור דדמי למקח וממכר והם כיון שהם מקפידים כל כלים הוי לגבייהו מדה לפי שמקפידין לידע שיעורו לשלם להם הכלי וכן משקל ששוקלים ומכוונים זה כנגד זה ביד ואמרינן בביצה* אין משגיחין במאזנים ביום טוב ומשום מנין כדאמר בביצה (דף כט:) הולך אדם אצל חנוני הרגיל אצלו ואומר לו תן לי כו' ובלבד שלא יזכיר לו שום מקח שאם היו נותנים מאה אגוזים בדינר ולקח כבר תשעים לא יאמר לו תן לי עשרים אגוזים שאתחייב לך עשרה אגוזים שנראה שעושה להשלים הדינר אבל יכול לומר לו תן לי כ' אגוזים סתם ובבני חבורה המקפידים אסור שיבא לידי איסור שיזכירו להשלים וכדברי (ו) בית הלל אף משום רבית דכשהם מחזירין זה לזה הם מקפידים מה ששוות יותר וקשה לפירוש

[תוספ' פי"ח]

[ברב אלפס איתא רבי מתיר וכו' וכ"א בבעל המאור ובמלחמות. אבל בהרא"ש אי' ר' יהודה מתיר וכו']

[עי' תוס' ע"ז כט. ד"ה המסתפר]

[וע"ע תוספות ע"ז נ. ד"ה כ"ג]

[דף כח.]

רבינו חננאל

דתנן אין מקדישין בשבת ולא ביום טוב בחובות שאין קבוע להן זמן. מונה אדם את אורחיו ואת פרפריותיו מפיו אבל לא מן הכתב. ואמרינן מן הכתב מ"ט לא. רב ביבי אמר גזירה שמא ימחוק אביי אמר גזירה שמא יקרא בשטרי הדיוטות ופירושו כיון שיראה אדם קורא כמה אורחים צריך להביא כמה פרפריות אצלו אף הוא אומר מותר לקרוא בשטרי הדיוטות מאי בינייהו דכתיב אכותל במקום גבוה שאינו יכול למחוק דרב ביבי בכי האי גוונא שרי. ואביי אסר. ואקשינן על רב ביבי והתנן לא יקרא לאור הנר ואמר רבה אפילו גבוה ב' קומות או ב' מרדעות ואפילו עשרה בתים זה ע"ג זה לא יקרא. והא הכא דליכא למיחש אלא שמא יטה ואפי' גבוה כמה אמר (רבא) [רבה] חיישינן ואסור. ואע"ג דסלקא כתנאי הלכתא (כרבא) [כרבה] דסתם מתניתין כוותיה ולא חיישינן אמחלוקות דברייתא הזורנו להביא טעם אחר לומר כי אינם חלוקים אלא אם הוא הכתב בכותל נמוך שמגעת לה ויכול למחוק דלרב ביבי אסור כטעמיה ולאביי שרי דכותל בשטר לא מיחלף. ואקשינן על אביי וליחוש שמא ימחוק הואיל והכותל נמוך הוא וגם זה הטעם נדחה ואתינן לאוקמי פלוגתיה בכתב דחייק אטבלא ופנקס וגם זה נדחה. וחזרנו על הטעם הראשון דכתוב אכותל ומידלי. לרב ביבי מותר ולאביי אסור. וזה שהקשינו לרב ביבי מדברי רבה שאמר אפילו גבוה כמה. אמר לך רב ביבי דרבה תנאי היא ואנא דאמרי כתנא דשרי. דתניא מונה אדם את אורחיו ואת פרפרותיו מפיו אבל לא מן הכתב. ר' אחא מתיר מן הכתב שעל גבי הכותל ואוקימנא דכתוב אכותל ומידלי. ואמרינן הני תנאי כי הני תנאי כלומר ר' אחא ות"ק חולקין במחלוקת ר' ות"ק דיליה דלר' אחא *צחצות הסיג מן המראה הוא מוחק לפיכך קתני אין רואין במראה ור' מתיר במראה הקבועה בכותל כת"ק דר' אחא ודמיא להא דאמרינן בכלל גדול (דף עה) דשף בין העמודים [חייב] משום **) מוחק שדישה למוחק כתב. ותלמוד א"י השף את העור ע"ג העמוד ר' אחא בשם ר' יהודה בן לוי משום מוחק ואקשינן עלה מ"ש מראה הקבועה בכותל דאדהכי והכי מדכר. ולא פירש מהו שיזכור וימנע. יש מי שאומר כי נאסר הראיה במראה בשבת שמא יראה בו כעין חלודה (וכעין חלודה) בזה המראה ויצחצחנו בשבת ונמצא מתקן מנא. גם נהיות המראה למטה במקום נמוך עד שיתעסק להביא סכין כדי לצחצח יזכור ששבת הוא וימנע ונדחה זה הטעם. ועמד כר"נ דאמר מפני מה אמרו מראה של מתכת אסורה מפני שאדם עשוי להשיר בה נימין המדולדלות ור' שמתיר אומר כיון שהיא גבוה לא גזרינן. ות"ק סבר גזרינן: **ת"ר** כתב של תחת הצורה של תחת דיוקני. פי' דיוקני צורת אדם והכתב שתחתיו אסור לקרותו בשבת ולא גרע משטרי הדיוטות דאסור בשבת. ודיוקני עצמה אסורה. אפילו בחול כטעמיה: **מפיס** אדם עם בניו ועם כו' פי' מפיס אדם מלשון פיוס כההיא דאמרי מי מפיס. וכמו שאמר על השכר (פסחים קז) מיסרו ומפיס. בניו ובני ביתו

*) לכאורה לפי גירסיה ז"ל לכיפך דר' אחא כרבי ואולי דגירסתו היא להכך ומההלה נעתק בטעות וצ"ע. **) לפנינו גם בגמ' איתא משום ממחק וצ"ע.

הגהות הב"ח

(א) רש"י ד"ה כל הני וכו' קאמר הס"ד ואח"כ מ"ה למ"ד שמא יקרא חיישינן ואפי' גבוה: (ב) תוס' ד"ה לעולם וכו' דר' אחא ורבנן בדרבה דא"כ: (ג) בא"ד והא לא מצי למימר דפליגי ר' אחא ורבנן בחייק מיחק ובגוד' בשטרא: (ד) בא"ד וקשה קצת לפי' זה דה"ל למימר דכ"ע אביי ורב ביבי לית להו דרבה ובגוד':(ה) ד"ה ודיוקנא וכו' אבל לשם נוי: (ו) ד"ה בני וכו' שיזכירו להשלים וכדברי הלל אף: ויגלחם במספרים כצ"ל רש"ל

גליון הש"ס

גמ' אין רואין במראה בשבת. עי' מ"ז כט ע"א תוס' ד"ה המסתפר: שם כתב המהלך תחת הצורה. עי' לעיל דף קטז ע"ב תוס' ד"ה וכ"ש בשטרי:

צ"ל והתנן לעיל יא.

ב"מ סב.

עין משפט
נר מצוה

יט א מיי' פכ"ג מהלכו' שבת הלכה יז סמג שם טוש"ע או"ח סימן שכב סעיף ו :

כ ב מיי' שם (ופ"ו מהל' גזילה ואבידה הל"ו) סמג שם ועשין ליד ולאוין עב טור שו"ע או"ח שם וטוש"ע חו"מ סימן שפ סעיף ב :

כא ג ד מיי' פ"ד מהל' י"ט הלכה כ סמג לאוין עה :

לפירוש זה דאם הלל לא איירי אלא במקפידין אם כן אמאי קאמר לעיל לימא מתניתין דלא כהלל והא הלל במקפידין איירי ומתניתין דלעיל אתי שפיר כוותיה דהא רישא באין מקפידין דקתני שואל דאילו למקפידין אסרינן שאלה לפי מה שפירש' להכי נראה לפרש עוברין משום מדה ומשום משקל כלומר קרובין לבא לידי כך שיעברו משום מדה שע"י שמקפידין זה ע"ז ורגילין ליקח במדה זה מזה גם ביו"ט יעשו כך וגם כל בני אדם הוי אסורין בכלי של מדה כדאמר בבילה (דף כט: ושם) אבל למקפידין נותן הוא עלה שלא ישתתפו שקרובים הן לבא לידי איסור מדה וכן לידי איסור משקל מתוך שרגילים לשקול על ידי הקפדתן גם ביו"ט לא ירגישו עד שישקלו ולידי מכין כשישאל אחד מהן ס' אגוזים יאמר לו תן לי מ' להשלים ק' כמו שרגילין לעשות ומשום לווין ופורעין ביו"ט כדאמר לעיל דלשון הלואה אסור והם מתוך שמקפידים יזכירו לשון הלואה לפי שיאמר השואל אם אזכיר לו לשון שאלה משמע דהדרא בעיניה לכך אומר לשון הלואה וכדברי הלל אף משום רבית דכשלוין זה מזה כבר באין לידי רבית לפי שפעמים שזה משלם יותר שאע"פ שמקפיד הוא בוש הוא שלא ישלם כמו שהלוהו בשביל שהגהו וכיון שאינו מוחל הוי רבית אבל שאר בני אדם מחלי ולא הוי רבית והשתא מתני' איירי במקפידין דסתם שכנים באינם חברים מקפידין ומ"מ דרך שאלה מותר ומה שדברו כאן על מקפידין לא אמרינן אלא גבי חבורה שרגילים לישאל זה מזה תדיר ואתי לידי איסור אבל שכנים שאין תדירין כל כך לשאול זה מזה מותרים ואין לגזור בהם שמא יבאו לידי איסור ולהכי לא משני כי אמר מתני' דלא כהלל דמתניתין איירי כשאין מקפידין משום דסתמא דמתני' איירי במקפידין כדפרישית. מ"ר: **מאי** טעמא משום קוביא · הייט כרבי יהודה בשם רבי טרפון דאמר אין אחד מהן נזיר שלא נתנה נזירות אלא להפלאה וסבירא ליה דלא מחית איניש לספיקא ולית הלכתא הכי אלא כאידך דר' יהודה כדפסקינן בסנהדרין בפרק זה בורר (דף כה· ושם) · מ"ר

***מטילין** חלשים על הקדשים ביו"ט · תימה דאמר בפרק ב' דקדושין (דף נג. ושם) דאין חולקין זבחים כנגד זבחים ומנחה כנגד מנחה ומפיק לה מלכל בני אהרן תהיה איש כאחיו ועוד דפריך התם מוהלגועים מושכין ידיהם והגרגרנים חולקין מאי חולקין חוטפין כו' ואומר רבי דאין מועלת בהם חלוקה וגורל שיהא ממוט לקדש בו את האשה ולהוליאו בדיינים אבל מ"מ מטילין היו חלשין לתת לכל א' חלקו פן יריבו ביחד כדכתיב (הושע ד) ועמך כמריבי כהן והא דמשני התם חולקין לאו דוקא אלא חוטפין ולא משני הכי משו' דחולקין משמע סופן לחלוק ע"כ מחמת שחוטפין אותן שאין שלהם · מ"ר

[נ"ל ברה ומשום שאינו לא היה כגון לפיכך לא סוכירו . כ"כ רש"י בעירובין פ. ד"ה כריס]

[נ"ל ברה]

[עייך לעיל קמה: במשנה]

וכדברי (*ב"ה) אף משום רבית אי הכי בניו ובני ביתו נמי בניו ובני ביתו היינו טעמא כדרב יהודה אמר רב *דאמר רב יהודה אמר רב מותר להלוות בניו ובני ביתו ברבית כדי להטעימן טעם רבית אי הכי מנה גדולה כנגד מנה קטנה נמי אין ה"נ וחסורי מיחסרא והכי קתני *מפיס אדם עם בניו ועם בני ביתו על השלחן אפי' מנה גדולה כנגד מנה קטנה מ"ט כדרב יהודה אמר רב עם בניו ועם בני ביתו אין עם אחרים לא מ"ט כדרב יהודה אמר שמואל "מנה גדולה כנגד מנה קטנה אף בחול לאחרים אסור מ"ט משום קוביא : "מטילין חלשין על וכו' : מאי אבל לא על המנות א"ר יעקב *בריה דבת יעקב אבל לא "על המנות של חול ביו"ט פשיטא מהו דתימא הואיל וכתיב °ועמך כמריבי כהן אפי' מנות דחול נמי קמ"ל וא"ר יעקב *בריה דבת יעקב °כל שחבירו נענש על ידו אין מכניסין אותו במחיצתו של הקב"ה מנלן אילימא משום דכתיב °ויאמר ה' מי יפתה את אחאב ויעל ויפול ברמות גלעד ויאמר זה בכה וזה אמר בכה ויצא הרוח ויעמוד לפני ה' ויאמר אני אפתנו וגו' ויאמר אצא והייתי רוח שקר בפי כל נביאיו ויאמר תפתה וגם תוכל צא ועשה כן ואמרינן מאי רוח *א"ר יוחנן זה רוחו של נבות ומאי צא אמר רב צא ממחיצתי ודילמא התם היינו טעמא דכתיב °דובר שקרים לא יכון אלא מהכא °שבעת קלון מכבוד שתה גם אתה והערל וגו' שבעת קלון מכבוד זה נבוכד נצר שתה גם אתה והערל זה צדקיה חדא דכוליה קרא בנבוכד נצר כתיב ועוד צדקיה צדיקא מאי הוה ליה למיעבד ליה דא"ר יהודה אמר רב בשעה שבקש אותו רשע לעשות לאותו צדיק כך וכו' אלא מהכא °גם ענוש לצדיק לא טוב אין לא טוב אלא רע וכתיב °כי לא אל חפץ רשע אתה לא יגורך רע *צדיק אתה ה' ולא יגור במגורך רע מאי משמע דהאי חלשים לישנא דפורא הוא דכתיב °איך נפלת משמים הילל בן שחר נגדעת לארץ חולש על גוים וגו' אמר רבה בר רב הונא מלמד שהיה מטיל פור על גדולי מלכות לידע איזה בן יומו של משכב זכור וכתיב °כל מלכי גוים כולם וגו' אמר רבי יוחנן שנחו ממשכב זכור וא"ר יוחנן כל ימיו של אותו רשע לא נמצא שחוק בפה כל בריה שנאמר °נחה שקטה כל הארץ פצחו רנה מכלל דעד השתא לא הוה רנה ואמר ר' יצחק אמר ר' יוחנן אסור לעמוד בביתו של אותו רשע שנא' °ושעירים ירקדו שם ואמר רב יהודה אמר רב בשעה שביקש אותו רשע לעשות לאותו צדיק כך נמשכה ערלתו שלש מאות אמה והיתה מחזרת על כל המסיבה כולה שנאמר שבעת קלון מכבוד שתה גם אתה והערל ערל בגימטריא שלש מאות הוי ואמר רב יהודה אמר רב בשעה שירד אותו רשע לגיהנם רעשו כל יורדי גיהנם אמרו שמא למשול עליהם הוא בא או *ליחלות כמותם הוא בא שנאמר °גם אתה חולית כמונו אלינו נמשלת יצאתה ב"ק ואמרה °ממי נעמת רדה והשכבה את ערלים °איך שבת נוגש שבתה מדהבה א"ר יהודה אמר רב שבתה אומה זו שאמרה מדוד

הושע ד · מלכים א כב · תהלים קא · חבקוק ב · משלי יז · תהלים ה · ישעיה יד · שם · שם · שם יד · שם יד · יחזקאל לב · ישעיה יד

וכדברי (בית) הלל דחיש שמא יוקירו חיטי בהלואת ככרות אף משום רבית: בניו ובני ביתו נמי. ליחוש לרבית וכל הני: להלוות · משלו : בניו ובני ביתו · הסמוכים על שלחנו דכיון דהכל משלו אין כאן רבית : להטעימן טעם רבית · שידעו כמה קשה אלמא כיון דמשלו הוא אין כאן איסור רבית והלכך גבי מדה ומשקל ומנין נמי לאו קפידא הוא אלא להשוותם בלא קנאה : אי הכי מנה גדולה כנגד מנה קטנה נמי. דמוקמינן טעמא לקמן משום קוביא ואפי' בחול אסור וכיון דהכל משלו אמאי אסור להטעימן טעמא קוביא בעלמא הוא : מאי טעמא מותר· ולא חייש לקוביא : כדרב יהודה אמר רב · דלהטעימן בעלמא הוא : עם אחר לא כדרב יהודה אמר שמואל · דכיון דמקפידין עוברין משום מדה ומשקל ומנין : משום קוביא · דגזל הוא דאסמכתא לא קניא והא אסמכתא דסמיך על הגורל אם יפול גורל אמנה הגדולה אזכה בה ולפיכך תלה עצמו אף לגורל הקטנה על הספק ואילו יודע מתחלה שכן לא היה מתרלה : של חול · של קדשים של אתמול : כמריבי כהן · ככהנים אלו שהם בעלי מריבה : אפי' דחול נמי · לישתרי להו להפיס ביו"ט כי היכי דלא לינלו : זה בכה · אני אפתנו בכה : שבעת קלון · בנבוכדנלר משתעי שהיה מטיל משכב זכור על המלכים וכשהגיע יומו של לדקיהו נמשכה ערלתו ג' מאות אמה והייט שבעת קלון : חדא דכוליה קרא בנבוכדנלר כתיב · שפיר מלית לאוקמי כוליה בנבוכדנלר וה"ק שתה גם אתה כאותם שהיית מקלה אותן והערל והתערל והתגנה : בשעה שעשה לו כו' · לקמן היא מדקאמר לאותו לדיק ש"מ אנוס היה : ענוש ללדיק לא טוב · לדיק המענים לא טוב וכיון דאינו טוב הרי הוא רע : וכתיב לא יגורך רע· אלמא אינו נכנס במחילתו: חולש על גוים · בנבוכדנלר כתיב : ושעירים ירקדו שם · ולא אנשים ובשביל הבריות מסתלקין המזיקין ונמלא מבטל גזירת המלך : המסיבה· מלכים שהיו מסובין ויושבין לפניו : גם אתה חולית כמונו אלינו וגו' · ביורדי גיהנם כתיב דכתיב לעיל מיניה שאול מתחת רגזה לך לקראת בואך וגו' (א) : חולית כמונו אלינו נמשלת · לשון ממשלה : נעמת · סבור אתה להיות בטעס מן האחרים : מדוד

תורה אור

מסורת הש"ס

[נ"ל הילל]

ב"מ עה. [ושם מסיק הש"ס ולאו' מילתא היא כו' ויישוב נכון על קושיא זו ביאר הט"ז באו"ח סימן שכ"ב ס"ק ד]

הגהות הב"ח

(א) רש"י ד"ה גם אתה וכו' וגו' חלית כמונו או אלינו כצ"ל וסד"א :

סנהדרין פט. קב:

גליון הש"ס

גמ' כל שחבירו נענש על ידו . עי' ב"ב דף כב ע"א תוס' ד"ה אגא ענשתיה :

[חגיגה יב: סוטה מב. סנהדרין קג.]

רבינו חננאל

ביתו אין אחרים לא . משמיה דר' יהודה אמר שמואל דאמר בני חבורה המקפידין זה על זה פי' שמדקדקין זה על זה שאומר אחד לחבירו המנה שלך שלקחתה גדולה תן לי אני כמותה והוא שוקלה בידו. ואם היה דג אומר לו לקחת דג או כדומה לו שהוא ארוך זרת צריך לתת לו (שמדתו) [תמורתו] זרת דגים או קישואין או אבטיחים וכדומה להן ואם היו אגוזים ושקדים וכדומה להן אומר לקחת עשרים או אומר לו בעת (שניטלו) [נוטלו] המתן עד שאשקול המנה ועד שאמדוד אורך הדגים והקישואים ואמנה הביצים והאגוזים והשקדים שאתה נוטל שאטול גם במשקלם וכמדתם וכמניינם . וכדברי ב"ה שאומרים לא תלוה אשה מחברתה ככרות כו' : ומטילין חלשים כו' . פירוש מטילין גורלות אבל לא על המנות אוקמוה על המנות של חול ביו"ט : נבוכדנאצר אנס צדקיהו בעברה וכיון שנענש נ"נ ע"י צדקיהו נענש גם הוא שנאמר שבעת קלון מכבוד זה נבוכדנאצר שתה גם אתה והערל זה צדקיהו ואמרינן האי קרא כוליה בנ"נ כתיב ועוד צדקיהו צדיקא מאי הוה ליה למעבד . אמר רב יהודה אמר רב בשעה שעשה אותו רשע לאותו צדיק כן

רב נסים גאון . פרק שואל . וכדברי הלל אף משום ריבית הוא שהוקדם זכרו בראש הפרק (דף קמח) וכן היה הלל אומר לא תלוה אשה ככר לחברתה עד שתעשנו דמים שמא יוקרו חטים או יוזלו ונמצאו באות לידי ריבית ועיקר זה במשנה בפרק אי זהו נשך (דף עה) :

number, borrowing and repaying on the Festival.[2] [149b] and according to Beth[3] Hillel, usury too.[4] If so, the same applies to his sons and household?—As for his sons and household, this is the reason, as Rab Judah [said] in Rab's name. For Rab Judah said in Rab's name: One may lend to his sons and household on interest, in order to give them experience thereof.[5] If so, a large portion [set off] against a small portion [should be permitted] too?—That indeed is so, and there is a lacuna, while it is thus taught: 'A MAN MAY CAST LOTS FOR HIS SONS AND HOUSEHOLD FOR THE TABLE, even [setting] a large portion against a small portion'. What is the reason?—As Rab Judah['s dictum] in Rab's name. Yet only for his sons and household, but not for strangers. What is the reason?—As Rab Judah['s dictum] in Samuel's name. [Further, 'setting] A LARGE PORTION AGAINST A SMALL PORTION is forbidden even on weekdays in the case of strangers'. What is the reason?—On account of gambling.[6]

AND [PRIESTS] MAY CAST LOTS FOR, etc. What does BUT NOT FOR THE PORTIONS mean?—Said R. Jacob the son of the daughter of Jacob: But [one must not cast lots] for the portions of weekday [sacrifices] on the Festivals. That is obvious? You might argue, since it is written, *for thy people are like the priests that quarrel*,[1] even the portions of weekdays too:[2] therefore he informs us [that it is not so].

R. Jacob son of Jacob's daughter also said: He through whom his neighbour is punished is not permitted to enter within the barrier [precincts] of the Holy One, blessed be He. How do we know this? Shall we say, because it is written, *And the Lord said, Who shall persuade Ahab, that he may go up and fall at Ramoth-gilead? And one said on this manner; and another said on that manner. And there came forth a spirit and stood before the Lord, and said, I will persuade him. And he said, I will go forth and be a lying spirit in the mouth of all his prophets. And He* [the Lord] *said, Thou shalt entice him, and shalt prevail also: go forth, and do so.*[3] Now we discussed, What spirit is meant? And R. Joḥanan answered: The spirit of Naboth the Jezreelite.[4] And what does '*go forth*' mean? Said Rab, Go forth from within My precincts![5] But perhaps there this is the reason, [viz.,] because it is written, *He that speaketh falsehood shall not be established before Mine eyes?*[6] Again, [if] it is derived from here: *Thou art filled with shame for glory: drink thou also, and be as one uncircumcised*, etc.;[7] and it is maintained: '*Thou art filled with shame for glory*' refers to Nebuchadnezzar: [whilst] '*drink thou also and be as one uncircumcised*', refers to Zedekiah,[8]—one [objection] is that the whole verse is written in reference to Nebuchadnezzar;[9] and further, what could the righteous Zedekiah have done to him, for Rab Judah said in Rab's name: When that wicked man [Nebuchadnezzar] wished to do thus to that righteous man
b [Zedekiah], etc.?[1] Rather [it follows] from this: *Also to punish the righteous is not good.*[2] Now, '*is not good*' can mean nought but [that he is] evil,[3] and it is written, *For thou art a God that hath no pleasure in wickedness, evil shall not sojourn with Thee*,[4] [which means], Thou art righteous, O Lord, thus evil shall not sojourn *in Thy habitation*.

How is it implied that HALASHIM[5] connotes lots?—Because it is written, *How art thou fallen from heaven, O day star, son of the morning! how art thou cut down to the ground, thou* ḥolesh [*who didst cast lots*][6] *over the nations*, etc.[7] Rabbah son of R. Huna said: This teaches that he [Nebuchadnezzar] cast lots over the royal chiefs[8] to ascertain whose turn[9] it was for pederasty. And it is written, *All the kings of the nations, all of them*, [*sleep in glory*, etc.].[10] R. Joḥanan said: That means that they rested from pederasty.[11]

R. Joḥanan also said: As long as that wicked man lived mirth was never heard[12] in the mouth of any living being, for it is written, *the whole world is at rest, and is quiet: they break forth into singing:*[13] whence it follows that hitherto[14] there was no singing.

R. Isaac also said in R. Joḥanan's name: One may not stand in that wicked man's palace, for it is said, *and satyrs shall dance there.*[15]

Rab Judah said in Rab's name: When that wicked man [Nebuchadnezzar] wished to treat that righteous one [Zedekiah] thus,[16] his membrum was extended three hundred cubits and wagged in front of the whole company [of captive kings], for it is said, *Thou art filled with shame for glory: drink thou also, and be as one uncircumcised* [he'orel]: the numerical value of '*orel* is three hundred.

Rab Judah also said in Rab's name: When that wicked man descended to Gehenna,[17] all who had [previously] descended thither trembled, saying, Does he come to rule over us, or to be as weak as we [are], for it is said, *Art thou also become weak as we?*
c *or art thou to rule over us?*[1] A Heavenly Echo went forth and declared, *Whom dost thou pass in beauty? go down, and be thou laid with the uncircumcised.*[2]

How hath the oppressor ceased! the golden city [madhebah] *ceased:*[3] Rab Judah said in Rab's name: This people hath ceased, that

(2) On Festivals one may borrow from his neighbour, but not by weight, measure or number. Likewise, he may not use the terms 'lend' and 'repay', for these belong to monetary transactions. When members of a company are particular with each other, they are likely to be led into a transgression of these prohibitions. (3) Var. lec. omit 'Beth', v. *supra* 148*b*. (4) When they are not particular with each other, and one borrows and returns the same amount after its price advances, there is no usury, since neither cares whether the exact amount is returned or not. But there every change in value is scrupulously noted, and therefore if it advances there is usury. This does not refer particularly to Festivals. (5) Lit., 'to let them know the taste of usury', i.e., the grief and anxiety it causes. (6) Which this resembles.

a (1) Hos. IV, 4 (E.V. '*for thy people are as they that strive with the priest*'). (2) To save them from quarrelling. (3) I Kings XXII, 20ff. (4) This is deduced from the employment of the def. art. in Hebrew: '*and* the *spirit came forth*', implying a particular one, viz., that of Naboth the Jezreelite, whom Ahab had turned from a living human being into a spirit—by judicial murder; v. ibid. ch. XXI. (5) Because he lured Ahab to destruction, which proves the dictum of R. Jacob. (6) Ps. CI, 7. Though God sought to lure Ahab to his doom, He nevertheless desired it to be done by arguments drawn from true facts (Maharsha in Sanh. 89*a*). (7) Hab. II, 16. (8) And the verse is interpreted in the sense that Zedekiah too is regarded as uncircumcised and not permitted to enter the precincts of the Almighty, because Nebuchadnezzar was punished on his account. (9) I.e., it can be so interpreted.

b (1) V. *infra* for the complete allusion. (2) Prov. XVII, 26. (3) Translating the verse thus: even the righteous, when made the cause or vehicle of punishment, is accounted evil. (4) Ps. V, 5 (E.V. 4). (5) The word used in the Mishnah. (6) *Which didst lay low*. (7) Isa. XIV, 12. (8) The kings he had captured in battle. (9) Lit., 'day'. (10) Ibid. 18. (11) The ascription of pederasty to Nebuchadnezzar may be a covert allusion to the fact that the Romans were addicted to this vice; v. Weiss, *Dor*, II, 21. (12) Lit., 'found'. (13) Isa. XIV, 7. (14) I.e., before Nebuchadnezzar's death. (15) Ibid. XIII, 21. (16) I.e., submit him to sexual abuse. (17) V. *supra* 33*a*, n. c8.

c (1) Isa. XIV, 10. This connects נמשלת with משל, to rule E.V.: *art thou become like unto us*. (2) Ezek. XXXII, 19. (3) Isa. XIV, 4.

demanded, [150a] Measure out [tribute] and bring it [to us]; others interpret: that demanded, Bring ever more and more, without measure.[4]

And excellent greatness was added to me:[5] Rab Judah said in R. Jeremiah b. Abba's name: This teaches that he rode upon a male lion to whose head he had tied a snake [for reins], in fulfilment of what is said, *and the beasts of the field also have I given him to serve him.*[6]

a *MISHNAH.* A MAN MUST NOT HIRE LABOURERS ON THE SABBATH, NOR INSTRUCT HIS NEIGHBOUR TO HIRE LABOURERS ON HIS BEHALF. ONE MUST NOT GO TO THE TEḤUM TO AWAIT NIGHTFALL[7] IN ORDER TO HIRE LABOURERS OR BRING IN PRODUCE; BUT ONE MAY DO SO IN ORDER TO WATCH [HIS FIELD], AND [THEN] HE CAN BRING [HOME] PRODUCE WITH HIM.[8] ABBA SAUL STATED A GENERAL PRINCIPLE: WHATEVER I HAVE A RIGHT TO INSTRUCT [THAT IT BE DONE], I AM PERMITTED TO GO TO AWAIT NIGHTFALL FOR IT [AT THE TEḤUM].

a *GEMARA.* Wherein does he differ from his neighbour?[1]—Said R. Papa: A Gentile neighbour [is meant]. R. Ashi demurred: [Surely] an order to a Gentile is [forbidden as] a *shebuth?*[2] Rather said R. Ashi: One may even say [that] an Israelite neighbour [is meant]. [Yet] he [the Tanna] informs us this: One may not say to his neighbour, 'Hire labourers for me,' but one may say to his neighbour, 'Well, we shall see[3] whether you join me[4] in the evening!'[5] And with whom does our Mishnah agree? With R. Joshua b. Ḳarḥah. For it was taught: One must not say to his neighbour, 'Well, we shall see whether you join me in the evening'! R. Joshua b. Ḳarḥah said: One may say to his neighbour, 'Well, we shall see whether you join me in the evening'! Rabbah b. Bar Ḥanah said in R. Joḥanan's name: The *halachah* is as R. Joshua b. Ḳarḥah. Rabbah b. Bar Ḥanah also said in R. Joḥanan's name: What is R. Judah b. Ḳarḥah's reason? Because it is written, *nor finding thine own pleasure nor* speaking *thine own words:*[6] [explicit] speech is forbidden, but thought is permitted.[7]

R. Aḥa son of R. Huna pointed out a contradiction to Raba. Did R. Joḥanan say: Speech is forbidden, thought is permitted, which shows that thought is not the same as speech? But surely Rabbah b. Bar Ḥanah said in R. Joḥanan's name: One may meditate [on learning] everywhere, except at the baths or in a privy?—There it is different, because [the fulfilment of] *and thy camp shall be holy*[8] is required, which is absent.[9] But it is also written, *that he see no indecent speech* [dabar] *in thee?*[10]—That is required for Rab Judah['s dictum]. For Rab Judah said: One may not recite the *shema'*[11] in the presence of a naked heathen. Why particularly a heathen: even an Israelite too?—He proceeds to a climax:[12] it is superfluous to state that it is forbidden [in the presence of a naked] Israelite; but as for a heathen, since it is written of him,
b *whose flesh is the flesh of asses,*[1] I might say that it is permitted; therefore he tells us [otherwise]. Yet perhaps that indeed is so?—Scripture saith, *and they saw not their father's nakedness.*[2]

Now, is speech forbidden? Surely R. Ḥisda and R. Hamnuna both said: Accounts in connection with religion may be calculated [discussed] on the Sabbath. And R. Eleazar said: One may determine charity [grants] to the poor on the Sabbath. Again, R. Jacob b. Idi said in R. Joḥanan's name: One may supervise matters of life and death and matters of communal urgency on the Sabbath, and one may go to the synagogues to attend to communal affairs on the Sabbath. Also, R. Samuel b. Naḥmani said in R. Joḥanan's name: One may go to theatres and circuses and basilicas to attend to communal affairs on the Sabbath. Further, the School of Manasseh taught: One may make arrangements on the Sabbath for the betrothal of young girls and the elementary education[3] of a child and to teach him a trade![4]—Scripture saith, *nor finding* thine own *affairs nor speaking* thine own *words:* thine affairs are forbidden, the affairs of Heaven [religious matters] are permitted.

Rab Judah said in Samuel's name: Unimportant accounts[5] and past expenditure accounts[6] may be calculated on the Sabbath. It was taught likewise: One may not calculate past or future

(4) These interpret *madhebah* either as *medod habeh* (count and bring) or *me'od habi* (*belo*) *middah* (bring much, without measure). (5) Dan. IV, 36. This was said by Nebuchadnezzar when he regained sanity after having lived seven years like a wild beast. (6) Jer. XXVII, 6. (7) Lit., 'for nightfall'. I.e., one may not go as far as the *teḥum* on the Sabbath in readiness to cross it immediately the Sabbath terminates. (8) Lit., 'in his hand'. Though he may not go to the *teḥum* in the first place for this purpose, yet since he did so primarily in order to watch his field, he may take advantage of the fact and bring home produce too.

a (1) It is obvious that if he must not engage labourers his neighbours must not either. (2) V. Glos. This is a well-known general principle, already taught in the Mishnah *supra* 121a, and it need not be repeated. (3) הנראה. The exact meaning of the expression is not established. (4) Lit., 'stand with me'. (5) Though both understand it as a hint that he desires to engage him. (6) Isa. LVIII, 13, q.v. (7) A hint is not explicit but left to the understanding. (8) Deut. XXIII, 15. (9) For speech is not mentioned in that passage. (10) Ibid. E.V.: '*that he see no unclean thing in thee*'. (11) V. Glos. (12) Lit., 'he states, "it is unnecessary"'.

b (1) Ezek. XXIII, 20. [I.e., nudity is common among them]. (2) Gen. IX, 23: This shows that it is indecent in all cases. (3) Lit., 'to teach him (the) book'. (4) All these involve actual speech. (5) Lit., 'accounts of what is it to thee'. Rashi. 'Aruch and R. Ḥan.: accounts of guests, i.e., how many guests will be present, etc. (6) Rashi. Lit., 'what (cost) lies in this'. *Aliter:* 'of no practical value'. Lit., 'of what is in it'.

תורה אור

מדוד והבא ואיכא דאמרי שאמרה מאד מאד הביא בלא מדה °ורבו יתירה הוספת לי אמר רב יהודה אמר רב ירמיה בר אבא מלמד שרכב על ארי זכר וקשר תנין בראשו לקיים מה שנא' °וגם את חית השדה נתתי לו לעבדו:

מתני' [א]לא ישכור אדם פועלים בשבת ולא יאמר אדם לחבירו לשכור לו פועלים *[ב]אין מחשיכין על התחום לשכור לו פועלים ולהביא פירות [ג]אבל מחשיך הוא לשמור ומביא פירות בידו כלל אמר אבא שאול כל שאני זכאי באמירתו רשאי אני להחשיך עליו:

גמ' (פשיטא) מ"ש הוא ומ"ש חבירו אמר רב פפא °חבר נכרי מתקיף לה רב אשי *[ד]אמירה לנכרי שבות אלא אמר רב אשי אפילו תימא חבירו ישראל הא קמ"ל לא יאמר אדם לחבירו שבור לי פועלים [ה]אבל אומר אדם לחבירו הנראה שתעמוד עמי לערב ומתני' מני כרבי יהושע בן קרחה דתניא *לא יאמר אדם לחבירו הנראה שתעמוד עמי לערב רבי יהושע בן קרחה אומר אומר אדם לחבירו הנראה שתעמוד עמי לערב אמר רבה בר בר חנה אמר רבי יוחנן הלכה כרבי יהושע בן קרחה ואמר רבה בר בר חנה אמר רבי יוחנן מ"ט דרבי יהושע בן קרחה דכתיב °ממצוא חפצך ודבר דבר *דיבור אסור הרהור מותר רמי ליה רב אחא בר רב הונא לרבא מי אמר ר' יוחנן דיבור אסור הרהור מותר *אלמא הרהור לאו כדיבור דמי *והאמר רבה בר בר חנה אמר רבי יוחנן בכל מקום מותר להרהר חוץ מבית המרחץ ומבית הכסא שאני התם דבעינן °והיה מחניך קדוש וליכא הכא נמי כתיב °ולא יראה בך ערות דבר ההוא מיבעי ליה לכדרב יהודה *דאמר רב יהודה [ו]עכו"ם ערום אסור לקרות קרית שמע כנגדו מאי איריא עכו"ם אפי' ישראל נמי לא מיבעיא קאמר לא מיבעיא ישראל דאסור אבל עכו"ם כיון דכתיב ביה °אשר בשר חמורים בשרם אימא שפיר דמי קמ"ל אימא הכי נמי אמר קרא °וערות אביהם לא ראו ודיבור מי אסיר *והא רב חסדא ורב המנונא דאמרי תרוייהו [ז]חשבונות של מצוה מותר לחשבן בשבת וא"ר אלעזר [ח]פוסקים צדקה לעניים בשבת וא"ר יעקב בר אידי אמר רבי יוחנן מפקחין פיקוח נפש ופיקוח רבים בשבת והולכין לבתי כנסיות לפקח על עסקי רבים בשבת [ט]וא"ר שמואל בר נחמני א"ר *יוחנן הולכין לטרטיאות ולקרקסאות ולבסילקאות לפקח על עסקי רבים בשבת ותנא דבי [י]מנשה משדכין על התינוקות ליארס בשבת ועל התינוק ללמדו ספר וללמדו אומנות *אמר קרא ממצוא חפצך ודבר דבר *חפציך אסורים חפצי שמים מותרין א"ר יהודה אמר שמואל חשבונות של [*מלך] ושל מה בכך מותר לחשבן בשבת תנ"ה *[כ]חשבונות שעברו ושעתידין להיו' אסור לחשבן של*) מלך ושל

*) כס"י מה לך

רש"י

מדוד · מעות ודינרי זהב והבא: ורבו יתירה הוספת לי · לאחר שהיה ז' שנים בהמה וחזר למלכותו היה משתבח כן ומהו התוספת שקשר תנין גדול כתם גדול בראשו של ארי כמין אפסר: מתני' לא ישכור אדם פועלים · דכתיב (ישעיה נח) ממצוא חפצך: ולא יאמר לחבירו כו' · בגמרא פריך פשיטא כיון דהוא אסור חבירו נמי אסור דהא ישראל הוא והשולחו עובר משום לפני עור לא תתן מכשול: אין מחשיכין על התחום · לקרב עצמו בשבת עד סוף התחום ולהחשיך שם שיהא קרוב למקום הפועלים או לפרדס להביא פירות דכל דבר שאסור לעשותו בשבת אסור להחשיך עליו: אבל מחשיך הוא · להיות קרוב לנאת לשמור פירותיו וזה דבר המותר בשבת לשמור פירותיו אם היו בתוך תחומו: ומביא פירות בידו · הואיל ועיקר מחשבתו לא היה לכך: כלל אמר אבא שאול · נותן היה כלל בדבר זה להוסיף דברים אחרים כיוצא בו ולקמיה מפרש לאתויי מאי: כל שאני זכאי באמירתו · שאני רשאי לאומרו להבירו או לנכרי בשבת לעשות למוצאי שבת רשאי אני להחשיך עליו: גמ' מאי שנא כו' · ופשיטא דכיון דאמר לא ישכור ה"ה לא יאמר לחבירו דהא ישראל הוא כמותו ולא מצי לאוגרינהו: אמירה לנכרי שבות · וכבר סתמה רבי למתני'* נכרי שבא לכבות אין אומרים לו כבה: הא קמ"ל · משנה יתירה בהדיא הוא דלא לימא ליה אבל סתמא שרי ליה למימר: הנראה · עכשיו נראה אם תעמוד עמי לערב אם תבא אלי לכשתחשך ושניהן יודעין שעל מנת לשוכרו לפעולתו הוא מזהירו וכיון דלא מפרש בהדיא שרי כדמפרש טעמא לקמן דבור אסור הרהור מותר: מותר להרהר · בדברי תורה: והיה מחניך קדוש · ולא כתיב ביה דבר אלא מקום חנייתך תהא בקדושה וטעמא משום דישראל מהרהרין תמיד בדברי תורה: ערות דבר · אלמא לא אסיר ליה אלא בשעת דבור: ההיא כדרב יהודה · כלומר לעולם והיה מחניך קדוש משום הרהור תורה ואפי' אין דבור ולא יראה בך ערות דבר במילתא אחריתי מיירי דאסור בשעת הדבור ולא בשעת הרהור כגון להסתכל בערוה: עכו"ם ערום · כ"ש ישראל כדמפרש ואזיל: אימא שפיר דמי · דכבהמה בעלמא הוא: וערות אביהם · אלמא ערוה היא בבן נח: ודבור מי אסור והא אמר רב חסדא כו' · וכל הני דבור הוא: פקוח נפש · בדבר שיש בו סכנה פקוח דיקומבימונ"ט: ופקוח דרבים · כגון לרשות: טרטייאות וקרקסאות ובסילקאות · מיני פלטין הן ששם נאספו לבית הוועד: ללמדו אומנות · דהא נמי מצוה היא דכל שאינו מלמדו אומנות מלמדו לסטות ומצוה ילפינן מקרא בקדושין בהאשה נקנית (ד' ל:): של מלך · של עצה שאינו שלו ואין צריך בכך כגון הרוצה לבנות בית כך וכך צריך להוציא בו ול"נ כמו מה לך מה לך ולחשבונות הללו הרי אין צורך בהן לא לך ולא לאחר כגון ההיא דפרישית: ושל

תוספות

מה לי הוא ומה לי חבירו · ואם תאמר ונימא דחבירו היינו דאמר ליה שכור לי פועלים למחר וי"ל דא"כ מאי איריא חבירו אפי' הוא נמי לא מצי למימר אשכור פועלים למחר דעד כאן לא קאמר רב יהודה אמר שמואל מותר לאדם לומר לחבירו לכרך פלוני אני הולך למחר אלא משום דשאם יש בורגנין הולך הא לאו הכי לא:

ורבי יהושע בן קרחה היא · יש מפרש דר"ע קרוי קרחה שהיה קרח כדתניא בפרק בתרא דבכורות (דף נח· וסם) אמר בן עזאי כל חכמי ישראל דומין לפני כקליפת השום חוץ מן הקרח הזה ואומר שזה היה ר"ע והיה לו בן ששמו יהושע כדאמר בפרק קמא דשבועות* א"ל ר' יהושע בנו של ר"ע לר"ע ואין נראה לר"ת דמה שקראו בן עזאי לר"ע קרח בבדיחותא בעלמא אין לנו לקרותו כן כל שעה דלשון גנות הוא שנא' עלה קרח עלה קרח (מלכים ב ב) ואמרינן נמי לקמן (דף קנב.) אמר ליה ההוא לדוקי לר' יהושע בן קרחה מהכא לקרחינאה כמה הוי הרי שהיה מגנה אותו על שהיה קרח ועוד אמרי' במגילה פרק בתרא (דף כח·) שאל רבי את רבי יהושע בן קרחה במה הארכת ימים כו' א"ל רבי ברכני א"ל יהי רצון שתגיע לחצי ימי ואי ר' יהושע בן קרחה בנו של ר"ע והא קיימא לן* דלא נשא ר"ע בת כלבא שבוע עד שקיבל עליו לעסוק בתורה ואז היה בן מ' דתניא בסוף ספרי מ' שנה שימש ת"ח מ' שנה פירנס את ישראל וכל ימיו ק"כ שנים ואמרי' בקידושין פרק בתרא (דף עב·) עד שלא מת ר"ע נולד רבי ואפילו נולד ר' יהושע בשנה ראשונה שנשאה לא נשאר כי אם פ' שנים מר"ע ורבי יהושע בשעה שבירך את רבי היה בן ק"מ שנים לכל הפחות שבפחות מע' שנה לא היה מברכו ואז היה רבי לכל הפחות בן ס' וא"כ לא היה מברכו רק מי' שנים ועוד נראה שלא נשאה עד שעסק בי רב תרי סרי ותרי סרי שנין נמצא כשהיה רבי יהושע בן קרחה בן ק"מ היה רבי יותר מחצי ימיו לכך נראה לר"ת דלא ר"ע היה אלא היניש אחרינא היה ששמו קרחה וקרחה הוא שם אדם כמו קרח ונולד הרבה קודם ר' יהושע בנו של ר"ע* · מ"ר:

אומר אדם לחבירו הנראה שתעמוד עמי לערב · י"א דדווקא לחבירו אבל לנכרי אסור לפי שהוא (א) [עושה] לדעת אותה [אמירה] ואינו נראה דהא שרינן ליה הכא משו' דדבור אסור והרהור מותר [א"כ] ל"ש נכרי ל"ש ישראל · מ"ר:

ודיבור מי אסור · פי' מן התורה דהא מדסרינן דיבור של מצוה מכלל דמדאורייתא שרי:

ואמר ר"א פוסקין צדקה לעניים בשבת · וא"ת מה צריך לאתויי (ב) הא ה"ל לאתויי מילתייהו דבית הלל [בפי"ז] (בתוספתא) דתני אין פוסקים צדקה אפי' להשיא יתום ויתומה ואין משדכין על התינוקות ליארס בו דברי בית שמאי ובית הלל מתירין ונ"ל דניחא ליה לאתויי מילתא דרבי אלעזר דמהתם לא הוה שמעינן פסיקת צדקה לעניים דהא לא שרי בית הלל אלא להשיא יתום ויתומה: ואין

רבינו חננאל

נמשכה ערלתו וכו': [מתני'] לא ישכור פועלים בשבת ולא יאמר לחבירו שכור לי פועלים: גמ' ואקשינן עלה מ"ש הוא ומ"ש חבירו. ובא רב פפא לאוקמיה למתני' בחבירו נכרי. רב אשי אמר אפילו תימא בחבירו ישראל הא קמ"ל דלשכור פועלים הוא דלא יאמר לו אבל אומר לו הנראה שתעמוד עמי לערב כלומר אסור שיאמר לו לערב לך לשכור לי פועלים או כיוצא בו. אבל אם יאמר לו הא נראה שתעמוד עמי לערב ובדעתו שיאמר לו לערב לך לשכור לי פועלים או עשה לי מלאכה כך וכך מותר כר' יהושע בן קרחה. ואמר ר' יוחנן הלכתא כר' יהושע בן קרחה ודייק ר' יוחנן ואמר טעמיה דר' יהושע בן קרחה דיבור בפירוש' אסור אבל הרהור מותר דכתיב ממצוא חפצך ודבר דבר. ואקשינן עליה והא הוא דאמר בכל מקום מותר להרהר חוץ ממרחץ ובית הכסא כו' ואמאי לא אמרינן הכא נמי הרהור מותר. ומפרקינן האי קרא מיבעי ליה לאסור אפילו ערותו של נכרי דאשכחנן קרא דאמר וערות אביהם לא ראו. ואקשי' תוב ודבור מי אסור והביאו ה' שמועות אחת שאפילו דבור אם' מותר בשבת ואלו הן חשבונות ופוסקין צדקה לעניים ומפקחין פיקוח רבים. והולכין לבתי כנסיות ולבתי מדרשות לפקח על עסקי רבים והולכין לבתי טאטראות ולבתי קרקסאות לפקח על עסקי רבים. ותנא משדכין על התינוקות ליארס ועל התינוק ללמדו ספר וללמדו אומנות. ומפרקי' אלא אמר קרא ממצוא חפצך ודבר דבר חפצך אסורין כדבור חפצי שמים מותרין. ואלו כולן חפצי שמים הן: חשבונות של מלך. פירוש מילך אורחים ובא הלך לאיש העשיר כלומר מותר לאדם לחשב אורחים הקרואים להסב אצלו בסעודה וכדתנן מונה אדם את אורחיו ואת פרפריותיו פי' חשבונות של מה בכך כמו שיחשב אדם חשבון כגון חיילות המלך כך וכך אלף וכיוצא בו אומ' לו מה בכך. כלומר מה הנאה יש לך ומה צורך לך בזה כגון אלו מותר בשבת. וזה שאומרים מחשבין חשבונות

עין משפט נר מצוה

כב א מיי' פכ"ד מהל' שבת הלכה יב סמג לאוין סה טור שו"ע או"ח סימן שז סעיף ב:
כג ב ג מיי' פכ"ד שם הלכה ג סמג שם טור שו"ע או"ח סימן שו סעיף א וסי' שז סעיף ח:
כד ד מיי' פ"ו שם הל"א סמג שם:
כה ה מיי' פכ"ד שם הל"ד וסמג שם טור שו"ע או"ח סימן שז סעיף ז:
[דף ו.]
כו ו מיי' פ"ג מהלכות ק"ש הלכה טז סמג עשין יח טור שו"ע או"ח סימן עה סעיף ד:
כז ז ח ט י מיי' פכ"ד מהלכות שבת הל"ה סמג לאוין סה טוש"ע או"ח סימן שו סעיף ו:
כח כ מיי' פכ"ד מהל' שבת הל"א סמג שם טור שו"ע או"ח סימן שז סעיף ז:
[כתובות סג. ועיין שם ובהלכות דר"נ פ"ו]
[וע"ע תוס' בכורות נח. ד"ה חוץ ותוס' ב"ב קיג. ד"ה ומטו ותוס' פסחים קיב. ד"ה צוה]

מסורת הש"ס

[עי' תוס' לקמן ע"ב ד"ה ואין]
[עירובין סז: גיטין ח: ב"ק פ: ב"מ צ.]
[לעיל קכא.]
לעיל קיג:
[ברכות כ:]
שם כד:
לעיל מ:
קידושין לג.
ע"ז מד:
זבחים קב.
ברכות כה: ע"ש
[תוספ' פי"ח]
כתובות ה.
[נ"ל יוחנן]
גי' רש"ל דאמר לעיל קיג.
[נ"ל מילך פי' אורחי' כלכתי' ויבא הלך כלומר מותר אדם לחשב אורחיו הקרואים. ערוך ערך חשב]
[בכ"י מה לך]

הגהות הב"ח

(א) תוס' ד"ה אומר וכו' לפי שהוא רוצה לדעת אותה מלאכה ואינו: (ב) ד"ה ואמר רבי אלעזר וכו' וא"ת מה צריך לאתויי מילתא דרבי אלעזר ה"ל לאתויי:

גליון הש"ס

גמ' חבר נכרי. עי' סוכה דף לט ע"א תוס' ד"ה הלוקח ועי' מג"א סימן תק ס"ק ג:

ושל מה בכך מותר לחושבן ורמינהו חושבין חשבונות שאינן צריכין ואין מחשבין חשבונות שצריכין בשבת כיצד אומר אדם לחבירו כך וכך פועלים (א) הוצאתי על שדה זו כך וכך דינרין הוצאתי על דירה זו אבל לא יאמר לו כך וכך הוצאתי וכך וכך אני עתיד להוציא ולטעמיך קשיא לך היא גופא אלא *הא דאיכא אגרא דאגירא גביה הא דליכא אגרא דאגירא גביה: אין מחשיכין: תנו רבנן מעשה בחסיד אחד שנפרצה לו פרץ בתוך שדהו ונמלך עליה לגודרה ונזכר ששבת הוא *ונמנע אותו חסיד ולא גדרה ונעשה לו נס ועלתה בו צלף וממנה היתה פרנסתו ופרנסת אנשי ביתו א"ר יהודה אמר שמואל [ג]מותר לאדם לומר לחבירו לכרך פלוני אני הולך למחר שאם יש בורגנין הולך תנן אין מחשיכין על התחום לשכור פועלים ולהביא פירות בשלמא לשכור פועלים דבשבת לא מצי אגר אלא להביא פירות לימא שאם יש שם מחיצות מביא [ג]משכחת לה בפירות המחוברים והתני ר' אושעיא אין מחשיכין על התחום להביא תבן וקש בשלמא קש משכחת לה במחובר אלא תבן היכי משכחת לה בתיבנא סריא ת"ש *[ד]מחשיכין על התחום לפקח על עסקי כלה ועל עסקי המת על עסקי כלה ומת אין על עסקי אחר לא בשלמא אחר דומיא דכלה משכחת לה למיגזא ליה אסא אלא מת מאי ניהו להביא לו ארון ותכריכין וקתני מת אין אבל אחר לא ואמאי לימא שאם יש שם מחיצו' מביא מת נמי משכחת לה *למיגזא ליה גלימא: אבל מחשיכין: ואע"ג דלא אבדיל והאמר רבי אלעזר בן אנטיגנוס משום רבי אליעזר בן יעקב [ה]אסור לו לאדם שיעשה חפציו קודם שיבדיל וכי תימא דאבדיל בתפלה והאמר רב יהודה אמר שמואל *[ו]המבדיל בתפלה צריך שיבדיל על הכוס וכי תימא דאבדיל על הכוס כוס בשדה מי איכא תרגמא רבי נתן בר אמי קמיה דרבא בין הגיתות שנו א"ל ר' אבא לרב אשי [ז]במערבא אמרינן הכי המבדיל בין קודש לחול ועבדינן צורכין אמר רב אשי כי הוינא בי רב כהנא הוה אמר המבדיל בין קודש לחול ומסלתינן סילתי: כלל אמר אבא שאול כל שאני וכו': (איבעיא להו) אבא שאול אהייא אילימא ארישא קאי אין מחשיכין על התחום לשכור פועלים להביא פירות האי

(לקמן קנא.)

רש"י

ושל מה בכך · כגון שכבר היו לצורך אלא שעברו כגון כך וכך הוצאתי בבנין זה: חשבונות שעברו· לקמן מוקי לה דלא עברו לגמרי שעדיין שכר הפועלים עליו שלא נתנו להן ושל מה בכך שעברו לגמרי ואין שכר פועלים עליו: כך וכך הוצאתי· אלמא עברו מותרין: תקשי לך היא גופא · ברייתא קמייתא רישא קתני שעברו אסורין וסיפא קתני של מה בכך מותרין דהיינו עברו: צלף · אילן גדול הוא ובעל ענפים הרבה ושלשה מיני אוכל יש בפירותיו אביונות קפריסין ועולבין: שאם יש בורגנין · מע' אמה לע' אמה הולך אפי' בשבת שהכל חשוב כעיר אחת וכל העיר כד' אמות כדאמרינן בעירובין (דף כא.) וכיון דהוא דבר שיש לו היתר על ידי תקנה בשבת מותר לאומרו אפילו במקום שאין שם ההיתר: המחוברים · שא"א לקוצן בשבת ע"י שום תקנה: קש · זנבות השבולים אשטרליי"א: בתיבנא סריא · שאפי' יש מחיצות אינו מביא משום דמוקצה הוא: על עסקי כלה ומת אין · דחפצי שמים הן אבל על עסקי אחר אפי' דומיא דכלה לא: בשלמא אחר דומיא דכלה משכחת לה · דאסור להחשיך כגון לחתוך מן המחובר: למיגז לה אסא · דעבדו לה גננא דאסא לכלתא: אלא עסקי מת מאי היא · הבאה דארון ותכריכין ואמאי לאחר לא לימא הואיל ואם יש שם מחיצות מביא: למיגז ליה גלימא · לתקן לו תכריכין דאין היתר לדבר היום כלל: ואע"ג דלא אבדיל · אסיפא דמתני' מתמה דקתני ומביא פירות בידו לקוצן מן המחובר בלא הבדלה: בין הגיתות שנו · דאיכא כוס בשדה: המבדיל בין קודש לחול · להיכרא בעלמא ללוות את המלך: ועבדינן צורכין · ואחר כך אנו מברכין על הכוס ברכה גמורה דהבדלה וכ"ש דאי אבדיל בתפלה מותר לעשות צרכיו וחוזר ומבדיל על הכוס: ומסלתינן סילתי · חוטבין עצים: אהייא · קאי ומשוי כללא: אי נימא ארישא · דקתני ת"ק לאיסורא וקאתי אבא שאול לשוויה בה כללא א"כ דכללא לאיסורא ה"ל למימר בהדיא כל שאינו זכאי באמירה כגון אנו שאינו רשאי לומר לחבירו שכור לי פועלים או הבא לי פירות למוצאי שבת אינו רשאי להחשיך מיבעי ליה: אלא

תוספות

*ואין מחשיכין על התחום לשכור פועלים ולהביא פירות · השתא משמע דוקא על התחום אבל בתוך התחום מחשיכין לשכור פועלי' ולהביא פירו' וקשה לרבי דבסוף פ' בכל מערבין (עירובין דל"ה:) תניא לא יהלך אדם לתוך שדהו לידע מה צריכה כיוצא בו לא יטייל אדם על פתח מדינה כדי שיכנס למרחץ מיד ואומר רבי דהתם מינכרא מילתא · דאינו מטייל אלא ליכנס למרחץ מיד אחר השבת שעל פתח מדינה רגילים להיות מרחצאות כדאמרי' בפ"ק *דמגילה (דף ו:) (ב)ה' מאות מעלות עשן חוץ לחומה אבל הכא אין הוכחה כ"כ בתוך התחום המחשיך לשכור פועלים ולהביא פירות וכי האי גוונא משני התם · מ"ר:

אבל מחשיך הוא לשמור ומביא פירות בידו · מתוך פירוש הקונטרס משמע לשמור חוץ לתחום וכן משמע פשט המשנה וקשה לרבי מהא דאמר שמואל בגמ' מותר לאדם לומר לחבירו לכרך פלוני אני הולך למחר ופריך תנן אין מחשיכין על התחום לשכור פועלים כו' והשתא מתניתין גופיה תיקשי ליה דמוכחא מילתא כוותיה דשמואל מדקתני בסיפא כלל אמר אבא שאול כל שאני זכאי באמירתו יכול אני להחשיך עליו וקא מפרש בגמ' דמה שמותר לומר מותר להחשיך וא"כ מדשרינן להחשיך לשמור חוץ לתחום אלמא שרי למימר חוץ לתחום אני הולך למחר דהא בהא תליא והיינו כשמואל ואיכי יודע מאי קשיא דאי לאו דשמואל מתני' אתיא שפיר דה"א אין לך דבר שלא יהא מותר לאדם לומר על עצמו ואפי' אשכור פועלים למחר או אבנה בנין זה יכול לומר בשבת דהוה אמירה דווקא לחבירו אסור לומר שכור לי פועלים למחר דמהני אמירתו אבל על עצמו יכול לומר כל מה שירצה דלא מהני אמירתו וכי תלי אבא שאול ההחשכה (ג)ה"מ באמירה לחבירו דיש אסורה ויש מותרת אבל אם איתא לדשמואל פריך שפיר דאסר כל אמירות אפילו על עצמו אלא דווקא לכרך פלוני אני הולך למחר משום טעמא דשאם יש שם בורגנין הולך והשתא פריך כיון דאי לאו האי טעמא הוה אסרת ליה אלא משום האי טעמא דווקא שרית ליה א"כ מתני' נמי תשתרי להביא פירות שאם יש מחיצות מביא · כ"ל:

לכרך פלוני אני הולך · תימה מאי איריא הוא אפילו לחבירו נמי יכול לומר לך לי לכרך פלוני למחר מהאי טעמא דקאמר

*מדשרי שמואל לקמן למר לחבירו שמור לי פירות שבתחומך אפילו בשבת כ"ש שיכול לומר שמור לי למחר ואין לפרש דשאני התם שהן בתחומו אבל אין יכול לומר לחבירו שמור לי פירות שחוץ לתחומך דנראה הוא שאפילו זה יכול לומר מכיון שמותר להחשיך וי"ל דלא נקט שמואל דוקא לכרך פלוני אני הולך דהוא הדין לחבירו יכול לומר לך לי לכרך פלוני למחר:

בשלמא קש במחובר משכחת לה · ה"נ הו"מ למימר מטעם מוקצה דהא אינו ראוי למאכל בהמה כדאמר לעיל (דף קמא.) הקש שע"ג המטה לא ינענעו כו' אלא רבותא קאמר דאפילו במחובר משכחת לה: במחובר משכחת לה · אומר רבי דלאו משום תלישה נקט לה דאע"ג שמחובר לארץ אין בו איסור תלישה כיון שיבש אינו יונק מן הארץ כדמוכח בחולין פרק העור והרוטב (דף קכז: ושם) דאמר תאנים שלמקו באביהן מטמאין טומאת אוכלין והתולש ממנה בשבת חייב חטאת דווקא למקו אבל יבשו לא וכן משמע בכל הסוגיא דיבשו הן ועוקציהן מטמא טומאת אוכלין ואין דינו כלל כמחובר והא דקאמר הכא במחובר. משכחת לה היינו משום איסור ייפוי קרקע כדאמר לעיל התולש עולשין בשבת חייב חטאת בפרק הבונה (לעיל דף קג.) והא דפריך בפרק המוציא תפילין (עירובין דף ק:) אאילן יבש הא קא כתרי פירי משמע שיש ביבש איסור תלישה אומר רבי דמיירי התם ביבשו הן ולא עוקציהן: בתיבנא סריא · והא דאמר לקמן פרק מי שהחשיך (דף קנה:) מפרכין תבן ואספסתא לפני בהמה ומוקי לה בתבנא סריא משמע דחזי לבהמה אומר רבי דמיירי כגון דלא סרי' כולי האי: אלא מת מאי ניהו להביא לו ארון ותכריכין · תימה אמאי לא קאמר למיגז ליה אסא שהיו רגילין להביא אסא למת כדאשכחן בנדה (דף לז.) דשור אסא מערסא לערסא וי"ל ע"כ ל"ל ארון ותכריכין כדקתני במתני' בהדיא · מ"ר:

רבינו חננאל

חשבונות שאין צריכין ואין מחשבין חשבונות שצריכין. כיצד אומר אדם לחבירו כך וכך פועלין כך וכך דינרין הוצאתי על שדה זו. אבל לא יאמר כך הוצאתי וכך אני עתיד להוציא. ואוקימנא אם נשאר עליו שכירות במה שעבר אסור לומר לו ואפילו כך הוצאתי שרצונו ליחשב ולידע סכום השכר הנשאר עליו והן חשבונות שצריכין ואסור. אמר רב יהודה אמר שמואל מותר לאדם לומר לחבירו לכרך פלוני אני הולך למחר שאם יש בורגנין הולך אפילו בשבת. תנן אין מחשיכין לשכור פועלין ולהביא פירות הרא משנה היא וקשיא אקשיא בהא. ומשנינן בשלמא לשכור פועלין היינו טעמא דאין מחשיכין על התחום ובשבת אסור לאגורי פועלין אלא פירות נימא שאם יש מחיצות מותר להביאו ומותר להחשיך ולהביאם. ומפרקינן הא דתני אין מחשיכין להביא פירות בפירות מחוברין שאסור להתחבן בשבת ועוד אקשינן מדתני ר' אושעיא ומפרקינן בתיבנא חדיא דלא חזי ותוב אמרינן ת"ש מחשיכין על התחום לפקח על עסקי כלה ועל עסקי המת כו' ומפרקינן לפקח על עסקי כלה למיגז לה אסא לבי גננא על עסקי המת נמי למיגז ליה גלימא לאתפור תכריכין והללו דמשום מצוה התירו רבנן. הא אחר כגון דברים הללו אסור. אבל מחשיך הוא לשמור ומביא פירות בידו ואקשינן ואע"ג דלא אבדיל כלומר עושה מלאכה קודם הבדלה והאמר ר' אלעזר וכו' אסור לעשות מלאכה קודם הבדלה. ואם יש לומר זה שמביא פירות התפלל הבדיל בתפלתו והאמר שמואל המבדיל בתפלה צריך שיבדיל על הכוס ואוקימנא מן הגיתות שנו. כלומר בשעת הגיתות מצוי בשדה בימי הבציר יין והבדיל על הכוס. וסלקא שמעתא שאסור לעשות מלאכה עד שהבדיל ואפילו לא אמר אלא המבדיל בין קודש לחול דיו. דהא רב אשי דהוא בתרא אמר כי הוינן בי רב כהנא הוה אמרינן המבדיל בין קודש לחול ואפכינן סלתי כלומר היינו מתעסקין במלאכה ולא [בא] רב אשי למעט אלא שאינו צריך לומר הבדלות. כאשר חלקו בפרק ערבי פסחים אבל צריך להזכיר ברכה בשם ומלכות דליח ורעה מברכת האירות וברכת המצות. וכן הלכה: כלל אמר אבא שאול. כל שאני זכאי באמירתו רשאי אני להחשיך עליו. והוצרכנו לדקדק לידע באיזה בבא דמתניתין אמר אבא שאול

עין משפט נר מצוה

[שייך לע"א משנה]

כט א טור ש"ע או"ח סימן שו סעיף ז:

ל ב ג מיי' פכ"ד מהלכות שבת הלכה ג סמג שם טוש"ע או"ח סימן שו סעיף ח ט:

לא ד מיי' שם הלכה ס סמג שם טור ש"ע או"ח סימן שו סעיף ג:

[בה"ס ליתא אבל בעין יעקב מצאתי ע"ש]

לב ה מיי' פכ"ט מהל' שבת הלכה ה סמג עשין כט טור ש"ע או"ח סימן רצט סעיף י:

לג ו מיי' שם הלכה ו ופ"ב מהלכות תפלה הלכה יב סמג שם טוש"ע או"ח סי' רצד סעיף א:

לד ז מיי' פכ"ט מהל' שבת הל"ג סמג שם טוש"ע או"ח סימן רצט סעיף י:

מסורת הש"ס

[עי' בע"ז סי' ש"ז ס"ק יד פירוש על זה]

ביצה ו.

[ערוך גרס למיגז להתור פי' לחתוך וי"ל לתפור]

[ברכות לג. ע"ש פסחים קה: ע"ש ודף קז.]

ועוד מדברי כצ"ל

הגהות הב"ח

(א) גמ' כך וכך פועלים הוצאתי על שדה: (ב) תוס' ד"ה ואין וכו' כדאמרינן פרק קמא דמגילה שלשת אלפים בני ביתו כו ולכל אחד ואחד ס' מאות תלוגות מעלות עשן: (ג) ד"ה אבל וכו' וכי תלי אבא שאול ההחשכה באמירה ס"ס:

accounts,[7] [but accounts] of unimportance [150*b*] or of past expenditure may be calculated. But the following contradicts it: One may reckon up accounts that are not required, but one may not reckon up on the Sabbath accounts that are necessary. E.g., a man may say to his neighbour, 'I hired so many labourers for this field,' 'I expended so many *denarii* for this residence.' But he must not say to him, 'I have expended so much and am [yet] to expend so much'!—Then according to your reasoning, that
a [Baraitha] itself presents a difficulty.[1] But in the one case he is [still] in possession of his employee's wages;[2] in the other he is not in possession of his employee's wages.

ONE MUST NOT GO TO THE TEḤUM TO AWAIT NIGHTFALL. Our Rabbis taught: It once happened that a breach was made in the field of a pious man and he decided to fence it about, when he recalled that it was the Sabbath, so he refrained and did not repair it; thereupon a miracle was performed for him, a caper bush grew up there, whence he and his household derived their livelihood.

Rab Judah said in Samuel's name: One may say to his neighbour [on the Sabbath], 'I am going to that town to-morrow,' for if there are stations [on the road] he may go [on the Sabbath itself].[3] We learnt: ONE MUST NOT GO TO THE TEḤUM TO AWAIT NIGHTFALL IN ORDER TO HIRE LABOURERS OR BRING IN PRODUCE. As for hiring labourers, it is well, since one may not hire them on the Sabbath; but to fetch produce, let us say [that it is permitted], for if there were walls [partitions] there he might bring [it even on the Sabbath]?[4]—This [ruling of our Mishnah] can refer to produce attached [to the soil].[5] But R. Oshaia taught: One must not go to the *teḥum* to await nightfall in order to bring straw or stubble. As for stubble, it is well: this can refer to attached; but to what can straw refer?[6]—Offensive smelling straw.[7]

Come and hear: One may go to the *teḥum* to await nightfall to
b attend to the affairs of a bride and the business of a corpse.[1] Thus, only for the affairs of a bride or a corpse, but not for the business of any other. As for another [with a purpose] analogous to [that of] a bride, it is well:[2] this is conceivable where one desires to cut a myrtle for him.[3] But what can the purpose in connection with a corpse be? [Presumably] in order to bring a coffin and shrouds; yet he [the Tanna] specifies a corpse, but not another;[4] yet why so: let us argue that [it is permissible for another too], for if there were walls there he might bring [articles even on the Sabbath]?—In the case of a corpse too, it is conceivable where the purpose is to cut out shrouds for him.[5]

BUT ONE MAY GO TO THE TEḤUM TO AWAIT NIGHTFALL, etc. Though he did not recite *habdalah*?[6] Surely R. Eleazar b. Antigonus said on R. Eliezer b. Jacob's authority: One is forbidden to attend to his affairs before reciting *habdalah*. And should you answer that he recites *habdalah* in the Prayer,[7] surely Rab Judah said in Samuel's name: He who recites *habdalah* in the Prayer must [also] recite it over a cup [of wine]?[8] And should you answer that he does recite *habdalah* over a cup,—[it may be asked] is a cup procurable in the fields?—R. Nathan b. Ammi explained this before Raba: They learnt this of the season of wine pressing.[9] R. Abba said to R. Ashi: In the West [Palestine] we say thus: 'He who makes a distinction between holy and profane', and then we attend to our affairs. R. Ashi related: When I was at R. Kahana's academy he used to recite, 'Who makest a distinction between holy and profane,' and then we chopped up logs.

ABBA SAUL STATED A GENERAL PRINCIPLE: WHATEVER I HAVE, etc. To what does Abba Saul refer? Shall we say that he refers to the first clause, [viz.,] ONE MUST NOT GO TO THE TEḤUM TO AWAIT NIGHTFALL IN ORDER TO HIRE LA-

(7) I.e., I have expended or will have to expend so much or so much.
a (1) The first Baraitha states in its first clause that one must not calculate past accounts, while the second clause states that past expenditure accounts are permitted. (2) Then it is forbidden, for though incurred in the past, it has still to be paid. (3) *Burgin*, pl. *burganim*, is an isolated residence on a road, often used as a station for travellers (Jast.). If the road to the town were dotted with these stations at intervals of less than seventy cubits the journey might be made even on the Sabbath. It is therefore permitted to mention it even in the absence of such stations. (4) I.e., if the road lay between walls it might technically be a private domain wherein carrying is permitted. (5) Which may not be detached under any circumstances. (6) Which straw can be meant which shall not be permitted by Rab Judah's logic? (7) Which may not be handled in any case, as it is *mukẓeh* on account of its repulsiveness (v. *supra* 46*a*).
b (1) E.g. to arrange for the funeral. (2) For the implication must be that for the same purpose where it is permitted in connection with a bride or a corpse it is forbidden in connection with another. (3) An overhead awning of myrtles was erected for a bride. Thus it is permitted for a bride, but not for another, since the myrtles are attached to the soil and may not be cut on the Sabbath. (4) Though bringing a coffin and shrouds is just the same as bringing any other article. (5) By analogy, another might desire to go to the *teḥum* in order to be ready to cut out a suit, and this is forbidden. (6) V. Glos. and *supra* 69*b*, n. b2. The difficulty is the last clause: surely he may not cut down produce before reciting *habdalah*? (7) The 'Prayer' always refers to the 'Eighteen Benedictions', in the fourth of which a *habdalah* passage is inserted; v. *P.B.* p. 94*d*; Elbogen, *Der Jüdische Gottesdienst*, pp. 46f; 120f. (8) *Habdalah* originally was not a statutory addition to the Sabbath evening Prayer; op. cit. (9) A cup of wine is then obtainable in the fields.

BOURERS OR BRING IN PRODUCE,—[151a] then instead of WHATEVER I HAVE A RIGHT TO INSTRUCT [THAT IT BE DONE], I AM PERMITTED TO GO TO AWAIT NIGHTFALL FOR IT, he should state, 'Whatever I have *no* right to instruct [that it be done], I am *not* permitted to await nightfall for it'.[1] Whereas if he bases himself on the second clause, BUT ONE MAY DO SO IN ORDER TO WATCH OVER HIS FIELDS, AND [THEN] HE CAN BRING [HOME] PRODUCE WITH HIM, then he should state, 'Whatever I have a right to await nightfall [at the *teḥum*], I am permitted to instruct [that it be done]'?—In truth he refers to the second clause, but Abba Saul bases himself on the following. For Rab Judah said in Samuel's name: One may say to his neighbour, 'Watch for me over the fruit in your *teḥum*, and I will watch for you over the fruit in my *teḥum*.' And thus Abba Saul argues with the first Tanna: Do you not admit that one may say to his neighbour, 'Watch for me over the fruit in your *teḥum* and I will watch for you over the fruit in my *teḥum?*' then say, WHATEVER I HAVE A RIGHT TO INSTRUCT [THAT IT BE DONE], I AM PERMITTED TO GO TO AWAIT NIGHTFALL FOR IT.[2]

What does the general principle add?[3]—It adds the following, which our Rabbis taught: One may not go to the *teḥum* to await nightfall in order to bring an animal. If it is standing without the *teḥum*, one may call it and it comes. Abba Saul stated a general principle: Whatever I have a right to say [that it shall be done],[1] I am permitted to await nightfall [at the *teḥum*] for it. And one may go to await nightfall in order to attend to the affairs of a bride or of a corpse, to bring a coffin and shrouds for him. And one may give instructions to another, 'Go to such and such a place, and if you cannot obtain them from there, bring them from elsewhere; if you cannot obtain them for a *maneh*, obtain them for two *manehs*.' R. Jose son of R. Judah said: Provided that he does not mention the exact price to him.[2]

MISHNAH. YOU MAY GO TO THE TEḤUM AGAINST NIGHTFALL IN ORDER TO ATTEND TO THE AFFAIRS OF A BRIDE OR OF A CORPSE, TO BRING A COFFIN AND SHROUDS FOR HIM. IF A GENTILE BRINGS REED-PIPES ON THE SABBATH,[3] ONE MUST NOT BEWAIL AN ISRAELITE ON THEM, UNLESS THEY CAME FROM A NEAR PLACE.[4] IF HE [A GENTILE] MADE A COFFIN FOR HIMSELF OR DUG A GRAVE FOR HIMSELF,[5] AN ISRAELITE MAY BE BURIED THEREIN. BUT IF [HE MADE IT] FOR THE SAKE OF AN ISRAELITE, HE MAY NEVER BE BURIED THEREIN.[6]

GEMARA. What does FROM A NEAR PLACE mean? Rab said: Literally from a near place.[7] While Samuel said: We conjecture that they [the reed-pipes] were [just] without the [city] wall during
c the night.[1] [Raba said,][2] The deduction of our Mishnah supports Samuel, for it is stated: IF HE [A GENTILE] MADE A COFFIN FOR HIMSELF OR DUG A GRAVE FOR HIMSELF, AN ISRAELITE MAY BE BURIED THEREIN. This proves that it is permitted on account of a doubt;[3] so here too, it is permitted on account of a doubt. And we learnt in accordance with Rab [too]: A city inhabited by Israelites and Gentiles which contains baths where there is bathing on the Sabbath, if the majority are Gentiles, one [an Israelite] may bathe therein immediately; if the majority are Israelites, one must wait until hot water could be heated;[4] if half and half, one must wait until hot water could be heated.[5] R. Judah said: In the case of a small bath, if there is there[6] [a man of authority],[7] he [an Israelite] may bathe therein immediately. What is '[a man of] authority?' Said Rab Judah in the name of R. Isaac son of Rab Judah: If there is there an important personage who possesses ten slaves who heat ten kettles [of water] for him simultaneously, then if it is a small bath he [the Israelite] may bathe therein immediately.[8]

IF HE [A GENTILE] MADE A COFFIN FOR HIMSELF OR DUG A GRAVE FOR HIMSELF, etc. Yet why so? here too, let him wait until it could be made?[9]—Said 'Ulla: It refers to one [a grave] that stands in an [army] camp.[10] That is well of a grave; [but] what can be said of a coffin? Said R. Abbahu: It refers to [a coffin] that is lying on his grave.[11]

MISHNAH. ALL THE REQUIREMENTS OF THE DEAD MAY BE DONE; HE MAY BE ANOINTED WITH OIL AND WASHED, PROVIDED THAT NO LIMB OF HIS IS MOVED. THE PILLOW MAY BE REMOVED FROM UNDER HIM, AND HE MAY BE PLACED

(1) So that the principle is parallel to the clause upon which it is based. (2) It is assumed that both accept Samuel's ruling. Hence the permission given by the first Tanna to go to the end of the *teḥum* to watch over produce would be included in Abba Saul's principle, and all other permitted cases likewise, and there is no need for the first Tanna to give a specific instance. (3) It is axiomatic that when a general principle is stated it is to add a case that is not explicitly taught.

(1) Which includes calling an animal from beyond the *teḥum*. (2) He may authorize him to pay a high price if he cannot buy them cheaply, but must not state the exact figures. (3) For playing at a Jew's funeral, which formed part of the obsequies, cf. B.M. 75*b*, n. c3. (4) I.e., within the *teḥum*. (5) Either for his own use or in order to sell.—The reference is to the Sabbath. (6) [According to Maim. the reference is to the Israelite for whom the grave was dug. He may not, that is to say, be buried even בכדי שיעשו i.e., after sufficient time has elapsed after the termination of the Sabbath for the grave to be dug.] (7) We must know this for certain, having seen that he had them in his house within the city.

c (1) Even if they were not in his house we may assume that they were only just without the city wall, yet within the *teḥum*, unless we know to the contrary. Lit., 'we apprehend lest'. The phrase is also used with lenient implications, v. Ḥag. 15*a* (Rashi). Normally the more stringent possibility is acted upon, but here it is the reverse, for the sake of the dead. (2) So text as emended by BaḤ. (3) For he might actually have made it for a Jew. [Tosaf. a.l. deletes this passage as in this Mishnah the question of doubt does not arise as explained in the Gemara *infra*.] (4) V. *supra* 122*a*, for notes. (5) Which shows that in a case of doubt we are stringent, and this agrees with Rab. (6) In the city. (7) Jast.: a Roman official. (8) As the water may have been thus prepared after the Sabbath. (9) For the Gentile may have had a Jew in mind. (10) *Aliter:* in the broad open street. It is unusual for Jews to be buried there. (11) *Sc.* the Gentile's grave dug in the camp.

האי כל שאני זכאי באמירתו רשאי אני בחשיכתו כל שאיני זכאי באמירתו איני רשאי בחשיכתו מיבעי ליה אלא אסיפא קאי אבל מחשיך הוא לשמור ומביא פירות בידו האי כל שאני זכאי בחשיכתו רשאי אני באמירתו מיבעי ליה לעולם אסיפא קאי ואבא שאול אהא קאי דאמר רב יהודה אמר שמואל *מותר לאדם לומר לחבירו שמור לי פירות שבתחומך ואני אשמור לך פירות שבתחומי וקאמר אבא שאול לת"ק מי לא מודית דמותר אדם לומר לחבירו שמור לי פירות שבתחומך ואני אשמור לך פירות שבתחומי ואימא כל שאני זכאי באמירתו רשאי אני להחשיך עליו כלל לאתויי מאי לאתויי הא דת"ר *אין מחשיכין על התחום להביא בהמה *היתה עומדת חוץ לתחום קורא לה והיא באה כלל אמר אבא שאול כל שאני זכאי באמירתו רשאי אני להחשיך עליו ומחשיכין לפקח על עסקי כלה ועל עסקי המת להביא לו ארון ותכריכין ואומרים לו לך למקום פלוני ואם לא מצאת במקום פלוני הבא ממקום פלוני לא מצאת במנה הבא במאתים ר' יוסי ברבי יהודה אומר ובלבד שלא יזכיר לו סכום מקח:

מתני' *מחשיכין על התחום לפקח על עסקי כלה ועל עסקי המת להביא לו ארון ותכריכים נכרי שהביא חלילין בשבת לא יספוד בהן ישראל אא"כ באו ממקום קרוב עשו לו ארון וחפרו לו קבר יקבר בו ישראל ואם בשביל ישראל לא יקבר בו עולמית:

גמ' מאי ממקום קרוב רב אמר ממקום קרוב ממש ושמואל אמר חיישינן שמא (א)חוץ לחומה לנו [א] דיקא מתניתין כוותיה דשמואל דקתני עשה לו ארון וחפר לו קבר יקבר בו ישראל אלמא מספיקא שרי הכא נמי מספיקא שרי *ותניא כוותיה [ב] דרב (ב) *עיר שישראל ונכרים דרים בה והיתה בה מרחץ המרחצת בשבת אם רוב נכרים לערב רוחץ בה מיד אם רוב ישראל ימתין עד כדי שיחמו חמין מחצה על מחצה *(אסור וימתין) עד כדי שיחמו חמין ר' יהודה אומר באמבטי קטנה אם יש בה רשות רוחץ בה מיד מאי רשות אמר רב יהודה אמר רב יצחק בריה דרב יהודה אם יש בה אדם חשוב שיש לו עשרה עבדים שמחממין לו י' קומקומין בבת אחת באמבטי קטנה מותר לרחוץ בה מיד: עשו לו ארון והפרו לו קבר וכו': אמאי הכא נמי ימתין בכדי שיעשו אמר עולא בעומד באסרטיא תינח קבר ארון מאי איכא למימר א"ר אבהו במוטל על קברו:

מתני' עושין כל צרכי המת סכין ומדיחין אותו ובלבד שלא יזיז בו אבר שומטין את הכר מתחתיו ומטילין אותו על החול בשביל שימתין

[תוספתא פי"ז] [לעיל קנ.] לעיל קנ: לעיל קכב. ע"ש מכשירין פ"ב מ"ה ע"ש · צ"ל ימתין [וכ"א במשנה]

רש"י

אלא אסיפא קאי · דקאמר ת"ק להיתרא אבל מחשיך הוא לשמור ולהא איהו ושוייה ביה כללא להביא כל כיוצא בהן: האי כל שאני זכאי להחשיך עליו זכאי אני באמירתו מיבעי ליה · (ג) דהיתר דחשיכה תנן היתר דאמירה לא תנן והיכי תלי תניא בדלא תניא: לעולם אסיפא קאי · כדקאמרת ודקשיא לך אמירה מהיכא קאמר ליה להיתירא דתלי בה החשכה אהא קאי דאמר רב יהודה כו' אלמא זכאי אני באמירתו ואבא שאול ות"ק כולהו פשיטא להו הא דשמואל וקאמר ליה אבא שאול לת"ק מי לא מודית בהא שאתה מתיר להחשיך דמותר הוא לומר כדשמואל אלמא הואיל ומותר לומר מותר להחשיך הלכך אמאי נקטת החשכה לשמור לחודא שוי כללא למילתא ואימא כל שאני זכאי באמירתו רשאי אני להחשיך עליו דש"מ הך וש"מ מת וכלה דהא נמי זכאי באמירתו הוא כדמפרש לקמן והלכך מחשיכין עליו וסיפא דמתני' דקתני מחשיכין על התחום לפקח על עסקי כלה אבא שאול היא: כלל אמר אבא שאול כו' · והאי נמי זכאי באמירתו כדקתני סיפא ואומר לו לך למקום פלוני: סכום מקח · מנה ומאתים: מתני' נכרי שהביא חלילין בשבת · בשביל ישראל: לא יספוד בהן ישראל · לעולם וקנסא הוא משום דמוכחא מילתא דבשבילו הובאו דאין דרך להביא חלילין אלא בשביל מת: ממקום קרוב · בתוך התחום: עשו לו ארון · בשביל נכרי או למכור: גמ' רב אמר ממקום קרוב ממש · כלומר שידוע לנו בירור הדבר דממקום קרוב באו שראינום שהיו בביתו: ושמואל אמר חיישינן שמא חוץ לחומה לנו · אפילו הביא מחוץ לעיר אנו תולין להתיר ואומרים שמא בתוך התחום לנו ערב שבת וסופדין בהן במוצ"ש מיד וחיישינן נמי אמרינן לקולא כדאמרי' במס' חגיגה (דף טו·) גבי בתולה שעיברה חיישינן שמא באמבטי עיברה ומותרת לכהונה ולשמואל הכי קאמר מתני' לא יספוד בהן ישראל אא"כ יש לתלות שבאו ממקום קרוב ולאפוקי בידוע דמחוץ לתחום באו: ה"ג דיקא מתני' כוותיה דשמואל ותניא כוותיה דרב: יקבר בו ישראל · דתלינן מספיקא שמא לצורך נכרי נעשה: תניא כוותיה דרב · דספיקא אסור דקתני מחצה על מחצה ימתין בכדי שיחמו חמין וא"ת בכדי שיחמו חמין מיהא שרי והכא תני לא יספוד בהן משמע לעולם הכא מוכחא מילתא אבל במרחץ לא מוכחא מילתא כולי האי הואיל ואיכא נכרים: באמבטי קטנה · שיש לתלות ולומר משחשיכה הוחמה על ידי עבדים וקומקמין הרבה: אם יש בה רשות · אדם חשוב שליט: רוחץ בה · ישראל מיד דיש לומר משחשיכה הוחמו חמין לאותו נכרי ליגלא אחריתא גרסינן תניא כוותיה דשמואל ולא גרסי' דייקא מתני' כו' עד מספיקא שרי ומייתי סייעתא לשמואל מדרבי יהודה דתלינן לקולא וריש לא קשיא ליה כיון דמחצה על מחצה ודאי בשביל ישראל ונכרים הוחמו שהרי לא לאדם אחד לבדו הוחמו דנימא ספיקא לנכרי ספק לישראל ולשון זה נראה לי עיקר ורבותי נמי לא גרסי לעיל להא דקתני עשה נכרי את הארון עד מספיקא שרי ומיהו לא מפרשי לה כדפרישית: ימתין בכדי שיעשו · נכי דלא מוכחא מילתא מיהו י"ל שמא בשביל ישראל נעשה: בעומד · הקבר באיסרטיא שאין דרך ישראל ליקבר שם דודאי לא נעשה בשביל ישראל: ארון מאי איכא למימר · להוכיח דלא בשביל ישראל נעשה: במוטל · הארון: על קברו · של נכרי באיסרטיא דמוכח דלשם אותו קבר נעשה הארון: מתני' ומדיחין · במים: שלא יזיז בו אבר · לא יגביה לו ידו או רגלו או ריסי עיניו:

שימתין

תוספות

האי כל שאני רשאי בחשיכתו רשאי אני באמירתו מיבעי ליה · תימה הא דכי פריך לעיל האי כל שאני רשאי באמירתו אני רשאי בחשיכתו מיבעי ליה מכלל דאי הוה תנן הכי הוה אתי שפיר אע"ג דתלי חשיכה באמירה וי"ל התם שאני דלא הוה תלי תניא בדלא תניא דאמירה נמי תניא לעיל לא יאמר אדם לחבירו שכור לי פועלים אבל החשכה תלי תניא בדלא תניא דהיתר אמירה לא תניא אבל היתר החשכה תניא: לעולם אסיפא קאי · (ד) דאמר רב יהודה אמר שמואל מותר אדם לומר לחבירו שמור לי פירות שבתחומך · אע"פ שהוא אינו יכול לילך לשומרן יכול לומר לחבירו לשמרן ומתניתין הכי קאמר כל שאני זכאי באמירתו כגון לפקח על עסקי כלה ועל עסקי מת ויכול לומר לחבירו לעשות למחר רשאי אני להחשיך עליו וכ"ש מה שאני זכאי לומר לעשות היום כמו שמור לי פירות שבתחומך אע"פ שאיני רשאי לילך שם היום דמותר להחשיך עליו:

אין מחשיכין על התחום להביא בהמה · יש ספרים דגרסי מחשיכים לפי שאם יש שם בורגנים הולך ומביאה ובתוספתא גרס אין מחשיכין וי"ל דאיירי בבהמה שאינה יכולה לבא ברגליה כגון טלה קטן אא"כ ישאהו בכתף שאפילו יש מחיצות אינו רשאי להביא דאסור לטלטל בעלי חיים שהם מוקצים:

נכרי שהביא חלילים בשבת לא יספוד בהן ישראל · לא כפי' הקונטרס שפירש עולמית מדפריך בגמרא גבי עשה נכרי ארון וחפר לו קבר יקבר בו ישראל אלמאי הכא נמי כימא ימתין בכדי שיעשו ואמאי קאמר נמי אי לאו דקאי אחלילים על כן נראה דלא יספוד בהן ישראל היינו עד כדי שיבואו דסתם חלילים אין מביאין אותן לשם אדם אחד אלא לשם כמה בני אדם:

אא"כ באו ממקום קרוב · תימה לרבי מה מהני שבאו ממקום קרוב הלא הביאם דרך רה"ר ומה לי ארון וקבר שנעשו בשבת ומה לי חלילים שהובאו דרך רה"ר וי"ל דהביא ממקום קרוב לא מהני כל כך הבאתו: דיקא מתניתין כוותיה דשמואל כו' יקבר בו ישראל אלמא מספיקא שרי · תימה היכי (ה) מוכיחנא מינה דמספיקא שרי והא מוקמי' לה בעומד באיסרטיא דודאי לצורך נכרי נעשה מיהו אומר רבי דל"ג ליה להא דקתני עשו לו ארון כו' ול"ג נמי בסמוך (ו) ת"כ גם כפי' הקונט' ל"ג אלא ה"ג דיקא נמי ממתני' עיר שישראל ונכרים דרים בה כו' ומשנה היא במסכת מכשירין (פ"ב משנה ה) ר' יהודה אומר אם יש בה רשות רוחץ בה מיד אלמא תלינן להתיר כמו כן גבי חלילין יש לתלות בהיתר ולומר חוץ לחומה לנו · מ"ר:

עד

עין משפט נר מצוה

לה א (מיי' פכ"ד מהל' שבת) סמג לאוין סה טוש"ע או"ח סימן שו סעיף י:

לו ב מיי' שם הלכה ג סמג שם טוש"ע או"ח סימן שו סעיף א:

לז ג מיי' שם טור ש"ע שם סעיף ג:

לח ד ה מיי' שם הל"ה טוש"ע שם סעיף ג וסימן שז סעיף ח:

לט ו ז מיי' פ"ו מהל' שבת הל"ו סמג שם טוש"ע או"ח סימן שכה סעיף טו:

מ ח מיי' שם הלכה ז טוש"ע שם סעיף טז:

מא ט י כ מיי' שם הל' ה טור ש"ע שם סעיף יד:

מב ל מיי' פכ"ו מהל' שבת הלכה כ סמג שם טוש"ע. או"ח סימן שיא סעיף ז:

רבינו חננאל

כלל זה. ואמרינן אם על רישא דקתני אין מחשיכין על התחום לשכור פועלין וכו'. כל (שאני) [שאיני] זכאי בחשיכתו (אני) [איני] זכאי באמירתו היה לו לומר כי אין מחשיכין אמרה משנתנו בפירוש ומכללו נלמד האמירה כלומר מאחר שאין לי להחשיך בתחום לשכור פועלין כן אין לי לומר לחבירו השכר לי פועלין עם חשכה. אלא אסיפא. אבל מחשיך הוא לשמור וכו' כלומר כשם שמותר לו להחשיך כך מותר לו לומר לחבירו החשיך והביא לי פירות האי כל שאיני זכאי בחשיכתו זכאי אני באמירתו היה לו לומר ואוקימנא כדרב פפא דאמר מותר לאדם לומר לחבירו שמור לי פירות שבתחומך וכו' כלומר כשם שאני זכאי לומר לחברו שמור לי פירות שבתחומך כך מותר לי לשמר פירות שבתחומי. ולהחשיך עליו ואמרינן עוד ולמה ליה כלל לתנייה בהדיא ופרקינן כלל להביא הא דת"ר מחשיכין על התחום להביא בהמה היתה עומדת חוץ לתחום קורא לה והיא באה. ולפקח על עסקי כלה ועל עסקי המת להביא לו ארון ותכריכין אומרים לו לך למקום פלוני לא מצאת במקום פלוני הבא ממקום פלוני לא מצאת במאה הבא במאתים ובלבד שלא יזכור את הדמים. ר' יוסי ב"ר יהודה [אומר] ובלבד שלא יזכור לי סכום המקח: מתני' מחשיכין על התחום. עד אא"כ באו ממקום קרוב מאי ממקום קרוב רב אמר קרוב ממש. ושמואל אמר חיישינן שמא חוץ לחומה לנו. *) ופירוש לן מרן דברי שמואל הללו והיאך מתני' דייקא כוותיה ומה טעם חלילים שהביאם גוי בשבת שלא יספוד בהם ישראל ולמה לא ימתין בכדי שיביאו או דלמא משום דלא ידעינן מהיכן באו ועוד המותר לספור בהן ביום ראשון ובשאר ימי החול או לאו מה פירק לו הלא אפילו אם המת מונח בדרך צריך להמתין בכדי שיחפור בקבר והדר קושיין לדוכתיה וכן בארון ליסברה לן מרן. ועוד אם הדברים הללו על עיר שרובן ישראל הם או לא. כי אם רובן גוים למה צריך להמתין והלא לענין מרחץ אמרו מותר לרחוץ בה מיד ושמואל אמר חיישינן שמא חוץ

*) נראה דזה הוא שאלה לרבינו וצ"ל יפרש לן מרן (ואולי שאל מאת רב האי גאון) והתשובה חסרה בה ובאמת שאלת התלמוד היא חצי תשובה

הגהות הב"ח

(א) גמ' חוץ לחומה לנו אמר רבא דיקא מתני': (ב) שם ותניא כותיה דרב דת"ר עיר: (ג) רש"י ד"ה האי כל וכו' דהיתרא דהחשכה תנן: (ד) תוס' ד"ה לעולם אסיפא קאי ואבא שאול אהא קאי דאמר רב יהודה: (ה) ד"ה דיקא וכו' היכי מוכח מינה: (ו) בא"ד ול"ג נמי בסמוך דתנו רבנן גם כפ"ה ל"ג ליה אלא ה"ג:

הגהות הגר"א

[א] גמ' (דיקא מתני' כו' עד ה"ג מספיקא שרי) תא"מ: [ב] שם כוותיה דרב צ"ל דשמואל:

עין משפט
נר מצוה

מג א מיי' פכ"ו מהל' שבת הלכה כ סמג שם טוש"ע או"ח סימן שיא סעיף ז:

מד ב מיי' פ"ד מהלכות אבל הלכה ה סמג עשין ב טוש"ע יו"ד סי' שלט סעיף א:

מה ג סמג עשין עט:

מו ד מיי' פ"י מהלכות תשובה הלכה א:

כז ה מיי' פ"י מהלכות מתנות עניים הל"ב [וכה' עבדים פ"ט הל"ח] טוש"ע יו"ד סימן רמז סעיף ג:

שימתין *קושרין את הלחי לא שיעלה אלא שלא יוסיף *וכן קורה שנשברה סומכין אותה בספסל או בארוכות המטה לא שתעלה אלא שלא תוסיף: גמ' *והאמר רב יהודה אמר שמואל מעשה בתלמידו של רבי מאיר שנכנס אחריו לבית המרחץ ביקש להדיח קרקע אמר לו אין מדיחין לסוך קרקע אמר לו אין סכין °קרקע בקרקע מחלפא מת בקרקע לא מיחלף כל לאתויי מאי לאתויי הא דת"ר מביאין כלי מיקר וכלי מתכות ומניחין על כריסו כדי שלא (א) תפוח ופוקקין את נקביו כדי שלא תיכנס בהן הרוח ואף שלמה אמר בחכמתו °עד *שלא ירתק חבל הכסף זה חוט השדרה ותרוץ גולת הזהב זה אמה ותשבר כד על המבוע זה הכרס ונרוץ הגלגל אל הבור זה פרש וכן הוא אומר °וזריתי פרש על פניכם פרש חגיכם אמר רב הונא ואמרי לה אמר רב חגא אלו בני אדם שמניחין דברי תורה ועושין כל ימיהם כחגים אמר רבי לוי אמר רב פפי א"ר יהושע לאחר שלשה ימים כריסו נבקעת ונופלת לו על פניו ואומרת לו טול מה שנתת בי: מתני' אין (א) מעצמין את המת בשבת ולא בחול עם יציאת נפש והמעצים עם יציאת הנפש הרי זה שופך דמים: גמ' תנו רבנן המעצמו עם יציאת הנפש הרי זה שופך דמים משל לנר שכבה והולכת אדם מניח אצבעו עליה מיד כבתה תניא *רשב"ג אומר הרוצה שיתעצמו עיניו של מת נופח לו יין בחוטמו ונותן שמן בין ריסי עיניו ואוחז בשני גודלי רגליו והן מתעצמין מאליהן תניא רשב"ג אומר תינוק בן יומו חי מחללין עליו את השבת דוד מלך ישראל מת אין מחללין עליו את השבת תינוק בן יומו חי מחללין עליו את השבת *אמרה תורה חלל עליו שבת אחד כדי שישמור שבתות הרבה דוד מלך ישראל מת אין מחללין עליו כיון שמת אדם בטל מן המצות והיינו *דא"ר יוחנן °במתים חפשי כיון שמת אדם נעשה חפשי מן המצות ותניא ר' שמעון בן אלעזר אומר תינוק בן יומו חי אין צריך לשומרו מן החולדה ומן העכברים אבל עוג מלך הבשן מת צריך לשומרו מן החולדה ומן העכברים שנאמר °ומוראכם וחתכם יהיה כל זמן שאדם חי אימתו מוטלת על הבריות כיון שמת בטלה אימתו אמר רב פפא *נקיטינן אריה אבי תרי לא נפיל הא קא חזינן דנפיל ההוא כדרמי בר אבא דאמר רמי בר אבא *אין חיה שולטת באדם עד שנדמה לו כבהמה שנאמר °אדם ביקר בל ילין נמשל כבהמות נדמו אמר רבי חנינא אסור לישן בבית יחידי וכל הישן בבית יחידי אחזתו לילית ותניא רשב"א אומר עשה עד שאתה מוצא ומצוי לך ועודך בידך ואף שלמה אמר בחכמתו °וזכור את בוראיך בימי בחורותיך עד [אשר] (ש) לא יבואו ימי הרעה אלו ימי הזקנה והגיעו שנים אשר תאמר אין לי בהם חפץ אלו ימי המשיח שאין בהם לא זכות ולא חובה ופליגא דשמואל *דאמר שמואל אין בין העולם הזה לימות המשיח אלא שיעבוד מלכיות בלבד שנא' °כי לא יחדל אביון מקרב הארץ תניא ר' אלעזר הקפר אומר לעולם יבקש אדם רחמים על מדה זו שאם הוא לא בא בא בנו ואם בנו לא בא בן בנו בא שנאמר °כי בגלל הדבר הזה תנא דבי ר' ישמעאל גלגל הוא שחוזר בעולם א"ר יוסף נקיטינן האי צורבא מרבנן לא מיעני והא קא חזינן דמיעני אם איתא דמיעני אהדורי אפתחא לא מיהדר אמר לה רבי חייא לדביתהו כי אתי עניא אקדימי ליה ריפתא כי היכי דלקדמו לבנין אמרה ליה מילט קא לייטת להו אמר לה קרא קא כתיב כי בגלל הדבר הזה ותנא דבי ר' ישמעאל גלגל הוא שחוזר בעולם תניא *ר' גמליאל ברבי אומר °ונתן לך רחמים ורחמך והרבך *כל המרחם על הבריות מרחמין עליו מן השמים וכל שאינו מרחם על הבריות אין מרחמין עליו מן השמים °עד אשר לא תחשך השמש והאור זו פדחת והחוטם והירח זו נשמה והכוכבים אלו הלסתות ושבו העבים אחר הגשם זו מאור עיניו של אדם שהולך אחר הבכי אמר שמואל האי דמעתא עד ארבעין שנין הדרא מכאן ואילך לא הדרא ואמר רב נחמן האי כוחלא עד ארבעין שנין מרווח מכאן ואילך אפילו מליא *כאביסנא דגירדאי אוקומי מוקים ארווחי לא מרווח מאי קא משמע לן דכמה דאלים מכוחלא טפי מעלי ר' חנינא שכיבא ליה ברתיה לא הוה קא בכי עלה אמרה ליה דביתהו תרנגולתא אפיקת מביתך אמר לה תרתי תכלא ועיורא סבר לה כי הא דאמר רבי יוחנן משום רבי יוסי בן קצרתה *שש דמעות הן שלש יפות ושלש רעות של עשן ושל בכי ושל

רש"י

שימתין · שלא יסריח מחמת חום הסדין והכרים: קושרין את הלחי · של מת שהיה פיו הולך ונפתח קושרין את לחייו כדי שלא יפתח פיו יותר: ולא שיעלה · להסגר ממה שנפתח דהייט מזיז אבר אלא שלא יוסיף ליפתח: סומכין אותה בספסל · שהרי תורת כלי עליו: לא שתעלה· דהוה ליה בונה: גמ' ואמר לו אין סכין · אלמא דבר האסור לטלטל אסור לסוך: קרקע בקרקע מיחלף · כלומר ההוא לאו משום טלטול הוא אלא משום אשויי גומות ואע"ג דמרחץ רצפת אבנים הוא וליכא למיחש לאשויי גומות מיחלף מיהא בקרקע אחר: כל לרכי המת לאתויי מאי · דלא תנן: כלי מיקר · שמביאים קרירות כגון זכוכית: ואף שלמה אמר בחכמתו · שכריסו של מת טופחת ונבקעת: זה חוט השדרה · שהוא כמין חבל ולבן ככסף: זו אמה · שהוא מעין של תולדה כמו גולות מים (יהושע טו): זה פרש · וגלגל לשון גלל (יחזקאל ד): אל הבור · שטפל לתוך פיו: כחגים. בתענוגים: מתני' אין מעצמין · את עיניו בשבת אפילו אחר יציאת הנפש דמזיז בו אבר: שופך דמים · כדמפרש בברייתא בגמ' שבטורח מועט מקרב מיתתו: גמ' ואוחז בשני גודלי רגליו· עולרן באלבעותיו: וחתכם· לשון חיותכם: אריה אבי תרי לא נפיל· להורגן כדכתי' ומוראכם תרי וכתיב על כל חית הארץ ואפי' ארי: כדרמי בר אבא · דנכנסה עליו מיתה ונדמה לארי כבהמה: נמשל · מי שחיה מושלת בו בידוע שכבהמה נדמה: עשה · לדקה: עד שאתה מולא · למי לעשות: ומלוי לך · ממון: ועודך בידך · עודך ברשותך קודם שתמות: תורה אור לא זכות · לא דבר לזכות בו שכולם עשירים: ולא חובה · לאמץ לב ולקפוץ יד: על מדה זו · שלא יבא לידי עניות דדבר המזומן הוא לבא או עליו או על בנו או על בן בנו: ונתן לך רחמים · שתרחם על הבריות: זו פדחת · המלח שהוא חלק ומאהיר יותר מכל הפרצוף: זה חוטם · שהוא תואר פני אדם: זו נשמה · כדכתיב נר אלהים נשמת אדם (משלי כ): הלסתות · לחיים: ושבו העבים · תשכת עינים יבא ויכסה המאור אחר שירבה בבכיה בזקנותו מהמת תשות כח וצרות רבות עליו: מרווח · מאור עינים: אפילו מליא · כחלא בעיניו כמכחול גדול: כאביסנא של גרדאי · כובד של גרדיים אינשובל"ש בלע"ז: אוקומי·(ב) המאור מוקים שלא יחשיך יותר ממה שהוא: מאי קמ"ל · בהא דאמר אפי' כאביסנא דגרדאי: אליס · עב: מכוחלא · עץ שהוא מכנים בשפופרת ונותן בעיניו וקורין לו מכחול: תיכלא ועיורא · שיכול בנים ועיורון הדמעה: של בכי · מתוך אבל וצרה: של

מסורת הש"ס: לעיל מג. · לעיל מג: · [יומא פה:] · תהלים פח · ברכות ט · תהלים מט · קהלת יב · דברים טו · שם · [ב"ב ט: ע"ש] · קהלת יב · [גי' הערוך כאבסנא] · [אדר"נ פמ"ח] · קהלת יב · מלאכי ב · בס"י איתא ר"ש בן אלעזר · לעיל ל. [נדה סא: ע"ש] · [עי' פרש"י בעירובין ס. ד"ה והאמר פירוש ע"ז] [סנהדרין לח: ע"ש] · ברכות לד: לעיל סג. פסחים סח. סנהדרין צא: צט. · [תוספתא דב"ק פ"ט]

הגהות הב"ח
(א) גמ' שלא יבא תפוח: (ב) רש"י ד"ה אוקומי. מוקים המאור שלא:

גליון הש"ס
גמ' קרקע בקרקע מיחלפא. כה"ג לעיל דף כט ע"ב ועי' בתוספות שם ד"ה גזירה:

א) [גי' הערוך אין מאמצין כו' וכל המאמץ כו' פירוש סותמין עיני המת לאחר המיתה כדי שלא יהיו עיניו פתוחות כענין שנאמר ויוסף ישית ידו על עיניך ע"כ ועי' לעיל דף עז: איבעיא להו מאמצין תנן או מעמצין וכו' ואשר ע"כ כתב דטעות הוא שהקדימו בדפוס ג' קודם למ' במשנה ובברייתא דהכא וגם בפרש"י דהכא אמנם בר"ף והרא"ש הגירסא במשנה ובברייתא על נכון המ' קודם לג' וכ"א במשנה שבמשניות ובפי' הרב וכתב התוי"ט אין מאמצין כמו עוצם עיניו כו']

רבינו חננאל
הרץ לחומה לנו ואע"ג דאיסורא הוא וקיי"ל הלכתא כרב באיסורי הכא הלכתא כשמואל דדיקא מתניתין כותיה דתנן במס' מכשירין עיר של ישראל ונכרים דרין בתוכה והיתה בה מרחץ המרחצת בשבת אם רוב נכרים מותר לרחוץ בה מיד אם רוב ישראל ימתין עד בכדי שיחמו חמין. מחצה על מחצה ימתין בכדי שיחמו חמין. ר' יהודה אומר באמבטי קטנה ואם יש רשות רוחץ בה מיד. ומפרש רב יצחק בריה דרב יהודה מאי רשות כגון אדם חשוב שיש לו עשרה עבדים שמחממין לו עשרה קומקמין בבת אחת מותר לרחוץ מיד: עשו לו ארון וחפרו לו קבר יקבר בהן ישראל ומקשינן אמאי והא ישראל ונכרי כמחצה על מחצה דמי ימתין בכדי שיעשו ומפרק עולא כגון בנכרי מת המוטל באיסטרטא דמוכחא מלתא שזה הקבר לזה הנכרי נחפר שדומה לרוב נכרים שאין צריך להמתין בכדי שיעשו תוב אקשינן תינח קבר ארון מאי ופריק ר' אבהו בארון המוטל על הקבר שנמצא הארון בקבר*)דאילו דברי ר"מ נסבייה בדרך גררה. בפרק כירה בענין דברים של (חול) [קדש] אסור לאומרם (בלשה"ק) [בלשון חול] אלא אם הוא לאפרושי מאיסורא כגון זה שא"ר מאיר לתלמידיו אין מדיחין ואין סכין בלשה"ק אבל הרואה שסכין ומדיחין המת לא יתיר הדחה וסיכה בקרקע ולפיכך התיר ר"מ הדחת המת וסיכתו ולא גזר סיכת המת והדחתו מפני סיכת מרחץ והדחתו. כל צרכי המת כלל זה להביא הא דת"ר מביאין כלי מיקר וכלי מתכות ומניחין לו על כרסו בשבת שלא תפוח ופוקקין נקביו בשביל שלא תכנס בהן הרוח ואף שלמה אמר בחכמתו עד אשר לא ירתק חבל הכסף ונו' ופשוטה היא: אין מאמצין את המת בשבת וכו'. פי' מאמצין סותמין את עיני המת. ת"ר המאמץ עם יציאת נפש אפילו בחול הרי זה שופך דמים משל לנר שכבה כו'. הניא ר"ש בן אלעזר אומר תינוק בן יומו חי מחללין עליו את השבת שעומד ומשמר שבתות הרבה. דוד מלך ישראל מת אין מחללין עליו את השבת

*) נראה דחסר כאן איזה תיבות ושייך להא דמקשינן כאן בגמ' והאמר ריא"ש מעשה בתלמידו של ר"מ

a ON SAND, IN ORDER THAT [151b] HE MAY BE ABLE TO KEEP.[1] THE JAW MAY BE TIED UP, NOT IN ORDER THAT IT SHOULD CLOSE[2] BUT THAT IT SHOULD NOT GO FURTHER [OPEN]. AND LIKEWISE, IF A BEAM IS BROKEN, IT MAY BE SUPPORTED BY A BENCH OR BED STAVES, NOT IN ORDER THAT IT [THE BREAK] SHOULD CLOSE UP, BUT THAT IT SHOULD GO NO FURTHER.

GEMARA. But surely Rab Judah related in Samuel's name: It once happened that a disciple of R. Meir followed him into the baths and wished to swill the ground for him, [but] he said to him, One may not swill; then he wished to oil the ground for him, but he said to him, One may not oil?[3]—Ground may be confused with ground, but a corpse cannot be confused with ground.[4]

What does ALL add? It adds the following, which our Rabbis taught: Cooling vessels and metal vessels may be brought and placed on his [the corpse's] stomach, in order that he should not swell, and his apertures may be stopped up, in order that the air should not enter. And [thus] said Solomon too in his wisdom: *'Or ever the silver cord be snapped asunder'*—this refers to the spinal cord; *'and the golden bowl be broken'*—this alludes to the membrum; *'and the pitcher be broken at the fountain'*—that means the stomach; *'and the wheel broken at the cistern'*—this refers to the excrements.[5] And thus it is said, *and I will spread dung on your faces,*
b *even the dung of your feasts.*[1] R. Huna—others state, R. Ḥaga—said: This refers to people who abandon study[2] and spend all their days at feasts. R. Levi said in R. Pappi's name in R. Joshua's name: After three days [from death] the stomach bursts and it [its contents] lies cast out before his face and exclaims, 'Take what you have put in me.'

MISHNAH. ONE MAY NOT CLOSE [THE EYES OF] A CORPSE ON THE SABBATH, NOR ON WEEKDAYS WHEN HE IS ABOUT TO DIE, AND HE WHO CLOSES THE EYES [OF A DYING PERSON] AT THE POINT OF DEATH[3] IS A MURDERER.[4]

GEMARA. Our Rabbis taught: He who closes [the eyes of a dying man] at the point of death is a murderer. This may be compared to a lamp that is going out: If a man places his finger upon it, it is immediately extinguished. It was taught, R. Simeon b. Gamaliel said: If one desires that a dead man's eyes should close, let him blow wine into his nostrils and apply oil between his two eyelids and hold his two big toes; then they close of their own accord.

It was taught, R. Simeon b. Gamaliel said: For a day-old infant the Sabbath is desecrated; for David, King of Israel, dead, the Sabbath must not be desecrated. 'For a day-old infant the Sabbath is desecrated': the Torah ordered, Desecrate one Sabbath on his account so that he may keep many Sabbaths. 'For David, King of Israel, dead, the Sabbath must not be desecrated': Once man dies he is free from [all] obligations, and thus R. Joḥanan interpreted: *Among the dead I am free:*[5] once a man is dead he is free from religious duties. It was further taught, R. Simeon b. Eleazar said: A day-old infant, alive, need not be guarded from weasels or mice, but Og, king of Bashan,[6] dead, needs guarding from weasels and mice, as it is said, *and the fear of you and the dread of you*

a (1) Until the funeral without putrefying. (2) Lit., 'go up'—to meet the top jaw. (3) V. *supra* 40b. This shows that whatever may not be handled may not be oiled. (4) The reason there is not because handling is forbidden, but lest he make ruts (v. *supra* 40b, n. c3); and though that is impossible, since baths are provided with stone flooring, yet it is forbidden lest it be thought that it may likewise be done to an earth flooring. But no one will think that if a corpse may be oiled, the ground may be oiled too. (5) Eccl. XII, 6. He translates *galgal* (E.V. *wheel*) as *galal* (dung).

b (1) Mal. II, 3. (2) Lit., 'words of the Torah'. (3) Lit., 'with the departure of the soul'. (4) Lit., 'he sheds blood'—because he hastens death. (5) Ps. LXXXVIII, 6 (E.V. 5: *cast off among the dead*). (6) V. Ber. 54b.

◁ *For the continuation of the English translation of this page see overleaf.*

עין משפט
נר מצוה

מג א מיי' פכ"ו מהל' שבת הלכה כ סמג שם טוש"ע או"ח סימן שיא סעיף ז :

מד ב מיי' פ"ד מהלכות אבל הלכה ה סמג עשין ב טוש"ע יו"ד סי' שלט סעיף א :

מה ג סמג עשין עט :

מו ד מיי' פ"י מהלכות תשובה הלכה א :

מז ה מיי' פ"י מהלכות מתנות עניים הל"ב [וה' עבדים פ"ט הל"ח] טוש"ע יו"ד סימן רמז סעיף ג :

שימתין *קושרין את הלחי לא שיעלה אלא שלא יוסיף *וכן קורה שנשברה סומכין אותה בספסל או בארוכות המטה לא שתעלה אלא שלא תוסיף : **גמ'** *והאמר רב יהודה אמר שמואל מעשה בתלמידו של רבי מאיר שנכנס אחריו לבית המרחץ ביקש להדיח קרקע אמר לו אין מדיחין לסוך קרקע אמר לו אין סכין °קרקע בקרקע מחלפא . מת בקרקע לא מיחלף כל לאתויי מאי לאתויי הא דת"ר מביאין כלי מיקר וכלי מתכות ומניחין על כריסו כדי שלא (א) תפוח ופוקקין את נקביו כדי שלא תיכנס בהן הרוח ואף שלמה אמר בחכמתו °עד *שלא ירתק חבל הכסף זה חוט השדרה ותרוץ גולת הזהב זה אמה ותשבר כד על המבוע זה הכרס ונרוץ הגלגל אל הבור זה פרש וכן הוא אומר °וזריתי פרש על פניכם פרש חגיכם אמר רב הונא ואמרי לה אמר רב חגא אלו בני אדם שמניחין דברי תורה ועושין כל ימיהם כחגים אמר רבי לוי אמר רב פפי א"ר יהושע לאחר שלשה ימים כריסו נבקעת ונופלת לו על פניו ואומרת לו טול מה שנתת בי : **מתני'** אין (א) מעצמין את המת בשבת ולא בחול עם יציאת נפש ב'והמעצים עם יציאת הנפש הרי זה שופך דמים : **גמ'** תנו רבנן המעצמו עם יציאת הנפש הרי זה שופך דמים משל לנר שכבה והולכת אדם מניח אצבעו עליה מיד כבתה תניא *רשב"ג אומר הרוצה שיתעצמו עיניו של מת נופח לו יין בחוטמו ונותן שמן בין ריסי עיניו ואוחז בשני גודלי רגליו והן מתעצמין מאליהן תניא רשב"ג אומר תינוק בן יומו חי מחללין עליו את השבת דוד מלך ישראל מת אין מחללין עליו את השבת תינוק בן יומו חי מחללין עליו את השבת *אמרה תורה חלל עליו שבת אחד כדי שישמור שבתות הרבה דוד מלך ישראל מת אין מחללין עליו כיון שמת אדם בטל מן המצות והיינו *דא"ר יוחנן °במתים חפשי כיון שמת אדם נעשה הפשי מן המצות ותניא ר' שמעון בן אלעזר אומר תינוק בן יומו חי אין צריך לשומרו מן החולדה ומן העכברים אבל עוג מלך הבשן מת צריך לשומרו מן החולדה ומן העכברים שנאמר °ומוראכם וחתכם יהיה כל זמן שאדם חי אימתו מוטלת על הבריות כיון שמת בטלה אימתו אמר רב פפא *נקיטינן אריה אבי תרי לא נפיל הא קא חזינן דנפיל ההוא כדרמי בר אבא דאמר רמי בר אבא *אין חיה שולטת באדם עד שנדמה לו כבהמה שנאמר °אדם ביקר בל ילין נמשל כבהמות נדמו אמר רבי חנינא ג'אסור לישן בבית יחידי וכל הישן בבית יחידי אחזתו לילית ותניא רשב"א אומר עשה עד שאתה מוצא ומצוי לך ועודך בידך ואף שלמה אמר בחכמתו °וזכור את בוראיך בימי בחורותיך עד [אשר] (ש) לא יבואו ימי הרעה ד'אלו ימי הזקנה והגיעו שנים אשר תאמר אין לי בהם חפץ אלו ימי המשיח שאין בהם לא זכות ולא חובה ופליגא דשמואל *דאמר שמואל אין בין העולם הזה לימות המשיח אלא שיעבוד מלכיות בלבד שנא' °כי לא יחדל אביון מקרב הארץ תניא ר' אלעזר הקפר אומר לעולם יבקש אדם רחמים על מדה זו שאם הוא לא בא בנו ואם בנו לא בא בן בנו בא שנאמר °כי בגלל הדבר הזה תנא דבי ר' ישמעאל גלגל הוא שחוזר בעולם א"ר יוסף נקיטינן האי צורבא מרבנן לא מיעני והא קא חזינן דמיעני אם איתא דמיעני אהדורי אפתחא לא מיהדר אמר לה רבי חייא לדביתהו כי אתי עניא אקדימי ליה ריפתא כי היכי דלקדמו לבנין אמרה ליה מילט קא לייטת להו אמר לה קרא קא כתיב כי בגלל הדבר הזה ותנא דבי ר' ישמעאל גלגל הוא שחוזר בעולם תניא *ר' גמליאל ברבי אומר °ונתן לך רחמים ורחמך והרבך ה'*כל המרחם על הבריות מרחמין עליו מן השמים וכל שאינו מרחם על הבריות אין מרחמין עליו מן השמים °עד אשר לא תחשך השמש והאור זו פדחת והחוטם והירח זו נשמה והכוכבים אלו הלסתות ושבו העבים אחר הגשם זו מאור עיניו של אדם שהולך אחר הבכי אמר שמואל האי דמעתא עד ארבעין שנין הדרא מכאן ואילך לא הדרא ואמר רב נחמן האי כוחלא עד ארבעין שנין מרווח מכאן ואילך אפילו מליא *כאביסנא דגירדאי אוקומי מוקים ארווחי לא מרווח מאי קא משמע לן דכמה דאלים מכוחלא טפי מעלי ר' חנינא שכיבא ליה ברתיה לא הוה קא בכי עלה אמרה ליה דביתהו תרנגולתא אפיקת מביתך אמר לה תרתי תכלא ועיורא סבר לה כי הא דאמר רבי יוחנן משום רבי יוסי בן קצרתה *שש דמעות הן שלש יפות ושלש רעות של עשן ושל בכי ושל

שימתין · שלא יסריח מחמת חום הסדין והכרים : קושרין את הלחי · של מת שהיה פיו הולך ונפתח קושרין את לחייו כדי שלא יפתח פיו יותר : ולא שיעלה · להסגר ממה שנפתח דהייט מזיז אבר אלא שלא יוסיף ליפתח : סומכין אותה בספסל · שהרי תורת כלי עליו : לא שתעלה · דהוה ליה בונה : **גמ'** ואמר לו אין סכין · אלמא דבר האסור לטלטל אסור לסוך : קרקע בקרקע מיחלף · כלומר ההוא לאו משום טלטול הוא אלא משום אשויי גומות ואע"ג דמרחץ רצפת אבנים הוא וליכא למיחש לאשויי גומות מיחלף מיהא בקרקע אחר : כל צרכי המת לאתויי מאי · דלא תנן : כלי מיקר · שמביאים קרירות כגון זכוכית : ואף שלמה אמר בחכמתו · שכריסו של מת טופחת ונבקעת : זה חוט השדרה · שהוא כמין חבל ולבן ככסף : זו אמה · שהוא מעין של תולדה כמו גולות מים (יהושע טו) : זה פרש · וגלגל לשון גלל (יחזקאל ד) : אל הבור · שטופל לתוך פיו : כחגים · בתענוגים : **מתני'** אין מעצמין · את עיניו בשבת אפילו אחר יציאת הנפש דמזיז בו אבר : שופך דמים · כדמפרש בברייתא בגמ' שבטורח מועט מקרב מיתתו : **גמ'** ואוחז בשני גודלי רגליו · עוקרן באצבעותיו : וחתכם · לשון חיותכם : אריה אבי תרי לא נפיל · להורגן כדכתי' ומוראכם תרי וכתיב על כל חית הארץ ואפי' ארי : כדרמי בר אבא · דנקנסה עליו מיתה ונדמה לארי כבהמה : נמשל · מי שחיה מושלת בו בידוע שכבהמה נדמה : עשה · צדקה : עד שאתה מוצא · למי לעשות : ומצוי לך · ממון : ועודך בידך · עודך ברשותך קודם שתמות : לא זכות · לא דבר לזכות בו שכולם עשירים : ולא חובה · לאמץ לב ולקפוץ יד : על מדה זו · שלא יבא לידי עניות דדבר המזומן הוא לבא או עליו או על בנו או על בן בנו : ונתן לך רחמים · שתרחם על הבריות : זו פדחת · המצח שהוא חלק ומצהיר יותר מכל הפרצוף : זה חוטם · שהוא תואר פני אדם : זו נשמה · כדכתיב נר אלהים נשמת אדם (משלי כ) : הלסתות · לחיים : ושבו העבים · חשכת עינים יבא ויכסה המאור אחר שירבה בבכיה בזקנותו מחמת תשות כח וצרות רבות עליו : מרווח · מאור עינים : אפילו מליא · כחלא בעיניו כמכחול גדול : כאביסנא של גרדאי · כובד של גרדיים אינשובל"ש בלע"ז : אוקומי · (ב) המאור מוקים שלא יחשיך יותר ממה שהוא : מאי קמ"ל · בהא דאמר אפי' כאביסנא דגרדאי : אלים · עב : מכוחלא · עץ שהוא מכניס בשפופרת ונותן בעיניו וקורין לו מכחול : תכלא ועיורא · שיכול בנים ועיורון הדמעה : של בכי · מתוך אבל וצרה : של

לעיל מב.
לעיל מב:

הגהות הב"ח
(א) גמ' שלא יפה תפוח : (ב) רש"י ד"ה אוקומי. מוקים המאור שלא :

בקרא אשר לא

גליון הש"ס
גמ' קרקע בקרקע מיחלפא. כה"ג לעיל דף כט ע"ב ועי' בתוספות שם ד"ה גוירס :

כס"י ליתא ר"ש בן אלעזר

[יומא פה:]

תהלים פח

בראשית ט

תהלים מט

קהלת יב

דברים טו

שם

שם יג

[ביצה לב: ע"ש]

קהלת יב

[גי' הערוך כאבסנא]

[אדר"נ פמ"א]

נדה ס. [נדה סא: ע"ש]

[עי' פרש"י בעירובין ה. ד"ה והאמר פירוקא ע"ז] [סנהדרין לח: ע"ש]

ברכות לד: לעיל סג. פסחים סח. סנהדרין צא: צט.

[תוספתא דב"ק פ"ט]

א) [גי' הערוך אין מאמצין כו' וכל המאמץ כו' פירוש סותמין עיני המת לאחר המיתה כדי שלא יהיו עיניו פתוחות כענין שנאמר ויוסף ישית ידו על עיניך ע"כ ועי' לעיל דף עז: איבעיא להו מאמצין תנן או מעמצין וכו' ואשר ע"כ ברור דטעות הוא שהקדימו בדפוס ל' קודם למ' במשנה ובברייתא דהכא וגם בפרש"י דהכא אמנם כרי"ף והרא"ש הגירסא במשנה ובברייתא על נכון המ' קודם לצ' וכ"א במשנה שבמשניות ובפי' הרב וכתב התוי"ט אין מאמצין כמו עוצם עיניו כו']

רבינו חננאל

הרץ לחומה לנו ואע"ג דאיסורא הוא וקיי"ל הלכתא כרב באיסורי הכא הלכתא כשמואל דדיקא מתניתין כותיה דתנן במס' מכשירין עיר של ישראל ונכרים דרין בתוכה והיתה בה מרחץ המרחצת בשבת אם רוב נכרים מותר לרחוץ בה מיד אם רוב ישראל ימתין עד בכדי שיחמו חמין. מחצה על מחצה ימתין בכדי שיחמו חמין . ר' יהודה אומר באמבטי קטנה ואם יש רשות רוחץ בה מיד . ומפרש רב יצחק בריה דרב יהודה מאי רשות כגון אדם חשוב שיש לו עשרה עבדים שמחממין לו עשרה קומקמין בבת אחת מותר לרחוץ מיד: עשו לו ארון וחפרו לו קבר יקבר בהן ישראל ומקשינן אמאי והא ישראל ונכרי כמחצה על מחצה דמי ימתין בכדי שיעשו ומפרק עולא כגון בנכרי מת המוטל באיסטרטא דמוכחא מלתא שזה הקבר לזה הנכרי נחפר שדומה לרוב נכרים שאין צריך להמתין בכדי שיעשו תוב אקשינן תינח קבר ארון מאי ופריק ר' אבהו בארון המוטל על הקבר שנמצא הארון בקבר*)דאילו דברי ר"מ נסבייה בדרך גררה. בפרק כירה בענין דברים של (חול) [קדש] אסור לאומרם (בלשה"ק) [בלשון חול] אלא אם הוא לאפרושי מאיסורא כגון זה שא"ר מאיר לתלמידיו אין מדיחין ואין סכין בלשה"ק אבל הרואה שסכין ומדיחין המת לא יתיר הדחה וסיכה בקרקע ולפיכך התיר ר"מ הדחת המת וסיכתו ולא גזר סיכת המת והדחתו מפני סיכת מרחץ והדחתו . כל צרכי המת כלל זה להביא הא דת"ר מביאין כלי מיקר וכלי מתכות ומניחין לו על כרסו בשבת שלא תפוח . ופוקקין נקביו בשביל שלא תכנס בהן הרוח ואף שלמה אמר בחכמתו עד אשר לא ירתק חבל הכסף וגו' ופשוטה היא : אין מאמצין את המת בשבת וכו' . פי' מאמצין סותמין את עיני המת . ת"ר המאמץ עם יציאת נפש אפילו בחול הרי זה שופך דמים משל לנר שכבה כו' . תניא ר"ש בן אלעזר אומר תינוק בן יומו חי מחללין עליו את השבת שעומד ומשמר שבתות הרבה . דוד מלך ישראל מת אין מחללין עליו אף השבת

*) נראה דחסר כאן איזה תיבות ושייך להא דמקשינן כאן בגמ' והאמר ריה"ש מעשה בתלמידו של ר"מ

Continuation of translation from previous page as indicated by ◁

c *shall be upon every beast of the earth:*[1] as long as a man is alive, his fear lies upon dumb creatures; once he dies his fear ceases. R. Papa said: We hold [as tradition] that a lion does not attack two persons [together]. But we see that it does?—That is [explained] as Rami b. Abba. For Rami b. Abba said: A beast has no power over man until it appears to it as an animal, for it is said, *Man that is in honour, and understandeth not, is like the beasts that perish.*[2]

R. Ḥanina said: One may not sleep in a house alone,[3] and whoever sleeps in a house alone is seized by Lilith.[4]

It was further taught, R. Simeon b. Eleazar said: Perform [righteousness and charity] whilst thou canst find [an object for thy charity], hast the opportunity,[5] and it is yet in thy power,[6] and Solomon in his wisdom too said: '*Remember also thy creator in the days of thy youth, or ever the evil days come*'—this refers to the days of old age; '*and the years draw nigh, when thou shalt say, I have no pleasure in them*'[7]—this refers to the Messianic era, wherein there is neither merit nor guilt. Now he disagrees with Samuel, who said: The only difference between this world and the Messianic era is in respect of servitude to [foreign] powers, for it is said, *For the poor shall never cease out of the land.*[8]

It was taught, R. Eleazar ha-Ḳappar said: Let one always pray to be spared this fate [poverty], for if *he* does not descend [to poverty] his son will, and if not his son, his grandson, for it is said, *because that for* [bi-gelal] *this thing,* [etc.].[9] The School of R. Ishmael taught: It is a wheel [*galgal*] that revolves in the world.[10] R. Joseph said: We hold [as tradition] that a Rabbinical student will not suffer poverty. But we see that he does suffer poverty?—Even if he suffers poverty, he [nevertheless] does not engage in
d begging.[1] R. Ḥiyya said to his wife: When a poor man comes, be quick to offer him bread, so that others may be quick to offer it to your children. You curse them! she exclaimed. A verse is written, he replied: '*because that for* [bi-gelal] *this thing*', whereon the School of R. Ishmael taught: It is a wheel that revolves in the world. It was taught, R. Gamaliel Beribbi[2] said: *And He shall give*[3] *thee mercy, and have compassion upon thee, and multiply thee:*[4] he who is merciful to others, mercy is shown to him by Heaven, while he who is not merciful to others, mercy is not shown to him by Heaven.[5]

'*Or ever the sun and the light be darkened*':[6] this refers to the forehead and the nose; '*and the moon*'—this is the soul; '*and the stars*'—these are the cheeks; '*and the clouds return after the rain*'—this is the light of man's eyes [his eyesight], which is lost after weeping.[7] Samuel said: For tears, until the age of forty there is a recovery, but thenceforth there is no recovery.[8] And R. Naḥman said: As for kohl,[9] until the age of forty it improves [the eyesight], but thereafter, even if the paint-stick is as thick [with paint] as a weaver's pin, it may indeed stay [the ravages of time], but will certainly not improve [the eyesight]. What does he inform us? That the thicker the paint-stick the more beneficial it is.

R. Ḥanina's daughter died, [but] he did not weep for her. Said his wife to him, 'Hast thou sent out a fowl from thy house?'[10] '[Shall I suffer] two [evils],' he retorted, 'bereavement and blindness?' He held as R. Joḥanan said in the name of R. Jose the son of a laundress: There are six kinds of tears, three being beneficial and three harmful: those caused by smoke, weeping,[11] [152a]

c (1) Gen. IX, 2. (2) Ps. XLIX, 14 and 21 (E.V. 20). He appears to translate: . . . not, he is ruled over (by wild beasts) when he appears (to them) like a beast.—This is a punishment for misdeeds. (3) *Aliter:* He who sleeps in a lonely (situated) house. (4) The night demon. V. *J.E.* art. *Lilith.* (5) Lit., 'it is found with thee'—*sc.* the means. (6) I.e., during thy lifetime. (7) Eccl. XII, 1. (8) Deut. XV, 11; v. *supra* 63a for notes. (9) Ibid. 10. (10) Coming to all people or their descendants; *Gelal* is thus connected with *galgal.*

d (1) Lit., 'going about the doors' (of houses). (2) V. *supra* 115a, n. b6. (3) E.V. *show.* (4) Deut. XIII, 17. (5) He translates the verse thus; and he shall give, i.e., inspire thee with mercy—towards others—then he shall have mercy upon thee. (6) Eccl. XII, 2. (7) The weeping of old age—caused by trouble and sickness—impairs or destroys the eyesight. (8) The eyes recover from the weakening effect of tears until one is forty years old, but not after. (9) An eye-salve. (10) Was she nothing more to you than that? (11) In grief.

and the privy[12] are harmful; those caused by chemicals, laughter, or plants[13] are beneficial.

In the day when the keeper of the house shall tremble; and the strong
a *men shall bow themselves*, etc.[1] *'In the day when the keeper of the house shall tremble'*—these are the flanks [sides] and the ribs; *'and the strong men shall bow themselves'*—the legs; *'and the grinders cease'*—the teeth; *'and those that look out of the windows darkened'*—the eyes. The emperor asked R. Joshua b. Hanania,[2] 'Why did you not attend the *Be Abedan?*'[3] 'The mountain is snowy, it is surrounded by ice,[4] the dog does not bark and the grinders do not grind,' he replied.[5] The School of Rab was wont to say: 'What I did not lose I seek.'[6]

It was taught, R. Jose b. Ḳisma said: Two are better than three,[7] and woe for the one thing that goes and does not return. What is that? Said R. Ḥisda: One's youth. When R. Dimi came,[8] he said: Youth is a crown of roses; old age is a crown of willow-rods.[9] It was taught in R. Meir's name: Chew well with your teeth, and you will find it in your steps, as it is said, *for then we had plenty of victuals, and were well, and saw no evil.*[10] Samuel said to Rab Judah: O keen scholar![11] open your mouth[12] and let your food enter. Until the age of forty food is more beneficial; thenceforth drink is more beneficial.

A certain eunuch [*gawzaah*] said to R. Joshua b. Ḳarḥah [Baldhead]: 'How far is it from here to Ḳarḥina [Baldtown]? 'As far as from here to Gawzania [Eunuchtown],' he replied.[13] Said the Sadducee to him, 'A bald buck is worth four *denarii*.' 'A goat, if castrated, is worth eight,' he retorted. Now, he [the Sadducee] saw that he [R. Joshua] was not wearing shoes, [whereupon] he remarked, 'He [who rides] on a horse is a king, upon an ass, is a free man, and he who has shoes on his feet is a human being; but
b he who has none of these, one who is dead[1] and buried is better off.' 'O eunuch, O eunuch,' he retorted, 'you have enumerated three things to me, [and now] you will hear three things: the glory of a face is its beard; the rejoicing of one's heart is a wife; *the heritage of the Lord is children;*[2] blessed be the Omnipresent, Who has denied you all these!' 'O quarrelsome baldhead,' he jeered at him. 'A castrated buck and [you will] reprove!'[3] he retorted.

Rabbi asked R. Simeon b. Ḥalafta: 'Why were we not permitted to receive you on the Festival, as my ancestors used to receive your ancestors?' 'The rocks have grown tall, the near have become distant, two have turned into three, and the peacemaker of the home has ceased, he replied.[4]

And the doors shall be shut in the streets:[5] this refers to the apertures of man; *'when the sound of the grinding is low'*—on account of the stomach's failing to digest;[6] *'and one shall rise up at the voice of a bird'*,—even a bird will awake him from sleep; *'and all the daughters of the music shall be brought low'*—even the voices of male

(12) I.e., through internal disorders. (13) E.g., onions or mustard.
a (1) Eccl. XII, 2. (2) V. *supra* 119*a*, n. c2. (3) V. *supra* 116*a* and notes a.l. (4) Lit., 'its surroundings are ice'. (5) My head is snowy white, my beard likewise, my voice feeble and my teeth do not function.—I am too old to attend. (6) This was their description of old age. One goes about bent and stooping, appearing to seek an article which he has not lost. (7) The two legs in youth are better than the three—i.e., the additional stick—of old age. (8) V. *supra* 5*a*, n. b9. (9) Heavy to bear. (10) Jer. XLIV, 17. (11) Or, man of long teeth.

(12) Lit., 'thy sack'. (13) Both fictitious places, of course, playfully formed from their names and persons.
b (1) Lit., 'one for whom a grave is dug'. (2) Ps. CXXVII, 3. (3) Rashi. R. Ḥan.: O castrated goat, I do but rebuke, not quarrel with thee. (4) I.e., I have grown old, even those near are as difficult to visit as those at a distance, my two legs need an additional stick for walking, and I can no longer exercise a man's functions. (5) Eccl. XII, 4. (6) Lit., 'grind'.

◁ *For the continuation of the English translation of this page see overleaf.*

הורה אור

ושל בית הכסא רעות של סם ושל שחוק ושל פירות יפות °ביום שיזועו שומרי הבית והתעותו וגו' ביום שיזועו שומרי הבית אלו הכסלים והצלעות והתעותו אנשי החיל אלו שוקים ובטלו הטוחנות אלו שינים וחשכו הרואות בארובות אלו עינים א"ל קיסר לר' יהושע בן חנניה מ"ט לא אתית לבי אבידן א"ל טור תלג סחרוני גלידין כלבוהי לא נבחין טחנוהי לא טוחנין בי רב אמרי אדלא אבידנא בחישנא *תניא רבי יוסי בר קיסמא אומר טבא תרי מתלת ווי לה להדא דאזלא ולא אתיא מאי היא א"ר חסדא ינקותא כי אתא רב דימי אמר ינקותא כלילא דוורדא סבותא כלילא *דחילפא תנא משמיה דרבי מאיר דוק בככי ותשכח בניגרי שנאמר °ונשבע לחם ונהיה טובים ורעה לא ראינו א"ל שמואל לרב יהודה *שיננא שרי שקיך ועייל לדמך עד ארבעין שנין מיכלא מעלי מכאן ואילך משתי מעלי א"ל ההוא גוזאה לר' יהושע בן קרחה מהכא לקרחינא כמה הוי א"ל כמהכא לגוזניא א"ל צדוקי ברחא קרחא בארבעה אמר ליה *עיקרא שליפא בתמניא חזייה דלא סיים מסאניה א"ל דעל סוס מלך דעל המור בן חורין ודמנעלי בריגלוהי בר איניש דלא הא ולא הא דדפיר וקביר טב מיניה א"ל גוזא גוזא תלת אמרת לי תלת שמעת הדרת פנים זקן שמדת לב אשה °נחלת ה' בנים ברוך המקום שמנעך מכולם א"ל קרחא מצויינא אמר ליה עיקרא שליפא תוכחה א"ל רבי לר' שמעון בן חלפתא מפני מה לא הקבלנו פניך ברגל כדרך שהקבילו אבותי לאבותיך א"ל סלעים נעשו גבוהים קרובים נעשו רחוקים משתים נעשו שלש משים שלום בבית בטל: °וסגרו דלתים בשוק וגו' אלו נקביו של אדם בשפל קול הטחנה בשביל קורקבן שאינו טוחן ויקום לקול הצפור שאפילו צפור מנערתו משנתו וישחו כל בנות השיר שאפילו (*קול שירים ושירות) דומות עליו כשוחה ואף ברזילי הגלעדי אמר לדוד °בן שמנים שנה אנכי היום האדע בין טוב לרע מכאן שדעותן של זקנים משתנות אם יטעם עבדך את אשר אוכל ואת אשר אשתה מכאן ששפתותיהן של זקנים מתרפטות אם אשמע עוד בקול שרים ושרות מכאן שאזניהם של זקנים מתכבדות אמר רב ברזילי הגלעדי שקרא הוה דההיא אמתא דהויא בי רבי בת תשעין ותרתין שנין והות טעמא קידרא רבא אמר ברזילי הגלעדי שטוף בזמה הוה °וכל השטוף בזמה *זקנה קופצת עליו תניא רבי ישמעאל ברבי יוסי אומר *תלמידי חכמים כל זמן שמזקינין חכמה נתוספת בהם שנאמר °בישישים חכמה ואורך ימים תבונה ועמי הארץ כל זמן שמזקינין טפשות נתוספת בהן שנאמר °מסיר שפה לנאמנים וטעם זקנים יקח גם מגבוה ייראו שאפילו גבשושית קטנה דומה עליו כהרי הרים וחתחתים בדרך בשעה שמהלך בדרך נעשו (א)לו *תוהים וינאץ *השקד זו קליבוסת ויסתבל החגב אלו עגבות ותפר האביונה זו חמדה רב כהנא הוה פסיק סידרא קמיה דרב כי מטא להאי קרא נגיד ואתנח אמר ש"מ בטל ליה המדיה דרב אמר רב כהנא מאי דכתיב °כי הוא אמר ויהי זו אשה הוא צוה ויעמוד אלו בנים תנא אשה חמת מלא צואה ופיה מלא דם והכל רצין אחריה °כי הולך האדם אל בית עולמו א"ר יצחק *מלמד שכל צדיק וצדיק נותנין לו מדור לפי כבודו משל למלך שנכנס הוא ועבדיו לעיר כשהן נכנסין כולן בשער אחד נכנסין כשהן לנין כל אחד ואחד נותנין לו מדור לפי כבודו ואמר רבי יצחק מאי דכתיב °כי הילדות והשחרות הבל דברים שאדם עושה בילדותו משחירים פניו לעת זקנתו *ואמר רבי יצחק קשה רימה למת כמחט בבשר החי שנאמר °אך בשרו עליו יכאב אמר רב חסדא נפשו של אדם מתאבלת עליו כל שבעה שנא' ונפשו עליו תאבל וכתיב °ויעש לאביו אבל שבעת ימים אמר רב יהודה *מת שאין לו מנחמין הולכין י' בני אדם ויושבין במקומו ההוא דשכיב בשבבותיה דרב יהודה לא היו לו מנחמין
כל

(רש"י) של בית הכסא · מתוך יסורין : של פירות · כגון ריח חרדל : הכסלים. ליפלאנק"ש : והצלעות · שהן שומרין בני המעיים וחיותו של אדם וסוגרין בעדם : אלו שוקיים · שכחו של אדם נסמך עליהם : לבי אבידן · מקום העשוי להתווכח שם לדוקים וביייתוסים עם ישראל במקראות : טור תלג · ההר נעשה שלג כלומר ראשי לבן : סחרוני גלידין · סביבותיו של הר מלאו קרח כלומר שפמי וזקני הלבינו: כלבוהי לא נבחין · קולי אינו נשמע : טחנוהי · השינים : אדלא אבידנא בחישנא · אחר מה שלא אבד ממני אני מפשפש מרוב זקנה אני הולך שחוח ומנענע ונראה כמי שמבקש דינר האבד לו : תרתי טבא מתלת · טובים ב' הרגלים של ימי בחרות מג' של זקנה שצריך משענת עם רגליו: ווי לה · חבל עליה כלומר יש לו להתאונן ולצעוק ווי ההולכת ואינה חוזרת : כלילא דוורדא · נזר של וורד : חילפי · אורטיא"ש : דוק בככי ותשכח בניגרי . לכוס הרבה ותמלא האכילה בפסיעותיך שיחזק כחך דוק כמו אכלה מדקה(דניאל ז) לשון כוסס: שרי שקיך · פתח פיך : גוזא · סרים ולדוקי היה: מהכא לקרחינא כמה הוי· כמה מהלך יש מכאן עד הקרח ולהקניטו על קרחתו נתכוון : כמהכא לגוזניא · כמו שמכאן עד הסרים: אמר ליה לדוקי ברחא קרחא בארבעה · שהקרח לקוח בארבע · ברחא קרחא הוא עז על שם שאינו מלובש בצמר כרחל קרוי קרחא : אמר ליה · רבי יהושע : עיקרא שליפא · שה שביציו עקורים ונתוקין לוקחין בשמנה: חזייה· לדוקי לרבי יהושע דלא סיים מסאניה: קרחא מצויינא · אתה הקרח במריבה אתה באת עמדי בתמיה : אמר לו רבי יהושע עיקרא שליפא תוכחה · אתה הסרים להקניטני ולהתווכח עמי באת : לא הקבלנו פניך · לא הקבלת פני ודרך ענוה קאמר ליה : סלעים · קטנים נעשו גבוהים שזקנתי : קרובים · נדמין לי כרחוקים : שתים נעשו לי שלש · שצריך אני משענת: משים שלום בבית · אבר תשמיש : לישנא אחרינא קרובים נעשו רחוקים מרוב חלשות של אדם כשמזקין צריך להרחיק רגליו זה מזה : שאינו טוחן · שאין בני מעיו טוחנין אכילתו : קורקבן · הוא המסס שקורין ליינפי"ל: כל בנות השיר . כל קולות של שיר הויין ליה שוחה: שדעתן של זקנים משתנות· דכתיב האדע בין טוב לרע ובזקנה מרובה קאמר : מתרפטות · מתבקעות כמו מנעל המרופט (לעיל דף קמא:) : מתכבדות· כמו ואזניו הכבד (ישעיה ו) : שטוף · כמו סוס שוטף במלחמה (ירמיה ח) להוט אחר הדבר ורודף: וטעם זקנים יקח · וע"כ מדקשי קראי אהדדי חד מתוקם בחכמים וחד בזקני השוק : מגבוה ייראו · יראים הם הזקנים מגבשושית שבדרכים ואומרים גבוהים הם : תוהים · פחדים : וינאץ השקד. אילן של שקדים ילין ויהיו בולטין גלים שלו : זו קליבוסת · עצם של הגק"א שהירך תקוע בו בולט ויוצא מרוב תשות כחו : ויסתבל החגב · דומה עליו כסבל משא כבד:ותפר האביונה · תבטל התאוה המדת תשמיש : פסיק סידרא · מסדר פרשיות של פסוקים : נגיד ואיתנח · רב : המדיה · תאותו : זו אשה · אם לא על פי גזרת המלך לא היתה ראויה להאוות לה שהיא כחמת מלאה מילום והכל רצים אחריה : מדור לפי כבודו · מדלא כתיב אל בית העולם ש"מ כל אחד ואחד לבית המוכן לו : בשער אחד . אף כאן הכל מתים בענין אחד: שאדם עושה בילדותו·רוב תשמיש: משחירים פניו· מתיש כחו:שאין לו מנחמים · אין לו אבלים שיהו צריכין לנחמו : במקומו · במקום שמת שם :
כל

רבינו חננאל

השבת לפי שבטל מן המצות והיינו דא"ר יוחנן מאי דכתיב במתים חפשי כיון שמת אדם נעשה חפשי מן המצות: א"ל קיסר לר' יהושע מ"ט לא אתית לבי אבידן. פי' בי אבידן בית שמתקבצין שם החכמים ונושאין ונותנין בדיני כל אומה ולשון השיבו ר' יהושע טור תלג סחרנוהי גלידין כלבוהי לא נבחין טחנוהי לא טחנן בבי רב אמרי (או לא או דן פי' בו) [אדלא אבדן בהשנא] ופירושו ההר כסהו שלג ודומה האדם להר כלומר ראשו כיסתו השיבה. וסביבותיה שהן הלחיים נעשו גלידין והוא הקרח שנקרא גליד. והגרון והלשון אינן מרימין קול. ככי שהן השניים אינן טוחנין המאכל. אדלא אבדן בחשנא. כלומר הזקן שאינו מביט מה שבפניו מתיירא שמא יכה ראשו באבן או בכיוצא בה וממשש בידו ונראה כאלו ממשש בדבר שאבד לו וזהו כמין משל ממשש הזקן מה שלא אבד. טבי תרי מתלת. פי' יותר הוא טוב המהלך על ב' רגליו מן הזקן שצריך משען כגון מקל אי שבט להישען עליו והוא כמו רגל שלישי. חבל על דאזלא ולא אתיא. פי' הבחרות הולכת כשמזקין האדם ואינה חוזרת אליו. ינקותא כלילא דוורדי. הבהרות כתר של וורד ריחו נודף ושל זקנה כתר של חילף שריחו מאוס. דוק בככי ותשכח בנגרי. טחון בככי בשניים כלומר אכול כדי שיהיה לך כח להלך ברגליך.א"ל ההוא גאזא התוך(הערוה) [הביצים]והוא סריס א"ל ר' יהושע בן קרחה מהכא לקרדוניא כמה.ביקש להודיעו שהוא קרח והן ביר לו דברים כמלעיג והשיבו ר' יהושע כמו הכא לגזוניא כלומר אתה גזוי. עוד אמר ליה ברחא קרחא בארבע. פי' (או)[עור] כבש גדול בד' כספים. השיבו ר' יהושע הדברים מוכיחין שגם אלו דברי הסרים הם שבקש להודיעו כי השלוף ביוקר יותר מן הקרח. ילמדנו רבינו איקא שליפא בתמניא. פי' עור תיש נתוק ביצים בשמונה כספים. שמבקשין אותו לעשותו נודות של שמן. חזייה דלא מסיים מסאניה. פירוש ראהו יחף כו'. א"ל קרחה מצוי. פי' א"ל קרחה מריבה סחרחר. כדכתיב הן לריב ומצה וגו' השיבו ר' יהושע תיש נתוק תוכחה אינם דברי ריב אלא דברי תוכחה. מפני מה לא הקבלנו פניך. למה לא באת אלינו להתראות פנים: מיכן ששפתותיהן של זקנים מתרפטות. פי' מתרפטות משתרבבות והוא מתרופפות אינם מתאמצת להסתם הפה בחוזקה. גבשושית פי' גב קטן של עפר. קליבוסת פירוש מן הפקוקלות ומפורש באלו מרפות. תרבא דאקליבוסתא. יתפר האביונה. זו חמדה (כמו) [כי] בטלה ממנו תאות אשה. פי' טלוניתא כמו על שאין בה ממש. נשייה שם ידו עליו מלשון נגששה:

רב נסים גאון

אמר ליה סלעים נעשין גבוהים כמו שנאמר אח"כ שאפילו גבשושית קטנה דומה עליו כהרי הרים ושאר הענין פירשוהו במקצת ההגדה וכך אמרו רחוקים נעשו קרובים אילין עיניא דהוון חמיין מרחוק אף מקרוב ליתנן חמאן קרובים נעשו רחוקים אילין אודניא דהוון שמעין בחד זמן כדו אף במאה זימנין ליתנן שמעין ב' נעשו ג' חוטרא ותרין ריגליא משים שלום בבית בטל זו תאוה שהיא מעלה שלום

(מסורת הש"ס) קהלת יב · מס' ד"א זוטא פ"י · [פי' מיני קמשונים ערוך] · ירמיה מד · [נ"ל איקא פי' בערוך] · תהלים קכז · קהלת יב · [נ"ל קול שרים ושרות] · שמואל ב יט · [תענית ה:] · איוב יב · [קנים פ"ג ע"ש ובמפרש] · שם · [תרגום של ויהרג יהוא ערוך] · עי' מ"ר ויקרא פ' י"ח · תהלים לג · קהלת יב · [ב"מ פג:] · קהלת · ברכות יח: לעיל יג: · איוב יד · ברכות · [לעיל נט. ברכות נו. עירובין כב. חגיגה טו: ר"ה כב: כתובות יב: יד: נג. קדושין לג. גיטין עח: ב"ק יד. טו: לו: ב"ב קנג: מ"ז מג: סנהדרין עו: כריתות יט: נדה יג. יז. כה.]

הגהות הב"ח (א) גמ' נעשה לבו תוהים. תוהים וינאץ השקד:

(עין משפט נר מצוה) מח א מיי' פ"ד מהלכות דעות הל"יט טור שו"ע או"ח סימן רמ סעיף יד : מט ב מיי' פי"ג מהל' אבל הלכה ד סמג עשין ב טוש"ע יו"ד סי' שעו סעיף ג [וברב אלפס מו"ק פ"ג דרל"ז] וברא"ש שם סימן פ"ט :

Continuation of translation from previous page as indicated by ◁

singers and female singers sound to him like a whisper. And thus too did Barzillai the Gileadite say to David: '*I am this day fourscore years old: can I discern between good and bad*'? This shows that the opinions of old men are changeable [changed]; '*can thy servant taste what I eat or drink*'? this shows that the lips of old men grow slack;[7] '*can I hear any more the voice of singing men and singing women*'?[8] this proves that the ears of old men are heavy.[9] Rab said: Barzillai the Gileadite was a liar. For there was a servant in Rab's house, ninety-two years old, who could taste the dish[es]. Raba said: Barzillai the Gileadite was steeped in lewdness, and whoever is steeped in lewdness, old age hastens upon him. It was taught, R. Ishmael son of R. Jose said: As for scholars, the older they grow the more wisdom they acquire, for it is said, *With aged men is*
c *wisdom, and in length of days understanding.*[1] But the ignorant, as they wax older, become more foolish, for it is said, *He removeth the speech of the trusty, and taketh away the understanding of the elders.*[2]

Yea, they shall be afraid of that which is high[3]—even a small knoll looks to him like the highest of mountains; '*and terrors shall be in the way*'—when he walks on a road his heart is filled with fears;[4] '*and the almond tree shall blossom*'—that refers to the coccyx[5] '*and the grasshopper shall be a burden*'[6]—the rump; '*and desire shall fail*'—the passions. R. Kahana was expounding a portion [of scripture][7] before Rab. When he came to this verse, he [Rab] uttered a long sigh. This shows that Rab's desires have ceased, observed he. R. Kahana said: What is meant by, '*For He decreed, and it was*':[8] this refers to a woman;[9] '*He commanded; and it did stand*'—this refers to children. A Tanna taught: Though a woman be as a pitcher full of filth and her mouth be full of blood, yet all speed after her.

Because man goeth to his long home.[10] R. Isaac observed: This teaches that every righteous person is given a habitation as befits his honour. This may be compared to a king who enters a town together with his servants. They all enter through the same gate, [yet] when they spend the night [there] each is given a lodging as befits his honour.

R. Isaac also said: What means the verse, *For youth and the prime of life are vanity?*[11] The things a man does in his youth blacken his face[12] in his old age.[13]

R. Isaac also said: Worms are as painful to the dead as a needle in the flesh of the living, for it is said, *But his flesh upon him hath pain.*[14] R. Ḥisda said: A man's soul mourns for him [after death] seven
d whole [days], for it is said, *And his soul mourneth for him;*[1] and it is written, *and he made a mourning for his father seven days.*[2]

Rab Judah said: If there are none to be comforted for a dead person,[3] ten people go and sit in his place.[4] A certain man died in the neighbourhood of Rab Judah. As there were none to be

(7) I.e., fall apart and cannot enjoy the taste of food. (8) II Sam. XIX, 35. (9) They are hard of hearing.
c (1) Job XII, 12. (2) Ibid. 20. (3) Eccl. XII, 5. (4) Yalḳuṭ Koheleth 989 reads: it (the road) becomes for him full of terrors. (5) The lowest end of the vertebrae—the extreme weakness of old age causes it to 'blossom', i.e., protrude and be moved from its place. (6) Or, *shall drag itself along*. (7) פסיק סדרא, v. *supra* 116b, n. a1. (8) Ps. XXXIII, 9. (9) It is God's decree that man shall desire woman. (10) Eccl. XII, 5. (11) Ibid. XI, 10. (12) Rashi: weaken him, the reference being to sexual indulgence. The passage may also refer to actions in general for which one in old age feels himself blackened with shame. (13) He derives *shaḥaruth* (E.V. *prime of life*) from *shaḥor*, black, and translates: 'for youth and the blackening (of old age) are vanity'. (14) Job XIV, 22.
d (1) Job XIV, 22. (2) Gen. L, 10. (3) I.e., there are no mourners. Lit., 'a dead person for whom there are no comforters'. (4) Where he died, and engage in religious exercises such as prayer and study.

הורה אור

ושל בית הכסא רעות של סם ושל שחוק ושל פירות יפות °ביום שיזועו שומרי הבית והתעותו וגו׳ ביום שיזועו שומרי הבית אלו הכסלים והצלעות והתעותו אנשי החיל אלו שוקים ובטלו הטוחנות אלו שינים וחשכו הרואות בארובות אלו עינים א״ל קיסר לר׳ יהושע בן חנניה מ״ט לא אתית לבי אבידן א״ל טור תלג סחרוני גלידין כלבוהי לא נבחין טחנוהי לא טוחנין בי רב אמרי אדלא אבידנא בחישנא *תניא רבי יוסי בר קיסמא אומר טבא תרי מתלת ווי לה להדא דאזלא ולא אתיא מאי היא א״ר חסדא ינקותא כי אתא רב דימי אמר ינקותא כלילא דוורדא סבותא כלילא *דחילפא תנא משמיה דרבי מאיר דוק בככי ותשכח בניגרי שנאמר °ונשבע לחם ונהיה טובים ורעה לא ראינו א״ל שמואל לרב יהודה *שיננא שרי שקיך ועייל לדמך עד ארבעין שנין מיכלא מעלי מכאן ואילך משתי מעלי א״ל ההוא גוזאה לר׳ יהושע בן קרחה מהכא לקרחינא כמה הוי א״ל כמהכא לגוזניא א״ל צדוקי ברחא קרחא בארבעה אמר ליה *עיקרא שליפא בתמניא הזייה דלא סיים מסאניה א״ל דעל סוס מלך דעל חמור בן חורין ודמנעלי בריגלוהי בר איניש דלא הא ולא הא דחפיר וקביר טב מיניה א״ל גוזא גוזא תלת אמרת לי תלת שמעת הדרת פנים זקן שמחת לב אשה °נחלת ה׳ בנים ברוך המקום שמנעך מכולם א״ל קרחא מצויינא אמר ליה עיקרא שליפא תוכחה א״ל רבי לר׳ שמעון בן חלפתא מפני מה לא הקבלנו פניך ברגל כדרך שהקבילו אבותי לאבותיך א״ל סלעים נעשו גבוהים קרובים נעשו רחוקים משתים נעשו שלש משים שלום בבית בטל: °וסגרו דלתים בשוק וגו׳ אלו נקביו של אדם בשפל קול הטחנה בשביל קורקבן שאינו טוחן ויקום לקול הצפור שאפילו צפור מנערתו משנתו וישחו כל בנות השיר שאפילו (*קול שירים ושירות) דומות עליו כשוחה ואף ברזילי הגלעדי אמר לדוד °בן שמנים שנה אנכי היום האדע בין טוב לרע מכאן שדעותן של זקנים משתנות אם יטעם עבדך את אשר אוכל ואת אשר אשתה מכאן ששפתותיהן של זקנים מתרפטות אם אשמע עוד בקול שרים ושרות מכאן שאזניהם של זקנים מתכבדות אמר רב ברזילי הגלעדי שקרא הוה דההיא אמתא דהויא בי רבי בת תשעין ותרתין שנין והות טעמא קידרא רבא אמר ברזילי הגלעדי שטוף בזמה הוה *וכל השטוף בזמה *זקנה קופצת עליו תניא רבי ישמעאל ברבי יוסי אומר *תלמידי חכמים כל זמן שמזקינין חכמה נתוספת בהם שנאמר °בישישים חכמה ואורך ימים תבונה ועמי הארץ כל זמן שמזקינין טפשות נתוספת בהן שנאמר °מסיר שפה לנאמנים וטעם זקנים יקח גם מגבוה ייראו שאפילו גבשושית קטנה דומה עליו כהרי הרים וחתחתים בדרך בשעה שמהלך בדרך נעשו (א)לו*תוהים וינאץ *השקד זו קליבוסת ויסתבל החגב אלו עגבות ותפר האביונה זו חמדה רב כהנא הוה פסיק סידרא קמיה דרב כי מטא להאי קרא נגיד ואתנח אמר ש״מ בטל ליה המדיה דרב אמר רב כהנא מאי דכתיב °כי הוא אמר ויהי זו אשה הוא צוה ויעמוד אלו בנים תנא אשה חמת מלא צואה ופיה מלא דם והכל רצין אחריה °כי הולך האדם אל בית עולמו א״ר יצחק *מלמד שכל צדיק וצדיק נותנין לו מדור לפי כבודו משל למלך שנכנס הוא ועבדיו לעיר כשהן נכנסין כולן בשער אחד נכנסין כשהן לנין כל אחד ואחד נותנין לו מדור לפי כבודו ואמר רבי יצחק מאי דכתיב °כי הילדות והשחרות הבל דברים שאדם עושה בילדותו משחירים פניו לעת זקנתו *ואמר רבי יצחק קשה רימה למת כמחט בבשר החי שנאמר °אך בשרו עליו יכאב אמר רב חסדא נפשו של אדם מתאבלת עליו כל שבעה שנא׳ ונפשו עליו תאבל וכתיב °ויעש לאביו אבל שבעת ימים אמר רב יהודה מת שאין לו מנחמין הולכין י׳ בני אדם ויושבין במקומו ההוא דשכיב בשבבותיה דרב יהודה לא היו לו מנרמין כל

רש״י

של בית הכסא · מתוך יסורין : של פירות · כגון ריח חרדל : הכסלים. ליפלאנק״ש : והצלעות · שהן שומרין בני המעיים וחיותו של אדם וסוגרין בעדם : אלו שוקיים · שכחו של אדם נסמך עליהם : לבי אבידן · מקום העשוי להתווכח שם לדוקים ובייתוסים עם ישראל במקראות : טור תלג · ההר נעשה שלג כלומר ראשי לבן : סחרוני גלידין · סביבותיו של הר מלאו קרח כלומר שפמי וזקני הלבינו: כלבוהי לא נבחין · קולי אינו נשמע : טחנוהי · השינים : אדלא אבידנא בחישנא · אחר מה שלא אבד ממני אני מפשפש מרוב זקנה אני הולך שחוח ומנענע ונראה כמי שמבקש דיבר האבד לו : תרתי טבא מתלת · טובים ב׳ הרגלים של ימי בחרות מג׳ של זקנה שצריך משענת עם רגליו: ווי לה · חבל עליה כלומר יש לו להתאונן ולצעוק ווי ההולכת ואינה חוזרת : כלילא דוורדא · נזר של וורד : חילפי · אורטיא״ש : דוק בככי ותשכח בניגרי. אכול הרבה ותמלא האכילה בפסיעותיך שיחזק כחך דוק כמו אכלה מדקה (דניאל ז) לשון כוסס: שרי שקיך · פתח פיך : גוזא · סרים ולדוקי היה: מהכא לקרחינא כמה הוי· כמה מהלך יש מכאן עד הקרח ולהקניטו על קרחתו נתכוון : כמהכא לגוזניא · כמו שמכאן עד הסריס: אמר ליה לדוקי ברחא קרחא בארבעה · שהקרח לקוח בארבע · ברחא קרחא הוא עז על שם שאינו מלובש בצמר כרחל קרוי קרחא : אמר ליה · רבי יהושע : עיקרא שליפא · שה שביציו עקורים ונתוקין לוקחין בשמנה: חזייה· לדוקי לרבי יהושע דלא סיים מסאניה: קרחא מצויינא · אתה הקרח במריבה אתה באת עמדי בתמיה : אמר לו רבי יהושע עיקרא שליפא תוכחה · אתה הסריס להקניטני ולהתווכח עמי באת : לא הקבלנו פניך · לא הקבלת פני ודרך ענוה קאמר ליה : סלעים · קטנים נעשו גבוהים שזקנתי : קרובים · נדמין לי כרחוקים : שתים נעשו לי שלש · שצריך אני משענת: משים שלום בבית · אבר תשמיש : לישנא אחרינא קרובים נעשו רחוקים מרוב חלשות של אדם כשמזקין צריך להרחיק רגליו זה מזה : שאינו טוחן · שאין בני מעיו טוחנין אכילתו : קורקבן · הוא המסס שקורין ליינפי״ל: כל בנות השיר. כל קולות של שיר הויין ליה שוחה: שדעתן של זקנים משתנות· דכתיב האדע בין טוב לרע ובזקנה מרובה קאמר : מתרפטות · מתבקעות כמו מנעל המרופט (לעיל דף קמא:) : מתכבדות· כמו ואזניו הכבד (ישעיה ו) : שטוף · כמו סוס שוטף במלחמה (ירמיה ח) להוט אחר הדבר ורודף: וטעם זקנים יקח · וע״כ מדקשי קראי אהדדי חד מתוקם בחכמים וחד בזקני השוק : מגבוה ייראו · יראים הם הזקנים מגבשושית שבדרכים ואומרים גבוהים הם : תוהים · פחדים : וינאץ השקד. אילן של שקדים ילין ויהיו בולטין נניס שלו : זו קליבוסת · עצם של הנק״א שהירך תקוע בו בולט ויוצא מרוב תשות כחו : ויסתבל החגב · דומה עליו כסבל משא כבד: ותפר האביונה · הבטל התאוה המדת תשמיש : פסיק סידרא · מסדר פרשיות של פסוקים : נגיד ואיתנח · רב : המדיה · האותו : זו אשה · אם לא על פי גזרת המלך לא היתה ראויה להאוות לה שהיא כחמת מלאה מילום והכל רצים אחריה : מדור לפי כבודו · מדלא כתיב אל בית העולם ש״מ כל אחד ואחד לבית המוכן לו : בשער אחד . אף כאן הכל מתים בענין אחד: שאדם עושה בילדותו· רוב תשמיש: משחירים פניו· מתיש כחו: שאין לו מנחמים · אין לו אבלים שיהו צריכין לנחמו : במקומו · במקום שמת שם : כל

מח א מיי׳ פ״ד מהלכות דעות הל״ט טוש״ע או״ח סימן רמ סעיף יד :

מט ב מיי׳ פי״ג מהל׳ אבל הלכה ד סמג עשין ב טוש״ע יו״ד סי׳ שעו סעיף ג [וברב אלפס מו״ק פ״ג דל״ז.] וברא״ש שם סימן פ״ט :

קהלת יב · [פס׳ ד״ה זוטא פ״י] · [פי׳ תיני ומשונים ערוך] · ירמיה מד · [נ״ל איקא עי׳ בערוך] · תהלים קכז

[לעיל נה. ברכות לו. עירובין נד. חגיגה טו: ר״ה כז: כתובות יג: יד. נג. קדושין לב. גיטין עח. ב״ק יד. טז: לו: ב״ב קנג: ע״ז מג: סנהדרין קו: כריתות יב: נדה יג. יז. כה:]

הגהות הב״ח

(א) גמ׳ נעשה לו תוהים תוהים וינאץ השקד :

קהלת יב · [נ״ל קול שרים ושרות] · שמואל ב יט · [תענית ה:] · [קנים פ״ג מ״ג ע״ש ובמפרש] · איוב יב · שם · [תרגום כל ויחרך ויתוש ערוך] · עי׳ מ״ר ויקרא פ׳ י״ח · תהלים לג · קהלת יב · [ב״מ פג:] · קהלת יא · ברכות יח: לעיל יג: נדרים ג · איוב יד

רבינו חננאל

השבת לפי שבטל מן המצות והיינו דא״ר יוחנן מאי דכתיב במתים חפשי כיון שמת אדם נעשה חפשי מן המצות : א״ל קיסר לר׳ יהושע מ״ט לא אתית לבי אבידן. פי׳ בי אבידן בית שמתקבצין שם החכמים ונושאין ונותנין בדיני כל אומה ולשון השיבו ר׳ יהושע טור תלג סחרנוהי גלידין כלבוהי לא נבהין טחנוהי לא טחנן בבי רב אמרי (או לא או דן פי׳ בו) [אדלא אבדן בהשנא] ופירושו ההר כסהו שלג ודומה האדם להר כלומר ראשו כיסתו השיבה . וסביבותיה שהן הלחיים נעשו גלידין והוא הקרח שנקרא גליד . והגרון והלשון אינן מריסין קול . ככי שהן השניים אינן טוחנין המאכל . אדלא אבדן בחשנא . כלומר הזקן שאינו מביט מה שבפניו מתיירא שמא יכה ראשו באבן או בכיוצא בה וממשש בידו ונראה כאלו ממשש בדבר שאבד לו וזהו כמין משל ממשש הזקן מה שלא אבד . טבי תרי מתלת. פי׳ יותר הוא טוב המהלך על ב׳ רגליו מן הזקן שצריך משען כגון מקל אי שבט להישען עליו והוא כמו רגל שלישי. חבל על דאזלא ולא אתיא . פי׳ הבהרות הולכת כשמזקין האדם ואינה חוזרת אליו . ינקותא כלילא דוורדי . הבדרות כתר של וורד ריחו נודף ושל זקנה כתר של חילף שריחו מאוס. דוק בככי ותשכח בנגרי. טחון בככי בשניים כלומר אכול כדי שיהיה לך כח להלך ברגליך. א״ל ההוא גוזא התוך (הערוה) [הביצים] והוא סרים א״ל ר׳ יהושע בן קרחה מהכא לקרדוניא כמה. ביקש להודיעו שהוא קרח והן ביר לו דברים כבלעיג והשיבו ר׳ יהושע כמו הבא לגזוניא כלומר אתה גזוי. עוד אמר ליה ברהא קרחא בארבע. פי׳ (או)[עור] כבש גדול בד׳ כספים. השיבו ר׳ יהושע הדברים מוכיחין שגם אלו דברי הסרים הם שבקשו להודיעו כי השלוף ביוקר יותר מן הקרח . ילמדנו רבינו איקא שליפא בתבניא . פי׳ עור תיש נתוק ביצים בשמונה כספים . שמבקשין אותו לעשותו נודות של שמן . חזייה דלא מסיים מסאניה . פירוש ראהו יחף כו׳ . א״ל קרחה מצוי. פי׳ קרחה מריבה סחרחר . כדכתיב הן לריב ומצה וגו׳ השיבו ר׳ יהושע תיש נתוק תוכחה אינם דברי ריב אלא דברי תוכחה . מפני מה לא הקבלנו פניך . למה לא באת אלינו להתראות פנים: מיכן ששפתותיהן של זקנים מתרפטות. פי׳ מתרפטות משתרבבות והוא מתרופפות אינם מתאמצות להסתם הפה בחזקה . גבשושית פי׳ גב קטן של עפר . קליבוסת פירוש מן הפקוקלות ומפורש באלו מרפות . תרבא דאקליבוסתא . יתפר האביונה. זו חמדה (כמו) [כי] בטלה ממנו תאות אשה. פי׳ טלוניתא כמו על שאין בה ממש . נשיה שם ידו עליו מלשון נגששה :

רב נסים גאון

אמר ליה סלעים נעשין גבוהים כמו שנאמר אח״כ שאפילו גבשושית קטנה דומה עליו כהרי הרים ושאר הענין פירשוהו במקצת ההגדה וכך אמרו רחוקים נעשו קרובים אילין עיניא דהוון חמיאן מרחוק אף מקרוב ליתנון המאן קרובים נעשו רחוקים אילין אודניא דהוון שמעין בחד זמן כדו אף במאה זימנין ליתנון שמעין ב׳ נעשו ג׳ חוטרא ותרין ריגליא משים שלום בבית בטל זו תאוה שהיא מעלה שלום

כל יומא הוה דבר רב יהודה בי עשרה ויתבי בדוכתיה לאחר שבעה ימים איתחזי ליה בחילמיה דרב יהודה ואמר ליה *תנוח דעתך שהנחת את דעתי א"ר אבהו ׳כל שאומרים בפני המת יודע עד שיסתם הגולל פליגי בה רבי חייא ור"ש ברבי חד אמר עד שיסתם הגולל וחד אמר עד שיתעכל הבשר מאן דאמר עד שיתעכל הבשר דכתיב °אך בשרו עליו יכאב ונפשו עליו תאבל מאן דאמר עד שיסתם הגולל דכתיב °וישוב העפר על הארץ כשהיה וגו' ת"ר °והרוח תשוב אל האלהים אשר נתנה תנה לו כמו שנתנה לך בטהרה אף אתה בטהרה משל למלך ב"ו שחלק בגדי מלכות לעבדיו פקחין שבהן קיפלום והניחום בקופסא טפשים שבהן הלכו ועשו בהן מלאכה לימים ביקש המלך את כליו פקחין שבהן החזירום לו כשהן מגוהצין טפשין שבהן החזירום לו כשהן מלוכלכין שמח המלך לקראת פקחין וכעס לקראת טפשין על פקחין אמר ינתנו כלי לאוצר והם ילכו לבתיהם לשלום ועל טפשין אמר כלי ינתנו לכובס והן יתחבשו בבית האסורים אף הקב"ה על גופן של צדיקים אומר °יבא שלום ינוחו על משכבותם ועל נשמתן הוא אומר °והיתה נפש אדוני צרורה בצרור החיים* על גופן של רשעים הוא אומר° °אין שלום אמר ה' לרשעים ועל נשמתן הוא אומר °ואת נפש אויביך יקלענה בתוך כף הקלע תניא ר' אליעזר אומר נשמתן של צדיקים גנוזות תחת כסא הכבוד שנאמר והיתה נפש אדני צרורה בצרור החיים ושל רשעים *זוממות והולכות [*ומלאך אחד עומד בסוף העולם ומלאך אחר עומד בסוף העולם ומקלעין נשמתן זה לזה] שנא' ואת נפש אויביך יקלענה בתוך כף הקלע א"ל רבה לר"נ של בינונים מאי א"ל *איכא (א) שכיבנא לא אמרי לכו האי מילתא הכי אמר שמואל אלו ואלו לדומה נמסרין הללו יש להן מנוח הללו אין להן מנוח אמר (ליה) רב מרי עתידים צדיקים דהוו עפרא דכתיב °וישוב העפר על הארץ כשהיה הנהו קפולאי דהוו קפלי בארעא דרב נחמן *) נחר בהו רב אחאי בר יאשיה אתו ואמרו ליה לרב נחמן נחר בן גברא אתא ואמר ליה מאן נינהו מר אמר ליה אנא אחאי בר יאשיה א"ל ולאו אמר רב מרי עתידי צדיקי דהוו עפרא א"ל ומני מרי דלא ידענא ליה א"ל והא קרא כתיב וישוב העפר על הארץ כשהיה אמר ליה דאקרייך קהלת לא אקרייך משלי דכתיב °ורקב עצמות קנאה °כל מי שיש לו קנאה בלבו עצמותיו מרקיבים כל שאין לו קנאה בלבו אין עצמותיו מרקיבים גששיה חזייה דאית ביה מששא אמר ליה ליקום מר לגוויה דביתא אמר ליה גלית אדעתך דאפילו נביאי לא קרית דכתיב °וידעתם כי אני ה' בפתחי *את קברותיכם א"ל והכתיב °כי עפר אתה ואל עפר תשוב א"ל ההוא שעה אחת קודם תחיית המתים א"ל ההוא צדוקי לר' אבהו אמריתו נשמתן של צדיקים גנוזות תחת כסא הכבוד אובא טמיא היכא אסקיה לשמואל *בנגידא א"ל התם בתוך שנים עשר חדש הוה דתניא כל י"ב חדש גופו קיים ונשמתו עולה ויורדת לאחר י"ב חדש הגוף בטל ונשמתו

*) [עי' פירושו ברש"י גיטין סח. ד"ה נחר]

מקורות: איוב יד · קהלת יב · שם · ישעיה נז · ש"א כה · ישעיה מח · שמואל א כה · [קהלת יב] · משלי יד · יחזקאל לז · בראשית ג

רש"י

כל יומא · ז' ימי אבילות : גולל · הוא כיסוי שנותנים על ארונו : ונפשו עליו תאבל · כל זמן שיש לו בשר יש לו לנפש לד חיות להבין : וישוב העפר · גופו קרוי עפר ומשב אל הארץ כשהיה מיד והרוח תשוב שאין בו רוח עוד : אשר נתנה · קרא יתירה הוא לידרש הוי זהיר שתשיבנה אליו כמה שנתנה לך נקייה בלי עון : כלי ינתנו לאוצר · להגניזן אף זו תינתן תחת כסא הכבוד : לכובס · ללבנן אף זו לגיהנם לצורפם שם : בבית האסורים · בחשך בלא אורה ושלוה: כף הקלע· רחב הרצועה שנותן האבן לתוכה לקלע עשויה כעין כף: בצרור החיים וגו'· את ה' אלהיך עמו בכסאו : זוממות · כמו בזממא דפרזלא (לעיל דף נא:) חבושות בבית הסוהר : אלו ואלו · רשעים ובינונים : לדומה · מלאך הממונה על הרוחות : דהוו עפרא · אפילו צדיקים נרקבים ונעשים אפר : קפולאי · חופרים : נחר בהו (ב) רבי אחאי · שהיה נקבר שם : דלא ידענא ליה · ואיני חש לדבריו : מי שיש לו קנאה · ותחרות על חברו : עצמותיו מרקיבים · ועליו נאמר וישוב אל העפר : ליקום מר לגוויה · (ג) יבא אדוני לבית : בפתחי · בהעלותי עד שיעלנו הקדוש ברוך הוא מקברותינו אין לנו רשות לעלות : והא כתיב ואל עפר תשוב · והאי ליכא למימר ברשעים לחודייהו דכל קללותיו של אדה"ר כל דורותיו שוין בהן : אובא טמיא · בעלת אוב שמשתמש בעצמות טמיא בלשון ארמי עצמות וכן פירש רב האי בפירושו של טהרות בית שהוא מלא טמיא מלא עצמות* : בנגידא · כן קורין למכשפות של אוב בלשון ארמי : אס

תוספות

עד שיסתם הגולל · בכל מקום מפרש רש"י דגולל הוא כיסוי ארונו של מת ודופק דף שנתון מלידו ונקרא דופק על שם שהמת דופק שם כמו חתיכה גופה תיהוי סימן אי דאדפקא אי דאטמא בפרק אלו מציאות (ב"מ דף כג:) שנקרא דופק לפי שהגשימה דופקת ואין נראה לר"ת מדאמר בברכות פרק מי שמתו (דף יט: ושם) מדלגים היינו ע"ג ארונות לקראת מלכי אומות העולם ואי ארון היינו גולל ודופק היאך היו מדלגין עליו והלא גולל ודופק מטמאין באהל כדאמר בחולין בפרק העור והרוטב (דף קכו:) גולל ודופק מטמא במגע ובאהל ואינו מטמא במשא ועוד דאמר בעירובין (דף מו:) כל דבר שיש בו רוח חיים אין עושין אותו לא גולל לקבר ולא דופן לסוכה ולא לחי למבוי ואי כפי' הקונט' וכי דרך לעשות כיסוי ארון מבעלי חיים ועוד בפרק בהמה המקשה (חולין עב·) מרבינן (ד) דופק דמטמא מדכתיב על פני השדה ולפי' הקונטרס הוא מונח בקרקע דהיינו ארון ולא על פני השדה ועוד דתנן במס' אהלות בפ"ב (משנה ד) דופק דופקים טהור ואי כפירוש הקונטרס וכי דרך להניח שני קרשים מימין המת ופירש ר"ת דגולל היינו אבן גדולה שעל ארונו של מת שקורין מצבה וגוללין אותה שם הקרובי' לסימן ולשון גולל נופל באבן כדכתיב (בראשית כט) וגללו את האבן וגולל אבן אליו תשוב (מש' כו) ודופק הם שתי אבני' שנותנין (ה) אחת לראשו ואחת לרגליו לציון ופעמים שעדיין האבן אינה מוכנת לשום שם נותנין שם בהמה או שום דבר לסימן עד שימצאו אבן והיינו דתנן בעירובין (דף טו·) דדבר שיש בו רוח חיים אין עושין כו' ובההיא דמדלגין היינו ע"ג ארונות שלא היה שם לא גולל ולא דופק ומאהל המת לא היינו מיטמאים כדמפרש התם שהיה ברוב ארונות (ו) חלל טפח ומרבי נמי שפיר גולל ודופק מעל פני השדה והא דקאמר דופק דופקים פעמים שמניחים הגולל ע"ג שתי אבנים ועוד מניחין לראש הגולל אבן אחת ולסופו אבן אחרת ולא תקשה לר' יהושע דאמר בפרק קמא דכתובות (דף ד: ושם) מאימתי חל אבילות משיסתם הגולל במקום שאין גולל מתי חל די"ל מכי אהדרי אפייהו מקברא כדאמר במו"ק (ד' כב·) בהגהו דלא אזלי בתר .שכבא מנו מכי אהדרי אפייהו ויש דוחין ראיה של ר"ת דמאי דמייתי ראיה מדמדלגין היינו אף על פי שהגולל מטמא באהל מ"מ יכולין היינו לדלג ולטמא עצמנו בגולל דהא תניא א) כל טומאה שאין הנזיר מגלח עליה אין כהן מוזהר עליו וגולל ודופק אין הנזיר מגלח עלייהו כדתנן במסכת נזיר פרק כ"ג (דף נד.) ואמר ר"ת דמשבשתא ההיא דמסכת שמחות דהא הש"ס ערוך דרביעית דם אין הנזיר מגלח עליו כדתנן התם בנזיר *וכהן מוזהר ואם הברייתא בהש"ס הוה פריך עלה ומשבש לה כדאשכחינן בכמה דוכתין דמשבש להו ואפילו הויא מתרצתא אכתי היאך מדלגין הלא מחמת המת היו מיטמאים והגולל ודופק לא היו חוצצין ומה שהביא ראיה מעירובין יש דוחין דאע"פ שאין רגילות לעשות כסוי ארון מבעלי חיים כמה דברים אשכחן דלא שכיחי ומיירי בהו הש"ס להראות לנו הדין ודרוש וקבל שכר כדאמרי' בבהמה המקשה (חולין דף ע.) בלעתו חולדה והוליאתו והכניסתו והקיאתו ויצא מאליו מהו הדביק שני רחמים ויצא מזה ונכנס לזה מהו ואף על פי שזה לא יהיה לעולם ועוד מקשין לפירוש ר"ת מדתני בהדיא בתוספתא דאהלות בפרק אמר רבי יהודה שתי אבנים גדולות שעשאן גולל לקבר המאהיל על גבי שתיהן טמא ניטלה אחת מהן המאהיל על גבי שנייה טהור מפני שיש לטומאה דרך שתצא ומה דרך שתצא שייך לפירוש ר"ת ובערוך פירש בענין אחר בערך גלל וכפירושו יתכן מה שבתוספתא* :

א) [במס' שמחות פ"ד הל' כ"א ע"ש]

עין משפט נר מצוה

נ א סמג עשין דרבנן ב :

רב נסים גאון

שלום בין איש לאשתו אלו ואלו נמסרין לדומה הללו יש להן מנוח והללו אין להן מנוח. בפרק כל ישראל יש להם חלק (סנהדרין דף לד) גרסינן א"ר יוחנן אותו מלאך שהוא ממונה על הרוחות דומה שמו וכבר הזכרנו אותו בברכות :

סליק שואל אדם

גליון הש"ס

גמ' על גופן של רשעים הוא אומר אין שלום אמר אלהי כצ"ל : שם כל מי שיש לו קנאה בלבו . עי' ב"ב דף יז ע"א תוס' ד"ה שבעה :

[נ"ל את ה' אלהיך על כו']

זוממות והולכות שנאמר ואת נפש כו' פי' דדייק מדלא אמרה יקלענה בכף הקלע ואמר בתוך כף הקלע משמע שהיא חבושה זכבושה בתוך כף הקלע ואינה יוצאת ממנו ומלאך ממלאכי הבלה מקלע אותה רצועה לכאן ולכאן וזהו לשון זוממות

[נ"ל את קברותיכם ובהעלותי אתכם מקברותיכם עמי וכ"א בע"י ובזה תבין פרש"י ד"ה בפתחי בהעלותי עד שיעלנו וכו']

מסורת הש"ס

[פסחים לב: יומא סו: סנהדרין לז: מנחות מה. ק.]

הגהות הב"ח

(א) גמ' איכא שכיבנא. נ"ב כלומר אי שכיבנא : (ב) רש"י ד"ה נחר בהו נער בהו רבי אחאי: (ג) ד"ה ליקום מר לגויה דביתא יבא : (ד) תוס' ד"ה עד שיסתום וכו' מרבינן גולל ודופק דמטמא : (ה) בא"ד שנותנין אחת לראשו. נ"ב פי' לראשו ולרגליו של גולל וכן הוא בתוספות פ"ק דכתובות דף ד' וע"ש בפרק מי שמתו בדף יט : (ו) בא"ד ברוב ארונות שהגהס חלל טפח :

ראה רש"י ברכות נט. ד"ה אובא

שמואל א כה

גי' רש"ל לא משמע כן מפי' רש"י שפי' שהן חבושין וגי' זו אין חבושי' ואולי מלא גי' כזו אבל גי' רש"י אינו כן מ"כ

[דף מד.]

[ערוך ערך בנגידא פי' בכישוף]

[וע"ש תוספות ברכות יט: ד"ה מדלגין ותוס' סוכה כג. ד"ה ולא ותוס' כתובות ד: ד"ה עד ותוס' סנהדרין מז : ד"ה משיסתום]

comforted, [152b] Rab Judah assembled ten men every day and they sat in his place. After seven days he [the dead man] appeared to him in a dream and said to him, 'Thy mind be at rest, for thou hast set my mind at rest.' R. Abbahu said: The dead man knows all that is said in his presence until the top-stone [*golel*] closes [the grave].[5] R. Ḥiyya and R. Simeon b. Rabbi differ therein: one maintains, until the top-stone closes [the grave]; whilst the other says, until the flesh rots away. He who says, until the flesh rots away,—because it is written, *But his flesh upon him hath pain and his soul within him mourneth.*[6] He who says, until the top-stone closes [the grave],—because it is written, *and the dust return to the earth as it was [and the spirit return unto God]*.[7]

Our Rabbis taught: [*'And the dust return to the earth as it was*], *and the spirit return unto God who gave it'*: Render it back to him as He gave it to thee, [viz.,] in purity, so do thou [return it] in purity. This may be compared to a mortal king[8] who distributed royal apparel to his servants. The wise among them folded it up and laid it away in a chest, whereas the fools among them went and did their work in them. After a time the king demanded his garments: the wise among them returned them to him immaculate, [but] the fools among them returned them soiled. The king was pleased with the wise but angry with the fools. Of the wise he said, 'Let my robes be placed in my treasury and they can go home in peace'; while of the fools he said, 'Let my robes be given to the fuller, and let them be confined in prison.' Thus too, with the Holy One, blessed be He: concerning the bodies of the right-
a eous He says, *He entereth into peace, they rest in their beds;*[1] while concerning their souls He says, *yet the soul of my lord shall be bound up in the bundle of life with the Lord thy God.*[2] But concerning the bodies of the wicked He says, *There is no peace saith the Lord, unto the wicked;*[3] while concerning their souls He says, *and the souls of thine enemies, them shall he sling out, as from the hollow of a sling.*[4]

It was taught, R. Eliezer said: The souls of the righteous are hidden under the Throne of Glory, as it is said, *yet the soul of my lord shall be bound up in the bundle of life.*[4] But those of the wicked continue to be imprisoned,[5] while one angel stands at one end of the world and a second stands at the other end, and they sling their souls to each other, for it is said, *and the souls of thine enemies, them shall he sling out, as from the hollow of a sling.* Rabbah asked R. Naḥman: What about those who are intermediate? Had I died I could not have told you this, he replied. Thus did Samuel say: Both these and those [the wicked and the intermediate] are delivered to Dumah;[6] these enjoy rest, whereas the others have no rest. R. Mari said: [Even] the righteous are fated to be dust, for it is written, *'and the dust return to the earth as it was'*. Certain diggers were digging in R. Naḥman's ground, [when] R. Aḥai b. Josiah[7] snorted at them. So they went and told R. Naḥman, 'A man snorted at us.' He went and asked him, 'Who are you?' 'I am Aḥai b. Josiah.' 'But did not R. Mari say, [Even] the righteous are fated to be dust?' said he. 'But who is Mari,' he retorted—'I do not know him.' Yet surely a verse is written, *'and the dust returns to the earth as it was'?* he urged. 'He who taught you Ecclesiastes did not teach you Proverbs,' he answered, 'for it is written,
b *But envy is the rottenness of the bones:*[1] he who has envy in his heart, his bones rot away, [but] he who has no envy in his heart, his bones do not rot away.' He then felt him and perceived that there was substance in him. 'Let my master arise [and come] to my house,' he invited him. 'You have thus disclosed that you have not even studied the prophets, for it is written, *And ye shall know that I am the Lord, when I open your graves,'*[2] said he to him, 'But it is written, *for dust art thou, and unto dust thou shalt return?'*[3] 'That means one hour before the resurrection of the dead', replied he.

A certain Sadducee said to R. Abbahu:[4] You maintain that the souls of the righteous are hidden under the Throne of Glory: then how did the bone [-practising] necromancer bring up Samuel by means of his necromancy?[5]—There it was within twelve months [of death], he replied. For it was taught: For full [twelve months] the body is in existence and the soul ascends and descends;

(5) R. Tam. Rashi: until the coffin-lid is closed, v. Nazir, 54*a*, n. b5. (6) I.e., he suffers pain and grief—a sign of consciousness—as long as his flesh is upon him. (7) Eccl. XII, 7. I.e., immediately the dust—*sc.* the body—returns to the earth, the spirit returns to God, and there is no further consciousness of earthly matters. (8) Lit., 'a king of flesh and blood'.

a (1) Isa. LVII, 2. (2) I Sam. XXV, 29. (3) Isa. XLVIII, 22. (4) I Sam. ibid. (5) Lit., 'muzzled'. Marginal translation: are eternally pressed down—*sc.* in the sling of destruction. (6) The guardian angel of the deceased. [The name is probably Silence, which is the meaning of Dumah, personified.] (7) Who was buried there.

b (1) Prov. XIV, 30. (2) Ezek. XXXVII, 13; i.e., God alone can free men from their graves. (3) Gen. III, 19. (4) MS.M. *min* (v. Glos.). This is preferable as there were no Sadducees in the time of R. Abbahu; cf. Sanh., 91*a*, n. 8. (5) V. I Sam. XXVIII, 7. Bones were used in necromancy.

after twelve months the body ceases to exist [153a] and the soul ascends but descends nevermore.

Rab Judah son of R. Samuel b. Shila said in Rab's name: From the funeral eulogy pronounced over a man it may be known whether the future world is his or not.[6] But that is not so? for Rab said to R. Samuel b. Shilath, 'Be fervent in my funeral eulogy, for I will be standing there'?[7]—There is no difficulty: in the one case a fervent lament is pronounced and one is deeply moved,[8] in the other a fervent lament is pronounced and one is not moved. Abaye asked Rabbah: 'You, for instance, whom the whole of the Pumbeditheans hate,[9] who will arouse lamentation for you?' 'You and Rabbah b. R. Ḥanan will suffice,' he replied.

R. Eleazar asked Rab: Which man has earned [enjoyment of] the future world? Said he to him, *And thine ears shall hear a word behind thee, saying, This is the way, walk ye in it; when ye turn to the right hand, and when ye turn to the left.*[1] R. Ḥanina said: He with whom his teachers are pleased.[2]

And the mourners go about the streets.[3] The Galileans said: Perform actions [which shall be lamented] in front of thy bier; the Judaeans said: Perform actions [to be lamented] behind thy bier. But they do not differ: each [spoke] in accordance with [the usage in] his locality.[4]

We learnt elsewhere, R. Eliezer said: Repent one day before your death.[5] His disciples asked him, Does then one know on what day he will die? Then all the more reason that he repent to-day, he replied, lest he die to-morrow, and thus his whole life is spent in repentance. And Solomon too said in his wisdom, *Let thy garments be always white; and let not thy head lack ointment.*[6] R. Joḥanan b. Zakkai said: This may be compared to a king who summoned his servants to a banquet without appointing a time. The wise ones adorned themselves and sat at the door of the palace, ['for,'] said they, 'is anything lacking in a royal palace?'[7] The fools went about their work, saying, 'can there be a banquet without preparations'?[8] Suddenly the king desired [the presence of] his servants: the wise entered adorned, while the fools entered soiled. The king rejoiced at the wise but was angry with the fools. 'Those who adorned themselves for the banquet,' ordered he, 'let them sit, eat and drink. But those who did not adorn themselves for the banquet, let them stand and watch.' R. Meir's son-in-law said in R. Meir's name: Then they too would [merely] look as being in attendance.[9] But both sit, the former eating and the latter hungering, the former drinking and the latter thirsting, for it is said, *Therefore thus saith the Lord God, Behold, My servants shall eat, but ye shall be hungry: behold, My servants shall drink, but ye shall be thirsty:* [*behold, My servants shall rejoice, but ye shall be ashamed:*] *behold, My servants shall sing for joy of heart, but ye shall cry for sorrow of heart.*[1] Another interpretation: '*Let thy garments be always white*'—this refers to fringes; '*and let not thy head lack ointment*'—to *tefillin*.

CHAPTER XXIV

MISHNAH. SHOULD DARKNESS FALL UPON A PERSON
c ON A ROAD,[1] HE ENTRUSTS HIS PURSE TO A GENTILE;[2] BUT IF THERE IS NO GENTILE WITH HIM, HE PLACES IT ON THE ASS. WHEN HE REACHES THE OUTERMOST COURTYARD[3] HE REMOVES THE OBJECTS WHICH MAY BE HANDLED ON THE SABBATH, WHILST AS FOR THOSE WHICH MAY NOT BE HANDLED ON THE SABBATH, HE UNTIES THE CORDS[4] AND THE SACKS FALL OFF AUTOMATICALLY.

GEMARA. Why did the Rabbis permit him to entrust his purse to a Gentile?[5]—The Rabbis knew for certain[6] that no man will restrain himself where his money is concerned; if you do not permit it to him, he will come to carry it four cubits in public ground.

Raba said: *His* purse only, but not something found. That is obvious, [for] we learnt HIS PURSE?—You might say, The same law applies even to a find, and why does he mention HIS PURSE—as a natural course:[7] therefore he informs us [that it is not so]. Yet we said this only where it did not come into his possession [before the Sabbath], but if it came into his possession, it is the same as his purse. Others state, Raba asked: What about a find that came into his possession [before nightfall]? since it came into this possession, it is the same as his purse; or perhaps since he had no trouble over it, it is not the same as his purse?—The question stands over.

IF THERE IS NO GENTILE WITH HIM, [etc.]. The reason is that there is no Gentile with him, but if there is a Gentile with him he
d must give it to him:[1] what is the reason?—As for an ass, you are under an obligation that it should rest;[2] but as for a Gentile, you are under no obligation [to ensure] that he should rest.

[If there is] an ass, and a deaf-mute, imbecile, or minor:[3] he must place it on the ass and not give it to the deaf-mute, imbecile or minor. What is the reason? The latter are human beings whereas the former is not. [In the case of] a deaf-mute and an imbecile: [he must give it] to the imbecile; [in the case of] an imbecile and a minor—to the imbecile. The scholars asked: What of a deaf-mute and a minor? On R. Eliezer's view there is no question, for it was taught: R. Isaac said in R. Eliezer's

(6) If it arouses widespread grief he must have been a good man who earned the enjoyment of the future world. (7) When it is pronounced. But if he felt certain that a funeral lament for a good man is spontaneously fervent and deep, what need of exhortation? (8) Lit., 'warmed'. (9) Rashi: because of his outspokenness, v. Ḥul. 127a.

(1) Isa. XXX, 21. I.e., if one hears a voice proclaiming thus after his death, he has earned the world to come. (2) Var. lec. our teachers. (3) Eccl. XII, 5. (4) In Galilee the professional mourners walked in front of the bier, in Judah behind. (5) A similar thought is expressed in the Book of Ben Sira, V, 8.

(6) Eccl. IX, 8. (7) The summons to enter may come at any moment. (8) Lit., 'trouble'. (9) Their punishment would not be so great.

b (1) Isa. LXV, 13f.

c (1) The Sabbath commences. (2) V. *supra* 17b. (3) Of the first town where he arrives. (4) Whereby they are fastened to the saddle. (5) Though that is tantamount to instructing the Gentile to carry it for him, which is forbidden. (6) Lit., 'it was established to the Rabbis'. (7) Finds are rare.

d (1) In preference. (2) V. Ex. XX, 10 (3) These three are frequently linked together as being the same in law.

ונשמתו עולה ושוב אינה יורדת אמר רב יהודה בריה דרב שמואל בר* שילת משמיה דרב מהספדו של אדם ניכר אם בן העוה"ב הוא אם לאו איני והאמר ליה רב לרב שמואל בר שילת אחים בהספידא דהתם קאימנא לא קשיא הא דמחמו ליה ואחים הא דמחמו ליה ולא אחים א"ל אביי לרבה כגון מר דסנו ליה כולהו פומבדיתאי מאן אחים הספידא א"ל מיסתיא את ורבה בר רב חנן בעא מניה רבי אלעזר מרב איזהו בן העוה"ב א"ל °ואזניך תשמענה דבר מאחריך לאמר זה הדרך לכו בו כי תאמינו וכי תשמאילו ר' חנינא אמר כל שדעת *רבותינו נוחה הימנו °וסבבו בשוק הסופדים °בני גלילא אמרי עשה דברים לפני מטתך בני יהודה אמרי עשה דברים לאחר מטתך ולא פליגי *מר כי אתריה ומר כי אתריה תנן התם רבי אליעזר אומר* ‏שוב יום אחד לפני מיתתך שאלו תלמידיו את ר"א וכי אדם יודע איזהו יום ימות אמר להן וכל שכן ישוב היום שמא ימות למחר ונמצא כל ימיו בתשובה ואף שלמה אמר בחכמתו °בכל עת יהיו בגדיך לבנים ושמן על ראשך אל יחסר א"ר יוחנן בן זכאי משל למלך שזימן את עבדיו לסעודה ולא קבע להם זמן פיקחין שבהן קישטו את עצמן וישבו על פתח בית המלך אמרו כלום חסר לבית המלך טיפשין שבהן הלכו למלאכתן אמרו כלום יש סעודה בלא טורח בפתאום ביקש המלך את עבדיו פיקחין שבהן נכנסו לפניו כשהן מקושטין והטיפשים נכנסו לפניו כשהן מלוכלכין שמח המלך לקראת פיקחים וכעס לקראת טיפשים אמר הללו שקישטו את עצמן לסעודה ישבו ויאכלו וישתו הללו שלא קישטו עצמן לסעודה יעמדו ויראו חתנו של ר"מ משום ר"מ אמר אף הן נראין כמשמשין אלא אלו ואלו יושבין הללו אוכלין והללו רעבין הללו שותין והללו צמאים שנאמר(א) °כה אמר ה' הנה עבדי יאכלו ואתם תרעבו הנה עבדי ישתו ואתם תצמאו הנה עבדי ירונו מטוב לב ואתם תצעקו מכאב לב ד"א בכל עת יהיו בגדיך לבנים אלו ציצית ושמן על ראשך אל יחסר אלו תפילין:

הדרן עלך שואל

*מי ‏שהחשיך(ה) בדרך נותן כיסו לנכרי ‏ואם אין עמו נכרי מניחו על החמור ‏הגיע לחצר החיצונה נוטל את הכלים הניטלין בשבת ושאינן ניטלין בשבת מתיר החבלים והשקין נופלין מאיליהם: **גמ'** מאי טעמא שרו ליה רבנן למיתב כיסיה לנכרי קים להו לרבנן ‏דאין אדם מעמיד עצמו על ממונו אי לא שרית ליה אתי לאיתויי ד' אמות ברה"ר אמר רבא ‏דוקא כיסו אבל מציאה לא פשיטא כיסו תנן מהו דתימא הוא הדין אפילו מציאה והאי דקתני כיסו אורחא דמילתא קתני קמ"ל ולא אמרן אלא ‏דלא אתי לידיה אבל אתי לידיה ככיסיה דמי איכא דאמרי בעי רבא מציאה הבאה לידו מהו כיון דאתא לידיה ככיסיה דמי או דילמא כיון דלא טרח בה לאו ככיסיה דמי תיקו: אין עמו נכרי: טעמא דאין עמו נכרי הא יש עמו נכרי לנכרי יהיב ליה מאי טעמא ‏חמור אתה מצווה על שביתתו נכרי אי אתה מצווה על שביתתו חמור. וחרש שוטה וקטן °אחמור מנח ליה לחרש שוטה וקטן לא יהיב ליה מ"ט הני אדם האי לאו אדם ‏חרש ושוטה לשוטה ‏שוטה וקטן לשוטה איבעיא להו ‏חרש וקטן מאי אליבא דר"א לא תיבעי לך דתניא *ר' יצחק אומר משום ר' *)אליעזר תרומת חרש לא

*) [ס"א אלעזר]

רש"י

אם בן עוה"ב הוא · שאם כשר היה הכל בוכין עליו ומורידין דמעות ומספידים שבחו: אחים בהספידא דהתם קאימנא · בשעת מיתתי התאמץ בהספד שלי שיתחממו ויכמרו רחמי העומדים ויבכו: דהתם קאימנא · בשעת הספד ואשמע איך תתחמם אלמא אילטריך לרב לאזהוריה אהספדא וכיון דרב גברא רבה ובן העולם הבא למה ליה לאזהוריה הא אמר מהספידו ניכר: הא דמחממין ליה · להספידא ואחים כו' לעולם חמומי בעי שאין בני אדם נכמרים כל כך על זקן ומיהו לאדם חסיד כי מחממו בהספידא מחממי ובכו כולהו ולמי שאינו חסיד כל כך מחממו ליה ולא מחממו: דסנו ליה כולהו פומבדיתאי · משום דמוכח להו במילי דשמיא(ב) ובני פומבדיתאי רמאין הן כדאמרינן בשחיטת חולין (חולין קכז·) פומבדיתאי לוייך שני אושפיזך: ואזניך תשמענה דבר מאחריך לאמר זה הדרך לכו בה · מאחרי מטתך כשתמות תשמע כשיאמרו זה הדרך שהלך בה זה לכו בה מובטח שהוא בן העוה"ב: נוחה הימנו · דעתם נוחה עליהם ממה ששומעין עליו ורואין בו: עשה דברים · שיאמרו לפני מטתך בהספדך: לאחר מטתך · היא היא אלא שבגליל היו הספדנין לפני המטה וביהודה לאחר המטה: וכ"ש · שמפני שאינו יודע איזה יום ימות(ד) וטובה תשובה יום אחד לפני מיתתו נמצא כל ימיו בתשובה יהיו: בגדיך לבנים · נשמתך טהורה ונקיה: כלום חסר בית המלך · בתמיה הכל מוכן ושמא יבהילנו לבא פתאום ואנו צריכין ליכנס לסעודה מקושטין: כלום יש סעודה בלא טורח · עדיין יצטרכו לטרוח לצורכי סעודה של בית המלך ויש לנו שהות הרבה להתקשט: יעמדו ויראו · ואף לעוה"ב צדיקים יושבים ואוכלים ורשעים עומדים ורואים: ר"מ אומר · אין עומדין ורואין שא"כ אף הם היו נראים מן הקרואים ולשמש שכן דרך המשרתים עומדים ואין כאן בושה: זה ציצית · שמלובן הבגד: אלו תפילין · שהם שם משמן טוב דכתיב וראו כל עמי הארץ כי שם וגו' ותניא ר"א הגדול אומר אלו תפילין שבראש (ברכות דף ו·):

הדרן עלך שואל

מי שהחשיך(ו)· נותן כיסו לנכרי · מבעוד יום: ואם אין עמו · הא יש עמו לנכרי עדיף כדמפרש בגמרא: לחצר החיצונה · של עיר שהוא מקום המשתמר ראשון ובא לפרק מן החמור: נוטל · בידו מעליו כלים הניטלין בשבת ושאין ניטלין מתיר החבלים של אוכף שהן קשורים בהן והשקין נופלין: **גמ'** מאי טעמא שרי ליה למיתב לנכרי · והרי הוא שלוחו לישאנו בשבת: מעמיד עצמו · מלהציל ממונו: דוקא כיסו · דכיון דטרח בה שע"י טורח הוא משתכר חיים עלה ואי לא שרית ליה הא אתי לאיתויי: ולא אמרן · דמציאה לא אלא דלא אתיא לידיה קודם שתחשך ולא הגביהה ולא זכה בה: האי אדם · ויש במינו שחייב במצות ואתי לאיתלופי: לשוטה · יהיב דלית ליה דעת כלל אבל חרש דעתא קלישתא אית ליה כדאמרי' ביבמות (דף קיג·):

תוספות

ונשמתו עולה ושוב אינה יורדת · אף על פי כן כשהיא רוצה היא יורדת כי ההיא דלעיל דרבי אחי בר יאשיה וכההיא מעשה דר' בנאה דחזקת הבתים (ב"ב דף נח· ושם) דהוה מציין מערתא כי מטא למערתא דאברהם אבינו אשכחיה לאליעזר עבד אברהם דקאי אבבא אמר ליה מאי קא עביד אברהם כו' אמר ליה ניעול וניתי כו' אע"פ שנשמתו היתה גנוזה מתחת כסא הכבוד · מ"ר:

הדרן עלך שואל

מי שהחשיך ט' חרש שוטה וקטן · אע"ג דאמר לעיל בפרק כל כתבי (דף קכא·) גבי קטן שבא לכבות דקטן העושה לדעת אביו אסור מיהו הכא לא מיירי כגון דעביד הקטן עקירה והנחה אלא כדאמרינן לקמן גבי חמור כשהיא מהלכת מניחו עליה וכשהיא עומדת נוטל הימנה · מ"ר:

כי

עין משפט נר מצוה

נא א מיי' פ"ז מהלכות תשובה הלכה ב:

א ב מיי' פ"ו מהלכות שבת הלכה כב סמג לאוין סה טוש"ע א"ח סי' רסו סעיף א וסעיף ח וסימן שמט סעיף ה:

ב ג מיי' פ"כ שם הלכה ו סמג שם טוש"ע א"ח סי' רסו סעיף ב:

ג ד מיי' פכ"א שם הל' י סמג שם טוש"ע שם סעיף ט:

ד ה מיי' פ"ו שם הלכה כב סמג שם:

ה ו ז מיי' שם ופ"כ שם הלכה ז סמג שם טוש"ע שם סעיף א:

ו ח מיי' פ"כ שם הלכה ו סמג שם טוש"ע שם סעיף א:

ז ט מיי' שם הלכה ז טוש"ע שם סעיף ג:

ח י מיי' שם טוש"ע שם סעיף ד:

ט כ ל מיי' שם טוש"ע שם סעיף ה:

רבינו חננאל

איזה בן עולם הבא כל שדעת רבותיו נוחה הימנו כך שמעתא דא סלקא:

הדרן עלך שואל אדם

פרק כד מי שהחשיך בדרך נותן כיסו לנכרי וכו' ואוקי' למתניתין דאין מעמיד עצמו על ממונו והתירו לו לתת כיסו לנכרי בשביל שלא ישאנו הוא בעצמו · ובא רבא ודקדק ואמר דוקא כיסו אבל מציאה דלא אתא לידיה לא התירו לו לתתו לנכרי ובמציאה דאתאי לידיה ללישנא בתרא עלתה בתיקו · וכל תיקו דאיסורא לחומרא והלכתא כרבא דאוקמא (לידיה) [למתני'] בכיסו ממש · אין עמו נכרי מניחו על חמור דייקינן מינה בעת שמצויין ביחד נכרי וחמור לנכרי יהיב ליה מפני שאינו מצווה על שביתתו של נכרי ולכן לא התירו לו לתת כיסו על החמור שהיא מצווה על שביתתו אלא אם אין שם נכרי אלא חמור · וישראל חרש או שוטה או קטן אינו נותן כיסו לאחד מהן אלא נותן כיסו על החמור ולעולם לגרוע שבהן נותן כגון חרש ושוטה לשוטה נותן שוטה וקטן לשוטה נותן והשוטה גרוע בבני אדם שאין הפרש בין אדם לבהמה אלא הדעת והתבונה וזה כיון שאין לו דעת כבהמה חשיב:

מסורת הש"ס

כ"א שילא וכן לקמן

[נ"ל רבותיו וכ"א ברי"ף ורא"ש]

[פסחים ג. וש"נ]

[אבות פ"ב מ"י]

[לעיל יז:]

[יבמות קיג.]

הגהות הב"ח

(א) גמ' שנאמר לכן כה אמר:
(ב) רש"י ד"ה דסנו וכו' דבני פומבדיתא:
(ג) ד"ה אזניך וכו' לכו בו מאחרי:
(ד) ד"ה וכ"ש שמפני וכו' ימות שישוב בתשובה:

פרק כד

(ה) במשנה מי שהחשיך לו בדרך: (ו) רש"י ד"ה מי שהחשיך לו נותן:

גליון הש"ס

גמרא בני גלילא אמרי עשה דברים לפני מטתך · מסכת שמחות פ"ג [illegible]:

גמרא

תורה אור

לא תצא לחולין מפני שהוא ספק כי תיבעי לך אליבא דרבנן דתנן* ‏א‏חמשה לא יתרומו ואם תרמו אין תרומתן תרומה אלו הן חרש שוטה וקטן והתורם את שאינו שלו *ונכרי שתרם את של ישראל אפילו ברשותו אין תרומתו תרומה מאי לחרש יהיב ליה דקטן אתי לכלל דעת או דילמא לקטן יהיב ליה דחרש אתי לאחלופי בגדול פיקח איכא דאמרי לחרש יהיב ליה איכא דאמרי לקטן יהיב ליה אין שם לא נכרי ולא חמור ולא חרש ולא שוטה ולא קטן מאי אמר רבי יצחק עוד אחרת היתה ולא רצו חכמים לגלותה מאי עוד אחרת היתה *‏ב‏מוליכו פחות פחות מד' אמות אמאי לא רצו חכמים לגלותה משום °כבוד אלהים הסתר דבר (משלי כה) וכבוד מלכים חקור דבר והכא מאי כבוד אלהים איכא דילמא אתי לאתויי ד' אמות ברה"ר תניא *ר"א אומר בו ביום גדשו סאה ר' יהושע אומר בו ביום מחקו סאה תניא משל דר"א למה הדבר דומה לקופה מלאה קישואין ודילועין אדם נותן לתוכה חרדל והיא מחזקת משל דר' יהושע למה הדבר דומה לעריבה מלאה דבש נותן לתוכה רימונים ואגוזים והיא מקיאה אמר מר אין עמו נכרי מניחו על החמור והלא מחמר ורחמנא אמר °לא תעשה כל מלאכה (שמות כ) א"ר אדא בר אהבה מניחו עליה כשהיא מהלכת והא אי אפשר דלא קיימא להשתין מים ולהטיל גללים ואיכא עקירה והנחה ‏ג‏כשהיא מהלכת מניחו עליה כשהיא עומדת נוטלו הימנה אי הכי אפילו חברו נמי אמר רב פפא ‏ד‏כל שבגופו חייב חטאת בחברו פטור אבל אסור כל שחברו פטור אבל אסור בחמורו מותר לכתחלה א"ר אדא בר אהבה ‏ה‏היתה חבילתו מונחת לו על כתיפו רץ תחתיה עד שמגיע לביתו דוקא רץ אבל קלי קלי לא מאי טעמא כיון דלית ליה היכירא אתי למיעבד עקירה והנחה סוף סוף כי מטא לביתיה אי אפשר דלא קאי פורתא וקמעייל מרשות הרבים לרה"י ‏ו‏דזריק ליה כלאחר יד אמר רמי בר חמא *המחמר אחר בהמתו בשבת בשוגג חייב חטאת במזיד חייב סקילה מאי טעמא אמר *רבא דאמר קרא לא תעשה כל מלאכה אתה ובהמתך בהמתו דומיא דידיה מה הוא בשוגג חייב חטאת במזיד חייב סקילה אף בהמתו נמי בשוגג חייב חטאת במזיד חייב סקילה אמר רבא שתי תשובות בדבר חדא דכתיב °תורה אחת יהיה לכם לעושה (במדבר טו) בשגגה והנפש אשר תעשה ביד רמה *הוקשה כל התורה כולה לע"ז מה ע"ז דעביד מעשה בגופיה ה"נ עד דעביד מעשה בגופיה ועוד *תנן ‏ז‏המחלל את השבת בדבר שחייבין על שגגתו חטאת ועל זדונו *סקילה מכלל דאיכא מידי דאין חייבין על שגגתו חטאת ולא על זדונו סקילה ומאי ניהו לאו דמחמר לא *תחומין ואליבא דר"ע והבערה אליבא דר' יוסי

רב

רש"י

לא תצא לחולין · והויא תרומה לאסור לזרים ויחזור ויתרום הפקח אחרת: שהוא ספק · אי דעת גנולתא היא אי לא ולר' יצחק ודאי לקטן יהיב ליה דלאו בר' מצות הוא ולא לחרש דספק חייב במצות הוא: אליבא דרבנן · דאמרי לאו דעתא צילתא היא ולענין מצות הרי הוא כקטן: והתורם את שאינו שלו · בלא רשות דכתיב (דברים יד) תבואת זרעך וחרש שוטה וקטן דכתיב אשר ידבנו לבו שיש לו לב להתנדב בהש"ס ירושלמי: אפילו ברשות · דשליחות מהיכא אתרבי מכן תרימו גם אתם גם לרבות שלוחכם ומה אתם בני ברית אף שלוחכם בני ברית: עוד אחרת היתה · תקנה לכיס להצילו: ואמאי לא רצו לגלותה · להעלים דברי תורה: כבוד אלהים הסתר דבר · מותר להסתיר דברי תורה לכבוד שמים: וכבוד מלכים חקור דבר · אין להסתיר לכבוד עושר אדם וחשיבותו אלא שב ותחקרהו: בו ביום גדשו סאה · ביום שעלו לעליית חנניה בן חזקיה וגזרו י"ח דבר וזו אחת מהן היתה כדאמרינן בפ"ק (דף יז:) נותן כיסו לנכרי בו ביום גזרו שלא יוליכנו פחות פחות מד"א אם יש שם נכרי אותו יום הרבו סייג לתורה במדה גדושה ויפה מדדו להרבות גדר בישראל: מחקו סאה · במדה מחוקה מדדו בו ביום שהרבו לגזור יותר מדאי ואין יכולין לעמוד בגזירתם ומתוך כך עוברין על דברי תורה כמלאת מדתם מחוקה מטפיפתה וטוב היה להם להיות מדתם טפופה ולא תבא לידי מחק מרוב גודשה: והיא מחזקת · את החרדל שנופל החרדל בין הקישואין אף כאן יפה תקנו והוסיפו דבר המתקיים: והיא מקיאה · את הדבש שהיה בה ראשון אף אלו ע"י גזירתם גרמו לעבור דשמא לא יאמין את הנכרי והם לא התירו להוליכו פחות פחות מארבע ואדם אינו מעמיד עצמו על ממונו ואתי לאיתויי ד' אמות: והלא מחמר · מנהיג חמור טעונה קרוי מחמר: ורחמנא אמר לא תעשה כל מלאכה אתה ובהמתך · ואיזוהי כתם מלאכה העשויה על ידי שניהם זו היא שהיא טעונה והוא מחמר: מניחו עליה כשהיא מהלכת · לאחר שנעקרה ללכת דלאו עקירה היא כדאמר בפ"ק (דף ג·) גבי הטעינו חברו אוכלין ומשקין וכיון דאדם לא מיחייב בה חטאת כי האי גוונא כאן מותר דהכא נמי מלאכה כתיב והא לאו מלאכה היא: וקאתי למיעבד עקירה והנחה · כשחוזרת ונעקרת ללכת אחר הטלת מים או גללים: נוטלו הימנה · ולאחר שתחזור ותעקור רגל יניחנו: אי הכי אפילו על חברו · יכול לעשות כן כיון דלאו איסורא דאורייתא היא גבי כיס שרי: כל שבגופו חייב חטאת · כי עביד ליה איהו כוליה כגון מעביר ד' אמות ברה"ר אפי' עקרו מן הארץ דרך הליכתו חייב דהא איכא עקירת חפץ בידים ולא בעינן עמידה אלא בטעון ועומד מבעוד יום או כשהטעינו חבירו דלא עקר ליה להאי חפץ אבל הכא הא עקר ליה הלכך כי עביד ליה חבריה הוי ליה שנים שעשאוה ואסור מדרבנן ולא שריוה גבי כיס: מונחת לו על כתיפו · מבעוד יום וקדש עליו היום: רץ תחתיה · וכל כמה דלא עמד לפוש אין כאן עקירה לאיסור: קלי קלי · מעט מעט כלומר בנחת: למיעבד עקירה והנחה · כלומר דזימנין דקאי ולאו אדעתיה אבל רץ היכרא איכא: כלאחר יד · שלא כדרך זריקה כגון מכתיפיו ולאחוריו: בשוגג · במלאכה שהוא עושה לבדו: אף בהמתו · אף מלאכה שעושה על ידי בהמתו דהיינו מחמר אחר חמור טעונה: חדא דכתיב תורה אחת יהיה לכם וגו' עד דעביד מעשה בגופיה · כדכתיב לעושה בשגגה והכא לא קא עביד *מלאכה אלא דבור בעלמא שמנהיג בקול הרי דבשוגג אינו חייב קרבן: ועוד · דקאמרת נמי במזיד חייב סקילה קשיא דתנן בסנהדרין (דף סו·) גבי נסקלים המחלל את השבת נסקל אם חללו בדבר שחייבים על שגגתו חטאת ועל זדונו סקילה: מכלל דאיכא · חילול דאין חייבין על שגגתו חטאת ולא על זדונו סקילה: ואליבא דר"ע · דאמר* דאורייתא נינהו והוי מחלל ומיהו אין חייבין לא על שגגתו חטאת כו': אליבא דר' יוסי · דאמר בפרק כלל גדול (לעיל דף ע·) הבערה ללאו יצאת:

רב

תוספות

כי תבעי לך אליבא דרבנן · הכא משמע דהלכה כרבנן ובמסכת יבמות פרק חרש (דף קיג·) משמע דהלכה כר"א דסבירא ליה לרב חייא בר אשי (*ומר) שמואל כוותיה · מ"ר: דחרש אתי לאיחלופי בגדול פקח · תימה א"כ לעיל נמי אמאי קאמר שוטה וקטן לשוטה הא אמרינן אתא לאיחלופי בגדול פקח: בו ביום גדשו סאה כו' נותן לתוכה חרדל והיא מחזקת · ה"נ כשגזרו י"ח דבר היתה חסרה גזירה זו של נותן כיסו לנכרי עד שגזרו עליה ומלאו הסאה לגמרי כמו שנתנו חרדל לתוכה: ר' יהושע אומר בו ביום מחקו סאה כו' נותן לתוכה אגוזים ורמונים והיא מקיאה· כמו כן קודם שגזרו על נתינת כיס לנכרי היו מותרין להוליכו פחות פחות מד' אמות מתוך כך אתי לאיתויי ד' אמות כעריבה שהיתה מקיאה עד שהסירו האגוזים והרמונים ואחר שהסירו האגוזים והרמונים שוב לא הקיאה יותר כך כשגזרו ליתן כיסו לנכרי אסרו נמי להוליך פחות פחות מד' אמות והשתא ר"א ורבי יהושע שניהם לשבח ולא כפירוש הקונטרס דפירש דרבי יהושע דאמר שלא עשו היטב שהרבו לגזור יותר מדאי דלא משמע הכי בירושלמי בפ"ק דמכילתין דאמר התם אמר ליה ר"א אלו היתה חסרה ומלאוה יאות חבית שהיא מלאה אגוזים כל מה שאתה נותן לתוכה שומשמין היא מחזקת א"ל ר' יהושע אלו היתה מליאה וחסרוה יאות חבית שהיא מלאה שמן כל מה שאתה נותן לתוכה מים היא מפזרת השמן · מ"ר: ואדרבה כ"ל שהירו' קשה לו דלא שייך למימר גבי מים כמו שמפר"י גבי נותן לתוכה אגוזים ורמונים: סוף סוף כי מטי לביתיה א"א דלא קאי וקא מעייל מרשות הרבים לרשות היחיד · תימה כדפרינן להוליכו פחות פחות מד' אמות תקשי ליה נמי הכי:

ואמרי

עין משפט נר מצוה

[נ"ל אמר]

י א מיי' פ"ד מהלכות תרומות הלכה ג סמג עשין קלד טוש"ע י"ד סימן שלא סעיף ל:

יא ב מיי' פ"כ מהלכות שבת הלכה ז סמג לאוין סה טוש"ע א"ח סי' רסו סעיף ז:

יב ג מיי' שם הלכה ו טוש"ע שם סעיף ב:

יג ד מיי' פי"ג שם הלכה יב:

יד ה ו מיי' פי"ג מהל' שבת הלכה ט סמג לאוין סה טוש"ע א"ח סי' רסו סעיף יא:

טו ז מיי' פ"א שם הלכה א ב:

רבינו חננאל

בזמן שאין עמו נכרי ולא חמור אלא חרש וקטן לאיזה מהן יתן כיסו יש מהן שאומר לחרש יש מהן שאומר לקטן ואם עשה כאחד מהן עשה· ואם אין עמו נכרי ולא חמור ולא חרש ולא שוטה ולא קטן · א"ר יצחק יש שם דרך להתיר לו להביאו במקום הראוי לשמירה והוא הבאתו פחות פחות מד' אמות ולא רצו חכמים לגלותה ואמרי' אמאי לא רצו חכמים לגלותה ואמרו גזירה דלמא אתו לאתויי ד' אמות ברה"ר· תניא ר' אליעזר אומר בו ביום גדשו סאה פי' בו ביום שהושיבו את רבי אלעזר בן עזריה בראש גדשו סאה· מדת הסאה ששת קבין והיא מחוקה הוסיפו רבותינו כמה דברים מדבריהם כגון הגדישה שהיא יתירה על העיקר והדברים שהוסיפו מהן להיתר ומהן לאיסור והכל להיות העיקר שמור ומוזהר והוא כמו זה ששנינו נותן כיסו התירו לו לתתו לנכרי שלא יביאהו בעצמו ויחלל את השבת · זה וכיוצא בו · ולאיסור כל גזירות שגזרו מקצת מן היתר המותר לעשות גדר לשאר שהוא אסור מן התורה · ורבי יהושע אומר בו ביום מחקו סאה פי' העמידו כל דבר על עיקרו לא פחתו ולא הוסיפו· אלא התירו העיקר המותר מן התורה · שאילו באו להוסיף מדבריהן חיששין שמא יפסדו גם דברי תורה שהן העיקר שיבוא אדם להרהר ולומר כשם שזה אינו מן התורה אלא מדרבנן גם זולתי זה יש מן המצות האחרות מדרבנן כמותן ובאו לגדור נמצאו פורצים: אמר מר [אין] עמו נכרי מניחו על החמור ואקשינן עלה והלא מחמר הוא ורחמנא אמר לא תעשה כל מלאכה · ואוקימנא כדתנא כשהיא מהלכת מניחו עליה · כשהיא עומדת נוטלו הימנה · אי הכי חבירו נמי שרי ולמה חמור ולא אמר חבירו ופירק רב פפא כל שבגופו חייב חטאת בחבירו פטור אבל אסור פי' כל מלאכה שהעושה חייב חטאת כגון מעונת משוי ד' אמות ברה"ר אם יטעון חבירו פטור אבל אסור ואם יטעון בהמתו מותר לכתחלה ובלבד שלא תהא עקירה והנחה וזה שאמר רב אדא בר אהבה היתה חבילה מונחת בין כתיפו רץ תחתיה עד שמגיע לביתו מדדייקינן לטימריה דווקא רץ ומפרקינן לטעמי' ש"מ הלכתא כוותיה ותו דליכא מאן דפליג עליה ופירוש' דוריק לה כלאחר יד לאו שמכניסה ומפרקה אלא מהלך בריצה וכשמגיע לפתחו מחזיר אחוריו כלפי פתח החצר ופניו לחוץ וזורק החבילה מעל כתיפו בהצר דרך הפתח ע"י ריצה בלא עמידה וזה פי' דוריק לה כלאחר יד שזורקה שלא כדרך מפרק ומכנס חבילות: אמר רמי בר חמא המחמר אחר בהמתו בשבת בשוגג חייב חטאת · במזיד חייב סקילה · פי' המחמר המנהיג בהמה טעונה משאוי כנושא משאוי על כתיפו מדכתיב לא תעשה כל מלאכה אתה ובהמתך הקיש בהמתו לו · והשיב רבא ב' תשובות בדבר חדא דכתיב תורה אחת יהיה לכם לעושה בשגגה · והנפש אשר תעשה ביד רמה הוקשה כל התורה לע"ז וכו' דעביד מעשה בגופה ופשוטה היא ומפורשת נמי בפרק כלל גדול ועוד תנן המחלל את השבת בדבר שחייבין על שגגתו חטאת ועל זדונו סקילה מאי לאו מכלל דאיכא מידי דאין חייבין לא על שגגתו חטאת ולא על זדונו סקילה ומאי נינהו מחמר ופריק ליה דלמא בתחומין

רב נסים גאון

פרק מי שהחשיך תניא ר' אליעזר אומר בו ביום גדשו סאה ר' יהושע אומר בו ביום מחקו סאה זה היום הוא היום שנסמך בו ר' אלעזר בן עזריה בישיבה כמו שאמרו בברכות בפרק תפלת השחר (דף כח) תנא עדיות בו ביום תיקנום וכל בו ביום דאמרינן הדוא יומא איתמר וי"ח דבר שגזרו בו ביום באותו היום נאמרו אחת מהן מי שהחשיך בדרך הסב מא* שדחו ביציאות השבת (דף יז) ולפיכך אמר בכאן בו ביום גדשו סאה נתכוונו בדבר זה למה שהוסיפו מן הגזירות שהזכירום: תחומין ואליבא דר' עקיבא· עיקר דברי ר' עקיבא במסכת סוטה (פרק כשם דף כז) וכבר פירשנו דבר זה בפרק במה בהמה שעברי הבערה ואליבא דר'

*) פירושו לפי מה

מסורת הש"ס

תרומות פ"א מ"א יבמות קיג.

גיטין נג:

[ע"ז ע. ועיין תוספ' עירובין לז: ד"ה רבי שמעון]

[תוספתא פ"א]

[ע"ז סו.]

[נ"ל רבה]

[מכות יג: לעיל סט.]

סנהדרין סו ע"ש בסנהדרין כרת [לעיל סט. וש"נ]

ס"א מעשה

סוטה כו:

name: The *terumah* of a deaf-mute[4] [153*b*] does not revert to *hullin*, because it is doubtful.[5] The question is on the Rabbis' view. For we learnt: Five must not separate *terumah*, and if they do their separation is not valid. And these are they: a deaf-mute, imbecile, minor, one who separates *terumah* on [produce] that is not his,[6] and a Gentile who separates *terumah* on an Israelite's [produce] even with [the latter's] permission, his separation is not valid. What then? must he give it to the deaf-mute, seeing that the minor will arrive at understanding;[7] or perhaps he must give it to the minor, because a deaf-mute may be confused with an intelligent adult?—Some rule: He must give it to the deaf-mute; others maintain: He must entrust it to the minor.

What if neither a Gentile, an ass, a deaf-mute, an imbecile nor a minor is there?—R. Isaac said: There was yet another [expedient], but the Sages did not wish to reveal it. What was the other [expedient]?—One may carry it in stretches of less than four cubits at a time.[8] Why were the Sages unwilling to reveal it? Because, *It is the glory of God to conceal a thing: But the glory of kings is to search*
a *out a matter.*[1] Yet what glory of God is there here?—Lest one come to carry it four cubits in public ground.

It was taught, R. Eliezer said: On that day[2] they overfilled the measure;[3] R. Joshua said: On that day they made the measure deficient.[4] It was taught, As an illustration, what does this resemble on R. Eliezer's view? A basket full of cucumbers and gourds: a man puts mustard [grain] therein and it holds it.[5] As an illustration, what does this resemble on R. Joshua's view? A tub full of honey: if one puts pomegranates and nuts therein, it [the tub] overflows.[6]

The Master said: 'If there is no Gentile with him, he places it on his ass'. But he [thereby] leads a [laden] ass, whereas Scripture saith, [*In it*] *thou shalt not do any work*, [*thou . . . nor thy cattle*]?[7]—Said R. Adda b. Ahabah: He places it upon her while she is walking.[8] But it is impossible that she shall not stop for the calls of Nature,[9] and so there is removing and depositing?—When she is walking he places it upon her, and when she stops he removes it from her. If so, [the same may be done] even [to] his neighbour too?—R. Papa answered: Where one is liable to a sin-offering in his own case, in the case of his neighbour though he is not culpable nevertheless it is forbidden;[10] and wherever in the case of one's neighbour he is not culpable though it is forbidden, in the case of one's ass it is permitted at the outset.

R. Adda b. Ahabah said: If one's bundle is lying on his shoulder, he must run with it until he arrives home. He may only run, but not walk leisurely. What is the reason?—Since he has nothing to mark a distinction, he will come to perform removing and depositing. Yet after all, when he arrives at the house it is impossible that he shall not stop for a moment, and so he carries it from public
b to private ground?—He throws it in a 'back-handed manner.'[1]

Rami b. Ḥama said: If one leads a laden ass on the Sabbath unwittingly, he is liable to a sin-offering; if deliberately, he is liable to stoning.[2] What is the reason? Said Rabbah, because Scripture said, *Thou shalt not do any work,—thou, . . . nor thy cattle:* his cattle is assimilated to himself. Just as when he [himself does work], if unwittingly, he is liable to a sin-offering: if deliberately, he is liable to stoning: so [when he works with] his cattle too, if unwittingly, he is liable to a sin-offering; if deliberately, he is liable to stoning. Raba observed, There are two objections to this. Firstly, because it is written, *Ye shall have one law for him that doeth aught unwittingly . . . But the soul that doeth aught with a high hand,* [etc.]:[3] all laws are assimilated to idolatry: just as in the case of idolatry, he *personally* performs an action, so here too [one does not incur a sin-offering] unless he *personally* performs work. Moreover, we learnt: He who desecrates the Sabbath [is stoned], provided that it is an offence punished by a sin-offering if unwitting, and by stoning[4] if deliberate. Hence it follows that there is an offence for which if done unwittingly one does not incur a sin-offering, nor stoning if deliberate: and what is that? Surely leading a laden ass?—No: [the violation of] *teḥumin*,[5] in accordance with R. Akiba's view,[6] or kindling, in accordance with R. Jose's view.[7]

(4) I.e., separated by him. (5) Whether his action is valid or not, as his mind may have been clear. On that view a minor stands lower, and the purse must certainly be given to the minor. (6) Without having been previously authorized. (7) Thus he is at least *potentially* an adult of intelligence. (8) V. *supra* 42*a*, n. a5.

a (1) Prov. XXV, 2. (2) When they entered the upper chambers of Hezekiah b. Garon for the eighteen enactments, v. *supra* 13*b* and n. a1. (3) They did well in enacting so many preventive laws, thereby safeguarding Israel from transgression. (4) Or, they just levelled the measure. I.e., they imposed so many prohibitions as to defeat their own object, for by a reaction Israel would be more likely to sin now than hitherto.—This is mentioned here because the entrusting of one's purse to a Gentile was one of those eighteen laws. (5) Though full it is still capable of receiving more. (6) Lit., 'it spews forth'—some of the honey itself. (7) Ex. XX, 10. (8) If one places a burden on a *man* while he is walking he is not culpable, because there is no 'removal' in a technical sense; v. *supra* 3*a*. Hence it does not constitute labour, and therefore the same applies here too. (9) And when she recommences there is 'removal', and when she stops again there is 'depositing', which together constitute 'work'. (10) For if a man carries an article four cubits in public ground, even if he picks it up while walking, he is culpable. Consequently one must not put a burden upon another person while walking, though there is no culpability.

b (1) V. *supra* 40*b*, n. b2. (2) In theory only. In actual practice the death penalty was restricted by so many conditions as to be non-existent in all but cases of murder (cf. Herzog, *Main Institutions of Jewish Law*, Vol. I, Introduction, XXI). (3) Num. XV, 29f, q.v. The latter refers to idolatry. (4) In Sanh. 66*a* the reading is: *kareth*. (5) *Teḥum*, pl. *teḥumin*, v. Glos. (6) Who regards the prohibition as Biblical, v. Soṭ. 36*b*. (7) V. *supra* 70*a*.

[154a] R. Zebid recited it thus: Rami b. Ḥama said: If one leads a laden ass on the Sabbath: if unwittingly, he does not incur a sin-offering: if deliberately, he is liable to stoning. Raba objected: He who desecrates the Sabbath by an offence for which, if unwitting, a sin-offering is incurred, if deliberate he is liable to stoning. Hence if one does not incur a sin-offering when it is unwitting, there is no stoning when it is deliberate?—Does he [the Tanna] then teach, 'Hence if one does not incur a sin-offering,' etc.? [Surely] he says thus: [Every] offence for which, if unwitting, one is liable to a sin-offering, if deliberate he is liable to stoning. Yet there is an offence for which, if unwitting, a sin-offering is *not* incurred, nevertheless if deliberate one is liable to stoning. And what is it? Leading a laden ass.

Raba, the brother of R. Mari b. Rachel, others state, the father of R. Mari b. Rachel—on the second version there is the difficulty that Rab declared R. Mari b. Rachel eligible [to hold office] and
a appointed him one of the collectors of Babylonia?[1]—(Perhaps there were two men of the name of Mari b. Rachel)[2] recited this discussion in R. Joḥanan's name, teaching non-culpability. [Thus:] R. Joḥanan said: If one drives a laden animal on the Sabbath he is not culpable at all. If it is unwitting he does not incur a sin-offering, because the whole Torah is assimilated to idolatry. If deliberate he is not culpable, because we learnt: He who desecrates the Sabbath [is stoned], provided that it is an offence for which a sin-offering is incurred if it is unwitting and stoning if it is deliberate:[3] hence if the unwitting offence does not involve a sin-offering, the deliberate offence does not involve stoning.
b Neither is he liable for [the violation of] a negative precept,[1] because it is a negative precept for which a warning of capital punishment at the hands of Beth din may be given, and for such there

(1) V. Yeb., 45*b* and n. b5. Such positions were only open to men of Jewish parentage, yet Rab declared him eligible because it was sufficient that his mother was a Jewess. That contradicts the present statement that his father too was a Jew. (2) BaḤ deletes the bracketed passage, and the same appears from Rashi and Tosaf. (3) This is the reading in cur. edd., and must be retained if the introductory phrase, 'we learnt', which always precedes a *Mishnah*, is correct, the Mishnah being that on Sanh. 66*a* (quoted *supra* 153*b* bottom). BaḤ however emends the text thus: if it is an offence for which a sin-offering is incurred if unwitting, stoning is incurred when deliberate. This suits the context better, this being the Baraitha quoted by Raba *supra*. But in that case the introductory phrase must be emended to 'it was taught'.

b (1) The penalty for which is flagellation.

רב זביד מתני הכי אמר רמי בר חמא המחמר אחר בהמה בשבת בשוגג אינו חייב חטאת במזיד חייב סקילה מתיב רבא *המחלל את השבת בדבר שחייבין על שגגתו חטאת חייבין על זדונו סקילה הא אין חייבין על שגגתו חטאת אין חייבין על זדונו סקילה מי קתני הא אין חייבין כו' הכי קאמר דבר שחייבין על שגגתו חטאת חייבין על זדונו סקילה ויש דבר שאין חייבין על שגגתו חטאת וחייבין על זדונו סקילה ומאי ניהו מחמר רבא אחוה דרב מרי בר רחל (א)ואמרי לה אבוה דרב מרי בר רחל ללישנא בתרא קשיא הא דרב *אכשריה לרב מרי בר רחל ומנייה בפורסיה דבבל דילמא תרי מרי בר רחל הוו הוה מתני לה להא שמעתיה משמיה דרבי יוחנן לפטור אמר רבי יוחנן *המחמר אחר בהמתו בשבת פטור מכלום בשוגג לא מחייב חטאת דהוקשה כל התורה כולה לע"ז במזיד נמי לא מיחייב דתנן *המחלל את השבת בדבר שחייבין על שגגתו חטאת(ג) ועל זדונו סקילה הא אין חייבין על שגגתו חטאת אין חייבין על זדונו סקילה בלאו נמי לא מיחייב דהוה ליה לאו שניתן לאזהרת מיתת ב"ד וכל[א] *לאו שניתן לאזהרת מיתת ב"ד אין לוקין עליו ואפילו

רש"י

רב זביד מתני · להא דרמי בר חמא הכי: איט חייב חטאת · דילפינן מע"ז דעד דעביד מעשה בגופיה: אבל במזיד חייב סקילה · מהיקישא דאתה ובהמתך דלעיל: מי קתני · הך דיוקא דדייקינן הא אין חייב כו' דילמא הכי קאמר המחלל בדבר שחייבין על שגגתו חטאת [חייבים על זדונו סקילה] הא דבר שאין חייבים על שגגתו חטאת יש מהן שחייבין על זדונו סקילה ויש שאין חייבין ומאי ניהו דחייבין [על זדונו] סקילה ואין חייבין על שגגתו חטאת מחמר: ואמרי לה אבוה דרב מרי בר רחל ל"ג דאבוה דרב מרי איסור גיורא שמיה ומאן דגרס ליה גרס בתריה הכי להך לישנא בתרא קשיא הך דרב אכשריה לרב מרי בר רחל ומניה בפורסי דבבל והך מילתא במסכת יבמות היא (דף מה:) בפורסי בלע"ז מנשטר"ל הן שוטרים ואף על גב דאמר מר כל משימות שאתה משים לא יהו אלא מקרב אחיך האי כיון דאמו מישראל מקרב אחיך קרינן ביה: לאזהרת מיתת בית דין · דשאר מלאכות דשבת נמי מהאי קרא נפקא להו אזהרה הלכך לאזהרת מיתת בית דין ניתן דלא ענש מיתה אלא אם כן הזהיר הלכך עיקר אזהרתו למקום שיש בו מיתה אתאי ולא למלקות:

תוספות

ואמרי לה רבא אבוה דרב מרי בר רחל · לא גרסינן ליה דהא מוכח ביבמות דאבוה דרב מרי גר הוה דאמר בהחולץ (יבמות מה: ושם) רב אכשריה לרב מרי בר רחל ומנייה אפורסיה דבבל וקאמר כיון דאמו מישראל מקרב אחיך קרינן ביה וליכא למימר דרבא אבוה דרב מרי נמי גר הוה דאם כן הוה ליה למימר רבא גיורא כדאמר הש"ס בעלמא איסור גיורא ועוד דאביו של רב מרי בר רחל משמע בבבא בתרא פרק מי שמת (דף קמט· ושם) דהייט איסור גיורא דאמרינן איסור גיורא הוה ליה תריסר אלפי זוזי בי רבא ורב מרי בריה הורתו שלא בקדושה ולידתו בקדושה הוה אע"ג דהתם לא גרסינן רב מרי בר רחל בריה דומה הוא שאותו היה מיהו אי אמרינן שהוא היה רב מרי בר רחל צריכא למימר דאיסור גיורא בא על רחל בת מר שמואל קודם שנתגייר דהא קאמר התם דהורתו שלא בקדושה הוה ורחל בת מר שמואל היתה כדאמר בכמה דוכתין רב מרי בר רחל בת מר שמואל ואמרינן בכתובות (דף כג·) דבנתיה דמר שמואל אישתביין ושמא אז בא עליה ואף על גב דאתו לקמיה דר"ח ואמרו נשביתי וטהורה אני לאו כולהו אמרו הכי מיהו תימה אי רב מרי בריה דאיסור גיורא הייט ההוא דיבמות איך חי איסור כל כך מימות רב עד רבא והא רב יהודה תלמידו של רב ואמרינן בקדושין (דף עב:) יום שמת רב יהודה נולד רבא ואפילו רב מרי בנו כבר היה גדול בתורה הרבה בימי רב מדמנייה אפורסיה דבבל ורב מרי נמי איך יתכן שחי כ"כ ונראה כפירוש ר"ח דגרסינן ביבמות דרב אשי אכשריה לרב מרי בר רחל ואע"ג דביום שמת רבא נולד רב אשי יכול להיות שהיה רב מרי קטן בימי רבא ובימי רב אשי כבר היה גדול בתורה וזקן ומינהו אפורסייה דבבל וכן ודאי נראה דיש בספרים רבים שכתוב בהם בשמעתא(ג) לאמרי לה והקשה דרב אשי אכשריה לרב מרי בר רחל ומשני תרי רב מרי הוו ופירוש הוא שנכתב בספרים · מ"ר* : **בלאו** נמי לא מיחייב דה"ל לאו שניתן לאזהרת מיתת ב"ד · תימה לר"י מה בכך מ"מ ילקה על לאו דלא תעשה כל מלאכה דכיון שבא להזהיר על מחמר ובמחמר ליכא מיתה אע"פ שבא להזהיר נמי על שאר מלאכות דשייך בהו מיתה מכל מקום יש לו ללקות כדאשכחן בבבא קמא (דף עד: ושם) דפליגי ר' יוחנן ור"א התם בעדים שהוכחשו בנפש ולבסוף הוזמו דחד אמר נהרגין וחד אמר אין נהרגין ואמרינן נמי תסתיים דר' אלעזר דאמר אין נהרגין דאמר ר"א עדים שהוכחשו בנפש לוקין ואי ס"ד ר"א דאמר נהרגין אמאי לוקין הוה ליה לאו שניתן לאזהרת מיתת ב"ד אלא ש"מ ר"א דאמר אין נהרגין הסתיים אלמא משום דאין נהרגין כשהוכחשו בתחילה לוקין ואע"ג דבעלמא ניתן לאו דלא תענה לאזהרת מיתת ב"ד היכא דהוזמו תחילה ועוד תימה לר"י דכל לאוין שבעולם שניתנו לאזהרת מיתת ב"ד יהיו לוקין עליהם כשלא התרו בהם למיתה אלא למלקות מההוא טעמא דלא ניתנו באותה שעה לאזהרת מיתת ב"ד ונראה לר"י דשאני לאו דלא תענה דגלי ביה קרא דניתן למלקות כדאשכחן גבי עדות בן גרושה כדמפקינן בריש מסכת מכות (דף ב: ושם)(ד) והרשיעו את הרשע והיה אם בן הכות הרשע וכיון דכתב בלא תענה מלקות בהדיא אע"ג דניתן לאזהרת מיתת ב"ד אית לן לאוקמי בכל מילי דלא מצי אתי לידי מיתה ומהאי טעמא נמי אתי שפיר הא דאמר במכות בגמרא מעידין אנו את איש פלוני שהוא חייב לחבירו מאתים זוז ונמצאו זוממים לוקין ומשלמין דברי ר' מאיר וחכמים אומרים כל המשלם איט לוקה דקאמר בשלמא לרבנן כדי רשעתו משום רשעה אחת אתה מחייבו כו' וקשה לר"י ל"ל למימר טעמא דרבנן משום כדי רשעתו תיפוק ליה דרבנן מוקמי לא תענה לאזהרה לעדים זוממין ולא למלקות כדמוכח התם על משנת מעידים אנו את איש פלוני שחייב מלקות ארבעים וקשה לר"י נמי היכי מצי למימר לרבנן דלאזהרה דעדים זוממים הוא דאתא ולא למלקות הא בהזמה דגלות ובן גרושה מודו רבנן דאיכא מלקות ולמאי דפרישית אתי שפיר דכי היכי דלא אתי לידי מיתה או לידי מלקות ע"י כאשר זמם לוקה משום לא תענה כיון דהתם לא צריך קרא דלא תענה לאזהרה לכאשר זמם משום הכי לקי במעידים אנו בפלוני שהוא בן גרושה או שחייב גלות ואתי נמי שפיר הא דתלי טעמא דרבנן התם משום כדי רשעתו דאי לאו משום כדי רשעתו היו לוקין משום לא תענה אפי' לרבנן דאע"ג דסבירא להו דלא תענה אזהרה לכאשר זמם הוא דאתא דלא ענש כאשר זמם אלא אם כן הזהיר והוי כלאו שניתן לאזהרת מיתת ב"ד שלא נכתב למלקות אלא לאזהרת מיתה ה"מ דוקא כשחייב מלקות מכאשר זמם כגון מעידים אנו באיש פלוני שחייב מלקות אבל כשאין חייבים מכאשר זמם אלא ממון לא מבעי התם לא תענה לאזהרה דכאשר זמם הוו מודו רבנן דלוקין משום לא תענה כמו בבן גרושה וגלות אי לאו משום כדי רשעתו וא"ת למאי דפירש דאי לאו דגלי קרא בהדיא מלקות בלא תענה מוהלדיקו את הלדיק לא הוה מחייבינן ביה משום דניתן לאזהרת מיתת ב"ד אם כן הא דמפיק עולא דעדים זוממים לוקין מוהלדיקו את הלדיק בריש מכות ופריך עלה תיפוק ליה מלא תענה ומשני משום דהוה ליה לאו שאין בו מעשה אמאי לא משני משום דהוה ליה לאו שניתן לאזהרת מיתת ב"ד ותירץ דההוא שטיא לא הוה אתי אלא לרבנן דלר' מאיר איכא תרי לאוי חד לאזהרה לכאשר זמם היכא דזמם מיתה או מלקות וחד למילקי עליה ולהכי ניחא טפי למימר טעמא דלאו שאין בו מעשה לאוקמא מילתא בין לרבנן בין לרבי מאיר דמתניתין דמכות אע"ג דטעמא דלאו שאין בו מעשה נמי לא אתי לר"י ולמאי דפי' איצטריך והלדיקו למלקות אפי' למאן דמחייב בלאו שאין בו מעשה ועוד היה רגיל לתרץ כיון דלא תענה סתם כתיב אכל מילי קאי ולהכי מיחייב מלקות כאילו נכתב אבן גרושה ואגלות וכאילו נכתב לא תענה שקר בממון ולבן גרושה וגלות שאז לא היה הנכתב לממון ניתן לאזהרה כאשר זמם ולכך היה ראוי ללקות עליו והכי נמי השתא אע"פ שזה לא היה ראוי ללקות על אותו הניתן לאזהרת מיתה אפי' כשאיט יכול לבא לידי מיתה עכשיו יש ללקות עליו כל זמן שלא יוכל לבא לידי מיתה הואיל ונכתב על מיתה וממון ביחד סתם וניתן להלקות עליו בהזמת מיתה נמי ניתן ללקות כל זמן שלא יוכל לבא לידי מיתה ולפי טעם זה לא היה יכול לתרץ בריש מכות משום דהוה ליה לאו שניתן לאזהרת מיתת ב"ד כי פריך ותיפוק ליה משום לא תענה דאע"פ שניתן לאזהרת מיתה יש ללקות עליו הואיל ונכתב סתם על מיתה ודברים אחרים כדפרישית ולפי לשון זה לא אתי דרשה דוהלדיקו אלא למאן דאית ליה לאו שאין בו מעשה אין לוקין עליו כדמשני בריש מכות אבל קשה דבכל הש"ס חשיב לאו דשבת ניתן לאזהרת מיתת ב"ד ואמאי הא קאי נמי אלאו דמחמר ואההיא דאיסי (לעיל דף ה:) דליכא מיתה וי"ל כיון דכתיב כל העושה בו מלאכה יומת משמע סתם מלאכה דשבת הייט שבמיתה ולהכי לא משמע לאו דמלאכה דאיסי אבל לאו דלא תעשה משמע שאר דברים שאין בהן מיתה ומלקות וכן לאו דמחמר דלא תעשה כל מלאכה אתה ובהמתך משמע אשאר חיובי שבת טפי ממחמר מדכתיב אתה כדקאמר הכא א"נ מדכתיב לא תעשה ולא כתיב לא תעשו והולאה נמי אע"ג דנפקא מאל ילא (עירובין יז:) בהדי תחומין דבמלקות אין לוקין עליו אפי' לא התרו בו למיתה דכל סתם הולאה דשבת איתא בקרא דויכלא העם מהביא ותירוץ ראשון נראה לר"י עיקר · מ"ר:

והא

עין משפט נר מצוה

טו א מיי' פ"ב מהלכות שבת הלכה א:

[טז] [א] [מיי' פ"ח מהלכות סנהדרין הלכה ב]:

מסורת הש"ס

[כריתות ד. ועי' תוס' לעיל ד"ה הא קנ"ג]

[יבמות מה: ע"ש]

[סנהדרין ס. ע"ש]

[עירובין יז: ב"ק עד: סנהדרין סה: מכות יג: שבועות ד.]

[עי' תוספות ב"מ צג: ד"ה רב]

רבינו חננאל

ואליבא דרבי עקיבא דסבר תחומין דאורייתא ועיקרו בסוטה פרק כשם שהמים בודקין אותו וחייב לאו כדכתי' אל יצא איש ממקומו ביום השביעי והבערה אליבא דר' יוסי דתניא הבערה ללאו יצאת דברי ר' יוסי ר' נתן אומר לחלק יצאת רב זביד מתני הכי אמר רמי בר חמא המחמר אחר בהמתו בשבת בשוגג פטור במזיד חייב סקילה ואקשי עליה רבא המחלל את השבת בדבר שחייבין על שגגתו חטאת חייבין על זדונו סקילה הא אין חייבין על שגגתו חטאת אין חייבין על זדונו סקילה ופריק ופשוטה היא · רבא אחוה דרב מרי בר רחל (אי') [ואמרי לה] כי רבא הוא אבוה דרב מרי בר רחל והוא מישראל קשיא ליה הא דרב אשי דאכשריה דכיון דאימיה מישראל מקרב אחיך קרינא ביה מכלל שלא היה אביו מישראל אלא אמו ומפורש בפרק החולץ ליבמתו · ומפרקי' דלמא תרי רב מרי בר רחל וזה אביו מישראל וכן תירוץ שמועה זו רבא אבוה דרב מרי בר רחל: א"ר יוחנן המחמר אחר בהמתו בשבת פטור מכלום בשוגג לא מחייב חטאת (והוקשה) [דהוקשה] כל התורה כולה לע"ז במזיד נמי לא מחייב (חטאת) [סקילה] · דתנן בפרק ארבע מיתות נמסרו לבית דין [המחלל את השבת וכו'] ואוקימנא התם בתחומין ואליבא דר"ע בהבערה ואליבא דר' יוסי *)דתנן המחלל את השבת בדבר שחייבין על שגגתו חטאת חייבין על זדונו סקילה הא אין חייבין על שגגתו חטאת אין חייבין על זדונו סקילה לאו נמי לא מיחייב דהוי לאו שניתן לאזהרת מיתת ב"ד וכל לאו שניתן לאזהרת מיתת ב"ד אין לוקין

*) נראה דנתחלפו שורות בכאן וכן צ"ל דתנן בפרק ד' מיתות נמסרו לב"ד המחלל את השבת בדבר שחייבין על שגגתו חטאת חייבין על זדונו סקילה הא אין חייבין על שגגתו חטאת אין חייבין על זדונו סקילה ואוקימנא התם בתחומין ואליבא דר"ע בהבערה אליבא דר"י לאו נמי וכו' ·

רב נסים גאון

דרבי יוסי גרסי לה. בפרק כלל גדול (דף ע) הבערה ללאו יצאת דברי רבי יוסי:

גליון הש"ס

תוס' ד"ה בלאו נמי וכו' בסה"ד נראה לר"י עיקר · עיין סנהדרין דף סג ע"א בתוספות ד"ה משום דסוי:

הגהות הב"ח

(א) גמ' רבא אחוה דרב מרי בר רחל (ואמרי לה רבא אבוה דרב וכו' תרי רב מרי בר רחל הוו) תא"מ · ונ"ב ס"א אין זה וכן רש"י *ותוספות לא גרסי ליה: (ב) שם על שגגתו חטאת חייבים על זדונו סקילה: (ג) תוס' ד"ה ואמרי לה וכו' בשמעתא לאמרי לה וקשיא הא דרב אשי: (ד) ד"ה בלאו וכו' בריש מס' מכות מוהצדיקו את הצדיק והרשיעו את:

עין משפט
נר מצוה

שייך אחר ד"ה בחיבור
יז א ב ג מיי' פכ"א מהלכות שבת הלכה י סמג לאוין סה טוש"ע א"ח סי' רסו סעיף ט :
יח ד ה מיי' שם טוש"ע שם וסימן שה סעיף יח :
יט ו מיי' פ"ד מהלכות סוכה הלכה ו טוש"ע א"ח סי' תרכח סעיף ג :

ואפי' למ"ד לוקין ליכתוב רחמנא לא תעשה כל מלאכה ובהמתך אתה למה לי הוא נידהו דמיחייב בהמתו לא מיחייב : הגיע לחצר החיצונה : אמר *רב הונא היתה בהמתו טעונה כלי זכוכית מביא כרים וכסתות ומניח תחתיה ומתיר החבלים והשקין נופלים והאנן תנן נוטל את הכלים הניטלין בשבת *כי קאמר רב הונא בקרני דאומנא דלא חזיא ליה והא קא מבטל כלי מהיכנו ׳בשליפי זוטרי מיתיבי היתה בהמתו טעונה *טבל ועששיות מתיר את החבלים והשקין נופלין ואע"פ שמשתברין התם בבולסא דיקא נמי דקתני דומיא דטבל מה טבל דלא חזי ליה אף הכא נמי לא חזי ליה ומאי אע"פ שמשתברין ׳מהו דתימא *להפסד מועט נמי חיישו קמ"ל תניא ר"ש בן יוחי אומר ׳היתה בהמתו טעונה שליף של תבואה מניח ראשו תחתיה ומסלקו לצד אחר והוא נופל מאליו חמורו של רבן גמליאל היתה טעונה דבש ולא רצה לפורקה עד מוצאי שבת למוצאי שבת מתה והאנן תנן נוטל כלים הניטלין כשהדביש *)הדביש למאי חזי לכתיתא דגמלי ויתיר חבלים ויפלו שקין מיצטרו זיקי ויביא כרים וכסתות ויניח תחתיהן מטנפי *וקמבטל כלי מהיכנו ׳והאיכא צער בעלי חיים קסבר *צער בעלי חיים דרבנן אביי אשכחיה לרבה דקא משפשף ליה לבריה אגבא דחמרא א"ל קא משתמש מר בבעלי חיים א"ל צדדין הן וצדדין לא גזרו בהו רבנן מנא תימרא דתנן מתיר(א) חבלים והשקין נופלין מאי לאו בחבר *גוולקי דהוו להו צדדין וצדדין לא גזרו בהו רבנן לא בחבר אגלווקי דלא הוו צדדין אי נמי בלכתא איתיביה *שתים בידי אדם ואחת באילן כשרה ואין עולין לה ביו"ט מאי לאו דהק ביה באילן דהוו להו צדדין *וצדדין אסורין לא דכפייה לאילן ואנח סיכוך עילויה (ב)דקמשמש באילן א"ה אימא סיפא שלש בידי אדם ואחת באילן כשרה ועולין לה ביו"ט ואי דכפייה לאילן אמאי עולין לה ביו"ט ואלא מאי צדדין אסורין סוף סוף אמאי עולין לה בי"ט אלא התם בגוואזא פרסבנא דאילן גופיה דופן בעלמא הוא דשוויה דיקא נמי דקתני זה הכלל ׳כל(ג) אילו שינטל האילן ויכולה לעמוד עולין לה ביו"ט ש"מ לימא כתנאי אין עולין לה ביו"ט *רשב"א אומר משום ר"מ עולין לה ביו"ט מאי לאו בהא קמיפלגי דמ"ס צדדין אסורין ומר סבר מותרין אמר אביי לא דכ"ע צדדין אסורין והכא בצדי צדדין קמיפלגי מ"ס צדי צדדין אסורין ומ"ס צדי צדדין מותרין רבא אמר מאן דאסר בצדדין אסר נמי בצדי צדדין מאן דשרי בצדי צדדין שרי נמי בצדדין איתיביה רב משרשיא לרבא נעץ

יתד

*) [עי' רש"י ב"מ לח. ד"ה הדביש וברש"י סנהדרין קא. ד"ה מדביש]

סוכה כב:

ואפי' למ"ד דלוקין · במסכת מכות (דף יג:) הכא אפי' לאו ליכא דלאי לאזהורי אמלאכה שעל ידו וע"י בהמתו אתא כגון מחמר ליכתוב לא תעשה כל מלאכה ובהמתך מאי אתה משמע אתה לבדך ובהמתך לבדה : בהמתו · במלאכה הנעשית ע"י בהמתו לא מיחייב לאו גמור ללקות עליו : טעונה כלי זכוכית · שאין ניטלין בידו להניחן לארץ : והאנן תנן נוטל את הכלים הניטלין · וכלי זכוכית ניטלין הן ולמה לי מתיר את החבלים : דאומני · מקיז דם שאין ראויין בשבת לכלום לפי שמאוסים : והא(ד) מבטל כלי · כרים וכסתות כשמניחן תחת דבר שאין ניטל מבטלן מהיכנן דשוב לא יטלם משם ודמי לסותר : בשליפי זוטרי · משואות קטנים ששומט הכר מתחתיהם ונופלין על הכר השני וכן עד שמגיען לארץ : עששיות של זכוכית · מש"ש בלע"ז ואע"פ שהעששיות משתברין אלמא אסור להניח כרים וכסתות תחתיהן : בכולסא · חתיכות רחבות של זכוכית שאינם כלים ועושין מהן חלונות וכיון דליכא פסידא בשבירתן וסופן להחתך בחתיכות קטנות לא שרו להביא כרים ולהניח תחתיהן : [טבל לא חזי ליה · דמוקצה הוא ואפילו לכהנים לא חזי] : ומאי אף על פי שמשתברין · הא ליכא פסידא : מהו דתימא להפסד מועט נמי חששו · ויביא כרים ויניח תחתיהם דהא ודאי אי אפשר בלא הפסד מועט שגילולות ניתזין בשבירתן שאינם ראוין לכלום : שליף · משוי של תבואה של טבל : והא אנן תנן כו' · ודבש ניטל בשבת ואמאי לא רצה לפורקה : כשהדביש · החמיץ : למאי חזי · ואמאי אייתי רבן גמליאל : לכתיתא דגמלי · לכתית של גמלים רדויישדוד"א : ויתיר החבלים ויפלו שקים · דהכי תנן במתניתין בדבר שאינו ניטל ומשני מצטרו זיקי נבקעים הנודות בנפילתן לארץ : מטנפי · בדבר הנשפך עליהם וקא מבטל כלי מהיכנו דשוב אין ראויין לבו ביום לכלום : והא איכא צער בעלי חיים · וליתי דאורייתא ולידחי דרבנן ביטול כלי מהיכנו : קסבר · ר"ג צער בעלי חיים דרבנן ופלוגתא היא באלו מציאות (ב"מ לב:): דמשפשף לבריה אגבא דחמרא · בשבת לשעשע התינוק : קא משתמש מר בבעלי חיים · ותנן (ביצה דף לו·) לא רוכבין על גבי בהמה וה"ה לכל תשמיש : צדדין · שאינו מרכיבו עליו אלא משפשפו על צדי גבו ואין זה דרך תשמישו ורבנן לא גזרו בה : מאי לאו בחבר גוולקי · דהוו להו צדדין גוואלקי עשקי"ם חבר גוואלקי שתים מחוברות יחד ברצועות ומרכיבין על החמור זו מכאן וזו מכאן וצריך לסלקן יחד וליקרב אצל החמור ומשפשף עצמו ונשען גופו בצדי החמור : בחבר אגלווקי · שתים שאין מחוברות יחד אלא על ידי טבעת מתכת שבראש הרצועה ובו מסמר קטן כעין שעושין לחבק שקורין ליגגל"א שאינו צריך אלא למשוך מעט והמסמר יוצא והן מתנתקות זו מזו : אי נמי בלכתא · כעין שעושין לדרדור יין שיש בהן טבעות של חבל לכל אחד ואחד ומכניס טבעת בטבעת ונוטל עץ כפוף קטן ומכניסו בפנימי ושוב אינו יוצא מחברו וכשבא לסלקו מושך העץ אליו והן מתנתקין זה מזה ונופלין : שתים בידי אדם ואחת באילן · גבי סוכה תנן שכשירה בג' דפנות ואם עשה שתים כהלכתן והשלישי עשה באילן כשירה דפנות לא איכפת לן אם מחוברות הם וה"ה אם כולן נקבעות באילן והא דנקט שתים בידי אדם רבותא אשמועינן דאפילו הכי אין עולין לה לאכול ולישן באותה סוכה בי"ט מפני שסככה קשור בדופניה ונשען עליה והוא משתמש על סככה ונותן כליו ונמצא משתמש באילן כל כניסה דסוכה נקיט בלשון עלייה במסכת סוכה לפי שרובן עושין סוכותיהן בראש גגן דבכמה דוכתין תנן בה הכי א)אין מטריחין אותו לעלות ב)אמר להם העלום לסוכה *אבל מוריד הוא את הכלים וכן הרבה : מאי לאו דחק ביה באילן · ואותיב ביה קנים של דפנות בנקבים שנקב הרבה בגופו של אילן וסיכך שוב על אותן דפנות ומ"מ אין כאן תשמיש אלא בצדי אילן : דכפייה לאילן · לענפיו העליונים הטה לצד אילן אחר וכן של זה לזה וקשרן אלו עם אלו ומהן נעשה הדופן : אמאי עולין לה בי"ט · הרי הסכך נשען עליו והוא משתמש בו : ה"ג אלא מאי צדדין אסורין סוף סוף אמאי עולין לה בי"ט אלא התם בגוואזא פרסכנא שאילן גופיה דופן בעלמא שוייה · גוואזא פרסכנא אילן שענפים הרבה יוצאין מצדדין ומתפשטין לכאן ולכאן ושויהו דופן בעלמא לסוכה ולא סמך הסכך עליהן ולהכי נקט גוואזא פרסכנא ולא שבקיה כדקא ס"ד בדכפייה ולישני כגון דלא סמך הסכך עליה משום דכיון דדופן רביעי הוא שאינו צריך לסוכה דהא בג' כשירה והסכך נמי לא סמך עליה לא טרח למעבד לו דופן להכי אוקמא בגוואזא פרסכנא וממילא הוא בלא טרחא : מאי לאו בהא קמיפלגי כו' · וכגון דחק באילן ומותיב קנים בצדדין וסיכך עליהן דהוה ליה משתמש בצדדין כשמשתמשין על ידי סככה דאי לא בהא פליגי במאי מוקמא פלוגתייהו דהא כולי עלמא סברי אסור להשתמש באילן : אמר אביי · א"כ בהכי פליגי ליכא למימר דסבירא ליה (לת"ק*) לצדדין מותרין דהכי לאו לצדדין נינהו אלא לצדי צדדים ג)שהקנים הנתונים בנקבים לצדדין והסיכוך הנתון על גבן לצדי צדדים ובצדי צדדים פליגי :

א) [ברייתא סוכה כט.] ב) [שם טו:] ג) ס"א שהגזע לצדדים והקנים הנתונים בנקבים לצדי לצדדים וגי' שלפנינו עיקר רש"ל

והא מבטל כלי מהיכנו · פירשנו למעלה בפרק כירה (דף מג·) : *שתים בידי אדם ואחת באילן · בסוכה בפ"ב דף כב: וכס) תנן העושה סוכתו בראש האילן יש לפרש בשני ענינים העושה סוכתו בראש האילן כגון שהסכך של סוכה על גבי האילן והאילן סומך אותה שאין יכול לעלות על אותו סכך אלא אם כן ישתמש באילן שרגילין היו לתת כליהן על הסכך א"נ יש לפרש שהתקרה סמוכה באילן שגגאה בגובה ותחתיה על האילן דהשתא כל שעה שהוא מהלך בסוכה משתמש באילן : בחיבור גוולקי · שני שקין אחד בימין החמור ואחד משמאלו ובראש כל אחד מן השקין רצועה אחת וקושרין אותן שתי הרצועות יחד ועכשיו מונח הקשר כנגד גבו של החמור והשקין מכבידין לכאן ולכאן ואי אפשר להתיר הקשר אם לא יגביהו השקין מעט ונסמכין שתי השקין בכריסו של החמור והוו להו כצדדים :

למטה

רבינו חננאל

עליו ואפי' למאן דאמר לוקין א"כ לכתוב קרא לא תעשה כל מלאכה ובהמתך אתה למה לי אלא לומר לך כל מלאכה ניהו דלי' עביד מיחייב בבהמתו לא מיחייב · והלכתא כר' יוחנן דהא דרמי ליתא דרבא אהדר עליה ופריק לטעמיה · ואע"ג דפריק לנפשיה לא שבקינן דברי רבא וסמכינן אשנוייה : הגיע לחצר החיצונה נוטל הכלים וכו' · אמר רב הונא היתה בהמתו טעונה כלי זכוכית מביא כרים וכסתות ומתיר הכלים והשקין נופלים ואקשינן עלה והתנן נוטל את הכלים הניטלין בשבת וכלי זכוכית ניטלין בשבת ולמה אין ניטלין בפני עצמן · ופריק רב הונא מי סברת הא דאמרי' היתה [בהמתו] טעונה כלי זכוכי' כבוסות ואשישות קאמינא דשרי לטלטלן בשבת קאמר בקרני (דאוני) [דאומנא] קאימנא שמוצצין בהן הדם שאסור לטלטלן ולמה אסור לטלטלן והא קיי"ל דדבר שמלאכתו לאיסור אפי' לצורך גופו ומקומו שרי · תוב אקשי' עליה הא אמרת מביא כרים וכסתות ומניח תחת משאוי הבהמה כדי שיפלו כלי זכוכית הללו על דבר רך שלא ישברו והלא אסור להשתמש באותן הכרים והכסתות כל זמן שאלו כלי זכוכית עליהן ואינו יכול לישן בהם והנה מבטל כלי מהיכנו ופריק רב אשי בשליפי זוטרי · פי' שמנער את הכר או את הכסת מעט והן נופלות כי הא דתנן מעות שעל הכר מנער את הכר והן נופלות · ואקשינן עליה היתה בהמתו טעונה עששיות מתיר חבלים והשקין נופלים · ואע"פ שמשתברין ופריק רב הונא אלו העששיות אינן כלי זכוכית עשוין אלא פולסא פי' חתיכות גדולות כדכתיב ברזל עשות ורוצה להכניסם לבור לעשות מהן כלי זכוכית והלכתא כרב הונא דאע"ג דאיתותב הא שני לה ושנוייא שינויין אינון דהא מתרץ לה מאן דמותבה ואמרינן דיקא נמי דקתני דומיא דטבל מה טבל דלא חזו ליה פי' אלא אחר שיתקנן אף האי נמי לא חזי ליה · והא דתניא רבי שמעון בן יוחי אומר היתה בהמתו טעונה שליף של תבואה מכנים ראשו תחתיו ומסלקו לצד אחר הלכתא כוותיה שאינו מפרק אלא מכביהו לצד אחר ונופל מעצמו ובאנו להקשות ממשנתנו אדרבן גמליאל שהיתה חמורו טעונה דבש דלא רצה לפרק חמורו · והא אנן תנן נוטל את הכלים הניטלין בשבת וזה הדבש הוא ראוי לאכילה היה לו לנוטלו ומפרקינן דבש זה הדביש פי' הפסד כדמפרש בפרק המפקיד · ותוב אקשינן עליה היה לו להתיר החבלים ומעצמו יפלו השקין · ופרקי' חייש דלמא כשיפלו השקין בקרקע מצטרו זיקו ופי' מתבקעין הנודות שהדבש בהן כדכתיב וילכו ויצטירו. ותוב אקשינן עליה היה לו להביא כרים וכסתות ויניח תחתיהן ויפלו השקין בהן ולא יתבקעו דהכי שרי למעבד כרב הונא ופרקי' אם יפלו זיקי אילין על הכסתות נמצא מבטל כלי מהיכנו ואם תאמר ינערם ויפול הכסתות כמו שאמרנו למעלה אע"פ שינערם אינן ראויין להשתמש בהן היום דקא מיטנפי· עוד אקשינן עליה ולמה הניח חמורו טעונה הא איכא צער ב"ח ופריק רשב"ג צער בעלי חיים דרבנן · אביי אשכחיה לרבה דקא משפשף לבריה אגבה דחמרא' פי' שפשוף כדאמרינן ואם מבערב ישפשף כלומר יוליך ויביא ידו על גופו שיוסר מעליו טינוף הקרי כן רבא היה מעלה ומוריד בנו כעין שפשוף ע"ג החמור מן הצד לא על שדרו של חמור כדרך רכיבה אלא היה מושיבו ע"ג החמור והתינוק ומתגדר ונחית ואביו מחזיק בו ומחזיקו שלא יפול לארץ · א"ל אביי משתמש מר בבעלי חיים · כלומר המשתמש בב"ח עובר משום הא דתנן ולא רוכבין על גבי בהמה השיבו רבה אינו שדרו של

רב נסים גאון

ואפי' למאן דאמר לוקין· כלו' שר' ישמעאל סבר כי לאו שניתן לאזהרת [מיתת] ב"ד לוקין עליו ור"ע סבר לאו שניתן לאזהרת [מיתת] ב"ד אין לוקין עליו: והא קא מבטל כלי מהיכנו' כבר פירשנו בפ' מפנין שעיקרו בפרק

מסורת הש"ס

[עמ"ש תוס' לעיל מג: ד"ה ככר]
[ע' תוס' שם ד"ה טבל]
[פסחים טו: כ: נה: ביצה לו. ב"ק קח. ב"מ לח:]
[לעיל מג. וש"נ]
[ב"מ לב: וש"נ]
[פי' שקים ערוך וע' בערך חבר פי' באריכות]
[עירובין לג.]
[תוספתא סוכה פ"א]
[סוכה מח.]
[נ"ל גר"מאיר] ויש גורסין לרשב"א

הגהות הב"ח

(א) גמ' ומאי תימרא דתנן מתיר החבלים: (ב) שם דקמשתמשים באילן: (ג) שם זה הכלל כל שאילו ינטל האילן : (ד) רש"י ד"ה והא קא מבטל כלי מהיכנו כרים :

is no flagellation.[2] [154b] And even on the view that we do flagellate [in such a case],[3] let the Divine Law write, *'Thou shalt not do any work nor thy cattle'*: why state *'thou'?* [To teach:] only [when] he personally [works] is he liable, but [if] his animal works, he is not liable.

WHEN HE REACHES THE OUTERMOST COURTYARD, etc. R. Huna said: If his animal is laden with glassware, he brings mattresses and pillows, places [them] under it, unties the cords, and the sacks fall off. But we learnt: HE REMOVES THE OBJECTS WHICH MAY BE HANDLED ON THE SABBATH?[4]—R. Huna spoke of surgeon's horns,[5] which are not fit for him.[6] But he makes a utensil lose its readiness [for use]?[7]—The reference is to small bags.[8]

An objection is raised: If one's animal is laden with *ṭebel* or glass balls,[9] he must untie the cords and the sacks fall off, though they are broken?—There it treats of glass lumps.[10] This may be proved too, for it is taught analogous to *ṭebel:* just as *ṭebel* is of no use to him, so here too [it means something] that is of no use to him. Then why state, 'though they are broken'?[11]—You might say that they [the Sages] were concerned even about a trifling loss: hence he informs us [otherwise].

It was taught, R. Simeon b. Yoḥai said: If the animal is laden with a bag of corn,[12] one places his head under it and moves it to the other side, so that it falls off automatically. R. Gamaliel's ass was laden with honey, but he would not unload it until the termination of the Sabbath. On the termination of the Sabbath it died. But we learnt: HE REMOVES THE OBJECTS WHICH
a MAY BE HANDLED?[1]—It had gone rancid. If it had gone rancid, of what use was it?[2]—For camels' sores.[3] Then he should have untied the cords so that the sacks would fall off?—The gourds [containers] would burst. Then he should have brought mattresses and pillows and placed them beneath them?—They would become soiled[4] and he would deprive a utensil of its readiness [for use]. But there was suffering of dumb animals?—He holds that the suffering of dumb animals is [only] Rabbinically [forbidden].[5]

Abaye found Rabbah letting his son glide down the back of an ass.[6] Said he to him, You are making use of dumb creatures [on the Sabbath]?—It is but on the sides [of the animal], he replied, and in that case the Rabbis did not impose an interdict.[7] How do you know it?—Because we learnt: HE UNTIES THE CORDS AND THE SACKS FALL OFF AUTOMATICALLY. Does that not refer to a pair of coupled haversacks,[8] when we must make use of its sides, thus showing that in such a case the Rabbis did not impose an interdict? No, a balanced load is meant,[9] where no use of the sides is made; alternatively, it means where [the sacks are fastened] by a bolt.[10]

He raised an objection: If two [walls] are [made] by man and a third is on a tree, it is valid, but one must not ascend [enter]
b therein on the Festival.[1] Does that not mean that one made grooves on the tree,[2] so that it is the sides [only that would be used], and thus the sides are forbidden?—No: it means that he bent over [the branches of] the tree and placed the roofing upon it, so that he makes use of the tree. If so, consider the second clause: If three are made by man and a fourth is in a tree, it is valid, and one may ascend therein on the Festival. But if he bent over the tree, why may he ascend therein on the Festival?[3]—Then what would you: that the sides are forbidden,[4]—then still the question remains: why may one ascend therein on the Festival? But there it treats of spreading branches, and the tree itself was merely made a wall.[5] This may be proved too, for he states, This is the general rule: wherever it [the *sukkah*] can stand if the tree were removed, one may ascend therein on the Festival.[6] This proves it.

Shall we say that this is dependent on Tannaim? [For it was taught.] One may not ascend therein on the Festival; R. Simeon b. Eleazar said in R. Meir's name: One may ascend therein on the Festival. Is that not [to be explained] that they differ in this, viz., one Master holds: The sides are forbidden; while the other
c Master holds: The sides are permitted?[1]—Said Abaye, No: All hold that the sides are forbidden, but here they differ in respect of the sides of the sides:[2] one Master holds: The sides of the sides are forbidden; while the other Master holds: The sides of the sides are permitted.

Raba maintained: He who forbids the sides forbids the sides of the sides too, while he who permits the sides of the sides permits the sides too. R. Mesharsheya raised an objection to Raba: If

(2) I.e., the offender could be formally warned against driving a laden ass on the grounds that it is punishable by death; in such a case there is no flagellation even if the death penalty is not imposed. (3) V. Mak. 13b. (4) Glassware may be handled. (5) Used in bleeding. (6) For handling on the Sabbath. (7) V. *supra* 43a. These pillows, etc. may be handled, but not when the sacks fall upon them. (8) The pillows can be pulled away from under them—which is permitted—without hurt, as they have not far to fall. (9) The word denotes lumps of glass, lanterns, etc. (10) Which may be broken without loss. (11) Seeing that no loss is incurred. (12) Of *ṭebel*.

a (1) Which includes honey. (2) Why did he trouble to bring it at all? (3) Caused by the chafing of the saddle. (4) If any of the honey were spilt. (5) This may seem non-humane, but it must be borne in mind that this was held long before other peoples gave the slightest consideration to animals. Cf. *supra* 128b, n. a2 and 117b, n. b6. (6) To amuse him. (7) It is not the normal way of employing an animal. (8) Coupled or tied together by a cord, a sack hanging down from each side of the animal. To make them fall one would have to lift them off and lean and rub against the animal in doing so, which is making use of its sides. Hence this shows that it is permitted. (9) Each sack being separately attached to a ring by a hook; a slight jerk would suffice to unhook it, and he would not make use of the animal. V. Jast s.v. חֶבֶר. (10) A wooden cross-bar which can easily be pulled out, letting the sacks drop.

b (1) V. Suk. 22a. A *sukkah* (q.v. Glos.) requires three walls only. Now if two are erected in the normal fashion, whilst the third is made of a tree (this may mean either that the tree constitutes the third wall or that the third wall is fastened to the tree), the *sukkah* is valid. Nevertheless, one may not enter it on the Festival itself but only during the intermediate days. For the roof is attached to the tree and various utensils, etc., were hung on the roof; thus indirectly one would be using the tree itself, which is forbidden on Festivals. 'Ascending' is mentioned because the *sukkah* was often built above the ground, e.g., on a roof (Rashi). (2) Wherein he fitted the third wall.—This assumes the second of the two meanings in n. b1. (3) He still makes use of the tree, in spite of the other three walls. (4) You wish to adhere to your original hypothesis, whence this follows. (5) I.e., the thick branches were allowed to form a fourth wall, the *sukkah* coming right up to them, but the roofing rested on the three other walls, not on the branches. The previous answer could have been retained, viz., that he bent over the branches of the tree, but rested the roofing on the other three walls. Since however a fourth wall is not required at all, it is assumed that one would not go to this trouble unless he meant the roofing to rest upon it (Rashi). (6) That is the reason of the second clause quoted above. Hence it must be assumed that the *sukkah* is so made that the roofing does not rest on the tree at all, as otherwise it could not stand if the tree were removed.

c (1) Assuming that grooves were made in the tree etc., as above. (2) The laths or canes fitted in the grooves are the sides, whilst the roofing which rests on the laths are the sides of the sides. I.e., they differ as to whether one may make *indirect* use of the sides.

one drives [155a] a peg in a tree and hangs a basket thereon[3] above ten handbreadths [from the ground], his *'erub* is not an *'erub;*[4] below ten handbreadths, his *'erub* is an *'erub*. Thus it is only because he fixed a peg in the tree, but if he did not, even if it is below ten handbreadths his *'erub* is not an *'erub*.[5] Thus this Tanna forbids the sides yet permits the indirect use of the sides? —Said R. Papa: Here we treat of a narrow-mouthed basket, so that in taking out the *'erub* he sways the tree, and thus makes use of the tree itself. Now the law is that the sides are forbidden, but the sides of the sides are permitted. R. Ashi said: Now that you have ruled that the sides are forbidden, one must not rest the lodge-ladder[6] on the palm tree, because that is tantamount to the [use of the] sides [of the trees;][7] but he must rest it on pegs without the tree,[8] and when he ascends he should place his foot not on the pegs but on the rungs.[9]

MISHNAH. BUNDLES [PEḲI'IN] OF SHEAVES MAY BE UNTIED FOR CATTLE AND BUNCHES [KIPPIN] MAY BE SPREAD
a OUT, BUT NOT SMALL BUNDLES [ZIRIN].[1] NEITHER FODDER[2] NOR CAROBS MAY BE CHOPPED UP FOR CATTLE, WHETHER SMALL OR LARGE;[3] R. JUDAH PERMITS IN THE CASE OF CAROBS FOR SMALL CATTLE.

GEMARA. R. Huna said: PEḲI'IN and KIPPIN are identical, [save that] *peḳi'in* are two [bunches tied together], while *kippin* are three; *zirin* are young shoots of cedar trees.[4] And this is what he [the Tanna] teaches: BUNDLES [PEḲI'IN] OF SHEAVES MAY BE UNTIED FOR CATTLE, AND THEY MAY BE SPREAD, and the same applies to KIPPIN, BUT NOT TO ZIRIN, which may neither be spread out nor untied. R. Ḥisda said, What is R. Huna's reason? He holds that we may indeed take trouble over [natural] foodstuffs,[5] but we may not turn something into foodstuffs.[6] Rab Judah said: *Peḳi'in* and *zirin* are identical, [save that] *peḳi'in* are two [bunches tied together], whilst *zirin* are three; *kippin* are young cedar shoots. And this is what he teaches: BUNDLES [PEḲI'IN] OF SHEAVES MAY BE UNTIED FOR CATTLE, but not spread out, but as for KIPPIN, [THEY] MAY [INDEED] BE SPREAD OUT; BUT NOT ZIRIN, [which it is not permitted] to spread out but [merely] to untie. Raba said, What is Rab Judah's reason? He holds that we may indeed turn something into fodder, but may not take trouble over fodder.[7]

We learnt: NEITHER FODDER NOR CAROBS MAY BE CHOPPED UP FOR CATTLE, WHETHER SMALL OR LARGE: [Surely it means] carobs like fodder: just as fodder is soft, so are soft carobs meant, thus proving that we may not take trouble over [what is] foodstuff [in any case], which refutes R. Huna?—R. Huna can answer you: No: fodder like carobs: just as carobs are hard,
b so hard fodder[1] is meant.[2] Where is that possible?[3] In the case of very young foals.

Come and hear: R. JUDAH PERMITS IN THE CASE OF CAROBS FOR SMALL CATTLE. Thus, only for small but not for large: now it is well if you agree that the first Tanna holds that we may not take trouble over foodstuffs, yet we may turn [something] into foodstuffs: hence R. Judah argues [that cutting up] carobs for small cattle is also [an act of] turning [it] into fodder. But if you maintain that the first Tanna holds that we may not turn [aught] into fodder, yet we may take trouble over fodder, then R. JUDAH PERMITS IN THE CASE OF CAROBS FOR SMALL CATTLE [only]? all the more so for large cattle![4]—Do you think that *daḳḳah* [small] is literally meant? [No] By *daḳḳah* large cattle is meant, yet why is it called *daḳḳah?* Because it grinds [*dayyḳa*] its food.[5] But since the first clause states, WHETHER SMALL OR LARGE, it follows that R. Judah means literally small? This is indeed a difficulty.

(3) And places his *'erub*—an *'erub* of boundaries (v. Glos.)—in it, intending to spend the Sabbath under the tree.—An *'erub* is not valid unless it is accessible on the Sabbath. (4) Because a basket is generally four handbreadths square, and if it is ten from the ground it is technically a private domain (cf. *supra* 6a), whereas the ground below is a public domain, and so one must not take the *'erub* from the basket; hence it is not accessible. (5) I.e., if he merely tied the basket to the tree. The *'erub* is invalid because in order to get at it he must make use of the side of the tree; where it is hanging on a peg, however, he only makes indirect use of the sides. (6) A ladder for ascending to a lodge set high up on poles near a tree. (7) When he ascends on the Sabbath. (8) I.e., pegs driven into the tree (Rashi). Jast.: on the branches spreading beyond the circumference of the tree. (9) Or, on the canes protruding from the poles on which the lodge is built.

a (1) The Gemara discusses the exact meaning of the terms used. (2) *Shaḥath* is corn not fully grown as fodder. (3) 'Small cattle'—sheep, goats, calves, etc.; large—cows and oxen. (4) Cut from the tree. While yet moist they are fit for fodder, though most people leave them to dry for fuel. (5) Such as bundles of sheaves. (6) Such as young shoots which are normally intended for fuel. (7) When the bundles are tied they are not fit for fodder, therefore they may be untied; but it is superfluous indulgence to spread them out, and that is forbidden. Bunches of young shoots, however, are unfit for fodder unless they are spread out; hence it is permitted.

b (1) E.g., if the corn has gone dry. (2) Without being cut up they are altogether unfit; hence they may not be cut up. (3) That unless cut up they are unfit.—Generally animals can eat them even when hard. (4) Since carobs are fit in any case, but are more easily eaten when cut up. 'All the more so'—because if they are fit in their present state for small cattle, they are certainly fit for large. (5) Chewing it until it is finely cut up.

יתד באילן ותלה בה כלכלה למעלה מעשרה טפחים אין עירובו עירוב למטה מי' טפחים עירובו עירוב טעמא דנעץ יתד באילן הא לא נעץ אפילו למטה מי' טפחים אין עירובו עירוב והא האי תנא דקאסר בצדדין וקשרי בצדי צדדין אמר רב פפא הכא בכלכלה דחוקה עסקינן דבהדי דשקיל ליה לעירוב קמניד ליה לאילן וקמשמש באילן גופיה °והלכתא *צדדין אסורין צדי צדדין מותרין אמר רב אשי השתא דאמרת צדדין אסורין האי דרגא דמדלא לא לינחיה איניש אדיקלא דהוו להו צדדין אלא לינחיה אגוואזי לבר מדיקלא וכי סליק לא לינח כרעיה אגוואזי אלא ליתנח אקנין:

מתני' מתירין פקיעי עמיר לפני בהמה ומפספסין את הכיפין אבל לא את (א) הזירין אין מרסקין לא את השחת ולא את החרובין לפני בהמה בין דקה ובין גסה רבי יהודה מתיר בחרובין לדקה:

גמ' אמר רב הונא הן הן פקיעין הן הן כיפין פקיעין תרי כיפין תלתא(ב) זירין דארזי וה"ק מתירין פקיעי עמיר לפני בהמה ומפספסין והוא הדין לכיפין אבל לא את הזירין לא לפספס ולא להתיר אמר רב חסדא מאי טעמא דרב הונא קא סבר למטרח באוכלא טרחינן לשויי אוכלא לא משוינן רב יהודה אמר הן הן פקיעין הן הן זירין פקיעין תרי זירין תלתא כיפין דארזי וה"ק ב מתירין פקיעי עמיר לפני בהמה אבל פספוסי לא וכיפין פספוסי נמי מפספסינן אבל לא הזירין לפספס [א] אלא להתיר אמר רבא מאי טעמא דרבי יהודה קסבר ג שווי אוכלא משוינן מטרח באוכלא לא טרחינן תנן ד אין מרסקין את השחת ואת החרובין לפני בהמה בין דקה ובין גסה מאי לאו חרובין דומיא דשחת מה שחת דרכיכי אף חרובין דרכיכי אלמא לא טרחינן באוכלא ותיובתיה דרב הונא אמר לך רב הונא לא שחת דומיא דחרובין מה חרובין דאקושי אף שחת דאקושי היכי משכחת לה בעילי זוטרי ת"ש רבי יהודה מתיר בחרובין לדקה לדקה אין לגסה לא אי אמרת בשלמא ת"ק סבר מיטרח באוכלא לא טרחינן שווי משוינן היינו דקא אמר ר' יהודה(ג) החרובין לדקה נמי שווי אוכלא הוא אלא אי אמרת ת"ק סבר שווי אוכלא לא משוינן מיטרח באוכלא מטרחינן רבי יהודה(ד) דמתיר בחרובין לדקה כל שכן לגסה מי סברת דקה דקה ממש מאי דקה גסה(ה) ומאי קרי לה דקה דדייקא באוכלא הא מדקתני רישא בין דקה ובין גסה מכלל דרבי יהודה דקה דקה ממש קאמר קשיא תא שמע *מתתבין את

רש"י

יתד · עץ : ותלה בה כלכלה · ונתן בה עירובו והוא נתכוון לשבות למטה תחת האילן : למטה מי' טפחים · אם הכלכלה בתוך י' לארץ עירובו עירוב דהוא ועירובו ברה"ר אבל למעלה מי' וסתם כלכלה רחבה ארבעה הויא לה כלכלה רשות היחיד והוא נתכוון לשבות ברשות הרבים ואינו יכול ליטלו שם ולאכלו וכיון דאיכא סעודה הראויה לו אינו קונה שביתה על ידה : טעמא דנעץ יתד · דכי שקיל לעירובו משתמש בצדי צדדין אבל לא נעץ יתד אלא קשרה בצדי אילן לא : הכא בכלכלה דחוקה · שפיה צר וקצרה היא ומכניס ידו לתוכה בדוחק הלכך אי ממש הוה קטר לה בצדי אילן כי שקיל ליה לעירוביה מניד ליה לאילן הלכך כי איכא יתד הוא דשרי ואי לא לא : האי דרגא דמדלא · סולם שעולין בו לסוכת עליה שעושין ע"ג קונדיסין גבוהין והיא סמוכה לאילן : לא לינחיה · ראש הסולם אדיקלא לא יסמוך ראש הסולם נגד דקל דכי סליק משתמש בצדדין : אלא לינחיה אגוואזי לבר מדיקלא · יתקע יתד בצדי האילן ויסמוך הסולם עליו דהוה ליה יתד צדדים וסולם צדי צדדין : וכי סליק לא לינח כרעיה על היתד אלא אקניא · על שליבות הסולם או קנים היוצאים מהקונדיסין: **מתני'** פקיעי עמיר · קשין של שבלים (שאותם) שאוגדים מתירין אותם שיהו נוחין לבהמה לאוכלה : מפספסין · שכן דרך שמפזרים לבהמה העשבים ויפין לה לאוכלן שכשהן דחוקין מתחממין ואינה מריחה ריחה כל כך וקצה בהן : את הכיפין · מפרש בגמרא וכן זירין : אין מרסקין · אין מחתכין : שחת · עשב של תבואה והוא אספסתא ומשום דטירחא דלא צריך הוא : רבי יהודה מתיר בחרובין לדקה · ששיניה דקות וקשין לה : **גמ'** הן הן פקיעין הן הן כיפין · כולן קשין של שבלין הן מיהו פקיעין תרי שאינן קשורין אלא בשני ראשים : כיפין תלת · קשורין ג' [אגודים] : זירין דארזא · ענפים לחין של ארז שמזרדין אותם ובעודם לחין ראויין לבהמה ורוב בני אדם מניחין אותם לעצים : וה"ק מתירין פקיעי עמיר ומפספסין . דכיון דמעיקרא אוכלא ניהו מותר לטרוח בהן להכשירם למתקן לה ואת הכיפין אף הן מתירין ומפספסין ואע"ג דנפיש טרחייהו אבל לא הזירין לא לפספס ולא להתיר דכיון דמעיקרא סתמייהו לאו אוכלא והשתא הוא דמשוי להו אוכלא ה"ל אולודי אוכלא בשבת : מיטרח באוכלא · בדבר שתחילתו אוכל קודם תיקון זה טרחינן ומכשרינן לייפותן לה : הן הן פקיעין הן הן זירין · שניהן בקשים של שבלים ומה שהתיר בזה התיר בזה ודקתני אבל לא הזירין אפספוס קאי : וה"ק מתירין פקיעי עמיר · דכל זמן שהוא קשור לאו אוכלא הוא ומתירו לשווי אוכלא ומשום צער בהמה שרי אבל פספוס לא דסגי ליה בהתרה ואיתעביד אוכלא ופספוסיה לתענוג בעלמא הוא ומטרח באוכל בדבר שהוא כבר אוכל בלא תיקון זה לא טרחינן ומפספסין את הכיפין דארזא דבלאו פספוס לא הוי אוכלא אבל לא את הזירין לפספס אלא להתיר שלשה אוגדין בפקיעין דהתרת אוגדין שווי אוכלא הוא : אין מרסקין · סיפא דמתניתין היא וחד טעמא : דרכיכי · כגון חרובין לחין דראויין למאכל בהמה בלא ריסוק וריסוק דידהו לתענוג בעלמא : דאקושי · קשין כגון שיבשו : בעילי זוטרי · עיירים קטנים שאף השחת קשה להם וצריכה ריסוק לשווי אוכלא : לדקה אין · דהוה ליה שווי אוכלא : לגסה לא · דהוה ליה מטרח באוכלא : אי אמרת בשלמא · שמע רבי יהודה לת"ק דאמר מיטרח באוכלין אסור ואין מרסקין ברכיכי קאמר אבל שווי אוכלא שרי היינו דקאמר ליה רבי יהודה חרובין לדקה לית לן למיסר דשווי אוכלא הוא ואע"ג דרכיכי אלא אי אמרת קסבר ת"ק מיטרח באוכלא שרי שווי אוכלא אסור ואין מרסקין דקאמר בדאקושי קאמר דשווי אוכלא הוי : רבי יהודה מתיר בחרובין לדקה · בתמיה הא כל שכן דלגסה למיטרח באוכלא הוא ושרי הכי ה"ל למיתני ור' יהודה מתיר בחרובין לגסה דהוה ליה מיטרח באוכלא והא ליכא למימר דר' יהודה מפיך דשווי אוכלא שרי מיטרח באוכלא אסיר דהא ת"ק בדאקושי קאמר וגבי גסה נמי שווי אוכלא הוא וה"ל למיתני ורבי יהודה מתיר סתמא בין דקה בין גסה ועוד הוה ליה למישרי נמי זירין להתיר ולפספס דשווי אוכלא נמי הוא : דדייקא · כוססת יפה ומדקת אוכלין בפיה : והא מדקתני רישא בין דקה בין גסה שמע מינה דקה ממש · ורבי יהודה את"ק קאי :

תוספות

למטה מי' טפחים עירובו עירוב · קשה אמאי עירובו עירוב והא כרמלית הוא כיון שרחבה ארבעה ואסור לטלטל לרה"ר וי"ל אין כרמלית בכלים כדפירש בקונטרס בפ"ק דמכילתין (דף ח:) גבי היתה קופתו מונחת כו' °אי נמי כרבי דאמר *כל דבר שהוא משום שבות לא גזרו עליו בין השמשות : אמר רב פפא הכא בכלכלה דחוקה עסקינן · מדמשני רב פפא הכי משמע דסבירא ליה צדדין מותרין ורב אשי משמע בסמוך דסבר דאסורין מדאמר רב אשי בסמוך השתא דאמרת צדדין אסורין וקשה לי הא איפכא שמעינן להו במסכת חגיגה בפ"ב (דף יז. ושם) דאמר רב פפא שמע מינה צדדין אסורין דאי סלקא דעתך צדדין מותרים נסמוך אריסא דצדדין ניכהו רב אשי אמר אפילו תימא צדדין מותרין, כל דלהדי גבה כגבה דמי* : והלכתא צדדין אסורין צדי צדדין מותרין · ותימה לרבי אמאי לא חשיב הני בהדי יע"ל קג"ס דהלכה כאביי (בבבא מציעא דף כב:) דאמר רבא מאן דאסר בצדדין אסר נמי בצדי צדדין ואביי אמר בצדדין כולי עלמא לא פליגי [דאסור] ובצדי צדדין פליגי : רב יהודה אמר הן הן פקיעין כו' וה"ק מתירים פקיעי עמיר כו' · פירש בקונטרס דהתרת פקיעים הויא שווי אוכלא וצריך לפרש(ו) נמי בהא דרב יהודה חשיב התרת פקיעין שווי אוכלא ורב הונא לא חשיב לה שווי אוכלא מדשרי לה ואין נראה לרבינו תם לאפלוגינהו בהכי אלא לתרוייהו לא הויא התרת פקיעי עמיר לא שויא אוכלא ולא מיטרח באוכלא דלא שייך טורח בהתרה והכי שריא לתרוייהו · מ"ר אין

*) ...פי' ולענ"ד י"ל דנ"מ בע"ש שחל להיות ביו"ט והניח עירוב בערב יו"ט בכלכלה זו שיהיה עירוב ליו"ט ושבת · ולפי דב' קדושות הן צריך שיהיה עירובו קיים ביה"ש דקודם שבת ובזה אם לא ... מהני עירובו לשבת דבה"ש אינו יכול ליטול עירובו דהא בממנ"פ אסור אי סוף יום והוא יו"ט או לילה והוא שבת אסור בשימוש במחובר אבל בנעץ יתד דמצד טלטול מכרמלית לרה"ר ליכא איסור סופא ביו"ט ובה"ש מותר דמשום שבות לא גזרינן בה"ש דדלמא עדיין יום וליכא איסור סופא :

עין משפט נר מצוה

[לעיל ח:]

כ א מיי' פכ"ה מהל' שבת הלכה ט סמג לאוין סה טוש"ע א"ח סימן שב סעיף יח :

כא ב ג מיי' פכ"א מהל' שבת הל' יח טוש"ע א"ח סי' שכד סעיף ד :

כב ד מיי' שם טוש"ע שם סעיף ח :

[ועי' תוספות חגיגה יז. ד"ה רב אשי דלא מקשה אלא דרב אשי אדרב אשי וכתבו תירוץ לזה]

רבינו חננאל

חמור אלא בצידי החמור אני משפשף (וינדלן)[וצדדין] לא גזרו בהו רבנן מדתנן מתיר החבלים והשקין נופלין מאי לאו כחבר גואלקי ולא גזרו בהו רבנן פי' חבר גואלקי כשטוענין הבהמה מביאין שק וטוענין אותו מצד אחד ושק האחר מצד השני ומביא חבל וקושרן ומחברן (ומשרכבן) [ומשכיבן] בצדי הבהמה וכשמבקשין לפרק משאוי מגביה השקין לרפרף קשר החבל להיות נוח להתיר ומתיר ומניח השקין והן יורדין מצדי הבהמה ויורדין לארץ נמצא מגביה ומוריד השקין בצידי החמור כאשר אני מגביה ע"ג החמור והוא יורד בדרך שפשף אמר לך אביי אינו אומר מתיר החבלים בחבר גואלקי אלא באבר גואלקי כדתנן כיצד מאברין את העדים ומפרשינן ליה מלשון אבר כן מוסיף כמין אבר בגואלקי והוא למעלה כדאמרי' בפ' לא יחפור (ב"ב כה:) באברורי הוו יתבי פי' אברורי למעלה מן המשאוי כגון שהיה צד המשאוי האחד כבד והשני קל ורצינו להשוות המשאוי שלא יהיה *)מטרטן ומוסיף על הצד הקל דבר להשוות המשקל שלא יהיה אחד מהן מכריע ועליו אמרה משנתנו מתיר החבלים והשקין נופלים שהקשר למעלה הוא' ואין צריך להגביה שק ולא להוריד אלא כשמתיר החבר נופלין אבר גואלקי נמצאו גואלקי על צידי בהמה ואם זה על גואלקי נמצא אבר זה צדי צדדין אי נמי בגואלקי דגואלקי עצמו אינן קשורין בחבלים אלא כמנהג שהי' לאורחים המהלכים בדרכים שעושין בראש השקין כמין קרסים ולולאות מן החבלים ומכניס הלולאות בקרסים אי נמי לולאות בלבד ומכנים בהן עץ ומחברן וכשרוצה לפרקן מושך העץ ההוא והן נופלים ונקרא עץ ההוא לכתא ואינו מניע לצדדין ואותו האבר נמי שמוסיפין על המשאוי הוא צדדי צדדין והוא מותר אבל הצדדין אסורין · ועוד אקשי ליה אביי לרבה הא ב' בידי אדם ואחת באילן כו' ופריק רבה התם דכפייה לאילן וסיכך על גביו שנמצא משתמש באילן עצמו · תוב אקשינן עליה מסיפא דקתני ג' בידי אדם ואחת באילן כשרה ועולין לה ביו"ט ואי כפייה לאילן וסיכך ע"ג אמאי עולין לה ביו"ט הא משתמש באילן ואסור ופריק ליה התם ופרסי כאנא פי' גיתא ופרסיכנא תרתב מאבקא **)עלה דייקינן זה הכלל כל שינטל האילן ויכולה לעמוד עולין לה ביו"ט ליטא כתנאי אין עולין לה ביו"ט כו' סברי לה כגון דחק באילן ונתן הנסרין שהן הסכך באותה החקיקה והן הצדדין זה אוסר להשתמש בצדדין וזה מתיר אמר אביי כולי עלמא צדדין אסורין והכא בצידי צדדין פליגי פי' כגון דחק באילן ונתן באותה החקיקה עץ חזק כמין קורה ושם ראשי הנסרים שהן הסכך על אותו העץ הנתון כמין קורה שנמצא העץ ההוא צדדי האילן והנסרים הנתונין על גביו צדדי צדדין רבא א' צדדין וצדדי צדדין דינם אחד האוסר בצדדין אוסר גם בצידי צדדין והמתיר צדדי צדדין גם בצדדין מתיר ובא רב משרשיא לאותובי לרבה דאמר המתיר בצידי צדדין גם בצדדין מתיר הא דתניא נעץ יתד באילן ותלה בו כלכלה למטה מעשרה עירובו עירוב למטה מי' טפחים אין עירובו עירוב · ודייקינן מינה טעמא דנעץ יתד באילן ותלה בו כלכלה פי' דהוה לה יתד צידי האילן והכלכלה צידי צדדין ולפיכך למטה מעשרה טפחים עירובו עירוב אבל אם לא נעץ יתד ותלה בו אלא תלה באמירי האילן אפילו למטה מעשרה אין עירובו עירוב דהוה לי' צדדין הדר נתברר כי

*) עיין ערוך ערך אכרוכי · **) פה הדברים משובשים בכ"י ומלוס לתקנם ועי' בערוך ערך גז האחרון ·

מסורת הש"ס

[חגיגה טז:]

לקמן קטו:

הגהות הב"ח

(א) במשנה את הכיפין אבל לא את הזורדין אין : (ב) גמ' כיפין תלתא זורדין דארזי וכו' אבל לא את הזורדין לא ליפספס וכו' למטרח באוכלא טרחינן לשווי אוכלא לא משוינן וכו' הן הן זורדין פקיעין תרי זורדין תלתא וכו' אבל לא הזורדין לפספסא : (ג) שם היינו דקא אמר ר' יהודה חרובין לדקה נמי שווי אוכלא: (ד) שם ר' יהודה מתיר כצ"ל ואות ד' נמחק: (ה) שם מאי דקה גסה ואמאי קרי : (ו) תוס' ד"ה ר' יהודה וכו' וצריך לפרש דפליגי נמי בהא :

הגהות הגר"א

[א] גמ' לפספס אלא להתיר · נ"ב גירסת הרי"ף ולא להתיר וכן מאד :

גליון הש"ס

גמ' והלכתא צדדים אסורין · עיין עירובין דף לג ע"א : תוס' ד"ה למטה מי' וכו'

רב נסים גאון

בפרק כירה (דף מג) ופירשנו כי החלוקה בצער בעלי חיים דאורייתא או דרבנן תמצא בפרק אלו מציאות (דף לג) :

עין משפט נר מצוה

כג א מיי' פכ"א מהל' שבת הלכה יח סמג לאוין סה טוש"ע א"ח סימן שכד סעיף ו :

כד ב ג מיי' שם טוש"ע שם סעיף ז :

כה ד ה מיי' שם הלכה לה טוש"ע שם סע"ט:

כו ו מיי' שם והלכה לו טוש"ע שם סעיף י :

כז ז ח"ט מיי' שם טוש"ע שם סעיף יא :

כח י מיי' פ"כ מהלכות טומאת מת הלכה ד :

כט כ מיי' פכ"א מהל' שבת הלכה לה :

ל ל מיי' פכ"א מהלכות שבת הלכה לד טוש"ע א"ח סי' שכד סע"ג :

רש"י

את הדלועין · התלושין ולא אמרינן מוקצין הן לבהמה דמאכל אדם הן : אשוני · קשין : א"נ · כלבים דקאמר בגורייתא זוטרי דכל נבלה קשה להן : ומערבין · התבן והאספסתא יחד והבהמה אוכלת התבן בשביל האספסתא : תבן בתיבנא סריא · דלא חזיא והשתא משוי לה אוכלא והאי סריא לאו סריא לגמרי דהויא לטינא קיימא ואסורה לטלטל : **מתני'** אין אובסין · מאכילין אותו הרבה על כ"חו ותוחבין לו בגרוט ובגמרא מפרש לשון אובסין עושין לה כמין אבוס בתוך מעיה : ולא דורסין · שדורס לה בתוך גרונה את השעורין ומיהו לא הוי כל כך כמו אובסין : אבל מלעיטין · מפרש בגמרא : אין מאמירין · מפרש בגמרא : מהלקטין · מפרש בגמרא : אין נותנין מים לפני דבורים · מפרש טעמא בגמרא אי משום דאין מזונותיהן עליו שיוצאין ואוכלין בשדה אי משום דמיא באגמא שכיח להו : הרדיסאות · על שם מקומן וניזונין בתוך הבית : **גמ'** כי האי גוונא · שיאכילנה כל כך שירחיבו מעיה כאבוס : אטענה טורא · על גבה למזונות לדרך לבד שאר משאות : למקום שאינה יכולה להחזיר · שתוחבו לה לפנים מבית הבליעה : בכלי · בתרווד : דספי בידים · תוחבו לתוך פיו : אלא יוני שובך וכו' · בתמיה ולמאי לא מאי טרחא איכא : אלא להו כו' · ומדמהלקטין דמתניתין למקום שאינה יכולה להחזיר נמי שרי שמע מינה מלעיטין דעגלים וגמלים למקום שאינה יכולה להחזיר ושרי אלא דגבי בהמה קרי ליה הלעטה וגבי עופות קרי ליה הילקוט ועל כרחך אין מאמירין דקאסר בכלי הוא : לעולם מהלקטין דספי ליה בידים · ולמקום שיכולה להחזיר : אין מזונותן עליך · דשכיחי להו בדברא : חזיר אין מזונותן עליך · דאסור יהודי *שיגדל חזירים : מתני' נמי דיקא · דאפילו שדי קמייהו נמי לא : דשכיחי באגמא · אבל מזונות לא שכיחי להו : שמזונותיו מועטין · שאין אדם חס עליו לתת לו מזונות הרבה : כמה תשהה במעיו · דהכלב שאכל בשר מת ומת הכלב בבית תוך ג' ימים מטמא באהל אבל בחיין לא מטמא דטומאה בלועה בבעלי חיים לא מיטמא כדאמר בבהמה המקשה (חולין דף עא:) : שמע מינה · מדקאמר שהקפיד הקדוש ברוך הוא על מזונותיו : משח אודניה · מעט כמות אזנו וקוטרא בתריה יכהו במקל מיד שלא יהא מרגילו אצלו : אבל במתא לא · ליתיב ליה מידי אי לאו דידיה הוא : משום דאתי למסרך · בתריה ויפסידו : לית דעתיר מחזירא · שכל מאכל ראוי לו ומוצא לאכול ואף מאכילין לו הרבה : כוותיה דרב יהודה · שהמראה למקום שאינו יכול להחזיר : פוקס את פיה · נותן חכה לתוך פיה שלא תוכל לסגור פיה : ומאכילה כרשינין ומים בבת אחת · והמים מבליעין הכרשינין לתוך בית בליעתה על כרחה : מאכילה מעומד · נותן לתוך פיה וכל זמן שאינו מרבילה אינו יכול לתחוב כל כך ויכול להחזירה : מתניתין מני · דקתני נותן מים לתוך המורסן דנתינת מים לא זהו גיבולו : אפי' רבי יוסי מודה · דזהו גיבולו : קלי · קמח של תבואה שנתייבשה כשהן קליות בתנור ואותו קמח לעולם מתוק והוא *קמחא דאבשונא ועושין ממנו שתיתא משמן ומים ומלח שמערבין בו :

רבי

תוספות

אין אובסין את הגמל וכו' · והא דאמרינן בעירובין פרק עושין פסין (דף כ: ושם) גמל שראשו ורובו מבפנים אובסין אותו מבפנים הך אביסה לאו היינו אביסה ממש דהא אמרינן הכא אין אובסין כו' וההיא אביסה היינו הלעטה וכן פירש רבינו שמואל: **אלא** קמח דבר גיבול הוא · פירשתי לעיל בפ"ק (דף יח· ושם*) :

גמרא

תורה אור

*את הדלועין לפני הבהמה ואת הנבלה לפני הכלבים °מאי לאו דלועין דומיא דנבלה מה נבלה דרכיכא אף דלועין דרכיכי אלמא טרחינן באוכלא ותיובתא דרב יהודה אמר לך רב יהודה לא נבלה דומיא דדלועין מה דלועין דאשוני אף נבלה דאשונא והיכי משכחת לה בבשר פילי א"נ בגורייאתא זוטרי תא שמע דתני רב חנן מנהרדעא *מפרכינן תבן ואספסתא ומערבין אלמא טרחינן באוכלא תבן בתיבנא סריא אספסתא בעילי זוטרי : **מתני'** אין אובסין את הגמל ולא דורסין אבל מלעיטין ואין מאמירין את העגלים אבל מלעיטין ומהלקטין לתרנגולין ונותנין מים למורסן אבל לא גובלין ואין נותנין מים לפני דבורים ולפני יונים שבשובך אבל נותנין לפני אווזין ותרנגולין ולפני יוני הרדיסיות : **גמ'** מאי אין אובסין אמר רב יהודה אין עושין לה אבוס בתוך מעיה מי איכא כי האי גוונא אין וכדאמר רב ירמיה מדיפתי לדידי חזי לי ההוא טייעא דאכלא כורא *ואטעינא כורא : אין מאמירין : איזו היא המראה ואיזו היא הלעטה אמר רב יהודה המראה למקום שאינה יכולה להחזיר הלעטה למקום שיכולה להחזיר רב חסדא אמר אידי ואידי למקום שאינה יכולה להחזיר והמראה בכלי הלעטה ביד מתיב רב יוסף *מהלקטין לתרנגולין ואין צריך לומר שמלקיטין ואין מלקיטין ליוני שובך וליוני עלייה ואין צריך לומר שאין מהלקטין מאי מהלקטין ומאי מלקיטין אילימא מהלקטין דספי ליה בידים מלקיטין דשדי ליה(א) קמייהו מכלל דיוני שובך ויוני עלייה מישדא קמייהו נמי לא אלא לאו מהלקטין למקום שאינה יכולה להחזיר מלקיטין למקום שיכולה להחזיר מכלל דהמראה בכלי ותיובתא דרב יהודה אמר לך רב יהודה לעולם מהלקטין דספי ליה בידים מלקיטין דשדי ליה קמייהו ודקא קשיא לך יוני שובך ויוני עלייה למישדא קמייהו נמי לא הני מזונותן עליך והני אין מזונותן עליך כדתניא נותנין מזונות לפני כלב ואין נותנין מזונות לפני חזיר ומה הפרש בין זה לזה זה מזונותיו עליך וזה אין מזונותיו עליך אמר רב אשי מתניתין נמי דיקא אין נותנין מים לפני דבורים ולפני יונים שבשובך אבל נותנין לפני אווזין ולפני תרנגולין ולפני יוני הרדיסיות מ"ט לאו משום דהני מזונותן עליך והני אין מזונותן עליך וליטעמיך מאי איריא מיא אפילו חיטי ושערי נמי לא אלא שאני מיא דשכיחי באגמא דרש רבי יונה אפיתחא דבי נשיאה מאי דכתיב °(*יודע) צדיק דין דלים יודע הקב"ה בכלב שמזונותיו מועטין לפיכך שוהה אכילתו במעיו ג' ימים *כדתנן כמה תשהה אכילתו במעיו ויהא טמא בכלב ג' ימים מעת לעת ובעופות ובדגים כדי שתפול לאור ותשרף אמר רב המנונא שמע מינה אורח ארעא למשדא אומצא לכלבא וכמה אמר רב מרי משח אודניה וחוטרא אבתריה הני מילי בדברא אבל במתא לא דאתא למסרך אמר רב פפא לית דעניא מכלבא ולית דעתיר מחזירא תניא כוותיה דרב יהודה *איזו היא המראה ואיזו היא הלעטה המראה מרביצה ופוקס את פיה ומאכילה כרשינין ומים בבת אחת הלעטה מאכילה מעומד ומשקה מעומד ונותנין כרשינין בפני עצמן ומים בפני עצמן : מהלקטין לתרנגולין כו' : אמר אביי אמריתה קמיה דמר מתניתין מני ואמר לי ר' יוסי בר יהודה היא דתניא *אחד נותן את הקמח ואחד נותן לתוכו מים האחרון חייב דברי רבי *ר' יוסי בר יהודה אומר אינו חייב עד שיגבל דילמא עד כאן לא קאמר רבי יוסי בר יהודה התם אלא קמח דבר גיבול הוא אבל מורסן דלאו בר גיבול הוא אפילו רבי יוסי בר יהודה מודה לא סלקא דעתך דתניא בהדיא אין נותנין מים למורסן דברי רבי ר' יוסי בר יהודה אומר נותנין מים למורסן ת"ר אין גובלין את הקלי וי"א גובלין *מאן י"א א"ר חסדא

רבי

מסורת הש"ס

משלי כט

[נ"ל מפרכין וכן העתיקו תוס' לעיל יח: וכן בתוס' ב"ב יט: ד"ה בתיבנא]

[עי' תוס' ב"מ פ: ד"ה שהם]

[תוספ' פי"ח]

[סוטה מט:]

[נקרא כתיב ידע חסר וי"ו]

[אהלות פי"א מ"ז]

[תוספ' פי"ח]

לעיל יח.

[לעיל יח. ע"ש רבי יוסי]

[עי' מ"ש תוס' ב"ב נג: ד"ה מאן]

[פסחים לט:]

הגהות הב"ח

(א) גמ' דשדי ליה קמיה אלא דיוני שובך :

רבינו חננאל

זה התנא אוסר בצדדין ומתיר בצידי צדדין · ופריק רב פפא אליבא דרבא הכא בכלכלה דהוקה וכו' · ודברי רב פפא פשוטין הן ומפקינן בה והלכתא צדדין אסורין צדדי צדדין מותרין: **דרגא** דמדלא סולם העשוי לעלות בו בערסל והוא (שכתוב) [שת"י] כמלונה במקשה [כעתל] . והוא סלונה לשומרי' פירות והקדק רב אשי מזו ההלכה שאסור להניח סולם על הדקל ולעלות בו שנמצא משתמש בצידי האילן ואסור · ופירוש שאם יהקוק באילן ויניח באותה חקיקה גואו שהן עצים יניח באותו העצים הסולם נמצא הסולם נתון בעצים כמין הכלכלה ביתד ושרי וגם אסור להניח רגלי העולה באותה סולם בעצים הנעוצין באילן מפני שהן צדדין והצדדין אסורין · וכי אינו מותר לו להשתמש ולעלות אלא בקנים שהן מעלות הסולם והן שליבותיו שהוודאי צדדי צדדין:[מתני'] מתירין פקיעי עמיר כו' · פי' פקיעי אגודות כדתנן פקעת גמי בא רב הונא לפרש משנתנו ואמר הפקיען והכיפין שניהם אגודות קשורות הן · אלא הפקיען ב' אגודות כפקיע והכפין ג' אגודות בכף זירין דארזי כשמתגזאין ומתקשין נקראין דארזי והן אחד אחד ואינן נאגדין באגודה · ואם אגדן בחזקתן עומדין ותרצה רב הונא למתניתין הכי מתירין פקיעי עמיר לפני בהמה ומפספסין פי' מפספסין מפרכין כעין פיתות (לרכנן לייתות) [לרכבן] לאכלה ומצינו בתלמוד א"י שאמרו בענין (תינוק פתילה) מפספסין ופי' מחרכין כדכתיב ושער ראשיהון לא התחרך ונראין הדברים שהחריכה מרככת כעין הפתיתה דהוא מעין פסיפה · כדאמרינן בידות האוכלין שכסמן לגורן וכשם שמתירין ומפספסין הפקיען הוא הדין לכפין אבל הזירין לא יפספס ולא להתיר אם נקשרו ובא רב חסדא ופי' טעמא דרב הונא ואמר שהעמידו למשנתנו שמתירין ומפספסין הפקיען והכפין שהן מקודם אוכל ויכולין להיאכל כמות שהן וכן התרה והפספוס לא להוסיף להם אלא הכשר לאכילה בלבד דייקינן מדבריו הללו דקסבר מותר למיטרח באוכל ומוסיף לו הכשר אבל אם אין יכול להיאכל כגון הזירין שהן דארזי אלא אחרי התר ופספוס אסור והוי לשויי אוכלי לא משוינן ורב יהודה חלק על רב הונא לדברי רבה דאוקמינהו לדברי רב יהודה שוויה אוכלא לא משווינן ואמר רבה מדתרצה למתניתין שהפקיען [והזירין שניהן אגודות מפספס למה הן מיהו הפקיען שתים באגודה והעמידן נ' מותר להתיר הפקיען שקשרן מתירן] ואם לא יתירם אינן נאכלין בטוב ושלש אין קשרן אמיץ ונאכלין וכיון שיכולים להיאכל קסבר אסורהי באכילה טרחינן ואם יש לומר מניין לנו ראיה שיש הפרש בין ב' לג' שאלו קשרם אמיץ יותר מאלו מצאנו לדבריהן שאומרים נימה אחת קשורה הוצצת ג' אין הוצצת ב' איני יודע פי' ג' אינן הוצצת שאין קשרן מתחוק ומרפרף הוא והמים באים בתוכו לפיכך אינן הוצצין אבל הכפים שהן דידי והן קשין כמו שאמרנו למעלה מפספסין כדי לשוותם אכל וכ"ש שמתירין ובאנו להקשות לרב הונא מסיפא דהא מתניתין דקתני אין מרסקין לא את השחת ולא את החרובין ופשוטה היא' ופריק רב הונא לא שהחרובין רכין הן כמות שהן (שהדות) [שהדהאה] שוק רכין ויכולין להיאכל אין מרסקין אותן אלמא לא מטרחינן באוכלא אלא שחת דומיא דחרובין מה חרובין דאשיני פירוש יבישין וקשין ואין יכולין להיאכל אף שחת כמותן שנתייבש ונתקשה ואינו אוכל והריסוק משווייהו אוכל ומתניתין כוותי דאמרי שויי אוכלא לא משווינן ואזו היא בהמה שאינה יכולה לאכול השחת אלא אחרי ריסוק ואמרנו בעילי זוטרי פי' עיירים קטנים ותוב אקשינן על רב הונא מדרב יהודה נשמע לרבנן לאו ר' יהודה מתיר בחרובין לדקה [אין] לגסה לא מכלל דרבנן סברי כיון שיכולין להיאכל כמות שהן לא טרחינן לדרוקינהו להו דמטרח באוכלא לא טרחינן · וא"ל רב יהודה לת"ק התינח לגסה שיכולה לאכול כמות שהיא בלא ריסוק אלא לדקה שאינה יכולה לאוכלה כמות שהיא בלא ריסוק שווי אוכלא הוא ושרי דאם נאמר כי ת"ק סבר מטרח טרחינן שווי אוכלא לא משוינן וריסוק זה שוויי אוכלא לדקה ולגסה הוא ואסור וא"ל ר' יהודה לדקה אוכלא הוא ומיטרח באוכל שרי ואם הוא אוכל לדקה כ"ש לגסה ולא היה צריך לומר אלא ר' יהודה מתיר סתם בין לדקה בין לגסה · ועלתה בקשיא לרב הונא וחזרנו להקשות על רב יהודה דתנן מחתכין את הדלועין לפני הבהמה ואת הנבלה לפני הכלבים ופריק ליה ופשוטה היא וכן הא דתני רב חנן מנהרדעא מפריכין תבן ואספסתא ומערבין אלמא טרחינן באוכלא ופריק גם זו ואע"ג דרוב סוגיא דשמעתא כרב הונא ריהשא הא איתותב ולא אשכח לה פירוקא ועלתה בה קושיא ותוב רב יהודה ורבה רישי מתיבתא הוו דאמרינן האי שיפורא מעיקרא בי רב יהודה ולבסוף בי רבה והלכתא כוותיה ומשונן אוכלא ולא קא טרחינן באוכלא מכלל דרב הונא לא הוה ריש מתיבתא והא אמרינן כי הוו מפטרי רבנן מבי רב הונא הוו פיישי כו' ואמרינן ואמרי במערבא קמא קמא לה מתיבתא דהונא בבלאה: [מתני'] אין אובסין את הגמל כו' · פי' אובסין מפטמין כדכתיב וברבורים אבוסים והוא מאכילין את הגמל הרבה כרב ירמיה דאמר אנא חזיתיה לההוא טייעא דאכלא כו' כורא ואטענה כורא וכן הלכה דאסור לפטם בהמה בשבת ולא אפילו עופות · אין ממרים את העגלים אבל מלעיטין איזו היא המראה ואיזו הלעטה · אמר רב יהודה המראה למקום שאינה יכולה להחזיר · פי' המראה שמוריד בידו המאכל בבלועו של עגלים במקום שאינו יכול להחזירו מתוך בלעו אבל ·חשוב הוא כבלוע כגון זה אסור להמרות · אבל להלעוטי כדכתיב הלעיטני נא' לתת המאכל בחך שלו מותר וזה וזה ביד · ורב חסדא אמר אידי ואידי למקום שאין יכול להחזיר והמראה בכלי והלעטה ביד ואותביה רב יוסף לרב יהודה מהלקטין לתרנגולין

ואין

גליון הש"ס גמרא מאי לאו דלועין · כעין זה בב"מ דף קט ע"ב ועיין שיטה מקובצת שם ד"ה ה"ג :

Come and hear: One may cut up [155b] gourds for cattle and a carcass for dogs. Surely [it means] gourds like a carcass: just as a carcass is soft, so are soft gourds meant, which proves that we may take trouble over foodstuffs,[6] which refutes Rab Judah?—Rab Judah can answer you: No. A carcass like gourds: just as gourds are hard, so a hard carcass [is meant].[7] And where is it possible?[8] In the case of split meat[9] or in the case of very young dogs.[10]

Come and hear: For R. Ḥanan of Nehardea recited: 'One may
a break up straw and corn fodder[1] and mix them together'. This proves that we may take trouble over fodder?—Straw means putrefying straw;[2] as for corn fodder [the reference is] to young foals.

MISHNAH. ONE MUST NOT STUFF A CAMEL [WITH FOOD] NOR CRAM [IT], BUT ONE MAY PUT FOOD INTO ITS MOUTH; AND ONE MUST NOT FATTEN CALVES,[3] BUT ONE MAY PUT FOOD INTO THEIR MOUTH. AND FOWLS MAY BE MADE TO TAKE UP FOOD. WATER MAY BE POURED INTO BRAN, BUT WE MAY NOT MIX IT [INTO A MASS]. AND WATER MAY NOT BE PLACED FOR BEES OR FOR DOVES IN A DOVE-COTE, BUT IT MAY BE PLACED BEFORE GEESE, FOWLS AND HARDISIAN DOVES.[4]

GEMARA. What does ONE MUST NOT STUFF [OBSIN] mean?—Said Rab Judah: One must not make a manger [*ebus*] in its stomach.[5] Is such possible?—Even so, and as R. Jeremiah of Difti[6] related: I myself saw a certain Arab feed it with a *kor* and load it with a *kor*.[7]

ONE MUST NOT FATTEN, [MA'AMIRIN]. What is *hamra'ah* and what is *hal'aṭah*?[8]—Said Rab Judah: *Hamra'ah* [is forcing the food] so far that it cannot return; *hal'aṭah* is [only] so far that it can return. R. Ḥisda said: Both mean so far that it cannot return, but *hamra'ah* is [done] with a utensil, [while] *hal'aṭah* is by hand.[9] R. Joseph objected: One may force fowls to take food [*mehalkiṭin*], and it is superfluous to state that we may fatten [*malkiṭin*] them; but one may not fatten [*malkiṭin*] the doves of the dove-cote or of the loft, and it is superfluous to state that we may not force them [*mehalkiṭin*]. What is *mehalkiṭin* and what is *malkiṭin?* Shall we say that *mehalkiṭin* is hand feeding, while *malkiṭin* is throwing [grain, etc.] in front of them? Whence it follows that one may not even cast [grain] before the doves
b of the dove-cote or of the loft![1] Hence *mehalkiṭin* is surely [forcing food] so far down that it cannot return, while *malkiṭin* is [only] so far that it can return. From this it follows that *hamra'ah* means [stuffing] with a utensil, which refutes Rab Judah?[2]—Rab Judah can answer you: In truth *mehalkiṭin* means feeding by hand, while *malkiṭin* means casting [the food] before

(6) For the gourds can be eaten even if not cut up. (7) They are uneatable unless cut up. (8) Cf. n. 3. (9) Meat that has gone so hard and dry that there are splits in it. (10) They cannot eat any flesh unless it is cut up.

a (1) I.e., *shaḥath*, v. *supra* 155a, n. a2. (2) Though not quite putrid, for that would be unfit and *mukẓeh*. (3) By stuffing them with food against their will. (4) A species of domesticated doves, probably so named from the manner of their fructification (Jast. s.v. הרדיסאות). *Aliter:* Herodian doves, a species of domesticated doves supposed to have been bred by Herod, v. Ḥul. 139b.—The Gemara discusses the various terms used in the Mishnah. (5) By excessively stuffing it. (6) V. *supra* 10a, n. b5. (7) Of fodder for the journey—this is a very great quantity indeed. (8) *Mal'iṭin* is the term used in the Mishnah for putting food into their mouth. (9) Hence not so forcible.

b (1) Surely that is incorrect! (2) For the Mishnah employs *mehalkiṭin* in respect of fowls and *mal'iṭin* i.e., *hal'aṭah* in respect of calves as parallel terms, and both are permissible. Hence *hamra'ah*, which is forbidden, must refer to feeding with a utensil.

◁ *For the continuation of the English translation of this page see overleaf.*

רש"י

את הדלועין · התלושין ולא אמרינן מוקצין הן לבהמה דמאכל אדם הן : אשוני · קשין : ה"ג · כלבים דקאמר בגורייתא זוטרי דכל נבלה קשה להן : ומערבין · התבן והאספסתא יחד והבהמה אוכלת התבן בשביל האספסתא : תבן בתיבנא סריא · דלא חזיא והשתא משוי לה אוכלא והאי סריא לאו סריא לגמרי דהויא לטינא קיימא ואסורה לטלטל : מתני' אין אובסין · מאכילין אותו הרבה על כרחו ותוחבין לו בגרוט ובגמרא מפרש לשון אובסין עושין לה כמין אבוס בתוך מעיה : ולא דורסין · שדורס לה בתוך גרונה את הורה אור השעורין ומיהו לא הוי כל כך כמו אובסין : אבל מלעיטין · מפרש בגמרא : אין מאמירין · מפרש בגמרא : מהלקטין · מפרש בגמרא : אין נותנין מים לפני דבורים · מפרש טעמא בגמרא אי משום דאין מזונותיהן עליו שיוצאין ואוכלין בשדה אי משום דמיא באגמא שכיח להו : הרדיסאות · על שם מקומן וניזונין בתוך הבית : גמ' כי האי גוונא · שיאכילנה כל כך שירחיבו מעיה כאבוס : אטענה כורא · על גבה למזונות לדרך לבד שאר משאות : למקום שאינה יכולה להחזיר · שתוחבו לה לפנים מבית הבליעה : בכלי · בתרווד : דספי בידים · תוחבו לתוך פיו : אלא יוני שובך וכו' · בתמיה והאי לא מאי פרחא איכא : אלא להו כו' · ומדמהלקטין דמתניתין למקום שאינה יכולה להחזיר נמי שרי שמע מינה מלעיטין דעגלים וגמלים למקום שאינה יכולה להחזיר ושרי אלא דגבי בהמה קרי ליה הלעטה וגבי עופות קרי ליה הילקוט ועל כרחך אין מאמירין דקאמר בכלי הוא : לעולם מהלקטין דספי ליה בידים · ולמקום שיכולה להחזיר : אין מזונותן עליך · דשכיחי להו בדברא : חזיר אין מזונותן עליך · דאסור יהודי *שיגדל חזירים : מתני' נמי דיקא · דאפילו שדי קמייהו נמי לא : דשכיחי באגמא · אבל מזונות לא שכיחי להו : שמזונותיו מועטין · שאין אדם חס עליו לתת לו מזונות הרבה : כמה תשהה במעיו · דהכלב שאכל בשר מת ומת הכלב בבית תוך ג' ימים מטמא באהל אבל בחייו לא מטמא דטומאה בלועה בבעלי חיים לא מיטמא כדאמר בבהמה המקשה (חולין דף עא:) : שמע מינה · מדקאמר שהקפיד הקדוש ברוך הוא על מזונותיו : משח אודניה · מעט כמות אוזנו וקוטרא בתריה יכהו במקל מיד שלא יהא מרגילו אצלו : אבל במתא לא · ליתיב ליה מידי אי לאו דידיה הוא : משום דאתי למסרך · בתריה ויפסידו : לית דעתיר מחזירא · שכל מאכל ראוי לו ומוגא לאכול ואף מאכילין לו הרבה : כוותיה דרב יהודה · שהמראה למקום שאינו יכול להחזיר : פוקס את פיה · נותן חכה לתוך פיה שלא תוכל לסגור פיה : ומאכילה כרשינין ומים בבת אחת · והמים מבליעין הכרשינין לתוך בית בליעתה על כרחה : מאכילה מעומד · נותן לתוך פיה וכל זמן שאינו מרביצה אינו יכול להחזיר כל כך ויכול להחזירה : מתניתין מני · דקתני נותן מים לתוך המורסן דנתינת מים לא זהו גיבולו : לפי' רבי יוסי מודה · דזהו גיבולו : קלי · קמח של תבואה שנתייבשה כשהן קלויות בתנור והוא קמח לעולם מתוק והוא *קמחא דאבשונא ועושין ממנו שתיתא משמן ומים ומלח שמערבין בו : רבי

גמרא

*את הדלועין לפני הבהמה [י]ואת הנבלה לפני הכלבים °מאי לאו דלועין דומיא דנבלה מה נבלה דרכיכא אף דלועין דרכיכי אלמא טרחינן באוכלא ותיובתא דרב יהודה אמר לך רב יהודה לא נבלה דומיא דדלועין מה דלועין [ד]דאשוני אף נבלה דאשונא והיכי משכחת לה בבשר פילי א"נ בגורייתא זוטרי תא שמע דתני רב חנן מנהרדעא *מפרכינן תבן ואספסתא ומערבין אלמא טרחינן באוכלא תבן בתיבנא סריא אספסתא בעילי זוטרי : **מתני'** אין אובסין את הגמל ולא דורסין אבל מלעיטין ואין מאמירין את העגלים אבל מלעיטין ומהלקטין לתרנגולין ונותנין מים למורסן אבל לא גובלין ואין נותנין מים לפני דבורים ולפני יונים שבשובך אבל נותנין לפני אווזין ותרנגולין ולפני יוני הרדיסיות : **גמ'** מאי אין אובסין אמר רב יהודה [ד]אין עושין לה אבוס בתוך מעיה מי איכא כי האי גוונא אין וכדאמר רב ירמיה מדיפתי לדידי חזי לי ההוא טייעא דאבלא כורא *ואטעינא כורא : אין מאמירין : איזו היא המראה ואיזו היא הלעטה אמר רב יהודה [ה]המראה למקום שאינה יכולה להחזיר הלעטה למקום שיכולה להחזיר רב חסדא אמר אידי ואידי למקום שאינה יכולה להחזיר והמראה בכלי הלעטה ביד מתיב רב יוסף *מהלקטין לתרנגולין ואין צריך לומר שמלקטין ליוני שובך וליוני עלייה ואין צריך לומר שאין מהלקטין מאי מהלקטין ומאי מלקטין אילימא מהלקטין דספי ליה בידים מלקטין דשדי ליה[(א)] קמיהו מכלל דיוני שובך ויוני עלייה מישדא קמיהו נמי לא אלא לאו מהלקטין למקום שאינה יכולה להחזיר מלקטין למקום שיכולה להחזיר מכלל דהמראה בכלי ותיובתא דרב יהודה אמר לך רב יהודה לעולם מהלקטין דספי ליה בידים מלקטין דשדי ליה קמיהו ודקא קשיא לך יוני שובך ויוני עלייה למישדא קמיהו נמי לא הני מזונותן עליך והני אין מזונותן עליך כדתניא [ו]נותנין מזונות לפני כלב ואין נותנין מזונות לפני חזיר ומה הפרש בין זה לזה זה מזונותיו עליך וזה אין מזונותיו עליך אמר רב אשי מתניתין נמי דיקא [ז]אין נותנין מים לפני דבורים ולפני יונים שבשובך אבל נותנין לפני אווזין ולפני תרנגולין ולפני יוני הרדיסיות מ"ט לאו [ט]משום דהני מזונותן עליך והני אין מזונותן עליך וליטעמיך מאי איריא מיא אפילו חיטי ושערי נמי לא אלא שאני מיא דשכיחי באגמא דרש רבי יונה אפיתחא דבי נשיאה מאי דכתיב °(*יודע) צדיק דין דלים יודע הקב"ה בכלב שמזונותיו מועטין לפיכך שוהה אכילתו במעיו ג' ימים *כדתנן כמה תשהה אכילתו במעיו ויהא טמא בכלב ג' ימים מעת לעת ובעופות ובדגים כדי שתפול לאור ותשרף אמר רב המנונא שמע מינה אורח ארעא למישדא אומצא לכלבא וכמה אמר רב מרי משח אודניה והוטרא אבתריה הני מילי בדברא אבל במתא לא דאתא למסרך אמר רב פפא לית דעניא מכלבא ולית דעתיר מחזירא תניא כוותיה דרב יהודה *[כ]איזו היא המראה ואיזו היא הלעטה המראה מרביצה ופוקס את פיה ומאכילה כרשינין ומים בבת אחת הלעטה מאכילה מעומד ומשקה מעומד ונותנין כרשינין בפני עצמן ומים בפני עצמן : מהלקטין לתרנגולין כו' : אמר אביי אמריתה קמיה דמר מתניתין מני ואמר לי ר' יוסי בר יהודה היא דתניא *אחד נותן את הקמח ואחד נותן לתוכו מים האחרון חייב דברי רבי *ר' יוסי בר יהודה אומר אינו חייב עד שיגבל דילמא עד כאן לא קאמר רבי יוסי בר יהודה התם אלא קמח דבר גיבול הוא אבל מורסן דלאו בר גיבול הוא אפילו רבי יוסי בר יהודה מודה לא סלקא דעתך דתניא בהדיא אין נותנין מים למורסן דברי רבי ר' יוסי בר יהודה אומר [ל]נותנין מים למורסן ת"ר אין גובלין את הקלי וי"א גובלין *מאן י"א א"ר חסדא רבי

תוספות

אין אובסין את הגמל וכו' · והא דאמרינן בעירובין פרק עושין פסין (דף כ: ושם) גמל שראשו ורובו מבפנים אובסין אותו מבפנים הך אביסה לאו היינו אביסה ממש דהא אמרינן הכא אין אובסין כו' והאי אביסה היינו הלעטה וכן פירש רבינו שמואל: **אלא** קמח דבר גיבול הוא · פירשתי לעיל בפ"ק (דף יח· ושם*) : מהו

עין משפט נר מצוה

כג א מיי' פכ"א מהל' שבת הלכה יה סמג לאוין סה טוש"ע א"ח סימן שכד סעיף ו :

כד ב ג מיי' שם טוש"ע שם סעיף ז :

כה ד ה מיי' שם הלכה לה טוש"ע שם סע"ט:

כו ו מיי' שם והלכה לו טוש"ע שם סעיף י :

כז ז ח ט מיי' שם טוש"ע שם סעיף יא :

כח י מיי' פ"כ מהלכות טומאת מת הלכה ד :

כט כ מיי' פכ"א מהל' שבת הלכה לה :

ל ל מיי' פכ"א מהלכות שבת הלכה לד טוש"ע א"ח סי' שכד סע"ג :

רבינו חננאל

זה התנא אוסר בצדדין ומתיר בצידי צדדין · ופריק רב פפא אליבא דרבא הכא בכלכלה הזוקה וכו' · ודברי רב פפא פשוטין הן ומפקינן בה והלכתא צדדין אסורין צדדי צדדין מותרין: **דרגא** דמדלא סילם העשוי לעלות בו בערסל והוא (שכתוב) [שת"י] כמלונה במקשה [בערסל] . והוא סלונה לשומרי' פירות והקדק רב אשי מזו ההלכה שאסור להניח סולם על הדקל ולעלות בו שנמצא משתמש בצידי האילן ואסור · ופירוש שאם יהקוק באילן ויניח באיתה הקיקה גיאוי שהן עצים ויניח באותו העצים הסולם נמצא הסולם נתון בעצים כמין הכלכלה ביתד ושרי וגם אסור להניח רגלי העולה באותה סולם בעצים הנעוצין באילן ספני שהן צדדין והצדדין אסורין · וכי אינו מותר לו להשתמש ולעלות אלא בקנים שהן מעלות הסילם והן שליבותיו שהוודאי צדדי צדדין:[מתני'] מתירין פקיעי עמיר כו' : פי' פקיעי אגודות כדתנן פקעת גמי בא רב הונא לפרש משנתנו ואמר הפקיעין והכיפין שניהם אגודות קשורות הן · אלא הפקיעין ב' אגודות כפקיע והכפין ג' אגודות בכף זירין דארזי כשמתגואין ומתקשין נקראין דארזי והן אחד אחד ואינן נאגדין באגודה · ואם אגדן בחזקתן עומדין ותרצה רב הונא למתניתין הכי מתירין פקיעי עמיר לפני בהמה ומפספסין פי' מפספסין מפרכין כעין פיתות (לרכנן לייתות) [לרכבן] לאכלה ומצינו בתלמוד א"י שאמרו בענין (תינוק פתילה) מפספסין ופי' מהרכין כדכתיב ושער ראשיהן לא התחרך ונראין הדברים שהחריכה מרככת כעין הפתיתה דהוא מעין פסיסה · כדאמרינן בידות האוכלין שכססן לגורן וכשם שמתירין ומפספסין הפקיעין הוא הדין לכפין אבל הזירין לא יפספס ולא להתיר אם נקשרו ובא רב חסדא ופי' טעמא דרב הונא ואמר שהעמידו למשנתנו שמתירין ומפספסין הפקיעין והכפין שהן מקודם אכל ויכולין להיאכל כמות שהן וכן התחת והפספוס לא להוסיף להם אלא הכשר לאכילה בלבד דייקינן מדבריו הללו דקסבר מותר למיטרח באוכל ומוסיף לו הכשר אבל אם אין יכול להיאכל כגון הזירין שהן דארזי אלא אחרי התר ופספוס אסור ודוד לשויי אוכלי לא משוינן ורב יהודה חלק על רב הונא לדברי רבה דאוקמינהו לדברי רב יהודה שוויה אוכלא לא משווינן ואמר רבה מדתרצה למתניתין שהפקיעין [והזירין שניהן אגודות מפספס לטה הן מירו הפקיעין שתים באגודה והעמירן ג' מותר להתיר הפקיעין שקשרן מתירן] ואם לא יתירם אינן נאכלין בטוב ושלש אין קשרן אמיץ ונאכלין וכיון שיכולים להיאכל קסבר אסורהי באכילה טרחינן ואם יש לומר מניין לנו ראיה שיש הפרש בין ב' לג' שאלו קישרם אמיץ יתר מאלו מצאני לדבריהן שאומרים נימה אחת קשורה הוצצת ג' אין הוצצת ב' אני יודע פי' ג' אינן דוצצת שאין קשרן מתחוק ומרפרף הוא והסים באים בתוכו לפיכך אינן הוצצין אבל הכפים שהן דידי והן קשין כמו שאמרנו למעלה מפספסין כדי לשותם אכל וכ"ש שמתירין ובאנו להקשות לרב הונא מסיפא דהא מתניתין דקתני אין מרסקין לא את השחת ולא את החרובין ופשוטה היא' ופריק רב הונא לא שהחרובין רכין הן כמות שהן (שהתתאה) [שהדות] שק רכין ויכולין להיאכל אין מרסקין אותן אלמא לא מטרחינן באוכלא אלא שחת דומיא דחרובין דאשיני פירוש יבישין וקשין ואין יכולין להיאכל אף שחת כמותן שנתייבש ונתקשה ואינו אוכל והריסוק משוייהו אוכל ומתניתין כוותי דאמרי שויי אוכלא לא משווינן ואזו היא בהמה שאינה לאכול השחת אלא אחרי ריסוק ואמרנו בעילי זוטרי פי' עיירים קטנים' ותוב אקשינן על רב הונא מדרב יהודה נשמע לרבנן לאו ר' יהודה מתיר בהרובין לדקה לדקה [אין] לגסה לא מכלל דרבנן סברי כיון שיכולין להיאכל כמות שהן לא טרחינן לדדוקינהו להו דמטרח באוכלא לא טרחינן · וא"ל רב יהודה לת"ק התינח לגסה שיכולה לאכול כמות שהיא בלא ריסוק אלא לדקה שאינה יכולה לאוכלה כמות שהיא בלא ריסוק איכלא הוא ושוי דאם נאמר כי ת"ק סבר מטרח טרחינן שויי אוכלא לא משוינן וריסוק זה שוויי אוכלא לדקה ולגסה הוא ואסור וא"ל ר' יהודה לדקה אוכלא הוא ומיטרח באוכל שרי ואם הוא אוכל לדקה כ"ש לגסה ולא היה צריך לומר אלא ר' יהודה מתיר סתם בין לדקה בין לגסה · ועלתה בקשיא לרב הונא והזרנו להקשות על רב יהודה דתנן מחתכין את הדלועין לפני הבהמה ואת הנבלה לפני הכלבים ופריק ליה ופשוטה היא וכן הא דתני רב חנן מנהרדעא מפריכין תבן ואספסתא ומערבין אלמא טרחינן באוכלא ופריק גם זו ואע"ג דרוב סוגיא דשמעתא כרב הונא ריהשא הא איתותב ולא אשכח לה פירוק בה קושיא ותוב רב יהודה ורבה רישי מתיבתא הוו דאמרינן האי שיפורא מעיקרא בי רב יהודה ולבסוף בי רבה והלכתא כוותיה ומשונין אוכלא ולא קא טרחינן באוכלא מכלל דרב הונא לא הוה ריש מתיבתא והוא אמרינן כי הוו מפטרי רבנן מבי רב הונא הוו פיישי כו' ואמרינן ואמרי במערבא קמא לה מתיבתא דהונא בבלאה: [מתני'] אין אובסין את הגמל כו' · פי' אובסין מפטמין כדכתיב ובהבורים אבוסים והוא את הגמל הרבה כרב ירמיה דאמר אנא חזיתיה לההוא טייעא דאכלא כו' כורא ואטענה כורא וכן הלכה דאסור לפטם בהמה בשבת ולא אפילו עופות · אין ממרים את העגלים אבל מלעיטין איזו היא המראה ואיזו היא הלעטה · אמר רב יהודה המראה למקום שאינה יכולה להחזיר · פי' המראה שמוריד בידו המאכל בבלועו של עגלים במקום שאינו יכול להחזירו מתוך בלעו אבל השוב הוא כבלוע כגון זה אסיר להמראה להלעוטי כדכתיב הלעיטני וגו' לתת המאכל בחך שלו מותר וזה וזה ביד · ורב חסדא אמר אידי ואידי למקום שאין יכול להחזיר והמראה בכלי והלעטה ביד ואותביה רב יוסף לרב יהודה מהלקטין לתרנגולין ואין

מסורת הש"ס

[נ"ל מפרכין וכן הערוך] [תוס' לעיל קנ: וכן בתוס' ב"ב יט: ד"ה בתיבנא] [עי' תוס' ב"מ פ: ד"ה סתם] [תוספתא פי"ח] [סוטה מט:] [בקרא כתיב ידע ועי' הסר וי"א אהלות פי"א מ"ז] [תוספתא פי"ח] לעיל יח. [לעיל יח. ע"ש רבי יוסי] [עי' מ"ש תוס' ב"ב לג: ד"ה מאן] [פסחים לט:] מגילה כט

הגהות הב"ח

(א) גמ' דשדי ליה קמיה אלא דיוני שובך :

Continuation of translation from previous page as indicated by ◁

them, but as to your difficulty, Is it then not even permitted to cast [food] before the doves of the dove-cote and of the loft,—[that indeed is so, for] you are responsible for the food of the former [*sc.* fowls], but not for that of the latter.[3] Even as it was taught: Food may be placed before a dog but not before a swine. And what is the difference between them? You are responsible for the food of the one, but you are not responsible for the food of the other. R. Ashi said, Our Mishnah too implies this: WATER MAY NOT BE PLACED FOR BEES OR FOR DOVES IN A DOVE-COTE, BUT IT MAY BE PLACED BEFORE GEESE, FOWLS, AND HARDISIAN DOVES. What is the reason? Is it not because you are responsible for the food of the latter, but you are not responsible for the food of the former?—But according to your reasoning, why particularly water: even wheat and barley too may not [be placed before them]? Rather [say] water is different, because it is found in pools.

R. Jonah lectured at the entrance to the Nasi's academy:[4] What is meant by the verse, *The righteous knoweth the cause of the*
c *poor?*[1] The Holy One, blessed be He, knoweth that a dog's food is scanty,[2] therefore He makes him retain his food in his stomach for three days. As we learnt: How long shall the food remain in its stomach and yet defile? In the case of a dog, three full days of twenty-four hours; while in the case of birds or fish, as long as it would take for it [the food] to fall into the fire and be burnt.[3] R. Hamnuna said: This proves[4] that it is the proper thing[5] to throw raw meat to a dog. And how much? Said R. Mari: Measure its ear and the stick [straight] after![6] But that is only in the fields but not in town, because it will come to follow him. R. Papa said: None are poorer than a dog and none richer than a swine.[7]

It was taught in accordance with Rab Judah: What is *hamra'ah* and what is *hal'aṭah? Hamra'ah:* one makes it [the animal] lie down, opens the mouth wide, and forces it to swallow vetches and water simultaneously; *hal'aṭah:* he feeds it standing and waters it standing, and puts vetches separately and water separately [into its mouth].[8]

FOWLS MAY BE MADE TO TAKE UP FOOD. Abaye said, I asked this before the Master [Rabbah]: With whom does our Mishnah agree?[9] And he answered me, With R. Jose b. Judah. For it was taught: If one pours in flour and another water, the second is liable: this is Rabbi's view. R. Jose b. Judah said: He is not liable unless he kneads [them].[10] Yet perhaps R. Jose b. Judah ruled thus only there, in respect of flour, which is used for kneading; but as for bran, which is not used for kneading, even R. Jose b. Judah may admit [that he is liable]?—You cannot think so, because it was explicitly taught: Water must not be poured into bran: this is Rabbi's view. R. Jose b. Judah ruled: Water may be poured into bran.

d Our Rabbis taught: Parched corn may not be mixed,[1] but others maintain, It may be mixed. Who are the 'others'?—Said R. Ḥisda:

(3) Because doves can fly about in the fields and find their own food. (4) Or, house. It would appear that popular lectures were given there in the open.

c (1) Prov. XXIX, 7. (2) Few people trouble about dogs.—Many of the dogs in the East are semi-savage, and this would account for their neglect; v. *J.E.* art. Dog. (3) If an animal consumes flesh of a corpse and then dies in a house before it is completely digested, the contents of the house are unclean. The Mishnah quoted states how long we are to regard the flesh as undigested. (4) *Sc.* the care that the Almighty takes over a dog's food. (5) Lit., 'the way of the world'. (6) Give it a little, only as large as its ear, then immediately drive it off. (7) Rashi: because the swine eats anything, and it is also given much food. (8) Obviously in the former case the food can be forced down so far that it will not return, but not in the latter case. (9) That the mere pouring in of water does not constitute kneading. (10) V. *supra* 18*a*.

d (1) With water and oil to make of it a beverage.

[156a] It is R. Jose son of R. Judah. But that is only if one does it in an unusual manner. How does one do it in an unusual manner?—Said R. Ḥisda: Little by little.[2] Yet they agree that *shatith*[3] may be stirred round on the Sabbath, and Egyptian beer may be drunk.[4] But you said that we must not mix?[5]—There is no difficulty: the one treats of a thick mass;[6] the other of a loose [one].[7] And that is only if he does it in an unusual manner. How does one do it in an unusual manner?—Said R. Joseph: During the week the vinegar is [first] poured in and then the *shatith*, whereas on the Sabbath the *shatith* is [first] poured in and then the vinegar.

Levi son of R. Huna b. Ḥiyya found [on Sabbath] the mixer of his father's household[8] mashing [up bran] and feeding the oxen. Thereupon he rebuked him. Then his father came and found him [there]. Said he to him. Thus did your maternal grandfather, viz., R. Jeremiah b. Abba, say in Rab's name: One may mash [bran] but not force it [on the animal]; and if it [the animal] cannot take it [the fodder] up with its tongue one may feed it;[9] provided, however, that it is done in an unusual manner. How does one do it in an unusual manner?—Said R. Yemar b. Shalmia in Abaye's name: [By stirring it] crosswise.[10] But he cannot mix it well [then]?—Said Rab Judah: He shakes up the vessel [itself].

It was recorded in Ze'iri's notebook: I asked my teacher, viz., R. Ḥiyya, What about kneading?[11] It is forbidden, replied he. What about emptying?[12] It is permitted, he answered.

R. Menassia said: It is well [to place] one [measure of food] for one animal, and two for two; but [to place] three [measures] for
a two [animals] is forbidden.[1] R. Jose said: A *ḳab* and even two *ḳabs* [may be set]. 'Ulla said: A *kor* and even two *kor*.[2]

It was recorded in Levi's notebook: I spoke to my teacher, viz., our holy Master,[3] about those who mix *shatitha* in Babylonia, and my teacher, viz., our holy Master, protested [vociferously] against the practice of mixing *shatitha*, but none heeded him, and he lacked the power to forbid it, on account of R. Jose b. Judah.[4]

It was recorded in R. Joshua b. Levi's notebook: He who [is born] on the first day of the week [Sunday] shall be a man without one [thing] in him. What does 'without one [thing] in him' mean? Shall we say, without one virtue?[5] Surely R. Ashi said: I was born on the first day of the week! Hence it must surely mean, one vice. But surely R. Ashi said: I and Dimi b. Ḳaḳuzta were born on the first day of the week: I am a king[6] and he is the captain of thieves![7]—Rather it means either completely virtuous or completely wicked.[8] [What is the reason? Because light and darkness were created on that day.][9] He who is born on the second day of the week will be bad-tempered. What is the reason? Because the waters were divided thereon.[10] He who is born on the third day of the week will be wealthy and unchaste. What is the reason? Because herbs were created thereon.[11] He who is born on the fourth day of the week will be wise and of a retentive
b memory.[1] What is the reason? Because the luminaries were suspended [thereon]. He who is born on the fifth day of the week will practise benevolence. What is the reason? Because the fishes and birds were created thereon.[2] He who is born on the eve of the Sabbath will be a seeker. R. Naḥman b. Isaac commented: A seeker after good deeds.[3] He who is born on the Sabbath will die on the Sabbath, because the great day of the Sabbath was desecrated on his account. Raba son of R. Shila observed: And he shall be called a great and holy man.[4]

R. Ḥanina said to them [his disciples]: Go out and tell the son of Levi, Not the constellation of the day but that of the hour is the determining influence. He who is born under the constellation of the sun[5] will be a distinguished[6] man: he will eat and drink of his own and his secrets will lie uncovered; if a thief, he will have no success. He who is born under Venus will be wealthy and unchaste [immoral]. What is the reason? Because fire was created therein.[7] He who is born under Mercury will be of a retentive memory and wise. What is the reason? Because it [Mercury] is the sun's scribe. He who is born under the Moon will be a man to suffer evil, building and demolishing, demolishing and building, eating and drinking that which is not his and his secrets will remain hidden: if a thief, he will be successful.[8] He who is born under Saturn will be a man whose plans will be frustrated.[9] Others say: All [nefarious] designs against him will be frustrated. He who is born under *Ẓedeḳ* [Jupiter] will be a right-doing man [*ẓadḳan*.] R. Naḥman b. Isaac observed: Right-doing in good deeds.[10] He who is born under Mars will be a shedder of blood. R. Ashi observed: Either a surgeon, a thief, a slaughterer, or a circumciser. Rabbah
c said: I was born under Mars.[1] Abaye retorted: You too inflict punishment and kill.[2]

It was stated, R. Ḥanina said: The planetary influence gives wisdom, the planetary influence gives wealth, and Israel stands under planetary influence. R. Joḥanan maintained: Israel is immune from planetary influence.[3] Now, R. Joḥanan is consistent with his view, for R. Joḥanan said: How do we know that Israel is immune from planetary influence? Because it is said, *Thus saith the Lord, Learn not the way of the nations, and be not dismayed at the signs of heaven, for the* nations *are dismayed at them:*[4] they are dismayed but not Israel.[5] Rab too holds that Israel is immune from planetary influence. For Rab Judah said in Rab's name: How do we know that Israel is immune from planetary influence? Because it is stated, *and He brought him forth abroad*.[6] Abraham pleaded before the Holy One, blessed be He, 'Sovereign of the Universe! *one born in mine house is mine heir*.'[7] 'Not so,' He replied, '*but he that shall come forth out of thine own bowels*.'[8] 'Sovereign of the Universe!' cried he, 'I have looked at my constellation and find that I am not fated to beget child.' 'Go forth from [i.e., cease] thy planet [gazing], for Israel is free from

(2) Lit., 'by hand, by hand'. (3) A drink prepared of flour and honey. (4) Though sometimes taken for medicinal purposes it is also imbibed as an ordinary beverage, and hence permitted; cf. *supra* 109*b*. (5) Stirring *shatith* is the same. (6) Such as a dough—that is forbidden. (7) Such as *shatith*. (8) It was his duty to mix the fodder for his father's cattle. (9) E.g., food may be put into the mouth of a young calf. (10) Instead of round and round. (11) Or, mashing—bran. (12) A mash from one vessel into another, in order to mix it (Tosaf.). Rashi: from the vessel standing in front of one animal and pouring it out for another animal.

a (1) One may set its usual quantity of food before an animal on the Sabbath, —i.e., as much as it generally consumes; similarly, a double quantity for two, if they both feed out of the same manger. But one may not set a treble quantity for two animals, since they do not eat so much during the week. (2) There is no limit. (3) R. Judah the Prince. (4) Who permits it *supra*. (5) Lit., 'one (thing) in (his) favour'. (6) I.e., the head of the academy. (7) An anticipation of gangsterdom? (8) I.e., he shall be a man complete in his mode of life, without any opposing principle within him. (9) Hence his nature shall be the one or the other.—Rashal, for some reason which is not clear, deletes the bracketed passage. (10) Division or disunity is caused by bad temper.—Rashi: so will he be estranged from other people (through his temper). (11) Herbs multiply very rapidly and also continually intermingle with other herbs.

b (1) 'Aruk. Rashi: bright, lustrous. (2) Which are fed by God's lovingkindness. (3) Just as on the eve of the Sabbath one seeks to complete the details necessary for the proper observance of the Sabbath. (4) Maharsha: Not all born on the Sabbath die on the Sabbath, but only those who are very holy. (5) I.e., when the sun, as one of the planets, wields its influence on man. (6) Or: bright, handsome. (7) During the hours ruled over by Venus. (8) Just like the moon, which waxes and wanes, has no light of its own but merely reflects the sun's light, and is in general dark. (9) בטל (to frustrate) is the Chaldaic equivalent of שבת. (10) Rashi: charitable.

c (1) And am none of these. (2) Not to be taken literally, of course. V. *supra* 153*a*. (3) Lit., there is no *mazzal* (planetary influence) to Israel. (4) Jer. X, 2. (5) Israel being uninfluenced by 'the signs of heaven'. (6) Gen. XV, 5, q.v. (7) Ibid. 3. (8) Ibid. 4.

רבי יוסי בר יהודה היא · (דאי רבי לא מהני ליה שינוי דמתניתא מים מיחייב אפילו במידי דלאו בר גיבול כדאמרינן גבי מורסן אבל לרבי יוסי בר יהודה) דאמר עד שיגבל הכא גובלין כלאחר יד כדמפרש ואזיל והנ"מ הוא דקא משני : שבוחשין · בתרווד דהיינו גובלין : ושותים זיתום המצרי · דבלאו רפואה נמי משקה הוא דתנן כל המשקין שותה אדם לרפואה (לעיל דף קט:) : בעבה · אין גובלין ברכה בוחשין שאין זו לישה : בחול נותן החומץ כו · כלומר כן דרכו בחול : לגבלא דבי נשיה · שומר בהמות אביו ומגבל מאכלן : דקא גביל · מורסן ע"י שינוי : בטש ביה · תורה אור

דהא לכולי עלמא אבל לא גובלין תנן : גובלין · מורסן ע"י שינוי כדמפרש ואזיל והוא דקא משני : ולא מספין · לתורי אין מאמירין אותן : ודלא לקיט בלישניה · עגל קטן שעדיין לא לומד לאכול : והני מילי · דאמרן דמותר לגבל מורסן : שתי וערב · פעם אחת מוליך המקל שתי ופעם אחת ערב : מנערו לכלי · והוא מתערב מאליו : אפינקסיה · לוחות קשורות זו עם זו כאותן של סוחרים : מהו לפרק · לתת מתוך כלי שלפני בהמה זו ולתת לפני חברתה : חדא קמי חדא · מילתא באפי נפשה היא חדא מדה שרגילין לתת לפני בהמה מותר לתת לפניה בשבת וכן תרתי קמי תרתי האוכלות באבוס אחד : אבל תלתא קמי תרתי · הואיל ובחול לא יהיב להו כי האי הוי טרחא דלא צריך וכ"ש תרתי קמי חדא : אמרית קמיה רבי · רבי לוי משתעי דהוא אמר קדם רבי על הנך איכפי דגבלין שתיתא : מדר' יוסי בר יהודה · בר פלוגתיה דהוה שרי לעיל אף בעבה ועל ידי שינוי והיו נוהגין כמותו : האי מאן דבחד בשבא · הנולד באחד בשבת : יהא גבר ולא חדא ביה · יהא אדם שלם במדה אחת יהא ולא אחת בו ממדה אחרת ולקמן מפרש לה ואזיל : והוא ריש גנבי · דמאן דבחד בשבא יהא ראש כמו שהיום ראש למעשה בראשית מיהו שמע מינה דנולדים בו לדיקים ורשעים : דאיפליגו מיא · כך הוא יבדל מכל אדם : זנאי · נואף : דאיברו ביה עשבים · דכתי' (בראשית א) תדשא הארץ והוא דבר שפרה ורבה מאד וממהר לגדל ולצמוח דהוא ענין פריצות אשוו"א בלע"ז [נ"א] דלא כתיב למינהו בעשבים בגוויים (ועוד) שיולאין בערבוביא ויונקין זו מזו : ונהיר · זיותן : דאיתלו ביה מאורות · וכתיב ותורה אור : דאיברו ביה דגים ועופות · שאין טורחין לאוכלין אלא ניזונים בחסדו של הקב"ה : חוזן · מחזר אחר מצות : חוזן במצות · שכן דרך ע"ש לחזר אחר מצות שבת : וקדישא רבה יתקרי · שיהא פרוש וקדוש דכתיב (שמות כ) ויקדשהו : אמר להו רבי חנינא · לתלמידים שקראו פנקסו של ר' יהושע : מזל שעה · ז' מזלות הן המשמשין את השעות חנכ"ל שצ"ם חמה היינו חמה ממש והוא אחד מן המזלות וכן לבנה והשאר הויין כוכבים : זיותן · כשמש המאיר : אכיל מדיליה · כשמש שאינו מסיג גבול רעהו למשול בלילה : ורזוהי גליין · אין לו רשות לכסות סודו ונסתרותיו אלא כשמש הזה שהוא פומבי לכל : דתלי ביה נורא · אם תלוי באותו מזל יצר של תשמיש בוער כתנור : מזל כוכב · הוא סופר של מזל חמה לכתוב דרך הילוכו ,תקופותיו ומלוי אלנו תמיד : סביל מרעין · כלבנה זו(ג) שמתכוונה והולכת : בנאי וסתיר · כלבנה זו שגדילה ומתמעטת : אכיל לא דיליה · כלבנה המסגת גבול החמה למשול אף ביום : ורזוהי כסיין · כלבנה שאינה מאירה : דבשבתאי · מזל כוכב ששמו שבתאי : בטלין · כמו לא ישבותו (בראשית ח) : לדקן במצות · לדקה לעניים דקרי ליה מצוה (בכל לשון אגדה) : גנבא · ליסטים ההורג נפשות : אומנא · מקיז דם : עניש · בני אדם העוברין על דבריו : מזל מחכים · לפי המזל היא החכמה כדאמר דבחמה נהיר וחכים ויש מזל לישראל שאין תפלה ולדקה משנה את המזל : אין מזל לישראל · דעל ידי תפלה וזכות משתנה מזלו לטובה : אילטגניות · חכמת המזלות : לא מאילטגניותך · היינו דכתיב ויולא אותו החולה חוץ מאילטגנינותו : דקאי

רבי יוסי בר' יהודה היא והנ"מ הוא [א]דמשני היכי משני א"ר חסדא על [ב]יד על יד *ושוין שבוהשין את השתית בשבת ושותים זיתום המצרי והאמרת אין גובלין ל"ק הא [ג]בעבה הא ברכה והני מילי הוא דמשני היכי משני אמר רב יוסף בחול נותן את החומץ ואח"כ נותן את השתית [ד]בשבת נותן את השתית ואח"כ נותן את החומץ לוי בריה דרב הונא בר חייא אשכחיה לגבלא דבי *נשיה דקא גביל וספי ליה לתוריה בטש ביה °אתא אבוה אשכחיה א"ל הכי אמר אבוה דאמך משמיה דרב ומנו רבי ירמיה בר אבא גובלין ולא מספין ודלא לקיט בלישניה מהלקיטין ליה וה"מ הוא דמשני היכי משני אמר רב ייִמר בר שלמיא משמיה דאביי שתי וערב והא לא מערב שפיר אמר רב יהודה מנערו לכלי כתיב אפינקסיה דזעירי אמרית קדם רבי ומנו רבי חייא מהו לגבל אמר אסור מהו לפרק אמר מותר אמר רב [*מנשיא] חד קמי חד תרי קמי תרי שפיר דמי תלתא קמי תרי אסור רב יוסף אמר קב ואפילו קביים עולא אמר כור ואפילו כוריים כתיב אפינקסיה דלוי אמרית קדם רבי ומנו רבינו הקדוש על דהוו גבלין שתיתא בבבל והוה צוח רבי ומנו רבינו הקדוש על דהוו גבלין שתיתא ולית דשמיע ליה ולית חילא בידיה למיסר מדרבי יוסי בר' יהודה כתיב אפינקסיה דרבי יהושע בן לוי האי מאן דבחד בשבא יהי גבר ולא חדא ביה מאי [ולא חדא ביה] אילימא ולא חד לטיבו והאמר רב אשי אנא בחד בשבא הואי אלא לאו חדא לבישו והאמר רב אשי אנא ודימי בר קקוזתא הווין בחד בשבא אנא מלך והוא הוה ריש גנבי אלא אי כולי לטיבו אי כולי לבישו (מאי טעמא דאיברו ביה אור והושך) האי מאן דבתרי בשבא יהי גבר רגזן מ"ט משום דאיפליגו ביה מיא האי מאן דבתלתא בשבא יהי גבר עתיר וזנאי יהא מ"ט משום דאיברו ביה עשבים האי מאן דבארבעה בשבא יהי גבר חכים *)ונהיר מ"ט משום דאיתלו ביה מאורות האי מאן דבחמשה בשבא יהי גבר גומל חסדים מ"ט משום דאיברו ביה דגים ועופות האי מאן דבמעלי שבתא יהי גבר חזרן אמר ר"נ בר יצחק חזרן במצות האי מאן דבשבתא יהי בשבתא ימות על דאחילו עלוהי יומא רבא דשבתא אמר רבא בר רב שילא וקדישא רבא יתקרי אמר להו רבי חנינא פוקו אמרו ליה לבר ליואי לא מזל יום גורם אלא מזל שעה גורם האי מאן דבחמה(א) יהי גבר זיותן יהי אכיל מדיליה ושתי מדיליה ורזוהי גליין אם גניב לא מצלח האי מאן דבכוכב נוגה יהי גבר עתיר וזנאי יהי מ"ט משום דאיתיליד ביה נורא האי מאן דבכוכב יהי גבר נהיר וחכים משום דספרא דחמה הוא האי מאן דבלבנה יהי גבר סביל מרעין בנאי וסתיר סתיר ובנאי אכיל דלא דיליה ושתי דלא דיליה ורזוהי כסיין אם גנב מצלח האי מאן דבשבתאי יהי גבר מחשבתיה בטלין ואית דאמרי כל דמחשבין עליה בטלין האי מאן דבצדק יהי גבר צדקן אמר ר"נ בר יצחק וצדקן במצות האי מאן דבמאדים יהי גבר אשיד דמא א"ר אשי אי אומנא אי גנבא אי טבחא אי מוהלא אמר רבה אנא במאדים הואי אמר אביי מר נמי עניש וקטיל איתמר רבי חנינא אומר מזל מחכים מזל מעשיר ויש מזל לישראל רבי יוחנן אמר אין מזל לישראל ואזדא רבי יוחנן לטעמיה *דא"ר יוחנן מניין שאין מזל לישראל שנאמר °כה אמר ה' אל דרך הגוים אל תלמדו ומאותות השמים אל תחתו כי יחתו הגוים מהמה *הם יחתו ולא ישראל ואף רב סבר אין מזל לישראל דאמר רב יהודה אמר רב מניין שאין מזל לישראל שנאמר *°ויוצא אותו החוצה אמר אברהם לפני הקב"ה רבש"ע °בן ביתי יורש אותי אמר לו לאו °כי אם אשר יצא ממעיך אמר לפניו רבש"ע נסתכלתי באיצטגנינות שלי ואיני ראוי להוליד בן אמר ליה צא מאיצטגנינות שלך שאין מזל לישראל מאי דעתיך דקאי

*) [פי' זכרן ערוך]

ירמיה י

בראשית טו

שם

שם

מהו לפרק · פירש בקונטרס לפרק מלפני בהמה זו וליתן לפני אחרת וכן פירש בערוך בערך פרק וקשה לר"י דהיינו מתניתין גבי בהמה (לעיל דף קנ:) ונראה לר"י לפרק היינו להריק המים וגם המורסן מכלי אל כלי שתגבל היטב ובערוך פירש כמה לשונות :

אין מזל לישראל · והא דאמר רבא בשילהי מו"ק (דף כח· ושם) בני חיי ומזוני לאו בזכותא תליא מילתא אלא במזלא תליא מילתא מכל מקום על ידי זכות גדול משתנה אבל פעמים שאין המזל משתנה כדאמר ביבמות פרק החולץ (דף נ· ושם) זכה מוסיפין לו לא זכה פוחתין לו (דאין מזל לישראל) : כלדאי

זמאי דלמא עד כאן לא קאמר ר' יוסי ב"ר יהודה עד שיגבל אלא בקמח דבר גיבול הוא' אבל מורסן. דלאו בר גיבול הוא אפי' ר' יוסי ב"ר יהודה מודי שנתינת מים למורסן אסור שזהו גיבולו ואשכחנן תניא בהדיא אין ותנין מים למורסןדברי ר' [ר'] יוסי ב"ר יהודה אומר נותנים מים למורסן ואע"ג דבבל :קום הלכתא כרבי מחבירו הכא הלכה כר' יוסי דתנינן מתניתין סתמא כוותיה' ותוב מהא דכתוב אפינקסיה דלוי אמרית קדם רבינו קדוש והוא רבי עד דהוו גבלין שתיתא בבבל והוא צווח רבי דלית דשמע ליה ולית היילא בידיה למיסר מדר' יוסי ב"ר יהודה מהא נמי שמעינן דהלכתא כר' יוסי ב"ר יהודה דהוא בר פלוגתיה לא אסר ונפק עובדא כוותיה: ר' אין גובלין את הקליא וי"א גובלין ואמרינן כאן י"א ואמר רב חסדא ר' יוסי ב"ר יהודה היא והוא דמשני היכי משני אמר רב חסדא על יד על יד פי' כעם מעט' מדמתרץ רב חסדא אליבא דר' יוסי ב"ר יהודה הלכתא

רבינו חננאל

ואין צ"ל שמלקטין כו' ופריק רב יהודה הכי לעולם פי' מתניתא דאמר כך היא מהלקטין דספו ליה בידיה והיא פחותה מהלעטה שאמרנו ומלקטין שמשליך לפניה שעורים וכיוצא בהן דברים שהן מאכל לעופות · ואין משליכין מאכל לפני יוני שובך ויוני [עליה] לפי שאינן [בני] תרבות ואין מזונותן עליך וכי [הא] דתניא נותנין מזונות לפני הכלב ואין נותנין מזונות לפני חזיר ומה הפרש בין זה לזה כלב מזונותיו עליך חזיר אין מזונותיו עליך ובא רב אשי לסייע דברי רב יהודה ולומר שנויא דשני שינויא היא מדוקיא דמתניתין דקתני אין נותנין מים לפני דבורים ולפני יונים שבשובך אבל נותנים לפני אווזים ותרנגולים ולפני יונים הרדוסיית מ"ט לאו משו' דהני מזונותיו עליך והני אין מזונותיו עליך ולא עמדו דברי רב אשי והלכה כרב יהודה דתניא כוותיה דתניא איזו היא המראה ואיזו היא הלעטה המראה מרביצה ופוקס את פיה ומאכילה כרשינין ומים בב"א · הלעטה מאכילה מעומד ומשקה מעומד ונותן לה כרשינין בפ"ע ומים בפ"ע : מהלקטין לתרנגולים ונותנין מים למורסן אבל לא גובלין אוקימנא לר' יוסי ב"ר יהודה דתניא אחד נותן את הקמח ואחד נותן לתוכו מים האחרון חייב דברי ר' ור' יוסי בר יהודה אומר עד שיגבל אלמא אמרינן [דנתינת מים זהו גיבולו]

לא א ב ג ד מיי' פ"ח מהל' שבת הל' לג סמג שם טוש"ע א"ח סימן שכד סעיף יד :

ר"מ מותק זה

[עי' תוספות חולין ד. ד"ה מכנים וכו' דגרסי' רב מנשה]

כתובות נח.

[נ"ל נשא ועמ"ש תוספ' לעיל כג: ד"ה דבי]

הגהות הב"ח

(א) גמ' מאן דבחמה יהא גבר כו' תהלת סדר הליכתן בש"ס חנכ"ל [נ"ל] לפי סדר סימני הימים כנ"ל :

גליון הש"ס

גמרא אתא אבוה דאשכחיה · עי' לעיל דף כב ע"ב תוס' ד"ה דבי כלה: רש"י ד"ה אכיל לא דיליה כלבנה שמכסה · עיין דבר נחמד בזה בתנות אור לבעל פמ"ג בפ' בראשית :

(סוכה כט.)

[סוכה כט.]

[מדרש לג.]

לב א טוש"ע י"ד סימן רמז סעיף ד:

לג ב טוש"ע א"ח סימן כ סעיף ו:

לד ג ד מיי' פכ"א מהלכות שבת הל' יח סמג שם טוש"ע א"ח סימן שכד סעיף ו ז:

לה ה מיי' פ"ב מהלכות י"ט הלכה טו סמג לאוין עה:

דקאי צדק במערב מהדרנא ומוקמינא ליה במזרח והיינו דכתיב °מי העיר ממזרח צדק יקראהו לרגלו ומדשמואל נמי אין מזל לישראל דשמואל ואבלט הוו יתבי והוו קאזלי הנך אינשי לאגמא א"ל אבלט לשמואל האי גברא אזיל ולא אתי טריק ליה חויא ומיית א"ל שמואל אי בר ישראל הוא אזיל ואתי אדיתבי אזיל ואתי קם אבלט שדיה לטוניה אשכח ביה חויא דפסיק ושדי בתרתי גובי א"ל שמואל מאי עבדת א"ל כל יומא הוה מרמינן ריפתא בהדי הדדי ואכלינן האידנא הוה איכא חד מינן דלא הוה ליה ריפתא הוה קא מיכסף אמינא להו אנא קאימנא וארמינא כי מטאי לגביה שואי נפשאי כמאן דשקילי מיניה כי היכי דלא ליכסיף א"ל מצוה עבדת *נפק שמואל ודרש °וצדקה תציל ממות ולא ממיתה משונה אלא ממיתה עצמה ומדר"ע נמי אין מזל לישראל דר"ע הויא ליה ברתא אמרי ליה כלדאי ההוא יומא דעיילה לבי גננא טריק לה חויא ומיתא הוה דאיגא אמילתא טובא ההוא יומא שקלתה למכבנתא דצתא בגודא איתרמי איתיב בעיניה דחויא לצפרא כי קא שקלה לה הוה קא סריך ואתי חויא בתרה אמר לה אבוה מאי עבדת אמרה ליה בפניא אתא עניא קרא אבבא והוו טרידי כולי עלמא בסעודתא וליכא דשמעיה קאימנא שקלתי (א)*לריסתנאי דיהבית לי יהבתיה ניהליה אמר לה מצוה עבדת נפק ר"ע ודרש וצדקה תציל ממות ולא ממיתה משונה אלא ממיתה עצמה ומדר"נ בר יצחק נמי אין מזל לישראל דאימיה דר"נ בר יצחק אמרי לה כלדאי בריך גנבא הוה לא שבקתיה גלויי רישיה אמרה ליה °כסי רישיך כי היכי דתיהוו עלך אימתא דשמיא ובעי רחמי לא הוה ידע אמאי קאמרה ליה יומא חד יתיב קא גריס תותי דיקלא נפל גלימא מעילויה רישיה דלי עיניה חזא לדיקלא אלמיה יצריה סליק פסקיה לקיבורא בשיניה: **מתני'** * °מחתכין את הדלועין לפני הבהמה °ואת הנבלה לפני הכלבים רבי יהודה אומר אם לא היתה נבלה מערב שבת אסורה לפי שאינה מן המוכן: **גמ'** איתמר (ער"ל שה"ז סימן) אמר עולא הלכה כרבי יהודה (*ושמואל אמר הלכה כר"ש) ואף רב סבר הלכה כרבי יהודה מדכרכי דזוזי *דרב אסר ושמואל שרי ואף לוי סבר הלכה כרבי יהודה כי הא דלוי כי הוו מייתי טריפתא לקמיה ביומא טבא לא הוה חזי לה אלא כי יתיב *אקילקליתא דאמר דילמא לא מתכשרא ואפילו לכלבים לא חזיא ושמואל אמר הלכה כרבי שמעון ואף זעירי סבר הלכה כר"ש דתנן *בהמה שמתה לא יזיזנה ממקומה ותרגמא זעירי °בבהמת קדשים אבל בחולין שפיר דמי ואף רבי יוחנן אמר הלכה כר"ש ומי א"ר יוחנן הכי *והא א"ר יוחנן הלכה כסתם משנה ותנן

אין

רש"י

דקאי לדק · שהוא מזל שלך: במערב · שהוא מקום מגונן ואין ראוי להוליד כך מצאתי בהש"ס רבינו הלוי: במזרחו · שהוא מקום חום: לדק · הקב"ה קראו להביאו למזרח: לרגלו · בשבילו: אבלט · שם חכם נכרי היה וחוזה בכוכבים: אזיל ואתי · דאין מזל לישראל ויועיל לו תפלה: בתרתי גובי · בשתי חתיכות שקללו עם הקנים בלא יודע: מרמינן בהדדי · מטילין פת [לסל] לכל החבורה כאחד ואוכלין יחד והאחד גובה מכולן: אנא קאימנא ומרמינא · אגבה ואשים בסל: שוואי נפשאי כמאן דשקלי מיניה · עשיתי עצמי כגובה ממנו ונתתי משלי חלקו: לא ממיתה משונה · ומיהו מיתה הגונה ימות אלא ממיתה עצמה מצלת ונותנת חיים: כלדאי · חוזים בכוכבים: דצתא · תחבתה: למכבנתא · [אישפינגלי"ז בלע"ז] נוסקא של זהב שיש כמו נס בראשה: ריסתנאי · אמנשטריישו"ן: ובעי רחמי · בקש רחמים שלא ישלוט בך יצר הרע: קיבורא · אשכול תמרים והדקל לא שלו היה: **מתני'** את הדלועין · התלושין ומיהו סתמן לאו למאכל בהמה קיימי אלא לאדם: ואת הנבלה · שנתנבלה היום ובין השמשות היתה עומדת לאדם ואפ"ה מחתכין: **גמ'** כר"ש · דלית ליה מוקצה: מדכרכי דזוזי · מחללות העשויות לספיטות לכסות פרקמטיא שבתוכן · זוזי ספיטות בלשון ארמי כך מצאתי בתשובת הגאונים: כי הוו מייתי טריפתא לקמיה · בהמה שנולד בה ספק טרפות וצריכה להוראת חכם: אקלקילתא · °על האשפה שאם יראנה טריפה יניחה שם: ואפילו לכלבים לא חזיא · דנשחטה היום ולא יוכלו לטלטל כרבי יהודה: תרגמא זעירי · במסכת ביצה בבהמת קדשים דאסורה בהנאה ולא חזיא לכלבים הא דחולין שפיר דמי להאכילה לכלבים:

אין

תוספות

כלדאי · בכולה סוגיא משמע דהייט חוזים בכוכבים ולא כמו שפירש"י בערבי פסחים (דף קיג:) מניין שאין שואלין בכלדאים שנאמר תמים תהיה וגו' ופירש דהייט אוב ועוד קשה דבהדיא כתיב אל תפנו וגו' ובספרי דרש מנין שאין שואלין בגורלות שנאמר תמים תהיה וגורל וחוזה בכוכבים חדא מילתא היא:

רבי יהודה אומר אם לא היתה נבלה מע"ש כו' · תימה היכי מוכח בפסחים פרק מקום שנהגו בסופו (דף נו: ושם) ובפ"ק דביצה (דף ו: ושם) מהך מתניתין דמוכן לאדם לא הוי מוכן לכלבים לעולם מוכן לאדם הוי מוכן לכלבים והכא הייט טעמא דאסירא לכלבים משום דהואי מוקצה מחמת איסור שלא היתה ראויה חיה (לא) לאדם (ולא לכלבים) ותירץ ר"י דיש דברים ראויים ליתן לפני הכלבים חיים כגון עופות וכיוצא בהן הלכך אי לאו דמוכן לאדם לא הוי מוכן לכלבים הוה שריא ליתן לכלבים וה"ר יצחק בן הר"ר מאיר גרים במתני' אם לא היתה נבלה מעיו"ט אסורה השתא אתי שפיר בפשיטות דמוכן שפיר לאדם ואיט מוקצה מחמת איסור ולא נהירא לי דבריש ביצה (דף ב:) דייק מינה דגבי שבת סתם לה תנא כר"ש אלמא גבי שבת מיתניא וה"ר פורת מפרש דממשנה יתירה דייק דה"ל למתני אם לא היתה נבלה מע"ש אסורה ותו לא דמאי ל"ל לפי שאינה מן המוכן אלא להכי תני לה דאפילו הוי מוכן לאדם לגמרי שלא היה מוקצה מחמת איסור לא הוי מוכן לכלבים · מ"ר:

ושמואל אמר הלכה כר"ש · תימה לר"י תרתי דשמואל למה לי דתיפוק ליה מההיא דכרכי דזוזי ועז לחלבה ורחל לגיזתה דשילהי פ"ק (דף יט: ושם) ותירץ ר"י דמוקצה דהתם קיל ממוקצה דהכא:

תרגמא זעירי בבהמת קדשים · תימה לר"י היכי מוכח מהכא דס"ל כר"ש ע"כ אילטריך לאוקמה בבהמת קדשים כדמוכח פרק אין לדין (ביצה דף כז:) משום דמתני' נמי דיקא דקתני עלה ולא החלה שנטמאת מה חלה דקדשים אף בהמה דקדשים ומכח האי דיוקא פריך התם למר בר אמימר דאמר מודה היה ר"ש בבעלי חיים שמתו שאסורין ודחיק ר"י לתרץ °דהכי קים ליה להש"ס שלא פירש זעירי כן אלא משום דבעי לאוקמה כר"ש · מ"ר:

והא א"ר יוחנן הלכה כסתם משנה ותנן אין מבקעין כו' · תימה לר"י היכי מוכח מהכא דלא ס"ל כר"ש דההיא ודאי כרבי יהודה דשמא אית ליה לרבי יוחנן מיגו דאיתקצאי לבין השמשות איתקצאי לכולי יומא וקורה שנשברה אפילו לר"ש איתקצאי בין השמשות קודם שבירתה דהואי מוקצה מחמת חסרון כיס דמודה ביה ר"ש אבל במתניתין לא איתקצאי בין השמשות דלית ליה ההיא מוקצה מה שהיא עומדת לאדם והיה רוצה רבי לתרץ דאי אית ליה לר' יוחנן מיגו דאיתקצאי היה אוסר ודאי לטלטל בהמה שנתנבלה בשבת שהרי נהי שהיתה ראויה לכלבים(ג) בלא שחיטה כדפירשית לעיל מיהו לטלטל היתה אסורה דכולי עלמא מודו דבעלי חיים הם מוקצים הוה לן למימר מיגו דאיתקצאי ודנתי לפני רבי כיון שהיא ראויה לכלבים משום שהיא מוקצה לטלטל אין לנו לאוסרה לטלטל נבלה בשבת מידי דהוה אפירות הנושרין דתלינן טעמא בריש ביצה (דף ג:) שמא יעלה ויתלוש ומשום מוקצה לא אסירי לטלטל כיון דחזו לעורבים בעודן מחוברין אע"פ (ג)שבעת חבורן היו אסורין לטלטל ותירץ רבי דמסתמא מתניתין בכל ענין איירי בין אותן שראויין לכלבים בעודן חיים בין שאינן ראויין לכלבים דבכולהו שרי ר"ש ואכולהו קאי רבי יוחנן דאמר הלכה כרבי שמעון דמתניתין ולא למחצה אלמא לית ליה מיגו דאיתקצאי · מ"ר:

והא אמר רבי יוחנן הלכה כסתם משנה · בריש ביצה (דף ב:) אמרינן גבי שבת דסתם לן תנא כר"ש משמע דחשיב לסתמא דמתני' סתמא · אמר רבי לאו משום סתמא קאמר דודאי לא חשיב כסתמא כיון דבמתניתין נמי פליג רבי יהודה וסתמא לאו דוקא אלא חשיב כרבים · מ"ר*):

*) [וע' תוספות ביצה ב: ד"ה גבי שבת]

אין

רבינו חננאל

הלכתא כוותיה ונתברר שהלכה כר' יוסי ב"ר יהודה שנותנין מים למורסן וגובלין את הקליא מעט מעט · ושוין שבוחשין את השתית בשבת· פי' השתית היא שתיתא דאמור רבנן בכיצד מברכין (דף ל"ח ע"א) ודברי הכל מותר לבחוש בשבת והוא נתינת השתית שהוא הקליא בכלי ואחר כך יתן בו חומץ ויערבנו שתי וערב בתרווד או כיוצא בו כלי הניטל בשבת וינער אח"כ את הכלי לכלי אחר אבל לא יערבנו כדרך מריסה שמריץ התרווד סביבות כל הכלי שבתוכו השתית אלא שתי וערב בלבד · והני מילי דבחיש בה רכה אבל לבוחשה עבה גיבול הוא ואסור · ואקשינן עלה היכי אמרת דשוין שבוחשין את השתית ומי שרי והא אמרת רישא אין גובלין את הקליא. כלומר ת"ק ור"י (אסור) [מתיר] גיבול הקליא וקתני סיפא דשוין שבוחשין את הקליא מכלל דאפי' [ת"ק] שרי ומפרקי' ל"ק הא דתני אין גובלין בעבה וסיפא דקתני ושוין שבוחשין ברכה והוא דמשני מעשה דחול שדרכו בחול נותן החומץ ואחר כך הקמח ובשבת ישנה יתן השתית ואחר כך יתן החומץ ואפילו נתינת מים למורסן כעין גיבול בשנוי שרי כדאמרי משמיה דרב ירמיה בר אבא גובלין ולא מספין ודלא לקיים בלשניה מלקיטין והני מילי גיבול בשנוי והוא עירוב שתי וערב וניעור מכלי אל כלי אחר אבל מירוס כעין טוחן ברחים של יד שמסבב ומוליך ומביא אסור · אמרו לו לרבי חנינא מהו לגבל אמר להו אסור לפרק מאי אמר [להו] מות' ולמה לא פירש מהו לפרק ומהו חד קמי הדא ותרי קמי תרתי כו' שראיתי בין הגאונים חילוקם בפירושם והלכתא כעולא דאמר אפילו כור אפילו כוריים שרי ואפילו לשלשה ועוד ובלבד ע"י שינוי כאשר פירשנו למעלה ושאר השמועה פשוטה היא: **אבלט** שהיה רבן שמואל אומר גוי הוא דאמרינן בפרק אין מעמידין בהמה בפונדקאות של גוים שמואל ואבלט הוו יתבי כו': **מתני'** מחתכין את הדלועין לפני הבהמה ואת הנבלה לפני הכלבים · רבי יהודה אומר אם לא היתה נבלה מע"ש אסורה: **אתמר** ע'ר'ל' אמר הלכה כר' יהודה · פי' ע'ר'ל' סימן שמות החכמים דאמרו דהלכה כר' יהודה והם ע'ולא ור'ב ול'וי אילו שלשתן כר' יהודה עולא בפירוש אמר הלכה כר' יהודה רב מכלל הלוקתו על שמואל בכראכי דזוני פי' מחצלאות הכרוכות זונות זונות העומדות לתפירה דרב אסר להתירן ולישב בהן שמעינן מינה כיון שהן לסחורה מוקצות הן מכלל דסבר הלכתא כר' יהודה לוי נמי מכללא דכי הוו מייתי טרפה לקמיה דלוי ביו"ט לא הוה חזי ליה אלא אקיקלתא סבר דלמא לא מכשרא ואפילו לכלבים לא חזי שמעינן מינה דכר' יהודה סבירא ליה דאמר לפי שאינה מן המוכן: ש'ו'ה' סימן והן שמואל זעירי ור' יוחנן: שמואל ור' יוחנן בהדיא אמרי הלכתא כר' שמעון זעירי מכללא מדחזינן ליה לזעירי דמתרגם להא דתנן בהמה שמתה לא יזיזנה ממקומה

מסורת הש"ס

גירסת הערוך לריסתנאי פי' חלק

ביצה ג: ו: כז: פסחים נו: חולין יד.

לעיל יט:

[ע' פרש"י ב"ק כח. ובע"ז כח. ד"ה ניקרא]

ביצה כב

[לעיל מו: וש"נ]

הגהות הב"ח

(א) גמרא שקלתיה לריסתנאי: נ"ב פירוש חלק סעודה שלי וע' בברכות דף מג: (ב) תוס' ד"ה והא א"ר יוחנן וכו' ראויה לכלבים בע"ש כדפי' לעיל: (ג) בא"ד אע"פ שבשעת חבורן:

גליון הש"ס

רש"י ד"ה אקלקילתא על האשפה · מאשפות ירים אביון (תהלים קיג) תרגום מקלקלתא מרים תשובת רשב"א ע"ג דף כח ע"א ד"ה ויקרא: תוס' ד"ה תרגמא וכו' דהכי קים ליה · עיין לעיל דף ט ע"ב תוספ' ד"ה הא לן וש"נ:

planetary influence. What is thy calculation? [156b] Because *Ẓedeḳ* [Jupiter][9] stands in the West?[10] I will turn it back and place it in the East.' And thus it is written, *Who hath raised up Ẓedeḳ from the east?*[11] *He hath summoned it for his sake.*[12]

From Samuel too [we learn that] Israel is immune from planetary influence. For Samuel and Ablaṭ were sitting, while certain people were going to a lake.[13] Said Ablaṭ[14] to Samuel: 'That man is going but will not return, [for] a snake will bite him and he will die.' 'If he is an Israelite,' replied Samuel, 'he will go and return.'[15] While they were sitting he went and returned. [Thereupon] Ablaṭ arose and threw off his [the man's] knapsack, [and] found a snake therein cut up and lying in two pieces. Said Samuel to
a him, 'What did you do?'[1] 'Every day we pooled our bread and ate it; but to-day one of us had no bread, and he was ashamed. Said I to them, "I will go and collect [the bread]".[2] When I came to him, I pretended to take [bread] from him, so that he should not be ashamed.' 'You have done a good deed,' said he to him. Then Samuel went out and lectured: *But charity*[3] *delivereth from death;*[4] and [this does not mean] from an unnatural death, but from death itself.

From R. Akiba too [we learn that] Israel is free from planetary influence. For R. Akiba had a daughter. Now, astrologers[5] told him, On the day she enters the bridal chamber a snake will bite her and she will die. He was very worried about this. On that day [of her marriage] she took a brooch [and] stuck it into the wall and by chance it penetrated [sank] into the eye of a serpent. The following morning, when she took it out, the snake came trailing after it. 'What did you do?' her father asked her. 'A poor man came to our door in the evening,' she replied, 'and everybody was busy at the banquet, and there was none to attend to him. So I took the portion which was given to me and gave it to him.' 'You have done a good deed,' said he to her. Thereupon R. Akiba went out and lectured: '*But charity delivereth from death*': and not [merely] from an unnatural death, but from death itself.

From R. Naḥman b. Isaac too [we learn that] Israel is free from planetary influence. For R. Naḥman b. Isaac's mother was told by astrologers, Your son will be a thief. [So] she did not let him [be] bareheaded, saying to him, 'Cover your head so that the fear of heaven may be upon you, and pray [for mercy]'. Now, he did not know why she spoke that to him. One day he was sitting and studying under a palm tree, when his head covering fell off. Raising his eyes, he saw the palm tree, whereupon the temptation[6] overcame him, he climbed up and bit off a cluster [of dates] with his teeth.[7]

b *MISHNAH*. GOURDS MAY BE CUT UP FOR CATTLE,[1] AND A CARCASE FOR DOGS. R. JUDAH SAID: IF IT WAS NOT NEBELAH BY THE EVE OF THE SABBATH IT IS FORBIDDEN, BECAUSE IT IS NOT MUKAN.[2]

GEMARA. It was stated: (Mnemonic: *'aReL SHaḤaZ*).[3] 'Ulla said; the *halachah* is as R. Judah. And Rab too holds [that] the *halachah* is as R. Judah; [this follows] from ship mattings,[4] which Rab forbids while Samuel permits. And Levi too holds [that] the *halachah* is as R. Judah. For when a *ṭerefah* was brought before him on a Festival,[5] he would not inspect it save when he sat by a dunghill, for he said, Perhaps it will not be found fit, in which case it is of no use even for dogs. But Samuel maintained: The *halachah* is as R. Simeon.[6] And Ze'iri too holds [that] the *halachah* is as R. Simeon, for we learnt: If an animal dies, it must not be moved from its place: and Ze'iri interpreted this as referring to a sacred animal,[7] but in the case of an ordinary animal it is permitted.[8] R. Joḥanan too said, The *halachah* is as R. Simeon. Yet did R. Joḥanan say thus: Surely R. Joḥanan ruled, The *halachah*

(9) Which is thy constellation. (10) Which is an unpropitious combination for begetting children. (11) E.V. '*righteousness*'. (12) *Sc.* for the sake of Abraham: Isa. XLI, 2. (13) Or, meadow. (14) V. *supra* 129a, n. b11. (15) Prayer can counteract his fate as determined by the planets (Rashi).

a (1) To escape your fate. (2) Lit., 'throw into the basket'. (3) E.V. *righteousness*. From the Jewish point of view the two are identical: One merely performs his duty (i.e., righteousness) in giving charity. (4) Prov. X, 2. (5) Lit., 'Chaldeans'. (6) Lit., 'the evil inclination'. (7) The tree did not belong to him. —This story shows that head-covering was not *de rigeur*, though regarded as conducive to piety.—From these stories we see that belief in planetary influence was not entirely rejected, but that these Rabbis held that it might be counteracted by good deeds.

b (1) Though normally they are for human consumption. (2) V. Glos. (3) V. *supra* 25a, n. b1. '=‘Ulla; *R*=*R*ab; *L*=*L*evi; *SH*=*SH*emuel (Samuel); *Ḥ*=Jo*Ḥ*anan; Z=Ze'iri. (4) V. *supra* 19b. (5) I.e., when a doubt arose whether an animal was *ṭerefah* (v. Glos.). (6) Who permits *mukẓeh*. (7) I.e., one sanctified for a sacrifice. When it dies all benefit thereof is forbidden and it may not even be thrown to the dogs. Hence it is *mukẓeh* on Festivals, with which this deals. (8) It can be thrown to the dogs, and is therefore not *mukẓeh*.

is as an anonymous Mishnah, and we learnt: [157a] One may not chop up wood from planks,[9] nor from a plank that is broken on a Festival?[10]—R. Johanan recited that as [the ruling of] R. Jose b. Judah.[11] Come and hear: One may commence with a heap of straw [for fuel supplies] but not with the timber stored in
a the shed?[1]—The reference there is to cedar and *ashuhe*[2] planks, for in the case of *mukzeh* on account of monetary loss even R. Simeon agrees.[3]

Come and hear: Pasture animals may not be watered and killed, but home animals may be watered and killed?[4]—R. Johanan found another [opposing] anonymous [Mishnah]: Beth Shammai say: One may remove bones and nutshells from the table; but Beth Hillel rule: One must take away the whole board and shake it. Whereon R. Nahman said: As for us, we have no other [view] but that Beth Shammai agree with R. Judah, and Beth Hillel with R. Simeon.[5]

R. Aha and Rabina differ therein: One maintains: In all [discussions on] the Sabbath the *halachah* is as R. Simeon, save in *mukzeh* on account of repulsiveness: and what is that? An old lamp.[6] While the other maintains: In respect of *mukzeh* on account of repulsiveness too the *halachah* is as R. Simeon, the exception being *mukzeh* on account of an interdict, and what is that? A lamp wherein a light had been lit on that self-same Sabbath.[7] But in the case of *mukzeh* on account of monetary loss even R. Simeon agrees, for we learnt: All utensils may be handled on the Sabbath, except a large saw and the pin of a plough.[8]

MISHNAH. VOWS CAN BE ANNULLED BY A HUSBAND ON THE SABBATH, AND ABSOLUTION MAY BE GRANTED[9] FOR VOWS WHEN THESE ARE NECESSARY FOR THE SABBATH. A SKYLIGHT MAY BE CLOSED UP,[10] AND A RAG MAY BE MEASURED,[11] AND A MIKWEH MAY BE MEASURED.[12] AND IT ONCE HAPPENED IN THE DAYS OF R. ZADOK'S FATHER AND THE DAYS OF ABBA SAUL THE SON OF BOTNITH THAT THEY CLOSED UP THE WINDOW WITH A PITCHER AND TIED AN [EARTHENWARE] POT WITH A REED ROPE TO ASCERTAIN WHETHER THERE WAS THE OPENING OF A HANDBREADTH OR
b NOT IN THE BARREL.[1] AND FROM THEIR WORDS WE LEARN THAT WE MAY CLOSE [A SKYLIGHT] AND MEASURE AND TIE ON THE SABBATH.

GEMARA. The scholars asked: Is annulment [permitted] whether it is required [for the Sabbath] or not, whereas absolution [may be granted] only when it is necessary, but not otherwise, and for that reason they are divided from each other;[2] or perhaps annulment too [is permitted] only when it is necessary [for the Sabbath] but not otherwise; the reason that they are divided being that annulment does not require a Beth din, whereas absolution requires a Beth din?[3]—Come and hear: For Zuti, of the School of R. Papa, recited: Vows may be annulled on the Sabbath when they are required for the Sabbath: thus, only when required for the Sabbath, but not otherwise.

Another version: The scholars asked: Does WHEN THESE ARE NECESSARY relate to both, but not when they are unnecessary, which proves that [for] the annulment of vows a period of twenty-four hours is given; or perhaps WHEN THESE ARE NECESSARY is stated in reference to absolution only, but the annulment of vows [is permitted] even when it is unnecessary, which proves that [for] the annulment of vows the whole day [only] is given?[4]—Come and hear: For Zuti of the School of R. Papa recited: Vows may be annulled on the Sabbath when they are required for the Sabbath. Only 'when required for the Sabbath', but not otherwise, which proves that [for] the annulment of vows a period of twenty-four hours is given. Said R. Ashi, But we learnt: [The period allowed for] annulment of vows is the whole day:
c this may result in greater stringency or greater leniency.[1] E.g., if she vows on Sabbath eve [Friday night], he can annul on the Sabbath eve and the Sabbath day; if she vows just before nightfall, he can annul only until the night, for if darkness falls and he has not annulled it, he can no longer do so?—It is dependent on Tannaim; for it was taught: [The period for] the annulling of vows is all day; R. Jose son of R. Judah and R. Eleazar son of R. Simeon maintain: Twenty-four hours.

AND ABSOLUTION MAY BE GRANTED FOR VOWS, etc. The scholars asked: Is that only if one had no time [before the Sabbath to seek absolution], or perhaps it holds good even if one had time?—Come and hear: For the Rabbis gave a hearing to R. Zutra b. R. Zera and absolved him of his vow, though he did have time.

THEY CLOSED UP THE WINDOW WITH A PITCHER AND TIED A POT WITH A REED ROPE. Rab Judah said in Rab's name: There was a small passage between two houses and an unclean

(9) Arranged in piles for building. (10) Because they are *mukzeh*, v. Bez. 31a. (11) But not as an anonymous Mishnah.

a (1) It is stored there for winter use and is *mukzeh*, Bez. 29b. This Mishnah is anonymous and agrees with R. Judah. (2) A genus of weak (female) cedar. *Aliter:* cypress. (3) Cf. *supra* 123b, n. a12. (4) V. *supra* 45b. This prohibits *mukzeh*. (5) V. *supra* 143a, n. a5. Beth Hillel's view is the same as an anonymous Mishnah, because it is always *halachah*. (6) V. *supra* 44a. (7) V. *supra* 44a, n. a9. (8) These are delicate tools that require careful handling and are not used for any purpose but their own, v. *supra* 123b. (9) Lit., 'may be sought'; *sc.* from a Sage or court of three laymen. (10) Cf. *supra* 125b. (11) Whether it is large enough to be defiled; v. *supra* 26b. E.g., if it came into contact with a *sherez* (q.v. Glos.) and then touched food. (12) To see whether it has the minimum for validity, i.e., one cubit square by three in breadth or its cubic equivalent.

b (1) This is discussed *infra*. (2) In the Mishnah, instead of stating, Vows may be annulled and absolution granted, etc. (3) A husband annuls his wife's vows and a father his daughter's, while a Sage or Beth din of three laymen can grant absolution to all. (4) A husband or a father can annul vows only on the day he hears them (Num. XXX, 5, 8, q.v.); and the question is whether 'day' means a calendar day, i.e., until the evening only, no matter when the vow is made, or full twenty-four hours? Now, where he hears of her vow first on Sabbath day, if annulment is permitted on the Sabbath only when it is necessary, it follows that full twenty-four hours are allowed so that he can annul after the termination of the Sabbath; for otherwise we deprive him of the right to annul at all.

c (1) By fixing a calender day, i.e., a night and a day, the period may be shorter or longer, as the case may be.

אין מבקעין עצים מן הקורות ולא מן הקורה שנשברה ביו"ט רבי יוחנן ההוא כרבי יוסי בר יהודה מתני לה תא שמע מתחילין בערימת התבן אבל לא בעצים שבמוקצה התם *בארזי ואשוחי דמוקצה מחמת חסרון כיס אפילו רבי שמעון מודה ת"ש *אין משקין ושוחטין את המדבריות אבל משקין ושוחטין את הבייתות ר' יוחנן סתמא אחרינא אשכח *ב"ש אומרים מגביהין מעל השלחן עצמות וקליפין וב"ה אומרים מסלק את הטבלה כולה ומנערה וא"ר נחמן אנו אין לנו אלא ב"ש כרבי יהודה וב"ה כר"ש פליגי בה רב אחא ורבינא חד אמר בכל השבת כולה הלכה כר"ש לבר ממוקצה מחמת מיאוס ומאי ניהו *נר ישן וחד אמר במוקצה מחמת מיאוס נמי הלכה כר"ש לבר ממוקצה מחמת איסור ומאי ניהו נר שהדליקו בה באותה שבת אבל *מוקצה מחמת חסרון כיס אפילו ר"ש מודה דתנן *כל הכלים ניטלין בשבת חוץ ממסר הגדול ויתד של מחרישה:

מתני' *מפירין נדרים בשבת ונשאלין לנדרים שהן לצורך השבת ופוקקין את המאור ומודדין את המטלית ומודדין את המקוה ומעשה בימי אביו של רבי צדוק ובימי אבא שאול בן בטנית שפקקו את המאור בטפיח [ה] וקשרו את המקידה בגמי לידע אם יש בגיגית פותח טפח אם לאו *ומדבריהם למדנו שפוקקין ומודדין וקושרין בשבת:

גמ' *איבעיא להו הפרה בין לצורך ובין שלא לצורך ושאלה לצורך אין שלא לצורך לא ומשום הכי קפלגינהו מהדדי או דילמא הפרה נמי לצורך אין שלא לצורך לא והא דקא פליג להו מהדדי משום דהפרה אין צריך ב"ד ושאלה צריכה ב"ד ת"ש דתני זוטי דבי רב פפא מפירין נדרים בשבת לצורך השבת לצורך השבת אין שלא לצורך השבת לא לישנא אחרינא איבעיא להו לצורך אתרוייהו קתני ושלא לצורך לא אלמא הפרת נדרים מעת לעת או דילמא כי קתני לצורך אשאלה הוא דקתני אבל הפרת נדרים אפילו שלא לצורך אלמא הפרת נדרים כל היום תא שמע דתני רב זוטי דבי רב פפי מפירין נדרים בשבת לצורך השבת לצורך השבת אין שלא לצורך השבת לא אלמא הפרת נדרים מעת לעת א"ר אשי והאנן *תנן הפרת נדרים כל היום ויש בדבר להקל ולהחמיר כיצד נדרה לילי שבת מיפר לילי שבת ויום השבת עד שתחשך נדרה עם חשכה מיפר עד שלא תחשך שאם לא הפר משחשכה אינו יכול להפר תנאי היא דתניא *הפרת נדרים כל היום ר' יוסי בר יהודה ורבי אלעזר ברבי שמעון אמרו מעת לעת: ונשאלים לנדרים: *איבעיא להו כשלא היה לו פנאי או דלמא אפילו היה לו פנאי תא שמע דאזדקיקו ליה רבנן לרב זוטרא בריה דרב זירא ושרו ליה נדריה ואף על גב דהוה ליה פנאי: שפקקו את המאור בטפיח וקשרו את המקידה בגמי: אמר רב יהודה אמר רב הילקטי קטנה היתה בין שני בתים [וטומאה היתה שם] וגיגית

רש"י

אין מבקעין עצים מן הקורות · סואר של הקורות המוקצות וסדורות לבנין: ולא מן קורה · הישנה שנשברה היום ומהשתא להסקה קיימא ואפ"ה אסור הואיל ובין השמשות לא איתכן להכי: מתחילין · להסיק בערימת התבן קא סלקא דעתך בתיבנא סריא דסתמיה להסקה: אבל לא בעצים שבמוקצה · שהגיחם ברחבה שאחורי ביתו והקצם לימות הגשמים · מוקצה רחבה שאחורי בתים שהקצה אחורי ביתו להכניס שם דבר לאוצר: בארזי ואשוחי · ארז זכר וארז נקבה שעומדין לבנין: משקין · אורחא דמילתא נקט משום סירכא דמשכא שתהא נוחה להפשיט: מדבריות ·(א) שרועות באפר תמיד ולנות בתוך התחום: סתמא אחרינא · בית הלל תשיב כסתמא: כל הכלים ניטלין · ואפי' מלאכתן לאיסור ורבי שמעון היא: חוץ מן המסר הגדול · מגירה שהיא לאומנין לקוץ בה עצים ומוקצה מחמת חסרון כיס הוא שלא ישתברו חריצים שהוא עשוי כסכין מלא פגימות: ויתד של מחרישה · החופר את הקרקע קולטר"א בלע"ז:

מתני' מפירין · בעל לאשתו: ונשאלין · לחכם: שהן לצורך השבת · כגון שנדר שלא לאכול [היום]: ופוקקין את המאור · כרבנן דאמרי (לעיל דף קכה:) פוקקין פקק החלון: ומודדין את המקוה · במדה שיהא שם עמוק שלש אמות מים ורוחב אמה על אמה: ואת המטלית ·(ב) שתהא שלש על שלש אצבעות כגון אם היתה טמאה ונגעה בטהרות: בטפיח · פך של חרס(ג) וחבירו בפי"ז (דף קכה:) זמורה שהיא קשורה בטפיח ממלאין בה בשבת: מקידה · כלי חרס: לידע אם יש בגיגית פותח טפח · בגמרא מפרש לה: וקושרין · קשר שאינו של קיימא אפילו לכתחילה: ומודדין · להתלמד על דבר הוראה:

גמ' איבעיא להו הפרה · דמתניתין בין לצורך [בין שלא לצורך] השבת דגבי הפרה ביום שמעו כתיב (במדבר ל) ואם לא מיפר האידנא שוב אינו מיפר: ושאלה לצורך אין שלא לצורך לא · דיכול לישאל למחר ומשום הכי מפליג להו מהדדי ולא קתני מפירין ונשאלין לנדרים שהן לצורך השבת דלא קאי לצורך אלא אשאלה: בית דין · חכם: הכי גרסי' ל"א איבעיא להו (במסכת נדרים דף עז:) לצורך אתרוייהו קאי · אהפרה והשאלה אבל הפרה שלא לצורך לא אלמא הפרת נדרים מעת לעת וזה ששמע בשבת יכול להפר משתחשך בתוך מעת לעת של שמיעה הלכך שלא לצורך לא שריגן בשבת: כל היום · עד שתחשך והו לא ואפילו שמע סמוך לחשיכה הלכך אפי' שלא לצורך *שאם לא יפר עכשיו לא יפר עוד: לצורך השבת · אלמא הפרת נדרים מעת לעת של שמיעה הלכך שלא לצורך(ד) לא מדלא שרי אלא לצורך: להקל ולהחמיר · כלומר פעמים שיש שהות גדול ופעמים שאינו אלא מעט: איבעיא להו · הא דקתני נשאלין לנדרים שהן לצורך: כשלא היה לו פנאי · לשאל מערב שבת קאמר או אפילו כשהיה לו פנאי: הילקטי קטנה · שביל קטן בין שני בתים: וגיגית

תוספות

אין משקין ושוחטין את המדבריות · הוה מצי למימר דהכי כגרוגרות וצמוקין דמיין כדאמר בפרק כירה (לעיל דף מה:):

לבר ממוקצה מחמת איסור · וכגון איסור דדחייה בידים כגון נר שהדליקו באותו שבת כדפירשתי בפ"ק בסופו:

והלכתא מעת לעת · לא גרס בפירוש ר"ח דבנדרים משמע דלית הלכתא הכי דאמר בפרק נערה המאורסה (כתובות דף עו:) אין הלכה כאותו הזוג · מ"ר:

הילקטי קטנה · מפרש בקונטרס שביל קטן היתה בין שני בתים והגיגית סדוקה מונחת על גבן והמת מוטל בהלקטי תחת הגיגית נגד הסדק וקשרו המקידה לידע אם יש בסדק פותח טפח ולהאי פירושא קשה לר"י דאפי' אין בסדק פותח טפח כיון שהמת נגדו לא חשבינן לה כמאהיל על המת כיון שאין [זה] דרך מאהיל(ה) כדמוכח במסכת אהלות (פ"י מ"ה) ומייתי לה בסוף פרק קמא דסוכה (דף יח: ושם) אין בארובה פותח טפח והמת בבית מה שבבית כנגד ארובה טהור המת כנגד ארובה מה שבבית טהור וכיון שהמת היה נגד הסדק מה היה להם לקשור המקידה ועוד פירש שלפני מות המת פקקו המאור בטפיח ולא הבין רבי לפירושו הלא אותו מת לא היה מת שלם שהרי לא ידעו אם למעלה הימנו היה פותח טפח והמת היה כולו תחת הסדק אלא ודאי כזית מן המת היה וא"כ לא היה לו לומר לפני מות המת אלא לפני שבא כזית מן המת לשם ומיהו יתכן לומר שהמת היה כולו מוטל תחת הגיגית שלא כנגד הסדק והגיגית היתה סדוקה באמצע מראשה לסופה ואילו היה באותו סדק על פני כולו פותח טפח לא היתה טומאה עוברת דלא חשיב כאהל אחד אבל אין בו פותח טפח כאלו אין כאן סדק וחשיב כאהל אחד ומביא את הטומאה לבית וקושיא ראשונה מכל מקום במקומה עומדת ונראה כפירוש ר"ח דמפרש דהלקטי היינו תל המתלקט ואותה הלקטי היתה בין שני בתים והמת היה בבית אחד ואותה הגיגית היתה למעלה מן התל עד לתקרה ואותה הגיגית לא היתה טמאה שהרי בטלה שם ואם לא היתה סדוקה לא היה הבית אחר טמא אלא הגיגית היתה סדוקה מלדה והשתא אתי שפיר דקתני סדוקה לפי שהיא מלדה אבל לפירוש הקונטרס לא אתי שפיר דכיון דפירש שהסדק למעלה מן הגיגית היה לו לומר פתוחה ולא סדוקה אבל לפר"ח אתי שפיר שהסדק היה מן הצד וקשרו את המקידה לידע אם יש פותח טפח ויש לנו לומר שאותו חור היה עשוי להשמיש דחור העשוי לתשמיש שיעורו בפותח טפח ואם היה פותח טפח הבית אחר טמא ואם לאו טהור ומיהו קשה לר"י לפירוש ר"ח דלא הוה ליה למימר על גבן אלא על גבה · מ"ר: באוגא

רבינו חננאל

מסקנא דבהמת קדשים [מיירי] מכלל דחולין שרי כר'[שמעון] דלית ליה מוקצה · ופקשינן על ר' יוחנן וכי סבר רבי יוחנן הלכה כרבי שמעון והא אמר ר' יוחנן הלכה כסתם משנה ותנן אין מבקעים עצים מן הקורות ולא מן הקורה שנשברה ופרקינן האי כר' יוסי ב"ר יהודה מתני לה רבי יוחנן ולית סתמא . ואמרינן תוב ת"ש מתחילין בערימת התבן אבל לא בעצים שבמוקצה ופרקינן התם בארזי ואשוחי [ואשוחי] דמוקצה מחמת חסרון כיס · דאפילו ר' שמעון מודה' פי' ארזי ואשוחי עצי ארזים וברושים העשויין לקורות שאין דעתו של אדם עליהן להסיקן תחת. תבשילו וגמר והקצה אותן · ואמרינן תוב אין משקין ושוחטין את המדבריות אבל משקין ושוחטין הבייתות והנה סתמא כר' יהודה ורבי יוחנן סבירא ליה הלכתא כסתם משנה קשיא הלכתא אהלכתא ופרקינן ר' יוחנן סתמא אחרינא אשכח בה"א מגביהין מעל השלחן עצמות וקליפין בש"א מסלק את הטבלא כולה ומנערה · ואמר רב נחמן אנו אין לנו אלא ב"ש כר' יהודה וב"ה כר' שמעון והלכתא כר' שמעון וכדפסק ר' יוחנן פליגי בה רב אחא ורבינא חד אמר בכולה שבת הלכתא כר' שמעון בר במוקצה מחמת מיאוס · וחד אמר במוקצה [מחמת] מיאוס נמי הלכתא כוותיה לבר ממוקצה מחמת איסורו כגון הנר שהדליקו בה באותה שבת וכיוצא בו אבל

רב נסים גאן

מפירין נדרים בשבת · אמרו [בתוספתא פ' י"ח] מפני מה נדרי שבת מפירין אותן בשבת שאם חשיכה ולא הפר אינו יכול להפר ורבי יוסי ב"ר יהודה ורבי אלעזר ברבי שמעון שאמרו הפרת נדרים מעת לעת אין הלכה כמותם כדגרסינן בנדרים בפרק נערה המאורסה (דף עו) אלא אמר רבי שמעון בן פזי אין הלכה כאותו הזוג לוי סבר למיעבד עובדא כי האי זוגא אמר ליה רב הכי אמר רב ביבי אין הלכה כאותו הזוג ואע"פ שהתירו הפרת נדרים בשבת ביארו בדבר זה תנאי והוא שאמרו לא יאמר אדם לאשתו מופר ליכי כדרך שאומר בחול אלא אומר לה [טלי ואכלי] טלי ושתי והנדר בטל מאליו א"ר יוחנן וצריך שיבטל בלבו תניא בית שמאי אומרים מבטל בלבו ובערב בחול מוציא בשפתיו וב"ה אומרים אחד זה ואחד זה מבטל בלבו ואינו צריך להוציא בשפתיו תמצאנו עוד בפרק נערה המאורסה (דף עז): אם

עין משפט נר מצוה

לו א מיי' פ"ב מהלכות יו"ט הלכה יב סמג לאוין עה טוש"ע א"ח סימן תקא סעיף א:

לז ב ג מיי' שם הלכה יא וסמג שם טוש"ע א"ח סי' תקיח סעיף ו:

לח ד מיי' שם הלכה יג סמג שם טוש"ע א"ח סימן תצו סעיף ב:

לט ה מיי' שם הלכה ב וסמג שם טוש"ע א"ח סי' תצ סעיף ג:

[ביצה מ. לעיל מה:]

[ה] [טוש"ע א"ח סימן שיז סעיף א]:

מ ו מיי' פכ"ד מהלכות שבת הלכה ו ופי"ג מהלכות נדרים הלכה ח וסמג לאוין סה טוש"ע א"ח סימן שמא סעיף א וטוש"ע י"ד סימן רלד סעיף כד:

מא ז מיי' פכ"ד מהל' שבת הלכה ו וסמג שם ומיי' פ"ו מהלכות שבועות הלכה ו סמג לאוין סה רסח טוש"ע שם וטוש"ע י"ד סי' רכח סעיף ג:

מב ח מיי' פי"ב מהל' נדרים הלכה טו סמג לאוין רמב טוש"ע י"ד סימן רלד סעיף כח:

מג ט מיי' פכ"ד מהל' שבת הלכה ו ופ"ו מהלכות שבועות הלכה ו סמג לאוין סה ולאוין רמב טוש"ע א"ח סימן שמא סעיף א וטוש"ע י"ד סימן רכח סעיף ג:

גי' רש"ל

הגהות הב"ח

(א) רש"י ד"ה מדבריות וכו' המיד הס"ד ואח"כ מה"ד בייתות ברועות חוץ לתחום ובאות ולנות בתוך התחום: (ב) ד"ה ואת המטלית לידע אם יש בה שלש על שלש: (ג) ד"ה בטפיח פך של חרס (וחבירו וכו' בשבת) תא"מ ונ"ב הג"ה היא: (ד) ד"ה לצורך השבת וכו' שלא לצורך הס"ד ואח"כ מה"ד והאנן תנן במס' נדרים הס"ד: (ה) תוס' ד"ה הלקטי וכו' שאין דרך מאהיל בכך כדמוכח: סליק מסכת שבת בס"ד

מד א מיי׳ פ״י מהל׳ שבת הלכה ו סמג לאוין סה טוש״ע א״ח סימן שיז סעיף א :

מה ב מיי׳ פכ״ד מהל׳ שבת הלכה ה סמג שם טוש״ע א״ח סימן שו סעיף ו :

וגיגית סדוקה מונחת על גביו · והמת מוטל בהילקטי תחת הגיגית [כנגד] הסדק ולפני מות המת פקקו בשבת המאור בטפיח שמא אין בסדק הגיגית פותח טפח ונמלא המת מוטל באהל שאין לו מקום לצאת דרך מעלה וחור שבין שני בתים מכנים את הטומאה לצד שני במלא אגרוף לפיכך סתמוהו בכלי חרס וגבו כנגד ההילקט וכלי חרס אינו מטמא מגבו וחוצן : וקשרו מקידה · שהיא רחבה טפח : בגמי לידע · אם תכנס בסדק הגיגית ובמסכת אהלות (פ״י) שנינו (דאין) חילוק בארובה שבתוך הבית וטומאה מקלתה כנגד ארובה ומקלתה בתוך הבית בין יש בארובה פותח טפח לאין בארובה פותח טפח ואכי לא יכולתי להבין בו ולהכי נקט גמי שראוי למאכל בהמה ולא מיבטל ליה להיות קשר של קיימא דמנתק כשיבש : באוונא · בגיגית מלאה מים : מתעסק · שלא לצורך אלא לאיעסוקי בעלמא :

באוונא דמיא · אמבטי של מים וכך פירש בערוך :

מדידה דמצוה דלאו דמצוה מי אמור כו׳ · בפקיקה לא בעינן של מצוה כדפירש׳ לעיל בשילהי כל הכלים (דף קכו:) אלא דווקא במדידה בעינן של מצוה :

הדרן עלך מי שהחשיך

וסליקא לה מסכת שבת

וגיגית סדוקה מונחת על גבן ופקקו את המאור בטפיח [א]וקשרו את המקידה בגמי לידע אם יש שם בגיגית פותח טפח אם לאו : ומדבריהם למדנו שפוקקין ומודדין וקושרין בשבת: עולא איקלע לבי ריש גלותא חזייה לרבה בר רב הונא דיתיב *באוונא דמיא וקא משח ליה אמר ליה [ב]אימר דאמרי רבנן מדידה דמצוה דלאו מצוה מי אמור אמר ליה מתעסק בעלמא אנא :

הדרן עלך מי שהחשיך

וסליקא לה מסכת שבת

[כרי״ף ובר״ן ליתא באגדה וכן הוא ברש״י שם וע׳ בערוך ערך אודנא וכן בברכות כג: ר׳ זירא הוה יתיב באגנא דמיא פרש״י באגנא גיגית]

הדרן עלך מי שהחשיך וסליקא לה מסכת שבת

רבינו חננאל

אבל מוקצה [מחמת] חסרון כיס אפילו ר״ש מודה דתנן כל הכלים ניטלין בשבת חוץ ממסר הגדול ויתד של מחרישה וקיי״ל דכל היכא דפליגי רב אחא ורבינא הלכתא כדברי המיקל ואסקינן בה הלכה למעשה · שהלכה כרבי שמעון בהלכות שבת כולן ואין הלכה כרבי יהודה אלא במוקצה מחמת איסורו ואשכחנן ר׳ יוחנן דאמר מודה ר׳ שמעון בזה · דגרסינן בפרק כירה א״ר חייא בר אבא א״ר יוחנן אין מוקצה לר׳ שמעון אלא כעין שמן שבנר בשעה שדולק הואיל והוקצה לאיסורו והוקצה למצותו ומוקצה מחמת חסרון כיס דברי הכל מוקצה הוא ואסור וקשיא לן הרא הלכתא דאמרינן בפ׳ כירה [ד׳ מ״ס] כי אתא ר׳ יצחק בר יוסף אמר הלכה כר׳ יהודה · וריב״ל אמר הלכה כר״ש וכו׳ וצריכא עיונא · (ואם) [ואבן] יש לומר הא ר׳ יצחק בר יוסף א״ר יוחנן הלכה כר׳ יהודה . הא ריב״ל פליג עליה ואמר הלכתא כר״ש ואע״ג [דאמר] רב יוסף [התם] היינו דאמר רבה בר בר חנה א״ר יוחנן אמרו הלכה כר׳ שמעון וליה לא ס״ל (דא״ל) [וא״ל] אביי לרב יוסף ואת לא תסברא דר׳ יוחנן כר׳ יהודה סבירא ליה הני כולהו שמעתתא לא דייקינן : מתני׳ מפירין נדרים בשבת ונשאלין לנדרים שהן לצורך השבת ומבעיא לן האי דקתני מפירין נדרים בשבת לצורך הוא אבל שלא לצורך השבת לא אלמא הפרת נדרים מעת לעת או דלמא כי קתני לצורך אשאלה בלבד · אבל הפרת נדרים אפילו שלא לצורך השבת מפירין · אלמא הפרת נדרים כל אותו היום בלבד וסלקא כתנאי דתניא הפרת נדרים כל היום · ר׳ יוסי בר יהודה ורבי אלעזר בר שמעון אומר מעת לעת והלכתא הפרת נדרים כל היום בלבד וגרסינן בפ׳ נערה המאורסה אביה ובעלה מפירין נדריה פי׳ שמועה זו והכי פסקה לה [התם] ר״ש בן פזי אריב״ל אין הלכה כאותו הזוג · ונשאלין לנדרים לצורך השבת · ומיבעיא לן בשלא היה לו פנאי מערב שבת או דלמא אפילו היה לו פנאי ופשטנא אפילו היה לו פנאי מערב (יום) [שבת] והוה אפשר להו לשאל נשאלין בשבת ושפיר דמי · מפירין נדרים שמפר הבעל לאשתו ונשאלין לנדרים שאלה לחכמים ומפרשינן בפרק נערה המאורסה סבר רב יוסף למימר נשאלין נדרים ביחיד מומחה בשבת אין [בשלשה הדיוטות] לא דמוריה בי דינא א״ל אביי כיון דסבירא לן אפילו מעומד ואפילו בקרובין ואפילו בלילה לא מחזי בי דינא · אמר רבא אמר רב נחמן הלכתא נשאלין נדרים מעומד יחידי ובלילה ובשבת ובקרובין ואפילו אפשר להן מבע״י: פוקקין את המאור· פירוש מניחין בגג מקום פתוח כגון זרת הן חסר הן יתיר ליכנס ממנו אור ונקרא מאור ותנן [פרק י״ג] העושה לו מאור בתחלה שיעורו מלא מקדח גדול של לשכה שירי המאור רום אצבעיים על רוחב גודל · ואם רוצה בשבת לסותמו מותר ועל זה שנינו פוקקין את המאור ופירושו סותמין את המאור כאשר פירשנו ומודדין את המטלית ואת המקוה אם הוא אמה על אמה ברום שלש ראוי לטבול בו: פקקו את המאור בטפיח.פי׳ טפיח כלי חרס קטן והוא כגון פתיא [וכרבים] נקראין פתוותא כדגרסינן בע״ז בגמרא אלו דברים של נכרים אסורין ואיסורן איסור הנאה [ד׳ ל״ג ע״ב] וכדתנן זמורה שהיא קשורה בטפיח ממלאין בה בשבת וקושרין את המקידה בגמי פי׳ מקידה כלי חרס כגון זה ששנינו בפ׳ היה מביא את מנחתה פיילי של (חדשה) [חרס] ונותן בתוכה חצי לוג מים מן הכיור*). וזו שאמר רב יהודה אמר רב הילקטי קטנה היתה בין ב׳ בתים וגיגית סדוקה מונחת על גבן ופקקו את המאור בטפיח וקשרו את המקידה בגמי לידע אם יש בגיגית פותח טפח אם לאו מדבריהם למדנו שפוקקין ומודדין וקושרין בשבת וכך פירושו היה שם ב׳ בתים · והילקטי מלשון תל המתלקט והוא כמין קיר חוצצין ביניהן : וגיגית כלי כמין פתיא סדוק או כמין כפושא מפולשת והיה קבוע בכותל (חלול) [חלון] פתוח ובאותה שבת היה המת מוטל בבית אחד ובבית האחר היו רוצים להכנס בו כהנים ולא היו יודעים בבירור אם יש בגיגית פותח טפח ומביא את הטומאה אם לאו שכך שנו במשנתנו. טפח על טפח על רום טפח מביא את הטומאה. ועוד שנינו פרק העושה מאור [פי״ג משנה ד׳] לזון את עיניו ולדבר עם חבירו ולתשמיש בפותח טפח וסתמו את המאור בטפיח הוא כמין כלי לכסות את המאור הפתוח שלא יאהילו העומדים על הגג באותו המאור ויטמאו מן הטומאה המוטלת בתוך הבית כנגד המאור שהיה נפתח המאור יתר ממלא מקדח גדול של לשכה שזה שיעורו ומפורש במשנתנו פרק [הנזכר] לפיכך הוצרכו לסותמו. ואותה הגיגית היתה בכותל גבוהה מקומת אדם ופישוט זרועותיו ולמטה מן הגג מכדי תליית אדם ופישוט זרועותיו ולקחו מקידה שהיא כלי חרס ויש בה בכולה טפח וקשרוה בגמי ושלשלוה והעמידה כנגד פי הגיגית לראות אם פי הגיגית נתמלאה הנה יש בה טפח ומביאה הטומאה מבית לבית ואם היא פחותה ממלא הגיגית נתברר שאין בגיגית פותח טפח ואינה מביאה הטומאה · ויש אומרים קשרו המקידה בגמי בראש הקנה ושיעור פתחה של גינית אם יש בה פותח טפח ואם לאו · עולא איקלע לבי ריש גלותא חזייה לרבה בר רב הונא דיתיב בארנא דמיא והיה מודד המים גובה במים ורוחבו · אמר לו אימר דאמרינן שהתירו חכמים מדידה דמצוה כגון מדידה של מקוה שצריך לטבילת מקוה מדידה דלאו מצוה מי אמור א״ל מתעסק בעלמא אנא כלומר אני מודד ולא מתכוון למדידה אני :

*) כמדומה שחסר כאן ונ״ל כמו שכתב בסוטה דף ט׳ דאיתא שם לפיכך הכהן משקה אותה במקידה של חרס וכו׳ ע״ש ג״כ שם דף ל״ב וכן מליין הערוך ערך קד.

הדרן עלך מי שהחשיך ברוך · תהלה לעל במתי עב דורך :

גירסא ירושלמי בר״ה פרק אם אין מכירין בתהלתו · אמר עד אחד נולד לאיש פלוני בשבת מלין אותו על פיו חשכה מוצאי שבת מטלטלין אותו על פיו · ר׳ חייא אמר מטלטלין אפומא (דימלותא) [דמלייתא] . רבי מתניאה מטלטל על אברתיה דיהרא · ר׳ (סמל) [אמי מל] על פי נשים דאמרי שמשא הות בסוטיתא :

סליקא לה מסכת שבת. משירי אהודנו צח דודי. כי כביר מצאה ידי.
מי שזיכני להתחיל והוא יזכני לסיים. חזק ונתחזק הכותב לעד לא יוזק.

רב נסים גאון

אם יש בגיגית · עיקר דיליה במס׳ אהלות (פרק ג משנה ו) כזית מן המת פתוח בטפח והמת פתוח בד׳ טפחים להציל את הטומאה על הפתחים אבל להוציא את הטומאה בפותח טפח · אמר ליה אנא מתעסק בעלמא אנא · עיקר שלו כבר פירשנו בפרק כלל גדול שהמתעסק פטור לענין שבת כמו שאמרו בכריתות בפרק אכל חלב (דף יט) אמר רב נחמן אמר שמואל מתעסק בחלבים ובעריות חייב שכבר נהנה מתעסק בשבת פטור מלאכת מחשבת אסרה תורה ובגמרא דהזורק דבני מערבא (סוף פירקא) גרסי המתעסק בשבת פטור היך עבידה אמר הריני קוצר חצי גרוגרת וקצר כגרוגרת פטור :

סליק מי שהחשיך וסליקא לה מסכתא דשבת בסייעתא דשמיא

אחר השלמת המסכת יאמר זה

ויועיל לשכחה בעזרת השם יתברך

הדרן עלך מסכת שבת והדרך עלן דעתן עלך מסכת שבת ודעתך עלן לא נתנשי מינך מסכת שבת ולא תתנשי מינן לא בעלמא הדין ולא בעלמא דאתי :

יאמר כן שלש פעמים ואחר כך יאמר

יהי רצון מלפניך יי אלהינו ואלהי אבותינו שתהא תורתך אומנותנו בעולם הזה ותהא עמנו לעולם הבא חנינא בר פפא רמי בר פפא נחמן בר פפא אחאי בר פפא אבא מרי בר פפא רפרם בר פפא רכיש בר פפא סורחב בר פפא אדא בר פפא דרו בר פפא :

הערב נא יי אלהינו את דברי תורתך בפינו ובפיפיות עמך בית ישראל ונהיה כולנו אנחנו וצאצאינו וצאצאי עמך בית ישראל כולנו יודעי שמך ולומדי תורתך : מאויבי תחכמני מצותך כי לעולם היא לי : יהי לבי תמים בחקיך למען לא אבוש : לעולם לא אשכח פקודיך כי בם חייתני : ברוך אתה יי למדני חקיך : אמן אמן אמן סלה ועד :

מודים אנחנו לפניך ה׳ אלהינו ואלהי אבותינו ששמת חלקנו מיושבי בית המדרש ולא שמת חלקנו מיושבי קרנות שאנו משכימים והם משכימים אנו משכימים לדברי תורה והם משכימים לדברים בטלים אנו עמלים והם עמלים אנו עמלים ומקבלים שכר והם עמלים ואינם מקבלים שכר אנו רצים והם רצים אנו רצים לחיי העולם הבא והם רצים לבאר שחת שנאמר ואתה אלהים תורדם לבאר שחת אנשי דמים ומרמה לא יחצו ימיהם ואני אבטח בך :

יהי רצון לפניך יי אלהי כשם שעזרתני לסיים מסכת שבת כן תעזרני להתחיל מסכתות וספרים אחרים ולסיימם ללמוד וללמד לשמור ולעשות ולקיים את כל דברי תלמוד תורתך באהבה וזכות כל התנאים ואמוראים ותלמידי חכמים יעמוד לי ולזרעי שלא תמוש התורה מפי ומפי זרעי וזרע זרעי עד עולם ותתקיים בי בהתהלכך תנחה אותך בשכבך תשמור עליך והקיצות היא תשיחך : כי בי ירבו ימיך ויוסיפו לך שנות חיים : אורך ימים בימינה בשמאלה עושר וכבוד : יי עוז לעמו יתן יי יברך את עמו בשלום :

יתגדל ויתקדש שמיה רבא בעלמא דהוא עתיד לאתחדתא ולאחיא מתיא ולאסקא לחיי עלמא ולמבני קרתא דירושלם ולשכלל היכליה בגוה ולמעקר פולחנא נוכראה מארעא ולאתבא פולחנא דשמיא לאתריה וימליך קודשא בריך הוא במלכותיה ויקריה בחייכון וביומיכון ובחיי דכל בית ישראל בעגלא ובזמן קריב ואמרו אמן : יהא שמיה רבא וכו׳ יתברך וכו׳ על ישראל וכו׳ יהא שלמא וכו׳ עושה שלום וכו׳ :

object lay there, [157b] and a split barrel[-shaped defective roofing] rested over them,—then they closed the window with a pitcher and tied a fire pot with a reed rope to ascertain whether the barrel[-shaped roofing] had an opening of a handbreadth or not.[2]

AND FROM THEIR WORDS WE LEARN THAT WE MAY CLOSE [A SKYLIGHT] AND MEASURE AND TIE ON THE SABBATH. 'Ulla visited the home of the Resh Galutha and saw Rabbah b. R. Huna sitting in a bath-tub of water and measuring it. Said he to him: Say that the Rabbis spoke thus of measuring in connection
a with a precept;[1] did they rule [thus] when it is not in connection with a precept?—I was merely occupying myself, he replied.[2]

מסכת שבת

הדרן עלך

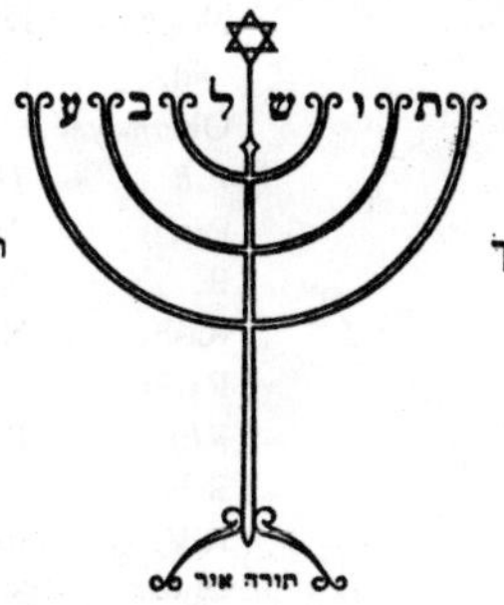

והדרך עלן

(2) The 'unclean object' was a corpse, which lay in the passage beneath the roofing under its split. Before the person died the window was closed up with the pitcher, for fear that the split was less than a handbreadth in width, in which case the corpse would be lying under a covering which contained no opening through which the uncleanness could pass out, and so it would spread to the rooms on its side through the window opening into the passage. Hence it was closed with an earthen pitcher, the back of which faced the passage; it then bars the progress of defilement. In order to know whether the split was a handbreadth in width they tied a fire-shard of that width with a reed, to see whether it could enter the split (Rashi). Tosaf. explains it differently.

a (1) *Sc.* the measuring of a *mikweh.* (2) But had no intention of actually measuring.

ABBREVIATIONS

Ab.	Aboth.
Alfasi	R. Isaac b. Jacob Alfasi (1013-1103).
'Aruch	Talmudic Dictionary by R. Nathan b. Jeḥiel of Rome (d. 1106).
Asheri	R. Asher b. Jeḥiel (1250-1327).
A.Z.	'Abodah Zarah.
b.	ben, bar; son of.
B.B.	Baba Bathra.
BaḤ.	Bayith Ḥadash, Glosses by R. Joel b. Samuel Sirkes (1561-1640).
Ber.	Berakoth.
Beẓ.	Beẓah.
B.Ḳ.	Baba Ḳamma.
B.M.	Baba Meẓi'a.
Cur. ed(d).	Current edition(s).
Dor	*Dor Dor Wedoreshaw*, by I. H. Weiss.
Doroth	*Doroth Harishonim*, by I. Halevy.
D.S.	*Diḳduḳe Soferim*, by R. Rabbinowicz.
'Er.	'Erubin.
E.V.	English Version.
Géogr.	*Géographie*, by A. Neubauer.
Giṭ.	Giṭṭin.
Glos.	Glossary.
Graetz	Graetz, H., *Geschichte der Juden* (4th ed.).
Ḥag.	Ḥagigah.
Ḥananel	R. Ḥananel b. Ḥushiel of Kairwan (about 990-1050).
Hor.	Horayoth.
Ḥul.	Ḥullin.
J.E.	*Jewish Encyclopedia.*
J.T.	Jerusalem Talmud.
Jast.	M. Jastrow's Dictionary of the Targumim, the Talmud Bible and Yerushalmi, and the Midrashic Literature.
Kel.	Kelim.
Keth.	Kethuboth.
Ḳid.	Ḳiddushin.
Ma'as.	Ma'asroth
Maharsha	R. Samuel Eliezer Halevi Edels (1555-1631).
Maim.	Moses Maimonides (1135-1204).
Mak.	Makkoth.
Maksh.	Makshirin.
Meg.	Megillah.
Men.	Menaḥoth.
MGWJ.	*Monatsschrift für Geschichte und Wissenschaft des Judentums.*
Miḳ.	Miḳwa'oth.
M.Ḳ.	Mo'ed Ḳaṭan.
MS.M.	Munich Codex of the Talmud.
Naz.	Nazir.
Ned.	Nedarim.
Neg.	Nega'im.
Nid.	Niddah.
Obermeyer	Obermeyer J., *Die Landschaft Babylonien.*
P.B.	*The Authorised Daily Prayer Book*, S. Singer.
Pes.	Pesaḥim.
R.	Rab, Rabban, Rabbenu, Rabbi.
Rashal	Notes and Glosses on the Talmud by R. Solomon Luria (d. 1573).
Rashi	Commentary of R. Isaac Yiẓḥaki (d. 1105).
REJ.	*Revue des Etudes Juives.*
R.H.	Rosh Hashanah.
R.V.	Revised version of the Bible.
Sanh.	Sanhedrin.
Shab.	Shabbath.
Sheb.	Shebi'ith.
Shebu.	Shebu'oth.
Sonc. ed.	English Translation of the Babylonian Talmud. Soncino Press, London.
Soṭ.	Soṭah.
Strashun.	Annotations by Samuel Strashun (1794-1872) in the Wilna editions of the Talmud.
Suk.	Sukkah.
Ta'an.	Ta'anith.
T.A.	*Talmudische Archäologie*, by S. Krauss.
Ṭoh.	Ṭoharoth.
Tosaf.	Tosafoth.
Tosef.	Tosefta.
Yeb.	Yebamoth.
Zeb.	Zebaḥim.

TRANSLITERATION OF HEBREW LETTERS

א (in middle of word)	= '
ב	= b
ו	= w
ח	= ḥ
ט	= ṭ
כ	= k
ע	= '
פ	= f
צ	= ẓ
ק	= ḳ
ת	= th

Full particulars regarding the method and scope of the translation are given in the Editor's Introduction in the first Shabbath volume (Mo'ed, Vol. I).

AGGADAH (Lit., 'tale', 'lesson'); the name given to those sections of Rabbinic literature which contain homiletic expositions of the Bible, stories, legends, folk-lore, anecdotes or maxims. Opposed to *halachah*, q.v.

'AM HA-AREẒ pl. *'amme ha-areẓ*, (lit., 'people of the land', 'country people'); the name given in Rabbinic literature to (*a*) a person who through ignorance was careless in the observance of the laws of Levitical purity and of those relating to the priestly and Levitical gifts. In this sense opposed to *ḥaber*, q.v.; (*b*) an illiterate or uncultured man, as opposed to *talmid ḥakam*, q.v.

AMORA. 'Speaker', 'interpreter'; originally denoted the interpreter who attended upon the public preacher or lecturer for the purpose of expounding at length and in popular style the heads of the discourse given to him by the latter. Subsequently (pl. Amoraim) the name given to the Rabbinic authorities responsible for the Gemara, as opposed to the Mishnah or Baraitha (v. Tanna).

BARAITHA (Lit., 'outside'); a teaching or a tradition of the Tannaim that has been excluded from the Mishnah and incorporated in a later collection compiled by R. Ḥiyya and R. Oshaiah, generally introduced by 'Our Rabbis taught', or, 'It has been taught'.

BETH DIN (Lit., 'house of law or judgment'); a gathering of three or more learned men acting as a Jewish court of law.

BETH HAMIDRASH. House of study; the college or academy where the study of the Torah was carried on under the guidance of a Rabbinical authority.

DEM'AI (Lit., 'dubious', 'suspicious'); produce concerning which there is a doubt as to whether the rules relating to the priestly and Levitical dues and ritual cleanness and uncleanness were strictly observed. Any produce bought from *'am ha-areẓ* (q.v.), unless the contrary is known, is treated as *dem'ai;* and *terumah gedolah* and *terumah* (q.v.) of the tithe must be separated from it.

DENAR. *Denarius*, a silver or gold coin, the former being worth one twenty-fourth (according to others one twenty-fifth) of the latter.

DUPONDIUM. A Roman coin of the value of two *issars*.

'ERUB (Lit., 'mixture'); a quantity of food, enough for two meals, placed (*a*) 2000 cubits from the town boundary, so as to extend the Sabbath limit by that distance; (*b*) in a room or in a court-yard to enable all the residents to carry to and fro in the court-yard on Sabbath.

GEZERAH SHAWAH (Lit., 'equal cut'); the application to one subject of a rule already known to apply to another, on the strength of a common expression used in connection with both in the Scriptures.

HABDALAH (Lit., 'separation'); the blessing (usually made over wine) by which the Sabbath or any other holy day is ushered out.

ḤABER. 'Fellow', 'associate', opp. to *'am ha-areẓ* (q.v.); one scrupulous in the observance of the law, particularly in relation to ritual cleanness and the separation of the priestly and Levitical dues.

HAFṬARAH (Lit., 'leave-taking'); a section from the Prophetical books recited after the reading from the Pentateuch on Sabbaths and Holy Days.

HALACHAH (Lit., 'step', 'guidance'), (*a*) the final decision of the Rabbis, whether based on tradition or argument, on disputed rules of conduct; (*b*) those sections of Rabbinic literature which deal with legal questions, as opposed to the *Aggadah*.

ḤALIẒAH (Lit., 'drawing off'); the ceremony of taking off the shoe of the brother of a husband who had died childless. (V. Deut. XXV, 5-9.)

ḤALLAH. The portion of the dough which belongs to the priest (v. Num. XV, 20f); in the Diaspora this is not given to the priest but burnt.

ḤALUẒAH. A woman who has performed *ḥaliẓah* (q.v.).

ḤANUKKAH. The Festival of Dedication (frequently designated the Feast of Lights); a minor eight days' festival, from the 25th of Kislev to the 2nd or 3rd of Tebeth, in commemoration of the rededication of the Temple in 165 B.C.E. after its desecration by Antiochus Epiphanes.

HEFḲER. Property which has no owner: a renunciation of ownership in favour of all and sundry. When used in reference to a court of law, it denotes an act of transfer of property from one person to another, in virtue of the power of the court to declare property ownerless, after which it can assign it to another.

HEḲDESH. Any object consecrated to the Sanctuary.

ḤELEB. The portion of the fat of a permitted domestic animal which may not be eaten; in sacrifices that fat was burnt upon the altar.

ḤULLIN (Lit., 'profane'); ordinary unhallowed food, as opposed to *terumah*, q.v.; unconsecrated animals, as opposed to *heḳdesh*, q.v.

ISSAR. A small Roman coin.

ḲAB. Measure of capacity equal to four *logs* or one sixth of a *se'ah*.

KARETH. 'Cutting off'; divine punishment for a number of sins for which no human penalty is specified. Sudden death is described as *'kareth* of days', premature death at sixty as *'kareth* of years'.

KARMELITH. An area which is neither a public nor a private domain, and which is subject to special laws in respect of the Sabbath and the legal acquisition of objects that happen to be within its limits.

KIL'AYIM (Lit., 'junction of diverse kinds'); the prohibition either (*a*) of seeds or plants for sowing; (*b*) of animals for propagation; and (*c*) of material containing wool and linen for wearing (v. Lev. XIX, 19; Deut. XXII, 9ff).

KOR. A measure of capacity = thirty *se'ahs* (q.v.).

ḲORBAN. An expression used in taking a vow of abstinence.

KUTAḤ. A preserve or relish made of bread crusts and sour milk.

LABUD (Lit., 'joined'). A legal fiction whereby a horizontal gap of certain prescribed dimensions is deemed to be closed up.

LOG. A liquid measure equal to a quarter of a *ḳab* (q.v.), or the space occupied by six eggs, c. 549 cubic centimetres.

LULAB. The palm-branch used in the ceremony of the Feast of Tabernacles (v. Lev. XXIII, 40).

MA'AH. The smallest current silver coin, weighing sixteen barleycorns, equal in value to two *dupondia*, a sixth of the silver *denar* or *zuz*.

MEZUZAH (Lit., 'doorpost'); a small case containing certain passages from the Scripture affixed to the post of a door (v. Deut. VI, 9).

MIḲWEH (Lit., 'a gathering [of water]'); a ritual bath containing not less than forty *se'ahs* of water.

MIN pl. *minim*, (lit., 'kind', 'species'); (*a*) a heretic, esp. (*b*) a member of the sect of the early Jewish Christians.

MINḤAH. The afternoon service, about two and a half hours before nightfall.

MISHNAH (rt. SHaNaH, 'to learn', 'to repeat'), (*a*) the collection of the statements, discussions and Biblical interpretations of the Tannaim in the form edited by R. Judah the Patriarch c. 200; (*b*) similar minor collections by previous editors; (*c*) a single clause or paragraph the author of which was a Tanna.

MUKAN (Lit., 'prepared', 'set in readiness'); a term describing an object as being in a state of preparedness and fitness before a Festival for use as may become desirable on the Festival.

MUḲẒEH (Lit., 'set aside'); that which may not be used or handled on the Sabbath or Festivals, though its use does not constitute actual labour.

NEBELAH (pl. *nebeloth*); an animal slaughtered in any manner other than that prescribed by Jewish ritual law; the least deviation therefrom, e.g., if the knife has the slightest notch, renders the animal *nebelah*.

NE'ILAH. The concluding service of the Day of Atonement.

NIDDAH. A woman in the period of her menstruation.

NOLAD (Lit., 'is born'). An object that made its first appearance or became available for use on the Sabbath or on any other holy day and the handling of which is forbidden in the days mentioned (cf. MUḲẒEH).

NOTHAR ('left over'); portions of sacrifices left over after the prescribed time within which they must be eaten.

OHEL (Lit., 'tent'); technical name for the uncleanness conveyed by a dead human body, or part of it, to men or utensils which are under the same tent or roof.

'OMER (Lit., 'sheaf'); the sheaf of barley offered on the sixteenth of Nisan, before which the new cereals of that year were forbidden for use (v. Lev. XXIII, 10).

ONEN. A mourner while his dead relative is awaiting burial; opposite to *abel*, a mourner from the time of burial for a period of seven or thirty days.

'ORLAH ('Uncircumcised'); applied to newly-planted trees for a period of three years during which their fruits must not be eaten (v. Lev. XIX, 23ff).

PE'AH ('corner'); the corner of a field that is being reaped, which must be left for the poor (v. Lev. XIX, 9ff).

PERUṬAH. The smallest copper coin, equal to one-eighth of an *issar* or one-sixteenth of a *dupondium*.

PIGGUL (Lit., 'abhorred'), flesh of the sacrifice which the officiating priest has formed the intention of eating at an improper time. V. Lev. VII, 18.

SANHEDRIN (συνέδριον); the council of state and supreme tribunal of the Jewish people during the century or more preceding the fall of the Second Temple. It consisted of seventy-one members, and was presided over by the High Priest. A minor court (for judicial purposes only) consisting of twenty-three members was known as the 'Small Sanhedrin'.

SE'AH. Measure of capacity, equal to six *kabs*.

SELA'. Coin, equal to four *denarii* (one sacred, or two common, *shekels*).

SHEBUTH (Lit., 'cessation'); an act forbidden by the Rabbis to be performed on the Sabbath.

SHECHINAH (Lit., 'abiding [of God]', 'Divine presence'); the spirit of the Omnipresent as manifested on earth.

SHECHITAH. Ritual slaughter, without which an animal is not fit for food.

SHEKEL. Coin or weight, equal to two *denarii* or ten *ma'ah* (q.v.). The sacred *shekel* was worth twenty *ma'ah* or *gerah* (cf. Ex. XXX, 13), twice the value of the common *shekel*.

SHEMA' (Lit., 'hear'); the biblical verse, '*Hear, O Israel*' etc. (Deut. VI, 4); also the three sections (Deut. VI, 5-9; Deut. XI, 13-20; and Num. XV, 37-41) which are recited after this verse in the morning and evening prayers.

SHEREẒ. Unclean reptile (including rodents).

SHOFAR (Lit., 'ram's horn'); a horn used as a trumpet for military and religious purposes, particularly in the service of the New Year and at the conclusion of the Day of Atonement.

SUKKAH. 'Booth'; esp. the festive booth for Tabernacles (Lev. XXIII, 34ff), the roof of which must be made of something that grows from the ground such as reeds, branches or leaves of a prescribed size, quantity and quality.

TALMID ḤAKAM (Lit., 'disciple of the wise'); scholar, student of the Torah.

TANNA (Lit., 'one who repeats' or 'teaches'); (*a*) a Rabbi quoted in the Mishnah or Baraitha (q.v.); (*b*) in the Amoraic period, a scholar whose special task was to memorize and recite Baraithas in the presence of expounding teachers.

ṬEBEL. Produce, already at the stage of liability to the levitical and priestly dues (v. *Terumah*), before these have been separated.

ṬEBILLAH. The act of taking a ritual bath in a *mikweh*, q.v.

ṬEBUL YOM (Lit., 'bathed during the day'); a person who has bathed to cleanse himself at the end of the period of his defilement, but who must wait until sunset to regain his ritual purity (Lev. XXII, 7).

TEFILLIN. Phylacteries; small cases containing passages from the Scripture and affixed to the forehead and arm during the recital of morning prayers, in accordance with Deut. VI, 8.

TEḤUM. The boundary beyond which one must not walk on the Sabbath, which is 2.000 cubits without the town limits; this can be extended by another 2.000 cubits by means of an '*erub*, q.v.

TEḲI'AH (Lit., 'blowing'); the plain blast made with the *Shofar*.

TERU'AH (Lit., 'shout'); the tremolo blast made with the *Shofar*.

TERUMAH. 'That which is lifted or separated'; the heave-offering given from the yields of the yearly harvests, from certain sacrifices, and from the *shekels* collected in a special chamber in the Temple (*terumath ha-lishkah*). *Terumah gedolah* (great offering): the first levy on the produce of the year given to the priest (v. Num. XVIII, 8ff). Its quantity varied according to the generosity of the owner, who could give one-fortieth, one-fiftieth, or one-sixtieth of his harvest. *Terumath ma'aser* (heave-offering of the tithe); the heave-offering given to the priest by the Levite from the tithes he receives (v. Num. XVIII, 25ff).

TORAH (Lit., 'teaching', 'learning', 'instruction'); (*a*) the Pentateuch (Written Law); (*b*) the Mishnah (Oral Law); (*c*) the whole body of Jewish religious literature.

ṬREFA or ṬEREFA (Lit., 'torn'): (*a*) an animal torn by a wild beast; (*b*) any animal suffering from a serious organic disease, whose meat is forbidden even if it has been ritually slaughtered.

ZAB (fem. ZABAH). The biblical term for a person who has experienced seminal emission (Lev. XV, 2).

ZAR (Lit., 'stranger'); an Israelite, as opposed to a priest, who may not eat of *terumah* or perform certain acts in connection with sacrifices.

ZUZ. A coin of the value of a *denarius*, six *ma'ah*, or twelve *dupondia*.

PRINTED IN THE NETHERLANDS
BY JOH. ENSCHEDÉ EN ZONEN, HAARLEM